# THE CATHOLIC BIBLE

## PERSONAL STUDY EDITION

**Jeanette Lucinio wrote the study materials for the following books:**

1 Chronicles 2 Chronicles Ezra Nehemiah Tobit Judith Esther 1 Maccabees 2 Maccabees Job Psalms Proverbs Ecclesiastes Song of Songs Wisdom Ben Sira Hebrews James 1 Peter 2 Peter 1 John 2 John 3 John Jude Revelation

She also wrote the following essays and produced the following diagrams:

Our Worship Heritage Relationship among Christian Churches Aramaic The Torah About Angels and Demons The Image of Women in the Church Hanukkah or Feast of Dedication Hellenization Why Do the Good Suffer? Experience and Tradition Wisdom, Who is She? What is Allegory? What About Life after Death? Christianity and the Book of Wisdom The Influence of Ben Sira on Jewish and Christian Communities Where Is Your God? What is Apocalyptic? Timeline: Postexilic Literature

**Cele Breen wrote the study materials for the following books:**

Daniel Hosea Joel Obadiah Jonah Micah Nahum Habakkuk Zephaniah Malachi Ephesians Philippians Colossians 1 Thessalonians 2 Thessalonians 1 Timothy 2 Timothy Titus Philemon

She also wrote the following essays:

Needed: Bible "Quadrafocals" to Correct 21st-Century Vision MSL: Metaphor as a Second Language Concentric Circle Thinking and Writing Reading Only One Side of Correspondence The Influence on Apocalyptic Thinking on Paul

**Graziano Marcheschi wrote the study materials for the following books:**

Genesis Exodus Leviticus Numbers Deuteronomy Joshua Judges Ruth 1 Samuel 2 Samuel 1 Kings 2 Kings Matthew Mark Luke John Acts of the Apostles

He also wrote the following essays and produced the following diagrams:

The Importance of Story Myth Did Moses Write the Pentateuch? How the Bible Has Been Read in History Are Some Genesis Stories Just Rewrites of Ancient Myths? YHWH The Apocrypha Slavery in the Bible Did It Really Happen? Holiness and Purity Holy War Obedience = Reward: Is It That Simple? Parables How Many Were There? Determining the Full Meaning of a Text Four Sources (of the Pentateuch) The Tribes of Israel Biblical Call-Patterns Kingship/Prophesy The Ten Plagues Ancient Treaties and the Sinai Covenant Sacrifices of the Old Testament Tribal Lists in the Book of Genesis, Numbers, and Deuteronomy Kings of Israel and Judah Kings of Judah Jesus' Resurrection The Four Gospels Parables in the Synoptic Gospels Differences Between John's Gospels and the Synoptics Biblical Numbers

**Biagio Mazza wrote the study materials for the following books:**

Isaiah Jeremiah Lamentations Baruch Ezekiel Romans 1 Corinthians 2 Corinthians Galatians

He also wrote the following essays:

Process of Transforming Life Experience into a Text and Beyond God and Suffering God and Universal Salvation

# The Catholic Bible

## Personal Study Edition


**Jean Marie Hiesberger**

EDITOR


## The New American Bible

### Revised Edition

*Translated from the Original Languages With*
*Critical Use of All the Ancient Sources*

*Authorized by the Board of Trustees of*
*the Confraternity of Christian Doctrine*
*And Approved by the Administrative Committee*
*of the United States Conference of Catholic Bishops*


OXFORD
UNIVERSITY PRESS

OXFORD
UNIVERSITY PRESS

Oxford University Press, Inc., publishes works that further Oxford University's objective of excellence in research, scholarship, and education.

Oxford New York
Auckland Cape Town Dar es Salaam Hong Kong Karachi Kuala Lumpur Madrid
Melbourne Mexico City Nairobi New Delhi Shanghai Taipei Toronto

With offices in
Argentina Austria Brazil Chile Czech Republic France Greece
Guatemala Hungary Italy Japan Poland Portugal Singapore
South Korea Switzerland Thailand Turkey Ukraine Vietnam



Published by Oxford University Press, Inc.
198 Madison Avenue, New York, New York 10016

http://www.oup.com



*Nihil Obstat*
Reverend John G. Lodge, S.S.L., S.T.D.
Censor Deputatis
Reverend Robert L. Schoenstene, M.A., S.S.L.
Censor Deputatis
October 2, 2006

*Imprimatur*
Reverend John F. Canary, S.T.L., D.Min.
Vicar General
Archdiocese of Chicago
October 4, 2006

The *Nihil Obstat* and *Imprimatur* are official declarations that a book is free of doctrinal and moral error. No implication is contained therein that those who have granted the *Nihil Obstat* and *Imprimatur* agree with the content, opinions, or statements expressed. Nor do they assume any legal responsibility associated with publication.

Scripture texts, prefaces, introductions, footnotes, and cross references used in this work constitute

The New American Bible
*Nihil Obstat*
Stephen J. Hartdegen, O.F.M., S.S.L.
Christian P. Ceroke, O. Carm., S.T.D.

*Imprimatur*
†Patrick Cardinal O'Boyle, D.D.
Archbishop of Washington
July 27, 1970

The Revised New Testament
*Nihil Obstat*
Stephen J. Hartdegen, O.F.M., S.S.L.
Censor Deputatis

*Imprimatur*
† James A. Hickey, S.T.D., J.C.D.
Archbishop of Washington
August 27, 1986

Revised Psalms
*Imprimatur*
Most Rev. Daniel E. Pilarczyk, President, National Conference of Catholic Bishops, October 10, 1991

RESCRIPT
In accord with canon 825 §1 of the Code of Canon Law, the United States Conference of Catholic Bishops hereby approves for publication The New American Bible, Revised Old Testament, a translation of the Sacred Scriptures authorized by the Confraternity of Christian Doctrine, Inc.

The translation was approved by the Administrative Committee of the United States Conference of Catholic Bishops in November 2008 and September 2010. It is permitted by the undersigned for private use and study.

Given in the city of Washington, the District of Columbia, on the Feast of Saint Jerome, Priest and Doctor of the Church, the 30th day of September, in the year of our Lord 2010.

Francis Cardinal George, O.M.I.
Archbishop of Chicago
President, USCCB



Interior typesetting by Blue Heron Bookcraft, Battle Ground, WA

Printed in Korea

7 9 8 6

# CONTENTS

## The New Testament of the *New American Bible*

# LIST OF ESSAYS, CHARTS, AND DIAGRAMS

*(List of Essays, Charts, and Diagrams, continued)*

# LIST OF MAPS

*(List of Maps, continued)*

# ALPHABETICAL LISTING OF THE BOOKS OF THE BIBLE

# ACKNOWLEDGMENTS

Any project of this scope requires the combined efforts of many people, and I will not be able to thank them all here. But I would like to thank, first of all, my editors at Oxford University Press, Donald Kraus and Elisabeth Nelson, who brought all of this material together and made sure that it was both accurate and readable. I also thank Peachtree Editorial and Proofreading Service for carefully checking all of the typeset pages.

This work builds on the earlier edition of this Bible, and I am grateful to all those who contributed to its development. This edition also has the benefit of treasures from other writers in *The Catholic Study Bible, The New Oxford Annotated Bible, The Jewish Study Bible, The Access Bible,* and *The Oxford Study Bible.*

Finally, for invaluable help in researching information and gathering the most relevant comments on the biblical text, I thank my husband, Robert Heyer. Any remaining errors in the text must remain my responsibility.

**Jean Marie Hiesberger**

October 4, 2006
The Feast of St. Francis of Assisi

# ABBREVIATIONS OF THE BOOKS OF THE BIBLE

## Old Testament

| | | | | | |
|---|---|---|---|---|---|
| Gn | Genesis | Tb | Tobit | Bar | Baruch |
| Ex | Exodus | Jdt | Judith | Ez | Ezekiel |
| Lv | Leviticus | Est | Esther | Dn | Daniel |
| Nm | Numbers | 1 Mc | 1 Maccabees | Hos | Hosea |
| Dt | Deuteronomy | 2 Mc | 2 Maccabees | Jl | Joel |
| Jos | Joshua | Jb | Job | Am | Amos |
| Jgs | Judges | Ps | Psalms | Ob | Obadiah |
| Ru | Ruth | Prv | Proverbs | Jon | Jonah |
| 1 Sm | 1 Samuel | Eccl | Ecclesiastes | Mi | Micah |
| 2 Sm | 2 Samuel | Sg | Song of Songs | Na | Nahum |
| 1 Kgs | 1 Kings | Wis | Wisdom | Hb | Habakkuk |
| 2 Kgs | 2 Kings | Sir | Ben Sira | Zep | Zephaniah |
| 1 Chr | 1 Chronicles | | (Ecclesiasticus) | Hg | Haggai |
| 2 Chr | 2 Chronicles | Is | Isaiah | Zec | Zechariah |
| Ezr | Ezra | Jer | Jeremiah | Mal | Malachi |
| Neh | Nehemiah | Lam | Lamentations | | |

## New Testament

| | | | | | |
|---|---|---|---|---|---|
| Mt | Matthew | Eph | Ephesians | Heb | Hebrews |
| Mk | Mark | Phil | Philippians | Jas | James |
| Lk | Luke | Col | Colossians | 1 Pt | 1 Peter |
| Jn | John | 1 Thes | 1 Thessalonians | 2 Pt | 2 Peter |
| Acts | Acts of the Apostles | 2 Thes | 2 Thessalonians | 1 Jn | 1 John |
| Rom | Romans | 1 Tm | 1 Timothy | 2 Jn | 2 John |
| 1 Cor | 1 Corinthians | 2 Tm | 2 Timothy | 3 Jn | 3 John |
| 2 Cor | 2 Corinthians | Ti | Titus | Jude | Jude |
| Gal | Galatians | Phlm | Philemon | Rev | Revelation |

# KEY TO REFERENCES

For greater clarity and convenience, the footnotes and cross references are printed at the bottom of each page and cross-indexed in the text itself. An *asterisk* (*) in the text indicates that there is a footnote to the text in question. Each footnote is in turn clearly marked with the number of the chapter and the verse to which it pertains. Similarly a *superior letter* ([a]) in the text indicates that there is a cross-reference to a particular verse. The reference itself is also clearly marked with the same letter. Hence, the reader is always aware of a footnote or a cross-reference simply by *reading the text*.

## Key to Scripture References

| | |
|---|---|
| Gn 1:1 | refers to Genesis, chapter one, verse one. |
| Gn 1:1a | refers to Genesis, chapter one, first part of verse one. |
| Gn 1:1f(f) | refers to Genesis, chapter one, verse one and the following verse (verses). |
| Gn 1:1–10 | refers to Genesis, chapter one, verses one through ten. |
| Gn 1:1–10, 24 | refers to Genesis, chapter one, verses one through ten and verse twenty-four. |
| Gn 1–5 | refers to Genesis, chapters one through five inclusive. |
| Gn 1:1–2:3 | refers to Genesis, chapter one, verse one through chapter two, verse three inclusive. |
| Gn 1:1; 2:3 | refers to Genesis, chapter one, verse one and chapter two, verse three. |

# READING GUIDE

# GENERAL INTRODUCTION

The book you hold in your hand contains one of humanity's greatest treasures. No one can deny that the Bible has had a profound impact on world civilization. Its epic stories, its powerful language, and its compelling images have left their imprint on human history, especially in cultures touched by Judaism and Christianity.

For the Christian, the Bible has an importance far more profound than its impact on culture. The Christian believes that through the turbulent and wonderful chapters of biblical history, God speaks to us. Although expressed in genuinely human terms and through very human authors, the Bible is, at the same time, the Word of God for us. Therefore, as Christians we revere and love the Scriptures. Because of that love, we seek to understand them as deeply as we can.

The purpose of *The Catholic Bible: Personal Study Edition* is to enable the reader to read the Scriptures with new understanding and depth. In writing and editing the study materials contained here, our primary aim has been to serve an audience of Roman Catholics. Some of the comments in the notes to the text, the Reference Articles, and the Reading Guides deliberately reflect Catholic experience and Catholic interests. However, the editors do not wish to exclude other Christian readers from the focus of this book. In most instances, the materials included here will be useful for all Christians who want to enter deeply into the mysteries and marvels of the Bible.

## Introducing the Bible

Although it is bound under one cover and bears a single title, the Bible is not a single, unified book. It is, in fact, a collection of some 73 different works by different authors, using very different styles and perspectives, composed over a span of many centuries, and in three different languages (Hebrew, Aramaic, and Greek). Most of the Old Testament (46 books) was written in Hebrew, but parts of the books of Daniel (2:4–7:28), Ezra (4:6–6:18; 7:12–26), and one verse from Jeremiah (10:11) were originally composed in Aramaic, a Middle Eastern language related to but different from Hebrew. Other Old Testament books, such as Tobit and the Wisdom of Solomon, were written in Greek. And all 27 of the New Testament books were composed in Greek.

The rich diversity of the Bible is one of its glories because it allows the story of God's people to be told from various perspectives. It also presents a challenge to the reader who should be aware of the different cultural, historical, and literary contexts of each biblical book. But there is a deeper unity to the Bible that binds together these individual pieces of literature. Through the many biblical books flows the continuing saga of God's love for Israel and for the Church. Each of the biblical authors, no matter how much separated in time, culture, and literary style, shares a conviction that God's presence is felt in human history and that God invites the human family to respond with faith and integrity.

### The Writing of the Bible

As its diverse makeup implies, the Bible was not written at a single point in history. The events covered in the Old Testament span nearly 2,000 years of history, from the time of Abraham and the patriarchs (around 1800 B.C.) to the period of the Maccabean wars (140 B.C.). If one includes the epic accounts of the creation and prepatriarchal stories such as Noah and the flood, then the reach of the biblical saga goes back to the beginning of time. But the actual formulation of the biblical accounts, although making use of earlier stories and traditions, is confined to a narrower period of time, probably beginning with the monarchy (around 1000 B.C.) and concluding in the century before the birth of Christ.

The New Testament books were all written during the latter half of the first century A.D. The letters of Paul were probably the earliest New Testament works to be put in writing, dating mainly from the decade of the fifties. The sayings of Jesus and the many stories about his ministry circulated in the Christian community all during these early decades of the Church but were probably not put in writing until shortly after A.D. 70, with Mark the first Gospel to be written. Matthew, Luke (and his second volume, the Acts of the Apostles), and John follow, with the compositions of their Gospels taking place sometime during the last quarter of the first century. The other non-Pauline letters and writings, including the book of Revelation or the Apocalypse, also date from this period.

### Forming a "Bible" from Diverse Books: The Story of the Canon

The gathering of these diverse writings into a single collection or "book" (the literal meaning of the word "Bible") was itself a long-term and laborious process. The technical term for the authoritative list of books belonging in the Bible is "canon" (which means "measuring rod"). Both Judaism and Christianity had to make choices about which books to include and which books to exclude from their respective "Bibles." Judaism would not make any official decision about which books belonged to its "Bible" until the end of the first century A.D. But that does not mean it was without a Bible for so much of its history. There was little or no dispute about the major books of the Old Testament, books which were constantly used in Jewish liturgy and teaching. But there was debate about the inclusion of later and less central works such as Esther or Ecclesiasticus (the Wisdom of Jesus ben Sira).

The Jewish or Hebrew canon ultimately recognizes 39 books, divided into three major categories:

1. The Law (sometimes referred to as the Pentateuch, or first five books of the Bible): Genesis, Exodus, Leviticus, Numbers, Deuteronomy.

2. The Prophets: Subdivided into the Former Prophets: Joshua, Judges, 1 and 2 Samuel, 1 and 2 Kings; and the Latter Prophets: Isaiah, Jeremiah, Ezekiel, and the Twelve (Hosea, Joel, Amos, Obadiah, Jonah, Micah, Nahum, Habakkuk, Zephaniah, Haggai, Zechariah, Malachi).

3. The Writings: Psalms, Proverbs, Job, Song of Songs, Ruth, Lamentations, Ecclesiastes, Esther, Daniel, Ezra-Nehemiah, 1 and 2 Chronicles.

As we shall explain below, not included in the official Jewish or Hebrew canon are seven other books that Roman Catholics (and Orthodox Christians) consider part of their Scriptures. Judaism reveres these books and considers them sacred, but they are not part of their canon or official list. These books are: Tobit, Judith, 1 and 2 Maccabees, Wisdom, Ecclesiasticus, and Baruch. There are also some additional passages in the books of Daniel and Esther.

The formation of the Christian canon also took place over a considerable period of time. In fact, the official Roman Catholic decision about the canon did not come until the Council of Trent in the sixteenth century, but by that time the choice of which writings were to be included in the Bible was well established. There were many sacred writings in the early decades of the Church that presumably could have been included in the Bible. We cannot always tell what criteria or decision-making processes were used to establish the canon. Some "gospels" evidently portrayed Jesus in a way unacceptable to the vast majority of Christians and so were not included. Other early writings, however, such as the Didache (Greek, "teaching")—a short handbook of moral behavior and church practice—seem perfectly acceptable in content and tone but nevertheless were not included. Probably the early Church considered a work's content, its authorship, and the frequency of its usage in the liturgy and teaching of the Churches as important criteria for judging if a sacred writing was inspired by God and worthy of inclusion in its official canon or Scriptures.

All Christians agree on the 27 books to be included in the New Testament. But there is a dispute about some of the books in the Old Testament. As noted above, Roman Catholics and Orthodox Christians agree on the 46 books that make up the Old Testament (the Orthodox include additional books in their canon: 1 and 2 Esdras; the prayer of Manasseh; Psalm 151; 3 Maccabees). Judaism and Protestant Christians hold for the shorter list of 39 books sketched above; the remaining seven or more are designated as the apocryphal books.

The reason for this divergence is that earliest Christianity used an ancient Greek translation of the Old Testament (called the Septuagint) as its Bible. This Greek version of the Bible included 46 books. Since most of the early Christians were Greek-speaking, this is the Bible they preferred. But when Judaism officially set out to determine its canon at the end of the first century, it drew up a shorter list of 39 books: those written in Hebrew. In the Reformation period, Protestants went back to this shorter Hebrew canon, considering it more authentic.

Today, many of the doctrinal tensions that separated Catholics and Protestants have eased. Some Protestant editions of the Bible include the "aprocryphal" (what Roman Catholics call "deuterocanonical") books in an appendix of their Bibles or in a special section between the Old and New Testaments. Following usual Catholic practice, the *New American Bible* integrates the deuterocanonical books into the order of the Old Testament canon. A table showing the different canons for each group—Jews, Protestant Christians, Catholic Christians, and Orthodox Christians—is on p. 1869.

## The Diverse Literary Forms and Historical Value of the Bible

The broad span of biblical history, and the fact that the Bible is a collection of various books, help to form its rich diversity. The reader of the Bible needs to be attentive not only to the historical context of a particular passage but to the varieties of literary forms and the specific style and intent of each biblical author. The prophetic oracles of Isaiah or Jeremiah are very different in literary style from the legal codes of Leviticus or the narratives of Exodus. The long lists of wise sayings in Proverbs are dramatically different in tone, style, and theology from the sweeping liturgical poetry of the Psalms. So, too, do the parables of the Gospels differ greatly from the letters of Paul or the dramatic apocalyptic scenes in the book of Revelation. The notes and Reading Guides found in this Study Bible help the reader to understand more about these various literary forms and their implications for interpreting the meaning of a particular biblical passage.

The presence of various literary forms or means of expression in the Bible also complicates the issue of the historical value of the Bible. Some Christians, particularly fundamentalist Christians, fear that admitting the Bible contains poetry, stories, and other literary forms is somehow an attack on the veracity of the Bible and dilutes its witness to history. They prefer to regard the story of creation in Genesis, or the episode of Jonah's sojourn in the belly of a great fish, as literally true.

Roman Catholic teaching—and that of many other Christian denominations—sees no incompatibility between recognizing the truth of the biblical witness and the fact that it is expressed in many forms of literature characteristic of human communication. Credible witness to the truth of history is not confined to an objective reporting of the facts in the manner of a police report or a mere factual description of what happened. All reporting of history involves a degree of interpretation. And such means as poetry, hymns, stories, myths, and other literary forms can also communicate historical truth about past events and the perspectives of our ancestors.

Undoubtedly, both the Old and New Testaments contain many accurate historical facts and descriptions reflecting the times and events of biblical history. But the biblical writers also wanted to interpret the *meaning* of that history and present it unabashedly from their perspectives. Previous traditions are given new interpretations and adapted to the circumstances of a different generation. In most instances their intent was not to provide a historical archive for subsequent generations but to see in the events of this history the presence of God's grace, and to communicate that conviction to their readers. The Bible is a witness to the vitality of the people who lived its events and pondered their meaning in a spirit of faith.

Each biblical passage, therefore, must be evaluated on its own terms in attempting to distinguish between factual historical data and the theological and historical interpretation provided by the biblical writer.

## The Transmission of the Biblical Text and its Modern Translations

Each modern reader of the Bible is in debt to countless numbers of people—Jewish and Christian—who faithfully handed on to the next generations the treasures of the Bible. For much of biblical history, such transmission of the biblical tradition was done orally, not in written form. Stories, sayings of great teachers and leaders, hymns and poetry were lovingly memorized and handed down from parents to children, teacher to disciple, from leader of prayer to congregation and, thereby, formed the growing body of the biblical heritage.

In ancient (and some modern) cultures, oral transmission of important literature was not a casual, haphazard affair. For our modern culture, so dependent on written means of communicating information, it is hard to realize that in oral cultures subtle and often unspoken rules govern how information is shaped, retained, and transmitted from one person and one generation to another.

But as styles of writing and writing materials became more sophisticated in Israel, and when it had the social organization under the monarchy to have archives and develop an educated class of scribes, then undoubtedly some parts of the Bible were preserved in written form as well.

In the New Testament, much of the Gospel materials were first preserved in oral form. Sayings of Jesus, his parables, the stories about his healings, his conflicts with opponents, and the narrative of his Passion would have been preserved and transmitted in a variety of settings such as the liturgy, instruction within the home or small Christian communities, or, perhaps even more formally, in some early centers of Christian learning. But eventually these oral materials were gathered and put in written form by the evangelists. It is likely that the oral transmission of the biblical materials, both Old and New Testaments, continued to exist and be employed even after the biblical text had been put into writing.

Paul's letters and other New Testament texts such as the catholic epistles and the book of Revelation were composed or dictated into written form immediately, although, as the study materials will show, some of these letters may be composites of several different writings. Nevertheless, it is important to recognize that some writings in the Bible—the book of Ezekiel, the Letter to the Romans, and others—were written by one author in the form in which we have them. Many other books, however—Genesis or Isaiah, for example—were put together from various separate writings created over a lengthy period.

Regardless of whether a biblical book was written at one time by one author or over a period of time by several writers, no original manuscript of any biblical book exists. Copyists from one generation to the next transcribed the biblical materials and enabled them to be available for subsequent generations. The earliest written manuscripts we have of some Old Testament biblical materials date from the first century B.C. These were part of the wealth of written materials discovered in 1948 on the northwest shore of the Dead Sea and thereafter named the "Dead Sea Scrolls." Most of the other surviving early written materials for both the Old and the New Testaments are papyrus fragments of biblical passages dating from the early second century A.D. and more complete manuscripts of the Bible on parchment from the third and fourth centuries A.D.

The hands of many copyists, with different personal interests and levels of skill, inevitably introduced some variations and errors into the numerous editions of the biblical text. Ancient translations (or versions) of manuscripts into other languages, such as Latin or Syriac or Coptic, could also introduce errors or varying interpretations not found in the original biblical language.

The science of textual criticism attempts to trace the relationships of ancient manuscripts to each other and to reestablish the most reliable form of the biblical text. The discovery of biblical texts among the Dead Sea Scrolls rolled back the age of extant biblical manuscripts several centuries. Surprisingly, although some variants exist, there is still remarkable correspondence between the state of the biblical text in the first century B.C. and the third or fourth century A.D.—testimony to the accuracy and care with which ancient peoples handed on the biblical tradition.

Besides recognizing that we do not have original manuscripts of the books of the Bible, we should also note that the biblical texts of the ancient Church did not have the neat format of our modern Bible. Division into the present system of chapters and verses was introduced only in the Middle Ages. Prior to that, demarcations between individual sentences and sections of a particular biblical book were much more casual and fluid.

## The New American Bible Translation

Most modern translations, including that found in the *New American Bible (NAB)*, are based on the most reliable texts of the Bible we have and are translated from the original biblical languages rather than using any intervening translations. Many previous Catholic translations had been based on the Vulgate, or Latin version of the Bible, first prepared by Jerome in the fifth century.

The translation of the *NAB* was a collaborative achievement of some 50 Catholic biblical scholars, determined to use the best of modern scholarship to bring a fresh and accurate translation of the Bible to the American Catholic community.

The first full edition of the *New American Bible* appeared in 1970. A revision of the New Testament appeared in 1986, and the *NAB Revised Edition* in 2011. It is this fully revised edition that is used in *The Catholic Bible: Personal Study Edition*. Every translation, no matter how accurate and faithful, falls short in attempting to communicate the subtlety and meaning of another language. All translators have to make decisions about the purpose and audience of their translation and the consequent principles they will use in translating the Bible from its original languages to a modern language such as American English. And, to some degree, every translation is a subtle interpretation of the biblical text.

The translators of the *New American Bible* wanted as much as possible to accurately reflect the nuance and form of biblical Hebrew and Greek, while recasting the language to make it compatible with the rules and style of modern English and in harmony with traditional Catholic interpretations of Scripture. The translators, however, wanted to avoid making the *NAB* a paraphrase or quasi-interpretation of the biblical text. Some modern translations attempt this. While such paraphrases perhaps make the biblical texts more palatable to a modern audience, they also risk a high degree of subjectivity in recasting the contents of the Bible. The *NAB* translation is faithful to the biblical text and takes its place alongside rigorously literal translations such as the Revised Standard Version. This makes it particularly suitable for deeper study of the biblical message, as well as its use in prayer and liturgy.

Accuracy of translation from one language to another also involves issues that are more than linguistic. For instance, the editors of the revised New Testament translation had to struggle with the question of inclusive language. This is a sensitive issue in modern American culture and in the Catholic Church in particular. The translators adopted a compromise stance here. Where the original biblical language clearly intended a generic reference to human beings, the translation is careful to use inclusive language. Where the original text uses a gender-specific reference, however, such as many references to God through male pronouns, the translation does not attempt to use inclusive language.

Modern political issues can also cause difficulties for the translator. Such geographical terms as Israel or Palestine have highly charged meanings in the political arena of today's Middle East. But their appearance in the biblical translation of the *New American Bible* implies no endorsement of any modern political stance on these difficult issues. So, too, can modern religious sensitivities come into play. Judaism in all its modern forms, out of reverence, avoids the use of the name Yahweh for God. Readers in the synagogue, for example, will substitute Adonai (My Lord) wherever the divine name appears in the biblical text. The modern translator and commentator have to make a decision on whether to try to respect this understandable religious sensitivity.

It should be noted that the Reading Guides and major Reference Articles included in the *Personal Study Edition* attempt throughout to use inclusive language, and, wherever possible, to avoid offense to modern religious, cultural, or political sensitivities. The editors believed that such a spirit is in accord with both the biblical witness and sound Catholic tradition. Some use of the geographical terms Israel and Palestine was unavoidable in some of the Reading Guides, but no reference to modern geopolitical realities is intended.

## Reading, Studying, and Praying the Scriptures

From the beginning of its existence, the Bible has been the object of intense study, prayerful reading, and even heated debate. The Bible is not meant to be a coffee-table book.

One could say that the Bible was formed in a context of prayer and reflection. The various biblical authors reflected on significant events in the life of Israel, of Jesus, and of the early Church. Their discovery of God's presence working within history gives the Bible its force. For all Christians the Bible has unique authority as writings inspired by God's Spirit working within the communities of Israel and the Church, and impelling the biblical writers to give expression in human words to their faith perspective. (For a Catholic view of biblical inspiration, see "The Bible in Catholic Life," RG 13.)

Judaism has always maintained a rich tradition of reflection on its Scriptures. The rabbis lovingly studied every detail of the biblical text and saw an infinite possibility of applications to everyday life. The Scriptures were reverenced as God's Word and took a central place within the prayer life of the synagogue. Christian tradition has had the same character. Until the late Middle Ages, almost all of the Church's theology and teaching was little more than an elaboration of the biblical text.

Some of this biblical focus was lost in the Catholic Church when philosophical analysis—always important—became over-dominant, and theological reflection could often be far distant in focus and spirit from our biblical foundations. While biblical symbols remained dominant in Catholic liturgical life and architecture, in popular preaching and much popular piety, the Bible was a more distant echo. In the past 50 years, that trend has been radically reversed. The Second Vatican Council gave a strong impetus to a biblical renewal in every dimension of Catholicism (see "The Bible in Catholic Life," RG 13).

One can approach reading and study of the Bible from several vantage points.

### The Historical Approach

One purpose in reading the Bible is to comb through the biblical books, seeking leads to the historical context of a given period or culture. While this is a legitimate historical enterprise, it does not correspond to the fundamentally religious character of the Bible. The Bible does have strong historical value; but its purpose is not simply to inform the reader about history but to probe the meaning of past history for the life of faith.

### The Theological Approach

Another way of entering the biblical world is to seek what the Bible, or a particular biblical book, has to say on a specific doctrinal or moral issue. What, for example, does the Bible say about violence? Or what is the biblical perspective on justice? Because the Bible is such a rich and diverse body of literature, we soon discover that the Bible will yield many perspectives on such important issues. There is seldom a single biblical viewpoint on any specific theological or moral issue. Only by first understanding the context of each biblical period and biblical book, and then interrelating the Bible's varied approaches to profound questions of faith, can one weave together a biblical theology.

### The Inspirational Approach

For most Christians, reading the Bible has a more modest, yet still important goal. They turn to the Scriptures for inspiration in living out their life of faith. Such inspiration can be gained in many different ways.

For some, the Scriptures are an important stimulant for prayer. The words of the Psalms, the challenge of the prophets, the compassionate mission of Jesus, the soaring words of Paul—all of these give form and expression to the longing of our own hearts as we seek the face of God.

Very often the biblical words are able to express the feelings and fears and hopes we could not put into words ourselves. And in reaching out to the Bible we unite ourselves with the faith of countless generations of Christians who found the same solace and strength in the Scriptures.

For others, probing the Scriptures either in private or with a group of Christians helps guide and illumine their daily lives. Study of the biblical text and discussion of its meaning with other thoughtful Christians can help us understand our own experience of faith and expand our perspective on what it means to be a believer in the modern world. This approach works best when the participant is not afraid to reflect on his or her own experience, and then relate that reflection to the ideas and images of the Bible. Very often the Bible opens its treasures when we bring to it questions and hopes that spring from our life of faith. Then, in turn, the biblical message can give new insight and nourishment to our faith experience.

A profound sense of grief or loss, for example, might lead a Christian to read with new understanding the lament psalms of the Old Testament or the passion of Jesus. And these biblical passages, in turn, can bring new strength to the one who suffers.

Whatever approach one takes to reading and praying the Bible, it is important from a Catholic perspective that it not be done in isolation. The Bible is the Church's book, not a private library. Only in the context of the Church's faith and tradition as a whole can the full meaning of the Bible be discovered. Some Christians who isolate themselves from common sense and from the sound wisdom of the Church community can interpret the Scriptures in a bizarre and even destructive manner. That is why the effort to understand the biblical text in its context, to sound out its possible meaning with other thoughtful Christians, and to be open to the guidance of the Church and its teaching forms the best context for full integration of the Bible into our lives (on this see the 1993 statement of the Pontifical Biblical Commission, *The Interpretation of the Bible in the Church,* which fully endorses the use of modern biblical methods).

*The Personal Study Edition* is designed to open the beauty and power of the Bible to the reader. The editors and the Oxford University Press hope that the guides, articles, and other resources provided in this unique volume will serve you well as you step into the marvelous world of the Bible.

**Donald Senior, C.P., Editor,**
***The Catholic Study Bible***
**(from which this essay is adapted)**

**Jean Marie Hiesberger, Editor,**
***The Catholic Bible:***
***Personal Study Edition***

# HOW TO USE *THE CATHOLIC BIBLE: PERSONAL STUDY EDITION*

We have included much information and many study aids in the *Catholic Bible: Personal Study Edition.* These aids will help you to use this study Bible in a great variety of ways and settings. This outline suggests some ways of starting your studies and reflections, using the features contained in this book. As you read further, we hope you will discover other approaches for yourself.

If your goal is to read and reflect on a single biblical book or major passage of the Bible, the two key sections of the Study Bible to use are the biblical text itself and the Reading Guides. These work together to help you grasp the overall character of a biblical book, its main themes, and specific issues that arise in a particular passage. In turning to the Gospel of Luke, for example, you can work through the Reading Guide for Luke, including the Discussion/Reflection questions, and then turn to the Bible section on p. 1494 and read the Introduction given there. Now when you go through the gospel itself, your reading will be much richer and more meaningful. You will not only have a better understanding of what you read, but with the Discussion/Reflection questions in mind, you will be reading it while attuned to their challenges. Of course, footnotes and sidebars, where they exist, will help "unpack" the text as you go.

## For Individual and Group Reading or Study

Whether you are using the Study Bible alone or in a group, learning about our "family history" in the biblical story can be a rich and, in some cases, life-changing experience. And, of course, we believe that Christ is among us where two or three gather in his name. A group can be the instrument of powerful insights helping us to make connections with our own story or applications to our life that we might miss otherwise. The Reading Guide is designed to walk us through the particular book of the Bible with a little background to "plow the ground" so that the seed of the scripture can take root in us more deeply and fruitfully.

The Reading Guide for each book follows a set pattern of three basic parts:

A section called "At a Glance" begins each guide with a kind of snapshot of the book to be read. It briefly addresses:

Who are the main players?
What should I look for?
When did this take place?
Where did these events occur?
Why was this book written?
What is the story?

Next comes a brief "walk through" the book, which gives important and helpful background information. This makes reading the actual biblical text much more understandable as well as meaningful.

Finally, the Reading Guide for each book ends with a set of discussion/reflection questions. These are meant for you to use after you have read and studied both the Reading Guide and the Bible text. These questions always follow the same three-part format, a format typically used with Catechumens and Candidates in the R.C.I.A. process:

• The first set of questions is *Group Sharing/ Discussion.* This set explores the Bible text itself, allowing for reviewing, digesting, and thinking about the story or the setting itself. Taking time for this step helps to synthesize and clarify what was read so that the next step will be easier and richer.

• The second set is *In Our Lives.* Here the questions push us to think about what might be called the "So what?" of reading the text. What is the lesson? What does it teach us? How does it apply to me or to us as a church community? As the first questions are about using our head, this set is for the heart also.

• The final set of questions is *Individual/Personal Reflection/Action.* Whether using the Study Guide alone or in a group, this is where we take time to decide on what we will do as a result of the lessons contained in this part of the Bible. This takes the scriptures one step beyond head and heart and helps us put them into our lives. And this, of course, is the whole point of scripture study.

Because scripture study is not learning an abstract or academic subject, but is about sharing faith and sharing personal insights and experience, the human dimension of our relationship with the others in Bible study groups needs attention. In addition to preparing for a group session by studying the Reading Guide and the Bible text, it is important for parish groups, R.C.I.A. sessions, or informal groups of any age to begin each session by welcoming everyone. When members are allowed to connect on the human level, catch up a bit on what has happened in their lives since the last meeting, perhaps share a cup of coffee and some refreshments, the relationships deepen and so does the ability to comfortably share insights and ideas. This "hospitality dimension" is the responsibility of everyone in the group, whether or not there is a designated leader. Most groups find that beyond 90 minutes there is little capacity for listening and learning, so it is important to respect the time frame agreed upon in advance. Some groups take a break in the middle of the session, others at the beginning or end.

The *Personal Study Edition* is also useful for the college or religious education classroom. It provides virtually a one-volume textbook and reference library on the Bible. Experienced and imaginative teachers will find their own way to best utilize a book like this. Here are some suggestions to get you started.

The Study Bible can certainly serve as a textbook for a course on the Bible as a whole or for introductions to the Old or New Testaments. Here again interplay between pertinent sections of the Reading Guides and the biblical text and notes is very important.

Teachers in a Catholic setting may want to give special attention to the Reference Article on "The Bible in Catholic Life" as an important summary of Catholic teaching on the role of the Bible in the Church's life and thought. The Reference Article on "The Bible in the Lectionary" will help Catholics (and Christians from other mainline denominations) understand how the liturgy is a major source of biblical inspiration for Roman Catholic tradition.

## Other Helpful Features of this Study Bible

Within this study Bible, you will find a full range of aids to help you discover the meaning of the Bible. The following description of its contents, and suggestions for using the book, might help you take full advantage of its unique resources.

### The *New American Bible*

Beginning on page 1, following the Reading Guides, you will find the full text and notes of the *New American Bible*. Each major section of the Bible and each biblical book has a brief introduction. Extensive notes explaining words or individual verses are found at the bottom of the page. An asterisk (*) alongside a particular word or verse signals to you that an explanatory note is provided for that biblical text. These notes provide a wealth of information for the studious reader.

The *New American Bible* also provides cross-references to other related biblical passages. These cross-references are signaled by a small italic letter printed in specific verses. The cross-reference is found at the bottom of the page.

There are sidebars set off within the text of the Bible. These contain information to make the text more understandable and meaningful as you read.

Finally, along the side margins there is another set of cross-references, directing you to the

Reading Guide for that particular biblical book. These cross-references are indicated by page numbers enclosed within a shaded box. Page numbers for the Reading Guides are preceded by the letters RG.

### General and Reference Articles

Another helpful feature of the *Catholic Bible: Personal Study Edition* is that it provides extensive and detailed studies of key issues for understanding and using the Bible. In addition to this introduction, the reader will find the following Reference Articles:

- The Bible in Catholic Life
- Catholics and Fundamentalism
- How to Read the Bible
- Understanding the Historical Background to the Biblical Texts
- The Catechism of the Catholic Church
- Catholic Beliefs in Scripture
- The Bible in the Lectionary
- Lectionary, Historical, and Canon Tables

### Glossary

The glossary provides clear explanations of the less familiar or more technical terms used in the Bible or in the Reading Guides and Reference Articles.

### Maps

Aside from maps dealing with specific matters in various points of the biblical text, there are full-color maps and a map index at the very end of the Bible. These will provide you with the entire geographical canvas on which the biblical drama is portrayed.

# THE BIBLE IN CATHOLIC LIFE

## DANIEL J. HARRINGTON

### Church Life Today

One of the great achievements of the Second Vatican Council (1962–1965) has been the renewal of interest in the Bible among Catholics. How dramatic this renewal has been can be grasped by comparing Catholic practice around 1950 and the situation in the early years of the twenty-first century.

At mid-twentieth century the Scriptures were read at Mass in Latin. There were few selections from the Old Testament, and a rather small number of New Testament passages dominated the one-year cycle. In response to the mandate of the Second Vatican Council we now have a three-year cycle of Sunday readings and a two-year weekday cycle. (See "The Bible in the Lectionary," p. 1849.) The Old Testament is very prominent, and almost the entire New Testament (Gospels and Epistles) is represented. The passages, of course, are read in the vernacular (English, Spanish, or whatever is the dominant local language).

In the 1950s study of Bible texts was not an integral part of the primary- or secondary-school curriculum in Catholic schools. At best Bible content was conveyed through summaries of the texts. Catholic college students might work through parts of the Bible with the aid of cautious and approved textbooks as guides. But now the texts of the Bible form a primary resource for Catholic religious education at all levels. And Bible courses and Bible-study groups have become especially popular forums for adult education.

At the mid-twentieth century, Catholic seminarians took most of their Scripture courses toward the end of their theology programs. In comparison with dogma and moral theology, Scripture study was considered a minor course. Now biblical studies are a major component of the seminary curriculum at all stages. And such courses are very popular. Students in Catholic seminaries assume that much of their preaching and teaching in the future will be devoted to the Bible, and so they study it with eagerness. There is also a lively dialogue and interdisciplinary cooperation between professors of Scripture and their theological colleagues.

Since Vatican II the Bible has become prominent not only in Catholic liturgy and education but also in popular piety. The revised prayers for the sacraments and other liturgical actions use biblical language almost entirely. Charismatic groups and base communities have found biblical reflection and prayer to be the source of great spiritual energy. Even traditional Catholic observances like the Rosary are (and always have been) thoroughly biblical. The language of Catholic prayer in almost every instance derives from the Bible.

The Scriptures have also been a major element in the ecumenical movement since the council. The serious historical and theological differences between the Christian churches remain. But the most progress has been made where the different Church groups have focused on the Bible as their common heritage and have reexamined their differences in light of the Bible's language and thought patterns. When this has occurred, the usual result has been the recognition that what unites the Christian churches is more important and fundamental than what divides them. In the new and more positive relationship that has emerged between Christians and Jews in recent years, Bible study has been a vital force toward greater mutual understanding and respect.

Catholic theology since the council gives far more attention to biblical sources and is likely to express itself more in biblical than in philosophical language. Official church documents on theological matters or current problems almost always begin from Scripture and try to ground their arguments in biblical texts. The Catholic Church today is far more "biblical" than it was in the mid-1950s.

## Bible Study in History

In order to understand the Bible's place in Catholic thinking today, it can be helpful to see how Christians in other times and places thought about and interpreted the Bible. The Bible has not always been studied according to the principles of modern historical criticism. Nor should scientific study of the Bible be understood as superseding, and thus making obsolete, all earlier approaches. A brief history of biblical interpretation will reveal important insights that remain valid today.

The Old Testament constituted the Bible for Jesus and the early Christians. According to the Gospels, Jesus sometimes quoted or alluded to Old Testament texts in order to establish a theological point or to suggest a way of acting. He clearly accorded these texts a certain degree of authority. Nevertheless, Jesus emerges from the New Testament as displaying flexibility toward the Old Testament and even asserting his authority over it. He distinguishes what comes from God and what comes from Moses (see Mk 10:1–12), goes beyond certain scriptural teachings (Mt 5:21–48), and rates love of God and neighbor (Mk 12:28–31) over strict observance of the Sabbath.

New Testament writers such as Paul and Matthew looked upon the Old Testament Scriptures as fulfilled in Jesus Christ. Basing themselves on what apparently was a widespread early Christian understanding, they interpreted the Old Testament Scriptures in the light of the life, death, and resurrection of Jesus. Like other Jews of the time, they understood the Old Testament to be a mystery—that is, something that could not be understood without guidance or explanation. Whereas the Qumran community (the Jewish group that gave us the Dead Sea Scrolls) found the key to the Scriptures in their own sect's history and life, the early Christians discovered Jesus to be the key that opened up the mystery of the Hebrew Bible.

By the time of the Fathers of the Church (the patristic period), the Christian Bible contained two Testaments—Old and New. These Fathers, or early theologians, generally adopted one or the other of two basic approaches to the reading and interpretation of Scripture: the allegorical and the literal methods.

The allegorical method, favored particularly by those theologians who lived in Alexandria in Egypt, emphasized uncovering the spiritual truths beneath the surface of the biblical stories. This method had been developed by Greek thinkers who interpreted the stories in Homer's *Iliad* and *Odyssey* as symbolizing emotional or spiritual struggles within the individual. It had also been adopted by Jewish interpreters, like Philo of Alexandria, who used the method on the Hebrew Bible in order to appeal to non-Jews and especially to Jews who had come under the influence of Greek philosophy and culture. Christian theologians who used this method included Origen and Clement of Alexandria.

In contrast to this method was the more literal reading of the Bible, favored by those Christian thinkers who lived in Antioch, the capital of Syria in Roman times. The literal approach focused more on the historical realities described in Scripture and insisted that any higher or deeper sense should be based firmly on the literal sense of the text. John Chrysostom and Theodore of Mopsuestia were among those who favored this approach.

It is important to recognize that these different emphases were not completely opposed to each other. Thus, the allegorical method did not deny the historical truth of events in Scripture, nor did the literal method deny the spiritual meaning of those events. Later theologians tended to blend the two approaches, although favoring one tendency or the other. Augustine, for instance, tended toward the allegorical and Jerome toward the literal.

Medieval interpreters, building on both these approaches, distinguished four senses in a scriptural text: literal (what took place), allegorical (the hidden theological meaning), anagogical (the heavenly sense), and moral or tropological (the significance for the individual's behavior). The classic example was the term "Jerusalem" (see Gal 4:22–31), which can refer to a city in Palestine (literal), the Church (allegorical), the heavenly home of us all (anagogical), and the human soul (moral). Since this wide-ranging approach to Scripture could easily degenerate into subjectivity, careful interpreters like Thomas Aquinas insisted that "nothing necessary to faith is contained under the spiritual sense that is not elsewhere put forward by Scripture in its literal sense." Thomas Aquinas also used human reason as a tool in explaining the Scriptures and tried to bring together philosophical truth (especially as proposed by Aristotle) and biblical truth.

With the Renaissance and the rise of Humanism came a new interest in studying the Scriptures in their original languages and their historical settings. Erasmus produced a new edition of the Greek New Testament to go along with his revision of the Latin Vulgate translation. He also used the Greek and Roman classics of paganism along with the writings of the Church Fathers to interpret the biblical texts. Catholic enthusiasm for the study of the Scriptures cooled, however, in response to the claims for the Bible (*sola scriptura* or Scripture alone) made by Martin Luther and other Protestant Reformers, especially their statements about the clarity of Scripture (so that there is no need for the Church as the final interpreter) and its sufficiency (so that there is no need for Church tradition).

The rationalist claims of the European Enlightenment made matters even more complicated for Catholic interpreters of the Bible. For example, the philosopher Baruch Spinoza maintained that when Scripture and philosophy come into conflict (as in the case of miracles), then Scripture is to be rejected in favor of reason. Thus the Catholic Church was backed into being the defender of biblical "truth," sometimes with unfortunate consequences.

This survey reveals some abiding principles of Catholic biblical interpretation: the central significance of Christ, the struggle to be faithful to the literal meaning while searching for spiritual meaning, the conviction that faith and reason are not opposed, the insistence that the Bible should be interpreted in the Church, and the emphasis on biblical truth against the attacks of rationalism.

## Modern Developments

The gradual Catholic acceptance of scientific biblical criticism (or the historical-critical method), while remaining true to the Church's heritage, can be traced with reference to a series of official Roman documents issued during the late nineteenth and the twentieth century. For a full collection of official Roman Catholic documents pertaining to the study of the Bible, see Dean R. Bechard (ed.), *The Scripture Documents: An Anthology of Official Catholic Teachings* (Collegeville, MN: Liturgical Press, 2002).

A cautious beginning was made with the papal encyclical *Providentissimus Deus* by Pope Leo XIII in 1893, only to be blunted by fears of Modernism under Pius X and by Benedict XV's encyclical *Spiritus Paraclitus,* issued in 1920. A new age dawned with the encyclical entitled *Divino Afflante Spiritu,* which was promulgated by Pius XII in 1943, in which the historical study of the Bible was given official approbation. The approach outlined by Pius XII was put into practice by the Pontifical Biblical Commission in its 1964 *Instruction Concerning the Historical Truth of the Gospels.*

The culmination of official Catholic pronouncements on biblical studies was the Second Vatican Council's *Dogmatic Constitution on Divine Revelation*. The nature of these documents is cumulative; that is, the latest document generally restates the teachings contained in previous documents and clarifies matters not discussed earlier in detail. However, the document of an ecumenical council has far more official weight than a papal encyclical or an instruction from the Pontifical Biblical Commission. Moreover, the council's document on Scripture was a "dogmatic constitution," the most authoritative kind issued by Vatican II. Thus Vatican II's *Dogmatic Constitution on Divine Revelation* can be taken as the authoritative climax of a long series of developments in the Church's attitude toward the Bible.

Vatican II was a "pastoral" council. It sought to address the needs of the Church and the world in the twentieth century and beyond. Its constitution on divine revelation (also known by its Latin title, *Dei verbum*) was addressed not so much to scholars or theologians as to the Church at large. In effect, the bishops were saying, "This is what the Catholic Church thinks and believes about the Bible and related matters." The document had a rocky history from its first draft in 1962 to its final form in 1965. Pope John XXIII's rejection of the initial draft, which favored a propositional understanding of revelation (revelation consists of statements of abstract truths) and a theory of two sources of revelation (Scripture and tradition), set the Second Vatican Council on its path of *aggiornamento* (Italian for "bringing up to date"). (All quotations are from the translation by Liam Walsh and Wilfrid Harrington in Austin Flannery [ed.], *Vatican Council II: The Conciliar and Post-Conciliar Documents* [Northport, NY: Costello, 1975] 750–65.)

The six chapters in *Dei verbum* treat divine revelation itself, the transmission of divine revelation, sacred Scripture—its divine inspiration and its interpretation, the Old Testament, the New Testament, and sacred Scripture in the life of the Church. What the constitution teaches on these topics will be taken up in the remaining parts of this essay. Here only what it teaches about scientific biblical criticism will concern us.

The conciliar statement about biblical criticism appears in paragraph 12, which is part of the chapter on the inspiration and interpretation of Scripture. It is prefaced by an acknowledgment that since God speaks in Scripture through human beings, and so in human fashion, interpreters should give careful attention to the ways in which the sacred writers thought and expressed themselves:

> In determining the intention of the sacred writers, attention must be paid, *inter alia,* to literary forms for the fact is that truth is differently presented and expressed in the various types of historical writing, in prophetical and poetical texts, and in other forms of literary expression. Hence the exegete must look for that meaning which the sacred writer, in a determined situation and given the circumstances of his time and culture, intended to express and did in fact express, through the medium of a contemporary literary form. Rightly to understand what the sacred author wanted to affirm in his work, due attention must be paid both to the customary and characteristic patterns of perception, speech and narrative which prevailed at the age of the sacred writer, and to the conventions which the people of his time followed in their dealings with one another.

The statement, which is really a condensation of Pius XII's 1943 encyclical *Divine Afflante Spiritu,* makes three points. First, it insists that we take into account the various literary forms in which the Bible is written, and it warns us against confusing historical, prophetic, and poetic texts. Next, it urges us to pay attention to the historical setting in which the sacred author wrote, suggesting that such historical awareness is necessary for grasping what the author intended. Finally, it recommends that we learn about the literary conventions and cultural assumptions that people accepted at the time when the biblical books were composed. Thus the conciliar document encourages the literary, historical, and sociological study of biblical texts.

The acceptance of biblical criticism, of course, does not reduce the Sacred Scriptures to the status of other, strictly human books. In fact, the very next sentence in the document affirms the divine authorship of the biblical texts and urges biblical interpreters to take that into consideration:

> But since sacred Scripture must be read and interpreted with its divine authorship in mind, no less attention must be devoted to the content and unity of the whole of Scripture, taking into account the Tradition of the entire Church and the analogy of faith, if we are to derive their true meaning from the sacred texts.

In this way the conciliar document achieves a balance between the human and the divine contributions to Scripture. Interpreters are thereby encouraged to apply all the tools of biblical criticism, while bearing in mind the Church's longstanding conviction that the Bible contains "the Word of God in the words of men."

In 1993, to mark the 100th anniversary of *Providentissimus Deus* and the 50th anniversary of *Divino Afflante Spiritu,* the Pontifical Biblical Commission, with the full approval of Pope John Paul II, issued a document entitled "The Interpretation of the Bible in the Church." Prepared by an international team of distinguished Catholic biblical scholars, this document describes various methods of and approaches to biblical interpretation, examines certain questions of a hermeneutical nature, reflects on the characteristic features of a Catholic interpretation of the Bible, and considers the place that biblical interpretation has in the life of the Church. This document spells out in some detail many of the directions recommended in the papal encyclicals and in Vatican II's *Dei verbum*.

The Pontifical Biblical Commission's document describes the historical-critical method as "the indispensable method for the scientific study of the meaning of ancient texts." While giving attention to the many possible contributions from certain "new" literary and social-scientific approaches, it criticizes fundamentalism as "dangerous" and even as inviting people to "a kind of intellectual suicide." And it insists on the pastoral significance of the whole exegetical enterprise when it states: "Exegesis produces its best results when it is carried out in the context of the living faith of the Christian community, which is directed toward the salvation of the entire world."

**Methods of Biblical Interpretation**

The term *biblical criticism* refers to various methods of scientific biblical study that have as their goal establishing the text, understanding the content and the literary style of biblical books, and determining their origin and authenticity. This undertaking is sometimes called the historical-critical method—historical because it focuses on the original historical settings of the biblical texts and the historical processes that gave rise to them, and critical because it applies reason to the texts and makes judgments about them in the effort to be as objective as possible. Biblical criticism aims to understand what a text was saying to its original audience and to make clear its significance then (and now).

*Textual criticism* (sometimes called lower criticism) seeks to establish the wording of the biblical text as the biblical authors wrote it. Since we no longer have direct access to the manuscripts written by the biblical authors (autographs), textual critics try to come as close as possible to the original form of the texts by gathering all the pertinent manuscript evidence (Hebrew and Aramaic for the Old Testament, Greek for the New Testament, ancient translations for both Testaments). When the evidence has been assembled, textual critics determine where the ancient manuscripts differ and proceed to decide which reading is original and to explain how the other readings arose. The rejected readings may have been unconscious mistakes (for example, confusing similar letters of the alphabet, omitting words or phrases, inserting marginal comments into the main text) or deliberate modifications (for example, harmonizing with parallel texts, "correcting" grammar or style, removing "offensive" material). The accepted readings should be consistent with the content and style of the document and follow the rules of grammar and good sense.

*Literary criticism* attends to the words and images, the characters and their relationships, the structure and progress of thought, the literary form, and the meaning. These processes are used today in studying all kinds of literature; they are by no means confined to biblical study. Bible concordances, dictionaries, and encyclopedias make it possible to trace the development of a word (for example, faith) or a theme (for example, covenant) and to locate a particular occurrence within such a framework. Careful inspection of a text enables one to chart out the interactions among the characters or to outline the progress of the argument. The biblical writers used many different literary forms. The Old Testament consists of law codes, narratives, psalms, prophecies, proverbs, visions, and even love poetry. The New Testament contains stories of Jesus' words and deeds (Gospels), the actions of some apostles (Acts), letters (Epistles), and visions (Revelation). Rather than stating theological truths in the form of theses or propositions, the biblical authors conveyed their message in artistic and memorable ways. Literary criticism helps us to read the biblical books on their own terms and thus to appreciate their artistry and their truth.

*Historical criticism* concerns the world behind the biblical texts; that is, the origin and growth of the biblical documents. Scholars assume that sometimes a complicated process of composition lies behind a finished book of the Bible. Smaller literary units—for example, a saying from Jesus, or a hymn—were told and retold, or used orally in worship. Later, perhaps, a collection of sayings or hymns was made. Still later, a writer created a longer narrative into which various sayings were fitted, or which quoted a hymn in order to make a point. At each stage, the original small unit was being used in a slightly different context, and it may have been changed in small ways in order to fit its new use better.

Scholars have various names for this sort of investigation of a biblical text, depending on what level they are examining. *Source criticism* attempts to establish where previously existing material (for example, a hymn, a saying, or a vision account) has been used by a later author in a longer work, either by accepting what is stated in the work itself or by noticing differences in content, vocabulary, and literary style. *Form criticism* seeks to classify literary genres or forms, and to isolate the historical settings in which the forms developed and functioned before they became part of the main text. A sermon, for instance, will have characteristics that are different from those of a letter or a story. *Redaction criticism* deals with the ways in which a biblical author or editor (redactor means editor) used sources, and sometimes changed them, to address problems and concerns facing his readers. So biblical criticism takes account of historical settings at three levels: the sources, the small units, and the finished document.

*Archaeological excavations and textual discoveries* such as the Ugaritic texts and the Dead Sea Scrolls can shed light on the material world and culture in which the biblical books were written. For example, ancient epics outside the Bible have helped us to appreciate the creation stories in the book of Genesis. And the Dead Sea Scrolls, besides providing the earliest extant manuscripts of the Hebrew Bible, have illumined the thought and organization of the early Church.

The interpretive process can also be enriched by the application of concepts and methods used in the *social sciences* such as sociology, cultural anthropology, and psychology. These approaches help in exposing the cultural assumptions about the human condition and the world that people in biblical times took for granted, and in explaining the development of ancient Israel into a nation and the early Christian communities into what we call the Church.

*Historical criticism* is sometimes defined narrowly to refer to the reality of the event behind the text, to determining what actually occurred at (for example) the first Passover or the first Easter. What really happened in detail is sometimes hard to discern, since the biblical authors were often more interested in the meaning of the events than in their precise details. Some historical critics (in the narrow sense) rule out the miraculous and divine intervention on philosophical grounds and make negative judgments about the communities that handed on the biblical texts. But this is not true of all historical critics, nor is it at all consistent with the Catholic approach to Scripture, which assumes that the biblical texts tell the "honest truth" about the events described in the texts.

While the classic historical-critical method is oriented mainly to illuminating the history of the text and the world behind the text, certain "new" methods of literary analysis focus more on the text as it now stands (the world of the text) and on its effects on the reader today (the world before or in front of the text). *Rhetorical analysis* explores the capacity of a biblical text to persuade and convince the reader, while *narrative analysis* investigates how a text works in the sense of its success in telling a story involving plot, characters, and point of view. *Structuralist analysis* and *semiotic analysis* are modern linguistic methods that examine the various temporal and spatial relationships in a text, with an eye toward revealing the deeper patterns of meaning underlying the text.

Another set of approaches to biblical interpretation privileges the interpreter and the social location of the interpreter. *Liberation theology* takes as its starting point the lived experience of poor people today and enters into conversation with biblical texts (e.g., Israel's Exodus from Egypt, or Mary's Magnificat in Lk 1:46–55) as a way of illumining both the biblical text and the present situation of the poor. *Feminist interpretation* calls attention to the prominence of certain women in the Bible, exposes the patriarchal or male-centered assumptions of the cultures in which the Bible was originally produced, and challenges interpreters to recognize the liberating contributions of women to the biblical story of salvation.

Other reader-oriented resources in biblical interpretation include the *history of interpretation* (how a text has been understood by Jewish and Christian readers throughout the centuries) and the *history of effects* (the impact or influence that a text has exercised in the course of history). Canonical criticism focuses on the final canonical form of a biblical text, explores its place within the biblical canon as a whole, and considers its significance for the Church's faith and way of life. *Hermeneutics* is concerned with discerning the present significance of a biblical text. While this is what preachers have always done, the hermeneutical phase of the interpretive task is open to and incumbent upon all Bible readers. It involves the fusion of horizons between the ancient text and the reader in the present and envisions a process by which the reader is changed intellectually and spiritually by encounter with the biblical text.

Two terms that have recently become prominent with regard to Catholic biblical interpretation and its practical impact in church life are *actualization* and *inculturation*. The Christian Scriptures are ancient texts, and so they need to be presented in ways in which they can speak to peoples of different times (actualization) and places or cultures (inculturation). The Scriptures are made "actual" whenever their spiritual insights are presented in such a way that they can address the problems and possibilities of the present day. Likewise, the Scriptures are "inculturated" whenever they are translated, interpreted, and applied in terms that peoples from outside the ancient Mediterranean world can understand and so live out their challenges and opportunities.

One traditional way of bringing together all these different methods in a simple and coherent framework is through the traditional Catholic approach developed in monastic circles and known as *lectio divina* (divine [or, spiritual] reading). There are four steps. The first step is *lectio* (reading); that is, a careful reading of the text from various critical perspectives (literary, historical, and theological) and the assimilation or appropriation of the text on both intellectual and emotional levels. The second step is *meditatio,* which explores what this text may be saying to me (or us) now. One can open up the text by focusing on a theme or a few phrases, by applying the senses (sight, hearing, smell, taste, touch) to the biblical scene, and by trying to make connections between the text and one's present situation. The third step is *oratio* (prayer) in which on the basis of reading and meditating one may speak words of praise, petition, adoration, and/or thanksgiving to God. The fourth step may take the form of *contemplatio* (relishing the religious experience generated by the encounter with the text and resting in the mystery of God) and/or *actio* (coming to a decision about one's life, or finding new ways to express what one has learned—through dance, drama, artwork, group sharing, homily, etc.).

### Scripture as Tradition

The official Catholic emphasis on attention to the literary forms, historical settings, and cultural assumptions of the biblical writings flows from the nature of the books themselves. Far from being individual creations generated in solitude, the biblical books include many ideas, traditions, and even small pieces that already existed before being integrated into the texts in which they now stand. Biblical literature is thoroughly and deliberately traditional.

The traditional character of the Old Testament has long been acknowledged. The first five books, which are customarily called the Pentateuch or Torah, are generally recognized to incorporate material from at least four different sources (Yahwist, Elohist, Deuteronomist, Priestly). See "Introduction to the Pentateuch," pp. 7–9. The historical books (Joshua to 2 Kings, Chronicles, Ezra, and Nehemiah) include earlier accounts, memoirs, genealogies, and so forth. The prophetic books are anthologies of short pieces of poetry and prose, and the wisdom books contain ideas and even sayings that circulated in the ancient Near East for centuries before. The Psalms are a collection of varied kinds of songs used mainly in the Jerusalem Temple; in the Psalms there may even be remnants of non-Jewish hymns (see Psalm 29). So complicated and so rich is the process of transmission that it is difficult in most cases to speak of *the* author of a biblical book as one may speak of an author today. The situation is further complicated by the fact that in biblical times personal creativity and originality were not important values. One displayed real creativity by using traditional ideas and expressions in new settings and in new combinations.

Given the nature of the Old Testament and the ancient concept of creativity, one would expect the New Testament to be thoroughly traditional also. And it is. The earliest complete documents in the New Testament are Paul's letters. Even these highly "original" and occasional pieces rely at key points on preexisting material (for example, Rom 1:3–4; 1 Cor 13:1–13; 15:3–5; Phil 2:6–11). Those epistles whose direct Pauline composition is doubtful (for example, the Pastorals, Ephesians, Colossians, 2 Thessalonians) are best understood as later attempts to bring the figure and teaching of Paul to bear on situations facing the churches in the late first century. We often regard Paul as a creative genius. However, not only did he use some traditional material, but also almost all his undisputed letters contain some indication of joint authorship (see 1 Thess 1:1; 1 Cor 1:1; Rom 16:22; etc.). Moreover, throughout his letters Paul gives credit to his "co-workers" and encourages the collection for the Jerusalem community as a sign of solidarity with the "mother church" there.

The complicated process of tradition and composition applies to the Gospels too. Most scholars today place the final composition of the four canonical Gospels in the late first century: Mark around A.D. 70, Matthew and Luke around A.D. 80–90, and John around A.D. 90–100. Yet all scholars acknowledge that the evangelists used already-existing material in their Gospels. For example, Matthew and Luke each seem to have read both Mark's Gospel and a collection of Jesus' sayings that modern scholars call "Q" (from the German word *Quelle,* which means "source"). John utilized a collection of miracle stories (signs) and perhaps also some "revelation discourses." The Markan and Johannine passion narratives surely contain much traditional information, accounts that had been passed from one person to another.

The Gospels and the traditions incorporated in them tell the story of Jesus of Nazareth, who was crucified around A.D. 30. Like other Jewish teachers of his time, Jesus taught by word (parables, proverbs, debates, other sayings) and deed (example, healings, symbolic gestures). His disciples remembered and retold his words and deeds, thus providing the basic materials for what became the Gospel tradition. Jesus did not write books. What we know of Jesus comes to us through the process of tradition from Jesus to the early Church and finally to the evangelists.

The nature of the Gospels demands that interpreters attend to three stages in their development. The *Dogmatic Constitution on Divine Revelation* (*Dei verbum* 19) captures that development in this marvelously concise statement:

> The sacred authors, in writing the four Gospels, selected certain of the many elements which had been handed on, either orally or already in written form, others they synthesized or explained with an eye to the situation of the churches, the while sustaining the form of preaching, but always in such a fashion that they have told us the honest truth about Jesus.

The council's document affirms that the Gospels tell us the "honest truth" about Jesus. It recognizes that there was an intermediary stage in which traditions about Jesus circulated in oral and written forms as "preaching" about the significance of Jesus. It acknowledges that the evangelists give us only a selection (see Lk 1:1–4; Jn 20:30–31; 21:25) of the traditions about Jesus. It also recognizes that the evangelists used the traditions about Jesus to address the situations of their own day. Therefore, Catholics must read the Gospels as traditional documents (because they are such) and attend to three stages in their development: Jesus, the early Church, and the evangelists.

Although in the past there has been some Catholic resistance to accepting the "traditional" character of the biblical books, this emphasis is perfectly compatible with the principles of Catholicism. There is no obligation for Catholics to be conservative historians of early Christianity (nor is there any obligation for them to be reckless or indifferent). As long as Catholic scholars make clear the link from Jesus through the early Church to the evangelists, they remain faithful to their theological heritage.

In fact, an emphasis on the traditional nature of the biblical writings is fully consistent with certain distinctively Catholic principles. The Catholic stress on the communal character of our way to God and God's way to us sensitizes Catholics to the complexity of early Christian tradition and to the role of the Church in shaping it and being formed by it. The Catholic emphasis that encounter with God is rooted in history and is a mediated experience helps us to see the continuity between Jesus and the early reflections on him, as well as the significance and correctness of those reflections. The Catholic sacramental approach, which sees God in and through all things, leads us to view the very human process of tradition as a vehicle for expressing, safeguarding, and adapting divine revelation.

### Scripture and Tradition

The Catholic Church does not restrict divine revelation to the biblical text. Against the Protestant Reformation's slogan of "Scripture alone," Catholic theologians insisted on "Scripture and tradition." The term "tradition" recognizes the fact that the living reality of the Church has the task of preserving the gospel as well as interpreting and applying it in new situations. Catholic Christianity is not simply a "religion of the Book."

While acknowledging the twofold reality of Scripture and tradition, Catholic theologians have long debated the precise relation between the two. One way of approaching the problem was to assume that Scripture and tradition constitute two separate sources of divine revelation. The Second Vatican Council rejected this view in the second chapter of its *Dogmatic Constitution on Divine Revelation* (*Dei verbum* 10): "Sacred Tradition and sacred Scripture make up a single sacred deposit of the Word of God, which is entrusted to the Church." In other words, the Word of God (or divine revelation) is the source of both tradition and Scripture.

How exactly Scripture and tradition are related remains a problem. The conciliar document uses the analogy of a wellspring or fountain to insist on their unity while preserving their diversity in *Dei verbum* 9:

> Sacred Tradition and sacred Scripture then, are bound closely together, and communicate one with the other. For both of them, flowing out from the same divine well-spring, come together in some fashion to form one thing, and move towards the same goal. Sacred Scripture is the speech of God as it is put down in writing under the breath of the Holy Spirit. And Tradition transmits in its entirety the Word of God which has been entrusted to the apostles by Christ the Lord and the Holy Spirit.

The same paragraph rejects the "Scripture alone" principle of the Reformation and preserves the Catholic approach of "Scripture and tradition" by insisting that the Church does not draw certainty about all revealed truths from the holy Scriptures alone. Hence, both Scripture and tradition must be accepted and honored with equal feelings of devotion and reverence. Thus the Second Vatican Council insisted that Scripture and tradition flow from the same divine wellspring and that both must be accepted and honored. Without endorsing any one theological approach to their relation, the council rejected the opinion of those who wished to keep the two separate.

The same tension appears when the *Dogmatic Constitution* addresses the issue of authoritative interpretation of the Scriptures in *Dei verbum* 10:

> . . . the task of giving an authentic interpretation of the Word of God, whether in its written form or in the form of Tradition, has been entrusted to the living teaching office of the Church alone. Its authority in this matter is exercised in the name of Jesus Christ. Yet this Magisterium is not superior to the Word of God, but is its servant. It teaches only what has been handed on to it. At the divine command and with the help of the Holy Spirit, it listens to this devotedly, guards it with dedication and expounds it faithfully. All that it proposes for belief as being divinely revealed is drawn from this single deposit of faith.

On the one hand, this statement entrusts authentic interpretation to the magisterium (the bishops with the pope). On the other hand, it insists that the magisterium is the servant of divine revelation and can only teach what is drawn from the single deposit of faith constituted by divine revelation.

The precise relation between Scripture and tradition also remains a problem. As a "pastoral" council, Vatican II avoided becoming an arbiter of theological disputes. Its insistence on the oneness of Scripture and tradition, however, did have a pastoral dimension. While not conceding to the "Scripture alone" position, it insisted that the Bible take again its rightful place in the center of Catholic life and that appeals to tradition be judged according to their consistency with Scripture.

### The Nature of the Bible

What is this book that it should be studied so intensely and guarded so carefully? The

*Dogmatic Constitution on Divine Revelation* made a theological formula that had become prominent before Vatican II: "the words of God, expressed in the words of men" (*Dei verbum* 13). That formula derives from the classical theological definitions of the divine and human natures in the person of Jesus Christ. In speaking about the Bible in this way, the Second Vatican Council sought to hold together the transcendent nature of Scripture and its human form. Although the Bible may look like other books and may be studied profitably as other books are studied (that is, with the techniques of biblical criticism), the Bible is different with regard to its origin and its nature. The "different" character of the Bible is expressed by means of some rather complicated terms: revelation, inspiration, inerrancy, and canon. As with "Scripture and tradition," the Second Vatican Council used these terms without adjudicating the theological disputes surrounding them. As a pastoral council it sought to express the significance of the words for the way in which the Bible is read within the Church.

Revelation is fundamentally God's self-revelation; it is the communication of the mystery of God to the world: "It pleased God, in his goodness and wisdom, to reveal himself and to make known the mystery of his will" (*Dei verbum* 2). The Christian theological tradition affirms that God's self-revelation comes to us through creation, history, persons, society, and reason. It is also customary to refer to the Bible as a privileged revealer of God—that is, a place where the divine revelation is particularly clear. This tradition appears prominently in *Dei verbum* 6:

> By divine Revelation God wished to manifest and communicate both himself and the eternal decrees of his will concerning the salvation of mankind.

The order adopted in this statement ("both himself and the eternal decrees") is significant, for it gives pride of place to the "personal" character of divine revelation without denying the content and the consequences. Although this point may seem obvious today, the council's emphasis on the personal dimension of revelation was correctly taken as a major step in clarifying Catholic attitudes toward Scripture. Through the Bible we encounter the mystery of God, not simply lists of commandments or interesting stories. The personal God makes those commandments and stories meaningful.

Two other theological terms for talking about the difference of the Bible from other books are "inspiration" and "inerrancy." Again the *Dogmatic Constitution on Divine Revelation* asserts the basic point expressed by these terms without arbitrating the very complicated theological debates surrounding them. On inspiration *Dei verbum* 11 states:

> The divinely revealed realities which are contained and presented in the text of sacred Scripture have been written down under the inspiration of the Holy Spirit. For Holy Mother Church relying on the faith of the apostolic age, accepts as sacred and canonical the books of the Old and the New Testaments, whole and entire, with all their parts, on the grounds that, written under the inspiration of the Holy Spirit (cf. Jn 20:31; 2 Tm 3:16; 2 Pt 1:19–21; 3:15–16), they have God as their author, and have been handed on as such to the Church herself. To compose the sacred books, God chose certain men who, all the while he employed them in this task, made full use of their powers and faculties so that, though he acted in them and by them, it was as true authors that they consigned to writing whatever he wanted written, and no more.

The same paragraph treats inerrancy:

> Since, therefore, all that the inspired authors, or sacred writers, affirm should be regarded as affirmed by the Holy Spirit, we must acknowledge that the books of Scripture firmly, faithfully and without error teach that truth which God, for the sake of our salvation, wished to see confided to the sacred Scriptures. Thus "all Scripture is inspired by God, and profitable for teaching, for reproof, for correction and for training in righteousness, so that the man of God may be complete, equipped for every good work" (2 Tm 3:16–17, Gk. text).

The key expression in this statement is "that truth which God, for the sake of our salvation, wished to see confided to the sacred Scriptures." Without explicitly embracing the theory of only limited inerrancy, that statement suggests that the Bible's inerrancy consists primarily in its being a trustworthy guide on the road to salvation. Thus it expresses "inerrancy" in a positive way, and avoids conceiving it as a defensive program of protecting the Bible against accusations of scientific or historical error.

The council's statement on inspiration refers to the books of the Bible as "sacred and canonical." The word "canon" (whose root meaning is "reed" or "measuring stick") originally meant the rule or characteristics that decided whether a particular book was judged to be part of Sacred Scripture. It now usually refers to the collection of books that are acknowledged to be authoritative in the Church and by which the Church's faith can be measured. The canon of Old Testament books traditional in Catholicism contains all the books of the Hebrew Bible (which is the same as the Protestant Old Testament canon) together with seven others that were part of the Greek and Latin Bible tradition (Judith, Tobit, Baruch, 1 and 2 Maccabees, Sirach/Ecclesiasticus, Wisdom). All Christians today share the same canon of 27 New Testament books. The history of the canon's development is quite complex. The final definitive list of biblical books (including the seven additional Old Testament books) for the Catholic Church was drawn up only at the Council of Trent in 1546, although there was little disagreement about the substance of the canon from the early centuries of the Christian era.

The Bible is different. How it is different has been expressed with the help of some traditional words: revelation, inspiration, inerrancy, and canon. The Second Vatican Council in its authoritative declaration on Scripture (*Dei verbum*) took over those hallowed terms. In interpreting the council's use of these words we must take account of the pastoral orientation of the council as a whole. Rather than working out theological subtleties or choosing among theological schools, the *Dogmatic Constitution on Divine Revelation* used those words to convey basic attitudes about how the Bible differs from other books. It affirmed that God's self-revelation comes to us through the Bible, that in some mysterious way God entered into the composition of these writings and inspired them, that the biblical books provide reliable guidance (inerrancy) for those who walk the way toward salvation with God, and that these books constitute the norm or rule (canon) by which the life of the Church is to be guided and measured in all ages. These are the basic "pastoral" meanings of revelation, inspiration, inerrancy, and canon.

### The Authority of the Bible

The terms by which Christians express the "difference" of the Bible indicate that it possesses great authority for them. The Bible is the "words of God, expressed in the words of men." It is revealed, inspired, inerrant, and canonical. The *Dogmatic Constitution on Divine Revelation* goes beyond the general assertions conveyed by the traditional theological vocabulary and speaks about the authority of various parts of the Bible.

The Old Testament (see *Dei verbum* 15) prepares for and declares in prophecy the coming of Christ. It conveys our basic understanding of God and the human situation: "how a just and merciful God deals with mankind." It provides "sound wisdom" and "a wonderful treasury of prayers." The document also mentions "matters imperfect and provisional" in the Old Testament, without specifying precisely what these are (presumably legislation about sacrifices and ritual purity, "vengeful" psalms, and other such material). The unity of the two Testaments is traced back to God who "in his wisdom has so brought it about that the New should be hidden in the Old and that the Old should be made manifest in the New" (*Dei verbum* 16).

The council accorded the Gospels a special place within the Bible "because they are our principal source for the life and teaching of the Incarnate Word, our Saviour" (*Dei verbum* 18). It insisted on the historicity and apostolicity of the Gospels, while recognizing the complex process of their composition from Jesus through the early Church to the Gospel texts. Catholics find a basic continuity between Jesus and the Gospel tradition under the guidance of the Spirit working in the Church. Their tendency is to insist that the tradition is basically historical. They assume that the modifications and reinterpretations made necessary by changing circumstances do not do violence to the original teaching or event. The "apostolic" character of the Gospels refers not so much to their direct composition by apostles as it does to the faithful transmission of the material in them by those who had experienced the risen Lord and bore witness to his resurrection. The term "apostolic" describes the generation between Jesus' death (about A.D. 30) and the composition of the New Testament books. The claim implied by the term is that those witnesses have told us the "honest truth" about Jesus.

The New Testament also contains Paul's letters and other writings (Hebrews, the catholic epistles, Revelation). After affirming their composition under the inspiration of the Holy Spirit, *Dei verbum* 20 describes the contributions that these writings make in the following way:

> In accordance with the wise design of God these writings firmly establish those matters which concern Christ the Lord, formulate more and more precisely his authentic teaching, preach the saving power of Christ's divine work and foretell its glorious consummation.

It would be a mistake, however, to conclude from this description that the epistles have a secondary status as supplements to the Gospels. In fact, Paul's authentic letters (1 Thessalonians, Galatians, 1 and 2 Corinthians, Philippians, Philemon, Romans) are the earliest complete documents in the New Testament from the standpoint of their dates of composition. Thus they give us precious information about how Paul and other early Christians in the fifties of the first century A.D. (some 25 years after the death of Jesus) understood the significance of Jesus' life, death, and resurrection. They show us how early Christians struggled to articulate their new faith in an environment that was often hostile and foreign to them. They reveal the kinds of problems that early Christians faced within their own communities (see especially 1 Corinthians) and so warn us against too easily viewing the apostolic period as a trouble-free and conflictless "golden age."

Enough has been said about the Bible in general (revelation, inspiration, inerrancy, and canon) and about its major parts (Old Testament, Gospels, Epistles) to indicate that it possesses great authority. But what kind of authority does the Bible have? It is surely not the coercive authority of a parent or the state or the police, which have the power to enforce a law or decision and to punish the uncooperative. It is not even the persuasive authority of the lawyer or the mathematician who convinces another by logic, arguments, proofs, and so forth. At some points in his epistles (for example, in 1 Corinthians 15) Paul does labor to make a convincing case on the basis of logic. But that is not his usual mode of presentation, nor is it the customary idiom of other biblical writers.

The authority that the Bible possesses can perhaps be best described as compelling. Compelling authority is the authority of the witness, the expert, the participant. Much of the Bible concerns what God's people say about God's action on their behalf. Without narrowing the testimony of the Bible to the concept of an eyewitness, it is possible to describe the Scriptures as a collection of testimonies to God. The biblical descriptions of creation, exodus, monarchy, exile, and return from exile all stress God's relatedness to Israel and Israel's responses of praise, confession, thanksgiving, and so forth. The New Testament writers portray Jesus as the revelation of God's power (and weakness). The proper response is faith, hope, and love. Thus the biblical documents contain the proclamation and articulation of people's faith about God and God's ways with creation.

God is the real basis of the Bible's authority. Insofar as the biblical books bear witness to God and thus enable us to understand better who God is and how God acts, and to grow in love for and trust in the God of the Scriptures, the Bible can be aptly called the "Word of God." And so Vatican II's *Dogmatic Constitution on Divine Revelation,* which so emphasizes God's self-communication, is appropriately titled from its initial two words *Dei verbum* (Latin for "Word of God").

### Scripture in Church Life

This essay began with a comparison regarding the Bible's place in church life of the 1950s and today. A look at Catholic liturgy, education, piety, and theology led to the conclusion that the Catholic Church today is far more "biblical" than it was in the 1950s. This development mirrors some powerful statements made in the final chapter of Vatican II's *Dogmatic Constitution on Divine Revelation.*

The centrality of Scripture in Catholic liturgy involves both preaching and sacramental practice. *Dei verbum* 21 insists that "all the preaching of the Church, as indeed the entire Christian religion, should be nourished and ruled by sacred Scripture." The same paragraph directly confronts and dissolves the opposition between word and sacrament that had been prominent since the Protestant Reformation. It does so with reference to the celebration of the Eucharist:

> The Church has always venerated the divine Scriptures as she venerated the Body of the Lord, in so far as she never ceases, particularly in the sacred liturgy, to partake of the bread of life and to offer it to the faithful from the one table of the Word of God and the Body of Christ.

The council document insists that Word and sacrament belong together in the Eucharist, to the point of asserting that they form "one table."

The popularity of Scripture in Catholic education and piety responds to a very strong statement in *Dei verbum* 22: "Access to sacred Scripture ought to be wide open to the Christian faithful." The document goes on to urge the production of modern-language translations made from the ancient biblical texts. It also encourages biblical exegetes to examine and explain the sacred texts so that preachers, teachers, and catechists "may be able to distribute fruitfully the nourishment of the Scriptures to the People of God" (*Dei verbum* 23).

The importance of Scripture for Catholic theology is stated in no uncertain terms: "The 'study of the sacred page' should be the very soul of sacred theology" (*Dei verbum* 24). The document mandates that all those officially engaged in the ministry of the Word should "immerse themselves in the Scriptures by constant sacred reading and diligent study" (*Dei verbum* 25). The same paragraph recommends the preparation of volumes such as the present one: "translations of the sacred texts which are equipped with necessary and really adequate explanations." There is overwhelming evidence that in response to the Second Vatican Council the Catholic Church has become much more "biblical." One of its most important documents was the *Dogmatic Constitution on Divine Revelation,* which has served as our principal guide in this article. At nearly every point the post-Vatican II Church has fulfilled the mandates of that council document and thus become more biblical.

The challenge facing the Catholic Church today is to look upon *Dei verbum* not only as the end of a long development (which it was) but also as the beginning of a process that has taken us into the twenty-first century and beyond. A still more biblical Church will paradoxically be better able to adjust to the rapid changes that the new millennium is already bringing upon us. A still more biblical Church will be better prepared to make common cause with other Christians, with Jews and Muslims, and with all truly religious people. A still more biblical Church will preserve its spiritual heritage and open its riches to others. An obvious step in the process toward a more biblical Church is an increase in knowledge and love of the Scriptures.

### Bibliography


Bechard, Dean R. (ed.). *The Scripture Documents: An Anthology of Official Catholic Teachings.* Collegeville, MN: Liturgical Press, 2002.

Brown, Raymond E. *Biblical Exegesis and Church Doctrine*. New York/Mahwah, NJ: Paulist, 1985.

———. *Responses to 101 Questions on the Bible*. New York/Mahwah, NJ: Paulist, 1990.

Brown, Raymond E., Joseph A. Fitzmyer, and Roland E. Murphy (eds.). *The New Jerome Biblical Commentary*. Englewood Cliffs, NJ: Prentice-Hall, 1990.

Fitzmyer, Joseph A. The Biblical Commission's Document "The Interpretation of the Bible in the Church": Text and Commentary. Rome: Editrice Pontificio Istituto Biblico, 1995.

———. *Scripture, the Soul of Theology*. New York/Mahwah, NJ: Paulist, 1994.

Hagen, Kenneth, et al. *The Bible in the Churches: How Various Christians Interpret the Scriptures*. 3rd ed. Milwaukee, WI: Marquette University Press, 1998.

Harrington, Daniel J. *Interpreting the New Testament*, rev. ed. Collegeville, MN: Liturgical Press, 1988.

———. *Interpreting the Old Testament*. Collegeville, MN: Liturgical Press, 1981.

Lienhard, Joseph T. *The Bible, the Church, and Authority*. Collegeville, MN: Liturgical Press, 1995.

Schneiders, Sandra M. *The Revelatory Text. Interpreting the New Testament as Sacred Scripture*, rev. ed. Collegeville, MN: Liturgical Press, 1999.

Williamson, Peter S. *Catholic Principles for Interpreting Scripture: A Study of the Pontifical Biblical Commission's* The Interpretation of the Bible in the Church. Rome: Editrice Pontificio Istituto Biblico, 2001.

# CATHOLICS AND FUNDAMENTALISM

In the years prior to the Second Vatican Council one often heard the difference between Protestants and Catholics described this way: "Protestants have the Bible and Catholics have the Sacraments." As with all such humorous generalizations, it contained a grain of truth. Catholics generally opened their Bibles only to record family milestones: baptisms, marriages, and deaths. In the renewal that the Church leaders brought about at Vatican Council II, one significant change was the direct encouragement of Catholics to rediscover the Bible. Among the strong statements in this regard is that the Scriptures are food for the soul *(Dei Verbum* 21) and that access to the scriptures ought to be open wide for the Christian faithful (*Dei Verbum* 22) since ignorance of the scriptures is ignorance of Christ (*Dei Verbum* 25). With this opening of the windows to the Scriptures and opening our eyes to the treasures of our faith therein, Catholics' relationship to the Scriptures has changed dramatically. In parishes all over the world there are Bible study groups; in living rooms and classrooms Catholics are unlocking these treasures and enriching their understanding and often changing how they live their faith. At the same time that the council sent us to our Bibles, it updated the source and summit of our faith, the liturgy, so that the Scriptures are now presented in an organized and more complete manner. Now, Catholics hear a wide variety of readings from both the Old Testament and the New Testament at Mass over the three-year liturgical cycle.

Since most Catholics have little experience and background in Bible study, responsible church leaders do well when they lead us in a Scripture learning process that is in tune with our Catholic tradition rather than one from a fundamentalist Protestant perspective. Many Catholics, who have no access to Scripture study groups in their own church, join such Bible study groups in other churches, many of whom have a fundamentalist rather than a Catholic perspective. While all who value the Bible share some beliefs, there are differences between Catholics and fundamentalists about some serious and basic views of scripture, about its interpretation and about how we use it for our lives. It is important to note that there are also vast differences between mainstream Protestants and many evangelical Protestants, on the one hand, and fundamentalist Protestants, on the other. It is the fundamentalist perspective that Catholics are cautioned about. It is also important to note that Catholic biblical scholarship has been indebted to the work of (non-fundamentalist) Protestant scholars over the years.

Both the Pontifical Biblical Commission and Pope Benedict VI, when he was head of the Vatican department that oversaw the Doctrine of the Faith, explained the Church's views:

> The fundamentalist approach is dangerous, for it is attractive to people who look to the Bible for ready answers to the problems of life. It can deceive these people, offering them interpretations that are pious but illusory, instead of telling them that the Bible does not contain an immediate answer to each and every problem. Without saying as much in so many words, fundamentalism actually invites people to an intellectual suicide. It injects into life a false certitude, for it unwittingly confuses the divine substance of the

Bible message with what are in fact its human limitations. (The Interpretation of the Bible in the Church [Rome: Pontifical Biblical Commission, 1993] # I.F.)

Fundamentalism is a danger. That is clear. It is absolutely incompatible with Catholic faith, because the Catholic faith supposes that I read the Bible in context of the community of faith and the community of all the centuries of faith. Thus I read the Bible with the Church and with the faith of all times. And I read it reasonably, in a reasonable manner. So we must strive to avoid fundamentalism. (Quoted in Richard John Neuhaus, Biblical Interpretation in Crisis [Grand Rapids, Mich.: Eerdmans, 1989] 140.)

| Fundamentalist Perspective on the Bible | Catholic Perspective on the Bible |
|---|---|
| The Bible is the Word of God | The Bible is God's Word in human words |
| Scripture *alone* | Scripture *and* Tradition |
| Emphasis on literalist reading of Bible | Emphasis on literal (not literalist) reading as well as deeper (and spiritual) meanings |
| Tendency to view inspiration narrowly | Tendency to take a broad view of inspiration |
| Inerrancy of the Bible in all matters | No errors in the Bible only on matters of faith and morals |
| Lack of historical perspective in interpretation | Historical perspective is essential for interpretation |
| Frequent interpretations out of context | Necessity of the interpretations in context, especially the context of the sacred canon |
| Direct and immediate applicability of most Biblical passages | Mostly indirect applicability of biblical passages |
| Denial of role of church in canonization of scripture | Recognition of role of Church in Canonization process |
| Tendency to ignore history of interpretation | History of interpretation essential |
| Narrow and precise prophetic eschatology often linked to a time line | Broad and imprecise eschatology not linked to any specific time line |
| Rejection of scientific historical-critical methods of interpretation | Acceptance of scientific historical-critical methods of interpretation (among others) |

# HOW TO READ THE BIBLE

The various books of the Bible, as most people know, were not written in English, but in languages now "dead": biblical Hebrew, Aramaic, and Koine Greek. To make these texts accessible today, translators have produced the *New American Bible* and other modern language translations. While we can be grateful for the benefits of such translations, we should also be aware that they share certain important limitations. All languages are deeply embedded in the cultural systems out of which they come. Therefore, if we wish to understand a text written in another language, we must understand that other culture as well, and simply reading an English translation does not provide that vital cultural information.

Therefore, although people taught to read English can easily read the *New American Bible*, if they were to do so as though it were a modern English text coming out of contemporary social experience, they would be seriously *mis*-reading the ancient stories, laws, letters, and poetry produced by the ancient authors and editors and understood by the first audiences of the Bible. A modern reader must *learn* something of the alien and long-dead cultures standing behind these texts; that is why publications such as this study Bible contain so much historical, religious, and literary background. If you sometimes think that explaining Isaiah's prophetic books or St. Paul's letters is complicated, imagine how much explanation St. Paul or Isaiah would need if they wanted to read one of *our* books!

## "Readers" Yesterday and Today

To speak of people *reading* the Bible in itself points to one of the most striking, yet often least recognized, differences between the modern reader and the ancient one. In the ancient world of the Hebrew people and even the later world of the Greeks, very few men—and almost no women—could read or write. Consequently, the authors of the biblical documents belonged to a tiny literate elite within largely illiterate societies. In addition, because the audience was illiterate, most of the biblical texts were written primarily to be heard with the ear rather than read with the eye. Those who could read would read aloud to a larger group. Hearing a text, rather than seeing it, affected the way ancient material was fashioned; repetition, puns, prologues, and summaries are all devices in biblical material because of the requirements of the ear.

Modern readers use chapter titles, tables of contents, paragraphing, and internal headings as ways of orienting themselves in books or articles. But such "eye helps" did not exist in ancient writings. The verse numbers in the Bible, for instance, were not added until the sixteenth century A.D. by the famous Parisian printer Stephanus. Where to stop and where to start, how to grasp the way the author organized the material, and what type of writing the author had chosen to use, had to be signaled in ways accessible to the ear for an ancient audience. Thus, repeated opening and closing patterns, proverbs, hymns, oracles, laws, letters, and straightforward, reliable narration are all important aspects of biblical literature. Such qualities are not so prevalent in modern writing.

But we must look deeper. It is not only the case that the writings of the Bible, in their final form, were meant to be read aloud. It is also the case that much of the material in those writings—the sayings of the prophets, the stories of Genesis, the accounts of events in the life of Jesus—circulated for years, perhaps centuries, as *oral* tradition before ever being written down. The stories were passed orally from one generation to the next, adapted to new occasions and altered to fit changing social and political circumstances. After a time, collections of these oral stories were made and written. Thus, the absence of widespread literacy in antiquity meant that *oral* communication was the medium of critical importance. Therefore, in order to understand the Bible as its first audiences did, modern readers must learn to *hear* its texts as well as read them.

Even referring to *the* Bible may encourage contemporary readers to *mis*-read, for *the* Bible is not one book but a collection of many books coming from many different countries and several quite distinct cultures. The Hebrew Bible contains books written from the tenth century B.C. to the second century B.C., almost a millennium of human history. The present shape of many of these books evolved over centuries of editing and reworking, from the early legends about the origins of the Hebrew people, most of which originally circulated as oral tradition, to the later apocalyptic visions of the end of the world in the book of Daniel. Because of this complex process of composition, these documents often reflect not only the evolving religious ideas of the Hebrew people but also their changing social and political fortunes. Yet, since the first audiences were themselves living that political and social history, it is in many places assumed that the reader or hearer will understand the context, and therefore that context is not explained. We can get an inkling of the need for explanation if we think about how *we* would explain, to an ancient Israelite or an early Christian, a contemporary news article that begins, "The White House announced today . . . ." And once we have thought about that—about what "the White House" means in contemporary America—we can also think about what we might expect if we are given various dates for this news article. Suppose the dateline were "Washington, D.C., October 1962. The White House announced today . . . ." Suppose it were 1982? Or 2002? What difference does it make if John F. Kennedy, Ronald Reagan, or George W. Bush is in the White House?

Although the New Testament books were written over a much shorter period—perhaps 60 or so years, from the mid-40s A.D. for Paul's earliest letters to as late as A.D. 100–110 for some of the later letters or the book of Revelation—the political history of that century, containing the war between Rome and the Jews, the subsequent fall of Jerusalem and Qumran, and the destruction of the Jerusalem Temple, as well as—probably—the destruction of the Christian community in Jerusalem, plays a crucial role in the outward growth of the Christian movement. Actually, the 27 separate letters and books that now compose the official New Testament canon are only a small selection from a much larger body of writings by Christians during the first several centuries B.C.

The Hebrew Bible and the New Testament, the two major divisions of the Bible, clearly display certain similarities in form and content: They both draw upon oral traditions; they are both made up of various types of literature, written at different times, directed to separate groups of people for a variety of reasons; and they both relate the continuing story of God's involvement with the Jewish people and the surrounding Gentile world. But we must also acknowledge that, because their audiences, aims, and backgrounds are so different, they often present moral and theological positions aimed at very different concerns. Therefore, to view the similarities as establishing a uniformity of perspective for *the* Bible would be a serious *mis*-reading of the material, for the cultural situation is fundamentally different. To grasp just how different, we can consider the differences in the various conceptions of the universe that are reflected in different parts of the Bible.

## The View of the Universe

In the ancient Near Eastern world of the Sumerians, Babylonians, and Hebrew people, the universe was an intimate and fairly compact affair, which might be visualized as three stories, separated by the solid firmament of the earth below and the heavens above. The top story, formed by the heavens, was the abode of the gods and was surrounded at its outermost limits by water, which the gods could allow to fall upon the earth by opening windows in the heavens—a fact that could cause considerable anxiety among the human population for fear that the gods might forget or decide not to close the windows and thus flood the earth. The second story, the space between earth and the heavens, was the location of humanity, while the bottom story with its limits also defined by water, which would rise to the earth above through rivers and oceans, belonged to the spirits of the underworld. All three stories were closely connected to each other. In such a small universe, encounters between the divine and the human worlds were expected and regular. Only when one element or another was out of place or not performing its assigned task (e.g., the gods were asleep or on a journey when they were needed [see 1 Kgs 18:27] or the king refused to rebuild the city walls or the farmer neglected the time of harvest) was the harmony of an entire system put at risk by an eruption of chaos. Order and a strong sense of place created a very secure world, and religion provided the map or contract set of rules needed to maintain the established order.

By the beginnings of Christianity, that secure, compact universe had exploded. Only a few other periods in the history of Western civilizations can rival the extensive change in perspective that occurred during the Greco-Roman era. The exact causes of that ancient transformation remain unclear, but it was surely influenced by the increasingly sophisticated developments in astronomy, science, and mathematics in Greek circles as well as the growth of large, multinational urban centers around the Mediterranean basin, where cultural, economic, and religious exchange could flourish. These intellectual and social innovations, along with the new mobility permitted by the widespread use of Koine Greek as a general language of commerce and the relative stability of Greek and then of Roman rule, extended the limits of the universe far beyond anything imaginable by earlier peoples.

The view of the universe in the Greco-Roman period, formally codified by Claudius Ptolemy in the second century A.D., might best be visualized as an expanding series of concentric spheres, all in eternal motion around a tiny, stationary earth. The first seven spheres contained the moon and the planets (including the sun), each moving in its appointed round and in the process, rubbing against the other spheres to produce musical notes. The outermost sphere contained the fixed stars. The planets were not the only inhabitants of each sphere, however, for the Greco-Roman people also believed that each sphere housed an order of angels or demons, constantly watching the activities of the human world below, and the closer the sphere to earth, the nastier were its tenants, with the demons responsible for illness, birth defects, and pains of all kinds lodging in the space between the moon and the earth. The intimate, secure universe of the earlier age had disappeared into the vast, threatening reaches of the cosmos, and God no longer dwelt a short distance away but instead resided out beyond the farthest sphere. Religion in such an age existed to help people escape the fears of daily life and to assure them of God's continued care in this world and the next across the outstretched spaces of the stars.

Today we neither live in the ancient three-story universe of the Hebrew people nor even in the Ptolemaic universe of the early Christians. In reading about worries over sleeping deities or threatening demonic powers, modern people probably think of metaphorical language or symbolic meanings, for in modern writings those images would surely function in that fashion. The Bible, however, is not a modern book or collection of modern books. The people who told, wrote, and heard these stories faced uncertain and dangerous worlds, which they attempted to understand as God's creation in ways their societies and theories pictured it. In order to read the Bible in a manner similar to the way they might have heard it, we must learn to appreciate the world in which they lived.

# UNDERSTANDING THE HISTORICAL BACKGROUND TO THE BIBLICAL TEXTS

DONALD SENIOR

The biblical writings were created over a lengthy period of time. That broad historical and cultural canvas is one important cause for the Bible's rich diversity. In this Study Bible, the Reading Guides (see RG 47) provided for each biblical book, and the introductions provided in the notes to the biblical text itself, offer specific information about the historical background of the individual books of the Bible. The following paragraphs sketch the relationship of the biblical books to the history out of which they grew.

The accounts of creation and the stories about the first ancestors of the human family, such as the tragic rivalry between Cain and Abel and the story of Noah and the flood, obviously do not have the same historical grounding that later traditions could. These stories answer the question about the origin of humanity and its plight in history. Firm historical traditions begin only with the forging of Israel into an identifiable people, an event that did not begin until probably around 1250 B.C. Traditions about the earlier patriarchal period starting around 1850 B.C. are much less certain historically, and even events from the time of Israel's sojourn in Egypt and during the period of the Exodus and early settlement in the land are sketchy, because there were few means of preserving historical archives.

## The Major Periods of Biblical History

### The Time of the Patriarchs (1850–1250 B.C.)

The period from Abraham to Joseph is recounted in Genesis 12–50. Historically, this was a period of vast migrations in the Middle East, with clans of herders moving freely from Mesopotamia down through the Fertile Crescent into present-day Israel. Egypt had been a dominant power in the Middle East for more than 2,000 years prior to that time. Egypt's might was counterbalanced by a succession of powerful dynasties at the eastern end of the Fertile Crescent, including the Persians, Assyrians, and Babylonians. Israel, located geographically between those two areas, would often be the battleground for those opposing forces.

Few firm historical traditions exist from this period but the general picture provided in the biblical traditions about the patriarchs does reflect something of the nomadic lifestyle and familial religion typical of the period.

### The Exodus, Wilderness Wandering, and Settlement in the Land (1250–1130 B.C.)

This period is covered in Exodus, Deuteronomy, Numbers, and Joshua. The story of Israel as a unified people begins in Egypt with the stories about Moses and the miraculous Exodus from Egypt. During a period of wandering in the desert, the covenant was formed with the LORD, the God of Israel. Under the leadership of Joshua, Israel finally breaks through into the Promised Land, driving the native Canaanites before them.

There is considerable debate about the historical background to this period. Some scholars, particularly conservative ones, are willing to accept the biblical portrayal at face value: namely that there was a mass migration of Hebrews from Egypt and that they invaded the regions of Israel with military force and thereby gained possession of the land.

The lack of clear archaeological evidence supporting such a vast military conquest and some ambiguity in the biblical traditions themselves have led other historians to surmise that both the migration from Egypt and the possession of the land took place over a longer period of time. Some Hebrew tribes may have already settled in Israel prior to the Exodus, and joined with the incoming tribes at a later period. While some Canaanite cities may have been taken by force, some of the land was probably settled in a peaceful fashion.

In any event, the Bible sees this process as a dramatic act of deliverance by God and as the historic beginning of the story of Israel.

**The Period of the Judges (1130–1020 B.C.)**

This early period of Israelite history is narrated in the book of Judges. It is clear that the Israelites at first resisted the idea of a strong central government. They preferred a loosely organized federation of clans or tribes ruled by charismatic leaders called judges. Only the LORD could claim the right to be called "King." This independent spirit and aversion to the monarchy goes deep into the consciousness of Israel.

**The Monarchy (1020–587 B.C.)**

This long, but in fact highly diverse, period of Israel's history is taken up in the books of 1 and 2 Samuel; 1 and 2 Kings; and a parallel account in 1 and 2 Chronicles.

The transition from the more informal and charismatic leadership under the judges to the more institutional form of the monarchy begins with Saul (about 1020–1000 B.C.) but reaches its zenith with David (1000–960 B.C.) and Solomon (960–930 B.C.). Threats from surrounding peoples and the need for more complex social organization gradually led Israel to adopt a monarchical form of government. David eventually unified diverse groups of people under a single government system, ruled from his new centrally located capital of Jerusalem. Under David and his son Solomon, Israel's territories greatly expanded.

The united kingdom forged by David did not last very long. Solomon strained it by increasing taxation and by lack of sensitivity to the old tribal loyalties. When Solomon's son Rehoboam ascended to the throne, the seams between north and south split and the separate kingdoms of Judah in the south and Israel in the north began. This divided monarchy would last until 724 B.C., when the Assyrian empire would crush the northern kingdom. Judah would survive until the Babylonian invasion of 587 B.C.

The biblical account has little respect for the northern rulers and takes a critical view of most of the kings of Judah as well, considering them unfaithful to the covenant. During this period the great prophetic movement would ignite in Israel. Elijah, Elisha, Amos, and Hosea were prophets in the northern kingdom. Isaiah served as court prophet to the kings of Judah.

**Exile and Return (587–332 B.C.)**

This crucial period of Israelite history is narrated in 2 Kings 24–25 and in the books of Ezra and Nehemiah. In the 590s B.C. the Babylonians took over Judah and installed a puppet king; when, in 587, that king attempted a rebellion, the Babylonians moved in with great force. They destroyed most of Jerusalem, pulled down the Temple, and forced all but the lowest members of society into exile.

The Babylonian captivity would last almost 50 years. Systematic deportation as a way of subduing conquered peoples had been used first by the Assyrians and then by the Babylonians. Only a small remnant of Israelites was left behind under the firm control of Babylonian officials. When the exiled Jews eventually returned, they considered the people who had stayed behind as somehow corrupt and would not allow them to take part in the reconstruction of Israel, a source of bitterness that would lead to the sharp divisions between Jews and Samaritans so obvious in the New Testament period.

Under the leadership of Ezra and Nehemiah, Jerusalem and its Temple were rebuilt. But Israel was now only a small and fragile nation, clustered around Jerusalem and very concerned with preserving its identity.

**The Greek Conquest and the Rise of the Hasmoneans (332–39 B.C.)**

This is a turbulent part of Israelite history, reflected in 1 and 2 Maccabees and Daniel.

Alexander conquered Palestine in 332 B.C., beginning a period in which Greek culture would have a strong impact on the life of Israel. After his death, the Middle Eastern portion of Alexander's empire was divided between the Seleucid dynasty, which ruled from Syria, and the Ptolemies, ruling from Egypt. The Ptolemaic dynasty controlled Israel from approximately 332 to 199 B.C. Their generally benign rule gave way to the Seleucids, who attempted to impose Greek culture and taxation in a more rigorous fashion. Seleucid ruthlessness eventually triggered the Maccabean revolt, which by 160 B.C. had thrown off the yoke of the Seleucids against incredible odds.

The Jewish dynasty of the Hasmonean family now began a 100-year reign. The Hasmonean kings proved to be as corrupt and ruthless as the foreigners who had preceded them. Reactions by pious Jews to the compromises of the Hasmoneans and their Jerusalem aristocracy would give rise to protest groups such as the Essenes and Pharisees. By 60 B.C. Roman influence was growing in the Middle East and brought pressure on Israel itself. The Hasmonean period came to an end with the emergence of Herod the Great, a vassal of the Romans, who would unify the country and hold it in his grip.

**The Roman Period (39 B.C.–A.D. 100)**

The New Testament writings emerge during this period of biblical history. With the death of Herod in 4 B.C., the Romans divided Israel among his three sons. Eventually the Romans removed the cruel and incompetent Archaelaus, taking over direct rule of Judah and Samaria.

Herod Philip and Herod Antipas would continue to govern in the regions of Upper Galilee, Lower Galilee, and the Transjordan (see Map 12).

Roman rule and its heavy taxation proved intolerable to the Jewish people. Tensions mounted all during the first half of the first century, exploding into revolution in A.D. 66. That revolt would be violently suppressed by the Romans, climaxing with the destruction of Jerusalem and its great Temple in A.D. 70. That event would change the complexion of Judaism forever. Another short-lived revolt would break out in A.D. 132. The Romans would continue to occupy Palestine until the time of the Byzantine empire. All of these events have left a profound impression on the writings of the New Testament.

# THE PENTATEUCH

## What Is the Pentateuch?

In the United States, the Declaration of Independence, the Constitution, and the Bill of Rights stand as the foundational documents on which the democratic system of government is based. No matter what new laws are written or policies are made, every piece of legislation, every judicial decision is ultimately judged in light of those original documents.

The foundation documents for the people of Israel are the books we now commonly refer to as the Pentateuch, the first five books of the Bible. These books do more than introduce the rest of the Bible: they are the very foundation on which the rest of the Scriptures stand. The Pentateuch serves as the blueprint or constitution by which all other Scripture is interpreted. By understanding the special nature and special role of these first five books of the Old Testament, we will have a better understanding of the entire Bible.

"Pentateuch" means "five scrolls." Rather than five distinct books, however, what we are really dealing with is one book in five volumes. Even in biblical times the Pentateuch was considered a single work. Jewish tradition calls it "Torah," which is often translated as "law" but really means "teaching" or "instruction." In the Torah we find the basic teachings of the Jewish faith. The chart below gives an overview of the Pentateuch.

Partly because the book of Deuteronomy leads into the books of Joshua and Judges, the Table of Contents of the New American Bible lists eight books under the heading "Pentateuch" and groups the books of the Old Testament into four categories: The Pentateuch, The Historical Books, The Wisdom Books, and the Prophetic Books. The Jewish Bible, which has its own

***The Pentateuch***

| | |
|---|---|
| Genesis | Origins: Creation and stories of primeval times. Abraham, Isaac, Jacob, Joseph: The great ancestors of the Jewish people. |
| Exodus | God chooses Moses to deliver Israelites from slavery in Egypt. The giving of the Law at Mt. Sinai. Many laws regarding daily life and religious practice. |
| Leviticus | Laws for the people of God relating to sacrifice, priesthood, and religious feasts. Recurring call to be "holy" as God is holy. |
| Numbers | More laws. Desert wanderings and military exploits on the way to the Promised Land. Repeated acts of unfaithfulness to God and Moses extend the wandering to 40 years. |
| Deuteronomy | A "second law" that sums up the significance of the Exodus. Moses' farewell speech delivered at the borders of the Promised Land, in which Moses warns people they must obey the covenant or risk losing the land. |

order, groups the biblical books differently, under three headings:

| *The Law (Torah)* | |
|---|---|
| Genesis; Exodus; Leviticus; Numbers; Deuteronomy | |
| ***The Prophets*** | ***The Writings*** |
| Former Prophets: Joshua; Judges; 1 and 2 Samuel (regarded as one book); Psalms; Job; Proverbs; 1 and 2 Kings (regarded as one book). | Ruth; Song of Songs; Ecclesiastes; Lamentations; Esther; Daniel; Ezra-Nehemiah; 1 and 2 Chronicles (regarded as one book). |
| Latter Prophets: Isaiah; Jeremiah; Ezekiel; The Book of the Twelve (minor prophets). | |

This arrangement helps us see that the Pentateuch is the source from which all the other books of the Old Testament flow. It may be surprising to find books of history together with those of prophetic writing in the "Prophets" column. But there is an important message in that fact: both the teaching of the prophets and Israel's life-experience call the people back to fidelity to the teachings of the Pentateuch. In our own lives, we often have to face unpleasant consequences of our own actions. Often, these experiences remind us of the differences between right and wrong that we learned when we were younger. In the same way, Israel had both the words of the prophets and their own history to help them determine how well or how poorly they had lived out the message of the Pentateuch in their life as a nation. Even when they were deaf to the prophets' words, the messes they frequently found themselves in were sufficient to remind them that they had indeed been unfaithful to God and the Law.

The Writings are a group of books that also flow out of the Pentateuch. Primarily they contain reflections and explanations intended to help us live the message of the Torah. In short, all the other books of the Old Testament are the result of Israel's reflection on the Torah.

**TaNaK** Modern Hebrew uses the acronym TNK (pronounced "Tenak") to refer to the Bible. The acronym consists of the first letters of the Hebrew words for the Law (Torah), the Prophets (Nebi'im), and the Writings (Ketubim).

## The Pentateuch and the Canon of Scripture

None of the books in the Bible got there by accident. Every decision about whether to include a certain book was carefully thought out, discussed, and probably hotly debated. The final decisions make a difference. When we read the books of the Bible we read them as part of a collection of books, and how we interpret the message of a book is determined, at least in part, by where that book stands in relation to other books. So as we begin to study the Old Testament we will want to determine why Genesis, Exodus, Leviticus, Numbers, and Deuteronomy appear in that order.

How do we do that? By asking questions about the books themselves, about the times during which they were written, and about their meaning for us today. For example:

1. Literary Shape: What kind of literature is this? Is it poetry, story, history, prophecy, myth, or some other form of writing?
2. Historical Development: How did separate pieces of writing composed by different authors come to be put together to make the present book?
3. Actual History: What was happening in Israel during the period this book describes?

**Canon** is the term used to refer to the list of officially approved books contained in the Bible. It comes from a Greek word meaning "reed, straight stick," that came to mean "ruler, measuring stick." Different groups—Jews, Catholics, Orthodox Christians, and Protestants—have different canons for their Bibles, but in each case there is an official "measure" for what is to be included.

4. Religious Significance: What is the religious message of the book for a modern reader?

## Story and Law

We said above that one of the first questions we put to a scripture text is "What kind of literature is it?" It is easy to see from just looking at the pages of the New American Bible that the bulk of the Pentateuch is prose rather than poetry. If you examine the five books carefully, you will soon find that two kinds of prose dominate: laws and stories (narratives). Generally, each book contains some of each, although either stories or laws might predominate. Sections of stories regularly alternate with sections of laws, but within every story segment you will find scattered laws and commands, and in every listing of laws you will find a healthy episode or two of story. The breakdown of laws and narratives is illustrated in the table below.

The stories of the Pentateuch are part of a larger story that continues into the books listed under the Former Prophets (Joshua, Judges, Samuel, Kings). The Pentateuch wraps its many laws in a package of stories that trace the "history" of the world from the moment of creation down to the time of the total collapse of the nation of Israel, just before the Babylonian Exile.

| Book | Content |
|---|---|
| Genesis | Nearly all stories (Gn 1–50) |
| Exodus | Half stories (Ex 1–10; 24; 31–34); half laws (Ex 20–23; 25–30; 35–40) |
| Leviticus | Nearly all laws (Lv 1–27) |
| Numbers | Half stories (Nm 1–19; 20–26; 31–33); half laws (Nm 1–10; 18–19; 27–30; 34–36) |
| Deuteronomy | Nearly all laws (Dt 1–34) |

## The Larger Picture

The Pentateuch ends with the chosen people standing on the borders of the Promised Land. But the story continues. The books of Joshua and Judges tell the story of the people's entry into the land: stories of conquest and the gradual settling of the land and stories of great military leaders called judges. The books of 1 and 2 Samuel recount how the people abandoned tribal rule and accepted kingship. The two books of Kings present stories of the life of Israel under the kings up to the time of the exile. All of them use the foundation of the Pentateuch to show how Israel's faithfulness to the laws affected its story.

The rich blending of laws and story in the Pentateuch was intentional. Its purpose was to help readers see the many laws as part of their unfolding story. They were not merely regulations tacked on to their life here and there; they were the very stuff of which their life as a nation was made. Without the Law, Israel would have had no story to tell.

A modern reader might be puzzled to find lists of the laws the Congress passed in a given period as part of a history of the United States. But in order to understand the history and culture of the country, we would have to know about the laws. Likewise, in biblical times awareness of the Law brought with it an awareness of how the lives of the ancestors were guided by the same laws. It made the Israelites aware of their continuity with

| | Stories | Laws |
|---|---|---|
| Genesis | From Creation to the days of the Patriarchs. | |
| Exodus | Leaving slavery in Egypt. | Laws delivered to Moses on Mt. Sinai that are to become the basis of the covenant between God and Israel, and many more laws Moses "receives" from God that govern every aspect of daily life. |
| Leviticus | Meeting God at Mt. Sinai. | |
| Numbers | Desert wanderings and reaching the borders of the Promised Land. | |
| Deuteronomy | | Moses sums up the Law and applies it to life in the land. |

those who went before them. They might think, "Our ancestors obeyed these laws, and we obey these laws, and as a result we are one people."

This sense of continuity helped the Hebrews see the Law as a gift from God. It not only taught them how to live, but, more importantly, it helped assure that they would live. By being faithful to the Law the people were maintaining their end of their relationship with God: "If you keep my commandments, I will be your God and you will be my people." Fidelity meant protection, and protection meant existence.

## The Structure of the Pentateuch

Try thinking about the structure of the Pentateuch as a plan within a plan. The plan begins in Genesis with God creating a good world so humanity can come to know and share in God's goodness. When humanity fails to live up to God's hopes (Gn 1–11), God chooses a family, Abraham's, that will be God's special means of revealing the divine goodness to all nations (Gn 12–50). This people will discover God's goodness through hardship (slavery) and deliverance (Exodus) and learn to be an obedient and holy people (Lv and Nm 1–10). Then God will lead them to a promised land (Nm 10–36), which they will keep only if they remain obedient and loyal (Deuteronomy). The diagram below illustrates this plan-within-a-plan structure.

## History in the Bible

Anywhere something of importance happens today newspaper and television reporters, photographers, and video cameras record every moment. We live in a world of instant replays where you don't have to wonder what someone said or did; you can even play it back in slow motion. In the ancient world, such technology, of course, was not available.

In a culture like ours, so dominated by science, we value exact observation and documentation for its own sake. We expect historians to prove the claims they make in their books with clear documentation. And we expect them to be unbiased reporters, not propaganda peddlers. That's a lot to ask in any age; even trained historians are never totally free of bias and have their own point of view that colors what they write. If modern historians are never entirely objective even when it's expected of them, then we certainly cannot hope for that kind of objectivity from ancient writers who never made it their goal.

Even if they had wanted that kind of accuracy, ancient writers had no way to get much of the historical information. The reason that little or no information was preserved for its own sake was that history was seen not as a record of "what happened," but as a lesson people were to learn from. History was written to teach that one kind of behavior or attitude was more appropriate than another. It was written more like newspaper editorials, which take sides and argue for their favorite causes.

The bottom line is that ancient "history" was more interested in explaining why something happened than in what happened. It was more concerned with the meaning of events than in an accurate record of those events.

God's Plan: Create Humanity to Praise and Share God's Goodness

| **First Plan** | | **New Plan:** Choose family-nation to teach all nations to praise and share God's goodness. | |
|---|---|---|---|
| *Creation.* Adam and Eve and all creation are created good. | Gn 1–2 | Promise to Patriarchs: Abraham, Isaac, Jacob, Joseph. | Gn 12–50 |
| *Sin.* Human sin and alienation grow. | Gn 3–11 | Escape from Egypt to Mt. Sinai. | Ex 1–15 |
| | | Laws given to teach Israel to be a holy people. | Ex 19–40<br>Lv 1–27<br>Nm 1–10 |
| | | Journey to the Promised Land. | Nm 10–36 |
| | | Summary of law. Ready to enter Land. | Dt 1–34 |

### History or Theology?

While the Pentateuch is a complete story, it is in no way a complete history. It picks and chooses the events and themes it wants to talk about. And it only talks about those things that will teach a religious lesson. What we have here is a handbook or rule book for right living, a theology book much more than any real history of the people. That is why laws are so generously sprinkled in among the stories. They were part of the lesson the stories were meant to teach.

Clearly, many of the stories in the Pentateuch are not at all about ordinary time in history. Genesis 1–11, for example, does not fit the category of history because it treats the creation of the world and the first events of human existence in a way that does not give them any definite context of place or time. By trying to answer universal questions—questions like: Why did God make humans this way? Why do we sin? Why do we die? Why is it hard to obey God? Why are men and women different?—the stories of Genesis 1–11 fall into the literary genre of myth. Even the stories of the patriarchs and matriarchs in Genesis 12–50 are not like modern history. Although based on real history, they resemble folktale hero stories, and it is hard to pin them down to exact locations and events.

Keep these insights in mind when you run into problems of logic in one of the books. For example, in Genesis 4 Cain and Abel are the only two children of Adam and Eve. Yet, after killing Abel, Cain is banished and, we are told, has "relations with his wife." If this were a real history, we would have to ask how Cain could have a wife when Adam and Eve were the only other living human beings at the time.

The author's intent obviously centers not on literal facts, but on a religious lesson, here concerning how the world came to be populated. Whether or not that lesson is consistent with what has previously been said does not concern the author.

But while it is important not to make the mistake of thinking that the Pentateuch is a record of history, it is also important not to think of it as just a clever story pulled from someone's imagination. It is a masterwork, a work of genius that makes God known to us. In beautiful language and powerful imagery it speaks of humanity's tendency toward sin, about the failure of most of the world to know God, and of God's choice of Israel to demonstrate to the world God's loving concern for humanity. The marvelous storytelling of the Pentateuch reveals God by focusing on a number of central events: the choice of the patriarchs, the giving of the Law, the making of a covenant, and the guidance through the wilderness to a promised land.

**Myth** "Myth" has many different meanings. Often it is used to refer to something that is false or unreliable: "The story of George Washington chopping down the cherry tree is a myth." But that familiar use of the word is misleading. Narrowly defined, the term refers to traditional stories about heroes, gods, or demi-gods. Defined very broadly, a myth is a story, factual or not, that people live by and that gives meaning to their lives. For instance, Americans have a national ideal of people from various parts of the world coming to this country and being able to participate in "the American dream" of a better life for themselves and their children. It is a powerful motivator in our country regardless of its "truth."

Scholars generally understand myths as attempts by ancient peoples to understand the mysteries of their existence, usually by explaining things as being the result of the actions of divine beings. Myths narrate a "sacred history" and are therefore special, sacred stories. But rather than providing answers, myths offer insights. They get at the core meaning of life and reality. For ancient peoples "myth" meant a "true story." What distinguishes myths is that they are stories that, although they may not be factual, convey a deeper truth about ultimate questions. Myths, therefore, do not contradict scientific knowledge, but rather answer a different question: not, "How did this happen?" but "What does this mean?"

**Patriarchs** The forefathers of the Israelites, that is, Abraham, Isaac, and Jacob. Because he figures so prominently in the Genesis patriarchal stories, Joseph is often designated a patriarch as well. The New Testament also refers to David and the twelve sons of Jacob as patriarchs. The term overlooks the significance of the wives of these men without whom God's plan would not have moved forward. These matriarchs, Sarah, Rebekah, Rachel, and Leah, can be included by the use of expressions like "forebears," "ancestors," or "patriarchs and matriarchs."

Good storytelling can give us pleasure, teach us about history, and give us philosophical and theological insights. As a great work of storytelling the Pentateuch is multilayered. It tells history, but it does not allow us to question it too closely about exact descriptions. It presents religious and theological lessons but warns us not to treat it like a catechism filled with lists of truths. Most of all it tells a story. The story teaches us by letting us compare our experience with that of the Hebrew people. As we read we begin to discover that their story and our story are intertwined, that the God who was at work in the lives of the Hebrew people works in similar ways in our own lives.

### Historical Dating of Pentateuch Traditions

Despite many difficulties, we are not completely in the dark when it comes to dating some of the events of the Pentateuch. Archaeological digs in ancient sites have produced tablets and other records that offer a good idea of what each different period in the second millennium B.C. was like, so we can date the major events of the Pentateuch with a fair degree of confidence.

The patriarchal narratives fall somewhere between 2000 and 1500 B.C., the Exodus event between 1450 and 1250 B.C., and the invasion of the land of Palestine around 1250 to 1200 B.C. Nonbiblical historical information makes some dates more likely than others: Since Egypt was governed by foreign rulers between 1750 B.C. and 1550 B.C., the story of how Joseph, a foreigner, rises to power best fits this time period. Exodus 1:11 says the enslaved Israelites built the cities of Pithom and Rameses, pointing to the reign of Seti I as the period of enslavement and the reign of Rameses II as the time of the Exodus.

### Did Moses Write the Pentateuch?

FOR MORE THAN 2,000 years Moses was considered the author of the Pentateuch even though no book of the Bible specifically names him as the author. The Pentateuch was often called "the Book of Moses," and throughout the Bible there are frequent references to the "Law of Moses." Jesus, like most of his contemporaries, took for granted that Moses authored the Pentateuch (see, for instance, Lk 16:29, 31; 20:37).

But even in the ancient world some questioned whether Moses could really have written the entire Pentateuch. How, for example could Moses have written about his own death as in Deuteronomy 34:5–12? Many of the laws supposedly written by Moses deal with situations that occurred much later than the time when Moses led the people through the desert. Other evidence in the Bible leads scholars to believe the Pentateuch did not exist in its present state until approximately 450 B.C.—nearly 800 years after Moses' death.

No one can say for certain who did write the Pentateuch, but there is no question that Moses played a unique and important role in the events recorded in these books. Modern scholars do not try to prove that Moses directly authored the written books of the Pentateuch. As Catholics, our belief that the Bible is divinely inspired makes the identity of its human author an issue of limited importance. Whatever else we may say, Moses may be regarded as the founder of the Israelite faith.

## How Scholars Study the Pentateuch: The Art of Interpretation

Studying the Bible is not easy. Because it was written over many centuries by people living in cultures very different from our own, we cannot simply expect to pick up a Bible and be able to grasp its meaning in its entirety. On the other hand, we must not be intimidated by the amount of scholarly knowledge it takes to understand the Bible properly, so that we start to feel it belongs only to some special caste. The reality lies somewhere in the middle. With some scholarly help, like that provided by this study guide and the excellent footnotes of the New American Bible, a layperson should be able to read the Bible intelligently and find in it religious meaning for his or her life.

When we read the Bible we are looking for two things: what the text meant to its original author and audience, and what it means now to us, its modern readers. (See "How to Read the Bible RG 28–30.) We must be careful, however, not to let one meaning cancel out the other. When we seek the original meaning of a text, we do not rule out the possibility that over the centuries a particular text may have taken on more meaning than even the author intended. So what it meant then and what it means now are not necessarily the same thing.

Some modern churchgoers have rejected scholarly theories and methods of study because they feel these have robbed the Bible of its status as God's inspired Word and have turned it into an ordinary literary document. Why so negative a reaction? Maybe because some scholars approach the Bible with the assumption that they may not use God as the explanation for anything. While they would not deny the possibility of miracles, they believe that what is called the "critical method" requires them to propose natural explanations whenever such explanations are plausible. Even discussions of inspiration are considered off-limits by some scholars. If you read the Bible only on this level, you might think it would tell you little of religious value.

But here is the heart of the matter: The critical method helps us to unlock and clarify what is going on in a text. How? First, by connecting the text to historical events that we may have learned about through nonbiblical sources; second, by helping us understand unusual cultural customs; and third, by helping us understand special literary styles of expression that are no longer in use today.

> **Exegesis** The critical or scholarly explanation of a Bible passage. (The term means "to bring out" and refers to the process of explaining meaning.)
>
> **Hermeneutics** is a term often used interchangeably with exegesis. While exegesis tries to discover what a passage meant in its original context (time and place of composition), hermeneutics uses exegesis to ask what the text means for us now. (The term comes from Hermes, the Greek messenger god, and means "interpretation.")

Without scientific study we would not comprehend those things that are not part of our culture. When archaeologists dig up clay tablets that contain long-lost information, biblical scholars become the bridge that connects that information with the Bible. They study how language works, how people hand down traditions, and how they record events and tell folk tales. All this helps us understand how biblical stories and laws were put together.

All writing is interpretation. The ancient authors interpreted what they thought God was communicating; the churches and synagogues interpret what these words of revelation mean for their congregations. Modern scholars and believing readers must also interpret and decide what relevance these long-ago stories and events have for their lives. Everyone who reads the Bible asks "What does it mean?" But we can find a full answer only if our reading is illuminated by the twin lights of faith and scientific knowledge of the past. And nowhere in the Bible is this more crucial than in reading the Pentateuch.

The study of the Pentateuch has a long history that can be traced back even to the time of Jesus as illustrated in the chart on the next page.

***How the Bible Has Been Read in History***

| | |
|---|---|
| New Testament Times (Jesus and writers of New Testament books) | Scripture viewed as prophecy of Jesus, and used to show connection between Jesus and what went before him. |
| Early Church (the time after the Apostles to the sixth century) | Scripture read allegorically. Literal meaning rejected because Bible contains deeper meanings put there (inspired) by God. Therefore Bible always says more than the author intended to say. |
| Medieval Period (from the seventh century through the Renaissance and Reformation) | Allegorical reading still predominates. Growing respect for literal meaning of text. But much of Old Testament still viewed as prediction of Jesus. |
| Modern Study (from the seventeenth century to the twentieth century) | Critical study of texts. Four-sources theory and source criticism developed. Development of form criticism—the search for literary genres and the earliest and smallest literary units of tradition—and transmission history—the account of how the current texts came to be. |

### New Testament Times

In New Testament times, Jesus and the authors of various New Testament books referred to texts from the Bible, which at that time was simply the Hebrew Scriptures, what Christians now call the Old Testament. Usually they were referring to stories that were cited as proofs for something Jesus or one of the apostles was teaching. Some stories from the Pentateuch were treated as what has been called a *type,* in which an Old Testament figure is seen as a foreshadowing of a later character—like Abraham, who was seen as a forerunner of the Christian believer, or Isaac, who was seen as a foreshadowing of Jesus. The New Testament treats many passages from the Pentateuch, the Prophets, and the Psalms as a type of prophecy that predicts Jesus and helps explain his suffering, death, and resurrection. It would be fair to say that the New Testament uses the Bible primarily to show the deep connection between Jesus and what went before him.

### Early Church

The early Church (the community of believers from about A.D. 100 to 300) saw the Bible operating on three levels of meaning. First, there was the literal or historical meaning of the text. Then there was the *spiritual* or *allegorical* sense: a deep, often hidden, layer that went beyond the literal. The third level expressed the *moral* lesson the text meant to teach.

Level two, the spiritual level, was considered most important. Since Scripture is inspired writing, pious believers thought it therefore must contain layers of meaning of which the author was not even aware. God, after all, was using the ancient author to point the way to Jesus. The meaning of a passage, then, could not be limited to what the author intended to say. The full meaning was much deeper, more spiritual, and not immediately obvious.

This attitude led to an almost total disregard for the literal meaning of the text. All the focus was on the so-called spiritual meaning intended by God. Because of the conviction that every word of Scripture contained a prophecy about Jesus, and thus always said more than it seemed to say, the allegorical method flourished in the early Church.

### The Medieval Period

The medieval world was largely a period in love with the allegorical approach, and students of the Bible relied heavily on the opinions of the early Church writers regarding each passage of Scripture. But the rise of scholasticism in the twelfth and thirteenth centuries shifted the focus toward a clear and literal interpretation of Bible texts. Medieval thinkers, however, lacked a knowledge of Hebrew and Greek with which to study the original words, and they still viewed the Bible as prophecy rather than as a history of a people's experience of God working in their lives. So they, too, read the Bible more as a book about Christ and the Church than about Israel.

**Modern Study**

Truly modern study of the Bible began with a French priest named Richard Simon (1678) who detected different literary styles within the book of Genesis. He concluded that Moses did not write the Pentateuch from scratch, but probably was quoting sources that existed before him. This insight earned him Church condemnation, but it also opened the door for further critical study.

In the next century scholars began investigating the biblical passages that regularly call God by the proper name "Yahweh" (the *New American Bible* renders it as "LORD"), and those that generally call God by the more generic term, "Elohim" (which the *NAB* renders as "God"). Even though the passages that use the two names are intermixed, they run through the entire Pentateuch (up to the book of Numbers) as two parallel stories.

New questions arose. Were these two separate written works that told the same history of Israel, or was one original story embellished and eventually turned into two different versions? The debate was intense. Then scholars began to notice that the so called "Elohist" passages really contained two separate accounts themselves. The one that was more narrative and interested in God's great interventions in history was called the Elohist strand, while the other, which was more concerned with priestly and ritual actions, was called the Priestly strand.

By the mid-1800s scholars generally agreed that there were in fact three independent versions of the Pentateuch's basic story, which could be labeled with the initials J (for "Jahvist," from the German spelling of Yahweh), E (for Elohist), and P (for Priestly). The book of Deuteronomy was considered a fourth and totally separate source of its own, and received the label D. These traditions have often been called "documents," but that name can be misleading if it leads us to think of fully written-out manuscripts containing the different traditions. Rather, these traditions were probably much more fragmentary, consisting of numerous materials, some written, some oral, that were combined into our current books over a lengthy period of time.

The reason that scholars think the first five books of the Bible were put together in this way is that it accounts for certain oddities in the text better than any other explanation that has been proposed.

J and E are generally seen as having been combined at an early stage (and some scholars doubt the existence of a fully-formed E source at all). As a separate source, J presumably dates from the time of David (approximately 1000–960 B.C.) or shortly thereafter, and the E material could have been added after the destruction of the northern kingdom in 722/721. P was assembled later, perhaps during the exile in Babylon (when the First Temple had been destroyed in 587/586), although it reflects materials that were known at least to the priests involved in Temple worship during the time from Solomon (960–920) to the exile. D dates from the reign of King Josiah (640–609) and seems to have been the basis for the Temple reform that was undertaken at the time of his reign.

The J source is marked by the use of the Hebrew word translated LORD in the *NAB:* YHWH or "Yahweh" (German spelling "Jahveh"). The E source, on the other hand, generally uses the word "God" ('Elohim). The Priestly source contains most of the rules for Temple worship, genealogical lists, and legal materials. D designates primarily the separate writer responsible for Deuteronomy. J, E, and P were combined into the first four books at some time during or after the exile in Babylon.

None of these sources have been discovered as separate documents or manuscripts. But scholars have concluded that the first five books, as they now exist, contain variations within particular sections that can best be accounted for by assuming that someone was trying to combine two or more versions of an event into one account.

For example, in the story of the flood (Genesis chapters 6–8), there seem to be two different timelines: one of 40 days plus a few weeks (Gn 7:17; 8:6, 8, 10, 12), and one of 150 days plus 150 days plus a few months (Gn 7:24; 8:3, 5) for a total of a year and 10 days (7:11; 8:13–14). There also seems to be a difference regarding the numbers of animals to be brought into the ark: one pair of each creature (6:19–20) or one pair of the unclean and seven pairs of the clean creatures (7:2–3). These differences can be

*Four Sources Theory*

| Source and Characteristics | Why Written |
|---|---|
| **J: Yahwist**<br>Written in tenth or ninth century B.C. Literary artist. Loves stories. Focus on the heart. Earthy, frank language. Emphasis on God's closeness with humanity. Uses name Yahweh for God (in German, spelled "Jahveh," hence the J). Favors strong leaders like David. Southern tradition. | Written in Jerusalem to show that promises to Abraham were fulfilled in the empire of David. |
| **E: Elohist**<br>Written after 900 B.C. Uses Elohim for God's name. Stresses role of the prophet. Contains strong tone of challenge and stress on morality. Emphasizes role of Jacob and the significance of northern kingdom ideas and places. Northern tradition reflecting anti-Jerusalem view. Like D it stresses that the covenant with Moses is more important than kingship. | After the division of the kingdom, this version gathered up traditions to support the legitimacy of northern kings and institutions. |
| **P: Priestly**<br>Much of the material dates to eight and seventh centuries B.C., but some materials probably written in sixth century B.C. Very strong interest in ritual and priesthood. Less focus on story and more on religious symbols. Style is more formal. God is more distant, less intimately involved with human beings. Stresses obedience to Law and permanence of God's blessing. The dominant tradition in Pentateuch. Reflects southern point of view. The P editors arranged the four sources into our present Pentateuch around 500 B.C. | Some of the P material reflects and responds to the needs of the exiles in the sixth century B.C. |
| **D: Deuteronomist**<br>Written in eighth and seventh centuries B.C. Emphasizes role of family (parents) for instruction and fidelity to covenant. Moralistic: stresses preaching and exhortation. Style is eloquent; many often-repeated verbal formulas. Emphasizes Jerusalem as sole place of worship. Northern tradition, which stresses covenant over kingship. | Reassess J and E traditions in light of pagan inroads and unfaithful kings. |

explained by the hypothesis that there were two accounts of the flood, and that a later compiler brought them both together. Instead of ironing out the differences, however, the compiler regarded at least some of them as important, so kept them in, even though they were contradictory.

Eventually a German scholar, Julius Wellhausen, proposed dates for the writing of each version and speculated on the historical situation that created the need for each different telling of the history. All this came to be known as the "four source theory," and the method of study is called *source criticism*. Each strand responds to

*The Four Sources and the Four Characteristics ("P's")*

| Who | What | How |
|---|---|---|
| Yahwist | Emphasizes role of **Poet** | Storytelling |
| Elohist | Emphasizes role of **Prophet** | Challenging |
| Priestly | Emphasizes role of **Priest** | Legislating |
| Deuteronomist | Emphasizes role of **Parents** | Exhorting |

a particular situation or need in the life of the nation, incorporates the particular worldview of its author-editor, and has a distinctive style. This theory is outlined in the table on RG 43.

J and E existed side by side while the two kingdoms lasted from 930 to 722 B.C. (See the guide to the historical books.) When the northern kingdom fell, its E story was carried down to Judah by refugees, and there it was eventually combined (around 700 B.C.) with J into a single account. Still later, when Judah itself fell in 587 B.C. and during its exile, D and P were combined with JE to make our final JEPD. Editors from the Priestly circles applied the final touches. Each of the sources has a distinctive style and emphasis, as described in the table above.

All this speculation on sources led to even more research into the original units that made up each source. Where did the individual incidents, poems, stories, and laws come from? This search for the earliest and smallest units of the tradition gave birth to a new way of studying the Bible called *form criticism*. By identifying the special form of a poem or hymn or law or narrative, scholars thought they could probably determine the cultural-historical situation from which it came.

Some scholars have focused on the *transmission history* of a text, looking at how traditions get passed on and grow or change. Before reaching the final form they have today, original statements, stories, and laws went through a process of being combined with other units, and then combined again in still larger works. Study of how collections grew and how stories were sometimes arranged into a new order helps us understand how they were used and the meaning they were given by different generations. For example, the story of Exodus was the story of escaping from an oppressive situation. However, later on, in the context of the Law and the land, the story of Exodus became a story about the celebration of a feast year after year: the Passover. The bread, the lamb, and the bitter herbs all became parts of the yearly ritual Passover celebration.

## Reflecting on the Message of the Pentateuch

Like navigating a vast ocean, finding our way through the vast array of materials in the Pentateuch can be challenging. A lighthouse now and then can make the going easier. The Pentateuch provides these in the form of themes and topics that recur over and over again. The demand for obedience to God's will, which is seen as a sign of faith, and God's giving of the covenant, which is seen as a sign of God's love, are examples of such lighthouses. Whether it is Adam and Eve's failure to obey, or Moses' own failure when striking the rock for water in Numbers 20, it is clear that obedience is a major issue. Many other examples could be given. In fact, it is difficult trying to limit the themes to a specific number. Every time we read, new themes may capture our imagination or move our hearts.

We will have an easier time understanding the major theological themes of the Pentateuch if we remember that more than being a book *of* or *by* God, the Bible is a book *about* God. Through its many themes and stories, the Pentateuch reveals a God whom Israel has come to know as the one God, who acts in human history, and who has chosen Israel in a special way. All the themes of the Pentateuch reveal God's intimate relationship with people, emphasizing the need for humanity to respond to God's initiative.

## Ten Central Themes

### God Created a Good World

When Genesis tells us God spoke the world into being, it means that creation was no accident, but part of a divine plan causing all things to work together in harmony. God judged all creation as "very good" (Gn 1:31). Thus, no matter how bad things get, we must remember that the original blessing is never fully lost and that, ultimately, goodness will prevail.

### God Has Blessed Human Life

Twice Genesis tells us that God blessed the human race (Gn 1:28; 9:1). If the world is good, so is all life within it.

### Humanity Has a Tendency to Sin

Much of the biblical story presents human beings as disobedient and sinful, ignoring God's will. Many of the laws, therefore, center on atonement (particularly in Leviticus) and on the need to repent and turn back to God (Deuteronomy particularly).

### God Is a God of Mercy

If humanity tends toward rebellion, God tends toward forgiveness and mercy. God spares Adam and Eve, Cain and Noah, and others in order to give the human race a new start each time after it sins. In the Exodus event, God is revealed above all else as a liberating God.

### God Keeps Promises

God promised Noah, Abraham, Isaac, Jacob, and Moses that they would become a great people, and repeatedly the Pentateuch stresses the fulfillment of that promise. Israel's God is a God of the future, not one patterned on the recurring cycles of nature. God inspires hope. Believers can expect that God can act in new and decisive ways.

### The Covenant Binds God to Israel

All people believe their god relates to them somehow, but only in Israel do we find a relationship based on love, permanent loyalty, and respect for the human partner. The covenant is the heart of biblical faith because it expresses a unique bond between God and people.

### The Law Expresses Israel's Bond to God

The covenant establishes a relationship, but the laws of the Pentateuch show how that relationship can be lived out by the people. Laws are not restrictive rules; they are a joyful way of living that expresses faith in actions as well as words.

### Worship Is Praise Is Thanksgiving

An odd way to express a simple but important idea: To pray is to praise, and to praise is to thank God. The Pentateuch constantly reminds Israel of what God has done for them, and the laws express the need to rejoice and give thanks to God in everything.

### Religious Life Is Life in Community

God chose a people, not a lot of all-star individuals. Single hearts and voices can't know and praise God properly. Only human minds and voices joined together can do that. God's many faces can be seen only if we share our memories and relate to one another in love.

### God Directs All of History

The central conviction of Israel—that there is one, and only one, God—leads to recognition of God's lordship over all peoples and all events. God blesses and punishes, sets obstacles and shows the way through them. All things are in God's hands, so the only thing that makes sense is to walk in the ways of the LORD.

## Ten Themes of Biblical Spirituality for Today

The theological themes of the Pentateuch offer rich implications for our own spiritual life as disciples of the one God we find there. Following are some of the important personal demands the message of the Pentateuch places on our lives.

### All Things in Our Life Must Flow From Faith

The stories of the Pentateuch reveal that no part of life is outside of God's plan. We must live believing that God's will can be known and followed in all of life's situations.

### Our Prayer and Our Daily Life Must Be One

We must not pray on Sunday and go to hell for what we do on Monday. Nothing is so secular that God cannot be a part of it. Our worship and prayer should relate to the real problems and decisions we face in daily life. There is not a single area of life where God is not present.

### We Must Respect God's Holiness

The Bible often speaks of God with beautiful human imagery, but it never allows us to forget that God is also the all-powerful creator of the universe who cannot be represented by idols or treated like just another human being. The Pentateuch balances notions of God's closeness to the world with the clear recognition that our job is to do God's will—not try to make God do our will.

### We Must Imitate God's Holiness

Since we are made in God's image and likeness, we have a responsibility to act like God. God cares for the poor, the widow, the alien, and the orphan—and so must we. (See how Leviticus 19 outlines our duties to our neighbor.)

### Holiness Must Be Translated into Compassion

Forgiveness is the hallmark of God's holiness. God claims to be a God who bestows "mercy down to the thousandth generation, on the children of those who love me" (Ex 20:6) and who forgives "wickedness and crime and sin" (Ex 34:7). Holiness is best expressed not in private prayer, but in our forgiving and merciful behavior toward each other.

### Life Is a Journey

Among the oldest of metaphors for human existence, this image is deeply rooted in the Pentateuch itself. Abraham is called to a new land; Jacob must find God far from home. Joseph must go to Egypt, and Israel must cross the desert to find a Promised Land. The journey motif not only stresses the future to which we go; even more, it emphasizes the value of the journey itself, for the God toward whom we move is already with us on the road.

### Life's Journey Requires Trust in God

What is needed on a risk-filled journey with God? Trust! The Pentateuch asserts that God's guidance never fails even when the people turn from God's way. Keeping God's commandments builds our courage and confidence; we learn to trust in God's promises and find peace.

### We Are People of the Land

The Promised Land dominates the stories of the Pentateuch. Israel was in love with her land and never lost her infatuation with it even when it was taken from her. Israel never wanted to be divorced from the concrete realities of everyday life and never embraced asceticism as an ideal. Its spirituality was hardheaded and included wrestling with the proper use of the land and its resources, working for justice in social settings, and molding politics and economics to the demands of God's Law. Genesis says that we are from the earth and to the earth we shall return (Gn 3:10). Then we must take the earth seriously!

### Faith Is a Family Affair

Much of Israel's religious practice was centered in the home: Sabbath observance, Passover, prayer, teaching children the Law. The home-centered religious practices narrated in the Pentateuch can teach us much about how our own families can celebrate together, teach one another about God, and give concrete witness to what we believe.

### Prayer Must Fill Our Lives

The Pentateuch provides numerous examples both of public prayer and of the private prayers of individuals responding to every experience of God's presence in their lives. Israel's need and ability to pray in all situations eventually gave birth to the Psalms, a collection of prayers and hymns that express the whole range of human feelings before God. Their boldness and yet humility provide modern believers with an example of how we can live our lives as prayer.

### Questions for Discussion and Reflection

***Group Sharing/Discussion***

1. Much of the Pentateuch is about the laws of the Israelites. What do we learn about the people from these laws? What would someone from another planet learn about us from our laws?

2. Explain the meaning of two words you will meet often in Bible study: exegesis and hermeneutics.

3. Have four people each explain how the Bible was read in one of the four periods of history: New Testament times, Early Church, Medieval Period, Modern Study. What was the same and what was different from age to age?

4. What do you understand "myth" to mean? Is it an appropriate term to use in reference to some of the stories of Genesis? Why or why not?

*In Our Lives*

1. Depending on the size of your study group, divide up the *Ten Themes for Biblical Spirituality Today,* explaining each one and giving suggestions of how we can put it into practice in our daily lives.

2. One of the 10 central themes in the Pentateuch is that our religious life is in community. What is our individual role in building up our own community? How do certain individuals in your own parish build up the community?

*Individual/Personal Reflection/Action*

1. See how many of the new words you encountered in this essay are in the glossary.

2. Read over the last two of the *Ten Themes of Biblical Spirituality for Today*. Decide on one thing you will do to more consciously live those themes.

FOR FURTHER STUDY

Lawrence Boadt, C.S.P. *Reading the Old Testament: An Introduction.* Mahway, NJ: Paulist Press, 1985. A readable overview of all the critical and theological issues of Old Testament study.

*The New Jerome Biblical Commentary*. Englewood Cliffs, NJ: Prentice-Hall, 1990. A superb one-volume commentary on all of Scripture with fine background articles for study of the Pentateuch.

Margaret Nutting Ralph. *"And God Said What?"* Mahway, NJ: Paulist Press, 1986. A very understandable introduction to literary forms in the Bible.

# GENESIS READING GUIDE

## *At a Glance*

| | |
|---|---|
| Who are the main players? | Adam and Eve Cain and Abel Noah Abraham and Sarah Isaac and Rebekah Jacob and Rachel Joseph |
| What should I look for? | Creation of the world Human rebellion and sin The beginning of the nation of Israel God's Promises: Covenants with Noah and Abraham |
| When did this take place? | Prehistory and c. 1800 B.C. to 1300 B.C. |
| Where did these events occur? | The area now called the Middle East: Egypt, Jordan, Lebanon, Israel, Syria, Turkey, Iraq, Saudi Arabia |
| Why was this book written? | To make the point that God created all things and created them good; that human beings broke faith with God and are responsible for evil in the world; that God never stops loving humanity and, through Abraham, formed a people to whom and through whom God has been revealed. |
| What is the story? | God creates a good world. Man and woman sin. Noah and family survive the flood. Abraham receives God's promises and trusts God even to the point of being willing to sacrifice his own son. Through Isaac and Jacob, Abraham's clan begins to grow. In Egypt, Joseph provides a safe-haven for the fledgling nation and it begins to prosper and multiply. |

When you first approach the book of Genesis, a helpful way to start is by quickly reading all 50 chapters to grasp the "plot" and the style of the book. Then, a second, more careful reading will reveal much more.

The date and setting for the creation of the final form of Genesis is probably the time when the people of Judah were in exile in Babylon (sixth century B.C.) or when the Babylonian exiles returned home to Judah under the Persian empire (fifth century B.C.). The time of exile and the return home forced Israel to think hard about its identity as a people and its mission as the people of God among the nations of the world. By remembering the Genesis stories about the beginnings of the world and Israel's earliest ancestors, they could return to their roots and think about who they were as an exiled people who were returning home to Judah. They could identify with their ancestors in Genesis, who were also a family on the move. Just as the family of Abraham and Sarah migrated back and forth from Mesopotamia to Canaan (see map p. 27) so the exiles would migrate from Babylon back to Judah. The key promise in the midst of this wandering and yearning to return home was the promise God made to Jacob: "I am with you and will protect you wherever you go, and bring you back to this land" (28:15).

## Structure of Genesis

The book of Genesis received its English name from the Greek translation of the Hebrew word *toledot* (generations, genealogy, account of origins, derived from a verb meaning "give birth" or "beget"), which is used 13 times in Genesis and is translated as "story" (2:4) or "descendants" (10:1). In Hebrew, Genesis is known, like many books in the Bible, by its first word, *bereishit,* which means, "In the beginning." Genesis is indeed a book about beginnings—the beginning of the natural world, the beginning of human culture, and the beginning of the people of Israel, whose story occupies most of this book and will dominate the rest of the Bible.

The book of Genesis is thus, in more senses than one, a primary source for Jewish theology. It presents its ideas on the relationship of God to nature, to the human race in general, and to the people of Israel in ways that are foreign to the expectations of most modern readers. It is therefore all too easy to miss the seriousness of its messages. For Genesis conveys its worldview neither as a theological tract nor a rigorous philosophical proof nor a confession of faith. Instead, it uses narrative or story.

Most often scholars divide Genesis into two parts: chapters 1–11 and 12–50. While the parts seem to constitute a single, continuous story, there are actually significant differences between them in both subject matter and in the kind of literature they contain. The first 11 chapters, often referred to as the "primeval history," discuss the creation of the world and the first human beings—the ancestors of all humanity. The second part, on the other hand, describes the very ancestors of Israel itself. Genesis 1–11 falls into the literary category of "myth" (see box, RG 38) in which every story seems to model the proper (or improper, in some cases) relationship between God and humans. The stories of the latter part of Genesis, however, relate specific events in the life of what came to be a particular nation, Israel.

The characters and worlds of the two sections are very different. The world of the primeval history bears little resemblance to the world we live in. In that world people lived incredibly long lives and spoke directly with God. In contrast, Abraham, Isaac, Jacob, and the other people described in chapters 12–50, seem to live out their joys and struggles in a world like ours, making decisions that affect the whole history of the nation.

***Differences between the Two Major Divisions of Genesis***

| Topic | Genesis 1–11 | Genesis 12–50 |
|---|---|---|
| Time | Set in time before human history | Set in historical times well known to ancient records |
| Place | Locations vague: somewhere to the East of Israel | Locations exact: Palestine and Egypt and Northern Mesopotamia |
| Persons | Characters seem like symbols; little is known of their lives | Characters behave like typical people of the second millennium B.C. |
| Stories | Many stories can be classified as myths; they resemble those known from Mesopotamia | Saga-like stories and epic history narratives similar to oral lore of tribal groups |
| Events | Most events seem to have supernatural quality | Major events resemble normal human experience |
| Purpose | Describes the origins of humanity long before Israel's time | Traces the direct tribal ancestors of Israel itself |

| Genesis 1–11<br>**Primeval History** | Genesis 12–50<br>**Folk History** |
|---|---|
| Genesis 1–3<br>The story of God's creation and the first human sin | Genesis 12–25<br>Abraham is chosen to receive God's special blessing. |
| Genesis 4–5<br>The evil sin grows and spreads through the world. | Genesis 21–27<br>The son, Isaac, inherits the promise and passes it on. |
| Genesis 6–10<br>Evil overwhelms the world; God must begin again with a new blessing. | Genesis 27–36; 48–50<br>Jacob in turn receives the promise; he is blessed with the 12 sons who will become Israel. |
| Genesis 10–11<br>People again multiply across the earth but sin persists. | Genesis 37–50<br>Joseph brings the promise to Egypt and remains completely faithful to God. |

The chart on the previous page illustrates some of the significant differences between the two parts.

### Subdivisions of Genesis 1–50

By breaking down the two-part division of the book of Genesis into smaller units, we can get a clearer picture of the relationship between the two parts.

Note in the chart above how the four major sections of the primeval history match the four sections of the folk history of Israel's founders. Each column reveals growth, for better or worse: In the primeval history, sin grows; in the folk history, Israel. The Genesis editors' effort to show that there are stages in the history of humanity, and of Israel in particular, clearly succeeds. Each period of history has major impact on those that follow; therefore, as we read Genesis, we should keep our eyes open for signs of growth and development.

Another way to organize Genesis is to break it down into four blocks of material that focus on major characters. When we do this, as the chart below illustrates, we see that the "plot" of Genesis centers on major decisions made by key individuals.

The reader may be surprised to find that Genesis ends with Abraham's descendants living in Egypt instead of in the land of promise. But the book's ending reminds us that the story will continue: God's promise is not forgotten and Israel's future lies elsewhere.

### Division by the Special *Toledoth* Lists

The *New American Bible* points out that Genesis contains internal markers that help divide and organize the material. These markers are the genealogical lists, *toledoth,* that always begin "these are the descendants of. . . ." (Note: the *NAB* sometimes varies the translation of that phrase, but in Hebrew it is always the same.) These lists help make the point that while generations come and go, God's plan moves ahead no matter what. Sometimes appearing at the beginning and sometimes at the end of a section, the lists group together all the members of a family line or tribe to signal a break with the events that have just been recounted. The chart on the next page illustrates where these lists appear and the purpose they serve.

***Division of Genesis into Four Blocks of Material***

| | |
|---|---|
| A. The Prologue: primeval history of humankind's original blessing and failure through sin | Gn 1–11 |
| B. The story of Abraham: his call and response; his blessing and promise | Gn 12–25 |
| C. The stories of Abraham's son Isaac and grandson Jacob and how they carry on the blessing | Gn 26–36 |
| D. The story of Joseph in Egypt: preparation for God's great self-revelation in the Exodus | Gn 37–50 |

*The Toledoth Lists*

| | |
|---|---|
| Gn 2:4a | Begins the second story of creation |
| Gn 5:1 | Introduces the long break between the first family and the days of Noah |
| Gn 6:9 | Introduces the story of the flood |
| Gn 10:1 | Marks the great expansion of people all over the world |
| Gn 11:10 | Marks the addition of a new list of the nations of the world by the P source |
| Gn 11:27 | Begins the story of Abraham |
| Gn 25:12 | Closes off the life of Abraham's "other" family through Hagar and Ishmael |
| Gn 25:19 | Opens the story of Jacob's birth and destiny |
| Gn 36:1 | Ends the role of Jacob's twin, Esau, and directs us to Jacob's children, especially Joseph |
| Gn 36:9 | A repetition within the Esau list that marks its conclusion |
| Gn 37:2 | The phrase "family history" marks the opening of the story of Joseph and his brothers that continues to the end of Genesis |

The way a writer organizes material, and the choices made regarding the overall shape of the writing, reveal much about the purpose of the writing. Our purpose in identifying the major outline of Genesis and of naming its various subdivisions is to show that what we have here is a continuous story that runs not only from the beginning to the end of Genesis, but through the entire Pentateuch as well. Once we grasp the overall outline, we can begin to see how individual incidents fit into it.

## The Primeval History of Genesis 1–11

In studying these chapters, several aspects should be noted.

1. They are generally described by *form criticism* as a combination of myths and genealogical tables.

2. They are described by the source critics as a combination of the materials from the Yahwist (J) and the Priestly (P) sources. (See the explanation of the source hypothesis in the introductory essay on the Pentateuch, RG 42.)

3. Many of the individual stories have parallels in the literatures of other ancient Near Eastern peoples. These are often much older than the biblical versions. While this means that they are possible sources for the versions of these stories in the Bible, the J and P accounts have a distinctive character that is very different from these ancient sources (see box, "Are Some Genesis Stories Just Rewrites of Ancient Myths?" RG 53).

### J and P Sources

If we remember that the J stories are much older (probably) than the P stories, and at first probably stood alone as the basic proclamation of the beginnings of the world, we can first glance at each group separately.

It might be noted that there are several duplications in these lists: both J and P have a list of great ancestors between Adam and Noah (4:17–26 versus 5:1–32); both have a flood story that is now hopelessly intermixed as a single account; and both have a Table of Nations that spread over the earth in Genesis 10–11, that is also interwoven as a single narrative list.

### The Theology of the Yahwist Source

The incidents chosen by the J author to tell the story of creation focus on the tension between God's goodness and human beings' disobedience. Adam and Eve, Cain and Abel, the wicked generation of the flood, the sons of Noah, and the builders of the tower of Babel all received plenty of evidence of God's love. Yet each generation chose to disobey by embracing one of the deadly vices: greed, envy, lust, pride.

Look at the pattern the Yahwist author uses to structure each story:

This repeated pattern conveys an overarching message: Because humanity repeatedly failed to respond to God's offering of intimate love, sin spread and contaminated all people. Now God must find a new way to demonstrate control over the earth and all of history, and to show love for humanity. As with Adam and Eve and Noah and his family, God begins this

| J (Tenth Century B.C.) | P (Seventh to Sixth Centuries B.C.) |
|---|---|
| | **Gn 1:1–2:4a**<br>The creation of the world |
| **Gn 2:4b–3:24**<br>The human condition at creation, and sin | |
| **Gn 4:1–26**<br>Cain and Abel: even the children sin but God continues to care | |
| | **Gn 5:1–32**<br>The list of long-lived ancestors from Adam to Noah |
| **Gn 6:1–4**<br>More evil caused by the sin of angels and humans | |
| **Gn 6:5–9:29**<br>The flood story with 40 days and 7 pairs of clean animals, etc. | **Gn 6:5–9:29**<br>The flood story based on 365 days and one pair of each animal only, etc. |
| **Gn 10:8–19, 25–30**<br>Table of Nations from a different source | **Gn 10:1–7, 20–24**<br>Table of all the nations |
| **Gn 11:1–9**<br>The story of the tower of Babel | |
| | **Gn 11:10–32**<br>The continuation of the Table of Nations down to Abraham |

new round by again choosing a single family, Abraham's, and giving them a special revelation of divine goodness to share with the world.

### The Theology of the Priestly Source

If later Israelites had only the version of their history given in the J Source—sin, punishment, mercy, and the promise of being formed into a chosen people—they might have misunderstood it as promising absolute control over the land and great power for Abraham's descendants. But by the time the Priestly writers were gathering their own accounts, Israel had already experienced military defeats and the loss of 10 of the 12 tribes. Israel was wondering if God really was in control and would stand by them in hard times.

| God . . . | People . . . |
|---|---|
| 1. . . . acts lovingly toward humanity | |
| | 2. . . . disobey God and sin |
| 3. . . . announces punishment | |
| | 4. . . . are punished |
| 5. . . . shows mercy and gives a new blessing | |

The Priestly writers apparently wanted to make sure the promises spoken in the creation stories would suggest two things: first, that God's control over world events was greater than any human power; and second, that it would be shown in ways besides Israel's political fortunes. In other words, Israel's misfortunes did not mean that God had lost control. P clearly states that humans are made in the image of God (Gn 1:27 and 9:6) to govern the earth and fill it, but P's stress is not on humanity's independent power; rather, an important element of being made in the image of God is humanity's responsibility to act as God would act.

The genealogies of chapters 5 and 10–11 are also part of P's insistence that God has a plan that cannot be derailed by human whims, nor even upset by human sin. God is always in charge—even when we are experiencing just punishment. God's blessing *can* be relied on. We must learn trust! By stressing the goodness of creation and God's blessing of humanity, P's larger vision brought hope to Israel at a time when circumstances could have led it to despair.

### The Overall Message of Genesis 1–11

The combining of J and P reveals the full range of Hebrew thought regarding the origins of humanity:

God is good and all God created is good.

Human beings are morally obligated to obey God's plan.

God alone is worthy of worship.

By the way they used and reshaped Canaanite myths and subtly attacked pagan religious practices, the J and P authors and editors made the point that Canaanite worship and beliefs pervert God's plan. The Israelites did use elements from beliefs of other Near Eastern peoples—for example, creation being a fight between God and Chaos. However, they always modified these in a way that made clear their belief in God's sovereignty over creation. In the same way they took over planting and harvesting celebrations but distanced themselves from the fertility cults they were rejecting.

### Two Different Creation Stories

The Bible begins with two different versions of the story of the beginning of the world. These two versions arose at different periods in Israel's history. Most scholars would date the story in Gn 2:4–25 earlier than the story in 1:1–2:3. The former, from the J tradition, was probably written during the time Israel had kings reigning in Jerusalem and before the exile to Babylon in 587 B.C. The usual scholarly designation for this earlier tradition, which extends intermittently throughout the Pentateuch (Genesis—Deuteronomy), is the Yahwist or J tradition. Most scholars would date the later creation story in Genesis 1 to a time after 587 B.C. during the Persian period. This later tradition is the P or Priestly tradition. Allowing two different versions of the creation story to stand side by side suggests that the ancient writers were not interested in defining precisely how the world began in a scientific sense. Rather, they were interested in exploring larger questions of meaning and purpose through multiple perspectives on the same events of creation.

## Notes on Individual Creation Passages

### Genesis 1:1–2:4a

The Priestly creation story contains patterns that structure the individual days and the entire week.

*Pattern One:* Each day contains a five-point framework:

*Opening:* "Then God said. . . ."

*Command:* "Let there be. . . ."

*Fulfillment:* "And so it happened. . . ."

*Judgment:* "And God saw that it was good. . . ."

*Naming:* "Evening came, and morning followed . . ."

*Pattern Two:* The six days of creation are divided into two matched sets of three days each as shown in the chart on RG 54. During the first three days of creation we see God building a vast stage of heavens, water, and land by separating one from the other. During the second three days God populates the stage with its primary actors, and the creation becomes one integrated whole. The goodness of the creation is celebrated on the climactic seventh day. This day becomes the model of rest and celebration of God's goodness that humans are to follow each week.

## Are Some Genesis Stories Just Rewrites of Ancient Myths?

SOMETIMES READERS POINT to the similarities between the biblical creation stories and myths of ancient Near Eastern people as a way of discrediting the Bible texts. Since they are derived from pagan myths, they argue, the Bible stories have no more than literary value. But the fact that a biblical writer may have borrowed legends from neighboring cultures in no way diminishes the theological value of the writing.

It is the biblical author's final product, not the original myth, that the Church believes is inspired and has canonized into the body of Scripture. And this final form differs significantly in purpose and theology from the myths the inspired writer not only may have borrowed, but perhaps was also trying to debunk.

To take just two examples: The story of the creation of humanity and the story of the flood both have parallels among ancient Mesopotamian myths. Many of the similarities are even quite striking. But their overall messages are clearly different, especially in their presentation and understanding of God.

The Babylonian creation story called *Enuma Elish* presumes the existence of many gods who haphazardly created the world while fighting among themselves. Their creation is therefore partly good and partly evil, and human beings are nothing more than their slaves. Against this view of creation the biblical writer presents a theology that asserts one, and only one, God who creates consciously and out of love. God's creation is all good and human beings are not slaves, but are made in God's own image and are given dominion over the earth.

The Noah flood story has a close parallel in the *Epic of Gilgamesh,* possibly the oldest of recorded human stories. In the tale, Gilgamesh sets out to find an ancestor who has achieved immortality. The ancestor tells of having survived a great flood and of how he helped save humanity. In details, this flood account is surprisingly similar to the Genesis story. But the two versions present very different images of God.

The Babylonians believed there was an ongoing struggle between gods and humans. Their unpredictable gods found humans annoying and often erupted in hostility toward them. Human beings could never be sure of how to please their gods, nor of what would anger them. Genesis, on the other hand, presents a God who never changes. God is eternally just, yet loving and faithful. Israel's God punishes only when human beings have committed real wrong. And their God is always eager to forgive.

It is important to remember that being related to and derived from similar stories of the ancient Near East in no way compromises the religious truth or value of the stories we find in Genesis.

The pattern of creation was not invented by the P authors. The same order is followed in the ancient creation myth from Babylon called the *Enuma Elish,* in which Marduk, the chief god of Babylon, and at the same time young king of all gods, fashions the world from the body of Tiamat, the mother goddess whom he had slain in battle. The *Enuma Elish* describes Marduk's creative actions in a sequence parallel to the account in Genesis 1:

• It begins with a conquest of chaos by order = The opening statement of Gn 1:1–2

• Heavens created and separated from water = Day 2, the creation of heavens and separation of the waters.

| *Prologue: Introductory Statement Asserting God's Control of Chaos* | | | |
|---|---|---|---|
| | **Three Days of Separation** | | **Three Days of Integration** |
| Day 1 | God creates heavens and separates light from darkness | Day 4 | Sun, moon, and stars join the sky |
| Day 2 | God separates waters above (rain) from waters below (oceans) | Day 5 | Birds and fish are added to sky and waters |
| Day 3 | God separates land from waters and adds vegetation to land | Day 6 | Animals populate the land and, finally, humans |
| Day 7 | Epilogue: God rests, fully in control of all creation | | |

- The earth is set over the waters = Day 3, the land appears from the waters
- Creation of sun and moon = Day 4, sun and moon are set in heaven
- (No mention of plants or animals) = (Days 5–6, the creation of fish, birds, and animals)
- Creation of human beings = Day 6, the creation of humans
- The gods rest and celebrate = Day 7, God rests

### Genesis 2:4b—3:24

This is the Yahwist account of creation, a much older story than the Priestly version of chapter 1. Although we can detect here some story themes borrowed from Mesopotamia, the biblical account is unique as a whole and more sophisticated in its vision than anything else found in the ancient world. In the ancient Near East the king was often said to be the "image" of the God and thus to act with divine authority. So here the creation of humanity in God's *image* and *likeness* carries with it a commission to rule over the animal kingdom (1:26).

Some have seen in that commission a license for ecological irresponsibility. The fact is, however, that the Bible presents humanity not as the owner of nature but as its steward, strictly accountable to its true Owner (see Lv 25:23–24). The garden of Eden is not a paradise of luxury but a place for human work. Humans will *till* the garden and keep it.

Whereas 1:1–2:3 presented a majestic God-centered scenario of creation, 2:4–25 presents a different but equally profound story of origins. This second account of creation is centered more on human beings and familiar experiences, and even its deity is conceived in more anthropomorphic terms. Here humans' ambition to be like God or like divine beings is the root of their expulsion from Eden. The command not to eat from the tree of knowledge of good and evil carries a grave consequence, which in Hebrew reads literally: "you shall surely die."

This account of creation and sin presents some key biblical insights: Man is created first, at the beginning of creation, and all other creatures are made for his companionship. He participates in shaping the character of the animals by giving them names. God tries a second strategy to satisfy the human's loneliness. God fashions a woman from the rib of the sleeping man. Woman alone, among God's other creatures, is equal to the man and is a suitable helper for him. The term *helper* does not imply an inferior assistant but a genuine partner who comes to the aid of another. God is often called a "helper" for those in need (Ps 10:14; 54:4). Unlike the animals, the woman instantly evokes a joyous response from the man. Humans are more than just another creature—they were created to "cultivate and care for" the rest of creation (2:15). Intimacy is the chief characteristic of the relationship between God and human beings. Sin is a pervasive reality, but it is the result of human choice, not God's.

### Genesis 4:1–16

The story of Cain and Abel tells a moral about how evil flourishes and leads even to fratricide. But it also builds on an age-old theme of the conflict between the farmer and the herder. The musical *Oklahoma* sings how the farmer and the cowman should be friends, but their interests conflict—the farmer wants to fence in and protect his plot of land, the cowman requires wide-open spaces over which the cattle or sheep can move to new pastures. This was a conflict well known to the early Israelites, who as nomadic shepherds came up against the protected and settled lands of the Canaanite farmers. It is no accident that the evil that is displeasing to the LORD just happens to come from the (Canaanite) farmer Cain!

### Genesis 4:17–22; 5:1–32

The genealogies of Genesis 4–5 with the enormous ages of the patriarchs are not intended to be taken literally. A Sumerian list of kings who lived before the flood ascribes even more astounding ages to its monarchs, some of them living 28,000 years and more. Such genealogy lists are typical of many people who keep largely oral traditions.

### Genesis 6:1–9:27

Two observations should be remembered during your study of the flood account. First, it must have been very important to the biblical writers, because both the Yahwist and Priestly traditions had their own version of the flood, and they considered each important enough to save. Second, the biblical story bears strong resemblance to other ancient flood stories told in Babylon and Syria. What makes the biblical account unique and religiously important is what it teaches us about God. In the pagan versions God's motives for destroying humanity are either left out or trivialized (human noisiness kept the gods awake). But the Genesis story insists that God acted out of justice and in response to people's moral evil. The relationship between God and people is not characterized by the constant tension of the pagan versions, but by intimate love that continues despite the flood. The story's final image of the rainbow promises hope and blessing.

### Genesis 9:28–10:32

By being placed after the flood story, this second set of genealogies links the prehistoric flood with the call of Abraham in the very real towns of Ur and Haran in Mesopotamia. Like the genealogy of Genesis 4:17–5:32 it connects major moments in the history of God's interventions in human life and tells how, after the flood, people spread out to fill the far corners of the earth. The genealogy is a composite of two separate lists, one from the P school and the other from J. Look at the text and see how easy it is to pick out the more colorful J list with its bits of stories (10:8–30) from the much drier P list which gives names and nothing more (9:29–10:7 and 10:21–24).

### Genesis 11:1–9

The J writer has crafted an ironic and even humorous story. Having ignored God's earlier command to "fill the earth" (Gn 1:28; 9:1), people are united and speak one language. In addition, they want to "make a name for themselves," that is, achieve greatness without any help from God. God attacks this arrogance and forces the people both to disperse and to populate the earth by confusing their language. Note that the great temple they were building to glorify themselves is so small by divine standards that God has to "come down" to see it. Several wordplays add to the humor and irony of this story that makes the point that the growth of sin even turns a people against itself.

### Genesis 11:10–32

In this genealogy the ages of the patriarchs are greatly reduced (compare with Gn 5:1–32), although still exaggerated. This device shows that growing sin has brought the "golden age" to an end. More sin means less life. Besides illustrating the disintegrating effects of sin, the genealogies show continuity in human history from the dawn of time to Abraham. The periods recorded in the genealogies were times of blessing sandwiched in between times of sin and punishment, as illustrated in the chart on RG 56.

## Church Use of the Genesis Story of Human Creation

It is well to note that the account of making humanity in the divine image figures significantly in a number of official Catholic Church documents.

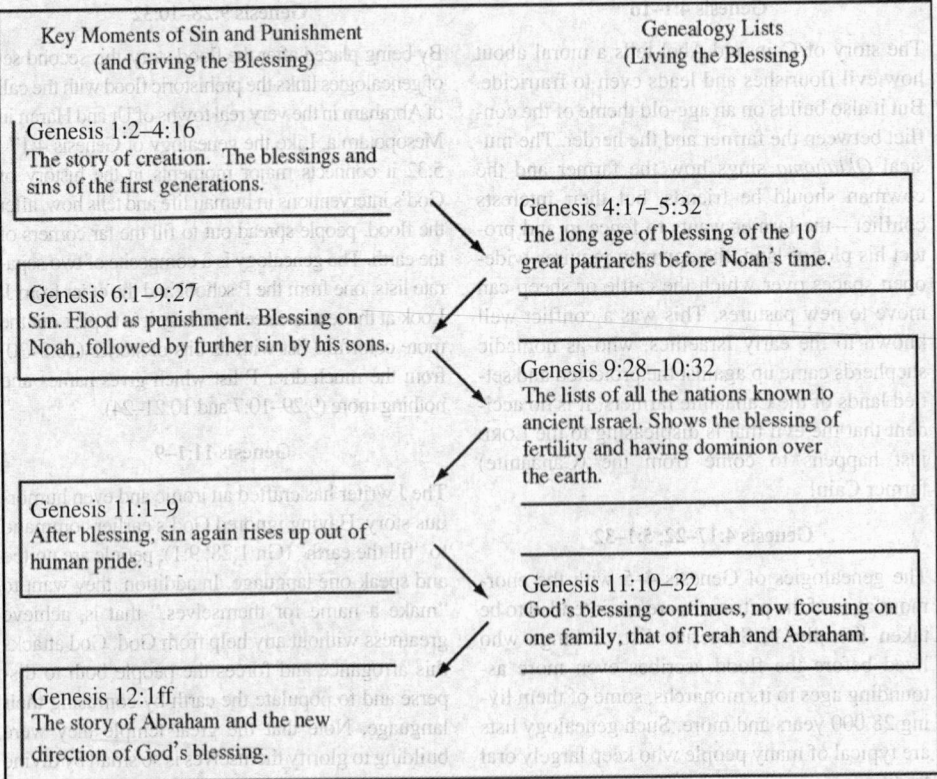

| Key Moments of Sin and Punishment (and Giving the Blessing) | Genealogy Lists (Living the Blessing) |
|---|---|
| **Genesis 1:2–4:16** The story of creation. The blessings and sins of the first generations. | |
| | **Genesis 4:17–5:32** The long age of blessing of the 10 great patriarchs before Noah's time. |
| **Genesis 6:1–9:27** Sin. Flood as punishment. Blessing on Noah, followed by further sin by his sons. | |
| | **Genesis 9:28–10:32** The lists of all the nations known to ancient Israel. Shows the blessing of fertility and having dominion over the earth. |
| **Genesis 11:1–9** After blessing, sin again rises up out of human pride. | |
| | **Genesis 11:10–32** God's blessing continues, now focusing on one family, that of Terah and Abraham. |
| **Genesis 12:1ff** The story of Abraham and the new direction of God's blessing. | |

For example, Pope Paul VI looked to Genesis 1:28 as a significant reference in his development of the responsibility to subdue the earth and its resources intelligently (*Populorum Progressio #22*). And along the same vein, John Paul II went to Genesis 1:26–30 for a reference to the "goodness" of creation in the Creator's eyes, and therefore grounding the claim that redemption is possible. (*Redemptor hominis*). Likewise, the United States bishops in their pastoral letter *Economic Justice for All* used Genesis 1:26f to show that all human relations must be based on the acknowledgement of the dignity of those created in God's image. This helps form the economic reflections of the letter.

### Questions for Discussion and Reflection

***Group Sharing/Discussion***

1. Explain how you would summarize the main ideas in this first section of Genesis to someone who is not familiar with them.

2. What is something helpful or something new you learned from reading the Reading Guide Notes on this section of Genesis?

3. Which part of these chapters is most significant to you? Explain what lesson could be learned from that part of scripture.

4. In this story of the beginning of the human race, God blesses his creatures and they then fail. What are some examples of how this pattern is repeated throughout our human history—God blesses humanity and humanity fails in some way?

***In Our Lives***

1. All of creation is good, God said, and God created humans in his image and likeness, saying that this was "very good." Share an example of when and how you see God's image in other people in your life.

2. Tell about an individual or organization working to keep the world of God's creation beautiful and good as it was created and intended to be.

3. In contrast to the story of Cain and Abel, what is an example of a person being their "brother's keeper?"

***Individual/Personal Reflection/Action***

1. Take time to be aware of the beauty of the created world around you, one of God's gifts.

2. Cain and Abel's story is an extreme example of jealousy and interpersonal conflict. Examine where you experience conflict in your life and reflect on what you might do to improve the situation.

## The Great Ancestor Narratives of Genesis 12–50

Since humanity as a whole proves stubbornly unresponsive to God's love, God shifts gears and chooses a single people who will respond to God's self-revelation and will testify about God's goodness to all nations. This second major part of Genesis tells the story of God's new plan by focusing on the lives of four patriarchal figures: Abraham, Isaac, Jacob, and Joseph. Through each character, God's plan moves a step further toward fulfillment. The blueprint for this new plan is contained in the story of Abraham's call at the beginning of chapter 12. The first three verses not only describe his call but also present the other major themes that will dominate Genesis and much of Israel's history:

| | |
|---|---|
| Verse 1 | The promise of a land for his family |
| Verse 2 | The promise of blessing through empire and fame, and probably children ("a great nation") |
| Verse 3 | The promise to rule other nations and to mediate God's blessing to them |

The promises of a son to carry on the name and a land of their own echo especially loudly in the stories that follow. But Israel did not read these promises as guarantees that life would be rosy. These stories record Israel's failures as well as successes, disobedience as well as obedience, lessons of deep faith and of sinful lack of trust. Because the Bible is the product of a faith-seeking community, Israel consistently found in its history evidence of God working even through their mistakes, guiding this people through all their troubles, helping them overcome obstacles, and bringing them blessing even in the land of their enemy, Egypt.

### The Literary Issues of Genesis 12–50

We can better appreciate what a masterpiece of storytelling Genesis is when we realize that whoever edited the book pulled together three different sources into one continuous story (see RG 42–44). Scholars have been able to identify many passages that came from J, and others that came from P. A third source, the Elohist, which is close to J in spirit but does not yet use the name Yahweh for God, has also been detected in these chapters. The three sources can be easily identified when they each tell their own version of the same story. The following chart shows how the three sources intertwine to tell the Abraham and Sarah story. In telling the story, each source stresses a different aspect of Abraham's personality. J extols his trust in the promise of land and a son, while E marvels at his obedience even to sacrificing his son. P stresses his fidelity to religious regulations, especially circumcision.

The stories of the great patriarchs and matriarchs existed in oral form long before J, E, or P ever wrote a word. The three literary sources did more than simply write down the stories, however. They carefully composed them in a way that revealed their religious value and more clearly pointed to the lessons in the stories. As you read, be aware that the writing contains two kinds of information: the original description of what happened, and Israel's later reflection on

***J, E, P Sources in the Abraham and Sarah Story***

| What Happened | J Version | E Version | P Version |
|---|---|---|---|
| Abraham receives promise of land and/or a son. | Gn 12:1–3 | Gn 15:1–6 | Gn 12:4–9 |
| God makes a covenant with Abraham. | Gn 15:7–12 | Gn 15:13–16 | Gn 17:1–14 |
| A son is born and the line of the promise is secured. | Gn 16:1–16; 18:1–19 | Gn 21:1–21 | Gn 17:15–27 |
| Abraham's life ends. | Gn 25:1–6 | Gn 22:1–13 | Gn 23:1–20 |
| Places stress on Abraham's . . . | Faith | Obedience | Fidelity |

what happened. As a people of faith, Israel saw many events as clear experiences of God's hand guiding them through history.

### The Historical Setting of the Patriarchal Stories

Scholars generally agree that the customs and events described in Genesis 12–50 best fit the period from 1900 to 1500 B.C. From what we know of the ancient world through nonbiblical sources, we can say that items like the names of the patriarchs, customs like the adoption of an heir (Gn 15:1–3) and marrying a sister (12:10–20), and Abraham's and Isaac's seminomadic lifestyle accurately reflect this period of history. The story of Joseph rising to the position of prime minister in Egypt is also most plausible in this period; Egypt was ruled by foreign invaders, the Hyksos, who may have been more likely to allow a fellow foreigner to assume power than the strong Egyptian leaders who took control around 1500 B.C.

These examples make the dating of the Genesis stories likely, but not certain. Archaeological finds, however, continue to present a picture of this part of the world that matches well with the descriptions found in Genesis.

### Abraham and Sarah, Genesis 12–25

There are several ways to get more out of the Abraham narrative. One way is to read it as the story of a man who is a homeless alien in chapter 12 and has become a wealthy landowner by the time he and Sarah are buried on their own land in chapters 23 and 25. Another way is to follow the series of promises made to Abraham and Sarah as they are slowly but surely fulfilled. Two sets of promises (see below) run parallel throughout these chapters.

A third and perhaps the most religiously fruitful way of reading Genesis 12–25 is to see it as a story of Abraham and Sarah's struggle to continue believing in and trusting God. They struggle because, like most believers, Abraham and Sarah create almost as many obstacles to God's plan as they do faith-filled responses (see next page). Remember, the Bible presents its lead characters honestly, warts and all.

### God's Promise to Abraham

God provides another version of the covenant promise, similar to the one made in Genesis 15. For the first time, however, God clearly names both Abraham and Sarah as the parents of the promised child. God also adds an element of assurance involving time: the covenant and God's relationship with the nation that will become Israel is everlasting, and Abraham's family will possess the land of Canaan perpetually. The names of Abram and Sarai are changed to mark the importance of this new promise. "Abraham" means "ancestor of a multitude," so the new name is another sign of the covenant. By also changing Sarai's name to Sarah, God indicates that she is now clearly part of the promise. God also introduces the ritual of circumcision as a physical sign of belonging to the covenant people of God. Circumcision involves cutting off the foreskin of the penis. The ritual was practiced by neighboring cultures around Israel as well as Israel itself and continues to be practiced by Jews, Muslims, and many Christians today.

Abraham laughs at the thought that he and Sarah will have a child at their ages of 100 and 90 years old. He pleads to God to keep Ishmael, who is now 13 years old, as the promised son rather than wait for yet another son (v. 18). But God

| Promise of a Son | | Promise of Land | |
|---|---|---|---|
| Gn 12:2 | I make you a great nation | Gn 12:1 | "Go to a land I will show you" |
| Gn 15:5 | At the night covenant | Gn 12:7 | At the terebinth of Moreh |
| Gn 17:4 | The P covenant | Gn 13:14 | At the departure of Lot |
| Gn 17:16 | The promise of Isaac | Gn 15:18 | At the night covenant |
| Gn 18:10 | The three angels | Gn 17:8 | The P covenant |
| Gn 18:18 | Recap of 12:2f | Gn 24:7 | The messenger for Isaac |
| Gn 21:12 | A promise to Isaac | Gn 26:4 | Repeated promise to Isaac |
| Gn 22:17 | At the sacrifice of Isaac | | |
| Gn 26:4 | Promise repeated to Isaac | | |

insists that Sarah will have a son, whose name will be Isaac, which means, "he laughs." The theme of laughter and Isaac will come up again (18:12–15; 21:5–6). God also responds to Abraham's concern for Ishmael. God promises to bless him, make him exceedingly numerous, and make him a great nation. These are the same promises that Abraham originally receives (12:1–3) and that now extend to Isaac as the child of promise.

The story of Abraham and Sarah climaxes in the great moment of the test in chapter 22. After Abraham proves himself fully obedient to God's will at that awful moment when he nearly sacrifices his son, the story comes to a rapid conclusion. The promise of a son is secured, Abraham's purchase of a tomb and a small piece of land foreshadows the eventual possession of the entire land God had promised, and so Abraham's role now passes on to Isaac.

### Isaac and Rebekah, Genesis 24–27

We may be surprised to find so little space given to the life of Isaac, one of the three great patriarchs of Israel. Although he plays an important role in the life of Abraham as the promised son, his role is primarily passive, even in the scene where he is nearly sacrificed. In Isaac, continuity with Abraham is clearly established, for God appears twice to Isaac, repeating to him the promises made to Abraham. But Isaac himself seems to do little to advance God's plan.

It would be easy to think of Isaac simply as a transitional character between Abraham and Jacob except for the presence in his life of his remarkable wife, Rebekah. The story of the messenger persuading Rebekah and her brother Laban to permit her to marry Isaac is a masterpiece of ancient writing (Gn 24). A total of 67 verses is given to describing this one event. Rebekah will become the key player in the next step of God's plan, the selection of her son Jacob over his older brother, Esau.

### Jacob, Genesis 27–36

The theme of promise that dominates the patriarchal stories continues here, but to it is added the theme of rivalry between brothers. When we see how that rivalry is played out, and the other forms of trickery and dishonesty that color Jacob's career, we might be surprised, even horrified that Jacob is God's choice to carry on the covenant. We will better appreciate the value and religious message of this part of the patriarchal history if we keep a few points in mind.

1. The overall purpose of Genesis 12–50 is to show God's promise being carried out despite all obstacles. We should not be surprised then that Jacob, like Abraham, is himself one of those obstacles.

2. These chapters consist of many hero-type folktales that had been told for generations. When these were gathered into written form and their religious meaning highlighted, even the less edifying details were kept and cherished.

3. We are dealing here with a world very different from our own, which did not share our refined sense of ethics. Craftiness and the ability to outfox an opponent were not incompatible with ancient people's standards of honesty and fair

| Trusting Responses | | Obstacles | |
|---|---|---|---|
| Gn 12:1–9 | Abraham leaves home | Gn 12:10–20 | Abraham pretends Sarah is his sister |
| Gn 14:1–24 | War and blessing of Melchizedek | Gn 13:1–8 | Lot allowed to choose the land |
| Gn 15:1–21 | The covenant with God | Gn 16:1–14 | Abraham has a son by his slave wife |
| Gn 17:1–27 | Abraham's covenant renewed | Gn 18:1–15 | Sarah doubts the promise of a son |
| Gn 18:16–33 | Abraham intercedes for Sodom | Gn 20:1–18 | Abraham nearly repeats his denial of Sarah |
| Gn 21:1–20 | The birth of Isaac | | |
| Gn 21:21–33 | Abraham establishes rights to water | | |
| Gn 22:1–14 | Abraham passes test of sacrificing Isaac | | |
| Gn 23:1–20 | Abraham buys land | | |

play. And we do not have to agree with or like all of what we find in these stories.

4. Israel is recounting its own history here, not the pious biography of a saint, and the central theme of this history is God's relationship with real people, not idealized characters.

Israel saw God working in the events of these stories. In them it recognized a God who had chosen to work through a people that was as imperfect as its leaders. And this very fact built their faith, for it proved that everything works for the good in God's plan. Israel realized God writes straight with crooked lines—including the choice of a younger son (Jacob) over the rightful leader, the older son (Esau), and following the advice of a mother (Rebekah) rather than the good judgment of a father of the promise, Isaac himself. These stories are reminders that despite their faults, the patriarchs never completely turned away from God, and that despite its faults, neither did Israel.

Jacob stands as a model for Israel in addition to being its founding father. Three times God appears to him. God passes on to Jacob the promise made to Abraham and Isaac, wrestles with him and changes his name, and assures him he will father a great nation. In turn, Jacob acknowledges God as the only god of Israel. But those encounters changed more than wily Jacob's name, for he emerged from them as a principled and decent human being. Israel found in Jacob's life a mirror of its own struggle to live out the covenant with God.

### Joseph, Genesis 37–50

Like those that precede it, Joseph's story can be read in two ways: to find the traditions and themes that reach far back into Israel's history, and to learn the theological purpose of the story as part of the overall religious message of Genesis. Scholars see the Yahwist and Elohist sources woven together to form this one unified story. The slight differences and inconsistencies found in the text are sure give-aways that two sources were blended into one. An obvious example occurs in chapter 37 where, in alternating sets of verses, J names Joseph's father *Israel,* states that his long *coat* caused his brothers' jealousy, that his brother *Judah* interceded for him,

## The Tribes of Israel

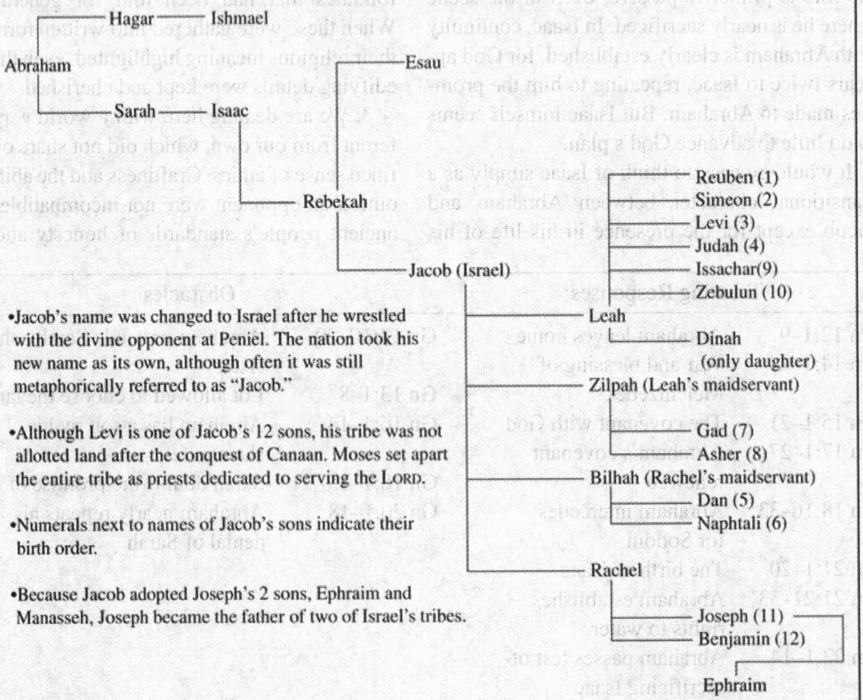


- Jacob's name was changed to Israel after he wrestled with the divine opponent at Peniel. The nation took his new name as its own, although often it was still metaphorically referred to as "Jacob."
- Although Levi is one of Jacob's 12 sons, his tribe was not allotted land after the conquest of Canaan. Moses set apart the entire tribe as priests dedicated to serving the LORD.
- Numerals next to names of Jacob's sons indicate their birth order.
- Because Jacob adopted Joseph's 2 sons, Ephraim and Manasseh, Joseph became the father of two of Israel's tribes.

and that *Ishmaelite* merchants bought him; while the E writer names the father *Jacob,* blames Joseph's *dreams* for causing the jealousy, credits *Reuben* with interceding for Joseph, and says 12 *Midianite* merchants carried him off to Egypt.

Scholars also agree that the Joseph story contains many elements of the Wisdom tradition of Israel. Joseph, once he is on his own in Egypt, fits the image of the ideal man offered by the book of Proverbs (for example, in chapter 4): He says only what is appropriate, keeps his own counsel, accepts misunderstandings, is hardworking and disciplined, is a fine administrator, interprets dreams, plays political games well, and avoids getting involved with foreign women. Most of all, Joseph is a devout, God-fearing man who knows God's ways are different from ours.

The Joseph story is more like a short novel than the string of saga-like stories that make up the previous chapters. There is a wonderful dramatic unity to the narrative: From start to finish, each part of the story fits into the whole like the pieces of a puzzle. If any piece were missing, the story simply wouldn't work. Some genius took all the old themes and separate traditions and created a literary work of art, the earliest such masterpiece that we know anywhere.

Again God has written straight with crooked lines. Joseph, one of the youngest of Jacob's 12 sons, is the instrument God uses to fulfill the promise to the patriarchs. The older and supposedly more deserving brothers are bypassed. What Joseph does is done entirely through divine guidance. Although his vanity caused him initial troubles, God's grace overcomes it and brings this lowly Palestinian shepherd to a position of power in Egypt second only to Pharaoh.

In the story of Joseph, as in all of Genesis, we see God working through flawed human beings, loving them despite their weaknesses, and bringing good even out of their mistakes and sins. At the end of Genesis Jacob's family is living off the fat of the land in Egypt. But this fact poses a question: What has happened to the promise to Israel that it would be a great people in possession of Canaan? Genesis ends with the message that for Israel, as in our own lives, God's work is far from finished.

**Questions for Discussion and Reflection**

***Group Sharing/Discussion***

1. The J, E, and P writers each wrote their version of the stories as they heard them passed down orally. Although they write about the same events, individually they stress either faith, obedience, or fidelity. Find examples of each of these virtues in the Genesis stories.

2. Abraham and Sarah continually struggled to believe and trust in God. (See the chart on RG 59.) Sometimes it was difficult because they could not see ahead and trust and other times it was difficult because of their own failures. Choose a particular time when they failed to believe or trust and tell what advice you would have given them to help them in that struggle.

3. The story of Joseph covers many chapters (37–50) and is a rich tale of youthful pride, sibling jealousy, making the best of an unexpected turn in life, brotherly forgiveness, and carrying out God's life-plan without understanding where it was leading. What is one part of Joseph's life with which you can identify?

4. Let different people in your group take on the part of one of Joseph's brothers and tell his side of the story, what he was thinking and feeling early on as well as when they meet again in Egypt. Do the same with Joseph.

5. In what ways is the book of Genesis helpful in understanding where we are today as the People of God?

***In Our Lives***

1. Jews, Christians, and Muslims (through Ishmael) all consider Abraham their father. Explaining this shared lineage to someone you know who has religious prejudices might help them be more open to their religious "relatives" in other traditions.

2. As you look over the entire book of Genesis, what is the most important lesson for your own life?

3. God is calling and leading us as a people today. Like the people in Genesis, we too sometimes miss the point, fail to trust, stubbornly go our own way, or just do not listen well. What are some ways we as a people can listen well and follow God's call?

***Individual/Personal Reflection/Action***

1. Have a conversation with someone you trust in which you tell them about how you are like one of the persons in Genesis at their time of failure. Ask for their advice and their support in prayer for you in this matter.

2. Choose a particular significant part of this family story and read it over by yourself slowly. Sit quietly and listen to your own thoughts and insights about it.

# EXODUS READING GUIDE

*At a Glance*

| | |
|---|---|
| Who are the main players? | Moses Miriam Aaron Zipporah Jethro Pharaoh Pharaoh's daughter Joshua Bezalel Oholiab |
| What should I look for? | Slavery Deliverance The Passover God's Guidance The Ten Commandments The covenant at Sinai Importance of laws and public worship |
| When did this take place? | Probably around 1270 B.C. Another possible date is 1440 B.C. |
| Where did these events occur? | Egypt, Midian (Modern Saudi Arabia), The Sinai Peninsula: The Sinai Desert and Mt. Sinai (also called Mt. Horeb) |
| Why was this book written? | To make sure Israel never forgot God's saving act of delivering them from slavery in Egypt; that it was God who made Israel a nation and swore, at Sinai, to be their God forever; that the Law is a sign of God's love and presence among them |
| What is the story? | Joseph's family settles and prospers in Egypt, but after his death the Israelites become so numerous that the Egyptians fear them and force them into slavery. God chooses Moses to lead the people from slavery to freedom in the Promised Land. It takes 10 plagues to convince Pharaoh to let the Israelites go. Finally, they escape across the Red Sea. After long wanderings in the desert, the Israelites make a covenant with God at Mt. Sinai and receive the Law to guide their life as a nation. |

## Structure of the Book of Exodus

Exodus begins where Genesis leaves off. It carries the story line from security in the land of Egypt through enslavement, deliverance, and escape through a desolate wilderness to a meeting with God at Mount Sinai. But this journey takes the reader only halfway through the book, to chapter 19. The second half dwells at length on two key activities that take place at the mountain. The first is the making of a covenant between God and the people, and the second is the description of the key elements of divine worship: the building of a sanctuary tent and an ark (a wooden chest) to serve as God's throne, and the establishment of priestly ministers. So the book is really an intricate mixture of narratives and legal regulations for the community. This did not happen by accident. The story of God's act of merciful liberation from slavery lays the foundation for his merciful guarantee to be with the people for all times, and that promise of presence is reflected in the laws and institutions for public worship.

### Overview

The book of Exodus, like the book of Genesis, is structured quite artistically and purposefully. It begins with a dramatic change—from success to terrible slavery. Is God's promise in doubt? It seems so; yet God is already setting a new plan in motion with the birth of Moses. Will Moses respond to God's plan as Joseph did? Will God overcome the power of Pharaoh? Will the people believe enough to leave Egypt? Will they follow Moses? During the trial in the desert, will they remain faithful? The following diagram illustrates how this story plays out.

Chapters 1–18 create an exciting action story that can keep the reader wondering whether the people will really reach their goal of freedom and a new security. This is achieved by returning to each theme again and again so that they are never quite resolved, and the tension remains—will God be successful? will the people continue to follow Moses?—right up to the moment they arrive at the mountain of God.

The second half of the book maintains this tension, as observed in the people's idolatry in chapter 32. More than in the first half, however, it establishes order and a state of security. God's Law is proclaimed and the people swear that they will keep the covenant. The detailed description of the sanctuary and its elements follows, balancing

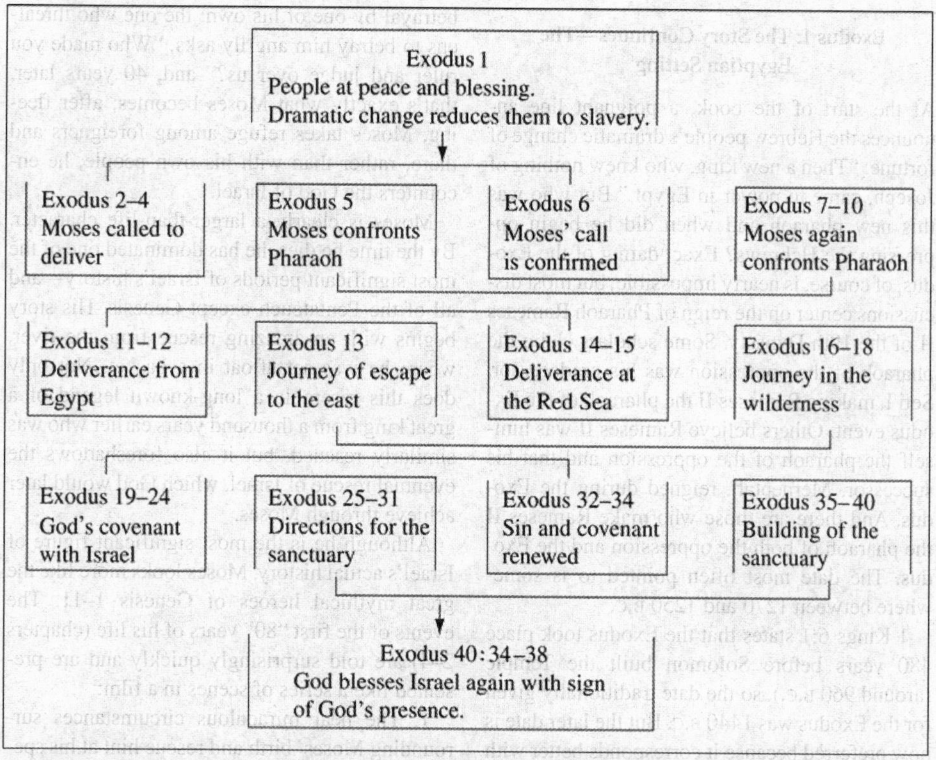


legal and liturgical matters. Finally, the descent of the glory of God into the sanctuary in 40:34–38 concludes this book, with the people now united to the divine presence in harmony just as they were at the beginning of chapter 1. Now, however, they are far from what their condition was there.

The three geographical regions in which God meets Israel, and that track the people's journey from slavery to freedom, provide another way of dividing the book, as illustrated below.

Throughout the book, we see God clearly in control of events. Moses is the leading character, but this is a story of God's power and authority exercised over every land and king. The book's novel-like structure surfaces in the many sudden and unexpected plot twists. Hopeless situations and near-defeats are suddenly transformed into hope and triumph. The book's structure follows that of the Psalms of Lament: A time of desperate need spurs the people to cry for help; God responds with mercy, and the people sing their thanks and praise (compare Pss 7, 10, and 53).

## Notes on Individual Passages

Because the final editor combined into one story the individual retelling of these events by each of the three major sources who recorded them (J, E, and P), you may notice some inconsistencies as well as some duplications in the book. But since this work was done so carefully and smoothly, you are not likely to notice them without careful examination. Where necessary, historical information that sheds light on particular passages will be provided.

| | | |
|---|---|---|
| Egypt | Exodus 1–12 | In Egypt God works wonders to free the people from slavery. |
| Wilderness | Exodus 13–18 | God guides the people safely through the wilderness to personal encounter with God. |
| Mount Sinai | Exodus 19–40 | At Mt. Sinai God establishes a community based on covenant, law, and worship. |

### Exodus 1: The Story Continues—The Egyptian Setting

At the start of the book, a poignant line announces the Hebrew people's dramatic change of fortune: "Then a new king, who knew nothing of Joseph, came to power in Egypt." But who was this new pharaoh and when did he begin oppressing the Hebrews? Exact dating of the Exodus, of course, is nearly impossible, but most discussions center on the reign of Pharaoh Rameses II of the 19th Dynasty. Some scholars claim the pharaoh of the oppression was his predecessor, Seti I, making Rameses II the pharaoh of the Exodus event. Others believe Rameses II was himself the pharaoh of the oppression and that his successor, Merneptah, reigned during the Exodus. And there are those who make Rameses II the pharaoh of both the oppression and the Exodus. The date most often pointed to is somewhere between 1270 and 1250 B.C.

1 Kings 6:1 states that the Exodus took place 480 years before Solomon built the Temple (around 960 B.C.), so the date traditionally given for the Exodus was 1440 B.C. But the later date is now preferred because it corresponds better with Exodus 12:40, which states that the Israelites had been in Egypt 430 years before Moses led them out. If Joseph and his family arrived in Egypt during the reign of the foreign invaders, the Hyksos (around 1700 B.C.—which is quite plausible), then the 1270 B.C. Exodus date is the most likely. In any case, biblical estimates of time cannot always be relied on, because they often use ideal numbers, such as 12 and 40, to arrive at a particular figure. Thus, "480 years" is 12 generations of 40 years each, representing a full (12) number of human lives from birth to death or to becoming a grandparent.

### Exodus 2–4: The Choice of Moses

The story of Moses presents some striking contrasts and fascinating ironies: He is an Israelite, but his name and upbringing are Egyptian; the pharaoh orders the killing of all male Israelite babies, but by doing so he sets in motion the very circumstances that bring Moses into the royal family; his mother abandons Moses in order to save him but later is hired to be his wet-nurse; Moses kills an Egyptian to protect one of his own people but soon is forced to flee because he fears betrayal by one of his own; the one who threatens to betray him angrily asks, "Who made you ruler and judge over us?" and, 40 years later, that's exactly what Moses becomes; after fleeing, Moses takes refuge among foreigners and there, rather than with his own people, he encounters the God of Israel.

Moses is clearly a larger-than-life character. By the time he dies, he has dominated one of the most significant periods of Israel's history—and all of the Pentateuch except Genesis. His story begins with an amazing rescue from the river, where he was set afloat in a basket. Not only does this resemble a long-known legend of a great king from a thousand years earlier who was similarly rescued, but it also foreshadows the eventual rescue of Israel, which God would later achieve through Moses.

Although he is the most significant figure of Israel's actual history, Moses looks more like the great mythical heroes of Genesis 1–11. The events of the first "80" years of his life (chapters 2–4) are told surprisingly quickly and are presented like a series of scenes in a film:

1. The near miraculous circumstances surrounding Moses' birth and rescue hint at his special mission.
2. The situation worsens—Moses is not respected by his own people and is forced to flee.
3. While Moses is living among foreigners, God asks him to do the near-impossible; very reluctantly, Moses accepts (Ex 3:1–12).
4. God communicates more intimately with Moses than with anyone else and even reveals to him the divine name, "I am who am" (Ex 3:12–22).
5. God reassures the insecure Moses and, grudgingly, assigns his brother, Aaron, as his spokesperson (Ex 4:1–22).
6. Persuaded by the miraculous signs he performed, the people believe Moses and accept his mission.

### God Calls Leaders

The call of Moses is the first instance of an oft-repeated biblical call-pattern that shows up in the call of other great prophets and leaders. This pattern is illustrated in the table below. Note the elements as they occur in the Moses story and see how they parallel the sequence of events in the other stories.

***Biblical Call-Patterns***

| | | |
|---|---|---|
| Apparition | God appears and speaks to Moses. | Ex 3:1–4 |
| Motive | God gives reason for issuing a call. | Ex 3:4–9 |
| Commission | God commissions Moses for his task. | Ex 3:10 |
| Objection | Moses protests he is unworthy and unqualified. | Ex 3:11 |
| Reassurance | God reassures Moses and insists he serve. | Ex 3:12 |
| Sign | God gives a sign or prediction. | Ex 3:12; 4:1–5 |

Listed below are places you can find the elements of this same pattern in the call of other prophets and leaders

| | Gideon | Isaiah | Jeremiah | Ezekiel |
|---|---|---|---|---|
| Apparition | Jgs 6:11f | Is 6:1f | Jer 1:4 | Ez 1:1–28a |
| Motive | Jgs 6:12f | Is 6:3–7 | Jer 1:5 | Ez 1:28b–2:2 |
| Commission | Jgs 6:14 | Is 6:8–10 | Jer 1:5 | Ez 2:3–5 |
| Objection | Jgs 6:15 | Is 6:11 | Jer 1:6 | Ez 2:6–8 |
| Reassurance | Jgs 6:16 | Is 6:11f | Jer 1:7f | Ez 2:6f |
| Sign | Jgs 6:17 | — | Jer 1:9f | Ez 2:8–3:11 |

The revelation of the divine name is an especially important moment in the story. God prepares Moses by first announcing, "I am the God of Abraham, the God of Isaac, and the God of Jacob," and by insisting that love and compassion are God's motives for coming to Moses and intervening in the lives of the Israelites. God then responds to Moses' question: If they ask me your name, what shall I say? God's answer is both surprising and mysterious, for God's is no ordinary name. Several versions of the divine name occur in the text: "I am who I am," "I AM," and "He who is" (or better, "He who causes to be"). Names, especially in the Bible, are handles one can use to control another (note that in C.B. radio jargon a person's broadcast nickname is called his or her "handle"). God's response makes it clear the Israelites will be given no handle on God. God's true identity is beyond their understanding, for God is pure power and being. But the name also suggests that God's existence has a purpose; here it is closely connected with the survival of Israel. By claiming to be the God of Abraham, Isaac, and Jacob, God is assuring Israel that "I am with you totally."

### Exodus 5–12: Confrontation with the Pharaoh

The biblical plagues dominate these chapters and contribute to the dramatic, even cinematic feel of this part of the story. There is no shortage of excitement and suspense. First Moses pleads with Pharaoh to allow the Israelites to go and worship the LORD (5:1–13). Pharaoh not only refuses, he increases the work of the slave laborers, prompting the Israelite foremen to grumble that Moses is making matters worse for them (5:14–21). An apparent repeat of the call of Moses opens chapter 6 in what is probably a retelling of the story by the P source. But instead of feeling redundant, the retelling serves to emphasize that Moses can rely on God to do exactly what God promised.

The fight for freedom shifts into high gear when God starts sending plagues upon Egypt. The following chart gives details regarding the plagues that should help us keep in mind two important points:

1. Each of the first nine plagues can be seen as an intensification of naturally occurring phenomena (e.g., small organisms still turn the Nile

**YHWH** (YAHWEH) In Hebrew only the consonants of words were originally written down; "points" (small marks surrounding the consonants) were later added to the word to indicate vowels. Hence the divine name is sometimes referred to as the *Tetragrammaton* (Greek for "four letters"). Much debate surrounds the meaning of the name, but most agree it is a form of the verb "to become."

As a sign of reverence, Jews from the time of the exile onward have refrained from speaking the name aloud (some of the Dead Sea Scrolls substitute four dots for the letters, refraining even from *writing* the name). In the Hebrew text, the letters *YHWH* were surrounded by vowel points for the word *Adonai* ("my Lord"), to indicate that when the text was read aloud, the reader should substitute *Adonai* for *Yahweh*. Misunderstanding of the significance of the vowel points used with the consonants for the divine name resulted, in the sixteenth century, in the word Yehowah, or the modern spelling "Jehovah." Today, pious Jews will frequently substitute the term *ha-shem*, or *has-sem* "the Name." The divine name occurs 6,823 times in the Old Testament. Only in Exodus 3:14 do we find the unique first person form "I am who I am." Everywhere else the divine name appears in the third person form, *Yahweh*.

Following the Jewish custom, Christians do not normally speak the name in prayer, but replace it with the title "LORD." Whenever you see the word in the *New American* Bible, printed with large and small capitals, it is replacing the Hebrew word *Yahweh*.

red during flood times; ancient Egyptian documents describe the calamity of being overrun by frogs; flies and gnats are a chronic nuisance in that area even today; sandstorms and desert dust are known to block out the sun's light [*see NAB* footnote at Ex 7:14–12:30]).

2. The Israelites saw the hand of God in the timing of these events and in the obvious control God exerted over them. In other words, the miracle was found not in the fact that the plagues happened (they could happen any time), but in when they happened. Such timing could only be explained as God's intervention.

The pharaoh is in a battle of wills with the LORD, and we might wonder if God's power can overcome Pharaoh's hardheartedness. The unfolding action is a little like the story of the Greek hero Sisyphus, who must push a boulder up a mountain only to have it roll down every time he reaches the summit. Each time Pharaoh starts to relent, he reneges at the last moment, and the hard work of pushing events in God's direction starts all over again.

The tenth and last plague, however, is decisive. Terrifying and chilling in our eyes, it was for Israel a clear sign of God's favor and protection. The firstborn males of the Egyptians perish while those of the Israelites are spared. In Israel's eyes this event marked God's clear choice of Israel as his favored nation, the firstborn of all the peoples of the earth. The Passover feast was developed as a celebration of the miracle of the "passing over" of the angel of death and the liberation of Israel from slavery.

So important was this ritual in the life of Israel that it is written into the account of the actual event. Instead of describing a fear-filled meal eaten in haste—as it probably occurred—the text describes the full liturgical ritual as it was *later* celebrated in memory of the original events. The theology of the book of Exodus (and Christian theology as well) stresses the oneness of later rituals and original events. The Hebrew concept of remembrance *(zakir)* emphasizes that remembering makes the past present again. What Israel's ancestors experienced in Egypt and the desert is relived and celebrated again in feasts and rituals. The Catholic Mass is a perfect example of the notion that ritual

### *The Ten Plagues*

| Plague<br>What Happened | Duplicated by Egyptians | Naturally Occurring Phenomenon | Pharaoh Starts to Relent |
|---|---|---|---|
| Blood<br>River Nile metaphorically "turned to blood" making most of Egypt's water undrinkable.*† | Yes | Yes | No |
| Frogs<br>Frogs came up out of the Nile and "covered the land."* | No | Yes | Yes |
| Gnats<br>The "dust of Egypt" turned into huge swarms of gnats.*† | No | Yes | No |
| Flies<br>Swarms of flies invaded every home in Egypt.* | No | Yes | Yes |
| Disease<br>Fatal disease afflicted all Egyptian livestock but none of the Israelites' animals.† | No | Yes | No |
| Boils<br>Festering boils broke out on all Egyptian people and animals.*† | No | Yes | No |
| Hail<br>Worst hail storm ever destroyed livestock and crops.*†‡ | No | Yes | Yes |
| Locusts<br>Countless locusts devoured what few crops were left.*‡ | No | Yes | Yes |
| Darkness<br>Total darkness covered Egypt for three days.* | No | Yes | Yes |
| Death of Firstborn<br>Firstborn son of every Egyptian family died also firstborn among livestock.* † | No | No | Yes |

*Plague affected humans; †Plague affected livestock; ‡Plague affected crops.

remembering makes past events present now, for we believe that when we remember what Jesus did, he becomes uniquely present among the assembly.

**Exodus 13–15: Escape through the Sea**

In addition to two tellings of the escape through the sea, these chapters list two additional practices the Israelites are to observe to remember how God delivered them from death and slavery: refraining from any food containing yeast, and consecration to God of all first-born males (13:1–16). These practices, in fact, may have existed among the Israelites and their pagan neighbors for generations before the time of the Exodus. But Israel's history persuaded them to give these practices a whole new meaning: They became reminders that Israel's life as a nation depended on the love and mercy of the God who delivered them from death.

The first telling of the flight through the sea (13:17–14:31) is a dramatic and detailed prose description. The second (15:1–21) is a poetic rendition, which probably derived from a feast-day hymn. It is also considered by many to be the oldest written text in the Bible, probably written during the 200-year period when Israel was ruled by judges, before the establishment of the monarchy. It presents God as a fierce warrior fighting on behalf of the people.

The first and older half of the song (vv. 1–12) recounts the actual battle God wages against Egypt, while the second half tells how God led Israel through the desert to the Promised Land. Verses 13–18 in the second half refer to events that have not yet happened at this point in the story (the eventual conquest and settlement of Canaan), leading scholars to conclude that the second half was probably composed later than the first part of the song.

**Exodus 16–18: Hardships in the Desert of Sinai**

The next stage of the journey takes the Israelites from the location of the sea to the foot of the mount of Sinai in two months. The itinerary of that two-month trek is listed for us, but unfortunately few of the places can be identified with any certainty: Even the place where the Israelites crossed the "Red Sea" and the location of Mt. Sinai are open to discussion. The Hebrew name for "Red Sea" has two other meanings: "reed sea" or the "sea of chaos." If the correct meaning is "Reed" Sea, then any of a number of marshy lakes might be the actual crossing site (although it is possible today's Red Sea was once called the "Sea of Reeds"). If "sea of chaos" is the correct reading, then anyone's guess might do since the name is symbolic, representing the place where God would destroy Pharaoh's army, the servants of chaotic evil.

While no definitive answer can be given about the route of the Exodus, scholars offer three possible options, which are shown on color Map 3 in the back of this book. Least likely is the northern and shortest route that would have led them through the so-called "Way to the Land of the Philistines" (13:17 notes God's decision to avoid the Philistines for fear that the possibility of conflict with them would turn the Israelites back toward Egypt). The second route would have traversed the Sinai peninsula, also in the northern area moving eastward. This was a major caravan route that passes near Kadesh-Barnea, where according to Deuteronomy 2:14 Israel camped for 38 years, and it went through territory known to be hospitable to nomadic groups. The map lists it as "The Way to Shur." Most favored and most probable, however, is the circular route along and around the southern part of the Sinai. What recommends this longest route is the fact that because Egyptians mined gems here, it is quite possible that Moses could have known it. Also, several of the mountain peaks found here are among the most impressive in Sinai and thus are likely candidates for being the mount of the covenant. The length of the route also makes plausible the Israelites' frequent moves as recorded in Exodus and Numbers.

But the book of Exodus is not as concerned with geography as modern scholars are. The reasons it gives for the route taken have little to do with the advantages of one route over another. Instead, the route serves the dual purpose of exposing the tension between Moses and the people and revealing God's protective presence among them throughout their long journey. Despite the people's habit of complaining about their hardships rather than giving thanks for their freedom, God remains present as *healer* (15:25f: at Marah God restores the water's sweetness), *provider* (16:16–36: God provides daily manna to feed them), and *reminder* (17:1–7: at Rephidim God turns the people's anger over lack of water into a reminder of the Red Sea crossing by making water miraculously issue from a rock). In addition, God is again experienced as protector (17:8–13) when the Israelites successfully fend off the attack of the Amalekites. Finally, Moses' father-in-law Jethro, a Midianite, helps organize judges and leaders to assist Moses, thus establishing a lasting bond between Israel and the Midianites (18:1–26).

**Questions for Discussion and Reflection**

***Group Sharing/Discussion***

1. Look back over the life of Moses. Which do you think are the three most significant moments or events in his life. Explain your choices.

2. Moses was not eager to be a leader. In fact he tried to argue his way out of it. Role-play each of Moses' excuses and the LORD's response each time. Different people could take the roles for each argument.

3. The night on which the Israelites finally were able to leave Egypt was so significant that

it is remembered to this day by the Passover ritual meal. It was this ritual meal that Jesus was celebrating at the Last Supper. During this meal the youngest person at the table asks, "Why is this night different from all other nights?" How would you answer that question?

4. Invite someone from the Jewish community to explain or even demonstrate the Passover Ritual. Or, look up "Passover" on the Web and choose one article to describe to your group.

*In Our Lives*

1. The Egyptians became afraid of the Israelites living in "their" country because the Israelites began to outnumber them. Eventually the Egyptians became ruthless. Where are there parallels today with regard to fear of other cultures in our own society or other lands?

2. When the daughter of Pharaoh rescued the baby Moses she had no idea what the long-term results of that act would be. She just did the right thing for someone in need. What are some specific ways our community can have an effect on the future by doing the right thing for someone in need?

3. Why is it important to continue the tradition of remembering our history in ritual celebrations as the Jews do in the Passover? What are ways we can make our community celebration of the Eucharist more effective in our lives?

4. Moses' father-in-law, Jethro, gave him the advice of looking among the community for trustworthy people to help lead them. How do we do this in our community? What can we do to encourage ourselves and others to be involved in community leadership?

***Individual/Personal Reflection/Action***

1. How might Moses as a "reluctant leader" be an inspiration and model for you?

2. The Israelites, under God's protection (*pesach,* which we usually translate "Passover," probably means "protect"), were safe from the death brought by the final plague, and the Jewish people remember that protection and rescue in their ritual meal to this day. How is Christ our Passover from death to life? What is similar to the Passover in our celebration of the Eucharist?

3. The Israelites sang and danced to praise and thank God for all he had done for them. At the end of each day, remember to look back and praise and thank God.

**Exodus 19–24: The Covenant with God**

To visualize how these five chapters constitute the high point of the entire Pentateuch, imagine a road starting at the Garden of Creation in Genesis 1:1 and ending at the borders of the Promised Land in Deuteronomy 34. The road, of course, climbs up and down hills and mountains, so imagine a sudden and steady climb through all of Genesis and Exodus 1–18 to the very top of Mt. Sinai. There the road levels out temporarily while God establishes a covenant with the people (Ex 19–24), and gives them laws that will enable them to live out the covenant (Ex 25–Nm 10). Then (at Nm 11) the road begins a sudden descent that sends it to the edge of the Jordan River (at the end of Deuteronomy). When the Israelites looked back at human history, that's the God-directed route they saw history following, with Israel playing a central role in the history.

Chapters 19 to 24 describe the high point of the Pentateuch. The events recounted here are divided into four stages:

1. Israel prepares to meet God and receive the Law (Ex 10:1–25).

2. God gives general laws (the Ten Commandments) (Ex 20:1–21).

3. God gives specific laws (Ex 21:22—23:33).

4. Israel accepts God's laws and seals the covenant with God (Ex 24:1–18).

Note the difference between the commandments and the more specific laws that follow. The commandments present the basic demands of a healthy relationship with God: loving God and neighbor. Limited to 10 (for easy memorizing

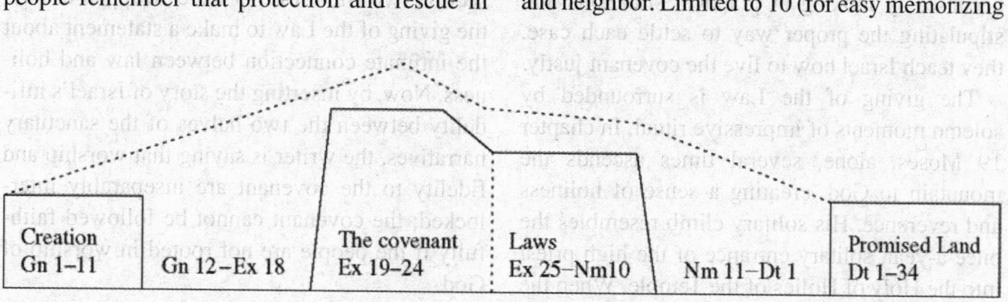

## Slavery in the Bible

IT MAY BE shocking to find in the Bible a reference to human beings as "property" (21:21). Remembering that all biblical literature arose out of the culture in which it was written may soften the blow a bit, but it may still be jarring to see apparent approval of slavery in the pages of scripture. Recalling that God's ways are gradually revealed to Israel throughout its history (e.g., the concept of life after death is a late development in their theology) may help put things in perspective. Christians believe that only in Jesus was God's self-revelation complete, yet even the New Testament made accommodation for slavery. God's people were still on the path of discovering God's ways and will.

It should be mentioned that the laws listed in Exodus represented an enlightened view of slavery. Other nations treated slaves as objects rather than as persons, according them no formal rights. Israel, aware of its own enslavement in Egypt, made laws to ensure humane treatment of slaves, provided for their rights, limited the time of enslavement (for Israelite slaves), and allowed slaves to assume positions of responsibility and prestige.

and counting on the fingers), they state simple demands but do not say what will happen if one disobeys them, while the laws of chapters 21–23 list the consequences of breaking each specific law. These laws are called "The Covenant Code" because, by looking at practical situations and stipulating the proper way to settle each case, they teach Israel how to live the covenant justly.

The giving of the Law is surrounded by solemn moments of impressive ritual. In chapter 19 Moses, alone, several times ascends the mountain to God, creating a sense of holiness and reverence. His solitary climb resembles the once-a-year, solitary entrance of the high priest into the Holy of Holies of the Temple. When the

**God's Self-Description** Chapter 34:6–7—the most quoted and alluded to passage in the Old Testament—provides a sublime understanding of who God is: "The LORD, the LORD, a God gracious and merciful, slow to anger and abounding in love and fidelity, continuing his love for a thousand generations, and forgiving wickedness, rebellion, and sin; yet not declaring the guilty guiltless."

people embrace the covenant in chapter 24, they seal the pact with two rituals: a sprinkling with blood (24:3–8), and a meal in which Moses, Aaron, and the 70 elders feast with God. Lawgiving and ritual thus combine in a setting of divine holiness and human sanctification to impress on the reader that the Law is the God-given means to becoming holy as God is holy.

### Exodus 25–40: Establishing God's Home in Israel

It may well be that there is more material describing the Tabernacle than there is about any other single topic in the Bible. This material helps emphasize one of the themes of Exodus: God is not only a transcendent and mighty warrior God, but also a gracious God who has chosen to live in the midst of the people.

Chapters 25–31 and 35–40 essentially repeat each other by giving directions for building and furnishing the Tabernacle and by describing in detail how the directions were carried out. In between, however, are stories of Israel's first failure to keep the covenant—the worship of the golden calf. This placement is probably no accident. Here, as in the previous section, structure reveals the writer's purpose: In the preceding section two ritual events were wrapped around the giving of the Law to make a statement about the intimate connection between law and holiness. Now, by inserting the story of Israel's infidelity between the two halves of the sanctuary narratives, the writer is saying that worship and fidelity to the covenant are inseparably interlocked; the covenant cannot be followed faithfully if the people are not rooted in worship of God.

| Exodus 19–24 covenant given | Exodus 25–31 sanctuary directions | Exodus 32–34 covenant renewed | Exodus 35–40 sanctuary built |
|---|---|---|---|

## The Theology of the Covenant

Because the giving of the covenant is the central moment of the entire Pentateuch, reflection on the meaning of the term "covenant" (the Hebrew word is *berit*) will yield a better understanding of Israel's faith. But first, some general points:

1. A covenant, like a contract, is a solemn agreement, legally binding on both parties, but made with a religious ritual.

2. Covenants can be made between individuals, between nations, between a superior and an inferior (king and vassal), or between a god and people.

3. Several types of royal covenants or treaties are known from the ancient Near East. A royal grant was an unconditional covenant between a king and a loyal servant. A parity treaty was made by equals who agreed to respect each other's rights and interests and accepted mutual responsibility. A Suzerain-vassal treaty was a covenant between a great king and the lesser kings of nations conquered or threatened by him. Vassal treaties were not an equal proposition; the vassal agreed to faithfully execute a long list of demands, while the king promised nothing more specific than kindness and protection.

4. Once solemnly made, these treaties were considered binding for all time.

5. The most common form of vassal treaty known from ancient times contains six parts, which, in a general way, can also be found in the Sinai covenant (Ex 19–24).

The similarities as outlined in the chart below are of interest, but they must not be pushed too far. Later in the tradition, legal treaty language

***Ancient Treaties and the Sinai Covenant***

| Typical Thirteenth-Century B.C. Hittite Vassal-Type Treaty | Elements of Typical Vassal-Type Treaty Found in the Sinai Covenant |
|---|---|
| A preamble stating names of the parties | Ex 20:2: "I am the LORD your God who brought you out of the land of Egypt, out of the house of slavery." |
| Historical listing of the good things the king has done | Ex 20:2 (19:4): "You have seen how I treated the Egyptians and how I bore you up on eagles' wings and brought you to myself." |
| Duties the vassal must perform | Ex 20:3–17; 20:23—23:17: The commandments and the laws governing daily life. |
| An order to save the document and read it publicly | Ex 24:3–8; 24:12: Blood-sprinkling ceremony and giving of the tablets of the Law to be kept among the people. |
| List of gods who witness the treaty | There are no divine witnesses because there is no other god who can testify to what the LORD does. |
| Lists of curses the gods will inflict on those who break the treaty and blessings for those who keep it | Ex 20:5f; 23:25: "I, the LORD your God, am a jealous God, inflicting punishment for their ancestors' wickedness on the children of those who hate me . . . but showing love down to the thousandth generation of those who love me and keep my commandments." |

**Literary Forms of the Bible**

WHAT IS THE Bible? From a literary point of view it is a collection of many types of literature. Broadly speaking we may classify the books of the Bible into five kinds of literature: (1) Narrative books (e.g. Genesis, Samuel, Kings, Maccabees, the Gospels, the Acts of the Apostles); (2) Poetry (e.g. Psalms, Song of Songs, Proverbs); (3) Prophetic books; (4) Epistles (e.g., the Letters of Paul); and (5) Apocalypses (Daniel, 2 Esdras [4 Ezra]; Revelation).

Of course, there are many types of literature that do not appear in the Bible, for example drama, satire, or autobiography. And none of the types of literature in the Bible are exclusively biblical. They are shared with nonbiblical literature as well. When we pay attention as we read it becomes clear that some books of the Bible contain more than one literary form. For example, Exodus contains narrative, laws, and poetry; Jeremiah contains narrative, poetry, and letters. Some of the Epistles contain poetic passages, such as 1 Corinthians, chapter 13. So, rather than just reading the text in a "flat" way, simply for plot or content, paying attention to the type of literature can deepen our appreciation and understanding of the particular part of the Bible we are reading.

became commonplace, such as in the covenant summary statement often found in the prophets, "You shall be my people and I will be your God" (Jer 7:23; 11:4; 24:7; Ez 11:20; 14:11; Hos 2:25, etc.). But Exodus is first of all a record of Israel's momentous encounter with God, and of her promise to worship the LORD, who was the savior and loving benefactor of this small and insignificant group of refugees.

The notion of covenant confirmed in Israel's mind the special and unique relationship they enjoyed with God. God had shown Israel special favor by revealing the divine name to them, saving them from slavery, choosing to live among them in the Tabernacle, and giving them laws to govern their life and ensure a just society among them. Initially the covenant was celebrated in worship with a sense of unalterable national destiny, a kind of "We can't lose because God is on our side" attitude. The later prophets like Jeremiah and Ezekiel, however, emphasized that while even disasters did not mean God had abandoned them, the people's faithlessness could bring punishment upon the nation.

### Questions for Discussion and Reflection

***Group Sharing/Discussion***

1. Imagine you are Moses and you come down from your mountain retreat and discover the people worshiping the golden calf. What would you say to them? Allow time in your group for each person to think about this, then take turns responding.

2. With which of the characters of Exodus can you most easily identify? Is it because of their strengths or their weaknesses? How does it feel to know you have some of the same strengths and weaknesses as these great characters of Exodus?

3. The Ten Commandments are very brief, but that does not mean they do not reach far into our daily living. Take each commandment, perhaps working in small groups, and write out as many "rules" contained in it as possible or ways that we live out the meaning of that commandment.

4. Why would God want the Sabbath to be honored? What is the wisdom in this?

***In Our Lives***

1. Which of the Ten Commandments do we as a society most need to pay serious attention to today? How can our parish community encourage that?

2. What does it say about Moses that, when the LORD was going to destroy the people and save only Moses, Moses begged God to save the people also? Who is someone in our day who is that selfless and puts the common good above individual wants?

3. The LORD had made a covenant, protected the people, and led them to safety. They seemed to forget all that and made a golden calf to worship. Sometimes people only turn to God when they are in need of help. What can help us to remember God in the good times as well as when things are difficult?

4. Some say the heart of the Old Testament is found in God's command to Moses when Pharaoh pursues the fleeing Israelites: "Go forward," God says. God tells them to move and pursue freedom; to yield to the call to greatness; to stop complaining, take action, and follow their dream. Has God ever given you that same command? When? Why? Can one be afraid of freedom? Why is slavery or dependence sometimes more attractive than freedom?

***Individual/Personal Reflection/Action***

1. God renewed the covenant after the Israelites failed. God's forgiveness is there for us too, when we fail or even when we just forget and betray our values. Sometimes we need to be forgiven. Sometimes we need to forgive. Where is forgiveness needed in your own life?

2. The Israelites were tempted to disobey the first commandment and failed. What temptations do you face against keeping God first over pursuing the "good life" by giving into the consumerism of our culture? Who or what helps you keep your priorities straight?

3. What are the ways you will "Remember the Sabbath day" this week?

# LEVITICUS READING GUIDE

### *At a Glance*

| | |
|---|---|
| Who are the main players? | Moses Aaron Aaron's sons: Abihu, Nadab, Eleazar, Ithamar |
| What should I look for? | Holiness of God and nation; relationship of Law and people's holiness Significance of physical perfection Religious ritual and worship Sacrificial offerings Levites and priesthood |
| When did this take place? | It is presented as perhaps two years after the Exodus from Egypt, during the Israelites' year-long stay camped at Mt. Sinai. (Possible date: around 1272 B.C. or 1442 B.C.) The laws were actually completed over a long period of time, perhaps 1000 B.C. to 600 B.C. |
| Where did these events occur? | In the Sinai peninsula, at the foot of Mt. Sinai (also called Mt. Horeb). |
| Why was this book written? | To answer the question: How can a sinful people serve a perfect and holy God? To teach the ways of holiness: observance of Law and religious ritual. To serve as a guidebook: teaching priests and people how to worship the LORD and live holy lives. |
| What is the story? | Leviticus contains few characters and almost no story line. The book is a very detailed compilation of rules and regulations governing worship and daily life. |

If you were working your way through the Bible one book at a time, your reading might come to a grinding halt at Leviticus. All the elements you might normally expect are missing here: plot, poetry, stories of suspense or deep emotion—even the characters are few. Yet the book holds a venerated place in Jewish tradition. That is because the book is rich with laws that define Jewish life and practice. Of the 613 binding commandments found in the Pentateuch, 247 are right here in Leviticus. Despite the fact that a major portion of the laws, those pertaining to temple sacrifice, became impossible to observe when the Jerusalem Temple was destroyed in A.D. 70, Leviticus remains the most important statement of Torah for Judaism. Its laws are much studied and debated, because Judaism has always found in their rich diversity the "teaching" or "way" it needed to follow to be faithful and beloved sons and daughters of God.

In Judaism Torah carries a positive and joyful connotation, not the narrow and restrictive meaning

"Law" often conjures among modern people. Because it means "teaching" or "guide," Torah is celebrated in Judaism as a gift from God that leads to God's favor and salvation. The best expression of this attitude can be found in Psalm 119, the longest Psalm in the Psalter, which, for 176 verses, exults in praise and gratitude for the Law.

## Differing Views of Law

Christians come to Leviticus with a very different attitude. Whether horrified by the details of animal sacrifice, or disgusted by the discussions of bodily emissions, or turned off by the many restrictive rules governing what can and cannot be eaten, Christians find little to celebrate here, preferring to emphasize instead the concept of "freedom from the law" that St. Paul stresses in his letters. What Christians who approach the book with these biases miss are the profound insights into the mystery of God that are woven into the fabric of Leviticus. Like golden thread, the insights into the holiness, majesty, power, and love of God shine through regularly and reveal the enduring value of the book. By keeping our eyes on the "big picture" rather than on individual laws, we can focus on the most important question the book raises: How would following these laws make Israel different from other nations?

To tap its fullest meaning, we must approach the book from two angles: First, we can ask what religious insights and meaning the ancient Israelites found in its various laws and practices. Second, we can explore how its major themes reveal the enduring character and purpose of God. Israel relied on these themes for their understanding of God, and Christianity has made them central in its own teaching. Take, for example, the concept of sacrifice. Knowing the importance of sacrifice in Leviticus as a means of relating to God can help Christians articulate the meaning of Jesus' death and an understanding of Eucharist.

## Structure of Leviticus

The style in Leviticus is of the Priestly (P) source, whose work is found throughout the Pentateuch—and who is always concerned with classifying and listing things in their proper place (see the P creation story in Genesis 1 and the list of nations in Genesis 11:10–32). Another major concern of the P writer is defining the difference between the world of the sacred and that of everyday life. Like wise parents teaching a child how to relate to fire, the P source knows God is not to be dealt with lightly. One must respect fire and understand its power if one is to deal with it and live. P deals directly with the life-and-death question of what is appropriate and inappropriate when relating to God.

Leviticus has two major divisions that are quite different in spirit. Chapters 1–16 live up to the name of the book, which basically means "That which pertains to the levitical priests." (The Hebrew title is the opening word of the text, *wayyiqra,* meaning "And he [the LORD] called"). Chapters 17–27, however, deal with larger areas of community behavior and public worship that express the unique identity of Israel and the call to holiness inherent in the covenant. A simple outline of the book is shown here.

**Outline of Leviticus**

**Part I**

A. Laws governing the five types of sacrifice (Lv 1–7)
B. The ceremony of ordination of Aaron and his sons (Lv 8–10)
C. Laws governing legal purity regarding animals, childbirth, leprosy, and sexuality (Lv 11–15)
D. The observance of the Day of Atonement (Lv 16)

**Part II**

A. Moral and ethical laws of holiness (Lv 17–20)
B. Ritual (liturgical) requirements for holiness (Lv 21–25)
C. Blessings and curses for following and breaking the covenant (Lv 26) (Serves as a conclusion to chapters 17–25 and to entire book)
D. Regulations for redeeming offerings vowed to God (Lv 27) (Added later to the book as an appendix)

In Part I of the outline we find a twice-repeated pattern of *laws* followed by *actions*. After the many regulations on sacrifice in chapters 1–7, there follows a narrative explanation of the

## Holiness and Purity

THE TWIN EMPHASES on holiness and ritual purity found in Leviticus reflect attitudes that on the surface might seem contradictory but, in actuality, are complementary.

The stress on holiness expressed the Israelites' belief that God lived among them. Holiness, in fact, might be defined as awareness of and respect for the divine presence that surrounds people everywhere. For Israel the implications were obvious: If a just and merciful God had chosen to "tabernacle" (make a home) among them, then they must be a just and merciful people. Over and over again in Leviticus we hear the refrain: "Be holy because I, the LORD your God, am holy." The expectation was that by living among them, God would rub off on the people.

A doubly opposite expectation is reflected in the stress on ritual purity: The people must not rub off on God. Yes, God was willing to live among them, but God's ways were still light-years away from human ways. People were not to approach God carelessly or take God for granted. Instead, the people were to foster an attitude of carefulness toward God, approaching God as worthily as possible. Keep in mind that ritual uncleanness in itself was not considered harmful or even sinful. Daily life, after all, made uncleanness impossible to avoid. God is the holy one; human beings of necessity fall short of God's holiness. The point, then, was not that one always had to be ritually clean, but that one could not approach God unless he or she was clean. Coming into the presence of God in an unclean state was truly dangerous, for God's holiness could not abide it. While Exodus taught the people how to make holy objects, Leviticus teaches them how to be holy people.

So all the laws regarding holiness and ritual purity point to the same reality: a holy, just, and loving God dwells among us calling us to be a holy, compassionate people; because our God is everywhere, even in ordinary day-to-day life, we must take care to keep our lives pure so that in every aspect of our lives we can stand worthily before the LORD, whose greatness so transcends our ordinary existence.

role of priests and a description of Aaron's first major sacrifice. Chapter 11 begins a new set of regulations, this time relating to proper use of food and respect for bodily functions. What follows in chapter 16 is an elaborate description of the annual Day of Atonement, the ritual that cleansed the people of guilt from all their sins. The message in this pattern of laws followed by actions is simple: Worship and daily life are closely connected—what we celebrate in worship flows out of how we live our lives.

Like Part I, Part II of Leviticus, often referred to as "The Law of Holiness," is dominated by the theme of holiness. This section of laws has a moralistic and preachy tone, which merely lists laws one after another. These later laws are of two types: Chapters 17–20 focus on moral laws that govern the way we relate as social beings living in community, while chapters 21–25 deal with regulations for priests and liturgical worship. Chapter 26 is an impressive chapter that caps the collection of laws and serves as a conclusion of the whole book.

All commentators agree that the viewpoint that dominates and unites Leviticus is Priestly. Those editors gathered together all the laws that governed the various activities that the priests were expected to monitor—everything from public worship to private matters like food and clothing, skin diseases, and sexual activity, as well as truly ethical questions about just and loving relationships among the people.

The laws of Leviticus were not written all at once. Groups of laws written at different times were joined by the Priestly editors into an ever-growing collection. Although three different

*Sacrifices of the Old Testament*

| Type of Sacrifice<br>What (elements) | Why (function) | Where (citation) |
|---|---|---|
| **Burnt Offering** | | |
| Male and unblemished cattle, sheep and goats, birds (pigeons for the poor) | Because wholly consumed, it acknowledges God as Lord of life: atones for sins; joyful worship | Lv 1:1–17; 6:8–13; **8:**18–21; 22:17 |
| **The Grain Offering** | | |
| Grain, flour, frankincense, oil, bread; only a symbolic portion burned, the rest eaten by priests | Substitute for expensive animal offering; thanksgiving for good crops; joyful worship | Lv 2:1–16; 6:14–23 |
| **The Communion Sacrifice** | | |
| Any unblemished animal—male or female (cattle or sheep and goats, but not birds since too small for group to eat) | A "well-being sacrifice"; not burned up, but eaten by offerers and families. Only fat parts (considered choicest) were burned to God | Lv 3:1–17; 7:11–34 |
| **Purification Offering** | | |
| If offender were whole people or a priest: bull; ordinary person: goat; poor: bird or some fine flour. Blood sprinkled on altar in outer courtyard if lay offender; in holy interior if priest or whole people offended | To atone for usually unintentional sin (violating something sacred); atone for loss of holiness; cleansing from impurity | Lv 4:1–5:13; 6:4–30 |
| **The Reparation Offering** | | |
| A ram sheep (its blood sprinkled on altar). The original wrong must be undone, then additional compensation must be offered to God. | While purification offering cleansed the defiled object or person, reparation offering is a "pay-back" to God for something we should have given or done—atonement to remove guilt | Lv 5:14–26; 7:1–6 |

sets of sacrifice laws, detected by their unique stylistic features, have been identified in chapters 1–7, and although the style of the first 16 chapters differs noticeably from that of the rest of the book, the editors, nevertheless, have blended these elements into a book that, after Deuteronomy, is the most unified of the five in the Pentateuch.

Because so much of the material in Leviticus is not a part of modern Christian religious practice, a look at each section of the outline on RG 74 should increase our understanding.

### Leviticus 1–7: The Topic of Sacrifice

The five types of sacrifice that are named in these chapters are described in the following

| Theology of Sacrifice |
|---|
| Expiation = dedication = fellowship<br>OR<br>Being forgiven = being committed = communion with God |

table. When more than one was presented, the sequence of offerings was as follows: first, the reparation or sin offering, which gave people a way of dealing with their sinfulness. The burnt offering followed, demonstrating the people's total dedication to God. Finally came the communion sacrifices, which established communion with God and others in the community. This sequence of expiation to dedication to fellowship reveals both the importance and the theology of Israel's system of sacrifice: To achieve communion with God one first had to be forgiven and totally committed to the LORD.

### Leviticus 8–10: The Anointing and Service of Aaron and His Sons

Chapters 25–31 of Exodus gave instructions about religious ritual that are finally put into practice in these chapters of Leviticus. (The instructions for the building of the tent and ark had already been followed by the end of Exodus, but those regarding sacrifice and the consecration of priests are not implemented until now.) Chapter 8 details the installation of Aaron and his descendants as priests of Israel. Chapter 9 narrates the first sacrifice, and chapter 10 deals with infractions of the sacrificial rules.

All three chapters reinforce the message that sacrifices must be approached with deadly seriousness. Close attention to the details of ritual is absolutely necessary, for ritual improperly done will not bring the glory of the LORD into their midst. So serious is this requirement that two of Aaron's sons are struck dead for failing to follow ceremonial rules and approaching God's presence carelessly.

Priests are reminded always to distinguish between the sacred and profane, the clean and unclean. Among other ways, they are to do this by refraining from customs that show disrespect for God's holiness such as improper dress, stepping outside the Tent of Meeting, and drinking alcoholic beverages. Even excess zeal that violates sacrificial regulations is dangerous. Aaron's sons Eleazar and Ithamar, for example, had refused to eat the portion of the sacrifice to which they, as priests, had been entitled. They allowed it to be burnt as an offering to God instead. They were permitted to get away with this transgression only because they had given up to God what was rightfully theirs. Had it been the other way around, however, they might well have been struck dead.

These chapters reinforce the belief that idolatry is very alluring and the holiness of God easily transgressed. The role of the priests, then, becomes extremely important, for by their careful observance of religious ritual they help preserve the people's relationship with God.

### Leviticus 11–15: The Laws of Purity

While the discussion of holiness and purity on RG 75 deals with this topic, some additional comments may aid our understanding of this area that is so foreign to modern Christian experience.

These chapters deal with four types of uncleanness:

1. Animals, Lv 11:1–47
2. Childbirth, Lv 12:1–8
3. Contagious disease, Lv 13:1–14:57
4. Genital discharges, Lv 15:1–33

The many regulations that fill these chapters govern (1) which animals are and are not fit for eating, (2) when quarantine is necessary to deal with contagious diseases or infected homes, and (3) how purification is achieved by both men and women following sexual emissions. Although other purity regulations controlled the nation's life (see Ex 12–13 and Dt 20), those listed here deal with matters that come under the direct supervision of the priests.

Reading through all the rules, you might begin to wonder why one animal is deemed clean and edible while another is not. Scholars vary in their opinions. Some say there is sound primitive science underlying the regulations reflected in such rules as the mandatory quarantine of persons with infectious diseases or the ban on pork—long recognized as a carrier of parasites. Others argue that the reason is religious. Some in this group insist certain animals are forbidden because they seem imperfect—freaks of nature perhaps, but certainly not what was intended in

### Clean and Unclean

VARIOUS REASONS ARE proposed for certain animals being designated clean and others unclean:

1. Medical: reducing exposure to infectious diseases and animals known to carry disease and parasites.
2. Religious: some animals are "defective" and fail to reflect God's original plan of creation.
3. Arbitrary: simply a means of setting Israel apart from its neighbors.

Note that chapter 10 of Acts of the Apostles indicates there is nothing inherently wrong with the animals Leviticus labels unclean.

the creation. Fish that swim, birds that fly, and animals that graze are fully in God's plan, but flightless birds like ostriches, sea creatures that walk like animals, and animals that crawl close to the ground like insects seem to be aberrations and must be shunned. Some scholars who hold for a religious basis for the division between clean and unclean think the divisions are mostly arbitrary—simply a way of making the Israelites different from other people. Canaanites used pigs in their worship, so for the Israelites they were forbidden. Sharing a meal was a very important part of Middle Eastern hospitality, but their strict dietary laws prevented the Israelites from being able to mix socially with their pagan neighbors. The best guess, perhaps, is that a blend of all these motivations influenced those who drew up the lists of clean and unclean foods.

The basis for all these laws is the belief that many areas of human life touch and express the mystery of God. Birth and death and sexuality are such holy areas because they are at the very heart of the divine mystery that controls our lives. As such, those areas cannot be defiled by anything impure or unworthy. Humans penetrate the set-apart world of the sacred not only on holy days, or when they enter a holy place or participate in rituals performed by a consecrated (and thus "holy") person, but also through common everyday moments that involve life and death—like eating to sustain life ("you are what you eat"), the awesome experience of sexual activity, and the sometimes dangerous loss of blood or other bodily fluids.

#### Leviticus 16: The Day of Atonement

The feast of the Day of Atonement described in chapter 16 was seen as a way of making up for all the instances of impurity that had defiled the land throughout the year. The description of this important ritual is the climax to all the preceding material from chapter 1 onward regarding sacrifice, priestly service, and purity. At one level or other, all those issues deal with the need for atonement. Note how atonement was at the center of most religious practice: The sacrifices always included some atoning function; ritual mistakes requiring atonement were a constant danger in priestly service; and, of course, daily life presented innumerable opportunities for intentional and especially unintentional impurity that required atoning. With this constant need for atonement, it was certainly reassuring that once a year the wickedness and rebellion of all the people could be laid onto a goat that would carry the sins off into the wilderness. Chapter 16 carefully describes each step. It lists first the proper procedures and clothing for Aaron and any future high priest to enter the presence of God in the holy of holies; then it outlines each step of the ritual, including the prayer and hand gestures over the goat; and finally it closes with a command to do this forever. Yom Kippur still occurs on the ninth day after Rosh Hashanah (New Year) each fall.

**Scapegoat** The term scapegoat is derived from the word Azazel (Lv 16:8), which may have been a name of Satan and is used nowhere but in this book and chapter. Ancient editions translated the word as "the escaping goat," which eventually became the English word "scapegoat." Today it means anyone who is blamed for wrongs committed by others.

### Leviticus 17–25: The Holiness Code

Chapters 1–16 dealt with ritual purity—all the behaviors and regulations that help overcome the natural barrier between God and humanity. Chapters 17–25 have a different focus: Rather than emphasizing what must be avoided in order to remain holy, they stress those positive things that must be done in order to grow in holiness.

While the long lists of laws in chapters 1–16 dealt mainly with liturgical requirements, the sermon-like verses of chapters 17–25 deal with the moral obligations of living in community. From how to worship a holy God, the focus has shifted to how to live a holy life. Because the Holiness Code of chapters 17–25 resembles the homiletic style of the book of Deuteronomy and the fiery oratory of the prophet Ezekiel, scholars think it may have been composed at the same time as these other writings, possibly during the Babylonian Exile (587–538 B.C.)

The Code itself can be divided into two parts: Chapters 17–20 cover laws for living a just and holy life binding on all members of the community, and chapters 21–25 deal mostly with priestly matters of public worship.

Although these lists might seem endless as you read them, remember that these (and the laws listed in Exodus, Numbers, and Deuteronomy) are the nation's entire collection of laws. Compared to modern law books, these are remarkably short and easy to understand. Read the laws and you will note they are not grouped in any systematic way—an inspiring law like the command to love your neighbor as yourself (Lv 19:18) stands beside one that tells you not to plant your field with two kinds of seed (Lv 19:19). A law forbidding turning your daughter into a prostitute is followed by one ordering observance of the Sabbath, which is followed by one about consulting mediums, and by another that says you should stand when an elderly person enters the room (Lv 19:30–32).

These laws comprise an *ideal* code, and it is likely that some of the laws were never really put into practice. For example, the Jubilee Year—which mandated that every 50 years debts were forgiven, Israelite slaves were set free, and all property leased or bought reverted to its original owners—may never actually have been practiced. But it does point to some remarkable characteristics of Israelite law.

These laws established Israel as a nation apart, different from all their neighbors. Israel protected the rights of the weak and the poor. Punishment was not allowed to be excessive, but had to be proportionate to the crime ("An eye for an eye"). Sexuality was to be treated as sacred and not allowed to degenerate into immorality. What went on inside a person was as important as what went on outside—that is, your heart had to be pure as well as your actions. The poor could get justice just as readily as the rich, and even foreigners were assured fair treatment. Property rights never took precedence over human rights. Encoded in this system of laws was the belief that the followers of a compassionate God who "led them out of Egypt" must be known, in turn, for their own compassion and justice.

### Leviticus 26–27: The Conclusion of the Holiness Code

This chapter ends both the Holiness Code and the entire book. The regulations regarding how to worship God and how to live as God's holy people have been spelled out. Blessings are promised for those who will obey the covenant, curses for those who will defy it.

The chapter reflects the postexilic attitude of the Priestly editors and shows signs of having been written with the benefits of hindsight: It predicts blessings but also the eventual curse of exile for disobedience. It also adds a promise of renewed blessing and assurance that God will not forget the covenant completely (Lv 26:45). The reference to "uncircumcised hearts" (Lv 26:41) also anticipates the spirit of the exilic prophets Jeremiah (see Jer 9:26) and Ezekiel, who announced that God was about to establish a new covenant that would be written on people's hearts. This covenant would be obeyed not out of fear of the Law, but out of love of the LORD.

The upbeat and hopeful final verses of chapter 26 were the original ending of Leviticus. Chapter 27 was added later to deal with the question of how to handle vows, sometimes rashly made, of dedicating certain people, animals, or objects to the LORD. When it was inappropriate to actually offer the vowed item, like a family member or an animal that was unclean, monetary value could be assigned to the item and the money, rather than the person or object itself, could be given over to the LORD.

**Circumcision** In Israel, the medical ritual practice of circumcision initiated a male into the covenant and nation and allowed him to participate in public worship. By speaking of "uncircumcised hearts," Leviticus is pointing out that more than a surgical procedure is needed to be a true follower of God. One's inner attitude is also critical. Moses (Dt 10:16) also calls the people to circumcise "the foreskin of your hearts" by loving the LORD and ending their disobedience. In essence, following the Law is a call to a deeper relationship with God.

**Questions for Discussion and Reflection**

*Group Sharing/Discussion*

1. What is an example of an important law in Leviticus? Which one(s) would you choose to leave out if you were making their laws?

2. The Hebrew people were putting themselves together as a nation, organizing how they would function. These numerous laws were a way to do that. At the founding of the United States as a country, much time and care were put into drawing up the Constitution to help organize us as a people. How would you compare and contrast those approaches?

3. Has your attitude toward Leviticus changed at all as a result of your reading? In what ways? What value, if any, do you find in reading through such long lists of laws?

*In Our Lives*

1. The laws of Leviticus are to help people be holy, to live and act as God's people. What in the Catholic tradition and liturgy is helpful to people today with regard to helping them live and act as God's people?

2. Why is it important to have laws? When might you decide not to follow a law?

3. The Day of Atonement was and is an important time for the ancient Israelites and modern Jews to reflect on their sins and failings and ask for pardon. When and how do we do this in our own tradition? What can help us do better at reflecting on our failings? Try to end each day by looking at how you've failed and succeeded.

*Individual/Personal Reflection/Action*

1. Name for yourself five "rules" or ways of living or worshiping in the Catholic tradition that are important to you. In the coming days think about what would help you pay attention to living them more fully.

2. Following the rules is not as important as understanding why we have the rule and choosing to honor that. What rules do you not understand in our Catholic tradition? Ask someone such as a parish staff person to help you understand their purpose.

# NUMBERS READING GUIDE

## *At a Glance*

| | |
|---|---|
| Who are the main players? | Moses, Aaron, and Miriam Joshua and Caleb Balaam, Korah, Eleazar |
| What should I look for? | Grumbling and rebellion of the people Characterizations of God's wrath God's faithfulness despite people's sin Importance of priests and Levites in developing fidelity through proper ritual and holiness God's use of foreign prophet/magician Balaam |
| When did this take place? | During the 38 years of Israel's wanderings in the desert following the sealing of the covenant at Sinai. |
| Where did these events occur? | Three main sites: Mt. Sinai—preparing to set out for the Promised Land; Kadesh—rebellion causes long delay, followed by eventual journey to Moab; the plains of Moab—readying to enter and conquer the Promised Land. |

Why was this book written? To show the consequences of Israel's murmuring and rebellion against the LORD; that God's wrath is to be taken seriously, but God's grace and mercy always prevail, and God will be faithful to the promises made to the Patriarchs; that God's plan for Israel and all peoples will not be thwarted; that the call to holiness and purity cannot be ignored, and that trust in God is a requirement for God's people.

What is the story? No sooner is the covenant at Sinai sealed, than the people start grumbling against the LORD. God punishes some, but Moses' prayers persuade God to spare the nation. Spies sent into the land of Canaan return with reports of giants and argue against invasion. Joshua and Caleb disagree, but the people refuse to move. Because of their lack of trust, God decides none of the generation that left Egypt will be allowed to enter the Promised Land. The "wandering" period begins and lasts until all adults who left Egypt have died in the desert (except Joshua and Caleb). God uses the pagan prophet Balaam to speak blessings on Israel as they prepare to enter the beautiful land of God's promise.

## Overview

The fourth book of the Pentateuch, Numbers, recounts memorable events of the Israelite wanderings from Sinai, God's mountain, to the plains of Moab, just opposite the Promised Land. Thus, Numbers continues the story begun in Exodus and continued in Leviticus of the escape from Egyptian servitude, the desert journey to Mount Sinai, the revelation at Sinai and giving of the Law, and the building of the Tabernacle with instruction on its operation.

Numbers is a complex collection of texts containing an assortment of interwoven kinds of literature: historical narratives, legal texts, ritual prescriptions, and poetic folk traditions. Its final form reflects a long and intricate literary history. Modern critical scholarship identifies separate sources underlying the final version of the book. Primarily, the texts derive from various layers of the Priestly school (P), with additional texts from the two older narrative sources, the Yahwist (J) and the Elohist (E). The predominant Priestly material often functions to expand, supplement, or recast the earlier (J and E) texts to fit the agenda of Priestly circles. The lengthy Balaam section (chs 22–24) in its entirety stands untouched by the Priestly writer.

The book of Numbers has three main sections.

1. Preparations for travel in the wilderness (chs 1–10)

This section is mainly prescriptive, telling how things are to be done. Its focus is the census and the arrangement of the camp of the Israelites (chs 1–2; 5:1–4); and the arrangement of the tribes and sanctuary when they are on the march (9:15–10:36). Interspersed in this are various instructions or descriptions concerning the reparation offering, suspected adultery, the Nazirite vow, the priestly blessing (5:5–6:27), and the delayed Passover (9:1–4). It is not always clear why these laws are placed where they are now found. The section is almost entirely Priestly in origin.

2. Travels in the wilderness (chs 11–25)

This part is mostly narrative, and combines Priestly and non-Priestly material. It tells of rebellions and complaints by Israelites, Miriam and Aaron, and the scouts (chs 11–14); the rebellion of Korah, Dathan, and Abiram (chs 16–17); Israel's encounters with various enemies; Balaam's blessing; and the Baal-Peor incident (chs 20–25). Sections of prescription interspersed among these chapters include rules on offerings, Sabbath violation, wearing fringes (ch 15); priesthood and Levitical duties (ch 18); and corpse contamination (ch 19).

3. The end of the wilderness travels and preparations for entering the land of Canaan (chs 26–36).

This section is mostly prescriptive, containing laws and rules. Portions that are closely connected with the story itself or the topic of acquiring the land of Canaan include the second census (ch 26); laws on female inheritance (27:1–11); the transfer of civil leadership to Joshua (27:12–23); revenge against the Midianites (ch 31); the distribution of the Transjordan land (ch 31); a summary of wilderness travels (ch 33); the boundaries of the land of Canaan (ch 34); Levitical cities and homicide laws (ch 35); and a supplement to laws of female inheritance (ch 36). Portions less visibly connected with the narrative context are the ritual calendar (chs 28–29) and the rules about women's vows (ch 30). This section is almost entirely Priestly in origin.

## Reading the Book of Numbers

A first reading of the book might begin with the main narrative, chs 1; 10–14; 16–17; 20–27; 31–33. The legal sections are more difficult to understand and may best be read according to different topics: the Levites (chs 3–4; 7–8; 18; 35); priestly and Levitical duties (chs 3–4; 16–17; 18; 35); the arrangement of camp (chs 2–3; 10); laws pertaining to women (ch 5; 27:1–11; chs 30–36); holy days (9:1–14; 15:32–36; chs 28–29); impurity and holiness (chs 6:1–4; 6:16–17; 19; 35); sacrifices and offerings (chs 7; 15; 28–29); and distribution of the land (chs 27:1–11; 32; 34–36). Numbers also contains a few poetic passages. Some of these are especially difficult and might be studied together in connection with the style of the Psalms.

There are few parallels to this type of writing in modern literature. We can learn to value and even enjoy this intense combining of laws and past lessons if we can forget our world a bit and imagine ourselves as one of those Israelites whose unique and passionate faith in a single God set them apart from other peoples. How do they preserve the ties back to the days of salvation and guidance in the desert without losing them in the culture of the people they conquer? They remember the ways in the desert and observe them!

## Major Religious Topics of Numbers

While keeping the journey story moving forward, the Priestly editors of Numbers emphasize certain themes over others. Ritual and worship matters are very important, as are questions regarding the duties of priests and Levites. Laws governing conflicts over land also receive attention. But the themes that dominate are theological, that is, issues that center on God's power to fulfill the promise made to Abraham and the other patriarchs. Of these topics four require more detailed attention:

1. The authority of Moses, Aaron, and the elders
2. The people's murmuring and lack of trust
3. God's use of the prophet Balaam
4. The use of war to advance God's plan for Israel

### Moses and Aaron

The leadership and importance of Moses in the Pentateuch can hardly be questioned. And yet that is exactly what the people often did during their journeys. Even his sister and brother questioned his right to sole authority. Moses says little in his own defense. He leaves that to God, and God does not disappoint. More than 150 times in Numbers we are told God spoke to Moses directly, and through him to Israel. Those who questioned Moses' role were reminded that God's relationship with Moses was unique.

Yet God did allow Moses to share the burden of leadership with Aaron and some elders of the community. Moses and Aaron were from the tribe of Levi, a tribe that was considered violent renegades in Genesis. Exodus, however, points out that the Levites were the only tribe that did not worship the golden calf, and Deuteronomy adds that the Levites alone were faithful at Massah and Meribah where Moses struck water from the rock.

### Priests and Levites

Levites and priests are distinct roles: Aaron is a Levite (Ex 4:14), but priests are supposedly limited to descendants of Aaron, a subgroup within the larger group of Levites. Levites assist in various Temple activities, and in Numbers their role (and its limits) are spelled out. They alone may carry the Ark and other sacred objects (1:49–53); they are the consecrated substitutes for each firstborn male from all other tribes (8:15–19); and they administer the cities of refuge, places where people suspected of crimes may go to avoid revenge-slayings until their cases could be heard (35:2–8). On the other hand, they may not be priests (chapters 16–17).

### *Instances of Grumbling and Rebellion*

| | |
|---|---|
| Nm 11:1 | At Taberah, the people grumble against Moses; God sends consuming fire, but the people are spared through Moses' prayer. |
| Nm 11:4 | At Kibroth-Hattaavah, people grumble over lack of meat; first God sends a plague, but then miraculous quail for food. |
| Nm 12:1–16 | Miriam and Aaron rebel against Moses' sole authority; Miriam is punished with leprosy, but later is healed by God. |
| Nm 14:1-38 | At the very edge of the Promised Land, the people cringe in fear, refusing to attack and take possession of the land; they accuse Moses of leading them to their deaths. God decides none of them will ever enter the Promised Land. |
| Nm 16:1–36 | Korah, Dathan, and Abiram lead 250 council members in open rebellion against Moses; they are destroyed by fire from heaven. |
| Nm 17:6–15 | The people grumble against Moses and Aaron; God's threatened punishment is averted by Aaron's ritual action. |
| Nm 17:27–28 | The Israelites express panic and despair. |
| Nm 20:2–13 | People grumble about lack of water; Moses strikes the rock and God sends water, but Moses won't be allowed to enter the Promised Land. |
| Nm 21:4–9 | More grumbling about food, so God sends poisonous snakes. Those who are bitten are saved by looking at a bronze serpent made by Moses. |

#### The Murmuring Tradition

In the desert, the people repeatedly grumbled and rebelled against God. (See a few examples above.) But all the instances of grumbling reflect the Priestly interest in showing how God punished the people and then allowed the leaders, Moses or Aaron, to intercede and save them. Through all these grumbling incidents, the Priestly editors emphasize that the community must atone for sin and seek purification through liturgy. Even the bronze serpent episode is an example of healing through ritual action.

#### The Balaam Oracles

Balaam, a person as mysterious as he is fascinating, takes the stage in chapters 22 through 24. Balaam is no typical biblical prophet. He is more a magician-for-hire, a foreigner belonging to a nomadic clan who is well known and well regarded even by the kings of his day. One king, Balak, tries to hire him to prophesy *against* Israel, but Balaam is able to utter only words of blessing for God's people: "How can I curse whom God has not cursed? It is a blessing I have been given to pronounce" (Nm 23:8–20) and curses their enemies.

Because the stories in Numbers seem to be a compilation of material from the J and E sources as well as the Priestly, we get two rather contradictory views of Balaam. Chapters 22–24 present him favorably as a true prophet to whom God speaks directly and who is willing to do what the LORD asks of him. Although even here there is a vague indication that Balaam was willing to be led more by greed than God's will, after being rebuked by his own donkey, he delivers four moving oracles about the destiny of Israel. God uses even this foreign prophet of questionable character to do the divine will.

In chapter 31, however, we learn Balaam was slaughtered by the Israelites because he had led the people into sexual immorality and the worship of false gods. Even New Testament books seem to pick up on a tradition that Balaam was a false teacher motivated by greed. In all, nine biblical books refer to Balaam, a sign of the importance given him and the events he dominates. His prophecies confirm Israel's eventual victory in its battle for the Promised Land.

#### Holy War

In Numbers 31 God tells Moses to take vengeance on the Midianites. Our ears may hear that order differently than did the writers and ancient readers of the Bible. To us it might sound like a random decision to punish innocent people for the sake of God's "chosen people," Israel. But the Israelites heard something different. In their view, the Canaanites were a wicked and sinful people who deserved punishment. What they heard was an expression of the life and death struggle between the LORD and the Canaanite gods. They were reminded that *in their founding days* God was a warrior who fought for them against their enemies. In Deuteronomy Moses bluntly tells the Israelites that "it is not because of your justice or the integrity of your heart that you are going in to take possession of their land; but it is because of their wickedness that the LORD, your God, is dispossessing these nations before you" (Dt 9:5). In thrusting aside the native people of Canaan, Israel also saw God fulfilling the promise of land made to the patriarchs.

But God did not victimize some innocent, unsuspecting nation. When, in Numbers 31, God ordered the destruction of all the Midianites, including the women, it was because they had been the ones who followed Balaam's advice and seduced the Israelites into fornication and idolatry of Baal at Peor. One of the primary purposes of Israel's dietary and purity regulations was ensuring that the nation would be different from all its neighbors. To be different, Israel had to be pure, and to be pure Israel had to avoid idolatry and sexual excess. The best way to prevent contamination was to remove all possible sources of these evils. Those are fierce standards. But Israel saw God inflicting equally brutal punishment on itself for its own unfaithfulness.

**Justifying Their War**

We must also recognize that the authors of these texts were trying to justify their conquests. It was therefore in their interest to emphasize that the war had God's command behind it, and that the inhabitants who were driven out deserved their fate. Some of the descriptions must be read bearing in mind that they were written by the winning side.

Deuteronomy 20 specifies restrictions for holy war that make it less than total massacre. Numbers, too, embodies some elements of this later attitude. Now, purity and obedience are to be the hallmarks of God's army, not vengeance. It seems as if the editors of Numbers were trying to soften the old stories of total war and call instead for a total commitment of life to God. The stories of old were plenty exciting, but they were not to be models for present behavior! Over the centuries Israel's theology of war developed, as reflected in the teachings of several prophets who said that war was not the way to do God's will (see Is 7:1–14; Hos 10:13f; Jer 21:3–10; Jer 34:1–5). In Numbers we find the earlier and later viewpoints on war mixed together.

**The Theology of the Priestly Writers**

The end of the book of Exodus already presented the Priestly writers' primary theology: God's presence in Israel will be found in the sanctuary (a tent during the desert years, a temple later). Israel's proper response to God's presence among them is observance of the laws of holiness and sacrifice. However, in Numbers, the P authors add important specifications about how this holiness is to be lived out: (1) through national institutions and (2) through relations among the tribes. Moreover, Israel must never neglect its system of religious worship no matter the circumstances. God will surely punish disobedience, but the intercession of priests and leaders can deter God's wrath and bring blessing; inevitably, God follows punishment with mercy. Most important, nothing can prevent God's will from being fulfilled and no one leader, not even Moses, is indispensable.

The end of Numbers finds the people still without a home, but equipped with all the tools of worship and obedience to enable them to hold on until God's promises are fulfilled. Now Moses can depart and the conquest can begin.

**Questions for Discussion and Reflection**

***Group Sharing/Discussion***

1. Choose various people who had a role in this part of the story. In your group, take turns telling their part (or highlights of it) from their point of view, explaining their role, defending what they did, and so on.

2. Describe the contradictory role of Balaam and tell how you would explain those contradictions to someone who asked you about them.

3. Compare/contrast the laws about women in the book of Numbers with those of our society in the past and today.

***In Our Lives***

1. Ritual and worship in the community are a central concern in Numbers. How do we mirror the importance of the community in worship in our own most important liturgical celebration, the Eucharist?

2. Could you use the words *holy* and *war* in the same sentence? How did Israel grow in their understanding of God's use of war? What insights does Christianity bring to that conversation?

3. Grumbling in the community did not stop with the Israelites. What ways do we have to bring our concerns to our religious and political leaders today, rather than grumble to each other?

***Individual/Personal Reflection/Action***

1. As you ponder the 40-year journey of the Israelites through the desert, what insights do you get about your own journey: the ebb and flow of your relationship with God, the ups and downs in your own commitment? Who or what helps you find your way when you need help?

2. Leaders cannot lead without followers. What are qualities that you look for in a leader you are willing to follow?

3. We can worship better as a community when we know and relate to those with whom we worship. What are some ways you can get to know members in your parish community better?

# DEUTERONOMY READING GUIDE

### *At a Glance*

| | |
|---|---|
| Who are the main players? | Moses and Joshua |
| What should I look for? | Review of Israel's history and God's saving activity Warm, personal tone of the writing Stress on God's love for the people Emphasis on laws and teaching of laws to children |
| When did this take place? | At the end of the 40 years of wandering, as Israel prepared to enter the Promised Land. |
| Where did these events occur? | The river Jordan's east bank, in the territory of Moab where the Jordan meets the Dead Sea. |
| Why was this book written? | To remind the Israelites of God's great love for them, of the mighty saving deeds God had performed for them, and that they must choose fidelity to the covenant in order to reap its benefits. |
| What is the story? | Poised to enter the land of promise, the Israelites hear three major speeches from Moses, who takes a final opportunity to admonish and instruct the people before his death. The book is a lengthy sermon in which Moses, like an elderly parent, tells his children what really matters and encourages them to choose carefully and well. Having done so, he blesses the tribes and goes off to die. |

## Reading the Book of Deuteronomy

We can start our examination of this last book of the Pentateuch by naming some of its special characteristics. First, the book is structured like one of the treaties typical of the ancient Near East. Second, the theology of Deuteronomy also runs through the historical books of Joshua, Judges, Samuel, and Kings, making Deuteronomy a kind of preface to these books. Third, Deuteronomy has a distinctive style that sets it apart from all the other writing in the Pentateuch: It reads like a sermon, spoken entirely by Moses, full of urgent pleas for obedience and thundering warnings about what will happen if the people don't obey the Law. Fourth, scholars believe Deuteronomy was written about the seventh century B.C., long after the time of Moses, so it is really looking backward at Israel's history even though it is written as if it were looking ahead to Israel's movement into the land.

Some commentators divide the book very simply into three major addresses of Moses:

1. First Address: Review of Israel's History (1:1–4:43)

2. Second Address: God's Covenant and Elaboration of the Law (4:44–26:19)

3. Third Address: Moses' Summary and Farewell (27:1–33:29); Death and Burial of Moses (34:1–10)

This simple outline makes clear that the core of the book is in fact a new presentation of the Law that restates many of the laws presented earlier in Exodus through Numbers (*Deuteronomos* is Greek for "second Law" or "repetition of the Law").

**The Unique Style of the Book**

From beginning to end, Deuteronomy has the feel of a first-person speech. Unlike the other books of the Pentateuch, which show evidence of being patchwork quilts of material drawn together from the J, E, and P sources, Deuteronomy stands alone as having an independent source. Even its vocabulary differs from that of the other books. Certain phrases that are repeated often throughout the book help establish Deuteronomy's special character. Note the following examples:

1. These are the ordinances, statutes, and decrees that the LORD, your God, has enjoined on you (cf. 4:45; 5:1; 6:20; etc.); take care to observe them (4:5; 5:1; 6:3; 7:12; 8:1; etc.)

2. You must learn them, or teach them in the land (5:1; 5:31; 11:19; etc.) and teach them to your children (4:9; 4:10; 11:19; etc.)

3. In the land you are about to enter to possess (5:31; 6:1; 6:10; 6:18; 9:5; etc.)

4. So that you might live long and prosper (4:40; 5:33; 6:2f; 6:24; 11:9; etc.)

5. You will love the LORD your God with all your heart and soul (6:5; 10:12; 11:13; etc.)

6. Do not turn aside after other gods to serve them (6:14; 7:4; 8:19; 11:16; etc.)

7. Do not forget the LORD (8:11; 6:12; etc.)

8. I set before you today a blessing and a curse (11:26; cf. 30:19)

9. The land, which the LORD swore to our fathers (6:10; 6:18; 6:23; 7:13; 10:11; etc.); a land flowing with milk and honey (6:3; 11:9; etc.)

10. Do what is right and good (6:18; cf. 12:28; 13:19; etc.)

The repeated use of these phrases sounds like a preacher working hard to get a message across. The goal is to make its audience choose and change. By referring constantly to the land as "flowing with milk and honey . . . a good land . . . a land that God swore to your ancestors," it also recalls God's good deeds toward Israel, especially God's help against foreign opposition. Deuteronomy's intense and repetitive language helps make the book's main point: The people must be obedient when they take possession of the land.

**The Historical Perspective of the Book**

Some people may assume that Israel was always run like a theocracy where knowledge and observance of the Law could be taken for granted. They may also assume that the Bible, as we know it today, was always available to guide the people of ancient Israel. The reality, of course, was much different. The books we now call the Pentateuch did not exist, as we now know them, until late in Israel's history; probably the J and E sources were not pulled together to form Genesis, Exodus, Leviticus, and Numbers until the reign of King Hezekiah (715–687 B.C.). What existed before the books were formalized and finalized were stories, traditions, laws, and legends that were mostly passed on orally and, if they were written at all, were available to very few people.

**The Story Continues**

The reign of the idolatrous King Manasseh was longer than any other king (687–642 B.C.). The king who followed him after a brief period, Josiah (640–609 B.C.), initiated a reform. He rejected the idolatry of Manasseh and called for renewed obedience of the Law. It was during his reign that the book of Deuteronomy first appeared. The story goes that during the rebuilding of the Temple a "Book of the Law" was found that greatly moved the young king: Upon hearing it read aloud, he tore his garments and wept. Immediately he consulted a well-known prophetess, Huldah, who declared the book's message authentic. Convinced more than ever, the king

**Obedience = Reward: Is it That Simple?**

DEUTERONOMY SEEMS TO offer a very simple formula for life: obey and you'll be rewarded; disobey and you'll be punished. The national history of Israel as presented by the biblical writers, although often with the benefit of hindsight, would indicate that the formula basically worked. It is hard to say whether the people of Israel would have received constant blessing if they had remained consistently faithful, rather than forgetful and unfaithful as they were. But what is clear is that Israel saw moments and enjoyed periods of great blessing only to watch them dissolve into times of tragic misfortune (a pattern that especially dominates the book of Judges).

Moses clearly says God had established a special relationship with Israel, and Israel's part of the bargain was to live by the covenant made at Sinai. In fact, even the understanding in Deuteronomy—that God will act on behalf of Israel only if the people keep their part of the treaty—is a positive development from earlier theologies that saw God as a warrior who would fight for Israel no matter what. In their infancy as God's people, Israel perhaps needed a mighty, warrior God who would destroy their enemies, solve their problems, and reward their every good deed. But, as time passed, they learned to view God differently.

Christians believe that Jesus continued God's self-revelation. From Jesus we learn that while peace is promised—a peace the world does not understand—it is also a peace that we can, indeed must, find even in the midst of trial, suffering, and possibly persecution. One of the important truths of the Christian tradition is that pain and suffering are an inevitable part of the journey to union with God.

fully embraced the book's program of reform and called the nation to repentance (2 Kings 22:1—23:25). Scholars theorize that this "Book of the Law" was in fact Deuteronomy, and that it was written shortly before this time in order to guide a reform of Israelite religion. Therefore, its concerns are those of the seventh century, and not those of five centuries or more earlier, when Moses lived.

Interestingly, a reform similar to Josiah's had been started in Judah nearly 100 years earlier by King Hezekiah, around 715 B.C. But did Hezekiah know about the teachings of Deuteronomy back then? It is just possible that the refugees who had fled the destruction of the northern kingdom only seven years earlier brought with them these same fundamental teachings, traditions, and laws, and that these influenced Hezekiah's reform.

### The Importance of the Covenant

While Deuteronomy has the shape of a vassal treaty between two people, it is also written like a speech of Moses, which reminds the people of God's miraculous care for them in the desert. It describes God in the role of a loving father caring for his son, and as a mother giving life to her child. This parent-child language is typical of covenant treaties of the times, which used love as the motivation for loyalty between the parties. In Deuteronomy, love and faithfulness are everything!

### The Law Is Not Simply Laws, but Total Commitment

In contrast with Exodus, Deuteronomy talks frequently about *why* laws need to be obeyed. And the reason is love. Before Deuteronomy, the Pentateuch seldom mentions that word as a motive for following the covenant, but this book repeatedly speaks of God's love for the people and their need to respond in kind. In Exodus obedience was a duty, in Deuteronomy it is an act of love. God gave the Law for the people's good, much the way a parent would lay out rules for a child out of concern for his or her welfare. The emphasis on knowing, teaching, reading, and writing the Law is not a sign of legalism, but a reflection of the deeper and more permanent commitment to the LORD that lies beneath.

### The Land and God's Blessing Are Conditional

Blessing and curse follow obedience and disobedience. The people of Israel learned that lesson from the events of their lives. Another lesson they had to learn was that even God's gift of the land could be taken away if they misused it or failed to create a just and honest society. By writing Deuteronomy as a farewell speech given by Moses in the desert, the authors make his warnings come from a period *before* the people took possession of Canaan. The writers are saying: Remember what it was like to have no land? Well, that could be the case again if you don't heed Moses' warnings. The book may have been most influential once the exile began (about 587 B.C.), since then readers could see that this tragedy resulted from their failure to obey the LORD as Moses had warned. It spoke to their misery and to their repentant hearts.

### There Is to Be One Sanctuary

One of the objectives of Deuteronomy is to focus the people's attention on Jerusalem as the central place of worship, so that they would not be distracted by local shrines and cult centers that often had pagan connections. But since, at the time that Moses is supposedly speaking, the choice of Jerusalem as the nation's capital by King David is still hundreds of years off, the city is never mentioned by name, only alluded to with such references as "the place which the LORD, your God, chooses as the dwelling place for his name" (12:11) and "the place which the LORD chooses in one of your tribal territories" (12:14).

### Deuteronomy Updates the Covenant Law

We've already mentioned that many of the laws listed in Deuteronomy are a restatement of the laws found in Israel's earliest law code, the "Covenant Code" found in Exodus 20:22—23:33. But there is also a difference. In Deuteronomy the laws are stated in a way that addresses the town and city life that had developed in Israel during the centuries since the Exodus. These laws have been fine-tuned to meet the needs of people living under conditions very different from those of the times when the laws were originally written. They accent the obligations of people to each other and especially to the weak and dispossessed, a need that became more visible and pressing once city life developed.

### Conclusion

By the time Deuteronomy was written, Israel was no longer a loose-knit alliance of desert tribes. It had become a kingdom. In this new life situation, Israel needed a reinterpretation and summary of the meaning of the events told in the other books of the Pentateuch. Deuteronomy provides this summary in the form of a "repetition of the Law." But Deuteronomy does more than look back at its history, it also anticipates its future in the land, which will be narrated in the historical books that follow. Thus Deuteronomy links those books written by historians from its own school of thought with the earlier Pentateuch traditions. The diagram below illustrates this relationship.

## Strong Words

The influence of Deuteronomy is seen in the

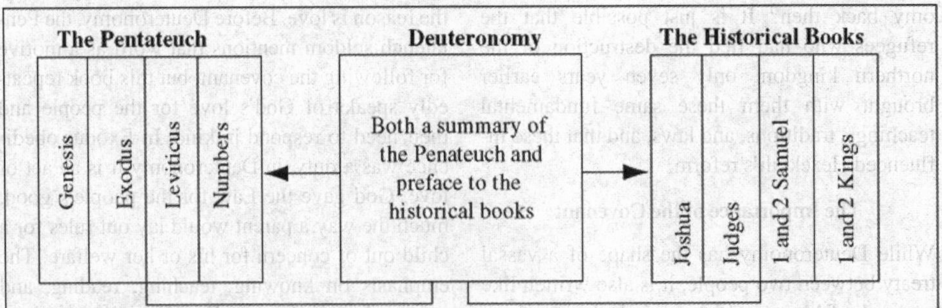

life of Jesus and the writings of the New Testament authors. Jesus' responses to Satan's three temptations all come from Deuteronomy (6:13; 6:16; 8:3). In the desert preparing for his mission, Jesus draws on the lessons Israel learned during its own desert experience to set the course of his journey. Jesus also quoted Deuteronomy when asked what was the greatest commandment.

Twenty-one New Testament books quote Deuteronomy almost 100 times in all, a testimony to its great influence. But that influence is found more in the basic themes of the New Testament than in any specific quotes. Jesus' whole ministry is an embodiment of the attitude in Deuteronomy of total dedication to God, God's love and fatherhood, doing more than the minimum the Law requires, and letting faith guide us to choose obedience over disobedience. The New Testament authors learned from Deuteronomy to see all of life as an integrated whole.

### Questions for Discussion and Reflection

***Group Sharing/Discussion***

1. Have each person name the five most important "teachings" of Moses in these three sermons at the end of his life.

2. What are some of the examples in Deuteronomy of the Law being very important? What are some examples of believing in God's love being very important?

3. What are three things about Jewish law or ritual that you learned from reading this book?

***In Our Lives***

1. Deuteronomy presents the motivation for obeying similar laws found in Exodus. That motivation is for obedience out of love rather than obedience out of duty. Which motivation is at the core of your own observance of our religious laws?

2. Moses reminds the people that God chose them not because of their merit, but out of pure love (see 7:7; 9:5; and 9:24). How would you explain this to someone who believes they can "earn" God's love?

3. Deuteronomy contains some strong messages about the importance of justice for the health of society. Concern for the poor and the weak is incorporated into the laws of the land. What contemporary laws have this same concern? Is it appropriate for civil laws to demand concern for the needy?

4. In chapter 4 Moses expresses concern for making sure the children learn the story so that their experiences are not forgotten. What are some ways Catholic Christians can help their children not forget the message of Christ?

***Individual/Personal Reflection/Action***

1. Imagine that like Moses, you were coming to the end of your life. Write what would be the most important messages you would want to leave for your family and friends?

2. In your own words, tell God how you know you are loved by God, and put your thanks for that love into your own words.

3. Name for yourself any important practices of our faith that you want to pay more attention to in your own life.

# THE HISTORICAL BOOKS

The story of the Israelite people is told in three major units of the Bible: the Pentateuch, the deuteronomistic history, and the chronicler's history. You will not find these designations used in the Bible itself, however, because they were originally defined by scholars who saw a unity among certain groups of books. By studying the writing style, subject matter, and major themes of each book, scholars are able to conclude that a collection of books was put together by one person or a small group working together.

Since each major section of the Bible covers centuries of history, no section can be a single person's eyewitness account. The ancient authors of the Bible usually began by collecting and organizing stories and oral traditions that already existed. The ancient writers turned those preexisting materials into the final form that became the Bible. Sometimes they did this by simply taking over the old stories with little or no change; other times they rewrote the original story. Scholars often can tell the difference between the older material the writer started with and its final form. Both are important. The *older* material tells us what had been valued by the ancient tradition. The *final form* tells us what the author thought was important and worth emphasizing at the time the collection was being shaped.

The reading guides up to this point have dealt with the Bible's first five books, the Pentateuch. The next section of the reading guide will deal with seven books (Joshua, Judges, 1 and 2 Samuel, 1 and 2 Kings, and Ruth, a later addition), which are called the *deuteronomistic history,* because the book of Deuteronomy serves as a kind of preface to the whole collection. The last group of historical books (1 and 2 Chronicles, Ezra, and Nehemiah) begins with the books of Chronicles, and therefore is called the *chronicler's history.* By telling the same story from different perspectives, the Bible gives us a clue that we have much to learn not just from the story itself, but also from its unique point of view.

## The Deuteronomistic History

### Joshua, Judges, 1 and 2 Samuel, and 1 and 2 Kings

The books we commonly refer to by these titles and treat as independent works are actually part of a continuous story that starts in Genesis and ends in 2 Kings. However, these six historical books existed as an independent unit, with the book of Deuteronomy as its preface, long before the Genesis-to-Kings collection was pulled together into its present form. But even before they became a unit, the individual works of this deuteronomistic history also existed independently as stories and traditions (also referred to as "sources"), which sometimes were written and sometimes were known only in oral form.

It is clear that the deuteronomistic writers who wrote the history of Israel used such sources. They even mention some of their sources (none of which have survived) in the history itself: "The Book of Jashar" (Jos 10:13), "The book of the chronicles of Solomon" (1 Kgs 11:41), "The book of the chronicles of the kings of Judah" (1 Kgs 14:29), and "The book of the chronicles of the kings of Israel" (1 Kgs 14:19).

***Deuteronomistic Vision of the Pattern of Israel's History***

1. God's offer of love
2. Israel's faithlessness and sin
3. God's just punishment
4. Israel's repentance and cry for help
5. God's forgiveness and mercy
6. Israel's renewed sinfulness

The deuteronomistic writers did not force their original sources to blend into one completely consistent story. They did not even try to blot out the contradictions, inconsistencies, or duplications that resulted from combining several sources. While they did impress an overall unity or perspective on the material they brought together, they also respected their sources and allowed them to speak for themselves, even if that meant letting them disagree with each other. For example, 1 Samuel chapter 8 shows God's displeasure at the request of the people for a king; chapter 9 presents the choice of Saul as God's idea. In 1 Samuel 17:48–51, David kills the Philistine warrior Goliath; in 2 Samuel 21:19, it is Elhanan who kills Goliath.

**Date and Purpose of the Deuteronomistic History**

The final edition of the deuteronomistic books was most likely put together during and after the exile that followed the destruction of Jerusalem in 586 B.C. Much of it, however, may already have been written down during the reign of Josiah, the reformer King of Judah (d. 609 B.C.). This dating helps us to understand, in part, the overall purpose of the history, which was to explain why the nation collapsed and why the people were led into exile. God did not abandon the covenant, says this history, the people did. Israel deserved destruction because of its sin. By refusing to heed God's constant warnings and shows of mercy, Israel sealed its fate. God was not obligated to stand by one particular country or king. Without the people's voluntary fidelity to the covenant, all bets were off.

***Typical Deuteronomistic Phrases***

"to follow other gods"

"you will know that the LORD alone is God"

"to serve other gods"

"to walk in the ways of the LORD"

"the city that the LORD has chosen"

"to keep all the commandments"

"to sacrifice and burn incense at high places"

"to provoke the LORD to anger"

The history, however, is not basically a pessimistic work. Signs of hope can be detected in the repeated calls for repentance and in the high value the authors place on God's promise to David of an everlasting dynasty. The recurring pattern in Israel's history—sin, punishment, cry for help, and deliverance—told the people that despite their sin and God's punishment, deliverance was possible again, if they returned to the LORD and asked for help.

**The Literary Character of the Deuteronomistic History**

The characteristic phrases and repetitions used by the writers of Deuteronomy make their style easy to recognize. These writers pulled together the sometimes detailed and well-written and sometimes sketchy stories of Israel's kings; then they added long speeches that would help readers understand the theological significance of each of the stages of Israel's history. The speeches (Jos 1:11–15; Jos 23; 1 Sm 12; 2 Sm 7; 1 Kgs 8:14–61), which usually are put into the mouths of main characters at critical moments of Israel's past, impose a religious interpretation on the events of Israel's history. They express the vision that God's initial offer of love was followed by Israel's sin, which was followed by God's mercy, only to be followed by more sin.

Besides *looking back* and explaining why things happened as they did, these speeches also *look forward* to Israel's future and urge the people to live differently. Past and future are viewed through the same glasses: If Israel obeys the Law, all goes well; if it does not, it is punished.

**Theological Concerns of the Deuteronomistic History**

It is important to recognize the theological concerns from which the writers of these books operate. Those concerns determine what they choose from their sources and how they use those sources. We do not have a complete history of Israel. We have Israel's history told from the theological perspective of these deuteronomistic writers: when Israel worshiped the LORD, and the LORD alone, all went well for the nation. However, because Israel chose to abandon the LORD and worship the gods of its neighbors, the LORD punished them with defeat and exile.

The book of Deuteronomy provides the key to understanding the deuteronomistic history. It sets forth the requirements of the Law (Dt 4:44–26:19), which will become the criteria by which the writers organize and evaluate Israel's history. According to the book of Deuteronomy, obedience to the laws of Moses brings covenant blessing (28:1–14), and disobedience brings curse (28:15–68). The deuteronomistic writers see in the events of Israel's history the realization of blessing or curse depending on Israel's obedience or disobedience to the laws of Moses.

The most important law for the writers is the first of the Ten Commandments: "I am the LORD your God . . . you shall not have other gods besides me" (Dt 5:6–7). Exclusive worship of the LORD is so crucial that virtually the entire history of Israel is told in terms of Israel's obedience to this one law. Although they frequently speak of obedience to the laws, statutes, and commandments, in reality all of these are reduced to one law: worship the LORD and the LORD alone. Even the writers' interest in centralized worship in the Jerusalem Temple is a reflection of their concern for obedience to this one law (see, for instance, 1 Kgs 12:26–30).

It is the word of the LORD that defines and determines the history of Israel. That word is expressed in the deuteronomic Law and repeated by the prophets. A true prophet is one who speaks the LORD's Law and warns the people of the consequences of disobedience (Dt 18:15–20).

### How to Read the Deuteronomistic History

Before beginning, see the "Understanding the Historical Background to the Biblical Texts" section on RG 31 and review the various levels of meaning that are found in the Bible, particularly in the histories.

In referring to this work as a history we must be clear about what we mean by that designation (see also RG 37). All history writing is a process of selection, organization, and interpretation. No history simply tells what happened. Every history tells some of the things that happened, while leaving out other things. That very selection process imposes an interpretation on the events. History is never objective in a strict sense because the facts it presents cannot exist in isolation from the way a historian uses them.

The deuteronomistic writers have taken many stories and combined them to form one story that communicates a fairly simple message to its audience: Learn from the past. Therefore, the focus of our study will not be on what actually happened, but on what the writers were trying to teach through the events they recounted.

### Questions for Discussion and Reflection

#### *Group Sharing/Discussion*

1. The seven books called the *deuteronomistic history* tell the story in a different way than does the final group of historical books (1 and 2 Chronicles, Ezra, and Nehemiah), called the *chronicler's history*. What is the value of repeating the same story in these different ways?

2. Have your group brainstorm about different perspectives you can use to understand the Bible. Talk about how these apply to studying the deuteronomistic history.

#### *In Our Lives*

1. It is the word of the LORD that defines and determines the history of Israel. The Word of the LORD in our Sunday Scriptures is an important way the LORD is present to us. How might we better prepare for, listen to, and live by the Word we hear in the Sunday liturgy readings?

2. The deuteronomistic writers were teaching their people to learn from the past. Specifically, what are some of the lessons we can learn from our past as Catholic Christians?

#### *Individual/Personal Reflection/Action*

1. Joshua had a chance to tell people what he believed were the most important things in life. Write down for yourself what message you would pass on to those you love about the most important things to you.

2. Share with another person in your life the parts of your family history that are most significant to you.

# JOSHUA READING GUIDE

### *At a Glance*

| | |
|---|---|
| Who are the main players? | Joshua Rahab, the prostitute Achan Caleb Eleazar, son of Aaron Phineas, the high priest |
| What should I look for? | The superiority of faith over military might Punishment of evil Reward of good Joshua's leadership Israel's God-given success The people's fidelity and careful observance of the Law The book's pervasive sense of hope |
| When did this take place? | During the period following the wandering in the desert, beginning around 1250 B.C. or 1406 B.C. |
| Where did these events occur? | In the land of Canaan, the land promised to Abraham, which is modern Israel |
| Why was this book written? | To record Israel's conquest of Canaan and the fulfillment of God's promise to give Israel the Promised Land |
| What is the story? | Still camped east of the Jordan River, the Israelites spy on Jericho, then prepare to march across the river. Joshua leads many successful campaigns of conquest in northern, southern, and central Canaan. Finally conquered, the land is allotted to the tribes. Joshua makes a farewell speech during which the covenant is renewed. Joshua dies and is buried. |

## Before Beginning

The book of Joshua is the sixth book of the Bible and carries on the story that begins in Genesis and continues through Deuteronomy. Abraham's descendants, who had been slaves in Egypt, are ready to take possession of the land promised to their ancestors. The land was not simply a gift of God to Israel—it was the gift that made God's power and presence in Israel's life something real and tangible. It was an act of grace like no other, for the gift of the land made it possible for the people of Israel to survive. The land provided Israel with its food, clothing, and shelter. Without it, Israel could not be a people. The land as God's gift to Israel was a central theme to the Israelites' faith. It was at the core of ancient Israel's stories, poetry, and prophecy. Refer to color Map 4 for an overview of the land.

Joshua is both the conclusion of one story and the beginning of another. It concludes the story of the liberation of the Hebrew slaves and their guidance through the wilderness to the Promised Land. It is also the first part of the story of Israel in that Promised Land. The books of Judges, Samuel, and Kings continue this story. The story begins with Joshua and the Israelite tribes taking control of the land, continues with stories about the judges who lead Israel in maintaining their presence in the land, and concludes with the stories of Israel's kings, who eventually lose control of that land. The story ends the same way it begins—with the Israelites outside the land. At the beginning they are ready to cross the Jordan and take control of the land; at the end they are in exile from the land, wondering about their future. It is a tragic story that begins with much promise and ends with great disappointment.

The ancient rabbis called the books that made up the story of Israel in its land "the Former Prophets" because they ascribed these books to prophetic authorship. Scholars have called these books the "Deuteronomistic History of Israel." But that name can be misleading, because these books are not histories—at least not in the modern sense. In the form we now have, the books date to about the middle of the sixth century while Israel was in exile. This story of Israel in the Promised Land turns Israel's past into a sermon in order to provide the exiles some basis for hope by affirming that Israel can have a future, despite the terrible losses it experienced when Jerusalem fell. The book of Deuteronomy provided the theological principles that guided the telling of the story of Israel in its land. The books of Joshua to 2 Kings show what happens when Israel is obedient and what happens when it is not. The story of Israel in its land, then, asserts that Israel can have a future if it chooses—because God has set before Israel the choice of life and death (Dt 30:15).

The book of Joshua answers two questions that were on the minds of its first readers, Israelites living in exile (see "The Historical Books" Reading Guide):

1. Is God able to restore Israel?
2. Is God willing to do so?

The answer that the book gives to the first question is a resounding yes. The book will tell the story of how Israel acquired its land ostensibly under Joshua's leadership. But as the story unfolds, it will become clear that it was God who was leading Israel all the while. The answer to the second question is a qualified yes. God has promised blessings to those who obey the Torah: if Israel chooses the path of obedience, it can expect to have a future in the land promised to its ancestors. If, however, Israel chooses the way of disobedience, there can be no hope.

## Reading Through the Book of Joshua

About 20 percent of the book's text describes the elaborate preparations for the entrance of the Israelite tribes into Canaan. Before the crossing of the Jordan begins, the book makes it clear that the land is a gift God is giving Israel (1:1–5). The way to ensure that Israel will be in a position to receive that gift is obedience to the Torah (1:6–9). The rest of the book simply illustrates these two assertions. First, under Joshua's leadership, the tribes will take the land with relative ease because God is handing the land to them. Second, because Israel was obedient, it easily succeeds in taking possession of the land, which is then distributed equitably among the tribes.

### Israel Enters the Promised Land (Jos 1:1–5:12)

The book's first chapter consists of four speeches: the LORD to Joshua (1:1–9); Joshua to the Israelite leadership (1:10–11); Joshua to the tribes from east of the Jordan (1:12–15); and the eastern tribes to Joshua (1:16–18). These speeches are the means of conveying the central religious affirmations of the book: the presence of God with Joshua and the Israelites, the importance of obedience to the Torah, the land as a gift from God, and Joshua as the successor of Moses. These affirmations provide a framework for understanding the stories that will follow. No military preparations are mentioned and none are necessary as long as Israel observes the Torah.

The episode with the two Israelite spies and Rahab, the prostitute from Jericho (2:1–21), betrays the book's purpose. Rahab's conversation with the two spies makes it seem as if she had been reading the book of Deuteronomy. Because she helps the Israelite spies, she is fulfilling the divine will and will escape the fate that the rest of Jericho's citizens will suffer (6:22–25). If Israel had followed her example, the fate of Jerusalem and its exiles would have been much different. If, like Rahab, Israel now chooses the way of obedience, it will return to its land to live in peace.

The scene depicting the crossing of the Jordan (3:1–4:24) underscores the book's intent to present the taking of the Promised Land as a wonder performed by God to fulfill the commitment made to Israel's ancestors. The book purposely describes the crossing of the Jordan River as a miracle like the crossing of the Red Sea (4:23), even though the Jordan is, in fact, easily fordable at several places. The miraculous crossing of the Jordan demoralizes the people of Canaan, robbing them of the will to resist (5:1). Again, it is clear that Israel's possession of the land was God's doing.

At God's instructions, the preparations to enter the land and face its inhabitants involve nothing of a military nature. In fact, these preparations actually render Israel's army quite vulnerable to attack because all the males have to be circumcised, making them temporarily ineffective as a fighting force. But the mass circumcision does, however, make the community fit to celebrate the Passover (5:2–12). Both these observances became important markers of Jewish identity during and after the exile. Certainly the book of Joshua intends to promote these practices.

## Violence in Joshua and the Bible

FOR MANY CONTEMPORARY readers, the most difficult aspect of the book of Joshua and its stories of conquest will not be understanding what happened, but rather accepting the level of violence and the apparent exaltation of annihilation that the book takes for granted. What is there to say about this aspect for those in our world, where many people think that military actions should be a "last resort" and others think we should not engage in such tactics at all? How do we regard the commands, attributed to God, that the people must eliminate everyone who lived in the land? (See, for instance, 6:21.)

First, we must acknowledge the great difference between our attitudes toward military action and the attitudes of those in the ancient world. To some extent, the book of Joshua is simply reflecting its own world. Those unwilling to fight and conquer in the ancient world ran the probable risk of being conquered themselves, and consequently of being oppressed by some outside invader.

Second, as with other issues, such as slavery, we have moved beyond where the Bible is. Just as all Christians now agree that slavery is wrong, even though the Bible condones it, we can agree that ruthless conquest and the extermination of native peoples is wrong, even though the book of Joshua presents such actions as being commanded by God.

Third, and finally, we must recognize that, whatever the book says about what happened, the conquest of Canaan was nowhere near so complete. In fact, even within the Bible itself there are indications that the inhabitants of the land continued to live there and were not wiped out by the invading Israelites. For instance, it took until King David's time—200 years or so later—for Jerusalem to be conquered (see 2 Sm 5:7). Since we know this, we can look at the picture of the conquest of Canaan in a different way: not as God's command to the people to conquer and kill all of the inhabitants of the land, but as the people's way of grasping that it was God, and only God, who "owned" the land and who ruled over it. It was God's to give or withhold. This was symbolized by accounts that suggested that all of the inhabitants were driven out or killed; this did not happen, but its meaning was what mattered.

### The Battle for the Promised Land (Jos 5:13–11:23)

Although the book of Joshua is often thought of as a chronicle of a massive invasion of Canaan by a united Israelite army under the leadership of Joshua, only one quarter of the book actually deals with the battles for the Promised Land. At the end of this section, the author comments that "Thus Joshua took the whole land" (11:23). But the account of the battles fought by the Israelite tribes focuses almost entirely on the central region of Canaan (6:1–10:27). Battles in the south (10:28–43) and the north (11:1–14) are treated in summary fashion. The two places that receive the most attention are Jericho (6:1–27) and Ai (7:2–8:29). But before Joshua begins the attack on Jericho, the mysterious "commander of the army of the LORD" arrives (5:14). Notice the similarity to the story of Moses' encounter with God at the burning bush (Ex 3:1–6). The true leader of Israel is someone other than Joshua.

Jericho was a town that had been abandoned for centuries before the time of Joshua, probably because its water source had become severely polluted, making its waters no longer drinkable. Ai had flourished in the Early Bronze Age—more than a thousand years before the Israelite tribes emerged in Canaan. It too had been abandoned for centuries before the Israelites made their appearance. The stories of the capture of Jericho and Ai in Joshua (6–8), then, are not historical records. But apparently, the people of Israel celebrated the gift of the land that they received from God at shrines near Jericho. Certainly, the story of Jericho's fall reads more like an account of a liturgical ceremony than that of a military adventure.

The book tells the tale of Jericho and Ai as object lessons for its readers. Neither Joshua's military leadership nor the bravery of the Israelite army was responsible for the fall of Jericho. The town was taken because Israel followed God's directions. The city's walls collapsed after an elaborate procession with the Ark—not because of any military operation. This led to a complete victory, but Israel was told not to enjoy the fruits of the victory: no one was to loot the city nor was there to be any Israelite settlement there. While Israel had no difficulty taking Jericho, Ai was another story (7:1–8:30). Because Joshua's spies misjudged the enemy's strength, Israel attacked Ai without sufficient force and suffered a grave defeat. The book accounts for this stunning setback by describing how Achan kept some of the booty from Jericho for himself, contrary to Joshua's instructions (6:17–21). After Joshua prayed and Achan was punished, God provided Joshua with tactical instructions for the defeat of Ai's army.

Joshua's detour to the north to build an altar on Mount Ebal, which flanks the valley in which Shechem is located (8:30–35), reminds readers of the significance of the Torah for the people's past and future. (For these locations and others mentioned in Joshua see Map 4 in the back of the book and "The Conquest of Canaan" on p. 262.) On the stones used to make the altar, Joshua wrote the Torah. He then read the Torah—complete with the blessings and curses contained in it—to the people, reminding them that they will shape their future by the choices they make.

### The Battle for Canaan

When the book returns to the story of the battle for Canaan, Joshua and his army are at Gilgal. Their victories led kings of the city-states in Canaan to form an alliance to stop the Israelite advance, while the people of Gibeon sought an alliance with the Israelites by falsely claiming to be, like the Israelites, newly arrived in Canaan (9:1–27). When the Israelites discovered that they were tricked by the Gibeonites, they suggested that the Gibeonites accept a low social status in the Israelite community as laborers in the temple.

Like Jericho and Ai, Gibeon was not inhabited in the thirteenth century B.C. This story serves as a warning to consult with the LORD in difficult circumstances, which the Israelites did not do in this situation—much to their regret (Jos 9:14). There will be several occasions in the monarchic period when Israel and Judah got into great difficulties because of the treaties they made with other nations, for example, Ahaz's alliance with Assyria (2 Kgs 16:7–9).

The theme of God making a gift of the land to the people continues when God enlists the sun and moon to seal Israel's victory (10:1–14). In the ancient Near East, the sun and the moon were gods in their own right, but here they are simply weapons in the LORD's arsenal, demonstrating God's dominion.

Following Joshua's defeat and execution of the kings allied against him, he moved against the south and brought that region under Israelite control (10:25–43). The story of Joshua's final victory, over a coalition led by Jabin of Hazor (11:1–23), is meant to account for the taking of the entire northern third of Canaan: the Jezreel Valley and the Sea of Galilee. The second section of Joshua ends with summary statements (11:15–23), the most important of which is that Joshua carried out the orders that God gave to Moses. The story of the battle for the Promised Land, then, is a story of the success that obedience brings.

The gift of the land is a motif that is woven throughout the Old Testament, but the references to how that land was acquired by Israel are not very specific. For example, although the story of Jericho's miraculous fall is an important part of Joshua, it is not mentioned elsewhere in the Old Testament. Precisely what experiences generated the first stories about Israel's acquisition of its land are unknown. But before they came to have their present form, they were shaped and reshaped by almost 600 years of life in that land. Ancient Israel's storytellers witnessed the rise and fall of the two Israelite national states. These experiences certainly left their mark on the story of Joshua and the emergence of the Israelite tribes in Canaan.

The story of the battle for the Promised Land

effectively turned the past into a sermon whose purpose was to stimulate the faith and hope of those who first heard or read it. They learned that there could be a future for the people of Israel if they, like Joshua's generation, were obedient to the Torah. The character of this story makes its use in reconstructing the early history of Israel problematic. Archaeological excavation supports the conclusion that the stories of conquest found in Joshua were not based on memories of actual battles that took place at Jericho, Ai, or in the environs of Gibeon. But archaeology has shown that people living in Canaan in the thirteenth century B.C. experienced serious disruptions. Towns and villages were destroyed and abandoned. The Israelite tribes emerged in the central highlands of Canaan precisely during this difficult period, so it is likely that Israel acquired the land that was to be the scene of its subsequent history, in part, by violence. It is difficult, from the evidence offered by the book of Joshua, to say much more. What the book does affirm unequivocally is that Israel came to possess the land because of God's power, and Israel was able to receive that land as God's gift because of its obedience. These affirmations, however, were meant to give Israel a vision of the future rather than information about the past.

**Israel's Inheritance (Jos 12:1–19:51)**

After listing the territories brought under Israelite control during the battle for the Promised Land (12:1–24), the book of Joshua has an extensive section dealing with the distribution of the land among the Israelite tribes (13:8–19:51). Working through this section is difficult for modern readers since it is full of geographical detail that is meaningless to many. While the precise borders of the various tribal allotments may have been very important to the people of ancient Israel, their significance today is exclusively historical. Still, there are some details in this part of the story that even contemporary readers should attend to.

It is important to remember that ancient Israel's economy was based on agriculture. Ownership of land was crucial to survival in such an economy. Possession of a plot of land enabled an Israelite to produce enough food for his family and livestock with a surplus to be used for replanting and for sacrificial offerings. Without land, a person had no access to the means of production. Such a person was dependent for survival on the charity of his fellow Israelites. Of course, there were some people who supported themselves as merchants and artisans, but they too ultimately depended on Israel's peasant farmers for their prosperity.

The account of the land distribution among the tribes begins with a reminder of the areas of Canaan that the Israelites did not control (13:1–6). This was a necessary correction to the exaggerations in the previous section of the book, which claimed that Joshua and the Israelites subdued "the entire land," and "the whole land" (Jos 9:24; 11:23). Then follows a review of the territories previously allotted by Moses to those Israelites who were going to live east of the Jordan River (13:7–33). Israel's control over this region was neither firm nor constant, but its inclusion among the tribal allotments expresses Israel's claim on that territory, even though Israel was not always able to support that claim. When Ezekiel described his vision of an Israel restored after the exile, he did not have any of the tribes living east of the Jordan (Ez 48:1–29).

When the account of the distribution of the land west of the Jordan begins in chapter 14, both Eleazar the priest and Joshua preside over the distribution (14:1; see also Nm 34:17). The preceding sections of the book did not emphasize the role of the priest except for liturgical actions (e.g., 3:6; 6:1–9). The priority given to Eleazar here may reflect the more significant role that the priests played in the leadership of the community after the state collapsed and the dynasty ended, as is evident from Haggai, Zechariah, and Ezra. Eleazar's presence may also be a consequence of having the land distributed by lot (14:2). Although Deuteronomy explicitly forbids attempts to determine the divine will through the techniques of divination (Dt 18:9–12), the casting of lots seems to have been widely practiced and accepted as legitimate. In this method of choosing something, the choice was limited to that between two things: two contending persons, two groups, an individual versus a group, or a "yes-or-no" question. Then a two-sided object was thrown to the ground. Depending on which side fell uppermost, the answer was "yes" or "no" or one of the two choices. It is the same as our "heads-or-tails" coin-toss method. The lot oracle was committed to the priests (Ex 28:30; Lv 8:5–9). To show that the distribution of the land was done according to God's will, it was accomplished by the use of lots in a procedure presided over by a priest. The New Testament gives evidence of the continuing popularity and acceptance of using lots to determine the divine will (Acts 1:26).

### Special Towns (Jos 20:1–21:45)

Two of ancient Israel's social institutions are the subject of the fourth section of the book of Joshua. The first is the city of refuge. There were six of these cities, three on each side of the Jordan. According to Numbers 35:9–34, it was Moses who announced God's plan to have such cities where a person who accidentally caused another's death could be safe from the victim's relatives, who might seek vengeance. Moses had already named the three cities east of the Jordan, and now Joshua designated three more west of the Jordan. The books of Samuel, Kings, and Chronicles never mention this institution since they were not needed following the centralization of authority by the monarchy. The book of Judges mentions two examples of private vengeance: 8:13–21 and 20:1–11. It is clear from these examples that the biblical tradition does not approve of such acts. A second set of 48 towns was set aside for the Levites. The tribe of Levi received no territory of its own because the men of that tribe served as priests, who were to teach the Torah to Israel and offer sacrifice to the LORD (see Dt 33:8–11). To fulfill these functions the priests needed to be available to the people; therefore the cities where the Levites had residential and grazing rights were scattered throughout the country.

### A Threat of Civil War (Jos 22:1–34)

The Israelites whose territory was east of the Jordan River had joined in the battle to take control of the area west of the river. Since that battle was successful, Joshua allowed them to return to their homes (vv. 1–9). This is a prelude to a conflict between the Israelites east of the river and those on the west (vv. 10–34). The tribes from the east side of the river built an altar near the Jordan, and this offended the Israelites from the west. War was averted because Phineas, Eleazar's son, succeeded in negotiating peace between the two groups of Israelites. The precise nature of the offense is not obvious, though it may reflect the deuteronomic belief that there was to be only one place where sacrifices were to be offered. Apparently, the book of Joshua assumed that this place was Shiloh. When the easterners explained that they did not intend to offer sacrifices, this defused the problem.

### An Era Ends (Jos 23:1–24:33)

The final testament of such an important person as Joshua was highly significant. The storyteller creates a speech for his hero that could have come right out of the book of Deuteronomy. Israel's continued presence in the land depends on its obedience to "all that is written in the book of the Law of Moses. . . ." (23:6). Joshua reminds Israel to love God (23:11), the Torah's greatest command. But then Joshua issues a warning that any failure on Israel's part to remain completely and exclusively loyal to God will have the gravest of consequences (23:15–16). While the land is a gift from God to Israel, the gift can be revoked. Of course, this is a theological conclusion that came from Israel's experience. By the time the book of Joshua took the form that it now has, Israel did "perish from the good land" that it had received from God (23:16). Israel's faith in God's fidelity, however, led to the hope that a new dedication to the Torah and a renewed commitment to the covenant would bring a reversal of the misfortune that Israel brought on itself. The book then describes an elaborate ceremony in which Israel of Joshua's day renews its commitment to God and the Torah. (24:1–28.) Like the ancestors in the days of Joshua, Israel must again commit itself to serve and obey God alone.

The burial notices with which the book ends (24:29–30, 32–33) are significant because of the prominence given to Eleazar, the priest. This is very likely another indication of the leadership role assumed by priests after the fall of the Israelite monarchy. Verse 31 is the verdict on the era of Joshua: it was an era marked by obedience and loyalty. That is the reason Israel came to possess the land: obedience brings God's blessing.

## The Continuing Significance of the Book of Joshua

The great irony of the book of Joshua was that its stories about the Israelite army conquering great cities and annihilating their populace were written at a time when ancient Israel was at its lowest ebb politically and militarily. The two Israelite national states no longer existed. Their territory was absorbed into the Babylonian provincial system. The leading citizens of Judah were taken to Babylon to prevent them from fomenting any resistance to the new order in the region. Those Judahites who remained in the land were subsistence farmers and not in a position to challenge Babylonian rule. Certainly the stories about the mighty Israelite army winning victory after victory under Joshua was a parody of the military and political impotence of Judah in the sixth century B.C. Unfortunately, the stories of the book of Joshua have served to provide support for the wars of conquest waged by Christians over the centuries. The Crusades, the wars against the Native Americans, and the Boer conquest of South Africa are just three examples of the lethal mixture of war and religion.

The book of Joshua was written not to stir a martial spirit in its readers but instead a spirit of obedience and commitment to the Torah. The book assumes that the exile of Israel from the land that God gave it was not due to any military disadvantages. Israel lost its land because of its failure to keep the Torah that God revealed to Moses. The only hope for restoration was for Judah to join their ancestors in recommitting themselves to their God: "Far be it from us to forsake the LORD to serve other gods. For it was the LORD, our God, who brought us and our ancestors up out of the land of Egypt, out of the house of slavery. He performed those great signs before our very eyes and protected us along our entire journey and among all the peoples through whom we passed. At our approach the LORD drove out all the peoples, including the Amorites who dwelt in the land. Therefore we also will serve the LORD, for he is our God" (Jos 24:16–18).

### Questions for Discussion and Reflection

*Group Sharing/Discussion*

1. Why is it important for Joshua to be the successor of Moses? What was unusual about the beginning of his leadership?

2. Where did the Israelites live when Joshua was written? How far was this from the Promised Land? Locate as many places as you can on the map.

3. Why does Rahab, the prostitute, escape the fate that the rest of Jericho's citizens suffer?

4. How does Joshua show that the distribution of the land was done according to God's will?

5. If you are in a group, have someone role-play Joshua's final message (ch 23), putting his most important messages into their own words. Then have another person take the same role for ch 24 with the rest of the group taking the role of the responses the people made to Joshua.

*In Our Lives*

1. God's gift of this Promised Land to Israel was a sign of God's presence in Israelite life. How are we today aware of God's presence in our lives?

2. What does it mean to be "obedient to the Torah?" What are the basic beliefs that we are to be "obedient to" or by which we are to try to live?

3. What do the rituals of circumcision and Passover symbolize? What are the most important rituals in our Catholic faith life? How might we improve our celebration of these key religious events?

4. Lots were cast to see what tribes would get which land. Describe an experience you have had or you know about when someone was trying to divide things fairly. What was similar and different to the casting of lots in Joshua?

*Individual/Personal Reflection/Action*

1. Joshua was a significant religious leader for his people. Who would you name as a significant religious leader today? Who in your own life helps you follow the pathway of your faith?

2. Rahab made a courageous decision to go against her own culture and follow what she believed in. Recalling your own hard decisions, who or what helps you have the courage of your convictions?

3. In their response to Joshua's challenges in his farewell address the people responded, "We will serve the LORD!" What challenges would you give yourself to show that your life, too, serves the LORD?

# JUDGES READING GUIDE

### *At a Glance*

| | |
|---|---|
| Who are the main players? | Othniel Ehud Deborah and Jael Gideon and his son Abimelech Jephthah and his daughter Samson and Delilah |
| What should I look for? | The issue of God's lordship over Israel Israel's repeated abandonment of the Lord The fourfold pattern of disobedience/oppression/cries for help/deliverance God's faithfulness despite the people's infidelity God's use of charismatic leaders to rescue Israel The imperfection of God's chosen leaders and lack of real heroes Sad, tragic, often ugly stories that seem out of place in the Bible |
| When did this take place? | During the period after the conquest of Canaan and before the establishment of the monarchy: probably the years between 1220 and 1000 B.C. |
| Where did these events occur? | Various locations in the land of Canaan |
| Why was this book written? | To document Israel's moral downfall and its inevitable consequences; to reiterate the deuteronomic theme that fidelity leads to blessing, but infidelity to certain and tragic punishment (including possible loss of land); and to help explain why God permitted Israel to change its system of government to monarchy. |
| What is the story? | The Israelites continue their conquest of the Promised Land. But the Canaanite natives who had not been driven out by the Israelites regroup and counterattack. In addition, the Israelites begin to adopt the customs and idolatrous worship of their pagan neighbors. A series of 12 leaders, each in a time of grave national crisis, arises to rouse the people and lead them against the threatening enemy. And every time, in response to the people's repentance, the LORD has mercy and rescues Israel. |

The book of Judges can be easily divided into three sections, as outlined on the following page.

## Before Beginning

The book of Judges is the second book in the collection the early rabbis called the "Former Prophets" and modern interpreters call the "Deuteronomistic History of Israel." It is a collection of stories about several Israelite heroes, set in the time between the settlement in Canaan under Joshua and the establishment of the Israelite monarchy. The title of the book comes from the designation of its principal characters. The judges were charismatic leaders of the Israelite community, especially in times of fierce competition over the land of Canaan. Their authority came from the LORD, and their duty was to enable Israel to live in faithful obedience. The judges had to deal with two problems:

1. The failure of Israel to serve the LORD alone
2. The competition for control of the land from other peoples.

The book presents these two problems as interrelated. When Israel failed to maintain its commitment to serve the LORD exclusively, then God allowed Israel's neighbors to make its life very difficult. The competition for control over the land of Canaan in the thirteenth century B.C. was stiff. In the course of that competition, individuals emerged who proved very capable of managing that competition to the benefit of the Israelite tribes. Stories about these individuals and their feats circulated among the Israelites and eventually found their way into the collection we know as the book of Judges. This collection, however, served a purpose beyond simply preserving the exploits of ancient heroes. The Israelites faced a practical and theological problem: the absence of the kind of leadership provided by Moses and Joshua. How should

| | | |
|---|---|---|
| I. Introduction<br>1:1–3:6 | 1. Israel's failure to fully conqure the land<br>2. Israel's disobedience as cause of their failure | |
| | **Major Judges** | **Minor Judges** |
| II. Exploits of the judges<br>3:7–16:31 | 1 Othniel (3:7–11) | |
| | 2 Ehud (3:12–30) | |
| | 3 | Shamgar (3:31) |
| | 4 Deborah (4:1–5:31) | |
| | 5 Gideon (6:1–8:35) | |
| | Abimelech, the illegitimate judge (9:1–57) | |
| | 6 | Tola (10:1–2) |
| | 7 | Jair (10:3–5) |
| | 8 Jephthah (10:6–12:7) | |
| | 9 | Ibzan (12:8–10) |
| | 10 | Elon (12:11–12) |
| | 11 | Abdon (12:13–15) |
| | 12 Samson (13:1–16:31) | |
| III. Appendices<br>17:1–21:25 | 1. Idol worship in the tribe of Dan<br>2. Outrage at the assult of a concubine and Israel's first civil war | |

Israel be governed? Who would insure that Israel would live according to the Torah in the land it had received from the LORD? Without a strong leader, the people abandoned their vow to serve the LORD (Jos 24:21–24). The book of Judges illustrates the consequences of Israel's failure.

## Three Significant Parts

The book of Judges has three parts. The first (1:1–3:6) gives a framework for understanding the significance of the stories about these ancient heroes. The second part (3:7–16:31) describes the exploits of the judges. The book concludes with a few supplementary stories (17:1–21:25) that show how the Israelite tribes were on a path of self-destruction. Originally the stories about the individual judges served to excite a certain measure of pride in the achievements of the tribes in maintaining control over the land of Canaan. But once these stories were put into their present context in the book of Judges, the effect was to show that there was something terribly wrong about the way the Israelite tribes were living their lives in the land that God had given them. Readers are led to conclude that matters could not go on like this—something had to be done, for the life of the Israelite tribes was degenerating into anarchy.

## Reading Through the Book of Judges

### Understanding the Time of the Judges (1:1–3:6)

The book begins by raising the question of leadership: "Who shall be first among us to attack the Canaanites and to do battle with them?" (1:1). The initial answer is Judah, the tribe that eventually became the nucleus of the southern kingdom. After some initial success, the tribes' progress bogged down. The first chapter concludes, then, with a list of areas over which the Israelites were not able to assert their control (1:27–35). The picture here is just the opposite of that given in the book of Joshua when Joshua "took the whole land, just as the LORD had said to Moses. Joshua gave it to Israel as their heritage, apportioning it among the tribes" (Jos 11:23). The process by which the Israelites achieved control over Canaan was clearly long and complicated.

The second chapter describes the price Israel had to pay for its style of leadership: the Israelite tribes found themselves in danger of being overcome by the other groups competing for the limited territory of Canaan. The reason for the tribes' inability to repeat Joshua's victories was their failure to keep their covenant with the LORD. Israel would have to deal with other contenders for the land by themselves. God's help would not be forthcoming. The contrast between the period of Joshua and that of the Judges could not be more absolute. Under Joshua's leadership, "the people served the LORD" (Jgs 2:7), and they had experienced victory after victory and came to possess "all the land." Without Joshua's leadership, the Israelite tribes were on the verge of annihilation because of their failure to obey the LORD. The Israelite response was lamentation at a place named Bochim (weepers) (Jgs 2:5).

## Religious Interpretation

The next section (2:6–3:6) elaborates on the religious interpretation of the problems the Israelite tribes had in maintaining a foothold in the land promised to their ancestors. The explanation given for Israel's difficulties is simple enough: "the Israelites did what was evil in the sight of the LORD. They served the Baals" (2:11). The Israelite worship of Baal, the title ("Lord" or "Owner") by which Hadad, the Canaanite god of the storm and fertility, was known, was incompatible with the exclusive service that Israel owed to its God.

One of the principal sources of anxiety for the Israelites was having enough food to eat. The problem was not the soil—it was fertile enough. The problem was water. The region had no river system as did Egypt and Mesopotamia. Israel was dependent on rain and worshiped the Canaanite deities Baal and Ashtaroth because rain and fertility were their specialties. Probably most Israelites did not consider their worship of Baal and Ashtaroth as incompatible with loyalty to the LORD, but certainly the author of Judges did. It took centuries for the people of Israel to be convinced of how critically important it was for them to serve the LORD alone. The book of Judges was an important contribution to this process.

## Pattern of Judges

The pattern for the way the stories of the judges will be told is set in 2:11–23. The book introduces the narrative of each of the judges with the formula found first in 2:11: "Israelites did what was evil in the sight of the LORD." The consequence of this infidelity was domination over the Israelite tribes by their rivals. But the period of the judges was marked not only by divine judgment but by divine mercy. The LORD always heard the sounds of Israel's pleading and responded by raising up a leader who rescued Israel from the oppression they were experiencing. Unfortunately, at the death of the judge who rescued them, the Israelites returned to their evil ways.

God determined, then, that Israel would have to continue facing the threat of extinction as long as it continued to serve the Baals (2:16–23). The introduction to the book ends with 3:1–6, which explains that Israel's competitors will remain in the land to test the loyalty of future generations. But one consequence of this intermingling will be that some Israelites will marry Canaanite spouses, which will often mean that the Israelite partners in such unions will abandon their ancestral religion.

Two final observations need to be made about the introduction. First, in the stories that follow, the threat and resistance are usually local. But Judges transforms the stories of local heroes into stories that have significance for all Israel. Second, as readers work their way though the stories of the judges, the question arises about how long God will continue to put up with Israel's infidelity. Is there some limit to God's patience?

## The Stories of the Judges (Jgs 3:7–15:20)

### Othniel (Jgs 3:7–11)

The book of Judges begins with a divine oracle that names the tribe of Judah as the leader of the

Israelites in the attempt to take control over Canaan (1:1–2), and the first of the judges, Othniel, is from Judah. He has already made an appearance in the book as the conqueror of Debir, a city in the southern hill country of Judah (1:11–13). Here Othniel's story is told with a minimum of detail, but it clearly follows the basic pattern of Judges: disobedience, oppression, repentance, and mercy. The spirit of the LORD empowered Othniel to accomplish extraordinary deeds.

### Ehud (Jgs 3:12–30)

Ehud came from the tribe of Benjamin, whose territory was immediately north of Judah. The first detail given about Ehud is that he was left-handed. While the people of the ancient world considered left-handedness abnormal, it was a distinct advantage in hand-to-hand combat because it provided an element of surprise and allowed the one who was left-handed to strike with a knife or sword behind his foe's shield. Although the name Benjamin means "the son of my right hand," the tradition behind the book associates this tribe with a high incidence of left-handedness. Judges 20:16 asserts that Benjamin could boast of 700 highly skilled left-handers.

Once again, Israel's sin was responsible for the oppression, which took the form of raids for 18 years, by Eglon, the king of Moab. Moab was a kingdom located directly across the river from Benjaminite territory, and "the City of Palms" was probably Jericho. Not only did the Moabites occupy Israelite territory, but they required the payment of tribute, a payment that signified the Israelites' submission to and dependence on Moab. Ehud, who was supposed to bring Benjamin's tribute to Eglon, instead assassinated him. After making his escape, Ehud was able to convince men from the tribe of Ephraim to join him in expelling the Moabites from Israelite territory. So total was Ehud's victory that Israel had peace for 80 years.

The story of Ehud's assassination of Eglon ridicules the Moabites. Certainly one can picture the Israelite audience having a good laugh at the expense of the Moabites. The book takes this entertaining story and makes it part of a comprehensive theological presentation about the importance of serving the LORD alone.

### Shamgar (Jgs 3:31)

There is some doubt whether Shamgar ought to be understood as a judge like the others in the book. His name is not Semitic nor does the text claim that God raised him up in response to Israel's cries. The Song of Deborah (Jgs 5) notes that the caravan trade was interrupted "in the days of Shamgar" (v. 6). Perhaps he was responsible for this disruption. While his service on Israel's behalf may have been indirect, he did make life easier for some Israelites by defeating the Philistines.

### Deborah and Barak (Jgs 4:1–5:31)

With the story of Deborah and Barak, the scene shifts northward to the vitally important Jezreel Valley. Once under Israelite control, communication between the tribes in Galilee and those in the highlands to the south became possible. Also significant was the agricultural and trade potential of the Jezreel Valley. Israel had to control this important piece of real estate. But standing in its way was Jabin, the king of Hazor, who wanted to keep the Jezreel Valley for himself. The story and poem about Deborah and Barak testify to the significance that the Jezreel Valley held. It is the celebration of a great and unexpected victory: that of an army of peasants over professional soldiers with the best of equipment. The book of Judges presents Deborah as the hero of the conflict with Sisera's army. Barak made his contributions with great reluctance.

The story labels Deborah as a prophetess and a judge (4:4) without further explanation. Because judges and prophets were charismatic leaders, these roles were open to women. The patriarchal structures of ancient Israelite society did not obstruct the "spirit of the LORD," and clearly people understood this. Deborah shamed Barak into raising a force from Naphtali and Zebulon to oppose Jabin's general Sisera and his chariots. Naphtali and Zebulon were Galilean tribes, and their territory was located just to the north of the Jezreel Valley. As the reader expects, God gave victory to the Israelites. Sisera escaped the rout only to be killed by the Kenite Jael while assuming she was protecting him from the pursuing Israelites. This event fulfilled, in an unforeseen way, Deborah's prophecy, which was intended to goad Barak into action (4:9).

The book of Judges preserves what many consider to be one of the oldest texts found in the Bible: the Song of Deborah (5). This hymn celebrates the victory of Israel over Sisera's army. Here readers find out how the victory was achieved—as in Joshua's victory over Gibeon (Jos 10:11–13), nature played a role in the battle. Verses 4 and 21 in particular suggest that sudden rain caused a flash flood in the valley and rendered the chariot force immobile, eliminating Sisera's advantage.

The poem contrasts two mothers: Deborah, mother of Israel, and Sisera's unnamed mother. Deborah was responsible for a great victory, while Sisera's mother came to realize that Sisera's failure to return promptly from the battle meant that she would never see her son again.

**Gideon (Jgs 6:1–8:35)**

No judge receives more attention from the book of Judges than Gideon. His story begins with Israel being harassed by the Midianites, who enjoyed a great advantage over Israel. The Midianites were mounted on camels when they raided Israelite territory at harvest time. These mounted attacks made them unstoppable. They simply confiscated the harvest that the Israelites produced, making life impossible for the Israelite peasants (6:1–6). To the angel sent to recruit Gideon to deliver Israel, the reluctant general pointed out his lack of suitability—a motif also found in the call of Moses (Ex 3:10), Isaiah (Is 6:5), and Jeremiah (Jer 1:6).

In Gideon's story, he is frequently called Jerubbaal, a name that seemingly honors Baal, the LORD's rival for Israel's loyalty. The meaning of that name (let Baal sue or take action), and the story of how Gideon earned it proves otherwise. Gideon's dismantling of an altar for sacrifices to Baal aroused the anger of the local people, and they were ready to kill Gideon for his sacrilege. Gideon's father suggested that they should leave the matter up to Baal—let Baal sue "since his altar had been dismantled" (Jgs 6:25–32).

The rest of Gideon's story describes his efforts to deal with the Midianites and others that were threatening the Israelite tribes in the central highlands. He rallied not only members of his own tribe (Manasseh) but the militia of three others (Asher, Zebulon, and Naphtali). But Gideon refused to proceed without receiving another sign that his mission was from God (6:36–40). Next came orders from God to dismiss most of Gideon's militia, including those who knelt to drink, leaving only 300 soldiers out of the original 32,000. This reduction in numbers ensured that the militia could not ascribe the coming victory to their military skills but to God. (7:1–8). The 300 vanquished the Midianites by a surprise nighttime attack without doing any actual fighting—again underscoring the divine origin of Israel's victory.

After the Midianites were subdued, Gideon's story takes a new twist as the Israelites asked Gideon to rule as king and establish a dynasty to provide ongoing protection from groups like the Midianites. Gideon refused, citing the Israelite notion that the LORD is king of Israel. Gideon then used part of the valuables confiscated from the Midianites to construct an ephod, a priestly vestment. The book does not consider this a positive development but notes that, nonetheless, Israel enjoyed peace for 40 years (8:22–28).

Gideon's story ends with a transition to what follows by introducing his many wives who bore him 70 children. The one child mentioned by name is Abimelech, who will be the principal character in the next story. After Gideon died, the people of Israel reverted to the worship of Baal and forgot both the LORD and Gideon's achievements (8:29–35).

**Abimelech (Jgs 9:1–36)**

Although it is in the middle of the book of Judges, the story of Abimelech is an oddity because Abimelech is not a judge. He did not free Israel from any oppression. Abimelech convinced the people of Shechem to accept him as the sole ruler of their city and its environs, replacing the more diffuse pattern of leadership as exercised by Jerubbaal's 70 sons. To solidify his one-man rule Abimelech murdered all his brothers except Jotham, who survived, cursed his brother, and then fled the Shechem area—never to be heard from again.

The book places on Jotham's lips a bitter diatribe against his brother (9:7–15). Jotham addresses Shechem's leadership in a fable about trees who were looking for a king but could persuade only a worthless thorn bush to accept the position. Is this a criticism of the monarchy as an institution or merely a criticism of Abimelech?

The book can barely hide its animosity toward Abimelech. It is important to remember that the book of Judges—in the form in which it now exists—was the product of someone who witnessed the fall of the Davidic dynasty and the end of the national state. Certainly the failure of the monarchy to prevent the disaster that came upon Jerusalem had to weigh heavily on the writer's mind. The role of the monarchy in Israelite life, then, was not simply a theoretical question. It is important to note that the setting of this story is Shechem, where earlier Israel had reaffirmed its covenant with the LORD (Jos 24). In Abimelech, Shechem accepts a human being as its lord. Such a choice will be disastrous. Ironically, Abimelech's very name contrasts with his ambitions: it means "my father [God] is king," a way of affirming the idea that God is the king of Israel. Abimelech wishes to establish himself, not God, as the ruler.

### Jephthah (Jgs 10:6–12:7)

Because Jephthah, as the son of a prostitute, had an even lower social standing than Gideon or Deborah, he too was at first an unlikely candidate for the leadership of the Israelite militia. He did, however, possess one advantage. As the leader of a group of raiders, Jephthah had military experience and was just the kind of man that the elders of Gilead were looking for when the Ammonites were trying to push their border northward into Gilead's territory. Gilead was an Israelite territory, which lay east of the Jordan; Ammon was a kingdom to the south of Gilead.

There are several unique features to Jephthah's story. First, before resorting to armed conflict, Jephthah tried to negotiate a settlement with the Ammonites (11:12–28). When the negotiations failed, the spirit of the LORD came upon Jephthah, empowering him. But then there is a second unusual detail in the story. Jephthah makes a hasty and carelessly worded vow before the battle. This promise to God might indicate that the judge was less than confident in the outcome of the approaching battle. When Jephthah handily defeated the Ammonites, it was time to act on the vow he made. Jephthah thought that he was trapped by the imprecise wording of his vow, and so he had to sacrifice the daughter, who ran out to meet him on his return from the battle with the Ammonites (11:34–35). The religious and cultural significance of the practice of lamenting for Jephthah's daughter (11:37–40) is not clear.

Although Jephthah did neutralize the Ammonite threat and judged Israel for six years, the impression left by the book is that Jephthah's career was marked by failure and tragedy. He was not able to successfully negotiate with either the Ammonites or the Ephraimites. He lost his daughter because of a carelessly spoken vow, and his victories ignited an intertribal war. The picture of Israel during the time of the judges is getting darker.

### Samson (Jgs 13:1–15:20)

Although Judges 15:20 states that Samson was a judge in Israel for 20 years, his career was different from that of the judges whose stories the book has told so far. Samson never led the Israelite tribal army. His was more of a solo act. The setting of Samson's story is the long conflict between the Israelites and the Philistines for control of Canaan. The Bible calls these people *pelishtim* (i.e., "inhabitants of Pelesheth," Philistines), that is, the people who live in the coastal plains. The Philistines organized themselves politically into a confederation of city-states: Gaza, Ashkelon, Ashdod, Ekron, and Gath. As the Philistines expanded to the north, they threatened the tribe of Dan, which was located on in the central part of the coastal plain. Samson was a Danite.

Samson's mother was told that the son she would conceive was to be a Nazirite. The word Nazirite comes from a Hebrew root that means "to separate, consecrate, abstain." Numbers 6 describes the lifestyle of the Nazirite. They were not to drink fermented beverages, wine, or vinegar. They were not even to drink grape juice or eat grapes or raisins. This prohibition probably was meant to insure that Nazirites would not lose the spirit of the LORD because of intoxication. Second, Nazirites were not to cut their hair. This prohibition likely reflects a belief that a person's hair was especially significant as a place where spirits dwelt. Finally, Nazirites were not to touch any corpse because they were to remain ritually pure, and contact with a corpse rendered a person impure. A person could take the vows of a Nazirite for a set time, or a person could become a permanent Nazirite.

Samson's conflicts with the Philistines appear to be private in nature. The first came as a result of a lost wager that Samson made with the Philistines during the celebration of his marriage to a Philistine woman (14:1–20). The second was a reaction to his wife being given to another man (15:1–7). The third involved an attempt by some Judahites to turn Samson over to the Philistines (15:8–20). The story affirms three separate times that the spirit of the LORD came upon Samson.

Each time the spirit gave Samson strength in situations when his life was in danger. The book implies that while Samson's struggles with the Philistines were personal, he caused the Philistines the type of setbacks that eased pressure on Dan for 20 years.

### Israel's Self-Destruction (Jgs 16:1–21:25)

The book of Judges concludes with a series of stories that show Israel clearly on the path of self-destruction. What God would not allow the Moabites, the Midianites, the Ammonites, or the Philistines to do, Israel seemed bent on doing to itself. The final chapters make it appear that the Israelites became addicted to chaos—chaos that threatened their continued existence as a people.

As the previous section ends with the stories of Samson's private vendettas easing the pressure that the Philistines were bringing to bear on Israel, so this final section begins with Samson's descent into self-destruction. What is even worse is that Samson nearly took Israel with him. In Judges 16:1–3, Samson's visit to a prostitute nearly cost him his life. Apparently, he learned nothing from that brush with death, and his affair with Delilah did end with his death. Delilah was from the Valley of Sorek, where the land was better for agriculture. Its one disadvantage was that it abutted Philistine territory; there was a constant threat of harassment hanging over the Israelite farmers in the Sorek because the Philistines too had moved into that valley. Delilah is never actually called a Philistine, but the implication is there.

The cutting of a Nazirite's hair was a public statement that he was released from his vows (see Acts 18:18). In Samson's case, it meant that he no longer had the LORD's support to defend Israel from the Philistine threat. His hair grew back, and Samson had one more opportunity to avenge himself, but at the cost of his life (Jgs 16:23–30). Samson's flaws proved fatal.

### Micah (Jgs 17:1–13)

The scene shifts from the fate of Samson to that of Israel as a whole. The story about Micah is a symptom of the disease that afflicted Israel—the failure to serve the LORD alone. Micah built himself a shrine and, with his mother's help, outfitted it with images. Micah had one of his sons serve as the priest of the shrine until a Levite happened to come by. Micah believed that as a result of his installing a Levite as a private priest, he would enjoy blessings from the LORD (Jgs 17:13). The only comment that the author of Judges makes on what he considers to be a warped notion of Israelite religious traditions is found in Judges 17:6: "In those days there was no king in Israel; everyone did what was right in their own eyes." Without some central authority, religious anarchy reigned in Israel.

Chapter 18 describes the migration of the tribe of Dan from the central part of the coastal plain to the far north of Galilee. The story begins by repeating the refrain, "In those days there was no king in Israel" (Jgs 18:1). The story continues to describe the religious anarchy among the tribes. The Danites stole the liturgical accessories from Micah's shrine and abducted his priest. After they took the city of Laish, they installed the Levite and the shrine in their new home, which they renamed Dan. Finally, the identity of the Levite is revealed. His name was Jonathan, and he was a grandson of Moses. The book of Judges regards this shrine as illegitimate because the "house of God" was located at Shiloh (Jgs 18:31). That Moses' grandson was associated with an illegal shrine so scandalized later scribes that they introduced another letter into the name of Moses in 18:30, changing it to Manasseh, which was also the name of the most notorious apostate of all Judah's kings (see 2 Kgs 21).

This story of the corrupting of a young Levite from Bethlehem is followed by the story of a well-established Levite from Ephraim (Jgs 19). This story, too, begins with the refrain: "In those days there was no king in Israel" (v. 1)—a warning that what follows is another example of the religious anarchy that plagued Israel in the time of the judges. On his way home from reclaiming his secondary wife (concubine), who had returned to her father in a fit of anger, the Levite and his concubine spent the night in Gibeah, a town in the territory of Benjamin. The town was not a model of hospitality, and it was finally a non-native who offered the Levite shelter for the night. In what has been characterized as a "text of terror," the Levite's wife was gang-raped and murdered (vv. 11–30; compare this story to that in Genesis 19:1–11). Despite his own guilt in facilitating this crime, the Levite summoned the Israelite militia for vengeance.

While the militia reassembled at Bethel, the people realized what they had done: virtually wiped out an entire Israelite tribe. When they sought an oracle from God to determine why one tribe had been virtually wiped out, none was forthcoming. Another rash vow—to not provide daughters in marriage to the remnants of Benjamin—led to yet more war and degeneracy, this time in the form of kidnapping. (The plot device of getting around the vow by acquiescing in this kidnapping scheme is probably meant to have comical overtones, although to us it seems simply cruel. We must remember that marriage in the ancient world was not primarily a matter of love between the married couple but of making sure that there were offspring.)

The author of Judges has painted a very bleak picture of the Israelite tribes. He leaves his readers with the by-now-familiar comment on the religious and civil anarchy that gripped the life of Israel in its land: "In those days there was no king in Israel; everyone did what was right in their own eyes" (Jgs 21:25). What follows is the story of Israel's experience with the monarchy, which ultimately proved just as incapable of forestalling disaster for the people of Israel. This ambivalence about the monarchy is reflected in Judges itself, which both bemoans the lack of a king and (in passages such as Jotham's parable, 9:7–21) warns against the dangers of kingship.

The book of Judges reflects the disordered state of life in Canaan at the end of the Late Bronze Age. It was a very unsettled time in the region, and certainly the book of Judges gives some idea of the chaos that affected the Israelite tribes who were trying to gain a foothold in the region. This is not to suggest that the book of Judges is a historical account of events as they happened. To some extent the narratives in Judges present an idealization of the early years of Israel's existence in Canaan: the stories of local heroes are arranged in what appears to be chronological order. What these stories show is that loyalty and commitment to the LORD are what stand between Israel's well-being and its destruction.

## Continuing Significance of the Book of Judges

If the modern religious reader of Judges is repulsed by its stories, the ancient author has been successful. The picture of Israel—especially at the end of the book—is far from attractive or edifying. But it does show what happens to a nation that ignores traditional ethical and moral values. Disaster inevitably follows. If the people of Judah would restore their community's life in the land promised to their ancestors, they needed to remember the centrality of the covenant that God made with those ancestors. The stipulations of that covenant require fidelity, commitment, and absolute loyalty to the LORD.

### Questions for Discussion and Reflection

***Group Sharing/Discussion***

1. In the book of Judges the meaning of "judge" is a tribal, charismatic leader. Would you add anything to that? What good or bad qualities of leadership did you recognize in their stories?

2. Scholars say the Song of Deborah (5:1–31) is the oldest part of the Bible. What does it celebrate?

3. What did Samson's Nazirite vow require of him? Did he live up to his vow?

***In Our Lives***

1. The purpose of the book of Judges is to illustrate Israel's failure to live in faithful obedience to the LORD. What might be described as similar signs of failure today?

2. A typical pattern in the book of Judges—sin, punishment, crying out to the LORD, deliverance—plays out both in communities and personally. Where do you recognize this pattern today?

3. Israel strayed in worshiping Baal, the Canaanite god of storm and fertility. What are false gods that are worshiped in our culture?

***Individual/Personal Reflection/Action***

1. The book of Judges shows what happens to a people that ignores ethical and moral values.

What message is here for the modern world? In your mind, what are some values we need to pay attention to today? In your life, who or what helps you stop and look at your own values from time to time?

2. Judges describes ongoing "holy war." Do you believe war can ever be "holy"? How would you describe your position to another person?

# RUTH READING GUIDE

## *At a Glance*

| | |
|---|---|
| Who are the main players? | Naomi Ruth, her daughter-in-law Boaz |
| What should I look for? | The loyalty of Ruth The felt but unseen presence of God The notion of redemption that runs throughout God's use of a non-Israelite to advance the divine plan. |
| When did this take place? | During the days of the judges, before the establishment of the monarchy (c 1200–1000 B.C.). The book, however, was probably written sometime during the period of the monarchy. |
| Where did these events occur? | In the land of Moab, east of the Dead Sea, and in Bethlehem. |
| Why was this book written? | To show that fidelity and integrity are possible even when faithlessness abounds; to illustrate God's faithfulness and protection; to demonstrate that kindness, piety, and loyalty bear good fruit. |
| What is the story? | Because of famine Naomi's family migrates to Moab where her sons marry Moabite women. Later, Naomi's husband and sons die, so she prepares to return home. One daughter-in-law, Ruth, insists on going back to Canaan with her. There she meets and marries Boaz, a kinsman. They bear a child, Obed, who will become the grandfather of King David. |

### *Ruth and the Rest of the Bible*

- The book of Ruth is one of only three books in the Bible that bears the name of a woman (the others are Esther and Judith).
- Ruth is one of the four women mentioned in Matthew's genealogy of Jesus.

## Before Beginning

The book of Ruth is a delightful story that continues to captivate its audience no matter how often it is read. Few can forget the loyalty of Ruth, the devastation of Naomi, the forthrightness of Boaz. The story has been of special interest to Christians because Matthew lists Ruth among the ancestors of Jesus (Mt 1:5).

## Ruth as Story

The book of Ruth is a short story, similar to the Joseph story in Genesis 37–50. It is an artistically told tale with a simple plot. While the story of Joseph is set at the court of Pharaoh and deals with important personages and events, Ruth's characters are ordinary people; its events, mundane. Its closeness to life enables us to identify with its characters, to sympathize with their situation, and to rejoice when their problems are solved. The plot of the book is controlled by the problems that Ruth and Naomi encounter as they adjust to their new status as widows—Ruth as a new widow, Naomi as a widowed mother who has lost both her sons. These problems are resolved through the interaction of the book's main characters: Ruth, Naomi, and Boaz, relieving the tension created by the uncertain future that the two women faced. The principal characters are people whose goodness is rewarded in the end, reinforcing the belief that human events are in some sense under the control of a power that insures that good triumphs. As a story, its purpose is to entertain and delight, and this it does, but at the same time it also instructs. Although God never directly speaks or acts in the story, nevertheless it is clear that the story has something to teach us of the way that God is present in life.

An important element in the story is Ruth's Moabite ancestry. It is especially significant because the book presents her as the great-grandmother of David. Although Deuteronomy 23:3 forbids a Moabite from becoming part of the Israelite community, Ruth not only does so but is a forebear of the great King David. Perhaps the author of the book made a connection between David and the Moabites because the story of David's rise to kingship has him place his parents in the safekeeping of the king of Moab while David is trying to elude capture by Saul (1 Sm 22:3). There is, of course, no possibility of verifying the details of Ruth's story.

## Place in the Canon

While there is universal agreement about Ruth's status in the canon of the books of the Bible, there is some disagreement about the book's placement within the canon. In Christian Bibles, including the *New American Bible,* the book of Ruth occupies a place after Judges and before 1 Samuel, following the order of books in the Septuagint, which was the version of the Old Testament read in the early Church. No doubt the Septuagint placed Ruth after Judges because the story is set "in the time of the judges" (Ru 1:1). It is important to note that despite its placement, the book of Ruth is not a part of the deuteronomistic history, the story of Israel from conquest to exile found in the books of Joshua, Judges, 1 and 2 Samuel, and 1 and 2 Kings. It does not reflect the thought or style of the deuteronomistic history; it does not have deuteronomistic theological overtones. In Jewish Bibles, the book of Ruth is placed in the third division of the Jewish Canon: the Writings, a collection of miscellaneous works. In the Jewish synagogue lectionary, Ruth is read on the Feast of Weeks (*Shavuoth*), the celebration of the spring harvest; *Shavuoth* occurs 50 days after Passover and is the basis of the Feast of Pentecost, since it was at *Shavuoth* after Jesus' resurrection that the apostles received the gift of the Holy Spirit.

## Theology in the Book of Ruth

In an age when the Torah was on the way to becoming the central religious symbol of early Judaism, the book of Ruth presents three characters, Ruth, Boaz, and Naomi, whose actions go beyond what is required of them. Ruth makes a commitment to her mother-in-law Naomi that ignores the claims of religious traditions and national origins. Naomi shows her loving concern for Ruth by devising a scheme to induce Boaz to marry Ruth, even though that scheme could have backfired on her. In spite of the fact that marrying Ruth means that her first child will be regarded not as Boaz's, but as Ruth's deceased husband Mahlon's, and that Naomi will be his responsibility as well (as she would have been her son's), Boaz ignores his self-interest to marry Ruth and redeem the property of Naomi's husband. The story shows how people who think of others' needs before their own find their truest happiness. God approves the conduct of these people by giving a son to Ruth and Boaz—a son who removes the emptiness and uncertainty that faced the widow Naomi. The author of Ruth is certainly saying to the book's readers: "Go you and do likewise."

## How to Proceed

Because a story conveys its meaning in terms of what is said of its actors and their actions, it is important to pay close attention to the characterization of Ruth, Naomi, and Boaz, and what they do. Pay particular attention to the subtle presence of God in the story. Notice, too, recurring motifs and patterns that will function as clues to meaning.

## The Book of Ruth in Outline

The story is worked out in scenes set between an introduction that presents the problem, and an epilogue that follows the resolution of the problem.

| | | |
|---|---|---|
| A. | 1:1–5 | Prologue: A Family Dies |
| B. | 1:6–22 | Naomi and Ruth in Bethlehem: Emptiness and Uncertainty |
| C. | 2:1–23 | Naomi, Ruth and Boaz (I): A Meeting with Possibilities |
| D. | 3:1–18 | Naomi, Ruth and Boaz (II): A Husband for Ruth |

E. 4:1–12 The Climax: Boaz Acts
F. 4:13–17 A Son for Naomi
G. 4:18–22 Epilogue: A Family's Genealogy

## Reading Through the Book of Ruth

### The Prologue: A Family Dies (Ru 1:1–5)

A family from Bethlehem that had been driven by hunger to Moab is now left without any hope of progeny, because the men of the family have recently died. This is a principal problem of the story: Naomi is left without husband or sons (1:5). The author makes a special note of identifying the family's origin in Bethlehem of Judah (1:1), noting more specifically that they were "Ephrathites from Bethlehem of Judah" (1:2). This detail, emphasized as it was, certainly led those who first read the story of Ruth to think of the most famous of all Ephrathites: David, the son of Jesse (see 1 Sm 17:12). Thus, the opening verses of the story hint at its eventual resolution.

### The Geographical and Cultural Setting

The events recounted in these opening verses reflect conditions typical of life in Canaan. Because the region did not have a river system that made large-scale irrigation possible, agriculture was completely dependent on rain. When the rainfall was inadequate, famine was the inevitable result. One way to cope was to move to areas unaffected by the famine—usually this meant Egypt (see Gn 12:10; 26:1). Moab was an unusual choice. It was located east of the Dead Sea and like the lands to the west, it too was entirely dependent on rain for agricultural produce. Presumably a drought that affected Bethlehem would have affected Moab as well. Also unusual is that no negative comments are made regarding the marriage of Naomi's sons to Moabite women. But these details, too, serve to prepare the reader for an even greater difference coming at the end of the story.

Childless widows were particularly vulnerable in the social and economic system of the societies of the ancient Near East. A husband and sons provided a woman with security. Naomi found herself without such protection in a foreign land. She bitterly lamented her fate (Ru 1:13), but in an unusual move, one of her daughters-in-law chose to ignore her own welfare and care for Naomi. Instead of attaching herself to a man to provide for her welfare, Ruth attaches herself to Naomi, who can offer her nothing.

### The Motif of Emptiness

Naomi's "emptiness" is the principal problem of the story. With great artistry the author of Ruth weaves into the story a motif of emptiness that sets the action of the story in motion and will be reversed by the end of the story. The emptiness of the land (famine) causes Naomi's family to leave the land. The emptiness of the land gives way to the emptiness of Naomi as she loses her husband and her sons. Naomi dismisses her daughters-in-law because her emptiness cannot be cured. She is too old to give birth again. Naomi's emptiness is accentuated when she contrasts her previous abundance with her present destitution (1:21). The story ends with Naomi no longer empty. She takes Ruth's child to her breast and cares for him. The neighboring women congratulate her: "A son has been born to Naomi" (Ru 4:17).

### God's Presence in the Story

It is important to note that in the story of Ruth, God is most often referred to in the blessings and oaths that are spoken by the main characters. Naomi blesses her two daughters-in-law (1:8f); Boaz blesses Ruth for her loyalty to Naomi (2:12) and her good character (3:10); Naomi blesses Boaz for his kindness to Ruth (2:20); the blessing of fertility is bestowed upon Ruth by the citizens at the city gate (4:11–12). All of these blessings are issued in God's name, but it is through the actions of the main characters that the blessings are fulfilled.

Other references to God in the story imply that God is the cause of all that happens. God is the one who has ended the famine in the land of Israel and filled it with food (1:6). God is blamed for Naomi's destitution (1:20f); God is also responsible for Naomi's abundance at the end of the story (4:14), by enabling Ruth to conceive and bear a child (4:13). The hand of God is to be found in all that happens in the lives of Naomi, Ruth, and Boaz. But there are no miracles, no appearances of God, no signs and wonders to illuminate Ruth's way. It is through the ordinary lives of ordinary people, who demonstrate extraordinary care for each other, that the divine is manifest.

**Naomi and Ruth in Bethlehem: Emptiness and Uncertainty (Ru 1:6–22)**

The length of this scene indicates its importance for the author of Ruth. Naomi decides to return home because the famine is over in the land of Israel. Also motivating her decision must be the realization that she will have a better chance of survival among her own people than as an Israelite widow living among Moabites. Naomi's words to her daughters-in-law accentuate the tragedy of her situation. She is too old to marry and can no longer bear children. She can hope for nothing. Her daughters-in-law share Naomi's desperate situation, but she advises them to return to their people. Among their own people they may be able to find husbands and thus secure their future. With Naomi there can be no future. Ruth's loyalty is shown in her refusal to abandon her mother-in-law in spite of the hopelessness of Naomi's future; she will stay with Naomi despite the prospect of poverty.

**The Character of Ruth**

By drawing out the hopelessness of Naomi's situation coupled with Ruth's refusal to leave her mother-in-law, the author highlights Ruth's character: she is faithful. While there is nothing wrong with Orpah's returning home, Ruth's virtue is shown in sharp relief by the contrasting actions of these two women. Ruth is willing to share the plight of Naomi. Ruth's character is spotlighted even more in its biblical context. She is not called by God. She receives no promises. No reward awaits her. She acts solely for the good of Naomi. Her loyalty will draw the attention of Boaz, which eventually will lead to the resolution of the problem facing Ruth and Naomi, and thus all in the story depends on this young widow.

**Ruth, Boaz, and Naomi (I): A Meeting with Possibilities (Ru 2:1–23)**

Ruth takes the initiative in this scene, requesting permission from her mother-in-law to glean in the fields. Picking the few stalks of grain left by the harvesters was one way that people without land were able to feed themselves. Both Leviticus and Deuteronomy require that harvesters not be so thorough as to leave nothing for the poor (Lv 19:9f; 23:22; Dt 24:19–21). Ruth, seemingly by chance, enters the fields of Boaz, a prominent relative of Naomi. Boaz has heard of Ruth's kindness to her mother-in-law and sees to it that she is protected and allowed to gather a considerable amount of barley.

**The Character of Boaz**

The story depicts Boaz as generous and noble. He insists that Ruth glean only in his fields, he extends his protection to her, he provides her with food and water, and he sees to it that she will prosper in her gleaning. The motive for his behavior toward Ruth is her kindness and loyalty to Naomi. We see in his gracious response to Ruth's faithfulness that Boaz is a person of integrity and honor.

**Naomi, Ruth, and Boaz (II): A Husband for Ruth (Ru 3:1–18)**

Naomi does not want Ruth to remain a widow, so she decides to take advantage of the positive encounter between Ruth and Boaz. She suggests a plan to Ruth that could lead to marriage with Boaz. Even though the writer uses euphemisms that reflect his culture's reticence about private matters, the sexual overtones of Ruth's actions are clear. Although her encounter with Boaz on the threshing floor could have turned out differently, Boaz's integrity and generosity leads in the direction Naomi hoped: Ruth will have a husband.

**The Climax: Boaz Acts (Ru 4:1–12)**

The storyteller introduces a new wrinkle into his tale to complicate matters just before the denouement. For the first time in the story, Naomi's husband Elimelech's land becomes an issue. Probably the story's first readers would have wondered when the storyteller was going to get around to dealing with this most important matter. Boaz assembles 10 of the town's elders to witness how the matter of the land was going to be settled among Elimelech's relatives. The presence of the elders ensured that the details of settlement became "public record." An unnamed relative who had a prior claim on the land was willing to buy it back, thus insuring that Elimelech's land would stay in the family. Of course, doing so would have benefited that man economically. But then Boaz adds that with the land came Ruth, Mahlon's widow. Any child born of Ruth and the relative in question would inherit the land; rights to it could not be controlled by the relative himself. It is at this point that he demurs and cedes his rights to Boaz. The storyteller implies that the unnamed relative was concerned solely about his own interests, unlike Naomi, Ruth, and Boaz, who, throughout the story, are concerned less about themselves and more about the welfare of others. With the tension brought on by this last complication resolved, the storyteller can proceed to the happy ending, which has Ruth acquire a husband, Boaz acquire both a wife and Elimelech's land, and Naomi acquire a son who will fill her emptiness.

#### Levirate Marriage and Land Redemption

Some interpreters suggest that the marriage of Boaz and Ruth represents a variation of the levirate marriage. A levirate marriage was the marriage of a woman with the brother of her deceased husband ("Levir" is the Latin word for "brother-in-law"). Such a union was mandated if the marriage was childless (Dt 25:5–10). The practice developed to ensure that the line of the deceased man would continue, in spite of the fact that he died before his wife bore him a child. Although Boaz claims Ruth as wife to raise up a family for her late husband, he is not her brother-in-law and thus the law of levirate marriage did not apply. The storyteller presents Boaz as going beyond his obligations in order to help two widows in need.

Land redemption was a strategy that developed to insure that circumstances that forced a man to sell his land would not lead his family into a permanent state of poverty. According to Leviticus 25:23–38, it was the responsibility of a relative to buy the land before it was sold outside the family or to buy it back if it already had been sold. The land remained the property of the relative who bought it back until the year of jubilee, when its ownership reverted to the descendants of the man who was forced to sell it.

#### A Son for Naomi (Ru 4:13–17)

Ruth's marriage to Boaz is blessed with a child. Naomi's loss is replaced by Ruth's gain; the tragedy of death, with which the story opened, is balanced by the joy of new life. Notice the women of the village congratulate Naomi as if she were the mother: "A son has been born to Naomi" (Ru 4:17). The storyteller thus solves the problem of Naomi's emptiness. The *NAB* translation obscures this point by calling the child Naomi's "grandson." While the child indeed was Naomi's grandson, the text nonetheless shows Naomi acting as if she were the mother (Ru 4:16) and being recognized as such by the women of her village (Ru 4:17).

#### The Epilogue: A Family's Genealogy (Ru 4:18–22)

The story's epilogue takes the reader back to the prologue, which identified Naomi's family as "Ephrathites from Bethlehem" (Ru 1:2), and informs the reader of the wider significance of this charming story of one family's problems. The most famous Ephrathite from Bethlehem was David, who, it turns out, was a descendant of Boaz and Ruth. Usually a genealogy serves to legitimate the status of the last person named. Here David, the last person named, serves to show the significance for all Israel of what happened to three people from the village of Bethlehem.

## Continuing Significance of the Story of Ruth

While Early Judaism came to regard careful observance of the Torah as the key to its future, the book of Ruth shows three people whose relationships with each other are based not on obligations but on love and concern for another in need. Such relationships have significance far beyond the lives of the three people involved directly. Jesus develops these insights in his Sermon on the Mount, in which he calls his followers to go beyond the commandments, as irreplaceable as they are. The charming story of Naomi, Ruth, and Boaz shows that an ethical system fulfills its purpose if those who accept it learn to go beyond its requirements. The Torah asserts that no Moabite is to be admitted into the Israelite community (Dt 23:3). But the book of Ruth presents a Moabite woman whose actions on behalf of her Israelite mother-in-law proceeded from love that ignored religious and ethnic boundaries. These boundaries keep people from responding to each other in love. The book of Ruth, then, presents this young Moabite woman to its readers and suggests that they follow her example. The ending of the book wishes readers to recognize that when people give of themselves for the sake of others they find their truest happiness. This paradox lies at the heart of the book of Ruth and makes it the charming and admirable story that it is.

**Questions for Discussion and Reflection**

***Group Sharing/Discussion***

1. It is important to be attentive to the characterization of Ruth, Naomi, and Boaz and to what they do. Have various people in the group focus on one of these characters and retell who they are and what they did. Explain what their actions say about their character. Besides loyalty, what other qualities do you see in each of them?

2. In ancient Palestine, a woman without a man in her life was destined for hardship. How does this shed light on the character of Ruth?

3. In the book of Ruth, what was the levirate law that Boaz chooses to follow?

4. Ruth, a Moabite; in *Joshua,* Rahab, a woman of Jericho; and Jael, a Kenite woman in *Judges,* are given important roles. Why do you think the writers of the Old Testament give critical roles to non-Israelites and women?

***In Our Lives***

1. The hand of God is found in all that happens in the ordinary lives of Naomi, Ruth, and Boaz. No signs and wonders! How do you look for the hand of God in your life? What does Ruth's story teach us concerning the way God is present in our own life?

2. During the exile many Jewish leaders were trying to restrict marriages and contact with foreigners. The story of Ruth challenges these racial and religious purity laws. Why is it significant that Ruth, the great-grandmother of King David, is a foreigner?

3. According to the Israelite Law the poor had the right to glean the fields and the farmers were required to leave part of the harvest for gleaning. Ruth gleans the fields of Boaz. Do we have any similar laws that protect the rights of the poor?

4. Life was difficult for widows such as Ruth. What are the challenges for widows and widowers in our midst? How can we better help with those challenges?

***Individual/Personal Reflection/Action***

1. Ruth is a woman of service. How much is service a part of your life? Your parish, your diocese, local hospitals, or service centers would be happy to help you with a plan for yourself.

2. So much of what we organize in our churches is couples- or family-centered. Reach out to include someone in the community who does not fit those categories.

# 1 AND 2 SAMUEL READING GUIDE

## *At a Glance*

| | |
|---|---|
| Who are the main players? | Eli Hannah Samuel Saul Jonathan David Goliath Bathsheba Joab, David's general Absalom, David's son |
| What should I look for? | The transition in Israel from theocracy to monarchy The system of checks and balances: the king's power is checked by God's Law and the voice of the prophet How Saul's and David's sins have both personal and national consequences The theme of obedience to God: "Obedience is better than sacrifice" (1 Sm 15:22) |
| When did this take place? | From the end of the age of the judges through the monarchy and death of David: approximately 1083 B.C. to 960 B.C. |
| Where did these events occur? | The land of Israel, especially Ramah, birthplace of Samuel; Shiloh, Israel's center of worship; the desert where David fled; Moab, where David moved his family; Ziklag, the city from which David conducted numerous raids; Mount Gilboa, site of Saul's final battle and death. |

| | |
|---|---|
| Why was this book written? | To depict Israel's transition from theocracy to democracy by narrating the life of Samuel and the reigns of Israel's first two kings, Saul and David. |
| What is the story? | Samuel, the last judge, anoints Saul as first king of Israel. Saul begins well but ends badly, becoming obsessed with jealousy and hatred of David. Saul turns to occult practices and eventually commits suicide. David succeeds him on the throne and unites Israel into a powerful kingdom. Although he never abandons the LORD, David's own sins bring strife to his family and nation. |

The books of Samuel were not written from start to finish by a single author or even a group of authors. Individual stories and blocks of material about the fascinating characters in these books had existed long before anyone pulled them together and gave them their present form. Although it is not as evident here as in the book of Judges, the same deuteronomistic editors who shaped that book shaped these.

As Israel changed, so did its literature. During the tribal era, it produced heroic sagas filled with astounding events. But when Israel became a state, *historical* writing developed. The books of Samuel combine sagas, like the story of David and Goliath, with historical writing, like the report in 2 Samuel 8 of David's conquest of the Moabites and Edomites. Yet, Samuel is not so much teaching history, as preaching the consequences of how Israel lives.

The books of Samuel offer a theological interpretation of how the monarchy was established in Israel. Their basic theological presupposition is this: David, who conquered Jerusalem and made it Israel's religious center, must have been God's chosen leader.

## Reading the Books of Samuel

The theological perspective of the editors colors their presentation of the lives of Samuel, Saul, and David (see the discussion of Understanding the Historical Background to the Biblical Texts on RG 31). Their viewpoint is this: Total obedience to God's Law brings success; disobedience brings failure. Since the deuteronomists see David succeed despite his sins, they conclude that he must have been loyal to the LORD. Saul, on the other hand, fails, so they conclude he must have been disloyal.

**Outline of 1 and 2 Samuel**

| | |
|---|---|
| 1 Sm 1:1–3:21 | Birth and youth of Samuel |
| 1 Sm 4:1–7 | Loss and return of the Ark of the Covenant |
| 1 Sm 7:2–17 | Samuel as judge |
| 1 Sm 8:1–12:25 | Establishment of the monarchy |
| 1 Sm 13:1–15:35 | Reign and rejection of Saul |
| 1 Sm 16:1–2 Sm 5:5 | David becomes king of Judah and Israel |
| 2 Sm 5:6–24:25 | Reign of King David |
| 2 Sm 21:1–24:25 | Appendices |

**Samuel's Birth and Youth (1 Sm 1:1–3:21)**

In Scripture, the circumstances of a child's birth often provide hints about the child's destiny. Samuel's destiny as one chosen by God for special service is foreshadowed by his mother Hannah's barrenness. Harassed by her husband's other wife who has borne numerous children, Hannah prays that God remove her misery by

**Deuteronomistic:** This term is used to refer to both the editors and the style of the history comprised in the books of Joshua, Judges, Samuel, and Kings, as prefaced by the book of Deuteronomy. These books reflect concern for such matters as obedience to the laws given in Deuteronomy, centralized worship in Jerusalem, and support for the Davidic dynasty.

**Barren Women** Besides Hannah, there are four other seemingly barren Old Testament women who were divinely blessed with a son: Sarah (Gn 11:30); Rebekah (Gn 25:21); Rachel (Gn 29:31); and Samson's mother (Jgs 13:3). In the New Testament, there is Mary's cousin Elizabeth (Lk 1:7).

**The Ark of the Covenant**

THE MOST SACRED of Israel's possessions, the Ark was a box of acacia wood measuring approximately 4′ x 2½′ x 2½′. Kept in the Holy of Holies of the moveable Tabernacle and later the Temple, it contained the Tablets of the Law (and possibly a jar of desert manna and Aaron's rod). It was considered God's throne and signified God's presence among people (at times it was virtually identified with God). Anyone who desecrated it was instantly struck down.

granting her a son. When her prayer for a son is answered, she fulfills her promise to dedicate the boy to God and raise him as a Nazirite (1:22) and leaves him in the care of Eli the priest at the shrine in Shiloh. Samuel is clearly a gift from God, special and destined for greatness.

After consecrating Samuel to God, Hannah prays a beautifully poetic prayer. Hannah praises God for reversing fortunes by bringing down the mighty and raising up the lowly, for making the barren fertile, and for defending the weak and lowly. Mary's Magnificat (Lk 1:46–55) resembles this prayer.

Hannah leaves Samuel in the care of Eli the priest at the shrine in Shiloh. While Samuel grew in stature and favor before God and people, the sons of Eli committed grave sins of greed and desecration, making them clearly unworthy for their service as priests of the LORD.

Samuel's special role in God's plan is highlighted by the story of his call (3:1–21). He is God's chosen servant: Reared as a priest, he is later given a prophetic ministry as well. He will also function as a military leader or judge, Israel's last and finest. Thus, the major institutions of ancient Israel—priest, prophet, and judge—are all manifested in this one man who also anointed Israel's first two kings.

### Loss and Return of the Ark (1 Sm 4:1–7:1)

In this story the Ark's primary significance is military. Its capture by the Philistines is a devastating blow. In Israel the Ark's presence in the battlefield signified God's presence fighting for the people. Is God's presence now lost? Ancient people believed that capturing an enemy's god and setting it up in your own temple indicated your gods were much more powerful than your enemy's. But this story shows that Israel's God works differently. Despite the Ark's capture, the LORD is still very much in control. This is pointedly (even humorously) demonstrated by the idol of the god Dagon twice falling down in worship before the Ark. Wherever it is held captive, the Ark causes disease and devastation. Every town to which it is sent experiences turmoil.

The Philistines soon learn whose god is most powerful and quickly resolve to return the Ark to Israel. But more than lampooning the god Dagon, the deuteronomistic writers use this story to illustrate that the prophecy God spoke through Samuel (that Eli's family would be punished for their wrongdoing [2:27–36]) is beginning to be fulfilled.

### Samuel as Judge (1 Sm 7:2–17)

When Samuel reappears in chapter 7, he is a military leader or judge leading the fight against the Philistines. The degree of his success is overstated (7:13), for the Philistines are not completely overcome until the reign of David. But by stressing Samuel's military victories—all of which were achieved not by Samuel but by God (7:10, 13)—the deuteronomistic writers make a point regarding kingship: Israel does not really need a king to lead its battles, for God can use

**Saul and David—First Impressions**

WE MEET SAUL chasing after donkeys—animals as stubborn as he turns out to be and possibly symbols of those who demanded a king despite God's displeasure. They were also a sign of his family's wealth. David, on the other hand, is introduced as a simple shepherd tending to his father's flock. Later he will shepherd Israel.

anyone at any time to bring the chosen people victory.

### Establishment of the Monarchy (1 Sm 8:1–12:25)

Throughout most of its history, Israel remained ambivalent about monarchy. One of the distinguishing characteristics of its literature is the fact that it preserves both strands of thinking: pro-monarchy and anti-monarchy. By mingling negative with positive overtones, the writers prepare the reader for the negative assessment of the whole institution of the monarchy presented in the books of Kings, and for the more immediate downfall of Israel's first king, Saul.

### Request for a King and Samuel's Opposition (1 Sm 8:1–22)

Because the Philistine military threat would not go away, Israel was in constant need of strong leadership. Other nations relied on kings, who would be succeeded by their sons when the king got old. Israel had no such assurance of continuity when a leader like Samuel died. So they asked for a king because they wanted to be "like all the nations" (8:20). But Israel was not supposed to be like other nations. Samuel resisted—perhaps because he was unhappy that his own sons were being rejected as potential future leaders. God instructed Samuel to warn the people that a king would bring higher taxes, forced labor, and a military draft.

Israel's king was the LORD; therefore the request for a human king was theologically repugnant. But in the end God relented. Since theological theory and historical practice seem to conflict, the text, accordingly, reflects ambivalence about God's decision. The editors, unable to deny the historical reality that monarchy existed for centuries in Israel, assume the theological position that therefore, God must have accepted it. The abandonment of God as king of Israel foreshadows the eventual collapse of Israel as a nation.

### Saul Anointed King by Samuel (1 Sm 10:1–11:15)

The story presents Saul in a positive light: His good looks and stature are signs of God's favor. Before his anointing, Saul had never heard of Samuel nor ever dreamed of kingship. Many folk stories depict their hero as someone on a mission to find something that is lost who instead finds something unexpected and better. Saul seeks out Samuel for help finding his asses but ends up with a crown. He is treated with honor at a feast, anointed as ruler, and sent away with three signs that will confirm his selection by God: Two men will tell him that the asses have been found (10:2); he will be offered bread intended for sacrifice (10:4); and most importantly, the Spirit of the LORD will come upon him as it had upon the judges (10:6). Note the existence of parallel accounts of how Saul became king: by Samuel's anointing him (10:1) and by lot (10:17–24). The ancient writers often preserved differing accounts of the same event from the sources available to them.

The ambivalence toward monarchy demonstrated in chapter 8 continues here: While the LORD accepts kingship and designates Saul the first king, nevertheless, by wanting a king the people have proven their lack of faith.

Saul seems to have returned to private life at the start of chapter 11. Led by the Spirit and acting more like a warrior judge than a king, he leads a victorious battle against the Ammonites.

### Samuel's Address and Acceptance of the Kingship (1 Sm 12:1–25)

Chapter 12 confirms the LORD's acceptance of kingship. After publicly asserting his own honesty, Samuel sets out to demonstrate how irrational is Israel's request for a king by telling how God always saved Israel in her times of need. The people have done evil in asking for a king, yet God permits it. However, the LORD is still the ultimate authority in Israel and failure to follow God's Law will bring just punishment.

The deuteronomistic writers present Samuel as the bridge between the eras of judges and kings. Samuel's speech brings the era of judges to an end and sets the stage for prophets to take on greater importance. The people will not have to depend solely on the king, for the prophet (whose power is here demonstrated by the thunderstorm [11:18]) will act on their behalf in four ways:

1. interceding and praying for them;
2. teaching them what is right;
3. exhorting them to worship the LORD alone;
4. warning them of punishment when they disobey. The prophet checks and balances the king's power and mediates the LORD's judgment.

### The Reign and Rejection of Saul (1 Sm 13:1–15:35)

In this section, the writers' main interest is in demonstrating why Saul failed as Israel's king.

#### Saul Is Rebuked for Disobeying Samuel (1 Sm 13:1–22)

Although eventually successful, primarily because of Saul's son Jonathan's heroics, Saul's campaign against the Philistines begins with Saul's disobedience. The crime seems trivial, but the consequences are serious. While waiting to attack the Philistines, Saul's soldiers begin to desert because Samuel does not arrive at the expected time. Overanxious, Saul disregards Samuel's order to wait for him and offers the sacrifice himself. Disobedience to the LORD's prophet is disobedience to the LORD; consequently Saul's kingdom will not endure.

#### Jonathan and the Defeat of the Philistines at Michmash (1 Sm 13:23–14:46)

Because of the Philistine monopoly on iron, the Israelites have no iron weapons, we are told, but the Philistines are armed with swords and spears. In light of this disparity of weapons, an Israelite victory can only be the LORD's doing.

The deuteronomistic editors continually reinforce the idea of the LORD as the giver of victory. Demonstrating amazing bravado, Jonathan, aided only by his armor-bearer, takes on and kills some 20 Philistines. At every stage, Jonathan reminds the reader that the LORD is responsible for his victory. It is Jonathan's victory that inspires Saul to attack. Saul leads a successful battle, but a rashly made decision threatens the safety of the army and demonstrates Saul's unfitness to reign as king. Saul had impulsively ordered his army to fast until nightfall on the day of battle, putting them at an unnecessary disadvantage. Knowing nothing of his father's order, Jonathan unwittingly breaks the fast.

Later, Saul is willing to kill his son for the inadvertent violation despite the fact that Jonathan had made the greatest contribution to the day's victory. Increasingly Saul seems ill-suited to lead God's people. Some commentators believe the story is also meant to indicate that Jonathan, too, is unacceptable as Saul's successor because, despite being uninformed, Jonathan did violate the oath and thus is guilty. Though Jonathan's life is spared (an animal is sacrificed in his place), a sense of doom remains.

#### War with the Amalekites and Rejection of Saul (1 Sm 14:47–15:35)

War continues, and Saul wins more victories and continues to have God's support, until he disobeys a command from God, delivered by Samuel. In violation of God's direct order, Saul refuses to enforce the ban against Israel's old enemies the Amalekites. He spares their king and refuses to slaughter the best of the herds of sheep and oxen. Instead he only destroys what is worthless. Because of Saul's disobedience—and subsequent lying about his disobedience, then passing the blame on to his soldiers—and greed, the LORD rejects Saul as king over Israel. He is still king for now, but the end is near. In fact, God sends Samuel to Bethlehem, where he will find and anoint David.

Jealousy of David becomes Saul's final downfall—although he was fond of David the harper and made him his armor-bearer, he resented David's military successes and the honors given him by the Israelites, as well as the LORD's favor. When Saul fails to kill David himself, he begins to plot against him, hoping that one of the many campaigns and tasks he gives David will result in his death. Saul both loves and hates David. He promises to make his daughter, Merob, David's wife, but then marries her to another man. He offers another daughter, Michal, but only on the condition that first David do the impossible: deliver to Saul the foreskins of a hundred Philistines. David not only meets the demand, he doubles it and wins a great military victory in the process. Instead of getting killed, David marries Michal, and Saul watches another plot to undermine his rival fail. Recognizing that the LORD's hand is upon David, Saul hates and fears him all the more.

### Saul's Pursuit of David and David's Escapes (1 Sm 19:1–28:2)

Saul is obsessed with David. He fears him and suspects disloyalty. These nine chapters chronicle both Saul's efforts to capture David and David's numerous escapes. Saul wants to kill David, although he allows his son Jonathan to persuade him to let David return to court. But soon his anger boils over again, and now it is Saul's daughter Michal who helps David escape. Even Samuel conspires to obstruct Saul's efforts against David. Throughout, David's innocence and loyalty are reaffirmed. David flees not because of any real crime, but because of Saul's obsessive attempts to destroy him.

David flees with his men and comes to the town of Nob, where the Tabernacle had been relocated after Shiloh's destruction. He lies to the priests in order to get food for himself and his men, an action that receives no comment from the narrator. The priests seek out God's will for David (22:10, 15) and allow him to take the sword of Goliath, indicating their approval of David as future king. By acting like a madman, David narrowly escapes capture by the king of Gath, then delivers his parents to the safety of the land of Moab (the home of his great-grandmother Ruth) to protect them from Saul's vengeance.

No negative judgment is made on any of David's actions (not even his lies to the priests). But Saul is depicted as becoming increasingly irrational. Although he had been unwilling to enforce the ban against his enemies, Saul now carries it out against his own people. He butchers the residents of Nob, including the priests David had tricked into helping him, and even the "children and infants." This tragic massacre fulfills the prophecy that Eli's family would be cut off from Israel's priesthood (2:31–36). Although one priest survives and gives his support to David, he, too, is later removed from the priesthood when Solomon sends him into exile, thus leaving no descendant of Eli serving as priest.

Saul keeps David on the run, but David does nothing without first consulting the LORD. God grants David much success in battle and in evading Saul. Even his fleeing reveals David's noble character: Twice he has an opportunity to secretly kill Saul but, despite the encouragement of his men, he refuses to harm the LORD's anointed. Chapters 24–26 emphasize David's innocence—even Saul recognizes it— and his selection as Israel's next king (24:21f).

In chapter 27 David makes a desperate and startling decision: Driven by Saul's incessant harassment, he joins forces with Israel's hated enemies, the Philistines. While working as a paid mercenary for the Philistines, David takes care never to attack Israel itself, but only her enemies, although he convinces the Philistines that he is attacking his own people.

### The Final Days of Saul's Reign (1 Sm 28:3–2 Sm 1:27)

Saul's last days are desperate and sad. When he receives no answers from God to his questions about how to handle a Philistine invasion, he panics and seeks out a sorceress to help him consult the ghost of Samuel. The dead prophet offers no comfort, but instead reminds Saul that God has rejected him as king and that he and his

**The Philistines** The fighting between Israel and her archenemies was constant. The books of 1 and 2 Samuel record at least 13 military encounters between Israel and the Philistines. Israel's success always depended on the degree of her faith in the LORD. Of the 13 battles, Israel was victorious 11 times and one battle was a draw.

sons will lose both the upcoming battle and their lives.

When David reappears, we find him in a serious predicament: He has sworn loyalty to the Philistine king, Achish, yet now that king wants to send David into battle against his own people. What will David do? Because of circumstances, David betrays neither side: The Philistine generals do not trust him, and they force him to leave. So David battles another of Israel's chief enemies, the Amalekites, and distinguishes himself in every way.

While David is enjoying every success, Saul has become a total failure. Rather than die at the hands of the Philistines like his three sons, Saul takes his own life. The once great and beloved leader is dead. As testimony to his former greatness, his soldiers march all night to retrieve and bury Saul's body. The first book of Samuel ends with the death of Israel's first king, who by his disobedience to the LORD doomed himself to failure as a ruler.

Interestingly, the start of the second book of Samuel presents a different version of Saul's death: An Amalekite youth, probably lying to win favor with David, claims that he killed Saul at the king's own request. The boy wins nothing from David but a death sentence.

One might expect David to rejoice, but instead Saul's death brings him great grief. The reader should remember that although Saul wanted David dead, David passed up opportunities to kill Saul and even desired genuine reconciliation. David expresses his sorrow in a mournful poem he chants for Saul and Jonathan (2 Sm 1:17–27).

**David Becomes King of Judah and Israel (2 Sm 2:1–5:5)**

After consulting the LORD, David travels to Hebron, where he is anointed king of Judah. But the northern territory is under the rule of Saul's son Ishbaal, who has been placed on the throne by Saul's general, Abner, the real power in Israel. A fight between representative warriors of each side—Joab's warriors representing David and Abner's representing Ishbaal—soon escalates into an all-out civil war between Israel and Judah. A series of murders and assassinations follows that results in the deaths of Abner and Ishbaal. The deuteronomistic writers make it very clear that David is innocent of the killings; he even punishes those who assassinated his rival, Ishbaal. But the result is that David benefits and becomes Israel's king (2 Sm 5:1–15).

**The Reign of King David (2 Sm 5:6–24:25)**

In this section the deuteronomistic writers advance their basic theological theme: because he is God's chosen, David found success in all his efforts, but he also suffered the consequences of all his sins. Interwoven with this dominant theme are concerns about who will rule after David dies, the activities of his children, and David's affection for Meribbaal, Jonathan's son.

The LORD is with David. Everything points to this fact: his choice as king of Israel, his military victories, the continued blessing of children in his life. David's first achievement as king of Judah and Israel is to take the city of Jerusalem, an act of the greatest political and theological significance. The city not only becomes the political capital of the empire, but, in the view of the deuteronomistic writers, the only legitimate place to worship the LORD.

**David Defeats the Philistines and Brings the Ark to Jerusalem (2 Sm 5:17–6:23)**

When they hear David has become king of both Israel and Judah, the Philistines immediately attack. But the LORD gives David the victory. This triumph, coupled with the previous conquest of Jerusalem, makes it possible for David to bring the Ark from the house of Abinadab, to the capital city, Jerusalem. A man named Uzzah tries to keep the Ark from falling during transport and is struck dead—harsh punishment for apparently well-intentioned behavior. But since the Ark represented God's very presence, only those who were consecrated could touch it. Uzzah's death emphasized the Ark's unparalleled holiness.

David dances naked before the Ark, and his wife, Michal (Saul's daughter), rebukes him for such undignified behavior. But David insists he will be even more enthusiastic (and undignified) in honoring the LORD, who chose him over Saul as Israel's king. Michal faces not only David's censure but the LORD's as well.

**God's Promise to David (2 Sm 7:1–29)**

2 Samuel 7 is an enormously significant text. God's promise to David of an eternal dynasty

**The Promise to David**

"YOUR HOUSE AND your kingdom shall endure forever before me; your throne shall stand firm forever." Like the covenants with Noah (Gn 9) and Abraham (Gn 15), the promise to David is unconditional, whereas the covenant with Moses at Sinai (Ex 19–24) contained a major condition ("*If* you obey my laws . . . ").

becomes the basis for Israel's expectation of a Messiah after the Davidic dynasty abruptly comes to an end with the destruction of Jerusalem in 586 B.C. The New Testament sees the prophecy fulfilled in Jesus, the Son of David and eternal king. This text climaxes the story of David's rise to power and prepares the way for the future that will be shaped largely by David's dynasty.

Ancient Near Eastern literature sees a connection between building a temple and establishing a dynasty. Nathan's prophecy contains an interesting play on words that may be inferring this connection. The Hebrew word for "house" can also mean both temple and dynasty. David wants to build God a house (temple); but the LORD insists on building a house (dynasty) for David.

### David's Exploits (2 Sm 8:1–10:19)

These episodes reveal David's noble character. He wins battles (8:1–18) and rules justly over all; he is the ideal king who shows mercy even to the family of his enemies. In ancient times new kings routinely killed all the relatives of the former king to eliminate any potential rival for the throne. But, because his love of Saul's family never wanes, David keeps his promise to Jonathan not to harm his relatives.

### David and Bathsheba (2 Sm 11:1–12:25)

One day David sees Bathsheba bathing and immediately decides he must have her. David is king, so what he wants he gets. We are told nothing of Bathsheba's feelings, but we know she is the wife of Uriah, one of David's generals who is away battling the Ammonites. After his lust conceives a child, David conceives a cover-up. He calls Uriah home from battle in the hope that he will have sexual relations with his wife and then think the child she carries is his. But Uriah spoils the plan: In keeping with the rules of holy war, he refuses to sleep with Bathsheba. David's plot turns drastic and cold-blooded. Uriah's murder, carried out by Joab, costs the lives of other men as well. Now David can marry Bathsheba and hide his double sin from all—but not from the LORD.

Enter Nathan with a heartrending story of abusive power. David does not hesitate in pronouncing judgment on the antagonist of Nathan's tale: "the man . . . deserves death!" But Nathan shocks him with the words, "You are the man!" David's uniqueness and true greatness is revealed in his sincere and humble repentance. God forgives him, but his sin will have consequences. The child born of his lust will die and he will live out his life in the shadow of a sword. The stories that follow (the rape of Tamar, the murder of Amnon, and the rebellions of Absalom and Sheba) embody the violence that now will never leave David's house. The second child of David and Bathsheba, however, will be a bright light that comes from their union. He will be Israel's next king, favored by the LORD.

### The Rape of Tamar and Absalom's Revenge (2 Sm 13:1–14:33)

Prior to David's sin with Bathsheba we heard nothing of problems in his reign. Now, as if set in motion by David's offense, problems multiply.

Like father, like son. Amnon lusts for his half-sister Tamar and will not rest until he has her. Although the customs of the times would have permitted a marriage between a half-brother and -sister, Amnon yields to lust rather than custom and rapes his sister. At times David's dealings with his sons were overindulgent, but taking no action against Amnon reveals a serious weakness, even blindness in David.

It falls to Absalom to avenge his sister. He waits two years, but eventually he slays his brother and in the process becomes next in line for the throne. Absalom goes into exile and David mourns the loss of both sons until Joab persuades him to bring Absalom back.

### Rebellions of Absalom and Sheba (2 Sm 15:1–20:26)

Absalom now consolidates his rebellious efforts, suggesting David is a poor enforcer of justice and claiming that if he were king, justice would reign. When he hears of Absalom's rebellion, David flees Jerusalem, barefoot and weeping, in a procession that resembles a penitential rite.

Absalom marches out in pursuit of his father and David is ready to meet him. But the soldiers will not let the king risk his life, so David asks them to deal gently with Absalom. The king's forces quickly rout the rebels, and Joab, in direct disobedience of David's orders, kills Absalom. David's reaction to his son's death (19:1) is one of Scripture's most moving passages. But the troops are shaken by David's bitter mourning. Joab warns the king he must set the example for the troops and let them rejoice in their victory. David listens and soon regains the support of his forces.

With the rebellion crushed, David returns triumphant to Jerusalem. But tension exists between the peoples of Judah and Israel, a fact that sets the stage for the next rebellion led by Sheba of the tribe of Benjamin. Joab pursues Sheba and quickly brings his rebellion to an end.

### Appendices (2 Sm 21:1–24:25)

Except that they all speak about David's reign, these final chapters seem to have no common thread.

### The Gibeonites Are Avenged; Battles with the Philistines (2 Sm 21:1–22)

Behind this story are ancient religious beliefs that national disasters are the result of sin. The famine here resulted from Saul's illegal slaughter of the Gibeonites, and such sins must be atoned in order to restore balance to nature. Seven sons and grandsons of Saul are executed to make atonement for his sin. Saul's concubine, Rizpah, protects their decaying bodies, moving David to provide belated proper burial for Saul, Jonathan, and the recently executed men.

What can we make of the claim in verse 19 that it was the warrior Elhanan who slew Goliath? Possible explanations include the following: perhaps the name Goliath became mistakenly associated with David's victim, who was actually a different Philistine; a later period may have romanticized Goliath's slaying as David's own doing; 1 Chronicles 20:5 credits Elhanan with the killing of Goliath's brother, which would mean David and Elhanan are both giant-killers.

### David's Song and Last Words (2 Sm 22–23)

David's hymn (which, with some variations, reappears as Psalm 18) gives thanks to the LORD for military victories. The song reasserts God's faithfulness, the need for obedience, and God's promise to David of an everlasting dynasty.

David's last words review his career and acknowledge him as God's favorite, the recipient of an eternal covenant.

### David Takes a Census (2 Sm 24:1–25)

Ancient writers sometimes confused primary and secondary causes. They believed that since God is all-powerful, God ultimately causes everything, no matter what the immediate causes might seem to be. Eventually they came to see that their all-loving God might permit but never "cause" evil. While this passage claims that God incited David to take the census, the same story retold in 1 Chronicles 21 blames it all on "Satan." The census is viewed as evil because it reflects arrogant pride, a willingness on David's part to put his trust in the size of his army rather than in the protection of the LORD. Even Joab feared angering the LORD by counting Israel's fighting forces.

## Continuing Significance of the Books of Samuel

As one reads the books of Samuel and their tales of jealousy, rape, murder, and revolution, one can almost hear their authors saying: "If you want a monarchy, this is what you get." The contemporary reader ought to recognize the folly of making any human institution absolute. The story of David's family shows what can happen when one is unable to keep in check the tendency to make absolute the institution of the monarchy. Second Samuel describes how Judah's royal family began to consume itself. Although monarchies are, for the most part, relics of another age, nations still succumb to the temptation of making their political, social, and economic institutions into absolutes. The story of Israel in its land shows what happens when a nation and its leader ignore the fundamental moral values.

**Questions for Discussion and Reflection**

*Group Sharing/Discussion*

1. In David's covenant with the LORD (2 Sm 7) what promises does the LORD make to David?

2. Why was David interested in having Michal, Saul's daughter, as his wife? For her part, why was Michal originally interested in David? What does this say about their culture and how does this compare to our culture?

3. Let different members of your group choose one of the main players in David's story—Saul, Jonathan, Samuel, Nathan, Michal, Abigail, Absalom, and so on—and explain why they were important and what lesson/s you learned from their relations with David.

4. In your view, what do you find admirable in David's life? How could this be imitated today?

*In Our Lives*

1. Dressed only in an ephod, David dances "with all his might" the whole night to celebrate the Ark of the Covenant's coming to Jerusalem. David sings, dances, and feasts with the people. Where and how does joy come into your life, into your religious experience? How do you plant seeds of joy?

2. Michal does not join the celebration. She is critical and uninvolved. She accuses David of fraternizing with the lowest element of society. How do you feel about Michal's reaction? In your life is it easy or difficult to fraternize with people from other lifestyles, economic classes? What is the message there?

*Individual/Personal Reflection/Action*

1. Reread the story of David and Bathsheba (2 Sm 11 and 12). David lusts after and kills for Bathsheba. His actions affect him, his family and friends, as well as the people. "Lead us not into temptation" becomes our daily prayer. Reflect upon how temptation of all different kinds touches your life.

2. By his story, Nathan, the wise prophet, reveals David to himself. David confesses he has sinned against the LORD. We all need wise prophets to help us see the way. Who are the persons you allow to nourish you on your way? Who is someone you would choose for that role?

3. In his Song of Thanksgiving (2 Sm 22:1–51) David prays to the LORD: "O LORD, my rock, my fortress, my deliverer." David built his life on the rock and foundation of the LORD. Who are people you know who clearly have the LORD as their rock and foundation, the main influence in how they live their lives? If you are comfortable doing so, let them know how you see them in this way.

# 1 AND 2 KINGS READING GUIDE

## *At a Glance*

| | |
|---|---|
| Who are the main players? | David Solomon Bathsheba Adonijah, half-brother of Solomon Rehoboam, son of Solomon and first king of Judah after the split Jeroboam, first king of Israel after the split Elijah, the prophet Elisha, his assistant and successor Ahab, a king of Israel Jezebel, his wife the Shunammite woman Naaman, general cured of leprosy Jehu, a king of Israel Hezekiah, a king of Judah Sennacherib, Assyrian king Isaiah, prophet in Judah Manasseh, worst king of Judah Josiah, reformer king of Judah Jehoiakim, a king of Judah Zedekiah, last king of Judah Nebuchadnezzar, king of Babylon |
| What should I look for? | How all kings are judged according to their faithfulness to the covenant, not by political, social, or economic standards How the authors pay most attention to the very faithful and |

| | |
|---|---|
| | very unfaithful kings or those who most interacted with one of God's prophets How the behavior of the king powerfully impacts the life of the nation, especially as regards idolatry The importance of the Temple in the nation's life How David's reign is used as a standard to measure the reigns of all later kings The importance given to the role of prophets The frequency with which events are seen as the fulfillment of prophecy |
| When did this take place? | During a period of 400 years, from approximately 960 B.C. to 586 B.C., that is, from the end of the reign of David to the Babylonian Exile. |
| Where did these events occur? | In the land of Israel, which becomes divided into two parts: Israel in the north and Judah in the south. |
| Why was this book written? | To help explain the exile; to tell the people that their infidelity to the covenant brought about the collapse of the nation, and to narrate the complete history of the monarchy. |
| What is the story? | David's reign comes to an end, and he is succeeded by his son Solomon, whose reign is described in great detail. After Solomon's reign the kingdom is divided in two: Israel in the north, with its own centers of worship to rival Jerusalem, and Judah in the south. Twenty kings, all judged unfaithful, rule the northern kingdom over a period of approximately 200 years until the north collapses in 722–721 B.C. and its population is led into exile. In the south David's descendants (20 in all, although one was a usurper) rule for a period of about 360 years, until the time of the Babylonian exile in 586 B.C. Several of the southern kings attempt reform but ultimately their efforts are too little, too late. |

In summarizing the character of the books of Kings, three distinct but interrelated features stand out. First, these books tell a story; they are narrative literature. Second, the story in Kings is about the past. We are dealing with the effort to write history, known as historiography. For all the artistry of the storytelling, there is a concern to write about a real past that is shared with other peoples in the Near East. Third, it is literature that teaches something about the God of Israel and his ways. There are three prominent theological themes in the story:

1. The LORD is indeed God and must not be confused with the various gods worshiped within Israel and outside, which are simply human creations (1 Kgs 12:25–30; 2 Kgs 19:14–19).

2. As the only God there is, the LORD demands exclusive worship. Much of Kings is therefore concerned to describe what is illegitimate in terms of worship. The main interest is the *content* of this worship (1 Kgs 11:12:13); there is also accompanying concern about the *place* of worship, which is ideally the Jerusalem Temple and not the "high places."

3. As giver of the Law that defines true worship, right thinking, and overall behavior, the LORD is also the one who executes judgment upon wrongdoers. The world of Kings is a moral world, in which wrongdoing is punished whether the sinner be king (11:19–13), prophet (13:7–25), or ordinary Israelite (2 Kgs 7:17–20).

## Before Beginning

First and Second Kings continue the story of Israel in its land. They are the final two components of the deuteronomistic history of Israel, which turns that story into a sermon that takes its theological principles from the book of

## Chronological Tables of Rulers

Problems of chronology of the kings of Israel and Judah permit no easy solution. The following tables are based upon two widely accepted systems of chronology, one developed by W. F. Albright, and the other by E. R. Thiele. The dates of Thiele's system (3rd ed.), which are enclosed within parentheses, are presented in simplified form apart from co-regencies and simultaneous claims to the throne. The two columns show the chronological relationships of the kings of the two kingdoms. The date shown is the year that ruler took the throne.

### The United Monarchy

The length of Saul's reign is not known; David and Solomon are each said to have ruled for 40 years, which is often used as a general and somewhat indefinite number. Their reigns must have fallen between about 1020 and 922 (931) B.C., perhaps as follows:

| | |
|---|---|
| Saul | 1020–1000 B.C. |
| David | 1000–961 (or 1000–965) B.C. |
| Solomon | 961–922 (or 965–931) B.C. |

### The Divided Monarchy, Judah and Israel

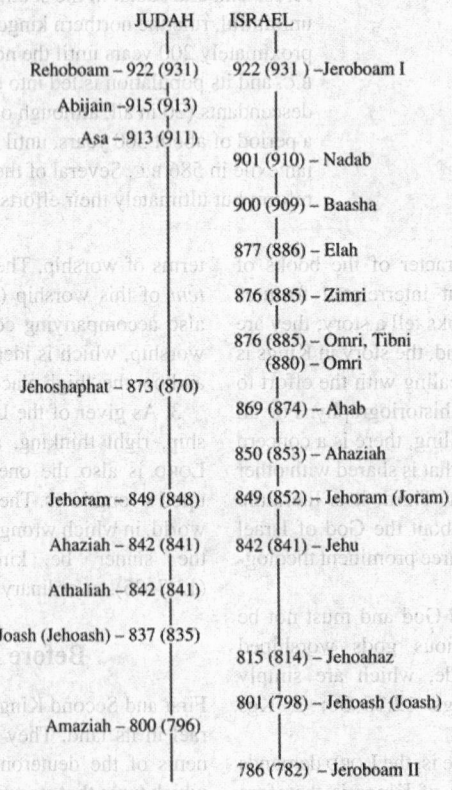

| JUDAH | ISRAEL |
|---|---|
| Rehoboam – 922 (931) | 922 (931) –Jeroboam I |
| Abijain –915 (913) | |
| Asa – 913 (911) | |
| | 901 (910) – Nadab |
| | 900 (909) – Baasha |
| | 877 (886) – Elah |
| | 876 (885) – Zimri |
| | 876 (885) – Omri, Tibni<br>(880) – Omri |
| Jehoshaphat – 873 (870) | |
| | 869 (874) – Ahab |
| | 850 (853) – Ahaziah |
| Jehoram – 849 (848) | 849 (852) – Jehoram (Joram) |
| Ahaziah – 842 (841) | 842 (841) – Jehu |
| Athaliah – 842 (841) | |
| Joash (Jehoash) – 837 (835) | |
| | 815 (814) – Jehoahaz |
| | 801 (798) – Jehoash (Joash) |
| Amaziah – 800 (796) | |
| | 786 (782) – Jeroboam II |

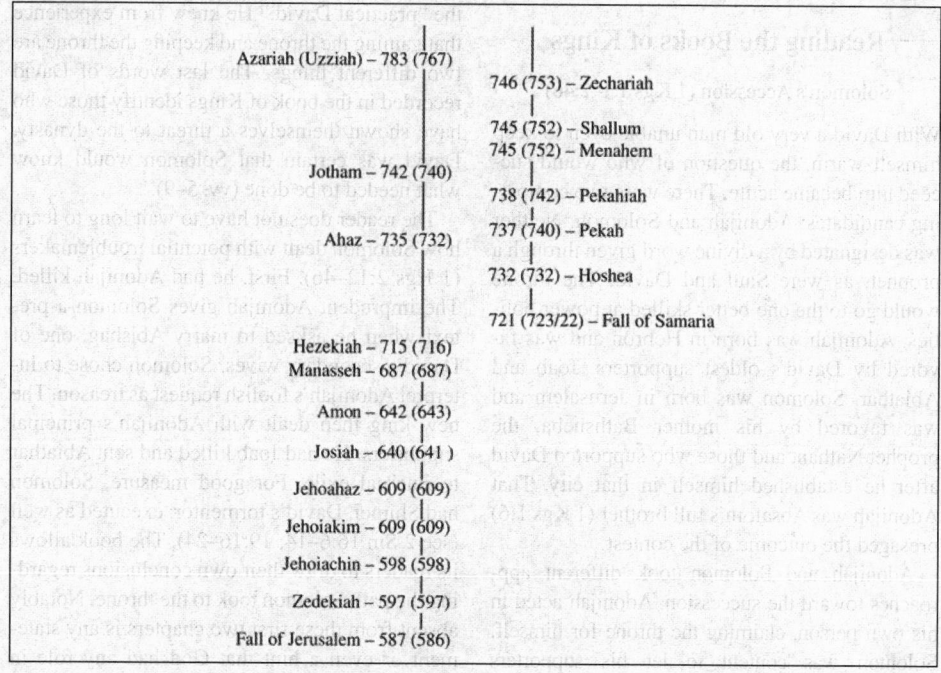

| | |
|---|---|
| Azariah (Uzziah) – 783 (767) | 746 (753) – Zechariah |
| | 745 (752) – Shallum |
| | 745 (752) – Menahem |
| Jotham – 742 (740) | |
| | 738 (742) – Pekahiah |
| | 737 (740) – Pekah |
| Ahaz – 735 (732) | |
| | 732 (732) – Hoshea |
| | 721 (723/22) – Fall of Samaria |
| Hezekiah – 715 (716) | |
| Manasseh – 687 (687) | |
| Amon – 642 (643) | |
| Josiah – 640 (641 ) | |
| Jehoahaz – 609 (609) | |
| Jehoiakim – 609 (609) | |
| Jehoiachin – 598 (598) | |
| Zedekiah – 597 (597) | |
| Fall of Jerusalem – 587 (586) | |

Deuteronomy. First Kings takes up where 2 Samuel 20 ended. It describes how the problem of the succession to David was resolved. The book then goes on to tell the story of the two Israelite kingdoms that arose following Solomon's death. The division between 1 and 2 Kings is artificial, because it is made in the middle of telling the story of King Ahaziah of Israel. Second Kings ends rather abruptly after telling of the parole of King Jehoiachin of Judah from prison in Babylon. The book allows readers to draw their own conclusions regarding the significance of this event. There is, then, no "happy ending" to the story of Israel in its land. What began with so much promise ends with great tragedy.

Certainly, the author of Kings used a variety of sources—from royal archives to prophetic legends—in composing his story. But in the form in which we read the book of Kings, it is probably the work of a single individual, writing during or shortly after the exile when the shape of Judah's future was unclear. The institutions that gave meaning to Israel's national and religious life were dead. The Temple of Jerusalem was in ruins and its priesthood scattered. The likelihood of a restoration of the Davidic dynasty seemed remote. The Israelite nation-states no longer existed. Their territory was simply incorporated into the conquering Mesopotamian empires. Imbued with the religious perspectives of the book of Deuteronomy, Kings clearly states that the downfall of Israel and Judah was a consequence of their disobedience; but it implies that Judah may still have a future—if it learns obedience.

The books of Kings are anything but objective. First, they reflect a clear bias in favor of Judah and so they write off the northern kingdom as a complete loss. Not a single monarch from the northern kingdom receives a positive evaluation. Second, Kings does praise a few kings of Judah although most are condemned. In the author's eyes, most kings promoted or at least allowed worship that did not reflect the uniqueness of Israel's God and the absolute loyalty that Israel owed to its divine patron. Third, the author was absolutely convinced of the centrality of the Torah in Israel's life with God. Every other religious institution is secondary to it. To make its theological points, the book uses speeches, prayers, and sometimes even editorial comments. Attention to these forms will help the reader become acquainted with the spin the book puts on the events it narrates.

## Reading the Books of Kings

### Solomon's Accession (1 Kgs 1:1–2:46)

With David a very old man unable even to keep himself warm, the question of who would succeed him became acute. There were two competing candidates: Adonijah and Solomon. Neither was designated by a divine word given through a prophet, as were Saul and David. The throne would go to the one better skilled at power politics. Adonijah was born in Hebron and was favored by David's oldest supporters, Joab and Abiathar. Solomon was born in Jerusalem and was favored by his mother Bathsheba, the prophet Nathan, and those who supported David after he established himself in that city. That Adonijah was Absalom's full brother (1 Kgs 1:6) presaged the outcome of the contest.

Adonijah and Solomon took different approaches toward the succession. Adonijah acted in his own person, claiming the throne for himself. Solomon was content to let his supporters manipulate his father into designating him as the successor to the throne. The book describes two simultaneous ceremonies, each of which was to inaugurate David's successor. The ceremonies took place near Jerusalem at two sites within shouting distance of each other. Adonijah chooses En-Rogel, a spring located at the juncture of the Hinnom and Kidron Valleys just south of Jerusalem, while Solomon had his ceremony at the Gihon Spring, Jerusalem's main water source, at the base of the eastern slope of David's city. Solomon was able to bring more people to his ceremony; after all, he was the candidate of the Jerusalem party. When Adonijah and his supporters heard the crowd acclaim Solomon as their king, they lost heart and fled. Adonijah submitted to Solomon's authority and begged for his life, which Solomon chose to spare.

With the succession settled, David makes his exit. Of course, a person as important as David must have some significant last words to say. The book provides David with a dual personality (1 Kgs 2:1–9). The first to speak is the "pious David" who charges his successor to be obedient to the written authoritative Torah, that is, the book of Deuteronomy. It will be through his obedience that Solomon will secure the throne for himself and his successors (vv. 2–4). Then it is the turn of the "practical David." He knew from experience that gaining the throne and keeping the throne are two different things. The last words of David recorded in the book of Kings identify those who have shown themselves a threat to the dynasty. David was certain that Solomon would know what needed to be done (vv. 5–9).

The reader does not have to wait long to learn how Solomon dealt with potential troublemakers (1 Kgs 2:12–46). First, he had Adonijah killed. The imprudent Adonijah gives Solomon a pretext when he asksed to marry Abishag, one of David's secondary wives. Solomon chose to interpret Adonijah's foolish request as treason. The new king then dealt with Adonijah's principal supporters. He had Joab killed and sent Abiathar to internal exile. For good measure, Solomon had Shimei, David's tormentor, executed as well (see 2 Sm 16:6–14; 19:16–24). The book allows its readers to draw their own conclusions regarding the path Solomon took to the throne. Notably absent from these first two chapters is any statement or even a hint that God had any role in Solomon's succession.

It is important to note the role that Bathsheba, Solomon's mother, played in his rise to the throne. After he became king, she enjoyed access to him and was seated near his throne at official functions (1 Kgs 2:19–20). The books of Kings name the mothers of 17 other kings: all but two kings of Judah (Jehoram and Ahaz) and two kings of Israel. This had led to the conclusion that the "queen mother" had an official position and exercised political and religious power. Unfortunately, the book does not provide the type of information that would permit firm conclusions to be drawn. That the author made it a point to mention the mother of 18 kings by name, however, makes it obvious that the "queen mother" enjoyed a specific rank and exercised some power—especially over domestic matters.

### Solomon's Reign (1 Kgs 3:1–11:43)

The account of Solomon's reign begins with an introductory statement that summarizes the book's ambivalence toward David's son (1 Kgs 3:1–3). On the one hand, the reader is told that Solomon "loved the LORD" (v. 3), fulfilling the great commandment of Deuteronomy (see Dt 6:5). But, on the other hand, he married a foreign princess and worshiped on the "high places."

The deuteronomic tradition takes a dim view of both patterns of behavior (see Dt 7:1–4; 1 Kgs 3:2–3, and 28 more times). Like Israel's life in the land, Solomon's reign will begin well enough but it will soon founder because of an unwillingness to be faithful to the most basic of the Torah's commands: absolute fidelity to Israel's God.

The book finally gets around to providing divine approval for Solomon's accession (1 Kgs 3:4–15). It does so by having God approve of Solomon's status as king through an appearance in a dream, which the Bible considers as one way that God communicates with human beings. The story reflects an ancient Near Eastern practice (called "incubation") of seeking an oracle by sleeping in a sanctuary after offering the prescribed sacrifices. Any dream experienced during this sleep was considered a revelation from the god honored at the sanctuary. The dream concerned Solomon's request for God's help in ruling Israel wisely. The request was granted. The book follows up the account of the dream with a tale illustrating Solomon's wisdom (1 Kgs 3:16–28). Solomon was able to settle a dispute between two women over an infant, because he knew that the true mother would sacrifice anything to ensure the welfare of her child.

The book pauses in its telling about Solomon's reign to include information about Solomon's administration, wealth, and wisdom (1 Kgs 4:1–5:14). In the past the people asked Samuel for a king to rule over them "like the nations." The book implies that the taxation, nepotism, and cronyism assure them that they have such a king. Deuteronomy requires that the king study the Torah so that he not "exalt himself over his kindred" (Dt 17:20). The list of the king's daily provisions (1 Kgs 5:1–5) certainly sounded more than extravagant to Judah's poor farmers. The divide between the royal establishment and the general population was becoming more pronounced. Still, 1 Kings 4:20 and 5:5 describe Solomon's reign as a time of peace and prosperity.

Just as Moses was associated with Torah and David with the Psalms, Solomon was remembered as a sage (see Prv 1:1; Sir 47:12). To conclude its initial portrait of Solomon, the book asserts that Solomon's wisdom was unsurpassed. His wisdom attracted admirers from all over the world (5:9–14). The reader recognizes that Solomon's court is far different from that of Saul—and even David.

**Building the Temple**

Next the book describes a project with which Solomon's name is always associated: the building of the Temple (1 Kgs 5:15–32). While the account implies that God ordained the project, building a temple was a royal prerogative in the ancient Near East. By erecting a temple to Israel's patron deity in Jerusalem, his capital, Solomon was asserting, in most dramatic form, his claim to Israel's throne. The book has Solomon explain that David did not build a temple because he was almost continuously at war (1 Kgs 5:17). Solomon also used good deuteronomic language as he said that he was going to build a temple "for the name of the LORD" (v. 19). The deuteronomic tradition usually avoided describing the Temple as God's dwelling place, preferring to speak of the Temple as the place for God's name (see Dt 12:11).

The book goes into some detail in describing the building of the Temple. It gives the date for both the beginning and the completion of the project (2 Kgs 6:1, 37) and describes the dimensions of the building and its three-part structure. The Temple was to have a porch, a nave, and a "holy of holies." The latter was a windowless room that was to contain the Ark of the Covenant, the symbol of the divine presence. In the holy of holies, there were to be two cherubim (1 Kgs 6:23–28). A cherub was a mythical, composite creature that had the face of a human being, the forequarters of a lion, the hindquarters of an ox, and wings of an eagle. (It is similar to the griffin or gryphon that is depicted in Western sculpture, including carvings on cathedrals.) The Ark of the Covenant would be placed between the two cherubim.

The Temple is presented as a most impressive building. Solomon spared no expense in its construction and ornamentation. He overlaid the entire structure with gold (1 Kgs 6:22). At the same time, however, the book offers an explanation for the eventual destruction of this structure. It presents God as warning Solomon that God will never forsake Israel, the dynasty, or the Temple if he keeps the commandments (1 Kgs 6:12). Kings will describe how Solomon and most of Israel's kings failed, leading God to abandon the Temple that Solomon built.

### Dedication of the Temple

With the Temple and its furnishings completed, all is ready for the building's dedication. The book provides an explanation (1 Kgs 8:1–9. 62–66) for a lengthy prayer that Solomon offers at the dedication. The framework describes the transfer of the Ark to the newly built Temple and the sacrifices offered there for the first time. The prayer, however, seems to prepare the reader for a world without a temple. The words of the prayer are, at times, in conflict with each other. Verses 10–13 speak about God's presence in the Temple, while verse 27 asserts that God cannot be contained in the building that Solomon has just built. The prayer also appears to transform the Temple from a place of sacrificial offerings (vv. 5 and 66) into a place of prayer where Israelite and non-Israelite alike can ask for forgiveness (vv. 42–43). Indeed, one does not even need to be present in the Temple to be heard by God. All that is necessary is that one prays in the direction of Jerusalem and its Temple (vv. 38:48; see Dn 6:11). The author of Kings composed this prayer to help his readers cope with the loss of the Temple.

The book uses another speech to reiterate its explanation for the disastrous end of the Davidic dynasty and the destruction of the Temple (1 Kgs 9:1–9). After all, the prayer of Solomon had just praised God for fulfilling the promise to David (1 Kgs 8:14–29) and celebrated the dedication of the Temple. God appears to Solomon and warns him that the future of the dynasty and the Temple depends on the fidelity of Israel's kings to the commandments and on Israel's exclusive loyalty to its ancestral God. The conclusion is obvious: the destruction of the Temple and the end of the dynasty did not occur because of any lack of fidelity on God's part. The people of Israel and their kings bear full responsibility for the fall of the two Israelite states and the exile of their people. Of course, the book wants its readers to recognize that the converse is true as well: obedience will bring God's blessing to the people and their land.

### Queen of Sheba

Next, the book describes the splendor of Solomon's reign by focusing on his wealth, wisdom, and chariot forces (1 Kgs 9:26–10:29). Eleven times the text mentions the gold that the king amassed. It also notes that the Queen of Sheba came to Jerusalem because of Solomon's renown as a sage. Sheba was located at the southwestern corner of the Arabian Peninsula and was likely one of Judah's trading partners. Goods passed between these two countries through the Red Sea port at Ezion Geber. According to an Ethiopian tradition, their country was Sheba and the results of the queen's visit to Solomon included her conversion to his religion and a son fathered by Solomon. This son visited his father and returned to Ethiopia with the Ark of the Covenant. While there is no biblical support for this tradition, it does explain the reason some people claim that the Ark of the Covenant is in Ethiopia.

### Judgment Against Solomon

From the book's perspective, the luster of all Solomon's achievements was tarnished by his failure to support the worship of the LORD alone. The reason offered for Solomon's infidelity was his marriage to non-Israelite women. Of course, the book is trying to promote marriage within the Judahite community as one way to maintain Judahite identity. To show the seriousness of Solomon's failure, the text has God speak to Solomon for a third and final time, announcing the end of the united Davidic-Solomonic kingdom and the rise of another Israelite national state, which will occur after Solomon's death (1 Kgs 11:1–13).

Kings concludes its story of Solomon's reign by mentioning three of Solomon's rivals (1 Kgs 11:14–40). The first is Hadad, king of Edom. Judah and Edom were perennial rivals for control of the southern part of the Levant, the eastern Mediterranean coast. The second was Rezon who was "king of Damascus," the capital of Aram (now in Syria). Israel and Aram struggled for many years for hegemony in the northern part of the Levant. The most serious threat, however, was an internal one. Jeroboam, one of Solomon's administrators, was supported in a bid for kingship by Egypt and with prophetic designation, threatening the rule of the Davidic dynasty. Although the rebellion was not successful at first, the book explains the origins of the two Israelite national states, Israel and Judah, as a

**Kingship** In the ancient Near East a king was viewed either as an "adopted" son of god (as in Mesopotamia) or as a god himself (as in Egypt). With absolute authority, kings maintained order, defended the nation from enemies, and dispensed justice. Kings also had important religious roles, so much so that kingship and priesthood were essentially flip sides of the same coin.

In many ways, Israel's kings resembled those of their neighbors: They led the military, upheld justice, maintained order, functioned as priests by offering sacrifice, and were considered the LORD's "adopted" sons. But in the area of absolute authority there was significant difference: Israel's kings were *not* absolute, for they too were under the law. In fact, the deuteronomistic writers define kingship as fearing the LORD and keeping the commandments. Israel's was more like a constitutional monarchy, in which the Law of Moses was the constitution that made demands even on the king.

**Prophecy** According to the book of Deuteronomy (18:9–22) prophets speak on God's behalf to both king and people. Primarily prophets *indict* and *warn*: they indict the king, and by extension the people, for not obeying God's commandments, and they warn the king and people of impending punishment in the hope of getting them to repent. The surest test of a true prophet, of course, is seeing whether or not the prophecy comes true (Dt 18:20–22). Consequently, the books of Kings repeatedly point out the fulfillment of specific prophecies. But while prophets may do miracles, their most important task is to motivate the people to worship only the one, true LORD (Dt 13).

consequence of Jeroboam's attempt to replace Solomon, who simply failed to observe the commandments and to worship the LORD alone. It is important to note that the book asserts that, despite Jeroboam, the Davidic dynasty continued in existence not only for the sake of David but also for the sake of Jerusalem. That city was destined to take on paramount importance for Judaism. The Temple, however, is not mentioned specifically. Also significant is the role played by the prophet Ahijah, who, like Samuel, pronounced words of judgment on the king. The book again was suggesting that Israel listen to the prophets sent to it.

### The Two Kingdoms
### (1 Kgs 12:1–2 Kgs 17:41)

The two Israelite national states arose in the Levant sometime in the ninth century B.C. Historians still have not arrived at a consensus as to the developments that led to their establishment. First Kings, however, describes the origins of the two Israelite states as the result of divine judgment on Solomon's rule, communicated by the prophet Ahijah. What Ahijah foretold was fulfilled almost immediately after Solomon's death and the accession of his son Rehoboam. But as it did with the origins of the monarchy, the book will describe the origins of the two Israelite national states in economic as well as religious terms (1 Kgs 12:1–25). Rehoboam refused to lighten the economic burdens that Solomon imposed on his subjects, and before Rehoboam was able to consolidate his hold on his father's realm, there was a revolution, which led to the establishment of the kingdom of Israel separate from the kingdom of Judah. When Rehoboam attempted to use military force against the rebellion, he was dissuaded by another prophetic word given through Shemiah.

While Kings implies that the Israelites had legitimate grievances, it does not approve of religious practices that it characterizes as obscuring the unity of Israel's ancestral deity, as violating the prohibition of images, and as ignoring the place that God chose. The book presents Jeroboam as fearing that the Jerusalem Temple would be a magnet, drawing the people to Jerusalem and to the Davidic dynasty. To counter this, Jeroboam built cultic centers at Dan at the extreme north of his kingdom and at Bethel in the extreme south (1 Kgs 12:26–33). The book makes its attitude toward these cultic centers absolutely clear when it depicts an unnamed "man of God" from Judah condemning the shrine at Bethel (1 Kgs 13:1–10). As the story of the northern kingdom unfolds, every king of Israel will be condemned for maintaining these shrines and continuing "the sin of Jeroboam."

First Kings concludes its treatment of Jeroboam by revisiting the theme of succession (1 Kgs 14:1–20). Abijah, Jeroboam's heir, fell ill and Jeroboam had his wife visit the prophet Ahijah in order to elicit a favorable oracle on behalf of the child. The prophet, however, predicted not only that the child was to die but also that Jeroboam's dynasty would end violently. Ahijah's speech is an intense and sometimes vulgar invective. While the prophet was not specific about Jeroboam's failures, he was quite specific about the king's future and that of the nation. He even blamed the exile on Jeroboam (v. 16).

The book intertwines narratives about the kings of the two Israelite national states until it tells of the fall of the northern kingdom to the Assyrians in 2 Kings 17. The two Israelite kingdoms were rivals at first. Disputes over their shared border were ongoing. The book notes that Israel and Judah fought continuously during the reigns of Jeroboam and Rehoboam (1 Kgs 14:30). Rehoboam also had to deal with a raid by Pharaoh Shishak, who had given asylum to Jeroboam during the reign of Solomon (1 Kgs 11:40). While the Egyptians were not in a position to reestablish their hegemony over the region, they raided 154 towns in the two kingdoms. Jerusalem was spared only because Rehoboam paid a large indemnity to Shishak (1 Kgs 14:26). The book characterizes Rehoboam's reign as a time of unfaithfulness (1 Kgs 14:21–24).

The book next turns its attention to the northern kingdom for most of the rest of 1 Kings (15:25–22:40).

### Elijah and Ahab

Ahab succeeded his father Omri as king in the northern kingdom. It was the first successful dynastic succession in the kingdom of Israel. From a military, economic, and political perspective, Ahab's reign was remarkably successful. His only defeat was the loss of Moab toward the end of his 22-year reign. Excavations at several cities in the north show that Ahab's reign was one of economic growth and military strength. His greatest military achievement took place at the battle of Qarqar, which the book ignores. Ahab led a coalition of small states that successfully engaged the Assyrians and prevented them from taking control of the region. Ahab led the largest force in the coalition. The book chooses to focus on Ahab's serious internal problems by introducing several stories about the prophets Elijah and Elisha. Both prophets were highly critical of the religious and social policies of Ahab and his successors.

Kings implies that his Phoenician wife Jezebel, who promoted the worship of Baal, caused Ahab's problems. The prophet Elijah forcefully opposed her. The conflict between Elijah and Ahab over Jezebel's activity dominates the portrait of Ahab in the Bible and makes it appear as if he were a weak and ineffective ruler, when in reality the opposite was true. The worship of Baal was attractive because this god was thought to provide the rain that made Israel's survival on its land possible. To show that Baal was unable to provide rain, Elijah announced a drought (1 Kgs 17:1). God's power to provide was obvious when a dry riverbed yielded water for the prophet and ravens brought him food. When the stream dried up again, the prophet went to beg in a Sidonian town. A poor widow from that town who took pity on the prophet never ran out of food despite the famine induced by the drought (1 Kgs 17:2–16). An even more remarkable demonstration of God's power occurred when the prophet brought the widow's deceased son back to life (1 Kgs 17:17–24).

Elijah finally met Ahab, who blamed the prophet for the drought. Of course, the reader knows that the fault lies with Ahab. While the confrontation with the prophets of Baal on Mt. Carmel was another indication of the power of Israel's God (1 Kgs 18:20–40), it was the prophet's prayer for rain that brought relief to the suffering people (1 Kgs 18:41–46). The rain that came on the land does not end the tension in the story, because Jezebel was determined to avenge Elijah's victory at Mt. Carmel. The prophet fled to the south, stopping at Beersheba, a town that abuts the Negev desert. After a brief pause, Elijah continued his journey until he reached Horeb, which is the name by which the deuteronomic tradition knows Mt. Sinai. At the place where the

Israelites experienced God's presence in a most dramatic way, the prophet experienced only God's absence until he realized God was present in a "light silent sound" (1 Kgs 19:12). God then commissioned the prophet to take specific steps to deal with the apostasy fomented by Israel's royal family. One of these steps was the anointing of a prophet to succeed him. Elijah found Elisha, whom the LORD had designated, and called him to his prophetic ministry (1 Kgs 19:13–21).

The book returns to the conflict between king and prophet as it tells the tale of Naboth's vineyard (1 Kgs 21:1–29). Again, it is Jezebel, Ahab's non-Israelite wife, who was responsible for the trouble. Ahab recognized that Naboth was within his rights in refusing to sell the king his vineyard. Jezebel, however, co-opted the elders of Naboth's city into convicting him on trumped up charges of blasphemy and treason. Naboth was executed and his property forfeited to the crown so Jezebel was able to present her husband with Naboth's vineyard. Of course, Elijah condemned this blatant injustice in God's name. Surprisingly, Ahab repented upon hearing the prophet's words of judgment and so God spared his life. Again, the book's message is obvious: if Israel listens to the prophets God sends to it, Israel's life will be spared as well.

But just as the book finished commending the prophetic word to Israel, it shows that discerning that word is not a simple matter. To do so the book describes preparations for a second war between Israel and Aram during the waning years of Ahab's reign (1 Kgs 22:1–28). This time Ahab sought help from Jehoshaphat, the king of Judah. Relations between the two Israelite states had steadily improved since the time of Ahab's father Omri. Indeed, Ahab offered his daughter in marriage to Jehoram, Jehoshaphat's son (2 Kgs 8:18). The king of Judah, however, suggested seeking a word from God before embarking on any campaign against the powerful Arameans. Ahab assembled 400 prophets to impress Jehoshaphat. After the 400 encouraged an attack, Jehoshaphat, apparently reluctant to fight the Arameans, asked if there were any more prophets who might be consulted. Ahab summoned Micaiah ben Imlah, who predicted an Aramean victory. Micaiah asserted that God put a "lying spirit" in the 400 prophets to insure that Ahab would be defeated. How then could prophecy be a reliable guide if God can inspire prophets to lie? The book assumes that the one reliable and unimpeachable guide to Israel's life is the written, authoritative Torah, the book of Deuteronomy. The attitude of Kings toward Ahab is evident from the description of what happened when Ahab's chariot was cleansed of the fallen king's blood (1 Kgs 22:38).

### Elisha

After describing the failures of Ahab and his son Ahaziah, at the very end of 1 Kings and the first chapter of 2 Kings, the author turns his attention back to Elijah and Elisha and the transition from the prophetic ministry of the former to that of the latter (2 Kgs 2:1–18). The book sees the succession of Elisha to the prophetic ministry as a genuine act of God. Perhaps a story with such spectacular details served to show that Elisha was a true witness to the God of Israel—as was Elijah—in contrast to the prophets that supported the house of Ahab (see 2 Kgs 3:13). Fifty "guild prophets" witnessed the passing of the prophetic mantle to Elisha (2 Kgs 2:15). Except for 1 Kings 20:35, these "guild prophets" are always mentioned in connection with Elisha and may have been his supporters against the king and his prophets. The book concludes its introduction to the cycle of stories about Elisha with two tales that encourage Israel to obey the prophets sent to it (2 Kgs 2:19–25).

The book shifts the focus of its story away from kings and international political conflicts to ordinary folk in need—people whose names are never given (2 Kgs 4:1–44). Elisha, whom this chapter refers to as a "man of God," responds to those needs with compassion. While the effect on the reader is to wonder at the miracle-working power of Elisha, the stories do not even hint that the man of God worked these miracles to establish his reputation. The book implies that Elisha did what the kings were supposed to do: respond to the needs of the lowly and poor. In fact, the reason ordinary people were in need was the economic and political policies of the monarchy. God redresses this injustice through Elisha. The prophetic task is not simply to speak words of judgment on injustice but to undo the effects of the greed that creates poverty.

### Story of Naaman

With the story of Naaman, Elisha moved back into the arena of international politics (2 Kgs 5:1–19). This is the second time the book has told a tale of someone searching for healing in a foreign country. In 2 Kings 1, it was King Ahaziah of Israel looking for healing in Ekron from Baal-Zebub. In 2 Kings 5, it is Naaman from Aram who looked for healing in Israel. Whereas the healings in 2 Kings 4 took place because of Elisha's compassion for those in need, here there is an overt apologetic purpose: The Aramean general Naaman was to learn that there was a prophet in Israel who could heal in the name of Israel's God. There is also a homiletic point to the story. Naaman is a model for Israel. Although reluctant at first, the Aramean general obeyed the prophet and was healed. Israel surely should obey the prophets sent to it. Two more stories with a clear homiletic thrust follow (2 Kgs 5:20–6:7). Both stories concern the prophet's followers. In the first, Gehazi seeks to reap a monetary profit from his association with Elisha and is duly punished for his avarice. In the second, Elisha's supporters find themselves in an embarrassing situation, which the prophet resolves. The book warns against corruption.

### Siege of Samaria

The circumstances change abruptly in the story of Ben-Hadad's siege of Samaria (2 Kgs 6:24–33). A siege sought to force surrender by cutting off the supply of food. Ben-Hadad's siege of the Israelite capital was working, as is evident from the horrific details that the book gives (vv. 28–29). The king, of course, did not accept responsibility for Samaria's troubles; he blamed the prophet whom the book describes as cowering behind a closed door in fear of the king's anger. The Aramean threat was a sign of things to come. Aram here is an instrument of divine judgment on Israel's abandonment of their faith, or apostasy—apostasy that continued ceaselessly. But Israel's time had not yet come, so 2 Kings 7:1–20 tells of the lifting of the Aramean siege of Samaria. The book makes it clear that the lifting of the siege and the relief of Samaria were not the work of Israel's military. God's power lifted the siege and four lepers by sheer happenstance opened the way to the city's relief from the famine. The book shows readers that Israel's God shapes human events through the prophetic word. Just as easily as God made Aram a threat to Israel, God removed that threat. This is another hint to the book's first readers that God could end their exile.

The epilogue to the story of Elisha and the woman of Shunem (2 Kgs 8:1–6; see 2 Kgs 5:8–37) is unusual on two counts. First, the prophet did not directly solve her problem. In fact, she was suffering economic privation precisely because she followed the prophet's instructions to relocate from Israel. Upon returning, she found her property had been confiscated. Still, just the power of the prophet's fame was enough to solve her problem. Second, it was the king who restored the woman's property. For once, an Israelite king did act for the benefit of those in need. The book illustrates the power of God to extricate people from difficult situations. That power is such that it can lead people to act contrary to their normal patterns to bring about the fulfillment of the divine will. In a sense, the woman of Shunem is Israel in microcosm. She experienced exile, loss, and eventually restoration. What happened to her, the book implies, can happen to Israel as well. It too can experience restoration after exile.

### Jehu's Revolution

To illustrate the disintegration of the kingdom of Israel, the book describes a revolution that brought an end to the house of Omri (2 Kgs 9:1–10:22)—a revolution so bloody that it was still remembered with horror a century later (see Hos 1:4–5). According to Kings, Jehu's revolution was set in motion by the apostasy and injustice practiced by Israel's kings, and the terrible end of these kings reflects the prophetic judgment on their actions (1 Kgs 14:11; 16:4; 21:19–24). The book then presents Jehu's revolution not in political but theological terms, so it begins with the prophet Elisha's naming of Jehu, an officer in Jehoram's army, as the one to replace the king. After Jehu assassinated Jehoram of Israel and Ahaziah of Judah, he turned to Jezebel, who taunted him as no better than Zimri, the assassin who was king of Israel for just seven days (see 1 Kgs 16:15–19). Jezebel shared the fate of her son Jehoram at Jehu's hand (1 Kgs 9:1–27).

Jehu had to eliminate claimants to the throne with better credentials. His revolutionary goals were to take Jehoram's place on the throne and end the Phoenician influence over the kingdom of Israel. To secure his throne, Jehu purged the entire royal family (10:1–11, 15–17) and to eliminate Phoenician influence, he killed the prophets of Baal and destroyed their temple (10:18–27). Because he also killed Ahaziah of Judah, Jehu had to deal with a force from the southern kingdom seeking to avenge Ahaziah. But the book does not tell the story of Jehu's action to give an accurate picture of the progress of his revolution. The book wishes to describe the religious significance of that revolution. From this perspective, for all his brutal thoroughness, Jehu was a failure. He did not follow the LORD when he was king but followed the pattern of apostasy as set by Jeroboam. Because of this sin, Jehu did not stop Israel's slide to oblivion. Like his predecessors, Jehu witnessed Israel's power diminishing. More territory was lost—probably to Aram. Israel's destruction was just a matter of time (2 Kgs 10:28–36).

### Kingdom of Israel

The downward spiral of the Kingdom of Israel continued during the 17-year reign of Jehoahaz (2 Kgs 13:1–9). Almost constant warfare between Israel and Aram led to the severe depletion of Israel's army (v. 7). Total disaster was averted by an unidentified "savior" (v. 5). It is likely that this savior came in the form of the Assyrian army that invaded Aram at the end of the ninth century, easing the pressure on Israel. With this account of Israel's deteriorating military power, the book begins its description of the fall of the house of Jehu. The end of Jehu's dynasty is inevitable because of the continuing apostasy of Israel's kings (v. 2).

Israel enjoyed a temporary respite from military reverses at the hand of the Arameans during the reign of Jehoash (2 Kgs 13:10–35). Before Elisha died, he predicted a revival of Israel's military fortunes. The short note about the revival of a corpse that touched the bones of the dead prophet illustrates how the prophetic word can bring life to the sick body of Israel, because God's saving will did not wish to bring the full force of judgment upon God's people. Tangible proofs of that were the victories of Jehoash and his recovery of Israelite territory lost to Aram.

### Reign of Jeroboam II

Although the book dismisses the 4-year reign of Jeroboam II in a few verses, it cannot ignore it completely (2 Kgs 14:23–29). Jeroboam had notable success in expanding the boundaries of his kingdom, which the book usually considers a sign of God's blessing. Here it asserts that Jeroboam's success was the fulfillment of a prophetic word given by Jonah. Although there is a book ascribed to Jonah in the collection of the prophets, the oracle given to Jeroboam is not preserved in that book or anywhere in the Bible. Kings goes on to explain the success of Jeroboam by claiming that it was the result of God's compassion on Israel (vv. 26–27). Although Jeroboam's reign is often described as a time of peace and prosperity, it was not. The expansion of Israel's territory had to come by way of war. His building projects put a strain on the country's resources that eventually led to the severe economic problems that Israel faced following Jeroboam's death. The chasm between rich and poor grew during Jeroboam's time.

Like Jeroboam II, Azariah of Judah enjoyed a very long reign, although it was marred by a skin disease that rendered him unable to perform rituals that were reserved to the king (2 Kgs 15:1–7). His son Jotham assumed many of Azariah's duties. Although the book praises Azariah, this praise is tempered by the comment that he did nothing about the high places, which the author of the book considered illegitimate. Under Azariah, the kingdom of Judah enjoyed a resurgence, which the book chooses to ignore because it does not reflect its notion of the direction in which Judah is heading.

Following the long reign of Jeroboam II, the northern kingdom began a rush to its total collapse. The text gives little more than the basic outline of a nation devolving into political chaos in the final years of its existence. The book provides few details about the reigns of these five kings, because it is more interested in the fate of Israel as a nation, whose doom it is describing. The five kings each receive the usual condemnation that is given to all the kings of the north, and their individual fates presage the disaster that the northern kingdom would experience.

### The Apostasy of Ahaz

The book has no regard for Ahaz, condemning him without reservation (2 Kgs 16:1–20). Ahaz's desperation in the face of the invasion by the combined forces of Aram and Israel is evident from his resorting to child sacrifice as a way to gain divine favor. Ahaz's situation was grievous, because he had to face hostilities on two fronts since the Edomites were moving in the south (v. 6) and Aram and Israel were coming from the north. This military pressure led Ahaz to align himself with Tiglath-Pileser, to whom he paid a large indemnity. The Assyrian king quickly put an end to the coalition seeking to depose Ahaz. Kings then describes in great detail changes that Ahaz made to the Temple and its altar, modeling the Temple after the Assyrians' altar in Damascus. These are regarded as acts of apostasy (vv. 10–20).

With the account of Ahaz's reign completed, the book returns to Israel, which was on the brink of total collapse. After narrating the events that led to the end of Israel's political existence (2 Kgs 17:1–6), the book launches into a long editorial comment to explain the fall of the northern kingdom as a consequence of its failure to shape its national life on the basis of the Torah (2 Kgs 17:7–23).

### The Final Years of the Kingdom of Judah (2 Kgs 18:1–25:30)

After describing the fall of the northern kingdom, the book details the last years of the southern kingdom. The account begins with the story of Hezekiah, a king that it greatly admired because of his obedience to the Torah and his destruction of the high places. Hezekiah was able to augment Judah's territories at the expense of the Philistines. In contrast to Israel, Judah and its king appeared to be prospering (2 Kgs 18:1–12). However, the Assyrians ended Hezekiah's peace by invading Judah and besieging Jerusalem. Although Hezekiah offered an indemnity to Sennacherib, the Assyrian king, the siege continued. Sennacherib demanded the surrender of Jerusalem, claiming that Judah's own patron deity had ordered him to conquer the country (2 Kgs 18:1–37, esp. v. 25).

In his despair, Hezekiah turned to the prophet Isaiah, who assured him that Sennacherib would lift the siege and return to his country (v. 7). For reasons that are not clear to historians, the Assyrian army did retreat and Sennacherib was assassinated later—just as the prophet predicted (2 Kgs 19:1–37). Of course, Kings sees the lifting of the siege as an act of God. The final episode in Hezekiah's story puts the king's reputation under a cloud. Although God healed him and promised him a longer reign, Hezekiah wanted proof that the promises made to him by Isaiah would be fulfilled. The arrival of an ambassador from Babylon gave Isaiah the opportunity to announce Judah's approaching defeat and exile. Instead of this announcement moving Hezekiah to repentance, the king expressed relief that the disaster would come after he was gone. It is as if Hezekiah learned nothing from the near disaster brought about by the Assyrians (2 Kgs 20:1–21).

His son Manasseh succeeded Hezekiah. From the point of view of Kings, Judah never fell so low as it did during the 55-year reign of this king. It accuses Manasseh of apostasy, idolatry, and murder, and explicitly identifies him as the Judahite Ahab, leading the southern kingdom to disaster as Ahab had in the northern kingdom. Unnamed prophets pronounced divine judgment on Manasseh's actions. There is no doubt that Manasseh kept his throne by demonstrating his loyalty to the Assyrians, in part by introducing Assyrian religious rituals to the Jerusalem Temple.

Manasseh was succeeded by his son Amon, who continued his father's policies. This led to his assassination by his own courtiers. Evidently the assassination of yet another king provoked the ordinary folk, who supported the Davidic dynasty. They likely believed that another round of assassinations would be the end of Judah, so they killed the conspirators and installed Amon's young son, Josiah, as king (2 Kgs 21:19–26). It was during Josiah's reign that Judah made one last attempt at reform, although it proved to be too late to avert divine judgment.

Josiah's reign was a short pause as Judah moved to the inevitable (2 Kgs 22:1–23:30). Kings describes Josiah as a monarch who "pleased the LORD" (2 Kgs 22:2). A critical event in Josiah's reign was the discovery of a book in the course of renovations that were being made on the Temple. The author of Kings wants readers to assume that the "book of the Law" was what we know as the book of Deuteronomy. Josiah responded to hearing the words of the book with a gesture of repentance. He had the book authenticated by a prophet. Although Jeremiah was active at this time, the prophet consulted was an otherwise unknown woman named Huldah. She authenticated the book but announced that the curses on the unfaithful found in the book would fall on Judah and Jerusalem, although not in Josiah's time.

Fortunately for Josiah, he came into power about the time Assyria's control over the Levant was waning, so he moved quickly to reclaim Judah's sovereignty in matters of religion and politics. The book concentrates on Josiah's actions in the sphere of religious practice. The king took action against all types of non-Yahwistic religious activity and promoted traditional practices such as the Passover. His move into the north was likely prompted by a determination to take advantage of Assyria's weakness to extend the territory under his control. Josiah's attempts to reassert and expand Judahite sovereignty ended when he died during an ill-advised attempt to involve himself in international politics. He endeavored to stop the Egyptian army as it was advancing into Mesopotamia and was killed in battle. Josiah's reform died with him, because Judah once again came under foreign domination. The Egyptians asserted their control over Judah by deposing Josiah's successor Jehoahaz and exiling him to Egypt. They placed another of Josiah's sons, Eliakim, on the throne, changing his name to Jehoiakim. (2 Kgs 23:31–35). Judah had to pay an indemnity to the Egyptians. This, of course, burdened Judah's economy, which had been already made fragile by Josiah's military adventures.

Jehoiachin succeeded his father just as the Babylonian siege of Jerusalem was about to end with the city's surrender and the sacking of the Temple. While Judah was able to maintain the appearance of sovereignty, it was more firmly under Babylon's control than ever. Jehoiachin was deposed and exiled along with many of Judah's leading citizens. The Babylonians placed Mattaniah, another of Josiah's sons, on the throne, changing his name to Zedekiah. The book lets the events speak for themselves, as Judah's final collapse appears to be imminent. Zedekiah was to be the last king of the Davidic line. He managed to keep his throne for 11 years. No longer able to resist calls to rebel against Babylonian domination, Zedekiah sealed the fate of the dynasty and the kingdom. The Babylonians responded to his rebellion by taking Jerusalem a second time, killing Zedekiah's sons, blinding the king, and leading him into exile. Zedekiah was never heard from again (2 Kgs 24:18–25:7).

Jerusalem too paid for Zedekiah's folly in revolting against Nebuchadnezzar. The city was put to the torch and its Temple was left in ruins. Many of Jerusalem's leading citizens were executed and the rest were deported to Babylon. And so ends the story of Israel in its land.

As an epilogue, Kings mentions the parole of Jehoiachin from prison in Babylon (2 Kgs 25:27–30). Unfortunately, the book does not reflect on the significance of the exiled king's new status for Judah's future. At the most critical moment in his story, the author of Kings is inexplicably reticent, leaving the reader to wonder what will become of Judah and Jerusalem. Is the divine judgment brought on by Judah's failure to be loyal to the LORD and shape its life according to Torah final? Perhaps Jehoiachin's parole is a harbinger of Judah's rehabilitation. Unfortunately, the book does not give an explicit answer to these questions. The books of Kings end on a most ambiguous note, requiring readers to make sense out of a tragic tale.

## Continuing Significance of the Books of Kings

Like the other books that make up the deuteronomistic history of Israel, the books of Kings put in sharp focus the consequences of failing to remain absolutely committed to the LORD and to the pattern of life given to Israel in the book of Deuteronomy. The book illustrates a continuing pattern of failure to live responsibly. Although Kings focuses almost exclusively on the actions of the ruling class, its message was certainly intended for a wider audience. These books remind believers today that they bear a responsibility to act on the Word. Election offers no guarantees; rather, it calls believers to greater commitment. The books of Joshua to 2 Kings tell a sad and tragic story. What began with so much hope ends in disaster. It is not a pleasant story—especially in 2 Kings when it becomes clear that the two Israelite kingdoms are headed toward self-destruction. But the reader today knows that Jerusalem's fall, the end of the national state, and the collapse of all Judahite religious and political institutions were not the end of the story. God's mercy triumphed over God's justice and a renewed Judah emerged from the exile. The story of Israel in its land makes it absolutely clear that God's moral demands must be taken seriously. Failing to do so brings disaster. But despite this, believers recognize that God is still love.

**Questions for Discussion and Reflection**

***Group Sharing/Discussion***

1. Newly anointed King Solomon prayed, "Give your servant, therefore, a listening heart to judge your people and to distinguish between good and evil." (1 Kgs 3:9) What are some signs of Solomon acting wisely in governing his people? When a leader today exercises power, what would be signs of wisdom in his leadership?

2. Despite his wisdom, Solomon slipped when he turned to false worship of foreign gods. (1 Kgs 11:1–2) What were the personal (internal) and social (external, cultural) reasons for his sin?

3. What parts of Kings do you find most interesting? Which are most lesson-filled for you? Explain.

***In Our Lives***

1. After Elijah walked 40 days and nights to the mountain of God, Horeb, the LORD said to him, "Go out and stand on the mountain before the LORD; the LORD will pass by" (1 Kgs 19:11ff). God could have come in the fire, or the wind, or the earthquake. But for Elijah God's presence came in the stillness of silence. In our lives, too, God is present. Reflect on when and how you recognize God's presence. How do such things as silence, retreat, and fasting help in this regard? How can our parish encourage such times of stillness for its busy community members?

2. Elijah and Elisha were passionate prophets proclaiming to the leaders and people of Israel that Yahweh is their God and keeping his covenant means not worshiping false gods. Who are the prophets in your world reminding you of God's love and commands? Remember, also, that at baptism you are called to become a prophet. How do you live this call in your world?

3. Israel's and Judah's kings and people were fascinated with worshiping false gods. What were the attractions of the pagan religions for God's chosen people? Why were they easily led astray? Where, in today's society, do you see signs of idolatry?

***Individual/Personal Reflection/Action***

1. Elijah, faithful to the LORD's covenant, lived in solidarity with the poor people. He denounced Queen Jezebel and Kings Ahab and Ahaziah for worshiping false gods. These powerful leaders wanted to kill and silence him for speaking out against them. Look at your world through the justice lenses of Elijah. What do you see? Whom would you support and whom would you denounce or challenge? What do you do to promote a just society? Talk with your parish staff about ways you could be more effective in this regard.

2. The story of Elisha feeding a hundred hungry men (2 Kgs 4:42–44) reminds us of the stories of Jesus feeding the hungry crowd (Mt 14:13ff; 15:32ff; Mk 6:30ff; Lk 9:10ff; Jn 6:1ff). It is important to feed the body. It is just as important to feed our soul, our spirit, with hope, with love, with faith. What are your times, the opportunities, and the resources for this spiritual feeding? How can you pay more attention to this care and feeding of yourself?

3. Were the LORD's expectations of the chosen people higher than the expectations of the other nations? Are God's expectations of you different from those of others in your life? What about the expectations of your country?

# THE CHRONICLER'S HISTORY AND THE LATER HISTORIES

## 1 AND 2 CHRONICLES READING GUIDE

### *At a Glance*

| | |
|---|---|
| Who are the main players? | David Solomon Hezekiah Josiah the chronicler |
| What should I look for? | Although the chronicler tells the story of Israel's past, the real purpose is to sketch out the prospects of Israel's future. The legitimacy of restored Judah's cultic institutions and continuity with the past are what count. |
| When did this take place? | From Adam to the fifth century B.C. following the restoration of the Jerusalem Temple after the Babylonian Exile, which lasted from 587 to 539 B.C. |
| Where did these events occur? | In the land of Israel, but mainly in Judah and Jerusalem. |
| Why was this book written? | Judah's religious institutions and their continuity with the past are critical for its future. The one aim of the work is to defend the legitimacy of the Temple of Jerusalem and the significance of its worship for Israel's life. |
| What is the story? | Although beginning with Adam, Chronicles' first nine chapters are genealogical lists without narrative material. The narrative begins with David, which is the chronicler's way of saying Israel's story really begins with David. His selected use and analysis of Israel's history reveals the chronicler's religious message: Israel will secure its future only by worshiping God according to the pattern set by David at God's direction. |

The first book of Chronicles is part of a larger work that includes the second book of Chronicles, Ezra, and Nehemiah. This "chronicler's history"—which was assembled after the return from exile, and which was probably not written by one person or one small group—begins with Adam (1 Chr 1:1) and concludes with the writer's own day, the fifth century, following the restoration of the Jerusalem Temple after the Babylonian Exile (587 to 539 B.C.).

Like Genesis 1, the chronicler's history begins with Adam, but it repeats none of the stories found in the priestly history. Chapters 1–9 are little more than genealogical lists taken from Bible texts and other sources available to the author. The narrative material begins with the story of Saul's death and burial (10:1–14). This, perhaps,

**Cult** The ritual and religious practices at a temple or other place of worship.

is the chronicler's way of stating that Israel's story really begins with David, Saul's successor as king.

Like the deuteronomistic history of Israel (Joshua, Judges, Samuel, and Kings, with Deuteronomy as its preface), the chronicler's history tells the story of the Israelite kingdoms and their fall. This second history tries to explain why they fell. Even though the chronicler tells the story of Israel's past, the author's real purpose is to sketch out the prospects for Israel's future.

For the chronicler, what really counts is the validity of Judah's cultic institutions and their continuity with the past. The author wanted to defend David's dynasty and the Temple of Jerusalem. By presenting the Judah of the chronicler's day as a worshiping community that was a direct extension of the community that God had established centuries before, the author aimed to show that Israel could secure its future by continuing to worship God according to the pattern set by David. Israel's hope, then, resided not in the revelation that a messiah could guarantee its future, but in the belief that careful observance of the cultic institutions, handed down by Judah's priests, would be its security. These cultic institutions were kept alive by the remnant that survived the exile and returned to Jerusalem. For the chronicler, the exile was just an unfortunate interruption in the otherwise unbroken history of the worshiping community of Judah.

The Septuagint (the ancient Greek translation of the Hebrew Bible) entitled the books of Chronicles "Paraleipomenon" ("that which was left out"). This was also the name used in the Douay-Rheims version and some other Roman Catholic versions. Those responsible for the Septuagint considered Chronicles a sort of supplement to the books of Samuel and Kings. The placement of these books differs in Bibles used by Jews. In Christian Bibles, the Old Testament ends with the prophets. The final text is Malachi's prophecy of the return of Elijah, who will announce the "day of the LORD" (Mal 3:23f). The Church reads a messianic meaning in this text and identifies John the Baptist, the precursor of Jesus, as the returning Elijah (Mt 1:1–14; 17:11–13). But in the Hebrew Bible arranged by the rabbis, the prophetic books follow the books of Moses (the Torah or the Pentateuch), because the early rabbis viewed the prophets as explainers of the Torah. The Hebrew Bible has a third part called the "Writings," a collection of books that belong to neither the Torah nor the Prophets. The last books of this collection are 1 and 2 Chronicles. Thus the Hebrew Bible ends with the decree of Cyrus (2 Chr 36:23) that calls for the people of Judah to return to Jerusalem and rebuild the Temple there.

## Reading the First Book of Chronicles

The first book of Chronicles has a very simple arrangement: Chapters 1–9:34 are extensive genealogy lists; chapters 9:35–29:30 tell the story of David.

### The Genealogies

The genealogies of Chronicles extend from Adam to the return from the Babylonian Exile. The author uses the genealogies from the book of Genesis in his own tables that begin with the descent from Adam to Abraham. From there the focus is on the 12 sons of Jacob. The chronicler arrives at the centerpiece of his presentation, the family of Judah, one of Jacob's 12 sons. The author traces Judah's descendants down to David and his relatives. Chapter 3 lists David's descendants, all the kings of the Davidic dynasty and their descendants, into the period after the Babylonian Exile. The genealogies of the other tribes follow but are not as extensive as the one for Judah, except for the tribe of Levi. The chronicler had a special interest in the priestly tribe of Levi and the cult that they administered. Finally, the genealogies of Saul's descendants frame a list of those who returned from the Babylonian Exile. From this reading one is left with the impression that the true beginning of Israel was not at Sinai with the giving of the Torah, as the priestly history would have it, but with the rise of David.

### The History of David's Reign

This section begins with a report on Saul's death and burial (10:1–12), along with a short editorial comment on the dangers Saul's reign posed for

Israel because Saul was not faithful to God. Saul is little more than a figure of contrast for David, whose portrait the chronicler painted with strokes of piety and fidelity.

The chronicler wanted to make David's rise to power more impressive than the version found in the deuteronomic history (2 Sm 1–20), one of the sources he used. For example, 2 Samuel states that only "the men of Judah" anointed David as king of their tribe following Saul's death; David ruled over Judah seven years before the elders of Israel chose him as king over the rest of the tribes (2 Sm 5:1–5). The chronicler, however, states that "all Israel" made David king immediately following Saul's death (1 Chr 11:1–3). And while the deuteronomic historian paints David's decision to bring the Ark into Jerusalem as a decision made by David alone, the chronicler portrays the same event as an act approved by all the people. The Ark's entrance into Jerusalem highlights the role of the Levites as David appoints them to carry it into the city. And since the king also commissions them to be singers in the Temple, they sing a psalm. The deuteronomic history does not contain these details. The rest of David's story is devoted to the plans for the building of the Temple, which Solomon, David's son, would eventually carry out. This makes Solomon a central figure in the chronicler's story.

The negative features of the story of David and Solomon that are recorded by the deuteronomic historian are omitted in the chronicler's version. Nothing is said about how Solomon succeeded David as king (2 Sm 12:1–12; 1 Kgs 1–2). Nothing is said about David's adultery with Bathsheba and the prophet Nathan's condemnation of David (2 Sm 12:1–12). Nor does the chronicler make mention of the two revolts against David (2 Sm 15–18; 20:1–22).

Solomon's role is to complete the work David began. This seems to be a deliberate effort by the chronicler to imitate the transition from Moses to Joshua (Dt 21 and Jos 1). The author considered Solomon's succession to David as important as Joshua's succession to Moses.

**Shalom** The Hebrew word for peace. It is reflected in the name Solomon, in Hebrew, *Shelomo.* A contrast is drawn between Solomon, the peaceful man, and David, who waged great wars. David was prevented from building the Temple not only because all his time was taken up in battle but also because he shed much blood, which made him ritually unfit for the task.

### The Establishment of the Temple

The chronicler paints the portraits of David and Solomon so as to underscore their respective roles in the establishment of the Temple and its liturgy. Worship then is one of the chronicler's principal concerns. The God who is present in Judah's experience evokes a response in worship from the people whose destiny this God guides. The chronicler tries to show that Judah's future is dependent upon its faithfulness to the proper forms of worship that God has revealed through David. There is a reciprocal relationship between God and Judah: God blesses Judah and Judah worships God.

For the chronicler, the Temple and its liturgy were symbols of God's continuing presence among the people of Judah. As long as the priests offered the correct sacrifices at the appropriate times in the presence of a grateful people, the LORD would dwell in Judah's midst. For the chronicler, the history of Israel was not a series of unrelated actions by kings and prophets. Its heart was the worship led by the priests appointed by Moses and David. The chronicler recognized that there were times when Judah's sin led to serious failures to offer proper worship, but Judah's sin was never fatal. Judah was always able to recover, resume proper liturgical services, and be certain of God's abiding presence. The fall of Jerusalem and the exile to Babylon formed an unfortunate interruption in an otherwise unbroken history of Judah as a community that offered legitimate worship to its ancestral deity. The only way to avoid a similar disaster in the future was to worship God in the Jerusalem Temple according to rituals that went back to those developed by David.

### The Importance of the Temple

For proper worship of the LORD, a Temple was indispensable. Like the books of Kings, Chronicles recognizes the legitimacy of only one temple—the Temple at Jerusalem. At the time of

| The Priests (chief religious officials) | The Levites ("lower clergy") |
|---|---|
| Duties: blow the trumpets, minister in inner sanctuary, offer sacrifice on the altar, burn incense | Duties: carry the Ark, singers, gatekeepers, judges, prophets, fund raisers |

| Temple Slaves |
|---|
| Duty: to help the Levites |

the composition of the chronicler's history, the worshipers of Israel's ancestral god were not unanimous in recognizing Jerusalem's Temple as the only legitimate place of worship. There was a temple dedicated to the LORD in Samaria, and at Elephantine (a Jewish military colony located on an island near the modern city of Aswan in Egypt). In telling the story of the northern kingdom, the chronicler does not even mention the sanctuaries at Dan or Bethel that Jeroboam I built (see 1 Kgs 12:26–29). For the chronicler there could be only one Temple. David planned and Solomon built this Temple under the same kind of divine guidance that led Moses to build the Tabernacle in the wilderness. The LORD gave David the plans for the Temple in Jerusalem (1 Chr 28:19). No other sanctuary could be a legitimate place to worship the God of Israel.

### The Temple Personnel

Chapters 23–27 are important for the chronicler's general purpose; proper worship and proper personnel to conduct the liturgy are described in detail. The division of duties among the priests, the Levites, and the Temple slaves is shown here.

First Chronicles concludes with David passing both the kingship and the responsibility for constructing the Temple on to Solomon. According to the chronicler, Solomon was anointed king even before David's death.

## Roman Catholic Priesthood

THE SACRAMENT OF Orders in the Roman Catholic Church is largely a part of our heritage from ancient Israel. The rituals of ordination recognize this heritage. The division of orders in the Roman Catholic Church into the episcopacy, presbyterate, and diaconate mirrors to some extent the chronicler's division of Temple personnel into priests, Levites, and Temple slaves. Of course the status, role, and interrelationships of the orders in the Church are different from those of the Old Testament's cultic personnel, since they descend from the leaders of the early church—bishops or overseers (*episcopos*), priests or elders (*presbyteres*), and deacons (*diakonos*). The church also sees a sacramental connection between the priesthood of Jesus and the ordained priesthood. The concern in the Church for a hierarchy among the people directly concerned with worship is similar to that of the chronicler.

There is not a single instance in the New Testament of anyone called a "priest" presiding at Christian worship. It is the chronicler (and even more the Priestly strand of the Pentateuch, especially Leviticus and Numbers) who tries to make the reader sensitive to the presence of God in the act of sacrificial worship led by "official" ministers. For the chronicler the priests and Levites were those through whom God's abiding presence among the people was evident. The rituals they conducted were a source of blessing for the people and an act of devotion to their God. The chronicler's God was not a hidden God. The people experienced God in worship more than anywhere else. It should be clear that the value that the Church places on the liturgy and priesthood finds a strong support in the chronicler's history.

## Reading the Second Book of Chronicles

### Chronicles and the Israelite Kingdoms

The second book of Chronicles continues the story of Israel with the accession of Solomon to the throne of David. Comparing the way Chronicles tells this story with the books of Kings helps to see the purpose of the chronicler. For example, after Solomon's death and the breakup of the Davidic-Solomonic empire into the two national states of Israel and Judah, the chronicler all but ignores the northern kingdom (Israel) and its kings. He focuses his attention on the southern kingdom (Judah). The chronicler mentions Israel only when the story of Judah makes it necessary to do so. The chronicler wishes to focus on the Davidic dynasty and its finest achievement: the Temple in Jerusalem. Also, the chronicler's treatment of Judah's kings focuses almost entirely on the promotion of legitimate worship and the performance of the proper ritual.

### Solomon

The story of Solomon (2 Chr 1–9) deals exclusively with the building of the Temple as envisioned by David. Again the chronicler does not repeat the negative aspects of Solomon's story that 1 Kings recounts. For example, the chronicler omits the details about how Solomon secured his throne by executing potential opponents, including his half brother Adonijah (1 Kgs 2). Also unmentioned is Solomon's marriage to the daughter of Pharaoh (1 Kgs 3:1) and other non-Israelite women (1 Kgs 11:1–13). Throughout the description of Solomon's achievement in building and dedicating the Temple, the chronicler reminds his readers of David's preparations (2:6, 13, 16; 3:1; 5:1; 6:3–11). In the eyes of the chronicler, the Temple was the combined enterprise of David and Solomon, who each made his own contribution to the completion of this great work.

### The Kingdom of Judah

The remaining chapters of the book (10–36) retell the history of Judah to the Babylonian Exile from the singular perspective of the chronicler. (Remember that after Solomon's death, the Davidic-Solomonic empire broke up into two national states of Israel in the north and Judah in the south.)

Chapters 29–31 describe a thoroughgoing reform of Judah's liturgy under Hezekiah. This reform included a confession of past neglect of proper worship (2 Chr 29:5–11), the cleansing of the Temple (29:16f) and the celebration of the Passover. Hezekiah invited the northerners who survived the Assyrian conquest to join the people of Judah in the renewal of the covenant (30:1–9). The account of Hezekiah's reign in 2 Kings 18–20 says little about Hezekiah's reform because 2 Kings wished to portray Josiah as a second David who restored the covenant (2 Kgs 22–23). Another striking contrast to 2 Kings is the chronicler's portrait of Manasseh, whom 2 Kings presents as the most evil of all Judah's kings. His sins were responsible for the fall of the southern kingdom (2 Kgs 21:1–18). The chronicler rehabilitates Manasseh by describing his conversion, which led to a reform of Judah's worship (2 Chr 33:11–17).

### The Purpose of the Chronicler

Why did the chronicler bother to retell the story of Judah's monarchy? After all, 2 Samuel to 2 Kings already told that story. Indeed, the chronicler derived much of his story from these books. Still, when we look more closely we can see that the basic purpose of this new version of the story of David and his dynasty was to guide the Jerusalem community as it was reestablishing itself following the exile. In the eyes of the chronicler, the one lasting contribution of the Davidic monarchy was the Temple, its rituals, and its priesthood. The Jewish community as a whole functioned as the successor of that dynasty. Once the people rebuilt the Temple and restored the proper form of its liturgy, the essential elements of Jewish life were in place. According to the chronicler, David and Solomon combined forces to establish a divinely ordained liturgy in Jerusalem. The people, led by Ezra and Nehemiah, resumed the service of God according to the pattern set by David. In the chronicler's scheme, the restoration of the national state and the Davidic dynasty was not as crucial as the reestablishment of the proper worship of the LORD in Jerusalem. The people who supported the Temple and resumed the authentic worship there fulfilled all the really important tasks of monarchy.

### Jews and Samaritans

The books of Chronicles reflect one stage in the division that arose between the Jews and the Samaritans, who lived in the northern kingdom. Historical reconstruction has not been able to identify any sudden and dramatic act that divided the two groups irrevocably. According to Samaritan sources, the division took place at the end of the period of the judges (eleventh century B.C.) when Eli left Shechem and established a high-priestly line at Shiloh. According to the biblical tradition (2 Kgs 17), the separation took place in the eighth century B.C. when the people of the former northern kingdom intermarried with foreign peoples whom the Assyrians introduced into their territory. Although it is not possible to treat either of these two accounts as straight history, they do point to important concerns. In the chronicler's perspective, the Samaritans did not have the true priesthood (2 Chr 13:9) and therefore their sacrificial worship was worthless.

The Samaritans were one example of the rich diversity in early Judaism. Their religious traditions developed independently of the leadership of the community that arose around the priests of Jerusalem. Other examples of the variety of religious perspectives in early Judaism include the Hasidim, the Essenes, and the Pharisees. An important moment in this development was the building of the Samaritan temple on Mt. Gerizim (near Shechem) sometime in the early Hellenistic period (late fourth century B.C.). It was the building of this temple by the Samaritans and its later destruction by the Jewish king John Hyrcanus in 128 B.C. that led to the definitive break between the Jews and the Samaritans.

It is within this context that one should read John 4, in which Jesus meets the Samaritan woman at the well in Shechem. Her comments reflect the religious and historical conflicts between her people and the Jews. Jesus, of course, says that there will come a day when true worship of God will transcend the conflict between Jew and Samaritan (Jn 4:21). The chronicler's attitude toward those outside the Jerusalem-centered worship community offers a striking example of an unwillingness to accept too great a diversity among those who considered themselves to be worshipers of the LORD. The reasons for the chronicler's attitude are complex. In part they were political and economic. Apparently the province of Samaria wanted to control Jerusalem, while the leadership of the Jerusalem community wished to remain independent of such control. In part the reasons were religious and liturgical. Although the people in the north wished to help with the rebuilding of the Jerusalem Temple (Ezr 4:2), the Judahites refused their help. Perhaps they did not believe that the northerners were sincere because of their continued use of the sanctuaries at Dan and Bethel. The Judahites considered the cult at these sanctuaries to be illegitimate. In part the reasons for the rift were historical. The Israelite tribes in the north and the south developed somewhat independently of one another, and the northerners cherished this independence fiercely. Whatever the reasons for the chronicler's attitude toward the northerners who considered themselves to be authentic worshipers of the LORD, it was decidedly negative. It contributed to the tension between Jews and Samaritans that has lasted into the present.

The chronicler's approach to the problem of religious diversity was understandable given the political and religious realities of the fourth century B.C. The rigid application of the directives of Ezra and Nehemiah and the intensity of the chronicler's rhetoric (see 2 Chr 13:4–12) made it difficult for succeeding generations to overcome the division between Jew and Samaritan. Indeed, further divisions occurred within the Jewish community. The Essenes opposed the Hasmoneans. The Pharisees disputed with the Sadducees. The Herodians fought with the Zealots. In the middle of all this, Christianity emerged. Eventually, because of historical circumstances, the Pharisaic party survived the fall of Jerusalem in A.D. 70 and was the precursor of rabbinic Judaism. The Kairites of Babylon refused to accept the authority of the rabbis. Even within Judaism today, some Orthodox rabbis do not accept the legitimacy of Conservative and Reform Judaism. The chronicler did not succeed in eliminating religious diversity among those who considered themselves worshipers of the LORD.

**Relationships among Christian Churches**

Until the Second Vatican Council, the attitude of Catholics toward other Christians was similar to the lack of tolerance that the chronicler showed toward religious diversity. One of the principal concerns of the council was promoting the restoration of unity among all Christians (*Decree on Ecumenism*, 1). Like the chronicler, who was in part responsible for the rift between Jew and Samaritan, the Catholic Church, according to the council, shares in responsibility for the divisions among Christian churches (*Decree on Ecumenism,* 3). One way to overcome these divisions is through dialogue that leads to a knowledge and appreciation of the doctrine and religious life of the many Christian churches.

Of the two main kinds of division within the Christian community, that which separates the East from the West resembles the separation between Jew and Samaritan that developed in the last four centuries before Christ. Although there were tensions between East and West for a long time, these came to a head in A.D. 1054 with the excommunication of the Patriarch of Constantinople by the papal legate and the patriarch's consequent excommunication of the pope's delegate. Four centuries later, other divisions arose in Western Christianity as a result of the Reformation. The differences between Christian churches are not simply theological but are also historical, political, sociological, cultural, and even psychological.

To help overcome these divisions within Christianity, the council suggested that dialogue among Christian churches focus first on elements which the various Christian churches share: the Scriptures, belief in Christ, baptism, and the Eucharist. The diversity of customs and doctrines will not then necessarily be obstacles to unity. We recognize them as contributing to the Church's beauty, helpful adaptations to differences of culture, necessary for the good of the faithful.

To the Christian churches that today are struggling with the project of restoring the Church's unity, the chronicler presents a lesson regarding what can happen when concern for the survival of one religious community leads to a type of narrow exclusivity that ignores the values of other people's approach to God. The tasks of Ezra and Nehemiah and the duty of the chronicler were clear: to ensure the survival of the small community of the LORD surrounding Jerusalem, whose continued existence was in doubt. They fulfilled their responsibilities. The responsibility of Christian churches is somewhat different today: to restore Christian unity. To make unity a possibility, Christians will need to be more willing to live with religious diversity than they have been. The chronicler's hesitancy regarding religious diversity is understandable. Judaism was struggling for its very survival. Christianity today is not as beleaguered as was Judaism in the chronicler's day. Achieving unity while respecting diversity should be easier for us.

**Questions for Discussion and Reflection**

***Group Sharing/Discussion***

1. Give some examples of the chronicler's reinterpretation of the materials from his sources in Samuel and Kings. Why did the chronicler make these adaptations?

2. The chronicler claimed that the Samaritans did not have true priesthood, and therefore their cult was worthless. Why do you think the author had this unwillingness to accept diversity among those committed to the LORD? What do you think of this attitude?

3. The chronicler describes in detail the roles of priests, Levites, and Temple "slaves" for proper worship. The division of the Roman Catholic Sacrament of Holy Orders (bishops, priests, deacons) mirrors to a certain extent the chronicler's division of Temple personnel. What are some of these similarities and some significant differences?

***In Our Lives***

1. Shalom, the Hebrew word for peace, is reflected in the name Solomon, in Hebrew *Shelomo*. In contrast to David, Solomon was a man of peace. What practices in living make a person a "person of peace"? How was Jesus a "man of peace"? What nourishes a peacemaker? Who are some examples of peacemakers in your parish, your town or city? How can you support them?

2. The Second Vatican Council emphasized that the *Church* is the entire people of God. For centuries the term Church tended to mean the clergy. In chapter five of Vatican II's *Constitution on the Church*, the council spoke of "the universal call of holiness."

How does this reverse the age-old idea that only "the ordained" have a vocation to holiness?

3. Since Vatican II lay ministers have become an accepted part of the liturgical life of the Roman Catholic Church. Today there are more lay ministers than ordained ministers in the United States. What does this lay ecclesial ministry mean for today's Church? What impact has this development had on the formation of church community?

*Individual/Personal Reflection/Action*

1. Take time to reflect upon your community worship experience. Recall the priests, the lay ministers, the ritual context, the customs and culture of your experience. What contributes to your full participation in community worship?

2. Until Vatican II the attitude of Catholics was similar to the lack of tolerance that the chronicler showed toward religious diversity. Restoration of Christian unity was one of the principle concerns of the Council's Decree on Ecumenism. The council suggested that the dialogue focus first on what we share: the Scriptures, Christ, baptism, and the Eucharist. Reflect on how you would share your Catholic beliefs on these parts of our faith.

# EZRA AND NEHEMIAH READING GUIDE

### *At a Glance*

| | |
|---|---|
| Who are the main players? | Ezra Nehemiah Cyrus the Great Artaxerxes I and II Zerubbabel Jeshua Sheshbazzar |
| What should I look for? | Restoring of the community and building of Jerusalem. Ezra, the Zadokite priest, was commissioned to reestablish Judahite society based on the Torah. Nehemiah's task was to rebuild the city and Temple. |
| When did this take place? | Between about 538 and 398 B.C. |
| Where did these events occur? | Jerusalem Judah Babylon Egypt Persia |
| Why was this book written? | The books of Ezra and Nehemiah are the only narrative accounts of the period after the Babylonian Exile (587–539 B.C.) that survived in the Hebrew Bible. Ezra provided the community with a source of stability and continuity—the Torah—which Jews came to see as encompassing the eternal order given to Moses by God. |
| What is the story? | The books of Ezra and Nehemiah deal with the restoration of Judah following years of exile in Babylonia. These books deal with the two phases of restoration: the first is rebuilding the Temple and the second is the reordering of Jewish life. Ezra speaks to a weak religious community on the brink of extinction. Assimilation is one of its main threats. He preaches the Torah as a source of identity and fosters an attitude of separation and exclusion. |

The book of Ezra deals with several episodes of the return to Jerusalem by Judeans after the Babylonian captivity; these episodes took place both in the sixth and fifth centuries.

The books of Ezra and Nehemiah are the only narrative accounts of the period after the Babylonian Exile (587–539 B.C.) that have survived in the Hebrew Bible. Originally Ezra and Nehemiah were a single work. In fact, Nehemiah does not even have its own title in Jewish Bibles.

The books of Ezra and Nehemiah do not give a reliable chronology of the restoration of Judah. They are more interested in presenting the religious dimension of the renewed life of Judah.

*The Kings of Persia*

| | | | |
|---|---|---|---|
| Cyrus | 538–529 B.C. | Darius II | 423–404 B.C. |
| Cambyses | 529–521 B.C. | Artaxerxes II | 404–358 B.C. |
| Darius I | 521–485 B.C. | Artaxerxes III | 358–337 B.C. |
| Xerxes | 485–464 B.C. | (Defeat of Darius III) | 336–330 B.C. |
| Artaxerxes I | 464–423 B.C. | End of the Persian Empire | 331 B.C. |

There are important political reasons why the Persian rulers were concerned about conditions in Judah. The beginning of both Nehemiah's and Ezra's missions coincided with Egyptian revolts against Persia's imperialism. It was important to have a sympathetic Judah at their back as they moved against rebellious Egypt. The above list of the Kings of Persia will be useful for dating the events mentioned in Ezra and Nehemiah.

## Reading the Book of Ezra

**Outline of the Book of Ezra**

Ezr 1:1–6:22 The Return from Exile
Ezr 7:1–10:44 The Deeds of Ezra

### The Return from Exile and Rebuilding of the Temple

The most striking feature of this section is not apparent to those who read it in translation. While the rest of the book of Ezra is in Hebrew, 4:7–6:18 are in Aramaic. This is because of the author's citing of a few official Persian documents relating to the restoration of Judah.

Chapters 1–3 cover the return from exile. Cyrus, the king of Persia, proclaimed that every exile from Judah who was ready to return to Jerusalem to rebuild its Temple should do so. The following verses describe the return itself. Chapter 2 gives a list of names of the returnees. At the top of the list is Zerubbabel, a member of the Davidic family, and Jeshua, a member of a prominent priestly family. These two play an important role in chapter 3 in the revival of worship in Jerusalem.

Although the rebuilding of the Temple begins immediately upon the return of the exiles, there were problems. Opposition came from "the enemies of Judah and Benjamin" and from "the people of the land." Both tried to convince the Persians that restoration of Jerusalem was an act of political disloyalty. In the end all opposition failed and the people of Judah completed their project with full support of Persian imperial authorities. The story of the rebuilding of the Temple concludes with a joyful account of the celebration of the Passover (6:19–22), a sure sign of the return from exile and echo of the Israelites deliverance from slavery in Egypt.

### Ezra's Mission

The genealogy in 7:1–5 shows that Ezra was a Zadokite priest. (The Zadokite priests were those associated with the Jerusalem Temple before the Babylonian Exile. Zadok was a priest who served David and Solomon.) Ezra was an expert in the Torah, which the priests who were in exile developed

**The Four Stages of Return from Exile**

1. Return under Cyrus (538 B.C.) led by Sheshbazzar, who began rebuilding the Temple but left it unfinished because of local opposition.
2. Return under Darius I (521–485 B.C.) led by Zerubbabel and Jeshua, who completed the Temple.
3. A group led by Ezra, who brought a copy of the Mosaic Law, in either 458 or 398 B.C.
4. Another group in 445 B.C. under Artaxerxes I (464–423 B.C.) led by Nehemiah to build the walls of Jerusalem and attempt to establish purity of community and worship. Nehemiah came as governor with his own retinue. He did not, strictly speaking, lead a group of returning exiles.

*Timeline: Postexilic Literature*

| OT Sources | Events in Jerusalem | Persian Rulers |
|---|---|---|
| | 586 B.C. to 500 B.C. | |
| | 586: Fall of Jerusalem to Babylon; second and final deportation; diaspora Jews in Babylon | 550–530: Cyrus II (the Great)<br>539: Fall of Babylonian Empire to Cyrus the Great |
| Ezra 1–6 | 538: First wave of the return to Jerusalem begins (groups continue to drift back over the next century); Zerubbabel begins rebuilding the Temple in Jerusalem; Samaritans thwart their efforts; rebuilding project halts. | 538: Cyrus the Great issues Edict of Toleration, allowing Jews to return home<br>530–522: Cambyses II |
| Haggai and Zechariah 1–8 | 520: The prophets Haggai and Zechariah call for the rebuilding of the Temple to continue; work begins.<br>515: In March, the second Temple is finished. | 522–486: Darius I |
| | 500 B.C. to 400 B.C. | |
| [Esther?]<br>Nehemiah's Memoirs: Neh 1–7 and Neh 11–13<br>[Jonah and Ruth?]<br>Malachi | 444–432: Nehemiah hears of the plight of Jerusalem while in Persia. He is appointed governor of Judah; the walls around Jerusalem are rebuilt. | 486–465: Xerxes I ("Ahasuerus" in the book of Esther)<br>465–423: Artaxerxes I (Age of Pericles in Athens)<br>423: Xerxes II<br>423–404: Darius II<br>404–358: Artaxerxes II |
| | 400 B.C. to 331 B.C. | |
| The "I" narrative: Ezr 7:11–9:15<br>The "he" narrative: Ezr 10 and Neh 8–10<br>The king's letter: Ezr 7:12–26<br>The lists: Ezr 8:1–14; Ezr 10:18–44; Neh 10:1–27 | 398(?): Ezra, priest and scribe, institutes reforms of worship.<br>End of OT history, c. 400 | 331: Alexander the Great conquers the Persian Empire (defeat of Darius III); age of Socrates, Plato, Aristotle; rise of Hellenism |

**Aramaic** is a Semitic language that is related to Hebrew. It was a common language of the diverse people that made up the Persian empire and was the official language of the administration. The use of Hebrew and Aramaic shows that the people were bilingual. Originally Aramaic was the language of the Arameans. Because Arameans were active in commercial affairs in the Near East, the language became widely known. By the sixth century B.C., it became the most commonly used Semitic language and was generally used in Palestine until Greek became the official language after the conquest of Alexander the Great in the fourth century B.C. Aramaic remained the language of the common people until the seventh century A.D., when Arabic replaced it. Aramaic was the language of Jesus, although he may have known Greek as well.

while in Babylon. An imperial commission given to Ezra from Artaxerxes II includes information about contributions to the Temple in Jerusalem and the order to reestablish Judahite society based on the "Law of God." By acceptance or rejection of the Torah, Judahites define themselves as belonging to or rejecting membership in the Jewish community. This means that in the view of the Persian government, the priestly version of ancient Israel's ancestral faith was the "official" religion of Judah. The author's account of Ezra's journey seems to have been modeled on the Exodus from Egypt, the crossing of the Jordan, and the occupation of the land.

Ezra's description of the journey to Jerusalem contains repeated descriptions of how the hand of the LORD was upon them, keeping the travelers safe on their journey. The amount of gold, silver, and other valuables they were carrying would have made them a tempting target for bandits and others. The protection of the LORD—not military might—was their safeguard.

### The Problem of Mixed Marriages

The final two chapters deal with Jews who have married outside their religious community. Ezra finds their behavior unacceptable and recites a long penitential prayer on their behalf. The people ask Ezra for help to set matters straight. The Hebrew text is unclear about the action taken in this matter, but some Jewish men probably divorced their non-Jewish wives in response to Ezra's urging.

## Exclusivism in Ezra

In denouncing mixed marriages, Ezra speaks of the Jews as a "holy race." He accuses the people of desecrating themselves with "the people of the land" (Canaanites, Hittites, Perizzites, Jebusites, Ammonites, Moabites, Egyptians, and Amorites). The Jewish community faced the same threats to its existence as did the Israelite tribes centuries before the establishment of the Israelite national state (thirteenth to eleventh centuries B.C.). At that time Israel faced hostile neighbors and was unable to defend herself adequately. There was little unity or even cooperation among the tribes in the eleventh century. As was shown in the books of Samuel, the response to these problems was to establish the monarchy. The king provided order and stability to the foundering Israelite tribes. The Davidic dynasty lasted from the eleventh to the fifth centuries B.C. and furnished a sense of continuity. But in the fifth century B.C. Persian imperialism made the reestablishment of Judah's native dynasty impossible. Ezra provided the community with another source of stability and continuity—the Torah, which the Jews came to see as encompassing an eternal order given to Moses by God. This notion made the Jewish community exclusive and led to the idea of a "holy race," which was to remain unsullied by contact with the nations. To counteract the danger of Jews being absorbed by the non-Jewish culture that surrounded them, Ezra taught that there was a very specific criterion for membership in the Jewish community—heredity. Mixed marriages were no longer permissible and, under Ezra, the community was not open to outsiders.

Elevating heredity to the position of defining the people of God is understandable, yet it separated Israel from other nations. The Samaritans whom Ezra's decrees excluded from the people of God considered him their archenemy. In contrast, the Talmud (the code of rabbinical teaching on the manner of observing the Law) considers Ezra to be a second Moses because he restored observance of the Torah when the people had forgotten about it. Early Christianity also had to deal with Ezra's legacy as it faced the consequences of its highly successful mission to the Gentiles (Acts 10:1–15:35). The early Church abandoned the views of Ezra on membership in the people of God.

We need to see Ezra's notion of a "holy race" against the backdrop of the cultural assumptions of ancient Near Eastern people. The key word here is *holy*. According to Ezra, part of observance of the Torah revolved around separation from all that was not *ritually* pure. Holy is a cultic term, not a moral one implying that the Jews were ethically superior to other nations. Books such as Jonah and Ruth reminded their readers among the Jews that Gentiles, too, could please God, showing that the Hebrew Bible affirms inclusive views as well as exclusive ones.

## Here and Now: The Call to Inclusion

The book of Ezra speaks to a beleaguered religious community on the brink of extinction. The circumstances faced by Ezra's community are not those faced by the human community today. In our time, the threat to human existence comes from ignorance, prejudice, and hatred that keeps the peoples of the world apart. The Second Vatican Council recognized this when it decided to issue a separate document dealing with non-Christian religions. The council declared that all peoples comprise a single community with a single final goal: God. All the religions of the world have come about from the universal attempt to probe the mystery of the divine. Catholics are encouraged to speak and work with followers of other religions. They are to acknowledge, preserve, and promote the spiritual and moral values found in these non-Christian religions. Judaism and Islam (the other two monotheistic faiths) are singled out by the council for special attention. Any form of persecution and hatred that existed between Christians and Jews at any time is condemned. The Church has rejected any type of discrimination directed at people because of their religion and calls upon all Catholics to maintain "good fellowship" with all peoples by living with them in peace.

## Reading the Book of Nehemiah

It is important to see the work of both Nehemiah and Ezra against the deplorable conditions that the prophet Malachi describes (see Mal 1–2). Without the strong communal structures that Ezra and Nehemiah provided for Judah, the people would have found it impossible to live according to the high ideals of their ancestral religion, because they lacked a healthy social and religious life. Nehemiah was a man of good practical sense, combined with deep faith in God. He was a layman, and his generous dedication of talents to the service of God and God's people remains an example for lay people today.

**Outline of the Book of Nehemiah**

Neh 1:1–7:22 The Deeds of Nehemiah
Neh 8:1–13:31 Promulgation of the Law

### The Rebuilding of Jerusalem

Because of bad reports that came to the Persian imperial court from Jerusalem, the emperor Artaxerxes I agreed to send Nehemiah, his cupbearer, to rebuild the city. There was great opposition from the governors of neighboring provinces, who even proposed military action against Jerusalem when they saw the wall being rebuilt. When their criticism and threats failed to dissuade Nehemiah, they began to plot against his life. Some within the Judahite community associated themselves with these plots against Nehemiah. This internal opposition came from the upper classes, who had a stake in maintaining the status quo. But despite all this opposition, Nehemiah completed the project of rebuilding the walls of the city in just 52 days.

From the time of David, Jerusalem was the central city of ancient Israel—at least for those devoted to the Davidic monarchy. David and Solomon wanted their Temple to solidify their capital's importance in the hearts of their people. But in spite of its great splendor, the Babylonians leveled the Temple and the city around it in 587 B.C. Although the Temple was rebuilt and Nehemiah refortified the city, the second Temple was never as elaborate as the one built by Solomon. Jerusalem was no longer a symbol of unity of north and south. It was, now, the center for preserving the particular worship of the Jewish community.

### The Promulgation of the Torah

At this point the Nehemiah memoirs break off and chapters 8–10 describe a ritual that Ezra conducted. This ceremony brought closure to the rebuilding of the city and the restoration of its religious life. The community heard the words of the Torah and responded by celebrating the Feast of Booths according to its prescriptions. Two weeks later they began a fast, and then Ezra made a great confession of sin in the name of the people.

### The Confession

Nehemiah 9:6–37 is one of the important creedal statements in the Old Testament. It recounts Israel's experience of God from the time of Abraham to the period of restoration. This remarkable act of faith acknowledges God's goodness and fidelity despite Israel's failure to keep the commandments. The similar prayer of confession in Ezra 9:7–15 suggests that these two confessions were originally parts of the same prayer.

### The Agreement of the People

Chapter 10 contains a written pledge made by those listed in verses lb–27 to observe the Torah of Moses. Among the specific points made in this pledge are the prohibition of marriage with Gentiles and the observance of the Sabbath. Those who made the pledge promised to provide firewood for the altar, first fruits for sacrifice, and tithes for the support of the Levites. Chapter 11 begins with a lottery used to resettle Jerusalem. Nehemiah 12 lists returning priests and Levites, followed by a description of the dedication of the walls. The book concludes with a list of the various reform measures that the people pledged themselves to observe.

## Ritual Purity

At first glance, the books of Ezra and Nehemiah may seem to be concerned with racial or ethnic discrimination. Although this issue could have been at work here, it is important to note that the emphasis on purity primarily involves cult and ritual. Mixing two peoples in marriage or in worship offends the Near Eastern notion of order. Exclusion of Gentiles from worship did not come from a belief in ethnic superiority but was associated with the rebuilding of the Temple and the restoration program led by both Ezra and Nehemiah. In order for the Jewish religion to continue and the worship of the LORD to be revived in Jerusalem, it was crucial that the practices and rituals not be watered down by those of other groups. Religion and ethnicity tended to parallel each other.

According to the Gospel of John in the New Testament, Christians worship in "Spirit and in truth" (Jn 4:23), transcending these ethnic patterns. Paul makes it clear that in Jesus there is "no Jew or Greek" (Gal 3:28). And Matthew writes that Jesus' final command was to "make disciples of all nations" (Mt 28:10). This did not occur to the first Christians automatically. The Acts of the Apostles shows that the inclusion of the Gentiles into the Christian community was a matter of spirited debate among Jewish Christians (Acts 15:1–35).

The synagogue also struggled with the question of inclusion or exclusion of the Gentiles. Some rabbis favored the more exclusive strain as found in Deuteronomy, Ezra, and Nehemiah. Others endorsed the more inclusive tendencies in texts such as Isaiah 56, which states that the Temple was to be "a house of prayer for all peoples."

### Questions for Discussion and Reflection

***Group Sharing/Discussion***

1. Ezra provided the community with a source of stability and continuity. He offered the Jewish community the Torah, which the Jews came to see as encompassing an eternal order given by God to Israel alone. This notion of Torah had some profound effects in the social order. What do you think were some signs of this in the community?

2. Ezra found "mixed marriages" unacceptable (chs 9–10) and elevated heredity to a position of defining the people of God. What are the effects of limiting Jewish identity to physical heredity?

***In Our Lives***

1. The teachings of the Torah are not considered a burden but as principles or a moral code given by a loving parent to the children. Tell about what teachings you view in this manner.

2. Ezra created an *exclusive* community. Explain the kind of exclusions you see or experience in your community, our country, the world.

## The Torah

AN IMPORTANT THEME in both Ezra and Nehemiah is the Torah as a written official guide for the life of the Jewish community. In Nehemiah 8–10, Ezra reads the Law, the people confess their failure to observe it, and then they agree to live according to its precepts. Unfortunately, too many Christians have very distorted notions of the Torah. These may have arisen because of the tense atmosphere in the Gospels, which recount Jesus' debates with the Pharisees regarding the interpretation of the Torah, and the bitter exchanges between Paul and some early Christians who thought that the Torah should be observed by everyone. But both Jesus and Paul often gave praise to the Torah: "Do you think that I have come to abolish the law or the prophets. . . . Whoever breaks one of the least of these commandments and teaches others to do so will be called the least in the kingdom of heaven. . . ." (Mt 5:17–19) and "So then the law is holy, and the commandment is holy and righteous and good" (Rom 7:12). Still the word "law" has a negative ring to it in the ears of most Christians.

The key to understanding and appreciating the Torah is to discover where it came from. Like most important words in the Hebrew Bible, *Torah* is used in several different ways. *Torah* could have come from the Hebrew word *yarah,* which means to cast lots, to point the way, or to instruct. Torah may have derived from the instructions priests gave to the people.

In the Bible, *Torah* usually refers to God's instructions to Moses at Sinai that he handed on to ancient Israel. In the book of Deuteronomy, *Torah* takes on a more extensive sense and becomes that which determines Israel's cultural, religious, and national identity. The prophets use Torah in several ways: cultic regulations, God's moral commands and ethical norms, and even the divine teachings given through the prophets. The Psalms praise both the Torah and those who live by it.

The early rabbis believed that they were responsible for transmitting not only the written Torah but also an oral Torah, which contained the teachings of revered sages who furthered the obligations of the Law beyond the words of the written Torah and made it much more difficult to violate the written Torah. Around A.D. 200, Rabbi Judah the Prince committed this oral Law to writing in a work called the Mishnah. This was the beginning of the Talmud (the code of rabbinical teaching on the manner of observing the Law). In Judaism today, *Torah* refers not only to the books of Moses but to the Talmud and the entire Jewish ethical tradition.

The Bible often speaks of Israel as God's children. Some people understood the Torah as the teaching given by the loving parent, God, to the child, Israel. In this light, the giving of Torah is an act of highest love. Jews of ancient Israel or modern times do not experience Torah as a burden, but as a way to life and as a source of joy. This devotion to ethical principles—the attitude of self-examination and self-correction that comes from loving observance and the preservation of identity through a specific moral code—are values that Christians could learn from Judaism, ancient and modern.

3. Ezra responded to the severe problems of his day with passionate commitment. To what do you have a passionate commitment? What calls Christians today to this kind of passionate commitment?

***Individual/Personal Reflection/Action***

1. In *Nostra Aetate* the Vatican Council encouraged Catholics to speak and work with followers of other religions. They are to acknowledge, preserve, and promote the spiritual and moral values found in non-Christian religions. Take some time to reflect on what this Church directive invites you to do.

2. In the *Declaration on the Relationship of the Church to Non-Christian Religions* the Church rejects any type of discrimination directed at people because of their religion. The bishops called upon all Catholics to maintain "good fellowship" with all peoples by living with them in peace. Examine your experience to recognize discrimination and to form attitudes of good fellowship. What can be done today to help people overcome prejudice against other people or religions?

3. The call for ritual purity and separation is pervasive in Ezra and Nehemiah. The New Testament affirms that the Christian worship transcends these patterns. According to John, Christians worship in "Spirit and truth" (Jn 4:23). Paul makes it clear that in Jesus there is "no Jew or Greek" (Gal 3:28). Matthew writes that Jesus' final command was to "make disciples of all nations" (Mt 28:19). This insight did not occur to the first Christians automatically. The Acts of the Apostles shows that the inclusion of the Gentiles into the Christian community was a matter of spirited debate among the Jewish Christians (Acts 25:1–35). Meditate on this contrast: exclusive/inclusive, in spirit and truth/ritually pure. Rejoice in Jesus' inclusiveness and Christian worship.

# TOBIT READING GUIDE

## *At a Glance*

| | |
|---|---|
| Who are the main players? | Tobit Sarah Tobiah |
| What should I look for? | This book is not history but a religious story. The purpose of this engaging tale is to show that God controls events and manages circumstances to ensure that God's purposes come to fruition. Reflect upon how God answers the prayers of the innocent Tobit and Sarah. |
| When did this take place? | Probably written in the early second century B.C. The author is unknown. |
| Where did these events occur? | Purportedly, in Nineveh, capital of Assyria, and Ecbatana, in Media. This book is a kind of religious novel. The historical and geographical details are there simply to provide setting for the story. |
| Why was this book written? | The book of Tobit reflects the importance that the book of Deuteronomy came to have in early Judaism. It maintains that the exile is not God's final judgment on Israel; rather there is hope for mercy, and the Temple in Jerusalem is the only legitimate place for worship. |
| What is the story? | This is the story of a pious Jew in exile who, after many misfortunes and trying events, finally sees the victory of God's providence in a happy family reunion and a peaceful end. Apart from the fascination of the tale itself, the book reflects aspects of Jewish piety during the Hellenistic period. The account is presented as history and as having taken place in Nineveh in the eighth century B.C. |

The book of Tobit is a complex literary work with a very simple moral. The book tells the tragedies and triumphs in the lives of three people: Tobit, Sarah, and Tobiah. The author, by weaving the stories together in three different but related plots, has a theological purpose: to show that God can manage the circumstances of people's lives to bring God's plans to fulfillment. The primary message is simple: God rewards those who are faithful.

## Approaching the Book: The Literary Form of Tobit

This book is a kind of religious novel. The historical and geographical details are there simply to provide a setting for the story. The author confuses the kings of Assyria, shows ignorance of the topography of Mesopotamia, and dates Tobit's exile earlier than it could have been. There is little to suggest that the author meant this work to be historical.

The book is the work of a single author and not the product of tradition. What is especially important to notice is how the author tells the stories of Tobit and his relative Sarah, both of whom suffer undeservedly. This cleverly told story is short enough to read in a single sitting. One key to understanding the purpose of the story is the unfolding of how God answers the prayers of the innocent Tobit and Sarah in a way they hardly expected. The story assumes God's determination to reward the just. When they suffer, there is a limit to that suffering. Once the limit is reached, God will intervene, sometimes miraculously.

## The Judaism of the Book

The book of Tobit was probably written in the second century B.C.; it is not known where. It reveals a form of Judaism that accepts magic and sees angels and demons as having important roles to play in the drama between God and human beings. This differs sharply from the books such as Judith and Esther, where human beings are in control of their own destiny without any intervention from angels or demons. The author of Tobit considers angels to be more than God's messengers: They mediate prayers in God's throne room; they oppose demons; and they authorize the writing of books. While angels expend efforts on behalf of good people, demons are malicious powers.

The book of Tobit reflects the importance that the book of Deuteronomy came to have in early Judaism. This is especially clear in Tobit 14:4–7, which claims that the exile happened because of Israel's infidelity. But it maintains that the exile is not God's final judgment on Israel; rather there is hope for mercy, and the Temple in Jerusalem is the only legitimate place for worship. Fidelity to God is measured in terms of fulfillment of the Torah, just as Deuteronomy preaches.

Finally, Tobit seems to reflect the circumstances of Jews in the diaspora (Jewish settlements outside Palestine). The book depicts Gentiles as unsympathetic to Tobit's activities and as persecutors. The book presents marriage within Judaism as a duty. It teaches that God is supreme over all people and is present to those in exile in the midst of their suffering. It emphasizes the need to preserve Jewish identity in the diaspora.

## Reading the Book of Tobit

The only way to savor the book's literary artistry and to appreciate its religious perspectives is to follow the way the author unfolds the events of Tobit's, Sarah's, and their families' lives. Notice how the stories of Tobit and Sarah parallel one another:

| | |
|---|---|
| Tobit's piety (2:1–7) | Sarah's innocence (3:14) |
| Tobit's blindness (2:9–10) | Sarah's demon (3:8) |
| Tobit's reproach (2:14) | Sarah's reproach (3:7–10) |
| Tobit's prayer (3:1–6) | Sarah's prayer (3:10–15) |

God hears these prayers but responds to them in a totally unexpected manner. Although Tobit and Sarah felt abandoned by God, God was, nonetheless, with them in the midst of their suffering. The reader should notice the movement in the book from despair to thanksgiving and praise.

### Questions for Discussion and Reflection

*Group Sharing/Discussion*

1. All the biblical short stories are told from the third-person point of view; that is, the

## About Angels and Demons

THE BOOK OF Tobit reflects the belief of early Judaism in angels and demons as supernatural beings. The first form of this belief seems to be "the messenger of the LORD," which belongs to the earliest narratives in the Hebrew Bible. In some of these stories the messenger is not different from the LORD (see Gn 16:13; 21:18; 31:13). Because God confronts people directly in many early stories, the appearance of angels is somewhat rare. As people begin to think of God as far beyond the human sphere, angels appear more regularly in the stories. Ideas develop about good angels and bad angels (demons), a hierarchy of angels, and the various duties of angels. It is possible to see popular imagination at work in the description of angels. They wear white garments and have wings. Around the time Tobit was written, there seems to be the belief in a few Jewish texts that it was permissible to portray figures from Israel's past, especially Adam and Jacob, as angels. Some Jews must have held that it was possible for a select few to transcend humanity and become angels. However, not all Jews believed in angels. The Acts of the Apostles asserts that the Pharisees, who represented more liberal, popular belief, acknowledged the existence of angels while the Sadducees rejected the existence of angels as well as belief in spirits and the resurrection from the dead.

narrator tells us about the characters by describing their actions through dialogue and speech. How would the story of the book of Tobit be affected if it were told by the characters themselves? (Note that Tobit begins in the first person [1:1–3:6]. Does this affect how you read it?) Choose a character who interests you and pick a particular scene or episode from the story. Allow that person to tell the story from his or her own point of view. Give lots of details, emotional reactions, and insights based on the story.

2. This story assumes God's control in people's lives and God's determination to reward the just. It says that when the just suffer, there is a limit to that suffering. Once that limit occurs, God will intervene and sometimes that intervention is miraculous. Share what you believe about suffering and God's relationship to it.

*In Our Lives*

The purpose of the book is to move its readers from despair to prayer. The most important message in this story is that God is with Tobit and Sarah even when they do not experience the divine presence. Mention how you perceive God's fidelity to you in time of suffering. Pray together Tobit's Song of Praise (13:1–18).

*Individual/Personal Reflection/Action*

1. Tobit is about how God answers the prayers of innocent Tobit and Sarah in an unexpected way. What experience have you had similar to Tobit's in your own life?

2. Tobit presents marriage within Judaism as a duty, for Jewish identity is important. It teaches God is sovereign over all people and is present to those in exile. Reflect on what you learned concerning marriage, God's sovereignty, and God's presence that is relatable to your own life.

# JUDITH READING GUIDE

### *At a Glance*

| | |
|---|---|
| Who are the main players? | Judith Holofernes |
| What should I look for? | Do not read this as history. It is a faith-filled meditation on God's providential care for Israel. The book attempts to show how the invisible hand of God rescues Israel through Judith. It also sets up a confrontation between the false |

| | |
|---|---|
| | belief that kings were the equivalent of gods on Earth, and faith in the one true God of Israel. |
| When did this take place? | May have been written as late as first century B.C., but in some ways it reflects the Maccabean revolt of the second century B.C. |
| Where did these events occur? | Although set in earlier times, the narrative reflects conditions prevalent during the turmoil of the Hellenistic period described in 1 and 2 Maccabees. |
| Why was this book written? | The name Judith is not a proper name; it means "Jewish woman." By rescuing her people from destruction at the hands of the Gentiles, Judith is a model for the Jewish woman as the preserver of tradition. Judith is a paradigm for the Jewish woman who protects her family from intrusions from the outside that threaten to dilute their loyalty to their ancestral religion. |
| What is the story? | Judith is a good story—a well-paced combination of description and action with purposeful realism. The heroine represents Israel's faith and spirit, strong and resourceful despite a weak appearance, which emerges triumphant in the confrontation with the great powers of the Near East. |

## The Book's Literary Form

There have been several attempts to classify the book of Judith according to its literary type. Clearly it is not history. It is useless to try to read it against the backdrop of Jewish history or that of other nations in the ancient world. There are just too many historical errors. Is it then a historical novel, *midrash*, or a fictional drama? None of these is completely satisfactory. The book is the result of a conscious, faith-filled meditation on God's providential care for Israel. The story shows how the invisible hand of God rescues Israel through the hand of Judith.

Over the centuries this story has attracted remarkable attention from writers, artists, and composers. Mozart chose Judith as the subject of his oratorio "La Betulia Liberata" ("The Liberation of Bethulia"). Painters, including Artemisia Gentileschi, have represented her story on canvas, and sculptors—Donatello is probably the most famous—have represented the story in bronze. Anonymous stonemasons even carved her story on the great cathedral of Chartres in France. The reason for all this attention is that Judith's story is such a good one. It is a heroic tale in which an unlikely character overcomes the cowardice of her own people in the face of the enemy.

The book of Judith is a piece of literature for difficult times. It was hoped that the reader would take to heart the lesson that God was still the master of history who could save Israel from her enemies. There is a parallel with the time of the Exodus: As God had delivered the people by the hand of Moses, so God could deliver them by the hand of the pious widow Judith.

The heroine's name is probably not a proper name. It simply means "Jewish woman." Judith is more than an individual: She is a composite of all the women who have saved Israel in the past by their piety, wisdom, and action. These heroines saved the people of ancient Israel when the more usual channels of leadership (the king, priests, and other notables) were not able to meet the challenges of faith. Some examples include Rahab (Joshua), Deborah (Judges), and Esther.

The first people to hear the story of Judith lived in a traditional society in which roles

> **Midrash** is the expansion, probing and exposition of biblical texts to bring out their full new meaning for changed circumstances.

## The Image of Women in the Church

A TYPE OF tension similar to that in Judith is visible in the U.S. Bishops' Pastoral Response to Women's Concerns for Church and Society, *Partners in the Mystery of Redemption* (1988). The first draft attempted to integrate the responses the bishops received from Catholic women through conversations that were part of the formulation of this first draft. Reading these responses makes it clear that there is great diversity among Catholic women. "The typical Catholic woman" does not exist. Like Judith, Catholic women see themselves as preservers of what is best in the tradition, although some are ready to cross what they perceive as artificial barriers set up by that tradition. The book of Judith offers a model for the process of contemporary theological reflection on the role and status of women in the Church. The book itself is a product of early Judaism's reflection on the role of women in its social and religious system. At the very least, the book sees women as, at times, better fit to be instruments of salvation than men—a conclusion that was most unexpected in the cultural milieu in which it arose.

assigned to men and women were clearly distinct. Change, if it took place at all, occurred very slowly. This story offers a surprising contradiction to what the culture assumed the role and status of women should be. In this story the men proved to be utter failures in the face of the threats of the king Nebuchadnezzar and Holofernes, the commander of his armies. The impact that this story made on a traditional society such as early Judaism is difficult for us to appreciate because we live in a society where change occurs much more quickly.

On the other hand, the book of Judith is quite conservative in its outlook. By rescuing her people from destruction at the hands of Gentiles, Judith is a model for the Jewish woman as the preserver of tradition. Judith is a paradigm for the Jewish woman who protects her family from intrusions from the outside that threaten to dilute their loyalty to their ancestral religion. The heroine of the book carries out the role assigned her by her culture but also surpasses that role.

## The Irony of the Book

The story of Judith is full of unexpected turns. The most obvious, especially to those who first heard or read the story, is that a woman—not a man—saved Judah in time of severe distress. Judith is more faithful and resourceful than any of the men of Bethulia. She is more eloquent than the king and more courageous than the leading citizens of the city. Yet Judith is a very unlikely heroine. As a childless widow, she occupied a very low place in the social hierarchy. While the king, priests, and leaders show themselves incapable of dealing with the crisis, Judith stands up to the threat posed by Holofernes and takes decisive action to end that threat.

The means she uses to accomplish her end may offend some. She uses her beauty to gain access to the enemy camp and to beguile Holofernes. Judith, though, is using the one weapon she has available to her. This leads to the second irony. Judith destroys the enemy not with military might but with her charm and disarming beauty.

Finally, Judith is a childless widow, yet the book portrays her as the mother of faith. That is why the high priests praise her so highly. The Latin hymn, *Tota pulchra es*, applies these words in praise of Mary. The story of Judith provides the liturgy with an appropriate image for the Virgin Mary as the Mother of the Church.

## The Judaism of the Book

The book of Judith affirms that the deliverance of the Jews of Bethulia depends not on power and might but on fidelity to the Law and guidance from the LORD. The author portrays Judith as living according to the Law as Jews interpreted it at the time. As a widow, she lives in a state of mourning marked by fasting. She prays daily at the hour of the incense offering in the

Temple. She observes Jewish dietary laws. She purifies herself by bathing in running water at the appropriate time. Judith criticizes the people for violating the law of first fruits and tithes. But while the book presents Judith's obedience to the Torah as the key to Israel's deliverance, it shows a type of flexibility that is able to respond to a person such as Achior the Ammonite, who wishes to join the Israelites in the service of God. According to Deuteronomy, Israel was never to admit an Ammonite into their community. The issue of inclusion and exclusion was a perplexing one for Judaism, as it was also for the first Christians (see Acts 10:1–49; 11:1–8; 15:1–12).

**Questions for Discussion and Reflection**

***Group Sharing/Discussion***

1. Judith is a model Jewish woman. What religious qualities show in her actions?

2. What are the role expectations out of which you live your life? Who have been your heroes or heroines? How does society's expectations influence the kind of man or woman you want to be?

3. Imagine a modern story of a religious Judith for a TV drama. Role-play the parts.

***In Our Lives***

1. How have experiences of women's faith nourished your life?

2. What are some ways that women's faith sustains the Church?

***Individual/Personal Reflection/Action***

1. Scripture uses both masculine and feminine images as revelatory of God. See how many of each you can name. Reflect on how thinking and speaking of God through masculine and feminine images make a difference in our sense of the divine.

2. Consider ways that you could bring to the attention of your parish the need and practice for both feminine and masculine images of God in nourishing spirituality.

# ESTHER READING GUIDE

## *At a Glance*

| | |
|---|---|
| Who are the main players? | Ahasuerus (Xerxes I) Vashti Esther Haman Mordecai. |
| What should I look for? | Esther is a novella on the theme of the persecuted righteous and their deliverance. The central concern of the book of Esther is the survival of the Jewish minority in the midst of a world that is growing hostile to it. The book makes it clear that God will act to preserve the Jewish community. |
| When did this take place? | At the end of the Persian empire toward the close of the fourth century B.C. |
| Where did these events occur? | The story describes the plot of Haman to destroy all Jews as happening in the Persian empire about 485 B.C. |
| Why was this book written? | The book was intended to console Israel and remind them that God's providence continually cares for them, never abandoning them when they serve God faithfully or turn to God, asking for forgiveness. God does not intervene directly to resolve the problem, but even though the divine action may be hidden, it is nonetheless real. |
| What is the story? | Set in the royal court of Persia, the book of Esther recounts how, through a series of dramatic events, a Jewish woman becomes queen and uses her influence to win for her people the right to fight off a threat of genocide. The Jewish holiday of Purim, described at the end of the book, celebrates this victory. |

The central concern of the book of Esther is the survival of the Jewish minority in the midst of a world that is growing more hostile to it. This book tells the story of Mordecai, a Jewish courtier in the service of the Persian emperors, and his beautiful and courageous niece, Esther, and how they averted one threat to Jewish survival. The book was intended to console Israel and remind them that God's providence continually cares for them, never abandoning them when they serve God faithfully or turn to God, asking for forgiveness. God does not intervene directly to resolve the problem, but even though the divine action may be hidden, it is nonetheless real.

## Structure of the Book

A confusing aspect to the arrangement of this book in the New American Bible is the order and numbering of its chapters and verses. Besides the familiar numbering common to the rest of the Bible, there are six chapters that have letter identifications scattered in the midst of chapters that have the usual number identifications. This is the result of the way the book of Esther has come down to us.

This book has survived in two forms: a shorter Hebrew text and a longer version preserved in the Septuagint (the ancient Greek version of the Hebrew Bible). The Greek has about 107 verses more than the Hebrew. When St. Jerome revised the Old Latin translation and compared these two ancient versions, he concluded that the extra verses in Greek were not inspired. Jerome took these verses out of their proper context and put them in an appendix at the end of the book. The Greek additions also did not become part of the Jewish canon, and their place in the canon of the Roman Catholic Church was not settled until the Council of Trent in the sixteenth century. Protestant churches do not accept the additions to Esther as canonical. The arrangement in this New American Bible attempts to follow the order of the Greek version without losing the arrangement of numbering of chapters and verses that is universally followed. The table below compares the two versions.

The purpose of the Greek additions to the Hebrew version of Esther is clear. They introduce a religious element into a secular story. The Hebrew version is a tale about how the Jews were able to outsmart their enemies and does not make a single reference to God (although the phrase in 4:14, "from another source," is interpreted by both Jewish and Christian writers as referring to God). The additions also lend an air of authenticity by introducing "documents" (B:107; E:1–24) that make the book read as if it were a historical work. This is important to encourage the celebration of the Feast of Purim with which the story became associated.

**Purim** The holiday named for the pur (lot) Haman cast to determine when the Jews would be destroyed. Purim is the feast celebrated on the 14th and 15th of Adar (around the first of March) commemorating the deliverance of the Jews from Haman's pogrom (an officially organized massacre).

| Hebrew Bible | Greek Septuagint |
|---|---|
| 1:1–3:13 | A. Mordecai's dream; the conspiracy against the king |
| 3:14–4:17 | B. The royal edict of Haman |
| | C. The prayers of Mordecai and Esther |
| 5:1–2 (omitted in Septuagint) | D. Expansion of the account of Esther's audience with the king |
| 5:3–8:12 | E. The royal edict of Mordecai |
| 8:13–10:3 | F. Explanation of Mordecai's dream, conclusion, and postscript |

## The Story and Its Personalities

The story takes place in the diaspora (the Jewish settlements outside of the land of Israel) and makes no reference to the homeland of the Jews. Two royal officials, Mordecai the Jew and Haman the Agagite, vie for power and position in the court of the Persian emperor. The rivalry between them soon sweeps up the entire Jewish community because of their particular customs and patterns of behavior. When Esther joins her relative, Mordecai, in a plan to frustrate Haman's murderous plots, the tension is resolved. What was to have been an officially organized massacre of the Jews becomes a celebration of the Jews because Haman and his conspiracy fail.

The story begins with the dethronement of Vashti, the queen of Persia. Vashti refused to obey the command of her drunken husband, Ahasuerus, king of Persia, when during a banquet he ordered her to "display her beauty" before his male courtiers. Because she refused to submit to this indignity, the king's officials advised him to remove her as queen. They feared that their own wives might imitate and refuse to obey their orders. The king issued a decree deposing Vashti and declaring that "every man should be lord in his own home."

Unlike Judith, Esther is hardly a model for feminists. She participates in the process to replace Vashti, who is the real heroine according to a feminist reading of this text. Vashti lost her crown but preserved her dignity. Esther betrayed the queen by seeking to replace her. While this story shows that the author was familiar with the royal court and the administrative system of Persia, the story of Esther is fictional and was not intended to report an actual event. It is an early Jewish novella on the theme of the persecuted righteous and their deliverance.

## The Book of Esther and the Feast of Purim

According to F:10, God wished the Jews to celebrate the feast on the 14th and 15th of Adar to celebrate their deliverance. The Bible mentions this feast nowhere else except a possible allusion in 2 Maccabees 15:36 that mentions Mordecai's day. Did the feast come first and the story of Esther later or did the feast come from the book? It may be that the Jews in the Persian diaspora adopted a local spring festival and attached a story of deliverance to it. Passover, the principal Jewish spring festival, shows a similar origin. Passover was a festival celebrated by nomads as they changed grazing areas for their flocks in spring. The Israelites attached the story of the deliverance from Egypt to this celebration. Since the Torah did not mandate the observance of Purim, the story of Esther serves to promote a religious celebration commemorating the story of a frustrated massacre and the secular triumph of the Jews over their enemies. Although a minor fast precedes Purim, the festival itself is a joyous one and includes a boisterous reading of the story of Esther, plenty of food and drink, and much merriment. Jews are also to give gifts of food and to support charity. These prescriptions symbolize the turning from sorrow to joy and give a religious dimension to what was a purely secular story. The Jews are to understand their survival not just in nationalistic terms but as a religious obligation.

The story of Esther describes intrigues and plots, power plays and schemes for murder. The Bible text does not approve the actions of either Esther or Mordecai but only the results. What God intended was the survival of the Jewish community. God did not dictate the means for that survival: The human personalities in the story controlled these. Perhaps the Hebrew version's refusal to speak about God directly in the story was an attempt to emphasize the importance of the Jews taking the matter of their survival into their

**Novella** A novella is a fictional piece of prose and is not meant to be historically accurate. A novella is shorter than a novel. It is written by a single author and meant to be read, not recited. The plot moves from tension to complication to resolution, concentrating on the development of characters and situations.

**The name Esther** The name Esther was a Mesopotamian name. Her Jewish name was Hadassah, which means "myrtle."

**Additions to the Book of Esther**

| | |
|---|---|
| Additions A and F | Mordecai's dream makes it clear that God controls the destiny of Israel. |
| Addition B | The decree of the Persian king against the Jews emphasizes the peculiarity of Jewish customs and alleges that they are not loyal to him. |
| Addition C | The deliverance of the Jews is in response to the prayers of Mordecai and Esther. |
| Addition D | The king's change of opinion regarding the Jews resulted from God's answer to Esther's prayer. |
| Addition E | God condemns the enemy of Israel. The Jews are innocent. The king acclaims the God of the Jews sovereign over all. |

own hands. The additions to the Greek version, however, show that some people saw this reticence as something that needed correction. The list above summarizes these additions.

How do Christians read a book so highly saturated with Jewish nationalism? The message of the book of Esther has an important role in the Christian canon. It offers an opportunity to check the tendency to spiritualize the people of ancient Israel and their descendants today. Where Vatican Council II declared that there is a spiritual bond between Jews and Christians, the book of Esther asserts that the preservation of the Jewish people is a *religious obligation.* The presence of the book of Esther in the Christian canon is a statement of the religious importance of the Jewish people as an ethnic group. It makes the sin of anti-Semitism even more shameful than the irrational injustice that most Christians understand it to be today.

**Questions for Discussion and Reflection**

***Group Sharing/Discussion***

1. This story begins with Queen Vashti's refusal to submit to indignity before the king's courtiers. Compare and contrast her response to the king with the courtiers' request.

2. The book of Esther makes it clear that God will act to preserve the Jewish community. What meaning does this story of Esther have for you and the Christian community?

***In Our Lives***

1. The central character in both Esther and Judith is a beautiful Jewish woman whose bravery and wiles save her people from certain destruction. Recall some stories of heroes or heroines throughout history and in your life today.

2. In the book of Esther, Haman practices anti-Semitism. Do you recognize this evil of anti-Semitism in your world? In Christian history?

3. Because they were living outside their land and faith community, the Jews in this story were "aliens." How does it feel to be aliens or alienated? Does the story of Esther speak to you about these experiences? What can you as an individual or your parish as a community do to help everyone feel welcome in your parish and your community?

***Individual/Personal Reflection/Action***

1. Vatican Council II declared there is a spiritual bond between Jews and Christians. Take time to reflect on how this is true both in the origin of Christianity and in our life today.

2. Both Esther and Judith are novellas in form, that is, they are fictional prose and not historical narratives. But they do have a spiritual message. How important is awareness of the literary form of a book in the Bible in receiving its message? Research some of the other forms of writing contained in the Bible.

# 1 MACCABEES READING GUIDE

## *At a Glance*

| | |
|---|---|
| Who are the main players? | Mattathias Judas and his brothers Antiochus Epiphanes |
| What should I look for? | Observance of the Torah Saving Jews from persecution |
| When did these events take place? | The first book of Maccabees is a historical narrative of events in the life of the Jewish community in and around Jerusalem from the reign of the Greek Antiochus IV (175–164 B.C.) to the accession of the Jewish ruler, John Hyrcanus (134–104 B.C.). |
| Why was this book written? | The first book of Maccabees is one of the main sources for reconstructing the history of the Jews in Palestine during the middle of the second century B.C. The purpose of the work was to assert the legitimacy of the Hasmonean high-priestly dynasty. The book implies that the right of the Hasmoneans to rule is clear from the achievements of their ancestors: (1) the Maccabees saved the Jews from persecution; (2) they restored observance of the Torah; and (3) they inaugurated an era of peace and prosperity. The author of this book believed that God willed that the Hasmoneans assume the mantle of leadership over the Jews of Palestine. |
| What is the story? | The story told in this book is a small part of a much larger story: Hellenization, the shifting of cultural orientation from East to West, in the eastern Mediterranean region. The Greek ruler and general Alexander the Great conquered this area in the fourth century B.C. It was his dream to take the culture of Greece and wed it to the cultures of the ancient Near East so that people could benefit from the best of each. Although Alexander's premature death in 323 B.C. prevented him from fulfilling that dream, the process of Hellenization proceeded in the cultural, political, and economic spheres. The response of the Jewish community to Hellenism was equivocal: some Jews resisted Hellenization; others eagerly accepted the new wave that was sweeping the world. |

By 326 B.C., Alexander the Great had conquered the lands surrounding the eastern end of the Mediterranean. At his sudden death in 323 B.C., however, his empire fell apart into three separate sections. One, which included Egypt and parts of present-day Israel, Jordan, and Lebanon, was ruled by Ptolemy, one of Alexander's generals. Another general, Seleucus, ruled a territory including what is now Syria, Iran, and Iraq, and extending eastward at one point as far as India. The portion of the empire centered on Greece was ruled (and fought over) by various members of Alexander's family and court.

The word "Maccabee" derives from the Hebrew word for hammer and was the nickname for Judas, a leader in the Jewish revolt against the Seleucid ruler Antiochus Epiphanes (165–161 B.C.). The nickname later became a designation for other members of Judas's family who succeeded him in the revolt. Judas and his brothers became known as "the Maccabees" and "Maccabean" came to designate the period of Jewish history that witnessed the successful revolt against the Seleucid Empire.

After the revolt, the descendants of the Maccabees took over religious and later political leadership of the Jewish community in Palestine. They ruled an independent Judah from about 164 B.C. (beginning with Judas Maccabee) until Pompey conquered Palestine for Rome in 63 B.C. This dynasty was called the "Hasmonean" dynasty. That name comes from the ancestor Asamonaeus whom Josephus (a first-century A.D. Jewish historian) identifies as the father of Mattathias and grandfather of Judas and his brothers. Mattathias started the revolt against Antiochus.

## What Is the Maccabean Literature?

There are four books of the Maccabees that have survived from early Judaism. None are in the Hebrew Bible and so are not included in Jewish or Protestant Bibles. An overview of the contents of these books can be found below.

**First Book of Maccabees** Historical narrative of events in life of Jewish community in and around Jerusalem from 175 B.C. to 104 B.C. (Included by Jerome in Vulgate; became part of the Catholic canon.)

**Second Book of Maccabees** Abridgement of a five-volume history of the Maccabees that no longer exists. Covers period in Palestine from 180 B.C. to 161 B.C. (Became part of Catholic canon.)

**Third Book of Maccabees** A misnamed work that has nothing to do with the exploits of the Maccabees. It is a first-century B.C. work that describes the persecution of the Jews in Egypt under Ptolemy IV (221–203 B.C.). (Included in the canon of Eastern Christianity.)

**Fourth Book of Maccabees** A first-century A.D. tract on religious reason as exemplified by Jewish martyrs during the Maccabean revolt. (No Christian tradition accepts this book as divinely inspired, although some Eastern churches include it as an appendix to the Bible, and it has had some influence in their spirituality.)

## History and Theology in First Maccabees

Unlike the books of Tobit, Judith, and Esther, which use historical events and persons as a backdrop for fictional tales, the first book of Maccabees is a historical story. The author tries to show the significance of the events in the middle of second century B.C. Palestine. But the book is more than a catalogue of events. Its purpose was to affirm the legitimacy of the Hasmonean high-priestly dynasty, whose right to rule was based on the achievements of their ancestors:

1. The Maccabees saved the Jews from persecution.
2. They restored observance of the Torah.
3. They set up an era of peace and prosperity.

The author believed that it was God's will that the Hasmoneans assumed leadership over the Jews of Palestine. The members of this dynasty were not without their opponents. After all, they ruled as kings when many Jews believed that the only legitimate political leaders ought to be descendants of David. As a priestly family the Hasmoneans were not of David's tribe (Judah), let alone part of his family. In addition, the Hasmoneans functioned as high priests even though they were not descendants of Aaron, as required by tradition. The chief opponents of the Hasmoneans were the Hasidim, who were the spiritual ancestors of the Essenes and the Pharisees.

The first book of Maccabees reflects a type of pragmatism that was incompatible with the religious zeal of the Hasidim. 1 Maccabees 8 is lavish in its praise of the Romans. This shows that the Hasmoneans were willing to compromise with foreigners when circumstances made it necessary. Later the Pharisees adopted the same

**Hasidim** were the "pious ones" who saw themselves as the careful observers of the Law. They were sometimes not very prudent in their self-styled devotion to the Torah (see 1 Mc 7:8–18).

position, and so did the early church (see Rom 13:1–7 and 1 Pt 2:13–17).

First Maccabees also shows that both Spartans and Romans, the major political powers of the day, recognized the Hasmoneans as the political leaders of the Jewish people.

## Reading the Book

The story told in this book is part of a much larger story: the Hellenization in the eastern Mediterranean. It was the dream of Alexander the Great, who conquered this area in the fourth century B.C., to take the culture of Greece and wed it to the cultures of the ancient Near East so that people could benefit from the best of each. But his premature death in 323 B.C. prevented him from fulfilling that dream. Alexander's generals divided his empire among themselves. The area of the former Israelite kingdoms came under the control of Ptolemy, who ruled from Egypt. Ptolemy permitted the Jews to practice their religion without much interference. The process of Hellenization grew in the other areas of Jewish cultural, political, and economic life. Some Jews resisted Hellenization while others eagerly accepted the new wave that was sweeping the world.

The region of the ancient Mesopotamian Empire fell to another of Alexander's generals: Seleucus. He thought that the territory of the old Judahite and Israelite kingdoms rightfully belonged to him. The Ptolemies and Seleucids fought over this region until it passed into the hands of the Seleucids in 200 B.C. At first the Jews were permitted to practice their religion. But circumstances changed in 168 B.C. when the Seleucid king Antiochus IV Epiphanes ("Epiphanes" means "[god] manifest," and indicates that Antiochus was supposed to be regarded in his own culture as a divine, or at least deified, being) seized upon the opportunity provided by divisions within the Jewish community. He favored the Jewish Hellenizers for reasons that were partly economic but also in some part cultural. To ensure the victory of the Jewish Hellenizers, Antiochus forbade the practice of the Jewish religion. Without anyone to resist his policies, the future of Judaism looked bleak.

> **Seleucid** was the name of the Greek dynasty that ruled in Syria following the death of Alexander the Great. The name derived from Seleucus, one of Alexander's generals.

### Mattathias (1 Mc 1:1–2:70)

The first chapter sets the scene for the bloody confrontation between the Jews and the Seleucids. It describes the Hellenization of Jerusalem, the military attacks on the city by two Seleucid armies, and the prohibition of Jewish religious practices. The king's efforts at destroying the Jewish religion culminated in the "horrible abomination," which was the setting up of an altar to Zeus Olympus upon the altar for daily sacrifice in the holy place in the Temple where burnt offerings were made (Dn 11:31; 12:11).

The second chapter importantly describes the specific type of opposition that the Maccabees and their followers mounted against the Hellenization of Antiochus and his Jewish collaborators. Not all Jews who opposed Antiochus responded in the same way. While some reacted with a type of passive resistance, the Maccabees, in the person of Mattathias, opposed these policies militantly. A key text is 2:23–46, which describes Mattathias's fury at the prospect of Jewish apostasy. By comparing Mattathias's response with that of Phinehas (see Nm 25:6–14), the author implies that Mattathias's action prevented God's anger from consuming the Jews because of their apostasy. This merited the high-priestly office for the Hasmoneans. Mattathias became the leader of a large guerilla force whose aim was to end the Seleucid military domination of the Jews and the banning of their religion.

### The Militancy of First Maccabees

The United States Bishops' Pastoral, *The Challenge of Peace*, asserts "the sacred scriptures provide the foundation for confronting war and peace today" (27). In trying to formulate a Christian response to these issues, one has to face the armed resistance of 1 Maccabees to the Seleucid persecution. Theologically, they were responding from the religious traditions of ancient Israel.

It is important to remember that the response of the Maccabees was not the only response among religious Jews in Palestine. Although there was an agreement that they ought to oppose Antiochus, there was a variety of viewpoints on how they ought to resist. While the Maccabees insisted on violent resistance, there were others who opted for martyrdom, nonviolent resistance, and even pacificism in the face of the threat of anti-Jewish laws.

While 2 Maccabees shares the militancy of 1 Maccabees, it expands the meaning of the revolution by adding martyrdom as another way the faithful may contribute to the final victory over their enemies. The blood of martyrs who died rather than violate the Torah cries to God for vengeance and thereby seals the victory for the Jews.

### Mattathias's Farewell

Chapter 2 ends with Mattathias's statement in which he turns over his military authority to his sons, commending to them the example of Israelite heroes of the past to support his militant ideology.

**Hanukkah, or the Feast of Dedication** is a Jewish feast celebrating the purification and rededication of the second Temple during the Maccabean revolt. Judas Maccabee mandated the observance of this festival. Three years to the day after Antiochus's "horrible abomination" of the Temple, the Maccabees gained control of the area, purified the Temple, and rebuilt the altar. Josephus calls this festival "the feast of lights": The rededication involved rekindling the Temple's menorah (a lamp stand with seven branches). Jews observe this festival at home by lighting one candle on a special Hanukkah menorah each night. According to a legend in the Talmud, the family is reminded of how one day's supply of oil lasted for the full eight days of the original festival until the priests could obtain more oil for the menorah in the Temple. This festival is glorification of the deeds of those who refused to give up their faith.

### Judas (1 Mc 3:1–9:22)

About 40 percent of the story centers on the exploits of Judas, who succeeded his father as leader of the Jewish guerilla forces. Although the text acclaims his exploits and praises his bravery, the author is careful to imply that Judas's victories came because of divine help. Judas prayed before every battle. He reminded his army of how God helped their ancestors in the face of overwhelming odds. Judas dismissed those that Deuteronomy exempts from war (3:56, see Dt 20:5–8). That, and the way he dealt with the defeated enemy and the spoils of war, shows a man who was certain that he was fighting in accord with a divine command. Finally, Judas praised God when he celebrated his victories.

### Jonathan (1 Mc 9:23–12:54)

Judas dies in battle and his brother Jonathan succeeds him. While the text hails Jonathan's military exploits, of particular importance is his acceptance of the appointment as high priest from the Seleucid king Alexander who succeeded Antiochus.

### Simon (1 Mc 13:1–16:24)

When the followers of Trypho, the pretender to the Syrian throne, assassinate Jonathan, the succession passes to his brother Simon. The first book of Maccabees reaches its climax with the succession of Simon as leader and high priest. Remember, the purpose of the book is the establishment of the Hasmonean house as the legitimate political and religious dynasty for the Jews in Palestine.

A poem in 14:4–15 is a combination of biblical themes suggesting that with Simon has come to the Jews a state of peace and prosperity not seen since the days of David and Solomon. A beleaguered minority stood up to a powerful empire for the sake of their religion. The author of 1 Maccabees believed that God was working through the Hasmonean family.

However, the book closes on a tragic note. Simon is murdered by a political rival who is captured and executed by John, Simon's son. The succession is safe and another Hasmonean, John Hyrcanus, continues the line of those "of the family through whom Israel's deliverance was given" (5:62).

**The Story of the Maccabees in Music**

GEORGE FREDERICK HANDEL'S oratorio *Judas Maccabeus* tells the story of the Maccabean revolt. It includes the famous chorus "Hallelujah, Amen."

### First Maccabees in Catholic Tradition

This book is not part of the Hebrew Bible. There is no evidence that it formed part of the Qumran library, and Josephus did not include it on the list of his sacred books. Reverence for the book by the early church's theologians was perhaps the reason that the Councils of Florence and Trent affirmed it canonically. But it has never had a real impact on Christian theology, and its use in the liturgy is minimal.

## 2 MACCABEES READING GUIDE

### *At a Glance*

| | |
|---|---|
| Who are the main players? | Onias Jason Menelaus Judas Maccabee Antiochus Greeks |
| What should I look for? | How God dealt with those who disregarded the divine will. Also, martyrs who would accept death rather than be disobedient |
| When did this take place? | The second book of Maccabees is an abridgement of a five-volume history of the Maccabees that no longer exists. It covers the period of Jewish history in Palestine from the time of the high priest Onias III (180 B.C.) to the victory of Judas Maccabee over the Greeks in 161 B.C. |
| Where did these events occur? | Palestine |
| Why was this book written? | Second Maccabees is intensely devoted to the Torah. Death, even suicide (2 Mc 14:37–46), is preferable to violating the Torah. The reward for such loyalty for the individual is resurrection, and for the community it is the possession of Jerusalem. Despite this opposition to Hellenization, it is impossible to escape the influence of Hellenistic culture. Second Maccabees itself uses rhetorical forms that come from Greek literature. |
| What is the story? | The story of 2 Maccabees overlaps with that of 1 Maccabees. While 2 Maccabees does not cover as much of the history of the Maccabees as does 1 Maccabees, it is a more polished literary work. Also 2 Maccabees is less of an apology for the Hasmonean dynasty and more of an attempt to illustrate an important theological theme: God's justice in rewarding the faithful and punishing the impious. The book provides an inventory of how God dealt with both Jews and Greeks who disregarded the divine will. Its focus, however, is on those Jews who accepted death rather than be guilty of an act of disobedience. Second Maccabees highlights the death of Jewish martyrs to affect the emotions of its readers so that they may recommit themselves to faithful observance. |

## The Relationship between 1 and 2 Maccabees

The second book of Maccabees does not continue the history of the Jewish revolt against the Seleucid Empire but is an abridgement of a five-volume work on the Maccabees by one Jason of Cyrene (2 Mc 2:23). This longer work has not come down to us. The unknown editor who is responsible for the present form of 2 Maccabees wished to simplify Jason's work so that readers could remember its most important features (2 Mc 2:25). The book is not simply a digest of a much longer work. There are portions of the book that do not come from Jason but were written by the person who made the abridgement.

Second Maccabees begins its story of the Jews in Palestine with the reign of the Syrian king Seleucus IV when Onias III was the high priest and ends with the defeat of the Syrian army by Judas Maccabee. The period extends from approximately 180 to 160 B.C. The story overlaps with that in 1 Maccabees 1:10–7:5, with great similarity between 2 Maccabees 8–15 and 1 Maccabees 3–7.

Second Maccabees is less defensive of the Hasmonean dynasty and gives more emphasis to God's justice in rewarding the faithful and punishing both Jews and Greeks who disregard the divine will. The book focuses on those Jews who accepted death rather than be guilty of an act of disobedience.

## Reading the Book

Second Maccabees begins with two letters directed to the Jewish community in Egypt, calling them to celebrate a festival in honor of the rededication of the Temple following the victory of the Maccabees over the Seleucids. Since the Torah could not mandate the celebration of the feast of Hanukkah, the leadership of the Jewish community had to take this special step to encourage its observance.

The Jewish community in Egypt built its own temple under the direction of Onias IV, the last legitimate high priest. Perhaps these letters were directed to the Jews in Egypt to keep them from forgetting their ties with Palestine. But it could be that the person responsible for the present form of 2 Maccabees added these letters to the story of the Maccabees in order to make the book into a festal scroll for Hanukkah as the book of Esther is for the Feast of Purim.

### The Story of the Maccabees (2 Mc 3:1–15:36)

The author has a theological purpose in the way the story of the Maccabees is presented. The events of Jewish history from the time of Onias the high priest to the time of Judas Maccabee show a God who cares for the Jewish people by rewarding the faithful and punishing evildoers. The author uses a scheme first devised by the authors of the deuteronomic history of Israel, who told how Israel came to own the land under Joshua and then how Israel lost the land under its kings. Infidelity transformed a blessing into a curse.

**Blessing—Sin—Punishment**

1. Period of *blessing* (3:1–40): during the time of Onias III when people observed the Torah
2. Period of *sin* (4:1–5:10): during the time of the high priests Jason and Menelaus when the

**Looking at the Past**

LEGEND, CHRONICLE, AND history are all ways of narrating the past. A *legend* is a popular story, often with a fantastic character. It may be based on an actual historical event, or it may be entirely fictitious. In the context of religious literature, legends are meant to edify rather than to convey factual information. A *chronicle* is a factual account of events in the order in which they occurred. It usually reads as a simple sequence of events, without interpretive comments. *History* or *historiography,* like a chronicle, attempts to give an accurate account of the past but includes discussions of causes and consequences. Historical writing normally involves the use of sources and the critical evaluation of evidence. Chronicles and legends, then, might serve as the source for the historian.

**Hellenization** is a term that describes Greek culture, ideals, and institutions that reached their peak in fifth-century B.C. when Athens came to have huge influence throughout the eastern Mediterranean. Until the time of Alexander the Great, the region was oriented culturally to the East: Assyria, Babylon, and Persia. Alexander effected a genuine cultural reorientation that lasted until the Muslim conquest in the seventh century A.D.

The city or "polis" with its marketplace *(agora),* colonnaded streets, temples, theaters, and gymnasium was the instrument of economic prosperity, and of the spread of Hellenism as well. Throughout Palestine the Greeks remade ancient cities. Even Jerusalem was made over (1 Mc 1:11–14).

It is not surprising that there was resistance among some Jews to Hellenization. After all, the Jews had a very traditional culture in which change occurred only gradually. There were people—especially among the upper class of Jewish society—who embraced the new cultural wave. At first the Hellenism the Jews faced was a mild type. Matters changed dramatically under the Seleucid king Antiochus IV, who imposed Hellenism upon the Jews. His policies sparked the Maccabean revolt.

Similar to 1 Maccabees, 2 Maccabees is opposed to the forced Hellenization program of Antiochus. It is intensely devoted to the Torah. Despite this opposition to Hellenism, it works in favor of the author when 2 Maccabees appeals to the emotions of its readers. The work does not hesitate to describe the death of Jewish martyrs in vivid detail. This approach is typical of Hellenistic history writing. It is impossible to escape the influence of Hellenistic culture. The miraculous episodes in 2 Maccabees are also comparable to episodes in Greek histories.

As opposed to the Greeks as 2 Maccabees is, it is not simplistic in the way it deals with Jews and Greeks. It presents some Greeks as sympathetic to the Jews. Antiochus even converts on his deathbed. The Jews do not object to the rule of the Greeks as such. The Jews can be good citizens. What they do object to are the abuses that came with Antiochus.

There comes a point when the pious must choose. With Hellenism there came a whole collection of gods and goddesses. There were even deified kings. But more subtle were the novelties in philosophy and ethics. For the pious Jew, Hellenism represented a religious ideology and practice that was completely foreign. But there was no escaping the influence of Greek culture at this time and on into the future. For example, almost 700 years later during the Byzantine period (fourth to sixth centuries A.D.) there were a few synagogues in Palestine that had decorative motifs that included a zodiac complete with the god Helios in the center of the mosaic floor.

Second Maccabees represents an earlier view that rejected any compromise with Hellenism. There are absolute values that do not allow any compromise. Even in the face of death, the righteous will choose fidelity to the Torah and be confident that such a choice is not in vain because of their belief in the resurrection.

people and the leaders violated the Torah and followed the customs of the Greeks

3. Period of *punishment* (5:11–6:17): Antiochus is the agent of God's judgment.

**Turning Point—Blessing**

1. The prayers of the people and the heroic death of the Jewish martyrs bring a change in circumstances. Although the book is aware of the victories of Judas Maccabee that ended the domination of Antiochus, it assumes that the death of the martyrs turned God's anger to mercy and made the victories possible.

2. The cycle is complete: *blessing* has returned to the Jewish community.

Another story runs parallel to this story of salvation: retribution. The enemies of the Jews come to a terrible end:

- Antiochus dies in agony (9:8).
- The Greek who murdered Onias is himself killed (4:38).
- The general who commanded the siege against Jerusalem is dead and his head hangs from the citadel of the city (15:35).
- The wicked among the Jews suffer under divine judgment.
- The high priests Jason and Menelaus both come to miserable ends (5:1–10 and 13:7f).

## The Book's Influence in Christian Theology

This section of the book has influenced the development of the notion in Christian theology that suffering can have a positive value. Suffering can be a form of divine education. God did not send suffering to destroy the Jewish people but to discipline them. God's people are never abandoned. The suffering of the innocent leads the author to affirm his belief in the resurrection of the dead (7:9; 7:11; 7:14; 7:23; 14:46). This enables the Jewish martyrs to accept their suffering, for God will deliver the faithful despite their death at the hands of the wicked.

One of the most important texts in this book for Roman Catholic theology is 12:42–46. The author tries to show that Judas Maccabee believed in the resurrection of the dead, because he ordered prayers and sacrifices for those who had fallen in battle. Such prayers would be useless unless Judas believed that they would rise again (12:44). This text is sometimes used as support for the Roman Catholic belief in purgatory and the power of prayers for the living and the dead. Another important text for Roman Catholics is 2 Maccabees 15:12–16. Here Judas Maccabee sees the prophet Jeremiah in a dream praying for the Jews and Jerusalem. Catholic tradition accepts this text as one support for the belief in the power of the intercession of the saints.

**Questions for Discussion and Reflection**

***Group Sharing/Discussion***

1. Hanukkah is a Jewish feast celebrating the rededication of the second Temple during the Maccabean revolt. Josephus calls this festival the "feast of lights." Why did Judas Maccabee mandate this celebration? Why was it called the "feast of lights"? What is the significance of Hanukkah for a pious Jew? Talk with Jews about how they celebrate Hanukkah or invite them to come to your group.

***In Our Lives***

1. The principle opponents of the priestly family of Hasmoneans were the Hasidim (the pious ones) who were the spiritual ancestors of the Essenes and the Pharisees. The Hasidim saw themselves as careful observers of the Law; they saw the Hasmonean high priests as illegitimate. Do you see any of their traits in the New Testament? How do they appear in modern Jewish life? What qualities are religiously attractive?

***Individual/Personal Reflection/Action***

1. One of the most significant texts in this book for Roman Catholic theology is 12:42–46. Here the author wished to show that Judas Maccabee believed in the resurrection of the dead since he ordered prayers and sacrifices for those who had fallen in battle. The author concludes that such prayers would be futile unless Judas believed that they would rise again (12:44). Take some time to meditate on the resurrection of the dead and praying for the departed.

2. Reflect upon the story of the Seven Brothers' (7:1–42) motives for going to martyrdom. What would you say to them about their decisions?

# THE WISDOM BOOKS

### *At a Glance*

| | |
|---|---|
| Job | A dramatic poem that treats the problem of suffering of the innocent, and of retribution. |
| Psalms | A collection of religious songs under the major headings of hymns, laments, and songs of thanksgiving. |
| Proverbs | An anthology of mostly short sayings in poetical form whose purpose is to teach wisdom for successful living. |
| Ecclesiastes | A treatise on the vanity, or emptiness, of all things. The book is concerned with the purpose and value of human life. |
| The Song of Songs | A collection of love poems full of sensuous imagery. It could be seen as a portrayal of ideal human love. |
| Wisdom | Oratory from the Jewish community of Alexandria about 100 years before the coming of Christ, explaining traditions and themes familiar to Judaism but reinterpreting them from the experience of living in a Greek or Hellenistic culture. |
| Ben Sira | A collection of proverbs dealing with moral instruction, written to show that real wisdom was to be found in the traditions of Israel and not in the godless philosophy of the day. |

Beginning around the time of the Davidic-Solomonic monarchy (tenth century B.C.) and continuing for centuries after that, writers and thinkers in ancient Israel developed the "wisdom" tradition in their literature. This literature shows how Israel encountered God *through* human experience, not *in addition to* it. A new question was being asked: What kind of role does God play in everyday life? The answers to that question form a "guide for successful living." Since every person in every culture must struggle with the questions of life, this literature has universal appeal. This might explain why, even today, people of other religious cultures can more easily identify with the teaching of the wisdom books than with the other books found in the Bible.

*Wisdom* is the ability to perceive the order of the universe and to live in harmony with it. The Israelites believed that their God was the great Creator-God, the one responsible for the world and everything in it. By observing the regularity in creation, they concluded that there was some kind of order in nature itself. If they could understand how this order operated and then attune their lives with it, they would be successful and at peace.

The writers of wisdom literature used various teaching techniques such as storytelling, exhortation, warning, and questioning. They also used proverbs, riddles, parables, and metaphors to instruct, advise, and persuade. Usually there were very definite lessons they wanted to teach, so it should not surprise us to come across what appears to be "the moral of the story."

The sages were humanists; that is, they were concerned with the study of human beings and attentive to human welfare, values, and dignity. They taught that whatever benefited humanity was a good to be pursued; and whatever was harmful should be avoided. The gauge for judging the value of any undertaking was the degree of success or happiness that it brought. Success was a concrete sign of the wisdom of the person who succeeded.

Although the wise woman or man believed that there was a right way of behaving, there was no insistence on a rigid standard that would fit everybody. Each case was unique. The wise person was the one who had a store of wisdom gained from experience and who knew which way of behaving was appropriate for each situation. The idea that the good shall be rewarded and the evil shall be punished undergirds most of the wisdom literature.

The wisdom tradition, unlike the Pentateuch, Historical books, and Prophetic books, does not refer to central aspects of the religious history of Israel, such as the Exodus; to religious practice as centered in the Temple; or to central concepts, such as covenant. It is more concerned with the human ability to discern pattern and stability in ordinary life, and to develop a religious understanding on that basis.

Israel's wisdom tradition did not develop in a vacuum. It was part of a much broader movement within the Near Eastern world. There is a remarkable similarity between the biblical wisdom material and some Egyptian, Mesopotamian, and Canaanite texts. The non-Israelite texts are significantly older, and more likely than not, Israel borrowed from its neighbors and adapted and reinterpreted when necessary.

# JOB READING GUIDE

## *At a Glance*

| | |
|---|---|
| Who are the main players? | Eliphaz Bildad Zophar Job Elihu the LORD |
| What should I look for? | Job's struggle with suffering is a universal and perennial problem. The universal appeal stems from the nature of the questions posed by the tormented Job. |
| When did this take place? | Evidence from the book itself is often given in support of a preexilic dating (seventh century B.C.), but there is no agreement regarding when it was written. Job is not a record of actual events, but a dramatic, philosophical dialogue. |
| Where did these events occur? | No location is given. Job's complaints are reminiscent of the laments of Jeremiah, and some consider the book an outcry against the destruction of Jerusalem and deportation. |
| Why was this written? | Job as wisdom literature asks the question: What kind of role does God play in everyday life, specifically in the sufferings of life? The innocent, good Job's sufferings will shed light on the meaning of suffering and the integrity of God. |
| What is the story? | Job, a good and upright man, loses his considerable wealth, health and family. Although he questions the cause of his suffering, and his supposed friends insist that he must have brought it on himself, he remains righteous and refuses to curse God. |

## About the Book of Job

Job's struggle with suffering is a universal problem. There are older Near Eastern accounts of innocent sufferers that may have influenced the author of Job. The names and places of origin of Job's three visitors suggest foreign influence. Still, whatever may have originated elsewhere has been used here with Israelite theology in mind. Israel's wisdom tradition is clearly in accord with its Yahwistic faith. It may not focus on specifics of religion, but it is highly ethical, fundamentally monotheistic, and, at times, equates wisdom with fidelity to the Law of Israel.

## When it Was Written

There is no agreement about the book's date, its place of origin, or the source of some of its parts. There is not even total agreement as to its principal theme. Evidence from the book itself is often given in support of a date before the Babylonian Exile (seventh century B.C.). Job's complaints are reminiscent of the lamentations of Jeremiah, and some consider the book an outcry of impending destruction of Jerusalem and deportation into exile. However, similarities with the theology and style of Deutero-Isaiah (the portion of Isaiah beginning with chapter 40) seem to tip the scale in favor of it being after the exile (sixth to fifth century B.C.). It certainly appeared before the third century B.C. when "Satan" appears as a proper name (1 Chr 21:1) instead of the designated role of an adversary in a court of justice, as is found in the book of Job.

Like most pieces of ancient literature, Job is a composite rather than the work of a single author. It appears to be a prose folktale (1:1–2:13; 42:7–17) into which extensive poetic speeches (3:1–42:6) have been inserted. Even within the speeches, we can detect units believed to have originated from someone other than the principal author. But regardless of when or from whom these different sections originated, they all belong to the final form, and it is this final form that has been handed down to us as sacred Scripture. Therefore we read it as a unified literary work.

The universal appeal of the book of Job stems from the nature of the questions by this innocent man. Who has not struggled with the dilemma of bewildering suffering? Who has not cried out to God, or at least wondered, "Why?"

As the drama unfolds, each section of the book of Job has its own dynamic. From the beginning, Job's innocence is established beyond any doubt and we see who is responsible for Job's misfortune. God permits this righteous man to suffer in order to test the quality of his integrity. Job never knows this, nor do his visitors. It is important that the reader know what took place in heaven as we listen to the theological debate that follows. By the many arguments of the poetic speeches adding layer upon layer of accusation and rebuttal, the author brings us into the very midst of the impasse of this pointless debate. Only God can resolve this.

## The Literary Style

The simple understanding of the story about the innocent man stricken and rewarded in the end for his faithfulness does not accurately represent the story of Job. It is merely the plot of the folktale that frames the poetic dialogues that compose the principal part of the book. The more we understand how the form of the book works, the more we will discover the message within it.

In the following ways, the literary style of the author contributes to the development of the book's message.

1. *The dialogues:* Speeches in Hebrew poetic form. Each time Job cries out about his sorry state, either Eliphaz, Bildad, or Zophar offer counsel or attempt to convince him of his error. The cycles of speech proceed in orderly fashion.

2. *The use of nature as means of instruction:* This is characteristic of the wisdom tradition. While it occurs throughout the entire book, nowhere else does it have the effect it does in God's speeches. By not directly addressing Job's question, God does not ignore Job's concerns. This is the way the author uses nature as a teaching tool.

3. *Poetry:* The kind found within the book is unlike classical or contemporary poetry. There is no rhyme and the rhythm follows tonal patterns that are lost when the original Hebrew is translated.

4. *Lawsuit:* Again and again Job demands that God meet him in court where his case will be tried and he will be found innocent (23:2–4).

5. *Lament:* Job cries out to God in complaint and laments the day of his birth (3:1–10) and life

itself (10:1–7), and he pleads for help (13:20–27).

## The Message

While the book of Job is a poetic narrative, it is also a theological statement made up of several themes. The way we understand this theology will influence the way we perceive the arguments in this book. The themes here are presented not in any order of importance but as they appear in the book.

### Reward and Punishment

The belief that goodness should be rewarded and evil punished undergirds most of the wisdom literature. This theory probably arose out of life experience itself. When in the natural course of events it does not happen, someone in authority steps in to see that justice is done. We need this in order to live with a certain degree of security.

Job's real agony, however, lies in the incomprehensibility of his situation. Because he is suffering, it is assumed that he must have sinned. Because his suffering is so intense, his sin must be great. Job's visitors argue this point and try to persuade him to repent because they assume he is guilty. This same kind of thinking prompted the apostles to ask Jesus whether it was the sin of the blind man or of his parents that resulted in the man's blindness (see Jn 9:2).

Job holds to this theory as well, but from a different point of view. Since he has done nothing to deserve such misfortune, he blames God. He believes that it is God who usually decides who will be rewarded and who will be punished and accomplishes this through the laws set at creation. When these laws fail, the tradition of Israel claims that God intervenes to enforce justice. So from Job's point of view, God has failed to do this in his case.

Since the speeches argue in defense of or in opposition to Job's innocence, one would think that when God finally does thunder from the whirlwind, everything would become clear. But the question of justice is not addressed. Instead, the issue is the creative wisdom and power of God. This is not an avoidance of the question. Remember that God is cast in the role of a wisdom teacher who asks rhetorical questions and makes reference to the natural world in order to make a point. God leads Job to see that just as there is much in nature he cannot understand, so there is much in human experience that is beyond him. In this way God reveals the inadequacy of the theory of retribution. Happiness and success are not rewards for righteous living, nor are grief and failure punishment for unfaithfulness. Suffering is not a sure sign of alienation from God.

> **Theodicy,** from the Greek for "justifying God," is the name given to our attempt to explain the problem of evil, while at the same time maintaining the belief that God is a moral creator who is in control and who loves those who suffer. For the wisdom tradition, theodicy was of particular importance because the standard view of wisdom was that right behavior in life generally led to prosperity. The book of Job argues against this standard view.

Once we are convinced that certain suffering is undeserved, we are faced with a very troubling question: Why does God seem to allow injustice to occur? If Job did not believe God is a moral God, the question of evil would take a totally different turn. If God is not righteous then Job's suffering might be just as difficult to bear but would not be the puzzle it is. He would know that he could not depend on God. Such a view was foreign to Israel's faith. Job's counselors never question God's integrity, and Job does so only reluctantly and at the risk of falsely accusing God.

Another view holds that God could be moral but not able to control evil completely. This is the theory held by some thinkers concerning the Holocaust when they cannot explain why God allowed so many millions of innocent people to be exterminated during World War II. This thinking is not found in the Bible. Israel believed its God was the undisputed creator (see Is 45:7; Am 3:6).

Some may think God is both moral and omnipotent but unconcerned about simple people. Surely the Almighty has more important things to do than worry about the fortunes or misfortunes of one person. The traditions of Israel contradict this notion as well. From the stories of their ancestors we see God portrayed as attentive to the most personal needs of the individual (see Genesis). This memory causes Job to lament his present situation. How could God, who cared for him in earlier years, turn against him now?

While theodicy is not an issue for Job or for his visitors, it is of major importance for the author of the book, who depicts God as all-powerful and provident and a God of unchallenged goodness. At the end, the question of suffering may be left unanswered but the integrity of God is no longer questioned.

**Reward or Vindication**

In a very real sense, the drama of the book stems from Satan's challenge found in 1:9: "Is it for nothing that Job is God-fearing?" It is easy to be loyal to God when things are going right and he is happy with life. Take away these good things, and Job will not only give up his way of integrity, he will actually curse God. God takes the dare.

Twice Job is assaulted and he neither curses God nor veers from his attachment to God. His confidence has not been shaken and he actually praises God. It is probable that he did expect to be blessed for being faithful. So the question remains: Was Job faithful for the sake of reward or was his piety really disinterested?

Job's laments and pleading show that he does not look for reward; he wants vindication. He is not concerned about possessions; he insists that his integrity be acknowledged. When he finally understands the lesson God set out to teach him, he is silent and seems content with his new insights. Now we know that the depth of Job's piety is based on his relationship with God, not on some promise of reward.

We must remember that at that time Israelites did not have a clear idea of reward or punishment in an afterlife, as Christian theology teaches. If justice was not received in this life, they had no hope at all for retribution.

**Suffering**

Although the customary way of understanding suffering was a punishment for sin, the book of Job does provide other explanations for it. The prologue itself tells us that God allowed Job's misfortunes to befall him so that Job's integrity might be tested (1:11; 2:3–5). In the book of Genesis "God put Abraham to the test" (Gn 22:1) and told him to sacrifice his son Isaac. The difference, however, is that in the end Abraham was told that he had been tested while Job never knows about God's dealings with Satan.

Suffering is sometimes seen as a source of moral discipline, a warning against sin and a defense against pride and self-satisfaction.

Other interpretations include suffering endured for others (the Suffering Servant: Is 52:13–53:12); undergoing purification (Ps 66:10); a necessary way of accomplishing the will of God (Joseph in Egypt: Gn 50:20). Only the first two explanations are found in the book of Job.

The ancient Near East offered another explanation referred to as the "curse of the evil deed." It claimed that those who engage in evil infect themselves in the process: "Whoever digs a pit falls into it" (Prv 26:27). God does not intervene to punish.

The writers appear to be more interested in the reason and purpose of suffering than in its origin. They offer temporary explanations to strengthen people in their struggle. Circumstances change and the advice might cease to be appropriate, which is precisely the case in Job. No one seems able to offer him an adequate explanation for his suffering.

**God in the Life of Humans**

Up to this point the themes have focused our attention on Job. Now we turn our gaze toward God. In his complaints, Job characterizes God as powerful and oppressive when near and unconcerned when at a distance. Job's companions describe God as a prosecuting judge. But the image unveiled in the speeches of the LORD is quite different.

God is indeed powerful, but it is a wondrous, awe-inspiring power. It is true that God is transcendent, but this does not prevent God from being attentive to the mountain goat about to kid (see 39:1). Finally, God does not assume the role of divine judge to find Job guilty. Instead, God as the divine teacher leads Job to new horizons of understanding. Now Job understands that he has been treading on mystery—"things too marvelous for me" (42:3). This provident yet mysterious God of creation is the same God who works in the life of each of us yet remains a mystery.

The enigma of the suffering of good people and the good fortune of the wicked was one addressed by Israelite literature, both in the Psalms and in other wisdom texts. Distinctive to the book of Job is the way it situates these issues. The book is neither a treatise on innocent suffering, as often supposed, nor an apology for God's justice in the face of inexplicable human suffering. Rather, the principal theological issue that the book raises is, ironically, the question posed by the adversary in the divine council (see 1:9): Will mortals be religious apart from rewards and punishment or do they act as they should simply because God will reward or punish them accordingly? As the dialogue develops, however, the questions of divine justice that torture Job's mind are not satisfactorily met by the arguments of his friends. Yet when God answers Job, it is neither as the friends have imagined God would speak nor as Job had hoped God would answer him.

The meaning and significance of the divine speeches continue to be among the most debated issues in the book. Some interpret the speeches as a repudiation of a human's right to question God. Others understand them as a necessary correction to Job's too-limited understanding of the world as a place where all suffering can be reduced to legal categories of guilt and innocence. All agree that the extraordinary beauty of the poetry is part of its meaning. Perhaps the very elusiveness of the divine speeches implies that no answer from God to Job's questions can satisfy the human intellect. Yet the ending suggests that there is a resolution to be found in the depth of a pious life lived before a mysterious God.

**Questions for Discussion and Reflection**

***Group Sharing/Discussion***

1. What are the most important lessons you can find in this book of the Bible?

2. In this literary tradition of the wisdom writings, Israel claimed that it encountered God *through* human experience, not *in addition to* it. Explain how Job is an example of this. How do you believe you encounter God in your human experience?

3. Israel's wisdom tradition is clearly in accord with its Yahwistic faith. It may not focus on specifics of religion, but it is highly ethical and fundamentally monotheistic, or believes in only one God. How is the faith of Christians today similar or different?

***In Our Lives***

1. Job remained faithful to God but did not hesitate to complain to God. He certainly can be a model to us of having the courage to remain faithful, but also a model of staying in conversation with God. Prayer is described as talking with God. We tell our joys and our troubles to our best friend, even lamenting, although not blaming them. How is Job's relationship with God similar or different to your relationship with God?

2. Some of Job's "friends" were hardly helpful when they came to visit him. There are people in pain of different kinds today who do not have anyone to even come visit them. How does our community look out for those who suffer alone? Sometimes, as in chapter 2:11–13 they just need someone to sit with them. How does our parish reach out to families at times of loss? What more might we consider doing?

3. Job's visitors accused him unjustly. They assumed he had sinned and was being punished. It can be hard to put aside our prejudices and assumptions about people or things we feel strongly about—issues in politics or Church or among our family members. Some people suggest checking yourself out by "arguing with yourself" from the opposite point of view as yours. When would it be helpful to you to put aside your prejudices and be more open? What will help you to do this?

***Individual/Personal Reflection/Action***

1. A young, talented priest with cancer was asked by a friend why was this happening to him of all people; his immediate response was, "Why not me?" Job's question was the opposite, "Why me?" How would you respond to each of those questions?

2. If you are suffering, have the courage and humility to ask for help, from God and from your friends. If you see people who are suffering, be the friend to them that Job could have used.

3. Spend a few minutes each morning or evening this week just talking with God, telling God what is on your mind and in your heart in a familiar way, such as Job did.

# PSALMS READING GUIDE

*At a Glance*

| | |
|---|---|
| Who are the main players? | David Korah Asaph |
| What should I look for? | Psalms are prayerful responses to life experiences. Types of psalms are mainly classified as lament, hymns, and thanksgiving, also wisdom poems and royal psalms. The fact that the psalmist cries out to God demonstrates Israel's belief that God has the power and will to deliver the nation in present distress. |
| When did this take place? | Different times. Depending upon the dating of a particular psalm, the events could have been the fall of the northern kingdom (c. 722 B.C.), the Babylonian Exile (c. 586 B.C.), or the Maccabean conflict (107 B.C.). |
| Where did these events occur? | In general in Israel. Our present book of Psalms was composed from earlier collections. Some are attributed to David in Jerusalem. Several in the second and third books are ascribed to Korah and Asaph, two guilds of Temple singers during the period of the second Temple. |
| Why was this book written? | The expressions of rich piety found in the book of Psalms give us an insight into the theology in ancient Israel. The portrait of God found in the Psalms draws together all the divine faces found in the rest of Israel's tradition. For Jews and Christians the Psalms are much more than profoundly moving poetry. They are voices of our respective faiths. |
| What is the story? | The Psalms reveal Israel's understanding of and relationship with God. For the early Christians the Psalms were not only prayer but contained statements of faith, statements that found fulfillment in the person and mission of Jesus. |

The book of Psalms, also known as the Psalter, is a collection of poetical prayers. Its title in Hebrew, "tehillim," means "praises," and the English title comes from the Greek word "psalmos," meaning a song that is accompanied by a stringed instrument. The Psalter is divided into books, each of which ends with a short hymn of praise called a doxology:

The First Book:
Psalms 1–41 end with a doxology in 41:14

The Second Book:
Psalms 42–72 end with 72:18f

The Third Book:
Psalms 73–89 end with 89:53

The Fourth Book: Psalms 90–106 end with 106:48

The Fifth Book:
Psalms 107–150 end with an entire psalm of praise (Ps 150)

## Who Wrote the Psalms?

Evidence within the book of Psalms itself indicates that it is made up of earlier collections. Several psalms, found principally in the first book, are attributed to David. (This may account for the popular but probably not historically accurate tradition that David himself wrote most of the psalms.) Several psalms in the second and third books are ascribed to Korah and Asaph, the two great guilds of Temple singers during the period of the second Temple (see 1 Chr 6:33f; 25:1f), a period that began around 400 B.C., six centuries after David's time. The fourth book also has possible references to the destruction of Jerusalem (587 or 586 B.C.); for instance, Psalm 102:13–22 fits with the time when Jerusalem lay in ruins and was about to be restored. Finally, the fifth book is made up of a number of Songs of Ascent—probably songs sung by those on pilgrimage to Jerusalem—and psalms of praise known as the Hallel ("praise") or Hallelujah collection. These groupings may have been the original collections around which other psalms clustered.

## Types of Psalms

The three major categories are: lament, hymn, and thanksgiving. There are also royal psalms, wisdom psalms, and some that might fit into more than one category.

### Laments

The most common type of psalm is the lament. Nearly a third of the psalms belong to this category. Depending on who the speaker is, they are further classified as either community or individual laments.

**Community Laments (Pss 12, 14, 44, 53, 58, 60, 74, 79, 80, 83, 85, 90, 94, 106, 123, 126, 137)**

- Apparently part of Israel's Temple liturgies
- Used when people were gathered to fast and pray because of national humiliation or distress
- Israel's rivals were viewed as opposed to the LORD
- A recital of the former deeds that God accomplished in the history of the nation
- Purpose: to remind God of past favors and encourage God to grant new ones
- Used to remind people of God's earlier blessings and to instill confidence in their hearts

**Individual Laments (Pss 3–7, 13, 17, 22, 25–28, 31, 35, 36, 38–40, 42, 43, 51, 52, 54–57, 59, 61, 63, 64, 67–71, 77, 86, 88, 102, 109, 120, 130, 140–143)**

- Prayerful responses to personal misfortunes such as illness or persecution
- An integral part of personal liturgical devotion
- Frequently suffering people went to the Temple or a shrine to request help or deliverance

The usual structure of the lament is an introduction, a plea for deliverance from misfortune, praise of God or an expression of confidence that God will come to the rescue, and a vow to perform an act of worship in gratitude for God's help. Some laments include an acknowledgment of guilt or a claim of innocence. Often the psalmist hurls a curse at those responsible for the situation that brought about the lament.

### Hymns

The hymn is a song praising God and can be either an individual's prayer or for the whole community to use in the liturgies of Israel's major festivals.

**Hymns of Praise (Pss 8, 19, 29, 33, 100, 103, 104, 111, 113, 114, 117, 135, 136, 145–150)**

The structure of a hymn is quite simple. It begins with a call to praise, which suggests that this type of psalm originated in a community setting, followed by an account of the wondrous acts of God, and ends with a repetition of the initial call to praise, some expression of exaltation of God, and a plea for God's blessing.

**Hymns of the Lord's Kingship (Pss 47, 93, 96–99)**

This is a distinct group among the psalms. Their focus is the LORD, the universal king. They were a way that perhaps helped the Israelites deal with the fact that creation is not always friendly and life does not always favor us. Nonetheless, the LORD was truly in charge.

**The Songs of Zion (Pss 46, 48, 76, 84, 87, 122)**

These psalms extol Zion as God's holy mountain and Jerusalem as the city God chose to inhabit. We are not certain about the setting at which the songs of Zion were sung.

### Thanksgiving

Thanksgiving psalms are similar to hymns in that they praise the marvelous works of God. Like the laments, they were probably part of the liturgy or personal prayer life of the people and were used when thanksgiving was in order. It is difficult to classify these psalms because expressions of confidence and gratitude are also often found within the laments. There are some psalms that might be considered explicit psalms of thanksgiving:

- Communal Psalms: Pss 115, 125, 129
- Individual Psalms: Pss 11, 16, 23, 62, 91, 121, 131
- Psalms of General Thanksgiving: Pss 9, 10, 30, 32, 41, 116, 138

### Royal Psalms

Israel was a nation that perceived its king as the representative of the whole people before God and as God's special envoy for the people. This assured the king of the special place he enjoyed. Various occasions in the king's life form the settings for these psalms: coronation hymns (Pss 2, 72, 101, 110), an anniversary hymn (Ps 132), a royal wedding song (Ps 45), petitions on behalf of the warrior-king (Pss 20, 144), and prayers of thanksgiving for his success (Pss 18, 21). These psalms are often referred to as "messianic psalms," since "messiah" means "anointed one" and that is what a king was. They take on new meaning in the Christian tradition when they are applied to Jesus, the supreme "anointed one" of God.

### Wisdom Poems

These psalms (1, 37, 49, 73, 112, 119, 127, 128) call people to listen and learn, rather than to pray. They are, in general, concerned with the problem of evil, the suffering of the righteous, and the justice of God. These psalms use the language and imagery of the wisdom tradition.

The sages of ancient Israel used several techniques that helped people learn. Some of these appear in the wisdom psalms. One of the most popular was the acrostic arrangement. In this form the letters of the alphabet in order determine the beginning letter of the first word of each successive line (Ps 37, 111, and 119). Because they follow this pattern, some commentators include them as wisdom poems rather than hymns (Ps 145), laments (Ps 125), or thanksgiving psalms (Pss 9, 10, 34).

### Various Psalms

These are other psalms, like Songs of Ascent (going up to the Temple) used during pilgrimage (Pss 120–134) or those for processions around Jerusalem (Pss 15, 24, 95). Since people frequently came to the Temple or to a shrine in search of some word from the LORD, some psalms trace their origin to a style of prophetic speech.

A few psalms do not fit into any of the categories we have mentioned. They are either stories about the feats of the LORD (Pss 78, 105), combinations of other psalm forms (Pss 108, 133, 139), or general liturgical songs (Ps 134).

## The Theology in the Psalms

The expressions of piety found within the book of Psalms give us insight into the theology of ancient Israel.

### The God of Israel

The portrait of God sketched in the Psalms draws together all of the divine traits found in the rest of the Israelite tradition. This God is

- the creator of the universe (Ps 8:4)
- the source of all life (Ps 36:10)
- enthroned in heaven (Ps 47:6)
- yet dwelling in Jerusalem (Ps 76:3)
- Israel's exclusive liberator (Ps 66:6)
- yet gradually seen as concerned for all people (Ps 117)

This majestic God inspires both fear (Ps 89:8) and confidence (Ps 23) and is demanding (Ps 75:83) as well as forgiving (Ps 85:3). Above everything God is "merciful and gracious . . . slow to anger, abounding in mercy" (Ps 103:8; see Ps 86:5). The LORD is the "covenant partner." Everything that is important to Israel flows from this perception of God.

### The Image of God

The human person is held in high regard in the Psalms. Honored as the culmination of creation, humanity is given responsibility for the other living creatures of the earth (Ps 8; see Gn 1). The psalmist marvels at this singular work of divine artistry.

Why should God be personally committed to such an insignificant being (Pss 8:5; 144:3f)? As extraordinary as they are, humans live a fleeting life (Ps 39:5f) and then perish like flowers in the field (Ps 103:15f). At the time the Psalms were written, Israelite religion did not include any clear notion of life after death. Human dignity was related to life in this world. In the Psalms

- God fully knows what human beings are, and they are totally dependent on God (Ps 139)
- God provides for their basic needs (Ps 65:10–14) and protects them from harm (Ps 121)
- God is the guardian of the poor and the afflicted (Ps 40:18), defenseless widows and orphans (Ps 68:6), and the *anawim* or lowly (Ps 147:6)

## The Piety of the Psalmist

The psalms generally speak *to* God rather than *about* God, but it is a particular kind of God that the psalms address. We can learn much about God by seeing how God is spoken to, and what the psalms expect of God. It will be helpful to return to the classifications (hymns, laments, thanksgiving, etc.) to look at the piety of Israel contained in the Psalms.

### Praise

Praise is the primary nature of psalms, and hymns of praise are the most common type of psalm in the Psalter. Most psalms are, in one way or another, aimed at praising God—for his power and assistance, for his creation of the world, and for his past acts of deliverance to Israel. Often the praise comes after the psalmist has prayed for help from sickness or enemies (the typical subject of complaints) and that prayer has been answered. As part of such a complaint, the psalmist promises to praise God when God has delivered from trouble one who prays. Thanksgiving for God's help is another form of praise. According to the outlook of Psalms, the main religious function of human beings is to offer praise to God, to proclaim God's greatness throughout the world. Thus, the Psalms encourage others to praise God, and they envision a world in which everyone and everything will praise God. This implies a relationship between God and humans, another important dimension of Psalms. God's character is one that hears prayers and responds. Worst of all is when he "hides his face" and refuses to pay attention to the psalmist, because this puts into question the power of prayer, one primary underlying assumption in the book of Psalms.

### The Songs of Zion

"Zion" seems originally to have meant the fortified hill that was the basis of the city of Jerusalem, originally a Canaanite settlement. It came to mean both Jerusalem as the religious center of Israelite life and the people who lived there. These songs contain some of the same images as the psalms in honor of the LORD King. In ancient Canaanite mythology, after the forces of evil have been conquered, a palace is built for the victor on the summit of the highest mountain, as was done by Solomon, David's son, after David conquered Jerusalem and made it his capital city. From this summit the hero holds sway over the entire universe.

Israel revered Zion as this sacred mountain and revered the Temple as the palace of the victorious creator God. God's creative power is now associated with the nation and, because of the close connection between Zion and David, specifically with the monarchy.

In these psalms God is praised as totally committed to the welfare of Israel. God is not distant from the people but lives in their midst, allowing them to approach the divine presence mysteriously dwelling in the Temple. Other nations were also allowed to worship the LORD in this holy place.

### Grief, Fear, Repentance, and Confidence

The conviction of God's special love and care led Israel to hope for security in a hostile world and a life of serenity and prosperity. This state of affairs is what the Bible refers to as *shalom*, or peace. Psalms of lament grew out of the absence of such peace.

Community laments apply to some national disaster that has already taken place. Depending on the date of the particular psalm, this calamity could have been:

- the fall of the northern kingdom of Israel (about 722 B.C.)
- the destruction of Jerusalem and the Babylonian Exile (about 586 B.C.)
- the desecration of the second Temple and the Maccabean revolt (about 167–164 B.C.)

The fact that the psalmist cries out to God indicates that Israel's belief in God's saving power is based on former saving events in the history of the people (Pss 44:2–4; 74:2; 83:10). Even as the people cried out in complaint, they were proclaiming God's all-encompassing power and declaring God's continued concern for them based on covenantal promises.

### Gratitude

Gratitude is obvious in the Psalms. The structure and content of thanksgiving psalms resemble those of the hymn. First the worshiper praises God's goodness and only then offers thanks.

### National Loyalty

Since the king was perceived as the representative of the whole people before God and as God's special envoy, loyalty to the king and to the nation was considered an act of devotion to God.

### An Understanding Heart

The wisdom psalms generally do not address God but are usually directed toward the community. The piety of the psalmist is shown in the way themes are presented.

The problem of evil, the suffering of the innocent, and the justice of God are all facets of the same issue: the right order of the universe. Evil that is clearly not a punishment for wrongdoing can challenge the sovereignty of God over creation. God either cannot repress evil or is unwilling to do so. While Job and Ecclesiastes live with the unanswered question of innocent suffering, the wisdom psalms do not challenge the prevailing situation. They presume that the suffering of the righteous is due to some legitimate purpose, which God will reveal at the appropriate time (see 1 Kgs 3:10–12).

### Enthusiasm, Humility, and Faithfulness

We can see these characteristics in the processional psalms, which invite the observant Israelite to participate with heart and soul in various liturgical celebrations. During the three "pilgrim feasts"—Passover or Unleavened Bread, Pentecost or Feast of Weeks, and Sukkoth or the Feast of Tabernacles—people traveled to Jerusalem, singing psalms as they approached the city. There were shouts of profound joy as well as humble acknowledgments of the need for pure hearts when approaching the holy city and the Temple of the LORD.

### Natural Creation

The Psalms reveal a special regard for creation as the handiwork of God (Ps 104). This view does not see nature itself as divine, or its mysterious powers as manifestations of many different gods, but rather shows nature to be a fellow creature along with humankind. God is revealed in the thunderstorm (Ps 29) and in the design of the natural world (Ps 65:7), where creation is no longer seen as a rival for the homage of the people but as a partner in the praise of God (Ps 148).

> **Sheol** The Psalms say very little about life beyond the grave, but they frequently mention a shadowy existence known as *Sheol* (Ps 49, 141). This was a place of neither reward nor punishment, but merely of darkness and dust, the abode of the dead. While Israel did not have a clear idea of a life after death, it entertained the possibility that the dead did not cease to exist.

### The Future

Ancient Israel was interested in both the future of the nation and the fate of the individual. The positive view it takes on this issue of *eschatology* stems from its faith in the goodness of God. Despite the struggles of attempting to live in a quarrelsome world, Israel believed that the final victory would be the LORD's. Individuals, too, clung to the conviction that God would right all wrongs and that they would enjoy the happiness that was their due.

An earlier theology taught that reward and punishment would be worked out in the community or down through the generations. But this theory was challenged when the wicked prospered, and even more when Jerusalem and the Temple were destroyed, leaving future generations without a place in which God could vindicate their trust. In response, the psalmist claimed that such prosperity would not last and the upright should not envy sinners (Ps 37:2). Still, the apparently peaceful death of the prosperous wicked and the suffering of the righteous remained an unresolved problem.

### The Psalms and the New Testament

It is clear that the early Christian community did not tend to distinguish between explicit theological statements on one hand and prayer on the other. For them, the Psalms were not only prayer but also contained important statements of faith, statements that found their fulfillment in the person and mission of Jesus (see Lk 24:44). The New Testament cites various psalms. Five seem to be referred to more than the rest:

- The messianic psalms 2 and 110: cited in discussions of Jesus' Messianic preeminence (Acts 13:33 and Heb 1:5)
- The individual laments 22 and 69: used in descriptions of Jesus' passion and death, suggesting that the psalmist was foretelling Jesus' suffering

• The communal thanksgiving Psalm 118: speaks of the rejected stone that becomes the cornerstone (v. 22; see Mt 21:42) and the blessedness of the one who comes in the name of the LORD (v. 26; see Mk 11:9)

### The Psalms Today

Most people are acquainted with the Psalms as they are used in the liturgy and the prayer life of the Church. Others may be more familiar through personal prayer and private devotion.

The Psalms are some of the most beautiful poetry that the human spirit has created. One need not be familiar with the historical situations from which the Psalms originated in order to appreciate them. Like all classic poetry they speak to every culture and every age. We may not come to the Psalms with hearts filled with praise, thanksgiving, or grief, but the world mirrored there relates to our own. We know that world, or at least we sense that we should know it, and we cry out with praise, thanksgiving, or grief. This poetic imagery can become a starting point of meditation on the Psalms.

For Jews and Christians the Psalms are the voice of their respective faith. Liturgy is not merely a celebration of some past event. It is an enactment through which promises and claims that were made in the past become present realities. Now these are *our* sentiments; this is *our* prayer.

### Questions for Discussion and Reflection

***Group Sharing/Discussion***

1. Allow time for each person in your group to choose a favorite psalm. Take turns reading them aloud and tell why you chose what you did.

2. Sheol is mentioned many times in the Psalms, such as Psalms 49 and 141, as the shadowy place where all the dead are. How does this compare with your own idea of heaven?

3. Lament, hymn and thanksgiving. Divide into three subgroups and have each choose a lament, a hymn, or a thanksgiving psalm. Before sharing it with the entire group, explain its meaning or significance to your group.

4. How would you describe this book of the Bible to someone who has never been exposed to it?

***In Our Lives***

1. Right after the first scripture reading at every Mass, we pray a psalm in community, so we hear many psalms over the three-year liturgical cycle. How will this study of the Psalms help you pray them better at Mass?

2. As we praise God for the splendor of creation and acknowledge it is God's gift to us, we are moved to profound respect for the world of which we are a part. The hymns of praise can instill in us a sense of responsibility to care for God's creation. What are ways in our own town or community that we can better care for the treasure of God's gift of the environment?

3. The songs of Zion honor the mountain as the dwelling place of God to which all nations are invited. The LORD is not in some distant, remote place, inaccessible to people, but in the midst of people, approachable, even inviting. Think of times you are aware of the LORD's presence. What would help you feel that God is inviting and approachable?

***Individual/Personal Reflection/Action***

1. Jesus prayed the Psalms at the last supper, and on the cross he prayed Psalm 22. The apostles and early Christians also used the Psalms as prayers. Commit yourself to spending a few minutes each day reading or praying one of the psalms.

2. Psalms of thanksgiving help us remember that whatever we enjoy has come to us from the hand of a gracious God and we would do well to be as generous with these gifts toward others as God has been toward us. Choose one concrete way you can put your generosity into action.

3. Solidarity with those who suffer is one way to enter into the world of the laments. As we share their suffering, their prayer becomes our own. Laments can strengthen us in our commitments to justice and peace. Learn about the peace efforts of our church and other religious organizations.

# PROVERBS READING GUIDE

*At a Glance*

| | |
|---|---|
| Who are the main players? | Solomon Hezekiah |
| What should I look for? | The Hebrew word translated as "proverb" embraces a broad category of literary forms: oracle (Nm 23:7); discourse (Jb 29:1); parable (Ps 78:2); taunt-song (Is 14:4). In each case there is a lesson to be learned. Proverbs describe how things work. Their purpose is not to indoctrinate, but to educate. They are not precepts that call for obedience, but adages that invite prudent response. The book of Proverbs clearly insists on the importance of living an ethical life. The ethics it promotes, however, issue from reflection on life rather than from conformity to Law. |
| When did this take place? | Although there is not enough information to reconstruct accurately its historical period, the Proverbs attests to both Hezekiah's influence and Solomon's reputation. |
| Where did these events occur? | Israel |
| Why was this book written? | Proverbs is probably the biblical book that best characterizes the wisdom tradition. It appears to be the "guide for successful living" referred to in the introduction. Its primary purpose is to teach wisdom. |
| What is the story? | It makes its appeal to various groups of people in different walks of life. It exhorts children (not necessarily or only young children) to heed the teaching of their parents (1:8), and it directs citizens to act with respect toward the king (16:10–15). It warns young men of the dangers of undisciplined living (5:1–14; 23:29–35), and it offers a portrait of the model wife for women to emulate (31:10–31). |

## Introduction

The book of Proverbs is an anthology—a collection of instructions plus speeches of wisdom (chs 1–9), two large collections of two-line sayings (chs 10–22 and 25–29), a booklet of counsels (22:17–24:34), and some poems (chs 30–31). The two chief literary types represented in the book are the instruction or lecture and the proverb or pithy saying. The instructional passages are examples of the instruction used in Mesopotamia, but especially favored in Egypt. In a typical instruction, a king, high official, or father instructs his son (or disciple or successor) how to live so as to enjoy the blessings of life and avoid unnecessary trouble. Despite their practical and common-sense approach, instructions were thoroughly religious, for they were written in the assumption that the world yields its blessings to those who respect the gods and direct their lives in accord with the order and rhythms of the divinely fashioned universe. The second type, the saying or proverb, was also very common in the ancient Near East. The two-line proverbs of Proverbs are broader than the modern proverb, which in one definition is "a concise statement of an apparent truth." Some verses in Proverbs are proverbs in this sense, but there are also witty sayings, paradoxes, and riddles. The sayings are hard to translate. In their original language, however, the sayings are incisive and witty, provoking readers to take a fresh look at life.

The universal truths of Proverbs remain relevant today. Proverbs proclaims that God's world is good, yielding its full blessings only to those who seek wisdom, do justice, and revere God. To those, however, who do not listen to the wisdom God has placed in the world and who are hostile to their neighbor, the world will prove a dangerous place: Evil comes back upon the wicked. The virtues of wisdom, justice, and piety are acquired through discipline, a process requiring sincerity, persistence, and openness to those more experienced. The book declares that right, wise, and reverent conduct is the only way to happiness, which God is invited to grant as a gift.

The book is difficult for some modern readers to enjoy. Some find the instructions without content and the sayings trite. It must be remembered that the instructions of chs 1–9 are concerned with forming character—developing an openhearted person who is faithful to the basic relationships of life (God, spouse, household, and neighbors) and who rejects easy compromises. They contain traditional insights that help us to grow in wisdom as we decode and ponder them.

**Outline of the Book of Proverbs**

| | |
|---|---|
| 1–9 | Collection of wisdom speeches and instructions |
| 10:1–22:16 | Proverbs of Solomon |
| 22:17–24:22 | The words of the wise |
| 24:23–34 | Appendix to words of the wise |
| 25–29 | Proverbs of Solomon edited by Hezekiah's scribes |
| 30:10–14 | The words of Agur |
| 30:15–33 | Numerical sayings |
| 31:1–9 | The words of Lemuel king of Massa |
| 31:10–31 | Praise of the capable wife |

## Who Wrote Proverbs?

That question is vigorously debated. Some believe the sayings and instructions originated with scribes in the royal court (or a scribal school), whereas others believe the materials originated with tribal elders instructing the young in ancestral traditions and customs, the material being written down later by scribes. Much material may be ultimately of folk origin, although the uniform and sophisticated style of the sayings and the foreign influence on the instructions suggests the book was essentially the work of palace scribes.

The first verse of the book states that Solomon is the author of the proverbs. There was a tradition that this king was not only versed in human wisdom (see 1 Kgs 3:16–18) but had encyclopedic knowledge as well (see 1 Kgs 3:4–14). Ancient people believed that wisdom belonged by right to the god, and since the king was the human representative of the god, it was the special possession of the king. Since Solomon ruled during a time of splendor and enlightenment, he became known in popular devotion as the wise man par excellence. His reputation gave credibility to wisdom writing and, as more wisdom writing was attributed to him, his reputation grew. Ascribing Solomonic authorship to Proverbs gives the book the status of official teaching and credits the king with comprehensive wisdom.

There is a possibility that the *real* royal authority behind the Proverbs is Hezekiah. Collections of proverbs could well have been compiled during the time of his religious reform and *he* could have ascribed them to Solomon. We do not have enough information to accurately reconstruct this historical period. The book of Proverbs, itself, however, attests to both Hezekiah's influence (25:1) and Solomon's reputation (1:1; 10:1; 25:1).

## About the Book

Proverbs is probably the biblical book that best characterizes the wisdom tradition. It appears to be the "guide for successful living" referred to in the Introduction. Its primary purpose is to teach wisdom. It makes an appeal to various groups of people in different walks of life. It teaches children (not necessarily or only young children) to heed the teaching of their parents (1:8), and it directs citizens to act with respect toward the king (16:10–15). It warns young men of the dangers of undisciplined living (5:1–14; 23:29–35), and it offers a portrait of the model wife for women to emulate (31:10–31).

The book itself is composed of eight collections of teaching. These are quite distinct sections. Several of them are identified within the biblical text itself. Others can be distinguished by their particular literary forms.

The first section consists of a general introduction to the entire book (1:1–7) and a collection of instruction (1:8–9:18). It is in this section that we find the student addressed again and again as "my son" and exhorted to listen to the teaching that is advanced. Fifteen of the 23 instances of this address appear in the first seven chapters of the book. The form clearly marks this section as instruction.

The second section (10:1–22:16) is explicitly

identified as "the Proverbs of Solomon" (10:1). Each verse in this section is a saying in its own right. Its meaning does not depend on what precedes it nor what follows it.

It is possible that the third section of the book (22:17–24:22), instructions entitled "The Words of the Wise," is patterned after a collection of an Egyptian scribe, Amen-em-Ope (22:19). If this is the case, it is probably the most obvious example in the wisdom tradition of Israel's literary borrowing from other ancient Near Eastern cultures.

The fourth section (24:23–34), a group of sentences designated "also . . . Words of the Wise" (24:23) is quite short. It is followed by a much longer collection of sentence literature (25:1–29:27) titled "the Proverbs of Solomon" (25:1). This collection is further linked with the sages of the court of Hezekiah, the Judean king who ruled around the turn of the seventh century B.C. It appears that he inaugurated a period of religious reform and literary activity. The mention of his name in a collection of proverbs may be evidence of this movement.

The sixth section, called "The words of Agur" (30:1), is the shortest (30:1–6). It is followed by a collection of proverbs that are distinguished by their literary form (30:7–33). The numerical proverbs, so named because of their use of numbers, have much in common with the riddle. The latter is a form mentioned in one of the introductory verses (1:6) and in other places of the Bible (see the riddle of Samson, Jgs 14:12, and the test of the queen of Sheba, 1 Kgs 10:1), but found nowhere in the book of Proverbs itself. The eighth and last section can be divided into two parts: instruction (31:1–9), entitled "The words of Lemuel" (31:1); and a poem describing the ideal wife (31:10–31).

## The Role of Wisdom Today

Proverbs may not be popular reading today because it seems to describe a world that does not exist—a world that has a proper order and in which events follow a cause-and-effect sequence. We know that life is very unpredictable and the events of life cannot be foreseen.

• Proverbs does not claim to describe everything, but each proverb does depict a snippet of life. Together they offer a collage, not a blueprint.

• The process that produces proverbs may be more important than the content of the proverbs themselves. It teaches us the importance of serious reflection on experience and the need to adjust our behavior as circumstances change.

Proverbs offers us an appreciation of life and encouragement to live it well.

### Questions for Discussion and Reflection

***Group Sharing***

1. Divide into two or more small groups. Let one "make the case" for each of the following proverbs. Do not criticize the other proverb but just explain why "yours" is good to follow.

The beginning of wisdom is: get wisdom (4:7)

The beginning of wisdom is the fear of the LORD (9:10).

2. Discuss how women are perceived or described in Proverbs. Compare that with today's views of women. Talk about the characterization of wisdom as a woman.

***In Our Lives***

1. Reflecting upon your ordinary experiences of this past week, think of an event that could be the basis for a contemporary proverb. Jot it down. Test out the wisdom of your proverb with the group. Does it resonate with others' experience?

2. Many people struggle with parenting today. Look through the book of Proverbs. Which ones offer valuable guidance for the training of children and youth in our contemporary world? If you are a parent, how might you apply them today? If you are a young person, how would you want them applied to you?

3. If you were writing your own book of Proverbs, what are some things you would absolutely want to include?

4. How can/does our parish share the wisdom of people within the community? How can we do this better rather than ignore these treasures in our midst?

***Individual/Personal Reflection/Action***

1. Remember a wise person you have encountered in your lifetime (a grandparent, parent, teacher, etc.). What bit of wisdom did they offer you or others? Think about how you can thank them for this.

2. Choose one or two of your favorite proverbs and copy them down. Put them on your desk or bathroom mirror or refrigerator door for a week or two.

# ECCLESIASTES READING GUIDE

## *At a Glance*

| | |
|---|---|
| Who are the main players? | Qoheleth |
| What should I look for? | Qoheleth is a wise teacher who searches for the meaning of all life. He sets out to discover everything of value in human experience. He is also troubled by the inevitability of death and the futility it imparts. |
| When did this take place? | The inclusion of several Aramaic words has led scholars to date the book around the third century B.C. |
| Where did these events occur? | The place of origin is more difficult to determine. Some say it was Phoenicia, others suggest Egypt. |
| Why was this book written? | Ecclesiastes manifests some of the characteristics of a Royal Testament, a common literature of the Near East intended for the education of the king's successor. |
| What is the story? | Qoheleth accomplished all he set out to do. He acquired wisdom and wealth; he enjoyed pleasure and prosperity. He achieved all his goals and yet he declares "All is vanity!" To suppose that the attainment of goals, even noble goals, can fulfill human longings, according to Qoheleth, is vanity. The wisdom of Qoheleth consists not only in a critical examination of everything that is supposed to bring happiness, but also in providing positive counsel. |

You may not be as familiar with the book of Ecclesiastes as you are with other writings from the wisdom tradition. But you are probably not unfamiliar with some of its expressions: "There's nothing new under the sun!" and "You can't take it with you!"

## About the Book

Ecclesiastes demonstrates some of the literary characteristics of a Royal Testament, a common type of literature in the ancient Near East intended for the instruction of the king's successor. It was written in the third person and claimed to be advice gleaned from the experience of life. Although the book begins and ends in the third person (12:9–14), everything else suggests but one speaker and, despite some conflicting statements, one point of view.

The language of the book resembles the kind of Hebrew that appeared during a very late biblical period and was used almost exclusively for literary purposes. The inclusion of several Aramaic words has led scholars to date the book around the 3rd century B.C. Some say it originated in Phoenicia; others suggest Egypt. Because the wisdom tradition was common to the ancient Near East, precise identification of origin is difficult.

Ecclesiastes is one of the five books that make up the *Megilloth* (see sidebar RG 184). It was read during the harvest celebration of Sukkoth, also known as the Feast of Tabernacles or Booths. This major pilgrim feast was so named because the harvesters lived in booths as they gathered their crops. It is not clear how this practice began or why Ecclesiastes was chosen. Perhaps the somber tone of the book fit the dreariness of autumn. Although reading the book was not always a consistent synagogue practice, Ecclesiastes continues to be considered part of the *Megilloth.*

## A Note About the Ending

The book clearly begins with the distinctive, "Vanity of vanities, says Qoheleth, vanity of vanities! All things are vanity!" (1:2) and ends on the same tone: "Vanity of vanities, says Qoheleth, all

### Who Was Qoheleth?

THE VERY FIRST verse identifies the speaker as "David's son, Qoheleth, king in Jerusalem." There is no biblical mention of a Davidic son by this name, so some other meaning must be intended. The exact meaning of Qoheleth is debated. It probably comes from the Hebrew word *qahal,* assembly, and refers to someone who calls forth or presides over a meeting, perhaps for the purpose of teaching. The form of the word *Qoheleth* suggests that it is not a name, but rather a participle that designates someone who does something. The Greek word used to translate *qahal* is *ekklesia,* a citizens' assembly in Greece. The one who presides over this particular assembly is called Ecclesiastes or Preacher.

The man is further designated as king of Israel. This is an obvious reference to Solomon, the one revered in popular devotion as the wise king. The author claims that Solomon is the speaker, and therefore his teaching has the authority of Solomon's wisdom. From the outset it has authority even though it may prove to be unorthodox. Because the author uses instruction, proverbial quotations, contrasting proverbs, rhetorical questions, parables, the words of the wise, and riddles, the characterization of Qoheleth is of a respected teacher of wisdom.

things are vanity!" (12:8). What some consider a kind of prologue (1:1–11) might well come from the original author. The epilogue (12:9–14) is different: At least one, possibly two people besides the main author have added something. Whoever added verses 9–11 plainly agreed with Qoheleth's conclusions. The tone changes with verse 12. This might be a second epilogue. The student is warned about too much speculation and is advised to trust in the punishing justice of God, a theme that Qoheleth, in contrast, consistently challenged.

**Megilloth or "Scrolls"** This is a special collection in the Hebrew Bible that also includes Song of Songs, Ruth, Lamentations, and Esther. These books were read during various liturgical festivals and were gathered together for the sake of convenience.

It appears that the author created a literary character, Qoheleth, and attributed Solomon-like authority to him to give his own instruction credibility. A later editor further authenticated this teaching by explicitly assuring the reader of Qoheleth's wisdom. However, with two short verses, a second editor tried to temper Qoheleth's statements. There are two possible explanations for this inconsistent ending:

1. The book was already well enough accepted so that the critics could not dismiss it. Still, someone added a caution to what might be considered questionable teaching.
2. If only one editor agreed with Qoheleth's teaching, that person realized that without some kind of tempering it would not be preserved. The last verses restate the traditional view of punishment and seem to return the entire teaching to the circle of orthodoxy.

## A Critical Point of View

There is a wide range of scholarly opinion regarding the meaning of the book. Qoheleth has been described as a skeptic, a cynic, or more positively, a pragmatist. His view of life has been called everything from pessimistic and fatalistic to realistic. Some judge his religious outlook as pleasure-seeking, while others think it is faithful to Israelite values. It is clear that he is disillusioned with certain parts of his society, yet he lacks the enthusiasm of a reformer or the vision of a mystic. Because of this some critics label him a frustrated man who is resigned to the

**Retribution** This theory claims that there is a direct relationship between the uprightness of one's behavior and the good fortune that one enjoys.

injustice and meaninglessness of life and has decided to make the most of fleeting pleasures. Careful reading of Qoheleth will show that he does not really despair of life but of the unrealistic expectations regarding it. His real struggle is with the meaning of life.

### A Chase after the Wind

Qoheleth sets out to discover everything within human experience (1:13). Since he is a king, he has both wealth and the leisure to embark on this quest. As one with extraordinary wisdom (1:16), he of all people is equipped to experience life to the fullest. But what he really sought was always beyond his grasp, "a chase after wind" (1:17). It is clear that in his search for wisdom, he was looking for something else as well. Qoheleth next turned to the search for self-gratification. In many ways he was successful, but still he was not satisfied (2:1–11). He accomplished everything he set his mind to in his search to answer the fundamental question:

> What profit have we from all the toil
> which we toil at under the sun? (1:3)

He constantly arrived at the same conclusion: There is no lasting gain, no tangible dividend, "no profit under the sun" (2:11).

According to the theory of retribution, Qoheleth's wisdom and wealth would be perceived as a concrete proof of his goodness and the guarantee of his future prosperity. But Qoheleth really does not enjoy his good fortune, so he questions its value. Since death comes to everyone, he wonders, "Why should I be wise? Where is the profit?" (2:15). It is not life, nor the search for fulfillment in life, that frustrates him. What he loathes is the unprofitability of human striving. It is not fulfilling. He is asking more of life than success and prosperity.

Since death comes to all, any advantage one might have because of righteousness, wisdom, or wealth is only temporary, and therefore questionable. Maybe the fool who disregards the rules of society may actually have an edge over the one who conforms to them at the cost of enjoyment. So he wonders if perhaps life itself is "a chase after wind."

> **Qoheleth's** term for the futility of life—"vanity"—is the Hebrew word *"hevel,"* which literally means a puff of air or vapor. In Jeremiah 10:15 the prophet calls idols *"hevel,"* translated "nothing" in the NAB. In Psalm 39:6, 12, "man" (human beings) are compared to a *"hevel"*—a "breath."

### Nothing is New under the Sun

We have already seen how the wisdom teachers appealed to the obvious order within the natural world as they urged people to live in obedience to the acceptable social custom. The author of Job used the same technique with a slightly different twist. Job was overwhelmed by the wonders of nature and led to acknowledge the incomprehensible dimension of life. The author of Ecclesiastes also directs our attention to the regularity in nature (1:2–11) but does so in order to highlight its monotony. The sun rises and sets day after day. Although the wind appears to be irregular, upon observation its paths can be predicted. Although the sea is constantly fed, it is never full. The regularity of the earth appears to be lacking any progress. There is nothing new under the sun.

What advantage does the earth have in being so constant? The sage urges us to learn another lesson from nature. Human striving for gain is nothing but wearisome labor that must be repeated and repeated with no promise of conclusion and no assurance of satisfaction. Human life is basically the same regardless of the society or the generation into which one is born. Life itself follows the same cycles, and experiences are quite similar. As nature repeats itself, so does human history. Nothing seems to have lasting significance.

### An Appointed Time

"There is an appointed time for everything . . . under the heavens." In what may be the most familiar section of the entire book, Qoheleth declares that each event of human life has its own appointed time. Each event is linked in poetic construction with its opposite. There are two ways of understanding the pattern:

1. Juxtaposing opposites is a way of expressing totality. It encompasses both poles and

everything in between. For examples, "knowledge of good and evil" (Gn 2:9–17) means comprehensive knowledge; "bone . . . flesh" (Gn 2:23) refers to the entire body.

2. A second poetic form is an expression of relativity. The circumstances of life determine what is fitting and what is not. What is appropriate at one time can be out of place when circumstances change. This may be the author's way of insisting that there are no absolutes; everything is relative to everything else. There is a time to die as well as a time to be born. Neither seems to have an advantage over the other. Still, we do not know the rules that govern these appointed times, so we are helpless and may feel that we are at their mercy.

The task of living is not easy. Qoheleth explains why in 3:11. This verse may be the most difficult one in the book because of the questions surrounding the translation and interpretation of the Hebrew word *olam*. Although some versions translate the word as "world," or "future," or even "ignorance," the *New American Bible* translates it as "the timeless." God has put *olam* in the human heart, and we want to know and understand, even to control everything in the world. It seems that while human beings are finite, their desires transcend the limits of time.

> You have made us for yourself, O Lord,
> and our hearts are restless
> until they rest in you. (St. Augustine)

**All Is Vanity**

Qoheleth accomplished all his goals and yet he declares, "All is vanity!" All the energy he put into his projects was pointless. We might expect him to advise others against ever trying to be happy but he does not. On the contrary, he urges people to enjoy what they have. Then what is it about life that he regards as vanity?

Qoheleth observed in the lives of others what Job experienced, that is, the inadequacy of the theory of retribution. The righteous do not always enjoy the good things of life, nor are the wicked always deprived of them (4:1; 8:10f). While Qoheleth shares this insight with Job, his dissatisfaction in the face of his own prosperity and success has led him a step further in challenging the theory. It is not only that a righteous person sometimes does not prosper; it is also that, even when one does realize some desired goal, there is no guarantee of fulfillment. To suppose that the attainment of goals, even noble ones, can fulfill human longings is, to Qoheleth, vanity.

## The Wisdom of the Sage

The wisdom of Qoheleth consists not only in a critical examination of everything that is supposed to bring happiness, but also in positive advice. Although he finds fault with some aspects of human striving, he encourages something that is often overlooked in busy lives. The key to true fulfillment may be to relish the simple pleasures of life that are at hand (2:24; 3:13–22; 5:19; 8:15; 9:9). These pleasures can be experienced in the very act of living: in eating, in drinking, in the work itself rather than in the wealth that one may hope to produce by it. The pleasure, like everything, has come from the hand of God and should be enjoyed.

Life is not a business transaction with a strict quid pro quo (this for that) return. Such a rigid interpretation of retribution will only end in disappointment. To wait in anticipation of something more is foolish, because the future is uncertain. Rather, people should value the present satisfaction that accompanies human activity.

Qoheleth objects to making human accomplishment the primary goal in life. He calls upon all to find pleasure in what they are doing and, if they are fortunate enough to become successful in the process, to see this as a gift from God as well.

**Questions for Discussion and Reflection**

***Group Sharing/Discussion***

1. A strict interpretation of retribution often expects God to respond to our actions with proper reward or punishment. Looking at the scripture itself, find passages where Qoheleth reminds us that God is not bound by these expectations that people may have.

2. Reread together the section above entitled: "A Critical Point of View." Let group members choose one of the words that describe Qoheleth and tell why they think it is an accurate description. Then let each person say how he or she would describe Qoheleth, having read Ecclesiastes.

3. What are some things in Ecclesiastes that you disagree with and things that you agree with?

*In Our Lives*

1. Our economic system feeds into the materialism that Qoheleth criticizes. What are ways you and your family protect yourselves against acquiring more and more things? What are some ways parents teach their children to resist the pressure of wanting more and "the latest" and "bigger and better" in such an atmosphere?

2. How does your parish community provide opportunities to follow Qoheleth and experience the joy and satisfaction of doing the right thing by sharing with those in need? How could it do more to preach and practice this?

3. Describe someone who does not have a lot of material possessions but is a happy and fulfilled person. What lessons does their life contain for us?

4. Many people spend a lifetime climbing the ladder of power. How would Qoheleth challenge the struggle for "upward mobility"?

***Individual/Personal Reflection/Action***

1. What are some pieces of advice you would want to take from Ecclesiastes? Write down three things to help you put them into effect in your life. Put them on the bathroom mirror or your desk or someplace you will see them each day.

2. Spend five or ten minutes each day this week writing down what advice and values you would pass along if you were today's Qoheleth.

# THE SONG OF SONGS READING GUIDE

## *At a Glance*

| | |
|---|---|
| Who are the main players? | The voices belong to a young woman, her lover, and the daughters of Jerusalem. The way one understands the meaning and function of this book will influence the way one identifies these characters. |
| What should I look for? | What is the book's theological value? What does it teach us? Think about this poetry as showing a figurative way of understanding our relationship with God, the conviction that death does not have final victory, and an example of faithful love. The literal understanding affirms sexuality as one of God's gifts. |
| When did this take place? | The appearance of the Persian word for orchard or park suggests a postexilic date (after 589 B.C.). |
| Where did these events occur? | The geographic references mentioned northern locations, places in Transjordan, and Judah. |
| Why was this book written? | This relatively short book is a collection of poems on the meaning of love. Song of Songs is read on the last day of the celebration of Passover. |
| What is the story? | A maiden takes the initiative in this romantic pursuit. This wisdom book teaches that human passion is both noble and ennobling. Furthermore, its attraction and vitality are natural to both women and men. As with the characters and theology, the interpretation of the romance depicted here depends greatly on how the reader approaches the book. |

## Language and Authorship

THIS SHORT BOOK has an unusually large number of uncommon words. Its 117 verses contain 49 words that appear nowhere else in the Old Testament. This adds to the difficulty of understanding the book, for we are prevented from comparing the meaning of a word in one context with its meaning in another. This unfamiliar vocabulary opens the poem to many interpretations, but it also allows for rich differences of understanding and meanings.

Like Proverbs and Ecclesiastes, the Song is associated with Solomon. Attribution to the famous king occurs only in the editorial introduction (1:1) and is preceded by a preposition that can be translated in various ways: "by" Solomon; "to" Solomon; "for" Solomon; "of" Solomon; "concerning" Solomon. This does not mean Solomon was the author. Connecting the king's name to the Song probably gave it credibility and linked it to the other wisdom traditions. Since the book includes other references to Solomon (3:7–11; 8:11f ) some interpreters identify Solomon as the amorous shepherd. But because the king never speaks in these passages, the references could be merely figurative allusions to fabulous wealth.

The Song of Songs presents many barriers to interpretation. It is clearly a collection of love poems full of sensuous imagery. It does not offer any apparent theological or moral values, and it never even mentions God. It is no wonder that both Jewish and Christian writers at various times have questioned its acceptance into the canon of inspired writings. The very character of the book has led to many distinct interpretations.

## About the Book

The Song of Songs is a collection of poems of various lengths, but scholars differ about how to arrange these poems into sections. Some see a pattern of separation, longing, and union. Others maintain that while these elements are present, they do not follow a particular pattern. Others see unity in verbal echoes, for instance the repetitions in 2:6–7; 3:5; 8:3–4. Since there is no narrative plot and the speakers are neither identified nor introduced, one can only speculate about the original intention of the compiler.

The geographic references are wide-reaching. Northern locations are mentioned (2:1; 3:9; 4:8; 6:4; 7:5–6), as are places to the east (4:1) and in Judah (1:14; 3:5). This variety may reflect the early northern Israelite source of some of the original poems and a later southern (perhaps Jerusalem) setting for the final edition. The appearance of the Persian word for orchard or park (4:13) suggests a date after the exile in Babylon (after 539 B.C.).

The Song of Songs is also found in the *Megilloth*, or the collection of five festal scrolls (the others are Ruth, Lamentations,

*Voices in the Song of Songs*

| | |
|---|---|
| Daughters of Jerusalem | A Chorus of Voices |
| Bride | Meaning is not clear. Hebrew text refers to a young woman betrothed but not yet married to a man. While the text alludes to the sexual union of the lovers, it never describes a marriage. The male partner is not necessarily a "groom." |
| Lover | There seem to be two distinct lovers, one a royal figure from Jerusalem (1:12–17; 3:6–11) and the other a rustic youth from the north (1:7f; 2:8–17). Nowhere is there a combination of the two. |

**Interpretation** When we talk about interpretation, it is important to distinguish between what the book meant in the past and what it means for the present. Those interpreters who use a strict historical-critical approach insist that the original sense must be the focus of our explanation. Discovering the earliest form and meaning of the book is crucial. It is this original meaning, they would argue, that continues to be revelatory for us today. Other commentators do not categorize methods as "right" or "wrong" but as "helpful" or "not helpful." They would be more open to various interpretations of the Song of Songs.

Ecclesiastes, and Esther), and is read on the last day of the celebration of Passover. Perhaps the announcement of the end of winter (2:11) made the poem suitable for a spring festival. Reference to horses and chariots of Pharaoh (1:9) is an allusion to Exodus, the event commemorated at Passover.

Several different voices are heard in the Song of Songs, as outlined in the table at the bottom of RG 188.

Who are these mysterious lovers? The way one understands the meaning and function of the book will influence the way one identifies the characters within it. If these are ancient wedding songs, then the lovers are bride and groom. The New American Bible takes this approach, labeling the "Lover's" words as those of a bridegroom. If it is love poetry, then the "bride" is understood in a figurative sense; her partner the man with whom she is intimately involved. He is called "lover," not "husband."

## Form and Meaning

For more than 2,000 years, the Song of Songs has been not only a source of fascination but also something of a riddle. Its very uniqueness has made understanding it a challenge. There are four ways of interpreting it: allegorical, cultic, dramatic, and literal. Each of these approaches reveals different possibilities for our religious enrichment. All of them have gained acceptance within Roman Catholic tradition. It is interesting to note that while the first and preferred method of interpreting the Bible has been the literal approach, the opposite has been true with this book. It seems that the suggestive sexual imagery offends the sensitivities of many of the faithful. Therefore commentators have presumed that the poems were not intended to be taken literally but must have some concealed religious meaning.

### Allegorical Interpretations

An allegorical method presumes that the surface meaning of a figure of speech, character, or image signifies some deeper spiritual truth. This approach was quite popular in Jewish circles around the time of Christ (Philo, 20 B.C.–A.D. 54) as well as among early Christian writers (Origen, A.D. 185–254). Jewish commentators who allegorize the Song interpret it as symbolizing God's

### What Is Allegory?

AN ALLEGORY IS a comparison between two areas of human experience, usually a concrete or everyday area and an abstract one more removed from ordinary experience. For example, justice in our courts is often represented as a beautiful woman wearing a blindfold and holding balancing scales. The woman's beauty symbolizes the attractions of justice: Just as we are drawn to beauty, so we should be drawn to justice. Her blindfold symbolizes the impartiality of justice. No matter how important or unimportant the person who appears before her, she is concerned only with the merits of the case. The balancing scales symbolize the idea that decisions are made according to public standards and anyone can observe how they are made. By using everyday images, the allegorical figure helps us understand our ideals of justice.

relationship with Israel, tracing it from the time of the Exodus to the coming of the Messiah. They believe it celebrates God's steadfast love bestowed on Israel and describes the fickleness that characterized Israel's attitude toward its divine lover.

As Christians began to read the Hebrew traditions in light of their faith in Christ, this allegorical method produced new meanings. They identified the lovers as Christ and the Church. Some read it as a description of the mystical union of God and the individual soul.

The bride has even been explained as the Virgin Mary. Although not easily accommodated to the poem, this interpretation has been quite prominent within the Roman Catholic tradition. One reason for this is the belief that Mary is the model of the individual soul in union with God. A stronger reason for this interpretation is the fact that sections of the Song are read during the liturgy on several Marian feasts. Thus by association this interpretation has become common in popular devotion to Mary.

### Cultic Interpretation

A second way of understanding the Song of Songs assumes that it was originally a liturgical reenactment of a drama that takes place in nature each spring. In a well-known fertility myth of the ancient Near Eastern world, the great god (the Canaanite Baal or the Babylonian Tammuz) dies after the harvest and is mourned by the fertility goddess (Anath or Ishtar respectively). She searches frantically for him during the barrenness of winter. Her efforts are successful and they are finally united. Nature is revived with the coming of spring and the cycle of life continues. The fact that this book was read during the springtime festival of Passover seems to support the theory that Israel was influenced by the agricultural celebrations of the era.

There is ample evidence in the Bible of Israel's use and reinterpretation of Canaanite cultic practices. A Canaanite nomadic festival took on historical meaning when it was used to commemorate God's deliverance of the people from Egyptian bondage. It was associated with the Feast of Unleavened Bread after the people had settled in Canaan and had moved from a nomadic to an agricultural form of life. These two festivals merged into one celebration, and elements of both became details of the standard story of the first Passover celebration. *Passover* is probably a combination of two festivals: an early nomadic celebration intended to ensure the fertility of the flock, and an agricultural one, the Feast of Unleavened Bread, intended to ensure the growth of the crop.

### Dramatic Interpretation

This third approach has had a long history in the Church's tradition. As early as the second century of the Christian era, Origen claimed that the Song was a wedding poem written in dramatic form by Solomon himself. Some interpreters today divide the book into a drama of five movements:

1. The anticipation and meeting of the lovers (1:1–2:17)
2. The separation (3:1–11)
3. Reunion (4:1–5:1)
4. A second separation (5:2–6:3)
5. Final union (6:4–8:14)

The commentators assign the speeches to the characters, as indicated in the New American Bible, and identify the various scenes by means of subtitles within the text.

The two major characters are the royal shepherd and the Shulammite maiden. A two-character interpretation has serious deficiencies. There is no dramatic development, and the book lacks ethical purpose. A three-character approach was developed to address these weaknesses. It distinguishes two male individuals, the king and the shepherd. The king tries to win the love of the maiden, but she remains faithful to her shepherd lover. In the first interpretation the royal shepherd is worthy of the faithful love of the Shulammite. This personage might well represent Solomon. In the second interpretation, the king is a villain who tries to seduce the maiden with the promise of luxury and comfort. One wonders how this disapproving portrait of Solomon could survive as part of the wisdom tradition, which ascribed wisdom to the very king who is depicted in this manner.

The weaknesses of this approach are obvious. Since the biblical text does not supply names for the speeches, the decisions about their identification are influenced by the biases of the interpreter. Stage directions are imposed from without rather than discovered within the poems themselves. Finally, there is neither story line nor character development, essential traits of good drama.

### Literal Interpretation

It may be that the original meaning of the Song is found in its literal interpretation. The Song of Songs is most likely a collection of love poems that neither symbolize divine love nor were developed from fertility rites. It teaches no lesson; it tells no story. It simply celebrates the passion of human love. While some believe that the poems are secular, others doubt that purely secular love songs would ever be admitted to the canon. These latter commentators believe that the poems are examples of Judean wedding songs. They also discover traces of a poetic form called *wasf:* an Arabic word meaning description. These are poems that use images from nature to describe parts of the male or female body. The *wasf* form uses one point of comparison between the image and the object being described (the whiteness of the woman's teeth compared to that of freshly washed sheep, for example), and often results in an extravagant or amusing combination. This may explain some of the strange imagery found in the Song (see 4:1–5; 7:2–6).

The Song's claim of Solomon as its author may be the main reason this book is part of the Bible. Each of the three books attributed to Solomon addresses a central issue of life basic to the wisdom thinking of the ancient Near East, Israel included.

• Proverbs provides directions on how to achieve peace and prosperity by coming to an understanding of order and stability in the world.

• In Ecclesiastes, Qoheleth addresses the search for meaning in life.

• The Song of Songs celebrates a fundamental human emotion—erotic love.

None of these books fits into the category of "salvation history," but each one is an example of the "way of wisdom."

Once the writings were associated with Solomon and the wisdom attributed to him, it was not long before they possessed their own authoritative significance. This seems to have been enough to ensure inclusion in the canon. Although the three books are quite distinct, they have come to represent different moments in the life of the same man.

The Song of Songs reveals a young, passionate, unguarded Solomon.

Proverbs shows a moderate but optimistic man who has learned from his experience of life.

The musings of Qoheleth in Ecclesiastes come from someone who comes to the end of life challenging the enduring value of human accomplishment.

The quality of these human, but nonetheless theological, concerns is evidence of their religious value. Ascribing them to Solomon provided them with canonical status.

### Questions for Discussion and Reflection

***Group Sharing/Discussion***

1. From each of the interpretive approaches described above, what does the Song of Songs teach us? What is its theological value? We have

**An Independent Woman in a Patriarchal Society**

THE PORTRAIT OF the maiden is exceptional for literature from a patriarchal and male-dominated society. This is not the image of a sexually naive and passive woman, dependent upon a man for protection and sustenance. It is the woman who takes the initiative in this romantic pursuit. She utters almost twice as much of the erotic poetry as does the man. Her language is quite explicit, and she shatters any stereotypes that suggest that women may be romantic but not sexually inclined. The Song of Songs does not portray male dominance and female subordination.

The maiden is an independent person. She tends vineyards (1:6) and shepherds flocks (1:8), occupations normally assigned to men. This wisdom book teaches that human passion can be both noble and ennobling, and its attraction and vitality are natural to both men and women.

considered four different methods of interpretation, so there are four distinct approaches to these questions. Read through these summaries and discuss what can be valued or learned from each of them.

A. The Allegorical Approach

A symbolic approach provides us with a figurative way of understanding the nature of our relationship with God, which is dynamic, energizing, and mutually loving. Contrary to an image of God as an impassive creator or avenging judge, the Song of Songs offers us a portrait of a passionate lover, one who desires union with us. Some may find this notion scandalous, but the wisdom tradition (especially Job and Ecclesiastes) repeatedly teaches something about God or human nature that has been unconventional.

B. The Cultic Interpretation

At the heart of the dying/rising ritual is the conviction that death does not have the final victory. The love of the grieving goddess is strong enough to bring her lover back to her and revitalize the lifeless earth.

C. The Dramatic Interpretation

Understanding the poem as a dialogue or interaction among various characters provides an example of faithful love. The fidelity of the bride is held up for all to admire and imitate. This image of a faithful woman conforms to the one found in other places in the wisdom tradition (see Prv 31:10–31).

D. The Literal Interpretation

Seeing the work as lyrical poetry makes no apology for its erotic interpretation. It affirms that sexuality is one of the gifts that God gave for our enjoyment (see Prv 5:15–21; Eccl 9:9). The sexual pleasure is not sought promiscuously but pursued only within the context of a faithful and exclusive commitment.

***In Our Lives***

1. What do you think is the message or lesson we can take from Song of Songs? If the most basic way of experiencing God's love and saving presence is through human friendship, what does this tell us about who God is?

2. What is our culture's attitude toward the human body? What is the different message proclaimed in the Song of Songs?

***Individual/Personal Reflection/Action***

1. Who are people you have known who are models of healthy love? Examine your own attitudes towards friendship/love/commitment and see how you want to deepen and mature them.

2. Pray each day this week for ways to spread a healthy and holy understanding of how God wants us to love each other as human beings.

# THE BOOK OF WISDOM READING GUIDE

## *At a Glance*

| | |
|---|---|
| Who are the main players? | The author, a Hellenized Jew |
| What should I look for? | The dimensions and facets of divine wisdom. Many passages of the first section are used in our liturgy (e.g., 3:1–8). The way that the Exodus is presented (11:2ff.) shows the special providence of God. |
| When did this take place? | About a hundred years before the coming of Christ. |
| Where did these events occur? | In the ancient Jewish community in Alexandria, Egypt. |
| Why was this book written? | Even during persecution the author attempts to exhort and inspire his readers to embrace wisdom through his flair with words and the way he uses biblical history in his preaching. |
| What is the story? | The book of Wisdom is divided into three parts: (a) chapters 1–6, rewards of living justly; (b) 7:1–11:1, reflections on wisdom by "Solomon"; (c) 11:2–19:22, the religious meaning of the Exodus. |

## Background for Understanding the Book of Wisdom

The last half of the fourth century saw rapid and sweeping changes in the ancient world. Alexander the Great had brought the entire eastern world under the influence of Greek culture, thereby unifying a diverse, disorganized world. This, however, threatened the integrity of other cultures and religious perspectives. With his death in 323 B.C., the empire was divided among his followers, and three independent kingdoms were formed. These kingdoms were hostile to each other. Two of these kingdoms played an important role in the affairs of the Jewish nation. Ptolemy gained control of Egypt and established himself in Alexandria; Seleucus triumphed over Babylon and made Antioch his center. Each kingdom contributed to the shaping of the biblical tradition.

Hellenization was forced upon the Jewish community by the ruler Antiochus Epiphanes. A large colony of Jews lived in Alexandria and adapted itself to Greek language and culture. This was the group that translated its religious traditions from Hebrew into Greek, producing what has come to be known as the Septuagint.

This Greek version was probably the one in popular use during the first century of the Christian era. During the same time, the Jewish community adopted the older Palestinian or Hebrew version of the Bible as its official text. The Christian practice of adding their own writings to the collection may have contributed to this decision.

Christians continued to revere the Alexandrian (Greek) tradition of the Septuagint. Scholars comparing Old Testament citations used by New Testament writers conclude that a good number, if not all of them, came from the Alexandrian rather than from the earlier Palestinian version.

At the time of the Reformation, the official version of the Old Testament became a point of disagreement among Christian denominations. Protestant churches kept the shorter, more ancient Hebrew canon, while the Roman Church accepted the wider Greek canon, preserving an early Church tradition. This explains why some Bibles include such books as Wisdom and Ben Sira, while others do not.

**Septuagint** The Latin for "seventy," frequently designated LXX, Septuagint is the name for the main ancient Greek translation of the Hebrew Bible with additions. Tradition claimed that 70 scribes, working independently of each other, labored over the translation of the Bible for 70 days in 70 different locations and produced identical versions. This was seen as evidence of the inspired nature of the translation. In reality, the translation probably took decades, but this did not detract from the reverence accorded the Septuagint over the years.

## About the Book

Over the centuries this book has been called "The Book of Wisdom" (from the Latin translations), "The Wisdom of Solomon" (from the Septuagint), or variations of either title. Although the author does not explicitly identify himself as Solomon, speaking in the first person, he does describe himself as such (7:5; 8:21; 9:7f; see I Kgs 3:5–15). The author may have presumed that the unconventional character of the book's ideas might need the authority of Solomon to be accepted as orthodox teaching.

The book suggests an origin from within the Jewish community of Alexandria. It is clear that the author was steeped in the history of the Exodus (11:2–16; 12:23–27; 16:2–19:22), was acquainted with the religious practices of Egypt (15:14–16:1), and was well versed in Hellenistic

**Deuterocanonical** ("second listing"). Those books accepted as Scripture by Catholics but not found in the Hebrew canon.

**Apocryphal** (originally meaning "hidden"). Understood as inspirational but not in the canon of official scripture.

philosophy and science (6:22–11:1). The author reinterpreted his own heritage and critiqued the traditions, practices, and insights of the other two cultures. He did this to support those Jews who were questioning the relevance of their ancient faith in the face of radical cultural changes they were undergoing.

#### Date of the Book

Most scholars date it somewhere during the first century B.C. The primary threat at this time did not arise from the Hellenizing Greeks but from the Hellenized Jews themselves. The outside oppression at the time of the Maccabean Revolt had given way to a subtle undermining of traditional teaching and values. Even religious leaders were not immune to this kind of worldliness. The author appears to have been concerned that:

1. The pious not be led astray
2. Those enthralled by Greek culture be convinced of the value of the work of their own religious heritage
3. Those already carried away by the currents of change be brought back.

#### Literary Features of the Book

Wisdom was originally written in Greek. The style is natural and free-flowing, not awkward, as might be the case if this were a translation from Hebrew.

1. The vocabulary reveals an author who possessed an extensive comprehension of Hellenistic (Greek) learning.
2. References to earlier religious tradition correspond to the style of the Alexandrian rather than the Palestinian version.
3. The thought is similar to what is found in Jewish-Alexandrian works of this period.
4. The author frequently used a form of expression that resembles the diatribe. The diatribe is a method of argument that creates imaginary opponents who raise questions that the philosopher then refutes.

Despite these Greek characteristics, this is basically a Jewish work. The description of God's care during the Exodus is a kind of midrash homily. Midrash is an interpretation that the Jewish community devised in order to apply the Bible to new situations. Thus a law (*halakah*) was restated or a narrative (*haggadah*) retold in such a way as to give new direction to a new generation. The Greeks, especially Philo, developed allegory as a principal method of interpreting traditions. It is significant that the author of Wisdom employed midrash rather than allegory. This further verifies the Jewish, rather than Greek, origin of the book.

## Wisdom Teaching

The unifying theme of this biblical book is "the praise of wisdom." Each of the three major sections addresses this theme from its own distinctive point of view. Each section will highlight the significant theological elements found there.

#### Immortality of the Soul

The soul's immortality is a central issue in the first half of the book of Wisdom. Virtually all the books contained in Hebrew Scripture assume that human life ends at death. During the Hellenistic period, many Jews came to believe in life after death. Generally speaking, there were two ways of thinking about life after death: resurrection of the body and immortality of the soul. New Testament texts assert belief in resurrection (for example, 1 Cor 15:12–58). Other Jewish texts outside the scriptural canon (such as the writings of Philo) reflect belief in the immortality of the soul, much like Wisdom. There was no agreement on the issue. The author of Ben Sira states repeatedly and with absolute certainty that life ends at death (38:21–23; 41:1–4). Ben Sira may be two centuries earlier than Wisdom, but even in the first century A.D., the Sadducees denied there was life after death (Mt 22:23–33; Acts 23:8). The debate is closely tied to the problem of theodicy, as is evident in the text of Wisdom. How does one believe in the goodness of God if there is evil and suffering in the world? If righteous people can be unjustly accused and wrongly condemned to death, where is justice? Belief in life after death allows for the possibility that wrongs may be set right, which is exactly what is described in 3:1–9.

#### The Reward of Justice (1:1–6:21)

The first section is often called "The Book of Eschatology." (Eschatology traditionally refers to the last or final things: the end of the age, death, judgment, reward, and punishment.) In this section we find the destinies of the righteous and of the wicked described in vivid contrast. The righteous, regardless of their obvious suffering, "are in the hand of God" (3:1), while the wicked "shall receive a punishment to match their thoughts" (3:10). This entire section serves as a call to be faithful to the religious traditions of Israel, a fidelity that will guarantee these rewards of wisdom.

This is a radical departure from the traditional understanding. Indeed, the author of Wisdom diverges from tradition on several topics.

1. The author insisted that childlessness, a condition that brought reproach in ancient society (see Gn 16:4; 1 Sm 1:7) is not a mark of divine displeasure (3:13f; 4:1). Moral goodness, not physical fruitfulness, is emphasized.

2. The author denied that suffering itself presumes that the person has sinned. In fact, an untimely death may be a righteous person's rescue from the wickedness of life (4:14). We are reminded of the popular saying: "The good die young." The author agreed with Job and Qoheleth that virtue is not always rewarded in this life, nor is evil punished. Whoever thinks that death of the righteous is an affliction or destruction is foolish (3:2f). It is rather a trial they must endure.

3. The author brought two earlier creation narratives together and reinterpreted them. The statement about being made in God's image (2:23), an allusion to Genesis 1:16, 28, is followed by the claim that the devil's envy brought death into the world 12:24), a reinterpretation of Genesis. Some think that the latter refers to Cain's envy, which resulted in the death of Abel (Gn 4:1–6). Another writer of this time says that Satan led Eve astray (Enoch 60:6). The author of Wisdom was the first biblical writer to identify the serpent of the Genesis account with the devil.

## What about Life after Death?

In the book of Wisdom, the reader is introduced for the first time to the Greek concept of *psyche* (soul, 1:11; 3:1). The Greeks held that human nature was a combination of a perishable material (body) and an eternal spiritual (soul). This combination was dissolved at death. We must be careful, however, not to take this Greek thought further than the author did. Nowhere does this book speak of an immortal soul. Rather, the author argues that God intended human life to continue without death (2:23); what survives is the full human being.

Life after death is quite different from the earlier perception of *Sheol*, the abode of the dead. There is just enough lack of clarity in the words "immortality" (3:4; 4:1; 8:13, 17; 15:3) and "incorruptibility" (2:23; 6:18f) to prevent us from making definite statements about the author's view. One thing seems clear. Immortality is not an automatic quality of human nature; it is the result of union with wisdom (8:13, 17; 15:3). Although 2:23 claims that God made humans to be imperishable, 6:18 suggests that it is possible only when one is faithful to wisdom.

We are not sure if the author was speaking of physical death, of physical death followed by spiritual death, or of spiritual death alone. The thought does seem to be directed to spiritual death. St. Paul will have to face the same question when dealing with the unexpected deaths of Christians (1 Thes 4:13–18). Unlike the author of Wisdom, his answer is quite specific.

### Praise of Wisdom by Solomon (6:22–11:1)

The second major section of the book is an address acclaiming the glories of wisdom. It is from this section that the book receives its name, and it is from here that we find a representation of personified Wisdom. This representation of Wisdom is quite different from that found in earlier tradition. The author may have realized that he needed to claim the authority of Solomon to gain acceptance for this reinterpretation. This section begins with an account of his humble origin, his own prayer for wisdom, and God's immeasurable gift in answering his plea (7:1–7; also see 9:1–18). This is an allusion to the prayer of Solomon (1 Kgs 3:5–15), and it characterizes the author as the wise king.

The description of Wisdom is composed of elements from:

• Israelite tradition (7:22a; see Prv 8:30).

• The cult of the Egyptian deity Isis (goddess of wisdom and patron of culture whose praises were in the form of listings similar to those found in 7:22–8:1).

• Hellenistic philosophy and science (see 8:7 for mention of the cardinal virtues of Plato). This may be the way the author argues for the superiority of the religion of Israel. The author confers on the figure of Wisdom the characteristics of Isis already found in the Israelite tradition and draws upon Hellenistic religious and scientific concepts to praise her as he argues that real wisdom is a gift from God bestowed on the faithful.

## Christianity and the Book of Wisdom

In this book wisdom is referred to as "the spirit of the LORD" (1:7). The theology of this verse functions significantly in the liturgy of Pentecost. Although spirit played a major role in Stoic philosophy, it was clearly a theme in Jewish tradition as well. The author ascribed to Wisdom what earlier writers attributed to the Spirit of the LORD:

• The creative power of the world (7:22a; see Jdt 16:14)

• The source of Joseph's honor in Egypt (10:13; see Gn 41:38)

• The inspiration that prepared Moses for the Exodus and led the people through the wilderness (10:16f; see Is 63:11, 14).

What is the influence of the figure of Wisdom on New Testament writings? Some scholars believe that the influence is direct. Others hold that there was a treasury of thought, imagery, and language that served as a common source. Whichever the case may be, early Christian theologians reinterpreted the figure of Wisdom as they struggled to understand Jesus the Christ.

Paul explicitly referred to Christ as the wisdom of God (1 Cor 1:24, 30). The most obvious example of this is found in the Gospel according to John. There we find Jesus described in ways that Wisdom had been depicted earlier: as being with God in the beginning before the world existed (Jn 1:1; 17:5; see Wis 2:22) and as sent from heaven to accomplish the will of God (Jn 6:38; see Wis 9:10). Current scholarship is only beginning to seek the implications of this imagery for Christology.

This section ends with a summary of the way Wisdom guided the ancestors of Israel by bringing them out of Egypt through the agency of Moses (see Hos 12:14); and by enabling them to prosper (Wis 10:1–11:1). It is clear that Wisdom, once thought to be the possession of the king, was now to be understood as the constant companion of true Israelites, those faithful ones of the past as well as committed Jews of the present.

### Special Providence of God during the Exodus (11:2–19:22)

At this point there is an observable shift in focus. The poem in praise of Wisdom gives way to midrash that praises the God of Israel. This version of the experience of the Exodus and the time in the wilderness illustrates two points:

1. The sufferings that befell the Egyptians were the direct result of their sinfulness (11:16).

2. The very elements that afflicted the Egyptians benefited the Israelites (11:51).

This reading of the past is done through creative selection of biblical data as well as addition of material not found anywhere else.

The author did not set out to recount historical facts but seemed intent on addressing the challenge raised by Hellenism. His goal was to remind the Alexandrian Jews that once before they had suffered at the hands of the Egyptians and, in the face of impossible odds, they had been rescued. This provides a "historical" basis for continued trust in the God of Israel.

There are two digressions within this third division of the book. Both of them are found in the second example of God's providence:

1. A testimony to God's mercy (11:17–12:22). Although it breaks the midrash style of thought, it may have been prompted by the mention of punishment in the preceding verses.

2. A condemnation of idolatry (13:1–15:17). It follows the claim that the Egyptians "saw and recognized the true God whom formerly they had refused to know" (12:27) but continued in their idolatry. The language used in the condemnation of nature worship (13:1–9) may be the best example of the author's broad grasp of scientific knowledge.

## Theology in a New Context

The author of Wisdom did not set out in search

of new theological insights. Since he was committed to proving the lasting value of the religion of Israel, he explained traditions and themes that were familiar to the Jews of his day. What made his contribution unique was the method that he employed as he went about his task.

Throughout its history, Israel had been forced by circumstances to deal with religious and cultural tensions of other societies. The Bible itself shows that these encounters were sometimes peaceful and at other times violent and destructive. Whatever the situation may have been, elements from those cultures found their way into the traditions of Israel. It was the religion of Israel that reinterpreted features of other cultures and then took these new ideas into their own perspective. Israel seldom took seriously the religious worldview of the other culture.

This attitude changed with the Hellenization of the world. It was precisely the attraction of Greek civilization itself that threatened Jewish faith. The community wrestled with an agonizing dilemma: Could one accept the Greek culture and remain faithful to the traditions of the ancestors? The author of Wisdom undertook the task of answering this question in the affirmative. He did not try to reconcile Judaism with Hellenism but used the ideas, the language, and the literary style of Greek culture to demonstrate the excellence of the Jewish faith.

In taking Greek culture seriously, this theologian did what theologians after him would have to do, which was not so different from the task facing us: that is, adapt and transfer a religious heritage that started in one cultural context into another. His purpose was to defend the ancestral faith. Ours is to proclaim the Word of God. We have much to learn from this wisdom teacher and his method of theological reinterpretation.

**Questions for Discussion and Reflection**

***Group Sharing/Discussion***

1. Why was the author concerned about the Hellenized Jews being influenced by the Greek culture?

2. What are some of the differences described in store for the righteous and the unrighteous?

3. Read aloud 11:17–26. Describe in your own words the kind of God described in this section.

***In Our Lives***

1. The first half of the book of Wisdom has as a central issue the immortality of the soul. What is your own description of life after death? What would change in the way you live if you did not believe in life after death?

2. Chapters 1:1–6:21 deal primarily with the differences between the treatment of the good and the wicked. What there do you agree with or disagree with?

3. The author describes himself as a seeker of wisdom in 7:1–22a. What are ways you seek wisdom? Describe someone you know who could be called a wisdom figure.

***Individual/Person Reflection/Action***

1. Write down five words that describe your own image of God. How do these compare with the description you had of God when you were a child? How has your image of God matured as you have aged?

2. Some parts of Wisdom explain why bad things happen to good people. How would you explain them? How does your faith help you deal with bad things in you life?

3. Name for yourself someone who has helped you by sharing their wisdom. Perhaps you have just observed how they handle life or you may even have had conversations with them about your life. Let them know what this has meant to you.

# BEN SIRA (ECCLESIASTICUS) READING GUIDE

*At a Glance*

| | |
|---|---|
| Who are the main players? | Jesus, son of Eleazar, son of Sira |
| What should I look for? | The careful maxims of a sage who loves and lives the Torah and wants to share his experience to maintain religious faith and integrity. |
| When did this take place? | Written in Hebrew around 180 B.C., the text was translated into Greek c. 132 B.C. by the author's grandson. |
| Where did these events occur? | A respected Jerusalem scribe wrote the Hebrew; the Greek was written in the Diaspora. |
| Why was this book written? | Both editions were written for those who wished to gain learning and were disposed to live according to the Law. |
| What is the story? | The book contains reflections grouped according to various subjects such as individual, family, and community relations. It treats of friendship, education, poverty and wealth, worship, and many religious and social customs. |

## About the Book

Over the years the book of Ben Sira has been known by different names: "The Wisdom of Jesus Ben Sira" (of which Sirach is the Greek form); "The Book of Sirach" (a shortened title); and "Ecclesiasticus" (from the Latin for book of the Church, a designation that probably stems from its frequent use as a catechetical aid in the early centuries of the Western Church).

The book appears to be a collection of proverbs organized in such a way as to resemble short essays. While there is no explicit arrangement in the book itself, one can divide the material into themes and according to literary form.

Ben Sira is the only biblical book that:

• Identifies its author (50:27)

• Refers to its translator (a grandson of Ben Sirach)

• Dates its translation ("the 38th year of the reign of King Euergetes," sometime after 132 B.C. (see the foreword preceding chapter 1).

Although the prophetic books claim to originate from the prophets and do locate their ministry during the reign of specific kings (for example, Hos 1:1; Is 1:1; Jer 1:2f; etc.), the references there are to the activity of the prophets, not to the books that bear the prophets' names. Here we have a clear reference to when the book was written.

The foreword also provides us with some interesting information about the composition of the biblical canon (the official list of inspired books). Three times the grandson of Ben Sira speaks of "the Law, the Prophets, and the authors" (or "the rest of the books"). This tells us that by the second century B.C. the Jewish community already had what came to be known as a tripartite (three-part) Bible. Scholars believe that the first two parts (the Law and the Prophets) most likely include the books as we have them today. The third part (the Writings) was probably quite fluid well into the Christian era.

Like the book of Wisdom, Ben Sira belongs to the collection called Deuterocanonical by Roman Catholics or Apocryphal by Protestants (see Glossary). The foreword, which is considered historical introduction and not inspired instruction, recounts the translator's arrival in Egypt, where he discovered that the Jews' "no little learning" had been rendered from Hebrew into Greek, the language of the day. This inspired him to undertake the translation of his grandfather's teachings. The Hebrew version from which he worked seems to have dropped out of sight until copies of it were found in 1806. Its absence from the Jewish list explains why it is missing from the Protestant canon.

The way the high priest Simon is described (50:1–21) leads one to conclude he had recently died. This would locate the writing of the original Hebrew version of Ben Sira sometime during the first quarter of the second century (200–175) B.C. The description of Simon's priestly performance suggests that the author was quite familiar with the Jerusalem ritual and perhaps was even a resident of the city and wrote there.

## The Reason for Writing

The Hellenization of the Near East had already taken hold among the educated upper classes by the time Ben Sira (meaning son of Sira) put his teachings into writing. Many Jews must have wondered whether their ancient traditions could match the breadth and depth of Greek thought. Being a well-traveled man (34:11) and an observant Jew, Ben Sira would have witnessed the decline in fervor that overtook his fellow Jews, and it would have troubled him. His object in writing was to show the Jews of his day that real wisdom was to be found in the traditions of Israel and not in the godless philosophy of the Greeks. He intended his work to be a guide to every circumstance of life:

• Ben Sira encouraged his readers to study the ancient traditions to find direction needed to cope with their new, challenging situation (2:10).

• He warned against trying to live according to the standards of both Judaism and Hellenism (2:12).

• He condemned those who chose Hellenism over Judaism (2:13f).

• He identified the wise ("those who fear the Lord") as those who were faithful to the religion of Israel (2:15–17).

Although most of Ben Sira's wisdom teaching is quite conventional, the way he blended it with Israel's history and legal and cultic traditions is distinctive. Earlier wisdom writing showed little interest in Israelite matters. Ben Sira's way of arguing in favor of faithfulness to Judaism was:

• To claim that true wisdom resided in Israel (24:1–21)

• To use history to support this claim (44:1–49:16)

• To identify Wisdom with the Law of Moses (24:22), giving this a place of honor above the traditions of other cultures

• To demonstrate a profound concern for the cult and role of the priesthood (46:6–20; 47:12f; 50:1–21).

## Wisdom Teaching

Like the book of Proverbs, the primary focus of Ben Sira's teaching is moral guidance. The book is like an instruction manual containing maxims, many of which are grouped according to topic. A series of short essays addresses topics such as duties toward God, toward one's parents, and toward rulers. There are instructions on how to train children, how to choose friends, and how to guard one's speech. There are warnings against excess, laziness, and foolishness. Whatever one needs to succeed in life, while at the same time remaining faithful to the traditions of the elders, is addressed in the instruction.

Like Proverbs, Ben Sira celebrates the glories of personified Wisdom (chapters 1 and 24). But it takes the characterization a step further than the earlier work. Here we see Wisdom searching for a place to dwell and finally pitching her tent in Jerusalem. Traces of this poetic characterization can be found in the Gospel of John where the Word, present with God from the beginning and involved in the creation of all things, "made his dwelling [literally "lived in a tent"] among us" (Jn 1:1–14).

Ben Sira's poems describing the role of divine wisdom in creation (16:22–17:18; 39:12– 35; 42:15–43:35) are really commentaries on the opening chapters of Genesis. The rather technical way he develops his thought shows us the extent to which Ben Sira was influenced by the scientific knowledge of his day.

The book contains some of the harshest statements about women found in the Bible. Proverbs may have warned the naive youth to beware of wily and seductive women, but this author seems to speak disparagingly against women in general. Ben Sira is the one who blames woman for sin and death (25:23). He expected wives to be subservient to their husbands, for he seems to be in favor of punishment, even including divorce, if they refuse to obey (25:24f). Perhaps the worst example of this is found in the description of the unwed daughter (42:9–14). The author considers her a liability, and his concern is exclusively with the reputation of the father. As with biblical passages about slavery and other practices of ancient society, we need to use care in present-day interpretation.

The author holds a traditional view of retribution (4:11–19; 7:1–3; 16:1–21; 21:1–10). Reward or punishment after death does not seem to be the concern of this wisdom teacher (14:15–19). He counsels mourning at the death of another but cautions his reader to moderation in the expression of grief. The reason the display should be temperate is that the dead are dead and nothing can be changed by uncontrolled sorrow (38:1–23).

While this view of death may be similar to earlier notions of retribution, it was not universally held in Israel at this time. Hope of reward after death for fidelity during persecution is found in other writings of this period (for example Dn 12:1–3; 2 Mc 7:9–29). Although Ben Sira probably lived before the Maccabean Revolt (events surrounding this period are recorded in other books), his grandson-translator certainly lived after the rebellion, and he upheld his ancestor's traditional view.

## The Influence of Sirach on Jewish and Christian Communities

The New Testament writers primarily used the ancient Greek version of the Hebrew Bible called the Septuagint, which contained additional works such as Ben Sira. It is not surprising that the influence of Ben Sira can be detected in some of their writings. The Letter of James is a clear example of this. Both books address questions of pride (Sir 10:7; Jas 4:6) and humility (Sir 3:18; Jas 1:9), of rich and poor (Sir 10:19–24; Jas 2:1–6), and of true wisdom (Sir 19:17–21; Jas 3:13–17), to name but a few.

There are also parallels between directives found in Ben Sira and those in the Gospels. This includes teaching on magnanimity (Sir 29:12; Mt 6:19) and forgiveness (Sir 28:2; Mk 11:25) and against placing false hope in possessions (Sir 11:18f; Lk 12:16–21).

From the time of its appearance Ben Sira has been very influential in both the Jewish and Christian communities. Over the years it has served as a kind of handbook of practical ethics, and its teachings can be found in the liturgical texts of both groups.

Although the canonical status of Ben Sira was and remains a question for debate in the larger Judeo-Christian community, for Catholics, Ben Sira is a canonical book. It continues to exercise its influence even today. Passages from Ben Sira are used as lectionary readings and, for many Catholics, the liturgical celebration is their primary exposure to the Bible.

### Questions for Discussion and Reflection

***Group Sharing/Discussion***

1. Choose several maxims from Ben Sira that especially appeal to you. Why do you think they are appropriate for life today?

2. Give examples from Ben Sira that are inappropriate for the way we live today.

3. If you were Ben Sira, what 10 teachings would you leave for your children and their children?

***In Our Lives***

1. Where do most people today find the principles by which they live?

2. How does our parish leadership take responsibility for helping our people follow the teachings of Christ in their daily lives?

3. Share ideas on passing along to children the principles by which a Christian lives.

***Individual/Personal Reflection/Action***

1. When you hear a particularly helpful homily, remember to tell the preacher you appreciate it.

2. Make a list for yourself of the 10 most important principles by which you live. After each one write down how you learned it, and who and what helped form in you that belief.

3. Ask helpful people to recommend a book you might use in your own life to stay encouraged and challenged to live by your principles.

# THE PROPHETS

If you are studying this in a group, it would be helpful to read this essay and the following one, "The Prophetic Books," together before beginning Isaiah and the other prophets.

## Prophetic Themes

Before getting into the individual characteristics and message of each of the prophetic books, it will be important to know a little about prophets and prophecies. For most people, the common understanding of a prophet is that a prophet is a person who predicts the future. This is not, however, what the Bible means.

A biblical prophet is a person deeply concerned and called by God to address the present-day events that affect the moral and spiritual lives of people. Having experienced God's presence and love in a profound way, the prophet becomes attuned to the wishes of God for individual lives and in the life of the community. Taking on the perspective of God awakens the prophet to concerns of faith and justice—especially concern for the poor, the afflicted, the alienated, and the marginalized. The prophet, having become a very intimate friend of God, consults with God on various matters, who then compels the prophet to share those insights and discussions with the rest of the community. The prophet uses all possible techniques to communicate with the people: symbols, stories, word plays, and speech forms and patterns common to that day.

## How Does a Prophet Come to Be?

Most biblical prophets are instructed by God in what to say, how to act, and whom to address. For some, such as Isaiah and Ezekiel, the initial call comes in the form of a dramatic vision; for others, all readers are told is that "The word of the LORD came" to the prophet. The prophet, through that personal relationship with God, takes on the role of God's messenger and sees the world around him in terms of how it relates to God. The prophet assesses people and events not on the basis of wealth, status, or possessions, but rather on the basis of the value and dignity of every single person created in the image and likeness of God. This viewpoint is so much the prophet's own that the prophet dares to speak for God, often using the phrase, "Thus says the LORD . . ." This conviction comes to the surface most clearly when the prophet perceives the lack of justice, faithfulness, or compassion in individual lives and especially in the life and actions of the community. These experiences of injustice call the prophet forth to speak, no matter what the cost. The prophet's challenge is hard to listen to, because the prophet speaks of matters that go counter to the accepted actions within the community, whether in religion, culture, or politics. Usually, the prophet's message concerns a movement away from being preoccupied with our own selfish concerns, to a movement toward being concerned for others—especially those who have no power: the poor, the widows, the afflicted, the outcasts, the alienated, the marginalized, the stranger.

As an integral member of this community, the prophet's own challenge is to renounce self-righteousness and to speak as one also in continual need of healing and conversion. Self-righteousness is not the true stance of the prophet, although that danger is ever present. Rather, the prophet speaks as a member of this sinful community. Despite this stance, the messenger is often clearly unpopular, because the message is difficult, even painful. Think about it for yourself: Would you want to live with someone who constantly pointed out your injustices or social evils, as if God were constantly watching you?

## Demands of the Prophet

Although the prophets differ from one another in what they emphasize and in the particular themes and applications of their prophetic words, one or more of three main subjects preoccupy almost all of the prophetic books. The prophets maintain that the social life of Israel or Judah is unjust; that the worship life of the people is corrupt; and that the relations between Israel or Judah and other countries are evidence of the lack of faith in God on the part of the people and their leaders. Social injustice is manifested in the treatment of the poor and marginalized, such as orphans and widows. Corruption in worship appears in the introduction of practices from other religions into Temple worship and in the belief that carrying out the form of sacrifice, while maintaining unjust or unfair social policies, is sufficient to satisfy God's demands. Faithlessness in foreign policy is shown when the leaders rely on treaties with the great powers of the day, and payment of tribute to emperors, rather than on following the commandments of God.

In speaking from the perspective of God, the prophet always laments over the injustices and points out and accuses the wrongdoers, hoping for repentance and reform. Usually, a warning is included, in which the prophet, in a general manner, tells of possible dire consequences if matters are not corrected, or if attitudes are not changed. The prophet's message always demands a change of heart, mind, and attitudes—aligning them to the mind, heart, and attitudes of God. Only in this manner can justice once again prevail and God be intimately present to the community.

However, the prophet's message is not always one of doom and gloom. Rather, the prophet continually reminds the people of God's faithful love and concern for them. In this context, the prophet offers the opportunity and the guidance for the community to realign itself with God's love, reconciliation, and peace. But the challenge is that this will only occur if the people continue to do the LORD's work, the work of justice. Just as God is faithful, the prophet spurs the people on to be faithful also. God's love and peace will be manifest if the people attend to the concerns of the poor and to the works of justice. Reform of self in order to be of service to others is the key message of all the prophets. In order for the reform to take place, the prophet continually reminds the people of God's loving arms and faithful care. If the people continue to remember God's love and fidelity toward them, then justice will indeed flourish in the land.

# THE PROPHETIC BOOKS

Many of the books of the Bible were written much later than the time period and the events they recount. This is true for the collection of the prophetic books. The prophetic books follow a pattern somewhat like this. First the prophet experiences life within a believing faith community. This community nourishes and sustains the prophet's relationship with God and enables the prophet to grow in intimacy with God and others. Sometime during the prophet's life, he experiences God intimately and profoundly, and the prophet feels called to help bridge the gap between God and the community. The prophet develops an acute sensitivity to violations of justice, especially toward the poor and rejected. The prophet has an inherent need to call these incidents to the attention of the community. Often, warnings of dire consequences accompany the prophet's words, challenging the community to action on behalf of those who are experiencing injustice.

Some in the community reject the prophet's message and try to out-shout, silence, imprison, exile, or even kill the prophet. Others see the wisdom in the prophet's words and begin to live and act accordingly. This segment of the community preserves the message and memory of the prophet by acting on the challenge and by passing the words and story on to anyone who will listen. Prophets were originally speakers rather than writers, but once their words were written down, the writings were brought together and edited so their lasting message could be kept alive and understood. In this process of handing on the stories, the words of the prophet are shaped and reshaped, so that they speak not only to the prophet's original audience but also to those presently in the community.

There is, nevertheless, a viewpoint for these prophetic collections. This viewpoint, the theology of the book, reflects the human relationship with God and tries to be faithful to the living memory of the original prophet. At the same time, it also continues to be relevant to changing times and experiences of the believing community. Thus, the words of the prophet still challenge our generation and times in the same way that they challenged the prophet's own generation and times.

**Questions for Discussion and Reflection**

***Group Sharing/Discussion***

1. In your own words, tell what a prophet is.
2. How is the role of the prophet helpful and important to the community?
3. Why would the prophet take such personal risk and share bad news?
4. Share something you learned or thought about as a result of these essays.

# ISAIAH READING GUIDE

### *At a Glance*

Scholars conclude three different authors at three different times were edited into this one book: I: chapters 1–39; II: chapters 40–55; III: chapters 56–66.

| | |
|---|---|
| Who are the main players? | I. Isaiah; super-power Assyria is dominant foreign power threatening Israel.<br>II. Written in Babylon for the exiled Hebrews, the poets/theologians were key authors; Cyprus, king of Persia<br>III. Israelites are back in Zion, intent upon rebuilding; the prophet's criticisms and promises center on Zion. |
| What should I look for? | In general the three-fold pattern (a) appearance of the LORD in power (b) requiring a response by the people or their representative, followed by (c) a divine intervention that implements justice. Look for the linkage of salvation and justice.<br>I. Denunciations of Zion and Judah; promises of blessings; announcements of God's judgments; oracles about foreign nations and narratives of the prophet.<br>II. No narratives, denunciations, or prophetic biography; rather carefully fashioned speeches announcing forgiveness to exiles in Babylon and inviting them to Zion; Servant Songs that note consolation and hope amid internal tensions.<br>III. Exclusively on internal affairs of the community—on deep religious, social, and economic divisions within the Judean community; also attention is projected to a future intervention of God in judgment and salvation; an apocalyptic vision of a purified people and Jerusalem as religious capital of the world. |
| When did it take place? | I. Preserves the preaching and deeds of Isaiah of Jerusalem of the late eighth century B.C.<br>II. Second Isaiah written in the mid-sixth century, about a century and a half after First Isaiah.<br>III. Third Isaiah written several decades later. |
| Where did these events occur? | I. In Palestine during occupation of Assyria<br>II. In Babylon while in exile<br>III. In Jerusalem after the Babylonian Exile |
| Why was this book written? | I. The prophet indicts the people and King Ahaz for refusing to trust in God's promises, tells of God's choosing Assyria as the punisher and gives promise of a better king.<br>II. The authors of Second Isaiah were poet-theologians who developed their ideas in new ways to persuade the people to certain modes of action.<br>III. The prophet announces that the LORD will rebuild the community in Zion, and Israel, to be authentic, needs to adhere to God's commands in worship and social justice. |

What is the story?

I. Isaiah tries to lead the people to trust in God's promises and to be faithful and just.

II. In Babylonia the prophet reminds the people of their religious identity in their teachings.

III. The prophet reveals the internal problems of the Israelite community. He urges them to follow the commands of worshiping God and doing justice. He nourishes the community with a vision of God's salvation.

The chapters of Isaiah comprise a "collection of collections." This complex structure might bewilder the reader unless you realize there are essentially three themes dominating Isaiah.

First is the unity and destiny of Israel as the people of the LORD God as they face the military threat of Mesopotamia (Assyria, Babylonia, and Persia).

Second, Jerusalem is the spiritual center and symbol of Israel's role among the nations of the world.

Third, the dynasty of David bears a special significance. David, the founder, had first established a united kingdom of Israel, with a capital in Jerusalem. The fate of this royal house plays a dominant role in the prophecies of chapters 6–12, but less so in later chapters. However, this link with the language and themes of the kingship of these Davidic leaders has made Isaiah the "messianic" prophet of the Old Testament.

## Three in One: The Book of Isaiah

Since the Bible presents us with a single work, under one title, it is natural to assume that the entire book of Isaiah was written by one person called Isaiah. Scholarly research, however, has shown that one person could not have written the entire book. Close analysis reveals that the people, places, and events in this book span several centuries. This is important to realize as you attempt to read this well-known and beloved book of the Bible. It is a book that has had a significant influence on both the Old and New Testaments, with Isaiah being one of the books most often quoted in the New Testament.

At least three different authors or communities, spanning three centuries, wrote and edited materials that were actually compiled into the one book we now know as Isaiah. Biblical scholars have assigned names to each of the three collections of materials in the book of Isaiah: First Isaiah, or *Isaiah of Jerusalem,* chapters 1–39; Second or *Deutero-Isaiah,* chapters 40–55; and Third or *Trito-Isaiah,* chapters 56–66. They are briefly described here and more detail follows.

### Isaiah of Jerusalem

First Isaiah, or Isaiah of Jerusalem (chs 1–39) is usually dated to a very turbulent period in the history of Israel, 740–687 B.C. First Isaiah witnessed the events that led Assyria to annihilate and exile the northern kingdom of Israel, in 721, as well as to place Judah itself under their control. Isaiah of Jerusalem was still ministering in 701 when Hezekiah, king of Judah, grew tired of being subject to Assyria and asked Egypt for help in rebelling against Assyria. In response to this rebellious league against him, Sennacherib, the king of Assyria, came back and captured all the key Judean towns, ultimately surrounding Jerusalem. In the biblical version of the story, a plague sent by God broke out, and Sennacherib retreated with the war spoils from the other cities. The Assyrian version of the story, found recorded in a recent archaeological discovery known as Taylor's prism (an inscribed stone, called a prism because of its shape), is that Hezekiah knew he was defeated, so he called a truce and agreed to pay a very large sum of money if Sennacherib would leave and not destroy the city. Sennacherib agreed, and the battle ended.

### Isaiah in Babylonia

Second or Deutero- (from the Greek word meaning second) Isaiah, chapters 40–55, covers the years 540–537 B.C., in Babylonia. Babylonia, roughly modern-day Iraq, had defeated the previous superpower, Assyria, in 612, when

**Steps of Transforming Life Experience into a Text and Beyond**

1. An experience—immediate or of long duration
2. Reflecting on that experience over time
3. Verbal articulation of that experience—storytelling and reshaping of story over a period of time
4. Written texts—collections of stories, sayings, rituals, insights, wisdom, proverbs, poetry, narration
5. Editing of the written material into a coherent whole with an overarching point of view or theology

This entire process is repeated every time an individual or a community reads or hears and experiences the text as speaking directly to them. Applying the text to one's own personal experience starts this process over and over. In this context, the text becomes a living document able to speak to those willing to listen and take it to heart.

At some point, certain texts were accepted as *final* or *canonical,* and no more changes could be made to the text. But up to that point, the text was still in a process of shaping and reshaping.

Babylonia captured Assyria's capital city, Nineveh. Nebuchadnezzar, the king of Babylonia, went on a campaign to capture as much territory as he could handle. In 587, he captured the southern kingdom of Judah, destroyed Jerusalem and its Temple, and exiled or deported the people of Judah to Babylonia. From 587 to 538, the people of Judah were in Babylonia, without land, temple, or roots. In 538, Cyrus, the king of the Persians, defeated the Babylonian empire and restored the people to their homeland. It was during the last few years of the Babylonian Exile, and the beginning of the return under Cyrus, that Second Isaiah spoke to the people in Babylonia.

### Isaiah of the Return from Exile

Third Isaiah, also known as Trito-Isaiah ("trito" is the Greek word meaning third), chapters 56–66, is dated to the period after the return of the people from Babylon, 537–500 B.C. There was great joy in returning, but soon worry, depression, and defeat set in because of the vast amount of work that needed to be done to rebuild the land, the city walls and structures, and the Temple. These preoccupations were further complicated by the attitude of some of those who returned to the land.

Even though they had come to see their exile as a consequence of their faithlessness, and their liberation as God's new mighty act that renewed the covenant relationship, people still sinned, acted from motives of greed, and showed injustice toward the poor and oppressed. These chapters presume the Temple had been rebuilt, dating them after 515 B.C. Judah had become a province of Persia, and the people were caught up in the frustrating process of rebuilding the land and their Jewish identities. It is in this context that Third Isaiah speaks to the people.

Editors, who gave them final shape, pulled these three blocks of material, each with its unique message, together. The description above helps us set a context for reading and understanding Isaiah. Unless we are familiar with the historical background, the prophet's words will not be clear, because we will not understand the specific references. God speaks and acts in and through human events and through people. To know what God is saying, therefore, we must be aware of the events, practices, and culture of the times. Only those who see matters from God's perspective will be true guides in reading the signs of the times.

## First Isaiah

### Overview of Chapters 1–39

First Isaiah, or Isaiah of Jerusalem, speaks from the very turbulent events of 742–700 B.C. In its final form, the work begins with a particular message to Jerusalem in chapters 1–12. It then addresses the nations as a whole in chapters 13–23, and finally speaks about the fate of the whole world in chapters 24–27, which probably do not go back to Isaiah of Jerusalem. Chapters 28–39 will be discussed later.

**Biblical Vocation Call Pattern**

1. God significantly enters a human life.
2. God gives the person a mandate or a mission.
3. The person being called usually objects.
4. God makes creative use of this objection.
5. God reassures the person.

Some Biblical Texts Indicative of this Pattern:

- Exodus 3:1–12
- Jeremiah 1:4–10
- Isaiah 6:1–8
- Isaiah 40:1–9
- Luke 1:28–38
- Acts 9:10–19

The account of the prophet's call usually provides significant clues to the prophet's perspective. (See the explanation above.) Chapter 6 of Isaiah recounts First Isaiah's call.

Isaiah experiences the LORD as king and glorious majesty during Temple worship and prayer. This majestic, overwhelming, holy presence is suffused in and through "all the earth." The prophet's experience of this presence leads to his understanding of himself as a person, like everyone else, full of imperfections, infidelities, and weaknesses. Yet, when the LORD touches and cleanses the mouth of the prophet with a fiery ember, the prophet is empowered to speak in spite of his weak and sinful human condition. The prophet sees the need for someone to speak to the people, feels called to respond to this need, and volunteers as the spokesperson for the LORD. Isaiah will speak the LORD's message but the people will not listen or understand. When Isaiah asks how long this will continue, he receives the answer: until all is destroyed, laid waste, and made desolate.

Thus, the message that Isaiah brings, the people will not listen to, and therefore destruction will come upon both the people and the land. Yet, throughout there is the ultimate hope for peace, harmony, and messianic salvation. No matter how stubborn the people are in their refusal to listen and repent, God will still work peace and future salvation in and through that very stubbornness and refusal. Suffering and punishment will prove to be a purifying, refining fire that will bring the community closer to God and that will make them more concerned with each other, especially the poor, the oppressed, and the alienated.

Remember, however, that the original prophetic material has been shaped and reshaped as it has been handed down and further modified by the final editors into a message that will be pertinent to their own particular community. These ancient editors even added material to stress a particular aspect of the original message. Therefore, while Isaiah's call is located in chapter 6, the editors have provided a summary section, chapters 1–6, showing what Isaiah's message was to be, and how the people would respond, along with how God would eventually work out the loving plan of salvation.

**Isaiah, Chapters 1–6**

Chapter 1 of Isaiah boldly states that unless the community repents its injustices and cares for the poor and defenseless in their midst, God will bring severe punishment upon the people. God punishes them (for instance, by the Assyrian conquest) not to destroy them, but rather to purify them, so that they will become a more just and loving community.

Isaiah 2:1–5 speaks of a vision of future peace in a passage that is one of the most quoted and best-known passages of all Scripture. It speaks of that ideal time when instruments of war are turned into tools of peace—tools that can be used for meeting the hungers of the human family. This is the ideal to which God has called Israel and the entire community, the vision that is integral to Isaiah's message as prophet. Yet chapter 2:6 to chapter 5 continue what must have been Isaiah's enduring, poorly received, and unheard message. In this section the prophet calls to mind the selfishness of the people, their lack of justice, their lack of concern for others, and their utter disregard for the loving relationship into which

## God and Suffering

A THEOLOGICAL PERSPECTIVE in Isaiah focuses on God as an impatient parent who is fed up with the sinful actions of the children. Punishment is seen by the parent as a means of redirecting or redefining the focus of the child. Isaiah seems to be saying that God punishes in order to purify the sinful actions and inclinations of the people. Other nations are used by God as instruments to accomplish this punishing and purifying process.

A question that needs to be asked is whether this is an image of God that makes sense to us today. Does this image of God speak to our experience and consciousness of what we have come to understand as God? Just as corporal punishment of children is no longer considered an appropriate form of punishment for misbehavior, so this image of God as child-punisher has to be also reevaluated. We have come to realize that suffering is not something that God causes to happen in order to help us learn a lesson. Rather, suffering is part and parcel of what it means to be human.

God is experienced as one who is always life-giving, life-enhancing, life-producing. All the experiences of our lives are means by which we can enter into a greater personal and loving relationship with God. Suffering and pain are key moments in our experience that help us to realize that we are not the center of the universe. It is at these particular moments that God invites us to an ever deeper relationship, challenging us to believe very firmly that new life will come out of this seemingly life-denying experience. God is always on the side of life, on our side, in the sense of a loved one who is faithful no matter what the sorrow or pain. It is this faithfulness of God toward the people that is truly Isaiah's message.

God brings about redemption in and through those very experiences of pain and sorrow that bring us to our knees. God does not cause the pain and suffering, but rather, God uses it to bring new life out of death. This is what we mean when we speak of the Christian life as one deeply imbedded in the Paschal Mystery, the mystery of death and resurrection that Jesus experienced and in which we participate. God does not cause the pain; neither does God free us from this very human experience. Rather, God transforms our very pain and sorrow into an occasion of greater understanding of self as human, of deeper sympathy with others in pain, and of greater depth in our personal, loving relationship with God and all of creation.

God called Israel. Chapter 6 relates Isaiah's vocation call experience, a willingness to devote himself to the work of the LORD despite the frustration, futility, and hardships that the work and message will bring.

### The Book of Immanuel

Chapters 7–12, usually referred to as the "Book of Immanuel" because it contains the famous verses of the Immanuel prophecy (Is 7:12), deal with salvation that comes only with reliance on God, and not on one's own strength or alliances for security. Isaiah 7:9 clearly expresses the intent of this whole section, as well as all of the book of Isaiah, when it states that "unless your faith is firm, you shall not be firm." Faith in God is the root that will maintain us no matter what comes along. Yet even if we are overwhelmed by what comes along, God will continue to be with us bringing new life, birth, and creation out of death, destruction, and pain. Although the material in these chapters comes from different times in Isaiah's ministry, it has been carefully arranged to stress the themes of reliance on God and God's fidelity to the promises made to the people.

### Oracles against the Nations

Chapters 13–23 make up a collection of oracles against the nations. The prophet uses these to show that God will not allow Israel to be unjust indefinitely. Just because the Israelites have an established relationship with God does not mean that they can do whatever they want. God will draw the line at some point, and Isaiah's message is exactly that: You cannot go on being unjust and expect to get away with it.

Usually, God's plan for punishment of the people was understood by the prophets to be the key reason that other nations were successful in defeating Israel. God uses other nations to accomplish his purifying purposes upon the community of Israel. However, God does not allow the other nations to overstep their bounds either. God makes sure that other nations merely accomplish the purifying punishment desired, and no more. The key to these oracles in Isaiah is that the final editors have inserted another revolutionary concept, that of universal salvation. They saw God's saving hand operative even in these foreign nations. Like Israel, they will not be completely destroyed. Rather, there is hope that they, too, after experiencing their own purification through suffering, will ultimately place their reliance on God, and God alone. They too, like Israel, will be saved.

### The Apocalypse of Isaiah

Chapters 24–27 are referred to as the "Apocalypse of Isaiah." Apocalypse, a style of writing, is a term meaning to reveal or to draw aside the veil of the mysteries of life, and discern God's plan at work, especially those experiences that are the most puzzling or opaque to such insights, like pain and suffering. Often such writings were intended primarily to offer encouragement and support to those suffering and oppressed. Highly symbolic language was used to reveal how God would ultimately accomplish the plan of salvation, especially how salvation would be brought out of the pain, suffering, and evil in the midst of the community.

These chapters of Isaiah provide a future vision, a peek into the end times, when all the ruin, destruction, and suffering will be put into perspective, and new life will come out of it. Those who have continually trusted in the LORD will be fully rewarded and recompensed with new life and the defeat of death (25:7f, 19). Full intimacy with God, explored here in the image of an eternal divine banquet on God's holy mountain (25:6ff), will be reestablished.

The defeat of death and the universal salvation of all nations are two of the most revolutionary concepts found in the book of Isaiah, if not in the entire Old Testament. Up to this time, future survival was seen exclusively in terms of the memory of an individual living on in the family, in the children, and in the survival of the nation of Israel.

### Later Addition to First Isaiah

Chapters 28–33 and 34–35 are later additions made by a second editor or group who were inspired by the words and tradition of Isaiah of Jerusalem. It is important to remember that inspiration applies to the entire process that resulted in the biblical text, not just to one author but also to those who collected and edited the material, as well as those who reflected upon and reshaped the original words or message of Isaiah. In other words, the final book that we know as Isaiah is the result of a whole tradition, begun by Isaiah and ending when the final editing touches were placed on the entire book. Chapters 28–33 and 34–35, although they are the work of a different group of editors, are consistent with the previous 27 chapters.

They stress once again the need to put away all injustice and to trust in God. Since the people will refuse to listen, God will punish the people, yet this punishment will lead to recognition of the need to place faith and trust completely in God. The vision of 35:5–6 focuses on the lame, deaf, and blind placing their trust in God, and establishing their home in the new Jerusalem that God has prepared for the faithful. After the pain and anguish caused by the purifying punishment, God will gather all the scattered and bring them back home to a new Jerusalem that will be faithful to the loving relationship God has initiated.

### Historical Appendix to First Isaiah

Chapters 36–39 are a historical appendix provided by the editors and based primarily on 2 Kings 18:13–20:19, giving a quick summary of the historical events surrounding the oracles of First Isaiah of Jerusalem. This quick summary is intended to provide a link back to the message of Isaiah and the actual historical events surrounding Hezekiah and Sennacharib. Also, this summary provides a link forward to the Babylonian attack and the destruction of Jerusalem, as well as the exile of the people to Babylon. The time that has elapsed between chapter 39 and chapter 40 is approximately 150 years. Second Isaiah, chapters 40–55, picks up the themes of First Isaiah, especially God's plan for universal salvation, and expands them significantly.

## Second Isaiah

Second Isaiah speaks to a community that has indeed experienced the terrifying, purifying punishment of God and still continues to do so. The Babylonians defeated Assyria, and in 583 B.C. they captured and destroyed Jerusalem and exiled its entire people. Second Isaiah speaks in the very midst of this exile, observing how it is about to end, with Cyrus, king of the Persians, referred to as God's anointed, coming to defeat the Babylonians and setting God's people free. The tone of Second Isaiah is one of comfort, hope, restoration, and of God's loving arms reaching out to comfort and console the people.

### Overture to Second Isaiah's Symphony

Like an overture to a good piece of music, chapter 40 summarizes, in beautiful poetry, all the key themes of chapters 40–55. At the time when Israel is most discouraged and ready to despair, Isaiah speaks God's word of comfort and love to the people. The setting for Second Isaiah's message is the entire world, for God's saving action on behalf of the people will be so evident that all will see and experience God's saving plan, love, and power. Greed, corruption, and reliance on false gods are again condemned, making their elimination the key condition upon which God's loving and saving activity will become realized.

### The Suffering Servant and God's Faithfulness

Chapters 41–48 take up several themes that are beautifully and poetically developed by Second Isaiah. The "servant" theme is one that has great meaning, both in its application to Israel as the suffering servant of God, and to Jesus, the ultimate model of the suffering servant of God. There are at least four servant passages in all of Second Isaiah: 42:1–4; 49:1–7; 50:4–11; 52:13–53:12.

Another rich theme that Second Isaiah explores concerns the comparison that is made between God's saving action on behalf of the people now in Babylon, and God's foundational saving action on behalf of the people in their Exodus from Egypt. Second Isaiah exhorts the people to be faithful to God, for God is about to unleash a new salvation experience for the people, just like the one their ancestors experienced in the desert. Second Isaiah uses the image of God as the master engineer who will design and build a wonderful road right through the desert so that Israel will be able to take a direct route back to its home. What God did for the people in the beginning of their relationship he will do again, to show his great love and fidelity toward the people. Second Isaiah emphasizes the fact that God is still faithful now, as God was in the infancy stages of Israel's growth. God continues to work those great and mighty deeds that were worked in the midst of their ancestors. Faith and reliance on God are the only key requirements for God's mighty deeds to take place.

### Salvation Involves Suffering

Chapters 49–55 have a less exalted, less hopeful tone, with more of a tragic sense of what is needed to bring about God's plan. One aspect of this deeper view is the prophet's identification of himself as the suffering servant. Another is in the recognition of the importance of suffering.

Salvation will come about, but often through one who suffers with and for the people, as an ultimate example and model of what suffering is all about. These passages about the suffering servant were identified with Second Isaiah and with the whole people of God. Most of all, however, they are identified with Jesus. In chapters 49–55 the hopeful message of joy and comfort is still there, but it is deepened through the realization that the very messenger of the good news must endure pain and suffering for the good news to take root in the minds and hearts of the community.

## Third Isaiah

### Isaiah of the Return

With these ideas in mind, we now move to Third Isaiah, whose melancholy tone is much more pronounced than that in Second Isaiah. Third Isaiah presumes a time when the people have returned from exile and have rebuilt the Temple. From a variety of sources, the date can be set any time after 515 B.C. The people are home; they are changed and purified by their experience of suffering, yet authentic worship and a concern for justice are not central to the lives of the restored people of God.

The author of Third Isaiah, whether one person or a community of persons, experiences this lack in the community and is moved to use the vision of the Isaiah tradition to address the current situation. The author reinterprets the message of Isaiah of Jerusalem and Isaiah of the exile to address the needs of the community of that time, resulting in the Isaiah of the return.

Chapters 56–59 pick up themes of the previous chapters, especially themes of salvation in and through suffering. Suffering has the potential to make the worshiping community more sensitive to the needs of others who suffer in their midst, especially the foreigner, the outcast, and the marginalized. These people are welcomed into the house of God—a radical proposal—because of the key insight developed in 56:7 that the house of God is a house of prayer for all peoples. Yet worship can also result in self-righteousness and complacency that says: We have done our part in worship, God. When are you going to do yours?

### Ritual and Life Are Related

Third Isaiah challenges this notion by connecting worship with actions that flow from worship. If worship does not lead to a greater concern for those who are in need, if it does not lead to justice for the oppressed and outcasts, then worship is indeed meaningless. Chapter 57:1–2 continues a theme central to the whole of Isaiah (see chapters 24–27, especially 25:7f, 19), a belief in the continuation of life after death, especially for the just, for those who have tried to rely on God, and who are concerned for the poor, the needy, and the alienated.

### Suffering as Purifying Fire

Chapters 60–62 form the heart of Third Isaiah's message. By using a variety of images that echo Second Isaiah, Third Isaiah speaks of the salvation that has come upon the community once the purifying punishment has ended. Because the community remained faithful to God during this time of testing and trial, God will more than reward the people. Not only will God restore the people to their former glory, but God will make them a light to all other nations. All the nations will see what God has done for the people, and they will stream toward Israel, and begin their own relationship with God.

Third Isaiah emphasizes that the clear sign of this salvation will be that of the Jubilee experience. The Jubilee (every 50 years) celebration, like the sabbatical experience (every 7 years), was a time of celebration and joy that spilled out into every facet of the community's life. During this time, the community is to remind itself forcibly that everything belongs to God. Thus, the land is to lie fallow, and what grows on it belongs to all people. Debts are to be wiped out, offenses are to be forgiven, the needy are to be taken care of, and all are to be at peace. Salvation is to spill into every facet of life and make itself visible to all people and nations. Jesus himself understood his mission and ministry in terms of the insights communicated here by Third Isaiah, even quoting them, and applying them to his own vocation as God's salvation to the people.

### Reliance on God Brings Eternal Rewards

Chapters 63–66 are parallel to the key themes in chapters 56–59. Sorrow is expressed over the sins of the community and the need of the community to be punished because of its sinfulness and injustice. This punishment is seen as the only way that God could curb the excesses, greed, and selfishness of this sinful people. Yet, once the punishment is accomplished, God reaches out with double the effort to restore the people and make them even better and greater than before. A universality is evident in the salvation theme, where Jew and Gentile will live as one and worship God together. Those who refuse to rely on God will be severely punished, but those who trust in God will be abundantly rewarded.

## Conclusion

Thus ends the book of Isaiah, a book that spans about 200 years. Throughout that period of turmoil, tension, and suffering, Isaiah focuses on one key theme: reliance, trust, faith, and confidence in God. This trust in God will lead to the recognition that God and others are the center of the universe, and not any individual person. Faith in God leads to reaching out to those in need, even when this might lead to conflict, frustration, and rejection. The book can probably be summed up by a phrase St. Paul uses in his letter to the Romans: "We know that all things work for good for those who love God. . . ." and another Pauline text that states that "What eye has not seen, and ear has not heard, and what has not entered the human heart, what God has prepared for those who love him."

### Questions for Discussion and Reflection

*Group Sharing/Discussion*

1. Isaiah uses many strong images to speak to the people of God, of their role, of the relationship between God and the people, and so on. These images include violence and war, a vineyard, brothers and sisters, wild and tame animals together, and tears being wiped away. Choose one image in Isaiah and tell why it was an appropriate image for the prophet to use at the time.

2. Chapter Six describes how a reluctant Isaiah was eventually able to agree to speak for the LORD. How would you explain the significance of the symbol of the live coal on his lips?

3. Throughout this book there are many threats and many promises. Choose a threat and a promise that strike you as most significant.

4. What is the significance of this book being edited over the course of many generations? What effect do you think that had on the message?

*In Our Lives*

1. First Isaiah's message was very hard on people's ears. They did not like the sound of its challenges to their life, such as caring for the poor, living a life that was fair and just, and worshiping God. If you were today's Isaiah, what challenges would you give to our society, our culture, and our religious groups?

2. How do you understand the role of the suffering servant as portrayed by Second Isaiah? How was this image applied to Jesus? What role does it play in the life of a Christian?

3. One message in this book is about being faithful and trusting in God even during difficulties, unfairness, and painful happenings in life. This can be a difficult message to hear when undergoing trials and suffering. How can our community "be Isaiah" to those undergoing hardship? What will help us do this better?

4. Recall an experience in which someone offered hope, comfort, and consolation to you while you were taken up with your pain and suffering. How did this make you feel? How did you respond to the person?

5. What in the message of Isaiah is especially relevant for our own life and times?

*Individual/Personal Reflection/Action*

1. Isaiah was at first reluctant to speak out but overcame his hesitation. What opportunities do you have to speak and offer Christ's message of hope or the message of the challenges that being a Christian brings with it? Who or what will help you have the courage to speak of these things?

2. Who is someone you might call a prophet today—someone who has the courage to challenge us, to question the way we live?

3. Our society today tempts us with many false gods such as power, money, materialism, self-centeredness. What is the hardest temptation for you to resist? What can you do to become stronger in recognizing and resisting it?

4. In the book of Isaiah, God's constant and tender love reaches out continually toward goodness, especially those who suffer. Try to remember to thank God each evening for this constant and tender love for you.

# JEREMIAH READING GUIDE

*At a Glance*

| | |
|---|---|
| Who are the main players? | Jeremiah Josiah Jehoiakim Nebuchadnezzar Jehoiachin Zedekiah Gedaliah |
| What should I look for? | Three views:<br>1. Jeremiah's poetry-sermons, focused on Exodus and covenant, very personal, agonizing, interacting with the community and God (chs 1–25; 30–33).<br>2. The "Confessions" of Jeremiah where he argues with God over his vocation and message (12:1–5; 15:10–21; 17:12–18; 18:18–23; 20:7–18).<br>3. Narrative sections regarding the theology of Jeremiah collected by Baruch, his secretary (chs 26–29; 34–35). |
| When did this take place? | Jeremiah began his prophetic ministry in 627 B.C. during the reform of Josiah and was last heard from as an unwilling exile in Egypt about 570 B.C. |
| Where did these events occur? | Jeremiah was born in Anathoth, just three miles from Jerusalem. He preached in Jerusalem and Israel. He was left behind when all were deported to Babylon, and he was dragged off to Egypt where he died. |
| Why was this book written? | Jeremiah's life spanned a tumultuous age in religion, politics, and war. During these times Jeremiah's message is the attitude of compassion and prayer. This is intimately linked to fidelity to a new covenant inscribed upon the heart. More than any other prophet Jeremiah made his own life the message. |
| What is the story? | Although his ministry began in a period of bright promise and reform, his recorded preaching focused on the disintegration of Judah from 609 B.C. forward, after King Josiah was killed and Babylon's assaults began. Especially noteworthy is his preaching during the grim period leading up to the destruction of Jerusalem and the Temple in 586. Four central themes are the new covenant, sin and atonement, faith and prayer, and true and false prophecy. |

## Jeremiah: The Person, the Message

Jeremiah's life speaks as loudly as his message. Both his life and his message thus need to be examined in order for the book to have its full impact.

Jeremiah hails from the town of Anathoth, 3.6 miles northeast of Jerusalem. His father, Hilkiah, may have been the one by that name who found the book of the Law of Moses (the book of Deuteronomy) during the repair of the Temple by King Josiah in 622 B.C. (2 Kgs 22:8). This fact partially explains the influence of Deuteronomy on Jeremiah.

Politics helped to form the message of Jeremiah. The words and actions of Jeremiah were intimately caught up with the political happenings of the day, particularly the demise of the Assyrian Empire and the rise of Babylon as the world power.

Jeremiah's ministry began in 627 B.C. With the collapse of the Assyrian Empire, he joyfully announced the return of the northern tribes. This is the context for chapters 30–31. Jeremiah also condemned idolatry at Jerusalem but was strangely silent during the deuteronomic reform under King Josiah. In 609 B.C. Josiah was killed in battle against the Egyptians. His son Jehoiakim succeeded him and revolted against the new world power, the Babylonians. They responded by capturing Jerusalem in 597 B.C., sacking the city and deporting many of its leading citizens.

King Zedekiah was warned by Jeremiah not to join with the Egyptians in another rebellion against the Babylonians. Zedekiah gave in to the rebellion temptation and the Babylonians once again stormed the city in July, 587 B.C. They burned Jerusalem and the Temple to the ground. The king and the people were all deported to Babylonia. Jeremiah was left behind, choosing to remain in the land as a sign of hope for the future (Jer 40:1–6). When the remaining few in Jerusalem rejected his advice to stay on the land and fled to Egypt, they dragged Jeremiah with them (Jer 42:1–43:7). There Jeremiah died, leaving behind a tradition and a book.

The character of Jeremiah shines brightly from any page of the book. Jeremiah manifests:

- Joyful optimism (ch 31)
- Honest, painful struggling with God (12:1–5; 15:10–21; 20:7–18)
- Courage in confronting kings (ch 37)
- Agony over the tragic fate of Jerusalem (8:18–9:10)
- Perseverance amid continuous rejection (20:9)
- Irritability and, at times, a desire for revenge, showing itself especially in his Confessions (12:1–5; 15:10–21; 17:12–18; 18:18–23; 20:7–18)
- Sensitivity to the beauties and wonder of nature (1:11; 2:13; 4:25)
- Celibacy, a hard choice from which he suffered much (16:1–4); yet at the same time it kept him in tune with the suffering of the people and their need to trust and have faith in God, leading to peace.

Jeremiah gave a solid focus to the piety of Israel. This focus centered on the laments against pain and evil, as well as the bold questioning of God and God's motives. Examples of laments and questioning existed before Jeremiah, but not to the extent or degree exemplified by him. Jeremiah's Confessions were such deep questionings of God that they became seared in the community's consciousness, never to be forgotten. They have the same effect on modern readers.

Jeremiah's name, in Hebrew, means, "The LORD raises up." It is the LORD who raises Jeremiah up to be a prophet and to communicate with God's people through his life and words. Yet Jeremiah sometimes struggled with his role. In Jeremiah's struggle to determine what God wanted and how God wanted it, we also see our own struggle in trying to live in a loving, faithful relationship to God. With Jeremiah, we realize that this is not easy. God's word comes to us not in clearly defined terms and directions, but rather in the messiness of life, with all its ambiguities and fuzziness.

Like Jeremiah, our struggle in relating to God is to be continually asking and discovering where God is in all of this. Where is God in the good times? Where is God in the bad times? Where is God at those times when I am in need? Why doesn't God leave me alone? It is not that Jeremiah wants to live without God. Jeremiah cannot live without God. Jeremiah cannot ignore God, either in his life or in the life of the community, and sometimes God's message to Jeremiah is unwelcome.

Jeremiah's life and message is continually intermixed with all these questions and concerns. While desiring to be faithful and obedient to God's message at work in his life, Jeremiah is continually overwhelmed by it. This feeling causes him to question God, to get angry with God, to doubt, to feel abandoned by God.

All of Jeremiah's reactions to God are most clearly expressed in passages scattered throughout his book, known as the Confessions of Jeremiah (12:1–5; 15:10–21; 17:12–18; 18:18–23; 20:7–18). In these passages Jeremiah vents his anger and frustration, yet he continually works through the anger by placing his reliance on God, who, no matter what the situation, is always faithful. Through the venting, Jeremiah arrives at a sense of peace and renewed commitment to that loving relationship with God, along with all that the relationship demands.

If Jeremiah the person is the message as much as his words are, then we need to look at the very human change and adaptation that Jeremiah endures in order to work out God's purpose in his life and in the life of the community. This discernment is as much our own journey with God

*Historical Background*

| | |
|---|---|
| Chapters 1–6 | Reign of King Josiah (640–609 B.C.).<br>Collapse of the Assyrian Empire.<br>Independence of many vassal states like Babylonia and Judah.<br>Deuteronomic reform at Jerusalem (2 Chr 34f).<br>Reunification of all Israel (2 Kgs 23).<br>Violent death of Josiah while attempting to block the Egyptian army at the pass of Megiddo (2 Chr 35:20–25).<br>Josiah's son, Jehoahaz, taken captive to Egypt; another son, Jehoiakim, installed as king (2 Chr 36:1–8). |
| Chapters 7–20 | Reign of Jehoiakim (609–597 B.C.), a ruthless tyrant despised by Jeremiah.<br>Nebuchadnezzar defeats Egypt at Carchemesh in Syria (605 B.C.), takes Jerusalem in 603 B.C. for the Babylonians and confirms Jehoiakim in office 601 B.C. Jehoiakim revolts. Babylonians return to Jerusalem in 597 B.C. Jehoiakim is dead; his son Jehoiachin is taken captive to Babylon and Zedekiah is installed as king (2 Chr 36:9f). |
| Chapters 21–29 | Reign of Zedekiah (597–587 B.C.); chapters 30–33 come from an earlier period, probably after the fall of Nineveh (612 B.C.). |
| Chapters 34–45 | Fall and last days of Jerusalem (587–583 B.C.).<br>City and Temple destroyed, August, 587 B.C.<br>Most of the people deported.<br>Gedaliah governor; Jeremiah remains at Jerusalem.<br>Gedaliah assassinated; people flee to Egypt, dragging Jeremiah with them, 583 B.C.<br>Third Babylonian deportation, 582 B.C.<br>Jeremiah dies in Egypt. |
| Chapters 46–51 | Oracles against the Nations. |
| Chapter 52 | Historical appendix. |

as it is Jeremiah's. Jeremiah's journey with God has often been compared with Jesus' journey with God. Jesus, like Jeremiah, had to struggle with faith, doubt, and feelings of abandonment to determine what the will of God was for him in his own life and community. Every person who tries to live in relationship with God and attempts to be continually faithful to God, no matter what the results, shares this process.

## Jeremiah, the Book

The table above gives the historical background to Jeremiah. However, the development of the book as a story, and as a collection of the words and actions of Jeremiah, follows a different format. This can be sketched out in the table of literary background, which follows.

The book of Jeremiah is clearly a tradition, begun by the prophet and also continued by disciples who composed a major part of what is entitled in 1:1 "the words of Jeremiah." "Words" mean actions as well as statements, disciples' response, as well as the master's leadership.

### Sources of the Book of Jeremiah

The organization of the book indicates a long, complex development. The sources of this development are the sermons of the prophet himself, often in poetic form. Jeremiah is usually associated with traditions that developed in the northern kingdom, especially the focus on the Exodus and the covenant. While working out of these traditions, Jeremiah is not a slave to them but rather stamps his words with his own uniqueness and individuality. Chapters 2–25 and 30–33 are uniquely Jeremiah: very personal, agonizing, and continually interacting with the community and God.

*Literary Background*

| | |
|---|---|
| Chapter 1 | The prologue, or Jeremiah's prophetic call from God. |
| Chapters 2–25 | The preaching of the prophet. The ordering of the material in this section remains close to the chronology of Jeremiah's life. |
| Chapters 26–45 | A disciple's justification of the prophet, with a message of hope from Jeremiah in chapters 30–33. Chapters 30–33 probably represent Jeremiah's earliest preaching. By placing it in the middle of the book, Jeremiah's followers showed that they never gave up on the hopeful message of the prophet, despite the tragic events of chapters 2–29. |
| Chapters 46–51 | The Oracles against the Nations. These balance well with Jeremiah's call to be "a prophet to the nations" at the beginning of the book (1:4f). |
| Chapter 52 | A fulfillment of Jeremiah's threats, concluding hopefully with the release from prison of King Jehoiachin. |

The ultimate example of Jeremiah's struggle with his vocation and mission from God is located in sections of the book called the "Confessions" of Jeremiah. In these Confessions Jeremiah argues with God and anguishes over his vocation and the message God has given him to proclaim to the community: 12:1–5; 15:10–21; 17:12–18; 18:18–23; 20:7–18. These Confessions might have originally been a diary of Jeremiah that was possibly split up and inserted into the text by an editor. The insertion of these Confessions at particular places in the text is confirmed by the fact that wherever they appear, the sequence of the verses is disturbed.

There are two long prose sections about Jeremiah (chs 26–29 and 34–45), which are generally considered to have been collected and edited by Jeremiah's secretary, Baruch. Even though they tell of Jeremiah, the key purpose of these sections is theological and not necessarily biographical.

The book of Jeremiah also contains sermons based on phrases from a number of discourses from the book of Deuteronomy. These sermons are evident in 7:1–8:3; 11:1–17; 16:1–13; 21:1–10. It is possible that these sermons were originally discourses preached by disciples of Jeremiah, reflecting upon the prophet's words or actions.

**The Editing of Jeremiah's Preaching**

The development of the text of the book of Jeremiah has an extensive and complex history. Scholars have arrived at several conclusions regarding this complex history of the text:

1. The prophet's words were originally preserved in separate booklets.
2. Several editions of the book were made during the prophet's lifetime; several more editions were made after his death.
3. The book contains not only the preaching of the prophet, but also extended accounts about him, as well as sermons based on his words.
4. Jeremiah might not have intended all of his words, most especially his confessions, to be made public.

We should not focus simply on Jeremiah as being inspired by God. Rather, we need to focus on an inspired Jeremiah tradition, in which inspiration was shared among prophet, disciples, editors, and community.

**Introduction and Call to Prophecy (ch 1)**

This chapter represents more than God's call to the prophet. Either Jeremiah or one of his disciples wrote his call into the accepted form for a prophet. (See other examples of this form in Ex 3; Is 6 and 40; Lk 1:5–38.) In doing this, the editors affirmed in the very beginning of the book what God wanted for the prophet and for the community. Two separate visions (vv. 11–16) anticipate the fulfillment of Jeremiah's prophecy about the destruction of Jerusalem.

**Oracles from the Reign of Josiah (chs 2–6)**

Jeremiah's preaching centered on the tender love of God as manifested in the covenant during the days of Moses (2:2f). Sin brings its own punishment, but this punishment can be purifying and transforming (2:19, 30; 4:14). Jeremiah 3:12–4:4 repeats one of Jeremiah's key themes: Return to the LORD. In these chapters Jeremiah makes several very radical observations. In 3:14–18 a whole new series of religious and civic leaders is called for, along with the removal of the necessity of the Ark of the Covenant, and the call to welcome foreigners to the new Temple.

**Oracles from the Reign of Jehoiakim (chs 7–20)**

In this section we meet the first of the famous sermons in the style and theological content of the book of Deuteronomy. These sermons were probably composed by disciples of Jeremiah, reflecting on earlier texts of Jeremiah. Chapter 7 is the most important of these sermons. When Jeremiah threatened the destruction of the Temple, the people shouted, "Blasphemy." Yet Jeremiah reminded them of such an occurrence at an earlier time, at Shiloh, done by an act of God. The preservation of the Temple did not depend blindly upon divine promises, nor upon more and better ceremonies. Rather, it depended on the following: "If you thoroughly reform your ways . . . if each of you deals justly with your neighbor; if you no longer oppress the resident alien, the orphan, and the widow, . . . will I let you continue to dwell in this place" (7:5–7).

The first of Jeremiah's Confessions occurs at 12:1–5. Jeremiah's complaint against God is courageous, tender, impatient, and obedient. God never answers Jeremiah's initial question but addresses his faith, basically encouraging him to continue his task even though things are going to get worse.

Many symbols and parables are used to communicate God's messages to the people of Israel: Jeremiah's celibacy (ch 16), the potter (chs 18–20), and the purchase of a field (ch 32). Visions and symbolic actions were key vehicles used by prophets to get people's attention and to communicate their message in a way that would make an impression and be remembered by the community.

**Oracles from the Last Years of Jerusalem (chs 21–25)**

Most of chapter 21, like chapter 7, is a sermon along the lines of the book of Deuteronomy, developed by Jeremiah's disciples as they reflected on his words to the community. In chapter 22, Jeremiah explodes in anger against the greedy, cruel, and devious King Jehoiakim, wishing for him "the burial of a donkey" (vv. 13–19). Along with this outburst, there is an elegy to Jehoiakim's successor, King Jehoiachin, a young man lost to the Babylonian Exile.

In chapter 23 Jeremiah reaffirms his loyalty to the dynasty of David, but only on the condition that the entire family tree be cut to the roots. From these roots, God will raise a new shoot to shepherd the people rightly. This chapter also severely denounces false prophets, individuals who claim insights into God's ways but only end up fostering their own greed and immorality. They condone sin in others to excuse their own sin.

Chapter 25 announces the "seventy years" of exile (v. 11). "Seventy years" is used several times in Jeremiah and in other parts of the Old Testament. This number, like seven, should be taken as a symbolic number indicating completion and fulfillment. In other words, it announces that the exile will run its full course, but it will also be completed and come to an end.

**Biographical Accounts about Jeremiah (chs 26–29 and 34–45)**

Baruch, Jeremiah's secretary, shows how true the prophecies of Jeremiah were, especially about the destruction of Jerusalem and its Temple. By showing us the eventual reality of the exile and its destruction, Baruch contrasts the truth of Jeremiah's message from God with the falsity of those prophets who chose to believe themselves and not God. In this fashion, Jeremiah is shown to be the prophet faithful to God, involved in the agony of the community, and yet already preparing for the restoration of the people, the land, and the coming of the messianic age.

**The Book of Consolation (chs 30–33)**

An editor gathered this material from various moments in the life of Jeremiah, especially from his earliest preaching. That editor placed it here between chapter 29, a letter of encouragement to those in exile since 597 B.C., and chapters 34–45, detailing in a gruesome fashion the end of Jerusalem and the second deportation to Babylonia in 587 B.C. As a result of this editing, words intended for a different context were reinterpreted to apply to this particular context. This process occurs often in Scripture, especially when a new context shows a new way of looking at the text and of applying that text to this new situation.

**Oracles against the Nations (chs 46–51; Appendix, ch 52)**

These oracles are intended to show that God is in control and that God will overcome all hostile powers. By doing this, God will ensure that the covenant and the divine plans will be fulfilled. Israel's exile into foreign lands does not mean the end of Israel. The appendix, chapter 52, ends with a ray of hope for all exiles: King Jehoiachin is released from prison. It is significant that a prophet of doom like Jeremiah ends on a hopeful note.

## The Message of Jeremiah

Central to Jeremiah's message is the attitude of compassion and prayer. This is intimately linked to faithfulness to a covenant inscribed upon the heart. Four crucial themes central to Jeremiah are the new covenant, sin and atonement, faith and prayer, and true and false prophecy.

**The New Covenant**

The key passage for this theme of the new covenant is Jeremiah 30–33, the Book of Consolation. These passages of hope were reinterpreted to apply to the context of restoration after exile. There are frequent references to "the days are coming" or "the coming days." Before Jeremiah, the Israelites thought mostly in terms of a future fulfillment of God's promises in a single great day of the LORD. Under Jeremiah's influence this future "day" began to appear in stages: first suffering; then "the coming days" or the in-between period; and finally, the definite completion of all the hopes and promises.

Jeremiah's "new" covenant written on the heart is closely tied with the Mosaic covenant of Mount Sinai. This covenant of Exodus 34:6f had already bonded Israel with a compassionate, forgiving God. Jeremiah's covenant was "new" in that it reminded people of the covenant terms they had forgotten or neglected. This idea of the new covenant, one which was taken into the personality or character of each person, greatly influenced Jesus and the early Church and continues to influence our current understanding of what it means to be a member of the people of God.

**Sin and Atonement**

Jeremiah rightly declares that sin brings its own sorrow. People are transformed, for good or bad, into those very things that they seek or desire. Yet the punishment resulting from sin can be a source of purification of our desires and a strengthening of our resolve to change our lives. All this is linked to God's compassion, leading us to hope in being forgiven and restored. This sequence of sin—suffering—repentance—forgiveness—new life undergirds the theology of the books of Joshua, Judges, 1 and 2 Samuel, and 1 and 2 Kings. By recovering this existing tradition and applying it to the present, Jeremiah makes this tradition new again, bringing it to life with new meaning and vigor.

**Faith and Prayer**

Jeremiah continually bares his heart and soul as he struggles in his relationship to God and to the community. This wrestling with God is most evident in his Confessions (12:1–5; 15:10–21; 17:12–18; 18:18–23; 20:7–18). In these prayer experiences, Jeremiah confronts God with defiant and bold questions. Yet, throughout the questioning and the doubts, Jeremiah never wavers from his reliance on God's faithfulness and God's concern for him and for the community. God never resolves Jeremiah's questions or concerns, yet this venting out to God seems to help Jeremiah in coming to grips with his own pain, anguish, and struggle.

Jeremiah arrives at the conviction that his relationship with God is the only one he can depend upon, and once again he finds peace and reassurance in that reality. The recounting of this human experience of Jeremiah proved to be very powerful and very attractive to the community, for it modeled for them a realistic relationship to God and to one another.

**True and False Prophecy**

Throughout his ministry Jeremiah had to struggle with the charge of being a false prophet, because the message that he proclaimed was neither acceptable nor popular. The criteria for determining a true prophet just did not fit the personality, mission, prayer life, or credentials that Jeremiah exhibited. Jeremiah is the classic example of the rejected prophet. Despite continuous rejection and persecution, Jeremiah eventually became one of the most popular and accepted prophets. His genuine expressions of piety made an impact on the community for generations to come. His spontaneous and continuous interaction with God, openly and honestly, authenticated the genuineness of his mission and message.

True prophecy is usually judged by the lasting impact that the prophet and the message have on the community. This long-term community acceptance of the prophet also determined which prophet's words and works were to be preserved in the collection of books that came to be known as the Bible. Jeremiah has proven to be a true prophet indeed.

**Questions for Discussion and Reflection**

***Group Sharing/Discussion***

1. Jeremiah experienced many emotions in the course of his message. Name as many as you can. Find examples of each of them in the text.

2. When the LORD called him, what excuse did Jeremiah give? How did God answer it?

3. Was Jeremiah a prophet of good news, bad news, or both? Explain your conclusion.

***In Our Lives***

1. Certainly Jeremiah's influence was greater after his death. Think of other people whose influence grew after they were no longer alive—persons in your own life, in our country's history. Why do you think this often happens?

2. Chapter 7:5–6 tells how God wants the people to reform. Read those verses slowly several times. How do those conditions apply today in our country and throughout the world? What might we do as a religious community to help, even in a small way, with such needed reforms?

3. When, like Jeremiah, have you been misjudged, ignored or falsely accused? How did you handle the situation?

***Individual/Personal Reflection/Action***

1. Jeremiah has a mission in life. The same can be said of each one of us. Ours is not necessarily to be a prophet but it is to use our gifts and talents to the best of our ability and in service of others. Discovering our mission gives purpose to our life, for it helps us answer the question, "Why was I born?" much as Jeremiah had that question answered for him. Spend time in reflection and prayer or talking with someone who knows you well to identify your life's mission for yourself.

2. Despite many setbacks and disappointments, Jeremiah maintained a hopeful stance in life. What are the things in life that give you hope? How do they do this? What role does your relationship to God play in the things that give you hope in life?

# LAMENTATIONS READING GUIDE

***At a Glance***

| | |
|---|---|
| Who are the main players? | It is important to understand that Lamentations are prayers asking God to do something for Israel. They are not merely expressions of personal or communal misery. |
| What should I look for? | Attentive readers will see subtle dramatic movement within each poem and between the poems; a range of emotions is fully expressed—grief, anger, near despair, glimmers of hope and joy, and the will to carry on. |
| When did this take place? | The early sixth century when the Temple and Jerusalem were destroyed. |
| Where did these events occur? | In Jerusalem. |

| | |
|---|---|
| Why was this book written? | In the two centuries before Lamentations were composed, Israel was in political decline and its religious and national traditions in crisis. Although the immediate cause of the composition was the destruction of the city and Temple in 586 B.C. the poems actually mourn a much longer period of divine absence and national humiliation. |
| What is the story? | Destruction of the Temple dealt a terrible blow to the ordinary way in which public prayer was carried out. For the people of Israel, the LORD dwelled on Zion (Jerusalem) and there received the praise and petitions of the people of Israel. Zion was the privileged place of encounter between Yahweh and the holy people. But with the Temple and city lying in ruins, Israelite worship changed profoundly. Lamentations is a reaction to that loss. |

## The Human Reality

Imagine your feelings if you experienced the loss of someone who had been of great significance in your life. It could be the death of a loved one, a mentor or guide, or a person who was supportive and kind when you needed it the most. Now imagine that, at the same time that this loss occurs, your home, your means of income, all your personal possessions, as well as all that was of material value to you, were also gone or destroyed. Add to this the fact that your church, your priests, and your community were no longer there to lend a helping hand in this time of sorrow.

Imagine the feelings that would stir in you. Imagine the anger, frustration, despair, and hopelessness that would overwhelm you. Imagine the questions that you might be asking of God. Imagine also the possible feelings of guilt. Was there something that you could have done to prevent or minimize this pain, suffering, or destruction? If you can imagine this overwhelming human experience of pain, suffering, and privation, then you can at least begin to understand the human context out of which the book of Lamentations was written.

## Prayer Poems

The book of Lamentations consists of five prayers of complaint and mourning about the destruction of Jerusalem and the Temple. Because Jerusalem and the Temple were destroyed by the Babylonians in 586 B.C. and a new Temple was constructed sometime after 515, the prayers must have been composed in the 70-year period when the Temple lay in ruins.

These poems have an interesting acrostic form. That is, the initial word of each verse or each stanza begins with a successive letter of the 22-letter Hebrew alphabet. Each poem, therefore, has either 22 stanzas or 22 verses. Although the fifth poem does not use initial letters of the alphabet, it also has 22 verses and so, in a broad sense, is influenced by the acrostic pattern.

First-time readers may find the five poems dreary, repetitive, and far too comfortable with the role of victim. Closer study reveals subtle dramatic movement within each poem and between the poems; they skillfully explore and express a range of emotions—grief, anger, something near despair, acceptance, glimmers of hope and joy, and an indomitable will to carry on.

## Historical Background

It is helpful to situate these poems in Israel's history. In the two centuries before the Lamentations were composed, Israel was in political decline, and its religious and national traditions in crisis. For most of those two centuries, the people lived under the control of two great empires, Assyria and then Babylon. The early sixth century, when Lamentations was written, was particularly difficult. That period witnessed Babylonian pressure, uncertain Judean leadership, the destruction of Jerusalem and the Temple, and large deportations to Babylon. The countryside was devastated, and the economy destroyed. Such dismal conditions called into question the national traditions that had provided earlier generations with meaning and helped them make sense of everyday life. The traditions proclaimed that Israel's God was supreme over all gods and nations and had liberated Israel from the Egyptians and given them the land of Canaan; the LORD made the land fertile and protected the people from their enemies. Now, the people were not liberated; their land belonged to others; many of them had been shipped off to servitude in Babylon. Where was the LORD in all this? What could the people hope for? Although the immediate cause of the composition of Lamentations was the destruction of the city and Temple in 586, the poems actually mourn a much longer period of divine absence and national humiliation.

Destruction of the Temple dealt a terrible blow to the ordinary way in which public prayer was carried out. Public prayer texts such as the psalms presupposed that the LORD chose to dwell on Zion (Jerusalem) and there receive the praise and petitions of Israel. Zion was the privileged place of encounter between Yahweh and the holy people. Modern people might assume that the LORD can appear equally at any time and any place, but ancients thought otherwise. Although the LORD, the God of Israel, might appear and act in other places, Zion was his preeminent place of disclosure and encounter with Israel; only here was Israel fully "before the LORD." Here the LORD was enthroned upon the cherubim (Pss 80:1; 99:1) and "judged," that is, governed Israel and the nations. Zion was the goal of the three annual feasts of pilgrimage. Although the universe might totter, Zion, it was believed, would remain unshaken and secure (Pss 46:2–3; 48:4–8; 76:3). With the Temple lying in ruins, Israelite worship changed profoundly. Lamentations attempted to find new modes of prayer in time of destruction.

## Genre of the Book

Two traditional genres (or types) of prayer influenced the book of Lamentations. One was the communal lament found in the Psalms, and the other was the city lament, common in Mesopotamian religious literature and found here and there in the Bible. A major difference between the Psalms and Lamentations is that the lament psalms *remember*, that is, tell in words (and perhaps in ritual actions) the divine act of God that installed the king, gave the land, or built the Temple in order that the LORD would renew the original act. With confidence in God's great acts of the past, they pray to God to renew those powerful acts now. Lamentations, on the other hand, does not remember or review in that sense; the poems do not work from the same confidence in the national traditions. Lamentations' poems explore the human emotions evoked by the catastrophe—the sorrow, guilt, anger, and hope—and bring them before the LORD. Just as the Psalms made it possible for every Israelite, even those far from Jerusalem, to participate in the worship carried out in the Temple, so Lamentations made it possible for all Israelites during the exile to explore and express their grief, anger, and hope concerning the Temple and the God who once dwelt there. Today, the book makes it possible for all Christians and Jews to explore and express their own sorrows and forms of exile.

It is important to underline that Lamentations are prayers asking God to *do* something for Israel. They are not merely expressions of personal and communal misery. Although their tone is disappointed and often bitter, they believe that the LORD is behind the present distress of the community and has the power to turn and bring healing and prosperity. The strategy of the prayers is to remind God of his failure to carry out his promises to protect the people and make them prosperous. Thus, they proclaim that they are miserable and abandoned in the hope (however dim) that God will finally come to their rescue. The prayers ask the LORD to turn from his callous ways.

## Poetic Style of the Book

Lamentations blends the fixed forms of Hebrew poetry with exceptionally free movement. The first four poems follow the alphabetic or acrostic arrangement: the first letters in the stanza follow the order of the letters of the alphabet. In the third Lamentation all three lines of a stanza start with the same letter.

An exceptional variety of attitudes are included: national and individual laments of misery (1:12–16; 3:43–45); prayer for help (1:9c); confidence in the LORD (3:22–25); faith in the wisdom of God to assure that all receive what they deserve (3:26–42); and a hymn of praise (5:19). Jerusalem is described by the congregation (1:1) and also speaks for herself (1:12–16).

While lamenting how chaos erupts everywhere, the poetry implies that God is still in control; all is not lost. Good order must return and Israel's theology must absorb and teach the lessons of Jerusalem's destruction and exile. Lamentations asks that this process not be hurried. Israel needs space for mourning. Theology too, cannot be hurried in unraveling an explanation of this redemptive suffering.

## Authorship and Place in the Bible

Despite later tradition, quite a few signs point to someone other than Jeremiah as the author. Lamentations speaks favorably of the Davidic kings (4:20, "The anointed one of the LORD, our breath of life, was caught in their snares, he in whose shadow we thought we could live on among the nations"), whereas Jeremiah suffered severely from them (Jer 22:13–19; 37) and did not put his hopes for the future on them. The vocabulary and religious perspective of the two books are quite different. The most ancient manuscripts of Lamentations do not mention Jeremiah as the author. Moreover, the two books are found in different parts of the Hebrew Bible (the Jewish arrangement of the Old Testament), Jeremiah among the Prophets, and Lamentations among the Writings. Ascribing the book to Jeremiah came much later, an example of the ancient practice of ascribing originally anonymous works to a famous hero. The statement in 2 Chronicles 35:25 that Jeremiah composed a lamentation over King Josiah, "which can be found written in the Lamentations," does not refer to the present book of Lamentations. In the Septuagint, the second-century B.C. Greek translation, this book and that of Baruch (see Jer 36) are found immediately after the prophecy of Jeremiah, and Christian Bibles have maintained that order (sometimes excluding Baruch, which does not exist in the Hebrew Bible, completely).

A Christian tradition points to a hillside cave north of the walled city of Jerusalem as the place where Jeremiah wept over the city and composed these laments. So common was the ascription to Jeremiah that the Council of Trent's enumeration of the inspired books of the Old Testament does not name Lamentations, but only "Jeremiah with Baruch" (Session IV, 8 April 1546). Lamentations became a part of the tradition of Jeremiah in reflecting upon suffering as a way of expiating sin.

Was there a single author of Lamentations? Even though the five poems of Lamentations have much in common, it is difficult to decide upon a single author. They are better explained by traditions of prayer amid Israelites struggling to survive in the rubble of Jerusalem.

## Praying with the Book

These five chapters are not intended to solve the problem of suffering; rather, they let us sorrow in God's presence. Prayer, like friendship, is not meant to accomplish something, only to be aware of the one we love. Nonetheless, we may find help in a few markers along the way.

The first lamentation begins with the sorrow of the author at the sight of the ruined city (vv. 1–11a). Then Jerusalem herself confesses her sins, her hopes, and her anger against the enemy (vv. 11b–22).

The second lamentation lays the devastated city before God (vv. 1–10). Technically this is the style of a lament: simply to present the situation as it is in its pain and horror. After revealing personal sorrow (vv. 11f), the poet addresses the city from the depths of compassion (vv. 13–22), beginning: "To what can I liken or compare you, O daughter Jerusalem?"

The third lamentation turns into an *individual* cry of sorrow. It begins with an assertiveness that startles us at a time when people's spirits, like their homes, are broken apart:

> I am one who has known affliction
> under the rod of God's anger.
> One whom he has driven and forced to walk
> in darkness, not in the light.

While the poet speaks during most of the poem, in verses 25–47 other voices speak from a group of sages or wise persons and other friends, baffled by the tragedy (vv. 40–47). Despite the torture and misery of verses 1–24, the poem ultimately expresses deep faith in God's grace and power. This poem is the most complex of all.

The fourth lamentation returns to the style and mood of the first two. The opening verses tell the end of nobles and children (vv. 1–10), followed by a meditation on Jerusalem (vv. 11f). After the responsibility is placed upon the religious leaders (vv. 13–20), the poem ends with a curse upon the enemy (vv. 21f). The fifth and last lamentation was entitled by the Latin Vulgate "The Prayer of Jeremiah." This liturgical prayer sustains its beauty and serenity despite its topic of rejection and tragedy. It asks very little, only that the LORD remember.

## Lamentations and Christianity

The Christian Church has used Lamentations in reference to Christ's passion. In the Roman Catholic Church, Lamentations played an important and memorable role in the Holy Week services prior to the reforms of Vatican II. They were sung during the ceremony of Tenebrae (darkness), probably named from the custom of extinguishing one candle after each psalm until the church was left in darkness. Several of the Tenebrae texts (although not Lamentations) have survived in the revised morning offices for Good Friday and Holy Saturday. In general, the Lamentations are used sparingly in the Roman Catholic lectionary; there are only three selections among the many Old Testament readings for masses for the dead and only one in the readings for masses "for any need." It remains a challenge for the Church to learn how to incorporate laments into its public prayer so that the pains and difficulties of Christian discipleship are represented as fully as the peace and joy of faith.

### Questions for Discussion and Reflection

*Group Sharing/Discussion*

1. In small groups or individually, list the various things being lamented in these poems. Share and discuss your lists with each other.

2. Give examples of the many attitudes toward God represented in this book.

3. How would you describe what it is the people want from God?

4. Find the poem or part of the poem with which you can most identify and explain why.

*In Our Lives*

1. Our Catholic tradition uses sign, gesture, music, ritual action, and words in our community prayer. Name something in our liturgies that helps people deal with grief in the face of loss or suffering.

2. What is the role of the community toward the person undergoing pain and suffering? How might we respond better in our parish?

3. When the whole community is suffering greatly from loss or disappointment, what are some appropriate ways for the community to respond to the crisis?

4. What is our role to those outside our community, even outside our country who are in pain? How are we "response-able" to them?

*Individual/Personal Reflection/Action*

1. Recall an experience of your own pain and sorrow. How did you respond to the experience? What supports were there to sustain you? What challenges did you need to address or confront?

2. When people blame God for their suffering, what kind of God does that say they believe in? How would you answer them?

3. Think about how you can be more responsive to others suffering pain or loss. Talk with someone who can help you do this.

# BARUCH READING GUIDE

### *At a Glance*

| | |
|---|---|
| Who are the main players? | "Baruch" Jeremiah |
| What should I look for? | Baruch is a guide for people who are separated or lost, physically and emotionally, from their normal environment. It shows that hope is in the LORD and in the scriptures. It provides a long prayer of lament and exalts wisdom, found in the Torah. |

| | |
|---|---|
| When did this take place? | The date of composition was some time in the late second or early first century B.C. |
| Where did these events occur? | Only a few books admit the possibility of an Israelite living permanently outside the Promised Land. Baruch is one. It does not refer to place. |
| Why was this book written? | With the disappearance of the old institutions of religion and government in Judea, questions arose about the divine presence and religious authority, as well as related questions about wisdom and authoritative teaching or *torah*. These concerns are addressed in the book of Baruch. |
| What is the story? | The postexilic period was a time of literary creativity. Some of these late books looked back at the preexilic period with awe and reverence, regarding its literature as a timeless standard. Baruch gives lessons on how to live in exile. Jeremiah attacks the worship of more than one God, ridiculing idols. |

Baruch is in the Orthodox and Roman Catholic canon of sacred scripture. However, since it is only in the ancient Greek version of the Bible, the Septuagint, and not in the Hebrew Bible, in the Protestant canon it is classed among the Apocrypha (this word means "hidden" in Greek). Catholic Bibles add the Epistle of Jeremiah to Baruch as its sixth chapter.

## Outline of the Book of Baruch

| | |
|---|---|
| 1:1–14 | Introduction recalling the Feast of Tabernacles and the renewal of the covenant |
| 1:15–3:8 | Offers to God a humble confession of sin |
| 3:9–4:4 | A reflection in the style of wisdom literature, acting as a bridge to conversion and renewed loyalty to God's Law |
| 4:5–5:9 | A response of consolation, forgiveness, and renewed hope to the humble confession of sin in 1:15–3:8 |
| 6:1–72 | In a letter format, idolatry is ridiculed with irony and sarcasm. There is a question concerning this chapter: Was it part of the original editing of the book, or was it added later on by another editor? |

## Reading the Book of Baruch

As the essay introducing the book of Baruch on page 1138 reminds us, Baruch was secretary to the great prophet, Jeremiah. He shared Jeremiah's fate as an exile in Egypt. Eventually, the Jewish exiles were allowed to return to Jerusalem. However, most of them did not return but, instead, stayed where they were living.

### Introduction (1:1–14)

The purpose of this section is not to provide details but to set a mood of exile and separation. Many of the details in this section are out of place both in time and situation, in fact. The exile provides a framework for those who are displaced or estranged, either physically or emotionally, to understand their situation. Displaced people need solidarity, religious assemblies, outreach in helping others, and a point of contact for unity. The wrath of God has not yet turned away from the exiles (1:13), and Baruch advises fervent prayer as well as teaching them how to seek wisdom in this less than perfect situation of exile.

### A Long Confession of Sin (1:15–3:8)

This is a style of prayer common in the Bible (Ezr 9:6–15; Neh 1:5–11; 9:5–37; Dn 9:4–19). These prayers were probably derived from a common collection of prayers for exiles. The prayer does not encourage violence to regain freedom but rather counsels acceptance of the government in control. Yet moral ideals and practices are not to be abandoned, even in such conditions. The prayer recalls God's fidelity to the people during their miseries in Egypt, and how God was compassionate and faithful during their sufferings and their desert journey. It acknowledges that the people have sinned and all their ills are deserved.

### In Praise of Divine Wisdom (3:9–4:5)

It is significant that this poem praising wisdom and urging Israel to walk "in the way of God" (v. 13) comes immediately after the community has confessed their helplessness and blindness. This section is parallel to Job 28 and Ben Sira 24, both books within the wisdom tradition of the Jewish people. Because of these parallels, and Baruch's influence on later works in Judaism, Baruch provides a key link between the earlier and the later development of the wisdom tradition in Judaism.

Where is wisdom to be found, especially when they are in exile? Human beings cannot lay hold of wisdom by their own means. It must be given by God, who has in fact given wisdom to Israel in the Torah or their Law: "[Wisdom] is the book of the precepts of God, the law that endures forever; All who cling to her will live, but those will die who forsake her. Turn, O Jacob, and receive her: walk by her light toward splendor" (4:1–2).

### A Poem of Encouragement (4:5–5:9)

In this section voices that provide needed hope for a desolate people surface slowly and repetitively. Meditating on the promises expressed in Isaiah 40–66, the people renew their hopes and are reminded once again of God's love and fidelity. In 4:5–8, the prophet talks encouragingly to the people Israel. In 4:9–16, Jerusalem addresses to her neighbors a lament about her lost children. In 4:17–29, Jerusalem turns and speaks to the children, her people in exile. In 4:30–5:9, the prophet addresses Jerusalem in words of hope and consolation based on Isaiah. God will manifest power and glory in and through Jerusalem, and she will rejoice greatly as God rescues the people once again and returns them to their land and their holy city.

### Letter of Jeremiah (6:1–72)

The author of this section is different from the author of the rest of the book. Often, this chapter is not included as part of the book of Baruch, but rather as a separate book altogether, referred to as the Letter of Jeremiah. However, for our purposes, this chapter is treated as an integral part of the final editing of the book of Baruch.

Drawing upon a tradition about Jeremiah as a letter writer (Jer 29) and a holder of divine secrets (2 Mc 2:2), the author, most probably a synagogue preacher, attacks idolatry with great irony and sarcasm. This attack seems to be modeled on earlier prophets (Jer 10:1–16 and Is 44:9–20). The gist of the attack focuses on the inability of these carved idols to do anything for themselves or for their human creators. Why fear or be threatened by such silliness? The sermon gathers momentum with its frequent refrain, which the gathered community would quickly learn and repeat: verses 14, 22, 28, 39, 44, 50, 56, 64, and the grand finale, 71f. Here, idolatry seems more foolish than threatening.

### Religious Teaching of Baruch

Because of the dangers of living in exile, several key themes are meant to reinforce the people's identity, as well as their core beliefs, values, and traditions. These themes are summarized in the table that follows.

### Questions for Discussion and Reflection

*Group Sharing/Discussion*

1. Read aloud chapter 3:24 to 4:4, letting different people in the group each read a few lines. What is the impression you get about who God is and who Wisdom (she/her) is from this part of the prayer?

2. In chapter 6 on idolatry, what are some of the negative things the author has to say about idols that are worshiped?

*In Our Lives*

1. Baruch insists that one must place all one's hope in the LORD; that one can find the LORD in the inspired scriptures. What are some ways you see us doing these things as a Church, especially since Roman Catholics' study of the scriptures is much more recent than many other denominations? What are particular places in scripture that have helped you "find" the LORD?

2. The prayer in Baruch was to be prayed not as an individual's prayer but as the prayer of the community. What is the value in your life of community prayer?

***Key Themes in Baruch's Religious Teaching***

| | |
|---|---|
| Monotheism | All other gods are to be scorned (ch 6). Israel's God created all of creation (3:32–35) and is enthroned in the highest heaven (3:3). God is the supreme source of wisdom (3:12–32), justice (1:15; 2:6–10), and mercy (2:27; 3:1; 5:9). |
| Sin | Sin is an act of rebellion (1:22; 4:7), which disrupts and repudiates God's wisdom for the universe (2:12). Sin is seen in terms of communal sin, not personal, individual sin (1:16–20; 2:1–6). Sin always brings suffering in its wake (1:13–15; 2:1–5). |
| Repentance | This is the principal reason for putting together the book of Baruch. Israel needs to be honest in confessing her faults (2:14; 3:2). She needs to return to the sole fount of goodness (2:8; 4:28). |
| Hope | Hope in the Lord is the dominant attitude in this book. Further, the Lord can be found in the inspired scriptures. God lives eternally (3:3) and establishes an eternal covenant with Israel (2:35). Salvation is from this eternal God (4:8). Eternity pervades God's consolation to Israel (4:10, 21–24, 35; 5:2–5) as well as announcements of eternal joy (4:23–29; 5:1–4). |

3. If you, like the exiles, were living in a foreign country, what kinds of support and encouragement would you need? Who are similar persons in your own area today? Why do you think more people do not reach out to them? What are some things you can do to support and encourage them?

*Individual/Personal Reflection/Action*

1. Each morning this week, spend a few minutes recalling someone who has been a sign of hope to you or encouraged you when you needed support. Send an email or note to one of them in thanks.

2. Think about the "idols" in our society that some people worship. Make a list of the top 10 things many people spend their time, energy and money working/hoping for. Make a list of your own potential idols and compare the two.

# EZEKIEL READING GUIDE

## *At a Glance*

| | |
|---|---|
| Who are the main players? | Ezekiel Leaders and the People the Temple |
| What should I look for? | Notice that Ezekiel, priest and prophet, demands both exactness in rituals and compassion toward one's neighbor. As a priest, his categories are purity and impurity. As a prophet, his purview included social justice and fidelity required by the covenant. Holiness implied social justice and social justice implied right worship. |
| When did this take place? | Ezekiel's prophetic ministry began with his call in July 593 B.C. near Nippur, a few miles south of the city of Babylon. The last dated formula in his book is 571. |
| Where did these events occur? | Babylon; Jerusalem; Israel |
| Why was this book written? | Ezekiel had a twofold task: to interpret the national traditions in the light of the ever-changing course of history and |

to persuade people to act in accord with the required changes. His message emphasizes the centrality of the Temple and the LORD's presence, the awesome wonder of God, and individual responsibility.

What is the story?

His public career was spent completely in dismal circumstances of the destruction of Jerusalem and the Temple and the exile in Babylon. Yet it is a tribute to his faith and imagination that the prophet's message is ultimately about the bright future God has in store for his people. With other exiles he settled in Nippur and occupied a prominent place in the transplanted community and was often consulted by them. To judge by his opposition to the community and his vigorous criticism of their opinions, he had a very different understanding of the exile than they did. He saw the exile as a long process of judgment that required faith. The people, however, saw themselves as hapless victims.

## Ezekiel, the Person

The book opens in 593/2 B.C. with Ezekiel already in exile at a village called Tel Abib (1:1; 3:15). It is not clear when Ezekiel made the journey northward from Israel, eastward across Syria, then southward down the Euphrates River into modern-day Iraq. The Babylonians may have deported him in 597 B.C., the year of their first attack on Jerusalem. Or he may have gone freely to join the exiles sometime before 593/2 B.C. The latest date in the book is 571 B.C. (29:17). Ezekiel was born into a priestly family (1:3), and was married (24:16–18).

Although the written text is the starting point, writing seems to have been of secondary importance to Ezekiel. The focus throughout the book is on symbolic actions, gestures, public demonstrations of faith, confrontations with others, and a total focus on God. Ezekiel is continually being ordered to: hear the word (6:2–3; 13:2; 34:2); prophesy and speak that word to his countrymen (14:4; 20:3); or raise a lament (19:1–3; 27:2f). This focus on action and speaking make Ezekiel truly a public person in the community. This may explain how he could be objective and distant, and yet intensely present with his audience.

Ezekiel continually speaks in the first person singular, yet it is not he who speaks but the LORD speaking through him. Ezekiel remains obedient to God, like clay in the hands of the potter, never questioning God's complete control over all things. Ezekiel's prophetic career was very colorful, even puzzling, with all kinds of strange symbolic actions. Gifted as well with visions and mystical insights, Ezekiel is an interesting and intriguing character.

No matter how we regard the prophet's unusual behavior and miraculous gifts, Ezekiel remained a strong, influential person in his community. Elders gathered round him (8:1; 14:1; 20:1); the messenger from Jerusalem came first to Ezekiel (32:21f), as did other people (33:30–33). Also, Ezekiel had an extraordinary influence on later prophecy and the history of Judaism.

### Theological Background

Ezekiel combined and spoke out of various theological traditions, like Hosea, Jeremiah, and other prophets usually associated with the northern part of Israel. Jeremiah and Ezekiel both speak of a new covenant written within each person (Jer 31:31–34; Ez 30:26f), leading to a more personal responsibility for the covenant itself (Jer 31:27–30; Ez 18). As Isaiah, Micah, and traditions associated with the south and Jerusalem did, Ezekiel emphasizes the importance of the holy city and its Temple.

The rituals and the traditions of the Temple greatly affected Ezekiel. This may explain his tendency to include many details in his account of events. It also may explain why he frequently expresses himself in symbolic actions and stories.

## Ezekiel, the Message

Ezekiel's message can be summarized under five topics:

1. The central importance of the Temple and the LORD's presence
2. The awesome wonder of God
3. Individual responsibility
4. Prophecy and beyond
5. The influence of Ezekiel on the New Testament

### The Centrality of the Temple and the LORD's Presence

Ezekiel's book of prophecy opens with a vision of the LORD enthroned as in the Temple. The book closes with the sacred stream flowing from the Temple altar (47:1–12) and with the proclamation of Jerusalem's new name, Yahweh Shamah, "the LORD is there" (48:35). In Ezekiel, God is portrayed either in the Temple, or in a style that is associated with the Temple.

Ezekiel's vision of God that begins the book also dominates the whole book. Significant events including God anointing Ezekiel as prophet (ch 1); God departing from the Temple and the city, setting it up for destruction (ch 10); God preparing for the resurrection of the people (37:1); and God reconsecrating the new Temple and city (43:1–9). These events are told with language involving priestly details and symbols. But Ezekiel the priest is also Ezekiel the prophet. Thus prophecy is evident throughout these priestly descriptions.

Ezekiel the prophet insists that the Temple is not holy of itself, but only because the LORD is present there. And significantly, the LORD's presence requires that the people practice justice. The LORD can therefore choose to depart from the Temple and reappear in foreign lands, areas that priests considered unclean. The announcement in chapter 34 of the destruction of Jerusalem and its Temple led to the second major period in Ezekiel's preaching, which focused on the new purified Israel.

### The Awesome Wonder of God

Ezekiel's God is overpowering and awesome, reaching beyond human relationships (24:15–24) and human explanations (20:25f). God is neither someone to be argued with, as in Jeremiah; nor someone agonizing over the fate of the people, as in Hosea. Ezekiel does not portray the LORD as parent or family member. For Ezekiel, God is close, yet also very distant.

A phrase constantly used by Ezekiel to portray God's majestic and overpowering presence is "the glory of the LORD" (1:28; 3:12–23; 8:4; 10:4). This phrase usually accompanies the vision of the cherubim or the four living creatures. Still another word is "holiness." The name of the LORD is usually qualified as holy. These two descriptions are usually associated with events that take us beyond normal human existence. Although the LORD is continually communicating through the prophet, the character of the prophet is lost within the overpowering message of the LORD.

### Individual Responsibility

Ezekiel is generally referred to in any discussions on the topic of individual responsibility. Like Jeremiah he quotes a well-known proverb, only to prove how wrong it really is: "Parents eat sour grapes, but the children's teeth are on edge" (Ez 18:2; Jer 31:29). Both prophets insist that this proverb is a denial of the actual reality of a situation, along with a refusal to take responsibility for one's actions. Ultimately, this proverb blames others for one's present condition. In a long chapter Ezekiel insists "only the one who sins shall die" (18:4).

For Ezekiel, the entire nation is God's chosen people. Thus each individual Israelite is personally responsible for living out the covenant. Each person lives or dies according to his or her virtuous or wicked way of life. Ezekiel focuses not only on exterior behavior, but also on interior change of heart (11:19; 18:31; 36:26f). Here, as well as with Ezekiel 18:2, we see important points of comparison with Jeremiah (see Jer 31:31–34). Both prophets speak of a new heart.

### Prophecy and Beyond

While remaining within the prophetic tradition of Israel that he inherited, Ezekiel also went beyond it. He changed the tradition in many ways; prophecy after him would never be the same. After the return from exile, prophets like Haggai, Zechariah, Joel, and Malachi seem as much priest as prophet. Their words and preaching seem to be more concerned with liturgical action in the Temple, or the Temple itself, than with social justice and compassion.

*Apocalyptic* means "drawing aside the veil" so

as to perceive mysteries hidden in God. Ezekiel had turned the style of prophecy in the direction of the apocalyptic movement. Apocalyptic prophets are often called "seers" rather than prophets because of the awesome mysteries they foresee about Israel's future. To communicate these mysteries, they resort to symbols rather than plain speech. At times, these symbols are so beyond human understanding that angels are needed to interpret the vision or the symbol. Apocalyptic prophets actually speak of present realities and situations in the context of the ultimate end of all things, using visions, dreams, and all sorts of symbols.

### Influence on the New Testament

Ezekiel's influence on the New Testament shows up in the Gospels whenever Jesus refers to himself as the "Son of Man" or "ben-Adam" in Hebrew. This title reflects someone absorbed within humanity (Adam) and overwhelmed before God's mighty presence (Ez 2:2f). Ezekiel's notion of the "son of man" seems to have been more influential on Jesus than the more exalted "son of man" in Daniel (Dn 7:13f, although Daniel's vision clearly influenced Jesus' statement to the high priest during his trial; see Mk 14:62). Ezekiel's image of the shepherd, in chapter 34, influenced Jesus' use of the image of the good shepherd (Jn 10).

It is in the book of Revelation that the influence of Ezekiel shows up consistently: the four living creatures (Ez 1; Rev 4:6–9); a voice like the sound of many waters (Ez 1:24; Rev 1:15); Gog from the land of Magog (Ez 38–39; Rev 20:8); the seer being carried to a high mountain (Ez 40:2; Rev 21:10). The book of Revelation tends to change or simplify the stranger features of Ezekiel's prophecy, but the connection between the two books is clear.

## Ezekiel, the Book

The overall plan of the book can be clearly seen from the way it is structured. There are two major sections to the book: one condemning Jerusalem to total destruction (chs 1–24) and the other announcing the resurrection of a new people and a new Jerusalem (chs 25–48). A second organizing structure, overlapping the first, can also be seen as dividing the book: Ezekiel the prophet (chs 1–39) and Ezekiel the priest (chs 40–48).

### Major Historical Developments

The format of the book follows national and world events as these affected Israel:

| | |
|---|---|
| Chapters 4–24 | The nations are God's instruments for punishing a sinful people. After the exile, the prophet prepares for the rebirth of his people. |
| Chapters 25–32 | The prophet gives oracles that proclaim the destruction of those foreign nations responsible for Israel's suffering and exile, especially Egypt and Tyre. |
| Chapters 33–37 | He also gives speeches and visions that announce Israel's religious renewal beyond anyone's expectations. |
| Chapters 38–39 | Because the restoration of the people was not final, Ezekiel foresees another victory for the LORD, against the most powerful of the world's forces. |
| Chapters 40–48 | Description of the LORD finally achieving the total peace of Jerusalem and the transformation of the Promised Land into paradise. |

- Chapters 1–39, Ezekiel the Prophet

| | |
|---|---|
| Chapters 1–3 | The call to prophesy |
| Chapters 4–24 | The condemnation of Jerusalem |
| Chapters 25–32 | The oracles against the nations |
| Chapters 33–37 | Israel's revival and transformation |
| Chapters 38–39 | The final defeat of world forces |

- Chapters 40–48, Ezekiel the Priest

| | |
|---|---|
| Chapters 40–43 | The new Temple |
| Chapters 44–46 | The new way of life |
| Chapters 47–48 | The new promised land |

### Literary Themes

In its final form, Ezekiel contains several key themes and repetitions that run throughout, giving it a sense of unity. Identical words and phrases appear at different places throughout the book, as illustrated by these examples:

- "the hand of the LORD came upon me" 1:3; 3:14–22; 8:1; 33:22; 37:1; 40:1
- "know that I am the LORD" 6:7, 10, 13, 14; 7:4, 9, 27; 11:10, 12; 32:15; 33:29; 38:23
- "I, the LORD, have spoken" 5:13, 15, 17; 12:25; 17:24; 21:22; 22:14; 34:24; 36:36
- "glory of the LORD," "glory of the God of Israel" 1:28; 3:12, 23; 8:4; 9:3; 10:4–19; 11:22, 23; 43:2, 4, 5; 44:4
- "rebellious house" 2:5–8; 3:9, 26, 27; 12:2, 3, 9, 15; 17:12; 24:3; 44:6
- "abominations" 5:9, 11; 6:9, 11; 7:3, 4, 8, 9; 8:6, 9, 13, 15, 17; 9:4; 11:18, 21; 12:16; 14:6; 16:2, 22, 43, 47, 51, 58; 20:4; 33:26, 29; 43:8; 44:6, 7, 13

### Visions

The book is bound together by a series of visions, starting with that of the four living creatures in chapter 1. Visions introduce key sections of Ezekiel's prophecy:

- The four living creatures (1:4–3:15): Vision of the witnesses to Ezekiel's call to be a prophet
- Idolatry in the Temple (chs 8–11): Vision of the activity that seals the ultimate destruction of Jerusalem
- The dry bones (ch 37): Vision that prepares for the resurrection of exiled Israel to new life
- New Jerusalem (chs 40 and 43): Vision that prepares for the resurrection of Jerusalem and the Temple to new splendor and glory
- Stream of water flowing from the altar (47:1–12): Vision of new life restored once more at the very heart of Israel, and also the vision that brings Ezekiel's prophecy to a close

## Major Sections of the Book of Ezekiel

### The Four Living Creatures (chs 1–3)

This opening vision sets the tone and scene for the entire book. The editors have united the entire prophecy of Ezekiel around the cherubim, the four living creatures who once upheld the throne of the LORD in the Holy of Holies of the Jerusalem Temple (Ex 25:17–22). The four living creatures appear first in 1:4–28. They reappear in 8:1–4; 10; 11:22f, providing the setting for the eventual destruction of the Temple.

### Symbolic Actions (chs 4–12)

Not only the visions but also many symbolic actions surround Ezekiel. Each symbolic action follows a precise pattern:

1. A command from the LORD
2. The carrying out of that command by Ezekiel, with all the care and attention required in response to God's command
3. The meaning that this action has for Israel

Because of this pattern, Ezekiel sometimes seems to be almost like a robot, acting blindly on divine orders. This strong preference for patterns may be Ezekiel's answer to the chaos that resulted from Israel's lack of faithfulness.

The first set of four symbolic actions occurs in 4:1–5:17. In these verses, the fiery destruction of Jerusalem and the people's long journey into exile are symbolically acted out by Ezekiel. This sequence of events is shown below. Symbols, words, and actions all combine to tell the community the reality of their fate, because of their infidelity and idolatry.

***Symbolic Actions of the Destruction and Exile of Israel***

| | |
|---|---|
| 4:1–3 | Siege of Jerusalem is acted out with a ramp, battering rams, and other actions of siege. |
| 4:4–8 | The long siege is symbolized by the prophet lying for 390 days on his left side, and 40 days on his right side, while bound with cords. |
| 4:9–17 | The hunger and thirst of the siege are acted out by the prophet in eating and drinking very little while lying on his side. |
| 5:1–17 | The shaving of his hair and beard (a very demeaning action for an Israelite male—2 Sm 10:4), and the burning of some of the hair, as well as the striking with the sword and the scattering of the hair, are all symbolic of the burning of Jerusalem and the dispersal of the survivors. |

Editors reinterpreted Ezekiel's symbolic actions and visions. Additions are inserted at different places. One example is in 5:3f, where a small amount of hair is preserved in the hem of the garment, to show that not all will be lost in the destruction and the exile. The symbolic action with the hair in 5:1–4 is given four related but separate interpretations: 5:7–10; 5:11–13; 5:14f; 5:16f.

There are other symbolic actions in the book that portray further the destruction of the city and the exile. Further symbols of exile are:

| | |
|---|---|
| 12:1–16 | Packing one's baggage and crawling through a hole in the city wall |
| 12:17–20 | Eating and drinking with trembling and horror |
| 21:11f | Groaning bitterly |
| 21:19–22 | Clapping hands and waving a sword |
| 24:15–17 | Ezekiel not mourning the death of his wife, just as the people are not to mourn the death of Jerusalem |

Symbolic actions also extend to hopeful prophecies for the future as in 37:15–28. Here the symbolic tying of two sticks together shows that the people from both the northern and southern kingdoms who survive the destruction will be united peacefully under a Davidic prince around the sanctuary.

### Other Literary Forms (chs 13–24)

The book of Ezekiel displays many literary forms as it tries in creative ways to get the message of destruction and exile across to the community. The following table shows some examples of the various literary forms used.

This ends the first major part of Ezekiel's prophecy, which emphasized the fact that God is determined to destroy Jerusalem, which is too wicked to be purified any further. Ezekiel will now await the news of the city's destruction in chapter 33 and then begin to reconstruct a new people. First, however, the editor records the oracles against the nations, chapters 25–32.

### Oracles against the Nations (chs 25–32)

Making prophetic speeches condemning foreign nations and singing mocking laments over their death are consistent biblical patterns (see Am 1:2–2:16; Is 13–23; Jer 46–51). This pattern probably has its source in Temple prayers for victory, as well as in ritual curses against the enemy.

*Variety of Literary Forms in Chapters 13–24*

| | |
|---|---|
| 13:1–23 | Two prophecies of woe against false prophets, both male and female |
| 14:1–23 | A legal case against idol-worshipers |
| 15:1–8 | A scornful disputation with the inhabitants of Jerusalem |
| 16:1–63 | An allegory about Jerusalem |
| 17:1–24 | A fable, featuring an eagle, a cedar, and a vine |
| 18:1–32 | A long disputation on personal responsibility |
| 19:1–14 | A funeral dirge, ridiculing Jerusalem, speaking to her as if already dead |
| 20:1–44 | A prophetic speech, about God's interventions to save Israel, with a litany of the people's infidelities |
| 21:1–37 | Three prophecies of doom linked by the image of a sword |
| 22:1–31 | Prophecy and allegory decreeing the punishment of Jerusalem, a city of blood and guilt |
| 23:1–49 | A long allegory about two immoral sisters |
| 24:1–14 | An allegory |
| 24:15–27 | A symbolic action |

Ezekiel concentrates his speeches against the nations of Egypt and Tyre, both of which represent forces that caused harm and division within Israel. There are seven oracles against the nations. Seven is a symbolic number representing perfection. Thus seven oracles represent the complete defeat of the enemy forces, as well as the seven nations of Palestine that Joshua was told to defeat so that Israel could gain the land (Dt 7:1–4).

### Message of Consolation (chs 33–37)

Chapter 33 recalls earlier passages and moves into a new age for Israel. The prophet as watchman (vv. 1–9) links with 3:16–21 and Ezekiel's initial call. The passage on individual responsibility for one's actions (vv. 10–20) links with chapter 18, a key passage in understanding

Ezekiel's notion of sin, guilt, and punishment. The arrival of the fugitive from Jerusalem and the end of Ezekiel's muteness (vv. 21f) links well with 3:22–27 and 24:25–27. The final verses 23–33 insist that salvation is reserved for those exiles who have been internally transformed, anticipating 36:16–38.

Chapter 34 comes from a long tradition of referring to kings as shepherds (2 Sm 5:2; Mi 5:4; Jer 2:8; 3:15; 23:1–6). Ezekiel's passage in turn influenced Zechariah 11:4–17, and together they helped to form New Testament readings like Mark 6:34 and John 10.

Chapter 36:16–38 makes an interesting study with Jeremiah 31:31–37. Both speak of an internal renewal, with Ezekiel introducing many external details or rituals to accompany the internal transformation.

Chapter 37:1–14 tells of Israel's revival. In verses 1–11, the dry bones in the valley come together to form living people. In verses 12–14, God explains how the similarly lifeless bones of Israel will rise out of their graves. Ezekiel's prophecy over the dead bones enables him to summon the spirit that brings them back to life.

### The LORD's World Victory (chs 38–39)

After the purifying renewal of Israel during the exile and the return to the Promised Land, why did Israel not experience the final glorious fulfillment of God's promises? The crisis behind chapters 38–39 may be the long, dreary, frustrating stretch of existence after the return from exile. This is the in-between period of time, between the initial renewal of Israel and the definitive, everlasting victory of peace that was still to come.

In this literary form the forces of good are always at war with the forces of evil. God's mighty intervention on behalf of the forces of good is the only way that the forces of evil will ever be finally defeated. During severe crises, preachers and writers turn to the final day of the LORD as a means of offering hope and consolation to those enduring pain or suffering.

For Ezekiel, the forces of Gog (the land of Magog) represent the forces of evil that have to be defeated before final and lasting peace can be experienced by Israel. The final verses of this section (39:21–29) may once have concluded the book of Ezekiel. They summarize well the goals of Ezekiel's preaching.

### Vision of the New Temple, Land, and Community (chs 40–48)

Visions surround this final section (40:1–44:3; 47:1–12). Between these visions and after 47:12, Ezekiel provides rules or instructions for the community and its leadership. Some of the outstanding passages are summarized below. The book of Ezekiel ends fittingly with the new name for Jerusalem, "The LORD is there" (48:35).

***Important Passages from Chapters 40–48***

| | |
|---|---|
| 43:1–9 | The glory of the LORD reverses the journey of chapter 10 and returns to its place above the Ark of the Covenant, between the wings of the cherubim. This return promises the Temple a place in the final age. |
| 44:4–31 | Ezekiel takes a strong stand against the more open positions of Deuteronomy and Third Isaiah (56–66). In verses 5–9 Ezekiel forbids all foreigners from entering the Temple. Also, Ezekiel favors the priestly family of the Zadokites over all the other Levite families. The Zadokites are "the only Levites who may come near to minister to the LORD" (40:46; 43:19). |
| 45:18–23 | This section includes a calendar of feasts. |
| 46:2 | This verse drops the title of king and reduces the heir of the Davidic royalty to the rank of a "prince." Royal privileges and power are being transferred to the high priest. The eternal promises made to David are no longer applied to his heirs but are understood as promises for the future Messiah. |
| 47:1–12 | This passage offers a vision of fresh water, flowing from the altar, down the Kidron Valley, into the Dead Sea. This is part of the biblical tradition that declares symbolically that all life flows from God, enthroned at the Temple. The Temple becomes a symbol of the messianic era and mirrors God's true and everlasting home in heaven. |

**Questions for Discussion and Reflection**

*Group Sharing/Discussion*

1. Ezekiel emphasized that God was acting in the life and history of the people. Give examples of positive and negative actions of God that Ezekiel describes.

2. Chapter 34 is the Parable of the Shepherds. How do(es) the message(s) here compare with the Parable of the Good Shepherd?

3. In your own words, describe the significance of Ezekiel and his main message.

*In Our Lives*

1. Is there a person or a group today who reminds you of Ezekiel? Explain why.

2. As a Jewish priest, Ezekiel spoke much about the Temple and his vision of it. How well do we honor our church buildings as the house of the Lord?

3. Chapter 18 describes the reflection of an individual's good works or sins upon family members. How does our society react to the family of those who do good or do evil? How does this compare with Ezekiel's description?

*Individual/Personal Reflection/Action*

1. In chapter 2, Ezekiel eats the scroll and is empowered and changed. How does "chewing on the scriptures" affect what you do and say? When has it especially made a difference for you in how you think or how you act?

2. The closing verse says that the name of the city is to be "The LORD is there." In what ways is that true of your city or town? In what ways is it not a description of where you live?

3. What is one quality of this prophet that you would like to imitate? How can you grow in that quality?

# DANIEL READING GUIDE

## *At a Glance*

| | |
|---|---|
| Who are the main players? | Daniel Hananiah Mishael Azariah |
| What should I look for? | Daniel is an example of apocalyptic writing. This type of literature is usually written in a time of distress and persecution; it points ahead to the day of the LORD, who is Lord of history. The stories of trials and triumphs of Daniel and his companions show how men of faith can resist temptation and conquer adversity. |
| When was this written? | This was written during the persecution of Antiochus IV Epiphanes in 167–165 B.C. |
| Where did these events occur? | The stories of Daniel are rooted in the history and myths of Judah and take place in Babylonia. |
| Why was this book written? | Written during persecution, these stories of its popular traditions strengthened and comforted the Jewish people in their ordeal. |
| What is the story? | Chapters 1–6 present Daniel and his companions in the Diaspora as wise, observant, and faithful Jews who adhere to their Jewish identity even in exile, thus demonstrating that God supports Jewish practice outside the land of Israel. The four visions, chapters 7–12, show the divine control over events and that the kingdom of God will ultimately triumph. |

As the NAB introduction says, the book of Daniel falls into three sections. The first (chs 1–6) consists of stories in which Daniel and his three companions are the heroes. The second (chs 7–12) is made up of revelations told by Daniel in the first person. The third (chs 13–14) contains short stories that are not found in the Hebrew/Aramaic text of Daniel, but only in the Greek and Latin versions. Jews and Protestant Christians do not accept these stories as canonical, but the

Protestants include them in the Apocrypha, a collection of ancient Jewish writings that they consider edifying even if not inspired. The different kinds of material in the three divisions of Daniel reflect the gradual growth of the book. The stories in 1–6 are the oldest part and may originally have been independent stories. We know that the revelations were composed during the persecution of the Jews by Antiochus IV Epiphanes of Syria in 168–164 B.C. The "appendix" was added some time later, probably before the beginning of the Christian era.

## The Authorship and Date of Daniel

The book of Daniel was written by an unknown author probably in the middle of the second century B.C., but it presents itself as the composition of a wise Israelite, Daniel, during the fifth century B.C. This false attribution of authorship was a common practice in the ancient world, when a composition needed the extra authority of a prominent author or of having been written a long time before.

Daniel therefore predicts a future that is already known to the author. This means that, in reading the book, we must concentrate on the lessons that the author thought were important for contemporary readers. If we do not pay attention to this, we will be misled into concentrating on Daniel as a predictor of the future.

## Outline of the Book of Daniel

| | |
|---|---|
| Dn 1–6 | Stories of Daniel and his companions. These may have once been independent stories. |
| Dn 7–12 | Revelations as told by Daniel and composed during the persecution of the Jews by Antiochus IV Epiphanes of Syria (168–164 B.C.). |
| Dn 13–14 | This "appendix" was added sometime later, probably before the Christian era. |

### The Tales (chs 1–6)

These stories are similar to historical novels: They mention historical names and places, but they are fictional. They are not concerned with historical accuracy but, instead, carry a religious message, like the parables of Jesus. Daniel, like Noah and Job, may never have existed, but that does not take away from the religious value of the stories.

The stories paint an ideal picture of the life of Jewish exiles in Babylon. The situation is idealized in order to express hope and define acceptable behavior. The modern situation of religious people living in the secular world is not so far removed from ancient Jews living in the pagan world of Babylon. The message has two facets: It affirms the possibility of living in a Gentile environment, and it insists on the importance of fidelity to the essentials of the Jewish tradition.

#### Affirmation of the Gentile Environment

This affirmation is demonstrated in the story in chapter 1 when Daniel and his companions are trained and even excel in "the language and literature of the Chaldeans." They express no reservations about this training. In chapter 2, Daniel, with God's assistance, is able to interpret the king's dream when the Babylonian wise men fail. There are more instances of Daniel's ability to interpret mysteries in chapters 4 and 5.

Several instances in these chapters reveal Daniel's attitude toward Gentile kingship. One dream foretells that all Gentile kingdoms will eventually be destroyed, but there is no urgency about this prophecy. God has willed a long Gentile rule and Jews can find fulfillment in the service of a pagan king. The stories about King Nebuchadnezzar and King Belshazzar make it clear that Gentile kings must be subject to God and not become too proud or arrogant. They must act with restraint. If they do this, Daniel has no objection to their rule. Only when the kings exceed their limits do they incur the judgment of God.

#### The Importance of Fidelity

This second facet of the message is presented in the actions of Daniel and his companions. They remain faithful to their Jewish religion even as they enjoy their success at the pagan court. They refuse to eat the king's food, because it is not kosher (ch 1). The three youths refuse to worship the king's statue, at the risk of death (ch 3). Daniel refuses to depart from his custom of daily prayer even at the cost of being thrown into the lions' den. Each time the Jews ultimately win the respect of their rulers and become more successful.

The stories of the fiery furnace and the lions' den, like all miracle stories, are meant to arouse a sense of wonder. They are not realistic stories. The essential point in Daniel's stories is that God has the power to save, or to do what is for the best. Daniel and his companions trust in God, and this liberates them to do whatever they ought to do regardless of the immediate circumstances. This attitude is expressed in the words of the three youths: "If our God, whom we serve, can save us from the white-hot furnace and from your hands, O king, may he save us! But even if he will not, you should know, O king, that we will not serve your god or worship the golden statue which you set up." Their fidelity is not conditional.

Daniel 1–6 conveys a sense that God is in control and that all will work out for the best. The will of God can be exercised through the rule of pagan kings. True religion does not require any particular political system.

## Apocalyptic Literature

Daniel's visions (chs 7–12) belong to a kind of literature called apocalyptic (see Glossary, apocalypse). This word is from the Greek for "revelation" and has come to be associated with a particular kind of revelation, with certain recurring characteristics. The table below lists some of those characteristics, some examples from Daniel, and a few of the ways the characteristics function.

These characteristics create numerous difficulties for the modern reader and call for some caution in interpreting books like Daniel.

1. *Heavy Use of Symbolism.* Apocalyptic authors do not speak directly but use symbols or images instead. For example, all scholars agree that King Antiochus is a major figure in Daniel, but his name is never mentioned. He appears as the eleventh horn on a beast. Sometimes this veiled language might be used to save the community from persecution from the king. It also strengthens the impression of supernatural origin and allows later generations to make their own interpretations. This characteristic can easily lead to misinterpretation and misapplications. Two hundred years later the eleventh horn might have been interpreted as the Roman emperor instead of Antiochus. In our own time the beasts rising out of the sea might be interpreted as meaning the outbreak of the Second World War. It is important to remember that the author of Daniel was speaking of persecution in the second century B.C. and not predicting any later event. The book of Daniel can help us understand our modern situation because it describes patterns that recur throughout history, but it cannot be used to predict specific events or persons in our world. The same can be said for the New Testament book of Revelation.

2. *Angels and Demons.* The first thing to remember when trying to interpret the meaning of

| **Characteristics** | **Function** |
|---|---|
| Heavy use of symbolism<br>Example: beasts = kingdoms; sea = chaos | Veils meaning; lack of specificity adds mystery, allows long-term interpretation |
| Angels and Demons<br>Example: Interpreting angel; Archangel Michael | Angels emphasize supernatural, add to sense of mystery, and dramatize divine control. |
| Pseudonymity<br>Example:second-century author writes as if living during exile | Antiquity adds to prestige of writings. Allows accurate "predictions" that foster hope and inspire right conduct. |
| Determinism<br>Example: History has fixed ratio (70 weeks of years or 490 years) | Divine control. Course of history is set with fate of righteous and wicked. Human decisions not predetermined. |
| Predictions of the End<br>Example: End of persecution (Daniel) or end of the world | During persecution, easier to keep going if the specific day of relief is known. |

the heavenly beings in Daniel is that, like other apocalypses, this is a work of imagination. The author is trying to build up hope in the people by saying that earthly war is not entirely under earthly control. To understand an apocalypse, we should ask, not, "Do these angels exist?" but, "What do they stand for?"

3. *Pseudonymity.* Many readers today consider the practice of claiming ancient authorship and, therefore, accurate predictions as deceptive and unethical. It was widely accepted in the ancient world, however, and helped the people believe in the real predictions of what was to come. The question is not whether Daniel really predicted all these things in advance, but whether his stance in the face of religious persecutions is a valid one.

4. *Determinism.* In dealing with the notion of fixed periods of history, the modern reader needs to remember that human decisions are not predetermined. On the contrary, the book of Daniel is basically a call for decision in a time of crisis. The fact that God has control over history strengthens the people's hope and their ability to make decisions.

5. *Predictions of the End.* Whether the end predicted was of persecution or of the world, the point of the specific predictions was, again, to encourage people to stand firm in their faith in the midst of suffering.

The problems of interpreting apocalyptic literature can be minimized if the believer reads for inspiration or exhortation rather than information. It has ethical value and relevance for modern times if the focus is placed on the attitudes and actions it was designed to support.

**A Symbolic Vision (ch 7)**

This vision of four human kingdoms that will be followed by a kingdom set up by God is one of the most famous and influential of all apocalyptic visions. In biblical poetry the sea is often a symbol of chaos, of all that is opposed to God; that is the point Daniel makes when he represents the pagan kingdoms as beasts from the sea. This is much more negative than the view of pagan kingdoms in Daniel 1–6. The experience of persecution colored the author's perception of all Gentile kingdoms.

After the vision of the four beasts, Daniel sees a judgment scene in which the "Ancient One" sits on a throne, the fourth beast is condemned to the fire, and "one like a son of man" appears on the clouds of heaven. There have been a variety of interpretations of this "son of man" figure. Early Christian tradition, beginning with the Gospels, identified this figure with Jesus Christ, but that could not have been the case in the second century B.C. Jewish tradition identified the "son of man" as the Messiah. Modern scholarship is divided between two interpretations: a symbol for Israel, or Michael the archangel. Either interpretation, however, can be understood as representing the triumph of the Jewish people over their persecutors under their heavenly patron.

The message of the vision is one of hope. Even when the opposing forces seem overwhelming, the power of God will eventually defeat them. The symbolism of the vision (beasts, fire, figure riding on the cloud) expresses the message with exceptional power and vividness. The image has been used over and over again in new situations. It provides language to express the power of evil that erupts from time to time in human affairs (for example, the Holocaust), and it can also express a hope that does not depend on human power. A similar symbolic vision is found in chapter 8 and, again, the message is one of hope.

**Prophecy Reinterpreted (ch 9)**

A prophecy of Jeremiah provides the basis for a different kind of revelation in this chapter. Jeremiah prophesied in the seventh century that the land would be subject to Babylon for 70 years. The second book of Chronicles credits Cyrus of Persia with fulfilling the prophecy (after 50 years had passed). Zechariah related it to the rebuilding of the Temple (after 66 years). The author of Daniel obviously does not think the prophecy has been fulfilled, but rather than discard it as a failure, he reinterprets it. Seventy years, he says, really means 70 weeks of years or 490 years. Like the dreams and visions of earlier chapters, Jeremiah's number is treated as a symbol. It is not meant to stand for an exact number of years. Rather, it reminds the readers that they can depend on God's promises even when the time of fulfillment is completely unknown.

Daniel's prayer in chapter 9 contains another important reminder: We should not expect our prayers to alter the course of events. Daniel receives a revelation in response to his prayer, but his prayer does not result in a shortening of the time of trial.

### Daniel's Apocalyptic View of History (chs 10–12)

This long vision explains to Daniel that the ongoing war between Judah and her enemies is not the whole picture. The earthly battle is only a reflection of the more important heavenly battle between the archangels Michael and Gabriel opposing the angelic princes of Persia and Greece. The vision shows that Michael will eventually be victorious (12:1) and the resurrection will follow. It is important to notice some key points about history in the vision.

1. The vision presumes that the outcome of warfare between human kingdoms depends on God's power, not human power (illustrated by the battle between the angelic powers).

2. The vision gives the impression that what happens in history is fixed in advance. It is written as if Daniel is writing during the exile, some 400 years before the actual events of persecution under Antiochus Epiphanes. This is done not to deceive, but to build up confidence in the prediction about the death of the king (11:40–55) and the resurrection (12:1–3).

3. The vision clearly affirms the resurrection of individuals (the only book of the Hebrew Bible to do so). Other books use the language of resurrection to refer to the restoration of the Jewish nation but not of individuals. This new emphasis was probably influenced by the experience of martyrdom in the time of persecution (see 2 Mc 7).

Belief in the resurrection made an enormous difference to Judaism and was essential to the beginnings of Christianity. Before this, Jewish religion taught that the reward for a just life was to see one's children's children to the fourth generation and the welfare of the nation as a whole. Now, however, pious Jews were being put to death for obeying the Law and were being cut off from the traditional reward. Just as the 70-year prediction of Jeremiah was reinterpreted in a new situation, so too, the reward of a just life had to be reinterpreted. Belief in life beyond the grave put martyrdom in a new perspective.

For Daniel, the Jews who remained faithful in the time of persecution were the wise persons (11:33–35). These put their trust in Michael and the heavenly world and apparently did not join in the fighting. The faithful stance of these wise teachers illustrates the ethical stance of the book of Daniel, which is the most enduring message of the book.

The apocalyptic message of chapters 10–12 has some basic beliefs in common with the older stories found in chapters 1–6, although the stories are more optimistic. Both affirm the belief that God rules all kingdoms and has the power to save, and that the individual must act with integrity even at the cost of life itself. This last is helped by the belief in the resurrection.

It is important to remember when reading Daniel that apocalyptic writing comes out of difficult, troubled times, and therefore the writer's position may be presented as the only right way of seeing things. Daniel presents one possible way in which a faithful person might respond to a situation of oppression and persecution. It would be a mistake to think that it is the only appropriate response. The Bible presents many different responses in a variety of situations.

### The Additions or Appendix (chs 13–14)

These are independent stories added here probably because Daniel happens to be one of the characters.

#### Susanna

This story may be described as a parable because it reverses our expectations. Daniel appears as a young but wise judge, as suggested by his name (Dan comes from the Hebrew verb "to judge"). Usually elders who have been appointed judges are the righteous ones, and the word of a young woman would carry little weight against theirs. However, it is characteristic of biblical narrative that the underdog prevails or is justified.

The story of Susanna is similar to the rest of Daniel in her response when she is trapped: "Yet it is better for me not to do it and to fall into your power than to sin before the Lord."

#### Bel and the Dragon

Daniel 14 contains two stories that make fun of pagan idolatry and are not meant to be taken as accurate descriptions of Babylonian religion. The Babylonians are portrayed as excessively stupid, and the stories are more fantastic than Daniel 6. Although the fantastic elements give the tale a lighthearted quality, the background here is more tense than Daniel 1–6. Bel and the Dragon allows for no ecumenical relations with pagan religion and reflects a more serious situation than indicated in Daniel 1–6. The present-day reader must remember that biblical stories are shaped by historical circumstances, and this affects how we read them.

**Questions for Discussion and Reflection**

***Group Sharing/Discussion***

1. Retell how Daniel and his companions remain faithful to their Jewish religion, in relation to food, worship, and prayer.

2. Give examples from the stories of the five characteristics of apocalyptic literature, that is, use of symbolism, angels and demons, pseudonymity, determinism, prediction of the end. Can you identify any apocalyptic characteristics in the way you express your faith?

***In Our Lives***

1. Daniel's stories affirm that God rules all kingdoms, that God has the power to save, and that the individual must act with integrity at the cost of life. What do your stories of God affirm? How is your integrity linked to these stories?

2. Daniel reminds us that God controls history even though human decisions are not predetermined. In times of crisis this inspiration strengthens people's hope and ability to decide. Reflect on your strengths, your hopes, your decisions. What are the convictions that strengthen your hope and enable you to make ethical decisions?

3. Daniel's vision of history (chs 11–12) affirms resurrection of the individual. This reflects also the beliefs of the New Testament. What does individual resurrection mean to you?

***Individual/Personal Reflection/Action***

1. Daniel's prayer (ch 9) teaches us not to expect our prayers to alter the course of events. Think about your patterns of prayer. Do you usually pray to change God, to change events or conditions, or to change yourself and strengthen your fidelity?

2. Take time to meditate on the situations that might affect your fidelity to God (e.g., your financial goals, government policies, job requirements, personal decisions, etc.).

# THE TWELVE MINOR PROPHETS

The authors of this collection of books (referred to as the Book of the Twelve) are called minor prophets because their writings are short compared to the four major prophets, Isaiah, Jeremiah, Ezekiel, and Daniel. Like the others, however, they were "here and now" kinds of people dealing with specific situations; so it is important to know as much as possible about the time and place of their activity (see the timeline on RG 146):

1. This collection covers a period of about 300 years of prophetic activity.

2. Amos, Hosea, and Micah were active in the eighth century B.C. at the same time Isaiah was beginning his career. Recall that there were two kingdoms at this time. Hosea was in the north and Micah in the south. Amos was from the southern kingdom but prophesied in the north.

3. Zephaniah, Nahum, and Habakkuk were active toward the end of the seventh century B.C. during the Babylonian period.

4. Haggai and Zechariah (chs 1–8) were involved in the rebuilding of the Temple in Jerusalem in 520 B.C.

5. Joel, Jonah, Obadiah, and Malachi are from the time after the exile (called the postexilic period) but are difficult to date more precisely.

Most of these books are made up of short poetic oracles or messages from God delivered through the prophets. The book of Jonah, a short story, is an exception.

We can discover a pattern in the content of these books: sin followed by judgment followed by salvation or the promise of restoration. Not all of the prophets get to the end of the pattern (Amos), while others focus primarily on restoration (Haggai and Zechariah). Within this overall pattern there is diversity, as well as some dominant themes:

1. Most of these prophets focus on the sins of their own people. There are a few exceptions, but generally you could say that these prophets are critical of those around them.

2. They concentrate on two kinds of sin. Social sin, the mistreatment of the poor, the weak, and the unprotected, is clearly denounced in Amos and Micah but is found throughout the collection. Cultic sin, the worship of false gods and abuses within their own religious rituals, is also condemned. We would expect the prophets to be hard on the people of Israel when they worship gods other than the LORD. They are even stronger when it comes to the worship of the LORD that is only empty ritual. Amos and Micah draw social and cultic sin together. They condemn the cult of their people because it makes them too comfortable and distracts them from the injustices of their society.

3. These prophets expand the common biblical belief that God acts in history. They teach that whatever actually happens is the work of God. They understood the destruction of the northern kingdom in 721 B.C. and the southern kingdom of Judah in 587/586 B.C. as acts of divine judgment.

Salvation and restoration become more prominent after the exile, but they are also evident in earlier prophets, most notably Hosea. It is appropriate to talk of restoration after a time of destruction. Very often the prophets imagine a situation that is very different from the present. This is the case especially with the postexilic prophets when they are trying to encourage the people in the rebuilding of the Temple. The phrase "on that day" often introduces prophecies of transformation. The reader needs to be aware that some of these messages of hope may have been added at a later date by the editors of the prophetic books.

Taken as a whole, the Book of the Twelve is both a reflection on the past and a lesson for the future. The editors of the prophetic books were heavily influenced by the theology of Deuteronomy: Sin does not go unpunished, but God is ultimately merciful and wants only the repentance and restoration of Israel. This call to repentance can be heard throughout this collection.

# HOSEA READING GUIDE

***At a Glance***

| | |
|---|---|
| Who are the main players? | Hosea Gomer |
| What should I look for? | Recognize the variety of ways in which the images of marital infidelity are employed to picture Israel's disloyalty. It is important also to notice how much of Hosea's message of faithlessness is directed against abuses in Israelite religion: its priesthood, rites, and sacred sites and altars. |
| When did this take place? | In the later part of the eighth century B.C. |
| Where did these events occur? | In the northern kingdom |
| Why was this book written? | Hosea began the tradition of describing the relationship between Yahweh and Israel in terms of marriage. His description of God's love for his people in chapter 11 is one of the high points in the Old Testament. |
| What is the story? | Hosea's primary image of Israel's disloyalty to God is the wife who is unfaithful to the husband and has become a prostitute. This image of the unfaithful wife gave him a strong image with which to criticize the abuses of Israel's elite. |

## Introduction

Hosea's central concern is Israel's loyalty to its God. He denounces Israel for worshiping other gods, in particular the Canaanite god Baal, and pleads with Israel to return to the faithful worship of its God alone. To gain his audience's attention and to make his message vivid, Hosea used the metaphor of marriage to describe Israel's relationship to God. God is pictured as a husband and Israel as his faithless and promiscuous wife. Israel, the disloyal wife, is urged to repent and return to her husband. The marriage metaphor is enacted by Hosea himself in chapters 1–3, when Hosea marries Gomer, described as a prostitute (2:2) and an adulteress (3:1). And Hosea uses the marriage metaphor repeatedly in the speeches in chapters 1–14, which make up the bulk of the book. A prophet fond of metaphors, Hosea also compares Israel's disloyalty to a barren tree (9:13–17), a stubborn heifer (4:16; 10:11–15), and a rebellious son (11:1–7).

Hosea's prophecy can be divided into two parts, the first a collection of narratives in chapters 1–3 that describes Israel's disloyalty in terms of Hosea's faithless wife. Narratives about prophets, such as these, typically take up less space in a prophetic book than the prophet's speeches themselves, and they frequently describe prophets acting out the message they wish to deliver. The second and larger part of Hosea is a collection of prophetic speeches (chs 4–14) that condemn Israel's deceit, predict God's punishment, and express hope for Israel's renewal. It is difficult to know where one speech ends and the next begins, but a dominant pattern can be detected in which indictments of sin are followed by sentences of judgment. In the brief speech that begins this collection, for example, an indictment listing Israel's crimes (4:1–2) is followed by a sentence describing God's punishment (4:3).

Much less common are speeches predicting Israel's restoration (11:8–11). Hosea's own speeches may have been supplemented at points by later editors who wished to relate Hosea's message to the southern kingdom of Judah or to the Judeans in exile (11:10–11).

Hosea lived and prophesied in the northern kingdom of Israel, also called Ephraim, at the time of the divided monarchy when Israel and Judah were separate kingdoms. Hosea was the only native northerner among the prophets, the rest of whom all lived in or came from Judah. His career covered the last 30 years of the kingdom of Israel (750–721 B.C.), when Israel was under the constant threat of Assyrian imperialism and was wracked by a series of violent coups in its own capital, Samaria. Hosea deplores the internal political violence of this period (7:5–7) and Israel's attempt to protect itself by international alliances (7:11), and he believes Israel's impending doom in the face of Assyrian expansion to be God's punishment for its social and religious corruption.

Hosea is especially critical of the religious scene in Israelite society during this period. His frequent references to Baal (2:8; 13; 16), indicate that many Israelites had turned from their own God to worship this Canaanite deity. This attraction to Baal-worship among the Israelites was an old and continual problem, as the contest between Elijah and the prophets of Baal a century earlier shows (2 Kgs 17–19). The Israelites believed that Baal, like Israel's own God, could deliver the rains and agricultural productivity on which their economy and survival depended. The calves that Hosea criticizes (8:5–6), although possibly pedestals or throne images for Israel's God, are also associated with Baal in this period, and Hosea regards them as idols of Baal.

Hosea's work appears first in the collection of minor prophets, sometimes called The Book of the Twelve. Although not chronologically first, Hosea provides a good introduction to these prophets. He is unrivaled for the beauty of his poetry and the emotional power of his oracles.

Hosea lived at a time of great difficulty and instability for the northern kingdom of Israel, caused by the westward expansion of the mighty Assyrian empire. During Hosea's time, Assyria moved from merely being a threat to actually bringing about the end of the northern kingdom in 722 B.C. Even before this tragic date, there was unrest in the kingdom. In the 14 years between the death of Jeroboam II and 722, five kings ruled.

We get an insight into the personal life of Hosea from his use of the metaphor of marriage. Like some of the other prophets, he uses metaphor not just as a matter of spoken or written words; his life itself conveys his message. This speaks clearly of his total involvement in his prophecy. Even his children are given symbolic names, "Not-Pitied" (Lo-ruhama, 1:6) and "Not-My-People" (Lo-ammi, 1:8). The prophet and his family are living signs of God's concern for the welfare of his people.

## Outline of the Book of Hosea

Hosea is usually divided into two parts:

| | |
|---|---|
| Hos 1–3 | The metaphor of marriage |
| Hos 4–14 | Oracles of Israel's destruction. Two exceptions: Prophecy of restoration 11:8–11; Invitation to repentance 14:2–9 |

### The Metaphor of Hosea's Marriage (chs 1–3)

The LORD's first recorded words to Hosea capture the power of this metaphor, "Get for yourself a woman of prostitution. . . ." It may be that Gomer was not a harlot at the time of her marriage to Hosea. However, many scholars see the choice of a harlot wife as a deliberate symbolic act on the part of the prophet. And if, as some think, Gomer was not only a prostitute, but a cult prostitute serving the pagan god Baal (see below), then Hosea's action is even more dramatic. In any case, the prophet's message is clear: Israel's behavior toward God is like that of an unfaithful spouse. This metaphor illustrates several significant insights:

**Covenant**

Hosea believes that God and Israel are bound together by the covenant given to Moses, symbolized here by the marriage covenant, an agreement that forms the basis of a relationship. Hosea's words, "you are my people" and "My God" (2:25), recall not only the standard marriage formula, but the covenant language of Exodus as well.

## Metaphor as a Second Language

THE STUDY OF any type of literature would be enhanced by a good course on metaphor. This is especially true for the study of the Bible. This need for the language of metaphor, image, or symbol comes from the Bible itself. To respond to the thinking of the biblical writers, to get to their message, one must be able to use this language because it was their language. The need also arises from our modern pragmatic, conceptual approach. As one participant in an adult Bible study class said, "Can't you skip the flowery stuff and cut to the bottom line? Tell us what it means."

Metaphor is especially appropriate to convey meaning in the Bible because it reminds us that we are dealing with the divine, with a reality that can never be fully understood. This is one way of describing mystery. A mystery is not something that our reason cannot grasp; it does not put an end to our efforts to comprehend it. Rather, it is a never-ending process of coming to new understanding. The love of God for us is a mystery, not because we cannot understand what love is, but because we cannot comprehend the fullness of God's love, no matter how hard we try. When Israel tried to put into words how God had entered into relationship with them or how God acted in their history, they were at a loss for words. The language of metaphor at least allowed them to point to the reality that is beyond what was tangible or measurable.

In Hosea we have a prime example of the beauty of metaphorical language and its power to convey meaning that is almost beyond our power to communicate. Perhaps his most famous is the "lived metaphor" of his marriage to Gomer, which portrays Israel as the unfaithful spouse. In other places he compares Israel to an "unturned cake" (7:8), a "wild ass" (8:9), or a "luxuriant vine" (10:1). These examples have an emotional effect that evokes a response in the reader because of the many associations they carry.

Another striking example is in chapter 11, which begins, "When Israel was a child I loved him." The reference is to the Exodus event, but the effect is very different from our response to the Pentateuch. By portraying Israel as a child, Hosea paints a vivid picture of God as the loving parent, teaching the infant to walk and lifting it up. The comparison strongly implies that Israel should have the same kind of bond with the LORD that a toddler has with its parents.

The metaphorical language of the Bible points the reader to something beyond our ability to completely understand, to the mystery of God.

### Idolatry and Infidelity

A major problem addressed by Hosea was idolatry, specifically the cult of the Canaanite god Baal. Baal was a real temptation for the people because he was a fertility god who was supposed to guarantee the productivity of the land, animals, and people. Think about how much farmers and ranchers depend on good weather for their livelihood, and you will understand the strength of this temptation.

The worship of Baal may have included sexual acts with prostitutes. If Gomer was such a prostitute, then Hosea's comparison was all the more pronounced: Israel's covenant with the LORD, understood as marriage, contrasted with the worship of Baal, understood as prostitution. Gomer exemplified the behavior of Israel by straying from the marital relationship.

Hosea was not concerned just with Israel's participation in the Baal fertility rites. Her infidelity was more pervasive, as he says in 4:1–3:

There is no fidelity, no loyalty,
  no knowledge of God in the land.
Swearing, lying, murder,
  stealing and adultery break out;
  bloodshed follows bloodshed.
Therefore, the land ddries up . . .

According to Hosea, one cannot pick and choose when it comes to the LORD. As we say of some things today, "It's a package deal." When the Israelites acknowledge the LORD as LORD, they have to accept the covenant code of ethics as well.

**Understanding of God**

Hosea understands God as the best in human nature, only more so. And, for him, a faithful marriage is the culmination of love between a man and a woman. Therefore, the love between the LORD and Israel is best understood as a faithful marriage.

## Concentric Circle Thinking and Writing

SOMETIMES READING THE Bible can be confusing. For example, you might be reading along focusing on one idea and a new image is introduced, and even another. Or, you are reading a text and you think, "Haven't I read this before?" What at first seems confusing can really be helpful to understanding the biblical message.

This could be called concentric circle thinking or writing. It is a way of organizing information that many of the biblical writers felt at home with, although it may seem strange to us. The way we've been taught to think or reason is more linear; you go through certain steps in a particular order to reach a conclusion. The people who produced the Bible generally thought in a more circular fashion. It doesn't mean that they weren't logical; it's a different kind of logic.

Picture someone throwing a rock into a pond or lake. When the rock hits the water, there is a splash—that's the main point of the writer. Then a circle appears and begins to expand—the development of the main point. Another circle appears and moves out—a related idea is added and developed. Soon there are several concentric circles all visible and moving at the same time.

Hosea is a good example of this; his images sometimes seem to be tumbling over one another. In chapter 2, Hosea is in the process of developing the marriage metaphor, comparing Israel to his own unfaithful wife. Then he brings in the image of the desert, then back to his harlot wife. Several lines later he is talking about laying waste her vines and fig trees, building a wall against her, then leading her into the desert to allure her. Later on there's talk of the covenant and more marriage talk and several more images in between. Finally the chapter ends with, "You are my people," and the response, "My God!"

By going around and around and bringing in many familiar words and images, Hosea is pleading with his people to be faithful once again to the LORD who is faithful to them. He has already said that God is like a faithful spouse; he brings up the desert to remind them of God's saving action on their behalf and of the covenant relationship. He warns them about how destructive unfaithfulness can be to a relationship. Even though he knows that they won't really listen and will suffer the consequences, he sows the seeds of hope.

When you are reading this circular kind of structuring, it is important to remember not to get caught up in trying to figure out what is first, second, or third. Let the images circle around. Through the use of a commentary, try to find out what the people of Hosea's time would have heard when these words were spoken or read to them. Let the message just sink in.

### Land and Desert

While Hosea is developing the marriage metaphor, he weaves in the familiar Exodus images of the promised land and the desert with all their rich associations. He recalls the foundational experience of Exodus/Covenant that gave Israel its identity as a people. This reminds the people of what is really important, their covenant with God.

The prophet focuses on the gift of the land "flowing with milk and honey," the primary symbol of salvation from ancient times. This is where the prophet delivers the threat with full force: The land will be reduced to a desert. Because there is no belief in an afterlife at this time, to lose the land is to undo the Exodus. The expression, "to have the rug pulled out from under you," is apt. For Israel it was that and more.

Hosea transforms the desert image; it is not only a place of wandering and death, but a place where a man might court a young woman in privacy. He is suggesting that away from the cult of Baal and other abuses, after being stripped down by the Assyrians, something new is possible, a new Exodus.

So, hope is introduced. It may not be full-fledged, flag-waving hope, but it is there. After all, Hosea is a realist. Second Isaiah (Is 40–55) will develop this new Exodus theme after the Exile, and it reappears in the Dead Sea Scrolls and in the New Testament.

### Questions for Discussion and Reflection

*Group Sharing/Discussion*

1. An important lesson we can learn from Hosea has to do with theological method, that is, that one way to knowledge of God is through observing human experience. How is God like a faithful spouse, a loving parent, a friend seeking a lasting relationship?

*In Our Lives*

1. What does infidelity do to human relationships? Would the same things apply to our relationship with God?

*Individual/Personal Reflection/Action*

1. Meditate on this passage from Hosea. How does this relate to "burning incense to idols" in modern life? Does this Old Testament depiction of God as healer shed light on your own image of God? (from Hos 11:1–4)

When Israel was a child, I loved him,
out of Egypt I called my son.
The more I called them,
the farther they went from me,
Sacrificing to the Baals
and burning incense to idols.
Yet it was I who taught Ephraim to walk,
who took them in my arms;
I drew them with human cords,
with bands of love;
I fostered them like those
who raise an infant to their cheeks;
I bent down to feed them.

# JOEL READING GUIDE

## *At a Glance*

| | |
|---|---|
| Who are the main players? | Joel |
| What should I look for? | Joel is unique among the prophets in his focus on a natural catastrophe, a locust plague. To appreciate the danger of the crisis Joel faced, one must recover a sense of the terrible destructiveness of a locust infestation for a preindustrial agricultural society. This prophecy is rich in apocalyptic imagery and is eschatological in tone. |
| When did this take place? | It was composed about 400 B.C. |
| Where did these events occur? | Judah |
| Why was this book written? | Joel's unique focus on the locust plague as an image of divine judgment offers some religious vision for the not-uncommon plagues, both natural and symbolic, that Israel experienced. |

What is the story? A plague of locusts ravages Judah. Joel sees this as a symbol of the coming of the LORD. He summons the people to repent and turn to the LORD with fasting. They convene a solemn assembly of prayer for deliverance. The LORD answers their prayer and promises to drive away the locusts and bless them with peace and prosperity.

## Outline of the Book of Joel

The book moves from specific concern with the plague of locusts to a more general prophecy of universal judgment:

| | |
|---|---|
| Joel 1:1–2:17 | The plague of locusts and prayer for deliverance |
| Joel 2:18–27 | Reply and reassurance from God |
| Joel 3 | Future time when God will intercede |
| Joel 4 | Final judgment of the nations and salvation for the elect |

## The Day of the LORD

The theme of the Day of the LORD runs through the book as a unifying thread. This theme with its two related aspects, the vision of plenty and the desire for vengeance, is important for understanding Joel's message.

In Amos (eighth century B.C.), the meaning of the Day of the LORD shifts from the original festive day to one of a day of darkness, not light. By the time the book of Joel was written, any great disaster might be called a "Day of the LORD."

In developing this theme, Joel starts with something specific, the plague of locusts. He takes something that was surely terrible and uses it to teach the people what the real disaster, the Day of the LORD, will be like. The locust plague is a rehearsal, an image of the end of the world, the day of judgment of the nations.

The locusts transform the land from being like the "garden of Eden" to a "desolate wilderness" (2:3). Joel also uses the similarity of the locust plague to an invasion to describe them as an invading army, with the LORD at their head (2:11), affirming the conviction that whatever happens is the work of God. The people respond to the plague in a way typical of the ancient world, by bringing offerings and libations. Joel also responds typically, like other Hebrew prophets, by turning the crisis into an occasion for reform and repentance. In 2:13 we find a classic expression of the prophetic view of proper ritual: "Rend your hearts, not your garments."

In our day we do not usually regard natural disasters as visitations from God, or seek relief primarily through rituals. But in Joel's time, the situation was beyond human control. The ritual was the only thing they could do. It was a way of expressing their desperation and their hope that God would give them relief. And the prophet, by urging reform, was trying to bring some good out of a bad situation. This is a good example of the "here and now" attitude of the prophets. For them, salvation is primarily concerned with the welfare of the people on earth.

In chapter 3, the Day of the LORD takes on a different meaning. It now refers to the Day of Judgment, and the passage suggests the end of the world: "The sun will darken, the moon turn blood-red, . . . " (3:4). We are dealing here with the language of metaphor. The darkening of the sun and moon is a way of expressing a time of tumult and confusion; the world as we have known it will be turned upside down. Unlike later apocalyptic writers, who took the image of the end of the world literally, Joel looks for a transformation of this world rather than a new creation.

### Vision of Plenty

Joel's hope for the transformation of the earth is captured in his prediction of a time of plenty. It is a natural reaction to the locust plague and also appeals to the universal hope for freedom from hunger. In a time of scarcity, Joel comforts his people with the promise that they will eat and be filled (2:26). This is very common in the prophets and serves two functions: It gives hope to the poor, and it gives a goal for people to work toward.

### Vengeance on the Nations

The occasional desire for vengeance in the Hebrew scriptures can be distasteful to Christians, although not unknown to their experience. Joel's presentation of Judah's desire for vengeance recalls the "eye for an eye" attitude. It is not enough that Judah flow with wine and milk; the hated neighbor Edom must be a desert waste (4:10). If their enemy sold Jews into slavery, then the enemy's children must be sold. Some prophets called for peace, calling the people to beat their swords into plowshares (Is 2:4; Mi 4:3); Joel calls for a showdown.

Vengeance is not noble, but it is understandable in some situations. We must not overlook the fact that the prophet's call for vengeance is a call for justice. In Joel it is a protest of the powerless who had seen their children sold into slavery.

### Questions for Discussion and Reflection

***Group Sharing/Discussion***

1. The plague of locusts transformed the land into "desert waste." The Israelites' rituals express their desperate concern and hope that God will bring relief. Joel comforts his people with the promise that they will eat and have their fill.

Share your insights on how the plague affected the people; on their views of what caused it; on the role of the prophet for his people; and on their views of their neighbors.

***In Our Lives***

1. It is not enough that Judah flow with milk and wine; their hated neighbor Edom must be a desert waste (4:19). Joel's presentation of Judah's desire for vengeance recalls the "eye for an eye" attitude.

Try this as an examination of conscience about vengeance. For one week be aware of all the people who might feel like "turning the tables" on you, or you might feel that way toward them. See how you can improve one of these situations.

***Individual/Personal Reflection/Action***

1. "Rend your hearts, not your garments." Think about what attitudes of your heart need to be changed to return to the LORD.

# AMOS READING GUIDE

## *At a Glance*

| | |
|---|---|
| Who are the main players? | Amos, Priest of Bethel |
| What should I look for? | Note that this is an anthology of Amos' oracles. Keep in mind the typical two-part form: indictment of sins followed by announcement of punishment. |
| When did this take place? | Amos was a shepherd of Tekoa in Judah, who exercised his ministry during the prosperous reign of Jeroboam II (786–746 B.C.). |
| Where did these events occur? | He prophesied in Israel at the great cult center of Bethel. |
| Why was this book written? | Amos proclaims that true religion requires not just ritual observances, but a moral life. |
| What is the story? | Amos preached against the northern kingdom and is the first of Israel's prophets to have his speeches preserved in a collection. He is a prophet of divine judgment during a time of political and economic stability and growth. Amos' harsh criticism of Israelite society and the expectation that its injustice would bring divine judgment seemed exaggerated and outlandish to his audience. A mere 25 years later, his predictions came true when Samaria fell to Assyrian armies. |

## Introduction

Amos is Israel's prophet of social justice, proclaiming that true religion consists not just of ritual observances, but in a moral life based on fair and equitable treatment of all members of society, powerful and powerless alike. This concern for justice lies at the heart of Israel's prophetic involvement, but no other prophet expresses it with more passion and substance. Amos demands justice in all areas of society: political (6:10), judicial (5:10, 12), and economic (8:4–6), and he mercilessly attacks Israel's elite for their abuse of power (4:1; 6:1). He believes Israel's religious assemblies, sacred music, and elaborate sacrifices are pointless without principled and ethical behavior in daily affairs (5:21–24). And he regards the demise of Israelite society as the inevitable outcome of its internal corruption and injustices (5:6–7). The power of social justice in the imagination of Western society derives in large part from Israel's prophets and from Amos' passionate appeals in particular.

## Amos, the Book

The book of Amos contains one brief narrative about an event in his career (7:10–17) and several reports of his visions (7:1–9; 8:1–3; 9:1–4), but the book is primarily made up of short judgment speeches with a simple two-part structure: an indictment listing Israel's sins and a sentence of judgment prescribing God's punishment for these sins. This structure is clearly visible, for example, in Amos' speech to the priest Amaziah at Bethel, in which Amos indicts Amaziah for restricting prophetic speech (7:16) and announces the divine sentence punishing Amaziah and his family (7:17). While judgment speeches against Israel predominate, the book of Amos actually begins with a series of judgment speeches, with this same two-part structure, directed against Israel's neighbors (1:3–2:5).

Amos must be read as an anthology of short, independent speeches rather than as a book with a single thesis developed from beginning to end. The reader must also be aware that Amos (and other prophets) composed speeches in a poetic form based on verse units of two parallel lines: "let justice surge like waters,/ and righteousness like an unfailing stream" (5:24). Keeping these two features of Amos' work in mind can help make sense of a book that might otherwise appear disorganized and repetitious.

## Amos, the Prophet

Only one episode of Amos' career is recounted in this book. Although he came from the southern kingdom of Judah, Amos proclaimed his oracles in the northern kingdom, especially around the temple of Bethel. (After the northern tribes split off from Judah to form their own kingdom, King Jeroboam set up two official sanctuaries at Dan and Bethel to discourage people from worshiping at the Jerusalem Temple.) Amaziah, the priest at Bethel, was worried because Amos was prophesying against the king in the temple precincts. The priest could not afford to offend the king, so he told Amos to go back to Judah. The reply of Amos (7:14) about not being a prophet, nor belonging to a company of prophets, until the LORD called him, points to his independence. He did not have to rely for support on the priest or the king. He could take care of himself working as a shepherd or a dresser of sycamores (a kind of fig tree).

This independence, added to his obvious personal conviction, gave rise to a style that is blunt and sometimes offensive. He calls the women of Samaria "cows of Bashan" (4:1) and tells the priest that his wife will be a harlot in the city (7:17). He had nothing to gain by soft pedaling his message. He was not a trusted adviser to the king, as the prophet Nathan was to David; and as an outsider, he had no hope of influencing the upper classes. He simply proclaims the doom that is coming.

## Amos and the Covenant

Amos consistently treats Israel the same as the other nations in the sight of God. Did the prophet consider Israel as a chosen nation and, therefore, special in any sense? Certainly Amos considered the Exodus as fundamental to Israel's identity, but this did not give the Israelites any guarantees, nor put them into a position of privilege. Rather, it gave them more responsibility.

Two passages make this very clear. Chapter 3, verse 2 says, "You alone I have known, among all the families of the earth." The modern-day reader is probably surprised to read the verse that follows: "Therefore I will punish you for all your iniquities." Amos' audience was no doubt shocked and maybe even angered. This was not what they wanted to hear. Similarly and even more bluntly, we read in 9:7: "Did I not bring the Israelites from the land of Egypt as I brought the Philistines from Caphtor and the Arameans from Kir?" Israel is special but so is every other nation.

## Organization of the Book

### Outline of the Book of Amos

| | |
|---|---|
| Amos 1–2 | Oracles against the nations ending with a denunciation of Israel |
| Amos 3:1–5:9 | "Words"—three long oracles (strings of short utterances). Note that 5:7–9 has been reordered by the NAB editors. |
| Amos 5:7–6:14 | Three "woes" against Israel and Judah |
| Amos 7:1–9:8b | Visions of destruction |
| Amos 9:8c–15 | An epilogue, probably added later |

### Oracles against the Nations (chs 1–2)

The book begins with oracles of judgment against Israel's immediate neighbors (present-day Lebanon, Syria, Jordan, and part of the occupied territory of Palestine). It is not unusual for a prophet to denounce other nations, but what is unusual is that Amos goes on to pronounce a similar judgment on Israel. He insists that Israel is no different from other nations in the eyes of God. According to Amos, any nation that sins against humanity deserves punishment. Moab is condemned for burning to lime the bones of the King of Edom (2:1); Israel is condemned for selling the just man for silver and the poor man for a pair of sandals (2:6).

The oracle in 2:6–16 is in the form of a speech in which a "lawsuit" is brought against Israel for failing to keep the Sinai covenant. This style of writing follows a pattern: recalling God's action on behalf of Israel in the Exodus; pointing out Israel's unfaithfulness in not keeping the commandments; usually issuing a threat. Many scholars think that this recollection of the Exodus may have been added by an editor of the prophetic books who wanted to put the prophetic preaching in the context of the theology of Deuteronomy as found in the Books of Joshua, Judges, Samuel, and Kings. This opinion seems reasonable because Amos' own focus was broader. He believed that people of any nation are bound by the requirements of justice, whether or not they know the law of Moses. In other words, Amos affirms the natural law as it was understood in the ancient Near East. Paul makes the same point in the first chapter of Romans when he says that pagan idolaters have no

### Editor at Work

AN EXAMPLE OF one way scholars discover the hand of an editor at work is found in the lawsuit speech (2:6–16). Here, one could say, the clue is theological. Throughout the oracles, Amos denounces Israel and the neighboring nations for behavior that is anti-human or against nature. The prophet's messages were not limited to those bound by the law of Moses. So, when the oracle is presented in a covenant pattern typical of the theology of Deuteronomy, a flag goes up for the interpreter with the question, "Is this Amos or a later editor fitting Amos into a specific theological view?"

Other clues that might attract attention have to do with vocabulary, writing style, and historical references. One who is thoroughly familiar with a particular biblical text in the original language will notice words, phrases, or ways of expression that are not typical of the work as a whole and will ask the question. Similarly, if something that seems more at home in the fifth century shows up in an eighth-century document, it is likely some editorial work has been done.

excuse, "for what can be known about God is evident to them."

### Words and Woes (3:1–6:14)

The three "words" of Amos are really a string of shorter oracles, mainly concerned with Israel's sins. There is a short section in 3:3–8, however, that is important because it focuses for the reader part of what Amos believes about God. This kind of insight helps the reader understand the rest of the prophet's work.

For Amos, everything that happens is God's doing. The order in nature is God's design. Nothing happens by chance. The acts of God in history are not confined to special events but take in everything, good as well as bad. (There was no devil in Israel's religion at this time to blame for the evil in the world.) This basic conviction about God accounts for Amos' interpretation of political events. For example, if Assyria is more powerful than Israel, this is not by chance; it is God's will. All this is another way of saying that Amos is a radical monotheist; he not only ignores other gods, but he attributes everything that happens to the God of Israel.

In both the "words" and the "woes," Amos criticizes the cult of Israel, its religious rituals and practices. In 4:4, he uses a play on words to make his point. The words for "sin offering" and "sin" in Hebrew are so similar that the people would, no doubt, understand Amos' implication, that they come to the sanctuary at Bethel to sin, rather than to make an offering for sin.

The prophet's sharpest critique of the cult is the "woe" against those who yearn for the Day of the LORD (5:18–25). This yearning was expressed in a major harvest festival in the fall, an occasion celebrating the victory of the God of Israel and the defeat of God's enemies. Amos turns a celebration into its opposite, a day of judgment. He was the first prophet to speak of the Day of the LORD as a day of judgment on Israel.

Amos goes on to issue a broadside against all the festivals of Israel. His point is not that all ritual is necessarily bad, but that ritual is not the essence of religion. The essence of religion is social justice. If ritual furthers justice, well and good, but too often it does not. Amos thought that ritual made the upper classes complacent, so much so that they thought that God would protect them no matter what and that they need not be concerned about the plight of the poor. They could leave the festival and go back to cheating in the marketplace (8:5). Amos labels all this as self-delusion.

In the final "woe" in chapter 6, Amos predicts that the upper classes of both kingdoms, "the complacent in Zion, [and] those who are secure on the mount of Samaria," would be the first to go into exile. They had sold the poor into slavery while they lived in luxury. Amos knew what he was talking about; he knew that the practice of the Assyrians was to take the upper classes into exile so there would be no one left to organize a revolt. In his view, it was a fate they richly deserved.

### Visions of Destruction (7:1–9:8b)

Amos is so moved by the enormity of the destruction he envisions that, at first, he intercedes and God relents. Once again, using a play on words, he makes the point that the time for forgiveness has run out. The vision is of a basket of

#### "They Hand Over the Just for Silver"

WITH THIS PHRASE, Amos strikes at the heart of Israel's guilt (2:6; 8:6). He criticizes not just an abuse here and an injustice there, but an economic system that condones the accumulation of great wealth in the hands of a few (6:1–6) and the growth in the gap between rich and poor (5:11). In Israel's traditional economy, families supported themselves by farming their ancestral lands, as Amos himself may have done (1:1; 7:14–15). But as the wealthy imposed heavy taxes (2:8; 5:11), took collateral for themselves (2:8), and cheated customers in the marketplace (8:5), the poor were eventually forced off their lands and reduced to debt-slavery, where they were bought and sold by the rich. Such an economic system was intolerable, according to Amos, for a society that had itself been once freed from slavery (2:10; 3:1).

ripe fruit. The Hebrew for "ripe fruit" is similar to the word for "end," so "the time is ripe" (8:2) can be translated "the end has come."

This was the first time that the idea of the "end" was proclaimed in ancient Israel. For Amos, the end was the end of Israel as an independent nation that had existed for 200 years. It was primarily the Israel of the upper classes that would end. The peasants would continue to suffer under Assyria, but, for them, it probably didn't make much difference whether they paid taxes to a foreign power or to oppressive Israelite landlords. For Amos and for the peasants, what mattered was not political identity, but the living conditions of the poor within society.

### Epilogue (9:8c–15)

Another example of the work of an editor is found in the epilogue. The force of Amos' prophecy was in its finality, as we read in the last line before the epilogue (9:8a and b), "The eyes of the LORD God are on this sinful kingdom: I will destroy it from off the face of the earth." In the very next line, a later editor adds, "But I will not destroy the house of Jacob completely, says the LORD."

The editor puts the prophecy of Amos in a broader historical perspective, that of the whole of Israel. The message of the prophets of Israel, in general, was not of destruction, but of hope. Death and destruction have their place and time, but hope remains. Ultimate optimism is an essential ingredient of biblical faith.

### Questions for Discussion and Reflection

*Group Sharing/Discussion*

1. Although Israel was special, why did Amos treat Israel the same as other nations?

*In Our Lives*

1. In the ancient world it was the role of the prophet to be the conscience of the nation and to speak up for the powerless.
   a. Who are the powerless of our day?
   b. Who speaks for them? Religious leaders? Social workers?
   c. Do you ever feel motivated to speak for the powerless? Who or what will help you act on this?

*Individual/Personal Reflection/Action*

1. Reflect on Amos' words on justice and worship (Am 5:23–24).

> Take away from me your noisy songs;
> The melodies of your harps, I will not listen to them
> Rather let justice surge like waters,
> and righteousness like an unfailing stream.

2. How is acting justly linked to prayer and worship in your life? In your parish? Who can you speak with to help make your parish worship more linked to acting justly?

# OBADIAH READING GUIDE

## *At a Glance*

| | |
|---|---|
| Who are the main players? | Obadiah |
| What should I look for? | The 21 verses of this book contain the strongest and sternest prophecy in the Old Testament. |
| When did this take place? | Sometime in the fifth century B.C. |
| Where did these events occur? | Judah |
| Why was this book written? | This book is unique because it contains only a single speech and that is directed against Edom, a neighboring nation, and not Israel. The Edomites entered Jerusalem when the Babylonians had invaded it, looting it and mistreating the people. See Psalm 137:7–8. |
| What is the story? | God's judgment of Edom is viewed as a fair punishment for the Edomites' disloyalty to their Israelite neighbors. Though their relations were often marked by conflict, Israel believed they were closely related as descendants of the two brothers, Jacob and Esau. |

## Outline of the Book of Obadiah

Obadiah is the shortest of the prophetic books with only 21 verses:

| | |
|---|---|
| Verses 1–14 | Short oracles against Edom |
| Verses 15–16 | An oracle against all the nations |
| Verses 17–21 | Prediction of restoration for Judah |

**Oracles against Edom and the Nations (1–16)**

Oracles of vengeance against Edom were common in the time after the Exile (compare Jer 49:7–22; Jl 4:19). Obadiah then extends this vengeance to all the nations. The basic message of these oracles is stated clearly in verse 15, "As you have done, so it shall be done to you."

Once more the reader is challenged to deal with the notion of vengeance. The prophet says that if you do violence to your neighbors and gloat over their distress, you deserve the same treatment. When the prophet extends the attack beyond Edom to all the nations, he uses the familiar motif of the Day of the LORD. Here it refers to the day of judgment, not the end of the world. The judgment is based on the law of retribution: As you have done, so it will be done to you.

**The Restoration of Judah (17–21)**

Modest hope is expressed at the end of Obadiah. Judah will rule over its neighbors, and this kingdom will be the LORD's. There is a slight notion of vengeance in this image of the kingdom, but the hope for the survival of the people is far more significant.

**Questions for Discussion and Reflection**

***Individual/Personal Reflection/Action***

The Edomites incurred the lasting hatred of the Jews by exploiting the weaknesses of Judah and pillaging its territory after the Babylonian invasion. Obadiah's oracle of vengeance is stated clearly: "As you have done, so shall it be done to you, your conduct will come back upon your own head."

1. Does this vengeance, which is similar to Amos', express the natural law of the punishment fits the crime?

2. How would you contrast this attitude with modern "hatred" of one country against another?

3. Does Jesus' teaching of "love your enemy, do good to those who hurt you" contrast with this attitude? Are they compatible? Is Jesus' teaching on love of neighbor limited to personal relations or does it also apply to groups and nations?

# JONAH READING GUIDE

### *At a Glance*

| | |
|---|---|
| Who are the main players? | Jonah People of Nineveh |
| What should I look for? | Look for the message of God's action through the disobedient prophet Jonah. Also notice the universality of God's mercy. |
| When did this take place? | Written in the postexilic era, probably in the fifth century B.C., this book is an instructive story with an important message. |
| Where did these events occur? | Nineveh, a great Assyrian city feared and hated by the Israelites |
| Why was this book written? | This prophecy strikes directly at the intolerant nationalism, which limited God's mercy to the chosen people of Israel. It is a parable of mercy, showing God's threatened punishments are but the expressions of a merciful will that moves all people to repent and seek forgiveness. |
| What is the story? | The book of Jonah is full of humor and irony. The author repeatedly undercuts expectations. Jonah is commanded to go in one direction and goes in the other; the sailors are more devout than the prophet; Jonah is disappointed when his mission succeeds; he is more concerned about a plant than about a populous city. God withheld his punishment and Jonah complained. From this humorous story a sublime lesson may be drawn. |

## Jonah the Book

Jonah is unique among the prophetic books. It is a story rather than a series of oracles. Jonah is himself a sort of anti-prophet: His actions are the opposite of what we expect of prophets. The story is more a fable, because of the role of the fish (like the animals in Aesop's fables). It's also a parable, a short story that goes against the expected. It is clearly meant to be humorous. It was written sometime in the postexilic period but has a different outlook from other writings of that period.

The chapter headings reveal the outline of the book. The long psalm in chapter 2 was probably added by a later editor, who focused on the miracle of Jonah's survival.

To appreciate Jonah, we need to consider that:

1. the book is deliberately humorous;
2. it is about the proper attitude to foreign nations, not about Jonah's miraculous escape from drowning;
3. the story is mildly critical of the religious zeal usually connected with prophecy.

## The Story's Humor

The humor is apparent from verse one: A prophet shamelessly disobeys a divine command; pagan sailors fear the LORD of Israel; a fish swallows a man and then spits him up on the shore; wicked Assyrians and even animals repent.

The author is not interested in historical plausibility; he uses this fantastic tale to teach a theological lesson. Ironically, in this "prophetic book," the prophet is not given the dignity usually associated with the office, nor are his convictions taken seriously. The reader is asked to reconsider the stereotype of both pagan and prophet.

## The Attitude to Foreign Nations

The wickedness of Assyria is the premise of this story, and Jonah is upset at being sent to preach to those who seem not to deserve God's mercy. Incredibly, the Assyrians repent, and Jonah questions whether they deserve divine forgiveness. One might react thus if the leaders of some dictatorial regime made a show of repentance for their crimes and were pardoned. It is not that Jonah is exceptionally narrow-minded but, rather, that his God is exceptionally tolerant. To God the Creator, Assyrians are as important as Israelites (or, in our terms, no racial or ethnic group is beyond redemption).

The last verse of the book recognizes that ordinary Assyrians are no more guilty of the crimes of their nation than are the cattle. In any case, guilt or innocence is not the point; the astonishing magnanimity of God is the message. The book of Jonah sees God in the same terms as the much later book of Wisdom 11:24: "For you love all things that are and loathe nothing that you have made; for you would not fashion what you hate." The penitent Assyrian is as great a contradiction as the "good Samaritan" of the Gospel, and as hard to accept, given the situation of the Jews of the postexilic period in which the book was written.

## The Perspective on Prophetic Zeal

Jonah reacts to God's mercy by sulking and praying for death (4:8). He is a prophet in the same mold as Elijah who, with great zeal for destroying sinners, had done the same in 1 Kings 10:4f. But the book of Jonah sees the limitations of prophetic zeal. Jonah is well-intentioned and acts out of a long tradition, but God rebukes him mildly. Earlier, Hosea had broadened the tradition by recognizing that it is more fitting for God to have mercy than to punish. This book goes further and extends that mercy to foreign nations. Even prophets must learn that reconciliation is a higher value than strict retribution. Not all the prophetic books reflect this insight, but it is the view affirmed for Christianity in the Gospels.

### The Sign of Jonah

The episode in the belly of the fish, a minor humorous motif in the story, acquires greater meaning in later tradition. It is taken to prefigure (Mt 12:39f) Jesus' time in the tomb. Jonah is a frequent symbol of the Resurrection in early Christian art. In chapter 2 the belly of the fish is equated with the netherworld, and Jonah's regret about being there is that he is separated from God's presence. Jonah asks to be restored to that presence, which is the fullness of life for most Old Testament writers.

### The Relevance of Jonah

Jonah's message is as urgent in today's world as it was in his time. It teaches us not only tolerance and understanding for those who are different from us, but also forgiveness for those who have truly behaved wickedly, if they are willing to accept it.

The sign of Jonah is a sign of hope that we can afford to forgive the injustices of life. The wicked deeds of the oppressor are not as final as they seem. Belief in resurrection is often associated with a hope for the damnation of the wicked. The book of Jonah, read in the light of the New Testament and Christian tradition, suggests that resurrection can also give a larger perspective on life, one that has room for tolerance and forgiveness.

### Questions for Discussion and Reflection

*Group Sharing/Discussion*

1. The prophet Jonah is often described as an anti-prophet. Retell some incidents when Jonah acts in the opposite manner of a prophet.

*In Our Lives*

1. The story is deliberately humorous: a disobedient prophet, sailing to a remote place to get away from the LORD; pagan sailors exhibiting more fear of the LORD than Jonah; fantastic Assyrian repentance, including the animals; the big fish saving and delivering Jonah to Nineveh. The ironic humor of the story invites us to reconsider our stereotypes of prophet and pagans.

Jonah's message of tolerance and forgiveness prompts us to recognize, practice, and pray for the grace to be tolerant and to forgive. Decide on ways to make this message part of your life.

2. Humor enriches life. How do you recognize it, nourish it in your life, and share it?

*Individual/Personal Reflection/Action*

1. For later generations and for us who have the New Testament, the sign of Jonah is the sign of hope. The book of Jonah suggests resurrection and hope, which teaches the message of tolerance and forgiveness. Reread the story of Jonah consciously in the light of the resurrection. Pray for the grace and light of hope that gives tolerance and forgiveness.

# MICAH READING GUIDE

## *At a Glance*

| | |
|---|---|
| Who are the main players? | Micah |
| What should I look for? | Micah must be read as an anthology of short speeches rather than as a unified narrative. It is especially important to distinguish the judgment speeches from the salvation speeches and to keep the historical context in mind. |
| When did this take place? | Micah's prophetic career spanned the latter part of the eighth century B.C. |
| Where did these events occur? | Micah's home was the small village of Moresheth, southwest of Jerusalem, but his speeches are directed to Samaria and Jerusalem, capital cities of the north and the south. |
| Why was this book written? | Micah, a contemporary of Amos, Hosea, and Isaiah, was largely preoccupied with the same issues of social justice and the coming Assyrian invasion. He accuses the ruling elite of corruption and misleading the people. He has little patience for false prophets. |
| What is the story? | His judgment speeches (chs 1–3; 6 and 7:1–7) focus on Samaria and Jerusalem and their ruling elite who were both corrupt and complacent. Rulers, judges, and prophets are accused of corruption and mistreating and misleading the people. His salvation speeches (chs 4–5, and 7:8–20) describe the misfortune their listeners have experienced and predict a period of renewal and restoration for them. He ends with a note of hope and promise. |

Micah, in his role as prophet, resembles Jeremiah. He spoke out against prophets who wanted to be popular. They said what people wanted to hear and were more concerned about their own well-being than that of the nation. Micah saw the role of the true prophet "to declare to Jacob his crimes and to Israel his sins" (3:8). Because of this position, Micah stands as a lonely figure. Like Jeremiah, he was not successful in reaching the people, but trusted that God would vindicate him (7:7–10).

## Outline of the Book of Micah

| | |
|---|---|
| Mi 1–3 | Impending judgment |
| Mi 4–5 | (Added later) Restoration |
| Mi 6 | Indictment of Israel |
| Mi 7 | The prophet's reflection |

### The Impending Judgment (chs 1–3)

Micah begins with a description of an apparition of God. In Israel's tradition, such appearances of God were associated with God's saving action, as on Sinai. But in Micah, God is not coming to save, but to judge. Eighth-century Israel experiences God's presence in the invasion of the Assyrian army rather than in Sinai's fire and earthquake. According to Micah, the destruction would center on Jerusalem and Samaria, home to royalty and the ruling classes.

In chapter 2, the prophet gives the reason for the coming destruction: The rich force the small property owners into debt and eventually seize their property. It is only right, says Micah, that the Assyrians will seize the land from the rich.

In chapter 3, Micah attacks the complacency and illusion of some religious teaching and practice. It is not enough to say that no evil can come upon Israel because the LORD is in its midst. Such faith is not virtue for Micah. Virtue is in the practice of justice and in facing reality honestly. Faith cannot be based on any religious institution, no matter how sacred. Micah's prophecy that Zion would be plowed like a field was not what people wanted to hear. The prophecy was not fulfilled in Micah's time, but his words were justified later.

### The Prophecies of Restoration (chs 4–5)

As indicated above, these prophecies of restoration were probably added to Micah after the Babylonian exile. Two of them in particular show us the work of the postexilic editor. The prophecy of the restoration of the house of the LORD in 4:1–3 is also found in Isaiah 2:24. The idea of nations streaming to Jerusalem is not new, but it speaks of the time after the exile when Jews who lived in other lands came to Jerusalem on pilgrimage. The placement of this prophecy immediately after the prediction that Zion would become a plowed field is typical of the editors of the prophetic books. They often spoke of hope after destruction or judgment. In the same way, the Temple and its rituals had taken on too much importance in the eighth century; now, after the exile, the Temple has a potential for uniting the people and strengthening faith.

The prophecy about Bethlehem in Micah 5:1–4 is familiar to Christians for obvious reasons. The postexilic editor had at least two reasons for inserting it here: first, to build up hope, suggesting that David's kingly line would be restored, and second, by mentioning Bethlehem rather than Jerusalem, the editor is pointing to a humbler, simpler monarchy free of big city corruption.

### The Indictment of Israel (ch 6)

Micah recalls the covenant, God's faithfulness, and Israel's failure in a speech that sounds like a courtroom scene (compare Am 2). The prophet returns to the themes of justice and honesty in his indictment of Israel's false religion, which included performing rituals to further their own interests.

Micah's solutions sound simple on the surface. Although offerings of thousands of animals, vats of expensive oil, and even first-born children sound impressive, God rejects these showy attempts at faithfulness. True religion is not based on certain rituals or beliefs, only this, "to do justice and to love goodness, and to walk humbly with your God" (6:8). Notice the emphasis on action and humility.

### The Concluding Indictment and Prayer (ch 7)

The first six verses of this chapter describe a society where corruption and lawlessness are prevalent. The only solution, according to Micah, is repentance and renewed reliance on the LORD. The confession and hope for ultimate victory in verses 8–10, spoken probably by a personified Jerusalem to the enemy, Assyria, is followed by the vision of a return from exile (vv. 12–13) and hope for the restoration of prosperity (vv. 14–15) and the downfall of enemies (vv. 16–17). Finally, Micah ends with the hope in a God who will forgive the sins of the people and restore them to divine favor.

**Questions for Discussion and Reflection**

***Group Sharing/Discussion***

1. In the eight century B.C., Israel experienced God through the invading and destroying Assyrian army. In chapter 2 Micah gives the reasons for this coming destruction. What does he say are the reasons that God destroys Zion?

***In Our Lives***

1. The rich devised ways of forcing smaller landowners into debt and then seized their land. Their greed would be in vain because of the Assyrian army. What parallels do you see in modern life? What makes greed so wrong?

2. A true prophet who points out the ills of a society is often not popular. What true prophets today are unpopular? How might we respond to them as individuals, as a church, as a nation?

3. Micah had little respect for the professional prophets who told people what they wanted to hear and led them astray. Who are the modern professional prophets who lack integrity and mislead us?

***Individual/Personal Reflection/Action***

1. An oracle of hope immediately follows Micah's prediction that Zion would become a plowed field. In 5:1–4 he speaks of a ruler who will come from Bethlehem, David's birthplace. Christians have treasured this prophecy. What did this mean for the early Christians? Does the fact that Jesus comes from Bethlehem have any significance for you?

# NAHUM READING GUIDE

*At a Glance*

| | |
|---|---|
| Who are the main players? | Nahum City of Nineveh |
| What should I look for? | The oracles of Nahum are concerned with a single event, the fall of Nineveh in 612 B.C. Because Assyria long dominated Israel with taxes and colonial acquisitions, the euphoria of the prophet is understandable. Yet behind these emotions lies a belief in God's just government of world affairs. |
| When did this take place? | Shortly before the fall of Nineveh in 612 B.C. |
| Where did these events occur? | In Nineveh, the capital of the Assyrian empire for one hundred years |
| What is the story? | Nineveh, an ancient and powerful Assyrian city, became the capital and symbol of the entire empire itself, until it fell to the armies of the Medes and the Babylonians in 612 B.C. These speeches predicting Nineveh's end were written by the prophet Nahum shortly before that fall. |

## Nahum's Message

Nahum's sole concern is the fall of the Assyrian capital city of Nineveh. The prophet is euphoric:

> At this moment on the mountains the footsteps of one bearing good news, announcing peace! Celebrate. . . . For never again with destroyers invade you . . . (2:1)

It is characteristic of biblical prophecy that the fall of one Gentile nation at the hands of another is assumed to be the work of the LORD.

## Outline of the Book of Nahum

Na 1:2–2:1:3 The LORD's coming in judgment

Na 2:2–3:19 The fall of Nineveh

## A Jealous God

The opening verse of Nahum's prophecy is somewhat shocking to modern ears: "A jealous and avenging God is the LORD" (1:2). However, this image of God is neither new nor incompatible with a God of mercy and love. In the book of

Exodus, the LORD is called a "warrior" (15:3) and described as jealous on Sinai (20:50). Even Nahum, in the very next verse after "jealous and avenging," says that "The LORD is slow to anger . . ." (1:3).

The modern reader could, no doubt, benefit by taking on the ancient Hebrew's ability to deal with ambiguity when it comes to God. This means letting diverse or seemingly contradictory statements about God stand side by side. It is an acknowledgment that God is beyond our ability to completely explain. It also allows God's wrath to be seen as an expression of justice.

**The Fall of Nineveh**

Nahum's description of Nineveh's destruction is a series of vibrant images showing the once-formidable city brought to its knees. The city once full of loot is now plundered and laid waste (2:10–11; 3:1); the strongest walls crumble at a mere shake (3:12); and those who are supposed to protect the city have fallen asleep on the job (3:18). Nineveh will suffer the same fate it brought to the cities conquered by Assyria.

Is it any wonder that "All who hear this news of you clap their hands over you; For who has not suffered under your malice?" (3:19).

**A Short-Sighted Prophecy**

Judah's freedom, proclaimed by Nahum, was short-lived. It was only 15 years before another oppressor would lay siege to Jerusalem. Nahum's short prophecy is a lesson in realistic hope; no power lasts forever, but neither is complete freedom attained in this life.

Nahum's influence can be seen in the book of Revelation. John uses the image of the harlot from Nahum (3:4) in anticipating the fall of Rome.

**Questions for Discussion and Reflection**

***Group Sharing/Discussion***

1. What event in history does the prophecy of Nahum deal with? How did Assyria treat the countries it conquered?

***In Our Lives***

1. What do you think of the opening verse of Nahum's prophecy, "A jealous and avenging God is the LORD"? This aspect of divinity was never thought to be incompatible with mercy and love. What do you think is the image of God in the minds of Nahum's listeners? Our image of God both personally and socially grows with experience and learning. Take time to reflect upon your personal image of God.

***Individual/Personal Reflection/Action***

1. The lesson of Nahum is two edged: The fall of Nineveh reminds us all tyrants fall sooner or later, which is cause for hope. But the fall of a particular tyrant is not the end of all tyrants. Nahum's exaltation over the fall of Nineveh is echoed in the New Testament in John's anticipation of the fall of Rome (Rev 17–19). Meditate on the rhythm of God's hope in the history of nations and peoples.

2. Words worth pondering and remembering from Nahum 1:2a, 3a, 7.

A jealous and avenging God is the LORD,
an avenger is the LORD, full of wrath; . . . (Na 1:2a)
The LORD is slow to anger, yet great in power,
the LORD will not leave the guilty
unpunished. . . . (Na 1:3a)
The LORD is good, a refuge on the day of
distress;
Taking care of those who look to him
for protection, . . . (Na 1:7)

Try the "both/and" approach when thinking about God. See how many times you can fill in the blanks: God is both ____ and ____.

# HABAKKUK READING GUIDE

*At a Glance*

| | |
|---|---|
| Who are the main players? | Habakkuk |
| What should I look for? | Note how the prophet calls God to account for his government of the world. Also, be enriched by the religious faith of the prophet, especially in chapter 3, Habakkuk's prayer that his vision be fulfilled. |
| When did this take place? | This prophecy dates from the years 605–597 B.C. |

| | |
|---|---|
| Where did these events occur? | In Judah where the situation was desperate at this time, with political intrigue and religious idolatry widespread in the small kingdom |
| Why was this book written? | The prophet Habakkuk is primarily concerned about believing in God's just rule over the world, which appears to be overwhelmingly unjust. |
| What is the story? | The prophecy of Habakkuk is considerably more reflective than that of Nahum. He prophesied a few years later. Habakkuk prophesied when the Babylonian threat had become obvious. He ponders not only that danger, but also the underlying problem of injustice and questions why God allows such a situation to prevail. |

## Outline of the Book of Habakkuk

| | |
|---|---|
| Habakkuk 1–2 | A dialogue between the prophet and the LORD |
| Habakkuk 3 | A hymn of faith |

### The Dialogue (chs 1–2)

Habakkuk's prophecy comes shortly after that of Nahum (see timeline for Nahum), when the Babylonian threat was even more obvious, but Habakkuk is more reflective than Nahum. He reacts to the immediate danger, but he also seeks to understand the problem. He asks the age-old questions: Why do the wicked prevail over the just? How can God allow such a situation to exist? Is God just? These types of questions, called theodicy, or the effort to explain the existence of evil, are more typical of wisdom literature (particularly Job) and apocalyptic (see Apocalypse in the glossary) literature than of prophecy.

Habakkuk was concerned first of all with the injustice within Jewish society. He applies the woes in chapter 2 to the arrogant and wealthy. This section is similar to chapter 22 of Jeremiah, written at about the same time (609–598 B.C.), accusing King Jehoiakim of oppression and exploitation. Habakkuk's woes could be directed to the king as well.

Habakkuk's answer to the questions of God's justice is not an explanation, but a promise that the situation will be set aright in the future. At first the solution seems worse than the problem: God will raise up the Babylonians (1:6–11) to conquer Israel. Just as Isaiah (ch 10) had spoken of Assyria as the rod of the LORD's anger, Babylon will bring about the downfall of King Jehoiakim. The comparison to Isaiah continues in the implied hope of Habakkuk; like the rod that would eventually be destroyed, so too will Babylon. It is unclear in the prophecy whether Habakkuk is referring to Babylon or the wicked in Judah because their behavior is similar (the wicked devouring the just). The lesson, however, is clear. Even though justice is not apparent in the world, one should trust in the LORD and be patient.

### Righteousness and Faith (ch 3)

Faith according to Habakkuk might be closer to the traditional Christian understanding of hope. For the prophet, faith is simply the trust in God that enables one to wait for the future. The person who only looks at the present and sees no justice in the world and, therefore, judges that God is not in control lacks faith. The righteous or faithful one takes a longer view, trusts that justice will prevail, and is content to wait for it.

This hope in the future is expressed poetically in the hymn in chapter 3. The image of God coming in triumph as a warrior stands in a long tradition of such hymns (see Dt 33; Jgs 5; Mi 1). The early hymns of this kind referred to God's past activity on behalf of Israel. Habakkuk expects this victory in the future. It will be directed against "the people who attack us" (3:16), presumably the Babylonians but maybe the Jewish oppressors as well. The prophet pictures a decisive intervention of God to wipe out all wickedness and oppression. This whole description of the future is close to what we find later in the apocalyptic literature and explains why Habakkuk was popular in apocalyptic circles; for example, the Dead Sea Scrolls include a commentary on Habakkuk.

**Questions for Discussion and Reflection**

***Group Sharing/Discussion***

1. The message of Habakkuk is clear. Even though justice is not apparent in the world, one should trust in the LORD and be patient. After some reflection share your view on this. Why are the wicked successful? Why does God allow the wicked to devour the righteous? Why should we be patient? What helps with being patient?

***In Our Lives***

1. The contrast in Habakkuk is between the rash man and one who is able to take the long view. His famous saying (2:4) reads, "the just one who is righteous because of his faith shall live." St. Paul builds on this in his reflections on faith (e.g., see Rom 1:17 and Gal 3:11.) Take time to compare Habakkuk's vision with Paul's development.

***Individual/Personal Reflection/Action***

1. The faith of Habakkuk is a faith against appearances (3:17ff). It is based on the conviction that God is just and so justice will ultimately prevail. The value of this faith does not depend upon its fulfillment, but on its power to transform the lives of the faithful. It is a faith that encourages us to trust in God's activity in our midst. It is a faith that also encourages us to work against oppression and exploitation. Reflect on your faith. What is its source and foundation? Its strength? Its expressions?

# ZEPHANIAH READING GUIDE

***At a Glance***

| | |
|---|---|
| Who are the main players? | Zephaniah |
| What should I look for? | In a time of religious decline, notice the worshiping of false gods in rites that are false to the monotheism of Moses. Yet, the LORD in His mercy will spare a holy remnant. |
| When did this take place? | During the reign of Josiah, who governed the southern kingdom of Judah during 640–609 B.C. |
| Where did these events occur? | In the kingdom of Judah |
| Why was this book written? | The emphasis of Zephaniah is not on the sins of Judah, but on the destructiveness of the Day of the LORD, the result of idolatry by the people. It is portrayed in cosmic terms: God will make an end of all who live on earth. The day of judgment is seen as the vindication of the majesty of God against the unworthiness of the people. |
| What is the story? | Zephaniah's prophecy has three sections: A Day of Judgment for Judah, A Day of Judgment on the Nations, and Reproach and Promise for Jerusalem. |

Zephaniah prophesied a little earlier than Nahum and Habakkuk and at the same time that Jeremiah was getting started, during the reign of Josiah who instituted the deuteronomic reform (2 Kgs 22–23). Idolatry is one of Zephaniah's themes because purifying Temple worship was the focus of the reform, but almost everything is expressed in terms of the Day of the LORD.

## A Day of Judgment for Judah (ch 1)

The first oracle on the Day of the LORD is directed against Judah for idolatry and lack of faith in the LORD (1:12). Zephaniah emphasizes not the sins of Judah, but the destructiveness of the Day of the LORD. It is portrayed in cosmic terms: God will make an end of all who live on earth. The day of judgment is a vindication of the majesty of God against the unworthiness of the people.

## A Day of Judgment on the Nations (ch 2)

Judah is not the only object of the LORD's wrath. Chapter 2 lists the surrounding nations and seems to build up to Assyria, the most arrogant of all. The prophet quotes Nineveh's boast: "I and there is no one else" (2:15), the same as that of Babylon (Is 47:10). The most fundamental human sin is self-divinization, and it is seen again and again throughout the Bible. Zephaniah's prophecies of the Day of the LORD dramatize the gulf between God and humanity and are basically a put-down of human pride.

## Reproach and Promise for Jerusalem (ch 3)

Chapter 3 does not use the phrase "Day of the LORD" but deals with related themes. The phrase "on that day" (3:11) refers to the Day of the LORD and is often used to introduce additions to the prophetic books in this period after the exile.

Jerusalem is denounced as the tyrannical city that accepts no correction (3:1–8), which may refer to the failure of the reform or the rejection of the prophet. Finally, the last oracle (3:11–20) promises restoration for Jerusalem, when God "will leave as a remnant in your midst a people humble and lowly." This reference to the remnant, familiar from the preaching of Isaiah, could be a sign of Isaiah's influence on Zephaniah, but it is more likely that it is another example of an optimistic oracle added on by an editor.

Whether or not these last words come from Zephaniah, they have their own validity. Just as the judgments on Assyria and Babylon were not God's last words to Israel, hope is still possible even after the destructive Day of the LORD.

**Questions for Discussion and Reflection**

***Group Sharing/Discussion***

1. One of Zephaniah's themes concerns idolatry (1:4–8). The prophet speaks against the king's sons for adopting foreign customs. Why is this considered idolatry?

***In Our Lives***

1. What idolatries does Zephaniah refer to in his first oracle?

***Individual/Personal Reflection/Action***

1. Self-divinization is a charge often made by the prophets. Meditate on the many forms of self-divinization in the world. What does it look like? How is it expressed?

2. Remember that God will send as a remnant in your midst a people humble and lowly. Who do you know who might fit the description in 3:12–13? What can you do to emulate them?

# HAGGAI READING GUIDE

*At a Glance*

| | |
|---|---|
| Who are the main players? | Haggai Zerubbabel |
| What should I look for? | Haggai preached to a people who returned from exile to a ruined land and are no longer in control of their own affairs. He encourages reconstructing the Temple. |
| When did this take place? | In the second year of Darius, 520 B.C. |
| Where did these events occur? | In Judah |
| Why was this book written? | At a time of defeatism, Haggai exhorted and encouraged the people to complete the great task of rebuilding the Temple. |
| What is the story? | His prophecy is divided into five oracles: (1) the call to rebuild the Temple; (2) the glory of the Temple; (3) an instruction on offering sacrifice; (4) the blessings of rebuilding the Temple; and (5) a pledge to Zerubbabel. |

There are two main emphases of Haggai's prophetic work, and they both have to do with the Temple and the difficult situation of the returned exiles (the "remnant of the people"). Along with Zechariah, Haggai encourages the people to complete the Temple (Ezr 5:1), and then he must help them deal with their disappointment after its completion.

## Exhortation to Rebuild (ch 1)

The reasons for delaying the completion of the Temple all make sense, whether in ancient or modern times. The returned exiles were poverty-stricken; in addition, they were suffering under drought and crop failure. It was obvious that they needed houses for shelter and God did not. Haggai's interpretation of this situation was that their difficulties were due to the fact that they had not rebuilt the Temple but had concentrated instead on rebuilding their own homes.

There is wisdom in the prophet's exhortation to rebuild the Temple. The morale of the community would also be built by working on a common project, especially one that would focus the people's attention on God. Recall the experience of the poor European immigrant communities in the United States in the late nineteenth and early twentieth centuries. They built impressive churches and schools at great sacrifice to themselves. Their value to these communities was enormous, not just economically, but as a sign of their faith in God and what they could accomplish by working together.

## The Reaction to the Finished Temple (ch 2)

The completion of the Temple was a disappointment. Those who could remember Solomon's Temple lamented because this new Temple was so puny by comparison (2:3). Not only that, the completion did not bring about the reversal of fortunes that Haggai had predicted. His reaction is typical of prophets whose predictions don't come to pass. He says it is delayed, and the reason for the delay is that the people are not observing the purity laws, and their offerings are unclean. He ends by reaffirming that God will shake the heavens and the earth when conditions are right.

This situation points out the problem with prophecies that make specific predictions. The hopes raised are good for the morale of the community, but only for a time. When they are not fulfilled, it leads to disillusionment. The same problem will tend to discredit apocalyptic and messianic expectations of later times.

## The Lessons of Haggai

There are two lessons to be learned from Haggai. One is that hope should not be focused on specific predictions, and the other is the value of religious symbols and ritual for bringing people together. The Temple may not have satisfied immediate expectations, but it contributed to Jewish life for the next 500 years and far outweighed the initial disappointments.

### Questions for Discussion and Reflection

***Group Sharing/Discussion***

1. The completion of the Temple did not bring dramatic reversal of their fortunes for the people that Haggai had predicted. He learned that hope should not be focused on a specific prediction. Give an example of how you have learned a similar lesson.

***In Our Lives***

1. The people had put building their own homes before the building of the Temple. Building the Temple helped their morale by focusing on the community project rather than their own problems. Why was this helpful? What were the values of religious symbols, for example, the Temple and rituals, for the people? Were there any long-term values? What role do religious symbols play in our life?

2. Describe a situation when you have experienced the value of people working together on a common project for the community. Is there a community project we should initiate for ourselves?

***Individual/Personal Reflection/Action***

1. Reflect upon and remember these words of Haggai (2:4c–5).

> For I am with you—oracle of the LORD of Hosts
> This is the commitment I made to you
> when you came out of Egypt,
> My spirit remains in your midst;
> do not fear!

Spend time reflecting on those expressions of your faith that sustain you through the difficulties and disappointments of life. Try writing them in your journal.

# ZECHARIAH READING GUIDE

## *At a Glance*

| | |
|---|---|
| Who are the main players? | Zechariah Joshua Zerubbabel |
| What should I look for? | Zechariah should be read as a book in two parts: the visions of Zechariah (chs 1–8) and the speeches of an anonymous prophetic figure of a later time (chs 9–12). The eight visions are meant to promote the rebuilding of the Temple and to encourage exiles to return. In the second section the messianic vision of the coming of the Prince of Peace begins with chapter 9, verse 9. These verses are used by the Evangelists to describe the entry of Christ into Jerusalem. |
| When did this take place? | Zechariah's initial prophecy is dated to 520 B.C., the same year that Haggai received the prophetic call. |
| Where did these events occur? | In Judah |
| Why was this book written? | The prophet encouraged the people to complete the Temple after their return from exile. |
| What is the story? | The original oracles of Zechariah are characterized by a series of visions, which disclose the prophet's view of what is really going on in the postexilic period. In all eight of these visions, the hidden, heavenly activity is assuring and a source of confidence for the fledgling Jewish community. In the second section the messianic coming is envisioned, and the oracle proclaiming the final victory of God's people over the heathens is proclaimed. |

The book of Zechariah contains the work of more than one prophet. It is named for the prophet who, along with Haggai, encouraged the people to complete the Temple after their return from the exile. His work is found in chapters 1–8. The prophet of chapters 9–14 comes from a much later time. Some scholars point to a third prophet as the author of chapters 12–14.

## The Original Zechariah (chs 1–8)

These oracles are a series of visions that are explained to the prophet by an angel. This is the first time that the interpreting angel appears in biblical literature; it becomes common in later apocalyptic writings. The visions show the prophet's view of what is really going on in these times after the exile, revealing something that is hidden from the ordinary person. It is God's activity that is hidden. The prophet wants to assure the returned exiles that God is active among them. For example, the first vision shows four horsemen sent by God to patrol the earth to indicate that God is in control, although not visible. Similarly, in chapter 2, four heavenly blacksmiths come to beat down the nations and an angelic "man" makes preparations for the restoration of Jerusalem. All this is aimed at building up the confidence of the struggling community.

### High Priest and Governor

When Zechariah prophesied to the returned exiles, the monarchy had been destroyed, and there was no king. The Persians ruled the area. Zerubbabel, a descendant of David, was governor, and Joshua was the High Priest. In the absence of a king, the High Priest had additional power and authority.

Up until the time of the Babylonian exile, the prophets had been sharply critical of the king and usually the priests as well. Prophets like Amos condemned the monarchy and its religious practices for making the people complacent and, therefore, unfaithful. In this new situation, Zechariah takes a different stance and comes to the defense of the leaders, in opposition to their critics.

In the vision in chapter 3, the High Priest, Joshua, stands before the angel of the LORD and is accused by Satan. This is one of the earliest appearances of Satan in the Old Testament (see Jb 1–2 and 1 Chr 21:1). Satan is not yet portrayed as the Devil; rather, he is an angel in the service of God, serving as a prosecuting attorney. In Zechariah's vision, Satan represents the people in the community who are criticizing Joshua and receives a stinging rebuke from the angel of the LORD. Zechariah's point is not that Joshua is without fault, but that criticism is not appropriate when the community is struggling.

The prophet is equally positive about Zerubbabel, the governor. In chapter 4, the two leaders are pictured as olive trees, because both priest and king were anointed with oil. This type of anointing, incidentally, which goes back to the earliest days of kingship (see 1 Sm 10) is the source of the title "messiah" or "anointed one." In chapter 6, the prophet goes further and says that he has been commanded to make a crown for Zerubbabel. To make a king of a Davidic prince would have been extremely dangerous because the Persian rulers would, no doubt, have seen this as an act of rebellion. We don't know whether Zechariah ever carried it out, but we do know that the understanding of the monarchy became more and more idealized in the minds of the people in this period after the exile. The people hoped for a future messiah-king, the anointed one who would make Jerusalem again a holy city (8:3). Zechariah's visions helped keep alive this dream of justice and freedom.

### The Appreciation of Ritual

A positive view of ritual is another contrast to earlier prophets that we see in Zechariah. He shows that ritual is powerful in expressing human desires because it engages the emotions and motivations of the people performing it. In 5:5–11, he relates a vision of wickedness, pictured as a woman, placed in a bushel container and shipped off to Babylon (similar to the Scapegoat ritual in Lv 16). The ritual action of getting rid of wickedness is meant to strengthen the people's resolve to rid society of evil and to move them to action.

Zechariah also appreciates the limits of ritual. After the experience of the exile and the destruction of the Temple, Zechariah knew the importance of sacrifice but still leaned more toward the position of Hosea; "It is loyalty that I desire, not sacrifice" (Hos 6:6).

## Messianic Oracle and Allegory of the Shepherds (chs 9–11)

The messianic oracle in chapter 9 is famous because of its association with the Palm Sunday passages in Matthew 21:5 and John 12:15. The donkey was not as humble an animal in the ancient world as in modern times and was used by the nobility in Genesis and Judges. Here, however, the image is used to recall an earlier, simpler time to express the hope for a ruler to restore Solomon's empire without the arrogance of the monarchy, symbolized by the horses and chariots. Although the messianic age is usually described as a time of universal disarmament, the messianic oracle in chapter 9 sounds very war-like. The point here, similar to what is found in later apocalyptic writing, is that the LORD will fight for Judah. The human role is to maintain purity and be obedient to the law. This role of the LORD as warrior is in accord with much of Israelite tradition (see Ex 15:3).

The allegory of the shepherds in chapter 11 must be read against the background of two passages in Ezekiel, because Zechariah 11 reverses this earlier prophet's predictions of salvation. Ezekiel 34 speaks against the shepherds of Israel who exploited their flock. The mood changes, however, from judgment to salvation as the LORD takes over as shepherd. In chapter 37, Ezekiel takes two sticks, representing the two kingdoms of Israel and Judah, and joins them together, signifying that they would be one nation under David their king. In Zechariah 11 there are also exploitive shepherds but no movement to salvation, only slaughter. Also in Zechariah there are two staffs symbolizing two covenants, one with the nations and one between Judah and Israel. Both are broken in the course of the prophecy.

It is not clear when this prophecy was written or what context it addressed, but it is clearly an expression of extreme dissatisfaction and disillusionment with the situation after the exile. There is not a hint of the support for the institutional leaders found in chapters 1–8 or of the dream of justice and freedom. This anonymous prophet (sometimes called Deutero-Zechariah or "Second" Zechariah) can only proclaim judgment and try to make the people see reality for what it is.

## Chapters 12–14

The last three chapters of Zechariah are even more confusing than chapters 9–11. There is persistent criticism of the rulers, especially in chapter 13: a "song of the sword" against the shepherd with a prediction that only a third of the people will be spared; and a surprising prediction of the end of prophecy. A motif of a final battle in Jerusalem runs through these chapters, especially 12 and 14, with the prophet expressing hope for reconciliation (between the leaders in Jerusalem and the people they oppressed) and a remarkable universalism (wanting to include the Egyptians in the worship of the true God).

After Haggai and Zechariah, prophets seemed to have lost status. This was partly due to the failure of predictions, the conflict between prophets themselves, and the willingness of some to mislead the people for their own gain. Although some of this could be said of some earlier times, these late postexilic prophets do not command the same respect as their predecessors; their real names are not even used (e.g., Deutero-Zechariah).

### Questions for Discussion and Reflection

***Group Sharing/Discussion***

1. Zechariah's first vision shows four horsemen whom the LORD has sent to patrol the earth. What do you see as the meaning or implication of this vision?

2. In chapter 2 the visions show four heavenly blacksmiths coming to beat down the "horns" of the nations. What understanding do you find in this vision?

***In Our Lives***

1. In chapter 7 Zechariah is asked about the proper number of fast days. He answers that motivation is more important than number. What do you think? Should there be specific fasting days? What motivates you to fast?

2. Zechariah's attitude toward the institutions and their leadership differed from the earlier prophets. He was more supportive because the community was struggling. Pick an institution to which you belong, such as your local church or local government, and list some ways in which you can be both supportive and yet constructively critical.

3. What values govern whether or not you give support to designated leaders?

***Individual/Personal Reflection/Action***

1. Zechariah thought that what is most important is "Judge with true justice, and show kindness and compassion toward each other" (7:9). He echoes Hosea's "it is loyalty that I desire, not sacrifice." Take some time to reflect and evaluate your life in respect to these qualities: living truthfully and showing kindness and compassion.

# MALACHI READING GUIDE

## *At a Glance*

| | |
|---|---|
| Who are the main players? | Malachi Priests People |
| What should I look for? | Malachi preached to a disillusioned people and a failed leadership. This challenge he faced must be kept in mind as you read his speeches. He is primarily concerned about a lack of devotion and seriousness in Temple worship and about a lack of fidelity in Judah's social relationships. |
| When did this take place? | This work was composed by an anonymous writer shortly before Nehemiah's arrival in Jerusalem (455 B.C.). |
| Where did these events occur? | Judah |
| Why was this book written? | The prophecy gives a picture of life in the Jewish community returned from Babylon; his criticism of the abuses and religious indifference prepare the way for reforms. |

What is the story? The prophet addresses these issues in a series of disputations: He blames the Temple Priesthood for its impure offerings and improper teachings and Judah's people for the meager contributions. Further, he blames the people for the lack of faithfulness in family relationships and in obligations to the poor. He replies to the question, "Where is the God of justice?" that the Day of the LORD is coming. But first the forerunner must clear the way for repentance and true worship.

We do not know who wrote these three chapters that make up the last prophetic book. "Malachi" is probably not a proper name but simply a characterization: "my messenger." The word is taken from 3:1, "Now I am sending my messenger," to designate the one through whom this word of the LORD is given. The book is made up of six oracles; all except the first are critical of Judah, the priesthood, and the people.

## The Priesthood (1:6–2:9)

Malachi, like many prophets before him, is critical of the priesthood. However, the prophet is not opposed to the priesthood as a whole; in fact, he has the greatest respect for the ideal of the priesthood. His problem with the priests is that they have been offering cheap sacrifices, sick and lame animals. His point is that an offering represents the person bringing it. No one would offer a sick animal to the governor, so why would the priests offer one to God?

A familiar and somewhat surprising line is found in 1:11, "from the rising of the sun to its setting, my name is great among the nations." It is not certain what the prophet had in mind, because the Gentiles did not worship the LORD explicitly. It could refer to those Jews who were spread out among all the nations (the Diaspora) or to the Persian kings who were generous in supporting the Temple. A third possibility would point to a decidedly broad-minded and liberal attitude. Because the LORD is called the God of Heaven (Ezr 6:10), then the High God of the Persians and other deities could also be acknowledged as "the God of Heaven." This would mean that the Gentiles worshiped the same God as the Jews!

## Breaches of Faith (2:10–17)

Another surprising phrase is found in the third oracle (2:10–17). The prophet begins with the question: "Have we not all one father?" Then he denounces two breaches of faith: Judah's marriage to a "daughter of a foreign god" (2:11) and the divorce of "the wife of your youth" (2:14).

The usual explanation for this passage is that Jewish men were divorcing the Jewish wives of their youth and marrying Gentile women, possibly for social reasons. This led to their involvement in the cult of pagan deities. So the question "Have we not all one Father?" is addressed only to Jews and does not reflect as universal an attitude as it seems.

Another interpretation is based on the fact that there is no other evidence that Jews in the postexilic period divorced their Jewish wives. Once a marriage had been entered into, it was sacred. The Jewish men should have seen to it that their offspring were "godly" (2:15). Conversion of the spouses, rather than divorce, was the solution. The "one Father," then, is the creator of all, Jews and Gentiles. Ethnic distinctions do not matter if one is willing to recognize the one God.

If this interpretation is correct, Malachi exhibits some of the spirit of St. Paul in his openness to the Gentiles. It also points to the diversity of opinion in Judaism at this time. Ezekiel (44:7) insisted that no "foreigners, uncircumcised in heart and flesh" be admitted to the Temple.

## The Day of the LORD (ch 3)

The final chapter of the book is dominated by the expectation that God will come in judgment, an adaptation of the traditional Day of the LORD. It is from this chapter that Handel borrowed the image of the refiner's fire for his *Messiah*. Malachi is also the source of the motif of the messenger who prepares the way and is first identified as Elijah the prophet. In the New Testament, John the Baptist is cast in this role (Mt 11:14; 17:12f). It is likely that the prophet we call Malachi saw himself in this role.

The final oracle of Malachi is also the conclusion of all the prophetic books. The editors refer to Moses as a way of reinforcing the laws of the Pentateuch. They also underline the theme of the coming judgment. The prophetic books not only remind us of the past, but motivate us in the present by making us look into the future.

**Questions for Discussion and Reflection**

***Group Sharing/Discussion***

1. The most startling statement in Malachi is the declaration that "from the rising of the sun to its setting, my name is great among the nations" (1:11). The Gentile nations did not worship the LORD explicitly, but what do you think the prophet had in mind?

2. Malachi stands in a long line of prophets who are critical of the priesthood who were offering "cheap sacrifices." What did this "cheap sacrifice" consist of? What did such a cheap sacrifice imply regarding the relationship with God?

***In Our Lives***

1. Malachi has the greatest respect for the ideal of priesthood. He mentions a covenant with Levi (2:4), which is never mentioned in the Pentateuch or historical books. What is your vision of the ideal priest? After reflecting on your own vision, compare this with what the Church teaches, for instance, in the Vatican II document, *Decree on the Ministry and Life of Priests*.

2. "For I hate divorce says the LORD" (2:16). Malachi states this categorically. This view contrasts with Ezra's strong policy for Jews to divorce their foreign wives. Malachi, despite his disapproval of those mixed marriages, thought once a marriage was entered into, it was sacred. How do you feel about Malachi's view of marriage and divorce?

***Individual/Personal Reflection/Action***

1. Malachi says that "one father" is creator for all, Jews and Gentiles. He believes if foreigners were willing to convert to Judaism, he would welcome them into the Temple. Ethnic distinctions don't matter. Ezekiel (44:7) believes that no foreigners were allowed into the Temple. In contrast, Isaiah had a more open attitude to foreigners, similar to Malachi's. The prophets in Israel had different religious views, for example, concerning foreigners in the Temple and the one God of all.

Do you see any modern parallels to the prophets' diversity? How can you ensure that all ethnic groups feel welcome in your church? In your workplace? In your home? What might you do to encourage such diversity in your church?

# THE GOSPELS

## The Synoptic Gospels

Because of their striking similarities, the three Gospels of Matthew, Mark, and Luke have traditionally been called the "synoptic" Gospels, from the Greek meaning to "view together." The observer of these three Gospels would, in fact, notice many parallels among these stories of Jesus if they were laid side by side. (See the "Harmony of the Gospels" that follows.)

At the same time, the synoptic Gospels are different from John's Gospel. For example, in each of the synoptic Gospels, Jesus begins his public ministry of teaching and healing in Galilee, travels with his disciples on a single purposeful journey to Jerusalem, and there experiences final rejection, death and, ultimately, resurrection. Jesus' sayings in these Gospels are generally either succinct and pointed or in the story form of the parable; his actions are characterized by marvelous healings and exorcisms; a major theme of his preaching is the advent of the "Rule of God." In John, on the other hand, Jesus moves back and forth between Galilee and Judea, and his teaching is often expressed in long, meditative discourses. There are no parables in John, no exorcisms, and fewer healing stories; the Rule of God motif plays a very minor role.

But the three synoptic Gospels develop their own distinct view of Jesus and his mission. Mark, for instance, begins his story of Jesus with his baptism at the Jordan, whereas Matthew, by means of the Infancy Narrative at the beginning of the Gospel, traces Jesus' origin back into the history of Israel. Luke, too, begins with an infancy narrative, but gives much more positive emphasis to Jerusalem than either Mark or Matthew. In Luke's Gospel the young Jesus goes to Jerusalem to listen to the teachers in the Temple courtyard, and the disciples of Jesus will gather to pray after his resurrection in the Jerusalem Temple. Luke also adds a second volume to his Gospel; the Acts of the Apostles picks up the story of Jesus and his apostles where the Gospel left off and shows its continuing force as the community of the Risen Christ moves out into the world.

Both the similarities and the differences among the synoptic Gospels have led to ongoing debate about their interrelationship. Analyses of the style and content of Mark led scholars to conclude that Mark was the first Gospel written, with Matthew and Luke directly dependent on Mark. The presence of other material in Matthew and Luke that was not found in Mark, such as the sayings of Jesus in the Sermon on the Mount, led to the hypothesis of an additional source for Matthew and Luke. This hypothetical source of material—which scholars call "Q" (from the German word *Quelle* or "source")—was probably a collection of sayings and parables of Jesus that circulated in the earliest Christian community. Independently of each other, if this hypothesis is correct, Matthew and Luke blended this source with their new renditions of Mark and perhaps with some other materials or traditions specific to their own communities.

Scholars assume, therefore, that Mark was the first Gospel to be written and that Mark, in fact, set the basic format for the story of Jesus, a format that both Matthew and Luke used as the starting point for their own narratives. This relationship accounts for the similarities among the Gospels. Each Gospel writer's particular interpretation of Mark, the use of other sources, and the unique pastoral and theological perspectives of the writers and their local churches lead to the distinctiveness of each of the synoptics.

The issue of the relationship of John's Gospel to the synoptics is more problematic. Until the midpoint of this century, most modern biblical scholars assumed that John knew of the synoptic Gospels and that his own Gospel was a very distinctive variation on the synoptic tradition. But more recently, a significant number of scholars speculate that John may represent an independent stream of tradition that had little, if any, contact with the synoptic Gospels.

*The Four Gospels at a Glance*

| **Matthew** | **Mark** | **Luke** | **John** |
|---|---|---|---|
| **DATE OF WRITING** | | | |
| A.D. 70–90 | A.D. 65–70 | A.D. 70–90 | A.D. 90–100 |
| **PLACE OF WRITING** | | | |
| Antioch in Syria | Rome | Greece | Syria or Palestine |
| **TARGET AUDIENCE** | | | |
| Jewish Christians | Gentiles | Greeks | All Christians |
| **PURPOSE FOR WRITING** | | | |
| To assert that Jesus is the long-awaited Messiah who fulfills Israel's hopes and the words of the prophets | To present the person of Jesus through his actions and miracles | To give an orderly account of the ministry of Jesus, so readers will rely on the gospel to build their faith | To lead to faith in Jesus as God's son, so those who believe will gain eternal life |
| **PORTRAIT OF JESUS** | | | |
| Promised Messiah | Suffering servant, hidden Messiah | Son of Man | Son of God/Word of God |
| **CHARACTER OF THE AUTHOR** | | | |
| Teacher/Catechist | Storyteller | Historian | Theologian |
| **MAJOR EMPHASIS** | | | |
| Jesus' teachings | Jesus' actions | Jesus' humanity | Jesus' teachings |
| **THEMES** | | | |
| Jesus fulfilled Old Testament prophecy | The identity of Jesus | Salvation is a joyous surprise | The role of "signs" in building faith |
| Jesus identifies with the lowly | The importance of the cross | Salvation is offered to everyone | Dualistic struggle between forces of light and darkness |
| Jesus is the world's savior, not just Israel's | Discipleship | Jesus identifies with the lowly and respects and defends the dignity of all | Faith in Jesus is necessary for eternal life |
| | | Mary is the first disciple | Jesus is the divine son of God |

## *Harmony of the Gospels*

| | Matthew | Mark | Luke | John |
|---|---|---|---|---|
| The Divinity of Jesus | | | | 1:1–5 |
| Announcement of the Birth of John the Baptist | | | 1:5–25 | |
| The Betrothal of the Virgin Mary | 1:18 | | 1:27 | |
| The Announcement of the Birth of Jesus | | | 1:26–38 | |
| Mary Visits Elizabeth | | | 1:39–56 | |
| Joseph's Dream | 1:20–25 | | | |
| The Birth of John the Baptist | | | 1:57–80 | |
| The Birth of Jesus | | | 2:1–7 | |
| The Visit by the Shepherds | | | 2:8–20 | |
| The Circumcision and Naming of Jesus | | | 2:21 | |
| The Presentation in the Temple | | | 2:22–29 | |
| The Genealogy of Jesus | 1:1–17 | | 3:23–38 | |
| The Visit of the Magi | 2:1–12 | | | |
| The Flight to Egypt | 2:13–15 | | | |
| The Massacre of the Infants | 2:16–18 | | | |
| The Return from Egypt | 2:19–23 | | 2:39 | |
| The Boy Jesus in the Temple | | | 2:41 | |
| With the Teachers in the Temple | | | 2:46–50 | |
| Youth of Jesus | | | 2:51 | |
| The Preaching of John the Baptist | 3:1–4 | 1:1–8 | 3:1–18 | 1:6–15 |
| Baptism by John | 3:6 | 1:5 | 3:21 | |
| The First Testimony of the Baptist to Christ | 3:11–12 | 1:7–8 | | 1:29–34 |
| The Baptism of Jesus | 3:13–17 | 1:9–11 | 3:21–22 | |
| The Temptation of Jesus | 4:1–11 | 1:12–13 | 4:1–13 | |
| John the Baptist's Testimony to Himself | | | | 1:19–35 |
| The Call of the First Disciples | 4:18–22 | 1:16–20 | 5:1–11 | 1:37–51 |
| First Miracle at Cana | | | | 2:1–11 |
| Visit to Capernaum | | | | 2:12 |
| Cleansing of the Temple | 21:12–13 | 11:15–17 | 19:45–46 | 2:13–23 |
| Nicodemus | | | | 3:1–21 |
| The Final Witness of the Baptist | | | | 3:22–36 |
| The Samaritan Woman | | | | 4:1–42 |
| The Return to Galilee | | | | 4:43–45 |
| The Second Sign at Cana | | | | 4:46–54 |
| The Cure on a Sabbath | | | | 5:1–47 |
| Imprisonment of John the Baptist | 4:12; 14:3 | 1:14–15 | | 3:24 |
| The Beginning of the Galilean Ministry | 4:12–17 | 1:14–15:4 | 14–15 | |
| The Rejection at Nazareth | 13:54–58 | 6:1–4 | 4:16–27 | |
| Jesus Preaches at Capernaum | 4:13–17 | | | |
| The Cure of a Demoniac | | 1:23–27 | 4:33–36 | |
| The Cure of Peter's Mother-in-law | 8:14–15 | 1:29–31 | 4:38–39 | |
| Other Healings | 8:16–17 | 1:32–34 | 4:40–41 | |
| Circuit through Galilee | | 1:38–39 | 4:42–44 | |
| The Cleansing of a Leper | 8:1–4 | 1:40–45 | 5:12–18 | |
| Retirement for Solitary Prayer | | 1:45 | 5:16 | |
| The Healing of a Paralytic | 9:1–8 | 2:1–12 | 5:18–25 | |

| | Matthew | Mark | Luke | John |
|---|---|---|---|---|
| Call of Matthew | 9:9–17 | 2:13–22 | 5:27–39 | |
| Ministering to a Great Multitude | 4:23–25 | | 6:17–19 | |
| Picking Grain on the Sabbath | 12:1–8 | 2:23–28 | 6:1–5 | |
| The Man with the Withered Hand | 12:9–14 | 3:1–6 | 6:6–11 | |
| Retirement for Solitary Prayer | | | 6:12 | |
| The Mission of the Twelve | 10:1–4 | 3:13–19 | 6:13–16 | |
| | | 6:7–13 | 9:1–6 | |
| The Sermon on the Mount | 5:1–12 | | 6:20–26 | |
| The Healing of the Centurion's Servant | 8:5–13 | | 7:1–10 | |
| The Raising of the Widow's Son | | | 7:11–17 | |
| The Messengers from John the Baptist | 11:2–19 | | 7:18–35 | |
| The Pardon of the Sinful Woman | | | 7:36–50 | |
| The Beatitudes | 5:2–12 | | 6:20–26 | |
| Galilean Women Follow Jesus | | | 8:1–3 | |
| Jesus and Beelzebul | 12:22–28 | 3:23–30 | 11:14–23 | |
| Blasphemy against the Holy Spirit | 12:31–32 | | | |
| The Return of the Unclean Spirit | 12:43–45 | | 11:24–26 | |
| The True Family of Jesus | 12:46–50 | 3:31–35 | 8:19–21 | |
| The Parable of the Sower | 13:1–9 | 4:1–9 | 8:6–8 | |
| | | 4:14–20 | 8:11–15 | |
| The Parable of the Weeds among the Wheat | 13:24–30 | | | |
| The Parable of the Mustard Seed | 13:31–32 | 4:30–32 | 13:18–19 | |
| The Parable of the Yeast | 13:33 | | 13:20–21 | |
| The Parable of the Lamp | 5:15 | 4:21 | 8:16; 11:33 | |
| The Parable of the Buried Treasure | 13:44 | | | |
| The Parable of the Fine Pearl | 13:45–46 | | | |
| The Parable of the Thrown Net | 13:47–48 | | | |
| The Calming of the Storm at Sea | 8:24–27 | 4:37–41 | 8:23–25 | |
| The Healing of the Gergesene Demoniacs | 8:28–34 | 5:1–20 | 8:26–39 | |
| The Parable of the Bridegroom | 9:15 | | | |
| The Parable of the New Cloth | 9:16 | 2:21 | 5:36 | |
| The Parable of the New Wine in Old Bottles | 9:17 | 2:22 | 5:37–38 | |
| Miracles: Jairus' Daughter and the Woman with a Hemorrhage | 9:18–26 | 5:22–43 | 8:41–56 | |
| The Healing of Two Blind Men | 9:27–31 | | | |
| The Healing of a Mute Person | 9:32–34 | | | |
| The Mission of the Twelve | 10:1–4 | 6:7–12 | 9:1–6 | |
| Herod's Opinion of Jesus | 14:1–12 | 6:14–29 | 9:7–9 | |
| The Return of the Twelve and the Feeding of the Five Thousand | 14:13–21 | 6:31–44 | 9:10–17 | 6:1–14 |
| The Walking on the Water | 14:22–33 | 6:47–52 | | 6:16–21 |
| The Bread of Life Discourse | | | | 6:22–65 |
| Retirement for Solitary Prayer | 14:23 | 6:46 | | |
| The Tradition of the Elders | 15:1–20 | 7:1–23 | | |
| The Canaanite Woman's Faith | 15:24–29 | 7:24–30 | | |
| The Healing of Many People | 15:29–31 | | | |
| The Feeding of the Four Thousand | 15:32–39 | 8:1–9 | | |

| | Matthew | Mark | Luke | John |
|---|---|---|---|---|
| The Demand for a Sign: Weather | 16:1–4 | 8:11–13 | 12:54–56 | |
| The Leaven of the Pharisees and Sadducees | | 16:5–12 | 8:14–21 | |
| Peter's Confession of Christ | 16:13–20 | 8:27–30 | 9:18–20 | |
| The First Prediction of the Passion | 16:21–23 | 8:31–38 | 9:22–27 | |
| The Transfiguration of Jesus | 17:1–8 | 9:2–8 | 9:28–36 | |
| The Healing of a Boy with a Demon | 17:14–21 | 9:14–25 | 9:37–43 | |
| The Second Prediction of the Passion | 17:22–23 | 9:30–32 | 9:43–45 | |
| Payment of the Temple Tax | 17:24–27 | | | |
| The Greatest in the Kingdom | 18:1–5 | 9:33–37 | 9:46–48 | |
| The Parable of the Lost Sheep | 18:10–14 | | 15:1–7 | |
| A Brother Who Sins | 18:15–20 | | 17:3–4 | |
| A Lesson on Self-denial | 18:18 | | | |
| The Parable of the Unforgiving Servant | 18:23–35 | | | |
| The Departure for Jerusalem | | | 9:51–52 | |
| The Jealousy of the Samaritans | | | 9:53 | |
| The Anger of James and John | | | 9:54–56 | |
| The Feast of Tabernacles | | | | 7:1–10 |
| The First Dialogue | | | | 7:14–31 |
| Officers Sent to Arrest Jesus | | | | 7:32–36 |
| The Woman Caught in Adultery | | | | 8:1–11 |
| The Light of the World | | | | 8:12–20 |
| Jesus Threatened with Stoning | | | | 8:59 |
| The Man Born Blind | | | | 9:1–41 |
| The Good Shepherd | | | | 10:1–21 |
| The Mission of the Seventy-two | | | 10:1–12 | |
| The Return of the Seventy-two | | | 10:17–20 | |
| The Parable of the Good Samaritan | | | 10:29–37 | |
| The Visit to Martha and Mary | | | 10:38–42 | |
| The Lord's Prayer | 6:9–13 | | 11:1–4 | |
| Jesus and Beelzebul | 12:22–45 | 3:23–30 | 11:14–23 | |
| The Demand for a Sign: Jonah | 12:38–42 | | 11:29–32 | |
| God's Providence to Birds and Flowers | 10:29–31 | | 12:6–7; 12:24; 12:27–28 | |
| The Parable of the Rich Fool | | | 12:16–20 | |
| A Call to Repentance | | | 13:1–5 | |
| The Parable of the Barren Fig Tree | | | 13:6–9 | |
| The Cure of the Crippled Woman on the Sabbath | | | 13:10–17 | |
| The Feast of Dedication | | | | 10:22–42 |
| The Attempt to Stone Jesus | | | | 10:31 |
| Jesus Retires across the Jordan | | | | 10:40 |
| Salvation and Rejection | 7:13–14; 7:21–23 | | 13:22–30 | |
| Herod's Desire to Kill Jesus | | | 13:31–33 | |
| The Healing of the Man with Dropsy on the Sabbath | | | 14:1–6 | |
| The Parable of the Great Feast | 22:1–14 | | 14:15–24 | |
| The Parable of the Lost Sheep | 18:10–14 | | 15:1–7 | |

| | Matthew | Mark | Luke | John |
|---|---|---|---|---|
| The Parable of the Lost Coin | | | 15:8–10 | |
| The Parable of the Prodigal Son | | | 15:11–32 | |
| The Parable of the Dishonest Steward | | | 16:1–8 | |
| The Parable of the Rich Man and Lazarus | | | 16:19–31 | |
| The Raising of Lazarus | | | | 11:38–44 |
| The Return of Jesus from Peraea to Bethany | | | | 11:11–16 |
| The Resurrection of Lazarus | | | | 11:38–44 |
| The Session of the Sanhedrin | | | | 11:45–54 |
| The Last Passover | | | | 11:55 |
| The Last Journey in Jerusalem | 19:1 | 10:1 | 17:11 | |
| The Cleansing of the Ten Lepers | | | 17:11–19 | |
| The Parable of the Persistent Widow | | | 18:1–8 | |
| The Parable of the Pharisee and the Tax Collector | | | 18:9–14 | |
| Marriage and Divorce | 10:1–12 | 10:1–12 | | |
| Blessing of the Children | 19:13–15 | 10:13–16 | 18:15–17 | |
| The Rich Young Man | 10:16–30 | 10:17–22 | 18:18–23 | |
| The Workers in the Vineyard | 20:1–16 | | | |
| The Third Prediction of the Passion | 20:17–19 | 10:32–34 | 18:31–34 | |
| The Request of James and John | 20:20–28 | 10:35–45 | | |
| The Healing of Two Blind Men | 20:29–34 | 10:46–52 | 18:35–43 | |
| Zacchaeus the Tax Collector | | | 19:1–10 | |
| The Parable of the Talents | 25:14–30 | | 10:11–27 | |
| The Supper in Simon's House | 26:6–13 | 14:3–9 | | 12:1–9 |
| Mary Anoints Jesus | 26:7–13 | 14:3–9 | 12:3–8 | |
| The Entry into Jerusalem | 21:1–11 | 11:1–10 | 19:29–44 | 12:12–19 |
| The Survey of the Temple | | 11:11 | | |
| The Cursing of the Fig Tree | 21:18–19 | 11:12–14 | | |
| The Cleansing of the Temple | 21:12–17 | 11:15–18 | | |
| The Lesson of the Fig Tree | 21:20–22 | 11:20–25 | | |
| The Authority of Jesus Questioned | 21:23–27 | 11:27–33 | 20:1–8 | |
| The Parable of the Two Sons | 21:28–32 | | | |
| The Parable of the Tenants | 21:33–46 | 12:1–12 | 20:9–19 | |
| The Wedding Feast | 22:1–14 | | 14:15–24 | |
| Paying Taxes to the Emperor | 22:15–22 | 12:13–17 | 20:20–26 | |
| The Question about the Resurrection | 22:23–33 | 12:18–27 | 20:27–39 | |
| The Greatest Commandment | 22:34–40 | 12:28–34 | 11:25–28 | |
| The Question about David's Son | 22:41–46 | 12:35–37 | 20:41–44 | |
| Denunciation of the Scribes and Pharisees | 23:1–33 | 12:38–40 | 11:37–54 | |
| The Poor Widow's Contribution | | 12:41–44 | 21:1–4 | |
| The Coming of Jesus' Hour | | | | 12:20–23 |
| The Destruction of the Temple Foretold | 24:1–2 | 13:1–3 | | |
| The Parable of the Ten Virgins | 25:1–13 | | 10:11–27 | |
| The Judgment of Nations | 25:31–46 | | | |
| The Conspiracy Against Jesus | 26:3–5 | 14:1–2 | 22:1–2 | |
| The Betrayal by Judas | 26:14–16 | 14:10–11 | 22:3–6 | 18:2–5 |
| Preparation of the Passover | 26:17–19 | 14:12–16 | 22:7–13 | |
| The Washing of the Disciples' Feet | | | | 13:1–17 |

| | Matthew | Mark | Luke | John |
|---|---|---|---|---|
| The Lord's Supper | 26:26 | 14:22 | 22:14 | |
| The Betrayal Foretold | 26:21 | 14:18 | 22:21 | 13:21 |
| The Giving of the Morsel | | | | 13:26–27 |
| The Departure of Judas | | | | 13:30 |
| Peter's Denial Predicted | 26:31–35 | 14:27–31 | 22:21–23 | 13:36 |
| Blessing the Cup | 26:27–28 | 14:23–24 | 22:17 | |
| Last Supper Discourses | | | | 14:1–14 |
| The Prayer of Jesus | | | | 17:1 |
| The Hymn | 26:30 | 14:26 | | |
| The Agony in the Garden | 26:36 | 14:32–42 | 22:39–46 | 18:1 |
| | 26:44 | | | |
| Jesus is Comforted by the Angel | | | 22:43–44 | |
| The Sleep of the Apostles | 26:40–45 | 14:37–41 | 22:45–46 | |
| The Betrayal and Arrest of Jesus | 26:47–50 | 14:43–46 | 22:47–54a | 18:1–13a |
| Peter Smites Malchus | 26:51 | 14:47 | 22:50 | 18:10 |
| Jesus Heals the Ear of Malchus | | | 22:51 | |
| Jesus Forsaken by His Disciples | 26:56 | 14:50 | | |
| Jesus Led to Annas | | | | 18:12–13 |
| Jesus Before the Sanhedrin | 26:57 | 14:53 | 22:66 | |
| Peter Follows Jesus | 26:58 | 14:54 | 22:55 | 18:15 |
| The High Priest's Adjuration | 26:63 | 14:61 | 22:66 | |
| Jesus Condemned | 26:66–67 | 14:64–65 | 22:70–71 | |
| Peter's Denial of Jesus | 26:69–75 | 14:66–72 | 22:54–62 | 18:17–27 |
| Jesus before Pilate | 27:1 | 15:1 | 23:1 | 18:28 |
| The Death of Judas | 27:3 | | | |
| Pilate Comes out to the People | | | | 18:29 |
| Pilate Speaks to Jesus Privately | | | | 18:33 |
| Mockery by the Soldiers | 27:27 | 15:15 | 22:63–65 | 19:1 |
| Jesus Crowned with Thorns | 27:29 | 15:17 | | 19:2 |
| Jesus Exhibited by Pilate | | | | 19:5 |
| Jesus Questioned by Pilate | 27:11 | 15:2 | 23:2 | |
| Jesus Sent by Pilate to Herod | | | 23:6–11 | |
| The Sentence of Death | 27:15 | 15:6 | 23:17 | 19:12–16 |
| Pilate Receives a Message from his Wife | 27:19 | | | |
| Pilate Washes his Hands | 27:24 | | | |
| Pilate Releases Barabbas | 27:26 | 15:15 | 23:25 | |
| Pilate Delivers Jesus to Be Crucified | 27:26 | 15:15 | 23:25 | 19:16 |
| The Way of the Cross | 27:32 | 15:21 | 23:26 | |
| The Crucifixion | 27:33–44 | 15:22–32 | 23:33–43 | 19:17–30 |
| The Death of Jesus | 27:45–56 | 5:33–41 | 23:44–49 | |
| The Burial of Jesus | 27:57–61 | 15:42–47 | 23:50–56 | 19:38–42 |
| The Guard at the Tomb | 27:62–66 | | | |
| The Resurrection of Jesus | 28:1–10 | 16:1–8 | 24:1–12 | 20:1–10 |
| The Report of the Guards | 28:11–15 | | | |
| The Appearance to Mary Magdalene | | 16:9 | | 20:14 |
| The Appearance to the Women | | | | |
| Returning Home | 28:9 | | | |
| The Appearance to Two Disciples | | | | |
| Going to Emmaus | | 16:12 | 24:13 | |

| | Matthew | Mark | Luke | John |
|---|---|---|---|---|
| The Appearance to Peter | | | 24:34 | |
| The Appearance to the Disciples in Jerusalem | | | 24:36 | 20:10 |
| The Appearance to the Eleven Apostles | | 16:14 | | |
| The Appearance to Thomas | | | | 20:27 |
| The Appearance to the Seven Disciples | | | | 21:1–22 |
| Jesus and Peter | | | | 21:15–19 |
| The Commissioning of the Disciples | 28:16–20 | 16:14 | | |
| The Ascension of Jesus | | 16:19–20 | 24:50–43 | |

## Parables

The word *parable* comes from a Greek word that means "to throw alongside" or "compare." A parable is a story about a situation, usually one that would be very familiar to the hearers. The story is told to make a point about another reality, moral or spiritual, that is not as easy to speak of in down-to-earth terms.

Jesus' parables are *similes* (statements comparing one thing with another by using *like* or *as*, such as, "The kingdom of heaven is like a mustard seed . . . " in Mt 13:31) or *metaphors* (statements identifying one thing with another, for instance, "Beware of false prophets, who come to you in sheep's clothing, but underneath are ravenous wolves" in Mt 7:15). Sometimes these comparisons grow into stories. They make their points by using everyday objects and characters drawn from real-life situations in families, farms, the marketplace, and the courts of kings. Jesus used parables as a main part of his teaching, and their primary purpose was to reveal some dimension of God's Kingdom.

As you read through the parables, keep in mind this combination of day-to-day reality and great spiritual insight. The parables are famous, rightly so, for their ability to take the most ordinary situations—cleaning house, growing grapes, the rivalry between two brothers, the preparations for a wedding, the story of a mugging in a bad part of town—and find in them an endless source of spiritual meaning.

The parables can be grouped into three categories according to their length and complexity.

1. Similes and metaphors that have minimal elaboration and are basically "one-liners." Some examples are the lamp under the basket (Mt 5:14–16); the mustard seed (Mt 13:31–32); and the two debtors (Lk 7:41–43).

2. Comparisons that are more extended; these are more elaborate than the simple metaphors above, but are not yet full-blown stories like those in category 3. Some examples are the two sons (Mt 21:28–32); the growing seed (Mk 4:26–29); the rich fool (Lk 12:16–21); and the unprofitable servants (Lk 17:7–10).

3. Stories that contain characters, dialogue, plot, and setting; these stories have a clear beginning, middle, and end. Some examples are the good Samaritan (Lk 10:30–37); the prodigal son (Lk 15:11–32); the wicked vinedressers (Mt 21:33–41); and the wise and foolish virgins (Mt 25:1–13).

Parables were used by Jesus to reveal the Kingdom he came to initiate through his life and ministry. But, ironically, Jesus also used them to obscure his teaching (Mk 4:11–12). Knowledge of the Kingdom is available to all who sincerely seek it, but this knowledge requires some effort. Parables make their points indirectly, so people will only discover their truths if their ears and eyes are open, and if they have the hearts of seekers. Even the disciples of Jesus did not always understand the significance of his parables. However, because they were committed to Jesus, they sought, and the doors of understanding were opened to them. Those who stand on the "outside" at a safe distance from Jesus, unwilling to make a commitment, are locked into misunderstanding. They are unable to "hear" the truth expressed in the parables because they are unwilling to open their ears and eyes and hearts.

For many centuries parables were viewed primarily as allegories in which every element carried some kind of symbolic significance or hidden meaning. For example, St. Augustine allegorized the parable of the Good Samaritan. He saw the victim as Adam, the robbers as Satan and his angels, the priest and Levite who walked by as representative of the Torah and the prophets, the Samaritan as Jesus, and the inn as the church, etc. But scholars would say Augustine went way

***Parables in the Synoptic Gospels***

| Parable | Matthew | Mark | Luke |
|---|---|---|---|
| The Weeds among the Wheat | 13:24–30 | | |
| The Buried Treasure | 13:44 | | |
| The Fine Pearl | 13:45–46 | | |
| The Thrown Net | 13:47–48 | | |
| The Unforgiving Servant | 18:21 | | |
| The Workers in the Vineyard | 20:1–16 | | |
| The Two Sons | 21:28–30 | | |
| The Wedding Feast | 22:2–14 | | |
| The Talents | 25:14–30 | | |
| The Judgment of Nations | 25:31–46 | | |
| Seed Grows of Itself | | 4:26–29 | |
| Need for Watchfulness | | 13:32–37 | |
| The Two Debtors | | | 7:41–42 |
| The Good Samaritan | | | 10:30–35 |
| The Persistent Friend | | | 11:5–8 |
| The Rich Fool | | | 12:16–20 |
| The Vigilant and Faithful Servants | | | 12:35–40 |
| The Faithful and Prudent Steward | | | 12:42–48 |
| The Barren Fig Tree | | | 13:6–9 |
| The Great Feast | | | 14:15–24 |
| The Tower | | | 14:28–30 |
| The King Marching into Battle | | | 14:31–33 |
| The Lost Coin | | | 15:8–10 |
| The Prodigal Son | | | 15:11–32 |
| The Dishonest Steward | | | 16:1–8 |
| The Rich Man and Lazarus | | | 16:19–31 |
| Attitude of a Servant | | | 17:7–10 |
| The Persistent Widow | | | 18:2–5 |
| The Pharisee and the Tax Collector | | | 18:9–14 |
| The Ten Gold Coins | | | 19:11–27 |
| The Two Foundations | 7:24–29 | | 6:46–49 |
| The Yeast | 13:33 | | 13:20–21 |
| The Lost Sheep | 18:10–14 | | 15:1–7 |
| The Lamp | 5:15 | 4:21 | 8:16<br>11:33 |
| The New Cloth | 9:16 | 2:21 | 5:36 |
| The New Wine in Old Wineskins | 9:17 | 2:22 | 5:37–38 |
| The Sower | 13:1–9 | 4:1–9 | 8:4–8 |
| The Mustard Seed | 13:31–32 | 4:30–34 | 13:18–19 |
| The Tenants | 21:33–46 | 12:1–12 | 20:9–19 |
| The Lesson of the Fig Tree | 24:32–35 | 13:28–31 | 21:29 |

beyond what Jesus intended. The point the parable was meant to make (that God's love is extravagant and unconditional) almost gets lost in the elaborate analogy. Modern scholarship has therefore turned away from that kind of interpretation, insisting that parables make only a single point. The details of the story have just one point of contact with the spiritual teaching the story is trying to convey.

Although modern readers have moved away from an overly allegorical reading of parables, avoiding allegorical interpretations entirely is not an absolute rule. Some parables, in fact, do have more than one point of contact with the teaching they convey. The parable of the sower is one of them. One must be careful, of course, to make sure that the points of contact they discover are coming *from* the text, not being read *into* the text. Besides the parable of the sower (Mk 4:14–20), see the parable of the wheat among the weeds (Mt 13:37–40) as another example of a parable that does have more than one point of contact with the teaching it presents. However, the general approach is that interpretation is derived from the story as a whole, rather than from its individual details.

The parables are designed to make us see differently. They don't just present moral teaching; they offer a whole new way of perceiving how God rules over and is present in our lives. They also help us understand how we are converted by this presence and thus how we enter God's Kingdom. Certain truths just cannot be explained directly. So we resort to imagination. Because they appeal to the imagination, parables can touch us in ways that an abstract explanation cannot. They supply jolts to the imagination, as for example Mt 13:33: "The kingdom of heaven is like yeast that a woman took and mixed with three measures of wheat flour until the whole batch was leavened." They penetrate deeper and plant their truths inside us.

But they do much more than provide folksy examples that make a point. They shake us up, make us ask questions. They challenge our categories and make us think our way through to a conclusion. Often they do this by reversing our expectations: A host who is stood up by the guests invites the poor, the lame, and the blind to his banquet (Lk 14:21); the owner of a vineyard pays those hired *last* the same amount as those hired *first* (Mt 20:8); a man acquires a treasure not because of his hard work, but out of dumb luck (Mt 13:44).

Most of us approach life with certain expectations or a particular worldview: The good are rewarded, and the bad are punished; those who work harder and longer get paid more than those who work fewer hours, and so on. Then we read a parable, and it shakes us up; it turns our world upside down: The *prodigal* got the party, not the good older brother; the workers hired last were paid as much as those hired first! We become disoriented by such a perspective. But if we do the work the parable calls for, we will be rewarded; if we seek, we will discover the profound truth the parable wants to teach us. For example, the parable of the good Samaritan is not a pious story about being compassionate, but a radical challenge to consider as "neighbor" those we had previously viewed as "enemy." Out of this seeking and struggle, a sense of reorientation emerges.

The parables invite us into a process of questioning. Within that process, we become an essential part of their meaning. They are incomplete in themselves. They invite and await a response. Our response completes the process that they initiate. Their truth does not stand alone. It combines with our efforts and springs to life in our hearts as a revelation of God's mysterious Kingdom.

# MATTHEW READING GUIDE

### *At a Glance*

| | |
|---|---|
| Who are the main players? | John the Baptist  Mary  Joseph  Herod  Jesus  the disciples  Mary Magdalene  the religious leaders  Caiaphas  the high priest  Pilate |
| What should I look for? | Matthew's Gospel is a dynamic story. Follow the story of Jesus' life and ministry. Notice how Matthew has organized the sayings of Jesus into discourses that contain the major themes of his Gospel. |
| When did this take place? | Jesus' life spanned the first three decades of the first century A.D. The probable date for Matthew's writing is between A.D. 70 and 90. His theology, his command of Greek, |

| | |
|---|---|
| | and rabbinic training indicate Matthew the evangelist was probably a second generation Jewish Christian. |
| Where did these events occur? | In Palestine |
| Why was this book written? | Matthew wrote to show the essential dependence of Jesus and the early church on Judaism. At the same time he is concerned with how the Jewish Jesus is the messiah for the whole world. |
| What is the story? | Matthew's work is a narrative of Jesus' life. It begins with the roots of Jesus' family tree, describes the circumstances of his birth, then turns to the events of his ministry, culminating in his death, resurrection and final appearances to his disciples. |

| | |
|---|---|
| **Healings in Matthew** | Cleansing a leper 8:2–4 (Mk, Lk)<br>The centurion's servant 8:5–13 (Lk)<br>Peter's mother-in-law 8:14–15 (Mk, Lk)<br>Evening time healing of the sick 8:16–17 (Mk, Lk)<br>The paralytic 9:2–8 (Mk, Lk)<br>The woman with a hemorrhage 9:20–22 (Mk, Lk)<br>Two blind men 9:27–31<br>The mute demoniac 9:32–34<br>The man with a withered hand 12:10–13 (Mk, Lk)<br>The blind and mute demoniac 12:22–32 (Lk)<br>The Canaanite woman's daughter 15:21–28 (Mk)<br>The boy with a demon 17:14–20 (Mk, Lk)<br>Two blind men 20:30–34 (Mk, Lk)<br>(Mk and Lk indicate the healing miracle is recounted in Mark and Luke as well.) |
| **Other miracles found in Matthew** | Calming the storm at sea 8:23–27 (Mk, Lk)<br>The Gadarene demoniacs cured 8:28–34 (Mk, Lk)<br>Raising the official's daughter 9:18, 23–26 (Mk, Lk)<br>Feeding the five thousand 14:13–21 (Mk, Lk, Jn)<br>Walking on the water 14:22–33 (Mk, Jn)<br>Feeding the four thousand 15:32–38 (Mk)<br>Finding tax payment in fish's mouth 17:24–27<br>Cursing the fig tree 21:18 (Mk)<br>(Mk; Lk and Jn indicate the miracle story also occurs in Mark, Luke, or John) |
| **Parables found only in Matthew** | Weeds and wheat 13:24–30<br>The hidden treasure 13:44<br>The pearl of great price 13:45–46<br>The dragnet 13:47–50<br>The lost sheep 18:12–14<br>The unforgiving servant 18:23–35<br>The workers in the vineyard 20:1–16<br>The two sons 21:28–32 |

| | |
|---|---|
| | The wedding feast 22:2–14<br>The wise and foolish virgins 25:1–13 |
| **Stories told only in Matthew** | Joseph's dream 1:20–24<br>The visit of the Magi 2:1–12<br>The flight to Egypt 2:13–15<br>The massacre of the infants 2:16–18<br>The death of Judas 27:3–10<br>The dream of Pilate's wife 27:19<br>The dead rise after Jesus' resurrection 27:52<br>Guards are posted at Jesus' tomb 27:62–66<br>The resurrection earthquake 28:2–4 |
| **When Jesus prays in Matthew** | The Lord's Prayer 6:9–15<br>Praising the Father 11:25<br>Blessing the children 19:13<br>When multiplying leaves and fishes 14:9; 15:36<br>At the Last Supper 26:26–27<br>In the garden of Gethsemane 26:36–44<br>On the cross 27:46 |
| **Matthew's portrait of Jesus** | Paints Jesus as a lawgiver and Messiah, the great teacher of Israel |
| **Matthew's unique perspective** | A convert to Christianity, Matthew traces Jesus' origins back into the history of Israel. He has great interest in showing that Jesus is the promised Messiah who fulfills Old Testament prophecy ("Son of David" and other messianic language is utilized throughout). His Jesus is a kind of catechist, teaching the law and preaching the kingdom of God. |

While all share common elements, each of the Gospels is unique. Matthew has traditionally held a place of honor among the four Gospels because it had long been considered the first written. Though that thinking has changed, it still contains elements that set it apart: Matthew contains more of Jesus' sayings than any of the other Gospels; more forcefully than the other Gospels, it connects the story of Jesus with the story of the people of Israel; and it does all this in the form of a powerful story.

## A Story

Matthew's Gospel contains an unfolding plot, fascinating characters, and various settings. In other words, it has all the elements of a good story. The plot traces Jesus' life from his birth, through his ministry of some success and much rejection, to his death and the final triumph of his resurrection. The characters are sometimes flat and one-dimensional (the Pharisees), and sometimes well developed (Jesus, Peter). And the settings, even though briefly described, help establish the drama and reality of the various scenes. These are characteristics of all good stories.

In describing Matthew's Gospel as a story, we are not implying that it has no historical basis. There is no doubt that Matthew uses materials rooted in history (most of which he draws from the Gospel of Mark, one of his principal

**Why Matthew Isn't Matthew Anymore**

SCHOLARS NO LONGER believe Matthew the apostle is Matthew the evangelist (Gospel writer). Why?

1. Because he uses 90 percent of Mark's Gospel: Why, ask the scholars, would one of the Twelve who was an eyewitness to the life of Jesus depend so heavily on the account of a non-eyewitness?
2. His theological perspective, his command of the Greek language, and his apparent rabbinic training all indicate Matthew the evangelist was probably a *second generation* Jewish Christian.

sources). But the evangelist, or Gospel writer, casts these traditions about Jesus into the form of a running story. A story or narrative helps catch up the reader into the dynamism and feeling of the events being recounted. This feature of the Gospel can engage us when we come to study or read it in more depth.

## A Source of Teaching

While Matthew's Gospel remains a dynamic story, it is also enriched—more than any of the other Gospels—with the sayings of Jesus. This feature has led commentators over the centuries to consider Matthew a kind of "catechism" or teacher's manual. In addition to the basic story of Jesus' life and ministry, which Matthew drew mainly from the Gospel of Mark, he also had a supply of the important sayings of Jesus (many of which he shares in common with the Gospel of Luke). The evangelist has organized many of these sayings into discourses or speeches of Jesus. These are not transcripts of actual talks given by Jesus because there is little logical progression found in the discourses as a whole. Rather, the evangelist has clustered the sayings of Jesus around basic themes. These discourses bring the reader of Matthew's Gospel into vital contact with the power of Jesus' teaching.

## The Jewish Heritage of Jesus and the Early Church

While all of the New Testament writings illustrate the essential dependence of Jesus and the early church on Judaism, none does it more forcefully than Matthew's Gospel. In fact, one of the primary purposes of this Gospel may have been the attempt to link the story of Jesus with the history of Israel. Any reader of Matthew who wants to go deeply into this Gospel must be alert to its Jewish background.

This feature of Matthew springs to our attention from the opening lines of the Gospel, which begin with a genealogy or family tree, tying Jesus into the history of Israel. The frequent use of Old Testament quotations, the concern with the Jewish law and customs of purity and prayer, the sharp critique of the Jewish leaders for their rejection of Jesus and for their failure to lead a life of holiness—all of these show that Matthew was absorbed with Jesus' Jewish heritage.

Strange as it may seem, Matthew's Jewish roots may also explain another difficult feature of his Gospel: his strong critique of the Jewish leaders. The Jesus of Matthew's Gospel blisters his opponents for their hypocrisy and lack of faith. They are held up to the reader of the Gospel as negative examples of what an authentic disciple should avoid becoming. The sharp edge to Matthew's critique may stem from the tragic division and hostility that grew between Judaism and Jewish Christianity in the early decades of the church. For Matthew, the fact that most of Israel did not accept Jesus or the Gospel—while many Gentiles did accept it—was a baffling and unexpected turn in salvation history, and his telling of the story of Jesus reflects this. Unfortunately, Matthew's characterization of the Jewish leaders also provided an opportunity for later anti-Semitism to develop (itself a violation of the Gospel's teaching).

## Messiah for the Whole World

But it is also apparent that Matthew is concerned with how this Jewish Jesus is messiah for the whole world. As we will indicate below, the universal mission of the church is also a prime motif of this Gospel. In fact, Matthew seems to be telling the story of Jesus so that it can help both the Jewish Christians and the Gentile converts of his community. After reading the Gospel they would be able to understand that Jesus fulfills the hopes and dreams God planted in the people of Israel, and He now extends the offer of God's salvation to all the world.

## Reading through Matthew's Gospel

The outline or major segments of Matthew's Gospel can be determined only by paying attention to his story.

• The Origin of Jesus (1:1–2:23). Here Matthew presents the events surrounding Jesus' birth and infancy.

• Preparation for the Ministry of Jesus (3:1–4:7). The test in the desert and the ministry of John the Baptist help prepare for the formal beginning of Jesus' mission.

• The Galilean Ministry of Jesus (4:7–16:12). This major section spans the ministry of Jesus from his entrance into Galilee until his announcement of the Passion and his intent to go to Jerusalem. It can be subdivided into other important segments:

1. The Sermon on the Mount (4:17–7:29)
2. Jesus the Healer (8:1–9:35)
3. The Mission Discourse (9:36–11:1)
4. Mounting Hostility to Jesus (11:2–12:50)
5. The Parable Discourse (13:1–53)
6. The Kingdom and the Disciples (13:54–16:12) This section includes the ongoing activity of Jesus and reaction to it, but with special emphasis on Jesus' relationship with Peter and the rest of the disciples.

• The Way to Jerusalem (16:13–20:34). Jesus' fateful journey to Jerusalem with his disciples dominates this section. Three times during this journey Jesus predicts his Passion and Resurrection (16:21; 17:22f; 20:17–19) and instructs his disciples on the cost of following him. There is also the important discourse on community life (18:1–35).

• Final Teaching in Jerusalem (21:1–25:46). This section of the Gospel takes place in Jerusalem. It concentrates on Jesus' final exchanges with his opponents (esp. 21:12–22:46), his condemnation of the scribes and Pharisees (23:1–39), and the long discourse on the final age and judgment (24:1–25:46).

• Death and Resurrection (26:1–28:20). The concluding segment of the narrative contains the Passion narrative and the account of Jesus' burial (26:1–27:66), the events surrounding the discovery of the empty tomb (28:1–15), and Jesus' final appearance to the eleven disciples on a Galilean mountaintop (28:16–20).

## The Origin of Jesus (1:1–2:23)

Right from the start Matthew underlines Jesus' Jewish heritage. He is "son of David, son of Abraham" (1:1). From this beginning to the end of the Gospel, Matthew announces repeatedly and loudly that Jesus is the promised Messiah through whom God's longed-for salvation would be realized.

### A Messiah Close to His People

The experiences of Jesus and his family evoke another theme important to this Gospel, namely Jesus' identification with the "least." Matthew's Christmas story has a sober mood to it. Jesus and his family are threatened with death by a tyrant. Innocent people are killed because they are identified with Jesus. The holy family is forced into exile (just as Israel had been in its tortured history). Even when they return from Egypt (a new exodus), they are unable to go home to Bethlehem but must become displaced persons, living in Nazareth (2:22f).

This identification with Israel's struggle to be free may help explain one of the names given Jesus in Matthew's story. He is to be called Emmanuel, that is, "God is with us" (1:23). As subsequent events of the Gospel will show, the Matthean Jesus has extraordinary compassion for the suffering (e.g., see the healings in chs 8 and 9), explicitly identifies himself with the "least" (see Mt 25:31–46; 10:42), and promises to remain with his church as it continues its mission in the world (28:20; 18:20).

### Messiah of Israel and Savior of the World

As Herod and the leaders of Jerusalem plot to destroy Jesus, the magi, Gentile wise men, come seeking to pay homage to him (2:1–12). The account of this visit may well be influenced by Isaiah

60:3: "Nations [i.e., non-Jews] shall walk by your light, kings by the radiance of your dawning." Even in the family tree of Jesus, Matthew may be hinting at the wider horizons of Jesus' mission. While most of the genealogy traces the male line of Jesus' ancestry, there are several women mentioned—Tamar, Rahab, Ruth, Bathsheba—all of whom were foreigners whose entry into Jewish history was under unusual, sometimes even scandalous, circumstances. Even Mary, the mother of Jesus, seems to be put in this category because her association with the royal Davidic line is not by natural means, but only through the initiative of the Holy Spirit—something that causes consternation to Joseph (1:18–19).

Thus, from the beginning outsiders were part of Jesus' history. This is a major theme of Matthew's Gospel. He will emphasize the rejection Jesus experiences from the Jewish leaders and at the same time provide scattered examples of Gentiles groping toward faith (e.g., the centurion in 8:5–13; the Gadarene demoniacs in 8:28–34; the Canaanite woman in 15:21–28). Matthew carefully notes that Jesus' historical ministry focused on Israel (10:5), but with the new age of resurrection, that mission of salvation would now extend to all nations (28:19).

### Who Jesus Is

The infancy narrative also hints at the kind of salvation Jesus will bring. Of all the Gospels, Matthew alone stresses the significance of the name "Jesus." The angel gives the divine instruction that the child is to be named Jesus (Hebrew Yehoshuah, "the LORD saves"—the name of Joshua, the leader of the Israelites after Moses) "because he will save his people from their sins." Jesus is depicted as savior throughout the Gospel as he delivers people from their burdens of sickness, oppression, and sin. This is a Jesus who thirsts for justice or righteousness (3:15) and blesses those who, like the prophets before them, suffer in the pursuit of justice (5:10). Jesus exercises divine power in forgiving sins (see 9:1–8) and urges his disciples to reflect this same sense of reconciliation in dealing with each other (see especially 5:43–48; 18:21–35).

### The Christmas Story

The overall mood of Matthew's Christmas story is quite different from that of Luke's. There are no triumphant angels, no picturesque gathering of shepherds, little focus on a tender vision of mother and child. Instead there are ominous plots against the child, outbreaks of violence, displacement, and exile. But throughout there is also the promise of God's abiding presence, bringing salvation in spite of sin and rejection. Perhaps we can think of Matthew's infancy Gospel as an "adult" Christmas story, one that has a special truth for the many people experiencing violence and persecution today. It tells a story that begins in the strength and beauty of a particular history and culture but will ultimately reach across boundaries to touch all peoples. In any case, these two chapters prepare us for the story that will follow, a story that will trace Jesus' mission of salvation through bitter rejection to ultimate triumph.

## Preparation for the Ministry of Jesus (3:1–4:17)

This brief section serves as a transition between the infancy narrative and the beginning of Jesus' ministry in Galilee. John the Baptist's preaching in the desert opens the section, and Jesus' entry into Galilee ends it. In between we find two of Matthew's major themes.

### The Dawn of the New Age

Israel had long awaited the return of the prophet Elijah whose coming would signal the end of the world and the appearance of the kingdom of God. Matthew sees the promise of Elijah's return fulfilled in the person of John the Baptist. John declares the nearness of God's kingdom and prepares the way for Jesus who, being greater than John, is the one who ushers in the kingdom. Matthew's awareness that the coming of Jesus represents the culmination of God's plan for salvation runs throughout the Gospel. Jesus, the "beloved son" (3:17) of God has come to dispel darkness and offer hope to all people who stumble in the dark of sin and death.

### Repentance and Good Deeds

In Matthew's Gospel repentance means a change in one's way of thinking and acting. Real change is evident in the good deeds that flow from it. When John and Jesus call for repentance, they are challenging their listeners not to rely on their status as children of Abraham (3:15), but to respond concretely to God's love offered in Jesus.

Jesus' temptations in the desert illustrate this same point. As he did in the details of his birth, Jesus here relives the experience of Israel in the desert. Only his story ends differently. Similarly tempted, Jesus does not yield to temptation and sin as Israel did in the desert. Jesus practices what he preaches. He demands fidelity to God and teaches how by being fiercely faithful himself.

## The Galilean Ministry of Jesus (4:17–16:12)

This major section of the Gospel begins with Jesus' entry into Galilee and the inauguration of his ministry of teaching and healing.

### The Sermon on the Mount (4:17–7:29)

The Sermon on the Mount, the first of Jesus' five great discourses in this Gospel, is perhaps the best-known passage of Matthew's Gospel. The sermon itself spans chapters 5 through 7, but preparation for this great discourse begins in chapter 4. After sounding the theme of the Kingdom of God (4:17), Jesus calls his first disciples to follow him and to share in his mission (4:18–22). Jesus is committed to teaching, proclaiming the Kingdom of God, and healing (4:23). That liberating mission draws a response from every point of the compass as throngs of broken and needy people surge toward Jesus and his message of God's mercy (4:24f). Jesus' teaching, Matthew implies, is not mere abstract truth. Jesus' words and his healing touch have the power to transform lives.

The Sermon on the Mount does not have a neat progressive structure; rather, sayings of Jesus are clustered around basic themes.

#### A New Teaching for a New Age.

Matthew's conviction that Jesus is the Messiah, and therefore the authoritative teacher of God's will, runs throughout the Sermon. With Jesus the final age of salvation dawns and with it, new insight into God's will. Matthew's Jesus sees the will of God as being in continuity with the revelation that came through the Law of Moses in the Old Testament, but now bringing that law to its fullest and most compelling expression. In the opening verses of the Sermon, Jesus states: "Do not think that I have come to abolish the law or the prophets. I have come not to abolish but to fulfill" (5:17).

The conviction that the end of the world will be a triumph of God's grace—a conviction based on belief in the life, death, and resurrection of Jesus—runs throughout the Sermon and gives it special force. The false values assumed by the world are crumbling. This is the message of the beatitudes (5:3–12): those who are "poor in spirit" or who "hunger and thirst for righteousness" or are "peacemakers" are blessed because God will vindicate their hopes. Similarly, because it is a new age with new possibilities, the old wisdom is no longer adequate. A series of six contrast statements mark off the difference between former interpretation of the Jewish law and Jesus' own radical teaching (see 5:21–48).

#### The Supreme Law of Love Expressed in Committed Action

Matthew's emphasis on good deeds, cited above (see comments on Preparation for the Ministry of Jesus), is clearly in evidence here. The words of Jesus at the conclusion of the Sermon are unequivocal: "Not everyone who says to me, 'Lord, Lord,' will enter the kingdom of heaven, but only the one who does the will of my Father in heaven" (7:21). But the Sermon demonstrates that Matthew's Jesus is not simply talking about frenetic action. The heart and soul of Jesus' teaching is the command to love. That comes to its fullest expression in the last of the contrast statements where Jesus tells his disciples they are to love even the enemy (5:44) because God's own love is lavish and indiscriminate, bathing both just and unjust in its light and refreshment (5:45). Matthew is consistent on this point throughout the Gospel (see 7:12; 22:34–40). Asking his disciples to strive for love of enemies—the most challenging demand that can be made on the human heart—expresses the ultimate spirit of all of Jesus' teaching on human relationships. For this reason, the disciple is to strive for complete honesty (5:33–37), avoid retaliation for injury (5:38–39), and not violate another through lust or manipulation (5:27–30).

Jesus' teaching roots all of this in God's relationship to us. The teaching on love of enemy and no retaliation is, therefore, not a minor part of the Gospel nor is it an abstract ideal. This fundamental teaching of Jesus remains a challenge for Christians who live in a violent world where the use of force is commonplace.

### Revelation of a Close and Compassionate God

Jesus' teaching in this part of the Gospel also gives a profound insight into the Gospel's image of God. God's boundary-breaking love is not based on merit but reaches out even to the unjust and the "enemy" (5:45–48). God cares for us more than for birds of the air or the wild flowers, whose freedom and beauty are signs of God's provident love (6:25–32). Therefore, the disciple is to have complete trust in God and to pray with confidence and without pretense (7:7–11). Jesus' model prayer (6:9–15) catches up much of the spirit of the entire sermon. There is a wonderful simplicity and honesty about the instructions on piety in the sermon (6:1–18); God's relationship to us is direct and close. There is no place for pretending before such a loving God.

### The Authority of the Sermon

How to live with the Sermon on the Mount has been a constant point of discussion in the church. Are these demanding words to be taken as impossible ideals, meant only for a perfect world or for perfect people? Or do they make sense only in the setting of Jesus' own times, when people thought the end of the world was near and so might be capable of responding heroically in such an emergency situation?

None of these solutions are adequate. The instructions of Jesus are not a system of clear-cut laws spelling out exactly how we are to act in every circumstance, nor are they abstract or impossible ideals. These teachings give us practical guidance as we seek to live a life faithful to the Gospel. They illustrate the core spirit of Jesus' teaching, a spirit we must embody in our own circumstances. The possibility of living in accord with the teaching of Jesus is based on God's grace; the Sermon illustrates the difference grace can make in a person's life and relationships. Within the array of moral choices that confront us, the examples Jesus gives in the Sermon—such as the call for integrity in our relationships, for nonretaliation, and for a commitment to reconciliation—help direct us in the right way.

### Jesus the Healer (8:1–9:35)

In this powerful section, Matthew presents Jesus the healer. Though he draws most of his material here from Mark's Gospel, Matthew significantly edits the material he borrows. He wants to concentrate on Jesus' most essential actions and words, so he shortens Mark's stories and eliminates some of Mark's most colorful details. Matthew arranges the stories of this section into three groups, each with its own dominant motif:

Group 1: 8:1–17 Emphasizes Jesus' healing power (the leper, centurion's servant, Peter's mother-in-law).

Group 2: 8:18–9:17 Emphasizes the demands of discipleship (calming the storm, healing the demoniacs, the paralytic).

Group 3: 8:18–34 Emphasizes the indispensable role of faith in the healing stories (the official's daughter, the woman with a hemorrhage, two blind men, the mute demoniac).

### Christology

By narrowing the spotlight on Jesus in the first three stories, Matthew emphasizes the divine power that works through the Messiah. Jesus cleanses the leper, heals the servant of a Gentile soldier, and dispels the fever of Simon's mother-in-law. Except in the case of the centurion, there is little attention to the plight or disposition of the sick person in these stories. The concluding verse of the section (8:17) makes Matthew's intended point; by his healing touch Jesus fulfills the prophetic promise of Isaiah 53:4: "Yet it was our pain that he bore, our suffereings he endured."

By their very nature the healing stories serve Matthew's purpose. All of us experience sickness or disability at one time or another in our life. We all experience our limitations and realize too well that death looms before us. Jesus is moved with compassion (9:36) and does not hesitate to stand in solidarity with those whose condition makes them "outsiders" (see his association with the leper, the Gentile, the tax collectors).

### The Conditions of Discipleship

In the second set of stories Matthew illustrates some of the demands of discipleship. Only those fully committed to proclaiming the Kingdom of

God and following Jesus are able to go with him across the sea (see 8:18–23). But even for those who remain, following Jesus can mean the threatening experience of the storm at sea (8:24–27) and strange encounters with the power of evil (8:28–34). The true disciple is one who learns that mercy and compassion drive Jesus, a lesson the Pharisees (whom Matthew consistently portrays in negative tones) seem unable to grasp (9:9–13).

**Faith**

The healing stories often serve to illustrate the meaning of faith. Faith is, first of all, trust in Jesus' power to heal and transform us. Such faith is evident in the leper who approaches Jesus (even though the law forbade him to do so), in the centurion who pleads on behalf of his servant (see 8:10), in the friends who bring the paralytic to Jesus (9:2), in the woman with the hemorrhage who touches the tassel of his cloak (9:22), and in the two blind men who trust that Jesus can do what no one else can (9:28f).

Note, too, that the faith illustrated in these stories often takes a very active form. The leper boldly comes up to Jesus; the woman dares to touch him; the Gentile swallows his pride and pleads with a Jewish healer; the friends of the paralytic gain him access to Jesus. For the characters in this story, trusting in God does not mean mere passivity, waiting for a bolt from heaven. Transformation comes when they exercise their trust in God, and commit their own resources to seeking a new life.

**The Mission Discourse (9:35–11:1)**

Now that Matthew has completed his portrait of Jesus as teacher and healer, he moves to a new segment of the Gospel. Using his own mission as a model, Jesus gathers his twelve apostles and commissions them to proclaim the Kingdom of God, and to heal. The motivation for their mission is the same that animated Jesus' own energetic healing in the previous two chapters: the crowds are "troubled and abandoned, like sheep without a shepherd" (see Mt 9:36–38).

This forms the second of the five great discourses of Matthew's Gospel. The evangelist draws some of the material in this discourse from chapter 13 of Mark's Gospel.

Note that the discourse can be read from two different perspectives: (1) as part of the unfolding story of Jesus' ministry and his relationship with his disciples; and (2) as an instruction for the post-Easter church. In the former time frame, Jesus tells his apostles to restrict their mission to Israel, the chosen people of God (10:5f); in the new age, when the gospel must be proclaimed to all the world (see 28:16–20), Jesus' words apply to the universal mission of the church.

Typical themes for Matthew run through the discourse. The Twelve (including Matthew the tax collector, 10:3) share in Jesus' own mission of proclaiming the Kingdom and healing those in need (10:7f). Note that the apostles are not yet commissioned to "teach"—that comes only after the Resurrection (see 28:20) when they have a deeper grasp of Jesus' mission. Any disciple who follows Jesus can expect to meet indifference, hostility, or rejection (e.g., see 10:16–25, 34–39). Jesus clearly warns the apostles about the cost of proclaiming the gospel in an authentic way.

But there is also strong affirmation of the power of the gospel and of the sense of confidence that should go with those on mission. They are not to be afraid of those who threaten their lives (10:26–28) or flinch before the divisions that may come. The loving God who has an eye for the sparrows and counts the hairs on our heads will not abandon those who follow the way of Jesus. Christians who live in circumstances of persecution and violence understand well these words of Jesus. Those who live in more comfortable circumstances need to ask themselves if the gospel values they reverence are not sometimes co-opted by the seductions of the dominant culture.

Matthew's concern with the mission of the church will reemerge in the final scene of the Gospel when the mission of Jesus, confined to Israel during his lifetime, bursts out into the world through the mission of the church (28:16–20).

**Mounting Hostility to Jesus and His Mission (11:2–12:50)**

Jesus warned that his message would be opposed. Now opposition hits him (and the Baptist) square in the face.

John is in prison awaiting death. He sends his

disciples to Jesus with the poignant question: "Are you the one who is to come, or should we look for another?" We can hear 2000 years of longing in that question. Jesus uses the inquiry to summarize his great deeds and to comment on John's ministry and his own. No one else in all the Gospels receives praise like Jesus gives John here.

One of the Gospel's most beautiful passages, which sheds light on the nature of the relationship between Jesus and his Father ("No one knows the Father except the son," 11:25–27), is juxtaposed against scenes of opposition from enemies who are unable to recognize Jesus for who he is and who attack him for violating the Sabbath.

Another of Matthew's themes now emerges: judgment. Opposition to Jesus will not go unnoticed. Those who reject him (like the unrepentant towns of 11:20–24) will bear responsibility. Matthew makes it very clear that good intentions alone are never enough. To avoid judgment, a tree must bear good fruit (12:33). And blood kinship alone does not make one a family member with Jesus, but doing God's will does (12:50).

### The Parable Discourse (13:1–50)

Parables were the trademarks of Jesus' teaching style. These pointed stories both reveal and veil the mystery of the Kingdom. Unless the listener is willing to probe beneath the surface of the parables, the true meaning of Jesus' words will escape them (13:14f).

Typical themes of Matthew's Gospel emerge again in this discourse. The certain triumph of the Kingdom, which was a strong theme of the Sermon on the Mount, dominates the parable of the sower (13:1–9) as well as the parables of the mustard seed (13:31f) and the yeast (13:33f). Discipleship motifs stand out in the parables of the treasure and the pearl (13:44–46): true followers of Jesus are to put aside everything and be fully committed to the compelling beauty of God's reign.

The Scribe who is instructed (literally: "discipled") in the kingdom of heaven (13:52) is like the householder who can bring from the storehouse "both the new and the old." Preserving the best of the past and yet making it come alive for a new generation seems to be one of the main purposes of Matthew's Gospel. Matthew was convinced that Jesus did not destroy the beautiful traditions of Judaism but gave them new meaning. Bridging past and present in an open and respectful manner is one of the greatest challenges of religious leadership in any age.

### The Kingdom and the Disciples (13:51–16:12)

It is difficult to characterize this long section of Matthew's story under any single heading. Jesus' ministry of teaching and healing continues but now begins to burst beyond the confines of Galilee into Gentile territory. Clashes with his opponents, mainly the Pharisees, also continue to erupt. But the haunting story of Jesus' walking on the water and Peter's awkward attempts to trust his master (14:22–33) may give us a clue to the special character of this section. With new intensity Jesus begins to instruct his disciples on the mystery of the Kingdom, and they begin to realize the awesome identity of the Messiah. Several motifs run through these chapters.

### The Inclusive Mission of Jesus

Following the lead of Mark's Gospel, Matthew begins to trace the boundary-breaking nature of Jesus' ministry After another conflict with the Pharisees (15:1–20), Jesus ventures near the Gentile region of Tyre and Sidon and there encounters a "Canaanite" woman (15:21–28). This is one of the most intriguing stories in the Gospel. At first Jesus resists the woman's entreaties on behalf of her daughter. The Matthean Jesus remains committed only to the people of Israel (see 10:5f). But the woman's insistence, an expression of her active faith, breaks down Jesus' resistance and seems to open the horizons of his own vision. Matthew uses this story to instruct his own church: they, too, may have had too narrow a concept of their mission, thinking that only Jews could become Christians. But the needs and genuine faith of the Gentiles showed the early church that God intended to extend the boundaries of the Kingdom to include all people.

The two stories of the miraculous feedings (14:13–21; 15:32–39) give a similar impression of expansiveness. Jesus will not let the vast crowds go hungry and uses the occasion to instruct his disciples. Another epic scene takes place on the mountaintop, a favorite place of revelation in Matthew's Gospel (15:29–31).

Similar to the vista at the beginning of the Sermon on the Mount (see 4:23–25), vast crowds of the sick and disabled surge toward Jesus, and he cures them. Once again the disciples can observe the boundless compassion that drives Jesus.

### Opposition and Rejection

Despite the mercy of Jesus, his opponents continue to resist and misunderstand his message. The Parable discourse had warned that some would prefer not to "see" and not to "hear" what Jesus preached. That prediction comes true in Nazareth (13:54–58) where Jesus' own people rebuff him and take offense at his "wisdom and mighty deeds." The story of Herod and the death of John the Baptist (14:1–12) are early warning signs about Jesus' own fate. His enemies were so immersed in their opposition that they would carry it to the point of trying to destroy Jesus.

In the conflict about the tradition of washing hands before eating (15:1–20), the Gospel offers one explanation of the stubbornness of Jesus' opponents. They have allowed their own traditions to "nullify the word of God" (15:6). In other words, they had lost a sense of priority, placing good but not essential values ahead of those that were most fundamental. Matthew continues to stress that Jesus was not opposed or indifferent to the Law, but he wanted to inject new life into its observance by insisting that the love command was the basis of all fidelity.

### The Disciples

The story of Peter walking on the water contains material unique to Matthew's Gospel and illustrates both the importance of traditions about Peter in this Gospel and the evangelist's view of discipleship. Peter begins to sink in the waves because he "doubted" or "hesitated" and because he has "little faith" (14:31). The latter phrase is particularly characteristic of Matthew's Gospel. Matthew's portrayal is sympathetic and realistic: The disciples believe, but their faith is weak. Deeper trust in Jesus is needed.

At the same time, the disciples are quite different from the opponents of Jesus. While the opponents reject Jesus and align him with Satan (12:24), the disciples acclaim Jesus as "the Son of God" (14:33). The enemies of Jesus cannot understand his teaching, but the disciples, although hesitantly, do "understand" (16:12; see also 13:16, 51).

## The Way to Jerusalem (16:13–20:34)

A dramatic shift in the setting of the gospel story is about to take place. Jesus goes with his disciples to the northernmost reaches of Israel, Caesarea Philippi (16:13). There he will ask the fundamental question of the gospel: "Who do you say that I am?" (16:15). Jesus' question and Peter's response represent a turning point in the story. "From now on" (16:21) Jesus will begin to speak openly about his approaching death, and the action of the gospel will point toward Jerusalem and the events of the Passion and Resurrection.

The announcement of Jesus' journey to Jerusalem (16:21) thus introduces the motif of a "journey," a theme already present in Mark's Gospel and one greatly expanded in the Gospel of Luke. The threefold prediction of the Passion (in Mt, see 16:21; 17:22f; 20:17–19) punctuates the journey and keeps the reader's attention directed to Jerusalem and Jesus' death and resurrection. That great climax to the gospel, already alluded to as early as the infancy narrative, dominates and gives urgency to Jesus' teaching. The transfiguration reflects this: Immediately after Jesus predicts his death for the first time, the light of resurrection glory seems to emanate from his person in a mountaintop scene reminiscent of the revelation given to Moses on Sinai.

During the journey narrative, the spotlight seems to fall with new intensity on Jesus' relationship with his disciples. Although some conflicts with the Pharisees take place (e.g., see the dispute about divorce, 19:1–12), most of Jesus' words are directed to his disciples, revealing to them what it means to follow a Crucified Messiah. Special traditions about Peter are present in this section, too, including his confession at Caesarea Philippi and Jesus' blessing upon him, his mediating role in paying the Temple tax on behalf of Jesus and himself (17:24–27), and his lead question about forgiveness in the discourse on community life (18:21).

### The Ministry of Leadership

In the scene at Caesarea Philippi (16:16), Peter does what the disciples had done before him: confess his faith in Jesus. Then, as he does

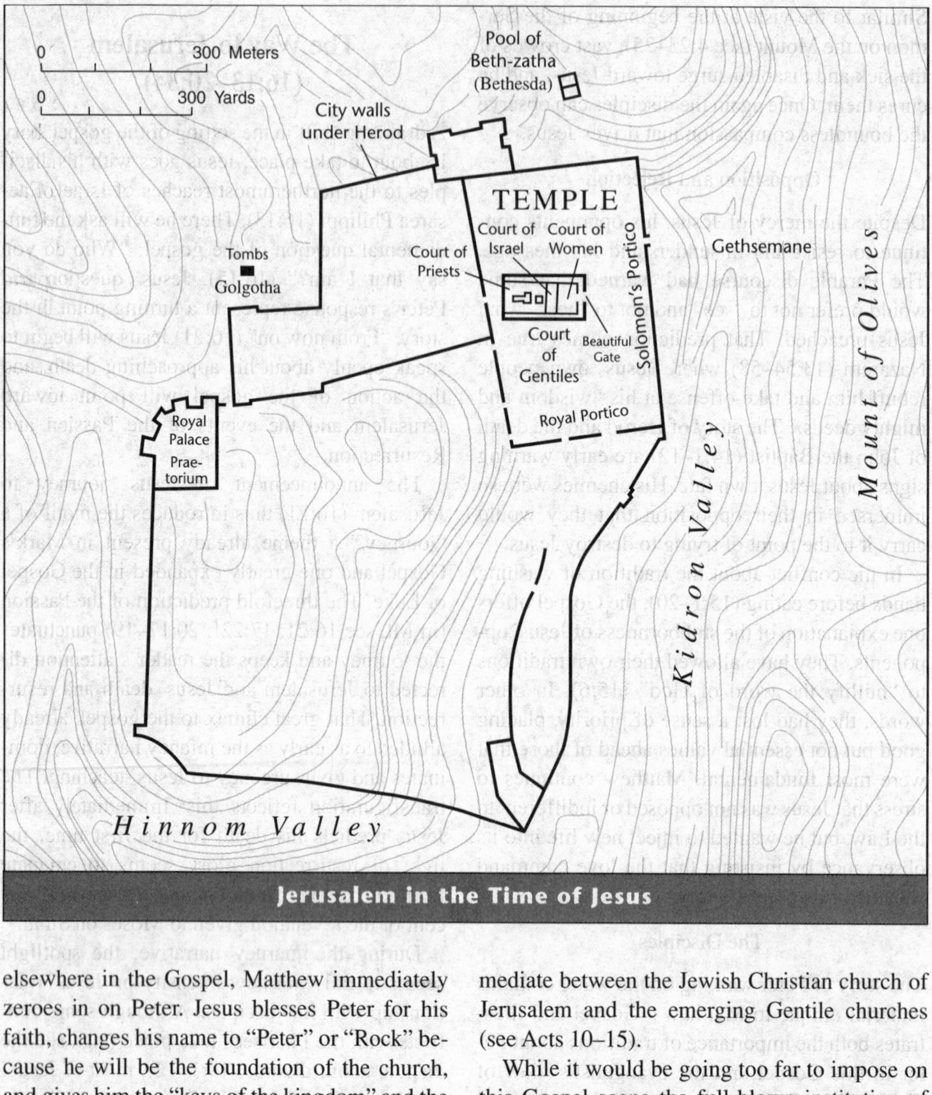


**Jerusalem in the Time of Jesus**

elsewhere in the Gospel, Matthew immediately zeroes in on Peter. Jesus blesses Peter for his faith, changes his name to "Peter" or "Rock" because he will be the foundation of the church, and gives him the "keys of the kingdom" and the power to "bind" and "loose" (giving the "keys" is a sign of the unique leadership role given to Peter).

Matthew will balance out this focus on Peter by also asserting the authority of the community in chapter 18, but at this point in the Gospel he is showing the important role entrusted to the leader of the community. Undoubtedly, this reflects a ministry of leadership already present in Matthew's church. The Gospel uses Peter as a model for leadership. Historically, Peter had been an important leader in the church. In the Acts of the Apostles, we are told that he helped mediate between the Jewish Christian church of Jerusalem and the emerging Gentile churches (see Acts 10–15).

While it would be going too far to impose on this Gospel scene the full-blown institution of the papal office, Roman Catholic tradition can legitimately see in the figure of Peter the founding model for the later emergence of this office in the church. Peter is blessed because of his strong faith in Jesus and because he served a key role in maintaining the unity of the church. Equally important to remember, however, is that the Gospel refuses to idealize Peter or to place him above the demands of the gospel. The same Peter that Jesus blesses lavishly here is also called "Satan" and "obstacle" (16:23), will underestimate the need for reconciliation (18:21), and will deny his discipleship in the face of the

Passion (26:69–75). Leaders within the community must remain disciples (see 23:10).

### Life in the Community

The Discourse on Community, the fourth of Matthew's major discourses, occurs here. It is built around two parables, the Lost Sheep (18:10–14) and the Unforgiving Servant (18:21–35), that communicate the two major themes of this discourse.

The Lost Sheep parable reveals God's great interest in the weak or alienated members of the community. Community members are to be humble and should never "scandalize" or shun those who are weak or living on the margins of the church (18:6–10).

The second half of the discourse concludes with another key saying: "So will my heavenly Father do to you, unless each of you forgives his brother (or sister) from the heart" (18:35). The need for reconciliation dominates the latter half of the discourse. Disputes are to be settled in a fair and practical manner (18:15–17), and even if strong discipline must be taken toward a recalcitrant member, he or she is to be treated "like a Gentile or a tax collector"—a poignant note in a Gospel where Jesus seeks out just such people (e.g., see 9:9–13). Those who have experienced limitless forgiveness from God should not put limits on reconciliation within the community. That is the radical message of Jesus' reply to Peter, and the concluding parable of the story. Its message is similar in content to Jesus' teaching on love of enemies in the Sermon on the Mount (see 5:43–48).

## Final Teaching in Jerusalem (21:1–25:46)

The Gospel drama now enters Jerusalem, the capital city, where Jesus will experience death and resurrection. The great temple of Herod dominated this city in the time of Jesus, and its shadow falls across the scenes Matthew narrates in these chapters.

Jesus the Messiah enters his city in triumph, but he is seated on a donkey's colt, which Matthew interprets as a sign of Jesus' humility. As a fearless prophet, Jesus cleanses the house of God, another sign of his God-given mission to call Israel to repentance. The next day Jesus returns to the Temple compound and begins to teach the crowds (21:13). There follows a number of key texts that reveal the heart of Jesus' message. But the Jewish authorities (the Pharisees now joined by the "chief priests and elders of the people," all members of the Sanhedrin, an informal ruling body whose base would, in fact, have been Jerusalem) remain hostile to Jesus and his message. This section of the Gospel is filled with sharp clashes between Jesus and his opponents.

Two important clusters of sayings and parables are found here. In the first, 23:1–39, Jesus excoriates the scribes and the Pharisees, portraying them in purely negative tones for their hypocrisy and lack of fidelity. This is Matthew's most intense assault on the Jewish leaders. The second collection of sayings and parables forms the fifth and final discourse of the Gospel, the so-called Eschatological Discourse or discourse on the end of the world. While gazing at the stunning Temple from the Mount of Olives, Jesus reflects on the fate of the Temple and the end of human history. This leads to a series of parables, some of them unique to Matthew, urging the disciples to remain faithful and to exemplify that fidelity through good deeds (see 24:36–25:46).

### The Authority of Jesus

Like a fine conductor, Matthew orchestrates the elements of this section to trumpet a grand Messiah chorus. Jesus' triumphant entry into Jerusalem shakes the entire city (21:10). Strength and authority accompany him wherever he goes. On his own authority this "Lord of the Sabbath" (12:8) drives the money changers from the Temple and reasserts the Temple's proper role as a house of prayer (21:12–27). And he backs down from none of the religious authorities who challenge him—not the scribes or the chief priests, not the elders of the people, nor the Sadducees. Matthew leaves no room for doubt about Jesus' status as Messiah and true Teacher of Israel.

And what is the source of Jesus' authority? He is the Son of God. For Matthew the evidence is clear and irresistible. Even the parable of the tenants affirms it (21:33–46). In that allegory Jesus describes himself as the vineyard owner's son and "heir." And later he asserts his preeminence even over King David who called the future Messiah his "Lord" (22:41–46).

When Jesus is questioned about the Law, his reaction is typical of Matthew's Gospel: He reinterprets, never rejects, the Law. Though surrounded by hostile opponents, Jesus fields their questions with the poise and ease of a master teacher, reminding them that the "whole law and the prophets" (22:40) depend on the command to love God and neighbor.

### Jesus and His Opponents

Suddenly the tone changes. The poised Jesus shifts into an offensive mode, hammering the scribes and Pharisees for their hypocrisy and infidelity. Jesus points to them as negative role models, the opposite of what disciples should be, Through the series of seven "woes" ("Woe to" was a phrase used by the prophets to express horror over sin and the punishment it will bring), Matthew reveals the values that really matter to Jesus:

- Practicing what you preach (23:3)
- Showing compassion rather than burdening others (23:4)
- Not using religion for self-glorification (23:5f)
- Letting mercy and justice guide interpretation of the law (23:23–38)
- Expecting religious leaders to show respect rather than arrogance toward the community (23:8–12)

This strong indictment of the failings of the leaders is not intended solely to pummel the opponents of Jesus. Rather, it is meant as a sober instruction for the Christian readers of the Gospel. Nevertheless, the negative stereotyping of the Jewish leaders, especially when it is read apart from its historical context in the Gospel, can have destructive effects. We who live in the horrible shadow of the Holocaust must be responsible readers of this Gospel and, while taking to heart the important lessons of this discourse, must not allow its negative image of the Jewish leaders to influence our attitude to Jews today. Every modern pope and the teaching of the Second Vatican Council has attacked anti-Semitism and reminded Catholics of their spiritual and historical roots in the living faith of Judaism (see particularly the 2002 statement of the Pontifical Biblical Commission, The Jewish People and their Sacred Scriptures in the Christian Bible).

## The Death and Resurrection of God's Son (26:1–28:20)

### The Passion (26:1–27:66)

The Passion story moves quickly from Jesus' prediction of the plot against him (26:1–5), through the last supper with his disciples (26:20–30), his anguished prayer and arrest in Gethsemane (26:36–56), the interrogation and trial before the Sanhedrin or Jewish Council (26:57–75), the Roman trial before Pilate (27:1–31), and the final scene of crucifixion, mockery, and death (27:32–56). The burial in Joseph of Arimathea's tomb and the Pharisees' demand that Pilate post a guard (27:57–66) prepare the reader for the explosive events of the resurrection.

The peculiar emphases Matthew gives the Passion story can be summarized under three major themes:

### The Majesty of Jesus

Even in the Passion story, Jesus remains the majestic Messiah of Israel. This is already true in Mark's account, but it is given particular emphasis by Matthew. Jesus is imbued with prophetic knowledge of the events about to take place: He predicts the plot of the leaders (26:1f), is fully aware of his impending death (26:12.18), knows the identity of his betrayer (26:25), and sees the certainty of Peter's denials (26:34). His captors cannot seize him until Jesus confronts Judas with his treachery (26:50). And when the high priest commands with an oath that Jesus reveal his identity, Jesus predicts with calm majesty his eventual triumph as the Son of Man who will be exalted at the right hand of God (26:64). Death cannot destroy or defeat God's Son—that is the heart of Matthew's message in the Passion story. The parade of mockers who file past the cross jeer Jesus and ridicule his claim to be God's Son (27:39–44). But as death comes, Jesus is acclaimed as the true Son of God, and nature itself erupts in testimony to Jesus' victory.

### The Dawn of the New Age

The death of Jesus is the center point of sacred history in Matthew's perspective. Matthew, along with all of the New Testament, considered Jesus as the coming of the final and decisive age of salvation promised by God to Israel. The death of Jesus was the climactic act of his entire mission: Here all of his love and commitment were compressed into one intense act of faithfulness to the will of his Father. Thus, the death of Jesus becomes in a special way the turning point between the old and the new age. With the death and resurrection of Jesus, the final age of human history had begun and, therefore, humanity must respond to God's grace in a new way.

Several features of Matthew's Passion story proclaim this theology of history. At the moment of death (27:51–57), signs of the new age break out: nature convulses, the tombs are split open, and the dead are liberated—just as the dream of the prophet Ezekiel had envisioned, with the dead bones of Israel's hopes taking flesh and escaping the tomb (see Ez 37). The age of death is over; the age of resurrection begins.

The attention Matthew gives to the response of the leaders and people of Israel to Jesus is another part of his theology of history (e.g., see 27:24f). Paradoxically, because Israel rejects Jesus, the way will now be open for the gospel to be proclaimed to the Gentiles. This does not mean that Matthew despairs of having the Jews accept the message of Jesus (he seems to offer some hope of this in 23:39), but he does believe that the mission to the Gentiles is now possible in the new and final age of salvation. One of the catalysts for that mission was the fact that the mission to Israel had failed. Paul, too, has a similar theology in Romans 9–11, where he reminds his readers that in the mystery of God's providence, the failure of Israel becomes a moment of grace for the Gentiles. For Paul, Israel remains special because God is faithful and will never forget the promises made to the chosen people. This biblical teaching is echoed in the theology of Vatican II where it is insisted that the Jewish people have a special place in the history of salvation (see decree on non-Christian religions), and therefore Christians should not impose conversion on the Jewish people.

### Examples and Counterexamples

The Passion story also serves Matthew's teaching about discipleship. In the crucible of suffering and death, one's true character is revealed. The Passion is filled with examples, both positive and negative, of how people respond to the gospel in crisis. The leaders remain implacably hostile to Jesus and demand his death. Peter and the rest of the disciples prove their "little faith," with Peter denying he knows Jesus and the others fleeing in panic. Judas betrays his master and gives in to despair rather than seeking repentance (27:3–10).

There are also bright moments: the woman of Bethany who performs a last kindness for Jesus, anointing him for burial despite the protests of the disciples (26:6–13); Pilate's wife who pleads on behalf of "that righteous man" (27:19); the centurion and his companions who acclaim the crucified Jesus as the "Son of God" (27:54); the women who stand by Jesus at the cross and see to his burial (27:56); and Joseph of Arimathea, the rich disciple, who risks his reputation by burying a publicly executed man in his own new tomb (27:57–61). And, of course, Jesus himself is the prime example of fidelity—seeking God's will despite the threat of death, refusing violence at the moment of his arrest, and trusting in God even as his life's breath is taken from him.

There is no doubt that Matthew intended the readers of the Passion to place themselves in the story and to ask the troubled question posed by the disciples: "Is it I, Lord?" (26:22).

### The Resurrection (28:1–20)

The Gospel concludes with the events surrounding the empty tomb and Jesus' appearances to his disciples. None of the Gospels attempts to describe the resurrection itself, but Matthew comes closest to that in mentioning an "earthquake" and an "angel of the Lord" who comes from heaven to roll back the stone from the tomb (28:2). Marvelous events such as these and the opening of the tombs at the moment of Jesus' death (see 27:51–53) continue to signal the final and glorious age when God's presence would be felt in a vivid way.

Mark's original ending does not include the report of any appearances of the Risen Christ; the discovery of the empty tomb, and the words of the heavenly messenger about Jesus' triumph over death are enough to proclaim the message (see Mk 16:1–8). But in Matthew's Gospel, Jesus appears first to the women as they leave the empty tomb (28:9f), and then to the eleven remaining disciples in Galilee (28:16–20). Matthew's denunciation of the Jewish leaders continues right to the end of the Gospel: when the chief priests and elders learn from the soldiers about the astounding events at the tomb, instead of believing in Christ's triumph, they concoct a false story about the disciples stealing the body of Jesus (28:11–15).

The final scene of the Gospel (28:16–20) is on a mountaintop, the favored site of special revelation throughout the Gospel (e.g., see the temptation, the Sermon on the Mount, the transfiguration, the healing of the crowds, 15:29–31). The Risen Christ comes in triumph, as he had predicted during his Passion, and commissions his disciples to go to "all nations," making disciples, baptizing them into the community, and teaching them to observe all that Jesus had commanded.

Major themes of the Gospel are compressed into this scene: Matthew's concern with the universal mission of the church; his emphasis on Jesus as teacher; his realistic portrayal of the disciples (who even now "hesitate" as they encounter the Risen Christ, see 28:17); his interest in the church. This scene has inspired countless Christian missionaries throughout the centuries to leave their homeland to bring the gospel to others. Above all, the gospel's majestic portrayal of Jesus as the church's firm foundation and abiding hope is reaffirmed. No matter how turbulent the church's future will be, the Risen Jesus will not abandon it. Matthew concludes his Gospel with the final promise of one who was named Emmanuel, "God is with us" (see 1:23): "I am with you always, until the end of the age" (28:20).

### Judgment

Here we find a theme we've seen before in Matthew: The true disciple is a doer of good deeds. Look at the many examples that state and restate that point:

- The "faithful and prudent servant" is the one caring for the house and doing good for the needy (24:45–51).
- The "wise virgins" are those who have their oil ready (25:1–13).
- The servant who is rewarded when the master returns is the one who used his or her talents (25:14–30).
- Those who inherit the Kingdom are those who live the law of love by feeding, clothing, visiting, and welcoming the needy (25:31–46).

There is no better lesson on the value of good deeds than the climactic parable of the sheep and goats. The "sheep" are blessed because in life they showed compassion even though they did not realize it was the risen Lord who was present in the needy they served. The good do good. Hypocrites just talk about it. Matthew's Jesus has little tolerance for that.

### Questions for Discussion and Reflection

***Group Sharing/Discussion***

1. Take time for members of the discussion group to re-read Jesus' sayings. Have each person choose their favorite two or three sayings and explain why those were chosen. Each person should take a turn with the first saying on his or her list before repeating.

2. Read as many references as you can find that connect Jesus' message with his Jewish heritage. Why is this an important message then and now?

3. What events in the story of the birth of Jesus have their echo in the history of the Jewish people or parallel later events in Jesus' life?

4. Imagine you are sitting on a hillside listening to the Sermon on the Mount for the very first time. Read aloud chapter 5:1–12. What would/did you find surprising? Explain why.

5. Look again at 15:21–28. Having read the Gospel of Matthew, how would you explain to someone what Jesus taught and who he cured?

***In Our Lives***

1. Read the familiar 6:9–13. How could we apply verse 11 today? How could we apply verse 12?

2. In 7:21, Jesus explains that Heaven is for those who do the Father's will. In the course of Matthew's Gospel, Jesus gives many lessons on how to do the Father's will. After the resurrection he told them to teach people "to observe all that I have commanded . . ." (28:20). Describe how you interpret this today.

3. Review The Last Supper (26:26–30). Discuss at least five ways our celebration of the Eucharist is the same as this event.

4. Read together The Greatest Commandment: 22:34–40. Give examples of someone who has followed the second part. Name one way you will try to more fully live that part of the commandment in the future.

*Individual/Personal Reflection/Action*

1. Each morning or evening, take one of the Beatitudes (5:3–10) and reflect on where you see examples of it lived and not lived today. Pray to remember that beatitude in the coming day.

2. The Parable of the Unforgiving Servant (18:21–35) can apply to individuals, groups, and nations. Watch for parallels in the news. Take a bit of time to write or e-mail to the news source or a political representative to encourage them to put this into action.

3. In 28:16–20 Jesus commissioned his disciples. How does this commissioning apply to you as a disciple? Reflect on this and, if possible, talk with a friend about specific ways you want to teach by your example. Ask for their support in your effort, perhaps by talking about it together regularly.

# MARK READING GUIDE

### *At a Glance*

| | |
|---|---|
| Who are the main players? | John the Baptist Jesus the twelve disciples, especially Peter, James, and John Pilate the religious opponents |
| What should I look for? | Three foci: (1) the good news of salvation, (2) the mystery of Jesus' identity, (3) what it means to follow Jesus as a disciple |
| When was this book written? | Scholars believe that Mark was the first Gospel written and that the probable date of composition was between A.D. 65 and 70. |
| Where was it written and by whom? | Possibly in Rome by a Gentile disciple of Peter. It was the unanimous opinion of the early church, and remains the opinion of many today, that the writer was John Mark, the companion of Paul first mentioned in Acts 12:12. |
| Why was this book written? | Mark paints Jesus as the hidden, suffering Messiah. His purpose was not only to preserve the church's memory about Jesus, but also to make that memory take on a new force in the lives of his readers. |
| What is the story? | Mark shaped the Christian message into the most effective and moving form, that of a story about Jesus. The evangelist knit together sayings of Jesus and stories about the ministry into a dynamic narrative, tracing the life of Jesus from the first encounter with John the Baptist at the Jordan to the dynamic mission in Galilee and on to his death and resurrection in Jerusalem. |

## Characteristics of Mark's Gospel

As you read, there are several themes of Mark's Gospel that you should be on the lookout for.

### A Theology in Narrative

One of the most obvious features of Mark's Gospel, but one that should not be overlooked, is the fact that it is a narrative, a "story," about Jesus. It is not a series of abstract statements, but a forceful and emotional story.

This was probably the first Gospel to be written, and the urgency in its tone and its strong language propel this shortest of the four Gospels toward its climax. Mark has no time for an infancy story, for elegant prose, or for lengthy discourses like those in Matthew. His purpose is clearly to tell that Jesus is the Son of God, and this is what he does.

Mark's urgency helps communicate his theological message: There is no time to waste in

| | |
|---|---|
| **Healings in Mark** | A leper 1:40 (Mt, Lk)<br>Peter's mother-in-law 1:30 (Mt, Lk)<br>Evening healings of the sick 1:32 (Mt, Lk)<br>A paralytic 2:3 (Mt, Lk)<br>A man with a withered hand 3:1 (Mt, Lk)<br>The woman with a hemorrhage 5:25 (Mt, Lk)<br>The Syrophoenician woman's daughter 7:24 (Mt)<br>A deaf-mute man 7:31 (only in Mk)<br>A blind paralytic at Bethsaida 8:22 (only in Mk)<br>The epileptic boy 9:17 (Mt, Lk)<br>The blind Bartimaeus 10:46 (Mt, Lk)<br>(Mt and Lk indicate the healing miracle is recounted in Matthew and Luke as well.) |
| **Other miracles found in Mark** | Cure of a demoniac in synagogue 1:23 (Lk)<br>Calming the storm 4:35 (Mt, Lk)<br>Curing the Gerasene demoniacs 5:1 (Mt, Lk)<br>Raising Jairus's daughter 5:22 (Mt, Lk)<br>Feeding the five thousand 6:30 (Mt, Lk, Jn)<br>Walking on the water 6:48 (Mt, Lk, Jn)<br>Feeding the four thousand 8:1 (Mt)<br>Withering the fig tree 11:12 (Mt)<br>(Mt, Lk, and Jn indicate the miracle story also occurs in Matthew, Luke or John) |
| **Miracles and parables found only in Mark** | Though all but 31 of Mark's verses are quoted by either Luke or Matthew, two parables and two miracles are found only in Mark:<br>Parables: The growing seed 4:26–29<br>The traveling householder 13:34–37<br>Healings: A deaf man 7:31–37<br>The blind man at Bethsaida 8:22–26<br>(Mark has fewer parables than the other synoptics: Matthew = 20, Luke = 28, Mark = 9) |
| **When Jesus prays in Mark** | In a deserted place 1:35<br>In the garden at Gethsemane 14:32–40<br>On the cross 15:34 |
| **Mark's portrait of Jesus** | Paints Jesus as the unrecognized (hidden), suffering Messiah |
| **Mark's unique perspective** | Though the shortest Gospel, Mark often contains more vivid detail than Matthew or Luke. Mark stresses Jesus' suffering: Jesus is the prophesied Messiah who came not as a king, but as a servant. Mark is a storyteller who focuses more on what Jesus did than on what he said; he thus reveals Jesus as a man of power and decisive action. Because he was rejected by the Jews to whom he went first, Jesus expanded his mission to Gentiles. Through his many miracles, Jesus manifests his divine status as God's only son. |

### Mark in the Liturgy

UNTIL VATICAN II revised the lectionary, the Gospel of Mark was rarely heard in Roman Catholic liturgy. Mark had been largely ignored because the Gospel was considered a poor condensation of Matthew's Gospel. His literary style is unsophisticated and at times blunt. Today, Mark's Gospel is used for an entire year (Year B) in the three-year cycle of the Sunday lectionary.

### The Messianic Secret

IT MAY SEEM curious that throughout Mark's Gospel (seven times in all) Jesus tries to keep his true identity a secret: He instructs those he heals, his disciples, and even demons not to talk about his miracles or reveal who he is. Jesus knows the kind of Messiah the people want and expect. He is not prepared to be that kind of Messiah—a military leader overthrowing Roman rule, or an easy Messiah who fills empty stomachs and relieves every burden. Jesus has come to be a suffering Messiah, not a king of glory and triumph. Jesus' consistent effort in Mark's Gospel to conceal his identity as Messiah is called the "Messianic Secret."

responding to the message and mission of Jesus. Mark's story is packed with conflicts between Jesus and his religious opponents and between Jesus and demonic forces. Mark wants to let his readers know that to follow Jesus demands radical changes that inevitably will put them, too, in conflict with the forces of this world.

#### Christology

Jesus himself poses the central question of Mark's Gospel: "Who do you say that I am?" (8:20). Yet, ironically, in this Gospel Jesus works very hard to keep his identity as the Messiah a secret. But the secret keeps "leaking" out through everything Jesus says and does: He heals, expels demons, argues with opponents, teaches his disciples, shares parables, and, most importantly, he dies and rises from the dead. All this proclaims Jesus' unmistakable identity as the Son of God and the Messiah.

Jesus' healings and exorcisms were evidence that God was breaking into human history, offering liberation and salvation. But for Mark the most convincing sign of that fact was the cross. Real faith in Jesus means embracing his cross. The liberation and salvation Jesus came to bring were only made possible by his death. Yes, he was "Messiah," "healer," and "Son of Man," but those titles can only be understood in the context of Jesus' redemptive death.

#### Discipleship

Mark is very intent on teaching what it means to be a disciple of Jesus. And yet the disciples, Jesus' inner circle, do no better than anyone else at understanding who Jesus is and what he came to do. First, they openly misunderstand Jesus, and then they totally abandon him.

In Mark the disciples are both historical figures and the subject of lessons. Mark wanted his readers to see themselves in the disciples, who failed Jesus but received his love and forgiveness nonetheless. The Gospel ends with hope and promise of renewal: The "young man" at the tomb asks the women to tell the disciples to go to Galilee where they will see Jesus again. The same hope is offered to the reader who, like the disciples, may have been slow to understand Jesus, and may even have failed him, but who now can hope for the same forgiveness and renewal Jesus offered the disciples.

## Reading through Mark's Gospel

It is very helpful to read all of Mark at one sitting; the compact story makes for compelling reading. Then you can begin to focus on individual passages.

Mark uses geography to organize his story of Jesus into four main parts:

1. The *Judean desert,* where Jesus is baptized by John;
2. *Galilee,* the locus of most of Jesus' ministry;
3. The *journey to Jerusalem,* as Jesus prepares to embrace his fate; and
4. *Jerusalem* itself, where the story climaxes in death and resurrection.

Thus, the basic outline of Mark's Gospel can be sketched simply in four parts:

I. Overture in the Desert (1:1–13). In the Judean desert John preaches a baptism of repentance. Jesus accepts John's baptism and, at that very moment, his identity as God's son is revealed. Jesus then goes off alone and is tempted by Satan.

II. The Galilean Ministry of Jesus (1:14–8:21). In Galilee, the northern region of Israel, Jesus embarks on his public ministry. The central events are:
   - A. Announcing the Kingdom of God (1:14–15)
   - B. Calling his first disciples (1:16–45)
   - C. Tangling with the religious leaders (2:1–3:6)
   - D. Experiencing continued opposition and misunderstanding (3:7–4:34)
   - E. Expanding his mission to include Gentile territory (4:35–8:21)

III. The Journey from Galilee to Jerusalem (8:22–10:52). Starting in Caesarea Philippi, where Peter acknowledges Jesus as the Christ, Jesus and the disciples travel down to Jerusalem for Jesus' upcoming Passion. Much teaching on discipleship is found in this section.

IV. Death and Resurrection in Jerusalem (11:1–16:8). The story climaxes in Jerusalem where Jesus:
   - A. Enters triumphantly into the city and then drives the money changers from the Temple (11:1–12:44)
   - B. Predicts the destruction of the Temple (13:1–37)
   - C. Is arrested, tried, flogged, and crucified (14:1–15:47)
   - D. Achieves victory over death and the grave (16:1–8)

The Gospel of Mark originally ended at chapter 16:8. Writers other than the evangelist added additional endings they felt made for a smoother, more suitable conclusion.

## Overture (1:1–13)

A desert can be many things. It can be a place of new beginnings—Israel, after all, was led into the desert, and there it was forged into a people covenanted to God. But it can also be a place of testing; it was in the desert that the Israelites first rebelled against the Lord and discovered their true character. In Mark's Gospel Jesus comes to the desert to inaugurate his mission, and in the desert, Satan puts him to the test. Like the overture of an orchestral piece, Mark's brief introduction announces the major themes that will surface again throughout the Gospel:

1. *A new age is beginning.* John, dressed like the long-awaited Elijah who was to return at the end of the world, comes as the herald of a new age. By casting John in this light, Mark indicates that God is doing something new. People must reform their lives to be ready for God's new dawn.

2. *Jesus is the Son of God.* At his baptism, God's voice announces Jesus' true identity; then God's Spirit descends on Jesus to fill him with power for his messianic mission. Christology (understanding the nature of Jesus) will remain a major concern of the Gospel.

3. *Jesus' ministry will be marked by conflict with the forces of darkness.* What Jesus experienced in the desert is but a preview of what is to come: In carrying out his mission, Jesus will often confront opponents and cast out demons. Struggle is a constant in any effort for true liberation.

## The Galilean Ministry of Jesus (1:14–8:21)

This major section, which constitutes half the Gospel, can be divided into five distinctive segments.

### The Keynote of Jesus' Mission (1:14–15)

A single verse, 1:15, announces three major themes of Mark's Gospel:

*"This is the time of fulfillment."* What Israel had longed for is finally here: the new and final age of salvation. And Jesus is the one who ushers it in. In this new age, old ways will have to yield to new responses, just like new wine must be poured into new wineskins (2:18–22).

*"The Kingdom of God is at hand."* The "Kingdom of God" is a biblical symbol that expresses Israel's hope for a time when God would rule the earth with justice and peace. Jesus not only announces the rule of God, he actually inaugurates

it by healing, working for justice, and freely giving his life for others.

*"Repent and believe in the gospel."* The gospel of Jesus demands a response, a turning around: repentance. Jesus asks his disciples to see, hear, and think differently, to view reality with eyes of faith and to change their lives accordingly.

**Immediately** Mark's succinct and simple style makes frequent use of a Greek word that can be translated as "at once," "quickly," "just then," and "immediately." The word is used more than 40 times in the short 16 chapters of the Gospel, adding to the urgency and immediacy of Mark's account and giving the impression that Jesus was constantly active.

### The Call of the Disciples and Jesus' First Day of Ministry (1:16–45)

In Mark's account, Jesus gets busy immediately. Set in the small fishing village of Capernaum where Mark situates most of Jesus' ministry, this section is typical of Mark's portrayal of Jesus: As soon as he's chosen his disciples, Jesus tackles sickness and pain and casts out demons wherever he meets them.

#### The Call of the Disciples (1:16–20)

The importance of discipleship is reinforced by the fact that Jesus' first act is the calling of his disciples to join him in his ministry. A theology of discipleship is compressed into this brief episode:

• Discipleship is a gift: Jesus calls them; the disciples don't volunteer.

• Disciples follow Jesus: that's the essence of the call; nothing is more important.

• Discipleship is a privilege, and it is defined here as "fishing" for people.

#### Exorcism and Healing (1:20–45)

Again the beginning is typical of the rest of Jesus' ministry. Jesus enters a synagogue and liberates a man tormented by an "unclean spirit" (called "unclean" because they separated their victim from the worship of God). The demons, unlike most of the humans in Mark's story, recognize Jesus and even announce his identity. That Jesus can expel the demon with words alone causes the crowd to marvel at his "authority." The exorcisms, which occur frequently in Mark, are an important part of his overall design. They demonstrate in the most dramatic terms the ultimate purpose of Jesus' mission: to free humanity from the power of death in all its forms.

### Conflict (2:1–3:6)

The more Jesus continues to heal, the greater the opposition builds against him. Five stories of conflict between Jesus and the scribes and Pharisees crowd this section. They culminate in the leaders' plot to kill Jesus. Though it is still far off, Mark has already set our sights on the Passion.

Note that Jesus and the leaders disagree on precisely the issues that are at the heart of Jesus' mission: healing and forgiveness of sins. The very things that make Jesus distinctive are what anger the Pharisees: Jesus associates with sinners and outcasts and refuses to allow the law to override compassion. For Jesus, healing on the Sabbath is simply putting the spirit of the law ahead of the letter of the Law, but for the Pharisees, it is the final straw.

In the discussion on fasting (2:18–22), Mark reiterates his message that Jesus has ushered in a new age that will operate by new standards. The images here are of newness and change. The arrival of the "bridegroom" calls for new ways of seeing and responding. When he describes faith in this new age, Mark uses images of perception—"hearing," "seeing," and "understanding"—and stresses the need to perceive differently.

The call of Levi reminds us that the call to discipleship is a gift that God can give to anyone—the sinner as well as the just. This point is lost on the Pharisees who criticize Jesus for eating with "tax collectors and sinners." But Jesus responds that it was precisely for sinners (the "sick") that he came (2:17).

Like Jesus, those who take the Gospel seriously had best be prepared for opposition and conflict, for those who live by the ways of the world will bitterly resent the Gospel's insistence

## The Company They Keep

IF IT IS true that a person can be known by the company he or she keeps, then here are some hints regarding the kind of person Jesus was. In Mark, he spent time with, healed and/or touched the following:

- A paralyzed man 2:1–12
- A demon-possessed man 5:1–15
- A leader of the synagogue 5:22
- A woman with a chronic bleeding problem 5:22
- A young girl 5:41
- A Gentile mother of a possessed child 7:25–30
- A boy with an evil spirit 9:17–27
- A group of little children 10:13–16
- A rich young man 10:17–23
- A blind beggar 10:46
- The Jewish religious authorities 12:13–37

on justice and compassion. And even the church needs the reminder of Jesus' example so that it does not neglect to care for the sick, disabled, and society's outcasts.

### The Mystery of the Kingdom (3:7–4:34)

Several elements—the portrayal of Jesus' family, the portrayal of the disciples, and the series of parables—all work together in this section to amplify Mark's message that the Kingdom is a mysterious reality that is beyond human control. God grants it to those who are called to be Jesus' disciples.

The disciples present a great irony: Though they are the privileged few called to be followers of Jesus, they are always out of step, unable to understand what Jesus is really all about (4:13).

One might expect that Jesus' family would be the first to express faith in him, yet two scenes here demonstrate the opposite. In 3:21 his "relatives" want to take Jesus home because they think "he is out of his mind." In a later scene of the same incident, Jesus' "mother and his brothers" also come to take him back home (3:31–35). Jesus responds by shunning his uncomprehending family and, pointing to the disciples gathered around him, announces "whoever does the will of God" is his brother and sister and mother (3:35).

The reason for all this misunderstanding is provided by the parable discourse (4:1–34). Jesus, like his parables, is a mysterious revelation of God's Kingdom. Understanding does not come easily. It is a gift given by God, not earned solely through our own effort. While Mark respects human freedom, his point is that God is always in control—even a person's rejection of Jesus is somehow part of God's overall will and plan.

The "seed" parables teach another important point. All three—the sower casting seed onto fertile and infertile ground (4:3–9), the tiny mustard seed (4:30–32), and the seed growing while the farmer sleeps (4:26–29)—make the point that the Kingdom has a life of its own. It grows unnoticed, even into our own lives. Because of this hidden but sure growth, the Kingdom's ultimate triumph is assured. No opposition can prevent the final harvest from being lavishly abundant, "thirty, sixty, and a hundredfold."

### The Universal Mission of Jesus (4:35–8:21)

In this section, which begins to bring to an end the Galilean ministry of Jesus, the Sea of Galilee takes on prominence as a symbolic boundary between Jew and Gentile (the western shore was mostly Jewish, while the eastern shore was mainly Gentile).

Crossing the Sea several times, Jesus and the disciples make excursions into Gentile territory. Among the Gerasenes (5:1) Jesus frees a man from a horrifying demon. Later, on another missionary journey that takes him through the Decapolis (on the eastern side of the Sea of Galilee), Jesus encounters the Syrophoenician woman whose daughter he heals (7:24–30).

**Decapolis** A loosely knit federation of Gentile cities north of the Dead Sea and east of the Sea of Galilee. Though the word is Greek for "ten cities," the actual number was greater and varied from time to time.

Several blocks of material give a missionary flavor to this section: Jesus sends the twelve disciples out to preach and expel unclean spirits, giving them full participation in his own ministry (6:7–13). Herod's murder of John the Baptist and Jesus' continuing disputes with his enemies are stark reminders that discipleship comes at a high cost (6:14–29). And the two miraculous feedings of the huge and hungry crowds, one on the Jewish side and one on the Gentile side of the lake, give insight into the universal nature of Jesus' mission.

Following are some of this section's major themes:

**The Universality of the Gospel**

Human beings tend to exclude outsiders. Mark's Gospel gives evidence of both the need to overcome these tendencies and the courage it takes to do so.

Jesus heals the Gerasene demoniac (5:1–20), the Greek woman's daughter (7:24–30), and the deaf-mute from the Decapolis (7:31–37), but to do so he and the disciples must endure the terror of the storm to get to the Gentile side of the lake. The sea and the storm can be seen as metaphors for the difficulty of crossing religious and cultural boundaries.

**Nourishing God's People**

The two feeding stories reveal the nature of Jesus' mission. He must feed God's hungry people (a lesson the disciples who want to send the crowd away hungry apparently need to learn). The feeding stories both recall the miraculous feeding of Israel with manna during the Exodus, and anticipate the Eucharistic meal (notice how Jesus takes, blesses, breaks, and gives the bread exactly as he does at the last supper, 14:22).

**The Struggle of the Disciples**

Jesus' ministry in Galilee draws to a close. The disciples have seen many wonders (calming the storm, 4:38–41; walking on water, 6:45–51) and have heard Jesus' parables and words of instruction. Yet they are still stumbling in the dark of misunderstanding about who Jesus is. After so much evidence, Jesus' question echoes with judgment and pathos: "Do you still not understand?" (8:21).

**Mark's Gentile Audience**

ONE INDICATION THAT Mark's Gospel is addressed to a Gentile audience is the fact that he often defines Aramaic words and explains Jewish customs to his readers. For examples, look up the following: *"Talitha koum"* 5:41; handwashing regulations 7:3; *"qorban"* 7:11; and *"Eloi, Eloi, lema sabachtani?"* 15:35.

## The Journey from Galilee to Jerusalem (8:22–10:52)

Significantly, Mark begins and ends this section with a healing of a blind man, symbols of the disciples' inability to see Jesus for who he is. From the northernmost section of Galilee, Caesarea Philippi, Jesus and the disciples journey to Jerusalem. But first Jesus asks the central question of the Gospel: "Who do you say that I am?" (8:29). Of course, the answer has been consistently given by the eloquent words and powerful healings that have accompanied Jesus' ministry. But those signs are not enough for either Jesus' opponents or his disciples to fully comprehend that Jesus is the Messiah.

Now Jesus begins to speak openly (8:31; 9:31; 10:33–34) about his impending death and resurrection. Understanding the cross becomes the key to understanding who Jesus is and what discipleship means. The journey toward Jerusalem becomes part of the instruction on the meaning of the cross. Jesus' trip to the holy city is very deliberate: He knows what awaits him there, and he willingly accepts the Father's call to this act of selfless love for others. All who would follow Jesus, Mark suggests, must be willing to travel the same road he walks. Because Jerusalem with its great Temple is the place where Jesus will be rejected and die, the Jerusalem Temple will be replaced by a new temple, Jesus himself.

The disciples become incredibly thick-headed. To each of Jesus' Passion predictions, they make inappropriate responses: Peter by scolding Jesus (8:32); the disciples by arguing over who is the greatest (9:33ff); and James and John by requesting places of special honor in the Kingdom (10:35–37). In addition, they misjudge Jesus' willingness to spend time with children (10:13) and can't even perform an exorcism on a sick boy (9:18)—despite having been given the power to do so (see 6:7).

Jesus intensifies his instruction on discipleship after each of the Passion predictions:

• Disciples must be as humble as their master, putting aside self-interest and becoming the "servant of all" (10:35f).

• The cross is an indispensable part of the formula for discipleship. It in no way represents failure.

• Rather than being concerned with their own importance or preoccupied with fears, disciples must be as willing as Jesus to give up their lives for others.

But the only way the disciples will overcome their stubborn, deep-seated spiritual blindness will be to imitate the physically blind Bartimaeus, who begs Jesus to make him see (10:51). Unless they ask Jesus for the light of faith, they will remain in a darkness far more disabling then Bartimaeus' lack of sight.

## Death and Resurrection in Jerusalem (11:1–16:8)

The final phase of Jesus' story can be subdivided into four sections. The first two focus on the Temple, the latter two on the Passion and the empty tomb.

### Jesus and the Temple (11:1–12:44)

For a glowing moment Jesus' true identity shines out clearly. But the exultant crowd that greets him will soon become the menacing mob that calls for his execution. The peculiar story of the fig tree (11:12–14:20f) introduces a somber note into this section. Mark wraps the fig tree story around the story of the cleansing of the Temple. Just like the tree that failed to produce fruit, the Temple has failed to produce just and contrite hearts and authentic worship of the Lord. Jesus not only cleanses the Temple, he declares the temple invalid. It will be replaced by a temple "not made by hands" (14:58) that will be Jesus himself and his future community of disciples. In that new temple, love of God and neighbor will replace burnt offerings and sacrifice as forms of worship. The hypocritical leaders who delight in the trappings of religion while "devouring the houses of widows" will have no place there; but the humble, like the poor widow who gives all she has to God, will be assured a place (12:38–44).

### Towards the End-time (13:1–37)

Set in the context of Jesus' prediction that the great Temple of Herod would be leveled (and it was, in A.D. 70 ), this final discourse of Jesus is one of the Gospel's most puzzling, but important, passages. It focuses on the future of the Christian community and how it will carry out its mission in history after Jesus' death and resurrection. From the sayings of Jesus and Old Testament quotations that Mark has woven together in this discourse, three main themes can be identified:

*Warnings of persecutions and divisions as the community carries out its mission.* The world cannot end until the gospel has been proclaimed throughout the world (13:10). But that evangelization effort will be met with opposition, persecution (13:9–11), and internal divisions (13:12f).

*The Christian must "stay awake."* Without becoming doomsayers endlessly speculating about the end of the world, Christians must be sober and alert, aware of God's presence breaking into human history. False prophets will say, "I am he," and, "There he is" (13:6, 21), but true disciples will faithfully proclaim the Gospel while anticipating God's soon-to-be-revealed presence in history.

*God's triumph in history.* Without denial or sugar-coating, Mark acknowledges that the Christian community will suffer and face crises, but ultimately grace will triumph and human history will be full of hope.

### The Passion (14:1–15:47)

In keeping with the important role that the Passion plays in Mark's understanding of Jesus, these chapters constitute the longest single narrative of the Gospel; yet the story moves quickly to its climax at the cross.

The opening scenes (14:1–11) set contrasting moods: While Judas and the leaders plot, a faithful woman anoints Jesus' body for death. The next section is dominated by the last supper, where the broken bread and shared cup become signs of Jesus' impending death for others. Gethsemane is a scene of profound pain and sorrow (14:32–52). As darkness closes in around Jesus, the disciples take a nap—disappointing Jesus' hope that they would keep watch with him (13:36). Then Jesus is arrested by an armed band led by one of his own disciples. The rest of the disciples flee, leaving Jesus alone to face his trials before the Sanhedrin (14:53–72) and Pilate (15:1–20), and deserting him at his crucifixion and death.

Two motifs dominate the Passion story: the crisis of discipleship and the revelation of Jesus as the Son of God.

**The Crisis of Discipleship**

Throughout the Gospel the disciples have come off rather badly, and now their behavior is even scandalous. They professed loyalty at the last supper (14:31), but in the midst of crisis they run like frightened rabbits. Peter, the leader of the lot, denies even knowing the man he so recently confessed as the Messiah. While suffering and persecution make a hero of Jesus, it makes cowards of his friends.

The only people who come off looking good are those one would least expect: the woman who anoints Jesus despite the objections of his disciples (14:3–9); a Roman centurion who proclaims his faith in Jesus (15:39); and Joseph of Arimathea who courageously recovers and buries the body of Jesus (15:42–47).

**The Revelation of Jesus Christ, the Son of God**

In the Passion story we learn the answer to this Gospel's chief question: Who is Jesus? Jesus himself makes the bold announcement before the Sanhedrin: he is the Christ, the Son of God (14:61f). This Messiah stands as a prisoner soon to be condemned to death. He came to liberate Israel, but he has no army or weapons. He liberates not with power and might, but by freely surrendering his life. Jesus is the son of a God who is revealed in the "weakness" of selfless giving. For Mark, it is in the shadow of the cross that Jesus is seen most clearly.

### The Empty Tomb (16:1–8)

This brief but important passage is probably the original ending of Mark's Gospel. Someone writing later than Mark added the longer ending.

**Jesus' Victory over Death**

The crucified Jesus has conquered death: The empty tomb proclaims the fact and so does the mysterious "young man" who greets the women there. It is the truth of the young man's announcement that "Jesus of Nazareth, the crucified, has been raised" that makes Mark's story "gospel"—good news.

**Reconciliation with the Disciples**

Jesus does not wait for the disciples to come seeking him. The women are told to "go tell his disciples and Peter, 'He is going before you to Galilee; there you will see him.'" As he had promised at the last supper (14:24), Jesus will be reunited with his disciples despite the fact that they deserted him. Significantly, the messenger at the tomb instructs the women to tell the disciples and Peter. Peter, who had not only abandoned Jesus but denied him, is singled out.

**Back to Galilee: The Mission Begins**

In Galilee, where Jesus began his ministry and first called the disciples to share it with him, is where the reunion of master and disciples will occur. But it is not clear what kind of reunion Mark has in mind. It may be a resurrection appearance, a final end-of-the-world meeting with the disciples, or perhaps a reunion in spirit—Jesus promising to be with the disciples as they go forth to spread the gospel. Mark doesn't say.

### Mark's Abrupt Ending

Why does Mark's Gospel end so suddenly? Some speculate that he may have been prevented from finishing the Gospel. More likely, the original ending has been lost, or perhaps Mark thought that after the empty tomb nothing more need be said. The vocabulary, literary style, and theological content of the longer ending differ enough from Mark to convince scholars it came from another's pen.

**The Longer Ending (16:9–20)**

A later writer added the longer ending that recounts Jesus' appearance to Mary Magdalene, who brings the message of Jesus' resurrection to the disciples. The report of Jesus' appearance to the eleven begins with rebukes for their lack of faith in his resurrection. It concludes with a commissioning of the disciples and with promises that signs and wonders will accompany their ministry. Finally, without mention of a mountaintop, Jesus is taken up into heaven. The disciples go forth to preach, and the risen Lord is with them.

**Questions for Discussion and Reflection**

***Group Sharing/Discussion***

1. Discuss how the beginning and end of this Gospel are different than those in the other Gospels.

2. In this Gospel Jesus teaches more by his actions than by his words. Give examples of what/how he was teaching.

3. In your group, let different people represent different disciples from the Gospel. Have them tell who they are, what they did according to this Gospel, and how that person might explain their actions.

4. What are examples of the fact that Mark was writing, not for Jews, but for non-Jews?

***In Our Lives***

1. Discuss which disciple with whom you can most identify.

2. Jesus' family publicly rejected him. Why do you imagine they did that? Is there an example of that behavior towards you or someone you know? How do you think Jesus would want people to handle it today?

3. What can we learn for our own lives from the kind of company Jesus kept: for example, a paralyzed man (2:1–12); a demon-possessed man (5:1–15); a leader of the synagogue (5:22); a young girl (5:41); a Gentile mother of a possessed child (7:25–30); a rich young man (10:17–23); and a blind beggar (10:46)? How does our church imitate Jesus in this regard? What might we do better?

4. Name the qualities of a disciple of Christ as portrayed by Mark. Choose one that you want to develop further for yourself. Talk about how you might "grow" that quality.

***Individual/Personal Reflection/Action***

1. The central question of Mark's Gospel is "Who do you say I am?" (8:20). After reading the Gospel, how would you answer that question?

2. The cross looms large in Mark's Gospel. Why is it so central to his understanding of who Jesus was? Paul said the cross was a scandal and a stumbling block. Yet Christianity has clung to the cross as a mark of faith and a sign of hope. What is the message of the cross? What meaning does it hold for you and your faith?

3. In your own words in your heart, thank Mark for what you appreciate in this presentation of Christ's life.

# LUKE READING GUIDE

## *At a Glance*

| | |
|---|---|
| Who are the main players? | Elizabeth an Angel of the Lord Zechariah John the Baptist Mary Joseph the disciples Zacchaeus Herod the Great Pilate Mary Magdalene |
| What should I look for? | Luke provides an account of Jesus' life and teaching for the universal mission. He was engaged in intercultural dialogue when he told the story of Jesus for Greek-speaking, non-Jewish converts. Also note his addition of Jesus praying at the major moments of his mission. |
| When was this book written? | Proposed dates vary between A.D. 63 and 90. Some evidence suggests a date between A.D. 80–85. |
| Who wrote this book? | The unanimous tradition of the church has held that Luke, "the beloved physician" of Colossians (4:14), is the author of the Gospel. Probably a well-educated member of a |

wealthy urban family, and very likely from Antioch of Syria, Luke was writing for a Hellenistic audience. The only Gentile among the four evangelists, he was a companion of Paul who accompanied him in his travels.

**Why was this book written?** The introduction suggests Luke is a second or third generation Christian looking back on the founding years of the movement. Luke provides an account of the life and mission of Jesus for the universal mission of the gospel. Luke's Gospel shows that the preaching of the church is rooted in the life of Jesus.

**What is the story?** Luke is interested in showing us how God's plan of salvation is fulfilled in the Christian movement. The infancy stories or narratives review the hopes of the faithful people of Israel. Later, as Jesus begins his journey up to Jerusalem, he knows he is going to be taken up from there in death. This journey is a time to prepare the disciples for the events in Jerusalem and for their future role as witnesses to Jesus' teaching. In the telling of Jesus' death and resurrection, Luke emphasizes the necessity for the Messiah to suffer and die in Jerusalem. The episode with the repentant criminal shows that the death of Jesus extends salvation and forgiveness to others.

---

**Healings in Luke**

A leper 5:12 (Mk, Mt)
The centurion's servant 7:1 (Mt)
Peter's mother-in-law 4:38 (Mk, Mt)
Evening healings of the sick 4:40 (Mk, Mt)
A paralytic 5:18 (Mk, Mt)
A man with a withered hand 6:6 (Mk, Mt)
The woman with a hemorrhage 8:42 (Mk, Mt)
A mute demoniac 11:14 (Mt)
An epileptic boy 9:38 (Mk, Mt)
Two blind men 18:35 (Mk, Mt)
The crippled woman 13:11
The man with dropsy 14:1
The ten lepers 17:11
Restoring the ear of the servant Malchus 22:50
(Mt and Mk indicate the healing miracle is reported in Matthew and Mark as well.)

**Other Miracles Reported in Luke**

Casting out an unclean spirit 4:33 (Mk)
Calming the storm at sea 8:22 (Mk, Mt)
Curing the Gerasene demoniacs 8:26 (Mk, Mt)
Raising of Jairus's daughter 8:40 (Mk, Mt)
Feeding the five thousand 9:10 (Mk, Mt)
Escape from hostile Nazareth crowd 4:30
The catch of fish 5:1
Raising of son of the widow of Nain 7:11–17
Luke is the only Gospel that does not report the miracle of walking on the sea.
(Mk, Mt, and Jn indicate the miracle story also occurs in Mark, Matthew, or John.)

**Parables Found Only in Luke**

The two debtors 7:41–43
The good Samaritan 10:29–37
A friend at midnight 11:5–13
The rich fool 12:16–21
Faithful servants 12:35–40
The vigilant steward 12:42–48
The barren fig tree 13:6–9
The great feast 14:16–24
Constructing a tower and a king preparing for war 14:25–35
The lost coin 15:8–10
The lost (prodigal) son 15:11–32
The dishonest steward 16:1–13
The rich man and Lazarus 16:19–31
The master and servants 17:7–10
The persistent widow 18:1–8
The Pharisee and the tax collector 18:9–14
The ten gold coins 19:11–27

**When Jesus Prays in Luke**

At the Jordan River 3:21
In desert places 5:16
On a mountain 6:12
In solitude 9:18
On the Mountain of Transfiguration 9:28
In a "certain place" and teaching the "Our Father" 11:1–4
The upper room 22:32
In the garden 22:39–46
From the cross 23:34, 46
With the Emmaus disciples 24:30
At the ascension 24:50
(Luke records more instances of Jesus at prayer than any other evangelist.)

**Luke's Portrait of Jesus**

Luke's Jesus is a man of mercy and compassion with a particular concern for the poor and outcast. His Jesus prays often, especially before important events. Though he is the son of God, Luke's Jesus is also fully human and his concern for all people makes him the universal Messiah.

**Luke's Unique Perspective**

Luke aims at a clear, orderly, and faith-affirming presentation of the words and deeds of Jesus. Wanting his readers to know the truth and reliability of the gospel, he pays attention to historical detail. He stresses Christian prayer and the value of renunciation. He sees the fulfillment of prophecy in Jesus and thus stresses the fidelity of the God of Jesus. His Jesus shows a special interest in sinners, women, and family

**Luke's Unique Perspective *(cont.)***

life. His Gospel expresses joy at the announcement of the "good news," makes frequent use of the title "Son of Man," and reveals the active participation of the Spirit in the ministry of Jesus.

**Some Accounts Found Only in Luke**

- Announcements of the birth of John (1:5–25) and Jesus (1:26–38)
- Canticles of Mary (1:46–55) and Zechariah (1:67–79)
- Birth in Bethlehem, visit of the shepherds, and presentation in the Temple (2:1–40)
- Twelve-year-old Jesus in the Temple (2:41–52)
- Imprisonment of John (3:19, 20)
- Jesus is rejected at Nazareth (4:16–30)
- A sinful woman washes Jesus' feet (7:36–50)
- Galilean women follow Jesus (8:1–3)
- The meeting with Zacchaeus (19:1–10)
- The trial before Herod (23:6–12)

## Before Beginning

Luke tells us that he was not an eyewitness to the events of Jesus' ministry. He is dependent upon others who did witness and have already given their testimony in writing (1:2). Scholars have identified three of the sources that Luke used: Mark's Gospel; a collection of Jesus' sayings that was also used by Matthew, called "Q"; and a source for additional material about Jesus, which scholars designate "L" (see the NAB introduction to Luke, p. 1495). The introduction suggests that Luke is a second- or third-generation Christian looking back on the founding years of the movement. Luke's ability to write in different styles—including that of the Septuagint (the Greek translation of the Hebrew Scriptures, which was the Bible for most of the early Christian communities)—and to use conventions of Greek literature, such as the opening dedication to a prominent patron, suggest a well-educated author. To have received a literary education of this sort, Luke probably came from a prosperous urban family. Unlike the other Gospel writers, Luke's account did not end with the Gospel. He wrote a second volume, Acts of the Apostles, which showed that God's salvation, begun in Jesus, moved beyond Jerusalem and the pious of Israel into the whole world.

Luke's Gospel provides an account of Jesus' life and teaching for that universal mission. Today, people sometimes think that Christianity and its Gospels belong to North American and European culture. But the story of Jesus originated in a Semitic culture. Luke and other early Christians were already engaged in intercultural dialogue when they retold the story of Jesus for the Greek-speaking, non-Jewish converts who inhabited cities in the eastern part of the Roman empire. Their example shows that the gospel message is not limited to any one culture.

## An Assured Teaching

Luke's desire to establish Christianity within the larger world of the Roman Empire is evident in references to Roman emperors and events. For example, he links the birth of Jesus to Caesar Augustus (2:1). People have sometimes thought that Luke was attempting to write what we would call a history of Jesus and the earliest disciples. Most of the "historical" references, however, are not accurate even by ancient standards. Luke calls his work a *diegesis,* meaning a "narrative account," not a history. He claims that it is thorough, accurate, and orderly. He has traced the events that have occurred among "us" (i.e., the Christian community) from the beginning (1:1–4). The purpose of his writing is to provide "assurance" for the instruction that Christians

### Luke's "History"

LUKE IS SOMETIMES characterized as the "historian" among the evangelists. While he does make historical references to Roman emperors and Jewish kings (2:1–3; 3:1–2), his details are vague and not always accurate. He also shows faulty knowledge of Palestine, for example, in describing its climate and the way homes were built. Clearly, he is not a historian by modern standards. His chief interest is theological.

give. In other words, Luke's book will show that what the church preaches is rooted in the ministry of Jesus and the preaching of the first apostles.

Luke takes patterns for his story from biblical history. We see this, for example, in the infancy narratives, which show God's promises of salvation being fulfilled in Jesus. When Luke claims that his narrative is "orderly," he refers to the literary order, which sets out the periods of salvation. In the second volume, Acts of the Apostles, he shows the same Spirit at work in the developments in the early community. Civic authorities were suspicious of new religious movements. Luke's work addresses those fears by highlighting the high moral standards and social value of Christianity.

## An Ordered Narrative

Luke has told us that he is dependent upon earlier accounts but that he has reworked his material to provide a more accurate and orderly account. This refers to Luke's desire to set forth the way in which God's plan of salvation is fulfilled in the Christian movement. Scholars have made detailed studies of additions, deletions, and changes that Luke has made in the order of material taken over from Mark. There are three major additions that even the beginning Gospel reader can spot. Mark begins abruptly with the appearance of John the Baptist. Luke (as does Matthew) begins with an account of Jesus' birth (1:5–2:40). He adds a tale about the child Jesus (2:41–52). Then, between the Baptism and Temptation stories, Luke reintroduces Jesus by giving his genealogy (3:23–38).

A long section in which Jesus is journeying toward Jerusalem with the disciples (9:51–19:27) contains much of the teaching of Jesus. It includes parables that Luke has taken from "Q" (and from his special tradition) and retold in a way that serves as instruction for the church. By contrast, Mark's Gospel has only a short section of instruction to the disciples on the trip to Jerusalem.

Finally, there are several differences in the Passion and the Resurrection section. Mark ends with the women running from the empty tomb. Luke 24, on the other hand, has accounts of appearances by the Risen Lord, as well as instructions to the disciples. Luke's Passion narrative differs from Mark (and Matthew) as well. Jesus is never formally tried by the Jewish court. There is an unusual episode in which Pilate sends Jesus to be investigated by Herod (23:6–12). Pilate persists in declaring that Jesus is innocent of the charges against him (23:4, 14f, 22). The dying Jesus prays for forgiveness for his enemies (23:34) and enacts the message of the gospel by promising salvation to a repentant criminal who dies with him (23:39–43). Each of the above contributes to our sense that God's plan of salvation is being carried out.

## The Tragedy of Israel

The infancy stories awaken the joyful expectation that Israel's messianic king has arrived to bring salvation. Through him, God's peace and blessings will come to both Jews and Gentiles (2:29–32). Yet, as the story unfolds, this promise will not be fulfilled. Persistent rejection, first of Jesus and then of the disciples' mission, leaves Israel excluded. Luke points out the tragedy of this situation in a series of prophetic laments that Jesus utters over Jerusalem and her inhabitants. The first is a "Q" tradition (13:34f; Mt 23:37–39), which Luke has attached to an episode from his special tradition (13:31–33). The episode contained a warning that Herod was seeking Jesus' life. Jesus connects the divine necessity that he die in Jerusalem (13:33) with a lament for the city. The second, from Luke's special tradition, occurs as Jesus is looking out over the city where he is to die (19:41–44). Jesus weeps at the thought of the peace that will elude the city and the terrible devastations of war that it is to suffer. The final lament, also from "L," occurs as Jesus is on the way to his death. He looks out at the weeping women of Jerusalem and warns them to weep for themselves instead (23:27–31).

The church has constantly reminded Catholics that, even though the ancestors of today's Jews chose not to accept Jesus as Messiah, Christians cannot reject or persecute Jews. The church has also insisted that Christians share a common heritage with the Jewish people that is rooted in the Hebrew Scriptures. Luke insists that the heritage of the Christian movement lies in the faithful and just persons of Israel. Jesus' own family are among the righteous ones who trust in God for salvation. Though Luke's Passion holds certain Jewish leaders responsible for some of the events, Jesus does not condemn them but asks God's forgiveness. Luke also presents us with a Jesus who is able to weep as he foresees the terrible fate of Jerusalem. The prosperous and beautiful city of his day will be reduced to the rubble of war. Jerusalem will not enjoy the peace that God so longs to give the people.

## Reading through Luke

Before you begin to study Luke, read through the whole Gospel. Many of the stories will be familiar, because Luke contains some of the best-loved stories in the Gospels. Luke is a gifted storyteller. Even in the parables of Jesus, he creates short episodes and switches from the third-person report into dialogue between the characters. Young children often enjoy the stories in Luke more than those in the other Gospels. As you are reading, you might note passages that particularly appeal to you. Do you find any common themes in those stories? Here are some of the themes that you will find running through the Gospel.

### Salvation Is a Joyous Surprise

Luke has many images of celebration and rejoicing. From the very beginning to the very last verse, people are praising and thanking God for the salvation that they experience in Jesus. Salvation is a "surprise" or gift because those who receive it could never have anticipated that it would come. Mary's Magnificat (1:46–55) sets the tone. God has come and rescued the humble, poor, oppressed, and lowly people of the land. Jesus begins his ministry (4:18) by quoting a promise from Isaiah: a threefold release from poverty, from sickness, and from sin. Luke drives home this point about salvation by showing that Jesus has the power to forgive sins and to heal people (see 5:17–26). Even the rich tax collector Zacchaeus hears the message, demonstrates his repentance by making restitution to those he had cheated, and shares his joy by throwing a banquet (19:1–10).

God's mercy is the source of this salvation. Christians are to show mercy in the same way that God is merciful (6:36). When Jesus gives examples of what God's mercy and forgiveness are like, he uses very active images. God is not waiting for people to come crawling back, begging forgiveness. God is out looking for people to help like the shepherd and the lost sheep, the woman and the lost coin, or the wayward son's father, who goes running out of the house and immediately orders a large celebration.

### Salvation Includes Everyone

In Acts, Luke will show us that God directed the disciples to take the gospel to all the peoples of the earth. The Gospel demonstrates the universality of God's love and salvation in a different way. It stresses the fact that Jesus reached out to all sorts of people, even to those who seemed to have no chance at salvation. Zacchaeus, the tax collector, was a sinner who had defrauded people to enrich himself (19:1–10). The Samaritans, traditional enemies of the Jews, turn out to be examples of Jesus' teaching. The mercy shown by the Good Samaritan (10:37) is so well known that we can speak of anyone who shows mercy or unmerited assistance to another as a "Samaritan." Less well known is the Samaritan leper (17:11–19) who is the only one of the group healed by Jesus to return and give him thanks. Women—often excluded from education, public leadership, and cultural events in those days—are constantly included in Jesus' ministry. A sinful woman provides a better demonstration of love and hospitality than the Pharisee. Her sins are forgiven (7:31–50). Mary is permitted to sit and listen to Jesus as a disciple. She does not have to busy herself with the business of serving the male guests that has her sister so distracted (10:38–42). When Jesus defended Mary's listening to his teaching, he was not condemning Martha's devotion to serving her guests or the traditional tasks of women in the home. Jesus was really issuing an invitation to her to join her sister. Martha was so busy that she was missing the one necessary thing, to hear Jesus' message about the Kingdom (10:41f).

### Special Concern for Those in Need

Salvation has very concrete aspects in Luke. Those who are poor, helpless, in prison, sick, and the like are promised release. Jesus and the apostles are able to relieve the suffering of the sick by healing. Acts contains many stories in which God intervenes to free the apostles from prison. To achieve this goal, however, miraculous events are not required. The story of the Good Samaritan (10:29–37) shows how this salvation can come about through concrete actions. The Samaritan uses his own resources to see that the man beaten up by robbers is restored to health, even though, as a Jew, the victim is his enemy. The parable of the Great Supper, in which the host replaces the friends who refused to come with the poor, and the sayings about showing aid to those who cannot repay (14:12–24) are other examples of how salvation can come to those in need.

Luke often returns to the theme of rich and poor. The rich often fail to receive salvation because they are trapped by their own desires for money or pleasure (see 12:13–21; 16:19–30). Even those who are good people like the Rich Ruler (18:18–24) are so locked in by possessions that they cannot achieve the eternal life they desire. That does not mean that Luke thinks all rich people are excluded from the Kingdom. The Samaritan, Zacchaeus, and anyone else who is willing to share his possessions generously with those who are in need can become a disciple of Jesus. Acts will return to this theme in its picture of sharing possessions in the early community. Luke also retains the sayings of Jesus that call upon followers to renounce material goods to become disciples (6:35; 9:3; 10:4; 12:33; 14:33; 16:13). By doing so, Jesus, and later the apostles, demonstrate that they are completely dedicated to God. But Luke knows that such discipleship is possible only if the basic needs of the group are met through the generosity of others. He reports that a group of women followers provided the necessary support (8:1–3). In Acts, he reports that Paul achieved the same end by laboring at his trade (Acts 20:33–35).

### Mary Is the First Disciple

Catholic Christians have always paid special honor to Mary, the mother of Jesus. Luke's Gospel provides the basis for the devotion to Mary. Her assent to God's work of salvation initiates the whole story. Her Magnificat is a strong statement of God's faithfulness and mercy. It is not just because of the miracle of Jesus' birth that Mary is honored. That is not Luke's picture. For Luke she is both the epitome of the faithful people of Israel who wait confidently for God's salvation and the beginning of the new life of those who will be disciples of Jesus. Jesus defines her role in 8:21. She is one who hears and does the word of God. He repeats this affirmation in 11:27f. The crowd praises Jesus' biological mother. Jesus corrects them by insisting that hearing and keeping the word of God constitutes the true source of blessing.

The infancy narrative demonstrates that Mary

**Discipleship** Luke's formula for discipleship is clear: Don't just hear the word of God; live it. Luke uses parables, more than the other evangelists, to teach about discipleship. Look at the following parables for what they teach about the way a disciple should behave:

- The good Samaritan (10:29–37)
- The rich fool (12:16–21)
- The lost sheep; lost coin; lost son (15:1–32)
- The dishonest steward (16:1–13)
- The rich man and Lazarus (16:19–31)
- The Pharisee and publican (18:9–14)

has this quality of true discipleship. She has accepted God's will in the Annunciation scene. Later she keeps in her heart words spoken to her about Jesus, as well as the extraordinary events she witnesses (2:19, 51). Simeon includes her in his prayer about the impact of Jesus' ministry in Israel (2:34f). Mary remains among the faithful disciples of Jesus. She was present among those disciples gathered in Jerusalem after Easter (Acts 1:14).

## An Outline of Luke

Luke's Gospel falls into a neat pattern that moves from the infancy narrative, through the ministry in Galilee, back to the Jerusalem Temple, and finally to Jesus' death and resurrection. The Gospel ends with the disciples in Jerusalem awaiting the coming of the Spirit. Acts will take the Gospel from Jerusalem out into the world. Jerusalem forms a symbolic center to the Gospel, as much of the narrative takes place either in or on the way to the holy city. The major divisions in the story are clearly marked transitions in the unfolding of the plot:

Prologue (1:1–4)
Infancy Narrative (1:5–2:52)
Preparation for the Public Ministry (3:1–4:13)
The Ministry in Galilee (4:14–9:50)
The Journey to Jerusalem (9:51–19:27)
Teaching Ministry in Jerusalem (19:28–21:38)
The Passion Narrative (22:1–23:56)
The Resurrection Narrative (24:1–53)

In reading through the Gospel of Luke in detail, notice how Luke develops a picture of Jesus, salvation, and Christian discipleship. Because Luke preserves important blocks of the teaching of Jesus, note also how Luke presents the teaching of Jesus for Christians in his time. Discipleship requires living the word of God as well as hearing it

## The Infancy Narrative (1:5–2:52)

This section is built on an elaborate similarity between Jesus and John the Baptist. In each case, Jesus is greater than the Baptist, who is only the forerunner of the Messiah. The most detailed parallels occur between the two angelic birth announcements (John: 1:5–25; Jesus: 1:26–38):

1. Neither parent is expecting a child;

2. An angel appears, the parent is troubled and told not to fear;

3. A child is announced, his name given, and a statement is made about his future greatness;

4. The parent raises a question about how this can happen;

5. The angel gives an assertion that it will happen, and a sign;

6. Zechariah is forced to be silent; Mary's spontaneous answer affirms God's will.

The birth announcements are followed by an episode that brings the two together and confirms the angel's statement to Mary, the Visitation (1:39–56). In this episode the Baptist testifies to the presence of Jesus as savior by moving in the womb.

The next cycle recounts the births (John: 1:57f; Jesus: 2:1–20) and circumcision/naming of the two children (John: 1:57–80; Jesus: 2:21–40). Each birth section includes mention of the joy at the birth. Each naming section concludes with an affirmation that the child grew. This cycle is followed by an episode that prefigures Jesus' last days, the Finding in the Temple (2:41–52). Jesus will return to the Temple to teach before his death (see the outline of the Gospel).

It is made clear that God is responsible for the origins of both children. For the Baptist, God has overcome the barrenness of his parents, just as other barren women in the Hebrew Bible, like Sarah and Hannah, had been given children. For Jesus, God has done something even greater by bringing the child into existence in the womb of his virgin mother.

### Songs of Salvation: The Canticles

These episodes contain several canticles, which have become a treasured part of Christian worship: Mary's Magnificat (1:46–55); Zechariah's Benedictus (1:68–79); the canticle of the angels (2:13f); and Simeon's Nunc Dimittis (2:29–32). Many scholars think that Luke has taken the Magnificat, the Benedictus, and perhaps the Nunc Dimittis from a Jewish Christian source. They use expressions taken from the Hebrew Bible and other Jewish psalms and hymns from the time of Jesus.

Mary's Magnificat is an individual song of

praise, which seems to be modeled on the Song of Hannah (1 Sm 2:1–10). After celebrating God's greatness toward the lowly handmaid (vv. 51–53), in a series of strong, active verbs, the song refers to God's past deeds of salvation. The final verses (54f) relate the career of Jesus to the covenant God had made with Abraham. Scholars think that this hymn originated among Jewish Christians who identified themselves with the "poor ones," the "anawim," of Israel. That term designated those who were unfortunate, lowly, sick, or downtrodden. The rich and powerful, those who feel no need of God, are opposed to the anawim (see Ps 149:4; Is 49:13; 66:2). The poor ones are the righteous remnant in Israel who know that they must look to God for salvation.

The Benedictus begins as a song of thanksgiving (vv. 71–75) recalling the dynasty expectation of the house of David (see 2 Sm 7:12f). The hymn affirms that Jesus will fulfill this messianic role. It then shifts to the form of an oracle concerning the destiny of the newborn (76–79). The Baptist will prepare God's people for the coming Messiah. We are reminded that God comes to save the people out of merciful compassion. Luke will make the theme of mercy a central theme in the ministry of Jesus.

The Nunc Dimittis draws upon two passages of Isaiah (Is 40:5; 49:6). Simeon has now seen the salvation that these two passages promised. The image of an elderly patriarch blessed with a glimpse of God's promise is rooted in the Hebrew Bible (see Joseph, Gn 46:30; Moses, Dt 32:49–50; 34:1–5; Anna and Tobit, Tb 11:9.14). Verses 31–32 point to another important theme in Luke: God's salvation is given for all peoples. The aged prophet Simeon not only recognizes the dawning of salvation; he also warns that Jesus' coming will bring about divisions. God's plan includes the rejection of the Messiah by his own people (see 4:29; 13:33–35; 19:44, 47f; 20:14, 17).

#### Virgin Birth and Christology in the Infancy Narrative

As mentioned, the canticles celebrate Jesus' coming as the fulfillment of all God's promises to the faithful people of Israel. The Benedictus pointed to Jesus as the anticipated Messiah of the Davidic house. The announcement of Jesus' birth by the angels is made in two stages. Verses 32f parallel 2 Samuel 7:9, 13, 14, 16. Jesus will inherit the throne of David and rule over Jacob's house forever as "son" of God. The second stage in the announcement moves beyond these promises of a messiah to the special sense in which Jesus is Son of God: Jesus is begotten through God's intervention. Some scholars suggest that Luke created this two-step process from older statements of Christ such as Romans 1:3f. There, Jesus is "Son of David" during his earthly life and is designated "Son of God" through the power of the Holy Spirit when he is exalted to God's right hand at the Resurrection. The announcement to Mary speaks of God's Spirit overshadowing her and bringing into being a child who is Son of God from the time he is conceived. For Luke, Jesus is fully human but is never just another ordinary human being.

Mary's virginity serves to sharpen the Christological focus: the child to be born is God's Son. Mary is not like the barren woman, someone whose womb could unexpectedly open and produce a child. As virgin, there is no human way for her to have a child without God's unique presence in that process. Ancient Greek biology taught that the spirit in a father's sperm gave shape to the material in a mother's womb. The more active the spirit, the more closely a child resembled its father. Thus, Mary's virginity indicates a relationship between Jesus and God unlike that of any other human being. The honor that Mary enjoys is not due to the fact of her virginity, but to her willingness to accept a role in God's plan for the salvation of humanity.

A second angelic announcement, that of the angels to the shepherds, accompanies the story of Jesus' birth (2:1–20). Luke introduces this section with a reference to Caesar Augustus and the expansion of Roman rule indicated by the census. Historically, there was no worldwide census under Quirinius. When the Romans took over administration of Judaea in A.D. 6–7, they took a census of that province. Residents of Galilee, which was still ruled by one of Herod's sons, would not have been obligated to return to their ancestors' village in Judaea. The tradition in the Gospel of Matthew claims that Jesus was born toward the end of the rule of Herod the Great, who died in 4 B.C. Though Luke lacks precise historical information in this scene, its Roman associations permit a symbolic contrast. The Roman emperor Augustus emphasized the fact that his rule had brought peace in the world. The doors to the temple of war, pictured on coins, were shown closed. Luke uses the announcement by the angels (2:10–14) to show that the true source of peace lies elsewhere: in the Messiah who has been born in David's town, Bethlehem.

## Preparation for the Public Ministry (3:1–4:13)

Before Luke begins to recount the public ministry, he introduces three additional blocks of material: (1) John the Baptist's mission in preparing the way for Jesus and Jesus' baptism; (2) a genealogy; and (3) the Temptation of Jesus.

### The Baptist's Ministry (3:1–22)

Luke has gathered together traditions about John the Baptist from different sources. John the Baptist is fulfilling the mission given him to serve as forerunner for God's Messiah. Luke has arranged his account so that the fiery preacher of repentance also serves as precursor to Jesus in what the message says about: (1) repentance and forgiveness, two of the effects of salvation in Luke, and (2) the requirements for dealing with material possessions. The ethical section of John's preaching (vv. 10–14) illustrates the "good fruit," which must come from repentance (v. 9).

As the episode comes to a conclusion, the Baptist separates himself clearly from the Messiah. John belongs to the age of prophets. Jesus will inaugurate the messianic age. Luke then completes the story by reporting the fact that John was imprisoned by Herod Antipas before Jesus appears on the scene. This order creates some chaos in the account of Jesus' baptism, which follows it (vv. 21f). For Luke, the baptism of Jesus can never suggest that Jesus was dependent upon the Baptist. Rather, the episode permits a divine affirmation that Jesus is son of God and provides the occasion for the Spirit to descend on Jesus and inaugurate his ministry.

### Genealogy of Jesus (3:23–38)

This unusual genealogy corrects a misapprehension about Jesus. People may think he is the son of Joseph. The Christian community knows better. It traces Jesus' ancestry back to the first "son of God," Adam, and thus links Jesus to the entire human race, not just to the house of David.

### Temptation of Jesus (4:1–13)

Jesus goes to the desert under the impulse of the Spirit. The temptations Satan poses are challenges to Jesus' identity as Son of God, which has been the central title in Luke's narrative to this point. Temptation, in this sense, is not toward some sinful act. Rather, as in the testing of Abraham by the demand that he sacrifice Isaac, temptation puts the person before a crisis that will demonstrate whether their faith in God can be destroyed. Jesus refuses to use his status as Son for personal gain. Though Satan is silenced, the story ends on an ominous note; though Jesus'

### The Evangelists Symbolized

SINCE ANCIENT TIMES, artists have used the four living creatures of the book of Revelation (Rev 4:7) to symbolize the four evangelists.

*Mark* is linked with the desert lion because his Gospel opens with John, the voice of one "crying out in the desert."

*Luke* is linked with the calf, a sacrificial animal, because his Gospel opens with Zechariah offering sacrifice in the Temple.

*Matthew* is associated with the human figure because his Gospel begins with a record of Jesus' human ancestors.

*John* is linked with the eagle because his Gospel starts with a hymn of praise to Jesus who uniquely can look on the face of God just as the eagle uniquely looks upon the sun.

ministry will undermine Satan's power (10:18; 13:16), Satan may yet return. In Luke 22:31f Jesus speaks of a confrontation with Satan on behalf of his disciples; though they will be seriously tested by the events of the Passion, Jesus has prayed that their faith will not fail. When the temptations are finished, Jesus has demonstrated that he is the obedient Son of God who will carry out God's plan of salvation—whatever the cost.

## The Ministry in Galilee (4:14–9:50)

The introduction to this section (4:14f) highlights the power of the Spirit active in the ministry of Jesus (1:35; 3:22; 4:1, 14, 18).

### In Nazareth and Capernaum (4:16–44)

Luke's sources had Jesus' ministry begin in Capernaum (see Mk 1:21–35). Luke has reordered events (v. 23 refers to the Capernaum tradition) to open with a sermon in Nazareth that depicts Jesus as the one who fulfills what the Hebrew prophets foretold (vv. 17–21). Throughout Luke and Acts, announcements occur in synagogues and at the Temple. Jesus announces the joyous freedom of the Year of Jubilee (combining Is 61:1–11 and Is 58:6). Once again, Luke previews the story yet to come. Jesus points to Hebrew prophets Elijah and Elisha, who were directed to assist persons who were not Israelites. These words provoke a deadly hostility in the hearers (vv. 25–30).

The rest of the chapter consists of healing stories that illustrate the liberation Jesus has just announced. The demons acknowledge that Jesus is "from God." However, the popular acclaim, which results from the miracles, makes it so difficult for Jesus even to move about that he leaves for synagogues in Judea (vv. 42–44).

### Jesus Gathers Disciples (5:1–39)

Jesus' activities in Nazareth and Capernaum come before he has any disciples. This arrangement provides those who are called with a reason for following Jesus. By the time he gathers his first disciples, Jesus already has a reputation as healer and teacher. Simon Peter's call to follow Jesus is linked with a story of a miraculous catch of fish. Peter, viewing the catch of fish, announces that he is unworthy to be in the presence of the divine (v. 8). Peter's acknowledgment that he is a "sinner" is also similar to the "fear" exhibited at the appearance of the angels in the birth announcement stories. Like the angel, Jesus first tells Peter not to be afraid. Then he states what Peter's future destiny is to be: "from now on you will be catching men" (v. 10). The Christian reader knows of Peter's role as missionary apostle in Acts. Peter and the sons of Zebedee, James and John, respond as exemplary disciples. They will leave everything to follow Jesus.

Jesus continues to establish his authority through healings, first of a leper (vv. 12–16), then of a paralyzed man (vv. 17–26). When Luke took over the account of the healing of the paralyzed man, it was already a controversy story—that is, an account of a controversy or conflict between Jesus and the religious authorities—over Jesus' authority to forgive sins (see Mk 2:1–12). The reader already knows that Jesus has the power to heal anyone he wishes. In this case, the miracle becomes both an occasion to free the man from sin through forgiveness and a demonstration of the authority by which Jesus can claim that the man's sins have been forgiven. The crowd goes home praising God, but the Pharisees and scribes become suspicious of Jesus. His offer of forgiveness appears to be a blasphemous attempt by a human being to claim power that belongs to God (v. 21). Luke's reader knows that Jesus is not just any human being, but the obedient Son of God. Jesus would never seize any power that rightly belongs to God (see 4:5–8).

As Jesus calls his next disciple, the toll collector Levi, the Pharisees and scribes complain further. They go to Jesus' disciples to ask why he eats with persons who are considered sinners. Jesus first cites a proverb in defense of his actions and then insists that the goal of his mission is to call sinners. He is not out to preach to the righteous.

Jesus is accused of not instructing his disciples in piety as a true teacher would do. The disciples of both the Baptist and the Pharisees fast. Jesus' disciples do not. Jesus' defense consists of a brief parable and a string of proverbs (5:33–39). The first uses a human analogy: It is impossible to fast at a wedding. The abundance of the wedding feast was also a common metaphor for the time of salvation. When Jesus is no longer present, Christians will fast (v. 35). The proverbs demonstrate the absurdity of trying to mix the old ways of life with the new time of salvation. Persons

**The Beatitudes** In contrast with Matthew, Luke lists only four beatitudes or "blessed" statements, which he contrasts with four "woes." *Blessed* refers to those who receive God's favor. The woes threaten God's wrath against those who value material wealth over the things of the Kingdom. Note that the future will see the hungry and weeping satisfied and laughing, while those who are filled and laughing will hunger and weep. It is especially noteworthy that while Matthew spiritualizes the beatitudes—blessed are the poor *in spirit* (Mt 5:5), those who hunger and thirst *for righteousness* (Mt 5:6)—Luke refers to very real economic and social circumstances.

used to the old way may find it difficult to accept the new (v. 39).

Jesus then defends his disciples against charges of breaking the Sabbath (6:1–5), first by appeal to Scripture (1 Sm 21:1–6), then by insisting on his authority as Son of Man (cf 5:24), and finally on humanitarian grounds: It is always right to preserve rather than destroy life (vv. 6–11). The section concludes with the choice of the Twelve from the larger group of disciples who will share Jesus' mission and serve as witnesses to what Jesus has done and said.

### Sermon on the Plain (6:17–49)

In Jesus' first major sermon (4:18), the Kingdom is good news for the poor and oppressed, and divine judgment is against the wealthy and prosperous. As the stories of Christian missionaries in Acts will demonstrate, Christians must expect rejection and persecution for preaching about Jesus (see Acts 7:52). The love command (vv. 27–30) covers all forms of mercy because it is to be modeled on the mercy of God. Examples point to general ethical precepts: give to one who asks; lend to those who cannot repay; treat others as you would be treated. Judgment sayings add strength to this ethical teaching: We are judged by the judgments we make about others (vv. 37–42).

### Jesus is the Promised Savior (7:1–9:18)

Jesus' ministry in Galilee continues with a series of traditional miracle stories told so that they testify to Jesus' identity: cure of the centurion's slave indicates that there is greater faith among the Gentiles than in Israel (7:9); the widow's son evokes the allusions to Elijah and Elisha in the opening sermon (4:25f); awestruck, the people acknowledge that a great prophet has arisen (7:16). Further miracles demonstrate the truth of Jesus' reply to the Baptist's disciples: he is indeed the one to come (vv. 18–23). Luke edits his sources to make a distinction between those who received John's baptism and also receive Jesus with praise, and those who reject the plan of God—the lawyers and Pharisees (vv. 28–30). The call of Levi (5:27–32) illustrated the conversion of tax collectors. This contrast prepares the reader for the sharp contrast between the Pharisee Simon, who failed to show Jesus the hospitality due an honored guest, and the sinful woman, who anoints Jesus and whose sins are forgiven (7:36–50). The parable of the Pharisee and the tax collector makes a similar point (18:9–14).

Examples of women who followed Jesus (8:1–3) and Jesus' mother as a model disciple, one who hears and keeps the word of God (8:19–21), frame the instruction about discipleship given in the parable of the sower (8:4–15), the lamp (8:16–17), and a general warning to be careful how one hears the word (v. 18). The interpretation of the sower parable indicates the threats to discipleship: some will not believe the initial preaching; some will be turned from discipleship by temptation, cares, riches, and pleasure; and still others will lack the patient endurance necessary to bring forth the harvest.

### Other Miracles

Another series of miracles emphasizes Jesus' power to save. The disciples are rescued from the storm (8:22–25); the Gerasene is saved from the multitude of demons that made it impossible for any human bonds to restrain him (vv. 26–37). The concluding instructions are pointed toward Christians as well: go and declare what God has done for you (vv. 38f). The healing of Jairus's daughter and the woman with the hemorrhage focus on the faith of the recipients (vv. 40–56). This section concludes with the feeding of the five thousand (9:13–17). As Luke shapes the story, this miracle represents food for the hungry (6:21), as well as a response to Satan's challenge to turn stones into bread (4:3f). Jesus does live by the word of God alone.

### The Messiah Who Must Suffer (9:18–50)

None of the opinions about Jesus' identity capture the truth that Jesus is the Messiah who must suffer. Luke applies this insight to the followers of Jesus by insisting that the disciple must be ready to take up the cross "daily" (9:23). Not only does God affirm Jesus' sonship at the Transfiguration (as in Mk 9:7), but Moses and Elijah also talk with Jesus about his coming departure from the world at Jerusalem (9:30f). Luke has omitted Mark's material that is critical of the disciples from the Passion prediction (Mk 8:33), the Transfiguration (Mk 9:6), and the healing of an epileptic boy (Mk 9:28–29). In doing so, Luke brings the dramatic Transfiguration closer to the predictions of the Passion. God prevents the disciples from understanding what Jesus has said to them. Their arguments over greatness and jealousy of a outsider who uses Jesus' name (9:46–50) show that they are not yet ready to follow Jesus in suffering.

## The Journey to Jerusalem (9:51–19:27)

The journey to Jerusalem is the time of preparation for the disciples. Teachings of Jesus dominate this section of the Gospel. Miracles underline Jesus' conflict with the Pharisee teachers over the merciful application of the Law (13:10–17; 14:1–6); they point to the virtues of faith and gratitude (shown by a Samaritan leper, 17:11–19), and they anticipate Jesus' triumphal entry into Jerusalem (18:35–43).

### Criticism of the Pharisee Opponents of Jesus

The shape of the Pharisees' criticism was anticipated by the story of the sinful woman in the house of a Pharisee (7:36–50). Luke sharpens the charges and also generalizes them to apply to Christians as well: it is hypocritical to use the Law to condemn in one case what one's actions in another approve; applications of purity regulations demonstrate this principle (11:37–44); and lack of love of God leads to self-aggrandizement and even persecution of those sent by God (11:45–52). The Pharisees are persistently pictured as driven by love of money, desire for honor, and self-justification that stems from their application of the Law. The first two characteristics (16:14f) reappear in Acts as typical of magicians and false prophets in paganism (see Acts 8:9–25).

### Warnings about Judgment

Luke does not anticipate the return of Jesus in judgment in the immediate future. Therefore, warnings to be watchful apply to both Jesus' opponents and Luke's Christian readers. Demands for a sign only prove that there was more wisdom among Gentiles in the past than among God's people in the present (11:29–32). Hypocrisy can never be hidden from God's judgment (12:1–3). The stories of faithful and unfaithful servants warn against presuming that the delay in Jesus' return means that all restraints are removed (12:35–48). Although they can read the signs of the weather, Jesus' contemporaries are unable to see what is before them in Jesus (12:54–56). People must not fall into false confidence because of the tragedies that happen to others. The fact that we have not suffered the disasters that happen to others does not mean that those who suffer are worse than we are, or that God is more pleased with us (13:1–5). The parable of the barren fig tree provides a different understanding of the situation. It could be that we are like the tree being given its one last chance (13:6–9). The narrow door and shut door warn that Jesus' audience could be excluded and replaced with foreigners in the Kingdom (13:22–30). Framing the parable of the servants entrusted with the master's wealth with the parable of the ruler who had gone into a distant country emphasizes the problem of discipleship in a time of delay (19:11–27). Delay doesn't necessarily mean the kingdom is absent. Luke preserves sayings that point out the presence of the Kingdom for Jesus' disciples as well as its sudden arrival (17:20–37). Luke expands the traditional saying about the coming of the Son of Man in judgment with another affirmation that the Son of Man must first suffer and be rejected by his own generation (17:25).

### Discipleship: Renunciation, Devotion, and Suffering

The journey to Jerusalem opens with sayings that warn would-be disciples that they must be completely devoted to the Kingdom (9:57–62). Such disciples renounce normal human ties to family. They are the ones sent to heal and to preach the approach of the Kingdom (10:9). Their words are equivalent to the words of Jesus (10:16). Luke 10:17–20 acknowledges the potential dangers that the disciples face. However, Satan's fall from heaven indicates that the mission is weakening evil's power over humanity. Stories of the apostles in Acts will illustrate the certainty of divine protection. Sayings against anxiety require the disciple to have confidence in the generosity of others (12:22–34). Luke's addition to the traditional saying—sell possessions, give alms, and so provide yourself with heavenly treasure (v. 22)—points to one way in which the material needs were met. The good news for the poor depends upon consistent efforts by Christians to help those in need. This should not make people feel looked down upon or rejected. Jesus and the early church welcomed such people into the community in addition to providing food and clothing for them.

The Martha and Mary story (10:38–42) also illustrates a discipleship that abandons the cares of this world, even the obligations of hospitality, for the one thing necessary to salvation—hearing and keeping the word of Jesus (also see 11:27–28).

Disciples must also expect division. Jesus' ministry brings division even within families (12:49–53; see also 2:34f). Jesus challenges disciples to recognize the full cost of being a disciple: both suffering and patient endurance to follow Jesus to the end are required (14:25–33). The slave can never tell the master, "I quit" (17:7–10).

### Discipleship and Material Possessions

Riches can be a major hurdle to becoming or remaining a disciple of Jesus (8:14; 18:18–25). Disciples have left everything to follow Jesus (18:26–30). Luke's parables demonstrate the folly of being possessed by wealth: The rich farmer dies before he can build his barns (12:13–21), and the rich man who cannot see the poor Lazarus at his door is so blind to his own sinful behavior that he thinks he can bargain even with Abraham from hell (16:19–31). Alongside the call for renouncing everything, Luke presents another way in which Christians can use material possessions: They can share them with the unfortunate as the Good Samaritan does (10:29–37). Instead of feasting friends, they can provide for those who have no resources (14:12–24). Luke presents the parable of the dishonest steward as a warning not to mix service to God with the pursuit of wealth (16:1–13). The final episode in the travel narrative, the parable of the ten gold coins (19:11–27), draws on a common experience in a world without instant communications, uncertainty about the fate or return of those on a journey. Luke recognizes that Jesus may not return in judgment for a long time. Disciples must remain faithful stewards of what God has given them.

### Prayer in the Life of Disciples

Jesus frequently turns to prayer (3:21; 6:12; 9:18, 28; 11:2; 22:32, 41; 23:46). Two times the disciples are instructed about prayer. The first is as a response to their request to be taught as the Baptist had taught his disciples (11:1; see also 5:33). Luke follows the Lord's Prayer (11:2–4) with the parable of the persistent friend (vv. 5–8) and instruction on the efficacy of prayer (vv. 9–13). In the parable of the importunate widow (18:1–6), if an unjust judge with no moral conscience can be badgered into hearing the widow, how much the more quickly will God respond to the pleas of the suffering lowly ones? After all, God is not withdrawn, waiting for humans to come begging, but is actively seeking those who are lost (see ch 15).

## Jesus' Teaching Ministry in Jerusalem (19:28–21:38)

Jesus' arrival in Jerusalem brings the narrative back to its beginning.

### The Messiah Comes to City and Temple (19:28–48)

The Messiah who should have brought peace to Jerusalem will not be able to do so (19:41–44). Luke has revised the story of Jesus' entry into Jerusalem (Mk 11:1–10) so that the crowd consists of followers testifying to the works Jesus has done in Galilee (v. 37). Jesus goes directly to the Temple so that his entry reflects the Greek version of Malachi 3:1, "the lord whom you seek will come suddenly to his temple." But Jesus has not come to set up the kingdom of David (19:11; Acts 1:4). The city is the object of a prophetic lament—peace comes in the heavens, not on earth (v. 38). Allusion to Habakkuk 2:11, the stones crying out from the walls against a nation that plunders the people (19:39f), heightens the sense of a city about to meet its divine destiny. Jesus purges the Temple so that it can be a place of prayer as well as the location for Jesus' teaching in Jerusalem (19:45–48).

**Jesus Teaches Daily in the Temple (20:1–21:4)**

A traditional series of pronouncement stories (Mk 11:27–12:44) provides the content of Jesus' teaching now that he has returned to "his Father's house" (2:49).

**The Authority for Jesus' Actions**

One day Jesus was teaching the people in the temple, and the Pharisees came and asked him, "Tell us by what authority are you doing these things?"(20:1–2). Jesus answers with a counter question hinting that those who reject him do not believe the Baptist either. Compare Jesus' answer (20:8) with his response to the Council when they demand to know whether Jesus is Messiah (22:67). If Jesus speaks, they do not believe; if Jesus asks a question, they do not answer.

**Wicked Tenants**

Christians have traditionally read this parable as an allegory for the replacement of Israel as God's covenant people. Today we recognize that neither Jesus nor Luke think that a faithful God would give up on the Jewish people. Jesus directs this tale at his opponents.

**Tribute Due God and Caesar**

Luke's addition of verse 20 intensifies the hostility implied in the question. Jesus' opponents are seeking evidence for charges of stirring up political rebellion to bring against Jesus at trial (see 23:2–5). The spies pose their malicious question under the guise of pious flattery. Jesus, they say, teaches the truth and exhibits a godlike impartiality toward persons. Again, Jesus responds with a question. He forces the opponents to acknowledge that they are carrying coins with Caesar's image, and they utter Caesar's name. Jesus' reply serves as a judgment against their failure to pay God the honor due God. Readers know that Jesus' disciples have left coins and human positions of honor behind. They recognize that only God claims our loyalty. Thus, this passage does not teach the doctrine of separate powers of church and state that has traditionally been attached to it.

**Resurrection of the Dead**

The final challenge receives a double answer. The absurd case that a man must marry his dead brother's wife if she had not yet borne children (see Dt 25:5; Gn 38:8) probably came from the debates between the Sadducees and Pharisees over resurrection. Jesus' first answer affirms that the "children of God" (note the contrast with the woman who dies childless) are resurrected to an angelic existence. His second answer (20:37f) points to the revelation of God to Moses. If God is God of the patriarchs, they must be living.

**Jesus Challenges the Opposition**

Having silenced those who came to question him, Jesus poses challenges of his own. The question about how David's Son can be greater than his ancestor draws upon Psalm 110:1, a text frequently used in early Christianity to speak of Jesus' exaltation. The warning about the scribes (20:45–47) invokes the contrast in Luke between the wealthy and the oppressed poor. Jesus emerges as advocate for the poor. Finally, the comment on the widow's offering (21:1–4) repeats the contrast between a poor person and the wealthy. The radical gift of the widow condemns

> **Apocalyptic** The term refers to the revelation of mysterious truth that was previously hidden regarding future events that deal with the end of human history and final judgment. Both "revelation" (from Latin *revelatio*) and "apocalypse" (from Greek *apokalypsis*) mean "take away the veil."

the abundance that stands behind the gifts of the rich. Jesus is not approving the poverty in which the widow lives, but he is asserting that her acts demonstrate a piety greater than that of the rich.

#### Fate of the Temple and the Coming End-time (21:5–38)

The Jerusalem teaching ends with Luke's version of the apocalyptic sayings in Mark 13. He has recast the traditional material to support the view that the end-time is not about to come. He does this by separating the destruction of the Temple (21:5–7) from events that signal the end-time.

Even traditional signs of the end, false messiahs and rebellions, do not point to an immediate second coming (vv. 8–11). They are part of a time of persecution. God protects the Christian who must face hostility or even death from Jews, Gentiles, and even family (21:12–19). The fall of Jerusalem does not lead to the end-time. Instead, it begins a new stage in salvation history. Jerusalem will be overrun until the age of the pagans reaches its conclusion (21:20–24). After all these events the Son of Man will return in glory (21:25–28). The Christian who lives in the world between Jesus' ascent to heaven and the second coming can remain confident that Jesus' words will never pass away (21:29–33). Christians remain watchful and pray for strength to endure and appear before the Son of Man (21:24–36).

## The Passion Narrative (22:1–23:56a)

The Passion narrative is not a court record of what happened, but a telling of what happened that is shaped by the belief that Jesus is the suffering Messiah, the obedient Son who has been raised by God. Political charges (23:2, 5, 18f) are false and recognized as such by Pilate, who declares Jesus innocent three times (vv. 4, 14f, 22). Pilate yields to pressure from Jewish leaders, to whom he hands over Jesus for crucifixion (23:23–26). In the conspiracy to kill Jesus (22:1–6), Luke blames only certain Jewish leaders for the plot that costs Jesus his life (22:1–2).

#### The Last Supper (22:7–38)

Jesus is aware of the suffering he is about to undergo. A new covenant will be made in the death of Jesus as symbolized by the interpretation of the cups of wine and the bread at the Passover meal. As the Jews had been told to remember the Exodus during Passover, Jesus tells his disciples to remember his death as the new focal point of salvation history.

The second element in the Last Supper scene is the farewell speech. Such speeches were delivered by dying patriarchs to their children, encouraging them to remember the ancestor's example by remaining faithful to the Law and then predicting their failures to do so. Luke creates Jesus' speech out of four independent sayings:

1. oracle against the betrayer (22:21–23);
2. the disciples' place in the Kingdom (vv. 24–30);
3. prophecy of Peter's denial and eventual restoration (vv. 31–34); and
4. a saying about two swords (vv. 35–38).

Jesus sets the disciples an example in his death. The worst sin committed by a disciple is Judas's betrayal, which is rendered even worse by the echoes of covenant sacrifice associated with the meal. Luke puts the disagreement about greatness (see Mk 10:42–45) here at the Supper, where it forms a contrast with Jesus' example as "one who serves" (22:27). Jesus' earlier instructions to invite persons to your banquet who cannot repay you rather than invite those, like you, who can afford to give banquets, and Jesus' own appearance as slave or servant rather than master, provide additional illustrations of the Lucan theme of reversal in the Kingdom.

Beyond the ominous events of Jesus' death, Judas's betrayal, and Peter's denial, there are images of fulfillment. The Twelve who stand by Jesus will occupy the twelve thrones of the tribes of Israel. (Judas will be replaced; see Acts 1:15–26.) The meal anticipates a future celebration with Jesus in glory—a communal celebration with Jesus, not the ranked banquets of those whose idea of greatness Jesus rejects. Before this banquet can occur, Jesus must suffer to enter glory. Satan makes the threatened return (4:13) in Judas (22:3) and in testing Peter.

#### Arrest of Jesus (22:39–53)

Jesus demonstrates his faithfulness as God's obedient Son in his prayer before his Passion. Luke deflects criticism of the disciples for failing to stay awake by alluding to their grief. They are warned that they must pray to avoid being tested.

Jesus exhibits his freedom from fear over his fate in his words to those who come to seize him. He is no robber in hiding. They could have taken him publicly in the Temple, but the present hour of darkness is permitted by God's plan (v. 53).

### Trial of Jesus (22:54–23:25)

Jesus' predictions are fulfilled, and this gives further evidence that God's will, not the plan of his enemies, controls the events around Jesus' death. Luke puts the story of Peter's denial before the trial of Jesus begins. Jesus reminds Peter of the earlier prediction by looking at him; Peter breaks down in tears. When Jesus' captors challenge him to prophesy as a form of mockery (22:64), readers have evidence from the Peter episode to show that Jesus is a true prophet. Luke does not report a legal trial by Jewish authorities. The false accusations and the verdict have been fixed before the Passion even begins. Jesus responds to the question about his messiahship with a judgment saying about the Son of Man. The Sanhedrin concludes that Jesus claims to be "Son of God" (22:66–71).

Luke's version of the trial before Pilate insists that Jesus was innocent of the charges of stirring up political rebellion, which was used as a reason to put him to death. Luke adds the geographical note, "from Galilee where he began even to here" (23:5), and then clears Jesus from guilt in Galilee by having him appear before Herod (vv. 6–12). That scene represents the climax of the earlier accounts of Herod's reaction to Jesus, which shifted from fascination to opposition (9:9; 13:31–33). Herod desires a miracle, but all he sees is the silent prisoner who is the object of violent accusations and mockery. Ironically, the incident creates peace between the old enemies, Herod and Pilate (v. 12). Even though Pilate persists in affirming Jesus' innocence, he is manipulated by the angry crowd into handing Jesus over for crucifixion. The leaders who orchestrated Jesus' death are really the ones fostering rebellion. They ask for the release of a known murderer and rebel (23:25).

### Crucifixion and Burial of Jesus (23:26–56a)

As he is led to his death, Jesus prophesies the terrible fate awaiting Jerusalem once more (23:26–32; 19:41–44). Scorned and considered a criminal, Jesus is able to offer salvation to the repentant sinner (23:39–43). The crowd challenges Jesus to save himself from his fate, which, as it turns out, is the entry into paradise both for him and for those who repent and are forgiven (see 22:28–30; the disciples who feast with Jesus in the Kingdom are those who have endured with him in his trials). This shows that God's mercy can be experienced even in the midst of brutal hostility. Apocalyptic signs accompany Jesus' death, which is witnessed by the women and other followers from Galilee. The centurion proclaims Jesus' innocence while the crowd laments (23:44–48).

Joseph, a member of the Council, buries Jesus as an act of piety. He represents the righteous of Israel who sought the Kingdom of God (v. 51). The women prepare to anoint the body, but they are interrupted by the Sabbath. The burial scene shows that Jesus was buried with honor, not like a criminal, and that the place was known to his followers. Luke is telling us that when the women return to complete the anointing, there can be no possibility that they have mistaken the place of burial.

## Resurrection of Jesus (23:56b–24:53)

Jesus' departure takes place in Jerusalem on the third day after the crucifixion (24:21, 51). Luke has rewritten traditional stories about the empty tomb and about mealtime appearances of the Risen Lord to create a sequence of three scenes. He arranges these scenes so that the Resurrection faith is more and more explicitly spelled out. The Gospel concludes with the disciples offering prayer and praise in Jerusalem while waiting for the Holy Spirit to initiate the next stage in the drama of salvation, the spread of the Gospel from Jerusalem to the whole world.

### The Women at the Tomb (23:56b–24:12)

The first of the three scenes opens when the women return to the tomb. Angels chide them for seeking the living among the dead (cf 20:38). Instead of a simple proclamation of the Easter faith as one finds in Mark 16:6b, Luke's angels remind the women of Jesus' predictions of the Passion and Resurrection. The women report that the angels said Jesus was alive (24:22f).

## Women in Luke

LUKE WAS ESPECIALLY sensitive to outcasts and outsiders. Women in his day could claim few of the rights men enjoyed. But Jesus often crossed social, religious, and political barriers; he treated all people with compassion and respect. Luke reflects this by introducing thirteen women who are mentioned in no other Gospel. He also includes five incidents involving women that are not reported by any of the other evangelists:

- Raising the widow's son (7:11–17)
- Pardon of a sinful woman (7:36–50)
- Galilean women follow Jesus (8:1–3)
- Visit to Martha and Mary (10:38–42)
- Cure of a crippled woman (13:10–17)

**Jesus Appears on the Road to Emmaus (24:13–35)**

In the second scene, Luke uses a folktale motif: the appearance of a divine being disguised as a stranger who must be shown hospitality. Jesus expands on what the angels at the tomb said, and he interprets Moses and the prophets to demonstrate that the suffering of the Messiah was God's plan. Then a new theme comes in: the manifestation of Jesus in the breaking of bread. (John 21:1–14 contains a variation of the manifestation of Jesus in the guise of a stranger at a meal.) The Messiah has suffered, entered into glory, and now renews his presence to the disciples in the meal.

**Jesus Appears to the Disciples in Jerusalem (24:36–49)**

Luke knows the tradition that Jesus had appeared to Peter (24:34; 1 Cor 15:5) but recounts only the appearance to the disciples at a meal. The third appearance confirms the fact that the Jesus who appears is the crucified one, raised up by God, not some ghost or other psychic phenomenon. The body that was missing from the tomb has been taken up by the risen Jesus.

**Jesus Commissions the Disciples (24:44–49)**

In this third scene, as in the previous two episodes, Luke reminds us that the Messiah had to suffer and die to fulfill Scripture (vv. 44–46). The story then takes up the central element in all resurrection appearance stories: commissioning the recipients. These stories all point to the future mission of the disciples and founding of Christian communities in which Jesus continues to be present. The commission in verses 47–49 is a prelude to the story of the first apostles, which Luke will tell in Acts. The disciples' mission to preach repentance and baptism to all nations in Jesus' name, beginning from Jerusalem, continues the

## Jesus' Resurrection

CHRISTIAN BELIEF IN the resurrection of Jesus cannot be supported by near-death experiences—well-intentioned as such efforts might be. Christians do not believe Jesus was *resuscitated* in the sense that his dead body came back to life in the same way as a near-death survivor's. Nor was his resurrection merely a spiritual phenomenon, that is, he rose in the minds and hearts of his followers who experienced his presence through his teachings and his "spirit" among them. Both attitudes miss the mark. Christian belief says God transformed Jesus, body and spirit. Lazarus was resuscitated or revivified, meaning he returned to the same state of life he had enjoyed previous to his death. But Jesus was truly and fully transformed. He experienced a bodily resurrection, which meant his body was now different from anything we know or understand. His body was freed from the limitations of time and space. Disciples who had known him in life now could not recognize him. Luke shows him needing to convince the apostles that he is Jesus and to prove he is no ghost by eating. The transformation of Jesus gives hope to all Christians that the ultimate fate of all creation is a like transformation in the fullness of the Kingdom.

preaching that occurred during Jesus' ministry and reflects a new stage in salvation history.

### Jesus Departs (24:50–53)

The ending of the Gospel reflects the departure that Jesus discussed with Moses and Elijah (9:31), as well as showing the Son of Man in glory at the right hand of God (22:69). Jesus' resurrection appearances are understood to be from his place of glory with God (24:26). The stories have introduced ways in which Jesus will now be present to the church, through the Spirit promised by the Father (v. 49) and in the breaking of the bread (v. 35). The church's mission will be to take Jesus' teaching throughout the world.

## Things We Have Learned from Luke

### Jesus Is Savior for All Peoples

From the very beginning, Luke shows that the hopes that poor, weak, suffering, righteous persons have are fulfilled in the coming of Jesus. The Gospel shows that women as well as men; foreigners and Gentiles as well as Israelites; sick, weak, sinful, and despised persons as well as the well-off and respected people can come to Jesus. God seeks to reverse the situation of the poor and suffering. Consequently, Jesus comes as a suffering, servant Messiah, not as a liberator or king, who will take his place with the powerful of this world. Jesus' parables reveal that the love and mercy of God prompts this gift of salvation.

### Disciples Participate in the Mission of Jesus

The disciples do not simply preach about Jesus or the Kingdom of God; they also participate in the reversal of roles, status, and concerns that the coming of salvation brings. Some disciples renounce everything that ties them to the social structures of the world. Others use their material resources in ways quite different from those around them. They do not seek exchanges between friends, which would create obligations. They do not try to pile up wealth or to indulge themselves and their friends in consuming luxurious goods. Their lives are not dominated by concern for acquiring and preserving material things. Instead, they aid people who will never be able to repay them. They give away wealth to meet the needs of other people. Their only "anxiety" is acquiring heavenly treasure. All disciples are willing to follow Jesus' example of suffering service rather than demanding that others honor and serve them.

### Prayer and Worship are the Center of Christian Life

Even acts of mercy and compassion would not establish a relationship with God if people did not praise God in worship and ask God's assistance in meeting the challenges that the life of discipleship poses. Throughout the Gospel, Jesus sets the example. He worships with others in the synagogue and withdraws for prayer at critical moments. The disciples turn to prayer and praise after the Resurrection. Luke also contains examples of prayer in the Lord's Prayer and the canticles of the infancy narrative. Jesus warned the disciples in the garden that they would have to pray to be spared testing, a reminder of the last petition of the Lord's Prayer.

### Questions for Discussion and Reflection

*Group Sharing/Discussion*

1. What are the three sources that Luke depended upon in writing his Gospel?

2. What is the main purpose of Luke's Gospel (1:1–4)?

3. Let each person select a story from Luke—for example, infancy narrative (1:4–2:52), Zacchaeus (19:1–10), Good Samaritan (10:29–37), Mary and Martha (10:35–42), Sinful Woman (7:31–50), and so on—and retell it in their own words, being sure to include how you think Luke was using the story.

4. Luke retains Jesus' call to renounce material goods to be a disciple (6:35; 9:3; 10:4; 12:33; 14:33; 16:13). Read each aloud and explain Jesus' teaching.

5. What role does John the Baptist play in Jesus' mission? What message does the Baptist preach?

6. Role-play the story of the Good Samaritan (10:29–37). Afterwards, let each person explain his or her actions and reactions afterwards.

*In Our Lives*

1. The parable of the sower (8:4–15) is an instruction for discipleship. Explain the meaning of the seeds and discipleship.

2. The meeting of Mary and Martha with Jesus (10:38–42) illustrates the demands of disci-

pleship—hearing the word and keeping the word of Jesus. Have individuals role-play the story, then discuss the meaning of this incident and lesson.

3. In Luke, riches are obstacles to becoming a disciple (8:14; 18:18–25). His parables show the folly of being possessed by wealth (12:13–21; 16:19–31). Read these sections aloud, give time for silent reflection, and then let each person tell how they interpret these teachings on wealth and discipleship and how they apply them to their lives.

4. Luke writes the traditional resurrection stories into three stories. What are these? Retell these aloud: 24:13–35, 36–43, 44–49. What do you discover as you hear this retelling?

5. In Luke Jesus is the advocate of the poor. He challenges the leaders about their wealth and oppression of the poor (20:25–47). Luke often focuses attention on the theme of the rich and the poor. Because the rich are trapped by their desires for money and pleasure, they often fail to receive salvation—for example, 12:13–21 and 16:19–30. However, this does not mean all rich people are excluded from the Kingdom. The Good Samaritan, Zacchaeus, and others who share their wealth with those in need can become disciples of Jesus. Where do you stand in regard to your wealth and your faith? How does your belief affect your attitude toward the poor? What actions for the poor should you take?

***Individual/Personal Reflection/Action***

1. Prayer and worship are center to Christian life. Jesus sets the example. Luke regularly presents Jesus at prayer during major moments in his ministry:

At his baptism (3:21)
At the choice of the Twelve (6:12)
Before Peter's confession (9:18)
At the Transfiguration (9:28)
When he teaches his disciples to pray (11:1)
At the Last Supper (22:32)
On the Mount of Olives (22:41)
On the cross (23:46)

Disciples must also ground their life of seeking justice in prayer and worship. At his disciples' request, Jesus instructs his disciples about praying, about persistence in prayer, and about its efficacy (11:1–13; 18:1–6). Prayer is essential to becoming a Christian disciple. Review your own habits of prayer and worship. What is positive in these habits? Decide what changes you might want to make.

2. Luke's beatitudes (Lk 6:20–26) differ in style as well as content from Matthew's (Mt 5:3–12). What significance do you find in Matthew's spiritualized beatitudes in contrast to Luke's more economically oriented beatitudes? Which do you find more challenging, which more comforting? Luke's version includes four "woes." How do these very real social and economic conditions impact your life and challenge your beliefs?

3. Women play an important role in Luke's Gospel. In a patriarchal culture, what did you find surprising or noteworthy about the roles that women play in this Gospel? Why do you think Luke includes this strong emphasis on women? What can you do and what can the church do to nourish women more effectively?

4. Mary is the first disciple because she is one who hears and does the word of God (8:21). Because Mary became the Mother of God, this is the ultimate foundation of all Marian devotions. Take some time to reflect on this by meditating on the Magnificat (1:46–55).

# JOHN READING GUIDE

### *At a Glance*

| | |
|---|---|
| Who are the main players? | Jesus John the Baptist the twelve disciples the beloved disciple Lazarus Martha Mary, Mother of Jesus Pilate Mary Magdalene Peter |
| What should I look for? | The Fourth Gospel uses symbols, signs, and metaphors to help present its message that Jesus is the unique Son of God. No one who reads Jesus' words solely on the literal level will understand the truth Jesus reveals. As you read |

the Gospel, you will see that Jesus often identifies with the great symbols like light, life, water, bread, shepherd, and vine. The author assumes that the reader will recognize these symbols have roots in Jewish scripture. The Fourth Gospel also often uses the expression "the Jews" as a symbol of all those who oppose Jesus.

When was this book written and by whom?

Most likely between A.D. 90 and 100. The author may have been a disciple of the Apostle John but almost certainly was not the Apostle himself, though that had been the belief from the second century on. Several things are clear: The Gospel shows the hand of more than one writer (several sources may have been combined into one Gospel); the Gospel contains many accurate details that argue for its being based on eyewitness testimony; the Beloved Disciple may be the source of that testimony, but the story was likely told and retold within the community before being written down.

Where was this book written?

Though the place of composition traditionally was considered to be Ephesus, some scholars today propose a location in Syria or Palestine.

Why was this book written?

The Fourth Gospel has a double conclusion (20:30ff and 21:24ff). Both conclusions remind the readers that the Gospel has been written to inspire and confirm their faith in Jesus. Also the readers faced being forced out of the Jewish communities, as well as conflict between the Petrine and Johanine communities. These tensions are answered in the Gospel.

What is the story?

Like the other Gospels, John tells the story of Jesus' life. However, John is very different from the other Gospels. The story is a theological narrative. Jesus speaks in long symbolic discourses, not in short sayings or episodes that end in short sayings. The only piece of ethical teaching is the love command. There are two major differences in order of events: Jesus' ministry extends for three Passovers, and the cleansing of the Temple comes at the beginning, not the end of Jesus' ministry, giving a context to the entire Gospel. Jesus' death is attributed to the followers coming after his raising of Lazarus. Many miracles are presented as claims about Jesus' relationship with God.

## Before Beginning

The Fourth Gospel has a double conclusion. After the Resurrection stories in Jerusalem, we are told that Jesus did many other signs, but those in this book seek to lead people to belief in Jesus as Son of God (20:30f). After the Resurrection stories in Galilee, we learn that the Beloved Disciple was the source of the Johannine tradition and that all the things Jesus did could not be written down (21:24f). Expanded or revised editions of a book were not uncommon in those times. This is to remind the people who read it that this Gospel has been written to inspire and confirm their faith in Jesus.

## Composition of the Fourth Gospel

The double ending of this Gospel indicates that there was an earlier version. Other additions to the story and some of the awkward transitions

***Differences between John's Gospel and the Synoptics***

| Synoptics | John |
|---|---|
| Jesus' teaching focuses on the Kingdom of God. | The Kingdom is not a focus of John's Gospel. He stresses instead Jesus' relationship with the Father. |
| Writing style makes use of proverbs, maxims, and parables. Sayings of Jesus are probably closer to their original form in these Gospels. Numerous ethical teachings are given. | Retells no parables and avoids use of proverbs. Instead, uses metaphor to describe Jesus' role ("I am the way," "I am the bread of life," etc.) Freely shapes and phrases the teachings of Jesus in his own style and imagery. The only ethical teaching here is the command to love one another. |
| Focuses on Jesus' human origins by recounting his conception, birth, and childhood. | Focuses on Jesus as the preexistent, divine Word who was with God from the beginning. |
| Jesus' ministry centers on Galilee, and scant time is spent in Judea. He makes only one trip to Jerusalem where he cleanses the Temple at the end of his ministry. | Jesus' ministry spans several years and includes three trips to Jerusalem in Judea. The Temple cleansing occurs at the beginning of his ministry. |
| The Last Supper is a Passover meal, which would take place on the evening of the first day of Passover. | The Last Supper takes place the evening of the day before Passover. Jesus dies on the cross at the time the lambs for the Passover meal are being killed. |
| The disciples only gradually realize the meaning of messiahship. | The disciples profess Jesus as Messiah from the start. |
| Miracles are recounted in rapid succession and tend to speak for themselves. | Miracles are related within extended narratives followed by discourses that explain their meaning and provide insight into the identity of Jesus. |
| Jesus starts his ministry just as John the Baptist comes to the end of his. No mention of Jesus baptizing. | John's and Jesus' ministries overlap. Jesus has a baptizing ministry at the same time as John. |

between sections also lead to this conclusion. For example, John 14:31 brings the discourse to an end. Yet the Gospel as we have it contains three more chapters of discourse material. In addition, John 12:44–50 appears to be tacked on at the end of chapter 12. Some of the additional material may have been added to the Gospel by later disciples of the author. As you read the Gospel, you will also see that Jesus often identifies with great religious symbols such as light, life, water, bread, shepherd, and vine. The author of the Gospel assumes that its readers will recognize that these symbols have roots in the Hebrew Scriptures. This symbolic way of speaking about Jesus was probably developed within a community of Christians, which included the Beloved Disciple, followers who compiled the final edition of the Gospel, and another teacher who wrote the Johannine letters.

## The Fourth Gospel and the Other Gospels

John's Gospel is very different from the other gospels. You will immediately notice that Jesus speaks in long symbolic discourses, not in short sayings or episodes that end in sayings. The only piece of ethical teaching in this Fourth Gospel is the love command. There are also major differences in the order of events. John pictures Jesus' ministry extending over three Passovers. The cleansing of the Temple comes at the beginning (2:13–22), not at the end of Jesus' ministry. Jesus' death is attributed to the reports to the Sanhedrin after he restored Lazarus to life. John attaches symbolic discourses to many of the miracles so that the miracle becomes a claim about Jesus' relationship to God. Most scholars think that John draws on traditions about Jesus that were independent of those preserved in the synoptic (Matthew, Mark, Luke) Gospels.

## Symbols, Irony, and Misunderstanding

The Fourth Gospel uses symbols to present its message that Jesus is the unique Son of God. No one who persists in taking Jesus' words literally can understand the truth that Jesus reveals (see the rejection of literal understandings of Jesus' words and deeds in 3:4–10; 4:10–15; 6:26–33). The reader knows the true meaning of Jesus' words when the characters in the story do not.

## The Fourth Gospel and the Jews

Though some Jews, like Nicodemus, are sympathetic to Jesus (3:1–11; 7:50–52; 12:42), the Gospel often uses the expression "the Jews" as a symbol for all those who oppose Jesus. They display a murderous desire to kill God's envoy and will be condemned by the founders of their own tradition, who testify to Jesus (Moses, 5:41–47; Abraham, 8:48–59). The hostility in the Johannine account may have had its roots in the expulsion of Christian Jews from the synagogues, referred to in John 9:27 and 16:1–4a.

If you read carefully, you will notice that John often does not bother to distinguish the various groups within Judaism at the time of Jesus, such as Sadducees, Herodians, scribes, lawyers, and Pharisees. He often speaks of "the Jews" as though summarizing a story in which Jesus is facing "the bad guys." This habit creates a tension between the fact that Jesus and his followers were also Jews and the way in which the Gospel is using "Jews" as a term for a role in the story. John 18:35f illustrates this tension. Pilate treats Jesus with scorn because Jesus is a Jew, handed over by fellow Jews. Jesus' answer distinguishes himself and his followers from "the Jews," that is, the group opposed to him. John is not making a statement about the Jewish people when he uses "the Jews" to fill the role of "bad guys." The Vatican has reminded Catholics that anti-Semitism is one of the worst forms of racism. We must acknowledge that in the past people have not distinguished between John's use of "the Jews" as characters and the Jewish people as a whole. Today, we must be very careful not to continue that misreading. In some contexts, it might be appropriate to substitute another phrase like "Jesus' enemies" or a more literal rendering of the term used for "the Jews," "the Judeans," when retelling the Johannine story to avoid confusion. Such substitutions are particularly important when working with young children who cannot make the distinction easily between "the Jews" as characters in a story and their Jewish classmates and neighbors.

## Reading through John

In reading John, we must be sensitive to the use of symbols, irony, and misunderstanding. The characters who interact with Jesus in the story are at different levels of understanding as to who Jesus is. The disciples begin with faith that Jesus fulfills the promise of a messiah given to Israel, but this faith is not yet knowledge of Jesus as this revelation of God. Their faith must be completed by the post-Easter process of coming to understand Jesus, the perspective that the evangelist shares with readers (16:25). Jewish sympathizers and the crowds have a vague idea that Jesus might be "from God" or even the Messiah. John often divides the opinions of the crowd in two. One opinion is wrong or literal-minded; the other is partially correct (12:27–29). Unlike the Jewish crowds, who sometimes accept Jesus, John also uses the expression "the Jews" to represent religious authorities hostile to Jesus. They reject all testimony to the truth that Jesus comes from God, and they are the ones responsible for his death.

## Signs and Faith in the Fourth Gospel

The symbolic perspective influences John's account of miracles (see the NAB introduction to John, p. 1547). Taken literally, they cannot lead a

**Miracles** are sometimes seen as events that transcend the ordinary laws of nature or even all the laws of nature. The Bible presents the marvelous or wonderful elements of miracles for a reason. God is active throughout our lives and history, but a miracle is an event in which God's participation is made clear to everyone.

Some modern scholars have dismissed the Gospel miracles as later additions to the original Gospel preaching. Their premise is that miracles just don't happen in the real world, so the miracles of Jesus must be made up. This position ignores Jesus as the unique manifestation of God. Though using miracles as a way of proving Jesus' identity misses the main point of the Gospel miracle stories, those stories must, nonetheless, be seen as authentic memories of the extraordinary presence of God in the ministry of Jesus.

person to faith (2:23–25), but seen as signs pointing to Jesus' identity with God, his "glory" (2:11), they may serve as the beginning point for faith. John embeds four of the miracles in discourses, which interpret their symbolic meaning. The symbols of life, light, and bread point to Jesus as the source of eternal life for all who believe.

## Dualism in the Fourth Gospel

The Gospel uses a number of dualistic or opposite expressions, such as light/dark, life/death, from above (heavenly)/from below (earthly), not judged/condemned. They show a process of division that occurs within the story. Persons confronted with Jesus' word either believe and become children of God who will inherit eternal life, or they reject Jesus and are condemned by God. This dualism gives John a certain harshness. There is no middle ground between belief and unbelief (12:44–50). Believers are united with Jesus and the Father. They may even experience the larger world as hostile (15:1–27). Dualistic imagery and a negative picture of the nonbelieving world often appear in sectarian groups.

## Belief and Eternal Life

Christians usually think of salvation or eternal life as a reward that comes in the future when they join Jesus in heaven (14:2f; 17:24) or when Jesus returns to judge the world (5:27–29). John retains this traditional language but introduces a new perspective on salvation. Belief brings persons into unity with Jesus. Therefore, they can be spoken of as already having passed through death to life (3:16–21; 5:24–26). Those who reject Jesus are already condemned. Judgment really occurs when Jesus, who has come into the world as light, is accepted or rejected. Though various sources provide testimony—John the Baptist, Scripture, and the deeds which Jesus does—the believer must accept Jesus' word about God. Only Jesus comes from heaven to reveal God (3:31–36).

## Jesus as God in the Fourth Gospel

The Gospel presents Jesus as "from above" by identifying him with the Word, which is always present to God and through which God created the world (1:1–5). John defends the claim that Jesus is equal to God in functional terms: (1) Jesus makes God known; (2) Jesus exercises functions attributed to God, giving life and judging; and (3) humans ought to respond to Jesus with the honor appropriate to God. John also emphasizes the special Father/Son relationship between Jesus and God. Jesus is obedient to the mission the Father has given him. Jesus' death will be a sign of God's love for humanity. The disputes between Jesus and "the Jews" (ch 5–12) turn on the issue of Jesus' relationship to God. This section ends with the ironic fact that Jesus' opponents seek to kill the source of life.

## An Outline of John

The plot of the Fourth Gospel follows a pattern of descent into the world and ascent to glory. Jesus comes into the world from the Father seeking "his own," those who will believe. Then, Jesus confronts the world. His ministry divides believers from unbelievers. The hostility of unbelief leads to the "hour" of his crucifixion, which John treats as an exaltation. Jesus then returns to the glory that he had enjoyed with the Father from the beginning. The Gospel is clearly divided into two parts: first, the account of Jesus' confrontation with the world, which many scholars refer to as the book of Signs (ch 1 through 12); and second, the account of Jesus' return to the Father when the destined hour arrives, referred to as the book of Glory (ch 13 through 20).

• Prologue (1:1–18). A hymnic section introduces us to Jesus as God's Word, which has come into the world.

• The book of Signs (1:19–12:50). Jesus' confrontation with the world represents God's judgment against unbelief. This section falls into two parts:

Gathering witnesses to Jesus (1:19–4:54). Jesus demonstrates his glory to disciples and others who will believe in him before the confrontation with unbelief begins.

Confrontation with the world (5:1–12:50). The light (Jesus) comes into the world for judgment. He confronts those who refuse to believe with testimony to his divine origin.

• The book of Glory (13:1–20:31). Jesus' whole life has been moving toward the hour of his glorification and return to the Father. This section falls into two parts:

Preparing the disciples for the hour (13:1–17:26). At the Last Supper, Jesus delivers lengthy discourses about his return to the Father and its meaning for the disciples.

Jesus' arrest, crucifixion, and resurrection (18:1–20:31). John understands the crucifixion as the moment of Jesus' life-giving exaltation and return to the Father.

• Epilogue: Resurrection Appearance in Galilee (21:1–25). The second conclusion reports further appearances of Jesus and points toward the destiny of two leading disciples, Peter and the Beloved Disciple.

## The Prologue (1:1–18)

### A Hymn to the Divine Word

The introduction to John is different from all of the other Gospels. It begins even before creation. John might even be following the opening words of Genesis 1, in which God creates the world out of formless chaos by speaking. Because of Jesus, John has a new insight about the divine Word. The Word is not simply speech or some abstract power that God can use to create. The Word actually became known to us in a person, Jesus. This is the Incarnation—God becoming human. This idea of God is the special revelation of Christianity. It differs from the monotheism of Judaism and Islam, which insists that the unity of God cannot be shared. The Christian claim that Jesus can be spoken of as God is at the core of the controversies in the Fourth Gospel. John makes it clear right at the beginning that we can speak about God under two distinct aspects: God as the ultimate source of all things (i.e., the Father) and as the Word, through whom God creates and sustains the world and guides humans (i.e., the Son). Later in the Gospel we will also learn that the Spirit comes from God to those who believe. Christians believe that the Father, Son, and Spirit are three distinct persons that make up the one God.

Notice that many of the verses in this section have a poetic quality made up of short parallel lines that use the symbols of life, light, darkness, and glory. Also notice that other verses speak of the role of John the Baptist as witness to the light (1:6–8, 15). Still other verses speak in the first person plural of what "we" have received from the coming of the light (vv. 12, 14b, 16). "We" clearly means the Christian community that believes in Jesus. They have received the power to become children of God thanks to Jesus (v. 12). Many scholars think that the poetic verses belonged to an early hymn, which John has used for the introduction. The NAB prints these verses in a poetic form so that you can distinguish them from the prose comments that the author inserted to create the introduction.

### Salvation, a Gift from the Word

This section makes it clear that only those people who receive Jesus as the incarnate Word can attain salvation. The Word actually existed before anything was created, but people may still fail to receive the Word when it comes to them. The Prologue contains several hints about the fate of the light when it comes into our world. People who should receive Jesus, do not. But those who do, receive the grace of becoming children of God and coming to know God as revealed by Jesus. The contrast between the Law that came through Moses and the "grace and truth" that comes through Jesus, probably meaning the Hebrew expression for God's love and fidelity to the covenant, anticipates the conflict between Jesus and the Jewish leaders. Jesus will establish a new covenant between God and those people who come to believe in him.

### The Book of Signs (1:19–12:50)

John uses the word "signs" to emphasize the symbolic role of Jesus' miracles in pointing to Jesus' true, divine origin. To understand the truth revealed by the signs, a person must think of their symbolism, not of the literal words or events. "The Jews" will be portrayed as persons who are unable to see the symbolic truth of Jesus' words.

**Gathering Witnesses to Jesus (1:19–4:54)**

The Prologue told us that the Baptist was sent to testify to Jesus. He opens this section with that testimony (1:19–34). Although there are hints of hostility to come, the first four chapters are generally positive. Jesus gathers followers who believe in his divine mission.

**John Testifies to Jesus (1:19–34)**

The Baptist testifies on different occasions to two different groups of officials that he himself is not the Messiah. He is simply preparing the way for the one who is coming (1:19–28). The Synoptic Gospels contain a scene in which Jesus is baptized and hears God announce that he is God's beloved Son (see Mk 1:9–11). Jesus has no need of such a revelation in the Fourth Gospel. The evangelist transforms the traditional scene into another example of testimony about Jesus. The Baptist sees the Spirit descend from heaven like a dove and remain on Jesus. God has given him that sign to identify the Messiah, who will baptize with the Spirit and will take away the sin of the world (1:29–34).

**Titles of Jesus**

BESIDES THE TITLES used in this section, Jesus gives himself other names in this Gospel that reveal his identity and mission:

Bread of life 6:35

Light of the world 8:12

Gate for the sheep 10:7

Good shepherd 10:11

The vine 15:1

He also calls himself "the resurrection and life" (11:25) and "the way and the truth and the life" (14:6).

**Jesus Gathers Disciples (1:35–51)**

A series of brief scenes shows us how Jesus gathered the rest of his disciples. They follow a set pattern. Persons who come to Jesus through the testimony of others have their own experience with Jesus, which makes them true disciples. The Baptist sends Jesus the first disciples (vv. 35–37). Notice that this chapter contains many of the titles that early Christians used to speak of Jesus: Lamb of God (v. 36); Messiah (v. 41); the one predicted by Moses and the prophets (v. 45); Son of God (v. 49); King of Israel (v. 49); and Son of Man (v. 51). The final verse is very enigmatic. It hints at the story of the ladder, which Jacob saw in a dream vision (Gn 28:12). But Jesus as the heavenly figure, the Son of Man, has replaced the ladder. According to John, no one sees God except through Jesus (see 1:18).

**Cana Miracle Manifests his Glory (2:1–12)**

Now that he has gathered the disciples, Jesus' first miracle reveals his divine glory to them. The real revelation of Jesus' glory, however, cannot come until the crucifixion. Therefore, Jesus first appears to reject his mother's request (vv. 4f). A wedding feast was often used as a symbol for the time of rejoicing that would follow God's judgment. Jesus has provided the wine for such a feast. We will see that Jesus replaces some of the most important Jewish feasts and customs.

Christians no longer follow traditional patterns of worship. Here, Jesus replaces the water, which was to be used for ritual purification.

**Cleansing of the Temple (2:13–25)**

Unlike the Synoptic Gospels, which include only one visit to Jerusalem in Jesus' ministry, John has three different Passover visits as well as episodes during other feasts. The other Gospels link the cleansing of the Temple with the Passover of Jesus' death. John puts that episode much earlier. It enables him to tell the Christian reader that Jesus will also replace the Temple. The evangelist reminds readers that Jesus' disciples could not have understood the saying until after the resurrection (2:22). The end of the chapter warns against faith that is based simply on miracles (vv. 23–25). Many attracted by Jesus' miracles will not remain faithful.

**Dialogue with Nicodemus (3:1–21)**

The next two dialogues, with Nicodemus and with the Samaritan woman, both use the technique of misunderstanding in which the person to whom Jesus speaks takes Jesus' words literally and thus provokes further comment from him. Jesus always responds with an even more difficult statement than the one that provoked the original misunderstanding. In this case, Jesus' words appear to leave Nicodemus behind, but he will reappear as someone sympathetic to Jesus (7:50–52). Since Jewish writings of the period also speak of a cleansing of the righteous by the Holy Spirit, Nicodemus might have been expected to understand that Jesus was speaking about a rebirth "from above," that is, through the Spirit rather than "again" (see note to 3:3). John's Christian readers probably saw a reference to baptism in the insistence that people had to be reborn to enter the Kingdom. The episode marks a clear distinction between the teacher of Israel who cannot understand the idea of spiritual rebirth, and Jesus who is, in fact, the very source of life.

A sudden shift to the plural "we" and "you people" echoes the confrontation between Christians and their synagogue opponents in the evangelist's time (v. 11). Verses 12–15 follow a pattern similar to 1:50f. Belief on the grounds of some "earthly" sign is challenged by the heavenly reality, which is to be revealed in Jesus. In both cases a saying about the Son of Man represents the higher truth. Drawing upon the story of Moses lifting up a bronze serpent in the wilderness (Nm 21:9), the evangelist asserts that Jesus will have to be lifted up (on the cross) to become a source of eternal life for all believers. Verses 16–21 speak to the Christian reader about the coming of Jesus. Elsewhere in the Gospel, "world" is a negative symbol for those who are hostile to the Word. Here the world refers to all humans as the object of God's love. The passage offers one explanation for the tragic fact that people will prefer darkness to light; they would rather hide their evil ways than "live the truth," a Semitic expression for following the will of God revealed in the Law.

**Jesus and John the Baptist (3:22–4:3)**

John once again testifies to Jesus as the one to come. The saying about the Bridegroom appears in the Synoptic Gospels as part of an exchange over fasting. John's disciples fast while Jesus' do not (see Mk 2:18–19). In John's Gospel the emphasis lies on the identity of the two men. The Baptist's role ends once he has given witness to Jesus. Verse 27 points to the importance of grace

**Samaritans** The animosity between Jews and Samaritans was long-standing. The books of Kings pass a consistently negative judgment on the northern kingdom of Israel for its infidelity to the Jerusalem Temple and the true worship of the LORD. Those who lived in the territory of the northern kingdom after the fall of the North at the hands of Assyria were non-Israelites settled there by the Assyrian overlords. These foreigners intermarried with the few Jews not carried into exile and adopted Jewish religion but mixed it with their own polytheism. Even after the Hebrew nation was restored under Ezra and Nehemiah, the Samaritans were considered outsiders and never assimilated. The mutual hatred was so great that when Jews traveled, they would take routes that bypassed Samaria even though that meant many extra miles of travel.

in the Gospel: no one can have anything that God has not given to that person. Verses 31–36 seem to be the evangelist's summary of the entire chapter. The contrast between the "one from heaven," who testifies to the truth and speaks the words of God, and those who belong to earth, who reject the Son, once again demonstrates that the coming of the Son also brings judgment (v. 36b).

**The Samaritan Woman (4:4–42)**

John has divided this story into a series of scenes that gradually reveal the truth about Jesus and his mission. Jesus comes to be known as greater than the patriarch Jacob, who met his future wife at a well. Jesus is more than a messiah figure who would vindicate the Jews by exalting Jerusalem. Jesus is more than the prophet whom the Samaritans expected to establish their version of the Law and place of worship against the claims of their Judean neighbors. We know that when Jesus speaks of a gift of living (i.e., flowing) water, he speaks symbolically of the gift of the Spirit (3:8). The woman persists in treating Jesus' words literally until Jesus' reference to her marital status persuades her that Jesus is a prophet. When Jesus responds to her challenge to settle the old dispute between Jews and Samaritans over where to worship God by speaking of worship in "spirit and truth," Jesus is alluding to himself as the replacement of the Temple (see 2:13–22). The woman finally accepts Jesus as Messiah. Like the disciples in chapter 1, she puts that insight into action by bringing others to Jesus (v. 29).

Jesus' dialogue with his disciples about mission and harvest (4:31–38) indicates that, like the woman, they too are sent to preach to others. Along with the previous episode, in which Jesus was said to be baptizing more people than John the Baptist, this story makes it clear that Jesus was able to convert people with his preaching. The hostile controversies of the next section might otherwise give the impression that Jesus' mission was largely a failure. The large numbers of Samaritans who come to Jesus indicate the truth of Jesus' words to the disciples about the rich harvest. The story concludes with the ringing affirmation that Jesus is "Savior of the world."

**Healing the Royal Official's Son (4:43–54)**

The section on gathering followers concludes with a second miracle in Cana. Jesus' word spoken at a distance is enough to heal the official's son (4:53).

Now that Jesus' identity as the Son sent from God to save the world has been established, we are ready for the confrontation between Jesus and those who do not believe.

**Confrontation with the World (5:1–12:50)**

The sharp confrontation with unbelief that makes up this section of the Gospel does not represent failure, because it leads to the hour of Jesus' exaltation and return to the Father. Jesus succeeds in gathering those persons who believe his words despite all the obstacles that others put in their way.

**Healing on the Sabbath: Jesus Gives Life and Judges (5:1–47)**

The tradition that Jesus provoked hostility among religious leaders by healing a paralyzed man on the Sabbath and associating that healing with the forgiveness of sins is well known (see Mk 2:1–12). John uses the discourse that follows the miracle story to draw out the real issue: Jesus' claim to equality with God (5:16–18). Opposing teachers could appeal to the Law of Moses to argue that no human being can claim to do things which are God's alone, to give life to the dead and to judge (see notes to 5:21, 22). Jesus defends his right to give life and to judge by appealing to the special relationship he enjoys with God. As Son, Jesus does what the Father has given him to do. He does not act on his own authority (v. 30). Furthermore, those who question his behavior should look to the witnesses he can bring forward: the Baptist (vv. 31–35), the deeds that God has enabled him to do (v. 36), and the witness that God has given through Scripture (vv. 37–39). Jesus accuses his opponents of failing to recognize that he is from God because they are not really concerned with the glory that belongs to God. They are only interested in the human glory they receive from other people. He warns them that their confidence in Moses is misplaced. Moses witnesses to Jesus and will condemn anyone who rejects that testimony (vv. 40–47).

**Jesus Is the Bread from Heaven (6:1–71)**

Chapter 6 is based upon a traditional cycle of material that included the feeding of the multitude, calming the storm at sea, a demand that Jesus give people a sign, a challenge to Jesus based on his human origins, and Peter's confession of faith in Jesus as Messiah. John reshapes this material by including a lengthy discourse on Jesus as the bread of life, which has come down from heaven (vv. 22–59). Those who fail to see the symbolism of the feeding miracle or who focus on earthly facts about Jesus will not receive Jesus as the bread of life. Just as Jesus had promised the Samaritan woman a gift of water that would lead to eternal life, he promises bread that will give life to the believer. But "the Jews" are going to copy the behavior of their ancestors, who murmured against Moses. John explains that those who do come to believe in Jesus have been brought to him by God (vv. 37–39, 44f). The comment that Jesus will not cast out those who come to him (v. 37) probably refers to the members of John's church who had been expelled from the Jewish community by officials. That experience is prefigured in the story of the blind man (9:22).

Jesus' words are the source of eternal life in the first part of the discourse. Christian tradition associates the manna and the "bread of life" with the Eucharist. This tradition appears in 6:51–59. It is necessary to eat the life-giving bread and wine, the flesh and blood of Jesus. This meal establishes a special relationship between Jesus and the believer: They "abide in" one another. Just as the Father is the source of Jesus' life, so Jesus becomes the source of life for the Christian. According to John, receiving eternal life is not the result simply of thinking that Jesus is God's Son. It really involves an entirely new relationship with God that is possible in Jesus. John 6:51–58 places the Eucharist at the center of that relationship. If Jesus' words about eating his flesh and blood were taken in too literal a fashion by his audience, they would consider it to be a blasphemous participation in a human sacrifice. The flesh and blood are real means of participating in the life that Jesus shares with God. Even if Jesus' audience understood that Jesus was speaking symbolically, they might be horrified at the idea that Jesus could identify himself with God so closely. Indeed, these words were too difficult for many to accept.

**Conflict and Division at the Feast of Tabernacles (7:1–8:59)**

The episodes in this section occur at the Feast of Tabernacles and at an unnamed feast that follows it. The symbolism of light and water were part of the Tabernacles ritual, and Jesus uses them to express his identity (7:37–39; 8:12). Throughout the section we are reminded that officials are seeking Jesus' death even when they deny that fact (7:1, 19f, 25; 8:39f). Jesus is accused of "leading the people astray." He is also accused of being possessed by a demon. Several scenes picture the divided opinion among the crowd. These scenes may also provide answers to Jewish objections against Jesus:

1. Jesus did not keep the Law in healing on the Sabbath, but the Law permits activities like circumcision on the Sabbath (7:19–24);
2. Jesus' origins make it impossible for him to be the Messiah, yet Jesus' real origins are "from heaven," and the signs he has done testify to that fact (7:25–31, 40–44);
3. Jesus is not an established teacher of the Law, yet Jesus has received his words and teaching from God so that he does not seek personal glory as human teachers do (7:15–18).

Jesus begins to prepare the reader for his departure. He speaks of it in a symbolic way, which the crowd cannot fully understand. Jesus will go to a place where they cannot follow him (7:32–36). The crowd thinks that Jesus will go to the Jewish communities outside Palestine. There is a symbolic truth in that statement: Christianity will spread in those communities. Or, perhaps, Jesus intends to commit the blasphemous act of killing himself (8:21f). The ironic truth of that statement is that Jesus will give up his life on behalf of others. He predicts that when his enemies have executed him, they will find that Jesus is the one who comes from the Father. Jesus even bears the divine name *I AM* (8:28). The bitter conflict between Jesus

**God's Mercy Revealed**

IN THIS STORY Jesus discredits the commonly held belief that physical suffering was the result of sin. Neither the man nor his parents sinned, Jesus says. His blindness was an opportunity for God's power and mercy to be revealed.

and the Jewish leaders in chapter 8 repeats this identification of Jesus with God's *I AM* in a dispute over his descent from Abraham. Those who seek to kill Jesus cannot be descendants of Abraham, because what Abraham saw and rejoiced in was Jesus. Therefore, they are branded children of Satan (8:39–59). The story acknowledges the difficulty of Jesus' words. He is asking us to identify a human being with the God revealed to Abraham and to Moses.

**The Blind Man Believes in Jesus (9:1–41)**

This story shows that it was possible for the blind man to move from the miracle by which Jesus restored his sight to true faith in Jesus. He does so as the religious authorities pressure him to condemn Jesus. He comes to recognize more and more clearly that Jesus cannot be a sinner and therefore Jesus must have come from God. The fear that "Jews" (authorities) will drive them out of the synagogue keeps the man's parents from testifying (9:22f). This story may represent the experience of members of the Johannine community. Jesus returns at the end of the story to show the man his identity and condemn the blindness of the Jewish leaders (vv. 39–41).

**True Shepherd Gives his Life (10:1–42)**

We already know that Jesus' death is an expression of God's love for the world (3:16). Religious authorities have said that Jesus deserves death for leading people astray (7:45–52). Here, parables of the shepherd and his sheep demonstrate that Jesus is the true leader of the people, at least for those whom God has enabled to respond to his call (10:1–30). Jesus will even give his life for the sheep, something that none of the hired hands who claim to lead the people will do. Offended by his claim to identity with the Father (vv. 30–39), the crowd again tries to stone Jesus. We are reminded that Jesus' death is a free offering on his part, not a victory for those allied against him (vv. 17f).

> **Shepherds** In first-century Palestine shepherds tended their flocks without dogs. The sheep knew the voice of the shepherd and responded only to that voice. Sheep were often herded together into a common pen with other flocks, but when a shepherd called his flock, only those sheep that belonged to him would come out.

**Raising Lazarus: Gift of Life Means Death (11:1–57)**

John has used the raising of Lazarus to bring out the irony of what the religious leaders are seeking to do. Jesus is the source of life (vv. 24–26), yet they think that they can silence Jesus by killing him. The Lazarus episode also serves to remind Christians that if they truly believe that Jesus is resurrection and life, then they should not mourn physical death as others do. Jesus often seems remote from others, but here Jesus displays his love for Lazarus and his sisters. Ironically, the following that Jesus gained from his greatest sign led to the formal decision of the Jewish Council to arrange his death (11:45–57). Although the high priest does not know the truth of his words, it will turn out to be a good thing that one person dies for the people, and, as the evangelist points out, for all the peoples of the world (vv. 50–52).

**The Light is Departing (12:1–50)**

John locates the traditional story of Jesus' anointing at Bethany (Mk 14:3–9) in the home of Lazarus and identifies the anonymous woman as his sister, Mary. She recognizes the approach of Jesus' death. Hints of the future Christian mission are evident in the Pharisees' response to the entry "the whole world has gone after him" (v. 19) and the coming of some Greeks to seek Jesus. Their arrival marks the hour of Jesus' death. He prophesies that when he is lifted up on the cross, he will draw all people to himself (vv. 20–32). The book of Signs concludes with reflections on the tragedy of disbelief (vv. 39–43 and 44–50).

## The Book of Glory (13:1–20:31)

We already know that Jesus offers his life out of love; that Jesus' crucifixion is the moment of his exaltation and return to the Father; and that this death is the source of eternal life for all who believe and the manifestation of a new relationship between believers and God. The truth about Jesus' death lies in the revelation that occurs on the cross, not in the plots of Jesus' enemies.

**The Supper Discourses (13:1–17:26)**

Jesus prepares the disciples for the events to come, as well as their future life as a community of believers. The foot-washing not only reflects the service Jesus is about to perform in his death, it also sets a pattern for relationships among disciples. They are going to be the ones sent to represent Jesus and must follow the model given by their teacher (13:1–20), being a servant as Jesus is to them. John has never let us forget that one of Jesus' disciples, Judas, does not really belong to Jesus. He is the agent of God's purpose even though he is in the grip of Satan (6:70f; 12:4–6; 13:2, 11, 21–30; 17:12). Throughout this section, the evangelist reminds us that the disciples understood the significance of what Jesus said and did only after he had been glorified (13:7; 14:29; 16:4, 25). As Judas is about to depart, a new character, the Beloved Disciple, appears in the narrative. He is closer to Jesus than any other disciple (13:23) and will show special insight into events of the Passion and resurrection. The Johannine community revered the Beloved Disciple as the source of its tradition.

The discourses in 13:31–17:26 may have been composed as independent units. John 13:36–14:31 treats the disciples' grief, Jesus' departure and return, and the coming of the Advocate. Jesus also promises to return to the disciples to dwell within them along with the Father (14:20). John 16:4b–33 also deals with the disciples' grief, Jesus' departure and return, and the coming of the Advocate. It lacks the development of the return theme, however, as the mutual indwelling of Father and Son. John 15:1–16:4a encourages the disciples to remain united with Jesus the true vine and to love one another. This unity may be severely tested, because the disciples must also expect hatred, persecution, and even death from the world (15:18–16:4a). Finally, John 17:1–26 contains a prayer in which Jesus speaks to the Father about the disciples he is leaving behind. They are the evidence that Jesus has completed the task he was sent into the world to accomplish (17:6–11a). Left in the world, the disciples are no more "of the world" than Jesus, but without Jesus they require God's protection (17:13–19). As the Father sent him, so Jesus is sending the disciples into the world. The prayer looks beyond the immediate community of disciples to the community that will be the result of their preaching. Jesus expresses a vision of Christian community that runs throughout these discourses. The community is to express the love and unity, which has its source in the love and unity that exists between the Father and the Son (17:20–26).

Mutual love and unity grounded in their vision of God are the focal points of the discourses. You may have noticed that the only explicit commandment given in the Fourth Gospel is the command to love one another (13:34f). This love expresses the love of God (14:21, 23f; 17:23) and of Jesus for "his own" (13:1; 14:21b; 15:11–15). These discourses also suggest that mutual love and unity will be severely tested. The disciples do not yet fully understand what Jesus has revealed to them. The Advocate, who comes from God, must continue the process of bringing understanding to the community (14:25f; 16:13–15). Hatred and persecution from outsiders may also take their toll, as the synagogue exclusion apparently did. The Advocate will help the disciples who have to stand trial (15:26f) and convict the world of its unrighteousness and sin

**The Trial of Jesus**

THERE ARE DIFFERENCES in the four evangelists' descriptions of Jesus' trial.

- Only John records a hearing before Annas (18:13–23).
- All four mention the hearing before Caiaphas (Mt 26; Mk 14; Lk 22; Jn 18).
- Only the synoptics record the hearing before the Sanhedrin (Mt 27; Mk 15; Lk 22).
- All recount the trial before Pilate (Mt 27; Mk 15; Lk 23; Jn 23).
- Only in Luke is the Pilate trial interrupted by an appearance before Herod (Lk 23), after which the Pilate trial resumes.

(16:8–11). The community may not remain in the "name of God," which Jesus has revealed (17:11). If you read 1 John, you will see that the Johannine churches suffered serious internal divisions. These discourses remind us that Jesus' revelation of God's love is the foundation of Christian unity.

**Jesus' Arrest, Crucifixion, and Resurrection (18:1–20:31)**

Throughout his Passion, Jesus remains in complete control of his destiny. Jesus himself lays down his life; others do not take it from him. When Jesus identifies himself with the name *I AM,* used of God in the Old Testament, all those who came to seize him fall to the ground (18:1–14). Jesus confronts his accusers with the evidence of his public teaching. He demands that they bring evidence against him, which they are unable to do (18:19–24). Jewish officials try to hand Jesus over to Pilate without a formal charge (18:28–32). Consequently, the inquiry that Pilate conducts picks up the theme of kingship. John's use of double meanings throughout the Gospel has prepared us for the dialogue that follows. Jesus both denies any earthly kingship and assents to the title "King of the Jews" (18:33–38). Nor are we surprised to find the soldiers' mockery turns Jesus into a king symbolically and then to see Pilate present the "king" to the Jewish people (19:1–5).

When Jesus is presented as "king," the trial scene breaks out into vicious hostility. Pilate knows Jesus is innocent but can only speak to the Jewish officials and to Jesus with bitterness and sarcasm. He knows nothing about truth (18:38). Jesus does not accept Pilate's claim to authority (19:10f). Pilate is the one who fears the political power of others. He will give in to the threats of being denounced to Caesar and execute an innocent man. At the same time, he retaliates against those responsible by insisting that the charge read "King of the Jews." The chief priests demonstrate how far away from God they are by proclaiming that they have no king but Caesar (19:12–22). The violent cruelty and bitterness of this scene show what brute force and political power are like when those in power have no awareness of their responsibilities toward God.

Pilate is interested only in asserting Roman control over the conquered Jews. The death of this obscure Galilean is of no concern to him. Details in the crucifixion scene, which fulfill passages of Scripture, demonstrate that everything is happening according to God's plan (19:23f, 28, 33–37). Jesus provides for those faithful to him by entrusting his mother to the Beloved Disciple as "son" (19:25–27).

Jesus' crucifixion and death are witnessed by friends and enemies alike. When Pilate releases the body to Joseph of Arimathea and Nicodemus for burial, we know that Jesus has really died and been buried according to accepted customs (19:38–42). Consequently, Mary's reaction to discovering the tomb open is to conclude that "they" (possibly hostile authorities) have taken the body (20:1f). Though the Beloved Disciple arrives at the tomb and is said to believe, all he and Peter discover are the grave wrappings in one pile and the face cloth rolled up in another place. The evangelist comments that they could not understand what had happened because they did not know the Scripture about Jesus' Resurrection (20:9).

Mary of Magdala's encounter with the Risen Lord combines the old tradition of an angelic appearance to the women at the tomb, announcing the Resurrection, with the tradition that Jesus himself appeared to the women in the vicinity of the tomb (20:11–18; see Mt 28:1–10). As in the other tomb stories, Mary receives a message for the disciples. She is not to cling to the Lord but to announce Jesus' return to God. John's account puts the occurrence of all the events—Resurrection, ascent to the Father, and bestowing the Spirit on the disciples—on Easter. When Jesus

**His Bones Were Not Broken**

THE LEG BONES of crucified men were broken to speed up their death: Because they could no longer support their weight with their legs, they slumped and suffocated. The urgency reported here was due to the need to remove the bodies before sundown and the start of the Passover feast. Because Jesus was already dead, his bones did not need to be broken, though his side was pierced—fulfilling Scripture (Ex 12:46; Zec 12:10).

appears among the disciples, the marks on his body prove that the Risen Lord is the one who had been crucified. The disciples are now officially sent to the world as Jesus had been, and they receive the promised gift of the Spirit, a sign that Jesus' mission has been completed (7:39; 3:34). Forgiveness of sins as an activity of the Spirit within the Christian community (21:23) appears only here in John's Gospel, but it is familiar from the Synoptics (see Lk 24:47; Mt 18:18). First John presupposes some form of "forgiveness" available within the community (see 1 Jn 1:8–2:2; 5:16f).

John creates a second episode from the tradition of Thomas's doubt. The demand for physical evidence is a sign of unbelief. Christians who have not seen and yet believed are the ones who are really blessed (20:28f).

**Epilogue (21:1–25)**

This chapter seems to have been added to the Gospel sometime after its completion (see NAB introduction to John). It elaborates on a tradition of Resurrection appearances in Galilee. The miraculous catch of fish has a parallel in the miracle associated with the calling of Peter in Luke 5:1–11. This chapter focuses upon the two heroes: Peter, who inherited Jesus' role as shepherd, and the Beloved Disciple, who established the Johannine tradition. Peter had died a martyr's death. The Beloved Disciple lived a long time but has also died. Johannine Christians can look back upon that generation of disciples as faithful witnesses to Jesus.

## Things We Have Learned from John

John has presented a unique story of Jesus. Instead of collecting sayings and parables in which Jesus spoke about the Kingdom of God, the evangelist focuses attention on the special relationship between Jesus and God. We need to remember this special relationship between Jesus and God, because we can slip into thinking of Jesus as though he were just another human religious leader. If we think that way, then Jesus becomes something of a hero, someone could just as easily be replaced by another person whose life and message seemed more inspiring at another time in our lives. We need to remember that Jesus is more than a great human being. Jesus is our revelation of God.

**Jesus Is the Unique Son of God**

No one can come away from this Fourth Gospel without recognizing that Jesus is identified with God. The Prologue described that relationship as the *Word,* which is always with God and through which God acts in the world. In the narrative, Jesus appears as the unique Son of the Father. The Son is the only one who can reveal the Father. Father and Son are united by a common love and the Son's obedience to everything the Father requires.

**Salvation Comes through Belief in the Son**

Salvation, which John usually describes as eternal life, requires belief in Jesus as God's Son. It cannot be delivered by human institutions such as those the Jewish leaders think will provide security. Salvation consists in a new relationship to God through Jesus. This relationship is open to anyone to whom God has given the grace to believe in Jesus. Sometimes we meet evangelical Christians who tell us that unless we accept Jesus Christ as our personal Lord and savior, we cannot be saved. They try to suggest that there is something wrong with the belief in Jesus that we have unless we go through the type of conversion experience typical of members of that church.

Reading the Gospel of John makes it clear that anyone who believes that his or her salvation has come through the revelation that Jesus brought has already accepted Jesus as Lord and Savior. That special relationship is what we mean when we talk about faith.

**Jesus' Death Expresses God's Love for Humanity**

Jesus is not the victim of human injustice. Jesus chose to offer his life for others so that they could see God's love revealed on the cross. When we see God's love on the cross, we are reminded that God identifies with the lowly, suffering people of the world by joining with them. God does not approve of the injustice that creates such suffering. Jesus reminded Pilate that Jesus' death was an "offering" and not the triumph of Pilate's power. Christians must look for ways of identifying with and helping the suffering, rather than expecting God to act through the powers of the world.

### Mutual Love and Unity in the Church Express the Love of God

The love shown by Christians is not simply an expression of a moral virtue. Christians always have the example of Jesus' love to follow. They also have the experience of the Father and Son dwelling in the community to inspire their efforts to achieve unity.

### Questions for Discussion and Reflection

*Group Sharing/Discussion*

1. Name some of the differences between John and the synoptic Gospels (Matthew, Mark and Luke). What is the significance of these differences?

2. Jesus defines himself more than thirty times in John's Gospel as "I am . . . "—I am bread, light, gate, the good shepherd, the resurrection, the way, the truth, the life, the vine, etc. Explore his meaning of "I am." Let different group members take one of these metaphors and describe what they think it signifies.

3. Discuss the meaning of "world," which occurs quite frequently in John, for example, John 2:16–21, where it is used as a symbol.

4. John 3:16, is famous on TV as a hanging banner in many sports events and may be the best-known verse in John. "For God so loved the world that he gave his only Son, so that everyone who believes in him may not perish, but may have eternal life." What does this mean?

5. Each person should tell what his or her favorite story in John is (e.g., Nicodemus, Woman at the Well, Cana, Man Born Blind, Lazarus, Feeding of the Multitude, etc.). Remember that John wrote to encourage faith in Jesus as the Son of God. Retell the story in your words accenting what happens to the faith of the person in the story.

6. Jesus places Eucharist in the center of the new relationship with God (6:51–58). Jesus' words about eating his flesh and drinking his blood caused some of his followers to leave. What would his words mean if taken literally? If taken symbolically?

7. Why does John see the crucifixion as the hour of glory?

*In Our Lives*

1. In John the word "Jews" is symbolic. It is not an ethnic group. But it sounds like it is when you hear John's Passion read in the Good Friday liturgy. As a symbol both in Scripture and liturgy, it means all those who oppose Jesus, the powers of darkness. If you read John carefully, you meet many good Jews; also you realize that the term "Jews" has different meanings, but generally it refers to those who oppose Jesus. The Vatican has reminded Catholics that this error of taking "Jews" as an ethnic group is wrong and the cause of anti-Semitism over the centuries, and this is evil racism. Recount the many good Jews you meet in John and in life. What are some ways you can live out and be a witness against anti-semitism?

2. "Washing feet" was a most demeaning task for anyone in that society. Only Gentile slaves were called to perform this work. If there was no Gentile slave, then each washed their own feet. Take time to prepare a role-play of the drama of the washing of the feet (Jn 13:1–38). After this, talk about Jesus' intentions in washing their feet and Peter's reluctance to let him. Notice that in John, Jesus washes feet but doesn't share the bread and wine as in the other Gospels. This gives serious significance to the washing of the feet as the way to be a disciple. How do we symbolically wash each other's feet in our own daily lives?

3. "Unless I wash you, you have no inheritance with me" (13:8b) is the fifth time John has Jesus make an "unless" statement. Together they spell out John's vision of Christian identity (3:3; 3:5; 6:53; 8:24; 13:8). Review these statements, having different people read them and explain their significance.

4. Reread 2:13–25. The Temple, the place of worship, had become a marketplace, and Jesus exorcized this. How did Jesus' purging of the Temple become a threat to the people and the authorities? What message could this have today?

5. In John's Gospel, Mary requested the first miracle at Cana; the Samaritan woman was the first convert and disciple; Mary of Magdala, a follower from the beginning, was the first witness of the risen Lord. In a patriarchal culture does John have a message here? What might this remind us of?

6. What is the only commandment in John's Gospel (13:34f)? Discuss whether this is the only commandment you need.

***Individual/Personal Reflection/Action***

1. The Samaritan Woman's "Come and see" (4:1–43) echoes Jesus' words to his first disciples. Why does John put Jesus' words on the lips of the Samaritan woman? Carefully, reread the story and note the stages of conversion you see in the dialogue. Compare this to the stages of conversion of the man born blind (9:1–41). This takes time, but it will nourish your understanding of your own stages of faith.

2. When you see the cross, are you reminded that God chose to identify with the lonely, suffering people of the world? Meditate on what you see in the cross. What does this say to you?

3. The supper discourses of Jesus (13:1–17, 26) are to prepare the disciples for their mission. They suggest also that their mutual love will be tested. But they remind us that Jesus' revelation of God's love is the foundation of Christian unity. Reflect on these passages. How can they nourish your own mission in life? Let them deepen your conviction that Jesus is God's revelation of love and the foundation of the mission.

# ACTS READING GUIDE

## *At a Glance*

| | |
|---|---|
| Who are the main players? | Peter Stephen Philip Paul Cornelius James Timothy Barnabus Lydia Titus Apollos Felix Festus King Agrippa Luke |
| What should I look for? | How the Spirit-led church spreads from Jerusalem to Rome, the center of the empire.<br>How the church thrived even during times of opposition, demonstrating its divine guidance.<br>The defense of Christianity that runs through the book.<br>The internal struggles present in and survived by the early church.<br>The continuing presence of Lukan themes first seen in his Gospel: the work of the Spirit; the importance of prayer; the pervasive presence of joy; the significance of women, including Mary, the mother of Jesus. |
| When did this take place? | Sometime after the destruction of Jerusalem and the Temple (A.D. 70 ), probably between A.D. 80 and 90. From the late second century onward, church tradition has held that Luke, the sometime companion of Paul and the author of the Gospel, is also the author of the book of Acts. He was a well-educated Syrian from Antioch who was himself a Gentile convert to Christianity. Luke addresses the book of Acts to Theophilus, the same individual to whom he addressed the Gospel and whose name means "one who loves God." But the book is also intended for all who love and fear God. |
| Where did these events occur? | In Jerusalem and various cities of what we now call the Middle East: Joppa, Antioch, Derbe, Lystra, Ephesus, Iconium, the island of Cyprus, Philippi, Thessalonica, Berea, Corinth, Athens, the island of Malta, Rome |
| Why was this book written? | To continue Luke's record of biblical or salvation history and to provide a historical account of the founding of the church. |

To explain that the salvation brought by Jesus has been extended to Gentiles.

To demonstrate the working of the Holy Spirit in the life of the early church.

To assert that the spread of the gospel was accomplished through the apostles who were chosen by God and commissioned by Jesus.

What is the story?

The book centers on the preaching and ministry of Peter and Paul. After the Ascension, Peter begins to preach boldly and to work many miracles. Though initially he resists preaching the gospel to Gentiles, he eventually realizes that God wants all people to come to know Jesus. Paul, a devout and zealous Jew, at first persecutes the followers of Jesus until a miraculous encounter with the risen Jesus changes his life. He becomes a missionary preaching about Jesus throughout much of the Roman Empire. After the church is established in Jerusalem, conflicts arise with Jewish authorities that climax in the martyrdom of Stephen and the imprisonment of Peter. The gospel spreads throughout the Gentile world largely due to the efforts of Paul, Barnabas, and others. Internal conflicts arise but are resolved. The book ends with Paul imprisoned in Rome where he has witnessed to the gospel in the very heart of the empire.

## Before Beginning

The Acts of the Apostles continues the story that began with Luke's Gospel. What began with Jesus' life did not end on Easter. God's plan requires another act: the gospel must spread beyond Jerusalem to all the peoples of the earth (Lk 24:47; Acts 1:8). Luke recounts the deeds of the first generation of apostles by which God took the movement out of the Galilean and Judean environment of its birth. He has not provided a detailed chronicle of everything that occurred during the period between the resurrection of Jesus and Paul's arrival in Rome (ca. A.D. 30–62). Peter disappears from the story once Paul's mission to the Gentiles is established as God's plan. Acts ends with Paul under benign house arrest in Rome, able to preach to visitors (28:17–31). We hear nothing of the martyrdom of Peter and Paul there under Nero, although allusions show that Luke's readers are expected to know of Paul's death (20:25; 21:13).

## A Story of God's Salvation

Acts has an unusual ending. One of its heroes is under arrest in Rome, and we never find out what happens to him. As soon as you read Paul's letter to the Romans, you find out that he was not the first missionary to reach Rome. There was an established Christian community before he arrived (1:8–15). Paul mentions a number of people associated with that church at the end of the letter (16:1–16). Luke knew about these people. He mentions the fact that two famous missionaries, Aquila and Priscilla (Acts 18:2; see Rom 16:3f), had to leave Italy when the Emperor Claudius expelled Jews from Rome. Roman sources tell us that the cause was riots over the name of "Chrestus" (Suetonius, Life of Claudius 25). This event may have taken place as early as A.D. 40 (see note to Acts 18:2). While Luke has not included all of the events in early Christian history that were known to his readers, he has adopted a literary style close to what the ancients would consider an "historical monograph." Unlike secular histories of great wars, lives of emperors, the founding of states, and the like, Luke has models for history writing in the Jewish Scriptures. Biblical history wants to show how God's plan of salvation worked out through special people and events. We use the expression "salvation history" for this type of writing.

## Understanding Salvation History

How do we even know what God's plan is? You will see as you read the stories in Acts that even the disciples did not know what God intended. They had certain guideposts. The most important was what they knew about Jesus. Jesus had also told them in very general terms that a new stage in God's plan was about to unfold and that they would be an essential part of carrying it out. They also knew passages from the Old Testament that helped them understand how Jesus' life and death fit into God's plan. Luke makes it very clear, however, that even with these resources the disciples would not have been able to figure out God's plan in advance. God intervenes through the Holy Spirit at the critical turning points in the story.

Though God's intervention is crucial to salvation history, human beings are not manipulated like puppets. You will notice that the disciples in the story have to figure out the significance of the unusual experiences that happen to them during their mission. They pray to God for further assistance. They also discuss the events that have occurred as they prepare to take new steps in preaching the gospel. Their ability to look back on past examples of God's action helps them understand what God is doing in the present. Sometimes they might even have taken the wrong step if God had not intervened. Acts 16:6–10 reports that the Spirit of Jesus actually caused Paul to change his travel plans in Asia Minor and then to go over to Greece. It was time for Paul to spread the word farther to the west.

**Preaching in Acts of the Apostles**

A LARGE PART of Acts, about one-fourth of the book, consists of sermons, 18 in all. These are Luke's reconstructions of sermons given by Peter, Paul, and other leaders of the early church. They are not verbatim reports, but they do communicate a good sense of the flavor and the content of the teachings of the early church.

## The Plan of Salvation History in Acts

The book uses a geographical plan for the spread of the gospel. It begins where the ministry of Jesus had ended, in Jerusalem. Moving west, it comes to the center of the empire that embraced the whole circle of the Mediterranean: Rome. By the end of the book, Christianity is no longer confined to the band of followers in Jerusalem. Christian churches dot the empire. The map of Paul's missionary journeys in Acts shows that Paul touches the major cities along the roads and sea routes of his time (see Map 14).

As you read through Acts, you will also notice another feature of the early mission. The disciples preach first to Jews and then to Gentiles. Apollos is active in the synagogues (Acts 18:26–28). Some of Luke's summaries refer to converts among both Jews and "Greeks," an expression used for non-Jews, or Gentiles, rather than purely for persons of Greek descent (see Acts 18:10). But often the mission to non-Jews begins only when influential people in the synagogue turn the audience against the missionaries (see Acts 13:44–52). Israel has first place in the plan of salvation. It receives another chance after the rejection of Jesus when the disciples begin to preach the gospel (see 3:11–26). The pattern of rejection by Jews followed by enthusiastic reception on the part of Gentiles, makes us aware of a turning point in the story of salvation. The Hebrew Scriptures and the public ministry of Jesus told of God's dealings with Israel. From now on, the story of salvation would involve all the peoples of the world. Luke's pattern of Jews first, then Gentiles, also reminds us that Christianity is indebted to Judaism. That link is not a trivial cultural accident but part of the divine plan of salvation.

## Reading through Acts

Before studying about Acts, read through the whole book. You will notice that there are some types of stories that occur again and again. The apostles are put in jail. They must make speeches before various courts and officials. Sometimes God rescues them from jail or another hostile action. Besides the legal speeches, Luke adds the drama of speeches that announce the gospel.

Often the apostles gain attention through miracles, which they are able to work in Jesus' name. Other times the apostles challenge the religious beliefs, superstitions, and magical practices of the Gentiles. As the gospel moves out from Jerusalem, these dramatic episodes fit into a pattern of journeys.

## Acts as Entertainment

As Luke tells the story of God's plan of salvation, he provides the reader with a number of entertaining incidents (e.g., confusing Paul and Barnabas with pagan gods in Acts 14:8–18). Persecutions, trials, imprisonments, journeys, and dramatic shipwrecks all had their counterparts in novels that were popular during this period. The novels usually had a romantic theme rather than a religious one, but the use of comparable tales reminds us that Acts provided readers with pleasure as well as instruction.

## Acts and the Early Community

There appears to be great harmony among Christians in the early communities. We know from Paul's letters that the early churches were sometimes torn by dissent and often needed encouragement by the apostle to demonstrate in their actions the love that Christians were to show one another.

Luke knows that the early communities were not always perfect. Acts shows us how the churches *ought* to live together. It even shows us how Christians should work out difficulties that they face. They are never to forget that their purpose is to thank God for the salvation they have received and to preach the same message to others. There is no place for the love of money, for the jealousy, maliciousness, and deceitful behavior that those who persecute the apostles.

## An Outline of Acts

• Preparation for the Christian Mission (1:1–2:13). This section includes all of the events between Easter and the first missionary sermon that Peter preaches on Pentecost.

Waiting in Jerusalem (1:1–14)
Replacing Judas (1:15–26)
Pentecost, the Coming of the Spirit (2:1–13)

• The Mission in Jerusalem (2:14–8:3).

Two Sermons by Peter (2:14–3:26)
Peter and John before the Sanhedrin (4:1–31)
Sharing Possessions in the Community (4:31–5:16)
Trial before the Sanhedrin (5:17–42)
Deacons for the Hellenists (6:1–7)
Trial and Death of Stephen (6:8–8:3)

• Mission in Judea and Samaria (8:4–9:43). The gospel begins to spread into areas around Jerusalem.

Philip Preaches Outside Jerusalem (8:4–40)
Conversion of Paul (9:1–30)
The Church Continues to Grow (9:31–43)

• Inauguration of the Gentile Mission (10:1–15:35). These chapters set the stage for the mission of Paul by showing that the Gentile mission began from Jerusalem itself.

Conversion of Cornelius (10:1–11:26)
Paul's First Missionary Journey (11:27–14:28)
Gentile Mission Confirmed in Jerusalem (15:1–35)

• Paul's Mission to the Ends of the Earth (15:36–28:31). Paul now fulfills the mission that God gave him by carrying the gospel throughout the Roman Empire from Jerusalem to Rome itself.

Second Missionary Journey (15:36–18:23)
Third Missionary Journey (18:24–21:14)
Paul's Arrest and Imprisonment at Jerusalem (21:17–26:32)
Paul's Journey to Rome (27:1–28:31)

Read through each section of Acts in detail, looking to see how Luke describes the development of the early church. Even though the apostles do not always know where God is leading, they remain open to the Spirit. The apostles experience hostility and some deaths, but they never cease to tell people about Jesus. God has shown them that Jesus came to be the savior for all the nations of the world.

### The Preparation for the Christian Mission (1:1–2:13)

#### Waiting in Jerusalem (1:1–14)

Acts continues the story that Luke's Gospel had ended with Easter (Lk 24:50–53). The New Testament refers to a number of different ap-

> **Casting Lots** This (1:23–26) is the last time casting of lots is mentioned in the Bible. From Pentecost on, the disciples seek the guidance of the Holy Spirit for important decisions.

pearances by the Risen Lord (see 1 Cor 15:3–7). Jesus did not continue to appear to his disciples indefinitely. Nor did he remain with them continuously as he had during his lifetime (see Jn 20:19–29). Luke has used the biblical number of 40 to set a time frame for the appearance of the Lord (see note to Acts 1:3). He insists that the risen Jesus is identical with the person who had died on the cross. Jesus' teaching during this interim period repeats the Kingdom theme of the gospel.

The disciples must wait in Jerusalem until the Holy Spirit comes on them as it had come on Jesus at the beginning of his mission (see Lk 3:22). This event will mark the transition to a new phase of the salvation story—the age of the church. The Ascension (vv. 6–12) also marks a change in the idea of how God will bring salvation. Jesus has not gone to heaven so that he can return with divine power and set up God's kingdom in Jerusalem as some people thought (1:6–7). After receiving the Holy Spirit, Jesus' disciples will become witnesses to Jesus throughout the world.

The apostles and other followers of Jesus, including his mother, Mary, and some other women, form the first community. Luke emphasizes the importance of prayer in the life of the church. Gathering for prayer and celebration of the meal together is one pillar of the church. We will see that the other is charity toward the poor.

**Replacing Judas (1:15–26)**

The number of apostles has to be restored to Twelve. The Twelve represented the twelve tribes of Israel (see Lk 22:30). The church was to become the new Israel (see note to 1:26). By using lots to determine which of two candidates would take Judas's place, the early Christians are permitting God to have the final say in this decision. The qualifications for the candidates—that they followed Jesus from the beginning to the end of his ministry—reflect Luke's understanding of the apostles as the "witnesses" who guarantee the validity of the gospel that is being preached in the churches (see Lk 24:48; Acts 1:8). Luke also takes this occasion to repeat a legend about the death of Judas (vv. 17–20; a different legend about Judas's death appears in Mt 27:3–10). Peter uses Scripture to show that Judas's betrayal did not destroy God's plan. Judas's death reflects divine punishment for a person who has committed a blasphemous act against God.

**Pentecost, the Coming of the Spirit (2:1–13)**

Fire and strong winds are typical elements in appearances of God (see notes to 2:2f). The Greek translation of Isaiah 66:15, 18 says of God's coming: "For see, the LORD will come in fire,/ . . . I am coming to gather all nations and tongues." The new turn in salvation history, represented by Acts, shows us that God is gathering the "nations and tongues" into one church through the Christian mission. Luke makes Pentecost a double miracle. Not only does the Spirit inspire the disciples' speech, but persons from different nations are able to understand their message. Pentecost anticipates the goal of the missionary effort that the Spirit will inspire in the Church.

### The Mission in Jerusalem (2:14–8:3)

**Two Sermons by Peter (2:14–3:26)**

Luke follows a similar pattern in all of Peter's sermons. His Pentecost Sermon is the most famous (2:14–36). It begins with the theme of prophetic fulfillment. The prophets anticipated a powerful outpouring of God's Spirit in the last days. Though the world is not ending, God has given that Spirit to the disciples. Peter uses several Old Testament quotations to demonstrate that the risen Jesus is the Messiah whom God had promised. God has established the crucified Jesus as Lord and Christ in heaven (v. 36).

Peter's speech has a profound impact on the crowd. The universality of the Christian mission is represented by these converts from the distant corners of the earth. Baptism is the rite though which the new converts receive forgiveness of sins and the gift of the Holy Spirit (2:37–41). Acts 2:42–47 describe the unity of the growing community. The fundamental elements of Christian community are presented: teaching, fellowship, breaking bread, and prayer.

Luke frequently uses miracles to provide evidence for the faith that people should have in Jesus. The healing of a crippled man (3:1–10) provides the occasion for Peter's second speech (3:11–26). Once again the speech is a brief telling of the salvation history, which has been fulfilled in Jesus. God's promise to Abraham has been realized in Jesus (3:25f).

**Peter and John before the Sanhedrin (4:1–31)**

This scene is the first of a number of trial scenes in Acts. A pattern is developed:

1. the miracle attracts attention;
2. the apostles teach those who have been attracted by the miracle;
3. arrest of the missionary by jealous (Jewish) officials;
4. trial of the missionary;
5. miraculous escape or vindication of the missionary.

At first, the trials are orderly. The judges take a moderate approach and only warn the disciples, but opposition to the Christian mission will increase until Stephen is murdered by an enraged mob. The apostles never claim any miraculous powers for themselves. Miracles are done in the name of Jesus (v. 10). All of the miracles have some connection with the mission to spread the gospel. Acts 4:12 expresses the belief that motivates preaching the gospel throughout the world: "There is no salvation through anyone else, nor is there any other name under heaven given to the human race by which we are to be saved."

The communal prayer that follows the apostles' release (4:23–31) shows that Christians never lost their confidence in God's power to rescue them from danger. What happened to Jesus, and will shortly happen to martyrs like Stephen, is not a defeat for Christians. God's plan for salvation can make use of such events. God responds to this prayer with a second Pentecost: The Holy Spirit comes to all who are present.

**Sharing Possessions in the Community (4:32–5:16)**

Christians demonstrate their care for one another by giving to the poor. The early church did not force members to renounce everything, as Peter and the others had done. Many would continue to own property and practice their trade. In this the church was different from groups like the Jewish sect called the Essenes, which expected members to turn over property to the sect as a condition of joining monastic-like groups. Essenes who lived in villages were required to turn over a set number of day's wages to the group's overseer. Ancient philosophers described the ideal relationship between friends as sharing all things in common. Acts depicts a Christian community that spontaneously fulfills such ideals.

Luke presents striking examples of generosity by persons who were willing to follow the sayings of Jesus, which encouraged people to sell all and become disciples (see Lk 12:33; 16:9, 11, 13). The story of Ananias and Sapphira provides an illustration—perhaps deliberately harsh to get the reader's attention—of what might happen to persons who attempt to pretend that they have the generosity of disciples while hiding money for their own use (compare the Rich Fool, Lk 12:16–21). Once again, death is viewed as God's judgment against persons who have done something blasphemous. They were not required to sell the property to be part of the community. Their sin was in the attempt to deceive the Holy Spirit. Human beings can be taken in by fraud, but God will always know what is in a person's heart. No one can cheat God. We may refuse to follow these examples of Christians helping those in need. We may even devise a scheme to appear to help the poor while keeping more for ourselves, but if we do, we will have to answer to God.

**Trial before the Sanhedrin (5:17–42)**

The miracles of the previous passage lead to jealousy and another imprisonment. This time we learn that no one could keep the apostles in jail if God wished them to continue preaching elsewhere. An angel takes them from prison to preach in the Temple area. This miraculous sign further enrages the opposition. The apostles are released thanks to Gamaliel, a Pharisee who demonstrates respect for God's plan (v. 39), but some people are now angry enough to kill the apostles (v. 33).

**Deacons for the Hellenists (6:1–7)**

This passage presents several difficulties, because it does not fit with what follows. The distinction between Hebrews and Hellenists seems to be based on an individual's mother tongue. The Hellenists would be Jewish converts to Christianity who spoke Greek. The description of the Seven as persons who would take care of the distribution of food, so that the apostles could devote themselves to prayer and preaching, suggests that the Seven were to be like deacons in the church at a later date. They must oversee the material arrangements and aid to the poor. Verse 6 describes the process, prayer and laying on of hands, by which persons were installed in offices in the church during Luke's time. In the next episode (v. 8) the most famous of the persons chosen engages in ministry of preaching like Peter and the other apostles.

**Trial and Death of Stephen (6:8–8:3)**

This trial scene is the longest in Acts. Stephen emphasizes Israel's past failures. His speech prepares the reader for the mission to the Gentiles as it develops in the plot of Acts. Luke creates a link between Stephen and the hero of that mission, Paul, by picturing Paul—who tells us that he had persecuted the church out of zeal for ancestral tradition (see Gal 1:13; 1 Cor 15:9b; Phil 3:6)—as a witness to Stephen's death (8:1). Luke uses the Stephen episode to tie the beginning of a non-Jewish Christianity to the ministry of Jesus. The charges against Stephen (6:13f) are similar to those brought against Jesus. False witnesses testify that Stephen attacks the Temple and the Law, and they predict that Jesus will destroy the Temple. The tradition that Jesus' predictions about the destruction of the Temple were brought into his Jewish trial is established in the Synoptic Gospels (see Mk 14:58; Mt 26:61; Mk 15:29; Mt 27:40). Luke omits this detail from the appearance of Jesus before the Council in his Gospel and places it here.

Predictions that God will destroy a corrupt Temple to establish one that is a holy place appear in the prophets (see Jer 7:11; Zec 14:21; Mal 3:1; Is 56:7). One Jewish sect (known as the Essenes) was severely critical of the corrupt priesthood and calendar used in the Temple. Their criticism stemmed from a concern for more exact observance of the Law. By contrast, the Stephen episode ties criticism of the Temple to an attack on the Law.

Later in Acts, similar suspicions will be voiced against Paul (see 22:20f). Like Stephen, he will be seized on the grounds that he is attacking the Temple (sometimes referred to as "this place") and the Law. Two further charges are made against Paul. He speaks against the Jewish people, and he has committed a sacrilegious act by bringing a Gentile into the area reserved for Jews (22:28). Luke's narrative shows that Stephen and Paul were not attacking the Law. Luke has shown that the Jerusalem Christians were constantly in the Temple praying. There is no basis for the accusations brought against either Stephen or Paul, just as there had been no basis for the charges against Jesus (see Lk 23:4f, 13–15, 22).

Many interpreters have suggested that Luke is using the trial scenes here to defend Christianity against the suspicions of outsiders (see NAB introduction to Acts). Political insurrection, disregard for ancestral traditions, and acts of impiety like defiling a temple were terrible deeds, all of which could stir local as well as Roman officials to punish those guilty. The Roman authorities were particularly suspicious of groups that they thought might lead rebellion among the people of the empire. At the same time, the Romans protected sacred places and traditional religious practices. Special edicts from the emperor prohibited local officials from taking advantage of their Jewish population by taking money collected for the Temple in Jerusalem, forcing Jews to appear in court on the Sabbath, and such things. Christians were particularly suspect, because their religious practices were not the traditions of an ancient people. Luke may be attempting to answer this objection by demonstrating that Christianity is the true heir of the Jewish tradition. Stephen's speech (7:2–53) recites salvation history to indict Israel for failure to obey God's commands. Such a speech would not be out of place in a Jewish context. One of the rule books of the Essene sect, The Damascus Document, begins in a similar way. It concludes that because Israel had been unfaithful, even though she had suffered punishment for various misdeeds, God had taken the promises away from the nation as a whole. They thought that only the small remnant of righteous Jews who made up the Essene sect would experience the blessings of salvation when the Messiah comes.

By implying that the audience shares hostility to God's prophets (vv. 51–53), Stephen fuels a rage that not only kills him, but also spawns persecution against other Christians. Because it scatters Christians outside Jerusalem (8:1), this hostility indirectly furthers God's plan. Stephen's vision of the risen Lord exalted in heaven recalls a saying that Mark reports Jesus using before the high priest (Mk 14:62). Visions of the heavenly Son of Man usually carry overtones of divine judgment in the New Testament (cf Rev 1:7–18). Another similarity between the death of Stephen and that of Jesus is that Stephen dies peacefully with words of forgiveness on his lips (cf Lk 23:34, 46). There is one important difference. Jesus had prayed to God, the Father; Stephen addresses his prayer to Jesus whom he has seen standing at God's right hand.

## Mission in Judea and Samaria (8:4–9:43)

### Philip Preaches outside Jerusalem (8:4–40)

The gospel begins to be spread outside Jerusalem to those who have some contact with Judaism: the Samaritans, who had their own version of the Law of Moses, and an Ethiopian, who was already interested in the traditions of the Jewish people. Several Lucan themes appear in this section. Philip's instruction about Isaiah (8:30–35) shows that Jesus is the fulfillment of what is written in the prophets. Unlike the Jerusalem crowd who had turned a deaf ear to such arguments, the Ethiopian demonstrates the proper response: He becomes a disciple of Jesus by being baptized. This story also introduces a minor theme: Prominent people become Christians, listen to the apostles' preaching with sympathy, and often ask them to return or provide some other form of assistance.

The conversion of the Samaritans and the conflict with Simon the magician introduce two more themes: the continuity of the new Christian mission with the apostles in Jerusalem and the superiority of Christianity to all forms of pagan superstition and religion. The gift of the Holy Spirit defines Christian baptism for Luke (Acts 2:38; 10:48), who contrasts it with the water baptism of John the Baptist (Lk 3:16; Acts 1:5; 11:16; 18:25; 19:3f). Christians are baptized in the name of Jesus. Baptism involves forgiveness of the past sins of a life without God, as well as receiving the Spirit. Acts 8:16 departs from the normal pattern, because Philip has baptized in the name of the Lord, but his converts did not receive the Spirit until Peter and John came from Jerusalem to lay hands on them (8:14–17).

This text has often been used as evidence to support the need for a second sacrament, confirmation, to confer the Spirit. Pentecostal Christians claim that persons who have not experienced the Spirit coming over them are not yet fully Christian. Neither development represents the view presented in Acts. Episodes in which the Spirit is separated from water baptism reflect unusual occurrences and not the norm. In the conversion of Cornelius (ch 10), the Spirit will indicate that God has accepted the new converts even before water baptism. Here, the separation between water baptism and receiving the Spirit allows Luke to show that the new mission takes place under the sponsorship of Jerusalem. Luke indicates that the Spirit always operates in and through the church.

The encounter with Simon the magician (sometimes called Simon Magus) allows Luke to address another possible objection to Christianity. Luke frequently uses miracle stories or references to miracle working to initiate interest in the Christian preaching. In the past, healings and other extraordinary events that occurred through assistance from a god or goddess might be called miracles, but a hostile bystander might accuse the miracle worker of being nothing more than a magician. The contest between Moses and the magicians at Pharaoh's court (Ex 7:8f, 12) provides a biblical pattern for evaluating magic. Even though they may duplicate some of Moses' miracles, no magician can duplicate or withstand the power that comes from the Lord. The conversion of Simon demonstrates the power of Christianity to destroy such superstitions. Luke mentions another common charge against religious charlatans: greed. The Christian mission is not driven by desire for money (3:1–10). Christians sell property and share their possessions.

### Conversion of Paul (9:1–30)

Paul's conversion demonstrates God's power to use everything, even the hostile persecutor, to achieve the divine purpose. Paul himself tells us little about the call from God that transformed him from being an enemy of the Jesus movement to being its advocate (see Gal 1:11–24). Luke presents the story of Paul's conversion three times (Acts 9:1–19; 22:4–16, 17–21; 26:12–18), with some differences. Each of the four accounts serves a purpose. Paul's own account in Galatians 1 belongs to an impassioned defense of his preaching to the Gentiles. He must show that, in telling them they could be saved through belief in Jesus without also taking on obligations of the Jewish Law, he is not distorting the gospel or breaking agreements made with Jerusalem. Acts 9 must vindicate Paul as the representative of God's offer of salvation to the Gentiles. The next two accounts (Acts 22 and 26) of Paul's conversion occur in speeches that Paul gives while imprisoned in Jerusalem.

Luke's accounts share a core of details: (a) letters from the high priest; (b) Saul is approaching Damascus; (c) light from heaven shines around Paul (and in #3, Acts 26, around those with him); (d) he (#3: we) falls to the ground; (e) hears a voice speaking to him (#3: in Hebrew); (f) "Saul, Saul, why are you persecuting me?" (#3: "hard for you to kick against the goad"); (f) Saul asks identity of speaker; and (g) "Jesus, whom you are persecuting." This core suggests a common story about Paul's conversion. After this point the three accounts diverge. Acts 9:12–16 expands on the theme of Paul's blindness. Ananias comes to Paul as "healer" (note the emphasis on the cure in v. 18). Acts 22:11a, 12f gives a more abbreviated account, and Acts 26 omits these details altogether as it does the details about the actions of Paul's companions after the appearance, the visit of Ananias, and Paul's baptism. In Acts 9:16, the Lord tells Ananias of Paul's commission. In Acts 22:14f, Ananias gives the commission to Paul, but in 26:16b–18, Paul receives the commission directly from the Lord.

The blinding/healing sequence in Acts 9:12–19 suggests that the blinding of Paul is an act of God's displeasure similar to the temporary blindness God inflicts on the magician Elymas (Acts 13:9–11). Paul's own version and the later stories in Acts emphasize Paul's commission, but this plays no role in the narrative about Paul. God uses it as an argument to persuade Ananias to go to Paul. Acts 9:15 has been phrased so that it reflects the commission given the disciples in 1:8. The ensuing versions of the story will relate the commission to Paul's vision of Christ and to the details of his specific role in the Gentile mission as it has unfolded in Acts. Here, Luke uses the story of the miraculous conversion of the persecutor of Christianity to initiate the preparation for that global mission, which is the subject of this section of the book.

**The Church Continues to Grow (9:32–43)**

Luke concludes the section with two stories from Peter's mission. The healing of Tabitha follows the same pattern as Jesus' own healing of the little girl, (see Mk 5:41). Tabitha indicates the important roles that women believers play in the growth of Christianity. Not only is she an example of piety and charity, but she also has a group of poor widows who assemble in her home. This period of peace and growth shows that the community has successfully weathered the storm of persecution that began with Stephen's martyrdom.

## Inauguration of the Gentile Mission (10:1–15:35)

**Conversion of Cornelius (10:1–11:26)**

Before Paul can fulfill his role as one who carries the gospel from Jerusalem to Rome, the leaders of the church must formally accept Gentiles into the Christian fellowship. The common meal was the basic expression of Christian unity. Paul reports an episode in which Jewish Christians from Jerusalem were unwilling to eat with the Gentile members of the Antioch church, presumably because they felt that such behavior would have violated the food laws that set Jews apart from other peoples. Paul says that before these people came, Peter himself was willing to share the meal with Gentile Christians, but that when the stricter Jewish Christians arrived, Peter, Barnabas, and other Jewish Christians began to celebrate a separate meal (see Gal 2:11–14). Peter may have been attempting to preserve harmony in the church by not offending Jewish Christians who could not bring themselves to change a whole lifetime of kosher food laws. The story of how Peter came to accept Gentile converts, which Luke repeats here, bears traces of that old dispute. God directs Peter in a vision to renounce his former understanding of what represented clean and unclean food.

**Christians** The followers of Jesus were not always known as Christians. The name originated in Antioch (Acts 11:26) where Jews and Gentiles worshiped together in a single Christian fellowship for the first time. Before that believers were known variously as "the Way" (9:2); "the sect of the Nazoreans" (24:5), and other improvised names. The name "Christians" was probably given by outsiders and may have carried a derogatory connotation (see 26:28).

Peter takes others with him to Cornelius's house so that he has witnesses to what has happened. His sermon acknowledges the fact that God is impartial. Anyone can receive salvation through Jesus if that person honors God and acts justly. The Spirit even demonstrates to Peter and the others that Gentiles are to be accepted into the church by granting Cornelius and his household a mini Pentecost before they are baptized (10:44–48). Upon his return to Jerusalem, Peter gains official approval for his actions from the other leaders there. He reports everything that had happened in connection with the Cornelius episode so that those in Jerusalem agree, "God has then granted life-giving repentance to the Gentiles too" (11:18).

The first church to include Jews and Gentiles in a single fellowship is founded by anonymous Christians in Antioch. Quickly, however, they obtain the services of two famous apostles, Barnabas and Paul. Barnabas is sent by the authorities in Jerusalem. He provides the link between Antioch and the church in Jerusalem (11:19–26). Acts 11:26 notes that the name "Christians" originated in Antioch. It appears that this name was first given to followers of Jesus by outsiders. It may have implied some scorn for the leader whom Christians worshiped, as appears to be the case when Agrippa uses it in Acts 26:28.

### Paul's First Missionary Journey (11:27–14:28)

The missionary efforts of Barnabas and Paul illustrate one of the principles of Luke's account of salvation history. *Jewish rejection* of the gospel leads the apostles to turn to the Gentiles, who receive God's salvation with joy. Paul's first missionary journey establishes the pattern of first preaching in Jewish synagogues and then turning to the Gentiles. Paul makes this principle explicit in his sermon at Pisidian Antioch (13:44–47).

*Persecution.* The Jerusalem church suffers yet another round of persecution. We are told that James, the son of Zebedee, was martyred by the Jewish king and that Peter was imprisoned. He would have been executed if God had not intervened to rescue him from jail (12:1–19).

*Death of Herod.* Herod Agrippa suffers a tortured death as divine punishment for his impiety (12:20–24). In ancient stories, being eaten by worms was a typical punishment for tyrants who scorned the gods. The historian Josephus has preserved a Jewish account of Herod's death. His version agrees with Luke that Herod had accepted divine honors from his subjects and so had been struck down.

*Superiority of Christian Faith.* Luke wishes to show that Christianity is superior to pagan superstition. Paul overcomes a Jewish magician who had influence with the Roman proconsul on Cyprus (13:4–12), and in keeping with Luke's interest in the conversion of prominent persons, the proconsul becomes a believer. Throughout this journey the apostles are plagued by hostility from Jews at the same time that they receive warm receptions from the Gentiles.

### Gentile Mission Confirmed in Jerusalem (15:1–35)

All of these events prove to the leaders of the church that God does want them to accept Gentiles into the church. They must face the objections of Jewish Christians, however, who feel that to admit Gentiles without requiring them to observe the Law contradicts the whole story of God's covenant with Israel. They insisted that Jesus was the Messiah for those who sought to be faithful children of Abraham and followers of Moses. In addition to Acts, we have Paul's report of the council in Jerusalem (Gal 2:1–10). The two versions of the meeting in Jerusalem do not agree in many of their details. Some scholars think that Paul is referring to an earlier meeting.

**The Council of Jerusalem**

THE GROWING NUMBER of Gentile converts posed challenges to the church that had started within Judaism and whose early members were all Jewish. It was approximately ten years since Peter had the vision that persuaded him to accept Cornelius into the church. By then there are probably more Gentile believers in the church than Jewish. But some of the Jewish disciples (called "Judaizers" by scholars) thought that non-Jewish Christians should be required to accept certain aspects of the Mosaic law (including circumcision) to be baptized. The Council of Jerusalem represents the first gathering of church elders to resolve a matter of faith or discipline. Their Spirit-led solution was a compromise of the two extreme positions.

When the agreement to divide missionary efforts, with Peter going to Jews and Paul to Gentiles, failed to resolve the difficulties that arose in mixed churches like Antioch, another meeting was held. At that meeting some restrictions were laid on the Gentiles. They had to avoid idolatry, avoid meat that Jewish law would have considered impure, and not enter into marriages that Jewish law considered incestuous. The decree is mentioned again in Acts 21:25. The list of prohibitions is based on rules in Leviticus 17–18 that regulate the behavior of non-Jews who live among Jews. Adopting these rules would make it possible for Jewish and Gentile Christians to enjoy table fellowship.

Luke knew of a letter sent by James to Antioch that stated these rules. He presumed that they came from the same meeting at which Paul and Barnabas received authorization for a mission to the Gentiles that would not require the Gentiles to observe Jewish practices. Paul insists that there were no rules imposed on the Gentiles (Gal 2:6). By Luke's time most churches were predominantly Gentile. The significance of the Jerusalem Council lies in the way in which church leaders were able to recognize and officially affirm the new direction in salvation history. The gospel could expand beyond the nation and culture in which it was born to all peoples of the earth.

## The Mission of Paul to the Ends of the Earth (15:36–28:31)

### Second Missionary Journey (15:36–18:23)

Paul now begins the journeys that will take the gospel throughout the rest of the empire. On this journey, he will take the decisive step of crossing from Asia Minor into Greece, where some of the most important Pauline churches would be founded. The New Testament contains Paul's own letters to churches in Thessalonica, Philippi, and Corinth. When Paul arrives in Europe, the narrative style suddenly changes from the third person to the first person "we." Sections in the "we" style appear throughout the rest of Acts (16:6–12 [beginning of the European mission]; 20:1–7, 13–16; 21:1–9, 15–17 [last journey to Jerusalem]; 27:1–28:16 [voyage to Rome]). Some scholars attribute the "we" sections to a travel diary kept by a companion of Paul. The content of these sections matches that of the journeys that Luke has already used to describe the Pauline mission. A shift into the first-person plural was often used by ancient authors for its literary effect. The change in style may represent Luke's way of telling us that we have now arrived at the mission for which the rest of the narrative has prepared us. The gospel is to be taken completely beyond Judaism. In time these Gentile Christians will be the sole keepers of a tradition, which God has been preparing since Abraham. It will be their responsibility to see to it that the gospel continues to be preached in all the nations of the earth.

### Philippi

A dream vision takes Paul into Macedonia (16:6–16). Dream visions were frequently cited as the source of divine guidance in the ancient world. Paul's first major foundation is at Philippi, a Roman colony that enjoyed the rights of an Italian city. Paul's letter to the Philippians indicates that he enjoyed close relationships with this church. They sent assistance to Paul when he was imprisoned or working in other areas, and both men and women from the Philippian church worked as missionaries (see Phil 1:14; 4:2f). Acts does not contain much information about the extensive periods of time that Paul lived in communities like Philippi, Thessalonica, and Corinth, nor does Luke refer to persons and issues mentioned in Paul's letters to those churches. There is no evidence in Acts that Luke was familiar with any of Paul's letters. If he had accompanied Paul on some part of his missionary work (see Phlm 24; Col 4:14), Luke cannot have been involved in the major events of Paul's mission in the way that Timothy, Titus, and Silvanus were.

Luke appears to have drawn upon anecdotal material for the major events in each of the cities. He then shapes that material to illustrate his understanding of the growth of the early church. The Philippi episode repeats themes that we have already encountered. Christian preaching is well received by wealthy, respectable citizens, in this case Lydia, a woman who trades in purple cloth (16:12–15). Christianity triumphs over pagan superstition and exploitation of the supernatural for personal gain when Paul exorcises the demon from a slave girl (16:16–18). Like the demons in the Gospel stories (see Lk 4:31–37), this demon recognizes the purpose for which the apostles have come.

**Thessalonica, Beroea**

The episodes at Thessalonica (17:1–9) and Beroea (17:10–15) repeat the patterns. Initial success, including prominent converts, leads to jealousy and charges that the apostles are destroying public order and encouraging revolt against Rome. Luke's readers already know that such accusations are false and that hostility will not impede the apostles' mission.

**Athens**

Paul tells us nothing of his stay in Athens except that he remained there alone after sending Timothy to strengthen the faith of the recent converts in Thessalonica (1 Thes 3:1f). Paul may not have succeeded in establishing a church there. Luke, however, uses the occasion to advance his case for the religious superiority of Christianity by showing it to be equal to the philosophical understanding of the divine principle governing the universe, and not simply another form of religious cult, magic, or superstition that sought to sway the masses for the financial gain of its preachers. Its reputation was built on its philosophic schools. Luke refers to the two most popular types of philosophy among the Romans, Epicurean and Stoic (17:18–21). The speech that Paul delivers at their request (17:22–34) touches on common themes in the philosophical account of religion, which was opposed to the superstitious beliefs about the gods found among the masses. God, the invisible, omnipresent creator and sustainer of the universe, is not swayed by rituals or is partial to one group of people over another. Hellenistic Jews had also taken over the language of philosophical monotheism to advocate the superiority of their religious tradition.

Those in Athens were well known for their piety and their curiosity. Following the practice of ancient rhetoric, the speech opens by seeking to render the audience friendly to the speaker. Paul praises them for these traits. In composing the speech, Luke has apparently modified a common type of altar inscription," . . . altars of the gods, names unknown, and heroes . . . " to the singular (v. 23). Paul then develops three claims about God that were philosophic commonplaces among both pagan and Jewish authors:

1. God is the creator of the entire universe and consequently has no need of human service or temples (vv. 24f);

2. God has allotted certain zones of the earth for the nations of human beings, who should be grateful for God's ordering of the universe and seek to serve God, who sustains and is present to all created things (vv. 26–28);

3. true worship of God will reject all superstitious practices, such as identifying the creator with the products of human artistry and imagination (v. 29).

The conclusion shifts from the common ground between the Christian preacher and philosophical enlightenment to an appeal for conversion (vv. 30f). It recalls the "unknown" taken from the altar inscriptions, which had served as an example of piety in Athens in verse 24. Inscriptions to unknown gods are a feature of those who believe in many gods, because they point to an anxiety to honor deities who might influence events but who are not "named" in the local traditions. Now is the time for a true monotheism. There is only one God, and God is not an abstract principle. God is the one who calls on Paul's listeners to repent (abandon even their philosophical paganism) and accept the message about Jesus as the one in whom all the nations of the earth are to receive salvation. As was the case in earlier missionary speeches, the Resurrection appears as evidence that Jesus is judge of all. This draws skepticism or, at best, a puzzled willingness to hear more.

**Corinth**

Luke's account of Paul's extensive work in Corinth (18:1–17) refers to the fact that Paul worked at his trade while preaching there, as he did in all of his churches (see 1 Thes 2:9; 1 Cor 4:12; 9) and supplies the additional information that his trade was that of tentmaker, probably someone who made tents of leather and rough cloth, as well as making other items such as harnesses. It mentions two of Paul's close associates from that mission, Priscilla and Aquila (1 Cor 16:19; Rom 16:3). After success in attracting influential persons, hostility from the Jews forces the apostle to turn to the Gentiles. They bring Paul before the Roman proconsul Gallio, who refuses to hear a charge involving Jewish religious law. Gallio's response (v. 14f) reflects what Luke considers to be the ideal response when Christians accused of disturbances, which are internal Jewish affairs, are brought before officials. His reference to Priscilla and Aquila's being exiled from Rome (18:2) shows that he knows that Romans often responded differently to disputes that Christian preaching caused within the Jewish community.

**Third Missionary Journey (18:24–21:14)**

**Ephesus**

This section of Acts builds on episodes about the mission in Ephesus, which was the residence of the governor of the province of Asia and the fourth largest city in the empire. Ephesus was also the location of a famous temple of the goddess Artemis, which was one of the wonders of the Hellenistic world. Silver coins from the city depict the temple with the statue of the goddess inside. Paul's confrontation with that cult occupies most of the account of his mission there (19:8–41). Later Paul delivers his farewell speech to leaders of the church in Ephesus (20:17–38). Luke's emphasis on Ephesus may have led him to locate two episodes there that seem to come from separate traditions: (1) the instruction of Apollos, who had received only the baptism of John (18:24–28) and (2) the conferring of the Spirit on persons who had received only the baptism of John (19:1–7). Luke's account assumes that Priscilla and Aquila have moved to Ephesus from Corinth and that Ephesian Christians urged Apollos to go to Corinth. Luke seems to assume that Apollos and Paul had not met (19:1), although Paul writes 1 Corinthians from Ephesus or its environs and says that Apollos was unwilling to return to Corinth (1 Cor 16:8, 12). And although Apollos had only received John's baptism, he is not rebaptized. Priscilla and Aquila are able to bring persons into full Christian discipleship. Yet, the disciples of 19:1–7 have not even heard of the Holy Spirit! Scholars have suggested that this episode would be more appropriate in the area of Syro-Palestine, where Jewish baptismal sects would continue to exist well into the third century.

The episode is similar to one in which Peter and John confer the Spirit on Samaritan converts (8:14–25). It serves two functions in Luke's schema for the expanding mission: (1) it shows that Paul is able to win over Jewish sectarians, and (2) it demonstrates the continuity between the Pauline mission and the activity of the Jerusalem church. He brings persons into the community that the Holy Spirit has been creating through the apostles since Pentecost.

Paul's mission in Ephesus is the last story of Paul's activity that is not shadowed by his impending arrest at Jerusalem. Luke's summary continues the pattern of synagogue preaching followed by withdrawal to a Gentile environment. Miracles draw attention to the new movement. They also demonstrate the power of Christianity to destroy superstition and magical practices among the people (19:8–20). The success of Christian preaching, however, awakens hostility from persons who exploit the presence of the temple of Artemis.

Demetrius's speech (see v. 26) to his fellow silversmiths alludes to the speech of Acts 17:24f. Christian preaching teaches people that human temples and artifacts do not represent God. As had been the case in earlier conflicts with magicians, fears for the economic loss that would

**More Blessed to Give . . .**

THE FAMOUS SAYING of Jesus, "It is more blessed to give than to receive," quoted everywhere from greeting cards to Hollywood movies, is never mentioned in any of the four Gospels. Only Paul quotes it (Acts 20:35) to encourage hard work for the sake of the weak and needy.

result from accepting the Christian gospel spark the hostility. As in the Gallio case, the local town clerk refuses to become involved. The Christians have not committed any impious acts such as robbing the temple or dishonoring the goddess. Demetrius is the one who is endangering public order by inciting the crowds.

This conclusion seems to represent an ideal rather than reality. As Luke fills out the rest of the journey with brief notices of stops and miracles performed by the apostle (20:1–16), he makes it appear that Paul left Ephesus of his own volition and that he avoided returning there to save time needed to reach Jerusalem by Pentecost (20:16). Yet the summons to the officials of the church in Ephesus for a farewell meeting at Miletus (20:17f) suggests that in fact Paul may have been banished from Ephesus. Paul's obscure reference to conflict in Ephesus (see 1 Cor 15:32a) implies that at one time he suffered imprisonment or punishment there.

Paul's farewell to the Ephesians (20:17–35) provides the occasion for Luke to reflect on the transition from the generation of the apostles to the church of his own day. The farewell speech of the dying patriarch was an established custom. The Old Testament contains a farewell speech from Moses to Israel (Dt 29–32). In such speeches, the dying patriarch advises his offspring to follow the Law, anticipates their future disobedience (in most cases), and sets before them the example of his own life. Moses also provides for the future leadership of the people by appointing Joshua as his successor. Luke has incorporated many of these elements in this speech. The Spirit has been warning Paul that he faces imprisonment and hardship in Jerusalem. He holds up his own life as an example of complete devotion to bearing witness to the gospel no matter what. Unlike the pagans, who sought to enrich themselves from the superstitions of the people, Paul has never sought money from his converts. He commends his own example of working at a trade, not only because it frees the apostle and his associates from suspicion of greed, but also because it provides the opportunity to give aid to the weak (v. 35). Thus, we find Paul's final word of advice returning to the example that the earliest Jerusalem community had set. Christians donate their property for support of the poor.

The farewell speech is also the time to look from the ideal of the past into the dangers of the future. Paul warns of divisions even within the ranks of the community's leaders. He admonishes the presbyters (v. 17; the Greek word means "elders") and "overseers" (v. 28; Greek *episkopoi;* see Phil 1:1), who have charge of the community left behind by the apostles, to watch over themselves as well as the church. They must continue proclaiming the gospel and exhorting others to faith and repentance. In Luke's writing we have now seen the completion of the apostolic period. Officials from local churches must take over the community. These persons have been appointed by apostles and commissioned by the laying on of hands (14:23). In that sense, they appear as successors to the apostles. But just as Joshua could not be another Moses, so they are not replacement apostles. The Spirit that has guided the church throughout the developments of the apostolic period must continue to direct her course.

**James**

THE JAMES OFTEN referred to in the book of Acts is not James, the brother of John, the son of Zebedee. He is, instead, James, "the brother of the Lord" (Mt 13:55; Mk 6:3; Acts 12:17), that is, one of four half-brothers or cousins of Jesus mentioned in the Gospels. James became the first leader or bishop of the Jerusalem community. He was killed at the instigation of the high priest and the Sanhedrin soon after the death of the Roman procurator, Festus.

Paul's dedication to his mission, even in the face of suffering, leads him to continue the journey (21:4). Even the Christian prophet Agabus, whom we know to be reliable because he predicted the famine under Claudius (see 11:28), warns Paul that in Jerusalem the Jews will bind him and hand him over to the Romans. See what Paul himself wrote to the Romans just before he left for Jerusalem (Rom 15:31). He was concerned about what he might suffer from unbelievers as well as the fact that the Jewish Christian church might reject the offering that he brings.

**Paul's Arrest and Imprisonment at Jerusalem (21:15–26:32)**

As soon as Paul arrives in Jerusalem, James warns him that devout Jewish Christians suspect Paul of leading Christians who are Jewish away from the traditions of their ancestors. James proposes that Paul demonstrate his own piety by paying the expenses for some persons who had taken a private vow. Ironically, Paul's participation in these rites leads to his arrest. Luke uses Paul's imprisonment in Jerusalem to provide speeches in which Paul defends and explains his mission. His first speech to the Jerusalem crowd (22:1–21) points to the extreme piety of his early life. Only the direct intervention of God could change Paul's behavior. Paul refers to his conversion as evidence for God's direction of his life and ministry. This theme is underlined by a second vision of Christ as Paul is praying in the Temple (22:17–21).

During his imprisonment at Philippi, Paul said nothing about his Roman citizenship until after he had been flogged (16:37). Here he stops the Roman commander as he is about to interrogate Paul under torture (22:25–29). Though Paul is able to stall the Sanhedrin by pitting the Pharisees against the Sadducees, the Romans must intervene by moving Paul to Caesarea under heavy guard (Acts 23). With the transfer to Caesarea, Paul is now in Roman hands. However sympathetically they listen to Paul's preaching, the Roman authorities take no steps to have him released. Paul's first speech before Felix, the Roman procurator of Judea, defends the Jewish character of his own personal conduct (24:10–21). He remains in prison through a change in the Roman administration. The Jews hope that the new procurator will turn Paul over to them. Faced with the possibility that he might be tried in Jerusalem, Paul invokes the ultimate privilege of a Roman citizen, the right to be heard by a court in Rome itself (25:1–12). The Roman procurator repeats the details of Paul's situation to the visiting Jewish king, Herod Agrippa II. Festus, the procurator, clearly understands that Paul has not been charged with any crime under Roman law. At best, the squabble concerns points of Jewish law. Felix arranges for a final speech by the apostle (26:1–23). Paul defends himself by repeating the circumstances of his life as a devout Jew who was converted by a divine vision, which no one could ignore. In this account of Paul's conversion, Luke focuses upon the divine commission to be a missionary to the Gentiles (26:16–18). After the hearing, both Festus and Agrippa agree that Paul is innocent. Luke may be following the pattern set out in Jesus' trial. Pilate and Herod both agree that Jesus is innocent. But Paul cannot be released, because he has demanded a hearing in the imperial court (26:30–32).

**Paul's Journey to Rome (27:1–28:31)**

The conclusion of Acts, in which Paul is preaching the gospel at Rome, though under house arrest (28:17–31), brings Luke's plot to a climax. The gospel has reached the capital of the civilized world. Luke's account of how Paul came to Rome makes use of another type of ancient adventure story, the sea voyage. Such voyages frequently included descriptions of how the hero escaped from shipwreck, pirates, and other such dangers. The story of Paul's journey is told with all the high drama of such tales. During the vicious storm that destroys the ship and has the survivors washed up on the beach at Malta, Paul demonstrates his own confidence in God and superiority to the fears of the ship's crew. Paul is even able to celebrate a meal of bread, which he has blessed (27:35f). The wording reminds Christians of the Eucharist (note to 27:35). It is impossible to sail across the Mediterranean in winter, so the group is forced to stay on Malta. The episode associated with that stay includes the drama of native peoples watching the shipwrecked party. When Paul is unharmed by a poisonous snake, they conclude that he must be a god (28:3–6). Paul wins more friends on the island by healing the sick, and they are provided with everything needed to continue the journey (vv. 7–10). Although clearly told with an eye toward entertaining the reader, the Malta story also points out that God will provide whatever is necessary for the apostle to fulfill his mission. The superstitious pagans had ignored Paul's prophetic warning that attempting to sail so close to winter would destroy both ship and cargo. The island natives thought that the snake was divine punishment for some evil Paul had committed until they saw that he escaped unharmed. In each case, the apostle comes through the threat to his life because he places all of his trust in the Lord.

## Things Learned from Acts

Luke has made striking use of traditions he inherited about the apostles—a plan of salvation history and the art of storytelling to instruct us about the development of God's plan of salvation in the apostolic age.

### Judaism Is the Inherited Tradition of the Church

The church developed according to a divine plan of salvation, which remains rooted in the experiences of Israel. When God led the church to turn toward the Gentiles, this heritage was not forgotten, although it was no longer necessary for a person to be culturally and legally a Jew to experience salvation.

### God Seeks the Salvation of All the Peoples on Earth

Acts shows us that the apostles had to venture beyond their own Jewish culture to take the gospel to the ends of the earth. Though they found this task difficult, because it often resulted in hostility from fellow Jews, all the apostles accepted this growth toward becoming a truly universal church as an expression of God's will. The task is not over. The church still must venture into other lands and cultures to fulfill the mission that is hers until the end of time: to bear witness to the gospel everywhere.

### The Church Is a Spirit-guided Institution

In Acts, the Spirit works in and through the official leaders and structures of the community. Developments like the admission of Gentiles were clearly difficult adjustments, but the leaders of the community in Jerusalem eventually came to express what is the will of God. Furthermore, as the apostle Paul leaves the scene, he has established "elders" or "overseers" in his churches. It is necessary that persons be designated as leaders now that the apostolic age has passed. Although many people think that an institution can never be the vehicle for the Spirit, Acts insists that the church is such a vehicle.

### Christians Must Be Willing to Suffer for the Gospel

Because the apostles overcome the sufferings and imprisonments they face, we may forget how relentless the onset of hostility is. No form of suffering causes any of the apostles to stray from the mission given by God and cease to proclaim the gospel. There is no instance in which preaching the gospel does not awaken some form of resistance.

### The Christian Fellowship Has Special Marks of Its Identity

Luke has presented us with ideal pictures of what the church should be. We see the harmonious gathering of diverse peoples for prayer, preaching by the apostles, and community meals. We also see a community in which concern for the weak and needy is one of the most important parts of its communal life.

### The Church Calls People to Religious Conversion

Because the church preaches religious conversion, it comes into conflict with all forms of pseudo-religion and superstition. Magical practices have no place in Christian life, nor do movements that use the religious sentiments of the masses to collect money from those who are taken in by the propaganda of such false cults. Christians give their resources to help those in need. They speak out against any false idea of God that would require buildings and other material goods for God or God's servants. Christians remain loyal to the basic institutions of their society, even when those institutions seem to be used against them by persons who do not like the criticism of false beliefs and behavior that comes from the gospel.

### Questions for Discussion and Reflection

*Group Sharing/Discussion*

1. What role does Peter play in Luke's Acts of the Apostles?

2. Prepare and role-play the meeting of Philip and the Ethiopian (8:26–40). Afterwards consider what each person in the Scripture story learned and what he taught.

3. Luke did not intend to include all events of early Christian history. He wrote Salvation history. What does this mean?

4. What is the link between Christianity and Judaism?

5. Why did the apostles use "drawing of lots" to determine the replacement for Judas?

6. How is Stephen's death similar to Jesus' trial and death?

7. Luke is clear about the differences between the water baptism of John the Baptist and Christian baptism. What is this difference?

8. Where did the name "Christians" originate (11:26)?

9. In their first missionary journey to Antioch Paul and Barnabas first visited the synagogues and then preached to the Gentiles. What were the results?

10. Demetrius of Ephesus spoke out against the Christians there. Why? (19:26)

11. Why did Paul evoke his privilege as a Roman citizen? What resulted from his exercising this right?

*In Our Lives*

1. Discuss the significance of the Jerusalem Council. Name some questions that they discussed: What was recognized in the early growth and affirmed as Salvation history? Why was the incorporation of the Gentiles into the new Christian community such a controversial issue? What problems and issues did it raise with the Jewish believers? What do you think of the solution that was offered by the Jerusalem leaders?

2. Read aloud the first sermon of Peter (2:14–3:6). Share the message concerning the fundamental elements of the Christian community. How do these look in the modern Church?

3. Were you surprised to learn there were struggles and disagreements in the apostolic church? What insights and inspiration can you draw from the knowledge of that experience? What is our role when disagreements arise in our church today?

4. Luke is clear and strong concerning riches and the mission of the Church. Read aloud 2:42–47 concerning how Christians sell their property and share their possessions. Reflect on how this basic element of charity to the poor is lived out in the Christian community today. What steps can our parish community take to come closer to this teaching? What can you personally do better?

*Individual/Personal Reflection/Action*

1. Recall how Luke presented the development of the early Church. Consider how even though the apostles did not know where God is leading, they remain open to the Spirit. Reflect on the gift of the Spirit and the need to be open to the Spirit's inspiration personally and as a community.

2. Through his storytelling Luke instructs us about the development of God's plan of salvation. We learn the following:

A. Judaism is the inherited tradition of the church.

B. God seeks the salvation of all peoples.

C. The Church is a Spirit-guided institution.

D. Christians must be willing to suffer for the gospel.

E. Catholic identity includes: prayer, preaching of the apostles, community meals and special concern for the poor and needy.

F. The Church calls the people to religious conversions from all sorts of forms of false religion and superstition.

Think about each of these learnings from reading and studying Acts. Make your own list of the three most important things you learned from the Acts of the Apostles. What difference will these make in your life?

# THE WRITINGS OF PAUL

According to the Acts of the Apostles, Paul was born in Tarsus, a city on the eastern end of the Mediterranean Sea, in what is now Turkey, around A.D. 10. He was a Roman citizen from birth, a status that carried certain privileges. He was also, according to Acts, a student of Gamaliel, a renowned rabbi. Paul was a Pharisee, that is, a member of a strictly observant Jewish party. His own writings indicate that he was well-educated in the Greek language and in methods of biblical interpretation used by the Pharisees. Both Paul and Acts of the Apostles tell that he was so zealous for the Jewish Law before his conversion that he persecuted those who, he believed, had strayed from the Law because they believed that Jesus was the Christ. During this earlier part of the sketch of Paul's life in Acts, he is called by his Jewish name, Saul. When in the narrative story, he begins to encounter the Roman world (13:9), Luke calls him by his Roman name, Paul.

After experiencing a revelation of the Risen Christ from God, however, Paul himself joined these followers of "the Way" as a young adult, about A.D. 34. He firmly believed that his conversion included a call to preach the Christian message of salvation to all people, including the Gentiles. Paul spent the rest of his life, about 30 years, in carrying out this mission. After 3 years in Arabia and a brief visit to Jerusalem, he embarked on his missionary career. After some years working in the Eastern Mediterranean area as far west as Greece, Paul visited Jerusalem to deliver relief funds collected in Asia Minor and Greece. He then intended to visit Rome and Spain, but in Jerusalem he met with increasing opposition from some Jewish leaders and was arrested and brought to Rome around A.D. 60. Between A.D. 48 and his death around A.D. 62, Paul wrote letters to communities with which he had worked, answering their questions, and preaching the gospel as he understood it to have been revealed to him.

## Sources

We learn about Paul's life from his own letters and from Luke's account in the Acts of the Apostles (cf. Acts 9:1–30; 11:1–28:31). There are some differences between what Paul says and what Luke records about certain incidents of Paul's career. For example, Luke and Paul do not agree about whether the Council of Jerusalem, around A.D. 50, decided that the Gentiles should keep some aspects of the Jewish Law (see Acts 15 and Gal 2:1–10). We must remember that when Luke writes about Paul's life, his account is a secondary source. It was written about A.D. 85, more than a generation after Paul lived. This was a time when the major issue of non-Jewish converts was no longer as pressing. Luke minimizes the tensions involved in integrating the Gentiles into the church.

## The Epistles of Paul

There are thirteen letters or epistles ascribed to Paul, but most commentators recognize only seven of these as definitely written by the apostle; the others are attributed to disciples of Paul. The seven letters certainly written by Paul himself are:

Romans
1 and 2 Corinthians
Galatians
Philippians
1 Thessalonians
Philemon

The remaining six letters (Ephesians, Colossians, 2 Thessalonians, 1 and 2 Timothy, and Titus) are often called "Deutero-Pauline." Among this latter group Paul's authorship of 2 Thessalonians and Colossians is most disputed.

For various reasons commentators believe that these six letters were not actually written by Paul but instead were written by later Christians familiar with his teachings. Disciples could have claimed to be writing in Paul's name to gain authority for their own adaptations of his teaching, an accepted practice among the ancients. In the New Testament, the Pauline writings are arranged in two groups: first, letters to communities; second, letters to individuals. Within each group they run roughly from the longest to the shortest. Thus, the letters are not arranged in the order in which they were written.

## Letters and Epistles

Paul's letters follow the fairly simple structure of a usual letter in Greek or Roman culture. Letters were not placed in envelopes, so the address is given right at the start. Then comes the body of the letter; finally, the conclusion which contains personal greetings and instructions. Some scholars have suggested a distinction between more formal, systematic "epistles" and informal "letters." In this way of thinking, Romans would be an example of a formal epistle, whereas Philemon or Titus would be examples of an informal letter. Even some of those letters supposedly written to individuals may really be formal "epistles" intended for wider circulation. Many interpreters have also noted that a fundamental structure can be seen in many of Paul's writings, but most clearly in Romans. Paul first outlines his most basic teachings in a section sometimes called the doctrinal or "indicative" part. This is followed by an application of these teachings in Paul's exhortations to the community, a section called the "imperative."

## The Apostle and His Gospel

Much of the Christian vocabulary we have become so familiar with and associate with the ministry of Jesus actually originated with Paul.

For example, Paul was, as far as we know, the first to coin a Christian meaning for the words apostle, gospel, charism, ministry, and many doctrinal phrases such as "justification by faith." As the first Christian writer, Paul began to develop specifically Christian terminology, even though many of the terms he uses will have roots in Judaism, or other meanings in secular Greek.

Paul's writings predate any of our written gospels. Paul is the first to speak about preaching the gospel, although he does not conceive this as a story about the life and ministry of Jesus. The idea of the gospel, which appears even in the Old Testament (e.g., see Is 61:1–2, "good news"), means the "good news." For Paul this is the message of salvation now accessible to all through faith in Jesus Christ. In Romans, Paul describes the gospel as the "power of God" to save all who believe (Rom 1:16). Thus, Paul does not think of the gospel as a story of the events in Jesus' life, nor even as a set of beliefs about Jesus. Rather, the gospel is the "good news" that all who believe in Jesus are already saved.

Paul rarely speaks of any actions or words of Jesus during his lifetime. Rather, he focuses on God's power, working through the death and resurrection of Jesus, to save Jews and Greeks (i.e., all people) alike. Keep in mind that for Paul, the term "gospel" means the proclamation of faith in God's forgiveness or realizing the "good news" that Jesus Christ has come to bring salvation to all people.

In his writings, Paul usually identifies himself as an apostle (Rom 1:1; 11:13; 1 Cor 1:1; 4:9; 9, lf, 5; 15:9; 2 Cor 1:1; 11:5, 13; 12:11, 12; etc.). The term apostle literally means "one sent," who represents the sender and is entrusted with the sender's authority and message. God is the source of Paul's apostleship.

## The Letters in Circulation

The apostle's authority was in his words and in his example. It became real when the community as a whole discerned Paul's meaning and decided on what actions they as believers should take as a result of Paul's words. In his letters, Paul teaches, exhorts, encourages, and corrects. The communities revered his instructions. They read them and preserved them. They also circulated his letters, sharing them with other communities. In this way the letters eventually gained the authority of Christian scriptures as the communities were increasingly strengthened, formed, and informed by a common tradition. Most people in Pauline communities probably could not read, so a reader would read Paul's letter aloud to the assembly of believers. There they reflected together on its contents. From Paul's writings we can get a picture how the early church operated, how it worshiped, how it governed itself, and how it grew.

When we read Paul's letters, we need to keep in mind that we are, in effect, reading one side of a conversation. Paul frequently seems to be responding to particular questions or concerns that Christians in various local churches have asked him about. Sometimes they have raised these questions with him on a visit, and sometimes they have written to him, and he is answering their letters. But we do not have any of this correspondence, so in many cases we have to deduce what they were asking from how Paul answers them.

# ROMANS READING GUIDE

### *At a Glance*

| | |
|---|---|
| Who are the main players? | Paul Roman church |
| What should I look for? | In Romans, Paul describes the gospel as the "power of God" to save all who believe, not as the life and ministry of Jesus. Much of the Christian vocabulary we are familiar with originated with Paul. For example, Paul coined the Christian meaning of the words *apostle, gospel, charism, ministry* and many doctrinal phrases such as "*justification by faith.*" |
| When did this take place? | Paul's writings predate any of our written gospels. He joined the "followers of the way" about A.D. 34. Between 48 and his death in 62, Paul wrote letters to communities. Romans was written between A.D. 56–58, most likely from Corinth. |
| Where did these events occur? | Paul was about to go to Jerusalem with money for the poor. After this he hopes to visit Rome. Meanwhile he writes this letter to the Romans to share the good news of Jesus Christ. |
| Why was this book written? | Romans is the longest of Paul's letters, but also it is the most important. More than any other Pauline writings, Romans is like a formal treatise, a summary of Paul's theology that serves as an introduction to Paul as well as a summary of the message Paul preached. |
| What is the story? | In no other authentic Pauline letter besides Romans does Paul write in his name alone. In the first section (chs 1–11), he describes his view of Christian life. He develops his teaching that justification by faith is already given in Christ and describes the life of freedom from sin, death, and the law. In the second section (chs 12–15) Paul derives some ethical conclusions from these teachings. |

## Before Beginning

Placing Paul's letter to the Romans at the beginning of the New Testament letters is appropriate not only because it is the longest of Paul's letters, but also because it may very well be his most important work. Romans has always held a special place among Paul's writings. Especially since the time of the Protestant Reformation in the sixteenth century, the importance of the doctrine of "justification by faith," which Paul develops in Romans (and, in a more succinct version, in Galatians), has been recognized by Catholics and Protestants alike as one of the most significant teachings of Paul and, in fact, of Christianity.

## Paul and the Roman Christians

The Roman Christian community must have been fairly large by the time Paul arrived there. It is estimated that the Jewish community of Rome in the early first century numbered 50,000. Among Christians, it seems from Paul's letter that there were both Jews and Gentiles.

Some of the information given in chapter 16 indicates quite a few house churches existed. Of course, Paul did not intend to arrive in Rome as a prisoner, as told in Acts, but as a free missionary.

Several unique characteristics of Romans distinguish this letter from the other writings of Paul. In this letter, Paul addresses a church he has not founded. He writes to introduce himself and his gospel and to seek the Roman community's acceptance and help. Before fulfilling his desire to come to Rome on the way to Spain (cf. Rom 15:22–33), Paul must first deliver the collection of money from the Gentile churches for the "poor saints of Jerusalem" (15:26), who have been suffering from a famine. When these funds are delivered, his sights will be set for Rome.

So it is that both the Jewish mission field represented by the church in Jerusalem and the open-ended Gentile mission represented by Rome and Spain are on Paul's mind as he writes this letter. Paul is concerned about unity among Christians. Although he has not founded the Roman church, he refers to the common faith he shares with believers there. He stresses the common fund of teaching from which both he and they draw. The issues of reconciliation and of being a community in faith go through all of Romans and contribute to its appeal to believers of every age.

Except for chapter 16, which may have been added later (cf. below), Romans lacks the personal tone of most of Paul's letters. Some manuscripts omit the words "in Rome" in 1:7 and 15. Without this designation and the greetings of chapter 16, Romans might be considered as a circular letter, a general development of Paul's most basic theological ideas. In Romans, Paul teaches about universal salvation, the notion of justification by faith, and on the relationship between Israel and the church as transformed by Christ. These are some of the most important and generally applicable aspects of all of Paul's theology. The general nature and universal applicability of Romans contribute to its wide appeal as an introduction to Paul.

## Romans as a "Diatribe"

More than any other Pauline writing, Romans is like a formal treatise, a summary of Paul's theology. It serves two purposes: as a self-introduction to a community not yet personally acquainted with Paul and as a summary for the message Paul preaches. Even though Romans has the formal features of an epistle, it can also be understood as a *diatribe* or a written exposé that tries to anticipate real or supposed objections or rebuttal. The diatribe, which was used by some ancient philosophers in teaching and writing, often interjected traces of dialogue to answer questions that opponents might offer. For example, Paul brings his arguments forward by sprinkling through Romans such imagined questions as "What advantage is there then in being a Jew?" (3:1) or "Well, then, are we better off?" (3:9) or "What then can we say that Abraham found, our ancestor according to the flesh?" (4:1). Thus, in comparison to Paul's other works, Romans is structured more as a philosophical treatise. Most of the other letters reflect more the give and take of real dialogue among people actually working and interacting together.

## Working through Romans

The typical Greco-Roman letter form applied to Romans yields the following divisions:

the address, consisting of a greeting and a thanksgiving, is contained in Rom 1:1–15; the body of the letter comprises 1:16–15:13. It contains the essential message of Paul, basically following what has helpfully been called the "indicative imperative" structure (see "Letters and Epistles"). The conclusion in 15:14–16:27 contains Paul's travelogue, his personal greetings, and a final doxology.

A working outline of Romans follows:

I. The Address (Rom 1:1–15)
II. The Body of the Letter (1:16–15:13)
  A. The Theme; the "Indicative" (1:16–17)
  B. The Common Predicament of Gentiles and Jews (1:18–3:20)
  C. Central Declaration of Justification by Faith (3:21–31)
  D. Abraham, Model of Faith (4:1–25)
  E. The Two Adams (5:1–21)
  F. A Preliminary "Imperative" (6:1–23)
  G. Life without the Spirit (7:1–25)
  H. Life in the Spirit (8:1–39)
  I. But what of Israel? (9:1–11:36)
  J. The Final "Imperative" (12:1–15:13)
III. Conclusion (15:14–16:27)

### The Address (1:1–15)

The address typically includes greetings and a thanksgiving, which is how Greco-Roman letters usually began. Here and in some other letters, notably Philippians, Paul has woven this brief feature into an extended prayer. In no other authentic Pauline letter besides Romans does Paul write in his name alone. He usually has with him some coworker known to the letter's recipients. In chapter 16, this is certainly the case. But even in Romans, Paul is not entirely independent. He needs the Romans' acceptance. He is grateful for their perseverance, and he looks forward to being strengthened by them through their common faith (1:11). Paul says that although he is personally unknown to the Romans, the gospel or Christian message he preaches is the same as that which they have received from other Christian missionaries.

Although Paul usually refers to his addressees as "the church in ________," he does not use the term "church" in the address of Romans. But he does remind the Roman Christians of their vocation to holiness. In developing a Christian terminology in the Greek language, Paul will consistently draw upon images and phrases that appear in the Hebrew Scriptures. An example is Paul's description of the believing community as holy, as saints, called and sanctified by God (e.g., 1 Cor 1:2). Israel is a "kingdom of priests, a holy nation," according to Exodus 19:6. The Law sets Israel apart, making it distinct from its neighbors because it has a covenant relationship with God. This holiness has nothing to do with the virtue of the members but arises from the fact of God's call. Their personal holiness is then a response to that call.

## The Body of the Letter (1:16–15:13)

### The Theme (1:16–17)

Romans 1:16–17 states the theme. In the chapters that follow, the gospel is described as the power of God for universal salvation. This theme is developed in both its positive and negative implications. Positively, Paul insists that faith is accessible to all through Christ. But Paul also realizes some negative implications, even of his belief that all are saved in Christ. For example, it is clear that all have sinned and are in need of salvation. The emphasis on universal sinfulness deserving of God's wrath is the negative pole of the theme of Romans. There is no human means of achieving salvation; it must be given to us.

***Paul's Fundamental Doctrine: Justification by Faith***

| Universal Sinfulness | Universal Salvation |
|---|---|
| Sinfulness of all is manifested in<br>• both Jews and Gentiles (1:18–3:31)?<br>• Sin of all since sin of Adam (5:12 –21)<br>• The human dilemma—knowing what is right (the Law) does not enable us to do what is right (7:13–25) | We are already justified by faith<br>• Exemplified by Abraham (4:1–25)<br>• Fulfilled in Christ (5:1–11; 6:1–23; 8:1–39) |

In Romans these two poles are in constant dynamic tension.

It is important to note that for Paul the starting point is not that all have sinned but, rather, that all have been saved. This is the conviction of faith. Paul considers sin to be an illustration of the universal need for salvation. This explains why Paul's hope, eloquently expressed especially in chapters 5, 8, and 15, is so deep and certain. No human sin is sufficient to separate us from the love of God that saves us.

**Paul's Fundamental Conviction**

The Greek words that we translate "just," "justice," "justify," and "righteousness" are all derived from the same root word, *dikaios* (just), *dikaiosyne* (justice, righteousness, or justification). Even more important, for Paul the concepts are closely linked. He connects the justice of God with God's power and will to "justify" all people, that is, to regard them as just.

The Scriptures show that God's justice is revealed, that is, it cannot be completely comprehended through human effort or study. Isaiah reminds us that God's thoughts are not human thoughts, and God's ways not our ways (see Is 55:7–8). Yet the Scriptures also tell us that we are to be just, that we must act in imitation of God, that we are to walk blamelessly before God and be perfect (see Gn 17:1; Hos 6:6). Thus, justice is not completely foreign to us. The God-fearing Israelite seeks to act justly, act in ways that are acceptable to God and in accord with God's covenant. These ways are also revealed through the Jewish Torah ("instruction") or Law. The Torah was handed down from Moses and interpreted throughout the history of the Jewish people, who reverenced it as the revealed will of God. So, for example, Abraham in Genesis (Gn 15:6) and Joseph in the infancy narrative (Mt 1:19) are described as "righteous" (*dikaios*) men. It is not that acting justly or keeping the Law earns salvation or God's approval but, rather, the opposite. The covenant is God's gift to Israel. Israel's response is to keep the Law. The Jewish person seeking justice is enjoined to study and to follow the Torah or the instruction of God. In the covenant is the hope of being justified, that is, "made just" in God's sight. Thus, for the Old Testament as for Paul, the related terms "justice," "just," and "justified" all originate in God, who reveals how we are to act and judges us accordingly. Although all people are sinners, Jewish theology teaches that we may expect to learn the way of justice through a faithful following of the Law in all things. This is the background for Paul's understanding of justification through Jesus Christ.

**Justification or Salvation**

There are two main ideas that we must understand if we are to grasp the argument about justification that Paul puts forth in Romans and in some of his other writings. The first is the meaning for him of trying to attain justification or salvation by obeying the Law. (This is dealt with particularly in chapter 3 of his Letter to the Galatians; see the Reading Guide to Galatians.) The second main idea pertains to Paul's explanation of how the Gentiles, or those who do not have the Law, are justified.

First, for Paul, justification through the works of the Law is a false hope for several reasons. The idea that the Law held the key to justification was the position of the Jews who did not become Christians, as well as of the Christian-Jewish group led by Peter and James. This was the majority of the church when Paul began his mission. The theological challenge Paul faces is that his experience of the Risen Christ and his mission to preach that justification is available to all, both Jews who have the Law and the Gentiles who do not, convinced Paul that justification is an act of God, given freely to all who believe. Like his Jewish contemporaries, Paul himself was zealous for the Law (cf. Rom 10:1–3; Phil 3:3–7; Gal 1:11–14), but now his experience has taught him that this is not the way to go. Now in his zeal to win people over to the way he is convinced is right, Paul argues that the Law is impossible to keep and can only lead to frustration and self-righteousness. This caricature of the Law must be understood as rhetorical attempts to persuade Gentiles attracted by Law observance to his point of view.

Second, justification through the Jewish Law is insufficient because it excludes the Gentiles, who, as Paul has described the situation in Romans 1:18–3:31, are in the same sinful predicament as are the Jews. But both Abraham and Christ show that the Gentiles, no less than the Jews, are now justified through faith. According to the Law, Jesus was condemned to death. But God overturned the Law's verdict in raising Jesus to life (see Gal 3:10–14). Thus, for Paul, the death and resurrection of Jesus has taken the place of the Law. As a result, the Gentiles are now included among the justified. By accepting Jesus' gift of justification, and consequently living in accord with God's will, Jews and Gentiles both are saved. Following the just requirements of the Law or the precepts of the church is not a prerequisite for but a result of being justified.

Paul thus understands justification as already having taken place through the death and resurrection of Christ. Salvation is in the future, promised to those who believe in Christ and live according to this belief. As Paul himself says it, "Indeed, if, while we were enemies, we were reconciled to God through the death of his Son, how much more, once reconciled, will we be saved by his life" (Rom 5:10).

**Faith and Salvation**

We must also understand Paul's idea of faith to understand the argument of Romans. It may seem that he is simply replacing one human action, obedience to the Law, with another human action, faith in Jesus Christ. But for Paul faith is trust: the belief that it is God's power, not our own, and our reliance on God, not on our own abilities, that saves us. Paul saw the obvious danger for sinful people: the danger that they would continue in their wrong behavior and close themselves off from God forever. But Paul also saw the danger for those people who seemed moral and upright: the danger that they would believe God was forced to save them because they had earned their way into God's love.

For Paul, this thinking is a fatal mistake. It assumes that we can manipulate God by our actions. Paul explains away this misunderstanding by the necessity of faith. Faith is our acknowledgment that it is God's power that saves us, not our own efforts. We are helpless, in that we are all sinners; and in spite of that, we can trust in God to save us.

Notice that Paul begins with the affirmation of faith in God's work of salvation to which everyone has access in Christ. He does not start with the premise of defeat nor emphasize that each person must individually become convicted of sin. Rather, Paul stresses first the goodness and power of God to save, and then tries to demonstrate the universal need for salvation to be given.

Paul uses terms such as "redeem" and "justify" and "reconcile" in relationship to one another and sometimes almost interchangeably (see Rom 5:9–11 and discussion on that passage below). These terms originally belonged to the world of finance; for Paul they appropriately illustrate the economy of salvation. The "debit" columns of sin and guilt and punishment are converted by God into the "credit" columns of forgiveness, redemption, and reconciliation. Through faith we are reconciled to God and to one another. We are redeemed by the blood of Christ, and our sins are forgiven.

Paul came to believe that the revelation of the Law was fulfilled by the death and resurrection of Christ. In Romans, Paul will develop a dichotomy between what was "formerly" and what is "now." For Paul, God's justice is only fully revealed in Jesus. The emphasis on "now" also implies an emphasis on the accessibility of God's justice to all through faith. The Law (or Torah) formerly divided humanity into "Jews and Gentiles," the latter not sharing in the promise represented by the Law. This division is overcome, and all now have equal access to God's revelation of justice expressed in Christ.

**The Common Predicament of Gentiles and Jews (1:18–3:20)**

Having stated his conviction that the gospel is God's power to save all people through faith (1:1–16f), Paul proceeds to demonstrate the need of all people for salvation. Universal sin illustrates this need. Paul shows that "all," both Gentiles and Jews, have sinned and incurred the wrath of God. The "wrath of God" is being revealed in that the Gentiles are experiencing disastrous consequences of their own behavior (Rom 1:18–32). The wrath of God is an image borrowed from the Old Testament prophets (see Is 9:8–12; 10:5; Jer 50:11–17; Ez 5:13; 36:5–6). It depicts God's rejection or "abandonment" (Rom 1:24, 26, 28) of people to their own sin. The story of Saul's disobedience to God in 1 Samuel 15 dramatizes this dynamic: From the moment when God no longer accepts Saul's kingship, Saul's downfall is certain.

Although the Gentiles could know God through creation, the evidence of their godless lives means that they have rejected knowledge of God. Belief in God is no mere intellectual affair but involves a conversion to "the living and true God" (see

1 Thes 1:9) expressed in a virtuous life. Paul adopts the Old Testament notion of the relationship between idolatry and immorality evident among the pagans. (But see the New American Bible [NAB] note on 1:18–32 that cautions that the lives of many in the Greco-Roman culture could serve as models for Christians today.) Paul speaks in generalities here, trying first to indict the Gentiles (1:18–31) and later (in 2:1–3:9) the Jews, in an effort to show the effects of universal sin and the need of all humanity for God's salvation.

**Central Declaration of Justification by Faith (3:21–31)**

Paul summarizes his previous demonstration of universal sinfulness (3:23) but prefaces it with the way out, accomplished by God through Christ, then makes the central assertion: we are justified by faith apart from the works of the Law (3:28). He emphasizes that God's just judgment comes upon all people, for God shows no partiality (2:11; see also Dt 10:17; 2 Chr 19:7; Sir 35:12f; Acts 10:34; Gal 2:6; Eph 6:9; Col 3:2, 5; 1 Pt 1:17). Having indicated that the Gentiles are sinners, Paul turns to concentrate throughout Romans 2:1–3:20 on the Jews. Here Paul adopts the language of the prophets, who not only charged sinfulness to the pagans, but also accused the Jews of having "a stubborn and impenitent heart."

**Abraham, Model of Faith (4:1–25)**

For Paul, Abraham is a type of Christ; that is, Abraham follows the pattern of Christ. Adam and Moses, on the other hand, are antitypes or reverse patterns. For Jews, circumcision, the ritual removal of the foreskin of the penis of infant boys, symbolizes the individual's membership in the people of God and, therefore, the individual's acceptance of God's law and teaching. Because Abraham was justified before his circumcision, he was justified independently of the Law. Therefore, Abraham is the ancestor of both Jews and Gentiles. Abraham's example illustrates the theme of Romans: All have access now to salvation through faith. (For further discussion of the image of Abraham for Paul, see the Reading Guide to Galatians.)

**The Two Adams (5:1–6:23)**

In chapter 5 Paul contrasts Christ's saving actions (i.e., his death and resurrection) with the devastating consequences of the sin of the first Adam. By the time of Paul, it was generally understood that the first human beings were created immortal (Wis 2:23f) but that their sin brought death into the world. Subsequent generations continue the sentence of death by continuing to sin (Rom 5:12). Adam represents all people under sin with its curse of death. But Adam is also a figure drawing out God's promise of redemption. The writer of Genesis portrays the situation of Adam as obviously in need of some divine action: even before the curse for sin is pronounced in Genesis 3:16–19, God promises to save the human family in the end (Gn 3:15). The early church fathers, above all St. Augustine, used these passages, especially Romans 5:12, as a basis for describing the devastating effects of original sin, although Paul does not use this term. Instead, he argues that if the first sin had such widespread effects that all people since Adam have been under its influence, how much more effective and powerful is the gift of salvation won through Jesus Christ. That gift is called "grace," which brings eternal life (5:21). The mode of argument here is a familiar pattern of argument: from lesser to greater. If so much damage was caused by the first human being, Adam, how much greater is the grace and redemption won by the ultimate human being, Christ. Paul's thinking is at the basis of the church's ecstatic thanksgiving, "O happy fault that has merited so great a redeemer!" The Roman liturgy recalls this prayer during the Easter Vigil each year in the singing of the Exsultet, which tells this story.

Salvation is a reality that Paul describes here and elsewhere (see 1 Cor 6:11; 2 Cor 5:10–15; 10:5–10), using words like "reconciliation," "redemption," "justification," and "sanctification." The verb "to save" refers to God's intervening action when human beings are in need. It connotes actual, sometimes physical, rescue as well as deliverance from spiritual distress. The Old Testament often refers to God as "Savior." Reference to God's saving action is one of the Bible's most frequent ways of referring to God, appearing literally hundreds of times. In the New Testament this term is often used in connection with Jesus. The disciples, for example, prayed "Lord, save us" (e.g., Mt 8:25). Paul assumes we are familiar with the long Old Testament tradition of God's saving actions on behalf of people. But Paul, in relating God's action to the death and resurrection

| Paul's "Justification by Faith" Argument in 5:1–8:39 |
|---|
| 5:1–21 Justification already given in Christ |
| 6:1–7:25 Baptism has freed us from sin and the Law now plays a different role |
| 8:1–39 The effects of the Spirit's work in us, giving us hope |

of Christ, gives a new emphasis in the theology of salvation or "soteriology." Many scholars point out that all of Paul's christology (or thinking about Christ) is really a soteriology or doctrine of how God saves through Christ.

Paul's view of humankind (i.e., his theological anthropology) is evident in this chapter. He considers all people to be under some dominant influence, living either for God under grace or living for sin. This is a different perspective from our contemporary one that considers human freedom as an autonomous, absolute ideal. For Paul, freedom is related to life for God (6:10) in contrast with slavery to sin (6:6). By means of the opposites of death and life, Paul contrasts the former condition of sin and death to the new life of freedom won by Christ and obtained by the believer through baptism.

The term baptism means "immersion," and Paul plays on this original sense even as he has the initiatory rite in view. He coins several expressions in chapter 6 that signify believers' solidarity with Christ. We have "died with" him and are "buried with" him; therefore we will be "raised with" him and now "live with" him. This incorporation into the death-resurrection of Christ by means of baptism necessarily has implications for the moral life. As a result of this incorporation, we "walk" (a term designating moral living) in the newness of life (6:4). Paul will postpone a fuller discussion of the implications of this "newness of life" until chapters 12 through 15.

### Life without the Spirit (7:1–25)

The major part of chapter 7 follows the style of a diatribe (see the NAB introduction and notes on ch 7). Paul anticipates the objections of real or imaginary opponents in a kind of dialogue designed to present his own ideas in an orderly fashion. The most important aspects of Paul's argument are three.

1. The Christian views the Law differently now, having been freed from its service (Paul says "bondage") by participation in the death of Christ.

2. The purpose of the Law is to name what is sinful. Thus, the Law did not encourage grace or freedom but only identified sin.

3. Anticipating an objection that the Law is therefore sin, Paul responds emphatically, "No!" Yet knowledge of what is good does not enable us to do what is good. The Law is one more factor, then, in the judgment against humanity, convicting all of sin. The Law concurs with human conscience, judging us as sinners. This is the meaning of the expression, "the good that I want to do I avoid and the evil I wish to avoid I do" (see 7:19–21).

But it is important to realize that his statements about this unhappy predicament are not expressions about him personally but of the situation of humanity without God.

### Life in the Spirit (8:1–39)

Chapter 8 celebrates the message of salvation. "There is no condemnation for those who are in Christ Jesus" (8:1). Nothing will "be able to separate us from the love of God in Christ Jesus our Lord" (8:38f). Nowhere is Paul's understanding of the role of the Spirit more eloquently expressed than here. Paul begins chapter 8 with a consideration of the opposition between the flesh and the spirit. He often tries to illustrate his meaning by opposing two poles of thought. This is a way of showing the mutually exclusive categories of sin and death versus grace and life. Paul adapts the Greek notion of the flesh to express the sinful condition of humanity before grace. In the Greek philosophical tradition, flesh, like spirit, had several connotations. "The flesh" means, of course, that which pertains to the body. But it can also mean the inferior aspect of human existence, whatever in human life is weak or limited. For the Greeks, the flesh referred to what they regarded as baser desires, which for them included sensual and sexual instincts. The flesh is mortal and must be controlled by the spirit (i.e., the mind and will), which in Greek thought is immortal. Paul adapts this notion to sometimes speak of the flesh as the moral equivalent of sin. For Paul, however, sins of the flesh include not just bodily sins, such as gluttony, but also spiritual sins, such as pride. Drawing on the same tradition, Paul uses the term "spirit" to refer to the new life accessible to all through Christ. In stressing the life of the spirit, Paul contrasts the present salvation with the past that was characterized by sin, death, and slavery to the dictates of the flesh.

The Holy Spirit is an advocate, coming to our aid and strengthening us. Like the Israelites in Egypt, we formerly could only groan in the suffering and weakness caused by sin. The Spirit converts our cries into a prayer that recognizes God as Father and ourselves as children of God. Thus, through the Spirit we are liberated from slavery to sin and enabled to pray as the children of God, saying "Abba" (8:15). From Paul's use of this prayer, we can assume that he is indirectly referring to the Gospel tradition that tells us that Jesus himself addressed God as "Abba, Father" (Mk 14:36). We are confident, too, that the suffering we experience and witness is as nothing compared to the glory that is to come. All creation shared in the sin of Adam and groans with humanity in its suffering. Now all creation awaits the revelation of the children of God (8:20–25).

At the end of chapter 8, Paul exclaims that nothing can separate us from the love of God. But he goes on to acknowledge in chapters 9 through 11 that the Jewish rejection of the Christian message is a challenge to this belief. Some may say that now God has run out of patience with Israel. But if Israel's rejection of Christ could limit God's fidelity to the covenant and God's justice, what does that mean not only for Israel but for the Christian church, which is adopting the prerogatives of Israel? Has God had a change of mind? These are some of the questions Paul puzzles out in these chapters in a remarkable review of the history of salvation.

**But what of Israel? (9:1–11:36)**

The form of this three-chapter unit is a philosophical diatribe. Paul responds to anticipated questions or challenges in the form of an artificial dialogue. In the course of developing his views, he makes abundant use of the Old Testament. Before dealing with some ethical conclusions to the doctrines in chapters 12 through 15, Paul senses the necessity of taking up this personally painful question about God's fidelity to the Jews. Israel's rejection of Christ was clearly a problem not only for Paul, but also for the early church. Paul's consideration of this question properly belongs with the doctrinal development of Romans.

Paul's summary of the privileges of Israel in Romans 9:1–5 prompts him to redefine the term Israel in chapters 9 through 11. Israel is not a mere ethnic or historical reality, but one that always had theological connotations. The Jewish scriptures show, Paul argued, that "not all of Israel are Israel" (9:6). The element of divine choice was operating throughout Jewish history, illustrating that God is free to show mercy as God wishes. Not all are children of Abraham simply because they descended from him, as the preference for Isaac over Ishmael shows (see 9:7–9; Gal 4:22–31). God chose Jacob over Esau (Rom 9:10–13). God hardens some, as in the case of Pharaoh; but divine mercy is shown to Moses and the Hebrews in Egypt (9:15–17). Paul also cites examples from the prophets, especially Jeremiah, Hosea, and Isaiah to support God's freedom to choose. For Paul, God's mercy is God's justice. Paul carefully builds his arguments to show how God is now including the Gentiles among the new "Israel of God" (Gal 6:16).

Paul begins chapter 10, as he had chapter 9, with a defense of his kinspeople. He testifies to Jewish zeal in conforming to the Law, as he himself was zealous for the Law prior to his faith in Christ (see Gal 1:14). But as the "end of the law" (Rom 10:4), Christ brings justification for all who believe. Thus, Christ renders the Law useless and eliminates the differences between Jew and Gentile. To support his assertion that Christ is the end of the Law, Paul develops an explanation of scripture in the style of a Jewish Midrash or "running commentary." Paul applies the Old Testament to Christ and so gives an example of how the "law and the prophets testify" to the righteousness given by God in Christ (cf. Rom 3:2ff). Paul argued that there is only one God of Jews and Gentiles in Romans 3:21–31. Similarly, here in chapter 10, Paul says that there is only one Lord over all and accessible to all who call upon him. That Lord is Christ. Near the end of the chapter, in 10:14–21, Paul echoes the traditional prophetic denunciation of Israel who alone is responsible for her infidelity. But God continues to reach out to a "disobedient people"(10:21).

God's fidelity, proven in the past and present (chs 9 and 10) will ultimately be for the salvation of "all Israel" in the future (Rom 11). God has not finally abandoned Israel because a remnant remains faithful to God as a sign of the ultimate salvation of "all Israel" (Rom 11:26). Paul cautions the Gentiles, included by the action of Christ into "all Israel," to remember that it is only by grace that they are saved. This is a mystery revealing God's infinite mercy. The power of God is the divine compassion by which all are enfolded into the salvation of "all Israel."

### The Heart of Paul's Ethics (12:1–15:13)

Paul's ethical conclusions apply his teaching, and form the "imperative" part of the letter. This can be subdivided into consideration of the church and the world (12:1–13:14) and a call for reconciliation and unity (14:1–15:13). Romans 12:1–2 has been called the heart of Pauline ethics. Here Christians, who do not yet have a sacrificial ritual like most of their neighbors in their temples or the Jews in Jerusalem, learn that their lives are their living sacrifice, purifying them to be able to live not in conformity to the world (seen as being in opposition to God), but with transformed understanding. In describing the Christian community, Paul adapts the image of the "body" (12:4–8), a popular image used by Stoic philosophers to illustrate the interdependence of members in a state. Older Catholics may be familiar with this image for the church and probably relate it to ideas developed by Pope Pius XII in an encyclical titled "The Mystical Body" (*Mystici Corporis*). This encyclical stressed the various ways members of the Christian community, both now and in past ages, are related to one another. We can also note that Paul develops the image to stress the very real mutual dependency of Christians who "ought not to think of themselves more highly than others" (12:3) but as "one body" (12:4) having many parts. The image of the body provides the transition between the liturgical language that describes Christians' behavior as "spiritual worship" (12:1), and the obligations of the mutual love that is to be characteristic of Christians.

### Christians and Government

Romans 13:1–7 takes up the question of the Christian community's relation to civil government. We must remember that Paul is speaking to a minority community within an alien state. At first glance his advice appears simplistic. Paul says that all authority is ordained by God and has its origin in God. Christians in Paul's time were trying simply to survive. Society expected citizens to follow the religion of the state. Paul instructs Christians to be good citizens while not being conformed to the standards of the world around them. Then, having spoken about giving society its due, Paul considers the question of the debt believers owe one another: Love is the fulfillment of the law. Apparently, Paul is acquainted with the love command of Jesus (see Rom 13:8–10). He reviews the commandments from adultery to covetousness, repeating finally in verse 10 what he stated in verse 8: "Love is the fulfillment of the law."

### Divisions over Observances and the Call to Unity (14:1–15:13)

Paul frequently says that Christians should be of one and the same mind (e.g., Phil 2:1–4). However, disagreements over ethical issues threaten the unity that should characterize the Christian church. The Roman Christians disagree over dietary matters and the observance of certain feast days. In a mixed community of Jewish and Gentile Christians, such questions could not help but arise.

Referring to the different sides of this debate, Paul speaks of those with "weak" and those with "strong" faith. His emphasis is not so much on the opinions or positions of individual believers but on the common attitudes to be cultivated among believers. He refers to the faith of the community and of members' responsibility to be united with the faith of the whole body. Paul exhorts the Christians to a fundamental harmony that is expressed in mutual respect and concern for one another. Paul reminds the Roman Christians, many of whom are Jewish, that the Scriptures are written for our instruction and encouragement. The term "encouragement" is linked to the hope that abounds in the community "by the power of the Holy Spirit" (15:13). Hope, joy, and peace are linked to belief. Faith is a confession about the meaning of Jesus' death and resurrection (see Rom 10:9). But it is also, according to 15:7–13, acceptance of other members of the Christian community.

### Conclusion (15:14–16:27)

Paul reminds the Romans again, as he did at the beginning of his letter, about their common faith as well as his confidence in them. In 15:14–33 the apostle speaks of his need for their hospitality soon; he requests prayers as he embarks on his mission to Jerusalem to take the collection there. Although Paul is not personally acquainted with the Romans, he has written "boldly" because he is a "minister" of Jesus Christ. He describes his ministry in liturgical language, as a "priestly" (*leitourgos*) duty (15:16). Paul is of course not referring to a sacramental priesthood, because Christians have not yet developed a theology of sacrificial cult, but to his mission to preach the Christian message to the Gentiles. He uses language common to the Jerusalem Temple priesthood and to other religious worship of the day.

Paul reports that his immediate plans include a visit to Rome in passing on the way to Spain, after taking the collection to Jerusalem. He understands the collection as a symbol linking Jews and Gentiles, the fulfillment of a responsibility he accepted at the Jerusalem council (Gal 2:10). The term *debt* occurred in Romans 13:8–10 where Paul described love as the only legitimate debt a believer can incur. Because spiritual blessings are much greater than material things, the Gentiles owe these lesser goods to the Jews as a consequence of their inheriting Israel's spiritual blessings now through Jesus Christ. Common faith makes kin of Jews and Gentiles and links both in mutual responsibility. Paul's strategy, then, is twofold: to ensure that the offering is sizable and that it is accepted as symbolic of the true faith and equal status of the Gentile Christians. If the Jewish Christians accept the gift, they are thereby accepting the mission to the Gentiles.

Chapter 16 consists mostly of greetings to and from various people known to Paul. It is possible that it was originally part of a letter intended for Ephesus and was for some reason later added to the preceding 15 chapters of Romans. This chapter seems almost like an afterthought, and further examination suggests it even contains some discrepancies to material stated or implied in the first 15 chapters. Paul commends Phoebe, bearer of the letter to the Romans, speaking of her as *diakonos* (the only named person in the New Testament who is a "deacon" of a particular church) and *prostatis,* that is, his patron and benefactor. Then he greets numerous people as if he is well known to them and as if he and the Romans have a number of mutual acquaintances. Until now the apostle has maintained a certain distance from the Roman Christians, insinuating that his introduction to himself and to his gospel could serve in place of the personal contact he usually has with communities he has founded. But if Paul knows as many Romans as this chapter indicates, the uncharacteristically general and impersonal tone of chapters 1 through 15 of the letter is strange. The note on 16:1–23 draws attention to the mixture of Jewish and Gentile names, representative of the mixed background of the Roman community. Much valuable social information about acquaintances and collaborators of Paul, both male and female, whether in Ephesus or Rome, is contained in these verses.

The placement and authorship of the final doxology or blessing is debated. But its appropriateness at the end of this epistle is not. The doxology echoes several themes developed in the letter. Paul speaks of "my gospel" (see 1:16–17), the mystery kept secret for long ages (11:25–32), manifested through prophetic writings (numerous allusions to the Old Testament throughout this epistle), and to the obedience of faith (see 1:5; 15:28). Paul has pronounced a blessing at various points (7:24; 8:35–39; 11:33–36), as if carried away by the abundance of God's wisdom and mercy. This reflects the Jewish custom of celebrating the wonders of God with praise. Nowhere is the doxology more fitting than after Paul has reviewed the fundamentals of his gospel, with emphasis on the universality of redemption and the imminence of God's victory over all evil in the triumph of Jesus Christ.

## Concluding Remarks

Thus important themes are: justification by faith, the emphasis on the present reality of justification contrasted with the former life of sin, and most importantly, the inclusion of all—Jews and Gentiles—in a new Israel of God, the church. The ethical section of Romans may be seen as a description of the church living in but not of the world. It would be hard to overestimate the influence of Romans in the development of Christian doctrine and morality throughout history.

**Questions for Discussion and Reflection**

***Group Sharing/Discussion***

1. The issues of community in faith and of reconciliation permeate the book of Romans. Discuss what these mean and why they were important for Paul.

2. Romans contains Paul's basic theological ideas. Some are: universal salvation, justification by faith, the relationship of Israel and the church as transformed by Christ. Let each person choose a theme to review and explain to the group.

3. According to Exodus 19:6 Israel is "a holy nation." Explain how the Law and God's covenant related to its holiness.

4. Jews and many Jewish Christians, including James and Peter, thought that following the Law held the key to justification. What convinced Paul that justification is an act of God given freely to all?

5. The God-fearing Israelite acted justly by living according to God's covenant. This way of living was revealed in the Torah. The covenant is God's gift to Israel and Israel's response is to keep the Law. Explain Paul's two reasons why this was an inadequate view of justification.

6. Paul shows all, both Gentiles and Jews, have sinned and incurred the "wrath of God" (Rm 1:18–32). What does this "wrath of God" mean and what does it refer to?

7. In light of time and experience, Paul redefines "Israel" (chs 9–11). For Paul, Israel is not a mere ethnic or historical reality but a reality that always had theological meaning. Explain what Paul is teaching regarding "Israel."

***In Our Lives***

1. "Following the just requirements of the Law or the precepts of the Church is not a prerequisite for but a result of being justified." Have some people explain what this means for Paul and others explain what it means and implies for Catholic doctrine.

2. Paul says that justification has already taken place through the death and resurrection of Christ. Salvation is in the future, promised to those who believe in Christ and live according to that belief. For Paul it is God's power, not our own, and our reliance on God, not on our own abilities that saves us. Explain this belief of Paul's in your own words. Reflect on this to make it your own.

3. In chapter 13 Paul instructs Christians to be good citizens while not being conformed to the standards of the world around them. Name the standards of the world around you. Spell out what it means to be Christian working for the common good in this world. How do you communicate this vision? How can you do it more effectively?

4. This is an important letter because it explains Paul's theology and views. What, if anything, was surprising to you? What is especially appealing or important for you? Was anything surprising to you?

5. Paul explains baptism (6:1–23) by a common preposition: "with," that is, we have "died with, are buried with, we are raised with and now live with" him. As a result, we walk in newness of life. Share what this all means in living your baptism.

***Individual/Personal Reflection/Action***

1. Look through Romans 8 again and choose part of it to re-read and reflect on. Think about the role of the Spirit in your life and in the life of the Christian community. The power of the Spirit enables us to work toward unity and a loving relationship with one another. How does this affect the way you relate to the Christian community? To people of other faiths? To the people of the world?

2. Paul's doctrine of "justification by faith" is central to his whole relationship with Jesus. What does "justification by faith" mean in Romans? Reflect on this essential Pauline doctrine. Then consider what it means in your life. Does it help you to grow in your relationship with Christ? What role does concern and care of others play in relationship to "justification by faith"?

# THE LETTERS TO THE CORINTHIANS

## Introduction

The letters to the Corinthians reveal Paul the pastoral theologian in ways that his other letters do not. The sheer number of pastoral problems posed and answered, especially in 1 Corinthians, leads us to think that here Paul was most challenged to apply the principles he knew to the lives of his community. The Corinthians could never be accused of lack of initiative. Rather, they seem to have taken (perhaps more seriously than Paul would have liked) his encouragement to find new freedom in Christ, so that his relationship with them was complex and tumultuous.

Corinth was the capital and central city of the Roman Province of Achaia, which comprised southern Greece. Its location near the isthmus dividing the Peloponnesus from mainland Greece made it a major seaport and trading center. It was also a Roman freedmen's colony, and therefore its population was made up of people of various groups, but with a heavy concentration of Roman citizens and Roman interests. With its mixture of national and religious groups, rich and poor, Jews, pagans, and Christians, and moral and immoral people, it was an exciting but difficult environment for the small Christian community, which was predominantly Gentile, but probably had a small Jewish minority.

The letters we call 1 and 2 Corinthians formed part of a larger collection that originally consisted of several letters Paul wrote to the community. He speaks in 1 Corinthians 5:9 of a previous letter written to the Corinthians instructing them to avoid immoral people. Such a letter no longer exists, and nowhere do we have this instruction from Paul, unless, as has been suggested, a piece of it survives as 2 Corinthians 6:14–7:1. Similarly, the reference to a letter written in "much affliction and anguish of heart" (2 Cor 2:4) hardly fits the tone of 1 Corinthians. Furthermore, 2 Corinthians is characterized by discontinuity, suggesting that it is actually composed of several letters put together (see NAB, introduction to 2 Cor).

We learn that the Corinthians also wrote to Paul (see 1 Cor 7:1), and that the Corinthian church, difficult as it was for Paul, preserved and honored his advice, undoubtedly reading his letters at liturgical gatherings as Paul had instructed them. We are left with the impression that the existing letters reflect an editing and combining of writings, compiled as the community processed and integrated the words of the apostle.

# 1 CORINTHIANS READING GUIDE

### *At a Glance*

| | |
|---|---|
| Who are the main players? | Paul Christian Community at Corinth Chloe Apollos Sosthenes |
| What should I look for? | 1 Corinthians is a particularly fruitful source of reflection because it raises many issues that are still relevant: divisions based on different world views, marriage and celibacy, theology of women and the participation of women in church, the Eucharist, charismatic gifts, and belief in the Resurrection. |
| When did this take place? | In writing this around A.D. 56, Paul was responding to disquieting reports he had received while he was in Ephesus. |
| Where did these events occur? | Corinth was a Roman freedmen's colony and therefore its population was made up of various peoples but with a heavy concentration of Roman citizens. With its mixture of national and religious groups, rich and poor, Jews, pagans, and Christians, it was an exciting but difficult environment for the small Christian community. |

| | |
|---|---|
| Why was this book written? | The Corinthians were not a single large community. Several small communities gathered at different houses. These communities represented different competitive factions and developed divergent expressions of Christian life and worship. Paul addresses these real situations. |
| What is the story? | The Corinthians disagreed about Christian life after baptism. Paul responds to these issues. Although our problems and divisions may be expressed somewhat differently, Paul's admonitions to the Corinthians on the importance of charity, unity, and mutual respect based upon a common faith provide us with a model of approaching our own problems. |

## Before Beginning

In writing 1 Corinthians around A.D. 56, Paul was responding to some disquieting reports he had received about the community. First Corinthians addresses real, not theoretical, situations. Paul's knowledge of what was going on was based on verbal accounts from reliable sources, letters from members of the community, and Paul's own 18-month experience of living in this community (Acts 18:11).

First Corinthians is a particularly fruitful source of reflection for our contemporary church because it raises so many issues that are still relevant: divisions based on ideologies or different world views, incest, lawsuits among Christians, scandal, marriage and celibacy, theology of woman and the participation of women in the church, the proper way to celebrate Eucharist, charismatic gifts, and belief in the Resurrection. We, like the Corinthians, are challenged to find the right role and qualifications of leadership in a pluralistic society. Like the Corinthians we need to recognize that how we live and behave is a sign of what we believe.

In a sense, the singular "community" might misrepresent the Corinthians. We may tend to think of the community as a specific group that met at the house of a particular individual in a city. But the Corinthians were not a single large community. It is likely that in that particular city there were several Christian communities that congregated at different houses. Apparently, these communities represented different competitive factions. Each community was developing divergent expressions of Christian life and worship. Some groups were homogeneous, preferring to worship with like-minded people from similar social and religious backgrounds, who followed certain diets and enjoyed certain prestigious spiritual gifts.

A variety of liturgical celebrations developed. The Corinthians disagreed about whether Christians ought to marry or, if married, should remain married after baptism. Paul responds to these issues among the Christians at Corinth. Although our problems and divisions may be expressed somewhat differently, Paul's admonitions to the Corinthians on the importance of unity, charity, and mutual respect based on a common faith provide us with a model for approaching our own problems. First Corinthians discloses to us the pastor, Paul, who encourages the Corinthians to imitate him as he imitates Christ (11:1).

## Working through 1 Corinthians

Our comments on the major themes and relevance of this epistle will follow the structure suggested in the NAB introduction to the book, with some rather minor adjustments. First Corinthians contains the usual letter format: an address in 1:1–9, the body of the letter in 1:10–15:58, and a conclusion in 16:1–24.

Because this letter is a response to the concerns of the Corinthians, there is not the same kind of objective, formal structure as in Romans. Yet in 1 Corinthians there is a structural pattern that helps shed some light on the emphasis and meaning of Paul's message. Paul's general approach to issues follows an A-B-A′ pattern by which Paul introduces and begins to develop a topic (A), disrupts his reflections by bringing up a second issue (B), and then returns to the original topic (A′). Often he uses this pattern to emphasize the middle, or B, statement. One illustration is Paul's discussion of abuses in the celebration of the Eucharist.

1. 11:17–22. Paul describes the abuses in 1 Corinthians (A).

2. 11:23–25 Paul interjects into the middle of this description his account of Jesus' Last Supper the night before he died (B).

3. 11:26–34. Paul's discussion of abuses continues (A).

In this way Paul tries to remedy the abuses at Corinth by recalling what Jesus did and reminding the Corinthians that they are to act "in memory of" Jesus. Further examples of Paul's use of the A-B-A′ pattern will be discussed as they appear in this letter. For the moment simply note that the pattern has the effect of emphasizing the B section as a corrective for the situations described in A and A′.

A working outline of 1 Corinthians is the following:

I. Address (1:1–9)
II. The Body of the Letter (1:10–15:58)
- A. Reported Divisions and Abuses (1:10–6:20)
  1. Factions (1:10–4:21)
  2. Immoral Behavior (5:1–6:20)
- B. Answers to the Corinthians' Questions (7:1–11:1)
  1. Marriage and Virginity (7:1–40)
  2. Food Offered to Idols (8:1–11:1)
     - a. Exercising Knowledge and Love (8:1–13; 10:1–11:1)
     - b. The Example of Paul (9:1–27)
- C. Problems in Liturgical Assemblies (11:2–14:40)
  1. Dress and Decorum in the Assembly (11:2–16)
  2. Celebration of the Eucharist (11:17–34)
  3. The Spiritual Gifts (12:1–14:40)
- D. The Resurrection (15:1–58)

III. Conclusion (16:1–24)

## Reading through 1 Corinthians

### The Address (1:1–9)

The address contains a greeting (1:1–3) and thanksgiving (1:4–9). In the greeting, Paul refers to himself as an "apostle of Jesus Christ" and identifies a "brother," Sosthenes, as co-author who, however, does not reappear in the letter. He is perhaps to be identified with the synagogue official of the same name in Acts 18:17. Paul addresses the community as a "church" (*ekklesia*), which has been "sanctified in Jesus Christ" and "called to be holy." Paul thus reminds the Corinthians that they have a common vocation (*ekklesia* literally means "called out of"). This is Paul's usual word for the assembly of believers, taken from the civic word for the assembly of citizens in a free city-state. It may also be a conscious translation of the Hebrew *qahal*, the biblical assembly of Israel. The Corinthians have a new identity, rooted in God, that distinguishes them from the world around them.

Paul's adaptation of the thanksgiving usually found in Hellenistic letters focuses on the blessings received by his addressees. The thanksgiving also announces themes Paul will develop in the letter. The Corinthians lack no spiritual gift (1:7). The factions among them that so concerned Paul are rooted precisely in their envy of and competition for extraordinary gifts.

### The Body of the Letter (1:10–15:58)

All of 1 Corinthians addresses specific issues that caused dissension and strained the fabric of the Corinthian community. In the first section of the body or main part of the letter, Paul discusses the divisions he has heard about among the Corinthians (1:10–6:20). He then turns to address matters that the Corinthians had themselves directed to him (see 7:1–11:1). Finally, Paul will consider other issues relevant to the Corinthian community; namely, appropriate ways of celebrating the Eucharist (11:2–14:40) and the meaning of the Resurrection (15:1–58).

#### Reported Divisions and Abuses (1:10–6:20)

Reports from Chloe's people (see 1:11) identified some problems at Corinth stemming from two matters: (a) factions (1:10–4:21) and (b) immoral behavior (5:1–6:20).

***Factions in Corinth (1:10–4:21).*** The variety of backgrounds of its members caused many problems in the community of Corinth. Various members of the community turned to different leaders, and groups began to vie with one another for superiority and recognition. Paul first takes up the slogans adopted by groups who profess allegiance to the various leaders. He names group leaders, specifically Cephas (i.e., Peter), Apollos, and himself. He shows the absurdity of divisions based on leadership, which is superficial compared to the common baptism by which all Christians are sanctified and saved.

The Corinthians disagreed among themselves about which leaders were the most important and which group of Christians was the most prestigious. They may have taken their lead from disagreements among the great figures themselves. James disagreed with Paul, for example, about whether any aspects of the Jewish Law were required of Gentile Christians (Gal 2). Peter favored at least minimal requirements, while Paul advocated complete freedom from the Jewish Law for Gentile converts. First Corinthians suggests that the leaders' disagreement affected the Corinthians and caused many to side with one leader against another. But the Corinthians also had their own divisions.

Another leader was Apollos who, for very different reasons, had a following that competed for the Corinthians' loyalty. Apollos attracted many Corinthians because of his eloquence in speaking (see Acts 18:24–28). Meanwhile, some of the Corinthians cited Paul's unimpressive physical presence and speaking abilities as reason to reject him (1 Cor 2:1–5; 2 Cor 1:10). Paul chided the Corinthians for judging by human standards, not by God's as revealed in the cross of Christ. Paul reminded them that neither he nor Peter nor Apollos were crucified for them. The Corinthians were baptized in Christ's name and belonged to Christ. The formation of competitive groups within the Christian community is absurd. Paul admonishes the Corinthians to remember who they are—that by worldly standards few among them have any reason to boast (1:26–31)—but that "in the Lord" they can boast that they are saved and form a "new creation" (2 Cor 5:17). They do not have wealth or nobility or education, but they are rich in the blessings of the Spirit of God. The "not many of you" in verse 26 has been read both ways: Paul is stressing the humble origins and status of most, but in saying this he suggests that some really were of higher social status and wealth.

The first part of this letter (1:10–4:21) may be summarized as the gospel paradox, the teaching that God's wisdom is greater than human wisdom, that the power of the cross outweighs all human power. The Corinthians portrayed themselves as sophisticated, mature, and truly wise. Paul describes them as rather immature, of the "flesh" rather than spiritual (3:1), deceiving themselves and therefore lacking in the most fundamental knowledge. They erroneously judged according to standards that are transitory rather than eternal. The riches and wisdom of God surpass all understanding and may be perceived only through wisdom that is revealed by the Spirit (2:10).

***Immoral Behavior (5:1–6:20).*** In chapters 5 and 6, Paul gives examples of when judgments on the appropriate behavior for believers would be necessary. The Christian message of salvation has many implications—doctrinal, liturgical, ethical. Certain behavior is inconsistent with belonging to the Christian community. Chapters 5 and 6 specifically mention incest, bringing lawsuits against other members of the community, and sexual promiscuity, as up to the community's judgment.

The Corinthians were complacent about keeping in their community someone who violated Jewish incest laws by living with his stepmother.

Paul uses a traditional image of "yeast" to help describe the impact of the presence of such a one in their midst. The proverb "a little yeast leavens all the dough" illustrates the extent to which the sinner's action corrupts the whole community. Jesus uses this same image to warn about the influence of the Pharisees on the disciples (Mt 16:6; Mk 8:15; Lk 12:1). Paul was concerned about the impact of the sinner on the community and the "contagion" of sinful actions. Throughout this letter, a fundamental point of Christian theology is emphasized: Namely, as Christians we cannot act alone without regard for one another. Our actions affect others, for good or evil. Paul sees conversion as a "turning from idols to worship of the one living and true God." (1 Thes 1:9). This conversion requires a readiness to change not only our hearts, but also our actions so that we may live in accordance with our baptism. Continuing the yeast image, Paul cites the formula of the Paschal Lamb and unleavened bread, pure and free from yeast. Yeast, as it is here, is usually a negative symbol. The connection is especially relevant at the time of the year in which Paul writes, the season of Passover (16:8).

It troubles Paul to hear that some in the community are bringing lawsuits against one another, when what they should be doing is suffering wrongs in imitation of Christ. At best, they should settle such disputes among themselves. He reminds them of the scenario in which God's holy ones will judge the earth. They therefore have no business submitting their grievances to unbelieving judges now. Nor do they know what they are doing by participating in prostitution. "All things are lawful" to the one who is free in Christ, but this does not mean all things are acceptable. The body of every believer is a temple of the Holy Spirit that cannot be profaned.

**Answers to the Corinthians' Questions (7:1–11:1)**

Paul then takes up the Corinthians' own questions about how daily life is an expression of their faith. The Corinthians themselves identified certain issues within their community that were disturbing their unity. They wrote to Paul about these two types of questions: those about marriage and virginity (see 7:1–40) and those pertaining to the eating of idol meats and participation at pagan meals (8:1–11:1).

***Marriage and Virginity (7:1–40).*** In chapter 7 Paul specifically discusses three life choices that many Christians believed were affected by baptism with an advantage on one side: marriage or virginity (7:1–7, 16), fidelity to Judaism signified by circumcision versus noncircumcision (vv. 18–20), and slavery versus freedom (vv. 21–24). According to 1 Corinthians 7, a specific question arose concerning whether married Christians ought to remain married. An understanding of baptism as initiation into the eschatological community seemed to imply that the baptized should renounce the constraints and responsibilities of marriage. Jesus' opposition to divorce is first attested here (7:10, 11). Some asked whether a Christian married to an unbeliever could or should remain in the marriage. Some men wondered if there was an advantage to circumcision. Some slaves thought, and perhaps expected, that they would be better off freed.

Paul's general advice is to "remain in the state in which you were called" (see 7:17, 20, 24). His reasoning is that the time is short (7:29, 31), too short for unnecessary social entanglements. It is debatable whether Paul believed literally that the end was imminent or whether this was his way of seeing all of life as dependent on the absolute power and will of God. Although Christians are "in" the world, they are not "of" it as John says (Jn 17:14–16). The particular circumstances of believers do not interfere with or lessen the effect of the new status of their identity in Christ. Christians have always sensed the need to express the implications of their new identity as baptized persons with an appropriate way of life.

Paul agreed with a position held by some in Corinth, that "it is a good thing . . . not to touch a woman" (1 Cor 7:1). Paul acknowledged his own preference for celibacy that leaves one "free of anxieties" (7:32). The Gospels record Jesus' saying that "in heaven there is neither giving nor taking in marriage" (see Mk 12:25 and parallel passages). Sexuality, circumcision, even slavery do not have significance in the new age. Indeed, the hope for a new society of equals was one of the reasons Christianity was so appealing to many "minority" groups, including women, slaves, and others who lacked status in the Greco-Roman world.

Paul's response is to advocate no change in social status because it is unimportant in the Christian context. Responding to those who challenge the right of Christians to marry, Paul drew on the word of Jesus regarding the indissolubility of marriage (7:10–11). Yet Paul added an exception that considerably weakens the effect of Jesus' statement. In the case of unwillingness of the unbelieving spouse to remain married to a baptized person, they may separate. Furthermore, Paul applied the exception to both men and women, giving women the same rights as men.

We should note Paul's remarkable freedom in relating Jesus' words to the pastoral situation of Corinth. In all of the questions with which he has to deal, Paul demonstrates a surprising creativity and flexibility.

***Food Offered to Idols (8:1–11:1).*** Here Paul responds to three very practical situations about which the Corinthians must make everyday decisions: whether they should (a) eat meat bought in the marketplace that was probably originally offered in sacrifice at a pagan temple; (b) accept dinner invitations in rented banquet rooms in pagan temples, during which there was a sacrificial libation to the god in whose temple they were; (c) accept dinner invitations to the homes of unbelievers. He asserts a basic theological position that these gods are not really gods at all, supports it with reference to Israel's history as recorded in the Scriptures (10:1–13) and with the example of his own experience. But the bottom line is the unity of the community. If anyone of weaker conscience will be scandalized, then it is not to be done.

***Exercising Knowledge and Love (8:1–7 and 10:23–11:1).*** Paul quotes a Corinthian slogan, acknowledging the truth that "all of us have knowledge" (8:1). The Corinthians apparently assumed that such knowledge made some of them superior to others. So, for example, it was their "knowledge" that allowed them to overlook incest in one of their members (see ch 5). It was the competition for the gifts considered superior that was disrupting their assemblies (14:20–33) and even the LORD's Supper (11:17–18). Paul proposes charity as a remedy for the rivalry of the various kinds of "knowledge" that inflate the ego and that were causing factions in the Corinthian church. Whereas knowledge divides, love unites, enabling the Corinthians' many gifts to supply various needs in the community, helping them to "build up" (see the description of the role of prophecy in 1 Cor 14:3), rather than destroy (1 Cor 11:17–34).

In discussing the factions between the "weak and the strong," Paul speaks of "conscience," a term that appears almost exclusively in Pauline writings with little impact on other New Testament authors (e.g., Rom 2:15; 9:1; 13:5; 1 Cor 8:7, 10, 12; 10:25, 27, 28, 29; 2 Cor 1:12; 1 Tm 1:5; 2 Tm 1:3; Ti 1:15; see also Acts 23:1; Heb 9:9, 14; 1 Pt 2:19; 3:16, 21). In biblical thinking, conscience never involves only the individual. It always has to do with how one sees oneself in relation to one's community. Paul gives a communal meaning to conscience and places it in a new Christian context. In this context, the personal consciences of both the "weak" and the "strong" are subordinate to the obligations of mutual charity. The weak must not judge the strong and the strong not scandalize the weak. For Paul, conscience is not autonomous. It cannot be the last court of appeal among Christians. It is subject to charity and concern for one "for whom Christ has died" (8:11).

In 1 Corinthians 10:23–11:1, Paul summarizes his discussion of knowledge of the specific issues regarding pagan meals and customs, and of imitation of his own example. Quoting another Corinthian slogan (as he did in 8:1 where he said "all of us have knowledge"), Paul agrees "Everything is lawful" (10:23). Yet, he continues, not everything is beneficial. The merit of an action is related to its effects on the community. Concrete questions about whether to eat or not should be resolved in view of their effect on the other members of the community. For Paul, the morality of a decision depends upon its impact on the conscience of other brothers and sisters. Paul's attempt to win others over rather than to alienate them keeps their salvation in view. Thus, he concludes that Corinthian Christians ought to imitate him as he does Christ (11:1).

***The Example of Paul (9:1–27).*** To support his argument about mutual love and avoidance of scandal, Paul inserts between the two parts of the argument the example of his own conduct (ch 9 represents B in the A-B-A' pattern discussed in the introduction.) Though he could demand material support, though he could exercise a great deal more freedom and authority, he instead tries to become all things to everyone by being as much like them as possible. The hint is clear: You too do not need to exercise all the freedom to which you have a right, but you can subordinate some of it for the good of the whole. The Corinthians' problems reflect their mixed makeup of predominantly Gentile but also partly Jewish members, as well as a certain level of education and intellectual refinement. Greek intellectual life valued gifts of mind and spirit, such as knowledge and eloquent reasoning. Such gifts contributed to the status of the individuals who possessed them, sometimes to the detriment of charity.

In many of his letters, Paul refers to the fact that he works with his hands and thus gives an example for his addressees to follow (1 Thes 2:9; 2 Thes 3:7–10). Paul freely forfeited the privilege of support "not to place an obstacle to the gospel of Christ" (1 Cor 9:12). He served all—Jews, Gentiles, the "strong and the weak"—so that through this service the gospel message would be available to them. No one should be denied the gospel because of inability to pay. This forfeiting of privilege makes Paul freer to serve.

Yet, as he will argue in 2 Corinthians 8:1–9:15, after receiving the gospel message, Christians have a responsibility to contribute to the support of other Christians in need. Here he ends this digression about his own example with an athletic image. Just like a professional athlete, he disciplines himself, training not for a perishable crown of laurel or celery, as did the athletes of the day, but for an imperishable one.

Asceticism has played an important role in Christian spirituality throughout the history of the church. Paul legitimizes asceticism or self-denial for apostolic reasons. Today we live in a world that encourages individual freedom without constraints and the pursuit of happiness almost to any length. Such a mentality is not so distant from the sophisticated world of the Corinthians. Paul's corrective view suggests another approach altogether. The community's pursuit of charity should be the focus of the individual's energies and form the individual's conscience. Freedom is for the service of the gospel message. A person's rights are subject to God's call to preach the gospel. The charity of God compels us, training us in the school of self-denial and the pursuit of God's will in our lives.

**Problems in Liturgical Assemblies (11:2–14:40)**

Paul now turns to issues affecting the ways that the Corinthians are worshiping together. They fall into three categories: decorum at assemblies (11:2–16), celebration of the Lord's Supper (11:17–34), and the unity and variety of spiritual gifts (12:1–14:40)

***Dress and Decorum in the Assembly (11:2–16).*** This is a problematic passage that has received much attention. Throughout the ancient Mediterranean world, among Jews, Greeks, and Romans alike, the subordination of women to men was a common part of the thinking, even though by this time women of sufficient wealth and status exercised a great deal of social and economic autonomy. It was common custom that respectable adult women veiled themselves in public, even though that custom was changing in social circles that were more sensitive to Roman customs. In more traditional circles, as is still the case in some cultures, the unveiled female head was a sign of sexual availability. It appears that some female members of the Corinthian church, however, were combining their knowledge of newer social customs with Paul's own preaching about freedom in the Spirit and concluded that the veil was no longer necessary in some circumstances, particularly the church assembly, where others, including Paul, judged that it was. While never questioning women's right to pray and prophesy publicly (11:5), he simply judged that it must be done with traditional dress. In his attempt to provide a theological explanation, Paul draws on traditional images of headship and subordination, using as illustration three parallel examples.

Christ and man, man and woman, God and Christ. He then goes on to appeal to "nature," which really means "common sense," that is, what people were used to. Finally, he realizes that he has not proved his case and simply withdraws to the position of authority: We just don't do it that way (11:16)! While affirming women's full position in the church, he capitulates on the question of dress in favor of something that will not cause scandal among conservative outsiders (and perhaps some insiders, too) who are undoubtedly watching this new movement.

***Celebration of the Eucharist (11:17–34).*** There were divisions among the Corinthians on social and economic grounds. Wealthy Christians apparently boasted great meals at which the poor were either not welcomed or were treated badly. Some people became drunk while others went away hungry (11:20–22, 33–34). Paul says that this is not the Lord's Supper and that the Corinthians are eating and drinking their own condemnation (see 11:27–29). Within the context of the discussion of abuses in the community's liturgical celebrations, Paul inserts his account of the institution of the Last Supper to put the troubles in the proper context. This is the earliest written account of the institution of the Lord's Supper in the New Testament (see the note on 11:23–25). Paul's version, also reflected in Luke 22:14–20, contains at least three significant differences from the version given in Mark 14:22–25 and in Matthew 26:26–29. These variants are in the additions of the words "for you," the command "Do this in remembrance of me" (v. 24), and the qualifier "new" before "covenant" in 11:25. These variants witness to several early versions of the eucharistic sayings.

By emphasizing that Jesus' body was given "for you," Paul reminds the Corinthians of Jesus' self-giving act in which they participate by receiving the bread and the cup. They are then warned that an "unworthy" reception would not bring salvation but rather condemnation. The command to do this in memory of Jesus calls the Christians to offer a fitting memorial, including calling to mind Jesus' self-offering and imitating him in this. The insertion of "new" before "covenant" reminds the Corinthians that Jeremiah's prophecy of a "new covenant" is fulfilled in Christ (see Jer 31:31; 2 Cor 3:3, 6). This is an inclusive covenant, one that is already proclaimed in ancient Israel and that will be extended to all, one that provides the basis for a new society and a new relationship with God. It is important to realize that Paul's critique of the Corinthian Eucharist is not primarily concerned with proper reverence toward the sacrament, but with proper reverence toward the poor and proper respect for all members of the community who participate in the celebration of the Eucharist.

***The Spiritual Gifts (12:1–14:40).*** The divisions among the Corinthians based on competition for the higher gifts continues to occupy Paul. He reminds the Corinthians that when they were pagans they were "attracted and led away" by idols (12:2). Idolatry attributes the honor and devotion that belongs to God to false gods. Paul advises the Corinthians that in true conversion to Jesus Christ, there is unity with others who also worship the same God.

The hymn of love in 1 Corinthians 13, inserted within the context of chapters 12 and 14 on the variety of gifts, may not be a Pauline composition but something borrowed from Stoic sources, which he found helpful to illustrate the unity that should characterize the Corinthians (see note on 13:1–13). In chapter 11, Paul alluded to the divisions between the wealthy and the poor at the common table. In chapters 12 and 14, it is not so much the social distinctions as striving for spiritual gifts that threatens the Corinthians' unity. As remedy, Paul offers reflections on the community as the body of Christ (12:12–27), a new adaptation of an old image of social unity. A very high estimation is placed on prophecy, the action of the Spirit through members of the community. But the new context Paul provides emphasizes that love is the highest spiritual gift, one to which all believers must aspire to achieve (13:13). Love remains the most important of all the spiritual gifts in the church. This is not to diminish faith and hope and the other spiritual gifts such as teaching and administration. Love is an expression of God's own love, enabling us to act mercifully and kindly toward one another. Love in action, at the service of others, is the essential message of the gospel.

**The Resurrection (15:1–58)**

For Paul, the death, burial, and resurrection of Christ make up the central mystery of the Christian life—but not in isolation. If we are to experience death and burial, we are also to experience resurrection. Paul claims to have met the Risen Christ directly, and we can assume that some of his assertions about the Resurrection are derived from that experience (Gal 1:12, 15–16). Others perhaps came from his meeting with Cephas (Gal 1:18), who had participated in the post-Easter appearances. Paul implies that if the Corinthians really grasped and accepted the Resurrection and its implications, many of the problems he has addressed throughout the letter would have been resolved. In the first part of this chapter (15:1–11), he states the fundamental teaching on the resurrection of Christ and recites the earliest surviving creed and list of appearances. He stresses the appearances of the Risen Christ that were the foundational experiences, beginning with Peter's and ending with his own.

A second section (11:12–28) states emphatically, "If Christ is not risen, our faith is in vain" (15:14, 17). The resurrection of Christ forms the basis of faith and causes believers to reassess all of life and death. By his resurrection, Christ is revealed as the "first fruits of those who have fallen asleep" (15:20). Christ is our hope, our assurance that we too will have the same experience. Without it, perseverance in faith, including the sacrifices involved in suffering persecution, is pointless.

In a third section (11:29–34), Paul is trying to shame the Corinthians by showing them the absurdities of some Christian practices and beliefs without faith in the Resurrection as the fate of all the faithful. The slogan quoted by Paul, "Let us eat and drink for tomorrow we die" (15:32) is the wisdom of those without hope in the life to come.

In the next section (11:35–50), he takes up those who speculate on the nature of resurrection and the risen body. He uses the example of dissimilar creatures, such as birds and fish, the sun and the moon, to show the qualitative difference between bodies as a way of stressing, without going into detail, the differences in our bodies before and after the resurrection. The seed sown in the ground is not the same as the green shoot that springs from it, yet the shoot is continuous with the life of the seed that must die to produce it. Paul draws a contrast between the first Adam, the earthly, corruptible one whose image we now bear, and the last Adam, Christ, the incorruptible and eternal one, whose image we will bear in the resurrection.

The last section of 1 Corinthians 15 (vv. 51–58) incorporates a hymn celebration of God's victory through Christ over sin and death, compiled from verses of Isaiah and Hosea. Conquered by Christ, sin and death have lost their sting. By the resurrection of Christ, God has shown us that sin and death are not the last word, but only lead to life. Therefore, Paul sings God's praises for the hope that the Resurrection gives. He reminds the Corinthians that their "labor is not in vain in the Lord" (1 Cor 15:58). The rousing message of the chapter is: hang on! The best is yet to come!

### Conclusion (16:1–24)

Finally, Paul speaks of the collection of money and how it is to alleviate the suffering of the saints (16:1–4). Paul then reports his travel plans, sends greetings to his friends, and concludes with a blessing. Comparison of the persons named with those mentioned in 1 Corinthians 1 and Acts 18 renders an interesting profile of the Corinthian community with its mixture of notable men and women, rich and poor, powerful and ordinary citizens. Paul greets representatives of all categories, personally demonstrating the acceptance and unity he has been advocating.

## Concluding Remarks

Some readers may find it surprising to realize that Paul deals in 1 Corinthians with some of the same questions that continue to challenge the church today. Christians still struggle with whether there are more limits on the freedom allowed to women than to men. The rights and responsibilities of ministers in the church are at the heart of the renewal of the priesthood initiated by Vatican II and continued in various important pastoral and ecclesial efforts locally and in the universal church. Issues such as the requirements for a sacramental marriage and qualifications for the ordained ministry, the possibilities for lay ministries, or the role of the sacraments (especially baptism and the Eucharist) in Christian life were not answered by Paul, or even by Vatican II, once and for all. But the church continues to use Paul's pastoral approach to guide and to respond to the needs of its members.

The Corinthians were a church like ours—real people with real problems. They struggled for charity in the midst of disagreements, for respect for leaders without exaggerating these leaders' roles. Paul stressed the role of ministers as servants of God and Jesus Christ. Paul recognizes the authority of the church to discipline its members, including the immoral, those in dispute, the strong as well as the weak. Paul tried to help remedy their problems by advising them to seek spiritual gifts, especially charity. Paul advocated a healthy respect for the body without failing to see the value of asceticism. Paul recognized roles for both women and men in the liturgy. He gave some concrete examples of practical implications of living the gospel message as a community of equals. He protests discrimination against the poor or those considered inferior because they possess lesser gifts. Further, Paul stresses already in 1 Corinthians, and more so in 2 Corinthians, the necessity of aiding the less fortunate. The first epistle to the Corinthians is truly an interpretation of the gospel message that continues to challenge us with its many implications.

### Questions for Discussion and Reflection

*Group Sharing/Discussion*

1. Where is Corinth? What was the make-up of the population of Corinth in Paul's time?
2. What was the occasion of Paul's writing 1 Corinthians?

3. Present a role-play dialogue between the following:

a. Peter and Paul;

b. Paul and Apollos. Have the players present the disputes that cause the frictions among the Corinthians, cf. 1:10–4:22. At the end have Paul present his solutions to these frictions.

4. In the United States today, describe a mature, sophisticated, wise person. In Paul's day Corinthians thought they were so! Paul considered them immature. Why?

5. Paul names incest, lawsuits against Christians, and sexual promiscuity as behavior inconsistent with belonging to the Christian community. Do you agree with this? Would you add or qualify this list?

6. Jesus' word on indissolubility of marriage and his opposition to divorce are attested to here (7:10–11). But Paul also allows for making exceptions to this. What are these?

7. Paul proposes charity as a cure for various kinds of "knowledge" (8:1–7; 10:23–11:1, 17–18; 14:20–33). Give some concrete examples of this principle that knowledge divides, charity unites.

8. Here are several principles of the Christian life as Paul taught in Corinthians. Have a person or team explain each in context of Corinthians and of today.

a. Conscience is never a merely individual function.

b. The morality of a decision depends upon its impact on others (11:1).

c. Forfeiting of privilege make one freer to serve (9:12).

d. Asceticism plays an important role in Christian spirituality.

e. Freedom is for the service of the gospel.

9. Paul emphasizes that love is the highest spiritual gift, one which all believers must aspire to achieve (13:13). Read aloud the hymn of love (1 Cor 13), each taking a part. Afterwards, spell out examples of these verses.

***In Our Lives***

1. For Paul, the death, burial, and resurrection of Christ make up the central mystery of the Christian life. "If Christ has not been raised, your faith is in vain" (15:14–17). Share what you understand by this central mystery. How does this impact your beliefs and behavior?

2. Paul emphasizes the importance of unity, charity, and mutual respect in solving problems. How can these provide a model for personal and community problem solving? When have you seen this in your life?

3. In Paul's account of the institution of the Last Supper (the earliest in writing), he notes three significant differences from versions in Matthew and Mark. These additions are: (a) "for you"; (b) "Do this in remembrance of me"; and (c) "new" before covenant. What do each mean? What do they mean to you?

4. Like the Corinthians we need to appreciate that our behavior is an indicator of what we believe. How does this express itself in your life and community?

***Individual/Personal Reflection/Action***

1. Remember that "in the Lord" we can boast that we are saved (1:26–31) and form a "new creation" (2 Cor 5:17). Reflect and pray that this may be your own expression of faith.

2. As Christians, we cannot act alone without regard for one another. This is a fundamental Christian belief according to Paul. Count the ways that you are called to show regard for others and the community. What can you do to become closer to your own parish community? Pray to nourish this commitment in your life.

3. Return to chapter 13. Take a few minutes a day for the next month and use this as food for mediation.

## The Influence of Apocalyptic Thinking on Paul

APOCALYPTIC LITERATURE (GREEK *apokalypsis* "unveiling"; Latin *revelatio*) contains mysterious revelations, usually veiled in symbolic language and delivered by a heavenly guide such as an angel. It intends to show the true meaning of history, current events, and the future, especially the final judgment. The book of Revelation and Daniel 7–12 are examples within the Bible. It was intended to encourage the people to remain faithful during times of suffering, oppression, and disappointment.

The list below shows some of the ways that apocalyptic thinking influenced Paul. It is based on four elements of Jewish apocalyptic thought that had significant impact on Paul and other New Testament writers. (For more about apocalyptic literature, see the Reading Guides to Daniel, RG 233, and Revelation, RG 455.)

### Four Elements of Jewish Apocalyptic Thought Found in Paul

1. Salvation is available to all. For the Jews all of history, good and bad, was tied to the divine plan for Israel's salvation. Paul extends this concern to all of humanity, saved in Christ.
   - God shows no partiality (Rom 1:16; 3:22 and 29; 10:12; Eph 2:14)
   - "neither Jew nor Greek . . . all one in Christ" (Gal 3:28)
   - The new Israel of God is inclusive of the Gentiles (Rom 9:6; Gal 6:15)
   - Christ eliminated the barrier between Jew and Gentile, establishing peace (Col 1:20; Eph 2:15–16)
2. Salvation of the Faithful and Punishment of the Wicked. This pattern is typical of apocalyptic writers. The basis for the judgment for Paul is acceptance or rejection of the gospel.
   - The "saved" and the perishing (1 Cor 1:18; 2 Thes 2:10)
   - Judgment according to "good and evil" (2 Cor 5:10)
   - The faithful delivered from the wrath (1 Thes 1:10) but not the "enemies of the cross" (Phil 3:18; 1 Thes 2:16)
3. Dualism—Two Powers (conflict between good and evil). This is a way of explaining the tension and even hostility between how things are now and the time of fulfillment to come. In apocalyptic writings, good will eventually triumph.
   - Christ is in the process of returning all things to God (1 Cor 15:28)
   - Dangers threaten the Christian community: factions (1 Cor 1:10–25; Gal 5:13–15; Phil 2:1–4); idleness 1 Thes 4:11f; 5:14; 2 Thes 3:6–15); persecution from outside (Phil 1:28–30)
   - All creation is involved in the conflict (Rom 8:20–25; Phil 3:21)
4. The End Will Be Soon. Apocalyptic writers used this as a way of encouraging people to "hold on."
   - This influenced Paul's views on marital and social status (1 Cor 7); prayerful vigilance (1 Thes 5:1–11); enduring suffering or oppression while striving to build up the community (Phil 2:12–18)

Paul adapts these elements, avoiding the extremes of some apocalyptic thinkers. His adaptations are due to his experience as an apostle to the Gentiles and his conviction that the end times have already begun in Christ.

# 2 CORINTHIANS READING GUIDE

## *At a Glance*

| | |
|---|---|
| Who are the main players? | Paul Timothy Titus Christian Community at Corinth. |
| What should I look for? | Note the problem relations Paul has with the Corinthians. Note also the qualities of his ministries to them; that is, his ministries are based upon Scripture and the new covenant in Christ. A paradox of appreciating God's mysterious ways as well as being "earthen vessels." A ministry of reconciliation and concern for the poor. |
| When did this take place? | In writing this around A.D. 57, Paul was responding to disquieting reports of dissension and distrust he had received. |
| Where did these events occur? | Corinth was a Roman freedmen's colony and therefore its population was made up of various peoples but with a heavy concentration of Roman citizens. With its mixture of national and religious groups, rich and poor, Jews, pagans, and Christians, and moral and immoral people, it was an exciting but difficult environment for the small Christian community. The Christian communities shared this diversity and the consequent conflicts. |
| Why was this book written? | Despite the many troubles and misunderstandings between Paul and them, the Corinthians seem to have respected Paul's authority enough to preserve his words, reflect upon them, and circulate them to other churches. In 2 Corinthians Paul reaffirms his love and concern for them and reviews his past relationship and the roots of his ministry with them. |
| What is the story? | The message of 2 Corinthians develops in three main dimensions:<br>A. Paul reviews his past relationship with the Corinthians (1:8–7:16);<br>B. Paul develops a theology of giving, specifically speaking of the generosity of the Corinthians as a symbol of the fruitfulness of the Gentile mission;<br>C. Paul revisits topics he raised in the first part and returns to the theme of his credentials as an apostle, accenting his weakness and the call of God. It is here that Paul develops a theology of suffering, speaking candidly and with great feeling about his own experience of the grace of God. |

## Before Beginning

Second Corinthians features some of the most profound moments of Paul's theology, but in a puzzling arrangement. If 1 Corinthians has a structure that is clear and easy to follow, his second letter to the same church is characterized by the opposite, to such a degree that many scholars think it is actually a composite of several letters Paul sent to the same church. The tone tends to be more defensive than most of his letters, and the flow of thought is choppy. Some fragments (e.g., 6:14–7:1) appear completely out of context. The transition from 2:13 to 2:14 is very rough, while 7:5 seems to pick up exactly where 2:13 left off. Further, chapters 8 and 9 seem to have been originally two separate letters, each dealing with the collection, but neither assuming the other nor influenced by chapters 1 through 7 and 10 through 13. Finally, chapters 10 through 13 could stand alone as an "apologia," an explanation in defense of Paul's own spiritual experience, his vocation, and apostolic credentials. Certainly, 2 Corinthians exhibits traces of an ongoing conversation.

Yet the lack of cohesion in Paul's thought may be only apparent. It is also possible that there is an order to the letter that demonstrates Paul's typical A-B-A′ pattern, which also influenced 1 Corinthians. So, for example, Paul begins and ends 2 Corinthians with personal testimony about the painful difficulties both he and the Corinthians have experienced in the course of their relationship (see 1:12–7:16 as A, and 10:1–13:10 as A′). Within this frame, the two middle chapters, 8 and 9, dealing with the collection for the poor in Jerusalem (B section) illustrate that for Paul, the generosity of the Corinthians symbolizes the success of the Gentile mission.

Older scholarship, with its emphasis on literary sources and redactions, tends to see the letter as composed of several fragments. In this view, a later editor combined the pieces into the whole that we now have, but the parts sometimes do not fit together well. Why not? Why did the editor do such a poor job? Newer scholarship tries to look at the letter as a unified whole. In this case, the disruptions in the flow of the text are due to Paul's deliberate digressions for effect.

Whichever may be the true situation, we need to work through 2 Corinthians in this final form, even if it also represents originally separate letters or letter fragments. We approach 2 Corinthians as part of the New Testament canon, a letter preserved by the early church and read at liturgical gatherings in spite of its criticisms of the Corinthians and the many challenges it raised for the church there. Lest we think that ours is the only age in which deep divisions appear in the church, this letter reveals that Christian community in the first years was no idyllic experience. The Corinthian letters will serve as a corrective to such mistaken idealism.

## Working through 2 Corinthians

Some initial observations about connection of parts of the text will help us read 2 Corinthians with better understanding. As already indicated, 2 Corinthians follows a rather disrupted and choppy sequence. Following the usual Greco-Roman letter structure, 2 Corinthians has the three main parts:

- the *address* in 1:1–7,
- the *body* of the letter in 1:8–13:10,
- and the *conclusion* in 13:11–13.

A working outline of 2 Corinthians is as follows:

I. The Address (1:1–7)
II. The Body of the Letter (1:8–13:10)
  A. Crisis between Paul and the Corinthians (1:8–7:16)
    1. Past Difficulties and Relationships (1:9–2:13)
    2. Paul's Ministry (2:14–7:4)
    3. Resolution of the Crisis (7:5–16)
  B. The Collection for Jerusalem (8:1–9:15)
  C. Paul's Defense of his Ministry (10:1–13:10)
III. Conclusion (13:11–13)

### The Address (1:1–7)

In the address Paul names Timothy as co-author. The Corinthians apparently trusted Timothy and Titus (2:13; 7:6; 8:16, 23; see also Gal 2:1) more than they trusted Paul. Timothy is not named again in 2 Corinthians, although some suppose he is the unnamed "brother" who accompanies Titus with the collection. Luke tells us that Timothy was a faithful companion of Paul, especially on the second and third missionary journeys (see discussion on The Pastoral Letters).

The greeting includes a doxology or prayer glorifying and praising God whose "encouragement" is strength in affliction (see 2 Cor 1:3–4).

This word encouragement (*paraklesis,* a Greek word that also is the basis for "Paraclete," the "Advocate" or Holy Spirit in Jn 16:7ff ) in noun or verbal form occurs ten times in five verses, 3 through 7. This addition gives us a hint as to the overriding mood of 2 Corinthians. Paul and the Corinthians have experienced much misunderstanding, but Paul wants to move it on to great consolation. Transcending all the pain is the certainty of God's presence with them and Paul's confidence that God is at work in their lives.

### The Body of the Letter (1:8–13:10)

The message of 2 Corinthians is developed in three main parts:

1. In the first part (1:8–7:16), Paul reviews his past relationship with the Corinthians;

2. Chapters 8 and 9 form a second part in which Paul develops a theology of giving, speaking of the collection among the Gentiles and specifically of the generosity of the Corinthians as a symbol of the fruitfulness of the Gentile mission (A′);

3. In the third part, 10:1–13:10, Paul revisits topics he raised in the first part and returns to the theme of his credentials as an apostle, accenting his own weakness and the call of God. It is here that Paul develops a theology of suffering, speaking candidly and with great feeling about his own experience of the grace of God. Many in the history of Christianity have seen in these chapters a spiritual reality by which they are helped to interpret their own personal experience of God: "My grace is sufficient for you, for power is made perfect in weakness" (12:9).

We can read through these three parts of the body of 2 Corinthians, reflecting on the relevance of this composite letter for our own experience as Christians.

### The Crisis between Paul and the Corinthians (1:8–7:16)

The relationship between Paul and the Corinthians seems to have been marked by crisis. This is evident in both 1 and 2 Corinthians. We shall focus now on the problems Paul mentions in the first part of 2 Corinthians. He first reviews his past relationship with the Corinthians and then his ministry with them. Paul mentions several instances of mistrust and tension between himself and the Corinthians in his review of their past relationship.

***Past Difficulties and Relationships (1:9–2:13).*** First, Paul reviews the difficulties he had in "Asia," meaning the Roman province that covered the western part of Asia Minor. He probably alludes to Ephesus, where because of this and 1 Corinthians 15:32, many scholars think he endured an imprisonment not recorded in Acts.

Paul then focuses on several areas—a change of plans and the Corinthians' subsequently accusing him of inconstancy and lack of sincerity; his confrontation with an offending member of the community and his plea for leniency in the punishment of this person whom he has forgiven; and Paul's anxiety about the lack of information about the Corinthians from Titus. Paul appears frustrated at the apparent lack of communication, sympathy, and confidence. The factions that were mentioned in 1 Corinthians could have made a simple change of mind such as this a source of strife. Paul's detractors accused him of being unreliable.

Paul appeals to God's own fidelity as part of his response (1:18), showing that his word is sincere and his care constant. Yet he decided to change his plans in view of the recent painful letter (2:4) that he had found it necessary to write to the Corinthians. He postponed a promised visit only to give time for healing (2:1–4). With sufficient reflection Paul is confident that the Corinthians would realize the abundant love he has for them (2:4).

Apparently someone in the community publicly offended Paul (2:5–11), though the nature of the offense remains obscure. As in 1 Corinthians 5, Paul advocates a judgment not by outsiders but within the church. The action by the majority was acceptable and judged sufficient by Paul. In the case of the incestuous man of 1 Corinthians, he recommended expulsion from the church (see 1 Cor 5:2, 4–5). But in 2 Corinthians 2:5–11 Paul says that the time has come for forgiveness and reintegration lest Satan be granted a victory in the offender. Like many other biblical writers, Paul sees the world as an arena where the conflict between good and evil forces is ongoing, each vying for human allegiance. The church is entrusted with the "ministry of reconciliation" as Paul describes it in 2 Corinthians 5:11–16. The forgiveness of the one who offended Paul is a specific example of that ministry in practice.

In 2:12–13 Paul mentions the anguish he felt at his inability to find Titus and receive news about the Corinthians. This anxiety is a further indication of Paul's sincere affection for the Corinthians. In 1:12–24 he defends his change of plans and insistence on his anxious concern for the Corinthians. It would seem that this was written before Paul received the happy news from Titus described in 7:5–16.

***Paul's Ministry (2:14–7:4).*** Paul interrupts his review of the events that troubled his relationship to the Corinthians in order to describe in more general theological terms his apostolic ministry. Within the overall A-B-A′ structure of

2 Corinthians, we see subsections like 1:12–7:16 also exhibiting this same pattern. In this instance, 2:14–7:4 (B), describing Paul's ministry, is framed by, and grounds theologically, the practical and painful experience of Paul's relationship with the community described in 1:12–2:13 (A) and 7:5–16 (A′ ). Paul's description of his ministry develops several important themes:

1. The New Covenant enacted by Christ (3:1–18)

2. The paradox of the ministry: strength in weakness (4:1–21)

3. The ministry of reconciliation entrusted to them (5:1–21)

This description begins (2:14–17) and ends (7:2–4) with expressions of confidence in God and in the Corinthians. We will briefly discuss each of the three Pauline themes.

### The New Covenant Enacted by Christ (3:1–18)

Here, Paul's reasoning is based on the Old Testament passages and on one of his favorite contrasts, between spirit and flesh (see Rom 8:1–10; Gal 2:3; 5:17–23). It exemplifies the method taught him in his biblical training, taking several passages from different sources and combining them to produce a new conclusion. Jeremiah's promise of a "new covenant" (31:31–34) is combined with Ezekiel's prophecy of God's promise to replace human hearts of stone with hearts of flesh and to give a covenant in the Spirit (Ez 36:26–36). Exodus 34 described the relationship between God and Moses as so glorious that Moses had to come down from Mount Sinai with a veil covering his head lest the Israelites die at the sight of his glowing face (Ex 34:33–35). These passages from the prophets and the Law provide the scriptural basis for Paul's argument that the ministry (*diakonia*) of the new covenant, to which Paul is devoted, is superior to that of Moses. Using the familiar rhetorical method from lesser to greater, Paul argues that if Moses' covenant was so spectacular yet was still written on stone, how much greater is Christ's covenant, which is the fulfillment of the prophetic promise of the Spirit!

Paul contrasts the Mosaic covenant written "in ink" or "on stone" with the "new covenant" written by the "spirit" on "hearts of flesh." In the process he uses the phrase "old covenant" (2 Cor 3:14), the only instance of this expression in the Scriptures. This "old" covenant was enacted by God with Moses. Jeremiah and Ezekiel had spoken of a new enactment of the covenant reality, in which intimate access to God would be realized. Paul picks up this theme to write that this promise of a "new covenant" is realized in the work of Jesus. The difference between the two covenants illustrates the contrast between Moses and Christ and indicates the superiority of the covenant in Christ. Paul and the Corinthians are ministers or agents (*diakonoi*) of the new covenant that brings life and the Spirit. In the last part of the passage, he switches the image of the veil to apply it not as a protection on Moses' face to prevent injury to the people, but as an obstacle to clear vision, now upon the faces of those who are unable to see the glory of the new covenant in Jesus (3:14–18). Christian readers today should remember that Paul was working within the Jewish context of biblical interpretation to work in a new way with familiar texts and images. While his message was definitely that a new thing had been done in Christ that would fully include the Gentiles, he was not drawing a contrast between an old Jewish covenant, now obsolete, and a new Christian covenant that would replace it. Rather, he wanted new Gentile members of the church to realize their debt to our Jewish brothers and sisters for the spiritual heritage they preserved and which we share with them. The Old Testament Scriptures continue to provide a fertile field for mutual reflection and understanding between Christians and Jews.

### The Paradox of the Ministry: Strength in Weakness (4:1–21)

Even though Paul is a minister of this great new covenant, he knows that the glory is God's, not his, and that the mystery of reception in faith is not within his control. He expresses the weakness and fragility of this ministry by the familiar image: "We hold this treasure in earthen vessels" (4:7), a poetic translation of meaning that could be said more prosaically: "We hold these treasures in clay pots," as a reminder that the power is from God, not from humans. Paul recalls the price to be paid: "We are afflicted in every way . . . perplexed . . . persecuted . . . constantly being given up to death for the sake of Jesus" (4:8–11). But Paul continuously alludes to God as the source of his own hope, confidence, and power.

Grace is given in greater and greater abundance through the mystery of Christ for the glory of God. Even while they experience diminishment of their "outer self," the "inner self" grows stronger. The afflictions they experience are passing, but the invisible power of God is what lasts forever.

**The Ministry of Reconciliation (5:1–21)**

Throughout 2 Corinthians 2:14–7:4 Paul wrestles with the redemptive aspects of suffering for the sake of the Christian message. This aspect has several implications: first, the negative is not overwhelming; rather, there is always some experience of rescue or salvation. Second, the experience of suffering ends not with the apostle but redounds to the good of the community and, beyond the community, relates to the will of God. Third, for Paul, redemption effects a radical change in believers, taking them out of a particular sinful mode of existence and introducing them into another mode of reality that is in Christ. Fourth and finally, Paul and the Corinthians, like all ministers of the gospel, are involved in the ministry of reconciliation of the whole world to God.

Earthly existence is fraught with difficulties. In Paul's words, we "groan and are weighed down" (5:4) by the difficulties of human existence and of fidelity to the work entrusted to us. We are longing to be covered not with a "tent" but with a heavenly dwelling not made with human hands. We walk by faith (5:7), trying to please the Lord by whom, in the end, we will be judged (5:10) not only on our own deeds, but also on the effect of those deeds on others' actions. Catholic interpretation has always emphasized the communal responsibility or the obligations believers have toward others. Paul goes on to explain in the remainder of chapter 5 (vv. 11–21) that Christ's work is a ministry of reconciling the world to God. But that work is not finished once and for all. Through Christ we have been given the astounding mission and responsibility of carrying on that work of reconciliation (5:17–20). In this context, Paul pleads with the Corinthians to be reconciled with God and thus, implicitly, with him.

**Resolution of the Crisis (7:5–16)**

Paul returns to the concrete situation in Corinth, alluding to his anguished wait until he encountered Titus. Paul's representative, Titus, had now furnished good news about the Corinthians' reception of Paul's difficult letter (2:4 and 7:8), which some argue is actually chapters 10 through 12 of the present letter. Now the conflict between Paul and the Corinthians was apparently resolved. Paul's exuberant gratitude overshadows all of the former sadness and anxiety. It appears as though all is completely restored, and there is no more reason for concern.

If we have been reading along with Paul, we have noted that some of the problems that afflict our church were present in the experience of the earliest Christians. Paul was an itinerant preacher who normally traveled from community to community preaching the gospel. But Paul lived among the Corinthians longer than with any other community—18 months (Acts 18:11). He invested enormous energy in this community and could not be indifferent to their problems and questions and mistakes. No one can doubt that this is a problematic relationship, yet it was not severed. The deliberate rhetorical contrast in this letter is between the apparently conflicting data of 2 Corinthians 1:12–7:16: the lofty statements about the ministry of the new covenant as well as the insinuations of distrust, discouragement, and anxiety between apostle and community. Paul describes the Christian ministry as a ministry of reconciliation, but he also reminds us of the fragility of the human agents, as earthen vessels holding the treasure. All the hardships are apparently forgotten in Paul's exuberant conclusion: "I rejoice, because I have confidence in you in every respect" (7:16).

**The Collection for Jerusalem (8:1–9:15)**

Chapters 8 and 9 appear originally to have been two independent "fund-raising letters" on the importance of a generous and substantial offering to the Jerusalem church. This collection for Jerusalem presumably was the condition for acceptance there of Paul's mission to the Gentiles in Galatians 2:10. Jerusalem may have been a collection center for distribution of relief to other churches of Palestine and Syria. This collection is important because it represents the full participation of the Gentile Christians in the community of the new Israel, the church. On the one hand Paul encourages the Corinthians to give generously, seeing this request as a "test [of] the genuineness of your love by your concern for others" (8:8). On the other hand Paul will see acceptance of the Gentiles' offering as evidence of the Jewish Christians', and specifically of the Jerusalem church's, willingness to accept the Gentile mission (Rom 15:22–33).

Paul uses the tactic of creating competition among the Gentile churches. He encourages the Corinthians to give as generously as the Macedonians (Philippi and Thessalonica), who were generous even when they themselves were "tested by affliction" (8:2). But in 9:2 Paul claims that he has boasted of the Corinthians' generosity to the Macedonians. In Romans he says that both the Achaians (the Corinthians) and the Macedonians were only too happy to contribute because they understood it as their obligation (Rom 15:27). The Gentiles were "indebted" to the mother church in Jerusalem and to the other Jewish Christian churches whose spiritual heritage they shared. The language of wealth and poverty in these passages is rhetorical and should not be taken as economic indicators. At the end of the chapter, Paul speaks of envoys or messengers from and to the churches, among whom is Titus. The others are unnamed but probably known to the recipients of the letter. They are in fact called "apostles" of the churches (8:23). Along with this title applied to Epaphroditus in Philemon 2:25 and to Andronicus and Junia in Romans 16:7, it shows that the title of "apostle" was held by many people in the Pauline churches.

Paul begins chapter 9 as if he has not written chapter 8. Although he has just encouraged generosity in the collection, he says in 9:1, "It is superfluous for me to write to you" about the collection. There are many other ideas repeated in chapter 9 that were raised in chapter 8. It would be very strange for Paul to say the difficult things he says to the Corinthians before and after these chapters and even deal with their accusations against him (ch 10), while here in the middle asking them for money! These arguments, and the apparent independence of these chapters not only from each other but also from the context of the rest of the letter, prompt many interpreters to consider them as originally separate letters or letter fragments. For us, however, they represent a crucial example of the importance of Paul's role as apostle to the Corinthians. This is the role he reviewed in chapters 1 through 7 and ardently defends in chapters 10 through 13, to which we now turn.

**Paul's Defense of his Ministry (10:1–13:10)**

In the course of defending his ministry again, Paul can be seen following the A-B-A′ pattern, by which he introduced arguments in 10:1–18 (A), which he will continue in a concluding section in 12:19–13:10 (A′). Between these he interjects 11:1–12:18 (B), his own experience with the Corinthians and his own sufferings as an apostle. Thus Paul's development includes responses to accusations that continue among the Corinthians: His is weak (10:1–2), not an eloquent speaker (10:10), and he is not supported by the community (11:7–10). Paul reminds the Corinthians at the beginning (10:2, 11) and end (12:20–13:2, 10) that he intends to visit them soon and deal with such issues in person. In the midst of his responses to charges, Paul develops in a famous and memorable passage (11:1–12:18) his own lived theology of the cross.

**Paul's Response (10:1–18; 12:19–13:10)**

Paul's impatient tone in chapters 10 through 13 suggests that he has already dealt with their accusations against him, and they ought to have been laid to rest. The Corinthians appear to be elitists, perceiving themselves to be superior in knowledge and moving toward those whom they think possess superior gifts. These gifts include eloquence and an impressive appearance. Some of the Corinthians apparently favored Apollos' eloquence over the "contemptible speech" of Paul (see 1 Cor 3:4–5; 4:6–7). They noted Peter's freedom, his authority, and the fact that he accepts support from the community (see 1 Cor 9:6), and they challenged Paul's reasons for refusing community support. Apparently, the Corinthians are offended by Paul's refusal to accept their patronage and continue to see this as an admission that Paul is not of the same stature as Peter.

The Corinthians' complaint that Paul is an impressive writer but that his presence and speech are disappointing (10:1, 10), is arrogant but perhaps speaks a truth that led him to rely so strongly on the written word. Oratory was highly prized; perhaps Paul did not measure up to expectations in that regard. In response, Paul warned that he was empowered by Christ to "act boldly." He would use spiritual weapons to subdue in the end every enemy and disobedient thought in all to make all things subject to Christ (10:2–6). Paul warned the Corinthians against false pride and conceits and jealousies. He had earlier told the Corinthians to decide whether he came peacefully or "with a rod" (1 Cor 4:21). Now he promises to visit again soon and warns that he shall not be lenient with them (13:1–10). The Corinthians should examine themselves and see whether Christ is in them. For his part Paul is confident that Christ is with him. This warning tone is difficult to imagine in the same letter with and following the reconciling tone of 7:5–10.

**Paul Boasts of His Labors and His Weakness (11:1–12:18)**

Because the Corinthians are attracted by knowledge, Paul proposes to speak of "foolishness" and asks their indulgence. Remember that in 1 Corinthians 1–3 Paul described the wisdom of God as folly for humans and added that God confounds the wise with the wisdom of the cross. In this section of 2 Corinthians, Paul talks about the role of the cross in his own life.

Again, it is Paul's opponents who draw out this vehement testimony about the source of his authority. There are those Paul sarcastically calls the "superapostles" (11:5); a few verses later, they are labeled for what Paul really thinks of them, as "false apostles" (11:13; see the "false brothers" of Gal 2:4). In any case, others are leading the Corinthians astray; Paul fears that the Corinthians are like Eve (11:3), deceived by the serpent's cunning. This little aside indicated Paul's acceptance of the prevailing male wisdom of his time, since Ben Sira 25:23, that Eve represented the more easily seduced segment of humankind. The comparison with Eve, so regarded, would be insulting to the lofty Corinthians, a strategy Paul uses to bring them back to humility.

Continuing his paradoxical development of knowledge and foolishness, Paul describes the wisdom he has learned through suffering. His beautiful testimony can hardly be adequately paraphrased. It must be read and reflected upon. The experiences that the Corinthians construe as "failures"—the beatings, humiliations, imprisonments, and dangers—are Paul's apostolic credentials. He has experienced visions and revelations and ecstasies. He might have been tempted to pride in these (as he suggests the Corinthians would be). But Paul also experienced a "thorn in the flesh . . . an angel of Satan to beat me" (2 Cor 12:7). The wisdom Paul learned from this suffering, so beautifully expressed, is that God's power is made perfect in his human weakness. In the end we can understand why Paul says, "I boast most gladly of my weaknesses, in order that the power of Christ may dwell with me" (12:9).

**Conclusion (13:11–13)**

The conclusion is brief and encouraging and could be the conclusion to any Pauline letter. It does not reveal the depth of pain involved in some of its earlier content. By following Paul's apparently circuitous arguments, we are enriched far beyond the effort of understanding the specific situation Paul addressed in Corinth centuries ago. An outcome of studying 2 Corinthians is the realization that all the suffering involved in creating the church among limited human beings bears fruit in fidelity and hope. From 2 Corinthians we are brought to a whole new appreciation of the role of the cross in the Christian vocation to holiness.

**Questions for Discussion and Reflection**

***Group Sharing/Discussion***

1. Who are the co-authors with Paul of Second Corinthians?

2. Paul's teaching uses a good deal of Old Testament scripture to communicate the Christian message to the Gentiles. Give an example. Why do you think Paul did this?

3. "We hold this treasure in earthen vessels" (4:7) Paul writes. To what paradox was Paul referring?

4. Suffering for the sake of the Christian message is important in Paul's life and teaching. Discuss the dimensions of this reality. Have four members of your group each present one implication of suffering for the sake of the Christian gospel (cf 5:1–21).

5. We "groan and are weighed down" (5:4) by the difficulties of human existence and of fidelity to the work entrusted to us. Paul states these clearly. What are these difficulties?

6. Why is the collection for the poor of Jerusalem so important to Paul?

7. Both Paul and Apollos were preachers in Corinth. Role-play their presentations to the community of Corinth on who has the qualities of a better leader (10:1–18; 12:19–13:10).

8. Name and describe what wisdom Paul learned through his suffering (11:1–12:18).

*In Our Lives*

1. In Second Corinthians Paul recalls the suffering he endured. "We are afflicted in every way . . . perplexed . . . persecuted . . . constantly being given up to death for the sake of Jesus" (4:8–11). Today people have their own trials and sufferings. How would you encourage someone to view and understand them as a Christian?

2. Paul inserted "new" before covenant in the words of consecration. This reference is to Jeremiah's promise (31:31–34) and Ezekiel's prophecy (Ez 36:26–36) of a new covenant. Reread Jeremiah and Ezekiel on this "new" covenant. How do you describe this new covenant? How does it affect the way you live?

3. Paul teaches that the ministry of reconciliation is essential for Christian living. How do you or how could you put this ministry into practice—in your own life; within your family; within your parish community; within the world?

*Individual/Personal Reflection/Action*

1. According to Paul, to be Christian means having real concern for the common good. Chapters 8 and 9 emphasize the financial responsibility of a Christian community for another Christian community that is in need. Reflect on the scripture that reinforces this responsibility. Consider how you may show concern for and affect the common good, not just for what is good for me and mine. How does your church community show regard for the common good of the local community and city?

2. For Paul, to experience the cross of Christ is the true beginning of wisdom needed to carry out the ministry of reconciliation. Name for yourself times when you experienced the cross of Christ in your life. What wisdom have you learned from these experiences? How has this wisdom helped you to relate to and understand others? Share this with others who might be helped or encouraged by your experience.

# GALATIANS READING GUIDE

## *At a Glance*

| | |
|---|---|
| Who are the main players? | Paul the Galatians the "Judaizers" |
| What should I look for? | The issues of freedom and faith, diversity of teachings and different understandings of the gospel message, and the relationship between Christianity and Judaism. These are as important today as in Paul's day. Also, it is essential to realize that this letter in which Paul talks the most about freedom is also the letter in which he most identifies with the cross of Christ. Freedom is for the sake of service. |
| When did this take place? | In writing this around A.D. 48–55, Paul was responding to the "Judaizers" who were undermining his authority. |
| Where did these events occur? | Galatia comprised central and northern Asia Minor, including Iconium, Lystra, and Derbe in which Paul had worked. |
| Why was this book written? | Paul sees the problem in Galatian communities as a threat to both his reputation and his mission. Other missionaries, the "Judaizers," claimed that Gentiles must follow some aspects of the Jewish law, including circumcision, to be fully Christian. They were undermining Paul's authority and the sufficiency of faith in Christ that Paul preached. |

What is the story?

We cannot adequately comprehend Galatians without recognition of an important historical issue that was at the basis of Paul's missionary perspective. That issue involves the relationship between Judaism and the infant church that struggled to integrate the non-Jews or Gentiles into a new "Israel of God" and between Jews and Gentiles in that church. The question "who shall belong?" had to be resolved differently than it was in Judaism, where circumcision was the sign of initiation. The "Judaizers" claimed the Gentiles should fulfill some basic requirements of the Jewish law, particularly circumcision and dietary restrictions, to demonstrate that they were actually converted from their pagan ways. But from the beginning of Christian preaching, faith in Jesus crucified and raised from the dead by God had been the only requirement for baptism.

## Before Beginning

Galatians is the only Pauline letter written as a circular letter to various churches of a geographical region rather than an urban center. The old territory of Galatia comprised a large central and northern area of Asia Minor. The Roman province of Galatia included some of the cities, such as Iconium, Lystra, and Derbe, in which Paul worked, according to Acts.

Paul's tone in the opening lines of Galatians is defensive and emotional, shown by the absence of the usual prayer of thanksgiving following the address, which is a common characteristic of Paul's letters. Paul sees the problem in the Galatian communities as a great threat, not only to his own reputation and mission, but to the gospel itself. Other missionaries, whom scholars commonly call "Judaizers," came into Galatia after Paul and claimed that Gentiles must follow some aspects of the Jewish law, including circumcision, to be fully Christian. They were undermining Paul's authority and the sufficiency of faith in Christ that Paul preached. Consequently, he writes heatedly to convince the recipients that he has the full truth. From the emotional tone of chapters 1 and 2, he passes to the complex biblical demonstrations of chapters 3 and 4, finally into the ethical teaching of chapters 5 and 6.

Today's reader of Galatians must see past the combative tone of this letter, the circumstances of its writing, and the historical context in which Paul first developed his dichotomy between faith and works. These tasks are well worth the effort if we are to understand this important epistle of Paul. It is also essential to realize that this letter in which Paul talks the most about freedom is also the letter in which he most identifies with the cross of Christ. Freedom is for the sake of service.

## Jews and Gentiles in the Pauline Churches

We cannot adequately comprehend Galatians without recognition of an important historical issue that was at the basis of Paul's missionary perspective. That issue was the relationship between Judaism and the infant church that struggled to integrate the non-Jews or Gentiles into a new "Israel of God" (Gal 6:16) and between Jews and Gentiles in that church. Although this may seem like a remote issue unrelated to the problems the church faces today, it is actually quite relevant for us with our increasing ethnic diversity and ecumenical concerns. The question of "Who shall belong?" had to be resolved differently than it was in Judaism, where circumcision was the sign of initiation, and obedience to the Mosaic Law signified membership.

Those Christians who were already ethnically and religiously Jewish saw the message of Jesus largely within the context of Judaism. Indeed, Christianity might have remained as a sect within Judaism had it revolved only around belief that Jesus was the Messiah. Early Christianity, however, was almost immediately open to the conversion of the Gentiles (sometimes called the "nations" or the "pagans" in translations). We must also remember that before his conversion to Christ, Paul the Pharisee was so zealous for the observance of the Law that he persecuted the church (Gal 1:13). According to Acts, Paul obtained authorization to hunt down and bring to trial in Jerusalem those fellow Jews who had become convinced that Jesus was the Messiah (Acts 9:1–2). As a strict Jew, Paul had perceived along with many others that the message of Christ was a threat to Jewish claims to a unique access to the one true God through the covenant.

The Pharisees to which Paul belonged were already open to Gentile membership, based on the universal vision of the later prophets, especially Second and Third Isaiah, but with the requirement that they convert to Judaism. After Paul had accepted the messianic identity of Jesus through revelation and had begun, as a missionary, to proclaim it (1:15–16), he held the conviction that this new movement must be able to absorb both Jews and Gentiles, but in a new way. His own special call, based on a personal revelation, was to preach the gospel to Gentiles, a call that he says the leaders in Jerusalem accepted (2:7–9). Importantly, through his pastoral experience, he had come to the conclusion that the only way to integrate Jews and Gentiles fully into the churches was to eliminate the need for conversion to Judaism on the part of the Gentiles.

In other words, Paul reassessed the role of the Jewish Law to which he had always been devoted. In light of his God-given vocation to preach the message of Christ to non-Jews, Paul began to see the Law as superseded. According to the Law as it was then understood, the Gentiles had been excluded from salvation. Through Christ, Paul taught, they are included—and on their own terms, not as converts to Judaism. As a result of a revelation from God, Paul identified himself as an apostle to the Gentiles. Consequently, Paul felt as committed to the Gentile mission as he ever had felt formerly with regard to the Jewish Law.

The Gentile mission, however, did not begin with Paul. Stephen (see Acts 6) and others, including Peter (Acts 10), had preached to Gentiles and baptized them before Paul. Nevertheless, not all of the early Christian leaders felt the same degree of freedom from the Jewish Law as Paul did. Nor did everyone agree that Gentiles who were becoming part of the church should neglect the requirements of the Jewish Law. Peter and James, for example, who were recognized Christian leaders, both felt that some observance of Jewish Law should be required of the Gentiles. James was a very significant figure in the Jerusalem mother church. Peter, of course, was one of the Twelve and a leader of the Jerusalem community, as well as a known authority in the predominantly Jewish Christian community at Antioch. Representatives from James apparently were preaching at least a minimal observance of Jewish law and gaining a significant hearing among the Gentile converts (see Acts 11:1–26; Gal 2:1–10).

The matter was confusing for several reasons. Christianity incorporated the belief in one God and the high ethical principles of Judaism, which were very attractive to many Gentiles. The appeal of these basics of Judaism made more reasonable the position of those who "Judaized" (a verb Paul uses only in Gal 2:14, where it is translated "live like Jews"). The "Judaizers" claimed that Gentiles should fulfill some basic requirements of the Jewish law, particularly circumcision and some dietary restrictions, to demonstrate that they had actually converted from pagan ways. But from the beginning the only requirement for baptism was faith in Jesus crucified and raised from death by God.

Even Peter testified that the Gentiles, like the Jews, were saved through faith and that "God shows no partiality" (Acts 15:9; Gal 2:6). Paul vehemently opposed any additional requirements for the Gentiles. He believed that these additions would, in fact, constitute deviation from the firm conviction that salvation is a work of God accomplished through grace that is accepted by faith in Jesus as the Christ.

## Working through Galatians

Galatians represents Paul's effort to defend his preaching against alternative interpretations and to correct some misrepresentations about the message he preaches. Galatians exhibits the three main parts of a letter: the *address* (1:1–5), the *body* (1:6–6:10), which contains teaching (1:6–4:31) and ethical applications (5:1–6:10), and a *conclusion* (6:11–18).

I. Address (1:1–5)

II. The Body of the Letter (1:6–6:10)

A. Defense of Paul's Gospel and Authority (1:6–2:21)
   1. Paul's vocation (1:6–24)
   2. Paul and the Jerusalem authorities (2:1–21)
B. Faith, Freedom, and the Scriptures (3:1–4:31)
   1. Abraham, father of faith (3:6–16)
   2. Example of the human will (3:17–23)
   3. Example of the child-minder (3:24–4:11)
   4. Assurance of Paul's affection (4:12–20)
   5. Allegory of the two wives of Abraham (4:21–31)
C. Exhortations for Christian Life (5:1–6:10)

III. Conclusion (6:11–18)

## Reading through Galatians

### The Address (1:1–5)

This address, in which Paul greets the recipients, is abbreviated and assertive. It lacks the usual thanksgiving characteristic of the opening of a Pauline letter. Perhaps Paul's eagerness to get to the heart of his message explains this omission. Perhaps, too, he is so distressed at what he has heard about the events in Galatia that he cannot feel thankful. He asserts from the beginning that his credentials are not from any human source, but from God and Jesus Christ.

### The Body of the Letter (1:6—6:10)

In Galatians we see Paul on the defensive, strongly insisting on his loyalty to the gospel. This defense is occasioned by accusations that he seeks only to please other human beings. He develops several themes as part of his defense of the message he preached and of the divine source of his authority. Key themes in this defense are Paul's vocation, the agreement of his message with that of Jerusalem, and the biblical proofs of the truth of his preaching.

#### Defense of Paul's Preaching and Authority (1:6–2:21)

Paul expresses amazement that the Galatians have so quickly deserted him who called them and who remains faithfully rooted in Christ, while they have deserted to "another gospel" (1:6). He is about to prove to them that they and those who have taught them this way are wrong.

#### Paul's Vocation (1:6–24)

Apparently, there were those who accused Paul of lying. They claimed that Paul neglected to inform the Gentiles that their baptism involved following prescriptions of the Jewish Law. According to these opponents, Paul did not fully explain the gospel to his converts. But Paul countered that it was the opponents, rather than he, who were perverting the message of Christ. There cannot be two versions of the true gospel message. Paul understood the challenge to his authority as also a threat to the message he preached. His appeal to the divine origin of his call serves to emphasize that there can only be one true gospel. Even if he himself or any other church leader or an "angel from heaven" (1:8) should teach otherwise, the one true gospel is the one the Galatians heard from Paul. It does not need to be augmented with certain prescriptions from the Jewish Law.

Although we often speak about his conversion, Paul himself describes what happened as a "vocation." This was not merely a personal call as we might think of vocation today. Paul's call from God involves also a mission specifically to the Gentiles. Paul insists that this call came from God and underlines its divine origin by contrasting it with the role played by human beings, including his own initial unwillingness to accept Christ. It is precisely because he was in conflict with many others, including leaders of the church, that Paul begins Galatians by emphasizing that his call is from God. Paul has received an "apocalypse" or "revelation." He did not even go to Jerusalem nor meet any other apostle until three years after his call (which most scholars date around A.D. 34–35).

Paul uses language from the great prophets to describe his call, suggesting that he stands in their line. He claims that he was called from his "mother's womb," echoing the description of Jeremiah's call (Jer 1:4; see also Is 49:1). Paul reviews his own efforts to destroy the church, insisting that it was zeal for the Jewish Law that caused him to seek the authority to bring to trial in Jerusalem his fellow Jews who believed in Christ. Paul insists that he did not consult nor compromise with "flesh and blood," referring to the church authorities such as Peter, whom he did not even meet until later.

**Paul and the Jerusalem Authorities (2:1–21)**

According to the authentic gospel preaching, faith in Jesus as the Christ is sufficient for salvation, without any other obligations to the Jewish Law. The single gospel message, Paul argues in Galatians 2:1–10, was confirmed by a meeting in Jerusalem with all the leaders of the church. Scholars place this meeting around A.D. 50 (see Acts 11 and 15). The only stipulation the leaders expressed was that Paul and the Gentiles be mindful of the poor, which probably refers to the collection of money from the Gentile churches for a common fund in Jerusalem. Paul insists that he was eager to do this. Nevertheless, the Gentiles probably needed to learn that concern for the poor was a priority of Christian life (see 2 Cor 8:1–9:15). The Gentiles would not have benefited from the long Jewish ethical tradition that mandated taking care of the poor. Although this just concern was part of Jewish Law, the Law is not the reason Paul gives for accepting this stipulation. Rather, he insists that there was neither discussion nor agreement about the Gentiles following any prescriptions of the Law. This account from Paul is quite at odds with the account of presumably the same Jerusalem meeting in Acts 15:20, 29, where observance of Jewish marital and sexual customs and basic dietary laws are enjoined on the Gentiles. Scholars have always had difficulty with the two versions, some assuming that Luke invented the cultic observances that the Gentiles were expected to observe, others assuming that Paul ignored them. Here Paul insists that no restrictions were part of the accord but were only added after the Jerusalem meeting and only because of pressure from the Jerusalem church headed by James. In Galatians 5:3 Paul will remind the Galatians that those who are circumcised must observe the whole Law, not just selected precepts.

The issue of imposing at least a minimal observance of the Jewish Law, including circumcision, on the Gentiles was introduced, Paul asserts, by "representatives from James," only after the Jerusalem Conference. Paul accuses them of bad faith, saying that they had come to "spy on our freedom in Christ Jesus" (2:4). The notion of Christian freedom will be more developed in Galatians 5. Here it is introduced as characteristic of Christians in the Pauline churches. Paul confronted Peter later in Antioch because Peter caved in to the pressure of the "Judaizing" delegation from James in Jerusalem. The picture Paul paints is of a change of mind on the part of James and Peter after the Jerusalem agreement, which had the impact of undermining Paul's authority in Galatia and elsewhere. The "Judaizers" of Galatia may have been witnesses to this discrepancy and thus felt authorized to challenge Paul's authority there. Paul had accused Peter of influencing the Gentiles to "live like Jews" in the observance of some basics of the Law, including circumcision. Peter, who had also baptized Gentiles (Acts 10), was beginning to compromise the Gentiles' freedom after the Jerusalem meeting.

**Historical Misinterpretation**

This historical conflict provides the context for Paul's important concept of "justification by faith." Within the framework of his conflict with Peter and James, Paul reminds Peter as a fellow Jew that "we who are Jews . . . know that a person is not justified by works of the [Jewish] law but through faith in Jesus Christ" (2:15–16). Paul appeals to the faith he has in common with Peter and with other Jewish Christians. All Christians of Jewish descent share the belief that Jesus is the Christ. It is Jesus rather than the Jewish Law that justifies all. Generations later in the church, when the preponderance of believers were of Gentile rather than Jewish origin, the historical context of this dispute was forgotten.

Since then, Christians have sometimes mistakenly interpreted Paul's message as somehow considering faith as opposed to works. Furthermore, the word "alone" was added to the formula "justification by faith," and the phrase was understood in an absolute sense. So, for example, Luther portrayed the gospel as "law-free" in his famous objection to indulgences, which were undoubtedly carried to extremes in his day. The Reformers used Paul's doctrine of justification by faith to oppose any notion of salvation as dependent on good works, such as they alleged the Catholic doctrine of salvation taught. They distorted the Catholic teaching of works as a response to faith. For their part, Catholics have sometimes exaggerated the role of good deeds to gain grace. Both Protestants and Catholics have based their arguments on Paul, especially on Galatians and Romans, and both have distorted the Jewish understanding of Law observance as the response of the faithful to the gift of the covenant. As a result, some Christians erroneously read into Paul's message a dichotomy between faith and works that does not accurately interpret Paul's original meaning, and a theological anti-Judaism that characterizes the Jewish way of life as oppressively bound in Law as contrasted to liberating Christian freedom.

We see in all of Paul's letters that his doctrine is consistently followed by ethical applications. Thus Paul teaches that faith is expressed in the moral life. Good works are a response to faith.

Even in passages where Paul speaks of freedom (e.g., in Gal 5), he advocates at the same time the practice of good works. Paul's understanding of Christianity includes a highly developed ethic or lifestyle. He would see no opposition between faith and freedom on one side and good works and obedience on the other, as he will show in the next major section of Galatians.

**Faith, Freedom, and the Scriptures (3:1–4:31)**

Here Paul begins his theological and biblical explanation of his gospel. He appeals first to the experience of the Galatians, then to the biblical exposition of several texts, then to several human examples.

Paul insists that his converts in Galatia have heard the true and complete gospel message from him and that, as a result of their conversion to Christ, they have received the Spirit of God. He asks them a question to which they all know the answer, to shame them into attention: Did you receive the Spirit through Law or through faith (3:2)? They know it was through his preaching of faith without Law. To emphasize the importance of continuing to live the life of faith, Paul employs a contrast between the "flesh" and the "spirit" designed to show that these are mutually exclusive. Today's reader will find such a contrast problematic unless we understand the Greek philosophical mindset of Paul's audience and the special meanings he attaches to the words.

Today we tend to equate "flesh" with body or material existence, and to affirm the body as a positive and even essential expression of self-fulfillment and human happiness. But the Greeks stressed the tension between the flesh and the spirit, which presupposed the superiority of the spirit and the inferiority of the flesh. For them, the spirit represented the immortal, life-giving aspect of human experience, whereas the body or flesh signified the weaker, sensual, mortal aspect that had to be subordinated to the spirit to find happiness. Though the Hebrews did not generally share this mindset, still earlier biblical language will sometimes use "flesh" or "flesh and blood" to mean the weakness and vulnerability of human existence without the assistance of God (see even 1 Cor 15:50).

This is usually Paul's meaning for "flesh": human arrogance that tries to live independently of God's grace. To further complicate our task of interpreting Paul's meaning, we note that Paul sometimes refers to the Spirit of God or Holy Spirit (at times simply called the "Spirit") and at other times he designates the human spirit. Often it is hard for the reader to distinguish the two. In English translations God's Spirit is usually capitalized, but that is the choice of the translator, and sometimes the difference is not clear. Paul asserts that the Spirit of God was conferred upon the Galatians by faith, not by "works of the flesh" such as circumcision. Paul therefore concludes that it would be an absurd regression to "end in the flesh" what had begun in the spirit. Faith had moved the Galatians and all believers from the domain of the flesh to that of the spirit. The Spirit of God enables us to share fully in the inheritance of the promise made to Abraham and fulfilled now in Christ. Thus Paul moves from a review of the Galatian experience of the gospel to an illustration of the validity of that experience taken from the Scriptures.

**Abraham, Father of Faith (3:6–16)**

Paul reinforces his teaching on justification by faith by giving examples from the Scriptures showing that faith in Christ is sufficient for salvation. Using the exegetical methods in which he was trained, he draws out several biblical passages from different places and puts them together into a new argument to show that Abraham received the promise and was considered to have been justified in God's sight before he was given the precept of circumcision (Gen 12:3; 15:6). Then the crucified Christ took upon himself the curse of the

Law by hanging on a tree (Dt 27:26; Hb 2:4; Lv 18:5; Dt 21:23). Paul relates the experience of Abraham and his sons to the experience of the Galatians. Through faith the Galatians (a predominantly Gentile community) became the "children of Abraham" (3:7). "Abraham believed God, and it was credited to him as righteousness" (3:6). God gave a promise to Abraham because of his faith. This promise included the "nations" or Gentiles who are blessed through Abraham. Now, Paul says, the Gentiles have received the blessing of Abraham. The promise has been fulfilled in Christ.

**Example of the Human Will (3:17–23)**

Paul then uses the example of a last will or testament (in Greek, the words, "will, testament, covenant" are all the same, *diatheke*, which helps make the analogy in a way that is lost in English). Once made and ratified, it cannot be changed by something that comes along later. In like manner, the covenant with Abraham could not be altered by the Mosaic Law that came later. The original covenant through faith is the prior one that cannot be annulled, and this is the one in which all persons of faith belong.

**Example of the Child-minder (3:24–4:11)**

The next human analogy that Paul uses would have been perfectly comprehensible to his contemporaries, but it needs some explanation today. The "custodian" was a slave in a wealthy family who had authority over the minor son and was responsible for his discipline and education. Once the son came of age and became the heir, the roles were reversed. Paul uses this example to argue that the Law was a temporary custodian until Christ came, which is the time set by the father for our spiritual coming of age. At that point, the Law has no more power over us.

As an example of this maturity in Christ that we now have, Paul uses one of his most famous sayings, probably a baptismal formula that he quotes for effect. "All who have been baptized in Christ have a new identity, so that there is no longer Jew or Greek, slave or free, male and female, but all are one in Christ Jesus (3:27–28)." We would like to know how seriously this proclamation was taken in Paul's day. The tension between Jew and Greek (i.e., Gentile) continued, but it was precisely to this that Paul was devoting much of his effort. Nevertheless, Christian persecution of Jews increased rather than decreased in following centuries. Slavery certainly continued for centuries in Christian households and states. Problems between men and women in the church have not yet subsided. Disparities in treatment based on ethnicity, social status, and gender are perennial. This prophetic text remains a challenge for the church in every age.

**Assurance of Paul's Affection (4:12–20)**

In spite of the harsh things Paul had to say to the Galatians in the beginning of the letter, he now softens a bit to express his continued affection for them and his remembrance of how well they treated him when he was there. Verse 15 leads some commentators to suppose that Paul had some kind of eye disease that made him less impressive in person (see 2 Cor 10:10), but this is speculation. He hopes to come again to be with them and to be able to speak more affectionately than he has been able to do in this letter.

**Allegory of the Two Wives of Abraham (4:21–31)**

Paul goes on to illustrate his teaching with yet another scriptural example, namely that of Abraham's two sons by two women. The first, Ishmael, is the son of a slave woman, Hagar, whose name never actually occurs here (but see Gn 21). Isaac is Sarah's son, born free. Ishmael and his mother were expelled from Abraham's sight and did not inherit the promise. Paul develops his commentary as an allegory, understanding Ishmael and Hagar to represent slavery to the covenant on Mount Sinai. Isaac represents the promise fulfilled in the freedom of faith without the restrictions of the Law. The words originally spoken to Sarah, who had been barren, are fulfilled in the believers who inherit the promise (4:27). Paul says of the Galatians that they, like Isaac, are children of the promise, that is, the promise of grace and with it, freedom from the Law. Thus Paul's reading of the Scriptures reinforces his insistence that the Galatians are justified without the Law and freed from the Law. Therefore, to return to the Law's restrictions would be a great foolishness (see 3:1).

### Exhortations for Christian Living (5:1–6:10)

Paul draws implications for Christian living from his teaching. While insisting on freedom, he shows how faith has its consequences in Christian life. Chapters 5 and 6 exhort believers to exercise their faith in their relationships with one another. These exhortations focus on the responsibilities Christians share for developing the community. We are struck by Paul's emphasis on social responsibility. Note that Paul does not dwell on a believer's personal, interior life so much as on the relationships that should characterize the Christian community, which is living the blessings of the Spirit of God (see 5:21–23).

The term "freedom" recurs here (5:1, 13). For Paul freedom is not lawlessness but the liberty to live for God (see Rom 6:4) and to serve one another through love (Gal 5:13). The choice between slavery and freedom is the choice between the works of the Law and the works of the Spirit. For Paul, all humans are under some power—either of "sin" and the "flesh" or of the Spirit of God and faith.

In 5:2–12 Paul refers again to the specific problem that occasioned this urgent letter. The Judaizers are agitating the Galatians, trying to convince them to be circumcised and follow some of the elements of the Jewish Law. Paul reminds the Galatians of a principle certainly upheld by Jews, that circumcision of itself is nothing if not a sign of commitment to follow the whole Law (5:3). The problem Paul confronts is the imposition of circumcision on the Gentiles. Galatians 5:11 implies that Paul, even as a Christian, did "preach circumcision" for Jews; perhaps he did at one time earlier in his career, and the Galatians have heard of it. Paul does not dispute the role of the Law in Jewish life. Although some accused Paul of undermining the Law for Jews, he considers himself innocent of that charge (see Rom 9:1–5; 1 Cor 9:20; Acts 21:20–26). The list of "works of the flesh" in 5:20–21 show that Paul does not equate flesh with the body; many of them are perversions of mind.

In Galatians 6:1–10 Paul continues to reflect on community life, advocating the virtues of charity, service, and humility. Christians are obliged to "bear one another's burdens." Although they are also called to "do good to all," even those outside the church, special priority is given to those in the family of faith (6:10).

### Conclusion (6:11–18)

Paul adds a final note for emphasis and concludes with a short prayer. He probably dictated this letter to a scribe. He adds his own closing remarks, beginning at verse 11. Here he adds a new dimension to the arguments against the agitators: They are insincere, because they themselves do not follow the Law. They are only trying to escape persecution by other Jews, or possibly the Romans (see note on 6:12–15). Paul contrasts their cowardice and insincerity with his own boldness and consistency, referring to the "marks of Jesus" on his body. All that matters, Paul says, is that we are created anew (6:15). He concludes with a prayer for peace and mercy, calling down a blessing on his brothers and sisters in Christ.

## Concluding Remarks

The letter to the Galatians may be one of the most difficult for us to approach without prior knowledge of the historical circumstances in which it was written, yet no one knows very much about those circumstances. Paul's message here is nevertheless especially appropriate today. Despite painful differences with other leaders, Paul focuses on a single gospel message that all authentic Christian missionaries preach. This message emphasizes the role of faith and the significance of community. Paul's use of Scripture illustrates that this is the same message that has been repeated and refined throughout the Old Testament. Faith is the expression of the bond between God and us, a bond lived out in relationships with others. Paul's exhortation to Christians is to "be free" and therefore responsible for one another. There is no conflict between faith and works, according to Paul. Faith is necessarily expressed in the everyday life of believers. Paul does, however, stress that the works of faith are a result of the gift of the Spirit and a response to it, not a requirement for receiving the Spirit or for meriting salvation.

### Questions for Discussion and Reflection

*Group Sharing/Discussion*

1. Paul's tone in the opening chapter of Gala-

tians is defensive. How is this shown? Why is Paul defensive?

2. Paul sees the problem in Galatia as a threat to his mission and to the gospel. The "Judaizers" are the cause of this. Who are they? What are they doing in Galatia?

3. Role play a scene in Galatia about A.D. 50 where a group in the market are talking about faith and freedom. The speakers are:

a. a Jewish-Christian convert of Paul
b. a Gentile-Christian convert of Paul
c. a disciple of James from Jerusalem
d. a Gentile convert of Peter.

4. Paul teaches: Freedom is for the sake of service. Give examples of his meaning.

5. For Jews in Galatia, circumcision was the sign of initiation into the people of God, obedience to the Torah signified membership. What was the sign and commitment required to be a Christian?

6. What did the Mosaic Law at the time of Galatians teach concerning salvation? What did Paul teach the Galatians concerning the source of salvation?

7. What did Paul mean by "flesh" (5:20–21)?

8. According to Paul, when he went to Jerusalem council, what was the only stipulation that the Church leaders expressed about his teaching (2:1–10)?

*In Our Lives*

1. The representatives of James from Jerusalem preached to the Galatians that they needed to follow the basics of Jewish Law—circumcision and cultic food observations. Explain why you think they sent disciples to do this? (Read Acts 15:20, 29 for an account of the Jerusalem council that is at odds with Paul's account.) Describe what you imagine might be Jewish/Christian differences today if Peter and James' rule had continued.

2. Paul's meaning for "flesh" is this: human arrogance that tries to live independently of God's grace. Where in our lives today do we see this kind of arrogance?

3. Catholics believe that good works are a response to faith—that, because we believe, we act. This means that good works are not something we store up to earn grace for a better place in heaven. Explain why we don't believe in this image of God who would "keep a list" of our good deeds like Santa Claus does for a child.

4. Invite someone from the Jewish community to explain their belief in good works and the requirements for being an active Jew.

*Individual/Personal Reflection/Action*

1. Paul teaches that all who have been baptized into Christ have a new identity, so that there is no longer Jew or Greek, slave or free, male or female, but all are one in Christ Jesus (3:27–28). Reflect upon the new identity you have been graced with and what it means in your daily actions.

2. The Judaizers were so attached to their approach and understanding of what was involved in being a follower of Christ that they lost sight of the authentic gospel message. How open are you to learning new ways of following Christ? What signs would you check out to see if this new way was authentic? What virtues and graces are required for one to be faithful to the gospel?

# EPHESIANS READING GUIDE

### *At a Glance*

| | |
|---|---|
| Who are the main players? | Paul Tychicus |
| What should I look for? | The Pauline vision of the universal church, Jews and Gentiles united under the headship of Christ with a mission to make God's plan of salvation known throughout the world. This saving plan is anchored in God's love. |
| When did this take place? | Probably written around A.D. 80, after Paul's death (A.D. 64–65). Some of the language is Paul's, but the theology is more developed. |
| Where did these events occur? | Probably written from Rome as a "circular" letter to the churches of Asia Minor |

Why was this book written? The resolution of the tensions between Jews and Gentiles called for an adaptation of Paul's theology to new times and circumstances. The mystery of the church, its unity and mission, was the focus of the answer.

What is the story? The body of the letter concerns the teaching on the Church, its unity and world mission. Then it considers some ethical applications of this teaching.

## Before Beginning

Ephesians displays a well-developed theology of the church. The four major epistles of Paul (Romans, 1 and 2 Corinthians, and Galatians) are all addressed to specific congregations or communities in various important locations in the Greco-Roman world. Ephesians envisions not a single congregation but the universal church seen as a spiritual reality entrusted with the worldwide mission of Christ. Here the word "church" *(ekklesia)* acquires that new meaning of universal reality.

There are significant parallels between Ephesians and Colossians. The well-developed theology of Christ (Christology) and of the church (ecclesiology), the apparent absence of Jewish-Gentile tensions, and, finally, the unusual vocabulary unique to these two epistles among the Pauline letters prompt many interpreters to assert that Ephesians and Colossians were written in an era after the death of Paul. If that is the case, the disciple who wrote these letters was familiar with Pauline theology and style and adapted Paul's message to new times and circumstances. In our comments we will follow the usual practice of referring to the author of Ephesians as "Paul," all the while keeping in mind that nearly all Pauline scholars think of Ephesians as not from Paul himself, and a majority think the same of Colossians.

## Working through Ephesians

Ephesians follows the pattern of a Greco-Roman letter, beginning with an *address* (1:1–14) and ending with a *conclusion* (6:21–24). Moreover, it follows the pattern of a Pauline letter, with initial blessing or prayer in the address and conclusion adapted to a liturgical assembly. These stylized elements enclose the *body* of the letter (1:15–6:20), which presents a teaching or doctrine on the church and then applies this teaching to the daily life of believers. The outline is as follows:

I. The Address (1:1–14)
II. The Body of the Letter (1:15–6:20)
   A. The Teaching on the Church (1:15–4:24)
      1. Unity of the Church (1:15–2:22)
      2. World Mission of the Church (3:1–4:24)
   B. Ethical Applications (4:25–6:20)
III. Conclusion (6:21–24)

### The Address (1:1–14)

Ephesians identifies the sender as "Paul, an apostle of Christ Jesus by the will of God." The absence from some manuscripts of the designation "in Ephesus" (1:1) is one reason why Ephesians is considered by some to be a circular letter—intended for a wider audience rather than for the specific community at Ephesus alone. No particularities regarding the Ephesian community are mentioned as is customary when Paul writes to a community he knows as well as he should have known the Ephesians (see Acts 19:10). The lack of a personalized greeting further supports the view that this is a letter to *all* the churches and written by a disciple of Paul.

A doxology or blessing of God replaces the usual personal thanksgiving characteristic of Paul's letters (Eph 1:3–6). As if conscious of the great mystery of the church he is about to describe, the author begins by proclaiming the blessedness of God. The recurrence of the term "blessed" and the many liturgical references suggest that this prayer of praise is inspired by the Jewish liturgies in which believers, mindful of the wondrous works of God, cannot but bless the Creator. The focus is on God's blessing in Christ in whom the divine plan for the salvation of all people is achieved. The Holy Spirit is described as the "first installment" (1:14) of our inheritance toward redemption.

### The Body of the Letter (1:15–6:20)

The message of Ephesians has two parts. The first or doctrinal section (1:15–4:24) unfolds the church as the fulfillment of God's plan for salvation, inaugurated in Christ. A second section (4:25–6:20) contains ethical "imperatives" concerning the daily conduct of believers, providing practical applications of Paul's teaching.

### The Teaching on the Church (1:15–4:24)

Ephesians develops the New Testament teaching about the unity of the church and the church's worldwide mission. Integral to this mission is the significant role of the apostle in its promotion. We shall briefly consider each of these teachings.

#### Unity of the Church (1:15–2:22)

The ecclesiology, or theology of the church, in Ephesians is integrally linked to its Christology. That is to say that its view of the church follows from its view of Christ and Christ's saving work. Therefore, to understand the emphasis on the unity of the church that occurs in Ephesians, we must see the perspective on Christ developed there. The Christology and ecclesiology in Ephesians and Colossians is developed beyond that in Paul's major letters to the Corinthians and the Romans. Yet this development has its roots in Paul, for whom the image of the church as the body of Christ helps to express the unity of Christians and the salvific work of Christ's death and resurrection.

The description of the church as the Body of Christ appears first in 1 Corinthians 12:12–27 and Romans 12:4–8. Paul urged the Christians in Corinth and Rome to express their unity in mutual love as members of the same body, Christ. But in Ephesians and Colossians, there is a major change in the image. Here Christ is referred to as the "head of the body, the church" (Eph 1:22–23; Col 1:18). This shift in the image leads away from the mutual participation and responsibility of all the members to centralized authority in the person of Christ, who is portrayed as above every principality, authority, and dominion (cf. Eph 1:21–22). Nevertheless, the recipients are still reminded that in the body of Christ, we are members of one another (4:15) and of Christ (5:30).

By his resurrection, Paul asserts, Jesus became Lord of all, Jews and Gentiles and every creature (see 1 Cor 12:3). This is so because in Christ's resurrection God has conquered sin and death; it is the beginning of a new era. Paul's writings speak of the humiliation (death) and exaltation (resurrection) of Christ by which God vindicated Jesus because of his obedience. Jesus now sits at God's right hand. At Jesus' name, every knee bends and every tongue proclaims that Jesus is Lord (Phil 2:6–11). This is one of the oldest Christological proclamations (Rom 10:9). Jesus' lordship is an expression of his sovereignty over all created things and his word reconciling the whole of creation to God. Yet even now the universal recognition of Jesus' lordship has not been completed. The mission of preaching Christ's lordship and bringing all creation under God's reign is entrusted to the church.

Some time after A.D. 50, when Paul was writing Galatians and Romans, it is clear that one of the major problems facing the church was the reconciliation of Jews and Gentiles under one God and one Lord. Distinctions between Jews and Gentiles were symbolized by such practices as circumcision, dietary laws, and restrictions regarding table fellowship, intermarriage, and other forms of social interaction. These, Paul insisted, were erased by Christ's death. Yet the apostle himself had to struggle to resolve the tensions between Israel and the Gentiles (e.g., see Rom 9–11). The teaching about the church in Ephesians seems to reflect a time or place in which these tensions are resolved. The Gentiles are portrayed as those who were once "far off . . . strangers to the covenants of promise." Now they have "become near by the blood of Christ" (2:13). The images of the church as the body of Christ and Christ as the head of the church serve to illustrate the intrinsic unity of the church of Jews and Gentiles, that is, of all people in Christ.

#### World Mission of the Church (3:1–4:24)

The author of Ephesians identifies himself as "Paul, a prisoner of Christ [Jesus] for you Gentiles" (3:1). He then abruptly interrupts this self-introduction to elaborate on his role in the mystery of God's plan for the salvation of the world. Now imprisoned, Paul continues the work of intercession. Through prayer Paul brings the Gentiles to God. The church—the body of Christ and the family of God—is entrusted with the work of salvation that is to fill all things "with the fullness of God" (3:19). Paul understands his work to be essential in God's plan, and yet he is unperturbed either by his own imprisonment or by the failure of some to accept the message of Christ. Salvation as well as creation is in God's hands, and God's plan is being fulfilled in inscrutable mystery.

Again the language reflects that introduced by Paul in his earlier writings. But the conception of the divine plan of salvation is more developed. The church, under the impetus of the Spirit, is bringing all to the "one God and Father of all, who is over all and through all and in all" (4:6). Paul's prayer is that "you may be filled with the fullness of God" (3:19). The mystery of God who ordained that "all Israel will be saved" (Rom 11:26) now prescribes that we "no longer live as the Gentiles do" (Eph 4:17), but "put on the new self, created in God's way in righteousness and holiness of truth" (4:24). Having described this mystery, Paul goes on to exhort the Ephesians to express their common call to holiness and unity in their daily life.

**Ethical Applications (4:25–6:20)**

Ephesians 5 illustrates how its teaching on the church has practical consequences in the daily lives of believers. Ephesians 5:1 says, "So be imitators of God, as beloved children, and live in love." This could be the summary of the whole of Christian life. The author of Ephesians draws out some implications of imitating God by living in love. Much of this section consists of general moral exhortation, description of what the ideal Christian life with one another should look like.

Christians relate to one another in ways already established and governed, at least to some extent, by outward society. So, for example, wives and husbands, children and parents, slaves and masters all follow Greco-Roman social norms, which give some direction about the rights and duties of people who are in these kinds of relationships. The author adopts and adapts the traditional philosophical approach to household life that is at least as old as Aristotle, which we call "household rules." In ordinary Greco-Roman society, the lines of authority and of subservience were clearly drawn. Husbands, parents, and masters all have great power over wives, children, and slaves in a rigid social hierarchy.

For Paul these rules or principles become practical applications of faith for members of the "household of God" (2:19), giving directives for various segments of society in their relationships to one another. Paul does not offer a radical critique of certain social contracts, such as slavery or male dominance. Yet for him, relationships among Christians must reflect a new perspective. Christians are motivated to a new way of thinking, determined by their common baptism. Christians share the conviction that all are one in Christ and saved by Christ. This leads to innovations in the usual treatment of household rules: Here both parties in a relationship are addressed, whereas in the traditional form, only the male authority would be addressed, and here the inferior party is even addressed first. The Ephesians are urged to "live in a manner worthy of the call you have received . . . bearing with one another through love" (Eph 4:1f). They are exhorted to "be subordinate to one another" (5:21), to "nourish and cherish" one another, because they are members of one body (5:29–30). The extra verses spent on the analogy of husband to Christ and wife to the church are the springboard for much later mysticism, even as they also have been justification for continued subordinate positions for women. Such a passage as this, along with the exhortations to slave obedience, are contradictions of beauty, grace, and what today can only be seen as social oppression in the name of faith. They require careful interpretation in the context both of the author's world and of ours.

If we do not let these thorny problems be major obstacles, reading Ephesians today can inspire us to a powerful vision of the church. It leads us to reassess the ordinary way of approaching one another as colleagues, family, clients, and the like. We, like the Ephesians, are urged to remember our real identity and to respect others by relating to everyone in a way worthy of members of the "household of God." The ordinary hierarchical system that obtains in the world is superseded by a new way of relating to one another in Christ.

Paul finally urges the Ephesians to "pray at every opportunity in the Spirit" (6:18). He again asks for prayers for himself, that he may speak "the mystery of the gospel" with boldness and courage even though he is in chains (6:19–20).

### Conclusion (6:21–24)

Ephesians does not exhibit the usual personal tone and greetings of Paul's authentic letters. In the conclusion, however, the author indicates that he sends the letter with Tychicus (6:21), the name of Paul's messenger of Colossians as well (Col 4:7). The final prayers are for peace and love and grace.

## Concluding Remarks

Ephesians strikes a balance between reflection on the church as a universal, spiritual reality and application in the daily lives of Christians of their new identity as members of this spiritual creation. The letter also emphasizes the congruence between Christians' personal spirituality and their responsibilities in relationships with one another. Through baptism we are renewed. We have put off the "old humanity," symbolized by Adam; we have been transformed into a "new humanity," in Christ. We are called to be imitators of God and to reflect God's love and compassion in our daily lives.

As part of our Christian Scriptures, Ephesians stands as a continual challenge calling us beyond the present to a deeper reality where all things are in the care of God. The present with its trials, temptations, failures, and limitations can indeed discourage us. The problems of resolving tensions and enduring suffering are temporary. Ephesians is a letter from prison, addressing a church afflicted with oppression from the outside, confusion and dissension from within. Ephesians testifies to the author's faith and by the hope of God's plan for the salvation of the entire world—a plan that will be fulfilled despite, and even by means of, apparent obstacles. When we are confronted by the limitations of our present circumstances or hampered by fear, Ephesians provides encouragement. For us as Christians, the liturgy celebrates a communion with God. Faith is conviction of things unseen, especially about the triumph of God in Christ.

Ephesians is one of the most hope-filled and confident of all the Pauline letters. It may lack the usual personal tone expected of communities Paul knew well. But Ephesians expresses fundamental Christian beliefs that continue to characterize the church today. For example, despite suffering and failures, the church celebrates the reality of salvation already experienced in the daily life of Christians. In our world, where many families are in crisis, we read Paul's advice about mutual relationships with members of God's household and take courage in the advice to serve one another in love. Like the writer of Ephesians, the church at Vatican II complemented reflection on the nature of the church with reconciling the whole of the church in the modern world. Each of us, as members of the Christ's body, no matter what its limitations, is church and has a role in this mission.

### Questions for Discussion and Reflection

*Group Sharing/Discussion*

1. Why do you think Ephesians is called a "catholic" letter, that is, a letter to the whole church and not just to Ephesus?

2. The focus of Ephesians is on God's blessings in Christ in whom the divine plan for salvation of all people is achieved. Share your views on how this focus is expressed in the letter.

3. In Corinthians (1 Cor 12:12–27) and Romans (12:4–8) Paul expressed the unity of members in Christ by the image of the body. In Ephesians there is a major change (Eph 1:22–23; also in Col 1:18) in this body image. What is this change and what do you feel is its meaning?

4. We are reminded that in the body of Christ we are members of one another (4:15) and of Christ (5:30). How would you explain the meaning of this? What is the relationship of this meaning and our behavior?

*In Our Lives*

1. Paul works passionately for the world mission of the church. Yet he knows that salvation as well as creation is in God's hands and that God's plan is being fulfilled in mystery. Take time to reflect and translate this into your own experience and your own mission.

2. Ephesians 5:1 says, "So be imitators of God, as beloved children, and live in love." Paint a picture of our life that shows the meaning of this in how you live. Share this with one other person in the group.

3. Paul applies these central religious beliefs to practical applications of living faith in your personal life. He failed to apply his critique and teaching to social evils such as slavery and male dominance. How would you take his principles and apply them to these social evils?

***Individual/Personal Reflection/Action***

1. Ephesians reminds us that we are called—called to reflect the love and compassion of God in our lives. Pray to see more clearly how this touches your personal home life, your social life, your work life and your commitments to bring compassion to the world beyond yours. Take some action from your prayer.

2. Accepting the challenge of faith helps us to remember a deeper reality where all things are in the care of God. Life always presents problems, failures, temptations, limitations, and suffering. Name your trials and pray for faith and hope. These are always temporary. Ephesians challenges us to live by faith and hope even when it is dark.

3. Faith is conviction of things unseen, especially the triumph of God in Christ. Pray with Paul that "you may be filled with all the fullness of God" (3:19).

# PHILIPPIANS READING GUIDE

*At a Glance*

| | |
|---|---|
| Who are the main players? | Paul Euodia Syntyche Clement Epaphroditus Community at Philippi |
| What should I look for? | The theme of joy. In Philippians Paul shows his human sensitivity and tenderness, his enthusiasm for Christ as the key to death and life, and his deep feeling for the community of Philippi. |
| When did this take place? | Probably, about A.D. 55 while Paul was in prison in Ephesus |
| Where did these events occur? | Philippi, in northeastern Greece, was a city of some importance in the Roman province of Macedonia. |
| Why was this book written? | Philippi was the first church Paul established in his mission to the Gentiles of ancient Macedonia. The relationship between Paul and this church was long and dear, for Paul mentions how often the community shared in a partnership with him. Lydia was his first convert at Philippi. But it is not clear where or why he wrote or whether it is a combination of several letters. |
| What is the story? | All the themes are related to the mission of the community to proclaim the gospel. Paul accents their partnership for the gospel and his confident joy in spite of suffering. He shows concern for external pressures (Judaizers) and internal divisions. |

## Before Beginning

Philippians is one of the most appealing of Paul's letters. Along with Ephesians, Colossians, and Philemon, Philippians is traditionally called a "captivity letter" because in all four the author refers to his imprisonment. The authentic Pauline authorship of Philippians and Philemon is never doubted, although there is disagreement regarding the authorship of Ephesians and Colossians.

There are several theories about the location and occasion of the imprisonment from which Paul writes. The oldest and traditional view is that he writes from Rome in his final imprisonment there; this would date the letter to the late 50s or early 60s of the first century. Some have questioned the feasibility of this location, given the apparent frequent exchanges implied in the letter and the great distance from Rome to Philippi. So a second location has been suggested, Caesarea Maritima on the Palestinian coast, during the two years of confinement recorded in Acts 24–26. Still, that is a great distance requiring a month or more of travel. A third suggestion is that Paul was imprisoned earlier in his life in Ephesus, and that Philippians and Philemon date from that time, perhaps in the middle years of the 50s. The mysterious references to trouble in Asia (Ephesus was the principal city of the Roman province of Asia) in 1 Corinthians 15:32 and 2 Corinthians 1:8–10 support this idea, as does Paul's avoidance of Ephesus on his journey to Jerusalem (Acts 20:16). In that case, travel back and forth from Paul's prison to Philippi would have been much easier and faster.

If the Pauline authorship of Philippians is unquestioned, the unity of the letter poses some challenges. The choppy nature of this letter has led many interpreters to suggest that Philippians was originally at least three letters. A later editor (according to this theory), adapting the initial and final greeting, combined the originally separate messages into one edited "letter" for the purpose of later circulation. On the other hand, many more recent interpreters, using methods derived from the principles of ancient rhetoric, argue for the unity of the letter in spite of the rough edges here and there. Whichever is the case, the end result, the "canonical letter," provides the rich spiritual legacy called Philippians so beloved in the Christian tradition.

## Themes of Philippians

Important Pauline themes are developed in Philippians, particularly that of unity. We see in the letter the deep love Paul feels for this community. Disregarding the dangers facing him, Paul focuses on the sufferings of the community caused by external persecution and internal divisions. We hear of Paul's gratitude for the material support he has received from the community. We witness his fears about the problems within the community and the pressure from outside, but he subordinates those concerns to expressions of joy for the strength of the Philippians' church. In a surprisingly vehement outburst against those who advocate a return to the Jewish Law, he reminds us that this issue, so central to Galatians and Romans, is not forgotten elsewhere.

## Working through Philippians

The basic letter contains the usual *address* (1:1–11), *body* (1:12–3:1), and *conclusion* (4:21–23). The main themes of Philippians are the following:

I. Address and Thanksgiving (1:1–11)
II. The Body of the Letter (1:12–3:1)
  A. Paul's situation and the progress of the gospel (1:12–26)
  B. Exhortations for community unity; example of Jesus (1:27–2:18)
  C. Travel of Paul and assistants (2:19–3:1)
  D. Digression and warning (3:1–4a)
  E. Example of Paul (3:4b–21)
  F. Specific appeal to unity (4:1–9)
  G. A thank-you note (4:10–20)
III. Conclusion (4:21–23)

### The Address (1:1–11)

The opening line names Paul and Timothy as senders of the letter, but the speaker quickly changes to "I" in verse 3, for Paul is really the author. Timothy will be mentioned as an ideal companion in 2:19–24. The address is unique among Pauline letters in its acknowledgment of local leaders by title, "overseers and ministers," which by using later meanings of the words could also mean "bishops and deacons," but there is no evidence that the connotations later brought to those words are active here. Nevertheless, the address shows the beginnings of official titles and functions in the church.

A thanksgiving (1:3–8) and a prayer (1:9–11) complete the address. This is one of the longest and most beautifully developed of the Pauline thanksgivings. It introduces the themes of joy and community, themes that recur throughout Philippians. The paradox expressed in this letter is that the intense suffering experienced by Paul and the Philippians pales in comparison to the confident joy they share. Although separated because of Paul's imprisonment, and threatened on all sides, Paul and the Philippians are "partners," participating together in the spread of the gospel message. Paul draws strength from the Philippians' affection and display of concern for him. He prays (1:9–11) that they will be strengthened and that their love will grow even amid hardships. Together they all await the "day of Christ," which Paul longs for and strains forward to obtain.

### The Body of the Letter (1:12–3:1)

**Paul's Situation and the Progress of the Gospel (1:12–26)**

Paul links faith in suffering and the spread of the gospel. Nowhere is this link more eloquently expressed than in Philippians 1:12–26 where he refers to the effect his own imprisonment has had on the progress of the gospel message. Paul rejoices that even his enemies are using the opportunity represented by his present circumstances to energetically pursue the spread of the Christian message. For him, the priority is that "in every way . . . Christ is being proclaimed" (1:18). This position stands in some contrast to his insistence elsewhere, even in 3:2–3 of this letter, that only he has the right gospel. Paul speaks of joy even though he is in prison and the outcome is uncertain. He could be facing death. As a committed and passionate apostle, Paul worked tirelessly to promote acceptance of the gospel message by Gentiles everywhere. Now, in prison, Paul is equally peaceful, knowing that even should he die, the preaching will be continued.

If 1 Corinthians, especially chapters 1 and 2, represents a theoretical development of Paul's theology of the cross, Philippians represents Paul's own faith as he lives this theology. The wisdom of the cross is that God's power is made perfect in weakness. By this transforming power of the cross, Paul's brothers and sisters take encouragement from his imprisonment and preach the gospel all the more fearlessly. By the wisdom of the cross, Paul considers death to be "gain," and what he formerly considered "gain" to be "rubbish" (see 3:7–8). Imprisoned, Paul draws strength from the community. He speaks with confidence and joy, expressing hope that is firmly rooted in God.

**Exhortations for Community Unity and the Example of Jesus (1:27–2:18)**

As he does in several other letters, Paul expresses concern that the opposition the Philippians experience will threaten their faith. He knows of internal divisions among these Christians. By appealing to them to "have a common mind and heart," Paul alludes first to his own suffering and imprisonment and then to the example of Christ.

The beautiful hymn about the abasement of Christ of 2:6–11 is probably taken from an already existing piece of early Christian poetry with which the Philippians are familiar. It recalls their source of encouragement and is a cherished expression of faith in the redemptive aspects of Christ's suffering and death. The example of Christ's death must, above all else, influence the believing community in its own practical acceptance of and obedience to God's will. Thus, Christ who "emptied himself" is the example of behavior for the Philippians who are having trouble preserving unity in the congregation. Further, Christ by his death became "Lord" so that all who profess his Lordship are subject to him. In homage they recognize that they are brothers and sisters, members with one another of one believing community. So Christ is the example and the empowerment of selfless, mutual service in the church. Following the hymn, Paul draws out some implications: The Philippians are to remain blameless and innocent in the midst of adversity and wickedness, waiting for the Day of Christ (2:16). Conceiving of the Christian life as a liturgical sacrifice, Paul says that even though he is "poured out as a libation" (wine that is offered in sacrifice), he rejoices. He asks only that the Philippians share his joy.

**Travel of Paul and Assistants (2:19–3:1)**

The travel account given here and other indications suggest relatively free and frequent exchanges between the prisoner, Paul, and the Philippians. This would be more easily understood with an imprisonment closer to Philippi than to Rome; thus, there is the Ephesian theory. The news about Epaphroditus's illness and recovery seems to indicate different visits. He probably came from Philippi and was not able to continue his apostolic work because of illness. Timothy is extolled as an ideal assistant, a second example of unity after Jesus. The trust among Paul, Timothy, and Epaphroditus stands in contrast to the squabbling between Euodia and Syntyche and other members of the Philippian community (4:2–3).

**Digression and Warning (3:2–4a)**

The abrupt change of tone and content between the first two chapters of Philippians and the strong warning in 3:2–4 is one of the strongest arguments that these were originally separate communications. Even so, a skilled rhetorician could also just as abruptly switch topic and tone to get his audience's attention. This sudden theme of resistance to those who agitate for the Gentiles to be circumcised, presented in an insulting tone, is brief and does not reappear in this letter.

**Example of Paul (3:4b–21)**

After presenting the example of Jesus and then in a lesser way of Timothy, Paul now proposes himself as example of one who knows how to give up privilege and status for the good of others. He gives us some of our best biographical information about himself and then reflects on the consequences of his encounter with Christ. Using athletic imagery, Paul encourages the Philippians to strain toward the goal of a "perfect maturity." He urges them not to regress into the past, seeking glory in shame (possible allusions to circumcision) or in other practices of the "flesh," such as observances of certain dietary rules. These, Paul says, are earthly things. Paul himself used to glory in his religious accomplishments, but since his conversion, he no longer regards these as significant. Indeed, his former system of valuing is "rubbish" compared with his new way of seeing things in Christ. This is the wisdom of the cross. Those who do not accept this wisdom are "enemies of the cross" (3:18).

**Specific Appeal to Unity (4:1–9)**

Paul turns to an internal crisis that is just as destructive and threatening to the community. He begins chapter 4 by urging the Philippians to live in harmony, a theme he had already developed in chapters 1 and 2. But now he is specific in his appeal to unity, and all the previous rhetoric on the subject may be leading to this climax. There is a conflict between some leading women of the community, Euodia and Syntyche, and Paul solemnly begs them to stop. What position these women occupy we do not know, but their division is obviously central to the community's problems, so they may be significant leaders. Paul addresses a comrade and enlists the help of an otherwise unknown man named Clement to aid in the reconciliation of these women for the betterment of the whole community.

**A Thank-you Note (4:10–20)**

Paul expresses thanks for the help received from the Philippians and sent with Epaphroditus. He adds, however, that his gratitude is not so much that he was personally aided as that the Philippians' generosity is "profit that accrues to your account" (4:17). Paul testifies to his own indifference and ability to do without. Yet he humbly accepted aid not only to alleviate his own need, but as a symbol of the affection that linked him to the Philippians. Paul speaks of this aid in liturgical terms, referring to it as "a fragrant aroma . . . a sacrifice, pleasing to God" (4:18–19; see also 2 Cor 2:14–16). This is the ancient language of liturgical offering and sacrifice. The idea of an offering of mutual love and aid by Christians to one another as a "liturgy" appears also in Romans 12:1–2 and 15:17–20.

**Conclusion (4:21–23)**

The conclusion of the letter sends greetings to everyone there from everyone here. The reference to "Caesar's household" is to the vast imperial network of civil servants that were present in every major city. We know from this reference that there were Christians among them.

## Concluding Remarks

Since the writing of Philippians, the Christian community has been inspired not only by the words of the apostle, but by the example of the imprisoned leader who speaks with such affection, hope, and faith. One of the most beautiful and well known of Paul's letters, Philippians represents a reflection on the meaning of fidelity in the midst of trial. Paul's confidence that in all things "Christ is . . . proclaimed" (1:18) transcends the threat of others' jealousy and rivalry.

The Christological hymn of Philippians 2 not only inspired the Philippians to greater unity, but also continues to invite believers of every age to imitate Christ. Paul's prayer for his fellow Christians is that they always be happy (Phil 4:4–9). This serves as a model for our prayers for one another. Paul puts his own life before the Philippians, encouraging them to follow him in everything that he does and says. Paul then promises that the "God of peace will be with you" (4:9). Such should be our prayer in attracting others to live the Christian life.

**Questions for Discussion and Reflection**

***Group Sharing/Discussion***

1. Paul writes this epistle from prison. Let each one in the group choose a theme of Paul's and explain it to the group.

2. Philippians is unique in Pauline letters in that it acknowledges local leaders by title, "overseers and ministers." What were their roles in this early church?

3. Paul links faith and suffering with the spread of the gospel (1:12–26). Read this aloud and share what you think Paul feels regarding his imprisonment. How does this relate to your experience?

4. The wisdom of the cross is that God's power is made perfect in weakness. Paul's imprisonment gives encouragement to the Philippians. Let each person share their reaction to this.

***In Our Lives***

1. For Paul the priority is that "in everything . . . Christ is being proclaimed" (1:18). Share how this faith priority speaks to you and your Christian vision.

2. Christ is the model and empowerment of selfless, mutual service in the Church (2:6–11). Where and in whom do you see this in your life, your parish community?

3. The trust among Paul, Timothy, and Epaphroditus contrasts with the squabbling between Euodia and Syntyche and the Philippians' community. Talk about the necessity of trust in building the Christian community; give examples. Explain what are the needs of increasing trust in your community and suggestions for doing that.

4. Paul proposes himself as an example of one who knows how to give up status and privilege for the good of others. Name this reality and need in your community.

5. Paul used to glory in his religious accomplishments but since his conversion no longer does. He grew in a new way of seeing things in Christ. What would be similar experiences in Christian history (e.g., St. Augustine, St. Ignatius Loyola) and in your life of experiencing of a new way of seeing things in Christ?

***Individual/Personal Reflection/Action***

1. Set aside time and meditate on the sufferings of Christ (2:6–11). Recall this is a source of encouragement and an expression of faith. Christ who "emptied himself" is still an example for our Christian life.

2. Philippians presents a reflection on the meaning of Christian faithfulness in the midst of trial. What is your experience of this? To whom can you look for encouragement in this?

3. Make Paul's prayer (4:4–9) your prayer. It is a treasure. "God of peace be with you" (4:9).

# COLOSSIANS READING GUIDE

*At a Glance*

| | |
|---|---|
| Who are the main players? | Paul Epaphras Timothy Christians of Colossae |
| What should I look for? | Paul encourages fidelity to foundational beliefs in Christ's person and redemptive work, while warning against false teachings concerning spirits and ascetical practices. |
| When did this take place? | If Paul wrote it, he was imprisoned several times during the decade of the A.D. 50s; if written by a disciple, it could be around A.D. 60–62. |
| Where did these events occur? | This is addressed to a Gentile congregation at Colossae in the Lycus Valley in Asia Minor. |
| Why was this book written? | The letter is a response to Epaphras, founder of the community, concerning false doctrines that are disrupting the congregation. |
| What is the story? | Without debating about angelic spirits, Paul affirms that Christ possesses full redemptive power and that spiritual renewal occurs through contact in baptism with Christ who died and rose again. It is unnecessary to placate spirits. True Christian asceticism consists in avoiding sin and practicing love of neighbor as Christ teaches. |

## Before Beginning

It is customary to refer to the author of Colossians as Paul, even though many interpreters question whether Paul himself wrote this brief letter. Many characteristics of the letter seem to suggest Paul's presence behind it. The lively style and personal greetings are typical of Paul. Most of the personal names mentioned here also appear in Philemon, a letter that has always been attributed to Paul himself. Yet there are strange expressions, new terms, and a new understanding of the church so that many scholars think it indicates a different author here, writing in Paul's name with the hope of using Paul's authority. A compromise position is that Paul entrusted the message to a secretary who composed it in his own terms and with his own style.

Paul himself did not establish the church at Colossae. Possibly Epaphras, a disciple of Paul, was the founding missionary there. The context is that erroneous teachers implied that Christ's work of redemption was incomplete and therefore that certain other religious practices were required to supplement Christ's saving death and resurrection. These suggested practices were drawn from Jewish as well as non-Jewish or pagan religions.

They amounted to ascetical and superstitious additions to the message Paul and Epaphras had taught. As in Galatians, but less emotionally, Paul adamantly insists in Colossians that adding to the gospel message is really subtracting from grace. Only as a member of Christ's body and under his headship can we fill up "what is lacking in the afflictions of Christ" (1:24), that is, continuing Christ's redemptive suffering in the world.

At issue in the discussion at Colossae is the primary role of Christ in the salvation of the world. The power and authority of Christ and his relation to the rest of creation are challenged. False teachings at Colossae suggested that other spiritual beings were rivals to Christ's role and that certain ascetical practices were a means of becoming more spiritual while also helping to appease these spiritual beings. Using categories and labels present in these false teachings, Paul insists on the primacy of Christ and that Christ's saving action on our behalf is sufficient. Ethical demands follow from this fundamental faith. It is not a matter of satisfying some angelic spirits or following some ascetical ideals.

## Working through Colossians

The *address and thanksgiving* (1:1–14) and *conclusion* (4:7–18) enclose the *body* of this letter in 1:15–4:6. The body of Colossians follows the basic indicative-imperative pattern characteristic of Paul. The structure of Colossians then is the following:

I. Address and Thanksgiving (1:1–14)
II. The Body of the Letter (1:15–4:6)
  A. Instruction about Christ and false teaching (1:15–2:23)
  B. Ethics characterizing the true Christian (3:1–4:6)
III. Conclusion (4:7–18)

### The Address (1:1–14)

The *address* includes not only the usual greeting (1:1–2) and thanksgiving (1:3–8), but also a prayer for the continued progress of the Colossians (1:9–14). Both the *address* and *conclusion* (4:7–18) contain greetings and personal references that are typical of Paul.

### The Body of the Letter (1:15–4:6)

Colossians' main message is correct teaching and warnings against false teachings (1:15–2:23). This is followed by exhortations to exercise fundamental beliefs in daily Christian living (3:1–4:6).

#### Instruction about Christ and False Teaching (1:15–2:23)

Paul is confident that Epaphras has given the community a solid foundation. He reminds the Colossians that by Christ's saving death, "[God] delivered us from the power of darkness and transferred us to the kingdom of his beloved Son" (1:13). This transference from the realm of sin and error into that of grace and truth is effected in baptism and must be lived out in the daily lives of Christians. The doctrinal presentation of the first major part of Colossians falls into three sections: the Christological hymn and its implications (1:15–23), Paul's own ministry and example (1:24–2:3), and warnings against false teachers and their teaching (2:4–23).

#### The Christological Hymn (1:15–23)

To teach a correct Christology and clarify errors, Paul quotes a liturgical hymn apparently familiar to the Colossians (1:15–20; see also Phil 2:6–11). Many interpreters believe that this hymn predates Paul and was already in use by the early Christian communities. The poetic rhythm and language suggest that it was a hymn and that it was at home in the liturgy. Because Paul generally writes in prose, the insertion of a hymn here is easily discerned in the Greek. In this hymn Christians profess and celebrate the authority of Christ in whom all "fullness was pleased to dwell, and through him to reconcile all things for him." Paul stresses the redemption and peace won for us through Christ. He does not badger or scold the Colossians for their errors, but presents Christ's role of reconciling the world to God as the basis of common faith among all believers. The text adapts a variety of traditions about the figure of Wisdom and a cosmic savior to the person of Christ, who begins, as in the prologue of John's Gospel, in the heavenly realm. But he is also the head of the church and first-born from the dead, so that his saving action works in our history.

**Paul's Ministry and Example (1:24–2:3)**

Emphasis on his own example is a remarkable trait of Paul's letters, one expected of a great teacher in his day (see further 1 Thes 1:6; 2 Cor 11–12). It is also significant that upon reviewing Christ's work of redemption, Paul immediately attaches his own example as a model for the Colossians to emulate. At first this advice may strike us as surprising and almost shocking. How can Paul claim to be a model for all to imitate (see 1 Cor 11:1; Phil 4:8)? It springs from the apostle's humility and transparent confidence. Paul is so firmly rooted in God that he dares to advise his addressees to follow his example. By studying Paul's life, others may know the power of God and be converted. Paul always reveals the source of his confidence, which is not self-reliance but hope in God. This hope is best expressed in Christ's gift of salvation evidenced in the life of the apostle. The apostle glories in his vocation and fidelity while also accentuating his sufferings in the service of the gospel.

In describing his own ministry, Paul adapts categories important to the Colossians and to the false teachers who are disturbing them. They are emphasizing "wisdom" and "perfection," so Paul speaks about the "knowledge of the mystery of God, Christ, in whom are hidden all the treasures of wisdom and knowledge" (2:2–3). Paul identifies the goal of his mission to "present everyone perfect in Christ" (1:28). For this he labors and struggles in accord with "God's power working within me" (1:29).

**Warnings against False Teachings (2:4–23)**

Paul encourages the Colossians in their faith, reminding them of their identity in Christ. He observes the "good order and the firmness of your faith in Christ." He celebrates this fidelity and encourages the Colossians to be grateful, with a thanksgiving rooted in faith. Finally, he warns against the seduction of false teaching that is according to mere human tradition and not grounded in Christ. The false teaching was probably a combination of Jewish and pagan philosophies and pagan ideals. Paul denounces the "circumcision administered by human hands" and the ascetical practices regarding "food and drink" alleged to be required at certain times and days (2:16). Some teachers flaunted their visions and self-abasement and were involved in complicated devotions to angelic beings. Paul labeled all these as passing fads, "shadows of things to come" and "things destined to perish." By contrast, in Christ dwells the fullness of God. All are members of Christ, who is the head of the body, the church. Here and in Ephesians, this specific role of Christ within the church is introduced. Christians are united in one church under one Lord who is Christ. Their common task is the reconciliation of the world to God under Christ.

**Ethics Characterizing the True Christian (3:1–4:6)**

Paul does not really present a new, uniquely Christian ethical system but draws from several existing systems. Often Paul lists vices or virtues similar to lists found in Stoic or other Greek philosophers. The "household rules" found in Colossians (see Eph 5:21–6:9; Ti 2:1–3:8; 1 Pt 2:11–3:7) have parallels in contemporary Greco-Roman literature where elements of household management are discussed. The submission of wives, children, and slaves to the male household head was an expected part of the social order. A fundamental difference for Paul is the motivation and the empowerment to fulfill these ethical principles. The church as the body of Christ distinguishes itself from the outside world in that the love command operates to create a new way for Christians to relate to one another. Paul says that the Colossians once conducted themselves as pagans who practiced immorality, greed, and passion (see 3:5–7). Now they have "put on the new self, which is being renewed . . . in the image of its creator" (3:10). In Christ the usual sexual, social, and ethnic distinctions do not exist, "but Christ is all and in all" (3:11).

**Conclusion (4:7–18)**

Tychicus is the messenger entrusted with the letter to the Colossians. Many think that the Onesimus mentioned as his companion (4:9) is the former slave who returned to Colossae with the letter from Paul to Philemon (see Reading Guide to Philemon). The other companions mentioned at the end of Colossians are well-known Christians named in other Pauline letters except for Nympha (4:15), a woman who hosts a house church. This list of personal references reminds us about the common Christian teaching upon which Paul depends and to which he urges the Colossians to hold firm.

## Concluding Remarks

Today no less than in the times of the Colossians, Christians are pulled in various directions, and people are still searching for spiritual guides and nourishment. The exotic, speculative language in Colossians does not seem so strange to us when we consider the attractions of undemanding spirituality, the ease with which we can adopt superstitious practices, or the popularity of "self-help" books that tell us we can accomplish anything if we "image" it correctly. The epistle to the Colossians stresses the reconciliation of all things in Christ as the fundamental faith assertion with enormous ethical repercussions. As the firstborn of all creation, Christ is a symbol of the value of all creation and a promise of the ultimate salvation of all. That truth translates into the church's responsibility for stewardship in the world, assuming that in preaching reconciliation the rights of all are respected. In carrying out its mission, the church must be a symbol of peace, because Christ is the head of the church, and Christ made peace by the blood of the cross.

**Questions for Discussion and Reflection**

***Group Sharing/Discussion***

1. The context of Colossians was false teaching in the community that Christ's work of redemption was incomplete. How were the false teachings expressed in Colossians?

2. What does Paul say about continuing Christ's redemptive sufferings in the world (1:24)?

3. Paul speaks and acts with a great deal of confidence. What is the source of this confidence?

4. The central issue in Colossians is the primary role of Christ in the salvation of the world. This involves the power and authority of Christ as well as his relation to all creation. Let each person share with the group what you believe is Christ's primary role and how this relates to the world and all creation. Also, what ethical issues follow from Christ's role?

5. Basically, the lists of virtues and vices that Paul presents are not new; they are found earlier in the Greek philosophers. What Paul did present that was different is the motivation for acting ethically. Explain this significant difference.

***In Our Lives***

1. Paul includes a liturgical hymn (1:15–23) that celebrates Christ in whom "all the fullness was pleased to dwell, and through him to reconcile all things for him." Paul stresses redemption and peace won for us by Christ. This is the foundation of his response to the false teachings and ethical problems. Share what this meant to the Colossians in their context. Share what this means today to you and with your friends or community.

2. Paul identifies the goal of his mission to "present everyone perfect in Christ" (1:28). Reflect and clarify what your mission is as a follower of Christ. Paul labored and struggled for his mission in accord with God's power "working within me" (1:19). Do you grow aware of God's power working within to face the struggles of being Christ in the world today?

3. In his letters Paul celebrates the faithful by thanksgiving. He gives thanks always. He celebrates their faith and encourages the Colossians to be grateful. Reflect upon your rhythm of living. How do you rise and give thanks each day? How often do you give thanks to God and to persons? Are you conscious at the liturgy that thanksgiving is central to your worship? Share ideas with each other on how to grow in giving thanks.

***Individual/Personal Reflection/Action***

1. Paul's trait of giving his own life as an ex-

ample for the Colossians to follow is remarkable and is common to his letters. Paul followed Christ and taught Christ. He calls his readers to follow Christ and teach Christ by their life. Who are your teachers? Who are your models or mentors? How and to whom are you a teacher or model? What values do you see and follow?

2. All are members of Christ, who is the head of the body, the church. Paul introduces this role of Christ within the church. Christians are united as members with Christ as the head. Their common task is the reconciliation of the world to God under Christ. Christ is head of the body, the Church. All are united in church under one head who is Christ. How are these part of your consciousness? Our common task: Reconcile the world to God under Christ. How do you keep this growing and maturing in your life?

# 1 THESSALONIANS READING GUIDE

### *At a Glance*

| | |
|---|---|
| Who are the main players? | Paul Timothy Silvanus |
| What should I look for? | Be aware of Paul's affectionate thanksgiving. Note the relationship between faith and charity as well as the teaching on the second coming of Christ. |
| When did this take place? | About A.D. 51, probably written from Corinth |
| Where did these events occur? | In Thessalonica, the capital of the Roman province of Macedonia. The Christian community there was one of the very first Paul established. |
| Why was this book written? | Paul sent Timothy back to Thessalonica to strengthen that community in its trials. Timothy's return with a report on the conditions there served as the occasion of Paul's first letter. |
| What is the story? | Paul experienced a great deal of persecution from the Jews and Gentiles because of his preaching. In this letter he expresses his gratitude to the community for their faith and defends his ministry. In addition he gives specific instructions on sexual conduct, death, and church order. |

## Before Beginning

Thessalonica was the capital and major city of the Roman province of Macedonia, about one hundred miles southwest of Philippi along a major Roman road. The communities at Thessalonica and Philippi were among Paul's first converts in Greece. This letter indicates that he encountered many troubles there from both Jews and Greeks. The beginning of Paul's ministry in Thessalonica was characterized by suffering and humiliation. He was "insolently treated at Philippi," an incident to which he does not allude in his letter there (see 2:2; see also Acts 20:34; 1 Cor 4:12; 9:3–18; 2 Thes 3:7–9). The Thessalonians, too, shared in some of that persecution (2:14–16). Persecution, illness, misunderstanding, and other forms of suffering plague Paul's ministry. Yet he constantly has hope of being found worthy by God to be entrusted with the preaching of the gospel (2:4).

## Working through 1 Thessalonians

Following the usual letter format, 1 Thessalonians has an address and thanksgiving (1:1–10) and conclusion (5:26–28), which envelop the body of Paul's message (2:1–5:25). This message falls into two parts: the indicative (2:1–3:13) followed by the ethical exhortations (4:1–5:25).

The structure of 1 Thessalonians can be outlined as follows:

I. The Address (1:1–10)

II. The Body of the Letter (2:1–5:25)

A. Paul's Account and Defense of his Ministry (2:1–3:13)

B. Specific Exhortations and Instructions (4:1–5:22)

III. Conclusion (5:23–28)

**The Address and Thanksgiving (1:1–10)**

The address contains a short greeting (1:1) and an extended thanksgiving (1:2–10). A distinctive feature of Paul's letters is that the thanksgiving focuses on what God has done for Paul's addressees. In other correspondence of the time, the thanksgiving normally centers on the health and benefits enjoyed by the sender and a wish for the prosperity of the recipient. Paul's co-authors are Silvanus and Timothy. Following his custom, Paul writes not only in his own name, but as a member of a team of Christian missionaries. Unlike many others of his letters that begin with several names, here the second person plural is maintained throughout the letter, Paul's "I" breaking through only at 2:18 and 5:27. In what we believe is the first extant letter from Paul, there is a greeting that will become Paul's trademark: "To the church of ______, grace and peace to you in (or from) God the Father and the Lord Jesus." This greeting is seen in its simplest form here; in later letters Paul will elaborate on this basic form.

A function of the thanksgiving in the address is often to anticipate the themes of a letter. In the case of 1 Thessalonians, thanksgiving itself is a major theme. Paul is grateful for the reception of the word of God by the Thessalonians and for the impact that their faith has had on other communities. Paul claims that he himself does not even have to testify to the fruitfulness of the Thessalonian mission because word of it has spread throughout the Greek world (Macedonia and Achaia include the whole of Greece, 1:8). Besides the initial thanksgiving of 1:2–10 that properly belongs to the address, two other thanksgivings appear in 2:13–16; 3:9–13. In all three places, Paul speaks of the relationship between faith and charity and of the expectation of the Parousia or second coming of Jesus Christ. These are the major themes of 1 Thessalonians.

**The Body of the Letter (2:1–5:25)**

The body contains Paul's main message in two parts; Paul's account and defense (2:1–3:13) followed by teachings and exhortation (4:1–5:25).

**Paul's Account and Defense of his Ministry (2:1–3:13)**

Paul states clearly that his motives are pure in his work with the Thessalonians. If we can read between the lines, we can surmise the accusations of unworthy motives on his part against which he defends himself. He stresses his gratitude to God for the success of this community and presents a defense of his ministry.

Thanksgiving is a persistent thread that runs throughout 1 Thessalonians. Yet Paul is not a naive optimist. He is aware that this community is experiencing several problems. Although he will return to the theme of gratitude, he launches into a defense of his own ministry with the Thessalonians, thereby implying that some have questioned his authority or actions. Throughout Paul's ministry career, he insists that he is an apostle, called by God to preach the gospel message. Paul's defense of himself and his authority are linked to the call he has from God. He is under a divine compulsion to preach the gospel, and his confidence derives from this vocation. His defense of his ministry is also prompted by some of the dangers represented by false teachers agitating the Thessalonians in Paul's absence. Although this is a painful and threatening problem, Paul interrupts this defense with thanksgivings, as if to say that he is confident in the Thessalonians' perseverance despite the interference of the agitators.

One of the most difficult yet persistent problems that faced the early church was that of false prophets or false teachers. In the ancient world, where travel was difficult and communications took time, often philosophers or religious teachers joined others who traveled for business or personal reasons. News was gathered and disseminated by such traveling groups; new converts were often made along the way. First Thessalonians reflects this kind of mobility where Paul speaks about his own past visits with the Thessalonians as well as his thwarted plans to return. He promises to visit again soon. He warns the Thessalonians about other types of ministers—those who are greedy or who flatter (2:5) or who rely on the community for support (2:9). Paul's own example stands out in contrast to these, for he has been "gentle as a nursing mother" among them (2:7).

Despite his grateful recognition of the sturdy faith of the Thessalonians, Paul found it necessary to remind them of the sacrifices and dedication they saw in him and his companions. Among his characteristic practices, Paul repeatedly notes that he is self-supporting. He "toiled day and night" among them and in so doing, he gave them an example that they ought to imitate. This practice of working with his hands and supporting himself was unusual. The Corinthians misinterpreted it, and he did accept gifts of support from the Philippians (Phil 4:10–20).

**Specific Exhortations and Instructions (4:1–5:22)**

Concrete ethical applications or "imperatives" follow from Paul's grateful description of the Christian community at Thessalonica. This exhortatory section may be considered a specific example of Paul's concern that faith be exercised in practical living, particularly as expressed in charity.

**Sexual Conduct (4:3–8)**

These verses refer to sexual morality, but it is not clear how. The text may refer to a man being faithful to his wife (the usual translation), or to the need for his own sexual control, with no wife mentioned, and verse 6 may refer again to marital fidelity against adultery, or to cheating in business matters. In any case, the text raises a variety of ethical concerns including sexual conduct and business ethics.

For their part, the Jews considered the obligations of marriage and the family to be linked to the covenant relationship with God. This link was an important one Paul wished to adopt for the Gentile Christians. Paul therefore stresses the obligation of believers to develop relationships worthy of them, reflecting respect for one another and for their call to holiness. Charity among believers, in turn, has an effect even on those outside the community who will be impressed with the example of high moral conduct of the Christians.

**Death and the Need for Vigilance (4:13–5:11)**

Paul and other early Christians seem to have believed that the Parousia or return of Jesus was very near. Now members of the Thessalonian community are dying before this event, which was a problem for their faith that Jesus would truly return. They wondered how the dead would participate in the triumphant day of Christ's return. Paul encourages the Thessalonians to persevere in faith and joins to this a warning about continued vigilance. Enthusiastic faith can often wane at the onslaught of opposition, suffering, and frustrated expectations. Paul fears that the death of fellow Christians will so shake the Thessalonians' faith that their grief will give way to doubt, discouragement, and even apostasy.

Paul's view of the second coming is influenced by perception that God is living in heaven, which is "above," beyond the clouds. An archangel and trumpets are standard images accompanying the end of the world and a call to judgment. The second coming of Christ, unlike the first, will be a show of power. It will be cosmic in effect, changing the entire order of creation, not only human existence.

Paul promises that the Christian dead have not been lost or forgotten. They, like us, will be gathered by Christ and judged. The righteous will be restored to God. Paul's emphasis is on the certainty of this event, not on times or manner. The exact manner of the resurrection and of judgment, Paul finally admits in 1 Corinthians 15, is unknown to us (see 1 Thes 5:1; 1 Cor 15:35–57).

The death of loved ones may pose painful faith questions for believers in any age. The death of beloved members of the community seems to have challenged the faith of the Christians at Thessalonica. Because the death of fellow Christians was so threatening, Paul admonished: "console one another with these words" (4:18; 5:11). He reinforced his warning to persevere by speaking again about the certainty of Christ's coming. The images of the pregnant woman and of the thief in the night are ones that appear in Jesus' own preaching, according to the Gospel accounts (see Mt 24:43; Lk 21:23). They stress at once the need for preparedness and vigilance, the certainty of the occurrence, and the threatening aspect of suffering. Continuing his use of stock apocalyptic imagery, Paul envisions a cosmic struggle that differentiates between those who are the children of light and those who remain in darkness.

**Spirit and Order (5:12–22)**

Paul teaches respect for those who minister among the faithful, an unusual reference to local leaders (see also Phil 1:1). But the more important points are about the way in which believers are to exercise mutual love, not returning evil for evil but consistently seeking the good of all. Joy, prayer, and gratitude characterize their lives as they live according to the Spirit, discerning between good and evil.

**Conclusion (5:23–28)**

The concluding prayer (5:23–25) and final greetings (5:26–28) suggest that this letter was intended for reading in a liturgical setting. Paul says that the Thessalonians will be kept holy and spotless as they wait for the LORD's return. The "holy kiss" with which they are to greet one another was probably the ritual exchange of peace done during the liturgical assembly.

## Concluding Remarks

Actions are an expression of faith. Behavior is a key to the way people think and what they believe. Therefore, if there is carelessness about others, or promiscuity, or indifference to one's role in creating a livable society and universe, we have to examine the underlying faith presuppositions to these actions or omissions. Charity, chastity, and an honest, humble bearing in this life are signs for Paul of conversion to the "living and true God." Paul exhorts Christians to live according to the gospel he preaches. It is not hard to see how the message of 1 Thessalonians is appropriate for today.

**Questions for Discussion and Reflection**

***Group Sharing/Discussion***

1. What are the main themes in 1 Thessalonians (1:2–10; 2:13–16; 3:9–13)?

2. What is Paul's view of the second coming of Jesus?

3. Paul repeatedly notes that he is self-supporting. Why? Share your views of the results and how this may or may not apply to the church today.

4. Paul notes that his vocation and his authority came from his call by God. Why does Paul feel he must defend his ministry?

5. In 4:3–8 Paul talks about sexual conduct. Read this aloud and each comment on how his teaching relates to modern life.

***In Our Lives***

1. Paul and the early Christians believed that the return of Jesus was very near. When members of the community died before this event, it became a problem of faith and of belief that Jesus would truly return. Remember what Paul said to help them. Reflect on how the second coming of Jesus relates to you and your faith. How would you help someone whose faith was weakened by the death of a dear one?

2. In 1 Thessalonians Paul advises, "do not quench the Spirit" (5:19). Share what this may mean in today's church. Share how you try to nourish the Spirit in your parish.

3. Paul asks for respect for the ministers and reminds us that there must be mutual care and trust. How do you contribute to this in your parish? How would you teach a group to respect ministers and vice versa?

***Individual/Personal Reflection/Action***

1. Pray and reflect carefully on 5:14–22. Make this a frequent examination of conscience. Who are the idle? The fainthearted? The weak? How do I do the following: Admonish? Cheer a person? Support those around us? Pray without ceasing? Give thanks? Recall that this is the will of God for you.

2. Like the Thessalonians, we may find the death of a loved one brings painful questions. Any death leaves a hole in the fabric of a community. How can the community work together to respond helpfully when someone dies? How does your faith respond? Does God seem closer or more remote? How do you nourish your faith and love so as to be helpful?

3. Charity among the community, in turn, has an effect on the outside community. Count the many ways you see this charity in your parish community. Reflect and plan on new ways of increasing this.

# 2 THESSALONIANS READING GUIDE

*At a Glance*

| | |
|---|---|
| Who are the main players? | Paul Silvanus Timothy Community of Thessalonians |
| What should I look for? | The apocalyptic message of consolation and hope, which does not cause fear but is a message of encouragement in the face of confusion and suffering. |
| When did this take place? | Probably written around A.D. 70 by a Pauline disciple |
| Where did these events occur? | In Thessalonica, the capital of the Roman province of Macedonia |
| Why was this book written? | This is a response to a letter allegedly sent by Paul containing false teaching that the day of the Lord is at hand. |
| What is the story? | The heart of the letter has to do with the message supposedly sent by Paul that the second coming of Christ is at hand. Thanksgiving, prayers, and teachings add encouragement at a time of fear and suffering. |

## Before Beginning

The apocalyptic, end of the world, perspective of 2 Thessalonians (see introduction to 1 Thes and the notes on apocalyptic elements in Paul preceding the Reading Guide to 2 Cor) is more pronounced here than in any other Pauline letter. The Pauline authorship of 2 Thessalonians is widely disputed. This letter may be written in Paul's name by someone other than Paul, probably a disciple or admirer. There is a studied attempt on the part of this disciple of Paul to copy Paul's style. For example, the greeting differs only slightly from the greeting of 1 Thessalonians, and the final greeting insists that the letter is based on Paul's authority. There is a rejection of other supposedly Pauline letters circulating (2:1). One could also say that these are signs of Paul's true authorship, but perhaps the insistence on Paul's authority seems more than a little defensive. Writing in Paul's name assured that a letter would be taken seriously. This practice of Paul's disciples was also an attempt to give continuity to the apostle's message, explicitly interpreting the Pauline traditions in a new context. Despite the reservations of interpreters about Paul's authorship, it is customary to refer to the writer of 2 Thessalonians as "Paul."

There is good reason to believe that 2 Thessalonians was written a decade or more after Paul's death. It is addressed to the same community as 1 Thessalonians but a community that is troubled by the mistaken preaching that the Day of the Lord had now arrived. The preoccupation of early Christians with the times and circumstances accompanying the return of Christ is a problem addressed by many of the New Testament writers, including the Gospels of Matthew, Mark, and Luke, and the book of Revelation. The "apocalyptic" message of 2 Thessalonians is not a frightening one that heightens with fear the anticipation of Christ's return, but is instead a message of consolation and hope for the Christians suffering persecution and confusion. The term "apocalyptic" has come into vogue again today when the future seems uncertain. We need to understand biblical apocalyptic as emphasizing hope for all those who persevere.

## Working through 2 Thessalonians

Second Thessalonians exhibits the usual letter characteristics of an address and thanksgiving (1:1–12) and conclusion (3:15–18) enclosing the message or body of the letter in 2:1–3:16.

I. The Address (1:1–12)
II. The Body of the Letter (2:1–3:15)
III. Conclusion (3:16–18)

### The Address and Thanksgiving (1:1–12)

The address includes a greeting (1:1–2), a thanksgiving (1:3–10), and a prayer (1:11–12). The greeting is an almost slavish imitation of the greeting of 1 Thessalonians. Paul joins himself with Silvanus and Timothy, fellow missionaries to the Thessalonians (see 1 Thes 1:1). Also similar to 1 Thessalonians is the fact that thanksgiving is not only a part of the initial address as a formal characteristic of a letter; gratitude is also a central theme in the development of Paul's teaching (see 2:13–17).

### The Body of the Letter (2:1–3:15)

Paul's message to the Thessalonians can be subdivided into instruction on right thinking (2:1–17) and right conduct in the daily life of the Christians who lived in Thessalonica (3:1–16).

#### Paul's Teaching on Right Thinking (2:1–17)

The early Christians' expectation of an imminent return of Christ needed to be adjusted and corrected as the community developed. Unforeseen crises arose, and answers had to be sought in the basics of Christian preaching. Time passed, and the danger was that Christians would become disenchanted and would lose faith, especially in the midst of adversity. First Thessalonians had warned the community about maintaining faith, hope, and love even amid trials such as the death of fellow Christians. There Paul focused on the day of the Lord, which, he assured them, was coming soon. This reminder served as a warning that behavior would be judged, and the faithful would be rewarded, whereas the unfaithful would be punished.

By the time of the writing of 2 Thessalonians, it seems the expectation was being taken too seriously, and this caused new problems. As time passed, the early Christians were wondering about the accuracy of their hope that Christ would return soon. They became alarmed by prophecies and by a letter that they thought came from Paul; it seems to have said that the expected "day of the Lord" had arrived (2:2). The author denies this and lists a number of events that must come first. This change in 2 Thessalonians 2:1–10 from the expectation of the near return of Christ seen in 1 Thessalonians is one of the main reasons interpreters suspect that 2 Thessalonians is from a later, second generation Pauline Christian. The early Christians had experienced persecution. History had already shown that any expectation that Christ would speedily return with power, to punish the oppressors of the Christians, was wrong.

The message underlying the apocalyptic references in 2 Thessalonians is "do not be alarmed." The writer avoids any kind of futile speculation concerning times and circumstances of the coming of Christ. He uses standard apocalyptic images portraying the conflict between good and evil, and the ultimate victory of God over evil. Yet he studiously avoids any specific description. It is enough that his readers focus on the hope of God's victory and that they remain vigilant against deception or alarm.

#### Paul's Teaching on Right Conduct (3:1–15)

The admonition in 3:10 not to feed anyone who will not work and the general exhortation against idleness is probably connected to the apocalyptic expectation discussed earlier. Some thought that there was no further point to building the human community if it would all end soon. But Paul warns that idlers only disrupt the peace of the community. Thus he connects idleness and a lack of charity. The apostle presents himself as a model to the contrary to be imitated. His work with his hands is apparently a topic of discussion among his converts. Perhaps, like the Corinthians, the Thessalonians despise labor and prefer the leisure that is considered more conducive to the development of the mind and spirit. Paul gives both social and theological reasons showing that he was not constrained to work but does so freely. Part of the legacy he left with the community was his example of working. This may have been a form of self-abasement Paul practiced to "be all things to all people" (see 1 Cor 9:21–22). Paul stresses that his aim is to make the gospel accessible to all.

### Conclusion (3:16–18)

The author adds a greeting "in his own hand," apparently to show that this is from Paul. Yet it is such characteristics that make Pauline authorship of 2 Thessalonians suspect. There are no personal greetings and no originality to the abrupt closing of this letter. The author seems to be copying Paul's style rather than adding a more personalized signature as Paul would have done.

## Concluding Remarks

Christians today can understand the need for restraint on the belief that the return of Christ was imminent. Perhaps more than ever before, we can appreciate the important balance introduced by 2 Thessalonians between faith that indeed the return of Christ would come and emphasis on the need to work diligently to create a better society. Second Thessalonians offers us a message of hope and encouragement. The events that must come to pass before the end of the world are opportunities inviting us to a change of heart, expressed in careful stewardship of our lives, of the church, and of the world.

**Questions for Discussion and Reflection**

***Group Sharing/Discussion***

1. What was the occasion for the writing of this letter?

2. What would you say is the main lesson here?

***In Our Lives***

1. The writer avoids useless guessing or speculation concerning the time and circumstances of the second coming of Christ. His message expresses the certainty of the coming and the victory of God. How do you focus your hope? Is it in the confidence of Christ's coming?

2. Events that must come to pass before the end of the world are opportunities inviting us to a change of heart. What are the problem areas in your life, your parish, your city, or the world that require the balance of intense prayer and energetic action? Have you given up on praying or working for solutions of these problems?

***Individual/Personal Reflection/Action***

1. Second Thessalonians offers us a message of hope and encouragement. Hope and encouragement are necessary for Christian living. To have hope and to act with encouragement require prayer and reflection. Take the time: be hopeful and share your hope; be encouraged by Christ and your many gifts and share this encouragement with those in need.

# THE PASTORAL LETTERS

## Introduction

The two letters to Timothy and the single letter to Titus have been called the "Pastoral Letters" because they deal largely with issues regarding pastoral care in Pauline communities. Most scholars consider them not to have been written by Paul, but by a later writer, because they reflect a degree of church organization not present in Paul's day. We are indebted to these communities for preserving this distinctive correspondence that describes the initial development of church offices and organization. The Pastorals might be read as reflections on Christian ministry. In keeping with the tradition of authorship by Paul, we will refer to the writer as "Paul," although most interpreters would agree that these letters are written at least a generation after Paul's death. In form they are personal letters written to one disciple, but in reality, they are open letters to communities covering church policy on various issues.

Paul himself traveled far and wide preaching the message of Christ, founding churches, and writing letters back to communities he had established. Throughout his missionary career, Paul was joined by others and worked with others. He depended upon others. He kept in touch with local leadership. His letters request prayers and sometimes aid for himself and for his mission. In writing letters, Paul often names coworkers as coauthors. He sends emissaries to communities, sometimes for diplomatic reasons and sometimes because he is prohibited from coming at the time and needs to send a messenger. Among his most trusted and reliable partners in the spread of Christianity were Timothy and Titus.

Both Timothy and Titus served Christian congregations in ancient Greece. The traditional understanding reflected in these letters is that Timothy later became a church leader in Ephesus (1 Tm 1:3) and Titus in Crete (Ti 1:5). Both were struggling with the challenge of those who offered alternatives to the teachings of Paul. Paul writes to reinforce the faith of these pastors and to encourage them, reminding them of their own Christian vocation.

# 1 TIMOTHY READING GUIDE

*At a Glance*

| | |
|---|---|
| Who are the main players? | Paul Timothy community of Ephesus |
| What should I look for? | The ongoing problem of false teaching and practical challenges of the developing communities, for example, relationship of members, authority, money are the two foci of this letter. Also notice what Paul calls the essentials of the Christian message. |

| | |
|---|---|
| When was this written? | Probably written by a disciple of Paul around the beginning of the second century |
| Where did these events occur? | The letter is addressed to Timothy, who administered the church of Ephesus. |
| Why was this book written? | To reinforce the faith of the pastors and community as well as to encourage them to guard the tradition of Pauline churches |
| What is the story? | The central message is to preserve authentic church doctrine from false teaching. It presents principles for relationships with older members, with presbyters, with widows, for charitable ministrations, for liturgical celebrations, for selections of deacons and bishops. This letter is addressed to Timothy, who administered the church at Ephesus. It speaks to the ongoing problem of false teaching that always threatened the church and the practical challenges of the developing communities and their ministries. As with other letters written in Paul's name, the author is referred to as "Paul" in this guide. |

## Before Beginning

Both of the letters addressed to Timothy struggle with the nagging threat of false teaching. This is a problem that afflicted the church from the beginning.

## Working through 1 Timothy

The content of this letter is diverse, and any particular outline seems arbitrary and artificial. Our discussion of 1 Timothy is based on the following structure:

I. The Address and Thanksgiving (1:l–2, l2–l7)
II. The Body of the Letter (1:3–11; 1:18–6:19)
 A. Paul's Message to Timothy (1:3–11; l:18–4:16)
 B. Duties Toward Others (5:1–6:19)
III. Conclusion (6:20–21)

### The Address and Thanksgiving (1:1–2, 12–17)

The address consists of a brief greeting in Pauline form (1:1–2) with the thanksgiving delayed until 1:12–17. A warning against false doctrines (1:3–11) appears between these two parts of the address. This intrusion breaks the usual structure of a letter but manifests the gravity of the author's concern. The thanksgiving (1:12–17) recalls Paul's former blasphemy and persecution of the church, evidence that his call was unmerited and unsolicited (1:12–17). Paul's example is a primary instance of the transforming power of grace. Because he sinned grievously (though in ignorance), the grace bestowed upon Paul had to be abundant. Notice that the author does not dwell on guilt or remorse. His allusion to Paul's sinful past only serves to illustrate the greatness of God's mercy. These reflections prompt him to praise God in a short doxology or blessing (1:17).

### The Body of the Letter (1:3–11; 1:18–6:19)

The message of 1 Timothy is primarily a warning against the dangers of false teaching. The writer reminds Timothy about the qualities he should look for in assistants who are true ministers of the gospel, and he discusses Christians' duties toward others.

#### Paul's Message to Timothy (1:3–11; 1:18–4:16)

***The Warning Against False Teaching (1:3–11, 18–20).*** The teaching attacked in 1 Timothy is a form of gnosis (knowledge) that involved "myths and . . . genealogies [and] . . . speculations" (1:4). All three Pastorals, but especially 1 Timothy, are aimed at secure knowledge of the truth and secure ways of acting it out. These are reflections on the genuine applications of a teaching or knowledge that Timothy knows well.

**Gnosis** is the Greek word for knowledge and is the root for the word Gnosticism (see the Glossary). Gnosticism was a kind of religion that claimed secret knowledge for its members. It developed during the second, third, and fourth centuries.

It is possible that the so-called knowledge attacked in 1 Timothy is a sign of the beginnings of gnostic influences during New Testament times. (See the note on 1 Tm 6:20 in the NAB text.)

The threat Paul combats in 1 Timothy is the pursuit of gnosis without any ethical or practical applications for living (1 Tm 1:4; see 2 Tm 2:14; 3:7; Ti 3:9). Thus, the practicalities of Christian living and church life together are emphasized, along with a pastorally oriented theology. This letter attacks those who would reduce Christianity to a mere doctrine or intellectual exercise, to the neglect of the ethical implications. The letter presumes a common fund of knowledge and emphasizes that authentic Christianity should work itself out in everyday life.

**Life and Leadership in the Community (2:1–4:16)**

The primary example of authentic Christian living is the minister of the gospel message. Timothy has a great responsibility entrusted to him by God and verified in the church (1:3, 18–20; 4:6–16; 6:11–16, 20–21). The writer impresses on Timothy the importance of his role as example for the church.

The advice to Timothy in this letter proceeds from the admonition to draw strength from the "prophetic words once spoken about you" (1:18) and the suggestion to "attend to yourself and to your teaching" (4:16). Timothy should concentrate on "righteousness, devotion, faith, love, patience, and gentleness" (6:11). He should ignore the seduction of "profane babbling and the absurdities of so-called knowledge" (6:20). Constancy and perseverance in the faith are required to attract and encourage other believers. Timothy is urged to demonstrate to all his reliance on God.

The discussion of how each group of persons should act toward others is an adaptation of the "household codes" used in Ephesians 5:21–6:9 and Colossians 3:18–4:1. Here men and women, young and old, male and female should treat each other with the respect due them in traditional society (also 5:1–2; 6:1–2). The duties of bishop and deacons (3:1–13) are drawn from typical descriptions of virtue. The text speaks of a single bishop and a number of deacons, both male and female (or, possibly, of male deacons and their wives, 3:11). We know from Philippians 1:1 that these titles were used very early on. Presbyters are not mentioned in this passage (3:1–7), but only in 5:17–19. It does not seem, therefore, that there is as yet a triple-tiered ministry of bishop, presbyters, and deacons, which will come in the next years.

In one way, 1 Timothy may be read as a list of rules for people in various offices and positions within the community. There is, however, a common theme in all of Paul's advice. Members of the Christian community should distinguish themselves by their love for and service to one another. Even the dress and decorum of men and women at the liturgy, for example, should contribute to the building up of the community (2:8–10).

**Advice Concerning Women**

The particular advice to women, which has been controversial throughout Christian history, should be understood in the context of charity and the importance of good example. False teachers advocating asceticism, especially in the form of renunciation of marriage or restrictions on certain foods (4:1–3), were particularly successful with women whom the author of 1 Timothy perceives as especially susceptible. The prevailing male wisdom taught that women were gullible and subject to error, as symbolized in the story of Eve who was seduced by the serpent. Contrary to the false teachers, Paul supports marriage and sees the family as conducive to holiness. He therefore advocates the "submission" of women, which was part of traditional views about the well-run family. This, he insists, is not a lifestyle unworthy of Christian women, but a way in which women may, like Timothy, "persevere in faith and love and holiness" (2:15).

The same thinking drives the advice to slaves in a later passage to honor and respect their owners (6:1–2), with the warning that believing slaves are not to think of themselves as equal to their owners but are to be even more respectful. This kind of thinking, as can be imagined, has caused difficulty in later centuries when those who resist social change appeal to the authority of the Bible. In his own context, however, Paul is simply trying to uphold human dignity within a social structure that he cannot change.

**Duties toward Others (5:1–6:19)**

This is really a rather artificial division, because the whole letter is preoccupied with community relationships. There is ambiguity in the discussion about widows (5:3–16), perhaps indicative of uneven editing. First, widows who have no other means of support are to be supported by the church (5:3–8, 16). Then, there is some kind of enrollment of widows who are at least 60 years old, distinguished for practicing virtue and resolved to remain unmarried—hardly issues to consider if a widow is starving. Some kind of service organization is envisioned in 5:9–15, returning again in verse 16 to the assistance of needy widows. Given lower life expectancy, few women would live beyond 60, and younger widows are to remarry, so they could not hope to qualify later to be enrolled as those married only once (5:9).

The concrete advice regarding bishops and deacons and other ministers to the community stresses the power of example. This is especially important in those offices that have visibility in the community and represent a community trust. Many interpreters assume that the degree of development of the offices mentioned suggests a late composition of 1 Timothy. It would seem to have taken some years for the church to develop such a variety of roles and recognized ministries. On the other hand, we know that these ministries were beginning to develop already in Paul's day. They pertain to basic needs that arose as the church struggled to respond to its mission in the world. The office of bishop or overseer developed out of the custom of holding all things in common so that the surplus of the rich would supply for the needs of the poor in the Christian community (see 2 Cor 8 and 9). The ministry of deacons reflected the priority of preaching the word, while not neglecting the physical and material needs of the church's members (Rom 16:2; Acts 6:1–6). The earliest writings of Paul, and in fact all of the New Testament, stress the social dimension of the Christian message. Therefore, the stewardships that would assure this dimension were created as soon as the priority was recognized.

**Conclusion (6:20–21)**

The conclusion (6:20–21) is in the form of a final recommendation and warning. First Timothy ends by restating the main message of the letter: "Guard the trust" (see 1:3–10; 4:7; 6:3–5). Authority is stewardship. Many have been deceived by gnosis or false knowledge. Timothy is urged to hold firm to what he knows and to live it quietly.

## Concluding Remarks

First Timothy represents several challenges for the modern interpreter. The author's view that women are more susceptible to error than men, for example, betrays the bias of a male dominated culture. Changing attitudes throughout history facilitated the education of women, and consequently the underlying premise of their greater gullibility has been proven false. First Timothy stresses the responsibility of leaders to interpret the essentials of the Christian message and to insure charity as a visible quality of the Christian community. Interpreters today distinguish between the culturally based bias against women and the essential message that included all in the life of charity to be lived by the community. This is a life in which all may grow and mature, women as well as men. The responsibility of leaders and pastors is to nurture that life, providing in their own lives a model of charity for other Christians to emulate.

**Questions for Discussion and Reflection**

***Group Sharing/Discussion***

1. What advice did Paul give to Timothy? (6:11; 4:16)

2. In the time of Timothy what were the roles of deacon and bishop?

3. *Gnosis* means knowledge in Greek. It is the root of gnosticism, the heresy that says special knowledge gives salvation, and that what you do

doesn't matter. Some roots of this heresy appear in Timothy. What are some examples of this false teaching that Paul talks about?

4. Paul encourages Timothy to focus on the basic teaching of Catholicism. How does Paul describe this in the letter to Timothy?

5. Paul advises slaves to honor and respect their owners (6:1–2). Does he mean that slavery, as an institution, is morally acceptable? How were his words used in Christian history to validate slavery?

*In Our Lives*

1. To understand clearly Paul's message to Timothy, you need to know his social context. What is the social context of his teaching on women? Concerning the community? Concerning slavery? Have each individual or team prepare an explanation of the social context of one of these issues. Contrast with your social culture.

2. Contrary to the false teaching, Paul supports marriage and sees family as conducive to holiness (2:15). Share your views on how to support marriage in our culture; on how to recognize and nourish holiness in today's family.

3. A common theme of Paul's advice to the community and leaders is to distinguish themselves by their love for one another and service. Allow for time to reflect and perhaps take some notes. Then let each person share how he or she has experienced this in the church. Answer the more difficult question: how can you increase this love and service in your life?

*Individual/Personal Reflection/Action*

1. Paul's teaching that women were more susceptible to error than men betrays the bias of the male-dominated culture. Over time attitudes are changing due to education and political changes. A symbol of this growth of tradition in the Church is that the majority of those receiving Catholic doctorates and graduate degrees in theology and scripture are women. Change has occurred. How do you see this change affecting you and affecting the church?

2. First Timothy stresses the responsibility of leaders to interpret the essentials of the Christian message and to ensure charity is distinctive of the Christian community. As a way of connecting this message to our lives, consider and reflect upon: What upsets me concerning the church? How is this related to spreading the gospel and building the community? What should I do about this?

# 2 TIMOTHY READING GUIDE

## *At a Glance*

| | |
|---|---|
| Who are the main players? | "Paul" Timothy community at Ephesus |
| What should I look for? | Like 1 Timothy, there is concern for false teaching and ministry. Here the tone of the reflections on ministry is more personal and focuses on Timothy. |
| When was this written? | Possibly at the beginning of the second century, probably written by a disciple of Paul |
| Where did these events occur? | Probably in Ephesus |
| Why was this book written? | The author, in Paul's name, seems to be giving the young pastor the benefit of his experience. The elder apostle speaks of his own life, his loneliness, his lack of confidence. Yet he is not discouraged because God is the source of his strength as he is for Timothy. |
| What is the story? | This letter addresses Timothy in vivid terms and depicts Paul's courage and hope in the face of discouragements; Paul is portrayed as a prisoner; it recalls the mission days with Timothy; it suggests Timothy prepare others to replace him; Paul urges him to persevere in preaching the Christian message with the resurrection of Jesus and his messianic role as the heart of the gospel. |

## Before Beginning

The same preoccupations appear here as in 1 Timothy: warnings about false teachings, and Paul's exhortation to Timothy as a minister of the gospel like himself. Second Timothy is written in a warmer, more personal tone than 1 Timothy, and therefore its lack of formal structure is understandable. It is really a testament in the form of a letter. Like Moses in Deuteronomy 29–30 or Jesus in John 14–16, the elder Paul, imprisoned in Rome (1:16–17), looks back on his life with the knowledge of his imminent death (4:6–8) and gives the younger man the benefit of his experience. He begins and ends the letter with references to his own experiences and the vocation of Timothy, thus linking the two. Their ties of affection and of common vocation are deep and very significant for Paul. The elder apostle speaks of his own life, his loneliness, his lack of confidence in other human beings. Yet he is not discouraged. God is the source of strength for both Paul and Timothy. The deeply personal tone of this letter has led some recent commentators to reevaluate the question of Pauline authorship and to suggest that while 1 Timothy and Titus are of a later era, perhaps 2 Timothy is not.

## Working through 2 Timothy

The address and thanksgiving (1:1–4) and conclusion (4:19–22) envelop the body of the letter in 1:5–4:18. The main themes of 2 Timothy are the minister's experience of God and warnings against false teaching.

I. The Address and Thanksgiving (1:1–5)
II. The Body of the Letter (1:6–4:18)
  A. Instructions to Timothy (1:6–2:13)
  B. Warnings about False Teaching (2:14–3:9)
  C. Final Advice (3:10–4:18)
III. Conclusion (4:19–22)

### The Address and Thanksgiving (1:1–5)

The address (1:1–5) consists of a greeting (1:1–2) and a thanksgiving (1:3–5), following the authentic Pauline style.

### The Body of the Letter (1:6–4:8)

We have noted previously that Paul generally follows a basic pattern of first presenting his fundamental teaching on various issues and then drawing ethical conclusions from this teaching, though these two parts do not always follow one another in neat order. First Timothy does not follow this pattern very well, and Second Timothy even less so, primarily because it is more of a personal communication that combines reminders about teaching with advice in an informal way. The informal structure of this letter focuses on two main themes that are developed here: the minister's experience of God and warnings against false teaching.

#### Instructions to Timothy (1:6–2:13)

Timothy is not to be ashamed of the gospel or his commission to testify to the truth at all times. He also has the responsibility to guard that truth intact as he has received it. The apostle often uses himself as example, as a source of inspiration and motivation. Paul lives with such integrity that he urges Christians to imitate him in everything (see Phil 4:8–10). Timothy is reminded that those who follow Christ will suffer persecution. This echoes Jesus' warning to his disciples (Mt 24:9–14; Mk 13:9–13; Lk 21:12–19; Jn 15:11–27). In the face of such pressure, Timothy is to remain constant.

#### False Teaching (2:14–3:9)

Like the other Pastorals, 2 Timothy is aimed at false teachings that promote a certain gnosis or knowledge and a consequent asceticism or strict discipline. The false teachings Paul attacks attach superior value to those who are "enlightened" with such knowledge and practice stringent customs regarding sexuality and diet. These practices set them apart from others, contributing to their sense of superiority. In all three letters, Paul was assuming that his addressees held the right beliefs so that it was not necessary to review the correct teaching or doctrine that the writer and recipient hold in common. Therefore, Paul spoke in vague and abstract terms about the false teaching, concentrating instead on the appropriate ethical applications that follow from true gospel preaching. Paul urges Timothy not to become embroiled in debates: "Charge [people] . . . to stop disputing about words . . . avoid profane [and] idle talk" (2:14, 16). One of the false teachings actually identified is that baptized Christians are already risen with Christ and that there is no future bodily resurrection (see note on 2:14–19). Paul understands Christians as living in the last days when there are many dangers and threats to faith.

**Warnings about False Teaching (3:1–9)**

While such warnings are also present in other parts of the letter, here they are concentrated and seem aimed at a specific group of people, although they could also be intended more generally. The disparagement of women's intellectual ability that we have seen surface in 1 Timothy is again present (3:6–7), with perhaps the opposite effect: In fact, the author is telling us that missions among women were very successful, which means that the women were intellectually alert and responsive.

**Final Advice (3:19–4:18)**

Paul describes his life and impending death as a liturgical sacrifice; he is being poured out like a libation, an offering of wine (4:6). He has run and finished the course (4:7). He awaits with longing the reward of God (4:6–8). Such confidence is based in God and meant to serve as encouragement to Timothy who still runs the course. Like other biblical heroes (including Moses and Jesus), Paul is represented in 2 Timothy as giving a kind of farewell address near the end of his life (4:6–8). In this speech the hero warns his followers about impending dangers and threats to fidelity. They are commissioned with authority and reminded about the source of their confidence. They are promised that God will remain with them and that they will endure. Paul reminds Timothy to hold to the essentials of sound doctrine: scripture and the example of Christ and of other Christians. He reminds Timothy that those who live the gospel message will be persecuted. Paul urges Timothy to be faithful in waiting for the appearance of Jesus Christ.

**Conclusion (4:19–22)**

The personal tone and greetings of 2 Timothy mark this as the closest Pastoral Letter to Paul's own style. Paul often experienced failure in his relationships with others. The author of 2 Timothy experiences similar problems. Like Paul, he says that such difficulties are the occasion for more converts to the gospel message. The letter ends with a prayer for God's spirit to be with Timothy (singular). The plural in the last line may indicate the letter's being read and reflected upon in the assembly.

## Concluding Remarks

The church is not a perfect society, nor are its ministers without human faults and failings. Conflicts over a variety of issues have plagued believers from the beginning, making it sometimes difficult to discern right from false teaching and practice. The church has experienced crises of leadership and problems with authority and obedience. Relationships among Christians have often been strained. Paul and other New Testament authors are not strangers to such tensions and problems. The author of 2 Timothy manifests a remarkable vulnerability to the strains in his own relationships with others, but this does not in any way detract from his visions or hopes for the church. In fact, with amazing confidence and humility, the author of 2 Timothy shows that even his failures are opportunities for the spread of the Christian message.

**Questions for Discussion and Reflection**

***Group Sharing/Discussion***

1. What are some of the indications in 2 Timothy that it is a more personal communication than the usual letter of Paul?

2. What are Paul's main instructions to Timothy in this letter? How did Paul encourage Timothy?

***In Our Lives***

1. The church is not a perfect society. What failings do you see in it ? What response or solutions would you offer?

2. Throughout its history the church has experienced crises of leadership or authority in its history. Can you name some? Councils and new religious communities (e.g., Benedict, St. Francis of Assisi, St. Ignatius Loyola, St. Theresa of Avila, etc.) often provided solutions and renewal. Each member of your group should read and share the story of a founder or a council to appreciate how the church grows and faces challenges.

***Individual/Personal Reflection/Action***

1. Paul urges Timothy not to become embroiled in debate (2:14–16). The warning in this letter against engaging in useless disputes may strike a cord. Recall some examples of situations where

arguing over words was a way of dodging the real issues. Reflect how debating or arguing sometimes is fruitful and sometimes a waste. What advice would you give others and yourself in such a situation?

2. Timothy often experienced problems in his relationships with others. This book suggests that such difficulties are the occasion to add more converts to the gospel. Good relations are the life and food of community. Take some time to make a list and examine your own relationships. Are they healthy? Plan how you can heal or grow them.

3. The author of 2 Timothy shows that even his failures are opportunities for spreading the Christian message. Take time to imagine how your failures could also be opportunities for spreading the Christian message.

# TITUS READING GUIDE

## *At a Glance*

| | |
|---|---|
| Who are the main players? | "Paul" Titus Christian community of Crete |
| What should I look for? | Along with 1 and 2 Timothy, these letters are called "Pastoral" because they deal with the ongoing care of the Pauline communities. All are concerned with choosing and forming Church leaders, virtuous practices of the community, and protecting against false teaching. |
| When did this take place? | Possibly around the beginning of the second century. Most interpreters agree these pastoral letters were written at least a generation after Paul's death. |
| Where did these events occur? | Probably sent to Titus, the administrator of the Christian community on the large Mediterranean island of Crete |
| Why was this book written? | The letter is very similar to 1 Timothy and shows the same concern for those entrusted to care for the local communities. Titus should be careful in appointing ministers who will present sound church teaching. |
| What is the story? | The first teaching concerns the appointment of reliable ministers to protect against false teachers. The main section concerns the content and motivation of the teaching and authority. |

## Before Beginning

The third Pastoral Letter is addressed to Titus, who is charged with the administration of the church in the large area of Crete (1:5). The letter to Titus has many parallels with 1 Timothy and manifests the same concerns for the maintenance duties of those entrusted with the care of the local communities. They are to give particular care to the appointment of reliable assistants and to the presentation of sound church teaching, protecting it from the many threats and dangers of false teaching.

## Working through Titus

The address in 1:1–4 is not followed by the usual thanksgiving, but the text goes directly into the body of the letter in 1:5–3:11. This message presents the pastoral charge or responsibilities, especially that of working with others in the preaching of the Christian message. The entire letter may be seen as an encouragement from one pastor to another. A short conclusion (3:12–15), giving personal information, brings the letter to a close. The simple structure is as follows:

I. Address (1:1–4)
II. The Body of the Letter (1:5–3:11)
A. Pastoral Charge (1:5–16)
B. Teaching the Christian Life (2:1–3:11)
III. Conclusion (3:12–15)

**The Address (1:1–4)**

The address follows the usual Pauline pattern, but here it consists of a greeting only. It is slightly more elaborate than Paul's usual greetings but exhibits many of the features of Paul's thinking. As in the other Pastorals, the author emphasizes the apostle's role in the spread of the worldwide mission of Christ. This mission is now entrusted to Paul's "child," Titus, a fellow worker encouraged through this letter to insure the continuing line of good pastors and to preserve the faithful teaching of Christian life. The great dangers that face Titus and the church of Crete are the false teachers and those who would corrupt the Christian message.

**The Body of the Letter (1:5–3:11)**

**Pastoral Charge (1:5–16)**

Verses 5 through 9 are parallel to the instruction of 1 Timothy 3:1–7. Paul is an itinerant preacher who, nevertheless, is keenly aware of the need for stabilized leadership, especially to protect the church against heretical or false teaching. Therefore, the instructions given to Titus concerning the administration of the church at Crete are related first to the appointment of trustworthy and reliable pastors for the various duties required for the growth and development of the church there.

One of the important offices was that of presbyter (elder, v. 5), a term that in meaning is quite close in this letter to *episkopos* (overseer or bishop, v. 7). The two statements seem to be about the same people, as they could also be in 1 Timothy 3:1–7; 5:17–20. The main function of the bishop was apparently the overseeing of the financial or material matters in the church. Again, as in Philemon 1:1, it is difficult to translate *episkopos* accurately, because the title "bishop" has such different connotations today. This bishop is God's "steward," entrusted with the distribution of goods and accountable to the members of the community. Therefore his own life ought to be exemplary. He must not only avoid excesses, but also represent a model Christian life in his own family. As in 1 Timothy 3:2–13, the description of the virtues of officeholders is taken from typical descriptions in Greek literature on the virtues necessary for leadership.

Leaders of the church are to offer an alternative example to that of the false teachers who preach for personal gain, living off the community and seeking personal recognition and recompense. These kinds of accusations against one's opponents are also part of traditional rhetoric and should not be taken at face value. The conduct of the presbyters or bishops should, however, be above reproach. Primary among the false teachers are the Judaizers who continue to advocate observance of some aspects of the Jewish Law, a custom that was attractive to some Christians for many centuries. The writer stoops to an ethnic slur by quoting an earlier author to the effect that Cretans are by their very nature prone to deceit, dishonesty, and laziness, thus making them all the more susceptible to falsehoods (1:12).

**Teaching the Christian Life (2:1–3:11)**

Titus is encouraged to hold on to sound faith in teaching, while resisting pressures from all sides. Because the imagery of moral preaching often depicted the church as the new family, its members are here taught to relate to one another as older and younger people would in a well-ordered family in which respect dominates. Groups singled out include older men and younger men, older and younger women, slaves, and those in authority. Christians must not act in accordance with the world around them. Yet they must survive in an alien world. Paul's instructions focus on how to survive in this world while offering an alternative lifestyle and developing integrity as Christians. The domestic role for women is reinforced. The author reminds them of their duties to be examples within the marital context. Likewise slaves are directed not to rebel against the control of their masters (2:9–10). The author urges them to fidelity and kindness within the context of slavery. Citizens were also inclined to see Christianity as an alternative to obedience to a corrupt state. The author of Titus advocates exemplary citizenship based on the status of Christians as already justified and relying on the mercy of God. Paul summarizes his advice to Titus, reminding him to avoid controversies and to maintain his integrity in the true faith. The false teachers disturb the community and its ministers. Paul exhorts to vigilance and constancy.

**Conclusion (3:12–15)**

The final lines include very specific travel directives and recommendations for travelers passing through Crete. Titus is told to come with an assistant whom he will send, to join Paul at Nicopolis, a common city name; probably the one in western Greece is intended. Mediterranean sea travel shut down from November 10 to March 10, and a traveler thus had to "winter" somewhere waiting out the passage of those months. Paul closes with personal greetings. The final greeting "grace be with you all" is the simplest of closing forms. Some manuscripts add "of the Lord" or "of God" and "Amen," which are closer to the usual elaborations of Paul himself.

**Pastoral Letters for Today**

CHRISTIANS CONTINUE TO wrestle with questions relating practice or behavior to belief. Christianity, like Judaism, has always emphasized the importance of deeds rather than mere knowledge or doctrine alone. Ministers of the gospel are entrusted with the responsibility to preserve teaching while also presenting exemplary lives. The letter to Titus reminds us of the difficulties, yet the importance, of working with others for the advance of the gospel message.

The challenge of the Pastoral Letters for today's church can hardly be overestimated. The Catholic view of Paul has long been unduly influenced by his portrait in these letters. Catholic Christians in particular have inherited a long tradition stressing the communal dimensions of Christian teaching. We do not receive the Christian message individually, nor can we live it in isolation from each other. This emphasis on communal responsibility is part of the legacy of the Pastoral Letters.

**Questions for Discussion and Reflection**

***Group Sharing/Discussion***

1. Where was Titus administrator of the Church?

2. What is the purpose of Paul's letter to Titus?

3. What were the dangers facing Titus in his church?

4. What was the main function of the elder or overseer in the church at that time?

***In Our Lives***

1. The writer expresses an ethnic slur (1:12) that Cretans are deceitful, dishonest, and lazy and therefore more receptive to false teaching. Where do you recognize ethnic slurs in your world? In your church? How do you deal with this in your own reactions and those individuals and institutions in your life?

2. Christians must not act in accordance with the world around them, Paul teaches. How would this teaching apply in your life? Each person should name at least one way of acting in the world that Catholic Christians should *not* imitate.

***Individual/Personal Reflection/Action***

1. Survive in the world while offering an alternative lifestyle and continue to develop integrity as Christians. This teaching of Paul to Titus applies to living in the world today. Reflect on what it takes to survive while offering an alternative lifestyle. What does/would your alternative lifestyle look like? Name the elements in your life needed to survive and the dimensions of your Christian lifestyle. Where are the difficulties and conflicts between these? How do leaders in the Church offer an example of an alternative lifestyle?

2. Paul's advice to Titus is to avoid controversies and maintain integrity in the faith. Is this good advice for your life? Consider the ways of nourishing your integrity in the faith and how to react to controversies. This requires prayer and reflection concerning your journey of faith in the community.

# PHILEMON READING GUIDE

*At a Glance*

| | |
|---|---|
| Who are the main players? | Paul Onesimus Philemon |
| What should I look for? | In a society that accepted slavery as an institution Paul presents a new way of relating to others, including slaves, based on baptism in Christ. |
| When did this take place? | Between A.D. 61 and 63 |
| Where did these events occur? | Maybe in Rome |
| Why was this book written? | This short letter to three individuals was written by Paul during imprisonment. It was sent as a plea for welcoming Onesimus, a slave from Colossae. |
| What is the story? | Onesimus, a slave, was converted to Christ by Paul who sends him back to his master, Philemon, with this letter asking that he be welcomed back not just as a slave but as a brother in Christ. |

## Before Beginning

Paul's letter to Philemon is a gem of early Christian communication and the only true personal letter that we have from Paul. No one seriously challenges Philemon as an authentic Pauline letter and an integral part of the New Testament. Philemon appears to be a letter between individuals, dealing with a very concrete matter rather than with generalized, abstract theological principles. Neither Paul nor the early Christian community intended to attack slavery directly, so we may well wonder why this letter was preserved at all and why it might be significant for us.

Despite being a brief letter, it is full of interpretive problems and has been intensively studied in recent years. The traditional understanding of it since the fourth century has been that Onesimus, a slave, had run away from his master, Philemon, and had come to Paul for protection. Paul had converted Onesimus to Christianity and now sent him back to Philemon, carrying this letter. But more recently, this interpretation has been questioned and several other possible scenarios proposed. One is that, according to Roman law, a slave who goes to a third party to mediate a dispute with his or her owner is not to be considered a fugitive. If one reads the letter from this perspective, it also fits. A third argument is that Onesimus is not a slave at all, but Philemon's brother, whom Philemon is treating like a slave (Phlm 16). Paul asks him to reconcile and treat him as he deserves. The interpretation that Onesimus is indeed a slave is the majority one, but why he went to Paul remains an open question, as does what Paul really wants Philemon to do. But it is clear that the relationship between Philemon and Onesimus is not good, and Paul is trying to patch it up.

The informal conversational tone does not detract from the letter's impressive significance within the Christian context. Each part of this letter underscores its community context and gives us a glimpse into the structure of relationship and exchange in the early Christian church. Because nearly all the names mentioned in the letter also occur in Colossians, the usual supposition is that Philemon's house church is located in Colossae.

## Working through Philemon

The letter to Philemon has the usual features of letters of Paul:

I. Address and Thanksgiving (1–6)
II. The Body of the Letter (7–22)
III. Conclusion (23–25)

### The Address and Thanksgiving (1–6)

It is not Philemon alone who is addressed, but Apphia, perhaps Philemon's wife, Archippus, another member of the household, and the whole "church [that meets] at your house" (1–2). The thanksgiving (4–6) notes the renowned love and faith Philemon has always shown the "holy ones," a reference to his fellow Christians. Paul also names Philemon a "partner" in faith, emphasizing the common life in Christ that they share, which is the basis for the new society that Paul envisions.

### The Body of the Letter (7–22)

The varied expressions of Paul's complex relationship with Philemon serve as a model for the new relationships Philemon now has with Onesimus. Their common baptism provides a basis for Philemon and Onesimus (as well as for the whole church) to create an entirely new way of relating to one another and to resolve the tensions between them. In no other Pauline letter is the relationship between the statement of Christian reality (signified by a common baptism) so bound up with the implications or exhortations that flow from this reality.

In 1 Corinthians 7:21–23, Paul says that slavery or freedom is indifferent in the Christian life. It is not clear in this letter whether Paul appeals to Philemon to free Onesimus from slavery. He may expect that the two of them now continue in a good relationship of master and slave. But if Onesimus is a runaway, the normal punishment against an errant slave (who perhaps also stole from his master, 18–19) is prohibited by Paul. Master and slave are fellow Christians. The community context should help them work out a new way of relating to one another as "brothers." Because of whatever way Onesimus has wronged Philemon, Philemon is in a delicate position. If he does not punish Onesimus, he is lacking in necessary discipline, and his social peers will think him weak. If he does insist on punishment, he will violate his Christian obligation to forgiveness and Paul's express desires. The whole house church is watching to see what he will do! Unfortunately, we do not know the answer.

Paul describes himself as a prisoner (9), as Philemon's brother (7, 20), and as father of Onesimus (10). Paul says he is an old man (9), an anticipated guest of Philemon (22) and one to whom Philemon is indebted (19). These descriptions illustrate the various ways in which the patronage system of the culture interacted with Christian expressions of interdependence and ultimately equality in Christ. They are a way of redefining Paul's relationship to Philemon and to the church in Colossae. They also serve as a model for Philemon to develop a new relationship between himself and Onesimus. The letter is a masterpiece of rhetorical strategy. Paul does not mandate any specific set of actions, but rather appeals to Philemon and to the whole community to read and reflect on this letter in light of their common baptism, and to discern a course of action toward Onesimus that will reflect the Christian faith they share.

### Conclusion (23–25)

The final greetings mention names of Paul's coworkers also found in Colossians (1:7; 2:1; 4:12–13) and 2 Timothy (4:9–13). Together with the liturgical blessing (Phlm 25), these greetings underscore once again the communal context in which this letter was written and in which it ought to be reflected and acted upon. Philemon draws out some implications of the baptismal formula quoted in Galatians 3:28: "There is neither Jew nor Greek, there is neither slave nor free person, there is not male and female; for you are all one in Christ Jesus" (see also Col 3:11).

## Concluding Remarks

The letter to Philemon raises interesting challenges for its original recipients and for us. Apparently, Onesimus himself is bearer of this letter from Paul to his master. The letter is to be read at the liturgy when the Christian community will help Philemon reintegrate Onesimus back into his household as a fellow Christian. The very fact that the community preserved this letter—and that it comes down to us included in the canon of the New Testament—testifies to the spirit of openness, humility, and generosity of Philemon and his congregation that must have successfully resolved this matter. Today the church as a whole and local churches are faced with perplexing social problems, especially with regard to social expectations and their clash with faith values. We can take hope that what was written long ago was written for our instruction. We can well afford to contemplate the role of such a Pastoral Letter and of the community's reflection on its contents.

**Questions for Discussion and Reflection**

***Group Sharing/Discussion***

1. Tell the story of the letter. Imagine Philemon as the content for a play, at the house church of Philemon and Apphia, with the community. Assign persons to take the roles of Paul, Onesimus, Philemon, Apphia (Philemon's wife), Archippus (a visitor from Galatia). Scenes:

a. Paul and Onesimus talking about their relations and matters in the letter.

b. Philemon and his wife talking about Onesimus' returning and the community.

c. Onesimus and Philemon when he arrives with the letter.

d. Archippus tells the community how they are identified in Galatia: "There is neither Jew nor Greek, there is neither slave nor free person, there is not male nor female; for you are all one in Christ Jesus" (Gal 3:28).

2. The letter to Philemon has the usual features of a Pauline letter: (1) Address and Thanksgiving; (2) The Body of the Letter; and (3) the Conclusion. Assign a person to read aloud each of these parts of the letter.

***In Our Lives***

1. Were Paul and the Christian community concerned with or attacking the institution of slavery? Where does slavery still exist in its different forms? When did American Catholics actively teach that slavery was wrong?

2. "The whole church that meets at your house," Paul writes to Philemon and his wife. Take some time to discover and read about the first communities in Paul. Our roots are in "house churches" (cf C. Osiek "Who Did What in the Church in the New Testament?" in *Lay Ministry in the Catholic Church,* Liguori, MO: Liguori Press, 2005).

3. Paul emphasizes the common life they share in Christ through baptism. This is the basis of the new society that Paul envisions. What are the essential qualities of this new community? Where do you see or experience these same qualities?

***Individual/Personal Reflection/Action***

1. What are the most pressing social problems facing your local church? What can you do to contribute energy in helping to solve some of these problems?

2. Meditate on being baptized in Christ. How do relationships created by baptism cause you to look at social problems in a different way?

# HEBREWS READING GUIDE

### *At a Glance*

| | |
|---|---|
| Who are the main players? | Author as preacher Christ |
| What should I look for? | This is not a letter, it is a written sermon. It is best approached by reading it from beginning to end aloud. Study its symbols carefully, because they are difficult to understand. The interpretation of Jesus as priest is unique in the New Testament. |
| When did this take place? | Some view the date as before A.D. 70, others as early second century, written by a person familiar with Greek philosophy, the scriptures, and allegorical logic. |
| Where did these events occur? | The exact audience, author, and place of composition have long been disputed. The audience is assumed to be Jewish Christians because of the use of scripture as argument and the Temple and its cult. |
| Why was this book written? | The author saw the audience in danger of losing their Christian faith due to weariness with the demands of Christian life. |

What is the story? The six movements are: (1) God's revelation in Jesus is superior to the covenant; (2) the Son is higher than the angels; (3) Jesus as faithful and compassionate high priest; (4) Jesus' eternal priesthood and sacrifice; (5) heroes and heroines of the past as examples to imitate; (6) Christians live in the world but are not defined by it or its values.

## Before Beginning

Hebrews is not a real letter but a sermon. The best way to experience Hebrews is by reading it out loud from beginning to end. Oral recitation helps to catch the sermonic rhythms of Hebrews, its use of "we" and "you" (so natural to the sermon), and its alternating pattern of exposition and exhortation. Reading straight through also enables the reader to grasp the powerful argument that is the outstanding characteristic of this early Christian writing.

## Toward Understanding Hebrews

Hebrews has significantly shaped the liturgy, doctrine, and spirituality of the church. Although other New Testament writings speak of Jesus' death as a sacrifice, Hebrews' unique reflection on Melchizedek (ch 7) and on Jesus as the Great High Priest have influenced the development of Catholic liturgy. Hebrews' insistence on Jesus' full divinity and equally full participation in human nature contributed to the understanding of Jesus' identity as God's Son (chs 1–2). And Hebrews' vision of faith as a pilgrimage toward God (chs 11–12) created a symbolic framework for the Christian understanding of discipleship as a "journey." For all its riches, Hebrews resists easy understanding for two reasons: first, it presents a sustained argument from beginning to end; second, its symbols are hard to understand.

Dealing with these difficulties clears the way to more intelligent and satisfactory reading.

### The Argument

Some parts of the New Testament, like the Gospel parables, can be read out of their original context and still make sense. But each part of Hebrews plays a role in a complicated interplay of argument and explanation concerning Jesus and Christian life. Hebrews resists being excerpted or taken out of context. It uses a form of argument, found both in Greek philosophy and rabbinic Judaism, called "from the lesser to the greater." The argument goes, "If something is true in a smaller matter, it is even more true in an analogous greater matter." In Hebrews, the contrast is between the partial revelation of God in the past through angels, law, and priesthood, and the perfect revelation "in the last of these days" through God's Son, Jesus, between that former "lesser" salvation and the present "greater" salvation.

The argument in Hebrews is not theoretical but practical. The real point is the contrast between the response to God's word by the people of the past and the response demanded of the people today. A greater blessing and hope require a greater degree of obedience and loyalty, just as disobedience carries a greater penalty. The stakes are higher all around.

### The Symbols

The symbols of Hebrews are sufficiently strange to shake any assumption that the New Testament world was "just like ours." Hebrews demands of its readers, for example, a more sophisticated grasp of Scripture than most Christians possess today. Much of its argument, in fact, is based on complex modes of scriptural interpretation. These are strange to us but were common in the first century. The version of Scripture used by Hebrews (as by other New Testament writings) was not Hebrew but Greek. Its citations and allusions are from the Septuagint. This study edition gives some assistance by providing complete Scripture references. Citations in the text are flagged with small letters; passages are identified at the bottom of each page. To fully appreciate Hebrews' virtuosity, study the citations in their original context as well as how Hebrews can turn them to fit its argument (as in 10:5–7).

Hebrews' view of the world is strikingly different from that of present-day Christians in an even more fundamental sense. Hebrews works within a philosophical tradition called

Platonism, which saw a great gulf between the spiritual realm and the material world. Spiritual things are eternal, unchanging; material things are transitory. As a result, spiritual things are both more real and better than the material. For Platonic Jews and Christians, the "spiritual" and "material" realms were understood in terms of "heaven" and "earth."

This is the framework for grasping Hebrews' point about the superiority of Jesus' priesthood. By his resurrection, Jesus entered heaven, where he is a "priest forever" (5:6), in contrast to the Jewish priesthood, which could only be temporary. Likewise the "heavenly sanctuary" is superior to the physical tent of worship described in Scripture (chs. 8–9). The symbolism at times becomes dense and requires patience to disentangle, but the basic point is clear. The human Messiah Jesus now shares God's life in heaven. His priesthood is therefore both the ultimate and eternal "cause of salvation" to others (5:9).

**The Readers**

The original hearers of this sermon had experienced the loss of property and friends (10:32–34). They were tempted to lose hope and seek a more stable framework than that offered by a crucified messiah. Hebrews addresses their longing for stability by offering the hope for "a better homeland, a heavenly one" (11:16). Their experience can be translated into that of every age: all of us in various ways experience loss, alienation, and despair. Hebrews' message to us is as sharp as it was to them: "Today if you hear his voice, harden not your hearts" (4:7). We also are called to go on pilgrimage through our troubled circumstances, looking to Jesus, who is still and always the "leader and perfecter of faith" (12:1).

**The Prologue (1:1–4)**

The opening sentence is elegantly constructed and introduces Hebrews' central themes. First is the contrast between God's partial revelation in the past ("to our fathers") and the perfect revelation now ("to us") made through God's Son, which establishes the basic thesis: Jesus is superior to the old dispensation, or Covenant (see 8:13). Second, Jesus' divine status is clearly expressed by calling him the "image of God." The exalted identity attributed to the Son is similar to that in John and Paul (e.g., see Jn 1:1–4 and 1 Cor 8:6). Third, the prologue states that the way God "spoke" in Jesus was through his death for others (the purification of sins) and his resurrection.

Note the image of enthronement: Jesus "takes his place at the right hand." This alludes to Psalm 110:1, the favorite resurrection psalm of early Christians: "The LORD says to my lord: 'Sit at my right hand while I make your enemies your footstool" (see also 1:13). Hebrews will also exploit the fourth verse of this psalm when the author develops the comparison between Jesus and Melchizedek in chapter 7. The image of enthronement runs throughout the sermon. Jesus is both priest and king. Finally, we notice that Jesus "inherits" a name better than that of the angels. Jesus is here portrayed as a forerunner. If they follow him, Christians also will enter into an inheritance (1:14; 6:12). The mention of angels, in turn, provides a transition to Hebrews' argument.

**The Son is Higher than the Angels (1:5–2:18)**

A series of Scripture citations proves that the Son is superior to angels. The pertinent question for us is, why do angels require putting in place, anyway? Our contemporary view of the world has small room for angels! But in the world of the New Testament, especially in the writings of Judaism, angels were regarded as the most powerful intermediaries between God and humans. The tendency to exalt their role is attested in Galatians 4:9 and Colossians 2:18. What concern does the author address? Jesus in his humanity did not appear so impressive as these "spiritual" beings. He was not only human; he suffered and died. Hebrews must overcome the scandal of a "lowly" Messiah.

Citations from Scripture do not by themselves demonstrate the point. As in other New Testament writings (e.g., Gal 3:1–5), Hebrews argues "the greater" from the fact of the readers' own experience. The work of God's Spirit among them is itself powerful "witness" to the salvation accomplished through Jesus (2:3f). And never content with the speculative, Hebrews drives home the exhortation. This "greater salvation" demands of the readers a greater response of alertness (2:1f).

From the perspective of the power of the Risen Lord, Hebrews takes up the issue of Jesus' "lowliness." On the basis of Psalm 8, the author asserts that Jesus was "lower than the angels" only temporarily. And the reason was so that he could "taste death for everyone," that is, act as priest. On the basis of a messianic reading of Isaiah 8:18f, Hebrews next affirms God's (and the Messiah's) solidarity with humanity. Then, Hebrews turns the tables, and makes Jesus' humanity a positive criterion for authentic priesthood. Because Jesus is one with those he represents before God—he shares the way they are "tested" and the way they "fear death"—he can be a compassionate and merciful priest. It is significant that Hebrews defines priesthood in terms of his personal identity and experience rather than in terms of religious ceremony. Hebrews thereby anticipates an important principle of later doctrine: "what is not assumed [by God] cannot be saved." Precisely because he is human, Jesus can save humanity.

### Jesus, Faithful and Compassionate High Priest (3:1–5:10)

Moses was so central a figure for Jews that he became a natural point of contrast for Christian claims about Jesus (e.g., see Jn 1:17). Hebrews now contrasts Moses as "the servant of [God's] House," and Jesus as "Son over the house" (3:4f). The real contrast in this section, however, is between the people that Moses led and the Christians the author of Hebrews addresses in terms of disobedience and obedient faith (3:7–13).

The argument here uses complex ancient rules for interpreting Scripture. Much is made, for example, of the occurrence of specific words, such as "rest" and "today," without regard for their original contexts. Hebrews asserts that the "rest" to which Moses led the people (the land) was not the "rest of God," namely, God's own life. For that matter, neither did people of old even succeed in entering that earthly rest because of their disobedience. Christians in contrast have hope for the real rest—of God's own life—won by Jesus' resurrection. The point? They are to obey the call of God and not fall away (4:6).

Hebrews has identified obedient faith as the fundamental response demanded by God. The comparison to the wandering Israelites also establishes Hebrews' basic image of the church as the people of God on pilgrimage. The image suggests that the church is not simply an institution like other institutions. It is never fully "at home" in the world. The church exists with reference to a higher goal—the "heavenly city"—toward which it must steadily move like a pilgrim, although this side of death the goal is never reached. Pilgrims need the sort of attentiveness, patience, obedience, and endurance demanded by Hebrews. Above all, they need hope (see 6:19). They can move lightly through this worldly existence only if convinced that their destination is truly "greater" than their present abode.

Hebrews points the reader again to the leader of the pilgrimage, the "apostle and high priest of our confession" (3:1). In the description of Jesus as priest (4:14–5:9), Hebrews combines what has come to be called both "high" and "low" Christologies (understandings of Jesus). Jesus is definitely "from above"; he is God's Son in the fullest sense, but he is also fully human, "from below." It is his human existence that defines the path "all the children" are to follow. As priest, he is exemplar. Jesus is not only "faithful" (3:1f) as all are called to be; he "learned obedience from what he suffered" (5:8). The full implications of this statement will become clear only later (see

#### Pilgrimage of the Church

VATICAN COUNCIL II, using this image of pilgrimage, suggested that the church is not simply an institution like other institutions. It is never fully "at home" in the world. The church is steadily moving toward the "heavenly city" like a pilgrim, although on this side of death the goal is never reached.

#### "High" and "Low" Christologies

*High:* Jesus is "from above," God's son in the fullest sense. The emphasis is on the divinity of Jesus.

*Low:* Jesus is also fully human, "from below." The emphasis is on Jesus' humanity.

12:1–11), but we already understand that Jesus' suffering deepened his faith, and his obedience was itself a form of suffering. Jesus progressively became, in his humanity, perfect Son of God, and therefore the "leader" of all who follow him.

### Jesus' Eternal Priesthood and Sacrifice (5:11–10:39)

The long middle section of the sermon argues for the superiority of Jesus' priesthood. It begins with an extended exhortation (5:11–6:20), and then focuses on Jesus' priestly identity and activity (7–10). Hebrews presupposes the readers' grasp of the basic teaching about Christ (6:1), but, in a rebuke as much as an exhortation, he urges them beyond the milk fit for babes to the meat meant for the mature (compare Paul's use of this imagery in 1 Cor 3:1–3). This "mature teaching" is by no means a matter of moving beyond Jesus or abandoning Jesus. Such apos-

**Jesus and Melchizedek (7:1–28)**

Both appearances of Melchizedek in Scripture point toward Christ:

Gn 14:17–20: Melchizedek was named a priest of God (although he was a Gentile), whom even Abraham acknowledged. A priest descended from Melchizedek would be superior to one descended from Abraham.

Psalm 110:4: Melchizedek's being without beginning or end (Scripture records neither his birth nor his death) is an anticipation of the Son of God whose priesthood is eternally valid.

In his resurrection, Jesus became priest, "by the power of a life that cannot be destroyed" (7:16). He remains "forever" (7:24). His sacrifice is "once for all" (7:27). "He lives forever to make intercession" (7:25). The Jewish priesthood descended from Abraham cannot compete.

**The Old and New Covenants (8:1–13)**

God's revelation in Jesus does not merely continue the former story, it raises it to a new plane. Jesus' death and resurrection mark an absolute beginning. Platonism is evident in 8:1–6: Moses' desert sanctuary is "the copy and shadow of the heavenly sanctuary" (8:5). Heaven is greater than earth. Hebrews turns this Platonism into an interpretation of history: The old covenant is a "shadow" of the new, pointing to but replaced by the work of Jesus. Hebrews exploits Jeremiah's promise of a new covenant "in the heart" to affirm that the old order has in fact passed.

**The Priestly Act of Jesus (9:1–10, 18)**

The contrast is between the ancient cult and Jesus' death and resurrection. The complicated imagery is daunting. It would be helpful to read through Exodus 25–27 (the Dwelling in the Wilderness) and Leviticus 16 (ritual for the Day of Atonement). Hebrews stresses two points: First, Jewish sacrifices had to be repeated, so they were not effective; Jesus entered "real" life, so his sacrifice is eternally valid. Second, the old cult sacrifices animals. Jesus gave his own life in obedience to God. Now all can enter the sanctuary.

**Exhortation to Fidelity (10:19–39)**

In the light of this "greater salvation," Hebrews warns again of the consequences of apostasy (10:26–31). Despite their losses and trials, Christians are called to a still deeper loyalty (10:32–30). By mentioning endurance and faith as requisites for receiving the promise (10:36–38), Hebrews prepares for its final stirring exhortation.

tasy from Christ Hebrews calls "recrucifying the Son of God" (6:5). Indeed, God's promise based on Jesus' resurrection is utterly reliable; Jesus is the "anchor of the soul" (6:19), to whose priesthood God has bound himself by oath (6:13). The nature and implications of Jesus' priesthood, however, are precisely what require explication. By it the Christian hope is made secure. By it Christians are able to become "imitators of those who, through faith and patience, are inheriting the promises" (6:12).

The consideration of Jesus as priest is the climax of the "lesser to the greater" argument. But because the procedures and symbols of Jewish cult are foreign to us today, this section makes for some of the hardest reading in the New Testament. It is important to remember from the start that Hebrews' argument is based on the Christian experience of the Spirit and conviction of the life of God (2:3–4). Only this premise makes Hebrews' reinterpretation of Scripture reasonable. Once that premise is granted, then the major turning points of the exposition make sense.

### Examples, Discipline, Disobedience (11:1–12:29)

The sermon's long argument reaches its climax in this exhortation to faith, understood as loyalty, endurance, and hope. The recital of heroes and heroines of the past serves to provide examples for the readers to imitate. Why? Just as the listeners had lost property and had been persecuted, so also had the believers who preceded them. Yet the ancestors persevered in the search for a better homeland (11:14). The repetition of the phrase "by faith" summons the readers to join ranks with those on pilgrimage to God's presence. Unlike the desert generation that fell by the way because of disobedience, they continued faithful, even though they themselves did not receive the full promise (11:29)! It was left to Jesus, the "leader and perfecter of faith" (12:2) to provide complete access to God through his death and resurrection. Because Christians can now look to him (12:2), there is solid reason to hope while still on the journey.

By summoning such a "cloud of witnesses" (12:1) to support the commitment of the readers, Hebrews states a conviction that eventually became an article of the Christian creed, "the communion of saints." Those struggling for God on earth are not alone. They are joined in a larger fellowship of faith with those who have died and who now support them with their prayers. The people of faith have solidarity in hope. This is not blind optimism: the alienation, suffering, and persecution experienced by the ancients is not trivialized. And Jesus, before he could sit on the throne, had to "endure the cross, despising its shame" (12:2). Jesus' human response to God is the perfect example for the faith of Christians. Faith is always "evidence of things not seen" (11:1), which means that it is always a risk taken in the face of a pain more palpably present than the promise. Thus, also, the Christian experience of prayer has as an essential component the "dark night" of the soul when God seems more absent than present.

The connection between Sonship and suffering continues in 12:5–13. The remarks about fathers disciplining their children at first seem banal if not regressive. But when we remember that Jesus, "although Son, learned obedience from what he suffered" (5:8), we come to appreciate the profound correspondence between Christology and Christian existence. What we suffer in our lives, if we can perceive and accept such suffering in faith, enables God to shape Jesus' own "sonship" in us. Being educated as children of God requires a painful transformation, for the goal is the holy God (12:10).

### Final Exhortation, Blessing, Greetings (13:1–25)

Although the final chapter is made up mainly of practical instructions, it is closely joined to the theological argument of chapters 1–12. Notice, for example, the plea to "imitate the faith" of leaders, the motivation of that faith being the eternal priesthood of Jesus who is "the same yesterday, today, and forever" (13:7–8).

The mix of advice about hospitality, marriage, and possessions, with the command to "go to Jesus outside the camp . . . for we have here no lasting city but seek the one that is to come" is typical of this sermon and of early Christianity's understanding of existence generally:

• Christians live in the world like other people and participate in its structures. But they are not defined by this world or its values, even its religious values (13:9–11).

• No institutional cult or sacrificial priesthood is made lawful by this severe writing; everything necessary has been accomplished already by Jesus.

• Christians are defined not by their liturgy, but by their following the one who suffered "outside the gate, to consecrate the people by his own blood" (13:12).

• Christians are never entirely at ease in this world or even in the church. They are pilgrims, struggling toward the "God of peace" into whose care the final blessing (13:20–21) entrusts the readers of this profound and powerful sermon.

### Questions for Discussion and Reflection

***Group Sharing/Discussion***

1. Why does the author address the issues of the difference between Jesus and the angels?

2. Hebrews describes the Church as the people of God on pilgrimage. Describe what this means in Hebrews.

3. Priesthood is described in Hebrews as identity and experience of Jesus, not ritually as in Jewish tradition. Why does Hebrews so define Jesus' priesthood?

4. Hebrews tells us that "our God is a consuming fire" (12:29). What might this mean?

5. Hebrews' approach to Jesus is considered containing both "low" and "high" Christology. Give an example of the "high" and "low" approach of studying Christ.

***In Our Lives***

1. Read Hebrews out loud from the beginning to the end. If you are in a group, share parts according to sections of the sermon.

2. Hebrews' view of the world is Platonic—there is a gulf between the spiritual realm and the material world. The spiritual things are more real and better than the material. How does this view influence the author's understanding of Jesus' priesthood? Do you see any effects of the Platonic influence in your world?

3. How is the Church as institution different from other institutions?

4. In that "cloud of witnesses" spoken of in Hebrews, who are some of these ancient witnesses who pray for the community on pilgrimage? Name some who support you in your pilgrimage.

5. Hebrews' original hearers of this sermon had suffered loss of friends and property. They were tempted to lose hope and look for new hope in a framework other than a crucified messiah. All of us may experience loss, alienation, and despair. How is your Christian faith a source of hope?

***Individual/Personal Reflection/Action***

1. Jesus "learned obedience from what he suffered." Reflect upon how suffering in faith opens us to God's action of shaping Jesus' own sonship in us.

2. Take some time to reflect on the difference between "being in the world but not of the world" and "enduring this life with an eye on heaven." What pilgrim steps could you take on this journey?

# THE CATHOLIC LETTERS AND THE BOOK OF REVELATION

## JAMES READING GUIDE

### *At a Glance*

| | |
|---|---|
| Who is the main player? | James, a relative of Jesus |
| What should I look for? | This is an exhortation concerned with ethical conduct in the tradition of Jewish wisdom literature such as in Proverbs or Ben Sira. James emphasized sound teaching and responsible moral behavior based on ethical norms derived from conversion, baptism, forgiveness and judgment. |
| When was this written? | This is a very Jewish work, written in excellent Greek style. Some attribute it to James of Jerusalem via a secretary, which would date it before A.D. 70; others think it is more like a pseudonymous work of a later period, around A.D. 90–100. |
| Where did these events occur? | Jerusalem (if James is author) or in the Greek Diaspora if later. |
| Why was this book written? | This is a "catholic," that is, universal letter. Unlike Paul's letters to specific churches, this is addressed more generally to the universal church. It is concerned with traditional values. |
| What is the story? | Six movements of this exhortation are: (1) worldly values, where competition reigns without God, versus wholeness of faith and works; (2) discrimination and the law of love; (3) faith without works is dead; (4) speech should conform to faith; (5) friendship with the world and friendship with God are opposing ways of life; and (6) three forms of arrogance and the proper uses of speech in the church. |

## Before Beginning

### James as Moral Exhortation

Letter writing was so popular in antiquity that the epistolary form became a package capable of holding many materials. In the case of James (as noted in the NAB introduction to James), the letter format is the frame for a moral exhortation intended for a general readership.

Before turning to an analysis of the text, it is helpful to consider some of its literary features and major themes. James is not terribly difficult to understand; its style is lucid, its message is straightforward.

### The Writing

The form of Greco-Roman moral exhortation called *parenesis* was concerned with reminding readers of traditional values rather than with constructing theory. Such reminders often took the form of short maxims. James's first chapter in particular has such maxims, which are less connected to each other than to other sections of the composition. Chapters 2 through 5 take the form of short essays. The maxims in chapter 1 set themes that are developed in those essays. Note how the "control of the tongue" in 1:26 is elaborated by 3:1–12. Moral exhortation also presented models of virtue for readers to imitate. In James, the figures of Abraham, Rahab, Job, and Elijah provide examples from Scripture of the practical virtue James encourages.

James, however, is more than a moral treatise. It is a religious writing that uses the symbols of Scripture. James resembles the Wisdom tradition in its use of maxims and in advocating a "wisdom from above" as the measure of life (3:13–18). James uses the language and perspective of the prophets in its attack on rich oppressors (5:1–6). James also uses the Law. For James, both the Decalogue (Ten Commandments) and the Law of Love are binding for Christians. They are to be understood, however, in light of the teachings of Jesus. James has many allusions to the words of Jesus (e.g., see 1:12; 2:5; 3:12; 5:12).

**The Message**

James advocates living faith and practical love. His concern is behavior. Like other moralists of his age, he is impatient with fine words that go nowhere (e.g., see 1:22–25). Above all, faith that is not expressed in love is a charade.

James's target is the Christian who is "of two minds" (1:8; 4:8). This person wants to live by two standards at once: that of God, and that of the world. James demands a choice. Not only speech but also the use of possessions and the practice of fairness within the community lie within the range of his concern. He especially attacks envy, which perfectly illustrates the morals of "the world" opposed to God (see esp. 3:13–4:10).

But James does not lack theology. He bases his exhortations on the one God who creates and judges all humanity. James centers attention on God rather than on Christ.

**The Two Measures (1:1–27)**

Although chapter 1 is made up of separate aphorisms with only loose internal connections, the chapter does more than simply provide a table of contents for the essays to follow. The opening statements also make clear that humans must live by either one sort of measure or another.

The first verses have some word-linkages, but they don't form an easily followed argument. The aphorisms are not, however, simply a random collection of wise sayings. The maxims in chapter 1 provide something of an index to the contents of chapters 2 through 5. The theme of enduring trials (1:2–4, 12–15) is developed in 5:7–11; the opposition between rich and poor (1:9–11) recurs in 4:13–5:6. Control of the tongue (1:19–21) is expanded in 3:1–12. Carrying out words in speech (1:22–26) is enlarged by 2:14–26. The theme of true wisdom (1:5–8, 16–18) is argued by 3:13–4:10. The prayer of faith (1:6f) is amplified by 5:12–18.

The aphorisms also introduce the basic pattern that structures the whole of James: the contrast between the measure of the world and the measure of God. The measure of the world is expressed by envy: "desire conceives and brings forth sin, and when sin reaches maturity, it gives birth to death" (1:15). The values of the world are self-deceptive (1:16, 27) and are expressed in wrathful behavior (1:19) and every sort of excess (1:21), especially the pursuit of illusory wealth (1:11). These values are based on the perception of life as a closed system; God has no part. Therefore all humans are in competition: one person's gain is another's loss.

The measure of faith is the opposite. All creation—life itself—is a gift: "all good giving and every perfect gift is from above, coming down from the Father of lights" (1:17). Because God has created humans by "the word of truth" (1:18), humans are able to receive the implanted word from him (1:21) and live in the way God does, giving "generously and ungrudgingly" (1:5). In the Greek, these words suggest the opposite of envy, which always grasps for more. Life by God's measure is expressed by "care for orphans and widows in their affliction" (1:27). One is thereby "unstained by the world" by living according to a different value system (1:27).

As in Hebrews and 1 Peter, Christians are regarded as pilgrims and sojourners. They are not hostile to the world but neither are they defined

**Shared Faith**

PAUL AND JAMES each interpret the same verse from the Old Testament—"Abram put his faith in the LORD, who attributed it to him as an act of righteousness" (Gn 15:6)—to support his own view (Paul in Gal 3:6–14, James in Jas 2:21–24). For Paul, the believer's justification comes through faith, not works (Rom 4:16–5:2); for James, "faith of itself, if it does not have works, is dead" (2:17). The conflict, however, is more apparent than real. For Paul, faith is primarily trust in God (Rom 4:5), a sense of the word that James also shares (1:5); but, in his critique of faith, James means by it essentially the assent to ideas about God without any personal relationship or commitment to inform them: "Even the demons believe" (2:19). James sees works as acts springing from the believer's love for God (2:14), whereas for Paul works are the external observances of ritual, like circumcision, regarded in isolation from any connection to one's relationship to God. For both, the key is understanding where the center is: one's relationship to God.

by it. James's whole effort is to persuade those "of two minds" (1:8) to live by God's measure, which is the perfect "wisdom from above" (see 3:15).

**Discrimination and the Law of Love (2:1–13)**

The first essay reveals a voice that resembles that of Paul in Galatians. James uses the same oral, dialogical style known as the diatribe. Vivid and lively, it is filled with rhetorical questions, exclamations, and abrupt transitions. The effect is a direct challenge to every reader—then and now. The challenge is even more clearly heard when the text is read aloud.

Christians, James says, must live consistently with their convictions. "Faith in our . . . Lord Jesus Christ" (2:1) is incompatible with any form of discrimination within the community. James sketches a lively scene that probably reflects a general situation rather than a local incident. The context is judgment within the community, like that carried out in the Diaspora synagogue to settle disputes. In the background is the injunction of Leviticus 19:15 that forbids partiality in judgment. How plausible and true to life is his portrayal of a community pandering to rich members and slighting their poor!

That James intends us to see discrimination as an offense against love as well as faith in his allusion to Leviticus 19:15 is shown immediately by his explicit citation of Leviticus 19:18 in 2:8. The "law of love" is also identified by Jesus as the summation of Scripture. James calls it the "royal" law, by which he means the standard regulating relations in the community. It is the "law of the kingdom." James spells out this commandment by alluding to the Ten Commandments (2:11) and also to the specific commandments found in the original context of Leviticus 19 that accompany the original exhortation "love your neighbor as yourself" (see Jas 4:11; 5:4, 9, 12, 20). James says that breaking any commandment means breaking the whole law, because sin is not against a law but against a lawgiver. In other words, committing a specific wrong is more than simply disobeying a rule; it is a break in a personal relationship. Faith in the one God excludes picking and choosing between commandments, just as it excludes picking and choosing between fellow Christians.

**Active Faith (2:14–26)**

The following section is often misunderstood. Because James speaks of "faith" and "works" (terms often used by Paul), people think James is responding to Paul's teaching. In fact, his perspective is entirely different. James speaks not of the commandments of the law, but of active faith. He is a moralist and is concerned with the way speech gets converted to action. Like all moralists, his concern is efficacy: "Of what use is it?" The examples of Abraham and Rahab illustrate James's point. Their faith expressed itself in effective action. Abraham was willing to sacrifice his son; Rahab showed hospitality to God's scouts. James is not debating with Paul over the question of how people are saved. His exhortation is intensely practical and arises from the situation pictured in 2:14–16: Pious talk does not feed or clothe the needy. Such faith is as "dead" as a corpse; such religion is fraudulent (see 1:26f).

We discover here two distinctive aspects of James. His teaching is not based on what is specifically Christian, but on faith in the one God shared by other monotheistic traditions. For James, the "faith of Christ" and teachings of Jesus do not oppose but refine Torah. James therefore also contains the beginning of a genuine social ethic. His moral teaching is not confined to the Christian community; it can be extended to the world. If there is no partiality in the community, based in the law of God, then forms of discrimination in the wider world can be combated on the same basis. If sister and brother in the community are to be fed, then the community as such should also feed the needy of the world in every changing circumstance.

James also warns us that this can cut both ways. If the Christian community does not live up to its own calling and is unjust, then it bears no witness to the world and is itself subject to condemnation (2:5–7).

### The Power of the Tongue (3:1–12)

James's concern for the proper use of speech (see 1:19, 26) now becomes thematic. Preoccupation with speech is typical of ancient moralists. Taciturnity as a sign of wisdom was proverbial (e.g., see Prv 10:19; 11:12). That such "control of the tongue" was almost insurmountably difficult to achieve was also well known. James therefore considers control of speech to be a mark of perfection (3:2).

James makes two related points using conventional imagery from Greek philosophy. The first compares the tongue to a horse's bit or a ship's rudder, showing not only how a small organ can direct a large body, but also how much that organ itself, with its disproportionate power, needs to be controlled by someone with a sense of direction and good judgment. James's second point concerns the potential for harm in uncontrolled speech. It is like a flame "setting the entire course of our lives on fire" (3:6).

The capacity of speech to do evil is more impressive than its power for good: "No human being can tame the tongue. It is a restless evil, full of deadly poison" (3:8). Sadly, the story of human discourse from the Garden of Eden to the latest garden party only confirms James's harsh judgment. No wonder the ancients valued taciturnity: Better no speech than destructive speech.

> **The Value of Silence**
>
> THE DANGERS INHERENT in speech also undergird the value of silence in the monastic/contemplative tradition of both the East and the West. Silence is the necessary precondition to "welcome the word that . . . is able to save your souls" (1:21).

The theological implications of speech are central to James's exhortation. In 3:9–12, he contrasts the speech that "blesses God" with that which "curses human beings" who are made in God's image. Once again James combats the "two-minded" person, who thinks that it is possible to have a relationship with God that disregards human obligations. As in 2:14–17, James insists that religious language and practical human care must go together. The same source cannot yield two kinds of water, and a Christian should not speak with two tongues. Action should follow conviction; speech should conform to faith.

### Friendship with God or the World (3:13–4:10)

Although the paragraph division of modern translations hides what is clearer in Greek, 3:13–4:10 is a self-contained essay stating the central theological framework for understanding James as a whole.

Formally, it is a call of conversion. In 3:13–4:6, James presents an indictment. In 4:7–10, he exhorts his readers to repentance. A powerful spatial metaphor governs both parts, a contrast between what comes "from above" (true wisdom, God's Gift), and that which originates "from below" (false wisdom, human arrogance). Correspondingly, the readers are told to "humble" themselves, so that God can "exalt" them (4:10). The spatial metaphor points to differing measures of reality. That "from below" James calls "the world." It treats life as though God had no claim; success is measured by human accomplishment and acquisition. But God's

> **Envy**
>
> ENVY COMES FROM the "wisdom from below." The point clearly is that God's spirit has nothing to do with envy. James associates with envy all the vices commonly attributed to it in Greek moral discourse, especially social unrest, murder, and war.
>
> Why is envy so singled out? Because its underlying assumption is that your gain is my loss. This is the opposite of the Spirit of community, where all gain by anyone's growth, and all rejoice in anyone's good fortune. Envy causes me to sorrow when another has something that I lack. And when life is measured simply in terms of what I possess—"I am what I have"—then for another to have and me to lack is intolerable. Envy drives the acquisitive instinct: "you covet" (4:2). It is a short step to conflict, war, and murder, between individuals and among nations. Like other Greek moralists, James assigns the cause of war to envy (4:1–3). It is remarkable that this passage, which alone in the New Testament analyzes the causes of human conflict, should play so little role in moral discussions of war and peace.

measure says that everything comes as a gift from "the Father of lights" (1:17), and that arrogance is empty pretense. James, as always, has as his main target the "two-minded" person (4:8) who wants to live by both measures at once. Within this call to conversion, James develops the theme of envy as exemplifying the measure of the world.

At the climax of the indictment (4:4), James accuses his readers of being "adulterers" because they have broken covenant both with God and with their fellow humans. The covenant is about loyalty and love. There is no connection between those attitudes and the self-seeking of envy. James also uses the language of Greek philosophy concerning "friendship." He contrasts "friendship with the world" and "friendship with God" as opposing ways of life. James is not condemning the world understood as the place of human activity or God's creation. Rather, it is a system of values that excludes consideration of God. To be "friends with the world" therefore means to live by a measure that leaves God's claim aside.

To this closed system James opposes the measure of faith: God is the source of "every good and perfect gift" (1:17). God "gives more grace" to the humble even while resisting the arrogant (4:6). God is not envious of humans but gives to all generously and without grudging (see 1:5). Those who submit to God are therefore also lifted up by God (4:10). Their tears of repentance will rapidly turn to joy, because—a remarkable statement—when humans draw near to God, God also draws near to them (4:8).

**Against Arrogance (4:11–5:6)**

James now turns to three forms of arrogance, which exemplify life according to the measure of the world. The first is the practice of slandering a neighbor (4:1f). Such critical speech naturally involves both a condemnation of the other and an implied assertion of one's own superiority: "I am in a position to judge." James insists that such judgment breaks the law of love (see Lv 19:16) and reminds his readers that the lawgiver is also the judge. God alone can both save and destroy life (see 1:21).

A second form of arrogance is demonstrated by those who make great business plans without ever considering the fragile nature of their own existence (4:13–17). Once more, their speech gives them away; they assume control over the present and the future. James comments: "You are boasting in your arrogance. All such boasting is evil" (4:16). The speech of one living by God's measure is also revealing: "If the LORD wills . . . ." This is more than pious talk; it refers all of life and all of life's projects to the one who gives and can alone sustain life. (Compare Jesus' parable of the Rich Fool, Lk 12:16–21.)

Finally, with a prophetic rage like that of Amos, James attacks the insolence of the rich who withhold wages from their laborers. The security gained by such fraud is illusory; the rich fatten themselves for the day of judgment (5:5). They "know the right thing to do but do not do it"

(4:17), which James defines as sin. How do they know? Because the scriptural context for the law of love in Leviticus 19:18 states plainly, "you shall not withhold overnight the wages of your laborer" (Lv 19:13).

**Patience, Plain Speech, Prayer (5:7–20)**

Having called the double-minded to conversion and excoriated the arrogant, James turns to the community's inner life. Speech is again the underlying theme, this time with reference to the proper uses of speech in the church.

Christians should speak plainly. In 5:12 James repeats the commandment of Jesus (Mt 5:33–37) that speech should be unadorned and straightforward, without oaths. And in his last exhortation, James encourages the sort of mutual correction that can build up the identity of the church (5:20).

Because the church is constituted by the word of truth (1:18), it should above all express that truth in its communal life of prayer. James enumerates the sorts of prayer that are appropriate to the community's diverse circumstances (5:13f) and then elaborates the prayer with anointing for a sick member. This ritual is the basis for the sacrament of anointing for the sick and has roots in the healing ministry of Jesus (see 5:15). James's last example from Torah is the prophet Elijah, whose prayer demonstrates the power of faith for those who live by God's measure (5:17f; cf. 1:6–8). These final exhortations, down to earth and humane, summarize beautifully the character of James, who from beginning to end finds wisdom in practical faith and active love.

**Questions for Discussion and Reflection**

***Group Sharing/Discussion***

1. James's epistle is a moral exhortation reminding readers of traditional values. What are some of the qualities of this form as seen in James?

2. James speaks to Christians who are of "two minds" (1:8; 4:8). Explain these two standards, the measure of the world and the measure of God. What are some examples of these?

3. James's first essay (2:1–13) is a diatribe. What are some qualities in James of this form of rhetoric?

4. For James breaking any commandment means breaking the whole law. What does he mean by this?

5. Why is proper control of speech a mark of perfection?

***In Our Lives***

1. James assigns the cause of war to envy (4:1–3). It is remarkable that this passage, which alone in the New Testament analyzes the causes of human conflict, should play so small a role in discussions of war and peace. Why is envy such a driving force for conflict among nations, family members, and ethnic groups?

2. "Faith in our . . . Lord Jesus Christ" is incompatible with any form of discrimination within the community says James. Who does our society judge should be kept on the fringes? What does our own community do about that? What else can our faith community do?

3. Read James's passage on control of the tongue (3:1–12). Recall experiences in your life or the life of others that confirm this strong message.

4. James contrasts "friendship with the world" and "friendship with God" (3:13–4:10). How would you describe these opposing ways of life in modern terms?

***Individual/Personal Reflection/Action***

1. James describes three forms of arrogance (4:11–5:6), that is, slandering your neighbor, "planning," and stealing from the wages of the poor. Take some time to reflect on these forms of arrogance as they touch your life.

2. James teaches, "Do not complain about one another that you may not be judged." Take time in the coming day to pray about this instruction and how it may fit into your life.

3. Those who submit to God are lifted up by God (4:10). Recall a time when you turned to God and reflect on the experience of listening for God in your heart. Whisper a prayer of thanks that God is with us always. Ask God to help you remember to listen often.

# 1 PETER READING GUIDE

***At a Glance***

| | |
|---|---|
| Who are the main players? | "Peter" Christian communities of Asia Minor |
| What should I look for? | Note the difference between social order and virtue. This letter is not an inspired blueprint of an ideal social order or family structure. What we find is the best moral teaching applied to the real world of that age. Social structures and related relationships of the past cannot be transferred to the present. But, then and now, virtues of good order, mutual respect, obedience and authority are very much needed. |
| When was this written? | Tradition regarded Peter as the author; therefore, the letter was dated prior to A.D. 67. Modern scholars, however, for good reasons would date this at the end of the first century or the beginning of the second. |
| Where did these events occur? | The letter was addressed to the Christian communities in the five provinces of Asia Minor, which is modern Turkey. |
| Why was this book written? | This is a letter of exhortation and encouragement to Gentile Christians who were recently converted from paganism. They find themselves still living among pagan symbols and social structures and are experiencing suffering and persecution. |
| What is the story? | Peter tries to inspire the "chosen sojourners" to live as God's people, remembering Christ's resurrection and future hope. He appeals to their experience of baptism as new birth and to the suffering and death of Christ as a source of salvation and example. He warns them to keep their distance from the values of the world, yet give witness to their neighbors. Be watchful, for the time for serious decision is now. Those who suffer will share Christ's glory. |

## Before Beginning

First Peter bears all the marks of a real letter. It was written to Christians scattered throughout the provinces of Asia Minor. Although written in clear and even elegant Greek, and although containing an exhortation and witness (5:12) at once simple and profound, 1 Peter is given far less attention than it deserves. Partly this is because many contemporary scholars think that the letter is pseudonymous and a product of second generation rather than primitive Christianity. There are, however, excellent reasons for considering Peter the apostle to have been the author of 1 Peter. In any case, the authority of New Testament writings does not derive from the identity of the author. Whether it was the apostle or someone writing in his name, this letter speaks powerfully to a situation of early believers and retains enduring value for readers in every age.

## A Letter to the Gentile Christians

### The Situation of the Readers

Because the letter is addressed to Christians spread over a large geographical area (1:1), we do not expect the detailed treatment of local problems. By reading between the lines, however, we are able to learn something about their shared characteristics.

#### Who Were They?

1. They seem to have been recently converted. Peter reminds them repeatedly of their former

life of vice (1:18–20; 4:3–4), as well as their initiation into the messianic community through baptism (1:3; 1:22–2:3).

2. They seem, furthermore, to be direct converts from paganism rather than from Judaism.

3. They continued to live among the symbols and social structures of the Empire. They inevitably felt pulled between an allegiance to their new calling and an attraction to the values of the world they had left.

4. They were, finally, converts who were experiencing suffering. On the basis of 4:12, some have considered this to be a state-sponsored persecution such as was later the lot of Christians. But Peter's positive view of the state (2:12–17) does not fit that reconstruction. It is more likely that Peter's readers were experiencing the sort of verbal abuse and social ostracism that Christians experienced from the beginning. The suffering was no less serious. Martyrdom is painful but swift. The corrosion of confidence is slower but terribly effective.

### Christian Apologetic

First Peter can best be understood as a form of apologetic literature. This form of writing originated among Diaspora Jews and was taken over by Christians. Ostensibly it explains one's distinctive beliefs to the wider world in terms outsiders can understand. Indirectly, it supports community identity. First Peter has many of the characteristics of this genre. It is positive and open to the dominant culture. Christians are not to flee the world or its structures. They are to be good citizens within those social structures. And they are to be ready to demonstrate by their behavior and their speech that they pose no threat to others (3:15–16).

At the same time, Peter works to build up the identity of the community.

1. He reminds his readers that they are called to holiness and a standard of behavior higher than that of their neighbors (2:11–12; 4:1–2).

2. He reminds them of the fundamental transformation they had undergone in their baptism.

3. He assures them that although they are "strangers" in the world (2:11), they are part of the "household of God" (2:4–5; 4:17).

In doing so, Peter appropriates for these new Gentile believers all the scriptural titles and symbols used of Israel, to give them a sense of continuity with God's people, even though once they were "no people." In 1 Peter we observe a thoroughly Gentile Christianity regarding itself as the "New Israel," taking up a place in the Diaspora not against the world but as a witness to the world.

### The Greeting (1:1–2)

The greeting of this circular letter establishes more than the simple identification of author and addressees. No need to elaborate the simple designation, "Peter, apostle of Jesus Christ," for Peter's authority is unquestioned (see, in contrast, 2 Pt). But the "dispersion" of Asia Minor has religious as well as geographical connotations. We see here a theme found also in James and Hebrews and in the Christian literature of the second century: Christians are in exile from their true homeland in heaven so long as they are on earth. They are, in fact, "sojourners" precisely because they have been "chosen" by God and have an identity distinct from that of their neighbors. They should therefore cultivate attitudes appropriate to exiles and pilgrims (e.g., see 2:11). The greeting also reminds the readers of the rich complexity of their experience of God: The Father has chosen them; the Son saved them by his obedient sacrifice; and the Spirit has sanctified them.

### The Gift and Call of God (1:3–21)

The opening prayer (1:3–9) is based on the blessing formula of Jewish worship: God is blessed for his gifts to humans. In this case, Peter gives thanks for the new life his readers have been granted through the resurrection of Jesus. Their new life is real, yet not complete. Their inheritance is one that is kept for them in heaven (1:4f). They, of course, still remain on earth. This tension establishes them as pilgrims and sojourners. As their salvation "waits for them," so also must they "wait for it." In the meantime, they must experience the trials and sufferings inherent to the life of faith (1:6f). Peter places his readers between the "already" of God's grace and the "not yet" of salvation fully achieved (1:9), in a manner typical of New Testament writings. But what they hope for is secure, a "living hope" (1:3), because it is based not simply on human longing, but in the "power of God" at work among them (1:4).

### Where Is the Place of the Historical Jewish People?

IT MUST BE confessed that 1 Peter simply does not take them into account. He appropriates the symbols of Torah for the exclusive use of Gentile believers. Readers today cannot expect to find in this text an answer to the many questions concerning the relations of Christians to Jews, for 1 Peter does not address them.

Despite the fact that his readers have converted from paganism, Peter inserts them into the story of Israel. In speaking of an "inheritance in heaven," Peter implies a contrast to the "inheritance of the land," which was the hope of Israel. Likewise, 1:10–12 develops a contrast between stages in the story. Peter asserts that the prophets of old did not speak of their own times (1:12), but spoke of the "sufferings destined for Christ and the glories to follow them" (1:11). Three aspects of this striking statement deserve notice.

1. The superiority of the Christians' present experience is clearly asserted; as in Hebrews, the claims of the earlier covenant are made secondary. What the Christians have received in the gospel transcends even what angels can know (1:12).

2. Scripture is taken over completely as messianic prophecy. Everything in Scripture points to Jesus.

3. As in Luke-Acts, the pattern of the Messiah is spelled out in terms of "suffering, then glory." That his readers must follow after this same pattern becomes explicit later in the letter.

Having asserted the reality of God's gift, Peter now sketches the demands it places on those who receive it (1:13–21). They are to direct their lives by the new form of existence given to them. This means a radical obedience to the giver of the gift, an obedience spelled out in terms of holiness (1:15f). As their lives have changed, so must their behavior. They must not act as they formerly did but are to become "different." They are to shape themselves in a manner in harmony with the one who "ransomed" them with the gift of the "precious blood of Christ" (1:18f). Peter again calls his readers "sojourners" (1:17). Jews of the Diaspora were to be different from pagans; Christians are to be "different" (holy) in the world as they wait for the fulfillment of their salvation (see 1:9). They are not defined by the norms of others (1:14, 18), but by their allegiance to God so that "your faith and hope are in God" (1:21).

#### A Gospel People (1:22–2:10)

To strengthen their grasp on their special identity, Peter reminds his readers of the basis of their new life in "the living and abiding word of God" (1:23). By this, Peter explicitly means the good news (1:25). This is the message of a crucified Messiah who was raised to new life. By the obedient acceptance of that strange proclamation, they were given "new birth" (1:23). Immediately, however, Peter asserts the need for them to grow. The "spiritual milk" they now imbibe is appropriate to new converts who have just "tasted and seen that the Lord is good" (see also 1 Cor 3:1–3; Heb 6:13); they are to mature "in Christ" by patterning their life according to a new standard of moral behavior. They must leave aside deceit in favor of truth, envy for love.

Peter is not only concerned with the transformation of individuals, but as much as Paul, with the identity of the community also. In 2:4–10, therefore, he reminds them of their communal identity as God's house and people. This section interweaves scriptural passages and allusions. The cross-references provided in the NAB provide valuable assistance. The choice of passages is strikingly similar to that in Romans 9:25–33. While it's possible that Peter used Romans, it is more likely that both Paul and Peter used community traditions of scriptural interpretation developed from the first days of the church.

The first set of quotations (2:6–8) portrays the paradox of Christian faith. The stone that God intended to be the basis for his people Israel was rejected by them; yet the rejected one became the basis of a new people, a "spiritual house" made up of living persons (2:4). The reference here is clearly to the crucified Jesus who was a scandal (a stone that caused stumbling) to his fellow Jews, who expected a messiah with more obvious and impressive credentials than suffering for others (see 1 Cor 1:18–23).

For the Christian community, however, the rejected Messiah is the basis for a new life and shared identity. In the second set of texts, Peter strings together the most precious epithets applied to Israel as God's people in Torah. Now they apply to these Gentiles "once no people, but now God's people." In the messianic community, these aliens have a home (see also Eph 2:19–22).

**Life within the World's Structures (2:11–3:7)**

Christians are to maintain distance from the values of this world as "aliens and sojourners" (2:11). At the same time, they must live within the social structures of the world. Peter is convinced that if they are good citizens, they will turn away slander and persecution. The practice of "good works" is the community's basic witness (2:12).

Peter uses the traditional form of "household ethics" to sketch the Christians' social obligations. Greek philosophy had elaborated the mutual duties of people who lived in a stratified social order. Over the empire as a whole, the emperor was considered head of the household. In individual families, husbands ruled wives, parents ruled children, and masters ruled slaves. This was simply the conventional arrangement of that time. Neither Paul (see Col 3:18–4:1) nor Peter thought that the Christian message demanded the dismantling of society's structures.

In 2:13–17, Peter portrays the empire and its agents in positive terms. Submission to legitimate authority is both right and expedient, because the state punishes only the wicked: Such an outlook is inconceivable if Christians were in fact being harassed by the state as such. Yet, even here, the relationship with God is primary. Social obligations, if they conflict with that relationship, must give way to it: "Be free, yet without using freedom as a pretext for evil, but as slaves of God" (2:16). Obedience to God comes before all; and before God, all are slaves.

We might expect in the next section exhortations to both masters and slaves (cf Col 3:22–4:1). Perhaps the absence of masters says something about the Christians' social status. But because Peter thinks of all Christians as slaves (2:16), this exhortation to servants becomes a general teaching to the community at large. The most striking aspect of this teaching is the invocation of Jesus as an explicit example to be imitated, for all who suffer unjustly (2:21–23). Jesus not only won salvation for others by his death on the cross. In his very manner of suffering, he provided the model for how Christians were to act. Not only what Jesus did but also how he did it becomes a source of life to the community.

**What Is Peter Getting At?**

THE EXHORTATION TO wives (3:1–6) is much more extensive than that to husbands (3:7). Traditional Jewish and Greek motifs, which stress the value of internal virtue over external adornment, are used to support the command to be submissive. Women are to be subordinate, we notice, not to all men, but to their husbands (3:1, 5). In return, men are to regard women as fully equal in their relationship before the Lord. Women are "joint heirs of the gift of life" (3:7).

In these instructions, we do not find a divinely inspired blueprint for the ideal social order or Christian family structure. What we find is the best available moral teaching applied to the real world of that age. Just as the social structures of the past cannot be transferred directly to the present, neither can the relationships appropriate to those structures be directly imitated. Yet for families both ancient and modern, for societies then and now, good order, mutual respect, obedience, and authority are very much required. The style of those structures, happily, is left to human creativity.

**Witness in a Hostile World (3:8–4:6)**

The Christians of Asia Minor were not suffering persecution, torture, and death. Their suffering was nevertheless real and painful. Social ostracism works a slow and insidious poison into a community's sense of identity. They were being "insulted" (3:9), maligned and defamed (3:16), and "vilified" (4:4). Why? Probably they were abused because they no longer followed the ways of their neighbors (4:3f ). They have become different (holy), and people who insist on being different generate resentment.

Peter's response to the community's experience of suffering is remarkable. He does not advocate withdrawal from society or hostility toward outsiders. Instead, Christians are to remain in the world (see 2:13–3:7) and are to engage outsiders in dialogue. They are to be ready to "give an explanation to anyone who asks you for a reason for your hope" (3:15). The expectation that such explanation would be helpful pays a high compliment to the basic reasonableness and goodwill of outsiders. Christians are also to follow the exhortation of Jesus to return a blessing for a curse (see Mt 5:44). To act in this way toward outsiders, they must cultivate the same qualities of sympathy and love toward each other in the community (3:8). Within their own hearts, furthermore, they are to "sanctify Christ as Lord" (3:15), which, Peter asserts, will free them from fear of outsiders (3:14). How will this happen?

1. They are to remember how Jesus not only "suffered for sins once" (3:18) but also how he was raised from the dead in power.

2. Using traditions found in apocalyptic literature (such as 1 Enoch), Peter symbolically expresses the conviction that the resurrection was not simply an event concerning the person Jesus but had cosmic extension.

3. "In the spirit," Jesus went to the spirits in prison to preach the good news (3:19–22). This dramatic announcement is the basis for the statement in the Apostles' Creed that says Jesus "descended into hell." It means that God's power to save reaches everywhere, even to the farthest reaches of human sin and alienation.

Peter's immediate point, however, is that by baptism (3:21), the Christians of Asia Minor have been given the same power. They need not fear human slander, for the power of God is at work among them. They are like those to whom Jesus preached after his resurrection, "though condemned in the flesh in human estimation . . . alive in the spirit in the estimation of God" (4:6).

### Community Attitudes (4:7–5:14)

First Peter does not portray the Christians' moral situation in stark black-and-white tones, but like most New Testament writings, it has a keen sense that the time for decision is now. The final exhortations are colored by the conviction that "the end of all things is at hand" (4:7). The time of judgment is soon (4:17). Therefore, Christian life means "resisting the devil" who through affliction such as they are experiencing "seeks to devour them" (5:8f ). Such circumstances call for a "serious, sober" attitude and one that is "vigilant" (4:7; 5:8). Those who experience affliction are to regard their sufferings as a share in Christ's own (5:13f), knowing that they will share in his glory (4:13; 5:10). Within the community, attitudes of mutual service are to prevail (4:9–11), demonstrated by good order and humility (5:1–16).

When exhorting the community's leaders, Peter forbids lording it over the flock. Leaders are rather to provide a positive example (5:3). The image of the shepherd recalls the portrayal of Jesus as the "shepherd and guardian of your souls" (2:25). The connection is made explicit in 5:4: with characteristic optimism, Peter promises such good leaders that "when the chief Shepherd is revealed, you will receive the unfading crown of glory."

The New Testament contains no writing more positive in its evaluation of the world yet more compelling in its call to holiness than 1 Peter. As Martin Luther correctly noted, it is one of the New Testament compositions that truly "show thee Christ."

### Questions for Discussion and Reflection

***Group Sharing/Discussion***

1. Describe the original audience of 1 Peter.

2. What was Peter's response to the community's experience of suffering?

3. Peter taught that what readers hope for is security, a "living hope" because it is based not simply in human longing, but in the "power of God" at work among them. Describe the hope of human longing and the "living hope" based on God's power.

4. Peter's exhortation was colored by his conviction that "the end of all things is at hand" (4:7). In this context Peter wrote this letter to urge Christians to live their faith. What virtues and attitudes for the communities did he suggest? If he were writing today what would he be asking Christians to do?

***In Our Lives***

1. Peter works to build the identity of the community by reminding them of their call to holiness, their transformation in baptism, and that

they are part of the "household of God." What do these three qualities mean in your world today? How would you nourish these in your life? In your community?

2. In his letter Peter teaches that Christians are to remain in the world and to engage outsiders in dialogue (2:13–3:7). He teaches: Be ready to give an explanation to anyone who asks you for the reason for your hope (3:15). How would you give a clear reason for your hope?

***Individual/Personal Reflection/Action***

1. Sometimes it is easier to love "outsiders" than those within "the household of faith." What are ways Catholics take one another for granted or fail to show appreciation? Choose one concrete action you can take this week to show your care, concern, and gratitude towards someone who shares your faith in Christ.

2. Newborns (the newly baptized) need "spiritual milk." But now you are mature in Christ. Read 1 Peter 2:1–3. Why is it easier to hold on to the spiritual sweetness of childhood faith than to accept the "solid food" that mature baptismal commitment requires? Describe how your image of God, of Christ, of the church and of Scriptures has changed since your childhood. Discuss the difficulty of letting go of secure religious images. Why do you think we are called to do this?

3. In this letter, Peter encourages civil obligations. Today, as in his day, families and society at large require good order. Read 1 Peter 2:13. Cite examples of breakdown in modern society where this is lacking. What are some creative ways of rebuilding the human spirit that will affect the quality of life for families, civil institutions, and international relationships?

# 2 PETER READING GUIDE

### *At a Glance*

| | |
|---|---|
| Who are the main players? | "Peter" the opponents |
| What should I look for? | This book is a general exhortation cast in the form of a letter. Notice Peter's response concerning the delay of the second coming of Christ. Also reflect upon the debate between living faith and practical atheism. |
| When was this writen? | 2 Peter is a pseudonymous work, written about the second quarter of the second century, forming a bridge between the apostolic period and the church of subsequent ages. |
| Where did these events occur? | The author is a Jewish Christian and the audience may be the churches of Asia Minor. |
| Why was this book written? | The principle problem of the author is the "scoffers" who deny the second coming of the Lord. |
| What is the story? | His message has three points: (1) he establishes the authority of the writer and of the Scripture that will be used as the source of his proof; (2) he attacks the opponents' "destructive teaching"; (3) he presents the proper understanding of the tradition concerning God's judgment. |

## Before Beginning

An appreciative understanding of 2 Peter demands more than the normal effort. Hard work is necessary to uncover the situation addressed by the letter. Perhaps even more difficult is the hurdle presented by the letter's sustained argumentative tone. Such effort finds its rewards, however, in the surprising discovery that the writing, which at first appears to be the New Testament's most irrelevant, can emerge as having perennial pertinence.

## A Defense of God's Judgment

The circumstances of 2 Peter's composition are obscure (see the NAB introduction to 2 Peter).

The same author did not write both 1 and 2 Peter. The style, outlook, and concerns of the two letters are too disparate for a common authorship. The main thing they have in common is the mention of Noah and the flood. Second Peter has far more in common with Jude (with which it shares the polemical material of chapter 2) than with 1 Peter. In all likelihood, 2 Peter is a pseudonymous composition. Despite the self-presentation of chapter 1, it is not "Symeon Peter" who writes, but someone who invokes his authority as a support for shared traditions being threatened by deviance. This sermon in the form of a letter may have been addressed to a single church, but it may also have been intended for a larger audience, all "those who have received a faith of equal value to ours" (1:1). It is thus considered a "general" epistle. The title "Catholic Epistles" was applied to 1 and 2 Peter; James; 1:2, and 3 John; and Jude because they were written for a broader audience than a local church (in Greek, "catholic" = "pertaining to the whole"). Some readers also consider 2 Peter "catholic" in another sense: Its concern for tradition anticipates the emergence of the Catholic Church in the second century.

At first reading, 2 Peter seems to be a loose collection of observations within which talk about Jesus' second coming plays a particularly significant part. Some scholars have therefore thought that the "delay of the Parousia" was the crisis that stimulated composition. Closer analysis, however, shows that "Peter" and his opponents are debating a deeper and more perennial problem: Does God judge the world? Underlying that issue, in turn, is a still more fundamental one concerning the reality of God and God's relationship to the world. The debate, in short, is between living faith and practical atheism. It is a debate still in progress. The contribution of 2 Peter is worth hearing.

Far from a random collection of statements, the letter as a whole presents a coherent argument. Chapter 1 establishes the authority of the writer and of the Scripture that will be used as the source of proof. Chapter 2 attacks the opponents' "destructive teachings" on the basis of Scripture. Chapter 3 presents the proper understanding of the tradition concerning God's judgment.

> **Pseudonymous** A *pseudonymous* work is one written by a later author who attributed it to an important person according to the literary convention popular at the time.

### The Common Tradition (1:1–21)

The first section of the letter establishes the authority of the writer and of the shared tradition (1:1) that the author represents. Extraordinary emphasis is put on the person of Peter and on the fact that he will soon die (1:13f). These touches recall the literary genre popular in early Christianity called the "Farewell Discourse." In this sort of composition, a figure from the past, speaking shortly before his death, predicts catastrophes to come and enjoins fidelity on his followers. We notice in this case, however, an equally strong emphasis on memory (1:9, 12, 13, 15). The opponents "forget" the proper knowledge, and Peter seeks to "remind" his readers of it. The emphasis on memory makes the letter resemble as well the form of moral exhortation called *parenesis*. The connection to parenesis is most obvious in 2 Peter 1:5–8. Parenesis spelled out moral obligations in terms of maxims. Here, Peter lists the sort of qualities that should follow upon the readers' faith. More important even than the specific items is the overall point made by the list: More than knowledge or faith is involved in being Christian. A whole way of life is demanded. Those who have "forgotten" this lead lives that are "idle and unfruitful" (1:8f ). There is a sharp polemical edge to this comment. In chapter 2, Peter will show that the opponents' "destructive heresies" bring about destructive behavior, which in turn brings down God's judgment.

A complex statement provides the basis for Peter's overall argument and a transition to his attack on his opponents (1:16–21). In a passage that clearly corresponds to the Synoptic Gospels' story of Jesus' transfiguration (see Mt 17:1–8), he asserts the reality of the Christian experience of God. The tradition out of which Peter writes is not speculation ("cleverly devised myths," 1:16), but is a power he and others experience personally; "we" saw and heard on the mountain (1:16–18). The community's tradition is based not in fancy, but in fact. The experience, moreover, was of "the power and coming" of the Lord Jesus Christ. As we will learn, the promise concerning Jesus' return is the bone of contention in chapter 3. Peter claims that the expectation of his return is based on the reality of his already having come.

The disciples' experience of Jesus also grounds the "prophetic message" about Jesus' return for judgment. Peter places this prophecy of Jesus (see Mt 24:29–31) among the prophecies of Scripture. As with scriptural prophecies, interpretation is not to be personal or idiosyncratic but a decision of the community that is guided by the same Spirit that gave utterance in the first place. With this alignment, Peter has provided the basis for arguing the whole issue of God's judgment (and therefore of Jesus' return) on the truthfulness of Scripture as properly interpreted by the tradition.

### Condemnation of False Teachers (2:1–22)

The claim to a true "prophetic message" in 1:19 provides a transition to the attack on "false teachers" (2:1) who are placed in the line of "false prophets." As we will learn more fully in chapter 3, the opponents are denying the power of God to judge, that is, to intervene in the affairs of the world (3:4). By denying God's ability to judge, they bring judgment on themselves. Their "destructive heresies" bring on them "destruction" (2:1). But their teaching has proven successful, convincing many (2:2); Peter's response must therefore be vigorous and pointed.

We saw in 1:5–8 that Peter was concerned with the moral consequences of faith. The ancient world knew what our world sometimes ignores, that people act on their ideas, and that bad ideas can lead to bad behavior. A real misconception of what life is about leads to a distorted existence. Showing how certain teachings lead to immoral behavior is a way of proving that the ideas are false. Peter therefore pays particular attention to the way of life generated by these doctrines. He attacks the "licentious ways" of the opponents (2:2), their "greed" and "lies" (2:3). They are people of "depraved desires" (2:10), are "irrational" (2:12) and "adulterous" (2:14). The catalogue of vices reaches a rhetorical climax in 2:17f, then takes a sharp turn: "They promise them freedom, though they themselves are slaves of corruption, for a person is a slave of whatever overcomes him" (2:19).

What sort of "freedom" did the opponents promise? Apparently, it was freedom from the fear of punishment. If God does not intervene in human affairs to punish the wicked and reward the good, then (they said) one can live immorally, looking out only for oneself, indulging in antisocial behavior.

Peter's first rebuttal is based on the nature of vice. They are slaves of their dominating appetite, which controls their behavior. They are not sophisticated or liberated. They are as compulsive as dogs returning to their vomit, these Christians who once knew righteousness but have now turned back to a novel version of an old atheism: "The fool says in his heart, 'There is no God'." (Ps 14:1).

The second part of Peter's rebuttal is based on the conviction that the Bible stories relate the facts of history. When Scripture says therefore that God did punish and reward, that is proof of God's ability still to do so. Peter relates the cases of the wicked angels (2:4), of Noah (2:5), of Sodom and Gomorrah (2:6–10) and of Balaam (2:15f) as evidence of God's intervention. In contrast to the letter of Jude (with which much of this material is shared), Peter does not just emphasize punishment; God also rewards those who are faithful. Here, the issue is whether God acts in human history at all. Peter's recitation from Scripture asserts that in fact God does.

### The Coming of the Lord (3:1–18)

The specific nature of the debate emerges for the first time in this final section. Here, not simply a question of fact but a matter of principle is at stake.

The question of fact is not really in dispute. Jesus clearly had not yet returned to judge the world as all Christians had been expecting. But quite different conclusions were being drawn from that undisputed fact. The "scoffers" challenge the very promise of his coming (3:4). They base their denial on the immutability of the world "from the beginning." They hold the position of the skeptics of the time, who denied divine providence. (See the box "Where Is Your God?" for more detailed discussion on both sides of this debate and how it continues today.) Because Jesus

## Where Is Your God?

WHAT OPPOSITION WERE the early Christians facing? Their neighbors in society ridiculed them for their faith in God's care for the world. The position held by the ancient skeptics such as the Epicureans and (among the Jews) Sadducees was a denial of divine providence. If there was a god, they said, he did not meddle with the world, which was a closed system of natural forces and human desires. God was not a factor to be considered, never had been, never would be. The failure of Jesus to return was only one more piece of evidence that all such prophecies were empty.

Though the debate about divine providence can obviously never be resolved—it has continued down to the present day—the side of those who believe in God is still strongly represented. Ultimately, believers can point to their own experience—the experience of prayer, of worship, of service—and identify that as one basis of their faith. Another basis is community—the sense of a fellowship of believers. A third basis is tradition—really a way of being in community with those who precede us. The debate will continue, but believers will also continue to have reason to maintain their position.

In this argument, both sides base their position on a claim of experience, which then interprets reality as a whole:

**The Skeptics**

Experience shows no evidence for God's activity: "Nothing has changed." How can you believe that God intervenes if he is so apparently absent?

**Peter**

Scripture proves that God does intervene, and the apostles experienced such an intervention in Jesus.

Trying to measure God's time on a human scale is impossible. God does not delay, but is waiting to ensure that people are prepared for the day of the Lord.

had yet to return, apparently supporting the scoffers' stance, theirs is a real threat to the whole structure of faith. They challenge not only the reality of the *Parousia,* but the very reality of a living God. Is God, then, merely a figment of the imagination, a projection of human longing? The whole concept of revelation is obviously challenged as well. There can be no real "promise" if there is no living God to speak, or to act.

In this argument, both sides base their position on a claim of experience, which then interprets reality as a whole. The skeptics say that experience shows no evidence for God's activity: "nothing has changed." Peter argues that Scripture (which is after all the record of human history) proves that God does intervene (see all of chapter 2). God created by a word and can destroy by a word (3:5f). Furthermore—and this is the significance of 1:16–19—Peter and his companions themselves experienced such an intervention in the transfiguration of Jesus. Thus, their tradition is based on the prophets, on the Lord Jesus, and on the apostles (3:2).

If God does intervene, how is his apparent absence to be interpreted? Peter invokes the arguments used by other defenders of divine providence. God's time cannot be measured by human time: There is an infinite distance between God and humans (3:7). God's apparent delay is to bring people to repentance (3:8f).

Ultimately, those whose experience is different are not likely to be convinced. Peter appeals not to the opponents, but to those attracted to their position. He reasserts the conviction that Jesus will come "like a thief in the night" (see Mt 24:43; 1 Thes 5:2; Rv 3:3) and that his coming will inaugurate "new heavens and a new earth in which righteousness dwells" (3:13; see Rv 21:1). His concern throughout this letter, however, has been most of all with the behavior of his readers, and he reasserts "what sort of persons they are to be" during this time of waiting (3:11). After all debate is over, only the truth of human existence validates doctrine.

The letter concludes with a reference to Paul's letters that the opponents are distorting (3:15f). The fact that the author refers to "all" of Paul's letters, that he makes them equivalent to "Scripture," and that there is already a history of interpreting (or misinterpreting) them are strong indications that this "Peter" is a writer of the second generation who defends a tradition common to the historical Peter and Paul against the threat of doctrinal and behavioral deviance.

**Questions for Discussion and Reflection**

***Group Sharing/Discussion***

1. Second Peter is known as a "Catholic Epistle." What does this title mean?

2. In all likelihood 2 Peter is a "pseudonymous" composition. What does that mean?

3. Second Peter resembles a form of moral exhortation called *parenesis* (cf. 2 Pt 1:5–8). What qualities of this form of moral exhortation are in 2 Peter?

4. In chapter 2, Peter shows that his opponents' "destructive heresies" bring destructive behavior. What was he talking about?

5. The promise concerning Jesus' return is the bone of contention in chapter 3. What does Peter argue regarding Jesus' return?

***In Our Lives***

1. Peter writes about the false teachers and skeptics who deny God's ability to judge or intervene in the affairs of this world (2:1–22). What happened as a result of this false teaching? Reflect upon what you believe concerning God's judgment and actions in the world today. Have you had experience in your religious world with false teachers or skeptics? What is their message? How can you respond?

2. "They promise them freedom, though they themselves are slaves of corruption, for a person is a slave of whatever overcomes him" (2:19). Give some examples of the truth of this statement in contemporary life. What does "freedom" feel like and mean to you? How do internal and external freedom differ?

***Individual/Personal Reflection/Action***

1. Peter shows concern about the relations of beliefs and behavior. Read and reflect on how he presents this in chapter 2.

2. In some Christian circles, a great emphasis is placed on "the Lord's second coming." What is the Catholic understanding of the *parousia*? How does this affect your understanding of divine providence?

3. This letter addresses the debate between living faith and practical atheism, a very contemporary subject. What is meant by "living faith" and "practical atheism"? Recall some examples of "practical atheism" at work in our society. Why is this culture so attractive and easy to be caught up in?

# 1 JOHN READING GUIDE

## *At a Glance*

| | |
|---|---|
| Who are the main players? | John Johannine community |
| What should I look for? | Two important values: the declaration of the humanity and divinity of Christ as an apostolic teaching and the development of the intrinsic connection between Christian moral conduct and Christian doctrine. |
| When was this written? | Early tradition identified this with John the apostle. It is agreed it resembles the Fourth Gospel, and both works are from the same Johannine Christianity. It may be dated toward the end of the first century. |
| Where did these events occur? | It is not tied to a particular place, but there is a tradition that locates the Johannine literature in and around Ephesus. |

Why was this book written? The community is divided by conflict. The purpose of the letter is to combat certain false ideas about Jesus and to deepen the spiritual and social awareness of the Christian community.

What is the story? This is more a theological treatise than a letter. Some former members of the community refuse to acknowledge Jesus as the Christ and thus deny that he was a true man. These theological errors are rejected by the author's declaring that authentic Christian love, ethics, and faith take place only within the historical revelation and sacrifice of Jesus Christ.

## Before Beginning

### Exhortation to a Divided Church

The New Testament contains three letters attributed to John. How these letters connect to the Gospel according to John and the book of Revelation is not easy to determine. Scholars agree that all came from a community of "Johannine Christianity" in the late first century, but neither their precise authorship nor sequence has been established. We are not even sure of the location of this "Johannine Christianity," although Asia Minor seems most likely. In such a state of uncertainty hypotheses abound. The introductions to each of these letters in the NAB give some sense of the options.

What we can learn of "Johannine Christianity" derives from the writings themselves. Apart from the connection to John, what common characteristics marked this version of messianism?

1. The figure of Jesus played a central role in the identity of the community.

2. These churches had experienced tragic division. In the Gospel and Revelation, there is conflict between these messianists and the Jews. In the letters and Revelation, there is also evidence of divisions within the churches.

3. This experience of division sharpened the community's symbols into a stark dualism: light and darkness, life and death, truth and falsehood, flesh and spirit.

### The Three Letters

In the three letters, we see conflict happening within the churches. Disputes involve the proper understanding of Jesus. These letters provide a window on this early Christian conflict, revealing at once both its multiple dimensions and its seriousness. It is impossible to say at this distance exactly how the letters relate to each other or to the situation. Second and Third John are real letters and claim to come from "the Elder." First John is anonymous and not really a letter so much as a sermon.

Some think that the three letters show three stages of the community's conflict. This hypothesis is possible, but a better one is that the three documents were written at the same time by the same author and sent to a single church. Each letter fulfills a specific function:

- 3 John recommends the mailman, Demetrius, to the church leader, Gaius.
- 2 John is a cover letter to be read publicly to the church.
- 1 John is the centerpiece, an exhortation to a community divided by conflict.

The Reading Guides for 2 and 3 John will describe how they fulfill their functions.

## The Character of 1 John

Because it is not so closely tied to the particulars of a specific community's life, 1 John lends itself more readily to every time and place. For a document generated by bitter conflict, it is amazingly positive and loving in tone. Christians through the ages have rightly considered it one of the great spiritual witnesses of the New Testament.

The structure of this writing is not obvious. Certainly it is not a genuine letter. Even as a sermon, it tends to wander a bit, repeating the same points. First John at times has the appearance of an argument but without giving the substance. Readers are sometimes shocked at the lack of consistency. What is stated positively is sometimes denied only a short time later. The reason for this alternation of ideal and real lies in the circumstances being addressed.

The Johannine Christians saw their lives defined by a choice. Their first and basic choice was to follow Jesus. They considered that truth, life, and light characterized them; while falsehood, darkness, and death characterized those who did not follow Jesus. The Christians were the community of true prophecy. But now, the community finds itself divided into two hostile camps, and the cause of division is precisely what should have been the centerpiece of this unity: the proper understanding of the nature and role of Jesus.

First John's apparent indecisiveness reflects the chastened perspective caused by the trauma of division. The symbols of unity and perfection need reshaping. The author urges his readers away from a smug sense of their own perfection, to an awareness of their need to repent. Not only "those who went out from us" have sinned; all have sinned and need the expiation offered by Jesus.

**Opening Exhortation (1:1–2:17)**

First John opens with a poetic prologue (1:1–4) that resembles the prologue to the Fourth Gospel (Jn 1:1–8) in its deliberate allusion to Genesis 1:1 ("in the beginning") and its emphasis on the "word of life." In the epistle's prologue, however, the stress is placed on the community's experience of the Word in Jesus. The writer testifies to what he has "seen and heard and touched" (cf Jn 19:35). The experience, furthermore, is one shared by the readers. The language of fellowship dominates 1:3f. The believers have fellowship with God the Father through Jesus. They are also, by that same agency, to have fellowship among themselves. A textual variant in 1:4 illustrates the dense interweaving: manuscripts differ on reading "your" joy, or "our" joy. For this writer, both meanings coincide.

The section closes with another deliberately rhetorical statement of purpose: "I am writing to you because" (2:12–14). Different groups in the community are addressed, but the message is basically one message and is more clearly spelled out by 2:15–17: The church is to live by the "will of God" and not by the standards of the "world." John's talk about "love of the world" here is very close to that in the letter of James about those who seek "friendship with the world" (Jas 4:4) and means much the same thing. The writer does not forbid love for humanity; he denounces the "worldliness" that denies God's claim on his creation and bases existence on "sensual lust, enticement for the eyes, and a pretentious life" (2:16).

Within the framework provided by the prologue and the statement of purpose, the rest of the opening section of this sermon serves to remind the readers of the need to live by the "message we have heard from him and proclaim to you" (1:5).

The community has, to be sure, already heard that "God is light and there is no darkness in him at all" (1:5). But now, because of the division in this community, a new sense of reality is required. Behavior must match their ideals. They can no longer simply assume that "we are the light" without hesitation. In fact, sin does occur among them, and they need to repent of it. They cannot claim to be "in the light" while their behavior shows that they "walk in darkness" (1:6). That is a lie. Likewise, they cannot claim to "know God" while not keeping God's commandments (2:4).

With a different vocabulary than James, but with a quite similar concern, John seeks to make his readers' actions conform to their convictions. And the great commandment of God that is to govern the life of the community is also, as in James, the law of love for neighbor, the test whether one is "in the light" or "in the darkness." For 1 John, it is not simply doctrinal correctness that spells true fellowship in the community, but ethical consistency.

First John places special emphasis on the role of Jesus as expiation for sin (1:7; 2:2) and advocate for believers (2:1). The community's failure, demonstrated in its division into hostile parties, makes the need for intercession clear. They cannot do it alone. It also makes clear that "love" is not simply a state of mind, but something to be performed. In an atmosphere of hurt and separation, such performance is difficult.

**The Divided Community (2:18–3:24)**

The severity of the community's crisis is indicated by the fact that the writer thinks the end of all things is at hand. The author calls those who have left the community "antichrists." In apocalyptic literature, the presence of antichrist is a sign of the final tribulation (see Mt 24:24). The theme of Jesus' return occurs again in 2:28 and 3:2. Typical of apocalyptic writing also is the exhortation to stand fast ("remain in him," 2:24, 27, 28; 3:6) and to avoid being deceived (2:26).

The threat to the community is the greater because former members make it: "They went out from us." It is impossible for this writer to acknowledge fully that they had ever been of one spirit with the community: "They were not really of our number." What proof does he have? "If they had been, they would have remained" (2:19). This is desperate logic. It indicates the shock given to a church devoted to unity and opposition to a world "out there" when it experiences conflict and division from within. The very identity of the community is called into question.

We cannot be sure exactly what the bone of contention was between those who left and those who stayed, only that it involved the proper understanding of Jesus. The author uses the language of "denial" and "confession" (2:22f), and it seems clear that a formal doctrinal issue is at stake (see also 2 Jn 7). The briefest description of the deviance is that they deny "Jesus is the Christ." This obviously qualifies them to be "anti-Christs" in the narrow sense, but it is hard to imagine how such people could ever have been part of the messianic community. Such a denial is more appropriate to those who rejected Jesus as Messiah and remained Jews. To complicate matters, the author adds other features in 3:23; 4:2f; 5:1, 10. These make it appear that outsiders deny either the full divine origin of Jesus (that he is "God's son") or his full humanity (that he "came in the flesh"). In short, John is convinced his party has the full understanding of Jesus and his opponents do not; beyond that general statement we cannot advance.

Characteristic of this writing, however, is its ability to combine a claim to possession of "the truth" (2:21), with a demand at the same time for transformation. The community is not yet perfect. They are indeed, to use one of their favorite expressions "children of God" (see Jn 1:12), but they still need to mature. Only when he appears will they become "like him, for we shall see him as he is" (3:2). Having the truth means living the truth, which demands strict ethical norms. In 3:4–18, John develops the strongest possible contrast between the way of the world governed by the devil (4:8; 5:19) and the way revealed by God through the Messiah, Jesus. The way of the world is driven by the envy that leads to murder (the example of Cain, 3:12; cf Jas 4:1–5). The way Jesus reveals is exactly the opposite. This way does not take away life but gives it and in the giving of life reveals love: "The way we came to know love was that he laid down his life for us." The moral correlative follows at once: "so we ought to lay down our lives for our brothers" (3:16). The New Testament contains no more direct connection between the work of the Messiah and the pattern of Christian existence. And lest anyone think the giving of life can be accomplished in attitude only or once for all, John spells it out in terms of the sharing of material possessions with the needy and concludes in a manner familiar to us from Paul and James: "Let us love not in word or speech but in deed and truth" (3:18).

> **Docetism** From a Greek word meaning "to seem," docetism is a heresy that claims Christ only seemed to be a human being, but was actually purely God.
>
> **Gnosticism** From a Greek word meaning "to know," gnosticism is a heresy that claims knowledge, particularly secret knowledge, is the key to salvation, and that actions are of little or no importance.

Finally, the claim to be in possession of the truth must be qualified by the deeper statement of humility in 3:19–21. It is because they are in the hands of the one who is "greater than our hearts and knows everything" that they know they belong to the truth. It is not their accomplishment but his gift; their adequate response is to act as he did, in love (3:23f).

### The Remnant Community (4:1–5:21)

Because the community is divided, shared symbols are now being interpreted by opposing parties to the dispute. More careful judgment is therefore required. John reminds his readers of the need to "test the spirits to see whether they belong to God" (4:1). As earlier he had spoken of

## Discernment

WITHIN THIS REMNANT community itself, discernment was also required. How could the church be sure it was living by the Spirit of God? Discernment, or "testing the spirits," has had a long tradition within Christianity. This is the process by which an individual or a community examines, in the light of the whole value structure of faith, what leads to God and a more perfect service of God and others and what detracts from this goal. Sometimes this is very difficult to distinguish.

That the Johannine community had the right confession of Jesus was taken for granted by its members. But John added the ethical dimension: Keeping the commandment of God showed their love for God (5:2f). What is that commandment? That they love one another. John joined love for God and love for neighbor in such a way that they could not be separated; doing one was doing the other. "If anyone says, 'I love God,' but hates his brother, he is a liar" (4:20).

There is a certain parallel to the beginning of Genesis in the Gospel of John when Christ breathes on the apostles and gives them the Holy Spirit (Jn 20:22). It is the Spirit that secures the unity of the body (1 Cor 12:13; Eph 2:16, 18; 4:4). The Spirit holds the body together. Divisions, factions, hurt, and separation are always suspect. However, even these can masquerade as truth. The only way a community can judge itself as being "in the truth" is to measure its members' love for one another. Because human beings do not have direct access to God (4:12; see Jn 1:18), their relationship to God is always mediated by their relationship with each other (4:12, 20–21).

the opponents as antichrists, now he applies to them the epithet "false prophets," another favorite designation in apocalyptic writing (see Mt 24:11). In this case, the proper confession of Jesus is the criterion for true and false prophecy, certifying whether the speaker belongs to God or to "the world" (4:2–4, 13–16).

Within the remnant community itself, discernment is also required. How can the church be sure that it lives by the Spirit of God? That it has the right confession of Jesus is taken for granted. But John adds the ethical dimension; keeping the commandment of God shows their love for God (5:2f). What is that commandment? It is that they are to love each other. John indissolubly joins love of God and neighbor; doing one is doing the other: "If anyone says 'I love God' but hates his brother, he is a liar" (4:20). As earlier in 3:15f, John grounds such love in the way God has revealed himself to be for humans in the sending of his son and Jesus' expiatory death: "In this is love, not that we have loved God, but that he loved us and sent his Son as expiation for our sins" (4:10). Because humans do not have direct access to God (4:12; see Jn 1:18), their relationship to God is mediated by their relationships with each other (4:12, 20f).

The last section of this sermon is filled with a mixture of confidence and caution. The community living by God's love and faith is sure of victory "over the world" (5:4f), even though "the whole world is under the power of the evil one" (5:19). This is because the community's testimony is not isolated. It is supported by the testimony of Father, Son, and Spirit, each working in and through the church (5:6–9). The community is confident of its gift of "eternal life" (2:25; 5:11, 13). But the victory over sin and death (see 3:7–14) is not yet complete.

- Idolatry is a temptation that needs to be avoided (5:21);
- Perfect love has not yet driven out fear (4:18);
- Mutual correction is required (5:16f).

For this divided community, nothing can any longer be taken for granted; division has given new urgency to discernment (5:20).

### Questions for Discussion and Reflection

*Group Sharing/Discussion*

1. What are the characteristics of Johannine Christianity?

2. What is the context in the community for this letter of John?

3. Johannine Christians saw their life defined by a choice. What was this basic choice?

4. What was the cause of the division of the community into hostile camps?

5. What is the difference between their understanding of "anti-Christ" and the common "modern" understanding?

6. According to John, how do you express your love for your neighbor?

*In Our Lives*

1. According to 1 John, "the whole world is under the power of the evil one" (5:19). Have you experienced this evil of the world? How has the Christian community, living by love and faith, nourished you to deal with this evil?

2. John reminds his readers of the need to "test the spirits to see whether they belong to God" (4:1). How do you test the "spirits" in living your life?

3. Our relation with God is not direct; it is mediated (4:12, 20f) by relationships with each other. Name some specific relationships where this is true for you, that is, some specific relationships where you meet God through other people.

***Individual/Personal Reflection/Action***

1. "The way we came to know love was that he laid down his life for us . . . so we ought to lay down our lives for" one another (3:16). The work of Jesus connects to the pattern of our Christian life. Have you come to know love by knowing "he laid down his life" for you? How do you nourish this love? How do you lay down your life for your neighbor?

2. For many Catholics, examination of conscience has been measured by a list of faults. What is the difference between awareness of sinfulness and simply making a "grocery list" of faults? How can a parish community discern whether it is "walking in the light"?

3. The Christian Churches of the East have a tradition of praying the "Jesus Prayer" below as a kind of mantra. It is said quietly over and over while leaving one's heart open to the action of the Holy Spirit. Try this prayer style each morning when you wake up:

"Lord, Jesus Christ, Son of the Living God, have mercy on me, a sinner."

# 2 JOHN READING GUIDE

### *At a Glance*

| | |
|---|---|
| Who is the main player? | John the Presbyter |
| What should I look for? | Note the concern for mutual love, truth, and integrity. These are the dimensions of establishing and maintaining the community. |
| When was this written? | At the end of the first century, probably written by a disciple of the apostle John |
| Where did these events occur? | Probably in Ephesus |
| Why was this book written? | Second John is a letter of introduction to the community to be read before the sermon is delivered. |
| What is the story? | The function of this letter is to identify the author, to emphasize its main teaching, and to suggest some practical actions to be taken by the community. |

## Before Beginning

### A Cover Letter to the Church

Unless 2 John and 3 John are connected to the same moment of crisis that generated 1 John, it is hard to explain their preservation by a local church, their exchange between churches, and their eventual inclusion in the New Testament canon. In the Reading Guide to 1 John (RG 444), the suggestion is made that all three letters were sent in a single packet by the emissary Demetrius to the local leader Gaius (see 3 Jn), who was still loyal to "the Elder" in the dispute dividing Johannine Christianity into hostile factions.

Whereas 1 John lacks all qualities of a letter or epistle and appears as a sermon to be delivered aloud to an assembly (or even a number of assemblies), 2 John bears the marks of a genuine letter. It has the formal elements of greeting (1–3), body (4–12), and farewell (13). It mentions the desire of the writer to visit the addressees (12). Unlike 3 John, however, which is addressed to an individual, 2 John is written to the "chosen Lady" and her children (1). The designation is almost certainly an honorary title for the church itself. The argument that it refers to a specific woman leader is doubtful, if the rest of the reconstruction here being suggested makes sense. The "children," of course, are the ones really being addressed; the second-person verbs are predominantly in the plural.

The symbols of Johannine Christianity are very much in evidence. Notice the emphasis on "truth" (1, 2, 3) and on "walking in the truth" (4); on "keeping the commandment," which is not new but from the beginning (5); on love for one another as the fulfillment of that commandment (6); on the creation of mutual joy as the mark of fellowship (12). Surely, such a cluster of distinctive themes makes best sense when read together with 1 John.

What distinguishes 2 John is its function. In 3 John 9, the Elder says that he "is writing" (or "wrote") something to the church. In all likelihood, this refers to 1 John, the exhortation to a remnant community. Second John, then, is undoubtedly a letter of introduction to the community, to be read before the sermon is delivered, to identify its author, to emphasize its main teaching, and to suggest some practical actions to be taken by the community. These may or may not be fully in accord with the spirit of 1 John, but they are certainly recognizable as a response to the crisis signaled by 3 John.

## Strategies for Survival

Again we meet the split between those who "walk in truth" and the "many deceivers who have gone out into the world" (7). As in 1 John, these are designated antichrists because they "do not acknowledge Jesus Christ as coming in the flesh." In the Reading Guide to 1 John, we suggest how difficult it is to determine precisely what this denial implies. For the Elder, however, the opponents appear as "progressives" who have gone too far in their interpretation and no longer "remain in the teaching of the Christ" (or "about" the Christ). The Elder's community is therefore portrayed as defending the traditional understanding of Jesus. The importance of right doctrine is underscored by the equation: having Christ is having God (see 1 Jn 4:3). For Johannine Christianity, the unique mediation of salvation by Jesus is axiomatic. He alone is the "way and the truth and the life" (Jn 14:6). The lesson is clear: Misconstruing the mediator means missing the good news entirely. If the Elder's readers do not hold to the proper understanding, they will "lose what they worked for."

The community crisis is so severe that the Elder calls for the extraordinary practice of excommunication. They are neither to offer heretics hospitality nor even to greet them as brothers (10). Notice the connection, everywhere assumed in the New Testament, between message and messenger. Physical fellowship implies spiritual unanimity. Thus, "whoever greets him shares in his evil works" (11). Only those who deliver the proper doctrine are to be welcomed. Here the Elder advocates the same practice of shunning and exclusion of which he accuses Diotrephes in 3 John. The battle is obviously a very bitter one.

It is difficult to know what positive instruction one should draw from these ancient fragments of hostile conflicts. Perhaps it is important for the church to remember that in every age it has never been easy to establish or to secure its identity; deviance and dispute are part of community life. Perhaps also, however, it is important for the church in every age to reflect whether proper doctrine is more important than the fellowship of love. Even in an age of ecumenism, that issue remains unresolved.

### Questions for Discussion and Reflection

***Group Sharing/Discussion***

1. The crisis is so severe that the Elder calls for excommunication of the dissidents. How would you describe excommunication?

***In Our Lives***

1. Only those who deliver the proper doctrine are to be welcomed into the Community. But

those who greet "heretics" share in their evil works (11). They are not even to be offered hospitality (10). What do you think are the reasons for these community rules? Do you agree with them? Would they be proper for the Church community today? Do they conflict with the message Jesus preaches? How?

*Individual/Personal Reflection/Action*

1. The task of establishing and maintaining the community identity is difficult for any age. In the epistles of John, the community faced critical difficulties from within the community in the form of two philosophies:

a. Docetism–the heresy that claims that Jesus only seemed to be human, but was actually purely God; and

b. Gnosticism–a heresy claiming that knowledge is the key to salvation and that actions are really not important.

Do you feel these heresies still infect the Catholic community? Reflect on your own image of Jesus and your understanding of salvation. Recall how these truths are talked about and taught in your parish.

# 3 JOHN READING GUIDE

### *At a Glance*

| | |
|---|---|
| Who are the main players? | John the Presbyter Demetrius Gaius |
| What should I look for? | Notice the hospitality and autonomy of the local church. |
| When was this written? | At the end of the first century |
| Where did these events occur? | Probably Ephesus |
| Why was this book written? | The author's purpose is to secure hospitality and material support for his missionaries. He is writing to another member of the church who welcomed them in the past. |
| What is the story? | The ancient world had protocol for letters such as these. It was natural for a missionary movement to certify its apostles with such letters to ensure their safety and the hospitality due such "co-workers in the truth." |

## Before Beginning

### A Letter of Recommendation

The New Testament contains two letters written explicitly to individuals: Paul's letter to Philemon, and the Elder's letter to Gaius, which we know as 3 John. Both Paul and John take up matters of community concern, while having the same specific function, that of recommending the bearer of the letter to the addressee. In 3 John, the Elder recommends to the local church leader his emissary Demetrius. He has a good reputation from all, and "we give our testimonial as well, and you know our testimony is true" (12).

The ancient world had conventions for these letters. They were widely used in early Christianity, as we learn elsewhere in Paul's correspondence (see 2 Cor 3:1; Rom 16). It was natural for a missionary movement to certify its agents (apostles) with such letters to ensure them a safe reception and the hospitality due such "co-workers in the truth" (8). Receiving such messengers, as we see also in 2 John, meant accepting their message as well, an understanding widespread in Judaism. This principle became problematic when the movement itself divided into hostile parties. Third John points us directly to such a situation.

Third John provides the key to the historical circumstances presupposed by 1 and 2 John (see the relevant reading guides for more). Without it, their religious emphasis would be less intelligible. And without 3 John, an appreciation for the travails of early Christianity would be appreciably diminished.

## The Politics of Ecclesial Power

Third John reveals clearly that the struggle for the soul of Johannine Christianity involved structure as much as symbol, power as much as piety. Indeed, the two levels of conflict were intimately connected. On one side we see the Elder writing to his loyal colleague Gaius. On the other side is Diotrephes, who "loves to dominate." Diotrephes not only asserts authority over Gaius at the local level, but he also refuses to acknowledge the authority of the Elder over the regional church. The author says that when he comes, he will "draw attention to what he is doing" (10), but this is a small threat to a rebellious local chieftain. The position of the Elder is threatened. He needs the personal loyalty of Gaius, and his financial assistance as well.

We are thereby brought to the political maneuvering at the heart of this battle. Diotrephes is not content to "spread evil nonsense" about the Elder. He takes positive action to suppress the Elder's authority. He refuses himself to receive the Elder's delegates, and, even more, Diotrephes expels from the church those who want to receive them (10). We can understand why the Elder appreciates Gaius's reception of Demetrius, and we can grasp the significance of verses 5–8. The Elder needs to provide an alternative source of hospitality and missionary outfitting, because Diotrephes has taken up a position among those who "went out from us" (1 Jn 2:19) and no longer supports the Elder's teaching.

Gaius is being asked to receive Demetrius (and his companions) as well as equip them for their next stage of travel. Perhaps by implication the Elder's future emissaries are also included in the request. Because the Johannine missionaries accept nothing from the "pagans" ("the world"), the need for a network of hospitality and financial support is obvious (7). As in 2 John, financial sharing is tantamount to spiritual fellowship. Helping such missionaries is being "co-workers in the truth" (8). It is clear as well that both parties to the dispute are using the same tactics. Here, Diotrephes is the one shunning and excommunicating. But in 2 John we find the Elder advocating the same actions among his followers.

The hurtful struggles of early Christianity are not terribly edifying, but they are instructive. Christians who long for a golden age of harmony should be reminded that there never was one. Among history's benefits is liberation from myth. And edifying or not, these letters testify to another truth. The struggle for identity is never simply a matter of ideas or even symbols. It inevitably involves the messy realities of money and political power.

**Questions for Discussion and Reflection**

***Group Sharing/Discussion***

1. Who was this letter written to?
2. Why was it written?
3. Explain the relations of the Elder, Gaius, and Diotrephes

***In Our Lives***

1. Third John reveals clearly that the struggle in the Johannine community was not limited to ideas but that politics and money were involved also. How does this letter show this complexity? How does this show its face in the church today? What can your parish do in the face of it today?

***Individual/Personal Reflection/Action***

1. St. Augustine said that Christians should manifest unity in essentials, diversity in all other things, and charity in everything. How can the Church experience diversity and still profess unity? What are the core essentials in your vision of your faith? How do you nourish this vision?
2. What has been your experience of diversity in the Catholic Church?

# JUDE READING GUIDE

### *At a Glance*

| | |
|---|---|
| Who is the main player? | "Jude" |
| What should I look for? | Take time to reflect on the Doxology, verse 24 of the letter; the letter is famous for this. Consider how behavior affects the unity of the Eucharistic community. |
| When was this written? | We do not know the author or his circumstance nor do we have a secure intellectual context. Many scholars consider |

Jude a pseudonym and date the work from the end of the first century or later. Some think that the author is Jude, named in the Gospels among the relatives of Jesus.

Where did these events occur? The content of the letter, including the discussion of ideas from Gnosticism, points to the Gentile world.

Why was this book written? Jude is an argument against false teachers and an exhortation to his readers to remain steadfast.

What is the story? Jude accuses his opponents of immoral behavior during the Eucharistic meals and also of being selfish and divisive. He charges them with sexual immorality, greed, slander, and living for themselves. In short they live on a worldly plane, devoid of the Spirit.

## Before Beginning

### The Obscurity of Jude

Although Jude is among the shortest writings in the New Testament, it bristles with difficulties. Some of these difficulties have to do with placing the composition in the historical development of early Christianity. Others involve grasping its language, which has a number of obscure allusions. The two sorts of problems are related. Our ignorance of the author and his circumstances prevents us from having a secure context for reading the letter. But because Jude so obviously was responding to some kind of specific crisis, every attempt must be made to construct such a context if the letter is to yield any sense at all.

The NAB introduction to Jude states the majority scholarly opinion on most of the questions concerning authorship and occasion. Jude is considered a general epistle of relatively late date. It is an attack on false teachers, probably representing some form of Gnosticism (an early deviant form of Christianity stressing "self-fulfillment"). Another reading of the evidence suggests that Jude could have been written at virtually any period and was concerned less with false teaching than with bad behavior. This minority view will be developed in the paragraphs to follow. The main point, of course, is to make as good sense as possible out of the letter.

## Literary Connections

Far more puzzling than the identity of Jude is the placement of his letter among other early Christian literature. The author mentions an earlier draft he had begun, when the crisis among his readers demanded his turning attention to the polemic now being read by them (3). What was that earlier version? A connected issue is the relation of Jude to 2 Peter. Everyone recognizes that the material in 2 Peter 2 is similar to that in Jude 5–13. Less clear is whether one author depended on the other, or both relied on a shared earlier tradition. Neither should the resemblance be overstated. Jude is not simply a source for 2 Peter or vice versa. Each author takes the same material and uses it in a way that is different from the other one.

Further puzzles are provided by Jude's literary allusions. He cites examples of sinners being punished. Some are readily apparent from the Bible, although a few (like Balaam) may derive as well from Jewish biblical interpretation. Jude also cites the apocryphal writing known as 1 Enoch as though it were Scripture (14). And his version of the dispute between Michael and Satan over the body of Moses appears to derive from another apocryphal writing, "The Assumption of Moses" (9). His reference to the "words spoken by the apostles" (17) is no clearer, because it is more an amalgam of early Christian statements on the end-time (e.g., see Mk 13:22; 1 Tm 4:1–3) than a specific citation.

That an author could assume familiarity with such sources among his readers seems to presuppose either a Jewish-Christian readership, or a Gentile one familiar with Jewish apocrypha. What the ancient readers presumably understood, we do not, and the lack of literary context continues to make this letter obscure to present-day readers.

## Historical Setting

Writings like 2 Peter and Jude remind us how little we know about early Christianity apart from the chronology provided by Acts and Paul's letters. We cannot fit these books into any development we know about and must rely on guesswork. Every hypothesis, furthermore, is based solely on the text itself. Precision concerning what the text does and does not say is obviously critical to the value of any reconstruction.

Jude clearly takes a polemical stand against opponents and exhorts its readers to remain steadfast. Contrary to the usual opinion, however, the text contains no clear indication that Jude was opposing "false teachers" or that they were teaching any "heresy." Their "scorning of Lordship" (vv. 4, 8) seems to have been practical rather than theoretical. Jude attacks immoral behavior rather than false teaching. So thorough is his disparagement that it is hard to know even what they were doing. He specifically accuses them of disrupting the community love feasts. The term is usually taken to mean eucharistic meals. They are also accused of carousing and of looking after only themselves (literally: "shepherding themselves," 12). He also calls their behavior divisive (19). Otherwise, Jude uses all the standardized charges common to the polemic of the ancient world: They are sexually immoral (7), greedy (11, 16), slanderous (15), and living for their own desires (16). In short, they "live on the natural plane, devoid of the Spirit" (19). They "pervert the grace of our God into licentiousness" (4).

## Living by God's Grace

Letters of Paul such as 1 Corinthians attest how difficult it was for the early Christians to translate the gift of God (grace) into consistent patterns of moral behavior. Legitimate disagreement could exist on matters of diet, work, use of possessions, and the like. It was not immediately obvious in all cases what "Life in the Spirit" meant behaviorally. In the case of Jude, however, it appears that disagreement has overstepped the boundary into true moral deviance, hence, the outrage of the author. The opponents are "perverting the gift."

Jude's first line of defense is an attack on the immoral people. He tries to demonstrate from Scripture how there have always been such troublemakers, and they have always been punished. These will be punished as well. In contrast to 2 Peter 2, in which the emphasis is on the power of God to judge the righteous and unrighteous, in Jude the stress is entirely on the punishment of the rebellious.

The polemic is not random but carefully argued, with some rhetorical polish. Notice the repetition of "these people" in verses 8, 10, 12, 16, and 19, which brings the examples of old to bear on the present circumstances. Jude also plays on the Greek words for "keep" in verses 1, 6, 13, 21, and 24. His opponents fail to "keep their place," but Jude's readers are to "keep themselves in the love of God" who is, in turn, able to "keep them from stumbling."

Jude's second line of defense is to edify ("build up") his readers in their "most holy faith" (20). He reminds them that God dealt with troubles like these from of old, and in fact the apostles of Jesus had foretold the emergence of such rebellious "scoffers" (17f). He reassures them that they are being "kept safe for Jesus Christ" despite this turmoil (1). Jude does not suggest that it is the believers' role to punish the reprobate. He exhorts them to avoid such immoral behavior (23) and to build up their own faith. If the opponents are "devoid of spirit," the believers are to "pray in the Spirit" (20). But their love for God is to be demonstrated in an attitude of mercy and care for those who waver and even for those who appear to be lost (22f).

Jude's witness is a limited one. But the use of moral outrage is not entirely exhausted by the circumstances of the first century. The tendency to turn grace into libertinism is a perennial one. Combining justifiable outrage at license with mercy for the licentious is a delicate and difficult art. Few writings have carried it off as well as Jude.

### Questions for Discussion and Reflection

*Group Sharing/Discussion*

1. Why is Jude obscure to present-day readers?
2. What does Jude teach concerning the attitude

of his community toward those who waver in their faith (22f)?

3. In the light of your reading of Jude, what is the difference between legitimate differences and moral deviances in a Christian community?

4. In an argumentative tone Jude accuses his opponents: They "live on the natural plane, devoid of the Spirit" (19). Name the specific actions that Jude condemns.

***In Our Lives***

1. Jude reminds his readers that "shepherding oneself" is a "division" (19) in the Eucharistic meal of the community (12). Discuss the meaning and importance of this statement both in his text and in today's world.

2. Share the experience of how the Eucharist is the sign and source of unity. Describe how individualism looks in our life and culture. Explain how this helps or weakens the unity of the Eucharistic community.

***Individual/Personal Reflection/Action***

1. Read verses 20–23. Take time to meditate on their personal meaning. Consider how these words of Jude are heard by present-day Catholics.

2. Pray and reflect upon Jude's ending doxology: "To the one who is able to keep you from stumbling and to present you unblemished and exultant, in the presence of his glory, to the only God, our savior, through Jesus Christ our Lord be glory, majesty, power, and authority from ages past, now, and for ages to come."

# REVELATION READING GUIDE

### *At a Glance*

| | |
|---|---|
| Who are the main players? | God Jesus Christ John People of the seven churches of Asia |
| What should I look for? | Do not read this literally, nor as a prediction of coming events. Understanding the literary form is very important in reaching the religious message of Revelation. This is apocalyptic literature, which contains an account of visions in symbolic and allegorical language borrowed extensively from the Old Testament. Look for the use of symbolic colors, metals, garments, and numbers (e.g., *four* signifies the world or wholeness [as in four directions], *six* imperfections, *seven* totality, *twelve* Israel's tribes or the apostles, *one thousand* immensity). |
| When was this written? | This is an exhortation to Christians to stand firm in their faith despite the threat of adversity and martyrdom. The date is probably near the end of Domitian's reign as Roman emperor, A.D. 81–96. |
| Who wrote this book? | Probably a disciple of John the apostle writing to the churches in Asia Minor |
| Why was this book written? | The book of Revelation can only adequately be understood against the historical background that occasioned its writing. It is composed as resistance literature to meet a crisis. The book suggests the crisis was ruthless persecution of the early church by Roman authorities. |
| What is the story? | John has been exiled to the rocky island of Patmos, a Roman penal colony, because of his Christian faith. The voice of his prophecy is directed to the seven Christian churches of Asia Minor. The author's message is that the |

What is the story? *(cont.)* victory of God over evil has been accomplished through the death and resurrection of Jesus, and the faithful who have been killed already share his victory in heaven. The religious message is simple: to the faithful, it says, "hold on"; to the wavering, it declares, "stand fast." It is a message of hope and consolation and challenge for all who dare to believe.

## Before Beginning

### A Book of Christian Prophecy

The book of Revelation makes for difficult reading. Many interpretations of it over the centuries have led to disastrous consequences both for individuals and communities. The fundamental error is to take Revelation as a literal set of predictions from the past about current events. Reading Revelation that way has been popular for a long time, but it has become an obsession for many contemporaries. Such readings have successively been disconfirmed by facts; the "end-time" has been awaited many times without occurring. Such readings have caused the distortion of lives. Many have abandoned livelihoods and loved ones to meet the New Jerusalem, only to have their dreams destroyed. Such readings also miss the real religious message of Revelation. They reduce its value to that of an astrological chart.

Although the text itself virtually calls out for such an interpretation, with its promise to reveal "what must happen soon" (22:18–19), it is critical to recognize that just such statements are standard features of a specific literary genre of the ancient world, called apocalyptic. Two convictions should guide faithful study of Revelation.

1. First, as with all the biblical writings, the Word of God was addressed first to the original audience; a text's "fuller" meaning for successive ages is secondary and never to be divorced from that first, historical, meaning.

2. Second, as in all literature, religious or otherwise, literary genre dictates the way meaning is conveyed.

Newspapers and poetry do not communicate their respective "truths" in identical ways. Knowing the conventions of a literary form is necessary to intelligent reading.

## Revelation as Apocalyptic

### What is Apocalyptic?

"APOCALYPSE" IS DERIVED from a Greek word, *apokalypsis,* that means "taking away the veil" (the Latin word for this is *revelatio*). The "veil" is the confusing flow of events in the reader's present-day environment, which the particular apocalyptic writing intends to interpret, so that the reader can learn the "true meaning" of history leading to the events of the present. In addition, because apocalyptic writings are often produced in conditions of political oppression, the message is delivered in a coded manner that will not be apparent to the outside reader, particularly one who is a member or agent of the oppressing group.

Beginning at least with the book of Daniel in the Old Testament, the apocalyptic style was widely used in Judaism during the New Testament period. Generated by persecution from without and the threat of apostasy from within, this "literature of the oppressed" quickly gained certain standard features:

1. Revelations about the future are experienced in dreams or visions.

2. The insights are communicated through a complex symbolism involving numbers, animals, and cosmic phenomena.
3. The element of prediction is actually a fiction.
4. The seer interprets events of his own age, using a figure of the past (such as Enoch) or an angelic being as a spokesperson.

These literary features serve to express an interpretation of history. Apocalyptic writing defends God's justice. Events appear to be under the control of evil people or even satanic powers, because those devoted to God are being persecuted. Such is the "present age." But apocalyptic literature places God's blessing in a future time, "the age to come." Just when things become humanly impossible on earth, God will intervene (as through a Messiah) to save his own, and thus inaugurate the "kingdom of God."

Apocalyptic literature reconciles the conviction that God controls history with the experience that suggests God does not. The religious message is simple. To the faithful, it says, "hold on"; to the wavering, "stand fast." It offers the hope of eventual vindication to those now oppressed but remaining loyal to the one God.

## Revelation as Prophecy

Revelation fits the apocalyptic genre well. It has visions, animals, numbers, and cosmic catastrophes. It has a two-age interpretation of history. And its basic religious message is a call for the "endurance of the holy ones" (13:10; 14:12). In other ways, however, Revelation transcends the genre. The author is not a fictional sage from the past but a leader well known to his readers. The voice of prophecy is directed explicitly (and not in coded fashion) to the seven churches of Asia Minor in chapters 2 and 3. Most importantly, the turn of the ages has already begun. The victory of God over evil has in principle been accomplished through the death and resurrection of Jesus; even more impressively, the faithful who have been killed already share in that victory in heaven.

The self-understanding of the church in this writing is thoroughly prophetic. Those who follow Jesus are "servants and prophets and saints" (11:18). Their witness is the "spirit of prophecy" (19:10). Jesus is the first and "faithful witness" (1:5) whose mission they continue. The nature of their prophecy is to bear witness to the reality of God in the world. In the letters of chapters 2 and 3, this is expressed as fidelity in face of corruption or apostasy. In the visions of chapters 4 through 21, it is expressed as loyalty in face of the idolatrous claims of the state and even of possible death.

## The Opening Vision (1:1–20)

The prologue (1:1–3) and the epilogue (22:6–21) provide an explicit prophetic framework for the entire work and reveal a self-conscious literary awareness as well (cf. 1:3; 22:18). The understanding of prophecy as witness, which becomes the major theme of the book, is sounded at once (1:2).

The popularity of letter writing in early Christianity is shown by the fact that this apocalyptic writing contains letters to the seven churches of Asia Minor (Rev 2–3), and even has an epistolary greeting to introduce the work (1:4–8). The author identifies himself as one known to his readers and recounts the vision that provides the basis for the rest of the book. The phrasing of 1:9 suggests that John is on the Greek island of Patmos as a punishment for his witness to Jesus. The vision that now comforts him becomes an exhortation to all who are likewise oppressed.

The Risen Jesus is encountered as the Son of Man (the central figure in much apocalyptic writing), described in the most transcendent terms available. The reader is now in the realm of visions, which means the realm of symbols. The terms are obviously not meant literally, any more than are the later fantastic descriptions of heaven. The terms used here and elsewhere are not fresh-minted but are the coinage of biblical

**Historical Dates to Assist Understanding of the Book of Revelation**

1. The death and resurrection of Jesus: the beginning of the 30s.
2. The martyrdom of Peter and Paul and Nero's persecution of the Christians: the 60s.
3. The capture of Jerusalem and the destruction of the Temple: 70–73.
4. After the destruction of the Temple, conflicts between Jews and Christians increased, resulting in a complete break around the year 90.
5. The Roman emperor Domitian (81–90) imposed the practice of emperor worship. Christians were often suspect and objects of persecution because of their refusal to participate in this ritual.

symbolism. Of all apocalyptic writings, Revelation most artfully weaves together the themes of classical prophecy, especially of the prophet Ezekiel. The footnotes and cross-references in the NAB will repay the effort required. One should quickly realize that Revelation is a self-conscious and complex literary construction.

The Son of Man appears with the stars in his hands, standing amid seven lampstands. Revelation makes clear from the start:

1. It is the risen and powerful Lord (in cosmic control) who reveals, and

2. That he is present to the churches (1:20), the concerns of which are taken up in the letters that follow.

## Letters to the Seven Churches (2:1–3:22)

In what are literally "spirit letters" (see chs 2, 7)

**What is the Spirit Saying to the Churches?**

**Read the Letters aloud and fill the spaces:**

| | Addressed to whom? | Christ described as . . . | Judgment? | Conversion? | What is promised? |
|---|---|---|---|---|---|
| **Ephesus 2:1–7** | | | | | |
| **Smyrna 2:8–11** | | | | | |
| **Pergamum 2:12–17** | | | | | |
| **Thyatira 2:18–29** | | | | | |
| **Sardis 3:1–6** | | | | | |
| **Philadelphia 3:7–13** | | | | | |
| **Laodicea 3:14–22** | | | | | |

**This activity is based on a chart in Jean-Pierre Prevost's book, *How to Read the Apocalypse* (New York: Crossroad, 1993), p. 70.**

from the Risen Jesus, seven churches of well known cities in Asia Minor receive individualized prophecies. Revelation understands "prophecy" not as predictions of the future but as exhortations to remain faithful to the integrity of their calling. The trials and lapses of the Christians in these communities are here put on remarkable display. We also hear fragments of sayings (such as in 2:3) that occur elsewhere in the New Testament literature (see 1 Thes 5:2 and Mk 13:33).

The letters all follow the same format. There is a greeting, followed by an elaborate designation of Jesus. The Risen Lord analyzes each community's spiritual condition and concludes with words of warning or of promise. The description of the church's struggles show how they faced opposition from without (as from the Jews), but even more, division within (as with the Nicolaitans). Corruption, too, appears as a vivid possibility. Typical for Johannine literature, the opposition is pictured in terms of false prophecy (2:20). The focus of praise and of persuasion in these letters is endurance.

The imagery of the letters is lush. Who can resist the almost fairy-tale quality of this statement: "I shall also give a white amulet upon which is inscribed a new name, which no one knows except the one who receives it" (2:17)? Beneath the poetry, however, lies grim reality. The difficulty in these letters of maintaining loyalty in the face of social exclusion and human laxity is raised, in the visions that follow, to the level of a cosmic conflict between the Lord and the forces of evil.

## God and the Lamb in Heaven (4:1–5:14)

John is "caught up in Spirit" (4:2), and the rest of Revelation consists in the visions he experienced in his ecstatic state. The vision is a staple of apocalyptic writing. It is found with equal frequency in early Jewish mysticism, called Merkabah, or "throne-chariot" mysticism (*merkabhah,* the Hebrew word for "chariot," comes from Ezekiel's vision of the heavenly chariot in Ez 1:4–28). In prayer, the adept ascended through the heavens to the throne of God's presence. Much of the celestial furniture here resembles that of the Merkabah writings: the jewel-encrusted throne room (4:3f); the sea of glass (4:6); the angelic creatures (4:6–9); and the numinous hymns sung in praise of God (5:9–13).

A dramatic departure from standard symbolism is the appearance of "the lamb that seemed to have been slain" (5:6). Jesus is also called "Lamb of God" in John's Gospel (1:29; see also Jn 19:36, a reference to the Passover lamb). It is a bold stroke to picture Jesus in such paradoxical animal terms, but this verse is in a sense the key to understanding Revelation. The salient aspect of the lamb is its sacrificial function: Jesus was slain. But this lamb is also "the lion of the tribe of Judah," who has triumphed over death (5:5). The ruling power of the universe is identified with self-sacrificing love. In a powerful assertion of Jesus' status after his resurrection, the lamb is at "the right hand of the one who sat on the throne" (5:7; see Ps 110:1). Both figures receive the praise of the heavenly creatures (5:9–11) and indeed of all creation (5:13f ).

The special character of the visions of Revelation is shown by the problem of "the scroll" (5:1). It contains the secrets to be revealed, and because of its use in Ezekiel, it is immediately recognizable as a symbol for prophecy (10:8–11, and Ez 2:9–3:4). Because of his resurrection, Jesus is empowered to open the scroll (5:5). What follows, therefore, is both a revelation of and from Jesus Christ (see 1:1). The visions will show "what must happen afterwards" (4:1), but the reader is not frightened, knowing from this first vision that the fundamental victory has already been accomplished.

## Visions of Cosmic Conflict (6:1–16:21)

The next section of Revelation is the most difficult to make sense of, and, not surprisingly, the most worked over for signs of the end. The candidates selected to fit the profile of the "Beast" with the number 666 (13:18) have ranged from Nero to Hitler.

The visions are so structured as to give the illusion of temporal sequence, linked together as they are by the phrase "and then I saw . . . " It is indeed tempting to translate a series of visions into a sequence of historical events, so readers have tried to compute the overlapping series of

**The Cosmic Conflict**

ON ONE SIDE we see all the "beasts" who oppose the faithful: the dragon (12:1–8), the first beast (13:1–10), and the second beast (13:11–17). These are not separate enemies but successive masks of the one force of evil. As in modern horror films, the destruction of one gives rise to another more horrifying still. Beneath the different manifestations, one visible enemy is most prevalent: the idolatrous state that persecutes the saints, enslaves them, and seeks to kill them (13:7–18).

On the other side are those loyal to God, the "servants, prophets, and saints" (11:18; 19:9f). They continue Jesus' own faithful witness to God by witnessing to Jesus. By so doing, they reject the idolatrous claims of the state on their obeisance. They suffer the consequences, some of them by shedding blood. Revelation establishes the connection between "witness" and "martyr" by the disciples' imitation of Jesus' death.

sevens: seals (6:1–17; 8:1), trumpets (8:1–9:21; 11:15), plagues (15:1–8), and bowls (16:1–20). But neither the events reported by headlines nor elaborate literary analyses have ever satisfactorily unlocked this dense poetry. It is in fact more likely that all the visions repeat the same basic message. The saints on earth, locked in conflict with hostile forces, find a cosmic counterpart in the struggle between God and Satan.

The prophetic self-consciousness of this church is most clearly stated in the account of the two witnesses (11:1–13). This earthly interlude shows two people, who both "witness" and "testify" (the terms are interchangeable). They are killed in imitation of Jesus (11:7). They are also called into heaven (11:12). The vignette describes the conviction of Revelation that those who share Jesus' death also share his triumph in heaven. Thus, alternating with scenes of suffering on earth below are serene descriptions of the saints in heaven celebrating the anticipated and certain victory of the Lamb (5:9f; 6:9–11; 7:4–7; 14:1–5; 15:2–4). In standard apocalyptic literature, history moves downward to ever more dismal circumstances, until God finally intervenes. In Revelation, however, the final outcome is not in doubt. Not only Jesus but also those "defeated" with him by evil already share in the resurrection triumph. The earthly conquest is just a matter of tidying up.

It is useless to tease such poetry into a train schedule for current events. The vision here is not one of history unfolding like clockwork; it is a religious vision of God's ultimate conquest despite current appearances. Once the reader lets go of the obsessive "need to know" that twists beauty into charts and tables, it is possible to wonder at the powerful poetic and religious imagination at work in these glorious images.

## Punishment of Babylon (17:1–20:15)

The masks fall away, revealing as the real enemy of God's people the Roman Empire, "the great harlot who lives near the many waters" (17:1). Rome is called Babylon (17:5) because in the biblical tradition it was Babylon above all that symbolized the desecration of the Temple and the exile of the people. In typical apocalyptic fashion, the sequence of events is laid out: God has given temporary rule to this evil empire to accomplish his ends. It does battle against the lamb and the people.

The persecution and suffering were undoubtedly real. These Christians were faced with the choices of all who suffer oppression. Were they to resist violently and seek the overthrow of Rome? That was futile as well as contrary to their ethos. Were they simply to cooperate? That would be to lose their identity. They chose the path of passive resistance. They did not fight the beast, but neither would they do its bidding. The path of martyrdom, however slow or fast, is not easy. For those who survive, the psychic toll is considerable. Anger at the enemy can easily turn inward; patient endurance is hard. They were convinced that "the lamb will conquer" (17:14), but in their earthly condition they had not yet seen it happen. Rome's fall is therefore described in delicious detail. The pent-up fury of the oppressed is released in glee over the degradation of the oppressor. Much of this is obviously and literally wish fulfillment, the stuff of fantasy. The anger of a downtrodden people is deflected to a punishing God.

The end-time reveals how "the words of God are accomplished" (17:17). The "Word of God" himself (19:13) leads the climactic battle and inaugurates the messianic age, when the saints "will reign with Christ for a thousand years" (20:4–6). But this is not yet the end. There is another outbreak of demonic destruction (20:7–10) and the tossing of the Devil into the fire, then the resurrection of the dead for final judgment (20:11–15). These stages lack poetry, but the final vision overcomes this deficiency.

## The New Creation (21:1–22:21)

The conclusion to Revelation is a fitting conclusion to the Bible as a whole. The vision of a new creation (21:1) is central to the New Testament (e.g., see 2 Cor 5:17). The Christian experience of Christ was an absolute beginning, rooted in the ever-new life of God himself. God can say, "Behold, I make all things new" (21:5) because God is "the Alpha and the Omega, the beginning and the end" of all things (21:6; 22:13). As Genesis began with the creation by a word, so the vision of the end-time recapitulates that beginning: Creation is renewed.

The hope expressed by Revelation is not simply that souls should be saved after death, or that evil should be conquered, or even that saints should reign for a thousand years over a burnt-out terrain. The hope is that creation itself will be transformed. So the sight of a "New Jerusalem coming down out of heaven from God" is the vision of a civilized order, one that is intrinsically holy in the proper sense. Human society is based on the recognition of God's power and presence. There is no place for those, now, who refuse the "dwelling place of God with the human race" (21:3, 7f).

In this city, there is not even need for "religion" as a separate compartment of life. The temple of the city is "the Lord God almighty and the Lamb" (21:22). And all the city's people will be priests of [the Lord] God (20:6), showing at last that the fundamental human vocation is praise of God (22:9). There need be no division between peoples. Nothing is here accursed (22:3). The nations will walk by the light of the Lamb (21:24), and the trees of the city "serve as medicine for the nations" (22:2). And what medicine! There will be "no more death or mourning, wailing or pain, [for] the old order has passed away" (21:4).

Great harm has come to those who have tried by force to make this vision a reality, and establish a thousand-year reign of the saints on earth. Great despair has come to the utopians who have tried on the basis of goodwill to construct a society like the New Jerusalem.

The vision has its value precisely as challenge, as ever-receding prophecy to all human effort for renewal. This renewal does not come about by human cunning but by God's gift. So compelling is the vision that no one who hears it can help joining in the plaintive cry of the epilogue, "Amen! Come, Lord Jesus!" The epilogue also reminds us that we are still in the in-between time when the world is not re-created. There is still need for the witness of prophecy and for endurance of the saints, for "the wicked still act wickedly, and the filthy still [are] filthy. The righteous must still do right, and the holy still be holy" (22:11).

### Questions for Discussion and Reflection

***Group Sharing/Discussion***

1. Why was John on the Isle of Patmos?

2. In Revelation Rome is called "Babylon." Why?

3. What are the qualities of the "New Jerusalem coming down out of heaven from God" (21:2–9f)?

4. Throughout Revelation Christ is given many new titles. Example: Jesus, Christ, the firstborn of the dead, who holds the key of David, and so on. Let each person choose one of these titles and explain its meaning.

5. Literary form dictates the meaning of Scripture. What are some qualities of apocalyptic literature as seen in Revelation?

***In Our Lives***

1. The persecution and suffering from Rome were undoubtedly real. The choices these Christians faced were also real. Should they simply cooperate? Resist Rome violently? Choose passive resistance? What did they choose? Why? (17:14)

| Number | Meaning | References |
|---|---|---|
| One or first | Primacy, excellence | 1:17; 2:8; 22:13 |
| Three or third | Limited | 8:1; 12:14; 11:9; 4:7; 6:5; 8:7–12 |
| Four | Whole, universality | 4:6–8; 5:6–8, 14; 6:1, 6; 7:11; 14:3; 15:7; 19:4 |
| Six | Imperfection | 13:18 |
| Seven | Fullness, perfection | 1:4, 12, 16; 4:5; 5:1 |
| Twelve | Continuity with the chosen people | 12:1; 21:12, 14, 20, 21 |
| Thousand | Superlative, very many | Chapters 7; 14; 20 |

2. According to Revelation, the Christian experiences Christ as the "Alpha and Omega" (21:6) who came to make all things new (21:5). How do you experience Christ in your family, your work, your friends, people in your community? How do you see Christ as the Alpha and Omega who comes to make all things new?

3. The Word of God is addressed to the original audience in their historical context. The fuller meaning for later ages is secondary and never divorced from the original meaning. Select a letter or vision in Revelation and explain this truth about God's revelation.

4. The religious message of Revelation is simple: Apocalyptic literature reconciles the conviction that God controls history with the experience that suggests that God does not. Reflect on how this applies to your experience and your community's experience.

5. The nature of prophecy is to bear witness to the reality of God in the world. Describe prophecy in Revelation (11:18; 19:10). Share with someone how this prophecy applies to your world.

***Individual/Personal Reflection/Action***

1. Take time to read carefully and pray the beautiful acclamations of Christ in the book of Revelation: 1:2–7; 5:1; 7:10; 19:6–7; 5:9–10; 5:13; and 11:15.

2. Pray the Seven Beatitudes of the book of Revelation: 1:3; 14:13; 16:15; 19:9; 20:6; 22:7; and 22:14.

3. Ancient peoples gave symbolism to special numbers. Look at the meaning of the numbers listed in the table above, then turn to the book of Revelation and reread the indicated passages. You may come to a better understanding of the poetic imagery.

# THE OLD TESTAMENT

NEW AMERICAN BIBLE

# PREFACE TO THE *NEW AMERICAN BIBLE*

## Old Testament

On September 30, 1943, His Holiness Pope Pius XII issued his now famous encyclical on scripture studies, *Divino Afflante Spiritu.* He wrote: "We ought to explain the original text which was written by the inspired author himself and has more authority and greater weight than any, even the very best, translation whether ancient or modern. This can be done all the more easily and fruitfully if to the knowledge of languages be joined a real skill in literary criticism of the same text."

Early in 1944, in conformity with the spirit of the encyclical, and with the encouragement of Archbishop Cicognani, Apostolic Delegate to the United States, the Bishops' Committee of the Confraternity of Christian Doctrine requested members of The Catholic Biblical Association of America to translate the sacred scriptures from the original languages or from the oldest extant form of the text, and to present the sense of the biblical text in as correct a form as possible.

The first English Catholic version of the Bible, the Douay-Rheims (1582–1609/10), and its revision by Bishop Challoner (1750) were based on the Latin Vulgate. In view of the relative certainties more recently attained by textual and higher criticism, it has become increasingly desirable that contemporary translations of the sacred books into English be prepared in which due reverence for the text and strict observance of the rules of criticism would be combined.

*The New American Bible* has accomplished this in response to the need of the church in America today. It is the achievement of some fifty biblical scholars, the greater number of whom, though not all, are Catholics. In particular, the editors-in-chief have devoted twenty-five years to this work. The collaboration of scholars who are not Catholic fulfills the directive of the Second Vatican Council, not only that "correct translations be made into different languages especially from the original texts of the sacred books," but that, "with the approval of the church authority, these translations be produced in cooperation with separated brothers" so that "all Christians may be able to use them."

The text of the books contained in *The New American Bible* is a completely new translation throughout. From the original and the oldest available texts of the sacred books, it aims to convey as directly as possible the thought and individual style of the inspired writers. The better understanding of Hebrew and Greek, and the steady development of the science of textual criticism, the fruit of patient study since the time of St. Jerome, have allowed the translators and editors in their use of all available materials to approach more closely than ever before the sense of what the sacred authors actually wrote.

Where the translation supposes the received text—Hebrew, Aramaic, or Greek, as the case may be—ordinarily contained in the best-known editions, as the original or the oldest extant form, no additional remarks are necessary. But for those who are happily able to study the original text of the scriptures at firsthand, a supplementary series of textual notes pertaining to the Old Testament was added originally in an appendix to the typical edition. (It is now obtainable in a separate booklet from The Catholic Biblical Association of America, The Catholic University of America, Washington, DC 20064.) These notes furnish a guide in those cases in which the editorial board judges that the manuscripts in the original languages, or the evidence of the ancient versions, or some similar source, furnish the correct reading of a passage, or at least a reading more true to the original than that customarily printed in the available editions.

The Massoretic text of 1 and 2 Samuel has in numerous instances been corrected by the more ancient manuscripts Samuel a, b, and c from Cave 4 of Qumran, with the aid of important evidence from the Septuagint in both its oldest form and its Lucianic recension. Fragments of the lost Book of Tobit in Aramaic and in Hebrew, recovered from Cave 4 of Qumran, are in substantial agreement with the Sinaiticus Greek recension used for the translation of this book. The lost original Hebrew text of 1 Maccabees is replaced by its oldest extant form in Greek. Judith, 2 Maccabees, and parts of Esther are also translated from the Greek.

# *Preface*

The basic text for the Psalms is not the Masoretic but one which the editors considered closer to the original inspired form, namely the Hebrew text underlying the new Latin Psalter of the Church, the *Liber Psalmorum* (1944[1], 1945[2]). Nevertheless they retained full liberty to establish the reading of the original text on sound critical principles.

The translation of Sirach, based on the original Hebrew as far as it is preserved and corrected from the ancient versions, is often interpreted in the light of the traditional Greek text. In the Book of Baruch the basic text is the Greek of the Septuagint, with some readings derived from an underlying Hebrew form no longer extant. In the deuterocanonical sections of Daniel (3:24–90; 13:1–14:42), the basic text is the Greek text of Theodotion, occasionally revised according to the Greek text of the Septuagint.

In some instances in the Book of Job, in Proverbs, Sirach, Isaiah, Jeremiah, Ezekiel, Hosea, Amos, Micah, Nahum, Habakkuk, and Zechariah there is good reason to believe that the original order of lines was accidentally disturbed in the transmission of the text. The verse numbers given in such cases are always those of the current Hebrew text, though the arrangement differs. In these instances the textual notes advise the reader of the difficulty. Cases of exceptional dislocation are called to the reader's attention by footnotes.

The Books of *Genesis to Ruth* were first published in 1952; the Wisdom Books, *Job to Sirach,* in 1955; the Prophetic Books, *Isaiah to Malachi,* in 1961; and the Historical Books, *Samuel to Maccabees,* in 1969. In the present edition of *Genesis to Ruth* there are certain new features: a general introduction to the Pentateuch, a retranslation of the text of Genesis with an introduction, cross-references, and revised textual notes, besides new and expanded exegetical notes which take into consideration the various sources or literary traditions.

The revision of *Job to Sirach* includes changes in strophe division in Job and Proverbs and in titles of principal parts and sections of Wisdom and Ecclesiastes. Corrections in the text of Sirach are made in 39:27–44:17 on the basis of the Masada text, and in 51:13–30 on the basis of the occurrence of this canticle in the Psalms scroll from Qumran Cave 11. In this typical edition, new corrections are reflected in the textual notes of Job, Proverbs, Wisdom, and Sirach. In the Psalms, the enumeration found in the Hebrew text is followed instead of the double enumeration, according to both the Hebrew and the Latin Vulgate texts, contained in the previous edition of this book.

In the Prophetic Books *Isaiah to Malachi,* only minor revisions have been made in the structure and wording of the texts, and in the textual notes.

The spelling of proper names in *The New American Bible* follows the customary forms found in most English Bibles since the Authorized Version.

The work of translating the Bible has been characterized as "the sacred and apostolic work of interpreting the word of God and of presenting it to the laity in translations as clear as the difficulty of the matter and the limitations of human knowledge permit" (A. G. Cicognani, Apostolic Delegate, in *The Catholic Biblical Quarterly,* 6, [1944], 389–90). In the appraisal of the present work, it is hoped that the words of the encyclical *Divino afflante Spiritu* will serve as a guide: "Let all the sons of the church bear in mind that the efforts of these resolute laborers in the vineyard of the Lord should be judged not only with equity and justice but also with the greatest charity; all moreover should abhor that intemperate zeal which imagines that whatever is new should for that very reason be opposed or suspected."

Conscious of their personal limitations for the task thus defined, those who have prepared this text cannot expect that it will be considered perfect; but they can hope that it may deepen in its readers "the right understanding of the divinely given Scriptures," and awaken in them "that piety by which it behooves us to be grateful to the God of all providence, who from the throne of his majesty has sent these books as so many personal letters to his own children" *(Divino afflante Spiritu).*

# PREFACE TO THE REVISED *NEW AMERICAN BIBLE*

## Old Testament

The first step in the genesis of *The New American Bible* was taken in 1936 when His Excellency, the Most Reverend Edwin V. O'Hara, D.D., chairman of the Episcopal Committee of the Confraternity of Christian Doctrine, invited a group of Catholic Scripture scholars to plan for a revised edition of the Challoner-Rheims New Testament, primarily on the basis of the Vulgate; the plans soon expanded to include the revision of the Old Testament. Archbishop O'Hara's initiative resulted in the formation of the Catholic Biblical Association, whose principal activity in its early years was this work of revision and translation. (For information on the work done on the New Testament, see the "Preface to *The New American Bible*: First Edition of the New Testament" and "Preface to the Revised Edition.") In 1943 His Holiness Pope Pius XII issued the encyclical *Divino afflante spiritu*, which encouraged Scripture scholars to translate the Scriptures from the original languages. He wrote: "We ought to explain the original text which was written by the inspired author himself and has more authority and greater weight than any, even the very best, translation whether ancient or modern. This can be done all the more easily and fruitfully if to the knowledge of languages be joined a real skill in literary criticism of the same text." Although at this point work on almost twenty of the Old Testament books was completed or near completion, that work was abandoned and the new project of translating from the Hebrew, Greek, and Aramaic was undertaken.

The completed books of the Old Testament were initially published, as they became available, in four volumes: Genesis–Ruth (1952), Job–Sirach (1955), Isaiah–Malachi (1961), and Samuel–Maccabees (1969). Some fifty scholars collaborated on this project; these were mainly Catholics, but, in accord with the suggestion of Vatican II that "with the approval of the church authority, these translations be produced in cooperation with separated brothers" so that "all Christians may be able to use them" (*Dei Verbum*, No. 22), non-Catholics also participated in the work. To this point the translation had been known under the name of the "Confraternity of Christian Doctrine" or CCD for short, but when these parts of the Old Testament were combined with the New Testament in a single volume, it was given the name "New American Bible," in part to reflect its ecumenical character. In producing the new volume certain changes were made from the original four volumes: a retranslation of the Book of Genesis, cross-references, new and expanded exegetical notes.

New translations and revision of existing translations are required from time to time for various reasons. For example, it is important to keep pace with the discovery and publication of new and better ancient manuscripts (e.g., the Dead Sea scrolls) so that the best possible textual tradition will be followed, as required by *Divino afflante spiritu*. There are advances in linguistics of the biblical languages which make possible a better understanding and more accurate translation of the original languages. And there are changes and developments in vocabulary and the cultural background of the receptor language. An obvious example of this is the abandonment in English of the second person singular (use of "thee," "thou," "sayest," "hearest"), which had a major impact on Bible translations. Other changes are less obvious but are nevertheless present. There have been changes in vocabulary; for example, the term "holocaust" is now normally reserved for the sacrilegious attempt to destroy the Jewish people by the Third Reich. Concerns such as these are reflected in what Pope John Paul II spoke of as the "three pillars" of good biblical translation: "A good translation is based on three pillars that must contemporaneously support the entire work. First, there must be a deep knowledge of the language and the cultural world at the point of origin. Next, there must be a good familiarity with the language and cultural context at the point where the work will arrive. Lastly, to crown the work with success, there must be an adequate mastery of the contents and meaning of what one is translating"—and he praised the translation that "utilizes the vocabulary and idioms of everyday speech" ("le parole e le forme della lingua di tutti i giorni"). (From an address to the United Bible Societies, November 26, 2001.)

This new edition is a thorough revision of the already excellent *New American Bible* Old Testament of 1970. Work on most books of the Old Testament, begun in 1994 and completed in 2001, was done by forty revisers and a board of eight editors. The 1991 revision of the Psalter, the work of thirty revisers and six editors, was further revised by seven revisers and two editors between 2009 and 2010. As suggested in the comments above, the revision aimed at making use of the best manuscript traditions available (see below), translating as accurately as possible, and rendering the result in good contemporary English. In many ways it is a more literal translation than the original NAB and has attempted to be more consistent in rendering Hebrew (or Greek) words and idioms, especially in technical contexts, such as regulations for sacrifices. In translating the Psalter special effort was made to provide a smooth, rhythmic translation for easy singing or recitation, and to retain the concrete imagery of the Hebrew.

Where the Old Testament translation supposes the received text—Hebrew, Aramaic, or Greek, as the case may be—ordinarily contained in the best-known editions, as the original or the oldest extant form, no additional remarks are necessary. Where the translators have departed from those received texts, e.g., by following the Septuagint rather than the Masoretic text, accepting a reading of what is judged to be a better textual tradition, as from a Qumran manuscript, or by emending a reading apparently corrupted in transmission, such changes are recorded in the revised edition of the *Textual Notes on The New American Bible*. Additional information on the textual tradition for some books may be found in the introduction to the book in the same *Textual Notes*.

In particular, important manuscripts from Cave 4 of Qumran, as well as the most useful recensions of the Septuagint, have been consulted in the preparation of 1 and 2 Samuel. Fragments of the lost Book of Tobit in Aramaic and in Hebrew, recovered from Cave 4 of Qumran, are in substantial agreement with the Sinaiticus Greek recension used for the translation of this book. The lost original Hebrew text of 1 Maccabees is replaced by its oldest extant form in Greek. Judith, 2 Maccabees, and parts of Esther are also translated from the Greek. The translation of The Wisdom of Ben Sira is based on the original Hebrew as far as it is preserved, with corrections from the ancient versions; otherwise, the Greek of the Septuagint is followed. In the Book of Baruch the basic text is the Greek of the Septuagint, with some readings derived from an underlying Hebrew form no longer extant. In the deuterocanonical sections of Daniel (3:24–90; 13:1–14:42), the basic text is the Greek text of so-called Theodotion, occasionally revised according to the Greek text of the Septuagint.

# THE PENTATEUCH

See RG 34–47

The Pentateuch (Greek for "five books") designates the first five books of the Jewish and Christian Bible (Genesis, Exodus, Leviticus, Numbers, and Deuteronomy). Jewish tradition calls the five books Torah (Teaching, Law) because of the centrality of the Sinai covenant and legislation mediated through Moses.

The unity of the Pentateuch comes from the single story it tells. God creates the world and destines human beings for the blessings of progeny and land possession (Gn 1–3). As the human race expands, its evil conduct provokes God to send the flood to wipe out all but righteous Noah's family. After the flood, the world is repopulated from his three sons, Ham, Shem, and Japheth (Gn 4–9). From them are descended the seventy nations of the civilized world whose offense this time (building a city rather than taking their assigned lands, Gn 10–11) provokes God to elect one family from the rest. Abraham and his wife, Sarah, landless and childless, are promised a child and the land of Canaan. Amid trials and fresh promises, a son (Isaac) is born to them and Abraham takes title to a sliver of Canaanite land, a kind of down payment for later possession (Gn 12–25). Gn 25–36 tells how their descendant Jacob becomes the father of twelve sons (because of which he is called "Israel"), and Gn 37–50 tells how the rejected brother Joseph saves the family from famine and brings them to Egypt.

In Egypt, a pharaoh who knew not Joseph subjects "the seventy sons of Jacob" ("the Hebrews") to hard labor, keeping them from their land and destroying their male progeny (Ex 1). Moses is commissioned to lead the people out of Egypt to their own land (Ex 2–6). In ten plagues, the Lord defeats Pharaoh. Free at last, the Hebrews leave Egypt and journey to Mount Sinai (Ex 7–18), where they enter into a covenant to be the people of the Lord and be shaped by the Ten Commandments and other laws (Ex 19–24). Though the people commit apostasy when Moses goes back to the mountain for the plans of the dwelling (tabernacle), Moses' intercession prevents the abrogation of the covenant by God (Ex 32–34). A principle has been established, however: even the people's apostasy need not end their relationship with God. The book ends with the cloud and the glory taking possession of the tent of meeting (Ex 36:34–38). "The sons of Israel" in Ex 1:1 are the actual sons of Jacob/Israel the patriarch, but at the end of the book they are the nation Israel, for all the elements of nationhood in antiquity have been granted: a god (and temple), a leader, a land, and an authoritative tradition.

Israel remains at the holy mountain for almost a year. The entire block of material from Ex 19:1 to Nm 10:11 is situated at Sinai. The rituals of Leviticus and Numbers are delivered to Moses at the holy mountain, showing that Israel's worship was instituted by God and part of the very fabric of the people's life. Priestly material in the Book of Exodus (chaps. 25–31, 35–40) describes the basic institutions of Israelite worship (the tabernacle, its furniture, and priestly vestments). Leviticus, aptly called in rabbinic tradition the Priests' Manual, lays down the role of priests to teach Israel the distinction between clean and unclean and to see to their holiness. In Nm 10:11–22:1, the journey is resumed, this time from Sinai through the wilderness to Transjordan; Nm 22:2–36:13 tells of events and laws in the plains of Moab.

The final book of the Pentateuch, Deuteronomy, consists of four speeches by Moses to the people who have arrived at the plains of Moab, ready to conquer the land: 1:1–4:43; 4:44–28:68; 29:1–32:52; 33:1–34:12. Each speech is introduced by the formula "This is the law/words/blessing."

The Priestly editor used literary formulas. The formula "These are the generations (the wording can vary) of . . ." occurs five times in the primordial history (Gn 2:4a; 5:1; 6:9; 10:1; 11:10) and five times in the ancestral history (11:27; 25:12; 25:19; 36:1 [v. 9 is secondary]; 37:2). In Exodus and Numbers the formula (with slight variations) "They departed from (place name) and encamped at (place name)" occurs in two groups of six: A. Ex 12:37a; 13:20; 14:1–2; 15:22a; 16:1; 17:1a; and B. 19:2; Nm 10:12; 20:1a; 20:22; 21:10–11; 22:1.

Who wrote the Pentateuch, and when? Up to the seventeenth century, the virtually unanimous answer of Jews and Christians was "Moses." Moses wrote the Pentateuch as David wrote the Psalter and Solomon wrote the wisdom literature. Though scholars had noted inconsistencies (compare Ishmael's age in Gn 16:16 and 21:5, 14) and duplications (Gn 12, 20, and 26), they assumed Mosaic authorship because of the prevalent theory of inspiration: God inspired authors while they wrote. With the rise of historical criticism, scholars began to use the doublets and inconsistencies as clues to different authors and traditions.

By the late nineteenth century, one theory of the sources of the Pentateuch had been worked out that proved acceptable in its main lines to the majority of scholars (apart from Christian and Jewish conservatives) then and now. It can be quickly sketched. In the premonarchic period of the Judges (ca. 1220–1020 B.C.), the twelve tribes had an oral form of their story from creation to the taking of the land. With the beginnings of monarchy in the late eleventh and tenth centuries, the oral material was written down, being known as the Yahwist account (from its use of the divine name Yhwh). Its abbreviation, "J," comes from the German spelling of the divine name. In the following century, another account took shape in the Northern Kingdom (called E after its use of Elohim as a divine name); some believe the E source is simply a supplement to J. After the fall of the Northern Kingdom in 722/721 B.C., the E version was taken to Jerusalem where it was combined with the J version to produce J-E. During the exile (conventionally dated 587–539 B.C.) or thereafter, an editor recast J-E to make it relevant for the exiled population. This editor is conventionally known as P (=Priestly) because of the chronological and ritual interests apparent in the work. P can also designate archival material and chronological notices. The audience for the Priestly edition no longer lived in the land and was deeply concerned about its survival and its claim on the land.

Deuteronomy (=D) stands alone in style, genre (preaching rather than narrative), and content. How did it come to be the fifth book of the Pentateuch? The J-E narrative actually ends in Numbers, when Israel arrives at the plains of Moab. Many scholars believe that Deuteronomy was secondarily attached to Numbers by moving the account of Moses' death from its original place in the J-E version in Numbers to the end of Deuteronomy (chap. 34). Deuteronomy was attached to Genesis–Numbers to link it to another great work, the Deuteronomistic History (Joshua to Kings). Deuteronomy is now the fifth book of the Pentateuch and the first book of the Deuteronomistic History.

In the last three decades, the above consensus on the composition of the Pentateuch has come under attack. Some critics are extremely skeptical about the historical value of the so-called early traditions, and a few doubt there ever was a preexilic monarchy of any substance. For such scholars, the Pentateuch is a retrojection from the fourth or third centuries B.C. Other scholars postulate a different sequence of sources, or understand the sources differently.

How should a modern religiously minded person read the Pentateuch? First, readers have before them the most significant thing, the text of the Pentateuch. It is accurately preserved, reasonably well understood, and capable of touching audiences of every age. Take and read! Second, the controversies are about the sources of the Pentateuch, especially their antiquity and character. Many details will never be known, for the evidence is scanty. Indeed, the origin of many great literary works is obscure.

The Pentateuch witnesses to a coherent story that begins with the creation of the world and ends with Israel taking its land. The same story is in the historical Ps 44, 77, 78, 80, 105, 114, and 149, and in the confessions Dt 26:5–9, Jos 24:2–13, and 1 Sm 12:7–13. Though the narrative enthralls and entertains, as all great literature does, it is well to remember that it is a theopolitical charter as well, meant to establish how and why descendants of the patriarchs are a uniquely holy people among the world's nations.

The destruction of the Jerusalem Temple and deportation of Israelites in the sixth century B.C. seemed to invalidate the charter, for Israel no longer possessed its land in any real sense. The last chapter of the ancient narrative—Israel dwelling securely in its land—no longer held true. The story had to be reinterpreted, and the Priestly editor is often credited with doing so. A preface (Gn 1) was added, emphasizing God's intent that human beings continue in existence through their progeny and possess their own land. Good news, surely, to a devastated people wondering whether they would survive and repossess their ancestral land. The ending of the old story was changed to depict Israel at the threshold of the promised land (the plains of Moab) rather than in it. Henceforth, Israel would be a people oriented toward the land rather than possessing it. The revised ending could not be more suitable for Jews and Christians alike. Both peoples can imagine themselves on the threshold of the promised land, listening to the word of God in order to be able to enter it in the future. For Christians particularly, the Pentateuch portrays the pilgrim people waiting for the full realization of the kingdom of God.

See RG 47–61

# The Book of Genesis

Genesis is the first book of the Pentateuch (Genesis, Exodus, Leviticus, Numbers, Deuteronomy), the first section of the Jewish and the Christian Scriptures. Its title in English, "Genesis," comes from the Greek of Gn 2:4, literally, "the book of the generation (*genesis*) of the heavens and earth." Its title in the Jewish Scriptures is the opening Hebrew word, *Bereshit*, "in the beginning."

The book has two major sections—the creation and expansion of the human race (2:4–11:9), and the story of Abraham and his descendants (11:10–50:26). The first section deals with God and the nations, and the second deals with God and a particular nation, Israel. The opening creation account (1:1–2:3) lifts up two themes that play major roles in each section—the divine command to the first couple (standing for the whole race) to produce offspring and to possess land (1:28). In the first section, progeny and land appear in the form of births and genealogies (chaps. 2–9) and allotment of land (chaps. 10–11), and in the second, progeny and land appear in the form of promises of descendants and land to the ancestors. Another indication of editing is the formulaic introduction, "this is the story; these are the descendants" (Hebrew *tōledôt*), which occurs five times in Section I (2:4; 5:1; 6:9; 10:1; 10:31) and five times in Section II (11:10; 25:12, 19; 36:1 [v. 9 is an addition]; 37:2).

***The Composition of the Book.*** For the literary sources of Genesis, see Introduction to the Pentateuch. As far as the sources of Genesis are concerned, contemporary readers can reasonably assume that ancient traditions (J and E) were edited in the sixth or fifth century B.C. for a Jewish audience that had suffered the effects of the exile and was now largely living outside of Palestine. The editor highlighted themes of vital concern to this audience: God intends that every nation have posterity and land; the ancestors of Israel are models for their descendants who also live in hope rather than in full possession of what has been promised; the ancient covenant with God is eternal, remaining valid even when the human party has been unfaithful. By highlighting such concerns, the editor addressed the worries of exiled Israel and indeed of contemporary Jews and Christians.

***Genesis 1–11.*** The seven-day creation account in Gn 1:1–2:3 tells of a God whose mere word creates a beautiful universe in which human beings are an integral and important part. Though Gn 2:4–3:24 is often regarded as "the second creation story," the text suggests that the whole of

2:4–11:9 tells one story. The plot of Gn 2–11 (creation, the flood, renewed creation) has been borrowed from creation-flood stories attested in Mesopotamian literature of the second and early first millennia. In the Mesopotamian creation-flood stories, the gods created the human race as slaves whose task it was to manage the universe for them—giving them food, clothing, and honor in temple ceremonies. In an unforeseen development, however, the human race grew so numerous and noisy that the gods could not sleep. Deeply angered, the gods decided to destroy the race by a universal flood. One man and his family, however, secretly warned of the flood by his patron god, built a boat and survived. Soon regretting their impetuous decision, the gods created a revised version of humankind. The new race was created mortal so they would never again grow numerous and bother the gods. The authors of Genesis adapted the creation-flood story in accord with their views of God and humanity. For example, they attributed the fault to human sin rather than to divine miscalculation (6:5–7) and had God reaffirm without change the original creation (9:1–7). In the biblical version God is just, powerful, and not needy.

How should modern readers interpret the creation-flood story in Gn 2–11? The stories are neither history nor myth. "Myth" is an unsuitable term, for it has several different meanings and connotes untruth in popular English. "History" is equally misleading, for it suggests that the events actually took place. The best term is creation-flood story. Ancient Near Eastern thinkers did not have our methods of exploring serious questions. Instead, they used narratives for issues that we would call philosophical and theological. They added and subtracted narrative details and varied the plot as they sought meaning in the ancient stories. Their stories reveal a privileged time, when divine decisions were made that determined the future of the human race. The origin of something was thought to explain its present meaning, e.g., how God acts with justice and generosity, why human beings are rebellious, the nature of sexual attraction and marriage, why there are many peoples and languages. Though the stories may initially strike us as primitive and naive, they are in fact told with skill, compression, and subtlety. They provide profound answers to perennial questions about God and human beings.

***Genesis 11–50.*** One Jewish tradition suggests that God, having been rebuffed in the attempt to forge a relationship with the nations, decided to concentrate on one nation in the hope that it would eventually bring in all the nations. The migration of Abraham's family (11:26–31) is part of the general movement of the human race to take possession of their lands (see 10:32–11:9). Abraham, however, must come into possession of his land in a manner different from the nations, for he will not immediately possess it nor will he have descendants in the manner of the nations, for he is old and his wife is childless (12:1–9). Abraham and Sarah have to live with their God in trust and obedience until at last Isaac is born to them and they manage to buy a sliver of the land (the burial cave at Machpelah, chap. 23). Abraham's humanity and faith offer a wonderful example to the exilic generation.

The historicity of the ancestral stories has been much discussed. Scholars have traditionally dated them sometime in the first half of the second millennium, though a few regard them as late (sixth or fifth century B.C.) and purely fictional. There is unfortunately no direct extra-biblical evidence confirming (or disproving) the stories. The ancestral stories have affinities, however, to late second-millennium stories of childless ancestors, and their proper names fit linguistic patterns attested in the second millennium. Given the lack of decisive evidence, it is reasonable to accept the Bible's own chronology that the patriarchs were the ancestors of Israel and that they lived well before the exodus that is generally dated in the thirteenth century.

Gn 25:19–35:43 are about Jacob and his twelve sons. The stories are united by a geographical frame: Jacob lives in Canaan until his theft of the right of the firstborn from his brother Esau forces him to flee to Paddan-Aram (alternately Aram-Naharaim). There his uncle Laban tricks him as he earlier tricked his brother. But Jacob is blessed with wealth and sons. He returns to Canaan to receive the final blessing, land, and on the way is reconciled with his brother Esau. As the sons have reached the number of twelve, the patriarch can be given the name Israel (32:28; 35:10). The blessings given to Abraham are reaffirmed to Isaac and to Jacob.

The last cycle of ancestor stories is about Jacob's son Joseph (37:1–50:26, though in chaps.

48–49 the focus swings back to Jacob). The Joseph stories are sophisticated in theme, deftly plotted, and show keen interest in the psychology of the characters. Jacob's favoring of Joseph, the son of his beloved wife Rachel, provokes his brothers to kill him. Joseph escapes death through the intercession of Reuben, the eldest, and of Judah, but is sold into slavery in Egypt. In the immediately following chap. 38, Judah undergoes experiences similar to Joseph's. Joseph, endowed by God with wisdom, becomes second only to Pharaoh in Egypt. From that powerful position, he encounters his unsuspecting brothers who have come to Egypt because of the famine, and tests them to see if they have repented. Joseph learns that they have given up their hatred because of their love for Israel, their father. Judah, who seems to have inherited the mantle of the failed oldest brother Reuben, expresses the brothers' new and profound appreciation of their father and Joseph (chap. 44). At the end of Genesis, the entire family of Jacob/Israel is in Egypt, which prepares for the events in the Book of Exodus.

***Genesis in Later Biblical Books.*** The historical and prophetic books constantly refer to the covenant with the ancestors Abraham, Isaac, and Jacob. Hos 10 sees the traits of Jacob in the behavior of the Israel of his own day. Is 51:2 cites Abraham and Sarah as a model for his dispirited community, for though only a couple, they became a great nation. Jn 1, "In the beginning was the word," alludes to Gn 1:1 (and Prv 8:22) to show that Jesus is creating a new world. St. Paul interprets Jesus as the New Adam in Rom 5:14 and 1 Cor 15:22, 24, whose obedience brings life just as the Old Adam's disobedience brought death. In Rom 4, Paul cites Abraham as someone who was righteous in God's eyes centuries before the Law was given at Sinai.

Outline of Genesis

- Preamble. The Creation of the World (1:1–2:3)
- I. The Story of the Nations (2:4–11:26)
  - A. The Creation of the Man and the Woman, Their Offspring, and the Spread of Civilization (2:4–4:26)
  - B. The Pre-flood Generations (5:1–6:8)
  - C. The Flood and the Renewed Blessing (6:9–9:29)
  - D. The Populating of the World and the Prideful City (10:1–11:9)
  - E. The Genealogy from Shem to Terah (11:10–26)
- II. The Story of the Ancestors of Israel (11:27–50:26)
  - A. The Story of Abraham and Sarah (11:27–25:18)
  - B. The Story of Isaac and Jacob (25:19–36:43)
  - C. The Story of Joseph (37:1–50:26)

---

# Preamble. The Creation of the World

## CHAPTER 1

See RG 52–54

***The Story of Creation.**** [1]In the beginning, when God created the heavens and the earth[a]— [2*] and the earth was without form

---

**1:1–2:3** This section, from the Priestly source, functions as an introduction, as ancient stories of the origin of the world (cosmogonies) often did. It introduces the primordial story (2:4–11:26), the stories of the ancestors (11:27–50:26), and indeed the whole Pentateuch. The chapter highlights the goodness of creation and the divine desire that human beings share in that goodness. God brings an orderly universe out of primordial chaos merely by uttering a word. In the literary structure of six days, the creation events in the first three days are related to those in the second three.

| | | | |
|---|---|---|---|
| 1. | light (day)/darkness (night) | = 4. | sun/moon |
| 2. | arrangement of water | = 5. | fish + birds from waters |
| 3. | a) dry land | = 6. | a) animals |
| | b) vegetation | | b) human beings: male/female |

The seventh day, on which God rests, the climax of the account, falls outside the six-day structure.

Until modern times the first line was always translated, "In the beginning God created the heavens and the earth." Several comparable ancient cosmogonies, discovered in recent times, have a "when . . . then" construction, confirming the translation "when . . . then" here as well. "When" introduces the pre-creation state and "then" introduces the creative act affecting that state. The traditional translation, "In the beginning," does not reflect the Hebrew syntax of the clause.

**1:2** This verse is parenthetical, describing in three phases the pre-creation state symbolized by the chaos out of which God brings order: "earth," hidden beneath the encompassing cosmic waters, could not be seen, and thus had no "form"; there was only darkness; turbulent wind swept over the waters. Commencing with the last-named elements (darkness

*a:* Gn 2:1, 4; 2 Mc 7:28; Ps 8:4; 33:6; 89:12; 90:2; Wis 11:17; Sir 16:24; Jer 10:12; Acts 14:15; Col 1:16–17; Heb 1:2–3; 3:4; 11:3; Rev 4:11.

**Days of Creation**

| | |
|---|---|
| LIGHT<br>day 1 (1:1–5) | LIGHTS *(i.e., sun, moon, and stars)*<br>day 4 (1:14–19) |
| SKY *(separating waters above from waters below)*<br>day 2 (1:6–8) | FISH/BIRDS<br>day 5 (1:20–23) |
| LAND AND PLANTS<br>day 3 (1:9–13) | LAND ANIMALS AND HUMANS<br>day 6 (1:24–31) |
| SABBATH<br>day 7 (2:1–3) | |

or shape, with darkness over the abyss and a mighty wind sweeping over the waters—[b]

3 Then God said: Let there be light, and there was light.[c] 4 God saw that the light was good. God then separated the light from the darkness. 5 God called the light "day," and the darkness he called "night." Evening came, and morning followed—the first day.*

6 Then God said: Let there be a dome in the middle of the waters, to separate one body of water from the other. 7 God made the dome,* and it separated the water below the dome from the water above the dome. And so it happened.[d] 8 God called the dome "sky." Evening came, and morning followed—the second day.

9 Then God said: Let the water under the sky be gathered into a single basin, so that the dry land may appear. And so it happened: the water under the sky was gathered into its basin, and the dry land appeared.[e] 10 God called the dry land "earth," and the basin of water he called "sea." God saw that it was good. 11[f] Then God said: Let the earth bring forth vegetation: every kind of plant that bears seed and every kind of fruit tree on earth that bears fruit with its seed in it. And so it happened: 12 the earth brought forth vegetation: every kind of plant that bears seed and every kind of fruit tree that bears fruit with its seed in it. God saw that it was good. 13 Evening came, and morning followed—the third day.

14 Then God said: Let there be lights in the dome of the sky, to separate day from night. Let them mark the seasons, the days and the years,[g] 15 and serve as lights in the dome of the sky, to illuminate the earth. And so it happened: 16 God made the two great lights, the greater one to govern the day, and the lesser one to govern the night, and the stars.[h] 17 God set them in the dome of the sky, to illuminate the earth, 18 to govern the day and the night, and to separate the light from the darkness. God saw that it was good. 19 Evening came, and morning followed—the fourth day.

20[i] Then God said: Let the water teem with an abundance of living creatures, and on the earth let birds fly beneath the dome of the sky. 21 God created the great sea monsters and all kinds of crawling living creatures

and water), vv. 3–10 describe the rearrangement of this chaos: light is made (first day) and the water is divided into water above and water below the earth so that the earth appears and is no longer "without outline." **The abyss**: the primordial ocean according to the ancient Semitic cosmogony. After God's creative activity, part of this vast body forms the salt-water seas (vv. 9–10); part of it is the fresh water under the earth (Ps 33:7; Ez 31:4), which wells forth on the earth as springs and fountains (Gn 7:11; 8:2; Prv 3:20). Part of it, "the upper water" (Ps 148:4; Dn 3:60), is held up by the dome of the sky (vv. 6–7), from which rain descends on the earth (Gn 7:11; 2 Kgs 7:2, 19; Ps 104:13). **A mighty wind**: literally, "spirit or breath [*ruah*] of God"; cf. Gn 8:1.

**1:5** In ancient Israel a day was considered to begin at sunset.

**1:7 The dome**: the Hebrew word suggests a gigantic metal dome. It was inserted into the middle of the single body of water to form dry space within which the earth could emerge. The Latin Vulgate translation *firmamentum*, "means of support (for the upper waters); firmament," provided the traditional English rendering.

*b:* Jer 4:23. *c:* 2 Cor 4:6. *d:* Prv 8:27–28; 2 Pt 3:5. *e:* Jb 38:8; Ps 33:7; Jer 5:22. *f:* Ps 104:14. *g:* Jb 26:10; Ps 19:2–3; Bar 3:33. *h:* Dt 4:19; Ps 136:7–9; Wis 13:2–4; Jer 31:35. *i:* Jb 12:7–10.

## It Is Good

SIX TIMES IN the first creation story, God observes the same thing about each part of creation: It is good. The seventh time these words are even stronger. When he surveys everything in creation, the sun and moon, the water and earth, the plants and creatures, and, finally, humans, God saw everything he had made and found it "very good." For this reason, according to the *Catechism of the Catholic Church*, the seventh commandment teaches that our dominion over inanimate creation and other living beings is not absolute but, rather, limited. In our use of natural resources, we are to consider the well being of others on our planet today and those who will be here in generations to come (CCC#2415). How do you conserve natural resources as an individual? How might we do better at this as a people?

with which the water teems, and all kinds of
winged birds. God saw that it was good,
22 and God blessed them, saying: Be fertile,
multiply, and fill the water of the seas; and
let the birds multiply on the earth.[j]
23 Evening came, and morning followed—
the fifth day.

24[k] Then God said: Let the earth bring
forth every kind of living creature: tame animals, crawling things, and every kind of
wild animal. And so it happened: 25 God
made every kind of wild animal, every kind
of tame animal, and every kind of thing that
crawls on the ground. God saw that it was
good. 26[l] Then God said: Let us make* human beings in our image, after our likeness.
Let them have dominion over the fish of the
sea, the birds of the air, the tame animals, all
the wild animals, and all the creatures that
crawl on the earth.

27 God created mankind in his image;
in the image of God he created them;
male and female* he created them.

28 God blessed them and God said to them:
Be fertile and multiply; fill the earth and
subdue it.* Have dominion over the fish of
the sea, the birds of the air, and all the living
things that crawl on the earth.[m] 29* [n] God also
said: See, I give you every seed-bearing
plant on all the earth and every tree that has
seed-bearing fruit on it to be your food;
30 and to all the wild animals, all the birds of
the air, and all the living creatures that crawl

**1:26 Let us make**: in the ancient Near East, and sometimes in the Bible, God was imagined as presiding over an assembly of heavenly beings who deliberated and decided about matters on earth (1 Kgs 22:19–22; Is 6:8; Ps 29:1–2; 82; 89:6–7; Jb 1:6; 2:1; 38:7). This scene accounts for the plural form here and in Gn 11:7 ("Let us then go down . . ."). Israel's God was always considered "Most High" over the heavenly beings. **Human beings**: Hebrew *'ādām* is here the generic term for humankind; in the first five chapters of Genesis it is the proper name Adam only at 4:25 and 5:1–5. **In our image, after our likeness**: "image" and "likeness" (virtually synonyms) express the worth of human beings who have value in themselves (human blood may not be shed in 9:6 because of this image of God) and in their task, dominion (1:28), which promotes the rule of God over the universe.

**1:27 Male and female**: as God provided the plants with seeds (vv. 11, 12) and commanded the animals to be fertile and multiply (v. 22), so God gives sexuality to human beings as their means to continue in existence.

**1:28 Fill the earth and subdue it**: the object of the verb "subdue" may be not the earth as such but earth as the territory each nation must take for itself (chaps. 10–11), just as Israel will later do (see Nm 32:22, 29; Jos 18:1). The two divine commands define the basic tasks of the human race—to continue in existence through generation and to take possession of one's God-given territory. The dual command would have had special meaning when Israel was in exile and deeply anxious about whether they would continue as a nation and return to their ancient territory. **Have dominion**: the whole human race is made in the "image" and "likeness" of God and has "dominion." Comparable literature of the time used these words of kings rather than of human beings in general; human beings were invariably thought of as slaves of the gods created to provide menial service for the divine world. The royal language here does not, however, give human beings unlimited power, for kings in the Bible had limited dominion and were subject to prophetic critique.

**1:29** According to the Priestly tradition, the human race was originally intended to live on plants and fruits as were the animals (see v. 30), an arrangement that God will later change (9:3) in view of the human inclination to violence.

*j:* Gn 8:17. *k:* Sir 16:27–28. *l:* Gn 5:1, 3; 9:6; Ps 8:5–6; Wis 2:23; 10:2; Sir 17:1, 3–4; Mt 19:4; Mk 10:6; Jas 3:7; Eph 4:24; Col 3:10. *m:* Gn 8:17; 9:1; Ps 8:6–9; 115:16; Wis 9:2. *n:* Gn 9:3; Ps 104:14–15.

**The Major Divisions of Genesis**

| | |
|---|---|
| First section: 1:1 to 11:9 | Primeval history, the origins of humankind, and failure through sin. |
| Second section: 11:10 to 25:34 | Abraham, his call and response, his blessing and promise, his son Isaac and Isaac's sons Jacob (Israel) and Esau |
| Third section: 26:1 to 36:43 | Isaac, Jacob, and the sons of Jacob (Israel) |
| Fourth section: 37:1 to 50:26 | The sons of Israel, and Jacob and the Israelites in Egypt |

on the earth, I give all the green plants for food. And so it happened. [31]God looked at everything he had made, and found it very good. Evening came, and morning followed—the sixth day.[o]

CHAPTER 2

See RG 52–54

[1]Thus the heavens and the earth and all their array were completed.[p] [2*] On the seventh day God completed the work he had been doing; he rested on the seventh day from all the work he had undertaken.[q] [3]God blessed the seventh day and made it holy, because on it he rested from all the work he had done in creation.[r]

## I. The Story of the Nations

***The Garden of Eden.*** [4]This is the story* of the heavens and the earth at their creation. When the LORD God made the earth and the heavens— [5]there was no field shrub on earth and no grass of the field had sprouted, for the LORD God had sent no rain upon the earth and there was no man* to till the ground, [6]but a stream* was welling up out of the earth and watering all the surface of the ground— [7]then the LORD God formed the man* out of the dust of the ground and blew into his nostrils the breath of life, and the man became a living being.[s]

**2:2** The mention of the seventh day, repeated in v. 3, is outside the series of six days and is thus the climax of the account. The focus of the account is God. The text does not actually institute the practice of keeping the Sabbath, for it would have been anachronistic to establish at this point a custom that was distinctively Israelite (Ex 31:13, 16, 17), but it lays the foundation for the later practice. Similarly, ancient creation accounts often ended with the construction of a temple where the newly created human race provided service to the gods who created them, but no temple is mentioned in this account. As was the case with the Sabbath, it would have been anachronistic to institute the temple at this point, for Israel did not yet exist. In Ex 25–31 and 35–40, Israel builds the tabernacle, which is the precursor of the Temple of Solomon.

**2:4 This is the story**: the distinctive Priestly formula introduces older traditions, belonging to the tradition called Yahwist, and gives them a new setting. In the first part of Genesis, the formula "this is the story" (or a similar phrase) occurs five times (2:4; 5:1; 6:9; 10:1; 11:10), which corresponds to the five occurrences of the formula in the second part of the book (11:27; 25:12, 19; 36:1[9]; 37:2). Some interpret the formula here as retrospective ("Such is the story"), referring back to chap. 1, but all its other occurrences introduce rather than summarize. It is introductory here; the Priestly source would hardly use the formula to introduce its own material in chap. 1.

The cosmogony that begins in v. 4 is concerned with the nature of human beings, narrating the story of the essential institutions and limits of the human race through their first ancestors. This cosmogony, like 1:1–3 (see note there), uses the "when . . . then" construction common in ancient cosmogonies. The account is generally attributed to the Yahwist, who prefers the divine name "Yhwh" (here rendered LORD) for God. God in this story is called "the LORD God" (except in 3:1–5); "LORD" is to be expected in a Yahwist account but the additional word "God" is puzzling.

**2:5 Man**: the Hebrew word *'adam* is a generic term meaning "human being." In chaps. 2–3, however, the archetypal human being is understood to be male (Adam), so the word *'adam* is translated "man" here.

**2:6 Stream**: the water wells up from the vast flood below the earth. The account seems to presuppose that only the garden of God was irrigated at this point. From this one source of all the fertilizing water on the earth, water will be channeled through the garden of God over the entire earth. It is the source of the four rivers mentioned in vv. 10–14. Later, with rain and cultivation, the fertility of the garden of God will appear in all parts of the world.

**2:7** God is portrayed as a potter molding the human body out of earth. There is a play on words in Hebrew between *'adam* ("human being," "man") and *'adama* ("ground"). It is not enough to make the body from earth; God must also breathe into the man's nostrils. A similar picture of divine

*o:* 1 Tm 4:4. *p:* Is 45:12; Jn 1:3. *q:* Ex 20:9–11; 31:17; Heb 4:4, 10. *r:* Ex 20:11; Dt 5:14; Neh 9:14. *s:* Gn 3:19; 18:27; Tb 8:6; Jb 34:15; Ps 103:14; 104:29; Eccl 3:20; 12:7; Wis 7:1; Sir 33:10; 1 Cor 15:45.

## A Second Creation Story—the Garden of Eden

GENESIS 2 BEGINS not with chaotic waters of the deep as in 1:1–2, but with a dry desert. Like the watery deep, the dry wilderness is a biblical image of evil and chaos (Is 21:1–3; 43:15–21). God's creative power turns the wilderness into a fertile garden with the trees of life and "knowledge of good and bad," that is to say, "all knowledge," at its center. Eating from the tree of life would give immortality, and eating from the tree of knowledge would provide wisdom, moral discernment, and the experience of pleasure and pain. The image of Eden is that of a lush garden at the center of the known world from which four major rivers flow to water the earth. We know the location of only two of the rivers, the Tigris and the Euphrates. They are in Mesopotamia. Havilah (v. 11) may be associated with Africa.

The garden of Eden is not a paradise of luxury, but a place for human work. The man is to cultivate the garden and care for it on God's behalf. God soon recognizes that the man needs a partner for this labor. Other translations use the word "helper," but it is important to remember that God's motivation in creating the woman is to provide a companion and someone who will come to his aid, not to provide a subservient assistant. The man's brief poetic response to the woman plays on Hebrew words *ish* (Man) and *ishshah* (Woman). They "become one body" (2:24) suggests not only sexual union, but also a unity through a common household and the raising of children. This story lays the foundation for marriage.

8 The LORD God planted a garden in Eden, in the east,* and placed there the man whom he had formed.[t] 9* Out of the ground the LORD God made grow every tree that was delightful to look at and good for food, with the tree of life in the middle of the garden and the tree of the knowledge of good and evil.[u]
10 A river rises in Eden* to water the garden; beyond there it divides and becomes four branches. 11 The name of the first is the Pishon; it is the one that winds through the

breath imparted to human beings in order for them to live is found in Ez 37:5, 9–10; Jn 20:22. The Israelites did not think in the (Greek) categories of body and soul.

**2:8 Eden, in the east**: the place names in vv. 8–14 are mostly derived from Mesopotamian geography (see note on vv. 10–14). Eden may be the name of a region in southern Mesopotamia (modern Iraq), the term derived from the Sumerian word *eden*, "fertile plain." A similar-sounding Hebrew word means "delight," which may lie behind the Greek translation, "The Lord God planted a paradise [= pleasure park] in Eden." It should be noted, however, that the garden was not intended as a paradise for the human race, but as a pleasure park for God; the man tended it for God. The story is not about "paradise lost."

The garden in the precincts of Solomon's Temple in Jerusalem seems to symbolize the garden of God (like gardens in other temples); it is apparently alluded to in Ps 1:3; 80:10; 92:14; Ez 47:7–12; Rev 22:1–2.

**2:9** The second tree, the tree of life, is mentioned here and at the end of the story (3:22, 24). It is identified with Wisdom in Prv 3:18; 11:30; 13:12; 15:4, where the pursuit of wisdom gives back to human beings the life that is made inaccessible to them in Gn 3:24. In the new creation described in the Book of Revelation, the tree of life is once again made available to human beings (Rev 2:7; 22:2, 14, 19). **Knowledge of good and evil**: the meaning is disputed. According to some, it signifies moral autonomy, control over morality (symbolized by "good and evil"), which would be inappropriate for mere human beings; the phrase would thus mean refusal to accept the human condition and finite freedom that God gives them. According to others, it is more broadly the knowledge of what is helpful and harmful to humankind, suggesting that the attainment of adult experience and responsibility inevitably means the loss of a life of simple subordination to God.

**2:10–14 A river rises in Eden**: the stream of water mentioned in v. 6, the source of all water upon earth, comes to the surface in the garden of God and from there flows out over the entire earth. In comparable religious literature, the dwelling of god is the source of fertilizing waters. The four rivers represent universality, as in the phrase "the four quarters of the earth." In Ez 47:1–12; Zec 14:8; Rev 22:1–2, the waters that irrigate the earth arise in the temple or city of God. The place names in vv. 11–14 are mainly from southern Mesopotamia (modern Iraq), where Mesopotamian literature placed the original garden of God. The Tigris and the Euphrates, the two great rivers in that part of the world, both emptied into the Persian Gulf. Gihon is the modest stream issuing from Jerusalem (2 Sm 5:8; 1 Kgs 1:9–10; 2 Chr 32:4), but is here regarded as one of the four

*t:* Is 51:3; Ez 31:9. *u:* Gn 3:22; Prv 3:18; Rev 2:7; 22:2, 14.

**How to Read the Account of the Fall**

THE *CATECHISM OF the Catholic Church* (CCC#390) reminds us that this account of the fall in Genesis 3 uses figurative language, by which it affirms that a choice at the beginning of human history marked the whole of that history, and that the choice was freely made.

whole land of Havilah, where there is gold.
[12]The gold of that land is good; bdellium and
lapis lazuli are also there. [13]The name of the
second river is the Gihon; it is the one that
winds all through the land of Cush.[v] [14]The
name of the third river is the Tigris; it is the
one that flows east of Asshur. The fourth
river is the Euphrates.
[15]The LORD God then took the man and
settled him in the garden of Eden, to cultivate and care for it.[w] [16]The LORD God gave
the man this order: You are free to eat from
any of the trees of the garden[x] [17]except the
tree of knowledge of good and evil. From
that tree you shall not eat; when you eat from
it you shall die.* [y]
[18]The LORD God said: It is not good for
the man to be alone. I will make a helper
suited to him.* [z] [19]So the LORD God formed
out of the ground all the wild animals and all
the birds of the air, and he brought them to
the man to see what he would call them;
whatever the man called each living creature
was then its name. [20]The man gave names to
all the tame animals, all the birds of the air,
and all the wild animals; but none proved to
be a helper suited to the man.
[21]So the LORD God cast a deep sleep on
the man, and while he was asleep, he took
out one of his ribs and closed up its place
with flesh.[a] [22]The LORD God then built the
rib that he had taken from the man into a
woman. When he brought her to the man,
[23]the man said:

"This one, at last, is bone of my bones
and flesh of my flesh;
This one shall be called 'woman,'
for out of man this one has been taken."*

[24b] That is why a man leaves his father and
mother and clings to his wife, and the two of
them become one body.*
[25]The man and his wife were both naked,
yet they felt no shame.*

## CHAPTER 3

See RG 54

*Expulsion from Eden.* [1]Now the snake
was the most cunning* of all the wild animals that the LORD God had made. He asked
the woman, "Did God really say, 'You shall
not eat from any of the trees in the garden'?"
[2]The woman answered the snake: "We may
eat of the fruit of the trees in the garden; [3c] it
is only about the fruit of the tree in the middle of the garden that God said, 'You shall
not eat it or even touch it, or else you will
die.'" [4]But the snake said to the woman:
"You certainly will not die![d] [5]God knows

great world rivers and linked to Mesopotamia, for Cush here seems to be the territory of the Kassites (a people of Mesopotamia) as in Gn 10:8. The word Pishon is otherwise unknown but is probably formed in imitation of Gihon. Havilah seems, according to Gn 10:7 and 1 Chr 1:9, to be in Cush in southern Mesopotamia though other locations have been suggested.

**2:17 You shall die**: since they do not die as soon as they eat from the forbidden tree, the meaning seems to be that human beings have become mortal, destined to die by virtue of being human.

**2:18 Helper suited to him**: lit., "a helper in accord with him." "Helper" need not imply subordination, for God is called a helper (Dt 33:7; Ps 46:2). The language suggests a profound affinity between the man and the woman and a relationship that is supportive and nurturing.

**2:23** The man recognizes an affinity with the woman God has brought him. Unlike the animals who were made from the ground, she is made from his very self. There is a play on the similar-sounding Hebrew words *'ishsha* ("woman," "wife") and *'ish* ("man," "husband").

**2:24 One body**: lit., "one flesh." The covenant of marriage establishes kinship bonds of the first rank between the partners.

**2:25 They felt no shame**: marks a new stage in the drama, for the reader knows that only young children know no shame. This draws the reader into the next episode, where the couple's disobedience results in their loss of innocence.

**3:1 Cunning**: there is a play on the words for "naked" (2:25) and "cunning/wise" (Heb. *'arum*). The couple seek to be "wise" but end up knowing that they are "naked."

*v:* Sir 24:25. *w:* Sir 7:15. *x:* Ps 104:14–15. *y:* Gn 3:2–3; Rom 6:23. *z:* Tb 8:6; Sir 36:24; 1 Cor 11:9; 1 Tm 2:13. *a:* Sir 17:1; 1 Cor 11:8–9; 1 Tm 2:13. *b:* Mt 19:5; Mk 10:7; 1 Cor 7:10–11; Eph 5:31. *c:* Gn 2:17; Rom 6:23. *d:* Wis 2:24; Sir 25:14; Is 14:14; Jn 8:44; 2 Cor 11:3.

THE *CATECHISM OF the Catholic Church* (CCC#289) underlines the importance of the first three chapters of Genesis. Although these texts have different sources, we read them as a unit in the light of what we know about Christ, as well as the overall unity of the Bible and our living tradition. These chapters thus are our principal source for catechesis on the basic issues of creation, fall, and the promise of salvation—salvation that has come about through the death and resurrection of Christ. In addition, we learn here about the significance of the Sabbath—rest from labor is not just a convenience but a divine mandate—that all creation is good, and that human beings are created in God's image.

Genesis in its final form probably dates to the time when the people of Judah were in exile in Babylon (sixth century B.C.) or when the Babylonian exiles returned home to Judah under the Persian empire (fifth century B.C.). The time of exile and the return home forced Israel to think hard about its identity as a people and its mission as the people of God among the nations of the world. Remembering the Genesis stories about the beginnings of the world and Israel's earliest ancestors was a way to return to their roots and think about who they were as an exiled people returning home to Judah. They could identify with their ancestors, who were also a family on the move. Just as the family of Abraham and Sarah migrated back and forth from Mesopotamia to Canaan, so the exiles would migrate from Babylon back to Judah. The key promise in the midst of this wandering and yearning to return home was God's promise to Jacob: "I am with you; I will protect you wherever you go, and bring you back to this land" (28:15).

well that when you eat of it your eyes will be
opened and you will be like gods, who
know* good and evil." 6The woman saw that
the tree was good for food and pleasing to
the eyes, and the tree was desirable for gaining wisdom. So she took some of its fruit
and ate it; and she also gave some to her husband, who was with her, and he ate it.[e] 7Then
the eyes of both of them were opened, and
they knew that they were naked; so they
sewed fig leaves together and made loin-
cloths for themselves.
8When they heard the sound of the LORD
God walking about in the garden at the
breezy time of the day,* the man and his wife
hid themselves from the LORD God among
the trees of the garden.[f] 9The LORD God then
called to the man and asked him: Where are
you? 10He answered, "I heard you in the garden; but I was afraid, because I was naked,
so I hid." 11Then God asked: Who told you
that you were naked? Have you eaten from
the tree of which I had forbidden you to eat?
12The man replied, "The woman whom you
put here with me—she gave me fruit from
the tree, so I ate it." 13The LORD God then
asked the woman: What is this you have
done? The woman answered, "The snake
tricked me, so I ate it."[g]
14Then the LORD God said to the snake:

Because you have done this,
cursed are you
among all the animals, tame or wild;
On your belly you shall crawl,
and dust you shall eat
all the days of your life.* [h]
15 I will put enmity between you and the
woman,
and between your offspring and hers;

**3:5 Like gods, who know**: or "like God who knows."

**3:8 The breezy time of the day**: lit., "the wind of the day." Probably shortly before sunset.

**3:14** Each of the three punishments (the snake, the woman, the man) has a double aspect, one affecting the individual and the other affecting a basic relationship. The snake previously stood upright, enjoyed a reputation for being shrewder than other creatures, and could converse with human beings as in vv. 1–5. It must now move on its belly, is more cursed than any creature, and inspires revulsion in human beings (v. 15).

*e:* Gn 3:22; 1 Tm 2:14. *f:* Jer 23:24. *g:* 2 Cor 11:3. *h:* Is 65:25; Mi 7:17; Rev 12:9.

They will strike at your head,
while you strike at their heel.* [i]

16 To the woman he said:

I will intensify your toil in childbearing;
in pain* you shall bring forth children.
Yet your urge shall be for your husband,
and he shall rule over you.

17 To the man he said: Because you listened to your wife and ate from the tree about which I commanded you, You shall not eat from it,

Cursed is the ground* because of you!
In toil you shall eat its yield
all the days of your life.[j]
18 Thorns and thistles it shall bear for you,
and you shall eat the grass of the field.
19 By the sweat of your brow
you shall eat bread,
Until you return to the ground,
from which you were taken;
For you are dust,
and to dust you shall return.[k]

20 The man gave his wife the name "Eve,"
because she was the mother of all the living.*

21 The LORD God made for the man and his
wife garments of skin, with which he
clothed them. 22 Then the LORD God said:
See! The man has become like one of us,
knowing good and evil! Now, what if he also
reaches out his hand to take fruit from the
tree of life, and eats of it and lives forever?[l]
23 The LORD God therefore banished him
from the garden of Eden, to till the ground
from which he had been taken. 24 He expelled the man, stationing the cherubim and
the fiery revolving sword east of the garden
of Eden, to guard the way to the tree of life.

## CHAPTER 4

See RG 55

*Cain and Abel.* 1 The man had intercourse with his wife Eve, and she conceived
and gave birth to Cain, saying, "I have produced a male child with the help of the
LORD."* 2 Next she gave birth to his brother
Abel. Abel became a herder of flocks, and
Cain a tiller of the ground.* 3 In the course of
time Cain brought an offering to the LORD
from the fruit of the ground, 4 while Abel, for
his part, brought the fatty portion* of the
firstlings of his flock.[m] The LORD looked
with favor on Abel and his offering, 5 but on

**3:15 They will strike . . . at their heel**: the antecedent for "they" and "their" is the collective noun "offspring," i.e., all the descendants of the woman. Christian tradition has seen in this passage, however, more than unending hostility between snakes and human beings. The snake was identified with the devil (Wis 2:24; Jn 8:44; Rev 12:9; 20:2), whose eventual defeat seemed implied in the verse. Because "the Son of God was revealed to destroy the works of the devil" (1 Jn 3:8), the passage was understood as the first promise of a redeemer for fallen humankind, the protoevangelium. Irenaeus of Lyons (ca. A.D. 130–200), in his *Against Heresies* 5.21.1, followed by several other Fathers of the Church, interpreted the verse as referring to Christ, and cited Gal 3:19 and 4:4 to support the reference. Another interpretive translation is *ipsa*, "she," and is reflected in Jerome's Vulgate. "She" was thought to refer to Mary, the mother of the messiah. In Christian art Mary is sometimes depicted with her foot on the head of the serpent.

**3:16 Toil . . . pain**: the punishment affects the woman directly by increasing the toil and pain of having children. **He shall rule over you**: the punishment also affects the woman's relationship with her husband. A tension is set up in which her urge (either sexual urge or, more generally, dependence for sustenance) is for her husband but he rules over her. But see Sg 7:11.

**3:17–19 Cursed is the ground**: the punishment affects the man's relationship to the ground (*'adam* and *'adamah*). **You are dust**: the punishment also affects the man directly insofar as he is now mortal.

**3:20** The man gives his wife a more specific name than "woman" (2:23). The Hebrew name *hawwa* ("Eve") is related to the Hebrew word *hay* ("living"); "mother of all the living" points forward to the next episode involving her sons Cain and Abel.

**4:1** The Hebrew name *qayin* ("Cain") and the term *qaniti* ("I have produced") present a wordplay that refers to metalworking; such wordplays are frequent in Genesis.

**4:2** Some suggest the story reflects traditional strife between the farmer (Cain) and the nomad (Abel), with preference for the latter reflecting the alleged nomadic ideal of the Bible. But there is no disparagement of farming here, for Adam was created to till the soil. The story is about two brothers (the word "brother" occurs seven times) and God's unexplained preference for one, which provokes the first murder. The motif of the preferred younger brother will occur time and again in the Bible, e.g., Isaac, Jacob, Joseph, and David (1 Sm 16:1–13).

**4:4 Fatty portion**: it was standard practice to offer the fat portions of animals. Others render, less satisfactorily, "the choicest of the firstlings." The point is not that Abel gave a more valuable gift than Cain, but that God, for reasons not given in the text, accepts the offering of Abel and rejects that of Cain.

---

*i:* Rom 16:20; 1 Jn 3:8; Rev 12:17. *j:* Gn 5:29; Rom 5:12; 8:20; Heb 6:8. *k:* Gn 2:7; Jb 10:9; 34:15; Ps 90:3; 103:14; Eccl 3:20; 12:7; Wis 15:8; Sir 10:9; 17:2; Rom 5:12; 1 Cor 15:21; Heb 9:27. *l:* Gn 2:9; Rev 22:2, 14. *m:* Ex 34:19; Heb 11:4.

Cain and his offering he did not look with favor. So Cain was very angry and dejected. 6 Then the LORD said to Cain: Why are you angry? Why are you dejected? 7 If you act rightly, you will be accepted;* but if not, sin lies in wait at the door: its urge is for you, yet you can rule over it.[n]

8 Cain said to his brother Abel, "Let us go out in the field."* When they were in the field, Cain attacked his brother Abel and killed him.[o] 9 Then the LORD asked Cain, Where is your brother Abel? He answered, "I do not know. Am I my brother's keeper?" 10 God then said: What have you done? Your brother's blood cries out to me from the ground! 11 Now you are banned from the ground* that opened its mouth to receive your brother's blood from your hand.[p] 12 If you till the ground, it shall no longer give you its produce. You shall become a constant wanderer on the earth. 13 Cain said to the LORD: "My punishment is too great to bear. 14 Look, you have now banished me from the ground. I must avoid you and be a constant wanderer on the earth. Anyone may kill me at sight." 15 Not so! the LORD said to him. If anyone kills Cain, Cain shall be avenged seven times. So the LORD put a mark* on Cain, so that no one would kill him at sight. 16 Cain then left the LORD's presence and settled in the land of Nod,* east of Eden.

*Descendants of Cain and Seth.* 17* Cain had intercourse with his wife, and she conceived and bore Enoch. Cain also became the founder of a city, which he named after his son Enoch. 18 To Enoch was born Irad, and Irad became the father of Mehujael; Mehujael became the father of Methusael, and Methusael became the father of Lamech. 19 Lamech took two wives; the name of the first was Adah, and the name of the second Zillah. 20 Adah gave birth to Jabal, who became the ancestor of those who dwell in tents and keep livestock. 21 His brother's name was Jubal, who became the ancestor of all who play the lyre and the reed pipe. 22 Zillah, on her part, gave birth to Tubalcain, the ancestor of all who forge instruments of bronze and iron. The sister of Tubalcain was Naamah. 23* Lamech said to his wives:

"Adah and Zillah, hear my voice;
wives of Lamech, listen to my utterance:
I have killed a man for wounding me,
a young man for bruising me.
24 If Cain is avenged seven times,
then Lamech seventy-seven times."

25* Adam again had intercourse with his wife, and she gave birth to a son whom she called Seth. "God has granted me another offspring in place of Abel," she said, "be-

**4:7 You will be accepted**: the text is extraordinarily condensed and unclear. "You will be accepted" is a paraphrase of one Hebrew word, "lifting." God gives a friendly warning to Cain that his right conduct will bring "lifting," which could refer to acceptance (*lifting*) of his future offerings or of himself (as in the Hebrew idiom "*lifting* of the face") or *lifting* up of his head in honor (cf. note on 40:13), whereas wicked conduct will make him vulnerable to sin, which is personified as a force ready to attack. In any case, Cain has the ability to do the right thing. **Lies in wait**: sin is personified as a power that "lies in wait" (Heb. *robes*) at a place. In Mesopotamian religion, a related word (*rabisu*) refers to a malevolent god who attacks human beings in particular places like roofs or canals.

**4:8 Let us go out in the field**: to avoid detection. The verse presumes a sizeable population which Genesis does not otherwise explain.

**4:11 Banned from the ground**: lit., "cursed." The verse refers back to 3:17 where the ground was cursed so that it yields its produce only with great effort. Cain has polluted the soil with his brother's blood and it will no longer yield any of its produce to him.

**4:15 A mark**: probably a tattoo to mark Cain as protected by God. The use of tattooing for tribal marks has always been common among the Bedouin of the Near Eastern deserts.

**4:16 The land of Nod**: a symbolic name (derived from the verb *nûd*, to wander) rather than a definite geographic region.

**4:17–24** Cain is the first in a seven-member linear genealogy ending in three individuals who initiate action (Jabal, Jubal, and Tubalcain). Other Genesis genealogies also end in three individuals initiating action (5:32 and 11:26). The purpose of this genealogy is to explain the origin of culture and crafts among human beings. The names in this genealogy are the same (some with different spellings) as those in the ten-member genealogy (ending with Noah), which has a slightly different function. See note on 5:1–32.

**4:23–24** Lamech's boast shows that the violence of Cain continues with his son and has actually increased. The question is posed to the reader: how will God's creation be renewed?

**4:25–26** The third and climactic birth story in the chapter, showing that this birth, unlike the other two, will have good results. The name Seth (from the Hebrew verb *shat*, "to place, replace") shows that God has replaced Abel with a worthy successor.

*n:* Sir 7:1; Jude 11. *o:* Wis 10:3; Mt 23:35; Lk 11:51; 1 Jn 3:12; Jude 11. *p:* Dt 27:24.

cause Cain killed him." 26 To Seth, in turn, a son was born, and he named him Enosh.

At that time people began to invoke the LORD by name.[q]

See RG 55

## CHAPTER 5

***Generations: Adam to Noah.**** 1 [r] This is the record of the descendants of Adam. When God created human beings, he made them in the likeness of God; 2 he created them male and female. When they were created, he blessed them and named them humankind.

3 [s] Adam was one hundred and thirty years old when he begot a son in his likeness, after his image; and he named him Seth.[t] 4 Adam lived eight hundred years after he begot Seth, and he had other sons and daughters. 5 The whole lifetime of Adam was nine hundred and thirty years; then he died.

6 When Seth was one hundred and five years old, he begot Enosh. 7 Seth lived eight hundred and seven years after he begot Enosh, and he had other sons and daughters. 8 The whole lifetime of Seth was nine hundred and twelve years; then he died.

9 When Enosh was ninety years old, he begot Kenan. 10 Enosh lived eight hundred and fifteen years after he begot Kenan, and he had other sons and daughters. 11 The whole lifetime of Enosh was nine hundred and five years; then he died.

12 When Kenan was seventy years old, he begot Mahalalel. 13 Kenan lived eight hundred and forty years after he begot Mahalalel, and he had other sons and daughters. 14 The whole lifetime of Kenan was nine hundred and ten years; then he died.

15 When Mahalalel was sixty-five years old, he begot Jared. 16 Mahalalel lived eight hundred and thirty years after he begot Jared, and he had other sons and daughters. 17 The whole lifetime of Mahalalel was eight hundred and ninety-five years; then he died.

18 When Jared was one hundred and sixty-two years old, he begot Enoch. 19 Jared lived eight hundred years after he begot Enoch, and he had other sons and daughters. 20 The whole lifetime of Jared was nine hundred and sixty-two years; then he died.

21 When Enoch was sixty-five years old, he begot Methuselah. 22 Enoch walked with God after he begot Methuselah for three hundred years, and he had other sons and daughters. 23 The whole lifetime of Enoch was three hundred and sixty-five years. 24 Enoch walked with God,* and he was no longer here, for God took him.[u]

25 When Methuselah was one hundred and eighty-seven years old, he begot Lamech.

cessor. From this favored line Enosh ("human being/humankind"), a synonym of Adam, authentic religion began with the worship of Yhwh; this divine name is rendered as "the LORD" in this translation. The Yahwist source employs the name Yhwh long before the time of Moses. Another ancient source, the Elohist (from its use of the term *Elohim*, "God," instead of *Yhwh*, "LORD," for the pre-Mosaic period), makes Moses the first to use Yhwh as the proper name of Israel's God, previously known by other names as well; cf. Ex 3:13–15.

**5:1–32** The second of the five Priestly formulas in Part I ("This is the record of the descendants . . ."; see 2:4a; 6:9; 10:1; 11:10) introduces the second of the three linear genealogies in Gn 1–11 (4:17–24 and 11:10–26). In each, a list of individuals (six in 4:17–24, ten in 5:1–32, or nine in 11:10–26) ends in three people who initiate action. Linear genealogies (father to son) in ancient societies had a communicative function, grounding the authority or claim of the last-named individual in the first-named. Here, the genealogy has a literary function as well, advancing the story by showing the expansion of the human race after Adam, as well as the transmission to his descendant Noah of the divine image given to Adam. Correcting the impression one might get from the genealogy in 4:17–24, this genealogy traces the line through Seth rather than through Cain. Most of the names in the series are the same as the names in Cain's line in 4:17–19 (Enosh, Enoch, Lamech) or spelled with variant spellings (Mahalalel, Jared, Methuselah). The genealogy itself and its placement before the flood shows the influence of ancient Mesopotamian literature, which contains lists of cities and kings before and after the flood. Before the flood, the ages of the kings ranged from 18,600 to 36,000 years, but after it were reduced to between 140 and 1,200 years. The biblical numbers are much smaller. There are some differences in the numbers in the Hebrew and Greek manuscripts.

**5:24** Enoch is in the important seventh position in the ten-member genealogy. In place of the usual formula "then he died," the change to "Enoch walked with God" implies that he did not die, but like Elijah (2 Kgs 2:11–12) was taken alive to God's abode. This mysterious narrative spurred much speculation and writing (beginning as early as the third century B.C.) about Enoch the sage who knew the secrets of heaven and who could communicate them to human beings (see Sir 44:16; 49:14; Heb 11:5; Jude 14–15 and the apocryphal work 1 Enoch).

*q:* 1 Chr 1:1; Lk 3:38. *r:* Gn 1:27; Wis 2:23; Sir 17:1; Jas 3:9. *s:* 1 Chr 1:1–4; Lk 3:36–38. *t:* Gn 4:25. *u:* Wis 4:10–11; Sir 44:16; 49:14; Heb 11:5.

**The *Toledoth* ("Generations") Lists**

IN THE TEXT of Genesis, the Hebrew word *toledoth* (pronounced "tole-uh-DOTE" and meaning "generations" or "descendants") serves as a marker for the end of one section of the narrative and the beginning of the next. Here are the places where the word occurs:

| | |
|---|---|
| 2:4a | The second creation story |
| 5:1 | Introduces the section between the first human family and the days of Noah |
| 6:9 | Introduces the story of the flood |
| 10:1 | The expansion of people over the earth |
| 11:10 | A new list of the nations of the earth |
| 11:27 | The beginning of Abraham's story |
| 25:12 | The end of the story of Hagar and Ishmael, Abraham's other family |
| 25:19 | Introduces Jacob's story |
| 36:1 | The end of Esau's story and the beginning of the story of Jacob's children |
| 36:9 | The conclusion of the list |
| 37:2 | The beginning of the story of Joseph and his brothers |

26 Methuselah lived seven hundred and eighty-two years after he begot Lamech, and he had other sons and daughters.
27 The whole lifetime of Methuselah was nine hundred and sixty-nine years; then he died.
28 When Lamech was one hundred and eighty-two years old, he begot a son
29 [v] and named him Noah, saying, "This one shall bring us relief from our work and the toil of our hands, out of the very ground that the LORD has put under a curse."*
30 Lamech lived five hundred and ninety-five years after he begot Noah, and he had other sons and daughters.
31 The whole lifetime of Lamech was seven hundred and seventy-seven years; then he died.
32 When Noah was five hundred years old, he begot Shem, Ham, and Japheth.* [w]

### CHAPTER 6

See RG 55

*Origin of the Nephilim.** 
1 When human beings began to grow numerous on the earth and daughters were born to them,
2 the sons of God* saw how beautiful the daughters of human beings were, and so they took for their wives whomever they pleased.[x]
3 Then the LORD said: My spirit shall not remain in human beings forever, because they are only flesh. Their days shall comprise one hundred and twenty years.
4 The Nephilim appeared on earth in those days, as well as later,* after the sons of God

**5:29** The sound of the Hebrew word *noah*, "Noah," is echoed in the word *yenahamenu*, "he will bring us relief"; the latter refers both to the curse put on the soil because of human disobedience (3:17–19) and to Noah's success in agriculture, especially in raising grapes for wine (9:20–21).

**5:32 Shem, Ham, and Japheth**: like the genealogies in 4:17–24 and 11:10–26, the genealogy ends in three individuals who engage in important activity. Their descendants will be detailed in chap. 10, where it will be seen that the lineage is political-geographical as well as "ethnic."

**6:1–4** These enigmatic verses are a transition between the expansion of the human race illustrated in the genealogy of chap. 5 and the flood depicted in chaps. 6–9. The text, apparently alluding to an old legend, shares a common ancient view that the heavenly world was populated by a multitude of beings, some of whom were wicked and rebellious. It is incorporated here, not only in order to account for the prehistoric giants, whom the Israelites called the Nephilim, but also to introduce the story of the flood with a moral orientation—the constantly increasing wickedness of humanity. This increasing wickedness leads God to reduce the human life span imposed on the first couple. As the ages in the preceding genealogy show, life spans had been exceptionally long in the early period, but God further reduces them to something near the ordinary life span.

**6:2 The sons of God**: other heavenly beings. See note on 1:26.

**6:4 As well as later**: the belief was common that human beings of gigantic stature once lived on earth. In some cultures, such heroes could make positive contributions, but the Bible generally regards them in a negative light (cf. Nm 13:33; Ez 32:27). The point here is that even these heroes,

*v:* Gn 3:17–19. *w:* Gn 6:10; 10:1. *x:* Mt 24:38; Lk 17:26–27.

had intercourse with the daughters of human beings, who bore them sons. They were the heroes of old, the men of renown.[y]

***Warning of the Flood.*** 5* When the LORD saw how great the wickedness of human beings was on earth, and how every desire that their heart conceived was always nothing but evil,[z] 6 the LORD regretted making human beings on the earth, and his heart was grieved.*

7 So the LORD said: I will wipe out from the earth the human beings I have created, and not only the human beings, but also the animals and the crawling things and the birds of the air, for I regret that I made them.* 8 But Noah found favor with the LORD.

9 These are the descendants of Noah. Noah was a righteous man and blameless in his generation;[a] Noah walked with God. 10 Noah begot three sons: Shem, Ham, and Japheth.

11 But the earth was corrupt* in the view of God and full of lawlessness.[b] 12 When God saw how corrupt the earth had become, since all mortals had corrupted their ways on earth,[c] 13 God said to Noah: I see that the end of all mortals has come, for the earth is full of lawlessness because of them. So I am going to destroy them with the earth.[d]

***Preparation for the Flood.*** 14 Make yourself an ark of gopherwood,* equip the ark with various compartments, and cover it inside and out with pitch. 15 This is how you shall build it: the length of the ark will be three hundred cubits, its width fifty cubits, and its height thirty cubits.* 16 Make an opening for daylight* and finish the ark a cubit above it. Put the ark's entrance on its side; you will make it with bottom, second and third decks. 17 I, on my part, am about to bring the flood waters on the earth, to destroy all creatures under the sky in which there is the breath of life; everything on earth shall perish.[e] 18 I will establish my covenant with you. You shall go into the ark, you and your sons, your wife and your sons' wives with you.[f] 19 Of all living creatures you shall bring two of every kind into the ark, one male and one female,* to keep them alive along with you. 20 Of every kind of bird, of every kind of ani-

filled with vitality from their semi-divine origin, come under God's decree in v. 3.

**6:5–8:22** The story of the great flood is commonly regarded as a composite narrative based on separate sources woven together. To the Yahwist source, with some later editorial additions, are usually assigned 6:5–8; 7:1–5, 7–10, 12, 16b, 17b, 22–23; 8:2b–3a, 6–12, 13b, 20–22. The other sections are usually attributed to the Priestly writer. There are differences between the two sources: the Priestly source has two pairs of every animal, whereas the Yahwist source has seven pairs of clean animals and two pairs of unclean; the floodwater in the Priestly source is the waters under and over the earth that burst forth, whereas in the Yahwist source the floodwater is the rain lasting forty days and nights. In spite of many obvious discrepancies in these two sources, one should read the story as a coherent narrative. The biblical story ultimately draws upon an ancient Mesopotamian tradition of a great flood, preserved in the Sumerian flood story, the eleventh tablet of the Gilgamesh Epic, and (embedded in a longer creation story) the Atrahasis Epic.

**6:6 His heart was grieved**: the expression can be misleading in English, for "heart" in Hebrew is the seat of memory and judgment rather than emotion. The phrase is actually parallel to the first half of the sentence ("the LORD regretted . . .").

**6:7** Human beings are an essential part of their environment, which includes all living things. In the new beginning after the flood, God makes a covenant with human beings and every living creature (9:9–10). The same close link between human beings and nature is found elsewhere in the Bible; e.g., in Is 35, God's healing transforms human beings along with their physical environment, and in Rom 8:19–23, all creation, not merely human beings, groans in labor pains awaiting the salvation of God.

**6:11 Corrupt**: God does not punish arbitrarily but simply brings to its completion the corruption initiated by human beings.

**6:14 Gopherwood**: an unidentified wood mentioned only in connection with the ark. It may be the wood of the cypress, which in Hebrew sounds like "gopher" and was widely used in antiquity for shipbuilding.

**6:15** Hebrew "cubit," lit., "forearm," is the distance from the elbow to the tip of the middle finger, about eighteen inches (a foot and a half). The dimensions of Noah's ark were approximately 440 × 73 × 44 feet. The ark of the Babylonian flood story was an exact cube, 120 cubits (180 feet) in length, width, and height.

**6:16 Opening for daylight**: a conjectural rendering of the Hebrew word *sohar*, occurring only here. The reference is probably to an open space on all sides near the top of the ark to admit light and air. The ark also had a window or hatch, which could be opened and closed (8:6).

**6:19–21 You shall bring two of every kind . . . , one male and one female**: For the Priestly source (P), there is no distinction between clean and unclean animals until Sinai (Lv 11), no altars or sacrifice until Sinai, and all diet is vegetarian (Gn 1:29–30); even after the flood P has no distinction between clean and unclean, since "any living creature that moves about" may be eaten (9:3). Thus P has Noah take the

*y:* Wis 14:6; Bar 3:26. *z:* Ps 14:2–3. *a:* Wis 10:4; Sir 44:17. *b:* Jb 22:15–17. *c:* Ps 14:2. *d:* Sir 40:9–10; 44:17; Mt 24:37–39. *e:* Gn 7:4, 21; 2 Pt 2:5. *f:* Gn 9:9; Wis 14:6; Heb 11:7; 1 Pt 3:20.

### Clean and Unclean Animals

THE DIFFERENCES BETWEEN clean animals (7:2) and animals that are not clean (7:8) involve a whole system of dividing animals and other parts of life into the categories of clean and unclean. Any animals that have two or more characteristics that usually go together are considered clean. For example, animals that live in the sea typically have fins and scales. Therefore, all fish are clean because they have the fins and scales that sea creatures usually have. However, other sea creatures such as clams or oysters are unclean because they live in the sea but do not have fins or scales. They are unclean because they are thought to cross created boundaries or mix characteristics that do not normally belong together (see Lv 11:1–47 and Dt 14:3–21). This system of dividing between clean and unclean underlies the Jewish dietary laws of kosher eating.

mal, and of every kind of thing that crawls on the ground, two of each will come to you, that you may keep them alive. [21]Moreover, you are to provide yourself with all the food that is to be eaten, and store it away, that it may serve as provisions for you and for them. [22]Noah complied; he did just as God had commanded him.*

## CHAPTER 7

See RG 55

[1]Then the LORD said to Noah: Go into the ark, you and all your household, for you alone in this generation have I found to be righteous before me.[g] [2]Of every clean animal, take with you seven pairs, a male and its mate; and of the unclean animals, one pair, a male and its mate; [3]likewise, of every bird of the air, seven pairs, a male and a female, to keep their progeny alive over all the earth. [4]For seven days from now I will bring rain down on the earth for forty days and forty nights, and so I will wipe out from the face of the earth every being that I have made.[h] [5]Noah complied, just as the LORD had commanded.

***The Great Flood.*** [6]Noah was six hundred years old when the flood came upon the earth. [7]Together with his sons, his wife, and his sons' wives, Noah went into the ark because of the waters of the flood.[i] [8]Of the clean animals and the unclean, of the birds, and of everything that crawls on the ground, [9]two by two, male and female came to Noah into the ark, just as God had commanded him.[j] [10]When the seven days were over, the waters of the flood came upon the earth.

[11]In the six hundredth year of Noah's life, in the second month, on the seventeenth day of the month: on that day

All the fountains of the great abyss* burst forth,
and the floodgates of the sky were opened.

[12]For forty days and forty nights heavy rain poured down on the earth.

[13]On the very same day, Noah and his sons Shem, Ham, and Japheth, and Noah's wife, and the three wives of Noah's sons had entered the ark, [14]together with every kind of wild animal, every kind of tame animal, every kind of crawling thing that crawls on the earth, and every kind of bird. [15]Pairs of all creatures in which there was the breath of life came to Noah into the ark. [16]Those that entered were male and female; of all creatures they came, as God had commanded Noah. Then the LORD shut him in.

minimum to preserve all species, one pair of each, without distinction between clean and unclean, but he must also take on provisions for food (6:21). The Yahwist source (J), which assumes the clean-unclean distinction always existed but knows no other restriction on eating meat (Abel was a shepherd and offered meat as a sacrifice), requires additional clean animals ("seven pairs") for food and sacrifice (7:2–3; 8:20).

**6:22 Just as God had commanded him**: as in the creation of the world in chap. 1 and in the building of the tabernacle in Ex 25–31, 35–40 (all from the Priestly source), everything takes place by the command of God. In this passage and in Exodus, the commands of God are carried out to the letter by human agents, Noah and Moses. Divine speech is important. God speaks to Noah seven times in the flood story.

**7:11 Abyss**: the subterranean ocean; see note on 1:2.

*g:* Wis 10:4; Sir 44:17; 2 Pt 2:5. *h:* Gn 6:17; 2 Pt 2:5. *i:* Wis 14:6; 1 Pt 3:20; 2 Pt 2:5. *j:* Gn 6:19.

17The flood continued upon the earth for forty days. As the waters increased, they lifted the ark, so that it rose above the earth. 18The waters swelled and increased greatly on the earth, but the ark floated on the surface of the waters. 19Higher and higher on the earth the waters swelled, until all the highest mountains under the heavens were submerged. 20The waters swelled fifteen cubits higher than the submerged mountains. 21All creatures that moved on earth perished: birds, tame animals, wild animals, and all that teemed on the earth, as well as all humankind.[k] 22Everything on dry land with the breath of life in its nostrils died. 23The LORD wiped out every being on earth: human beings and animals, the crawling things and the birds of the air; all were wiped out from the earth. Only Noah and those with him in the ark were left.

24And when the waters had swelled on the earth for one hundred and fifty days,

## CHAPTER 8

See RG 55

1God remembered Noah and all the animals, wild and tame, that were with him in the ark. So God made a wind sweep over the earth, and the waters began to subside. 2The fountains of the abyss and the floodgates of the sky were closed, and the downpour from the sky was held back. 3Gradually the waters receded from the earth. At the end of one hundred and fifty days, the waters had so diminished 4that, in the seventh month, on the seventeenth day of the month, the ark came to rest on the mountains of Ararat.* 5The waters continued to diminish until the tenth month, and on the first day of the tenth month the tops of the mountains appeared.

6At the end of forty days Noah opened the hatch of the ark that he had made, 7* and he released a raven. It flew back and forth until the waters dried off from the earth. 8Then he released a dove, to see if the waters had lessened on the earth. 9But the dove could find no place to perch, and it returned to him in the ark, for there was water over all the earth. Putting out his hand, he caught the dove and drew it back to him inside the ark. 10He waited yet seven days more and again released the dove from the ark. 11In the evening the dove came back to him, and there in its bill was a plucked-off olive leaf! So Noah knew that the waters had diminished on the earth. 12He waited yet another seven days and then released the dove; but this time it did not come back.

13* In the six hundred and first year, in the first month, on the first day of the month, the water began to dry up on the earth. Noah then removed the covering of the ark and saw that the surface of the ground had dried. 14In the second month, on the twenty-seventh day of the month, the earth was dry.

15Then God said to Noah: 16Go out of the ark, together with your wife and your sons and your sons' wives. 17Bring out with you every living thing that is with you—all creatures, be they birds or animals or crawling things that crawl on the earth—and let them abound on the earth, and be fertile and multiply on it.[l] 18So Noah came out, together with his sons and his wife and his sons' wives; 19and all the animals, all the birds, and all the crawling creatures that crawl on the earth went out of the ark by families.

20Then Noah built an altar to the LORD, and choosing from every clean animal and every clean bird, he offered burnt offerings on the altar. 21When the LORD smelled the sweet odor, the LORD said to himself: Never again will I curse the ground because of human beings, since the desires of the human heart are evil from youth; nor will I ever again strike down every living being, as I have done.[m]

**8:4 The mountains of Ararat**: the mountain country of ancient Arartu in northwest Iraq, which was the highest part of the world to the biblical writer. There is no Mount Ararat in the Bible.

**8:7–12** In the eleventh tablet of the Gilgamesh Epic, Utnapishtim (the equivalent of Noah) released in succession a dove, a swallow, and a raven. When the raven did not return, Utnapishtim knew it was safe to leave the ark. The first century A.D. Roman author Pliny tells of Indian sailors who release birds in order to follow them toward land.

**8:13–14** On the first day of the first month, the world was in the state it had been on the day of creation in chap. 1. Noah had to wait another month until the earth was properly dry as in 1:9.

*k:* Jb 22:16; Mt 24:39; Lk 17:27; 2 Pt 3:6. *l:* Gn 1:22, 28. *m:* Sir 44:18; Is 54:9; Rom 7:18.

THIS COVENANT WITH Noah was made with all of humankind while other covenants were with individuals or the Hebrew people.

22 All the days of the earth,
seedtime and harvest,
cold and heat,
Summer and winter,
and day and night
shall not cease.[n]

## CHAPTER 9

See RG 55

*Covenant with Noah.* 1* God blessed
Noah and his sons and said to them: Be fertile and multiply and fill the earth.[o] 2* Fear
and dread of you shall come upon all the animals of the earth and all the birds of the air,
upon all the creatures that move about on the
ground and all the fishes of the sea; into your
power they are delivered. 3[p] Any living creature that moves about shall be yours to eat; I
give them all to you as I did the green plants.
4[q] Only meat with its lifeblood still in it you
shall not eat.* 5Indeed for your own lifeblood
I will demand an accounting: from every animal I will demand it, and from a human being, each one for the blood of another, I will
demand an accounting for human life.[r]

6 * Anyone who sheds the blood of a
human being,
by a human being shall that one's
blood be shed;
For in the image of God
have human beings been made.[s]

7Be fertile, then, and multiply; abound on
earth and subdue it.[t]
8* God said to Noah and to his sons with
him: 9See, I am now establishing my covenant with you and your descendants after
you[u] 10and with every living creature that
was with you: the birds, the tame animals,
and all the wild animals that were with
you—all that came out of the ark. 11I will establish my covenant with you, that never
again shall all creatures be destroyed by the
waters of a flood; there shall not be another
flood to devastate the earth.[v] 12God said:
This is the sign of the covenant that I am
making between me and you and every living creature with you for all ages to come:
13[w] I set my bow in the clouds to serve as a
sign of the covenant between me and the
earth. 14When I bring clouds over the earth,
and the bow appears in the clouds, 15I will
remember my covenant between me and you
and every living creature—every mortal being—so that the waters will never again become a flood to destroy every mortal being.[x]
16When the bow appears in the clouds, I will
see it and remember the everlasting covenant between God and every living creature—every mortal being that is on earth.
17God told Noah: This is the sign of the covenant I have established between me and
every mortal being that is on earth.

**9:1** God reaffirms without change the original blessing and mandate of 1:28. In the Mesopotamian epic Atrahasis, on which the Genesis story is partly modeled, the gods changed their original plan by restricting human population through such means as childhood diseases, birth demons, and mandating celibacy among certain groups of women.

**9:2–3** Pre-flood creatures, including human beings, are depicted as vegetarians (1:29–30). In view of the human propensity to violence, God changes the original prohibition against eating meat.

**9:4** Because a living being dies when it loses most of its blood, the ancients regarded blood as the seat of life, and therefore as sacred. Jewish tradition considered the prohibition against eating meat with blood to be binding on all, because it was given by God to Noah, the new ancestor of all humankind; therefore the early Christian Church retained it for a time (Acts 15:20, 29).

**9:6** The image of God, given to the first man and woman and transmitted to every human being, is the reason that no violent attacks can be made upon human beings. That image is the basis of the dignity of every individual who, in some sense, "represents" God in the world.

**9:8–17** God makes a covenant with Noah and his descendants and, remarkably, with all the animals who come out of the ark: never again shall the world be destroyed by flood. The sign of this solemn promise is the appearance of a rainbow.

*n:* Jer 33:20, 25. *o:* Gn 1:22, 28; 8:17. *p:* Gn 1:29–30; Dt 12:15. *q:* Lv 7:26–27; 17:4; Dt 12:16, 23; 1 Sm 14:33; Acts 15:20. *r:* Gn 4:10–11; Ex 21:12. *s:* Gn 1:26–27; Lv 24:17; Nm 35:33; Jas 3:9. *t:* Gn 1:28; 8:17; 9:2; Jas 3:7. *u:* Gn 6:18. *v:* Sir 44:18; Is 54:9. *w:* Sir 43:12. *x:* Is 54:9.

*Noah and His Sons.* 18* The sons of Noah
who came out of the ark were Shem, Ham
and Japheth. Ham was the father of Canaan.[y]
19These three were the sons of Noah, and
from them the whole earth was populated.
20Noah, a man of the soil, was the first to
plant a vineyard. 21He drank some of the
wine, became drunk, and lay naked inside
his tent.[z] 22Ham, the father of Canaan, saw
his father's nakedness, and he told his two
brothers outside. 23Shem and Japheth, however, took a robe, and holding it on their
shoulders, they walked backward and covered their father's nakedness; since their
faces were turned the other way, they did not
see their father's nakedness. 24When Noah
woke up from his wine and learned what his
youngest son had done to him, 25he said:

"Cursed be Canaan!
The lowest of slaves
shall he be to his brothers."[a]

26He also said:

"Blessed be the LORD, the God of Shem!
Let Canaan be his slave.
27 May God expand Japheth,*
and may he dwell among the tents of
Shem;
and let Canaan be his slave."

28Noah lived three hundred and fifty years
after the flood. 29The whole lifetime of Noah
was nine hundred and fifty years; then he
died.

## CHAPTER 10

See RG 55

*Table of the Nations.** 1These are the
descendants of Noah's sons, Shem, Ham and
Japheth, to whom children were born after
the flood.
2b The descendants of Japheth: Gomer,*
Magog, Madai, Javan, Tubal, Meshech and
Tiras.[c] 3The descendants of Gomer: Ashkenaz,* Diphath and Togarmah. 4The descendants of Javan: Elishah,* Tarshish, the Kittim and the Rodanim. 5From these branched
out the maritime nations.
These are the descendants of Japheth by
their lands, each with its own language, according to their clans, by their nations.
6The descendants of Ham: Cush,* Mizraim,

**9:18–27** The character of the three sons is sketched here. The fault is not Noah's (for he could not be expected to know about the intoxicating effect of wine) but Ham's, who shames his father by looking on his nakedness, and then tells the other sons. Ham's conduct is meant to prefigure the later shameful sexual practices of the Canaanites, which are alleged in numerous biblical passages. The point of the story is revealed in Noah's curse of Ham's son Canaan and his blessing of Shem and Japheth.

**9:27** In the Hebrew text there is a play on the words *yapt* ("expand") and *yepet* ("Japheth").

**10:1–32** Verse 1 is the fourth of the Priestly formulas (2:4; 5:1; 6:9; 11:10) that structure Part I of Genesis; it introduces 10:2–11:9, the populating of the world and the building of the city. In a sense, chaps. 4–9 are concerned with the first of the two great commands given to the human race in 1:28, "Be fertile and multiply!" whereas chaps. 10–11 are concerned with the second command, "Fill the earth and subdue it!" ("Subdue it" refers to each nation's taking the land assigned to it by God.) Gn 9:19 already noted that all nations are descended from the three sons of Noah; the same sentiment is repeated in 10:5, 18, 25, 32; 11:8. The presupposition of the chapter is that every nation has a land assigned to it by God (cf. Dt 32:8–9). The number of the nations is seventy (if one does not count Noah and his sons, and counts Sidon [vv. 15, 19] only once), which is a traditional biblical number (Jgs 8:30; Lk 10:1, 17). According to Gn 46:27 and Ex 1:5, Israel also numbered seventy persons, which shows that it in some sense represents the nations of the earth.

This chapter classifies the various peoples known to the ancient Israelites; it is theologically important as stressing the basic family unity of all peoples on earth. It is sometimes called the Table of the Nations. The relationship between the various peoples is based on linguistic, geographic, or political grounds (v. 31). In general, the descendants of Japheth (vv. 2–5) are the peoples of the Indo-European languages to the north and west of Mesopotamia and Syria; the descendants of Ham (vv. 6–20) are the Hamitic-speaking peoples of northern Africa; and the descendants of Shem (vv. 21–31) are the Semitic-speaking peoples of Mesopotamia, Syria and Arabia. But there are many exceptions to this rule; the Semitic-speaking peoples of Canaan are considered descendants of Ham, because at one time they were subject to Hamitic Egypt (vv. 6, 15–19). This chapter is generally considered to be a composite from the Yahwist source (vv. 8–19, 21, 24–30) and the Priestly source (vv. 1–7, 20, 22–23, 31–32). Presumably that is why certain tribes of Arabia are listed under both Ham (v. 7) and Shem (vv. 26–28).

**10:2 Gomer**: the Cimmerians; **Madai**: the Medes; **Javan**: the Greeks.

**10:3 Ashkenaz**: an Indo-European people, which later became the medieval rabbinic name for Germany. It now designates one of the great divisions of Judaism, Eastern European Yiddish-speaking Jews.

**10:4 Elishah**: Cyprus; **the Kittim**: certain inhabitants of Cyprus; **the Rodanim**: the inhabitants of Rhodes.

**10:6 Cush**: biblical Ethiopia, modern Nubia. **Mizraim**:

*y:* Gn 5:32; 10:1. *z:* Lam 4:21; Hb 2:15. *a:* Dt 27:16; Wis 12:11. *b:* 1 Chr 1:5–10. *c:* Ez 38:2.

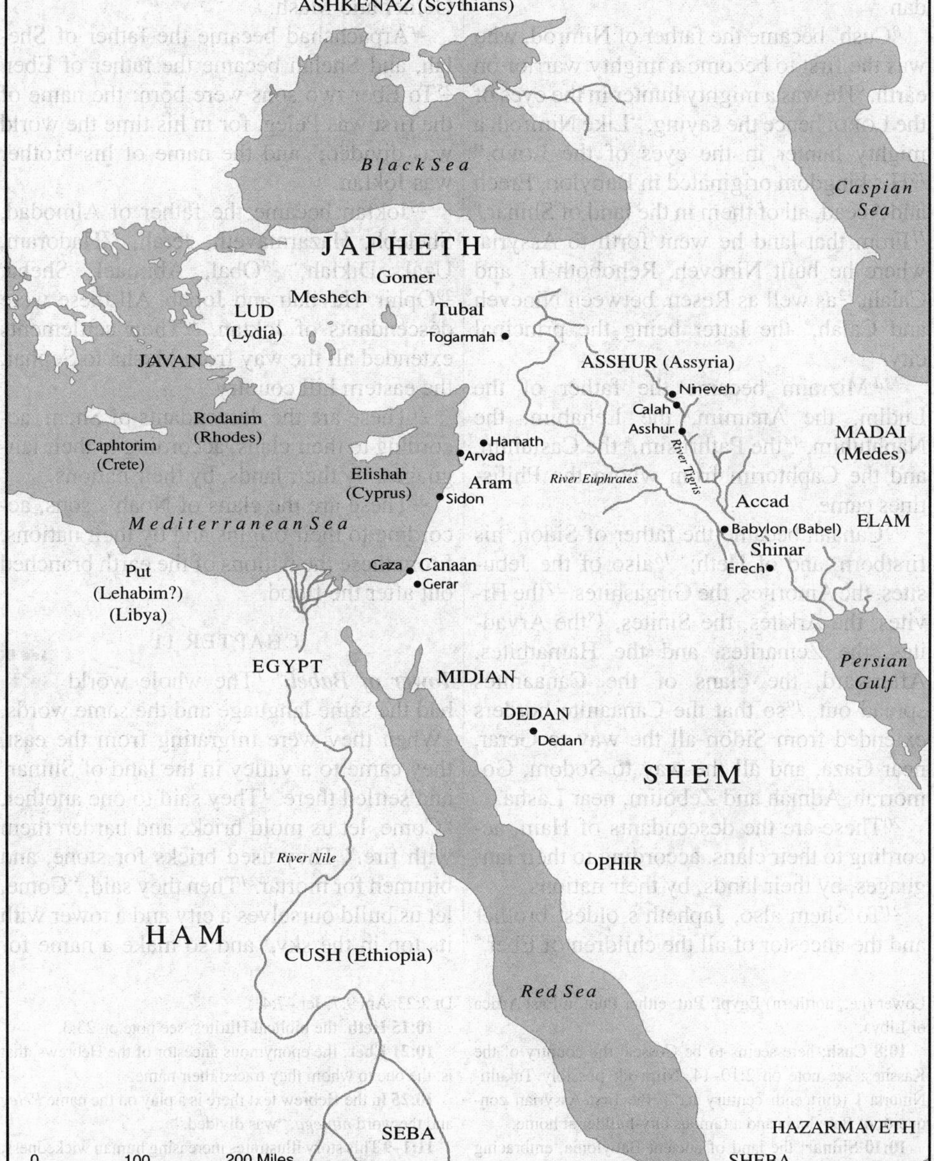


Table of Nations

Put and Canaan. [7]The descendants of Cush: Seba, Havilah, Sabtah, Raamah and Sabteca. The descendants of Raamah: Sheba and Dedan.

[8]Cush* became the father of Nimrod, who was the first to become a mighty warrior on earth. [9]He was a mighty hunter in the eyes of the LORD; hence the saying, "Like Nimrod, a mighty hunter in the eyes of the LORD." [10]His kingdom originated in Babylon, Erech and Accad, all of them in the land of Shinar.* [11]From that land he went forth to Assyria, where he built Nineveh, Rehoboth-Ir* and Calah, [12]as well as Resen, between Nineveh and Calah,* the latter being the principal city.

[13][d] Mizraim became the father of the Ludim, the Anamim, the Lehabim, the Naphtuhim, [14]the Pathrusim,* the Casluhim, and the Caphtorim from whom the Philistines came.

[15]Canaan became the father of Sidon, his firstborn, and of Heth;* [16]also of the Jebusites, the Amorites, the Girgashites, [17]the Hivites, the Arkites, the Sinites, [18]the Arvadites, the Zemarites, and the Hamathites. Afterward, the clans of the Canaanites spread out, [19]so that the Canaanite borders extended from Sidon all the way to Gerar, near Gaza, and all the way to Sodom, Gomorrah, Admah and Zeboiim, near Lasha.

[20]These are the descendants of Ham, according to their clans, according to their languages, by their lands, by their nations.

[21]To Shem also, Japheth's oldest brother and the ancestor of all the children of Eber,* children were born. [22][e] The descendants of Shem: Elam, Asshur, Arpachshad, Lud and Aram. [23]The descendants of Aram: Uz, Hul, Gether and Mash.

[24]Arpachshad became the father of Shelah, and Shelah became the father of Eber. [25]To Eber two sons were born: the name of the first was Peleg, for in his time the world was divided;* and the name of his brother was Joktan.

[26]Joktan became the father of Almodad, Sheleph, Hazarmaveth, Jerah, [27]Hadoram, Uzal, Diklah, [28]Obal, Abimael, Sheba, [29]Ophir, Havilah and Jobab. All these were descendants of Joktan. [30]Their settlements extended all the way from Mesha to Sephar, the eastern hill country.

[31]These are the descendants of Shem, according to their clans, according to their languages, by their lands, by their nations.

[32]These are the clans of Noah's sons, according to their origins and by their nations. From these the nations of the earth branched out after the flood.

## CHAPTER 11

See RG 55

*Tower of Babel.** [1]The whole world had the same language and the same words. [2]When they were migrating from the east, they came to a valley in the land of Shinar* and settled there. [3]They said to one another, "Come, let us mold bricks and harden them with fire." They used bricks for stone, and bitumen for mortar. [4]Then they said, "Come, let us build ourselves a city and a tower with its top in the sky,* and so make a name for

Lower (i.e., northern) Egypt; **Put**: either Punt in East Africa or Libya.

**10:8 Cush**: here seems to be Cossea, the country of the Kassites; see note on 2:10–14. **Nimrod**: possibly Tukulti-Ninurta I (thirteenth century B.C.), the first Assyrian conqueror of Babylonia and a famous city-builder at home.

**10:10 Shinar**: the land of ancient Babylonia, embracing Sumer and Akkad, present-day southern Iraq, mentioned also in 11:2; 14:1.

**10:11 Rehoboth-Ir**: lit., "wide-streets city," was probably not the name of another city, but an epithet of Nineveh; cf. Jon 3:3.

**10:12 Calah**: Assyrian Kalhu, the capital of Assyria in the ninth century B.C.

**10:14 The Pathrusim**: the people of Upper (southern) Egypt; cf. Is 11:11; Jer 44:1; Ez 29:14; 30:13. **Caphtorim**: Crete; for Caphtor as the place of origin of the Philistines, cf. Dt 2:23; Am 9:7; Jer 47:4.

**10:15 Heth**: the biblical Hittites; see note on 23:3.

**10:21 Eber**: the eponymous ancestor of the Hebrews, that is, the one to whom they traced their name.

**10:25** In the Hebrew text there is a play on the name *Peleg* and the word *niplega*, "was divided."

**11:1–9** This story illustrates increasing human wickedness, shown here in the sinful pride that human beings take in their own achievements apart from God. Secondarily, the story explains the diversity of languages among the peoples of the earth.

**11:2 Shinar**: see note on 10:10.

**11:4 Tower with its top in the sky**: possibly a reference to the chief ziggurat of Babylon, *E-sag-ila*, lit., "the house that raises high its head."

*d:* 1 Chr 1:11–16. *e:* 1 Chr 1:17–23.

ourselves; otherwise we shall be scattered
all over the earth."
[5]The LORD came down to see the city and
the tower that the people had built. [6]Then the
LORD said: If now, while they are one people
and all have the same language, they have
started to do this, nothing they presume to do
will be out of their reach. [7]Come, let us go
down and there confuse their language, so
that no one will understand the speech of another. [8]So the LORD scattered them from
there over all the earth, and they stopped
building the city. [9]That is why it was called
Babel,* because there the LORD confused the
speech of all the world. From there the LORD
scattered them over all the earth.

***Descendants from Shem to Abraham.****
[10][f]These are the descendants of Shem.
When Shem was one hundred years old, he
begot Arpachshad, two years after the flood.
[11]Shem lived five hundred years after he begot Arpachshad, and he had other sons and
daughters. [12]When Arpachshad was thirty-
five years old, he begot Shelah.* [13]Arpach-
shad lived four hundred and three years after
he begot Shelah, and he had other sons and
daughters.
[14]When Shelah was thirty years old, he
begot Eber. [15]Shelah lived four hundred and
three years after he begot Eber, and he had
other sons and daughters.
[16]When Eber* was thirty-four years old,
he begot Peleg. [17]Eber lived four hundred
and thirty years after he begot Peleg, and he
had other sons and daughters.
[18]When Peleg was thirty years old, he begot Reu. [19]Peleg lived two hundred and nine
years after he begot Reu, and he had other
sons and daughters.
[20]When Reu was thirty-two years old, he
begot Serug. [21]Reu lived two hundred and
seven years after he begot Serug, and he had
other sons and daughters.
[22]When Serug was thirty years old, he begot Nahor. [23]Serug lived two hundred years
after he begot Nahor, and he had other sons
and daughters.
[24]When Nahor was twenty-nine years old,
he begot Terah. [25]Nahor lived one hundred
and nineteen years after he begot Terah, and
he had other sons and daughters.
[26]When Terah was seventy years old, he
begot Abram,* Nahor and Haran.[g]

## II. The Story of the Ancestors of Israel

***Terah.*** [27]These are the descendants of Terah.* Terah begot Abram, Nahor, and Haran,
and Haran begot Lot. [28]Haran died before
Terah his father, in his native land, in Ur of
the Chaldeans.* [29]Abram and Nahor took

**11:9 Babel**: the Hebrew form of the name "Babylon"; the Babylonians interpreted their name for the city, *Bab-ili*, as "gate of god." The Hebrew word *balal*, "he confused," has a similar sound.

**11:10–26** The second Priestly genealogy goes from Shem to Terah and his three sons Abram, Nahor, and Haran, just as the genealogy in 5:3–32 went from Adam to Noah and his three sons Shem, Ham, and Japheth. This genealogy marks the important transition in Genesis between the story of the nations in 1:1–11:26 and the story of Israel in the person of its ancestors (11:27–50:26). As chaps. 1–11 showed the increase and spread of the nations, so chaps. 12–50 will show the increase and spread of Israel. The contrast between Israel and the nations is a persistent biblical theme. The ages given here are from the Hebrew text; the Samaritan and Greek texts have divergent sets of numbers in most cases. In comparable accounts of the pre-flood period, enormous life spans are attributed to human beings. It may be an attempt to show that the pre-flood generations were extraordinary and more vital than post-flood human beings.

**11:12** The Greek text adds Kenan (cf. 5:9–10) between Arpachshad and Shelah. The Greek listing is followed in Lk 3:36.

**11:16 Eber**: the eponymous ancestor of the Hebrews, "descendants of Eber" (10:21, 24–30); see note on 14:13.

**11:26** Abram is a dialectal variant of Abraham. God will change his name in view of his new task in 17:4.

**11:27 Descendants of Terah**: elsewhere in Genesis the story of the son is introduced by the name of the father (25:12, 19; 36:1; 37:2). The Abraham-Sarah stories begin (11:27–32) and end with genealogical notices (25:1–18), which concern, respectively, the families of Terah and of Abraham. Most of the traditions in the cycle are from the Yahwist source. The so-called Elohist source (E) is somewhat shadowy, denied by some scholars but recognized by others in passages that duplicate other narratives (20:1–18 and 21:22–34). The Priestly source consists mostly of brief editorial notices, except for chaps. 17 and 23.

**11:28 Ur of the Chaldeans**: Ur was an extremely ancient city of the Sumerians (later, of the Babylonians) in southern Mesopotamia. The Greek text has "the land of the Chaldeans." After a millennium of relative unimportance, Ur underwent a revival during the Neo-Babylonian/Chaldean empire (625–539 B.C.). The sixth-century author here identified the place by its contemporary name. As chap. 24 shows, Haran in

*f:* 1 Chr 1:24–27; Lk 3:34–36. *g:* Jos 24:2; 1 Chr 1:26–27.

wives; the name of Abram's wife was Sarai,*
and the name of Nahor's wife was Milcah,
daughter of Haran, the father of Milcah and
Iscah.[h] 30 Sarai was barren; she had no child.
31 Terah took his son Abram, his grandson
Lot, son of Haran, and his daughter-in-law
Sarai, the wife of his son Abram, and
brought them out of Ur of the Chaldeans, to
go to the land of Canaan. But when they
reached Haran, they settled there.[i] 32 The
lifetime of Terah was two hundred and five
years; then Terah died in Haran.*

## CHAPTER 12

See RG 58-59

***Abram's Call and Migration.*** 1 The
LORD said to Abram: Go forth* from your
land, your relatives, and from your father's
house to a land that I will show you.[j] 2* I will
make of you a great nation, and I will bless
you; I will make your name great, so that
you will be a blessing.[k] 3[l] I will bless those
who bless you and curse those who curse
you. All the families of the earth will find
blessing in you.*
4[m] Abram went as the LORD directed him,
and Lot went with him. Abram was seventy-
five years old when he left Haran. 5* Abram
took his wife Sarai, his brother's son Lot, all
the possessions that they had accumulated,
and the persons they had acquired in Haran,
and they set out for the land of Canaan. When
they came to the land of Canaan, 6* Abram
passed through the land as far as the sacred
place at Shechem, by the oak of Moreh. The
Canaanites were then in the land.
7 The LORD appeared to Abram and said:
To your descendants I will give this land. So
Abram built an altar there to the LORD who
had appeared to him.[n] 8 From there he moved
on to the hill country east of Bethel, pitching
his tent with Bethel to the west and Ai to the
east. He built an altar there to the LORD and
invoked the LORD by name. 9 Then Abram
journeyed on by stages to the Negeb.*

northern Mesopotamia is in fact the native place of Abraham. In the Genesis perspective, the human race originated in the East (3:24; 4:16) and migrated from there to their homelands (11:2). Terah's family moved from the East (Ur) and Abraham will complete the journey to the family's true homeland in the following chapters.

**11:29 Sarai**: like Abram, a dialectal variant of the more usual form of the name Sarah. In 17:15, God will change it to Sarah in view of her new task.

**11:32** Since Terah was seventy years old when his son Abraham was born (v. 26), and Abraham was seventy-five when he left Haran (12:4), Terah lived in Haran for sixty years after Abraham's departure. According to the tradition in the Samaritan text, Terah died when he was one hundred and forty-five years old, therefore, in the same year in which Abraham left Haran. This is the tradition followed in Stephen's speech: Abraham left Haran "after his father died" (Acts 7:4).

**12:1–3 Go forth . . . find blessing in you**: the syntax of the Hebrew suggests that the blessings promised to Abraham are contingent on his going to Canaan.

**12:2** The call of Abraham begins a new history of blessing (18:18; 22:15–18), which is passed on in each instance to the chosen successor (26:2–4; 28:14). This call evokes the last story in the primeval history (11:1–9) by reversing its themes: Abraham goes forth rather than settle down; it is God rather than Abraham who will make a name for him; the families of the earth will find blessing in him.

**12:3 Will find blessing in you**: the Hebrew conjugation of the verb here and in 18:18 and 28:14 can be either reflexive ("shall bless themselves by you" = people will invoke Abraham as an example of someone blessed by God) or passive ("by you all the families of earth will be blessed" = the religious privileges of Abraham and his descendants ultimately will be extended to the nations). In 22:18 and 26:4, another conjugation of the same verb is used in a similar context that is undoubtedly reflexive ("bless themselves"). Many scholars suggest that the two passages in which the sense is clear should determine the interpretation of the three ambiguous passages: the privileged blessing enjoyed by Abraham and his descendants will awaken in all peoples the desire to enjoy those same blessings. Since the term is understood in a passive sense in the New Testament (Acts 3:25; Gal 3:8), it is rendered here by a neutral expression that admits of both meanings.

**12:5** The ancestors appear in Genesis as pastoral nomads living at the edge of settled society, and having occasional dealings with the inhabitants, sometimes even moving into towns for brief periods. Unlike modern nomads such as the Bedouin, however, ancient pastoralists fluctuated between following the herds and sedentary life, depending on circumstances. Pastoralists could settle down and farm and later resume a pastoral way of life. Indeed, there was a symbiotic relationship between pastoralists and villagers, each providing goods to the other. **Persons**: servants and others who formed the larger household under the leadership of Abraham; cf. 14:14.

**12:6** Abraham's journey to the center of the land, Shechem, then to Bethel, and then to the Negeb, is duplicated in Jacob's journeys (33:18; 35:1, 6, 27; 46:1) and in the general route of the conquest under Joshua (Jos 7:2; 8:9, 30). Abraham's journey is a symbolic "conquest" of the land he has been promised. In building altars here (vv. 7, 8) and elsewhere, Abraham acknowledges his God as Lord of the land.

**12:9 The Negeb**: the semidesert land south of Judah.

*h:* Gn 17:15. *i:* Jos 24:3; Neh 9:7; Jdt 5:6–9; Acts 7:4. *j:* Acts 7:3; Heb 11:8. *k:* Gn 17:6; Sir 44:20–21; Rom 4:17–22. *l:* Gn 18:18; 22:18; Acts 3:25; Gal 3:8. *m:* Gn 11:31; Jos 24:3; Acts 7:4. *n:* Ex 33:1; Dt 34:4; Acts 7:5.

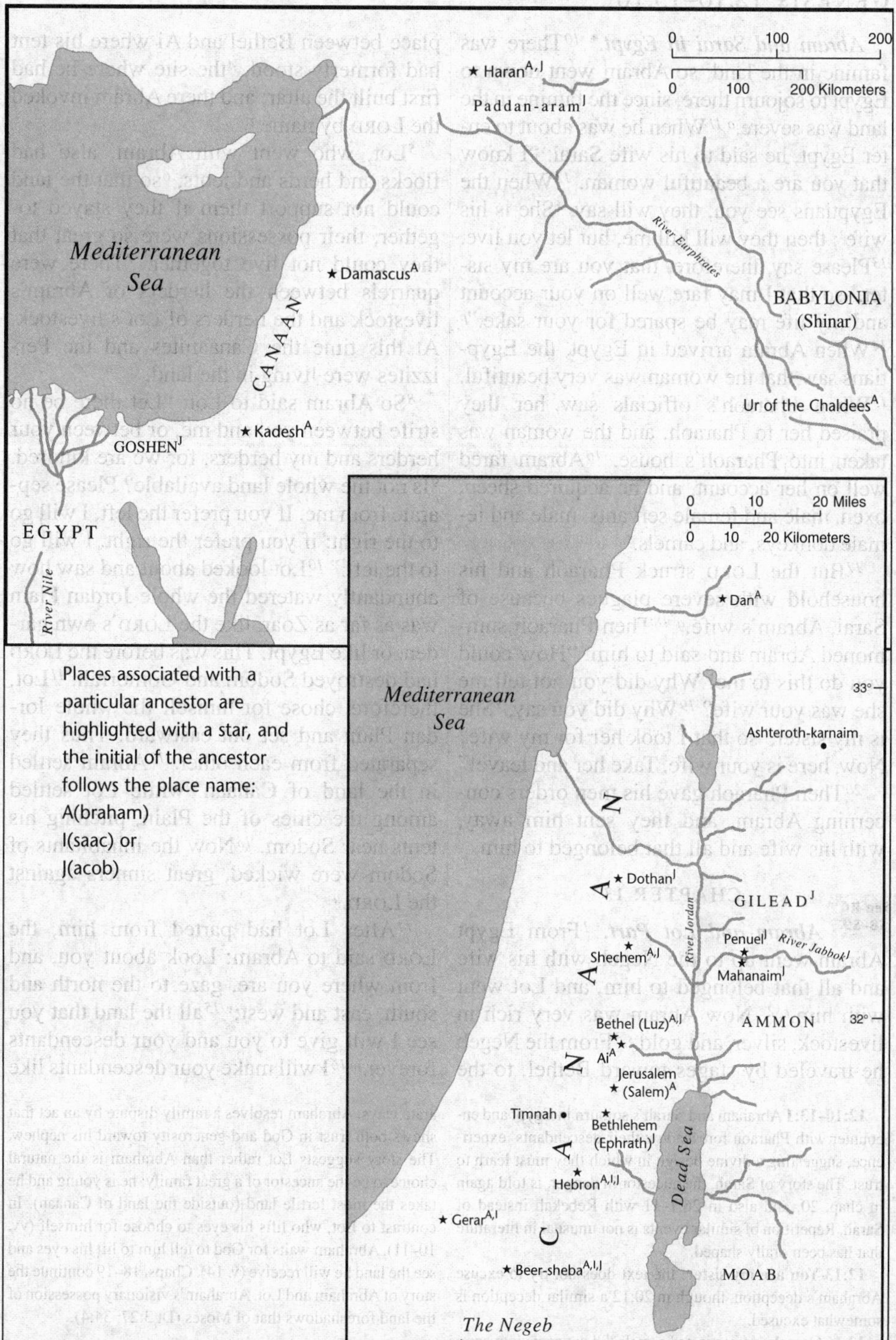
Mediterranean Sea
CANAAN
EGYPT
GOSHEN J
River Nile
Kadesh A
Damascus A
Haran A, J
Paddan-aram J
River Euphrates
BABYLONIA (Shinar)
Ur of the Chaldees A
0 100 200 Miles
0 100 200 Kilometers
0 10 20 Miles
0 10 20 Kilometers
Places associated with a particular ancestor are highlighted with a star, and the initial of the ancestor follows the place name:
A(braham)
I(saac) or
J(acob)
Mediterranean Sea
CANAAN
Dan A
Ashteroth-karnaim
Dothan J
GILEAD J
River Jordan
Shechem A,J
Penuel J
River Jabbok J
Mahanaim J
AMMON
Bethel (Luz) A,J
Ai A
Jerusalem (Salem) A
Timnah
Bethlehem (Ephrath) J
Hebron A,I,J
Dead Sea
Gerar A,I
Beer-sheba A,I,J
MOAB
The Negeb
Kadesh A
EDOM
33°
32°
31°
35°
36°

## Geography of Ancestral Narratives

*Abram and Sarai in Egypt.** 10 There was famine in the land; so Abram went down to Egypt to sojourn there, since the famine in the land was severe.[o] 11 When he was about to enter Egypt, he said to his wife Sarai: "I know that you are a beautiful woman. 12 When the Egyptians see you, they will say, 'She is his wife'; then they will kill me, but let you live. 13 Please say, therefore, that you are my sister,* so that I may fare well on your account and my life may be spared for your sake."[p] 14 When Abram arrived in Egypt, the Egyptians saw that the woman was very beautiful. 15 When Pharaoh's officials saw her they praised her to Pharaoh, and the woman was taken into Pharaoh's house. 16 Abram fared well on her account, and he acquired sheep, oxen, male and female servants, male and female donkeys, and camels.*

17 But the LORD struck Pharaoh and his household with severe plagues because of Sarai, Abram's wife.[q] 18 Then Pharaoh summoned Abram and said to him: "How could you do this to me! Why did you not tell me she was your wife? 19 Why did you say, 'She is my sister,' so that I took her for my wife? Now, here is your wife. Take her and leave!"

20 Then Pharaoh gave his men orders concerning Abram, and they sent him away, with his wife and all that belonged to him.

See RG 58–59

## CHAPTER 13

*Abram and Lot Part.* 1 From Egypt Abram went up to the Negeb with his wife and all that belonged to him, and Lot went with him.[r] 2* Now Abram was very rich in livestock, silver, and gold.[s] 3 From the Negeb he traveled by stages toward Bethel, to the place between Bethel and Ai where his tent had formerly stood, 4 the site where he had first built the altar; and there Abram invoked the LORD by name.[t]

5 Lot, who went with Abram, also had flocks and herds and tents, 6 so that the land could not support them if they stayed together; their possessions were so great that they could not live together. 7 There were quarrels between the herders of Abram's livestock and the herders of Lot's livestock. At this time the Canaanites and the Perizzites were living in the land.

8 So Abram said to Lot: "Let there be no strife between you and me, or between your herders and my herders, for we are kindred. 9 Is not the whole land available? Please separate from me. If you prefer the left, I will go to the right; if you prefer the right, I will go to the left." 10 Lot looked about and saw how abundantly watered the whole Jordan Plain was as far as Zoar, like the LORD's own garden, or like Egypt. This was before the LORD had destroyed Sodom and Gomorrah. 11 Lot, therefore, chose for himself the whole Jordan Plain and set out eastward. Thus they separated from each other. 12 Abram settled in the land of Canaan, while Lot settled among the cities of the Plain, pitching his tents near Sodom. 13 Now the inhabitants of Sodom were wicked, great sinners against the LORD.[u]

14 After Lot had parted from him, the LORD said to Abram: Look about you, and from where you are, gaze to the north and south, east and west;[v] 15 all the land that you see I will give to you and your descendants forever.[w] 16 I will make your descendants like

**12:10–13:1** Abraham and Sarah's sojourn in Egypt and encounter with Pharaoh foreshadow their descendants' experience, suggesting a divine design in which they must learn to trust. The story of Sarah, the ancestor in danger, is told again in chap. 20, and also in 26:1–11 with Rebekah instead of Sarah. Repetition of similar events is not unusual in literature that has been orally shaped.

**12:13 You are my sister**: the text does not try to excuse Abraham's deception, though in 20:12 a similar deception is somewhat excused.

**12:16 Camels**: domesticated camels did not come into common use in the ancient Near East until the end of the second millennium B.C. Thus the mention of camels here (24:11–64; 30:43; 31:17, 34; 32:8, 16; 37:25) is seemingly an anachronism.

**13:2–18** In this story of Abraham and Lot going their separate ways, Abraham resolves a family dispute by an act that shows both trust in God and generosity toward his nephew. The story suggests Lot rather than Abraham is the natural choice to be the ancestor of a great family; he is young and he takes the most fertile land (outside the land of Canaan). In contrast to Lot, who lifts his eyes to choose for himself (vv. 10–11), Abraham waits for God to tell him to lift his eyes and see the land he will receive (v. 14). Chaps. 18–19 continue the story of Abraham and Lot. Abraham's visionary possession of the land foreshadows that of Moses (Dt 3:27; 34:4).

---

*o:* Gn 26:1. *p:* Gn 20:12–13; 26:7. *q:* Ps 105:14. *r:* Gn 12:9. *s:* Ps 112:1–3; Prv 10:22. *t:* Gn 12:8. *u:* Gn 18:20; Ez 16:49; 2 Pt 2:6–8; Jude 7. *v:* Gn 28:14. *w:* Gn 12:7; Mt 5:5; Lk 1:55, 73; Acts 7:5; Rom 4:13; Gal 3:16.

the dust of the earth; if anyone could count the dust of the earth, your descendants too might be counted.[x] 17 Get up and walk through the land, across its length and breadth, for I give it to you. 18 Abram moved his tents and went on to settle near the oak of Mamre, which is at Hebron. There he built an altar to the LORD.[y]

## CHAPTER 14

See RG 58–59

*The Four Kings.* 1* When Amraphel king of Shinar, Arioch king of Ellasar, Chedorlaomer king of Elam, and Tidal king of Goiim 2 made war on Bera king of Sodom, Birsha king of Gomorrah, Shinab king of Admah, Shemeber king of Zeboiim, and the king of Bela (that is, Zoar), 3 all the latter kings joined forces in the Valley of Siddim (that is, the Salt Sea*). 4 For twelve years they had served Chedorlaomer, but in the thirteenth year they rebelled. 5 In the fourteenth year Chedorlaomer and the kings allied with him came and defeated the Rephaim in Ashteroth-karnaim, the Zuzim in Ham, the Emim in Shaveh-kiriathaim, 6 and the Horites in the hill country of Seir, as far as El-paran, close by the wilderness.[z] 7 They then turned back and came to En-mishpat (that is, Kadesh), and they subdued the whole country of both the Amalekites and the Amorites who lived in Hazazon-tamar. 8 Thereupon the king of Sodom, the king of Gomorrah, the king of Admah, the king of Zeboiim, and the king of Bela (that is, Zoar) marched out, and in the Valley of Siddim they went into battle against them: 9 against Chedorlaomer king of Elam, Tidal king of Goiim, Amraphel king of Shinar, and Arioch king of Ellasar—four kings against five. 10 Now the Valley of Siddim was full of bitumen pits; and as the king of Sodom and the king of Gomorrah fled, they fell into these, while the rest fled to the mountains. 11 The victors seized all the possessions and food supplies of Sodom and Gomorrah and then went their way. 12 They took with them Abram's nephew Lot, who had been living in Sodom, as well as his possessions, and departed.[a]

13 A survivor came and brought the news to Abram the Hebrew,* who was camping at the oak of Mamre the Amorite, a kinsman of Eshcol and Aner; these were allies of Abram. 14 When Abram heard that his kinsman had been captured, he mustered three hundred and eighteen of his retainers,* born in his house, and went in pursuit as far as Dan. 15 He and his servants deployed against them at night, defeated them, and pursued them as far as Hobah, which is north of Damascus. 16 He recovered all the possessions. He also recovered his kinsman Lot and his possessions, along with the women and the other people.

17 When Abram returned from his defeat of Chedorlaomer and the kings who were allied with him, the king of Sodom went out to greet him in the Valley of Shaveh (that is, the King's Valley).

18 Melchizedek, king of Salem,* brought

**14:1** Abraham plays a role with other world leaders. He defeats a coalition of five kings from the east (where, later, Israel's enemies lived) and is recognized by a Canaanite king as blessed by God Most High. The historicity of the events is controverted; apart from Shinar (Babylon), Tidal (Hittite Tudhaliya), and Elam, the names and places cannot be identified with certainty. The five cities were apparently at the southern end of the Dead Sea, and all but Bela (i.e., Zoar) were destined for destruction (19:20–24; Hos 11:8). The passage belongs to none of the traditional Genesis sources; it has some resemblance to reports of military campaigns in Babylonian and Assyrian royal annals.

**14:3 The Salt Sea**: the Dead Sea.

**14:13 Abram the Hebrew**: "Hebrew" was used by biblical writers for the pre-Israelite ancestors. Linguistically, it is an ethnic term; it may be built on the root Eber, who is the eponymous ancestor of the Israelites, that is, the one to whom they traced their name (10:21, 24–25; 11:14–17), or it may reflect the tradition that the ancestors came from beyond (*eber*) the Euphrates. It is used only by non-Israelites, or by Israelites speaking to foreigners.

**14:14 Retainers**: the Hebrew word *hanik* is used only here in the Old Testament. Cognate words appear in Egyptian and Akkadian texts, signifying armed soldiers belonging to the household of a local leader.

**14:18** Melchizedek, king of Salem (Jerusalem, cf. Ps 76:3), appears with majestic suddenness to recognize Abraham's great victory, which the five local kings were unable to achieve. He prepares a feast in his honor and declares him blessed or made powerful by God Most High, evidently the highest God in the Canaanite pantheon. Abraham acknowledges the blessing by giving a tenth of the recaptured spoils as a tithe to Melchizedek. The episode is one of several allu-

*x:* Gn 22:17; Nm 23:10. *y:* Gn 14:13. *z:* Dt 2:12. *a:* Gn 13:10–12.

**Hagar, Sarai, and the Birth of Ishmael**

BECAUSE SARAI COULD have no children on her own, ancient custom allowed her to have a child through one of her women servants. Hagar receives a promise (16:10) that is virtually identical to the promise the Lord made to Abram (15:5).

out bread and wine. He was a priest of God Most High. 19He blessed Abram with these words:[b]

> "Blessed be Abram by God Most High,
> the creator of heaven and earth;
> 20 And blessed be God Most High,
> who delivered your foes into your hand."

Then Abram gave him a tenth of everything.

21The king of Sodom said to Abram, "Give me the captives; the goods you may keep." 22But Abram replied to the king of Sodom: "I have sworn to the LORD, God Most High,* the creator of heaven and earth, 23that I would not take so much as a thread or a sandal strap from anything that is yours, so that you cannot say, 'I made Abram rich.' 24Nothing for me except what my servants have consumed and the share that is due to the men who went with me—Aner, Eshcol and Mamre; let them take their share."

## CHAPTER 15

See RG 58–59

*The Covenant with Abram.** 1Some time afterward, the word of the LORD came to Abram in a vision: Do not fear, Abram! I am your shield; I will make your reward very great.

2But Abram said, "Lord GOD, what can you give me, if I die childless and have only a servant of my household, Eliezer of Damascus?" 3Abram continued, "Look, you have given me no offspring, so a servant of my household will be my heir." 4Then the word of the LORD came to him: No, that one will not be your heir; your own offspring will be your heir.[c] 5He took him outside and said: Look up at the sky and count the stars, if you can. Just so, he added, will your descendants be.[d] 6[e] Abram put his faith in the LORD, who attributed it to him as an act of righteousness.*

7He then said to him: I am the LORD who brought you from Ur of the Chaldeans to give you this land as a possession.[f] 8"Lord GOD," he asked, "how will I know that I will possess it?" 9* He answered him: Bring me a three-year-old heifer, a three-year-old female goat, a three-year-old ram, a turtledove, and a young pigeon.[g] 10He brought him all these, split them in two, and placed

sions to David, king at Jerusalem, who also exercised priestly functions (2 Sm 6:17). Heb 7 interprets Melchizedek as a prefiguration of Christ. **God Most High**: in Heb. *El Elyon*, one of several "El names" for God in Genesis, others being *El Olam* (21:33), *El* the God of Israel (33:20), *El Roi* (16:13), *El Bethel* (35:7), and *El Shaddai* (the usual P designation for God in Genesis). All the sources except the Yahwist use El as the proper name for God used by the ancestors. The god El was well-known across the ancient Near East and in comparable religious literature. The ancestors recognized this God as their own when they encountered him in their journeys and in the shrines they found in Canaan.

**14:22** In vv. 22–24, Abraham refuses to let anyone but God enrich him. Portrayed with the traits of a later Israelite judge or tribal hero, Abraham acknowledges that his victory is from God alone.

**15:1–21** In the first section (vv. 1–6), Abraham is promised a son and heir, and in the second (vv. 7–21), he is promised a land. The structure is similar in both: each of the two promises is not immediately accepted; the first is met with a complaint (vv. 2–3) and the second with a request for a sign (v. 8). God's answer differs in each section—a sign in v. 5 and an oath in vv. 9–21. Some scholars believe that the Genesis promises of progeny and land were originally separate and only later combined, but progeny and land are persistent concerns especially of ancient peoples and it is hard to imagine one without the other.

**15:6** Abraham's act of faith in God's promises was regarded as an act of righteousness, i.e., as fully expressive of his relationship with God. St. Paul (Rom 4:1–25; Gal 3:6–9) makes Abraham's faith a model for Christians.

**15:9–17** Cutting up animals was a well-attested way of making a treaty in antiquity. Jer 34:17–20 shows the rite is a form of self-imprecation in which violators invoke the fate of the animals upon themselves. The eighth-century B.C. Sefire treaty from Syria reads, "As this calf is cut up, thus Matti'el shall be cut up." The smoking fire pot and the flaming torch (v. 17), which represent God, pass between

*b:* Ps 110:4; Heb 5:6, 10; 7:1. *c:* Gn 17:16. *d:* Gn 22:17; 28:14; Ex 32:13; Dt 1:10; Sir 44:21; Rom 4:18; Heb 11:12. *e:* 1 Mc 2:52; Rom 4:3, 9, 22; Gal 3:6–7; Jas 2:23. *f:* Gn 11:31; 12:1; Ex 32:13; Neh 9:7–8; Acts 7:2–3. *g:* Lv 1:14.

each half opposite the other; but the birds he did not cut up. [11]Birds of prey swooped down on the carcasses, but Abram scared them away. [12]As the sun was about to set, a deep sleep fell upon Abram, and a great, dark dread descended upon him.

[13]* Then the LORD said to Abram: Know for certain that your descendants will reside as aliens in a land not their own, where they shall be enslaved and oppressed for four hundred years.[h] [14]But I will bring judgment on the nation they must serve, and after this they will go out with great wealth.[i] [15]You, however, will go to your ancestors in peace; you will be buried at a ripe old age. [16]In the fourth generation* your descendants will return here, for the wickedness of the Amorites is not yet complete.[j]

[17]When the sun had set and it was dark, there appeared a smoking fire pot and a flaming torch, which passed between those pieces. [18]* On that day the LORD made a covenant with Abram, saying: To your descendants I give this land, from the Wadi of Egypt to the Great River, the Euphrates,[k] [19][l] the land of the Kenites, the Kenizzites, the Kadmonites, [20]the Hittites, the Perizzites, the Rephaim, [21]the Amorites, the Canaanites, the Girgashites, and the Jebusites.

## CHAPTER 16

See RG 58–59

*Birth of Ishmael.** [1]Abram's wife Sarai had borne him no children. Now she had an Egyptian maidservant named Hagar.[m] [2]Sarai said to Abram: "The LORD has kept me from bearing children. Have intercourse with my maid; perhaps I will have sons through her." Abram obeyed Sarai.* [n] [3]Thus, after Abram had lived ten years in the land of Canaan, his wife Sarai took her maid, Hagar the Egyptian, and gave her to her husband Abram to be his wife. [4]He had intercourse with her, and she became pregnant. As soon as Hagar knew she was pregnant, her mistress lost stature in her eyes.* [o] [5][p] So Sarai said to Abram: "This outrage against me is your fault. I myself gave my maid to your embrace; but ever since she knew she was pregnant, I have lost stature in her eyes. May the LORD decide between you and me!" [6]Abram told Sarai: "Your maid is in your power. Do to her what you regard as right." Sarai then mistreated her so much that Hagar ran away from her.

[7]The LORD's angel* found her by a spring in the wilderness, the spring on the road to Shur,[q] [8]and he asked, "Hagar, maid of Sarai, where have you come from and where are

the pieces, making God a signatory to the covenant.

**15:13–16** The verses clarify the promise of the land by providing a timetable of its possession: after four hundred years of servitude, your descendants will actually possess the land in the fourth generation (a patriarchal generation seems to be one hundred years). The iniquity of the current inhabitants (called here the Amorites) has not yet reached the point where God must intervene in punishment. Another table is given in Ex 12:40, which is not compatible with this one.

**15:16 Generation**: the Hebrew term *dor* is commonly rendered as "generation," but it may signify a period of varying length. A "generation" is the period between the birth of children and the birth of their parents, normally about twenty to twenty-five years. The actual length of a generation can vary, however; in Jb 42:16 it is thirty-five and in Nm 32:13 it is forty. The meaning may be life spans, which in Gn 6:3 is one hundred twenty years and in Is 65:20 is one hundred years.

**15:18–21** The **Wadi**, i.e., a gully or ravine, **of Egypt** is the Wadi-el-'Arish, which is the boundary between the settled land and the Sinai desert. Some scholars suggest that the boundaries are those of a Davidic empire at its greatest extent; others that they are idealized boundaries. Most lists of the ancient inhabitants of the promised land give three, six, or seven peoples, but vv. 19–21 give a grand total of ten.

**16:1–16** In the previous chapter Abraham was given a timetable of possession of the land, but nothing was said about when the child was to be born. In this chapter, Sarah takes matters into her own hands, for she has been childless ten years since the promise (cf. 12:4 with 16:16). The story is about the two women, Sarah the infertile mistress and Hagar the fertile slave; Abraham has only a single sentence. In the course of the story, God intervenes directly on the side of Hagar, for she is otherwise without resources.

**16:2** The custom of an infertile wife providing her husband with a concubine to produce children is widely attested in ancient Near Eastern law; e.g., an Old Assyrian marriage contract states that the wife must provide her husband with a concubine if she does not bear children within two years.

**16:4** Because barrenness was at that time normally blamed on the woman and regarded as a disgrace, it is not surprising that Hagar looks down on Sarah. Ancient Near Eastern legal practice addresses such cases of insolent slaves and allows disciplining of them. Prv 30:23 uses as an example of intolerable behavior "a maidservant when she ousts her mistress."

**16:7 The LORD's angel**: a manifestation of God in human form; in v. 13 the messenger is identified with God. See note on Ex 3:2.

*h:* Ex 12:40; Nm 20:15; Jdt 5:9–10; Is 52:4; Acts 13:20; Gal 3:17. *i:* Ex 3:8, 21–22. *j:* 1 Kgs 21:26. *k:* Ex 32:13; Neh 9:8; Ps 105:11; Sir 44:21. *l:* Dt 7:1. *m:* Gn 11:30. *n:* Gn 21:8–9; Gal 4:22. *o:* 1 Sm 1:6; Prv 30:23. *p:* Gn 21:10–19. *q:* Ex 15:22.

you going?" She answered, "I am running
away from my mistress, Sarai." 9But the
LORD's angel told her: "Go back to your
mistress and submit to her authority. 10I will
make your descendants so numerous,"
added the LORD's angel, "that they will be
too many to count."[r] 11Then the LORD's angel said to her:

"You are now pregnant and shall bear a son;
you shall name him Ishmael,*
For the LORD has heeded your affliction.
12 He shall be a wild ass of a man,
his hand against everyone,
and everyone's hand against him;
Alongside* all his kindred
shall he encamp."[s]

13To the LORD who spoke to her she gave
a name, saying, "You are God who sees
me";* she meant, "Have I really seen God
and remained alive after he saw me?"[t] 14That
is why the well is called Beer-lahai-roi.* It is
between Kadesh and Bered.

15Hagar bore Abram a son, and Abram
named the son whom Hagar bore him Ishmael.[u] 16Abram was eighty-six years old
when Hagar bore him Ishmael.

## CHAPTER 17

See RG 58–59

*Covenant of Circumcision.** 1When
Abram was ninety-nine years old, the LORD
appeared to Abram and said: I am God the
Almighty. Walk in my presence and be
blameless.[v] 2Between you and me I will establish my covenant, and I will multiply you
exceedingly.[w]

3Abram fell face down and God said to
him: 4For my part, here is my covenant with
you: you are to become the father of a multitude of nations.[x] 5No longer will you be
called Abram; your name will be Abraham,*
for I am making you the father of a multitude
of nations.[y] 6I will make you exceedingly
fertile; I will make nations of you; kings will
stem from you. 7I will maintain my covenant
between me and you and your descendants
after you throughout the ages as an everlasting covenant, to be your God and the God of
your descendants after you.[z] 8I will give to
you and to your descendants after you the
land in which you are now residing as aliens,
the whole land of Canaan, as a permanent
possession; and I will be their God.[a] 9God
said to Abraham: For your part, you and
your descendants after you must keep my
covenant throughout the ages. 10This is the

**16:11 Ishmael**: in Hebrew the name means "God has heard." It is the same Hebrew verb that is translated "heeded" in the next clause. In other ancient Near Eastern texts, the name commemorated the divine answer to the parents' prayer to have a child, but here it is broadened to mean that God has "heard" Hagar's plight. In vv. 13–14, the verb "to see" is similarly broadened to describe God's special care for those in need.

**16:12 Alongside**: lit., "against the face of"; the same phrase is used of the lands of Ishmael's descendants in 25:18. It can be translated "in opposition to" (Dt 21:16; Jb 1:11; 6:28; 21:31), but here more likely means that Ishmael's settlement was near but not in the promised land.

**16:13 God who sees me**: Hebrew *el-ro'i* is multivalent, meaning either "God of seeing," i.e., extends his protection to me, or "God sees," which can imply seeing human suffering (29:32; Ex 2:25; Is 57:18; 58:3). It is probable that Hagar means to express both of these aspects. **Remained alive**: for the ancient notion that a person died on seeing God, see Gn 32:31; Ex 20:19; Dt 4:33; Jgs 13:22.

**16:14 Beer-lahai-roi**: possible translations of the name of the well include: "spring of the living one who sees me"; "the well of the living sight"; or "the one who sees me lives." See note on v. 13.

**17:1–27** The Priestly source gathers the major motifs of the story so far and sets them firmly within a covenant context; the word "covenant" occurs thirteen times. There are links to the covenant with Noah (v. 1 = 6:9; v. 7 = 9:9; v. 11 = 9:12–17). In this chapter, vv. 1–8 promise progeny and land; vv. 9–14 are instructions about circumcision; vv. 15–21 repeat the promise of a son to Sarah and distinguish this promise from that to Hagar; vv. 22–27 describe Abraham's carrying out the commands. **The Almighty**: traditional rendering of Hebrew *El Shaddai*, which is P's favorite designation of God in the period of the ancestors. Its etymology is uncertain, but its root meaning is probably "God, the One of the Mountains."

**17:5** Abram and Abraham are merely two forms of the same name, both meaning, "the father is exalted"; another variant form is Abiram (Nm 16:1; 1 Kgs 16:34). The additional *-ha-* in the form Abraham is explained by popular etymology as coming from *ab-hamon goyim*, "father of a multitude of nations."

**17:10 Circumcised**: circumcision was widely practiced in the ancient world, usually as an initiation rite for males at puberty. By shifting the time of circumcision to the eighth day

*r:* Gn 17:20; 21:13, 18; 25:12–18. *s:* Gn 21:20; 25:18. *t:* Gn 24:62. *u:* Gn 16:2; Gal 4:22. *v:* Gn 35:11; Ex 6:3. *w:* Gn 12:2; 13:16; Ex 32:13. *x:* Sir 44:21; Rom 4:17. *y:* Neh 9:7. *z:* Ps 105:42; Lk 1:72–73; Gal 3:16. *a:* Ex 32:13; Dt 1:8; 14:2; Lk 1:55; Acts 7:5.

covenant between me and you and your descendants after you that you must keep: every male among you shall be circumcised.* [b] 11 Circumcise the flesh of your foreskin. That will be the sign of the covenant between me and you.[c] 12 Throughout the ages, every male among you, when he is eight days old, shall be circumcised, including houseborn slaves and those acquired with money from any foreigner who is not of your descendants.[d] 13 Yes, both the houseborn slaves and those acquired with money must be circumcised. Thus my covenant will be in your flesh as an everlasting covenant. 14 If a male is uncircumcised, that is, if the flesh of his foreskin has not been cut away, such a one will be cut off from his people; he has broken my covenant.

15 God further said to Abraham: As for Sarai your wife, do not call her Sarai; her name will be Sarah.* 16 I will bless her, and I will give you a son by her. Her also will I bless; she will give rise to nations, and rulers of peoples will issue from her.[e] 17 Abraham fell face down and laughed* as he said to himself, "Can a child be born to a man who is a hundred years old? Can Sarah give birth at ninety?"[f] 18 So Abraham said to God, "If only Ishmael could live in your favor!" 19 God replied: Even so, your wife Sarah is to bear you a son, and you shall call him Isaac. It is with him that I will maintain my covenant as an everlasting covenant and with his descendants after him.[g] 20 Now as for Ishmael, I will heed you: I hereby bless him. I will make him fertile and will multiply him exceedingly. He will become the father of twelve chieftains, and I will make of him a great nation.[h] 21 But my covenant I will maintain with Isaac, whom Sarah shall bear to you by this time next year.[i] 22 When he had finished speaking with Abraham, God departed from him.

23 Then Abraham took his son Ishmael and all his slaves, whether born in his house or acquired with his money—every male among the members of Abraham's household—and he circumcised the flesh of their foreskins on that same day, as God had told him to do. 24 Abraham was ninety-nine years old when the flesh of his foreskin was circumcised,[j] 25 and his son Ishmael was thirteen years old when the flesh of his foreskin was circumcised. 26 Thus, on that same day Abraham and his son Ishmael were circumcised; 27 and all the males of his household, including the slaves born in his house or acquired with his money from foreigners, were circumcised with him.

## CHAPTER 18

See RG 58–59

***Abraham's Visitors.*** 1* The LORD appeared to Abraham by the oak of Mamre, as he sat in the entrance of his tent, while the day was growing hot. 2 Looking up, he saw three men standing near him. When he saw them, he ran from the entrance of the tent to greet them; and bowing to the ground,[k] 3 he said: "Sir,* if it please you, do not go on past your servant. 4 Let some water be brought, that you may bathe your feet, and then rest under the tree. 5 Now that you have come to your servant, let me bring you a little food, that you may refresh yourselves; and afterward you may go on your way." "Very well," they replied, "do as you have said."

6 Abraham hurried into the tent to Sarah

after birth, biblical religion made it no longer a "rite of passage" but the sign of the eternal covenant between God and the community descending from Abraham.

**17:15** Sarai and Sarah are variant forms of the same name, both meaning "princess."

**17:17 Laughed**: *yishaq*, which is also the Hebrew form of the name "Isaac"; similar explanations of the name are given in Gn 18:12 and 21:6.

**18:1** Chapters 18 and 19 combined form a continuous narrative, concluding the story of Abraham and his nephew Lot that began in 13:2–18. The mysterious men visit Abraham in Mamre to promise him and Sarah a child the following year (18:1–15) and then visit Lot in Sodom to investigate and then to punish the corrupt city (19:1–29). Between the two visits, Abraham questions God about the justice of punishing Sodom (18:16–33). At the end of the destruction of Sodom, there is a short narrative about Lot as the ancestor of Moab and the Ammonites (19:30–38).

**18:3** Abraham addresses the leader of the group, whom he does not yet recognize as the Lord; in the next two verses he speaks to all three men. The other two are later (Gn 19:1) identified as angels. The shifting numbers and identification of the visitors are a narrative way of expressing the mysterious presence of God.

*b:* Jn 7:22; Acts 7:8; Rom 4:11. *c:* Sir 44:20. *d:* Lv 12:3; Lk 1:59; 2:21. *e:* Gn 18:10; Gal 4:23. *f:* Rom 4:19; Heb 11:11–12. *g:* Gn 11:30; 21:2; Ex 32:13; Sir 44:22. *h:* Gn 16:10; 21:13, 18; 25:12–16. *i:* Gn 18:14; 21:2; 26:2–5; Rom 9:7. *j:* Gn 17:10; Rom 4:11. *k:* Heb 13:1–2.

and said, "Quick, three measures* of bran
flour! Knead it and make bread." 7He ran to
the herd, picked out a tender, choice calf,
and gave it to a servant, who quickly prepared it. 8Then he got some curds* and milk,
as well as the calf that had been prepared,
and set these before them, waiting on them
under the tree while they ate.
9"Where is your wife Sarah?" they asked
him. "There in the tent," he replied. 10One of
them* said, "I will return to you about this
time next year, and Sarah will then have a
son." Sarah was listening at the entrance of
the tent, just behind him.[l] 11Now Abraham
and Sarah were old, advanced in years, and
Sarah had stopped having her menstrual periods.[m] 12So Sarah laughed* to herself and said,
"Now that I am worn out and my husband is
old, am I still to have sexual pleasure?" 13But
the LORD said to Abraham: "Why did Sarah
laugh and say, 'Will I really bear a child, old
as I am?' 14Is anything too marvelous for the
LORD to do? At the appointed time, about this
time next year, I will return to you, and Sarah
will have a son."[n] 15Sarah lied, saying, "I did
not laugh," because she was afraid. But he
said, "Yes, you did."
***Abraham Intercedes for Sodom.*** 16With
Abraham walking with them to see them on
their way, the men set out from there and
looked down toward Sodom. 17The LORD
considered: Shall I hide from Abraham what
I am about to do, 18now that he is to become
a great and mighty nation, and all the nations
of the earth are to find blessing in him?[o] 19In-
deed, I have singled him out that he may direct his children and his household in the future to keep the way of the LORD by doing
what is right and just, so that the LORD may
put into effect for Abraham the promises he
made about him. 20[p] So the LORD said: The
outcry against Sodom and Gomorrah is so
great, and their sin so grave,* 21that I must go
down to see whether or not their actions are
as bad as the cry against them that comes to
me. I mean to find out.
22As the men turned and walked on toward Sodom, Abraham remained standing
before the LORD. 23Then Abraham drew near
and said: "Will you really sweep away the
righteous with the wicked? 24Suppose there
were fifty righteous people in the city;
would you really sweep away and not spare
the place for the sake of the fifty righteous
people within it? 25Far be it from you to do
such a thing, to kill the righteous with the
wicked, so that the righteous and the wicked
are treated alike! Far be it from you! Should
not the judge of all the world do what is
just?"[q] 26The LORD replied: If I find fifty
righteous people in the city of Sodom, I will
spare the whole place for their sake. 27Abra-
ham spoke up again: "See how I am presuming to speak to my Lord, though I am
only dust and ashes![r] 28What if there are five
less than fifty righteous people? Will you destroy the whole city because of those five?"
I will not destroy it, he answered, if I find
forty-five there. 29But Abraham persisted,
saying, "What if only forty are found there?"
He replied: I will refrain from doing it for
the sake of the forty. 30Then he said, "Do not
let my Lord be angry if I go on. What if only
thirty are found there?" He replied: I will refrain from doing it if I can find thirty there.
31Abraham went on, "Since I have thus presumed to speak to my Lord, what if there are
no more than twenty?" I will not destroy it,
he answered, for the sake of the twenty.
32But he persisted: "Please, do not let my

**18:6 Three measures**: Hebrew *seah*; three seahs equal one ephah, about half a bushel.

**18:8 Curds**: a type of soft cheese or yogurt.

**18:10 One of them**: i.e., the Lord.

**18:12 Sarah laughed**: a play on the verb "laugh," which prefigures the name of Isaac; see note on 17:17.

**18:20** The immorality of the cities was already hinted at in 13:13, when Lot made his choice to live there. The "outcry" comes from the victims of the injustice and violence rampant in the city, which will shortly be illustrated in the treatment of the visitors. The outcry of the Hebrews under the harsh treatment of Pharaoh (Ex 3:7) came up to God who reacts in anger at mistreatment of the poor (cf. Ex 22:21–23; Is 5:7). Sodom and Gomorrah became types of sinful cities in biblical literature. Is 1:9–10; 3:9 sees their sin as lack of social justice, Ez 16:46–51, as disregard for the poor, and Jer 23:14, as general immorality. In the Genesis story, the sin is violation of the sacred duty of hospitality by the threatened rape of Lot's guests.

*l:* Gn 17:19; 21:1; 2 Kgs 4:16; Rom 9:9. *m:* Gn 17:17; Rom 4:19; Heb 11:11–12. *n:* Mt 19:26; Mk 10:27; Lk 1:37; 18:27; Rom 4:21. *o:* Lk 1:55. *p:* Gn 19:13; Is 3:9; Lk 17:28; Jude 7. *q:* Dt 32:4; Jb 8:3, 20; Wis 12:15. *r:* Sir 10:9; 17:27.

Lord be angry if I speak up this last time. What if ten are found there?" For the sake of the ten, he replied, I will not destroy it.[s]

33 The LORD departed as soon as he had finished speaking with Abraham, and Abraham returned home.

See RG 58–59

## CHAPTER 19

***Destruction of Sodom and Gomorrah.**** 1 The two angels reached Sodom in the evening, as Lot was sitting at the gate of Sodom. When Lot saw them, he got up to greet them; and bowing down with his face to the ground, 2 he said, "Please, my lords,* come aside into your servant's house for the night, and bathe your feet; you can get up early to continue your journey." But they replied, "No, we will pass the night in the town square."[t] 3 He urged them so strongly, however, that they turned aside to his place and entered his house. He prepared a banquet for them, baking unleavened bread, and they dined.

4[u] Before they went to bed, the townsmen of Sodom, both young and old—all the people to the last man—surrounded the house. 5 They called to Lot and said to him, "Where are the men who came to your house tonight? Bring them out to us that we may have sexual relations with them." 6 Lot went out to meet them at the entrance. When he had shut the door behind him, 7 he said, "I beg you, my brothers, do not do this wicked thing! 8 I have two daughters who have never had sexual relations with men. Let me bring them out to you,* and you may do to them as you please. But do not do anything to these men, for they have come under the shelter of my roof." 9 They replied, "Stand back! This man," they said, "came here as a resident alien, and now he dares to give orders! We will treat you worse than them!" With that, they pressed hard against Lot, moving in closer to break down the door.[v] 10 But his guests put out their hands, pulled Lot inside with them, and closed the door; 11 they struck the men at the entrance of the house, small and great, with such a blinding light* that they were utterly unable to find the doorway.

12 Then the guests said to Lot: "Who else belongs to you here? Sons-in-law, your sons, your daughters, all who belong to you in the city—take them away from this place![w] 13 We are about to destroy this place, for the outcry reaching the LORD against those here is so great that the LORD has sent us to destroy it."[x] 14 So Lot went out and spoke to his sons-in-law, who had contracted marriage with his daughters.* "Come on, leave this place," he told them; "the LORD is about to destroy the city." But his sons-in-law thought he was joking.

15 As dawn was breaking, the angels urged Lot on, saying, "Come on! Take your wife with you and your two daughters who are here, or you will be swept away in the punishment of the city." 16 When he hesitated, the men, because of the LORD's compassion for him, seized his hand and the hands of his wife and his two daughters and led them to safety outside the city. 17 As soon as they had brought them outside, they said: "Flee for your life! Do not look back or stop anywhere on the Plain. Flee to the hills at once, or you will be swept away."[y] 18 "Oh, no, my lords!" Lot replied to them. 19 "You have already shown favor to your servant, doing me the great kindness of saving my life. But I cannot flee to the hills, or the disaster will overtake and kill me. 20 Look, this town ahead is

**19:1–29** The story takes place in one day (counting a day from the previous evening): evening (v. 1), dawn (v. 15), and sunrise (v. 23). The passage resembles Jgs 19:15–25, which suggests dependence of one story on the other.

**19:2 My lords**: Lot does not yet know that the men are God's messengers; cf. 18:3.

**19:8 Let me bring them out to you**: the authority of a patriarch within his house was virtually absolute. Lot's extreme response of offering his daughters to a violent mob seems to be motivated by the obligation of hospitality.

**19:11 Blinding light**: an extraordinary flash that temporarily dazed the wicked men and revealed to Lot the true nature of his guests.

**19:14** It is uncertain whether Lot's sons-in-law were fully married to his daughters or only "engaged" to them (Israelite "engagement" was the first part of the marriage ceremony), or even whether the daughters involved were the same as, or different from, the two daughters who were still in their father's house.

*s*: Jer 5:1; Ez 22:30. *t*: Heb 13:1–2. *u*: Jgs 19:22–25; Jude 7. *v*: Gn 13:12; 2 Pt 2:7–8. *w*: 2 Pt 2:7–9. *x*: Is 1:7, 9; Ez 16:49–50; Zep 2:9. *y*: Wis 10:6.

near enough to escape to. It is only a small place.* Let me flee there—is it not a small place?—to save my life.” 21“Well, then,” he replied, “I grant you this favor too. I will not overthrow the town you have mentioned. 22Hurry, escape there! I cannot do anything until you arrive there.” That is why the town is called Zoar.[z]

23The sun had risen over the earth when Lot arrived in Zoar, 24and the LORD rained down sulfur upon Sodom and Gomorrah, fire from the LORD out of heaven.[a] 25He overthrew* those cities and the whole Plain, together with the inhabitants of the cities and the produce of the soil.[b] 26But Lot’s wife looked back, and she was turned into a pillar of salt.[c]

27The next morning Abraham hurried to the place where he had stood before the LORD. 28As he looked down toward Sodom and Gomorrah and the whole region of the Plain,* he saw smoke over the land rising like the smoke from a kiln.[d]

29When God destroyed the cities of the Plain, he remembered Abraham and sent Lot away from the upheaval that occurred when God overthrew the cities where Lot had been living.

***Moabites and Ammonites.**** 30Since Lot was afraid to stay in Zoar, he and his two daughters went up from Zoar and settled in the hill country, where he lived with his two daughters in a cave. 31The firstborn said to the younger: “Our father is getting old, and there is not a man in the land to have intercourse with us as is the custom everywhere. 32Come, let us ply our father with wine and then lie with him, that we may ensure posterity by our father.” 33So that night they plied their father with wine, and the firstborn went in and lay with her father; but he was not aware of her lying down or getting up. 34The next day the firstborn said to the younger: “Last night I lay with my father. Let us ply him with wine again tonight, and then you go in and lie with him, that we may ensure posterity by our father.” 35So that night, too, they plied their father with wine, and then the younger one went in and lay with him; but he was not aware of her lying down or getting up.

36Thus the two daughters of Lot became pregnant by their father. 37The firstborn gave birth to a son whom she named Moab, saying, “From my father.”* He is the ancestor of the Moabites of today.[e] 38The younger one, too, gave birth to a son, and she named him Ammon, saying, “The son of my kin.”* He is the ancestor of the Ammonites of today.[f]

## CHAPTER 20

See RG 58–59

***Abraham at Gerar.**** 1From there Abraham journeyed on to the region of the Negeb, where he settled between Kadesh and Shur.* While he resided in Gerar as an alien, 2Abraham said of his wife Sarah, “She is my sister.” So Abimelech, king of Gerar, sent and took Sarah. 3But God came to Abimelech in a dream one night and said to him: You are about to die because of the

**19:20 A small place**: the Hebrew word *misar*, lit., “a little thing,” has the same root consonants as the name of the town Zoar in v. 22.

**19:25 Overthrew**: this term, lit., “turned upside down,” is used consistently to describe the destruction of the cities of the Plain. The imagery of earthquake and subsequent fire fits the geology of this region.

**19:28–29** In a deft narrative detail, Abraham looks down from the height east of Hebron, from which he could easily see the region at the southern end of the Dead Sea, where the cities of the Plain were probably located.

**19:30–38** This Israelite tale about the origin of Israel’s neighbors east of the Jordan and the Dead Sea was told partly to ridicule these ethnically related but rival nations and partly to give popular etymologies for their names. The stylized nature of the story is seen in the names of the daughters (“the firstborn” and “the younger”), the ease with which they fool their father, and the identical descriptions of the encounters.

**19:37 From my father**: in Hebrew, *me’abi*, similar in sound to the name “Moab.”

**19:38 The son of my kin**: in Hebrew, *ben-ammi*, similar in sound to the name “Ammonites.”

**20:1–18** Abraham again passes off his wife Sarah as his sister to escape trouble in a foreign land (cf. 12:10–13:1, the J source). The story appears to be from a different source (according to some, E) and deals with the ethical questions of the incident. Gn 26:6–11 is yet another retelling of the story, but with Isaac and Rebekah as characters instead of Abraham and Sarah.

**20:1 Kadesh and Shur**: Kadesh-barnea was a major oasis on the southernmost border of Canaan, and Shur was probably the “way to Shur,” the road to Egypt. Gerar was a royal city in the area, but has not been identified with certainty.

*z:* Wis 10:6. *a:* Ps 9:6; 11:6; 107:34; Wis 10:7; Sir 16:8; Is 1:9; Lk 17:29; 2 Pt 2:6. *b:* Dt 29:22; Is 13:19; Jer 50:40; Lam 4:6; Am 4:11. *c:* Wis 10:7; Lk 17:32. *d:* Rev 9:2; 14:10–11. *e:* Dt 2:9. *f:* Dt 2:19.

woman you have taken, for she has a husband. [4]Abimelech, who had not approached
her, said: "O Lord, would you kill an innocent man? [5]Was he not the one who told me,
'She is my sister'? She herself also stated,
'He is my brother.' I acted with pure heart
and with clean hands." [6]* God answered him
in the dream: Yes, I know you did it with a
pure heart. In fact, it was I who kept you
from sinning against me; that is why I did
not let you touch her. [7]So now, return the
man's wife so that he may intercede for you,
since he is a prophet,* that you may live. If
you do not return her, you can be sure that
you and all who are yours will die.

[8]Early the next morning Abimelech called
all his servants and informed them of everything that had happened, and the men were
filled with fear. [9]Then Abimelech summoned Abraham and said to him: "What
have you done to us! What wrong did I do to
you that you would have brought such great
guilt on me and my kingdom? You have
treated me in an intolerable way. [10]What did
you have in mind," Abimelech asked him,
"that you would do such a thing?" [11]Abra-
ham answered, "I thought there would be no
fear of God* in this place, and so they would
kill me on account of my wife. [12]Besides,
she really is my sister,* but only my father's
daughter, not my mother's; and so she became my wife. [13]When God sent me wandering from my father's house, I asked her:
'Would you do me this favor? In whatever
place we come to, say: He is my brother.' "[g]
[14]Then Abimelech took flocks and herds
and male and female slaves and gave them
to Abraham; and he restored his wife Sarah
to him. [15]Then Abimelech said, "Here, my
land is at your disposal; settle wherever you
please." [16]To Sarah he said: "I hereby give
your brother a thousand shekels of silver.
This will preserve your honor before all who
are with you and will exonerate you before
everyone." [17]Abraham then interceded with
God, and God restored health to Abimelech,
to his wife, and his maidservants, so that
they bore children; [18]for the LORD had
closed every womb in Abimelech's household on account of Abraham's wife Sarah.

## CHAPTER 21

See RG 58–59

*Birth of Isaac.** [1]The LORD took note of
Sarah as he had said he would; the LORD did
for her as he had promised.[h] [2]Sarah became
pregnant and bore Abraham a son in his old
age, at the set time that God had stated.[i]
[3]Abraham gave the name Isaac to this son of
his whom Sarah bore him.[j] [4]When his son
Isaac was eight days old, Abraham circumcised him, as God had commanded.[k] [5]Abra-
ham was a hundred years old when his son
Isaac was born to him. [6]Sarah then said, "God
has given me cause to laugh,* and all who
hear of it will laugh with me.[l] [7]Who would
ever have told Abraham," she added, "that
Sarah would nurse children! Yet I have borne
him a son in his old age." [8]The child grew and
was weaned, and Abraham held a great banquet on the day of the child's weaning.

**20:6** Abimelech is exonerated of blame, but by that fact not cleared of the consequences of his act. He is still under the sentence of death for abducting another man's wife; the consequences result from the deed not the intention.

**20:7 Prophet**: only here is Abraham explicitly called "prophet," Hebrew *nabi* (cf. Ps 105:15).

**20:11 Fear of God** is the traditional though unsatisfactory rendering of Hebrew *yir'at YHWH*, literally, "revering Yahweh." The phrase refers neither to the emotion of fear nor to religious reverence of a general kind. Rather it refers to adherence to a single deity (in a polytheistic culture), honoring that deity with prayers, rituals, and obedience. The phrase occurs again in 26:24; 43:23; and 50:19. It is very common in the wisdom literature of the Bible.

**20:12 My sister**: marrying one's half sister was prohibited later in Israel's history.

**21:1–21** The long-awaited birth of Isaac parallels the birth of Ishmael in chap. 16, precipitating a rivalry and expulsion as in that chapter. Though this chapter is unified, the focus of vv. 1–7 is exclusively on Sarah and Isaac, and the focus of vv. 8–21 is exclusively on Hagar and Ishmael. The promise of a son to the barren Sarah and elderly Abraham has been central to the previous chapters and now that promise comes true with the birth of Isaac. The other great promise, that of land, will be resolved, at least in an anticipatory way, in Abraham's purchase of the cave at Machpelah in chap. 23. The parallel births of the two boys has influenced the Lucan birth narratives of John the Baptist and Jesus (Lk 1–2).

**21:6 Laugh**: for the third time (cf. 17:17 and 18:12) there is laughter, playing on the similarity in Hebrew between the pronunciation of the name Isaac and words associated with laughter.

*g:* Gn 12:13. *h:* Gn 17:19; 18:10. *i:* Gal 4:23; Heb 11:11. *j:* Mt 1:2; Lk 3:34. *k:* Gn 17:10–14; Acts 7:8. *l:* Gn 17:17.

### Hagar and Ishmael Are Sent Away

THE EPISODE IN 21:8–21 contains elements similar to the earlier story of Hagar and Ishmael (16:1–16): conflict between Sarah and Hagar, journey into the desert, encounter with a divine angel, a well of water, and promises that Ishmael too would have a great future.

9Sarah noticed the son whom Hagar the
Egyptian had borne to Abraham playing
with her son Isaac; 10so she demanded of
Abraham: "Drive out that slave and her son!
No son of that slave is going to share the inheritance with my son Isaac!"[m] 11Abraham
was greatly distressed because it concerned
a son of his.* 12But God said to Abraham: Do
not be distressed about the boy or about your
slave woman. Obey Sarah, no matter what
she asks of you; for it is through Isaac that
descendants will bear your name.[n] 13As for
the son of the slave woman, I will make a nation of him also,* since he too is your offspring.
14Early the next morning Abraham got
some bread and a skin of water and gave
them to Hagar. Then, placing the child on
her back,* he sent her away. As she roamed
aimlessly in the wilderness of Beer-sheba,
15the water in the skin was used up. So she
put the child down under one of the bushes,
16and then went and sat down opposite him,
about a bowshot away; for she said to herself, "I cannot watch the child die." As she
sat opposite him, she wept aloud. 17God
heard the boy's voice, and God's angel
called to Hagar from heaven: "What is the
matter, Hagar? Do not fear; God has heard
the boy's voice in this plight of his.[o] 18Get
up, lift up the boy and hold him by the hand;
for I will make of him a great nation."
19Then God opened her eyes, and she saw a
well of water. She went and filled the skin
with water, and then let the boy drink.
20God was with the boy as he grew up. He
lived in the wilderness and became an expert
bowman. 21He lived in the wilderness of Paran. His mother got a wife for him from the
land of Egypt.

***The Covenant at Beer-sheba.*** 22* At that
time Abimelech, accompanied by Phicol, the
commander of his army, said to Abraham:
"God is with you in everything you do. 23So
now, swear to me by God at this place* that
you will not deal falsely with me or with my
progeny and posterity, but will act as loyally
toward me and the land in which you reside
as I have acted toward you." 24Abraham
replied, "I so swear."
25Abraham, however, reproached Abimelech about a well that Abimelech's servants
had seized by force. 26"I have no idea who
did that," Abimelech replied. "In fact, you
never told me about it, nor did I ever hear of
it until now."
27Then Abraham took sheep and cattle
and gave them to Abimelech and the two
made a covenant. 28Abraham also set apart
seven ewe lambs of the flock, 29and Abimelech asked him, "What is the purpose of
these seven ewe lambs that you have set

**21:11 A son of his**: Abraham is the father of both boys, but Sarah is the mother only of Isaac. Abraham is very concerned that Ishmael have a sufficient inheritance.

**21:13 I will make a nation of him also**: Ishmael's descendants are named in 25:12–18.

**21:14 Placing the child on her back**: a reading based on an emendation of the traditional Hebrew text. In the traditional Hebrew text, Abraham put the bread and the waterskin on Hagar's back, while her son apparently walked beside her. In this way the traditional Hebrew text harmonizes the data of the Priestly source, in which Ishmael would have been at least fourteen years old when Isaac was born; compare 16:16 with 21:5; cf. 17:25. But in the present Elohist (?) story, Ishmael is obviously a little boy, not much older than Isaac; cf. vv. 15, 18.

**21:22** Of the two related promises of progeny and land, that of progeny has been fulfilled in the previous chapter. Now the claim on the land begins to be solidified by Abimelech's recognition of Abraham's claim on the well at Beer-sheba; it will be furthered by Abraham's purchase of the cave at Machpelah in chap. 23. Two levels of editing are visible in the story: (1) vv. 22–24, 27, 32, the general covenant with Abimelech; (2) vv. 25–26, 28–30, 31, Abraham's claim on the well. Both versions play on the root of the Hebrew word *sheba'*, which means "seven" and "swear," and the place name Beer-sheba.

**21:23 This place**: Beer-sheba (v. 31). Abimelech had come from Gerar (20:2), about thirty miles west of Beer-sheba.

*m:* Jgs 11:2; Gal 4:30. *n:* Rom 9:7; Heb 11:18. *o:* Gn 16:7.

**Ready!**

GOD CALLED ABRAHAM, and he responded, "Here I am!" (22:1). There are other times in the Bible when we read of someone responding to God's call: for example, Samuel (1 Sm 3) and Isaiah (Is 43:1). This pattern continues in our own time: God calls each person. We listen, with our hearts and minds, to hear that call. The response is up to each one of us.

apart?" 30Abraham answered, "The seven
ewe lambs you shall accept from me that
you may be my witness that I dug this well."
31This is why the place is called Beer-sheba;
the two of them took an oath there. 32When
they had thus made the covenant in Beer-
sheba, Abimelech, along with Phicol, the
commander of his army, left to return to the
land of the Philistines.*

33Abraham planted a tamarisk at Beer-
sheba, and there he invoked by name the
LORD, God the Eternal.* 34Abraham resided
in the land of the Philistines for a long time.

## CHAPTER 22

See RG 58–59

*The Testing of Abraham.** 1Some time
afterward, God put Abraham to the test and
said to him: Abraham! "Here I am!" he
replied.[p] 2Then God said: Take your son
Isaac, your only one, whom you love, and go
to the land of Moriah. There offer him up as
a burnt offering on one of the heights that I
will point out to you.[q] 3Early the next morning Abraham saddled his donkey, took with
him two of his servants and his son Isaac,
and after cutting the wood for the burnt offering, set out for the place of which God
had told him.

4On the third day Abraham caught sight of
the place from a distance. 5Abraham said to
his servants: "Stay here with the donkey,
while the boy and I go on over there. We will
worship and then come back to you." 6So
Abraham took the wood for the burnt offering
and laid it on his son Isaac, while he himself
carried the fire and the knife. As the two
walked on together, 7Isaac spoke to his father
Abraham. "Father!" he said. "Here I am," he
replied. Isaac continued, "Here are the fire and
the wood, but where is the sheep for the burnt
offering?" 8"My son," Abraham answered,
"God will provide the sheep for the burnt offering." Then the two walked on together.

9When they came to the place of which
God had told him, Abraham built an altar
there and arranged the wood on it. Next he
bound* his son Isaac, and put him on top of
the wood on the altar.[r] 10Then Abraham
reached out and took the knife to slaughter
his son.[s] 11But the angel of the LORD called
to him from heaven, "Abraham, Abraham!"
"Here I am," he answered. 12"Do not lay

**21:32 Philistines**: one of the Sea Peoples, who migrated from Mycenaean Greece around 1200 B.C. and settled on the coastland of Canaan, becoming a principal rival of Israel. Non-biblical texts do not use the term "Philistine" before ca. 1200 B.C.; it is probable that this usage and those in chap. 26 are anachronistic, perhaps applying a later ethnic term for an earlier, less-known one.

**21:33 God the Eternal**: in Hebrew, *'el 'olam*, perhaps the name of the deity of the pre-Israelite sanctuary at Beer-sheba, but used by Abraham as a title of God; cf. Is 40:28.

**22:1–19** The divine demand that Abraham sacrifice to God the son of promise is the greatest of his trials; after the successful completion of the test, he has only to buy a burial site for Sarah and find a wife for Isaac. The story is widely recognized as a literary masterpiece, depicting in a few lines God as the absolute Lord, inscrutable yet ultimately gracious, and Abraham, acting in moral grandeur as the great ancestor of Israel. Abraham speaks simply, with none of the wordy evasions of chaps. 13 and 21. The style is laconic; motivations and thoughts are not explained, and the reader cannot but wonder at the scene. In vv. 15–18, the angel repeats the seventh and climactic promise. **Moriah**: the mountain is not given a precise geographical location here, though 2 Chr 3:1 identifies Moriah as the mountain of Jerusalem where Solomon built the Temple; Abraham is thus the first to worship there. The word "Moriah" is a play on the verb "to see" (Heb. *ra'ah*); the wordplay is continued in v. 8, "God will provide (lit., "see")" and in v. 14, Yahweh-yireh, meaning "the Lord will see/provide."

**22:9 Bound**: the Hebrew verb is *'aqad*, from which is derived the noun Akedah, "the binding (of Isaac)," the traditional Jewish name for this incident.

*p*: Sir 44:20. *q*: 2 Chr 3:1; 1 Mc 2:52; Heb 11:17. *r*: Jas 2:21. *s*: Wis 10:5.

your hand on the boy," said the angel. "Do not do the least thing to him. For now I know that you fear God, since you did not withhold from me your son, your only one."[t] 13 Abraham looked up and saw a single ram caught by its horns in the thicket. So Abraham went and took the ram and offered it up as a burnt offering in place of his son.* 14 Abraham named that place Yahweh-yireh;* hence people today say, "On the mountain the LORD will provide."

15* A second time the angel of the LORD called to Abraham from heaven 16[u] and said: "I swear by my very self—oracle of the LORD—that because you acted as you did in not withholding from me your son, your only one, 17 I will bless you and make your descendants as countless as the stars of the sky and the sands of the seashore; your descendants will take possession of the gates of their enemies,[v] 18 and in your descendants all the nations of the earth will find blessing, because you obeyed my command."[w]

19 Abraham then returned to his servants, and they set out together for Beer-sheba, where Abraham lived.

***Nahor's Descendants.**** 20 Some time afterward, the news came to Abraham: "Milcah too has borne sons to your brother Nahor: 21 Uz, his firstborn, his brother Buz, Kemuel the father of Aram, 22 Chesed, Hazo, Pildash, Jidlaph, and Bethuel." 23 Bethuel became the father of Rebekah. These eight Milcah bore to Nahor, Abraham's brother. 24 His concubine, whose name was Reumah, also bore children: Tebah, Gaham, Tahash, and Maacah.

## CHAPTER 23

See RG 58–59

***Purchase of a Burial Plot.**** 1 The span of Sarah's life was one hundred and twenty-seven years. 2 She died in Kiriath-arba—now Hebron—in the land of Canaan, and Abraham proceeded to mourn and weep for her. 3 Then he left the side of his deceased wife and addressed the Hittites:* 4 "Although I am a resident alien* among you, sell me from your holdings a burial place, that I may bury my deceased wife."[x] 5 The Hittites answered Abraham: "Please, 6 sir, listen to us! You are a mighty leader among us. Bury your dead in the choicest of our burial sites. None of us would deny you his burial ground for the

**22:13** While the Bible recognizes that firstborn males belong to God (Ex 13:11–16; 34:19–20), and provides an alternate sacrifice to redeem firstborn sons, the focus here is on Abraham's being tested by God (v. 1). But the widely attested practice of child sacrifice underscores, for all its horror today, the realism of the test.

**22:14 Yahweh-yireh**: a Hebrew expression meaning "the Lord will see/provide." See note on vv. 1–19.

**22:15–19** The seventh and climactic statement of the blessings to Abraham. Unlike the other statements, which were purely promissory, this one is presented as a reward for Abraham's extraordinary trust.

**22:20–24** The descendants to the second generation of Nahor, Abraham's brother, who married Milcah. Of Terah's three sons (11:27), the oldest, Abraham, fathered Isaac (21:1–7), and the youngest, Haran (who died in Ur), fathered Lot. Abraham is now told that Nahor had eight children by Milcah and four by his concubine Reumah. Apart from the notice about the children born to Abraham by his second wife, Keturah (25:1–6), all the information about Terah's family to the second generation is now complete. It is noteworthy that Jacob will, like Nahor, have eight children by his wives and four by his concubines.

**23:1–20** The occasion for purchasing the land is the need for a burial site for Sarah, for it would be unthinkable to bury Sarah outside of the promised land. One of the two great promises to Abraham, that of progeny, has been fulfilled (21:1–7). And now the promise of land is to be fulfilled, through a kind of down payment on the full possession that will take place only with the conquest under Joshua and during the reign of David. This purchase has been prepared for by Abimelech's recognition of Abraham's claim to the well at Beer-sheba (21:22–34). Among the ancestral stories this narrative is one of two that are entirely from the P source (chap. 17 being the other). The Priestly writers may have intended to encourage the generation of the exile to a renewed hope of repossessing their land.

**23:3 The Hittites**: in the Bible the term is applied to several different groups—inhabitants of the second-millennium Hittite empire in Asia Minor and northern Syria, residents of the Neo-Hittite kingdoms in northern Syria in the first part of the first millennium, and (following Assyrian terminology) the inhabitants of Syria and Palestine. The third group is meant here.

**23:4 A resident alien**: such a one would normally not have the right to own property. The importance of Abraham's purchase of the field in Machpelah, which is worded in technical legal terms, lies in the fact that it gave his descendants their first, though small, land rights in the country that God had promised the patriarch they would one day inherit as their own. Abraham therefore insists on purchasing the field and not receiving it as a gift.

*t:* Rom 8:32; 1 Jn 4:9. *u:* Gn 15:5; Ex 32:13; Lk 1:73; Rom 4:13; Heb 6:13–14; 11:12. *v:* Gn 24:60. *w:* Gn 12:3; 18:18; 26:4; Sir 44:21; Acts 3:25; Gal 3:16. *x:* Gn 33:19; Acts 7:16; Heb 11:9.

**The Family Tree of Abraham**

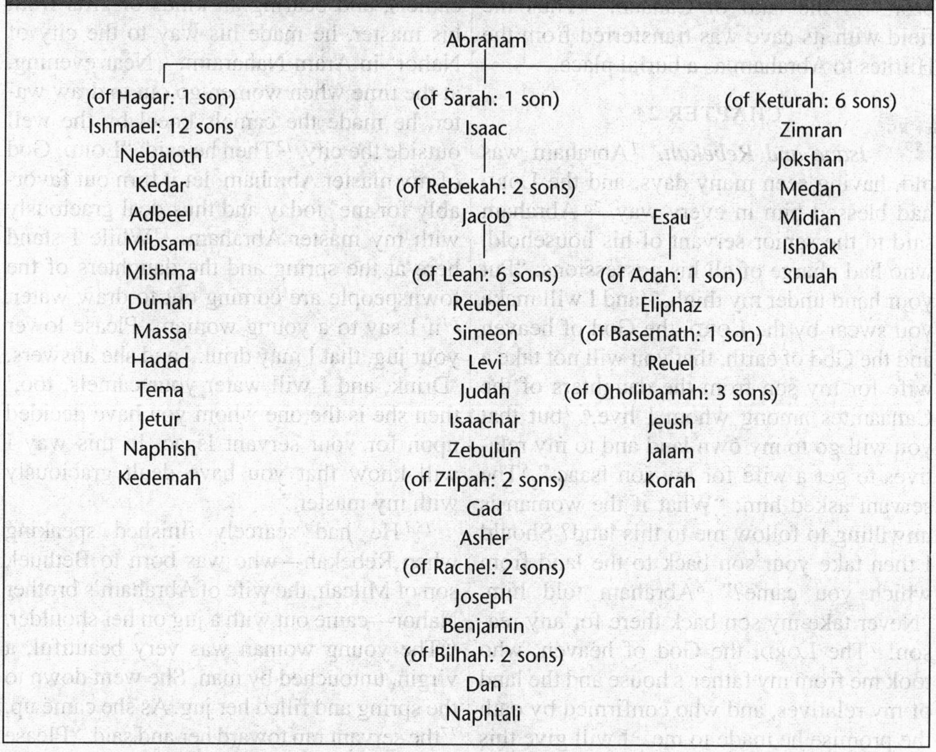


burial of your dead." [7]Abraham, however,
proceeded to bow low before the people of
the land, the Hittites, [8]and said to them: "If
you will allow me room for burial of my
dead, listen to me! Intercede for me with
Ephron, son of Zohar, [9]so that he will sell me
the cave of Machpelah that he owns; it is at
the edge of his field. Let him sell it to me in
your presence at its full price for a burial
place."

[10]Now Ephron was sitting with the Hittites. So Ephron the Hittite replied to Abraham in the hearing of the Hittites, all who
entered the gate of his city: [11]"Please, sir, listen to me! I give you both the field and the
cave in it; in the presence of my people I
give it to you. Bury your dead!" [12]But Abraham, after bowing low before the people of
the land, [13]addressed Ephron in the hearing
of these men: "If only you would please listen to me! I will pay you the price of the
field. Accept it from me, that I may bury my
dead there." [14]Ephron replied to Abraham,
"Please, [15]sir, listen to me! A piece of land
worth four hundred shekels* of silver—what
is that between you and me? Bury your
dead!" [16][y] Abraham accepted Ephron's
terms; he weighed out to him the silver that
Ephron had stipulated in the hearing of the
Hittites, four hundred shekels of silver at the
current market value.*

[17][z] Thus Ephron's field in Machpelah,
facing Mamre, together with its cave and all
the trees anywhere within its limits, was
conveyed [18]to Abraham by purchase in the
presence of the Hittites, all who entered the
gate of Ephron's city. [19]After this, Abraham
buried his wife Sarah in the cave of the field

**23:15 Four hundred shekels**: probably an exorbitant sum; Jeremiah (32:9) paid only seventeen shekels for his field in Anathoth, though the Babylonian invasion no doubt helped to reduce the price.

**23:16 The current market value**: the standard weight called a shekel varied according to time and place.

*y*: Acts 7:16. *z*: Gn 49:29–30.

of Machpelah, facing Mamre—now Hebron—in the land of Canaan. [20]Thus the field with its cave was transferred from the Hittites to Abraham as a burial place.

See RG 59

## CHAPTER 24

***Isaac and Rebekah.*** * [1]Abraham was old, having seen many days, and the LORD had blessed him in every way. [2][a] Abraham said to the senior servant of his household, who had charge of all his possessions: "Put your hand under my thigh,* [3]and I will make you swear by the LORD, the God of heaven and the God of earth, that you will not take a wife for my son from the daughters of the Canaanites among whom I live,[b] [4]but that you will go to my own land and to my relatives to get a wife for my son Isaac." [5]The servant asked him: "What if the woman is unwilling to follow me to this land? Should I then take your son back to the land from which you came?" [6]Abraham told him, "Never take my son back there for any reason! [7]The LORD, the God of heaven, who took me from my father's house and the land of my relatives, and who confirmed by oath the promise he made to me, 'I will give this land to your descendants'—he will send his angel before you, and you will get a wife for my son there.[c] [8]If the woman is unwilling to follow you, you will be released from this oath to me. But never take my son back there!" [9]So the servant put his hand under the thigh of his master Abraham and swore to him concerning this matter.

[10]The servant then took ten of his master's camels, and bearing all kinds of gifts from his master, he made his way to the city of Nahor* in Aram Naharaim. [11]Near evening, at the time when women go out to draw water, he made the camels kneel by the well outside the city. [12]Then he said: "LORD, God of my master Abraham, let it turn out favorably for me* today and thus deal graciously with my master Abraham. [13]While I stand here at the spring and the daughters of the townspeople are coming out to draw water, [14]if I say to a young woman, 'Please lower your jug, that I may drink,' and she answers, 'Drink, and I will water your camels, too,' then she is the one whom you have decided upon for your servant Isaac. In this way I will know that you have dealt graciously with my master."

[15][d] He had scarcely finished speaking when Rebekah—who was born to Bethuel, son of Milcah, the wife of Abraham's brother Nahor—came out with a jug on her shoulder. [16]The young woman was very beautiful, a virgin, untouched by man. She went down to the spring and filled her jug. As she came up, [17]the servant ran toward her and said, "Please give me a sip of water from your jug." [18]"Drink, sir," she replied, and quickly lowering the jug into her hand, she gave him a drink. [19]When she had finished giving him a drink, she said, "I will draw water for your camels, too, until they have finished drinking." [20]With that, she quickly emptied her jug into the drinking trough and ran back to the

**24:1–67** The story of Abraham and Sarah is drawing to a close. The promises of progeny (21:1–7) and land (chap. 23) have been fulfilled and Sarah has died (23:1–2). Abraham's last duty is to ensure that his son Isaac shares in the promises. Isaac must take a wife from his own people (vv. 3–7), so the promises may be fulfilled. The extraordinary length of this story and its development of a single theme contrast strikingly with the spare style of the preceding Abraham and Sarah stories. It points ahead to the Jacob and Joseph stories.

The length of the story is partly caused by its meticulous attention to the sign (vv. 12–14), its fulfillment (vv. 15–20), and the servant's retelling of sign and fulfillment to Rebekah's family to win their consent (vv. 34–49).

**24:2 Put your hand under my thigh**: the symbolism of this act was apparently connected with the Hebrew concept of children issuing from their father's "thigh" (the literal meaning of "direct descendants" in 46:26; Ex 1:5). Perhaps the man who took such an oath was thought to bring the curse of sterility on himself if he did not fulfill his sworn promise. Jacob made Joseph swear in the same way (Gn 47:29). In both these instances, the oath was taken to carry out the last request of a man upon his death.

**24:10 Nahor**: it is uncertain whether this is the place where Abraham's brother Nahor (11:27) had lived or whether it is the city Nahur, named in the Mari documents (nineteenth and eighteenth centuries B.C.), near the confluence of the Balikh and Middle Euphrates rivers. **Aram Naharaim**: lit., "Aram between the two rivers," is the Yahwist designation for Terah's homeland. The two rivers are the Habur and the Euphrates. The Priestly designation for the area is Paddan-aram, which is from the Assyrian *padana,* "road or garden," and Aram, which refers to the people or land of the Arameans.

**24:12 Let it turn out favorably for me**: let me have a favorable sign; cf. end of v. 14.

*a:* Gn 47:29. *b:* Gn 24:37; 28:1–2; Jgs 14:3; Tb 4:12. *c:* Gn 12:7; Ex 6:8; Tb 5:17; Gal 3:16. *d:* Gn 22:23.

well to draw more water, until she had drawn enough for all the camels. 21The man watched her the whole time, silently waiting to learn whether or not the LORD had made his journey successful. 22When the camels had finished drinking, the man took out a gold nose-ring weighing half a shekel, and two gold bracelets weighing ten shekels for her wrists. 23Then he asked her: "Whose daughter are you? Tell me, please. And is there a place in your father's house for us to spend the night?" 24She answered: "I am the daughter of Bethuel the son of Milcah, whom she bore to Nahor. 25We have plenty of straw and fodder," she added, "and also a place to spend the night." 26The man then knelt and bowed down to the LORD, 27saying: "Blessed be the LORD, the God of my master Abraham, who has not let his kindness and fidelity toward my master fail. As for me, the LORD has led me straight to the house of my master's brother."

28Then the young woman ran off and told her mother's household what had happened. 29[e] Now Rebekah had a brother named Laban. Laban rushed outside to the man at the spring. 30[*] When he saw the nose-ring and the bracelets on his sister's arms and when he heard Rebekah repeating what the man had said to her, he went to him while he was standing by the camels at the spring. 31He said: "Come, blessed of the LORD! Why are you standing outside when I have made the house ready, as well as a place for the camels?" 32The man then went inside; and while the camels were being unloaded and provided with straw and fodder, water was brought to bathe his feet and the feet of the men who were with him. 33But when food was set before him, he said, "I will not eat until I have told my story." "Go ahead," they replied.

34"I am Abraham's servant," he began. 35"The LORD has blessed my master so abundantly that he has become wealthy; he has given him flocks and herds, silver and gold, male and female slaves, and camels and donkeys. 36My master's wife Sarah bore a son to my master in her old age, and he has given him everything he owns. 37My master put me under oath, saying: 'You shall not take a wife for my son from the daughters of the Canaanites in whose land I live; 38instead, you must go to my father's house, to my own family, to get a wife for my son.' 39When I asked my master, 'What if the woman will not follow me?' 40he replied: 'The LORD, in whose presence I have always walked, will send his angel with you and make your journey successful, and so you will get a wife for my son from my own family and my father's house.[f] 41Then you will be freed from my curse. If you go to my family and they refuse you, then, too, you will be free from my curse.'[*]

42"When I came to the spring today, I said: 'LORD, God of my master Abraham, please make successful the journey I am on. 43While I stand here at the spring, if I say to a young woman who comes out to draw water, 'Please give me a little water from your jug,' 44and she answers, 'Drink, and I will draw water for your camels, too—then she is the woman whom the LORD has decided upon for my master's son.'

45"I had scarcely finished saying this to myself when Rebekah came out with a jug on her shoulder. After she went down to the spring and drew water, I said to her, 'Please let me have a drink.' 46She quickly lowered the jug she was carrying and said, 'Drink, and I will water your camels, too.' So I drank, and she watered the camels also. 47When I asked her, 'Whose daughter are you?' she answered, 'The daughter of Bethuel, son of Nahor, borne to Nahor by Milcah.' So I put the ring on her nose and the bracelets on her wrists. 48Then I knelt and bowed down to the LORD, blessing the LORD, the God of my master Abraham, who had led me on the right road to obtain the daughter of my master's kinsman for his son. 49Now, if you will act with kindness and

**24:30** Laban becomes hospitable only when he sees the servant's rich gifts, which is in humorous contrast to his sister's spontaneous generosity toward the servant. Laban's opportunism points forward to his behavior in the Jacob stories (31:14–16).

**24:41 Curse**: this would be the consequence of failing to carry out the oath referred to in v. 3.

*e:* Gn 27:43. *f:* Tb 5:17; 10:13.

fidelity toward my master, let me know; but
if not, let me know that too. I can then proceed accordingly."
50[g] Laban and Bethuel said in reply: "This
thing comes from the LORD; we can say
nothing to you either for or against it. 51 Here
is Rebekah, right in front of you; take her
and go, that she may become the wife of
your master's son, as the LORD has said."
52 When Abraham's servant heard their answer, he bowed to the ground before the
LORD. 53 Then he brought out objects of silver and gold and clothing and presented
them to Rebekah; he also gave costly presents to her brother and mother. 54 After he
and the men with him had eaten and drunk,
they spent the night there.

When they got up the next morning, he
said, "Allow me to return to my master."[h]
55 Her brother and mother replied, "Let the
young woman stay with us a short while, say
ten days; after that she may go." 56 But he
said to them, "Do not detain me, now that
the LORD has made my journey successful;
let me go back to my master." 57 They answered, "Let us call the young woman and
see what she herself has to say about it."
58 So they called Rebekah and asked her,
"Will you go with this man?" She answered,
"I will."* 59 At this they sent off their sister
Rebekah and her nurse with Abraham's servant and his men. 60 They blessed Rebekah
and said:

"Sister, may you grow
into thousands of myriads;
And may your descendants gain
possession
of the gates of their enemies!"[i]

61 Then Rebekah and her attendants started
out; they mounted the camels and followed
the man. So the servant took Rebekah and
went on his way.
62 Meanwhile Isaac had gone from Beer-lahai-roi and was living in the region of the
Negeb.[j] 63 One day toward evening he went
out to walk in the field, and caught sight of
camels approaching. 64 Rebekah, too, caught
sight of Isaac, and got down from her camel.
65 She asked the servant, "Who is the man
over there, walking through the fields toward
us?" "That is my master," replied the servant.
Then she took her veil and covered herself.
66 The servant recounted to Isaac all the
things he had done. 67 Then Isaac brought
Rebekah into the tent of his mother Sarah.
He took Rebekah as his wife. Isaac loved her
and found solace after the death of his
mother.

## CHAPTER 25

See RG 59

### *Abraham's Sons by Keturah.*

1* [k] Abraham took another wife, whose name
was Keturah. 2 She bore him Zimran, Jokshan, Medan, Midian, Ishbak, and Shuah.*
3 Jokshan became the father of Sheba and Dedan. The descendants of Dedan were the
Asshurim, the Letushim, and the Leummim.[l]
4 The descendants of Midian were Ephah,
Epher, Hanoch, Abida, and Eldaah. All of
these were descendants of Keturah.
5 Abraham gave everything that he owned
to his son Isaac.* 6 To the sons of his concubines, however, he gave gifts while he was
still living, as he sent them away eastward,
to the land of Kedem,* away from his son
Isaac.

**24:58** Marriages arranged by the woman's father did not require the woman's consent, but marriages arranged by the woman's brother did. Laban is the brother and Rebekah is therefore free to give her consent or not.

**25:1–11** As with the story of Terah in 11:27–32, this section lists all the descendants of Abraham as a means of concluding the story. The Jacob story ends similarly with the listing of the twelve sons (35:22–26), the death of Isaac (35:27–29), and the descendants of Esau (chap. 36). **Abraham took another wife**: though mentioned here, Abraham's marriage to a "concubine," or wife of secondary rank, is not to be understood as happening chronologically after the events narrated in the preceding chapter.

**25:2** Three of the six names can be identified: the Midianites are a trading people, mentioned in the Bible as dwelling east of the Gulf of Aqaba in northwest Arabia; Ishbak is a north Syrian tribe; Shuah is a city on the right bank of the Middle Euphrates. The other names are probably towns or peoples on the international trade routes.

**25:5** Amid so many descendants, Abraham takes steps that Isaac will be his favored heir.

**25:6 The land of Kedem**: or "the country of the East," the region inhabited by the Kedemites or Easterners (29:1; Jgs 6:3, 33; Jb 1:3; Is 11:14). The names mentioned in vv. 2–4, as far as they can be identified, are those of tribes in the Arabian desert.

*g:* Tb 7:11–12. *h:* Tb 7:14; 8:20. *i:* Gn 22:17. *j:* Gn 16:13–14; 25:11. *k:* 1 Chr 1:32–33. *l:* Is 21:13.

***Death of Abraham.*** [7]The whole span of
Abraham's life was one hundred and seventy-five years. [8]Then he breathed his last,
dying at a ripe old age, grown old after a full
life; and he was gathered to his people. [9]His
sons Isaac and Ishmael buried him in the
cave of Machpelah, in the field of Ephron,
son of Zohar the Hittite, which faces
Mamre,[m] [10]the field that Abraham had
bought from the Hittites; there he was buried
next to his wife Sarah. [11]After the death of
Abraham, God blessed his son Isaac, who
lived near Beer-lahai-roi.

***Descendants of Ishmael.*** [12][*] These are the
descendants of Abraham's son Ishmael,
whom Hagar the Egyptian, Sarah's slave,
bore to Abraham. [13][n] These are the names of
Ishmael's sons, listed in the order of their
birth: Ishmael's firstborn Nebaioth, Kedar,
Adbeel, Mibsam,[o] [14]Mishma, Dumah,
Massa, [15]Hadad, Tema, Jetur, Naphish, and
Kedemah. [16]These are the sons of Ishmael,
their names by their villages and encampments; twelve chieftains of as many tribal
groups.[p]

[17]The span of Ishmael's life was one hundred and thirty-seven years. After he had
breathed his last and died, he was gathered
to his people. [18]The Ishmaelites ranged from
Havilah, by Shur, which is on the border of
Egypt, all the way to Asshur; and they
pitched camp[*] alongside their various kindred.[q]

***Birth of Esau and Jacob.*** [19][*] These are the
descendants of Isaac, son of Abraham;
Abraham begot Isaac. [20]Isaac was forty
years old when he married Rebekah, the
daughter of Bethuel the Aramean of Paddan-aram[*] and the sister of Laban the Aramean.[r] [21]Isaac entreated the LORD on behalf
of his wife, since she was sterile. The LORD
heard his entreaty, and his wife Rebekah became pregnant. [22]But the children jostled
each other in the womb so much that she exclaimed, "If it is like this,[*] why go on living!" She went to consult the LORD, [23]and
the LORD answered her:

Two nations are in your womb,
two peoples are separating while still
within you;
But one will be stronger than the other,
and the older will serve the younger.[*] [s]

[24]When the time of her delivery came, there
were twins in her womb.[t] [25]The first to
emerge was reddish,[*] and his whole body
was like a hairy mantle; so they named him
Esau. [26]Next his brother came out, gripping

**25:12** Like the conclusion of the Jacob story (chap. 36), where the numerous descendants of the rejected Esau are listed, the descendants of the rejected Ishmael conclude the story.

**25:18 Pitched camp**: lit., "fell"; the same Hebrew verb is used in Jgs 7:12 in regard to the hostile encampment of desert tribes. The present passage shows the fulfillment of the prediction contained in Gn 16:12.

**25:19–36:43** The Jacob cycle is introduced as the family history of Isaac (Jacob's father), just as the Abraham stories were introduced as the record of the descendants of Terah (Abraham's father, 11:27). The cycle, made up of varied stories, is given unity by several recurring themes: birth, blessing and inheritance, which are developed through the basic contrasts of barrenness/fertility, non-blessing/blessing, and inheritance/exile/homeland. The large story has an envelope structure in which Jacob's youth is spent in Canaan striving with his older brother Esau (25:19–28:22), his early adulthood in Paddan-aram building a family and striving with his brother-in-law Laban (chaps. 29–31), and his later years back in Canaan (chaps. 32–36).

**25:20 Paddan-aram**: the name used by the Priestly tradition for the northwest region of Mesopotamia, between the Habur and the Euphrates rivers. In Assyrian, *padana* is a road or a garden, and Aram refers to the people or the land of the Arameans. The equivalent geographical term in the Yahwist source is Aram Naharaim, "Aram between two rivers."

**25:22 If it is like this**: in Hebrew, the phrase *lamah zeh* is capable of several meanings; it occurs again in v. 32 ("What good . . . ?"), 32:30 ("Why do you want . . . ?"), and 33:15 ("For what reason?"). It is one of several words and motifs that run through the story, suggesting that a divine pattern (unknown to the actors) is at work.

**25:23 The older will serve the younger**: Rebekah now knows something that no one else knows, that God favors Jacob over Esau. The text does not say if she shared this knowledge with anyone or kept it to herself, but, from their actions, it seems unlikely that either Isaac or Esau knew. That fact must be borne in mind in assessing Rebekah's role in chap. 27, the theft of Esau's blessing.

**25:25 Reddish**: in Hebrew, *'admoni*, a reference to Edom, another name for Esau (v. 30; 36:1). Edom was also the name of the country south of Moab (southeast of the Dead Sea) where the descendants of Esau lived. It was called the "red" country because of its reddish sandstone. Moreover, "red" points ahead to the red stew in the next scene. **Hairy**: in Hebrew, *se'ar*, a reference to Seir, another name for Edom (36:8).

---

*m:* Gn 23:3–20. *n:* 1 Chr 1:29–31. *o:* Is 60:7. *p:* Gn 17:20. *q:* Gn 16:12. *r:* Gn 24:67. *s:* Gn 27:29; Nm 24:18; Mal 1:2–5; Rom 9:10–13. *t:* Hos 12:4.

## Jacob Steals Esau's Blessing

JACOB DECEIVES HIS old and blind father Isaac by pretending to be his older brother Esau. In this way, he receives the blessing and inheritance that belongs to the first-born son. The grief and anger of Isaac and Esau presuppose that the words and power of a blessing cannot be taken back once they have been spoken. Esau can only receive the opposite of what Jacob already received. Jacob will receive of (the Hebrew preposition *min*) the fertility of the earth (27:28) while Esau will live far from (the same preposition *min*) the fertile earth (v. 39). The land of Edom was not an agriculturally rich area. The last words we hear from Esau concerning Jacob until they meet many years later (ch 33) are "I may kill my brother Jacob" (27:41). Rebekah's excuse to Isaac for sending Jacob away is to avoid Jacob's marrying one of the Hittite or Canaanite women of the land as Esau had done (26:34–35), but her real reason is to stop Esau from murdering his brother Jacob (27:42–45). Isaac instructs Jacob to return to the original homeland of Abram and of his mother Rebekah in Mesopotamia to obtain a wife as Isaac had done (ch 24).

Esau's heel;* so he was named Jacob. Isaac
was sixty years old when they were born.[u]
27 When the boys grew up, Esau became a
skillful hunter, a man of the open country;
whereas Jacob was a simple* man, who
stayed among the tents.[v] 28 Isaac preferred
Esau, because he was fond of game; but Rebekah preferred Jacob. 29 Once, when Jacob
was cooking a stew, Esau came in from the
open country, famished. 30 He said to Jacob,
"Let me gulp down some of that red stuff;* I
am famished." That is why he was called
Edom. 31 But Jacob replied, "First sell me
your right as firstborn."*[w] 32 "Look," said
Esau, "I am on the point of dying. What
good is the right as firstborn to me?" 33 But
Jacob said, "Swear to me first!" So he sold
Jacob his right as firstborn under oath.[x] 34 Jacob then gave him some bread and the lentil
stew; and Esau ate, drank, got up, and went
his way. So Esau treated his right as firstborn
with disdain.

### CHAPTER 26

See RG 59

***Isaac and Abimelech.*** 1*[y] There was a
famine in the land, distinct from the earlier
one that had occurred in the days of Abraham, and Isaac went down to Abimelech,
king of the Philistines in Gerar.[z] 2 The LORD
appeared to him and said: Do not go down to
Egypt, but camp in this land wherever I tell
you. 3 Sojourn in this land, and I will be with
you and bless you; for to you and your descendants I will give all these lands, in fulfillment of the oath that I swore to your father Abraham.[a] 4 I will make your
descendants as numerous as the stars in the
sky, and I will give them all these lands, and
in your descendants all the nations of the
earth will find blessing—[b] 5 this because
Abraham obeyed me, keeping my mandate,
my commandments, my ordinances, and my
instructions.
6* So Isaac settled in Gerar. 7 When the

**25:26 Heel**: in Hebrew *'aqeb*, a wordplay on the name Jacob; cf. 27:36. The first of three scenes of striving with Esau. The second is vv. 27–34, and the third, chap. 27. In all the scenes, Jacob values the blessing more than his ardent but unreflective brother Esau does.

**25:27 Simple**: the Hebrew word denotes soundness, integrity, health, none of which fit here. Whatever its precise meaning, it must be opposite to the qualities of Esau.

**25:30 Red stuff**: in Hebrew, *'adom*; another play on the word Edom, the "red" land.

**25:31 Right as firstborn**: the privilege that entitled the firstborn son to a position of honor in the family and to a double share in the possessions inherited from the father. There is a persistent wordplay between *bekorah*, "right of the first-born," and *berakah*, "the blessing." Contrary to custom, the preference here is for the younger son, as it was in the choice of Isaac over Ishmael.

**26:1** The promise of land and numerous descendants given to Abraham (12:1–3; 15; 17; 22:17–18) is renewed for his son Isaac. The divine blessing to Isaac is mentioned also in vv. 12, 24, and 29.

**26:6–11** This scene is the third version of the wife-in-danger

*u:* Mt 1:2. *v:* Gn 27:6–7. *w:* Dt 21:17. *x:* Heb 12:16. *y:* Gn 12:10–20. *z:* Gn 12:10. *a:* Gn 12:7; 15:18; Ex 32:13; Ps 105:9; Sir 44:22; Heb 11:9. *b:* Gn 12:3; 22:17–18; 28:14; Ex 32:13.

men of the place asked questions about his wife, he answered, "She is my sister." He was afraid that, if he called her his wife, the men of the place would kill him on account of Rebekah, since she was beautiful. [8]But when they had been there for a long time, Abimelech, king of the Philistines, looked out of a window and saw Isaac fondling his wife Rebekah. [9]He called for Isaac and said: "She must certainly be your wife! How could you have said, 'She is my sister'?" Isaac replied, "I thought I might lose my life on her account." [10]"How could you have done this to us!" exclaimed Abimelech. "It would have taken very little for one of the people to lie with your wife, and so you would have brought guilt upon us!" [11]Abimelech then commanded all the people: "Anyone who maltreats this man or his wife shall be put to death."

[12]* Isaac sowed a crop in that region and reaped a hundredfold the same year. Since the LORD blessed him, [13c] he became richer and richer all the time, until he was very wealthy. [14]He acquired flocks and herds, and a great work force, and so the Philistines became envious of him. [15d] The Philistines had stopped up and filled with dirt all the wells that his father's servants had dug back in the days of his father Abraham. [16]So Abimelech said to Isaac, "Go away from us; you have become far too numerous for us." [17]Isaac left there and camped in the Wadi Gerar where he stayed. [18]Isaac reopened the wells which his father's servants had dug back in the days of his father Abraham and which the Philistines had stopped up after Abraham's death; he gave them names like those that his father had given them. [19]But when Isaac's servants dug in the wadi and reached spring water in their well, [20]the shepherds of Gerar argued with Isaac's shepherds, saying, "The water belongs to us!" So he named the well Esek,* because they had quarreled there. [21]Then they dug another well, and they argued over that one too; so he named it Sitnah.* [22]So he moved on from there and dug still another well, but over this one they did not argue. He named it Rehoboth,* and said, "Because the LORD has now given us ample room, we shall flourish in the land."

[23]From there Isaac went up to Beer-sheba. [24]The same night the LORD appeared to him and said: I am the God of Abraham, your father. Do not fear, for I am with you. I will bless you and multiply your descendants for the sake of Abraham, my servant.[e] [25]So Isaac built an altar there and invoked the LORD by name. After he had pitched his tent there, Isaac's servants began to dig a well nearby.

[26f] Then Abimelech came to him from Gerar, with Ahuzzath, his councilor, and Phicol, the general of his army. [27]Isaac asked them, "Why have you come to me, since you hate me and have driven me away from you?" [28]They answered: "We clearly see that the LORD has been with you, so we thought: let there be a sworn agreement between our two sides—between you and us. Let us make a covenant with you: [29]you shall do no harm to us, just as we have not maltreated you, but have always acted kindly toward you and have let you depart in peace. So now, may you be blessed by the LORD!" [30]Isaac then made a feast for them, and they ate and drank. [31]Early the next morning they exchanged oaths. Then Isaac sent them on their way, and they departed from him in peace.

[32]That same day Isaac's servants came and informed him about the well they had been digging; they told him, "We have

story (cf. chaps. 12 and 20). The mention of the famine in 26:1 recalls the famine in 12:10; the name Abimelech, king of the Philistines in Gerar, recalls 20:2. The deception, according to all the stories, is the claim that the wife is a sister. This story (from the Yahwist source) departs from the two previous accounts in that the wife is not taken into the harem of the foreign king.

**26:12–33** The dispute is over water rights. In a sparsely watered land, wells were precious and claims on water could function as a kind of claim on the land. Scholars generally judge the account of the dispute over water rights and its settlement by a legal agreement between Isaac and Abimelech to be a Yahwist version of the similar story about Abraham in 21:22–34. Here, Abimelech realizes that Isaac has brought blessing to his people and thus desires a covenant with him. The feast in v. 30 is part of the covenant ceremony.

**26:20 Esek**: "quarrel."

**26:21 Sitnah**: "opposition."

**26:22 Rehoboth**: "wide spaces," i.e., ample room to live; site is probably SW of modern day Beer-sheba.

*c:* Jb 1:3. *d:* Gn 21:25–31. *e:* Gn 46:3. *f:* Gn 21:22–31; Prv 16:7.

reached water!" 33He called it Shibah;[*]
hence the name of the city is Beer-sheba to
this day. 34[*] When Esau was forty years old,
he married Judith, daughter of Beeri the Hittite, and Basemath, daughter of Elon the Hivite.[g] 35But they became a source of bitterness to Isaac and Rebekah.

See RG 59–60

## CHAPTER 27

***Jacob's Deception.***[*] 1When Isaac was
so old that his eyesight had failed him, he
called his older son Esau and said to him,
"My son!" "Here I am!" he replied. 2Isaac
then said, "Now I have grown old. I do not
know when I might die. 3So now take your
hunting gear—your quiver and bow—and
go out into the open country to hunt some
game for me. 4Then prepare for me a dish in
the way I like, and bring it to me to eat, so
that I may bless you[*] before I die."

5Rebekah had been listening while Isaac
was speaking to his son Esau. So when Esau
went out into the open country to hunt some
game for his father,[h] 6Rebekah said to her
son Jacob, "Listen! I heard your father tell
your brother Esau, 7'Bring me some game
and prepare a dish for me to eat, that I may
bless you with the LORD's approval before I
die.' 8Now, my son, obey me in what I am
about to order you. 9Go to the flock and get
me two choice young goats so that with
these I might prepare a dish for your father
in the way he likes. 10Then bring it to your
father to eat, that he may bless you before he
dies." 11But Jacob said to his mother Rebekah, "But my brother Esau is a hairy man
and I am smooth-skinned![i] 12Suppose my father feels me? He will think I am making fun
of him, and I will bring on myself a curse instead of a blessing." 13His mother, however,
replied: "Let any curse against you, my son,
fall on me! Just obey me. Go and get me the
young goats."

14So Jacob went and got them and brought
them to his mother, and she prepared a dish
in the way his father liked. 15Rebekah then
took the best clothes of her older son Esau
that she had in the house, and gave them to
her younger son Jacob to wear; 16and with
the goatskins she covered up his hands and
the hairless part of his neck. 17Then she gave
her son Jacob the dish and the bread she had
prepared.

18Going to his father, Jacob said, "Father!" "Yes?" replied Isaac. "Which of my
sons are you?" 19Jacob answered his father:
"I am Esau, your firstborn. I did as you told
me. Please sit up and eat some of my game,
so that you may bless me." 20But Isaac said
to his son, "How did you get it so quickly,
my son?" He answered, "The LORD, your
God, directed me." 21Isaac then said to Jacob, "Come closer, my son, that I may feel
you, to learn whether you really are my son
Esau or not." 22So Jacob moved up closer to
his father. When Isaac felt him, he said, "Although the voice is Jacob's, the hands are
Esau's." 23(He failed to identify him because
his hands were hairy, like those of his
brother Esau; so he blessed him.) 24Again
Isaac said, "Are you really my son Esau?"
And Jacob said, "I am." 25Then Isaac said,
"Serve me, my son, and let me eat of the
game so that I may bless you." Jacob served
it to him, and Isaac ate; he brought him wine,
and he drank. 26Finally his father Isaac said

**26:33 Shibah**: the place name Shibah is a play on two Hebrew words, *shebu'ah*, "oath," and *shwebaa'*, "seven." In v. 31, they exchanged oaths.

**26:34–35** These verses from the Priestly source introduce the next section on Esau's loss of his right as firstborn by suggesting a motivation for this in Isaac's and Rebekah's dislike for Esau's Canaanite wives.

**27:1–45** The chapter, a literary masterpiece, is the third and climactic wresting away of the blessing of Esau. Rebekah manages the entire affair, using perhaps her privileged information about Jacob's status (25:23); Jacob's only qualm is that if his father discovers the ruse, he will receive a curse instead of a blessing (vv. 11–12). Isaac is passive as he was in chaps. 22 and 24. The deception is effected through clothing (Jacob wears Esau's clothing), which points ahead to a similar deception of a patriarch by means of clothing in the Joseph story (37:21–33). Such recurrent acts and scenes let the reader know a divine purpose is moving the story forward even though the human characters are unaware of it.

**27:4 I may bless you**: Isaac's blessing confers fertility (vv. 27–28) and dominion (v. 29). The "dew of heaven" is rain that produces grain and wine, two of the principal foodstuffs of the ancient Near East. The "fertility of the earth" may allude to oil, the third basic foodstuff. The full agricultural year may be implied here: the fall rains are followed by the grain harvests of the spring and the grape harvest of late summer, and then the olive harvest of the fall (cf. Dt 11:14; Ps 104:13–15).

*g:* Gn 27:46. *h:* Gn 25:28. *i:* Gn 25:25.

to him, "Come closer, my son, and kiss me."
27 As Jacob went up to kiss him, Isaac
smelled the fragrance of his clothes. With
that, he blessed him, saying,

"Ah, the fragrance of my son
is like the fragrance of a field
that the LORD has blessed![j]
28 May God give to you
of the dew of the heavens
And of the fertility of the earth
abundance of grain and wine.
29 [k] May peoples serve you,
and nations bow down to you;
Be master of your brothers,
and may your mother's sons bow
down to you.
Cursed be those who curse you,
and blessed be those who bless you."

30 Jacob had scarcely left his father after
Isaac had finished blessing him, when his
brother Esau came back from his hunt.
31 Then he too prepared a dish, and bringing
it to his father, he said, "Let my father sit up
and eat some of his son's game, that you may
then give me your blessing." 32 His father
Isaac asked him, "Who are you?" He said, "I
am your son, your firstborn son, Esau."
33 Isaac trembled greatly. "Who was it, then,"
he asked, "that hunted game and brought it
to me? I ate it all just before you came, and I
blessed him. Now he is blessed!" 34 As he
heard his father's words, Esau burst into
loud, bitter sobbing and said, "Father, bless
me too!" 35 When Isaac said, "Your brother
came here by a ruse and carried off your
blessing," 36 Esau exclaimed, "He is well
named Jacob, is he not! He has supplanted
me* twice! First he took away my right as
firstborn, and now he has taken away my
blessing." Then he said, "Have you not
saved a blessing for me?"[l] 37 Isaac replied to
Esau: "I have already appointed him your
master, and I have assigned to him all his
kindred as his servants; besides, I have sustained him with grain and wine. What then
can I do for you, my son?" 38 But Esau said
to his father, "Have you only one blessing,
father? Bless me too, father!" and Esau wept
aloud.[m] 39 His father Isaac said in response:

"See, far from the fertile earth
will be your dwelling;
far from the dew of the heavens above![n]
40 By your sword you will live,
and your brother you will serve;
But when you become restless,
you will throw off his yoke from your
neck."[o]

41 Esau bore a grudge against Jacob because of the blessing his father had given him.
Esau said to himself, "Let the time of mourning for my father come, so that I may kill my
brother Jacob."[p] 42 When Rebekah got news
of what her older son Esau had in mind, she
summoned her younger son Jacob and said to
him: "Listen! Your brother Esau intends to
get his revenge by killing you. 43 So now, my
son, obey me: flee at once to my brother Laban in Haran, 44 and stay with him a while until your brother's fury subsides— 45 until your
brother's anger against you subsides and he
forgets what you did to him. Then I will send
for you and bring you back. Why should I
lose both of you in a single day?"

***Jacob Sent to Laban.*** 46 Rebekah said to
Isaac: "I am disgusted with life because of
the Hittite women. If Jacob also should
marry a Hittite woman, a native of the land,
like these women, why should I live?"[q]

## CHAPTER 28

See RG 59–60

1* Isaac therefore summoned Jacob
and blessed him, charging him: "You shall

**27:36 He has supplanted me**: in Hebrew, *wayyaqebeni*, a wordplay on the name Jacob, *ya'aqob*; see Jer 9:3 and Gn 25:26. There is also a play between the Hebrew words *bekorah* ("right of the firstborn") and *berakah* ("blessing").

**28:1–9** A glimpse of Rebekah's shrewdness is provided by 27:42–28:2. She is aware of Esau's murderous plot against Jacob (27:42–45) but realizes the episode of the stolen blessing is still painful to Isaac; she therefore uses another motive to persuade Isaac to send Jacob away—he must marry within the family (endogamy), unlike Esau. Esau, unreflective as usual, realizes too late he also should marry within the family but, significantly, marries from Abraham's rejected line. At this point in the story, Jacob (and his mother) have taken the blessing for themselves. Their actions have put Jacob in a precarious position: he must flee the land because of his

*j:* Gn 22:17–18; Heb 11:20. *k:* Gn 25:23; 49:8; Nm 24:9. *l:* Gn 25:26, 29–34; Hos 12:4. *m:* Heb 12:17. *n:* Heb 11:20. *o:* 2 Kgs 8:20, 22; 2 Chr 21:8. *p:* Wis 10:10; Ob 10. *q:* Gn 26:34–35.

not marry a Canaanite woman![r] 2Go now to Paddan-aram, to the home of your mother's father Bethuel, and there choose a wife for yourself from among the daughters of Laban, your mother's brother.[s] 3May God Almighty bless you and make you fertile, multiply you that you may become an assembly of peoples. 4May God extend to you and your descendants the blessing of Abraham, so that you may gain possession of the land where you are residing, which he assigned to Abraham."[t] 5Then Isaac sent Jacob on his way; he went to Paddan-aram, to Laban, son of Bethuel the Aramean, and brother of Rebekah, the mother of Jacob and Esau.[u]

6Esau noted that Isaac had blessed Jacob when he sent him to Paddan-aram to get himself a wife there, and that, as he gave him his blessing, he charged him, "You shall not marry a Canaanite woman," 7and that Jacob had obeyed his father and mother and gone to Paddan-aram. 8Esau realized how displeasing the Canaanite women were to his father Isaac, 9so Esau went to Ishmael, and in addition to the wives he had, married Mahalath, the daughter of Abraham's son Ishmael and sister of Nebaioth.[v]

***Jacob's Dream at Bethel.**** 10Jacob departed from Beer-sheba and proceeded toward Haran. 11When he came upon a certain place,* he stopped there for the night, since the sun had already set. Taking one of the stones at the place, he put it under his head and lay down in that place. 12Then he had a dream: a stairway* rested on the ground, with its top reaching to the heavens; and God's angels were going up and down on it.[w] 13And there was the LORD standing beside him and saying: I am the LORD, the God of Abraham your father and the God of Isaac; the land on which you are lying I will give to you and your descendants.[x] 14Your descendants will be like the dust of the earth, and through them you will spread to the west and the east, to the north and the south. In you and your descendants all the families of the earth will find blessing.[y] 15I am with you and will protect you wherever you go, and bring you back to this land. I will never leave you until I have done what I promised you.[z]

16When Jacob awoke from his sleep, he said, "Truly, the LORD is in this place and I did not know it!" 17He was afraid and said: "How awesome this place is! This is nothing else but the house of God, the gateway to heaven!" 18Early the next morning Jacob took the stone that he had put under his head, set it up as a sacred pillar,* and poured oil on top of it.[a] 19He named that place Bethel,* whereas the former name of the town had been Luz.[b]

20Jacob then made this vow:* "If God will be with me and protect me on this journey I

brother's murderous intent and find a wife in a far country. One might ask how God's blessing can be given to such an unworthy schemer. There is a biblical pattern of preferring the younger brother or sister over the older—Isaac over Ishmael, Jacob over Esau, Rachel over Leah, Joseph over his older brothers, Ephraim over Manasseh (Gn 48:14), David over his older brothers.

**28:10–22** As Jacob is leaving the land on his way to an uncertain future in Paddan-aram, God appears to him at a sacred place that Jacob had visited only to take a night's rest. Jacob's unawareness of the holiness of the place underscores the graciousness of the gift. On his return to Canaan, he will again encounter a divine visitor in the form of the mysterious attacker (32:23–33) and, after his return and reconciliation with Esau, he will again go to Bethel (35:1–15).

**28:11 Place**: the Hebrew word is often used specifically of a sacred site. The ambiguous word "place" is used here, for the text emphasizes that Jacob has no idea the place he has come upon is sacred; only when he wakes up does he realize it is sacred. The place was Bethel (v. 19), a sacred site as early as the time of Abraham (12:8).

**28:12 Stairway**: in Hebrew, *sullam*, traditionally but inaccurately translated as "ladder." The corresponding verb, *salal*, means "to heap up" something, such as dirt for a highway or a ramp. The imagery in Jacob's dream may be derived from the Babylonian ziggurat or temple tower, "with its top in the sky" (11:4), and with brick steps leading up to a small temple at the top.

**28:18 Sacred pillar**: in Hebrew, *masseba*, a stone which might vary in shape and size, set upright and usually intended for some religious purpose. The custom of erecting such sacred pillars in Palestine went back to its pre-Israelite period; but since their polytheistic associations were often retained, later Israelite religion forbade their erection (Lv 26:1; Dt 16:22) and ordered the destruction of those that were associated with other religions (Ex 34:13; Dt 12:3).

**28:19 Bethel**: i.e., "house of God"; the reference is to the house of God in v. 17.

**28:20 This vow**: knowing well that Esau's murderous wrath stands between him and the possession of the land

*r:* Gn 24:3–4; 26:35. *s:* Gn 22:22. *t:* Ex 32:13. *u:* Jdt 8:26. *v:* Gn 36:2–3. *w:* Jn 1:51. *x:* Dt 1:8; Mi 7:20. *y:* Gn 12:3; 13:14–15; 15:5–6; 18:18; 22:17–18; 26:4; Dt 19:8; Sir 44:21. *z:* Gn 31:3. *a:* Gn 31:13; 35:14–15. *b:* Gn 35:6; 48:3; Jos 18:13; Jgs 1:23; Hos 12:5.

am making and give me food to eat and clothes to wear, 21 and I come back safely to my father's house, the LORD will be my God. 22 This stone that I have set up as a sacred pillar will be the house of God. Of everything you give me, I will return a tenth part to you without fail."

## CHAPTER 29

See RG 59–60

***Arrival in Haran.*** * 1[c] After Jacob resumed his journey, he came to the land of the Kedemites. 2 Looking about, he saw a well in the open country, with three flocks of sheep huddled near it, for flocks were watered from that well. A large stone covered the mouth of the well.[d] 3 When all the shepherds were assembled there they would roll the stone away from the mouth of the well and water the sheep. Then they would put the stone back again in its place over the mouth of the well.

4 Jacob said to them, "My brothers, where are you from?" "We are from Haran," they replied. 5 Then he asked them, "Do you know Laban, son of Nahor?" "We do," they answered.[e] 6 He inquired further, "Is he well?" "He is," they answered; "and here comes his daughter Rachel with the sheep." 7 Then he said: "There is still much daylight left; it is hardly the time to bring the animals home. Water the sheep, and then continue pasturing them." 8 They replied, "We cannot until all the shepherds are here to roll the stone away from the mouth of the well; then can we water the flocks."

9 While he was still talking with them, Rachel arrived with her father's sheep, for she was the one who tended them. 10 As soon as Jacob saw Rachel, the daughter of his mother's brother Laban, and the sheep of Laban, he went up, rolled the stone away from the mouth of the well, and watered Laban's sheep. 11 Then Jacob kissed Rachel and wept aloud. 12 Jacob told Rachel that he was her father's relative, Rebekah's son. So she ran to tell her father. 13 When Laban heard the news about Jacob, his sister's son, he ran to meet him. After embracing and kissing him, he brought him to his house. Jacob then repeated to Laban all these things, 14 and Laban said to him, "You are indeed my bone and my flesh."*

***Marriage to Leah and Rachel.*** After Jacob had stayed with him a full month, 15* Laban said to him: "Should you serve me for nothing just because you are a relative of mine? Tell me what your wages should be." 16 Now Laban had two daughters; the older was called Leah, the younger Rachel. 17 Leah had dull eyes,* but Rachel was shapely and beautiful. 18 Because Jacob loved Rachel, he answered, "I will serve you seven years for your younger daughter Rachel."* 19 Laban replied, "It is better to give her to you than to another man. Stay with me." 20 So Jacob served seven years for Rachel, yet they seemed to him like a few days because of his love for her.[f]

21 Then Jacob said to Laban, "Give me my

promised him, Jacob makes his vow very precise. He vows to make the God who appeared to him his own if the God guides him safely to Paddan-aram and back to this land.

**29:1–14** Jacob's arrival in Haran. The sight of Rachel inspires Jacob to the superhuman feat of rolling back the enormous stone by himself. The scene evokes the meeting of Abraham's steward and Jacob's mother Rebekah at a well (24:11–27).

The verse begins the story of Jacob's time in Mesopotamia (29:1–31:54), which is framed on either side by Jacob's time in Canaan, 25:19–28:22 and 32:1–36:43. In these chapters, Jacob suffers Laban's duplicity as Esau had to suffer his, though eventually Jacob outwits Laban and leaves Mesopotamia a wealthy man. An elaborate chiastic (or envelope) structure shapes the diverse material: (A) Jacob's arrival in Haran in 29:1–4; (B) contract with Laban in 29:15–20; (C) Laban's deception of Jacob in 29:21–30; (D) the center, the birth of Jacob's children in 29:31–30:24; (C') Jacob's deception of Laban in 30:25–43; (B') dispute with Laban in 31:17–42; (A') departure from Laban in 31:43–54. As the chiasm reverses, so do the fortunes of Laban and Jacob. **Kedemites**: see note on 25:6.

**29:14 Bone and . . . flesh**: the Hebrew idiom for English "flesh and blood" (cf. 2:23; Jgs 9:2; 2 Sm 5:1 = 1 Chr 11:1).

**29:15–30** Laban's deception and Jacob's marriages. There are many ironies in the passage. Jacob's protest to Laban, "How could you do this to me?" echoes the question put to Abraham (20:9) and Isaac (26:10) when their deceptions about their wives were discovered. The major irony is that Jacob, the deceiver of his father and brother about the blessing (chap. 27), is deceived by his uncle (standing in for the father) about his wife.

**29:17 Dull eyes**: in the language of beauty used here, "dull" probably means lacking in the luster that was the sign of beautiful eyes, as in 1 Sm 16:12 and Sg 4:1.

**29:18** Jacob offers to render service (Jos 15:16–17; 1 Sm 17:25; 18:17) to pay off the customary bridal price (Ex 22:15–16; Dt 22:29).

*c:* Wis 10:10. *d:* Gn 24:11–12. *e:* Tb 7:4. *f:* Hos 12:13.

wife, that I may consummate my marriage
with her, for my term is now completed."
[22]So Laban invited all the local inhabitants
and gave a banquet. [23]At nightfall he took
his daughter Leah and brought her to Jacob,
and he consummated the marriage with her.
[24]Laban assigned his maidservant Zilpah to
his daughter Leah as her maidservant. [25]In
the morning, there was Leah! So Jacob said
to Laban: "How could you do this to me!
Was it not for Rachel that I served you?
Why did you deceive me?" [26]Laban replied,
"It is not the custom in our country to give
the younger daughter before the firstborn.
[27]Finish the bridal week* for this one, and
then the other will also be given to you in return for another seven years of service with
me."[g]
[28]Jacob did so. He finished the bridal
week for the one, and then Laban gave him
his daughter Rachel as a wife. [29]Laban assigned his maidservant Bilhah to his daughter Rachel as her maidservant. [30]Jacob then
consummated his marriage with Rachel
also, and he loved her more than Leah. Thus
he served Laban another seven years.[h]
***Jacob's Children.**** [31]When the LORD saw
that Leah was unloved, he made her fruitful,
while Rachel was barren. [32]Leah conceived
and bore a son, and she named him Reuben;*
for she said, "It means, 'The LORD saw my
misery; surely now my husband will love
me.' "[i] [33]She conceived again and bore a
son, and said, "It means, 'The LORD heard
that I was unloved,' and therefore he has
given me this one also"; so she named him
Simeon.* [34]Again she conceived and bore a
son, and she said, "Now at last my husband
will become attached to me, since I have
now borne him three sons"; that is why she
named him Levi.* [35]Once more she conceived and bore a son, and she said, "This
time I will give thanks to the LORD"; therefore she named him Judah.* Then she
stopped bearing children.[j]

## CHAPTER 30

See RG 59–60

[1]When Rachel saw that she had not
borne children to Jacob, she became envious
of her sister. She said to Jacob, "Give me
children or I shall die!"[k] [2]Jacob became angry with Rachel and said, "Can I take the
place of God, who has denied you the fruit of
the womb?"[l] [3]She replied, "Here is my
maidservant Bilhah. Have intercourse with
her, and let her give birth on my knees,* so
that I too may have children through her."[m]
[4]So she gave him her maidservant Bilhah as
wife,* and Jacob had intercourse with her.
[5]When Bilhah conceived and bore a son for
Jacob, [6]Rachel said, "God has vindicated
me; indeed he has heeded my plea and given
me a son." Therefore she named him Dan.*
[7]Rachel's maidservant Bilhah conceived
again and bore a second son for Jacob, [8]and
Rachel said, "I have wrestled strenuously

**29:27 The bridal week**: an ancient wedding lasted for seven days; cf. Jgs 14:12, 17.

**29:31–30:24** The note of strife, first sounded between Jacob and Esau in chaps. 25–27, continues between the two wives, since Jacob loved Rachel more than Leah (29:30). Jacob's neglect of Leah moves God to make her fruitful (29:31). Leah's fertility provokes Rachel. Leah bears Jacob four sons (Reuben, Levi, Simeon, and Judah) and her maidservant Zilpah, two (Gad and Asher). Rachel's maidservant Bilhah bears two (Dan and Naphtali). After the mandrakes (30:14–17), Leah bears Issachar and Zebulun and a daughter Dinah. Rachel then bears Joseph and, later in the land of Canaan, Benjamin (35:18).

**29:32 Reuben**: the literal meaning of the Hebrew name is disputed. One interpretation is *re'u ben,* "look, a son!", but here in Genesis (as also with the names of all the other sons of Jacob), it is given a symbolic rather than an etymological interpretation. Name and person were regarded as closely interrelated. The symbolic interpretation of Reuben's name, according to the Yahwist source, is based on the similar-sounding *ra'a be'onyi*, "he saw my misery." In the Elohist source, the name is explained by the similar-sounding *ye'ehabani*, "he will love me."

**29:33 Simeon**: in popular etymology, related to *shama'*, "he heard."

**29:34 Levi**: related to *yillaweh*, "he will become attached."

**29:35 Judah**: related to *'odeh*, "I will give thanks, praise."

**30:3 On my knees**: in the ancient Near East, a father would take a newborn child in his lap to signify that he acknowledged it as his own; Rachel uses the ceremony in order to adopt the child and establish her legal rights to it.

**30:4 As wife**: in 35:22 Bilhah is called a "concubine" (Heb. *pilegesh*). In v. 9, Zilpah is called "wife," and in 37:2 both women are called wives. The basic difference between a wife and a concubine was that no bride price was paid for the latter. The interchange of terminology shows that there was some blurring in social status between the wife and the concubine.

**30:6 Dan**: explained by the term *dannanni*, "he has vindicated me."

*g:* Hos 12:13. *h:* Dt 21:15–17. *i:* Gn 49:3. *j:* Mt 1:2; Lk 3:33. *k:* Prv 30:16. *l:* 2 Kgs 5:7. *m:* Gn 16:2–4.

with my sister, and I have prevailed." So she
named him Naphtali.*
[9]When Leah saw that she had ceased to
bear children, she took her maidservant Zilpah and gave her to Jacob as wife. [10]So
Leah's maidservant Zilpah bore a son for Jacob. [11]Leah then said, "What good luck!" So
she named him Gad.* [12]Then Leah's maidservant Zilpah bore a second son to Jacob;
[13]and Leah said, "What good fortune, because women will call me fortunate!" So she
named him Asher.*
[14]One day, during the wheat harvest, Reuben went out and came upon some mandrakes* in the field which he brought home
to his mother Leah. Rachel said to Leah,
"Please give me some of your son's mandrakes." [15]Leah replied, "Was it not enough
for you to take away my husband, that you
must now take my son's mandrakes too?"
Rachel answered, "In that case Jacob may
lie with you tonight in exchange for your
son's mandrakes." [16]That evening, when Jacob came in from the field, Leah went out to
meet him. She said, "You must have intercourse with me, because I have hired you
with my son's mandrakes." So that night he
lay with her, [17]and God listened to Leah; she
conceived and bore a fifth son to Jacob.
[18]Leah then said, "God has given me my
wages for giving my maidservant to my husband"; so she named him Issachar.* [19]Leah
conceived again and bore a sixth son to Jacob; [20]and Leah said, "God has brought me
a precious gift. This time my husband will
honor me, because I have borne him six
sons"; so she named him Zebulun.* [21]After-
wards she gave birth to a daughter, and she
named her Dinah.
[22]Then God remembered Rachel. God listened to her and made her fruitful. [23]She
conceived and bore a son, and she said,
"God has removed my disgrace."[n] [24]She
named him Joseph,* saying, "May the LORD
add another son for me!"

***Jacob Outwits Laban.**** [25]After Rachel
gave birth to Joseph, Jacob said to Laban:
"Allow me to go to my own region and land.
[26]Give me my wives and my children for
whom I served you and let me go, for you
know the service that I rendered you." [27]La-
ban answered him: "If you will please! I
have learned through divination that the
LORD has blessed me because of you." [28]He
continued, "State the wages I owe you, and I
will pay them." [29]Jacob replied: "You know
what work I did for you and how well your
livestock fared under my care; [30]the little
you had before I came has grown into an
abundance, since the LORD has blessed you
in my company. Now, when can I do something for my own household as well?" [31]La-
ban asked, "What should I give you?" Jacob
answered: "You do not have to give me anything. If you do this thing for me, I will again
pasture and tend your sheep. [32]Let me go
through your whole flock today and remove
from it every dark animal among the lambs
and every spotted or speckled one among the
goats.* These will be my wages. [33]In the fu-

**30:8 Naphtali**: explained by the Hebrew term *naftulim*, lit., "contest" or "struggle."

**30:11 Gad**: explained by the Hebrew term *begad*, lit., "in luck," i.e., "what good luck!"

**30:13 Asher**: explained by the term *be'oshri*, lit., "in my good fortune," i.e., "what good fortune," and by the term *ye'ashsheruni*, "they call me fortunate."

**30:14 Mandrakes**: an herb whose root was thought to promote conception. The Hebrew word for mandrakes, *duda'im*, has erotic connotations, since it sounds like the words *daddayim* ("breasts") and *dodim* ("sexual pleasure").

**30:18 Issachar**: explained by the terms, *sekari*, "my reward," and in v. 16, *sakor sekartika*, "I have hired you."

**30:20 Zebulun**: explained by the terms, *zebadani . . . zebed tob*, "he has brought me a precious gift," and *yizbeleni*, "he will honor me."

**30:24 Joseph**: explained by the words *yosep*, "may he add," and in v. 23, *'asap*, "he has removed."

**30:25–43** Jacob's deception of Laban. Jacob has been living in Laban's household as an indentured worker paying off the bride price. Having paid off all his obligations, he wants to settle his accounts with Laban. His many children attest to the fulfillment of the Lord's promise of numerous progeny; the birth of Joseph to his beloved Rachel signals the fulfillment in a special way. To enter into the Lord's second promise, the land, he must now return to Canaan.

**30:32 Dark . . . lambs . . . spotted or speckled . . . goats**: in the Near East the normal color of sheep is light gray, whereas that of goats is dark brown or black. A minority of sheep in that part of the world have dark patches, and a minority of goats, white markings. Laban is quick to agree to the offer, for Jacob would have received only a few animals. But Jacob gets the better of him, using two different means: (1) he separates out the weaker animals and then provides visual impressions to the stronger animals at mating time (a folkloric belief); (2) in 31:8–12, he transmits the preferred

*n:* Lk 1:25.

ture, whenever you check on my wages, my honesty will testify for me: any animal that is not speckled or spotted among the goats, or dark among the lambs, got into my possession by theft!" 34 Laban said, "Very well. Let it be as you say."

35 That same day Laban removed the streaked and spotted he-goats and all the speckled and spotted she-goats, all those with some white on them, as well as every dark lamb, and he put them in the care of his sons.* 36 Then he put a three days' journey between himself and Jacob, while Jacob was pasturing the rest of Laban's flock.

37 Jacob, however, got some fresh shoots of poplar, almond and plane* trees, and he peeled white stripes in them by laying bare the white core of the shoots. 38 The shoots that he had peeled he then set upright in the watering troughs where the animals came to drink, so that they would be in front of them. When the animals were in heat as they came to drink, 39 the goats mated by the shoots, and so they gave birth to streaked, speckled and spotted young. 40 The sheep, on the other hand, Jacob kept apart, and he made these animals face the streaked or completely dark animals of Laban. Thus he produced flocks of his own, which he did not put with Laban's flock. 41 Whenever the hardier animals were in heat, Jacob would set the shoots in the troughs in full view of these animals, so that they mated by the shoots; 42 but with the weaker animals he would not put the shoots there. So the feeble animals would go to Laban, but the hardy ones to Jacob. 43 So the man grew exceedingly prosperous, and he owned large flocks, male and female servants, camels, and donkeys.

## CHAPTER 31

See RG 59–60

***Flight from Laban.*** 1* Jacob heard that Laban's sons were saying, "Jacob has taken everything that belonged to our father, and he has produced all this wealth from our father's property." 2 Jacob perceived, too, that Laban's attitude toward him was not what it had previously been. 3 Then the LORD said to Jacob: Return to the land of your ancestors, where you were born, and I will be with you.[o]

4 So Jacob sent for Rachel and Leah to meet him in the field where his flock was. 5 There he said to them: "I have noticed that your father's attitude toward me is not as it was in the past; but the God of my father has been with me. 6 You know well that with all my strength I served your father; 7 yet your father cheated me and changed my wages ten times. God, however, did not let him do me any harm.[p] 8 Whenever your father said, 'The speckled animals will be your wages,' the entire flock would bear speckled young; whenever he said, 'The streaked animals will be your wages,' the entire flock would bear streaked young. 9 So God took away your father's livestock and gave it to me. 10 Once, during the flock's mating season, I had a dream in which I saw he-goats mating that were streaked, speckled and mottled. 11 In the dream God's angel said to me, 'Jacob!' and I replied, 'Here I am!' 12 Then he said: 'Look up and see. All the he-goats that are mating are streaked, speckled and mottled, for I have seen all the things that Laban has been doing to you. 13 I am the God of Bethel, where you anointed a sacred pillar and made a vow to me. Get up now! Leave this land and return to the land of your birth.' "[q]

characteristics through controlled propagation. It should be noted that Jacob has been told what to do in a dream (31:10) and that God is behind the increase in his flocks.

**30:35** By giving the abnormally colored animals to his sons, Laban not only deprived Jacob of his first small wages, but he also schemed to prevent the future breeding of such animals in the flock entrusted to Jacob.

**30:37 Plane**: also called the Oriental Plane, a deciduous tree found in riverine forests and marshes.

**31:1–54** Jacob flees with his family from Laban. The strife that has always accompanied Jacob continues as Laban's sons complain, "he has taken everything that belonged to our father"; the brothers' complaint echoes Esau's in 27:36. Rachel and Leah overcome their mutual hostility and are able to leave together, a harbinger of the reconciliation with Esau in chap. 33.

**31:15 Outsiders**: lit., "foreign women"; they lacked the favored legal status of native women. **Used up**: lit., "eaten, consumed"; the bridal price that a man received for giving his daughter in marriage was legally reserved as her inalienable dowry. Perhaps this is the reason that Rachel took the household images belonging to Laban.

*o:* Gn 26:3; 28:15; 32:10. *p:* Jdt 8:26. *q:* Gn 28:18.

14 Rachel and Leah answered him: "Do we still have an heir's portion in our father's house? 15 Are we not regarded by him as outsiders?* He not only sold us; he has even used up the money that he got for us! 16 All the wealth that God took away from our father really belongs to us and our children. So do whatever God has told you."[r] 17 Jacob proceeded to put his children and wives on camels, 18 and he drove off all his livestock and all the property he had acquired in Paddan-aram, to go to his father Isaac in the land of Canaan.

19 Now Laban was away shearing his sheep, and Rachel had stolen her father's household images.*[s] 20 Jacob had hoodwinked* Laban the Aramean by not telling him that he was going to flee. 21 Thus he fled with all that he had. Once he was across the Euphrates, he headed for the hill country of Gilead.

22 On the third day, word came to Laban that Jacob had fled. 23 Taking his kinsmen with him, he pursued him for seven days* until he caught up with him in the hill country of Gilead. 24 But that night God appeared to Laban the Aramean in a dream and said to him: Take care not to say anything to Jacob.[t]

***Jacob and Laban in Gilead.*** 25 When Laban overtook Jacob, Jacob's tents were pitched in the hill country; Laban also pitched his tents in the hill country of Gilead. 26 Laban said to Jacob, "How could you hoodwink me and carry off my daughters like prisoners of war?* 27 Why did you dupe me by stealing away secretly? You did not tell me! I would have sent you off with joyful singing to the sound of tambourines and harps. 28 You did not even allow me a parting kiss to my daughters and grandchildren! Now what you have done makes no sense. 29 I have it in my power to harm all of you; but last night the God of your father said to me, 'Take care not to say anything to Jacob!' 30 Granted that you had to leave because you were longing for your father's house, why did you steal my gods?" 31 Jacob replied to Laban, "I was frightened at the thought that you might take your daughters away from me by force. 32 As for your gods, the one you find them with shall not remain alive! If, with our kinsmen looking on, you identify anything here as belonging to you, take it." Jacob had no idea that Rachel had stolen the household images.

33 Laban then went in and searched Jacob's tent and Leah's tent, as well as the tents of the two maidservants; but he did not find them. Leaving Leah's tent, he went into Rachel's. 34* Meanwhile Rachel had taken the household images, put them inside the camel's saddlebag, and seated herself upon them. When Laban had rummaged through her whole tent without finding them,[u] 35 she said to her father, "Do not let my lord be angry that I cannot rise in your presence; I am having my period." So, despite his search, he did not find the household images.

36 Jacob, now angered, confronted Laban and demanded, "What crime or offense have I committed that you should hound me? 37 Now that you have rummaged through all my things, what have you found from your household belongings? Produce it here before your kinsmen and mine, and let them decide between the two of us.

**31:19 Household images**: in Hebrew, *teraphim*, figurines used in divination (Ez 21:26; Zec 10:2). Laban calls them his "gods" (v. 30). The traditional translation "idols" is avoided because it suggests false gods, whereas Genesis seems to accept the fact that the ancestors did not always live according to later biblical religious standards and laws.

**31:20 Hoodwinked**: lit., "stolen the heart of," i.e., lulled the mind of. **Aramean**: the earliest extra-biblical references to the Arameans date later than the time of Jacob, if Jacob is dated to the mid-second millennium; to call Laban an Aramean and to have him speak Aramaic (Jegar-sahadutha, v. 47) is an apparent anachronism. The word may have been chosen to underscore the growing estrangement between the two men and the fact that their descendants will be two different peoples.

**31:23 For seven days**: lit., "a way of seven days," a general term to designate a long distance; it would actually have taken a camel caravan many more days to travel from Haran to Gilead, the region east of the northern half of the Jordan. The mention of camels in this passage is apparently anachronistic since camels were not domesticated until the late second millennium.

**31:26 Prisoners of war**: lit., "women captured by the sword"; the women of a conquered people were treated as part of the victor's spoil; cf. 1 Sm 30:2; 2 Kgs 5:2.

**31:34** As in chap. 27, a younger child (Rachel) deceives her father to gain what belongs to him.

*r:* Wis 10:10–11. *s:* Gn 31:34; 1 Sm 19:13. *t:* Wis 10:12. *u:* Gn 31:19.

38 "In the twenty years that I was under you, no ewe or she-goat of yours ever miscarried, and I have never eaten rams of your flock. 39[v] I never brought you an animal torn by wild beasts; I made good the loss myself. You held me responsible for anything stolen by day or night.* 40 Often the scorching heat devoured me by day, and the frost by night, while sleep fled from my eyes! 41 Of the twenty years that I have now spent in your household, I served you fourteen years for your two daughters and six years for your flock, while you changed my wages ten times. 42 If the God of my father, the God of Abraham and the Fear of Isaac, had not been on my side, you would now have sent me away empty-handed. But God saw my plight and the fruits of my toil, and last night he reproached you."[w]

43* Laban replied to Jacob: "The daughters are mine, their children are mine, and the flocks are mine; everything you see belongs to me. What can I do now for my own daughters and for the children they have borne? 44* Come, now, let us make a covenant, you and I; and it will be a treaty between you and me."

45 Then Jacob took a stone and set it up as a sacred pillar.[x] 46 Jacob said to his kinsmen, "Gather stones." So they got stones and made a mound; and they ate there at the mound. 47 Laban called it Jegar-sahadutha,* but Jacob called it Galeed. 48 Laban said, "This mound will be a witness from now on between you and me." That is why it was named Galeed— 49 and also Mizpah,* for he said: "May the LORD keep watch between you and me when we are out of each other's sight. 50 If you mistreat my daughters, or take other wives besides my daughters, know that even though no one else is there, God will be a witness between you and me."

51 Laban said further to Jacob: "Here is this mound, and here is the sacred pillar that I have set up between you and me. 52 This mound will be a witness, and this sacred pillar will be a witness, that, with hostile intent, I may not pass beyond this mound into your territory, nor may you pass beyond it into mine. 53 May the God of Abraham and the God of Nahor, the God of their father, judge between us!" Jacob took the oath by the Fear of his father Isaac.* 54 He then offered a sacrifice on the mountain and invited his kinsmen to share in the meal. When they had eaten, they passed the night on the mountain.

## CHAPTER 32

See RG 59–60

1* Early the next morning, Laban kissed his grandchildren and his daughters and blessed them; then he set out on his journey back home. 2 Meanwhile Jacob continued on his own way, and God's angels encountered him. 3 When Jacob saw them he said, "This is God's encampment." So he named that place Mahanaim.*

***Envoys to Esau.*** 4 Jacob sent messengers ahead to his brother Esau in the land of Seir,

**31:39** Jacob's actions are more generous than the customs suggested in the Code of Hammurabi: "If in a sheepfold an act of god has occurred, or a lion has made a kill, the shepherd shall clear himself before the deity, and the owner of the fold must accept the loss" (par. 266); cf. Ex 22:12.

**31:43–54** In this account of the non-aggression treaty between Laban and Jacob, the different objects that serve as witness (sacred pillar in v. 45, cairn of stones in v. 46), their different names (Jegar-sahadutha in v. 47, Mizpah in v. 49), and the two references to the covenant meal (vv. 46, 54) suggest that two versions have been fused. One version is the Yahwist source, and another source has been used to supplement it.

**31:44–54** The treaty is a typical covenant between two parties: Jacob was bound to treat his wives (Laban's daughters) well, and Laban was bound not to cross Jacob's boundaries with hostile intent.

**31:47–48 Jegar-sahadutha**: an Aramaic term meaning "mound of witness." **Galeed**: in Hebrew, "the mound of witness."

**31:49 Mizpah**: a town in Gilead; cf. Jgs 10:17; 11:11, 34; Hos 5:1. The Hebrew name *mispa* ("lookout") is allied to *yisep yhwh* ("may the Lord keep watch"), and also echoes the word *masseba* ("sacred pillar").

**31:53 Fear of . . . Isaac**: an archaic title for Jacob's God of the Father.

**32:1–22** Jacob's negotiations with Esau. Laban kisses his daughters and grandchildren good-bye but not Jacob. On leaving Mesopotamia, Jacob has an encounter with angels of God (vv. 2–3), which provokes him to exclaim, "This is God's encampment," just as he exclaimed upon leaving Canaan, "This is the house of God, the gateway to heaven" (28:11–17).

**32:3 Mahanaim**: a town in Gilead (Jos 13:26, 30; 21:38; 2 Sm 2:8; etc.). The Hebrew name means "two camps." There are other allusions to the name in vv. 8, 11.

*v:* Ex 22:12. *w:* Gn 31:24, 29. *x:* Gn 28:18; 35:14.

### Jacob Prepares to Meet His Brother Esau

RECALL THAT the last words we heard from Esau twenty years before were, "I may kill my brother Jacob" (27:41). Jacob's preparations to meet Esau exhibit great anxiety about whether Esau still carries this threat with him (32:11). Forgiveness can be one of life's major challenges. It is also one of the most powerful and life changing acts, whether between individuals, among groups, or between nations.

the country of Edom,[y] 5 ordering them: "Thus you shall say to my lord Esau: 'Thus says your servant Jacob: I have been residing with Laban and have been delayed until now. 6 I own oxen, donkeys and sheep, as well as male and female servants. I have sent my lord this message in the hope of gaining your favor.' " 7 When the messengers returned to Jacob, they said, "We found your brother Esau. He is now coming to meet you, and four hundred men are with him."

8 Jacob was very much frightened. In his anxiety, he divided the people who were with him, as well as his flocks, herds and camels, into two camps. 9 "If Esau should come and attack one camp," he reasoned, "the remaining camp may still escape." 10 Then Jacob prayed: "God of my father Abraham and God of my father Isaac! You, LORD, who said to me, 'Go back to your land and your relatives, and I will be good to you.'[z] 11 I am unworthy of all the acts of kindness and faithfulness that you have performed for your servant: although I crossed the Jordan here with nothing but my staff, I have now grown into two camps. 12 Save me from the hand of my brother, from the hand of Esau! Otherwise I fear that he will come and strike me down and the mothers with the children. 13 You yourself said, 'I will be very good to you, and I will make your descendants like the sands of the sea, which are too numerous to count.' "[a]

14 After passing the night there, Jacob selected from what he had with him a present for his brother Esau: 15 two hundred she-goats and twenty he-goats; two hundred ewes and twenty rams; 16 thirty female camels and their young; forty cows and ten bulls; twenty female donkeys and ten male donkeys. 17 He put these animals in the care of his servants, in separate herds, and he told the servants, "Go on ahead of me, but keep some space between the herds." 18 He ordered the servant in the lead, "When my brother Esau meets you and asks, 'To whom do you belong? Where are you going? To whom do these animals ahead of you belong?' 19 tell him, 'To your servant Jacob, but they have been sent as a gift to my lord Esau. Jacob himself is right behind us.' " 20 He also ordered the second servant and the third and all the others who followed behind the herds: "Thus and so you shall say to Esau, when you reach him; 21 and also tell him, 'Your servant Jacob is right behind us.' " For Jacob reasoned, "If I first appease him with a gift that precedes me, then later, when I face him, perhaps he will forgive me." 22 So the gifts went on ahead of him, while he stayed that night in the camp.

***Jacob's New Name.**** 23 That night, however, Jacob arose, took his two wives, with the two maidservants and his eleven children, and crossed the ford of the Jabbok. 24 After he got them and brought them across the wadi and brought over what belonged to him, 25 Jacob was left there alone. Then a

**32:23–33** As Jacob crosses over to the land promised him, worried about the impending meeting with Esau, he encounters a mysterious adversary in the night with whom he wrestles until morning. The cunning Jacob manages to wrest a blessing from the night stranger before he departs. There are folkloric elements in the tale—e.g., the trial of the hero before he can return home, the nocturnal demon's loss of strength at sunrise, the demon protecting its river, the power gained by knowledge of an opponent's name—but these have been worked into a coherent though elliptical narrative. The point of the tale seems to be that the ever-striving, ever-grasping Jacob must eventually strive with God to attain full possession of the blessing.

*y:* Gn 36:6. *z:* Gn 31:3. *a:* Gn 28:14; 48:16; Ex 32:13; Heb 11:12.

man* wrestled with him until the break of
dawn. 26When the man saw that he could not
prevail over him, he struck Jacob's hip at its
socket, so that Jacob's socket was dislocated
as he wrestled with him.[b] 27The man then
said, "Let me go, for it is daybreak." But Jacob said, "I will not let you go until you
bless me." 28"What is your name?" the man
asked. He answered, "Jacob."[c] 29Then the
man said, "You shall no longer be named Jacob, but Israel,* because you have contended
with divine and human beings and have prevailed." 30Jacob then asked him, "Please tell
me your name." He answered, "Why do you
ask for my name?" With that, he blessed
him. 31Jacob named the place Peniel,* "because I have seen God face to face," he said,
"yet my life has been spared."[d]
32At sunrise, as he left Penuel, Jacob
limped along because of his hip. 33That is
why, to this day, the Israelites do not eat the
sciatic muscle that is on the hip socket, because he had struck Jacob's hip socket at the
sciatic muscle.

See RG 59–60

## CHAPTER 33

*Jacob and Esau Meet.** 1Jacob looked
up and saw Esau coming, and with him four
hundred men. So he divided his children
among Leah, Rachel, and the two maidservants, 2putting the maidservants and their
children first, Leah and her children next, and
Rachel and Joseph last. 3He himself went on
ahead of them, bowing to the ground seven
times, until he reached his brother. 4Esau ran
to meet him, embraced him, and flinging himself on his neck, kissed him as he wept.
5Then Esau looked up and saw the women
and children and asked, "Who are these with
you?" Jacob answered, "They are the children
with whom God has graciously favored your
servant." 6Then the maidservants and their
children came forward and bowed low; 7next,
Leah and her children came forward and
bowed low; lastly, Joseph and Rachel came
forward and bowed low. 8Then Esau asked,
"What did you intend with all those herds that
I encountered?" Jacob answered, "It was to
gain my lord's favor." 9Esau replied, "I have
plenty; my brother, you should keep what is
yours." 10"No, I beg you!" said Jacob. "If you
will do me the favor, accept this gift from me,
since to see your face is for me like seeing the
face of God—and you have received me so
kindly. 11Accept the gift I have brought you.
For God has been generous toward me, and I
have an abundance." Since he urged him
strongly, Esau accepted.
12Then Esau said, "Let us break camp and
be on our way; I will travel in front of you."
13But Jacob replied: "As my lord knows, the
children are too young. And the flocks and
herds that are nursing are a concern to me; if
overdriven for even a single day, the whole
flock will die. 14Let my lord, then, go before
his servant, while I proceed more slowly at
the pace of the livestock before me and at the
pace of my children, until I join my lord in
Seir." 15Esau replied, "Let me at least put at
your disposal some of the people who are
with me." But Jacob said, "Why is this that I
am treated so kindly, my lord?" 16So on that
day Esau went on his way back to Seir, 17and
Jacob broke camp for Succoth.* There Jacob

**32:25 A man**: as with Abraham's three visitors in chap. 18, who appear sometimes as three, two, and one (the latter being God), this figure is fluid; he loses the match but changes Jacob's name (v. 29), an act elsewhere done only by God (17:5, 15). A few deft narrative touches manage to express intimate contact with Jacob while preserving the transcendence proper to divinity.

**32:29 Israel**: the first part of the Hebrew name *Yisrael* is given a popular explanation in the word *saritha*, "you contended"; the second part is the first syllable of *'elohim*, "divine beings." The present incident, with a similar allusion to the name Israel, is referred to in Hos 12:5, where the mysterious wrestler is explicitly called an angel.

**32:31 Peniel**: a variant of the word Penuel (v. 32), the name of a town on the north bank of the Jabbok in Gilead (Jgs 8:8–9, 17; 1 Kgs 12:25). The name is explained as meaning "the face of God," *peni-'el*. **Yet my life has been spared**: see note on 16:13.

**33:1–20** The truly frightening confrontation seems to have already occurred in Jacob's meeting the divine stranger in the previous chapter. In contrast, this meeting brings reconciliation. Esau, impulsive but largehearted, kisses the cunning Jacob and calls him brother (v. 9). Jacob in return asks Esau to accept his blessing (*berakah*, translated "gift," v. 11), giving back at least symbolically what he had taken many years before and responding to Esau's erstwhile complaint ("he has taken away my blessing," 27:36). Verses 12–17 show that the reconciliation is not total and, further, that Jacob does not intend to share the ancestral land with his brother.

**33:17 Succoth**: an important town near the confluence of

*b*: Hos 12:5. *c*: Gn 35:10; 1 Kgs 18:31; 2 Kgs 17:34. *d*: Jgs 13:22.

built a home for himself and made booths
for his livestock. That is why the place was
named Succoth.
[18]Jacob arrived safely at the city of Shechem, which is in the land of Canaan, when
he came from Paddan-aram. He encamped
in sight of the city.[e] [19]The plot of ground on
which he had pitched his tent he bought for
a hundred pieces of money* from the descendants of Hamor, the father of Shechem.[f]
[20]He set up an altar there and invoked "El,
the God of Israel."[g]

See RG 59–60

## CHAPTER 34

*The Rape of Dinah.* [1]* Dinah, the
daughter whom Leah had borne to Jacob,
went out to visit some of the women of the
land. [2]When Shechem, son of Hamor the Hivite,* the leader of the region, saw her, he
seized her and lay with her by force. [3]He was
strongly attracted to Dinah, daughter of Jacob, and was in love with the young woman.
So he spoke affectionately to her. [4]Shechem
said to his father Hamor, "Get me this young
woman for a wife."
[5]Meanwhile, Jacob heard that Shechem
had defiled his daughter Dinah; but since his
sons were out in the field with his livestock,
Jacob kept quiet until they came home.
[6]Now Hamor, the father of Shechem, went
out to discuss the matter with Jacob, [7]just as
Jacob's sons were coming in from the field.
When they heard the news, the men were indignant and extremely angry. Shechem had
committed an outrage in Israel by lying with
Jacob's daughter; such a thing is not done.[h]
[8]Hamor appealed to them, saying: "My son
Shechem has his heart set on your daughter.
Please give her to him as a wife. [9]Intermarry
with us; give your daughters to us, and take
our daughters for yourselves. [10]Thus you
can live among us. The land is open before
you. Settle and move about freely in it and
acquire holdings here."* [11]Then Shechem
appealed to Dinah's father and brothers: "Do
me this favor, and whatever you ask from
me, I will give. [12]No matter how high you
set the bridal price and gift, I will give you
whatever you ask from me; only give me the
young woman as a wife."
*Revenge of Jacob's Sons.* [13]Jacob's sons
replied to Shechem and his father Hamor
with guile, speaking as they did because he
had defiled their sister Dinah. [14]They said to
them, "We are not able to do this thing: to
give our sister to an uncircumcised man. For
that would be a disgrace for us. [15]Only on
this condition will we agree to that: that you
become like us by having every male among
you circumcised. [16]Then we will give you
our daughters and take your daughters in
marriage; we will settle among you and become one people. [17]But if you do not listen
to us and be circumcised, we will take our
daughter and go."
[18]Their proposal pleased Hamor and his
son Shechem. [19]The young man lost no time
in acting on the proposal, since he wanted
Jacob's daughter. Now he was more highly
regarded than anyone else in his father's
house. [20]So Hamor and his son Shechem
went to the gate of their city and said to the
men of their city: [21]"These men are friendly
toward us. Let them settle in the land and
move about in it freely; there is ample room
in the land for them. We can take their
daughters in marriage and give our daughters to them. [22]But only on this condition

the Jabbok and the Jordan (Jos 13:27; Jgs 8:5–16; 1 Kgs 7:46). **Booths**: in Hebrew, *sukkot*, of the same sound as the name of the town.

**33:19 Pieces of money**: in Hebrew, *qesita*, a monetary unit of which the value is unknown. **Descendants of Hamor**: Hamorites, "the people of Hamor"; cf. Jgs 9:28. Hamor was regarded as the eponymous ancestor of the pre-Israelite inhabitants of Shechem.

**34:1–31** The story of the rape of Dinah and the revenge of Jacob's sons on the men of the city of Shechem may reflect the relations of the tribes of Simeon and Levi to their Canaanite neighbors around Shechem; the tribes are represented by their eponymous ancestors. Jacob's farewell testament (49:5–7) cites this incident as the reason for the decline of the tribes of Simeon and Levi. Ominously, vv. 30–31 leave the situation unresolved, with Jacob concerned about the welfare of the whole family, and Simeon and Levi concerned only about the honor of their full sister. The danger to the family from narrow self-interest will continue in the Joseph story.

**34:2 Hivite**: the Greek text has "Horite"; the terms were apparently used indiscriminately to designate the Hurrian or other non-Semitic elements in Palestine.

**34:10** Hamor seems to be making concessions to Jacob's family in the hope of avoiding warfare between the two families.

*e:* Gn 12:6; Jn 4:5. *f:* Jos 24:32; Jn 4:5; Acts 7:16. *g:* Jgs 6:24. *h:* 2 Sm 13:12.

will the men agree to live with us and form one people with us: that every male among us be circumcised as they themselves are. 23 Would not their livestock, their property, and all their animals then be ours? Let us just agree with them, so that they will settle among us."

24 All who went out of the gate of the city listened to Hamor and his son Shechem, and all the males, all those who went out of the gate of the city,* were circumcised. 25 On the third day, while they were still in pain, two of Jacob's sons, Simeon and Levi, brothers of Dinah, each took his sword, advanced against the unsuspecting city and massacred all the males.[i] 26 After they had killed Hamor and his son Shechem with the sword, they took Dinah from Shechem's house and left.[j] 27 Then the other sons of Jacob followed up the slaughter and sacked the city because their sister had been defiled. 28 They took their sheep, cattle and donkeys, whatever was in the city and in the surrounding country. 29 They carried off all their wealth, their children, and their women, and looted whatever was in the houses.[k]

30 Jacob said to Simeon and Levi: "You have brought trouble upon me by making me repugnant to the inhabitants of the land, the Canaanites and the Perizzites. I have so few men that, if these people unite against me and attack me, I and my household will be wiped out." 31 But they retorted, "Should our sister be treated like a prostitute?"

See RG 59-60

## CHAPTER 35

***Bethel Revisited.*** 1* God said to Jacob: Go up now to Bethel. Settle there and build an altar there to the God who appeared to you when you were fleeing from your brother Esau.[l] 2 So Jacob told his household and all who were with him: "Get rid of the foreign gods* among you; then purify yourselves and change your clothes. 3 Let us now go up to Bethel so that I might build an altar there to the God who answered me in the day of my distress and who has been with me wherever I have gone." 4 They gave Jacob all the foreign gods in their possession and also the rings they had in their ears* and Jacob buried them under the oak that is near Shechem. 5 Then, as they set out, a great terror fell upon the surrounding towns, so that no one pursued the sons of Jacob.

6 Thus Jacob and all the people who were with him arrived in Luz (now Bethel) in the land of Canaan.[m] 7 There he built an altar and called the place El-Bethel,* for it was there that God had revealed himself to him when he was fleeing from his brother.[n] 8 Deborah, Rebekah's nurse, died. She was buried under the oak below Bethel, and so it was named Allon-bacuth.*

9 On Jacob's arrival from Paddan-aram, God appeared to him again and blessed him. 10 God said to him:

Your name is Jacob.
You will no longer be named Jacob,
  but Israel will be your name.[o]

So he was named Israel. 11 Then God said to him: I am God Almighty; be fruitful and multiply. A nation, indeed an assembly of nations, will stem from you, and kings will issue from your loins. 12 The land I gave to Abraham and Isaac I will give to you; and to your descendants after you I will give the land.[p]

**34:24 All those who went out of the gate of the city**: apparently meaning all the residents. By temporarily crippling the men through circumcision, Jacob's sons deprived the city of its defenders.

**35:1–7** Jacob returns to Bethel and founds the sanctuary, an event that forms a "bookend" to the first visit to Bethel in 28:10–22. To enter the Lord's sanctuary, one must purify oneself and get rid of all signs of allegiance to other gods (Jos 24:23; Jgs 10:16). Jacob also seems to initiate the custom of making a pilgrimage to Bethel (see Ps 122:1 and Is 2:3, 5).

**35:2 Foreign gods**: divine images, including those of household deities (see note on 31:19), that Jacob's people brought with them from Paddan-aram.

**35:4 Rings . . . their ears**: the earrings may have belonged to the gods because earrings were often placed on statues.

**35:7 El-Bethel**: probably to be translated "the god of Bethel." This is one of several titles of God in Genesis that begin with *El* (= God), e.g., *El Olam* (21:33), *El Elyon* (14:18), *El* the God of Israel (33:20), *El Roi* (16:13), and *El Shaddai*. Most of these (except *El Shaddai*) are tied to specific Israelite shrines.

**35:8 Allon-bacuth**: the Hebrew name means "oak of weeping."

*i:* Gn 49:6. *j:* Jdt 9:2. *k:* Jdt 9:3–4. *l:* Gn 28:12–13. *m:* Gn 28:19; Jos 18:13; Jgs 1:22–23. *n:* Gn 28:12–13. *o:* 1 Kgs 18:31; 2 Kgs 17:34. *p:* Ex 32:13; Heb 11:9.

[13]Then God departed from him. [14]In the place where God had spoken with him, Jacob set up a sacred pillar, a stone pillar, and upon it he made a libation and poured out oil.[q] [15]Jacob named the place where God spoke to him Bethel.

***Jacob's Family.*** [16]Then they departed from Bethel; but while they still had some distance to go to Ephrath, Rachel went into labor and suffered great distress. [17]When her labor was most intense, the midwife said to her, "Do not fear, for now you have another son." [18]With her last breath—for she was at the point of death—she named him Ben-oni;* but his father named him Benjamin. [19]Thus Rachel died; and she was buried on the road to Ephrath (now Bethlehem).*[r] [20]Jacob set up a sacred pillar on her grave, and the same pillar marks Rachel's grave to this day.

[21]Israel moved on and pitched his tent beyond Migdal-eder. [22]While Israel was encamped in that region, Reuben went and lay with Bilhah, his father's concubine. When Israel heard of it, he was greatly offended.*[s]

The sons of Jacob were now twelve. [23]The sons of Leah: Reuben, Jacob's firstborn, Simeon, Levi, Judah, Issachar, and Zebulun; [24]* the sons of Rachel: Joseph and Benjamin; [25]the sons of Rachel's maidservant Bilhah: Dan and Naphtali; [26]the sons of Leah's maidservant Zilpah: Gad and Asher. These are the sons of Jacob who were born to him in Paddan-aram.

[27]Jacob went home to his father Isaac at Mamre, in Kiriath-arba (now Hebron), where Abraham and Isaac had resided. [28]The length of Isaac's life was one hundred and eighty years; [29]then he breathed his last. He died as an old man and was gathered to his people. After a full life, his sons Esau and Jacob buried him.

## CHAPTER 36

See RG 59–60

***Edomite Lists.**** [1]These are the descendants of Esau (that is, Edom). [2]* Esau took his wives from among the Canaanite women: Adah, daughter of Elon the Hittite; Oholibamah, the daughter of Anah the son of Zibeon the Hivite;[t] [3]and Basemath, daughter of Ishmael and sister of Nebaioth. [4]Adah bore Eliphaz to Esau; Basemath bore Reuel;[u] [5]and Oholibamah bore Jeush, Jalam and Korah. These are the sons of Esau who were born to him in the land of Canaan.[v]

[6]Esau took his wives, his sons, his daughters, and all the members of his household, as well as his livestock, all his cattle, and all the property he had acquired in the land of Canaan, and went to the land of Seir, away from his brother Jacob.[w] [7]Their possessions had become too great for them to dwell together, and the land in which they were residing could not support them because of their livestock. [8]So Esau settled in the highlands of Seir. (Esau is Edom.)[x] [9]These are

**35:18 Ben-oni**: means either "son of my vigor" or, more likely in the context, "son of affliction." **Benjamin**: "son of the right hand," meaning a son who is his father's help and support.

**35:19 Bethlehem**: the gloss comes from a later tradition that identified the site with Bethlehem, also called Ephrath or Ephratha (Jos 15:59; Ru 4:11; Mi 5:1). But Rachel's grave was actually near Ramah (Jer 31:15), a few miles north of Jerusalem, in the territory of Benjamin (1 Sm 10:2).

**35:22** The genealogy in vv. 23–29 is prefaced by a notice about Reuben's sleeping with Bilhah, his father's concubine. Such an act is a serious challenge to the authority of the father (cf. 2 Sm 3:7 and 16:21). In his final testament in chap. 49, Jacob cites this act of Reuben as the reason for Reuben's loss of the authority he had as firstborn son (49:4). Reuben's act is one more instance of strife in the family and of discord between father and son.

**35:24–26** Benjamin is here said to have been born in Paddan-aram, apparently because all twelve sons of Jacob are considered as a unit.

**36:1–43** The line of Esau. In the preceding chapter (35:22–26), the list of Jacob's children completes the narrative of Jacob; in this chapter, the narrative of Esau is complete when his descendants are listed. The notice of Abraham's death and burial in 25:7–10 was followed by a list of the line of his elder son Ishmael (25:12–18) and here Isaac's death and burial are followed by the line of Esau. The lines of both Ishmael and Esau are introduced by the same double formula, "These are the descendants of . . ." (25:12; 36:9) and "These are the names of the sons of . . ." (25:13; 36:10). The chapter consists of diverse material: vv. 1–3, Esau's wives; vv. 9–14, Esau's descendants; vv. 15–19, the clans of Esau; vv. 20–30, the Horites of Seir; vv. 31–39, the Edomite kings; vv. 40–43, the Edomites.

**36:2–14** The names of Esau's wives and of their fathers given here differ considerably from their names cited from other old sources in 26:34 and 28:9. **Zibeon the Hivite**: in v. 20 he is called a "Horite"; see note on 34:2.

*q:* Gn 28:18; 31:45. *r:* Gn 48:7; 1 Sm 10:2; Mi 5:1. *s:* Gn 49:4; 1 Chr 5:1. *t:* Gn 26:34. *u:* 1 Chr 1:35. *v:* 1 Chr 1:35. *w:* Gn 32:4. *x:* Dt 2:4–5; Jos 24:4.

the descendants of Esau,* ancestor of the Edomites, in the highlands of Seir.

10 These are the names of the sons of Esau: Eliphaz, son of Adah, wife of Esau, and Reuel, son of Basemath, wife of Esau. 11[y] The sons of Eliphaz were Teman, Omar, Zepho, Gatam, and Kenaz. 12 Timna was a concubine of Eliphaz, the son of Esau, and she bore Amalek to Eliphaz. Those were the sons of Adah, the wife of Esau. 13 These were the sons of Reuel: Nahath, Zerah, Shammah, and Mizzah. Those were the sons of Basemath, the wife of Esau.[z] 14 These were the sons of Esau's wife Oholibamah—the daughter of Anah, son of Zibeon—whom she bore to Esau: Jeush, Jalam, and Korah.[a]

15 These are the clans of the sons of Esau. The sons of Eliphaz, Esau's firstborn: the clans of Teman, Omar, Zepho, Kenaz, 16 Korah, Gatam, and Amalek. These are the clans of Eliphaz in the land of Edom; they are the sons of Adah. 17 These are the sons of Reuel, son of Esau: the clans of Nahath, Zerah, Shammah, and Mizzah. These are the clans of Reuel in the land of Edom; they are the sons of Basemath, wife of Esau. 18 These were the sons of Oholibamah, wife of Esau: the clans of Jeush, Jalam, and Korah. These are the clans of Esau's wife Oholibamah, daughter of Anah. 19 These are the sons of Esau—that is, Edom—according to their clans.

20 These are the sons of Seir the Horite,* the inhabitants of the land: Lotan, Shobal, Zibeon, Anah,[b] 21 Dishon, Ezer, and Dishan; those are the clans of the Horites, sons of Seir in the land of Edom. 22[c] The sons of Lotan were Hori and Hemam, and Lotan's sister was Timna. 23 These are the sons of Shobal: Alvan, Mahanath, Ebal, Shepho, and Onam. 24 These are the sons of Zibeon: Aiah and Anah. He is the Anah who found water in the desert while he was pasturing the donkeys of his father Zibeon. 25 These are the children of Anah: Dishon and Oholibamah, daughter of Anah. 26 These are the sons of Dishon: Hemdan, Eshban, Ithran, and Cheran. 27 These are the sons of Ezer: Bilhan, Zaavan, and Akan. 28 These are the sons of Dishan: Uz and Aran. 29 These are the clans of the Horites: the clans of Lotan, Shobal, Zibeon, Anah, 30 Dishon, Ezer, and Dishan; those are the clans of the Horites, clan by clan, in the land of Seir.

31[d] These are the kings who reigned in the land of Edom before any king reigned over the Israelites.* 32 Bela, son of Beor, became king in Edom; the name of his city was Dinhabah. 33 When Bela died, Jobab, son of Zerah, from Bozrah, succeeded him as king. 34 When Jobab died, Husham, from the land of the Temanites, succeeded him as king. 35 When Husham died, Hadad, son of Bedad, succeeded him as king. He is the one who defeated Midian in the country of Moab; the name of his city was Avith. 36 When Hadad died, Samlah, from Masrekah, succeeded him as king. 37 When Samlah died, Shaul, from Rehoboth-on-the-River, succeeded him as king. 38 When Shaul died, Baal-hanan, son of Achbor, succeeded him as king. 39 When Baal-hanan, son of Achbor, died, Hadad succeeded him as king; the name of his city was Pau. His wife's name was Mehetabel, the daughter of Matred, son of Mezahab.

40 These are the names of the clans of Esau identified according to their families and localities: the clans of Timna, Alvah, Jetheth, 41 Oholibamah, Elah, Pinon, 42 Kenaz, Teman, Mibzar, 43 Magdiel, and Iram. Those are the clans of the Edomites, according to their settlements in their territorial holdings—that is, of Esau, the ancestor of the Edomites.

**36:9 These are the descendants of Esau**: the original heading of the genealogy is preserved in v. 10 ("These are the names of the sons of Esau"). This use of the Priestly formula is secondary and should not be counted in the list of ten such formulas in Genesis.

**36:20 Seir the Horite**: according to Dt 2:12, the highlands of Seir were inhabited by Horites before they were occupied by the Edomites.

**36:31 Before any king reigned over the Israelites**: obviously this statement was written after the time of Saul, Israel's first king. According to 1 Sm 14:47, Saul waged war against the Edomites; according to 2 Sm 8:2, 13–14 and 1 Kgs 11:14–17, David made Edom a vassal state and nearly wiped out the royal line. These events reflect the words of the Lord to Rebekah at the birth of the boys, "the older shall serve the younger" (25:23).

*y:* 1 Chr 1:36. *z:* 1 Chr 1:37. *a:* 1 Chr 1:35. *b:* 1 Chr 1:38. *c:* 1 Chr 1:39–42. *d:* 1 Chr 1:43–54.

See RC 60-61

## CHAPTER 37

***Joseph Sold into Egypt.*** 1 Jacob settled
in the land where his father had sojourned,
the land of Canaan.* 2 This is the story of the
family of Jacob.* When Joseph was seventeen years old, he was tending the flocks
with his brothers; he was an assistant to the
sons of his father's wives Bilhah and Zilpah,
and Joseph brought their father bad reports
about them. 3 Israel loved Joseph best of all
his sons, for he was the child of his old age;
and he had made him a long ornamented tunic.* 4 When his brothers saw that their father
loved him best of all his brothers, they hated
him so much that they could not say a kind
word to him.

5* Once Joseph had a dream, and when he
told his brothers, they hated him even more.[e]
6 He said to them, "Listen to this dream I had.
7 There we were, binding sheaves in the field,
when suddenly my sheaf rose to an upright
position, and your sheaves formed a ring
around my sheaf and bowed down to it." 8 His
brothers said to him, "Are you really going to
make yourself king over us? Will you rule
over us?" So they hated him all the more because of his dreams and his reports.[f]

9 Then he had another dream, and told it to
his brothers. "Look, I had another dream,"
he said; "this time, the sun and the moon and
eleven stars were bowing down to me."
10 When he told it to his father and his brothers, his father reproved him and asked,
"What is the meaning of this dream of
yours? Can it be that I and your mother and
your brothers are to come and bow to the
ground before you?" 11 So his brothers were
furious at him but his father kept the matter
in mind.

12 One day, when his brothers had gone to
pasture their father's flocks at Shechem,
13 Israel said to Joseph, "Are your brothers
not tending our flocks at Shechem? Come
and I will send you to them." "I am ready,"
Joseph answered. 14 "Go then," he replied;
"see if all is well with your brothers and the
flocks, and bring back word." So he sent him
off from the valley of Hebron. When Joseph
reached Shechem, 15 a man came upon him
as he was wandering about in the fields.
"What are you looking for?" the man asked
him. 16 "I am looking for my brothers," he
answered. "Please tell me where they are
tending the flocks." 17 The man told him,
"They have moved on from here; in fact, I
heard them say, 'Let us go on to Dothan.' "
So Joseph went after his brothers and found
them in Dothan. 18 They saw him from a distance, and before he reached them, they plotted to kill him. 19 They said to one another:
"Here comes that dreamer! 20 Come now, let
us kill him and throw him into one of the cisterns here; we could say that a wild beast devoured him. We will see then what comes of
his dreams."[g]

**37:1** The statement points ahead to 47:27, "Thus Israel settled in the land of Egypt, in the region of Goshen." These two statements frame the Joseph narrative; the later material (47:28–49:33) is about Jacob; chap. 50 brings to a conclusion themes remaining from the earlier story. One aim of the Joseph story is to explain how Israel came to Egypt after sojourning so long in Canaan.

**37:2** The Joseph story is great literature not only in its themes but in its art. The stories show an interest in the psychology of the characters; everyone acts "in character" yet there is never a doubt that a divine purpose is bringing events to their conclusion. According to a literary analysis, vv. 1–4 set the scene; vv. 5–36 introduce the dramatic tension in the form of a conflict within the family; chaps. 38–41 describe the journeys away from their family of the eponymous ancestors of the two great tribes of later times, Judah (chap. 38) and Joseph (chaps. 39–41) and their preliminary conclusions; chaps. 42–44 detail the famine and journeys for food (chaps. 42, 43) that bring the brothers and (indirectly) the father into fresh contact with a mature Joseph who now has the power of life and death over them; 45:1–47:27 is the resolution (reconciliation of Joseph to his brothers) and the salvation of the family.

**37:3** Jacob's favoring Joseph over his other sons is a cause of the brothers' attempt on his life. Throughout the story, Jacob is unaware of the impact of his favoritism on his other sons (cf. vv. 33–35; 42:36). **Long ornamented tunic**: the meaning of the Hebrew phrase is unclear. In 2 Sm 13:18–19, it is the distinctive dress of unmarried royal daughters. The "coat of many colors" in the Septuagint became the traditional translation. Ancient depictions of Semites in formal dress show them with long, ornamented robes and that is the most likely meaning here. Possibly, the young Joseph is given a coat that symbolizes honor beyond his years. Later, Pharaoh will clothe Joseph in a robe that symbolizes honor (41:42).

**37:5–10** Joseph's dreams of ruling his brothers appear at first glance to be merely adolescent grandiosity, and they bring him only trouble. His later successes make it clear, however, that they were from God. Another confirmation of their divine source is the doubling of dreams (cf. 41:32).

*e:* Gn 42:9. *f:* Gn 50:17–18. *g:* Gn 44:28.

21* But when Reuben heard this, he tried
to save him from their hands, saying: "We
must not take his life." 22Then Reuben said,
"Do not shed blood! Throw him into this cistern in the wilderness; but do not lay a hand
on him." His purpose was to save him from
their hands and restore him to his father.[h]
23So when Joseph came up to his brothers,
they stripped him of his tunic, the long ornamented tunic he had on; 24then they took him
and threw him into the cistern. The cistern
was empty; there was no water in it.
25Then they sat down to eat. Looking up,
they saw a caravan of Ishmaelites coming
from Gilead, their camels laden with gum,
balm, and resin to be taken down to Egypt.[i]
26Judah said to his brothers: "What is to be
gained by killing our brother and concealing
his blood?[j] 27Come, let us sell him to these
Ishmaelites, instead of doing away with him
ourselves. After all, he is our brother, our
own flesh." His brothers agreed.
28Midianite traders passed by, and they
pulled Joseph up out of the cistern. They
sold Joseph for twenty pieces of silver* to
the Ishmaelites, who took him to Egypt.[k]
29When Reuben went back to the cistern and
saw that Joseph was not in it, he tore his garments,* 30and returning to his brothers, he
exclaimed: "The boy is gone! And I—where
can I turn?" 31They took Joseph's tunic, and
after slaughtering a goat, dipped the tunic in
its blood. 32Then they sent someone to bring
the long ornamented tunic to their father,
with the message: "We found this. See
whether it is your son's tunic or not." 33He
recognized it and exclaimed: "My son's tunic! A wild beast has devoured him! Joseph
has been torn to pieces!"[l] 34Then Jacob tore
his garments, put sackcloth on his loins, and
mourned his son many days. 35Though his
sons and daughters tried to console him, he
refused all consolation, saying, "No, I will
go down mourning to my son in Sheol."*
Thus did his father weep for him.[m]
36The Midianites, meanwhile, sold Joseph
in Egypt to Potiphar, an official of Pharaoh
and his chief steward.[n]

## CHAPTER 38

See RG 60-61

***Judah and Tamar.**** 1About that time
Judah went down, away from his brothers,
and pitched his tent near a certain Adullamite named Hirah. 2There Judah saw the
daughter of a Canaanite named Shua; he
married her, and had intercourse with her.[o]
3She conceived and bore a son, whom she
named Er. 4Again she conceived and bore a
son, whom she named Onan. 5Then she bore
still another son, whom she named Shelah.
She was in Chezib* when she bore him.[p]
6Judah got a wife named Tamar for his

**37:21–36** The chapter thus far is from the Yahwist source, as are also vv. 25–28a. But vv. 21–24 and 28b–36 are from another source (sometimes designated the Elohist source). In the latter, Reuben tries to rescue Joseph, who is taken in Reuben's absence by certain Midianites; in the Yahwist source, it is Judah who saves Joseph's life by having him sold to certain Ishmaelites. Although the two variant forms in which the story was handed down in early oral tradition differ in these minor points, they agree on the essential fact that Joseph was brought as a slave into Egypt because of the jealousy of his brothers.

**37:28 They sold Joseph . . . silver**: editors tried to solve the confusion, created by different sources, by supposing that it was the Midianite traders who pulled Joseph out of the pit and sold him to Ishmaelites. In all probability, one source had the brothers selling Joseph to Ishmaelites, whereas the other had them cast him into the pit whence he was taken by Midianite traders.

**37:29 Tore his garments**: the traditional sign of mourning in the ancient Near East.

**37:35 Sheol**: see note on Ps 6:6.

**38:1–30** This chapter has subtle connections to the main Joseph story. It tells of the eponymous founder of the other great tribe of later times, Judah. Having already been introduced as one of the two good brothers in 37:26–27, he appears here as the father-in-law of the twice-widowed Tamar; he has reneged on his promise to provide his son Shelah to her in a levirate marriage. Unjustly treated, Tamar takes matters into her own hands and tricks Judah into becoming the father of her children, Perez and Zerah. Judah ultimately acknowledges that his daughter-in-law was right ("She is in the right rather than I," v. 26). In contrast to Judah's expectations, the family line does not continue through his son Shelah, but through the children of Tamar. Similarities relate this little story to the main narrative: the deception involving an article of clothing (the widow's garments of Tamar, Judah's seal, cord, and staff) point back to the bloody tunic that deceives Jacob in 37:31–33; a woman attempts the seduction of a man separated from his family, for righteous purposes in chap. 38, for unrighteous purposes in chap. 39.

**38:5 Chezib**: a variant form of Achzib (Jos 15:44; Mi 1:14), a town in the Judean Shephelah.

*h:* Gn 42:22. *i:* Gn 43:11. *j:* Jb 16:18. *k:* Ps 105:17; Wis 10:13; Acts 7:9. *l:* Gn 44:28. *m:* Gn 42:38. *n:* Ps 105:17. *o:* 1 Chr 2:3. *p:* 1 Chr 4:21.

firstborn, Er. [7]But Er, Judah's firstborn, greatly offended the LORD; so the LORD took his life.[q] [8r] Then Judah said to Onan, "Have intercourse with your brother's wife, in fulfillment of your duty as brother-in-law, and thus preserve your brother's line."* [9]Onan, however, knew that the offspring would not be his; so whenever he had intercourse with his brother's wife, he wasted his seed on the ground, to avoid giving offspring to his brother. [10]What he did greatly offended the LORD, and the LORD took his life too. [11]Then Judah said to his daughter-in-law Tamar, "Remain a widow in your father's house until my son Shelah grows up"—for he feared that Shelah also might die like his brothers. So Tamar went to live in her father's house.

[12]Time passed, and the daughter of Shua, Judah's wife, died. After Judah completed the period of mourning, he went up to Timnah, to those who were shearing his sheep, in company with his friend Hirah the Adullamite. [13]Then Tamar was told, "Your father-in-law is on his way up to Timnah to shear his sheep." [14]So she took off her widow's garments, covered herself with a shawl, and having wrapped herself sat down at the entrance to Enaim, which is on the way to Timnah; for she was aware that, although Shelah was now grown up, she had not been given to him in marriage.[s] [15]When Judah saw her, he thought she was a harlot, since she had covered her face. [16]So he went over to her at the roadside and said, "Come, let me have intercourse with you," for he did not realize that she was his daughter-in-law. She replied, "What will you pay me for letting you have intercourse with me?" [17]He answered, "I will send you a young goat from the flock." "Very well," she said, "provided you leave me a pledge until you send it." [18]Judah asked, "What pledge should I leave you?" She answered, "Your seal and cord,* and the staff in your hand." So he gave them to her and had intercourse with her, and she conceived by him. [19]After she got up and went away, she took off her shawl and put on her widow's garments again.

[20]Judah sent the young goat by his friend the Adullamite to recover the pledge from the woman; but he did not find her. [21]So he asked the men of that place, "Where is the prostitute,* the one by the roadside in Enaim?" But they answered, "No prostitute has been here." [22]He went back to Judah and told him, "I did not find her; and besides, the men of the place said, 'No prostitute has been here.' " [23]"Let her keep the things," Judah replied; "otherwise we will become a laughingstock. After all, I did send her this young goat, but you did not find her."

[24]About three months later, Judah was told, "Your daughter-in-law Tamar has acted like a harlot and now she is pregnant from her harlotry." Judah said, "Bring her out; let her be burned." [25]But as she was being brought out, she sent word to her father-in-law, "It is by the man to whom these things belong that I am pregnant." Then she said, "See whose seal and cord and staff these are." [26]Judah recognized them and said, "She is in the right rather than I, since I did not give her to my son Shelah." He had no further sexual relations with her.

[27]When the time of her delivery came, there were twins in her womb.[t] [28]While she was giving birth, one put out his hand; and the midwife took and tied a crimson thread on his hand, noting, "This one came out first." [29u] But as he withdrew his hand, his brother came out; and she said, "What a breach you have made for yourself!" So he was called Perez.* [30]Afterward his brother,

**38:8 Preserve your brother's line**: lit., "raise up seed for your brother": an allusion to the law of levirate, or "brother-in-law," marriage; see notes on Dt 25:5; Ru 2:20. Onan's violation of this law brought on him God's punishment (vv. 9–10).

**38:18 Seal and cord**: the cylinder seal, through which a hole was bored lengthwise so that it could be worn from the neck by a cord, was a distinctive means of identification. Apparently one's staff could also be marked with some sign of identification (cf. Nm 17:17–18).

**38:21 Prostitute**: the Hebrew term *qedesha*, lit., "consecrated woman," designates a woman associated with a sanctuary whose activities could include prostitution; cf. Dt 23:18; Hos 4:14, where the same Hebrew word is used. In 38:15 and 24 the common word for prostitute, *zona*, is used.

**38:29 He was called Perez**: the Hebrew word means "breach."

*q:* 1 Chr 2:3. *r:* Dt 25:5; Mt 22:24; Mk 12:19; Lk 20:28. *s:* Prv 7:10. *t:* 1 Chr 2:4. *u:* Ru 4:12; Mt 1:3; Lk 3:33.

who had the crimson thread on his hand, came out; he was called Zerah.*[v]

## CHAPTER 39

See RG 60-61

***Joseph's Temptation.*** [1]When Joseph was taken down to Egypt, an Egyptian, Potiphar, an official of Pharaoh and his chief steward, bought him from the Ishmaelites who had brought him there. [2][w]The LORD was with Joseph and he enjoyed great success and was assigned to the household of his Egyptian master. [3]When his master saw that the LORD was with him and brought him success in whatever he did, [4]he favored Joseph and made him his personal attendant; he put him in charge of his household and entrusted to him all his possessions.[x] [5]From the moment that he put him in charge of his household and all his possessions, the LORD blessed the Egyptian's house for Joseph's sake; the LORD's blessing was on everything he owned, both inside the house and out. [6]Having left everything he owned in Joseph's charge, he gave no thought, with Joseph there, to anything but the food he ate.

Now Joseph was well-built and handsome. [7]After a time, his master's wife looked at him with longing and said, "Lie with me." [8]But he refused and said to his master's wife, "Look, as long as I am here, my master does not give a thought to anything in the house, but has entrusted to me all he owns. [9]He has no more authority in this house than I do. He has withheld from me nothing but you, since you are his wife. How, then, could I do this great wrong and sin against God?" [10]Although she spoke to him day after day, he would not agree to lie with her, or even be near her.[y]

[11]One such day, when Joseph came into the house to do his work, and none of the household servants were then in the house, [12]she laid hold of him by his cloak, saying, "Lie with me!" But leaving the cloak in her hand, he escaped and ran outside. [13]When she saw that he had left his cloak in her hand as he escaped outside, [14]she cried out to her household servants and told them, "Look! My husband has brought us a Hebrew man to mock us! He came in here to lie with me, but I cried out loudly. [15]When he heard me scream, he left his cloak beside me and escaped and ran outside."

[16]She kept the cloak with her until his master came home. [17]Then she told him the same story: "The Hebrew slave whom you brought us came to me to amuse himself at my expense. [18]But when I screamed, he left his cloak beside me and escaped outside." [19]When the master heard his wife's story in which she reported, "Thus and so your servant did to me," he became enraged. [20]Joseph's master seized him and put him into the jail where the king's prisoners were confined.[z] And there he sat, in jail.

[21]But the LORD was with Joseph, and showed him kindness by making the chief jailer well-disposed toward him.[a] [22]The chief jailer put Joseph in charge of all the prisoners in the jail. Everything that had to be done there, he was the one to do it. [23]The chief jailer did not have to look after anything that was in Joseph's charge, since the LORD was with him and was bringing success to whatever he was doing.

## CHAPTER 40

See RG 60-61

***The Dreams Interpreted.*** [1]* Some time afterward, the royal cupbearer and baker offended their lord, the king of Egypt. [2]Pharaoh was angry with his two officials, the chief cupbearer and the chief baker, [3]and he put them in custody in the house of the chief steward, the same jail where Joseph was confined. [4]The chief steward assigned Joseph to them, and he became their attendant.

After they had been in custody for some time, [5]the cupbearer and the baker of the king of Egypt who were confined in the jail both had dreams on the same night, each his

**38:30 He was called Zerah:** a name connected here by popular etymology with a Hebrew word for the red light of dawn, alluding apparently to the crimson thread.

**40:1** Joseph interprets the dreams of the Pharaoh's two officials. His ability to interpret the dreams shows that God is still with him and points forward to his role of dream interpreter for Pharaoh in chap. 41.

*v:* Nm 26:20; 1 Chr 2:4; Mt 1:3. *w:* 1 Sm 3:19; 10:7; 18:14; 2 Sm 5:10; 2 Kgs 18:7; Acts 7:9. *x:* Dn 1:9. *y:* 1 Mc 2:53. *z:* Ps 105:18. *a:* Acts 7:9–10.

own dream and each dream with its own meaning. 6When Joseph came to them in the morning, he saw that they looked disturbed. 7So he asked Pharaoh's officials who were with him in custody in his master's house, "Why do you look so troubled today?" 8They answered him, "We have had dreams, but there is no one to interpret them." Joseph said to them, "Do interpretations not come from God? Please tell me the dreams."[b]

9Then the chief cupbearer told Joseph his dream. "In my dream," he said, "I saw a vine in front of me, 10and on the vine were three branches. It had barely budded when its blossoms came out, and its clusters ripened into grapes. 11Pharaoh's cup was in my hand; so I took the grapes, pressed them out into his cup, and put it in Pharaoh's hand." 12Joseph said to him: "This is its interpretation. The three branches are three days; 13within three days Pharaoh will single you out* and restore you to your post. You will be handing Pharaoh his cup as you formerly did when you were his cupbearer. 14Only think of me when all is well with you, and please do me the great favor of mentioning me to Pharaoh, to get me out of this place. 15The truth is that I was kidnapped from the land of the Hebrews, and I have not done anything here that they should have put me into a dungeon."

16When the chief baker saw that Joseph had given a favorable interpretation, he said to him: "I too had a dream. In it I had three bread baskets on my head; 17in the top one were all kinds of bakery products for Pharaoh, but the birds were eating them out of the basket on my head." 18Joseph said to him in reply: "This is its interpretation. The three baskets are three days; 19within three days Pharaoh will single you out and will impale you on a stake, and the birds will be eating your flesh."

20And so on the third day, which was Pharaoh's birthday, when he gave a banquet to all his servants, he singled out the chief cupbearer and chief baker in the midst of his servants. 21He restored the chief cupbearer to his office, so that he again handed the cup to Pharaoh; 22but the chief baker he impaled—just as Joseph had told them in his interpretation. 23Yet the chief cupbearer did not think of Joseph; he forgot him.

## CHAPTER 41

See RG 60–61

***Pharaoh's Dream.*** 1* After a lapse of two years, Pharaoh had a dream. He was standing by the Nile, 2when up out of the Nile came seven cows, fine-looking and fat; they grazed in the reed grass. 3Behind them seven other cows, poor-looking and gaunt, came up out of the Nile; and standing on the bank of the Nile beside the others, 4the poor-looking, gaunt cows devoured the seven fine-looking, fat cows. Then Pharaoh woke up.

5He fell asleep again and had another dream. He saw seven ears of grain, fat and healthy, growing on a single stalk. 6Behind them sprouted seven ears of grain, thin and scorched by the east wind; 7and the thin ears swallowed up the seven fat, healthy ears. Then Pharaoh woke up—it was a dream!

8Next morning his mind was agitated. So Pharaoh had all the magicians* and sages of Egypt summoned and recounted his dream to them; but there was no one to interpret it for him. 9Then the chief cupbearer said to Pharaoh: "Now I remember my negligence! 10Once, when Pharaoh was angry with his servants, he put me and the chief baker in custody in the house of the chief steward. 11Later, we both had dreams on the same night, and each of our dreams had its own meaning. 12There was a Hebrew youth with us, a slave of the chief steward; and when we told him our dreams, he interpreted them for us and explained for each of us the meaning of his dream.[c] 13Things turned out just as he had told us: I was restored to my post, but the other man was impaled."

**40:13 Single you out**: lit., "lift up your head" (see also vv. 19, 20).

**41:1–57** Joseph correctly interprets Pharaoh's dream and becomes second in command over all Egypt.

**41:8 Magicians**: one of the tasks of the "magicians" was interpreting dreams. The interpretation of dreams was a long-standing practice in Egypt. A manual of dream interpretation has been found, written in the early second millennium and re-published later in which typical dreams are given ("If a man sees himself in a dream . . .") followed by a judgment of "good" or "bad." Interpreters were still needed for dreams, however, and Pharaoh complains that none of his dream interpreters can interpret his unprecedented dream. The same term will be used of Pharaoh's magicians in Exodus.

*b:* Gn 41:16. *c:* Dn 1:17.

[14]Pharaoh therefore had Joseph summoned, and they hurriedly brought him from the dungeon. After he shaved and changed his clothes, he came to Pharaoh.[d] [15]Pharaoh then said to Joseph: "I had a dream but there was no one to interpret it. But I hear it said of you, 'If he hears a dream he can interpret it.' " [16]"It is not I," Joseph replied to Pharaoh, "but God who will respond for the well-being of Pharaoh."[e]

[17]Then Pharaoh said to Joseph: "In my dream, I was standing on the bank of the Nile, [18]when up from the Nile came seven cows, fat and well-formed; they grazed in the reed grass. [19]Behind them came seven other cows, scrawny, most ill-formed and gaunt. Never have I seen such bad specimens as these in all the land of Egypt! [20]The gaunt, bad cows devoured the first seven fat cows. [21]But when they had consumed them, no one could tell that they had done so, because they looked as bad as before. Then I woke up. [22]In another dream I saw seven ears of grain, full and healthy, growing on a single stalk. [23]Behind them sprouted seven ears of grain, shriveled and thin and scorched by the east wind; [24]and the seven thin ears swallowed up the seven healthy ears. I have spoken to the magicians, but there is no one to explain it to me."

[25]Joseph said to Pharaoh: "Pharaoh's dreams have the same meaning. God has made known to Pharaoh what he is about to do. [26]The seven healthy cows are seven years, and the seven healthy ears are seven years—the same in each dream. [27]The seven thin, bad cows that came up after them are seven years, as are the seven thin ears scorched by the east wind; they are seven years of famine. [28]Things are just as I told Pharaoh: God has revealed to Pharaoh what he is about to do. [29]Seven years of great abundance are now coming throughout the land of Egypt; [30]but seven years of famine will rise up after them, when all the abundance will be forgotten in the land of Egypt. When the famine has exhausted the land, [31]no trace of the abundance will be found in the land because of the famine that follows it, for it will be very severe. [32]That Pharaoh had the same dream twice means that the matter has been confirmed by God and that God will soon bring it about.

[33]"Therefore, let Pharaoh seek out a discerning and wise man and put him in charge of the land of Egypt. [34]Let Pharaoh act and appoint overseers for the land to organize it during the seven years of abundance. [35]They should collect all the food of these coming good years, gathering the grain under Pharaoh's authority, for food in the cities, and they should guard it. [36]This food will serve as a reserve for the country against the seven years of famine that will occur in the land of Egypt, so that the land may not perish in the famine."

[37]This advice pleased Pharaoh and all his servants.[f] [38]"Could we find another like him," Pharaoh asked his servants, "a man so endowed with the spirit of God?" [39]So Pharaoh said to Joseph: "Since God has made all this known to you, there is no one as discerning and wise as you are. [40]You shall be in charge of my household, and all my people will obey your command. Only in respect to the throne will I outrank you."[g] [41]Then Pharaoh said to Joseph, "Look, I put you in charge of the whole land of Egypt." [42]With that, Pharaoh took off his signet ring* and put it on Joseph's finger. He dressed him in robes of fine linen and put a gold chain around his neck. [43]He then had him ride in his second chariot, and they shouted "Abrek!"* before him.

Thus was Joseph installed over the whole land of Egypt. [44]"I am Pharaoh," he told Joseph, "but without your approval no one shall lift hand or foot in all the land of Egypt." [45]Pharaoh also bestowed the name of Zaphenath-paneah* on Joseph, and he

**41:42 Signet ring**: a finger ring in which was set a stamp seal, different from the cylinder seal such as Judah wore; see note on 38:18. By receiving Pharaoh's signet ring, Joseph was made vizier of Egypt (v. 43); the vizier was known as "seal-bearer of the king of Lower Egypt." The gold chain was a symbol of high office in ancient Egypt.

**41:43 Abrek**: apparently a cry of homage, though the word's derivation and actual meaning are uncertain.

**41:45 Zaphenath-paneah**: a Hebrew transcription of an

*d:* Ps 105:20. *e:* Gn 40:8. *f:* Acts 7:10. *g:* 1 Mc 2:53; Ps 105:21; Wis 10:14; Acts 7:10.

gave him in marriage Asenath, the daughter of Potiphera, priest of Heliopolis. And Joseph went out over the land of Egypt. 46Joseph was thirty years old when he entered the service of Pharaoh, king of Egypt.

After Joseph left Pharaoh, he went throughout the land of Egypt. 47During the seven years of plenty, when the land produced abundant crops, 48he collected all the food of these years of plenty that the land of Egypt was enjoying and stored it in the cities, placing in each city the crops of the fields around it. 49Joseph collected grain like the sands of the sea, so much that at last he stopped measuring it, for it was beyond measure.

50Before the famine years set in, Joseph became the father of two sons, borne to him by Asenath, daughter of Potiphera, priest of Heliopolis.[h] 51Joseph named his firstborn Manasseh,* meaning, "God has made me forget entirely my troubles and my father's house"; 52and the second he named Ephraim,* meaning, "God has made me fruitful in the land of my affliction."

53When the seven years of abundance enjoyed by the land of Egypt came to an end, 54the seven years of famine set in, just as Joseph had said. Although there was famine in all the other countries, food was available throughout the land of Egypt.[i] 55When all the land of Egypt became hungry and the people cried to Pharaoh for food, Pharaoh said to all the Egyptians: "Go to Joseph and do whatever he tells you." 56When the famine had spread throughout the land, Joseph opened all the cities that had grain and rationed it to the Egyptians, since the famine had gripped the land of Egypt. 57Indeed, the whole world came to Egypt to Joseph to buy grain, for famine had gripped the whole world.

## CHAPTER 42

See RG 60–61

### *The Brothers' First Journey to Egypt.**

1When Jacob learned that grain rations were for sale in Egypt, he said to his sons: "Why do you keep looking at one another?" 2He went on, "I hear that grain is for sale in Egypt. Go down there and buy some for us, that we may stay alive and not die."[j] 3So ten of Joseph's brothers went down to buy grain from Egypt. 4But Jacob did not send Joseph's brother Benjamin with his brothers, for he thought some disaster might befall him. 5And so the sons of Israel were among those who came to buy grain, since there was famine in the land of Canaan.[k]

6Joseph, as governor of the country, was the one who sold grain to all the people of the land. When Joseph's brothers came, they bowed down to him with their faces to the ground.[l] 7He recognized them as soon as he saw them. But he concealed his own identity from them and spoke harshly to them. "Where do you come from?" he asked them. They answered, "From the land of Canaan, to buy food."

8When Joseph recognized his brothers, although they did not recognize him, 9he was reminded of the dreams he had about them. He said to them: "You are spies.[m] You have come to see the weak points* of the land." 10"No, my lord," they replied. "On the contrary, your servants have come to buy food. 11All of us are sons of the same man. We are honest men; your servants have never been

Egyptian name meaning "the god speaks and he (the newborn child) lives." **Asenath**: means "belonging to (the Egyptian goddess) Neith." **Potiphera**: means "he whom Ra (the Egyptian god) gave"; a shorter form of the same name was borne by Joseph's master (37:36). **Heliopolis**: in Hebrew, *On*, a city seven miles northeast of modern Cairo, site of the chief temple of the sun god; it is mentioned also in v. 50; 46:20; Ez 30:17.

**41:51 Manasseh**: an allusion to this name is in the Hebrew expression, *nishshani*, "he made me forget."

**41:52 Ephraim**: related to the Hebrew expression *hiphrani*, "(God) has made me fruitful." The name originally meant something like "fertile land."

**42:1–38** The first journey of the brothers to Egypt. Its cause is famine, which was also the reason Abraham and Sarah undertook their dangerous journey to Egypt. The brothers bow to Joseph in v. 6, which fulfills Joseph's dream in 37:5–11. Endowed with wisdom, Joseph begins a process of instruction or "discipline" for his brothers that eventually forces them to recognize the enormity of their sin against him and the family. He controls their experience of the first journey with the result that the second journey in chaps. 43–44 leads to full acknowledgment and reconciliation.

**42:9, 12 Weak points**: lit., "the nakedness of the land"; the military weakness of the land, like human nakedness, should not be seen by strangers.

*h:* Gn 46:20; 48:5. *i:* Ps 105:16; Acts 7:11. *j:* Acts 7:12. *k:* Jdt 5:10; Acts 7:11. *l:* Ps 105:21. *m:* Gn 37:5.

spies." 12But he answered them: "Not so! It is the weak points of the land that you have come to see." 13"We your servants," they said, "are twelve brothers, sons of a certain man in Canaan; but the youngest one is at present with our father, and the other one is no more."[n] 14"It is just as I said," Joseph persisted; "you are spies. 15This is how you shall be tested: I swear by the life of Pharaoh that you shall not leave here unless your youngest brother comes here. 16So send one of your number to get your brother, while the rest of you stay here under arrest. Thus will your words be tested for their truth; if they are untrue, as Pharaoh lives, you are spies!" 17With that, he locked them up in the guardhouse for three days.

18On the third day Joseph said to them: "Do this, and you shall live; for I am a God-fearing man. 19If you are honest men, let one of your brothers be confined in this prison, while the rest of you go and take home grain for your starving families. 20But you must bring me your youngest brother. Your words will thus be verified, and you will not die." To this they agreed.[o] 21To one another, however, they said: "Truly we are being punished because of our brother. We saw the anguish of his heart when he pleaded with us, yet we would not listen. That is why this anguish has now come upon us."[p] 22Then Reuben responded, "Did I not tell you, 'Do no wrong to the boy'? But you would not listen! Now comes the reckoning for his blood."[q] 23They did not know, of course, that Joseph understood what they said, since he spoke with them through an interpreter. 24But turning away from them, he wept. When he was able to speak to them again, he took Simeon from among them and bound him before their eyes. 25Then Joseph gave orders to have their containers filled with grain, their money replaced in each one's sack, and provisions given them for their journey. After this had been done for them, 26they loaded their donkeys with the grain and departed.

27At the night encampment, when one of them opened his bag to give his donkey some fodder, he saw his money there in the mouth of his bag. 28He cried out to his brothers, "My money has been returned! Here it is in my bag!" At that their hearts sank. Trembling, they asked one another, "What is this that God has done to us?"

29When they got back to their father Jacob in the land of Canaan, they told him all that had happened to them. 30"The man who is lord of the land," they said, "spoke to us harshly and put us in custody on the grounds that we were spying on the land. 31But we said to him: 'We are honest men; we have never been spies. 32We are twelve brothers, sons of the same father; but one is no more, and the youngest one is now with our father in the land of Canaan.' 33Then the man who is lord of the land said to us: 'This is how I will know if you are honest men: leave one of your brothers with me, then take grain for your starving families and go. 34When you bring me your youngest brother, and I know that you are not spies but honest men, I will restore your brother to you, and you may move about freely in the land.' "

35When they were emptying their sacks, there in each one's sack was his moneybag! At the sight of their moneybags, they and their father were afraid. 36Their father Jacob said to them: "Must you make me childless? Joseph is no more, Simeon is no more, and now you would take Benjamin away! All these things have happened to me!" 37Then Reuben told his father: "You may kill my own two sons if I do not return him to you! Put him in my care, and I will bring him back to you." 38But Jacob replied: "My son shall not go down with you. Now that his brother is dead, he is the only one left. If some disaster should befall him on the journey you must make, you would send my white head down to Sheol in grief."[r]

## CHAPTER 43

See RG 60–61

*The Second Journey to Egypt.** 1Now the famine in the land grew severe. 2So

**43:1–34** The second journey to Egypt. Joseph the sage has carefully prepared the brothers for a possible reconciliation. In this chapter and the following one Judah steps forward as the hero, in contrast to chaps. 37 and 42 where Reuben was the hero. Here Judah serves as guarantee for Benjamin.

*n:* Gn 44:20. *o:* Gn 43:5. *p:* Gn 37:18–27. *q:* Gn 37:22. *r:* Gn 37:35.

when they had used up all the grain they had brought from Egypt, their father said to them, "Go back and buy us a little more food." 3But Judah replied: "The man strictly warned us, 'You shall not see me unless your brother is with you.'[s] 4If you are willing to let our brother go with us, we will go down to buy food for you. 5But if you are not willing, we will not go down, because the man told us, 'You shall not see me unless your brother is with you.' "[t] 6Israel demanded, "Why did you bring this trouble on me by telling the man that you had another brother?" 7They answered: "The man kept asking about us and our family: 'Is your father still living? Do you have another brother?' We answered him accordingly. How could we know that he would say, 'Bring your brother down here'?"

8Then Judah urged his father Israel: "Let the boy go with me, that we may be off and on our way if you and we and our children are to keep from starving to death.[u] 9I myself will serve as a guarantee for him. You can hold me responsible for him. If I fail to bring him back and set him before you, I will bear the blame before you forever.[v] 10Had we not delayed, we could have been there and back twice by now!"

11Israel their father then told them: "If it must be so, then do this: Put some of the land's best products in your baggage and take them down to the man as gifts: some balm and honey, gum and resin, and pistachios and almonds.[w] 12Also take double the money along, for you must return the amount that was put back in the mouths of your bags; it may have been a mistake. 13Take your brother, too, and be off on your way back to the man. 14May God Almighty grant you mercy in the presence of the man, so that he may let your other brother go, as well as Benjamin. As for me, if I am to suffer bereavement, I shall suffer it."

15So the men took those gifts and double the money and Benjamin. They made their way down to Egypt and presented themselves before Joseph. 16When Joseph saw them and Benjamin, he told his steward, "Take the men into the house, and have an animal slaughtered and prepared, for they are to dine with me at noon." 17Doing as Joseph had ordered, the steward conducted the men to Joseph's house. 18But they became apprehensive when they were led to his house. "It must be," they thought, "on account of the money put back in our bags the first time, that we are taken inside—in order to attack us and take our donkeys and seize us as slaves." 19So they went up to Joseph's steward and talked to him at the entrance of the house. 20"If you please, sir," they said, "we came down here once before to buy food.[x] 21But when we arrived at a night's encampment and opened our bags, there was each man's money in the mouth of his bag—our money in the full amount! We have now brought it back.[y] 22We have brought other money to buy food. We do not know who put our money in our bags." 23He replied, "Calm down! Do not fear! Your God and the God of your father must have put treasure in your bags for you. As for your money, I received it." With that, he led Simeon out to them.

24The steward then brought the men inside Joseph's house. He gave them water to wash their feet, and gave fodder to their donkeys. 25Then they set out their gifts to await Joseph's arrival at noon, for they had heard that they were to dine there. 26When Joseph came home, they presented him with the gifts they had brought inside, while they bowed down before him to the ground. 27After inquiring how they were, he asked them, "And how is your aged father, of whom you spoke? Is he still alive?"[z] 28"Your servant our father is still alive and doing well," they said, as they knelt and bowed down. 29Then Joseph looked up and saw Benjamin, his brother, the son of his mother. He asked, "Is this your youngest brother, of whom you told me?" Then he said to him, "May God be gracious to you, my son!"[a] 30With that, Joseph hurried out, for he was so overcome with affection for his brother that he was on the verge of tears. So he went into a private room and wept there.

31After washing his face, he reappeared

*s:* Gn 44:23. *t:* Gn 42:20. *u:* Gn 42:37. *v:* Gn 44:32. *w:* Gn 45:23. *x:* Gn 42:3. *y:* Gn 42:27–28. *z:* Tb 7:4. *a:* Gn 42:13.

and, now having collected himself, gave the order, "Serve the meal." [32]It was served separately to him,* to the brothers, and to the Egyptians who partook of his board. Egyptians may not eat with Hebrews; that is abhorrent to them. [33]When they were seated before him according to their age, from the oldest to the youngest, they looked at one another in amazement; [34]and as portions were brought to them from Joseph's table, Benjamin's portion was five times as large as* anyone else's. So they drank freely and made merry with him.

## CHAPTER 44

See RG 60–61

***Final Test.**** [1]Then Joseph commanded his steward: "Fill the men's bags with as much food as they can carry, and put each man's money in the mouth of his bag. [2]In the mouth of the youngest one's bag put also my silver goblet, together with the money for his grain." The steward did as Joseph said. [3]At daybreak the men and their donkeys were sent off. [4]They had not gone far out of the city when Joseph said to his steward: "Go at once after the men! When you overtake them, say to them, 'Why did you repay good with evil? Why did you steal my silver goblet? [5]Is it not the very one from which my master drinks and which he uses for divination?* What you have done is wrong.' "

[6]When the steward overtook them and repeated these words to them, [7]they said to him: "Why does my lord say such things? Far be it from your servants to do such a thing! [8]We even brought back to you from the land of Canaan the money that we found in the mouths of our bags. How could we steal silver or gold from your master's house? [9]If any of your servants is found to have the goblet, he shall die, and as for the rest of us, we shall become my lord's slaves." [10]But he replied, "Now what you propose is fair enough, but only the one who is found to have it shall become my slave, and the rest of you can go free." [11]Then each of them quickly lowered his bag to the ground and opened it; [12]and when a search was made, starting with the oldest and ending with the youngest, the goblet turned up in Benjamin's bag. [13]At this, they tore their garments. Then, when each man had loaded his donkey again, they returned to the city.

[14]When Judah and his brothers entered Joseph's house, he was still there; so they flung themselves on the ground before him. [15]"How could you do such a thing?" Joseph asked them. "Did you not know that such a man as I could discern by divination what happened?" [16]Judah replied: "What can we say to my lord? How can we plead or how try to prove our innocence? God has uncovered your servants' guilt.* Here we are, then, the slaves of my lord—the rest of us no less than the one in whose possession the goblet was found." [17]Joseph said, "Far be it from me to act thus! Only the one in whose possession the goblet was found shall become my slave; the rest of you may go back unharmed to your father."

[18]Judah then stepped up to him and said: "I beg you, my lord, let your servant appeal to my lord, and do not become angry with your servant, for you are the equal of Pharaoh. [19]My lord asked his servants,* 'Have you a fa-

**43:32 Separately to him**: that Joseph did not eat with the other Egyptians was apparently a matter of rank.

**43:34 Five times as large as**: probably an idiomatic expression for "much larger than." Cf. 45:22.

**44:1–34** Joseph's pressure on his brothers and Judah's great speech. Judah has the longest speech in the Book of Genesis; it summarizes the recent past (vv. 18–29), shows the pain Joseph's actions have imposed on their aged father (vv. 30–32), and ends with the offer to take the place of Benjamin as servant of Joseph (vv. 33–34). The role of Judah in the entire story is exceedingly important and is easily underrated: he tries to rescue Joseph (37:26–27), his "going down away from the brothers" is parallel to Joseph's (chap. 38) and prepares him (as it prepares Joseph) for the reconciliation, his speech in chap. 44 persuades Joseph to reveal himself and be reconciled to his brothers. Here, Judah effectively replaces Reuben as a spokesman for the brothers. Jacob in his testament (chap. 49) devotes the most attention to Judah and Joseph. In one sense, the story can be called the story of Joseph and Judah.

**44:5 Divination**: seeking omens through liquids poured into a cup or bowl was a common practice in the ancient Near East; cf. v. 15. Even though divination was frowned on in later Israel (Lv 19:31), it is in this place an authentic touch which is ascribed to Joseph, the wisest man in Egypt.

**44:16 Guilt**: in trying to do away with Joseph when he was young.

**44:19 My lord asked his servants**: such frequently re-

*b:* Gn 42:13.

ther, or another brother?' 20So we said to my lord, 'We have an aged father, and a younger brother, the child of his old age. This one's full brother is dead, and since he is the only one by his mother who is left, his father is devoted to him.'[b] 21Then you told your servants, 'Bring him down to me that I might see him.' 22We replied to my lord, 'The boy cannot leave his father; his father would die if he left him.' 23But you told your servants, 'Unless your youngest brother comes down with you, you shall not see me again.'[c] 24When we returned to your servant my father, we reported to him the words of my lord.

25"Later, our father said, 'Go back and buy some food for us.' 26So we reminded him, 'We cannot go down there; only if our youngest brother is with us can we go, for we may not see the man if our youngest brother is not with us.' 27Then your servant my father said to us, 'As you know, my wife bore me two sons. 28One of them, however, has gone away from me, and I said, "He must have been torn to pieces by wild beasts!" I have not seen him since.[d] 29If you take this one away from me too, and a disaster befalls him, you will send my white head down to Sheol in grief.'

30"So now, if the boy is not with us when I go back to your servant my father, whose very life is bound up with his, he will die as soon as he sees that the boy is missing; 31and your servants will thus send the white head of your servant our father down to Sheol in grief. 32Besides, I, your servant, have guaranteed the boy's safety for my father by saying, 'If I fail to bring him back to you, father, I will bear the blame before you forever.'[e] 33So now let me, your servant, remain in place of the boy as the slave of my lord, and let the boy go back with his brothers. 34How could I go back to my father if the boy were not with me? I could not bear to see the anguish that would overcome my father."

## CHAPTER 45

See RG 60-61

***The Truth Revealed.**** 1Joseph could no longer restrain himself in the presence of all his attendants, so he cried out, "Have everyone withdraw from me!" So no one attended him when he made himself known to his brothers. 2But his sobs were so loud that the Egyptians heard him, and so the news reached Pharaoh's house. 3[f]"I am Joseph," he said to his brothers. "Is my father still alive?" But his brothers could give him no answer, so dumbfounded were they at him.

4"Come closer to me," Joseph told his brothers. When they had done so, he said: "I am your brother Joseph, whom you sold into Egypt. 5But now do not be distressed, and do not be angry with yourselves for having sold me here. It was really for the sake of saving lives that God sent me here ahead of you.[g] 6The famine has been in the land for two years now, and for five more years cultivation will yield no harvest. 7God, therefore, sent me on ahead of you to ensure for you a remnant on earth and to save your lives in an extraordinary deliverance. 8So it was not really you but God who had me come here; and he has made me a father to Pharaoh,* lord of all his household, and ruler over the whole land of Egypt.

9* "Hurry back, then, to my father and tell him: 'Thus says your son Joseph: God has made me lord of all Egypt; come down to me without delay.[h] 10You can settle in the region of Goshen,* where you will be near me—you and your children and children's children, your flocks and herds, and everything that you own. 11I will provide for you there in the five years of famine that lie ahead, so that you and your household and all that are

peated expressions in Judah's speech show the formal court style used by a subject in speaking to a high official.

**45:1–28** Joseph reveals his identity and the family is reconciled.

**45:8 Father to Pharaoh**: a term applied to a vizier in ancient Egypt.

**45:9–15** In these verses, as in 46:31–47:5a, all from the Yahwist source, Joseph in his own name invites his father and brothers to come to Egypt. Only after their arrival is Pharaoh informed of the fact. On the other hand, in 45:16–20, which scholars have traditionally attributed to the Elohist source, it is Pharaoh himself who invites Joseph's family to migrate to his domain.

**45:10 The region of Goshen**: the meaning of the term is unknown. It is found in no Egyptian source. It is generally thought to be in the modern Wadi Tumilat in the eastern part of the Nile Delta.

---

*c:* Gn 43:3. *d:* Gn 37:20, 33. *e:* Gn 43:9. *f:* Acts 7:13. *g:* Gn 50:20. *h:* Acts 7:14.

## Joseph Discloses His Identity

A CENTRAL TEACHING of the Joseph story now unfolds: Despite the evil intent of Joseph's brothers, God has worked to ensure the realization of the divine promise (45:7–8). The lesson here is that final judgment cannot be passed on unfavorable events of the moment. Sometimes people find that when they look back over what seemed like a terrible situation at the time, much good came from it.

yours will not suffer want.’ 12Surely, you can
see for yourselves, and Benjamin can see for
himself, that it is I who am speaking to you.
13Tell my father all about my high position
in Egypt and all that you have seen. But
hurry and bring my father down here.”
14Then he threw his arms around his brother
Benjamin and wept on his shoulder. 15Jo-
seph then kissed all his brothers and wept
over them; and only then were his brothers
able to talk with him.

16The news reached Pharaoh's house: “Joseph's brothers have come.” Pharaoh and his
officials were pleased. 17So Pharaoh told Joseph: “Say to your brothers: ‘This is what
you shall do: Load up your animals and go
without delay to the land of Canaan. 18There
get your father and your households, and
then come to me; I will assign you the best
land in Egypt, where you will live off the fat
of the land.’[i] 19Instruct them further: ‘Do
this. Take wagons from the land of Egypt for
your children and your wives and bring your
father back here. 20Do not be concerned
about your belongings, for the best in the
whole land of Egypt shall be yours.’ ”

21The sons of Israel acted accordingly. Joseph gave them the wagons, as Pharaoh had
ordered, and he supplied them with provisions for the journey. 22He also gave to each
of them a set of clothes, but to Benjamin he
gave three hundred shekels of silver and five
sets of clothes. 23Moreover, what he sent to
his father was ten donkeys loaded with the
finest products of Egypt and another ten
loaded with grain and bread and provisions
for his father's journey. 24As he sent his
brothers on their way, he told them, “Do not
quarrel on the way.”

25So they went up from Egypt and came to
the land of Canaan, to their father Jacob.
26When they told him, “Joseph is still
alive—in fact, it is he who is governing all
the land of Egypt,” he was unmoved, for he
did not believe them. 27But when they recounted to him all that Joseph had told them,
and when he saw the wagons that Joseph had
sent to transport him, the spirit of their father
Jacob came to life. 28“Enough,” said Israel.
“My son Joseph is still alive! I must go and
see him before I die.”

### CHAPTER 46

See RG 60–61

*Migration to Egypt.* 1* Israel set out
with all that was his. When he arrived at
Beer-sheba, he offered sacrifices to the God
of his father Isaac. 2There God, speaking to
Israel in a vision by night, called: Jacob! Jacob! He answered, “Here I am.” 3Then he
said: I am God,* the God of your father. Do
not be afraid to go down to Egypt, for there I
will make you a great nation. 4I will go down
to Egypt with you and I will also bring you
back here, after Joseph has closed your eyes.

5So Jacob departed from Beer-sheba, and
the sons of Israel put their father and their
wives and children on the wagons that Pharaoh had sent to transport him. 6They took
with them their livestock and the possessions they had acquired in the land of Canaan. So Jacob and all his descendants came
to Egypt.[j] 7His sons and his grandsons, his
daughters and his granddaughters—all his
descendants—he took with him to Egypt.

**46:1–47:26** Jacob and his family settle in Egypt. Joseph's economic policies.

**46:3 I am God**: more precisely according to the Hebrew text, “I am El.” “El” is here a divine name, not the common noun “god.”

**46:9–27** This genealogical list is based on the clan lists

*i:* Acts 7:14. *j:* Ex 1:1; Jos 24:4; Jdt 5:10; Acts 7:15.

## Shepherds Are Abhorrent

GOSHEN IS A pasture land in the Nile River delta isolated from the rest of Egypt. Shepherds were abhorrent (46:34) because Egyptian agriculture was based more on crops and field agriculture that would be ruined by their wandering herds of grazing animals.

[8]These are the names of the Israelites, Jacob and his children, who came to Egypt.

Reuben, Jacob's firstborn,[k] [9]* and the sons of Reuben: Hanoch, Pallu, Hezron, and Carmi.[l] [10]The sons of Simeon: Jemuel, Jamin, Ohad, Jachin, Zohar, and Shaul, son of a Canaanite woman.[m] [11]The sons of Levi: Gershon, Kohath, and Merari.[n] [12]The sons of Judah: Er, Onan, Shelah, Perez, and Zerah—but Er and Onan had died in the land of Canaan; and the sons of Perez were Hezron and Hamul.[o] [13]The sons of Issachar: Tola, Puah, Jashub, and Shimron.[p] [14]The sons of Zebulun: Sered, Elon, and Jahleel.[q] [15]These were the sons whom Leah bore to Jacob in Paddan-aram, along with his daughter Dinah—thirty-three persons in all, sons and daughters.

[16]The sons of Gad: Zephon, Haggi, Shuni, Ezbon, Eri, Arod, and Areli.[r] [17]The sons of Asher: Imnah, Ishvah, Ishvi, and Beriah, with their sister Serah; and the sons of Beriah: Heber and Malchiel.[s] [18]These are the children of Zilpah, whom Laban had given to his daughter Leah; these she bore to Jacob—sixteen persons in all.

[19]The sons of Jacob's wife Rachel: Joseph and Benjamin. [20]In the land of Egypt Joseph became the father of Manasseh and Ephraim, whom Asenath, daughter of Potiphera, priest of Heliopolis, bore to him.[t] [21]The sons of Benjamin: Bela, Becher, Ashbel, Gera, Naaman, Ahiram, Shupham, Hupham, and Ard.[u] [22]These are the sons whom Rachel bore to Jacob—fourteen persons in all.

[23]The sons of Dan: Hushim.[v] [24]The sons of Naphtali: Jahzeel, Guni, Jezer, and Shillem.[w] [25]These are the sons of Bilhah, whom Laban had given to his daughter Rachel; these she bore to Jacob—seven persons in all.

[26]Jacob's people who came to Egypt—his direct descendants, not counting the wives of Jacob's sons—numbered sixty-six persons in all.[x] [27]Together with Joseph's sons who were born to him in Egypt—two persons—all the people comprising the household of Jacob who had come to Egypt amounted to seventy persons* in all.[y]

[28]Israel had sent Judah ahead to Joseph, so that he might meet him in Goshen. On his arrival in the region of Goshen, [29]Joseph prepared his chariot and went up to meet his father Israel in Goshen. As soon as Israel made his appearance, Joseph threw his arms around him and wept a long time on his shoulder. [30]And Israel said to Joseph, "At last I can die, now that I have seen for myself that you are still alive."

[31]Joseph then said to his brothers and his father's household: "I will go up and inform Pharaoh, telling him: 'My brothers and my father's household, whose home is in the land of Canaan, have come to me. [32]The men are shepherds, having been owners of livestock;* and they have brought with them their flocks and herds, as well as everything

(Nm 26:5–50) from the Mosaic period.

**46:27 Seventy persons**: it is difficult to get this exact number by adding up the persons mentioned in the preceding genealogies. One might assume it refers to Jacob and sixty-nine descendants, excluding Er and Onan but including Dinah. Ex 1:5 repeats the number but excludes Jacob. Dt 10:22 refers to seventy persons descending to Egypt. The best solution is to take the number as expressing totality. Since there are seventy nations in chap. 10, it is likely that the text is drawing a parallel between the two entities and suggesting that Israel "represents" the nations before God.

**46:32 Owners of livestock**: the phrase occurs only here and in v. 34. The difference between this term and "shepherds" is not clear, for the brothers do not mention it to Pharaoh in 47:3.

*k:* Ex 1:2. *l:* Ex 6:14; Nm 26:5; 1 Chr 5:3. *m:* Ex 6:15; Nm 26:12; 1 Chr 4:24. *n:* Ex 6:16; Nm 3:17; 26:57; 1 Chr 6:1. *o:* Gn 38:3–10, 29–30; Nm 26:19; Ru 4:12; 1 Chr 2:5. *p:* Nm 26:23–24; 1 Chr 7:1. *q:* Nm 26:26. *r:* Nm 26:15–16. *s:* Nm 26:44; 1 Chr 7:30–31. *t:* Gn 41:50; Nm 26:28, 35. *u:* Nm 26:38; 1 Chr 7:6; 8:1–4. *v:* Nm 26:42. *w:* Nm 26:48–49; 1 Chr 7:13. *x:* Ex 1:5. *y:* Ex 1:5; Dt 10:22; Acts 7:14.

else they own.' [33]So when Pharaoh summons you and asks what your occupation is,
[34]you must answer, 'We your servants, like
our ancestors, have been owners of livestock
from our youth until now,' in order that you
may stay in the region of Goshen, since all
shepherds are abhorrent to the Egyptians."

## CHAPTER 47

See RG 60–61

***Settlement in Goshen.*** [1]Joseph went
and told Pharaoh, "My father and my brothers have come from the land of Canaan, with
their flocks and herds and everything else
they own; and they are now in the region of
Goshen." [2]He then presented to Pharaoh five
of his brothers whom he had selected from
their full number. [3]When Pharaoh asked
them, "What is your occupation?" they answered, "We, your servants, like our ancestors, are shepherds. [4]We have come," they
continued, "in order to sojourn in this land,
for there is no pasture for your servants'
flocks, because the famine has been severe
in the land of Canaan. So now please let your
servants settle in the region of Goshen."[z]
[5]Pharaoh said to Joseph, "Now that your father and your brothers have come to you,
[6]the land of Egypt is at your disposal; settle
your father and brothers in the pick of the
land. Let them settle in the region of Goshen. And if you know of capable men
among them, put them in charge of my livestock." [7]Then Joseph brought his father Jacob and presented him to Pharaoh. And Jacob blessed Pharaoh. [8]Then Pharaoh asked
Jacob, "How many years have you lived?"
[9]Jacob replied: "The years I have lived as a
wayfarer amount to a hundred and thirty.
Few and hard have been these years of my
life, and they do not compare with the years
that my ancestors lived as wayfarers."*
[10]Then Jacob blessed Pharaoh and withdrew
from his presence.

[11]Joseph settled his father and brothers
and gave them a holding in Egypt on the
pick of the land, in the region of Rameses,*
as Pharaoh had ordered. [12]And Joseph provided food for his father and brothers and his
father's whole household, down to the
youngest.

***Joseph's Land Policy.*** [13]Since there was no
food in all the land because of the extreme
severity of the famine, and the lands of
Egypt and Canaan were languishing from
hunger, [14]Joseph gathered in, as payment for
the grain that they were buying, all the
money that was to be found in Egypt and Canaan, and he put it in Pharaoh's house.
[15]When all the money in Egypt and Canaan
was spent, all the Egyptians came to Joseph,
pleading, "Give us food! Why should we
perish in front of you? For our money is
gone." [16]"Give me your livestock if your
money is gone," replied Joseph. "I will give
you food in return for your livestock." [17]So
they brought their livestock to Joseph, and
he gave them food in exchange for their
horses, their flocks of sheep and herds of
cattle, and their donkeys. Thus he supplied
them with food in exchange for all their livestock in that year. [18]That year ended, and
they came to him in the next one and said:
"We cannot hide from my lord that, with our
money spent and our livestock made over to
my lord, there is nothing left to put at my
lord's disposal except our bodies and our
land. [19]Why should we and our land perish
before your very eyes? Take us and our land
in exchange for food, and we will become
Pharaoh's slaves and our land his property;
only give us seed, that we may survive and
not perish, and that our land may not turn
into a waste."

[20]So Joseph acquired all the land of Egypt
for Pharaoh. Each of the Egyptians sold his
field, since the famine weighed heavily upon
them. Thus the land passed over to Pharaoh,
[21]and the people were reduced to slavery,
from one end of Egypt's territory to the
other. [22]Only the priests' lands Joseph did
not acquire. Since the priests had a fixed allowance from Pharaoh and lived off the allowance Pharaoh had granted them, they did
not have to sell their land.

**47:9 Wayfarer . . . wayfarers**: human beings are merely sojourners on earth; cf. Ps 39:13.

**47:11 The region of Rameses**: same as the region of Goshen; see note on 45:10.

**47:28–50:26** Supplements to the Joseph story. Most of the material in this section centers on Jacob—his blessing of Jo-

*z:* Ex 23:9; Dt 23:8.

23 Joseph told the people: "Now that I have acquired you and your land for Pharaoh, here is your seed for sowing the land. 24 But when the harvest is in, you must give a fifth of it to Pharaoh, while you keep four-fifths as seed for your fields and as food for yourselves and your households and as food for your children." 25 "You have saved our lives!" they answered. "We have found favor with my lord; now we will be Pharaoh's slaves." 26 Thus Joseph made it a statute for the land of Egypt, which is still in force, that a fifth of its produce should go to Pharaoh. Only the land of the priests did not pass over to Pharaoh.

***Israel Blesses Ephraim and Manasseh.*** 27 Thus Israel settled in the land of Egypt, in the region of Goshen. There they acquired holdings, were fertile, and multiplied greatly.[a] 28* Jacob lived in the land of Egypt for seventeen years; the span of his life came to a hundred and forty-seven years. 29 When the time approached for Israel to die, he called his son Joseph and said to him: "If it pleases you, put your hand under my thigh as a sign of your enduring fidelity to me; do not bury me in Egypt. 30 When I lie down with my ancestors, take me out of Egypt and bury me in their burial place."[b] "I will do as you say," he replied. 31 But his father demanded, "Swear it to me!" So Joseph swore to him. Then Israel bowed at the head of the bed.*

See RG 60–61

## CHAPTER 48

1* Some time afterward, Joseph was informed, "Your father is failing." So he took along with him his two sons, Manasseh and Ephraim. 2 When Jacob was told, "Your son Joseph has come to you," Israel rallied his strength and sat up in bed.

3[c] Jacob then said to Joseph: "God Almighty appeared to me at Luz* in the land of Canaan, and blessing me, 4 he said, 'I will make you fertile and multiply you and make you into an assembly of peoples, and I will give this land to your descendants after you as a permanent possession.' 5 So now your two sons who were born to you in the land of Egypt before I joined you here, shall be mine; Ephraim and Manasseh shall be mine as much as Reuben and Simeon are mine. 6 Progeny born to you after them shall remain yours; but their heritage shall be recorded in the names of their brothers. 7[d] I do this because, when I was returning from Paddan, your mother Rachel died, to my sorrow, during the journey in Canaan, while we were still a short distance from Ephrath; and I buried her there on the way to Ephrath [now Bethlehem]."*

8 When Israel saw Joseph's sons, he asked, "Who are these?" 9 "They are my sons," Joseph answered his father, "whom God has given me here." "Bring them to me," said his father, "that I may bless them." 10 Now Israel's eyes were dim from age; he could not see well. When Joseph brought his sons close to him, he kissed and embraced them. 11 Then Israel said to Joseph, "I never expected to see your face again, and now God has allowed me to see your descendants as well!"

12 Joseph removed them from his father's knees and bowed down before him with his

seph's sons, his farewell testament, and his death and burial in Canaan. Only the last verses (50:15–26) redirect attention to Jacob's sons, the twelve brothers; they are assured that the reconciliation will not collapse after the death of the patriarch.

**47:31 Israel bowed at the head of the bed**: meaning perhaps that he gave a nod of assent and appreciation as he lay on his bed. The oath and gesture are the same as Abraham's in 24:2. Israel's bowing here suggests the fulfillment of Joseph's dreams in 37:9–10, when parents and brothers bowed down to Joseph (cf. 42:6; 43:26). By using different vowels for the Hebrew word for "bed," the Greek version translated it as "staff," and understood the phrase to mean that he bowed in worship, leaning on the top of his staff; it is thus quoted in Heb 11:21.

**48:1–22** Jacob continues his preparations for death. In a scene that evokes the nearly blind Isaac blessing Jacob and Esau (chap. 27), Jacob blesses Joseph's two sons. He adopts them, elevating them to a status equal to that of Jacob's first sons Reuben and Simeon (cf. 1 Chr 5:1). The adoption is one more instance of Jacob's favoring Rachel and those born of her. The mention of Jacob's failing eyesight and his selection of the younger son over the older evokes the great deathbed scene in chap. 27. He reaffirms to Joseph the ancient divine promise of progeny and land.

**48:3 Luz**: an older name of Bethel (28:19).

**48:7** Since her early death prevented Rachel from bearing more than two sons, Jacob feels justified in treating her two grandsons as if they were her own offspring.

*a:* Ex 1:7. *b:* Gn 50:5. *c:* Gn 28:12–15; 35:6. *d:* Gn 35:19.

face to the ground. 13 Then Joseph took the
two, Ephraim with his right hand, to Israel's
left, and Manasseh with his left hand, to Israel's right, and brought them up to him.
14 But Israel, crossing his hands, put out his
right hand and laid it on the head of
Ephraim, although he was the younger, and
his left hand on the head of Manasseh, although he was the firstborn. 15 Then he
blessed them with these words:

"May the God in whose presence
my fathers Abraham and Isaac walked,
The God who has been my shepherd
from my birth to this day,[e]
16 The angel who has delivered me from all
harm,
bless these boys
That in them my name be recalled,
and the names of my fathers, Abraham
and Isaac,
And they may become teeming
multitudes
upon the earth!"

17 When Joseph saw that his father had laid
his right hand on Ephraim's head, this
seemed wrong to him; so he took hold of his
father's hand, to remove it from Ephraim's
head to Manasseh's, 18 saying, "That is not
right, father; the other one is the firstborn;
lay your right hand on his head!" 19 But his
father refused. "I know it, son," he said, "I
know. That one too shall become a people,
and he too shall be great. Nevertheless, his
younger brother shall surpass him, and his
descendants shall become a multitude of nations." 20 So he blessed them that day and
said, "By you shall the people of Israel pronounce blessings, saying, 'God make you
like Ephraim and Manasseh.'" Thus he
placed Ephraim before Manasseh.[f]

21 Then Israel said to Joseph: "I am about
to die. But God will be with you and will restore you to the land of your ancestors. 22 [g] As
for me, I give to you, as to the one above his
brothers, Shechem, which I captured from
the Amorites with my sword and bow."*

## CHAPTER 49

See RG 60-61

*Jacob's Testament.** 1 Jacob called his
sons and said: "Gather around, that I may
tell you what is to happen to you in days to
come.

2 "Assemble and listen, sons of Jacob,
listen to Israel, your father.

3 "You, Reuben, my firstborn,
my strength and the first fruit of my
vigor,
excelling in rank and excelling in
power!
4 Turbulent as water, you shall no longer
excel,
for you climbed into your father's bed
and defiled my couch to my sorrow.[h]

5 * "Simeon and Levi, brothers indeed,
weapons of violence are their knives.*
6 Let not my person enter their council,
or my honor be joined with their
company;

**48:22** Both the meaning of the Hebrew and the historical reference in this verse are obscure. By taking the Hebrew word for Shechem as a common noun meaning shoulder or mountain slope, some translators render the verse, "I give you one portion more than your brothers, which I captured . . ." The reference may be to the capture of Shechem by the sons of Jacob (34:24–29). Shechem lay near the border separating the tribal territory of Manasseh from that of Ephraim (Jos 16:4–9; 17:1–2, 7).

**49:1–27** The testament, or farewell discourse, of Jacob, which has its closest parallel in Moses' farewell in Dt 33:6–25. From his privileged position as a patriarch, he sees the future of his children (the eponymous ancestors of the tribes) and is able to describe how they will fare and so gives his blessing. The dense and archaic poetry is obscure in several places. The sayings often involve wordplays (explained in the notes). The poem begins with the six sons of Leah (vv. 2–15), then deals with the sons of the two secondary wives, and ends with Rachel's two sons, Joseph and Benjamin. Reuben, the oldest son, loses his position of leadership as a result of his intercourse with Bilhah (35:22), and the words about Simeon and Levi allude to their taking revenge for the rape of Dinah (chap. 34). The preeminence of Judah reflects his rise in the course of the narrative (mirroring the rise of Joseph). See note on 44:1–34.

**49:5–7** This passage probably refers to their attack on the city of Shechem (Gn 34). Because there is no indication that the warlike tribe of Levi will be commissioned as a priestly tribe (Ex 32:26–29; Dt 33:11), this passage reflects an early, independent tradition.

**49:5 Knives**: if this is the meaning of the obscure Hebrew word here, the reference may be to the knives used in circumcising the men of Shechem (34:24; cf. Jos 5:2).

*e:* Heb 11:21. *f:* Heb 11:21. *g:* Jos 17:14, 17–18; Jn 4:5. *h:* Gn 35:22; 1 Chr 5:1–2.

For in their fury they killed men,
at their whim they maimed oxen.[i]
7 Cursed be their fury so fierce,
and their rage so cruel!
I will scatter them in Jacob,
disperse them throughout Israel.

8 "You, Judah, shall your brothers praise
—your hand on the neck of your enemies;
the sons of your father shall bow down to you.
9 Judah is a lion's cub,
you have grown up on prey, my son.
He crouches, lies down like a lion,
like a lioness—who would dare rouse him?[j]
10 The scepter shall never depart from Judah,
or the mace from between his feet,
Until tribute comes to him,*
and he receives the people's obedience.
11 He tethers his donkey to the vine,
his donkey's foal to the choicest stem.
In wine he washes his garments,
his robe in the blood of grapes.*
12 His eyes are darker than wine,
and his teeth are whiter than milk.

13 "Zebulun shall dwell by the seashore;
he will be a haven for ships,
and his flank shall rest on Sidon.

14 "Issachar is a rawboned donkey,
crouching between the saddlebags.
15 When he saw how good a settled life was,
and how pleasant the land,
He bent his shoulder to the burden
and became a toiling serf.

16 "Dan shall achieve justice* for his people
as one of the tribes of Israel.
17 Let Dan be a serpent by the roadside,
a horned viper by the path,
That bites the horse's heel,
so that the rider tumbles backward.

18 "I long for your deliverance, O LORD!*

19 "Gad shall be raided by raiders,
but he shall raid at their heels.*

20 "Asher's produce is rich,
and he shall furnish delicacies for kings.

21 "Naphtali is a hind let loose,
which brings forth lovely fawns.

22 "Joseph is a wild colt,
a wild colt by a spring,
wild colts on a hillside.
23 Harrying him and shooting,
the archers opposed him;
24 But his bow remained taut,
and his arms were nimble,
By the power of the Mighty One of Jacob,
because of the Shepherd, the Rock of Israel,
25 The God of your father, who helps you,*
God Almighty, who blesses you,
With the blessings of the heavens above,
the blessings of the abyss that crouches below,
The blessings of breasts and womb,
26 the blessings of fresh grain and blossoms,
the blessings of the everlasting mountains,
the delights of the eternal hills.
May they rest on the head of Joseph,
on the brow of the prince among his brothers.

27 "Benjamin is a ravenous wolf;
mornings he devours the prey,
and evenings he distributes the spoils."

**49:10 Until tribute comes to him**: this translation is based on a slight change in the Hebrew text, which, as it stands, would seem to mean, "until he comes to Shiloh." A somewhat different reading of the Hebrew text would be, "until he comes to whom it belongs." This last has been traditionally understood in a messianic sense. In any case, the passage aims at the supremacy of the tribe of Judah and of the Davidic dynasty.

**49:11 In wine . . . the blood of grapes:** Judah's clothes are poetically pictured as soaked with grape juice from trampling in the wine press, the rich vintage of his land; cf. Is 63:2.

**49:16** In Hebrew the verb for "achieve justice" is from the same root as the name Dan.

**49:18** This short plea for divine mercy has been inserted into the middle of Jacob's testament.

**49:19** In Hebrew there is assonance between the name Gad and the words for "raided," "raiders," and "raid."

**49:25–26** A very similar description of the agricultural riches of the tribal land of Joseph is given in Dt 33:13–16.

*i:* Gn 34:25. *j:* 1 Chr 5:2.

***Farewell and Death.*** [28]All these are the twelve tribes of Israel, and this is what their father said about them, as he blessed them. To each he gave a suitable blessing. [29]Then he gave them this charge: "Since I am about to be gathered to my people, bury me with my ancestors in the cave that lies in the field of Ephron the Hittite, [30]the cave in the field of Machpelah, facing on Mamre, in the land of Canaan, the field that Abraham bought from Ephron the Hittite for a burial ground.[k] [31]There Abraham and his wife Sarah are buried, and so are Isaac and his wife Rebekah, and there, too, I buried Leah— [32]the field and the cave in it that had been purchased from the Hittites."

[33]When Jacob had finished giving these instructions to his sons, he drew his feet into the bed, breathed his last, and was gathered to his people.

## CHAPTER 50

See RG 60–61

***Jacob's Funeral.*** [1]Joseph flung himself upon his father and wept over him as he kissed him. [2]Then Joseph ordered the physicians in his service to embalm his father. When the physicians embalmed Israel, [3]they spent forty days at it, for that is the full period of embalming; and the Egyptians mourned him for seventy days. [4]When the period of mourning was over, Joseph spoke to Pharaoh's household. "If you please, appeal to Pharaoh, saying: [5]My father made me swear: 'I am dying. Bury me in my grave that I have prepared for myself in the land of Canaan.' So now let me go up to bury my father. Then I will come back."[l] [6]Pharaoh replied, "Go and bury your father, as he made you promise on oath."

[7]So Joseph went up to bury his father; and with him went all of Pharaoh's officials who were senior members of his household and all the other elders of the land of Egypt, [8]as well as Joseph's whole household, his brothers, and his father's household; only their children and their flocks and herds were left in the region of Goshen. [9]Chariots, too, and horsemen went up with him; it was a very imposing retinue.

[10]When they arrived at Goren-ha-atad,* which is beyond the Jordan, they held there a very great and solemn memorial service; and Joseph observed seven days of mourning for his father. [11]When the Canaanites who inhabited the land saw the mourning at Goren-ha-atad, they said, "This is a solemn funeral on the part of the Egyptians!" That is why the place was named Abel-mizraim. It is beyond the Jordan.

[12]Thus Jacob's sons did for him as he had instructed them. [13]They carried him to the land of Canaan and buried him in the cave in the field of Machpelah, facing on Mamre, the field that Abraham had bought for a burial ground from Ephron the Hittite.[m]

[14]After Joseph had buried his father he returned to Egypt, together with his brothers and all who had gone up with him for the burial of his father.

***Plea for Forgiveness.*** [15]* Now that their father was dead, Joseph's brothers became fearful and thought, "Suppose Joseph has been nursing a grudge against us and now most certainly will pay us back in full for all the wrong we did him!" [16]So they sent to Joseph and said: "Before your father died, he gave us these instructions: [17]'Thus you shall say to Joseph: Please forgive the criminal wrongdoing of your brothers, who treated you harmfully.' So now please forgive the

**50:10–11 Goren-ha-atad**: "Threshing Floor of the Brambles." **Abel-mizraim**: although the name really means "watercourse of the Egyptians," it is understood here, by a play on the first part of the term, to mean "mourning of the Egyptians." The site has not been identified through either reading of the name. But it is difficult to see why the mourning rites should have been held in the land beyond the Jordan when the burial was at Hebron. Perhaps an earlier form of the story placed the mourning rites beyond the Wadi of Egypt, the traditional boundary between Canaan and Egypt (Nm 34:5; Jos 15:4, 47).

**50:15–26** The final reconciliation of the brothers. Fearful of what may happen after the death of their father, the brothers engage in a final deception, inventing the dying wish of Jacob. Again, Joseph weeps, and, again, his brothers fall down before him, offering to be his slaves (44:16, 33). Joseph's assurance is also a summation of the story: "Even though you meant harm to me, God meant it for good, to achieve this present end, the survival of many people" (v. 20). Joseph's adoption of the children of Manasseh's son Machir recalls Jacob's adoption of his grandchildren (48:5, 13–20); the adoptions reflect tribal history (cf. Jgs 5:14).

*k:* Gn 23:17. *l:* Gn 47:30. *m:* Gn 23:16; Jos 24:32; Acts 7:16.

**Good and Evil**

THE BROTHERS' WORDS "We are your slaves!" (50:18) unintentionally anticipate the slavery of the Israelites in Egypt. Joseph's words in v. 20 sound the overriding theme of the Joseph story: the divine ability to guide events and to turn evil into good.

crime that we, the servants of the God of
your father, committed." When they said
this to him, Joseph broke into tears. 18Then
his brothers also proceeded to fling themselves down before him and said, "We are
your slaves!" 19But Joseph replied to them:
"Do not fear. Can I take the place of God?
20Even though you meant harm to me, God
meant it for good, to achieve this present
end, the survival of many people.[n] 21So now,
do not fear. I will provide for you and for
your children." By thus speaking kindly to
them, he reassured them.[o]
22Joseph remained in Egypt, together with
his father's household. He lived a hundred
and ten years. 23He saw Ephraim's children
to the third generation, and the children of
Manasseh's son Machir were also born on
Joseph's knees.[p]
*Death of Joseph.* 24Joseph said to his
brothers: "I am about to die. God will surely
take care of you and lead you up from this
land to the land that he promised on oath to
Abraham, Isaac and Jacob."[q] 25Then, putting
the sons of Israel under oath, he continued,
"When God thus takes care of you, you must
bring my bones up from this place."[r] 26Joseph died at the age of a hundred and ten. He
was embalmed and laid to rest in a coffin in
Egypt.[s]

*n:* Gn 45:5. *o:* Gn 47:12. *p:* Nm 32:39; Jos 17:1. *q:* Ex 3:8; Heb 11:22. *r:* Ex 13:19; Heb 11:22. *s:* Sir 49:15.

See RG 62–73

# The Book of Exodus

The second book of the Pentateuch is called Exodus, from the Greek word for "departure," because its central event was understood by the Septuagint's translators to be the departure of the Israelites from Egypt. Its Hebrew title, *Shemoth* ("Names"), is from the book's opening phrase, "These are the names . . .." Continuing the history of Israel from the point where the Book of Genesis leaves off, Exodus recounts the Egyptian oppression of Jacob's ever-increasing descendants and their miraculous deliverance by God through Moses, who led them across the Red Sea to Mount Sinai where they entered into a covenant with the Lord. Covenantal laws and detailed prescriptions for the tabernacle (a portable sanctuary foreshadowing the Jerusalem Temple) and its service are followed by a dramatic episode of rebellion, repentance, and divine mercy. After the broken covenant is renewed, the tabernacle is constructed, and the cloud signifying God's glorious presence descends to cover it.

These events made Israel a nation and confirmed their unique relationship with God. The "law" (Hebrew *torah*) given by God through Moses to the Israelites at Mount Sinai constitutes the moral, civil, and ritual legislation by which they were to become a holy people. Many elements of it were fundamental to the teaching of Jesus (Mt 5:21–30; 15:4) as well as to New Testament and Christian moral teaching (Rom 13:8–10; 1 Cor 10:1–5; 1 Pt 2:9).

The principal divisions of Exodus are:

I. Introduction: The Oppression of the Israelites in Egypt (1:1–2:22)
II. The Call and Commission of Moses (2:23–7:7)
III. The Contest with Pharaoh (7:8–13:16)
IV. The Deliverance of the Israelites from Pharaoh and Victory at the Sea (13:17–15:21)
V. The Journey in the Wilderness to Sinai (15:22–18:27)
VI. Covenant and Legislation at Mount Sinai (19:1–31:18)
VII. Israel's Apostasy and God's Renewal of the Covenant (32:1–34:35)

VIII. The Building of the Tabernacle and the Descent of God's Glory upon It (35:1–40:38)

---

## I. Introduction: The Oppression of the Israelites in Egypt

### CHAPTER 1

See RG 64

***Jacob's Descendants in Egypt.*** [1]These are the names of the sons of Israel* who, accompanied by their households, entered into Egypt with Jacob: [2]* Reuben, Simeon, Levi and Judah; [3]Issachar, Zebulun and Benjamin; [4]Dan and Naphtali; Gad and Asher. [5]The total number of Jacob's direct descendants* was seventy.[a] Joseph was already in Egypt.

[6]Now Joseph and all his brothers and that whole generation died.[b] [7]But the Israelites were fruitful and prolific. They multiplied and became so very numerous that the land was filled with them.*

***The Oppression.*** [8c] Then a new king, who knew nothing of Joseph,* rose to power in Egypt. [9]He said to his people, "See! The Israelite people have multiplied and become more numerous than we are! [10]Come, let us deal shrewdly with them to stop their increase;* otherwise, in time of war they too may join our enemies to fight against us, and so leave the land."

[11]Accordingly, they set supervisors over the Israelites to oppress them with forced labor.[d] Thus they had to build for Pharaoh* the garrison cities of Pithom and Raamses. [12]Yet the more they were oppressed, the more they multiplied and spread, so that the Egyptians began to loathe the Israelites. [13]So the Egyptians reduced the Israelites to cruel slavery, [14]making life bitter for them with hard labor, at mortar* and brick and all kinds of field work—cruelly oppressed in all their labor.

***Command to the Midwives.*** [15]The king of Egypt told the Hebrew midwives, one of whom was called Shiphrah and the other Puah, [16]"When you act as midwives for the Hebrew women, look on the birthstool:* if it is a boy, kill him; but if it is a girl, she may live." [17]The midwives, however, feared God; they did not do as the king of Egypt had ordered them, but let the boys live. [18]So the king of Egypt summoned the midwives and asked them, "Why have you done this, allowing the boys to live?" [19]The midwives answered Pharaoh, "The Hebrew women are not like the Egyptian women. They are robust and give birth before the midwife arrives." [20]Therefore God dealt well with the midwives; and the people multiplied and grew very numerous. [21]And because the

**1:1 Sons of Israel**: here literally the first-generation sons of Jacob/Israel. Cf. v. 5. However, beginning with v. 7 the same Hebrew phrase refers to Jacob's more remote descendants; hence, from there on, it is ordinarily rendered "the Israelites." **Households**: the family in its fullest sense, including wives, children and servants.

**1:2** Jacob's sons are listed here according to their respective mothers. Cf. Gn 29:31; 30:20; 35:16–26.

**1:5 Direct descendants**: lit., "persons coming from Jacob's loins"; hence, wives of Jacob's sons and servants are not included. Cf. Gn 46:26. **Seventy**: Gn 46:26, along with the Septuagint for the verse, agrees on a total of sixty-six coming down to Egypt with Jacob, but in v. 27 the Hebrew text adds the two sons born to Joseph in Egypt and presupposes Jacob himself and Joseph for a total of seventy; the Septuagint adds "nine sons" born to Joseph to get a total of seventy-five. This is the figure the Septuagint and 4QEx[a] have here in Ex 1:5.

**1:7 Fruitful . . . multiplied . . . the land was filled with them**: the language used here to indicate the fecundity of the Israelite population echoes the divine blessing bestowed upon humanity at creation (Gn 1:28) and after the flood (Gn 9:1) as well as suggesting fulfillment of the promises to the ancestors Abraham, Isaac, and Jacob (Gn 12:2; 13:16; 15:5; 28:14; passim).

**1:8 Who knew nothing of Joseph**: the nuance intended by the Hebrew verb "know" here goes beyond precise determination. The idea may be not simply that a new king came to power who had not heard of Joseph but that this king ignored the services that Joseph had rendered to Egypt, repudiating the special relationship that existed between Joseph and his predecessor on the throne.

**1:10 Increase**: Pharaoh's actions thereby immediately pit him against God's will for the Israelites to multiply; see note on v. 7 above.

**1:11 Pharaoh**: not a personal name, but a title common to all the kings of Egypt.

**1:14 Mortar**: either the wet clay with which the bricks were made, as in Na 3:14, or the cement used between the bricks in building, as in Gn 11:3.

**1:16 Birthstool**: apparently a pair of stones on which the mother is seated for childbirth opposite the midwife. The Hebrew word elsewhere is used to refer to the stones of a potter's wheel.

---

*a:* Gn 46:26–27; Dt 10:22; Acts 7:14. *b:* Gn 50:26. *c:* Acts 7:18–19. *d:* Dt 26:6.

midwives feared God, God built up families for them. [22]Pharaoh then commanded all his people, "Throw into the Nile every boy that is born,[e] but you may let all the girls live."

See RG 64–65

## CHAPTER 2

***Birth and Adoption of Moses.*** [1]Now a man* of the house of Levi married a Levite woman,[f] [2]and the woman conceived and bore a son. Seeing what a fine child he was, she hid him for three months.[g] [3]But when she could no longer hide him, she took a papyrus basket,* daubed it with bitumen and pitch, and putting the child in it, placed it among the reeds on the bank of the Nile. [4]His sister stationed herself at a distance to find out what would happen to him.

[5]Then Pharaoh's daughter came down to bathe at the Nile, while her attendants walked along the bank of the Nile. Noticing the basket among the reeds, she sent her handmaid to fetch it. [6]On opening it, she looked, and there was a baby boy crying! She was moved with pity for him and said, "It is one of the Hebrews' children." [7]Then his sister asked Pharaoh's daughter, "Shall I go and summon a Hebrew woman to nurse the child for you?" [8]Pharaoh's daughter answered her, "Go." So the young woman went and called the child's own mother. [9]Pharaoh's daughter said to her, "Take this child and nurse him for me, and I will pay your wages."* So the woman took the child and nursed him. [10]When the child grew,* she brought him to Pharaoh's daughter, and he became her son.[h] She named him Moses; for she said, "I drew him out of the water."

***Moses' Flight to Midian.*** [11][i] On one occasion, after Moses had grown up,* when he had gone out to his kinsmen and witnessed their forced labor, he saw an Egyptian striking a Hebrew, one of his own kinsmen. [12]Looking about and seeing no one, he struck down the Egyptian and hid him in the sand. [13]The next day he went out again, and now two Hebrews were fighting! So he asked the culprit, "Why are you striking your companion?" [14]But he replied, "Who has appointed you ruler and judge over us? Are you thinking of killing me as you killed the Egyptian?" Then Moses became afraid and thought, "The affair must certainly be known." [15]When Pharaoh heard of the affair, he sought to kill Moses. But Moses fled from Pharaoh and went to the land of Midian.* [j] There he sat down by a well.

**2:1 Now a man**: the chapter begins abruptly, without names for the man or woman (in contrast to the midwives of 1:15), who in 6:20 are identified as Amram and Jochebed.

**2:3 Basket**: the same Hebrew word is used in Gn 6:14 and throughout the flood narrative for Noah's ark, but nowhere else in the Bible. Here, however, the "ark" or "chest" was made of papyrus stalks. Presumably the allusion to Genesis is intentional. Just as Noah and his family were preserved safe from the threatening waters of the flood in the ark he built, so now Moses is preserved from the threatening waters of the Nile in the ark prepared by his mother. **Among the reeds**: the Hebrew noun for "reed" is overwhelmingly used in the phrase "Reed Sea," traditionally translated "Red Sea."

**2:9 And I will pay your wages**: the idea that the child's mother will be paid for nursing her child—and by Pharaoh's own daughter—heightens the narrative's irony.

**2:10 When the child grew**: while v. 9 implies that the boy's mother cared for him as long as he needed to be nursed (presumably, between two and four years), the same verb appears in v. 11 to describe the attainment of adulthood. **And he became her son**: Pharaoh's daughter adopts Moses, thus adding to the irony of the account. The king of Egypt had ordered the killing of all the sons of the Hebrews, and one now becomes the son of his own daughter! **Moses**: in Hebrew, *mosheh*. There is a play on words here: Hebrew *mosheh* echoes *meshithihu* ("I drew him out"). However, the name Moses actually has nothing to do with that Hebrew verb, but is probably derived from Egyptian "beloved" or "has been born," preserved in such Pharaonic names as Thutmoses (meaning approximately "Beloved of the god Thoth" or "The god Thoth is born, has given birth to [the child]"). The original meaning of Moses' name was no longer remembered (if it was Egyptian, it may have contained an Egyptian divine element as well, perhaps the name of the Nile god Hapi), and a secondary explanation was derived from this story (or gave rise to it, if the drawing from the water of the Nile was intended to foreshadow the Israelites' escape from Egypt through the Red Sea).

**2:11 After Moses had grown up**: cf. 7:7, where Moses is said to be eighty years old at the time of his mission to Pharaoh. **Striking**: probably in the sense of "flogging"; in v. 12, however, the same verb is used in the sense of "killing."

**2:15 Land of Midian**: the territory under the control of a confederation made up, according to Nm 31:8, of five Midianite tribes. According to Gn 25:1–2, Midian was a son of Abraham by Keturah. In view of the extreme hostility in later periods between Israel and Midian (cf. Nm 31; Jgs 6–8), the relationship is striking, as is the account here in Exodus of good relations between Moses and no less than a Midianite priest.

*e:* Acts 7:19. *f:* Ex 6:20; Nm 26:59. *g:* Acts 7:20; Heb 11:23. *h:* Acts 7:21; Heb 11:24. *i:* Acts 7:23–28. *j:* Acts 7:29; Heb 11:27.

### Moses Is Born and Saved from the Nile River

THIS STORY OF Moses' birth and rescue from the river includes parallels to other birth stories of heroes, especially the Legend of King Sargon of Akkad (ninth century B.C.). Moses is born of parents from the Israelite tribe of Levi. The Levites became a tribe of priests or servants dedicated to the worship of God (32:25–29). The family tree for the tribe of Levi in Exodus 6:14–27 names Moses' parents as Amram and Jochebed, his brother as Aaron, and his sister as Miriam. Micah 6:4 lists these three siblings—Moses, Aaron, and Miriam—as the leaders of Israel in their wilderness trek from Egypt to the Promised Land of Canaan.

Pharaoh's own daughter conspires with Hebrew women to resist her father's vicious program against Israelite children (2:10). In a satisfying twist of fate, Pharaoh's daughter will pay wages to Moses' mother for nursing the mother's own child (v. 9). The name Moses (*Mosheh*) plays on the verb "to draw out" (*mashah*).

[16]Now the priest of Midian had seven
daughters, and they came to draw water and
fill the troughs to water their father's flock.
[17]But shepherds came and drove them away.
So Moses rose up in their defense and watered their flock. [18]When they returned to
their father Reuel,* he said to them, "How is
it you have returned so soon today?" [19]They
answered, "An Egyptian* delivered us from
the shepherds. He even drew water for us
and watered the flock!" [20]"Where is he?" he
asked his daughters. "Why did you leave the
man there? Invite him to have something to
eat." [21]Moses agreed to stay with him, and
the man gave Moses his daughter Zipporah
in marriage. [22]She conceived and bore a son,
whom he named Gershom;* for he said, "I
am a stranger residing in a foreign land."[k]

## II. The Call and Commission of Moses

***The Burning Bush.*** [23]A long time passed,
during which the king of Egypt died. The Israelites groaned under their bondage and
cried out, and from their bondage their cry
for help went up to God.[l] [24]God heard their
moaning and God was mindful of his
covenant[m] with Abraham, Isaac and Jacob.
[25]God saw the Israelites, and God knew . . .*

### CHAPTER 3

See RG 64–65

[1]* Meanwhile Moses was tending the
flock of his father-in-law Jethro, the priest of
Midian. Leading the flock beyond the wilderness, he came to the mountain of God, Horeb.*

**2:18 Reuel**: also called Jethro. Cf. 3:1; 4:18; 18:1.

**2:19 An Egyptian**: Moses was probably wearing Egyptian dress, or spoke Egyptian to Reuel's daughters.

**2:22 Gershom**: the name is explained unscientifically as if it came from the Hebrew word *ger*, "sojourner, resident alien," and the Hebrew word *sham*, "there." **Stranger residing**: Hebrew *ger*, one who seeks and finds shelter and a home away from his or her own people or land.

**2:25 God knew**: in response to the people's cry, God, mindful of the covenant, looks on their plight and acknowledges firsthand the depth of their suffering (see 3:7). In vv. 23–25, traditionally attributed to the Priestly writer, God is mentioned five times, in contrast to the rest of chaps. 1–2, where God is rarely mentioned. These verses serve as a fitting transition to Moses' call in chap. 3.

**3:1–4:17** After the introduction to the narrative in 2:23–25, the commissioning itself falls into three sections: God's appearance under the aspect of a burning bush (3:1–6); the explicit commission (3:7–10); and an extended dialogue between Moses and God, in the course of which Moses receives the revelation of God's personal name. Although in the J source of the Pentateuch people have known and invoked God's personal name in worship since the time of Seth (Gn 4:26), for the E and P sources (see 6:2–4) God first makes this name publicly available here through Moses.

**3:1 The mountain of God, Horeb**: traditionally, "Horeb" is taken to be an alternate name in E source material and Deuteronomy (e.g., Dt 1:2) for what in J and P is known as Mount Sinai, the goal of the Israelites' journey after leaving Egypt and the site of the covenant God makes with Israel. However, it is not clear that originally the two names reflect the same mountain, nor even that "Horeb" refers originally to a mountain and not simply the dry, ruined region (from Hebrew *horeb*, "dryness, devastation") around the mountain. Additionally, the position of "Horeb" at the end of the verse may indicate that the identification of the "mountain of God" with Horeb (= Sinai?) represents a later stage in the evolution

*k:* Ex 18:3. *l:* Ex 3:7, 9; Dt 26:7. *m:* Ex 6:5; Ps 105:8–9; 106:44–45.

[2]There the angel of the LORD* appeared to
him as fire flaming out of a bush.[n] When he
looked, although the bush was on fire, it was
not being consumed. [3]So Moses decided, "I
must turn aside to look at this remarkable
sight. Why does the bush not burn up?"
[4]When the LORD saw that he had turned
aside to look, God called out to him from the
bush: Moses! Moses! He answered, "Here I
am." [5]God said: Do not come near! Remove
your sandals from your feet, for the place
where you stand is holy ground.[o] [6]I am the
God of your father,* he continued, the God
of Abraham, the God of Isaac, and the God
of Jacob.[p] Moses hid his face, for he was
afraid to look at God.

***The Call and Commission of Moses.*** [7]But
the LORD said: I have witnessed the affliction of my people in Egypt and have heard
their cry against their taskmasters, so I know
well what they are suffering. [8]Therefore I
have come down* to rescue them from the
power of the Egyptians and lead them up
from that land into a good and spacious land,
a land flowing with milk and honey, the
country of the Canaanites, the Hittites, the
Amorites, the Perizzites, the Girgashites,
the Hivites and the Jebusites.[q] [9]Now indeed
the outcry of the Israelites has reached me,
and I have seen how the Egyptians are oppressing them. [10]Now, go! I am sending you
to Pharaoh to bring my people, the Israelites,
out of Egypt.

[11]But Moses said to God, "Who am I* that
I should go to Pharaoh and bring the Israelites out of Egypt?" [12]God answered: I will be
with you; and this will be your sign* that I
have sent you. When you have brought the

of the tradition about God's meeting with Moses. The phrase "mountain of God" simply anticipates the divine apparitions which would take place there, both on this occasion and after the Israelites' departure from Egypt; alternatively, it means that the place was already sacred or a place of pilgrimage in pre-Israelite times. In any case, the narrative offers no indications of its exact location.

**3:2 The angel of the LORD**: Hebrew *mal'ak* or "messenger" is regularly translated *angelos* by the Septuagint, from which the English word "angel" is derived, but the Hebrew term lacks connotations now popularly associated with "angel" (such as wings). Although angels frequently assume human form (cf. Gn 18–19), the term is also used to indicate the visual form under which God occasionally appeared and spoke to people, referred to indifferently in some Old Testament texts either as God's "angel," *mal'ak*, or as God. Cf. Gn 16:7, 13; Ex 14:19, 24–25; Nm 22:22–35; Jgs 6:11–18. **The bush**: Hebrew *seneh*, perhaps "thorny bush," occurring only here in vv. 2–4 and in Dt 33:16. Its use here is most likely a wordplay on Sinai (Hebrew *sinay*), implying a popular etymology for the name of the sacred mountain.

**3:6 God of your father**: a frequently used epithet in Genesis (along with the variants "my father" and "your father") for God as worshiped by the ancestors. As is known from its usage outside of the Bible in the ancient Near East, it suggests a close, personal relationship between the individual and the particular god in question, who is both a patron and a protector, a god traditionally revered by the individual's family and whose worship is passed down from father to son. **The God of Abraham . . . Jacob**: this precise phrase (only here and in v. 15; 4:5) stresses the continuity between the new revelation to Moses and the earlier religious experience of Israel's ancestors, identifying the God who is now addressing Moses with the God who promised land and numerous posterity to the ancestors. Cf. Mt 22:32; Mk 12:26; Lk 20:37. **Afraid to look at God**: the traditions about Moses are not uniform in regard to his beholding or not being able to look at God (cf. 24:11; 33:11, 18–23; 34:29–35). Here Moses' reaction is the natural and spontaneous gesture of a person suddenly confronted with a direct experience of God. Aware of his human frailty and the gulf that separates him from the God who is holy, he hides his face. To encounter the divine was to come before an awesome and mysterious power unlike any other a human being might experience and, as such, potentially threatening to one's very identity or existence (see Gn 32:30).

**3:8 I have come down**: cf. Gn 11:5, 7; 18:21. **Flowing with milk and honey**: an expression denoting agricultural prosperity, which seems to have been proverbial in its application to the land of Canaan. Cf. Ex 13:5; Nm 13:27; Jos 5:6; Jer 11:5; 32:22; Ez 20:6, 15.

**3:11 Who am I**: this question is always addressed by an inferior to a superior (to the ruler in 1 Sm 18:18; to God in 2 Sm 7:18 and its parallel, 1 Chr 17:16; 1 Chr 29:14; 2 Chr 2:5). In response to some special opportunity or invitation, the question expresses in a style typical of the ancient Near East the speaker's humility or gratitude or need of further assistance, but never unwillingness or an outright refusal to respond. Instead the question sets the stage for further support from the superior should that be needed (as here).

**3:12 Sign**: a visible display of the power of God. The ancient notion of a sign from God does not coincide with the modern understanding of "miracle," which suggests some disruption in the laws governing nature. While most any phenomenon can become a vehicle for displaying the purposes and providence of God, here the sign intended to confirm Moses' commission by God seems to be the burning bush itself. Since normally the giving of such a sign would follow the commission rather than precede it (see Jgs 6:11–24), some see Israel's service of God at Sinai after the exodus from Egypt as the confirmatory sign, albeit retroactively. It is more likely, however, that its mention here is intended to establish the present episode with Moses alone as a prefigurement of God's fiery theophany to all Israel on Mount Sinai.

*n:* Acts 7:30–35. *o:* Jos 5:15. *p:* Ex 4:5; Mt 22:32; Mk 12:26; Lk 20:37. *q:* Gn 15:19–21.

people out of Egypt, you will serve God at
this mountain. 13“But,” said Moses to God,
“if I go to the Israelites and say to them, ‘The
God of your ancestors has sent me to you,’
and they ask me, ‘What is his name?’ what
do I tell them?” 14God replied to Moses: I
am who I am.* Then he added: This is what
you will tell the Israelites: I AM has sent me
to you.

15God spoke further to Moses: This is
what you will say to the Israelites: The
LORD, the God of your ancestors, the God of
Abraham, the God of Isaac, and the God of
Jacob, has sent me to you.

This is my name forever;[r]
  this is my title for all generations.

16Go and gather the elders of the Israelites, and tell them, The LORD, the God of
your ancestors, the God of Abraham, Isaac,
and Jacob, has appeared to me and said: I
have observed you and what is being done to
you in Egypt; 17so I have decided to lead you
up out of your affliction in Egypt into the
land of the Canaanites, the Hittites, the Amorites, the Perizzites, the Girgashites, the Hivites and the Jebusites, a land flowing with
milk and honey. 18They will listen to you.
Then you and the elders of Israel will go to
the king of Egypt and say to him:[s] The LORD,
the God of the Hebrews, has come to meet
us. So now, let us go a three days’ journey in
the wilderness to offer sacrifice to the LORD,
our God. 19Yet I know that the king of Egypt
will not allow you to go unless his hand is
forced. 20So I will stretch out my hand and
strike Egypt with all the wondrous deeds I
will do in its midst. After that he will let you
go. 21[t]I will even make the Egyptians so
well-disposed toward this people that, when
you go, you will not go empty-handed.
22Every woman will ask her neighbor and
the resident alien in her house for silver and
gold articles* and for clothing, and you will
put them on your sons and daughters. So you
will plunder the Egyptians.

## CHAPTER 4

See RG 64–65

1“But,” objected Moses, “suppose
they do not believe me or listen to me? For
they may say, ‘The LORD did not appear to
you.’ ” 2The LORD said to him: What is in
your hand? “A staff,” he answered. 3God
said: Throw it on the ground. So he threw it
on the ground and it became a snake,[u] and
Moses backed away from it. 4Then the LORD
said to Moses: Now stretch out your hand
and take hold of its tail. So he stretched out
his hand and took hold of it, and it became a
staff in his hand. 5That is so they will believe
that the LORD, the God of their ancestors, the
God of Abraham, the God of Isaac, and the
God of Jacob, did appear to you.

6Again the LORD said to him: Put your
hand into the fold of your garment. So he put
his hand into the fold of his garment, and
when he drew it out, there was his hand covered with scales, like snowflakes. 7Then
God said: Put your hand back into the fold of
your garment. So he put his hand back into
the fold of his garment, and when he drew it
out, there it was again like his own flesh. 8If

**Serve God**: Hebrew *‘-b-d*, “serve,” includes among its meanings both the notion of “serving or working for another” and the notion of “worship.” The implication here is that the Israelites’ service/worship of God is incompatible with their service to Pharaoh.

**3:14 I am who I am**: Moses asks in v. 13 for the name of the One speaking to him, but God responds with a wordplay which preserves the utterly mysterious character of the divine being even as it appears to suggest something of the inner meaning of God’s name: *’ehyeh* “I am” or “I will be(come)” for “*Yhwh*,” the personal name of the God of Israel. While the phrase “I am who I am” resists unraveling, it nevertheless suggests an etymological linking between the name “Yhwh” and an earlier form of the Hebrew verbal root *h-y-h* “to be.” On that basis many have interpreted the name “Yhwh” as a third-person form of the verb meaning “He causes to be, creates,” itself perhaps a shortened form of a longer liturgical name such as “(God who) creates (the heavenly armies).” Note in this connection the invocation of Israel’s God as “LORD (*Yhwh*) of Hosts” (e.g., 1 Sm 17:45). In any case, out of reverence for God’s proper name, the term *Adonai*, “my Lord,” was later used as a substitute. The word LORD (in small capital letters) indicates that the Hebrew text has the sacred name (*Yhwh*), the tetragrammaton. The word “Jehovah” arose from a false reading of this name as it is written in the current Hebrew text. The Septuagint has *egō eimi ho ōn*, “I am the One who is” (*ōn* being the participle of the verb “to be”). This can be taken as an assertion of God’s aseity or self-existence, and has been understood as such by the Church, since the time of the Fathers, as a true expression of God’s being, even though it is not precisely the meaning of the Hebrew.

**3:22 Articles**: probably jewelry.

*r:* Ps 135:13. *s:* Ex 5:3. *t:* Ex 11:2–3; 12:35–36. *u:* Ex 7:10.

they do not believe you or pay attention to
the message of the first sign, they should believe the message of the second sign. 9 And if
they do not believe even these two signs and
do not listen to you, take some water from
the Nile and pour it on the dry land. The water you take from the Nile will become blood
on the dry land.[v]

***Aaron's Office as Assistant.*** 10 Moses,
however, said to the LORD, "If you please,
my Lord, I have never been eloquent, neither
in the past nor now that you have spoken to
your servant; but I am slow of speech and
tongue."[w] 11 The LORD said to him: Who
gives one person speech? Who makes another mute or deaf, seeing or blind? Is it not
I, the LORD? 12 Now go, I will assist you in
speaking* and teach you what you are to say.
13 But he said, "If you please, my Lord, send
someone else!"* 14 Then the LORD became
angry with Moses and said: I know there is
your brother, Aaron the Levite, who is a
good speaker; even now he is on his way to
meet you. When he sees you, he will truly be
glad. 15 You will speak to him and put the
words in his mouth. I will assist both you
and him in speaking and teach you both
what you are to do. 16 He will speak to the
people for you: he will be your spokesman,*
and you will be as God to him.[x] 17 Take this
staff* in your hand; with it you are to perform the signs.

***Moses' Return to Egypt.*** 18 After this Moses returned to Jethro* his father-in-law and
said to him, "Let me return to my kindred in
Egypt, to see whether they are still living."
Jethro replied to Moses, "Go in peace."
19 Then the LORD said to Moses in Midian:
Return to Egypt, for all those who sought
your life are dead. 20 So Moses took his wife
and his sons, mounted them on the donkey,
and started back to the land of Egypt. Moses
took the staff of God with him. 21 The LORD
said to Moses: On your return to Egypt, see
that you perform before Pharaoh all the
wonders I have put in your power. But I will
harden his heart* and he will not let the people go. 22[y] So you will say to Pharaoh, Thus
says the LORD: Israel is my son, my firstborn. 23 I said to you: Let my son go, that he
may serve me. Since you refused to let him
go, I will kill your son, your firstborn.[z]

24* On the journey, at a place where they
spent the night, the LORD came upon Moses
and sought to put him to death. 25[a] But Zipporah took a piece of flint and cut off her

**4:12 Assist you in speaking**: lit., "be with your mouth"; cf. v. 15, lit., "be with your mouth and with his mouth."

**4:13 Send someone else**: lit., "send by means of him whom you will send," that is, "send whom you will."

**4:16 Spokesman**: lit., "mouth"; Aaron was to serve as a mouthpiece for Moses, as a prophet does for God; hence the relation between Moses and Aaron is compared to that between God and his prophet: Moses "will be as God to," i.e., lit., "will become God for him." Cf. 7:1.

**4:17 This staff**: probably the same as that of vv. 2–4; but some understand that a new staff is now given by God to Moses.

**4:18 Jethro**: the Hebrew text has "Jether," apparently a variant form of "Jethro" found in the same verse. **To see whether they are still living**: Moses did not tell his father-in-law his main reason for returning to Egypt.

**4:21 Harden his heart**: in the biblical view, the heart, whose actual function in the circulation of blood was unknown, typically performs functions associated today more with the brain than with the emotions. Therefore, while it may be used in connection with various emotional states ranging from joy to sadness, it very commonly designates the seat of intellectual and volitional activities. For God to harden Pharaoh's heart is to harden his resolve against the Israelites' desire to leave. In the ancient world, actions which are out of character are routinely attributed not to the person but to some "outside" superhuman power acting upon the person (Jgs 14:16; 1 Sm 16:10). Uncharacteristically negative actions or states are explained in the same way (1 Sm 16:14). In this instance, the opposition of Pharaoh, in the face of God's displays of power, would be unintelligible to the ancient Israelites unless he is seen as under some divine constraint. But this does not diminish Pharaoh's own responsibility. In the anthropology of the ancient Israelites there is no opposition between individual responsibility and God's sovereignty over all of creation. Cf. Rom 9:17–18.

**4:24–26** This story continues to perplex commentators and may have circulated in various forms before finding its place here in Exodus. Particularly troublesome is the unique phrase "spouse of blood." Nevertheless, v. 26, which apparently comes from the hand of a later commentator on the original story, is intended to offer some clarification. It asserts that when Zipporah used the problematic expression (addressing it either to Moses or her son), she did so with reference to the circumcision performed on her son—the only place in the Bible where this rite is performed by a woman. Whatever the precise meaning of the phrase "spouse of blood," circumcision is the key to understanding it as well as the entire incident. One may conclude, therefore, that God was angry with Moses for having failed to keep the divine command given to Abraham in Gn 17:10–12 and circumcise his son. Moses' life is spared when his wife circumcises their son.

*v:* Ex 7:17, 19–20. *w:* Ex 6:12. *x:* Ex 7:1. *y:* Sir 36:11. *z:* Ex 11:5; 12:29. *a:* Is 6:2; 7:20.

**Moses and Aaron Confront Pharaoh for the First Time**

PHARAOH'S WORDS "I do not know the LORD" (5:2) introduce a theme that recurs throughout this book of the Bible (7:5, 17; 8:6; 9:14; 14:18); hints of things to come are common in ch 5. The threat of pestilence or sword points indirectly to the plagues that will begin soon. The need to stop working to worship the LORD (v. 5) will become a defining practice of the Israelite community with the commandment concerning the Sabbath (20:9–11; Dt 5:12–15). Bad odor with the Pharaoh (v. 21) foreshadows the bad odor that will accompany the first two plagues (7:21; 8:13–14). Verses 22–23 give an example of Moses' bold willingness to speak words of resistance, correction, or complaint to God (chs 3–4; 32:11–14; 33:12–23).

son's foreskin and, touching his feet,* she
said, "Surely you are a spouse of blood to
me." 26 So God let Moses alone. At that time
she said, "A spouse of blood," in regard to
the circumcision.

27 The LORD said to Aaron: Go into the
wilderness to meet Moses. So he went; when
meeting him at the mountain of God, he
kissed him. 28 Moses told Aaron everything
the LORD had sent him to say, and all the
signs he had commanded him to do. 29 Then
Moses and Aaron went and gathered all the
elders of the Israelites. 30 Aaron told them
everything the LORD had said to Moses, and
he performed the signs before the people.
31 The people believed, and when they heard
that the LORD had observed the Israelites and
had seen their affliction,* they knelt and
bowed down.

## CHAPTER 5

See RG 65–67

*Pharaoh's Hardness of Heart.* 1 Afterwards, Moses and Aaron went to Pharaoh
and said, "Thus says the LORD, the God of
Israel: Let my people go, that they may hold
a feast* for me in the wilderness." 2 Pharaoh
answered, "Who is the LORD, that I should
obey him and let Israel go? I do not know the
LORD,* and I will not let Israel go." 3 They
replied, "The God of the Hebrews has come
to meet us. Let us go a three days' journey in
the wilderness, that we may offer sacrifice to
the LORD, our God,[b] so that he does not
strike us with the plague or the sword." 4 The
king of Egypt answered them, "Why, Moses
and Aaron, do you make the people neglect
their work? Off to your labors!" 5 Pharaoh
continued, "Look how they are already more
numerous* than the people of the land, and
yet you would give them rest from their
labors!"

6 That very day Pharaoh gave the taskmasters of the people and their foremen* this order: 7 "You shall no longer supply the people
with straw for their brickmaking* as before.
Let them go and gather their own straw! 8 Yet
you shall levy upon them the same quota of
bricks as they made previously. Do not reduce it. They are lazy; that is why they are
crying, 'Let us go to offer sacrifice to our

**4:25 Touching his feet**: a euphemism most probably for the male sexual organ (see 2 Kgs 18:27; Is 7:20); whether the genitals of the child (after Zipporah circumcised him) or of Moses (after the circumcision of his son) is not clear.

**4:31 Observed . . . their affliction**: the same phrases used in God's dialogue with Moses in 3:16–17.

**5:1 Hold a feast**: the Hebrew verb used here, *hagag* ("to celebrate a feast or a festival"; see 12:14; 23:14), refers to a community celebration marked above all by a procession to the sanctuary. It is used especially of three major feasts: Unleavened Bread, Pentecost (in 23:16, "the Feast of Harvest," but customarily "the Feast of Weeks" [*Shavuot*]), and Succoth/Sukkoth (in 34:16, "the Feast of Ingathering," but more frequently "of Booths, or Tabernacles," as in Dt 16:13, 16; 31:10; Lv 23:34; Zec 14:16; passim) and—along with the related noun *hag*—the Passover in 12:14. See 23:14–18; 34:18–25.

**5:2 I do not know the LORD**: whether or not he had heard of the Lord, the God of Israel, Pharaoh here refuses to acknowledge the Lord's authority. See note on 1:8.

**5:5 They are already more numerous**: a recollection of Pharaoh's earlier words to his subjects in 1:9.

**5:6 The taskmasters of the people and their foremen**: the former were higher officials and probably Egyptians; the latter were lower officials (perhaps recordkeepers or clerks), chosen from the Israelites themselves. Cf. v. 14.

**5:7** Straw was mixed with clay to give sun-dried bricks greater cohesion and durability.

*b:* Ex 3:18.

## Genealogy

THE GENEALOGY OR family tree in ch 6 traces the family line of Jacob's three oldest sons: Reuben (v. 14), Simeon (v. 15), and Levi (vv. 16–25). The focus is clearly on the descendants of Levi, a family of priests. The family tree of Levi has two functions: to identify Moses and Aaron as Levites and brothers, and to trace the priestly line through Aaron to his son Eleazar (vv. 23–24) and his grandson Phinehas (v. 25). Eleazar takes over Aaron's role as high priest in Numbers 20:22–29. God commissions Phinehas and his descendants as priests in Numbers 25:6–13.

God.’ 9Increase the work for the men, so that they attend to it and not to deceitful words.” 10So the taskmasters of the people and their foremen went out and told the people, “Thus says Pharaoh,* ‘I will not provide you with straw. 11Go and get your own straw from wherever you can find it. But there will not be the slightest reduction in your work.’ ” 12The people, then, scattered throughout the land of Egypt to gather stubble for straw, 13while the taskmasters kept driving them on, saying, “Finish your work, the same daily amount as when the straw was supplied to you.” 14The Israelite foremen, whom the taskmasters of Pharaoh had placed over them, were beaten, and were asked, “Why have you not completed your prescribed amount of bricks yesterday and today, as before?”

***Complaint of the Foremen.*** 15Then the Israelite foremen came and cried out to Pharaoh:* “Why do you treat your servants in this manner? 16No straw is supplied to your servants, and still we are told, ‘Make bricks!’ Look how your servants are beaten! It is you who are at fault.” 17He answered, “Lazy! You are lazy! That is why you keep saying, ‘Let us go and offer sacrifice to the LORD.’ 18Now off to work! No straw will be supplied to you, but you must supply your quota of bricks.”

19The Israelite foremen realized they were in trouble, having been told, “Do not reduce your daily amount of bricks!” 20So when they left Pharaoh they assailed Moses and Aaron, who were waiting to meet them, 21and said to them, “The LORD look upon you and judge! You have made us offensive to Pharaoh and his servants, putting a sword into their hands to kill us.”

***Renewal of God's Promise.*** 22Then Moses again had recourse to the LORD and said, “LORD, why have you treated this people badly? And why did you send me? 23From the time I went to Pharaoh to speak in your name, he has treated this people badly, and you have done nothing to rescue your people.”

### CHAPTER 6

See RG 65–67

1The LORD answered Moses: Now you will see what I will do to Pharaoh. For by a strong hand, he will let them go; by a strong hand,* he will drive them from his land.

***Confirmation of the Promise to the Ancestors.*** 2* Then God spoke to Moses, and said to him: I am the LORD. 3As God the Almighty* I appeared[c] to Abraham, Isaac, and Jacob, but by my name, LORD, I did not make myself

**5:10 Thus says Pharaoh**: the standard formula for prophetic oracles, but with Pharaoh rather than the Lord as the subject. This heightens the sense of personal conflict between Pharaoh, who acts as if he were God, and the Lord, whose claims are spurned by Pharaoh.

**5:15 Cried out to Pharaoh**: the Hebrew verb translated “cry out” and its related noun are normally used of appeals to God by Moses (8:8; 14:15; 15:25; 17:4), the people (3:7, 9; 14:10), or an oppressed individual (22:22, 26). Here, by implication, these minor Israelite officials appeal to Pharaoh as if he were their God. See v. 10.

**6:1 By a strong hand**: by God's hand or Pharaoh's hand? The Hebrew is ambiguous; although it may be an allusion to God's hand of 3:19–20, both interpretations are possible.

**6:2–7:7** According to the standard source criticism of the Pentateuch, 6:2–7:7 represents a Priestly version of the JE call narrative in 3:1–4:17. But in context the present account does more than simply repeat the earlier passage. See note below.

**6:3 God the Almighty**: in Hebrew, *El Shaddai*. This traditional translation does not have a firm philological basis. **But by my name . . . I did not make myself known to them**: although the text implies that the name LORD was unknown previously, in context the emphasis in the passage falls on the

*c:* Gn 17:1; 35:11.

## The Ten Plagues

THE NUMBER "TEN" is nowhere explicitly stated, and the ten plagues are the result of the combination of several overlapping plague accounts, none of which narrated all ten plagues. Alternative traditions, with fewer plagues, in different order, are preserved in Psalms 78:44–51; 105:28–36. Some of the plagues could be natural phenomena. Yet for the biblical writers they are clearly extraordinary manifestations of divine power (see Ex 9:18, 24; 10:6, 14; 11:6).

known to them. 4I also established my covenant with them, to give them the land of Canaan, the land in which they were residing as aliens.[d] 5Now that I have heard the groaning of the Israelites, whom the Egyptians have reduced to slavery, I am mindful of my covenant.[e] 6Therefore, say to the Israelites: I am the LORD. I will free you from the burdens of the Egyptians and will deliver you from their slavery. I will redeem you by my outstretched arm and with mighty acts of judgment. 7I will take you as my own people, and I will be your God;[f] and you will know that I, the LORD, am your God who has freed you from the burdens of the Egyptians 8and I will bring you into the land which I swore to give to Abraham, Isaac, and Jacob. I will give it to you as your own possession—I, the LORD! 9But when Moses told this to the Israelites, they would not listen to him because of their dejection and hard slavery.

10Then the LORD spoke to Moses: 11Go, tell Pharaoh, king of Egypt, to let the Israelites leave his land. 12However, Moses protested to the LORD, "If the Israelites did not listen to me, how is it possible that Pharaoh will listen to me, poor speaker* [g] that I am!" 13But the LORD spoke to Moses and Aaron regarding the Israelites and Pharaoh, king of Egypt, and charged them to bring the Israelites out of the land of Egypt.

*Genealogy of Moses and Aaron.* 14These are the heads of their ancestral houses.* The sons of Reuben,[h] the firstborn of Israel: Hanoch, Pallu, Hezron and Carmi; these are the clans of Reuben. 15The sons of Simeon:[i] Jemuel, Jamin, Ohad, Jachin, Zohar and Shaul, the son of a Canaanite woman; these are the clans of Simeon. 16These are the names of the sons of Levi,[j] in their genealogical order: Gershon, Kohath and Merari. Levi lived one hundred and thirty-seven years.

17The sons of Gershon,[k] by their clans: Libni and Shimei. 18The sons of Kohath:[l] Amram, Izhar, Hebron and Uzziel. Kohath lived one hundred and thirty-three years. 19The sons of Merari:[m] Mahli and Mushi. These are the clans of Levi in their genealogical order.

20Amram married his aunt* Jochebed,[n] who bore him Aaron, Moses, and Miriam. Amram lived one hundred and thirty-seven years. 21The sons of Izhar: Korah, Nepheg and Zichri. 22The sons of Uzziel: Mishael, Elzaphan and Sithri. 23Aaron married Elisheba, Amminadab's[o] daughter, the sister of Nahshon; she bore him Nadab, Abihu, Eleazar and Ithamar. 24The sons of Korah: Assir, Elkanah and Abiasaph. These are the clans of the Korahites. 25Eleazar, Aaron's son, married one of Putiel's daughters, who bore him Phinehas.* These are the heads of the ances-

understanding of God that comes with knowledge of the name. In this way God responds to the worsening plight of the Israelites and Moses' complaint in 5:23 that God has done nothing at all to rescue them.

**6:12 Poor speaker**: lit., "uncircumcised of lips": a metaphor expressing the hindrance of good communication expressed as "slow of speech and tongue" (4:10). Also used as a metaphor for impeded "heart" (Lv 26:41; Dt 10:16).

**6:14** The purpose of the genealogy here is to give the line from which Moses and Aaron sprang, with special emphasis placed on the line of Aaron. Reuben and Simeon are mentioned first because, as older brothers of Levi, their names occur before his in the genealogy.

**6:20 His aunt**: more exactly, "his father's sister." Later on such a marriage was forbidden. Cf. Lv 18:12. Hence, the Greek and Latin versions render here, "his cousin."

**6:25 Phinehas**: according to Nm 25:13, Phinehas was given by God "the covenant of an everlasting priesthood" because of

*d:* Gn 15:18; 17:4–8. *e:* Ex 2:24. *f:* Lv 26:12. *g:* Ex 4:10. *h:* Nm 26:5–6; 1 Chr 5:3. *i:* Nm 26:12; 1 Chr 4:24. *j:* Nm 3:17; 1 Chr 6:1; 23:6. *k:* Nm 3:21; 1 Chr 6:2; 23:7. *l:* Nm 3:27; 1 Chr 6:3, 18. *m:* Nm 3:20; 1 Chr 6:4, 14; 23:21. *n:* Nm 26:59. *o:* Ru 4:19–20; 1 Chr 2:10.

> **The First Plague: The Nile Turns to Blood**
>
> THE NILE RIVER was the primary source of water and life for Egypt. However, the Egyptians had earlier used the Nile as an instrument of death when Pharaoh ordered every Hebrew baby boy to be thrown into the river (1:22). This first plague recalls that previous atrocity. The plague also foreshadows one of the first miraculous signs God gave to Moses to convince the Israelites of God's power (4:9).

tral houses of the Levites by their clans. 26 These are the Aaron and the Moses to whom the LORD said, "Bring the Israelites out from the land of Egypt, company by company." 27 They are the ones who spoke to Pharaoh, king of Egypt, to bring the Israelites out of Egypt—the same Moses and Aaron.

28 When the LORD spoke to Moses in the land of Egypt 29 the LORD said to Moses: I am the LORD. Say to Pharaoh, king of Egypt, all that I tell you. 30 But Moses protested to the LORD, "Since I am a poor speaker, how is it possible that Pharaoh will listen to me?"

## CHAPTER 7

See RG 65–67

1 The LORD answered Moses: See! I have made you a god to Pharaoh,[p] and Aaron your brother will be your prophet.* 2 You will speak all that I command you. In turn, your brother Aaron will tell Pharaoh to let the Israelites go out of his land. 3 Yet I will make Pharaoh so headstrong that, despite the many signs and wonders that I work in the land of Egypt, 4 Pharaoh will not listen to you. Therefore I will lay my hand on Egypt and with mighty acts of judgment I will bring my armies, my people the Israelites, out of the land of Egypt. 5 All Egyptians will know that I am the LORD, when I stretch out my hand against Egypt and bring the Israelites out of their midst.

6 This, then, is what Moses and Aaron did. They did exactly as the LORD had commanded them. 7 Moses was eighty years old, and Aaron eighty-three, when they spoke to Pharaoh.

## III. The Contest with Pharaoh

***The Staff Turned into a Serpent.*** 8 The LORD spoke to Moses and Aaron: 9 When Pharaoh demands of you, "Produce a sign or wonder," you will say to Aaron: "Take your staff and throw it down before Pharaoh, and it will turn into a serpent."[q] 10 Then Moses and Aaron went to Pharaoh and did just as the LORD had commanded. Aaron threw his staff down before Pharaoh and his servants, and it turned into a serpent. 11 Pharaoh, in turn, summoned the wise men and the sorcerers, and they also, the magicians[r] of Egypt, did the same thing by their magic arts. 12 Each one threw down his staff, and they turned into serpents. But Aaron's staff swallowed their staffs. 13 Pharaoh, however, hardened his heart and would not listen to them, just as the LORD had foretold.

***First Plague: Water Turned into Blood.**** 14 Then the LORD said to Moses: Pharaoh is obstinate* in refusing to let the people go. 15 In the morning, just when he sets out for the water, go to Pharaoh and present yourself by the bank of the Nile, holding in your

his zeal for God when the Israelites committed apostasy by worshiping the Baal of Peor in the plains of Moab (see Nm 25:1–18).

**7:1 Prophet**: Hebrew *nabi*, one who can legitimately speak for God and in God's name to another or others. Just as God spoke to Moses, so Moses will speak to Aaron, who will be a "prophet" to Pharaoh. Cf. 4:16.

**7:14–12:30** After a brief preface (vv. 8–13) drawn from the Priestly source, a narrative depicting the series of ten disasters that God brings upon Pharaoh because of his stubbornness ensues. Although most of these disasters, known traditionally as the "ten plagues of Egypt," could be interpreted as naturally occurring phenomena, they are clearly represented by the biblical authors as extraordinary events indicative of God's intervention on behalf of Israel and as occurring exactly according to Moses' commands. See Ps 78:43–51 and 105:27–36 for poetic versions of these plagues, which also differ significantly from the account here.

**7:14 Pharaoh is obstinate**: lit., "Pharaoh's heart is heavy" (*kabed*); thus not precisely the same Hebrew idiom as found in vv. 13 and 22, "stubborn," lit., "Pharaoh's heart was hard(ened)" (*hazaq*) (cf. the related idiom with Pharaoh as the object, e.g., 4:21).

*p*: Ex 4:15–16. *q*: Ex 4:3. *r*: 2 Tm 3:8.

hand the staff that turned into a snake.* 16 Say to him: The LORD, the God of the Hebrews, sent me to you with the message: Let my people go to serve me in the wilderness. But as yet you have not listened. 17 Thus says the LORD: This is how you will know that I am the LORD. With the staff here in my hand, I will strike the water in the Nile and it will be changed into blood.[s] 18 The fish in the Nile will die, and the Nile itself will stink so that the Egyptians will be unable to drink water from the Nile.

19 The LORD then spoke to Moses: Speak to Aaron: Take your staff and stretch out your hand over the waters of Egypt—its streams, its canals, its ponds, and all its supplies of water—that they may become blood. There will be blood throughout the land of Egypt, even in the wooden pails and stone jars.

20 This, then, is what Moses and Aaron did, exactly as the LORD had commanded. Aaron raised his staff and struck the waters in the Nile in full view of Pharaoh and his servants, and all the water in the Nile was changed into blood. 21 The fish in the Nile died, and the Nile itself stank so that the Egyptians could not drink water from it. There was blood throughout the land of Egypt. 22 But the Egyptian magicians did the same* by their magic arts. So Pharaoh hardened his heart and would not listen to them, just as the LORD had said. 23 Pharaoh turned away and went into his house, with no concern even for this. 24 All the Egyptians had to dig round about the Nile for drinking water, since they could not drink any water from the Nile.

*Second Plague: the Frogs.* 25 Seven days passed after the LORD had struck the Nile. 26 Then the LORD said to Moses: Go to Pharaoh and tell him:[t] Thus says the LORD: Let my people go to serve me. 27 If you refuse to let them go, then I will send a plague of frogs over all your territory. 28 The Nile will teem with frogs. They will come up and enter into your palace and into your bedroom and onto your bed, into the houses of your servants, too, and among your people, even into your ovens and your kneading bowls. 29 The frogs will come up over you and your people and all your servants.

## CHAPTER 8

See RG 65–67

1 The LORD then spoke to Moses: Speak to Aaron: Stretch out your hand with your staff over the streams, the canals, and the ponds, and make frogs overrun the land of Egypt. 2 So Aaron stretched out his hand over the waters of Egypt, and the frogs came up and covered the land of Egypt. 3 But the magicians did the same by their magic arts and made frogs overrun the land of Egypt.

4 Then Pharaoh summoned Moses and Aaron and said, "Pray to the LORD to remove the frogs from me and my people, and I will let the people go to sacrifice to the LORD." 5 Moses answered Pharaoh, "Please designate for me the time when I am to pray for you and your servants and your people, to get rid of the frogs from you and your houses. They will be left only in the Nile." 6 "Tomorrow," he said. Then Moses replied, "It will be as you have said, so that you may know that there is none like the LORD, our God. 7 The frogs will leave you and your houses, your servants and your people; they will be left only in the Nile."

8 After Moses and Aaron left Pharaoh's presence, Moses cried out to the LORD on account of the frogs that he had inflicted on Pharaoh; 9 and the LORD did as Moses had asked. The frogs died off in the houses, the courtyards, and the fields. 10 Heaps of them were piled up, and the land stank. 11 But when Pharaoh saw there was a respite, he became obstinate and would not listen to them, just as the LORD had said.

*Third Plague: the Gnats.* 12 Thereupon the LORD spoke to Moses: Speak to Aaron:

**7:15 The staff that turned into a snake**: the allusion is to 4:2–4 rather than 7:9–12. The latter comes from the hand of the Priestly writer and features Aaron—with his staff—as the principal actor.

**7:22 The Egyptian magicians did the same**: this is an exaggeration, presumably influenced by the similar statement in v. 11; whereas the magicians could turn their staffs into snakes after Aaron had done so, after Aaron's sign there should not have been any water in Egypt still unchanged to blood for the magicians "to do the same" with it (cf. v. 24).

*s:* Ex 4:9; Ps 78:44; 105:29; Wis 11:5–7. *t:* Ps 78:45; 105:30.

Stretch out your staff and strike the dust of the earth, and it will turn into gnats* [u] throughout the land of Egypt. 13They did so. Aaron stretched out his hand with his staff and struck the dust of the earth, and gnats came upon human being and beast alike. All the dust of the earth turned into gnats throughout the land of Egypt. 14Though the magicians did the same thing to produce gnats by their magic arts, they could not do so.[v] The gnats were on human being and beast alike, 15and the magicians said to Pharaoh, "This is the finger of God."* Yet Pharaoh hardened his heart and would not listen to them, just as the LORD had said.

***Fourth Plague: the Flies.*** 16Then the LORD spoke to Moses: Early tomorrow morning present yourself to Pharaoh when he sets out toward the water, and say to him: Thus says the LORD: Let my people go to serve me. 17For if you do not let my people go, I will send swarms of flies upon you and your servants and your people and your houses. The houses of the Egyptians and the very ground on which they stand will be filled with swarms of flies. 18But on that day I will make an exception of the land of Goshen, where my people are, and no swarms of flies will be there, so that you may know that I the LORD am in the midst of the land. 19I will make a distinction* between my people and your people. This sign will take place tomorrow. 20This the LORD did. Thick swarms of flies entered the house of Pharaoh and the houses of his servants; throughout Egypt the land was devastated on account of the swarms of flies.[w]

21Then Pharaoh summoned Moses and Aaron and said, "Go sacrifice to your God within the land." 22But Moses replied, "It is not right to do so, for what we sacrifice to the LORD, our God, is abhorrent to the Egyptians.* If we sacrifice what is abhorrent to the Egyptians before their very eyes, will they not stone us? 23We must go a three days' journey in the wilderness and sacrifice to the LORD, our God, as he commands us." 24Pharaoh said, "I will let you go to sacrifice to the LORD, your God, in the wilderness, provided that you do not go too far away. Pray for me." 25Moses answered, "As soon as I leave you I will pray to the LORD that the swarms of flies may depart tomorrow from Pharaoh, his servants, and his people. Pharaoh, however, must not act deceitfully again and refuse to let the people go to sacrifice to the LORD." 26When Moses left Pharaoh, he prayed to the LORD; 27and the LORD did as Moses had asked, removing the swarms of flies from Pharaoh, his servants, and his people. Not one remained. 28But once more Pharaoh became obstinate and would not let the people go.

## CHAPTER 9

See RG 65–67

***Fifth Plague: the Pestilence.*** 1Then the LORD said to Moses: Go to Pharaoh and tell him: Thus says the LORD, the God of the Hebrews: Let my people go to serve me. 2For if you refuse to let them go and persist in holding them, 3the hand of the LORD will strike your livestock in the field—your horses, donkeys, camels, herds and flocks—with a very severe pestilence. 4But the LORD

**8:12, 17 Gnats, flies**: it is uncertain what species of troublesome insects are meant here in vv. 12–14 and then in vv. 17–27, the identification as "gnat" (vv. 12–14) and as "fly" (vv. 17–27) being based on the rendering of the Septuagint. Others suggest "lice" in vv. 12–14, while rabbinic literature renders Hebrew *'arob* in vv. 17–27 as a "mixture of wild animals." In the Hebrew of the Old Testament, the word occurs only in the context of the plagues (see also Ps 78:45 and 105:31).

**8:15 The finger of God**: previously the magicians had, for the most part, been able to replicate the signs and wonders Moses performed to manifest God's power—turning their staffs into snakes (7:11–12), turning water into blood (7:22), and producing frogs to overrun the land of Egypt (8:3). But now for the first time they are unable to compete, and confess a power greater than their own is at work. Cf. Lk 11:20.

**8:19 A distinction**: while some uncertainty surrounds the Hebrew here rendered as "distinction," it is clear that now the Israelites begin to be set apart from the Egyptians, a separation that reaches a climax in the death of the Egyptian firstborn (11:7).

**8:22** Perhaps Moses is deceiving the Pharaoh much like the "God-fearing" midwives (1:16–20), although ancient historians writing about Egypt some time after the period in which the exodus is set do note Egyptian prohibitions on sacrificing cattle or slaughtering sacred animals. As such, the Egyptians might well have fiercely resented certain sacrificial practices of the Israelites. Certain animals were held sacred in Egypt, as the representations of various deities.

*u:* Ps 105:31. *v:* Wis 17:7. *w:* Ps 78:45; 105:31; Wis 16:9.

will distinguish between the livestock of Israel and that of Egypt, so that nothing belonging to the Israelites will die. 5And the LORD set a definite time, saying: Tomorrow the LORD will do this in the land. 6And on the next day the LORD did it. All the livestock of the Egyptians died,[x] but not one animal belonging to the Israelites died. 7But although Pharaoh found upon inquiry that not even so much as one of the livestock of the Israelites had died, he remained obstinate and would not let the people go.

***Sixth Plague: the Boils.*** 8So the LORD said to Moses and Aaron: Each of you take handfuls of soot from a kiln, and in the presence of Pharaoh let Moses scatter it toward the sky. 9It will turn into fine dust over the whole land of Egypt and cause festering boils* on human being and beast alike throughout the land of Egypt.

10So they took the soot from a kiln and appeared before Pharaoh. When Moses scattered it toward the sky, it caused festering boils on human being and beast alike. 11Because of the boils the magicians could not stand in Moses' presence, for there were boils on the magicians as well as on the rest of the Egyptians. 12But the LORD hardened Pharaoh's heart, and he would not listen to them, just as the LORD had said to Moses.

***Seventh Plague: the Hail.*** 13Then the LORD spoke to Moses: Early tomorrow morning present yourself to Pharaoh and say to him: Thus says the LORD, the God of the Hebrews: Let my people go to serve me, 14for this time I will unleash all my blows upon you and your servants and your people, so that you may know that there is none like me anywhere on earth. 15For by now I should have stretched out my hand and struck you and your people with such pestilence that you would have vanished from the earth. 16But this is why I have let you survive: to show you* my power and to make my name resound throughout the earth![y] 17Will you continue to exalt yourself over my people and not let them go? 18At this time tomorrow, therefore, I am going to rain down such fierce hail as there has never been in Egypt from the day it was founded up to the present. 19Therefore, order your livestock and whatever else you have in the open fields to be brought to a place of safety. Whatever human being or animal is found in the fields and is not brought to shelter will die when the hail comes down upon them. 20Those of Pharaoh's servants who feared the word of the LORD hurried their servants and their livestock off to shelter. 21But those who did not pay attention to the word of the LORD left their servants and their livestock in the fields.

22The LORD then said to Moses: Stretch out your hand toward the sky, that hail may fall upon the entire land of Egypt, on human being and beast alike and all the vegetation of the fields in the land of Egypt. 23So Moses stretched out his staff toward the sky, and the LORD sent forth peals of thunder and hail.[z] Lightning flashed toward the earth, and the LORD rained down hail upon the land of Egypt. 24There was hail and lightning flashing here and there through the hail, and the hail was so fierce that nothing like it had been seen in Egypt since it became a nation. 25Throughout the land of Egypt the hail struck down everything in the fields, human being and beast alike; it struck down all the vegetation of the fields and splintered every tree in the fields. 26Only in the land of Goshen, where the Israelites were, was there no hail.

27Then Pharaoh sent for Moses and Aaron and said to them, "I have sinned this time! The LORD is the just one, and I and my people are the ones at fault. 28Pray to the LORD! Enough of the thunder* and hail! I will let you go; you need stay no longer." 29Moses replied to him, "As soon as I leave the city I will extend my hands to the LORD; the thunder will cease, and there will be no more hail

**9:9 Boils**: the exact nature of the disease is not clear. Semitic cognates, for example, suggest the Hebrew root means "to be hot" and thus point to some sort of inflammation. The fact that soot taken from the kiln is the agent of the disease would point in the same direction. See further Lv 13:18–23; Dt 28:35; 2 Kgs 20:7.

**9:16 To show you**: some ancient versions such as the Septuagint read, "to show through you." Cf. Rom 9:17.

**9:28 Thunder**: lit., "divine voices," "voices of God," or the like.

*x:* Ps 78:48. *y:* Rom 9:17. *z:* Ps 78:47; 105:32–33.

so that you may know that the earth belongs to the LORD. [30]But as for you and your servants, I know that you do not yet fear the LORD God."

[31]Now the flax and the barley were ruined, because the barley was in ear and the flax in bud. [32]But the wheat and the spelt were not ruined, for they grow later.

[33]When Moses had left Pharaoh and gone out of the city, he extended his hands to the LORD. The thunder and the hail ceased, and the rain no longer poured down upon the earth. [34]But Pharaoh, seeing that the rain and the hail and the thunder had ceased, sinned again and became obstinate, both he and his servants. [35]In the hardness of his heart, Pharaoh would not let the Israelites go, just as the LORD had said through Moses.

See RG 65–67

## CHAPTER 10

***Eighth Plague: the Locusts.*** [1]Then the LORD said to Moses: Go to Pharaoh, for I have made him and his servants obstinate in order that I may perform these signs of mine among them [2]and that you may recount to your son and grandson how I made a fool of the Egyptians and what signs I did among them, so that you may know that I am the LORD.[a]

[3]So Moses and Aaron went to Pharaoh and told him, "Thus says the LORD, the God of the Hebrews: How long will you refuse to submit to me? Let my people go to serve me. [4]For if you refuse to let my people go, tomorrow I will bring locusts into your territory. [5]They will cover the surface of the earth, so that the earth itself will not be visible. They will eat up the remnant you saved undamaged from the hail, as well as all the trees that are growing in your fields. [6]They will fill your houses and the houses of your servants and of all the Egyptians—something your parents and your grandparents have not seen from the day they appeared on this soil until today." With that he turned and left Pharaoh.

[7]But Pharaoh's servants said to him, "How long will he be a snare for us? Let the people go to serve the LORD, their God. Do you not yet realize that Egypt is being destroyed?" [8]So Moses and Aaron were brought back to Pharaoh, who said to them, "Go, serve the LORD, your God. But who exactly will go?" [9]Moses answered, "With our young and old we must go; with our sons and daughters, with our flocks and herds we must go. It is a pilgrimage feast of the LORD for us." [10]"The LORD help you,"* Pharaoh replied, "if I let your little ones go with you! Clearly, you have some evil in mind. [11]By no means! Just you men go and serve the LORD.* After all, that is what you have been asking for." With that they were driven from Pharaoh's presence.

[12][b]The LORD then said to Moses: Stretch out your hand over the land of Egypt for the locusts, that they may come upon it and eat up all the land's vegetation, whatever the hail has left. [13]So Moses stretched out his staff over the land of Egypt, and the LORD drove an east wind* over the land all that day and all night. When it was morning, the east wind brought the locusts. [14]The locusts came up over the whole land of Egypt and settled down over all its territory. Never before had there been such a fierce swarm of locusts, nor will there ever be again. [15]They covered the surface of the whole land, so that it became black. They ate up all the vegetation in the land and all the fruit of the trees the hail had spared. Nothing green was left on any tree or plant in the fields throughout the land of Egypt.

[16]Pharaoh hurriedly summoned Moses and Aaron and said, "I have sinned against the LORD, your God, and against you. [17]But now, do forgive me my sin only this once, and pray to the LORD, your God, only to take this death from me." [18]When Moses left Pharaoh, he prayed to the LORD, [19]and the LORD caused the wind to shift to a very

**10:10 The LORD help you . . .**: lit., "May the Lord be with you in the same way as I let you . . ."; a sarcastic blessing intended as a curse.

**10:11** Pharaoh realized that if the men alone went they would have to return to their families. He suspected that the Hebrews had no intention of returning.

**10:13 East wind**: coming across the desert from Arabia, the strong east wind brings Egypt the burning sirocco and, at times, locusts. Cf. 14:21.

*a:* Dt 6:20–25. *b:* Ps 78:46; 105:34–35.

**Moses Insists**

PHARAOH WILL PERMIT the people to go but not their flocks (10:24), as if to undermine the purpose for which the Israelites are leaving—to sacrifice, which requires animals from the flocks. Moses counters by demanding that Pharaoh provide the sacrificial animals from his own livestock, while continuing to insist that the Israelite livestock also go with them. Moses seeks Pharaoh's total capitulation to God.

strong west wind, which took up the locusts
and hurled them into the Red Sea.* Not a single locust remained within the whole territory of Egypt. 20Yet the LORD hardened
Pharaoh's heart, and he would not let the Israelites go.

*Ninth Plague: the Darkness.* 21[c] Then the
LORD said to Moses: Stretch out your hand
toward the sky, that over the land of Egypt
there may be such darkness* that one can
feel it. 22So Moses stretched out his hand toward the sky, and there was dense darkness
throughout the land of Egypt for three days.
23People could not see one another, nor
could they get up from where they were, for
three days. But all the Israelites had light
where they lived.

24Pharaoh then summoned Moses and
Aaron and said, "Go, serve the LORD. Only
your flocks and herds will be detained. Even
your little ones may go with you." 25But Moses replied, "You also must give us sacrifices
and burnt offerings to make to the LORD, our
God. 26Our livestock also must go with us.
Not an animal must be left behind, for some
of them we will select for service* to the
LORD, our God; but we will not know with
which ones we are to serve the LORD until
we arrive there." 27But the LORD hardened
Pharaoh's heart, and he was unwilling to let
them go. 28Pharaoh said to Moses, "Leave
me, and see to it that you do not see my face
again! For the day you do see my face you
will die!" 29Moses replied, "You are right! I
will never see your face again."

## CHAPTER 11

See RG 65-67

*Tenth Plague: the Death of the First-
born.* 1Then the LORD spoke to Moses: One
more plague I will bring upon Pharaoh and
upon Egypt. After that he will let you depart.
In fact, when he finally lets you go, he will
drive you away. 2[d] Instruct the people that
every man is to ask his neighbor, and every
woman her neighbor, for silver and gold articles and for clothing. 3The LORD indeed
made the Egyptians well-disposed toward
the people; Moses himself was very highly
regarded by Pharaoh's servants and the people in the land of Egypt.

4Moses then said, "Thus says the LORD:
About midnight I will go forth through
Egypt.[e] 5[f] Every firstborn in the land of
Egypt will die, from the firstborn of Pharaoh
who sits on his throne to the firstborn of the
slave-girl who is at the handmill,* as well as
all the firstborn of the animals. 6Then there
will be loud wailing throughout the land of
Egypt, such as has never been, nor will ever
be again. 7But among all the Israelites,

**10:19 The Red Sea**: the traditional translation, cf. Septuagint and other Versions; but the Hebrew literally means "sea of reeds" or "reedy sea," which could probably be applied to a number of bodies of shallow water, most likely somewhat to the north of the present deep Red Sea.

**10:21 Darkness**: commentators note that at times a storm from the south, called the *khamsin*, blackens the sky of Egypt with sand from the Sahara; the dust in the air is then so thick that the darkness can, in a sense, "be felt." But such observations should not obscure the fact that for the biblical author what transpires in each of the plagues is clearly something extraordinary, an event which witnesses to the unrivaled power of Israel's God.

**10:26 Service**: as is obvious from v. 25, the service in question here is the offering of sacrifice. The continued use of the verb *'bd* "to serve" and related nouns for both the people's bondage in Egypt and their subsequent service to the Lord dramatizes the point of the conflict between Pharaoh and the God of Israel, who demands from the Israelites an attachment which is exclusive. See Lv 25:55.

**11:5 Handmill**: two pieces of stone were used to grind grain. A smaller upper stone was moved back and forth over a larger stationary stone. This menial work was done by slaves and captives.

*c:* Ps 105:28. *d:* Ex 3:21–22; 12:35–36. *e:* Ex 12:12. *f:* Ex 12:29–30.

## The LORD Provides Instructions for the Annual Festivals of Passover and Unleavened Bread

THE FLOW OF the exodus story is interrupted in ch 12 by instructions for celebrating the two festivals of Passover and Unleavened Bread. The immediate purpose of the Passover is to mark every Israelite home with blood so that it will be protected from the effects of the final plague, the death of all Egyptian first-born. After Israel leaves Egypt, the annual festivals of Passover and Unleavened Bread will enable future generations to remember and identify the story of the exodus as their own (vv. 14–17). Passover comes from the smearing of the lamb's blood on the doorposts and lintel, or upper door frame, to mark the house as Israelite and thus protect it from the plague, which will kill all the Egyptian first-born (vv. 12–13. 21–23). The verb pass over (*pasaḥ*) is the basis for the festival's name, Passover (*pesaḥ*, v. 11). Unleavened bread, or biscuits without yeast, is quickly baked bread. Verses 33–34 provide the connection with the exodus: The Israelites could not wait for their bread dough to rise. The bitter herbs recall the bitterness of Israel's slavery. The lamb is to be roasted rather than eaten raw or boiled to ensure all of its blood is drained. The blood is the essence of life and must be returned to the deity and not eaten in recognition that life belongs to God (Gn 9:4; Lv 17:10–14).

among human beings and animals alike, not even a dog will growl, so that you may know that the LORD distinguishes between Egypt and Israel. [8]All these servants of yours will then come down to me and bow down before me, saying: Leave, you and all your followers![g] Then I will depart." With that he left Pharaoh's presence in hot anger.

[9]The LORD said to Moses: Pharaoh will not listen to you so that my wonders may be multiplied in the land of Egypt. [10]Thus, although Moses and Aaron performed all these wonders in Pharaoh's presence, the LORD hardened Pharaoh's heart, and he would not let the Israelites go from his land.

### CHAPTER 12

See RG 65–67

*The Passover Ritual Prescribed.** [1]The LORD said to Moses and Aaron in the land of Egypt: [2]* This month will stand at the head of your calendar; you will reckon it the first month of the year.[h] [3]Tell the whole community of Israel: On the tenth of this month every family must procure for itself a lamb, one apiece for each household. [4]If a household is too small for a lamb, it along with its nearest neighbor will procure one, and apportion the lamb's cost* in proportion to the number of persons, according to what each household consumes. [5]Your lamb must be a year-old male and without blemish. You may take it from either the sheep or the goats. [6]You will keep it until the fourteenth day of this month, and then, with the whole community of Israel assembled, it will be slaughtered during the evening twilight. [7]They will take some of its blood and apply it to the two doorposts and the lintel of the houses in which they eat it. [8]They will consume its meat that same night, eating it roasted with unleavened bread and bitter herbs. [9]Do not eat any of it raw or even boiled in water, but roasted, with its head and shanks and inner organs. [10]You must not keep any of it beyond the morning; whatever is left over in the morning must be burned up.

[11]This is how you are to eat it: with your loins girt, sandals on your feet and your staff

**12:1–20** This section, which interrupts the narrative of the exodus, contains later legislation concerning the celebration of Passover.

**12:2** As if to affirm victory over Pharaoh and sovereignty over the Israelites, the Lord proclaims a new calendar for Israel. **This month**: Abib, the month of "ripe grain." Cf. 13:4; 23:15; 34:18; Dt 16:1. It occurred near the vernal equinox, March–April. Later it was known by the Babylonian name of Nisan. Cf. Neh 2:1; Est 3:7.

**12:4 The lamb's cost**: some render the Hebrew, "reckon for the lamb the number of persons required to eat it." Cf. v. 10.

*g:* Ex 12:31–33. *h:* Lv 23:5–8; Nm 9:2–5; 28:16–25; Dt 16:1–8.

in hand, you will eat it in a hurry. It is the
LORD's Passover. 12 For on this same night I
will go through Egypt, striking down every
firstborn in the land, human being and beast
alike, and executing judgment on all the
gods of Egypt—I, the LORD![i] 13 But for you
the blood will mark the houses where you
are. Seeing the blood, I will pass over you;
thereby, when I strike the land of Egypt, no
destructive blow will come upon you.[j]

14 This day will be a day of remembrance
for you, which your future generations will
celebrate with pilgrimage to the LORD; you
will celebrate it as a statute forever. 15 For
seven days you must eat unleavened bread.
From the very first day you will have your
houses clear of all leaven. For whoever eats
leavened bread from the first day to the seventh will be cut off* from Israel. 16 On the first
day you will hold a sacred assembly, and
likewise on the seventh. On these days no
sort of work shall be done, except to prepare
the food that everyone needs. 17 Keep, then,
the custom of the unleavened bread,[k] since it
was on this very day that I brought your armies out of the land of Egypt. You must observe this day throughout your generations as
a statute forever. 18 From the evening of the
fourteenth day of the first month until the
evening of the twenty-first day of this month
you will eat unleavened bread. 19 For seven
days no leaven may be found in your houses;
for anyone, a resident alien or a native, who
eats leavened food will be cut off from the
community of Israel. 20 You shall eat nothing
leavened; wherever you dwell you may eat
only unleavened bread.

***Promulgation of the Passover.*** 21 Moses
summoned all the elders of Israel and said to
them, "Go and procure lambs for your families, and slaughter the Passover victims.
22 [l] Then take a bunch of hyssop,* and dipping it in the blood that is in the basin, apply
some of this blood to the lintel and the two
doorposts. And none of you shall go outdoors until morning. 23 For when the LORD
goes by to strike down the Egyptians, seeing
the blood on the lintel and the two doorposts,
the LORD will pass over that door and not let
the destroyer come into your houses to strike
you down.

24 "You will keep this practice forever as a
statute for yourselves and your descendants.
25 Thus, when you have entered the land
which the LORD will give you as he promised, you must observe this rite. 26 [m] When
your children ask you, 'What does this rite
of yours mean?' 27 you will reply, 'It is the
Passover sacrifice for the LORD, who passed
over the houses of the Israelites in Egypt;
when he struck down the Egyptians, he delivered our houses.' "

Then the people knelt and bowed down,
28 and the Israelites went and did exactly as
the LORD had commanded Moses and Aaron.

***Death of the Firstborn.*** 29 [n] And so at midnight the LORD struck down every firstborn
in the land of Egypt, from the firstborn of
Pharaoh sitting on his throne to the firstborn
of the prisoner in the dungeon, as well as all
the firstborn of the animals. 30 Pharaoh arose
in the night, he and all his servants and all
the Egyptians; and there was loud wailing
throughout Egypt, for there was not a house
without its dead.

***Permission to Depart.*** 31 During the night
Pharaoh summoned Moses and Aaron and
said, "Leave my people at once, you and the
Israelites! Go and serve the LORD as you
said. 32 Take your flocks, too, and your herds,
as you said, and go; and bless me, too!"*

33 The Egyptians, in a hurry to send them
away from the land, urged the people on, for
they said, "All of us will die!" 34 The people,
therefore, took their dough before it was
leavened, in their kneading bowls wrapped

**12:15 Cut off**: a common Priestly term, not easily reduced to a simple English equivalent, since its usage appears to involve a number of associated punishments, some or all of which may come into play in any instance of the term's use. These included the excommunication of the offender from the Israelite community, the premature death of the offender, the eventual eradication of the offender's posterity, and finally the loss by the offender of all ancestral holdings.

**12:22 Hyssop**: a plant with many small woody branches that was convenient for a sprinkling rite.

**12:32 Bless me, too**: in a final and humiliating admission of defeat, once again Pharaoh asks Moses to intercede for him (cf. 8:24). However, Pharaoh may be speaking sarcastically.

*i:* Nm 33:4. *j:* Heb 11:28. *k:* Ex 13:3. *l:* Ex 12:7, 13. *m:* Ex 13:8, 14–15; Dt 6:20–25. *n:* Ex 11:4–6; Nm 33:4; Ps 78:51; 105:36; 136:10; Wis 18:10–16.

in their cloaks on their shoulders. 35[o] And the Israelites did as Moses had commanded: they asked the Egyptians for articles of silver and gold and for clothing. 36 Indeed the LORD had made the Egyptians so well-disposed toward the people that they let them have whatever they asked for. And so they despoiled the Egyptians.

*Departure from Egypt.* 37 The Israelites set out from Rameses[p] for Succoth, about six hundred thousand men on foot, not counting the children. 38 A crowd of mixed ancestry* also went up with them, with livestock in great abundance, both flocks and herds. 39 The dough they had brought out of Egypt they baked into unleavened loaves. It was not leavened, because they had been driven out of Egypt and could not wait. They did not even prepare food for the journey.

40 The time the Israelites had stayed in Egypt* was four hundred and thirty years.[q] 41 At the end of four hundred and thirty years, on this very date, all the armies of the LORD left the land of Egypt. 42 This was a night of vigil for the LORD, when he brought them out of the land of Egypt; so on this night all Israelites must keep a vigil for the LORD throughout their generations.

*Law of the Passover.* 43 The LORD said to Moses and Aaron: This is the Passover statute. No foreigner may eat of it. 44 However, every slave bought for money you will circumcise; then he may eat of it. 45 But no tenant or hired worker may eat of it. 46 It must be eaten in one house; you may not take any of its meat outside the house.[r] You shall not break any of its bones.* 47 The whole community of Israel must celebrate this feast. 48 If any alien[s] residing among you would celebrate the Passover for the LORD, all his males must be circumcised, and then he may join in its celebration just like the natives. But no one who is uncircumcised may eat of it. 49 There will be one law* for the native and for the alien residing among you.

50 All the Israelites did exactly as the LORD had commanded Moses and Aaron. 51 On that same day the LORD brought the Israelites out of the land of Egypt company by company.

## CHAPTER 13

See RG 67-68

*Consecration of Firstborn.* 1 The LORD spoke to Moses and said: 2 Consecrate to me every firstborn; whatever opens the womb among the Israelites,[t] whether of human being or beast, belongs to me.

3[u] Moses said to the people, "Remember this day on which you came out of Egypt, out of a house of slavery. For it was with a strong hand that the LORD brought you out from there. Nothing made with leaven may be eaten. 4 This day on which you are going out is in the month of Abib.* 5 Therefore, when the LORD, your God, has brought you into the land of the Canaanites, the Hittites, the Amorites, the Perrizites, the Girgashites, the Hivites, and the Jebusites, which he swore to your ancestors to give you, a land flowing with milk and honey, you will perform the following service* in this month. 6 For seven days you will eat unleavened bread, and the seventh day will also be a festival to the LORD. 7 Unleavened bread may be eaten during the seven days, but nothing leavened and no leaven may be found in your possession in all your territory. 8 And on that day you will explain to your son, 'This is because of what

**12:38 Mixed ancestry**: not simply descendants of Jacob; cf. Nm 11:4; Lv 24:10–11.

**12:40 In Egypt**: according to the Septuagint and the Samaritan Pentateuch "in Canaan and Egypt," thus reckoning from the time of Abraham. Cf. Gal 3:17.

**12:46 You shall not break any of its bones**: the application of these words to Jesus on the cross (Jn 19:36) sees the Paschal lamb as a prophetic type of Christ, sacrificed to free men and women from the bondage of sin. Cf. also 1 Cor 5:7; 1 Pt 1:19.

**12:49 One law**: the first appearance of the word torah, traditionally translated as "law," though it can have the broader meaning of "teaching" or "instruction." Elsewhere, too, it is said that the "alien" is to be accorded the same treatment as the Israelite (e.g., Lv 19:34).

**13:4 Abib**: lit., "ear (of grain)," the old Canaanite name for this month; Israel later called it "Nisan." It was the first month in their liturgical calendar (cf. Ex 12:2).

**13:5 The following service**: the celebration of the feast of Unleavened Bread now constitutes the Israelites' service, in contrast to the "service" they performed for Pharaoh as his slaves.

*o:* Ex 3:21–22; 11:2–3; Ps 105:37–38. *p:* Nm 33:3–5. *q:* Gn 15:13; Acts 7:6; Gal 3:17. *r:* Nm 9:12; Jn 19:36. *s:* Nm 9:14. *t:* Ex 13:12–15. *u:* Ex 12:2–20.

the LORD did for me when I came out of
Egypt.’ 9It will be like a sign* on your hand
and a reminder on your forehead,[v] so that the
teaching of the LORD will be on your lips:
with a strong hand the LORD brought you out
of Egypt. 10You will keep this statute at its
appointed time from year to year.
11“When the LORD, your God, has brought
you into the land of the Canaanites, just as he
swore to you and your ancestors, and gives it
to you, 12[w] you will dedicate to the LORD
every newborn that opens the womb; and
every firstborn male of your animals will belong to the LORD. 13Every firstborn of a donkey you will ransom with a sheep. If you do
not ransom it, you will break its neck. Every
human firstborn of your sons you must ransom. 14And when your son asks you later on,
‘What does this mean?’ you will tell him,
‘With a strong hand the LORD brought us out
of Egypt, out of a house of slavery. 15When
Pharaoh stubbornly refused to let us go, the
LORD killed every firstborn in the land of
Egypt, the firstborn of human being and
beast alike. That is why I sacrifice to the
LORD every male that opens the womb, and
why I ransom every firstborn of my sons.’
16It will be like a sign on your hand and a
band on your forehead that with a strong
hand the LORD brought us out of Egypt.”[x]

## IV. The Deliverance of the Israelites from Pharaoh and Victory at the Sea

***Toward the Red Sea.*** 17Now, when Pharaoh
let the people go, God did not lead them by
way of the Philistines’ land,* though this was
the nearest; for God said: If the people see
that they have to fight, they might change
their minds and return to Egypt. 18Instead,
God rerouted them toward the Red Sea by
way of the wilderness road, and the Israelites went up out of the land of Egypt arrayed
for battle. 19Moses also took Joseph’s bones[y]
with him, for Joseph had made the Israelites
take a solemn oath, saying, “God will surely
take care of you, and you must bring my
bones up with you from here.”
20Setting out from Succoth, they camped
at Etham[z] near the edge of the wilderness.
21[a] The LORD preceded them, in the daytime by means of a column of cloud to show
them the way, and at night by means of a column of fire* to give them light. Thus they
could travel both day and night. 22Neither
the column of cloud by day nor the column
of fire by night ever left its place in front of
the people.

### CHAPTER 14

See RG 67–68

1Then the LORD spoke to Moses:
2Speak to the Israelites: Let them turn about
and camp before Pi-hahiroth, between Migdol and the sea.[b] Camp in front of Baal-zephon,* just opposite, by the sea. 3Pharaoh
will then say, “The Israelites are wandering
about aimlessly in the land. The wilderness
has closed in on them.” 4I will so harden
Pharaoh’s heart that he will pursue them.
Thus I will receive glory through Pharaoh
and all his army, and the Egyptians will
know that I am the LORD.
This the Israelites did. 5[c] When it was reported to the king of Egypt that the people
had fled, Pharaoh and his servants had a
change of heart about the people. “What in
the world have we done!” they said. “We

**13:9 Sign**: while here observance of the feast of Unleavened Bread is likened only metaphorically to a physical sign of one’s piety that can be worn as a kind of badge in commemoration of the exodus, from ancient times Jews have seen in this verse also the basis for the wearing of phylacteries. These are small receptacles for copies of biblical verses which Jewish men bind to the arms and forehead as a kind of mnemonic device for the observance of the Law.

**13:17 By way of the Philistines’ land**: the most direct route from Egypt to Palestine, along the shore of the Mediterranean.

**13:21 A column of cloud . . . a column of fire**: probably one and the same extraordinary phenomenon, a central nucleus of fire surrounded by smoke; only at night was its luminous nature visible; cf. 40:38.

**14:2 Pi-hahiroth . . . Migdol . . . Baal-zephon**: these places have not been definitively identified. Even the relative position of Pi-hahiroth and Baal-zephon is not clear; perhaps the former was on the west shore of the sea, where the Israelites were, and the latter on the opposite shore.

*v:* Ex 13:16; Dt 6:8; 11:18. *w:* Ex 13:2; 22:28–29; 34:19–20; Nm 3:12–13; 8:16–17; 18:15; Dt 15:19. *x:* Ex 13:9. *y:* Gn 50:25; Jos 24:32. *z:* Nm 33:6. *a:* Ex 40:38; Nm 9:15–22; Dt 1:33; Neh 9:19; Ps 78:14; 105:39; Wis 10:17. *b:* Nm 33:7–8. *c:* Wis 19:3; 1 Mc 4:9.

have released Israel from our service!” [6]So Pharaoh harnessed his chariots and took his army with him. [7]He took six hundred select chariots and all the chariots of Egypt, with officers* on all of them. [8]The LORD hardened the heart of Pharaoh, king of Egypt, so that he pursued the Israelites while they were going out in triumph. [9]The Egyptians pursued them—all Pharaoh’s horses, his chariots, his horsemen,* and his army—and caught up with them as they lay encamped by the sea, at Pi-hahiroth, in front of Baal-zephon.

***Crossing the Red Sea.*** [10]Now Pharaoh was near when the Israelites looked up and saw that the Egyptians had set out after them. Greatly frightened, the Israelites cried out to the LORD. [11]To Moses they said, “Were there no burial places in Egypt that you brought us to die in the wilderness? What have you done to us, bringing us out of Egypt? [12]Did we not tell you this in Egypt, when we said, ‘Leave us alone that we may serve the Egyptians’? Far better for us to serve the Egyptians than to die in the wilderness.” [13]But Moses answered the people, “Do not fear! Stand your ground and see the victory the LORD will win for you today. For these Egyptians whom you see today you will never see again. [14]The LORD will fight for you; you have only to keep still.”

[15]Then the LORD said to Moses: Why are you crying out to me? Tell the Israelites to set out. [16]And you, lift up your staff and stretch out your hand over the sea, and split it in two, that the Israelites may pass through the sea on dry land. [17]But I will harden the hearts of the Egyptians so that they will go in after them, and I will receive glory through Pharaoh and all his army, his chariots and his horsemen. [18]The Egyptians will know that I am the LORD, when I receive glory through Pharaoh, his chariots, and his horsemen.

[19]The angel of God,* who had been leading Israel’s army, now moved and went around behind them. And the column of cloud, moving from in front of them, took up its place behind them, [20]so that it came between the Egyptian army and that of Israel. And when it became dark, the cloud illumined the night; and so the rival camps did not come any closer together all night long.* [21][d] Then Moses stretched out his hand over the sea; and the LORD drove back the sea with a strong east wind all night long and turned the sea into dry ground. The waters were split, [22]so that the Israelites entered into the midst of the sea on dry land, with the water as a wall to their right and to their left.

***Rout of the Egyptians.*** [23]The Egyptians followed in pursuit after them—all Pharaoh’s horses and chariots and horsemen—into the midst of the sea. [24]But during the watch just before dawn, the LORD looked down from a column of fiery cloud upon the Egyptian army and threw it into a panic; [25]and he so clogged their chariot wheels that they could drive only with difficulty. With that the Egyptians said, “Let us flee from Israel, because the LORD is fighting for them against Egypt.”

[26]Then the LORD spoke to Moses: Stretch out your hand over the sea, that the water may flow back upon the Egyptians, upon their chariots and their horsemen. [27]So Moses stretched out his hand over the sea, and at daybreak the sea returned to its normal flow. The Egyptians were fleeing head on toward it when the LORD cast the Egyptians

**14:7 Officers**: cf. 1 Kgs 9:22; Ez 23:15. The Hebrew word *shalish*, rendered in 1 Kgs 9:22 as “adjutant,” has yet to have its meaning convincingly established. Given the very possible etymological connection with the number “three,” others suggest the translation “three-man crew” or, less likely, the “third man in the chariot” although Egyptian chariots carried two-man crews. The author of the text may have been describing the chariots of his experience without direct historical knowledge of Egyptian ways.

**14:9 Horsemen**: the usage here may be anachronistic, since horsemen, or cavalry, play a part in warfare only at the end of the second millennium B.C.

**14:19 Angel of God**: Hebrew *mal’ak ha’elohim* (Septuagint *ho angelos tou theou*) here refers not to an independent spiritual being but to God’s power at work in the world; corresponding to the column of cloud/fire, the expression more clearly preserves a sense of distance between God and God’s creatures. The two halves of the verse are parallel and may come from different narrative sources.

**14:20** The reading of the Hebrew text here is uncertain. The image is of a darkly glowing storm cloud, ominously bright, keeping the two camps apart.

*d:* Ex 15:19; Ps 66:6; 78:13; 136:13–14; Wis 10:18; 19:7–8; Is 63:12–13; Heb 11:29.

into the midst of the sea. 28[e] As the water
flowed back, it covered the chariots and the
horsemen. Of all Pharaoh's army which had
followed the Israelites into the sea, not even
one escaped. 29 But the Israelites had walked
on dry land through the midst of the sea,
with the water as a wall to their right and to
their left. 30 Thus the LORD saved Israel on
that day from the power of Egypt. When Israel saw the Egyptians lying dead on the
seashore 31 and saw the great power that the
LORD had shown against Egypt, the people
feared the LORD. They believed in the LORD[f]
and in Moses his servant.

## CHAPTER 15

See RG 67–68

1 Then Moses and the Israelites sang[g]
this song to the LORD:*

I will sing to the LORD, for he is
  gloriously triumphant;
horse and chariot he has cast into the
  sea.
2 My strength and my refuge is the LORD,
  and he has become my savior.[h]
This is my God, I praise him;
  the God of my father, I extol him.
3 The LORD is a warrior,
  LORD is his name!
4 Pharaoh's chariots and army he hurled
  into the sea;
the elite of his officers were drowned
  in the Red Sea.*
5 The flood waters covered them,
  they sank into the depths like a stone.[i]
6 Your right hand, O LORD, magnificent in
  power,
your right hand, O LORD, shattered the
  enemy.
7 In your great majesty you overthrew your
  adversaries;
you loosed your wrath to consume
  them like stubble.
8 At the blast of your nostrils the waters
  piled up,
the flowing waters stood like a mound,
  the flood waters foamed in the midst
  of the sea.
9 The enemy boasted, "I will pursue and
  overtake them;
I will divide the spoils and have my
  fill of them;
I will draw my sword; my hand will
  despoil them!"
10 When you blew with your breath, the sea
  covered them;
like lead they sank in the mighty
  waters.
11 Who is like you among the gods,
  O LORD?
Who is like you, magnificent among
  the holy ones?
Awe-inspiring in deeds of renown,
  worker of wonders,
12 when you stretched out your right
  hand, the earth swallowed them!
13 In your love* you led the people you
  redeemed;
in your strength you guided them to
  your holy dwelling.

**15:1–21** This poem, regarded by many scholars as one of the oldest compositions in the Bible, was once an independent work. It has been inserted at this important juncture in the large narrative of Exodus to celebrate God's saving power, having miraculously delivered the people from their enemies, and ultimately leading them to the promised land.

Although the victory it describes over the Egyptians at the sea bears a superficial resemblance in v. 8 to the preceding depiction of the water standing like a wall (14:22), the poem (as opposed to the following prose verse, v. 19) suggests a different version of the victory at sea than that found in chap. 14. There is no splitting of the sea in an act reminiscent of the Lord's combat at creation with the sea monsters Rahab and Leviathan (Jb 9:13; 26:12; Ps 74:13–14; 89:11; Is 51:9–10); nor is there mention of an east wind driving the waters back so that the Israelites can cross. In this version it is by means of a storm at sea, caused by a ferocious blast from his nostrils, that the Lord achieves a decisive victory against Pharaoh and his army (vv. 1–12). The second half of the poem (vv. 13–18) describes God's guidance into the promised land.

**15:4 Red Sea**: the traditional translation of the Hebrew *yam suph*, which actually means "Sea of Reeds" or "reedy sea." The location is uncertain, though in view of the route taken by the Israelites from Egypt to Sinai, it could not have been the Red Sea, which is too far south. It was probably a smaller body of water south of the Gulf of Suez. The term occurs also in Exodus at 10:19; 13:18; and 23:31.

**15:13 Love**: the very important Hebrew term *hesed* carries a variety of nuances depending on context: love, kindness, faithfulness. It is often rendered "steadfast love." It implies a relationship that generates an obligation and therefore is at home in a covenant context. Cf. 20:6.

*e:* Dt 11:4; Ps 106:11. *f:* Ex 4:31; Ps 106:12; Wis 10:20. *g:* Ex 15:21. *h:* Ps 118:14; Is 12:2. *i:* Neh 9:11.

**Moses and Miriam Sing Songs of Victory**

THE SONGS OF Moses and Miriam in ch 15 represent some of the earliest traditions of the Bible. The elevated language of Hebrew poetry in the songs contains many examples of parallelism, or doubling of thoughts and images in consecutive lines. A recurring image in the poem is the stone. Israel's enemy sinks or freezes in fear like a stone (vv. 5, 10, 16) in contrast to being "planted" in the eternal security of God's mountain sanctuary (vv. 17–18). The Song of Moses (vv. 1–18) retells the story of ch 14 with some differences in details. For example, Israel's crossing the sea on dry land (14:22) is not described in the song.

14 The peoples heard and quaked;
anguish gripped the dwellers in Philistia.
15 Then were the chieftains of Edom dismayed,
the nobles of Moab seized by trembling;
All the inhabitants of Canaan melted away;
16 [j] terror and dread fell upon them.
By the might of your arm they became silent like stone,
while your people, LORD, passed over,
while the people whom you created passed over.*
17 You brought them in, you planted them
on the mountain that is your own—
The place you made the base of your throne, LORD,
the sanctuary, LORD, your hands established.
18 May the LORD reign forever and ever!

19 When Pharaoh's horses and chariots and
horsemen entered the sea, the LORD made
the waters of the sea flow back upon them,
though the Israelites walked on dry land
through the midst of the sea.[k] 20 Then the
prophet Miriam, Aaron's sister, took a tambourine in her hand, while all the women
went out after her with tambourines, dancing; 21 and she responded* to them:

Sing to the LORD, for he is gloriously triumphant;
horse and chariot he has cast into the sea.[l]

## V. The Journey in the Wilderness to Sinai

***At Marah and Elim.*** 22[m] Then Moses led Israel forward from the Red Sea,* and they
marched out to the wilderness of Shur. After
traveling for three days through the wilderness without finding water, 23 they arrived at
Marah, where they could not drink its water,
because it was too bitter. Hence this place
was called Marah. 24 As the people grumbled
against Moses, saying, "What are we to
drink?" 25 he cried out to the LORD, who
pointed out to him a piece of wood. When he
threw it into the water, the water became
fresh.[n]

It was here that God, in making statutes
and ordinances for them, put them to the
test. 26 He said: If you listen closely to the
voice of the LORD, your God, and do what is
right in his eyes: if you heed his commandments and keep all his statutes, I will not afflict you with any of the diseases with which
I afflicted the Egyptians;[o] for I, the LORD,
am your healer.

27 Then they came to Elim, where there
were twelve springs of water and seventy

**15:16 Passed over**: an allusion to the crossing of the Jordan River (cf. Jos 3–5), written as if the entry into the promised land had already occurred. This verse suggests that at one time there was a ritual enactment of the conquest at a shrine near the Jordan River which included also a celebration of the victory at the sea.

**15:21 She responded**: Miriam's refrain echoes the first verse of this song and was probably sung as an antiphon after each verse.

**15:22 Red Sea**: see note on Ex 15:4.

*j:* Ps 78:53–55. *k:* Ex 14:21–29. *l:* Ex 15:1. *m:* Nm 33:8. *n:* Sir 38:5. *o:* Dt 7:15.

### Quail and Manna

QUAIL MIGRATING, OFTEN in great numbers, between Africa and Europe in the spring and fall often drop exhausted in the Sinai and are caught by hunters. This provision of meat was repeated in Numbers 11:31–32 but was not a daily occurrence, as was the occurrence of manna. The quail were also not a miraculous phenomenon, but the Israelites saw their timely appearance at God's promise as an instance of divine providence. The manna (named in 16:31) was a fine and flaky substance. If there is a natural explanation for manna, it is probably the sweet, edible honeydew (still called "manna" in Arabic) found in parts of the Sinai in June and July.

palm trees, and they camped there near the water.[p]

See RG 68

## CHAPTER 16

*The Wilderness of Sin.* [1]Having set out from Elim, the whole Israelite community came into the wilderness of Sin, which is between Elim and Sinai, on the fifteenth day of the second month* after their departure from the land of Egypt. [2]Here in the wilderness the whole Israelite community grumbled against Moses and Aaron. [3]The Israelites said to them, "If only we had died at the LORD's hand in the land of Egypt, as we sat by our kettles of meat and ate our fill of bread! But you have led us into this wilderness to make this whole assembly die of famine!"

*The Quail and the Manna.* [4]Then the LORD said to Moses:[q] I am going to rain down bread from heaven* for you. Each day the people are to go out and gather their daily portion; thus will I test them, to see whether they follow my instructions or not. [5]On the sixth day, however, when they prepare what they bring in, let it be twice as much as they gather on the other days. [6]So Moses and Aaron told all the Israelites,[r] "At evening you will know that it was the LORD who brought you out of the land of Egypt; [7]and in the morning you will see the glory of the LORD, when he hears your grumbling against him. But who are we that you should grumble against us?" [8]And Moses said, "When the LORD gives you meat to eat in the evening and in the morning your fill of bread, and hears the grumbling you utter against him, who then are we? Your grumbling is not against us, but against the LORD."

[9]Then Moses said to Aaron, "Tell the whole Israelite community: Approach the LORD, for he has heard your grumbling." [10]But while Aaron was speaking to the whole Israelite community, they turned in the direction of the wilderness, and there the glory of the LORD appeared in the cloud! [11]The LORD said to Moses: [12]I have heard the grumbling of the Israelites. Tell them: In the evening twilight you will eat meat, and in the morning you will have your fill of bread, and then you will know that I, the LORD, am your God.

[13]In the evening, quail[s] came up and covered the camp. In the morning there was a layer of dew all about the camp, [14]and when the layer of dew evaporated, fine flakes were on the surface of the wilderness, fine flakes like hoarfrost on the ground. [15]On seeing it, the Israelites asked one another, "What is this?"* for they did not know what it was. But Moses told them, "It is the bread which the LORD has given you to eat.[t]

**16:1 On the fifteenth day of the second month**: just one full month after their departure from Egypt. Cf. 12:2, 51; Nm 33:3–4. The Septuagint takes the date to be the beginning of the Israelites' grumbling.

**16:4 Bread from heaven**: as a gift from God, the manna is said to come down from the sky. Cf. Ps 78:24–25; Wis 16:20. Perhaps it was similar to a natural substance that is still found in small quantities on the Sinai peninsula—probably the honey-like resin from the tamarisk tree—but here it is, at least in part, clearly an extraordinary sign of God's providence. With reference to Jn 6:32, 49–52, the Christian tradition has regarded the manna as a type of the Eucharist. **Test**: as the text stands, it seems to leave open the question whether the test concerns trusting in God to provide them with the daily gift of food or observing the sabbath instructions.

*p:* Nm 33:9. *q:* Ps 78:24–25; 105:40; Jn 6:31–32; 1 Cor 10:3. *r:* Ex 16:12. *s:* Nm 11:31; Ps 78:27–28. *t:* Dt 8:3.

*Regulations Regarding the Manna.*
16 "Now, this is what the LORD has commanded. Gather as much of it as each needs
to eat, an omer[*] for each person for as many
of you as there are, each of you providing for
those in your own tent." 17 The Israelites did
so. Some gathered a large and some a small
amount. 18[*] But when they measured it out
by the omer, the one who had gathered a
large amount did not have too much, and the
one who had gathered a small amount did
not have too little. They gathered as much as
each needed to eat. 19 Moses said to them,
"Let no one leave any of it over until morning." 20 But they did not listen to Moses, and
some kept a part of it over until morning, and
it became wormy and stank. Therefore Moses was angry with them.

21 Morning after morning they gathered it,
as much as each needed to eat; but when the
sun grew hot, it melted away. 22 On the sixth
day they gathered twice as much food, two
omers for each person. When all the leaders
of the community came and reported this to
Moses, 23 he told them, "That is what the
LORD has prescribed. Tomorrow is a day of
rest, a holy sabbath of the LORD. Whatever
you want to bake, bake; whatever you want
to boil, boil; but whatever is left put away
and keep until the morning." 24 When they
put it away until the morning, as Moses
commanded, it did not stink nor were there
worms in it. 25 Moses then said, "Eat it today,
for today is the sabbath of the LORD. Today
you will not find any in the field. 26 Six days
you will gather it, but on the seventh day, the
sabbath, it will not be there." 27 Still, on the
seventh day some of the people went out to
gather it, but they did not find any. 28 Then
the LORD said to Moses: How long will you
refuse to keep my commandments and my
instructions? 29 Take note! The LORD has
given you the sabbath. That is why on the
sixth day he gives you food for two days.
Each of you stay where you are and let no
one go out on the seventh day. 30 After that
the people rested on the seventh day.

31 The house of Israel named this food
manna.[u] It was like coriander seed,[*] white,
and it tasted like wafers made with honey.
32 Moses said, "This is what the LORD has
commanded. Keep a full omer of it for your
future generations, so that they may see the
food I gave you to eat in the wilderness
when I brought you out of the land of
Egypt." 33 Moses then told Aaron, "Take a
jar[*] and put a full omer of manna in it. Then
place it before the LORD to keep it for your
future generations." 34 As the LORD had commanded Moses, Aaron placed it in front of
the covenant[*] to keep it.

35 The Israelites ate the manna for forty
years, until they came to settled land;[v] they
ate the manna until they came to the borders
of Canaan. 36 (An omer is one tenth of an
ephah.)[*]

## CHAPTER 17

See RG 68

*Water from the Rock.* 1 From the
wilderness of Sin the whole Israelite community journeyed by stages, as the LORD directed, and encamped at Rephidim.[w]

But there was no water for the people to
drink, 2[x] and so they quarreled with Moses
and said, "Give us water to drink." Moses
replied to them, "Why do you quarrel with
me? Why do you put the LORD to a test?"
3 Here, then, in their thirst for water, the
people grumbled against Moses, saying,
"Why then did you bring us up out of
Egypt? To have us die of thirst with our
children and our livestock?" 4 So Moses
cried out to the LORD, "What shall I do with
this people? A little more and they will
stone me!" 5 The LORD answered Moses:
Go on ahead of the people, and take along

**16:15 What is this**: the Hebrew *man hu* is thus rendered by the ancient versions, which understood the phrase as a popular etymology of the Hebrew word *man*, "manna"; but some render *man hu*, "This is manna."

**16:16 Omer**: a dry measure of approximately two quarts.

**16:18** Paul cites this passage as an example of equitable sharing (2 Cor 8:15).

**16:31 Coriander seed**: small, round, aromatic seeds of bright brown color; the comparison, therefore, refers merely to the size and shape, not to the taste or color of the manna.

**16:33 Jar**: according to the Greek translation, which is followed in Heb 9:4, this was a golden vessel.

**16:34 The covenant**: i.e., the ark of the covenant, in which were placed the two tablets of the Ten Commandments. Cf. 25:16, 21–22.

**16:36 Omer . . . ephah**: see note on Is 5:10.

*u:* Nm 11:7. *v:* Jos 5:12. *w:* Nm 33:12–14. *x:* Nm 20:2–13.

with you some of the elders of Israel, holding in your hand, as you go, the staff with which you struck the Nile. [6]I will be standing there in front of you on the rock in Horeb. Strike the rock, and the water will flow from it for the people to drink.[y] Moses did this, in the sight of the elders of Israel. [7]The place was named Massah and Meribah,* because the Israelites quarreled there and tested the LORD, saying, "Is the LORD in our midst or not?"[z]

***Battle with Amalek.*** [8]Then Amalek* came and waged war against Israel in Rephidim.[a] [9]So Moses said to Joshua, "Choose some men for us, and tomorrow go out and engage Amalek in battle. I will be standing on top of the hill with the staff of God in my hand." [10]Joshua did as Moses told him: he engaged Amalek in battle while Moses, Aaron, and Hur climbed to the top of the hill. [11]As long as Moses kept his hands raised up, Israel had the better of the fight, but when he let his hands rest, Amalek had the better of the fight. [12]Moses' hands, however, grew tired; so they took a rock and put it under him and he sat on it. Meanwhile Aaron and Hur supported his hands, one on one side and one on the other, so that his hands remained steady until sunset. [13]And Joshua defeated Amalek and his people with the sword.

[14]Then the LORD said to Moses: Write this down in a book as something to be remembered, and recite it to Joshua:[b] I will completely blot out the memory of Amalek from under the heavens. [15]Moses built an altar there, which he named Yahweh-nissi;* [16]for he said, "Take up the banner of the LORD!* The LORD has a war against Amalek through the ages."

## CHAPTER 18

See RG 68

***Meeting with Jethro.*** [1]Now Moses' father-in-law Jethro, the priest of Midian, heard of all that God had done for Moses and for his people Israel: how the LORD had brought Israel out of Egypt. [2]So his father-in-law Jethro took along Zipporah, Moses' wife—now this was after Moses had sent her back—* [3]and her two sons. One of these was named Gershom;[c] for he said, "I am a resident alien in a foreign land." [4]The other was named Eliezer; for he said, "The God of my father is my help; he has rescued me from Pharaoh's sword." [5]Together with Moses' wife and sons, then, his father-in-law Jethro came to him in the wilderness where he was encamped at the mountain of God,* [6]and he sent word to Moses, "I, your father-in-law Jethro, am coming to you, along with your wife and her two sons."

[7]Moses went out to meet his father-in-law, bowed down, and then kissed him. Having greeted each other, they went into the tent. [8]Moses then told his father-in-law of all that the LORD had done to Pharaoh and the Egyptians for the sake of Israel, and of all the hardships that had beset them on their journey, and how the LORD had rescued them. [9]Jethro rejoiced over all the goodness that the LORD had shown Israel in rescuing them from the power of the Egyptians. [10]"Blessed be the LORD," he said, "who has rescued you from the power of the Egyptians and of Pharaoh. [11]Now I know that the LORD is greater than all the gods; for he rescued the people from the power of the Egyptians when they treated them arrogantly." [12]Then Jethro, the father-in-law of Moses, brought a burnt offering* and sacrifices for God, and Aaron came with

**17:7 Massah . . . Meribah**: Hebrew words meaning, respectively, "the place of the test" and "the place of strife, of quarreling."

**17:8 Amalek**: the Amalekites appear in the Bible as early inhabitants of southern Palestine and the Sinai peninsula prior to the appearance of the Israelites in the region. Cf. Nm 24:20.

**17:15 Yahweh-nissi**: meaning, "the Lord is my banner."

**17:16 Take up the banner of the LORD**: lit., "a hand on the LORD's banner," apparently a war cry for the Israelite troops in the conduct of Holy War; however, the Hebrew text is difficult to interpret.

**18:2 Moses had sent her back**: a later gloss which attempts to harmonize Zipporah's presence with Jethro here in this story and the account of Moses' return to Egypt with Zipporah in 4:20.

**18:5** The allusion to meeting Moses encamped at the mountain of God, prior to the arrival of the Israelites at Sinai in chap. 19, might well suggest a different narrative context for this story from an earlier stage of the biblical tradition's development. It is noteworthy that immediately after the Sinai pericope (Ex 19:1–Nm 10:28), recounting the theophany at Sinai and the giving of the law, the narrative of Israel's march through the wilderness resumes with an apparent doublet of the visit by Moses' father-in-law (Nm 10:29–32).

*y:* Dt 8:15; Ps 78:15–16; 105:41; Wis 11:4; Is 43:20; 48:21. *z:* Ps 95:8–9. *a:* Dt 25:17–19; 1 Sm 15:2. *b:* Nm 24:20; 1 Sm 15:3, 20. *c:* Ex 2:22.

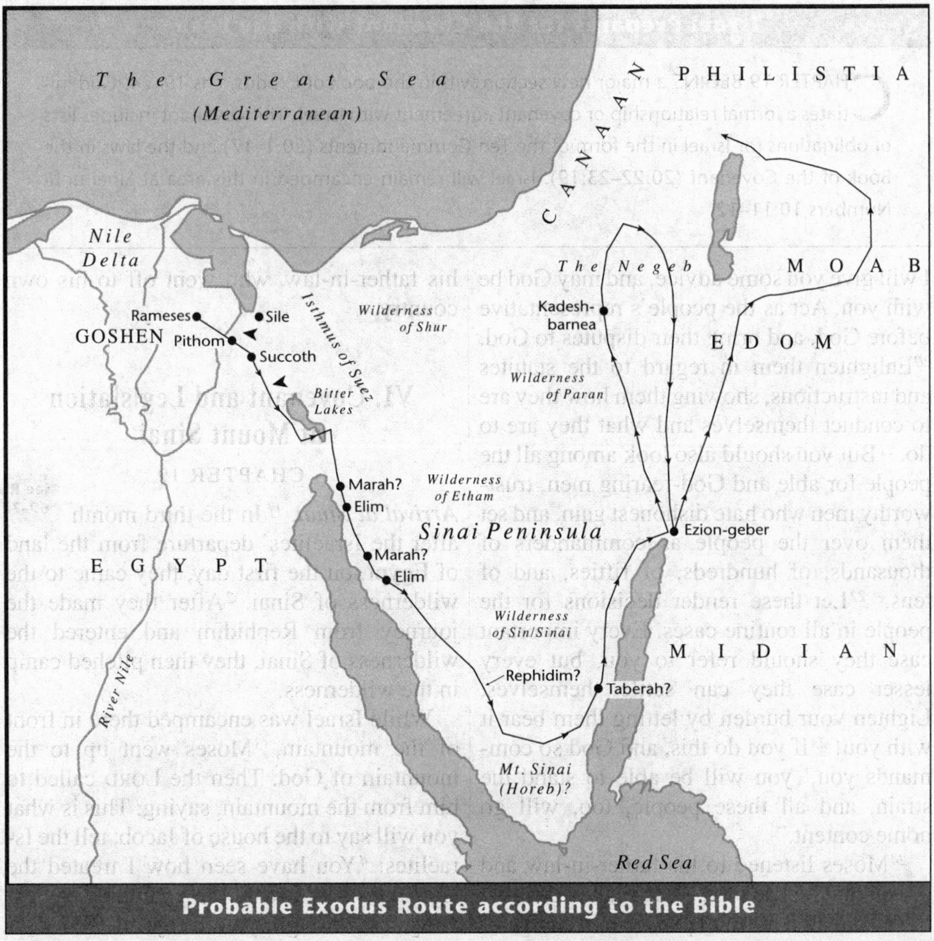

Probable Exodus Route according to the Bible

all the elders of Israel to share with Moses' father-in-law in the meal before God.

***Appointment of Minor Judges.*** [13]The next day Moses sat in judgment for the people, while they stood around him from morning until evening. [14]When Moses' father-in-law saw all that he was doing for the people, he asked, "What is this business that you are conducting for the people? Why do you sit alone while all the people have to stand about you from morning till evening?"

[15]Moses answered his father-in-law, "The people come to me to consult God. [16]Whenever they have a disagreement, they come to me to have me settle the matter between them and make known to them God's statutes and instructions."

[17]"What you are doing is not wise," Moses' father-in-law replied. [18]"You will surely wear yourself out, both you and these people with you. The task is too heavy for you;[d] you cannot do it alone. [19]* Now, listen to me, and

**18:12** That a non-Israelite, such as Jethro, should bless Israel's God by way of acknowledging what God had done for Israel (v. 10) is not entirely surprising; but the Midianite priest's sacrifice to the God of Israel, including his presiding over a sacrificial meal with Aaron and the elders of Israel, is unusual, suggesting that he was himself already a worshiper of Yhwh, Israel's God. Note further in this connection the role Jethro takes in the following narrative (vv. 13–27) in instituting a permanent judiciary for the Israelites. **Burnt offering:** a sacrifice wholly burnt up as an offering to God.

**18:19–20** By emphasizing Moses' mediatorial role for the people before God in regard to God's statutes and instructions,

*d:* Nm 11:14.

**Israel Prepares for the Covenant with the LORD**

CHAPTER 19 BEGINS a major new section within the book of Exodus, chs 19–24. God initiates a formal relationship or covenant agreement with Israel. This covenant includes lists of obligations for Israel in the form of the Ten Commandments (20:1–17) and the laws in the Book of the Covenant (20:22–23:19). Israel will remain encamped in this area at Sinai until Numbers 10:11–12.

I will give you some advice, and may God be
with you. Act as the people's representative
before God, and bring their disputes to God.
20 Enlighten them in regard to the statutes
and instructions, showing them how they are
to conduct themselves and what they are to
do. 21 But you should also look among all the
people for able and God-fearing men, trustworthy men who hate dishonest gain, and set
them over the people as commanders of
thousands, of hundreds, of fifties, and of
tens.[e] 22 Let these render decisions for the
people in all routine cases. Every important
case they should refer to you, but every
lesser case they can settle themselves.
Lighten your burden by letting them bear it
with you! 23 If you do this, and God so commands you,* you will be able to stand the
strain, and all these people, too, will go
home content."

24 Moses listened to his father-in-law and
did all that he had said. 25 He picked out able
men from all Israel and put them in charge of
the people as commanders of thousands, of
hundreds, of fifties, and of tens. 26 They rendered decisions for the people in all routine
cases. The more difficult cases they referred
to Moses, but all the lesser cases they settled
themselves. 27 Then Moses said farewell to
his father-in-law, who went off to his own
country.

## VI. Covenant and Legislation at Mount Sinai

### CHAPTER 19

See RG 69–70

*Arrival at Sinai.* 1[f] In the third month
after the Israelites' departure from the land
of Egypt, on the first day, they came to the
wilderness of Sinai. 2 After they made the
journey from Rephidim and entered the
wilderness of Sinai, they then pitched camp
in the wilderness.*

While Israel was encamped there in front
of the mountain, 3 Moses went up to the
mountain of God. Then the LORD called to
him from the mountain, saying: This is what
you will say to the house of Jacob; tell the Israelites: 4 You have seen how I treated the
Egyptians and how I bore you up on eagles'
wings and brought you to myself.[g] 5 Now, if
you obey me completely and keep my covenant,* you will be my treasured possession
among all peoples,[h] though all the earth is
mine. 6 You will be to me a kingdom of
priests,* a holy nation.[i] That is what you
must tell the Israelites. 7 So Moses went and

this story about the institution of Israel's judiciary prepares for Moses' role in the upcoming revelation of the law at Sinai.

**18:23 And God so commands you**: i.e., and God approves.

**19:2** Apparently from a different source (P) than v. 1, which notes the date, v. 2 from the J source includes a second notice of the arrival in the wilderness of Sinai. The Israelites now will be camped at Sinai from this point on all the way to Nm 10:10. This is a striking indication of the centrality and importance of the Sinai narrative in the overall composition of the Pentateuch.

**19:5 Covenant**: while covenants between individuals and between nations are ubiquitous in the ancient Near East, the adaptation of this concept to express the relationship that will henceforth characterize God's relationship to Israel represents an important innovation of biblical faith. Other gods might "choose" nations to fulfill a special destiny or role in the world; but only Israel's God is bound to a people by covenant. Thereby Israel's identity as a people is put upon a foundation that does not depend upon the vicissitudes of Israelite statehood or the normal trappings of national existence. Israel will be a covenant people.

**19:6 Kingdom of priests**: inasmuch as this phrase is parallel to "holy nation," it most likely means that the whole Israelite nation is set apart from other nations and so consecrated to God, or holy, in the way priests are among the people (cf. Is 61:6; 1 Pt 2:5, 9).

*e:* Dt 1:15; 16:18. *f:* Nm 33:15. *g:* Dt 32:11–12. *h:* Dt 7:6; 14:2; 26:18–19; 32:8–9. *i:* 1 Pt 2:9.

summoned the elders of the people. When he set before them all that the LORD had ordered him to tell them, 8all the people answered together, "Everything the LORD has said, we will do." Then Moses brought back to the LORD the response of the people.

9The LORD said to Moses: I am coming to you now in a dense cloud,[j] so that when the people hear me speaking with you, they will also remain faithful to you.

When Moses, then, had reported the response of the people to the LORD, 10the LORD said to Moses: Go to the people and have them sanctify themselves today and tomorrow. Have them wash their garments 11and be ready for the third day; for on the third day the LORD will come down on Mount Sinai in the sight of all the people. 12Set limits for the people all around,[k] saying: Take care not to go up the mountain, or even to touch its edge. All who touch the mountain must be put to death. 13No hand shall touch them, but they must be stoned to death or killed with arrows. Whether human being or beast, they must not be allowed to live. Only when the ram's horn sounds may they go up on the mountain.* 14Then Moses came down from the mountain to the people and had them sanctify themselves, and they washed their garments. 15He said to the people, "Be ready for the third day. Do not approach a woman."

***The Great Theophany.*** 16* On the morning of the third day there were peals of thunder and lightning, and a heavy cloud over the mountain, and a very loud blast of the shofar,* so that all the people in the camp trembled. 17But Moses led the people out of the camp to meet God, and they stationed themselves at the foot of the mountain. 18Now Mount Sinai was completely enveloped in smoke, because the LORD had come down upon it in fire. The smoke rose from it as though from a kiln, and the whole mountain trembled violently. 19The blast of the shofar grew louder and louder, while Moses was speaking and God was answering him with thunder.

20* When the LORD came down upon Mount Sinai, to the top of the mountain, the LORD summoned Moses to the top of the mountain, and Moses went up. 21Then the LORD told Moses: Go down and warn the people not to break through to the LORD in order to see him; otherwise many of them will be struck down. 22For their part, the priests, who approach the LORD must sanctify themselves; else the LORD will break out in anger against them. 23But Moses said to the LORD, "The people cannot go up to Mount Sinai, for you yourself warned us, saying: Set limits around the mountain to make it sacred." 24So the LORD said to him: Go down and come up along with Aaron. But do not let the priests and the people break through to come up to the LORD; else he will break out against them." 25So Moses went down to the people and spoke to them.

## CHAPTER 20

See RG 69–70

***The Ten Commandments.**** 1Then God spoke all these words:

2m I am the LORD your God, who brought you out of the land of Egypt,[n] out of the

**19:13 May they go up on the mountain**: in vv. 12–13a, a later Priestly reshaping of an earlier version of the instructions governing how the people are to prepare for the encounter with God (vv. 10–11, 13b), the people are to be restrained from ascending the mountain, which is suffused with the holiness of God and too dangerous for their approach. In the earlier version, as v. 13b suggests, the sanctified people must come near, in order to hear God speaking with Moses (v. 9) and in this way receive confirmation of his special relationship with God.

**19:16 Shofar**: a ram's horn used like a trumpet for signaling both for liturgical and military purposes.

**19:20–25** At this point the Priestly additions of vv. 12–13a are elaborated with further Priestly instructions, which include the priests' sanctifying themselves apart from the people (v. 22) and Aaron accompanying Moses to the top of the mountain (v. 24).

**20:1–17** The precise numbering and division of these precepts into "ten commandments" is somewhat uncertain. Traditionally among Catholics and Lutherans vv. 1–6 are considered as only one commandment, and v. 17 as two. The Anglican, Greek Orthodox, and Reformed churches count vv. 1–6 as two, and v. 17 as one. Cf. Dt 5:6–21. The traditional designation as "ten" is not found here but in 34:28 (and also Dt 4:13 and 10:4), where these precepts are alluded to literally as "the ten words." That they were originally written on two tablets appears in Ex 32:15–16; 34:28–29; Dt 4:13; 10:2–4.

The present form of the commands is a product of a long development, as is clear from the fact that the individual precepts vary considerably in length and from the slightly dif-

*j:* Ex 20:21; 24:15–18. *k:* Ex 34:3; Heb 12:18–19. *l:* Dt 4:10–12. *m:* Dt 5:6–21. *n:* Lv 26:13; Ps 81:11; Hos 13:4.

### The Decalogue

THE DECALOGUE IS the initial stipulation of the covenant. (*Decalogue*, Greek for "ten words" or "ten statements," is a more literal rendition of the Hebrew *aseret hadevarim* than "Ten Commandments"; see Ex 34:28.) It is addressed directly to the people. No punishments are stated; obedience is motivated not by fear, but by God's absolute authority and the people's desire to live in accordance with his will.

The items in the Decalogue are arranged in two groups. Duties to God come first. Each commandment in this group contains the phrase, "the LORD, your God." The second group contains duties toward fellow humans, which are depicted as being of equal concern to God. The first five are accompanied by explanatory comments or exhortations. The remaining five, as widely recognized ethical requirements, need no such support.

house of slavery. [3]You shall not have other
gods beside me.* [4]You shall not make for
yourself an idol[o] or a likeness of anything* in
the heavens above or on the earth below or
in the waters beneath the earth; [5]you shall
not bow down before them or serve them.[p]
For I, the LORD, your God, am a jealous
God, inflicting punishment for their ancestors' wickedness on the children of those
who hate me, down to the third and fourth
generation*; [6]but showing love down to the
thousandth generation of those who love me
and keep my commandments.

[7]You shall not invoke the name of the
LORD, your God, in vain.* [q] For the LORD
will not leave unpunished anyone who invokes his name in vain.

[8]Remember the sabbath day—keep it
holy.* [9]Six days you may labor and do all
your work, [10]but the seventh day is a sabbath
of the LORD your God.[r] You shall not do any
work, either you, your son or your daughter,
your male or female slave, your work animal, or the resident alien within your gates.
[11]For in six days the LORD made the heavens
and the earth, the sea and all that is in them;

ferent formulation of Dt 5:6–21 (see especially vv. 12–15 and 21). Indeed they represent a mature formulation of a traditional morality. Why this specific selection of commands should be set apart is not entirely clear. None of them is unique in the Old Testament and all of the laws which follow are also from God and equally binding on the Israelites. Even so, this collection represents a privileged expression of God's moral demands on Israel and is here set apart from the others as a direct, unmediated communication of God to the Israelites and the basis of the covenant being concluded on Sinai.

**20:3 Beside me**: this commandment is traditionally understood as an outright denial of the existence of other gods except the God of Israel; however, in the context of the more general prohibitions in vv. 4–5, v. 3 is, more precisely, God's demand for Israel's exclusive worship and allegiance.

The Hebrew phrase underlying the translation "beside me" is, nonetheless, problematic and has been variously translated, e.g., "except me," "in addition to me," "in preference to me," "in defiance of me," and "in front of me" or "before my face." The latter translation, with its concrete, spatial nuances, has suggested to some that the prohibition once sought to exclude from the Lord's sanctuary the cult images or idols of other gods, such as the asherah, or stylized sacred tree of life, associated with the Canaanite goddess Asherah (34:13). Over the course of time, as vv. 4–5 suggest, the original scope of v. 3 was expanded.

**20:4 Or a likeness of anything**: compare this formulation to that found in Dt 5:8, which understands this phrase and the following phrases as specifications of the prohibited idol (Hebrew *pesel*), which usually refers to an image that is carved or hewn rather than cast.

**20:5 Jealous**: demanding exclusive allegiance. **Inflicting punishment . . . the third and fourth generation**: the intended emphasis is on God's mercy by the contrast between punishment and mercy ("to the thousandth generation"—v. 6). Other Old Testament texts repudiate the idea of punishment devolving on later generations (cf. Dt 24:16; Jer 31:29–30; Ez 18:2–4). Yet it is known that later generations may suffer the punishing effects of sins of earlier generations, but not the guilt.

**20:7 In vain**: i.e., to no good purpose, a general framing of the prohibition which includes swearing falsely, especially in the context of a legal proceeding, but also goes beyond it (cf. Lv 24:16; Prv 30:8–9).

**20:8 Keep it holy**: i.e., to set it apart from the other days of the week, in part, as the following verse explains, by not doing work that is ordinarily done in the course of a week. The special importance of this command can be seen in the fact that, together with vv. 9–11, it represents the longest of the Decalogue's precepts.

*o:* Ex 34:17; Lv 26:1; Dt 4:15–19; 27:15. *p:* Ex 34:7, 14; Nm 14:18; Dt 4:24; 6:15. *q:* Lv 19:12; 24:16. *r:* Ex 23:12; 31:13–16; 34:21; 35:2; Lv 23:3.

but on the seventh day he rested.[s] That is why the LORD has blessed the sabbath day and made it holy.*

[12]* [t] Honor your father and your mother, that you may have a long life in the land the LORD your God is giving you.[u]

[13]You shall not kill.* [v]

[14]You shall not commit adultery.[w]

[15]You shall not steal.[x]

[16]You shall not bear false witness against your neighbor.[y]

[17]You shall not covet your neighbor's house. You shall not covet your neighbor's wife, his male or female slave, his ox or donkey, or anything that belongs to your neighbor.[z]

***Moses Accepted as Mediator.*** [18]Now as all the people witnessed the thunder and lightning, the blast of the shofar and the mountain smoking, they became afraid and trembled.[a] So they took up a position farther away [19]and said to Moses, "You speak to us, and we will listen; but do not let God speak to us, or we shall die." [20]Moses answered the people, "Do not be afraid, for God has come only to test you and put the fear of him upon you so you do not sin." [21]So the people remained at a distance, while Moses approached the dark cloud where God was.

***The Covenant Code.*** [22]* The LORD said to Moses: This is what you will say to the Israelites: You have seen for yourselves that I have spoken to you from heaven. [23]You shall not make alongside of me gods of silver, nor shall you make for yourselves gods of gold.[b] [24]An altar of earth make for me, and sacrifice upon it your burnt offerings and communion sacrifices, your sheep and your oxen.[c] In every place where I cause my name to be invoked* I will come to you and bless you. [25]But if you make an altar of stone for me,[d] do not build it of cut stone, for by putting a chisel to it you profane it. [26]You shall not ascend to my altar by steps, lest your nakedness be exposed.

## CHAPTER 21

See RG 69–70

***Laws Regarding Slaves.*** [1]These are the ordinances* you shall lay before them. [2][e] When you purchase a Hebrew slave,* he is to serve you for six years, but in the seventh year he shall leave as a free person without any payment. [3]If he comes into service alone, he shall leave alone; if he comes with a wife, his wife shall leave with him. [4]But if his master gives him a wife and she bears him sons or daughters, the woman and her children belong to her master and the man shall leave alone. [5]If, however, the slave declares, 'I love my master and my wife and children; I will not leave as a free person,'

**20:11** Here, in a formulation which reflects Priestly theology, the veneration of the sabbath is grounded in God's own hallowing of the sabbath in creation. Compare 31:13; Dt 5:15.

**20:12–17** The Decalogue falls into two parts: the preceding precepts refer to God, the following refer primarily to one's fellow Israelites.

**20:13 Kill**: as frequent instances of killing in the context of war or certain crimes (see vv. 12–18) demonstrate in the Old Testament, not all killing comes within the scope of the commandment. For this reason, the Hebrew verb translated here as "kill" is often understood as "murder," although it is in fact used in the Old Testament at times for unintentional acts of killing (e.g., Dt 4:41; Jos 20:3) and for legally sanctioned killing (Nm 35:30). The term may originally have designated any killing of another Israelite, including acts of manslaughter, for which the victim's kin could exact vengeance. In the present context, it denotes the killing of one Israelite by another, motivated by hatred or the like (Nm 35:20; cf. Hos 6:9).

**20:22–23:33** This collection consists of the civil and religious laws, both apodictic (absolute) and casuistic (conditional), which were given to the people through the mediation of Moses. They will be written down by Moses in 24:4.

**20:24 Where I cause my name to be invoked**: i.e., at the sacred site where God wishes to be worshiped. Dt 12 will demand the centralization of all sacrificial worship in one place chosen by God.

**21:1 Ordinances**: judicial precedents to be used in settling questions of law and custom. More than half of the civil and religious laws in this collection (20:22–23:33), designated in 24:7 as "the book of the covenant," have parallels in the cuneiform laws of the ancient Near East. It is clear that Israel participated in a common legal culture with its neighbors.

**21:2 Slave**: an Israelite could become a slave of another Israelite as a means of paying a debt, or an Israelite could be born into slavery due to a parent's status as a slave. Here a time limit is prescribed for such slavery; other stipulations (vv. 20–21, 26–27) tried to reduce the evils of slavery, but slavery itself is not condemned in the Old Testament.

*s:* Ex 31:17; Gn 2:2–3. *t:* Mt 19:18–19; Mk 10:19; Lk 18:20; Rom 13:9. *u:* Lv 20:9; Mt 15:4; Mk 7:10; Eph 6:2–3. *v:* Mt 5:21. *w:* Lv 18:20; 20:10; Dt 22:22; Mt 5:27. *x:* Lv 19:11. *y:* Ex 23:1; Dt 19:16–19; Prv 19:5, 9; 24:28. *z:* Rom 7:7. *a:* Dt 4:11; 5:22–27; 18:16; Heb 12:18–19. *b:* Ex 20:3–4. *c:* Dt 12:5, 11; 14:23; 16:6. *d:* Dt 27:5; Jos 8:31. *e:* Lv 25:39–55; Dt 15:12–18; Jer 34:14.

[6]his master shall bring him to God* and there, at the door or doorpost, he shall pierce his ear with an awl, thus keeping him as his slave forever.

[7]When a man sells his daughter as a slave, she shall not go free as male slaves do. [8]But if she displeases her master, who had designated her* for himself, he shall let her be redeemed. He has no right to sell her to a foreign people, since he has broken faith with her. [9]If he designates her for his son, he shall treat her according to the ordinance for daughters. [10]If he takes another wife, he shall not withhold her food, her clothing, or her conjugal rights. [11]If he does not do these three things for her, she may leave without cost, without any payment.

***Personal Injury.*** [12]* Whoever strikes someone a mortal blow must be put to death.[f] [13]However, regarding the one who did not hunt another down, but God caused death to happen by his hand, I will set apart for you a place to which that one may flee. [14]But when someone kills a neighbor after maliciously scheming to do so, you must take him even from my altar and put him to death. [15]Whoever strikes father or mother shall be put to death.*

[16]A kidnapper, whether he sells the person or the person is found in his possession, shall be put to death.[g]

[17]Whoever curses* father or mother shall be put to death.[h]

[18]When men quarrel and one strikes the other with a stone or with his fist, not mortally, but enough to put him in bed, [19]the one who struck the blow shall be acquitted, provided the other can get up and walk around with the help of his staff. Still, he must compensate him for his recovery time and make provision for his complete healing.

[20]When someone strikes his male or female slave with a rod so that the slave dies under his hand, the act shall certainly be avenged. [21]If, however, the slave survives for a day or two, he is not to be punished, since the slave is his own property.

[22]* When men have a fight and hurt a pregnant woman, so that she suffers a miscarriage, but no further injury, the guilty one shall be fined as much as the woman's husband demands of him, and he shall pay in the presence of the judges. [23][i] But if injury ensues, you shall give life for life, [24]eye for eye, tooth for tooth, hand for hand, foot for foot, [25]burn for burn, wound for wound, stripe for stripe.

[26]When someone strikes his male or female slave in the eye and destroys the use of the eye, he shall let the slave go free in compensation for the eye. [27]If he knocks out a tooth of his male or female slave, he shall let the slave go free in compensation for the tooth.

[28]When an ox gores a man or a woman to death, the ox must be stoned; its meat may

**21:6 To God**: the ritual of the piercing of the slave's ear, which signified a lifetime commitment to the master, probably took place at the door of the household, where God as protector of the household was called upon as a witness. Another possible location for the ritual would have been the door of the sanctuary, where God or judges would have witnessed the slave's promise of lifetime obedience to his master.

**21:8 Designated her**: intended her as a wife of second rank.

**21:12–14** Unintentional homicide is to be punished differently from premeditated, deliberate murder. One who kills unintentionally can seek asylum by grasping the horns of the altar at the local sanctuary. In later Israelite history, when worship was centralized in Jerusalem, cities throughout the realm were designated as places of refuge. Apparently the leaders of the local community were to determine whether or not the homicide was intentional.

**21:15** The verb used most often signifies a violent, sometimes deadly, attack. The severe penalty assigned is intended to safeguard the integrity of the family.

**21:17 Curses**: not merely an angrily uttered expletive at one's parents, but a solemn juridical formula of justifiable retribution which was considered to be legally binding and guaranteed by God.

**21:22–25** This law of talion is applied here in the specific case of a pregnant woman who, as an innocent bystander, is injured by two fighting men. The law of talion is not held up as a general principle to be applied throughout the book of the covenant. (But see note on Lv 24:19–20.) Here this principle of rigorous accountability aimed to prevent injury to a woman about to give birth by apparently requiring the assailant to have his own wife injured as she was about to bring new life into his family. However, it is debatable whether talion was ever understood or applied literally in Israel. In his Sermon on the Mount, Jesus challenges his audience to find a deeper form of justice than the supposed equilibrium offered by talion (Mt 5:38–40).

*f:* Lv 24:17; Nm 35:15–29; Dt 4:41–42; 19:2–5. *g:* Dt 24:7. *h:* Lv 20:9; Prv 20:20; Mt 15:4; Mk 7:10. *i:* Lv 24:18–21; Dt 19:21; Mt 5:38.

not be eaten. The owner of the ox, however, shall be free of blame. 29But if an ox was previously in the habit of goring people and its owner, though warned, would not watch it; should it then kill a man or a woman, not only must the ox be stoned, but its owner also must be put to death. 30If, however, a fine is imposed on him, he must pay in ransom[*] for his life whatever amount is imposed on him. 31This ordinance applies if it is a boy or a girl that the ox gores. 32But if it is a male or a female slave that it gores, he must pay the owner of the slave thirty shekels of silver, and the ox must be stoned.

***Property Damage.*** 33When someone uncovers or digs a cistern and does not cover it over again, should an ox or a donkey fall into it, 34the owner of the cistern must make good by restoring the value of the animal to its owner, but the dead animal he may keep.

35When one man's ox hurts another's ox and it dies, they shall sell the live ox and divide this money as well as the dead animal equally between them. 36But if it was known that the ox was previously in the habit of goring and its owner would not watch it, he must make full restitution, an ox for an ox; but the dead animal he may keep.

37When someone steals an ox or a sheep and slaughters or sells it, he shall restore five oxen for the one ox, and four sheep for the one sheep.[j]

See RG 69–70

## CHAPTER 22

1[If a thief is caught[*] in the act of housebreaking and beaten to death, there is no bloodguilt involved. 2But if after sunrise he is thus beaten, there is bloodguilt.] He must make full restitution. If he has nothing, he shall be sold to pay for his theft. 3If what he stole is found alive in his possession, be it an ox, a donkey or a sheep, he shall make twofold restitution.

4When someone causes a field or a vineyard to be grazed over, by sending his cattle to graze in another's field, he must make restitution with the best produce of his own field or vineyard. 5If a fire breaks out, catches on to thorn bushes, and consumes shocked grain, standing grain, or the field itself, the one who started the fire must make full restitution.

***Trusts and Loans.*** 6When someone gives money or articles to another for safekeeping and they are stolen from the latter's house, the thief, if caught, must make twofold restitution. 7If the thief is not caught, the owner of the house shall be brought to God,[*] to swear that he himself did not lay hands on his neighbor's property. 8In every case of dishonest appropriation, whether it be about an ox, or a donkey, or a sheep, or a garment, or anything else that has disappeared, where another claims that the thing is his, the claim of both parties shall be brought before God; the one whom God convicts must make twofold restitution to the other.

9When someone gives an ass, or an ox, or a sheep, or any other animal to another for safekeeping, if it dies, or is maimed or snatched away, without anyone witnessing the fact, 10there shall be an oath before the LORD between the two of them that the guardian did not lay hands on his neighbor's property; the owner must accept the oath, and no restitution is to be made. 11But if the guardian has actually stolen from it, then he must make restitution to the owner. 12If it has been killed by a wild beast, let him bring it as evidence; he need not make restitution for the mangled animal.[k]

13When someone borrows an animal from a neighbor, if it is maimed or dies while the owner is not present, that one must make restitution. 14But if the owner is present, that one need not make restitution. If it was hired, this was covered by the price of its hire.

***Social Laws.*** 15[l] When a man seduces a

**21:30 Ransom**: the amount of money or material goods required to restore the relationship between the relatives of the victim and the negligent owner of the goring ox.

**22:1–2 If a thief is caught**: this seems to be a fragment of what was once a longer law on housebreaking, which has been inserted here into the middle of a law on stealing animals. At night the householder would be justified in killing a burglar outright, but not so in the daytime, when the burglar could more easily be caught alive. **He must make full restitution**: this stood originally immediately after 21:37.

**22:7 Brought to God**: either within the household or at the sanctuary, the owner of the house is required to take an oath before God.

*j:* 2 Sm 12:6. *k:* Gn 31:39. *l:* Dt 22:28–29.

virgin who is not betrothed, and lies with her, he shall make her his wife by paying the bride price. 16If her father refuses to give her to him, he must still pay him the bride price for virgins.*

17You shall not let a woman who practices sorcery live.[m]

18Anyone who lies with an animal shall be put to death.[n]

19Whoever sacrifices to any god, except to the LORD alone, shall be put under the ban.[o]

20You shall not oppress or afflict a resident alien, for you were once aliens residing in the land of Egypt.[p] 21You shall not wrong any widow or orphan. 22If ever you wrong them and they cry out to me, I will surely listen to their cry. 23My wrath will flare up, and I will kill you with the sword; then your own wives will be widows, and your children orphans.

24[q] If you lend money to my people, the poor among you, you must not be like a money lender; you must not demand interest from them. 25If you take your neighbor's cloak as a pledge, you shall return it to him before sunset; 26for this is his only covering; it is the cloak for his body. What will he sleep in? If he cries out to me, I will listen; for I am compassionate.[r]

27You shall not despise God,* nor curse a leader of your people.[s]

28You shall not delay the offering of your harvest and your press. You shall give me the firstborn of your sons. 29You must do the same with your oxen and your sheep; for seven days the firstling may stay with its mother, but on the eighth day you must give it to me.[t]

30You shall be a people sacred to me. Flesh torn to pieces in the field you shall not eat; you must throw it to the dogs.[u]

## CHAPTER 23

See RG 69–70

1You shall not repeat a false report. Do not join your hand with the wicked to be a witness supporting violence.[v] 2You shall not follow the crowd in doing wrong. When testifying in a lawsuit, you shall not follow the crowd in perverting justice. 3You shall not favor the poor in a lawsuit.[w]

4When you come upon your enemy's ox or donkey going astray, you must see to it that it is returned.[x] 5When you notice the donkey of one who hates you lying down under its burden, you should not desert him; you must help him with it.

6You shall not pervert justice for the needy among you in a lawsuit. 7You shall keep away from anything dishonest. The innocent and the just you shall not put to death, for I will not acquit the guilty. 8Never take a bribe, for a bribe blinds the clear-sighted and distorts the words of the just.[y] 9You shall not oppress a resident alien; you well know how it feels to be an alien, since you were once aliens yourselves in the land of Egypt.[z]

***Religious Laws.*** 10[a] For six years you may sow your land and gather in its produce. 11But the seventh year you shall let the land lie untilled and fallow, that the poor of your people may eat of it and their leftovers the wild animals may eat. So also shall you do in regard to your vineyard and your olive grove. 12For six days you may do your work, but on the seventh day you must rest,[b] that your ox and your donkey may have rest, and that the son of your maidservant and the resident alien may be refreshed. 13Give heed to all that I have told you.

You shall not mention the name of any other god; it shall not be heard from your lips. 14[c] Three times a year you shall celebrate a pilgrim feast to me.* 15You shall keep the feast of Unleavened Bread. As I have commanded you, you must eat unleavened bread for seven days at the appointed time in the month of Abib, for it was then that you came

**22:16 The bride price for virgins**: fifty shekels according to Dt 22:29.

**22:27 Despise God**: a turning away from God's authority and so failing to honor God (cf. 1 Sm 2:30).

**23:14** These three feasts—Passover/Unleavened Bread, Weeks (Pentecost), and Booths (Tabernacles or Succoth/Sukkoth)—are also listed in 34:18–26; Lv 23; Dt 16.

*m:* Lv 19:26, 31; 20:6, 27; Dt 18:10–11. *n:* Lv 18:23; Dt 27:21. *o:* Dt 13; 17:2–7. *p:* Ex 23:9; Lv 19:33–34; Dt 10:18–19; 24:17–18; 27:19; Zec 7:10. *q:* Lv 25:35–38; Dt 23:19–20; 24:10–13; Ez 18:7–8, 17–18. *r:* Dt 24:10–13; Jb 22:6; Prv 20:16; 27:13; Am 2:8. *s:* Acts 23:5. *t:* Ex 13:2; 34:19; Lv 22:27; Dt 15:19. *u:* Lv 7:24; 17:15; 22:8. *v:* Dt 19:16–21. *w:* Lv 19:15. *x:* Dt 22:1–4. *y:* Dt 16:19; 27:25; Sir 20:28. *z:* Ex 22:20. *a:* Lv 25:3–7. *b:* Ex 20:8–10. *c:* Ex 34:18, 22–24; Lv 23; Dt 16:1–17.

out of Egypt. No one shall appear before me*
empty-handed. 16You shall also keep the
feast of the grain harvest with the first fruits
of the crop that you sow in the field; and finally, the feast of Ingathering at the end of
the year, when you collect your produce
from the fields. 17Three times a year shall all
your men appear before the LORD God.

18You shall not offer the blood of my sacrifice with anything leavened;[d] nor shall the
fat of my feast be kept overnight till the next
day. 19The choicest first fruits of your soil
you shall bring to the house of the LORD,
your God.

You shall not boil a young goat in its
mother's milk.*

***Reward of Fidelity.*** 20See, I am sending an
angel[e] before you, to guard you on the way
and bring you to the place I have prepared.
21Be attentive to him and obey him. Do not
rebel against him, for he will not forgive
your sin. My authority is within him.* 22If
you obey him and carry out all I tell you, I
will be an enemy to your enemies and a foe
to your foes.

23My angel will go before you and bring
you to the Amorites, Hittites, Perizzites,
Canaanites, Hivites and Jebusites; and I will
wipe them out. 24Therefore, you shall not
bow down to their gods and serve them, nor
shall you act as they do; rather, you must demolish them and smash their sacred stones.*[f]
25You shall serve the LORD, your God; then
he will bless your food and drink, and I will
remove sickness from your midst; 26no
woman in your land will be barren or miscarry; and I will give you a full span of life.

27I will have the terror of me precede you,
so that I will throw into panic every nation
you reach.[g] I will make all your enemies turn
from you in flight, 28and ahead of you I will
send hornets* to drive the Hivites, Canaanites and Hittites out of your way. 29But I will
not drive them all out before you in one year,
lest the land become desolate and the wild
animals multiply against you. 30Little by little I will drive them out before you, until you
have grown numerous enough to take possession of the land. 31[h] I will set your boundaries from the Red Sea to the sea of the Philistines,* and from the wilderness to the
Euphrates; all who dwell in this land I will
hand over to you and you shall drive them
out before you. 32You shall not make a covenant with them or their gods. 33They must
not live in your land. For if you serve their
gods, this will become a snare to you.[i]

## CHAPTER 24

See RG 69–70

***Ratification of the Covenant.*** 1Moses
himself was told: Come up to the LORD, you
and Aaron, with Nadab, Abihu, and seventy
of the elders of Israel. You shall bow down
at a distance. 2Moses alone is to come close
to the LORD; the others shall not come close,
and the people shall not come up with them.

3When Moses came to the people and related all the words and ordinances of the
LORD, they all answered with one voice,
"We will do everything that the LORD has
told us."[j] 4Moses then wrote down all the
words of the LORD and, rising early in the
morning, he built at the foot of the mountain
an altar and twelve sacred stones* for the

**23:15 Appear before me**: the original expression was "see my face"; so also in several other places, as 23:17; 34:23–24; Dt 16:16; 31:11.

**23:19 Boil a young goat in its mother's milk**: this command, repeated in 34:26 and Dt 14:21, is difficult to understand. It may originate from a taboo that forbade killing the young that were still nursing from the mother, or that forbade the mixing of life and death: the slaughtered young goat with the milk that previously had nourished its life. The Jewish dietary custom of keeping meat and dairy products separate is based on this command.

**23:21 My authority is within him**: lit., "My name is within him."

**23:24 Sacred stones**: objects that symbolized the presence of Canaanite deities. In general, standing stones served as memorials for deities, persons, or significant events such as military victories or covenant-making. See 24:4.

**23:28 Hornets**: the Hebrew *sir'ah* is a disputed term, but according to ancient interpreters it refers to hornets that were unleashed against the enemy to sting them and cause panic (cf. Dt 7:20; Jos 24:12; Wis 12:8). Others associate the word with plagues or troublesome afflictions.

**23:31 The sea of the Philistines**: the Mediterranean. Only in the time of David and Solomon did the territory of Israel come near to reaching such distant borders.

**24:4 Sacred stones**: stone shafts or slabs, erected as symbols of the fact that each of the twelve tribes had entered into this covenant with God; see 23:24; Gn 28:18.

*d:* Ex 34:25–26. *e:* Ex 14:19; 32:34; 33:2. *f:* Ex 34:10–16; Nm 33:51–52; Dt 7:24–26. *g:* Dt 2:25; 7:20–22. *h:* Gn 15:18; Dt 11:24; Jos 1:4. *i:* Ex 34:12–16; Dt 7:2–6. *j:* Ex 19:8.

twelve tribes of Israel. 5[k] Then, having sent young men of the Israelites to offer burnt offerings and sacrifice young bulls as communion offerings to the LORD, 6 Moses took half of the blood and put it in large bowls; the other half he splashed on the altar. 7 Taking the book of the covenant, he read it aloud to the people, who answered, "All that the LORD has said, we will hear and do." 8 Then he took the blood and splashed it on the people, saying, "This is the blood of the covenant which the LORD has made with you according to all these words."

9 Moses then went up with Aaron, Nadab, Abihu, and seventy elders of Israel, 10 and they beheld the God of Israel. Under his feet there appeared to be sapphire tilework, as clear as the sky itself. 11 Yet he did not lay a hand on these chosen Israelites. They saw God,* and they ate and drank.

***Moses on the Mountain.*** 12 The LORD said to Moses: Come up to me on the mountain and, while you are there, I will give you the stone tablets[l] on which I have written the commandments intended for their instruction. 13 So Moses set out with Joshua, his assistant, and went up to the mountain of God. 14 He told the elders, "Wait here for us until we return to you. Aaron and Hur are with you. Anyone with a complaint should approach them." 15 Moses went up the mountain. Then the cloud covered the mountain. 16 The glory of the LORD settled upon Mount Sinai. The cloud covered it for six days, and on the seventh day he called to Moses from the midst of the cloud.[m] 17 To the Israelites the glory of the LORD was seen as a consuming fire on the top of the mountain.[n] 18 But Moses entered into the midst of the cloud and went up on the mountain. He was on the mountain for forty days and forty nights.[o]

## CHAPTER 25

See RG 70

***Collection of Materials.*** 1 The LORD spoke to Moses:[p] 2 Speak to the Israelites: Let them receive contributions for me. From each you shall receive the contribution that their hearts prompt them to give me. 3 These are the contributions you shall accept from them: gold, silver, and bronze;[q] 4 violet, purple, and scarlet yarn; fine linen and goat hair; 5 rams' skins dyed red, and tahash* skins; acacia wood; 6 oil for the light; spices for the anointing oil and for the fragrant incense; 7 onyx stones and other gems for mounting on the ephod and the breastpiece. 8 They are to make a sanctuary for me, that I may dwell in their midst.[r] 9 According to all that I show you regarding the pattern of the tabernacle and the pattern of its furnishings, so you are to make it.[s]

***Plan of the Ark.*** 10 You shall make an ark of acacia wood,[t] two and a half cubits* long, one and a half cubits wide, and one and a half cubits high. 11 Plate it inside and outside with pure gold, and put a molding of gold around the top of it. 12 Cast four gold rings and put them on the four supports of the ark, two rings on one side and two on the opposite side. 13 Then make poles of acacia wood and plate them with gold. 14 These poles you are to put through the rings on the sides of the ark, for carrying it; 15 they must remain in the rings of the ark and never be withdrawn. 16 In the ark you are to put the covenant which I will give you.

17 You shall then make a cover* of pure gold, two and a half cubits long, and one and a half cubits wide. 18 Make two cherubim* of

**24:11 They saw God**: the ancients thought that the sight of God would bring instantaneous death. Cf. 33:20; Gn 16:13; 32:31; Jgs 6:22–23; 13:22. **Ate and drank**: partook of the sacrificial meal.

**25:5 Tahash**: perhaps a kind of specially finished leather. The Greek and Latin versions took it for the color hyacinth.

**25:10 Cubits**: the distance between the elbow and tip of the middle finger of an average-size person, about eighteen inches. The dimensions of the ark of the covenant were approximately 3 3/4 feet long, 2 1/4 feet wide, and 2 1/4 feet high.

**25:17 Cover**: the Hebrew term, *kapporet*, has been connected with *kippur*, as in the feast of Yom Kippur or Day of Atonement (Lv 16; 23:26–32): hence, influenced by the Greek and Latin versions, and Luther's German, English translations have rendered it "propitiatory," "mercy seat," and the like.

**25:18–20 Cherubim**: probably in the form of human-headed winged lions. The cherubim over the ark formed the throne for the invisible Lord. Cf. Ps 80:2. For a more detailed

*k:* Heb 9:18–20. *l:* Ex 31:18; 32:15–16; Dt 5:22. *m:* Sir 45:5. *n:* Ex 19:18; Heb 12:18. *o:* Ex 34:28; Dt 9:9. *p:* Ex 35:4–9, 20–29. *q:* Ex 35:4–9. *r:* Ex 26:1–30; 36:8–38. *s:* Acts 7:44. *t:* Ex 37:1–9; Heb 9:1–5.

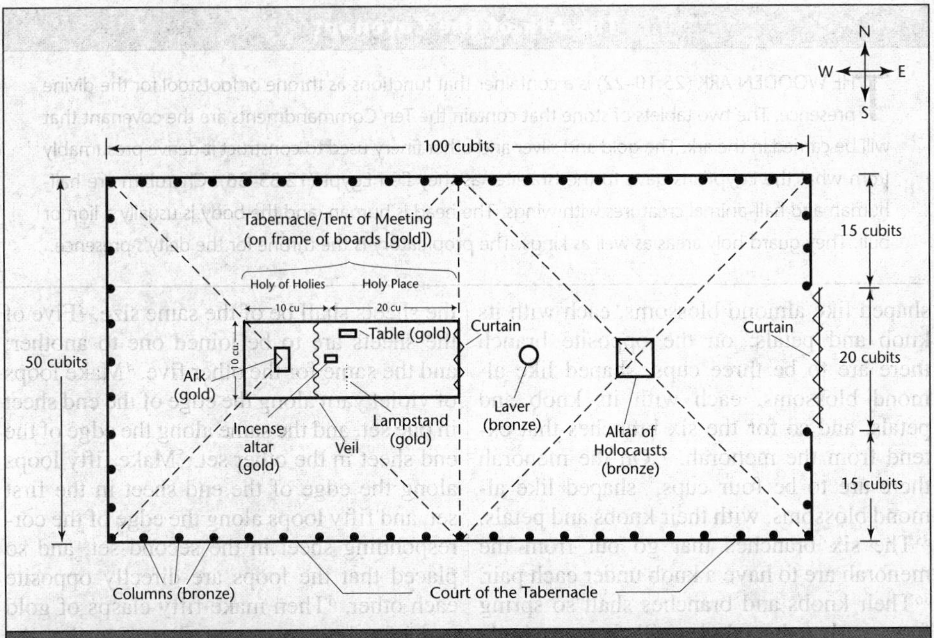


**Structure of the Tabernacle**

beaten gold for the two ends of the cover; [19]make one cherub at one end, and the other at the other end, of one piece with the cover, at each end. [20]The cherubim shall have their wings spread out above, sheltering the cover with them; they shall face each other, with their faces looking toward the cover. [21]This cover you shall then place on top of the ark. In the ark itself you are to put the covenant which I will give you. [22]There I will meet you and there, from above the cover, between the two cherubim on the ark of the covenant, I will tell you all that I command you regarding the Israelites.

***The Table.*** [23]You shall also make a table of acacia[u] wood, two cubits long, a cubit wide, and a cubit and a half high. [24]Plate it with pure gold and make a molding of gold around it. [25]Make a frame* for it, a handbreadth high, and make a molding of gold around the frame. [26]You shall also make four rings of gold for it and fasten them at the four corners, one at each leg. [27]The rings shall be alongside the frame as holders for the poles to carry the table. [28]These poles for carrying the table you shall make of acacia wood and plate with gold. [29]You shall make its plates* and cups, as well as its pitchers and bowls for pouring libations; make them of pure gold. [30]On the table you shall always keep showbread set before me.[v]

***The Menorah.*** [31]You shall make a menorah* of pure beaten gold[w]—its shaft and branches—with its cups and knobs and petals springing directly from it. [32]Six branches are to extend from its sides, three branches on one side, and three on the other. [33]* On one branch there are to be three cups,

description of the somewhat different cherubim in the Temple of Solomon, see 1 Kgs 6:23–28; 2 Chr 3:10–13.

**25:25 A frame**: probably placed near the bottom of the legs to keep them steady. The golden table of Herod's Temple is pictured thus on the Arch of Titus.

**25:29–30** The plates held the showbread, that is, the holy bread which was placed upon the table every sabbath as an offering to God, and was later eaten by the priests. The cups held the incense which was strewn upon the bread. Cf. Lv 24:5–9. The libation wine was poured from the pitchers into the bowls. All these vessels were kept on the golden table.

**25:31 Menorah**: this traditional lampstand is still used today in Jewish liturgy.

**25:33** In keeping with the arrangement of the ornaments on the shaft, the three sets of ornaments on each branch were probably so placed that one was at the top and the other two

*u*: Ex 37:10–16. *v*: Lv 24:5–9. *w*: Ex 37:17–24.

## The Ark of the Covenant

THE WOODEN ARK (25:10–22) is a container that functions as throne or footstool for the divine presence. The two tablets of stone that contain the Ten Commandments are the covenant that will be carried in the ark. The gold and silver and other finery used to construct it derive presumably from what the Egyptians gave to the Israelites as they fled Egypt (12:35–36). Cherubim are half-human and half-animal creatures with wings. The head is human, and the body is usually a lion or bull. They guard holy areas as well as kings. The propitiatory is the throne for the deity's presence.

shaped like almond blossoms, each with its knob and petals; on the opposite branch there are to be three cups, shaped like almond blossoms, each with its knob and petals; and so for the six branches that extend from the menorah. 34On the menorah there are to be four cups,* shaped like almond blossoms, with their knobs and petals. 35The six branches that go out from the menorah are to have a knob under each pair. 36Their knobs and branches shall so spring from it that the whole will form a single piece of pure beaten gold. 37* You shall then make seven lamps[x] for it and so set up the lamps that they give their light on the space in front of the menorah. 38These, as well as the trimming shears and trays,* must be of pure gold. 39Use a talent* of pure gold for the menorah and all these utensils. 40See that you make them according to the pattern shown you on the mountain.[y]

### CHAPTER 26

See RG 70

*The Tent Cloth.* 1The tabernacle itself you shall make out of ten sheets* woven of fine linen twined and of violet, purple, and scarlet yarn, with cherubim embroidered on them.[z] 2The length of each shall be twenty-eight cubits, and the width four cubits; all the sheets shall be of the same size. 3Five of the sheets are to be joined one to another; and the same for the other five. 4Make loops of violet yarn along the edge of the end sheet in one set, and the same along the edge of the end sheet in the other set. 5Make fifty loops along the edge of the end sheet in the first set, and fifty loops along the edge of the corresponding sheet in the second set, and so placed that the loops are directly opposite each other. 6Then make fifty clasps of gold and join the two sets of sheets, so that the tabernacle forms one whole.

7Also make sheets woven of goat hair for a tent* over the tabernacle. Make eleven such sheets; 8the length of each shall be thirty cubits, and the width four cubits: all eleven sheets shall be of the same size. 9Join five of the sheets into one set, and the other six sheets into another set. Use the sixth sheet double at the front of the tent.* 10Make fifty loops along the edge of the end sheet in one set, and fifty loops along the edge of the end sheet in the second set. 11Also make fifty bronze clasps and put them into the loops, to join the tent into one whole. 12There will be an extra half sheet of tent covering, which shall be allowed to hang down over the rear of the tabernacle. 13Likewise, the sheets of

equally spaced along the length of the branch. **Knob**: the cup-shaped seed capsule at the base of a flower.

**25:34–35** Of the four ornaments on the shaft, one was at the top and one was below each of the three sets of side branches.

**25:37** The lamps were probably shaped like small boats, with the wick at one end; the end with the wick was turned toward the front of the menorah.

**25:38 Trays**: small receptacles for the burnt-out wicks.

**25:39 Talent**: Heb. *kikkar*. The largest unit of weight used in the Bible, equivalent to 3,000 shekels (see 38:24). It is difficult to be precise about biblical weights; the Israelite talent may have weighed between 75–80 pounds.

**26:1 Sheets**: strips of tapestry, woven of white linen, the colored threads being used for the cherubim which were embroidered on them. These sheets were stretched across the top of the tabernacle to form a roof, their free ends hanging down inside the framework that formed the walls.

**26:7 Tent**: the cloth made of sheets of goat hair to cover the tabernacle.

**26:9** Half the width of the end strip was folded back at the front of the tabernacle, thus leaving another half-strip to hang down at the rear. Cf. v. 12.

*x*: Lv 24:2–4; Nm 8:2. *y*: Heb 8:5. *z*: Ex 36:8–19.

the tent will have an extra cubit's length to be left hanging down on either side of the tabernacle to cover it. [14]Over the tent itself make a covering of rams' skins dyed red, and above that, a covering of tahash skins.

*The Framework.* [15][a] You shall make frames for the tabernacle, acacia-wood uprights. [16]The length of each frame is to be ten cubits, and its width one and a half cubits. [17]Each frame shall have two arms* joined one to another; so you are to make all the frames of the tabernacle. [18]Make the frames of the tabernacle as follows: twenty frames on the south side, [19]with forty silver pedestals under the twenty frames, two pedestals under each frame for its two arms; [20]twenty frames on the other side of the tabernacle, the north side, [21]with their forty silver pedestals, two pedestals under each frame. [22]At the rear of the tabernacle, to the west, six frames, [23]and two frames for the corners of the tabernacle, at its rear. [24]These two shall be double at the bottom, and likewise double at the top, to the first ring. That is how both corner frames are to be made. [25]Thus, there shall be eight frames, with their sixteen silver pedestals, two pedestals under each frame. [26]Also make bars of acacia wood: five for the frames on one side of the tabernacle, [27]five for those on the other side, and five for those at the rear, to the west. [28]The center bar, at the middle of the frames, shall reach across from end to end. [29]Plate the frames with gold, and make gold rings on them as holders for the bars, which are also to be plated with gold. [30]You shall set up the tabernacle according to its plan, which you were shown on the mountain.

*The Veils.* [31]You shall make a veil woven of violet, purple, and scarlet yarn,[b] and of fine linen twined, with cherubim embroidered on it.[c] [32]It is to be hung on four gold-plated columns of acacia wood, which shall have gold hooks* and shall rest on four silver pedestals. [33]Hang the veil from clasps. The ark of the covenant you shall bring inside, behind this veil which divides the holy place from the holy of holies. [34]Set the cover on the ark of the covenant in the holy of holies.

[35]Outside the veil you shall place the table and the menorah, the latter on the south side of the tabernacle, opposite the table, which is to be put on the north side. [36]For the entrance of the tent make a variegated* curtain of violet, purple, and scarlet yarn and of fine linen twined. [37]Make five columns of acacia wood for this curtain; plate them with gold, with their hooks of gold; and cast five bronze pedestals for them.

## CHAPTER 27

See RG 70

***The Altar for Burnt Offerings.*** [1]You shall make an altar[d] of acacia wood, on a square, five cubits long and five cubits wide; it shall be three cubits high. [2]At the four corners make horns* that are of one piece with the altar. You shall then plate it with bronze. [3]Make pots for removing the ashes, as well as shovels, basins, forks, and fire pans; all these utensils you shall make of bronze. [4]Make for it a grating,* a bronze network; make four bronze rings for it, one at each of its four corners. [5]Put it down around the altar, on the ground. This network is to be half as high as the altar. [6]You shall also make poles of acacia wood for the altar, and plate them with bronze. [7]These poles are to be put through the rings, so that they are on either side of the altar when it is carried. [8]Make the altar itself in the form of a hollow* box. Just as it was shown you on the mountain, so it is to be made.

**26:17 Arms**: lit., "hands." According to some, they served as "tongue and groove" to mortise the structural elements; according to others, they were pegs that fitted into sockets in the pedestals.

**26:32 Hooks**: probably placed near the tops of the columns, to hold the rope from which the veils and curtains hung.

**26:36 Variegated**: without definite designs such as the cherubim on the inner veil.

**27:2 Horns**: the horn of a ram, goat or ox is a common Old Testament figure for strength and dignity; they represent the divine character of the altar itself or the deity worshiped there.

**27:4 Grating**: it is not clear whether this was flush with the altar or at some small distance from it; in the latter case the space between the altar and the grating would be filled with stones and serve as a platform around the altar, which would otherwise be too high for the priest to reach conveniently.

**27:8 Hollow**: probably filled with earth or stones when in use. Cf. 20:24–25.

*a:* Ex 36:20–34. *b:* 2 Chr 3:14. *c:* Ex 36:35–38. *d:* Ex 38:1–7.

*Court of the Tabernacle.* 9[e] You shall also make a court for the tabernacle. On the south side the court shall have hangings, of fine linen twined, a hundred cubits long, 10 with twenty columns and twenty pedestals of bronze; the hooks and bands on the columns shall be of silver. 11 On the north side there shall be similar hangings, a hundred cubits long, with twenty columns and twenty pedestals of bronze; the hooks and bands on the columns shall be of silver. 12 On the west side, across the width of the court, there shall be hangings, fifty cubits long, with ten columns and ten pedestals. 13 The width of the court on the east side shall be fifty cubits. 14 On one side there shall be hangings to the extent of fifteen cubits, with three columns and three pedestals; 15 on the other side there shall be hangings to the extent of fifteen cubits, with three columns and three pedestals.

16 At the gate of the court there shall be a variegated curtain, twenty cubits long, woven of violet, purple, and scarlet yarn and of fine linen twined. It shall have four columns and four pedestals.

17 All the columns around the court shall have bands and hooks of silver, and pedestals of bronze. 18 The court is to be one hundred cubits long, fifty cubits wide, and five cubits high. Fine linen twined must be used, and the pedestals must be of bronze. 19 All the fittings of the tabernacle, whatever be their use, as well as all its tent pegs and all the tent pegs of the court, must be of bronze.

*Oil for the Lamps.* 20 You shall command the Israelites to bring you clear oil of crushed olives, to be used for the light, so that you may keep lamps burning always.[f] 21 From evening to morning Aaron and his sons shall maintain them before the LORD in the tent of meeting, outside the veil which hangs in front of the covenant. This shall be a perpetual statute for the Israelites throughout their generations.

## CHAPTER 28

See RG 70

*The Priestly Vestments.* 1[g] Have your brother Aaron, and with him his sons, brought to you, from among the Israelites, that they may be my priests: Nadab and Abihu, Eleazar and Ithamar, Aaron's sons. 2 For the glorious adornment of your brother Aaron you shall have sacred vestments made. 3 Therefore, tell the various artisans whom I have endowed with skill* to make vestments for Aaron to consecrate him as my priest. 4 These are the vestments they shall make: a breastpiece, an ephod, a robe, a brocade tunic, a turban, and a sash. In making these sacred vestments which your brother Aaron and his sons are to wear in serving as my priests, 5 they shall use gold, violet, purple, and scarlet yarn and fine linen.

*The Ephod and Breastpiece.* 6 The ephod* they shall make of gold thread and of violet, purple, and scarlet yarn, embroidered on cloth of fine linen twined.[h] 7 It shall have a pair of shoulder straps joined to its two upper ends. 8 The embroidered belt of the ephod shall extend out from it and, like it, be made of gold thread, of violet, purple, and scarlet yarn, and of fine linen twined.

9 Get two onyx stones and engrave on them the names of the sons of Israel: 10 six of their names on one stone, and the names of the remaining six on the other stone, in the order of their birth. 11 As a gem-cutter engraves a seal, so shall you have the two stones engraved with the names of the sons of Israel and then mounted in gold filigree work. 12 Set these two stones on the shoulder straps of the ephod as memorial stones of the sons of Israel. Thus Aaron shall bear their names on his shoulders as a reminder before the LORD. 13 Make filigree rosettes of gold,[i] 14 as well as two chains of pure gold, twisted like cords, and fasten the cordlike chains to the filigree rosettes.

**28:3 Artisans . . . endowed with skill**: lit., "wise of heart," and "filled with a spirit of wisdom." In Hebrew wisdom includes practical skills. Cf. 35:35; 36:1–2.

**28:6 Ephod**: this Hebrew word is retained in the translation because it is the technical term for a peculiar piece of the priestly vestments, the exact nature of which is uncertain. It seems to have been a sort of apron that hung from the shoulders of the priest by shoulder straps (v. 7) and was tied around his waist by the loose ends of the attached belt (v. 8).

*e:* Ex 38:9–20. *f:* Lv 24:1–4. *g:* Ex 39:1; Sir 45:7. *h:* Ex 39:2–7; Sir 45:8–14. *i:* Ex 28:22, 25; 39:15, 18.

15[j] The breastpiece* of decision you shall also have made, embroidered like the ephod with gold thread and violet, purple, and scarlet yarn on cloth of fine linen twined. 16 It is to be square when folded double, a span high and a span wide. 17[*] On it you shall mount four rows of precious stones: in the first row, a carnelian, a topaz, and an emerald; 18 in the second row, a garnet, a sapphire, and a beryl; 19 in the third row, a jacinth, an agate, and an amethyst; 20 in the fourth row, a chrysolite, an onyx, and a jasper. These stones are to be mounted in gold filigree work, 21 twelve of them to match the names of the sons of Israel, each stone engraved like a seal with the name of one of the twelve tribes.

22 When the chains of pure gold, twisted like cords, have been made for the breastpiece, 23 you shall then make two rings of gold for it and fasten them to the two upper ends of the breastpiece. 24 The gold cords are then to be fastened to the two rings at the upper ends of the breastpiece, 25 the other two ends of the cords being fastened in front to the two filigree rosettes which are attached to the shoulder straps of the ephod. 26 Make two other rings of gold and put them on the two lower ends of the breastpiece, on its edge that faces the ephod. 27 Then make two more rings of gold and fasten them to the bottom of the shoulder straps next to where they join the ephod in front, just above its embroidered belt. 28 Violet ribbons shall bind the rings of the breastpiece to the rings of the ephod, so that the breastpiece will stay right above the embroidered belt of the ephod and not swing loose from it.

29 Whenever Aaron enters the sanctuary, he will thus bear the names of the sons of Israel on the breastpiece of decision over his heart as a constant reminder before the LORD. 30 In this breastpiece of decision[k] you shall put the Urim and Thummim,* that they may be over Aaron's heart whenever he enters the presence of the LORD. Thus he shall always bear the decisions for the Israelites over his heart in the presence of the LORD.

***Other Vestments.*** 31 The robe of the ephod[l] you shall make entirely of violet material. 32 It shall have an opening for the head in the center, and around this opening there shall be a selvage, woven as at the opening of a shirt, to keep it from being torn. 33 At the hem at the bottom you shall make pomegranates, woven of violet, purple, and scarlet yarn and fine linen twined, with gold bells between them; 34 a gold bell, a pomegranate, a gold bell, a pomegranate, all around the hem of the robe. 35 Aaron shall wear it when ministering, that its sound may be heard as he enters and leaves the LORD's presence in the sanctuary; else he will die.

36 You shall also make a plate of pure gold and engrave on it, as on a seal engraving, "Sacred to the LORD." 37 This plate is to be tied over the turban with a violet ribbon in such a way that it rests on the front of the turban,[m] 38 over Aaron's forehead. Since Aaron bears whatever guilt the Israelites may incur in consecrating any of their sacred gifts, this plate must always be over his forehead, so that they may find favor with the LORD.

39[n] The tunic of fine linen shall be brocaded. The turban shall be made of fine linen. The sash shall be of variegated work.

40 Likewise, for the glorious adornment of Aaron's sons you shall have tunics and sashes and skullcaps made, for glorious splendor. 41 With these you shall clothe your brother Aaron and his sons. Anoint and install them,* consecrating them as my priests. 42 You must also make linen pants for them,

**28:15–30 Breastpiece**: an approximately nine-inch square, pocketlike receptacle for holding the Urim and Thummim (v. 30). It formed an integral part of the ephod, to which it was attached by an elaborate system of rings and chains. Both the ephod and its breastpiece were made of brocaded linen. **Span**: Heb. *zeret*, the distance between the top of the little finger and the thumb; one half a cubit, approximately nine inches.

**28:17–20** The translation of the Hebrew names of some of these gems is quite conjectural.

**28:30 Urim and Thummim**: both the meaning of these Hebrew words and the exact nature of the objects so designated are uncertain. They were apparently lots of some kind which were drawn or cast by the priest to ascertain God's decision on particular questions. Hence, the pocket in which they were kept was called "the breastpiece of decision."

**28:41 Install them**: lit., "fill their hands," a technical expression used for the installation of priests.

*j:* Ex 39:15–21. *k:* Lv 8:8; Sir 45:11. *l:* Ex 39:20–25; Lv 8:9; Sir 45:10. *m:* Ex 39:31; Lv 8:9. *n:* Ex 39:27–31.

to cover their naked flesh from their loins to their thighs.[o] 43 Aaron and his sons shall wear them whenever they go into the tent of meeting or approach the altar to minister in the sanctuary, lest they incur guilt and die. This shall be a perpetual ordinance for him and for his descendants.

See RG 70

## CHAPTER 29

***Consecration of the Priests.*** 1 This is the rite you shall perform in consecrating them as my priests.[p] Procure a young bull and two unblemished rams. 2 With bran flour make unleavened cakes mixed with oil, and unleavened wafers spread with oil, 3 and put them in a basket. Take the basket of them along with the bull and the two rams. 4 Aaron and his sons you shall also bring to the entrance of the tent of meeting, and there wash them with water. 5 Take the vestments and clothe Aaron with the tunic, the robe of the ephod, the ephod itself, and the breastpiece, fastening the embroidered belt of the ephod around him. 6 Put the turban on his head, the sacred diadem on the turban. 7 Then take the anointing oil and pour it on his head, and anoint him. 8 Bring forward his sons also and clothe them with the tunics, 9 gird them with the sashes, and tie the skullcaps on them.[q] Thus shall the priesthood be theirs by a perpetual statute, and thus shall you install Aaron and his sons.

***Installation Sacrifices.*** 10[r] Now bring forward the bull in front of the tent of meeting. There Aaron and his sons shall lay their hands on its head. 11 Then slaughter the bull before the LORD, at the entrance of the tent of meeting. 12 Take some of its blood and with your finger put it on the horns of the altar. All the rest of the blood you shall pour out at the base of the altar. 13 All the fat that covers its inner organs, as well as the lobe of its liver and its two kidneys, together with the fat that is on them, you shall take and burn on the altar. 14 But the meat and hide and dung of the bull you must burn up outside the camp, since this is a purification offering.[s]

15 Then take one of the rams, and after Aaron and his sons have laid their hands on its head, 16 slaughter it. The blood you shall take and splash on all the sides of the altar. 17 Cut the ram into pieces; you shall wash its inner organs and shanks and put them with the pieces and with the head. 18 Then you shall burn the entire ram on the altar, since it is a burnt offering, a sweet-smelling oblation to the LORD.

19 After this take the other ram, and when Aaron and his sons have laid their hands on its head, 20 slaughter it. Some of its blood you shall take and put on the tip of Aaron's right ear and on the tips of his sons' right ears and on the thumbs of their right hands and the great toes of their right feet. Splash the rest of the blood on all the sides of the altar. 21 Then take some of the blood that is on the altar, together with some of the anointing oil, and sprinkle this on Aaron and his vestments, as well as on his sons and their vestments, that he and his sons and their vestments may be sacred.

22 Now, from this ram you shall take its fat: its fatty tail,* the fat that covers its inner organs, the lobe of its liver, its two kidneys with the fat that is on them, and its right thigh, since this is the ram for installation; 23 then, out of the basket of unleavened food that you have set before the LORD, you shall take one of the loaves of bread, one of the cakes made with oil, and one of the wafers. 24 All these things you shall put into the hands of Aaron and his sons, so that they may raise them as an elevated offering* before the LORD. 25 After you receive them back from their hands, you shall burn them on top of the burnt offering on the altar as a sweet-smelling oblation to the LORD. 26 Finally, take the brisket of Aaron's installation ram and raise it as an elevated offering before the LORD; this is to be your own portion.

**29:22 Fatty tail**: the thick layer of fat surrounding the tails of sheep and rams bred in the Middle East. It is regarded as a choice food. Cf. Lv 3:9.

**29:24–26 Elevated offering**: the portions of a communion offering, brisket and right thigh, which the officiating priest raised in the presence of the Lord. They were reserved for Aaron and his sons.

*o:* Ez 44:18. *p:* Lv 8:1–9. *q:* Lv 8:13. *r:* Lv 8:14–30. *s:* Heb 13:11.

27* Thus shall you set aside the brisket of whatever elevated offering is raised,[t] as well as the thigh of whatever contribution is raised up, whether this be the installation ram or anything else belonging to Aaron or to his sons. 28 Such things are due to Aaron and his sons from the Israelites by a perpetual statute as a contribution. From their communion offerings, too, the Israelites shall make a contribution, their contribution to the LORD.

29 The sacred vestments[u] of Aaron shall be passed down to his sons after him, that in them they may be anointed and installed. 30 The son who succeeds him as priest and who is to enter the tent of meeting to minister in the sanctuary shall be clothed with them for seven days.

31[v] You shall take the installation ram and boil its meat in a holy place. 32 At the entrance of the tent of meeting Aaron and his sons shall eat the meat of the ram and the bread that is in the basket. 33 They themselves are to eat of these things by which atonement was made at their installation and consecration; but no unauthorized person may eat of them, since they are sacred. 34 If some of the meat of the installation sacrifice or some of the bread remains over on the next day, this remnant you must burn up; it is not to be eaten, since it is sacred.

35 Carry out all these commands in regard to Aaron and his sons just as I have given them to you.[w] Seven days you shall spend installing them, 36[x] sacrificing a bull each day as a purification offering, to make atonement. Thus you shall purify the altar* by purging it, and you shall anoint it in order to consecrate it. 37 Seven days you shall spend in purging the altar and in consecrating it. Then the altar will be most sacred, and whatever touches it will become sacred.

38* Now, this is what you shall regularly offer on the altar: two yearling lambs[y] as the sacrifice established for each day; 39 one lamb in the morning and the other lamb at the evening twilight. 40 With the first lamb there shall be a tenth of an ephah of bran flour mixed with a fourth of a hin* of oil of crushed olives and, as its libation, a fourth of a hin of wine. 41 The other lamb you shall offer at the evening twilight, with the same grain offering and libation as in the morning. You shall offer this as a sweet-smelling oblation to the LORD. 42 Throughout your generations this regular burnt offering shall be made before the LORD at the entrance of the tent of meeting, where I will meet you and speak to you.

43 There, at the altar, I will meet the Israelites; hence, it will be made sacred by my glory.[z] 44 Thus I will consecrate the tent of meeting and the altar, just as I also consecrate Aaron and his sons to be my priests. 45 I will dwell in the midst of the Israelites and will be their God. 46 They shall know that I, the LORD, am their God who brought them out of the land of Egypt, so that I, the LORD, their God, might dwell among them.

## CHAPTER 30

See RG 70

***Altar of Incense.*** 1 For burning incense you shall make an altar of acacia wood,[a] 2 with a square surface, a cubit long, a cubit wide, and two cubits high, with horns that are of one piece with it. 3 Its grate on top, its walls on all four sides, and its horns you shall plate with pure gold. Put a gold molding around it. 4 Underneath the molding you shall put gold rings, two on one side and two on the opposite side, as holders for the poles used in carrying it. 5 Make the poles, too, of acacia wood and plate them with gold. 6 This altar you are to place in front of the veil that hangs before the ark of the covenant where I will meet you.[b]

**29:27–30** These verses are a parenthetical interruption of the installation ritual; v. 31 belongs logically immediately after v. 26.

**29:36–37 Purify the altar**: the purpose of the purification offering here is to cleanse, or purify, the newly constructed altar of any defilement resulting from presumably minor and inadvertent sins, but the text is not explicit about what the offenses were or who committed them. So various theories have been proposed to explain the cause of the altar's contamination. Note, however, that the offering appears to be demanded of Aaron and his sons; they are the ones who lay hands upon it (v. 10).

**29:38–42** A parenthesis inserted into the rubrics for consecrating the altar; v. 43 belongs directly after v. 37.

**29:40 Hin**: see note on Ez 45:24.

*t:* Lv 7:31–34; 10:14–15; Nm 18:18–19; Dt 18:3. *u:* Nm 20:26, 28. *v:* Lv 8:31–32. *w:* Lv 8:36. *x:* Lv 8:33–35. *y:* Nm 28:3–8. *z:* Ex 25:22. *a:* Ex 37:25–28. *b:* Ex 40:26.

7 On it Aaron shall burn fragrant incense. Morning after morning, when he prepares the lamps, 8 and again in the evening twilight, when he lights the lamps, he shall burn incense. Throughout your generations this shall be the regular incense offering before the LORD. 9 On this altar you shall not offer up any profane incense, or any burnt offering or grain offering; nor shall you pour out a libation upon it. 10 Once a year Aaron shall purge its horns.[c] Throughout your generations he is to purge it once a year with the blood of the atoning purification offering. This altar is most sacred to the LORD.

***Census Tax.*** 11 The LORD also told Moses: 12 When you take a census[d] of the Israelites who are to be enrolled, each one, as he is enrolled, shall give the LORD a ransom for his life, so that no plague may come upon them for being enrolled. 13 This is what everyone who is enrolled must pay: a half-shekel, according to the standard of the sanctuary shekel—twenty gerahs to the shekel—a half-shekel contribution to the LORD.[e] 14 Everyone who is enrolled, of twenty years or more, must give the contribution to the LORD. 15 The rich need not give more, nor shall the poor give less, than a half-shekel in this contribution to the LORD to pay the ransom for their lives. 16[f] When you receive this ransom money from the Israelites, you shall donate it to the service of the tent of meeting, that there it may be a reminder of the Israelites before the LORD of the ransom paid for their lives.

***The Basin.*** 17 The LORD told Moses: 18 For ablutions you shall make a bronze basin with a bronze stand. Place it between the tent of meeting and the altar, and put water in it.[g] 19 Aaron and his sons shall use it in washing their hands and feet.[h] 20 When they are about to enter the tent of meeting, they must wash with water, lest they die. Likewise when they approach the altar to minister, to offer an oblation to the LORD, 21 they must wash their hands and feet, lest they die. This shall be a perpetual statute for him and his descendants throughout their generations.

***The Anointing Oil.*** 22 The LORD told Moses: 23 Take the finest spices: five hundred shekels of free-flowing myrrh; half that amount, that is, two hundred and fifty shekels, of fragrant cinnamon; two hundred and fifty shekels of fragrant cane; 24 five hundred shekels of cassia—all according to the standard of the sanctuary shekel; together with a hin of olive oil; 25 and blend them into sacred anointing oil,[i] perfumed ointment expertly prepared.[j] With this sacred anointing oil 26 you shall anoint the tent of meeting and the ark of the covenant, 27 the table and all its utensils, the menorah and its utensils, the altar of incense 28 and the altar for burnt offerings with all its utensils, and the basin with its stand. 29 When you have consecrated them, they shall be most sacred; whatever touches them shall be sacred. 30 Aaron and his sons you shall also anoint and consecrate as my priests.[k] 31 Tell the Israelites: As sacred anointing oil this shall belong to me throughout your generations. 32 It may not be used in any ordinary anointing of the body, nor may you make any other oil of a like mixture. It is sacred, and shall be treated as sacred by you. 33 Whoever prepares a perfume like this, or whoever puts any of this on an unauthorized person, shall be cut off from his people.

***The Incense.*** 34[l] The LORD told Moses: Take these aromatic substances: storax and onycha and galbanum, these and pure frankincense in equal parts; 35 and blend them into incense. This fragrant powder, expertly prepared, is to be salted and so kept pure and sacred. 36 Grind some of it into fine dust and put this before the covenant in the tent of meeting where I will meet you. This incense shall be treated as most sacred by you. 37 You may not make incense of a like mixture for yourselves; you must treat it as sacred to the LORD. 38 Whoever makes an incense like this for his own enjoyment of its fragrance, shall be cut off from his people.

---

*c:* Lv 16:18. *d:* Nm 1:2–3; 26:2. *e:* Mt 17:24–27. *f:* Ex 38:25. *g:* Ex 38:8; 40:7, 30. *h:* Ex 40:31–32. *i:* Ex 37:29. *j:* Ex 40:9–11; Lv 8:10; Nm 7:1. *k:* Ex 29:7; Lv 8:12. *l:* Ex 25:6; 37:29.

### CHAPTER 31

See RG 70

*Choice of Artisans.* 1[m] The LORD said to Moses: 2 See, I have singled out* Bezalel, son of Uri, son of Hur, of the tribe of Judah, 3 and I have filled him with a divine spirit of skill and understanding and knowledge in every craft: 4 in the production of embroidery, in making things of gold, silver, or bronze, 5 in cutting and mounting precious stones, in carving wood, and in every other craft. 6 As his assistant I myself have appointed Oholiab, son of Ahisamach, of the tribe of Dan. I have also endowed all the experts with the necessary skill to make all the things I have commanded you: 7[n] the tent of meeting, the ark of the covenant with its cover, all the furnishings of the tent, 8 the table with its utensils, the pure gold menorah with all its utensils, the altar of incense, 9 the altar for burnt offerings with all its utensils, the basin with its stand, 10 the service cloths,* the sacred vestments for Aaron the priest, the vestments for his sons in their ministry, 11 the anointing oil, and the fragrant incense for the sanctuary. According to all I have commanded you, so shall they do.

*Sabbath Laws.* 12[o] The LORD said to Moses: 13 You must also tell the Israelites: Keep my sabbaths, for that is to be the sign between you and me throughout the generations, to show that it is I, the LORD, who make you holy. 14* Therefore, you must keep the sabbath for it is holiness for you. Whoever desecrates it shall be put to death. If anyone does work on that day, that person must be cut off from the people. 15 Six days there are for doing work, but the seventh day is the sabbath of complete rest, holy to the LORD. Anyone who does work on the sabbath day shall be put to death. 16 So shall the Israelites observe the sabbath, keeping it throughout their generations as an everlasting covenant. 17 Between me and the Israelites it is to be an everlasting sign; for in six days the LORD made the heavens and the earth, but on the seventh day he rested at his ease.

18 When the LORD had finished speaking to Moses on Mount Sinai, he gave him the two tablets of the covenant, the stone tablets inscribed by God's own finger.[p]

## VII. Israel's Apostasy and God's Renewal of the Covenant

### CHAPTER 32

See RG 70

*The Golden Calf.* 1 When the people saw that Moses was delayed in coming down from the mountain, they gathered around Aaron and said to him, "Come, make us a god who will go before us; as for that man Moses who brought us out of the land of Egypt, we do not know what has happened to him."[q] 2 Aaron replied, "Take off the golden earrings that your wives, your sons, and your daughters are wearing, and bring them to me." 3 So all the people took off their earrings and brought them to Aaron. 4 He received their offering, and fashioning it with a tool, made a molten calf. Then they cried out, "These are your gods, Israel, who brought you* up from the land of Egypt."[r] 5 On seeing this, Aaron built an altar in front of the calf and proclaimed, "Tomorrow is a feast of the LORD." 6 Early the next day the people sacrificed burnt offerings and brought communion sacrifices. Then they sat down to eat and drink, and rose up to revel.[s]

7[t] Then the LORD said to Moses: Go down at once because your people, whom you brought out of the land of Egypt, have acted corruptly. 8 They have quickly turned aside from the way I commanded them, making for themselves a molten calf and bowing down to it, sacrificing to it and crying out,

**31:2 Singled out**: lit., "called by name"; cf. 35:30.

**31:10 The service cloths**: so the Greek. They were perhaps the colored cloths mentioned in Nm 4:4–15.

**31:14–15** For the distinction between work proscribed on certain festivals and weekly Sabbaths, see note on Lv 23:3.

**32:4–5 Who brought you . . . a feast of the LORD**: it seems that the golden calf was intended as an image, not of another god, but of the Lord, whose strength was symbolized by the strength of a young bull. The Israelites, however, had been forbidden to represent the Lord under any visible form. Cf. 20:4. In the tenth century Jeroboam made golden calves for the shrines at Bethel and Dan, presumably to function as thrones for the Lord as the ark did in Jerusalem (see 1 Kgs 12:27–30).

*m:* Ex 35:30–35. *n:* Ex 35:10–19. *o:* Ex 20:8–11; 35:1–3. *p:* Ex 24:12; 32:15–16; Dt 5:22. *q:* Ex 32:23; Acts 7:40. *r:* Ex 32:8; 1 Kgs 12:28. *s:* 1 Cor 10:7. *t:* Dt 9:12, 16.

"These are your gods, Israel, who brought
you up from the land of Egypt!" 9[u] I have
seen this people, how stiff-necked they are,
continued the LORD to Moses. 10 Let me
alone, then, that my anger may burn against
them to consume them. Then I will make of
you a great nation.
11* But Moses implored the LORD, his
God, saying,[v] "Why, O LORD, should your
anger burn against your people, whom you
brought out of the land of Egypt with great
power and with a strong hand? 12 Why
should the Egyptians say, 'With evil intent
he brought them out, that he might kill them
in the mountains and wipe them off the face
of the earth'? Turn from your burning wrath;
change your mind about punishing your
people. 13 Remember your servants Abraham, Isaac, and Israel, and how you swore to
them by your own self, saying,[w] 'I will make
your descendants as numerous as the stars in
the sky; and all this land that I promised, I
will give your descendants as their perpetual
heritage.' " 14 So the LORD changed his mind
about the punishment he had threatened to
inflict on his people.
15 Moses then turned and came down the
mountain with the two tablets of the covenant in his hands,[x] tablets that were written
on both sides, front and back. 16 The tablets
were made by God; the writing was the writing of God, engraved on the tablets.[y] 17 Now,
when Joshua heard the noise of the people
shouting, he said to Moses, "That sounds
like a battle in the camp." 18 But Moses answered,

"It is not the noise of victory,
it is not the noise of defeat;
the sound I hear is singing."

19 As he drew near the camp, he saw the calf
and the dancing. Then Moses' anger burned,
and he threw the tablets down and broke
them on the base of the mountain.[z] 20 Taking
the calf they had made, he burned it in the
fire and then ground it down to powder,
which he scattered on the water* and made
the Israelites drink.[a]
21* Moses asked Aaron, "What did this
people do to you that you should lead them
into a grave sin?" 22 Aaron replied, "Do not
let my lord be angry. You know how the people are prone to evil. 23 They said to me,
'Make us a god to go before us; as for this
man Moses who brought us out of the land
of Egypt, we do not know what has happened to him.' 24 So I told them, 'Whoever is
wearing gold, take it off.' They gave it to me,
and I threw it into the fire, and this calf came
out."
25 Moses saw that the people were running
wild because Aaron had lost control—to the
secret delight of their foes. 26 Moses stood at
the gate of the camp and shouted, "Whoever
is for the LORD, come to me!" All the Levites[b] then rallied to him, 27 and he told them,
"Thus says the LORD, the God of Israel:
Each of you put your sword on your hip! Go
back and forth through the camp, from gate
to gate, and kill your brothers, your friends,
your neighbors!" 28 The Levites did as Moses
had commanded, and that day about three
thousand of the people fell. 29 Then Moses
said, "Today you are installed as priests* for
the LORD, for you went against your own
sons and brothers, to bring a blessing upon
yourselves this day."
***The Atonement.*** 30 On the next day Moses
said to the people,[c] "You have committed a
grave sin. Now I will go up to the LORD; perhaps I may be able to make atonement for
your sin." 31 So Moses returned to the LORD
and said, "Ah, this people has committed a
grave sin in making a god of gold for them-

**32:11–13** Moses uses three arguments to persuade the Lord to remain faithful to the Sinai covenant even though the people have broken it: (1) they are God's own people, redeemed with God's great power; (2) God's reputation will suffer if they are destroyed; (3) the covenant with Abraham still stands. The Lord's change of mind is a testimony to Israel's belief in the power of intercessory prayer.

**32:20 The water**: according to Dt 9:21, this was the stream that flowed down Mount Sinai.

**32:21–24** Aaron attempts to persuade Moses not to act in anger, just as Moses persuaded the Lord. He also shifts the blame from himself to the people.

**32:29 Installed as priests**: lit., "fill your hands," a term for the ordination of priests (see 28:41; 29:9, 29, 33, 35; Nm 3:3). Because of their zeal for the true worship of the Lord, the Levites were chosen to be special ministers of the ritual service.

*u:* Dt 9:13. *v:* Nm 14:13–19; Dt 9:28–29; Ps 106:23. *w:* Gn 22:16–17. *x:* Dt 9:15. *y:* Ex 31:18. *z:* Dt 9:16–17. *a:* Dt 9:21. *b:* Dt 33:8–9. *c:* Dt 9:18–19.

selves! 32 Now if you would only forgive their sin! But if you will not, then blot me out of the book that you have written."* 33 The LORD answered Moses: Only the one who has sinned against me will I blot out of my book. 34 Now, go and lead the people where I have told you. See, my angel will go before you. When it is time for me to punish, I will punish them for their sin.

35 Thus the LORD struck the people for making the calf, the one that Aaron made.

## CHAPTER 33

See RG 70

1 The LORD spoke to Moses: Go! You and the people whom you have brought up from the land of Egypt are to go up from here to the land about which I swore to Abraham, Isaac, and Jacob: I will give it to your descendants.[d] 2 Driving out the Canaanites, Amorites, Hittites, Perizzites, Hivites and Jebusites, I will send an angel before you[e] 3 to a land flowing with milk and honey. But I myself will not go up in your company, because you are a stiff-necked people; otherwise I might consume you on the way. 4 When the people heard this painful news, they mourned, and no one wore any ornaments.

5 The LORD spoke to Moses: Speak to the Israelites: You are a stiff-necked people. Were I to go up in your company even for a moment, I would destroy you. Now off with your ornaments! Let me think what to do with you. 6 So, from Mount Horeb onward, the Israelites stripped off their ornaments.

***Moses' Intimacy with God.*** 7 Moses used to pitch a tent[f] outside the camp at some distance. It was called the tent of meeting. Anyone who wished to consult the LORD would go to the tent of meeting outside the camp. 8 Whenever Moses went out to the tent, the people would all rise and stand at the entrance of their own tents, watching Moses until he entered the tent. 9 As Moses entered the tent, the column of cloud would come down and stand at its entrance while the LORD spoke with Moses. 10 On seeing the column of cloud stand at the entrance of the tent, all the people would rise and bow down at the entrance of their own tents. 11 The LORD used to speak to Moses face to face,[g] as a person speaks to a friend. Moses would then return to the camp, but his young assistant, Joshua, son of Nun, never left the tent.

12 Moses said to the LORD, "See, you are telling me: Lead this people.[h] But you have not let me know whom you will send with me. Yet you have said: You are my intimate friend;* You have found favor with me. 13 Now, if I have found favor with you, please let me know your ways so that, in knowing you, I may continue to find favor with you. See, this nation is indeed your own people. 14 The LORD answered: I myself* will go along, to give you rest. 15 Moses replied, "If you are not going yourself, do not make us go up from here. 16 For how can it be known that I and your people have found favor with you, except by your going with us? Then we, your people and I, will be singled out from every other people on the surface of the earth." 17 The LORD said to Moses: This request, too, which you have made, I will carry out, because you have found favor with me and you are my intimate friend.

18 Then Moses said, "Please let me see your glory!" 19 The LORD answered: I will make all my goodness pass before you, and I will proclaim my name, "LORD," before you; I who show favor to whom I will, I who grant mercy to whom I will.[i] 20 But you cannot see my face,[j] for no one can see me and live.* 21 Here, continued the LORD, is a place near me where you shall station yourself on the rock. 22 When my glory passes I will set you in the cleft of the rock and will cover you with my hand until I have passed by.

**32:32 The book that you have written**: a symbolic reference to the list of God's faithful people.

**33:12 Intimate friend**: lit., "know by name." The root word meaning "know" or "make known" appears four times in vv. 12–13.

**33:14 I myself**: lit., "my face," that is, "my presence." The making of the calf (32:1–4) is an attempt to control the Lord's presence. In response the Lord refuses to accompany the people (33:3) until Moses persuades him.

**33:20 No one can see me and live**: reflecting the tradition that to see God meant instant death. This is contradicted by the statements that Hagar (Gn 16:13), Jacob (Gn 32:31), and Manoah and his wife (Jgs 13:22) all "see God" and yet live (see also Ex 24:10–11).

*d:* Gn 12:7. *e:* Ex 23:23. *f:* Ex 29:42–43. *g:* Nm 12:8; Dt 34:10; Sir 45:4–5. *h:* Ex 32:34. *i:* Rom 9:15. *j:* Jn 1:18; 1 Tm 6:16.

## Accenting God's Mercy over God's Judgment

ISRAEL'S WORSHIP OF the golden calf (32:8) broke the covenant with God. The new covenant between God and Israel revealed a deeper aspect of God's character: God's mercy and compassion. This deeper revelation is evident when we compare the description of God's character in Exodus 20:5–6 with that in Exodus 34:6–7:

> For I, the LORD, your God, am a jealous God, inflicting punishment for their ancestors' wickedness on the children of those who hate me, down to the third and fourth generation; but showing love down to the thousandth generation of those who love me and keep my commandments. (20:5–6)

> The LORD, the LORD, a God gracious and merciful, slow to anger and abounding in love and fidelity, continuing his love for a thousand generations, and forgiving wickedness, rebellion, and sin; yet not declaring the guilty guiltless, but bringing punishment for their parents' wickedness on children and children's children to the third and fourth generation! (34:6–7)

We can see a number of differences between these two similar texts. The excerpt from ch 20 emphasizes God's punishment as the first element of God's character, whereas the excerpt from ch 34 puts this aspect in second place. The love and mercy of God, in second place in ch 20, moves to the front in ch 34. Chapter 34 also expands the description of God's compassionate nature: slow to anger, abounding in love and fidelity. The condition that God loves "those who love" God in ch 20 is removed in ch 34, where also God forgives wickedness.

Variations of this important description of God's nature occur elsewhere: Nm 14:18; Neh 9:17; Ps 103:8; Jl 2:13; Jon 4:2. Because it appears in so many places, this description seems to have been a creed or confession of faith in God for the ancient Israelites.

23 Then I will remove my hand, so that you may see my back; but my face may not be seen.

### CHAPTER 34

See RG 70

***Renewal of the Tablets.*** 1 The LORD said to Moses: "Cut two stone tablets like the former,[k] that I may write on them the words* which were on the former tablets that you broke. 2 Get ready for tomorrow morning, when you are to go up Mount Sinai and there present yourself to me on the top of the mountain. 3 No one shall come up with you, and let no one even be seen on any part of the mountain;[l] even the sheep and the cattle are not to graze in front of this mountain." 4 Moses then cut two stone tablets like the former, and early the next morning he went up Mount Sinai as the LORD had commanded him, taking in his hand the two stone tablets. 5 The LORD came down in a cloud and stood with him there and proclaimed the name, "LORD." 6 So the LORD passed before him and proclaimed: The LORD, the LORD, a God gracious and merciful, slow to anger and abounding in love and fidelity,* 7 continuing his love for a thousand generations, and forgiving wickedness, rebellion, and sin; yet not declaring the guilty guiltless, but bringing punishment for their parents' wickedness on children and children's children to the third and fourth generation![m] 8 Moses at once knelt and bowed down to the ground. 9 Then he said, "If I find favor with you, Lord, please, Lord, come along in our company. This is indeed a stiff-necked people;

**34:1 Words**: a common term for commandments, especially the Decalogue (see v. 28). In v. 27 "words" connotes the commands given in vv. 11–26.

**34:6 Gracious . . . fidelity**: this succinct poetic description of God is an often-repeated statement of belief (see Nm 14:18; Ps 103:8; 145:8; Jl 2:13; Jon 4:2). All the terms describe God's relationship to the covenant people.

*k:* Dt 10:1–2. *l:* Ex 19:12–13, 21. *m:* Ex 20:5–6; Nm 14:18; Dt 5:9–10; Jer 32:18.

yet pardon our wickedness and sins, and claim us as your own."

***Religious Laws.*** 10 The LORD said: Here is the covenant I will make. Before all your people I will perform marvels never before done* in any nation anywhere on earth, so that all the people among whom you live may see the work of the LORD. Awe-inspiring are the deeds I will perform with you! 11 As for you, observe what I am commanding you today.[n]

See, I am about to drive out before you the Amorites, Canaanites, Hittites, Perizzites, Hivites and Jebusites. 12 [o] Take care not to make a covenant with the inhabitants of the land that you are to enter; lest they become a snare among you. 13 Tear down their altars; smash their sacred stones, and cut down their asherahs.* 14 You shall not bow down to any other god, for the LORD—"Jealous"* his name—is a jealous God. 15 Do not make a covenant with the inhabitants of the land; else, when they prostitute themselves with their gods and sacrifice to them, one of them may invite you and you may partake of the sacrifice. 16 And when you take their daughters as wives for your sons, and their daughters prostitute themselves with their gods, they will make your sons do the same.

17 You shall not make for yourselves molten gods.[p]

18 You shall keep the festival of Unleavened Bread.[q] For seven days at the appointed time in the month of Abib you are to eat unleavened bread, as I commanded you; for in the month of Abib you came out of Egypt.

19 To me belongs every male that opens the womb among all your livestock, whether in the herd or in the flock.[r] 20 The firstling of a donkey you shall redeem with a lamb; if you do not redeem it, you must break its neck. The firstborn among your sons you shall redeem.

No one shall appear before me empty-handed.

21 Six days you may labor,[s] but on the seventh day you shall rest; even during the seasons of plowing and harvesting you must rest. 22 [t] You shall keep the feast of Weeks with the first fruits of the wheat harvest, likewise, the feast of the Ingathering at the close of the year.* 23 Three times a year all your men shall appear before the Lord, the LORD God of Israel. 24 Since I will drive out the nations before you and enlarge your territory, no one will covet your land when you go up three times a year to appear before the LORD, your God.

25 You shall not offer me the blood of sacrifice with anything leavened, nor shall the sacrifice of the Passover feast be kept overnight for the next day.

26 The choicest first fruits of your soil you shall bring to the house of the LORD, your God.

You shall not boil a young goat in its mother's milk.[u]

***Radiance of Moses' Face.*** 27 Then the LORD said to Moses: Write down these words, for in accordance with these words I have made a covenant with you and with Israel. 28 So Moses was there with the LORD for forty days and forty nights,[v] without eating any food or drinking any water, and he wrote on the tablets the words of the covenant, the ten words.

29 As Moses came down from Mount Sinai with the two tablets of the covenant in his hands, he did not know that the skin of his face had become radiant* while he spoke with

**34:10 Never before done**: lit., "created." The verb used here (Heb. *bara'*) is predicated only of God (see Gn 1:1, 21, 27; Ps 51:12). These wonders are a new creation and can be performed only by God.

**34:13** Asherah was the name of a Canaanite goddess. In her honor wooden poles (*asherot*) were erected, just as stone pillars (*massebot*) were erected in honor of the god Baal. Both were placed near the altar in a Canaanite shrine.

**34:14 Jealous**: see note on 20:5. Some, by a slight emendation, render, "The Lord is jealous for his name." Cf. Ez 39:25.

**34:22 Feast of Weeks**: the festival of thanksgiving for the harvest, celebrated seven weeks or fifty days after the beginning of the harvest. It was also called Pentecost (fiftieth) and coincided with the giving of the law on Mount Sinai, fifty days after the offering of the first fruits; cf. Lv 23:10–11; Dt 16:9. **Feast of the Ingathering**: feast of Booths.

**34:29 Radiant**: the Hebrew word translated "radiant" is spelled like the term for "horns." Thus the artistic tradition of portraying Moses with horns.

*n:* Ex 13:5; 33:2. *o:* Ex 23:32–33; Dt 7:1–5; 12:2–3. *p:* Lv 19:4; Dt 5:8–9. *q:* Ex 12:15–20; 13:3–4. *r:* Ex 13:2, 12–13; 23:15. *s:* Ex 20:9–10. *t:* Ex 23:16–17; Dt 16:10, 13, 16. *u:* Ex 23:18–19. *v:* Ex 24:18; Dt 9:9, 18; 10:2, 4.

the LORD. 30 When Aaron, then, and the other
Israelites saw Moses and noticed how radiant
the skin of his face had become, they were
afraid to come near him. 31 Only after Moses
called to them did Aaron and all the leaders of
the community come back to him. Moses
then spoke to them. 32 Later, all the Israelites
came up to him, and he enjoined on them all
that the LORD had told him on Mount Sinai.
33 When Moses finished speaking with them,
he put a veil over his face. 34 Whenever Moses
entered the presence of the LORD to speak
with him, he removed the veil until he came
out again.[w] On coming out, he would tell the
Israelites all that he had been commanded.
35 Then the Israelites would see that the skin
of Moses' face was radiant; so he would again
put the veil over his face until he went in to
speak with the LORD.

## VIII. The Building of the Tabernacle and the Descent of God's Glory upon It

### CHAPTER 35

See RG 70

*Sabbath Regulations.* 1 Moses assembled the whole Israelite community and said
to them,[x] "These are the words the LORD has
commanded to be observed. 2 On six days
work may be done, but the seventh day shall
be holy to you as the sabbath of complete
rest to the LORD. Anyone who does work on
that day shall be put to death. 3 You shall not
even light a fire in any of your dwellings on
the sabbath day."

*Collection of Materials.* 4 Moses said to
the whole Israelite community, "This is what
the LORD has commanded: 5[y] Receive from
among you contributions for the LORD.
Everyone, as his heart prompts him, shall
bring, as a contribution to the LORD, gold,
silver, and bronze; 6 violet, purple, and scarlet yarn; fine linen and goat hair; 7 rams'
skins dyed red, and tahash skins; acacia
wood; 8 oil for the light; spices for the anointing oil and for the fragrant incense; 9 onyx
stones and other gems for mounting on the
ephod and on the breastpiece.

*Call for Artisans.* 10[z] "Let every artisan
among you come and make all that the LORD
has commanded: 11 the tabernacle, with its
tent, its covering, its clasps, its frames, its
bars, its columns, and its pedestals; 12 the ark,
with its poles, the cover, and the curtain veil;
13 the table, with its poles and all its utensils,
and the showbread; 14 the menorah, with its
utensils, the lamps, and the oil for the light;
15 the altar of incense, with its poles; the
anointing oil, and the fragrant incense; the
entrance curtain for the entrance of the tabernacle; 16 the altar for burnt offerings, with
its bronze grating, its poles, and all its utensils; the basin, with its stand; 17 the hangings
of the court, with their columns and
pedestals; the curtain for the gate of the
court; 18 the tent pegs for the tabernacle and
for the court, with their ropes; 19 the service
cloths for use in the sanctuary; the sacred
vestments for Aaron, the priest, and the vestments for his sons in their ministry."

*The Contribution.* 20 When the whole Israelite community left Moses' presence, 21 all,
as their hearts moved them and their spirit
prompted, brought a contribution to the
LORD for the work of the tent of meeting, for
all its services, and for the sacred vestments.
22 Both the men and the women, all as their
heart prompted them, brought brooches, earrings, rings, necklaces, and various other
gold articles.[a] Everyone who could presented an offering of gold to the LORD.
23 Everyone who happened to have violet,
purple, or scarlet yarn, fine linen or goat
hair, rams' skins dyed red or tahash skins,
brought them. 24 Whoever could make a contribution of silver or bronze offered it to the
LORD; and everyone who happened to have
acacia wood for any part of the work,
brought it. 25 All the women who were expert
spinners brought hand-spun violet, purple,
and scarlet yarn and fine linen thread. 26 All
the women, as their hearts and skills moved
them, spun goat hair. 27 The tribal leaders
brought onyx stones and other gems for
mounting on the ephod and on the breastpiece; 28 as well as spices, and oil for the
light, anointing oil, and fragrant incense.

*w:* 2 Cor 3:13, 16. *x:* Ex 31:13–17. *y:* Ex 25:2–7. *z:* Ex 31:6–11. *a:* Ex 25:3–7.

[29]Every Israelite man and woman brought to the LORD such voluntary offerings as they thought best, for the various kinds of work which the LORD, through Moses, had commanded to be done.

***The Artisans.*** [30]Moses said to the Israelites:[b] "See, the LORD has singled out Bezalel, son of Uri, son of Hur, of the tribe of Judah, [31]and has filled him with a divine spirit of skill and understanding and knowledge in every craft: [32]in the production of embroidery, in making things of gold, silver, or bronze, [33]in cutting and mounting precious stones, in carving wood, and in every other craft. [34]He has also given both him and Oholiab, son of Ahisamach, of the tribe of Dan, the ability to teach others. [35]He has endowed them with skill to execute all types of work: engraving, embroidering, the making of variegated cloth of violet, purple, and scarlet yarn and fine linen thread, weaving, and all other arts and crafts.

## CHAPTER 36

See RG 70

[1]"Bezalel, therefore, will set to work with Oholiab and with all the artisans whom the LORD has endowed with skill and understanding in knowing how to do all the work for the service of the sanctuary, just as the LORD has commanded."[c]

[2]Moses then called Bezalel and Oholiab and all the other artisans whom the LORD had endowed with skill, men whose hearts moved them to come and do the work. [3]They received from Moses all the contributions which the Israelites had brought for the work to be done for the sanctuary service. Still, morning after morning the people continued to bring their voluntary offerings to Moses. [4]Thereupon all the artisans who were doing the work for the sanctuary came from the work each was doing, [5]and told Moses, "The people are bringing much more than is needed to carry out the work which the LORD has commanded us to do." [6]Moses, therefore, ordered a proclamation to be made throughout the camp: "Let neither man nor woman make any more contributions for the sanctuary." So the people stopped bringing their offerings; [7]there was already enough at hand, and more than enough, to complete the work to be done.

***The Tent Cloth and Coverings.*** [8][d] The various artisans who were doing the work made the tabernacle with its ten sheets woven of fine linen twined, having cherubim embroidered on them with violet, purple, and scarlet yarn. [9]The length of each sheet was twenty-eight cubits, and the width four cubits; all the sheets were the same size. [10]Five of the sheets were joined together, edge to edge; and the other five sheets likewise, edge to edge. [11]Loops of violet yarn were made along the edge of the end sheet in the first set, and the same along the edge of the end sheet in the second set. [12]Fifty loops were thus put on one inner sheet, and fifty loops on the inner sheet in the other set, with the loops directly opposite each other. [13]Then fifty clasps of gold were made, with which the sheets were joined so that the tabernacle formed one whole.

[14]Sheets of goat hair were also woven as a tent over the tabernacle. Eleven such sheets were made. [15]The length of each sheet was thirty cubits and the width four cubits; all eleven sheets were the same size. [16]Five of these sheets were joined into one set, and the other six sheets into another set. [17]Fifty loops were made along the edge of the end sheet in one set, and fifty loops along the edge of the corresponding sheet in the other set. [18]Fifty bronze clasps were made with which the tent was joined so that it formed one whole. [19]A covering for the tent was made of rams' skins dyed red and, above that, a covering of tahash skins.

***The Framework.*** [20][e] Frames were made for the tabernacle, acacia-wood uprights. [21]The length of each frame was ten cubits, and the width one and a half cubits. [22]Each frame had two arms, fastening them one to another. In this way all the frames of the tabernacle were made. [23]The frames for the tabernacle were made as follows: twenty frames on the south side, [24]with forty silver pedestals under the twenty frames, two pedestals under each frame for its two arms;

*b:* Ex 31:1–6. *c:* Ex 31:1, 6. *d:* Ex 26:1–14. *e:* Ex 26:15–29.

[25]twenty frames on the other side of the tabernacle, the north side, [26]with their forty silver pedestals, two pedestals under each frame. [27]At the rear of the tabernacle, to the west, six frames were made, [28]and two frames were made for the corners of the tabernacle, at its rear. [29]These were double at the bottom, and likewise double at the top, to the first ring. That is how both corner frames were made. [30]Thus, there were eight frames, with their sixteen silver pedestals, two pedestals under each frame. [31]Bars of acacia wood were also made, five for the frames on one side of the tabernacle, [32]five for those on the other side, and five for those at the rear, to the west. [33]The center bar, at the middle of the frames, was made to reach across from end to end. [34]The frames were plated with gold, and gold rings were made on them as holders for the bars, which were also plated with gold.

***The Veil.*** [35][f] The veil was made of violet, purple, and scarlet yarn, and of fine linen twined, with cherubim embroidered on it. [36]Four gold-plated columns of acacia wood, with gold hooks, were made for it, and four silver pedestals were cast for them.

[37]The curtain for the entrance of the tent was made of violet, purple, and scarlet yarn, and of fine linen twined, woven in a variegated manner. [38]Its five columns, with their hooks as well as their capitals and bands, were plated with gold; their five pedestals were of bronze.

## CHAPTER 37

See RC 70

***The Ark.*** [1]Bezalel made the ark of acacia wood, two and a half cubits long, one and a half cubits wide, and one and a half cubits high. [2]The inside and outside were plated with gold, and a molding of gold was put around it. [3]Four gold rings were cast for its four supports, two rings on one side and two on the opposite side. [4]Poles of acacia wood were made and plated with gold; [5]these poles were put through the rings on the sides of the ark, for carrying it.

[6]The cover was made of pure gold, two and a half cubits long and one and a half cubits wide. [7]Two cherubim of beaten gold were made for the two ends of the cover; [8]one cherub was at one end, the other at the other end, made of one piece with the cover, at each end. [9]The cherubim had their wings spread out above, sheltering the cover. They faced each other, with their faces looking toward the cover.[g]

***The Table.*** [10][h] The table was made of acacia wood, two cubits long, a cubit wide, and a cubit and a half high. [11]It was plated with pure gold, and a molding of gold was put around it. [12]A frame a handbreadth high was also put around it, with a molding of gold around the frame. [13]Four rings of gold were cast for it and fastened at the four corners, one at each leg. [14]The rings were alongside the frame as holders for the poles to carry the table. [15]These poles for carrying the table were made of acacia wood and plated with gold. [16]The vessels that were set on the table, its plates and cups, as well as its pitchers and bowls for pouring libations, were made of pure gold.

***The Menorah.*** [17][i] The menorah was made of pure beaten gold—its shaft and branches—with its cups and knobs and petals springing directly from it. [18]Six branches extended from its sides, three branches on one side and three on the other. [19]On one branch there were three cups, shaped like almond blossoms, each with its knob and petals; on the opposite branch there were three cups, shaped like almond blossoms, each with its knob and petals; and so for the six branches that extended from the menorah. [20]On the menorah there were four cups, shaped like almond blossoms, with their knobs and petals. [21]The six branches that went out from the menorah had a knob under each pair. [22]The knobs and branches so sprang from it that the whole formed but a single piece of pure beaten gold. [23]Its seven lamps, as well as its trimming shears and trays, were made of pure gold. [24]A talent of pure gold was used for the menorah and its various utensils.

***The Altar of Incense.*** [25][j] The altar of incense was made of acacia wood, on a square, a cubit long, a cubit wide, and two cubits

*f:* Ex 26:31–37. *g:* Ex 25:10–22. *h:* Ex 25:23–30. *i:* Ex 25:31–39. *j:* Ex 30:1–5.

high, having horns that sprang directly from it. 26 Its grate on top, its walls on all four sides, and its horns were plated with pure gold; and a gold molding was put around it. 27 Underneath the molding gold rings were placed, two on one side and two on the opposite side, as holders for the poles used in carrying it. 28 The poles, too, were made of acacia wood and plated with gold.

29 The sacred anointing oil and the fragrant incense were prepared in their pure form by a perfumer.[k]

See RG 70

## CHAPTER 38

***The Altar for Burnt Offerings.*** 1 The altar for burnt offerings[l] was made of acacia wood, on a square, five cubits long and five cubits wide; its height was three cubits. 2 At the four corners horns were made that sprang directly from the altar. It was then plated with bronze. 3 All the utensils of the altar, the pots, shovels, basins, forks and fire pans, were likewise made of bronze. 4 A grating, a bronze network, was made for the altar and placed around it, on the ground, half as high as the altar itself. 5 Four rings were cast for the four corners of the bronze grating, as holders for the poles, 6 which were made of acacia wood and plated with bronze. 7 The poles were put through the rings on the sides of the altar for carrying it. The altar was made in the form of a hollow box.

8 The bronze basin,[m] with its bronze stand, was made from the mirrors of the women who served* at the entrance of the tent of meeting.

***The Court of the Tabernacle.*** 9[n] The court was made as follows. On the south side the hangings of the court were of fine linen twined, a hundred cubits long, 10 with twenty columns and twenty pedestals of bronze, the hooks and bands of the columns being of silver. 11 On the north side there were similar hangings, a hundred cubits long, with twenty columns and twenty pedestals of bronze; the hooks and bands of the columns were of silver. 12 On the west side there were hangings, fifty cubits long, with ten columns and ten pedestals; the hooks and bands of the columns were of silver. 13 On the east side the court was fifty cubits. 14 On one side there were hangings to the extent of fifteen cubits, with three columns and three pedestals; 15 on the other side, beyond the gate of the court, there were likewise hangings to the extent of fifteen cubits, with three columns and three pedestals. 16 The hangings on all sides of the court were woven of fine linen twined. 17 The pedestals of the columns were of bronze, while the hooks and bands of the columns were of silver; the capitals were silver-plated, and all the columns of the court were banded with silver.

18 At the gate of the court there was a variegated curtain, woven of violet, purple, and scarlet yarn and of fine linen twined, twenty cubits long and five cubits wide, in keeping with the hangings of the court. 19 There were four columns and four pedestals of bronze for it, while their hooks were of silver, and their capitals and their bands silver-plated. 20 All the tent pegs for the tabernacle and for the court around it were of bronze.

***Amount of Metal Used.*** 21 The following is an account of the various amounts used on the tabernacle, the tabernacle of the covenant, drawn up at the command of Moses by the Levites under the direction of Ithamar, son of Aaron the priest. 22 However, it was Bezalel, son of Uri,[o] son of Hur, of the tribe of Judah, who made all that the LORD commanded Moses, 23 and he was assisted by Oholiab, son of Ahisamach, of the tribe of Dan, who was an engraver, an embroiderer, and a weaver of variegated cloth of violet, purple, and scarlet yarn and of fine linen.

24 All the gold used in the entire construction of the sanctuary, having previously been given as an offering, amounted to twenty-nine talents and seven hundred and thirty shekels, according to the standard of the sanctuary shekel. 25 The silver of those of the community who were enrolled was one hundred talents and one thousand seven hundred and seventy-five shekels, according to the standard of the sanctuary shekel; 26 one

**38:8** The reflecting surface of ancient mirrors was usually of polished bronze. **The women who served**: cf. 1 Sm 2:22.

*k:* Ex 30:23–25, 34–36. *l:* Ex 27:1–8; 2 Chr 1:5. *m:* Ex 30:18–21. *n:* Ex 27:9–19. *o:* Ex 31:2, 6; 35:30, 34; 36:1.

bekah apiece, that is, a half-shekel, according to the standard of the sanctuary shekel,
was received from everyone who was enrolled, of twenty years or more, namely, six
hundred and three thousand five hundred
and fifty men.[p] [27]One hundred talents of silver were used for casting the pedestals of the
sanctuary and the pedestals of the veil, one
talent for each pedestal, or one hundred talents for the one hundred pedestals. [28]The remaining one thousand seven hundred and
seventy-five shekels were used for making
the hooks on the columns, for plating the
capitals, and for banding them with silver.
[29]The bronze, given as an offering,
amounted to seventy talents and two thousand four hundred shekels. [30]With this were
made the pedestals at the entrance of the tent
of meeting, the bronze altar with its bronze
gratings, and all the utensils of the altar,
[31]the pedestals around the court, the
pedestals at the gate of the court, and all the
tent pegs for the tabernacle and for the court
around it.

## CHAPTER 39

See RG 70

***The Priestly Vestments.*** [1]With violet,
purple, and scarlet yarn were woven the service cloths for use in the sanctuary, as well
as the sacred vestments[q] for Aaron, as the
LORD had commanded Moses.
[2r] The ephod was woven of gold thread
and of violet, purple, and scarlet yarn and of
fine linen twined. [3]Gold was first hammered
into gold leaf and then cut up into threads,
which were woven with the violet, purple,
and scarlet yarn into an embroidered pattern
on the fine linen. [4]Shoulder straps were
made for it and joined to its two upper ends.
[5]The embroidered belt on the ephod extended out from it, and like it, was made of
gold thread, of violet, purple, and scarlet
yarn, and of fine linen twined, as the LORD
had commanded Moses. [6]The onyx stones
were prepared and mounted in gold filigree
work; they were engraved like seal engravings with the names of the sons of Israel.
[7]These stones were set on the shoulder
straps of the ephod as memorial stones of the
sons of Israel, just as the LORD had commanded Moses.
[8s] The breastpiece was embroidered like
the ephod, with gold thread and violet, purple, and scarlet yarn on cloth of fine linen
twined. [9]It was square and folded double, a
span high and a span wide in its folded form.
[10]Four rows of precious stones were
mounted on it: in the first row a carnelian, a
topaz, and an emerald; [11]in the second row, a
garnet, a sapphire, and a beryl; [12]in the third
row a jacinth, an agate, and an amethyst; [13]in
the fourth row a chrysolite, an onyx, and a
jasper. They were mounted in gold filigree
work. [14]These stones were twelve, to match
the names of the sons of Israel, and each
stone was engraved like a seal with the name
of one of the twelve tribes.
[15t] Chains of pure gold, twisted like cords,
were made for the breastpiece, [16]together
with two gold filigree rosettes and two gold
rings. The two rings were fastened to the two
upper ends of the breastpiece. [17]The two
gold chains were then fastened to the two
rings at the ends of the breastpiece. [18]The
other two ends of the two chains were fastened in front to the two filigree rosettes,
which were attached to the shoulder straps
of the ephod. [19]Two other gold rings were
made and put on the two lower ends of the
breastpiece, on the edge facing the ephod.
[20]Two more gold rings were made and fastened to the bottom of the two shoulder
straps next to where they joined the ephod in
front, just above its embroidered belt. [21]Vio-
let ribbons bound the rings of the breastpiece
to the rings of the ephod, so that the breastpiece stayed right above the embroidered
belt of the ephod and did not swing loose
from it. All this was just as the LORD had
commanded Moses.
***Other Vestments.*** [22]The robe of the ephod
was woven entirely of violet yarn, [23]with an
opening in its center like the opening of a
shirt, with selvage around the opening to
keep it from being torn. [24]At the hem of the
robe pomegranates were made of violet, purple, and scarlet yarn and of fine linen
twined; [25]bells of pure gold were also made

---

*p:* Nm 1:46. *q:* Ex 31:10. *r:* Ex 28:6–12. *s:* Ex 28:15–21. *t:* Ex 28:31–35.

and put between the pomegranates all around the hem of the robe: [26]a bell, a pomegranate, a bell, a pomegranate, all around the hem of the robe which was to be worn in performing the ministry—all this, just as the LORD had commanded Moses.

[27]For Aaron and his sons there were also woven tunics of fine linen;[u] [28]the turban of fine linen; the ornate skullcaps of fine linen; linen pants of fine linen twined; [29]and sashes of variegated work made of fine linen twined and of violet, purple, and scarlet yarn, as the LORD had commanded Moses. [30][v] The plate of the sacred diadem was made of pure gold and inscribed, as on a seal engraving: "Sacred to the LORD." [31]It was tied over the turban with a violet ribbon, as the LORD had commanded Moses.

***Presentation of the Work to Moses.*** [32]Thus the entire work of the tabernacle of the tent of meeting was completed. The Israelites did the work just as the LORD had commanded Moses; so it was done. [33]They then brought to Moses the tabernacle, the tent with all its furnishings, the clasps, the frames, the bars, the columns, the pedestals, [34]the covering of rams' skins dyed red, the covering of tahash skins, the curtain veil; [35]the ark of the covenant with its poles, the cover, [36]the table with all its utensils and the showbread, [37]the pure gold menorah with its lamps set up on it and with all its utensils, the oil for the light, [38]the golden altar, the anointing oil, the fragrant incense; the curtain for the entrance of the tent, [39]the altar of bronze with its bronze grating, its poles and all its utensils, the basin with its stand, [40]the hangings of the court with their columns and pedestals, the curtain for the gate of the court with its ropes and tent pegs, all the equipment for the service of the tabernacle of the tent of meeting; [41]the service cloths for use in the sanctuary, the sacred vestments for Aaron the priest, and the vestments to be worn by his sons in their ministry. [42]Just as the LORD had commanded Moses, so the Israelites had carried out all the work. [43]So when Moses saw that all the work was done just as the LORD had commanded, he blessed them.

## CHAPTER 40

See RG 70

***Setting up the Tabernacle.*** [1]Then the LORD said to Moses: [2][w] On the first day of the first month* you shall set up the tabernacle of the tent of meeting.[x] [3]Put the ark of the covenant in it, and screen off the ark with the veil.[y] [4]Bring in the table and set it. Then bring in the menorah and set up the lamps on it. [5]Put the golden altar of incense in front of the ark of the covenant, and hang the curtain at the entrance of the tabernacle. [6]Put the altar for burnt offerings in front of the entrance of the tabernacle of the tent of meeting. [7]Place the basin between the tent of meeting and the altar, and put water in it. [8]Set up the court round about, and put the curtain at the gate of the court.

[9][z] Take the anointing oil and anoint the tabernacle and everything in it, consecrating it and all its furnishings, so that it will be sacred. [10]Anoint the altar for burnt offerings and all its utensils, consecrating it, so that it will be most sacred. [11]Likewise, anoint the basin with its stand, and thus consecrate it.

[12][a] Then bring Aaron and his sons to the entrance of the tent of meeting, and there wash them with water. [13]Clothe Aaron with the sacred vestments and anoint him, thus consecrating him as my priest. [14]Bring forward his sons also, and clothe them with the tunics. [15]As you have anointed their father, anoint them also as my priests. Thus, by being anointed, shall they receive a perpetual priesthood throughout all future generations.

[16]Moses did just as the LORD had commanded him. [17]On the first day of the first month of the second year the tabernacle was set up. [18]It was Moses who set up the tabernacle. He placed its pedestals, set up its frames, put in its bars, and set up its columns. [19]He spread the tent over the tabernacle and put the covering on top of the tent, as the LORD had commanded him. [20][b] He took the covenant and put it in the ark; he

**40:2 On the first day of the first month**: almost a year after the departure of the Israelites from Egypt. Cf. v. 17.

*u:* Ex 28:39–42. *v:* Ex 28:36–37. *w:* Ex 40:16–33. *x:* Ex 26:30. *y:* Ex 26:33–37. *z:* Ex 30:26–29. *a:* Ex 28:41; 29:4–9; Lv 8:1–13. *b:* Ex 25:16, 21; 26:33–37.

**The Climax of the Book**

NOW THAT MOSES has carried out all of God's instructions (40:33), everything is finally ready so that God may reside among the people (cf. Ex 25:8; 29:42–46). The cloud and the glory are signs of God's presence "tabernacling," that is, dwelling, with Israel. The column of cloud by day and the column of fire by night that have led Israel thus far (Ex 13:21–22) take their place over the tabernacle, because they will accompany Israel on the rest of its journey (Nm 9:15–23). As the cloud covered the top of Mount Sinai (Ex 24:15–18), so it now covers the tabernacle and will guide Israel to the Promised Land. God is on the march.

placed poles alongside the ark and set the cover upon it. [21]He brought the ark into the tabernacle and hung the curtain veil, thus screening off the ark of the covenant, as the LORD had commanded him. [22]He put the table in the tent of meeting, on the north side of the tabernacle, outside the veil, [23]and arranged the bread on it before the LORD, as the LORD had commanded him.[c] [24]He placed the menorah in the tent of meeting, opposite the table, on the south side of the tabernacle, [25]and he set up the lamps before the LORD, as the LORD had commanded him. [26]He placed the golden altar in the tent of meeting, in front of the veil, [27]and on it he burned fragrant incense, as the LORD had commanded him. [28]He hung the curtain at the entrance of the tabernacle. [29]He put the altar for burnt offerings in front of the entrance of the tabernacle of the tent of meeting, and sacrificed burnt offerings and grain offerings on it, as the LORD had commanded him. [30d]He placed the basin between the tent of meeting and the altar, and put water in it for washing. [31]Moses and Aaron and his sons used to wash their hands and feet there, [32]for they washed themselves whenever they went into the tent of meeting or approached the altar, as the LORD had commanded Moses. [33]Finally, he set up the court around the tabernacle and the altar and hung the curtain at the gate of the court.

Thus Moses finished all the work.

***God's Presence in the Tabernacle.*** [34e]Then the cloud covered the tent of meeting, and the glory of the LORD filled the tabernacle. [35]Moses could not enter the tent of meeting, because the cloud settled down upon it and the glory of the LORD filled the tabernacle. [36]Whenever the cloud rose from the tabernacle, the Israelites would set out on their journey. [37]But if the cloud did not lift, they would not go forward; only when it lifted did they go forward. [38]The cloud of the LORD was over the tabernacle by day, and fire in the cloud at night, in the sight of the whole house of Israel in all the stages of their journey.

*c:* Ex 25:30. *d:* Ex 30:18–21. *e:* Nm 9:15–22.

See RG 73-80

# The Book of Leviticus

The name "Leviticus" was given to the third book of the Pentateuch by the ancient Greek translators because a good part of this book deals with concerns of the priests, who are of the tribe of Levi.

The book mainly treats cultic matters (i.e., sacrifices and offerings, purity and holiness, the priesthood, the operation of the sanctuary, and feast days) but is also interested in various behavioral, ethical, and economic issues (e.g., sexual practices, idolatrous worship, treatment of others, the sale of land, slavery). The goal of the laws is not merely legislative. For the most part they cohere as a system and attempt to inculcate a way of life in the book's hearers and readers. In addition to these concerns, Leviticus, comprising as it does the center of the Pentateuch, carries forward the narrative of Exodus (cf. chaps. 1, 8–9, 10, 16, 24).

The book is part of the Priestly tradition (P) of the Pentateuch, to which belong various narratives and legal passages (e.g., Gn 1:1–2:4; 9:1–17; 17:1–27; Ex 12:1–20, 40–50; 25:1–31:18; 35:1–40:38; Nm 1:1–10:28; 15:1–14; 17:1–19:22; 25:6–31:54). Within the Priestly material itself there are signs of variant traditions and development.

The main divisions of Leviticus are:

- I. Ritual of Sacrifices (1:1–7:38)
  - A. Instructions for the Israelites (1:1–5:26)
  - B. Instructions for the Priests (6:1–7:38)
- II. Ceremony of Ordination (8:1–10:20)
- III. Laws Regarding Ritual Purity (11:1–16:34)
- IV. Holiness Laws (17:1–26:46)
- V. Redemption of Offerings (27:1–34)

# I. Ritual of Sacrifices

## A. Instructions for the Israelites

### CHAPTER 1

See RG 76–77

*Burnt Offerings.* 1The LORD called Moses, and spoke to him from the tent of meeting:[a] 2Speak to the Israelites and tell them: When any one of you* brings an offering of livestock to the LORD, you shall bring your offering from the herd or from the flock.[b]

3* [c] If a person's offering is a burnt offering* from the herd, the offering must be a male without blemish.[d] The individual shall bring it to the entrance of the tent of meeting to find favor with the LORD, 4and shall lay a hand* on the head[e] of the burnt offering, so that it may be acceptable[f] to make atonement[g] for the one who offers it. 5The bull shall then be slaughtered* before the LORD, and Aaron's sons, the priests, shall offer its blood by splashing it on all the sides of the altar which is at the entrance of the tent of meeting.[h] 6Then the burnt offering shall be flayed and cut into pieces. 7After Aaron's sons, the priests, have put burning embers on the altar and laid wood on them, 8they shall lay the pieces of meat, together with the head and the suet, on top of the wood and the embers on the altar; 9but the inner organs and the shanks shall be washed with water. The priest shall then burn all of it on the altar as a burnt offering, a sweet-smelling oblation to the LORD.[i]

10If a person's burnt offering is from the flock, that is, a sheep or a goat, the offering must be a male without blemish. 11It shall be slaughtered on the north side of the altar before the LORD, and Aaron's sons, the priests, shall splash its blood on all the sides of the altar. 12When it has been cut into pieces, the priest shall lay these, together with the head and suet, on top of the wood and the embers on the altar; 13but the inner organs and the shanks shall be washed with water. The priest shall then offer all of it, burning it on the altar. It is a burnt offering, a sweet-smelling oblation to the LORD.

**1:2 Any one of you**: women as well as men bring sacrifices (see 12:6–8; 15:28–30) and are explicitly obligated in other ritual matters (e.g., 13:29, 38; Nm 5:6; 6:2; Lk 2:24). Thus, though the Hebrew formulates sacrificial and other law with male reference, the translation reflects the inclusion of women in ritual requirements. **From the herd or from the flock**: the only animals which could be used as sacrificial victims were domestic animals either of the bovine class (bulls, cows and calves) or the ovine class (sheep and lambs, goats and kids). Excluded, therefore, were not only all wild animals, but also such "unclean" domestic animals as the camel and the donkey (cf. 11:1–47; 27:26–27).

**1:3–5 Entrance of the tent of meeting . . . before the LORD**: probably the forecourt from the entrance of the court to the entrance of the tent (cf. Ex 27). Thus the altar in front of the tent was entirely accessible to the laity.

**1:3** The burnt offering is used for regular daily (6:1–6) offerings, public festivals (Nm 28–29), purification rituals (Lv 12:6–8; 14:19–20; 15:15, 30), and individuals' vows and voluntary offerings (22:18–20).

**1:4 Lay a hand**: the imposition of a single hand for the sacrifices in chaps. 1–5 may be a means of designating the animal as belonging to the offerer. See note on 16:21. **Atonement**: see note on 16:6.

**1:5 Shall then be slaughtered**: lit., "he shall slaughter the bull." Slaughtering is not something the offerer must do (as opposed to, for example, hand placement [v. 4] or the presentation of sacrificial portions as an elevated offering [7:29–34]). Thus the verb is construed impersonally here.

*a:* Ex 40. *b:* Lv 1:3, 10; 3:1, 6, 12. *c:* Lv 6:1–6; 22:18–19; *d:* Lv 22:17–25; Ex 12:5. *e:* Lv 3:2, 8, 13; 4:4, 15, 24, 29, 33; 8:14, 18, 22; Nm 8:12; 2 Chr 29:23; cf. Lv 16:21; 24:14; Nm 27:18, 23; Dt 34:9. *f:* Lv 19:5; 22:19–29; Gn 4:3–5; Mal 1:8–14. *g:* Lv 9:7; 14:20; Jb 1:5; 42:8; cf. Gn 32:21; Ex 29:36–37; 30:15; Lv 16:16–20; 17:11; Ez 43:20, 26. *h:* Lv 1:11, 15; 3:2, 8, 13; cf. Lv 4:5–7, 25. *i:* Lv 2:2; 3:5; 4:31; 26:31; Gn 8:20–21; Nm 28:2; cf. Lv 3:11; 21:6, 21; 22:25.

EVEN AFTER THE destruction of the temple and the cessation of sacrificial worship and temple ritual, Leviticus remains at the foundation of Jewish life. Among the institutions still central to Judaism, which have their biblical origins in Leviticus, are most of the dietary laws (the permitted and forbidden animals and the blood prohibition); many of the festival rituals; most of the laws regulating sex, marriage, and family purity; and the commandments governing the seventh year, still applicable in the land of Israel. Moreover, the religious life of the congregation, centered upon the synagogue and the daily prayers offered at fixed times and in precisely ordained ritual forms, is a direct outgrowth of, and according to rabbinic tradition a substitute for, the temple ritual as envisioned in Leviticus.

All the institutions that ultimately shaped Israel's national and religious existence—the law, the priesthood, the forms of temple worship, and the tribal foundations of its society—are said to have been ordained and established during the years immediately after the exile.

[14] If a person offers a bird as a burnt offering to the LORD, the offering brought must be a turtledove or a pigeon.[j] [15] Having brought it to the altar, the priest shall wring its head off and burn it on the altar. The blood shall be drained out against the side of the altar.[k] [16] He shall remove its crissum* by means of its feathers and throw it on the ash heap at the east side of the altar. [17] Then, having torn the bird open by its wings without separating the halves, the priest shall burn it on the altar, on the wood and the embers. It is a burnt offering, a sweet-smelling oblation to the LORD.

## CHAPTER 2

See RG 76–77

*Grain Offerings.* [1] *[l] When anyone brings a grain offering to the LORD, the offering must consist of bran flour. The offerer shall pour oil on it and put frankincense[m] over it, [2] and bring it to Aaron's sons, the priests. A priest shall take a handful of the bran flour and oil, together with all the frankincense, and shall burn it on the altar as a token of the offering,* a sweet-smelling oblation to the LORD.[n] [3] The rest of the grain offering belongs to Aaron and his sons,[o] a most holy[p] portion from the oblations to the LORD.

[4] When you offer a grain offering baked in an oven, it must be in the form of unleavened cakes made of bran flour mixed with oil, or of unleavened wafers spread with oil.[q] [5] If your offering is a grain offering that is fried on a griddle,[r] it must be of bran flour mixed with oil and unleavened. [6] Break it into pieces, and pour oil over it. It is a grain offering. [7] If your offering is a grain offering that is prepared in a pan, it must be made of bran flour, fried in oil. [8] A grain offering that is made in any of these ways you shall bring to the LORD. It shall be presented to the priest, who shall take it to the altar. [9] The priest shall then remove from the grain offering a token and burn it on the altar as a sweet-smelling oblation to the LORD. [10] The rest of the grain offering belongs to Aaron and his sons, a most holy portion from the oblations to the LORD.

[11] * Every grain offering that you present to

**1:16 Crissum**: the area around the anus of the bird, lying beneath the bird's tail.

**2:1** Grain offerings are used as independent offerings (those in this chapter and cf. 6:12–16; 8:26–27; 23:10–11), as substitutes for other offerings in a case of poverty (5:11–13), and as accompaniments to animal offerings (cf. Nm 15:1–12; 28:1–29:39; Lv 14:20; 23:12, 18, 37). Chapter 2 describes two basic types of grain offering: uncooked (vv. 1–3) and cooked (vv. 4–10). The flour (*sōlet*) used was made of wheat (Ex 29:2) and Jewish tradition and Semitic cognates indicate that it is a coarse rather than a fine flour.

**2:2 Token of the offering**: lit., "reminder." Instead of burning the whole grain offering, only this part is burned on the altar.

**2:11–12** No grain offering that is leavened can be offered on the altar. Those in 7:13 and 23:17 are leavened but not offered on the altar. The Hebrew word for "honey" may refer to fruit syrup as well as to bee honey.

*j:* Lv 5:7; 12:8; 15:14–15; Lk 2:24. *k:* Lv 5:8–9. *l:* Lv 5:11–13; 6:7–16; 7:9–14; 24:5–9; Nm 15:1–21; cf. Gn 4:3–5. *m:* Cf. Ex 30:1–10; Lv 16:11–13; Prv 27:9. *n:* Lv 1:9. *o:* Lv 6:9; 7:9–10. *p:* Lv 6:10, 18, 22; 10:12, 17; 24:9. *q:* 1 Chr 23:29. *r:* Lv 6:14.

the LORD shall be unleavened, for you shall not burn any leaven or honey as an oblation to the LORD.[s] 12Such you may present to the LORD in the offering of the first produce that is processed,[t] but they are not to be placed on the altar for a pleasing odor. 13You shall season all your grain offerings with salt. Do not let the salt of the covenant with your God* be lacking from your grain offering. On every offering you shall offer salt.[u]

14If you offer a grain offering of first ripe fruits to the LORD, you shall offer it in the form of fresh early grain, roasted by fire and crushed as a grain offering of your first ripe fruits. 15You shall put oil on it and set frankincense on it. It is a grain offering. 16The priest shall then burn some of the groats and oil, together with all the frankincense, as a token of the offering, an oblation to the LORD.

See RG 76–77

## CHAPTER 3

***Communion Sacrifices.*** 1*[v] If a person's offering is a communion sacrifice, if it is brought from the herd, be it a male or a female animal, it must be presented without blemish[w] before the LORD. 2The one offering it shall lay a hand on the head[x] of the offering. It shall then be slaughtered at the entrance of the tent of meeting. Aaron's sons, the priests, shall splash its blood on all the sides of the altar. 3[y] From the communion sacrifice the individual shall offer as an oblation to the LORD the fat* that covers the inner organs, and all the fat that adheres to them, 4as well as the two kidneys, with the fat on them near the loins, and the lobe of the liver, which is removed with the kidneys. 5Aaron's sons shall burn this on the altar with the burnt offering that is on the wood and the embers, as a sweet-smelling oblation to the LORD.[z]

6If the communion sacrifice one offers to the LORD is from the flock, be it a male or a female animal, it must be presented without blemish. 7If one presents a lamb as an offering, that person shall bring it before the LORD, 8and after laying a hand on the head of the offering, it shall then be slaughtered before the tent of meeting. Aaron's sons shall splash its blood on all the sides of the altar. 9From the communion sacrifice the individual shall present as an oblation to the LORD its fat: the whole fatty tail, which is removed close to the spine, the fat that covers the inner organs, and all the fat that adheres to them, 10as well as the two kidneys, with the fat on them near the loins, and the lobe of the liver, which is removed with the kidneys. 11The priest shall burn this on the altar as food,[a] an oblation to the LORD.

12If a person's offering is a goat, the individual shall bring it before the LORD, 13and after laying a hand on its head, it shall then be slaughtered before the tent of meeting. Aaron's sons shall splash its blood on all the sides of the altar. 14From this the one sacrificing shall present an offering as an oblation to the LORD: the fat that covers the inner organs, and all the fat that adheres to them, 15as well as the two kidneys, with the fat on them near the loins, and the lobe of the liver, which is removed with the kidneys. 16The priest shall burn these on the altar as food, a sweet-smelling oblation.

All the fat belongs to the LORD. 17This shall be a perpetual ordinance for your descendants wherever they may dwell. You shall not eat any fat or any blood.*[b]

**2:13 The salt of the covenant with your God**: partaking of salt in common was an ancient symbol of friendship and alliance. Cf. Mark 9:49–50 and Col 4:6.

**3:1** The exact meaning of Hebrew *shelamim*, "communion sacrifice," is not clear. It has also been rendered "gift," "(re)payment," "peace," "well-being," or "covenant" offering. This offering may be brought for a vow or voluntary offering (cf. 22:21). A distinct version of the communion sacrifice is the thanksgiving offering (7:11–15 vis-à-vis vv. 16–18).

**3:3–5 Fat**: only part of the offering is devoted to God, as opposed to the burnt offering (chap. 1), which is wholly burnt (except for the skin). The meat is distributed among the offerer (and the offerer's party) and the priests (cf. 7:11–36).

**3:17 Any fat or any blood**: this prohibition is mentioned here because portions of this offering could be eaten by lay Israelites, who may not be entirely familiar with the prohibition (cf. 7:22–27; 19:26). The fat prohibited is only the visceral fat mentioned in 3:9–10, 14–15, not muscular fat.

*s:* Mt 16:12; Mk 8:15; Lk 12:1; 1 Cor 5:7; Gal 5:9. *t:* Nm 18:12–13, 27; 15:20–21. *u:* Nm 18:19; Ezr 6:9; 7:22; Ez 43:24. *v:* Lv 7:11–36. *w:* Lv 22:21. *x:* Lv 1:4. *y:* Lv 3:9–10, 14–16; 4:8–9, 31, 35; 6:5; 7:3–4, 30–31; 8:16, 25; 16:25; 17:6; Ex 29:13, 22; cf. Ez 44:15. *z:* Lv 1:9. *a:* Lv 9:19. *b:* Lv 17:10.

## CHAPTER 4

See RG 76–77

***Purification Offerings.*** 1The LORD said to Moses: 2[c] Tell the Israelites: When a person inadvertently* does wrong by violating any one of the LORD's prohibitions—

***For the Anointed Priest.*** 3If it is the anointed priest* who thus does wrong and thereby makes the people guilty, he shall offer to the LORD an unblemished bull of the herd as a purification offering for the wrong he committed. 4Bringing the bull to the entrance of the tent of meeting, before the LORD, he shall lay his hand on its head[d] and slaughter it before the LORD. 5* The anointed priest shall then take some of the bull's blood and bring it into the tent of meeting, 6where, dipping his finger in the blood, he shall sprinkle some of it seven times before the LORD, toward the veil of the sanctuary.[e] 7The priest shall also put some of the blood on the horns of the altar of fragrant incense which stands before the LORD in the tent of meeting. The rest of the bull's blood he shall pour out at the base of the altar for burnt offerings which is at the entrance of the tent of meeting. 8He shall remove all the fat of the bull of the purification offering: the fat that covers the inner organs, and all the fat that adheres to them, 9as well as the two kidneys, with the fat on them near the loins, and the lobe of the liver, which is removed with the kidneys, 10just as the fat pieces are removed from the ox of the communion sacrifice.[f] The priest shall burn these on the altar for burnt offerings. 11* But the hide of the bull and its meat, with its head, shanks, inner organs and dung, 12that is, the whole bull, shall be brought outside the camp to a clean place* where the ashes are deposited and there be burned in a wood fire. At the place of the ash heap, there it must be burned.[g]

***For the Community.*** 13If the whole community of Israel errs* inadvertently and without even being aware of it violates any of the LORD's prohibitions, and thus are guilty, 14when the wrong that was committed becomes known, the community shall offer a bull of the herd as a purification offering. They shall bring it before the tent of meeting. 15The elders of the community shall lay their hands on the bull's head before the LORD. When the bull has been slaughtered before the LORD, 16the anointed priest shall bring some of its blood into the tent of meeting, 17and dipping his finger in the blood, he shall sprinkle it seven times before the LORD, toward the veil. 18He shall also put some of the blood on the horns of the altar which is before the LORD in the tent of meeting. The rest of the blood he shall pour out at the base of the altar for burnt offerings which is at the entrance of the tent of meeting. 19He shall remove all of its fat and burn it on the altar, 20doing with this bull just as he did with the other bull of the purification offering; he will do the same thing. Thus the priest shall make atonement[h] on their behalf, that they may be forgiven. 21This bull shall also be brought outside the camp and burned,[i] just as the first bull. It is a purification offering for the assembly.

***For the Tribal Leader.*** 22Should a tribal leader[j] do wrong inadvertently by violating

**4:2 Inadvertently**: the concern in this chapter, and much of chap. 5, is wrongs done unintentionally. Intentional ("high-handed") sins are punished with being "cut off" from the people (Nm 15:30–31). See note on Lv 7:20. **LORD's prohibitions**: not included in the faults figured here is failure to perform positive commandments. Failing to perform positive commands, however, still renders the individual liable to other punishment (e.g., failing to observe the Passover, Nm 9:13). Cf. Nm 15:22–31.

**4:3 The anointed priest**: the chapter presents four cases of inadvertent wrong, arranged in descending order according to the status of the wrongdoer: high priest (vv. 3–12), entire community (vv. 13–21), tribal leader (vv. 22–26), and general populace (vv. 27–35). The higher one's position, the more deeply the sin affects the sanctuary (vv. 5–7, 17–18 versus vv. 25, 29, 34). See note on 16:6. **Purification offering**: the Hebrew verb *ḥiṭṭēʾ* means "remove sin, purify" (Lv 8:15; Ez 43:20–23; 45:18–19; cf. Ex 29:36). The offering cleansed the various places to which the blood was applied or the rooms in which it was sprinkled.

**4:5–7** On the structure of the sanctuary, see Ex 26–27.

**4:11–12** See note on 6:17–23.

**4:12 Clean place**: i.e., ritually "clean" or pure. It has nothing to do with the presence of dirt or waste. See 6:4.

**4:13 Whole community . . . errs**: this case probably complements that of vv. 3–12. There the high priest sins so that the people become guilty. Those verses deal with his requirements for atonement; vv. 13–21 deal with the people's requirements.

---

*c:* Lv 6:17–23; Nm 15:22–31. *d:* Lv 1:4. *e:* Lv 4:17–18; 16:16; cf. 4:25. *f:* Lv 3:3. *g:* Lv 6:23. *h:* Lv 1:4. *i:* Lv 6:23. *j:* Nm 10:4; 25:14.

## Holiness and Sacrifice

TWO CONNECTED CONCEPTS give the meaning and significance for both the codes of law and the practices of worship in the Temple. These concepts are *holiness* and *sacrifice.*

The Hebrew word for "holy"—*qadosh*—comes from a root that means "separate" or "set apart." Something holy is set apart from other, ordinary things. The original and definitive holy being is God: although God made the creation, God is separate from it. Ultimately, the Israelite people as a whole are to be holy, set apart from the other nations of the world because of their service to God and their status as God's people: "Be holy, for I, the LORD your God, am holy" (Lv 19:2). Something can become holy by being associated with God in some way. The established way to do that, in Hebrew worship, is to offer it to God by setting it apart and putting it beyond the use of the person offering it.

This making holy or setting apart is a "sacrifice," from the Latin words that mean "to make holy." Something could be sacrificed by burning it (Lv 1:9); giving it to someone else (the priest) to eat (Lv 2:3); chasing it into the wilderness (Lv 16:22); and, in the case of liquids, splashing them against the altar (Lv 1:11) or pouring them on the ground (Lv 4:18; see also Dt 12:16). In each case, the offering had become God's possession; the particular action was a way of demonstrating this.

The Hebrew words for the different kinds of sacrifices indicate how the sacrifice is carried out or what its aim is. One word—*zebach*—means "slaughter [for sacrifice]," and is the term used in "communion sacrifice." (See NAB note on 3:1 for alternate translations.) Another—*olah*—is translated "burnt offering" in the New American Bible. In this sacrifice, the entire animal (except the skin) is consumed by fire. The name comes from a verb that means "ascend, go up" because the smoke from the sacrifice rises to the presence of God. The word *minchah* means "gift" or "tribute" as from an inferior to a superior, and refers to the "grain offering" where cakes made of oil and flour were burnt or eaten by the priests.

These sacrifices—communion sacrifice, burnt offering, and grain offering—are voluntary offerings from the individual to praise God, give thanks for a blessing, fulfill a vow, pray for healing or deliverance, and so on. The first three chapters deal with these.

In chs 4–5 the sacrifices are those brought about by wrongdoing, either deliberate or accidental, and are required, not voluntary. The first is *chattat* (NAB "purification offering" [4:3]). This means "that which misses," like an arrow that falls short of its target. The point of the sacrifice, however, is to restore the right relationship between God and the person offering it, and to remove the sin. This atonement (Hebrew *kipper,* which means "wipe clean"; the same word names the Jewish holiday Yom Kippur, "Day of Atonement") is brought about by the sacrifice, which purges or purifies the offerer. (See NAB note on 4:3, suggesting that this is an "offering [that] cleansed the various places to which the blood was applied.") The second type of sacrifice for wrongdoing is the *asham,* which originally meant a penalty incurred and came to mean "offense" or "guilt." The emphasis, however, is not so much on the guilt of the offender but on the restoration (Lv 5:16) or restitution (Lv 5:24) of what has been wrongfully taken. That is the basis for the translation "reparation offering" (Lv 5:15). The one who is offering is trying to make up for a past offense.

Thus, the Israelites maintained their relationship with God by offering sacrifices: setting something aside for God (making it holy), whether in thanksgiving or penitence.

any one of the prohibitions of the LORD his God, and thus be guilty, 23 when he learns of the wrong he committed, he shall bring as his offering an unblemished male goat. 24 He shall lay his hand on its head and it shall be slaughtered in the place where the burnt offering is slaughtered, before the LORD. It is a purification offering. 25 The priest shall then take some of the blood of the purification offering on his finger and put it on the horns[k] of the altar for burnt offerings. The rest of the blood he shall pour out at the base of the altar. 26 All of its fat he shall burn on the altar like the fat of the communion sacrifice. Thus the priest shall make atonement on the tribal leader's behalf for his wrong, that he may be forgiven.

***For the General Populace.*** 27 If anyone of the general populace does wrong inadvertently by violating one of the LORD's prohibitions, and thus is guilty, 28 upon learning of the wrong committed, that person shall bring an unblemished she-goat as the offering for the wrong committed. 29 The wrongdoer shall lay a hand on the head of the purification offering, and the purification offering shall be slaughtered at the place of the burnt offerings. 30 The priest shall then take some of its blood on his finger and put it on the horns of the altar for burnt offerings. The rest of the blood he shall pour out at the base of the altar. 31 He shall remove all the fat, just as the fat is removed from the communion sacrifice. The priest shall burn it on the altar for a sweet odor to the LORD. Thus the priest shall make atonement, so that the individual may be forgiven.

32 If, however, a person brings a lamb as a purification offering, that person shall bring an unblemished female, and 33 lay a hand on its head. It shall be slaughtered as a purification offering in the place where the burnt offering is slaughtered. 34 The priest shall then take some of the blood of the purification offering on his finger and put it on the horns of the altar for burnt offerings. The rest of the blood he shall pour out at the base of the altar. 35 He shall remove all its fat just as the fat is removed from the lamb of the communion sacrifice. The priest shall burn these on the altar with the other oblations for the LORD. Thus the priest shall make atonement on the person's behalf for the wrong committed, that the individual may be forgiven.

## CHAPTER 5

See RG 76–77

***Special Cases for Purification Offerings.**** 1 If a person, either having seen or come to know something, does wrong by refusing as a witness under oath to give information,[l] that individual shall bear the penalty; 2 or if someone, without being aware of it, touches any unclean thing, such as the carcass of an unclean wild animal, or an unclean domestic animal, or an unclean swarming creature,* and thus is unclean and guilty;[m] 3 or if someone, without being aware of it, touches some human uncleanness,[n] whatever kind of uncleanness this may be, and then subsequently becomes aware of guilt; 4 or if someone, without being aware of it, rashly utters an oath with bad or good intent,[o] whatever kind of oath this may be, and then subsequently becomes aware of guilt in regard to any of these matters— 5 when someone is guilty in regard to any of these matters, that person shall confess the wrong committed, 6 and make reparation to the LORD for the wrong committed: a female animal from the flock, a ewe lamb or a she-goat, as a purification offering. Thus the priest shall make atonement on the individual's behalf for the wrong.

7 If, however, the person cannot afford an animal of the flock,[p] that person shall bring

**5:1–13** This differs from the prescriptions for purification offerings in chap. 4 by listing four specific wrongs for which a purification offering is brought and allowing the substitution of birds and grain offerings in the case of poverty.

**5:2 Swarming creature**: a rather imprecise categorization that includes various small creatures in the seas, such as fish that go about in large groups or swarms (Gn 1:20; Lv 11:10); or, similarly, various winged insects that mass in the skies (Lv 11:20; Dt 14:19); and, finally, various small creatures that move in swarms on land, whether crawlers, quadrupeds, or of the multilegged variety (Lv 11:41–42). According to 11:29–30, even various rodents and lizards can be included in this category.

*k:* Lv 4:30, 34; 8:15; 9:9; 16:18; Ex 29:12; Ez 43:20; cf. Lv 4:7. *l:* Jgs 17:2–3; Prv 29:24. *m:* Lv 11:1–45; 15:31; 17:15–16. *n:* Lv 12:4; 13:35–36; 15:2–12, 19–27; Nm 19:14–22. *o:* Nm 30:3; Jgs 11:30–36; 1 Sm 14:24–30; Mk 6:23–26; Acts 23:12. *p:* Cf. Lv 5:11; 12:8; 14:21.

to the LORD as reparation for the wrong
committed two turtledoves or two pigeons,
one for a purification offering and the other
for a burnt offering. 8The guilty party shall
bring them to the priest, who shall offer the
one for the purification offering first.[q]
Wringing its head at the neck, yet without
breaking it off, 9he shall sprinkle some of the
blood of the purification offering against the
side of the altar. The rest of the blood shall
be drained out against the base of the altar. It
is a purification offering. 10The other bird he
shall offer as a burnt offering according to
procedure. Thus the priest shall make atonement on the person's behalf for the wrong
committed, so that the individual may be
forgiven.

11If the person is unable to afford even
two turtledoves or two pigeons, that person
shall bring as an offering for the wrong committed one tenth of an ephah* of bran flour
for a purification offering. The guilty party
shall not put oil or place frankincense on it,
because it is a purification offering.[r] 12The
individual shall bring it to the priest, who
shall take a handful as a token of the offering
and burn it on the altar with the other oblations for the LORD. It is a purification offering. 13Thus the priest shall make atonement
on the person's behalf for the wrong committed in any of the above cases, so that the
individual may be forgiven. The rest of the
offering, like the grain offering, shall belong
to the priest.

***Reparation Offerings.**** 14The LORD said to
Moses: 15[s] When a person commits sacrilege
by inadvertently misusing any of the LORD's
sacred objects,[t] the wrongdoer shall bring to
the LORD as reparation an unblemished ram
from the flock, at the established value* in
silver shekels according to the sanctuary
shekel, as a reparation offering. 16The
wrongdoer shall also restore what has been
misused of the sacred objects, adding a fifth
of its value,[u] and give this to the priest. Thus
the priest shall make atonement for the person with the ram of the reparation offering,
so that the individual may be forgiven.

17If someone does wrong and violates one
of the LORD's prohibitions without realizing
it, that person is guilty[v] and shall bear the
penalty. 18The individual shall bring to the
priest an unblemished ram of the flock, at
the established value, for a reparation offering. The priest shall then make atonement on
the offerer's behalf for the error inadvertently and unknowingly committed so that
the individual may be forgiven. 19It is a reparation offering. The individual must make
reparation to the LORD.

20The LORD said to Moses: 21When someone does wrong and commits sacrilege
against the LORD by deceiving[w] a neighbor
about a deposit or a pledge or a stolen article, or by otherwise retaining a neighbor's
goods unjustly;[x] 22or if, having found a lost
article, the person lies about it, swearing
falsely about any of the things that a person
may do wrong— 23when someone has thus
done wrong and is guilty, that person shall
restore the thing that was stolen, the item unjustly retained, the item left as deposit, or the
lost article that was found 24or whatever else
the individual swore falsely about. That person shall make full restitution of the thing itself, and add one fifth of its value to it, giving it to its owner at the time of reparation.
25Then that person shall bring to the priest as
reparation to the LORD an unblemished ram
of the flock, at the established value, as a
reparation offering. 26The priest shall make
atonement on the person's behalf before the
LORD, so that the individual may be forgiven
for whatever was done to incur guilt.

**5:11 Ephah**: see note on Is 5:10.

**5:14–26** This last half of the chapter deals with a distinct sacrifice, the reparation offering (Heb. *'asham*). The Hebrew root for this term has a basic meaning of "be guilty." The noun can have a consequential sense of "that which is due from guilt," i.e., "compensation, indemnification, reparation"; hence the translation "reparation offering," rather than the alternatives "guilt offering" or "trespass offering." This offering is brought most often in cases of sacrilege.

**5:15 At the established value**: the Hebrew term *'erkĕkā*, which in context means "(established) value," may indicate that a person could bring the monetary equivalent of a ram instead of an actual animal. See vv. 18, 25.

*q:* Lv 1:14–17. *r:* Lv 2:1–3; Nm 5:15. *s:* Lv 7:1–6; Nm 5:5–8. *t:* Lv 22:14. *u:* Lv 22:14; 27:13, 15, 19, 27. *v:* Ps 19:13; Jb 1:5. *w:* Ps 59:13; Hos 4:2. *x:* Ex 22:6–12.

## B. Instructions for the Priests

### CHAPTER 6

See RG 76-77

***The Daily Burnt Offering.*** 1The LORD said to Moses: 2* [y] Give Aaron and his sons the following command: This is the ritual* for the burnt offering—the burnt offering that is to remain on the hearth of the altar all night until the next morning, while the fire is kept burning on the altar. 3The priest, clothed in his linen robe and wearing linen pants underneath, shall take away the ashes to which the fire has reduced the burnt offering on the altar, and lay them at the side of the altar. 4Then, having taken off these garments and put on other garments, he shall carry the ashes to a clean place outside the camp. 5The fire on the altar is to be kept burning; it must not go out. Every morning the priest shall put firewood on it. On this he shall lay out the burnt offering[z] and burn the fat of the communion offering. 6The fire is to be kept burning continuously on the altar; it must not go out.

***The Grain Offering.**** 7This is the ritual of the grain offering. Aaron's sons shall offer it before the LORD, in front of the altar. 8A priest shall then take from the grain offering a handful of bran flour and oil, together with all the frankincense that is on it,[a] and this he shall burn on the altar as a token of the offering, a sweet aroma to the LORD. 9The rest of it Aaron and his sons may eat; but it must be eaten unleavened in a sacred place:[b] in the court of the tent of meeting they shall eat it. 10It shall not be baked with leaven. I have given it to them as their portion from the oblations for the LORD; it is most holy,[c] like the purification offering and the reparation offering. 11Every male of Aaron's descendants may eat of it perpetually throughout your generations as their rightful due from the oblations for the LORD. Whatever touches the oblations becomes holy.

***High Priest's Daily Grain Offering.**** 12The LORD said to Moses: 13This is the offering that Aaron and his sons shall present to the LORD on the day he is anointed: one tenth of an ephah of bran flour for the regular grain offering, half of it in the morning and half of it in the evening. 14You shall bring it well kneaded and fried in oil on a griddle.[d] Having broken the offering into pieces, you shall present it as a sweet aroma to the LORD. 15The anointed priest descended from Aaron who succeeds him shall do likewise. This is the LORD's due forever. The offering shall be wholly burned.[e] 16Every grain offering of a priest shall be a whole offering; it may not be eaten.

***Purification Offerings.**** 17The LORD said to Moses: 18[f] Tell Aaron and his sons: This is the ritual for the purification offering. At the place where the burnt offering is slaughtered, there also, before the LORD, shall the purification offering be slaughtered. It is most holy.[g] 19The priest who offers the purification offering shall eat of it; it shall be eaten in a sacred place,[h] in the court of the tent of meeting. 20Whatever touches its flesh becomes holy. If any of its blood spatters on a garment, the stained part must be washed in a sacred place. 21A clay vessel in which it has been boiled shall be broken; if it is boiled in a copper vessel, this shall be scoured afterward and rinsed with water.[i] 22Every male of the priestly line may eat it.

**6:2–6** This passage may have reference to the burnt offering that is offered in the morning and late afternoon each day (cf. Ex 29:38–42; Nm 28:3–8).

**6:2 Ritual**: Hebrew *torah*, which also has the broader meaning of "instruction." The treatment of sacrifices in chaps. 6–7 recapitulates the offerings treated in 1–5 but now with more emphasis on priestly duties and prerogatives.

**6:7–11** The passage is apparently concerned with the raw grain offering of 2:1–3.

**6:12–16** This seems to refer to a grain offering offered twice daily by the high priest, perhaps identical to the regular grain offering in Nm 4:16 (cf. Neh 10:34). This offering is distinct from the grain offering that accompanies the daily burnt offering.

**6:17–23** There are two types of purification offering: one whose blood is used inside the tent sanctuary (4:1–12, 13–21) and another whose blood was only used at the outer sacrificial altar (4:22–26, 27–31, 32–35). The carcasses of the former, as well as of purification offerings brought by the priests themselves (cf. 8:14–17; 9:8–11), are not eaten by priests but disposed of at the ash heap outside the camp, which itself is set up around the sanctuary (Ex 29:14; Lv 4:11–12, 21; 6:23; 8:17; 9:11; 16:27). The Letter to the Hebrews compares Jesus' suffering "outside the gate" to the disposal of purification offering carcasses outside the camp (Heb 13:11–13).

*y:* Lv 1. *z:* Lv 9:17. *a:* Lv 2:1–3. *b:* Lv 6:19; 7:6; 10:13, 17; 24:9. *c:* Lv 2:3. *d:* Lv 2:5. *e:* Lv 2:9. *f:* Lv 4:1–5:13. *g:* Lv 2:3. *h:* Lv 6:9. *i:* Lv 11:32–33; 15:12.

It is most holy. [23]But no purification offering of which some blood has been brought into the tent of meeting[j] to make atonement in the sanctuary shall be eaten; it must be burned with fire.[k]

### CHAPTER 7

See RG 76–77

*Reparation Offerings.* [1*l] This is the ritual for the reparation offering. It is most holy. [2]At the place where the burnt offering is slaughtered, the reparation offering shall also be slaughtered.[m] Its blood shall be splashed on all the sides of the altar. [3n] All of its fat shall be offered: the fatty tail, the fat that covers the inner organs, and all the fat that adheres to them, [4]as well as the two kidneys with the fat on them near the loins, and the lobe of the liver, which is removed with the kidneys. [5]The priest shall burn these on the altar as an oblation to the LORD. It is a reparation offering. [6]Every male of the priestly line may eat of it; but it must be eaten in a sacred place.[o] It is most holy.[p]

[7]Because the purification offering and the reparation offering are alike, both have the same ritual. The reparation offering belongs to the priest who makes atonement with it. [8]As for the priest who offers someone's burnt offering, to him belongs the hide of the burnt offering that is offered. [9*q] Also, every grain offering that is baked in an oven or made in a pan or on a griddle shall belong to the priest who offers it, [10]whereas all grain offerings[r] that are mixed with oil or are dry shall belong to all of Aaron's sons without distinction.

*Communion Sacrifices.** [11s] This is the ritual for the communion sacrifice that is offered to the LORD. [12*] If someone offers it for thanksgiving, that person shall offer it with unleavened cakes mixed with oil, unleavened wafers spread with oil, and cakes made of bran flour mixed with oil and well kneaded. [13]One shall present this offering together with loaves of leavened bread along with the thanksgiving communion sacrifice. [14]From this the individual shall offer one bread of each type of offering as a contribution* to the LORD; this shall belong to the priest who splashes the blood of the communion offering.

[15*t] The meat of the thanksgiving communion sacrifice shall be eaten on the day it is offered; none of it may be kept till the next morning.[u] [16]However, if the sacrifice offered is a votive or a voluntary offering,* it shall be eaten on the day the sacrifice is offered, and on the next day what is left over may be eaten.[v] [17]But what is left over of the meat of the sacrifice on the third day must be burned in the fire. [18]If indeed any of the flesh of the communion sacrifice is eaten on the third day, it shall not be accepted; it will not be reckoned to the credit of the one offering it. Rather it becomes a desecrated meat. Anyone who eats of it shall bear the penalty.*

[19*] Should the meat touch anything unclean, it may not be eaten, but shall be burned in the fire.[w] As for other meat, all who are

**7:1–6** These prescriptions may appear here rather than in 5:14–26 where this offering is first treated because the monetary equivalent of the offering might have been brought instead of an actual animal. See note on 5:15.

**7:9–10** For the distinction between uncooked and cooked grain offerings, see 2:1–10 and note on 2:1. The contradiction between v. 9 and 2:10 may reflect a development in custom, with the distribution in v. 9 coming from earlier times, when sanctuary personnel was more limited.

**7:11–36** This section discusses three types of communion sacrifice: the thanksgiving offering (vv. 12–15), a votive offering, and a voluntary offering (vv. 16–18). The latter two are similar and are thus mentioned together. Verses 19–36 apply to all types of communion sacrifice.

**7:12–13** Four types of breads accompany the thanksgiving offering. Three types are cooked grain offerings comparable to those in 2:4–10. Also required are loaves of leavened bread (see 2:11).

**7:14 Contribution**: Hebrew *terumah*. This does not indicate a particular ritual action. The word simply means "gift, something set apart."

**7:15–18** Sacrifices must be properly consumed for them to be effective (cf. also 19:5–8; 22:30). Similar rules obtain for the Passover offering (Ex 12:10; Nm 9:12; cf. Ex 23:18; 34:25; Dt 16:4) and the ordination offering (Ex 29:34; Lv 8:32).

**7:16 Votive or a voluntary offering**: these are not specific types of offerings but rather motivations for bringing the communion sacrifice (cf. 22:18). A votive offering is brought as the consequence of a promise (vow) made to God. A voluntary offering is a spontaneous gift to God independent of a prior promise. See note on 27:2–13.

**7:18 Bear the penalty**: this refers in many cases to punishment by God (cf. 17:16; 19:8; 20:17, 19; Nm 18:1, 23; 30:16).

**7:19–21** For ritual impurity, see note on 11:1–15:33.

*j:* Lv 4:5; Heb 13:11. *k:* Lv 4:11–12, 21; 8:17; 9:11; 16:27. *l:* Lv 5:14–26. *m:* Lv 6:18. *n:* Lv 3:4. *o:* Lv 6:9. *p:* Lv 2:3. *q:* Lv 2:3–10; Nm 18:9; Ez 44:29. *r:* Lv 2:14–15. *s:* Lv 3. *t:* Lv 19:6–7. *u:* Lv 22:29–30. *v:* Lv 19:5–8. *w:* Lv 12:4.

**The Consecration of Aaron and His Sons**

IN CH 8, Aaron and his sons are consecrated to the priesthood. According to the priestly source, God, many months earlier, had informed Moses that Aaron and his sons were to become his priests (Ex 28) and outlined the details of this ceremony (Ex 29). Now the consecration is to take place.

clean may eat of it. [20]If, however, someone in a state of uncleanness eats the meat of a communion sacrifice belonging to the LORD, that person shall be cut off* [x] from the people. [21]Likewise, if someone touches anything unclean, whether it be human uncleanness or an unclean animal or an unclean loathsome creature, and then eats the meat of the communion sacrifice belonging to the LORD, that person, too, shall be cut off from the people.

***Prohibition Against Blood and Fat.*** [22]The LORD said to Moses: [23]Tell the Israelites: You shall not eat the fat of any ox or sheep or goat.[y] [24]Although the fat of an animal that has died a natural death or has been killed by wild beasts may be put to any other use, you may not eat it.[z] [25]If anyone eats the fat of an animal from which an oblation is made to the LORD, that person shall be cut off from the people. [26a]Wherever you dwell, you shall not eat any blood, whether of bird or of animal. [27]Every person who eats any blood shall be cut off from the people.

***Portions from the Communion Sacrifice for Priests.*** [28]The LORD said to Moses: [29]Tell the Israelites: The person who offers a communion sacrifice to the LORD shall be the one to bring from it the offering to the LORD. [30]The offerer's own hands shall carry the oblations for the LORD: the person shall bring the fat together with the brisket, which is to be raised as an elevated[b] offering* before the LORD. [31]The priest shall burn the fat on the altar,[c] but the brisket belongs to Aaron and his sons. [32]Moreover, from your communion sacrifices you shall give to the priest the right leg as a contribution. [33]The one among Aaron's sons who offers the blood and the fat of the communion offering shall have the right leg as his portion, [34]for from the communion sacrifices of the Israelites I have taken the brisket that is elevated and the leg that is a contribution, and I have given them to Aaron, the priest, and to his sons as their due from the Israelites forever.[d]

[35]This is the priestly share from the oblations for the LORD, allotted to Aaron and his sons on the day they were brought forth to be the priests of the LORD, [36]which the LORD ordered to be given them from the Israelites on the day they were anointed, as their due throughout their generations forever.

***Summary.*** [37]This is the ritual for the burnt offering, the grain offering, the purification offering, the reparation offering, the ordination offering,[e] and the communion sacrifice, [38]which the LORD enjoined on Moses at Mount Sinai at the time when he commanded the Israelites in the wilderness of Sinai to bring their offerings to the LORD.[f]

# II. Ceremony of Ordination

## CHAPTER 8

See RG 77

***Ordination of Aaron and His Sons.**** [1g]The LORD said to Moses: [2]Take Aaron

**7:20 Cut off**: a common term in the Priestly source that cannot always be reduced to a simple English equivalent, since its usage appears to involve a number of associated punishments, some or all of which may come into play in any one instance (see Ex 12:15 and note). All the same, as a punishment from God, to be "cut off" (from one's people) frequently appears to refer to termination of the offender's family line (and perhaps in some cases an early death); see Lv 20:2–3, 20–21; Ru 4:10; Ps 109:13; Mal 2:12.

**7:30 Raised as an elevated offering**: these portions of the sacrifices were specially dedicated by lifting them in presentation before God's abode. The sanctifying effect of this action is clearly seen in 23:17–20; Nm 6:19–20.

**8:1–2** This chapter presents the fulfillment of the commands in Ex 28–29; 30:26–30; and 40:9–15.

*x:* Lv 17:4, 9–10, 14; 18:29; 20:3, 5–6, 17–18; Gn 17:14; Ex 30:33; Nm 15:31; Ps 37:9, 28, 34; 109:13. *y:* Lv 3:17. *z:* Lv 22:8. *a:* Lv 17:10. *b:* Lv 8:27, 29; 9:21; 10:15; 14:12, 21, 24; 23:17, 20; Nm 6:20; 8:13; 18:18. *c:* Lv 3:11, 16. *d:* Ex 29:27–28. *e:* Lv 8:22. *f:* Lv 26:46; 27:34. *g:* Cf. Ex 28–29; 39; 40:12–15.

along with his sons, the vestments, the anointing oil, the bull for a purification offering, the two rams, and the basket of unleavened bread, 3 then assemble the whole community* at the entrance of the tent of meeting. 4 Moses did as the LORD had commanded. When the community[h] had assembled at the entrance of the tent of meeting, 5 Moses told them: "This is what the LORD has ordered to be done." 6 Bringing forward Aaron and his sons, Moses first washed them with water. 7* Then he put the tunic on Aaron,[i] girded him with the sash, clothed him with the robe, placed the ephod on him, and girded him with the ephod's embroidered belt, fastening the ephod on him with it. 8 He then set the breastpiece on him, putting the Urim and Thummim* in it. 9 He put the turban on his head, attaching the gold medallion, the sacred headband,* on the front of the turban, as the LORD had commanded Moses to do.

10* Taking the anointing oil, Moses anointed and consecrated the tabernacle and all that was in it.[j] 11 Then he sprinkled some of the oil seven times on the altar, and anointed the altar, with all its utensils, and the laver, with its base, to consecrate them. 12 He also poured some of the anointing oil on Aaron's head and anointed him, to consecrate him.[k] 13 Moses likewise brought forward Aaron's sons, clothed them with tunics, girded them with sashes, and put skullcaps on them, as the LORD had commanded him to do.

***Ordination Sacrifices.*** 14 He brought forward the bull for a purification offering, and Aaron and his sons laid their hands on its head. 15 When it was slaughtered, Moses took the blood* and with his finger he put it on the horns around the altar, thus purifying the altar.[l] He poured out the rest of the blood at the base of the altar. Thus he consecrated it so that atonement could be made on it. 16 Taking all the fat that was over the inner organs, as well as the lobe of the liver and the two kidneys with their fat,[m] Moses burned them on the altar. 17 The bull, however, with its hide and flesh and dung he burned in the fire outside the camp, as the LORD had commanded Moses to do.[n]

18 He next brought forward the ram of the burnt offering,[o] and Aaron and his sons laid their hands on its head. 19 When it was slaughtered, Moses splashed the blood on all sides of the altar. 20 After the ram was cut up into pieces, Moses burned the head, the cut-up pieces and the suet. 21 After the inner organs and the shanks were washed with water, Moses burned these remaining parts of the ram on the altar. It was a burnt offering for a sweet aroma, an oblation to the LORD, as the LORD had commanded Moses.

22* Then he brought forward the second ram, the ordination ram,[p] and Aaron and his sons laid their hands on its head. 23 When it was slaughtered, Moses took some of its blood and put it on the lobe of Aaron's right ear, on the thumb of his right hand, and on the big toe* of his right foot.[q] 24 Moses had

**8:3–4 Community**: this word (Heb. *'edah*) may refer to tribal leaders, all adult males, or the entire nation. The last is probably intended here.

**8:7–9, 13** On the priestly clothing, see Ex 28–29. **Ephod**: according to Ex 28:6–14, the term for one of Aaron's special vestments made of gold thread, with multicolored woolen thread woven into it as well as fine linen. In appearance it resembled a kind of apron, hung on the priest by shoulder straps and secured by an embroidered belt. A somewhat simpler "apron" was presumably worn by other priests (1 Sm 22:18).

**8:8 The Urim and Thummim**: see Ex 28:30 and note there. Although these terms and the object(s) they refer to are still unexplained, they appear to be small objects that functioned like dice or lots to render a decision for those making an inquiry of God, perhaps originally in legal cases where the guilt of the accused could not otherwise be determined (cf. Ex 28:30; Nm 27:21; Dt 33:8; 1 Sm 28:6; Ezr 2:63; Neh 7:65).

**8:9 Headband**: see Ex 39:30–31. The gold medallion, together with its cords, comprises the sacred headband.

**8:10–12** Anointing with the specially prepared oil (cf. Ex 30:22–33) is one of the means of making objects and persons holy by setting them apart for a special function or purpose.

**8:15 Moses took the blood**: Moses is acting as a priest in this chapter.

**8:22–32** The priestly ordination offering is a unique type of sacrifice but similar in many respects to the communion sacrifice (chap. 3; 7:11–34).

**8:23–24 Lobe . . . thumb . . . toe**: these parts of the body are meant to represent the body as a whole. The application of the blood symbolizes the priests' passing from a profane to a holy state. Cf. 14:14–17.

*h:* Nm 27:19. *i:* Sir 45:8–13; Heb 5:1–4; 7:1–28. *j:* Ex 30:26. *k:* Sir 45:15. *l:* Heb 9:22. *m:* Lv 3:4–5; 4:8–11. *n:* Lv 6:23. *o:* Lv 1:10–13. *p:* Lv 7:37. *q:* Lv 14:14, 17.

the sons of Aaron also come forward, and he put some of the blood on the lobes of their right ears, on the thumbs of their right hands, and on the big toes of their right feet. The rest of the blood he splashed on all the sides of the altar. 25He then took the fat: the fatty tail and all the fat over the inner organs, the lobe of the liver and the two kidneys with their fat, and likewise the right thigh; 26from the basket of unleavened bread that was set before the LORD he took one unleavened cake, one loaf of bread made with oil, and one wafer; these he placed on top of the portions of fat and the right thigh. 27He then put all these things upon the palms of Aaron and his sons, whom he had raise them as an elevated offering before the LORD.[r] 28When Moses had removed them from their palms, he burned them on the altar with the burnt offering. They were an ordination offering for a sweet aroma, an oblation to the LORD. 29He then took the brisket and raised it as an elevated offering before the LORD; this was Moses' own portion of the ordination ram, as the LORD had commanded Moses. 30Taking some of the anointing oil and some of the blood that was on the altar, Moses sprinkled it upon Aaron and his vestments, as well as his sons and their vestments, thus consecrating both Aaron and his vestments and his sons and their vestments.[s]

31Moses said to Aaron and his sons, "Boil the meat at the entrance of the tent of meeting, and there eat it with the bread that is in the basket of the ordination offering, in keeping with the command I have received: 'Aaron and his sons shall eat of it.' 32What is left over of the meat and the bread you shall burn in the fire. 33Moreover, you are not to depart* from the entrance of the tent of meeting for seven days, until the days of your ordination are completed; for your ordination is to last for seven days. 34What has been done today the LORD has commanded be done, to make atonement for you. 35You must remain at the entrance of the tent of meeting day and night for seven days, carrying out the prescriptions of the LORD, so that you do not die, for this is the command I have received."[t] 36So Aaron and his sons did all that the LORD had commanded through Moses.

## CHAPTER 9

See RG 77

***Octave of the Ordination.*** 1On the eighth day* [u] Moses summoned Aaron and his sons, together with the elders of Israel, 2and said to Aaron, "Take a calf of the herd for a purification offering and a ram for a burnt offering, both without blemish, and offer them before the LORD. 3* Tell the Israelites, too: Take a he-goat for a purification offering, a calf and a lamb, both unblemished yearlings, for a burnt offering, 4and an ox and a ram for a communion sacrifice, to sacrifice before the LORD, along with a grain offering mixed with oil; for today the LORD will appear to you." 5So they brought what Moses had ordered before the tent of meeting. When the whole community had come forward and stood before the LORD, 6* Moses said, "This is what the LORD orders you to do, that the glory of the LORD may appear to you. 7Approach the altar," Moses then told Aaron, "and make your purification offering and your burnt offering in atonement for yourself and for your household;* then make the offering of the people in atonement for them, as the LORD has commanded."[v]

8Approaching the altar, Aaron first slaughtered the calf of the purification offering that was his own offering. 9When his sons presented the blood to him, he dipped his finger in the blood and put it on the horns of the altar.[w] The rest of the blood he poured out at the base of the altar. 10He then burned on the altar the fat, the kidneys and the lobe of the

**8:33–35 You are not to depart**: the tenor and context of this requirement in vv. 33 and 35 seem to indicate that the priests are not to leave the sanctuary precincts for any reason. **Your ordination is to last for seven days . . . what has been done today . . . be done**: the consecration rites in Exodus are to be performed every day for seven days (cf. Ex 29:30, 35–37).

**9:1 Eighth day**: this is the conclusion of the priestly initiation ceremony.

**9:3–4** The seven-day consecration of the priests in chap. 8 did not require sacrifices from the community. Now communal sacrifices as well as priestly sacrifices are required.

**9:6–21** Aaron and his sons now perform the offerings, instead of Moses (see note on 8:15).

**9:7 For your household**: unlike the Septuagint, the Hebrew reads *be'ad ha'am*, "for the people."

*r:* Lv 7:30. *s:* Ex 40:15. *t:* Lv 10:7. *u:* Lv 8:33. *v:* Lv 16:3–5. *w:* Lv 4:25, 30, 34.

liver from the purification offering, as the LORD had commanded Moses; 11 but the flesh and the hide he burned in the fire outside the camp.[x] 12 Then Aaron slaughtered the burnt offering. When his sons brought him the blood, he splashed it on all sides of the altar. 13 They then brought him the pieces and the head of the burnt offering, and he burned them on the altar. 14 Having washed the inner organs and the shanks, he burned these also with the burnt offering on the altar.[y]

15 Then he had the people's offering brought. Taking the goat that was for the people's purification offering, he slaughtered it and offered it as a purification offering as before. 16 Then he brought forward the burnt offering and offered it according to procedure. 17 He then presented the grain offering; taking a handful of it, he burned it on the altar, in addition to the morning burnt offering.[z] 18 Finally he slaughtered the ox and the ram, the communion sacrifice of the people. When his sons brought him the blood, Aaron splashed it on all sides of the altar.[a] 19 The portions of fat from the ox and from the ram, the fatty tail, the covering fat, the kidneys, and the lobe of the liver 20 they placed on top of the briskets. Aaron burned the fat pieces on the altar, 21 but the briskets and the right thigh he raised as an elevated offering[b] before the LORD, as the LORD had commanded Moses.

***Revelation of the Lord's Glory.*** 22* Aaron then raised his hands over the people and blessed[c] them. When he came down from offering the purification offering, the burnt offering, and the communion offering, 23 Moses and Aaron went into the tent of meeting. On coming out they blessed the people. Then the glory of the LORD appeared to all the people. 24* Fire came forth from the LORD's presence and consumed the burnt offering and the fat on the altar.[d] Seeing this, all the people shouted with joy and fell prostrate.

## CHAPTER 10

See RG 77

***Nadab and Abihu.*** 1* Aaron's sons Nadab and Abihu took their censers and, putting incense on the fire they had set in them,[e] they offered before the LORD unauthorized fire, such as he had not commanded. 2 Fire therefore came forth from the LORD's presence and consumed them,[f] so that they died in the LORD's presence. 3 Moses then said to Aaron, "This is as the LORD said:

> Through those near to me I will be sanctified;
> in the sight of all the people I will obtain glory."* [g]

But Aaron said nothing. 4* Then Moses summoned Mishael and Elzaphan, the sons of Aaron's uncle Uzziel, with the order, "Come, carry your kinsmen from before the sanctuary to a place outside the camp." 5 So they drew near and carried them by means of their tunics outside the camp, as Moses had commanded.

***Conduct of the Priests.*** 6 Moses said to Aaron and his sons Eleazar and Ithamar, "Do not dishevel your hair[h] or tear your garments,[i] lest you die and bring God's wrath also on the whole community. While your kindred, the rest of the house of Israel, may mourn for those whom the LORD's fire has burned up, 7 you shall not go beyond the entrance of the tent of meeting,[j] else you shall die; for the anointing oil of the LORD is upon you." So they did as Moses told them.

**9:22–23** The people are blessed twice. For the possible content of the blessing, compare the priestly blessing in Nm 6:22–27. Solomon offers a double blessing at the dedication of the Temple (1 Kgs 8:14–21, 55–61).

**9:24** The theophany consists of a fire that apparently comes from the tent of meeting. God's fiery glory is also manifested in the pillar of cloud and fire that led the Israelites and rested over the tent of meeting (Ex 13:21; 40:38; Nm 9:15–23; 10:11). On God's fiery glory, see also Ex 24:17; Ez 1:27–28.

**10:1–2** Nadab and Abihu are the older sons of Aaron (Ex 6:23–24). Their sin apparently involves using embers from an unapproved source instead of the altar (cf. 16:12). The fire that destroys them is the same type found in 9:24.

**10:3** The explanation for the divine reaction indicates that improper cultic actions desecrate God and compromise God's glory. Desecration evokes divine punishment (cf. Ex 28:43; Nm 4:15, 19–20). **Those near to me**: i.e., cultic officials.

**10:4–5** Moses has lay people remove the bodies so that the priests can continue their cultic activities free of contamination by a corpse (cf. Nm 19).

*x:* Lv 6:23. *y:* Lv 1:5–9. *z:* Nm 28:23; 2 Kgs 16:15; Ez 46:13–15. *a:* Lv 3:2. *b:* Lv 7:30–34. *c:* Nm 6:22–27. *d:* 1 Kgs 18:38; 2 Chr 7:1; 2 Mc 2:10; cf. Ex 24:16–17. *e:* Lv 16:1; Nm 3:4; 26:61; 1 Chr 24:2. *f:* Nm 16:35; cf. Lv 9:24. *g:* Lv 21:17, 21; Nm 20:12. *h:* Lv 13:45. *i:* Lv 21:5–6, 10–12. *j:* Lv 8:33–35; 21:12.

8 The LORD said to Aaron: 9 When you are
to go to the tent of meeting, you and your
sons are forbidden, by a perpetual statute
throughout your generations, to drink any
wine or strong drink, lest you die.[k] 10 You
must be able to distinguish between what is
sacred and what is profane, and between
what is clean and what is unclean;*[l] 11 and
you must be able to teach the Israelites all
the statutes that the LORD has given them
through Moses.

***The Eating of the Priestly Portions.*** 12 Moses said to Aaron and his surviving sons, Eleazar and Ithamar, "Take the grain offering*
left over from the oblations to the LORD, and
eat it beside the altar in the form of unleavened cakes, since it is most holy. 13 You must
eat it in a sacred place because it is your and
your sons' due from the oblations to the
LORD; such is the command I have received.
14[m] The brisket of the elevated offering and
the leg* of the contribution, however, you
and your sons and daughters may eat, in a
clean place; for these have been assigned to
you and your children as your due from the
communion sacrifices of the Israelites.
15 The leg of the contribution and the brisket
of the elevated offering shall be brought in
with the oblations of fat to be raised as an elevated offering before the LORD. They shall
belong to you and your children as your due
forever, as the LORD has commanded."

16 Moses inquired closely about the goat of
the purification offering* and discovered
that it had all been burned. So he was angry
with the surviving sons of Aaron, Eleazar
and Ithamar, and said, 17[n] "Why did you not
eat the purification offering in the sacred
place, since it is most holy? It has been given
to you that you might remove the guilt of the
community and make atonement for them
before the LORD. 18 Since its blood was not
brought inside the sanctuary, you should certainly have eaten the offering in the sanctuary, as I was commanded." 19 Aaron answered Moses, "Even though they presented
their purification offering and burnt offering
before the LORD today, still this misfortune
has befallen me. Had I then eaten of the purification offering today, would it have been
pleasing to the LORD?" 20 On hearing this,
Moses was satisfied.

## III. Laws Regarding Ritual Purity*

### CHAPTER 11

See RG 77–78

***Clean and Unclean Meats.**** 1[o] The
LORD said to Moses and Aaron: 2 Speak to
the Israelites and tell them: Of all land animals these are the ones you may eat: 3 Any
animal that has hoofs you may eat, provided
it is cloven-footed and chews the cud. 4 But

**10:10 Sacred and . . . profane . . . clean and . . . unclean**: something or someone may be either sacred or profane (i.e., ordinary, not set apart), and at the same time clean or unclean. Priests would be particularly concerned about keeping what is unclean away from the sacred.

**10:12–13 Grain offering**: this is the grain offering of the people of 9:4, 17. Only the token offering had been offered; the rest was for the priests' consumption.

**10:14 Brisket . . . leg**: these are from the Israelites' communion sacrifices in 9:4, 18–21.

**10:16–20 Goat of the purification offering**: this is the people's purification offering of 9:3, 15. Since its blood is not brought into the sanctuary, then, according to 6:17–23, this is the type of purification offering which is to be eaten by the priests in a holy place. **Eleazar and Ithamar**: they burned the entire goat of the people's purification offering (9:15) instead of eating it in a sacred place (6:19) to remove ritually the sin of the community by the ingestion of the meat of the offering. Aaron's defense of this action of his sons is somewhat vague; he merely alludes to the loss suffered in the death of Nadab and Abihu, without giving an explicit reason for Eleazar and Ithamar's not eating the people's purification offering, as required.

**11:1–15:33** Priestly legislation manifests two types of impurity or uncleanness: tolerated and prohibited. Prohibited impurity arises from various sins (e.g., 4:1–5; 5:2–3; 18:6–23; 20:2–5; Nm 5:13–14; 6:6–7). Tolerated impurity has three main sources: certain dead bodies (animal and human; cf. Lv 11 and Nm 19), various regular and abnormal genital discharges (Lv 12; 15), and diseases (specifically "scaly infection," chaps. 13–14). An additional tolerated impurity is that generated by the cult in order to rectify the effect of these impurities or sins (cf. chap. 4; 16:26, 28).

**11:1–47** Apart from the introduction and conclusion (vv. 1–2a, 46–47), this chapter has three sections: (1) prohibitions against eating certain land, water, and air animals (vv. 2b–23); (2) consequences of contact with various animals (vv. 24–41); (3) a prohibition against eating small land animals, which is motivated by the requirement that Israel be holy as God is holy (vv. 41–45). These animals are impure only when dead. Cf. Dt 14:3–21.

*k:* Ez 44:21. *l:* Lv 11:47; 20:25; Ez 22:26; 44:23. *m:* Lv 7:34. *n:* Lv 6:18–19. *o:* Lv 27:11, 27; Gn 7:2–3, 8–9; Dt 14:3–21.

you shall not eat[p] any of the following from among those that only chew the cud or only have hoofs: the camel, which indeed chews the cud, but does not have hoofs and is therefore unclean for you; 5the rock hyrax,* which indeed chews the cud, but does not have hoofs and is therefore unclean for you; 6the hare, which indeed chews the cud, but does not have hoofs and is therefore unclean for you; 7and the pig,[q] which does indeed have hoofs and is cloven-footed, but does not chew the cud and is therefore unclean for you. 8You shall not eat their meat, and you shall not touch their carcasses; they are unclean for you.

9Of the various creatures that live in the water, you may eat the following: whatever in the seas or in river waters that has both fins and scales you may eat.[r] 10But of the creatures that swarm in the water or of animals that otherwise live in the water, whether in the sea or in the rivers, all those that lack either fins or scales are loathsome for you, 11and shall always be loathsome to you. Their meat you shall not eat, and their carcasses you shall loathe. 12Every water creature that lacks fins or scales is loathsome for you.

13Of the birds,* these you shall loathe; they shall not be eaten, they are loathsome: the griffon vulture, the bearded vulture, the black vulture, 14the kite, the various species of falcons, 15the various species of crows, 16the eagle owl, the kestrel, the long-eared owl, the various species of hawks, 17the little owl, the cormorant, the screech owl, 18the barn owl, the horned owl, the osprey, 19the stork, the various species of herons, the hoopoe, and the bat.

20The various winged insects that walk on all fours are loathsome for you. 21But of the various winged insects that walk on all fours you may eat those that have legs jointed above their feet for leaping on the ground; 22hence of these you may eat the following: the various kinds of locusts, the various kinds of bald locusts, the various kinds of crickets, and the various kinds of grasshoppers.[s] 23All other winged insects that have four legs are loathsome for you.

24You become unclean by the following—anyone who touches their carcasses shall be unclean until evening,[t] 25and anyone who carries any part of their carcasses shall wash his garments and be unclean until evening—26by all hoofed animals that are not cloven-footed or do not chew the cud; they are unclean for you; anyone who touches them becomes unclean. 27Also by the various quadrupeds that walk on paws; they are unclean for you; anyone who touches their carcasses shall be unclean until evening, 28and anyone who carries their carcasses shall wash his garments and be unclean until evening. They are unclean for you.

29Of the creatures that swarm on the ground, the following are unclean for you: the rat, the mouse, the various kinds of lizards, 30the gecko, the spotted lizard, the agama, the skink, and the chameleon. 31Among the various swarming creatures, these are unclean for you. Everyone who touches them when they are dead shall be unclean until evening. 32Everything on which one of them falls when dead becomes unclean, including any article of wood, cloth, leather or goat hair—any article of which use can be made. It must be immersed in water and remain unclean until evening, when it again becomes clean. 33Should any of these creatures fall into a clay vessel, everything in it becomes unclean, and the vessel itself you must break. 34Any food that can be eaten which makes contact with water, and any liquid that may be drunk, in any such vessel become unclean. 35Any object on which any part of their carcasses falls becomes unclean; if it is an oven or stove, this

**11:5–6** According to modern zoology, **the rock hyrax** (*hyrax Syriacus*) is classified as an ungulate, and **the hare** as a rodent; neither is a ruminant. They appear to chew their food as the true ruminants do, and it is upon this appearance that the classification in the text is based.

**11:13–23, 30 Birds**: the term is broader, including all animals that fly (including bats, v. 19, and flying insects, vv. 20–23). The identification of the various Hebrew names for these birds and reptiles is in many cases uncertain.

*p:* Jgs 13:4, 7; Is 66:17; Ez 4:12–14. *q:* Prv 11:22; Is 65:4; 66:17; Mt 7:6; 8:30–32; Mk 5:11–16; Lk 8:32–33; 15:15–16. *r:* Jn 21:9–13. *s:* Mt 3:4; Mk 1:6. *t:* Lv 5:2; 7:21.

## Purity, Cleanliness, and Ritual

IN THE THINKING of the ancient Israelites, there were certain boundaries within nature that should not be crossed or confused. These boundaries separated things of one kind from things of another kind, and things that went together were seen to have certain characteristics in common. Take, for instance, the category of "creatures that live in the water" (11:9): along with living in the water, these creatures were supposed to have fins and scales. If a creature—such as an oyster or a lobster—lived in the waters but did not have fins and scales, it did not fulfill all of the characteristics of its kind, and it therefore confused the boundaries of "creatures that live in the water" and was unclean. In the same way, the Israelites believed that animals that chewed the cud—ruminants, such as the cow—should have cloven, or divided, hoofs. The cow has divided hoofs, so it is clean. But the pig, which has divided hoofs, does not chew the cud, so it is unclean. It has confused a natural category, and is therefore to be avoided. See also Deuteronomy 14:3-21.

The clearest and strongest boundary was the one between life and death, and one had to be very careful when dealing with anything that was dead.

must be broken to pieces; they are unclean
and shall always be unclean to you. [36]How-
ever, a spring or a cistern for collecting water remains clean; but whoever touches such
an animal's carcass becomes unclean. [37]If
any part of their carcasses falls on any sort of
grain that is to be sown, it remains clean;
[38]but if the grain has become moistened, it
becomes unclean to you when any part of
their carcasses falls on it.
[39]* [u] When one of the animals that you
could otherwise eat dies of itself, anyone
who touches its carcass shall be unclean until evening; [40]and anyone who eats any part
of its carcass shall wash his garments and be
unclean until evening;[v] so also, anyone who
carries its carcass shall wash his garments
and be unclean until evening.
[41]All the creatures that swarm on the
ground are loathsome and shall not be eaten.
[42]Whether it crawls on its belly, goes on all
fours, or has many legs—any creature that
swarms on the earth—you shall not eat
them; they are loathsome. [43]Do not make
yourselves loathsome by any swarming
creature nor defile yourselves with them and
so become unclean by them.[w] [44]For I, the
LORD, am your God. You shall make and
keep yourselves holy,* because I am holy.[x]
You shall not make yourselves unclean,
then, by any swarming creature that crawls
on the ground. [45]Since I, the LORD, am the
one who brought you up from the land of
Egypt that I might be your God, you shall be
holy, because I am holy.
[46]This is the instruction for land animals,
birds, and all the creatures that move about
in the water, as well as any animal that
swarms on the ground, [47]that you may distinguish between the clean and the unclean,
and between creatures that may be eaten and
those that may not be eaten.[y]

### CHAPTER 12

See RG 77–78

*Uncleanness of Childbirth.* [1]The
LORD said to Moses: [2]Tell the Israelites:
When a woman has a child, giving birth to a
boy, she shall be unclean* for seven days,

**11:39–40** These animals create uncleanness, but are not prohibited as food (cf. 17:15–16). Priests who have a higher degree of holiness than other Israelites may not eat these animals (22:8; cf. Ez 44:31). Cf. Ex 22:30; Dt 14:21.

**11:44–45 Keep yourselves holy . . . you shall be holy:** a similar idea is expressed in 20:25–26. There, distinguishing between the animals is compared to God's distinguishing between the peoples and choosing Israel.

**12:2–5** The mother has two stages of uncleanness or impurity: the first where her uncleanness is as severe as during her menstrual period and is contagious to profane persons and objects (cf. 15:19–24), and the second where she does not contaminate persons and objects but is still impure to what is holy, such as the sanctuary (12:4) or sacrifices. The implication is that in the second stage she may resume sexual relations with her husband (which would be prohibited in the first stage according to 18:19).

*u:* Lv 17:15–16; 22:8; Ex 22:30; Ez 4:12–14; 44:31. *v:* Lv 17:15; 22:8. *w:* Lv 20:25–26. *x:* Lv 19:2; 20:7, 26; Mt 5:48; 1 Pt 1:16. *y:* Lv 10:10.

with the same uncleanness as during her menstrual period.[z] [3]On the eighth day, the flesh of the boy's foreskin shall be circumcised,*[a] [4]and then she shall spend thirty-three days more in a state of blood purity; she shall not touch anything sacred nor enter the sanctuary till the days of her purification are fulfilled. [5]If she gives birth to a girl, for fourteen days she shall be as unclean as during her menstrual period, after which she shall spend sixty-six days* in a state of blood purity.

[6]* When the days of her purification for a son or for a daughter are fulfilled,[b] she shall bring to the priest at the entrance of the tent of meeting a yearling lamb for a burnt offering and a pigeon or a turtledove for a purification offering. [7]The priest shall offer them before the LORD to make atonement for her, and thus she will be clean again after her flow of blood. Such is the ritual for the woman who gives birth to a child, male or female. [8]If, however, she cannot afford a lamb,[c] she may take two turtledoves or two pigeons,[d] the one for a burnt offering and the other for a purification offering. The priest shall make atonement for her, and thus she will again be clean.

## CHAPTER 13

See RG 77–78

***Scaly Infection.**** [1]The LORD said to Moses and Aaron: [2][e] When someone has on the skin a mark, lesion, or blotch which appears to develop into a scaly infection, the person shall be brought to Aaron, the priest, or to one of the priests among his sons. [3]If the priest, upon examination of the skin's infection, finds that the hair on the infection has turned white and the infection itself appears to be deeper than the skin,* it is indeed a scaly infection; the priest, on seeing this, shall declare the person unclean. [4]* If, however, the blotch on the skin is white, but does not seem to be deeper than the skin, nor has the hair turned white, the priest shall quarantine the afflicted person for seven days.* [5]Should the priest, upon examination on the seventh day, find that the infection has remained unchanged in color and has not spread on the skin, the priest shall quarantine the person for another seven days. [6]Should the priest, upon examination again on the seventh day, find that the infection is now faded and has not spread on the skin, the priest shall declare the person clean; it was merely a scab. The person shall wash his garments* and so become clean. [7]But if,

**12:3** Circumcision is the sign of the covenant between God and Israel (Gn 17:1–27) and allows full participation in the religious community (Ex 12:43–49; Jos 5:2–10). This command was fulfilled after Jesus' birth (Lk 2:21).

**12:5 If she gives birth to a girl . . . sixty-six days**: while the longer period of uncleanness following the birth of a girl, compared to that following the birth of a boy, might reflect the relative disparity in social status between men and women in ancient Israel (and attested in other cultures), this is by no means certain. There is no simple correlation in the Bible between the worth of something and the degree of impurity it can occasion.

**12:6–8** Certain tolerated impurities (see note on 11:1–15:33) are strong enough to pollute the sanctuary and require purification offerings, including the parturient (see also 14:10–32; 15:13–15, 28–30). Cf. note on 4:3. Mary fulfilled the command of bringing sacrifices after the birth of Jesus (Lk 2:22–24).

**13:1–14:57** These chapters deal with scaly or fungal infections (Hebrew *sāraʻat*). The older translation "leprosy" is misleading because *sāraʻat* refers to not just one but several chronic and enduring skin diseases in human beings. The disease known as "leprosy" (Hansen's disease) is probably not included among the conditions described in the chapter. Also the term *sāraʻat* refers to fungal growths in fabrics and on the walls of houses. The reason why these conditions, and not other diseases, were considered unclean may be that they were quite visible, associated with death (cf. Nm 12:9–12), and traditionally connected with punishment by the deity (Lv 14:34; Dt 28:27, 35; 2 Sm 3:29; 2 Kgs 5:26–27; 2 Chr 26:16–21).

**13:3** The symptoms of white hair and depth (perhaps a subcutaneous lesion) do not clearly correlate with known skin diseases or lesions. It may be that the symptoms are a hybrid ideal that do not reflect reality and are the result of priestly systematization. The same judgment applies to the conditions in vv. 10–11, 20, 25; cf. note on vv. 12–17.

**13:4–8** The symptoms here involve a flaky patch of skin that spreads after one week or stays the same after two. This correlates with many skin diseases, such as psoriasis, seborrhoeic dermatitis, certain mycotic infections, patchy eczema, and pityriasis rosea.

**13:4 Quarantine . . . seven days**: unless lesions have unmistakable symptoms of scaly infection, time is needed to distinguish disease from a condition which is following the natural course of healing and remission. Cf. vv. 5, 21, 26, 27, 31, 33, 50, 54; 14:38.

**13:6 Wash his garments**: even suspected scaly infections create some impurity, not just diagnosed infections (vv. 45–46).

*z:* Lv 15:19. *a:* Gn 17:12; Jn 7:22. *b:* Lk 2:22–24. *c:* Lv 14:21–22. *d:* Lv 1:14; Lk 2:24. *e:* Lv 22:4; Ex 4:6; Nm 5:2–3; Dt 24:8; 2 Sm 3:29; 2 Kgs 5:1, 3–7, 11, 27; Mk 1:40–45.

after the person was examined by the priest
and declared clean, the scab spreads at all on
the skin, the person shall once more be examined by the priest. [8]Should the priest, upon examination, find that the scab has indeed
spread on the skin, he shall declare the person
unclean; it is a scaly infection.

[9]When someone is afflicted with a scaly
infection, that person shall be brought to the
priest. [10]Should the priest, upon examination, find that there is a white mark on the
skin which has turned the hair white and that
there is raw flesh in it, [11]it is a chronic scaly
infection on the skin. The priest shall declare
the person unclean without quarantine, since
the individual is certainly unclean. [12]* If the
scaly infection breaks out on the skin and, as
far as the priest can see, covers all the skin of
the afflicted person from head to foot,
[13]should the priest then, upon examination,
find that the scaly infection does cover the
whole body, he shall declare the afflicted
person clean; since the person has turned
completely white; that individual is clean.
[14]But as soon as raw flesh appears, the individual is unclean; [15]on observing the raw
flesh, the priest shall declare the person unclean, because raw flesh is unclean; it is a
scaly infection. [16]If, however, the raw flesh
again turns white, the person shall return to
the priest; [17]should the latter, upon examination, find that the infection has indeed turned
white, he shall declare the afflicted person
clean; the individual is clean.

[18]If a boil appeared on a person's skin
which later healed, [19]should now in the place
of the boil a white mark or a reddish white
blotch develop, the person shall be examined
by the priest. [20]If the latter, upon examination,
finds that it is deeper than the skin and that the
hair has turned white, he shall declare the person unclean; it is a scaly infection that has
broken out in the boil. [21]But if the priest, upon
examination, finds that there is no white hair
in it and that it is not deeper than the skin and
is faded, the priest shall quarantine the person
for seven days. [22]If it has then spread on the
skin, the priest shall declare the person unclean; it is an infection. [23]But if the blotch remains the same without spreading, it is
merely the scar of the boil; the priest shall
therefore declare the person clean.

[24]If there was a burn on a person's skin,
and the burned area now becomes a reddish
white or a white blotch, [25]when the priest,
upon examination, finds that the hair has
turned white in the blotch and this seems to
be deeper than the skin, it is a scaly infection
that has broken out in the burn; the priest
shall therefore declare the person unclean; it
is a scaly infection. [26]But if the priest, upon
examination, finds that there is no white hair
in the blotch and that this is not deeper than
the skin and is faded, the priest shall quarantine the person for seven days. [27]Should the
priest, upon examination on the seventh day,
find that it has spread at all on the skin, he
shall declare the person unclean; it is a scaly
infection. [28]But if the blotch remains the
same without spreading on the skin and is
faded, it is merely the spot of the burn; the
priest shall therefore declare the person
clean, since it is only the scar of the burn.

[29]* When a man or a woman has an infection on the head or in the beard, [30]should the
priest, upon examination, find that the infection appears to be deeper than the skin and
that there is fine yellow hair in it, the priest
shall declare the person unclean; it is a scall.
It is a scaly infection of the head or beard.
[31]But if the priest, upon examining the scall
infection, finds that it does not appear to be
deeper than the skin, though the hair in it may
not be black, the priest shall quarantine the
scall-stricken person for seven days. [32]Should
the priest, upon examining the infection on
the seventh day find that the scall has not
spread and has no yellow hair in it and does
not seem to be deeper than the skin, [33]the person shall shave, but not the scall spot. Then
the priest shall quarantine the scall-diseased
person for another seven days. [34]If the priest,
upon examining the scall on the seventh day,
finds that it has not spread on the skin and that

**13:12–17** This is not a paradox, namely where a limited lesion is impure but one that covers the whole body is pure. Rather, a white lesion that lacks ulcerated skin ("raw flesh") is pure, even if it covers the whole body. This formulation reflects priestly interest in systematization.

**13:29–37** The symptoms in this unit may include either favus (a mycotic infection) or a protein deficiency syndrome (Kwashiorkor) where the hair may be fine and copper-red to yellow.

it does not appear to be deeper than the skin, he shall declare the person clean; the latter shall wash his garments, and will thus be clean. [35]But if the scall spreads at all on the skin after the person has been declared clean— [36]should the priest, upon examination, find that the scall has indeed spread on the skin, he need not look for yellow hair; the individual is unclean. [37]If, however, the scall has remained unchanged in color and black hair has grown in it, the disease has been healed; the person is clean, and the priest shall declare the individual clean.

[38]* When the skin of a man or a woman is spotted with several white blotches, [39]if the priest, upon examination, finds that the blotches on the skin are pale white, it is only tetter that has broken out on the skin, and the person therefore is clean.

[40]When a man loses the hair of his head, he is simply bald on the crown and not unclean.[f] [41]So too, if he loses the hair on the front of his head, he is simply bald on the forehead and not unclean. [42]But when there is a reddish white infection on his bald crown or bald forehead, it is a scaly infection that is breaking out there. [43]If the priest, upon examination, finds that the infection spot on the bald area on the crown or forehead has the same reddish white appearance as that of a scaly infection of the skin, [44]the man has a scaly infection and is unclean. The priest shall declare him unclean; his infection is on his head.

[45]* The garments of one afflicted with a scaly infection shall be rent and the hair disheveled,[g] and the mustache covered.[h] The individual shall cry out, "Unclean, unclean!" [46]As long as the infection is present, the person shall be unclean. Being unclean, that individual shall dwell apart, taking up residence outside the camp.[i]

***Fungal Infection of Fabrics and Leather.*** [47]When a fungal infection is on a garment of wool or of linen, [48]or on the warp and woof* of linen or wool, or on a hide or anything made of leather, [49]if the infection on the garment or hide, or on the warp or woof, or on any leather article is greenish or reddish, the thing is indeed a fungal infection and must be examined by the priest. [50]Having examined the infection, the priest shall quarantine the infected article for seven days. [51]If the priest, upon inspecting the infection on the seventh day, finds that it has spread on the garment, or on the warp or woof, or on the leather, whatever be its use, the infection is a harmful fungus; the article is unclean. [52]He shall therefore burn up the garment, or the warp or woof, be it of wool or linen, or any leather article which is infected; since it is a harmful fungus, it must be destroyed by fire. [53]But if the priest, upon examination, finds that it has not spread on the garment, or on the warp or woof, or on the leather article, [54]he shall give orders to have the infected article washed and then quarantined for another seven days. [55]If the priest, upon examination after the infection was washed, finds that it has not changed its color, even though it may not have spread, the article is unclean. You shall burn it with fire. It is a fray, be it on its inner or outer side. [56]But if the priest, upon examination, finds that the infection has faded after the washing, he shall cut it out of the garment, or the leather, or the warp or woof. [57]If, however, the infection again appears on the garment, or on the warp or woof, or on the leather article, it is still virulent and you shall burn the thing infected with fire. [58]But if, after the washing, the infection has disappeared from the garment, or the warp or woof, or the leather article, the thing shall be washed a second time, and

**13:38–39** This may refer to vitiligo, where patches of the skin and hair lose pigmentation.

**13:45–46** The symbolic association with death is found in the mourning activities in which those diagnosed with these afflictions engage: rending clothes, disheveling the hair, and covering the mouth. They are also excluded from the camp. Cf. examples of exclusion in Nm 5:1–4; 12:14–15; 2 Kgs 7:3–10; 15:5; 2 Chr 26:21. Persons with scaly infections must have been able to pollute others in the priestly system, though this is not stated. Hence, they must cry out "Unclean, unclean!" to warn others of their presence.

**13:48 Warp and woof**: it is possible that the nature of the weave allowed fungus to grow separately along warp or woof. Otherwise, this may refer to the yarns before they are woven together.

*f:* 2 Kgs 2:23. *g:* Lv 10:6. *h:* Mi 3:7. *i:* Lv 14:3; Nm 5:2; 12:14–15; 2 Kgs 7:3–10; 15:5; 2 Chr 26:21; Mt 26:6; Mk 14:3; Lk 17:11–19.

thus it will be clean. 59 This is the instruction for a fungal[j] infection on a garment of wool or linen, or on a warp or woof, or on any leather article, to determine whether it is clean or unclean.

## CHAPTER 14

See RG 77-78

### *Purification After Scaly Infection.*

1* The LORD said to Moses: 2[k] This is the ritual for someone that had a scaly infection at the time of that person's purification.[l] The individual shall be brought to the priest, 3 who is to go outside the camp.[m] If the priest, upon inspection, finds that the scaly infection has healed in the afflicted person, 4 he shall order that two live, clean birds,* as well as some cedar wood, scarlet yarn, and hyssop be obtained for the one who is to be purified.[n] 5* The priest shall then order that one of the birds be slaughtered over an earthen vessel with fresh water in it. 6 Taking the living bird with the cedar wood, the scarlet yarn and the hyssop, the priest shall dip them, including the live bird, in the blood of the bird that was slaughtered over the fresh water, 7 and then sprinkle seven times on the person to be purified from the scaly infection. When he has thus purified that person, he shall let the living bird fly away over the countryside.[o] 8 The person being purified shall then wash his garments, shave off all hair, and bathe in water,* and so become clean. After this the person may come inside the camp, but shall still remain outside his or her tent for seven days.[p] 9 On the seventh day this individual shall again shave off all hair, of the head, beard, and eyebrows—all hair must be shaved—and also wash his garments and bathe the body in water, and so become clean.

10 On the eighth day the individual shall take two unblemished male lambs, one unblemished yearling ewe lamb, three tenths of an ephah of bran flour mixed with oil for a grain offering, and one log* of oil. 11 The priest who performs the purification ceremony shall place the person who is being purified, as well as all these offerings, before the LORD at the entrance of the tent of meeting. 12 Taking one of the male lambs, the priest shall present it as a reparation offering,[q] along with the log of oil, raising them as an elevated[r] offering before the LORD. 13 This lamb shall be slaughtered in the sacred place where the purification offering and the burnt offering are slaughtered, because the reparation offering is like the purification offering; it belongs to the priest and is most holy. 14*[s] Then the priest shall take some of the blood of the reparation offering and put it on the lobe of the right ear, the thumb of the right hand, and the big toe of the right foot of the person being purified. 15 The priest shall also take the log of oil and pour some of it into the palm of his own left hand; 16 then, dipping his right finger in the oil on his left palm, he shall sprinkle some of it with his finger seven times before the LORD. 17 Of the oil left in his hand the priest shall put some on the lobe of the right ear, the thumb of the right hand, and the big toe of the right foot of the person being purified, over the blood of the reparation offering. 18 The rest of the oil in his hand the priest

**14:1–32** The rites here are for purification from human scaly infections after recovery, not for healing (but cf. 2 Kgs 5:10–14).

**14:4–7** The bird rite is also found for purifying a house from a fungus (vv. 49–53). The rite apparently removes impurity from the individual and, by means of the live bird, sends it away to unpopulated areas (v. 7). This is similar to the dispatch of a goat laden with sins on the Day of Atonement (16:21–22).

**14:5–7** The blood from the bird serves as a ritual detergent, much like the blood from the purification offering (see notes on 4:3). It is not a sacrifice, however, since it is not performed at the sanctuary. **Fresh water**: lit., "living water," taken from some source of running water, not from a cistern.

**14:8 Bathe in water**: This phrase occurs frequently in Lv 14–16 and is imprecise. It can refer to both ordinary and cultic washing. The context will determine the meaning. At this early period in Israel's history it is probably not a reference to cultic immersion in a Mikveh—a Second Temple period ritual.

**14:10 Log**: a liquid measure of capacity attested in the Bible only here. It is apparently equal in capacity to one-half liter.

**14:14–17** The application of blood and oil here facilitates the movement of the person from the severely impure to the pure profane sphere; it reintegrates him or her into the community. Cf. 8:23–24.

*j:* Lv 14:54–57. *k:* 2 Kgs 5:10, 14; Mt 8:4; 10:8; Mk 1:44; Lk 4:27; 5:14. *l:* Lv 14:48–53. *m:* Lv 13:46. *n:* Nm 19:6. *o:* Lv 16:21–22. *p:* Lv 15:13, 28. *q:* Lv 7:1–10. *r:* Lv 7:30. *s:* Lv 8:23–24.

shall put on the head[t] of the one being purified. Thus shall the priest make atonement for the individual before the LORD. 19 The priest shall next offer the purification offering,[u] thus making atonement on behalf of the one being purified from the uncleanness. After this the burnt offering shall be slaughtered. 20 The priest shall offer the burnt offering[v] and the grain offering on the altar before the LORD. Thus shall the priest make atonement for the person, and the individual will become clean.

***Poor Person's Sacrifices.*** 21 If a person is poor and cannot afford so much,[w] that person shall take one male lamb for a reparation offering, to be used as an elevated offering in atonement, one tenth of an ephah of bran flour mixed with oil for a grain offering, a log of oil, 22 and two turtledoves or pigeons, which the individual can more easily afford, the one as a purification offering and the other as a burnt offering. 23 On the eighth day of purification the person shall bring them to the priest, at the entrance of the tent of meeting before the LORD. 24 Taking the lamb of the reparation offering, along with the log of oil, the priest shall raise them as an elevated offering before the LORD. 25 When the lamb of the reparation offering has been slaughtered, the priest shall take some of its blood, and put it on the lobe of the right ear, on the thumb of the right hand, and on the big toe of the right foot of the person being purified. 26 The priest shall then pour some of the oil into the palm of his own left hand 27 and with his right finger sprinkle some of the oil in his left palm seven times before the LORD. 28 Some of the oil in his hand the priest shall also put on the lobe of the right ear, the thumb of the right hand, and the big toe of the right foot of the person being purified, where he had sprinkled the blood of the reparation offering. 29 The rest of the oil in his hand the priest shall put on the head of the one being purified. Thus shall he make atonement for the individual before the LORD. 30 Then, of the turtledoves or pigeons, such as the person can afford, 31 the priest shall offer one as a purification offering and the other as a burnt offering,[x] along with the grain offering. Thus shall the priest make atonement before the LORD for the person who is being purified. 32 This is the ritual for one afflicted with a scaly infection who has insufficient means for purification.

***Fungal Infection of Houses.*** 33* The LORD said to Moses and Aaron: 34 When you come into the land of Canaan, which I am giving you to possess, if I put[y] a fungal infection in any house of the land you occupy, 35 the owner of the house shall come and report to the priest, "Something like an infection has appeared in my house." 36 The priest shall then order the house to be cleared out before he goes in to examine the infection, lest everything in the house become unclean. Only after this is he to go in to examine the house. 37 If the priest, upon inspection, finds that the infection on the walls of the house consists of greenish or reddish spots[z] which seem to go deeper than the surface of the wall, 38 he shall go out of the house to the doorway and quarantine the house for seven days. 39 On the seventh day the priest shall return. If, upon inspection, he finds that the infection has spread on the walls, 40 he shall order the infected stones to be pulled out and cast in an unclean place outside the city. 41 The whole inside of the house shall then be scraped, and the mortar that has been scraped off shall be dumped in an unclean place outside the city. 42 Then other stones shall be brought and put in the place of the old stones, and new mortar obtained and plastered on the house. 43 If the infection breaks out once more in the house after the stones have been pulled out and the house has been scraped and replastered, 44 the priest shall come; and if, upon inspection, he finds that the infection has spread in the

**14:33–53** Discussion of fungi in houses is probably delayed until here because it deals with a case pertaining to living in the land (v. 34) as opposed to the foregoing cases which apply even in the wilderness. The rules on fabrics (13:47–58) apply to the tent dwellings in the wilderness.

---

*t:* Lv 8:12, 30. *u:* Lv 4. *v:* Lv 1. *w:* Lv 5:7, 11; 12:8. *x:* Lv 1:14–17; 5:7–10. *y:* Nm 12:9–15; 2 Kgs 15:4–5; 2 Chr 26:16–21. *z:* Lv 13:49.

house, it is a corrosive fungus in the house, and it is unclean. [45]It shall be pulled down, and all its stones, beams and mortar shall be hauled away to an unclean place outside the city. [46][a] Whoever enters a house while it is quarantined shall be unclean until evening. [47]Whoever sleeps or eats in such a house shall also wash his garments.

[48][b] If the priest finds, when he comes to the house, that the infection has in fact not spread in the house after the plastering, he shall declare the house clean, since the infection has been healed. [49]To purify the house, he shall take two birds, as well as cedar wood, scarlet yarn, and hyssop. [50]One of the birds he shall slaughter over an earthen vessel with fresh water in it. [51]Then, taking the cedar wood, the hyssop and the scarlet yarn, together with the living bird, he shall dip them all in the blood of the slaughtered bird and the fresh water, and sprinkle the house seven times. [52]Thus he shall purify the house with the bird's blood and the fresh water, along with the living bird, the cedar wood, the hyssop, and the scarlet yarn. [53]He shall then let the living bird fly away over the countryside outside the city. Thus he shall make atonement for the house, and it will be clean.

[54]This is the ritual for every kind of human scaly infection and scall, [55]and for fungus diseases in garments and houses— [56]for marks, lesions and blotches— [57]to give direction when there is a state of uncleanness and when a state of cleanness. This is the ritual for scaly infection.

## CHAPTER 15

See RG 77–78

***Sexual Uncleanness.**** [1]The LORD said to Moses and Aaron: [2]* Speak to the Israelites and tell them: When any man has a genital discharge, he is thereby unclean.[c] [3]Such is his uncleanness from this discharge, whether his body* drains freely with the discharge or is blocked up from the discharge. His uncleanness is on him all the days that his body discharges or is blocked up from his discharge; this is his uncleanness. [4]Any bed on which the man with the discharge lies is unclean, and any article on which he sits is unclean. [5]Anyone who touches his bed shall wash his garments, bathe in water, and be unclean until evening. [6]Whoever sits on an article on which the man with the discharge was sitting shall wash his garments, bathe in water, and be unclean until evening. [7]Whoever touches the body of the man with the discharge shall wash his garments, bathe in water, and be unclean until evening. [8]If the man with the discharge spits on a clean person, the latter shall wash his garments, bathe in water, and be unclean until evening. [9]Any saddle on which the man with the discharge rides is unclean. [10]Whoever touches anything that was under him shall be unclean until evening; whoever carries any such thing shall wash his garments, bathe in water, and be unclean until evening.[d] [11]Anyone whom the man with the discharge touches with his unrinsed hands shall wash his garments, bathe in water, and be unclean until evening. [12]Earthenware touched by the man with the discharge shall be broken; and every wooden article shall be rinsed with water.

[13]When a man with a discharge becomes clean* of his discharge, he shall count seven days[e] for his purification. Then he shall wash his garments and bathe his body in fresh water, and so he will be clean. [14]On the eighth day he shall take two turtledoves or two pigeons,[f] and going before the LORD, to the entrance of the tent of meeting, he shall give them to the priest, [15]who shall offer them up, the one as a purification offering and the other as a burnt offering. Thus shall the priest make atonement before the LORD for the man because of his discharge.

[16]* When a man has an emission of semen, he shall bathe his whole body in water

**15:1–33** Sexual discharges may be unclean partly because they involve the loss of life fluids or are otherwise involved with phenomena at the margins of life and death.

**15:2–3** The uncleanness here is perhaps a discharge of pus because of urethritis (often but not solely associated with gonorrhea).

**15:3 Body**: here a euphemism in the Hebrew for "penis."

**15:13 Becomes clean**: i.e., when his discharge ceases. The rite that follows is for purification, not a cure; see note on 14:1–32.

**15:16–18** Menstrual blood, semen, and other impurities in

*a:* cf. Lv 15:10. *b:* Lv 14:2–9. *c:* Nm 5:2. *d:* Lv 11:24–25, 27–28, 39–40; 14:46–47. *e:* Lv 14:8. *f:* Lv 12:8; 14:22.

and be unclean until evening.[g] 17 Any piece
of cloth or leather with semen on it shall be
washed with water and be unclean until
evening.
18 If a man has sexual relations with a
woman, they shall both bathe in water and
be unclean until evening.
19* When a woman has a flow of blood
from her body, she shall be in a state of menstrual uncleanness for seven days. Anyone
who touches her shall be unclean until
evening.[h] 20 Anything on which she lies or
sits during her menstrual period shall be unclean. 21 Anyone who touches her bed shall
wash his garments, bathe in water, and be unclean until evening. 22 Whoever touches any
article on which she was sitting shall wash
his garments, bathe in water, and be unclean
until evening. 23 Whether an object* is on the
bed or on something she sat upon, when the
person touches it, that person shall be unclean until evening. 24 If a man lies with her,
he contracts her menstrual uncleanness and
shall be unclean for seven days;[i] every bed
on which he then lies also becomes unclean.
25* When a woman has a flow of blood for
several days outside her menstrual period, or
when her flow continues beyond the ordinary
period, as long as she suffers this unclean
flow she shall be unclean, just as during her
menstrual period.[j] 26 Any bed on which she
lies during such a flow becomes unclean, as
it would during her menstrual period, and
any article on which she sits becomes unclean just as during her menstrual period.
27 Anyone who touches them becomes unclean; that person shall wash his garments,
bathe in water, and be unclean until evening.
28[k] When she becomes clean from her
flow, she shall count seven days; after this
she becomes clean. 29 On the eighth day she
shall take two turtledoves or two pigeons
and bring them to the priest at the entrance
of the tent of meeting. 30 The priest shall offer one of them as a purification offering and
the other as a burnt offering. Thus shall the
priest make atonement before the LORD for
her because of her unclean flow.
31 You shall warn the Israelites of their uncleanness, lest they die through their uncleanness by defiling my tabernacle,[l] which
is in their midst.
32 This is the ritual for the man with a discharge, or who has an emission of semen,
and thereby becomes unclean; 33 as well as
for the woman who has her menstrual period; or one who has a discharge, male or female; and also for the man who lies with an
unclean woman.

## CHAPTER 16

See RG 78

*The Day of Atonement.* 1* After the
death of Aaron's two sons,[m] who died when
they encroached on the LORD's presence, the
LORD spoke to Moses 2 and said to him: Tell
your brother Aaron that he is not to come
whenever he pleases* into the inner sanctuary,
inside the veil,[n] in front of the cover on the
ark, lest he die, for I reveal myself in a cloud
above the ark's cover. 3 Only in this way may

Lv 11–15 are considered "impure" either because they are force of life whose "loss" represents death or because, as uniquely human conditions, they are symbolically incompatible with the deity and the divine abode, the sanctuary. Lv 15:16 refers to a spontaneous nocturnal emission, and either because this marks life and death boundaries or because of its uniquely human (versus divine) character, any contact with it renders the object or person ritually unclean. Thus, in 15:18 it is not the marital act itself that is polluting, but only semen.

**15:19–24** This is normal menstruation.

**15:23 An object**: the Hebrew is unclear. This translation means that even an object on the woman's unclean bed or chair can mediate uncleanness to another, but only if all the object touched is still on the bed or article sat upon, thus forming a chain of simultaneous contact.

**15:25–30** This is menstruation outside the normal cycle or for periods longer than normal. A woman with a chronic blood flow was healed by touching the tassel of Jesus' cloak (Mt 9:20–22; Mk 5:25–34; Lk 8:43–48).

**16:1–34** This is the narrative sequel of the story in chap. 10. The ritual in chapter 16 originally may have been an emergency rite in response to unexpected pollution of the sanctuary.

**16:2 Not to come whenever he pleases**: access to the various parts of the sanctuary is strictly controlled. Only the high priest can enter the most holy place, and only once a year. **The veil**: the Letter to the Hebrews makes use of the imagery of the Day of Atonement (in Hebrew *Yom Kippur*) to explain Jesus' sacrifice (Heb 9:1–14, 23–28). **Ark's cover**: the meaning of *kappōret* is not certain. It may be connected with the verb *kipper* "to atone, purge" (see note on v. 6) and thus refer to this part of the ark as a focus of atonement or purification.

*g:* Ex 19:15; Dt 23:11–12; 1 Sm 21:6. *h:* Lv 12:2, 5; 2 Sm 11:4; Ez 36:17. *i:* Lv 18:19; 20:18; Ez 18:6. *j:* Mt 9:20–22; Mk 5:25–34; Lk 8:43–48. *k:* Lv 15:13–15. *l:* Lv 5:2–3; 22:9; Nm 19:13, 20. *m:* Lv 10:1–5. *n:* Lv 23:26–32; Nm 29:7–11; Heb 9:6–28.

Aaron enter the inner sanctuary. He shall bring a bull of the herd for a purification offering and a ram for a burnt offering. 4He shall wear the sacred linen tunic, with the linen pants underneath, gird himself with the linen sash and put on the linen turban.[o] But since these vestments are sacred, he shall not put them on until he has first bathed his body in water.[p] 5From the Israelite community he shall receive two male goats for a purification offering and one ram for a burnt offering.

6Aaron shall offer the bull, his purification offering, to make atonement* for himself and for his household. 7Taking the two male goats and setting them before the LORD at the entrance of the tent of meeting, 8he shall cast lots[q] to determine which one is for the LORD and which for Azazel.* [r] 9The goat that is determined by lot for the LORD, Aaron shall present and offer up as a purification offering. 10But the goat determined by lot for Azazel he shall place before the LORD alive, so that with it he may make atonement by sending it off to Azazel in the desert.

11Thus shall Aaron offer his bull for the purification offering, to make atonement for himself and for his family. When he has slaughtered it, 12he shall take a censer full of glowing embers from the altar before the LORD, as well as a double handful of finely ground fragrant incense, and bringing them inside the veil, 13there before the LORD he shall put incense on the fire, so that a cloud of incense may shield the cover that is over the covenant, else he will die. 14Taking some of the bull's blood, he shall sprinkle it with his finger on the front of the ark's cover and likewise sprinkle some of the blood with his finger seven times in front of the cover.

15Then he shall slaughter the goat of the people's purification offering, and bringing its blood inside the veil, he shall do with it as he did with the bull's blood, sprinkling it on the ark's cover and in front of it. 16Thus he shall purge the inner sanctuary* of all the Israelites' impurities and trespasses, including all their sins. He shall do the same for the tent of meeting,[s] which is set up among them in the midst of their uncleanness. 17No one else may be in the tent of meeting from the time he enters the inner sanctuary to make atonement until he departs. When he has made atonement for himself and his household, as well as for the whole Israelite assembly, 18* he shall come out to the altar before the LORD and purge it also. Taking some of the bull's and the goat's blood, he shall put it on the horns around the altar, 19and with his finger sprinkle some of the blood on it seven times.[t] Thus he shall purify it and sanctify it from the impurities of the Israelites.

***The Scapegoat.*** 20When he has finished purging the inner sanctuary, the tent of meeting and the altar, Aaron shall bring forward the live goat. 21Laying both hands* on its head, he shall confess over it all the iniquities of the Israelites and their trespasses, including all their sins, and so put them on the goat's head.[u] He shall then have it led into the wilderness by an attendant. 22The goat will carry off all their iniquities to an isolated region.[v]

**16:6 Make atonement**: the Hebrew verb *kipper* refers specifically to the removal of sin and impurity (cf. Ex 30:10; Lv 6:23; 8:15; 16:16, 18, 20, 27, 33; Ez 43:20, 26; 45:20), thus "to purge" in vv. 16, 18, 20, and 33, and more generally to the consequence of the sacrificial procedure, which is atonement (cf. Lv 17:11). "Atonement" is preeminently a function of the purification sacrifice, but other sacrifices, except apparently for the communion sacrifice, achieve this as well.

**16:8 Azazel**: a name for a demon (meaning something like "angry/fierce god"). See note on 17:7.

**16:16 Inner sanctuary**: this refers to the most holy room (vv. 2, 11–15). **Trespasses, including all their sins**: the term for "trespasses" (Heb. *pesha'im*), which has overtones of rebellion, and the phrase "all their sins" indicate that even sins committed intentionally are included (such as when the sinner "acts defiantly," as in Nm 15:30–31). This complements the scheme found in Lv 4 (see note on 4:3): intentional sins pollute the sanctuary more and penetrate even further than inadvertent sins, namely to the most holy place. **The same for the tent of meeting**: this rite may be that found in 4:5–7, 16–18 where blood is sprinkled in the anterior room and blood is placed on the horns of the incense altar there. Cf. Ex 30:10.

**16:18–19** Thus a third locale in the sanctuary complex, the open-air altar, is purified. See the summaries in 16:20, 33.

**16:21 Both hands**: this gesture is for transferring sins to the head of the goat and is apparently different in meaning from the one-handed gesture that precedes the slaughtering of sacrificial animals (1:4; 3:2; 4:4; see note on 1:4).

*o:* Lv 8:7; Ex 28:1–40. *p:* Lv 8:6. *q:* Jos 7:14–20; Acts 1:26. *r:* Lv 17:7. *s:* Lv 4:5–7, 16–18. *t:* Lv 4:25, 30, 34. *u:* Is 53:6; 2 Cor 5:21. *v:* Lv 14:7, 53; Is 53:11–12; Jn 1:29; 1 Pt 2:24.

When the goat is dispatched into the wilderness, [23]Aaron shall go into the tent of meeting, strip off the linen vestments he had put on when he entered the inner sanctuary, and leave them in the tent of meeting. [24]After bathing his body with water in a sacred place, he shall put on his regular vestments, and then come out and offer his own and the people's burnt offering, in atonement for himself and for the people, [25]and also burn the fat of the purification offering on the altar.

[26]The man who led away the goat for Azazel shall wash his garments and bathe his body in water; only then may he enter the camp. [27]The bull and the goat of the purification offering whose blood was brought to make atonement in the inner sanctuary, shall be taken outside the camp,[w] where their hides and flesh and dung shall be burned in the fire. [28]The one who burns them shall wash his garments and bathe his body in water; only then may he enter the camp.

***The Fast.*** [29x] This shall be an everlasting statute for you: on the tenth day of the seventh month every one of you, whether a native or a resident alien, shall humble yourselves* and shall do no work. [30]For on this day atonement is made for you to make you clean; of all your sins you will be cleansed before the LORD. [31]It shall be a sabbath of complete rest for you, on which you must humble yourselves—an everlasting statute.

[32]This atonement is to be made by the priest who has been anointed and ordained to the priesthood in succession to his father. He shall wear the linen garments, the sacred vestments, [33]and purge the most sacred part of the sanctuary, as well as the tent of meeting, and the altar. He shall also make atonement for the priests and all the people of the assembly. [34]This, then, shall be an everlasting statute for you: once a year atonement shall be made on behalf of the Israelites for all their sins. And Moses did as the LORD had commanded him.

## IV. Holiness Laws

### CHAPTER 17

See RG 79

***Sacredness of Blood.*** [1]The LORD said to Moses: [2]Speak to Aaron and his sons, as well as to all the Israelites, and tell them: This is what the LORD has commanded: [3]* Any Israelite who slaughters an ox or a sheep or a goat, whether in the camp or outside of it, [4]without first bringing it to the entrance of the tent of meeting to present it as an offering to the LORD in front of the LORD's tabernacle, shall be judged guilty of bloodshed* [y]—that individual has shed blood, and shall be cut off[z] from the people. [5]This is so that such sacrifices as they used to offer in the open field the Israelites shall henceforth bring to the LORD at the entrance of the tent of meeting, to the priest, and sacrifice them there as communion sacrifices to the LORD.[a] [6]The priest will splash the blood on the altar of the LORD at the entrance of the tent of meeting and burn the fat for an odor pleasing to the LORD. [7]No longer shall they offer their sacrifices to the demons* with whom they prostituted themselves.[b] This shall be an everlasting statute for them and their descendants.

[8]Tell them, therefore: Anyone, whether of the house of Israel or of the aliens residing among them, who offers a burnt offering or sacrifice [9]without bringing it to the entrance of the tent of meeting to offer it to the LORD, shall be cut off from the people. [10c] As for

**16:29 Humble yourselves**: also v. 31. The idiom used here (Heb. *'innâ nephesh*) involves mainly fasting (Ps 35:13), but probably prohibits other activities such as anointing (Dn 10:3) and sexual intercourse (2 Sm 12:15–24). Such acts of self-denial display the need for divine favor. Fasting is often undertaken in times of emergency and mourning (cf. 1 Sm 14:24; 2 Sm 1:12; 3:35; cf. Mk 2:18–22).

**17:3–4** Any animal slaughtered must be brought to the tent of meeting as an offering. This differs from Dt 12:15–28, which allows those living too far from the temple to slaughter an animal for food at home without offering it as a sacrifice.

**17:4 Guilty of bloodshed**: human beings and animals can incur blood guilt for killing human beings (cf. Gn 9:5–6); human beings can incur blood guilt for killing animals (see note on Lv 24:17–22).

**17:7 Demons**: for Hebrew *śe'îrîm*, lit., "goats." Like the demon Azazel (cf. 16:8, 10, 21–22), they dwell in the open country (17:5). Cf. Is 13:21; 34:14.

*w:* Lv 4:11–12; 6:23; Heb 13:11–13. *x:* Lv 23:27, 32; Nm 29:7. *y:* Lv 24:18. *z:* Lv 7:20. *a:* Lv 3:1–2, 7–8, 13. *b:* Ex 34:15; Dt 32:17; 2 Chr 11:15; 1 Cor 10:20. *c:* Lv 3:17; 7:26–27; Gn 9:4; Dt 12:16, 23–24.

anyone, whether of the house of Israel or of the aliens residing among them, who consumes any blood, I will set myself against that individual and will cut that person off from among the people, 11 since the life of the flesh is in the blood,[d] and I have given it to you to make atonement* on the altar for yourselves, because it is the blood as life that makes atonement. 12 That is why I have told the Israelites: No one among you, not even a resident alien, may consume blood.

13 Anyone hunting,* whether of the Israelites or of the aliens residing among them, who catches an animal or a bird that may be eaten, shall pour out its blood and cover it with earth,[e] 14 since the life of all flesh is its blood. I have told the Israelites: You shall not consume the blood of any flesh. Since the life of all flesh is its blood, anyone who consumes it shall be cut off.

15 Everyone, whether a native or an alien, who eats of an animal that died of itself or was killed by a wild beast, shall wash his garments, bathe in water, and be unclean until evening, and then become clean.[f] 16 If one does not wash his garments and bathe, that person shall bear the penalty.

See RG 79

## CHAPTER 18

*Laws Concerning Sexual Behavior.* 1 The LORD said to Moses: 2 Speak to the Israelites and tell them: I, the LORD, am your God.* 3 You shall not do as they do in the land of Egypt, where you once lived, nor shall you do as they do in the land of Canaan, where I am bringing you; do not conform to their customs.[g] 4 My decrees you shall carry out, and my statutes you shall take care to follow. I, the LORD, am your God. 5 Keep, then, my statutes and decrees, for the person who carries them out will find life* through them. I am the LORD.[h]

6* None of you shall approach a close relative* to have sexual intercourse. I am the LORD. 7* You shall not disgrace your father by having intercourse with your mother.[i] She is your own mother; you shall not have intercourse with her. 8 You shall not have intercourse with your father's wife, for that would be a disgrace to your father. 9 You shall not have intercourse with your sister,*[j] your father's daughter or your mother's daughter, whether she was born in your own household or born elsewhere. 10 You shall not have intercourse with your son's daughter or with your daughter's daughter,* for that would be a disgrace to you. 11 You shall not have intercourse with the daughter whom your father's wife bore to him in his household,[k] since she, too, is your sister. 12 You shall not have intercourse with your father's sister,[l] since she is your father's relative. 13 You shall not have intercourse with your mother's sister, since she is your mother's relative. 14 You shall not disgrace your father's brother by having sexual relations with his wife,[m] since she, too, is your aunt. 15 You shall not have intercourse with your daughter-in-law;*[n] she is your son's wife; you shall not have intercourse with

**17:11 To make atonement**: this is probably to be understood in the context of liability for shedding animal blood (cf. v. 4). Placing the blood on the altar exonerates the slaughterer from guilt for the killing. See note on 16:6.

**17:13 Hunting**: game animals are not permitted as offerings. One nonetheless has to treat the blood of these animals carefully by covering it with earth. Cf. Dt 12:16, 24.

**18:2 I, the LORD, am your God**: this declaration appears frequently elsewhere throughout chaps. 17–26, sometimes with a statement of God's holiness or his sanctifying activity. It emphasizes the importance of the laws and the relationship of the divine lawgiver to the people.

**18:5 Find life**: in Dt 30:15–20 Moses sets before the people life and death. The alternatives are set out in detail in Lv 26 and Dt 28. Cf. Ez 20:11, 13, 21.

**18:6–23** These laws deal with illicit sexual behavior. Lv 20:10–21 reiterates most of these cases, with penalties. Cf. also Dt 27:15–26; Ez 22:7–12. The ordering of the cases in Lv 18 seems to be: blood relatives (vv. 6–13), those related by marriage (vv. 14–18), then other cases (vv. 19–23).

**18:6 Close relative**: this refers to a blood relative and includes those not specifically mentioned in the list, such as one's own daughter and a full sister. **Have sexual intercourse**: lit., "to uncover nakedness."

**18:7–8** Cf. the story of Reuben lying with Bilhah, his father's concubine and Rachel's maid (Gn 35:22; 49:4).

**18:9, 11** Cf. actual or possible marriage to a half sister in Gn 20:12 and 2 Sm 13:13.

**18:10** Daughter incest is found in the story of Lot (Gn 19:30–38).

**18:15** Judah had intercourse with his daughter-in-law Tamar (Gn 38), but did not know her true identity until her pregnancy was discovered.

*d:* Gn 9:4. *e:* Dt 12:15–16. *f:* Lv 11:39–40; 22:8. *g:* Lv 20:22–23. *h:* Ez 20:11, 13, 21; Gal 3:12. *i:* Lv 20:11; Dt 23:1; 27:20; 1 Cor 5:1. *j:* Lv 20:17; Dt 27:22. *k:* Lv 20:17. *l:* Lv 20:19. *m:* Lv 20:20. *n:* Lv 20:12.

her. 16 You shall not have intercourse with your brother's wife;* [o] that would be a disgrace to your brother. 17 You shall not have intercourse with a woman and also with her daughter, nor shall you marry and have intercourse with her son's daughter or her daughter's daughter;[p] they are related to her. This would be shameful. 18 While your wife is still living you shall not marry her sister as her rival and have intercourse with her.[q]

19 You shall not approach a woman to have intercourse with her while she is in her menstrual uncleanness.[r] 20 You shall not have sexual relations with your neighbor's wife,* [s] defiling yourself with her. 21 [t] You shall not offer any of your offspring for immolation to Molech,* thus profaning the name of your God. I am the LORD. 22 You shall not lie with a male as with a woman;[u] such a thing is an abomination. 23 You shall not have sexual relations with an animal, defiling yourself with it; nor shall a woman set herself in front of an animal to mate with it; that is perverse.[v]

24 Do not defile yourselves by any of these things, because by them the nations whom I am driving out of your way have defiled themselves. 25 And so the land has become defiled, and I have punished it for its wickedness, and the land has vomited out its inhabitants.[w] 26 You, however, must keep my statutes and decrees, avoiding all these abominations, both the natives and the aliens resident among you— 27 because the previous inhabitants did all these abominations and the land became defiled; 28 otherwise the land will vomit you out also for having defiled it, just as it vomited out the nations before you. 29 For whoever does any of these abominations shall be cut off from the people. 30 Heed my charge, then, not to observe the abominable customs that have been observed before your time, and thus become impure by them.[x] I, the LORD, am your God.

## CHAPTER 19

See RG 79

*Various Rules of Conduct.* 1 The LORD said to Moses: 2 Speak to the whole Israelite community and tell them: Be holy, for I, the LORD your God, am holy.* [y] 3* Each of you revere your mother and father,[z] and keep my sabbaths.[a] I, the LORD, am your God.

4 Do not turn aside to idols, nor make molten gods for yourselves.[b] I, the LORD, am your God.

5 When you sacrifice your communion sacrifice to the LORD, you shall sacrifice it so that it is acceptable on your behalf. 6 It must be eaten on the day of your sacrifice or on the following day. Whatever is left over until the third day shall be burned in fire. 7 If any of it is eaten on the third day, it will be a desecrated offering and not be accepted;[c] 8 whoever eats of it then shall bear the penalty for having profaned what is sacred to the LORD. Such a one shall be cut off[d] from the people.

9* When you reap the harvest of your land, you shall not be so thorough that you reap the field to its very edge, nor shall you gather the

**18:16** This refers to cohabiting with one's sister-in-law not only while the brother is alive, but also after he is dead. Dt 25:5–10 allows for the marriage to the wife of a brother when that brother died without a male heir. Cf. Gn 38:6–14. It was the violation of this law of Leviticus which aroused the wrath of John the Baptist against Herod Antipas (Mt 14:4; Mk 6:18).

**18:20** Adultery in the Hebrew Bible and the ancient Near East is intercourse between a married or betrothed woman and any male. In the Bible it is generally punishable by the death of both individuals (20:10; cf. Dt 22:22–27). Intercourse with an unmarried or unbetrothed woman is not prohibited but carries responsibilities and fines (cf. Ex 22:15–16; Dt 22:28–29). Cf. Lv 19:20–22.

**18:21 Immolation to Molech**: the reference is to the custom of sacrificing children to the god Molech. Cf. Ez 16:20–21; 20:26, 31; 23:37. See note on Lv 20:1–5.

**19:2 Be holy, for I . . . am holy**: in the writings commonly attributed to the Priestly collection, Israel is called to be holy through obeying God's precepts (11:44–45; 20:7–8, 24–26; Nm 15:40–41). Cf. Dt 14:2, 21; 26:19; and Ex 19:6.

**19:3–4** Cf. the Decalogue laws on revering parents (Ex 20:12; Dt 5:16), keeping sabbaths (Ex 20:8–11; Dt 5:12–15), and not making or worshiping idols (Ex 20:2–6; Dt 5:7–10).

**19:9–10** The Israelites maintain the poor in part by letting them gather unharvested portions of fields and vineyards. Cf. 23:22; Ru 2:1–10.

*o:* Lv 20:21; Dt 25:5–10; Mt 14:3–4; Mk 6:18. *p:* Lv 20:14; Dt 27:23. *q:* Gn 29:27–28. *r:* Lv 15:24, 33; 20:18; Ez 18:6; 22:10. *s:* Lv 20:10; Ex 20:14; Dt 5:18; 22:22; Mt 5:27–30; Jn 8:4–5. *t:* Lv 20:2–5; Dt 18:10; 1 Kgs 11:7; 2 Kgs 16:3. *u:* Lv 20:13; Gn 19:4–11; Jgs 19:22–30; Rom 1:27; 1 Cor 6:9. *v:* Lv 20:15–16; Ex 22:18; Dt 27:21. *w:* Lv 20:22. *x:* Lv 20:23; Dt 18:9. *y:* Lv 11:44. *z:* Lv 20:9; Ex 20:12. *a:* Lv 23:3. *b:* Lv 26:1; Ex 20:3–5; 34:17; Dt 5:8; 27:15. *c:* Lv 7:15–18. *d:* Lv 7:20.

gleanings of your harvest.[e] 10 Likewise, you shall not pick your vineyard bare, nor gather up the grapes that have fallen. These things you shall leave for the poor and the alien. I, the LORD, am your God.

11* You shall not steal. You shall not deceive or speak falsely to one another.[f] 12 You shall not swear falsely by my name, thus profaning the name of your God.[g] I am the LORD.

13 You shall not exploit your neighbor. You shall not commit robbery. You shall not withhold overnight the wages of your laborer.[h] 14* You shall not insult the deaf, or put a stumbling block in front of the blind, but you shall fear your God. I am the LORD.

15 You shall not act dishonestly in rendering judgment. Show neither partiality to the weak nor deference to the mighty, but judge your neighbor justly.[i] 16 You shall not go about spreading slander among your people; nor shall you stand by idly when your neighbor's life is at stake. I am the LORD.

17* You shall not hate any of your kindred in your heart. Reprove your neighbor openly so that you do not incur sin because of that person.[j] 18 Take no revenge and cherish no grudge against your own people. You shall love your neighbor as yourself. I am the LORD.[k]

19* Keep my statutes: do not breed any of your domestic animals with others of a different species; do not sow a field of yours with two different kinds of seed; and do not put on a garment woven with two different kinds of thread.[l]

20* [m] If a man has sexual relations with a female slave who has been acquired by another man but has not yet been redeemed or given her freedom, an investigation shall be made. They shall not be put to death, because she has not been freed. 21 The man shall bring to the entrance of the tent of meeting as his reparation to the LORD a ram as a reparation offering.[n] 22 With the ram of the reparation offering the priest shall make atonement before the LORD for the wrong the man has committed, so that he will be forgiven for the wrong he has committed.

23 When you come into the land and plant any fruit tree there,[o] first look upon its fruit as if it were uncircumcised. For three years, it shall be uncircumcised for you; it may not be eaten. 24 In the fourth year, however, all of its fruit shall be dedicated to the LORD in joyous celebration. 25 Not until the fifth year may you eat its fruit, to increase the yield for you. I, the LORD, am your God.

26 Do not eat anything with the blood still in it.[p] Do not recite charms or practice soothsaying.* [q] 27 Do not clip your hair at the temples, nor spoil the edges of your beard. 28 Do not lacerate your bodies for the dead, and do not tattoo yourselves.* [r] I am the LORD.

29 You shall not degrade your daughter by making a prostitute of her;[s] otherwise the land will prostitute itself and become full of lewdness. 30 Keep my sabbaths, and reverence my sanctuary.[t] I am the LORD.

31 Do not turn to ghosts or consult spirits,

**19:11–13** Cf. the Decalogue commandments against stealing (Ex 20:15; Dt 5:19), wrongly using God's name (Ex 20:7; Dt 5:11), and swearing falsely against another (Ex 20:16; Dt 5:20).

**19:14** In Dt 27:18 a curse falls on the head of the one who misleads the blind.

**19:17–18** These verses form a unit and describe different attitudes and actions towards one's fellow Israelites. A separate passage is necessary to advise a similar attitude toward aliens (vv. 33–34). Cf. 25:39–46. The admonition at the end of v. 18 came to be viewed in Judaism and Christianity as one of the central commandments. (See Mt 22:34–40; Mk 12:28–34; Lk 10:25–28; cf. Mt 19:19; Rom 13:8–10; Gal 5:14). The New Testament urges love for enemies as well as neighbors (Mt 5:43–48; Lk 6:27–36; cf. Prv 25:21–22).

**19:19** One reason why mixtures are prohibited seems to be that they are holy (see Dt 22:9, 10–11). Israelites are allowed mixtures in the wearing of fringes on the edges or corners of their clothing (Nm 15:37–41; Dt 22:12). Some mixtures are considered abominations (cf. Lv 18:23; Dt 22:5).

**19:20–22** On adultery, see note on 18:20. Here it is not adultery in the technical sense since the woman is not free. A reparation offering is required as a penalty (see 5:14–26).

**19:26 Recite charms . . . soothsaying**: methods of divination (cf. Gn 44:5, 15; Is 2:6; Ez 21:26–28). Legitimate means of learning the future or God's will were through the Urim and Thummim stones (see Lv 8:8), lots (see Lv 16:8) and prophets (cf. Dt 18:9–22; 1 Sm 28:6–7).

**19:28 Do not tattoo yourselves**: see note on Gn 4:15. This prohibition probably refers only to the common ancient Near Eastern practice of branding a slave with its owner's name as well as branding the devotees of a god with its name.

*e:* Lv 23:22; Dt 24:19–22. *f:* Ex 20:15–16. *g:* Ex 20:7; Mt 5:33–37. *h:* Dt 24:14–15. *i:* Ex 23:2–3; Dt 1:17; 16:19; Ps 82:2; Prv 24:23. *j:* Mt 18:15; Lk 17:3; Gal 6:1. *k:* Mt 5:43; 19:19; 22:39; Mk 12:31; Rom 13:9; Gal 5:14; Jas 2:8; 1 Jn 3:14. *l:* Dt 22:9–12. *m:* Dt 22:22–29. *n:* Lv 5:14–26. *o:* Dt 20:19–20. *p:* Lv 17:10. *q:* Dt 18:10; 2 Kgs 17:17; 21:6; 2 Chr 33:6. *r:* Lv 21:5. *s:* Lv 21:7, 14. *t:* Lv 19:3.

by which you will be defiled.[u] I, the LORD,
am your God.
32 Stand up in the presence of the aged,
show respect for the old, and fear your God.
I am the LORD.
33 When an alien resides with you in your
land, do not mistreat such a one.[v] 34 You shall
treat the alien who resides with you no differently than the natives born among you;
you shall love the alien as yourself; for you
too were once aliens in the land of Egypt.[w] I,
the LORD, am your God.
35 Do not act dishonestly in using measures
of length or weight or capacity. 36 You shall
have a true scale and true weights, an honest
ephah and an honest hin.*[x] I, the LORD, am
your God, who brought you out of the land of
Egypt. 37 Be careful, then, to observe all my
statutes and decrees. I am the LORD.

## CHAPTER 20

See RG 79

*Penalties for Various Sins.* 1* The
LORD said to Moses: 2 Tell the Israelites:
Anyone, whether an Israelite or an alien residing in Israel, who gives offspring to Molech shall be put to death.[y] The people of
the land shall stone that person. 3[z] I myself
will turn against and cut off[a] that individual
from among the people; for in the giving of
offspring to Molech, my sanctuary was defiled[b] and my holy name was profaned. 4 If
the people of the land condone the giving of
offspring to Molech, by failing to put the
wrongdoer to death, 5 I myself will turn
against that individual and his or her family, and I will cut off from their people both
the wrongdoer and all who follow this person by prostituting themselves with Molech.
6 Should anyone turn to ghosts and spirits
and prostitute oneself with them,[c] I will turn
against that person and cut such a one off
from among the people. 7 Sanctify yourselves, then, and be holy; for I, the LORD,
your God,[d] am holy. 8 Be careful, therefore,
to observe my statutes. I, the LORD, make
you holy.
9 Anyone who curses father or mother
shall be put to death;*[e] and having cursed father or mother, such a one will bear the
bloodguilt.* 10* If a man commits adultery
with his neighbor's wife,[f] both the adulterer
and the adulteress shall be put to death. 11 If
a man disgraces his father by lying with his
father's wife,[g] the two of them shall be put to
death; their bloodguilt is upon them. 12 If a
man lies with his daughter-in-law,[h] both of
them shall be put to death; they have done
what is perverse; their bloodguilt is upon
them. 13 If a man lies with a male as with a
woman,[i] they have committed an abomination; the two of them shall be put to death;
their bloodguilt is upon them. 14 If a man
marries a woman and her mother also,[j] that
is shameful conduct; the man and the two
women as well shall be burned to death, so
that shamefulness may not be found among
you. 15 If a man has sexual relations with an
animal,[k] the man shall be put to death, and
you shall kill the animal. 16 If a woman goes
up to any animal to mate with it,[l] you shall
kill the woman and the animal; they shall
both be put to death; their bloodguilt is upon
them. 17 If a man marries his sister,[m] his fa-

**19:36 Ephah**: see note on Is 5:10; **hin**: see note on Ez 45:24.

**20:1–5** The term Molech may refer to a deity, perhaps with an underworld association, and the activity forbidden here may be connected with divination. Cf. Dt 18:10; 2 Kgs 17:17; 21:6. In the kingdom of Judah the cult appears to have been practiced in the Valley of Hinnom, just outside Jerusalem on the west and south (2 Kgs 23:10; Jer 32:35).

**20:9 Curses father or mother . . . put to death**: this is more than a simple expletive uttered in anger against one's parents. See note on Ex 21:17.

**20:9–21 Bloodguilt**: these penalties, beginning with cursing one's parents, reflect the concerns of a patriarchal society that the breakdown of one's relations with one's parents can lead to the breakdown of all other familial relationships, resulting in the breakdown of society.

**20:10–21** See 18:6–23 and notes there. It appears that the inclusion of various penalties in 20:10–21 accounts for the different order of the cases here compared to the order found in 18:6–23. The reason why the offenses in 20:10–21 carry different penalties, however, is not clear. Perhaps the cases in vv. 17–21 were considered slightly less serious, being condemned but not criminally prosecuted.

*u:* Lv 20:6, 27; Dt 18:11; Is 8:19. *v:* Ex 22:20; 23:9; Jer 22:3; Mal 3:5. *w:* Dt 10:19. *x:* Dt 25:13–16; Prv 16:11; Am 8:5; Mi 6:10–11. *y:* Lv 18:21; Dt 12:31; 18:10; 2 Kgs 16:3; 17:17; 21:6; 23:10; Jer 32:35. *z:* Ez 23:39. *a:* Lv 7:20. *b:* Lv 15:31. *c:* Lv 19:31. *d:* Lv 11:44. *e:* Lv 19:3; Ex 21:17; Dt 21:18–21; Prv 20:20; Mt 15:4; Mk 7:10. *f:* Lv 18:20. *g:* Lv 18:8. *h:* Lv 18:15. *i:* Lv 18:22. *j:* Lv 18:17. *k:* Lv 18:23. *l:* Lv 18:23. *m:* Lv 18:9.

ther's daughter or his mother's daughter, and
they have intercourse with each other, that is
disgraceful; they shall be publicly cut off*
from the people; the man shall bear the
penalty of having had intercourse with his
own sister. 18 If a man lies with a woman during her menstrual period and has intercourse
with her, he has laid bare the source of her
flow and she has uncovered it.[n] The two of
them shall be cut off from the people. 19 You
shall not have intercourse with your
mother's sister or your father's sister,[o] because that dishonors one's own flesh; they
shall bear their penalty. 20 If a man lies with
his uncle's wife, he disgraces his uncle;[p]
they shall bear the penalty; they shall die
childless. 21 If a man takes his brother's wife,
it is severe defilement and he has disgraced
his brother;[q] they shall be childless.
22 Be careful to observe all my statutes and
all my decrees; otherwise the land where I
am bringing you to dwell will vomit you
out.[r] 23 Do not conform, therefore, to the customs of the nations[s] whom I am driving out
of your way, because all these things that
they have done have filled me with disgust
for them. 24 But to you I have said:[t] You shall
take possession of their land. I am giving it
to you to possess, a land flowing with milk
and honey. I, the LORD, am your God, who
have set you apart from other peoples.
25[u] You, too, must set apart, then, the clean
animals from the unclean, and the clean
birds from the unclean, so that you do not
make yourselves detestable through any
beast or bird or any creature which creeps on
the ground that I have set apart for you as unclean. 26 To me, therefore, you shall be holy;
for I, the LORD, am holy,[v] and I have set you
apart from other peoples to be my own.
27 A man or a woman who acts as a medium or clairvoyant[w] shall be put to death.
They shall be stoned to death; their bloodguilt is upon them.

## CHAPTER 21

See RG 79

*Sanctity of the Priesthood.* 1* The
LORD said to Moses: Speak to the priests,
Aaron's sons, and tell them: None of you
shall make himself unclean for any dead person among his kindred,[x] 2 except for his nearest relatives, his mother or father, his son or
daughter, his brother[y] 3 or his unmarried sister, who is of his own family while she remains single; for these he may make himself
unclean. 4 But as a husband among his kindred* he shall not make himself unclean and
thus profane himself.
5 The priests shall not make bald the
crown of their head, nor shave the edges of
their beard, nor lacerate their body.[z] 6 They
shall be holy to their God, and shall not profane their God's name, since they offer the
oblations of the LORD, the food of their God;
so they must be holy.
7* A priest shall not marry a woman debased by prostitution, nor a woman who has
been divorced by her husband; for the priest
is holy to his God.[a] 8 Honor him as holy for
he offers the food[b] of your God; he shall be
holy to you, because I, the LORD, am holy
who make you holy.
9 If a priest's daughter debases herself by
prostitution, she thereby debases her father;
she shall be burned with fire.[c]
10 The most exalted of the priests, upon
whose head the anointing oil has been
poured and who has been ordained to wear
the special vestments, shall not dishevel his
hair or rend his garments, 11 nor shall he go

**20:17 Cut off**: see note on 7:20.

**21:1–12** While off duty the regular priests are not to become corpse-contaminated except for the close relatives listed in vv. 2–3. While on duty they presumably could not become impure at all. The high priest is restricted from all corpse contamination, on or off duty (vv. 11–12). Lay Israelites are not restricted from corpse contamination, except when in contact with what is holy (cf. Dt 26:14). See note on Lv 11:39–40. Israelites who undertake a nazirite vow enter into a sanctified state and cannot contact corpses (Nm 6:6–12). Cf. Ez 44:25–27.

**21:4 Husband among his kindred**: this probably refers to relatives by marriage and may even include his wife.

**21:7** The ideal seems to be that a priest marry a virgin. This is explicitly stated for the high priest (cf. vv. 13–14; so also Ez 44:22, except there priests may marry widows of priests). The high priest has the added limitation that his wife must come from his kindred, i.e., the priestly family (cf. Ez 44:22).

*n:* Lv 18:19. *o:* Lv 18:12–13. *p:* Lv 18:14. *q:* Lv 18:16. *r:* Lv 18:25, 28. *s:* Lv 18:30. *t:* Ex 3:8, 17. *u:* Lv 11:2–47; Dt 14:4–20. *v:* Lv 11:44. *w:* Lv 19:31; Ex 22:17; Dt 18:11. *x:* Ez 44:25–27. *y:* Lv 10:6–7. *z:* Lv 19:27–28; Ez 44:20. *a:* Lv 19:29; Ez 44:22. *b:* Lv 1:9. *c:* Gn 38:24.

**Worship and Holiness**

WHEREAS EARLIER CHAPTERS were concerned with the proper procedure for sacrifice (chs 1–7, 17) and with the prompt disposal of impurity (chs 11–16), this section revolves primarily around holiness, that of the priests (ch 21) and that of sacrificial offerings (22:1–16). The sacred, which belongs to the divine sphere and has been saturated with holiness is vulnerable to attack and is subject to desecration if not kept apart from impurity, disqualifying imperfections, and unauthorized contact or use. Desecration of the holy redounds to God, profaning his abode and his holy name, and brings disastrous consequences in its wake.

near any dead person.[d] Not even for his father or mother may he thus become unclean;
12nor shall he leave the sanctuary and profane the sanctuary of his God, for the consecration of the anointing oil of his God is
upon him.[e] I am the LORD.
13He shall marry only a woman who is a
virgin. 14He shall not marry a widow or a
woman who has been divorced or one who
has been debased by prostitution, but only a
virgin, taken from his kindred, he shall
marry,[f] 15so that he not profane his offspring
among his kindred. I, the LORD, make him
holy.
***Priestly Blemishes.**** 16The LORD said to
Moses: 17Say to Aaron: None of your descendants, throughout their generations,
who has any blemish shall come forward to
offer the food of his God. 18Anyone who has
any of the following blemishes may not
come forward:[g] he who is blind, or lame, or
who has a split lip, or a limb too long, 19or a
broken leg or arm, 20or who is a hunchback
or dwarf or has a growth in the eye, or who
is afflicted with sores, scabs, or crushed testicles. 21No descendant of Aaron the priest
who has any such blemish may draw near to
offer the oblations of the LORD; on account
of his blemish he may not draw near to offer
the food of his God. 22He may, however, eat
the food of his God: of the most sacred as
well as sacred offerings.[h] 23Only, he may not
enter through the veil nor draw near to the
altar on account of his blemish; he shall not
profane my sacred precincts, for it is I, the
LORD, who make them holy.
24Moses, therefore, told this to Aaron and
his sons and to all the Israelites.

## CHAPTER 22

See RG 79

***Priestly Purity.**** 1The LORD said to
Moses: 2Tell Aaron and his sons to treat with
respect the sacred offerings which the Israelites consecrate to me; otherwise they will
profane my holy name. I am the LORD.
3* Tell them: If any one of you, or of your
descendants in any future generation, dares,
while he is in a state of uncleanness, to draw
near the sacred offerings which the Israelites
consecrate to the LORD, such a one shall be
cut off from my presence.[i] I am the LORD.
4No descendant of Aaron who is stricken
with a scaly infection,[j] or who suffers from a
genital discharge,[k] may eat of the sacred offerings, until he again becomes clean. Moreover, if anyone touches a person who has become unclean by contact with a corpse,[l] or if
anyone has had an emission of semen,[m] 5or
if anyone touches any swarming creature[n]
whose uncleanness is contagious or any person whose uncleanness, of whatever kind it
may be, is contagious—[o] 6the one who
touches such as these shall be unclean until
evening and may not eat of the sacred por-

**21:16–23** Though priests with certain bodily imperfections cannot serve at the altar (vv. 18–20), they are not impure, since they may still eat of the offerings, which are holy, and do so within the sanctuary precincts since it is there the most holy offerings are to be eaten (v. 22).

**22:1–16** While priests with bodily imperfections may eat the holy sacrifices (21:16–23), those impure and those not of the priestly household may not.

**22:3–8** On uncleanness, see chaps. 11–15 and notes there.

*d:* Lv 10:4–7. *e:* Lv 10:7. *f:* Ez 44:22. *g:* Lv 22:19–25; Dt 23:2–9. *h:* Lv 2:3, 10; 6:29; 7:6, 34. *i:* Lv 7:20–21. *j:* Lv 13–14. *k:* Lv 15:2–18. *l:* Nm 19:14–22. *m:* Lv 15:16. *n:* Lv 11:29–31. *o:* Lv 15:2–12, 18–27.

tions until he has first bathed his body in water.[p] [7]Then, when the sun sets, he shall be clean.[q] Only then may he eat of the sacred offerings, for they are his food. [8*] He shall not make himself unclean by eating of any animal that has died of itself or has been killed by wild beasts.[r] I am the LORD.

[9]They shall keep my charge so that they will not bear the punishment in this matter and die[s] for their profanation. I am the LORD who makes them holy.

[10]Neither an unauthorized person nor a priest's tenant or laborer may eat of any sacred offering.[t] [11]But a slave* whom a priest acquires by purchase or who is born in his house may eat of his food. [12*] A priest's daughter who is married to an unauthorized person may not eat of the sacred contributions. [13]But if a priest's daughter is widowed or divorced and, having no children, returns to her father's house, she may then eat of her father's food as in her youth. No unauthorized person, however, may eat of it. [14u] If such a one eats of a sacred offering through inadvertence, that person shall make restitution to the priest for the sacred offering, with an increment of one fifth of the amount. [15]The priests shall not allow the sacred offerings which the Israelites contribute to the LORD to be profaned[v] [16]nor make them incur a penalty when they eat their sacred offerings. For I, the LORD, make them holy.

***Unacceptable Victims.*** [17*] The LORD said to Moses: [18]Speak to Aaron and his sons and to all the Israelites, and tell them: When anyone of the house of Israel, or any alien residing in Israel, who presents an offering, brings a burnt offering[w] as a votive offering or as a voluntary offering to the LORD, [19]if it is to be acceptable for you, it must be an unblemished male of the herd, of the sheep or of the goats.[x] [20]You shall not offer one that has any blemish, for such a one would not be acceptable on your behalf.[y] [21]When anyone presents a communion sacrifice[z] to the LORD from the herd or the flock in fulfillment of a vow, or as a voluntary offering, if it is to find acceptance, it must be unblemished; it shall not have any blemish. [22]One that is blind or lame or maimed, or one that has running lesions or sores or scabs, you shall not offer to the LORD; do not put such an animal on the altar as an oblation to the LORD. [23*] An ox or a sheep that has a leg that is too long or is stunted you may indeed present as a voluntary offering, but it will not be acceptable as a votive offering. [24]One that has its testicles bruised or crushed or torn out or cut off you shall not offer to the LORD. You shall neither do this in your own land [25]nor receive from a foreigner any such animals to offer up as the food of your God; since they are deformed or blemished, they will not be acceptable on your behalf.

[26*] The LORD said to Moses: [27]When an ox or a lamb or a goat is born, it shall remain with its mother for seven days; only from the eighth day onward will it be acceptable, to be offered as an oblation to the LORD.[a] [28]You shall not slaughter an ox or a sheep on one and the same day with its young. [29]Whenever you offer a thanksgiving sacrifice to the LORD, so offer it that it may be acceptable on your behalf; [30]it must be eaten on the same day; none of it shall be left over until morning.[b] I am the LORD.

[31]Be careful to observe my commandments. I am the LORD. [32]Do not profane my

**22:8** See note on 11:39–40.

**22:11 Slave**: in contrast to the tenant or hired worker of v. 10, the slave, who is by definition a foreigner, is part of the priest's household and therefore may eat of sacrifices.

**22:12–13** A priest's daughter, when a dependent of her father, may eat of the lesser holy offerings.

**22:17–25** This passage complements the section on the bodily imperfections of priests in 21:16–23. The laws taken together indicate that whoever and whatever approaches and contacts the altar needs to be physically unimpaired.

**22:23** Burnt offerings and communion sacrifices brought as voluntary offerings may have slight defects, probably because they are freely given and do not depend upon a prior promise as do votive offerings.

**22:26–30** Other activities and procedures that would impair sacrifice are appended here. The rules in vv. 27–28 are reminiscent of the rule not to boil a young goat in its mother's milk (Ex 23:19; 34:26; Dt 14:21) and not to take a bird and its eggs (Dt 22:6–7), all of which have a humanitarian tenor.

**23:1–44** This is paralleled by another calendar from the

*p:* Lv 17:15; Nm 19:7–8, 19; Heb 10:22. *q:* Dt 23:12. *r:* Lv 11:39–40; Ez 44:31. *s:* Lv 15:31. *t:* Mt 12:4. *u:* Lv 5:15–16. *v:* Lv 19:8; Nm 18:32. *w:* Lv 1:3. *x:* Lv 21:16–23. *y:* Dt 15:21; 17:1; Mal 1:7–14. *z:* Lv 3:1; 7:11. *a:* Ex 22:29; 23:19. *b:* Lv 7:15.

**Sacred Times**

IN LV 23, God conveys to Moses, in five speeches, the laws of the weekly Sabbath and the annual holy days. Each of the Torah law collections contains a calendar of annual festivities, and most include a Sabbath law (some mention the Sabbath more than once). The command to abstain from labor on the Sabbath is found in all the collections, as is the tradition of festivals coinciding with the major events in the agricultural year: the early grain ripening, the reaping of the first produce, and the final gathering.

holy name, that in the midst of the Israelites I may be hallowed. I, the LORD, make you holy, [33]who led you out of the land of Egypt to be your God. I am the LORD.

## CHAPTER 23

See RG 79

*Holy Days.** [1]The LORD said to Moses: [2]Speak to the Israelites and tell them: The following are the festivals[c] of the LORD, which you shall declare holy days. These are my festivals:

[3]For six days work may be done; but the seventh day is a sabbath of complete rest,* a declared holy day; you shall do no work. It is the LORD's sabbath wherever you dwell.[d]

*Passover.* [4]These are the festivals of the LORD, holy days which you shall declare at their proper time.[e] [5]The Passover of the LORD* falls on the fourteenth day of the first month, at the evening twilight.[f] [6]The fifteenth day of this month is the LORD's feast of Unleavened Bread. For seven days you shall eat unleavened bread.[g] [7]On the first of these days you will have a declared holy day; you shall do no heavy work. [8]On each of the seven days you shall offer an oblation to the LORD. Then on the seventh day you will have a declared holy day; you shall do no heavy work.

[9]* The LORD said to Moses: [10]Speak to the Israelites and tell them: When you come into the land which I am giving you, and reap its harvest, you shall bring the first sheaf of your harvest to the priest, [11]who shall elevate[h] the sheaf before the LORD that it may be acceptable on your behalf.[i] On the day after the sabbath* the priest shall do this. [12]On this day, when your sheaf is elevated, you shall offer to the LORD for a burnt offering an unblemished yearling lamb. [13]Its grain offering shall be two tenths of an ephah of bran flour mixed with oil, as a sweet-smelling oblation to the LORD; and its libation shall be a fourth of a hin of wine. [14]You shall not eat any bread or roasted grain or fresh kernels until this day, when you bring the offering for your God. This shall be a perpetual statute throughout your generations wherever you dwell.

*Pentecost.* [15]Beginning with the day after the sabbath, the day on which you bring the sheaf for elevation, you shall count seven full weeks;[j] [16]you shall count to the day after the seventh week, fifty days.* [k] Then you shall

Priestly tradition, in Nm 28–29. Non-Priestly resumes of festal and holy observances are found in Ex 23:10–17; 34:18–24 and Dt 16:1–17.

**23:3 Sabbath of complete rest**: the sabbath and the Day of Atonement are called "sabbaths of complete rest" (Ex 16:23; 31:15; 35:2; Lv 16:31; 23:32). Work of any sort is prohibited on these days (Lv 23:3, 28; Nm 29:7) as opposed to other holy days where only laborious work is prohibited but light work, such as preparing food, is allowed (Ex 12:16; cf. Lv 23:7, 8, 21, 25, 35, 36; Nm 28:18, 25, 26; 29:1, 12, 35).

**23:5–6 The Passover of the LORD . . . feast of Unleavened Bread**: the two occasions were probably separate originally. Combined they celebrate the exodus from Egypt. Cf. Ex 12:1–20, 43–49; Nm 28:16–25.

**23:9–14** Around Passover a first fruits offering is to be brought (see 2:14), consisting of a sheaf of barley, the crop that matures at this time of year.

**23:11 Day after the sabbath**: the singular term *shabbat* "sabbath" may mean "week" here and refer to the seven-day period of the feast of Unleavened Bread. According to this interpretation, the barley sheaf is offered the day after the week of Unleavened Bread. Others understand it as referring to the first or last day of Unleavened Bread.

**23:16–21 Fifty days**: Pentecost. This festival occurs on a single day, fifty days after the feast of Unleavened Bread, elsewhere called the "feast of the Harvest" (Ex 23:16), "Day

*c:* Nm 28–29; Dt 16:1–17. *d:* Lv 19:3; 26:2; Ex 20:8–11; 23:12; 31:14–15; 34:21; Nm 28:9–10; Dt 5:12–15; Lk 13:14. *e:* Ex 23:14–19. *f:* Ex 12:1–51; Nm 9:1–8; 28:16–25; Dt 16:1–8. *g:* Ex 12:18; 13:3–10; 23:15; 34:18. *h:* Lv 7:30. *i:* Dt 26:2. *j:* Ex 23:16; 34:22; Nm 28:26–31; Dt 16:9–12. *k:* Acts 2:1.

present a new grain offering to the LORD. [17]For the elevated offering of your first-ripened fruits to the LORD, you shall bring with you from wherever you live two loaves of bread made of two tenths of an ephah of bran flour and baked with leaven. [18]Besides the bread, you shall offer to the LORD a burnt offering of seven unblemished yearling lambs, one bull of the herd, and two rams, along with their grain offering and libations, as a sweet-smelling oblation to the LORD. [19]One male goat shall be sacrificed as a purification offering, and two yearling lambs as a communion sacrifice. [20]The priest shall elevate them—that is, the two lambs—with the bread of the first-ripened fruits as an elevated offering before the LORD; these shall be sacred to the LORD and belong to the priest. [21]On this same day you shall make a proclamation: there shall be a declared holy day for you; no heavy work may be done. This shall be a perpetual statute through all your generations wherever you dwell.

[22][l] When you reap the harvest of your land, you shall not be so thorough that you reap the field to its very edge, nor shall you gather the gleanings of your harvest. These things you shall leave for the poor and the alien. I, the LORD, am your God.

*New Year's Day.* [23]The LORD said to Moses: [24]Tell the Israelites: On the first day of the seventh month*[m] you will have a sabbath rest, with trumpet blasts as a reminder, a declared holy day; [25]you shall do no heavy work, and you shall offer an oblation to the LORD.

***The Day of Atonement.*** [26]The LORD said to Moses: [27]Now the tenth day of this seventh month is the Day of Atonement.*[n] You will have a declared holy day. You shall humble yourselves and offer an oblation to the LORD. [28]On this day you shall not do any work, because it is the Day of Atonement, when atonement is made for you before the LORD, your God. [29]Those who do not humble themselves on this day shall be cut off from the people. [30]If anyone does any work on this day, I will remove that person from the midst of the people. [31]You shall do no work; this is a perpetual statute throughout your generations wherever you dwell; [32]it is a sabbath of complete rest for you. You shall humble yourselves. Beginning on the evening of the ninth of the month, you shall keep your sabbath from evening to evening.

***The Feast of Booths.*** [33]The LORD said to Moses: [34]Tell the Israelites: The fifteenth day of this seventh month is the LORD's feast of Booths,*[o] which shall continue for seven days. [35]On the first day, a declared holy day, you shall do no heavy work. [36]For seven days you shall offer an oblation to the LORD, and on the eighth day you will have a declared holy day. You shall offer an oblation to the LORD. It is the festival closing. You shall do no heavy work.

[37]* These, therefore, are the festivals of the LORD which you shall declare holy days, in order to offer as an oblation to the LORD burnt offerings and grain offerings, sacrifices and libations, as prescribed for each day, [38]in addition to the LORD's sabbaths, your donations, your various votive offerings, and the voluntary offerings that you present to the LORD.

[39]On the fifteenth day, then, of the seventh month, when you have gathered in the produce of the land, you shall celebrate the feast of the LORD* for a whole week. The first and

of First Fruits" (Nm 28:26), and "feast of Weeks" (Ex 34:22; Dt 16:10, 16). The name Pentecost comes from the later Greek term for the holy day (cf. Acts 2:1; 20:16; 1 Cor 16:8), referring to the fiftieth day. This is the occasion for bringing the first fruits of the wheat harvest.

**23:24 First day of the seventh month**: the seventh new moon is counted from a new year beginning in the spring (cf. v. 5). Like the seventh day in the week, it is preeminent among the new moon days (cf. Nm 28:11–15; 29:1–6).

**23:27 Day of Atonement**: see chap. 16 and notes there.

**23:34 Feast of Booths**: this is the final harvest festival of the year celebrating the remaining harvest. It is called the "feast of Ingathering" (Ex 23:16; 34:22), the "feast of Booths" (Lv 23:34; Dt 16:13), or simply the "feast" (1 Kgs 8:65). It is a seven-day festival with an eighth closing day. The first and eighth days are rest days (see note on v. 3).

**23:37–38** This appears to be the original conclusion of the chapter.

**23:39–43 The feast of the LORD**: the feast of Booths, the preeminent festival. This section supplements vv. 33–36 by prescribing the popular activities for the festival.

**23:40–43 Fruit . . . branches . . . boughs**: the fruit and/or foliage from these trees is to be gathered, but it is not said

*l:* Lv 19:9–10. *m:* Nm 29:1–6. *n:* Lv 16:1–34; 25:9; Nm 29:7–11. *o:* Ex 23:16; 34:22; Dt 16:13–15; 31:10; 2 Mc 1:9, 18; Jn 7:2.

the eighth day shall be days of rest. [40]On the first day you shall gather fruit of majestic trees, branches of palms, and boughs* of leafy trees and valley willows. Then for a week you shall make merry before the LORD, your God. [41]You shall keep this feast of the LORD for one whole week in the year. By perpetual statute throughout your generations in the seventh month of the year, you shall keep it. [42]You shall dwell in booths for seven days; every native-born Israelite shall dwell in booths, [43]that your descendants may realize that, when I led the Israelites out of the land of Egypt, I made them dwell in booths. I, the LORD, am your God.

[44]Thus did Moses announce to the Israelites the festivals of the LORD.

## CHAPTER 24

See RG 79

***The Sanctuary Light.**** [1]The LORD said to Moses: [2]Order the Israelites to bring you clear oil of crushed olives for the light, so that you may keep the lamp burning regularly.[p] [3]In the tent of meeting, outside the veil that hangs in front of the covenant, Aaron shall set up the lamp to burn before the LORD regularly, from evening till morning, by a perpetual statute throughout your generations. [4]He shall set up the lamps on the pure gold menorah to burn regularly before the LORD.

***The Showbread.**** [5]You shall take bran flour and bake it into twelve cakes,[q] using two tenths of an ephah of flour for each cake. [6]These you shall place in two piles, six in each pile, on the pure gold table before the LORD. [7]With each pile put some pure frankincense, which shall serve as an oblation to the LORD, a token of the bread offering. [8]Regularly on each sabbath day the bread[r] shall be set out before the LORD on behalf of the Israelites by an everlasting covenant. [9]It shall belong to Aaron and his sons, who must eat it in a sacred place, since it is most sacred,[s] his as a perpetual due from the oblations to the LORD.

***Punishment of Blasphemy.**** [10]A man born of an Israelite mother and an Egyptian father went out among the Israelites, and in the camp a fight broke out between the son of the Israelite woman and an Israelite man. [11]The son of the Israelite woman uttered the LORD's name in a curse and blasphemed. So he was brought to Moses—now his mother's name was Shelomith, daughter of Dibri, of the tribe of Dan—[12]and he was kept in custody till a decision from the LORD should settle the case for them.[t] [13]The LORD then said to Moses: [14]Take the blasphemer outside the camp, and when all who heard him have laid their hands* on his head,[u] let the whole community stone him. [15]Tell the Israelites: Anyone who blasphemes God shall bear the penalty; [16]whoever utters the name of the LORD in a curse shall be put to death.[v] The whole community shall stone that person; alien and native-born alike must be put to death for uttering the LORD's name in a curse.

[17]* Whoever takes the life of any human being shall be put to death;[w] [18]whoever takes the life of an animal shall make restitution of another animal, life for a life.[x] [19]* Anyone who inflicts a permanent injury on his or her

how they are used. The command to make merry suggests they may have been used in a procession or even circumambulation of the altar (cf. Ps 26:6). Later tradition understood these prescriptions as referring to making the booths out of the foliage (Neh 8:15).

**24:1–4** On the lamp, see Ex 25:31–40; 26:35; 27:20–21; 37:17–24; 40:24–25; Nm 8:1–4. It occupies the south side of the anterior room of the sanctuary tent and provides light for that room.

**24:5–9** On the bread table, see Ex 25:23–29; 26:35; 37:10–16; 40:22–23. It occupies the north side of the anterior room of the sanctuary tent. The bread is a type of grain offering (see note on 2:1).

**24:10–22** This is a narrative where an offense leads to clarifying revelation similar to the cases in Lv 10:1–7 and 16:1–34; Nm 9:6–14 and 15:32–36.

**24:14 Laid their hands**: see notes on 1:4 and 16:21. It may be that blasphemy generated a type of pollution which the hearers return to the culprit by this gesture.

**24:17–22** A digression dealing with bodily injury follows the blasphemy rules. It may have been appended since the first case is another example of the death penalty. But the section develops according to its own logic. All legal traditions require death for homicide: Gn 9:5–6; Ex 21:12–14; Nm 35:9–34; Dt 19:1–13; cf. Ex 20:13 and Dt 5:17.

**24:19–20** The phrase "life for a life" in v. 18 leads to in-

*p:* Ex 25:31–40; 27:20–21. *q:* Ex 25:23–30; 1 Kgs 7:48; 2 Chr 13:11; Heb 9:2. *r:* 1 Chr 9:32. *s:* 1 Sm 21:5. *t:* Nm 15:34. *u:* Lv 16:21. *v:* Ex 22:27; 1 Kgs 21:10, 13; Mt 26:65–66; Jn 10:33. *w:* Gn 9:5–6; Ex 21:12–14; Nm 35:9–34; Dt 19:11–13. *x:* Ex 21:33–34; cf. Lv 17:4.

neighbor shall receive the same in return: 20 fracture for fracture, eye for eye, tooth for tooth. The same injury that one gives another shall be inflicted in return.[y] 21 Whoever takes the life of an animal shall make restitution, but whoever takes a human life shall be put to death. 22 You shall have but one rule, for alien and native-born alike.[z] I, the LORD, am your God.

23 When Moses told this to the Israelites, they took the blasphemer outside the camp and stoned him;[a] they did just as the LORD commanded Moses.

See RG 79

## CHAPTER 25

***The Sabbatical Year.*** 1 The LORD said to Moses on Mount Sinai: 2* Speak to the Israelites and tell them: When you enter the land that I am giving you, let the land, too, keep a sabbath for the LORD. 3 For six years you may sow your field, and for six years prune your vineyard, gathering in their produce.[b] 4 But during the seventh year the land shall have a sabbath of complete rest, a sabbath for the LORD,[c] when you may neither sow your field nor prune your vineyard. 5 The aftergrowth of your harvest you shall not reap, nor shall you pick the grapes of your untrimmed vines. It shall be a year of rest for the land. 6 While the land has its sabbath, all its produce will be food to eat for you yourself and for your male and female slave, for your laborer and the tenant who live with you, 7 and likewise for your livestock and for the wild animals on your land.

***The Jubilee Year.*** 8* You shall count seven weeks of years—seven times seven years—such that the seven weeks of years amount to forty-nine years. 9 Then, on the tenth day of the seventh month* let the ram's horn resound; on this, the Day of Atonement,[d] the ram's horn blast shall resound throughout your land. 10 You shall treat this fiftieth year as sacred. You shall proclaim liberty in the land for all its inhabitants.[e] It shall be a jubilee for you, when each of you shall return to your own property, each of you to your own family. 11 This fiftieth year is your year of jubilee; you shall not sow, nor shall you reap the aftergrowth or pick the untrimmed vines, 12 since this is the jubilee. It shall be sacred for you. You may only eat what the field yields of itself.

13 In this year of jubilee, then, each of you shall return to your own property. 14 Therefore, when you sell any land to your neighbor or buy any from your neighbor, do not deal unfairly with one another. 15 On the basis of the number of years since the last jubilee you shall purchase the land from your neighbor;[f] and so also, on the basis of the number of years of harvest, that person shall sell it to you. 16 When the years are many, the price shall be so much the more; when the years are few, the price shall be so much the less. For it is really the number of harvests that the person sells you. 17 Do not deal unfairly with one another, then; but stand in fear of your God. I, the LORD, am your God.

18 Observe my statutes and be careful to keep my ordinances, so that you will dwell securely in the land. 19 The land will yield its fruit and you will eat your fill, and live there securely.[g] 20 And if you say, "What shall we

troducing the law of talion in vv. 19–20. Some have interpreted the law here and the similar expressions in Ex 21:23–25 and Dt 19:21 to mean that monetary compensation equal to the injury is to be paid, though the wording of the law here and the context of Dt 19:21 indicate an injury is to be inflicted upon the injurer.

**25:2–7** As every seventh day is to be a day of rest (cf. 23:3), so every seventh year is a year of rest (cf. 26:34–35, 43). The rest consists in not doing agricultural work. The people are to live off what grows naturally in the fields (vv. 6–7). Verses 19–22 add insurance by saying that God will make the sixth-year crop abundant such that its excess will stretch over the seventh sabbatical year as well as the eighth year when new crops are not yet harvested (cf. 26:10). Cf. Ex 23:10–11.

**25:8–17** The fiftieth year is the jubilee, determined by counting off "seven weeks of years." It is sacred, like the sabbath day. Specifically, in it indentured Israelites return to their own households and land that has been sold returns to its original owner. Different laws are found in Ex 21:1–6; Dt 15:1–3, 12–18 (cf. Jer 34:8–22).

**25:9 Seventh month**: the priestly laws reflect the use of two calendars, one starting in the spring (cf. chap. 23) and one in the fall. The jubilee is calculated on the basis of the latter. **Ram's horn**: Hebrew *shophar*. The name for the year, jubilee (Heb. *yobel*), also means "ram's horn" and comes from the horn blown to announce the occasion.

*y:* Ex 21:23–25; Dt 19:21; Mt 5:38. *z:* Lv 19:34; Ex 12:49; Nm 15:16. *a:* Acts 7:57–58. *b:* Ex 23:10–11. *c:* Lv 26:34; 1 Mc 6:49, 53. *d:* Lv 16:29. *e:* Nm 36:4; Is 61:2; Jer 34:8–22; Ez 46:17; Lk 4:19. *f:* Lv 27:18, 23. *g:* Lv 26:5–6.

eat in the seventh year, if we do not sow or reap our crop?"[h] [21]I will command such a blessing for you in the sixth year that there will be crop enough for three years, [22]and when you sow in the eighth year, you will still be eating from the old crop; even into the ninth year, until the crop comes in, you will still be eating from the old crop.[i]

***Redemption of Property.**** [23]The land shall not be sold irrevocably; for the land is mine, and you are but resident aliens and under my authority. [24]Therefore, in every part of the country that you occupy, you must permit the land to be redeemed. [25]When one of your kindred is reduced to poverty and has to sell some property, that person's closest relative,* who has the duty to redeem it, shall come and redeem what the relative has sold.[j] [26]If, however, the person has no relative to redeem it, but later on acquires sufficient means to redeem it, [27]the person shall calculate the years since the sale, return the balance to the one to whom it was sold, and thus regain the property.[k] [28]But if the person does not acquire sufficient means to buy back the land, what was sold shall remain in the possession of the purchaser until the year of the jubilee, when it must be released and returned to the original owner.[l]

[29]* When someone sells a dwelling in a walled town, it can be redeemed up to a full year after its sale—the redemption period is one year. [30]But if such a house in a walled town has not been redeemed at the end of a full year, it shall belong irrevocably to the purchaser throughout the generations; it shall not be released in the jubilee. [31]However, houses in villages that are not encircled by walls shall be reckoned as part of the surrounding farm land; they may be redeemed, and in the jubilee they must be released.

[32]* In levitical cities[m] the Levites shall always have the right to redeem the houses in the cities that are in their possession. [33]As for levitical property that goes unredeemed—houses sold in cities of their possession shall be released in the jubilee; for the houses in levitical cities are their possession in the midst of the Israelites. [34]Moreover, the pasture land[n] belonging to their cities shall not be sold at all; it must always remain their possession.

[35]When one of your kindred is reduced to poverty and becomes indebted to you, you shall support that person like a resident alien; let your kindred live with you. [36]Do not exact interest in advance or accrued interest,* but out of fear of God let your kindred live with you. [37][o] Do not give your money at interest or your food at a profit. [38]I, the LORD, am your God, who brought you out of the land of Egypt to give you the land of Canaan and to be your God.

[39]* When your kindred with you, having been so reduced to poverty, sell themselves to you, do not make them work as slaves.[p] [40]Rather, let them be like laborers or like your tenants, working with you until the jubilee year, [41]when, together with any children, they shall be released from your service and return to their family and to their ancestral property. [42]Since they are my servants, whom I brought out of the land of Egypt, they shall not sell themselves as

**25:23–55** This is a series of laws dealing mainly with situations of poverty in which one has to sell land, obtain a loan, or become indentured. Many of the laws are connected with the release of debts in the jubilee year.

**25:25** A close family member is responsible for redemption. Some of these are specified in v. 49.

**25:29–31** Not being able to redeem a house in a walled city after one year is probably due to the demographic and economic situation of large towns as opposed to small villages and open agricultural areas. The agricultural lands associated with the latter were the foundation for the economic viability of the Israelite family, and as such, God—who is the ultimate owner of the land (25:23)—has assigned them to the Israelites as permanent holdings.

**25:32–34** An exception to the rule in vv. 29–31 is made for levitical cities (Nm 35:1–8), since the Levites have no broad land holdings. Their houses can be redeemed and are to be released in the jubilee year.

**25:36 Interest in advance or accrued interest**: two types of interest are mentioned here. The former may refer to interest subtracted from the loaned amount in advance, and the latter, to interest or a payment in addition to the loaned amount.

**25:39–43** Here the individual Israelite has no assets and must become indentured to another Israelite for economic survival. No provision is given for redemption before the jubilee year, though such is probably allowed.

*h:* Mt 6:25, 31–34; Lk 12:22, 29. *i:* Lv 26:10. *j:* Ru 2:20; 4:4, 6; Jer 32:7–8. *k:* Lv 27:18, 23. *l:* Lv 27:24. *m:* Nm 35:1–8. *n:* Nm 35:3. *o:* Ex 22:24; Dt 23:20. *p:* Ex 21:2–11; Dt 15:12–18; 1 Kgs 9:22; Jer 34:8–22.

slaves are sold. 43Do not lord it over them harshly, but stand in fear of your God.

44* The male and female slaves that you possess—these you shall acquire from the nations round about you.[q] 45You may also acquire them from among the resident aliens who reside with you, and from their families who are with you, those whom they bore in your land. These you may possess, 46and bequeath to your children as their hereditary possession forever. You may treat them as slaves. But none of you shall lord it harshly over any of your fellow Israelites.[r]

47When your kindred, having been so reduced to poverty, sell themselves to a resident alien who has become wealthy or to descendants of a resident alien's family, 48even after having sold themselves, they still may be redeemed by one of their kindred, 49by an uncle or cousin, or by some other relative from their family; or, having acquired the means, they may pay the redemption price themselves. 50With the purchaser they shall compute the years from the sale to the jubilee, distributing the sale price over these years as though they had been hired as laborers. 51The more years there are, the more of the sale price they shall pay back as the redemption price; 52the fewer years there are before the jubilee year, the more they have as credit; in proportion to the years of service they shall pay the redemption price. 53The tenant alien shall treat those who sold themselves as laborers hired on an annual basis, and the alien shall not lord it over them harshly before your very eyes. 54And if they are not redeemed by these means, they shall nevertheless be released, together with any children, in the jubilee year. 55For the Israelites belong to me as servants; they are my servants, whom I brought out of the land of Egypt, I, the LORD, your God.

## CHAPTER 26

See RG 79

***The Reward of Obedience.*** 1* Do not make idols for yourselves. You shall not erect a carved image or a sacred stone for yourselves, nor shall you set up a carved stone for worship in your land;[s] for I, the LORD, am your God. 2Keep my sabbaths,[t] and reverence my sanctuary. I am the LORD.

3* [u] If you live in accordance with my statutes and are careful to observe my commandments, 4I will give you your rains in due season, so that the land will yield its crops, and the trees their fruit;[v] 5your threshing will last till vintage time, and your vintage till the time for sowing, and you will eat your fill of food, and live securely in your land.[w] 6I will establish peace in the land, and you will lie down to rest with no one to cause you anxiety. I will rid the country of ravenous beasts, and no sword shall sweep across your land. 7You will rout your enemies, and they shall fall before your sword. 8Five of you will put a hundred of your foes to flight, and a hundred of you will put to flight ten thousand, till your enemies fall before your sword.[x] 9I will look with favor upon you, and make you fruitful and numerous,[y] as I carry out my covenant with you. 10You shall eat the oldest stored harvest, and have to discard it to make room for the new.[z] 11[a] I will set my tabernacle in your midst, and will not loathe you. 12Ever present in your midst, I will be your God, and you will be my people; 13I, the LORD, am your God, who brought you out of the land of Egypt to be their slaves no more, breaking the bars of your yoke and making you walk erect.[b]

***The Punishment of Disobedience.**** 14[c] But if you do not heed me and do not keep all these commandments, 15if you reject my statutes and loathe my decrees, refusing to

**25:44–46** While Israelites may not be held as permanent slaves (vv. 39–43, 47–55), foreigners may be. They are not released in the jubilee, but may be bequeathed to one's children. They may be treated as "slaves," i.e., harshly (cf. Ex 21:20–21).

**26:1–46** This chapter concludes the revelation of laws at Mount Sinai (cf. v. 46). Blessings and curses are also found at the end of Deuteronomy's law collection (Dt 28). Similar lists of blessings and curses appear in the conclusions of ancient Near Eastern treaties.

**26:3–13** The blessings are concerned with the well-being of the nation and its land and involve agricultural bounty, national security, military success and population growth.

**26:14–46** To encourage obedience, the list of punishments

*q:* Dt 21:10–14. *r:* Is 14:1–2. *s:* Lv 19:4; Nm 33:52. *t:* Lv 23:3. *u:* Dt 28:1–69. *v:* Dt 11:14; Ps 85:13; Ez 34:26–27. *w:* Lv 25:18–19; Dt 12:10. *x:* Dt 32:30; Jos 23:10. *y:* Gn 1:28; Ex 1:7. *z:* Lv 25:22. *a:* Ex 29:45; Ez 37:26–28; 2 Cor 6:16. *b:* Ez 34:27; Na 1:13. *c:* Dt 28:15–69.

obey all my commandments and breaking my covenant, 16 then I, in turn, will do this to you: I will bring terror upon you—with consumption and fever to dim the eyes and sap the life. You will sow your seed in vain, for your enemies will consume the crop. 17 I will turn against you, and you will be beaten down before your enemies[d] and your foes will lord it over you. You will flee though no one pursues you.

18 If even after this you do not obey me, I will increase the chastisement for your sins sevenfold,[e] 19 to break your proud strength. I will make the sky above you as hard as iron, and your soil as hard as bronze, 20 so that your strength will be spent in vain; your land will bear no crops, and its trees no fruit.

21 If then you continue hostile, unwilling to obey me, I will multiply my blows sevenfold, as your sins deserve. 22 I will unleash wild beasts against you, to rob you of your children and wipe out your livestock, till your population dwindles away and your roads become deserted.

23 If, with all this, you still do not accept my discipline and continue hostile to me, 24[f] I, too, will continue to be hostile to you and I, for my part, will smite you for your sins sevenfold. 25 I will bring against you the sword, the avenger of my covenant. Though you then huddle together in your cities, I will send pestilence among you, till you are delivered to the enemy. 26 When I break your staff of bread, ten women will need but one oven for baking your bread, and they shall dole it out to you by weight;[g] and though you eat, you shall not be satisfied.

27 If, despite all this, you disobey and continue hostile to me, 28 I will continue in my hostile rage toward you, and I myself will discipline you for your sins sevenfold, 29 till you begin to eat the flesh of your own sons and daughters.[h] 30 I will demolish your high places, overthrow your incense stands, and cast your corpses upon the corpses of your idols.[i] In my loathing of you, 31 I will lay waste your cities and desolate your sanctuaries, refusing your sweet-smelling offerings. 32 So devastated will I leave the land that your enemies who come to live there will stand aghast at the sight of it.[j] 33 And you I will scatter among the nations[k] at the point of my drawn sword, leaving your countryside desolate and your cities deserted. 34 Then shall the land, during the time it lies waste, make up its lost sabbaths, while you are in the land of your enemies; then shall the land have rest and make up for its sabbaths[l] 35 during all the time that it lies desolate, enjoying the rest that you would not let it have on your sabbaths when you lived there.

36 Those of you who survive in the lands of their enemies, I will make so fainthearted that the sound of a driven leaf will pursue them, and they shall run as if from the sword, and fall though no one pursues them; 37 stumbling over one another as if to escape a sword, while no one is after them—so helpless will you be to take a stand against your foes! 38 You shall perish among the nations, swallowed up in your enemies' country. 39 Those of you who survive will waste away in the lands of their enemies, for their own and their ancestors' guilt.[m]

40* They will confess[n] their iniquity and the iniquity of their ancestors in their treachery against me and in their continued hostility toward me, 41 so that I, too, had to be hostile to them and bring them into their enemies' land. Then, when their uncircumcised hearts are humbled and they make amends for their iniquity, 42 I will remember my covenant with Jacob, and also my covenant with Isaac; and also my covenant with Abraham I will remember.[o] The land, too, I will remember. 43 The land will be forsaken by them, that in its desolation without them,

is longer than the blessings (cf. a similar proportion in Dt 28). The punishments are presented in waves (vv. 14–17, 18–20, 21–22, 23–26, 27–39), one group following another if the people do not return to obedience. Punishments involve sickness, pestilence, agricultural failure and famine, attack of wild animals, death of the people's children, destruction of illicit and even licit cults, military defeat, panic, and exile.

**26:40–45** Even though the people may be severely punished, God will remember the covenant when the people repent.

*d:* 2 Kgs 8:33–34. *e:* Ps 79:12; Prv 6:31. *f:* Jer 2:30; Ez 5:17; 14:17. *g:* Is 9:19; Ez 4:16; 5:16; 14:13; Mi 6:14. *h:* Lam 2:20. *i:* 2 Chr 14:5; 34:3–4, 7; Ez 6:3–6. *j:* 1 Kgs 9:8; Jer 9:11; 18:16; 19:8; 25:18. *k:* Ps 44:12; Jer 15:7; Ez 6:8. *l:* Lv 25:2; 2 Chr 36:21. *m:* Ez 4:17; 24:23; 33:10. *n:* Lv 16:21; Nm 5:7; Neh 1:6. *o:* Ex 6:5; 2 Kgs 13:23; Ps 106:45; Ez 16:60.

it may make up its sabbaths, and that they, too, may make good the debt of their guilt for having spurned my decrees and loathed my statutes. 44Yet even so, even while they are in their enemies' land, I will not reject or loathe them to the point of wiping them out, thus making void my covenant with them; for I, the LORD, am their God. 45I will remember for them the covenant I made with their forebears, whom I brought out of the land of Egypt before the eyes of the nations,[p] that I might be their God. I am the LORD.

46These are the statutes, decrees and laws which the LORD established between himself and the Israelites through Moses on Mount Sinai.[q]

## V. Redemption of Offerings

### CHAPTER 27

See RG 79

*Votive Offerings and Dedications.* 1The LORD said to Moses: 2* Speak to the Israelites and tell them: When anyone makes a vow to the LORD[r] with respect to the value of a human being, 3the value for males between the ages of twenty and sixty shall be fifty silver shekels, by the sanctuary shekel; 4and for a female, the value shall be thirty shekels. 5For persons between the ages of five and twenty, the value for a male shall be twenty shekels, and for a female, ten shekels. 6For persons between the ages of one month and five years, the value for a male shall be five silver shekels, and for a female, three shekels. 7For persons of sixty or more, for a male the value shall be fifteen shekels, and ten shekels for a female. 8However, if the one who made the vow is too poor to meet the sum,[s] the person must be set before the priest, who shall determine a value; the priest will do this in keeping with the means of the one who made the vow.

9If the offering vowed to the LORD is an animal that may be sacrificed, every such animal given to the LORD becomes sacred.[t] 10The offerer shall not substitute or exchange another for it, either a worse or a better one. If the offerer exchanges one animal in place of another, both the original and its substitute shall become sacred. 11If any unclean animal which is unfit for sacrifice[u] to the LORD is vowed, it must be set before the priest, 12who shall determine its value* in keeping with its good or bad qualities, and the value set by the priest shall stand. 13If the offerer wishes to redeem the animal, the person shall pay one fifth more than this valuation.[v]

14* When someone dedicates a house as sacred to the LORD,* the priest shall determine its value in keeping with its good or bad qualities, and the value set by the priest shall stand. 15A person dedicating a house who then wishes to redeem it shall pay one fifth more than the price thus established, and then it will again belong to that individual.[w]

16If someone dedicates to the LORD a portion of hereditary land, its valuation shall be made according to the amount of seed required to sow it, the acreage sown with a homer* of barley seed being valued at fifty sil-

**27:2–13** Vows are conditional promissory oaths. One covenants to do something for the benefit of God, usually to make a dedication, if God fulfills the individual's accompanying request (cf. Gn 28:20–21; Jgs 11:30–31; 1 Sm 1:11; 2 Sm 15:7–8; Ps 56:13–14). Vows must be fulfilled (Nm 30:3; Dt 23:22; cf. Ps 66:13–15). Verses 2–8 deal with votive offerings involving human beings. Actual dedication of human beings (cf. Jgs 11:30–31, 34–40; 1 Sm 1:11, 24–28) is obviated by payment of the person's value (mentioned in the temple income in 2 Kgs 12:5). The values reflect the different economic and administrative roles of people in different age and gender groups within ancient Israelite society. Verses 9–13 concern the bringing of animals for a vow.

**27:12 Determine its value**: in contrast to human beings (vv. 3–7) there are no set values for unclean animals, and the condition of the animal is taken into consideration (cf. vv. 14, 27).

**27:14–24** These verses deal with dedications. They take effect when uttered and, unlike vows, they are not conditional. They are related to the jubilee year laws in 25:23–31.

**27:14 House as sacred to the LORD**: the house becomes sanctuary property and presumably may be sold to another if the owner does not redeem it (cf. notes on vv. 20 and 21). While 25:31 requires that unredeemed houses in unwalled towns be returned to the original owners at the jubilee, in the laws here such houses apparently become the property of the sanctuary (cf. v. 21). It is likely that dedicated houses in a walled city needed to be redeemed within one year, following 25:29–30.

**27:16 Homer**: see note on Is 5:10.

*p:* Ex 12:51. *q:* Lv 7:38; Nm 36:13. *r:* Dt 23:22–24; Jgs 11:30–31; Eccl 5:3–4. *s:* Lv 5:7, 11. *t:* Lv 27:11, 27. *u:* Lv 11:2–8; Ex 13:13; 34:20. *v:* Lv 5:16, 24. *w:* Lv 22:14.

ver shekels. [17]If the dedication of a field is made at the beginning of a jubilee period, the full valuation shall hold; [18]but if it is some time after this, the priest shall estimate its money value according to the number of years left until the next jubilee year, with a corresponding reduction on the valuation.[x] [19]A person dedicating a field who then wishes to redeem*[y] it shall pay one fifth more than the price thus established, and so reclaim it. [20]If, instead of redeeming such a field, one sells it* to another, it may no longer be redeemed; [21]but at the jubilee it shall be released[z] as sacred* to the LORD; like a field that is put under the ban, it shall become priestly property.

[22]If someone dedicates to the LORD a field that was purchased and was not part of hereditary property, [23]the priest shall compute its value in proportion to the number of years until the next jubilee, and on the same day the person shall pay the price thus established, a sacred donation to the LORD; [24]at the jubilee the field shall revert to the hereditary owner of this land from whom it had been purchased.*

[25]Every valuation shall be made according to the standard of the sanctuary shekel. There are twenty gerahs to the shekel.

***Irredeemable Offerings.*** [26]* Note that a firstborn animal,[a] which as such already belongs to the LORD, may not be dedicated. Whether an ox or a sheep, it is the LORD's. [27]But if it is an unclean animal,* it may be redeemed by paying one fifth more than its value. If it is not redeemed, it shall be sold at its value.

[28]Note, also, that any possession which someone puts under the ban* for the LORD, whether it is a human being, an animal, or a hereditary field, shall be neither sold nor redeemed; everything that is put under the ban becomes most holy to the LORD.[b] [29]All human beings that are put under the ban cannot be redeemed; they must be put to death.[c]

[30]* All tithes of the land, whether in grain from the fields or in fruit from the trees, belong to the LORD; they are sacred to the LORD.[d] [31]If someone wishes to redeem any of the tithes, the person shall pay one fifth more than their value. [32]The tithes of the herd and the flock, every tenth animal that passes under the herdsman's rod, shall be sacred to the LORD. [33]It shall not matter whether good ones or bad ones are thus chosen, and no exchange may be made. If any exchange is made, both the original animal and its substitute become sacred and cannot be redeemed.

[34]These are the commandments which the LORD gave Moses on Mount Sinai for the Israelites.[e]

**27:19 Redeem**: the person apparently can redeem the land up to the jubilee year, following 25:23–28. See note on v. 21.

**27:20 If . . . one sells it**: the verse is difficult since the person should not be able to sell the land after it is dedicated. The verb "sells" may be construed impersonally here: "If . . . it is sold," i.e., by the sanctuary.

**27:21 Released as sacred**: the dedication changes the ownership of the land. It now belongs to the sanctuary. It returns to the sanctuary's possession after leasing it out (v. 20). Presumably if the land remained in the sanctuary's possession until the jubilee, and it was not redeemed, the land would belong permanently to the sanctuary and priests.

**27:24** In contrast to the cases in vv. 14–15 and 16–21, this land returns to the original owner since that individual did not personally make the dedication. The principle is that one cannot permanently dedicate what one does not own. Cf. 2 Sm 24:22–25.

**27:26** Firstborn animals and human beings already belong to God (cf. Ex 13:1–2, 12; 34:19); they cannot be vowed or dedicated. Cf. Nm 18:15–18; Dt 15:19–23.

**27:27 An unclean animal**: such as the firstborn of a donkey, which was unfit for sacrifice. According to Ex 13:13; 34:20, a firstborn donkey was to be redeemed by offering a sheep in its stead, or was to have its neck broken.

**27:28 Puts under the ban**: this is a higher form of dedication to God than that found in vv. 14–24. Anything so dedicated is beyond redemption and cannot be sold by the sanctuary and priests (contrast vv. 15, 19, 20). This type of dedication is found mostly in contexts of war (e.g., Jos 6:17–21; 8:26; 10:1, 28). Lv 27:28 shows that the ban can apply to one's own property.

**27:30–33** On the regulation concerning the tithes see Dt 14:22–29.

*x:* Lv 25:15–16, 26–27, 50–52. *y:* Lv 25:25. *z:* Lv 25:28, 31. *a:* Ex 13:2. *b:* Nm 18:14; Dt 7:26; Jos 7:1; 1 Sm 15:21; Ez 44:29. *c:* 1 Kgs 20:42. *d:* Nm 18:25–32; Dt 14:22–24; Mal 3:8, 10. *e:* Lv 7:38.

See RG 80–85

# The Book of Numbers

The Book of Numbers derives its name from the account of the two censuses taken of the Hebrew people, one near the beginning and the other toward the end of the journey in the wilderness (chaps. 1 and 26). It continues the story of that journey begun in Exodus, and describes briefly the experiences of the Israelites for a period of thirty-eight years, from the end of their encampment at Sinai to their arrival at the border of the promised land. Numerous legal ordinances are interspersed in the account, making the book a combination of law and history.

The book divides neatly into two parts. Each part begins with a census of the people (chaps. 1 and 26) and inaugurates a period of preparation prior to entering the promised land. In the first case these preparations come to a tragic end when scouts are sent forth to survey the promised land (chaps. 13–14). Upon their return, the people are so disheartened by the description of the native inhabitants and the seemingly impossible task that lies in front of them that they refuse to enter the land. This results in a decision to doom that entire generation to death and to allow another generation the chance to enter. After the death of the first generation, then, a second census is taken (chap. 26) and again preparations are made to enter the land. In this case, however, the birth of a new generation suggests these preparations will not be in vain. The book ends with the Israelites across the Jordan outside the land of Canaan, underscoring a chief theme of the Pentateuch as a whole: the people anticipating the fulfillment of God's promise of the land.

In the New Testament numerous allusions to incidents in the Book of Numbers appear: the bronze serpent (Jn 3:14–15), the sedition of Korah and its consequences (1 Cor 10:10), the prophecies of Balaam (2 Pt 2:15–16), and the water gushing from the rock (1 Cor 10:4).

The chief divisions of the Book of Numbers are as follows:

I. Census and Preparation for the Departure from Sinai (1:1–10:10)
II. Departure, Rebellion, and Wandering in the Wilderness for Forty Years (10:11–25:18)
III. Second Census of a New Generation and Preparation to Enter the Promised Land (25:19–36:13)

## I. Census and Preparation for the Departure from Sinai

### CHAPTER 1

See RG 80–85

*The Census.* 1 In the second year after
the Israelites' departure from the land of
Egypt, on the first day of the second month,
the LORD said to Moses at the tent of meeting in the wilderness of Sinai: 2* Take a census of the whole community of the Israelites,[a] by clans and ancestral houses,
registering by name each male individually.
3 You and Aaron shall enroll in companies all
the men in Israel of twenty years or more
who are fit for military service.

*Moses' Assistants.* 4 With you there shall
be a man from each tribe, each the head of
his ancestral house. 5[b] These are the names
of those who are to assist you:

from Reuben: Elizur, son of Shedeur;
6 from Simeon: Shelumiel, son of Zurishaddai;
7 from Judah:[c] Nahshon, son of Amminadab;
8 from Issachar: Nethanel, son of Zuar;
9 from Zebulun: Eliab, son of Helon;
10 for the descendants of Joseph: from Ephraim: Elishama, son of Ammihud; and from Manasseh: Gamaliel, son of Pedahzur;
11 from Benjamin: Abidan, son of Gideoni;

**1:2** All Israel was divided into tribes, each tribe into clans, and each clan into ancestral houses.

---

*a:* Nm 14:29; 26:2–51. *b:* Nm 10:14–28. *c:* Mt 1:4; Lk 3:32–33.

12 from Dan: Ahiezer, son of Ammishaddai;
13 from Asher: Pagiel, son of Ochran;
14 from Gad: Eliasaph, son of Reuel;
15 from Naphtali: Ahira, son of Enan.

16[d] These were the elect of the community, leaders of their ancestral tribes, heads
of the clans of Israel. 17So Moses and Aaron
took these men who had been designated by
name, 18and assembled the whole community on the first day of the second month.
Every man of twenty years or more then registered individually his name and lineage according to clan and ancestral house, 19as the
LORD had commanded Moses. So he enrolled them in the wilderness of Sinai.

***Count of the Twelve Tribes.*** 20Of the descendants of Reuben, the firstborn of Israel,
registered individually by name and lineage according to their clans and ancestral houses, every male of twenty years or more,
everyone fit for military service: 21those enrolled from the tribe of Reuben were forty-six thousand five hundred.

22Of the descendants of Simeon, registered individually by name and lineage according to their clans and ancestral houses, every male of twenty years or more, everyone fit for military service: 23those enrolled
from the tribe of Simeon were fifty-nine thousand three hundred.

24Of the descendants of Gad, registered by name and lineage according to their clans and ancestral houses, every male of twenty years or more, everyone fit for military service: 25those enrolled from the tribe of Gad
were forty-five thousand six hundred and fifty.

26Of the descendants of Judah, registered by name and lineage according to their clans and ancestral houses, every male of twenty years or more, everyone fit for military service: 27those enrolled from the tribe of Judah
were seventy-four thousand six hundred.

28Of the descendants of Issachar, registered by name and lineage according to their clans and ancestral houses, every male of twenty years or more, everyone fit for military service: 29those enrolled from the tribe of Issachar were fifty-four thousand four hundred.

30Of the descendants of Zebulun, registered by name and lineage according to their clans and ancestral houses, every male of twenty years or more, everyone fit for military service: 31those enrolled from the tribe
of Zebulun were fifty-seven thousand four hundred.

32Of the descendants of Joseph:

Of the descendants of Ephraim, registered by name and lineage according to their clans and ancestral houses, every male of twenty years or more, everyone fit for military service: 33those enrolled from the tribe of
Ephraim were forty thousand five hundred.

34Of the descendants of Manasseh, registered by name and lineage according to their clans and ancestral houses, every male of twenty years or more, everyone fit for military service: 35those enrolled from the tribe
of Manasseh were thirty-two thousand two hundred.

36Of the descendants of Benjamin, registered by name and lineage according to their clans and ancestral houses, every male of twenty years or more, everyone fit for military service: 37those enrolled from the tribe
of Benjamin were thirty-five thousand four hundred.

38Of the descendants of Dan, registered by name and lineage according to their clans and ancestral houses, every male of twenty years or more, everyone fit for military service: 39those enrolled from the tribe of Dan
were sixty-two thousand seven hundred.

40Of the descendants of Asher, registered by name and lineage according to their clans and ancestral houses, every male of twenty years or more, everyone fit for military service: 41those enrolled from the tribe of Asher
were forty-one thousand five hundred.

42Of the descendants of Naphtali, registered by name and lineage according to their clans and ancestral houses, every male of twenty years or more, everyone fit for military service: 43those enrolled from the tribe
of Naphtali were fifty-three thousand four hundred.

*d:* Ex 18:21, 25.

[44]It was these who were enrolled, each according to his ancestral house, by Moses and Aaron and the twelve leaders of Israel. [45]The total enrollment of the Israelites of twenty years or more, according to their ancestral houses, everyone fit for military service in Israel— [46]the total enrollment was six hundred and three thousand, five hundred and fifty.

*Levites Omitted in the Census.* [47]Now the Levites were not enrolled[e] by their ancestral tribe with the others.* [48]For the LORD had told Moses, [49]The tribe of Levi alone you shall not enroll nor include in the census along with the other Israelites. [50]You are to give the Levites charge of the tabernacle of the covenant with all its equipment and all that belongs to it. It is they who shall carry the tabernacle with all its equipment and who shall be its ministers;[f] and they shall camp all around the tabernacle. [51]When the tabernacle is to move on, the Levites shall take it down; when the tabernacle is to be pitched, it is the Levites who shall set it up. Any unauthorized person who comes near* it shall be put to death.[g] [52]The other Israelites shall camp according to their companies, each in their own divisional camps,[h] [53]but the Levites shall camp around the tabernacle of the covenant to ensure that God's wrath will not fall upon the Israelite community. The Levites shall keep guard over the tabernacle of the covenant.[i] [54]The Israelites complied; they did just as the LORD had commanded Moses.

## CHAPTER 2

See RG 80-85

*Arrangement of the Tribes.* [1]The LORD said to Moses and Aaron: [2]The Israelites shall camp, each in their own divisions, under the ensigns of their ancestral houses.[j] They shall camp at some distance all around the tent of meeting.

[3]* Encamped on the east side, toward the sunrise, shall be the divisional camp of Judah, arranged in companies. The leader of the Judahites is Nahshon, son of Amminadab, [4]and the enrollment of his company is seventy-four thousand six hundred. [5]Encamped beside it is the tribe of Issachar. The leader of the Issacharites is Nethanel, son of Zuar, [6]and the enrollment of his company is fifty-four thousand four hundred. [7]Also the tribe of Zebulun. The leader of the Zebulunites is Eliab, son of Helon, [8]and the enrollment of his company is fifty-seven thousand four hundred. [9]The total enrollment of the camp of Judah by companies is one hundred and eighty-six thousand four hundred. They shall be first on the march.

[10]The divisional camp of Reuben shall be on the south side, by companies. The leader of the Reubenites is Elizur, son of Shedeur, [11]and the enrollment of his company is forty-six thousand five hundred. [12]Encamped beside it is the tribe of Simeon. The leader of the Simeonites is Shelumiel, son of Zurishaddai, [13]and the enrollment of his company is fifty-nine thousand three hundred. [14]Next is the tribe of Gad. The leader of the Gadites is Eliasaph, son of Reuel, [15]and the enrollment of his company is forty-five thousand six hundred and fifty. [16]The total enrollment of the camp of Reuben by companies is one hundred and fifty-one thousand four hundred and fifty. They shall be second on the march.

[17]Then the tent of meeting and the camp of the Levites shall set out in the midst of the divisions. As they camp, so also they will march, each in place, by their divisions.

[18]The divisional camp of Ephraim shall be on the west side, by companies. The leader of the Ephraimites is Elishama, son of Ammihud, [19]and the enrollment of his company is forty thousand five hundred. [20]Beside it shall be the tribe of Manasseh. The leader of the Manassites is Gamaliel, son of Pedahzur, [21]and the enrollment of his company is

**1:47** The Levites were not enrolled in this census, which was principally for military purposes, but a separate census was made of them. Cf. 3:15–16, 39.

**1:51 Comes near**: here and in 3:10, 38; 17:5; 18:4, 7 the Hebrew word rendered "comes near" is very nearly a technical term for someone who intrudes upon or violates a space set apart as holy and for which they have not been qualified by priesthood.

**2:3–31** A similar arrangement of the tribes around the central sanctuary in the ideal Israel is given in Ez 48.

*e:* Nm 2:33; 3:14–39; 26:57–62. *f:* Nm 3:7–8; 4:2–49; 1 Chr 6:33. *g:* Nm 3:10, 38; 18:7; 2 Sm 6:6–7; 1 Chr 13:10. *h:* Nm 2:2, 34. *i:* Nm 3:7–8, 38; 8:19; 18:4–5. *j:* Nm 1:52.

thirty-two thousand two hundred. [22]Also the tribe of Benjamin. The leader of the Benjaminites is Abidan, son of Gideoni, [23]and the enrollment of his company is thirty-five thousand four hundred. [24]The total enrollment of the camp of Ephraim by companies is one hundred and eight thousand one hundred. They shall be third on the march.

[25]The divisional camp of Dan shall be on the north side, by companies. The leader of the Danites is Ahiezer, son of Ammishaddai, [26]and the enrollment of his company is sixty-two thousand seven hundred. [27]Encamped beside it shall be the tribe of Asher. The leader of the Asherites is Pagiel, son of Ochran, [28]and the enrollment of his company is forty-one thousand five hundred. [29]Also the tribe of Naphtali. The leader of the Naphtalites is Ahira, son of Enan, [30]and the enrollment of his company is fifty-three thousand four hundred. [31]The total enrollment of the camp of Dan is one hundred and fifty-seven thousand six hundred. They shall be the last on the march, by divisions.

[32k] These are the enrollments of the Israelites according to their ancestral houses. The total enrollment of the camps by companies is six hundred and three thousand five hundred and fifty. [33]The Levites, however, were not enrolled with the other Israelites, just as the LORD had commanded Moses. [34]The Israelites did just as the LORD had commanded Moses; both in camp and on the march they were in their own divisions, everyone by clan and according to ancestral house.

## CHAPTER 3

See RG 80-85

*The Sons of Aaron.* [1]These are the offspring of Aaron and Moses at the time the LORD spoke to Moses on Mount Sinai. [2]These are the names of Aaron's sons: Nadab, the firstborn, Abihu, Eleazar, and Ithamar.[l] [3]These are the names of Aaron's sons, the anointed priests whom he ordained to serve as priests. [4]But Nadab and Abihu died[m] in the presence of the LORD when they offered unauthorized fire before the LORD in the wilderness of Sinai; and they left no sons. So only Eleazar and Ithamar served as priests during the lifetime of their father Aaron.

*Levites in Place of the Firstborn.* [5]Now the LORD said to Moses: [6]Summon the tribe of Levi and station them before Aaron the priest to serve him.[n] [7]They shall discharge his obligations and those of the whole community before the tent of meeting[o] by maintaining the tabernacle. [8]They shall have responsibility for all the furnishings of the tent of meeting and discharge the obligations of the Israelites by maintaining the tabernacle. [9]You shall assign the Levites to Aaron and his sons;[p] they have been assigned unconditionally to him from among the Israelites. [10]But you will appoint only Aaron and his descendants to exercise the priesthood.[q] Any unauthorized person who comes near shall be put to death.

[11]The LORD said to Moses: [12]I hereby take the Levites from the Israelites in place of every firstborn that opens the womb among the Israelites.[r] The Levites, therefore, are mine, [13]because every firstborn is mine. When I struck down all the firstborn in the land of Egypt, I consecrated to me every firstborn in Israel, human being and beast alike. They belong to me; I am the LORD.

*Census of the Levites.* [14]The LORD said to Moses in the wilderness of Sinai: [15]Enroll the Levites by their ancestral houses and clans, enrolling every male of a month or more.[s] [16]Moses, therefore, enrolled them at the direction of the LORD, just as the LORD had charged.

[17t] These were the sons of Levi by name: Gershon, Kohath and Merari. [18]These were the names of the sons of Gershon, by their clans: Libni and Shimei. [19]The sons of Kohath, by their clans, were Amram, Izhar, Hebron and Uzziel. [20]The sons of Merari, by their clans, were Mahli and Mushi. These were the clans of the Levites by their ancestral houses.

*Duties of the Levitical Clans.* [21]To Gershon belonged the clan of the Libnites and the clan of the Shimeites; these were the

*k:* Nm 1:44–49. *l:* Ex 6:23; 1 Chr 24:1. *m:* Nm 26:61; Lv 10:1–2; 1 Chr 24:2. *n:* Nm 18:2. *o:* Nm 8:24. *p:* Nm 8:19. *q:* Nm 1:51; 18:7. *r:* Nm 3:41; 8:16–18; Ex 13:2, 12, 15. *s:* Nm 3:39; 26:62. *t:* Nm 26:57; Gn 46:11; Ex 6:16–19; 1 Chr 6:1–2, 16–19.

clans of the Gershonites. 22 Their enrollment, registering every male of a month or more, was seven thousand five hundred. 23 The clans of the Gershonites camped behind the tabernacle, to the west. 24 The leader of the ancestral house of the Gershonites was Eliasaph, son of Lael. 25[u] At the tent of meeting their responsibility was the tabernacle:[*] the tent and its covering, the curtain at the entrance of the tent of meeting, 26 the hangings of the court, the curtain at the entrance of the court enclosing both the tabernacle and the altar, and the ropes—whatever pertained to their maintenance.

27 To Kohath belonged the clans of the Amramites, the Izharites, the Hebronites, and the Uzzielites; these were the clans of the Kohathites. 28 Their enrollment, registering every male of a month or more, was eight thousand three hundred. They were the ones who performed the duties of the sanctuary. 29 The clans of the Kohathites camped on the south side of the tabernacle. 30 And the leader of their ancestral house of the clan of the Kohathites was Elizaphan, son of Uzziel. 31 Their responsibility was the ark, the table, the menorah, the altars, the utensils of the sanctuary with which the priests minister, the veil, and everything pertaining to their maintenance.[*] 32 The chief of the leaders of the Levites, however, was Eleazar, son of Aaron the priest; he was in charge of those who performed the duties of the sanctuary.

33 To Merari belonged the clans of the Mahlites and the Mushites; these were the clans of Merari. 34 Their enrollment, registering every male of a month or more, was six thousand two hundred. 35 The leader of the ancestral house of the clans of Merari was Zuriel, son of Abihail. They camped at the north side of the tabernacle. 36[*] The Merarites were assigned responsibility for the boards of the tabernacle, its bars, columns, pedestals, and all its fittings—and everything pertaining to their maintenance, 37 as well as the columns of the surrounding court with their pedestals, pegs and ropes.

38 East of the tabernacle, that is, in front of the tent of meeting, toward the sunrise, were camped Moses and Aaron and the latter's sons, performing the duties of the sanctuary incumbent upon the Israelites. Any unauthorized person who came near was to be put to death.

39 The total enrollment of the Levites whom Moses and Aaron enrolled at the direction of the LORD, by clans, every male a month old or more, was twenty-two thousand.

***Census and Ransom of Firstborn.*** 40 The LORD then said to Moses: Enroll every firstborn male of the Israelites a month old or more, and count the number of their names. 41 Then take the Levites for me—I am the LORD—in place of all the firstborn of the Israelites, as well as the Levites' cattle, in place of all the firstborn among the cattle of the Israelites. 42 So Moses enrolled all the firstborn of the Israelites, as the LORD had commanded him. 43 All the firstborn males, registered by name, of a month or more, numbered twenty-two thousand two hundred and seventy-three.

44 The LORD said to Moses: 45 Take the Levites in place of all the firstborn of the Israelites, and the Levites' cattle in place of their cattle, that the Levites may belong to me. I am the LORD. 46 As a redemption-price for the two hundred and seventy-three firstborn of the Israelites over and above the number of the Levites, 47 you shall take five shekels for each individual, according to the sanctuary shekel, twenty gerahs to the shekel.[v] 48 Give this money to Aaron and his sons as a redemption-price for the extra number. 49 So Moses took the redemption money for those

**3:25–26** The Gershonites had two wagons for transporting these things; cf. 7:7. For a description of the tabernacle, see Ex 26:1–6; the tent, Ex 26:7–13; its covering, Ex 26:14; the curtain at the entrance, Ex 26:36; the hangings of the court, Ex 27:9–15; the curtain at the entrance of the court, Ex 27:16; the ropes of the tabernacle, Ex 35:18.

**3:31** The Kohathites had to carry these sacred objects on their shoulders; cf. 7:9. For a description of the ark, see Ex 25:10–22; the table, Ex 25:23–30; the menorah, Ex 25:31–40; the altars, Ex 27:1–8; 30:1–10.

**3:36–37** The Merarites had four wagons for transporting this heavy material; cf. 7:8. For a description of the boards, bars, etc., of the tabernacle, see Ex 26:15–30; the columns, pedestals, etc., of the court, Ex 27:9–19.

*u:* Ex 26:7, 14, 36; 36:14. *v:* Nm 18:16; Ex 30:13; Lv 27:25; Ez 45:12.

### The Ark of the Commandments

THE ARK IS a wooden box holding the stone tablets of the Ten Commandments that also serves as a throne or footstool for the divine presence (Ex 25:10–22). The ark is housed in the inner room of the tabernacle within the meeting tent (see Ex 25–27; 30). The warning concerning the special danger to the Kohathites (Nm 4:17–20) stems from their responsibility to handle the most holy things (4:4).

over and above the ones redeemed by the Levites. [50]From the firstborn of the Israelites he took the money, one thousand three hundred and sixty-five shekels according to the sanctuary shekel. [51]He then gave this redemption money to Aaron and his sons, at the direction of the LORD, just as the LORD had commanded Moses.

## CHAPTER 4

See RG 80–85

***Duties Further Defined.*** [1]The LORD said to Moses and Aaron: [2]Take a census among the Levites of the Kohathites, by clans and ancestral houses, [3]all between thirty* and fifty years of age, who will join the personnel for doing tasks in the tent of meeting.[w]

[4]This is the task of the Kohathites in the tent of meeting: the most sacred objects. [5]In breaking camp, Aaron and his sons shall go in and take down the screening curtain* and cover the ark of the covenant with it. [6]Over these they shall put a cover of yellow-orange skin, and on top of this spread an all-violet cloth and put the poles in place. [7]On the table of the Presence they shall spread a violet cloth and put on it the plates and cups, as well as the bowls and pitchers for libations; the established bread offering shall remain on the table. [8]Over these they shall spread a scarlet cloth and cover it with a covering of yellow-orange skin, and put the poles in place. [9]They shall use a violet cloth to cover the menorah of the light with its lamps, tongs, and trays, as well as the various containers of oil from which it is supplied. [10]The menorah with all its utensils they shall then put in a covering of yellow-orange skin, and place on a litter. [11]Over the golden altar* they shall spread a violet cloth, and cover this also with a covering of yellow-orange skin, and put the poles in place. [12]Taking the utensils of the sanctuary service, they shall put them all in violet cloth and cover them with a covering of yellow-orange skin. They shall then place them on a litter. [13]After cleansing the altar* of its ashes, they shall spread a purple cloth over it. [14]On this they shall put all the utensils with which it is served: the fire pans, forks,* shovels, basins, and all the utensils of the altar. They shall then spread a covering of yellow-orange skin over this, and put the poles in place.

[15]Only after Aaron and his sons have finished covering the sacred objects and all their utensils on breaking camp, can the Kohathites enter to carry them. But they shall not touch the sacred objects; if they do they will die.[x] These, then, are the objects in the tent of meeting that the Kohathites shall carry.

[16]Eleazar, son of Aaron the priest, shall be in charge of the oil for the light, the fragrant incense, the established grain offering, and the anointing oil. He shall be in charge of the whole tabernacle with all the sacred objects and utensils that are in it.

[17]The LORD said to Moses and Aaron: [18]Do not let the group of Kohathite clans perish from among the Levites. [19]That they

**4:3 Thirty**: according to other passages the Levites began to serve when they were twenty-five (8:24) or even only twenty years old (1 Chr 23:24, 27; 2 Chr 31:17; Ezr 3:8; but cf. 1 Chr 23:3).

**4:5 The screening curtain**: the veil between the inner and the outer rooms of the sanctuary. Cf. Ex 26:31–33.

**4:11 The golden altar**: the altar of incense. Cf. Ex 30:1–6.

**4:13 The altar**: the bronze altar for animal sacrifices. Cf. Ex 27:1–8.

**4:14 Forks**: used in turning over the sacrificed animal on the fire of the altar. **Basins**: to receive the sacrificial blood; cf. Zec 9:15.

*w*: Nm 8:24; 1 Chr 23:24–27. *x*: 2 Sm 6:6–7; 1 Chr 13:9–10.

may live and not die when they approach the most sacred objects, this is what you shall do for them: Aaron and his sons shall go in and assign to each of them his task and what he must carry; [20]but the Kohathites shall not go in to look upon the sacred objects even for an instant, or they will die.[y]

[21]The LORD said to Moses: [22]Take a census of the Gershonites also, by ancestral houses and clans, [23]enrolling all between thirty and fifty years of age who will join the personnel to do the work in the tent of meeting. [24]This is the task of the clans of the Gershonites, what they must do and what they must carry: [25]they shall carry the curtains of the tabernacle, the tent of meeting with its covering and the outer wrapping of yellow-orange skin, the curtain at the entrance of the tent of meeting, [26]the hangings of the court, the curtain at the entrance to the gate of the court that encloses both the tabernacle and the altar, together with their ropes and all other objects necessary for their use. Whatever is to be done to maintain these things, they shall do. [27]The service of the Gershonites shall be entirely under the direction of Aaron and his sons, with regard to what they must carry and what they must do; you shall list for them by name what they are to carry. [28]This, then, is the task of the clans of the Gershonites in the tent of meeting; and they shall be under the supervision of Ithamar, son of Aaron the priest.

[29]The Merarites, too, you shall enroll by clans and ancestral houses, [30]enrolling all between thirty and fifty years of age who will join the personnel to maintain the tent of meeting. [31][z] This is what they shall be responsible for carrying, with respect to all their service in the tent of meeting: the boards of the tabernacle with its bars, columns and pedestals, [32]and the columns of the surrounding court with their pedestals, pegs and ropes, including all their accessories and everything for their maintenance. You shall list by name the objects they shall be responsible for carrying. [33]This, then, is the task of the clans of the Merarites with respect to all their service in the tent of meeting under the supervision of Ithamar, son of Aaron the priest.

***Number of Adult Levites.*** [34]So Moses and Aaron and the leaders of the community enrolled the Kohathites, by clans and ancestral houses, [35]all between thirty and fifty years of age who will join the personnel to work in the tent of meeting; [36]their enrollment by clans was two thousand seven hundred and fifty. [37]Such was the enrollment of the clans of the Kohathites, everyone who was to serve in the tent of meeting, whom Moses enrolled, together with Aaron, as the LORD directed through Moses.

[38]As for the enrollment of the Gershonites, by clans and ancestral houses, [39]all between thirty and fifty years of age who will join the personnel to work in the tent of meeting— [40]their enrollment by clans and ancestral houses was two thousand six hundred and thirty. [41]Such was the enrollment of the clans of the Gershonites, everyone who was to serve in the tent of meeting, whom Moses enrolled, together with Aaron, as the LORD directed.

[42]As for the enrollment of the clans of the Merarites, by clans and ancestral houses, [43]all from thirty up to fifty years of age who will join the personnel to work in the tent of meeting— [44]their enrollment by clans was three thousand two hundred. [45]Such was the enrollment of the clans of the Merarites, whom Moses enrolled, together with Aaron, as the LORD directed through Moses.

[46]As for the total enrollment of the Levites, which Moses and Aaron and the Israelite leaders had made, by clans and ancestral houses, [47]all between thirty and fifty years of age who were to undertake tasks of service or transport for the tent of meeting— [48]their total enrollment was eight thousand five hundred and eighty. [49]As the LORD directed through Moses, they gave each of them their assignments for service and for transport; just as the LORD had commanded Moses.

## CHAPTER 5

See RG 80–85

***The Unclean Expelled.*** [1]The LORD said to Moses: [2]Order the Israelites to expel

*y:* 1 Sm 6:19–20. *z:* Nm 3:36–37.

from camp everyone with a scaly infection, and everyone suffering from a discharge, and everyone who has become unclean by contact with a corpse.* [a] 3 Male and female alike, you shall expel them. You shall expel them from the camp so that they do not defile their camp, where I dwell in their midst.[b] 4 This the Israelites did, expelling them from the camp; just as the LORD had commanded Moses, so the Israelites did.

***Unjust Possession.*** * 5 The LORD said to Moses: 6 [c] Tell the Israelites: If a man or a woman commits any offense against another person, thus breaking faith with the LORD, and thereby becomes guilty, 7 that person shall confess the wrong that has been done, make restitution in full, and in addition give one fifth of its value to the one that has been wronged. 8 However, if there is no next of kin,* one to whom restitution can be made, the restitution shall be made to the LORD and shall fall to the priest; this is apart from the ram of atonement with which the priest makes atonement for the guilty individual. 9 Likewise, every contribution among the sacred offerings that the Israelites present to the priest will belong to him.[d] 10 Each shall possess his own sacred offerings; what is given to a priest shall be his.[e]

***Ordeal for Suspected Adultery.*** 11 The LORD said to Moses: 12 Speak to the Israelites and tell them: If a man's wife goes astray and becomes unfaithful to him 13 by virtue of a man having intercourse with her[f] in secret from her husband and she is able to conceal the fact that she has defiled herself for lack of a witness who might have caught her in the act; 14 or if a man is overcome by a feeling of jealousy that makes him suspect his wife, and she has defiled herself; or if a man is overcome by a feeling of jealousy that makes him suspect his wife and she has not defiled herself— 15 then the man shall bring his wife to the priest as well as an offering on her behalf, a tenth of an ephah* of barley meal. However, he shall not pour oil on it nor put frankincense over it, since it is a grain offering of jealousy, a grain offering of remembrance which recalls wrongdoing.

16 The priest shall first have the woman come forward and stand before the LORD. 17 In an earthen vessel he shall take holy water,* as well as some dust from the floor of the tabernacle and put it in the water.[g] 18 Making the woman stand before the LORD, the priest shall uncover her head and place in her hands the grain offering of remembrance, that is, the grain offering of jealousy, while he himself shall hold the water of bitterness that brings a curse. 19 Then the priest shall adjure the woman, saying to her, "If no other man has had intercourse with you, and you have not gone astray by defiling yourself while under the authority of your husband, be immune to this water of bitterness that brings a curse. 20 But if you have gone astray while under the authority of your husband, and if you have defiled yourself and a man other than your husband has had intercourse with you"— 21 so shall the priest adjure the woman with this imprecation—"may the LORD make you a curse and malediction* among your people by causing your uterus to fall and your belly to swell! 22 May this water, then, that brings a curse, enter your bowels to make your belly swell and your uterus fall!"[h] And the woman shall say, "Amen, amen!"* 23 The priest shall put these curses in writing and shall then wash them off into the water of bitterness, 24 and he will have the woman

**5:2** For the laws regarding victims of skin disease, see Lv 13–14; those suffering from a discharge, Lv 15; those unclean by contact with a corpse, Nm 19:11–22; Lv 21:1–4.

**5:5–10** The basic law on unjust possession is given in Lv 5:14–26. The new item here concerns the case where the injured party has died and left no heirs, in which case the restitution must be made to the priest.

**5:8 Next of kin**: Hebrew *go'el* ("redeemer"), a technical term denoting the nearest relative, upon whom devolved the obligation of "redeeming" the family property, in order to keep it within the family. Cf. Lv 25:25; Ru 4:1–6.

**5:15 Ephah**: see note on Is 5:10.

**5:17 Holy water**: water from the basin that stood in the court of the tabernacle.

**5:21 Curse and malediction**: the woman's name would be used in curses and oaths to invoke a similar misfortune on another person or on oneself. Cf. Is 65:15; Jer 29:22.

**5:22 Amen**: a Hebrew word meaning "certainly, truly," used to give assent to a statement, a curse, a blessing, a prayer, or the like, in the sense of "so be it."

*a:* Nm 19:11, 13; Lv 13:46; 21:1; 22:4. *b:* Nm 35:34. *c:* Lv 5:21–25. *d:* Dt 18:3–4; Ez 44:29–30. *e:* Lv 10:12–15. *f:* Lv 18:20; Jn 8:4. *g:* Nm 19:17. *h:* Ps 109:18.

drink the water of bitterness that brings a curse, so that the water that brings a curse may enter into her to her bitter hurt. 25 But first the priest shall take the grain offering of jealousy from the woman's hand, and having elevated the grain offering before the LORD, shall bring it to the altar, 26 where he shall take a handful of the grain offering as a token offering and burn it on the altar.[i] Only then shall he have the woman drink the water. 27 Once he has had her drink the water, if she has defiled herself and been unfaithful to her husband, the water that brings a curse will enter into her to her bitter hurt, and her belly will swell and her uterus will fall, so that she will become a curse among her people. 28 If, however, the woman has not defiled herself, but is still pure, she will be immune and will still be fertile.

29 This, then, is the ritual for jealousy when a woman goes astray while under the authority of her husband and defiles herself, 30 or when such a feeling of jealousy comes over a man that he becomes suspicious of his wife; he shall have her stand before the LORD, and the priest shall perform this entire ritual for her. 31 The man shall be free from punishment,* but the woman shall bear her punishment.

## CHAPTER 6

See RG 80–85

***Laws Concerning Nazirites.*** 1 The LORD said to Moses: 2 Speak to the Israelites and tell them: When men or women solemnly take the nazirite* vow to dedicate themselves to the LORD, 3 they shall abstain from wine and strong drink;[j] they may neither drink wine vinegar, other vinegar, or any kind of grape juice, nor eat either fresh or dried grapes. 4 As long as they are nazirites they shall not eat anything of the produce of the grapevine; not even the seeds or the skins. 5 While they are under the nazirite vow, no razor shall touch their hair.[k] Until the period of their dedication to the LORD is over, they shall be holy, letting the hair of their heads grow freely. 6 As long as they are dedicated to the LORD, they shall not come near a dead person.[l] 7 Not even for their father or mother, sister or brother, should they defile themselves, when these die, since their heads bear their dedication to God. 8 As long as they are nazirites they are holy to the LORD.

9 If someone dies very suddenly in their presence, defiling their dedicated heads, they shall shave their heads on the day of their purification, that is, on the seventh day. 10 On the eighth day they shall bring two turtledoves or two pigeons to the priest at the entrance of the tent of meeting. 11 The priest shall offer up the one as a purification offering and the other as a burnt offering, thus making atonement for them for the sin they committed with respect to the corpse. On the same day they shall reconsecrate their heads 12 and rededicate themselves to the LORD for the period of their dedication, bringing a yearling lamb as a reparation offering. The previous period is not valid, because they defiled their dedicated heads.

13 This is the ritual for the nazirites:[m] When the period of their dedication is complete they shall go to the entrance of the tent of meeting, 14 bringing their offerings to the LORD, one unblemished yearling lamb for a burnt offering, one unblemished yearling ewe lamb for a purification offering, one unblemished ram as a communion offering, 15 and a basket of unleavened cakes of bran flour mixed with oil and of unleavened wafers spread with oil, along with their grain offerings and libations. 16 The priest shall present them before the LORD, and shall offer

**5:31 Free from punishment**: the point is that a husband will not suffer a harmful consequence if his accusation is not borne out by the ordeal; if he's right, his wife's punishment vindicates him. For her part, the woman (if guilty) must bear her punishment.

**6:2–21 Nazirite**: from the Hebrew word *nazir*, meaning "set apart as sacred, dedicated, vowed." The nazirite vow could be either for a limited period or for life. Those bound by this vow had to abstain from all the products of the grapevine, from cutting or shaving their hair, and from contact with a corpse. They were regarded as men and women of God like the prophets; cf. Am 2:11–12. Examples of lifelong nazirites were Samson (Jgs 13:4–5, 7; 16:17), Samuel (1 Sm 1:11), and John the Baptist (Lk 1:15). At the time of Jesus the practice of taking the nazirite vow for a limited period seems to have been quite common, even among the early Christians; cf. Acts 18:18; 21:23–24, 26.

*i:* Lv 5:12. *j:* Jgs 13:7, 14. *k:* Jgs 13:5; 16:17; 1 Sm 1:11. *l:* Nm 19:11, 16; Lv 21:11. *m:* Acts 21:24, 26.

**The Priestly Blessing**

PRIESTS CONCLUDED COMMUNAL worship with the words of blessing and peace in 6:24–26. Two silver cylinders discovered by archaeologists and dated to 600 B.C. contain portions of this ancient priestly blessing written in Hebrew. To let one's face shine and look upon someone kindly (lit. "lift up the face") are images of protection, favor, and graciousness (6:25–26; see Ps 67:1–2; Jb 34:29). Peace ("shalom") connotes well-being and wholeness in all aspects of one's life (6:26). Putting the divine name upon the Israelites implies that they belong exclusively to the LORD and that the LORD will care for them.

up the purification offering and the burnt offering for them. 17He shall then offer up the
ram as a communion sacrifice to the LORD,
along with the basket of unleavened cakes,
and the priest will offer the grain offering and
libation. 18Then at the entrance of the tent of
meeting the nazirite shall shave his or her
dedicated head, take the hair of the dedicated
head, and put it in the fire under the communion sacrifice. 19After the nazirite has
shaved off the dedicated hair, the priest shall
take a boiled shoulder of the ram, as well as
one unleavened cake from the basket and one
unleavened wafer, and shall put them in the
hands of the nazirite. 20The priest shall then
elevate them as an elevated offering before
the LORD. They are an offering belonging to
the priest, along with the brisket of the elevated offering and the leg of the contribution.
Only after this may the nazirite drink wine.

21This, then, is the law for the nazirites,
that is, what they vow as their offering to the
LORD in accord with their dedication, apart
from anything else which their means may
allow. In keeping with the vow they take so
shall they do, according to the law of their
dedication.

***The Priestly Blessing.*** 22The LORD said to
Moses: 23Speak to Aaron and his sons and
tell them: This is how you shall bless the Israelites. Say to them:

24 The LORD bless you and keep you!
25 The LORD let his face shine upon you,
and be gracious to you!
26 The LORD look upon you kindly and give
you peace!*

27So shall they invoke my name upon the Israelites, and I will bless them.

## CHAPTER 7

See RG 80–85

***Offerings of the Tribal Leaders.*** 1Now,
when Moses had completed the erection of
the tabernacle, he anointed and consecrated
it with all its equipment,[n] as well as the altar
with all its equipment. After he anointed and
consecrated them, 2an offering was made by
the tribal leaders of Israel, who were heads
of ancestral houses, the same leaders of the
tribes who supervised those enrolled. 3The
offering they brought before the LORD consisted of six wagons for baggage and twelve
oxen, that is, a wagon for every two tribal
leaders, and an ox for each. These they presented before the tabernacle.

4The LORD then said to Moses: 5Accept
their offering, that these things may be put to
use to maintain the tent of meeting. Assign
them to the Levites, to each according to his
duties. 6So Moses accepted the wagons and
oxen, and assigned them to the Levites. 7He
gave two wagons and four oxen to the Gershonites[o] according to their duties, 8and four
wagons and eight oxen to the Merarites according to their duties, under the supervision
of Ithamar, son of Aaron the priest. 9He gave
none to the Kohathites, because they were responsible for maintenance of the sacred objects that had to be carried on their shoulders.[p]

**6:26 Peace**: the Hebrew word *Shalom* includes the idea of happiness, good health, prosperity, friendship, and general well-being. To use this term as a greeting was to pray for all these things upon the one greeted.

*n:* Ex 40:17. *o:* Nm 4:24–33. *p:* Nm 3:31; 4:4–15.

10For the dedication of the altar also, the
tribal leaders brought offerings when it was
anointed;[q] the leaders presented their offering before the altar. 11But the LORD said to
Moses: Let one leader each day present his
offering for the dedication of the altar.
12* The one who presented his offering on
the first day was Nahshon, son of Amminadab, of the tribe of Judah. 13His offering
consisted of one silver plate weighing a hundred and thirty shekels and one silver basin
weighing seventy shekels according to the
sanctuary shekel, both filled with bran flour
mixed with oil for a grain offering; 14one
gold cup of ten shekels' weight filled with
incense; 15one bull from the herd, one ram,
and one yearling lamb for a burnt offering;
16one goat for a purification offering; 17and
two bulls, five rams, five he-goats, and five
yearling lambs for a communion sacrifice.
This was the offering of Nahshon, son of
Amminadab.
18On the second day Nethanel, son of
Zuar, tribal leader of Issachar, made his offering. 19He presented as his offering one silver plate weighing a hundred and thirty
shekels and one silver basin weighing seventy shekels according to the sanctuary
shekel, both filled with bran flour mixed
with oil for a grain offering; 20one gold cup
of ten shekels' weight filled with incense;
21one bull from the herd, one ram, and one
yearling lamb for a burnt offering; 22one
goat for a purification offering; 23and two
bulls, five rams, five he-goats, and five yearling lambs for a communion sacrifice. This
was the offering of Nethanel, son of Zuar.
24On the third day it was the turn of the
tribal leader of the Zebulunites, Eliab, son of
Helon. 25His offering consisted of one silver
plate weighing a hundred and thirty shekels
and one silver basin weighing seventy
shekels according to the sanctuary shekel,
both filled with bran flour mixed with oil for
a grain offering; 26one gold cup of ten
shekels' weight filled with incense; 27one
bull from the herd, one ram, and one yearling lamb for a burnt offering; 28one goat for
a purification offering; 29and two bulls, five
rams, five he-goats, and five yearling lambs
for a communion sacrifice. This was the offering of Eliab, son of Helon.
30On the fourth day it was the turn of the
tribal leader of the Reubenites, Elizur, son of
Shedeur. 31His offering consisted of one silver plate weighing a hundred and thirty
shekels and one silver basin weighing seventy shekels according to the sanctuary
shekel, both filled with bran flour mixed
with oil for a grain offering; 32one gold cup
of ten shekels' weight filled with incense;
33one bull from the herd, one ram, and one
yearling lamb for a burnt offering; 34one
goat for a purification offering; 35and two
bulls, five rams, five he-goats, and five yearling lambs for a communion sacrifice. This
was the offering of Elizur, son of Shedeur.
36On the fifth day it was the turn of the
tribal leader of the Simeonites, Shelumiel,
son of Zurishaddai. 37His offering consisted
of one silver plate weighing a hundred and
thirty shekels and one silver basin weighing
seventy shekels according to the sanctuary
shekel, both filled with bran flour mixed with
oil for a grain offering; 38one gold cup of ten
shekels' weight filled with incense; 39one
bull from the herd, one ram, and one yearling
lamb for a burnt offering; 40one goat for a purification offering; 41and two bulls, five
rams, five he-goats, and five yearling lambs
for a communion sacrifice. This was the offering of Shelumiel, son of Zurishaddai.
42On the sixth day it was the turn of the
tribal leader of the Gadites, Eliasaph, son of
Reuel. 43His offering consisted of one silver
plate weighing a hundred and thirty shekels
and one silver basin weighing seventy
shekels according to the sanctuary shekel,
both filled with bran flour mixed with oil for
a grain offering; 44one gold cup of ten
shekels' weight filled with incense; 45one
bull from the herd, one ram, and one yearling lamb for a burnt offering; 46one goat for
a purification offering; 47and two bulls, five

**7:12–88** The repetitious account of the same offerings brought by each of the twelve tribal leaders and the summary of them are characteristic of an official registration.

*q:* Nm 7:84.

rams, five he-goats, and five yearling lambs
for a communion sacrifice. This was the offering of Eliasaph, son of Reuel.
[48]On the seventh day it was the turn of the
tribal leader of the Ephraimites, Elishama,
son of Ammihud. [49]His offering consisted of
one silver plate weighing a hundred and
thirty shekels and one silver basin weighing
seventy shekels according to the sanctuary
shekel, both filled with bran flour mixed with
oil for a grain offering; [50]one gold cup of ten
shekels' weight filled with incense; [51]one
bull from the herd, one ram, and one yearling
lamb for a burnt offering; [52]one goat for a purification offering; [53]and two bulls, five
rams, five he-goats, and five yearling lambs
for a communion sacrifice. This was the offering of Elishama, son of Ammihud.
[54]On the eighth day it was the turn of the
tribal leader of the Manassites, Gamaliel, son
of Pedahzur. [55]His offering consisted of one
silver plate weighing a hundred and thirty
shekels and one silver basin weighing seventy shekels according to the sanctuary
shekel, both filled with bran flour mixed with
oil for a grain offering; [56]one gold cup of ten
shekels' weight filled with incense; [57]one
bull from the herd, one ram, and one yearling
lamb for a burnt offering; [58]one goat for a purification offering; [59]and two bulls, five
rams, five he-goats, and five yearling lambs
for a communion sacrifice. This was the offering of Gamaliel, son of Pedahzur.
[60]On the ninth day it was the turn of the
tribal leader of the Benjaminites, Abidan,
son of Gideoni. [61]His offering consisted of
one silver plate weighing a hundred and
thirty shekels and one silver basin weighing
seventy shekels according to the sanctuary
shekel, both filled with bran flour mixed
with oil for a grain offering; [62]one gold cup
of ten shekels' weight filled with incense;
[63]one bull from the herd, one ram, and one
yearling lamb for a burnt offering; [64]one
goat for a purification offering; [65]and two
bulls, five rams, five he-goats, and five yearling lambs for a communion sacrifice. This
was the offering of Abidan, son of Gideoni.
[66]On the tenth day it was the turn of the
tribal leader of the Danites, Ahiezer, son of
Ammishaddai. [67]His offering consisted of
one silver plate weighing a hundred and
thirty shekels and one silver basin weighing
seventy shekels according to the sanctuary
shekel, both filled with bran flour mixed with
oil for a grain offering; [68]one gold cup of ten
shekels' weight filled with incense; [69]one
bull from the herd, one ram, and one yearling
lamb for a burnt offering; [70]one goat for a purification offering; [71]and two bulls, five
rams, five he-goats, and five yearling lambs
for a communion sacrifice. This was the offering of Ahiezer, son of Ammishaddai.
[72]On the eleventh day it was the turn of
the tribal leader of the Asherites, Pagiel, son
of Ochran. [73]His offering consisted of one
silver plate weighing one hundred and thirty
shekels and one silver basin weighing seventy shekels according to the sanctuary
shekel, both filled with bran flour mixed
with oil for a grain offering; [74]one gold cup
of ten shekels' weight filled with incense;
[75]one bull from the herd, one ram, and one
yearling lamb for a burnt offering; [76]one
goat for a purification offering; [77]and two
bulls, five rams, five he-goats, and five yearling lambs for a communion sacrifice. This
was the offering of Pagiel, son of Ochran.
[78]On the twelfth day it was the turn of the
tribal leader of the Naphtalites, Ahira, son of
Enan. [79]His offering consisted of one silver
plate weighing a hundred and thirty shekels
and one silver basin weighing seventy
shekels according to the sanctuary shekel,
both filled with bran flour mixed with oil for
a grain offering; [80]one gold cup of ten
shekels' weight filled with incense; [81]one
bull from the herd, one ram, and one yearling lamb for a burnt offering; [82]one goat for
a purification offering; [83]and two bulls, five
rams, five he-goats, and five yearling lambs
for a communion sacrifice. This was the offering of Ahira, son of Enan.
[84]These were the offerings for the dedication of the altar, given by the tribal leaders of
Israel on the occasion of its anointing: twelve
silver plates, twelve silver basins, and twelve
gold cups. [85]Each silver plate weighed a hundred and thirty shekels, and each silver basin
seventy, so that all the silver of these vessels
amounted to two thousand four hundred
shekels, according to the sanctuary shekel.

[86]The twelve gold cups that were filled with incense weighed ten shekels apiece, according to the sanctuary shekel, so that all the gold of the cups amounted to one hundred and twenty shekels. [87]The animals for the burnt offerings were, in all, twelve bulls, twelve rams, and twelve yearling lambs, with their grain offerings; those for the purification offerings were twelve goats. [88]The animals for the communion sacrifices were, in all, twenty-four bulls, sixty rams, sixty he-goats, and sixty yearling lambs. These, then, were the offerings for the dedication of the altar after it was anointed.

*The Voice.* [89]When Moses entered the tent of meeting to speak with God, he heard the voice addressing him from above the cover[r] on the ark of the covenant, from between the two cherubim; and so it spoke to him.

## CHAPTER 8

See RG 80–85

*The Menorah.* [1]The LORD said to Moses: [2]Speak to Aaron and say: "When you set up the menorah-lamps,[s] have the seven lamps throw their light in front of the menorah."* [3]Aaron did so, setting up the menorah-lamps to face the area in front of the menorah, just as the LORD had commanded Moses. [4]This is the construction of the menorah: hammered gold,[t] from its base to its bowls* it was hammered; according to the pattern which the LORD had shown Moses, so he made the menorah.

*Purification of the Levites.* [5]The LORD said to Moses: [6]Take the Levites from among the Israelites and cleanse them.* [7]This is what you shall do to them to cleanse them. Sprinkle them with the water of purification, have them shave their whole bodies and wash their garments, and so cleanse themselves. [8]Then they shall take a bull from the herd, along with its grain offering of bran flour mixed with oil; and you shall take another bull from the herd for a purification offering. [9]Bringing the Levites before the tent of meeting, you shall assemble also the whole community of the Israelites. [10]When you have brought the Levites before the LORD, the Israelites shall lay their hands upon them. [11]Aaron shall then present the Levites before the LORD as an elevated offering from the Israelites, that they may perform the service of the LORD. [12]The Levites in turn shall lay their hands on the heads of the bulls, offering one as a purification offering and the other as a burnt offering to the LORD, to make atonement for the Levites. [13]Then you shall have the Levites stand before Aaron and his sons, and you shall present them as an elevated offering to the LORD; [14]thus you shall separate the Levites from the rest of the Israelites, and the Levites shall belong to me.[u]

[15]Only then shall the Levites enter upon their service in the tent of meeting, when you have cleansed them and presented them as an elevated offering. [16]For they, among the Israelites, are totally dedicated to me; I have taken them for myself in place of everyone that opens the womb, the firstborn of all the Israelites.[v] [17]Indeed, all the firstborn among the Israelites, human being and beast alike, belong to me; I consecrated them to myself on the day I killed all the firstborn in the land of Egypt.[w] [18]But I have taken the Levites in place of all the firstborn Israelites; [19]and from among the Israelites I have given to Aaron and his sons these Levites, who are to be dedicated,[x] to perform the service of the Israelites in the tent of meeting and to make atonement for them, so that no plague may strike among the Israelites should they come too near the sanctuary.

[20]This, then, is what Moses and Aaron and the whole community of the Israelites did with respect to the Levites; the Israelites did exactly as the LORD had commanded Moses concerning them. [21]When the Levites had purified themselves* and washed their gar-

**8:2 Menorah**: a seven-branched lampstand; see Ex 25:31–40; 37:17–24.

**8:4 Bowls**: lit., "blossom," a designation for the blossom-shaped cups holding the lamps of the menorah.

**8:6 Cleanse them**: in the language of the Pentateuch only the priests were "consecrated," that is, made sacred or set aside for the Lord, in an elaborate ceremony described in Ex 29 and in this chapter. The Levites were "cleansed," that is, made ritually clean for their special work.

**8:21 Purified themselves**: by having the "water of purification" sprinkled on them as prescribed in v. 7.

*r:* Ex 25:22. *s:* Ex 25:37. *t:* Ex 25:31, 40. *u:* Nm 3:45. *v:* Nm 3:12, 45. *w:* Nm 3:13; Lk 2:23. *x:* Nm 3:9–10.

ments, Aaron presented them as an elevated offering before the LORD, and made atonement for them to cleanse them. 22 Only then did they enter upon their service in the tent of meeting under the supervision of Aaron and his sons. Exactly as the LORD had commanded Moses concerning the Levites, so it was done with regard to them.

***Age Limits for Levitical Service.*** 23 The LORD said to Moses: 24 This is the rule for the Levites. Everyone twenty-five years old or more shall join the personnel in the service of the tent of meeting.[y] 25 But everyone fifty on up shall retire from the work force and serve no more. 26 They shall assist their fellow Levites in the tent of meeting in performing their duties, but they shall not do the work. This, then, is how you are to regulate the duties of the Levites.

See RG 80–85

## CHAPTER 9

***Second Passover.*** 1 The LORD said to Moses in the wilderness of Sinai, in the first month of the second year following their departure from the land of Egypt: 2 Tell the Israelites to celebrate the Passover at the prescribed time. 3 In the evening twilight of the fourteenth day of this month[z] you shall celebrate it at its prescribed time, in accord with all its statutes and regulations. 4 So Moses told the Israelites to celebrate the Passover, 5 and they did celebrate the Passover on the fourteenth day of the first month during the evening twilight in the wilderness of Sinai. Just as the LORD had commanded Moses, so the Israelites did.

6 There were some, however, who were unclean because of a human corpse and so could not celebrate the Passover that day. These men came up to Moses and Aaron that same day 7 and they said to them, "Although we are unclean because of a human corpse, why should we be deprived of presenting the LORD's offering at its prescribed time along with other Israelites?" 8 Moses answered them, "Wait so that I can learn what the LORD will command in your regard."

9 The LORD then said to Moses: 10 Speak to the Israelites: "If any one of you or of your descendants is unclean because of a human corpse, or is absent on a journey, you may still celebrate the LORD's Passover. 11 But you shall celebrate it in the second month,[a] on the fourteenth day of that month during the evening twilight, eating it with unleavened bread and bitter herbs, 12 and not leaving any of it over till morning, nor breaking any of its bones,[b] but observing all the statutes of the Passover. 13 However, anyone who is clean and not away on a journey, who yet fails to celebrate the Passover, shall be cut off from the people, for not presenting the LORD's offering at the prescribed time. That person shall bear the consequences of this sin.

14 "If an alien* who lives among you would celebrate the LORD's Passover, it shall be celebrated according to the statutes and regulations for the Passover. You shall have the same law for the resident alien as for the native of the land."[c]

***The Fiery Cloud.*** 15 On the day when the tabernacle was erected, the cloud* covered the tabernacle, the tent of the covenant; but from evening until morning it took on the appearance of fire over the tabernacle.[d] 16 It was always so: during the day the cloud covered the tabernacle and at night had the appearance of fire. 17 Whenever the cloud rose from the tent, the Israelites would break camp; wherever the cloud settled, the Israelites would pitch camp.[e] 18 At the direction of the LORD the Israelites broke camp, and at the LORD's direction they pitched camp.[f] As long as the cloud stayed over the tabernacle, they remained in camp.

19 Even when the cloud lingered many days over the tabernacle, the Israelites kept the charge of the LORD and would not move on. 20 Yet if it happened the cloud was over the tabernacle only for a few days, at the di-

**9:14 An alien**: compare this passage with the Passover legislation in Ex 12:48, where circumcision is required of the alien who would celebrate the feast.

**9:15 The cloud**: already mentioned at the departure from Egypt; cf. Ex 13:21–22.

---

*y:* Nm 4:3, 23. *z:* Ex 12:6; Lv 23:5. *a:* 2 Chr 30:2–15. *b:* Ex 12:46; Jn 19:36. *c:* Ex 12:48–49. *d:* Ex 13:21. *e:* Wis 18:3. *f:* 1 Cor 10:1.

**The Two Silver Trumpets**

THE TWO SILVER trumpets (ch 10) are sacred instruments blown by priests for four purposes: to call together the whole congregation or the leaders for an assembly (vv. 3–4), to provide a signal to set out from camp on the wilderness sojourn (vv. 5–6), to sound an alarm at the time of war (v. 9), and to call a celebration on "your festivals" (v. 10). According to the ancient Jewish historian Josephus and as depicted on ancient Jewish coins, the silver trumpets are about twelve inches long with a slender body and wide mouth.

rection of the LORD they stayed in camp; and at the LORD's direction they broke camp. 21If it happened the cloud remained there only from evening until morning, when the cloud rose in the morning, they would break camp. Whether the cloud lifted during the day or the night they would then break camp. 22Whether the cloud lingered over the tabernacle for two days or for a month or longer, the Israelites remained in camp and did not break camp; but when it lifted, they broke camp. 23At the direction of the LORD they pitched camp, and at the LORD's direction they broke camp; they kept the charge of the LORD, as the LORD directed them through Moses.

See RG 80–85

### CHAPTER 10

*The Silver Trumpets.* 1The LORD said to Moses: 2Make two trumpets of silver, making them of hammered silver, for you to use in summoning the community and in breaking camp. 3When both are blown, the whole community shall gather round you at the entrance of the tent of meeting; 4but when one of them is blown, only the tribal leaders, the heads of the clans of Israel, shall gather round you. 5When you sound the signal, those encamped on the east side shall break camp; 6when you sound a second signal, those encamped on the south side shall break camp; when you sound a third signal, those encamped on the west side shall break camp; when you sound a fourth signal, those encamped on the north side shall break camp. Thus shall the signal be sounded for them to break camp. 7But in calling forth an assembly you are to blow a blast, without sounding the signal.

8The sons of Aaron, the priests, shall blow the trumpets; this is prescribed forever for you and your descendants. 9[g] When in your own land you go to war against an enemy that is attacking you, you shall sound the alarm on the trumpets, and you shall be remembered before the LORD, your God, and be saved from your foes. 10And when you rejoice* on your festivals, and your new-moon feasts, you shall blow the trumpets over your burnt offerings and your communion sacrifices,[h] so that this serves as a reminder of you before your God. I, the LORD, am your God.

## II. Departure, Rebellion, and Wandering in the Wilderness for Forty Years

***Departure from Sinai.*** 11In the second year, on the twentieth day of the second month, the cloud rose from the tabernacle of the covenant, 12and the Israelites moved on from the wilderness of Sinai by stages, until the cloud came to rest in the wilderness of Paran.

13The first time that they broke camp at the direction of the LORD through Moses, 14[i] the divisional camp of the Judahites, arranged in companies, was the first to set out. Over its whole company was Nahshon, son of Amminadab, 15with Nethanel, son of Zuar, over the company of the tribe of Issacharites, 16and Eliab, son of Helon, over the company of the tribe of Zebulunites. 17Then, after the

**10:10 When you rejoice**: cf. Dt 16:14. **Festivals**: the great annual feasts of the Passover, Pentecost and Booths described in Lv 23; Nm 28–29.

*g:* 2 Chr 13:14. *h:* Nm 29:1; 2 Chr 29:26–28. *i:* Nm 2:3, 5, 7.

tabernacle was dismantled, the Gershonites and Merarites who carried the tabernacle set out. [18]The divisional camp of the Reubenites, arranged in companies, was the next to set out. Over its whole company was Elizur, son of Shedeur, [19]with Shelumiel, son of Zurishaddai, over the company of the tribe of Simeonites, [20]and Eliasaph, son of Reuel, over the company of the tribe of Gadites. [21]The Kohathites, who carried the sacred objects, then set out. Before their arrival the tabernacle would be erected. [22]The divisional camp of the Ephraimites set out next, arranged in companies. Over its whole company was Elishama, son of Ammihud, [23]with Gamaliel, son of Pedahzur, over the company of the tribe of Manassites, [24]and Abidan, son of Gideoni, over the company of the tribe of Benjaminites. [25]Finally, as rear guard for all the camps, the divisional camp of the Danites set out, arranged in companies. Over its whole company was Ahiezer, son of Ammishaddai, [26]with Pagiel, son of Ochran, over the company of the tribe of Asherites, [27]and Ahira, son of Enan, over the company of the tribe of Naphtalites. [28]This was the order of march for the Israelites, company by company, when they set out.

***Hobab as Guide.*** [29]Moses said to Hobab,* son of Reuel the Midianite, Moses' father-in-law, "We are setting out for the place concerning which the LORD has said, 'I will give it to you.' Come with us, and we will be generous toward you, for the LORD has promised prosperity to Israel." [30]But he answered, "No, I will not come. I am going instead to the land of my birth." [31]Moses said, "Please, do not leave us; you know where we can camp in the wilderness, and you can serve as our guide. [32]If you come with us, we will share with you the prosperity the LORD will bestow on us."

***Into the Wilderness.*** [33j]From the mountain of the LORD* they made a journey of three days, and the ark of the covenant of the LORD went before them for the three-day journey to seek out a resting place for them. [34]And the cloud of the LORD was over them by day when they set out from camp.

[35]Whenever the ark set out, Moses would say,

> "Arise, O LORD, may your enemies be
> scattered,
> and may those who hate you flee
> before you."

[36]And when it came to rest, he would say,

> "Bring back, O LORD, the myriads of
> Israel's troops!"

## CHAPTER 11

See RG 80–85

***Discontent of the People.*** [1]Now the people complained bitterly in the hearing of the LORD;[k] and when he heard it his wrath flared up, so that the LORD's fire burned among them and consumed the outskirts of the camp. [2]But when the people cried out to Moses, he prayed to the LORD and the fire died out. [3]Hence that place was called Taberah,* because there the fire of the LORD burned among them.

[4]The riffraff among them were so greedy for meat that even the Israelites lamented again,[l] "If only we had meat for food! [5]We remember the fish we used to eat without cost in Egypt, and the cucumbers, the melons, the leeks, the onions, and the garlic. [6]But now we are famished; we have nothing to look forward to but this manna."[m]

[7n]Manna was like coriander seed* and had the appearance of bdellium. [8]When they had gone about and gathered it up, the people would grind it between millstones or

**10:29–32 Hobab**: one of three names for the father-in-law of Moses (see Ex 2:18; 4:18; 18:6; Jgs 4:11). Here perhaps Hobab's initial refusal indicates he wished to be coaxed before granting the favor. From Jgs 1:16 it seems probable that he did accede to Moses' request. However, Ex 18:27 suggests Moses' father-in-law returned to his own land. Indeed, to the extent Nm 10:29–32 appears to repeat Ex 18:27, it may indicate a resumption of the narrative of Israel's march through the wilderness after the "digression" formed by the Israelite sojourn at Sinai, Ex 19:1–Nm 10:28.

**10:33 The mountain of the LORD**: Sinai (Horeb), elsewhere always called "the mountain of God."

**11:3 Taberah**: means "the burning."

**11:7 Coriander seed**: see note on Ex 16:31. **Bdellium**: a transparent, amber-colored gum resin, which is also mentioned in Gn 2:12.

*j*: Dt 1:33. *k*: Dt 9:22. *l*: Ps 78:18. *m*: Nm 21:5; Ex 16:3; Acts 7:39. *n*: Ex 16:14–15, 31; Ps 78:24; Wis 16:20; Jn 6:31.

pound it in a mortar, then cook it in a pot and
make it into loaves, with a rich creamy taste.
[9]At night, when the dew fell upon the camp,
the manna also fell.[o]
[10]When Moses heard the people, family
after family, crying at the entrance of their
tents, so that the LORD became very angry,
he was grieved. [11]"Why do you treat your
servant so badly?" Moses asked the LORD.
"Why are you so displeased with me that
you burden me with all this people? [12]Was it
I who conceived all this people? or was it I
who gave them birth, that you tell me to
carry them at my breast, like a nurse carrying an infant, to the land you have promised
under oath to their fathers? [13]Where can I get
meat to give to all this people? For they are
crying to me, 'Give us meat for our food.' [14]I
cannot carry all this people by myself, for
they are too heavy for me. [15]If this is the way
you will deal with me, then please do me the
favor of killing me at once, so that I need no
longer face my distress."
*The Seventy Elders.* [16]Then the LORD said
to Moses: Assemble for me seventy of the
elders of Israel, whom you know to be elders and authorities among the people, and
bring them to the tent of meeting. When they
are in place beside you, [17]I will come down
and speak with you there. I will also take
some of the spirit that is on you and will confer it on them, that they may share the burden of the people with you. You will then not
have to bear it by yourself.
[18]To the people, however, you shall say:
"Sanctify yourselves for tomorrow, when
you shall have meat to eat. For in the hearing
of the LORD you have cried, 'If only we had
meat for food! Oh, how well off we were in
Egypt!' Therefore the LORD will give you
meat to eat, [19]and you will eat it, not for one
day, or two days, or five, or ten, or twenty
days, [20]but for a whole month—until it
comes out of your very nostrils and becomes
loathsome to you. For you have rejected the
LORD who is in your midst, and in his presence you have cried, 'Why did we ever leave
Egypt?' "
[21]But Moses said, "The people around me
include six hundred thousand soldiers; yet
you say, 'I will give them meat to eat for a
whole month.' [22]Can enough sheep and cattle be slaughtered for them? If all the fish of
the sea were caught for them, would they
have enough?" [23]The LORD answered Moses: Is this beyond the LORD's reach? You
shall see now whether or not what I have
said to you takes place.
*The Spirit on the Elders.* [24]So Moses went
out and told the people what the LORD had
said. Gathering seventy elders of the people,
he had them stand around the tent. [25]The
LORD then came down in the cloud and
spoke to him. Taking some of the spirit that
was on Moses, he bestowed it on the seventy
elders; and as the spirit came to rest on them,
they prophesied* but did not continue.
[26]Now two men, one named Eldad and the
other Medad, had remained in the camp, yet
the spirit came to rest on them also. They too
had been on the list, but had not gone out to
the tent; and so they prophesied in the camp.
[27]So, when a young man ran and reported to
Moses, "Eldad and Medad are prophesying
in the camp," [28]Joshua, son of Nun, who
from his youth had been Moses' aide, said,
"My lord, Moses, stop them." [29]But Moses
answered him, "Are you jealous for my
sake? If only all the people of the LORD were
prophets! If only the LORD would bestow his
spirit on them!" [30]Then Moses retired to the
camp, along with the elders of Israel.
*The Quail.* [31]There arose a wind[p] from the
LORD that drove in quail from the sea and
left them all around the camp site, to a distance of a day's journey and at a depth of two
cubits upon the ground.* [32][q] So all that day,
all night, and all the next day the people set

**11:25 They prophesied**: in the sense, not of foretelling the future, but of speaking in enraptured enthusiasm. Such manifestations are mentioned in the early days of Hebrew prophecy (1 Sm 10:10–12; 19:20–21; Jl 3:1) and in the first years of the Church (Acts 2:6–11, 17; 19:6; 1 Cor 12–14).

**11:31** The heaps of quail lying upon the ground all around the Israelites' camp suggest the ambiguity of God's response to the people's lament for meat in v. 4 and foreshadow the plague which God will now bring upon Israel (v. 33). Their request had been nothing less than a rejection of what God has done for them (v. 20).

*o:* Ex 16:14–15. *p:* Ps 78:26–28. *q:* Ps 78:26–31.

about to gather in the quail. Even the one who got the least gathered ten homers* of them. Then they spread them out all around the camp. 33 But while the meat was still between their teeth, before it could be chewed, the LORD's wrath flared up against the people, and the LORD struck them with a very great plague. 34 So that place was named Kibroth-hattaavah,* because it was there that the greedy people were buried.

35 From Kibroth-hattaavah the people set out for Hazeroth, where they stayed.

See RG 80–85

## CHAPTER 12

***Jealousy of Aaron and Miriam.*** 1 Miriam and Aaron spoke against Moses on the pretext of the Cushite woman he had married; for he had in fact married a Cushite woman.* 2 They complained,* "Is it through Moses alone that the LORD has spoken? Has he not spoken through us also?" And the LORD heard this. 3[r] Now the man Moses was very humble, more than anyone else on earth. 4 So at once the LORD said to Moses and Aaron and Miriam: Come out, you three, to the tent of meeting. And the three of them went. 5 Then the LORD came down in a column of cloud, and standing at the entrance of the tent, called, "Aaron and Miriam." When both came forward, 6 the LORD said: Now listen to my words:

If there are prophets among you,
in visions I reveal myself to them,
in dreams I speak to them;
7 Not so with my servant Moses!
Throughout my house he is worthy of trust:*[s]
8 face to face I speak to him,[t]
plainly and not in riddles.
The likeness of the LORD he beholds.

Why, then, do you not fear to speak against my servant Moses? 9 And so the LORD's wrath flared against them, and he departed.

***Miriam's Punishment.*** 10 Now the cloud withdrew from the tent, and there was Miriam,[u] stricken with a scaly infection, white as snow!* When Aaron turned toward Miriam and saw her stricken with snow-white scales, 11 he said to Moses, "Ah, my lord! Please do not charge us with the sin that we have foolishly committed! 12 Do not let her be like the stillborn baby that comes forth from its mother's womb with its flesh half consumed." 13 Then Moses cried to the LORD, "Please, not this! Please, heal her!" 14 But the LORD answered Moses: Suppose her father had spit in her face, would she not bear her shame for seven days? Let her be confined outside the camp for seven days; afterwards she may be brought back. 15 So Miriam was confined outside the camp for seven days, and the people did not start out again until she was brought back.

16 After that the people set out from Hazeroth and encamped in the wilderness of Paran.

## CHAPTER 13

See RG 80–85

***The Twelve Scouts.*** 1 The LORD said to Moses: 2 Send men to reconnoiter the land of Canaan, which I am giving the Israelites. You shall send one man from each ancestral tribe, every one a leader among them. 3[v] So Moses sent them from the wilderness of Paran, at the direction of the LORD. All of them were leaders among the Israelites. 4 These were their names:

from the tribe of Reuben, Shammua, son of Zaccur;
5 from the tribe of Simeon, Shaphat, son of Hori;
6 from the tribe of Judah, Caleb, son of Jephunneh;

**11:32 Homers**: see note on Is 5:10. **They spread them out**: to cure by drying.

**11:34 Kibroth-hattaavah**: means "graves of greed."

**12:1 Cushite woman**: apparently Zipporah, the Midianite, is meant; cf. Ex 2:21.

**12:2** The apparent reason for Miriam's and Aaron's quarrel with their brother Moses was jealousy of his authority; his Cushite wife served only as an occasion for the dispute.

**12:7 Worthy of trust**: the text is open to a variety of interpretations. Thus, the word of Moses may be relied upon by Israel because God speaks to him directly; or, Moses alone is worthy of God's trust in God's household (heavenly or earthly). An alternative translation, however, is: "with all my house he is entrusted."

**12:10 Stricken with a scaly infection, white as snow**: see note on Lv 13:1–14:47. The point of the simile lies either in the flakiness or the whiteness of snow.

*r:* Sir 45:1–2. *s:* Heb 3:2, 5. *t:* Ex 33:1; Dt 34:10; Sir 45:3. *u:* Dt 24:9. *v:* Dt 1:22–28.

7 from the tribe of Issachar, Igal;
8 for the Josephites, from the tribe of
Ephraim, Hoshea, son of Nun;
9 from the tribe of Benjamin, Palti, son of
Raphu;
10 from the tribe of Zebulun, Gaddiel, son
of Sodi;
11 for the Josephites, from the tribe of
Manasseh, Gaddi, son of Susi;
12 from the tribe of Dan, Ammiel, son of
Gemalli;
13 from the tribe of Asher, Sethur, son of
Michael;
14 from the tribe of Naphtali, Nahbi, son of
Vophsi;
15 from the tribe of Gad, Geuel, son of
Machi.

16 These are the names of the men whom
Moses sent to reconnoiter the land. But Hoshea, son of Nun, Moses called Joshua.*
17 In sending them to reconnoiter the land
of Canaan, Moses said to them, "Go up there
in the Negeb, up into the highlands, 18 and
see what kind of land it is and whether the
people living there are strong or weak, few
or many. 19 Is the country in which they live
good or bad? Are the towns in which they
dwell open or fortified? 20 Is the soil fertile or
barren, wooded or clear? And do your best to
get some of the fruit of the land." It was then
the season for early grapes.
21 So they went up and reconnoitered the
land from the wilderness of Zin* as far as
where Rehob adjoins Lebo-hamath. 22 [w] Going up by way of the Negeb, they reached
Hebron, where Ahiman, Sheshai and Talmai,
descendants of the Anakim,* were. (Now
Hebron had been built seven years before
Zoan in Egypt.) 23 They also reached the
Wadi Eshcol,* where they cut down a branch
with a single cluster of grapes on it, which
two of them carried on a pole, as well as
some pomegranates and figs. 24 It was because of the cluster the Israelites cut there
that they called the place Wadi Eshcol.[x]

***Their Report.*** 25 They returned from reconnoitering the land forty days later.
26 [y] Proceeding directly to Moses and Aaron
and the whole community of the Israelites in
the wilderness of Paran at Kadesh, they
made a report to them and to the whole community, showing them the fruit of the land.
27 They told Moses: "We came to the land to
which you sent us. It does indeed flow with
milk and honey, and here is its fruit. 28 However, the people who are living in the land
are powerful, and the towns are fortified and
very large.[z] Besides, we saw descendants of
the Anakim there. 29 Amalekites live in the
region of the Negeb; Hittites, Jebusites and
Amorites dwell in the highlands, and
Canaanites along the sea and the banks of
the Jordan."
30 Caleb, however, quieted the people before Moses and said, "We ought to go up
and seize the land, for we can certainly prevail over it." 31 But the men who had gone
up with him said, "We cannot attack these
people; they are too strong for us." 32 They
spread discouraging reports[a] among the Israelites about the land they had reconnoitered, saying, "The land that we went
through and reconnoitered is a land that
consumes its inhabitants. And all the people
we saw there are huge. 33 [b] There we saw the
Nephilim* (the Anakim are from the Nephilim); in our own eyes we seemed like mere
grasshoppers, and so we must have seemed
to them."

**13:16 Joshua**: in Hebrew, "Jehoshua," which was later modified to "Jeshua," the Hebrew name for "Jesus." Hoshea and Joshua are variants of one original name meaning "the LORD saves." Cf. Mt 1:21.

**13:21 The wilderness of Zin**: north of Paran and southwest of the Dead Sea. It is quite distinct from "the wilderness of Sin" near the border of Egypt (Ex 16:1; 17:1; Nm 33:11). **Lebo-hamath**: a town near Riblah (Jer 39:5–6) at the southern border of Hamath, an independent kingdom in southern Syria. David's conquests extended as far as Hamath (2 Sm 8:9–11), and Lebo-hamath thus formed the northern border of the ideal extent of Israel's possessions (Nm 34:7–9; Ez 47:15; 48:1). This may suggest that this verse was inserted precisely to extend the scope of the reconnaissance; cf. Dt 1:24.

**13:22, 28 Anakim**: an aboriginal race in southern Palestine, largely absorbed by the Canaanites. Either because of their tall stature or because of the massive stone structures left by them, the Israelites regarded them as giants.

**13:23 Eshcol**: means "cluster."

**13:33 Nephilim**: i.e., "fallen ones" (in the Septuagint, "giants"), a reference to fallen heroes of old. Cf. Gn 6:4.

*w*: Jos 11:21–22. *x*: Nm 32:9; Dt 1:24–25. *y*: Ex 3:8, 17. *z*: Dt 9:1–2. *a*: Nm 32:9; Jos 14:8. *b*: Dt 2:10.

**The Decisive Rebellion: The Previous Generation's Refusal to Enter the Promised Land**

THIS KEY NARRATIVE forms the basis for the overall structure of the book of Numbers, which divides into the death of the old generation of the wilderness (chs 1–25) and the birth of a new generation of hope on the edge of the Promised Land (chs 26–36). The old rebellious generation is condemned to wander for forty years and die in the wilderness (14:22–23, 29–30). Only the new generation of "little ones" (along with the two faithful spies Caleb and Joshua) will be allowed to enter the land of Canaan (vv. 24, 30–31).

## CHAPTER 14

See RG 80–85

***Threats of Revolt.*** [1]At this, the whole community broke out with loud cries, and the people wept into the night. [2][c] All the Israelites grumbled against Moses and Aaron, the whole community saying to them, "If only we had died in the land of Egypt," or "If only we would die here in the wilderness! [3]Why is the LORD bringing us into this land only to have us fall by the sword? Our wives and little ones will be taken as spoil. Would it not be better for us to return to Egypt?" [4]So they said to one another, "Let us appoint a leader and go back to Egypt."

[5]But Moses and Aaron fell prostrate before the whole assembled community of the Israelites; [6]while Joshua, son of Nun, and Caleb, son of Jephunneh, who had been among those that reconnoitered the land, tore their garments [7]and said to the whole community of the Israelites,[d] "The land which we went through and reconnoitered is an exceedingly good land. [8]If the LORD is pleased with us, he will bring us in to this land and give it to us, a land which flows with milk and honey. [9][e] Only do not rebel against the LORD! You need not be afraid of the people of the land, for they are but food for us!* Their protection has left them, but the LORD is with us. Do not fear them."

***The Lord's Sentence.*** [10]The whole community threatened to stone them. But the glory of the LORD appeared at the tent of meeting to all the Israelites. [11]And the LORD said to Moses: How long will this people spurn me? How long will they not trust me, despite all the signs I have performed among them?[f] [12]I will strike them with pestilence and disown them. Then I will make of you a nation greater and mightier than they.[g]

[13][h] But Moses said to the LORD: "The Egyptians will hear of this, for by your power you brought out this people from among them. [14]They will tell the inhabitants of this land, who have heard that you, LORD, are in the midst of this people; you, LORD, who directly revealed yourself! Your cloud stands over them, and you go before them by day in a column of cloud and by night in a column of fire.[i] [15]If now you slay this people all at once, the nations who have heard such reports of you will say, [16]'The LORD was not able to bring this people into the land he swore to give them; that is why he slaughtered them in the wilderness.'[j] [17]Now then, may my Lord's forbearance be great, even as you have said, [18][k] 'The LORD is slow to anger and abounding in kindness, forgiving iniquity and rebellion; yet certainly not declaring the guilty guiltless, but punishing children to the third and fourth generation for their parents' iniquity.' [19]Pardon, then, the iniquity of this people in keeping with your great kindness, even as you have forgiven them from Egypt until now."[l]

[20]The LORD answered: I pardon them as you have asked. [21]Yet, by my life and the

**14:9 They are but food for us**: lit., "for they are our bread." "Bread" (Heb. *lechem*) is here used in the sense of "prey, spoils" to be consumed by an invader. This is the answer to the pessimistic report that this land "consumes its inhabitants" (13:32).

*c:* Ex 16:3; Ps 106:25. *d:* Dt 1:25. *e:* Dt 7:18. *f:* Ps 78:22, 32. *g:* Ex 32:10. *h:* Ex 32:12; Dt 9:26–29; Ps 106:23. *i:* Ex 13:21; Jos 2:9–10. *j:* Ex 32:12; Dt 9:28. *k:* Ex 20:5; 34:6–7; Ps 103:8; 145:8. *l:* Ps 78:38.

LORD's glory that fills the whole earth, 22 of
all the people who have seen my glory and
the signs I did in Egypt and in the wilderness,[m] and who nevertheless have put me to
the test ten times already and have not
obeyed me, 23 not one shall see the land
which I promised on oath to their ancestors.
None of those who have spurned me shall
see it. 24 But as for my servant Caleb, because he has a different spirit and follows me
unreservedly,[n] I will bring him into the land
which he entered, and his descendants shall
possess it. 25 But now, since the Amalekites
and Canaanites are living in the valleys,*
turn away tomorrow and set out into the wilderness by way of the Red Sea road.

26 The LORD also said to Moses and Aaron:
27 How long will this wicked community
grumble against me?[o] I have heard the grumblings of the Israelites against me. 28 Tell
them:* "By my life"—oracle of the LORD—
"I will do to you just what I have heard you
say. 29 Here in the wilderness[p] your dead
bodies shall fall. Of all your men of twenty
years or more, enrolled in your registration,
who grumbled against me, 30 not one of you
shall enter the land where I solemnly swore
to settle you, except Caleb, son of Jephunneh, and Joshua, son of Nun. 31 Your little
ones, however, who you said would be taken
as spoil, I will bring in, and they shall know
the land you rejected.[q] 32 But as for you, your
bodies shall fall here in the wilderness,
33 while your children will wander for forty
years, suffering for your infidelity, till the
last of you lies dead in the wilderness.[r]
34 Corresponding to the number of days you
spent reconnoitering the land—forty days—
you shall bear your punishment one year for
each day: forty years. Thus you will realize
what it means to oppose me. 35 I, the LORD,
have spoken; and I will surely do this to this
entire wicked community that conspired
against me: here in the wilderness they shall
come to their end and there they will die."

36 And the men whom Moses had sent to
reconnoiter the land[s] and who on returning
had set the whole community grumbling
against him by spreading discouraging reports about the land— 37 these men who had
spread discouraging reports about the land
were struck down by the LORD and died.
38 Only Joshua, son of Nun, and Caleb, son
of Jephunneh, survived of all the men who
had gone to reconnoiter the land.[t]

***Unsuccessful Invasion.*** 39 When Moses repeated these words to all the Israelites, the
people mourned greatly. 40 Early the next
morning they started up high into the hill
country, saying, "Here we are, ready to go
up to the place that the LORD spoke of:[u] for
we did wrong." 41 But Moses said, "Why are
you now transgressing the LORD's order?
This cannot succeed. 42 Do not go up, because the LORD is not in your midst; do not
allow yourself to be struck down by your
enemies.[v] 43 For there the Amalekites and
Canaanites will face you, and you will fall
by the sword. You have turned back from
following the LORD; therefore the LORD will
not be with you."

44 Yet they dared to go up high into the hill
country,[w] even though neither the ark of the
covenant of the LORD nor Moses left the
camp. 45 And the Amalekites and Canaanites
who dwelt in that hill country came down
and defeated them, beating them back as far
as Hormah.*

## CHAPTER 15

See RG 80–85

***Secondary Offerings.*** 1 The LORD
spoke to Moses: 2* Speak to the Israelites and
say to them: When you enter the land that I
am giving you for your settlements, 3 if you

**14:25 The valleys**: the low-lying plains in the Negeb and along the seacoast and in the Jordan depression, as well as the higher valleys in the mountains farther north: cf. v. 45.

**14:28–29** God punished the grumblers by giving them their wish; cf. v. 2. Their lack of trust in God is cited in 1 Cor 10:10 and Heb 3:12–18 as a warning for Christians.

**14:45 Hormah**: one of the Canaanite royal cities in southern Judah, according to the tradition attested in Jos 12:14, although Nm 21:1–3 gives it as the new name for the city of Arad when it was destroyed by Israel. According to the list of conquered cities preserved in Jgs 1, the earlier name for the city of Hormah was Zephath. The precise location is unknown.

**15:2–16** These laws on sacrifice are complementary to those of Lv 1–3. Since the food of the Israelites consisted not

*m:* Dt 1:35. *n:* Jos 14:8–9. *o:* Ex 16:7, 12. *p:* Dt 1:35; Heb 3:17. *q:* Dt 1:39. *r:* Nm 13:26; 32:13; Ps 95:10; Ez 4:6. *s:* Nm 13:17, 32–33; 1 Cor 10:10. *t:* Nm 26:65. *u:* Nm 13:18; Dt 1:41. *v:* Dt 1:42. *w:* Dt 1:43. *x:* Ez 44:30.

make to the LORD an oblation from the herd or from the flock—either a burnt offering or a sacrifice, to fulfill a vow, or as a voluntary offering, or for one of your festivals—to produce a pleasing aroma for the LORD, [4]the one presenting the offering shall also present to the LORD a grain offering, a tenth of a measure* of bran flour mixed with a fourth of a hin of oil, [5]as well as wine for a libation, a fourth of a hin. You will do this with the burnt offering or the sacrifice, for each lamb. [6]Alternatively for a ram you shall make a grain offering of two tenths of a measure of bran flour mixed with a third of a hin of oil, [7]and for a libation, a third of a hin of wine, thereby presenting a pleasing aroma to the LORD. [8]If you make an offering from the herd—either a burnt offering, or a sacrifice, to fulfill a vow, or as a communion offering to the LORD, [9]with it a grain offering of three tenths of a measure of bran flour mixed with half a hin of oil will be presented; [10]and you will present for a libation, half a hin of wine—a sweet-smelling oblation to the LORD. [11]The same is to be done for each ox, ram, lamb or goat. [12]Whatever the number you offer, do the same for each of them.

[13]All the native-born shall make these offerings in this way, whenever they present a sweet-smelling oblation to the LORD. [14]Likewise, in any future generation, any alien residing with you or anyone else in your midst, who presents an oblation of pleasing aroma to the LORD, must do as you do. [15]There is but one statute for you and for the resident alien, a perpetual statute throughout your generations. You and the resident alien will be alike before the LORD; [16]you and the alien residing with you will have the same rule and the same application of it.

[17]The LORD spoke to Moses: [18]Speak to the Israelites and say to them: When you enter the land into which I am bringing you [19]and eat of the bread of the land, you shall offer the LORD a contribution. [20]A round loaf from your first batch of dough* you shall offer as a contribution. Just like a contribution from the threshing floor you shall offer it.[x] [21]Throughout your generations you shall give a contribution to the LORD from your first batch of dough.

***Purification Offerings.**** [22]If through inadvertence you fail to do any of these commandments which the LORD has given to Moses—[y] [23]anything the LORD commanded you through Moses from the time the LORD first gave the command down through your generations— [24]if it was done inadvertently without the community's knowledge, the whole community shall sacrifice one bull from the herd as a burnt offering of pleasing aroma to the LORD, along with its prescribed grain offering and libation, as well as one he-goat as a purification offering. [25][z] Then the priest shall make atonement for the whole Israelite community; and they will be forgiven, since it was inadvertence, and for their inadvertence they have brought their offering: an oblation to the LORD as well as their purification offering before the LORD. [26]Not only the whole Israelite community but also the aliens residing among you shall be forgiven, since the inadvertent fault affects all the people.

[27]If it is an individual who sins inadvertently,[a] this person shall bring a yearling she-goat as a purification offering. [28]And the priest shall make atonement before the LORD for the one who erred, since the sin was inadvertent, making atonement for the person to secure forgiveness. [29]You shall have but one rule for the person who sins inadvertently, whether a native-born Israelite or an alien residing among you.

[30]But anyone who acts defiantly,[b] whether a native or an alien, reviles the LORD, and

only of meat but also of bread, oil and wine, they offered flour, wine and oil in sacrifice to the Lord besides the animal oblations.

**15:4 Measure**: the word, supplied from the context, does not appear in the Hebrew (as also in vv. 6, 9; 28:9, 12, 20, 28; 29:3, 9, 14). Probably the ephah (which is named in 5:15; 28:5) is intended. **Hin**: see note on Ez 45:24.

**15:20 Dough**: the meaning of the Hebrew term is uncertain; some render, "baking utensils." This word is used elsewhere only in Ez 44:30 and Neh 10:33; a related Hebrew word is used in Lv 2:14.

**15:22–31** See note on Lv 4:2. Although Lv 4–5 and Nm 15:22–31 both concern inadvertent sins, the emphasis here, as opposed to Lv 4–5, is on the failure of the community to perform "positive commands" rather than on doing what is prohibited.

*y:* Lv 4:13–14. *z:* Lv 4:20. *a:* Lv 4:27–28. *b:* Dt 17:12.

shall be cut off from among the people. 31[c] For having despised the word of the LORD and broken his commandment, he must be cut off entirely and bear the punishment.

*The Sabbath-breaker.* 32 While the Israelites were in the wilderness, a man was discovered gathering wood on the sabbath day. 33 Those who caught him at it brought him to Moses and Aaron and the whole community. 34 But they put him in custody, for there was no clear decision* as to what should be done with him.[d] 35 Then the LORD said to Moses: This man shall be put to death; let the whole community stone him outside the camp. 36 So the whole community led him outside the camp and stoned him to death, as the LORD had commanded Moses.

*Tassels on the Cloak.* 37 The LORD said to Moses: 38 Speak to the Israelites and tell them that throughout their generations they are to make tassels* for the corners of their garments, fastening a violet cord to each corner.[e] 39 When you use these tassels, the sight of the cord will remind you of all the commandments of the LORD and you will do them, without prostituting yourself going after the desires of your hearts and your eyes. 40 Thus you will remember to do all my commandments and you will be holy to your God. 41 I, the LORD, am your God who brought you out of the land of Egypt to be your God: I, the LORD your God.[f]

## CHAPTER 16

See RG 80–85

*Rebellion of Korah.* 1* Korah, son of Izhar, son of Kohath, son of Levi, and the Reubenites Dathan and Abiram, sons of Eliab, and On, son of Peleth,* son of Reuben took 2 two hundred and fifty Israelites who were leaders in the community, members of the council and men of note, and confronted Moses. 3 Holding an assembly against Moses and Aaron, they said,[g] "You go too far! The whole community, all of them, are holy; the LORD is in their midst. Why then should you set yourselves over the LORD's assembly?"

4 When Moses heard this, he fell prostrate. 5 Then he said to Korah and to all his faction, "May the LORD make known tomorrow morning who belongs to him and who is the holy one and whom he will have draw near to him! The one whom he chooses, he will have draw near to him. 6 Do this: take your censers, Korah and all his faction, 7 and put fire in them and place incense in them before the LORD tomorrow. He whom the LORD then chooses is the holy one. You Levites go too far!"

8 Moses also said to Korah, "Hear, now, you Levites! 9[h] Are you not satisfied that the God of Israel has singled you out from the community of Israel, to have you draw near him to maintain the LORD's tabernacle, and to attend upon the community and to serve them? 10 He has allowed you and your Levite kinsmen with you to approach him, and yet you seek the priesthood too. 11 It is therefore against the LORD that you and all your faction are conspiring. As for Aaron, what has he done that you should grumble against him?"

*Rebellion of Dathan and Abiram.* 12 Moses

**15:34 No clear decision**: either it was not clear that gathering wood constituted "work" and as such a willful violation of the sabbath and a capital offense; or they did not yet know how the death penalty was to be inflicted.

**15:38 Tassels**: at the time of Jesus these tassels were worn by all pious Jews, including Jesus (Mt 9:20–21; Mk 6:56); some Pharisees wore very large ones in a display of their zeal for the law (Mt 23:5).

**16:1–3** The evidence seems to show that accounts of two, if not more, distinct rebellions have been combined in this chapter. The most obvious are the rebellions of Korah and his faction (Nm 27:3) and of Dathan and Abiram (Dt 11:6); cf. Ps 106. The present account combines both events into one narrative; but even here it is rather easy to separate the two. The rebellion of the Reubenites, Dathan and Abiram, was more political in character, against Moses alone as the civil leader (cf. v. 13); these rebels were punished by being swallowed alive in an earthquake. The rebellion of Korah was more religious in character, directed primarily against the religious leadership of Aaron (though in vv. 19–22 it is Korah and the whole community against both Moses and Aaron). About two hundred and fifty malcontents joined Korah's faction, and they are punished by fire. The parts of the present section which refer to the rebellion of Dathan and Abiram are vv. 12–15 and vv. 25–34 of chap. 16; the rest of chap. 16 and all of chap. 17 chiefly concern the rebellion of Korah.

**16:1 The Reubenites . . . son of Peleth**: some suggest on the basis of 26:5, 8 and Gn 46:9 reading instead of the traditional Hebrew text: "son of Levi, and Dathan and Abiram, sons of Eliab, son of Pallu, son of Reuben."

---

*c:* Prv 13:13. *d:* Lv 24:12. *e:* Dt 22:12. *f:* Lv 22:32–33. *g:* Ps 106:16–18; Sir 45:19. *h:* Dt 10:8.

summoned Dathan and Abiram, sons of
Eliab, but they answered, “We will not go.*
13Are you not satisfied that you have brought
us here from a land flowing with milk and
honey to have us perish in the wilderness,
that now you must also lord it over us? 14Far
from bringing us to a land flowing with milk
and honey, or giving us fields and vineyards
for our inheritance, will you gouge out our
eyes?* No, we will not go.”

15Then Moses became very angry and said
to the LORD, “Pay no attention to their offering. I have never taken a single donkey from
them, nor have I wronged any one of them.”[i]

***Korah.*** 16Moses said to Korah, “You and
all your faction shall appear before the LORD
tomorrow—you and they and Aaron too.
17Then each of you take his own censer, put
incense in it, and present it before the LORD,
two hundred and fifty censers; and you and
Aaron, each with his own censer, do the
same.” 18So each of them took their censers,
and laying incense on the fire they had put in
them, they took their stand by the entrance
of the tent of meeting along with Moses and
Aaron. 19Then, when Korah had assembled
all the community against them at the entrance of the tent of meeting, the glory of the
LORD appeared to the entire community,
20and the LORD said to Moses and Aaron:
21Stand apart from this community, that I
may consume them at once. 22But they fell
prostrate and exclaimed, “O God, God of the
spirits of all living creatures, if one man sins
will you be angry with the whole community?” 23The LORD answered Moses:
24Speak to the community and tell them:
Withdraw from the area around the tent* of
Korah, Dathan and Abiram.

***Punishment of Dathan and Abiram.*** 25Mo-
ses, followed by the elders of Israel, arose
and went to Dathan and Abiram.* 26Then he
spoke to the community, “Move away from
the tents of these wicked men and do not
touch anything that is theirs: otherwise you
too will be swept away because of all their
sins.” 27So they withdrew from the area
around the tents of Korah, Dathan and Abiram. When Dathan and Abiram had come out
and were standing at the entrance of their
tents with their wives, their children, and
their little ones, 28Moses said, “This is how
you shall know that the LORD sent me to do
all I have done, and that it was not of my own
devising: 29if these die an ordinary death,
merely suffering the fate common to all humanity, the LORD has not sent me. 30But if the
LORD makes a chasm, and the ground opens
its mouth and swallows them with all belonging to them, and they go down alive to
Sheol,* then you will know that these men
have spurned the LORD.” 31[j]No sooner had
he finished saying all this than the ground beneath them split open, 32and the earth opened
its mouth and swallowed them and their families and all of Korah’s people* with all their
possessions. 33They went down alive to
Sheol with all belonging to them; the earth
closed over them, and they disappeared from
the assembly. 34But all the Israelites near
them fled at their shrieks, saying, “The earth
might swallow us too!”

***Punishment of Korah.*** 35And fire from the
LORD came forth which consumed the two
hundred and fifty men who were offering the
incense.

## CHAPTER 17

See RG 80-85

1The LORD said to Moses: 2Tell Eleazar, son of Aaron the priest, to remove the
censers from the embers; and scatter the fire
some distance away, for they have become

**16:12 We will not go**: to appear before Moses’ “tribunal.”

**16:14 Gouge out our eyes**: blind us to the real state of affairs.

**16:24 Withdraw from the area around the tent**: the word for “tent,” *mishkan*, here and in v. 27, is otherwise used in the singular only for the tent of meeting, suggesting possibly the erection of a rival sanctuary by the rebels. Note further, as an indication of the fact that various accounts of rebellion have been fused here, that in v. 19 the entire community had been assembled by Korah at the tent of meeting.

**16:25** Since Dathan and Abiram had refused to go to Moses (vv. 12–14), he, with the elders as witnesses, was obliged to go to their tents.

**16:30 Sheol**: see note on Ps 6:6.

**16:32 And all of Korah’s people**: the implication of this secondary addition to the text is, on the one hand, that Korah met his death elsewhere, presumably with the two hundred and fifty offering incense (vv. 16–17, 35); or, on the other hand, he died along with Dathan and Abiram in the splitting of the earth.

*i:* 1 Sm 12:3. *j:* Nm 26:10; Lv 10:2; Dt 11:6; Ps 106:17–18.

holy— [3]* the censers of those who sinned at
the cost of their lives. Have them hammered
into plates to cover the altar, because in being
presented before the LORD they have become
holy. In this way they shall serve as a sign to
the Israelites. [4]So taking the bronze censers
which had been presented by those who were
burned, Eleazar the priest had them hammered into a covering for the altar, [5]just as
the LORD had directed him through Moses.
This was to be a reminder to the Israelites
that no unauthorized person, no one who was
not a descendant of Aaron, should draw near
to offer incense before the LORD, lest he meet
the fate of Korah and his faction.

[6]The next day the whole Israelite community grumbled against Moses and Aaron,
saying, "You have killed the people of the
LORD." [7]But while the community was assembling against them, Moses and Aaron
turned toward the tent of meeting, and the
cloud now covered it and the glory of the
LORD appeared. [8]Then Moses and Aaron
came to the front of the tent of meeting, [9]and
the LORD said to Moses: [10]Remove yourselves from this community, that I may consume them at once. But they fell prostrate.

[11]Then Moses said to Aaron, "Take your
censer, put fire from the altar in it, lay incense on it, and bring it quickly to the community to make atonement for them; for
wrath has come forth from the LORD and the
plague has begun."[k] [12]Aaron took his censer
just as Moses directed and ran in among the
assembly, where the plague had already begun among the people. Then he offered the
incense and made atonement for the people,
[13]while standing there between the living
and the dead. And so the scourge was
checked. [14]There were fourteen thousand
seven hundred dead from the scourge, in addition to those who died because of Korah.
[15]When the scourge had been checked,
Aaron returned to Moses at the entrance of
the tent of meeting.

***Aaron's Staff.*** [16]The LORD now said to
Moses: [17]Speak to the Israelites and get from
them a staff* for each ancestral house,
twelve staffs in all, from all the leaders of
their ancestral houses. Write each man's
name on his staff; [18]and write Aaron's name
on Levi's staff.* For each head of an ancestral house shall have a staff. [19]Then deposit
them in the tent of meeting, in front of the
covenant, where I meet you. [20]The staff of
the man whom I choose shall sprout. Thus I
will rid myself of the Israelites' grumbling
against you.

[21]So Moses spoke to the Israelites, and all
their leaders gave him staffs, twelve in all,
one from each leader of their ancestral
houses; and Aaron's staff was among them.
[22]Then Moses deposited the staffs before the
LORD in the tent of the covenant. [23]The next
day, when Moses entered the tent of the covenant, Aaron's staff, representing the house
of Levi, had sprouted. It had put forth
sprouts, produced blossoms, and borne ripe
almonds! [24]So Moses brought out all the
staffs from the LORD's presence to all the Israelites, and each one identified his own
staff and took it. [25]Then the LORD said to
Moses: Put back Aaron's staff in front of the
covenant, for safe keeping as a sign to the rebellious, so that their grumbling against me
may cease and they might not die. [26]Moses
did this. Just as the LORD had commanded
him, so he did.

***Charge of the Sacred Things.*** [27]* Then the
Israelites exclaimed to Moses, "We will per-

**17:3** Whatever was brought into intimate contact with something holy shared in its holiness. See note on 19:20.

**17:17** The staff was not merely an article of practical use, but also a symbol of authority; cf. Gn 49:10; Nm 24:17; Jer 48:17. Therefore, the staff of a leader of a tribe was considered the emblem of the tribe; in fact, certain Hebrew words such as *matteh*, the word for "staff" here, also mean "tribe." Perhaps for this reason, to avoid confusion, the author here uses the term *bet'ab*, "ancestral house," for "tribe" instead of one of the ordinary words for "tribe."

**17:18** **Levi's staff**: it is not clear whether this is considered as one of the twelve mentioned in the preceding verse, or as a thirteenth staff. Sometimes Levi is reckoned as one of the twelve tribes (e.g., Dt 27:12–13), but more often the number twelve is arrived at by counting the two sub-tribes of Joseph, i.e., Ephraim and Manasseh, as distinct tribes. In this passage also it seems probable that the tribe of Levi is considered apart from the other twelve tribes.

**17:27–28** The people's distress here echoes their panic in 16:34, and may be heightened further by the death of the two hundred and fifty leaders offering incense in 16:35.

*k:* Wis 18:20–21.

**The Duties and Support of the Priests and Levites**

CHAPTER 18 MAKES a crucial distinction between Aaron and his sons as the Levites who serve as high priests and the other members of the tribe of Levi, who serve as assistants to Aaron and his sons (Nm 3:5–10).

ish; we are lost, we are all lost! 28 Anyone who
approaches the tabernacle of the LORD will
die! Will there be no end to our perishing?"

See RG 80–85

## CHAPTER 18

1 The LORD said to Aaron:* You and
your sons as well as your ancestral house
with you* shall be responsible for any sin
with respect to the sanctuary; but only you
and your sons with you shall be responsible
for any sin with respect to your priesthood.
2 You shall also present with you your kinsmen of the tribe of Levi, your ancestral tribe,
that they may be joined to you* and assist
you, while you and your sons with you are in
front of the tent of the covenant. 3 They shall
discharge your obligations and those with
respect to the whole tent; however, they
shall not come near the utensils of the sanctuary or the altar, or else both they and you
will die. 4 They will be joined to you to perform the duties associated with the tent of
meeting, all the labor pertaining to the tent.
But no unauthorized person* shall come near
you. 5 You shall perform the duties of the
sanctuary and of the altar, that wrath may not
fall again upon the Israelites.
6 I hereby take your kinsmen, the Levites,
from among the Israelites; they are a gift to
you,[l] dedicated to the LORD for the labor
they perform for the tent of meeting. 7[m] But
you and your sons with you must take care to
exercise your priesthood in whatever concerns the altar and the area within the veil.* I
give you your priesthood as a gift. Any
unauthorized person who comes near shall
be put to death.

***The Priests' Share of the Sacrifices.*** 8 The
LORD said to Aaron:* I hereby give to you
charge of the contributions made to me, including the various holy offerings of the Israelites;[n] I assign them to you and to your
sons as a perquisite, a perpetual due. 9 This is
what you shall have from the oblations that
are most holy: every offering of theirs—
namely, all their grain offerings, purification
offerings, and reparation offerings which
they must return to me—shall be most holy
for you and for your sons. 10 You shall eat
them in a most holy place;* every male may
partake of them. As holy, they belong to you.
11 This also you shall have: the contributions that are their gifts, including the elevated offering* of the Israelites; I assign them
to you and to your sons and daughters with
you as a perpetual due.[o] All in your household who are clean may eat them. 12 I also assign to you all the best[p] of the new oil and of
the new wine and grain that they give to the
LORD as their first produce that has been
processed. 13 The first-ripened fruits of whatever is in their land, which they bring to the
LORD, shall be yours; all of your household
who are clean may eat them. 14 Whatever is

**18:1–3** This law, which kept unqualified persons from contact with holy things, is in response to the Israelites' cry in 17:28. It is followed by other laws concerning priests and Levites.

**18:1 With you**: not only in the present but also those of his house in the future.

**18:2 Be joined to you**: in Hebrew a pun on the popular etymology of the name "Levi." Cf. Gn 29:34.

**18:4 Unauthorized person**: here, "one who is not a Levite"; in v. 7, "one who is not a priest."

**18:7 Veil**: the outer veil, or "curtain," is probably meant.

**18:8–10** Two classes of offerings are here distinguished: the most holy offering, which only the male members of the priestly families could eat (vv. 8–10), and the other offerings, which the women of the priestly families could eat (vv. 11–19).

**18:10 In a most holy place**: in the court of the tabernacle, according to Lv 6:9, 19.

**18:11 Elevated offering**: this included the brisket and right thigh (v. 18), the shoulder of the peace offering (Lv 7:30–34), and portions of the nazirite sacrifice (Nm 6:19–20). **With you**: see note on v. 1. Aaron had no daughters; see also v. 19.

*l:* Nm 3:9; 8:19. *m:* Nm 3:10. *n:* Nm 5:9. *o:* Ex 29:27–28; Lv 7:34; 10:14. *p:* Dt 18:4; 26:2.

under the ban* in Israel shall be yours. 15Every living thing that opens the womb, human being and beast alike, such as are to be offered to the LORD, shall be yours;[q] but you must redeem the firstborn of human beings, as well as redeem the firstborn of unclean animals. 16For the redemption price of a son, when he is a month old, you shall pay the equivalent of five silver shekels according to the sanctuary shekel, that is, twenty gerahs. 17But the firstborn of cattle, or the firstborn of sheep or the firstborn of goats you shall not redeem; they are holy. Their blood you must splash on the altar and their fat you must burn as an oblation of pleasing aroma to the LORD. 18[r] Their meat, however, shall be yours, just as the brisket of the elevated offering and the right thigh belong to you. 19As a perpetual due I assign to you and to your sons and daughters with you all the contributions of holy things which the Israelites set aside for the LORD; this is a covenant of salt* to last forever before the LORD, for you and for your descendants with you. 20[s] Then the LORD said to Aaron:* You shall not have any heritage in their land nor hold any portion among them; I will be your portion and your heritage among the Israelites.

***Tithes Due the Levites.*** 21To the Levites, however, I hereby assign all tithes in Israel as their heritage in recompense for the labor they perform, the labor pertaining to the tent of meeting.[t] 22The Israelites may no longer approach the tent of meeting, thereby incurring the penalty of death. 23Only the Levites are to perform the labor pertaining to the tent of meeting, and they shall incur the penalty for the Israelites' sin;* this is a permanent statute for all your generations. But they shall not have any heritage among the Israelites, 24for I have assigned to the Levites as their heritage the tithes which the Israelites put aside as a contribution to the LORD. That is why I have said, they will not have any heritage among the Israelites.

***Tithes Paid by the Levites.*** 25The LORD said to Moses: 26Speak to the Levites and say to them: When you take from the Israelites the tithes I have assigned you from them as your heritage, you are to make a contribution from them to the LORD, a tithe of the tithe; 27and your contribution will be credited to you as if it were grain from the threshing floor or new wine from the vat. 28Thus you too shall make a contribution to the LORD from all the tithes you take from the Israelites, handing over to Aaron the priest the contribution to the LORD. 29From all the gifts to you, you shall make every contribution due to the LORD—from their best parts, that is the part to be consecrated from them. 30Say to them also: Once you have made your contribution from the best part, the rest of the tithe will be credited to the Levites as if it were produce of the threshing floor or the produce of the vat. 31You and your households may eat it anywhere, since it is your recompense in exchange for labor in the tent of meeting. 32You will incur no punishment when you contribute the best part of it. But do not profane the holy offerings of the Israelites or else you shall die.

## CHAPTER 19

See RG 80–85

***Ashes of the Red Heifer.*** 1The LORD spoke to Moses and Aaron: 2This is the statute for the ritual which the LORD has commanded. Tell the Israelites to procure for you a red heifer without defect and free from every blemish and on which no yoke has ever been laid. 3You will give it to Eleazar the priest, and it will be led outside the camp*

**18:14 Under the ban**: in Hebrew, *herem*, which means here "set aside from profane use and made sacred to the Lord." Cf. Lv 27:21, 28.

**18:19 A covenant of salt**: cf. 2 Chr 13:5. The reference may perhaps be to the preservative power of salt (cf. Mt 5:13); but more likely the phrase refers to the custom of eating salt together to render a contract unbreakable. See note on Lv 2:13.

**18:20** The priests and Levites were forbidden to own hereditary land such as the other Israelites possessed; therefore in the allotment of the land (chap. 34) they did not receive any portion of it. Certain cities, however, were assigned to them for their residence; cf. 35:1–8.

**18:23 Incur the penalty for the Israelites' sin**: the Levites are responsible for protecting the sanctuary from illegitimate encroachment and in this sense pay the penalty for the Israelites' iniquity. This responds further to the fears of the people expressed in 17:27–28.

**19:3 Outside the camp**: several early Christian writers saw in this a prefiguring of the sacrificial death of Jesus out-

*q:* Ex 13:2. *r:* Lv 7:31–34. *s:* Dt 10:9; 18:1–2; Jos 13:33; Ez 44:28. *t:* Heb 7:5.

and slaughtered in his presence. [4]Eleazar the priest will take some of its blood on his finger and sprinkle it seven times toward the front of the tent of meeting.[*] [5]Then the heifer will be burned in his sight; it will be burned with its hide and flesh, its blood and dung; [6]and the priest will take cedar wood, hyssop and scarlet yarn and throw them into the fire in which the heifer is being burned. [7]The priest shall then wash his garments and bathe his body in water, afterward he may enter the camp. The priest remains unclean until the evening. [8]Likewise, the one who burned the heifer shall wash his garments in water, bathe his body in water, and be unclean until evening. [9]Then somebody who is clean shall gather up the ashes of the heifer and deposit them in a clean place outside the camp. There they are to be kept to prepare purification water for the Israelite community. This is a purification offering. [10]The one who has gathered up the ashes of the heifer shall also wash his garments and be unclean until evening. This is a permanent statute, both for the Israelites and for the alien residing among them.

*Use of the Ashes.* [11]Those who touch the corpse of any human being will be unclean for seven days; [12]they shall purify themselves with the water on the third and on the seventh day, and then be clean. But if they fail to purify themselves on the third and on the seventh day, they will not become clean. [13][u] Those who touch the corpse of a human being who dies and who fail to purify themselves defile the tabernacle of the LORD and these persons shall be cut off from Israel. Since the purification water has not been splashed over them, they remain unclean: their uncleanness is still on them.

[14]This is the ritual: When someone dies in a tent, everyone who enters the tent, as well as everyone already in it, will be unclean for seven days; [15]and every open vessel with its lid unfastened will be unclean. [16]Moreover, everyone who in the open country touches a person who has been slain by the sword or who has died naturally, or who touches a human bone or a grave, will be unclean for seven days. [17]For anyone who is thus unclean, ashes shall be taken from the burnt purification offering, and spring water will be poured on them from a vessel.[v] [18]Then someone who is clean will take hyssop, dip it in this water, and sprinkle it on the tent and on all the vessels and persons that were in it, or on the one who touched the bone, the slain person or the other corpse, or the grave. [19]The clean will sprinkle the unclean on the third and on the seventh day, and thus purify them on the seventh day. Then they will wash their garments and bathe in water, and in the evening be clean. [20][*] Those who become unclean and fail to purify themselves—those people will be cut off from the assembly, because they defile the sanctuary of the LORD. The purification water has not been splashed over them; they remain unclean. [21]This will be a permanent statute for you.

Those who sprinkle the purification water will wash their garments, and those who come in contact with the purification water will be unclean until evening. [22]Moreover, anything that the unclean person touches becomes unclean itself, and the one who touches such a person becomes unclean until evening.

## CHAPTER 20[*]

See RG 80–85

*Death of Miriam.* [1]The Israelites, the whole community, arrived in the wilderness of Zin[*] in the first month, and the people stayed at Kadesh. It was here that Miriam died, and here that she was buried.

*Need for Water at Kadesh.* [2]Since the

side the walls of Jerusalem; cf. Jn 19:20; Heb 13:12; in the purifying water, into which the ashes of the red heifer were put, they saw a type of the water of Baptism.

**19:4 Toward the front of the tent of meeting**: since the tabernacle faced the east (Ex 26:15–30), the killing of the heifer would take place east of the camp; in later times it was done on the Mount of Olives, east of the Temple.

**19:20** Ritual uncleanness is, as it were, contagious; so also sacredness; see note on 17:3.

**20:1–29** In this chapter the deaths of the three wilderness leaders are either intimated or explicitly reported: Miriam, v. 1; Moses, v. 12; Aaron, vv. 12, 22–29.

**20:1 The wilderness of Zin**: a barren region with a few good oases, southwest of the Dead Sea. See note on 13:21. **The first month**: we would expect the mention also of the day and of the year (after the exodus) when this took place; cf. similar dates in 1:1; 10:11; 33:38; Dt 1:3. Here the full date is left unspecified. According to one chronology, the Israel-

*u:* Lv 15:31. *v:* Heb 9:13–14.

## Water from the Rock and the LORD's Anger

THE LORD'S ANGRY response and punishment of Moses and Aaron in Nm 20:12ff is surprising and difficult to explain. Commentators have offered many possible solutions, but no clear explanation emerges out of the narrative itself. Did Moses' act of striking the rock disobey the LORD's instructions only to "order the rock" (v. 8)? Did Moses and Aaron in some way take credit themselves and away from the LORD (v. 10)? Did Moses and Aaron in some way imply that the LORD was unable or unwilling to give water to the people (v. 10)? Both Moses and Aaron are condemned to join the older generation in death outside the Promised Land of Canaan. Aaron's death is recorded in Numbers 20:22–29, and Moses' death is recorded in Deuteronomy 34:1–8.

community had no water, they held an assembly against Moses and Aaron. 3The people quarreled with Moses, exclaiming, "Would that we had perished when our kindred perished before the LORD! 4Why have you brought the LORD's assembly into this wilderness for us and our livestock to die here? 5Why have you brought us up out of Egypt, only to bring us to this wretched place? It is not a place for grain nor figs nor vines nor pomegranates! And there is no water to drink!" 6But Moses and Aaron went away from the assembly to the entrance of the tent of meeting, where they fell prostrate.

*Sin of Moses and Aaron.* Then the glory of the LORD appeared to them, 7and the LORD said to Moses: 8Take the staff and assemble the community, you and Aaron your brother, and in their presence command the rock to yield its waters. Thereby you will bring forth water from the rock for them, and supply the community and their livestock with water. 9So Moses took the staff from its place before the LORD, as he was ordered. 10Then Moses and Aaron gathered the assembly in front of the rock, where he said to them,[w] "Just listen, you rebels! Are we to produce water for you out of this rock?" 11[x]Then, raising his hand, Moses struck the rock twice* with his staff, and water came out in abundance, and the community and their livestock drank. 12*But the LORD said to Moses and Aaron: Because you did not have confidence in me, to acknowledge my holiness before the Israelites, therefore you shall not lead this assembly into the land I have given them.

13These are the waters of Meribah,[y] where the Israelites quarreled with the LORD, and through which he displayed his holiness.

*Edom's Refusal.* 14From Kadesh Moses sent messengers to the king of Edom: "Thus says your brother Israel:* You know of all the hardships that have befallen us, 15how our ancestors went down to Egypt, and we stayed in Egypt a long time, and the Egyptians treated us and our ancestors harshly. 16When we cried to the LORD,[z] he heard our cry and sent an angel who led us out of Egypt. Now here we are at Kadesh, a town at the edge of your territory. 17Please let us pass through your land. We will not cross any fields or vineyards, nor drink any well water, but we will go straight along the King's Highway* without turning to the right or to the left, until we have passed through your territory."

18But Edom answered him, "You shall not

ites arrived in Kadesh in the third year after the exodus (cf. Dt 1:46). But the itinerary in chap. 33 would suggest the fortieth year, the year in which Aaron died (33:38).

**20:11 Twice**: perhaps because he did not have sufficient faith to work the wonder with the first blow. Cf. v. 12.

**20:12–13** What lay behind Moses and Aaron's lack of confidence is not made explicit in the text. **Holiness**: an allusion to the name of the place, Kadesh, which means "holy, sanctified, sacred." Meribah means "contention." Cf. Ex 17:7.

**20:14 Your brother Israel**: according to biblical tradition, the Edomites were descended from Esau, the brother of Jacob. Their country, to the southeast of the Dead Sea, was also known as Seir; cf. Gn 25:24–26; 36:1, 8–9.

**20:17 The King's Highway**: an important highway, running north and south along the plateau east of the Dead Sea. In ancient times it was much used by caravans and armies; later it was improved by the Romans, and large stretches of it are still clearly recognizable.

*w:* Ex 17:5–6. *x:* Ps 78:15–16; Wis 11:4; 1 Cor 10:4. *y:* Nm 27:14; Ex 17:7. *z:* Ex 2:23.

pass through here; if you do, I will advance against you with the sword." [19]The Israelites said to him, "We will go up along the highway. If we or our livestock drink any of your water, we will pay for it. It is nothing—just let us pass through on foot." [20]But Edom replied, "You shall not pass through,"[a] and advanced against them with a large and heavily armed force. [21]Therefore, since Edom refused to let Israel pass through their territory, Israel turned away from them.

*Death of Aaron.* [22][b] Setting out from Kadesh, the Israelites, the whole community, came to Mount Hor.* [23]There at Mount Hor, on the border of the land of Edom, the LORD said to Moses and Aaron: [24]Let Aaron be gathered to his people, for he shall not enter the land I have given to the Israelites, because you both rebelled against my directions at the waters of Meribah. [25]Take Aaron and Eleazar his son and bring them up on Mount Hor.[c] [26]Then strip Aaron of his garments and put them on Eleazar, his son; but there Aaron shall be gathered up in death.

[27]Moses did as the LORD commanded. When they had climbed Mount Hor in view of the whole community, [28]Moses stripped Aaron of his garments and put them on Eleazar his son. Then Aaron died there on top of the mountain.[d] When Moses and Eleazar came down from the mountain, [29]all the community understood that Aaron had breathed his last; and for thirty days the whole house of Israel mourned Aaron.

See RG 80–85

## CHAPTER 21

***Victory over Arad.*** [1]When the Canaanite, the king of Arad,* who ruled over the Negeb,[e] heard that the Israelites were coming along the way of Atharim, he engaged Israel in battle and took some of them captive. [2]Israel then made this vow to the LORD: "If you deliver this people into my hand, I will put their cities under the ban."[f] [3]The LORD paid attention to Israel and delivered up the Canaanites,[g] and they put them and their cities under the ban. Hence that place was named Hormah.*

***The Bronze Serpent.*** [4]From Mount Hor they set out by way of the Red Sea, to bypass the land of Edom, but the people's patience was worn out by the journey; [5]so the people complained[h] against God and Moses, "Why have you brought us up from Egypt to die in the wilderness, where there is no food or water? We are disgusted with this wretched food!"*

[6]So the LORD sent among the people seraph* serpents, which bit[i] the people so that many of the Israelites died. [7]Then the people came to Moses and said, "We have sinned in complaining against the LORD and you. Pray to the LORD to take the serpents from us." So Moses prayed for the people, [8]and the LORD said to Moses: Make a seraph and mount it on a pole, and everyone who has been bitten will look at it and recover.* [9]Accordingly Moses made a bronze serpent* and mounted it on a pole, and whenever the serpent bit someone, the person looked at the bronze serpent and recovered.[j]

***Journey Around Moab.*** [10]The Israelites moved on and encamped in Oboth.[k] [11]Then they moved on from Oboth and encamped in Iye-abarim* in the wilderness facing Moab on the east. [12]Moving on from there, they encamped in the Wadi Zered. [13]Moving on from there, they encamped on the other side

**20:22 Mount Hor**: not definitively identified, but probably to be sought in the vicinity of Kadesh. According to Dt 10:6, Aaron died at Moserah (cf. "Moseroth" in Nm 33:30–31), which is apparently the name of the region in which Mount Hor is situated.

**21:1–3** The account of this episode seems to be a later insertion here, since logically v. 4 belongs immediately after 20:29. Perhaps this is the same event as that mentioned in Jgs 1:16–17.

**21:3 Hormah**: related to the Hebrew word *herem*, meaning "put under the ban." See notes on 14:45; 18:14.

**21:5 This wretched food**: apparently the manna is meant.

**21:6 Seraph**: the Hebrew name for a certain species of venomous snake; etymologically the word might signify "the fiery one." Compare the winged throne guardians in Is 6:2, 6; see also Is 14:29; 30:6.

**21:8 Everyone who has been bitten will look at it and recover**: in the Gospel of John this scene is regarded as a type for the crucifixion of Jesus (Jn 3:14–15).

**21:9** King Hezekiah, in his efforts to reform Israelite worship, "smashed the bronze serpent Moses had made" (2 Kgs 18:4).

**21:11 Iye-abarim**: probably means "the ruins in the Abarim (Mountains)." See note on 27:12.

*a:* Jgs 11:17. *b:* Nm 33:37. *c:* Dt 32:50. *d:* Nm 33:38. *e:* Nm 33:40. *f:* Jos 6:17; Jgs 1:17. *g:* Nm 14:45. *h:* Nm 11:6; Ex 16:3. *i:* Dt 8:15; Wis 16:5; 1 Cor 10:9. *j:* Wis 16:6–7, 10; Jn 3:14–15. *k:* Nm 33:43–44.

of the Arnon, in the wilderness that extends
from the territory of the Amorites; for the
Arnon forms Moab's boundary, between
Moab and the Amorites. 14 Hence it is said in
the "Book of the Wars of the LORD":*

"Waheb in Suphah and the wadies,
15 Arnon and the wadi gorges
That reach back toward the site of Ar*
and lean against the border of Moab."

16 From there they went to Beer,* which is the
well of which the LORD said to Moses,
Gather the people together so that I may give
them water. 17 Then Israel sang this song:

Spring up, O well!—so sing to it—
18 The well that the princes sank,
that the nobles of the people dug,
With their scepters and their staffs—
from the wilderness, a gift.

19 From Beer to Nahaliel, from Nahaliel to
Bamoth, 20 from Bamoth to the valley in the
country of Moab at the headland of Pisgah
that overlooks Jeshimon.*

***Victory over Sihon.*** 21 Now Israel sent
messengers to Sihon, king of the Amorites,
with the message, 22 "Let us pass through
your land. We will not turn aside into any
field or vineyard, nor will we drink any well
water, but we will go straight along the
King's Highway until we have passed
through your territory." 23 Sihon,[l] however,
would not permit Israel to pass through his
territory, but mustered all his forces and advanced against Israel into the wilderness.
When he reached Jahaz, he engaged Israel in
battle. 24 But Israel put him to the sword, and
took possession of his land from the Arnon
to the Jabbok and as far as Jazer of the Ammonites, for Jazer is the boundary of the
Ammonites. 25[m] Israel seized all the towns
here, and Israel settled in all the towns of the
Amorites, in Heshbon and all its dependencies. 26 For Heshbon was the city of Sihon,
king of the Amorites, who had fought
against the former king of Moab and had
taken all his land from him as far as the Arnon. 27 That is why the poets say:

"Come to Heshbon, let it be rebuilt,
let Sihon's city be firmly constructed.
28 For fire went forth from Heshbon
and a blaze from the city of Sihon;
It consumed Ar of Moab
and swallowed up the high places of
the Arnon.
29 Woe to you, Moab!
You are no more, people of Chemosh!*
He let his sons become fugitives
and his daughters be taken captive by
the Amorite king Sihon.
30 From Heshbon to Dibon their dominion
is no more;
Ar is laid waste; fires blaze as far as
Medeba."

31 So Israel settled in the land of the Amorites. 32 Moses sent spies to Jazer; and the Israelites captured it with its dependencies and
dispossessed the Amorites who were there.

***Victory over Og.*** 33[n] Then they turned and
went up along the road to Bashan. But Og,
king of Bashan, advanced against them with
all his forces to give battle at Edrei. 34 The
LORD, however, said to Moses: Do not fear
him; for into your hand I deliver him with all
his forces and his land. You will do to him as
you did to Sihon, king of the Amorites, who
reigned in Heshbon.[o] 35 So they struck him
down with his sons and all his forces, until
not a survivor was left to him, and they took
possession of his land.

**21:14 The "Book of the Wars of the LORD"**: an ancient collection of Israelite songs, now lost. **Waheb in Suphah**: since neither place is mentioned elsewhere, it is uncertain whether these Hebrew words are to be considered as place names; some Hebrew words, now lost, must have preceded this phrase.

**21:15 Ar**: a city or district in Moab, located on the Arnon; see v. 28; Dt 2:18.

**21:16 Beer**: "a well," here used as a place name.

**21:20 Jeshimon**: "the wasteland"; in 1 Sm 23:19, 24 and 26:1, 3, this is the wilderness of Judah on the western side of the Dead Sea, but here and in Nm 23:28, it seems to refer to the southern end of the Jordan valley where Beth-jeshimoth was situated.

**21:29 Chemosh**: the chief god of the Moabites, mentioned in the famous inscription of Mesha, king of Moab, who ruled at the same time as the Omrides in Israel. Cf. 1 Kgs 11:7, 33; 2 Kgs 23:13; Jer 48:7, 13.

*l:* Dt 2:32; Jgs 11:20. *m:* Jos 21:39; Jgs 11:26. *n:* Dt 3:1–7. *o:* Ps 136:17–22.

See RG 80–85

## CHAPTER 22

[1]Then the Israelites moved on and encamped in the plains of Moab* on the other side of the Jordan opposite Jericho.

***Balaam Summoned.*** [2]Now Balak, son of Zippor, saw all that Israel did to the Amorites, [3]and Moab feared the Israelites greatly because they were numerous. Moab was in dread of the Israelites. [4]So Moab said to the elders of Midian, "Now this horde will devour everything around us as an ox devours the grass of the field." At that time Balak, son of Zippor, was king of Moab; [5]and he sent messengers to Balaam, son of Beor, at Pethor on the river, in the land of the Ammonites,* to summon him with these words, "A people has come out of Egypt! They have covered up the earth and are settling down opposite me! [6]Now come, curse this people for me,* since they are stronger than I am. Perhaps I may be able to defeat them and drive them out of the land. For I know that whoever you bless is blessed and whoever you curse is cursed." [7]So the elders of Moab and the elders of Midian, themselves experts in divination,* left and went to Balaam, to whom they gave Balak's message. [8]He said to them, "Stay here overnight, and I will give you whatever answer the LORD gives me." So the princes of Moab lodged with Balaam.

[9]Then God came to Balaam and said: Who are these men with you? [10]Balaam answered God, "Balak, son of Zippor, king of Moab, sent me the message: [11]'This people that has come out of Egypt has covered up the earth. Now come, lay a curse on them for me; perhaps I may be able to fight them and drive them out.' " [12]But God said to Balaam: Do not go with them and do not curse this people, for they are blessed. [13]The next morning Balaam arose and told the princes of Balak, "Go back to your own country, for the LORD has refused to let me go with you." [14]So the princes of Moab went back to Balak with the report, "Balaam refused to come with us."

***Second Appeal to Balaam.*** [15]Balak yet again sent princes, who were more numerous and more distinguished than the others. [16]On coming to Balaam they told him, "Thus says Balak, son of Zippor: Please do not refuse to come to me. [17]I will reward you very handsomely and will do anything you ask of me. Come, lay a curse on this people for me." [18p] But Balaam replied to Balak's servants, "Even if Balak gave me his house full of silver and gold, I could not do anything, small or great, contrary to the command of the LORD, my God. [19]But, you too stay here overnight, so that I may learn what else the LORD may say to me." [20]That night God came to Balaam and said to him: If these men have come to summon you, go back with them; yet only on the condition that you do exactly as I tell you. [21]So the next morning when Balaam arose, he saddled his donkey,* and went off with the princes of Moab.

***The Talking Donkey.*** [22]But now God's anger flared up* at him for going, and the angel of the LORD took up a position on the road as his adversary. As Balaam was riding along on his donkey, accompanied by two of his servants, [23]the donkey saw the angel of the LORD standing in the road with sword

**22:1 The plains of Moab**: the lowlands to the northeast of the Dead Sea, between the Jordan and the foothills below Mount Nebo. Here the Israelites remained until they crossed the Jordan, according to Jos 1–4. Jericho lay to the west of the Jordan.

**22:5 In the land of the Ammonites**: the translation rests on a slight emendation of the traditional Hebrew text in accordance with the tradition represented by the Vulgate. While Pethor remains unidentified, this verse supports an identification of Balaam's homeland in the Transjordan (cf. the Deir 'Alla Inscriptions), over against other traditions in the text which connect Balaam with Syria (23:7; Dt 23:5).

**22:6 Curse this people for me**: Balak believed that Balaam, known in the tradition as a diviner (cf. Jos 13:22), could utter a curse upon Israel which would come to pass.

**22:7 Experts in divination**: lit., "divination was in their hand," i.e., "in their possession"; cf. Ezr 7:25.

**22:21 Donkey**: technically a she-donkey; Heb. *aton*.

**22:22 God's anger flared up**: God's apparent change of mind became a source of much speculation in the tradition. So, for example, God was angry, not merely because Balaam was going to Balak, for he had God's permission for the journey (v. 20), but perhaps because he was tempted by greed to curse Israel against God's command (cf. 2 Pt 2:15; Jude 11; compare Nm 22:32). **Adversary**: Heb. *satan*; see also v. 32; cf. 1 Sm 29:4; 2 Sm 19:22; 1 Kgs 11; Jb 1–2; Ps 109:6; Zec 3:1–2; 1 Chr 21:1.

*p:* Nm 24:13.

drawn. The donkey turned off the road and went into the field, and Balaam beat the donkey to bring her back on the road. 24 Then the angel of the LORD stood in a narrow lane between vineyards with a stone wall on each side. 25 When the donkey saw the angel of the LORD there, she pressed against the wall; and since she squeezed Balaam's leg against the wall, he beat her again. 26 Then the angel of the LORD again went ahead, and stood next in a passage so narrow that there was no room to move either to the right or to the left. 27 When the donkey saw the angel of the LORD there, she lay down under Balaam. Balaam's anger flared up and he beat the donkey with his stick.

28[q] Then the LORD opened the mouth of the donkey, and she asked Balaam, "What have I done to you that you beat me these three times?" 29 "You have acted so willfully against me," said Balaam to the donkey, "that if I only had a sword at hand, I would kill you here and now." 30 But the donkey said to Balaam, "Am I not your donkey, on which you have always ridden until now? Have I been in the habit of treating you this way before?" "No," he replied.

31 Then the LORD opened Balaam's eyes, so that he saw the angel of the LORD standing on the road with sword drawn; and he knelt and bowed down to the ground. 32 But the angel of the LORD said to him: "Why have you beaten your donkey these three times? I have come as an adversary because this rash journey of yours is against my will. 33 When the donkey saw me, she turned away from me these three times. If she had not turned away from me, you are the one I would have killed, though I would have spared her." 34 Then Balaam said to the angel of the LORD, "I have sinned. Yet I did not know that you took up a position to oppose my journey. Since it has displeased you, I will go back home." 35 But the angel of the LORD said to Balaam: "Go with the men; but you may say only what I tell you." So Balaam went on with the princes of Balak.

36 When Balak heard that Balaam was coming, he went out to meet him at Ar-Moab on the border formed by the Arnon, at its most distant point. 37 And Balak said to Balaam, "Did I not send an urgent summons to you? Why did you not come to me? Did you think I could not reward you?" 38 Balaam answered Balak, "Well, I have come to you after all. But what power have I to say anything? I can speak only what God puts in my mouth." 39 Then Balaam went with Balak, and they came to Kiriath-huzoth. 40 Here Balak sacrificed oxen and sheep, and sent portions to Balaam and to the princes who were with him.

***The First Oracle.*** 41 The next morning Balak took Balaam up on Bamoth-baal, and from there he could see some of the people.

## CHAPTER 23

See RG 80-85

1 Then Balaam said to Balak, "Build me seven altars here, and here prepare seven bulls and seven rams for me." 2 So Balak did as Balaam had ordered, and Balak and Balaam offered a bull and a ram on each altar. 3 Balaam said to Balak, "Stand here by your burnt offering while I go over there. Perhaps the LORD will meet me, and then I will tell you whatever he lets me see." And so he went out on the barren height. 4 Then God met Balaam, and Balak said to him: "I have erected the seven altars, and have offered a bull and a ram on each altar." 5 The LORD put an utterance in Balaam's mouth, and said: Go back to Balak, and speak accordingly. 6 So he went back to Balak, who was still standing by his burnt offering together with all the princes of Moab. 7 Then Balaam recited his poem:

From Aram* Balak has led me here,
Moab's king, from the mountains of
Qedem:[r]
"Come, curse for me Jacob,
come, denounce Israel."
8 How can I lay a curse on the one whom
God has not cursed?

**23:7 Aram**: the ancient name of the region later known as Syria. **The mountains of Qedem**: Qedem is the name for a region in northern Syria. Qedem also means "eastern." Perhaps this designates the low ranges in the Syrian desert. The "mountains of old" is also a possible translation.

*q*: 2 Pt 2:15–16. *r*: Nm 22:6.

How denounce the one whom the
LORD has not denounced?
9 For from the top of the crags I see him,
from the heights I behold him.
Here is a people that lives apart*
and does not reckon itself among the
nations.
10 Who has ever counted the dust of Jacob,
who numbered Israel's dust-cloud?*
May I die the death of the just,
may my end be like theirs!

11 "What have you done to me?" cried Balak to Balaam. "It was to lay a curse on my
foes that I brought you here; but instead, you
have blessed them!" 12 Balaam replied, "Is it
not what the LORD puts in my mouth that I
take care to repeat?"

*The Second Oracle.* 13 Then Balak said to
him, "Please come with me to another place*
from which you can see them; but you will
see only some, not all of them, and from
there lay a curse on them for me." 14 So he
brought him to a lookout post on the top of
Pisgah, where he built seven altars and offered a bull and a ram on each of them. 15 Balaam then said to Balak, "Stand here by your
burnt offering, while I seek a meeting over
there." 16 Then the LORD met Balaam, and,
having put an utterance in his mouth, said to
him: Return to Balak, and speak accordingly. 17 So he went to Balak, who was still
standing by his burnt offering together with
the princes of Moab. When Balak asked
him, "What did the LORD say?" 18 Balaam recited his poem:

Rise, Balak, and listen;
give ear to my testimony, son of
Zippor!
19 God is not a human being who speaks
falsely,
nor a mortal, who feels regret.
Is God one to speak and not act,
to decree and not bring it to pass?
20 I was summoned to bless;
I will bless; I cannot revoke it!
21 Misfortune I do not see in Jacob,
nor do I see misery* in Israel.
The LORD, their God, is with them;
among them is the war-cry of their
King.
22 They have the like of a wild ox's horns:*
God who brought them out of Egypt.[s]
23 No, there is no augury against Jacob,
nor divination against Israel.
Now it is said of Jacob,
of Israel, "Look what God has done!"
24 Here is a people that rises up like a
lioness,
and gets up like a lion;
It does not rest till it has devoured its
prey
and has drunk the blood of the slain.[t]

25 "Neither lay a curse on them nor bless
them," said Balak to Balaam. 26 But Balaam
answered Balak, "Did I not tell you, 'Everything the LORD tells me I must do'?"

*The Third Oracle.* 27 Then Balak said to
Balaam, "Come, let me bring you to another
place; perhaps God will approve of your laying a curse on them for me from there." 28 So
he took Balaam to the top of Peor, that overlooks Jeshimon. 29 Balaam then said to Balak, "Build me seven altars here; and here
prepare for me seven bulls and seven rams."
30 And Balak did as Balaam had ordered, offering a bull and a ram on each altar.

## CHAPTER 24

See RG 80–85

1 Balaam, however, perceiving that
the LORD was pleased to bless Israel, did not
go aside as before to seek omens, but turned
his gaze toward the wilderness. 2 When Balaam looked up and saw Israel encamped,
tribe by tribe, the spirit of God came upon
him, 3 and he recited his poem:

**23:9 A people that lives apart**: that is, "securely"; cf. Dt 33:28.

**23:10 The dust of Jacob . . . Israel's dust-cloud**: the Israelites will be as numerous as the dust kicked up by Israel in its march through the wilderness.

**23:13 To another place**: Balak thought that if Balaam would view Israel from a different site, he could deliver a different kind of omen.

**23:21 Misfortune . . . misery**: Balaam states that he is unable to see any evils for Israel.

**23:22 A wild ox's horns**: Israel possesses the strength of a wild ox because of God's presence among them. Compare the claim by the psalmist, the Lord is "my rock . . . my saving horn" (Ps 18:3).

*s:* Nm 24:8. *t:* Nm 24:9; Gn 49:9.

The oracle of Balaam, son of Beor,
the oracle of the man whose eye is true,
4 The oracle of one who hears what God says,
and knows what the Most High knows,
Of one who sees what the Almighty sees,
in rapture* and with eyes unveiled:
5 How pleasant are your tents, Jacob;
your encampments, Israel!
6 Like palm trees spread out,
like gardens beside a river,
Like aloes the LORD planted,
like cedars beside water;
7 Water will drip from their buckets,
their seed will have plentiful water;
Their king will rise higher than Agag*
and their dominion will be exalted.
8 They have the like of a wild ox's horns:
God who brought them out of Egypt.
They will devour hostile nations,
break their bones, and crush their loins.[u]
9 Crouching, they lie like a lion,
or like a lioness; who will arouse them?
Blessed are those who bless you,
and cursed are those who curse you![v]

10 In a blaze of anger at Balaam, Balak
clapped his hands* and said to him, "It was
to lay a curse on my foes that I summoned
you here; yet three times now you have actually blessed them![w] 11 Now flee to your
home. I promised to reward you richly, but
the LORD has withheld the reward from
you!" 12 Balaam replied to Balak, "Did I not
even tell the messengers whom you sent to
me, 13 'Even if Balak gave me his house full
of silver and gold, I could not of my own accord do anything, good or evil, contrary to
the command of the LORD'? Whatever the
LORD says I must say.[x]

*The Fourth Oracle.* 14 "But now that I am
about to go to my own people, let me warn
you what this people will do to your people
in the days to come." 15 Then he recited his
poem:

The oracle of Balaam, son of Beor,
the oracle of the man whose eye is true,
16 The oracle of one who hears what God says,
and knows what the Most High knows,
Of one who sees what the Almighty sees,
in rapture and with eyes unveiled.
17 I see him, though not now;
I observe him, though not near:
A star shall advance from Jacob,
and a scepter* shall rise from Israel,
That will crush the brows of Moab,[y]
and the skull of all the Sethites,
18 Edom will be dispossessed,
and no survivor is left in Seir.
Israel will act boldly,
19 and Jacob will rule his foes.

20 Upon seeing Amalek, Balaam recited his
poem:

**24:4 In rapture**: lit., "falling," therefore possibly "in a trance." However, this interpretation is uncertain.

**24:7 Agag**: during Saul's reign, king of Amalek (1 Sm 15:8), fierce enemy of Israel during the wilderness period; see v. 20 (Ex 17:8–16).

**24:10 Balak clapped his hands**: a gesture suggesting contempt or derision, apparently made in anger (cf. Jb 27:23; Lam 2:15).

**24:17 A star . . . a scepter**: some early Christian writers, as well as rabbinic interpreters, understood this prophecy in messianic terms. So, for example, Rabbi Akiba designates Bar Kosiba the messiah in the early second century A.D. by calling him Bar Kokhba, i.e., son of the star, alluding to this passage. Although this text is not referred to anywhere in the New Testament, in a Christian messianic interpretation the star would refer to Jesus, as also the scepter from Israel; cf. Is 11:1. But it is doubtful whether this passage is to be connected with the "star of the Magi" in Mt 2:1–12. **The brows of Moab, and the skull of all the Sethites**: under the figure of a human being, Moab is specified as the object of conquest by a future leader of Israel. The personification of peoples or toponyms is common enough in the Old Testament; see, e.g., Hos 11:1; Ps 98:8. In Jer 48:45, which paraphrases the latter part of our verse, Moab is depicted as someone whose boasting warrants its ruin. In view of the use of Heb. *pe'ah* (here "brows") in Nm 34:3 to indicate a boundary, some see in the "brows" of Moab and the "skull" of the Sethites a representation of features of Moab's topography, i.e., the borderlands and the interior plateau. **The Sethites**: cf. Gn 4:25; here probably a general designation for nomadic/tribal groups on the borders of Palestine, unless they are to be identified with the Shutu mentioned in Execration texts of the early second millennium B.C. and the fourteenth century Amarna tablets from Egypt; however, the Shutu are not attested in Moab. On the basis of Gn 4:25 and Gn 25, one might also think of a reference to humanity in general.

*u:* Nm 23:22. *v:* Nm 23:24; Gn 12:3; 27:29; 49:9. *w:* Nm 23:11. *x:* Nm 22:18. *y:* 2 Sm 8:2.

First* of the nations is Amalek,
but their end is to perish forever.[z]

21 Upon seeing the Kenites,* he recited his
poem:

Though your dwelling is safe,
and your nest is set on a cliff;
22 Yet Kain will be destroyed
when Asshur* takes you captive.

23 Upon seeing* [the Ishmaelites?] he recited
his poem:

Alas, who shall survive of Ishmael,
24 to deliver them from the hands of the
Kittim?
When they have conquered Asshur and
conquered Eber,
They too shall perish forever.

25 Then Balaam set out on his journey
home; and Balak also went his way.

## CHAPTER 25

See RG 80–85

***Worship of Baal of Peor.*** 1 While Israel
was living at Shittim,* the people profaned
themselves by prostituting themselves with
the Moabite women.[a] 2 These then invited
the people to the sacrifices of their god, and
the people ate of the sacrifices[b] and bowed
down to their god. 3 Israel thereby attached
itself to the Baal of Peor,[c] and the LORD's
anger flared up against Israel. 4[d] The LORD
said to Moses: Gather all the leaders of the
people, and publicly execute them* before
the LORD, that the blazing wrath of the LORD
may turn away from Israel. 5 So Moses told
the Israelite judges, "Each of you kill those
of his men who have attached themselves to
the Baal of Peor."*

***Zeal of Phinehas.*** 6 At this a certain Israelite came and brought in a Midianite woman*
to his kindred in the view of Moses and of
the whole Israelite community, while they
were weeping at the entrance of the tent of
meeting. 7[e] When Phinehas, son of Eleazar,
son of Aaron the priest, saw this, he rose up
from the assembly, and taking a spear in his
hand, 8 followed the Israelite into the tent
where he pierced the two of them, the Israelite and the woman. Thus the plague upon the
Israelites was checked; 9 but the dead from
the plague were twenty-four thousand.

10 Then the LORD said to Moses: 11 Phinehas, son of Eleazar, son of Aaron the priest,
has turned my anger from the Israelites by
his being as jealous among them as I am;
that is why I did not put an end to the Israelites in my jealousy.* 12[f] Announce, therefore,
that I hereby give him my covenant of
peace,* 13 which shall be for him and for his

**24:20 First**: lit., "the beginning." In the Bible, Amalek is a people indigenous to Palestine and therefore considered as of great antiquity. There is a deliberate contrast here between the words "first" and "end."

**24:21 The Kenites** lived in high strongholds in the mountains of southern Palestine and the Sinai Peninsula, and were skilled in working the various metals found in their territory. Their name is connected, at least by popular etymology, with the Hebrew word for "smith"; of similar sound to *qayin*, i.e., "Kain" or "smith," is the Hebrew word for "nest," *qen*—hence the play on words in the present passage.

**24:22 Asshur**: the mention of Asshur, i.e., Assyria, is not likely before the ninth or eighth centuries B.C.

**24:23–24 Upon seeing**: this phrase, lacking the Hebrew text, is found in the Septuagint, but without "the Ishmaelites" designated as the subject of the oracle. The Hebrew text of the oracle itself shows considerable disarray; the translation therefore relies on reconstruction of the putative original and is quite uncertain.

**25:1 Shittim**: the full name was Abel-shittim, a locality at the foot of the mountains in the northeastern corner of the plains of Moab (33:49). **Prostituting themselves**: the application to men of such traditional language for apostasy clearly suggests apostasy was taken to be an inevitable consequence of intermarriage with the Midianite women.

**25:4 Publicly execute them**: the same phrase occurs in 2 Sm 21:6–14, where the context shows that at least a part of the penalty consisted in being denied honorable burial. In both passages, dismemberment or impalement (perhaps subsequent to the actual execution) as a punishment for the breaking of covenant pledges, is a possible interpretation of the Hebrew phrase.

**25:5** Thereby Moses apparently alters the Lord's command to execute all the leaders.

**25:6 Midianite woman**: according to 22:4, 7, the Midianites were allied with the Moabites in opposing Israel, while 31:16 claims that Balaam had induced the Midianite women to lure the Israelites away from the Lord. **They were weeping**: on account of the plague that had struck them; cf. v. 8.

**25:11 My jealousy**: God's desire to maintain an exclusive hold on the allegiance of the Israelites.

**25:12 Covenant of peace**: by means of this covenant between God and Phinehas, Phinehas can expect God's protection, especially from any threat of reprisal for his action; cf. Is 54:10; Ez 34:25; 37:26.

---

*z:* Ex 17:14; 1 Sm 15:3. *a:* Nm 31:16. *b:* Ex 34:15–16. *c:* Ps 106:28; Hos 9:10. *d:* Dt 4:3. *e:* Ps 106:30. *f:* 1 Mc 2:26, 54; Ps 106:31; Sir 45:23–24.

descendants after him the covenant of an everlasting priesthood, because he was jealous on behalf of his God and thus made expiation for the Israelites.

14* The name of the slain Israelite, the one slain with the Midianite woman, was Zimri, son of Salu, prince of a Simeonite ancestral house. 15 The name of the slain Midianite woman was Cozbi, daughter of Zur, who was head of a clan, an ancestral house, in Midian.

***Vengeance on the Midianites.*** 16* The LORD then said to Moses: 17[g] Treat the Midianites as enemies and strike them, 18 for they have been your enemies by the deceitful dealings they had with you regarding Peor and their kinswoman Cozbi, the daughter of a Midianite prince, who was slain at the time of the plague because of Peor.

## III. Second Census of a New Generation and Preparation to Enter the Promised Land

### CHAPTER 26

See RG 80–85

***The Second Census.*** 19 After the plague 1 the LORD said to Moses and Eleazar, son of Aaron the priest: 2 Take a census, by ancestral houses, throughout the community of the Israelites of all those of twenty years or more who are eligible for military service in Israel.[h] 3 So on the plains of Moab along the Jordan at Jericho, Moses and Eleazar the priest enrolled them, 4 those of twenty years or more, as the LORD had commanded Moses.

The Israelites who came out of the land of Egypt were as follows:*

5[i] Reuben, the firstborn of Israel. The descendants of Reuben by their clans were: through Hanoch, the clan of the Hanochites; through Pallu, the clan of the Palluites; 6 through Hezron, the clan of the Hezronites; through Carmi, the clan of the Carmites. 7 These were the clans of the Reubenites, and those enrolled numbered forty-three thousand seven hundred and thirty.

8 From Pallu descended Eliab. 9 The sons of Eliab were Nemuel, Dathan, and Abiram[j]—the same Dathan and Abiram, ones designated by the community, who contended with Moses and Aaron as part of Korah's faction when they contended with the LORD. 10 The earth opened its mouth and swallowed them, along with Korah, as a warning. The faction was destroyed when the fire consumed two hundred and fifty men. 11 The descendants of Korah, however, did not die out.

12 The descendants of Simeon by clans were: through Nemuel,* the clan of the Nemuelites; through Jamin, the clan of the Jaminites; through Jachin, the clan of the Jachinites; 13 through Zerah, the clan of the Zerahites; through Shaul, the clan of the Shaulites. 14 These were the clans of the Simeonites, twenty-two thousand two hundred.

15 The descendants of Gad by clans were: through Zephon, the clan of the Zephonites; through Haggi, the clan of the Haggites; through Shuni, the clan of the Shunites; 16 through Ozni, the clan of the Oznites; through Eri, the clan of the Erites; 17 through Arod, the clan of the Arodites; through Areli, the clan of the Arelites. 18 These were the clans of the descendants of Gad, of whom there were enrolled forty thousand five hundred.

19 The sons of Judah were Er and Onan. Er and Onan died in the land of Canaan.[k] 20 The descendants of Judah by their clans were: through Shelah, the clan of the Shelahites; through Perez, the clan of the Perezites; through Zerah, the clan of the Zerahites. 21 The descendants of Perez were: through Hezron, the clan of the Hezronites; through Hamul, the clan of the

**25:14–15** The noble lineage of the slain couple is mentioned in order to stress the courage of Phinehas in punishing them. The zeal of Phinehas became proverbial; cf. Ps 106:30; Sir 45:23; 1 Mc 2:26, 54.

**25:16–18** The account of the execution of this command is given in 31:1–18.

**26:4** This introduction to the census seems to contradict vv. 64–65 by including those who came out of Egypt.

**26:12 Nemuel**: so also in 1 Chr 4:24. In Gn 46:10 and Ex 6:15, a son of Simeon with the same position in the genealogy bears the name "Jemuel"; it is uncertain which form is correct. See above, v. 9, where the name "Nemuel" occurs for a person descended from Pallu. Some speculate this name was inserted from v. 12 to provide a continuing line for Pallu.

*g*: Nm 31:2–12. *h*: Nm 1:2–3. *i*: 1 Chr 5:3. *j*: Nm 16:1, 32. *k*: Gn 38:7, 10; 46:12; 1 Chr 2:3.

Hamulites. 22 These were the clans of Judah, of whom there were enrolled seventy-six thousand five hundred.

23 The descendants of Issachar by their clans were: through Tola, the clan of the Tolaites; through Puvah, the clan of the Puvahites; 24 through Jashub, the clan of the Jashubites; through Shimron, the clan of the Shimronites. 25 These were the clans of Issachar, of whom there were enrolled sixty-four thousand three hundred.

26 The descendants of Zebulun by their clans were: through Sered, the clan of the Seredites; through Elon, the clan of the Elonites; through Jahleel, the clan of the Jahleelites. 27 These were the clans of the Zebulunites, of whom there were enrolled sixty thousand five hundred.

28 The sons of Joseph were Manasseh and Ephraim. 29 The descendants of Manasseh by clans were: through Machir, the clan of the Machirites. Now Machir begot Gilead: through Gilead, the clan of the Gileadites. 30 The descendants of Gilead were: through Iezer, the clan of the Iezrites; through Helek, the clan of the Helekites; 31 through Asriel, the clan of the Asrielites; through Shechem, the clan of the Shechemites; 32 through Shemida, the clan of the Shemidaites; through Hepher, the clan of the Hepherites. 33[l] As for Zelophehad, son of Hepher—he had no sons, but only daughters. The names of the daughters of Zelophehad were Mahlah, Noah, Hoglah, Milcah and Tirzah. 34 These were the clans of Manasseh, and those enrolled numbered fifty-two thousand seven hundred.

35 These were the descendants of Ephraim by their clans: through Shuthelah, the clan of the Shuthelahites; through Becher, the clan of the Becherites; through Tahan, the clan of the Tahanites. 36 These were the descendants of Shuthelah: through Eran, the clan of the Eranites. 37 These were the clans of the Ephraimites, of whom there were enrolled thirty-two thousand five hundred.

These were the descendants of Joseph by their clans.

38 The descendants of Benjamin by their clans were: through Bela, the clan of the Belaites; through Ashbel, the clan of the Ashbelites; through Ahiram, the clan of the Ahiramites; 39 through Shupham, the clan of the Shuphamites; through Hupham, the clan of the Huphamites. 40 The sons of Bela were Ard and Naaman: through Ard, the clan of the Ardites; through Naaman, the clan of the Naamites. 41 These were the descendants of Benjamin by their clans, of whom there were enrolled forty-five thousand six hundred.

42 These were the descendants of Dan by their clans: through Shuham the clan of the Shuhamites. These were the clans of Dan, 43 of whom there were enrolled sixty-four thousand four hundred.

44 The descendants of Asher by their clans were: through Imnah, the clan of the Imnites; through Ishvi, the clan of the Ishvites; through Beriah, the clan of the Beriites; 45 through Heber, the clan of the Heberites; through Malchiel, the clan of the Malchielites. 46 The name of Asher's daughter was Serah. 47 These were the clans of the descendants of Asher, of whom there were enrolled fifty-three thousand four hundred.

48 The descendants of Naphtali by their clans were: through Jahzeel, the clan of the Jahzeelites; through Guni, the clan of the Gunites; 49 through Jezer, the clan of the Jezerites; through Shillem, the clan of the Shillemites. 50 These were the clans of Naphtali, of whom there were enrolled forty-five thousand four hundred.

51 These were the Israelites who were enrolled: six hundred and one thousand seven hundred and thirty.

***Allotment of the Land.**** 52 The LORD said to Moses: 53[m] Among these the land shall be divided as their heritage in keeping with the number of people named. 54[n] To a large tribe you shall assign a large heritage, to a small

**26:52–56** The division of Canaan among the various tribes and clans and families was determined not only by the size of each group but also by lot. Perhaps the lots determined the respective locality of each tribal land and the section reserved for each clan, while the relative size of the allotted locality and section depended on the numerical strength of each group. The Israelites considered the outcome of the drawing of lots as an expression of God's will; cf. Lv 16:8–10; Jos 14:2; 15:1; etc.; Acts 1:23–26.

*l:* Nm 27:1; 36:11; Jos 17:3. *m:* Jos 11:23. *n:* Nm 33:54; 35:8.

**The Daughters of Zelophehad and the Inheritance of the Land**

THE LEGAL CASE PRESENTED in Nm 27:1–11, involves the conflict between two principles. On one hand, Israelite land normally passed from father to son and not to daughters. On the other hand, a high priority was given to maintaining a given land allotment within a particular family or clan to maintain a fair distribution of the land among family groups. On the basis of priority of this latter principle, the five daughters of a man named Zelophehad argue that they ought to receive their father's allotment of land as an inheritance. In the end, the LORD and Moses agree. In Numbers 36, the case is taken up again with some restrictions on whom the daughters of Zelophehad can marry to preserve the land in the family group.

tribe a small heritage, each receiving its heritage in proportion to the number enrolled in
it. 55But the land shall be divided by lot, all
inheriting according to the lists of their ancestral tribes. 56As the lot falls the heritage of
each tribe, large or small, will be assigned.

*Census of the Levites.* 57These were the
Levites enrolled by clans: through Gershon,
the clan of the Gershonites; through Kohath, the clan of the Kohathites; through
Merari, the clan of the Merarites. 58These
were clans of Levi: the clan of the Libnites,
the clan of the Hebronites, the clan of the
Mahlites, the clan of the Mushites, the clan
of the Korahites.*

Now Kohath begot Amram, 59whose wife
was named Jochebed. She was the daughter
of Levi, born to Levi in Egypt. To Amram
she bore Aaron and Moses and Miriam their
sister. 60To Aaron were born Nadab and
Abihu, Eleazar and Ithamar. 61But Nadab
and Abihu died when they offered unauthorized fire before the LORD. 62The Levites enrolled were twenty-three thousand, every
male one month or more of age.[o] They were
not enrolled with the other Israelites, however, for no heritage was given them among
the Israelites.

63These, then, were those enrolled by Moses and Eleazar the priest, when they enrolled the Israelites on the plains of Moab
along the Jordan at Jericho. 64Among them
there was not one of those who had been enrolled by Moses and Aaron the priest, when
they enrolled the Israelites in the wilderness
of Sinai. 65[p] For the LORD had told them that
they would surely die in the wilderness, and
not one of them was left except Caleb, son of
Jephunneh, and Joshua, son of Nun.

## CHAPTER 27

See RG 80–85

*Zelophehad's Daughters.* 1The daughters of Zelophehad, son of Hepher, son of
Gilead, son of Machir, son of Manasseh,
came forward. (Zelophehad belonged to the
clans of Manasseh, son of Joseph.) The
names of his daughters were Mahlah, Noah,
Hoglah, Milcah and Tirzah.[q] 2Standing before Moses, Eleazar the priest, the princes,
and the whole community at the entrance of
the tent of meeting, they said: 3"Our father
died in the wilderness. Although he did not
join the faction of those who conspired
against the LORD,* Korah's faction, he died
for his own sin without leaving any sons.
4But why should our father's name be cut off
from his clan merely because he had no son?
Give us land among our father's kindred."

*Laws Concerning Heiresses.** 5So Moses
laid their case before the LORD, 6and the
LORD said to him: 7The plea of Zelophehad's
daughters is just; you shall give them hereditary land among their father's kindred and
transfer their father's heritage to them. 8Tell

**26:58** Compare 3:18–20 for a different listing.

**27:3 He did not join . . . against the LORD**: had he done so, he and his heirs could have been deprived of a portion in the promised land.

**27:5–11** The purpose of this law, as also that of the related laws in 36:2–10 (marriage within the same tribe), Dt 25:5–10 (levirate marriage), and Lv 25:10 (return of property in the jubilee year), was to keep the landed property within the proper domain of each tribe.

*o:* Nm 3:39. *p:* Nm 14:22–24, 29. *q:* Nm 26:33; Jos 17:3.

the Israelites: If a man dies without leaving a son, you shall transfer his heritage to his daughter; [9]if he has no daughter, you shall give his heritage to his brothers; [10]if he has no brothers, you shall give his heritage to his father's brothers; [11]if his father had no brothers, you shall give his heritage to his nearest relative in his clan, who shall then take possession of it.

This will be the statutory procedure for the Israelites, as the LORD commanded Moses.[r]

***Joshua to Succeed Moses.*** [12]The LORD said to Moses: Go up into this mountain of the Abarim range* and view the land that I have given to the Israelites.[s] [13]When you have viewed it, you will be gathered to your people, as was Aaron your brother.[t] [14]For in the rebellion of the community in the wilderness of Zin you both rebelled against my order to acknowledge my holiness before them by means of the water.[u] (These were the waters of Meribah of Kadesh in the wilderness of Zin.)

[15]Then Moses said to the LORD, [16]"May the LORD, the God of the spirits of all humanity,* set over the community someone [17]who will be their leader in battle and who will lead them out and bring them in, that the LORD's community may not be like sheep without a shepherd." [18]And the LORD replied to Moses: Take Joshua, son of Nun,[v] a man of spirit,* and lay your hand upon him. [19]Have him stand before Eleazar the priest and the whole community, and commission him in their sight. [20]Invest him with some of your own power, that the whole Israelite community may obey him. [21]He shall present himself to Eleazar the priest, who will seek for him the decision of the Urim* in the LORD's presence; and as it directs, Joshua, all the Israelites with him, and the whole community will go out for battle; and as it directs, they will come in.

[22]Moses did as the LORD had commanded him. Taking Joshua and having him stand before Eleazar the priest and the whole community, [23]he laid his hands on him and commissioned him, as the LORD had directed through Moses.

## CHAPTER 28

See RG 80–85

***General Sacrifices.*** [1]The LORD said to Moses: [2]Give the Israelites this commandment: At their prescribed times, you will be careful to present to me the food offerings that are due me, oblations of pleasing aroma to me.

***Each Morning and Evening.*** [3][w] You will tell them therefore: This is the oblation which you will offer to the LORD: two unblemished yearling lambs each day as the regular burnt offering,* [4]offering one lamb in the morning and the other during the evening twilight, [5]each with a grain offering of one tenth of an ephah of bran flour mixed with a fourth of a hin of oil of crushed olives.* [6]This is the regular burnt offering that was made at Mount Sinai for a pleasing aroma, an oblation to the LORD. [7]And as the libation for the first lamb, you will make a libation to the LORD in the sanctuary* of a fourth of a hin of strong drink. [8]The other lamb you will offer during the evening twilight, making the same grain offering and the same libation as in the morning, as an oblation of pleasing aroma to the LORD.

**27:12 The Abarim range**: the mountains on the eastern side of the Dead Sea. The peak of this chain is Mount Nebo where Moses views the promised land before he dies (Dt 32:49).

**27:16 The God of the spirits of all humanity**: the sense is that God knows the character and abilities of all people and therefore knows best whom to appoint (cf. Jgs 6:34; 11:29; 1 Sm 16:13); see the same phrase in Nm 16:22, where "spirit" evidently means the life principle.

**27:18 A man of spirit**: lit., "a man in whom there is spirit," that is, probably one who is endowed with a courageous spirit (Jos 2:11); compare Gn 41:38; Dt 34:9.

**27:21 The Urim**: certain sacred objects which Israelite priests employed to discern the divine will, probably by obtaining a positive or negative answer to a given question. The full expression was "the Urim and Thummim"; cf. Ex 28:30; Lv 8:8; Dt 33:8; Ezr 2:63; Neh 7:65. Joshua ordinarily did not receive direct revelations from God as Moses had received them.

**28:3 The regular burnt offering**: "the *tamid* burnt offering," the technical term for the daily sacrifice. The lambs—as well as the goats for the purification offering (vv. 15, 22, 30)—are all specified as males.

**28:5 Oil of crushed olives**: this oil, probably made in a mortar, was purer and more expensive than oil extracted in the olive press.

**28:7 In the sanctuary**: i.e., the tent of meeting. But according to Sir 50:15, the libation was poured at the base of the outer altar.

*r:* Jer 32:6–9. *s:* Dt 3:27; 32:49; 34:1. *t:* Nm 20:12, 24. *u:* Dt 32:51. *v:* Dt 34:9. *w:* Ex 29:38–42.

*On the Sabbath.* [9]On the sabbath day: two unblemished yearling lambs, with a grain offering of two tenths of an ephah of bran flour mixed with oil, and its libation. [10]This is the sabbath burnt offering each sabbath, in addition to the regular burnt offering and its libation.

*At the New Moon Feast.* [11]On your new moons* you will offer as a burnt offering to the LORD two bulls of the herd, one ram, and seven unblemished yearling lambs, [12]with three tenths of an ephah of bran flour mixed with oil as the grain offering for each bull, two tenths of an ephah of bran flour mixed with oil as the grain offering for the ram, [13]and one tenth of an ephah of bran flour mixed with oil as the grain offering for each lamb, a burnt offering with a pleasing aroma, an oblation to the LORD. [14]Their libations will consist of a half a hin of wine for each bull, a third of a hin for the ram, and a fourth of a hin for each lamb. This is the burnt offering for the new moon, for every new moon through the months of the year. [15]Moreover, there will be one goat for a purification offering to the LORD; it will be offered in addition to the regular burnt offering and its libation.

*At the Passover.* [16]The fourteenth day* of the first month is the Passover of the LORD,[x] [17]and the fifteenth day of this month is the pilgrimage feast. For seven days unleavened bread is to be eaten. [18]On the first day you will declare a holy day, and you shall do no heavy work.*[y] [19]You will offer an oblation, a burnt offering to the LORD: two bulls of the herd, one ram, and seven yearling lambs that you are sure are unblemished. [20]Their grain offerings will be of bran flour mixed with oil; you will offer three tenths of an ephah for each bull and two tenths for the ram. [21]You will offer one tenth for each of the seven lambs; [22]and one goat as a purification offering to make atonement for yourselves. [23]These offerings you will make in addition to the morning burnt offering which is part of the regular burnt offering. [24]You will make exactly the same offerings each day for seven days as food offerings, oblations of pleasing aroma to the LORD; they will be offered in addition to the regular burnt offering with its libation. [25]On the seventh day you will declare a holy day: you shall do no heavy work.[z]

*At Pentecost.* [26]On the day of first fruits,* on your feast of Weeks,[a] when you present to the LORD an offering of new grain, you will declare a holy day: you shall do no heavy work. [27]You will offer burnt offering for a pleasing aroma to the LORD: two bulls of the herd, one ram, and seven yearling lambs that you are sure are unblemished. [28]Their grain offerings will be of bran flour mixed with oil: three tenths of an ephah for each bull, two tenths for the ram, [29]and one tenth for each of the seven lambs. [30]One goat will be for a purification offering to make atonement for yourselves. [31]You will make these offerings, together with their libations, in addition to the regular burnt offering with its grain offering.

## CHAPTER 29

See RG 80–85

*On New Year's Day.* [1]In the seventh month on the first day* you will declare a holy day, and do no heavy work; it shall be a day on which you sound the trumpet.[b] [2]You will offer a burnt offering for a pleasing aroma to the LORD: one bull of the herd, one ram, and seven unblemished yearling lambs. [3]Their grain offerings will be of bran flour mixed with oil: three tenths of an ephah for

**28:11 On your new moons**: beginning on the evening when the crescent of the new moon first appeared. The beginning of the month is reckoned according to the new moon.

**28:16 The fourteenth day**: toward evening at the end of this day; cf. Ex 12:6, 18.

**28:18 Heavy work**: apparently, some sorts of activity are permitted on a day such as this, whereas "any work" is prohibited by 29:7 on the Day of Atonement. See note on Lv 23:3.

**28:26 The day of first fruits**: a unique term for this feast, which is usually called "the feast of Weeks"; it was celebrated as a thanksgiving for the wheat harvest seven weeks after the barley harvest (Passover). In the time of Jesus it was commonly known by the Greek word "Pentecost," that is, "fiftieth" (day after the Passover); see note on Lv 23:16–21.

**29:1 In the seventh month on the first day**: (about September–October) now the Jewish New Year's Day. In the older calendar the year began with the first of Nisan (March–April), which is still known as the first month; cf. Ex 12:2.

*x:* Ex 12:18; Lv 23:5; Dt 16:1. *y:* Ex 12:16; Lv 23:7. *z:* Ex 12:16; 13:6; Lv 23:8. *a:* Ex 34:22. *b:* Nm 10:10; Lv 23:24.

the bull, two tenths for the ram, 4and one
tenth for each of the seven lambs. 5One goat
will be a purification offering to make atonement for yourselves. 6These are in addition
to the burnt offering for the new moon with
its grain offering, and in addition to the regular burnt offering with its grain offering, together with the libations prescribed for
them, for a pleasing aroma, an oblation to
the LORD.

***On the Day of Atonement.*** 7On the tenth
day of this seventh month* you will declare
a holy day, humble yourselves, and do no
sort of work.[c] 8You will offer a burnt offering to the LORD, a pleasing aroma: one bull
of the herd, one ram, and seven yearling
lambs that you are sure are unblemished.
9Their grain offerings of bran flour mixed
with oil: three tenths of an ephah for the bull,
two tenths for the one ram, 10and one tenth
for each of the seven lambs. 11One goat will
be a purification offering. These are in addition to the purification offering for purging,*
the regular burnt offering with its grain offering, and their libations.

***On the Feast of Booths.*** 12* On the fifteenth day of the seventh month you will declare a holy day:[d] you shall do no heavy
work. For the following seven days you will
celebrate a pilgrimage feast to the LORD.
13You will offer a burnt offering, an oblation
of pleasing aroma to the LORD: thirteen
bulls* of the herd, two rams, and fourteen
yearling lambs that are unblemished. 14Their
grain offerings will be of bran flour mixed
with oil: three tenths of an ephah for each of
the thirteen bulls, two tenths for each of the
two rams, 15and one tenth for each of the
fourteen lambs. 16One goat will be a purification offering. These are in addition to the
regular burnt offering with its grain offering
and libation.

17On the second day: twelve bulls of the
herd, two rams, and fourteen unblemished
yearling lambs, 18with the grain offerings
and libations for the bulls, rams and lambs in
their prescribed number, 19as well as one
goat as a purification offering, besides the
regular burnt offering with its grain offering
and libation.

20On the third day: eleven bulls, two rams,
and fourteen unblemished yearling lambs,
21with the grain offerings and libations for
the bulls, rams and lambs in their prescribed
number, 22as well as one goat for a purification offering, besides the regular burnt offering with its grain offering and libation.

23On the fourth day: ten bulls, two rams,
and fourteen unblemished yearling lambs,
24the grain offerings and libations for the
bulls, rams and lambs in their prescribed
number, 25as well as one goat as a purification offering, besides the regular burnt offering, its grain offering and libation.

26On the fifth day: nine bulls, two rams,
and fourteen unblemished yearling lambs,
27[e] with the grain offerings and libations for
the bulls, rams and lambs in their prescribed
number, 28as well as one goat as a purification offering, besides the regular burnt offering with its grain offering and libation.

29On the sixth day: eight bulls, two rams,
and fourteen unblemished yearling lambs,
30with the grain offerings and libations for
the bulls, rams and lambs in their prescribed
number, 31as well as one goat as a purification offering, besides the regular burnt offering, its grain offering and libation.

32On the seventh day: seven bulls, two
rams, and fourteen unblemished yearling
lambs, 33with the grain offerings and libations for the bulls, rams and lambs in their
prescribed number, 34as well as one goat as a
purification offering, besides the regular
burnt offering, its grain offering and libation.

35On the eighth day[f] you will hold a public assembly:* you shall do no heavy work.

**29:7 The tenth day of this seventh month**: the Day of Atonement. **Humble yourselves**: that is, with fasting.

**29:11 The purification offering for purging**: the bull prescribed in Lv 16:11–12 for the purging of the tent sanctuary.

**29:12** This feast of Booths (Tabernacles or Sukkot) celebrating the vintage harvest was the most popular of all and therefore had the most elaborate ritual. See note on Lv 23:34.

**29:13 Thirteen bulls**: the number of bulls sacrificed before the octave day was seventy, arranged on a descending scale so that the number on the seventh day was the sacred number seven.

**29:35 A public assembly**: the Hebrew word is the technical term for the closing celebration of the three major feasts of the

*c:* Lv 16:29; 23:27–28, 32. *d:* Lv 23:34–35. *e:* Nm 29:30, 37. *f:* Lv 23:36; Jn 7:37.

36 You will offer a burnt offering, an oblation
of pleasing aroma to the LORD: one bull, one
ram, and seven unblemished yearling lambs,
37 with the grain offerings and libations for
the bulls, rams and lambs in their prescribed
number, 38 as well as one goat as a purification offering, besides the regular burnt offering with its grain offering and libation.
39 These are the offerings you will make to
the LORD on your festivals, besides your votive or voluntary offerings of burnt offerings, grain offerings, libations, and communion offerings.

## CHAPTER 30

See RG 80–85

1 So Moses instructed the Israelites
exactly as the LORD had commanded him.
***Validity and Annulment of Vows.*** 2 Moses
said to the heads of the Israelite tribes, "This
is what the LORD has commanded: 3 When a
man makes a vow to the LORD or binds himself under oath to a pledge,* he shall not violate his word, but must fulfill exactly the
promise he has uttered.[g]
4 "When a woman makes a vow to the
LORD, or binds herself to a pledge, while still
in her father's house in her youth, 5 and her
father learns of her vow or the pledge to
which she bound herself and says nothing to
her about it, then any vow or any pledge to
which she bound herself remains valid. 6 But
if on the day he learns of it her father opposes her, then any vow or any pledge to
which she bound herself becomes invalid;
and the LORD will release her from it, since
her father opposed her.
7 "If she marries while under a vow or under a rash pledge to which she bound herself,
8 and her husband learns of it, yet says nothing to her on the day he learns it, then the
vows or the pledges to which she bound herself remain valid. 9 But if on the day her husband learns of it he opposes her, he thereby
annuls the vow she had made or the rash
pledge to which she had bound herself, and
the LORD will release her from it. 10 (The
vow of a widow or of a divorced woman,
however, any pledge to which such a woman
binds herself, is valid.)
11 "If it is in her husband's house* that she
makes a vow or binds herself under oath to a
pledge, 12 and her husband learns of it yet
says nothing to her to oppose her, then all her
vows remain valid or any pledge to which
she has bound herself. 13 But if on the day he
learns of them her husband annuls them, then
whatever she has expressly promised in her
vows or in her pledge becomes invalid; since
her husband has annulled them, the LORD
will release her from them.
14 "Any vow or any pledge that she makes
under oath to humble herself, her husband
may either confirm or annul. 15 But if her
husband, day after day, says nothing at all to
her, he thereby confirms all her vows or all
the pledges incumbent upon her; he has confirmed them, because on the day he learned
of them he said nothing to her. 16 If, however,
he annuls them* some time after he first
learned of them, he will be responsible for
her guilt."
17 These are the statutes which the LORD
commanded Moses concerning a husband
and his wife, as well as a father and his
daughter while she is still in her youth in her
father's house.

## CHAPTER 31

See RG 80–85

***Campaign Against the Midianites.***
1 The LORD said to Moses:* 2 Avenge the Israelites on the Midianites, and then you will
be gathered to your people. 3 So Moses told
the people, "Arm some men among you for
the campaign, to attack Midian and to execute the LORD's vengeance on Midian.
4 From each of the tribes of Israel you will

Passover, Pentecost and Booths, or of other special feasts that lasted for a week. Cf. Lv 23:36; Dt 16:8; 2 Chr 7:9; Neh 8:18.

**30:3 A vow . . . a pledge**: here the former signifies the promise to dedicate either a person, an animal, or a thing or their equivalent to the sanctuary upon the fulfillment of some specified conditions (Lv 27:1–13); the latter signifies the assumption of either a positive or a negative obligation—that is, the promise either to do something or to abstain from something; cf. v. 14.

**30:11 In her husband's house**: after her marriage. This contrasts with the case given in vv. 7–9.

**30:16 He annuls them**: he prevents their fulfillment. Since he has first allowed the vows to remain valid, he can no longer annul them.

**31:1–3** The narrative of Israel's campaign against Midian, which was interrupted after 25:18, is now resumed.

*g:* Dt 23:22; Eccl 5:3–4.

send a thousand men to the campaign."
5From the contingents of Israel, therefore, a
thousand men of each tribe were levied, so
that there were twelve thousand men armed
for war. 6Moses sent them out on the campaign, a thousand from each tribe, with
Phinehas, son of Eleazar, the priest for the
campaign, who had with him the sacred vessels and the trumpets for sounding the alarm.
7They waged war against the Midianites, as
the LORD had commanded Moses, and killed
every male. 8Besides those slain in battle,
they killed the kings of Midian: Evi, Rekem,
Zur, Hur and Reba, the five kings of Midian;* and they also killed Balaam, son of
Beor, with the sword. 9But the Israelites took
captive the women of the Midianites with
their children, and all their herds and flocks
and wealth as loot, 10while they set on fire all
the towns where they had settled and all
their encampments. 11Then they took all the
plunder, with the people and animals they
had captured, and brought the captives, together with the spoils and plunder, 12to Moses and Eleazar the priest and to the Israelite
community at their camp on the plains of
Moab by the Jordan opposite Jericho.

*Treatment of the Captives.* 13When Moses
and Eleazar the priest, with all the leaders of
the community, went outside the camp to
meet them, 14Moses became angry with the
officers of the army, the commanders of
thousands and the commanders of hundreds,
who were returning from the military campaign. 15"So you have spared all the
women!" he exclaimed. 16"These are the
very ones who on Balaam's advice were behind the Israelites' unfaithfulness to the
LORD in the affair at Peor,[h] so that plague
struck the LORD's community. 17* Now kill,
therefore, every male among the children
and kill every woman who has had sexual
relations with a man. 18But you may spare
for yourselves all the girls who have not had
sexual relations.

*Purification After Combat.* 19"Moreover,
remain outside the camp for seven days;
every one of you who has killed anyone or
touched someone killed will purify yourselves on the third and on the seventh day—
both you and your captives. 20You will also
purify every garment, every article of
leather, everything made of goats' hair, and
every article of wood."

21Eleazar the priest told the soldiers who
had taken part in the battle: "This is the prescribed ritual which the LORD has commanded Moses: 22gold, silver, bronze, iron,
tin and lead— 23whatever can stand fire—
you shall put into the fire, that it may become
clean; however, it must also be purified with
water of purification.* But whatever cannot
stand fire you must put into the water. 24On
the seventh day you will wash your garments, and then you will again be clean. After that you may enter the camp."

*Division of the Spoils.* 25The LORD said to
Moses: 26With the help of Eleazar the priest
and of the heads of the ancestral houses of
the community, inventory all the spoils captured, human being and beast alike; 27then
divide the spoils* between the warriors who
went on the campaign and the whole community. 28You will levy a tax for the LORD on
the soldiers who went on the campaign: one
out of every five hundred persons, oxen,
donkeys, and sheep. 29From their half you
will take it and give it to Eleazar the priest as
a contribution to the LORD. 30From the Israelites' half you will take one captive from
every fifty human beings, oxen, donkeys,
and sheep—all the animals—and give them
to the Levites, who perform the duties of the
LORD's tabernacle. 31So Moses and Eleazar
the priest did this, as the LORD had commanded Moses.

**31:8 The five kings of Midian**: they are called Midianite princes, Sihon's vassals, in Jos 13:21.

**31:17** There are later references to Midian in Jgs 6–8; 1 Kgs 11:18; Is 60:6. The present raid was only against those Midianites who were dwelling at this time near the encampment of the Israelites.

**31:23 Water of purification**: water mixed with the ashes of the red heifer as prescribed in 19:9.

**31:27 Divide the spoils**: for a similar division of the plunder into two equal parts, between those who engaged in the battle and those who stayed with the baggage, cf. 1 Sm 30:24. But note that here the tax on the plunder of the noncombatants is ten times as much as that on the soldiers' plunder.

*h:* 2 Pt 2:15; Rev 2:14.

***Amount of the Plunder.*** 32 This plunder, what was left of the loot which the troops had taken, amounted to six hundred and seventy-five thousand sheep, 33 seventy-two thousand oxen, 34 sixty-one thousand donkeys, 35 and thirty-two thousand women who had not had sexual relations.

36 The half-share that fell to those who had gone out on the campaign was in number: three hundred and thirty-seven thousand five hundred sheep, 37 of which six hundred and seventy-five fell as tax to the LORD; 38 thirty-six thousand oxen, of which seventy-two fell as tax to the LORD; 39 thirty thousand five hundred donkeys, of which sixty-one fell as tax to the LORD; 40 and sixteen thousand persons, of whom thirty-two persons fell as tax to the LORD. 41 Moses gave the taxes contributed to the LORD to Eleazar the priest, exactly as the LORD had commanded Moses.

42 As for the Israelites' half, which Moses had taken from the men who had fought— 43 the community's half was three hundred and thirty-seven thousand five hundred sheep, 44 thirty-six thousand oxen, 45 thirty thousand five hundred donkeys, 46 and sixteen thousand persons. 47 From the Israelites' half, Moses took one captive from every fifty, from human being and beast alike, and gave them to the Levites, who performed the duties of the LORD's tabernacle, exactly as the LORD had commanded Moses.

***Gifts of the Officers.*** 48 Then those who were officers over the contingents of the army, commanders of thousands and commanders of hundreds, came up to Moses 49 and said to him, "Your servants have counted the soldiers under our command, and not one of us is missing. 50* So, we have brought as an offering to the LORD articles of gold that each of us has picked up—anklets, bracelets, rings, earrings, or pendants—to make atonement for ourselves before the LORD." 51 Moses and Eleazar the priest accepted the gold from them, all fashioned pieces. 52 The gold that was given as a contribution to the LORD—from the commanders of thousands and the commanders of hundreds—amounted in all to sixteen thousand seven hundred and fifty shekels. 53 What the common soldiers had looted each one kept for himself.* 54 So Moses and Eleazar the priest accepted the gold from the commanders of thousands and of hundreds, and put it in the tent of meeting as a reminder on behalf of the Israelites before the LORD.

## CHAPTER 32

See RG 80–85

***Request of Gad and Reuben.*** 1 Now the Reubenites and Gadites had a very large number of livestock. Noticing that the land of Jazer and of Gilead* was a place suited to livestock, 2 the Gadites and Reubenites came to Moses and Eleazar the priest and to the leaders of the community and said, 3* "The region of Ataroth, Dibon, Jazer, Nimrah, Heshbon, Elealeh, Sebam, Nebo and Baal-meon— 4 the land which the LORD has laid low before the community of Israel, is a land for livestock, and your servants have livestock." 5 They continued, "If we find favor with you, let this land be given to your servants as their possession. Do not make us cross the Jordan."

***Moses' Rebuke.*** 6 But Moses answered the Gadites and Reubenites: "Are your kindred, then, to go to war, while you remain here? 7 Why do you wish to discourage the Israelites from crossing to the land the LORD has given them? 8 That is just what your ancestors did when I sent them from Kadesh-barnea to reconnoiter the land.[i] 9 They went up to the Wadi Eshcol and reconnoitered the land, then so discouraged the Israelites that they would not enter the land the LORD had given them. 10[j] At that time the anger of the LORD flared up, and he swore: 11 None of the men twenty years old or more who have come up from

**31:50** The precise nature and use of some of these articles of gold is not certain.

**31:53** Apparently because of the commanders' generosity the common troops were under no sort of obligation to make their own offerings and could keep their loot.

**32:1 Gilead**: the name of the western part of the plateau east of the Jordan, sometimes signifying the whole region from the Yarmuk to the Jordan, sometimes only the northern part of this region, and sometimes, as here, only its southern part. Jazer lay to the east of southern Gilead.

**32:3** The places named in this verse, as well as the additional ones given in vv. 34–38, were all in the former kingdom of Sihon, that is, in the region between the Jabbok and the Arnon. Cf. 21:23–24; Jos 13:19–21, 24–27.

*i:* Nm 13:31–33; Dt 1:22. *j:* Dt 1:34–35.

Egypt will see the land I promised under oath to Abraham and Isaac and Jacob, because they have not followed me unreservedly—[12][k] except the Kenizzite* Caleb, son of Jephunneh, the Kenizzite, and Joshua, son of Nun, since they have followed the LORD unreservedly. [13]So the anger of the LORD flared up against the Israelites and he made them wander in the wilderness forty years, until the whole generation that had done evil in the sight of the LORD had disappeared. [14]And now here you are, offspring of sinful stock, rising up in your ancestors' place to add still more to the LORD's blazing anger against the Israelites. [15]If you turn away from following him, he will again abandon them in the wilderness, and you will bring about the ruin of this entire people."

***Counter Proposal.*** [16]But they approached him and said: "We will only build sheepfolds here for our flocks and towns for our families; [17]but we ourselves will march as troops in the vanguard before the Israelites,[l] until we have led them to their destination. Meanwhile our families will remain in the fortified towns because of the land's inhabitants. [18]We will not return to our homes until all the Israelites have taken possession of their heritage. [19][m] But we will not claim any heritage with them across the Jordan and beyond, because we have received a heritage for ourselves on the eastern side of the Jordan."

***Agreement Reached.*** [20]* Moses said to them in reply: "If you do this—if you march as troops before the LORD into battle [21]and cross the Jordan in full force before the LORD until he has driven his enemies out of his way [22]and the land is subdued before the LORD, then you may return here, free from every obligation to the LORD and to Israel, and this land will be your possession before the LORD.[n] [23]But if you do not do this, you will have sinned against the LORD, and you can be sure that the consequences of your sin will overtake you. [24]Build the towns, then, for your families, and the folds for your flocks, but fulfill what you have promised."

[25]The Gadites and Reubenites answered Moses, "Your servants will do as my lord commands. [26][o] While our wives and children, our livestock and other animals remain there in the towns of Gilead, [27]all your servants will go across as armed troops before the LORD to battle, just as my lord says."

[28]So Moses gave this command in their regard to Eleazar the priest, to Joshua, son of Nun, and to the heads of the ancestral houses of the Israelite tribes: [29]He said to them, "If all the Gadites and Reubenites cross the Jordan with you in full force before the LORD into battle, the land will be subdued before you, and you will give them Gilead as a possession. [30]But if they will not go across in force with you before the LORD, you will bring their wives and children and livestock across before you into Canaan, and they will possess a holding among you in the land of Canaan."

[31]To this the Gadites and Reubenites replied, "We will do what the LORD has ordered your servants. [32]We ourselves will go across in force before the LORD into the land of Canaan, but we will retain our hereditary property on this side of the Jordan."* [33]So Moses gave them—*the Gadites and Reubenites, as well as half the tribe of Manasseh, son of Joseph—the kingdom of Sihon, king of the Amorites, and the kingdom of Og, king of Bashan, the land with its towns, and the districts of the surrounding towns.[p]

[34]The Gadites rebuilt the cities of Dibon, Ataroth, Aroer, [35]Atroth-shophan, Jazer, Jogbehah, [36]Beth-nimrah and Beth-haran—fortified cities—and sheepfolds. [37]The Reubenites rebuilt Heshbon, Elealeh, Kiriathaim, [38]Nebo, Baal-meon (names to be

**32:12 Kenizzite**: a member of the clan of Kenaz, which, according to Gn 36:11, 15, 42, was Edomite; but, according to Nm 13:6; 34:19, Caleb belonged to the tribe of Judah; cf. also Jos 14:6, 14.

**32:20–22** Since the ark of the Lord was carried into battle with the Israelite army, the vanguard was said to march before the Lord (see Jos 6:6–9).

**32:32 This side of the Jordan**: lit., "beyond the Jordan"; the perspective in Hebrew is from the west bank looking toward the east bank where the Reubenites and Gadites finally settled.

**32:33** The preceding is concerned solely with the two tribes of Gad and Reuben and with the land of the former kingdom of Sihon; it seems probable that the sudden reference here to the half-tribe of Manasseh and to their territory in Bashan, the former kingdom of Og, is a later addition to the text.

*k:* Nm 14:24; Dt 1:36. *l:* Jos 4:12–13. *m:* Jos 13:8. *n:* Jos 1:15. *o:* Jos 1:14. *p:* Dt 3:12; 29:7; Jos 12:6; 13:8.

changed!),* and Sibmah. These towns,
which they rebuilt, they called by their old
names.

*Other Conquests.* 39The descendants of
Machir, son of Manasseh, went to Gilead
and captured it, dispossessing the Amorites
who were there. 40(Moses gave Gilead to
Machir,[q] son of Manasseh, and he settled
there.) 41Jair,[r] a descendant of Manasseh,
went and captured their tent villages, and
called them Havvoth-jair.* 42Nobah went
and captured Kenath with its dependencies
and called it Nobah after his own name.

See RG 80–85

## CHAPTER 33

*Stages of the Journey.* 1The following
are the stages by which the Israelites went
out by companies from the land of Egypt under the guidance of Moses and Aaron.* 2Mo-
ses recorded the starting points of the various stages at the direction of the LORD.
These are the stages according to their starting points: 3They set out from Rameses in
the first month, on the fifteenth day of the
first month. On the day after the Passover
the Israelites went forth in triumph, in view
of all Egypt, 4while the Egyptians buried
those whom the LORD had struck down,
every firstborn; on their gods, too, the LORD
executed judgments.[s]

*From Egypt to Sinai.* 5Setting out from
Rameses, the Israelites camped at Succoth.
6Setting out from Succoth, they camped at
Etham near the edge of the wilderness. 7Set-
ting out from Etham, they turned back to Pi-
hahiroth, which is opposite Baal-zephon,
and they camped opposite Migdol.[t] 8Setting
out from Pi-hahiroth, they crossed over
through the sea into the wilderness,[u] and after they traveled a three days' journey in the
wilderness of Etham, they camped at Marah.
9Setting out from Marah, they came to Elim;
at Elim there were twelve springs of water
and seventy palm trees, and they camped
there.[v] 10Setting out from Elim, they camped
beside the Red Sea. 11Setting out from the
Red Sea, they camped in the wilderness of
Sin. 12Setting out from the wilderness of Sin,
they camped at Dophkah. 13Setting out from
Dophkah, they camped at Alush. 14Setting
out from Alush, they camped at Rephidim,
where there was no water for the people to
drink.[w] 15Setting out from Rephidim, they
camped in the wilderness of Sinai.[x]

*From Sinai to Kadesh.* 16Setting out from
the wilderness of Sinai, they camped at Kibroth-hattaavah. 17Setting out from Kibroth-
hattaavah, they camped at Hazeroth.[y] 18Set-
ting out from Hazeroth, they camped at
Rithmah. 19Setting out from Rithmah, they
camped at Rimmon-perez. 20Setting out
from Rimmon-perez, they camped at Libnah. 21Setting out from Libnah, they camped
at Rissah. 22Setting out from Rissah, they
camped at Kehelathah. 23Setting out from
Kehelathah, they camped at Mount Shepher.
24Setting out from Mount Shepher, they
camped at Haradah. 25Setting out from Haradah, they camped at Makheloth. 26Setting
out from Makheloth, they camped at Tahath.
27Setting out from Tahath, they camped at
Terah. 28Setting out from Terah, they
camped at Mithkah. 29Setting out from
Mithkah, they camped at Hashmonah.
30* Setting out from Hashmonah, they
camped at Moseroth. 31Setting out from Moseroth, they camped at Bene-jaakan. 32Set-
ting out from Bene-jaakan, they camped at

**32:38** The phrase in parentheses is probably a gloss, warning the reader perhaps to substitute some other word for Nebo and Baal, the names of foreign deities mentioned in the last two city names. **They called by their old names**: lit., "they called by their names"; however, some understand the current Hebrew text to mean, "they called by new names," or "their own names."

**32:41 Havvoth-jair**: that is, "villages of Jair."

**33:1–3** According to v. 2, this list of camping sites was drawn up by Moses as an itinerary recording Israel's trek through the wilderness. Comparison with the more detailed accounts of the journey as given elsewhere suggests that the list is not necessarily comprehensive. It records just forty camping sites, not counting the starting place, Rameses, and the terminus, the plains of Moab. This number, which corresponds exactly to the forty years of wandering in the wilderness, is probably a schematic device. Moreover, it seems that in its present form the order of some of the names here has been disturbed. Several names listed here are not recorded elsewhere.

**33:30–36** Moseroth is mentioned in Dt 10:6 (in the form of "Moserah") as the place where Aaron died, apparently a variant of the tradition here in v. 38 regarding the place of Aaron's death; so also Nm 20:22–24 and Dt 32:50. Perhaps Moseroth was close to Mount Hor.

*q:* Dt 3:15. *r:* Dt 3:14. *s:* Ex 12:12, 29, 37. *t:* Ex 14:2. *u:* Ex 15:22. *v:* Ex 15:27. *w:* Ex 17:1. *x:* Ex 19:2. *y:* Nm 11:34–35.

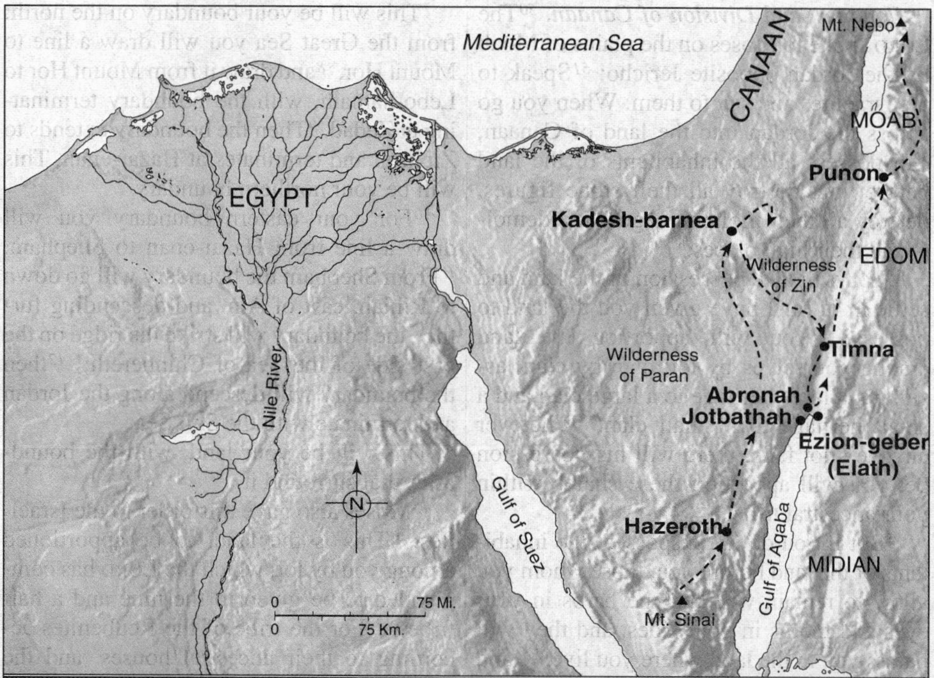


**Journey from the Wilderness to Canaan**

Mount Gidgad. [33]Setting out from Mount
Gidgad, they camped at Jotbathah. [34]Setting
out from Jotbathah, they camped at Abronah. [35]Setting out from Abronah, they
camped at Ezion-geber.* [36]Setting out from
Ezion-geber, they camped in the wilderness
of Zin, that is, Kadesh.[z]

***From Kadesh to the Plains of Moab.*** [37]Set-
ting out from Kadesh, they camped at Mount
Hor on the border of the land of Edom.

[38]Aaron the priest ascended Mount Hor[a]
at the LORD's direction, and there he died in
the fortieth year after the departure of the Israelites from the land of Egypt, on the first
day of the fifth month. [39]Aaron was a hundred and twenty-three years old when he
died on Mount Hor.

[40]* When the Canaanite, the king of Arad,
who ruled over the Negeb in the land of Canaan, heard that the Israelites were coming . . . .

[41]* Setting out from Mount Hor, they
camped at Zalmonah. [42]Setting out from Zalmonah, they camped at Punon. [43]Setting out
from Punon, they camped at Oboth. [44]Setting
out from Oboth, they camped at Iye-abarim
on the border of Moab. [45]Setting out from
Iye-abarim, they camped at Dibon-gad. [46]Set-
ting out from Dibon-gad, they camped at Al-
mon-diblathaim. [47]Setting out from Almon-
diblathaim, they camped in the Abarim range
opposite Nebo. [48]Setting out from the Abarim
range, they camped on the plains of Moab by
the Jordan opposite Jericho. [49]They camped
by the Jordan on the plains of Moab extended
from Beth-jeshimoth to Abel-shittim.

**33:35 Ezion-geber**: Solomon conducted sea trade with Ophir from this port (1 Kgs 9:26), today probably identified on the northern coast of the Gulf of Elath between the Jordanian city of Aqabah and the Israeli city of Elath.

**33:40** The verse repeats almost verbatim the same introduction to the account of the victory over Arad as is given in 21:1–3, where it also follows the account of Aaron's death. Perhaps the isolated verse here is intended by the editor(s) of Numbers to point the reader to the fuller account given there.

**33:41b–49** It seems that this section stood originally immediately after v. 36a.

*z:* Nm 20:1, 22. *a:* Nm 20:25; Dt 32:50.

***Conquest and Division of Canaan.*** 50The
LORD spoke to Moses on the plains of Moab
by the Jordan opposite Jericho: 51Speak to
the Israelites and say to them: When you go
across the Jordan into the land of Canaan,
52dispossess all the inhabitants of the land
before you; destroy all their stone figures,
destroy all their molten images, and demolish all their high places.[b]
53You will take possession of the land and
settle in it, for I have given you the land to
possess. 54You will apportion the land
among yourselves by lot, clan by clan, assigning a large heritage to a large clan and a
small heritage to a small clan.[c] Wherever
anyone's lot falls, there will his possession
be; you will apportion these shares within
your ancestral tribe.
55But if you do not dispossess the inhabitants of the land before you, those whom you
allow to remain will become barbs in your
eyes and thorns in your sides, and they will
harass you in the land where you live,[d] 56and
I will treat you as I had intended to treat them.

## CHAPTER 34

See RG 80–85

***The Boundaries.*** 1The LORD spoke to
Moses: 2Give the Israelites this order: When
you enter the land of Canaan, this is the territory that shall fall to you as your heritage—the land of Canaan with its boundaries:
3Your southern boundary will be at the
wilderness of Zin along the border of
Edom;[e] on the east your southern boundary
will begin at the end of the Salt Sea. 4Then
your boundary will turn south of the Akrabbim Pass and cross Zin. Terminating south
of Kadesh-barnea, it extends to Hazar-addar
and crosses to Azmon.[f] 5Then the boundary
will turn from Azmon to the Wadi of Egypt
and terminate at the Sea.[g]
6For your western boundary you will have
the Great Sea* with its coast; this will be
your western boundary.
7This will be your boundary on the north:
from the Great Sea you will draw a line to
Mount Hor,* 8and draw it from Mount Hor to
Lebo-hamath, with the boundary terminating at Zedad. 9Then the boundary extends to
Ziphron and terminates at Hazar-enan. This
will be your northern boundary.
10For your eastern boundary you will
draw a line from Hazar-enan to Shepham.
11From Shepham the boundary will go down
to Riblah, east of Ain, and descending further, the boundary will strike the ridge on the
east side of the Sea of Chinnereth;* 12then
the boundary will descend along the Jordan
and terminate with the Salt Sea.
This will be your land, with the boundaries that surround it.
13Moses also gave this order to the Israelites: "This is the land, to be apportioned
among you by lot, which the LORD has commanded to be given to the nine and a half
tribes. 14For the tribe of the Reubenites according to their ancestral houses, and the
tribe of the Gadites according to their ancestral houses, as well as half of the tribe of Manasseh, have already received their heritage;
15these two and a half tribes have received
their heritage across the Jordan opposite Jericho, in the east, toward the sunrise."
***Supervisors of the Allotment.*** 16The LORD
spoke to Moses: 17These are the names of
the men who shall apportion the land among
you: Eleazar the priest, and Joshua, son of
Nun; 18[h] and you will designate one leader
from each of the tribes to apportion the land.
19These are the names of the men:

from the tribe of Judah: Caleb, son of
Jephunneh,
20 from the tribe of the Simeonites: Samuel,
son of Ammihud;
21 from the tribe of Benjamin: Elidad, son
of Chislon;
22 from the tribe of the Danites: a leader,
Bukki, son of Jogli;

**34:6 The Great Sea**: the Mediterranean.

**34:7–8 Mount Hor**: different from the one where Aaron died; cf. 20:22; 33:37–38.

**34:11 Sea of Chinnereth**: in the New Testament known as the Sea of Galilee; today called Lake Kinneret.

---

*b:* Ex 23:31; 34:13; Dt 7:5; 12:3. *c:* Nm 26:53–56. *d:* Jos 23:13; Jgs 2:3. *e:* Jos 15:1–2. *f:* Jos 15:3. *g:* Jos 15:4. *h:* Nm 1:4.

23 for the descendants of Joseph: from the
tribe of the Manassites: a leader,
Hanniel, son of Ephod; and
24 from the tribe of the Ephraimites: a
leader, Kemuel, son of Shiphtan;
25 from the tribe of the Zebulunites: a
leader, Elizaphan, son of Parnach;
26 from the tribe of the Issacharites: a
leader, Paltiel, son of Azzan;
27 from the tribe of the Asherites: a leader,
Ahihud, son of Shelomi;
28 from the tribe of the Naphtalites: a
leader, Pedahel, son of Ammihud.

29 These are the ones whom the LORD
commanded to apportion to the Israelites
their heritage in the land of Canaan.

## CHAPTER 35

See RG 80–85

***Cities for the Levites.*** 1 The LORD spoke
to Moses on the plains of Moab by the Jordan
opposite Jericho: 2 [i] Command the Israelites
out of the heritage they possess to give the Levites cities to dwell in; you will also give the
Levites the pasture lands around the cities.
3 The cities will be for them to dwell in, and the
pasture lands will be for their cattle, their
flocks, and all their other animals. 4 The pasture
lands of the cities to be assigned the Levites
shall extend a thousand cubits out from the city
walls in every direction. 5 You will measure out
two thousand cubits outside the city along the
east side, two thousand cubits along the south
side, two thousand cubits along the west side,
and two thousand cubits along the north side,
with the city lying in the center. These will be
the pasture lands of their cities.

6 [j] Now these are the cities you will give to
the Levites: the six cities of asylum which
you must establish for the homicide to run
to, and in addition forty-two other cities— 7 a
total of forty-eight cities with their pasture
lands which you will assign to the Levites.
8* In assigning the cities from what the Israelites possess, take more from a larger group
and fewer from a smaller one, so that each
will cede cities to the Levites in proportion
to the heritage which it receives.

***Cities of Asylum.*** 9 [k] The LORD spoke to
Moses: 10 Speak to the Israelites and say to
them: When you go across the Jordan into
the land of Canaan, 11 select for yourselves
cities to serve as cities of asylum, where a
homicide who has killed someone inadvertently may flee. 12 These cities will serve you
as places of asylum from the avenger of
blood,* so that a homicide will not be put to
death until tried before the community. 13 As
for the cities you assign, you will have six
cities of asylum: 14 you will designate three
cities beyond the Jordan, and you will designate three cities in the land of Canaan. These
will be cities of asylum. 15 These six cities
will serve as places of asylum for the Israelites, and for the resident or transient aliens
among them, so that anyone who has killed
a person inadvertently may flee there.

***Murder and Manslaughter.*** 16* If someone
strikes another with an iron instrument and
causes death, that person is a murderer, and
the murderer must be put to death.[l] 17 If someone strikes another with a death-dealing stone
in the hand and death results, that person is a
murderer, and the murderer must be put to
death. 18 Or if someone strikes another with a
death-dealing club in the hand and death results, that person is a murderer, and the murderer must be put to death. 19 The avenger of
blood is the one who will kill the murderer,
putting the individual to death on sight.

20 If someone pushes another out of hatred, or throws something from an ambush,
and death results,[m] 21 or strikes another with
the hand out of enmity and death results, the
assailant must be put to death as a murderer.
The avenger of blood will kill the murderer
on sight.

22 [n] However, if someone pushes another

**35:8** This provision was hardly observed in the actual assignment of the levitical cities as narrated in Jos 21.

**35:12 The avenger of blood**: Hebrew, *go'el*, often translated as "redeemer," one who, as next of kin to the slain (2 Sm 14:7), and here, as executor of public justice, had the right and duty to take the life of the murderer; cf. Dt 19:6, 12; Jos 20:3, 5, 9.

**35:16–25** Here, as also in Dt 19:1–13, there is a casuistic development of the original law as stated in Ex 21:12–14.

*i:* Jos 14:3–4; 21:2. *j:* Dt 4:41–42; Jos 20:2. *k:* Dt 19:2; Jos 20:2–6. *l:* Ex 21:12; Lv 24:17. *m:* Ex 21:14; Dt 19:11. *n:* Jos 20:3.

without malice aforethought, or without lying in ambush throws some object at another, [23]or without seeing drops upon another some death-dealing stone and death results, although there was neither enmity nor malice— [24]then the community will judge between the assailant and the avenger of blood in accordance with these norms. [25]The community will deliver the homicide from the avenger of blood and the community will return the homicide to the city of asylum where the latter had fled;[o] and the individual will stay there until the death of the high priest who has been anointed with sacred oil. [26]If the homicide leaves at all the bounds of the city of asylum to which flight had been made, [27]and is found by the avenger of blood beyond the bounds of the city of asylum, and the avenger of blood kills the homicide, the avenger incurs no bloodguilt; [28]for the homicide was required to stay in the city of asylum until the death of the high priest. Only after the death of the high priest may the homicide return to the land of the homicide's possession.

[29]This is the statute for you throughout all your generations, wherever you live, for rendering judgment.

***Judgment.*** [30]Whenever someone kills another, the evidence of witnesses is required to kill the murderer.[p] A single witness does not suffice for putting a person to death.

***No Indemnity.*** [31]You will not accept compensation in place of the life of a murderer who deserves to die, but that person must be put to death. [32]Nor will you accept compensation to allow one who has fled to a city of asylum to return to live in the land before the death of the high priest. [33]You will not pollute the land where you live. For bloodshed pollutes the land, and the land can have no expiation for the blood shed on it except through the blood of the one who shed it. [34]Do not defile the land in which you live and in the midst of which I dwell;[q] for I the LORD dwell in the midst of the Israelites.

## CHAPTER 36

See RG 80–85

***Inheritance of Daughters.*** [1]The heads of the ancestral houses in a clan of the descendants of Gilead, son of Machir, son of Manasseh—one of the Josephite clans—came up and spoke before Moses and Eleazar the priest and before the leaders who were the heads of the ancestral houses of the Israelites. [2]They said: "The LORD commanded my lord to apportion the land by lot for a heritage among the Israelites;[r] and my lord was commanded by the LORD to give the heritage of Zelophehad our kinsman to his daughters. [3]But if they marry into one of the other Israelite tribes, their heritage will be withdrawn from our ancestral heritage and will be added to that of the tribe into which they marry; thus the heritage that fell to us by lot will be diminished. [4]When the Israelites celebrate the jubilee year,* the heritage of these women will be added to that of the tribe into which they marry and their heritage will be withdrawn from that of our ancestral tribe."

[5]* So Moses commanded the Israelites at the direction of the LORD: "The tribe of the Josephites are right in what they say. [6]This is what the LORD commands with regard to the daughters of Zelophehad: They may marry anyone they please, provided they marry into a clan of their ancestral tribe, [7]so that no heritage of the Israelites will pass from one tribe to another, but all the Israelites will retain their own ancestral heritage. [8]Every daughter who inherits property in any of the Israelite tribes will marry someone belonging to a clan of her own ancestral tribe, in order that all the Israelites may remain in possession of their own ancestral heritage. [9]Thus, no heritage will pass from one tribe to another, but all the Israelite tribes will retain their own ancestral heritage."

[10]The daughters of Zelophehad did exactly as the LORD commanded Moses. [11]Mahlah, Tirzah, Hoglah, Milcah and Noah, Zelophe-

**36:4** Before the jubilee year various circumstances, such as divorce, could make such property revert to its original tribal owners; but in the jubilee year it became irrevocably attached to its new owners.

**36:5–9** This is a supplement to the law given in 27:5–11.

*o:* Jos 20:6. *p:* Dt 17:6; 19:15; Jn 8:17; 2 Cor 13:1; 1 Tm 5:19. *q:* Ex 29:45. *r:* Nm 26:55; 27:6; Jos 17:3–4.

had's daughters, married sons of their uncles on their father's side. 12They married within the clans of the descendants of Manasseh, son of Joseph; hence their heritage remained in the tribe of their father's clan.

*Conclusion.* 13These are the commandments and decisions which the LORD commanded the Israelites through Moses, on the plains of Moab beside the Jordan opposite Jericho.

See RG 85–89

# The Book of Deuteronomy

The title of Deuteronomy in Hebrew is *Debarim*, "words," from its opening phrase. The English title comes from the Septuagint of 17:18, *deuteronomion*, "copy of the law"; this title is appropriate because the book replicates much of the legal content of the previous books, serving as a "second law." It brings to a close the five books of the Torah or Pentateuch with a retrospective account of Israel's past—the exodus, the Sinai covenant, and the wilderness wanderings—and a look into Israel's future as they stand poised to enter the land of Canaan and begin their life as a people there.

The book consists of three long addresses by Moses. Each of these contains narrative, law, and exhortation, in varying proportions. In an expansion of the first commandment of the decalogue (Ex 20:5–6; Dt 5:9–10), Moses tells the Israelites how to make a success of their life as a people once they are settled in the land. The choice presented to Israel is to love the Lord and keep his commandments, or to serve "other gods." That choice will determine what kind of life they will make for themselves in the land. Whichever choice they make as a people carries consequences, which Deuteronomy terms "blessing" and "curse." Thus the book can be seen as a kind of survival manual for Israel in their life as a people: how to live and what to avoid. This gives the book its hortatory style and tone of life-or-death urgency.

One defining concern of the book is centralization of worship. As Israel's God is one (6:4–5), so its worship must be focused in one place, which the Lord "will choose from among your tribes"; there the Lord will "make his name dwell" (see note on 12:5). Thus the privileged status of the Jerusalem Temple is asserted; all other places and all other modes of worship of the God of Israel (the local shrines, the "high places," "under every green tree") are proscribed.

The book was probably composed over the course of three centuries, from the eighth century to the exile and beyond. It bears some relation to "the Book of the Law" discovered in the Jerusalem Temple around 622 B.C. during the reign of King Josiah (2 Kgs 22:8–13). It gives evidence of later editing: cf. the references to exile in 4:1–40; 28:63–68; 29:21–28; 30:1–10.

Over the book looms the disaster of 722/721, the fall of the Northern Kingdom, Israel. The detailed description of siege (28:49–57) especially echoes the fate the North suffered at the hands of the Assyrian invader. The book draws the minds of its intended readers back to a time before disastrous mistakes were made and their disastrous effects felt, and serves to explain the political and theological dynamics that led to the destruction of the North as well as to warn the surviving Southern Kingdom, Judah, to reform by keeping faith with Israel's covenant Lord.

The characteristic and highly recognizable language and theology of Deuteronomy are seen in editorial comments structuring the works that follow it in the Hebrew canon, the Books of Joshua, Judges, Samuel, and Kings. Together with Deuteronomy, these present a history of Israel from Moses to the time of the Babylonian exile. Conventionally this great multivolume work is termed the Deuteronomistic History. The Book of Deuteronomy itself was also incorporated into the Torah as its fifth volume.

The book presents three discourses by Moses, as follows:

I. First Address (1:1–4:43)
II. Second Address (4:44–28:69)
    A. The Lord's Covenant with Israel (4:44–11:32)
    B. The Deuteronomic Code (12:1–28:69)
III. Third Address (29:1–33:29)
IV. The Death of Moses (34:1–12)

THE STORY BEGINS just as the Israelites, encamped on the plains of Moab, stand poised finally to enter the Promised Land. The entry into Canaan would provide the long-awaited climax of the story that had begun with the promises to the ancestors in Genesis. The enslavement in Egypt and the wandering in the wilderness had delayed its fulfillment. Now, Moses, on the eve both of his death and of the nations' entry into the land without him, is portrayed as Deuteronomy's speaker. He delivers a series of three speeches, grouped together as a long address. He reviews the nation's history, expounds upon their laws, and instructs them about the importance of loyalty to God. He also tells the nation to uphold this combination of law and theological instruction as a covenant upon the plans of Moab, one that supplements the one previously sworn at Horeb (Deuteronomy's name for Sinai; 28:69). Only after the conclusion of these three discourses and a following appendix (chs 31–34) does the story line resume with the account of the nation's entry into Canaan in Joshua and Judges.

## I. First Address

### CHAPTER 1

See RG 85–89

*Introduction.* [1*] These are the words that Moses spoke to all Israel beyond the Jordan in the wilderness, in the Arabah, opposite Suph, between Paran and Tophel, Laban, Hazeroth, and Dizahab. [2]It is a journey of eleven days from Horeb* to Kadesh-barnea by way of the highlands of Seir.

[3]In the fortieth year,* on the first day of the eleventh month, Moses spoke to the Israelites according to all that the LORD had commanded him to speak to them, [4]after he had defeated Sihon, king of the Amorites, who reigned in Heshbon,[a] and Og, king of Bashan, who reigned in Ashtaroth and in Edrei. [5]Beyond the Jordan, in the land of Moab, Moses undertook to explain this law:

*Departure from Horeb.* [6*] [b] The LORD, our God, said to us at Horeb:* You have stayed long enough at this mountain. [7]Leave here and go to the hill country of the Amorites* and to all the surrounding regions, the Arabah, the mountains, the Shephelah, the Negeb and the seacoast—the land of the Canaanites and the Lebanon as far as the Great River, the Euphrates. [8]See, I have given that land over to you.[c] Go now and possess the land that the LORD swore to your ancestors, Abraham, Isaac, and Jacob, to give to them and to their descendants after them.

*Appointment of Elders.* [9d] At that time I said to you, "I am unable to carry you by myself.[e] [10]The LORD, your God, has made you numerous, and now you are as numerous as the stars of the heavens.[f] [11]May the LORD, the God of your ancestors, increase you a thousand times over, and bless you as he promised! [12]But how can I, by myself,

**1:1** The entire book of Deuteronomy is set "beyond the Jordan," in the land of Moab (cf. v. 5; Nm 36:13), on the eve of the Israelites' crossing of the Jordan (Jos 3). **The Arabah**: the valley of the Jordan and the depression south of the Dead Sea.

**1:2 Horeb**: an alternative name for Mount Sinai, the wilderness mountain where the Israelites received revelation from God (cf. Ex 3; 19). **Kadesh-barnea**: the southern gateway to the land of Canaan, from which Moses sent spies to reconnoiter the land (cf. Nm 13:26; 32:8). **Seir**: Edom, the land just south of Moab.

**1:3 Fortieth year**: counting from the exodus from Egypt (cf. Ex 12:2; 13:20–22).

**1:6–3:29** Throughout this section Moses is reviewing the events following the departure from Horeb, as a basis for the exhortation beginning in 4:1. Most of these events are narrated with some variation in the Book of Numbers.

**1:6 Horeb**: the name given to the mountain of revelation in the Elohist and Deuteronomic traditions; this mountain is called Sinai in the Yahwist and Priestly traditions.

**1:7 The hill country of the Amorites**: the central mountain range of Palestine. **The Negeb**: the arid land in southern Palestine. **The Lebanon**: the mountain range of Phoenicia, north of Palestine. This is an idealized presentation of the land the Israelites were to occupy; Israel never held power as far as the "Great River" (the Euphrates). The Amorites and the Canaanites were only two of several different peoples occupying the land (cf. 7:1).

*a:* Dt 2:24–3:11; Nm 21:21–35. *b:* Ex 32:34–33:3. *c:* Dt 6:10, 23; 9:5, 27; 29:13; 30:20; 34:4; Gn 12:7; 13:14–15; 15:18–21; 17:8; 26:3–5; 28:13–14. *d:* Ex 18:13–26; Nm 11:16–30. *e:* Dt 1:31. *f:* Dt 10:22; Gn 15:5; 22:17; 26:3–4; Ex 32:13.

bear the weight, the contentiousness of you?
13 Provide wise, discerning, and reputable
persons for each of your tribes, that I may
appoint them as your leaders." 14 You answered me, "What you have proposed is
good." 15 So I took the leaders of your tribes,
wise and reputable, and set them as leaders
over you, commanders over thousands, over
hundreds, over fifties and over tens, and
other tribal officers. 16[g] I charged your
judges at that time, "Listen to complaints
among your relatives, and administer true
justice to both parties even if one of them is
a resident alien. 17 In rendering judgment, do
not consider who a person is; give ear to the
lowly and to the great alike, fearing no one,
for the judgment is God's. Any case that is
too difficult for you bring to me and I will
hear it." 18 Thus I charged you, at that time,
with all the things you were to do.

*The Twelve Scouts.* 19[h] Then we set out
from Horeb and journeyed through that
whole vast and fearful wilderness that you
have seen, in the direction of the hill country
of the Amorites, as the LORD, our God, had
commanded; and we came to Kadesh-barnea.[i] 20 I said to you, "You have come to the
hill country of the Amorites, which the LORD,
our God, is giving us. 21 See, the LORD, your
God, has given this land over to you. Go up
and take possession of it, as the LORD, the
God of your ancestors, has promised you. Do
not fear or be dismayed." 22 Then all of you
approached me and said, "Let us send men
ahead to spy out the land for us and report to
us on the road we should follow and the cities we will come upon." 23 Agreeing with the
proposal, I took twelve men from your number, one from each tribe. 24 They set out into
the hill country as far as the Wadi Eshcol, and
explored it. 25 Then, taking along some of the
fruit of the land, they brought it down to us
and reported, "The land the LORD, our God,
is giving us is good."

*Threats of Revolt.* 26[j] But you refused to
go up;[k] you defied the command of the
LORD, your God. 27 You set to murmuring in
your tents, "Out of hatred for us the LORD
has brought us out of the land of Egypt,[l] to
deliver us into the power of the Amorites
and destroy us. 28 What shall we meet with
up there? Our men have made our hearts
melt by saying, 'The people are bigger and
taller than we, and their cities are large and
fortified to the sky; besides, we saw the
Anakim* there.' "[m]

29 But I said to you, "Have no dread or fear
of them. 30[n] The LORD, your God, who goes
before you, is the one who will fight for you,
just as he acted with you before your very
eyes in Egypt, 31 as well as in the wilderness,
where you saw how the LORD, your God,
carried you, as one carries his own child, all
along your journey until you arrived at this
place." 32 Despite this, you would not trust
the LORD, your God, 33 who journeys before
you to find you a place to camp—by night in
the fire, and by day in the cloud, to show you
the way to go.[o] 34 When the LORD heard your
words, he was angry, and took an oath: 35 Not
a single one of this evil generation shall look
upon the good land I swore to give to your
ancestors, 36 except Caleb,* son of Jephunneh. He shall see it, for to him and to his descendants I will give the land he trod upon,[p]
because he has fully followed the LORD.

37 The LORD was angered against me also
on your account, and said, You shall not enter there either,[q] 38 but Joshua,[r] son of Nun,
your attendant, shall enter. Encourage him,
for he is the one who is to give Israel its possession. 39 Your little ones, who you said
would become plunder, and your children,
who as yet do not know good from evil—
they shall enter there; to them I will give it,
and they shall take possession of it. 40 But as
for yourselves: turn back and proceed into
the wilderness on the Red Sea road.

**1:28 Anakim**: a people proverbially notable for height, mentioned in pre-Israelite Egyptian texts, and in the biblical tradition associated with the region of Hebron and the hill country of Judah (Nm 13:22, 28, 33; Jos 11:21; 14:12, 15).

**1:36 Except Caleb**: and Joshua (v. 38).

---

*g:* Dt 10:17–18; 16:18–20. *h:* Nm 13:1–27. *i:* Nm 11:11–36. *j:* Nm 13:28–14:38. *k:* Dt 9:23. *l:* Dt 9:28. *m:* Dt 1:28; 2:10–11, 21; 9:2; Nm 13:22, 28, 33; Jos 11:21–22; 14:12, 15; 15:13–14; 21:11; Jgs 1:20. *n:* Dt 3:22; 8:15; 32:10; Ex 14:13–14. *o:* Ex 13:21; 40:38; Nm 9:15–16; 10:33–34; 14:14. *p:* Jos 14:6–14. *q:* Dt 4:21; 34:4; Nm 20:12. *r:* Dt 31:3, 7–8; Nm 27:18–23; 34:17; Jos 1:1–9.

***Unsuccessful Invasion.*** 41[s] In reply you said to me, "We have sinned against the LORD. We will go up ourselves and fight, just as the LORD, our God, commanded us." And each of you girded on his weapons, making light of going up into the hill country. 42 But the LORD said to me, Warn them: Do not go up and fight—for I will not be in your midst—lest you be beaten down before your enemies. 43 I gave you this warning but you would not listen. You defied the LORD's command and arrogantly went off into the hill country. 44 Then the Amorites living in that hill country came out against you and put you to flight the way bees do, cutting you down in Seir as far as Hormah. 45 On your return you wept before the LORD, but the LORD did not listen to your voice or give ear to you. 46 That is why you had to stay as long as you did at Kadesh.

## CHAPTER 2

See RG 85-89

***Northward Along Edom.*** 1[t] Then we turned and proceeded into the wilderness on the Red Sea road,[u] as the LORD had told me, and circled around the highlands of Seir for a long time. 2 Finally the LORD said to me, 3 You have wandered round these highlands long enough; turn and go north. 4 Command the people: You are now about to pass through the territory of your relatives, the descendants of Esau, who live in Seir. Though they are afraid of you, be very careful 5 not to come in conflict with them, for I will not give you so much as a foot of their land, since I have already given Esau possession of the highlands of Seir.[v] 6 You shall purchase from them with money the food you eat; even the water you drink you shall buy from them with money. 7 Surely, the LORD, your God, has blessed you in all your undertakings; he has been concerned* about your journey through this vast wilderness. It is now forty years that the LORD, your God, has been with you, and you have lacked nothing.[w] 8 So we passed by our relatives, the descendants of Esau who live in Seir, leaving behind us the Arabah route, Elath, and Ezion-geber.

***Along Moab.*** Then we turned and passed on toward the wilderness of Moab. 9[x] And the LORD said to me, Do not show hostility to the Moabites or engage them in battle, for I will not give you possession of any of their land, since I have given Ar to the descendants of Lot as their possession.[y] 10 (Formerly the Emim lived there, a people great and numerous and as tall as the Anakim;[z] 11 like the Anakim they are considered Rephaim, though the Moabites call them Emim.[a] 12 In Seir, however, the former inhabitants were the Horites;[b] the descendants of Esau dispossessed them, clearing them out of the way and dwelling in their place, just as Israel has done in the land of its possession which the LORD gave it.) 13 Now get ready to cross the Wadi Zered.

So we crossed the Wadi Zered. 14[c] Now thirty-eight years had elapsed between our departure from Kadesh-barnea and the crossing of the Wadi Zered; in the meantime the whole generation of soldiers had perished from the camp, as the LORD had sworn they should. 15 Indeed the LORD's own hand was against them, to rout them from the camp completely.

***Along Ammon.*** 16[d] When at length death had put an end to all the soldiers among the people, 17 the LORD said to me, 18 You are now about to leave Ar and the territory of Moab behind. 19 As you come opposite the Ammonites,[e] do not show hostility or come in conflict with them, for I will not give you possession of any land of the Ammonites, since I have given it to the descendants of Lot as their possession. 20 (This also is considered a country of the Rephaim; formerly the Rephaim dwelt there. The Ammonites call them Zamzummim,[f] 21 a people great and numerous and as tall as the Anakim. But these, too, the LORD cleared out of the way for the Ammonites, so that they dispossessed

**2:7 Concerned**: lit., "known"; cf. Ex 2:25.

*s:* Nm 14:39–45. *t:* Nm 20:14–21; Jgs 11:15–17. *u:* Dt 1:40; Nm 14:25. *v:* Gn 36:6–8. *w:* Dt 8:2–5. *x:* Nm 21:12–15; Jgs 11:17–18. *y:* Gn 19:36–38. *z:* Dt 1:28. *a:* Dt 2:20; 3:11, 13; Gn 14:5; 15:20; Jos 12:4; 13:12; 17:15. *b:* Gn 14:6; 36:20–30. *c:* Nm 14:28–35. *d:* Nm 21:24. *e:* Gn 19:36–38. *f:* Dt 2:11; 3:11, 13; Gn 14:5; 15:20; Jos 12:4; 13:12; 17:15.

them and dwelt in their place.[g] 22 He did the same for the descendants of Esau, who live in Seir, by clearing the Horites out of their way, so that they dispossessed them and dwelt in their place down to the present.[h] 23 As for the Avvim, who once lived in villages in the vicinity of Gaza,* the Caphtorim, migrating from Caphtor, cleared them away and dwelt in their place.)[i]

***Defeat of Sihon.*** 24[j] Advance now across the Wadi Arnon. I now deliver into your power Sihon, the Amorite king of Heshbon, and his land. Begin to take possession; engage him in battle.[k] 25 This day I will begin to put a fear and dread of you into the peoples everywhere under heaven, so that at the mention of your name they will quake and tremble before you.

26 So I sent messengers from the wilderness of Kedemoth to Sihon, king of Heshbon, with this offer of peace: 27 "Let me pass through your country. I will travel only on the road. I will not turn aside either to the right or to the left. 28 The food I eat you will sell me for money, and the water I drink, you will give me for money. Only let me march through, 29 as the descendants of Esau who dwell in Seir and the Moabites who dwell in Ar have done, until I cross the Jordan into the land the LORD, our God, is about to give us."[l] 30 But Sihon, king of Heshbon, refused to let us pass through his land, because the LORD, your God, made him stubborn in mind and obstinate in heart that he might deliver him into your power, as indeed he has now done.

31 Then the LORD said to me, Now that I have already begun to give over to you Sihon and his land, begin to take possession. 32 So Sihon and all his people advanced against us to join battle at Jahaz; 33 but since the LORD, our God, had given him over to us, we defeated him and his sons and all his people. 34[m] At that time we captured all his cities and put every city under the ban,* men, women and children; we left no survivor. 35 Our only plunder was the livestock and the spoils of the captured cities. 36 From Aroer on the edge of the Wadi Arnon and from the town in the wadi itself, as far as Gilead,[n] no city was too well fortified for us. All of them the LORD, our God, gave over to us. 37 However, just as the LORD, our God, commanded us, you did not encroach upon any of the Ammonite land, neither the region bordering on the Wadi Jabbok, nor the cities of the highlands.[o]

## CHAPTER 3

See RG 85–89

***Defeat of Og.*** 1 Then we turned and proceeded up the road to Bashan. But Og, king of Bashan,[p] came out against us with all his people to give battle at Edrei. 2 The LORD said to me, Do not be afraid of him, for I have delivered him into your power with all his people and his land. Do to him as you did to Sihon, king of the Amorites, who reigned in Heshbon. 3 And thus the LORD, our God, delivered into our power also Og, king of Bashan, with all his people. We defeated him so completely that we left him no survivor. 4 At that time we captured all his cities; there was no town we did not take: sixty cities in all, the whole region of Argob, the kingdom of Og in Bashan— 5 all these cities were fortified with high walls and gates and bars—besides a great number of unwalled towns. 6[q] As we had done to Sihon, king of Heshbon, so also here we put all the towns under the ban, men, women and children; 7 but all the livestock and the spoils of each city we took as plunder for ourselves.

8 And so at that time we took from the two kings of the Amorites beyond the Jordan the territory from the Wadi Arnon to Mount Hermon 9 (the Sidonians call Hermon Sirion and the Amorites call it Senir), 10 all the towns of the plateau, all of Gilead, and all of Bashan

**2:23 Gaza**: later a stronghold of the Philistines (cf. Jos 13:3). **Caphtor**: the island of Crete.

**2:34 Under the ban**: in Hebrew, *herem,* which means to devote to the Lord (cf. 7:1–5; 20:10–18). The biblical text often presents *herem* as the total extermination of a population as a manifestation of the will of the Lord. It is historically doubtful that Israel ever literally carried out this theological program.

*g:* Dt 1:28. *h:* Gn 14:6; 36:6–8, 20–30. *i:* Gn 10:14; Jos 13:3; 18:23; 1 Chr 1:12; Jer 47:4; Am 9:7. *j:* Dt 1:4; 29:7; 31:4; Jos 2:10; 9:10; 12:1–6; Neh 9:22; Ps 135:10–12; 136:17–22. *k:* Nm 21:21–32; Jgs 11:19–22. *l:* Dt 2:4–9. *m:* Dt 3:6; 7:2, 26; 13:16, 18; 20:16–18; Jos 10:40; 11:11–12. *n:* Dt 3:12–13; Jos 13:8–13, 15–23. *o:* Nm 21:24; Jos 12:2. *p:* Nm 21:33–35. *q:* Dt 2:34–35; 7:2, 26; 13:16, 18; 20:16–18; Jos 10:40; 11:11–12.

as far as Salecah and Edrei, towns of the
kingdom of Og in Bashan. 11(Og, king of Bashan, was the last remaining survivor of the
Rephaim. He had a bed of iron,* nine regular
cubits long and four wide, which is still preserved in Rabbah of the Ammonites.)[r]

***Allotment of the Conquered Lands.*** 12[s] As
for the land we took possession of at that
time, I gave Reuben and Gad the territory
from Aroer, on the edge of the Wadi Arnon,
halfway up into the highlands of Gilead, with
its cities. 13The rest of Gilead and all of Bashan, the kingdom of Og, I gave to the half-
tribe of Manasseh. (The whole Argob region,
all that part of Bashan, was once called a land
of the Rephaim.[t] 14Jair, a Manassite,[u] took all
the region of Argob as far as the border of the
Geshurites and Maacathites, and named
them—Bashan, that is—after himself, Havvoth-jair, the name it bears today.) 15To
Machir* I gave Gilead, 16and to Reuben and
Gad the territory from Gilead to the Wadi
Arnon—the middle of the wadi being its
boundary—and to the Wadi Jabbok, which is
the border of the Ammonites, 17as well as the
Arabah with the Jordan and its banks from
Chinnereth* to the Salt Sea of the Arabah, under the slopes of Pisgah on the east.

18[v] At that time I charged you: The LORD,
your God, has given you this land as your
possession. But all your troops equipped for
battle must cross over in the vanguard of
your fellow Israelites. 19But your wives and
children, as well as your livestock, of which
I know you have a large number, shall remain behind in the towns I have given you,
20until the LORD has settled your relatives as
well, and they too possess the land which the
LORD, your God, will give them on the other
side of the Jordan. Then you may all return
to the possessions I have given you.

21And I charged Joshua as well, "Your
own eyes have seen all that the LORD, your
God, has done to both these kings; so, too,
will the LORD do to all the kingdoms into
which you will cross over. 22Do not fear
them, for it is the LORD, your God, who will
fight for you."[w]

***Moses Excluded from the Promised Land.***
23[x] It was then that I entreated the LORD,
24"Lord GOD, you have begun to show to
your servant your greatness and your mighty
hand. What god in heaven or on earth can
perform deeds and powerful acts like yours?
25Ah, let me cross over and see the good land
beyond the Jordan, that fine hill country, and
the Lebanon!" 26But the LORD was angry
with me on your account* and would not hear
me.[y] The LORD said to me, Enough! Speak to
me no more of this. 27Go up to the top of Pisgah and look out to the west, and to the north,
and to the south, and to the east. Look well,
for you shall not cross this Jordan.[z] 28Com-
mission Joshua,[a] and encourage and
strengthen him, for it is he who will cross at
the head of this people and he who will give
them possession of the land you are to see.
29So we remained in the valley opposite
Beth-peor.

## CHAPTER 4

See RG 85-89

***Advantages of Fidelity.*** 1Now therefore, Israel, hear the statutes and ordinances
I am teaching you to observe, that you may
live, and may enter in and take possession of
the land which the LORD, the God of your
ancestors, is giving you.[b] 2In your observance of the commandments of the LORD,
your God,[c] which I am commanding you,
you shall not add to what I command you
nor subtract from it. 3You have seen with
your own eyes what the LORD did at Baal-

**3:11 Bed of iron**: some translate, "a sarcophagus of basalt"; its dimensions would be approximately thirteen and a half feet by six feet.

**3:15 Machir**: a clan of the tribe of Manasseh (cf. Gn 50:23).

**3:17 Chinnereth**: later known as the Lake of Gennesaret and the Sea of Galilee. **The Salt Sea**: the Dead Sea. **Pisgah**: a mountain range to the northeast of the Salt Sea; Mount Nebo, from which Moses viewed the promised land, is in this range (cf. v. 27; 34:1).

**3:26 On your account**: that Moses saw but never entered the promised land is attested by every Pentateuchal tradition, but different reasons are given in different places. Nm 20:12 and Dt 32:51 present Moses as being at fault. Here, as in 1:37 and 4:21, the fault lies in the people but affects Moses.

*r:* Dt 2:11, 20; 3:13; Gn 14:5; 15:20; Jos 12:4; 13:12; 17:15. *s:* Nm 32:1–42; Jos 13:8–33. *t:* Dt 2:11, 20; 3:11; Gn 14:5; 15:20; Jos 12:4; 13:12; 17:15. *u:* Nm 32:41; Jgs 10:4; 1 Chr 2:23. *v:* Jos 1:12–15; 4:12; 22:1–4. *w:* Dt 1:30; Ex 14:13–14. *x:* Nm 27:12–23. *y:* Dt 4:21. *z:* Dt 3:17; 32:48–52; 34:1–4. *a:* Dt 1:38; 31:7–8. *b:* Dt 4:45; 5:1, 31; 6:1, 17, 20; 11:32; 12:1; 26:16. *c:* Dt 13:1.

### The New Generations

THE PAIRED INSTRUCTIONS not to forget the powerful experience of God's actions and to undertake the education of "your children," so that the past becomes "present" also to them, represent a prominent aim of Deuteronomy: to overcome the historical distance of the past and to maintain it as a source of identity (Dt 4:23, 25; 6:2, 7, 20–25; 8:11; 9:7; 31:13; 32:18). The actual generation of the exodus had died off and been replaced by this new one, who had experienced none of the events here being recounted (Dt 2:14–15). Moses addresses those who had not witnessed the events as if they had, while insisting that they pass on the events to posterity (Dt 5:3–4, 23; 11:7; 29:13–14). Deuteronomy's theology of history treats all members of the community as if they were present when the community underwent its formative experiences. This may seem paradoxical to us, but we can find an analogy in our experience of the Mass, where we recount and relive the sacrifice of Jesus Christ as the followers of Jesus experienced it at the Last Supper and on Calvary.

peor:[d] the LORD, your God, destroyed from your midst everyone who followed the Baal of Peor; [4]but you, who held fast to the LORD, your God, are all alive today. [5]See, I am teaching you the statutes and ordinances as the LORD, my God, has commanded me, that you may observe them in the land you are entering to possess. [6]Observe them carefully, for this is your wisdom and discernment in the sight of the peoples, who will hear of all these statutes and say, "This great nation is truly a wise and discerning people."[e] [7][f] For what great nation is there that has gods so close to it as the LORD, our God, is to us whenever we call upon him? [8]Or what great nation has statutes and ordinances that are as just as this whole law which I am setting before you today?[g]

***Revelation at Horeb.*** [9]However, be on your guard and be very careful not to forget the things your own eyes have seen, nor let them slip from your heart as long as you live, but make them known to your children[h] and to your children's children, [10]that day you stood before the LORD, your God, at Horeb, when the LORD said to me: Assemble the people for me, that I may let them hear my words, that they may learn to fear* me as long as they live in the land and may so teach their children. [11][i] You came near and stood at the foot of the mountain, while the mountain blazed to the heart of the heavens with fire and was enveloped in a dense black cloud. [12]Then the LORD spoke to you from the midst of the fire.[j] You heard the sound of the words, but saw no form; there was only a voice. [13]He proclaimed to you his covenant, which he commanded you to keep: the ten words,* which he wrote on two stone tablets.[k] [14]At that time the LORD charged me to teach you the statutes and ordinances for you to observe in the land you are about to cross into and possess.

***Danger of Idolatry.*** [15]Because you saw no form at all on the day the LORD spoke to you at Horeb from the midst of the fire, be strictly on your guard [16]not to act corruptly by fashioning an idol for yourselves to represent any figure, whether it be the form of a man or of a woman,[l] [17]the form of any animal on the earth, the form of any bird that flies in the sky, [18]the form of anything that crawls on the ground, or the form of any fish in the waters under the earth. [19]And when you look up to the heavens and behold the sun or the moon or the stars, the whole heav-

**4:10 Fear**: not in the sense of "be terrified," but rather "manifest reverence or awe."

**4:13 Ten words**: the ten commandments, or decalogue (cf. 5:22; Ex 34:28).

*d:* Nm 25:1–13; Ps 106:28; Hos 9:10. *e:* Dt 26:5; Gn 12:2; 18:18; 46:3; Ex 32:10. *f:* 2 Sm 7:23. *g:* Dt 4:44. *h:* Dt 6:7, 20–25; 11:19–21; 29:29; 31:12–13; Ps 78:3–6. *i:* Ex 19:7–20:21. *j:* Dt 4:33, 36; 5:4. *k:* Dt 5:6–21; 10:4; Ex 20:1–17; 24:12; 31:18; 34:27–28. *l:* Dt 5:8; Ex 20:4.

enly host, do not be led astray into bowing down to them and serving them.[m] These the LORD, your God, has apportioned to all the other nations under the heavens; [20]but you the LORD has taken and led out of that iron foundry, Egypt, that you might be his people, his heritage, as you are today.[n] [21]But the LORD was angry with me on your account[o] and swore that I should not cross the Jordan nor enter the good land which the LORD, your God, is giving you as a heritage. [22]I myself shall die in this country; I shall not cross the Jordan; but you are going to cross over and take possession of that good land.[p] [23]Be careful, therefore, lest you forget the covenant which the LORD, your God, has made with you, and fashion for yourselves against his command an idol in any form whatsoever.[q] [24]For the LORD, your God, is a consuming fire, a jealous God.* [r]

***God's Fidelity and Love.*** [25][s] When you have children and children's children, and have grown old in the land, should you then act corruptly by fashioning an idol in the form of anything, and by this evil done in his sight provoke the LORD, your God, [26]I call heaven and earth this day to witness against you, that you shall all quickly perish from the land which you are crossing the Jordan to possess. You shall not live in it for any length of time but shall be utterly wiped out.[t] [27]The LORD will scatter you among the peoples, and there shall remain but a handful of you among the nations to which the LORD will drive you. [28]There you shall serve gods that are works of human hands, of wood and stone, gods which can neither see nor hear, neither eat nor smell.[u] [29]Yet when you seek the LORD, your God, from there, you shall indeed find him if you search after him with all your heart and soul.[v] [30]In your distress, when all these things shall have come upon you, you shall finally return to the LORD, your God, and listen to his voice. [31]Since the LORD, your God, is a merciful God, he will not abandon or destroy you, nor forget the covenant with your ancestors that he swore to them.[w]

[32]Ask now of the days of old, before your time, ever since God created humankind upon the earth; ask from one end of the sky to the other: Did anything so great ever happen before? Was it ever heard of? [33]Did a people ever hear the voice of God speaking from the midst of fire, as you did, and live?[x] [34]Or did any god venture to go and take a nation for himself from the midst of another nation, by testings, by signs and wonders,[y] by war, with strong hand and outstretched arm, and by great terrors, all of which the LORD, your God, did for you in Egypt before your very eyes? [35]All this you were allowed to see that you might know that the LORD is God; there is no other.[z] [36]Out of the heavens he let you hear his voice to discipline you; on earth he let you see his great fire, and you heard him speaking out of the fire. [37]For love of your ancestors he chose their descendants after them and by his presence and great power led you out of Egypt, [38]dispossessing before you nations greater and mightier than you, so as to bring you in and to give their land to you as a heritage, as it is today. [39]This is why you must now acknowledge, and fix in your heart, that the LORD is God in the heavens above and on earth below, and that there is no other.[a] [40]And you must keep his statutes and commandments which I command you today, that you and

**4:24 A jealous God**: Hebrew *'el qanna*. The root of the adjective *qanna* expresses the idea of intense feeling focused on solicitude for someone or something; see, e.g., Ps 69:10; Sg 8:6; Is 9:6; 37:32; Ez 39:25. The Septuagint translated the adjective as *zelotes*, and the Vulgate followed suit; hence the traditional English rendering "jealous" (and sometimes "zealous") found in the Douai-Rheims and King James versions. In modern usage, however, "jealous" denotes unreasonable, petty possessiveness, a meaning, even as nuance, wanting in the Hebrew. In the first commandment (5:6–10; Ex 20:2–6) and passages derived from it (like 4:24; 6:15; Ex 34:14; Jos 24:19; Na 1:2), Israel's God is represented as totally committed to his purpose, and Israel is put on notice to take him and his directives for their life as a people with equal seriousness.

*m:* Dt 17:3; Jb 31:26–28. *n:* 1 Kgs 8:51; Is 48:10; Jer 11:4. *o:* Dt 1:37; 3:26. *p:* Dt 3:27; 34:1–12; Jos 1–12. *q:* Dt 4:16; 9:12–14; Ex 32:1–10. *r:* Dt 5:9; 6:15; 9:3; Ex 24:17; 34:14. *s:* Dt 28:64–67. *t:* Dt 30:19; 31:28; 32:1; Is 1:2. *u:* Dt 28:64; 29:17; Lv 26:30–39; Ps 115:4–8; 135:15–18; Is 44:9–20. *v:* Dt 6:5; Jer 29:13–14. *w:* Dt 31:8; Gn 9:9–17; 15:18–21; 17:1–21; Ex 34:6–7. *x:* Dt 4:36; 5:24, 26; Ex 20:19. *y:* Dt 7:19; 26:8; 29:2; Ex 7:3; 15:3–10; Jer 32:21. *z:* Dt 4:39; 32:39; 1 Kgs 8:60; Is 43:10–13; Jl 2:27. *a:* Dt 4:35; 32:39; 1 Kgs 8:60; Is 43:10–13; Jl 2:27.

your children after you may prosper, and that you may have long life on the land which the LORD, your God, is giving you forever.[b]

*Cities of Refuge.* 41[c] Then Moses set apart three cities in the region east of the Jordan, 42 to which a homicide might flee who killed a neighbor unintentionally, where there had been no hatred previously, so that the killer might flee to one of these cities and live: 43 Bezer in the wilderness, in the region of the plateau, for the Reubenites; Ramoth in Gilead for the Gadites; and Golan in Bashan for the Manassites.

## II. Second Address

### A. The Lord's Covenant with Israel

***Introduction.*** 44 This is the law* which Moses set before the Israelites.[d] 45 These are the decrees, and the statutes and ordinances* which Moses proclaimed to the Israelites after they came out of Egypt,[e] 46[f] beyond the Jordan in the valley opposite Beth-peor, in the land of Sihon, king of the Amorites, who reigned in Heshbon, whom Moses and the Israelites defeated after they came out of Egypt.[g] 47 They took possession of his land and the land of Og, king of Bashan, as well—the land of these two kings of the Amorites in the region beyond the Jordan to the east: 48 from Aroer on the edge of the Wadi Arnon to Mount Sion* (that is, Hermon) 49 and all the Arabah beyond the Jordan to the east, as far as the Arabah Sea* under the slopes of Pisgah.

#### CHAPTER 5

See RG 85–89

***The Covenant at Horeb.*** 1 Moses summoned all Israel and said to them, Hear, O Israel, the statutes and ordinances which I proclaim in your hearing this day, that you may learn them and take care to observe them.[h] 2 The LORD, our God, made a covenant with us at Horeb; 3 not with our ancestors* did the LORD make this covenant, but with us, all of us who are alive here this day. 4[i] Face to face, the LORD spoke with you on the mountain from the midst of the fire,[j] 5 while I was standing between the LORD and you at that time, to announce to you these words of the LORD, since you were afraid of the fire and would not go up the mountain:

***The Decalogue.*** 6[k] I am the LORD your God, who brought you out of the land of Egypt,[l] out of the house of slavery. 7[m] You shall not have other gods beside me. 8 You shall not make for yourself an idol or a likeness of anything in the heavens above or on the earth below or in the waters beneath the earth; 9* you shall not bow down before them or serve them. For I, the LORD, your God, am a jealous* God, bringing punishment for their parents' wickedness on the children of those who hate me, down to the third and fourth generation, 10 but showing love down to the thousandth generation of those who love me and keep my commandments.

11 You shall not invoke the name of the

**4:44 Law**: Hebrew *torah,* meaning "instruction," "law," "teaching"; the standard translation "law" comes from the influence of the Septuagint's *nomos,* "law," and the extensive legislation in Ex 20–Nm 10.

**4:45 Statutes and ordinances**: terms referring to the legal corpus in 12:1–26:19.

**4:48 Sion**: another name for Mount Hermon, besides those mentioned in 3:9 (to be distinguished from the Mount Zion of Jerusalem).

**4:49 The Arabah Sea**: the Dead Sea, cf. 3:17.

**5:3 Not with our ancestors**: in fact, the covenant was made with the ancestors, but these had died out during the "forty" years. The covenant is considered to be ongoing—for Israel in Moab and beyond.

**5:9–10** Israel is confronted with a choice, to "love" or to "hate" the Lord, and with the consequences of each choice. "Wickedness" works destruction not only on those who do it but also down the generations, in a sort of ripple effect. Yet, if Israel keeps the commandments, they will experience the Lord's *hesed* ("love") down to the thousandth generation. Thus the Lord's merciful love is disproportionate to the evil results of iniquity ("down to the third and fourth generation"). **To the thousandth generation**: lit., "to thousands"; cf. 7:9.

**5:9 Jealous**: see note on 4:24.

*b:* Dt 6:3; 12:28. *c:* Dt 19:1–13; Nm 35:10–28; Jos 20:1–9. *d:* Dt 4:8; 17:18–19; 30:10; 31:11–12. *e:* Dt 4:1; 5:1, 31; 6:1, 17, 20; 11:32; 12:1; 26:16; Ps 25:10. *f:* Dt 2:24–3:29. *g:* Dt 3:29; 34:6. *h:* Dt 4:1, 45; 5:31; 6:1, 17, 20; 11:32; 12:1; 26:16. *i:* Ex 19:3–25; 20:18–19; 24:2. *j:* Dt 34:10; Nm 12:8. *k:* Ex 20:2–17. *l:* Ex 20:2; Ps 81:11. *m:* Dt 4:23–24, 31; 6:4–5; 7:9–10; 12:2–13:18; 17:3; 18:20; 24:16; 27:15; Ex 20:3–6; 34:6–7, 14; Lv 26:1; Nm 14:18; Ps 81:10; 97:7; Jer 7:9; 31:29–30; 32:18–19; Ez 18:1–24.

**The Analysis of the Decalogue in Deuteronomy 5:6–21**

| Command | Rabbinic Judaism | Hellenistic Judaism and Church Fathers | Catholic/Lutheran |
|---|---|---|---|
| 1 | Self-Identification of God as separate command (v. 6) | Other Gods (vv. 6–7) | Other Gods + Images (vv. 6–10) |
| 2 | Other Gods + Images (vv. 7–10) | Images (vv. 8–10) | False Oath (v. 11) |
| 3 | False Oath (v. 11) | False Oath (v. 11) | Sabbath (vv. 12–15) |
| 4 | Sabbath (vv. 12–15) | Sabbath (vv. 12–15) | Parents (v. 16) |
| 5 | Parents (v. 16) | Parents (v. 16) | Murder (v. 17) |
| 6 | Murder (v. 17) | Murder (v. 17) | Adultery (v. 18) |
| 7 | Adultery (v. 17) | Adultery (v. 17) | Theft (v. 19) |
| 8 | Theft (v. 17) | Theft (v. 17) | False Witness (v. 20) |
| 9 | False Witness (v. 17) | False Witness (v. 17) | Coveting Wife (v. 21) |
| 10 | Coveting (v. 18) | Coveting (v. 18) | Coveting Property (v. 21) |

LORD, your God, in vain.[n] For the LORD will not leave unpunished anyone who invokes his name in vain.

12o Observe the sabbath day—keep it
holy, as the LORD, your God, commanded
you. 13Six days you may labor and do all
your work, 14but the seventh day is a sabbath
of the LORD your God. You shall not do any work, either you, your son or your daughter, your male or female slave, your ox or donkey or any work animal, or the resident alien within your gates, so that your male and female slave may rest as you do. 15Remember
that you too were once slaves in the land of Egypt, and the LORD, your God, brought you out from there with a strong hand and outstretched arm. That is why the LORD, your God, has commanded you to observe the sabbath day.

16p Honor your father and your mother, as
the LORD, your God, has commanded you, that you may have a long life and that you may prosper in the land the LORD your God is giving you.

17q You shall not kill.*

18r You shall not commit adultery.

19s You shall not steal.

20t You shall not bear dishonest witness against your neighbor.

21u You shall not covet your neighbor's wife.

You shall not desire your neighbor's house or field, his male or female slave, his ox or donkey, or anything that belongs to your neighbor.

***Moses as Mediator.*** 22These words the
LORD spoke with a loud voice to your entire assembly on the mountain from the midst of the fire and the dense black cloud, and added no more. He inscribed them on two stone

**5:17 Kill**: see note on Ex 20:13.

*n:* Dt 6:13; 10:20; 18:20; 23:21–23; Ex 20:7; Lv 19:12; 24:10–23; Ps 24:4; Jer 29:23; Mt 5:33–37. *o:* Dt 14:22–16:17; 24:18, 22; Ex 20:8–11; 23:12; 31:12–17; 34:21; Is 58:13–14; Jer 17:21–27; Mt 12:1–14; Mk 2:23–3:6; Lk 6:1–11; 13:10–17; 14:1–6; Jn 5:2–18; 7:22–23. *p:* Dt 21:18–21; 27:16; Ex 20:12; 21:15, 17; Sir 3:1–16; Mt 10:34–39; 12:46–50; 15:4; 19:19; Mk 3:31–35; 7:10; 10:19; Lk 8:19–21; 14:26; 18:20, 28–30; Eph 6:1–4. *q:* Dt 4:41–43; 19:1–13; 20:1–21:9; 21:18–23; Gn 4:8–16; Ex 20:13; 21:12–14; Nm 35:16–34; Jer 7:9; Hos 4:2; Mt 5:21–26; 19:18; Mk 10:19; Lk 18:20; Jas 2:11. *r:* Dt 22:13–23:1; Gn 20:1–18; 39:7–20; Ex 20:14; Lv 18:20; 20:10; 2 Sm 11:1–12:25; Jer 7:9; Hos 4:2; Mt 5:27–30; 19:18; Mk 10:19; Lk 18:20; Jas 2:11. *s:* Dt 23:24; 24:7; Gn 40:15; Ex 20:15; 21:16, 37; 22:1–3, 12; Lv 19:11, 13; 1 Kgs 21:1–19; Jer 7:9; Hos 4:2; Mt 19:18; Mk 10:19; Lk 18:20. *t:* Dt 19:15–19; Ex 20:16; 23:1–3; Lv 19:11, 15–16; 1 Kgs 21:1–19; Ps 5:6–10; 10:7–9; 27:12; Prv 25:18; 30:8–10; Jer 7:9; Hos 4:2; Mt 19:18; 26:59–60; Mk 10:19; Lk 18:20. *u:* Dt 7:25; Ex 20:17; Jos 7:21; 2 Sm 11:1–12:25; 1 Kgs 21:1–19; Is 5:8; Mi 2:2; Mt 5:27–30; Lk 12:13–21; Eph 5:5; Col 3:5.

**"Hear, O Israel"**

THIS STATEMENT OF belief (6:4–9) is the most important one for Israel, and is also partly quoted in the New Testament by Jesus (Mark 12:29-30). It is known as the *Shema,* from its first word in Hebrew, the command "Hear!"

tablets and gave them to me.[v] 23 But when you heard the voice from the midst of the darkness, while the mountain was ablaze with fire, you came near to me, all your tribal heads and elders, 24 and said, "The LORD, our God, has indeed let us see his glory and his greatness, and we have heard his voice from the midst of the fire.[w] Today we have found out that God may speak to a mortal and that person may still live. 25 Now, why should we die? For this great fire will consume us. If we hear the voice of the LORD, our God, any more, we shall die.[x] 26 For what mortal has heard the voice of the living God speaking from the midst of fire, as we have, and lived? 27 You go closer and listen to all that the LORD, our God, will say, and then tell us what the LORD, our God, tells you; we will listen and obey."[y]

28 The LORD heard your words as you were speaking to me and said to me, I have heard the words these people have spoken to you, which are all well said.[z] 29 Would that they might always be of such a mind, to fear me and to keep all my commandments! Then they and their descendants would prosper forever. 30 Go, tell them: Return to your tents. 31 Then you stand here near me and I will give you all the commandments, the statutes and the ordinances; you must teach them, that they may observe them in the land I am giving them to possess.[a] 32 Be careful, therefore, to do as the LORD, your God, has commanded you, not turning aside to the right or to the left, 33 but following exactly the way that the LORD, your God, commanded you that you may live and prosper, and may have long life in the land which you are to possess.[b]

## CHAPTER 6

See RG 85-89

1 This then is the commandment, the statutes and the ordinances,[c] which the LORD, your God, has commanded that you be taught to observe in the land you are about to cross into to possess, 2 so that you, that is, you, your child, and your grandchild, may fear the LORD, your God, by keeping, as long as you live, all his statutes and commandments[d] which I enjoin on you, and thus have long life. 3 Hear then, Israel, and be careful to observe them, that it may go well with you and that you may increase greatly; for the LORD, the God of your ancestors, promised you a land flowing with milk and honey.[e]

***The Great Commandment.**** 4[f] Hear, O Israel!* The LORD is our God, the LORD alone! 5 Therefore, you shall love the LORD, your God, with your whole heart, and with your whole being, and with your whole strength.[g] 6[h] Take to heart these words which I command you today.[i] 7 Keep repeating them to your children. Recite them when you are at home and when you are away, when you lie

**6:4–5** This passage, an expansion of the first commandment (5:6–10), contains the basic principle of the whole Mosaic law, the keynote of the Book of Deuteronomy: since the Lord alone is God, Israel must love him with an undivided heart. Jesus cited these words as "the greatest and the first commandment," embracing in itself the whole law of God (Mt 22:37–38; Mk 12:29–30; Lk 10:27).

**6:4 Hear, O Israel!**: in Hebrew, *shema yisra'el*; hence this passage (vv. 4–9), containing the Great Commandment, is called the Shema. In later Jewish tradition, 11:13–21 and Nm 15:37–41 were added to form a prayer recited every evening and morning. **The LORD is our God, the LORD alone**: other possible translations are "the Lord our God is one Lord"; "the Lord our God, the Lord is one"; "the Lord is our God, the Lord is one."

*v:* Dt 4:13; 9:9–11, 17; 10:1–5; Ex 24:12; 31:18; 32:15–20; 34:1–5. *w:* Dt 4:33, 36; Ex 20:19. *x:* Dt 18:16. *y:* Ex 20:19. *z:* Dt 18:17. *a:* Dt 4:1, 45; 5:1; 6:1, 17, 20; 11:32; 12:1; 26:16. *b:* Dt 4:40. *c:* Dt 4:1, 45; 5:1, 31; 6:17, 20; 11:32; 12:1; 26:16. *d:* Dt 4:10, 40; 5:29; 6:24; 10:12–13. *e:* Ex 3:8. *f:* Dt 4:35, 39; 5:6–10; 6:13–14; 10:17; 1 Kgs 8:60; 18:39; 2 Kgs 5:15; 19:15, 19; Is 44:6; 45:5–6; Mt 22:37–38; Mk 12:29–30; Lk 10:27. *g:* Dt 4:29; 10:12; 11:13; 13:4; 26:16; 30:2, 10; 1 Sm 7:3; 2 Kgs 23:3, 25. *h:* Dt 11:18–21. *i:* Dt 11:18; 30:14; 32:46; Ps 37:31; Prv 3:3; Is 51:7; Jer 31:33.

down and when you get up.[j] [8]Bind them on your arm as a sign* and let them be as a pendant on your forehead.[k] [9]Write them on the doorposts of your houses and on your gates.[l]

***Fidelity in Prosperity.*** [10][m] When the LORD, your God, brings you into the land which he swore to your ancestors, to Abraham, Isaac, and Jacob, that he would give you, a land with fine, large cities that you did not build,[n] [11]with houses full of goods of all sorts that you did not garner, with cisterns that you did not dig, with vineyards and olive groves that you did not plant; and when, therefore, you eat and are satisfied,[o] [12][p] be careful not to forget the LORD, who brought you out of the land of Egypt, that house of slavery. [13][q] The LORD, your God, shall you fear; him shall you serve,* and by his name shall you swear. [14][r] You shall not go after other gods, any of the gods of the surrounding peoples— [15]for the LORD, your God who is in your midst, is a passionate God—lest the anger of the LORD, your God, flare up against you and he destroy you from upon the land.

[16]You shall not put the LORD, your God, to the test, as you did at Massah.[s] [17]But keep the commandments of the LORD, your God, and the decrees and the statutes he has commanded you. [18]Do what is right and good in the sight of the LORD, that it may go well with you, and you may enter in and possess the good land which the LORD promised on oath to your ancestors, [19]driving all your enemies out of your way, as the LORD has promised.[t]

***Instruction to Children.*** [20][u] Later on, when your son asks you, "What do these decrees and statutes and ordinances mean?"[v] which the LORD, our God, has enjoined on you, [21][w] you shall say to your son, "We were once slaves of Pharaoh in Egypt, but the LORD brought us out of Egypt with a strong hand[x] [22]and wrought before our eyes signs and wonders, great and dire, against Egypt and against Pharaoh and his whole house. [23]He brought us from there to bring us in and give us the land he had promised on oath to our ancestors.[y] [24][z] The LORD commanded us to observe all these statutes in fear of the LORD, our God, that we may always have as good a life as we have today. [25]This is our justice before the LORD, our God: to observe carefully this whole commandment he has enjoined on us."

## CHAPTER 7

See RG 85–89

***Destruction of the Nations in the Land.*** [1][a] When the LORD, your God, brings you into the land which you are about to enter to possess, and removes many nations before you—the Hittites, Girgashites, Amorites, Canaanites, Perizzites, Hivites, and Jebusites,[b] seven nations more numerous and powerful than you— [2]and when the LORD, your God, gives them over to you and you defeat them, you shall put them under the ban. Make no covenant with them[c] and do not be gracious to them. [3][d] You shall not intermarry with them, neither giving your daughters to their sons nor taking their daughters for your sons. [4]For they would turn your sons from following me to serving other gods, and then the anger of the LORD would flare up against you and he would quickly destroy you.

[5]But this is how you must deal with them:[e] Tear down their altars, smash their sacred pillars, chop down their asherahs,*

**6:8 Bind them . . . as a sign**: these injunctions were probably meant merely in a figurative sense; cf. Ex 13:9, 16. In the late postexilic period, they were taken quite literally, and devout Jews tied on their arms and foreheads "phylacteries," boxes containing strips of parchment on which these words were inscribed; cf. Mt 23:5.

**6:13 Him shall you serve**: the verb could be translated as either "serve" or "worship" (cf. 5:9).

**7:5 Sacred pillars . . . asherahs**: cut or uncut stones and wooden poles or trees (cf. 16:21) that had some cultic function. Fairly common religious artifacts, their association with the non-Israelite cults of Canaan and perhaps with Canaanite gods

*j:* Dt 4:9–10; 6:20–25; 11:1–7, 19; 31:13; 32:46; Prv 6:22. *k:* Dt 11:18; Ex 13:9, 16; Prv 3:3; 6:21. *l:* Dt 11:20. *m:* Dt 5:6–10. *n:* Dt 1:8. *o:* Dt 8:7–14; 32:11–14; Jos 24:13; Neh 9:25. *p:* Dt 5:6. *q:* Dt 10:20; Is 48:1; Jer 4:2; 12:16; Mt 4:10; Lk 4:8. *r:* Dt 4:23–26; 8:19–20; 11:16–17, 28; 29:18–28; 30:17–18; 2 Kgs 17:7–18. *s:* Ex 17:1–7; Ps 95:8–9; Mt 4:7; Lk 4:12. *t:* Ex 23:27; 34:11; Jos 1–12. *u:* Dt 6:6–9. *v:* Ex 12:26; 13:14; Jos 4:6, 21. *w:* Dt 26:5–10. *x:* Dt 5:3, 6. *y:* Dt 1:8. *z:* Dt 4:1–4; 30:15–20. *a:* Ex 23:23–33; 34:11–16; Nm 33:51–56. *b:* Dt 1:7; Gn 10:16–17; 13:7; 15:19–21; 23:3–20; 34:2, 30; 49:29–30; Ex 3:8; 23:23; 33:2; Nm 13:29; Jos 1:4; 3:10; 9:1–7; 15:63; 17:15; 24:11; Jgs 1:4–5; 3:3, 5; 2 Sm 5:6–10; 1 Kgs 9:20; Ez 16:3, 45. *c:* Dt 2:34–35; 3:6; 7:26; 13:16, 18; 20:16–18; Ex 23:32–33; 34:12, 15; Jos 9:3–27; 10:40; 11:11–12; Jgs 2:2. *d:* Gn 34:9–10; Ex 34:16; Jos 23:12–13; Jgs 3:5–6; 1 Kgs 11:1–6. *e:* Dt 12:2–3, 29–31; 16:21–22; Ex 34:13; 2 Kgs 18:4; 23:4–24.

and destroy their idols by fire. [6]For you are a people holy to the LORD, your God; the LORD, your God, has chosen you from all the peoples on the face of the earth to be a people specially his own.[f] [7]It was not because you are more numerous than all the peoples that the LORD set his heart on you and chose you; for you are really the smallest of all peoples.[g] [8]It was because the LORD loved you and because of his fidelity to the oath he had sworn to your ancestors, that the LORD brought you out with a strong hand and redeemed you from the house of slavery, from the hand of Pharaoh, king of Egypt.[h] [9][i] Know, then, that the LORD, your God, is God: the faithful God who keeps covenant mercy to the thousandth generation toward those who love him and keep his commandments,[j] [10]but who repays with destruction those who hate him; he does not delay with those who hate him, but makes them pay for it. [11]Therefore carefully observe the commandment, the statutes and the ordinances which I command you today.

***Blessings of Obedience.*** [12][k] As your reward for heeding these ordinances and keeping them carefully, the LORD, your God, will keep with you the covenant mercy he promised on oath to your ancestors. [13]He will love and bless and multiply you; he will bless the fruit of your womb and the produce of your soil, your grain and wine and oil, the young of your herds and the offspring of your flocks, in the land which he swore to your ancestors he would give you. [14]You will be blessed above all peoples; no man or woman among you shall be childless nor shall your livestock be barren. [15]The LORD will remove all sickness from you; he will not afflict you with any of the malignant diseases that you know from Egypt, but will leave them with all those who hate you.

[16]You shall consume all the peoples which the LORD, your God, is giving over to you. You are not to look on them with pity, nor serve their gods, for that would be a snare to you.[l] [17][m] If you say to yourselves, "These nations are more numerous than we. How can we dispossess them?" [18]do not be afraid of them. Rather, remember clearly what the LORD, your God, did to Pharaoh and to all Egypt: [19]the great testings which your own eyes have seen, the signs and wonders, the strong hand and outstretched arm with which the LORD, your God, brought you out. The same also will he do to all the peoples of whom you are now afraid. [20]Moreover, the LORD, your God, will send hornets among them, until those who are left and those who are hiding from you are destroyed.[n] [21]Therefore, do not be terrified by them, for the LORD, your God, who is in your midst, is a great and awesome God. [22]He will remove these nations before you little by little. You cannot finish with them quickly, lest the wild beasts become too numerous for you.[o] [23]The LORD, your God, will give them over to you and throw them into utter panic until they are destroyed.[p] [24]He will deliver their kings into your power, that you may make their names perish from under the heavens. No one will be able to stand up against you,[q] till you have destroyed them. [25][r] The images of their gods you shall destroy by fire. Do not covet the silver or gold on them, nor take it for yourselves, lest you be ensnared by it; for it is an abomination to the LORD, your God.[s] [26]You shall not bring any abominable thing into your house, so as to be, like it, under the ban; loathe and abhor it utterly for it is under the ban.*

## CHAPTER 8

See RG 85-89

***God's Care.*** [1]Be careful to observe this whole commandment[t] that I enjoin on you today, that you may live and increase,

and goddesses, specifically the goddess Asherah, led to their condemnation in the Deuteronomic reform and possibly earlier.

**7:26 Under the ban**: and therefore doomed to destruction; see note on 2:34.

---

*f:* Dt 14:2, 21; 26:18–19; 32:8–14; Ex 19:5–6; Ps 135:4; Mal 3:17. *g:* Dt 10:15. *h:* Dt 5:6; 9:26; 13:5; 15:15; 21:8; 24:18; Ps 78:42. *i:* Dt 4:31; 5:9–10; 24:16; Ex 20:5–6; 34:6–7; Nm 14:18; Jer 31:29–30; 32:18–19; Ez 18:1–24; Jn 9:1–3. *j:* Dt 5:9–10; 7:12; 32:4; 1 Kgs 8:23–24; Neh 1:5; 9:32; Ps 89:1–2, 24, 28, 33–34; 98:3; Is 49:7; 54:10; 55:3; Dn 9:4; Jon 4:2; Mi 7:20. *k:* Dt 15:6; 28:1–14; 30:1–10; Ex 23:22–33; Lv 26:3–13. *l:* Dt 5:7–10. *m:* Dt 1:28–31; 3:22; 4:34, 37–38; 9:1–3; 20:1; 29:2–3; Jos 23:3, 9–10. *n:* Ex 23:28. *o:* Ex 23:29–30; Jgs 3:1–6. *p:* Dt 7:2. *q:* Dt 11:25; Jos 12:7–24. *r:* Dt 5:8–9; 9:21; Jos 6:18–19; 7:1, 20–21; Jgs 8:24–27; 17:2–4; 1 Kgs 15:13; 2 Kgs 23:4. *s:* Dt 12:31; 17:1; 18:12; 22:5; 23:18; 24:4; 25:16; Prv 6:16; 15:8–9, 26. *t:* Dt 4:1; 6:1.

and may enter in and possess the land which the LORD promised on oath to your ancestors. 2Remember how for these forty years the LORD, your God, has directed all your journeying in the wilderness,[u] so as to test you by affliction, to know what was in your heart: to keep his commandments, or not. 3He therefore let you be afflicted with hunger, and then fed you with manna,[v] a food unknown to you and your ancestors, so you might know that it is not by bread alone* that people live, but by all that comes forth from the mouth of the LORD. 4The clothing did not fall from you in tatters, nor did your feet swell these forty years.[w] 5So you must know in your heart that, even as a man disciplines his son, so the LORD, your God, disciplines you.[x] 6Therefore, keep the commandments of the LORD, your God, by walking in his ways and fearing him.

*Cautions About Prosperity.* 7[y] For the LORD, your God, is bringing you into a good country, a land with streams of water, with springs and fountains welling up in the hills and valleys, 8a land of wheat and barley, of vines and fig trees and pomegranates, of olive trees and of honey, 9a land where you will always have bread and where you will lack nothing, a land whose stones contain iron and in whose hills you can mine copper. 10But when you have eaten and are satisfied, you must bless the LORD, your God, for the good land he has given you. 11[z] Be careful not to forget the LORD, your God, by failing to keep his commandments and ordinances and statutes which I enjoin on you today: 12lest, when you have eaten and are satisfied, and have built fine houses and lived in them, 13and your herds and flocks have increased, your silver and gold has increased, and all your property has increased, 14you then become haughty of heart and forget the LORD, your God, who brought you out of the land of Egypt, that house of slavery; 15he guided you through the vast and terrible wilderness with its saraph* serpents and scorpions, its parched and waterless ground; he brought forth water for you from the flinty rock[a] 16and fed you in the wilderness with manna, a food unknown to your ancestors, that he might afflict you and test you, but also make you prosperous in the end. 17Otherwise, you might say in your heart,[b] "It is my own power and the strength of my own hand that has got me this wealth." 18Remember then the LORD, your God, for he is the one who gives you the power to get wealth, by fulfilling, as he has now done, the covenant he swore to your ancestors. 19But if you do forget the LORD, your God, and go after other gods, serving and bowing down to them,[c] I bear witness to you this day that you will perish utterly. 20Like the nations which the LORD destroys before you, so shall you too perish for not listening to the voice of the LORD, your God.

## CHAPTER 9

*Unmerited Success.* 1Hear, O Israel! You are now about to cross the Jordan to enter in and dispossess nations greater and stronger than yourselves, having large cities fortified to the heavens,[d] 2the Anakim, a people great and tall.[e] You yourselves know of them and have heard it said of them, "Who can stand up against the Anakim?" 3Know, then, today that it is the LORD, your God, who will cross over before you as a consuming fire; he it is who will destroy them and subdue them before you, so that you can dispossess and remove them quickly, as the LORD promised you.[f] 4After the LORD, your God, has driven them out of your way, do not say in your heart, "It is because of my justice the LORD has brought me in to possess this land,[g] and because of the wickedness of these nations the LORD is dis-

See RG 85–89

**8:3 Not by bread alone**: Deuteronomic theology puts the good things promised faithful Israel into the context of the Lord's gratuitous love. As in 6:10–12, the goods of life must be seen as gift. Israel is to seek what really matters; all else will be added (cf. Mt 6:33).

**8:15 Saraph**: see note on Nm 21:6.

*u:* Dt 1:3; 2:7; 29:4; Ps 95:10; Am 2:10. *v:* Ex 16:11–36; Nm 11:5–9; Jos 5:12; Mt 4:4; Lk 4:4. *w:* Dt 29:4; Neh 9:21. *x:* Dt 4:36; 11:2; 21:18–21; Ps 94:12; Prv 3:11–12. *y:* Dt 1:25; 11:10–12; 32:13–14; 33:28. *z:* Dt 6:10–12. *a:* Dt 32:13; Ex 17:6; Nm 20:8–11; 21:6–9; Ps 114:8; Wis 11:4. *b:* Dt 9:4–5. *c:* Dt 4:25–26; 30:18; 2 Kgs 17:7–18. *d:* Dt 1:28; 4:38. *e:* Dt 1:28; 2:10–11, 21; Nm 13:22, 28, 33; Jos 11:21–22; 14:12, 15; 15:13–14; 21:11; Jgs 1:20. *f:* Dt 4:24; 31:3. *g:* Dt 8:17.

possessing them before me."* 5 No, it is not because of your justice or the integrity of your heart that you are going in to take possession of their land; but it is because of their wickedness that the LORD, your God, is dispossessing these nations before you and in order to fulfill the promise he made on oath to your ancestors, Abraham, Isaac, and Jacob.[h] 6 Know this, therefore: it is not because of your justice that the LORD, your God, is giving you this good land to possess, for you are a stiff-necked people.[i]

***The Golden Calf.*** 7 Remember and do not forget how you angered the LORD, your God, in the wilderness. From the day you left the land of Egypt until you came to this place, you have been rebellious toward the LORD.[j] 8 [k] At Horeb you so provoked the LORD that he was angry enough to destroy you,[l] 9 when I had gone up the mountain to receive the stone tablets of the covenant which the LORD made with you.[m] Meanwhile I stayed on the mountain forty days and forty nights; I ate no food and drank no water. 10 The LORD gave me the two stone tablets inscribed, by God's own finger,[n] with a copy of all the words that the LORD spoke to you on the mountain from the midst of the fire on the day of the assembly. 11 Then, at the end of the forty days and forty nights, when the LORD had given me the two stone tablets, the tablets of the covenant, 12 [o] the LORD said to me, Go down from here now, quickly, for your people whom you have brought out of Egypt are acting corruptly; they have already turned aside from the way I commanded them and have made for themselves a molten idol. 13 I have seen now how stiff-necked this people is, the LORD said to me. 14 Let me be, that I may destroy them and blot out their name from under the heavens. I will then make of you a nation mightier and greater than they.

15 When I had come down again from the blazing, fiery mountain, with the two tablets of the covenant in both my hands,[p] 16 I saw how you had sinned against the LORD, your God, by making for yourselves a molten calf. You had already turned aside from the way which the LORD had commanded you.[q] 17 I took hold of the two tablets and with both hands cast them from me and broke them before your eyes.[r] 18 Then, as before, I lay prostrate before the LORD for forty days and forty nights; I ate no food, I drank no water, because of all the sin you had committed in the sight of the LORD, doing wrong and provoking him.[s] 19 For I dreaded the fierce anger of the LORD against you: his wrath would destroy you.[t] Yet once again the LORD listened to me. 20 With Aaron, too, the LORD was deeply angry, and would have destroyed him; but I prayed for Aaron also at that time.[u] 21 Then, taking the calf, the sinful object you had made, I burnt it and ground it down to powder as fine as dust, which I threw into the wadi that went down the mountainside.[v]

22 At Taberah, at Massah, and at Kibroth-hattaavah likewise, you enraged the LORD.[w] 23 And when the LORD sent you up from Kadesh-barnea saying, Go up and take possession of the land I have given you, you rebelled against this command of the LORD, your God, and would not believe him or listen to his voice.[x] 24 You have been rebels against the LORD from the day I first knew you.

25 [y] Those forty days, then, and forty nights, I lay prostrate before the LORD, because he had threatened to destroy you. 26 And I prayed to the Lord and said: O Lord GOD, do not destroy your people, the heritage you redeemed in your greatness and have brought out of Egypt with your strong hand.[z] 27 Remember your servants, Abraham, Isaac, and Jacob. Do not look upon the stubbornness of this people nor upon their wickedness and sin,[a] 28 lest the land from which you have brought us say, "The LORD

**9:4 Before me**: Hebrew reads "before you."

*h:* Dt 1:8. *i:* Dt 9:13; 10:16; 31:27; Ex 32:9; 33:3; 34:9; Is 48:4; Jer 17:23; 19:15. *j:* Dt 31:27; Ex 14:10–14; 2 Kgs 21:15; Jer 7:25–26. *k:* Ex 32:1–34:29. *l:* Ex 32:10. *m:* Dt 4:13–14; 5:22; 9:11, 18, 25; 10:10; Ex 24:12–18; 34:28. *n:* Dt 5:22; 10:4; Ex 31:18. *o:* Dt 5:6–10; Ex 32:7–10. *p:* Ex 32:15. *q:* Dt 5:6–10; Ex 32:1–6; Ps 106:19–22. *r:* Ex 32:19. *s:* Dt 10:10; Ex 32:31; 34:28. *t:* Dt 10:10; Ex 32:11–14. *u:* Ex 32:1–6, 21–25, 35. *v:* Ex 32:20. *w:* Dt 6:16; Ex 17:1–7; Nm 11:1–34. *x:* Dt 1:19–33. *y:* Ex 32:11–14. *z:* Dt 4:20; 7:8. *a:* Dt 7:8.

was not able to bring them into the land he
promised them, and out of hatred for them,
he brought them out to let them die in the
wilderness."[b] [29]They are your people and
your heritage, whom you have brought out
by your great power and with your outstretched arm.[c]

## CHAPTER 10

See RG 85-89

[1][d] At that time the LORD said to me,
Cut two stone tablets like the first ones[e] and
come up the mountain to me. Also make an
ark out of wood. [2]I will write upon the
tablets the words that were on the tablets that
you broke, and you shall place them in the
ark. [3]So I made an ark of acacia wood, and
cut two stone tablets like the first ones, and
went up the mountain with the two tablets in
my hand.[f] [4][g] The LORD then wrote on the
tablets, as he had written before, the ten
words* that the LORD had spoken to you on
the mountain from the midst of the fire on
the day of the assembly; and the LORD gave
them to me. [5]Then I turned and came down
from the mountain, and placed the tablets in
the ark I had made.[h] There they have remained, as the LORD commanded me.
[6][i] The Israelites set out from Beeroth
Bene-jaakan for Moserah; Aaron died there
and was buried. His son Eleazar succeeded
him as priest.[j] [7]From there they set out for
Gudgodah, and from Gudgodah for Jotbathah, a region where there is water in the
wadies. [8]At that time the LORD set apart the
tribe of Levi to carry the ark of the covenant
of the LORD,[k] to stand before the LORD to
minister to him, and to bless in his name, as
they have done to this day. [9]For this reason,
Levi has no hereditary portion with his relatives;[l] the LORD himself is his portion, as the
LORD, your God, promised him.
[10]Meanwhile I stayed on the mountain as
I did before, forty days and forty nights, and
once again the LORD listened to me. The
LORD was unwilling to destroy you. [11]The
LORD said to me, Go now and set out at the
head of the people,[m] that they may enter in
and possess the land that I swore to their ancestors I would give them.

### *The Lord's Majesty and Compassion.*

[12][n] Now, therefore, Israel, what does the
LORD, your God, ask of you but to fear the
LORD, your God, to follow in all his ways, to
love and serve the LORD, your God, with
your whole heart and with your whole being,[o] [13]to keep the commandments and statutes of the LORD that I am commanding you
today for your own well-being?[p] [14]Look, the
heavens, even the highest heavens, belong to
the LORD, your God, as well as the earth and
everything on it.[q] [15]Yet only on your ancestors did the LORD set his heart to love them.
He chose you, their descendants, from all the
peoples, as it is today.[r] [16]Circumcise therefore the foreskins of your hearts,* and be
stiff-necked no longer. [17]For the LORD, your
God, is the God of gods, the Lord of lords,
the great God, mighty and awesome, who
has no favorites, accepts no bribes,[s] [18]who
executes justice for the orphan and the
widow, and loves the resident alien, giving
them food and clothing.[t] [19]So you too should
love the resident alien, for that is what you
were in the land of Egypt.[u] [20]The LORD, your
God, shall you fear, and him shall you serve;
to him hold fast and by his name shall you
swear.[v] [21]He is your praise; he is your God,
who has done for you those great and awesome things that your own eyes have seen.[w]
[22]Seventy strong your ancestors went down
to Egypt,[x] and now the LORD, your God, has
made you as numerous as the stars of heaven.

**10:4 Ten words**: the ten commandments (cf. 4:13).

**10:16 Circumcise therefore the foreskins of your hearts**: cf. 30:6; Jer 4:4; Rom 2:29. The "uncircumcised heart" (Lv 26:41; Jer 9:25; Ez 44:7, 9) is closed and unreceptive to God, just as "uncircumcised ears" (Jer 6:10) are closed to the word of the Lord, and "uncircumcised lips" (Ex 6:12, 30) are a hindrance to speaking on behalf of the Lord.

---

*b:* Dt 32:26–27; Nm 14:13–16. *c:* Dt 4:20; Ex 6:6–7. *d:* Ex 34:1–28. *e:* Ex 34:1. *f:* Ex 34:4. *g:* Dt 4:13; 5:22; Ex 20:1–17; 34:1–4, 27–29. *h:* Ex 40:20; 1 Kgs 8:9. *i:* Nm 33:31–33. *j:* Nm 3:1–4, 32; 20:22–29. *k:* Dt 21:5; 33:8–11; Ex 32:25–29; Nm 3:6–10; 6:22–27; 8:23–26. *l:* Dt 18:1–8; Nm 18:20. *m:* Dt 1:6; Ex 32:34; 33:1. *n:* Ps 15; 24:3–5; Mi 6:6–8. *o:* Dt 6:5, 13; 8:6; 11:13. *p:* Dt 4:1; 5:10, 29–33; 6:2; 7:9; 11:1, 13, 22. *q:* 1 Kgs 8:27; Neh 9:6; Ps 148:4. *r:* Dt 7:6–8; Ex 19:5–6. *s:* Dt 1:17; 16:19; Ex 15:11; 2 Chr 19:7; Jb 34:19; Ps 47:2; 136:2–3; Dn 2:47; Acts 10:34; Rom 2:11; Gal 2:6; 1 Tm 6:15; Rev 17:14; 19:16. *t:* Ps 68:5–6; 99:4; 146:7–9. *u:* Dt 24:17–22; Ex 22:21–24; 23:9; Lv 19:33–34. *v:* Dt 6:13; Mt 4:10; Lk 4:8. *w:* Ps 109:1; Jer 17:14. *x:* Dt 1:10; Gn 46:8–27; Ex 1:5; Acts 7:14.

**Community Responsibility**

LOYALTY TO THE covenant provides the condition for life in Canaan. The punishments and rewards in chapter 11 are predominantly addressed to a plural "you," stressing communal rather than individual responsibility.

## CHAPTER 11

See RG 85-89

***Recalling the Wonders of the Lord.*** [1]Love the LORD, your God, therefore, and keep his charge, statutes, ordinances, and commandments always.[y] [2]Recall today that it was not your children, who have neither known nor seen the discipline of the LORD, your God—his greatness, his strong hand and outstretched arm;[z] [3]the signs and deeds he wrought in the midst of Egypt, on Pharaoh, king of Egypt, and on all his land;[a] [4]what he did to the Egyptian army and to their horses and chariots, engulfing them in the waters of the Red Sea* as they pursued you,[b] so that the LORD destroyed them even to this day; [5]what he did for you in the wilderness until you came to this place; [6]and what he did to the Reubenites Dathan and Abiram, sons of Eliab, when the earth opened its mouth and swallowed them up out of the midst of Israel, with their families and tents and every living thing that belonged to them—[c] [7]but it was you who saw with your own eyes all these great deeds that the LORD has done.

***The Gift of Rain.*** [8][d] So keep all the commandments I give you today, that you may be strong enough to enter in and take possession of the land that you are crossing over to possess, [9]and that you may have long life on the land which the LORD swore to your ancestors he would give to them and their descendants, a land flowing with milk and honey. [10]The land you are to enter and possess is not like the land of Egypt from which you have come, where you would sow your seed and then water it by hand,* as in a vegetable garden. [11][e] No, the land into which you are crossing to take possession is a land of mountains and valleys that drinks in rain from the heavens, [12]a land which the LORD, your God, looks after; the eyes of the LORD, your God, are upon it continually through the year, from beginning to end.

[13]* [f] If, then, you truly listen to my commandments which I give you today, loving and serving the LORD, your God, with your whole heart and your whole being, [14]I will give the seasonal rain to your land, the early rain* and the late rain, that you may have your grain, wine and oil to gather in; [15]and I will bring forth grass in your fields for your animals. Thus you may eat and be satisfied. [16][g] But be careful lest your heart be so lured away that you serve other gods and bow down to them.[h] [17]For then the anger of the LORD will flare up against you and he will close up the heavens, so that no rain will fall, and the soil will not yield its crops, and you will soon perish from the good land the LORD is giving you.

***Need for Fidelity.*** [18][i] Therefore, take these words of mine into your heart and soul. Bind them on your arm as a sign, and let them be as a pendant on your forehead. [19]Teach them to your children, speaking of them when you are at home and when you are away, when you lie

**11:4 The Red Sea**: Hebrew *yam suph*, that is, "sea of reeds" or "reedy sea."

**11:10 By hand**: lit., "by foot," probably referring to a kind of mechanism for irrigation from the Nile.

**11:13–15** Here as elsewhere Moses shifts between speaking of the Lord in the third person and speaking for the Lord in the first person.

**11:14 The early rain**: the rains which begin in October or November and continue intermittently throughout the winter. **The late rain**: the heavy showers of March and April. In Palestine crops are sown in autumn and harvested in spring and summer.

*y:* Gn 26:5; 1 Kgs 2:3. *z:* Dt 4:9; 6:20–25. *a:* Dt 6:22; 7:18–19; 26:8; 29:1–2; 34:11; Ps 78:42–51. *b:* Ex 14:26–31; 15:1–10; Jos 24:6–7; Ps 78:53; 106:9–11. *c:* Nm 16:1–35; Ps 106:16–17. *d:* Dt 5:33; 6:1–3. *e:* Dt 8:7–10. *f:* Dt 7:12–14; 10:12–13; 28:1–14; Lv 26:3–5; Ps 104:14; Jer 5:24. *g:* Dt 4:25–27; 6:14–15; 28:15–68. *h:* Dt 5:6–10; 7:1–6; 13:2–19; 1 Kgs 8:35–36. *i:* Dt 6:6–9.

down and when you get up, [20]and write them on the doorposts of your houses and on your gates, [21]so that, as long as the heavens are above the earth, you and your children may live on in the land which the LORD swore to your ancestors he would give them.

[22][j] For if you are careful to observe this entire commandment I am giving you, loving the LORD, your God, following his ways exactly, and holding fast to him, [23]the LORD will dispossess all these nations before you, and you will dispossess nations greater and mightier than yourselves. [24][k] Every place where you set foot shall be yours: from the wilderness and the Lebanon, from the Euphrates River to the Western Sea,* shall be your territory. [25]None shall stand up against you; the LORD, your God, will spread the fear and dread of you through any land where you set foot, as he promised you.[l]

***Blessing and Curse.*** [26][m] See, I set before you this day a blessing and a curse: [27]a blessing for obeying the commandments of the LORD, your God, which I give you today; [28]a curse if you do not obey the commandments of the LORD, your God, but turn aside from the way I command you today, to go after other gods, whom you do not know.[n] [29]When the LORD, your God, brings you into the land which you are to enter and possess, then on Mount Gerizim you shall pronounce the blessing,[o] on Mount Ebal, the curse.* [30](These are beyond the Jordan, on the other side of the western road in the land of the Canaanites who live in the Arabah, opposite Gilgal beside the oak of Moreh.)[p] [31]Now you are about to cross the Jordan to enter and possess the land which the LORD, your God, is giving you. When, therefore, you take possession of it and settle there, [32]be careful to observe all the statutes and ordinances that I set before you today.

## B. The Deuteronomic Code

### CHAPTER 12

See RG 85–89

***One Center of Worship.*** [1]These are the statutes and ordinances which you must be careful to observe in the land which the LORD, the God of your ancestors, has given you to possess, throughout the time you live on its soil.[q] [2][r] Destroy entirely all the places where the nations you are to dispossess serve their gods, on the high mountains, on the hills, and under every green tree.[s] [3]Tear down their altars, smash their sacred pillars, burn up their asherahs, and chop down the idols of their gods, that you may destroy the very name of them from that place.

[4]That is not how you are to act toward the LORD, your God. [5]Instead,[t] you shall seek out the place which the LORD, your God, chooses out of all your tribes and designates as his dwelling to put his name there.* [u] There you shall go, [6]bringing your burnt offerings and sacrifices, your tithes and personal contributions, your votive and voluntary offerings, and the firstlings of your herds and flocks.[v] [7]There, too, in the presence of the LORD, your God, you and your families shall eat and rejoice in all your undertakings, in which the LORD, your God, has blessed you.[w]

[8]You shall not do as we are doing here to-

**11:24 The Western Sea**: the Mediterranean.

**11:29** For the full ceremony of blessing and curse, see chaps. 27–28. Gerizim and Ebal are mountains in Samaria, separated by a deep ravine.

**12:5 The place . . . to put his name there**: Moses thus designates Jerusalem (Mt. Zion), in accordance with the Deuteronomic doctrine that the Lord "chooses" Zion, as the place where eventually the Temple will be built, as he chooses the house of David to reign over Israel; see 2 Sm 7; 1 Kgs 8; Ps 132. But the Lord's presence in Jerusalem consists in putting his "name" there (12:11, 21; 14:23–24; 16:2, 6, 11; 26:2; 1 Kgs 8:44, 49; 9:3; 11:36; 14:21; 2 Kgs 17:34; 21:4, 7; 23:27). The Lord himself "cannot be contained" in an earthly dwelling (1 Kgs 8:27), but because he says of the Jerusalem Temple that "my name will be there" (1 Kgs 8:16, 29; 2 Kgs 23:27), he is present. This theology allows God in a way to dwell with Israel and at the same time preserves divine transcendence. See note on 1 Kgs 8:12–13.

*j:* Dt 7:1; 9:1–3; 10:12–13. *k:* Dt 1:7; Ex 23:31; Jos 1:3. *l:* Dt 2:25; 7:23–24; Ex 23:27. *m:* Dt 28:1–68; 30:1, 15–20; Lv 26:3–45. *n:* Dt 32:16–18. *o:* Dt 27:12–13; Jos 8:30–35. *p:* Gn 12:6; 35:4. *q:* Dt 4:44–45. *r:* Dt 5:7–10; Ex 20:24–26; 2 Kgs 18:3–6, 22; 23:4–9. *s:* Dt 7:5, 24–25; Ex 23:23–24; 34:11–14; Nm 33:51–52; Jgs 17:3–5; 1 Kgs 12:28–30; 14:22–24; 2 Kgs 16:4; 17:7–12; Jer 2:20; 3:6–10; Hos 4:12–13. *t:* Dt 12:11–12; 14:22–26; 15:19–20; 16:2, 6, 10–11, 14–15; 26:2. *u:* 2 Sm 7:13; 1 Kgs 8:16–21, 27–30. *v:* Dt 14:22–27; 15:19–23; 23:21–23; 26:12–15; Lv 1:3–17; 3:1–17; 6:2–6; 7:29–36; 27:1–8; Nm 15:18–21; 28:2–8; 30:2–15; Am 4:4–5; 5:22. *w:* Dt 12:12, 18–19; 14:26–27; 15:20; 16:11, 14; 26:11.

**Worship at a Central Sanctuary**

HAVING A CENTRAL place for sacrifice is Deuteronomy's most distinctive demand. Sacrificial worship was to take place only at a single, central sanctuary and at a location to be chosen by the LORD (Dt 12:5, 11, 14, 18, 26). Earlier practice had permitted sacrifice at many local altars scattered around the country (Ex 20:24). Deuteronomy never identifies the site of this central sanctuary because at the time Moses was supposedly speaking, the conquest of the land, and particularly of Jerusalem, had not yet taken place. This radical reform of centralized worship was imposed on Judah by King Josiah, who considered Jerusalem to be the LORD's chosen place (2 Kgs 23:4–20).

day, everyone doing what is right in their
own sight,[x] 9since you have not yet reached
your resting place, the heritage which the
LORD, your God, is giving you. 10But after
you have crossed the Jordan and dwell in the
land which the LORD, your God, is giving
you as a heritage, when he has given you rest
from all your enemies round about and you
live there in security,[y] 11* [z] then to the place
which the LORD, your God, chooses as the
dwelling place for his name you shall bring
all that I command you: your burnt offerings
and sacrifices, your tithes and personal contributions, and every special offering you
have vowed to the LORD. 12You shall rejoice
in the presence of the LORD, your God, with
your sons and daughters, your male and female slaves, as well as with the Levite
within your gates, who has no hereditary
portion with you.

13[a] Be careful not to sacrifice your burnt
offerings in any place you like, 14but offer
them in the place which the LORD chooses in
one of your tribal territories; there you shall
do what I command you.

***Profane and Sacred Slaughter.*** 15* However, in any of your communities you may
slaughter and eat meat freely, according to
the blessing that the LORD, your God, has
given you; the unclean as well as the clean
may eat it, as they do the gazelle or the deer.[b]
16* Only, you shall not eat of the blood, but
must pour it out on the ground like water.[c]
17Moreover, you may not, in your own communities, partake of your tithe of grain or
wine or oil, of the firstborn of your herd or
flock, of any offering you have vowed, of
your voluntary offerings, or of your personal
contributions. 18These you must eat in the
presence of the LORD, your God, in the place
that the LORD, your God, chooses, along
with your son and daughter, your male and
female slave, and the Levite within your
gates; and there, in the presence of the LORD,
you shall rejoice in all your undertakings.
19Be careful, also, that you do not neglect the
Levite as long as you live in your land.[d]

20[e] After the LORD, your God, has enlarged
your territory, as he promised you,[f] and you
think, "I will eat meat," as it is your desire to
eat meat, you may eat it freely; 21and if the
place where the LORD, your God, chooses to
put his name is too far, you may slaughter in
the manner I have commanded you any of
your herd or flock that the LORD has given
you, and eat it freely in your own community.
22You may eat it as you would the gazelle or
the deer: the unclean and the clean eating it
together. 23[g] But make sure that you do not
eat of the blood; for blood is life; you shall
not eat that life with the flesh. 24Do not eat of
the blood, therefore, but pour it out on the

**12:11** Sacrifice is to be confined to the single place that the Lord has chosen; eventually this was Jerusalem.

**12:15** At this point a distinction is being made between cultic sacrifice and slaughter of animals for food. **In any of your communities**: lit., "within your gates."

**12:16** The blood was understood to be the source or vehicle of life and so was not to be consumed. Cf. Gn 9:4.

*x:* Dt 6:18; 12:28; Jgs 17:6; 21:25. *y:* Dt 3:18–20; 11:22–25; Jos 23:1; 2 Sm 7:1; 1 Kgs 5:17–18; 8:56. *z:* Dt 12:5–7; 14:22–26; 15:19–20; 16:2, 6, 10–11, 14–15; 26:2. *a:* Jos 22:10–34. *b:* Dt 12:20–22; 15:22; Lv 7:19–21. *c:* Dt 12:23–27; 15:23; Gn 9:4; Lv 3:17; 17:10–14; 19:26; 1 Sm 14:31–35. *d:* Dt 14:27. *e:* Lv 17:3–9. *f:* Dt 19:8; Gn 28:14; Ex 34:24. *g:* Dt 12:16; 15:23; Gn 9:4; Lv 3:17; 17:10–14; 19:26; 1 Sm 14:31–35.

ground like water. 25 Do not eat of it, that you and your children after you may prosper for doing what is right in the sight of the LORD. 26 However, any sacred gifts or votive offerings that you may have, you shall bring with you to the place which the LORD chooses, 27 and there you must sacrifice your burnt offerings, both the flesh and the blood, on the altar of the LORD, your God; of your other sacrifices the blood indeed must be poured out against the altar of the LORD, your God,[h] but their flesh you may eat.

28 Be careful to heed all these words I command you today, that you and your descendants after you may forever prosper for doing what is good and right in the sight of the LORD, your God.[i]

***Warning Against Abominable Practices.*** 29[j] When the LORD, your God, cuts down from before you the nations you are going in to dispossess, and you have dispossessed them and are settled in their land, 30 be careful that you not be trapped into following them after they have been destroyed before you. Do not inquire regarding their gods, "How did these nations serve their gods, so I might do the same." 31 You shall not worship the LORD, your God, that way, because they offered to their gods every abomination that the LORD detests, even burning their sons and daughters to their gods.[k]

## CHAPTER 13

See RG 85-89

***Penalties for Enticing to Idolatry.*** 1 Every word that I command you, you shall be careful to observe, neither adding to it nor subtracting from it.

2[l] If there arises in your midst a prophet or a dreamer* who promises you a sign or wonder, 3 saying, "Let us go after other gods," whom you have not known, "and let us serve them," and the sign or wonder foretold to you comes to pass, 4 do not listen to the words of that prophet or that dreamer; for the LORD, your God, is testing you to know whether you really love the LORD, your God, with all your heart and soul.[m] 5 The LORD, your God, shall you follow, and him shall you fear; his commandments shall you observe, and to his voice shall you listen; him you shall serve, and to him you shall hold fast.[n] 6 But that prophet or that dreamer shall be put to death, because, in order to lead you astray from the way which the LORD, your God, has commanded you to take, the prophet or dreamer has spoken apostasy against the LORD, your God, who brought you out of the land of Egypt and redeemed you from the house of slavery. Thus shall you purge the evil from your midst.[o]

7 If your brother, your father's child or your mother's child, your son or daughter, your beloved spouse, or your intimate friend entices you secretly, saying, "Come, let us serve other gods," whom you and your ancestors have not known, 8 any of the gods of the surrounding peoples, near to you or far away, from one end of the earth to the other: 9 do not yield or listen to any such person; show no pity or compassion and do not shield such a one,[p] 10[q] but kill that person. Your hand shall be the first raised to put such a one to death; the hand of all the people shall follow. 11 You shall stone that person to death, for seeking to lead you astray from the LORD, your God, who brought you out of the land of Egypt, out of the house of slavery. 12 And all Israel shall hear of it and fear, and never again do such evil as this in your midst.[r]

13 If you hear it said concerning one of the cities which the LORD, your God, gives you to dwell in, 14 that certain scoundrels have sprung up in your midst and have led astray the inhabitants of their city, saying, "Come, let us serve other gods," whom you have not known, 15 you must inquire carefully into the matter and investigate it thoroughly. If you find that it is true and an established fact that

**13:2, 4, 6 Dreamer**: a false prophet who pretended to have received revelations from God in a dream; cf. Jer 23:25–32; 27:9; Zec 10:2. But dreams could also be a means of true prophecy (Nm 12:6; Jl 3:1) and of genuine revelations (Gn 20:3, 6; 31:11, 24; 37:5, 9; Mt 1:20; 2:12, 13, 19; etc.).

*h:* Lv 17:11. *i:* Dt 4:40; 5:29; 6:2–3, 17–18; 12:25. *j:* Dt 7:1–5, 25; Ex 23:33; 34:12; Jgs 2:2–3. *k:* Dt 18:10; Lv 18:21; 20:2–5; 2 Kgs 3:27; 16:3; 21:6; 23:10; Jer 7:31; 19:5. *l:* Dt 6:4, 14–15; 17:2–7. *m:* Dt 8:2, 16. *n:* Dt 6:4–5; 10:20; 11:22. *o:* Dt 17:7, 12; 19:19; 21:21; 22:21–22, 24; 24:7; Jer 28:16; 29:32. *p:* Dt 7:16; 19:13, 21; 25:12. *q:* Dt 17:5–7; 21:21; 22:20–24; Jos 7:25–26; 1 Kgs 21:13–14. *r:* Dt 17:13; 21:21.

**Ritual Purity**

ISRAEL'S PURITY SYSTEM categorized persons, objects, and foods (14:3–21). It had nothing to do with modern notions of hygiene. Those who ate unclean food became ritually unclean. They were excluded from social contact and the worship assembly until their impurity was removed. A similar list of clean and unclean animals is given in Leviticus 11.

this abomination has been committed in your midst,[s] [16t] you shall put the inhabitants of that city to the sword, placing the city and all that is in it, even its livestock, under the ban. [17]Having heaped up all its spoils in the middle of its square, you shall burn the city with all its spoils as a whole burnt offering to the LORD, your God. Let it be a heap of ruins forever, never to be rebuilt. [18]You shall not hold on to anything that is under the ban; then the LORD will turn from his burning anger and show you mercy, and in showing you mercy multiply you as he swore to your ancestors, [19]because you have listened to the voice of the LORD, your God, keeping all his commandments, which I give you today, doing what is right in the sight of the LORD, your God.

## CHAPTER 14

See RG 85–89

***Improper Mourning Rites.*** [1]You are children of the LORD, your God. You shall not gash yourselves nor shave the hair above your foreheads for the dead.[u] [2]For you are a people holy to the LORD, your God; the LORD, your God, has chosen you from all the peoples on the face of the earth to be a people specially his own.[v]

***Clean and Unclean Animals.*** [3]You shall not eat any abominable thing.[w] [4x] These are the animals you may eat: the ox, the sheep, the goat, [5]the deer, the gazelle, the roebuck, the wild goat, the ibex, the antelope, and the mountain sheep. [6]Any among the animals that has divided hooves, with the foot cloven in two, and that chews the cud you may eat. [7]But you shall not eat any of the following that chew the cud or have cloven hooves: the camel, the hare, and the rock badger, which indeed chew the cud, but do not have divided hooves; they are unclean for you. [8]And the pig, which indeed has divided hooves, with cloven foot, but does not chew the cud, is unclean for you. Their flesh you shall not eat, and their dead bodies you shall not touch.

[9]These you may eat, of all that live in the water: whatever has both fins and scales you may eat, [10]but all those that lack either fins or scales you shall not eat; they are unclean for you.

[11]You may eat all clean birds. [12*] But you shall not eat any of the following: the griffon vulture, the bearded vulture, the black vulture, [13]the various kites and falcons, [14]all kinds of crows, [15]the eagle owl, the kestrel, the long-eared owl, all species of hawks, [16]the little owl, the screech owl, the barn owl, [17]the horned owl, the osprey, the cormorant, [18]the stork, any kind of heron, the hoopoe, and the bat. [19*] All winged insects are also unclean for you and shall not be eaten. [20]Any clean winged creatures you may eat.

[21]You shall not eat the carcass of any animal that has died of itself; but you may give it to a resident alien within your gates to eat, or you may sell it to a foreigner. For you are a people holy to the LORD, your God.[y]

You shall not boil a young goat in its mother's milk.*

***Tithes.*** [22]Each year you shall tithe all the

**14:12–18** The identification of several of the birds in these verses is uncertain.

**14:19–20** Lv 11:20–23 suggests that the unclean winged insects are those that walk on the ground; the clean winged creatures are those that leap on the ground, such as certain species of locusts.

**14:21 Boil a young goat in its mother's milk**: the meaning of this regulation is obscure but it may have a humane concern similar to the prohibitions against slaughtering an animal and its young on the same day (Lv 22:27–28) and capturing a mother bird along with her fledgling or eggs (Dt 22:6–7). See note on Ex 23:19.

*s:* Dt 17:4; 19:18. *t:* Dt 20:16–18; Jos 6:17, 24; 7:25–26; 8:28. *u:* Dt 32:5–6, 18–20; Lv 19:27–28; 21:5; Ps 103:13; Is 1:2, 4; 30:1; Jer 3:14, 19, 22; 16:6; 31:9, 20; 41:4–5; Hos 2:1; 11:1–4. *v:* Dt 7:6; Ex 19:5–6. *w:* Acts 10:14. *x:* Lv 11:2–23. *y:* Ex 22:30; 23:19; 34:26; Lv 17:15; 22:8; Ez 44:31.

### Feeding the Disadvantaged

ONE OUT OF every three years, the tithe law is shifted away from the central sanctuary to focus on the needs of the disadvantaged and the marginalized in the local community, to ensure they too may eat their fill (14:29).

produce of your seed that grows in the field;[z]
23 then in the place which the LORD, your
God, chooses as the dwelling place of his
name[a] you shall eat in his presence the tithe
of your grain, wine and oil, as well as the
firstlings of your herd and flock, that you
may learn always to fear the LORD, your
God. 24[b] But if, when the LORD, your God,
blesses you, the journey is too much for you
and you are not able to bring your tithe, because the place which the LORD, your God,
chooses to put his name is too far for you,
25 you may exchange the tithe for money, and
with the money securely in hand, go to the
place which the LORD, your God, chooses.
26 You may then exchange the money for
whatever you desire, oxen or sheep, wine or
beer, or anything else you want, and there in
the presence of the LORD, your God, you
shall consume it and rejoice, you and your
household together.[c] 27 But do not neglect the
Levite within your gates, for he has no
hereditary portion with you.[d]
28[e] At the end of every third year you shall
bring out all the tithes of your produce for
that year and deposit them within your own
communities, 29 that the Levite who has no
hereditary portion with you, and also the resident alien, the orphan and the widow within
your gates, may come and eat and be satisfied; so that the LORD, your God, may bless
you in all that you undertake.

See RG 85–89

## CHAPTER 15

*Debts and the Poor.* 1 At the end of
every seven-year period* you shall have a remission of debts,[f] 2 and this is the manner of
the remission. Creditors shall remit all
claims on loans made to a neighbor, not
pressing the neighbor, one who is kin, because the LORD's remission has been proclaimed. 3 You may press a foreigner, but you
shall remit the claim on what your kin owes
to you.[g] 4[h] However, since the LORD, your
God, will bless you abundantly in the land
the LORD, your God, will give you to possess
as a heritage, there shall be no one of you in
need 5 if you but listen to the voice of the
LORD, your God, and carefully observe this
entire commandment which I enjoin on you
today. 6 Since the LORD, your God, will bless
you as he promised, you will lend to many
nations, and borrow from none;[i] you will
rule over many nations, and none will rule
over you.
7[j] If one of your kindred is in need in any
community in the land which the LORD, your
God, is giving you, you shall not harden your
heart nor close your hand against your kin
who is in need. 8 Instead, you shall freely open
your hand and generously lend what suffices
to meet that need.[k] 9 Be careful not to entertain
the mean thought, "The seventh year, the year
of remission, is near," so that you would begrudge your kin who is in need and give nothing, and your kin would cry to the LORD
against you and you would be held guilty.[l]
10 When you give, give generously and not
with a stingy heart; for that, the LORD, your
God, will bless you in all your works and undertakings. 11 The land will never lack for
needy persons; that is why I command you:

**15:1 At the end of every seven-year period**: in every seventh, or sabbatical, year. Cf. 15:9; 31:10; and compare Jer 34:14 with Dt 15:12. **A remission of debts**: it is debated whether a full cancellation of debts is meant, or merely a suspension of payment on them or on their interest, but the former is more likely. Cf. Ex 23:11 where the same Hebrew root is used of a field that is "let lie fallow" in the sabbatical year.

*z:* Gn 14:20; 28:22; Lv 27:30–33; Nm 18:21–32; 1 Sm 8:15, 17; 2 Chr 31:2–19; Neh 12:44; Am 4:4. *a:* Dt 12:5–7, 11–12, 17–18; 15:19–20. *b:* Mk 11:15; Jn 2:13–14. *c:* Dt 12:7. *d:* Dt 12:12, 19. *e:* Dt 26:12–15. *f:* Dt 31:10; Lv 25:1–55; Neh 10:31. *g:* Dt 23:20. *h:* Dt 7:12–14; 28:1–14. *i:* Dt 28:12. *j:* Ex 22:25. *k:* Dt 24:19; Lv 25:35; Ps 37:21–22; Prv 19:17; Sir 29:1–2; Mt 5:42. *l:* Dt 24:15; Ex 22:23–24, 27.

"Open your hand freely to your poor and to your needy kin in your land."[m]

***Hebrew Slaves.*** 12[n] If your kin, a Hebrew man or woman, sells himself or herself to you, he or she is to serve you for six years, but in the seventh year you shall release him or her as a free person. 13[o] When you release a male from your service, as a free person, you shall not send him away empty-handed, 14 but shall weigh him down with gifts from your flock and threshing floor and wine press; as the LORD, your God, has blessed you, so you shall give to him. 15 For remember that you too were slaves in the land of Egypt, and the LORD, your God, redeemed you. That is why I am giving you this command today.[p] 16[q] But if he says to you, "I do not wish to leave you," because he loves you and your household, since he is well off with you, 17 you shall take an awl and put it through his ear* into the door, and he shall be your slave forever. Your female slave, also, you shall treat in the same way. 18 Do not be reluctant when you let them go free, since the service they have given you for six years was worth twice a hired laborer's salary; and the LORD, your God, will bless you in everything you do.

***Firstlings.*** 19[r] You shall consecrate to the LORD, your God, every male firstling born in your herd and in your flock. You shall not work the firstlings of your cattle, nor shear the firstlings of your flock. 20 In the presence of the LORD, your God, you shall eat them year after year, you and your household, in the place that the LORD will choose.[s] 21[t] But if a firstling has any defect, lameness or blindness, any such serious defect, you shall not sacrifice it to the LORD, your God, 22 but in your own communities you may eat it, the unclean and the clean eating it together, as you would a gazelle or a deer. 23 Only, you must not eat of its blood; you shall pour it out on the ground like water.

## CHAPTER 16

See RG 85–89

***Feast of the Passover.*** 1 Observe the month of Abib* by keeping the Passover of the LORD, your God,[u] since it was in the month of Abib that the LORD, your God, brought you out of Egypt by night. 2 You shall offer the Passover sacrifice from your flock and your herd to the LORD, your God, in the place the LORD will choose as the dwelling place of his name.[v] 3[w] You shall not eat leavened bread with it. For seven days you shall eat with it only unleavened bread, the bread of affliction, so that you may remember as long as you live the day you left the land of Egypt; for in hurried flight you left the land of Egypt. 4 No leaven is to be found with you in all your territory for seven days, and none of the meat which you sacrificed on the evening of the first day shall be kept overnight for the next day.

5 You may not sacrifice the Passover in any of the communities which the LORD, your God, gives you; 6 only at the place which the LORD, your God, will choose as the dwelling place of his name, and in the evening at sunset, at the very time when you left Egypt, shall you sacrifice the Passover.[x] 7 You shall cook and eat it at the place the LORD, your God, will choose; then in the morning you may return to your tents. 8 For six days you shall eat unleavened bread, and on the seventh day there shall be a solemn assembly for the LORD, your God; on that day you shall do no work.[y]

***Feast of Weeks.*** 9[z] You shall count off seven weeks; begin to count the seven weeks from the day when the sickle is first put to the standing grain. 10 You shall then keep the feast of Weeks* for the LORD, your God, and the

**15:17 His ear**: cf. Ex 21:6 and note there.

**16:1 Abib**: "ear of grain, ripe grain," the name of the month in which the barley harvest fell, corresponding to our March and April; at a later period this month received the Babylonian name of "Nisan."

**16:10 Feast of Weeks**: a celebration of the grain harvest, later known as "Pentecost"; cf. Acts 2:1.

*m:* Dt 15:8; Mt 26:11. *n:* Ex 21:2–11; Jer 34:8–22. *o:* Ex 3:21–22; 12:35–36. *p:* Dt 5:15; 10:19; 16:12; 24:18, 22. *q:* Ex 21:5–6. *r:* Ex 13:2, 11–16; 22:29–30; 34:19–20; Lv 22:27; 27:26; Nm 18:15–18. *s:* Dt 12:6–7, 17–18; 14:23. *t:* Dt 12:15–16, 22–24; 17:1; Lv 22:17–25; Mal 1:8. *u:* Ex 12:2–13:10; 23:15; 34:18; Lv 23:5–8; Nm 28:16–25; Jos 5:10–12; 2 Kgs 23:21–23; 2 Chr 30:1–27; 35:1–19; Ez 45:21–24. *v:* Dt 12:5, 11; 16:6. *w:* Ex 12:34, 39; 13:6–7; 34:18. *x:* Dt 12:5, 11; 16:2. *y:* Ex 13:6; Lv 23:36; Nm 29:35; Is 1:13; Am 5:21. *z:* Ex 23:16; 34:22; Lv 23:15–21; Nm 28:26–31.

measure of your own voluntary offering which you will give shall be in proportion to the blessing the LORD, your God, has given you. 11 You shall rejoice in the presence of the LORD, your God, together with your son and daughter, your male and female slave, and the Levite within your gates, as well as the resident alien, the orphan, and the widow among you, in the place which the LORD, your God, will choose as the dwelling place of his name.[a] 12 Remember that you too were slaves in Egypt, so carry out these statutes carefully.

***Feast of Booths.*** 13[b] You shall celebrate the feast of Booths* for seven days, when you have gathered in the produce from your threshing floor and wine press. 14 You shall rejoice at your feast,[c] together with your son and daughter, your male and female slave, and also the Levite, the resident alien, the orphan and the widow within your gates. 15 For seven days you shall celebrate this feast for the LORD, your God, in the place which the LORD will choose; since the LORD, your God, has blessed you in all your crops and in all your undertakings, you will be full of joy.

16 Three times a year,[d] then, all your males shall appear before the LORD, your God, in the place which he will choose: at the feast of Unleavened Bread, at the feast of Weeks, and at the feast of Booths. They shall not appear before the LORD empty-handed, 17 but each with his own gift, in proportion to the blessing which the LORD, your God, has given to you.

***Justice.*** 18[e] In all the communities which the LORD, your God, is giving you, you shall appoint judges and officials throughout your tribes to administer true justice for the people. 19 You must not distort justice: you shall not show partiality;[f] you shall not take a bribe, for a bribe blinds the eyes even of the wise and twists the words even of the just. 20 Justice, justice alone shall you pursue, so that you may live and possess the land the LORD, your God, is giving you.

***Illicit Worship.*** 21[g] You shall not plant an asherah* of any kind of wood next to the altar of the LORD, your God, which you will build;[h] 22 nor shall you erect a sacred pillar, such as the LORD, your God, hates.

## CHAPTER 17

See RG 85–89

1 You shall not sacrifice to the LORD, your God, an ox or a sheep with any serious defect;[i] that would be an abomination to the LORD, your God.

2[j] If there is found in your midst, in any one of the communities which the LORD, your God, gives you, a man or a woman who does evil in the sight of the LORD, your God, and transgresses his covenant,[k] 3 by going to serve other gods, by bowing down to them, to the sun or the moon or any of the host of heaven, contrary to my command;[l] 4 and if you are told or hear of it, you must investigate it thoroughly. If the truth of the matter is established that this abomination has been committed in Israel, 5 you shall bring the man or the woman who has done this evil deed out to your gates* and stone the man or the woman to death. 6 Only on the testimony of two or three witnesses shall a person be put to death;[m] no one shall be put to death on the testimony of only one witness. 7 The hands of the witnesses shall be the first raised to put the person to death, and afterward the hands of all the people.[n] Thus shall you purge the evil from your midst.

***Judges.*** 8[o] If there is a case for judgment which proves too baffling for you to decide,

**16:13 Feast of Booths**: also called Tabernacles; a harvest festival at the end of the agricultural year. In later times, during the seven days of the feast the Israelites camped in booths made of branches erected on the roofs of their houses or in the streets in commemoration of their wanderings in the wilderness, where they dwelt in such temporary shelters.

**16:21–22 Asherah . . . sacred pillar**: see note on 7:5; Ex 34:13.

**17:5 Out to your gates**: outside the gates, so as not to defile the city; cf. Lv 24:14; Nm 15:36; Acts 7:58; Heb 13:12.

---

*a:* Dt 12:5–7, 11–12, 18. *b:* Dt 31:10–13; Ex 23:16; 34:22; Lv 23:34–43; Nm 29:12–38; 1 Kgs 8:2, 62–66; Ezr 3:4; Neh 8:14; Ez 45:25. *c:* Dt 16:11. *d:* Dt 12:7; 16:11, 14; Ex 23:14–15, 17; 34:23–24; 2 Chr 8:13. *e:* Dt 1:13–17; 17:8–13; 19:17; 21:5; Ex 18:13–26; 2 Chr 19:5–11. *f:* Dt 1:16–17; 10:17–18; Ex 23:2–3, 6–8; Lv 19:15; Prv 17:23; 18:5; 24:23; Is 1:23; Mi 7:3; Jn 7:24; Jas 2:9. *g:* Dt 5:7–10; 6:4–5; 12:29–14:2. *h:* Dt 7:5; Ex 34:13; 1 Kgs 14:15; 2 Kgs 23:6, 15; 2 Chr 33:3. *i:* Lv 22:20. *j:* Dt 13:2–19. *k:* Jos 7:11, 15; 23:16; Jgs 2:20; 2 Kgs 18:12; Jer 34:18; Hos 6:7; 8:1. *l:* Dt 4:19; 2 Kgs 17:16; 21:3; 23:5; Jer 8:2; Ez 8:16. *m:* Dt 19:15; Nm 35:30; Jn 8:17; 2 Cor 13:1. *n:* Dt 13:6, 10. *o:* Ex 18:13–26.

**Solomon's Offenses**

THE OFFENSES SPECIFIED in Dt 17:16–18, allude to the warnings against royal autocracy outlined in the very founding of the monarchy (1 Sm 8:10–18). They almost certainly presuppose Solomon's trade in horses (1 Kgs 10:26–29) and his multiple marital alliances with foreign wives (1 Kgs 11:1–8). Here, the author understood those marriages to lead to the corruption of Israelite religion, with the breakup of the united monarchy the divine punishment for these transgressions (1 Kgs 11:9–13).

in a matter of bloodshed or of law or of injury, matters of dispute within your gates, you shall then go up to the place which the LORD, your God, will choose, [9]to the levitical priests or to the judge who is in office at that time. They shall investigate the case and then announce to you the decision.[p] [10]You shall act according to the decision they announce to you in the place which the LORD will choose, carefully observing everything as they instruct you. [11]You shall carry out the instruction they give you and the judgment they pronounce, without turning aside either to the right or left from the decision they announce to you. [12]Anyone who acts presumptuously and does not obey the priest* who officiates there in the ministry of the LORD, your God, or the judge, shall die. Thus shall you purge the evil from Israel. [13]And all the people, on hearing of it, shall fear, and will never again act presumptuously.[q]

***The King.*** [14r] When you have come into the land which the LORD, your God, is giving you, and have taken possession of it and settled in it, should you then decide, "I will set a king over me, like all the surrounding nations,"[s] [15]you may indeed set over you a king whom the LORD, your God, will choose.[t] Someone from among your own kindred you may set over you as king; you may not set over you a foreigner, who is no kin of yours. [16*] But he shall not have a great number of horses; nor shall he make his people go back again to Egypt to acquire many horses, for the LORD said to you, Do not go back that way again.[u] [17]Neither shall he have a great number of wives, lest his heart turn away,[v] nor shall he accumulate a vast amount of silver and gold. [18]When he is sitting upon his royal throne, he shall write a copy of this law* upon a scroll from the one that is in the custody of the levitical priests.[w] [19* x] It shall remain with him and he shall read it as long as he lives, so that he may learn to fear the LORD, his God, and to observe carefully all the words of this law and these statutes, [20]so that he does not exalt himself over his kindred or turn aside from this commandment to the right or to the left, and so that he and his descendants may reign long in Israel.

## CHAPTER 18

See RG 85–89

***Priests.*** [1]The levitical priests, the whole tribe of Levi, shall have no hereditary portion with Israel; they shall eat the fire offerings of the LORD and the portions due to him.[y] [2]They shall have no heritage among

**17:12 The priest**: the high priest; **the judge**: a layman. The court system here, involving lay and priestly officials, resembles the one whose establishment is attributed to King Jehoshaphat in 2 Chr 19:8–11 (cf. Ex 18:17–23 and Dt 1:17).

**17:16–17** This restriction on royal acquisitions may have in mind the excesses of Solomon's reign mentioned in 1 Kgs 10:1–11:6. **Horses**: chariotry for war. Egypt engaged in horse trading, and the danger envisioned here is that some king might make Israel a vassal of Egypt for military aid.

**17:18 A copy of this law**: the source of the name Deuteronomy, which in Hebrew is literally "double" or "copy"; in the Septuagint translated as *deuteronomion*, literally "a second law." In Jerome's Latin Vulgate as *deuteronium*.

**17:19** The only positive requirement imposed upon the king is strict adherence to the Mosaic or Deuteronomic law. In that respect, the king's primary task was to be a model Israelite.

*p:* Dt 21:5; 2 Chr 19:8; Ezr 7:25. *q:* Dt 13:12. *r:* 1 Sm 10–25. *s:* Dt 26:1; 1 Sm 8:5, 19–20. *t:* 1 Sm 9:16; 10:24; 16:1–13; 1 Kgs 19:15–16; 2 Kgs 9:1–13. *u:* Dt 28:68; 1 Sm 8:10–12; 1 Kgs 4:26; 10:26–29; Is 2:7. *v:* 1 Kgs 10:10–25; 11:1–8; Neh 13:26; Is 2:7. *w:* Dt 31:9, 24–26; Jos 8:32. *x:* Dt 5:32–6:3; 2 Sm 7:12–16; 1 Kgs 2:4; Ps 132:11–18. *y:* Nm 18:8–9, 20–24; Jos 13:14; 18:7; 2 Chr 31:2–19; 1 Cor 9:13.

their kindred; the LORD himself is their heritage, as he has told them.[z] 3This shall be the due of the priests from the people: those who are offering a sacrifice, whether an ox or a sheep, shall give the priest the shoulder, the jowls and the stomach. 4The first fruits of your grain, your wine, and your oil,[a] as well as the first shearing of your flock, you shall also give him. 5For the LORD, your God, has chosen him out of all your tribes to be in attendance to minister in the name of the LORD, him and his descendants for all time.[b]

6When a Levite goes from one of your communities anywhere in Israel in which he has been residing, to visit, as his heart may desire, the place which the LORD will choose, 7and ministers there in the name of the LORD, his God, like all his fellow Levites who stand before the LORD there, 8he shall receive the same portions to eat, along with his stipends and patrimony.*

***Prophets.*** 9When you come into the land which the LORD, your God, is giving you, you shall not learn to imitate the abominations of the nations there.[c] 10[d] Let there not be found among you anyone who causes their son or daughter to pass through the fire,* or practices divination, or is a soothsayer, augur, or sorcerer, 11or who casts spells, consults ghosts and spirits, or seeks oracles from the dead. 12Anyone who does such things is an abomination to the LORD, and because of such abominations the LORD, your God, is dispossessing them before you.[e] 13You must be altogether sincere with the LORD, your God. 14Although these nations whom you are about to dispossess listen to their soothsayers and diviners, the LORD, your God, will not permit you to do so.

15A prophet like me* will the LORD, your God, raise up for you from among your own kindred; that is the one to whom you shall listen.[f] 16This is exactly what you requested of the LORD, your God, at Horeb on the day of the assembly, when you said, "Let me not again hear the voice of the LORD, my God, nor see this great fire any more, or I will die."[g] 17And the LORD said to me, What they have said is good. 18I will raise up for them a prophet like you from among their kindred, and will put my words into the mouth of the prophet; the prophet shall tell them all that I command.[h] 19Anyone who will not listen to my words which the prophet speaks in my name, I myself will hold accountable for it.[i] 20But if a prophet presumes to speak a word in my name[j] that I have not commanded, or speaks in the name of other gods, that prophet shall die.

21Should you say to yourselves, "How can we recognize that a word is one the LORD has not spoken?", 22if a prophet speaks in the name of the LORD but the word does not come true, it is a word the LORD did not speak. The prophet has spoken it presumptuously; do not fear him.

## CHAPTER 19

See RG 85-89

***Cities of Refuge.*** 1[k] When the LORD, your God, cuts down the nations whose land the LORD, your God, is giving you, and you have dispossessed them and settled in their cities and houses,[l] 2you shall set apart three cities* in the land the LORD, your God, is

**18:8 His stipends and patrimony**: meaning of the Hebrew is uncertain.

**18:10–11 Causes their son or daughter to pass through the fire**: to Molech. See note on Lv 18:21. Such human sacrifices are classed here with various occult and magical practices because they were believed to possess powers for averting a calamity; cf. 2 Kgs 3:27. Three other categories of magic are listed here: divination of the future (by a soothsayer or augur); black magic (by a sorcerer or one who casts spells); and necromancy (by one who consults ghosts and spirits, or seeks oracles from the dead to divine the future).

**18:15 A prophet like me**: from the context (opposition to the practices described in vv. 10–11) it seems that Moses is referring in general to all the true prophets who were to succeed him. This passage came to be understood in a quasi-Messianic sense in the New Testament (Mt 17:5; Jn 6:14; 7:40; Acts 3:22; 7:37).

**19:2 Set apart three cities**: the Israelites were to have at least six cities of refuge, three in the land east of the Jordan and three in the land of Canaan west of the Jordan (Nm 35:9–34); but since the three cities east of the Jordan had now

*z:* Nm 18:20; Jos 13:33. *a:* Dt 26:1–11; Nm 18:12; 2 Chr 31:5; Neh 13:10–13. *b:* Dt 10:8; Jer 33:18. *c:* Dt 12:29–31; Lv 18:24–30. *d:* Dt 12:31; Ex 22:18; Lv 18:21; 19:31; 20:6, 27; 1 Sm 28:7–19; 2 Kgs 17:17; 21:6; 23:10, 24; Is 8:19–20; Ez 21:21. *e:* Dt 9:4. *f:* Mt 17:5; Mk 9:7; Lk 9:35; Jn 1:45; 6:14; 7:40; Acts 3:22; 7:37. *g:* Ex 20:19. *h:* Ex 4:10–16; Jer 1:9; 15:19; Ez 3:1–4. *i:* Jer 11:21–23; Am 7:10–17; Acts 3:23. *j:* Dt 13:2–6; 1 Kgs 22:1–40; Jer 14:13–16; 23:9–40; 28:1–17; Ez 13:1–23. *k:* Dt 4:41–43; Ex 21:12–14; Nm 35:9–34; Jos 20:1–9. *l:* Dt 6:10–11; 12:29.

giving you to possess. [3]You shall measure the distances and divide into three regions the land of which the LORD, your God, is giving you possession, so that every homicide will be able to find a refuge.

[4]This is the case of a homicide who may take refuge there and live: when someone strikes down a neighbor unintentionally and not out of previous hatred. [5]For example, if someone goes with a neighbor to a forest to cut wood, wielding an ax to cut down a tree, and its head flies off the handle and hits the neighbor a mortal blow, such a person may take refuge in one of these cities and live. [6]Should the distance be too great, the avenger of blood* might in hot anger pursue, overtake, and strike the killer dead, even though that one does not deserve the death penalty since there had been no previous hatred; [7]for this reason I command you: Set apart three cities.

[8][m] But if the LORD, your God, enlarges your territory, as he swore to your ancestors, and gives you all the land he promised your ancestors he would give, [9]because you carefully observe this whole commandment which I give you today, loving the LORD, your God, and ever walking in his ways, then add three more cities to these three. [10]Thus, in the land which the LORD, your God, is giving you as a heritage, innocent blood will not be shed and you will not become guilty of bloodshed.[n]

[11]However, if someone, hating a neighbor, lies in wait, attacks, and strikes the neighbor dead, and then flees to one of these cities, [12]the elders of the killer's own city shall send and have the killer taken from there, to be handed over to the avenger of blood and slain. [13]Do not show pity, but purge from Israel the innocent blood, so that it may go well with you.[o]

***Removal of Landmarks.*** [14]You shall not move your neighbor's boundary markers* erected by your forebears in the heritage that will be allotted to you in the land the LORD, your God, is giving you to possess.[p]

***False Witnesses.*** [15][q] One witness alone shall not stand against someone in regard to any crime or any offense that may have been committed; a charge shall stand only on the testimony of two or three witnesses.[r]

[16]If a hostile witness rises against someone to accuse that person of wrongdoing, [17]the two parties in the dispute shall appear in the presence of the LORD, in the presence of the priests and judges in office at that time,[s] [18][t] and the judges must investigate it thoroughly. If the witness is a false witness and has falsely accused the other,[u] [19]you shall do to the false witness just as that false witness planned to do to the other. Thus shall you purge the evil from your midst. [20]The rest shall hear and be afraid, and never again do such an evil thing as this in your midst.[v] [21]Do not show pity. Life for life,* eye for eye, tooth for tooth, hand for hand, and foot for foot![w]

## CHAPTER 20

See RG 85–89

***Courage in War.*** [1]When you go out to war against your enemies and you see horses and chariots and an army greater than your own, you shall not be afraid of them, for the LORD, your God, who brought you up from the land of Egypt, will be with you.

[2]When you are drawing near to battle, the priest shall come forward and speak to the army, [3]and say to them, "Hear, O Israel! Today you are drawing near for battle against your enemies. Do not be weakhearted or afraid, alarmed or frightened by them. [4]For it is the LORD, your God, who goes with you to fight for you against your enemies and give you victory."[x]

[5]Then the officials shall speak to the

been appointed (Dt 4:41–43), reference is made here only to the three west of the Jordan. The execution of this command is narrated in Jos 20.

**19:6 The avenger of blood**: see note on Nm 35:12.

**19:14 Move your neighbor's boundary markers**: a prohibition against furtively extending one's property by moving a neighbor's boundary stone.

**19:21 Life for life . . .**: this phrasing of the *lex talionis* may seem exaggerated, but the law itself is meant to ensure equity and proportional punishment; cf. note on Ex 21:22–25.

*m:* Dt 11:22–25; 12:20; Gn 15:18–21; 28:14; Ex 23:31. *n:* Dt 21:8–9. *o:* Dt 13:6, 9. *p:* Dt 27:17; Jb 24:2; Prv 22:28; 23:10; Hos 5:10. *q:* Dt 5:20; Ex 20:16; 23:1. *r:* Dt 17:6; Nm 35:30; Mt 18:16; Jn 8:17; 2 Cor 13:1. *s:* Dt 1:17; 17:8–12. *t:* Dn 13:61–62. *u:* Dt 13:15; 17:4. *v:* Dt 13:11. *w:* Ex 21:23–25; Lv 24:19–20; Mt 5:38. *x:* Dt 1:30; 3:22; Ex 14:14; 15:3; Jos 23:10; Jgs 4:14.

**Rules for Waging Holy War**

IN CONTRAST TO other legal collections, which include only brief sections concerning military engagement (Ex 23:23–33; 34:11–16), Deuteronomy concerns itself extensively with the laws of holy war. God as divine warrior directly confronts the adversary on behalf of the nation, and God's presence in the camp imposes additional purity requirements on the people (Dt 23:10–14).

army:[y] "Is there anyone who has built a new house and not yet dedicated it? Let him return home, lest he die in battle and another dedicate it. [6]Is there anyone who has planted a vineyard and not yet plucked its fruit? Let him return home, lest he die in battle and another pluck its fruit. [7]Is there anyone who has betrothed a woman and not yet married her? Let him return home, lest he die in battle and another marry her."[z] [8]The officials shall continue to speak to the army: "Is there anyone who is afraid and weakhearted?[a] Let him return home, or else he might make the hearts of his fellows melt as his does."

[9]When the officials have finished speaking to the army, military commanders shall be appointed over them.

***Cities of the Enemy.*** [10b] When you draw near a city to attack it, offer it terms of peace. [11]If it agrees to your terms of peace and lets you in, all the people to be found in it shall serve you in forced labor. [12c] But if it refuses to make peace with you and instead joins battle with you, lay siege to it, [13]and when the LORD, your God, delivers it into your power, put every male in it to the sword; [14]but the women and children and livestock and anything else in the city—all its spoil—you may take as plunder for yourselves, and you may enjoy this spoil of your enemies, which the LORD, your God, has given you.

[15*] That is how you shall deal with any city at a considerable distance from you, which does not belong to these nations here. [16d] But in the cities of these peoples that the LORD, your God, is giving you as a heritage, you shall not leave a single soul alive. [17]You must put them all under the ban—the Hittites, Amorites, Canaanites, Perizzites, Hivites, and Jebusites—just as the LORD, your God, has commanded you, [18]so that they do not teach you to do all the abominations that they do for their gods, and you thus sin against the LORD, your God.

***Trees of a Besieged City.*** [19e] When you are at war with a city and have to lay siege to it for a long time before you capture it, you shall not destroy its trees by putting an ax to them. You may eat of them, but you must not cut them down. Are the trees of the field human beings, that they should be included in your siege? [20]However, those trees which you know are not fruit trees you may destroy. You may cut them down to build siegeworks against the city that is waging war with you, until it falls.

## CHAPTER 21

See RG 85–89

***Absolution of Untraced Murder.**** [1]If the corpse of someone who has been slain is found lying in the open, in the land the LORD, your God, is giving you to possess, and it is not known who killed the person, [2]your elders and judges shall go out and measure the distances to the cities that are in the neighborhood of the corpse. [3f] When it is established which city is nearest the corpse, the elders of that city shall take a heifer that has never been put to work or worn a yoke; [4]the elders of that city shall bring the heifer

**20:15** Deuteronomy makes a distinction between treatment of nations far away and those close at hand whose abhorrent religious practices might, or did, influence Israel's worship. This harsh policy was to make sure the nations nearby did not pass their practices on to Israel (cf. chap. 7).

**21:1–9** This law has to do with absolving the community of bloodguilt that accrues to it and to the land when a homicide occurs and the murderer cannot be identified and punished.

*y:* 1 Mc 3:56. *z:* Dt 24:5. *a:* Jgs 7:3. *b:* Jos 9:23–27; 11:19; 2 Sm 10:19. *c:* Nm 31:7, 9, 11; Jos 22:8. *d:* Dt 7:1–2; 12:29–31; Jos 10:40; 11:11, 14. *e:* 2 Kgs 3:18, 25. *f:* Nm 19:2–3.

**The Rebellious Son**

WHILE THE DECALOGUE requirement to honor the parents (Dt 5:16; Ex 20:12) carries no explicit punishment, in Dt 21:18–21, flagrant and sustained disobedience is a capital offense.

down to a wadi with an everflowing stream
at a place that has not been plowed or sown,
and shall break the heifer's neck there in the
wadi. 5 The priests, the descendants of Levi,
shall come forward, for the LORD, your God,
has chosen them to minister to him and to
bless in the name of the LORD, and every
case of dispute or assault shall be for them to
decide. 6 Then all the elders of that city nearest the corpse shall wash their hands* over
the heifer whose neck was broken in the
wadi, 7 and shall declare, "Our hands did not
shed this blood,* and our eyes did not see the
deed. 8 Absolve, O LORD, your people Israel,
whom you have redeemed, and do not let the
guilt of shedding innocent blood remain in
the midst of your people Israel." Thus they
shall be absolved from the guilt of bloodshed, 9 and you shall purge the innocent
blood from your midst, and do what is right
in the eyes of the LORD.[g]

***Marriage with a Female Captive.*** 10[h] When
you go out to war against your enemies and
the LORD, your God, delivers them into your
power, so that you take captives, 11 if you see
a beautiful woman among the captives and
become so enamored of her that you wish to
have her as a wife, 12 and so you take her
home to your house, she must shave her
head,* cut her nails, 13 lay aside her captive's
garb, and stay in your house, mourning her
father and mother for a full month. After that,
you may come to her, and you shall be her
husband and she shall be your wife. 14 If later
on you lose your liking for her, you shall give
her her freedom, if she wishes it; you must
not sell her for money. Do not enslave her,
since you have violated her.[i]

***Rights of the Firstborn.*** 15[j] If a man has
two wives, one loved and the other unloved,
and if both the loved and the unloved bear
him sons, but the firstborn is the son of the
unloved wife: 16 when he comes to bequeath
his property to his sons he may not consider
as his firstborn the son of the wife he loves,
in preference to the son of the wife he does
not love, the firstborn. 17 On the contrary, he
shall recognize as his firstborn the son of the
unloved wife, giving him a double share of
whatever he happens to own, since he is the
first fruits of his manhood, and to him belong the rights of the firstborn.[k]

***The Stubborn and Rebellious Son.*** 18[l] If
someone has a stubborn and rebellious son
who will not listen to his father or mother,
and will not listen to them even though they
discipline him,[m] 19 his father and mother
shall take hold of him and bring him out to
the elders at the gate* of his home city,
20 where they shall say to the elders of the
city, "This son of ours is a stubborn and rebellious fellow who will not listen to us; he
is a glutton and a drunkard."[n] 21 Then all his
fellow citizens shall stone him to death.
Thus shall you purge the evil from your
midst, and all Israel will hear and be afraid.[o]

***Corpse of a Criminal.*** 22[p] If a man guilty
of a capital offense is put to death and you
hang him on a tree,* 23 his corpse shall not remain on the tree overnight.[q] You must bury

**21:6 Wash their hands**: a symbolic gesture in protestation of one's own innocence when human blood is unjustly shed; cf. Mt 27:24.

**21:7 This blood**: the blood of the slain, or the bloodguilt effected by the killing.

**21:12–13 Shave her head . . .**: these symbolic actions probably signified the transition or change of status of the woman or perhaps the end of her period of mourning for her previous husband or family.

**21:19 The gate**: in the city walls. This open space served as the forum for the administration of justice. Cf. 22:15; 25:7; Ru 4:1, 2, 11; Is 29:21; Am 5:10, 12, 15.

**21:22 You hang him on a tree**: some understand, "impaled on a stake." In any case the hanging or impaling was not the means used to execute the criminal; he was first put

*g:* Dt 19:13. *h:* Dt 20:14. *i:* Dt 15:12–18; 22:13–19, 28–29; 24:1–3; Jer 34:15–16. *j:* Gn 21:9–13; 1 Kgs 1:5–21. *k:* Gn 49:3–4. *l:* Dt 5:16; 27:16; Ex 20:12; 21:15, 17; Lv 20:9. *m:* Ps 78:8; Jer 5:23. *n:* Prv 23:20–21; 28:7; Mt 11:19; Lk 7:34. *o:* Dt 13:6, 11–12; 22:21, 24; Lv 20:2; 24:14–16. *p:* Jos 8:29; 10:26–27; 1 Sm 31:8–13; 2 Sm 4:12. *q:* Gal 3:13.

it the same day; anyone who is hanged is a curse of God.* You shall not defile the land which the LORD, your God, is giving you as a heritage.

## CHAPTER 22

See RG 85-89

***Concern for the Neighbor.*** 1[r] You shall not see your neighbor's ox or sheep going astray and ignore it; you must bring it back. 2If this neighbor does not live near you, or you do not know who the owner may be, take it to your own house and keep it with you until your neighbor claims it; then return it. 3You shall do the same with a donkey; you shall do the same with a garment; and you shall do the same with anything else which your neighbor loses and you happen to find. You may not ignore them.

4You shall not see your neighbor's donkey or ox fallen on the road and ignore it; you must help in lifting it up.

***Various Precepts.*** 5A woman shall not wear a man's garment, nor shall a man put on a woman's clothing; for anyone who does such things is an abomination to the LORD, your God.[s]

6[t] If, while walking along, you come across a bird's nest with young birds or eggs in it, in any tree or on the ground, and the mother bird is sitting on them, you shall not take away the mother bird along with her brood. 7You must let the mother go, taking only her brood, in order that you shall prosper and have a long life.

8When you build a new house, put a parapet around the roof, so that you do not bring bloodguilt upon your house if someone falls off.[u]

9* [v] You shall not sow your vineyard with two different kinds of seed, or else its produce shall become forfeit, both the crop you have sown and the yield of the vineyard. 10You shall not plow with an ox and a donkey harnessed together. 11You shall not wear cloth made from wool and linen woven together.

12You shall put tassels on the four corners of the cloak that you wrap around yourself.[w]

***Marriage Legislation.*** 13If a man, after marrying a woman and having relations with her, comes to dislike her,[x] 14and accuses her of misconduct and slanders her by saying, "I married this woman, but when I approached her I did not find evidence of her virginity," 15the father and mother of the young woman shall take the evidence of her virginity* and bring it to the elders at the city gate. 16There the father of the young woman shall say to the elders, "I gave my daughter to this man in marriage, but he has come to dislike her, 17and now accuses her of misconduct, saying: 'I did not find evidence of your daughter's virginity.' But here is the evidence of my daughter's virginity!" And they shall spread out the cloth before the elders of the city. 18Then these city elders shall take the man and discipline him,* 19and fine him one hundred silver shekels, which they shall give to the young woman's father, because the man slandered a virgin in Israel. She shall remain his wife, and he may not divorce her as long as he lives. 20But if this charge is true, and evidence of the young woman's virginity is not found, 21they shall bring the young woman to the entrance of her father's house and there the men of her town shall stone her to death, because she committed a shameful crime in Israel by prostituting herself in her father's house. Thus shall you purge the evil from your midst.[y]

22If a man is discovered lying with a woman who is married to another, they both shall die, the man who was lying with the woman as well as the woman.[z] Thus shall you purge the evil from Israel.

23If there is a young woman, a virgin who

to death by the ordinary means, stoning, and his corpse was then exposed on high as a warning for others. Cf. Jos 8:29; 10:26; 1 Sm 31:10; 2 Sm 21:9.

**21:23** Gal 3:13 applies these words to the crucifixion of Jesus, who "redeemed us from the curse of the law, becoming a curse for us."

**22:9–11** Some understand these laws as serving to preserve distinctions set by God in the creation. **Become forfeit**: to the sanctuary; lit., "be holy"; cf. Lv 19:19; Jos 6:19.

**22:15 The evidence of her virginity**: the bridal garment or sheet stained with blood from the first nuptial relations.

**22:18 Discipline him**: whip him, as prescribed in 25:1–3.

*r*: Ex 23:4–5. *s*: Dt 7:25–26. *t*: Lv 22:28. *u*: Dt 19:10. *v*: Lv 19:19. *w*: Nm 15:38–41; Mt 23:5. *x*: Dt 24:1. *y*: Dt 13:6; Gn 34:7; 2 Sm 13:12. *z*: Dt 5:18; Ex 20:14; Lv 20:10; Ez 16:38–40; Jn 8:3–5.

is betrothed,* and a man comes upon her in
the city and lies with her, [24]you shall bring
them both out to the gate of the city and there
stone them to death: the young woman because she did not cry out though she was in
the city, and the man because he violated his
neighbor's wife. Thus shall you purge the
evil from your midst. [25]But if it is in the open
fields that a man comes upon the betrothed
young woman, seizes her and lies with her,
only the man who lay with her shall die.
[26]You shall do nothing to the young woman,
since the young woman is not guilty of a
capital offense. As when a man rises up
against his neighbor and murders him, so in
this case:* [a] [27]it was in the open fields that he
came upon her, and though the betrothed
young woman may have cried out, there was
no one to save her.

[28b] If a man comes upon a young woman,
a virgin who is not betrothed, seizes her and
lies with her, and they are discovered, [29]the
man who lay with her shall give the young
woman's father fifty silver shekels and she
will be his wife, because he has violated her.
He may not divorce her as long as he lives.

## CHAPTER 23

See RG 85-89

[1]A man shall not marry his father's
wife,* nor shall he dishonor his father's bed.[c]

***Membership in the Assembly.*** [2]* No one
whose testicles have been crushed or whose
penis has been cut off may come into the assembly of the LORD.[d] [3]No one born of an illicit union may come into the assembly of
the LORD, nor any descendant of such even
to the tenth generation may come into the assembly of the LORD.[e] [4f] No Ammonite or
Moabite may ever come into the assembly of
the LORD, nor may any of their descendants
even to the tenth generation come into the
assembly of the LORD, [5]because they would
not come to meet you with food and water
on your journey after you left Egypt, and because they hired Balaam, son of Beor, from
Pethor in Aram Naharaim, to curse you.
[6]The LORD, your God, would not listen to
Balaam but turned his curse into a blessing
for you, because the LORD, your God, loves
you. [7]Never seek their welfare or prosperity
as long as you live.[g] [8h] Do not abhor the
Edomite: he is your brother. Do not abhor
the Egyptian: you were a resident alien in his
country. [9]Children born to them may come
into the assembly of the LORD in the third
generation.

***Cleanliness in Camp.*** [10]When in camp
during an expedition against your enemies,
you shall keep yourselves from anything
bad. [11i] If one of you becomes unclean because of a nocturnal emission, he shall go
outside the camp; he shall not come back
into the camp. [12]Toward evening, he shall
bathe in water; then, when the sun has set, he
may come back into the camp. [13]Outside the
camp you shall have a place set aside where
you shall go. [14]You shall keep a trowel in
your equipment and, when you go outside to
relieve yourself, you shall dig a hole with it
and then cover up your excrement. [15]Since
the LORD, your God, journeys along in the
midst of your camp to deliver you and to
give your enemies over to you, your camp
must be holy, so that he does not see anything indecent in your midst and turn away
from you.[j]

***Various Precepts.*** [16k] You shall not hand
over to their master any slaves who have
taken refuge with you from their master.
[17]Let them live among you in any place they
choose, in any one of your communities* that
seems good to them. Do not oppress them.

**22:23 A young woman, a virgin who is betrothed**: a girl who is married but not yet brought to her husband's home and whose marriage is therefore still unconsummated.

**22:26 So in this case**: in the absence of witnesses ("in the open field"), the presumption must be that the woman is the victim, and so guiltless.

**23:1 Father's wife**: stepmother.

**23:2** Exclusion of an emasculated male may have had to do with association of emasculation with the practices of other peoples, or it may have been rejection of someone with a significant blemish who was thus not suitable for participation in the sacral assembly.

**23:17 In any one of your communities**: from this it would seem that the slave in question is a fugitive from a foreign country.

*a:* Dt 19:4–6. *b:* Dt 22:19; Ex 22:16–17. *c:* Dt 27:20; Gn 9:20–27; 49:4; Lv 18:6–19; 20:11; Ez 22:10. *d:* Lv 21:16–24. *e:* Gn 19:30–38; Lv 18:6–18. *f:* Nm 22:1–24:25; Ru 4:9–17; Ezr 10:10–44; Neh 13:1–3, 23–27. *g:* Ezr 9:12. *h:* Dt 2:2–8; 26:5; Gn 12:10–20; 25:19–26; 36:6–9; 46:5–7; 47:27. *i:* Lv 15:16–17. *j:* Dt 1:30; 20:4; 31:6, 8; 2 Sm 7:6. *k:* 1 Kgs 2:39–40.

[18]There shall be no temple prostitute*
among the Israelite women, nor a temple
prostitute among the Israelite men.[l] [19]You
shall not offer a prostitute's fee or a dog's
pay* as any kind of votive offering in the
house of the LORD, your God; both these
things are an abomination to the LORD, your
God.[m]

[20n] You shall not demand interest from
your kindred on a loan of money or of food
or of anything else which is loaned. [21]From
a foreigner you may demand interest, but
you may not demand interest from your kindred, so that the LORD, your God, may bless
you in all your undertakings on the land you
are to enter and possess.

[22o] When you make a vow to the LORD,
your God, you shall not delay in fulfilling it;
for the LORD, your God, will surely require
it of you and you will be held guilty.
[23]Should you refrain from making a vow,
you will not be held guilty. [24]But whatever
your tongue utters you must be careful to do,
just as you freely vowed to the LORD, your
God, with your own mouth.

[25]When you go through your neighbor's
vineyard, you may eat as many grapes as
you wish, until you are satisfied, but do not
put them in your basket. [26]When you go
through your neighbor's grainfield, you may
pluck some of the ears with your hand, but
do not put a sickle to your neighbor's grain.

See RG 85–89

## CHAPTER 24

***Marriage Legislation.**** [1p] When a
man, after marrying a woman, is later displeased with her because he finds in her
something indecent, and he writes out a bill
of divorce and hands it to her, thus dismissing her from his house, [2]if on leaving his
house she goes and becomes the wife of another man, [3]and the second husband, too,
comes to dislike her and he writes out a bill
of divorce and hands it to her, thus dismissing her from his house, or if this second man
who has married her dies, [4]then her former
husband, who dismissed her, may not again
take her as his wife after she has become defiled. That would be an abomination before
the LORD, and you shall not bring such guilt
upon the land the LORD, your God, is giving
you as a heritage.[q]

[5r] When a man is newly wed, he shall not
go out on a military expedition, nor shall any
duty be imposed on him. He shall be exempt
for one year for the sake of his family, to
bring joy to the wife he has married.

***Pledges and Kidnappings.*** [6]* No one shall
take a hand mill or even its upper stone as a
pledge for debt, for that would be taking as a
pledge the debtor's life.

[7]If anyone is caught kidnapping a fellow
Israelite, enslaving or selling the victim, that
kidnapper shall be put to death.[s] Thus shall
you purge the evil from your midst.

***Skin Diseases.*** [8t] In an attack of scaly infection* you shall be careful to observe exactly and to carry out all the instructions the
levitical priests give you, as I have commanded them: observe them carefully. [9u] Remember what the LORD, your God, did to
Miriam on the journey after you left Egypt.

**23:18–19 Temple prostitute**: Heb. *qedesha*, lit., "holy one," a title of the goddess of fertility. The role or function of the *qedesha* is debated; some see this as simply a term for a prostitute (Heb. *zona*). Others see it as designating a cultic role but not necessarily one involving sexual activity. The evidence is insufficient to give a final answer.

**23:19 Dog's pay**: "dog" is a derogatory term for a male temple prostitute.

**24:1–4** This law is directly concerned only with forbidding a divorced man from remarrying his former wife, and indirectly with checking hasty divorces, by demanding sufficient cause and certain legal formalities. Divorce itself is taken for granted and tolerated as an existing custom whose potential evils this law seeks to lessen. Cf. 22:19, 29; Mal 2:14–16. **Something indecent**: a rather indefinite phrase, meaning perhaps "immodest conduct," but possibly including any kind of objectionable conduct. By New Testament times Jewish opinion differed concerning what was sufficient ground for divorce; cf. Mt 19:3.

**24:6** Since the Israelites ground their grain into flour only in sufficient quantity for their current need, to deprive a debtor of his hand mill was equivalent to condemning him to starvation.

**24:8 Scaly infection**: the Hebrew word seems to have to do with one or more skin diseases that produce scales, such as psoriasis. Its precise meaning is uncertain. See note on Lv 13:1–14:57.

*l:* Gn 38:21–22; 1 Kgs 14:24; 15:12; 22:46; 2 Kgs 23:7; Hos 4:14. *m:* Dt 7:25–26; Is 23:17–18. *n:* Dt 15:1–11; 24:10–13; Ex 22:25; Lv 25:35–38; Ez 18:8, 13, 17; 22:12; Lk 6:34–35. *o:* Gn 28:20–22; Nm 21:2–3; 30:1–15; Jgs 11:30–40; 1 Sm 1:11; Ps 56:12–13; 66:13–15; 132:1–5; Eccl 5:3–5. *p:* Dt 22:13–19, 28–29; Sir 7:26; Jer 3:1; Mt 5:31–32; 19:3–9. *q:* Dt 7:25–26. *r:* Dt 20:7. *s:* Dt 13:6; Ex 21:16. *t:* Lv 13:1–14:57. *u:* Nm 12:10–15.

***Loans and Wages.*** [10]When you make a loan of any kind to your neighbor, you shall not enter the neighbor's house to receive the pledge, [11]but shall wait outside until the person to whom you are making the loan brings the pledge outside to you. [12]If the person is poor, you shall not sleep in the pledged garment, [13]but shall definitely return it at sunset, so that your neighbor may sleep in the garment[v] and bless you. That will be your justice before the LORD, your God.

[14w] You shall not exploit a poor and needy hired servant, whether one of your own kindred or one of the resident aliens who live in your land, within your gates.[x] [15]On each day you shall pay the servant's wages before the sun goes down, since the servant is poor and is counting on them. Otherwise the servant will cry to the LORD against you, and you will be held guilty.[y]

***Individual Responsibility.*** [16]Parents shall not be put to death for their children, nor shall children be put to death for their parents; only for one's own crime shall a person be put to death.[z]

***Rights of the Unprotected.*** [17a] You shall not deprive the resident alien or the orphan of justice, nor take the clothing of a widow as pledge. [18]For, remember, you were slaves in Egypt, and the LORD, your God, redeemed you from there; that is why I command you to do this.

[19b] When you reap the harvest in your field and overlook a sheaf in the field, you shall not go back to get it; let it be for the resident alien, the orphan, and the widow, so that the LORD, your God, may bless you in all your undertakings. [20]When you knock down the fruit of your olive trees, you shall not go over the branches a second time; let what remains be for the resident alien, the orphan, and the widow. [21]When you pick your grapes, you shall not go over the vineyard a second time; let what remains be for the resident alien, the orphan, and the widow. [22]For remember that you were slaves in the land of Egypt; that is why I command you to do this.

## CHAPTER 25

See RG 85–89

***Limits on Punishments.*** [1]When there is a dispute and the parties draw near for judgment, and a decision is given, declaring one party in the right and the other in the wrong, [2]if the one in the wrong deserves whipping, the judge shall have him lie down and in the presence of the judge receive the number of lashes the crime warrants. [3]Forty lashes* may be given, but no more;[c] or else, if more lashes are added to these many blows, your brother will be degraded in your sight.

***Treatment of Oxen.**** [4]You shall not muzzle an ox when it treads out grain.[d]

***Levirate Marriage.*** [5e] When brothers live together* and one of them dies without a son, the widow of the deceased shall not marry anyone outside the family; but her husband's brother shall come to her, marrying her and performing the duty of a brother-in-law.[f] [6]The firstborn son she bears shall continue the name of the deceased brother, that his name may not be blotted out from Israel. [7]But if a man does not want to marry his brother's wife, she shall go up to the elders at the gate and say, "My brother-in-law refuses to perpetuate his brother's name in Israel and does not intend to perform his duty toward me." [8]Thereupon the elders of his city shall summon him and speak to him. If he persists in saying, "I do not want to marry her," [9*] his sister-in-law, in the presence of

**25:3 Forty lashes**: while the punishment is severe, the law seeks to limit it from being overly harsh and inhumane. Later Jewish practice limited the number to thirty-nine; cf. 2 Cor 11:24.

**25:4** This is comparable in spirit to 22:6–7; Israelites are not to be grasping and calculating. St. Paul argues from this verse that laborers have the right to live on the fruits of their labor; cf. 1 Cor 9:9; 1 Tm 5:18.

**25:5 When brothers live together**: when relatives of the same clan, though married, hold their property in common. It was only in this case that the present law was to be observed, since one of its purposes was to keep the property of the deceased within the same clan. Such a marriage of a widow with her brother-in-law is known as a "levirate" marriage from the Latin word *levir*, meaning "a husband's brother."

**25:9–10** The penalty decreed for a man who refuses to

*v:* Dt 6:25; Ex 22:25–26; Am 2:8. *w:* Lv 19:13; Sir 34:26–27; Jer 22:13. *x:* Dt 1:16. *y:* Dt 15:9; Mt 20:1–16. *z:* Dt 7:10; 2 Kgs 14:6; 2 Chr 25:4; Jer 31:29–30; Ez 18:20. *a:* Dt 10:17–19; 15:15; 24:22; 27:19; Ex 22:21–24; 23:9. *b:* Ex 23:10–11; Lv 19:9–10; 23:22; Ru 2:1–23. *c:* 2 Cor 11:24. *d:* Prv 12:10; 1 Cor 9:9; 1 Tm 5:18. *e:* Gn 38:1–30; Ru 4:5–10; Lk 20:27–33. *f:* Mt 22:24; Mk 12:19; Lk 20:28.

the elders, shall go up to him and strip his
sandal from his foot and spit in his face, declaring, "This is how one should be treated
who will not build up his brother's family!"
10 And his name shall be called in Israel, "the
house of the man stripped of his sandal."

*Various Precepts.* 11 When two men are
fighting and the wife of one intervenes to
save her husband from the blows of his opponent, if she stretches out her hand and
seizes the latter by his genitals, 12 you shall
chop off her hand; show no pity.

13[g] You shall not keep two differing
weights in your bag, one heavy and the other
light; 14 nor shall you keep two different
ephahs* in your house, one large and the
other small. 15 But use a full and just weight,
a full and just ephah, so that you may have a
long life on the land the LORD, your God, is
giving you. 16 For everyone who does these
things, everyone who does what is dishonest,
is an abomination to the LORD, your God.[h]

17* [i] Bear in mind what Amalek did to you
on the journey after you left Egypt, 18 how he
surprised you along the way, weak and
weary as you were, and struck down at the
rear all those who lagged behind; he did not
fear God. 19 Therefore, when the LORD, your
God, gives you rest from all your enemies
round about in the land which the LORD,
your God, is giving you to possess as a heritage, you shall blot out the memory of Amalek from under the heavens. Do not forget!

## CHAPTER 26

See RG 85-89

*Thanksgiving for the Harvest.* 1[j] When
you have come into the land which the LORD,
your God, is giving you as a heritage, and
have taken possession and settled in it, 2 you
shall take some first fruits[k] of the various
products of the soil which you harvest from
the land the LORD, your God, is giving you;
put them in a basket and go to the place
which the LORD, your God, will choose as
the dwelling place for his name. 3 There you
shall go to the priest in office at that time and
say to him, "Today I acknowledge to the
LORD, my God, that I have indeed come into
the land which the LORD swore to our ancestors to give us."[l] 4 The priest shall then take
the basket from your hands and set it in front
of the altar of the LORD, your God. 5 Then
you shall declare in the presence of the
LORD, your God, "My father was a refugee
Aramean* who went down to Egypt with a
small household and lived there as a resident
alien.[m] But there he became a nation great,
strong and numerous. 6[n] When the Egyptians
maltreated and oppressed us, imposing harsh
servitude upon us, 7 we cried to the LORD, the
God of our ancestors, and the LORD heard
our cry and saw our affliction, our toil and
our oppression. 8 Then the LORD brought us
out of Egypt with a strong hand and outstretched arm, with terrifying power, with
signs and wonders,[o] 9 and brought us to this
place, and gave us this land, a land flowing
with milk and honey.[p] 10 Now, therefore, I
have brought the first fruits of the products
of the soil which you, LORD, have given me."
You shall set them before the LORD, your
God, and you shall bow down before the
LORD, your God. 11 Then you and your
household, together with the Levite and the
resident aliens who live among you, shall
celebrate with all these good things which
the LORD, your God, has given you.[q]

*Declaration Concerning Tithes.* 12 When
you have finished setting aside all the tithes of
your produce in the third year,[r] the year of the
tithes, and have given them to the Levite, the
resident alien, the orphan and the widow, that

comply with this law of family loyalty is public disgrace; the widow is to spit in his face. Some commentators connect this symbolic act with the ceremony mentioned in Ru 4:7, 8.

**25:14 Ephahs**: see note on Is 5:10.

**25:17–19** This attack on Israel by Amalek is not mentioned elsewhere in the Old Testament, although it probably was connected with the battle mentioned in Ex 17:8. A campaign against Amalek was carried out by Saul; cf. 1 Sm 15.

**26:5 Aramean**: probably in reference to the origin of the patriarchs from Aram Naharaim (cf. Gn 24:10; 25:20; 28:5; 31:20, 24).

**26:14** These are allusions to foreign religious practices. **To the dead**: to feed the spirits of the dead, or perhaps to worship Baal.

*g:* Lv 19:35–36; Prv 16:11; 20:23; Ez 45:10; Hos 12:7; Mi 6:11. *h:* Dt 7:25–26. *i:* Ex 17:8–16; 1 Sm 15:2–33. *j:* Dt 14:22–29; 16:1–17; Ex 22:29; Lv 23:9–21; Nm 28:26–31. *k:* Dt 12:5, 11; 18:4; Ex 23:19; 34:26; Tb 1:6–7. *l:* Dt 1:8, 20–21. *m:* Gn 46:5–7, 26–27; Ex 1:7, 9; Acts 7:14–15. *n:* Ex 1:8–22; 2:23–25; 3:7–10; 6:9; Nm 20:15–16; 1 Kgs 12:4. *o:* Dt 4:34; 6:21–22; Ex 12:51. *p:* Ex 3:8. *q:* Dt 12:7, 12. *r:* Dt 14:28–29.

they may eat and be satisfied in your own communities, [13]you shall declare before the LORD, your God, "I have purged my house of the sacred portion and I have given it to the Levite, the resident alien, the orphan and the widow, just as you have commanded me. I have not transgressed any of your commandments, nor forgotten any. [14*] I have not eaten any of the tithe while in mourning; I have not brought any of it while unclean; I have not offered any of it to the dead. I have thus obeyed the voice of the LORD, my God, and done just as you have commanded me.[s] [15]Look down, then, from heaven, your holy abode, and bless your people Israel and the fields you have given us, as you promised on oath to our ancestors, a land flowing with milk and honey."[t]

***The Covenant.*** [16u] This day the LORD, your God, is commanding you to observe these statutes and ordinances. Be careful, then, to observe them with your whole heart and with your whole being. [17]Today you have accepted the LORD's agreement: he will be your God, and you will walk in his ways, observe his statutes, commandments, and ordinances, and obey his voice. [18]And today the LORD has accepted your agreement: you will be a people specially his own, as he promised you, you will keep all his commandments, [19]and he will set you high in praise and renown and glory above all nations he has made, and you will be a people holy to the LORD, your God, as he promised.

See RG 85-89

## CHAPTER 27

***The Altar on Mount Ebal.*** [1]Then Moses, with the elders of Israel, commanded the people, saying: Keep this whole commandment which I give you today. [2]On the day you cross the Jordan into the land which the LORD, your God, is giving you, set up some large stones and coat them with plaster. [3]Write on them,[v] at the time you cross, all the words of this law, so that you may enter the land which the LORD, your God, is giving you, a land flowing with milk and honey, just as the LORD, the God of your ancestors, promised you. [4]When you cross the Jordan, on Mount Ebal you shall set up these stones concerning which I command you today, and coat them with plaster, [5w] and you shall build there an altar to the LORD, your God, an altar made of stones that no iron tool has touched. [6]You shall build this altar of the LORD, your God, with unhewn stones, and shall offer on it burnt offerings to the LORD, your God. [7]You shall also offer communion sacrifices* and eat them there, rejoicing in the presence of the LORD, your God. [8]On the stones you shall inscribe all the words of this law very clearly.

[9]Moses, with the levitical priests, then said to all Israel: Be silent, Israel, and listen! This day you have become the people of the LORD, your God.[x] [10]You shall obey the voice of the LORD, your God, and keep his commandments and statutes which I am giving you today.

***Preparation for Blessings and Curses.*** [11]That same day Moses commanded the people, saying: [12y] When you cross the Jordan, these shall stand on Mount Gerizim to bless the people: Simeon, Levi, Judah, Issachar, Joseph and Benjamin. [13]And these shall stand on Mount Ebal for the curse: Reuben, Gad, Asher, Zebulun, Dan and Naphtali.

***The Twelve Curses.*** [14]The Levites shall proclaim in a loud voice to all the Israelites: [15*] "Cursed be anyone who makes a carved or molten idol,[z] an abomination to the LORD, the work of a craftsman's hands, and sets it up in secret!" And all the people shall answer, "Amen!"

**27:7 Communion sacrifices**: The principal feature of this ritual (see Lv 3:1–17) is the sharing of the sacrifice with God, the priest and the person offering the sacrifice, who eat it as a holy thing (cf. Ex 24:5).

**27:15–26** The ceremony described here reflects the structure of covenant. The people assent to the directives their covenant Lord sets forth; their "Amen" ratifies the proscription of idolatry, injustice, incest, murder, and infidelity in general. Thus the "love" of the Lord which is at the heart of Israel's existence as his covenant people (6:4–5) is spelled out in terms of particular actions. The "Amen" is an acceptance of the curses or sanctions entailed by breaking faith with the Lord. Cf. 30:15–20, a concise statement of covenant theology.

*s:* Dt 14:1; Lv 11:24–25; 22:3; Jer 16:7. *t:* 1 Kgs 8:39, 43, 49; Ps 102:19. *u:* Dt 7:6; 8:6; 10:12–13; 11:22; 14:2; 27:9; 28:1, 9; 29:12–13; Ex 6:7; 19:5–6; 24:7; Lv 26:12; 2 Sm 7:24; Jer 7:23; 31:33; Ez 11:20; Hos 2:23. *v:* Jos 8:32. *w:* Ex 20:24–25; Jos 8:30–31. *x:* Dt 26:17–19. *y:* Dt 11:26–29; Jos 8:33–35. *z:* Dt 4:15–20; 5:8–9; Ex 20:4, 23; 34:17; Lv 19:4; 26:1; Ps 115:4–8; Wis 14:8.

16 "Cursed be anyone who dishonors father or mother!"[a] And all the people shall answer, "Amen!"

17 "Cursed be anyone who moves a neighbor's boundary markers!"[b] And all the people shall answer, "Amen!"

18 "Cursed be anyone who misleads the blind on their way!"[c] And all the people shall answer, "Amen!"

19 "Cursed be anyone who deprives the resident alien, the orphan or the widow of justice!"[d] And all the people shall answer, "Amen!"

20 "Cursed be anyone who has relations with his father's wife, for he dishonors his father's bed!"[e] And all the people shall answer, "Amen!"

21 "Cursed be anyone who has relations with any animal!"[f] And all the people shall answer, "Amen!"

22 "Cursed be anyone who has relations with his sister, whether his father's daughter or his mother's daughter!"[g] And all the people shall answer, "Amen!"

23 "Cursed be anyone who has relations with his mother-in-law!"[h] And all the people shall answer, "Amen!"

24 "Cursed be anyone who strikes down a neighbor in secret!"[i] And all the people shall answer, "Amen!"

25 "Cursed be anyone who accepts payment to kill an innocent person!"[j] And all the people shall answer, "Amen!"

26 "Cursed be anyone whose actions do not uphold the words of this law!"[k] And all the people shall answer, "Amen!"

## CHAPTER 28

See RG 85-89

***Blessings for Obedience.*** 1 Now,[l] [m] if you diligently obey the voice of the LORD, your God, carefully observing all his commandments which I give you today, the LORD, your God, will set you high above all the nations of the earth.[n] 2 All these blessings will come upon you and overwhelm you when you obey the voice of the LORD, your God:

3 [o] May you be blessed in the city,
and blessed in the country!
4 Blessed be the fruit of your womb,
the produce of your soil and the
offspring of your livestock,
the issue of your herds and the young
of your flocks![p]
5 Blessed be your grain basket and your
kneading bowl!
6 May you be blessed in your coming in,
and blessed in your going out!* [q]

***Victory and Prosperity.*** 7 The LORD will beat down before you the enemies that rise up against you; they will come out against you from one direction, and flee before you in seven.* [r] 8 The LORD will affirm the blessing upon you, on your barns and on all your undertakings; he will bless you in the land that the LORD, your God, is giving you. 9 The LORD will establish you as a holy people, as he swore to you,[s] if you keep the commandments of the LORD, your God, and walk in his ways. 10 All the peoples of the earth will see that the name of the LORD is proclaimed over you,* and they will be afraid of you.[t] 11 The LORD will generously increase the fruit of your womb, the offspring of your livestock, and the produce of your soil, upon the land which the LORD swore to your ancestors he would give you.[u] 12 The LORD will open up for you his rich storehouse, the heavens, to give your land rain in due season and to bless all the works of your hands. You will lend to many nations but borrow from

**28:6 In your coming in . . . in your going out**: at the beginning and end of every action, or in all actions in general. The rhetorical figure is called merismus. See also 6:7.

**28:7 From one direction . . . in seven**: in one disciplined body, contrasted with many scattered groups.

**28:10 The name of the LORD is proclaimed over you**: an expression signifying ownership and protection. Cf. 2 Sm 12:28; 1 Kgs 8:43; Is 4:1; 63:19; Jer 7:10–11; 14:9; 15:16; 25:29; Am 9:12.

*a:* Dt 5:16; 21:18–21; Ex 20:12; 21:17; Lv 20:9. *b:* Dt 19:14. *c:* Lv 19:14. *d:* Dt 24:17–18; Ex 22:21–24; 23:9; Lv 19:33–34. *e:* Dt 23:1; Lv 18:7–8; 20:11. *f:* Ex 22:18; Lv 18:23; 20:15–16. *g:* Lv 18:9; 20:17. *h:* Lv 18:17; 20:14. *i:* Dt 5:17; 21:1; Ex 20:13; 21:12; Nm 35:20–21. *j:* Dt 16:19; Ex 23:7–8. *k:* Jer 11:3; Gal 3:10. *l:* Lv 26:3–45. *m:* Dt 7:12–16; 11:13–15. *n:* Dt 26:19; Ps 89:27; Is 55:3–5. *o:* Dt 28:16–19. *p:* Dt 7:13–14; 30:9; Ex 23:26; Lv 26:9. *q:* Ps 121:8. *r:* Dt 9:1–3; Ex 23:27–28; Lv 26:6–8. *s:* Dt 26:18–19; Ex 19:5–6. *t:* Dt 2:25; 11:25; Is 61:9. *u:* Dt 28:4.

**Curses**

THE PREPONDERANCE OF curses over blessings in Dt 28 emphasizes the urgent need to reform. Note how the curses in vv. 16–19 correspond to the blessings of vv. 3–6; vv. 23–24 oppose the blessing of v. 12; and vv. 43–44 counter vv. 12–13. In vv. 45–46, a temporary conclusion is reached, summing up both the cause and effect of this long litany (disobedience leads to destruction), but even more curses follow.

none.[v] [13]The LORD will make you the head not the tail, the top not the bottom, if you obey the commandments of the LORD, your God, which I am giving you today, observing them carefully, [14]not turning aside, either to the right or to the left, from any of the words which I am giving you today, following other gods and serving them.[w]

***Curses for Disobedience.*** [15]But if you do not obey the voice of the LORD, your God,[x] carefully observing all his commandments and statutes which I give you today, all these curses shall come upon you and overwhelm you:

[16][y]May you be cursed in the city, and cursed in the country! [17]Cursed be your grain basket and your kneading bowl! [18]Cursed be the fruit of your womb, the produce of your soil and the offspring of your livestock, the issue of your herds and the young of your flocks! [19]May you be cursed in your coming in, and cursed in your going out!

***Sickness and Defeat.*** [20]The LORD will send on you a curse, panic, and frustration in everything you set your hand to, until you are speedily destroyed and perish for the evil you have done in forsaking me. [21][z]The LORD will make disease cling to you until he has made an end of you from the land you are entering to possess. [22]The LORD will strike you with consumption, fever, and inflammation, with fiery heat and drought, with blight and mildew, that will pursue you until you perish. [23]The heavens over your heads will be like bronze and the earth under your feet like iron.[a] [24]For rain the LORD will give your land powdery dust, which will come down upon you from the heavens until you are destroyed. [25]The LORD will let you be beaten down before your enemies; though you advance against them from one direction, you will flee before them in seven,* so that you will become an object of horror to all the kingdoms of the earth.[b] [26]Your corpses will become food for all the birds of the air and for the beasts of the field, with no one to frighten them off.[c] [27]The LORD will strike you with Egyptian boils[d] and with tumors, skin diseases and the itch, from none of which you can be cured. [28][e]And the LORD will strike you with madness, blindness and panic, [29]so that even at midday you will grope in the dark as though blind, unable to find your way.

***Despoilment.*** You will be oppressed and robbed continually, with no one to come to your aid. [30]Though you betroth a wife, another will have her. Though you build a house, you will not live in it. Though you plant a vineyard, you will not pluck its fruits.[f] [31][g]Your ox will be slaughtered before your eyes, but you will not eat its flesh. Your donkey will be stolen in your presence, but you will never get it back. Your flocks will be given to your enemies, with no one to come to your aid. [32]Your sons and daughters will be given to another people while you strain your eyes looking for them every day, having no power to do anything. [33]A people you do not know will consume the fruit of your soil and of all your labor, and you will be thoroughly oppressed and continually crushed, [34]until you are driven mad by what your eyes must look upon. [35]The LORD will strike you

**28:25 From one direction . . . in seven**: see note on v. 7.

*v:* Dt 15:6. *w:* Dt 5:32. *x:* Bar 1:20; Dn 9:11; Mal 2:2. *y:* Dt 28:3–6. *z:* Lv 26:16, 25; Jer 14:12; Am 4:9–10; Hg 2:17. *a:* Lv 26:19. *b:* Dt 1:44; 28:7; Lv 26:17, 37. *c:* Ps 79:2; Jer 7:33; 34:20. *d:* Dt 7:15; 28:60; Ex 9:8–12. *e:* Is 59:10. *f:* Dt 20:5–7; Am 5:11. *g:* Jer 5:17; Lam 5:1–18; Am 7:17.

with malignant boils of which you cannot be cured, on your knees and legs, and from the soles of your feet to the crown of your head.

***Exile.*** [36h] The LORD will bring you, and your king whom you have set over you, to a nation which you and your ancestors have not known, and there you will serve other gods, of wood and stone, [37]and you will be a horror, a byword, a taunt among all the peoples to which the LORD will drive you.

***Fruitless Labors.*** [38i] Though you take out seed to your field, you will harvest but little, for the locusts will devour it. [39]Though you plant and cultivate vineyards, you will not drink or store up the wine, for the worms will eat them. [40]Though you have olive trees throughout your country, you will have no oil for ointment, for your olives will drop off. [41]Though you beget sons and daughters, they will not remain with you, for they will go into captivity. [42]Buzzing insects will take possession of all your trees and the crops of your soil. [43j] The resident aliens among you will rise above you higher and higher, while you sink lower and lower. [44]They will lend to you, not you to them. They will become the head, you the tail.

[45]All these curses will come upon you, pursuing you and overwhelming you, until you are destroyed, because you would not obey the voice of the LORD, your God, by keeping his commandments and statutes which he gave you.[k] [46]They will be a sign and a wonder* for you and your descendants for all time. [47]Since you would not serve the LORD, your God, with heartfelt joy for abundance of every kind, [48]in hunger and thirst, in nakedness and utter want, you will serve the enemies whom the LORD will send against you. He will put an iron yoke on your neck, until he destroys you.[l]

***Invasion and Siege.*** [49m] The LORD will raise up against you a nation from afar, from the end of the earth, that swoops down like an eagle, a nation whose language you do not understand, [50]a nation of fierce appearance, that shows neither respect for the aged nor mercy for the young. [51]They will consume the offspring of your livestock and the produce of your soil, until you are destroyed; they will leave you no grain or wine or oil, no issue of herd, no young of flock, until they have brought about your ruin. [52]They will besiege you in each of your communities, until the great, fortified walls, in which you trust, come tumbling down all over your land. They will besiege you in every community throughout the land which the LORD, your God, has given you, [53n] and because of the siege and the distress to which your enemy subjects you, you will eat the fruit of your womb, the flesh of your own sons and daughters whom the LORD, your God, has given you. [54]The most refined and fastidious man among you will begrudge his brother and his beloved wife and his surviving children, [55]any share in the flesh of his children that he himself is using for food because nothing else is left him—such the siege and distress to which your enemy will subject you in all your communities. [56]The most fastidious woman among you, who would not venture to set the sole of her foot on the ground, so refined and fastidious is she, will begrudge her beloved husband and her son and daughter [57]the afterbirth that issues from her womb and the infants she brings forth because she secretly eats them for want of anything else—such the siege and distress to which your enemy will subject you in your communities.

***Plagues.*** [58]If you are not careful to observe all the words of this law which is written in this book, and to fear this glorious and awesome name, the LORD, your God,[o] [59p] the LORD will bring upon you and your descendants wondrous calamities, severe and constant calamities, and malignant and constant sicknesses. [60]He will bring back upon you all the diseases of Egypt* which you dread,

**28:46 A sign and a wonder**: an ominous example, attracting attention; cf. 29:21–28.

**28:60 He will bring back upon you all the diseases of Egypt**: such as the Lord had promised to remove from the people (7:15); cf. v. 27.

*h:* Dt 4:27–28; 1 Kgs 9:6–9; 2 Kgs 25:6–7, 11; 2 Chr 7:19–22; 33:11; 36:6, 20; Jer 16:13; 24:8–9; 25:8–11; Ez 17:12. *i:* Dt 28:18; Lv 26:20; Lam 1:5; Mi 6:15; Zep 1:13; Hg 1:6. *j:* Dt 15:6; 28:12–13. *k:* Dt 28:15. *l:* Jer 28:14. *m:* Jer 5:15–17; 6:22–26; Bar 4:15–16. *n:* Lv 26:29; 2 Kgs 6:28–29; Jer 19:9; Lam 2:20; 4:10; Bar 2:3. *o:* Dt 6:13; Jos 24:14. *p:* Dt 7:15; 28:21–22, 27.

and they will cling to you. [61]Even any sickness or calamity not written in this book of the law, that too the LORD will bring upon you until you are destroyed. [62]You who were numerous as the stars of the heavens[q] will be left few in number, because you would not obey the voice of the LORD, your God.

***Exile.*** [63][r] Just as the LORD once took delight in making you prosper and grow, so will the LORD now take delight in ruining and destroying you, and you will be plucked out of the land you are now entering to possess. [64]The LORD will scatter you among all the peoples from one end of the earth to the other, and there you will serve other gods, of wood and stone, which you and your ancestors have not known. [65]Among these nations you will find no rest, not even a resting place for the sole of your foot, for there the LORD will give you an anguished heart and wearied eyes* and a trembling spirit. [66]Your life will hang in suspense and you will stand in dread both day and night, never sure of your life. [67]In the morning you will say, "Would that it were evening!" and in the evening you will say, "Would that it were morning!" because of the dread that your heart must feel and the sight that your eyes must see. [68]The LORD will send you back in ships to Egypt, by a route which I told you that you would never see again;[s] and there you will offer yourselves for sale to your enemies as male and female slaves, but there will be no buyer.

[69]These are the words of the covenant which the LORD commanded Moses to make with the Israelites in the land of Moab, in addition to the covenant he made with them at Horeb.

## III. Third Address

### CHAPTER 29

See RG 85–89

***Past Favors Recalled.*** [1]Moses summoned all Israel and said to them, You have seen with your own eyes all that the LORD did in the land of Egypt to Pharaoh and all his servants and to all his land, [2]the great testings your own eyes have seen, and those great signs and wonders.[t] [3]But the LORD has not given you a heart to understand, or eyes to see, or ears to hear until this day.[u] [4][v] I led you for forty years in the wilderness. Your clothes did not fall from you in tatters nor your sandals from your feet; [5]it was not bread that you ate, nor wine or beer that you drank—so that you might know that I, the LORD, am your God. [6][w] When you came to this place, Sihon, king of Heshbon, and Og, king of Bashan, came out to engage us in battle, but we defeated them [7]and took their land, and gave it as a heritage to the Reubenites, Gadites, and the half-tribe of Manasseh.[x] [8]Observe carefully the words of this covenant, therefore, in order that you may succeed in whatever you do.[y]

***All Israel Bound by Covenant.*** [9]You are standing today, all of you, in the presence of the LORD, your God—your tribal heads, elders, and officials, all of the men of Israel, [10]your children, your wives, and the resident alien who lives in your camp, from those who cut wood to those who draw water for you— [11]to enter into the covenant of the LORD, your God, which the LORD, your God, is making with you today, with its curse, [12]so that he may establish you today as his people and he may be your God, as he promised you and as he swore to your ancestors, to Abraham, Isaac and Jacob. [13][z] But it is not with you alone that I am making this covenant, with its curse, [14]but with those who are standing here with us today in the presence of the LORD, our God, and with those who are not here with us* today.

***Warning Against Idolatry.*** [15]You know that we lived in the land of Egypt and that we passed through the nations, that you too passed through [16]and saw the loathsome things and idols of wood and stone, of gold and silver, that they possess. [17]There may be

**28:65 Wearied eyes**: cf. v. 32.

**29:14 Not here with us**: this includes future generations. This attitude appears also in 5:3.

*q:* Dt 1:10; 10:22; 26:5; Jer 42:2. *r:* Dt 4:26–28; 30:9; Lv 26:33–39. *s:* Jer 42–44; Hos 8:13; 9:3, 6; 11:5. *t:* Dt 4:34, 37–38; 6:21–23; 7:19; 26:5–9. *u:* Is 6:9–10; Jer 5:21; Ez 12:2; Mt 13:14–15; Mk 4:12; Lk 8:10; Jn 12:40; Acts 28:26–27. *v:* Dt 8:2–4. *w:* Dt 1:4; 2:31–33; 3:1–3; Nm 21:23–24, 33–35. *x:* Dt 3:16–17; Nm 32:33. *y:* Jos 1:7–8; 1 Kgs 2:3. *z:* Dt 5:3.

**Covenant Responsibility**

STIPULATING THAT THE Torah is taught to women, minors, and aliens (Dt 29:10), the law does not restrict the responsibility to observe the covenant to males (contrast Ex 19:15).

among you a man or woman, or a clan or tribe, whose heart is now turning away from the LORD, our God, to go and serve the gods of these nations; there may be among you a root bearing poison and wormwood; [18]if any such persons, after hearing the words of this curse, should congratulate themselves, saying in their hearts, "I am safe, even though I walk in stubbornness of heart," thereby sweeping away moist and dry alike,* [a] [19]the LORD will never consent to pardon them. Instead, the LORD's burning wrath will flare up against them; every curse written in this book will pounce on them, and the LORD will blot out their names from under the heavens.[b] [20]The LORD will single them out from all the tribes of Israel for doom, in keeping with all the curses of the covenant written in this book of the law.

*Punishment for Idolatry.* [21c] Future generations, your descendants who will rise up after you, as well as the foreigners who will come here from distant lands, when they see the calamities of this land and the ills the LORD has inflicted upon it— [22]all its soil burned out by sulphur and salt, unsown and unfruitful, without a blade of grass, like the catastrophe of Sodom and Gomorrah,[d] Admah and Zeboiim,* which the LORD overthrew in his furious wrath— [23e] they and all the nations will ask, "Why has the LORD dealt thus with this land? Why this great outburst of wrath?" [24]And they will say, "Because they abandoned the covenant of the LORD, the God of their ancestors, which he had made with them when he brought them out of the land of Egypt, [25]and they went and served other gods and bowed down to them, gods whom they did not know and whom he had not apportioned to them.[f] [26g] So the anger of the LORD flared up against this land and brought on it every curse written in this book. [27]The LORD uprooted them from their soil in anger, fury, and great wrath, and cast them out into another land, as they are today." [28]The hidden things* belong to the LORD our God, but the revealed things are for us and for our children forever, to observe all the words of this law.

## CHAPTER 30

*Compassion for the Repentant.* See RG 85-89

[1* h] When all these things, the blessing and the curse which I have set before you, come upon you,[i] and you take them to heart in any of the nations where the LORD, your God, has dispersed you, [2j] and return to the LORD, your God, obeying his voice, according to all that I am commanding you today, you and your children, with your whole heart and your whole being, [3]the LORD, your God, will restore your fortunes and will have compassion on you; he will again gather you from all the peoples where the LORD, your God, has scattered you. [4]Though you may have been dispersed to the farthest corner of the heavens, even from there will the LORD, your God, gather you; even from there will he bring you back.[k] [5]The LORD, your God, will then bring you into the land your ances-

**29:18 Sweeping away moist and dry alike**: possibly a proverbial expression: because of Israel's infidelity the Lord will punish the just with the wicked (cf. Gn 18:25), rooting out good plants in irrigated soil, together with worthless plants growing in dry ground.

**29:22 Admah and Zeboiim**: neighboring cities of Sodom and Gomorrah in the Jordan Plain and identified in the tradition as destroyed with them. Cf. Hos 11:8; Jer 50:40.

**29:28 The hidden things**: probably the events of the future. **The revealed things**: the covenant and its provisions, including the sanctions of blessing and curse. This aphorism may mean: leave "hidden things" to God; what matters is to keep the law.

**30:1–5** Text such as this suggests a postexilic perspective; cf. also chaps. 31–32.

*a:* Jer 7:10. *b:* Dt 9:14; 25:19. *c:* Dt 4:25–28. *d:* Gn 19:24–25; Hos 11:8. *e:* 1 Kgs 9:8–9; Jer 5:19; 9:12–16; 16:10–13; 22:8–9. *f:* Dt 4:19; 32:8–9. *g:* Dt 29:20–21; Dn 9:11–14. *h:* Dt 4:29–31; Lv 26:40–45. *i:* Dt 11:26–28; 27:11–28:69. *j:* Dt 4:29–30; 6:5; 30:10; 1 Kgs 8:47–48; Jer 24:7; 29:14; 33:26; Ez 39:25; Am 9:14; Zep 3:20. *k:* Neh 1:9; Is 43:5–7; Jer 31:10; 32:37; Ez 36:24; 37:21.

tors once possessed, that you may possess it; and he will make you more prosperous and numerous than your ancestors.[l] 6The LORD, your God, will circumcise your hearts* and the hearts of your descendants,[m] so that you will love the LORD, your God, with your whole heart and your whole being, in order that you may live. 7The LORD, your God, will put all those curses on your enemies and the foes who pursued you.[n] 8You, however, shall again obey the voice of the LORD and observe all his commandments which I am giving you today. 9Then the LORD, your God, will generously increase your undertakings, the fruit of your womb, the offspring of your livestock, and the produce of your soil;[o] for the LORD, your God, will again take delight in your prosperity, just as he took delight in your ancestors', 10because you will obey the voice of the LORD, your God, keeping the commandments and statutes that are written in this book of the law, when you return to the LORD, your God, with your whole heart and your whole being.

11[p] For this command which I am giving you today is not too wondrous or remote for you. 12It is not in the heavens, that you should say, "Who will go up to the heavens to get it for us and tell us of it, that we may do it?" 13Nor is it across the sea, that you should say, "Who will cross the sea to get it for us and tell us of it, that we may do it?" 14No, it is something very near to you, in your mouth* and in your heart, to do it.

***The Choice Before Israel.*** 15See, I have today set before you life and good, death and evil.[q] 16If you obey the commandments of the LORD, your God, which I am giving you today, loving the LORD, your God, and walking in his ways, and keeping his commandments, statutes and ordinances, you will live and grow numerous, and the LORD, your God, will bless you in the land you are entering to possess.[r] 17[s] If, however, your heart turns away and you do not obey, but are led astray and bow down to other gods and serve them, 18I tell you today that you will certainly perish; you will not have a long life on the land which you are crossing the Jordan to enter and possess. 19I call heaven and earth today to witness against you:[t] I have set before you life and death, the blessing and the curse. Choose life, then, that you and your descendants may live, 20by loving the LORD, your God, obeying his voice, and holding fast to him. For that will mean life for you, a long life for you to live on the land which the LORD swore to your ancestors, to Abraham, Isaac, and Jacob, to give to them.[u]

## CHAPTER 31

See RG 85–89

***The Lord's Leadership.*** 1When Moses had finished speaking these words to all Israel, 2he said to them, I am now one hundred and twenty years old[v] and am no longer able to go out and come in; besides, the LORD has said to me, Do not cross this Jordan. 3It is the LORD, your God, who will cross before you; he will destroy these nations before you, that you may dispossess them.[w] (It is Joshua who will cross before you, as the LORD promised.) 4[x] The LORD will deal with them just as he dealt with Sihon and Og, the kings of the Amorites, and with their country, when he destroyed them. 5When, therefore, the LORD delivers them up to you, you shall deal with them according to the whole commandment which I have given you.[y] 6Be strong and steadfast; have no fear or dread of them, for it is the LORD, your God, who marches with you; he will never fail you or forsake you.[z]

***Call of Joshua.*** 7Then Moses summoned Joshua and in the presence of all Israel said to him,[a] "Be strong and steadfast, for you shall bring this people into the land which the

**30:6 Circumcise your hearts**: see note on 10:16.

**30:14 In your mouth**: that is, memorized and recited; cf. 6:7; 11:19. **And in your heart**: internalized and appropriated; cf. 6:6; 11:18.

*l:* Jer 23:3. *m:* Dt 6:5; 10:16; Ez 11:19–20; 36:26–28. *n:* Dt 7:15. *o:* Dt 28:4, 11; 30:2. *p:* Dt 6:6; 11:18; Jer 1:9; Bar 3:29–31; Rom 10:6–8. *q:* Dt 11:26–28; Jer 21:8. *r:* Dt 4:1; 8:1; 11:22. *s:* Dt 5:7; 6:4; 8:19–20. *t:* Dt 4:26; 11:26–28; 28:2, 15; 31:28. *u:* Dt 1:8; 4:1, 40. *v:* Dt 1:37; 3:23–28; 4:21–24; 34:7; Gn 6:3; Ex 7:7; Nm 20:12; Acts 7:23, 30. *w:* Dt 1:30–33; 3:22, 28; 9:3. *x:* Dt 2:26–3:7; 3:21–22; Nm 21:21–35. *y:* Dt 7:1–5; 20:16–18. *z:* Dt 1:29; 20:3–4. *a:* Dt 1:21; 31:23; Jos 1:6–9; 10:25.

LORD swore to their ancestors he would give them; it is you who will give them possession of it. 8 It is the LORD who goes before you; he will be with you and will never fail you or forsake you. So do not fear or be dismayed."[b]

***The Reading of the Law.*** 9 [c] When Moses had written down this law, he gave it to the levitical priests who carry the ark of the covenant of the LORD, and to all the elders of Israel.[d] 10 Moses commanded them, saying, On the feast of Booths,[e] at the prescribed time in the year for remission* which comes at the end of every seven-year period, 11 when all Israel goes to appear before the LORD, your God, in the place which he will choose, you shall read this law aloud in the presence of all Israel. 12 Assemble the people—men, women and children, as well as the resident aliens who live in your communities—that they may hear and so learn to fear the LORD, your God, and to observe carefully all the words of this law. 13 Their children also, who do not know it yet, shall hear and learn to fear the LORD, your God, as long as you live on the land which you are about to cross the Jordan to possess.

***Commission to Joshua.*** 14 [f] The LORD said to Moses, The time is now approaching for you to die. Summon Joshua, and present yourselves at the tent of meeting that I may commission him. So Moses and Joshua went and presented themselves at the tent of meeting. 15 And the LORD appeared at the tent in a column of cloud; the column of cloud stood at the entrance of the tent.

***A Command to Moses.*** 16 The LORD said to Moses, Soon you will be at rest with your ancestors, and then this people will prostitute themselves* by following the foreign gods among whom they will live in the land they are about to enter.[g] They will forsake me and break the covenant which I have made with them. 17 [h] At that time my anger will flare up against them; I will forsake them and hide my face from them; they will become a prey to be devoured, and much evil and distress will befall them. At that time they will indeed say, "Is it not because our God is not in our midst that these evils have befallen us?" 18 Yet I will surely hide my face at that time because of all the evil they have done in turning to other gods. 19 Now, write out this song[i] for yourselves. Teach it to the Israelites and have them recite it, so that this song may be a witness for me against the Israelites. 20 For when I have brought them into the land flowing with milk and honey which I promised on oath to their ancestors, and they have eaten and are satisfied and have grown fat, if they turn to other gods and serve them, despising me and breaking my covenant, 21 then, when great evil and distress befall them, this song will speak to them as a witness, for it will not be forgotten if their descendants recite it. For I know what they are inclined to do even at the present time, before I have brought them into the land which I promised on oath. 22 So Moses wrote this song that same day, and he taught it to the Israelites.

***Commission of Joshua.*** 23 Then he commissioned Joshua, son of Nun, and said to him, Be strong and steadfast, for it is you who will bring the Israelites into the land which I promised them on oath.[j] I myself will be with you.

***The Law Placed in the Ark.*** 24 When Moses had finished writing out on a scroll the words of this law in their entirety, 25 Moses gave the Levites[k] who carry the ark of the covenant of the LORD this order: 26 Take this book of the law and put it beside the ark of the covenant of the LORD, your God, that there it may be a witness against you.[l] 27 For I already know how rebellious and stiffnecked you will be. Why, even now, while I am alive among you, you have been rebels against the LORD! How much more, then, af-

**31:10 The year for remission**: cf. 15:1–3 and note there.
**31:16 Prostitute themselves**: lit., "whore after," a play on the phrase "go after," viz. after other gods.

---

*b:* Ex 3:12; Jos 1:5, 17; 3:7; 2 Sm 7:9. *c:* Dt 31:24–27. *d:* Dt 10:1–5, 8. *e:* Dt 12:5; 15:1–11; 16:13–15; 2 Kgs 23:2; Neh 8:1–8. *f:* Ex 33:7–11; Nm 12:5. *g:* Dt 32:16–17; Ex 34:15–16; Jgs 2:11–23; 8:27, 33; 1 Kgs 11:1–10; 2 Kgs 17:7–41; Jer 11:9–10; Hos 4:12; 9:1. *h:* Dt 1:42; 32:19–25; Nm 14:42. *i:* Dt 6:6–9; 31:21; 32:1–43. *j:* Dt 31:7–8; Nm 27:15–23; Jos 1:1–9. *k:* Dt 31:9. *l:* Dt 10:1–5; Ex 40:20; 1 Kgs 8:9.

ter I am dead![m] 28[n] Assemble all your tribal
elders and your officials before me, that I
may speak these words for them to hear and
so may call heaven and earth to witness
against them. 29[o] For I know that after my
death you are sure to act corruptly and to
turn aside from the way along which I commanded you, so that evil will befall you in
time to come because you have done what is
evil in the LORD's sight, and provoked him
by your deeds.

***The Song of Moses.*** 30 Then Moses recited
the words of this song in their entirety, for
the whole assembly of Israel to hear:

## CHAPTER 32

See RG 85-89

1* Give ear, O heavens, and let me speak;
let the earth hear the words of my mouth![p]
2 May my teaching soak in like the rain,
and my utterance drench like the dew,
Like a downpour upon the grass,
like a shower upon the crops.
3 For I will proclaim the name of the LORD,
praise the greatness of our God!

4 The Rock—how faultless are his deeds,
how right all his ways!
A faithful God, without deceit,
just and upright is he![q]

5 Yet his degenerate children have treated him basely,
a twisted and crooked generation![r]
6 Is this how you repay the LORD,
so foolish and unwise a people?
Is he not your father who begot you,
the one who made and established you?[s]
7 Remember the days of old,
consider the years of generations past.
Ask your father, he will inform you,
your elders, they will tell you:[t]
8 When the Most High allotted each nation its heritage,
when he separated out human beings,[u]
He set up the boundaries of the peoples
after the number of the divine beings;*
9 But the LORD's portion was his people;
his allotted share was Jacob.[v]

10 He found them in a wilderness,
a wasteland of howling desert.
He shielded them, cared for them,
guarded them as the apple of his eye.[w]
11 As an eagle incites its nestlings,
hovering over its young,
So he spread his wings, took them,
bore them upon his pinions.[x]
12 The LORD alone guided them,
no foreign god was with them.[y]

13 [z] He had them mount the summits of the land,*
fed them the produce of its fields;
He suckled them with honey from the crags
and olive oil from the flinty rock;
14 Butter from cows and milk from sheep,
with the best of lambs;
Bashan* bulls and goats,
with the cream of finest wheat;
and the foaming blood of grapes you drank.

15 So Jacob ate and was satisfied,
Jeshurun* grew fat and kicked;
you became fat and gross and gorged.
They forsook the God who made them

**32:1–43** The whole song is a poetic sermon, having for its theme the Lord's benefits to Israel (vv. 1–14) and Israel's ingratitude and idolatry in turning to the gods of the nations; these sins will be punished by the nations themselves (vv. 15–29); in turn, the foolish pride of the nations will be punished, and the Lord's honor will be vindicated (vv. 30–43).

**32:8 Divine beings**: lit., "sons of God" (see also v. 43); members of the divine assembly; cf. 1 Kgs 22:19; Jb 1:6; 2:1; 38:7; Ps 82; 89:6–7. The nations are portrayed as having their respective tutelary deities.

**32:13 The land**: Canaan.

**32:14 Bashan**: a fertile grazing land east of the Jordan, famous for its sleek, strong cattle. Cf. Ps 22:13; Ez 39:18; Am 4:1.

**32:15 Jeshurun**: a term for Israel from *yashar*, meaning "upright"; its use here is possibly ironic.

*m:* Dt 9:6–7, 22–24. *n:* Dt 31:12–13, 19–22; 30:19; 32:1–43. *o:* Jgs 2:11–23. *p:* Dt 4:26; 30:19; 31:28. *q:* Dt 7:9; 32:15, 18, 30–31; 2 Sm 22:3; Ps 18:2, 31, 46; 92:15; Is 17:10; Hb 1:12; Rev 15:3. *r:* Dt 9:12; 14:1; 31:29; Ps 78:8; Is 1:2–4; Lk 9:41. *s:* Ex 4:22–23; Is 63:16; 64:8; Jer 31:9; Hos 11:1–4. *t:* Dt 4:32–34. *u:* Gn 14:18–22; Nm 24:16; Jb 1:6; 2:1; Ps 29:1; 47:2; 82:6; 83:18; 89:5–7; Is 14:14; Acts 17:26. *v:* Dt 7:6; Ex 19:5–6; Ps 33:12; Sir 17:17; Jer 10:16; Zec 2:16. *w:* Dt 1:31; 2:7; 8:15; Ps 17:8; Prv 7:2; Jer 2:2–3, 6; Hos 2:15; 13:5–6; Zec 2:12. *x:* Ex 19:4. *y:* Ex 15:13; Is 43:12; Hos 13:4. *z:* Dt 8:7–10; Ps 81:16.

and scorned the Rock of their
salvation.[a]
16 With strange gods they incited him,
with abominations provoked him to
anger.[b]
17 They sacrificed to demons, to "no-gods,"
to gods they had never known,
Newcomers from afar,
before whom your ancestors had never
trembled.
18 You were unmindful of the Rock that
begot you,
you forgot the God who gave you birth.[c]
19 The LORD saw and was filled with
loathing,
provoked by his sons and daughters.[d]
20 He said, I will hide my face from them,
and see what becomes of them.
For they are a fickle generation,
children with no loyalty in them![e]
21 Since they have incited me with a
"no-god,"
and provoked me with their empty
idols,
I will incite them with a "no-people";*
with a foolish nation I will provoke
them.[f]
22 For by my wrath a fire is kindled
that has raged to the depths of Sheol,
It has consumed the earth with its yield,
and set on fire the foundations of the
mountains.[g]
23 I will heap evils upon them
and exhaust all my arrows against
them:[h]
24 Emaciating hunger and consuming fever
and bitter pestilence,
And the teeth of wild beasts I will send
among them,
with the venom of reptiles gliding in
the dust.[i]
25 Out in the street the sword shall bereave,
and at home the terror
For the young man and the young
woman alike,
the nursing babe as well as the gray
beard.[j]
26 I said: I will make an end of them
and blot out their name from human
memory,
27 Had I not feared the provocation by the
enemy,
that their foes might misunderstand,
And say, "Our own hand won the victory;
the LORD had nothing to do with any
of it."[k]
28 For they are a nation devoid of reason,*
having no understanding.
29 If they had insight they would realize
this,
they would understand their end:
30 "How could one rout a thousand,
or two put ten thousand to flight,
Unless it was because their Rock sold
them,
the LORD delivered them up?"
31 Indeed, their "rock" is not like our Rock;
our enemies are fools.
32 For their vine is from the vine of Sodom,
from the vineyards of Gomorrah.
Their grapes are grapes of poison,
and their clusters are bitter.[l]
33 Their wine is the venom of serpents,
the cruel poison of vipers.
34 Is not this stored up with me,
sealed up in my storehouses?
35 Vengeance is mine and recompense,
for the time they lose their footing;

**32:21 "No-god" . . . "no-people"**: worship of the gods of the nations brings destruction at the hands of a foreign invader. A false god cannot sustain or protect (cf. Jer 14:22); and though the nations seem "foolish" (see their characterization in such passages as Ps 114:1; Is 28:11; 33:19), they will prove to be anything but nonentities when the Lord stirs them up against Israel (Is 9:10–12). For the "no-" or "not-" construction, see Hos 1:6, 9; 2:1, 25.

**32:28–35** The reference is to the nations, not to Israel.

**32:36 Neither bond nor free**: an all-inclusive expression; cf. 1 Kgs 14:10; 2 Kgs 9:8.

**32:44 Hoshea**: a variant of "Joshua." Cf. note on Nm 13:16.

**32:49 Abarim**: probably the mountain range to the east of the Dead Sea.

**32:50 Mount Hor**: on the western border of Seir or Edom; cf. Nm 20:23–28; 33:37–38. Dt 10:6 locates elsewhere the place of Aaron's death.

**32:51** Cf. note on 3:26.

*a:* Dt 8:12–18; 31:20; 33:5, 26; Neh 9:25; Is 44:2. *b:* Dt 31:16; Ps 78:58; 81:9; 106:34–39. *c:* Is 49:15; Jer 2:32. *d:* Dt 4:24. *e:* Dt 31:17–18; Nm 6:25–26. *f:* Dt 28:49–50; Jgs 2:14–15; Is 9:11–12; Rom 10:19. *g:* Dt 4:24; Ps 18:7–8; 50:3; Lam 4:11. *h:* Dt 32:42; Ps 7:12–13; 18:14; Ez 5:16. *i:* Dt 28:21–22. *j:* Lv 26:25; Jer 6:11; Lam 1:20; 2:21; Ez 7:15. *k:* Dt 9:26–29; Ex 32:11–14; Ps 74:18. *l:* Dt 29:23.

Because the day of their disaster is at
hand
and their doom is rushing upon them![m]

36 Surely, the LORD will do justice for his
people;
on his servants he will have pity.
When he sees their strength is gone,
and neither bond nor free* is left,[n]
37 He will say, Where are their gods,[o]
the rock in whom they took refuge,
38 Who ate the fat of their sacrifices
and drank the wine of their libations?
Let them rise up now and help you!
Let them be your protection!
39 See now that I, I alone, am he,
and there is no god besides me.
It is I who bring both death and life,
I who inflict wounds and heal them,
and from my hand no one can deliver.[p]
40 For I raise my hand to the heavens
and will say: As surely as I live forever,
41 When I sharpen my flashing sword,
and my hand lays hold of judgment,
With vengeance I will repay my foes
and requite those who hate me.[q]
42 I will make my arrows drunk with blood,
and my sword shall devour flesh—
With the blood of the slain and the
captured,
from the long-haired heads of the
enemy.

43 Exult with him, you heavens,
bow to him, all you divine beings!
For he will avenge the blood of his
servants,
take vengeance on his foes;
He will requite those who hate him,
and purge his people's land.[r]

44 So Moses, together with Hoshea,* son of
Nun, went and spoke all the words of this
song in the hearing of the people.[s]

*Final Appeal.* 45 When Moses had finished
speaking all these words to all Israel, 46 he
said to them,[t] Take to heart all the words that
I am giving in witness against you today,
words you should command your children,
that they may observe carefully every word
of this law. 47 For this is no trivial matter for
you, but rather your very life; by this word
you will enjoy a long life on the land you are
crossing the Jordan to possess.[u]

*Moses Looks upon Canaan.* 48 On that
very day the LORD said to Moses, 49 Ascend
this mountain of the Abarim,* Mount Nebo
in the land of Moab facing Jericho, and view
the land of Canaan, which I am giving to the
Israelites as a possession.[v] 50 Then you shall
die on the mountain you are about to ascend,
and shall be gathered to your people, just as
your brother Aaron died on Mount Hor* and
there was gathered to his people,[w] 51 because
both of you broke faith with me among the
Israelites at the waters of Meribath-kadesh
in the wilderness of Zin: you did not manifest my holiness among the Israelites.*[x]
52 You may indeed see the land from a distance, but you shall not enter that land which
I am giving to the Israelites.[y]

## CHAPTER 33

See RG 85–89

*Blessing upon the Tribes.** 1 This is the
blessing with which Moses, the man of God,
blessed the Israelites before he died.[z]
2[a] He said:

The LORD came from Sinai
and dawned on his people from Seir;
he shone forth from Mount Paran.
With him were myriads of holy ones;
at his right hand advanced the gods.*

**33:1–29** This poem, called the Blessing of Moses, consists of a series of poetic characterizations of each of the tribes of Israel (vv. 6–25), introduced (vv. 2–3) and concluded (vv. 26–27) by a theophany; vv. 4–5 lead into the blessing proper; and the poem ends with a blessing on Israel as a whole (vv. 28–29). This catalog of the tribal units of the people Israel resembles the Blessing of Jacob (Gn 49) and the Song of Deborah (Jgs 5, especially vv. 14–18); all three poems seem to date from the early premonarchic period.

**33:2 Gods**: the divine beings who constitute the armies of the Lord, the heavenly hosts (Sabaoth); see note on 32:8. These "holy ones" (v. 3) are the retinue of the Lord, the warrior God, in his march from the southern mountains (Sinai, Seir, Paran).

*m:* Ps 94:1; Is 59:18; 61:2; Hos 9:7. *n:* 2 Mc 7:6; Ps 9:8; 135:14. *o:* Jgs 10:14; 1 Kgs 18:27; Jer 2:28. *p:* Dt 4:35; 6:4; 1 Sm 2:6–8; Tb 13:2; Jb 5:18; Wis 16:13; Is 30:26; 43:10–13; 44:6; Hos 6:1–2. *q:* Is 1:24; Na 1:2. *r:* Dt 32:1, 8; Is 49:13. *s:* Dt 31:14–15, 23. *t:* Dt 4:9. *u:* Dt 4:40; 6:1–2. *v:* Dt 34:1; Nm 27:12. *w:* Dt 10:6; Nm 20:23–29; 27:13; 33:38–39. *x:* Ex 17:1–7; Nm 20:1–13; 27:14; Ps 106:32–33. *y:* Dt 3:27; 34:4. *z:* Jos 14:6; Ps 90:1. *a:* Ex 15:14–17; 19:18–20; Nm 10:36; Jgs 5:4–5; Ps 68:7–8, 17; 89:7; Hb 3:3–6.

3 Indeed, lover of the peoples,
all the holy ones are at your side;
They follow at your heels,
carry out your decisions.
4 Moses charged us with the law,
as a possession for the assembly of Jacob.[b]
5 A king arose* in Jeshurun
when the chiefs of the people assembled,
and the tribes of Israel united.[c]

6 May Reuben live and not die out,[d]
but let his numbers be few.

7 Of Judah he said this:

Hear, LORD, the voice of Judah,
and bring him to his people.*
His own hands defend his cause;
be a help against his foes.[e]

8 Of Levi he said:[f]

Give to Levi your Thummim,
your Urim* to your faithful one;
Him you tested at Massah,
contended against him at the waters of Meribah.[g]
9 * He said of his father and mother,
"I have no regard for them";
His brothers he would not acknowledge,
and his own children he did not recognize.
For they kept your words,
and your covenant they upheld.[h]
10 [i] They teach your ordinances to Jacob,
your law to Israel.
They bring incense to your nostrils,
and burnt offerings to your altar.
11 Bless, LORD, his strength,
be pleased with the work of his hands.
Crush the loins of his adversaries
and of his foes, that they may not rise.

12 Of Benjamin he said:

The beloved of the LORD,
he abides in safety beside him;
He shelters him all day long;
the beloved abides at his breast.* [j]

13 Of Joseph he said:[k]

Blessed by the LORD is his land
with the best of heaven above
and of the abyss crouching beneath;
14 With the best of the produce of the sun,
and the choicest yield of the months;
15 With the finest gifts of the ancient mountains
and the best from the everlasting hills;
16 With the best of the earth and its fullness,
and the favor of the one who dwells on Sinai.
Let these come upon the head of Joseph
and upon the brow of the prince among his brothers.[l]
17 His firstborn bull, majesty is his!
His horns are the horns of a wild ox;
With them he gores the peoples,
attacks the ends of the earth.
These are the myriads of Ephraim,
and these the thousands of Manasseh.

18 Of Zebulun he said:[m]

Rejoice, Zebulun, in your expeditions,
exult, Issachar, in your tents!
19 They invite peoples to the mountain
where they offer right sacrifices,
Because they suck up the abundance of the seas*
and the hidden treasures of the sand.

**33:5 A king arose**: it is unclear whether this refers to divine kingship or the beginning of the monarchy in Israel. **Jeshurun**: see note on 32:15.

**33:7 Bring him to his people**: this probably refers to the isolated position of the tribe of Judah (cf. Jgs 1:17–19); according to some commentators the reference is to the divided kingdom.

**33:8 Thummim . . . Urim**: devices priests used for divination (cf. note on Ex 28:30).

**33:9** The reference is probably to the Levites' slaughter of other Israelites after the incident of the golden calf; cf. Ex 32:27–29.

**33:12 Abides at his breast**: an image of security under divine protection.

**33:19 The abundance of the seas**: perhaps the wealth that comes from sea trade or from fishing. **The hidden treasures of the sand**: possibly an allusion to the valuable purple dye extracted from certain marine shells found on the coast of northern Palestine.

*b:* Dt 4:44; Jn 1:17; 7:19. *c:* Dt 32:15. *d:* Gn 49:3–4. *e:* Gn 49:8–12. *f:* Gn 49:5–7. *g:* Dt 6:16; 9:22; 32:51; Ex 17:1–7; 28:30; Lv 8:8; Nm 20:1–13; 1 Sm 14:41–42. *h:* Lk 14:26. *i:* Dt 10:8; 17:9–11; 18:1–8; Ex 30:7–8; Lv 10:11; 2 Kgs 17:27–28; Mal 2:4–9. *j:* Gn 49:27. *k:* Gn 49:22–26. *l:* Ex 3:1–6; Jgs 5:6. *m:* Gn 49:13–15.

20 Of Gad he said:[n]

Blessed be the one who has made Gad so
vast!
He lies there like a lion;
he tears the arm, the head as well.
21 He saw that the best should be his,
for there the commander's portion was
assigned;
he came at the head of the people.
He carried out the justice of the LORD
and his ordinances for Israel.[o]

22 Of Dan he said:

Dan is a lion's cub,[p]
that springs away from a viper!

23 Of Naphtali he said:

Naphtali, abounding with favor,
filled with the blessing of the LORD,
take possession of the west and south.[q]

24 Of Asher he said:[r]

Most blessed* of sons be Asher!
May he be the favorite among his
brothers,
and may he dip his foot in oil!
25 May the bolts of your gates be iron and
bronze;
may your strength endure through all
your days!
26 There is none like the God of Jeshurun,
who rides the heavens in his power,
who rides the clouds in his majesty;[s]
27 The God of old is a refuge;
a support are the arms of the Everlasting.
He drove the enemy out of your way
and he said, "Destroy!"[t]
28 Israel abides securely,
Jacob dwells apart,
In a land of grain and wine,
where the heavens drip with dew.[u]
29 Happy are you, Israel! Who is like you,
a people delivered by the LORD,
Your help and shield,
and the sword of your glory.
Your enemies cringe before you;
you stride upon their backs.[v]

## IV. The Death of Moses

### CHAPTER 34

See RG 85–89

1 Then Moses went up from the plains
of Moab to Mount Nebo,[w] the peak of Pisgah
which faces Jericho, and the LORD showed
him all the land—Gilead, and as far as Dan,
2 all Naphtali, the land of Ephraim and Manasseh, all the land of Judah as far as the Western
Sea,[x] 3 the Negeb, the plain (the valley of Jericho, the City of Palms), and as far as Zoar.
4 The LORD then said to him, This is the land[y]
about which I promised on oath to Abraham,
Isaac, and Jacob, "I will give it to your descendants." I have let you see it with your own
eyes, but you shall not cross over. 5 So there, in
the land of Moab, Moses, the servant of the
LORD, died[z] as the LORD had said; 6 and he was
buried in a valley in the land of Moab, opposite Beth-peor; to this day no one knows the
place of his burial.[a] 7 Moses was one hundred
and twenty years old[b] when he died, yet his
eyes were undimmed and his vigor unabated.
8 The Israelites wept for Moses in the plains of
Moab for thirty days, till they had completed
the period of grief and mourning for Moses.
9 Now Joshua, son of Nun,[c] was filled with
the spirit of wisdom, since Moses had laid
his hands upon him; and so the Israelites
gave him their obedience, just as the LORD
had commanded Moses.
10[d] Since then no prophet has arisen in Israel like Moses, whom the LORD knew face
to face, 11[e] in all the signs and wonders the
LORD sent him to perform in the land of
Egypt against Pharaoh and all his servants
and against all his land, 12 and all the great
might and the awesome power that Moses
displayed in the sight of all Israel.

**33:24 Most blessed**: Hebrew *baruk*; but the name Asher may suggest a play on the Hebrew *'ashre*, "happy"; cf., e.g., v. 29; Ps 1:1. **Oil**: the land of the tribe of Asher was covered with olive groves.

*n:* Gn 49:19. *o:* Nm 32:1–32; Jos 1:12–15; 1 Chr 5:18–22; 12:8–15. *p:* Gn 49:16–17. *q:* Gn 49:21; Jos 19:32–39. *r:* Gn 49:20. *s:* Dt 32:15; Ps 18:10; 68:4, 33; 104:3; Is 19:1. *t:* Dt 7:1, 17–24. *u:* Dt 7:12–16; Gn 27:28; Nm 23:9. *v:* Dt 4:7–8; Gn 15:1; 2 Sm 22:3; Ps 28:7; 119:114. *w:* Dt 3:27; 32:49. *x:* Dt 11:24. *y:* Dt 1:8; 3:27; 32:52; Gn 12:7; 15:18–21. *z:* Dt 32:50; Ex 14:31; Nm 12:7–8; Jos 1:1–2, 7, 13, 15; 1 Kgs 8:53, 56; Mal 3:22. *a:* Dt 3:29. *b:* Dt 31:2. *c:* Nm 27:18–23; Jos 1:17. *d:* Dt 5:4; 18:15; Ex 33:11; Nm 12:8; Sir 45:5. *e:* Dt 4:34; Ex 4:21; 7:1, 8–12.

See RG 93–99

# The Historical Books

Where the Hebrew Bible comprises three sections—Torah or Pentateuch; Prophetic Books, both the Former and the Latter Prophets; and the Writings, including everything else in the Hebrew Canon—the Christian Old Testament has traditionally been arranged along different lines. After the Pentateuch comes a series of books that continue, in roughly chronological order, the history of Israel. The Book of Joshua depicts Israel taking possession of the land of Canaan. Judges collects stories about the leaders of early Israel in the two hundred years before the emergence of the monarchy. After the tale of Ruth, a sort of interlude in the narrative sweep of these books, 1 and 2 Samuel tell of the rise and fall of Saul, Israel's first king, and the succession and successes of David. The Books of Kings take us from the death of David and the enthronement of Solomon, through the division of the people into the two kingdoms of Israel and Judah, to the destruction of the Northern Kingdom, Israel, at the hands of the Assyrian invader (722/721 B.C.), and the fall of Judah, the Southern Kingdom, to the Babylonians (587 B.C.) and its ensuing exile, the Babylonian captivity.

Except for Ruth, these writings bear the marks of a specific theological outlook, that of the Book of Deuteronomy, and together with that book as its introductory volume constitute what is called the Deuteronomistic History. In this theology, what has characterized Israel's history, in the six hundred years from Moses to the Babylonian exile, has been a dynamic of fidelity or infidelity to Israel's covenant Lord, and the consequent destiny Israel forges for itself of covenant blessing or covenant curse. This dynamic of choice and consequences serves to explain the disasters Israel incurs throughout its history, from the so-called conquest and the days of the Judges to the fall of the North. In its preexilic edition, the Deuteronomistic History would have stood also as warning and wake-up call to the surviving Southern Kingdom.

The Books of Chronicles recycle much of the material found in the previous works, but the author ("the Chronicler") treats it selectively, with a characteristic theological point of view; its focus is the Jerusalem Temple and its cultic arrangements, which by way of legitimation are attributed to David, the ideal king. The Chronicler's interests carry through the Books of Ezra and Nehemiah, which recount the restoration of Jewish worship and life in the period of Persian rule following release from exile in Babylon.

The Books of Maccabees give us two overlapping but somewhat differing accounts of Jewish resistance to Seleucid persecution in the early second century B.C., and the assumption of power by the leaders of the resistance, the Maccabees or Hasmoneans.

The traditional designation of these books as "historical" describes their scope and contents, and is not meant to assert factual verifiability; while they contain much valuable historical information, in the narrow sense, their purpose is theological rather than historiographic.

The Books of Tobit, Judith, and Esther are sometimes reckoned among the historical books, but they differ from the writings sketched above, and call for special treatment; see the introduction to those books.

See RG 93–99

# The Book of Joshua

The Book of Joshua presents a narrative of the way Israel took possession of the land of Canaan, making it the land of Israel. This process is swift and inexorable, and is followed by an orderly division and disposition of the land among the twelve tribes, with a concluding ceremony of covenant renewal.

The theological message of the book is unmistakable. God has been faithful to the promise of the land. If Israel relies totally on the Lord for victory; if Israel is united as a people; if the law of *herem* is kept and no one grows rich from victory in war—then and only then will Israel possess the land.

The Israelites are led by Joshua, the successor of Moses, and the book is at pains to show not only how Joshua carries on the work of Moses but how the "conquest" of Canaan is continuous with the exodus from Egypt. This is seen in the repeated insistence that, as the Lord was with Moses, so he is with Joshua; and, especially, in the crossing of the Jordan River, which is patterned after the crossing of the Red Sea.

The book preserves older traditions of Israel's settlement in the land, especially in the division of the land among the tribes. As with Deuteronomy and the whole Deuteronomistic History (see introduction to Deuteronomy), the fall of the Northern Kingdom in 722/721 B.C. shows its influence throughout. As addressed to the needs of a late preexilic audience, then, the book should be read not so much as imparting information about how Israel took over the land of Canaan, many centuries before the composition of the book, as teaching a lesson about how Israel is to avoid losing the land.

Modern readers may be put off by the description of battles and their aftermath, the destruction of everyone and everything in the cities taken under the "ban" (*herem*). The ban was practiced in the ancient Near East, in Israel and elsewhere, but in Joshua the wholesale destruction of the Canaanites is an idealization of the deuteronomic idea that pagans are to be wiped out so they will not be an occasion for apostasy from the Lord (cf. Dt 7:1–6); note in particular the artificial, formalized description of destruction of towns in Jos 10:28–39. It should be remembered that by the time the book was written, the Canaanites were long gone. Progressive revelation throughout Israel's history produced far more lofty ideals, as when the prophets see all the nations embracing faith in Yahweh, being joined to Israel, and living in peace with one another (Is 2:2–4; 19:23–25; 45:22–25; Zec 8:22–23), and the New Testament teaches us to love even our enemies (Mt 5:43–45).

A comparison of Joshua with the account of Israel's early history found in the first chapter of the Book of Judges shows that Israel's emergence as the dominant presence in the land was a slow and piecemeal affair, not achieved at one stroke and with great ease: the Book of Joshua, with its highly idealized depiction of the "conquest," is a theologically programmatic cautionary tale about what the people are to do and not do in order to avoid the fate of the Northern Kingdom in losing the land.

The Book of Joshua may be divided as follows:



# I. Conquest of Canaan

## CHAPTER 1

See RG 94

*Divine Promise of Assistance.* 1 After
Moses, the servant of the LORD, had died,
the LORD said to Moses' aide Joshua, son of
Nun: 2* Moses my servant is dead. So now,
you and the whole people with you, prepare
to cross the Jordan to the land that I will give
the Israelites. 3[a] Every place where you set
foot I have given you, as I promised Moses.
4* All the land of the Hittites, from the
wilderness and the Lebanon east to the great
river Euphrates and west to the Great Sea,
will be your territory.[b] 5 No one can withstand
you as long as you live. As I was with
Moses, I will be with you:[c] I will not leave
you nor forsake you. 6 Be strong and steadfast,
so that you may give this people possession
of the land I swore to their ancestors
that I would give them. 7[d] Only be strong
and steadfast, being careful to observe the
entire law which Moses my servant enjoined
on you. Do not swerve from it either to the
right or to the left, that you may succeed
wherever you go. 8 Do not let this book of the
law depart from your lips. Recite it by day
and by night,[e] that you may carefully ob-

**1:2–9** The beginning of the Book of Joshua strongly emphasizes the credentials of Joshua as Moses' worthy successor (vv. 2, 3, 4, 7; cf. v. 17; 3:7; 4:14; 5:15). The movement Joshua leads, whereby the Israelites take possession of the land of Canaan, is thus made continuous with the exodus from Egypt, even though (except for Joshua and Caleb) the generation that left Egypt under Moses' leadership has died out (5:4, 6), and the people who will make the land of Canaan the land of Israel are a new generation. Thus the book is at pains to establish the continuity between exodus and conquest.

**1:4** The frontiers are as follows: in the south the wilderness of Sinai, in the north the Lebanon range, in the east the Euphrates, and in the west the Great Sea, the Mediterranean. These boundaries are ideal rather than actual.

*a:* Jos 14:9; Gn 15:18; Dt 11:24–25; 34:4. *b:* Gn 10:19; Nm 13:17, 21–22; 34:3–12. *c:* Dt 3:21–22; 31:8, 23; Heb 13:5. *d:* Dt 2:27; 5:29; 17:11, 20; 28:14; Ps 1:1–3. *e:* Ps 1:2.

**Do not fear nor be dismayed, for the LORD, your God, is with you wherever you go.**

THIS THOUGHT FROM Joshua 1:9 has been treasured through the years by readers of this passage. When you are uncertain about what to do, or challenged to do something difficult, it can be a source of courage and comfort at the same time.

serve all that is written in it; then you will attain your goal; then you will succeed. [9]I command you: be strong and steadfast! Do not fear nor be dismayed, for the LORD, your God, is with you wherever you go.

[10f]So Joshua commanded the officers of the people: [11]"Go through the camp and command the people, 'Prepare your provisions, for three days from now you shall cross the Jordan here, to march in and possess the land the LORD, your God, is giving as your possession.' "

***The Transjordan Tribes.*** [12g]Joshua addressed the Reubenites, the Gadites, and the half-tribe of Manasseh: [13]"Remember what Moses, the servant of the LORD, commanded you when he said, 'The LORD, your God, is about to give you rest; he will give you this land.' [14]Your wives, your children, and your livestock may remain in the land Moses gave you here beyond the Jordan. But all the warriors among you must cross over armed, ahead of your kindred, and you must help them [15]until the LORD has settled your kindred, and they like you possess the land the LORD, your God, is giving them. Afterward you may return and possess your own land, which Moses, the servant of the LORD, has given you east of the Jordan."[h] [16]They answered Joshua, "We will do all you have commanded us, and we will go wherever you send us. [17]As completely as we obeyed Moses, we will obey you. Only, may the LORD, your God, be with you as God was with Moses. [18]Anyone who rebels against your orders and does not obey all your commands shall be put to death. Only be strong and steadfast."

## CHAPTER 2

See RG 94

***Spies Saved by Rahab.*** [1]Then Joshua, son of Nun, secretly sent out two spies from Shittim, saying, "Go, reconnoiter the land and Jericho." When the two reached Jericho, they went into the house of a prostitute named Rahab,[i] where they lodged. [2]But a report was brought to the king of Jericho: "Some men came here last night, Israelites, to spy out the land." [3]So the king of Jericho sent Rahab the order, "Bring out the men who have come to you and entered your house, for they have come to spy out the entire land." [4]The woman[j] had taken the two men and hidden them, so she said, "True, the men you speak of came to me, but I did not know where they came from. [5]At dark, when it was time to close the gate, they left, and I do not know where they went. You will have to pursue them quickly to overtake them." [6]Now, she had led them to the roof, and hidden them among her stalks of flax spread out* there. [7]But the pursuers set out along the way to the fords of the Jordan. As soon as they had left to pursue them, the gate was shut.

[8]Before the spies lay down, Rahab went up to them on the roof [9]and said:* "I know that the LORD has given you the land, that a dread of you has come upon us, and that all the inhabitants of the land tremble with fear because of you.[k] [10]For we have heard how

**2:6 Stalks of flax spread out**: to dry in the sun, after they had been soaked in water, according to the ancient process of preparing flax for linen-making. In the Near East the flax harvest occurs near the time of the feast of the Passover (4:19; 5:10); cf. Ex 9:31.

**2:9–11** Rahab's speech is Deuteronomic in content and style. Through her, the author expresses a theological conviction: the Lord, the God of Israel, is God above all gods; the formation of the people Israel and its success is the Lord's doing; and all the rulers of the neighboring nations do well to panic at what the Lord is doing (cf. 5:1). Rahab the prostitute is pointedly mentioned in the Matthean genealogy of Jesus (Mt 1:5) and in Jas 2:25.

*f:* Dt 20:5–9. *g:* Nm 32; Dt 3:12–20. *h:* Jos 22:4; Dt 3:20. *i:* Dt 1:22; Mt 1:5; Jas 2:25. *j:* Jos 6:17; Heb 11:31. *k:* Ex 15:15–16; 23:27.

the LORD dried up the waters of the Red Sea
before you when you came out of Egypt,[l]
and what you did to Sihon and Og, the two
kings of the Amorites beyond the Jordan,
whom you destroyed under the ban. 11We
heard, and our hearts melted within us;
everyone is utterly dispirited because of you,
since the LORD, your God, is God in heaven
above and on earth below.[m] 12[n] Now then,
swear to me by the LORD that, since I am
showing kindness to you, you in turn will
show kindness to my family.[o] Give me a reliable sign 13that you will allow my father
and mother, brothers and sisters, and my
whole family to live, and that you will deliver us from death." 14"We pledge our lives
for yours," they answered her. "If you do not
betray our mission, we will be faithful in
showing kindness to you when the LORD
gives us the land."

15Then she let them down through the window with a rope; for she lived in a house built
into the city wall.* 16"Go up into the hill
country," she said, "that your pursuers may
not come upon you. Hide there for three
days, until they return; then you may go on
your way." 17They answered her, "We are
free of this oath that you made us take, unless, 18when we come into the land, you tie
this scarlet cord in the window through
which you are letting us down. Gather your
father and mother, your brothers, and all your
family into your house. 19Should any of them
pass outside the doors of your house, their
blood will be on their own heads, and we will
be guiltless. But if anyone in your house is
harmed, their blood will be on our heads.
20If, however, you betray our mission, we
will be free of the oath you have made us
take." 21"Let it be as you say," she replied,
and sent them away. When they were gone,
she tied the scarlet cord in the window.

22They went up into the hill country, where
they stayed three days until their pursuers,
who had sought them all along the road without finding them, returned. 23Then the two
came back down from the hills, crossed the
Jordan to Joshua, son of Nun, and told him all
that had happened to them. 24They assured
Joshua, "The LORD has given all this land into
our power; indeed, all the inhabitants of the
land tremble with fear because of us."

## CHAPTER 3

See RG 94

### *Preparations for Crossing the Jordan.*

1Early the next morning, Joshua and all the
Israelites moved from Shittim and came to
the Jordan, where they stayed before crossing over. 2[p] Three days later the officers went
through the camp 3[q] and issued these commands to the people: "When you see the ark
of the covenant of the LORD, your God,
which the levitical priests will carry, you
must break camp and follow it, 4that you may
know the way to take, for you have not gone
over this road before. But let there be a space
of two thousand cubits between you and the
ark: do not come nearer to it." 5Joshua also
said to the people, "Sanctify yourselves, for
tomorrow the LORD will perform wonders
among you." 6And he told the priests, "Take
up the ark of the covenant and cross ahead of
the people"; so they took up the ark of the
covenant and went before the people.

7[r] Then the LORD said to Joshua: Today I
will begin to exalt you in the sight of all Israel, that they may know that, as I was with
Moses, so I will be with you.[s] 8Now command the priests carrying the ark of the covenant, "When you come to the edge of the
waters of the Jordan, there take your stand."

9So Joshua said to the Israelites, "Come
here and listen to the words of the LORD,
your God." 10He continued: "By this you
will know that there is a living God in your
midst: he will certainly dispossess before
you the Canaanites, Hittites, Hivites, Perizzites, Girgashites, Amorites, and Jebusites.[t] 11The ark of the covenant of the Lord
of the whole earth will cross the Jordan be-

**2:15 A house built into the city wall**: the city wall formed the back wall of the house; remains of such houses have been found at ancient sites. The upper story of Rahab's house was evidently higher than the city wall. It was through the window of such a house that St. Paul escaped from Damascus; cf. Acts 9:25; 2 Cor 11:33.

*l:* Jos 4:23; Ex 14:21; Nm 21:23–26, 33–35. *m:* Jos 5:1; Dt 4:39; Rom 10:9. *n:* Jgs 1:22–26. *o:* Jos 2:18; 6:23, 25. *p:* Jos 2:1. *q:* Nm 10:33. *r:* Jos 1:5; Dt 31:23. *s:* Jos 1:5; 4:14. *t:* Ex 33:2; Dt 7:1.

## The Ark and Crossing the Jordan

THE ARK OF the Covenant served as a container for the scroll of the law according to Deuteronomy 31:26. As the powerful physical symbol of God's presence among the people, it could be protective in battle (see Nm 10:33–35; 1 Sm 4:3–5). The Jordan symbolizes all the borders of the Promised Land, and crossing a river into Israel's territory echoes the people's passage through water (the Red Sea) under the leadership of Moses at the outset of the journey. This strengthens the depiction of Joshua as a new Moses, with great authority. The Jordan also functions primarily as a symbol representing the boundary between landlessness and settled peoplehood.

fore you. 12Now choose twelve men,[u] one
from each of the tribes of Israel. 13When the
soles of the feet of the priests carrying the
ark of the LORD, the Lord of the whole earth,
touch the waters of the Jordan, it will cease
to flow; the water flowing down from upstream will halt in a single heap."*
*The Crossing Begun.* 14The people set out
from their tents to cross the Jordan, with the
priests carrying the ark of the covenant ahead
of them. 15When those bearing the ark came
to the Jordan and the feet of the priests bearing the ark were immersed in the waters of the
Jordan—which overflows all its banks during
the entire season of the harvest—* 16the waters flowing from upstream halted, standing
up in a single heap[v] for a very great distance
indeed, from Adam, a city in the direction of
Zarethan; those flowing downstream toward
the Salt Sea of the Arabah disappeared entirely.* Thus the people crossed over opposite
Jericho. 17The priests carrying the ark of the
covenant of the LORD stood on dry ground in
the Jordan riverbed[w] while all Israel crossed
on dry ground, until the whole nation had
completed the crossing of the Jordan.

See RG 94

### CHAPTER 4

*Memorial Stones.* 1After the entire nation had completed the crossing of the Jordan, 2the LORD said to Joshua: Choose
twelve men[x] from the people, one from each
tribe, 3and command them, "Take up twelve
stones from this spot in the Jordan riverbed
where the priests have been standing.[y] Carry
them over with you, and place them where
you are to stay tonight."
4Summoning the twelve men he had selected from among the Israelites, one from
each tribe, 5Joshua said to them: "Go to the
Jordan riverbed in front of the ark of the
LORD, your God; lift to your shoulders one
stone apiece, so that they will equal in number the tribes of the Israelites. 6In the future,
these are to be a sign among you. When your
children ask you,* 'What do these stones
mean to you?'[z] 7you shall answer them, 'The
waters of the Jordan ceased to flow before
the ark of the covenant of the LORD when it
crossed the Jordan.'[a] Thus these stones are
to serve as a perpetual memorial to the Israelites." 8The twelve Israelites did as Joshua
had commanded: they took up twelve stones
from the Jordan riverbed as the LORD had
said to Joshua, one for each of the tribes of
the Israelites. They carried them along to the
camp site, and there they placed them.
9Joshua set up the twelve stones that had
been in the Jordan riverbed on the spot
where the priests stood who were carrying

**3:13 Heap**: Heb. *nēd*, the same word found in Ex 15:8; the narrative echoes the ancient Song of Miriam (Ex 15:1–18), which celebrates the crossing of the Red Sea. Thus the language provides another parallel between Joshua and Moses, conquest and exodus.

**3:15 Season of the harvest**: toward the end of March and the beginning of April, when the barley and other crops that grew during the rainy season of winter were reaped. The crossing took place "on the tenth day of the first month" of the Hebrew year, which began with the first new moon after the spring equinox; cf. 4:19. At this time of the year the Jordan would be swollen as a result of the winter rains and the melting snow of Mount Hermon.

**3:16** Some scholars have suggested that this account may reflect an annual ritual reenactment of the event near the sanctuary of Gilgal.

**4:6 When your children ask you**: reminiscent of the question and response at the Passover meal, Ex 12:26–27.

*u:* Jos 4:2, 4. *v:* Ps 114:3. *w:* Jos 4:7, 22. *x:* Jos 3:12. *y:* Jos 3:13; 4:8–9; Dt 27:2. *z:* Ex 12:26–27; Dt 6:7, 20–25. *a:* Jos 3:13, 16.

the ark of the covenant. They are there to this day.

10* The priests carrying the ark stood in the Jordan riverbed until everything had been done that the LORD had commanded Joshua to tell the people, just as Moses had commanded Joshua. The people crossed over quickly, 11 and when all the people had completed the crossing, the ark of the LORD also crossed; and the priests were now in front of them. 12 The Reubenites, Gadites, and half-tribe of Manasseh, armed, marched in the vanguard of the Israelites, as Moses had ordered. 13 About forty thousand troops, equipped for battle, crossed over before the LORD to the plains of Jericho for war.

14 That day the LORD exalted Joshua in the sight of all Israel,[b] and so during his whole life they feared him as they had feared Moses.

15 Then the LORD said to Joshua: 16 Command the priests carrying the ark of the covenant to come up from the Jordan. 17 Joshua commanded the priests, "Come up from the Jordan," 18 and when the priests carrying the ark of the covenant of the LORD had come up from the Jordan riverbed, as the soles of their feet regained the dry ground, the waters of the Jordan resumed their course and as before overflowed all its banks.

19 The people came up from the Jordan on the tenth day of the first month, and camped in Gilgal on the eastern limits of Jericho.[c] 20 At Gilgal Joshua set up the twelve stones that had been taken from the Jordan, 21 saying to the Israelites, "In the future, when your children ask their parents, 'What do these stones mean?' 22 you shall inform them, 'Israel crossed the Jordan here on dry ground.' 23 For the LORD, your God, dried up the waters of the Jordan in front of you until you crossed over, just as the LORD, your God, had done at the Red Sea, drying it up in front of us until we crossed over,[d] 24 in order that all the peoples of the earth may know that the hand of the LORD is mighty, and that you may fear the LORD, your God, forever."[e]

## CHAPTER 5

See RG 94–97

*Rites at Gilgal.* 1 When all the kings of the Amorites to the west of the Jordan and all the kings of the Canaanites by the sea heard that the LORD had dried up the waters of the Jordan before the Israelites until they crossed over, their hearts melted and they were utterly dispirited because of the Israelites.

2[f] On this occasion the LORD said to Joshua: Make flint knives and circumcise Israel for the second time. 3 So Joshua made flint knives and circumcised the Israelites at Gibeath-haaraloth.* 4 This was the reason for the circumcision: Of all the people who had come out of Egypt, every male of military age had died in the wilderness[g] during the journey after they came out of Egypt. 5 Though all the men who came out were circumcised, none of those born in the wilderness during the journey after the departure from Egypt were circumcised. 6 Now the Israelites wandered forty years in the wilderness, until all the warriors among the people that came forth from Egypt died off because they had not listened to the voice of the LORD. For the LORD swore[h] that he would not let them see the land he had sworn to their ancestors to give us, a land flowing with milk and honey. 7[i] It was the children God raised up in their stead whom Joshua circumcised, for these were yet with foreskins, not having been circumcised on the journey. 8 When the circumcision of the entire nation was complete, they remained in camp where they were, until they recovered. 9 Then the LORD said to Joshua: Today I have removed the reproach of Egypt from you.[j] Therefore the place is called Gilgal* to the present day.

10[k] While the Israelites were encamped at

**4:10–18** After the digression about the memorial stones, the author resumes the narrative by briefly repeating the story of the crossing, which had already been told in 3:14–17.

**5:3 Gibeath-haaraloth**: "Hill of the Foreskins."

**5:9 The place is called Gilgal**: by popular etymology, because of the similarity of sound with the Hebrew word *gallothi*, "I have removed." Gilgal probably means "circle," i.e., the place of the circle of standing stones. Cf. 4:4–8.

*b:* Jos 3:7. *c:* Ex 12:2–3. *d:* Ex 14:21. *e:* Ex 9:3; 14:31; 16:3. *f:* Gn 17; 34; Ex 4:24–26. *g:* Nm 14:29; 26:64–65; 1 Cor 10:5. *h:* Nm 14:33–34; Heb 3:11, 17. *i:* Gn 17:8–14. *j:* Jos 4:19; Eph 2:11–22. *k:* Ex 12:6; Nm 9:3–5.

Gilgal on the plains of Jericho, they celebrated the Passover on the evening of the fourteenth day of the month.* 11 On the day after the Passover they ate of the produce of the land in the form of unleavened cakes and parched grain. On that same day 12 after they ate of the produce of the land, the manna ceased. No longer was there manna for the Israelites, who that year ate of the yield of the land of Canaan.[l]

***Siege at Jericho.*** 13* While Joshua was near Jericho, he raised his eyes and saw one who stood facing him, drawn sword in hand.[m] Joshua went up to him and asked, "Are you one of us or one of our enemies?" 14 He replied, "Neither. I am the commander* of the army of the LORD: now I have come." Then Joshua fell down to the ground in worship, and said to him, "What has my lord to say to his servant?" 15 The commander of the army of the LORD replied to Joshua, "Remove your sandals from your feet, for the place on which you are standing is holy."[n] And Joshua did so.

## CHAPTER 6

See RG 95–97

1 Now Jericho was in a state of siege because of the presence of the Israelites. No one left or entered. 2 And to Joshua the LORD said: I have delivered Jericho, its king, and its warriors into your power. 3[o] Have all the soldiers circle the city, marching once around it. Do this for six days, 4 with seven priests carrying ram's horns ahead of the ark. On the seventh day march around the city seven times, and have the priests blow the horns. 5 When they give a long blast on the ram's horns and you hear the sound of the horn, all the people shall shout aloud. The wall of the city will collapse, and the people shall attack straight ahead.

6 Summoning the priests, Joshua, son of Nun, said to them, "Take up the ark of the covenant with seven of the priests carrying ram's horns in front of the ark of the LORD." 7 And he ordered the people, "Proceed and surround the city, with the picked troops marching ahead of the ark of the LORD." 8 When Joshua spoke to the people, the seven priests who carried the ram's horns before the LORD marched and blew their horns, and the ark of the covenant of the LORD followed them. 9 In front of the priests with the horns marched the picked troops; the rear guard followed the ark, and the blowing of horns was kept up continually as they marched. 10 But Joshua had commanded the people, "Do not shout or make any noise or outcry until I tell you, 'Shout!' Then you must shout." 11 So he had the ark of the LORD circle the city, going once around it, after which they returned to camp for the night.

12 Early the next morning, Joshua had the priests take up the ark of the LORD. 13 The seven priests bearing the ram's horns marched in front of the ark of the LORD, blowing their horns. Ahead of these marched the picked troops, while the rear guard followed the ark of the LORD, and the blowing of horns was kept up continually. 14 On this second day they again marched around the city once before returning to camp; and for six days in all they did the same.

15 On the seventh day, beginning at daybreak, they marched around the city seven times in the same manner; on that day only did they march around the city seven times. 16 The seventh time around, the priests blew the horns and Joshua said to the people, "Now shout, for the LORD has given you the city. 17[p] The city and everything in it is under the ban. Only Rahab the prostitute and all who are in the house with her are to live, because she hid the messengers we sent. 18[q] But be careful not to covet or take anything that

**5:10 The month**: the first month of the year, later called Nisan; see note on 3:15. The crossing of the Jordan occurred, therefore, about the same time of the year as did the crossing of the Red Sea; cf. Ex 12–14.

**5:13–6:26** The account of the siege of Jericho embraces: (1) the command of the Lord to Joshua (5:13–6:5); (2) Joshua's instructions to the Israelites, with a brief summary of how these orders were carried out (6:6–11); (3) a description of the action on each of the first six days (6:12–14); (4) the events on the seventh day (6:15–26).

**5:14 Commander**: the leader of the heavenly army of the Lord of hosts is either the Lord or an angelic warrior; if the latter, he is a messenger who speaks in the person of the one who sent him. **I have come**: the solemn language of theophany; cf., e.g., Ps 50:3; 96:13.

*l*: Ex 16:35. *m*: Ex 23:20. *n*: Ex 3:5; Acts 7:33. *o*: Nm 10:2–9; 2 Sm 6:15–16. *p*: Jos 2:4; Dt 20:17; Heb 11:31. *q*: Jos 7:12, 25; Dt 13:18.

is under the ban;* otherwise you will bring upon the camp of Israel this ban and the misery of it. 19 All silver and gold, and the articles of bronze or iron, are holy to the LORD. They shall be put in the treasury of the LORD."

*The Fall of Jericho.* 20 As the horns blew, the people began to shout. When they heard the sound of the horn, they raised a tremendous shout. The wall collapsed,* and the people attacked the city straight ahead and took it.[r] 21 They observed the ban by putting to the sword all living creatures[s] in the city: men and women, young and old, as well as oxen, sheep and donkeys.

22[t] To the two men who had spied out the land, Joshua said, "Go into the prostitute's house and bring out the woman with all her family, as you swore to her you would do." 23 The spies entered and brought out Rahab, with her father, mother, brothers, and all her family; her entire family they led forth and placed outside the camp of Israel. 24 The city itself they burned with all that was in it;[u] but the silver, gold, and articles of bronze and iron they placed in the treasury of the house of the LORD. 25* Because Rahab the prostitute had hidden the messengers whom Joshua had sent to reconnoiter Jericho, Joshua let her live, along with her father's house and all her family, who dwell in the midst of Israel to this day.

26[v] On that occasion Joshua imposed the oath: Cursed before the LORD be the man who attempts to rebuild this city, Jericho. At the cost of his firstborn will he lay its foundation, and at the cost of his youngest son will he set up its gates.*

27 Thus the LORD was with Joshua so that his fame spread throughout the land.[w]

See RG 95–97

## CHAPTER 7

*Defeat at Ai.* 1 But the Israelites acted treacherously with regard to the ban; Achan, son of Carmi, son of Zabdi, son of Zerah of the tribe of Judah, took goods that were under the ban,[x] and the anger of the LORD flared up against the Israelites.

2[y] Joshua next sent men from Jericho to Ai, which is near Beth-aven and east of Bethel, with the order, "Go up and reconnoiter the land." When they had explored Ai, 3 they returned to Joshua and advised, "Do not send all the people up; if only about two or three thousand go up, they can attack and overcome Ai. You need not tire all the people: the enemy there are few." 4 About three thousand of the people made the attack, but they fled before the army at Ai, 5 who killed some thirty-six of them. They pursued them from the city gate to the Shebarim, and defeated them on the descent, so that the confidence of the people melted away like water.

6 Joshua, together with the elders of Israel, tore their garments and fell face down before the ark of the LORD until evening; and they threw dust on their heads. 7 "Alas, Lord GOD," Joshua prayed, "why did you ever allow this people to cross over the Jordan, delivering us into the power of the Amorites, that they might destroy us? Would that we had been content to dwell on the other side of the Jordan. 8 Please, Lord, what can I say, now that Israel has turned its back to its enemies? 9 When the Canaanites and the other inhabitants of the land hear of it, they will close in around us and efface our name from the earth. What will you do for your great name?"[z]

10 The LORD replied to Joshua: Stand up. Why are you lying there? 11[a] Israel has sinned: they have transgressed the covenant* which I enjoined on them. They have taken goods subject to the ban. They have stolen and lied, placing the goods in their baggage. 12 If the Israelites cannot stand up to their enemies, but must turn their back to them, it is

**6:18 Under the ban**: doomed to destruction; see notes on Lv 27:28; Nm 18:14; 21:3.

**6:20** The blowing of the horns and the shouting, features of the ritual procession with the ark of the covenant (cf. 1 Chr 15:28; 2 Chr 5:11–14), are the people's counterpart of the Lord's theophany; cf. note on Jgs 5:4–5; and Jgs 7:15–22; 2 Chr 13:15. The Lord gives the victory; this is the theological point of the story.

**6:25** The genealogy of Jesus in Matthew (1:2–16) presents Rahab the prostitute as the wife of Salmon (1:5) and so the ancestor of David (Ru 4:18–22) and of Jesus.

**6:26 At the cost of his firstborn . . . its gates:** this curse was fulfilled when Hiel rebuilt Jericho as a fortified city during the reign of Ahab, king of Israel; cf. 1 Kgs 16:34.

**7:11 Transgressed the covenant**: the Hebrew word trans-

*r:* 2 Mc 12:15; Heb 11:30. *s:* Gn 15:16; Dt 7:2. *t:* Jos 2:13–14. *u:* Jos 8:2. *v:* Jos 9:23; 1 Kgs 16:34. *w:* Jos 1:5. *x:* Jos 6:18; 22:20; 1 Chr 2:7. *y:* Nm 13:17–20. *z:* Nm 14:13–19. *a:* Jos 6:17–19.

**The Destruction of Jericho**

THE LORD GIVES specific instructions to Joshua in language combining ritual with warfare. Joshua then carries out the commands, defeating Jericho and instituting the "herem," the complete annihilation of the enemy, but sparing Rahab and her family. In this way the story of Jericho makes clear that it is God who is leading the conquest; the deliverance of the land to the Israelites is God's gift, not something they earned by their own efforts.

because they are under the ban. I will not continue to be with you unless you remove that which is banned from among you. 13 Get up, sanctify the people.[b] Tell them, "Sanctify yourselves before tomorrow, for thus says the LORD, the God of Israel: That which is banned is in your midst, Israel. You cannot stand up to your enemies until you remove it from among you. 14 In the morning you must come forward by tribes. The tribe which the LORD designates shall come forward by clans; the clan which the LORD designates shall come forward by families; the family which the LORD designates shall come forward one by one. 15 Whoever is designated as having incurred the ban shall be destroyed by fire, with all that is his, because he has trangressed the covenant of the LORD and has committed a shameful crime in Israel."[c]

***Achan's Guilt and Punishment.*** 16 Early the next morning Joshua had Israel come forward by tribes, and the tribe of Judah was designated.* 17 Then he had the clans of Judah come forward, and the clan of Zerah was designated. He had the clan of Zerah[d] come forward by families, and Zabdi was designated. 18 Finally he had that family come forward one by one, and Achan, son of Carmi, son of Zabdi, son of Zerah of the tribe of Judah, was designated. 19 Joshua said to Achan, "My son, give glory to the LORD, the God of Israel, and praise him by telling me what you have done; do not hide it from me." 20 Achan answered Joshua, "I have indeed sinned against the LORD, the God of Israel. This is what I have done: 21 Among the spoils, I saw a beautiful Babylonian mantle, two hundred shekels of silver, and a bar of gold fifty shekels in weight; I coveted them and I took them. They are now hidden in the ground inside my tent, with the silver underneath." 22 Joshua sent messengers and they ran to the tent and there they were, hidden in the tent, with the silver underneath. 23 They took them from the tent, brought them to Joshua and all the Israelites, and spread them out before the LORD.

24 Then Joshua and all Israel took Achan, son of Zerah, with the silver, the mantle, and the bar of gold, and with his sons and daughters, his ox, his donkey and his sheep, his tent, and all his possessions, and led them off to the Valley of Achor. 25 Joshua said, "What misery have you caused us? May the LORD bring misery upon you today!"[e] And all Israel stoned him to death. They burnt them with fire and they stoned them. 26 Over Achan they piled a great heap of stones, which remains to the present day.[f] Then the LORD turned from his anger. That is why the place is called the Valley of Achor* to this day.

## CHAPTER 8

See RG 95-97

***Capture of Ai.*** 1[g] The LORD then said to Joshua: Do not be afraid or dismayed. Take all the army with you and prepare to attack Ai.[h] I have delivered the king of Ai into your power, with his people, city, and land. 2 Do to Ai and its king what you did to Jericho and its king—except that you may take its spoil and livestock as plunder.[i] Set an am-

lated "transgressed" appears frequently in the first five chapters where it is used to describe how Israel "crossed" the Jordan River. There is a wordplay here to emphasize Israel's responsibility to follow God to the promised land and so to obey and not transgress the divine command.

**7:16–18 Was designated**: probably by means of the Urim and Thummim; cf. 1 Sm 14:38–42. See note on Ex 28:30.

**7:26 Achor**: "misery," or "disaster." The reference is to the saying of Joshua in v. 25, with an allusion also to the similar-sounding name of Achan.

*b:* Jos 3:5; Lv 20:7; 1 Sm 16:5. *c:* Dt 13:15–16. *d:* Nm 26:20. *e:* Jos 6:18; 22:20; Dt 13:15–16; 1 Chr 2:7. *f:* Jos 8:29; Dt 13:18. *g:* Jgs 20:20–38. *h:* Jos 2:24; Dt 1:21. *i:* Jos 6:21, 24; Dt 20:14.

bush behind the city. 3So Joshua and all the
soldiers prepared to attack Ai. Picking out
thirty thousand warriors,* Joshua sent them
off by night 4with these orders: "See that you
ambush the city from the rear. Do not be
very far from the city. All of you must be
ready. 5The rest of the people and I will
come up to the city, and when they make a
sortie against us as they did the last time, we
will flee from them. 6They will keep coming
out after us until we have drawn them away
from the city, for they will think, 'They are
fleeing from us as they did the last time.'
When we flee, 7then you rise from ambush
and take possession of the city, which the
LORD, your God, will deliver into your
power. 8When you have taken the city, set it
on fire in obedience to the LORD's command. These are my orders to you."[j] 9Then
Joshua sent them away. They went to the
place of ambush, taking up their position to
the west of Ai, toward Bethel. Joshua, however, spent that night with the army.

10Early the next morning Joshua mustered
the army and went up to Ai at its head, with
the elders of Israel. 11When all the troops he
led were drawn up in position before the
city, they pitched camp north of Ai, on the
other side of the ravine. 12He took about five
thousand warriors and set them in ambush
between Bethel and Ai, west of the city.
13Thus the people took up their stations, with
the main body north of the city and the ambush west of it, and Joshua waited overnight
in the valley. 14The king of Ai saw this, and
he and all his army came out very early in
the morning to engage Israel in battle at the
place in front of the Arabah, not knowing
that there was an ambush behind the city.
15Joshua and the main body of the Israelites
fled toward the wilderness, pretending defeat, 16until the last of the soldiers in the city
had been called out to pursue them. Since
they were drawn away from the city, with
everyone pursuing Joshua, 17not a soldier remained in Ai or Bethel. They abandoned the
city, leaving it open, as they pursued Israel.

18Then the LORD directed Joshua: Stretch
out the javelin in your hand toward Ai, for I
will deliver it into your power. Joshua
stretched out the javelin in his hand toward
the city, 19and as soon as he did so, the men
in ambush rose from their post, rushed in,
captured the city, and immediately set it on
fire. 20By the time the army of Ai looked
back, the smoke from the city was going up
to the heavens. Escape in any direction was
impossible, because the Israelites retreating
toward the wilderness now turned on their
pursuers; 21for when Joshua and the main
body of Israelites saw that the city had been
taken by ambush and was going up in smoke,
they struck back at the forces of Ai. 22Since
those in the city came out to intercept them,
Ai's army was hemmed in by Israelites on
both sides, who cut them down without any
fugitives or survivors[k] 23except the king,
whom they took alive and brought to Joshua.

24When Israel finished killing all the inhabitants of Ai in the open, who had pursued
them into the wilderness, and all of them to
the last man fell by the sword, then all Israel
returned and put to the sword those inside
the city. 25There fell that day a total of
twelve thousand men and women, the entire
population of Ai. 26[l] Joshua kept the javelin
in his hand stretched out until he had carried
out the ban on all the inhabitants of Ai.
27However, the Israelites took for themselves as plunder the livestock and the spoil
of that city, according to the command of the
LORD issued to Joshua. 28Then Joshua destroyed Ai by fire, reducing it to an everlasting mound of ruins, as it remains today.[m]
29He had the king of Ai hanged on a tree until evening;[n] then at sunset Joshua ordered
the body removed from the tree and cast at
the entrance of the city gate, where a great
heap of stones was piled up over it, which remains to the present day.

**8:3 Thirty thousand warriors**: this figure of the Hebrew text, which seems extremely high, may be due to a copyist's error; some manuscripts of the Septuagint have "three thousand," which is the number of the whole army in the first, unsuccessful attack (7:4); the variant reading in v. 12 mentions "five thousand." More likely, the word for "thousand" here and in other military contexts may designate a squad or fighting unit, itself composed of significantly fewer warriors.

*j:* Jos 6:24. *k:* Dt 7:2. *l:* Ex 17:11–13. *m:* Dt 13:16. *n:* Jos 10:26–27; Dt 21:22–23; Jn 19:31.

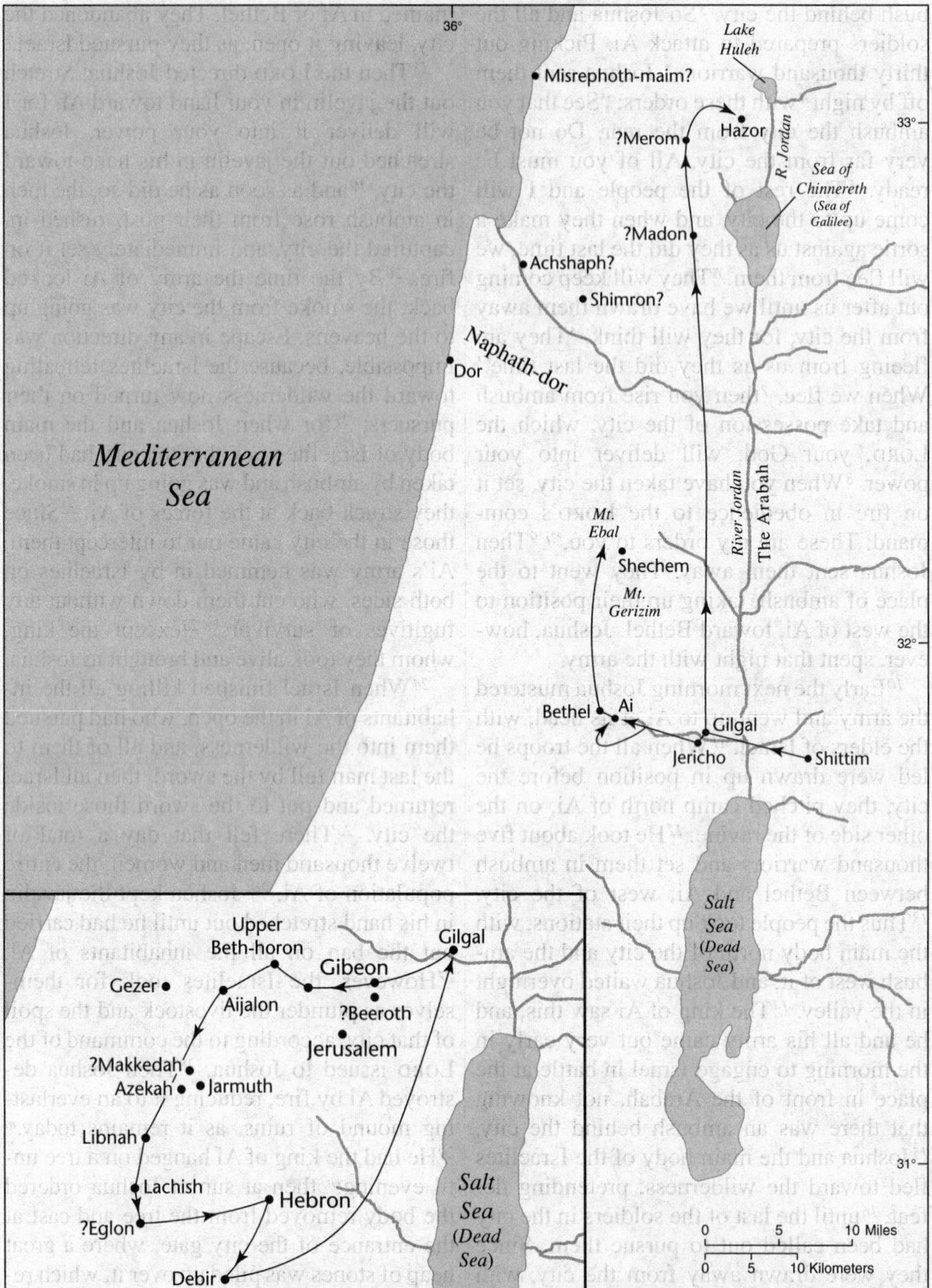


**Conquest of Canaan according to the Book of Joshua**

*Altar on Mount Ebal.* 30*[o] Later, on Mount Ebal, Joshua built to the LORD, the God of Israel, an altar 31 of unhewn stones on which no iron tool had been used,[p] just as Moses, the servant of the LORD, had commanded the Israelites, as recorded in the book of the law. On this altar they sacrificed burnt offerings to the LORD and made communion sacrifices. 32 There, in the presence of the Israelites, Joshua inscribed upon the stones a copy of the law written by Moses. 33 And all Israel, resident alien and native alike, with their elders, officers, and judges, stood on either side of the ark facing the levitical priests who were carrying the ark of the covenant of the LORD.[q] Half of them were facing Mount Gerizim and half Mount Ebal, just as Moses, the servant of the LORD, had first commanded for the blessing of the people of Israel. 34[r] Then were read aloud all the words of the law, the blessings and the curses, exactly as written in the book of the law. 35[s] Every single word that Moses had commanded, Joshua read aloud to the entire assembly, including the women and children, and the resident aliens among them.

## CHAPTER 9

See RG 95–97

*Confederacy Against Israel.* 1 When the news reached all the kings west of the Jordan, in the mountain regions and in the Shephelah, and all along the coast of the Great Sea as far as the Lebanon: Hittites, Amorites, Canaanites, Perizzites, Hivites, and Jebusites,[t] 2 they gathered together to launch a common attack against Joshua and Israel.

*The Gibeonite Deception.* 3 On hearing what Joshua had done to Jericho and Ai, the inhabitants of Gibeon[u] 4 formed their own scheme. They chose provisions for a journey, making use of old sacks for their donkeys, and old wineskins, torn and mended. 5 They wore old, patched sandals and shabby garments; and all the bread they took was dry and crumbly. 6 Thus they journeyed to Joshua in the camp at Gilgal, where they said to him and to the Israelites, "We have come from a far-off land; now, make a covenant with us."[v] 7 But the Israelites replied to the Hivites,* "You may be living in land that is ours. How, then, can we make a covenant with you?" 8 But they answered Joshua, "We are your servants." Then Joshua asked them, "Who are you? Where do you come from?" 9 They answered him, "Your servants have come from a far-off land, because of the fame of the LORD, your God. For we have heard reports of all that he did in Egypt[w] 10 and all that he did to the two kings of the Amorites beyond the Jordan,[x] Sihon, king of Heshbon, and Og, king of Bashan, who lived in Ashtaroth. 11 So our elders and all the inhabitants of our land said to us, 'Take along provisions for the journey and go to meet them. Say to them: "We are your servants; now make a covenant with us." ' 12 This bread of ours was still warm when we brought it from home as provisions the day we left to come to you, but now it is dry and crumbly. 13 Here are our wineskins, which were new when we filled them, but now they are torn. Look at our garments and sandals; they are worn out from the very long journey." 14 Then the Israelite leaders partook of their provisions, without inquiring of the LORD.[y] 15 So Joshua made peace with them and made a covenant to let them live,[z] which the leaders of the community sealed with an oath.

*Gibeonites Made Vassals.* 16 Three days after the covenant was made, the Israelites heard that these people were from nearby, and would be living in Israel. 17 The third day on the road, the Israelites came to their cities of Gibeon, Chephirah, Beeroth, and Kiriath-jearim, 18 but did not attack them, because the leaders of the community had sworn to them by the LORD, the God of Israel. When the en-

**8:30–35** These ceremonies were prescribed in Dt 11:29 and 27:2–26.

**9:7 The Hivites**: apparently the Gibeonites belonged to this larger ethnic group (cf. also 11:19), although in 2 Sm 21:2 they are classed as Amorites; both groups are listed among the seven nations of Canaan whom, according to Dt 7:1–2, the Israelites were to dispossess.

*o:* Dt 27:1–8, 12–13. *p:* Ex 20:24–25. *q:* Jos 3:3; Dt 11:27; 31:9, 12. *r:* Dt 28:2–68; 30:19; 31:11; Neh 8:2–3. *s:* Dt 31:12. *t:* Jos 3:10; 5:1; Ex 3:8, 17; 23:23; Dt 1:7. *u:* Jos 6:21, 24. *v:* Ex 23:32; Dt 7:2. *w:* Jos 2:10–11. *x:* Nm 21:25, 33–35; Dt 1:4. *y:* Nm 27:21. *z:* Jos 11:19; 2 Sm 21:2.

tire community grumbled against the leaders, 19 these all remonstrated with the community, "We have sworn to them by the LORD, the God of Israel, and so we cannot harm them. 20 Let us therefore let them live, and so deal with them that no wrath fall upon us because of the oath we have sworn to them."[a] 21 Thus the leaders said to them, "Let them live, and become hewers of wood and drawers of water* for the entire community." So the community did as the leaders advised them.[b]

22 Joshua summoned the Gibeonites and said to them, "Why did you deceive us and say, 'We live far off from you'?—You live among us! 23 Now are you accursed: every one of you shall always be a slave, hewers of wood and drawers of water, for the house of my God." 24 They answered Joshua, "Your servants were fully informed of how the LORD, your God, commanded Moses his servant that you be given the entire land and that all its inhabitants be destroyed before you. Since, therefore, at your advance, we were in great fear for our lives, we acted as we did.[c] 25 And now that we are in your power, do with us what is good and right in your eyes." 26* Joshua did what he had decided: while he saved them from being killed by the Israelites, 27 on that day he made them, as they still are, hewers of wood and drawers of water for the community and for the altar of the LORD, in the place the LORD would choose.

See RG 95–97

## CHAPTER 10

***The Siege of Gibeon.*** 1 Now when Adonizedek, king of Jerusalem, heard that Joshua had captured Ai and put it under the ban, and had done to that city and its king as he had done to Jericho and its king,[d] and that the inhabitants of Gibeon had made their peace with Israel, remaining among them, 2 there was great fear abroad, because Gibeon was a great city, like one of the royal cities, greater even than Ai, and all its men were warriors. 3 So Adonizedek, king of Jerusalem, sent to Hoham, king of Hebron, Piram, king of Jarmuth, Japhia, king of Lachish, and Debir, king of Eglon, with this message: 4 "Come and help me attack Gibeon, for it has made peace with Joshua and the Israelites."[e] 5 The five Amorite kings, of Jerusalem, Hebron, Jarmuth, Lachish, and Eglon,* gathered with all their forces, and marched against Gibeon to make war on it. 6 Thereupon, the Gibeonites sent an appeal to Joshua in his camp at Gilgal: "Do not abandon your servants. Come up here quickly and save us. Help us, because all the Amorite kings of the mountain country have joined together against us."[f]

***Joshua's Victory.*** 7 So Joshua marched up from Gilgal with all his army and all his warriors. 8 The LORD said to Joshua: Do not fear them, for I have delivered them into your power. Not one of them will be able to withstand you. 9 After an all-night march from Gilgal, Joshua made a surprise attack upon them, 10 and the LORD threw them into disorder before Israel. The Israelites inflicted a great slaughter on them at Gibeon and pursued them down the Beth-horon slope, attacking them as far as Azekah and Makkedah.

11 While they fled before Israel along the descent of Beth-horon, the LORD hurled great stones from the heavens* above them all the way to Azekah, killing many.[g] More died from these hailstones than the Israelites killed with the sword. 12 It was then, when the LORD delivered up the Amorites to the Israelites, that Joshua prayed to the LORD, and said in the presence of Israel:

Sun, stand still at Gibeon,  
Moon, in the valley of Aijalon!  
13 The sun stood still,  
the moon stayed,  
while the nation took vengeance on its foes.[h]

**9:21 Hewers of wood and drawers of water**: proverbial terms for those who do menial work; cf. Dt 29:10–11.

**9:26–27** Later on, Saul violated the immunity of the Gibeonites, but David vindicated it; cf. 2 Sm 21:1–9.

**10:5 Hebron . . . Eglon**: these four cities were to the south and southwest of Jerusalem.

**10:11 Great stones from the heavens**: the hailstones mentioned in the next sentence.

*a:* Jos 22:20. *b:* Dt 29:11. *c:* Ex 23:27–28; Dt 7:1–2. *d:* Jos 6:21, 24; 8:26–29. *e:* Jos 9:15. *f:* Jos 9:6. *g:* Jb 38:22–23. *h:* Sir 46:4; Is 28:21.

This is recorded* in the Book of Jashar. The
sun halted halfway across the heavens; not
for an entire day did it press on. 14Never before or since was there a day like this, when
the LORD obeyed the voice of a man; for the
LORD fought for Israel. 15Then Joshua and
all Israel returned to the camp at Gilgal.

*Execution of Amorite Kings.* 16The five
kings who had fled hid in the cave at Makkedah. 17When Joshua was told, "The five
kings have been found, hiding in the cave at
Makkedah," 18he said, "Roll large stones to
the mouth of the cave and post guards over
it. 19But do not remain there yourselves. Pursue your enemies, and harry them in the rear.
Do not allow them to reach their cities, for
the LORD, your God, has delivered them into
your power."

20Once Joshua and the Israelites had finally inflicted the last blows in this very
great slaughter, and the survivors had escaped from them into the fortified cities,
21all the army returned to Joshua and the
camp at Makkedah in victory; no one uttered
a sound against the Israelites. 22Then Joshua
said, "Open the mouth of the cave and bring
me those five kings from the cave." 23They
did so; they brought out to him from the cave
the five kings, of Jerusalem, Hebron, Jarmuth, Lachish, and Eglon. 24When they
brought the five kings out to Joshua, he summoned all the army of Israel and said to the
commanders of the soldiers who had
marched with him, "Come forward and put
your feet on the necks of these kings." They
came forward and put their feet upon their
necks. 25[i] Then Joshua said to them, "Do not
be afraid or dismayed, be firm and steadfast.
This is what the LORD will do to all the enemies against whom you fight." 26[j] Thereupon Joshua struck and killed the kings, and
hanged them on five trees, where they remained hanging until evening. 27At sunset
Joshua commanded that they be taken down
from the trees and be thrown into the cave
where they had hidden; over the mouth of
the cave large stones were placed, which remain until this very day.

*Conquest of Southern Canaan.* 28[k] Makkedah, too, Joshua captured and put to the
sword at that time. He put the city, its king,
and every person in it under the ban, leaving
no survivors. Thus he did to the king of
Makkedah what he had done to the king of
Jericho. 29Joshua then passed on with all Israel from Makkedah to Libnah, and attacked
it, 30and the LORD delivered it, with its king,
into the power of Israel. He put it to the
sword with every person there, leaving no
survivors. Thus he did to its king what he
had done to the king of Jericho. 31Joshua
next passed on with all Israel from Libnah to
Lachish, where they set up a camp during
the attack. 32The LORD delivered Lachish
into the power of Israel, so that on the second day Joshua captured it and put it to the
sword with every person in it, just as he had
done to Libnah. 33At that time Horam, king
of Gezer, came up to help Lachish, but
Joshua defeated him and his people, leaving
him no survivors. 34From Lachish, Joshua
passed on with all Israel to Eglon; encamp-
ing near it, they attacked it 35and captured it
the same day, putting it to the sword. On that
day he put under the ban every person in it,
just as he had done at Lachish. 36From Eglon, Joshua went up with all Israel to Hebron, which they attacked 37and captured.
They put it to the sword with its king, all its
cities, and every person there, leaving no
survivors, just as Joshua had done to Eglon.
He put it under the ban and every person in
it. 38Then Joshua and all Israel turned back
to Debir and attacked it, 39capturing it with
its king and all its cities. They put them to
the sword and put under the ban every person in it, leaving no survivors. Thus he did to
Debir and its king what he had done to Hebron, as well as to Libnah and its king.

40[l] Joshua conquered the entire land; the

**10:13 This is recorded**: the reference is to the preceding poetic passage. Evidently the *Book of Jashar*, like the *Book of the Wars of the Lord* (Nm 21:14), recounted in epic style the exploits of Israel's early heroes. **The sun halted**: lit., "the sun stood"; this obscure passage may suppose a longer than natural day caused when the sun stopped moving across the sky, or it may refer to the sun stopping its light-giving function, perhaps through an eclipse. In any case it was seen as a sign that God fought Israel's battle (v. 42; cf. Ex 14:14).

*i:* Jos 1:9. *j:* Jos 8:29; Dt 21:22–23. *k:* Jos 6:21. *l:* Dt 20:16–17.

mountain regions, the Negeb, the Shephelah, and the mountain slopes, with all their kings. He left no survivors, but put under the ban every living being, just as the LORD, the God of Israel, had commanded. 41 Joshua conquered them from Kadesh-barnea to Gaza, and all the land of Goshen* to Gibeon. 42 All these kings and their lands Joshua captured all at once, for the LORD, the God of Israel, fought for Israel. 43 Thereupon Joshua with all Israel returned to the camp at Gilgal.

## CHAPTER 11

See RG 95–97

*Northern Confederacy.* 1 When Jabin, king of Hazor,* learned of this, he sent a message to Jobab, king of Madon, to the king of Shimron, to the king of Achshaph, 2 and to the northern kings in the mountain regions and in the Arabah near Chinneroth, in the Shephelah, and in Naphath-dor to the west.[m] 3 These were Canaanites to the east and west, Amorites, Hittites, Perizzites, and Jebusites in the mountain regions, and Hivites at the foot of Hermon in the land of Mizpah.[n] 4 They came out with all their troops, an army numerous as the sands on the seashore, and with a multitude of horses and chariots.[o] 5 All these kings made a pact and together they marched to the waters of Merom,* where they encamped to fight against Israel.

6 The LORD said to Joshua, "Do not fear them, for by this time tomorrow I will present them slain to Israel. You must hamstring their horses and burn their chariots." 7 Joshua with his whole army came upon them suddenly at the waters of Merom and fell upon them. 8 The LORD delivered them into the power of the Israelites, who defeated them and pursued them to Greater Sidon, to Misrephoth-maim,[p] and eastward to the valley of Mizpeh. They struck them all down, leaving no survivors. 9 Joshua did to them as the LORD had commanded: he hamstrung their horses and burned their chariots.

*Conquest of Northern Canaan.* 10 At that time Joshua, turning back, captured Hazor and struck down its king with the sword; for Hazor formerly was the chief of all those kingdoms. 11 He also struck down with the sword every person there, carrying out the ban, till none was left alive. Hazor itself he burned. 12 All the cities of those kings, and the kings themselves, Joshua captured and put to the sword, carrying out the ban on them, as Moses, the servant of the LORD, had commanded.[q] 13 However, Israel did not destroy by fire any of the cities built on their mounds, except Hazor, which Joshua burned. 14 All the spoil and livestock of these cities the Israelites took as plunder; but the people they put to the sword, until they had destroyed the last of them, leaving none alive. 15 As the LORD had commanded his servant Moses, so Moses commanded Joshua, and Joshua acted accordingly.[r] He left nothing undone that the LORD had commanded Moses should be done.

*Survey of the Conquest.* 16 So Joshua took all this land: the mountain regions, the entire Negeb, all the land of Goshen, the Shephelah, the Arabah, as well as the mountain regions and Shephelah of Israel,[s] 17 from Mount Halak that rises toward Seir[t] as far as Baal-gad in the Lebanon valley at the foot of Mount Hermon. All their kings he captured and put to death. 18 Joshua waged war against all these kings for a long time. 19 With the exception of the Hivites who lived in Gibeon, no city made peace with the Israelites; all were taken in battle.[u] 20 For it was the LORD's doing to make their hearts obstinate to meet Israel in battle, that they might be put under the ban without mercy, and be destroyed as the LORD had commanded Moses.[v]

21* At that time Joshua penetrated the mountain regions and exterminated the

**10:41 Goshen**: a town and its surrounding district at the southern end of the Judean mountains (cf. 11:16; 15:51); not to be confused with the land of Goshen in northeastern Egypt (Gn 45:10).

**11:1–3 Hazor, Madon, Shimron,** and **Chinneroth**: cities and their surrounding districts in eastern Galilee. **Achshaph** and **Naphath-dor**: southwest of Galilee. **The mountain regions**: in central and northern Galilee.

**11:5 The waters of Merom**: of uncertain identification, perhaps Tel Qarnei Hittin, about seven and a half kilometers west of modern Tiberias.

**11:21–23** Most of the land assigned to the tribe of Judah was not conquered by it until the early period of the Judges. See note on Jgs 1:1–36.

*m:* Jos 12:3. *n:* Jos 3:10. *o:* Ex 15:1, 21. *p:* Jos 13:6. *q:* Dt 7:2; 20:16–17. *r:* Dt 7:2; 31:7–8. *s:* Jos 10:41; 12:8. *t:* Jos 12:7; Dt 7:24. *u:* Jos 9:3, 7, 15. *v:* Dt 2:30; 20:16–17.

Anakim in Hebron,[w] Debir, Anab, the entire mountain region of Judah, and the entire mountain region of Israel. Joshua put them and their cities under the ban, 22 so that no Anakim were left in the land of the Israelites. However, some survived in Gaza, in Gath, and in Ashdod. 23[x] Thus Joshua took the whole land, just as the LORD had said to Moses. Joshua gave it to Israel as their heritage, apportioning it among the tribes. And the land had rest from war.*

## CHAPTER 12*

See RG 97-98

*Lists of Conquered Kings.* 1 These are the kings of the land whom the Israelites conquered and whose lands they occupied, east of the Jordan, from the River Arnon to Mount Hermon, including all the eastern section of the Arabah: 2[y] First, Sihon, king of the Amorites, who lived in Heshbon. His domain extended from Aroer, which is on the bank of the Wadi Arnon, to include the wadi itself, and the land northward through half of Gilead to the Wadi Jabbok at the border with the Ammonites, 3 as well as the Arabah from the eastern side of the Sea of Chinnereth, as far south as the eastern side of the Salt Sea of the Arabah in the direction of Beth-jeshimoth,[z] southward under the slopes of Pisgah. 4 Secondly, the border of Og, king of Bashan, a survivor of the Rephaim, who lived at Ashtaroth and Edrei.[a] 5 He ruled over Mount Hermon, Salecah, and all Bashan as far as the boundary of the Geshurites and Maacathites, and over half of Gilead as far as the territory of Sihon, king of Heshbon. 6 It was Moses, the servant of the LORD, and the Israelites who conquered them; Moses, the servant of the LORD, gave possession of their land to the Reubenites, the Gadites, and the half-tribe of Manasseh.[b]

7 This is a list of the kings of the land whom Joshua and the Israelites conquered west of the Jordan, from Baal-gad in the Lebanon valley to Mount Halak which rises toward Seir; Joshua apportioned their land and gave possession of it to the tribes of Israel; 8 it included the mountain regions and Shephelah, the Arabah, the slopes, the wilderness, and the Negeb, belonging to the Hittites, Amorites, Canaanites, Perizzites, Hivites, and Jebusites: 9 The king of Jericho, one;[c] the king of Ai, which is near Bethel, one; 10 the king of Jerusalem, one; the king of Hebron, one; 11 the king of Jarmuth, one; the king of Lachish, one;[d] 12 the king of Eglon, one; the king of Gezer, one;[e] 13 the king of Debir, one; the king of Geder, one;[f] 14 the king of Hormah, one; the king of Arad, one; 15 the king of Libnah, one; the king of Adullam, one;[g] 16 the king of Makkedah, one; the king of Bethel, one;[h] 17 the king of Tappuah, one; the king of Hepher, one;[i] 18 the king of Aphek, one; the king of Lasharon, one;[j] 19 the king of Madon, one; the king of Hazor, one;[k] 20 the king of Shimron, one; the king of Achshaph, one;[l] 21 the king of Taanach, one; the king of Megiddo, one;[m] 22 the king of Kedesh, one; the king of Jokneam, at Carmel, one;[n] 23 the king of Dor, in Naphath-dor, one; the king of Goyim at Gilgal, one;[o] 24 and the king of Tirzah, one—thirty-one kings in all.

# II. Division of the Land

## CHAPTER 13

See RG 97-98

*Division of Land Commanded.* 1 When Joshua was old and advanced in years, the LORD said to him:[p] Though now you are old and advanced in years, a very large part of the land still remains to be possessed. 2 This is the remaining land: all Geshur* and all the districts of the Philistines 3 (from the stream

**11:23 The land had rest from war**: later passages (15:13–17; 17:12–13) show individual tribes still fighting against the remaining Canaanites. This verse forms the conclusion to the first part of the book.

**12:1–24** This chapter, inserted between the two principal parts of the book (chaps. 1–11 and 13–21), resembles the lists of conquered cities which are inscribed on monuments of Egyptian and Assyrian rulers. Perhaps this list was copied here from some such public Israelite record.

**13:2 Geshur**: not to be confused with the large Aramean district of the same name in Bashan (vv. 11–13; Dt 3:14); here it is a region to the south of the Philistine country, since vv. 2–5 list the unconquered lands along the coast from south to north; cf. also 1 Sm 27:8.

*w:* Jos 15:13–14; Nm 13:22; Dt 1:28; 9:1–3. *x:* Jos 14:1–19:51; Nm 34:2–12; Heb 4:8–10. *y:* Nm 21:21–35; Dt 1:4; 2:24–37. *z:* Jos 13:20. *a:* Nm 34:11–12. *b:* Nm 32:33; Dt 3:12–13. *c:* Jos 6:2; 8:23. *d:* Jos 10:23. *e:* Jos 10:23, 33. *f:* Jos 10:38–39; 15:36. *g:* Jos 10:29–30; 15:35. *h:* Jos 8:17; 10:28. *i:* Jos 15:34. *j:* Jos 15:53. *k:* Jos 11:1, 10. *l:* Jos 11:1. *m:* Jos 17:11. *n:* Jos 19:37. *o:* Jos 11:2. *p:* Jos 23:1.

adjoining Egypt to the boundary of Ekron in the north is reckoned Canaanite territory, though held by the five lords of the Philistines in Gaza, Ashdod, Ashkelon, Gath, and Ekron); 4also where the Avvim are in the south;[q] all the land of the Canaanites from Mearah of the Sidonians to Aphek, and the boundaries of the Amorites;[r] 5and the Gebalite territory; and all the Lebanon on the east, from Baal-gad at the foot of Mount Hermon to Lebo-hamath. 6All the inhabitants of the mountain regions between Lebanon and Misrephoth-maim, all Sidonians, I will drive out before the Israelites;[s] at least include these areas in the division of the Israelite heritage, just as I have commanded you. 7Now, therefore, apportion among the nine tribes and the half-tribe of Manasseh the land which is to be their heritage.

***The Eastern Tribes.*** 8[t] Now the other half of the tribe of Manasseh, as well as the Reubenites and Gadites, had taken as their heritage what Moses, the servant of the LORD, had given them east of the Jordan: 9from Aroer on the bank of the Wadi Arnon and the city in the wadi itself, through the tableland of Medeba and Dibon, 10with the rest of the cities of Sihon, king of the Amorites, who reigned in Heshbon, to the boundary of the Ammonites; 11also Gilead and the territory of the Geshurites and Maacathites, all Mount Hermon, and all Bashan as far as Salecah, 12the entire kingdom in Bashan of Og, who was king at Ashtaroth and Edrei (he was a holdover from the remnant of the Rephaim). These Moses defeated and dispossessed. 13But the Israelites did not dispossess the Geshurites and Maacathites, so that Geshur and Maacath dwell in the midst of Israel to this day. 14[u] However, Moses assigned no heritage to the tribe of Levi; the LORD, the God of Israel, is their heritage, as the LORD had promised them.

***Reuben.*** 15[v] This is what Moses gave to the tribe of the Reubenites by their clans:[w] 16Their territory reached from Aroer, on the bank of the Wadi Arnon, and the city in the wadi itself, through the tableland about Medeba, 17to include Heshbon and all its towns on the tableland, Dibon, Bamoth-baal, Beth-baal-meon, 18Jahaz, Kedemoth, Mephaath, 19Kiriathaim, Sibmah, Zereth-shahar on the knoll within the valley, 20Beth-peor, the slopes of Pisgah, Beth-jeshimoth, 21and the other cities of the tableland and of the whole kingdom of Sihon. This Amorite king, who reigned in Heshbon, Moses had defeated, with the princes of Midian, vassals of Sihon who were settled in the land: Evi, Rekem, Zur, Hur, and Reba;[x] 22Balaam, son of Beor, the diviner, the Israelites killed with the sword, together with those they struck down.[y] 23The boundary of the Reubenites was the Jordan. These cities and their villages were the heritage of the Reubenites by their clans.

***Gad.*** 24[z] This is what Moses gave to the tribe of the Gadites by their clans: 25Their territory included Jazer, all the cities of Gilead, and half the land of the Ammonites as far as Aroer, toward Rabbah 26(that is, from Heshbon to Ramath-mizpeh and Betonim, and from Mahanaim to the boundary of Lo-debar); 27and in the Jordan valley: Beth-haram, Beth-nimrah, Succoth, Zaphon, the other part of the kingdom of Sihon, king of Heshbon, with the bank of the Jordan to the southeastern tip of the Sea of Chinnereth. 28These cities and their villages were the heritage of the clans of the Gadites.

***Manasseh.*** 29[a] This is what Moses gave to the half-tribe of Manasseh; the half-tribe of the Manassites, by their clans, had 30territory including Mahanaim, all of Bashan, the entire kingdom of Og, king of Bashan, and all the villages of Jair, which are sixty cities in Bashan. 31Half of Gilead, with Ashtaroth and Edrei, royal cities of Og in Bashan, fell to the descendants of Machir, son of Manasseh, to half the Machirites, by their clans.

32These are the heritages which Moses gave when he was in the plains of Moab, beyond the Jordan east of Jericho. 33But Moses gave no heritage to the tribe of Levi: the LORD, the God of Israel, is their heritage, as he had promised them.[b]

---

*q:* Jgs 3:3. *r:* Jos 1:4. *s:* Jos 11:8. *t:* Jos 12:6; Nm 32:33. *u:* Jos 14:3–4; Nm 18:20–24. *v:* Dt 3:12–17. *w:* Nm 21:25–31; 32:37–38. *x:* Nm 21:24; 31:8; Dt 3:10. *y:* Nm 31:8. *z:* Nm 32:34–36. *a:* Nm 32:39–42. *b:* Jos 18:7; Nm 18:20.

**Land Distribution**

JOSHUA IS JOINED by the priest Eleazar in 14:1 because casting the sacred lot could only be done by a priest (Dt 33:8). Distribution by lot confirms that the results are in accordance with divine will. The total number of allotments comes out to twelve because Joseph gave rise to two tribes and Levi received no territory. In the practice of casting lots, two options (groups, people, or answers) would be presented and the lot would be cast, not unlike flipping a coin, to indicate one of the two options over the other. Subsequent castings would gradually narrow the results until the final answer was determined. See 1 Samuel 14:40–42 for such a progression.

## CHAPTER 14

See RG 97-98

*The Western Tribes.* [1]These are the portions which the Israelites received as heritage in the land of Canaan.[c] Eleazar the priest, Joshua, son of Nun, and the heads of families in the tribes of the Israelites determined [2]their heritage by lot, as the LORD had commanded through Moses concerning the remaining nine and a half tribes.[d] [3]To two and a half tribes Moses had already given a heritage beyond the Jordan; to the Levites he had given no heritage among them:[e] [4]the descendants of Joseph formed two tribes, Manasseh and Ephraim. But the Levites were given no share of the land except cities to live in, with their pasture lands for the herds and flocks.[f]

[5]As the LORD had commanded Moses, so the Israelites did: they apportioned the land.

*Caleb's Portion.* [6][g] When the Judahites approached Joshua in Gilgal, the Kenizzite Caleb, son of Jephunneh, said to him: "You know the word the LORD spoke to Moses, the man of God, concerning you and concerning me in Kadesh-barnea. [7][h] I was forty years old when Moses, the servant of the LORD, sent me from Kadesh-barnea to reconnoiter the land; and I brought back to him a frank report. [8][i] My fellow scouts who went up with me made the people's confidence melt away, but I was completely loyal to the LORD, my God. [9]On that occasion Moses swore this oath, 'The land where you have set foot shall become your heritage and that of your descendants forever, because you have been completely loyal to the LORD, my God.' [10]Now, as he promised, the LORD has preserved me these forty-five years since the LORD spoke thus to Moses while Israel journeyed in the wilderness; and now I am eighty-five years old,[j] [11]but I am still as strong today as I was the day Moses sent me forth, with no less vigor whether it be for war or for any other tasks.* [k] [12]Now give me this mountain region which the LORD promised me that day, as you yourself heard. True, the Anakim are there, with large fortified cities, but if the LORD is with me I shall be able to dispossess them, as the LORD promised."[l] [13]Joshua blessed Caleb, son of Jephunneh, and gave him Hebron as his heritage.[m] [14]Therefore Hebron remains the heritage of the Kenizzite Caleb, son of Jephunneh, to the present day, because he was completely loyal to the LORD, the God of Israel. [15]Hebron was formerly called Kiriath-arba, for Arba, the greatest among the Anakim.[n] And the land had rest from war.

## CHAPTER 15

See RG 97-98

*Boundaries of Judah.* [1]The lot for the tribe of Judah by their clans fell toward the boundary of Edom, the wilderness of Zin in the Negeb, in the extreme south.[o] [2][p] Their southern boundary ran from the end of the Salt Sea,* from the tongue of land that faces

**14:11 War . . . other tasks**: lit., "to go forth and to come in," i.e., to conduct military expeditions and to return after victory; cf. 1 Sm 18:16; 2 Sm 5:2.

**15:2 Salt Sea**: the Dead Sea. The "tongue," a prominent feature of the landscape, is a spit of land thrusting into the Dead Sea from its eastern shore; it is now called by its Arabic name, *'el lisân*, "tongue."

*c:* Jos 17:4; 21:1; Nm 27:19–22; 34:17–18. *d:* Nm 26:55; 33:54; 34:13. *e:* Jos 13:8, 14, 33. *f:* Jos 21:3–40; Gn 48:5. *g:* Nm 14:24, 30; 32:12; Dt 1:36, 38. *h:* Nm 14:6–9. *i:* Nm 13:31–33; 14:24; 32:12; Dt 1:36. *j:* Nm 14:30. *k:* Sir 46:1–10. *l:* Jos 11:21–22. *m:* Jos 10:36–37; 15:13–19; 21:11–12. *n:* Jgs 1:10. *o:* Nm 34:3. *p:* Nm 34:3–12.

the Negeb, [3]and went southward below the pass of Akrabbim, across through Zin, up to a point south of Kadesh-barnea, across to Hezron, and up to Addar; from there, looping around Karka, [4]it crossed to Azmon and then joined the Wadi of Egypt* before coming out at the sea. (This is your southern boundary.) [5]The eastern boundary was the Salt Sea as far as the mouth of the Jordan.

The northern boundary climbed northward from the tongue of the sea, toward the mouth of the Jordan, [6q] up to Beth-hoglah, and ran north of Beth-arabah, up to Eben-Bohan-ben-Reuben. [7]Thence the boundary climbed to Debir, north of the Valley of Achor,[r] in the direction of the Gilgal that faces the pass of Adummim, on the south side of the wadi; from there it crossed to the waters of En-shemesh and emerged at En-rogel. [8]Climbing again to the Valley of Ben-hinnom* on the southern flank of the Jebusites (that is, Jerusalem), the boundary rose to the top of the mountain at the northern end of the Valley of Rephaim,[s] which bounds the Valley of Hinnom on the west. [9]From the top of the mountain it ran to the fountain of waters of Nephtoah,[t] extended to the cities of Mount Ephron, and continued to Baalah, or Kiriath-jearim. [10]From Baalah the boundary curved westward to Mount Seir and passed north of the ridge of Mount Jearim (that is, Chesalon); it descended to Beth-shemesh, and ran across to Timnah. [11]It then extended along the northern flank of Ekron, continued through Shikkeron, and across to Mount Baalah, from there to include Jabneel, before it came out at the sea. [12]The western boundary was the Great Sea* and its coast. This was the complete boundary of the Judahites by their clans.

***Conquest by Caleb.*** [13u] As the LORD had commanded, Joshua gave Caleb, son of Jephunneh,[v] a portion among the Judahites, namely, Kiriath-arba (Arba was the father of Anak), that is, Hebron. [14w] And Caleb dispossessed from there the three Anakim, the descendants of Anak: Sheshai, Ahiman, and Talmai. [15]From there he marched up against the inhabitants of Debir,[x] which was formerly called Kiriath-sepher. [16]Caleb said, "To the man who attacks Kiriath-sepher and captures it, I will give my daughter Achsah in marriage." [17*] Othniel captured it, the son of Caleb's brother Kenaz; so Caleb gave him his daughter Achsah in marriage. [18]When she came to him, she induced him to ask her father for some land. Then, as she alighted from the donkey, Caleb asked her, "What do you want?" [19]She answered, "Give me a present! Since you have assigned to me land in the Negeb, give me also pools of water." So he gave her the upper and the lower pools.

***Cities of Judah.**** [20]This is the heritage of the tribe of Judahites by their clans: [21]The cities of the tribe of the Judahites in the extreme southern district toward Edom were: Kabzeel, Eder, Jagur, [22]Kinah, Dimonah, Adadah, [23]Kedesh, Hazor, and Ithnan; [24]Ziph, Telem, Bealoth, [25]Hazor-hadattah, and Kerioth-hezron (that is, Hazor); [26]Amam, Shema, Moladah, [27]Hazar-gaddah, Heshmon, Beth-pelet, [28]Hazar-shual, Beer-sheba, and Biziothiah; [29]Baalah, Iim, Ezem, [30]Eltolad, Chesil, Hormah, [31]Ziklag, Madmannah, Sansannah, [32]Lebaoth, Shilhim, and Ain and Rimmon; a total of twenty-nine cities with their villages.

[33]In the Shephelah: Eshtaol, Zorah, Ashnah, [34]Zanoah, Engannim, Tappuah, Enam, [35]Jarmuth, Adullam, Socoh, Azekah, [36]Sharaim, Adithaim, Gederah, and Gederothaim; fourteen cities and their villages.

**15:4 Wadi of Egypt**: the natural boundary between Gaza and the Sinai Peninsula.

**15:8 The Valley of Ben-hinnom**: the southern limit of Jerusalem. *Ben-hinnom* means "son of Hinnom." The place was also called Valley of Hinnom, in Hebrew *ge-hinnom*, whence the word "Gehenna" is derived.

**15:12 Great Sea**: the Mediterranean.

**15:17–19** The story of Othniel is told again in Jgs 1:13–15; cf. also Jgs 3:9–11.

**15:20–62** This elaborate list of the cities of Judah was probably taken from a document made originally for administrative purposes; the cities are divided into four provincial districts, some of which have further subdivisions. For similar lists of the cities of Judah, cf. 19:2–7; 1 Chr 4:28–32; Neh 11:25–30. This list has suffered in transmission, so that the totals given in vv. 32 and 36 are not exact; many of the cities cannot be identified.

*q:* Jos 18:18–19, 22. *r:* Jos 7:26; 18:16–18. *s:* Jos 18:16. *t:* Jos 18:15. *u:* Jgs 1:10–15. *v:* Jos 14:13–15. *w:* Nm 13:22; Jgs 1:20. *x:* Jos 10:38.

[37]Zenan, Hadashah, Migdal-gad, [38]Dilean,
Mizpeh, Joktheel, [39]Lachish, Bozkath, Eglon, [40]Cabbon, Lahmas, Chitlish, [41]Gede-
roth, Beth-dagon, Naamah, and Makkedah;
sixteen cities and their villages. [42]Libnah,
Ether, Ashan, [43]Iphtah, Ashnah, Nezib,
[44]Keilah, Achzib, and Mareshah; nine cities
and their villages. [45]Ekron and its towns and
villages; [46]from Ekron to the sea, all the
towns that lie alongside Ashdod, and their
villages; [47]Ashdod and its towns and villages; Gaza and its towns and villages, as far
as the Wadi of Egypt and the coast of the
Great Sea.

[48]In the mountain regions: Shamir, Jattir,
Socoh, [49]Dannah, Kiriath-sannah (that is,
Debir), [50]Anab, Eshtemoh, Anim, [51]Goshen,
Holon, and Giloh; eleven cities and their vil-
lages. [52]Arab, Dumah, Eshan, [53]Janim,
Beth-tappuah, Aphekah, [54]Humtah, Kiriath-
arba (that is, Hebron), and Zior; nine cities
and their villages. [55]Maon, Carmel, Ziph,
Juttah, [56]Jezreel, Jokdeam, Zanoah, [57]Kain,
Gibbeah, and Timnah; ten cities and their
villages. [58]Halhul, Beth-zur, Gedor, [59]Maa-
rath, Beth-anoth, and Eltekon; six cities and
their villages. Tekoa, Ephrathah (that is,
Bethlehem), Peor, Etam, Kulom, Tatam,
Zores, Karim, Gallim, Bether, and Manoko;
eleven cities and their villages. [60]Kiriath-
baal (that is, Kiriath-jearim) and Rabbah;
two cities and their villages.[y]

[61]In the wilderness:* Beth-arabah, Middin, Secacah, [62]Nibshan, Ir-hamelah, and
En-gedi; six cities and their villages. [63]But
the Jebusites who lived in Jerusalem the Judahites could not dispossess; so the Jebusites dwell in Jerusalem beside the Judahites
to the present day.[z]

## CHAPTER 16

See RG 97–98

***The Joseph Tribes.**** [1]The lot that fell
to the Josephites extended from the Jordan at
Jericho to the waters of Jericho east of the
wilderness; then the boundary went up from
Jericho to the heights at Bethel.* [2]Leaving
Bethel for Luz, it crossed the ridge to the
border of the Archites at Ataroth, [3]and descended westward to the border of the
Japhletites, to that of the Lower Beth-horon,
and to Gezer, and from there to the sea.[a]

***Ephraim.*** [4]Within the heritage of Manasseh and Ephraim, sons of Joseph, [5]the dividing line* for the heritage of the Ephraimites
by their clans ran from east of Ataroth-addar
to Upper Beth-horon[b] [6]and thence to the sea.
From Michmethath[c] on the north, their
boundary curved eastward around Taanath-
shiloh, and continued east of it to Janoah;
[7]from there it descended to Ataroth and Naarah, and reaching Jericho, it ended at the
Jordan. [8]From Tappuah the boundary ran
westward to the Wadi Kanah and ended at
the sea. This was the heritage of the
Ephraimites by their clans, [9]including the
villages that belonged to each city set aside
for the Ephraimites within the heritage of the
Manassites. [10]But they did not dispossess
the Canaanites living in Gezer;[d] they live
within Ephraim to the present day, though
they have been put to forced labor.

## CHAPTER 17

See RG 97–98

***Manasseh.*** [1][e] Now as for the lot that
fell to the tribe of Manasseh[f] as the firstborn
of Joseph: since Manasseh's eldest son,
Machir, the father of Gilead, was a warrior,
who had already obtained Gilead and Bashan, [2]the allotment was now made to the
rest of the Manassites by their clans: the descendants of Abiezer, Helek, Asriel, Shechem, Hepher, and Shemida; these are the
other male children of Manasseh, son of Joseph, by their clans.

[3][g] Furthermore, Zelophehad, son of Hepher, son of Gilead, son of Machir, son of
Manasseh, had no sons, but only daughters,
whose names were Mahlah, Noah, Hoglah,

**15:61 In the wilderness**: in the Jordan rift near the Dead Sea.

**16:1–17:18** After the boundaries and cities of Judah, the most important tribe, are given, the land of the next most important group, the two Joseph tribes of Ephraim and Manasseh, is described, though it was separated from Judah by the territories of Benjamin (18:11–20) and Dan (19:40–48).

**16:1–3** This line formed the southern boundary of Ephraim and the northern boundaries of Benjamin and of Dan.

**16:5 The dividing line**: separating Ephraim from Manasseh. Ephraim's northern border (v. 5) is given in an east-to-west direction; its eastern border (vv. 6–7) in a north-to-south direction.

---

*y:* Jos 18:14. *z:* Jgs 1:21; 2 Sm 5:6. *a:* Jos 10:10, 33. *b:* Jos 18:13. *c:* Jos 17:7–9. *d:* Jgs 1:29. *e:* Nm 26:29–33. *f:* Gn 41:51; 46:20; 48:18; 50:23; Dt 3:13, 15. *g:* Nm 27:1–7; 36:2.

Milcah, and Tirzah. 4These presented themselves to Eleazar the priest, to Joshua, son of Nun, and to the leaders, saying, "The LORD commanded Moses to give us a heritage among our relatives." So in accordance with the command of the LORD a heritage was given them among their father's relatives. 5Thus ten shares fell to Manasseh apart from the land of Gilead and Bashan beyond the Jordan,[h] 6since these female descendants of Manasseh received each a portion among his sons. The land of Gilead fell to the rest of the Manassites.

7Manasseh bordered on Asher.* From Michmethath, near Shechem, another boundary ran southward to include the inhabitants of En-Tappuah, 8because the district of Tappuah belonged to Manasseh, although Tappuah itself was an Ephraimite city on the border of Manasseh. 9This same boundary continued down to the Wadi Kanah.[i] The cities that belonged to Ephraim from among the cities in Manasseh were those to the south of that wadi; thus the territory of Manasseh ran north of the wadi and ended at the sea. 10The land on the south belonged to Ephraim and that on the north to Manasseh; with the sea as their common boundary, they reached Asher on the north and Issachar on the east.

11[j] Moreover, in Issachar and in Asher Manasseh was awarded Beth-shean and its towns, Ibleam and its towns, the inhabitants of Dor and its towns, the inhabitants of Endor and its towns, the inhabitants of Taanach and its towns, the inhabitants of Megiddo and its towns (the third is Naphath-dor). 12Since the Manassites were not able to dispossess these cities, the Canaanites continued to inhabit this region. 13When the Israelites grew stronger they put the Canaanites to forced labor, but they did not dispossess them.

***Protest of Joseph Tribes.*** 14The descendants of Joseph said to Joshua, "Why have you given us only one lot and one share as our heritage?[k] Our people are too many, because of the extent to which the LORD has blessed us." 15Joshua answered them, "If you are too many, go up to the forest and clear out a place for yourselves there in the land of the Perizzites and Rephaim, since the mountain regions of Ephraim are so narrow." 16For the Josephites said, "Our mountain regions are not enough for us; on the other hand, the Canaanites living in the valley region all have iron chariots, in particular those in Beth-shean and its towns, and those in the valley of Jezreel." 17Joshua therefore said to Ephraim and Manasseh, the house of Joseph, "You are a numerous people and very strong. You shall not have merely one share, 18for the mountain region which is now forest shall be yours when you clear it. Its adjacent land shall also be yours if, despite their strength and iron chariots, you dispossess the Canaanites."

## CHAPTER 18

See RG 97–98

1The whole community of the Israelites assembled at Shiloh, where they set up the tent of meeting; and the land was subdued before them.[l]

***The Seven Remaining Portions.*** 2There remained seven tribes among the Israelites that had not yet received their heritage. 3Joshua therefore said to the Israelites, "How much longer will you put off taking steps to possess the land which the LORD, the God of your ancestors, has given you? 4Choose three representatives from each of your tribes; I will send them to go throughout the land and describe it for purposes of acquiring their heritage. When they return to me 5you shall divide it into seven parts. Judah is to retain its territory in the south,[m] and the house of Joseph its territory in the north. 6You shall bring to me here the description of the land in seven sections. I will then cast lots for you here before the LORD, our God. 7For the Levites have no share among you,[n]

**17:7 Manasseh bordered on Asher**: only at the extreme northwestern section of Manasseh's territory. The boundary given in the following sentences (vv. 7–10) is a more detailed description of the one already mentioned in 16:5–7, as separating Manasseh from Ephraim.

*h:* Nm 13:30–31. *i:* Jos 16:8–9. *j:* 1 Chr 7:29. *k:* Jos 16:4; Gn 48:19–22. *l:* Jos 11:23; 14:15; 19:51. *m:* Jos 15:1–17:18. *n:* Jos 13:8, 33.

because the priesthood of the LORD is their heritage; while Gad, Reuben, and the half-tribe of Manasseh have already received the heritage east of the Jordan which Moses, the servant of the LORD, gave them."

[8]When those who were to describe the land were ready for their journey, Joshua commanded them, "Go throughout the land and describe it; return to me and I will cast lots for you here before the LORD in Shiloh." [9]So they went through the land, described its cities in writing in seven sections, and returned to Joshua in the camp at Shiloh. [10]Joshua then cast lots for them before the LORD in Shiloh, and divided up the land for the Israelites into their separate shares.

***Benjamin.*** [11]One lot fell to the tribe of Benjaminites by their clans. The territory allotted them lay between the descendants of Judah and those of Joseph. [12][o] Their northern boundary* began at the Jordan and went over the northern flank of Jericho, up westward into the mountains, until it reached the wilderness of Beth-aven. [13]From there it crossed over to the southern flank of Luz (that is, Bethel). Then it ran down to Ataroth-addar, on the mountaintop south of Lower Beth-horon.[p] [14]For the western border, the boundary line swung south from the mountaintop opposite Beth-horon until it reached Kiriath-baal (that is, Kiriath-jearim; this city belonged to the Judahites). This was the western boundary. [15]The southern boundary began at the limits of Kiriath-jearim and projected to the spring at Nephtoah. [16][q] It went down to the edge of the mountain on the north of the Valley of Rephaim, where it faces the Valley of Ben-hinnom; and continuing down the Valley of Hinnom along the southern flank of the Jebusites, reached En-rogel. [17]Inclining to the north, it extended to En-shemesh, and thence to Geliloth, opposite the pass of Adummim. Then it dropped to Eben-Bohan-ben-Reuben, [18]across the northern flank of the Arabah overlook, down into the Arabah. [19]From there the boundary continued across the northern flank of Beth-hoglah and extended northward to the tongue of the Salt Sea, toward the southern end of the Jordan. This was the southern boundary. [20]The Jordan bounded it on the east. This was how the heritage of the Benjaminites by their clans was bounded on all sides.

[21]Now the cities belonging to the tribe of the Benjaminites by their clans were: Jericho, Beth-hoglah, Emek-keziz, [22]Beth-arabah, Zemaraim, Bethel, [23]Avvim, Parah, Ophra, [24]Chephar-ammoni, Ophni, and Geba; twelve cities and their villages. [25]Also Gibeon, Ramah, Beeroth, [26]Mizpeh, Chephirah, Mozah, [27]Rekem, Irpeel, Taralah, [28]Zela, Haeleph, the Jebusite city (that is, Jerusalem), Gibeah, and Kiriath; fourteen cities and their villages. This was the heritage of the clans of Benjaminites.

## CHAPTER 19

See RG 97–98

***Simeon.*** [1]The second lot fell to Simeon. The heritage of the tribe of Simeonites by their clans lay within that of the Judahites. [2][r] For their heritage they received Beer-sheba, Shema, Moladah, [3]Hazar-shual, Balah, Ezem, [4]Eltolad, Bethul, Hormah, [5]Ziklag, Bethmar-caboth, Hazar-susah, [6]Beth-lebaoth, and Sharuhen; thirteen cities and their villages. [7]Also Ain, Rimmon, Ether, and Ashan; four cities and their villages, [8]besides all the villages around these cities as far as Baalath-beer (that is, Ramoth-negeb). This was the heritage of the tribe of the Simeonites by their clans. [9]This heritage of the Simeonites was within the confines of the Judahites; for since the portion of the latter was too large for them, the Simeonites obtained their heritage within it.

***Zebulun.*** [10]* The third lot fell to the Zebulunites by their clans. The boundary of their

**18:12–20** Benjamin's northern boundary (vv. 12–13) corresponded to part of the southern boundary of Ephraim (16:1–2). Their western border (v. 14) was the eastern border of Dan (cf. 19:40–47). Their southern boundary (vv. 15–19) corresponded to part of the northern boundary of Judah (15:5–9).

**19:10–16** Zebulun's territory was in the central section of the Jezreel Valley and of southern Galilee; it was bounded on the south by Manasseh, on the southeast by Issachar, on the northeast and north by Naphtali, and on the west by Asher. The site of the later city of Nazareth was within its borders. Bethlehem of Zebulun was, of course, distinct from the city of the same name in Judah. **Twelve cities**: apparently seven of the names are missing from v. 15, unless some of the places mentioned in vv. 12–14 are to be included in the number.

*o:* Jos 16:1–5. *p:* Gn 28:19. *q:* Jos 15:6–8. *r:* 1 Chr 4:28–33.

heritage was at Sarid. 11 Their boundary went up west and through Mareal, reaching Dabbesheth and the wadi that is near Jokneam. 12 From Sarid eastward it ran to the district of Chisloth-tabor, on to Daberath, and up to Japhia. 13 From there it continued eastward to Gath-hepher and to Eth-kazin, extended to Rimmon, and turned to Neah. 14 Skirting north of Hannathon, the boundary ended at the valley of Iphtahel. 15 Thus, with Kattath, Nahalal, Shimron, Idalah, and Bethlehem, there were twelve cities and their villages. 16 This was the heritage of the Zebulunites by their clans, these cities and their villages.

*Issachar.* 17* The fourth lot fell to Issachar. The territory of the Issacharites by their clans 18 included Jezreel, Chesulloth, Shunem, 19 Hapharaim, Shion, Anaharath, 20 Rabbith, Kishion, Ebez, 21 Remeth, En-gannim, En-haddah, and Beth-pazzez. 22 The boundary reached Tabor, Shahazumah, and Beth-shemesh, ending at the Jordan: sixteen cities and their villages. 23 This was the heritage of the Issacharites by their clans, these cities and their villages.

*Asher.* 24* The fifth lot fell to the Asherites by their clans. 25 Their territory included Helkath, Hali, Beten, Achshaph, 26 Allammelech, Amad, and Mishal, and reached Carmel on the west, and Shihor-libnath. 27 In the other direction, it ran eastward of Beth-dagon, reached Zebulun and the valley of Iphtahel; then north of Beth-emek and Neiel, it extended northward to Cabul, 28 Ebron, Rehob,[s] Hammon, and Kanah, near Greater Sidon. 29 Then the boundary turned back to Ramah and to the fortress city of Tyre; thence it cut back to Hosah and ended at the sea. Thus, with Mahalab, Achzib, 30 Ummah, Acco, Aphek, and Rehob, there were twenty-two cities and their villages. 31 This was the heritage of the tribe of the Asherites by their clans, these cities and their villages.

*Naphtali.* 32* The sixth lot fell to the Naphtalites. 33 Their boundary extended from Heleph, from the oak at Zaanannim, including Adami-nekeb and Jabneel, to Lakkum, and ended at the Jordan. 34 In the opposite direction, westerly, it ran through Aznoth-tabor and from there extended to Hukkok; it reached Zebulun on the south, Asher on the west, and the Jordan on the east. 35 The fortified cities were Ziddim, Zer, Hammath, Rakkath, Chinnereth, 36 Adamah, Ramah, Hazor, 37 Kedesh, Edrei, En-hazor, 38 Yiron, Migdal-el, Horem, Beth-anath, and Beth-shemesh;[t] nineteen cities and their villages. 39 This was the heritage of the tribe of the Naphtalites by their clans, these cities and their villages.

*Dan.* 40* The seventh lot fell to the tribe of Danites by their clans. 41 Their heritage was the territory of Zorah, Eshtaol, Ir-shemesh, 42 Shaalabbin, Aijalon, Ithlah,[u] 43 Elon, Timnah, Ekron, 44 Eltekoh, Gibbethon, Baalath, 45 Jehud, Bene-berak, Gath-rimmon, 46 Me-jarkon, and Rakkon, with the coast at Joppa. 47[v] But the territory of the Danites was too small for them; so the Danites marched up and attacked Leshem,* which they captured and put to the sword. Once they had taken possession of Leshem, they dwelt there and named it after their ancestor Dan. 48 This was the heritage of the tribe of the Danites by their clans, these cities and their villages.

*Joshua's City.* 49 When the last of them had received the portions of the land they were to inherit, the Israelites assigned a heritage in their midst to Joshua, son of Nun. 50 According to the command of the LORD, they gave him the city he requested, Timnah-serah[w] in the mountain region of Ephraim. He rebuilt the city and made it his home.

**19:17–23** Issachar's land was on the eastern watershed of the Jezreel Valley, but also included the southeastern end of the Galilean mountains. It was surrounded by Manasseh on the south and east, by Naphtali on the north, and by Zebulun on the west. Jezreel (v. 18) dominated the valley to which it gave its name, the later form of which was Esdraelon.

**19:24–31** Asher inherited the western slope of the Galilean hills as far as the Mediterranean, with Manasseh to the south, Zebulun and Naphtali to the east, and Phoenicia to the north.

**19:32–39** Naphtali received eastern Galilee; Asher was to the west and Zebulun and Issachar were to the south, while the upper Jordan and Mount Hermon formed the eastern border. Part of the tribe of Dan later on occupied the northern extremity of Naphtali's lands, at the sources of the Jordan (v. 47).

**19:40–46** The original territory of Dan was a small enclave between Judah, Benjamin, Ephraim, and the Philistines.

**19:47 Leshem**: called Laish in Jgs 18, where the story of the migration of the Danites is told at greater length.

*s:* Jgs 1:31. *t:* Jgs 1:33. *u:* Jgs 1:35. *v:* Jgs 18:27–29. *w:* Jos 24:30; Jgs 2:9.

[51]These are the heritages which Eleazar the priest, Joshua, son of Nun, and the heads of families in the tribes of the Israelites apportioned by lot in the presence of the LORD, at the door of the tent of meeting in Shiloh. Thus they finished dividing the land.

## CHAPTER 20

See RG 98

*Cities of Refuge.* [1][x] The LORD said to Joshua:* [2]Tell the Israelites: Designate for yourselves the cities of refuge of which I spoke to you through Moses, [3]to which anyone guilty of inadvertent and unintentional homicide may flee for asylum from the avenger of blood. [4]To one of these cities the killer shall flee, and standing at the entrance of the city gate, shall plead his case in the hearing of the elders of the city, who must receive him and assign him a place in which to live among them. [5]Though the avenger of blood pursues him, they shall not deliver up to him the one who killed a neighbor unintentionally, when there had been no hatred previously. [6]Once he has stood judgment before the community, he shall live on in that city until the death of the high priest who is in office at the time. Then the killer may return home to the city from where he originally fled.

*List of Cities.* [7]So they set apart Kedesh in Galilee in the mountain region of Naphtali, Shechem in the mountain region of Ephraim, and Kiriath-arba (that is, Hebron) in the mountain region of Judah.[y] [8]And beyond the Jordan east of Jericho they designated Bezer in the wilderness on the tableland in the tribe of Reuben, Ramoth in Gilead in the tribe of Gad, and Golan in Bashan in the tribe of Manasseh.[z] [9]These are the designated cities to which any Israelite or alien residing among them who had killed a person unintentionally might flee to escape death at the hand of the avenger of blood, until the killer could appear before the community.

## CHAPTER 21

See RG 98

*Levitical Cities.* [1]The heads of the Levite families* approached Eleazar the priest, Joshua, son of Nun, and the heads of families of the other tribes of the Israelites[a] [2]at Shiloh in the land of Canaan, and said to them, "The LORD commanded, through Moses, that cities be given us to dwell in, with pasture lands for our livestock."[b] [3]Out of their own heritage, according to the command of the LORD, the Israelites gave the Levites the following cities with their pasture lands.

[4]When the first lot among the Levites fell to the clans of the Kohathites, the descendants of Aaron the priest obtained by lot from the tribes of Judah, Simeon, and Benjamin, thirteen cities. [5]From the clans of the tribe of Ephraim, from the tribe of Dan, and from the half-tribe of Manasseh, the rest of the Kohathites obtained by lot ten cities.[c] [6]From the clans of the tribe of Issachar, from the tribe of Asher, from the tribe of Naphtali, and from the half-tribe of Manasseh, the Gershonites obtained by lot thirteen cities. [7]From the tribes of Reuben, Gad, and Zebulun, the clans of the Merarites obtained twelve cities. [8]These cities with their pasture lands the Israelites gave by lot to the Levites, as the LORD had commanded through Moses.

*Cities of the Priests.* [9][d] From the tribes of the Judahites and Simeonites they gave the following cities [10]and assigned them to the descendants of Aaron in the Kohathite clan of the Levites, since the first lot fell to them: [11]first, Kiriath-arba (Arba was the father of Anak), that is, Hebron, in the mountain region of Judah, with the adjacent pasture lands, [12]although the open country and vil-

**20:1–9** The laws concerning the cities of refuge are given in Nm 35:9–28; Dt 19:1–13; see notes on Nm 35:16–25; Dt 19:2.

**21:1** The order to establish special cities for the Levites is given in Nm 35:1–8. The forty-eight cities listed here were hardly the exclusive possession of the Levites; at least the more important of them, such as Hebron, Shechem, and Ramoth in Gilead, were certainly peopled for the most part by the tribe in whose territory they were situated. But in all these cities the Levites had special property rights which they did not possess in other cities; cf. Lv 25:32–34.

*x:* Ex 21:12–14; Nm 35:9–15; Dt 4:41–43; 19:1–10. *y:* Jos 15:13; 19:37; 21:21. *z:* Jos 21:27, 36. *a:* Ex 6:16–19; Nm 3:17–20. *b:* Nm 35:1–8. *c:* Gn 46:11. *d:* 1 Chr 6:39–66.

lages belonging to the city had been given to Caleb, son of Jephunneh, as his holding.[e] 13 Thus to the descendants of Aaron the priest were given the city of refuge for homicides at Hebron, with its pasture lands; also, Libnah with its pasture lands, 14 Jattir with its pasture lands, Eshtemoa with its pasture lands, 15 Holon with its pasture lands, Debir with its pasture lands, 16 Ain with its pasture lands, Juttah with its pasture lands, and Beth-shemesh with its pasture lands: nine cities from these two tribes. 17 From the tribe of Benjamin they obtained Gibeon with its pasture lands, Geba with its pasture lands, 18 Anathoth[f] with its pasture lands, and Almon with its pasture lands: four cities. 19 These cities which with their pasture lands belonged to the priestly descendants of Aaron, were thirteen in all.

*Cities of the Other Kohathites.* 20[g] The rest of the Kohathite clans among the Levites obtained by lot, from the tribe of Ephraim, four cities. 21 They were assigned, with its pasture lands, the city of refuge for homicides at Shechem in the mountain region of Ephraim; also Gezer with its pasture lands, 22 Kibzaim with its pasture lands, and Beth-horon with its pasture lands. 23 From the tribe of Dan they obtained Elteke with its pasture lands, Gibbethon with its pasture lands, 24 Aijalon with its pasture lands, and Gath-rimmon with its pasture lands: four cities. 25 From the half-tribe of Manasseh, Taanach with its pasture lands, and Gath-rimmon with its pasture lands: two cities. 26 These cities which with their pasture lands belonged to the rest of the Kohathite clans were ten in all.

*Cities of the Gershonites.* 27[h] The Gershonite clan of the Levites received from the half-tribe of Manasseh the city of refuge for homicides at Golan in Bashan, with its pasture lands; and also Beth-Astharoth with its pasture lands: two cities. 28 From the tribe of Issachar they obtained Kishion with its pasture lands, Daberath with its pasture lands, 29 Jarmuth with its pasture lands, and En-gannim with its pasture lands: four cities. 30 From the tribe of Asher, Mishal with its pasture lands, Abdon with its pasture lands, 31 Helkath with its pasture lands, and Rehob with its pasture lands: four cities. 32 From the tribe of Naphtali, the city of refuge for homicides at Kedesh in Galilee, with its pasture lands; also Hammath with its pasture lands, and Kartan with its pasture lands: three cities. 33 The cities which belonged to the Gershonite clans, with their pasture lands, were thirteen in all.

*Cities of the Merarites.* 34[i] The Merarite clans, the last of the Levites, received, from the tribe of Zebulun, Jokneam with its pasture lands, Kartah with its pasture lands, 35 Dimnah with its pasture lands, and Nahalal with its pasture lands: four cities. 36 Also, across the Jordan, from the tribe of Reuben, the city of refuge for homicides at Bezer with its pasture lands, Jahaz with its pasture lands, 37 Kedemoth with its pasture lands, and Mephaath with its pasture lands: four cities. 38 From the tribe of Gad, the city of refuge for homicides at Ramoth in Gilead with its pasture lands, Mahanaim with its pasture lands, 39 Heshbon with its pasture lands, and Jazer with its pasture lands: four cities in all. 40 The cities allotted to the Merarite clans, the last of the Levites, were therefore twelve in all.

41 Thus the total number of cities[j] within the territory of the Israelites which, with their pasture lands, belonged to the Levites, was forty-eight. 42 With each and every one of these cities went the pasture lands round about it.

43 And so the LORD gave Israel the entire land he had sworn to their ancestors he would give them.[k] Once they had taken possession of it, and dwelt in it, 44 the LORD gave them peace on every side, just as he had promised their ancestors. Not one of their enemies could withstand them; the LORD gave all their enemies into their power. 45 Not a single word of the blessing[l] that the LORD had promised to the house of Israel failed; it all came true.

---

*e:* Jos 14:14; 15:13. *f:* Jer 1:1. *g:* 1 Chr 6:51–55. *h:* 1 Chr 6:56–61. *i:* 1 Chr 6:62–66. *j:* Nm 35:7. *k:* Gn 12:7; 13:15; 15:18; 26:3; 28:4, 13. *l:* Jos 23:14–15.

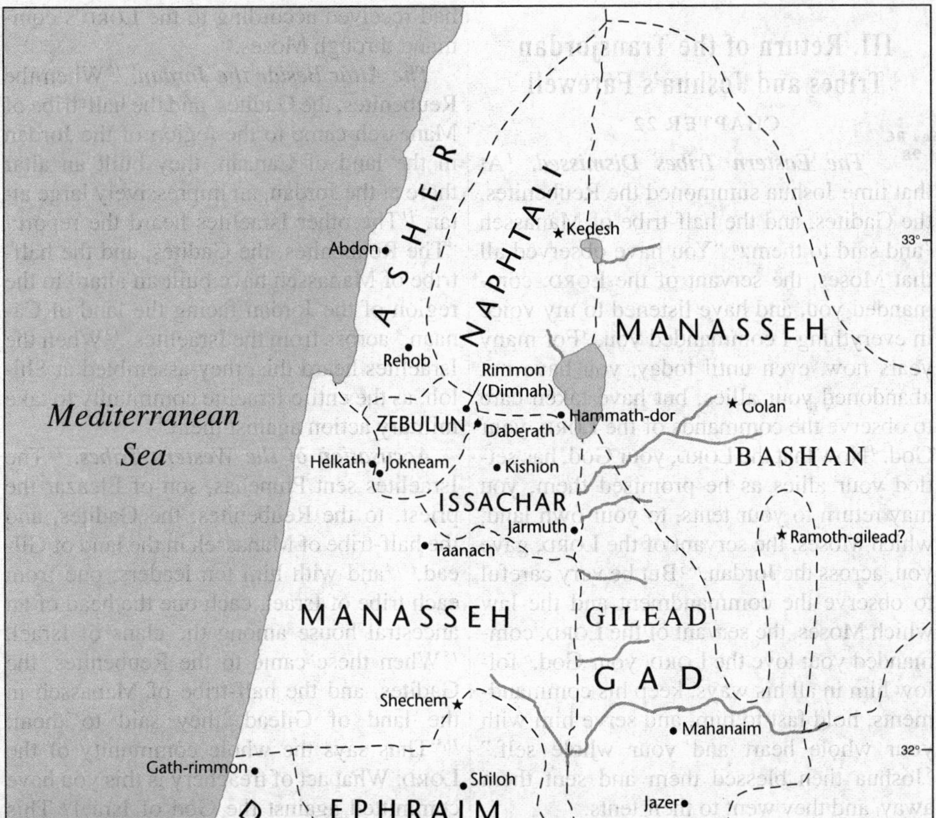

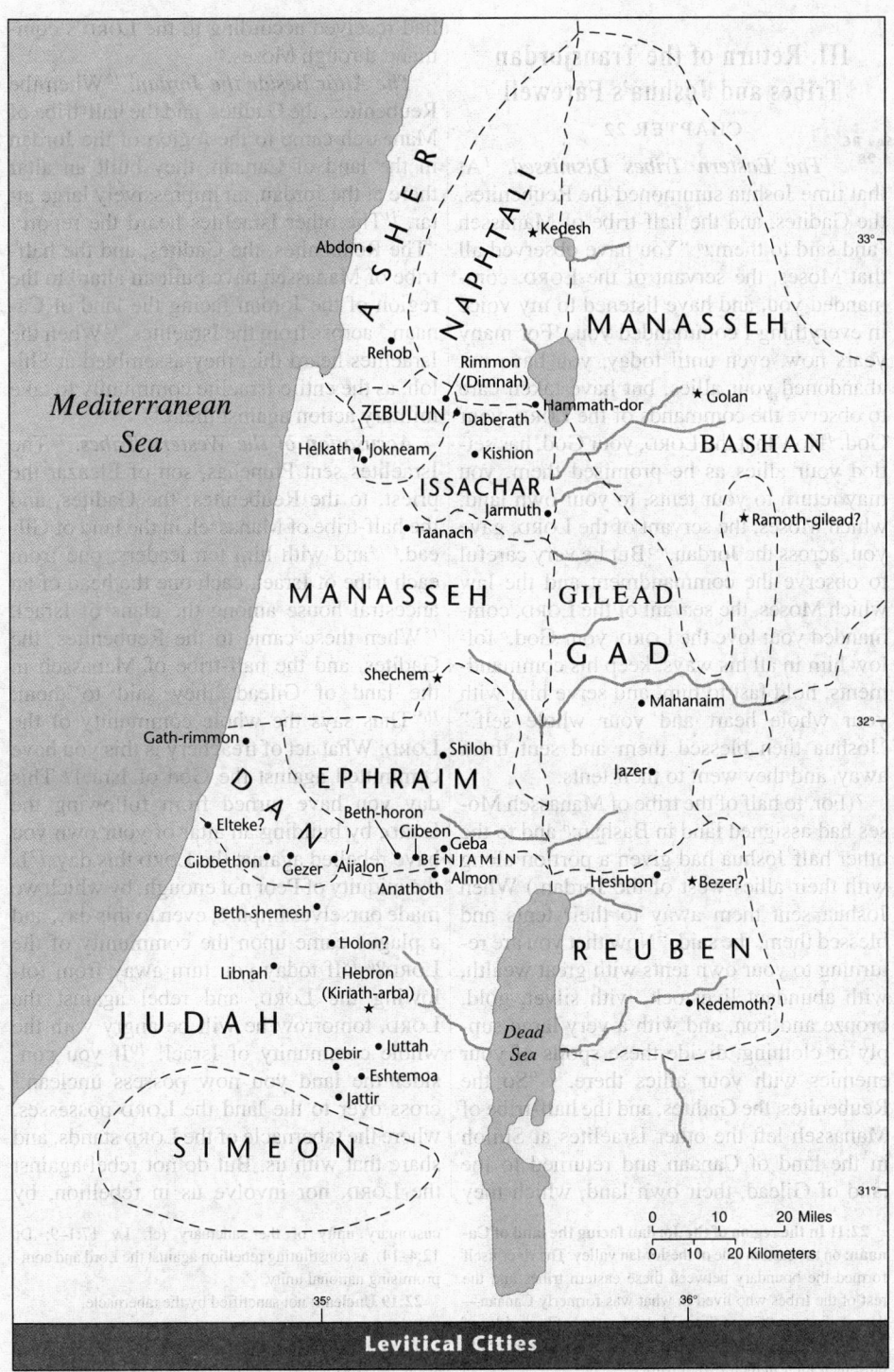


**Levitical Cities**

## III. Return of the Transjordan Tribes and Joshua's Farewell

### CHAPTER 22

See RG 98

*The Eastern Tribes Dismissed.* 1At that time Joshua summoned the Reubenites, the Gadites, and the half-tribe of Manasseh 2and said to them:[m] "You have observed all that Moses, the servant of the LORD, commanded you, and have listened to my voice in everything I commanded you. 3For many years now, even until today, you have not abandoned your allies, but have taken care to observe the commands of the LORD, your God. 4Now that the LORD, your God, has settled your allies as he promised them, you may return to your tents, to your own land, which Moses, the servant of the LORD, gave you, across the Jordan.[n] 5But be very careful to observe the commandment and the law which Moses, the servant of the LORD, commanded you: love the LORD, your God,[o] follow him in all his ways, keep his commandments, hold fast to him, and serve him with your whole heart and your whole self." 6Joshua then blessed them and sent them away, and they went to their tents.

7(For, to half of the tribe of Manasseh Moses had assigned land in Bashan;[p] and to the other half Joshua had given a portion along with their allies west of the Jordan.) When Joshua sent them away to their tents and blessed them, 8he said, "Now that you are returning to your own tents with great wealth, with abundant livestock, with silver, gold, bronze and iron, and with a very large supply of clothing, divide these spoils of your enemies with your allies there."[q] 9So the Reubenites, the Gadites, and the half-tribe of Manasseh left the other Israelites at Shiloh in the land of Canaan and returned to the land of Gilead, their own land, which they had received according to the LORD's command through Moses.[r]

*The Altar Beside the Jordan.* 10When the Reubenites, the Gadites, and the half-tribe of Manasseh came to the region of the Jordan in the land of Canaan, they built an altar there at the Jordan, an impressively large altar. 11The other Israelites heard the report:[s] "The Reubenites, the Gadites, and the half-tribe of Manasseh have built an altar" in the region of the Jordan facing the land of Canaan,* across from the Israelites. 12When the Israelites heard this, they assembled at Shiloh, as the entire Israelite community to take military action against them.*

***Accusation of the Western Tribes.*** 13The Israelites sent Phinehas, son of Eleazar the priest, to the Reubenites, the Gadites, and the half-tribe of Manasseh in the land of Gilead,[t] 14and with him ten leaders, one from each tribe of Israel, each one the head of an ancestral house among the clans of Israel. 15When these came to the Reubenites, the Gadites, and the half-tribe of Manasseh in the land of Gilead, they said to them: 16"Thus says the whole community of the LORD: What act of treachery is this you have committed against the God of Israel? This day you have turned from following the LORD; by building an altar of your own you have rebelled against the LORD this day. 17Is the iniquity of Peor not enough, by which we made ourselves impure, even to this day, and a plague came upon the community of the LORD?[u] 18If today you turn away from following the LORD, and rebel against the LORD, tomorrow he will be angry with the whole community of Israel! 19If you consider the land you now possess unclean,* cross over to the land the LORD possesses, where the tabernacle of the LORD stands, and share that with us. But do not rebel against the LORD, nor involve us in rebellion, by

**22:11 In the region of the Jordan facing the land of Canaan**: on the eastern side of the Jordan valley. The river itself formed the boundary between these eastern tribes and the rest of the tribes who lived in what was formerly Canaan—though the term "Canaan" could also be used of both sides of the Jordan valley (cf. v. 10). The Transjordan tribes naturally built their altar in their own territory.

**22:12 To take military action against them**: the western Israelites considered this altar, which seemed to violate the customary unity of the sanctuary (cf. Lv 17:1–9; Dt 12:4–14), as constituting rebellion against the Lord and compromising national unity.

**22:19 Unclean**: not sanctified by the tabernacle.

*m:* Jos 1:12–17; Nm 32:20–32; Dt 3:18–20. *n:* Jos 13:8. *o:* Dt 6:5–6, 17; 10:12; 11:1, 13, 22. *p:* Jos 17:5. *q:* Nm 31:27. *r:* Jos 18:1; Nm 32:1, 26, 29. *s:* Dt 12:5, 11–14; 13:13–17. *t:* Ex 6:25; Sir 45:23–24. *u:* Nm 25:3–4; Dt 4:3.

building an altar of your own in addition to
the altar of the LORD, our God. [20]When
Achan, son of Zerah,[v] acted treacherously by
violating the ban, was it not upon the entire
community of Israel that wrath fell? Though
he was but a single man, he did not perish
alone* for his guilt!"

***Reply of the Eastern Tribes.*** [21]The Reubenites, the Gadites, and the half-tribe of Manasseh replied to the heads of the Israelite
clans: [22]"The LORD is the God of gods. The
LORD, the God of gods,* knows and Israel
shall know. If now we have acted out of rebellion or treachery against the LORD, our
God, do not try to save us this day, [23]and if
we have built an altar of our own to turn from
following the LORD, or to sacrifice burnt offerings, grain offerings, or communion sacrifices upon it, the LORD himself will exact the
penalty. [24]We did it rather out of our anxious
concern lest in the future your children
should say to our children: 'What have you
to do with the LORD, the God of Israel? [25]For
the LORD has placed the Jordan as a boundary between you and us, you Reubenites and
Gadites. You have no share in the LORD.'
Thus your children would prevent ours from
revering the LORD. [26]So we thought, 'Let us
act for ourselves by building this altar of our
own'—not for burnt offerings or sacrifice,
[27][w] but as witness between us and you and
our descendants, that we have the right to
provide for the service of the LORD in his
presence with our burnt offerings, sacrifices,
and communion sacrifices. Now in the future
your children cannot say to our children,
'You have no share in the LORD.' [28]Our
thought was that, if in the future they should
speak thus to us or to our descendants, we
could answer: 'Look at the copy of the altar
of the LORD which our ancestors made, not
for burnt offerings or for sacrifices, but to
witness* between you and us.' [29]Far be it
from us to rebel against the LORD or to turn
now from following the LORD by building an
altar for burnt offering, grain offering, or sacrifice in addition to the altar of the LORD, our
God, which stands before his tabernacle."

[30]When Phinehas the priest and the leaders of the community, the heads of the Israelite clans, heard what the Reubenites, the
Gadites, and the Manassites had to say, they
were satisfied. [31]Phinehas, son of Eleazar
the priest, said to the Reubenites, the Gadites, and the Manassites, "Today we know
that the LORD is in our midst. Since you have
not rebelled against the LORD by this act of
treachery, you have delivered the Israelites
from the hand of the LORD."

[32]Phinehas, son of Eleazar the priest, and
the leaders returned from the Reubenites and
the Gadites in the land of Gilead to the Israelites in the land of Canaan, and reported the
matter to them. [33]The report satisfied the Israelites, who blessed God and decided not to
take military action against the Reubenites
and Gadites nor to ravage the land where
they lived.

[34]The Reubenites and the Gadites gave
the altar its name* as a witness among them
that the LORD is God.

## CHAPTER 23

See RG 98

***Joshua's Final Plea.*** [1]Many years
later, after the LORD had given the Israelites
rest from all their enemies round about
them, and when Joshua was old and advanced in years,[x] [2]he summoned all Israel,
including their elders, leaders, judges, and
officers, and said to them: "I am old and advanced in years.[y] [3]You have seen all that the
LORD, your God, has done for you against all
these nations; for it has been the LORD, your
God, who fought for you. [4][z] See, I have apportioned among your tribes as their heritage the nations that survive, as well as

**22:20 Achan . . . did not perish alone**: his guilt caused the failure of the first attack on Ai (7:4–23); this fact is adduced as an argument for the solidarity and mutual responsibility of all the Israelites.

**22:22 The LORD, the God of gods**: the Hebrew, which cannot be adequately rendered in English here, adds to the divine name Yhwh ("the LORD") two synonymous words for "God," *'el* and *'elohim*. The repetition of these three sacred words adds force to the protestations of fidelity and innocence.

**22:28 To witness**: far from being destined to form a rival sanctuary, the copy of the altar is intended by the eastern tribes solely as a means of teaching their children to be faithful to the one true sanctuary beyond the Jordan.

**22:34** The name of this altar was the Hebrew word for "witness," *'ed*.

*v:* Jos 7:1, 5. *w:* Ex 27:1–8; Dt 12:5–6, 11–14. *x:* Jos 13:1. *y:* Dt 29:10. *z:* Jos 13:2–7; 14:2; 18:10; Ps 78:55.

those I destroyed, between the Jordan and the Great Sea in the west. 5The LORD, your God, will drive them out and dispossess them at your approach, so that you will take possession of their land as the LORD, your God, promised you. 6Therefore be strong and be careful to observe all that is written in the book of the law of Moses, never turning from it right or left,[a] 7or mingling with these nations that survive among you. You must not invoke their gods by name, or swear by them, or serve them, or bow down to them,[b] 8but you must hold fast to the LORD, your God, as you have done up to this day. 9At your approach the LORD has dispossessed great and strong nations; not one has withstood you up to this day. 10One of you puts to flight a thousand, because it is the LORD, your God, himself who fights for you,[c] as he promised you. 11As for you, take great care to love the LORD, your God. 12For if you ever turn away from him and join with the remnant of these nations that survive among you, by intermarrying and intermingling with them,[d] 13know for certain that the LORD, your God, will no longer dispossess these nations at your approach. Instead they will be a snare and a trap for you, a scourge for your sides and thorns for your eyes, until you perish from this good land which the LORD, your God, has given you.[e]

14"Today, as you see, I am going the way of all the earth.* So now acknowledge with your whole heart and soul that not one of all the promises the LORD, your God, made concerning you has failed. Every one has come true for you; not one has failed. 15[f] But just as every promise the LORD, your God, made to you has come true for you, so will he bring upon you every threat,* even so far as to exterminate you from this good land which the LORD, your God, has given you. 16If you transgress the covenant of the LORD, your God, which he enjoined on you, to go and serve other gods and bow down to them, the anger of the LORD will flare up against you and you will quickly perish from the good land he has given you."

## CHAPTER 24

See RG 98

*Covenant Ceremony.* 1[g] Joshua gathered together all the tribes of Israel at Shechem, summoning the elders, leaders, judges, and officers of Israel. When they stood in ranks before God, 2Joshua addressed all the people: "Thus says the LORD, the God of Israel: In times past your ancestors, down to Terah,[h] father of Abraham and Nahor, lived beyond the River* and served other gods. 3But I brought your father Abraham from the region beyond the River and led him through the entire land of Canaan.[i] I made his descendants numerous, and gave him Isaac. 4To Isaac I gave Jacob and Esau.[j] To Esau I assigned the mountain region of Seir to possess, while Jacob and his children went down to Egypt.

5"Then I sent Moses and Aaron, and struck Egypt with the plagues and wonders that I wrought in her midst.[k] Afterward I led you out. 6And when I led your ancestors out of Egypt, you came to the sea, and the Egyptians pursued your ancestors to the Red Sea with chariots and charioteers.[l] 7When they cried out to the LORD,[m] he put darkness between you and the Egyptians, upon whom he brought the sea so that it covered them. Your eyes saw what I did to Egypt. After you dwelt a long time in the wilderness, 8[n] I brought you into the land of the Amorites who lived east of the Jordan. They fought against you, but I delivered them into your power. You took possession of their land, and I destroyed them at your approach. 9[o] Then Balak, son of Zippor, king of Moab, prepared to war against Israel. He summoned Balaam, son of Beor, to curse you, 10[p] but I would not listen to Balaam. Instead, he had to bless you, and

**23:14 Going the way of all the earth**: drawing near to death, the inevitable end of all; cf. 1 Kgs 2:1–2.

**23:15 Every threat**: mentioned especially in the list of curses in Dt 28:15–68.

**24:2 Beyond the River**: east of the Euphrates; cf. Gn 11:28–31.

*a:* Jos 1:7. *b:* Ex 20:3–6; Dt 5:7–10; 7:2–11. *c:* Ex 14:14; Lv 26:8; Dt 3:22. *d:* Ex 34:16; Dt 7:3. *e:* Nm 33:55. *f:* Lv 26:14–39; Dt 28:15–68. *g:* Ex 19:17. *h:* Gn 11:26, 31; 31:53. *i:* Gn 12:1; Acts 7:2–4. *j:* Gn 36:8; 46:1, 6; Acts 7:15. *k:* Ex 3:10; 7:14; 12:30. *l:* Ex 12:37, 51; 14:9. *m:* Ex 14:10, 20, 27–28. *n:* Nm 21:21–35. *o:* Nm 22:2–5. *p:* Nm 23:1–24:25.

I delivered you from his power. 11 Once you
crossed the Jordan[q] and came to Jericho, the
citizens of Jericho fought against you, but I
delivered them also into your power. 12 And I
sent the hornets* ahead of you which drove
them—the Amorites, Perizzites, Canaanites,
Hittites, Girgashites, Hivites, and Jebusites—out of your way; it was not your
sword or your bow.[r] 13 I gave you a land you
did not till and cities you did not build, to
dwell in; you ate of vineyards and olive
groves you did not plant.[s]

14[t] "Now, therefore, fear the LORD and
serve him completely and sincerely. Cast out
the gods your ancestors served beyond the
River and in Egypt, and serve the LORD.
15[u] If it is displeasing to you to serve the
LORD, choose today whom you will serve,
the gods your ancestors served beyond the
River or the gods of the Amorites in whose
country you are dwelling. As for me and my
household, we will serve the LORD."

16 But the people answered, "Far be it from
us to forsake the LORD to serve other gods.
17 For it was the LORD, our God, who brought
us and our ancestors up out of the land of
Egypt, out of the house of slavery. He performed those great signs before our very
eyes and protected us along our entire journey and among all the peoples through
whom we passed. 18 At our approach the
LORD drove out all the peoples, including
the Amorites who dwelt in the land. Therefore we also will serve the LORD, for he is
our God."

19 Joshua in turn said to the people, "You
may not be able to serve the LORD, for he is
a holy God; he is a passionate God[v] who will
not forgive your transgressions or your sins.
20 If you forsake the LORD and serve strange
gods, he will then do evil to you and destroy
you, after having done you good."

21 But the people answered Joshua, "No!
We will serve the LORD." 22 Joshua therefore
said to the people, "You are witnesses
against yourselves that you have chosen to
serve the LORD." They replied, "We are witnesses!" 23 "Now, therefore, put away the
foreign gods that are among you and turn
your hearts to the LORD, the God of Israel."
24 Then the people promised Joshua, "We
will serve the LORD, our God, and will listen
to his voice."

25 So Joshua made a covenant with the
people that day and made statutes and ordinances for them at Shechem. 26 Joshua wrote
these words in the book of the law of God.
Then he took a large stone and set it up there
under the terebinth that was in the sanctuary
of the LORD.[w] 27 And Joshua said to all the
people, "This stone shall be our witness,[x] for
it has heard all the words which the LORD
spoke to us. It shall be a witness against you,
should you wish to deny your God." 28 Then
Joshua dismissed the people, each to their
own heritage.[y]

*Death of Joshua.* 29[z] After these events,
Joshua, son of Nun, servant of the LORD,
died at the age of a hundred and ten, 30 and
they buried him within the borders of his
heritage at Timnath-serah[a] in the mountain
region of Ephraim north of Mount Gaash.*
31 Israel served the LORD during the entire
lifetime of Joshua, and of those elders who
outlived Joshua and who knew all the work
the LORD had done for Israel. 32[b] The bones
of Joseph,* which the Israelites had brought
up from Egypt, were buried in Shechem in
the plot of ground Jacob had bought from
the sons of Hamor, father of Shechem, for a
hundred pieces of money. This was a heritage of the descendants of Joseph. 33 When
Eleazar, son of Aaron, also died, he was
buried on the hill which had been given to
his son Phinehas[c] in the mountain region of
Ephraim.

**24:12 The hornets**: see note on Ex 23:28.

**24:30** Following this verse the Greek translation of the Bible (the Septuagint) adds: "They laid with him there, in the tomb where they buried him, the flint knives with which he had circumcised the Israelites at Gilgal, when he brought them out of Egypt, as Yhwh commanded them. There they are to this very day."

**24:32** Joseph's bones (Gn 50:24–26) and Jacob's purchase of the burial ground (Gn 33:18–20) relate Joshua with Genesis. **A hundred pieces of money**: see note on Gn 33:19.

*q:* Jos 3:14; 6:1. *r:* Jos 3:10; 11:20; Ex 23:28; Dt 7:20; Ps 44:3. *s:* Dt 6:10–11. *t:* Dt 10:12; 1 Sm 7:3; 12:24; Tb 14:9. *u:* Dt 30:15–19; Jgs 2:11–13. *v:* Ex 20:5; 23:21; 34:14; Lv 19:2; Dt 5:9. *w:* Gn 28:18; 31:45; Jgs 9:6. *x:* Jos 4:1–9; Gn 31:48, 52; Dt 31:19, 21, 26. *y:* Jgs 2:6. *z:* Jgs 2:7–9. *a:* Jos 19:50. *b:* Gn 33:19; 50:24; Ex 13:19. *c:* Jos 22:13.

See RG 100-107

# The Book of Judges

The Hebrew word translated "Judges" in the English title of the book refers not to specialized judicial officers or magistrates but to leaders in general. According to the biblical narrative these judges led Israel from the end of the conquest of Canaan until the beginning of the monarchy. The period of the Judges, therefore, extended from the death of Joshua (Jos 24:29–31; cf. Jgs 1:1) until the installation of Saul as Israel's first king by the prophet Samuel, who was also the last judge (see 1 Sm 7:15–17).

The Book of Judges begins with two introductory passages. The first (chap. 1) gives a description of the situation in Canaan after the Israelite conquest. It emphasizes the continued existence of the indigenous inhabitants of Canaan in many parts of the land because of Israel's inability to drive them out completely. The second passage (2:1–3:6) is a thematic introduction to the period of the Judges, describing a cyclical pattern of infidelity, oppression, "crying out," and deliverance (see note on 2:10–19).

The main part of the book (3:7–16:31) consists of a series of stories about thirteen leaders whose careers are described in greater or lesser detail. The exploits of six of these—Othniel, Ehud, Deborah, Gideon, Jephthah, and Samson—are related at length, and all are shown to have delivered Israel from oppression or danger. They are customarily called "major judges," whereas the other six—Shamgar, Tola, Jair, Ibzan, Elon, and Abdon—who appear only in brief notices, are designated "minor judges." The thirteenth, Abimelech, is included in neither group, since his story is essentially a continuation of that of Gideon and his career is presented as deplorable, a cautionary tale of royal ambition.

The final section of the book consists of two episodes, one about the migration of the tribe of Dan (chaps. 17–18) and the other about an intertribal war directed against the tribe of Benjamin (chaps. 19–21). These stories illustrate the religious and political disorder that prevailed at the time when, as yet, "there was no king in Israel" (see note on 17:6).

The principal contribution of the Deuteronomistic historian to the Book of Judges is the thematic introduction to—and theological evaluation of—the period of the Judges in 2:1–3:6, as well as editorial comments structuring the narrative throughout, e.g., 3:7; 4:1; etc. The historian drew the stories of the judges themselves from older sources, which could have existed in written form but derive ultimately from oral tradition.

Thus the principal divisions of the book in outline are as follows:

I. The Situation in Canaan Following the Israelite Conquest (1:1–3:6)
II. Stories of the Judges (3:7–16:31)
III. Further Stories of the Tribes of Dan and Benjamin (17:1–21:25)

## I. The Situation in Canaan Following the Israelite Conquest

### CHAPTER 1

See RG 101-102

*Canaanites in Palestine.* [1]* After the
death of Joshua the Israelites consulted the
LORD, asking, "Who shall be first among us
to attack the Canaanites and to do battle with
them?" [2]The LORD answered: Judah shall attack: I have delivered the land into his
power.[a] [3]Judah then said to his brother Simeon, "Come up with me into the territory allotted to me, and let us do battle with the
Canaanites. I will likewise go with you into
the territory allotted to you." So Simeon
went with him.[b]

**1:1–36** The chapter depicts the Israelite settlement of Canaan as a gradual and incomplete process (cf. Ex 23:29–30; Dt 7:22). This picture contrasts sharply with that found in Joshua, where the conquest is rapid and total. Accordingly, some scholars believe that Jgs 1 derives from an early account, which is less idealized and more realistic than that on which Joshua is based. Others, noting that Judah is presented as the only tribe that was completely successful in driving foreigners from its territory, think that the account was written at a late date and reflects suspicion in Judah about foreign elements in the Israelite populations of outlying areas (cf. 2 Kgs 17:24–33).

*a:* Jgs 20:18. *b:* Jgs 1:17.

*J*udges: The judges of the Bible were not people who wore black robes and presided over a court. Rather, they were spirit-led, charismatic leaders who rose up in times of crisis to lead the nation in battle against a threatening enemy. A better term might be "warlords" or "military heroes." The personalities of these freedom fighters were often seriously flawed. The term "judge" is also applied to local elders who settled disputes among the tribes.

[4]When Judah attacked, the LORD delivered the Canaanites and Perizzites into their power, and they struck down ten thousand of them in Bezek. [5c]They came upon Adonibezek in Bezek and fought against him. When they struck down the Canaanites and Perizzites, [6]Adonibezek fled. They pursued him, and when they caught him, they cut off his thumbs and big toes. [7]"Seventy kings," said Adonibezek, "used to pick up scraps under my table with their thumbs and big toes cut off. As I have done, so has God repaid me." He was brought to Jerusalem, and he died there. [8*] The Judahites fought against Jerusalem, captured it, and put it to the sword, setting the city itself on fire.[d]

[9]Afterward the Judahites went down to fight against the Canaanites who lived in the mountain region, in the Negeb, and in the foothills.[e] [10]Judah also marched against the Canaanites who lived in Hebron, which was formerly called Kiriath-arba, and defeated Sheshai, Ahiman, and Talmai.[f] [11]They marched from there against the inhabitants of Debir, which was formerly called Kiriath-sepher. [12]Caleb said, "To the man who attacks Kiriath-sepher and captures it, I will give my daughter Achsah in marriage." [13g] Othniel captured it, the son of Caleb's younger brother Kenaz; so Caleb gave him his daughter Achsah in marriage. [14]When she came to him, she induced him to ask her father for some land. Then, as she alighted from the donkey, Caleb asked her, "What do you want?" [15]She answered, "Give me a present. Since you have put me in the land of the Negeb, give me pools of water." So Caleb gave her what she wanted, both the upper and the lower pool.

[16h] The descendants of Hobab the Kenite, Moses' father-in-law,* came up with the Judahites from the City of Palms to the wilderness of Arad, which is in the Negeb, and they settled among the Amalekites. [17i] Then Judah went with his brother Simeon, and they defeated the Canaanites who lived in Zephath. They put the city under the ban and renamed it Hormah.* [j] [18]Judah captured Gaza with its territory, Ashkelon with its territory, Ekron with its territory, and Ashdod* with its territory.[k] [19]The LORD was with Judah, so they gained possession of the mountain region. But they could not dispossess those who lived on the plain, because they had iron chariots. [20l] As Moses had commanded, they gave Hebron to Caleb, who then drove the three sons of Anak away from there.

[21*] As for the Jebusites dwelling in Jerusalem, the Benjaminites did not dispossess

**1:8** See note on 1:21 below.

**1:16 Hobab the Kenite, Moses' father-in-law**: as in 4:11. However, in Nm 10:29 Hobab is identified as Moses' brother-in-law, while Reuel is identified as Moses' father-in-law (see also Ex 2:18). The more common name of Moses' father-in-law is Jethro, also a Midianite (e.g., Ex 3:1). It is impossible to sort out the relationships among these three men in the ancient traditions. **City of Palms**: Jericho (cf. Dt 34:3) or a town in the Negeb.

**1:17 The ban . . . Hormah**: the narrator relates the city-name "Hormah" to "the ban" (Hebrew *herem*), which commanded the Israelites to devote to the Lord—and thus to destroy—whatever was captured within the land (cf. Dt 20:10–18).

**1:18 Gaza . . . Ashkelon . . . Ekron . . . Ashdod**: four of the five major cities of the Philistines (see note on 3:3). Since these cities were on the coastal plain, the statement that Judah captured them is contrary to v. 19, which notes Judah's failure to drive out the inhabitants of the lowlands. In the Septuagint the problem is removed by changing the beginning of this verse to read "Judah did not dispossess . . . ."

**1:21** According to Jos 18:16, Jerusalem was assigned to the tribe of Benjamin. According to the notice in 1:8 above, the city was burned by the Judahites, but elsewhere (2 Sm 5:6–9) we learn that it was not actually taken from the Jebusites until David captured it and made it his capital.

*c:* Jos 10:1. *d:* Jos 10:1–27; 2 Sm 5:6–9. *e:* Jos 10:40; 11:16; 12:8. *f:* Jos 15:13–19; Nm 13:22; Jos 14:15. *g:* Jgs 3:9. *h:* Jgs 4:11; Nm 10:29–32. *i:* Jos 1:3. *j:* Nm 21:3; Jos 12:14. *k:* Jos 11:22. *l:* Jos 14:6–15.

them, so that the Jebusites live with the Benjaminites in Jerusalem to the present day.[m]
22 The house of Joseph, too, went up
against Bethel, and the LORD was with them.
23 The house of Joseph reconnoitered Bethel,
which formerly was called Luz.[n] 24 The
scouts saw a man coming out of the city and
said to him, "Tell us the way into the city, and
we will show you mercy." 25 He showed them
the way into the city, and they put the city to
the sword; but they let the man and his whole
clan go free. 26 The man then went to the land
of the Hittites, where he built a city and
called it Luz, which is its name to this day.
27[o] Manasseh did not take possession of
Beth-shean with its towns or of Taanach
with its towns. Nor did they dispossess the
inhabitants of Dor and its towns, those of Ibleam and its towns, or those of Megiddo and
its towns. The Canaanites continued to live
in this district. 28 When Israel grew stronger,
they conscripted the Canaanites as laborers,
but did not actually drive them out.
29[p] Ephraim did not drive out the Canaanites
living in Gezer, and so the Canaanites lived
among them in Gezer.
30[q] Nor did Zebulun dispossess the inhabitants of Kitron or those of Nahalol; the
Canaanites lived among them and became
forced laborers.
31[r] Nor did Asher dispossess the inhabitants of Acco or those of Sidon, or take possession of Mahaleb, Achzib, Helbah, Aphik,
or Rehob. 32 So the Asherites settled among
the Canaanite inhabitants of the land, for
they had not dispossessed them.
33[s] Nor did Naphtali drive out the inhabitants of Beth-shemesh or those of Beth-
anath. They settled among the Canaanite inhabitants of the land and the inhabitants of
Beth-shemesh and Beth-anath became
forced laborers for them.
34 The Amorites hemmed in the Danites in
the mountain region, not permitting them to
come down onto the plain. 35 So the Amorites
continued to live in Harheres, Aijalon, and
Shaalbim, but as the power of the house of Joseph grew, they were conscripted as laborers.
36 The territory of the Amorites extended
from the Akrabbim pass, from Sela and upward.

## CHAPTER 2

See RG 101–102

*Infidelities of the Israelites.* 1 A messenger of the LORD went up from Gilgal to
Bochim and said, I brought you up from
Egypt and led you into the land which I
promised on oath to your ancestors. I said, I
will never break my covenant with you, 2 but
you must not make a covenant with the inhabitants of this land; you must pull down
their altars.[t] But you did not listen to me.
Look what you have done! 3 For I also said,*
I will not clear them out of your way; they
will become traps for you, and their gods a
snare for you.[u]
4 When the messenger of the LORD had
spoken these things to all the Israelites, the
people wept aloud. 5 They named that place
Bochim,* and they offered sacrifice there to
the LORD.
6[v] Then Joshua dismissed the people, and
the Israelites went, each to their own heritage, to take possession of the land. 7 The
people served the LORD during the entire lifetime of Joshua, and of those elders who outlived Joshua and who had seen all the great
work the LORD had done for Israel. 8 Joshua,
son of Nun, the servant of the LORD, died at
the age of a hundred and ten, 9 and they
buried him within the borders of his heritage
at Timnath-heres in the mountain region of
Ephraim north of Mount Gaash.[w]
10* When the rest of that generation were

**2:3 I also said**: the Lord explicitly warned the Israelites of the consequences of disobedience; see Nm 33:55 and especially Jos 23:13.

**2:5 Bochim**: Hebrew for "weepers."

**2:10–19** This long thematic passage establishes the cyclical pattern for the stories found in the rest of the book. When the Israelites are secure, they forsake the Lord and worship other gods. In punishment the Lord places them in the power of a foreign oppressor. But when they cry out in distress, the Lord takes pity on them and raises up a judge, who delivers them from the oppressor. The Israelites remain faithful to the Lord during the lifetime of the judge, but when the judge dies they again abandon the Lord, and the cycle begins anew.

*m:* Jos 15:63; 18:16; 2 Sm 5:6–9. *n:* Gn 28:19; Jos 18:13. *o:* Jos 17:11–13. *p:* Jos 16:10. *q:* Jos 19:10–16. *r:* Jos 19:24–31. *s:* Jos 19:32–39. *t:* Ex 23:32; 34:12–13; Dt 7:2, 5; 12:2–3. *u:* Ex 23:33; Dt 7:16; Jos 23:13. *v:* Jos 24:28–31. *w:* Jos 19:49–50.

also gathered to their ancestors, and a later generation arose that did not know the LORD or the work he had done for Israel, [11][x] the Israelites did what was evil in the sight of the LORD. They served the Baals,* [12]and abandoned the LORD, the God of their ancestors, the one who had brought them out of the land of Egypt. They followed other gods, the gods of the peoples around them, and bowed down to them, and provoked the LORD.

[13]Because they had abandoned the LORD and served Baal and the Astartes,* [14]the anger of the LORD flared up against Israel, and he delivered them into the power of plunderers who despoiled them. He sold them into the power of the enemies around them, and they were no longer able to withstand their enemies. [15]Whenever they marched out, the hand of the LORD turned against them, as the LORD had said, and as the LORD had sworn to them;[y] and they were in great distress. [16]But the LORD raised up judges to save them from the power of their plunderers; [17]but they did not listen to their judges either, for they prostituted themselves by following other gods, bowing down to them. They were quick to stray from the way their ancestors had taken, who obeyed the commandments of the LORD; but these did not. [18]When the LORD raised up judges for them, he would be with the judge and save them from the power of their enemies as long as the judge lived. The LORD would change his mind when they groaned in their affliction under their oppressors. [19]But when the judge died, they would again do worse than their ancestors, following other gods, serving and bowing down to them, relinquishing none of their evil practices or stubborn ways.[z]

[20][a] The anger of the LORD flared up against Israel, and he said: Because this nation has transgressed my covenant, which I enjoined on their ancestors, and has not listened to me, [21]I for my part will not clear away for them any more of the nations Joshua left when he died. [22][b] They will be made to test Israel, to see whether or not they will keep to the way of the LORD and continue in it as their ancestors did. [23]Therefore the LORD allowed these nations to remain instead of expelling them immediately. He had not delivered them into the power of Joshua.

### CHAPTER 3

See RG 101–103

[1]These are the nations the LORD allowed to remain, so that through them he might test Israel, all those who had not experienced any of the Canaanite wars— [2]to teach warfare to those generations of Israelites who had never experienced it: [3][c] the five lords of the Philistines,* and all the Canaanites, the Sidonians, and the Hivites who lived in the mountain region of the Lebanon between Baal-hermon and Lebo-hamath. [4]These served as a test for Israel, to know whether they would obey the commandments the LORD had enjoined on their ancestors through Moses. [5]So the Israelites settled among the Canaanites, Hittites, Amorites, Perizzites, Hivites, and Jebusites.[d] [6]They took their daughters in marriage, and gave their own daughters to their sons in marriage,[e] and served their gods.

## II. Stories of the Judges

***Othniel.*** [7][f] Then the Israelites did what was evil in the sight of the LORD; they forgot the LORD, their God, and served the Baals and the Asherahs,* [8]and the anger of the LORD

**2:11 The Baals**: the title "Baal," meaning "lord" or "master," belonged to a large number of Canaanite, Phoenician, and Syrian deities, including especially the great storm god Hadad Baal, widely revered as lord of the earth. The plural form, which occurs here, was used by the biblical writers to refer to foreign gods in general.

**2:13 The Astartes**: Ashtoreth, or Astarte, was an important Canaanite and Phoenician goddess. The plural form used here probably refers to foreign goddesses in general.

**3:3 The Philistines**: a people of Aegean origin who settled on the coastal plain of southern Canaan in the twelfth century B.C.; from their name derives the geographic designation Palestine. Israel competed for control of the country against a group of their cities: Gaza, Ashkelon, Ashdod, Gath, and Ekron.

**3:7 The Asherahs**: Asherah was an important goddess, whose presence in the cult was represented by a wooden pole, also called an "asherah"; see notes on Ex 34:13 and Dt 7:5. Here the plural is used to refer to goddesses in general.

*x:* Jgs 3:7–8, 12; 4:1–2; 6:1; 10:6–8; 13:1. *y:* Lv 26:14–39; Dt 28:15–68. *z:* Jgs 3:12; 4:1; 8:33–34. *a:* Jos 23:13; Jgs 2:2–3. *b:* Jgs 3:1, 4. *c:* Jos 13:2–5. *d:* Ex 3:8, 17; 23:23; 33:2; 34:11; Dt 7:1; 20:17; Jos 3:10; 24:11. *e:* Ex 34:16; Dt 7:3; Jos 23:12. *f:* Jgs 2:11–14.

THE STORIES IN the book of Judges show how the people repeat the same pattern of unfaithfulness:

1. Israel sins by turning to other gods;
2. The LORD punishes Israel by allowing an enemy to conquer it;
3. The people repent and beg God for help;
4. The LORD sends a deliverer (a judge) who rescues Israel from their foe.

This "sin-punishment-cry for help-deliverance" pattern is the theological frame that surrounds the entire book. The pattern is repeated in the story of each judge.

flared up against them. He sold them into the power of Cushan-rishathaim,* king of Aram Naharaim; and the Israelites served Cushan-rishathaim for eight years. 9But when the Israelites cried out to the LORD,[g] he raised up a savior for them, to save them. It was Othniel, son of Caleb's younger brother Kenaz.[h] 10The spirit of the LORD came upon him,[i] and he judged Israel. When he marched out to war, the LORD delivered Cushan-rishathaim, king of Aram, into his power, and his hold on Cushan-rishathaim was firm. 11So the land was at rest for forty years,[j] until Othniel, son of Kenaz, died.

*Ehud.* 12Again the Israelites did what was evil in the sight of the LORD, so he strengthened Eglon, king of Moab, against Israel because they did what was evil in the sight of the LORD. 13Taking the Ammonites and Amalek as allies, he went and defeated Israel, taking possession of the City of Palms. 14So the Israelites served Eglon, king of Moab, for eighteen years.

15But when the Israelites cried out to the LORD, he raised up for them a savior, Ehud, son of Gera, a Benjaminite who was left-handed.* The Israelites would send their tribute to Eglon, king of Moab, by him. 16Ehud made himself a two-edged dagger a foot long, and strapped it under his clothes on his right thigh. 17He presented the tribute to Eglon, king of Moab; now Eglon was a very fat man. 18When he had finished presenting the tribute, he dismissed the troops who had carried the tribute. 19But he himself turned back at the sculptured stones near Gilgal, and said, "I have a secret message for you, O king." And the king said, "Silence!" Then when all his attendants had left his presence, 20Ehud went in to him where he sat alone in his cool upper room. Ehud said, "I have a word from God for you." So the king rose from his throne. 21Then Ehud with his left hand drew the dagger from his right thigh, and thrust it into Eglon's belly. 22The hilt also went in after the blade, and the fat closed over the blade because he did not withdraw the dagger from the body.

23Then Ehud went out onto the porch, shutting the doors of the upper room on Eglon and locking them. 24When Ehud had left and the servants had come, they saw that the doors of the upper room were locked, and thought, "He must be easing himself in the cool chamber." 25They waited until they were at a loss when he did not open the doors of the upper room. So they took the key and opened them, and there was their lord lying on the floor, dead.

26During their delay Ehud escaped and, passing the sculptured stones, took refuge in Seirah. 27On his arrival he sounded the horn in the mountain region of Ephraim, and the Israelites went down from the mountains with him as their leader. 28"Follow me," he said to them, "for the LORD has delivered your enemies the Moabites into your power."[k] So they followed him down and

**3:8 Cushan-rishathaim**: this king is not known from other biblical or extrabiblical sources. His title, "king of Aram Naharaim," indicates that he was a Mesopotamian ruler.

**3:15 Left-handed**: this detail is important because it shows why Ehud is able to conceal a weapon on his right thigh (3:16). There is also a wordplay involved, since "Benjaminite" in Hebrew could also mean "right-handed man."

*g:* Jgs 3:15; 4:3; 6:6, 7; 10:10; 1 Sm 12:8, 10. *h:* Jgs 1:13. *i:* Jgs 6:34; 11:29; 13:25; 14:6, 19; 15:14; 1 Sm 11:6. *j:* Jgs 3:30; 5:31; 8:28. *k:* Nm 21:34; Dt 2:24; Jos 2:24; Jgs 4:7, 14; 7:7, 9, 15.

seized the fords of the Jordan against the Moabites, permitting no one to cross. 29 On that occasion they slew about ten thousand Moabites, all of them strong warriors. Not one escaped. 30 So Moab was brought under the power of Israel[l] at that time; and the land had rest for eighty years.[m]

***Shamgar.*** 31 After him there was Shamgar,* son of Anath,[n] who slew six hundred Philistines with an oxgoad.[o] He, too, was a savior for Israel.

## CHAPTER 4

See RG 103–104

***Deborah and Barak.*** 1 [p] The Israelites again did what was evil in the sight of the LORD; Ehud was dead. 2 So the LORD sold them into the power of the Canaanite king, Jabin, who reigned in Hazor. The general of his army was Sisera, who lived in Harosheth-ha-goiim.[q] 3 [r] But the Israelites cried out to the LORD; for with his nine hundred iron chariots Jabin harshly oppressed the Israelites for twenty years.

4 At that time the prophet Deborah, wife of Lappidoth, was judging Israel. 5 She used to sit under Deborah's palm tree, between Ramah and Bethel in the mountain region of Ephraim, where the Israelites came up to her for judgment. 6 She had Barak, son of Abinoam,[s] summoned from Kedesh of Naphtali. She said to him, "This is what the LORD, the God of Israel, commands: Go, march against Mount Tabor, and take with you ten thousand men from Naphtali and Zebulun. 7 I will draw Sisera, the general of Jabin's army, out to you at the Wadi Kishon,[t] together with his chariots and troops, and I will deliver them into your power." 8 But Barak answered her, "If you come with me, I will go; if you do not come with me, I will not go." 9 "I will certainly go with you," she replied, "but you will not gain glory for the expedition on which you are setting out, for it is into a woman's power that the LORD is going to sell Sisera." So Deborah arose and went with Barak and journeyed with him to Kedesh.

10 Barak summoned Zebulun and Naphtali to Kedesh, and ten thousand men followed him.[u] Deborah also went up with him. 11 * Now Heber the Kenite had detached himself from Cain, the descendants of Hobab, Moses' father-in-law,[v] and had pitched his tent by the terebinth of Zaanannim, which was near Kedesh.

12 It was reported to Sisera that Barak, son of Abinoam, had gone up to Mount Tabor. 13 So Sisera called out all nine hundred of his iron chariots and all his forces from Harosheth-ha-goiim to the Wadi Kishon. 14 Deborah then said to Barak, "Up! This is the day on which the LORD has delivered Sisera into your power. The LORD marches before you." So Barak went down Mount Tabor, followed by his ten thousand men. 15 And the LORD threw Sisera and all his chariots and forces into a panic before Barak.[w] Sisera himself dismounted from his chariot and fled on foot, 16 but Barak pursued the chariots and the army as far as Harosheth-ha-goiim. The entire army of Sisera fell beneath the sword, not even one man surviving.

17 Sisera fled on foot to the tent of Jael, wife of Heber the Kenite, for there was peace between Jabin, king of Hazor, and the family of Heber the Kenite. 18 Jael went out to meet Sisera and said to him, "Turn aside, my lord, turn aside with me; do not be afraid." So he went into her tent, and she covered him with a rug. 19 He said to her, "Please give me a little water to drink. I am thirsty." So she opened a skin of milk, gave him a drink, and then covered him.[x] 20 "Stand at the entrance of the tent," he said to her. "If anyone comes and asks, 'Is there someone here?' say, 'No!' " 21 Jael, wife of Heber, got a tent peg and took a mallet in her hand. When Sisera was in a deep sleep from exhaustion, she approached him stealthily and

**3:31** Shamgar is the first of the so-called minor judges; cf. Introduction.

**4:11** It was characteristic of the Kenites that they encamped alongside or among other nomadic groups, such as the Amalekites (cf. 1:16; 1 Sm 15:6). They are most often mentioned in connection with tribes living in the southern part of Judah, but Heber's group seems to have moved north and pitched its tents in the lower Galilee. **Cain**: in this case a collective term for the Kenites. For Hobab, see 1:16.

*l:* Jgs 8:28; 11:23; 1 Sm 7:13. *m:* Jgs 3:11; 5:31; 8:28. *n:* Jgs 5:6. *o:* Jgs 15:15; 2 Sm 23:8, 18. *p:* Jgs 2:19; 3:12; 8:33–34. *q:* Jos 11:1–15; Ps 83:10; 1 Sm 12:9. *r:* Jgs 3:9, 15; 6:6, 7; 10:10; 1 Sm 12:8, 10. *s:* Heb 11:32. *t:* Jgs 5:21; Ps 83:10. *u:* Jgs 5:18. *v:* Nm 10:29; Jgs 1:16. *w:* Ex 14:24; Jos 10:10; 1 Sm 7:10. *x:* Jgs 5:25.

### Deborah, Jael, and Barak

DEBORAH THE PROPHETESS, Barak the army commander, and Jael wife of Heber the Kenite all contributed to achieving delivery from the Canaanite enemy. None of them is called the deliverer, because each of these human figures made only a partial contribution to the victory; in practice, the true deliverer was God (4:23).

drove the peg through his temple and down
into the ground, and he died.[y] 22 Then when
Barak came in pursuit of Sisera, Jael went
out to meet him and said to him, "Come, I
will show you the man you are looking for."
So he went in with her, and there lay Sisera
dead, with the tent peg through his temple.
23 Thus on that day God humbled the
Canaanite king, Jabin, before the Israelites;
24 their power weighed ever more heavily on
him, until at length they finished off the
Canaanite king, Jabin.

## CHAPTER 5

See RG 103–104

*Song of Deborah.* 1[z] On that day Deborah sang this song—and Barak, son of
Abinoam:

2 * When uprising broke out in Israel,
when the people rallied for duty—
bless the LORD!
3 Hear, O kings! Give ear, O princes!
I will sing, I will sing to the LORD,
I will make music to the LORD, the
God of Israel.
4 * [a] LORD, when you went out from Seir,
when you marched from the plains of
Edom,
The earth shook, the heavens poured,
the clouds poured rain,
5 The mountains streamed,
before the LORD, the One of Sinai,
before the LORD, the God of Israel.
6 In the days of Shamgar, son of Anath,[b]
in the days of Jael, caravans ceased:
Those who traveled the roads
now traveled by roundabout paths.[c]
7 Gone was freedom beyond the walls,
gone indeed from Israel.
When I, Deborah, arose,
when I arose, a mother in Israel.*
8 New gods were their choice;
then war was at the gates.
No shield was to be found, no spear,
among forty thousand in Israel!
9 My heart is with the leaders of Israel,
with the dedicated ones of the
people—bless the LORD;
10 Those who ride on white donkeys,
seated on saddle rugs,
and those who travel the road,
Sing of them
11 to the sounds of musicians at the wells.
There they recount the just deeds of the
LORD,
his just deeds bringing freedom to
Israel.
12 Awake, awake, Deborah!
Awake, awake, strike up a song!
Arise, Barak!
Take captive your captors, son of
Abinoam!
13 Then down went Israel against the mighty,
the army of the LORD went down for
him against the warriors.
14 * From Ephraim, their base in the valley;
behind you, Benjamin, among your
troops.

**5:2–31** This canticle is an excellent example of early Hebrew poetry, even though some of its verses are now obscure.

**5:4–5** The Lord himself marches to war in support of Israel. Storm and earthquake are part of the traditional imagery of theophany; cf. Ex 19:16, 18–20; Dt 33:2–3; Ps 18:7–15; 77:17–20; 144:5–7.

**5:7 A mother in Israel**: the precise meaning of the term "mother" is unclear, except that it seems to indicate Deborah's position of leadership, and so may be a title (cf. 2 Sm 20:19).

**5:14–22** The poet praises the tribes that participated in the war against Sisera: Ephraim, Benjamin, Machir (later regarded as a clan of Manasseh), Zebulun, Issachar, and Naphtali, the tribe of Barak (cf. 4:6). By contrast, the tribes of Reuben, Gilead (elsewhere a region occupied by Reubenites and Gadites), Dan, and Asher are chided for their lack of participation. The more distant tribes of Judah and Simeon are not

*y:* Jgs 5:26. *z:* Ex 15:1. *a:* Dt 33:2; Ps 68:8–9; Hb 3:3–15. *b:* Jgs 3:31. *c:* Is 33:8.

## The Poem: Song of Deborah

THE POETIC COUNTERPART to the prose of Judges 4:1–24, chapter 5 provides a more emotional celebration of the victory. Many scholars believe that this song is one of the oldest texts in the Bible. It is also one of the most obscure and difficult. It celebrates the LORD's role in the victory over Sisera through a sudden downpour that disabled the chariots in battle. Its primary attribution to a woman fits the role women have elsewhere in victory celebrations (Ex 15:20–21; Jgs 11:34; 1 Sm 18:6–7).

From Machir came down commanders,
from Zebulun wielders of the marshal's staff.
15 The princes of Issachar were with Deborah,
Issachar, faithful to Barak;
in the valley they followed at his heels.
Among the clans of Reuben
great were the searchings of heart!
16 Why did you stay beside your hearths
listening to the lowing of the herds?
Among the clans of Reuben
great were the searchings of heart!
17 Gilead stayed beyond the Jordan;
Why did Dan spend his time in ships?
Asher remained along the shore,
he stayed in his havens.
18 Zebulun was a people who defied death,
Naphtali, too, on the open heights![d]
19 The kings came and fought;
then they fought, those kings of Canaan,
At Taanach by the waters of Megiddo;
no spoil of silver did they take.
20 From the heavens the stars* fought;
from their courses they fought against Sisera.[e]
21 The Wadi Kishon swept them away;
the wadi overwhelmed them, the Wadi Kishon.[f]
Trample down the strong!*
22 Then the hoofs of the horses hammered,
the galloping, galloping of steeds.
23 "Curse Meroz,"* says the messenger of the LORD,
"curse, curse its inhabitants!
For they did not come when the LORD helped,
the help of the LORD against the warriors."
24 Most blessed of women is Jael,[g]
the wife of Heber the Kenite,
blessed among tent-dwelling women!
25 He asked for water, she gave him milk,
in a princely bowl she brought him curds.[h]
26 [i] With her hand she reached for the peg,
with her right hand, the workman's hammer.
She hammered Sisera, crushed his head;
she smashed, pierced his temple.
27 At her feet he sank down, fell, lay still;
down at her feet he sank and fell;
where he sank down, there he fell, slain.

28 * From the window she looked down,
the mother of Sisera peered through the lattice:
"Why is his chariot so long in coming?
why are the hoofbeats of his chariots delayed?"
29 The wisest of her princesses answers her;
she even replies to herself,
30 "They must be dividing the spoil they took:
a slave woman or two for each man,

mentioned, and some historians believe they were not part of Israel at this time.

**5:20–21 Stars**: the heavenly host, or angelic army. The roles played by the stars and the flash floods underscore the divine involvement in the battle (cf. 5:4–5).

**5:21 Trample down the strong!**: the meaning of these words is obscure. If this interpretation is correct, Deborah is the one addressed.

**5:23 Meroz**: an unknown locality in which Israelites probably resided, since its inhabitants are cursed for their failure to participate in the battle.

**5:28–30** The scene shifts to the household of the slain Canaanite general, where the anxious foreboding of Sisera's mother is countered by the assurances of the noblewomen.

*d:* Jgs 4:10. *e:* Jgs 4:15. *f:* Jgs 4:7, 13; Ps 83:10. *g:* Jgs 4:17; Jdt 13:18; Lk 1:42. *h:* Jgs 4:19. *i:* Jgs 4:21.

Spoil of dyed cloth for Sisera,
spoil of ornate dyed cloth,
a pair of ornate dyed cloths for my
neck in the spoil."
31 So perish all your enemies, O LORD![j]
But may those who love you be like
the sun rising in its might!

And the land was at rest for forty years.[k]

## CHAPTER 6

See RG 104

*The Call of Gideon.* 1 The Israelites
did what was evil in the sight of the LORD,
who therefore delivered them into the power
of Midian for seven years, 2 so that Midian
held Israel subject. From fear of Midian the
Israelites made dens in the mountains, the
caves, and the strongholds.[l] 3 For it used to
be that whenever the Israelites had completed sowing their crops, Midian, Amalek,
and the Kedemites* would come up, 4 encamp against them, and lay waste the produce of the land as far as the outskirts of
Gaza, leaving no sustenance in Israel, and no
sheep, ox, or donkey. 5 For they would come
up with their livestock, and their tents would
appear as thick as locusts. They would be
too many to count when they came into the
land to lay it waste. 6 [m] Israel was reduced to
utter poverty by Midian, and so the Israelites
cried out to the LORD.

7 When Israel cried out to the LORD because of Midian, 8 [n] the LORD sent a prophet
to the Israelites who said to them: Thus says
the LORD, the God of Israel: I am the one
who brought you up from Egypt; I brought
you out of the house of slavery. 9 I rescued
you from the power of Egypt and all your
oppressors. I drove them out before you and
gave you their land. 10 And I said to you: I,
the LORD, am your God; you shall not fear
the gods of the Amorites in whose land you
are dwelling. But you did not listen to me.

11 Then the messenger of the LORD came
and sat under the terebinth in Ophrah that
belonged to Joash the Abiezrite. Joash's son
Gideon[o] was beating out wheat in the wine
press to save it from the Midianites, 12 and
the messenger of the LORD appeared to him
and said: The LORD is with you, you mighty
warrior! 13 "My lord," Gideon said to him,
"if the LORD is with us, why has all this happened to us? Where are his wondrous deeds
about which our ancestors told us when they
said, 'Did not the LORD bring us up from
Egypt?' For now the LORD has abandoned us
and has delivered us into the power of Midian." 14 [p] The LORD turned to him and said:
Go with the strength you have, and save Israel from the power of Midian. Is it not I
who send you? 15 But he answered him,
"Please, my Lord, how can I save Israel? My
family is the poorest in Manasseh, and I am
the most insignificant in my father's
house."[q] 16 The LORD said to him: I will be
with you,* and you will cut down Midian to
the last man. 17 He answered him, "If you
look on me with favor, give me a sign that
you are the one speaking with me. 18 Please
do not depart from here until I come to you
and bring out my offering and set it before
you." He answered: I will await your return.

19 So Gideon went off and prepared a
young goat and an ephah* of flour in the
form of unleavened cakes. Putting the meat
in a basket and the broth in a pot, he brought
them out to him under the terebinth and presented them. 20 [r] The messenger of God said
to him: Take the meat and unleavened cakes
and lay them on this rock; then pour out the
broth. When he had done so, 21 the messenger of the LORD stretched out the tip of the
staff he held. When he touched the meat and
unleavened cakes, a fire came up from the
rock and consumed the meat and unleavened
cakes. Then the messenger of the LORD disappeared from sight. 22 * Gideon, now aware
that it had been the messenger of the LORD,

**6:3 Midian, Amalek, and the Kedemites**: three groups of camel nomads, whose raids were a constant threat to settled peoples like the Israelites during the period of the Judges.

**6:16 I will be with you**: narratives telling how the Lord commissions someone for a task depict the person's reactions of reluctance, confusion, or sense of inadequacy, and the Lord's reassurance ("I will be with you"), sometimes accompanied by a sign (cf. Ex 3:12; Jer 1:8). Lk 1:28–37 is modeled on this pattern.

**6:19 Ephah**: see note on Is 5:10.

**6:22** Ancient Israel thought that seeing God face to face meant mortal danger, as Ex 33:20 indicates and as Gideon's

*j:* Ps 83. *k:* Jgs 3:11, 30; 8:28. *l:* 1 Sm 13:6. *m:* Jgs 3:9, 15; 4:3; 10:10; 1 Sm 12:8, 10. *n:* Jgs 2:1–3; 10:11–14. *o:* Heb 11:32. *p:* Ex 3:10–12. *q:* 1 Sm 9:21. *r:* Jgs 13:19–22.

THE "ASHERAH" (6:25) is a symbol of the goddess Asherah. Using it as firewood would be a calculated desecration.

said, "Alas, Lord GOD, that I have seen the messenger of the LORD face to face!"[s] [23]The LORD answered him: You are safe. Do not fear. You shall not die. [24]So Gideon built there an altar to the LORD and called it Yahweh-shalom.* [t] To this day it is still in Ophrah of the Abiezrites.

[25]That same night the LORD said to him: Take your father's bull, the bull fattened for seven years, and pull down your father's altar to Baal. As for the asherah* beside it, cut it down [26]and build an altar to the LORD, your God, on top of this stronghold with the pile of wood. Then take the fattened bull and offer it as a whole-burnt sacrifice on the wood from the asherah you have cut down. [27]So Gideon took ten of his servants and did as the LORD had commanded him. But he was too afraid of his family and of the townspeople to do it by day; he did it at night. [28]Early the next morning the townspeople found that the altar of Baal had been dismantled, the asherah beside it cut down, and the fattened bull offered on the altar that was built. [29]They asked one another, "Who did this?" They inquired and searched until they were told, "Gideon, son of Joash, did it." [30]So the townspeople said to Joash, "Bring out your son that he may die, for he has dismantled the altar of Baal and cut down the asherah that was beside it." [31]But Joash replied to all who were standing around him, "Is it for you to take action for Baal, or be his savior? Anyone who takes action for him shall be put to death by morning. If he is a god, let him act for himself,[u] since his altar has been dismantled!" [32]So on that day Gideon was called Jerubbaal,* [v] because of the words, "Let Baal take action against him, since he dismantled his altar."

[33]Then all Midian and Amalek and the Kedemites mustered and crossed over into the valley of Jezreel, where they encamped. [34]And Gideon was clothed with the spirit of the LORD,*[w] and he blew the horn summoning Abiezer to follow him. [35]He sent messengers throughout Manasseh, and they, too, were summoned to follow him; he also sent messengers throughout Asher, Zebulun, and Naphtali, and they advanced to meet the others. [36]Gideon said to God, "If indeed you are going to save Israel through me, as you have said, [37]I am putting this woolen fleece on the threshing floor, and if dew is on the fleece alone, while all the ground is dry, I shall know that you will save Israel through me, as you have said." [38]That is what happened. Early the next morning when he wrung out the fleece, he squeezed enough dew from it to fill a bowl. [39]Gideon then said to God, "Do not be angry with me if I speak once more. Let me make just one more test with the fleece. Let the fleece alone be dry, but let there be dew on all the ground." [40]That is what God did that night: the fleece alone was dry, but there was dew on all the ground.

## CHAPTER 7

See RG 104

***Defeat of Midian.*** [1]Early the next morning Jerubbaal[x] (that is, Gideon) encamped by the spring of Harod with all his soldiers. The camp of Midian was north of him, beside the hill of Moreh in the valley. [2]The LORD said to Gideon: You have too many soldiers with you for me to deliver Midian into their power, lest Israel vaunt it-

reaction here shows. Compare the reaction of Samson's parents (13:22–23) when they realize they have been conversing with the Lord.

**6:24 Yahweh-shalom**: a reference to the Lord's words, "You are safe" (v. 23), lit., "Peace be to you!"

**6:25 The asherah**: see note on Ex 34:13.

**6:32 Jerubbaal**: similar in sound to the Hebrew words meaning, "Let Baal take action."

**6:34 Clothed with the spirit of the LORD**: narratives about the selection of leaders in early Israel typically attribute their prowess to "the spirit of the Lord," not to their own qualities (cf. v. 15). The Lord's spirit "comes upon" them (3:10; 11:29; 13:25) or "rushes upon" them (14:6, 19; 15:14; 1 Sm 11:6), and they are transformed into effective leaders. Here, Gideon is "clothed" with the Lord's spirit; cf. the clothing or vesture imagery in Is 59:17; 61:10; Ez 16:10–14; Jb 29:14.

*s:* Gn 32:31; Dt 5:24–26; Jgs 13:22. *t:* Gn 33:20; 35:7; Ex 7:15. *u:* 1 Kgs 18:27. *v:* 1 Sm 12:11. *w:* Jgs 3:10; 11:29; 13:25; 14:6, 19; 15:14; 1 Sm 11:6. *x:* Jgs 6:32.

self against me and say, “My own power
saved me.”* [y] 3So announce in the hearing of
the soldiers, “If anyone is afraid or fearful,
let him leave![z] Let him depart from Mount
Gilead!”* Twenty-two thousand of the soldiers left, but ten thousand remained. 4The
LORD said to Gideon: There are still too
many soldiers. Lead them down to the water
and I will test them for you there. If I tell you
that a certain man is to go with you, he must
go with you. But no one is to go if I tell you
he must not. 5* When Gideon led the soldiers
down to the water, the LORD said to him:
Everyone who laps up the water as a dog
does with its tongue you shall set aside by
himself; and everyone who kneels down to
drink raising his hand to his mouth you shall
set aside by himself. 6Those who lapped up
the water with their tongues numbered three
hundred, but all the rest of the soldiers knelt
down to drink the water. 7The LORD said to
Gideon: By means of the three hundred who
lapped up the water I will save you and deliver Midian into your power. So let all the
other soldiers go home. 8They took up such
supplies as the soldiers had with them, as
well as their horns, and Gideon sent the rest
of the Israelites to their tents, but kept the
three hundred men. Now the camp of Midian was below him in the valley.

9That night the LORD said to Gideon: Go,
descend on the camp, for I have delivered it
into your power. 10If you are afraid to attack,
go down to the camp with your aide Purah
11and listen to what they are saying. After
that you will have the courage to descend on
the camp. So he went down with his aide Purah to the outposts of the armed men in the
camp. 12[a] The Midianites, Amalekites, and
all the Kedemites were lying in the valley,
thick as locusts. Their camels could not be
counted, for they were as many as the sands

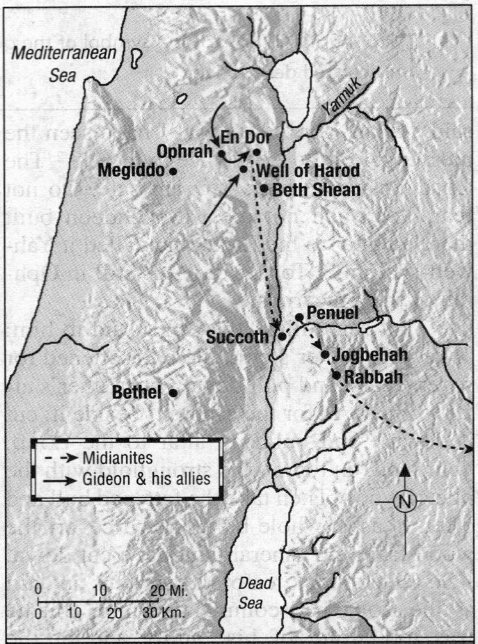

**Battles of Gideon**

on the seashore. 13* When Gideon arrived,
one man was telling another about a dream.
“I had a dream,” he said, “that a round loaf
of barley bread was rolling into the camp of
Midian. It came to a certain tent and struck it
and turned it upside down, and the tent collapsed.” 14“This can only be the sword of the
Israelite Gideon, son of Joash,” the other
replied. “God has delivered Midian and all
the camp into his power.” 15When Gideon
heard the account of the dream and its explanation, he bowed down. Then returning
to the camp of Israel, he said, “Arise, for the
LORD has delivered the camp of Midian into
your power.”

16He divided the three hundred men into
three companies, and provided them all with

**7:2 My own power saved me**: Deuteronomic theology constantly warns Israel against attributing success to their own efforts; cf. Dt 6:10–12; 8:17.

**7:3 Mount Gilead**: since the well-known highlands of Gilead were east of the Jordan River, some other hill of Gilead must be intended here. Perhaps its name is preserved in Ain Jalud (or Galud), the modern Arabic name of the spring of Harod, where Gideon's army is encamped (v. 1). The narrator plays on the Hebrew word “fearful” (*hared*) and the name of the spring, *harod*.

**7:5** The point of this selection process is clear: the battle against the nomadic raiders is going to be won not because of the numerical superiority of the Israelite troops but because of the power of the Lord.

**7:13** The dream seems to foretell the victory of the agricultural Israelites (the barley loaf) over the nomadic Midianites (the tent).

*y:* Dt 8:17; 9:4. *z:* Dt 20:8. *a:* Jgs 6:3.

horns and with empty jars and torches inside
the jars. 17“Watch me and follow my lead,”
he told them. “I shall go to the edge of the
camp, and as I do, you must do also. 18When
I and those with me blow horns, you too
must blow horns all around the camp and cry
out, ‘For the LORD and for Gideon!’ ” 19So
Gideon and the hundred men who were with
him came to the edge of the camp at the beginning of the middle watch,* just after the
posting of the guards. They blew the horns
and broke the jars they were holding.
20When the three companies had blown their
horns and broken their jars, they took the
torches in their left hands, and in their right
the horns they had been blowing, and cried
out, “A sword for the LORD and for Gideon!”
21They all remained standing in place
around the camp, while the whole camp began to run and shout and flee. 22When they
blew the three hundred horns, the LORD set
the sword of one against another throughout
the camp, and they fled as far as Beth-shittah
in the direction of Zeredah, near the border
of Abel-meholah at Tabbath.

23b The Israelites were called to arms from
Naphtali, from Asher, and from all Manasseh, and they pursued Midian. 24Gideon also
sent messengers throughout the mountain
region of Ephraim to say, “Go down to intercept Midian, and seize the water courses
against them as far as Beth-barah, as well as
the Jordan.” So all the Ephraimites were
called to arms, and they seized the water
courses as far as Beth-barah, and the Jordan
as well. 25c They captured the two princes of
Midian, Oreb and Zeeb, killing Oreb at the
rock of Oreb and Zeeb at the wine press of
Zeeb. Then they pursued Midian, but they
had the heads of Oreb and Zeeb brought to
Gideon beyond the Jordan.

See RG 104

## CHAPTER 8

1d But the Ephraimites said to him,
“What have you done to us, not summoning
us when you went to fight against Midian?”
And they quarreled bitterly with him. 2But
he answered them, “What have I done in
comparison with you? Is not the gleaning of
Ephraim better than the vintage of Abiezer?[e]
3It was into your power God delivered the
princes of Midian, Oreb and Zeeb.[f] What
have I been able to do in comparison with
you?” When he said this, their anger against
him subsided.

4When Gideon reached the Jordan and
crossed it, he and his three hundred men
were exhausted and famished. 5So he said to
the people of Succoth, “Will you give my
followers some loaves of bread? They are
exhausted, and I am pursuing Zebah and
Zalmunna, kings of Midian.” 6But the
princes of Succoth replied, “Are the hands
of Zebah and Zalmunna already in your possession, that we should give food to your
army?”* 7Gideon said, “Very well; when the
LORD has delivered Zebah and Zalmunna
into my power, I will thrash your bodies with
desert thorns and briers.” 8He went up from
there to Penuel and made the same request
of them, but the people of Penuel answered
him as had the people of Succoth. 9So to the
people of Penuel, too, he said, “When I return in peace, I will demolish this tower.”

10Now Zebah and Zalmunna were in Karkor with their force of about fifteen thousand
men; these were all who were left of the
whole Kedemite army, a hundred and twenty
thousand swordsmen having fallen. 11Gid-
eon went up by the route of the tent-dwellers
east of Nobah and Jogbehah, and attacked
the force when it felt secure. 12Zebah and
Zalmunna fled and Gideon pursued them.
He captured the two kings of Midian, Zebah
and Zalmunna, terrifying the entire force.

13Then Gideon, son of Joash, returned
from battle by the pass of Heres. 14He captured a young man of Succoth and questioned
him, and he wrote down for him the seventy-
seven princes and elders of Succoth. 15So he
went to the princes of Succoth and said,
“Here are Zebah and Zalmunna, with whom

**7:19 At the beginning of the middle watch**: at the start of the second of the three watches into which the night was divided. The sentinels were changed at the beginning of a watch, thus making the camp momentarily vulnerable.

**8:6 Are the hands . . . already in your possession . . . ?**: i.e., can you already boast of victory? The hands of slain enemies were sometimes cut off and counted as trophies.

*b:* Jgs 6:35. *c:* Ps 83:12; Is 10:26. *d:* Jgs 12:1. *e:* Jgs 6:34. *f:* Jgs 7:25.

you taunted me, 'Are the hands of Zebah and
Zalmunna already in your possession, that we
should give food to your weary men?' " [16]He
seized the elders of the city, and with desert
thorns and briers he thrashed the people of
Succoth. [17]He also demolished the tower of
Penuel and killed the people of the city.
[18]Then he said to Zebah and Zalmunna,
"What about the men you killed at Tabor?"
"They were all like you," they replied.
"They appeared to be princes." [19]"They
were my brothers, my mother's sons," he
said. "As the LORD lives, if you had spared
their lives, I would not kill you." [20]Then he
said to his firstborn, Jether, "Go, kill them."
But the boy did not draw his sword, for he
was afraid, for he was still a boy. [21][g] Zebah
and Zalmunna said, "Come, kill us yourself,
for as a man is, so is his strength." So Gideon stepped forward and killed Zebah and
Zalmunna. He also took the crescents that
were on the necks of their camels.
[22][h] The Israelites then said to Gideon,
"Rule over us—you, your son, and your
son's son—for you saved us from the power
of Midian." [23]But Gideon answered them, "I
will not rule over you, nor shall my son rule
over you. The LORD must rule over you."[i]
[24]Gideon went on to say, "Let me make a
request of you. Give me, each of you, a ring
from his spoils." (Since they were Ishmaelites,* the enemy had gold rings.) [25]"We will
certainly give them," they replied, and they
spread out a cloak into which everyone
threw a ring from his spoils. [26]The gold rings
he had requested weighed seventeen hundred gold shekels, apart from the crescents
and pendants, the purple garments worn by
the kings of Midian, and apart from the trappings that were on the necks of their camels.
[27][j] Gideon made an ephod out of the gold
and placed it in his city, Ophrah. All Israel
prostituted themselves there, and it became a
snare to Gideon and his household.
[28]Midian was brought into subjection by
the Israelites; they no longer held their heads
high, and the land had rest for forty years,[k]
during the lifetime of Gideon.
***Gideon's Son Abimelech.*** [29]Then Jerubbaal, son of Joash, went to live in his house.
[30][l] Now Gideon had seventy sons, his own
offspring, for he had many wives. [31]His concubine* who lived in Shechem also bore him
a son, whom he named Abimelech. [32]At a
good old age Gideon, son of Joash, died and
was buried in the tomb of Joash his father in
Ophrah of the Abiezrites. [33][m] But after Gideon was dead, the Israelites again prostituted
themselves by following the Baals, making
Baal-berith* their god. [34]The Israelites did
not remember the LORD, their God, who had
delivered them from the power of their enemies all around them. [35]Nor were they loyal
to the house of Jerubbaal (Gideon) for all the
good he had done for Israel.

## CHAPTER 9

See RG 104–105

[1]Abimelech, son of Jerubbaal, went to
his mother's kin in Shechem,[n] and said to
them and to the whole clan to which his
mother's family belonged, [2]"Put this question to all the lords of Shechem: 'Which is
better for you: that seventy men, all Jerubbaal's sons, rule over you, or that one man
rule over you?' You must remember that I
am your own flesh and bone."[o] [3]When his
mother's kin repeated these words on his behalf to all the lords of Shechem, they set
their hearts on Abimelech, thinking, "He is
our kin." [4]They also gave him seventy
pieces of silver from the temple of Baal-berith, with which Abimelech hired worthless
men and outlaws as his followers. [5]He then
went to his father's house in Ophrah, and
killed his brothers, the seventy sons of
Jerubbaal, on one stone. Only the youngest
son of Jerubbaal, Jotham, escaped, for he
was hidden. [6]Then all the lords of Shechem

**8:24 Ishmaelites**: evidently used here as a general term for nomads, whose wealth was in the form of gold and flocks. The genealogies in Genesis place the Midianites as descendants of Abraham and his wife Keturah (Gn 25:1–2), and the Ishmaelites as the descendants of Ishmael, son of Abraham and Hagar, Sarah's Egyptian slave (Gn 25:12–16).

**8:31 Concubine**: a wife of secondary rank.

**8:33 Baal-berith**: a divine epithet meaning "lord of the covenant." The same deity is called El-berith, "god of the covenant," in 9:46.

*g:* Ps 83:12. *h:* 1 Sm 8:5; Hos 13:10. *i:* 1 Sm 8:7; 10:19; 12:12. *j:* Jgs 17:5; 18:14. *k:* Jgs 3:11, 30; 5:31. *l:* Jgs 9:2, 5; 10:4; 12:9, 14. *m:* Jgs 2:19; 3:12; 4:1. *n:* Jgs 8:31. *o:* 2 Sm 5:1; 19:12, 13.

### Ambivalence to Monarchy

THE BIBLE CONTAINS much evidence that Israel was always divided about the institution of the monarchy: Some saw it as a practical, logical, and necessary development in the nation's history; others saw it as evidence of an abandonment of the LORD, the one true king of Israel. The story of Abimelech clearly preserves some of the negative attitude toward kingship. But the observation that everyone "did as he thought best" indicates that strong leadership became increasingly necessary.

and all Beth-millo came together and made
Abimelech king by the terebinth at the memorial pillar in Shechem.
7When this was reported to Jotham, he
went and stood at the top of Mount Gerizim
and cried out in a loud voice:

"Hear me, lords of Shechem,
and may God hear you!
8 One day the trees went out
to anoint a king over themselves.
So they said to the olive tree,
'Reign over us.'
9 But the olive tree answered them,
'Must I give up my rich oil,
whereby gods and human beings are
honored,*
and go off to hold sway over the
trees?'
10 Then the trees said to the fig tree,
'Come; you reign over us!'
11 But the fig tree answered them,
'Must I give up my sweetness
and my sweet fruit,
and go off to hold sway over the
trees?'
12 Then the trees said to the vine,
'Come you, reign over us.'
13 But the vine answered them,
'Must I give up my wine
that cheers gods* and human beings,
and go off to hold sway over the
trees?'
14 Then all the trees said to the buckthorn,
'Come; you reign over us!'
15 The buckthorn answered the trees,
'If you are anointing me in good faith,
to make me king over you,
come, and take refuge in my shadow.
But if not, let fire come from the
buckthorn
and devour the cedars of Lebanon.'[p]

16"Now then, if you have acted in good
faith and integrity in appointing Abimelech
your king, if you have acted with good will
toward Jerubbaal and his house, and if you
have treated him as he deserved— 17for my
father fought for you at the risk of his life
when he delivered you from the power of
Midian, 18but you have risen against my father's house today and killed his seventy
sons upon one stone and made Abimelech,
the son of his maidservant,[q] king over the
lords of Shechem, because he is your kin—
19if, then, you have acted in good faith and
integrity toward Jerubbaal and his house today, then rejoice in Abimelech and may he in
turn rejoice in you! 20But if not, let fire come
forth from Abimelech and devour the lords
of Shechem and Beth-millo, and let fire
come forth from the lords of Shechem and
Beth-millo and devour Abimelech." 21Then
Jotham fled and escaped to Beer, where he
remained for fear of his brother Abimelech.
22When Abimelech had ruled Israel for
three years, 23God put an evil spirit[r] between
Abimelech and the lords of Shechem, and the
lords of Shechem broke faith with the house
of Abimelech. 24This was to repay the violence done to the seventy sons of Jerubbaal
and to avenge their blood upon their brother

**9:9 Whereby gods and human beings are honored**: olive oil had a variety of cultic uses (e.g., Lv 2:1, 6, 15; 24:2), and it was also used in the consecration of priests and kings for office (e.g., Ex 30:25, 30; 1 Sm 10:1; 16:13).

**9:13 Cheers gods**: wine was part of a number of types of offerings in the Israelite cult (cf. Ex 29:40; Lv 23:13; Nm 15:7, 10), and it was also used widely in the worship of foreign gods (cf. Dt 32:37–38; Is 65:11).

*p*: 2 Kgs 14:9. *q*: Jgs 8:31. *r*: 1 Sm 16:14; 18:10; 19:9; 1 Kgs 22:19–23.

Abimelech, who killed them, and upon the lords of Shechem, who encouraged him to kill his brothers. 25 The lords of Shechem then set men in ambush for him on the mountaintops, and they robbed all who passed them on the road. It was reported to Abimelech.

26 Now Gaal, son of Ebed, and his kin came, and when they passed through Shechem, the lords of Shechem put their trust in him. 27 They went out into the fields, harvested the grapes from their vineyards, trod them out, and held a festival. Then they went to the temple of their god, where they ate and drank and cursed Abimelech. 28 [s] Gaal, son of Ebed, said, "Who is Abimelech? And who is Shechem that we should serve him? Did not the son of Jerubbaal and his lieutenant Zebul serve the men of Hamor, father of Shechem?[t] So why should we serve him? 29 Would that these troops were entrusted to my command! I would depose Abimelech. I would say to Abimelech, 'Get a larger army and come out!' "

30 When Zebul, the ruler of the city, heard what Gaal, son of Ebed, had said, he was angry 31 and sent messengers to Abimelech in Arumah to say, "Gaal, son of Ebed, and his kin have come to Shechem and are stirring up the city against you. 32 So take action tonight, you and the troops who are with you, and set an ambush in the fields. 33 Promptly at sunrise tomorrow morning, make a raid on the city. When he and the troops who are with him come out against you, deal with him as best you can."

34 During the night Abimelech went into action with all his soldiers and set up an ambush outside of Shechem in four companies. 35 Gaal, son of Ebed, went out and stood at the entrance of the city gate. When Abimelech and his soldiers rose from their place of ambush, 36 Gaal saw the soldiers and said to Zebul, "There are soldiers coming down from the mountaintops!" But Zebul answered him, "It is the shadow of the hills that you see as men." 37 But Gaal went on to say, "Soldiers are coming down from the region of Tabbur-haarez, and one company is coming by way of Elon-meonenim." 38 Zebul said to him, "Where now is your boast, when you said, 'Who is Abimelech that we should serve him?' Are these not the troops for whom you expressed contempt? Go out now and fight with them." 39 So Gaal went out at the head of the lords of Shechem to fight against Abimelech; 40 but when Abimelech went after him, he fled from him. Many fell slain right up to the entrance of the gate. 41 Abimelech returned to Arumah, and Zebul drove Gaal and his kin away so that they could no longer remain at Shechem.

42 The next day, the army marched out into the field, and it was reported to Abimelech. 43 He divided the troops he had into three companies, and set up an ambush in the fields. He watched until he saw the army leave the city and then went on the attack against them. 44 Abimelech and the company with him rushed in and stood by the entrance of the city gate, while the other two companies rushed upon all who were in the field and attacked them. 45 That entire day Abimelech fought against the city. He captured it, killed the people who were in it, and demolished the city itself, sowing it with salt.* [u]

46 When they heard of this, all the lords of the Migdal-shechem went into the crypt of the temple of El-berith. 47 It was reported to Abimelech that all the lords of the Migdal-shechem were gathered together. 48 So he went up Mount Zalmon with all his soldiers, took his ax in his hand, and cut down some brushwood. This he lifted to his shoulder, then said to the troops with him, "Hurry! Do just as you have seen me do." 49 So all the soldiers likewise cut down brushwood and, following Abimelech, placed it against the crypt. Then they set the crypt on fire over them, so that every one of the people of the Migdal-shechem, about a thousand men and women, perished.

50 Abimelech proceeded to Thebez, encamped, and captured it. 51 Now there was a strong tower in the middle of the city, and all the men and women and all the lords of the city fled there, shutting themselves in and

**9:45 Sowing it with salt**: a severe measure, since it rendered the soil barren and useless.

*s:* 1 Sm 25:10. *t:* Gn 33:19; 34:2. *u:* Dt 29:23; Jer 17:6; Ps 107:34.

going up to the roof of the tower. 52 Abimelech came up to the tower and fought against it. When he came close to the entrance of the tower to set it on fire, 53 a certain woman cast the upper part of a millstone* down on Abimelech's head, and it fractured his skull.[v] 54 He immediately called his armor-bearer and said to him, "Draw your sword and put me to death so they will not say about me, 'A woman killed him.' "[w] So his attendant ran him through and he died. 55 When the Israelites saw that Abimelech was dead, they all left for their homes.

56 Thus did God repay the evil that Abimelech had done to his father in killing his seventy brothers. 57 God also brought all the wickedness of the people of Shechem back on their heads, for the curse of Jotham, son of Jerubbaal, overtook them.

## CHAPTER 10

See RG 105

***Tola.*** 1 After Abimelech, Tola,* son of Puah, son of Dodo, a man of Issachar, rose up to save Israel; he lived in Shamir in the mountain region of Ephraim. 2 When he had judged Israel twenty-three years, he died and was buried in Shamir.

***Jair.*** 3 Jair the Gileadite came after him and judged Israel twenty-two years. 4[x] He had thirty sons who rode on thirty donkeys* and possessed thirty cities in the land of Gilead (these are called Havvoth-jair to the present day).[y] 5 Jair died and was buried in Kamon.

***Oppression by the Ammonites.*** 6[z] The Israelites again did what was evil in the sight of the LORD, serving the Baals and Ashtarts, the gods of Aram, the gods of Sidon, the gods of Moab, the gods of the Ammonites, and the gods of the Philistines. Since they had abandoned the LORD and would not serve him, 7 the LORD became angry with Israel and he sold them into the power of the Philistines and the Ammonites. 8 For eighteen years

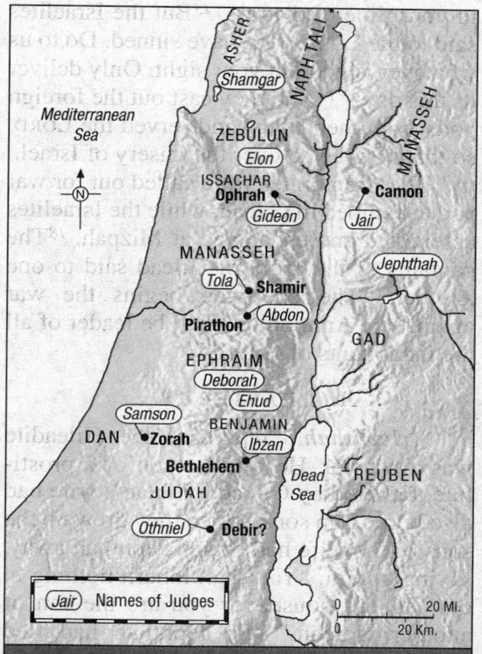

The Twelve Judges

they afflicted and oppressed the Israelites in Bashan, and all the Israelites in the Amorite land beyond the Jordan in Gilead. 9 The Ammonites also crossed the Jordan to fight against Judah, Benjamin and the house of Ephraim, so that Israel was in great distress. 10[a] Then the Israelites cried out to the LORD, "We have sinned against you, for we have abandoned our God and served the Baals." 11[b] The LORD answered the Israelites: Did not the Egyptians, the Amorites,[c] the Ammonites, the Philistines, 12 the Sidonians, the Amalekites, and the Midianites[d] oppress you? Yet when you cried out to me, and I saved you from their power, 13 you still abandoned me and served other gods. Therefore I will save you no more.[e] 14 Go and cry out to the gods you have chosen; let them save you

**9:53 The upper part of a millstone**: a common hand mill consisted of a large flat stone base and a smaller upper stone (cf. Dt 24:6) shaped so that it could be held in the hands and rolled or ground against the lower stone. It is an upper stone that the woman hurls over the wall to kill Abimelech.

**10:1–5 Tola . . . Jair**: two more of the so-called "minor judges"; see Introduction.

**10:4 Donkeys**: mounts signifying rank and wealth; cf. 5:10; 12:14.

*v:* 2 Sm 11:21. *w:* 1 Sm 31:4; 2 Sm 1:9; 1 Chr 10:4. *x:* Jgs 8:30; 9:2, 5; 12:9, 14. *y:* Dt 3:14. *z:* Jgs 2:11–14; 3:7–8, 12; 4:1–2; 6:1; 13:1. *a:* Jgs 3:9, 15; 4:3; 6:6, 7; 1 Sm 12:8, 10. *b:* Jgs 2:1–3; 6:8–10. *c:* Nm 21:21–32. *d:* Jgs 6:1–6. *e:* Jgs 2:21.

in your time of distress. [15]But the Israelites
said to the LORD, "We have sinned. Do to us
whatever is good in your sight. Only deliver
us this day!" [16]And they cast out the foreign
gods from their midst and served the LORD,
so that he grieved over the misery of Israel.
[17]The Ammonites were called out for war
and encamped in Gilead, while the Israelites
assembled and encamped at Mizpah. [18]The
captains of the army of Gilead said to one
another, "The one who begins the war
against the Ammonites shall be leader of all
the inhabitants of Gilead."[f]

## CHAPTER 11

See RG 105

***Jephthah.*** [1]Jephthah[g] the Gileadite
was a warrior. He was the son of a prostitute, fathered by Gilead. [2]Gilead's wife had
also borne him sons. When they grew up the
sons of the wife had driven Jephthah away,
saying to him, "You shall inherit nothing in
our father's house, for you are the son of
another woman." [3]So Jephthah had fled
from his brothers and taken up residence in
the land of Tob.[h] Worthless men had joined
company with him, and went out with him
on raids.[i]
[4]Some time later, the Ammonites went to
war with Israel. [5]As soon as the Ammonites
were at war with Israel, the elders of Gilead
went to bring Jephthah from the land of Tob.
[6]"Come," they said to Jephthah, "be our
commander so that we can fight the Ammonites." [7]"Are you not the ones who hated
me and drove me from my father's house?"
Jephthah replied to the elders of Gilead,
"Why do you come to me now, when you are
in distress?" [8][j] The elders of Gilead said to
Jephthah, "This is the reason we have come
back to you now: if you go with us to fight
against the Ammonites, you shall be the
leader of all of the inhabitants of Gilead."
[9]Jephthah answered the elders of Gilead, "If
you bring me back to fight against the Ammonites and the LORD delivers them up to
me, I will be your leader." [10]The elders of
Gilead said to Jephthah, "The LORD is witness between us that we will do as you say."
[11]So Jephthah went with the elders of Gilead, and the army made him their leader and
commander. Jephthah gave all his orders in
the presence of the LORD in Mizpah.
[12]Then he sent messengers to the king of
the Ammonites to say, "What do you have
against me that you come to fight with me in
my land?" [13]The king of the Ammonites answered the messengers of Jephthah, "Israel
took away my land from the Arnon to the
Jabbok and the Jordan when they came up
from Egypt.[k] Now restore it peaceably."
[14]Again Jephthah sent messengers to the
king of the Ammonites, [15]saying to him,
"This is what Jephthah says: 'Israel did not
take the land of Moab or the land of the Ammonites.[l] [16]For when they came up from
Egypt, Israel went through the wilderness to
the Red Sea and came to Kadesh. [17]Israel
then sent messengers to the king of Edom
saying, "Let me pass through your land."
But the king of Edom did not give consent.[m]
They also sent to the king of Moab, but he
too was unwilling. So Israel remained in Kadesh.[n] [18]Then they went through the wilderness, and bypassing the land of Edom and
the land of Moab, they arrived east of the
land of Moab and encamped across the Arnon.[o] Thus they did not enter the territory of
Moab, for the Arnon is the boundary of
Moab.[p] [19][q] Then Israel sent messengers to
the Amorite king Sihon, who was king of
Heshbon. Israel said to him, "Let me pass
through your land to my own place." [20]But
Sihon refused to let Israel pass through his
territory. He gathered all his soldiers, and
they encamped at Jahaz and fought Israel.
[21]But the LORD, the God of Israel, delivered
Sihon and his entire army into the power of
Israel, who defeated them and occupied all
the land of the Amorites who lived in that
region. [22]They occupied all of the Amorite
territory from the Arnon to the Jabbok and
the wilderness to the Jordan.[r] [23]Now, then, it
was the LORD, the God of Israel, who dispossessed the Amorites for his people, Israel. And you are going to dispossess them?
[24]Should you not take possession of that

*f:* Jgs 11:5–11. *g:* Heb 11:32. *h:* 2 Sm 10:6, 8. *i:* Jgs 9:4; 1 Sm 22:2. *j:* Jgs 10:18. *k:* Nm 21:24. *l:* Dt 2:9, 19. *m:* Nm 21:14–21. *n:* Dt 1:46. *o:* Nm 20:21; 21:4, 10–12; Dt 2:8. *p:* Nm 21:13; 22:36. *q:* Nm 21:21–26; Dt 2:26–36. *r:* Jgs 11:13.

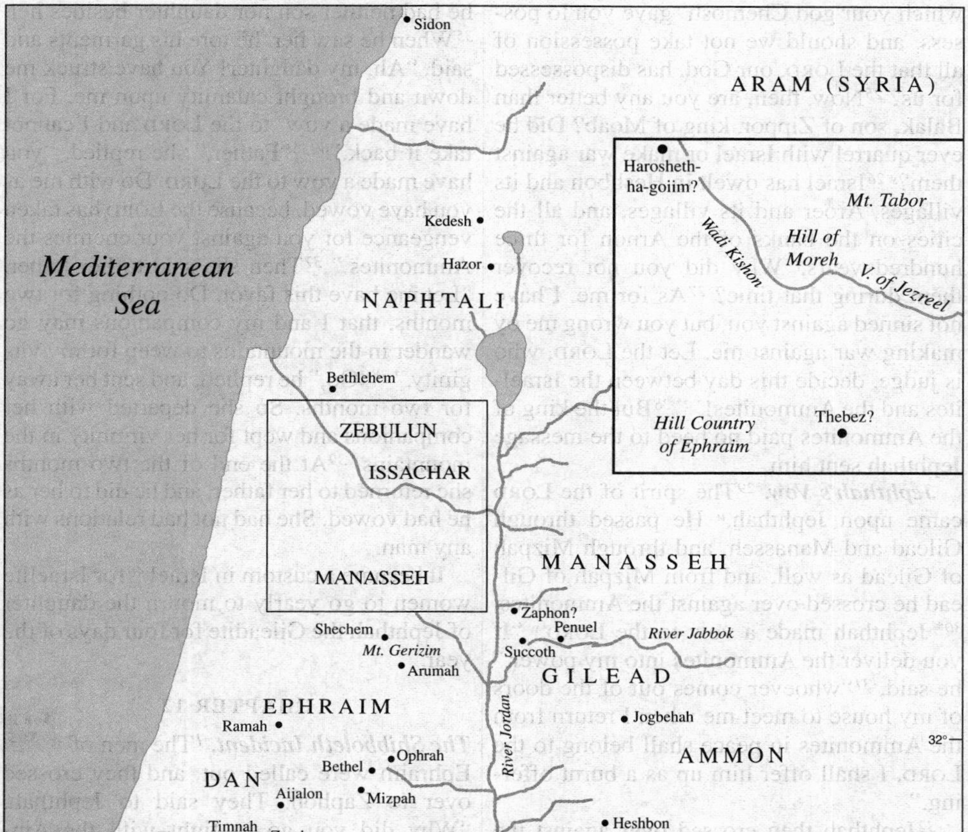

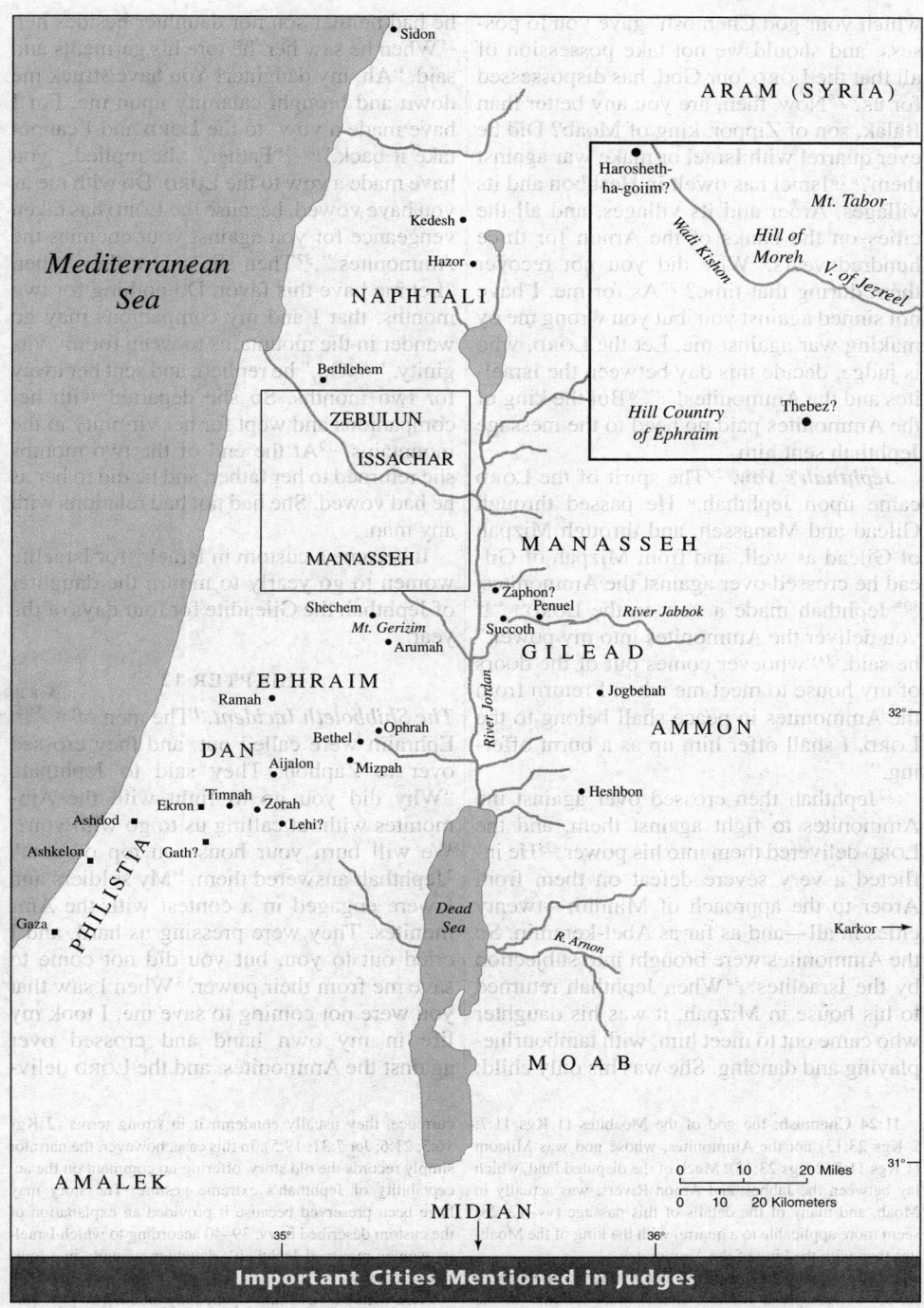


Important Cities Mentioned in Judges

which your god Chemosh* gave you to possess, and should we not take possession of all that the LORD, our God, has dispossessed for us? 25 Now, then, are you any better than Balak, son of Zippor, king of Moab? Did he ever quarrel with Israel or make war against them?[s] 26 Israel has dwelt in Heshbon and its villages, Aroer and its villages, and all the cities on the banks of the Arnon for three hundred years.[t] Why did you not recover them during that time? 27 As for me, I have not sinned against you, but you wrong me by making war against me. Let the LORD, who is judge, decide this day between the Israelites and the Ammonites!' " 28 But the king of the Ammonites paid no heed to the message Jephthah sent him.

***Jephthah's Vow.*** 29 The spirit of the LORD came upon Jephthah.[u] He passed through Gilead and Manasseh, and through Mizpah of Gilead as well, and from Mizpah of Gilead he crossed over against the Ammonites. 30* Jephthah made a vow to the LORD.[v] "If you deliver the Ammonites into my power," he said, 31 "whoever comes out of the doors of my house to meet me when I return from the Ammonites in peace shall belong to the LORD. I shall offer him up as a burnt offering."

32 Jephthah then crossed over against the Ammonites to fight against them, and the LORD delivered them into his power. 33 He inflicted a very severe defeat on them from Aroer to the approach of Minnith—twenty cities in all—and as far as Abel-keramin. So the Ammonites were brought into subjection by the Israelites. 34 When Jephthah returned to his house in Mizpah, it was his daughter who came out to meet him, with tambourine-playing and dancing. She was his only child: he had neither son nor daughter besides her. 35 When he saw her, he tore his garments and said, "Ah, my daughter! You have struck me down and brought calamity upon me. For I have made a vow* to the LORD and I cannot take it back."[w] 36 "Father," she replied, "you have made a vow to the LORD. Do with me as you have vowed, because the LORD has taken vengeance for you against your enemies the Ammonites." 37 Then she said to her father, "Let me have this favor. Do nothing for two months, that I and my companions may go wander in the mountains to weep for my virginity." 38 "Go," he replied, and sent her away for two months. So she departed with her companions and wept for her virginity in the mountains. 39 At the end of the two months she returned to her father, and he did to her as he had vowed. She had not had relations with any man.

It became a custom in Israel 40 for Israelite women to go yearly to mourn the daughter of Jephthah the Gileadite for four days of the year.

## CHAPTER 12

See RG 105

***The Shibboleth Incident.*** 1 The men of Ephraim were called out, and they crossed over to Zaphon. They said to Jephthah, "Why did you go to fight with the Ammonites without calling us to go with you?[x] We will burn your house on top of you." 2 Jephthah answered them, "My soldiers and I were engaged in a contest with the Ammonites. They were pressing us hard, and I cried out to you, but you did not come to save me from their power. 3 When I saw that you were not coming to save me, I took my life in my own hand and crossed over against the Ammonites, and the LORD deliv-

**11:24 Chemosh**: the god of the Moabites (1 Kgs 11:7; 2 Kgs 23:13) not the Ammonites, whose god was Milcom (1 Kgs 11:5; 2 Kgs 23:13). Much of the disputed land, which lay between the Jabbok and Arnon Rivers, was actually in Moab, and many of the details of this passage (vv. 12–28) seem more applicable to a quarrel with the king of the Moabites than with the king of the Ammonites.

**11:30–40** Jephthah's rash vow and its tragic consequences reflect a widespread folklore motif, most familiar in the Greek story of Iphigenia and her father, Agamemnon. The sacrifice of children was strictly forbidden by Mosaic law (Lv 18:21; 20:2–5), and when the biblical writers report its occurrence, they usually condemn it in strong terms (2 Kgs 16:3; 21:6; Jer 7:31; 19:5). In this case, however, the narrator simply records the old story, offering no comment on the acceptability of Jephthah's extreme gesture. The story may have been preserved because it provided an explanation of the custom described in vv. 39–40 according to which Israelite women mourned Jephthah's daughter annually in a four-day ceremony.

**11:35 Made a vow**: lit., "opened my mouth"; so in v. 36.

*s:* Nm 22–24; Jos 24:9–10; Mi 6:5. *t:* Nm 21:25; Dt 2:36. *u:* Jgs 3:10; 6:34; 13:25; 14:6, 19; 15:14; 1 Sm 11:6.

ered them into my power. Why, then, should you come up against me this day to fight with me?"

4 Then Jephthah gathered together all the men of Gilead and fought against Ephraim. The men of Gilead defeated Ephraim, 5 and Gilead seized the fords of the Jordan against Ephraim. When any of the fleeing Ephraimites said, "Let me pass," the men of Gilead would say to him, "Are you an Ephraimite?" If he answered, "No!" 6 they would ask him to say "Shibboleth."* If he said "Sibboleth," not pronouncing it exactly right, they would seize him and kill him at the fords of the Jordan. Forty-two thousand Ephraimites fell at that time.

7 Jephthah judged Israel for six years, and Jephthah the Gileadite died and was buried in his city in Gilead.[y]

***Ibzan.*** 8 After him Ibzan* of Bethlehem judged Israel. 9[z] He had thirty sons and thirty daughters whom he gave in marriage outside the family, while bringing in thirty wives for his sons from outside the family. He judged Israel for seven years. 10 Ibzan died and was buried in Bethlehem.

***Elon.*** 11 After him Elon the Zebulunite judged Israel; he judged Israel for ten years. 12 Elon the Zebulunite died and was buried at Aijalon in the land of Zebulun.

***Abdon.*** 13 After him Abdon, son of Hillel, the Pirathonite, judged Israel. 14[a] He had forty sons and thirty grandsons, who rode on seventy donkeys. He judged Israel for eight years. 15 Abdon, son of Hillel, the Pirathonite, died and was buried in Pirathon in the land of Ephraim in the mountain region of the Amalekites.

## CHAPTER 13

See RG 105-106

***The Birth of Samson.*** 1[b] The Israelites again did what was evil in the sight of the LORD, who therefore delivered them into the power of the Philistines for forty years.

2 There was a certain man from Zorah, of the clan of the Danites,* whose name was Manoah. His wife was barren and had borne no children.[c] 3[d] An angel of the LORD appeared to the woman and said to her: Though you are barren and have had no children, you will conceive and bear a son. 4[e] Now, then, be careful to drink no wine or beer and to eat nothing unclean, 5 for you will conceive and bear a son. No razor shall touch his head, for the boy is to be a nazirite for God* from the womb. It is he who will begin to save Israel from the power of the Philistines.

6 The woman went and told her husband, "A man of God came to me; he had the appearance of an angel of God, fearsome indeed. I did not ask him where he came from, nor did he tell me his name. 7 But he said to me, 'You will conceive and bear a son. So drink no wine or beer, and eat nothing unclean. For the boy shall be a nazirite for God from the womb, until the day of his death.' " 8 Manoah then prayed to the LORD. "Please, my Lord," he said, "may the man of God whom you sent return to us to teach us what to do for the boy who is to be born."

9 God heard the prayer of Manoah, and the angel of God came again to the woman as she was sitting in the field; but her husband Manoah was not with her. 10 The woman ran quickly and told her husband. "The man who came to me the other day has appeared to me," she said to him; 11 so Manoah got up and followed his wife. When he reached the man, he said to him, "Are you the one who spoke to my wife?" "I am," he answered. 12 Then Manoah asked, "Now, when what you say comes true, what rules must the boy follow? What must he do?" 13 The angel of the LORD answered Manoah: Your wife must

**12:6 Shibboleth**: Hebrew meaning "ear of grain" or "torrent of water." Though the Ephraimites probably spoke the same dialect of Hebrew as their Gileadite neighbors, there was enough regional variation in their pronunciation of the initial sound of this word to betray them to their enemies.

**12:8–15 Ibzan . . . Elon . . . Abdon**: three more of the so-called "minor judges"; see Introduction.

**13:2 The clan of the Danites**: before the migration described in chap. 18 the tribe of Dan occupied a small territory west of Benjamin, adjacent to the Philistine plain; see note on 3:3.

**13:5 A nazirite for God**: according to the rules for nazirites set forth in Nm 6:2–8, Samson's vows would have obliged him to abstain from wine and other products of the vine and to keep his hair uncut. As the story that follows shows, the last requirement proved especially fateful in Samson's life.

*v:* Gn 28:20–22; 1 Sm 1:11; 2 Sm 15:7–8. *w:* Nm 30:3; Dt 23:22; Eccl 5:4. *x:* Jgs 8:1. *y:* Jgs 10:2, 5; 12:10, 12, 15; 15:20. *z:* Jgs 8:30; 9:2, 5; 10:4; 12:14. *a:* Jgs 9:2, 5; 10:4; 12:9. *b:* Jgs 2:11–14; 3:7–8, 12; 4:1–2; 6:1; 10:6–8. *c:* 1 Sm 1:2; Lk 1:7. *d:* 1 Sm 1:20; Lk 1:13, 31. *e:* Nm 6:1–5; 1 Sm 1:11; Lk 1:15.

### Nazirite Vows

NAZIRITES, WHO COULD be male or female, took their three vows for a designated period of time or for life (Nm 6:2–8):

1. Abstain from wine and strong drink;
2. Avoid contact with any dead body;
3. Refrain from cutting the hair.

Though he was best at vow number three, Samson breaks all the vows, for by revealing his secret he becomes indirectly responsible for having his hair cut by Delilah.

be careful about all the things of which I
spoke to her. [14]She must not eat anything
that comes from the vine, she must not drink
wine or beer, and she must not eat anything
unclean. Let her observe all that I have commanded her. [15]Then Manoah said to the angel of the LORD, "Permit us to detain you, so
that we may prepare a young goat for you."
[16]But the angel of the LORD answered Manoah: Though you detained me, I would not
eat your food. But if you want to prepare a
burnt offering, then offer it up to the LORD.
For Manoah did not know that he was the
angel of the LORD. [17]* Then Manoah said to
the angel of the LORD, "What is your name,
that we may honor you when your words
come true?" [18][f] The angel of the LORD answered him: Why do you ask my name? It is
wondrous. [19][g] Then Manoah took a young
goat with a grain offering and offered it on
the rock to the LORD, who works wonders.
While Manoah and his wife were looking
on, [20]as the flame rose to the heavens from
the altar, the angel of the LORD ascended in
the flame of the altar. When Manoah and his
wife saw this, they fell on their faces to the
ground; [21]but the angel of the LORD was seen
no more by Manoah and his wife.[h] Then Manoah, realizing that it was the angel of the
LORD, [22]said to his wife, "We will certainly
die,* for we have seen God." [23]But his wife
said to him, "If the LORD had meant to kill
us, he would not have accepted a burnt offering and grain offering from our hands!
Nor would he have let us see all this, or hear
what we have heard."

[24]The woman bore a son and named him
Samson, and when the boy grew up the
LORD blessed him. [25]The spirit of the LORD
came upon him for the first time[i] in Mahaneh-dan, between Zorah and Eshtaol.

## CHAPTER 14

See RG 105–106

*Marriage of Samson.* [1]Samson went
down to Timnah where he saw one of the
Philistine women. [2]On his return he told his
father and mother, "I saw in Timnah a
woman, a Philistine. Get her for me as a
wife." [3][j] His father and mother said to him,
"Is there no woman among your kinsfolk or
among all your people, that you must go and
take a woman from the uncircumcised Philistines?" But Samson answered his father, "Get
her for me, for she is the one I want." [4][k] Now
his father and mother did not know that this
had been brought about by the LORD, who
was seeking an opportunity against the Philistines;* for at that time they ruled over Israel.[l]

shows, the last requirement proved especially fateful in Samson's life.

**13:17–19** Manoah asks for a name so that he will know how to acknowledge the help of the visitor, but the angel will say only that his name is "wondrous," i.e., beyond human comprehension. Manoah's response is to dedicate his offering to "the Lord, who works wonders."

**13:22 We will certainly die**: seeing God face to face was believed to be fatal, as explained in note on 6:22, where Gideon's reaction is similar to that of Manoah here.

**14:4 An opportunity against the Philistines**: although the story of Samson's first love might be taken as an illustration of the danger of foreign marriages, the narrator explains it differently. Samson's infatuation with the Timnite woman was the Lord's way of creating an opportunity to punish the Philistines for their oppression of Israel.

*f:* Gn 32:30. *g:* Jgs 6:19–21. *h:* Jgs 6:22–23. *i:* Jgs 3:10; 6:34; 11:29; 14:6, 19; 15:14; 1 Sm 11:6. *j:* Gn 24:3–4; 26:34–35; 28:1–2, 6–9. *k:* 1 Sm 10:14–16; Lk 2:41–51. *l:* 2 Kgs 5:7.

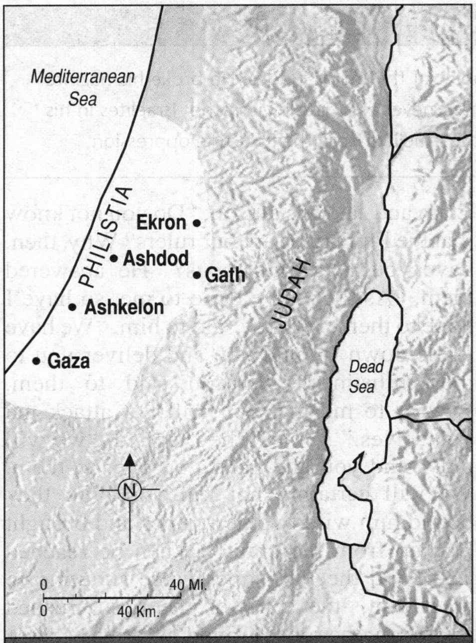

Five Cities of the Philistines

5So Samson went down to Timnah with
his father and mother. When he turned aside
to the vineyards of Timnah, a young lion
came roaring out toward him. 6[m] But the
spirit of the LORD rushed upon Samson, and
he tore the lion apart barehanded,[n] as one
tears a young goat. Without telling his father
or mother what he had done, 7he went down
and spoke to the woman. He liked her.
8Later, when he came back to marry her, he
turned aside to look at the remains of the
lion, and there was a swarm of bees in the
lion's carcass, and honey. 9So he scooped
the honey out into his hands and ate it as he
went along. When he came to his father and
mother, he gave them some to eat, but he did
not tell them that he had scooped the honey
from the lion's carcass.
10His father also went down to the
woman, and Samson gave a feast there,
since it was customary for the young men to
do this. 11Out of their fear of him, they
brought thirty men to be his companions.
12Samson said to them, "Let me propose a
riddle to you. If within the seven days of the
feast you solve it for me, I will give you
thirty linen tunics and thirty sets of garments. 13But if you cannot answer it for me,
you must give me thirty tunics and thirty sets
of garments." "Propose your riddle," they
responded, "and we will listen to it." 14So he
said to them,

"Out of the eater came food,
out of the strong came sweetness."

For three days they were unable to answer the
riddle, 15and on the fourth day they said to
Samson's wife,[o] "Trick your husband into
solving the riddle for us, or we will burn you
and your family.[p] Did you invite us here to reduce us to poverty?" 16* [q] So Samson's wife
wept at his side and said, "You just hate me!
You do not love me! You proposed a riddle to
my people, but did not tell me the answer."
He said to her, "If I did not tell even my father
or my mother, must I tell you?" 17But she
wept beside him during the seven days the
feast lasted, and on the seventh day, he told
her the answer, because she pressed him, and
she explained the riddle to her people.[r]
18On the seventh day, before the sun set,
the men of the city said to him,

"What is sweeter than honey,
what is stronger than a lion?"

He replied to them,

"If you had not plowed with my heifer,
you would not have solved my riddle."

19[s] The spirit of the LORD rushed upon
him, and he went down to Ashkelon, where
he killed thirty of their men and stripped
them; he gave their garments to those who
had answered the riddle. Then he went off to
his own family in anger, 20and Samson's

**14:16** The story of Samson and the Timnite woman is very similar in its narrative structure to the better-known story of Samson and Delilah (16:1–22). In both, Samson's success in his conflict with the Philistines depends on keeping a secret. In both stories Samson is betrayed by the Philistine woman he loves when she importunes him to reveal the secret to her and then, when he gives in, divulges it to her people.

*m:* Jgs 3:10; 6:34; 11:29; 13:25; 14:19; 15:14; 1 Sm 11:6. *n:* 1 Sm 17:34–36; 2 Sm 23:20. *o:* Jgs 16:5. *p:* Jgs 15:6. *q:* Jgs 16:15. *r:* Jgs 16:16–18. *s:* Jgs 3:10; 6:34; 11:29; 13:25; 14:6; 15:14; 1 Sm 11:6.

### Samson

THE FINAL "DELIVERER" is the lowest moral point of the major judges. He broke his nazirite vows, had intercourse with non-Israelite women, never associated with other Israelites in his conflicts with the Philistines, and did not deliver the Israelites from the Philistine oppression.

wife was married to the companion who had been his best man.[t]

## CHAPTER 15

See RG 105–106

*Samson Defeats the Philistines.* 1 After some time, in the season of the wheat harvest, Samson visited his wife, bringing a young goat. But when he said, "Let me go into my wife's room," her father would not let him go in. 2 He said, "I thought you hated her, so I gave her to your best man. Her younger sister is better; you may have her instead." 3 Samson said to him, "This time I am guiltless if I harm the Philistines." 4 So Samson went and caught three hundred jackals, and turning them tail to tail, he took some torches and tied one between each pair of tails. 5 He then kindled the torches and set the jackals loose in the standing grain of the Philistines, thus burning both the shocks and standing grain, the vineyards and olive groves.

6[u] When the Philistines asked, "Who has done this?" they were told, "Samson, the son-in-law of the Timnite, because his wife was taken and given to his best man." So the Philistines went up and destroyed her and her family by fire.[v] 7 Samson said to them, "If this is how you act, I will not stop until I have taken revenge on you." 8 And he struck them hip and thigh—a great slaughter. Then he went down and stayed in a cleft of the crag of Etam.

9 The Philistines went up and encamped in Judah, deploying themselves against Lehi.[w] 10 When the men of Judah asked, "Why have you come up against us?" they answered, "To take Samson prisoner; to do to him as he has done to us." 11 Three thousand men of Judah went down to the cleft of the crag of Etam and said to Samson, "Do you not know that the Philistines are our rulers? Why, then, have you done this to us?" He answered them, "As they have done to me, so have I done to them." 12 They said to him, "We have come down to bind you and deliver you to the Philistines." Samson said to them, "Swear to me that you will not attack me yourselves." 13 "No," they replied, "we will only bind you and hand you over to them. We will certainly not kill you." So they bound him with two new ropes and brought him up from the crag. 14 When he reached Lehi, and the Philistines came shouting to meet him,[x] the spirit of the LORD rushed upon him: the ropes around his arms became like flax that is consumed by fire, and his bonds melted away from his hands. 15 Coming upon the fresh jawbone of an ass, he reached out, grasped it, and with it killed a thousand men.[y] 16 Then Samson said,

"With the jawbone of an ass
I have piled them in a heap;
With the jawbone of an ass
I have slain a thousand men."

17 As he finished speaking he threw the jawbone from him; and so that place was named Ramath-lehi.* 18 Being very thirsty, he cried to the LORD and said, "You have put this great victory into the hand of your servant. Must I now die of thirst and fall into the hands of the uncircumcised?" 19 Then God split the cavity in Lehi, and water issued from it, and Samson drank till his spirit returned and he revived. Hence it is called En-hakkore* in Lehi to this day.

20 Samson judged Israel for twenty years in the days of the Philistines.[z]

**15:17 Ramath-lehi**: "Jawbone Height"; in Hebrew *lehi* means "jawbone."

**15:19 En-hakkore**: understood as "the spring of the crier," an allusion to Samson's cry in v. 18. The story is used to explain the name of a well-known spring in Lehi. The Hebrew also means "Partridge Spring."

*t:* Jgs 15:2, 6. *u:* Jgs 14:20. *v:* Jgs 14:15. *w:* 2 Sm 23:11–12. *x:* Jgs 3:10; 6:34; 11:29; 13:25; 14:6, 19; 1 Sm 11:6. *y:* Jgs 3:31; 2 Sm 23:12. *z:* Jgs 10:2, 5; 12:7, 10, 12, 15; 16:31.

## CHAPTER 16

See RG 106–107

[1]Once Samson went to Gaza, where
he saw a prostitute and visited her. [2]The
people of Gaza were told, "Samson has
come here," and they surrounded him with
an ambush at the city gate all night long.
And all the night they waited, saying, "At
morning light we will kill him." [3]Samson
lay there until midnight. Then he rose at
midnight, seized the doors of the city gate
and the two gateposts, and tore them loose,
bar and all. He hoisted them on his shoulders and carried them to the top of the ridge
opposite Hebron.

***Samson and Delilah.*** [4]After that he fell in
love with a woman in the Wadi Sorek whose
name was Delilah. [5][a] The lords of the Philistines came up to her and said, "Trick him
and find out where he gets his great strength,
and how we may overcome and bind him so
as to make him helpless. Then for our part,
we will each give you eleven hundred pieces
of silver."

[6]So Delilah said to Samson, "Tell me
where you get your great strength and how
you may be bound so as to be made helpless." [7]"If they bind me with seven fresh
bowstrings that have not dried," Samson answered her, "I shall grow weaker and be like
anyone else." [8]So the lords of the Philistines
brought her seven fresh bowstrings that had
not dried, and she bound him with them.
[9]She had men lying in wait in the room, and
she said to him, "The Philistines are upon
you, Samson!" But he snapped the bowstrings as a thread of tow is snapped by a
whiff of flame; and his strength remained unexplained.

[10]Delilah said to Samson, "You have
mocked me and told me lies. Now tell me
how you may be bound." [11]"If they bind me
tight with new ropes, with which no work
has been done," he answered her, "I shall
grow weaker and be like anyone else." [12]So
Delilah took new ropes and bound him with
them. Then she said to him, "The Philistines
are upon you, Samson!" For there were men
lying in wait in the room. But he snapped the
ropes off his arms like thread.

[13]Delilah said to Samson again, "Up to
now you have mocked me and told me lies.
Tell me how you may be bound." He said to
her, "If you weave the seven locks of my hair
into the web and fasten them with the pin, I
shall grow weaker and be like anyone else."
[14]So when he went to bed, Delilah took the
seven locks of his hair and wove them into
the web, and fastened them with the pin.
Then she said, "The Philistines are upon you,
Samson!" Awakening from his sleep, he
pulled out both the loom and the web.

[15][b] Then she said to him, "How can you
say 'I love you' when your heart is not mine?
Three times already you have mocked me,
and not told me where you get your great
strength!" [16][c] She pressed him continually
and pestered him till he was deathly weary
of it. [17]So he told her all that was in his heart
and said, "No razor has touched my head,
for I have been a nazirite for God from my
mother's womb.[d] If I am shaved, my
strength will leave me, and I shall grow
weaker and be like anyone else." [18]When
Delilah realized that he had told her all that
was in his heart, she summoned the lords of
the Philistines, saying, "Come up this time,
for he has told me all that is in his heart." So
the lords of the Philistines came to her and
brought the money with them.[e] [19]She put
him to sleep on her lap, and called for a man
who shaved off the seven locks of his hair.
He immediately became helpless, for his
strength had left him.* [20]When she said "The
Philistines are upon you, Samson!" he woke
from his sleep and thought, "I will go out as
I have done time and again and shake myself
free." He did not realize that the LORD had
left him. [21]But the Philistines seized him and
gouged out his eyes. Then they brought him
down to Gaza and bound him with bronze
fetters, and he was put to grinding grain in
the prison. [22]But the hair of his head began
to grow as soon as it was shaved.

***The Death of Samson.*** [23][f] The lords of the
Philistines assembled to offer a great sacrifice

**16:19** See note on 13:5.

*a:* Jgs 14:15. *b:* Jgs 14:16. *c:* Jgs 14:17. *d:* Jgs 13:5. *e:* Jgs 16:5. *f:* 1 Sm 5:2–5.

to their god Dagon* and to celebrate. They
said, "Our god has delivered Samson our enemy into our power." 24When the people saw
him, they praised their god. For they said,

"Our god has delivered into our power
our enemy, the ravager of our land,
the one who has multiplied our slain."

25When their spirits were high, they said,
"Call Samson that he may amuse us." So
they called Samson from the prison, and he
provided amusement for them. They made
him stand between the columns, 26and Samson said to the attendant who was holding
his hand, "Put me where I may touch the
columns that support the temple, so that I
may lean against them." 27The temple was
full of men and women: all the lords of the
Philistines were there, and from the roof
about three thousand men and women
looked on as Samson provided amusement.
28Samson cried out to the LORD and said,
"Lord GOD, remember me! Strengthen me
only this once that I may avenge myself on
the Philistines at one blow for my two eyes."
29Samson grasped the two middle columns
on which the temple rested and braced himself against them, one at his right, the other
at his left. 30Then saying, "Let me die with
the Philistines!" Samson pushed hard, and
the temple fell upon the lords and all the
people who were in it. Those he killed by his
dying were more than those he had killed
during his lifetime.

31His kinsmen and all his father's house
went down and bore him up for burial in the
grave of Manoah his father between Zorah
and Eshtaol. He had judged Israel for twenty
years.[g]

## III. Further Stories of the Tribes of Dan and Benjamin

### CHAPTER 17

See RG 106–107

***Micah and the Levite.*** 1There was a
man from the mountain region of Ephraim
whose name was Micah. 2* He said to his
mother, "The eleven hundred pieces of silver
that were taken from you, about which you
pronounced a curse and even said it in my
hearing—I have that silver. I took it. So now
I will restore it to you." Then his mother said,
"May my son be blessed by the LORD!"
3When he restored the eleven hundred pieces
of silver to his mother, she said, "I consecrate
the silver to the LORD from my own hand on
behalf of my son to make an idol overlaid
with silver."*[h] 4So when he restored the silver to his mother, she took two hundred
pieces and gave them to the silversmith, who
made of them an idol overlaid with silver. So
it remained in the house of Micah. 5The man
Micah had a shrine, and he made an ephod
and teraphim,*[i] and installed one of his sons,
who became his priest.[j] 6* In those days there
was no king in Israel; everyone did what was
right in their own eyes.[k]

7There was a young man from Bethlehem
of Judah, from the clan of Judah; he was a
Levite residing there.[l] 8The man set out from
the city, Bethlehem of Judah, to take up residence wherever he could find a place. On
his journey he came into the mountain region of Ephraim as far as the house of Micah. 9"Where do you come from?" Micah
asked him. He answered him, "I am a Levite,
from Bethlehem in Judah, and I am on my
way to take up residence wherever I can find

**16:23 Dagon**: an ancient Syrian grain deity (cf. Hebrew *dagan*, "grain") whom the Philistines adopted as their national god after their arrival on the coast of Canaan.

**17:2** The narrator picks up the story after a number of events, including a theft and a mother's curse, have already taken place.

**17:3 An idol overlaid with silver**: two nouns in Hebrew, one indicating a wooden image and the other denoting an image cast from metal. The probable interpretation is that the woman intends for her silver to be recast as a covering for an image of a god, possibly the Lord. This was forbidden in Mosaic law (cf. Ex 20:4 and Dt 5:8).

**17:5 An ephod and teraphim**: cultic paraphernalia. An ephod was a priestly garment, especially that worn by the high priest (cf. Ex 28 and 39), which contained a pocket for objects used for divination. Teraphim were household idols (Gn 31:19, 34–35; 1 Sm 19:13), which may also have had a divinatory function.

**17:6** This refrain, which will be repeated fully or in part three more times (18:1; 19:1; 21:25), calls attention to the disorder and lawlessness that prevailed before the establishment of kingship in Israel. In this case the problem is cultic impropriety, seen not only in the making of an idol but in the establishment of a local temple, complete with an ephod and teraphim.

---

*g:* Jgs 10:2, 5; 12:7, 10, 12, 15; 15:20. *h:* Ex 20:4; Lv 19:4; Dt 5:8. *i:* Jgs 18:14, 18. *j:* 1 Sm 7:1. *k:* Jgs 18:1; 19:1; 21:25. *l:* Jgs 19:1.

## Micah's House of God and the Temple of Dan

THIS STORY (17:1–18:31), focused upon cultic sites, serves to criticize the period of the judges by representing it as an age of anarchy: "In those days there was no king in Israel; everyone did what was right in their own eyes." (This statement is repeated, in whole or in part, in Judges 17:6; 18:1; 19:1; 21:25.) In terms of chronology, the story is set at the beginning of the age of the judges (see Jgs 18:30) but is placed at the end of the book to emphasize that the end of the period was similar to its beginning, and the judges were unable to correct the situation.

a place." 10"Stay with me," Micah said to him. "Be father and priest to me,[m] and I will give you ten silver pieces a year, a set of garments, and your living." He pressed the Levite, 11and he agreed to stay with the man. The young man became like one of his own sons. 12* Micah installed the Levite, and the young man became his priest, remaining in the house of Micah. 13Then Micah said, "Now I know that the LORD will prosper me, since I have the Levite as my priest."

### CHAPTER 18

See RG 106–107

***Migration of the Danites.*** 1In those days there was no king in Israel.[n] In those days the tribe of the Danites were in search of a heritage to dwell in, for up to that time no heritage had been allotted* to them among the tribes of Israel.[o]

2So the Danites sent from their clans five powerful men of Zorah and Eshtaol, to reconnoiter the land and scout it. "Go, scout the land," they were told. They went into the mountain region of Ephraim, and they spent the night there. 3While they were near the house of Micah,[p] they recognized the voice* of the young Levite,[q] so they turned aside. They asked him, "Who brought you here? What are you doing here? What is your interest here?" 4"This is what Micah has done for me," he replied to them. "He has hired me and I have become his priest."[r] 5They said to him, "Consult God, that we may know whether the journey we are making will lead to success."[s] 6The priest said to them, "Go in peace! The journey you are making is under the eye of the LORD."

7So the five men went on and came to Laish. They saw the people there living securely after the manner of the Sidonians, quiet and trusting, with no lack of any natural resource. They were distant from the Sidonians and had no dealings with the Arameans.* 8When the five returned to their kin in Zorah and Eshtaol, they were asked, "What do you have to report?" 9They replied, "Come, let us attack them, for we have seen the land and it is very good. Are you going to hesitate? Do not be slow to go in and take possession of the land! 10When you go you will come to a trusting people. The land stretches out in both directions, and God has indeed given it into your power—a place where no natural resource is lacking."[t]

11So six hundred of the clan of the Danites, men armed with weapons of war, set out from Zorah and Eshtaol. 12They marched up into Judah and encamped near Kiriath-jea-

**17:12–13** Previously one of Micah's sons served as priest (v. 5). But Micah's family were probably Ephraimites (cf. v. 1) rather than Levites, and the story reflects a sense that only Levites were to be consecrated as priests; cf. Nm 18:7, where descent from Aaron is further specified as a requirement to be a priest. Thus Micah believes it will be to his advantage to retain the itinerant Levite.

**18:1 No heritage . . . allotted**: according to Jos 19:40–48, the Danites received an allotment in the central part of the country (cf. note on 13:2 above). The point here may be that since they were unable to take full possession of that original allotment, as indicated by the notice in Jgs 1:34, they are now seeking territory elsewhere.

**18:3 Recognized the voice**: this might indicate that the Danite scouts were personally acquainted with the young Levite, but it is more likely to mean that, being originally from Judah, his dialect or accent was noticeably different from others in Micah's household.

**18:7 The Sidonians . . . the Arameans**: the people of Laish were not in regular contact with their neighbors, including the Sidonians or Phoenicians in the coastal district to the west and the Arameans in the regions to the north and east. This isolation is mentioned to underscore the vulnerability of the peaceful and unfortified city.

*m:* Jgs 18:19. *n:* Jgs 17:6; 19:1; 21:25. *o:* Jgs 1:34; Jos 19:40–48. *p:* Jgs 17:1. *q:* Jgs 17:7–12. *r:* Jgs 17:10. *s:* Jgs 1:1; 1 Sm 14:18–19, 36–44; 23:2, 4, 9–12; 30:7–8. *t:* 1 Chr 5:40.

rim; for this reason the place is called Mahaneh-dan* to this day (it lies west of Kiriath-
jearim).[u]
13From there they passed on into the
mountain region of Ephraim and came to the
house of Micah. 14Then the five men who
had gone to reconnoiter the land spoke up
and said to their kindred, "Do you know that
in these houses there are an ephod, teraphim,
and an idol overlaid with silver?[v] Now decide what you must do!" 15So turning in that
direction, they went to the house of the
young Levite at the home of Micah and
greeted him. 16The six hundred Danites stationed themselves at the entrance of the gate
armed with weapons of war. 17The five men
who had gone to reconnoiter the land went
up 18and entered the house of Micah with the
priest standing there. They took the idol, the
ephod, the teraphim and the metal image.
When the priest said to them, "What are you
doing?" 19they said to him, "Be still! Put
your hand over your mouth! Come with us
and be our father and priest.[w] Is it better for
you to be priest for the family of one man or
to be priest for a tribe and a clan in Israel?"
20The priest, agreeing, took the ephod, the
teraphim, and the idol, and went along with
the troops. 21As they turned to depart, they
placed their little ones, their livestock, and
their goods at the head of the column.
22[x] When the Danites had gone some distance from the house of Micah, Micah and
the men in the houses nearby mustered and
overtook them. 23They called to the Danites,
who turned and said to Micah, "What do you
want that you have called this muster?"
24"You have taken my god, which I made for
myself, and you have gone off with my priest
as well," he answered. "What is left for me?
How, then, can you ask me, 'What do you
want?' " 25The Danites said to him, "Do not
let your voice be heard near us, or aggravated
men will attack you, and you will have forfeited your life and the lives of your family!"
26Then the Danites went on their way, and
Micah, seeing that they were too strong for
him, turned back and went home.
27[y] Having taken what Micah had made
and his priest, they marched against Laish, a
quiet and trusting people; they put them to
the sword and destroyed the city by fire.
28No one came to their aid, since the city was
far from Sidon and they had no dealings
with the Arameans; the city was in the valley
that belongs to Beth-rehob. The Danites then
rebuilt the city and occupied it. 29They
named it Dan after their ancestor Dan, who
was born to Israel.[z] But Laish was the name
of the city formerly. 30* The Danites set up
the idol for themselves, and Jonathan, son of
Gershom, son of Moses,[a] and his descendants were priests for the tribe of the Danites
until the time the land went into captivity.
31They maintained the idol Micah had made
as long as the house of God was in Shiloh.*

## CHAPTER 19

See RG 106–107

*The Levite from Ephraim.* 1In those
days, when there was no king in Israel,* [b]
there was a Levite residing in remote parts
of the mountain region of Ephraim[c] who had
taken for himself a concubine from Bethlehem of Judah. 2But his concubine spurned
him and left him for her father's house in
Bethlehem of Judah, where she stayed for

**18:12 Mahaneh-dan**: Hebrew, "camp of Dan."

**18:30** Micah's shrine is now reinstalled at Laish-Dan. In the time of the kings of Israel and Judah, Dan was the site of one of the two national sanctuaries of the Northern Kingdom, both of which are strongly condemned by the editors of the Books of Kings, who regarded Jerusalem as the only acceptable place for a temple (1 Kgs 12:26–30). This verse draws a direct connection between Micah's temple and the later royal sanctuary at Dan. Seen in this light the account of the establishment of Micah's shrine, with its idol cast from stolen silver, becomes a highly polemical foundation story for the temple at Dan. **Jonathan, son of Gershom, son of Moses**: Micah's Levite is now identified as the son or descendant of Gershom, Moses' eldest son (Ex 2:22; 18:3). In the traditional Hebrew text an additional letter has been suspended over the name "Moses" to alter it to "Manasseh," thus protecting Moses from association with idol worship. **Captivity**: although Samaria fell in 722/721 B.C., much of the northern part of the country, probably including Dan, had been subjugated about a decade earlier by the Assyrian emperor Tilgath-pileser III.

**18:31 Shiloh**: a major sanctuary which has a role in the final episode of Judges (21:12, 21).

**19:1 No king in Israel**: see note on 17:6. The violent story that follows is offered as another example of the disorder that prevailed before the inauguration of the monarchy.

*u:* Jgs 13:25. *v:* Jgs 17:4–5. *w:* Jgs 17:10. *x:* Gn 31:22–32:1. *y:* Jos 19:47. *z:* Gn 30:5–6. *a:* Ex 2:22; 18:3. *b:* Jgs 17:6; 18:1; 21:25. *c:* Jgs 17:7.

some four months. 3Her husband then set out with his servant and a pair of donkeys, and went after her to soothe her and bring her back. He arrived at her father's house, and when the young woman's father saw him, he came out joyfully to meet him. 4His father-in-law, the young woman's father, urged him to stay, and so he spent three days eating and drinking and passing the night there. 5On the fourth day they rose early in the morning and he prepared to go. But the young woman's father said to his son-in-law, "Fortify yourself with a little food; you can go later on." 6So they stayed and the two men ate and drank together. Then the young woman's father said to the husband, "Why not decide to spend the night here and enjoy yourself?" 7The man made a move to go, but when his father-in-law pressed him he went back and spent the night there.

8On the fifth morning he rose early to depart, but the young woman's father said, "Fortify yourself!" He coaxed him, and he tarried until the afternoon, and the two of them ate. 9Then when the husband was ready to go with his concubine and servant, the young woman's father said to him, "See, the day is wearing on toward evening. Stay for the night. See, the day is coming to an end. Spend the night here and enjoy yourself. Early tomorrow you can start your journey home." 10The man, however, refused to stay another night; he and his concubine set out with a pair of saddled donkeys, and traveled until they came opposite Jebus, which is Jerusalem. 11Since they were near Jebus with the day far gone, the servant said to his master, "Come, let us turn off to this city of the Jebusites and spend the night in it." 12But his master said to him, "We will not turn off to a foreigner's city,[d] where there are no Israelites. We will go on to Gibeah. 13Come," he said to his servant, "let us make for some other place and spend the night in either Gibeah or Ramah."[e] 14So they continued on their way until the sun set on them when they were opposite Gibeah of Benjamin.

15* There they turned off to enter Gibeah for the night.[f] The man went in and sat down in the town square, but no one took them inside to spend the night. 16In the evening, however, an old man came from his work in the field; he was from the mountain region of Ephraim, though he was living in Gibeah where the local people were Benjaminites. 17[g] When he noticed the traveler in the town square, the old man asked, "Where are you going, and where have you come from?" 18He said to him, "We are traveling from Bethlehem of Judah far up into the mountain region of Ephraim, where I am from. I have been to Bethlehem of Judah, and now I am going home; but no one has taken me into his house. 19We have straw and fodder for our donkeys, and bread and wine for myself and for your maidservant and the young man who is with your servant; there is nothing else we need." 20"Rest assured," the old man said to him, "I will provide for all your needs, but do not spend the night in the public square." 21So he led them to his house and mixed fodder for the donkeys. Then they washed their feet, and ate and drank.[h]

***The Outrage at Gibeah.*** 22* [i] While they were enjoying themselves, the men of the city, a bunch of scoundrels, surrounded the house and beat on the door. They said to the old man who was the owner of the house, "Bring out the man who has come into your house, so that we may get intimate with him." 23The man who was the owner of the house went out to them and said, "No, my brothers; do not be so wicked. This man has come into my house; do not commit this terrible crime. 24Instead, let me bring out my virgin daughter and this man's concubine. Humiliate them, or do whatever you want; but against him do not commit such a terrible crime." 25But the men would not listen to him. So the man seized his concubine and thrust her out-

**19:15–21** The narrative casts a very unfavorable light on Gibeah of Benjamin, the town from which Israel's first king would come (cf. 1 Sm 9:1–2). No Benjaminite offers hospitality to the Levite and his travel party, who are obliged to wait at night in the town square until an Ephraimite residing in Gibeah welcomes them into his home.

**19:22–25** This part of the grim story closely parallels that of the assault on Lot's angelic visitors in Gn 19:4–8.

*d:* Jgs 1:21; 2 Sm 5:6. *e:* Jos 18:25. *f:* Jgs 20:4. *g:* Gn 19:1–3. *h:* Gn 18:4; 24:32; 43:24. *i:* Gn 19:4–9.

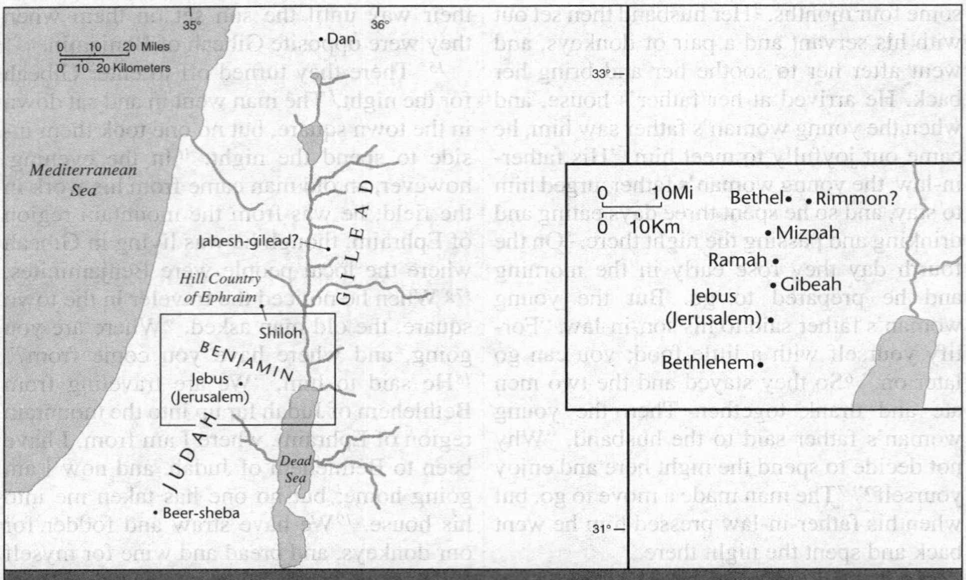


**Sites Mentioned in Benjaminite War**

side to them. They raped her and abused her
all night until morning, and let her go as the
sun was coming up. 26 At the approach of
morning the woman came and collapsed at
the entrance of the house in which her husband was, and lay there until morning.
27 When her husband rose in the morning and
opened the door of the house to start out
again on his journey, there was the woman,
his concubine, collapsed at the entrance of
the house with her hands on the threshold.
28 "Come, let us go," he said to her, but there
was no answer. So the man placed her on a
donkey and started out again for home.
29* On reaching home, he got a knife and
took hold of the body of his concubine. He
cut her up limb by limb into twelve pieces
and sent them throughout the territory of Israel.[j] 30 He instructed the men whom he sent,
"Thus you shall say to all the men of Israel:
'Has such a thing ever happened from the
day the Israelites came up from the land of
Egypt to this day?* [k] Take note of it; form a
plan and give orders.' "

## CHAPTER 20

See RG 106–107

*Assembly of Israelites.* 1 So all the Israelites came out as one, from Dan to Beer-
sheba* [l] including the land of Gilead, and the
assembly gathered to the LORD at Mizpah.
2 The leaders of all the people, all the staff-
bearers of Israel,* presented themselves in
the assembly of the people of God—four
hundred thousand foot soldiers who carried
swords. 3 Meanwhile, the Benjaminites
heard that the Israelites had gone up to Mizpah. The Israelites asked, "How did this evil
thing happen?" 4 and the Levite, the husband
of the murdered woman, testified: "It was at
Gibeah of Benjamin, which my concubine
and I had entered for the night.[m] 5[n] The lords
of Gibeah rose up against me and sur-

**19:29** The Levite's gruesome way of summoning the tribes is a drastic version of that used by Saul in 1 Sm 11:7, where he dismembers a yoke of oxen.

**19:30 Has such a thing ever happened . . . ?**: the outrage became a byword in Israel, so that in the eighth century the prophet Hosea could invoke "the days of Gibeah" (Hos 9:9; cf. 10:9) to signify corruption and wrongdoing.

**20:1 From Dan to Beer-sheba**: the entire country, from north to south. **The land of Gilead**: Israelite territory east of the Jordan.

**20:2 The staff-bearers of Israel**: the tribal leaders.

*j:* 1 Sm 11:7. *k:* Hos 9:9; 10:9. *l:* 1 Sm 3:20; 2 Sm 3:10; 17:11; 24:2, 15; 1 Kgs 5:5. *m:* Jgs 19:15. *n:* Jgs 19:22–28.

rounded me in the house at night. I was the
one they intended to kill, but they abused my
concubine and she died. 6[o] So I took my concubine and cut her up and sent her through
every part of the territory of Israel, because
of the terrible thing they had done in Israel.
7So now, all you Israelites, give your judgment and counsel in this matter."[p] 8All the
people rose as one to say, "None of us will
leave for our tents or return to our homes.
9Now as for Gibeah, this is what we will do:
We will go up against it by lot, 10taking from
all the tribes of Israel ten men for every hundred, a hundred for every thousand, a thousand for every ten thousand, and procuring
supplies for the soldiers who will go to exact
from Gibeah of Benjamin the full measure
of the terrible thing it committed in Israel."
11So all the men of Israel gathered against
the city, united as one. 12The tribes of Israel
sent men throughout the tribe of Benjamin to
say, "What is this evil that has occurred
among you? 13Now give up the men, the
scoundrels who are in Gibeah, that we may
put them to death and thus purge the evil
from Israel." But the Benjaminites refused
to listen to their kindred, the Israelites. 14In-
stead, the Benjaminites assembled from
their cities at Gibeah, to march out to battle
with the Israelites. 15On that day the Benjaminites mustered from their cities twenty-
six thousand swordsmen, in addition to the
inhabitants of Gibeah, who mustered seven
hundred picked men 16* who were left-
handed, every one of them able to sling a
stone at a hair without missing. 17The men of
Israel, without Benjamin, mustered four
hundred thousand swordsmen, all of them
warriors. 18They went up to Bethel and consulted God. When the Israelites asked, "Who
shall go up first for us to do battle with the
Benjaminites?" the LORD said: Judah first.* [q]
19* The Israelites rose in the morning and
encamped against Gibeah.

*War with Benjamin.* 20The men of Israel
marched out to do battle with Benjamin and
drew up in battle array against them at Gibeah. 21The Benjaminites marched out of
Gibeah that day and felled twenty-two thousand men of Israel. 22* But the army of the
men of Israel took courage and again drew
up for battle in the place where they had
drawn up on the previous day. 23Then the Israelites went up and wept before the LORD
until evening. "Shall I again engage my
brother Benjamin in battle?" they asked the
LORD; and the LORD answered: Attack!
24When the Israelites drew near to the Benjaminites on the second day, 25Benjamin
marched out of Gibeah against them again
and felled eighteen thousand Israelites, all of
them swordsmen. 26So the entire Israelite
army went up and entered Bethel, where
they sat weeping before the LORD. They
fasted that day until evening and presented
burnt offerings and communion offerings
before the LORD. 27The Israelites consulted
the LORD (for the ark of the covenant of the
LORD was there in those days, 28and Phinehas, son of Eleazar, son of Aaron,* was
standing in his presence in those days), and
asked, "Shall I again go out to battle with my
brother Benjamin, or shall I stop?" The
LORD said: Attack! For tomorrow I will deliver him into your power. 29* [r] So Israel set
men in ambush around Gibeah.
30When the Israelites went up against the
Benjaminites on the third day, they drew up

**20:16** The strange notice that the Gibeahite warriors were left-handed was probably added here under the influence of the Ehud story; cf. 3:15 and the note there.

**20:18 Judah first**: as in 1:2, where the enemy is the Canaanites. This time the attack is against fellow Israelites, an indication of how far things have deteriorated in these days when as yet "there was no king in Israel"; see note on 17:6.

**20:19–25** The Israelites are defeated twice by the Benjaminites.

**20:22–23** These two verses seem to be transposed. The day of supplication described in v. 23 must have preceded the assembly for battle reported in v. 22.

**20:28 Phinehas, son of Eleazar, son of Aaron**: the main line of the priesthood was traced through a grandson of Aaron by this name; see Ex 6:25 and Nm 25:10–13. Whether the priest identified here is the same man or his lineal descendant, the mention of his name adds authority to the sanctuary at Bethel. The reference to the ark of the covenant in the preceding verse has the same effect.

**20:29–46** The Israelites are successful in their third attempt to defeat Benjamin. Leaving an ambush behind, they decoy the enemy troops out of the city by pretending to be routed as on the two previous occasions. The stratagem is strongly reminiscent of that employed in the conquest of Ai (Jos 8). Two accounts of the present battle against Gibeah are preserved, one in 20:29–36a and another in 20:36b–46.

*o:* Jgs 19:29. *p:* Jgs 19:30. *q:* Jgs 1:1–2. *r:* Jos 8:3–24.

against Gibeah as on other occasions.
31 When the Benjaminites marched out to
meet the army, they began, as on other occasions, to strike down some of the troops
along the highways, one of which goes up to
Bethel and one to Gibeah in the open country; about thirty Israelites were slain. 32 The
Benjaminites thought, "They are routed before us as previously." The Israelites, however, were thinking, "We will flee and draw
them out from the city onto the highways."
33 And then all the men of Israel rose from
their places, forming up at Baal-tamar, and
the Israelites in ambush rushed from their
place west of Gibeah 34 and advanced against
Gibeah with ten thousand picked men from
all Israel. The fighting was severe, but no
one knew that a disaster was closing in.
35 The LORD defeated Benjamin before Israel; and on that day the Israelites killed
twenty-five thousand one hundred men of
Benjamin, all of them swordsmen.
36 Then the Benjaminites saw that they
were defeated. The men of Israel gave
ground to Benjamin, trusting in the ambush
they had set at Gibeah. 37 Then the men in
ambush, having made a sudden dash against
Gibeah, marched in and put the whole city to
the sword. 38 The arrangement the men of Israel had with the men in ambush was that
they would send up a smoke signal from the
city, 39 and the men of Israel would then
wheel about in the battle. Benjamin, having
begun by killing off some thirty of the men
of Israel, thought, "Surely they are completely routed before us, as in the earlier
fighting." 40 But when the signal, the column
of smoke, began to rise up from the city,
Benjamin looked back and there was the
whole city going up in smoke toward
heaven. 41 Then when the men of Israel
wheeled about, the men of Benjamin were
thrown into confusion, for they realized that
disaster was closing in on them. 42 They retreated before the men of Israel in the direction of the wilderness, but the fighting kept
pace with them, and those who had been in
the city were spreading destruction in between. 43 They surrounded the men of Benjamin, pursued them from Nohah and drove
them along to a point east of Gibeah. 44 Eighteen thousand from Benjamin fell, all of
them warriors. 45 They turned and fled into
the wilderness to the crag of Rimmon. The
Israelites picked off five thousand men on
the highways and kept pace with them as far
as Gidom, where they struck down another
two thousand of them. 46 The total of those
from Benjamin who fell that day was
twenty-five thousand swordsmen, all of
them warriors. 47 Six hundred men turned
and fled into the wilderness to the crag of
Rimmon, where they remained for four
months.[s]
48 Then the men of Israel turned back
against the Benjaminites, putting them to the
sword—the inhabitants of the cities, the
livestock, and all they came upon.[t] Moreover they destroyed by fire all the cities they
came upon.

## CHAPTER 21

See RG 106–107

*Ensuring a Future for Benjamin.*
1* The men of Israel took an oath at Mizpah:
"None of us will give his daughter in marriage to anyone from Benjamin." 2 So the
people went to Bethel and remained there before God until evening, raising their voices in
bitter weeping.[u] 3 They said, "LORD, God of
Israel, why has this happened in Israel that
today one tribe of Israel should be lacking?"
4 Early the next day the people built an altar
there and offered burnt offerings and communion offerings. 5 Then the Israelites asked,
"Are there any among all the tribes of Israel
who did not come up to the LORD for the assembly?" For there was a solemn oath that
anyone who did not go up to the LORD at
Mizpah should be put to death.[v]
6 The Israelites were disconsolate over
their brother Benjamin and said, "Today one
tribe has been cut off from Israel. 7 What can

**21:1–7** The victorious Israelites now become concerned about the survival of the tribe they have defeated. Despite the large number of Benjaminites killed in the final battle (20:46) and the general carnage that followed (20:48), there does not seem to be a shortage of men. The problem is rather a shortage of wives for the surviving men, the result of a previously unmentioned vow the Israelites took not to permit their daughters to marry Benjaminites.

*s:* Jgs 21:13. *t:* Dt 13:15–17. *u:* Jgs 20:26. *v:* Jgs 20:8–10.

we do about wives for the survivors, since
we have sworn by the LORD not to give them
any of our daughters in marriage?” 8 And
when they asked, “Is there one among the
tribes of Israel who did not come up to the
LORD in Mizpah?” they found that none of
the men of Jabesh-gilead had come to the
encampment for the assembly. 9 A roll call of
the people was taken, and none of the inhabitants of Jabesh-gilead[w] was present. 10 So
the assembly sent twelve thousand warriors
there with orders, “Go put the inhabitants of
Jabesh-gilead to the sword. 11 This is what
you are to do: Every male and every woman
who has had relations with a male you shall
put under the ban.”* [x] 12 Finding among the
inhabitants of Jabesh-gilead four hundred
young virgin women, who had not had relations with a man, they brought them to the
camp at Shiloh, in the land of Canaan.[y]
13 Then the whole assembly sent word to the
Benjaminites at the crag of Rimmon,[z] offering them peace. 14* So Benjamin returned at
that time, and they were given as wives the
women of Jabesh-gilead who had been
spared; but these proved to be not enough
for them.
15 The people had regrets about Benjamin
because the LORD had made a breach among
the tribes of Israel.[a] 16 The elders of the assembly said, “What shall we do for wives for
the survivors? For the women of Benjamin
have been annihilated.”[b] 17 They said, “There
must be heirs for the survivors of Benjamin,
so that a tribe will not be wiped out from Israel. 18 Yet we cannot give them any of our
daughters in marriage.” For the Israelites
had taken an oath, “Cursed be he who gives
a wife to Benjamin!” 19 Then they thought of
the yearly feast of the LORD at Shiloh,[c] north
of Bethel, east of the highway that goes up
from Bethel to Shechem, and south of Lebonah. 20 And they instructed the Benjaminites,
“Go and set an ambush in the vineyards.
21 When you see the women of Shiloh come
out to join in the dances, come out of the
vineyards and catch a wife for each of you
from the women of Shiloh; then go on to the
land of Benjamin. 22 When their fathers or
their brothers come to complain to us, we
shall say to them, ‘Release them to us as a
kindness, since we did not take a woman for
every man in battle. Nor did you yourselves
give your daughters to them, thus incurring
guilt.’ ”*
23 The Benjaminites did this; they carried
off wives for each of them from the dancers
they had seized, and they went back each to
his own heritage, where they rebuilt the cities and settled them. 24 At that time the Israelites dispersed from there for their own
tribes and clans; they set out from there each
to his own heritage.
25* In those days there was no king in Israel; everyone did what was right in their
own sight.[d]

**21:11 Under the ban**: see note on 1:17. In this case the sanction is imposed not because of the rules for the conquest of the promised land (cf. Dt 20:10–18) but because of the failure of the men of Jabesh-gilead to honor their oath and report for the assembly.

**21:14** Very strong political ties existed between the people of Jabesh-gilead and the Benjaminites, especially those involving Saul, the Benjaminite king of Israel. See 1 Sm 11, where Saul rescues Jabesh from an Ammonite siege, and 1 Sm 31:11–13, where the people of Jabesh exert themselves to ensure that the bodies of Saul and his sons should receive honorable burial.

**21:22 Release them . . . guilt**: this verse is difficult. Evidently the elders intend to make two arguments in support of their request that the men of Shiloh release their claims on the abducted women. The first argument seems to be that an insufficient number of women were taken “in battle”—i.e., the raid on Jabesh-gilead—to provide “a woman for every man”—i.e., a wife for every Benjaminite. The second argument is that since the women have been kidnapped, the men of Shiloh will not be guilty of having violated the oath mentioned above in 21:1, 7, and 18.

**21:25** See note on 17:6. This final editorial comment calls attention to the chaos that followed the Benjaminite civil war and the near anarchy that characterized the various efforts to meet the need for wives for the Benjaminites.

*w:* 1 Sm 11:1–11; 31:11–13; 2 Sm 2:4–7; 21:11–14. *x:* Nm 31:17. *y:* Jos 21:2; 22:9. *z:* Jgs 20:47. *a:* 2 Sm 6:8. *b:* Jgs 20:48. *c:* 1 Sm 1:3, 21. *d:* Jgs 17:6; 18:1; 19:1.

See RG 108–113

# The Book of Ruth

The Book of Ruth is named for the Moabite woman who commits herself to the Israelite people by an oath to her mother-in-law Naomi and becomes the great-grandmother of David by marriage to Boaz of Bethlehem. Thus she is an ancestor in the messianic line that leads to Jesus (Mt 1:5).

The book portrays the love and loyalty of human beings in working their way through tragic circumstances to participation in the community of the faithful people of God. The key is responsible and loving decision-making: Ruth's loyalty (2:11), her generosity (1:15–17; 2:2, 7) and her willingness to take risks for the sake of righteousness set in motion a chain of beneficial events, while behind the scenes God blesses each step in the developing drama. Ruth is so frequently designated "the Moabite" in the book that the audience of the story is constantly reminded of the universality of the embrace of salvation.

In the Greek and Latin canons, Ruth follows Judges, to which it is related by its opening time reference ("Once back in the time of the judges . . ."), and precedes Samuel, serving as transition from Israel as tribal union to monarchy. In the present sequence of the Hebrew canon it is placed among the "Writings" immediately after the Book of Proverbs, which ends with a powerful portrayal of "the woman of worth" (Prv 31:10–31; cf. Ru 3:11). Ruth is the primary liturgical text in Judaism for the celebration of the feast of Weeks (Shabuot).

The beauty of the story's construction, its use of dialogue (nearly two thirds of the text), and the sheer drama of its content mark it as one of the classic short stories of world literature. Based on the recollection of an historical figure, a story is developed which grips its audience with profound insight into divine and human relationships. The story is presented from a point some time after the course of events, as is indicated by the explanation of an obscure custom in 4:7. Wherever and whenever it was told, its claim of God's universal concern for humankind and the attractiveness of caring human responsibility shines forth.

The date of composition is disputed. Many authors date it early in the monarchy, and valid arguments can be presented for that position. Others argue for a postexilic date; they see the favorable presentation of a Moabite woman who became David's grandmother as a counter to the stringent measures of Ezra and Nehemiah against marriage with Moabites and other non-Jews (Ezr 9–10; Neh 13:23–29).

## CHAPTER 1

See RG 110–111

*Naomi in Moab.* [1]Once back in the time of the judges* there was a famine in the land; so a man from Bethlehem of Judah left home with his wife and two sons to reside on the plateau of Moab. [2]The man was named Elimelech, his wife Naomi, and his sons Mahlon and Chilion; they were Ephrathites from Bethlehem of Judah. Some time after their arrival on the plateau of Moab, [3]Elimelech, the husband of Naomi, died, and she was left with her two sons. [4]They married Moabite women, one named Orpah, the other Ruth. When they had lived there about ten years, [5]both Mahlon and Chilion died also, and the woman was left with neither her two boys* nor her husband.

[6]She and her daughters-in-law then prepared to go back from the plateau of Moab because word had reached her there that the LORD had seen to his people's needs* and given them food. [7]She and her two daughters-in-law left the place where they had

**1:1–2 Back in the time of the judges**: the story looks back three generations before King David (4:17) into the time of the tribal confederation described in the Book of Judges. David's Moabite connections are implied in 1 Sm 22:3–4. **Bethlehem of Judah**: Bethlehem, a town in which part of the Judean clan-division called Ephrathah lived; cf. 1 Chr 2:50–51; 4:4; Mi 5:1. Jos 19:15 mentions a different Bethlehem in the north. **The plateau of Moab**: on the east side of the Jordan valley rift, where the hills facing west get more rain, and where agricultural conditions differ from those in Judah. **Ephrathites**: a reminder of David's origins; cf. Mi 5:1.

**1:5 Boys**: the way the storyteller chooses certain words as guides is shown here; "boy" will not appear again until 4:16.

**1:6 Had seen to his people's needs**: lit., "had visited his people."

**1:8 Mother's house**: the women's part of the home, but

been living. On the road back to the land of
Judah, 8 Naomi said to her daughters-in-law,
"Go back, each of you to your mother's
house.* May the LORD show you the same
kindness as you have shown to the deceased
and to me. 9[a] May the LORD guide each of
you to find a husband and a home in which
you will be at rest." She kissed them good-
bye, but they wept aloud, 10 crying, "No! We
will go back with you, to your people." 11 Naomi replied, "Go back, my daughters. Why
come with me? Have I other sons in my
womb who could become your husbands?*
12 Go, my daughters, for I am too old to
marry again. Even if I had any such hope, or
if tonight I had a husband and were to bear
sons, 13 would you wait for them and deprive
yourselves of husbands until those sons
grew up? No, my daughters, my lot is too
bitter for you, because the LORD has extended his hand against me." 14 Again they
wept aloud; then Orpah kissed her mother-
in-law good-bye, but Ruth clung to her.

15 "See now," she said, "your sister-in-law
has gone back to her people and her god. Go
back after your sister-in-law!" 16* But Ruth
said, "Do not press me to go back and abandon you!

Wherever you go I will go,
  wherever you lodge I will lodge.
Your people shall be my people
  and your God, my God.
17 Where you die I will die,
  and there be buried.

May the LORD do thus to me, and more, if
even death separates me from you!" 18 Naomi then ceased to urge her, for she saw she
was determined to go with her.

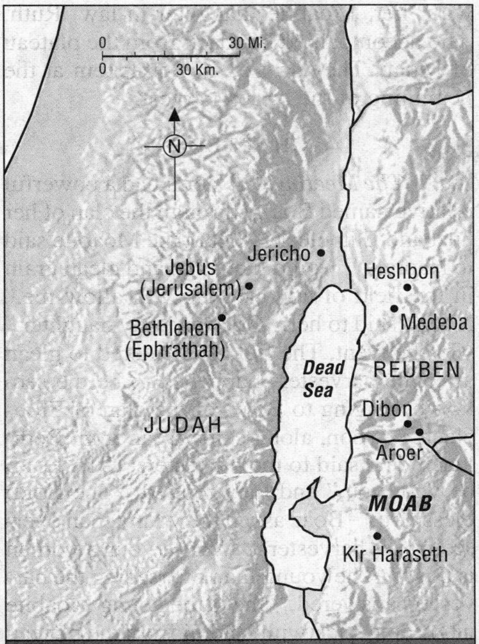

**Places in Ruth**

***The Return to Bethlehem.*** 19 So they went
on together until they reached Bethlehem.
On their arrival there, the whole town was
excited about them, and the women asked:
"Can this be Naomi?" 20[b] But she said to
them, "Do not call me Naomi ['Sweet']. Call
me Mara ['Bitter'], for the Almighty has
made my life very bitter. 21*[c] I went away
full, but the LORD has brought me back
empty. Why should you call me 'Sweet,'
since the LORD has brought me to trial, and
the Almighty has pronounced evil sentence
on me." 22 Thus it was that Naomi came back

also perhaps the proper location for arranging marriage; Sg 3:4; 8:2; Gn 24:28. **Kindness**: Hebrew *hesed*. The powerful relationship term used here will recur in 2:20 and 3:10; kindness operates on both the divine-human and human-human level in Ruth.

**1:11 Other sons . . . husbands**: a reference to a customary practice known from Dt 25:5–10, levirate marriage, which assigns responsibility to the brother-in-law to produce heirs in order to perpetuate the name and hold the patrimonial land of a man who died childless. How far the responsibility extended beyond blood brothers is unclear; cf. Gn 38:8 and the upcoming scene in Ru 4:5–6. Naomi imagines the impossible: were she to have more sons they could take Ruth and Orpah as their wives.

**1:16–17** Ruth's adherence to her mother-in-law in 1:14 is now expressed in a profound oath of loyalty, culminating in a formulary found frequently in Samuel and Kings; cf. especially 1 Sm 20:13. **Even death**: burial in Naomi's family tomb means that not even death will separate them.

**1:21** Naomi's despair is made clear by her play on the meaning of her name in v. 20 and now by her accusation, like that in many psalms and in Job, that God has acted harshly toward her. The language belongs to the realm of judicial proceedings. By crying out in this way, the faithful Israelite opens the door to change, since the cry assumes that God hears and will do something about such seemingly unjust circumstances.

*a:* Ru 3:1. *b:* Ex 15:23. *c:* Ru 3:17; 1 Kgs 17:20.

with her Moabite daughter-in-law Ruth, who accompanied her back from the plateau of Moab. They arrived in Bethlehem at the beginning of the barley harvest.*

## CHAPTER 2

See RG 111

*The Meeting.* 1* Naomi had a powerful relative named Boaz,[d] through the clan of her husband Elimelech. 2* Ruth the Moabite said to Naomi, "I would like to go and glean grain in the field of anyone who will allow me." Naomi said to her, "Go ahead, my daughter." 3So she went. The field she entered to glean after the harvesters happened to be the section belonging to Boaz, of the clan of Elimelech. 4* Soon, along came Boaz from Bethlehem and said to the harvesters, "The LORD be with you," and they replied, "The LORD bless you." 5Boaz asked the young man overseeing his harvesters, "Whose young woman is this?" 6The young man overseeing the harvesters answered, "She is the young Moabite who came back with Naomi from the plateau of Moab.[e] 7* She said, 'I would like to gather the gleanings into sheaves after the harvesters.' Ever since she came this morning she has remained here until now, with scarcely a moment's rest."

8Boaz then spoke to Ruth, "Listen, my daughter. Do not go to glean in anyone else's field; you are not to leave here. Stay here with my young women. 9Watch to see which field is to be harvested, and follow them. Have I not commanded the young men to do you no harm? When you are thirsty, go and drink from the vessels the young people have filled." 10Casting herself prostrate upon the ground, she said to him, "Why should I, a foreigner, be favored with your attention?" 11f Boaz answered her: "I have had a complete account of what you have done for your mother-in-law after your husband's death; you have left your father and your mother and the land of your birth, and have come to a people whom previously you did not know. 12g May the LORD reward what you have done! May you receive a full reward from the LORD, the God of Israel, under whose wings you have come for refuge." 13She said, "May I prove worthy of your favor, my lord. You have comforted me. You have spoken to the heart of your servant*—and I am not even one of your servants!" 14At mealtime Boaz said to her, "Come here and have something to eat; dip your bread in the sauce." Then as she sat near the harvesters, he handed her some roasted grain and she ate her fill and had some left over. 15As she rose to glean, Boaz instructed his young people: "Let her glean among the sheaves themselves without scolding her, 16and even drop some handfuls and leave them for her to glean; do not rebuke her."

17She gleaned in the field until evening, and when she beat out what she had gleaned it came to about an ephah* of barley, 18which she took into the town and showed to her mother-in-law. Next she brought out what she had left over from the meal and gave it to her. 19So her mother-in-law said to her, "Where did you glean today? Where did you go to work? May the one who took notice of

**1:22** Barley and wheat harvests come in succession, from as early as April–May into June–July; Dt 16:9–12 suggests that the grain harvest lasts about seven weeks. The time reference leads effectively to the next episode.

**2:1** Kinship ties and responsibilities now become very important. Boaz is introduced as one of a group surrounding Naomi through her husband's kin who are expected to extend care. The particular term used here (*moda'*, "relative") is picked up in 3:2; otherwise, most of the terminology about this responsibility to care will use the vocabulary of redeeming (*go'el*, "redeemer").

**2:2** Israelite custom made provision for the poor, the widow, the stranger and the orphan to gather what was left behind by the harvesters, and instructed farmers not to cut to the edges of their fields, for the sake of these marginalized; Lv 19:9–10; 23:22; Dt 24:19–22.

**2:4** The story brings Boaz upon the scene quickly, but he moves among his workers with the grace of a man of prominence, greeting them and being received with courtesy. The Hebrew blessing formulas used are frequent in Jewish and Christian liturgies.

**2:7** The verse is somewhat garbled, but the points are clear that Ruth has been appropriately deferential in seeking permission to glean, and has worked steadily since arriving. Or perhaps she has waited patiently until Boaz arrives to gain permission.

**2:13 Servant**: only here is the language of servanthood used. Ruth has spoken with very deferential words to Boaz, but then seems to think that she has assumed too much.

**2:17 Ephah**: see note on Is 5:10.

*d:* Ru 3:2, 12; Mt 1:5. *e:* Ru 1:22. *f:* Ru 1:14–17. *g:* Ru 3:9; Dt 32:37; Ps 91:4.

you be blessed!" Then she told her mother-in-law with whom she had worked. "The man at whose place I worked today is named Boaz," she said. [20][h] "May he be blessed by the LORD, who never fails to show kindness to the living and to the dead," Naomi exclaimed to her daughter-in-law. She continued, "This man is a near relative of ours, one of our redeemers."* [21]"He even told me," added Ruth the Moabite, "Stay with my young people until they complete my entire harvest." [22]"You would do well, my daughter," Naomi rejoined, "to work with his young women; in someone else's field you might be insulted." [23]So she stayed gleaning with Boaz's young women until the end of the barley and wheat harvests.

## CHAPTER 3

See RG 111

***Ruth Again Presents Herself.*** When Ruth was back with her mother-in-law, [1]Naomi said to her, "My daughter, should I not be seeking a pleasing home for you?[i] [2]* Now! Is not Boaz,[j] whose young women you were working with, a relative of ours? This very night he will be winnowing barley at the threshing floor. [3]Now, go bathe and anoint yourself; then put on your best attire and go down to the threshing floor. Do not make yourself known to the man before he has finished eating and drinking. [4]But when he lies down, take note of the place where he lies; then go uncover a place at his feet* and you lie down. He will then tell you what to do." [5]"I will do whatever you say," Ruth replied. [6]She went down to the threshing floor and did just as her mother-in-law had instructed her.

[7]Boaz ate and drank to his heart's content, and went to lie down at the edge of the pile of grain. She crept up, uncovered a place at his feet, and lay down. [8]Midway through the night, the man gave a start and groped about, only to find a woman lying at his feet. [9]"Who are you?" he asked. She replied, "I am your servant Ruth. Spread the wing of your cloak* over your servant, for you are a redeemer." [10]He said, "May the LORD bless you, my daughter! You have been even more loyal now than before in not going after the young men, whether poor or rich. [11]Now rest assured, my daughter, I will do for you whatever you say; all my townspeople know you to be a worthy woman.* [12][k] Now, I am in fact a redeemer, but there is another redeemer closer than I.* [13]Stay where you are for tonight, and tomorrow, if he will act as redeemer for you, good. But if he will not, as the LORD lives, I will do it myself. Lie there until morning."[l] [14]So she lay at his feet until morning, but rose before anyone could recognize another, for Boaz had said, "Let it not be known that this woman came to the threshing floor." [15]Then he said to her, "Take off the shawl you are wearing; hold it firmly." When she did so, he poured out six measures of barley and helped her lift the bundle; then he himself left for the town.

[16]She, meanwhile, went home to her mother-in-law, who asked, "How did things go, my daughter?" So she told her all the man had done for her, [17]and concluded, "He gave

**2:20** For the first time, the story uses the Hebrew word *go'el*, "redeemer," for the responsibilities of the circle of kinship surrounding Naomi and Ruth and their deceased relatives. Involved are the recovery or retention of family land (Lv 25:25; 27:9–33; Jer 32:6–25), release of a relative from voluntary servitude to pay debts (Lv 25:47–55), and "redeeming blood" or vengeance, attested in passages which regulate such vengeance. No explicit connection is made elsewhere in the Bible between marriage responsibilities and redeeming.

**3:2** Ruth's determined action to bring relief to Naomi's and her own circumstances now impels Naomi to move, using means available in Israelite custom which no one in the story has up to this point brought into play.

**3:4 Uncover a place at his feet**: Naomi advocates a course of action that will lead Boaz to act. Israelite custom and moral expectations strongly suggest that there is no loss of virtue involved in the scene.

**3:9 Spread the wing of your cloak**: Ez 16:8 makes it clear that this is a request for marriage. Ruth connects it to "redeemer" responsibility. A wordplay on "wing" links what Boaz is asked to do to what he has asked God to do for Ruth in 2:12.

**3:11 Worthy woman**: the language corresponds to the description of Boaz in 2:1 (lit., "strong and worthy"); the two worthy people are linked in character to one another, as they have already proven to be in their generous behavior toward the ones in need of their care. The townspeople, lit., "all the gate of my people," will ratify this at the gate in the sequel.

**3:12 Another redeemer closer than I**: Boaz knows of a closer relative who would have a prior right to buy the field and marry Ruth.

*h:* Gn 24:27; Lv 25:25; 27:9–33. *i:* Ru 1:9. *j:* Ru 2:1. *k:* Ru 4:1. *l:* Ru 1:16; 4:5.

## The Well and the Gate

IN VARIOUS BIBLE scenes, meeting places play an important role. In Ruth, for instance, the climax of the story comes with the actions of Boaz in bringing about his betrothal to Ruth. The text makes clear that this takes place "at the gate" of the city (Ru 4:1–12).

The gate was a narrow passageway through the defensive wall of a town or city. It was usually covered, with a barrier at one or both ends. Walls were thick because they were the main defense against invasion, and the passageway was narrow to impede the progress of any invaders who succeeded in getting past the outer barrier: They would have to walk in a narrow column through the passage. Often, a guardroom was built into the wall at one side of the passage, and places for the guards or others to sit outside lined both sides of the passage.

This gate would have been relatively shaded and cool and therefore was a pleasant place to gather. Because it was small, those of higher status would be favored for a place, and anyone of lower status would have to give way to a higher status person who came later. All of the people who gathered at the gate were men, and because of the presence of so many important members of the town, the gate became the place where the elders could pass judgment on questions put to them. In effect, the gate could become the town's court of justice, particularly for what we would call "civil actions": property disputes, debt collections, and the like.

In Ruth, Boaz brings up the complicated situation of the property of Naomi's family and the status of Ruth. The other relative with a claim on the property makes his declaration that he is abandoning the claim in the presence of the elders of the town, who serve as witnesses to make sure the declaration is binding. In Psalm 127:5 the reference to contending "at the gate," as the New American Bible notes point out, does not mean fighting off an invasion but, rather, making one's case in a legal dispute. In the book of Wisdom (6:14), Wisdom herself (personified as a woman) is to be met "at [the] gate" where the wise gather. It may have been a slight shock to read about meeting a woman in the gate in this passage, because women did not gather there.

Women gathered at a different place: the well. Drawing and transporting water for household use was considered women's work, and this was so clearly understood that Jesus could tell his followers to go with "a man . . . carrying a jar of water" (Mk 14:13; Lk 22:10) to find the place of the Last Supper. A man with a water jar would have been a very distinctive figure, a signal that this guide had been arranged in advance. In Genesis 24:10–14, Abraham's servant has been told to go to find a wife for Isaac, Abraham's son, in Abraham's ancestral land. The servant goes to the well to meet the local women, because he knows that that is where they will most likely be found. Saul and his servant, looking for the prophet Samuel, meet "some young women coming out to draw water" from whom they can ask directions (1 Sm 9:11). And in the Gospel of John, Jesus' encounter with the woman of Samaria takes place at the well, where she had come to draw water (Jn 4:7). The woman is drawing water at noon, rather than in the evening, which is unusual—perhaps because she wishes to avoid any meetings with the other women of the place, because her marital status is irregular. In her case, the social aspect of drawing water—the chance to meet and speak with other women—is a disadvantage.

me these six measures of barley and said, 'Do not go back to your mother-in-law empty.' "[m] [18]Naomi then said, "Wait here, my daughter, until you learn what happens, for the man will not rest, but will settle the matter today."

See RG 111–12

## CHAPTER 4

***Boaz Marries Ruth.*** [1]Boaz went to the gate* and took a seat there. Along came the other redeemer[n] of whom he had spoken. Boaz called to him by name, "Come, sit here." And he did so. [2]Then Boaz picked out ten of the elders* of the town and asked them to sit nearby. When they had done this, [3]he said to the other redeemer: "Naomi, who has come back from the plateau of Moab, is putting up for sale the piece of land that belonged to our kinsman Elimelech. [4*] So I thought I would inform you. Before those here present, including the elders of my people, purchase the field; act as redeemer.[o] But if you do not want to do it, tell me so, that I may know, for no one has a right of redemption prior to yours, and mine is next." He answered, "I will act as redeemer."

[5*] Boaz continued, "When you acquire the field from Naomi, you also acquire responsibility for Ruth the Moabite,[p] the widow of the late heir, to raise up a family for the deceased on his estate." [6]The redeemer replied, "I cannot exercise my right of redemption for that would endanger my own estate. You do it in my place, for I cannot." [7q] Now it used to be the custom in Israel that, to make binding a contract of redemption or exchange, one party would take off a sandal* and give it to the other. This was the form of attestation in Israel. [8]So the other redeemer, in saying to Boaz, "Acquire it for yourself," drew off his sandal. [9]Boaz then said to the elders and to all the people, "You are witnesses today that I have acquired from Naomi all the holdings of Elimelech, Chilion and Mahlon. [10]I also acquire Ruth the Moabite, the widow of Mahlon, as my wife, in order to raise up a family for her late husband on his estate, so that the name of the deceased may not perish from his people and his place. Do you witness this today?" [11r] All those at the gate, including the elders, said, "We do. May the LORD make this woman come into your house like Rachel and Leah, who between them built up the house of Israel. Prosper in Ephrathah! Bestow a name in Bethlehem! [12]With the offspring the LORD will give you from this young woman, may your house become like the house of Perez, whom Tamar bore to Judah."*

[13]Boaz took Ruth. When they came together as husband and wife, the LORD enabled her to conceive and she bore a son. [14]Then the women said to Naomi, "Blessed is the LORD who has not failed to provide you today with a redeemer. May he become famous in Israel! [15]He will restore your life and be the support of your old age, for his mother is the daughter-in-law who loves you. She is worth more to you than seven sons!" [16]Naomi took the boy, cradled him*

**4:1** The gate of an Israelite town was the place where commercial and other legal matters were dealt with in publicly witnessed fashion.

**4:2 Ten of the elders**: to serve as judges in legal matters as well as witnesses of the settlement of business affairs; cf. Dt 25:7–9.

**4:4** Although the laws governing inheritance by Israelite widows are not specified in the Bible, Naomi seems to have the right of disposal of a piece of Elimelech's land. The redemption custom in Lv 25:25 would then guide the procedure.

**4:5–6** Although redemption and levirate practices are not otherwise linked in the Bible, they belong in the same area of need. Boaz claims that buying Elimelech's field obligates the other redeemer to produce an heir for Mahlon, who would then inherit the land. That would jeopardize this redeemer's overall holdings, since he would lose the land he had paid for. He can afford the first step but not the second, and cedes his responsibility to Boaz, who is willing to do both.

**4:7 Take off a sandal**: the legislation in Dt 25:8–10 provides that if a "redeemer" refuses to carry out the obligation of marrying his brother's wife, the woman shall strip off his sandal as a gesture of insult. In later years, when the obligation of carrying out this function of the "redeemer" was no longer keenly felt, the removal of the sandal may have become a formalized way of renouncing the rights/obligations of the "redeemer," as in this text.

**4:12** Gn 38 contains a story about Tamar similar to Ruth's in levirate marriage. Judah, under less laudable circumstances, fulfills the same role as Boaz will, and Perez, son of Judah and Tamar, perpetuates the line. Thus two non-Israelite women, Tamar and Ruth, are important links in David's genealogy.

**4:16 Cradled him**: the child belongs to Naomi in the sense that he now becomes the redeemer in the family, as stated in 4:14. This tender act by Naomi is not necessarily adoptive and differs from the relationship in Gn 30:3; cf. Nm 11:12. Naomi now has a "boy" to replace her two lost "boys" in 1:5.

*m:* Ru 1:21. *n:* Ru 3:12. *o:* Lv 25:25. *p:* Ru 3:13. *q:* Dt 25:9. *r:* Gn 29:31–30:24; 35:16–19.

against her breast, and cared for him. 17 The neighbor women joined the celebration: “A son has been born to Naomi!”[s] They named him Obed. He was the father of Jesse, the father of David.

18[t] These are the descendants of Perez: Perez was the father of Hezron,[u] 19 Hezron was the father of Ram, Ram was the father of Amminadab, 20[v] Amminadab was the father of Nahshon, Nahshon was the father of Salma, 21 Salma was the father of Boaz, Boaz was the father of Obed, 22[w] Obed was the father of Jesse, and Jesse became the father of David.

*s:* Lk 1:58. *t:* 1 Chr 2:4–15; Mt 1:3–6. *u:* Gn 46:12; Nm 26:21; 1 Chr 4:1. *v:* Ex 6:23; Nm 1:7; 2:3; 7:12–17; 10:14. *w:* 1 Sm 16:2–13.

See RG 113–22

# The Books of Samuel

These books describe the rise and development of kingship in Israel. Samuel is a pivotal figure. He bridges the gap between the period of the Judges and the monarchy, and guides Israel’s transition to kingship. A Deuteronomistic editor presents both positive and negative traditions about the monarchy, portraying it both as evidence of Israel’s rejection of the Lord as their sovereign (1 Sm 8:6–22; 12:1–25) and as part of God’s plan to deliver the people (1 Sm 9:16; 10:17–27; 2 Sm 7:8–17). Samuel’s misgivings about abuse of royal power foreshadow the failures and misdeeds of Saul and David and the failures of subsequent Israelite kings.

Although the events described in 1 and 2 Samuel move from the last of the judges to the decline of David’s reign and the beginning of a legendary “Golden Age” under Solomon’s rule, this material does not present either a continuous history or a systematic account of this period. The author/editor developed a narrative timeline around freely composed speeches, delivered by prophets like Samuel (e.g., 1 Sm 15:10–31; 28:15–19) and Nathan (2 Sm 12:1–12), who endorse Deuteronomistic perspectives regarding the establishment of the monarchy, the relationship between worship and obedience, and the divine covenant established with the house of David.

These books include independent blocks (e.g., the Ark Narrative [1 Sm 4:1–7:1], Saul’s rise to power [1 Sm 9:1–11:15], David’s ascendancy over Saul [1 Sm 16–31], the Succession Narrative [2 Sm 9–20; 1 Kgs 1–2]), which the editor shaped into three narrative cycles, the last two marked by transitional passages in 1 Sm 13:1 and 2 Sm 1:1. Each section focuses on a major figure in the development of the monarchy: Samuel, the reluctant king maker (1 Sm 1–12); Saul, the king whom the Lord rejects (1 Sm 13–31); David, the king after the Lord’s own heart (2 Sm 1–24). A common theme unites these narratives: Israel’s God acts justly, prospering those who remain faithful and destroying those who reject his ways (1 Sm 2:9). Along with the rest of the Deuteronomistic History, the Books of Samuel become an object lesson for biblical Israel as it tries to re-establish its religious identity after the destruction of Jerusalem and the loss of its homeland (587/586 B.C.).

The contents of the Books of Samuel may be divided as follows:

I. The Last Judges, Eli and Samuel (1 Sm 1:1–7:17)
II. Establishment of the Monarchy (1 Sm 8:1–12:25)
III. Saul and David (1 Sm 13:1–2 Sm 2:7)
IV. The Reign of David (2 Sm 2:8–20:26)
V. Appendixes (2 Sm 21:1–24:25)

# The First Book of Samuel

## I. The Last Judges, Eli and Samuel

### CHAPTER 1

See RG 114–15

***Elkanah and His Family at Shiloh.*** [1]There was a certain man from Ramathaim, a Zuphite from the hill country of Ephraim. His name was Elkanah, the son of Jeroham, son of Elihu, son of Tohu, son of Zuph, an Ephraimite.[a] [2]He had two wives, one named Hannah, the other Peninnah; Peninnah had children, but Hannah had no children. [3]Each year this man went up from his city to worship and offer sacrifice to the LORD of hosts at Shiloh, where the two sons of Eli, Hophni and Phinehas, were ministering as priests of the LORD.[b] [4]When the day came for Elkanah to offer sacrifice, he used to give portions to his wife Peninnah and to all her sons and daughters, [5]but he would give a double portion to Hannah because he loved her, though the LORD had closed her womb.[c] [6]Her rival,* to upset her, would torment her constantly, since the LORD had closed her womb.[d] [7]Year after year, when she went up to the house of the LORD, Peninnah would provoke her, and Hannah would weep and refuse to eat.* [8]Elkanah, her husband, would say to her: "Hannah, why are you weeping? Why are you not eating? Why are you so miserable? Am I not better for you than ten sons?"[e]

***Hannah's Prayer.*** [9]Hannah rose after one such meal at Shiloh, and presented herself before the LORD; at the time Eli the priest was sitting on a chair near the doorpost of the LORD's temple. [10]In her bitterness she prayed to the LORD, weeping freely, [11]and made this vow: "O LORD of hosts, if you look with pity on the hardship of your servant, if you remember me and do not forget me, if you give your handmaid a male child, I will give him to the LORD all the days of his life. No razor shall ever touch his head."*[f] [12]As she continued praying before the LORD, Eli watched her mouth, [13]for Hannah was praying silently; though her lips were moving, her voice could not be heard. Eli, thinking she was drunk, [14]said to her, "How long will you make a drunken spectacle of yourself? Sober up from your wine!" [15]"No, my lord!" Hannah answered. "I am an unhappy woman. I have had neither wine nor liquor; I was only pouring out my heart to the LORD. [16]Do not think your servant a worthless woman; my prayer has been prompted by my deep sorrow and misery." [17]Eli said, "Go in peace, and may the God of Israel grant you what you have requested." [18]She replied, "Let your servant find favor in your eyes," and left. She went to her quarters, ate and drank with her husband, and no longer appeared downhearted. [19]Early the next morning they worshiped before the LORD, and then returned to their home in Ramah. When they returned Elkanah had intercourse with his wife Hannah, and the LORD remembered her.

***Hannah Bears a Son.*** [20]She conceived and, at the end of her pregnancy, bore a son whom she named Samuel.* "Because I asked the LORD for him." [21]The next time her husband Elkanah was going up with the rest of

**1:6 Her rival**: Hebrew *sara*, "rival wife, co-wife"; in the Talmud, a technical term for a second or co-wife.

**1:7** In biblical narrative, the social status gained by producing children, especially males, often set woman against woman; cf. e.g., Gn 16, 21, 30. Peninnah's provocations may be the arrogant boasting mentioned in 2:3.

**1:11 No razor . . .** : the Septuagint adds "he shall drink neither wine nor liquor." This addition is a further suggestion that Samuel is dedicated to God under a nazirite vow (Nm 6:4–5); see note on v. 22.

**1:20 Samuel**: Hannah's explanation associates her son's name with the narrative's wordplay on the Hebrew verbs *s'l* ("ask," vv. 17, 27), *his'il* ("hand over, dedicate," v. 28), *sa'ul* ("dedicated," v. 28), and the noun *se'elah* ("request," vv. 17, 27). The name, however, is related to the Hebrew root *s'l* only through assonance. It means "his name is El/God," not "the one requested of or dedicated (*sa'ul*) to God" (v. 28), which is the meaning of the name Saul. The author may have lifted the *s'l* wordplay from a narrative about Saul to portray Samuel as God's gracious answer to Hannah's request.

*a:* 1 Chr 6:19–20. *b:* Ex 23:14–17; 34:23; Dt 16:16; Jgs 21:19. *c:* Dt 21:15–17. *d:* Gn 16:4–5; 29:31; Jgs 13:2; Lk 1:7. *e:* Ru 4:15. *f:* Nm 6:1–5; Jgs 13:2–5; 16:17; Lk 1:15.

**The Song of Hannah**

BIBLICAL WRITERS SOMETIMES inserted poems into prose books where they seemed appropriate. In this case (2:1–10) the poem seems to be considerably later than the surrounding context. It is a psalm of national thanksgiving, but its thankful tone appropriately reflects Hannah's sentiments. It was later used as a model for Mary's song in Luke 1:46–55.

his household to offer the customary sacrifice to the LORD and to fulfill his vows, 22 Hannah did not go, explaining to her husband, "Once the child is weaned, I will take him to appear before the LORD and leave him there forever."* 23 Her husband Elkanah answered her: "Do what you think best; wait until you have weaned him. Only may the LORD fulfill his word!" And so she remained at home and nursed her son until she had weaned him.[g]

***Hannah Presents Samuel to the Lord.*** 24 Once he was weaned, she brought him up with her, along with a three-year-old bull, an ephah* of flour, and a skin of wine, and presented him at the house of the LORD in Shiloh. 25 After they had slaughtered the bull, they brought the child to Eli. 26 Then Hannah spoke up: "Excuse me, my lord! As you live, my lord, I am the woman who stood here near you, praying to the LORD. 27 I prayed for this child, and the LORD granted my request. 28 Now I, in turn, give him to the LORD; as long as he lives, he shall be dedicated to the LORD." Then they worshiped there before the LORD.

See RG 114–15

## CHAPTER 2

1 And Hannah prayed:*

"My heart exults in the LORD,
my horn is exalted by my God.
I have swallowed up my enemies;
I rejoice in your victory.[h]
2 There is no Holy One like the LORD;
there is no Rock like our God.[i]
3 Speak boastfully no longer,
Do not let arrogance issue from your mouths.*
For an all-knowing God is the LORD,
a God who weighs actions.[j]
4 "The bows of the mighty are broken,
while the tottering gird on strength.[k]
5 The well-fed hire themselves out for bread,
while the hungry no longer have to toil.
The barren wife bears seven sons,
while the mother of many languishes.[l]
6 "The LORD puts to death and gives life,
casts down to Sheol and brings up again.[m]
7 The LORD makes poor and makes rich,
humbles, and also exalts.
8 He raises the needy from the dust;
from the ash heap lifts up the poor,
To seat them with nobles
and make a glorious throne their heritage.
"For the pillars of the earth are the LORD's,
and he has set the world upon them.[n]
9 He guards the footsteps of his faithful ones,
but the wicked shall perish in the darkness;
for not by strength does one prevail.
10 The LORD's foes shall be shattered;
the Most High in heaven thunders;

**1:22 Leave him there forever**: a Qumran manuscript adds "I will give him as a nazirite forever"; it interprets v. 11 to mean that Hannah dedicates Samuel under a nazirite vow (cf. Nm 6:4–5).

**1:24 Ephah**: see note on Is 5:10.

**2:1–10** Hannah appeals to a God who maintains order by keeping human affairs in balance, reversing the fortunes of the arrogant, who, like Peninnah, boast of their good fortune (vv. 1, 3, 9) at the expense of those like Hannah who receive less from the Lord. Hannah's admission places her among the faithful who trust that God will execute justice on their behalf. The reference "his king . . . his anointed" (v. 10) recalls the final sentence of the Book of Judges and introduces the kingship theme that dominates the Books of Samuel.

**2:3 Speak . . . mouths**: addressed to the enemies mentioned in v. 1.

*g:* Dt 9:5; 2 Sm 7:25; 1 Kgs 2:4. *h:* Dt 33:17; 2 Sm 22:3; Ps 18:2; 89:18; Is 61:10; Lk 1:47, 69. *i:* 2 Sm 22:3; Ps 18:2. *j:* Ps 75:5–6. *k:* Is 40:29. *l:* Ru 4:15; Jer 15:9. *m:* Dt 32:39; Tb 4:19; Jb 5:11; Ps 30:4; Wis 16:13; Lk 1:52. *n:* Jb 9:6; 38:6; Ps 75:4; 104:5; 113:8; 121:3.

the LORD judges the ends of the earth.
May he give strength to his king,
and exalt the horn of his anointed!"[o]

11 When Elkanah returned home to Ramah,
the child remained in the service of the LORD
under the priest Eli.

***Wickedness of Eli's Sons.*** 12 Now the sons
of Eli were wicked; they had respect neither
for the LORD 13 nor for the priests' duties toward the people. When someone offered a
sacrifice, the priest's servant would come
with a three-pronged fork, while the meat
was still boiling,[p] 14 and would thrust it into
the basin, kettle, caldron, or pot. Whatever
the fork brought up, the priest would take for
himself. They treated all the Israelites who
came to the sanctuary at Shiloh in this way.
15 In fact, even before the fat was burned, the
priest's servant would come and say to the
one offering the sacrifice, "Give me some
meat to roast for the priest. He will not accept boiled meat from you, only raw meat."
16 And if this one protested, "Let the fat be
burned first, then take whatever you wish,"
he would reply, "No, give it to me now, or
else I will take it by force."[q] 17 Thus the
young men sinned grievously in the presence of the LORD, treating the offerings to
the LORD with disdain.

***The Lord Rewards Hannah.*** 18 Meanwhile
the boy Samuel, wearing a linen ephod,* was
serving in the presence of the LORD. 19 His
mother used to make a little garment for
him, which she would bring him each time
she went up with her husband to offer the
customary sacrifice. 20 And Eli would bless
Elkanah and his wife, as they were leaving
for home. He would say, "May the LORD repay you with children from this woman for
the gift she has made to the LORD!" 21 The
LORD favored Hannah so that she conceived
and gave birth to three more sons and two
daughters, while young Samuel grew up in
the service of the LORD.[r]

***Eli's Futile Rebuke.*** 22 When Eli was very
old, he kept hearing how his sons were treating all Israel, and that they were behaving
promiscuously* with the women serving at
the entry of the meeting tent. 23 So he said to
them: "Why are you doing such things? I
hear from everyone that your behavior is depraved. 24 Stop this, my sons! The report that
I hear the LORD's people spreading is not
good. 25 If someone sins against another,
anyone can intercede for the sinner with the
LORD; but if anyone sins against the LORD,
who can intercede* for the sinner?" But they
disregarded their father's warning, since the
LORD wanted them dead. 26 Meanwhile,
young Samuel was growing in stature and in
worth in the estimation of the LORD and the
people.[s]

***The Fate of Eli's House.**** 27 A man of God
came to Eli and said to him: "Thus says the
LORD: I went so far as to reveal myself to
your father's house when they were in Egypt
as slaves to the house of Pharaoh. 28 I chose
them out of all the tribes of Israel to be my
priests, to go up to my altar, to burn incense,
and to wear the ephod* in my presence; and I
assigned all the fire offerings of the Israelites
to your father's house.[t] 29 Why do you stare
greedily at my sacrifices and at the offerings
that I have prescribed? Why do you honor
your sons more than you honor me, fattening

**2:18 Linen ephod**: not the same as the high priest's ephod (Ex 28:6–14) or the ephod used in divination (v. 28). Samuel wore the same kind of a ceremonial garment as the priests did (1 Sm 22:18). David also wore an ephod when he danced before the ark (2 Sm 6:14).

**2:22 Behaving promiscuously**: this part of the verse, which recalls Ex 38:8, is a gloss; it is lacking in the oldest Greek translation, and in 4QSam[a].

**2:25 Who can intercede**: Eli's sons fail to understand that their crime is directly against God and that God will punish them for it. Their behavior is set in sharp contrast to Samuel's, which meets with God's approval.

**2:27–36** These verses describe the punishment of Eli from a point of view contemporary with the reform of Josiah (2 Kgs 23:9; cf. v. 36); they hint at the events recorded in 1 Sm 22:18–23 and 1 Kgs 2:27. The older story of this divine warning occurs in 1 Sm 3:11–14. **A man of God**: often an anonymous figure whose speech foreshadows events in the near future. Cf. 1 Sm 9:6; 1 Kgs 13:1; 2 Kgs 23:16–17.

**2:28 Ephod**: a portable container, presumably of cloth, for the lots used in ritual consultation of God during the days of the Judges (Jgs 17:5; 18:14–15) and into the time of David (1 Sm 14:3; 23:6–9; 30:7–8). Attached to the ephod of the high priest described in Ex 28:6–8 is a "breastpiece of decision" which symbolized, but did not facilitate, such consultation. The Exodus text codifies a later form of the tradition.

*o:* Ps 98:9. *p:* Ex 29:27–28; Lv 7:29–36; Dt 18:3. *q:* Lv 3:3–5; Nm 18:17. *r:* 1 Sm 3:19. *s:* Lk 2:52. *t:* 1 Sm 23:9; 30:7–8; Jgs 17:5.

yourselves with the choicest part of every offering of my people Israel? [30][u]This, therefore, is the oracle of the LORD, the God of Israel: I said in the past that your family and your father's house should minister in my presence forever. But now—oracle of the LORD: Far be it from me! I will honor those who honor me, but those who despise me shall be cursed. [31]Yes, the days are coming when I will break your strength and the strength of your father's house, so that no one in your family lives to old age. [32]You shall witness, like a disappointed rival, all the benefits enjoyed by Israel, but no member of your household shall ever grow old. [33]I will leave you one man at my altar to wear out his eyes and waste his strength, but the rest of your family shall die by the sword. [34]This is a sign for you—what happens to your two sons, Hophni and Phinehas. Both of them will die on the same day.[v] [35]I will choose a faithful priest who shall do what I have in heart and mind. I will establish a lasting house for him and he shall serve in the presence of my anointed forever. [36]Then whoever is left of your family will grovel before him for a piece of silver or a loaf of bread, saying: Please assign me a priestly function, that I may have a crust of bread to eat."[w]

## CHAPTER 3

See RG 114–15

***Revelation to Samuel.*** [1]During the time young Samuel was minister to the LORD under Eli, the word of the LORD was scarce and vision infrequent. [2]* One day Eli was asleep in his usual place. His eyes had lately grown so weak that he could not see. [3]The lamp of God was not yet extinguished,* and Samuel was sleeping in the temple of the LORD where the ark of God was.[x] [4]The LORD called to Samuel, who answered, "Here I am." [5]He ran to Eli and said, "Here I am. You called me." "I did not call you," Eli answered. "Go back to sleep." So he went back to sleep. [6]Again the LORD called Samuel, who rose and went to Eli. "Here I am," he said. "You called me." But he answered, "I did not call you, my son. Go back to sleep." [7]Samuel did not yet recognize the LORD, since the word of the LORD had not yet been revealed to him. [8]The LORD called Samuel again, for the third time. Getting up and going to Eli, he said, "Here I am. You called me." Then Eli understood that the LORD was calling the youth. [9]So he said to Samuel, "Go to sleep, and if you are called, reply, 'Speak, LORD, for your servant is listening.' " When Samuel went to sleep in his place, [10]the LORD came and stood there, calling out as before: Samuel, Samuel! Samuel answered, "Speak, for your servant is listening." [11]The LORD said to Samuel: I am about to do something in Israel that will make the ears of everyone who hears it ring.[y] [12]On that day I will carry out against Eli everything I have said about his house, beginning to end. [13]I announce to him that I am condemning his house once and for all, because of this crime: though he knew his sons were blaspheming God, he did not reprove them.[z] [14]Therefore, I swear to Eli's house: No sacrifice or offering will ever expiate its crime.* [15]Samuel then slept until morning, when he got up early and opened the doors of the temple of the LORD. He was afraid to tell Eli the vision, [16]but Eli called to him, "Samuel, my son!" He replied, "Here I am." [17]Then Eli asked, "What did he say to you? Hide nothing from me! May God do thus to you, and more,* if you hide from me a single thing he told you." [18]So Samuel told him everything, and held nothing back. Eli answered, "It is the LORD. What is pleasing in the LORD's sight, the LORD will do."

***Samuel Acknowledged as Prophet.*** [19]Samuel grew up, and the LORD was with him, not

**3:2–18** The call of Samuel: This section may be divided as follows: 1. the triple summons (vv. 2–9); 2. God's revelation (vv. 10–14); 3. Samuel informs Eli (vv. 15–18).

**3:3 Not yet extinguished**: referring to the nighttime setting of this narrative (cf. Ex 27:20–21) and foreshadowing a permanently extinguished lamp when the ark is captured and Shiloh destroyed.

**3:14** Lv 4:3–12 presents another view: the offering of a bull can expiate priestly sin.

**3:17 May God do thus to you, and more**: an oath formula which strengthens Eli's demand by threatening divine punishment if Samuel does not obey. Cf. 14:44; 20:13; 25:22; 2 Sm 3:9, 35; 19:14.

*u:* 2 Sm 22:26; 1 Kgs 2:27; Ps 18:25. *v:* 1 Sm 4:11. *w:* 2 Kgs 23:9. *x:* Ex 27:20–22. *y:* 2 Kgs 21:12. *z:* 1 Sm 2:27–36.

## Samuel's Call

SAMUEL'S ROLE AS a prophet had not yet been established because "the word of the LORD had not yet been revealed to him." In this story (3:2–18), Samuel becomes "familiar with the LORD" by learning to recognize God's revelations. Samuel's bed was inside the temple near the inner sanctuary where the ark of God, representing God's presence, was kept. The lamp of God, which burned at night (Ex 27:21), "was not yet extinguished," hence it was just before dawn when the LORD called to Samuel.

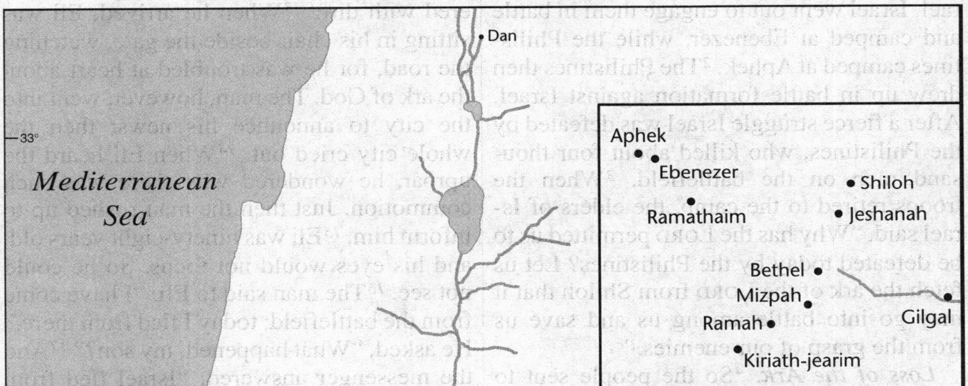

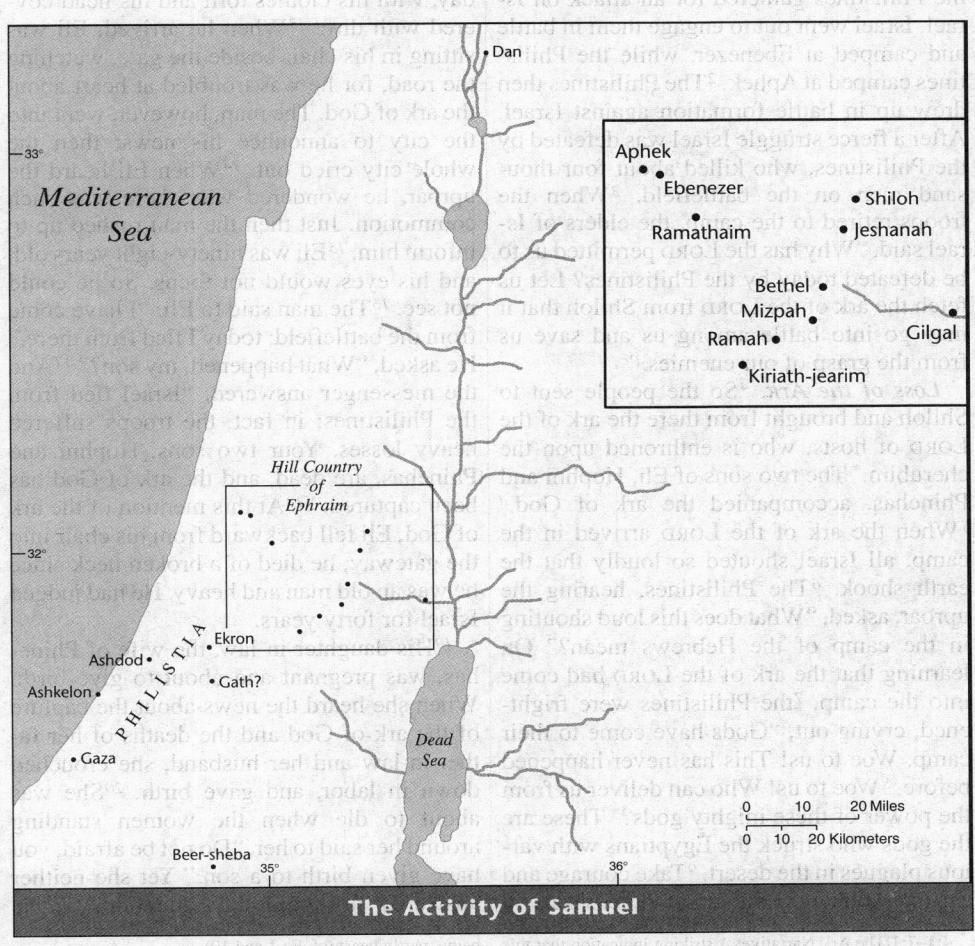


**The Activity of Samuel**

permitting any word of his to go unfulfilled.[a] [20b] Thus all Israel from Dan to Beer-sheba came to know that Samuel was a trustworthy prophet of the LORD. [21]The LORD continued to appear at Shiloh, manifesting himself to Samuel at Shiloh through his word. Samuel's word spread throughout Israel.

## CHAPTER 4

See RG 115

***Defeat of the Israelites.**** [1]At that time, the Philistines gathered for an attack on Israel. Israel went out to engage them in battle and camped at Ebenezer, while the Philistines camped at Aphek. [2]The Philistines then drew up in battle formation against Israel. After a fierce struggle Israel was defeated by the Philistines, who killed about four thousand men on the battlefield. [3]When the troops retired to the camp, the elders of Israel said, "Why has the LORD permitted us to be defeated today by the Philistines? Let us fetch the ark of the LORD from Shiloh that it may go into battle among us and save us from the grasp of our enemies."[c]

***Loss of the Ark.*** [4]So the people sent to Shiloh and brought from there the ark of the LORD of hosts, who is enthroned upon the cherubim.* The two sons of Eli, Hophni and Phinehas, accompanied the ark of God.[d] [5]When the ark of the LORD arrived in the camp, all Israel shouted so loudly that the earth shook. [6]The Philistines, hearing the uproar, asked, "What does this loud shouting in the camp of the Hebrews mean?" On learning that the ark of the LORD had come into the camp, [7]the Philistines were frightened, crying out, "Gods have come to their camp. Woe to us! This has never happened before. [8]Woe to us! Who can deliver us from the power of these mighty gods?* These are the gods who struck the Egyptians with various plagues in the desert. [9]Take courage and act like soldiers, Philistines; otherwise you will become slaves to the Hebrews, as they were your slaves. Fight like soldiers!" [10]The Philistines fought and Israel was defeated; everyone fled to their own tents.* It was a disastrous defeat; Israel lost thirty thousand foot soldiers. [11]The ark of God was captured, and Eli's two sons, Hophni and Phinehas, were dead.[e]

***Death of Eli.*** [12]A Benjaminite fled from the battlefield and reached Shiloh that same day, with his clothes torn and his head covered with dirt.[f] [13]When he arrived, Eli was sitting in his chair beside the gate, watching the road, for he was troubled at heart about the ark of God. The man, however, went into the city to announce his news; then the whole city cried out. [14]When Eli heard the uproar, he wondered why there was such commotion. Just then the man rushed up to inform him. [15]Eli was ninety-eight years old, and his eyes would not focus. So he could not see. [16]The man said to Eli: "I have come from the battlefield; today I fled from there." He asked, "What happened, my son?" [17]And the messenger answered: "Israel fled from the Philistines; in fact, the troops suffered heavy losses. Your two sons, Hophni and Phinehas, are dead, and the ark of God has been captured." [18]At this mention of the ark of God, Eli fell backward from his chair into the gateway; he died of a broken neck since he was an old man and heavy. He had judged Israel for forty years.

[19]His daughter-in-law, the wife of Phinehas, was pregnant and about to give birth. When she heard the news about the capture of the ark of God and the deaths of her father-in-law and her husband, she crouched down in labor, and gave birth. [20]She was about to die when the women standing around her said to her, "Do not be afraid, you have given birth to a son." Yet she neither answered nor paid any attention.[g] [21]She

**4:1–7:1** The Ark Narrative: A striking indication that this is an independent narrative is the absence of any mention of Samuel. **The Philistines**: one of the Sea Peoples, of Aegean origin, who occupied the coastal plain of Palestine and threatened the Israelites who settled the inland hills.

**4:4 Enthroned upon the cherubim**: this divine title first occurs in the Old Testament at the sanctuary at Shiloh (cf. 2 Sm 6:2); God is represented seated upon a throne borne through the heavens by cherubim, creatures partly human being, partly beast (cf. Ez 1 and 10).

**4:8 These mighty gods**: the Philistines, who were polytheists, presume that the Israelites also honored several gods.

**4:10 To their own tents**: the defeat is so catastrophic that the soldiers abandon the army for home; cf. 2 Sm 18:17.

*a:* 1 Sm 2:21. *b:* Jgs 20:1; 2 Sm 3:10; 17:11; 24:2. *c:* Nm 10:35; 14:42–44. *d:* Ex 25:21–22. *e:* 1 Sm 2:34. *f:* Jos 7:6; 2 Sm 1:2; Jer 7:12. *g:* 1 Sm 14:3; Gn 35:16–20.

### The Ark Troubles the Philistines

IN THE ANCIENT Near East, wars between nations were interpreted as contests between their respective gods. This story (5:1–12) explains that although the Philistines defeated Israel, the LORD was superior to Dagon, a Philistine god.

named the child Ichabod, saying, "Gone is the glory from Israel," referring to the capture of the ark of God and to her father-in-law and her husband. 22 She said, "Gone is the glory from Israel," because the ark of God had been captured.[h]

## CHAPTER 5

See RG 115

***The Ark in the Temple of Dagon.*** 1* [i] The Philistines, having captured the ark of God, transferred it from Ebenezer to Ashdod.[j] 2 They then took the ark of God and brought it into the temple of Dagon, placing it beside Dagon. 3 When the people of Ashdod rose early the next morning, Dagon was lying face down on the ground before the ark of the LORD. So they picked Dagon up and put him back in his place. 4 But early the next morning, when they arose, Dagon lay face down on the ground before the ark of the LORD, his head and hands broken off and lying on the threshold, his trunk alone intact. 5 For this reason, neither the priests of Dagon nor any others who enter the temple of Dagon tread on the threshold of Dagon in Ashdod to this very day.

***The Ark Is Carried About.*** 6 Now the hand of the LORD weighed heavily on the people of Ashdod, ravaging them and afflicting the city and its vicinity with tumors.* [k] 7 On seeing how matters stood, the people of Ashdod decided, "The ark of the God of Israel must not remain with us, for his hand weighs heavily on us and Dagon our god." 8 So they summoned all the Philistine leaders and inquired of them, "What shall we do with the ark of the God of Israel?" The people of Gath replied, "Let them move the ark of the God of Israel to us." So they moved the ark of the God of Israel to Gath. 9 But after it had been brought there, the hand of the LORD was against the city, resulting in utter turmoil: the LORD afflicted its inhabitants, young and old, and tumors broke out on them. 10 The ark of God was next sent to Ekron; but as it entered that city, the people there cried out, "Why have they brought the ark of the God of Israel here to kill us and our kindred?" 11 Then they, too, sent a summons to all the Philistine leaders and pleaded: "Send away the ark of the God of Israel. Send it back to its place so it does not kill us and our kindred." A deadly panic had seized the whole city, since the hand of God lay heavy upon it. 12 Those who escaped death were afflicted with tumors. Thus the outcry from the city went up to the heavens.

## CHAPTER 6

See RG 115

***The Ark Is Returned.*** 1 The ark of the LORD had been in the land of the Philistines seven months 2 when they summoned priests and diviners to ask, "What shall we do with the ark of the LORD? Tell us what we should send back with it." 3 They replied: "If you intend to send back the ark of the God of Israel, you must not send it alone, but must, by all means, make amends to God through a reparation offering.* Then you will be healed, and will learn why God continues to afflict you." 4 When asked further, "What reparation offering should be our amends to

**5:1–12** The Philistines take the ark to Dagon's temple in Ashdod to confirm their victory. Their action, however, underscores Dagon's impotence and the Lord's power. The narrator relates the transfer of the ark from Ashdod to Gath and then Ekron as the progress of a conquering warrior king through the Philistine cities along the central plain. The Philistines' humiliation recalls the climax of the Samson story (Jgs 16:13–21).

**5:6 Tumors**: the Septuagint adds that mice, suggestive of bubonic plague, infested their fields, thus anticipating the golden mice in 6:4–5. One symptom of bubonic plague is swollen lymph nodes ("tumors").

**6:3 A reparation offering**: an offering to make amends for unwitting transgressions against holy things or property rights; cf. Lv 6:1–3.

*h:* Ps 78:61. *i:* Jgs 16:23–30; Is 45:5–6, 20–21. *j:* Jos 13:3. *k:* Ps 32:4.

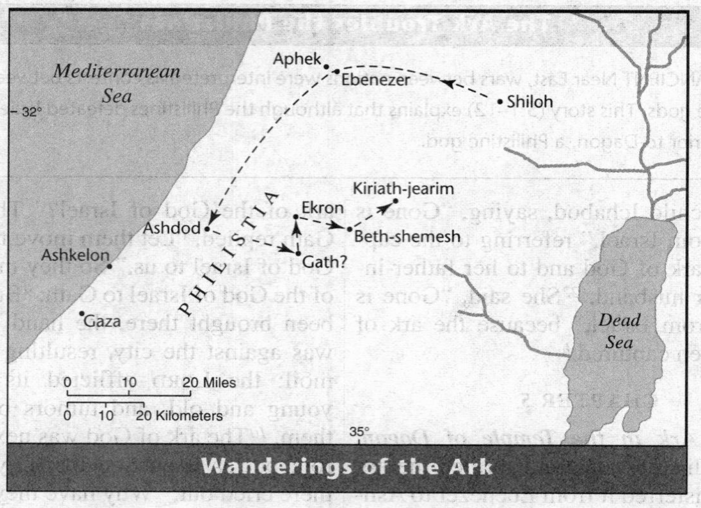


**Wanderings of the Ark**

God?" they replied: "Five golden tumors
and five golden mice to correspond to the
number of Philistine leaders, since the same
plague has struck all of you and your leaders. 5 Therefore, make images of the tumors
and of the mice that are devastating your
land and so give glory to the God of Israel.
Perhaps then God will lift his hand from
you, your gods, and your land. 6 Why should
you become stubborn, the way the Egyptians
and Pharaoh were stubborn? Was it not after
he had dealt ruthlessly with them that the Israelites were released and departed?[l] 7 So
now set to work and make a new cart. Then
take two milk cows that have not borne the
yoke; hitch them to the cart, but drive their
calves indoors away from them.* [m] 8 You
shall next take the ark of the LORD and place
it on the cart, putting the golden articles that
you are offering as reparation for your guilt
in a box beside it. Start it on its way, and let
it go. 9 Then watch! If it goes up to Beth-shemesh* along the route to the LORD's territory,
then it was the LORD who brought this great
calamity upon us; if not, we will know that it
was not the LORD's hand, but a bad turn, that
struck us."

***The Ark in Beth-shemesh.*** 10 They acted
upon this advice. Taking two milk cows,
they hitched them to the cart but shut up
their calves indoors. 11 Then they placed the
ark of the LORD on the cart, along with the
box containing the golden mice and the images of the tumors. 12 The cows went straight
for the route to Beth-shemesh and continued
along this road, mooing as they went, turning neither right nor left. The Philistine leaders followed them as far as the border of
Beth-shemesh. 13 The people of Beth-shemesh were harvesting the wheat in the valley. They looked up and rejoiced when they
saw the ark. 14 The cart came to the field of
Joshua the Beth-shemite and stopped there.
At a large stone in the field, the wood of the
cart was split up and the cows were offered
as a burnt offering to the LORD.[n] 15 The Levites, meanwhile, had taken down the ark of
God and the box beside it, with the golden
articles, and had placed them on the great
stone. The people of Beth-shemesh also offered other burnt offerings and sacrifices to
the LORD that day.[o] 16 After witnessing this,
the five Philistine leaders returned to Ekron
the same day.

**6:7 But drive their calves indoors away from them**: a test to confirm the source of the Philistines' trouble. Left to their instincts, milk cows would remain near their calves rather than head for the road to Beth-shemesh.

**6:9 Beth-shemesh**: a border city (about twenty-four miles west of Jerusalem) between Philistine and Israelite territory.

*l:* Ex 7:14; 8:15; 9:34. *m:* Nm 19:2; Dt 21:3; 2 Sm 6:3. *n:* 2 Sm 24:21–25. *o:* Dt 31:25; 1 Chr 15:2.

17 The golden tumors the Philistines sent back as a reparation offering to the LORD were as follows: one for Ashdod, one for Gaza, one for Ashkelon, one for Gath, and one for Ekron. 18 The golden mice, however, corresponded to the number of all the cities of the Philistines belonging to the five leaders, including fortified cities and open villages.* The large stone on which the ark of the LORD was placed is still in the field of Joshua the Beth-shemite at the present time.[p]

***Penalty for Irreverence.*** 19 The descendants of Jeconiah did not join in the celebration with the inhabitants of Beth-shemesh when they saw the ark of the LORD, and seventy of them were struck down. The people mourned over this great calamity which the LORD had inflicted upon them. 20 The men of Beth-shemesh asked, "Who can stand in the presence of the LORD, this Holy God? To whom can the ark go so that we are rid of it?" 21 They then sent messengers to the inhabitants of Kiriath-jearim, saying, "The Philistines have returned the ark of the LORD; come down and get it."

## CHAPTER 7

See RG 115–16

1 So the inhabitants of Kiriath-jearim came for the ark of the LORD and brought it into the house of Abinadab on the hill, appointing his son Eleazar as guardian of the ark of the LORD.

***Samuel the Judge.*** 2 From the day the ark came to rest in Kiriath-jearim, a long time, twenty years, elapsed, and the whole house of Israel turned to the LORD. 3 Then Samuel addressed the whole house of Israel: "If you would return to the LORD with your whole heart, remove your foreign gods and your Astartes, fix your hearts on the LORD, and serve him alone, then the LORD will deliver you from the hand of the Philistines."[q] 4 So the Israelites removed their Baals and Astartes,* and served the LORD alone. 5 Samuel then gave orders, "Gather all Israel to Mizpah, that I may pray to the LORD for you."[r] 6 When they had gathered at Mizpah, they drew water and poured it out* on the ground before the LORD, and they fasted that day, saying, "We have sinned against the LORD." It was at Mizpah that Samuel began to judge the Israelites.[s]

***Rout of the Philistines.*** 7 When the Philistines heard that the Israelites had gathered at Mizpah, their leaders went up against Israel. Hearing this, the Israelites became afraid of the Philistines 8 and appealed to Samuel, "Do not stop crying out to the LORD our God for us, to save us from the hand of the Philistines."[t] 9 Samuel therefore took an unweaned lamb and offered it whole as a burnt offering to the LORD.[u] He cried out to the LORD for Israel, and the LORD answered him. 10 While Samuel was sacrificing the burnt offering, the Philistines drew near for battle with Israel. That day, however, the LORD thundered loudly against the Philistines, and threw them into such confusion that they were defeated by Israel.[v] 11 Thereupon the Israelites rushed out from Mizpah and pursued the Philistines, striking them down even beyond Beth-car. 12 Samuel then took a stone and placed it between Mizpah and Jeshanah; he named it Ebenezer,* explaining, "As far as this place the LORD has been our help." 13 Thus were the Philistines subdued, never again to enter the territory of Israel, for the hand of the LORD was against them as long as Samuel lived.[w] 14 The cities from Ekron to Gath which the Philistines had taken from Israel were restored to them. Israel also freed the territory of these cities from Philistine domination.

**6:18 Open villages**: the plague devastated both fortified cities and villages, an indication of the Lord's power over the Philistines.

**7:4 Baals and Astartes**: a Deuteronomistic phrase; cf. Jgs 2:13; 10:6; 1 Sm 12:10. Baal and Astarte were Canaanite divinities.

**7:6 Drew water and poured it out**: this ritual act does not appear elsewhere in the Old Testament. Linked with fasting and admission of sin, it seems to function as a purification ritual that washes away the guilt incurred by worshiping the Canaanite Baal and his consort Astarte. Its effectiveness is immediately evident when the Lord thunders a response to Samuel's offering.

**7:12 Ebenezer**: "stone of the helper," i.e., the Lord.

*p:* 1 Sm 7:12; Gn 31:52; Jos 24:27. *q:* 1 Sm 12:10, 20, 24; Jos 24:23; Jgs 6:6–10; 10:10–16. *r:* 1 Sm 10:17; Jgs 20:1. *s:* Jgs 20:26; Ps 22:14; Lam 2:19. *t:* Jos 24:7; Jgs 3:9, 15; 6:6; 10:15. *u:* 2 Sm 22:14–15; Sir 46:16–18. *v:* Ex 9:23; 2 Sm 22:14. *w:* Jgs 3:20; 8:28; 11:33.

**The Foundation of the Monarchy**

NO LESS THAN five chapters (8–12) are devoted to the foundation of the monarchy, which shows the importance attached to the subject. The attitude toward kingship is not consistent—in chapters 8; 10:17–27; and 12 it is negative; in the other chapters, positive.

There was also peace between Israel and the Amorites.*

15 Samuel judged Israel as long as he lived. 16 He made a yearly circuit, passing through Bethel, Gilgal and Mizpah* and judging Israel at each of these places. 17 Then he used to return to Ramah, for that was his home. There, too, he judged Israel and built an altar to the LORD.[x]

## II. Establishment of the Monarchy

### CHAPTER 8

See RG 116

***Request for a King.*** 1* In his old age Samuel appointed his sons judges over Israel.[y] 2 His firstborn was named Joel, his second son, Abijah; they judged at Beer-sheba. 3 His sons did not follow his example, but looked to their own gain, accepting bribes and perverting justice.[z] 4 Therefore all the elders of Israel assembled and went to Samuel at Ramah 5 and said to him, "Now that you are old, and your sons do not follow your example, appoint a king over us, like all the nations, to rule us."[a]

6 Samuel was displeased when they said, "Give us a king to rule us." But he prayed to the LORD. 7 The LORD said: Listen to whatever the people say. You are not the one they are rejecting. They are rejecting me as their king.[b] 8 They are acting toward you just as they have acted from the day I brought them up from Egypt to this very day, deserting me to serve other gods. 9 Now listen to them; but at the same time, give them a solemn warning and inform them of the rights of the king who will rule them.

***The Governance of the King.*** 10 Samuel delivered the message of the LORD in full to those who were asking him for a king. 11 He told them: "The governance of the king who will rule you will be as follows: He will take your sons and assign them to his chariots and horses, and they will run before his chariot.[c] 12 He will appoint from among them his commanders of thousands and of hundreds. He will make them do his plowing and harvesting and produce his weapons of war and chariotry.[d] 13 He will use your daughters as perfumers, cooks, and bakers. 14 He will take your best fields, vineyards, and olive groves, and give them to his servants.[e] 15 He will tithe your crops and grape harvests to give to his officials* and his servants.[f] 16 He will take your male and female slaves, as well as your best oxen and donkeys, and use them to do his work. 17 He will also tithe your flocks. As for you, you will become his slaves.[g] 18 On that day you will cry out because of the king whom you have chosen, but the LORD will not answer you on that day."

***Persistent Demand.*** 19 The people, however, refused to listen to Samuel's warning and said, "No! There must be a king over us.[h] 20 We too must be like all the nations, with a king to rule us, lead us in warfare, and fight our battles." 21 Samuel listened to all the concerns of the people and then repeated

**7:14 The Amorites**: enemies in Transjordan. Israel is now secure, safe from external and internal threat.

**7:16 Bethel, Gilgal and Mizpah**: Bethel and Mizpah are located about five and eight miles north of Jerusalem respectively, in the district around Ramah, Samuel's home. Perhaps Gilgal, which has not been definitively located, was also in this area.

**8:1–22** From this chapter on, the editors of 1 Samuel provide two and sometimes three perspectives on the same event: e.g., the selection of Saul as king is recounted in chap. 8; 10:17–24; chap. 12.

**8:15 Officials**: lit., eunuchs. These high-ranking administrators were not necessarily emasculated.

*x:* 1 Sm 9:12; 14:35. *y:* 1 Chr 6:13. *z:* 1 Sm 2:12–17; Ex 23:8; Dt 16:19; Prv 17:23. *a:* Dt 17:14–15; Hos 13:10; Acts 13:21. *b:* 1 Sm 12:1, 12–13; Jgs 8:22–23; 10:13; 1 Kgs 9:9. *c:* 1 Sm 10:25; Dt 17:14–20; 1 Kgs 12. *d:* 2 Sm 15:1; 1 Kgs 1:5. *e:* Dt 14:22–23. *f:* 1 Sm 22:7; 1 Kgs 21:1–24; Ez 46:18. *g:* 1 Kgs 12:4. *h:* 1 Sm 10:19.

them to the LORD. [22]The LORD said: Listen to them! Appoint a king to rule over them. Then Samuel said to the people of Israel, "Return, each one of you, to your own city."*

See RG 116

## CHAPTER 9

*Saul.* [1]There was a powerful man from Benjamin named Kish, who was the son of Abiel, son of Zeror, son of Becorath, son of Aphiah, a Benjaminite.[i] [2]He had a son named Saul, who was a handsome young man. There was no other Israelite more handsome than Saul; he stood head and shoulders above the people.[j]

*The Lost Donkeys.* [3]Now the donkeys of Saul's father, Kish, had wandered off. Kish said to his son Saul, "Take one of the servants with you and go out and hunt for the donkeys." [4]So they went through the hill country of Ephraim, and through the land of Shalishah. Not finding them there, they continued through the land of Shaalim without success. They also went through the land of Benjamin, but they failed to find the animals. [5]When they came to the land of Zuph, Saul said to the servant who was with him, "Come, let us turn back, lest my father forget about the donkeys and become anxious about us." [6]The servant replied, "Listen! There is a man of God in this city, a man held in high esteem; everything he says comes true. Let us go there now! Perhaps he can advise us about the journey we have undertaken." [7k] But Saul said to his servant, "If we go, what can we offer the man? The food in our bags has run out; we have no present to give the man of God. What else do we have?" [8]Again the servant answered Saul, "I have a quarter shekel of silver.* If I give that to the man of God, he will advise us about the journey." [9l] (In former times in Israel, anyone who went to consult God used to say, "Come, let us go to the seer." For the one who is now called prophet was formerly called seer.) [10]Saul then said to his servant, "You are right! Come on, let us go!" So they headed toward the city where the man of God lived.

*Meeting the Young Women.* [11m] As they were going up the path to the city, they met some young women coming out to draw water and they asked them, "Is the seer in town?" [12n] The young women answered, "Yes, there—straight ahead. Hurry now; just today he came to the city, because the people have a sacrifice today on the high place.* [13]When you enter the city, you may reach him before he goes up to the high place to eat. The people will not eat until he arrives; only after he blesses the sacrifice will the invited guests eat. Go up immediately, for you should find him right now."

*Saul Meets Samuel.* [14]So they went up to the city. As they entered it—there was Samuel coming toward them on his way to the high place. [15]The day before Saul's arrival, the LORD had revealed to Samuel:[o] [16]At this time tomorrow I will send you a man from the land of Benjamin whom you are to anoint as ruler of my people Israel. He shall save my people from the hand of the Philistines. I have looked upon my people; their cry has come to me.[p] [17]When Samuel caught sight of Saul, the LORD assured him: This is the man I told you about; he shall govern my people. [18]Saul met Samuel in the gateway and said, "Please tell me where the seer lives." [19]Samuel answered Saul: "I am the seer. Go up ahead of me to the high place and eat with me today. In the morning, before letting you go, I will tell you everything on your mind. [20]As for your donkeys that were lost three days ago, do not worry about them, for they have been found. Whom should Israel want if not you and your father's family?" [21]Saul replied: "Am I not a Benjaminite, from the smallest of the tribes of Israel,* and is not my clan the least among

**8:22 To your own city**: Samuel will later reassemble the people at Mizpah (10:17) to acclaim Saul as their king.

**9:8 A quarter shekel of silver**: about a tenth of an ounce of silver.

**9:12 On the high place**: the local sanctuary on the top of a hill, where the sacrifice was offered and the sacrificial meal eaten.

**9:21 Smallest of the tribes of Israel**: Saul's objection is a common element in call narrative, e.g., Ex 3:11; 4:10; Jgs 6:15.

*i:* 1 Sm 14:51; 1 Chr 8:33. *j:* 1 Sm 10:23; 16:12. *k:* Nm 22:7; 1 Kgs 14:3; 2 Kgs 4:42; 5:15; 8:8–9. *l:* Sir 46:15. *m:* Gn 24:11–14; Ex 2:16. *n:* 1 Sm 7:17; 16:2, 5; 20:6, 29; Dt 12:13; 1 Kgs 3:2, 4. *o:* Acts 13:21. *p:* 1 Sm 10:1; Jgs 6:14.

*Anointing:* the rite that raised a commoner to kingship in Israel. Saul and David were anointed in secret (cf. 1 Sm 9:26–10:1; 16:1–13) Later, it was a more formal and public act (see 1 Kings 1:32–40).

the clans of the tribe of Benjamin? Why say such things to me?"[q]

***The Meal.*** * [22]Samuel then took Saul and his servant and brought them into the room. He seated them at the head of the guests, of whom there were about thirty. [23]He said to the cook, "Bring the portion I gave you and told you to put aside." [24]So the cook took up the leg and what went with it, and placed it before Saul. Samuel said: "This is a reserved portion that is set before you. Eat, for it was kept for you until this time; I explained that I was inviting some guests." Thus Saul dined with Samuel that day. [25]When they came down from the high place into the city, a mattress was spread for Saul on the roof, [26]and he slept there.

***Saul's Anointing.*** At daybreak Samuel called to Saul on the roof, "Get up, and I will send you on your way." Saul got up, and he and Samuel went outside the city together. [27]As they were approaching the edge of the town, Samuel said to Saul, "Tell the servant to go on ahead of us, but you stay here for a moment, that I may give you a word from God."

## CHAPTER 10

See RG 116

[1]Then, from a flask he had with him, Samuel poured oil on Saul's head and kissed him, saying: "The LORD anoints you ruler over his people Israel. You are the one who will govern the LORD's people and save them from the power of their enemies all around them.[r]

***The Signs Foretold.*** "This will be the sign* for you that the LORD has anointed you ruler over his heritage: [2]When you leave me today, you will meet two men near Rachel's tomb* at Zelzah in the territory of Benjamin. They will say to you, 'The donkeys you went to look for have been found. Now your father is no longer worried about the donkeys, but is anxious about you and says: What shall I do about my son?'[s] [3]Farther on, when you arrive at the oak of Tabor,* three men will meet you as they go up to God at Bethel; one will be bringing three young goats, another three loaves of bread, and the third a skin of wine. [4]They will greet you and offer you two elevated offerings of bread, which you should accept from them. [5][t] After that you will come to Gibeath-elohim, where the Philistine garrison* is located. As you enter that city, you will meet a band of prophets coming down from the high place. They will be preceded by lyres, tambourines, flutes, and harps, and will be in prophetic ecstasy. [6]The spirit of the LORD will rush upon you, and you will join them in their prophetic ecstasy and will become a changed man.[u] [7]When these signs have come to pass, do whatever lies to hand, because God is with you. [8][v] Now go down ahead of me to Gilgal, for I shall come down to you, to offer burnt offerings and to sacrifice communion offerings. Wait seven days until I come to you; I shall then tell you what you must do."*

**9:22–24** At this ritual meal, Samuel treats the youthful Saul as if he were already king. Saul receives the part of the sacrificed animal reserved for the priest and his family, perhaps the sheep's fat tail. Legal texts (Ex 29:22; Lv 3:9; 7:3–4) require the priest to burn this portion of the sheep on the altar.

**10:1 The sign**: the role of the new ruler is confirmed by specific signs; cf. Ex 7:9.

**10:2** Here, as in Jer 31:15, Rachel's tomb is placed at Ramah, north of Jerusalem. Later tradition understood Ephrath (Gn 35:19–20) as Bethlehem and placed the tomb farther south (Mt 2:16–18).

**10:3 Oak of Tabor**: or terebinth. Such a tree often indicates a shrine.

**10:5 The Philistine garrison**: the Hebrew word for "garrison" has been explained alternatively to mean a stele established to mark the Philistine occupation, or an inspector or officer for the collection of taxes. **Prophetic ecstasy**: a condition of religious enthusiasm often induced by communal rituals of music and dancing.

**10:8** By inserting this verse, with its seven days, an editor has named in the very context of Saul's anointing the condi-

*q*: 1 Sm 15:17. *r*: 1 Sm 9:16–17; 16:13; 24:7; Jgs 9:9; 1 Kgs 1:39; Acts 13:21. *s*: Jer 31:15; Mk 14:13. *t*: 1 Sm 13:3; 16:13; 19:20–21. *u*: 1 Sm 11:6; 16:13; Jgs 14:6, 19; 15:14; 2 Kgs 3:15. *v*: 1 Sm 13:8; Lv 3:1.

***The Signs Come to Pass.*** [9]As Saul turned to leave Samuel, God changed his heart. That very day all these signs came to pass. . . . [10*] From there they arrived at Gibeah, where a band of prophets met Saul, and the spirit of God rushed upon him, so that he joined them in their prophetic ecstasy.[w] [11]When all who had known him previously saw him in a prophetic state among the prophets, they said to one another, "What has happened to the son of Kish? Is Saul also among the prophets?"[x] [12]And someone from that district responded, "And who is their father?" Thus the saying arose, "Is Saul also among the prophets?" [13]When he came out of the prophetic ecstasy, he went home.

***Silence About the Kingship.*** [14]Saul's uncle asked him and his servant, "Where have you been?" Saul replied, "Looking for the donkeys. When we could not find them, we went to Samuel." [15]Saul's uncle said, "Tell me, then, what Samuel said to you." [16]Saul said to his uncle, "He assured us that the donkeys had been found." But Saul told him nothing about what Samuel had said about the kingship.

***Saul Chosen King.*** [17]Samuel called the people together to the LORD at Mizpah[y] [18]and addressed the Israelites: "Thus says the LORD, the God of Israel: It was I who brought Israel up from Egypt and delivered you from the power of the Egyptians and from the power of all the kingdoms that oppressed you.[z] [19]But today you have rejected your God, who saves you from all your evils and calamities, by saying, 'No! You must appoint a king over us.' Now, therefore, take your stand before the LORD according to your tribes and families."[a] [20]So Samuel had all the tribes of Israel come forward, and the tribe of Benjamin was chosen.* [21]Next he had the tribe of Benjamin come forward by clans, and the clan of Matri was chosen, and finally Saul, son of Kish, was chosen. But when they went to look for him, he was nowhere to be found. [22][b] Again they consulted the LORD, "Is there still someone else to come forward?" The LORD answered: He is hiding among the baggage. [23]They ran to bring him from there; when he took his place among the people, he stood head and shoulders above all the people.[c] [24]Then Samuel addressed all the people, "Do you see the man whom the LORD has chosen? There is no one like him among all the people!" Then all the people shouted out, "Long live the king!"[d] [25]Samuel next explained to the people the rules of the monarchy,* wrote them in a book, and placed them before the presence of the LORD. Samuel then sent the people back to their own homes.[e] [26]Saul also went home to Gibeah, accompanied by warriors whose hearts the LORD had touched. [27]But some worthless people said, "How can this fellow save us?" They despised him and brought him no tribute.*[f]

## CHAPTER 11

See RG 116

***Defeat of the Ammonites.*** [1*] About a month later, Nahash the Ammonite went up and besieged Jabesh-gilead. All the people of Jabesh begged Nahash, "Make a treaty with us, and we will serve you."[g] [2]But Nahash the Ammonite replied, "This is my condition for making a treaty with you: I will gouge out the right eye of every man,* and thus bring shame on all Israel." [3]The elders of Jabesh said to him: "Give us seven days to

tion which in a later narrative will be the grounds for the rejection of the dynastic character of Saul's kingship (13:8–15).

**10:10** An editor has abridged a longer version of this story by omitting mention of the first two signs Samuel has given (vv. 2–4).

**10:20 Was chosen**: probably by casting lots; cf. 14:40–42; Jos 7:14, 17.

**10:25 Rules of the monarchy**: a charter describing the relationship between the king and the people.

**10:27 Tribute:** a gift to honor a new ruler as a pledge of one's loyalty; see Gn 32:14; Jgs 3:15; 2 Sm 8:2.

**11:1** A text from Qumran (1QSam[a]) introduces this chapter with the report that Nahash, king of the Ammonites, had attacked the Gadites and the Reubenites, gouging out their right eyes. Seven thousand of them had fled to Jabesh-gilead. This additional information would explain why Nahash besieged Jabesh-gilead. There is no consensus among scholars whether the Qumran text represents an original reading or a secondary expansion.

**11:2 Right eye of every man**: thus rendering them incapable of military action.

*w:* 1 Sm 19:20–24; Nm 11:25. *x:* 1 Sm 19:24. *y:* 1 Sm 7:5. *z:* Ex 20:2; Lv 11:45; 25:38; Nm 15:41; Dt 5:6; Jgs 6:8–9. *a:* 1 Sm 8:19. *b:* 1 Sm 30:24. *c:* 1 Sm 9:2; 16:7. *d:* 2 Sm 16:16; 1 Kgs 1:25; 2 Kgs 11:12. *e:* 1 Sm 8:11; Dt 17:14–20. *f:* 1 Sm 11:12. *g:* 1 Sm 12:12; 31:11; 2 Sm 10:2.

send messengers throughout the territory of
Israel. If there is no one to save us, we will
surrender to you." [4]When the messengers arrived at Gibeah of Saul and reported the
news in the people's hearing, they all wept
aloud. [5]Just then Saul came in from the field,
behind his oxen. "Why are the people weeping?" he asked. They repeated the message
of the inhabitants of Jabesh for him. [6]As he
listened to this report, the spirit of God
rushed upon him and he became very angry.[h]
[7]Taking a yoke of oxen, he cut them into
pieces and sent them throughout the territory
of Israel* by messengers saying, "If anyone
does not come out to follow Saul and Samuel, the same thing will be done to his oxen!"
The dread of the LORD came upon the people and they went forth as one.[i] [8]When Saul
reviewed them in Bezek,* there were three
hundred thousand Israelites and seventy
thousand Judahites.

[9]To the messengers who had come he
said, "Tell the inhabitants of Jabesh-gilead
that tomorrow, when the sun grows hot, they
will be saved." The messengers went and reported this to the inhabitants of Jabesh, and
they rejoiced. [10]The men of Jabesh said to
Nahash, "Tomorrow we will surrender to
you, and you may do with us whatever you
want." [11]The next day, Saul arranged his
troops in three companies and invaded the
camp during the dawn watch. They slaughtered Ammonites until the day had gotten
hot; by then the survivors were so scattered
that no two of them were left together.

***Saul Accepted as King.*** [12]* The people
then said to Samuel: "Who questioned
whether Saul should rule over us? Hand
them over and we will put them to death."[j]
[13]But Saul objected, "No one will be put to
death this day, for today the LORD has rescued Israel."[k] [14]Samuel said to the people,
"Come, let us go to Gilgal to renew the kingship there." [15]So all the people went to Gilgal, and there they made Saul king in the
LORD's presence. They also sacrificed communion offerings there before the LORD, and
Saul and all the Israelites rejoiced greatly.

## CHAPTER 12*

See RG 116–17

***Samuel's Integrity.*** [1]* Samuel addressed all Israel: "I have granted your request in every respect," he said. "I have set a
king over you[l] [2]and now the king will lead
you. As for me, I am old and gray, and my
sons are among you. I was your leader from
my youth to the present day. [3]Here I stand!
Answer me in the presence of the LORD and
the LORD's anointed. Whose ox have I
taken? Whose donkey have I taken? Whom
have I cheated? Whom have I wronged?
From whom have I accepted a bribe and shut
my eyes because of it? I will make restitution to you."[m] [4]They replied, "You have neither cheated us, nor oppressed us, nor accepted anything from anyone." [5]So he said
to them, "The LORD is witness against you
this day, and the LORD's anointed is witness,
that you have found nothing in my possession." "The LORD is witness," they said.

***Samuel Admonishes the People.*** [6]Samuel
continued: "The LORD is witness, who appointed Moses and Aaron and brought your
ancestors up from the land of Egypt.[n] [7]Now
take your stand, that I may judge you in the
presence of the LORD according to all the
gracious acts that the LORD has done for you
and your ancestors. [8]When Jacob and his

**11:7 Throughout the territory of Israel**: Saul's gesture summons the Israelite confederacy to a coordinated response against Nahash; cf. Jgs 19:29 for a similar action. **Dread of the LORD**: often a panic that immobilizes Israel's enemies; here, however, it has the opposite effect and incites the Israelites to battle.

**11:8 Bezek**: probably modern Khirbet Ibziq, northeast of Shechem, on the west slope of the Jordan valley, opposite Jabesh-gilead.

**11:12–14** With the defeat of the Ammonites, Saul demonstrates his ability to command Israel's army and defend the land. At Gilgal, Saul's kingship is ratified; ironically, he loses his kingship at the same place (13:7).

**12:1–25** This chapter narrates the transition from the leadership of the judges to the rule of the king. The Deuteronomistic redactor has Samuel contrast the wickedness of Israel's ancestors with the Lord's gracious deliverance (vv. 6–12). The people realize that their demand for a king has compounded that wickedness. Now that the Lord has given them a king, Samuel urges the people and their king to serve the Lord wholeheartedly (vv. 13–25).

**12:1–5** Samuel's upright leadership is set in sharp contrast to the despotic powers of the king described in chap. 8. By their testimony, the people witness to Samuel's righteousness.

*h:* 1 Sm 16:13; Jgs 14:6, 19; 15:14. *i:* 1 Kgs 11:30; 2 Kgs 13:18. *j:* 1 Sm 10:27. *k:* 2 Sm 19:23. *l:* 1 Sm 8:7, 9, 22. *m:* Ex 20:17; 23:8; Nm 16:15; Dt 16:19; Sir 46:19. *n:* Mi 6:4.

sons went to Egypt and the Egyptians oppressed them, your ancestors cried out to the LORD. The LORD then sent Moses and Aaron to bring them out of Egypt and settled them in this place.[o] 9But they forgot the LORD their God; and so the LORD sold them into the power of Sisera, the captain of the army of Hazor, the power of the Philistines, and the power of the king of Moab, who made war against them.[p] 10They cried out to the LORD and said, 'We have sinned because we abandoned the LORD and served the Baals and Astartes. Now deliver us from the power of our enemies, and we will serve you.'[q] 11The LORD sent Jerubbaal, Barak, Jephthah, and Samuel; he delivered you from the power of your enemies on every side, so that you could live in security.[r] 12Yet, when you saw Nahash, king of the Ammonites, advancing against you, you said to me, 'No! A king must rule us,' even though the LORD your God is your king.[s]

***Warnings for People and King.*** 13"Now here is the king you chose. See! The LORD has given you a king.[t] 14If you fear and serve the LORD, if you listen to the voice of the LORD and do not rebel against the LORD's command, if both you and the king, who rules over you, follow the LORD your God—well and good. 15But if you do not listen to the voice of the LORD and if you rebel against the LORD's command, the hand of the LORD will be against you and your king. 16Now then, stand ready to witness the great marvel the LORD is about to accomplish before your eyes. 17Are we not in the harvest time for wheat?* Yet I will call upon the LORD, and he will send thunder and rain. Thus you will see and understand how great an evil it is in the eyes of the LORD that you have asked for a king."[u] 18Samuel called upon the LORD, and the LORD sent thunder and rain that day.

***Assistance Promised.*** Then all the people feared the LORD and Samuel. 19They said to Samuel, "Pray to the LORD your God for us, your servants, that we may not die for having added to all our other sins the evil of asking for a king." 20"Do not fear," Samuel answered them. "You have indeed committed all this evil! Yet do not turn from the LORD, but serve him with your whole heart. 21Do not turn aside to gods who are nothing,* who cannot act and deliver. They are nothing.[v] 22For the sake of his own great name* the LORD will not abandon his people, since the LORD has decided to make you his people.[w] 23As for me, far be it from me to sin against the LORD by ceasing to pray for you and to teach you the good and right way.[x] 24But you must fear the LORD and serve him faithfully with all your heart, for you have seen the great things the LORD has done among you. 25If instead you continue to do evil, both you and your king shall be swept away."

## III. Saul and David

### CHAPTER 13

See RG 117

1[Saul was . . . years old when he became king and he reigned . . . -two years over Israel.]*

***Saul Offers Sacrifice.*** 2Saul chose three thousand of Israel, of whom two thousand remained with him in Michmash and in the hill country of Bethel, and one thousand were with Jonathan in Gibeah of Benjamin. He sent the rest of the army back to their tents. 3Now Jonathan struck the Philistine garrison* in Gibeah, and the Philistines got

**12:17 Harvest time for wheat**: in May–June. Since this is a period of little or no rainfall in Israel, the people will not mistake the sign for a natural phenomenon.

**12:21 Gods who are nothing**: Hebrew *tohu*, lit., "emptiness," cf. Gn 1:2 ( . . . *webohu*); here, idols without power or substance, as in Is 41:29.

**12:22 His own great name**: were the Lord to abandon his people, even if they abandon him, he would diminish his stature or reputation in the divine council or among the nations (e.g., Ez 20:9). Throughout the Old Testament the Lord is encouraged to deliver Israel, despite its evil, "for the sake of his name."

**13:1** A formula like that of 2 Sm 5:4 was introduced here at some time; but the age of Saul when he became king remains a blank, and the two years assigned for his reign in the Masoretic text cannot be correct. Acts 13:21 offers the round number of forty years.

**13:3–4 The Philistine garrison**: see note on 10:5. **Let the**

*o:* Gn 46:5; Ex 1:11; 2:23–25. *p:* Jgs 3:12–15; 4:2–3; 10:7; 13:1. *q:* 1 Sm 7:3–4; Jgs 10:10. *r:* Jgs 6:14, 32; 11:1. *s:* 1 Sm 8:6–7, 19; 11:1–2; Jgs 8:23. *t:* 1 Sm 8:7. *u:* Ex 9:23, 28–30; 1 Kgs 18:1. *v:* Dt 32:37–39; Is 41:29; 44:9–10. *w:* Ex 18:10; Dt 4:34; Jos 7:9; Is 48:9; Jer 14:21; Dn 3:34. *x:* Ex 32:11.

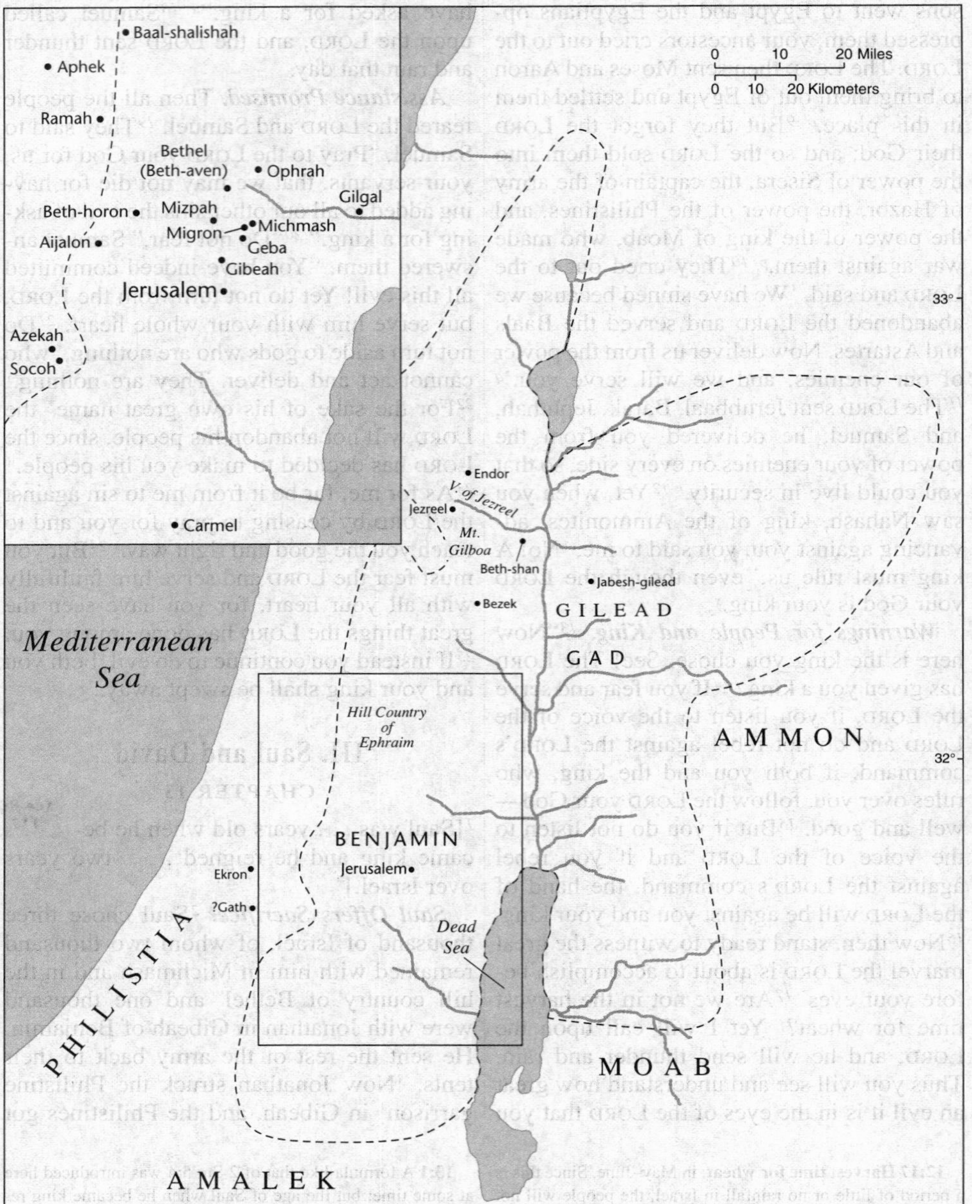

The Kingdom of Saul according to 1 Samuel

word of it. Then Saul sounded the horn
throughout the land, saying, “Let the Hebrews hear!”[y] 4 Then all Israel heard the report, “Saul has struck the garrison of the Philistines! Israel has become odious to the
Philistines!” Then the army was called up to
Saul in Gilgal. 5 The Philistines also assembled for battle against Israel, with thirty
thousand chariots,* six thousand horsemen,
and foot soldiers as numerous as the sand on
the seashore.[z] They came up and encamped
in Michmash, east of Beth-aven.[a] 6 When the
soldiers saw they were in danger because the
army was hardpressed, they hid themselves
in caves, thickets, rocks, caverns, and cisterns. 7 Other Hebrews crossed the Jordan
into the land of Gad and Gilead. Saul, however, held out in Gilgal, all his army trembling in fear behind him.* 8 He waited seven
days, until the appointed time Samuel had
set, but Samuel did not come, and the army
deserted Saul.[b] 9 He then said, “Bring me the
burnt offering and communion offerings!”
Then he sacrificed the burnt offering.

***King Saul Reproved.*** 10 As he finished sacrificing the burnt offering, there came Samuel! So Saul went out toward him in order to
greet him. 11 Samuel asked him, “What have
you done?” Saul explained: “When I saw
that the army was deserting me and you did
not come on the appointed day, and that the
Philistines were assembling at Michmash,
12 I said to myself, ‘Now the Philistines will
come down against me at Gilgal, and I have
not yet sought the LORD’s blessing.’ So I
thought I should sacrifice the burnt offering.” 13 Samuel replied to Saul: “You have
acted foolishly! Had you kept the command
the LORD your God gave you, the LORD
would now establish your kingship in Israel
forever; 14 but now your kingship shall not
endure. The LORD has sought out a man after his own heart* to appoint as ruler over his
people because you did not observe what the
LORD commanded you.”[c]

***Philistine Invasion.*** 15 Then Samuel set out
from Gilgal and went his own way; but what
was left of the army went up after Saul to
meet the soldiers, going from Gilgal to Gibeah of Benjamin. Saul then counted the soldiers he had with him, about six hundred.[d]
16 Saul, his son Jonathan, and the soldiers
they had with them were now occupying
Geba of Benjamin, and the Philistines were
encamped at Michmash. 17 Meanwhile,
raiders left the camp of the Philistines in
three bands.[e] One band took the Ophrah road
toward the district of Shual; 18 another turned
in the direction of Beth-horon; and the third
took the road for Geba that overlooks the
Valley of the Hyenas toward the desert.

***Disarmament of Israel.**** 19 Not a single
smith was to be found anywhere in Israel,
for the Philistines had said, “Otherwise the
Hebrews will make swords or spears.”[f] 20 All
Israel, therefore, had to go down to the Philistines to sharpen their plowshares, mattocks, axes, and sickles. 21 The price for the
plowshares and mattocks was two thirds of a
shekel, and a third of a shekel for sharpening
the axes and for setting the ox-goads. 22 And
so on the day of battle neither sword nor
spear could be found in the hand of any of
the soldiers with Saul or Jonathan. Only
Saul and his son Jonathan had them.

***Jonathan’s Exploit.*** 23 An outpost of the
Philistines had pushed forward to the pass of
Michmash.[g]

## CHAPTER 14

See RG 117–18

1 One day Jonathan, son of Saul, said
to his armor-bearer, “Come, let us go over to

**Hebrews hear**: a different reading of these verses, based on the Greek, would yield: “And the Philistines heard that the Hebrews (or: the slaves) had revolted. Saul in the meantime sounded the trumpet throughout all the land (v. 4), and all Israel heard that Saul . . . .”

**13:5 Thirty thousand chariots**: some Greek manuscripts read “three thousand chariots.”

**13:7–15** These verses, like 10:8, anticipate the rejection of Saul; a different occasion and motivation for this are given in chap. 15 and 28:17–18.

**13:14 After his own heart**: i.e., of his choosing, for his purpose. While the verse undoubtedly refers to David, it concerns the Lord’s decision to continue the kingship, even though he has rejected Saul, by selecting the heir to Saul’s throne.

**13:19–22** These details emphasize the Philistines’ military power and superior technology, a reminder that an Israelite victory depends on God.

*y:* 1 Sm 14:1–15; Jgs 3:27; 6:34; 2 Sm 20:1–2. *z:* Gn 22:17; 41:49; Jgs 7:12. *a:* 1 Sm 14:22. *b:* 1 Sm 10:8. *c:* 1 Sm 15:28; 25:30; 2 Sm 7:15–16; Ps 78:70; Acts 13:22. *d:* 1 Sm 14:2. *e:* 1 Sm 14:15. *f:* Jgs 5:8. *g:* 1 Sm 14:15.

the Philistine outpost on the other side." But he did not inform his father—[h] 2 Saul was sitting under the pomegranate tree in Migron on the outskirts of Gibeah; with him were about six hundred men. 3 Ahijah, son of Ahitub, brother of Ichabod, the son of Phinehas, son of Eli, the priest of the LORD at Shiloh, was wearing the ephod—nor did the soldiers know that Jonathan had gone.[i] 4 Flanking the ravine through which Jonathan intended to cross to the Philistine outpost were rocky crags on each side, one named Bozez and the other Seneh. 5 One crag was to the north, toward Michmash; the other to the south, toward Geba. 6 Jonathan said to his armor-bearer: "Come, let us go over to that outpost of the uncircumcised. Perhaps the LORD will help us, because it is no more difficult for the LORD to grant victory by means of a few than it is by means of many."[j] 7 His armor-bearer replied, "Do whatever you think best; I am with you in whatever you decide." 8 Jonathan continued: "When we cross over to those men, we will be visible to them. 9 If they say to us, 'Stay there until we can come to you,' we will stop where we are; we will not go up to them. 10 But if they say, 'Come up to us,' we will go up, because the LORD has delivered them into our hand. That will be our sign."* [k] 11 When the two of them came into the view of the Philistine outpost, the Philistines remarked, "Look, some Hebrews* are coming out of the holes where they have been hiding." 12 The men of the outpost called to Jonathan and his armor-bearer. "Come up here," they said, "and we will teach you a lesson." So Jonathan said to his armor-bearer, "Climb up after me, for the LORD has delivered them into the hand of Israel." 13 Jonathan clambered up with his armor-bearer behind him. As the Philistines fell before Jonathan, his armor-bearer, who followed him, would finish them off. 14 In this first attack Jonathan and his armor-bearer killed about twenty men within half a furlong. 15 Then terror spread through the camp and the countryside; all the soldiers in the outpost and in the raiding parties shuddered in terror. The earth shook with an awesome shuddering.* [l]

***Rout of the Philistines.*** 16 Saul's sentinels in Gibeah of Benjamin saw that the enemy camp had scattered and were running in all directions. 17 Saul said to those around him, "Count the troops and find out if any of us are missing." When they had taken the count, they found Jonathan and his armor-bearer missing. 18 Saul then said to Ahijah, "Bring the ephod here." (Ahijah was wearing the ephod before the Israelites at that time.) 19 While Saul was speaking to the priest, the uproar in the Philistine camp kept increasing. So he said to the priest, "Withdraw your hand." 20 And Saul and all his men rallied and rushed into the fight, where the Philistines, wholly confused, were thrusting swords at one another.[m] 21 The Hebrews who had previously sided with the Philistines and had gone up with them to their camp turned to join the Israelites under Saul and Jonathan.[n] 22 Likewise, all the Israelites who were hiding in the hill country of Ephraim, hearing that the Philistines were fleeing, kept after them in the battle.[o] 23* Thus the LORD saved Israel that day.

***Saul's Oath.*** The battle continued past Beth-aven. 24 Even though the Israelites were exhausted that day, Saul laid an oath on them, saying, "Cursed be the one who takes food before evening, before I am able to avenge myself on my enemies." So none of the people tasted food. 25 Now there was a honeycomb lying on the ground, 26 and when the soldiers came to the comb the honey was flowing; yet no one raised a hand from it to his mouth, because the people feared the oath.

**14:10 That will be our sign**: Jonathan acknowledges that the battle is in God's hands.

**14:11 Hebrews**: while this term is often used by foreigners of Israelites, in this verse it seems to be a derogatory epithet for soldiers who deserted Saul's army while he was waiting for Samuel to arrive in Gilgal.

**14:15 Awesome shuddering**: lit., "shuddering caused by God"; the panic in the Philistine camp is the work of Israel's warrior God.

**14:23** The victory apparently cleared the Philistines off the main ridge of mountains in the territories of Benjamin and Ephraim.

---

*h:* 1 Sm 13:3. *i:* 1 Sm 2:28; 4:21; 14:18; 23:9; 30:7. *j:* 1 Sm 17:26, 36, 47; Jgs 14:3; Sir 39:18; 1 Mc 3:19. *k:* Jos 8:1; 10:8; Jgs 12:3. *l:* 2 Sm 22:8; Jl 2:10–11. *m:* Jgs 7:22. *n:* 1 Sm 29:4. *o:* 1 Sm 13:6.

***Violation of the Oath.*** 27 Jonathan, who had not heard that his father had put the people under oath, thrust out the end of the staff he was holding and dipped it into the honeycomb. Then he raised it to his mouth and his eyes brightened. 28 At this, one of the soldiers spoke up: "Your father put the people under a strict oath, saying, 'Cursed be the one who takes food today!' As a result the people are weakened." 29[p] Jonathan replied: "My father brings trouble to the land. Look how bright my eyes are because I had this little taste of honey. 30 What is more, if the army had eaten freely of the enemy's plunder when they came across it today, surely the slaughter of the Philistines would have been the greater by now!"

***Consuming the Blood.*** 31 After the Philistines were routed that day from Michmash to Aijalon, the people were completely exhausted. 32 So the army pounced upon the plunder and took sheep, oxen, and calves, slaughtering them on the ground and eating the meat with the blood in it.[q] 33 Informed that the army was sinning against the LORD by eating the meat with blood in it, Saul said: "You have broken faith. Roll a large stone here for me." 34 He continued: "Mingle with the people and tell each of them, 'Bring an ox or sheep to me. Slaughter them here and then eat. But you must not sin against the LORD by eating meat with blood in it.'" So that night they all brought whatever oxen they had seized, and they slaughtered them there; 35 and Saul built an altar to the LORD—this was the first time he built an altar to the LORD.[r]

***Jonathan in Danger of Death.*** 36 Then Saul said, "Let us go down in pursuit of the Philistines by night, to plunder them until daybreak and leave no one alive." They replied, "Do what you think best." But the priest said, "Let us consult God." 37 So Saul inquired of God: "Shall I go down in pursuit of the Philistines? Will you deliver them into the hand of Israel?" But he received no answer on this occasion.[s] 38 "All officers of the army," Saul announced, "come forward. Find out how this sin was committed today. 39 As the LORD lives who has given victory to Israel, even if my son Jonathan has committed it, he shall surely die!" But none of the people answered him. 40 So he said to all Israel, "Stand on one side, and my son Jonathan and I will stand on the other." The people responded, "Do what you think best."[t] 41 And Saul said to the LORD, the God of Israel: "Why did you not answer your servant this time? If the blame for this resides in me or my son Jonathan, LORD, God of Israel, respond with Urim; but if this guilt is in your people Israel, respond with Thummim."* Jonathan and Saul were designated, and the people went free.[u] 42 Saul then said, "Cast lots between me and my son Jonathan." And Jonathan was designated. 43 Saul said to Jonathan, "Tell me what you have done." Jonathan replied, "I only tasted a little honey from the end of the staff I was holding. Am I to die for this?" 44 Saul declared, "May God do thus to me, and more, if you do not indeed die, Jonathan!"[v]

***Rescue of Jonathan.*** 45 But the soldiers protested to Saul: "Is Jonathan to die, the man who won this great victory for Israel? This must not be! As the LORD lives, not a single hair of his head shall fall to the ground, for God was with him in what he did today!" Thus the soldiers rescued* Jonathan and he did not die.[w] 46 After that Saul gave up the pursuit of the Philistines, who returned to their own territory.

***Saul's Victories.*** 47 After taking possession of the kingship over Israel, Saul waged war on its enemies all around—Moab, the Ammonites, Edom, the kings of Zobah, and the Philistines. Wherever he turned, he was successful[x] 48 and fought bravely. He defeated

**14:41 Urim . . . Thummim**: objects, one representing a positive response and the other a negative response, kept in the front pocket of the priest's ephod, a garment worn as a breastplate, and used to ascertain God's will in certain instances, e.g., whether Saul should help rout the Philistines. Saul consults the priest but is too impatient to finish the consultation and hurries impulsively into battle.

**14:45 Rescued**: the Hebrew word used is that for the "redemption" of the firstborn (Ex 13:13–15).

*p:* Jos 7:25; 1 Kgs 18:17–18. *q:* 1 Sm 15:19, 21; Gn 4:9; Lv 3:17; 7:26–27; 17:10–14; Acts 15:20, 29. *r:* 1 Sm 7:17; Jgs 6:24. *s:* 1 Sm 28:6, 15. *t:* Jos 7:13–15. *u:* 1 Sm 10:20; 28:6; Ex 28:30; Dt 33:8. *v:* 1 Sm 3:17; Ru 1:17. *w:* 2 Sm 14:11; 1 Kgs 1:52. *x:* 2 Sm 1:22; 8:2–5.

Amalek and delivered Israel from the hand of those who were plundering them.[y]

*Saul's Family.* 49 The sons of Saul were Jonathan, Ishvi, and Malchishua; the name of his firstborn daughter was Merob; the name of the younger was Michal.[z] 50 The name of Saul's wife was Ahinoam, daughter of Ahimaaz. The name of his general was Abner, son of Ner, Saul's uncle; 51 Kish, Saul's father, and Ner, Abner's father, were sons of Abiel.[a]

52 There was heavy fighting with the Philistines during Saul's lifetime. Whenever Saul saw any strong or brave man, he took him into his service.

See RG 117-18

## CHAPTER 15*

***Disobedience of Saul.*** 1 Samuel said to Saul: "It was I the LORD sent to anoint you king over his people Israel. Now, therefore, listen to the message of the LORD.[b] 2 Thus says the LORD of hosts: I will punish what Amalek did to the Israelites when he barred their way as they came up from Egypt.[c] 3 Go, now, attack Amalek, and put under the ban* everything he has. Do not spare him; kill men and women, children and infants, oxen and sheep, camels and donkeys."[d]

4 Saul alerted the army, and at Telaim reviewed two hundred thousand foot soldiers and ten thousand men of Judah.* 5 Saul went to the city of Amalek and set up an ambush in the wadi. 6[e] He warned the Kenites: "Leave Amalek, turn aside and come down so I will not have to destroy you with them, for you were loyal to the Israelites when they came up from Egypt."* After the Kenites left, 7 Saul routed Amalek from Havilah to the approaches of Shur, on the frontier of Egypt.[f] 8 He took Agag, king of Amalek, alive, but the rest of the people he destroyed by the sword, putting them under the ban. 9 He and his troops spared Agag and the best of the fat sheep and oxen, and the lambs. They refused to put under the ban anything that was worthwhile, destroying only what was worthless and of no account.

*Samuel Rebukes Saul.* 10 Then the word of the LORD came to Samuel: 11 I regret having made Saul king, for he has turned from me and has not kept my command. At this Samuel grew angry and cried out to the LORD all night.[g] 12 Early in the morning he went to meet Saul, but was informed that Saul had gone to Carmel, where he set up a monument in his own honor, and that on his return he had gone down to Gilgal. 13 When Samuel came to him, Saul greeted him: "The LORD bless you! I have kept the command of the LORD." 14 But Samuel asked, "What, then, is this bleating of sheep that comes to my ears, the lowing of oxen that I hear?" 15 Saul replied: "They were brought from Amalek. The people spared the best sheep and oxen to sacrifice to the LORD, your God; but the rest we destroyed, putting them under the ban." 16 Samuel said to Saul: "Stop! Let me tell you what the LORD said to me last night." "Speak!" he replied. 17 Samuel then said: "Though little in your own eyes, are you not chief of the tribes of Israel? The LORD anointed you king of Israel[h] 18 and sent you on a mission, saying: Go and put the sinful Amalekites under a ban of destruction. Fight against them until you have exterminated them.[i] 19 Why then have you disobeyed the LORD? You have pounced on the spoil, thus doing what was evil in the LORD's sight."[j] 20 Saul explained to Samuel: "I did indeed obey the LORD and fulfill the mission on which the LORD sent me. I have brought back Agag, the king of Amalek, and, carrying out the ban, I have destroyed the Amalekites. 21 But from the spoil the army took sheep and oxen, the best of what had been banned, to sacrifice to the LORD your God in Gilgal."[k] 22[l] But Samuel said:

**15:1–35** The rejection of Saul sets the stage for the remainder of 1 Samuel. The audience knows that, in the ensuing struggle between David and Saul, David will triumph as king.

**15:3 Put under the ban**: this terminology mandates that all traces of the Amalekites (people, cities, animals, etc.) be exterminated. No plunder could be seized for personal use. In the light of Dt 20:16–18, this injunction would eliminate any tendency toward syncretism. The focus of this chapter is that Saul fails to execute this order.

**15:4** The numbers here are not realistic; compare 14:2.

**15:6** The Kenites honored the terms of an alliance with Israel.

*y:* 1 Sm 15:7. *z:* 1 Sm 18:20, 25; 31:2; 1 Chr 8:33; 9:39; 10:2. *a:* 1 Sm 9:1. *b:* Jos 3:9; 2 Kgs 20:16; Is 28:14. *c:* Ex 17:8–10, 16; Dt 25:17–19. *d:* 1 Sm 27:8; 30:17; Ex 17:16; Nm 24:20; Jos 6:17. *e:* Nm 24:21. *f:* 1 Sm 27:8. *g:* 1 Sm 15:35; Gn 6:6–7. *h:* 1 Sm 9:21. *i:* 1 Sm 28:18. *j:* 1 Sm 14:32. *k:* Lv 27:28. *l:* Prv 21:3; Hos 6:6; Am 5:21–25; Zec 10:2; Mt 9:13; 12:7; Heb 10:9.

"Does the LORD delight in burnt
offerings and sacrifices
as much as in obedience to the LORD's
command?
Obedience is better than sacrifice,
to listen, better than the fat of rams.*
23 For a sin of divination is rebellion,
and arrogance, the crime of idolatry.
Because you have rejected the word of
the LORD,
the LORD in turn has rejected you as
king."[m]

*Rejection of Saul.* 24 Saul admitted to Samuel: "I have sinned, for I have transgressed
the command of the LORD and your instructions. I feared the people and obeyed them.[n]
25 Now forgive my sin, and return with me,
that I may worship the LORD." 26 But Samuel
said to Saul, "I will not return with you, because you rejected the word of the LORD and
the LORD has rejected you as king of Israel."[o]
27 As Samuel turned to go, Saul seized a loose
end of his garment, and it tore off.[p] 28 So Samuel said to him: "The LORD has torn the kingdom of Israel from you this day, and has
given it to a neighbor of yours, who is better
than you.[q] 29 The Glory of Israel neither deceives nor repents,* for he is not a mortal who
repents."[r] 30 But Saul answered: "I have
sinned, yet honor me now before the elders
of my people and before Israel. Return with
me that I may worship the LORD your God."
31 And so Samuel returned with him, and Saul
worshiped the LORD.

*Samuel Executes Agag.* 32 Afterward Samuel commanded, "Bring Agag, king of Amalek, to me." Agag came to him struggling
and saying, "So it is bitter death!" 33 And
Samuel said,

"As your sword has made women
childless,
so shall your mother be childless
among women."

Then he cut Agag to pieces before the LORD
in Gilgal.[s] 34 Samuel departed for Ramah,
while Saul went up to his home in Gibeah of
Saul. 35 Never again, as long as he lived, did
Samuel see Saul. Yet he grieved over Saul,
because the LORD repented that he had made
him king of Israel.[t]

## CHAPTER 16

See RG 114

*Samuel Is Sent to Bethlehem.* 1[u] The
LORD said to Samuel: How long will you
grieve for Saul, whom I have rejected as king
of Israel? Fill your horn with oil, and be on
your way. I am sending you to Jesse of Bethlehem, for from among his sons I have decided on a king.* 2 But Samuel replied: "How
can I go? Saul will hear of it and kill me." To
this the LORD answered: Take a heifer along
and say, "I have come to sacrifice to the
LORD." 3 Invite Jesse to the sacrifice, and I
myself will tell you what to do; you are to
anoint for me the one I point out to you.[v]

*Samuel Anoints David.* 4 Samuel did as the
LORD had commanded him. When he entered
Bethlehem, the elders of the city came trembling to meet him and asked, "Is your visit
peaceful, O seer?" 5 He replied: "Yes! I have
come to sacrifice to the LORD. So purify
yourselves and celebrate with me today." He
also had Jesse and his sons purify themselves
and invited them to the sacrifice.[w] 6 As they
came, he looked at Eliab and thought,
"Surely the anointed is here before the
LORD." 7 But the LORD said to Samuel: Do
not judge from his appearance or from his
lofty stature, because I have rejected him.
God does not see as a mortal, who sees the
appearance. The LORD looks into the heart.[x]
8[y] Then Jesse called Abinadab and presented

**15:22** Samuel's reprimand echoes that of the prophets. Cultic practice is meaningless, even hypocritical, unless accompanied by an attentiveness to God's will.

**15:29 Nor repents**: the apparent contradiction between this verse and vv. 11, 35 leads some scholars to consider it a gloss (cf. Nm 23:19). However, this phrase can be understood to underscore the definitive character of Samuel's declaration that Saul has lost the kingship.

**16:1** David is anointed two more times after Saul's death (2 Sm 2:4; 5:3). In 17:28, his brother Eliab is not aware of David's selection. These repetitions and inconsistencies reflect the final editor's use of multiple sources.

*m:* Dt 18:10. *n:* 1 Sm 26:21. *o:* 1 Kgs 11:11, 30–31. *p:* 1 Sm 24:6; 1 Kgs 11:29–31. *q:* 1 Sm 28:17; 2 Sm 7:15–16. *r:* Nm 23:19. *s:* Ex 21:23; Jgs 8:21. *t:* 1 Sm 28:15. *u:* Ru 4:17–22; 1 Kgs 1:39; 1 Chr 11:3; Is 11:1; Mt 2:6; Lk 2:4. *v:* 1 Sm 9:13, 22, 24. *w:* 1 Sm 9:12–13; 20:26; Ex 19:10; Jb 1:5. *x:* 1 Sm 10:23–24; 1 Kgs 11:4; 1 Chr 28:9; Prv 15:11; Jer 17:10; 20:12; Lk 16:15; Acts 1:24. *y:* 1 Sm 17:12–13; 1 Chr 2:13–15.

## David's Anointing

IN THIS FIRST story about David in ch 16:1–13, he still plays a passive role. Even his name is not mentioned until the last verse. His being chosen, though the youngest and the least esteemed of eight brothers, agrees with the biblical motif of the younger being preferred to the elder: Abel to Cain (Gn 4:2–5), Isaac to Ishmael (Gn 21:9–13), Jacob to Esau (Gn 27:28–40), Joseph to Reuben (Gn 37:3–11; 49:3–4, 22–26). This indicates that not seniority, but suitability, is the decisive factor.

him before Samuel, who said, "The LORD has not chosen him." [9]Next Jesse presented Shammah, but Samuel said, "The LORD has not chosen this one either." [10]In the same way Jesse presented seven sons before Samuel, but Samuel said to Jesse, "The LORD has not chosen any one of these." [11]Then Samuel asked Jesse, "Are these all the sons you have?" Jesse replied, "There is still the youngest, but he is tending the sheep." Samuel said to Jesse, "Send for him; we will not sit down to eat until he arrives here."[z] [12]Jesse had the young man brought to them. He was ruddy, a youth with beautiful eyes, and good looking. The LORD said: There—anoint him, for this is the one![a] [13]Then Samuel, with the horn of oil in hand, anointed him in the midst of his brothers, and from that day on, the spirit of the LORD rushed upon David. Then Samuel set out for Ramah.[b]

***David Wins Saul's Approval.*** [14]* [c] The spirit of the LORD had departed from Saul, and he was tormented by an evil spirit from the LORD. [15]So the servants of Saul said to him: "Look! An evil spirit from God is tormenting you. [16]If your lordship will order it, we, your servants here attending to you, will look for a man skilled in playing the harp. When the evil spirit from God comes upon you, he will play and you will feel better." [17]Saul then told his servants, "Find me a good harpist and bring him to me." [18][d] One of the servants spoke up: "I have observed that a son of Jesse of Bethlehem is a skillful harpist. He is also a brave warrior, an able speaker, and a handsome young man. The LORD is certainly with him."

***David Made Armor-Bearer.*** [19]Accordingly, Saul dispatched messengers to ask Jesse to send him his son David, who was with the flock. [20]Then Jesse took five loaves of bread, a skin of wine, and a young goat, and sent them to Saul with his son David.[e] [21]Thus David came to Saul and entered his service. Saul became very fond of him and made him his armor-bearer.[f] [22]Saul sent Jesse the message, "Let David stay in my service, for he meets with my approval." [23]Whenever the spirit from God came upon Saul, David would take the harp and play, and Saul would be relieved and feel better, for the evil spirit would leave him.

### CHAPTER 17

See RG 114

***The Challenge of Goliath.*** [1]The Philistines rallied their forces for battle at Socoh in Judah and camped between Socoh and Azekah at Ephes-dammim. [2]Saul and the Israelites rallied and camped in the valley of the Elah, drawing up their battle line to meet the Philistines. [3]The Philistines were stationed on one hill and the Israelites on an opposite hill, with a valley between them.

[4]A champion named Goliath of Gath came out from the Philistine camp; he was six cubits and a span* tall. [5]He had a bronze

**16:14–23** These verses explain Saul's loss of divine favor and David's rise to power. By approving the young man, Saul identifies David as his legitimate successor. Of the two traditions in the Hebrew text about David's entry into Saul's service, the Greek translation retains only the one found in vv. 14–23; 17:1–11, 32–54. **An evil spirit from the LORD**: Saul's erratic behavior is attributed to a change in the Lord's relationship with him. Cf. Jgs 9:23, where the Lord puts an evil spirit between Abimelech and the citizens of Shechem.

**17:4 Six cubits and a span**: about nine feet nine inches (a cubit equals about eighteen inches; a span equals about eight inches). The Greek text and 4QSam[a] read: "four cubits and a span" (six feet nine inches). The description of the Philistine's might and his powerful weapons contrasts with the picture of the youthful David who trusts in God.

*z:* 1 Sm 17:15, 28, 34; 2 Sm 7:8; Ps 78:70–71. *a:* 1 Sm 9:2. *b:* 1 Sm 10:6; 11:6; Jgs 3:10; 9:9; Sir 46:13. *c:* 1 Sm 18:10–11. *d:* 1 Sm 18:12, 14, 28; 2 Sm 5:10; 17:8; Jn 3:2. *e:* 1 Sm 9:7–8; 10:3–4; 16:1; 17:17–19. *f:* 1 Sm 18:2.

helmet on his head and wore a bronze breastplate of scale armor weighing five thousand shekels, [6]bronze greaves, and had a bronze scimitar slung from his shoulders. [7]The shaft of his javelin was like a weaver's beam, and its iron head weighed six hundred shekels.* His shield-bearer went ahead of him.[g] [8]He stood and shouted to the ranks of Israel: "Why come out in battle formation? I am a Philistine, and you are Saul's servants. Choose one of your men, and have him come down to me. [9]If he beats me in combat and kills me, we will be your vassals; but if I beat him and kill him, you shall be our vassals and serve us." [10]The Philistine continued: "I defy the ranks of Israel today. Give me a man and let us fight together." [11]When Saul and all Israel heard this challenge of the Philistine, they were stunned and terrified.

***David Comes to the Camp.**** [12]David was the son of an Ephrathite named Jesse from Bethlehem in Judah who had eight sons. In the days of Saul Jesse was old and well on in years.[h] [13]The three oldest sons of Jesse had followed Saul to war; the names of these three sons who had gone off to war were Eliab the firstborn; Abinadab the second; and Shammah the third. [14]David was the youngest. While the three oldest had joined Saul, [15]David would come and go from Saul's presence to tend his father's sheep at Bethlehem.[i]

[16]Meanwhile the Philistine came forward and took his stand morning and evening for forty days.

[17]Now Jesse said to his son David: "Take this ephah of roasted grain and these ten loaves for your brothers, and bring them quickly to your brothers in the camp. [18]Also take these ten cheeses for the field officer. Greet your brothers and bring home some token from them. [19]Saul and your brothers, together with all Israel, are at war with the Philistines in the valley of the Elah." [20]Early the next morning, having left the flock with a shepherd, David packed up and set out, as Jesse had commanded him. He reached the barricade of the camp just as the army, on their way to the battleground, were shouting their battle cry.[j] [21]The Israelites and the Philistines drew up opposite each other in battle array. [22]David entrusted what he had brought to the keeper of the baggage and hastened to the battle line, where he greeted his brothers.[k] [23]While he was talking with them, the Philistine champion, by name Goliath of Gath, came up from the ranks of the Philistines and spoke as before, and David listened. [24]When the Israelites saw the man, they all retreated before him, terrified. [25]The Israelites had been saying: "Do you see this man coming up? He comes up to insult Israel. The king will make whoever kills him a very wealthy man. He will give his daughter to him and declare his father's family exempt from taxes in Israel."[l] [26]David now said to the men standing near him: "How will the man who kills this Philistine and frees Israel from disgrace be rewarded? Who is this uncircumcised Philistine that he should insult the armies of the living God?"[m] [27]They repeated the same words to him and said, "That is how the man who kills him will be rewarded." [28]When Eliab, his oldest brother, heard him speaking with the men, he grew angry with David and said: "Why did you come down? With whom have you left those sheep in the wilderness? I know your arrogance and dishonest heart. You came down to enjoy the battle!"[n] [29]David protested, "What have I done now? I was only talking." [30]He turned from him to another and asked the same question; and everyone gave him the same answer as before. [31]The words that David had spoken were overheard and reported to Saul, who sent for him.

***David Challenges Goliath.*** [32]Then David spoke to Saul: "My lord should not lose heart. Let your servant go and fight this

**17:7 Six hundred shekels**: over fifteen pounds.

**17:12–31** Here the final editor begins an alternative account of David's encounter with the Philistine hero, which continues in vv. 50–51 and concludes in 17:55–18:5.

*g:* 2 Sm 21:19; 1 Chr 11:23; 20:5. *h:* 1 Sm 16:1, 10; Ru 1:2. *i:* 1 Sm 16:11; 18:2; 2 Sm 7:8; Ps 78:70–71. *j:* 1 Sm 26:5. *k:* 1 Sm 25:13. *l:* 1 Sm 18:17; Jos 15:16. *m:* 1 Sm 18:25; Dt 5:26; Jgs 15:18; 2 Kgs 19:4; Is 37:4; Jer 10:10. *n:* 1 Sm 16:6.

Philistine." [33]But Saul answered David, "You cannot go up against this Philistine and fight with him, for you are only a youth, while he has been a warrior from his youth." [34][o] Then David told Saul: "Your servant used to tend his father's sheep, and whenever a lion or bear came to carry off a sheep from the flock, [35]I would chase after it, attack it, and snatch the prey from its mouth. If it attacked me, I would seize it by the throat, strike it, and kill it. [36]Your servant has killed both a lion and a bear. This uncircumcised Philistine will be as one of them, because he has insulted the armies of the living God."

[37]David continued: "The same LORD who delivered me from the claws of the lion and the bear will deliver me from the hand of this Philistine." Saul answered David, "Go! the LORD will be with you."[p]

***Preparation for the Encounter.*** [38]Then Saul dressed David in his own tunic, putting a bronze helmet on his head and arming him with a coat of mail. [39]David also fastened Saul's sword over the tunic. He walked with difficulty, however, since he had never worn armor before. He said to Saul, "I cannot go in these, because I am not used to them." So he took them off. [40]Then, staff in hand, David selected five smooth stones from the wadi and put them in the pocket of his shepherd's bag. With his sling in hand, he approached the Philistine.

***David's Victory.*** [41]* With his shield-bearer marching before him, the Philistine advanced closer and closer to David. [42]When he sized David up and saw that he was youthful, ruddy, and handsome in appearance, he began to deride him. [43]He said to David, "Am I a dog that you come against me with a staff?" Then the Philistine cursed David by his gods [44]and said to him, "Come here to me, and I will feed your flesh to the birds of the air and the beasts of the field."[q] [45]David answered him: "You come against me with sword and spear and scimitar, but I come against you in the name of the LORD of hosts, the God of the armies of Israel whom you have insulted. [46]Today the LORD shall deliver you into my hand; I will strike you down and cut off your head. This very day I will feed your dead body and the dead bodies of the Philistine army to the birds of the air and the beasts of the field; thus the whole land shall learn that Israel has a God. [47]All this multitude, too, shall learn that it is not by sword or spear that the LORD saves. For the battle belongs to the LORD, who shall deliver you into our hands."[r]

[48]The Philistine then moved to meet David at close quarters, while David ran quickly toward the battle line to meet the Philistine. [49]David put his hand into the bag and took out a stone, hurled it with the sling, and struck the Philistine on the forehead. The stone embedded itself in his brow, and he fell on his face to the ground. [50]Thus David triumphed over the Philistine with sling and stone; he struck the Philistine dead, and did it without a sword in his hand.[s] [51]Then David ran and stood over him; with the Philistine's own sword which he drew from its sheath he killed him, and cut off his head.[t]

***Flight of the Philistines.*** When the Philistines saw that their hero was dead, they fled. [52]Then the men of Israel and Judah sprang up with a battle cry and pursued them to the approaches of Gath and to the gates of Ekron, and Philistines fell wounded along the road from Shaaraim as far as Gath and Ekron. [53]When they returned from their pursuit of the Philistines, the Israelites looted their camp. [54][u] David took the head of the Philistine and brought it to Jerusalem; but he kept Goliath's armor in his own tent.*

***David Presented to Saul.*** [55]As Saul watched David go out to meet the Philistine, he asked his general Abner, "Abner, whose son is that young man?" Abner replied, "On your life, O king, I have no idea."[v] [56]And the king said, "Find out whose son the lad is." [57]So when David returned from slaying the Philistine, Abner escorted him into Saul's

**17:41–47** The two combatants trade theological taunts. God uses the most unlikely opponent to destroy Goliath.

**17:54** Jerusalem was a Jebusite city; it came under Israelite control only at the beginning of David's rule. As a young shepherd, David would not have had a military tent. In 21:10, Goliath's sword is in the Nob temple.

*o:* Jgs 14:6; Sir 47:3. *p:* Prv 28:1. *q:* Dt 28:26; Ps 79:2–3; Is 18:6; Jer 7:33; 15:3. *r:* 1 Sm 14:6, 10; Ps 33:16. *s:* 1 Mc 4:30; Sir 47:4. *t:* 1 Sm 21:10. *u:* 1 Sm 31:9. *v:* 1 Sm 14:50.

presence. David was still holding the Philistine's head. [58]Saul then asked him, "Whose son are you, young man?" David replied, "I am the son of your servant Jesse of Bethlehem."

## CHAPTER 18

See RG 114

***David and Jonathan.*** [1]By the time David finished speaking with Saul, Jonathan's life became bound up with David's life; he loved him as his very self.[w] [2]Saul retained David on that day and did not allow him to return to his father's house.[x] [3]Jonathan and David made a covenant, because Jonathan loved him as his very self. [4]Jonathan took off* the cloak he was wearing and handed it over to David, along with his military dress, even his sword, bow, and belt.[y] [5]David then carried out successfully every mission on which Saul sent him. So Saul put him in charge of his soldiers; this met with the approval of the whole army, even Saul's officers.

***Saul's Jealousy.*** [6]At the approach of Saul and David, on David's return after striking down the Philistine, women came out from all the cities of Israel to meet Saul the king, singing and dancing, with tambourines, joyful songs, and stringed instruments.* [z] [7]The women played and sang:

"Saul has slain his thousands,
  David his tens of thousands."[a]

[8]Saul was very angry and resentful of the song, for he thought: "They give David tens of thousands, but only thousands to me. All that remains for him is the kingship." [9]From that day on, Saul kept a jealous eye on David.

[10][b]The next day an evil spirit from God rushed upon Saul, and he raged in his house. David was in attendance, playing the harp as at other times, while Saul was holding his spear. [11]Saul poised the spear, thinking, "I will nail David to the wall!" But twice David escaped him. [12]Saul then began to fear David because the LORD was with him but had turned away from Saul. [13]Saul sent him out of his presence and appointed him a field officer. So David led the people on their military expeditions [14]and prospered in all his ways, for the LORD was with him. [15]Seeing how he prospered, Saul feared David. [16]But all Israel and Judah loved David, since he led them on their expeditions.* [c]

***Saul Plots Against David.*** [17]Saul said to David, "Look, I will give you my older daughter, Merob, in marriage if you become my warrior and fight the battles of the LORD." Saul thought, "I will not lay a hand on him. Let the hand of the Philistines strike him."[d] [18]But David answered Saul: "Who am I? And who are my kindred or my father's clan in Israel that I should become the king's son-in-law?" [19]But when the time came for Saul's daughter Merob to be given to David, she was given as wife to Adriel the Meholathite instead.[e]

[20]Now Saul's daughter Michal loved David. When this was reported to Saul, he was pleased.[f] [21]He thought, "I will offer her to him as a trap, so that the hand of the Philistines may strike him." So for the second time Saul said to David, "You shall become my son-in-law today." [22]Saul then ordered his servants, "Speak to David privately and say: The king favors you, and all his officers love you. You should become son-in-law to the king." [23]But when Saul's servants mentioned this to David, he said: "Is becoming the king's son-in-law a trivial matter in your eyes? I am poor and insignificant." [24]When his servants reported David's answer to him, [25]Saul commanded them, "Say this to David: The king desires no other price for the bride than the foreskins of one hundred Philistines, that he may thus take vengeance on his enemies." Saul intended to have David

**18:4 Jonathan took off**: with the details in this verse, the narrator identifies David as Jonathan's replacement and Saul's heir to the throne. Cf. 23:17 and Gn 41:39–43.

**18:6 Stringed instruments**: perhaps a lute-like instrument with three strings; the Hebrew word, *shalshim*, perhaps related to the root *shlsh* ("three"), occurs only here in the Old Testament.

**18:16 Led them on their expeditions**: lit., "go out and come in," i.e., through the city gates; an idiom for military victory.

*w:* 1 Sm 19:1–7; 20:17; 23:16; 2 Sm 1:26; 9:1. *x:* 1 Sm 16:21; 17:15. *y:* 2 Sm 1:22. *z:* Ex 15:20–21; Jgs 11:34; Jdt 15:12. *a:* 1 Sm 21:12; 29:5; Ps 91:7; Sir 47:6–7. *b:* 1 Sm 16:14; 19:9–10; 20:33; 22:6; 26:8. *c:* 2 Sm 5:2. *d:* 1 Sm 14:49; 17:25. *e:* 1 Sm 21:8; 24:16. *f:* 1 Sm 14:49; 25:44; 26:23; 2 Sm 3:13.

fall into the hands of the Philistines.[g] 26 When the servants reported this offer to David, he was pleased with the prospect of becoming the king's son-in-law. Before the year was up, 27 David arose and went with his men and slew two hundred Philistines. He brought back their foreskins and counted them out before the king that he might become the king's son-in-law. So Saul gave him his daughter Michal as wife. 28 Then Saul realized that the LORD was with David and that his own daughter Michal loved David. 29 So Saul feared David all the more and was his enemy ever after.

30 The Philistine chiefs continued to make forays, but each time they took the field, David was more successful against them than any of Saul's other officers, and his name was held in great esteem.

## CHAPTER 19

See RG 118

***Persecution of David.*** 1 Saul discussed his intention to kill David with his son Jonathan and with all his servants. But Saul's son Jonathan, who was very fond of David,[h] 2 told him: "My father Saul is trying to kill you. Therefore, please be on your guard tomorrow morning; stay out of sight and remain in hiding. 3 I, however, will go out and stand beside my father in the countryside where you are, and will speak to him about you. If I learn anything, I will let you know." 4 Jonathan then spoke well of David to his father Saul, telling him: "The king should not harm his servant David. He has not harmed you, but has helped you very much by his deeds.* 5 When he took his life in his hands and killed the Philistine, and the LORD won a great victory for all Israel, you were glad to see it. Why, then, should you become guilty of shedding innocent blood by killing David without cause?"[i] 6 Saul heeded Jonathan's plea and swore, "As the LORD lives, he shall not be killed." 7 So Jonathan summoned David and repeated the whole conversation to him. He then brought David to Saul, and David served him as before.

***David Escapes from Saul.*** 8 When war broke out again, David went out to fight against the Philistines and inflicted such a great defeat upon them that they fled from him. 9[j] Then an evil spirit from the LORD came upon Saul as he was sitting in his house with spear in hand while David was playing the harp nearby. 10 Saul tried to pin David to the wall with the spear, but David eluded Saul, and the spear struck only the wall, while David got away safely.

11 The same night, Saul sent messengers to David's house to guard it, planning to kill him in the morning. David's wife Michal informed him, "Unless you run for your life tonight, tomorrow you will be killed."* 12 Then Michal let David down through a window, and he made his escape in safety.[k] 13 Michal took the teraphim* and laid it in the bed, putting a tangle of goat's hair at its head and covering it with a blanket.[l] 14 When Saul sent officers to arrest David, she said, "He is sick." 15 Saul, however, sent the officers back to see David and commanded them, "Bring him up to me in his bed, that I may kill him." 16 But when the messengers entered, they found the teraphim in the bed, with the tangle of goat's hair at its head. 17 Saul asked Michal: "Why did you lie to me like this? You have helped my enemy to get away!" Michal explained to Saul: "He threatened me, saying 'Let me go or I will kill you.' "

***David and Saul in Ramah.*** 18 When David got safely away, he went to Samuel in Ramah, informing him of all that Saul had done to him. Then he and Samuel went to stay in Naioth.* 19 When Saul was told that David was at Naioth in Ramah, 20 he sent officers to arrest David. But when they saw the band of prophets presided over by Samuel in a prophetic state, the spirit of God came upon them and

**19:4** Jonathan reminds Saul that David has served him loyally and done nothing to earn a traitor's death. Cf. 24:18–20.

**19:11** This story may have originally followed 18:29, placing the episode of David's escape on the night of his marriage with Michal.

**19:13 Teraphim**: a life-sized image of a household god in human form; cf. also note on Gn 31:19. Elsewhere in the Deuteronomistic History, use of teraphim is condemned (15:23; 2 Kgs 23:24).

**19:18 Naioth**: meaning "the pastures." This place appears only in chaps. 19–20 and is associated with Ramah.

*g:* 1 Sm 17:26; Gn 34:12. *h:* 1 Sm 18:1; 20:1–3. *i:* 1 Sm 17:55–56; Dt 19:10; Ps 119:109. *j:* 1 Sm 16:14; 18:10–11. *k:* Jos 2:15; Acts 9:25; 2 Cor 11:33. *l:* Gn 31:19; Jgs 17:5; 18:14, 18, 20; Ez 21:26.

they too fell into the prophetic ecstasy.[m] [21]Informed of this, Saul sent other messengers, who also fell into the prophetic ecstasy. For the third time Saul sent messengers, but they too fell into a prophetic ecstasy.

***Saul Among the Prophets.*** [22]Finally Saul went to Ramah himself. Arriving at the large cistern in Secu, he asked, "Where are Samuel and David?" Someone answered, "At Naioth in Ramah." [23]As he walked from there to Naioth in Ramah, the spirit of God came upon him also, and he continued on, acting like a prophet until he reached Naioth in Ramah. [24]Then he, too, stripped himself of his garments and remained in a prophetic state in the presence of Samuel;* all that day and night he lay naked. That is why they say, "Is Saul also among the prophets?"[n]

## CHAPTER 20

See RG 118

***David Consults with Jonathan.*** [1]David fled from Naioth in Ramah, and went to Jonathan. "What have I done?" he asked him. "What crime or what offense does your father hold against me that he seeks my life?"[o] [2]Jonathan answered him: "Heaven forbid that you should die! My father does nothing, great or small, without telling me. Why, then, should my father conceal this from me? It cannot be true!" [3]But David replied: "Your father is well aware that I am favored with your friendship, so he has decided, 'Jonathan must not know about this or he will be grieved.' Nevertheless, as the LORD lives and as you live, there is only a step between me and death." [4]Jonathan then said to David, "I will do whatever you say." [5]David answered: "Tomorrow is the new moon, when I should in fact dine with the king. Let me go and hide in the open country until evening.[p] [6]If it turns out that your father misses me, say, 'David urged me to let him go on short notice to his city Bethlehem, because his whole clan is holding its seasonal sacrifice there.'[q] [7]If he says, 'Very well,' your servant is safe. But if he becomes quite angry, you can be sure he has planned some harm. [8r] Do this kindness for your servant because of the LORD's covenant into which you brought us: if I am guilty, kill me yourself! Why should you give me up to your father?" [9]But Jonathan answered: "Not I! If ever I find out that my father is determined to harm you, I will certainly let you know." [10]David then asked Jonathan, "Who will tell me if your father gives you a harsh answer?"

***Mutual Agreement.*** [11]Jonathan replied to David, "Come, let us go out into the field." When they were out in the open country together, [12]Jonathan said to David: "As the LORD, the God of Israel, lives, I will sound out my father about this time tomorrow. Whether he is well disposed toward David or not, I will inform you. [13s] Should it please my father to bring any harm upon you, may the LORD do thus to Jonathan and more,* if I do not inform you of it and send you on your way in peace. May the LORD be with you even as he was with my father. [14]Only this: if I am still alive, may you show me the kindness of the LORD. But if I die, [15]never cut off your kindness from my house. And when the LORD cuts off all the enemies of David from the face of the land, [16]the name of Jonathan must never be cut off from the family of David, or the LORD will make you answer for it." [17]And in his love for David, Jonathan renewed his oath to him, because he loved him as he loved himself.

[18]Jonathan then said to him: "Tomorrow is the new moon; you will be missed, since your place will be vacant. [19]On the third day you will be missed all the more. Go to the spot where you hid on the other occasion and wait near the mound there.[t] [20]On the third day of the month I will shoot arrows to the side of it, as though aiming at a target. [21]I

**19:24 In the presence of Samuel**: this verse, which disagrees with 15:35, is further evidence of the diverse origins of these accounts. **"Is Saul also among the prophets?"**: although similar to the story of Saul's prophetic ecstasy in 10:10–13, this account offers a more disparaging portrait of Saul.

**20:13** See note on 3:17.

*m:* 1 Sm 10:5–6, 10; Nm 11:25. *n:* 1 Sm 10:10–12; 2 Sm 6:20. *o:* 1 Sm 19:1–7, 11–17; 21:11; 27:4; Gn 31:36. *p:* Nm 10:10; 28:11–15; Ezr 3:5; Neh 10:34. *q:* 1 Sm 17:12. *r:* 1 Sm 18:3; 23:17–18. *s:* 1 Sm 10:7; 17:37; 18:12, 14; 24:22–23; 2 Sm 9:1–13; 21:7. *t:* 1 Sm 19:1–7.

will then send my attendant to recover the arrows. If in fact I say to him, 'Look, the arrow is this side of you; pick it up,' come, for you are safe. As the LORD lives, there will be nothing to fear. 22 But if I say to the boy, 'Look, the arrow is beyond you,' go, for the LORD sends you away. 23 However, in the matter which you and I have discussed, the LORD shall be between you and me forever." 24 So David hid in the open country.

***David's Absence.*** On the day of the new moon, when the king sat down at the feast to dine, 25 he took his usual place against the wall. Jonathan sat facing him, while Abner sat at the king's side. David's place was vacant. 26[u] Saul, however, said nothing that day, for he thought, "He must have become unclean by accident."* 27 On the next day, the second day of the month, David's place was still vacant. So Saul asked his son Jonathan, "Why has the son of Jesse not come to table yesterday or today?" 28 Jonathan explained to Saul: "David pleaded with me to let him go to Bethlehem. 29 'Please let me go,' he begged, 'for we are having a clan sacrifice in our city, and my brothers insist on my presence. Now then, if you think well of me, give me leave to visit my brothers.' That is why he has not come to the king's table." 30 But Saul grew angry with Jonathan and said to him: "Son of a rebellious woman, do I not know that, to your own disgrace and to the disgrace of your mother's nakedness, you are the companion of Jesse's son? 31 For as long as the son of Jesse lives upon the earth, you cannot make good your claim to the kingship!* Now send for him, and bring him to me, for he must die."[v] 32 But Jonathan argued with his father Saul: "Why should he die? What has he done?" 33 At this Saul brandished his spear to strike him, and thus Jonathan learned that his father was determined to kill David.[w] 34 Jonathan sprang up from the table in a rage and ate nothing that second day of the month, because he was grieved on David's account, and because his father had humiliated him.

***Jonathan's Farewell.*** 35 The next morning Jonathan, accompanied by a young boy, went out into the field for his appointment with David. 36 There he said to the boy, "Run and find the arrows." And as the boy ran, he shot an arrow past him. 37 When the boy made for the spot where Jonathan had shot the arrow, Jonathan called after him, "The arrow is farther on!" 38 Again he called to the boy, "Hurry, be quick, don't delay!" Jonathan's boy picked up the arrow and brought it to his master. 39 The boy suspected nothing; only Jonathan and David knew what was meant. 40 Then Jonathan gave his weapons to his boy and said to him, "Go, take them to the city." 41 When the boy had gone, David rose from beside the mound and fell on his face to the ground three times in homage. They kissed each other and wept aloud together. 42[x] At length Jonathan said to David, "Go in peace, in keeping with what the two of us have sworn by the name of the LORD: 'The LORD shall be between you and me, and between your offspring and mine forever.' "

## CHAPTER 21

See RG 118

1 Then David departed on his way, while Jonathan went back into the city.

***The Holy Bread.*** 2 David went to Ahimelech, the priest of Nob, who came trembling to meet him. He asked, "Why are you alone? Is there no one with you?"* [y] 3 David answered the priest: "The king gave me a commission and told me, 'Do not let anyone know anything about the business on which I have sent you or the commission I have given you.' For that reason I have arranged a particular meeting place with my men. 4[z] Now what do you have on hand? Give me five loaves, or whatever you can find." 5* But the priest

**20:26** The meal on the first day of the month would have had religious overtones, and a ritual impurity (Lv 15:16; Dt 23:10–12) would have barred David from sharing in it.

**20:31 Your claim to the kingship**: Saul admits his intention that Jonathan should succeed him and that David is a threat to his lineage (cf. 23:17). However Jonathan has already acknowledged David's kingship (18:3–4) and his own subservient role (20:13–16).

**21:2** Ahimelech realizes that he risks incurring Saul's anger if David has come to Nob as a fugitive.

*u:* 1 Sm 16:5; Lv 7:20–21; 15:1–3. *v:* 2 Sm 12:5. *w:* 1 Sm 18:11. *x:* 2 Sm 9:1; 21:7. *y:* 1 Sm 16:4; Is 10:32; Mk 2:26. *z:* Lv 24:5, 9.

replied to David, "I have no ordinary bread on hand, only holy bread; if the men have abstained from women, you may eat some of that." 6David answered the priest: "We have indeed stayed away from women. In the past whenever I went out on a campaign, all the young men were consecrated—even for an ordinary campaign. All the more so are they consecrated with their weapons today!" 7So the priest gave him holy bread, for no other bread was on hand except the showbread which had been removed from before the LORD and replaced by fresh bread when it was taken away.[a] 8One of Saul's servants was there that day, detained before the LORD;* his name was Doeg the Edomite, the chief of Saul's shepherds.[b]

***The Sword of Goliath.*** 9David then asked Ahimelech: "Do you have a spear or a sword on hand? I brought along neither my sword nor my weapons, because the king's business was urgent." 10The priest replied: "The sword of Goliath the Philistine, whom you killed in the Valley of Elah, is here wrapped in a garment behind an ephod.* If you wish to take it, do so; there is no sword here except that one." "There is none like it," David cried, "give it to me!"[c]

***David a Fugitive.*** 11That same day David fled from Saul, going to Achish, king of Gath.[d] 12But the servants of Achish said to him, "Is this not David, the king of the land? Is it not for him that during their dances they sing out,

'Saul has slain his thousands,
David his tens of thousands'?"[e]

13David took note of these remarks and became very much afraid of Achish, king of Gath.* 14So, he feigned insanity in front of them and acted like a madman in their custody, drumming on the doors of the gate and drooling onto his beard. 15Finally Achish said to his servants: "You see the man is mad. Why did you bring him to me? 16Do I not have enough madmen, that you bring this one to rant in my presence? Should this fellow come into my house?"

## CHAPTER 22

See RG 118

1David left Gath and escaped to the cave of Adullam. When his brothers and the rest of his family heard about it, they came down to him there.[f] 2He was joined by all those in difficulties or in debt, or embittered,* and became their leader. About four hundred men were with him.

3From there David went to Mizpeh of Moab and said to the king of Moab, "Let my father and mother stay with you, until I learn what God will do for me." 4He left them with the king of Moab; they stayed with him as long as David remained in the stronghold.*

5But Gad the prophet said to David: "Do not remain in the stronghold! Leave! Go to the land of Judah." And so David left and went to the forest of Hereth.[g]

***Doeg Betrays Ahimelech.*** 6Now Saul heard that David and his men had been located. At the time he was sitting in Gibeah under a tamarisk tree on the high place, holding his spear, while all his servants stood by him.[h] 7So he said to them: "Listen, men of Benjamin! Will the son of Jesse give all of you fields and vineyards? Will he appoint any of you an officer over a thousand or a hundred men?[i] 8Is that why you have all

**21:5–6** According to Lv 24:5–9, the showbread consisted of twelve loaves that were replaced each sabbath. Since the old bread was to be consumed by the priests, Ahimelech questions David regarding the ritual purity of his men (see 2 Sm 11:11). David's answer supposes the discipline of a military campaign under the conditions of "holy war" (Dt 23:10–15).

**21:8 Detained before the LORD**: perhaps to fulfill a ritual obligation. David's arrival at Nob seems to coincide with a festival day, since the showbread has recently been replaced with fresh bread. **Shepherds**: i.e., Saul's palace guard. Cf. 22:9–10, where Doeg has easy access to Saul.

**21:10 Ephod**: here an object or image large enough to conceal Goliath's sword. Cf. Gideon's ephod in Jgs 8:27.

**21:13 Gath**: a Philistine city (see note on 5:1–12), the home of Goliath.

**22:2 Embittered**: Hebrew *mar-nephesh*, "bitter of spirit," used of Hannah, deprived of a child, in 1:10, and of David's soldiers, whose women and children the Amalekites had seized (30:6). Cf. also 2 Sm 17:8. David becomes a hero for those who have endured loss or deprivation.

**22:4–5 Stronghold**: seemingly connected with the cave complex in v. 1.

*a:* Lv 24:5–9; Mt 12:3–4; Mk 2:26; Lk 6:3–5. *b:* 1 Sm 22:9. *c:* 1 Sm 17:51, 54. *d:* 1 Sm 27:2; 29:5. *e:* 1 Sm 18:7; 29:5. *f:* 2 Sm 23:13; Ps 63; Mi 1:15. *g:* 2 Sm 24:11–13. *h:* 1 Sm 14:2; Jgs 4:5. *i:* 1 Sm 8:14.

conspired against me? Why no one told me that my son had made a pact with the son of Jesse? None of you has shown compassion for me by revealing to me that my son has incited my servant to ambush me, as is the case today.”[j] 9[k] Then Doeg the Edomite, who was standing with Saul’s officers, spoke up: “I saw the son of Jesse come to Ahimelech, son of Ahitub, in Nob. 10He consulted the LORD for him, furnished him with provisions, and gave him the sword of Goliath the Philistine.”

***Slaughter of the Priests.*** 11So the king summoned Ahimelech the priest, son of Ahitub, and all his family, the priests in Nob. They all came to the king. 12“Listen, son of Ahitub!” Saul declared. “Yes, my lord,” he replied. 13Saul questioned him, “Why have you conspired against me with the son of Jesse by giving him food and a sword and by consulting God for him, that he might rise up against me in ambush, as is the case today?” 14Ahimelech answered the king: “Who among all your servants is as loyal as David, the king’s son-in-law, captain of your bodyguard, and honored in your own house? 15Is this the first time I have consulted God for him? No indeed! Let not the king accuse his servant or anyone in my family of such a thing. Your servant knows nothing at all, great or small, about the whole matter.” 16But the king said, “You shall certainly die, Ahimelech, with all your family.” 17The king then commanded his guards standing by him: “Turn and kill the priests of the LORD, for they gave David a hand. They knew he was a fugitive and yet failed to inform me.” But the king’s servants refused to raise a hand to strike the priests of the LORD.[l]

18The king therefore commanded Doeg, “You, turn and kill the priests!” So Doeg the Edomite himself turned and killed the priests that day—eighty-five who wore the linen ephod. 19Saul also put the priestly city of Nob to the sword, including men and women, children and infants, and oxen, donkeys and sheep.

***Abiathar Escapes.*** 20One son of Ahimelech, son of Ahitub, named Abiathar,* escaped and fled to David.[m] 21When Abiathar told David that Saul had slain the priests of the LORD, 22David said to him: “I knew that day, when Doeg the Edomite was there, that he would certainly tell Saul. I am responsible for the slaughter of all your family. 23Stay with me. Do not be afraid; whoever seeks your life must seek my life also. You are under my protection.”*

## CHAPTER 23

See RG 118

***Keilah Liberated.*** 1David was informed that the Philistines were attacking Keilah and plundering the threshing floors.[n] 2So he consulted the LORD, asking, “Shall I go and attack these Philistines?” The LORD answered, Go, attack them, and free Keilah.[o] 3But David’s men said to him: “Even in Judah we have reason to fear. How much more so if we go to Keilah against the forces of the Philistines!” 4Again David consulted the LORD, who answered: Go down to Keilah, for I will deliver the Philistines into your power.[p] 5So David went with his men to Keilah and fought against the Philistines. He drove off their cattle and inflicted a severe defeat on them, and freed the inhabitants of Keilah.

6Abiathar, son of Ahimelech, who had fled to David, went down with David to Keilah, taking the ephod with him.[q]

***Flight from Keilah.*** 7When Saul was told that David had entered Keilah, he thought: “God has put him in my hand, for he has boxed himself in by entering a city with gates and bars.” 8Saul then called all the army to war, in order to go down to Keilah and besiege David and his men. 9When David found out that Saul was planning to harm him, he said to the priest Abiathar, “Bring

**22:20 Abiathar**: the sole survivor of Eli’s household (2:27–36). David now has in his service the only priest of the Lord left in the land and exclusive access to the ephod for consulting the Lord (cf. 23:9–13). David later appoints Abiathar co-high priest with Zadok in Jerusalem (2 Sm 20:25), but Solomon exiles Abiathar to Anathoth when the priest does not support his bid for the throne. Cf. 1 Kgs 2:26–27.

**22:23 You are under my protection**: once again a sharp contrast is drawn between Saul, who kills the Lord’s priests, and David, who protects the lone survivor.

*j:* 1 Sm 18:3; 20:8; 23:18. *k:* 1 Sm 21:2–10; Ps 52. *l:* 1 Sm 2:31, 33; 21:7. *m:* 1 Sm 23:6; 30:7; 2 Sm 20:25; 1 Kgs 2:26–27. *n:* Jos 15:44. *o:* 1 Sm 28:6. *p:* 1 Sm 17:47. *q:* 1 Sm 22:20; 30:7.

the ephod here."[r] [10]"LORD God of Israel," David prayed, "your servant has heard that Saul plans to come to Keilah, to destroy the city on my account. [11]Will they hand me over? Will Saul come down as your servant has heard? LORD God of Israel, tell your servant." The LORD answered: He will come down. [12]David then asked, "Will the citizens of Keilah deliver me and my men into the hand of Saul?" The LORD answered: They will deliver you. [13]So David and his men, about six hundred in number, left Keilah and wandered from place to place. When Saul was informed that David had fled from Keilah, he did not go forth.

*David and Jonathan in Horesh.* [14]David now lived in the strongholds in the wilderness, or in the barren hill country near Ziph. Though Saul sought him continually, the LORD did not deliver David into his hand. [15]While David was in the wilderness of Ziph at Horesh he was afraid that Saul had come out to seek his life. [16]Then Saul's son, Jonathan, came down to David at Horesh and encouraged him in the LORD.[s] [17]He said to him: "Have no fear, my father Saul shall not lay a hand to you. You shall be king of Israel* and I shall be second to you. Even my father Saul knows this."[t] [18]The two of them made a covenant before the LORD in Horesh, where David remained, while Jonathan returned to his home.[u]

*Treachery of the Ziphites.* [19]Some of the Ziphites went up to Saul in Gibeah and said, "David is hiding among us in the strongholds at Horesh on the hill of Hachilah, south of Jeshimon.[v] [20]Therefore, whenever the king wishes to come down, let him do so. It will be our task to deliver him into the king's hand." [21]Saul replied: "The LORD bless you for your compassion toward me.[w] [22]Go now and make sure once more! Take note of the place where he sets foot for I am told that he is very cunning. [23]Look around and learn in which of all the various hiding places he is holding out. Then come back to me with reliable information, and I will go with you. If he is in the region, I will track him down out of all the families of Judah." [24]So they went off to Ziph ahead of Saul. At this time David and his men were in the wilderness below Maon, in the Arabah south of the wasteland.[x]

*Escape from Saul.* [25]When Saul and his men came looking for him, David got word of it and went down to the gorge in the wilderness below Maon. Saul heard of this and pursued David into the wilderness below Maon. [26]As Saul moved along one side of the gorge, David and his men took to the other. David was anxious to escape Saul, while Saul and his men were trying to outflank David and his men in order to capture them. [27]Then a messenger came to Saul, saying, "Come quickly, because the Philistines have invaded the land." [28]Saul interrupted his pursuit of David and went to meet the Philistines. This is how that place came to be called the Rock of Divisions.

## CHAPTER 24

See RG 118

*David Spares Saul.** [1]David then went up from there and stayed in the strongholds of Engedi. [2]When Saul returned from the pursuit of the Philistines, he was told that David was in the desert near Engedi. [3]So Saul took three thousand of the best men from all Israel and went in search of David and his men in the direction of the wild goat crags. [4]When he came to the sheepfolds along the way, he found a cave, which he entered to relieve himself. David and his men were occupying the inmost recesses of the cave.[y]

[5]David's servants said to him, "This is the day about which the LORD said to you: I will deliver your enemy into your hand; do with him as you see fit." So David moved up and stealthily cut off an end of Saul's robe. [6]Afterward, however, David regretted that he had cut off an end of Saul's robe.[z] [7]He said

**23:17 King of Israel**: to emphasize the inevitability of the Lord's plan, the narrator frames Jonathan's statement with two accounts of David's mercy toward Saul.

**24:1** The first of two accounts (see chap. 26) in which David spares Saul's life. The two accounts, which do not make reference to each other, are probably alternative versions of the same story.

---

*r:* 1 Sm 2:28. *s:* 1 Sm 18:1. *t:* 1 Sm 20:14–16. *u:* 1 Sm 18:3; 20:8. *v:* 1 Sm 26:1–3; Ps 54. *w:* 2 Sm 2:5. *x:* 1 Sm 25:2. *y:* Ps 57. *z:* 1 Sm 15:27.

to his men, "The LORD forbid that I should do such a thing to my master, the LORD's anointed, to lay a hand on him, for he is the LORD's anointed."[a] [8]With these words David restrained his men and would not permit them to attack Saul. Saul then left the cave and went on his way. [9]David also stepped out of the cave, calling to Saul, "My lord the king!" When Saul looked back, David bowed, his face to the ground in homage, [10]and asked Saul: "Why do you listen to those who say, 'David is trying to harm you'? [11]You see for yourself today that the LORD just now delivered you into my hand in the cave. I was told to kill you, but I took pity on you instead. I decided, 'I will not raise a hand against my master, for he is the LORD's anointed.' [12]Look here, my father. See the end of your robe which I hold. I cut off an end of your robe and did not kill you. Now see and be convinced that I plan no harm and no rebellion. I have done you no wrong, though you are hunting me down to take my life.[b] [13]May the LORD judge between me and you. May the LORD exact justice from you in my case. I shall not lay a hand on you. [14]As the old proverb says, 'From the wicked comes wickedness.' Thus I will not lay a hand on you. [15]What is the king of Israel attacking? What are you pursuing? A dead dog! A single flea![c] [16]The LORD will be the judge to decide between us. May the LORD see this, defend my cause, and give me justice against you!"[d]

***Saul's Remorse.*** [17]When David finished saying these things to Saul, Saul answered, "Is that your voice, my son David?" And he wept freely. [18]Saul then admitted to David: "You are more in the right than I am. You have treated me graciously, while I have treated you badly. [19]You have declared this day how you treated me graciously: the LORD delivered me into your hand and you did not kill me. [20]For if someone comes upon an enemy, do they send them graciously on their way? So may the LORD reward you graciously for what you have done this day. [21]And now, since I know that you will certainly become king and that the kingship over Israel shall come into your possession,[e] [22]swear to me by the LORD that you will not cut off my descendants and that you will not blot out my name from my father's house."[f] [23]David gave Saul his oath and Saul returned home, while David and his men went up to the stronghold.

## CHAPTER 25

See RG 118

***Death of Samuel.*** [1]Samuel died, and all Israel gathered to mourn him; they buried him at his home in Ramah.[g] Then David went down to the wilderness of Paran.

***Nabal and Abigail.*** [2]There was a man of Maon who had property in Carmel; he was very wealthy, owning three thousand sheep and a thousand goats. At the time, he was present for the shearing of his flock in Carmel.[h] [3]The man's name was Nabal and his wife was Abigail. The woman was intelligent and attractive, but Nabal, a Calebite, was harsh and bad-mannered.[i] [4]While in the wilderness, David heard that Nabal was shearing his flock, [5]so he sent ten young men, instructing them: "Go up to Carmel. Pay Nabal a visit and greet him in my name. [6]Say to him, 'Peace be with you, my brother, and with your family, and with all who belong to you. [7]I have just heard that shearers are with you. Now, when your shepherds were with us, we did them no injury, neither did they miss anything while they were in Carmel. [8]Ask your servants and they will tell you. Look kindly on these young men, since we come at a festival time. Please give your servants and your son David* whatever you can.' "

[9]When David's young men arrived, they delivered the entire message to Nabal in David's name, and then waited. [10]But Nabal answered the servants of David: "Who is David? Who is the son of Jesse? Nowadays there are many servants who run away from their masters. [11]Must I take my bread, my

**25:8 Your son David**: this kinship language may reflect a political or social relationship between Nabal and David. Nabal, however, does not acknowledge it.

*a:* 1 Sm 10:1; 26:9; 31:4; 2 Sm 1:14. *b:* Rom 12:19. *c:* 2 Sm 9:8; 16:9. *d:* 1 Sm 18:19, 31; 26:19; Ps 35:1–3; 43:1. *e:* 1 Sm 26:25. *f:* 2 Sm 9:1–3. *g:* 1 Sm 28:3; Sir 46:13–20. *h:* 1 Sm 23:24; Jos 15:55. *i:* 1 Sm 27:3; Dt 1:35–36; Jos 14:6–15; 1 Chr 2:42, 45.

wine, my meat that I have slaughtered for my own shearers, and give them to men who come from who knows where?" 12 So David's young men retraced their steps and on their return reported to him all that had been said. 13 Thereupon David said to his men, "Let everyone strap on his sword." And everyone did so, and David put on his own sword. About four hundred men went up after David, while two hundred remained with the baggage.

14 Abigail, Nabal's wife, was informed of this by one of the servants, who said: "From the wilderness David sent messengers to greet our master, but he screamed at them. 15 Yet these men were very good to us. We were not harmed, neither did we miss anything all the while we were living among them during our stay in the open country. 16 Day and night they were a wall of protection for us, the whole time we were pasturing the sheep near them. 17 Now, see what you can do, for you must realize that otherwise disaster is in store for our master and for his whole house. He is such a scoundrel that no one can talk to him." 18 Abigail quickly got together two hundred loaves, two skins of wine, five dressed sheep, five seahs of roasted grain, a hundred cakes of pressed raisins, and two hundred cakes of pressed figs, and loaded them on donkeys. 19 She then said to her servants, "Go on ahead; I will follow you." But to her husband Nabal she said nothing.

20 Hidden by the mountain, she came down riding on a donkey, as David and his men were coming down from the opposite direction. When she met them, 21 David had just been saying: "Indeed, it was in vain that I guarded all this man's possessions in the wilderness, so that nothing of his was missing. He has repaid good with evil. 22 May God do thus to David, and more, if by morning I leave a single male alive among all those who belong to him."[j] 23 As soon as Abigail saw David, she dismounted quickly from the donkey and, falling down, bowed low to the ground before David in homage.

24 As she fell at his feet she said: "My lord, let the blame be mine. Please let your maidservant speak to you; listen to the words of your maidservant.[k] 25 My lord, do not pay any attention to that scoundrel Nabal, for he is just like his name. His name means fool,* and he acts the fool. I, your maidservant, did not see the young men whom my lord sent. 26 Now, therefore, my lord, as the LORD lives, and as you live, the LORD has kept you from shedding blood and from avenging yourself by your own hand. May your enemies and those who seek to harm my lord become as Nabal!*[l] 27 Accept this gift, then, which your maidservant has brought for my lord, and let it be given to the young men who follow my lord. 28 Please forgive the offense of your maidservant, for the LORD shall certainly establish a lasting house for my lord, because my lord fights the battles of the LORD. Let no evil be found in you your whole life long.[m] 29 If any adversary pursues you to seek your life, may the life of my lord be bound in the bundle of the living* in the care of the LORD your God; may God hurl out the lives of your enemies as from the hollow of a sling.[n] 30 And when the LORD fulfills for my lord the promise of success he has made concerning you, and appoints you as ruler over Israel,[o] 31 you shall not have any regrets or burdens on your conscience, my lord, for having shed innocent blood or for having rescued yourself. When the LORD bestows good on my lord, remember your maidservant." 32 David said to Abigail: "Blessed is the LORD, the God of Israel, who sent you to meet me today. 33 Blessed is your good judgment and blessed are you yourself. Today you have prevented me from shedding blood and rescuing myself with my own hand.

**25:25** Hebrew *nabal* means "fool" (cf. Is 32:5–7). Abigail, on the other hand, acts wisely to save herself and her household by offering prudent counsel to the future king of Israel.

**25:26** Abigail, encouraging David to trust in God's promise, anticipates that some misfortune will shortly overtake Nabal, as in fact it does (vv. 37–38).

**25:29 The bundle of the living**: the figure is perhaps taken from the practice of tying up valuables in a kerchief or bag for safekeeping. Abigail desires that David enjoy permanent peace and security, but that his enemies be subject to constant agitation and humiliation like a stone whirled about, cast out of the sling, and thereafter disregarded.

*j:* 1 Kgs 16:11; 21:21; 2 Kgs 9:8. *k:* 2 Sm 14:9. *l:* Dt 20:4; Jgs 7:2. *m:* 1 Kgs 11:38. *n:* Ps 69:28. *o:* 1 Sm 13:14; 2 Sm 3:10.

**Abigail**

THE PLACEMENT OF this story between the two accounts of David's chances to kill Saul (chs 24 and 26) is significant. While David avoids shedding Saul's blood, he is almost guilty of killing many innocent people in Nabal's household. Nabal is like Saul in many ways. He is "rich as a king" and was probably the chieftain among the Calebites, one of the leading clans of Judah. The name Nabal means "fool" or "brute." His wife, Abigail, on the other hand, is his complete opposite. The only other Abigail in the Bible is David's sister (1 Chr 2:16).

34 Otherwise, as the LORD, the God of Israel, lives, who has kept me from harming you, if you had not come so promptly to meet me, by dawn Nabal would not have had so much as one male left alive." 35 David then took from her what she had brought him and said to her: "Go to your home in peace! See, I have listened to your appeal and have granted your request."

*Nabal's Death.* 36 When Abigail came to Nabal, he was hosting a banquet in his house like that of a king, and Nabal was in a festive mood and very drunk. So she said not a word to him until daybreak the next morning. 37 But then, when Nabal was sober, his wife told him what had happened. At this his heart died within him, and he became like a stone. 38 About ten days later the LORD struck Nabal and he died. 39 Hearing that Nabal was dead, David said: "Blessed be the LORD, who has defended my cause against the insult from Nabal, and who restrained his servant from doing evil, but has repaid Nabal for his evil deeds."

*David Marries Abigail and Ahinoam.* David then sent a proposal of marriage to Abigail.[p] 40 When David's servants came to Abigail in Carmel, they said to her, "David has sent us to make his proposal of marriage to you." 41 Rising and bowing to the ground, she answered, "Let your maidservant be the slave who washes the feet of my lord's servants." 42 She got up immediately, mounted a donkey, and followed David's messengers, with her five maids attending her. She became his wife. 43[q] David also married Ahinoam of Jezreel. Thus both of them were his wives. 44 But Saul gave David's wife Michal, Saul's own daughter, to Palti, son of Laish, who was from Gallim.[r]

## CHAPTER 26

See RG 118

*David Spares Saul Again.** 1[s] Men from Ziph came to Saul in Gibeah, reporting that David was hiding on the hill of Hachilah at the edge of Jeshimon. 2 So Saul went down to the wilderness of Ziph with three thousand of the best warriors of Israel, to search for David in the wilderness of Ziph. 3 Saul camped beside the road on the hill of Hachilah, at the edge of Jeshimon. David, who was living in the wilderness, saw that Saul had come into the wilderness after him 4 and sent out scouts, who confirmed Saul's arrival. 5 David then went to the place where Saul was encamped and saw the spot where Saul and his general, Abner, son of Ner, had their sleeping quarters. Saul was lying within the camp, and all his soldiers were bivouacked around him.[t] 6 David asked Ahimelech the Hittite, and Abishai, son of Zeruiah and brother of Joab, "Who will go down into the camp with me to Saul?" Abishai replied, "I will."[u] 7 So David and Abishai reached Saul's soldiers by night, and there was Saul lying asleep within the camp, his spear thrust into the ground at his head and Abner and his troops sleeping around him.

8 Abishai whispered to David: "God has delivered your enemy into your hand today. Let me nail him to the ground with one thrust of the spear; I will not need to strike him twice!"[v] 9 But David said to Abishai,

**26:1** The second account of David sparing Saul's life; cf. note on 24:1.

*p:* 1 Kgs 2:44. *q:* 1 Sm 27:3. *r:* 1 Sm 18:20; 27:3; 30:5; 2 Sm 2:2, 13–16; 1 Chr 3:1. *s:* 1 Sm 23:19–20; Ps 54. *t:* 1 Sm 17:20. *u:* 2 Sm 3:30; 1 Chr 2:16. *v:* 1 Sm 18:11; 19:10; 20:33.

"Do not harm him, for who can lay a hand on
the LORD's anointed and remain innocent?
10 As the LORD lives," David declared, "only
the LORD can strike him: either when the
time comes for him to die, or when he goes
out and perishes in battle.* [w] 11 But the LORD
forbid that I lay a hand on the LORD's
anointed! Now take the spear at his head and
the water jug, and let us be on our way." 12 So
David took the spear and the water jug from
their place at Saul's head, and they withdrew
without anyone seeing or knowing or awakening. All remained asleep, because a deep
slumber* from the LORD had fallen upon
them.[x]

***David Taunts Abner.*** 13 Crossing over to an
opposite slope, David stood on a distant hilltop. With a great distance between them
14 David called to the army and to Abner, son
of Ner, "Will you not answer, Abner?" Then
Abner shouted back, "Who is it that calls
me?" 15 David said to Abner: "Are you not a
man? Who in Israel is your equal? Why were
you not guarding your lord the king when
one of his subjects came to assassinate the
king, your lord? 16 What you have done is not
right. As the LORD lives, you people deserve
death because you have not guarded your
lord, the anointed of the LORD. Go, look:
where are the king's spear and the water jug
that was at his head?"

***Saul Admits His Guilt.*** 17 Saul recognized
David's voice and asked, "Is that your voice,
David my son?"* David answered, "Yes, my
lord the king." 18 He continued: "Why does
my lord pursue his servant? What have I
done? What evil am I planning? 19 Please,
now, let my lord the king listen to the words
of his servant. If the LORD has incited you
against me, may an offering please the
LORD. But if it is the people who have done
so, may they be cursed before the LORD.
They have driven me away so that today I
have no share in the LORD's heritage,* but
am told: 'Go serve other gods!'[y] 20 Do not let
my blood spill on the ground far from the
presence of the LORD. For the king of Israel
has come out to seek a single flea as if he
were hunting partridge* in the mountains."
21 Then Saul said: "I have done wrong. Come
back, David, my son! I will not harm you
again, because you considered my life precious today even though I have been a fool
and have made a serious mistake." 22 But
David answered: "Here is the king's spear.
Let an attendant come over to get it. 23 The
LORD repays everyone's righteousness and
faithfulness. Although the LORD delivered
you into my hands today, I could not lay a
hand on the LORD's anointed.[z] 24 Just as I regarded your life as precious today, so may
the LORD regard my life as precious and deliver me from all dangers." 25 Then Saul said
to David: "Blessed are you, my son David!
You shall certainly succeed in whatever you
undertake." David went his way, and Saul
returned to his place.[a]

## CHAPTER 27

See RG 118

***David Flees to the Philistines.*** 1 David
said to himself: "I shall perish some day at
the hand of Saul. I have no choice but to escape to the land of the Philistines; then Saul
will give up his continual search for me
throughout the land of Israel, and I will be
out of his reach." 2 Accordingly, David departed with his six hundred soldiers and
went over to Achish, son of Maoch, king of
Gath.[b] 3 David and his men lived in Gath
with Achish; each one had his family, and

**26:10 Perishes in battle**: David's words foreshadow how Saul will die (31:3–4). They also emphasize that David, unlike Saul, knows his proper place before God. David comes to the kingship innocent of Saul's blood, although the king pursues him like an enemy and David has had two opportunities to kill him.

**26:12 Deep slumber**: as in Gn 2:21; 15:12; Is 29:10. The Lord aids David's foray into Saul's camp and allows David to come and go undetected.

**26:17 David my son**: Saul's reference to David as his son, which appears three times in this chapter (vv. 17, 21, 25), alludes to David's role as his successor.

**26:19 The LORD's heritage**: the land and people of Israel (Dt 32:8–9; Ps 33:12). If driven from the land, David could not take part in worship of Israel's God; nonetheless, God has blessed David (cf. v. 25).

**26:20 Partridge**: lit., "the caller." The metaphor is built on clever wordplay: in v. 14, David calls out to the army and Abner asks the caller's identity. David calls out the answer: "the caller" is the object of the king's pursuit.

*w:* Ps 37:13. *x:* Gn 2:21; 15:12. *y:* 1 Sm 24:16. *z:* 1 Sm 18:20. *a:* 1 Sm 18:14; 24:21. *b:* 1 Sm 21:11–16.

**Three Ways of Divining**

THREE MEANS OF divining (1 Sm 28:6) were dreams, or incubation, in which one slept at a holy place, anticipating the answer to an inquiry; Urim or lots, used earlier in 14:41; and prophets like the man of God in 9:1–10:16.

David had his two wives, Ahinoam from
Jezreel and Abigail, the widow of Nabal
from Carmel.[c] 4When Saul learned that David had fled to Gath, he no longer searched
for him.
5David said to Achish: "If I meet with
your approval, let me have a place to live in
one of the country towns. Why should your
servant live with you in the royal city?"
6That same day Achish gave him Ziklag,
which has, therefore, belonged to the kings
of Judah* up to the present time.[d] 7In all, David lived a year and four months in Philistine
territory.[e]
***David Raids Israel's Foes.*** 8David and his
men went out on raids against the Geshurites, Girzites, and Amalekites—peoples living in the land between Telam, on the approach to Shur, and the land of Egypt.[f] 9In
attacking the land David would not leave a
man or woman alive, but would carry off
sheep, oxen, donkeys, camels, and clothes.
Then he would return to Achish, 10who
would ask, "Against whom did you raid this
time?" David would reply, "Against the
Negeb of Judah,"* or "Against the Negeb of
Jerahmeel," or "Against the Negeb of the
Kenites."[g] 11David never left a man or
woman alive to be brought to Gath. He
thought, "They will betray us and say, 'This
is what David did.'" This was his custom as
long as he lived in Philistine territory.
12Achish trusted David, thinking, "His people Israel must certainly detest him. I shall
have him as my vassal forever."

## CHAPTER 28

See RG 118–19

1In those days the Philistines mustered their military forces to fight against Israel. So Achish said to David, "You realize,
of course, that you and your warriors* must
march out for battle with me." 2David answered Achish, "Good! Now you shall learn
what your servant can do." Then Achish said
to David, "I shall appoint you as my permanent bodyguard."
3Now, Samuel was dead. All Israel had
mourned him and buried him in his city, Ramah. Meanwhile Saul had driven mediums
and diviners out of the land.[h]
***Saul in Despair.*** 4The Philistines rallied
and, coming to Shunem, they encamped.
Saul, too, mustered all Israel; they camped
on Gilboa. 5When Saul saw the Philistine
camp, he grew afraid and lost heart completely. 6He consulted the LORD; but the
LORD gave no answer, neither in dreams nor
by Urim nor through prophets.[i] 7Then Saul
said to his servants, "Find me a medium*
through whom I can seek counsel." His servants answered him, "There is a woman in
Endor who is a medium."[j]
***The Medium at Endor.*** 8So he disguised
himself, putting on other clothes, and set out
with two companions. They came to the
woman at night, and Saul said to her, "Divine for me; conjure up the spirit I tell you."[k]
9But the woman answered him, "You know
what Saul has done, how he expelled the mediums and diviners from the land. Then why

**27:6** Ziklag was a royal city and not part of Israel's tribal land holdings. Jerusalem later enjoyed a similar status (2 Sm 5:7–9).

**27:10 The Negeb of Judah**: David deceives Achish by assuring him that he has attacked Israelite territory.

**28:1 You and your warriors**: David is faced with a potentially dangerous dilemma: either to reveal his continuing loyalty to his own people or to obey Achish and fight against his own people.

**28:7 A medium**: Saul's own prohibition of necromancy and divination (v. 3) was in keeping with the consistent teaching of the Old Testament (cf. Lv 19:31; 20:6, 27; Dt 18:10).

*c:* 1 Sm 25:3, 44; 30:3–5; 2 Sm 2:3. *d:* 1 Sm 30:1. *e:* 1 Sm 29:3. *f:* 1 Sm 15:3, 7; Jos 13:2–3. *g:* 1 Sm 30:14, 29; 1 Chr 2:9, 25, 42. *h:* 1 Sm 25:1; Sir 46:20. *i:* 1 Sm 14:37, 41; Ex 28:30; Lv 8:8. *j:* Lv 19:31; 20:27; Dt 18:10–12; 2 Kgs 21:6; 1 Chr 10:13–14; Acts 16:16. *k:* 1 Sm 15:23; 1 Kgs 14:2.

are you trying to entrap me and get me killed?" 10But Saul swore to her by the LORD, "As the LORD lives, you shall incur no blame for this." 11"Whom do you want me to conjure up?" the woman asked him. "Conjure up Samuel for me," he replied.

*Samuel Appears.* 12When the woman saw Samuel, she shrieked at the top of her voice and said to Saul, "Why have you deceived me? You are Saul!" 13But the king said to her, "Do not be afraid. What do you see?" "I see a god rising from the earth," she replied. 14"What does he look like?" asked Saul. "An old man is coming up wrapped in a robe," she replied. Saul knew that it was Samuel, and so he bowed his face to the ground in homage.

*Saul's Doom.* 15* Samuel then said to Saul, "Why do you disturb me by conjuring me up?" Saul replied: "I am in great distress, for the Philistines are waging war against me and God has turned away from me. Since God no longer answers me through prophets or in dreams, I have called upon you to tell me what I should do."[l] 16To this Samuel said: "But why do you ask me, if the LORD has abandoned you for your neighbor?[m] 17The LORD has done to you what he declared through me: he has torn the kingdom from your hand and has given it to your neighbor David.

18"Because you disobeyed the LORD's directive and would not carry out his fierce anger against Amalek, the LORD has done this to you today.[n] 19Moreover, the LORD will deliver Israel, and you as well, into the hands of the Philistines. By tomorrow you and your sons will be with me, and the LORD will have delivered the army of Israel into the hands of the Philistines."[o]

20Immediately Saul fell full length on the ground, in great fear because of Samuel's message. He had no strength left, since he had eaten nothing all that day and night. 21Then the woman came to Saul and, seeing that he was quite terror-stricken, said to him: "Remember, your maidservant obeyed you: I took my life in my hands and carried out the request you made of me. 22Now you, in turn, please listen to your maidservant. Let me set out a bit of food for you to eat, so that you are strong enough to go on your way." 23But he refused, saying, "I will not eat." However, when his servants joined the woman in urging him, he listened to their entreaties, got up from the ground, and sat on a couch. 24The woman had a stall-fed calf in the house, which she now quickly slaughtered. Then taking flour, she kneaded it and baked unleavened bread. 25She set the meal before Saul and his servants, and they ate. Then they got up and left the same night.

## CHAPTER 29

See RG 118–19

*David's Aid Rejected.* 1Now the Philistines had mustered all their forces in Aphek, and the Israelites were encamped at the spring in Jezreel.[p] 2As the Philistine lords were marching their units of a hundred and a thousand, David and his warriors were marching in the rear guard with Achish. 3The Philistine commanders asked, "What are those Hebrews doing here?" Achish answered them: "Why, that is David, the officer of Saul, king of Israel. He has been with me for a year or two, and from the day he came over to me until now I have never found fault in him."[q] 4But the Philistine commanders were angered at this and said to him: "Send that man back! Let him return to the place you picked out for him. He must not go down into battle with us; during the battle he might become our enemy. For how else can he win back his master's favor, if not at the expense of our soldiers?[r] 5Is this not the David for whom they sing during their dances,

'Saul has slain his thousands,
David his tens of thousands'?"[s]

6So Achish summoned David and said to him: "As the LORD lives, you are honest, and I would want you with me in all my battles.

**28:15–19** The consultation with the medium serves to remind the reader that the Lord's plan for David marches onward; no sorcery can thwart it.

---

*l:* 1 Sm 14:37; Sir 46:20. *m:* 1 Sm 15:27–28. *n:* 1 Sm 15:18–19, 26. *o:* 1 Sm 31:2–6; Sir 46:20. *p:* 1 Sm 4:1. *q:* 1 Sm 27:7. *r:* 1 Chr 12:19–20. *s:* 1 Sm 18:6–7; 21:12.

To this day I have found nothing wrong with you since you came to me. But in the view of the chiefs you are not welcome. [7]Leave peacefully, now, and do nothing that might displease the Philistine chiefs." [8]But David said to Achish: "What have I done? What fault have you found in your servant from the day I entered your service until today, that I cannot go to fight against the enemies of my lord the king?" [9]"I recognize," Achish answered David, "that you are trustworthy, like an angel of God. But the Philistine commanders are saying, 'He must not go with us into battle.' [10]So the first thing tomorrow, you and your lord's servants who came with you, go to the place I picked out for you. Do not take to heart their worthless remarks; for you have been valuable in my service. But make an early morning start, as soon as it grows light, and be on your way." [11]So David and his warriors left early in the morning to return to the land of the Philistines, and the Philistines went on up to Jezreel.

## CHAPTER 30

See RG 118–19

***Ziklag in Ruins.*** [1]Before David and his men reached Ziklag on the third day, the Amalekites had raided the Negeb and Ziklag. They stormed Ziklag, and set it on fire.[t] [2]They took captive the women and all who were in the city, young and old, killing no one, and they herded them off when they left. [3]David and his men arrived at the city to find it burned to the ground and their wives, sons, and daughters taken captive. [4]Then David and those who were with him wept aloud until they could weep no more. [5]David's two wives, Ahinoam of Jezreel and Abigail, the widow of Nabal from Carmel, had also been carried off.[u] [6]Now David found himself in great danger, for the soldiers spoke of stoning him, so bitter were they over the fate of their sons and daughters. David took courage in the LORD his God [7][v] and said to Abiathar, the priest, son of Ahimelech, "Bring me the ephod!" When Abiathar brought him the ephod, [8]David inquired of the LORD, "Shall I pursue these raiders? Can I overtake them?" The LORD answered him: Go in pursuit, for you will certainly overtake them and bring about a rescue.

***Raid on the Amalekites.*** [9]So David went off with his six hundred as far as the Wadi Besor, where those who were to remain behind halted. [10]David continued the pursuit with four hundred, but two hundred were too exhausted to cross the Wadi Besor and remained behind. [11]An Egyptian was found in the open country and brought to David. They gave him food to eat and water to drink; [12]they also offered a cake of pressed figs and two cakes of pressed raisins. When he had eaten, he revived, for he had not taken food nor drunk water for three days and three nights. [13]Then David asked him, "To whom do you belong? Where did you come from?" "I am an Egyptian, the slave of an Amalekite," he replied. "My master abandoned me three days ago because I fell sick. [14]We raided the Negeb of the Cherethites, the territory of Judah, and the Negeb of Caleb; and we set Ziklag on fire."[w] [15]David then asked him, "Will you lead me down to these raiders?" He answered, "Swear to me by God that you will not kill me or hand me over to my master, and I will lead you down to the raiders." [16]So he led them down, and there were the Amalekites lounging all over the ground, eating, drinking, and celebrating because of all the rich plunder they had taken from the land of the Philistines and from the land of Judah.

***The Plunder Recovered.*** [17]From dawn to sundown the next day David attacked them, allowing no one to escape except four hundred young men, who mounted their camels and fled.[x] [18]David recovered everything the Amalekites had taken, and he rescued his two wives. [19]Nothing was missing, small or great, plunder or sons or daughters, of all that the Amalekites had taken. David brought back everything. [20]Moreover, David took all the sheep and oxen, and as they drove these before him, they shouted, "This is David's plunder!"

***Division of the Plunder.*** [21]When David

*t:* 1 Sm 15:2; 27:6, 10; 1 Chr 12:21. *u:* 1 Sm 25:42; 27:3; 30:5. *v:* 1 Sm 2:28; 23:6; Ex 28:30. *w:* 1 Sm 27:10; Ez 25:16. *x:* 1 Sm 15:3; Jos 6:17; Jgs 7:12.

came to the two hundred men who had been too exhausted to follow him, whom he had left behind at the Wadi Besor, they came out to meet David and the men with him. As David approached, he greeted them. 22 But all the greedy and worthless among those who had accompanied David said, "Since they did not accompany us, we will not give them anything from the plunder, except for each man's wife and children." 23 But David said: "You must not do this, my brothers, after what the LORD has given us. The LORD has protected us and delivered into our hands the raiders that came against us.[y] 24 Who could agree with this proposal of yours? Rather, the share of the one who goes down to battle shall be the same as that of the one who remains with the baggage—they share alike."[z] 25 And from that day forward he made this a law and a custom in Israel, as it still is today.[a]

***David's Gifts to Judah.*** 26 When David came to Ziklag, he sent part of the plunder to his friends, the elders of Judah,* saying, "This is a gift to you from the plunder of the enemies of the LORD," namely, 27 to those in Bethel, Ramoth-negeb, Jattir, 28 Aroer, Siphmoth, Eshtemoa, 29 Racal, Jerahmeelite cities and Kenite cities,[b] 30 Hormah, Borashan, Athach, 31 Hebron, and to all the places that David and his men had frequented.[c]

## CHAPTER 31

See RG 118-19

***Death of Saul and His Sons.*** 1[d] Now the Philistines went to war against Israel, and the Israelites fled before them, and fell, slain on Mount Gilboa. 2 The Philistines pressed hard after Saul and his sons. When the Philistines had struck down Jonathan, Abinadab, and Malchishua, sons of Saul,[e] 3 the fury of the battle converged on Saul. Then the archers hit him, and he was severely wounded. 4 Saul said to his armor-bearer, "Draw your sword and run me through; otherwise these uncircumcised will come and abuse me." But the armor-bearer, badly frightened, refused, so Saul took his own sword and fell upon it.[f] 5[g] When the armor-bearer saw that Saul was dead, he too fell upon his sword and died with him. 6 Thus Saul, his three sons, and his armor-bearer died together on that same day. 7 When the Israelites on the slope of the valley and those along the Jordan saw that the men of Israel had fled and that Saul and his sons were dead, they abandoned their cities and fled. Then the Philistines came and lived in those cities.

8 On the following day, when the Philistines came to strip the slain, they found Saul and his three sons fallen on Mount Gilboa. 9 They cut off Saul's head and stripped him of his armor; these they sent throughout the land of the Philistines to bring the good news to the temple of their idols and to the people.[h] 10 They put his armor in the temple of Astarte but impaled his body on the wall of Beth-shan.

***Burial of Saul.*** 11[i] When the inhabitants of Jabesh-gilead heard what the Philistines had done to Saul, 12 all their warriors set out and traveled through the night; they removed the bodies of Saul and his sons from the wall of Beth-shan, and, returning to Jabesh, burned them.* 13 Then they took their bones and buried them under the tamarisk tree in Jabesh, and fasted for seven days.

**30:26 Elders of Judah**: David consolidates his power in southern Judah in preparation for his anointing at Hebron (2 Sm 5:3).

**31:12 Burned them**: cremation was not an Israelite custom. The people of Jabesh-gilead repay Saul's victory over the Ammonites on their behalf (chap. 11) by providing burial and funeral rites for him and his sons. Probably the damaged state of the corpus necessitated cremation.

*y:* Dt 20:4, 14. *z:* 1 Sm 17:22; 25:13. *a:* Nm 31:27. *b:* 1 Sm 27:10. *c:* 2 Sm 2:1–4. *d:* 2 Sm 1:1–16; 4:4; 1 Chr 10:1–12. *e:* 1 Sm 14:49; 28:19; 1 Chr 10:2–3. *f:* 1 Sm 24:6; Jgs 9:54; 1 Chr 10:4. *g:* 1 Sm 10:1; 26:9; 2 Mc 14:42. *h:* 1 Sm 17:54; 2 Sm 1:20; 2 Mc 15:35. *i:* 1 Sm 11:1–11; 2 Sm 2:4–7; 21:12–14.

See RG 113–22

# The Second Book of Samuel

See RG 118–19

## CHAPTER 1

***Report of Saul's Death.*** 1After the
death of Saul, David returned from his victory over the Amalekites and stayed in Ziklag
two days.[a] 2On the third day a man came from
the field of battle, one of Saul's people, with
his garments torn and his head covered with
dirt. Going to David, he fell to the ground in
homage. 3David asked him, "Where have you
come from?" He replied, "From the Israelite
camp: I have escaped." 4"What happened?"
David said. "Tell me." He answered that the
soldiers had fled the battle and many of them
had fallen and were dead; and that Saul and
his son Jonathan were dead. 5Then David said
to the youth who was reporting to him, "How
do you know that Saul and his son Jonathan
are dead?" 6[b] The youth reporting to him
replied: "I happened to find myself on Mount
Gilboa and saw Saul leaning on his spear,
with chariots and horsemen closing in on
him. 7He turned around and saw me, and
called me to him. When I said, 'Here I am,'
8he asked me, 'Who are you?' and I replied,
'An Amalekite.' 9Then he said to me, 'Stand
over me, please, and put me to death, for I am
in great suffering, but still alive.' 10So I stood
over him and put him to death, for I knew that
he could not survive his wound. I removed
the crown from his head and the armlet from
his arm and brought them here to my lord."
11David seized his garments and tore
them, and so did all the men who were with
him.[c] 12They mourned and wept and fasted
until evening for Saul and his son Jonathan,
and for the people of the LORD and the house
of Israel, because they had fallen by the
sword.[d] 13David said to the youth who had
reported to him, "Where are you from?" He
replied, "I am the son of a resident alien, an
Amalekite." 14David said to him, "How is it
that you were not afraid to put forth your
hand to desecrate the LORD's anointed?"[e]
15David then called one of the attendants and
said to him, "Come, strike him down"; so he
struck him and he died. 16David said to him,
"Your blood is on your head, for you testified against yourself when you said, 'I put
the LORD's anointed to death.'"

***Lament for Saul and Jonathan.*** 17Then
David chanted this lament for Saul and his
son Jonathan 18(he commanded that it be
taught to the Judahites; it is recorded in the
Book of Jashar):[f]

19 Alas! the glory of Israel,
  slain upon your heights!
How can the warriors have fallen!
20 Do not report it in Gath,
  as good news in Ashkelon's streets,
Lest Philistine women rejoice,
  lest the women of the uncircumcised
    exult![g]
21 O mountains of Gilboa,
  upon you be neither dew nor rain,
  nor surging from the deeps!*
Defiled there the warriors' shields,
  the shield of Saul—no longer anointed
    with oil![h]
22 From the blood of the slain,
  from the bodies of the warriors,
The bow of Jonathan did not turn back,
  nor the sword of Saul return
    unstained.*[i]
23 Saul and Jonathan, beloved and dear,
  separated neither in life nor death,
  swifter than eagles, stronger than
    lions!
24 Women of Israel, weep over Saul,
  who clothed you in scarlet and in
    finery,

**1:21 Surging from the deeps**: this conjectural reading of the Hebrew yields a parallelism with dew and rain: the mountains where the warriors have fallen in battle are to be desiccated, deprived of water from above (rain, dew) and below (the primordial deeps).

**1:22 Unstained**: lit., "empty." The sword was conceived as a devouring mouth; see, e.g., 2:26.

*a:* 1 Sm 30:17–20; 31:1–13. *b:* 2 Sm 4:10; 1 Sm 31:1–4; 1 Chr 10:1–4. *c:* 2 Sm 13:31. *d:* 1 Sm 31:13. *e:* 1 Sm 10:1; 24:7; Ps 105:15. *f:* Jos 10:13. *g:* Jgs 16:23; 1 Sm 31:9; Mi 1:10. *h:* Gn 27:28. *i:* 1 Sm 14:47.

**David's Wives' Influence**

DAVID'S TWO WIVES, Ahinoam and Abigail (2 Sm 2:2) were both from the area around Hebron and were therefore important political assets for his gaining the throne of Judah. Through his marriage to Abigail, David had assumed the wealth and position of a prominent Calebite leader, perhaps their chieftain (1 Sm 25).

covered your clothing with ornaments
of gold.
25 How can the warriors have fallen
in the thick of battle!
Jonathan—slain upon your heights!
26 I grieve for you, Jonathan my brother!
Most dear have you been to me;
More wondrous your love to me
than the love of women.[j]
27 How can the warriors have fallen,
the weapons of war have perished!

### CHAPTER 2

See RG 119

*David Is Anointed King.* 1 After this, David inquired of the LORD, "Shall I go up into one of the cities of Judah?" The LORD replied to him: Go up. Then David asked, "Where shall I go?" He replied: To Hebron. 2 So David went up there, with his two wives, Ahinoam of Jezreel and Abigail, the wife of Nabal of Carmel.[k] 3 David also brought up his men with their families, and they dwelt in the towns of Hebron. 4 Then the men of Judah came there and anointed David king over the house of Judah.

A report reached David that the people of Jabesh-gilead had buried Saul.[l] 5 So David sent messengers to the people of Jabesh-gilead and said to them: "May you be blessed by the LORD for having done this kindness to your lord Saul in burying him. 6 And now may the LORD show you kindness and fidelity. For my part, I will show generosity to you for having done this. 7 So take courage and prove yourselves valiant, for though your lord Saul is dead, the house of Judah has anointed me king over them."

## IV. The Reign of David

*Ishbaal King of Israel.* 8 Abner, son of Ner, captain of Saul's army, took Ishbaal,* son of Saul, and brought him over to Mahanaim,[m] 9 where he made him king over Gilead, the Asherites, Jezreel, Ephraim, Benjamin, and the rest of Israel. 10 Ishbaal, son of Saul, was forty years old when he became king over Israel, and he reigned two years; but the house of Judah followed David. 11 In all, David was king in Hebron over the house of Judah seven years and six months.[n]

*Combat near Gibeon.* 12 Now Abner, son of Ner, and the servants of Ishbaal, Saul's son, set out from Mahanaim for Gibeon. 13 Joab, son of Zeruiah, and the servants of David also set out and encountered them at the pool of Gibeon. And they sat down, one group on one side of the pool and the other on the opposite side. 14 Then Abner said to Joab, "Let the young men rise and perform for us."* Joab replied, "All right." 15 So they rose and were counted off: twelve of the Benjaminites of Ishbaal, son of Saul, and twelve of David's servants. 16 Then each one grasped his opponent's head and thrust his sword into his opponent's side, and they all fell down together.* And so that place was named the Field of the Sides; it is in Gibeon.

*Death of Asahel.* 17 The battle that day was very fierce, and Abner and the men of Israel were defeated by David's servants. 18 The three sons of Zeruiah were there—Joab, Abishai, and Asahel.[o] Asahel, who was as fleet of foot as a gazelle in the open

**2:8 Ishbaal**: here and elsewhere in the Hebrew text, his name appears as "Ishbosheth"; the second part of Ishbaal, *-baal*, refers to the Canaanite god Baal, and is therefore suppressed, replaced by *bosheth*, "shame."

**2:14 Perform**: lit., "play."

**2:16** The nature of this gruesome game is not clear, and the place name is variously given in the older texts.

*j:* 1 Sm 18:1–4. *k:* 1 Sm 25:42–43. *l:* 1 Sm 31:11–13. *m:* 1 Sm 14:50. *n:* 2 Sm 5:5; 1 Kgs 2:11. *o:* 2 Sm 23:24; 1 Chr 2:16; 27:7.

field, 19 set out after Abner, turning neither right nor left in his pursuit. 20 Abner turned around and said, "Is that you, Asahel?" He replied, "Yes." 21 Abner said to him, "Turn right or left; seize one of the young men and take what you can strip from him." But Asahel would not stop pursuing him. 22 Once more Abner said to Asahel: "Stop pursuing me! Why must I strike you to the ground? How could I show my face to your brother Joab?"[p] 23 Still he refused to stop. So Abner struck him in the abdomen with the heel of his spear, and the weapon protruded from his back. He fell there and died on the spot. All who came to the place where Asahel had fallen and died, halted. 24 But Joab and Abishai continued the pursuit of Abner. The sun had gone down when they came to the hill of Ammah which lies east of the valley toward the wilderness near Geba.

***Truce Between Joab and Abner.*** 25 Here the Benjaminites rallied around Abner, forming a single group, and made a stand on a hilltop. 26 Then Abner called to Joab and said: "Must the sword devour forever? Do you not know that afterward there will be bitterness? How long before you tell the people to stop pursuing their brothers?" 27 Joab replied, "As God lives, if you had not spoken, it would be morning before the people would be stopped from pursuing their brothers." 28 Joab then sounded the horn, and all the people came to a halt, pursuing Israel no farther and fighting no more. 29 Abner and his men marched all night long through the Arabah, crossed the Jordan, marched all through the morning, and came to Mahanaim. 30 Joab, coming from the pursuit of Abner, assembled all the men. Nineteen other servants of David were missing, besides Asahel. 31 But David's servants had struck down and killed three hundred and sixty men of Benjamin, followers of Abner. 32 They took up Asahel and buried him in his father's tomb in Bethlehem. Joab and his men made an all-night march, and dawn found them in Hebron.

## CHAPTER 3

See RG 119

1 There followed a long war between the house of Saul and the house of David, in which David grew ever stronger, but the house of Saul ever weaker.

***Sons Born in Hebron.*** 2[q] Sons were born to David in Hebron: his firstborn, Amnon, of Ahinoam from Jezreel; 3 the second, Chileab, of Abigail the wife of Nabal of Carmel; the third, Absalom, son of Maacah, who was the daughter of Talmai, king of Geshur;[r] 4 the fourth, Adonijah, son of Haggith; the fifth, Shephatiah, son of Abital;[s] 5 and the sixth, Ithream, by David's wife Eglah. These were born to David in Hebron.

***Ishbaal and Abner Quarrel.*** 6 During the war between the house of Saul and the house of David, Abner was gaining power in the house of Saul. 7 Now Saul had had a concubine, Rizpah, the daughter of Aiah. And Ishbaal, son of Saul, said to Abner, "Why have you slept with my father's concubine?"*[t] 8 Enraged at the words of Ishbaal, Abner said, "Am I a dog's head from Judah? As of today, I have been loyal to the house of Saul your father, to his brothers and his friends, and I have kept you out of David's clutches; and today you charge me with a crime involving a woman! 9 May God do thus to Abner, and more, if I do not carry out for David what the LORD swore to him—[u] 10 that is, take away the kingdom from the house of Saul and establish the throne of David over Israel as well as Judah, from Dan to Beersheba."[v] 11 Ishbaal was no longer able to say a word to Abner, he feared him so.

***Abner and David Reconciled.*** 12 Then Abner sent messengers to David in Telam, where he was at the moment, to say, "Make a covenant with me, and you have me on your side, to bring all Israel over to you." 13 He replied, "Good, I will make a covenant with you. But one thing I require of you. You must not appear before me unless you bring back Michal, Saul's daughter, when you come to present yourself to me."[w] 14 At the

**3:7** Asserting a right to the late king's harem was tantamount to claiming his kingship; cf. 16:21–22; 1 Kgs 2:21–22.

*p:* 2 Sm 3:27–28, 30. *q:* 1 Chr 3:1–4. *r:* 2 Sm 13:37; 15:8. *s:* 1 Kgs 1:5. *t:* 2 Sm 16:21–22; 21:8–10; 1 Kgs 2:21–22. *u:* Ru 1:17. *v:* 2 Sm 5:2; 1 Sm 25:30. *w:* 1 Sm 18:20–27.

same time David sent messengers to Ishbaal,
son of Saul, to say, "Give me my wife Michal, whom I betrothed by paying a hundred
Philistine foreskins." 15 Ishbaal sent for her
and took her away from her husband Paltiel,
son of Laish,[x] 16 who followed her weeping
as far as Bahurim. But Abner said to him,
"Go back!" So he turned back.

17 Abner then had a word with the elders of
Israel: "For some time you have been wanting David as your king. 18 Now take action,
for the LORD has said of David: By David my
servant I will save my people Israel from the
power of the Philistines and from the power
of all their enemies." 19 Abner also spoke
with Benjamin, and then went to speak with
David in Hebron concerning all that would
be agreeable to Israel and to the whole house
of Benjamin. 20 When Abner, accompanied
by twenty men, came to David in Hebron,
David prepared a feast for Abner and for the
men who were with him. 21 Then Abner said
to David, "I will now go to assemble all Israel for my lord the king, that they may make
a covenant with you; you will then be king
over all whom you wish to rule." So David
let Abner go on his way in peace.

***Death of Abner.*** 22 Just then David's servants and Joab were coming in from an expedition, bringing much plunder with them.
Abner, having been dismissed by David, was
no longer with him in Hebron but had gone
on his way in peace. 23 When Joab and the
whole force he had with him arrived, he was
informed, "Abner, son of Ner, came to David, and he let him go on his way in peace."
24 So Joab went to the king and said: "What
have you done? Abner came to you! Why did
you let him get away? 25 Don't you know Abner? He came to trick you, to learn your com-
ings and goings, to learn everything you do."
26 Joab then left David and sent messengers
after Abner to bring him back from the cistern of Sirah; but David did not know.
27 When Abner returned to Hebron, Joab took
him aside within the city gate to speak with
him privately. There he stabbed him in the
abdomen, and he died for the blood of Asahel, Joab's brother.[y] 28 Later David heard of it
and said: "Before the LORD, I and my kingdom are forever innocent.[z] 29 May the blood
of Abner, son of Ner, be on the head of Joab
and all his family. May Joab's family never
be without one suffering from a discharge, or
one with a skin disease, or a man who holds
the distaff, or one falling by the sword, or one
in need of food!"* 30 Joab and Abishai his
brother had been lying in wait for Abner because he killed Asahel their brother in battle
at Gibeon.

***David Mourns Abner.*** 31 Then David said
to Joab and to all the people who were with
him, "Tear your garments, put on sackcloth,
and mourn over Abner." King David himself
followed the bier.[a] 32 When they had buried
Abner in Hebron, the king wept aloud at the
grave of Abner, and all the people wept.
33 And the king sang this lament over Abner:

Should Abner have died like a fool?
34 Your hands were not bound with chains,
nor your feet placed in fetters;
As one falls before the wicked, you fell.

And all the people continued to weep for him.
35 Then they went to console David with food
while it was still day. But David swore, "May
God do thus to me, and more, if before the sun
goes down I eat bread or anything else."[b]
36 All the people noted this with approval, just
as everything the king did met with their approval. 37 So on that day all the people and all
Israel came to know that it was not the king's
doing that Abner, son of Ner, was put to
death. 38 The king then said to his servants:
"Do you not know that a prince, a great man,
has fallen today in Israel. 39 Although I am the
anointed king, I am weak this day, and these
men, the sons of Zeruiah, are too ruthless for
me. May the LORD repay the evildoer in accordance with his evil deed."[c]

## CHAPTER 4

See RG 119

***Death of Ishbaal.*** 1 When Ishbaal, son
of Saul, heard that Abner was dead in Hebron, he lost his resolve and all Israel was
alarmed. 2 Ishbaal, son of Saul, had two com-

**3:29** An assortment of imprecations, consisting of physical ailments, weakness, violent death, and poverty.

*x:* 1 Sm 25:44. *y:* 2 Sm 2:17–23; 1 Kgs 2:5, 31–33. *z:* 2 Sm 2:22–23. *a:* 2 Sm 21:10. *b:* Ru 1:17. *c:* Ps 28:4; Is 3:11.

pany leaders named Baanah and Rechab, sons of Rimmon the Beerothite, of the tribe of Benjamin—Beeroth, too, was ascribed to Benjamin:[d] [3]the Beerothites fled to Gittaim, where they have been resident aliens to this day.[e] [4](Jonathan, son of Saul, had a son with crippled feet. He was five years old when the news about Saul and Jonathan came from Jezreel; his nurse took him and fled, but in their hasty flight, he fell and became lame. His name was Meribbaal.)* [f] [5]The sons of Rimmon the Beerothite, Rechab and Baanah, came into the house of Ishbaal during the heat of the day, while he was lying on his bed in the afternoon. [6]The gatekeeper of the house had dozed off while sifting wheat, and was asleep. So Rechab and his brother Baanah slipped past her [7]and entered the house while Ishbaal was lying asleep in his bedroom. They struck and killed him, and cut off his head. Then, taking the head, they traveled on the Arabah road all night long.

***The Murder Avenged.*** [8]They brought the head of Ishbaal to David in Hebron and said to the king: "This is the head of Ishbaal, son of your enemy Saul, who sought your life. Thus has the LORD this day avenged my lord the king on Saul and his posterity." [9]But David replied to Rechab and his brother Baanah, sons of Rimmon the Beerothite: "As the LORD lives, who rescued me from every distress: [10]the man who reported to me, 'Saul is dead,' and thought he was bringing good news, that man I seized and killed in Ziglag: that was the reward I gave him.[g] [11]How much more now, when wicked men have slain an innocent man in bed at home, must I require his blood from you and purge you from the land!" [12]So at David's command, the young men killed them and cut off their hands and feet, hanging them up near the pool in Hebron. But he took the head of Ishbaal and buried it in Abner's grave in Hebron.[h]

## CHAPTER 5

See RG 119

***David King of Israel.*** [1][i] All the tribes of Israel came to David in Hebron, and they said: "Look! We are your bone and your flesh. [2]In days past, when Saul was still our king, you were the one who led Israel out in all its battles and brought it back. And the LORD said to you: You shall shepherd my people Israel; you shall be ruler over Israel."[j] [3]Then all the elders of Israel came to the king in Hebron, and at Hebron King David made a covenant with them in the presence of the LORD; and they anointed David king over Israel. [4]David was thirty years old when he became king, and he reigned forty years: [5]in Hebron he was king over Judah seven years and six months, and in Jerusalem he was king thirty-three years over all Israel and Judah.[k]

***Capture of Zion.**** [6][l] Then the king and his men went to Jerusalem against the Jebusites who inhabited the land. They told David, "You shall not enter here: the blind and the lame will drive you away!" which was their way of saying, "David shall not enter here."[m] [7]David nevertheless captured the fortress of Zion, which is the City of David. [8]On that day David said: "All who wish to strike at the Jebusites must attack through the water shaft. The lame and the blind shall be the personal enemies of David." That is why it is said, "The blind and the lame shall not enter the palace."[n] [9]David took up residence in the fortress which he called the City of David. David built up the city on all sides, from the Millo toward the center.[o] [10]David

**4:4 Meribbaal**: Hebrew has *mephiboseth*; see note on 2:8. His name, in fact, is Meribbaal; cf. 1 Chr 8:34; 9:40. He is the subject of chap. 9 below. The text of this verse may owe its present place to the fact that ancient copies of the Books of Samuel tended to confuse his name with that of his uncle Ishbaal, Saul's son and successor, a principal figure in chaps. 2–4.

**5:6–12** David's most important military exploit, the taking of Jerusalem, is here presented before his battles with the Philistines, vv. 17–25, which took place earlier. The sense of vv. 6 and 8 is in doubt. Perhaps the Jebusites boasted that Jerusalem was impregnable, using a metaphorical or proverbial expression that claimed the city was defensible even by people not suited for military action. The saying then received a different sense (v. 8), to the effect that "the blind and the lame" were David's enemies. Mt 21:14 and Lk 14:13 seem to play off, and transform, this saying.

*d:* 2 Sm 9:3; Jos 9:17–18. *e:* Jos 18:25. *f:* 2 Sm 9:3; 19:25. *g:* 2 Sm 1:6–10, 14, 16. *h:* Dt 21:22–23; 1 Sm 31:10. *i:* 1 Chr 11:1–3. *j:* 2 Sm 3:10; Dt 17:15; 1 Sm 18:16. *k:* 2 Sm 2:11; 1 Kgs 2:11; 1 Chr 3:4. *l:* 1 Chr 11:4–9. *m:* Jos 15:63; Jgs 1:19, 21; Is 29:3. *n:* Lv 21:18; Mt 21:14–15. *o:* 1 Kgs 3:1; 9:15; 11:27.

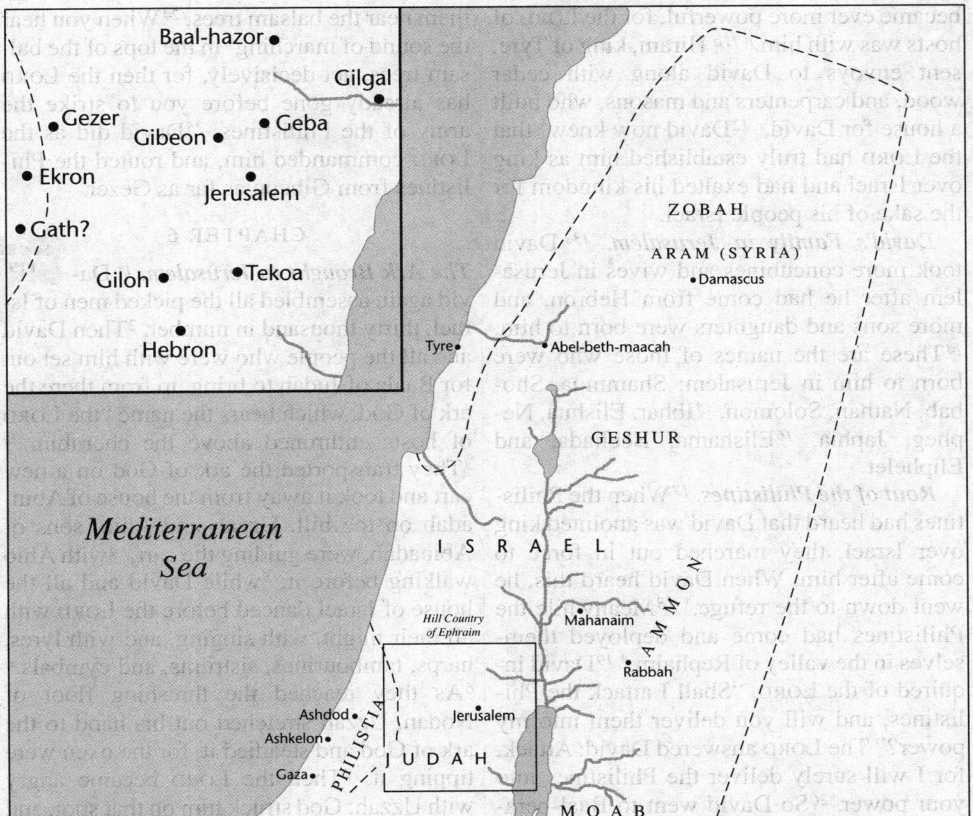


**The Kingdom of David according to 2 Samuel**

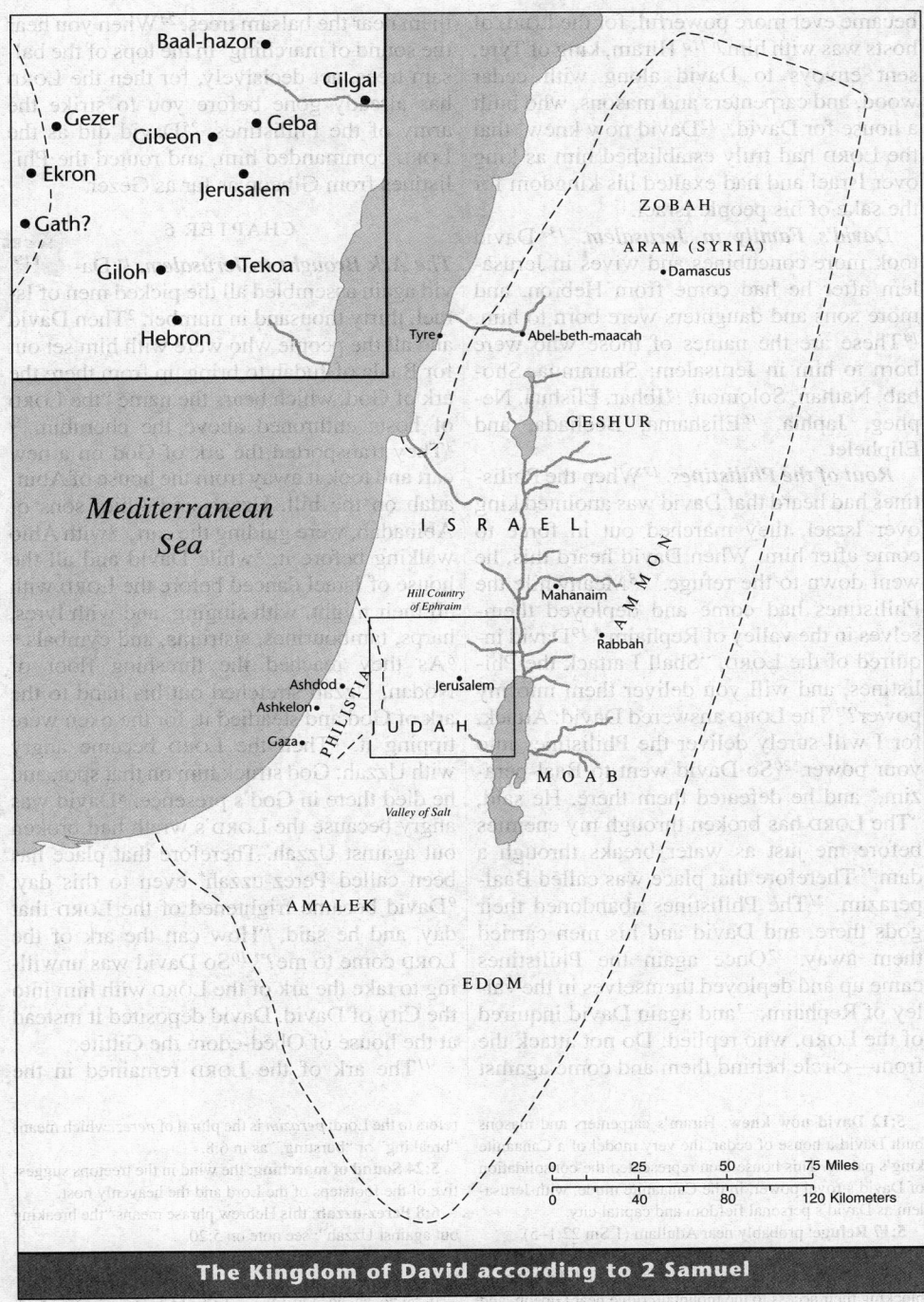

became ever more powerful, for the LORD of hosts was with him.[p] 11[q] Hiram, king of Tyre, sent envoys to David along with cedar wood, and carpenters and masons, who built a house for David.[r] 12 David now knew* that the LORD had truly established him as king over Israel and had exalted his kingdom for the sake of his people Israel.

***David's Family in Jerusalem.*** 13[s] David took more concubines and wives in Jerusalem after he had come from Hebron, and more sons and daughters were born to him. 14 These are the names of those who were born to him in Jerusalem: Shammua, Shobab, Nathan, Solomon, 15 Ibhar, Elishua, Nepheg, Japhia, 16 Elishama, Beeliada, and Eliphelet.

***Rout of the Philistines.*** 17 When the Philistines had heard that David was anointed king over Israel, they marched out in force to come after him. When David heard this, he went down to the refuge.* 18 Meanwhile the Philistines had come and deployed themselves in the valley of Rephaim.* 19 David inquired of the LORD, "Shall I attack the Philistines, and will you deliver them into my power?" The LORD answered David: Attack, for I will surely deliver the Philistines into your power. 20 So David went to Baal-perazim,* and he defeated them there. He said, "The LORD has broken through my enemies before me just as water breaks through a dam." Therefore that place was called Baal-perazim. 21 The Philistines abandoned their gods there, and David and his men carried them away. 22 Once again the Philistines came up and deployed themselves in the valley of Rephaim, 23 and again David inquired of the LORD, who replied: Do not attack the front—circle behind them and come against them near the balsam trees. 24 When you hear the sound of marching* in the tops of the balsam trees, act decisively, for then the LORD has already gone before you to strike the army of the Philistines. 25 David did as the LORD commanded him, and routed the Philistines from Gibeon as far as Gezer.

## CHAPTER 6

See RG 119

***The Ark Brought to Jerusalem.*** 1[t] David again assembled all the picked men of Israel, thirty thousand in number. 2 Then David and all the people who were with him set out for Baala of Judah to bring up from there the ark of God, which bears the name "the LORD of hosts enthroned above the cherubim."[u] 3 They transported the ark of God on a new cart and took it away from the house of Abinadab on the hill. Uzzah and Ahio, sons of Abinadab, were guiding the cart,[v] 4 with Ahio walking before it, 5 while David and all the house of Israel danced before the LORD with all their might, with singing, and with lyres, harps, tambourines, sistrums, and cymbals.[w] 6 As they reached the threshing floor of Nodan, Uzzah stretched out his hand to the ark of God and steadied it, for the oxen were tipping it. 7 Then the LORD became angry with Uzzah; God struck him on that spot, and he died there in God's presence. 8 David was angry because the LORD's wrath had broken out against Uzzah. Therefore that place has been called Perez-uzzah* even to this day. 9 David became frightened of the LORD that day, and he said, "How can the ark of the LORD come to me?" 10 So David was unwilling to take the ark of the LORD with him into the City of David. David deposited it instead at the house of Obed-edom the Gittite.

11 The ark of the LORD remained in the

**5:12 David now knew**: Hiram's carpenters and masons built David a house of cedar, the very model of a Canaanite king's palace. This house then represented the consolidation of David's royal power, in the Canaanite mode, with Jerusalem as David's personal fiefdom and capital city.

**5:17 Refuge**: probably near Adullam (1 Sm 22:1–5).

**5:18–25** The successive defeats of the Philistines in the valley of Rephaim southwest of Jerusalem had the effect of blocking their access to the mountain ridge near Gibeon, and confining them to their holdings on the coast and in the foothills beyond Gezer to the west and south.

**5:20 Baal-perazim**: here the title *ba'al*, "master, lord," refers to the Lord; *perazim* is the plural of *perez*, which means "breaking" or "bursting," as in 6:8.

**5:24 Sound of marching**: the wind in the treetops suggestive of the footsteps of the Lord and the heavenly host.

**6:8 Perez-uzzah**: this Hebrew phrase means "the breaking out against Uzzah"; see note on 5:20.

*p:* Ps 78:70–72; 89; 132:13. *q:* 1 Chr 14:1–16. *r:* 1 Kgs 5:15; 1 Chr 14:1–2. *s:* 1 Chr 3:5–8; 14:3–7. *t:* 1 Chr 13:1–14. *u:* Ex 25:10; Jos 15:9; 1 Chr 13:6; Ps 132:8–10. *v:* 1 Sm 4:3–4; 6:7–8; 7:1; Dn 3:55. *w:* Ps 68:24–25; 150:3–5.

**Holy City**

DAVID BRINGS THE ark of God to Jerusalem in 2 Sm 6, making the city not only his administrative center, but also his religious center. Thus, Jerusalem becomes the holy city, first in Judaism, where it is still the direction of prayer, and later also in Christianity and Islam, though for different reasons.

house of Obed-edom the Gittite for three months, and the LORD blessed Obed-edom and all his household.[x] 12[y] When it was reported to King David that the LORD had blessed the household of Obed-edom and all that he possessed because of the ark of God, David went to bring up the ark of God from the house of Obed-edom into the City of David with joy.[z] 13 As soon as the bearers of the ark of the LORD had advanced six steps, he sacrificed an ox and a fatling. 14 Then David came dancing before the LORD with abandon, girt with a linen ephod.* [a] 15 David and all the house of Israel were bringing up the ark of the LORD with shouts of joy and sound of horn. 16 As the ark of the LORD was entering the City of David, Michal, daughter of Saul, looked down from her window, and when she saw King David jumping and dancing before the LORD, she despised him in her heart. 17[b] They brought in the ark of the LORD and set it in its place within the tent which David had pitched for it. Then David sacrificed burnt offerings and communion offerings before the LORD. 18 When David had finished sacrificing burnt offerings and communion offerings, he blessed the people in the name of the LORD of hosts, 19 and distributed among all the people, the entire multitude of Israel, to every man and every woman, one loaf of bread, one piece of meat, and one raisin cake. Then all the people returned to their homes.

20* When David went home to bless his own house,[c] Michal, the daughter of Saul, came out to meet him and said, "How well the king of Israel has honored himself today, exposing himself to the view of the slave girls of his followers, as a commoner might expose himself!" 21 But David replied to Michal: "I was dancing before the LORD. As the LORD lives, who chose me over your father and all his house when he appointed me ruler over the LORD's people, Israel, not only will I make merry before the LORD,[d] 22 but I will demean myself even more. I will be lowly in your eyes, but in the eyes of the slave girls you spoke of I will be somebody." 23 Saul's daughter Michal was childless to the day she died.

## CHAPTER 7

See RG 119–20

*The Oracle of Nathan.* 1[e] After the king had taken up residence in his house, and the LORD had given him rest from his enemies on every side,[f] 2 the king said to Nathan the prophet, "Here I am living in a house of cedar, but the ark of God dwells in a tent!"[g] 3 Nathan answered the king, "Whatever is in your heart, go and do, for the LORD is with you."[h] 4 But that same night the word of the LORD came to Nathan: 5 Go and tell David my servant, Thus says the LORD: Is it you who would build me a house to dwell in?[i] 6 I have never dwelt in a house from the day I brought Israel up from Egypt to this day, but I have been going about in a tent or a tabernacle. 7 As long as I have wandered about among the Israelites, did I ever say a word to any of the judges whom I commanded to shepherd my people Israel: Why have you not built me a house of cedar?

**6:14 Girt with a linen ephod**: the ephod was some sort of priestly vestment (probably like an apron); cf. Ex 28:4; Jgs 17:5; 1 Sm 2:18, 28; 14:3; 22:18; 23:6. The cultic procession that accompanies the ark to the holy mountain, Zion, is led by King David, dancing ecstatically and wearing a priestly vestment.

**6:20–23** Michal's reaction to David's dancing comes from her conception of how a king should comport himself. David rejects this understanding, saying he needs no instruction from the house of the failed king, Saul.

*x:* 1 Chr 26:4. *y:* 1 Chr 15:1–29; Ps 24:7–10. *z:* 1 Kgs 8:1. *a:* 1 Sm 2:18. *b:* Lv 1:1–17; 3:1–17; 1 Chr 16:1–3. *c:* 1 Chr 16:43. *d:* 1 Sm 13:14; 15:28. *e:* 1 Chr 17:1–27. *f:* Dt 12:10; 25:19; 1 Kgs 5:4. *g:* Ex 39:32. *h:* Ps 132:1–5. *i:* 1 Kgs 5:3; 8:16, 27; 1 Chr 22:8; 28:3; Is 66:1; Acts 7:48–49.

## A Dynasty for David

THERE IS A play throughout ch 7 on the word "house." The house David proposes to build is a temple. But the LORD declines David's offer and says instead that he will build David a house, that is, a dynasty.

8Now then, speak thus to my servant David, Thus says the LORD of hosts:* I took you
from the pasture, from following the flock,
to become ruler over my people Israel.[j] 9I
was with you wherever you went, and I cut
down all your enemies before you. And I
will make your name like that of the greatest
on earth.[k] 10I will assign a place for my people Israel and I will plant them in it to dwell
there; they will never again be disturbed, nor
shall the wicked ever again oppress them, as
they did at the beginning, 11and from the day
when I appointed judges over my people Israel. I will give you rest from all your enemies. Moreover, the LORD also declares to
you that the LORD will make a house for
you:[l] 12[m] when your days have been completed and you rest with your ancestors, I
will raise up your offspring after you, sprung
from your loins, and I will establish his
kingdom. 13He it is* who shall build a house
for my name, and I will establish his royal
throne forever. 14I will be a father to him,
and he shall be a son to me. If he does
wrong, I will reprove him with a human rod
and with human punishments;[n] 15but I will
not withdraw my favor from him as I withdrew it from Saul who was before you.[o]
16Your house and your kingdom are firm forever before me; your throne shall be firmly
established forever.*[p] 17In accordance with
all these words and this whole vision Nathan
spoke to David.

***David's Thanksgiving.*** 18Then King David
went in and sat in the LORD's presence and
said, "Who am I, Lord GOD, and what is my
house, that you should have brought me so
far?[q] 19And yet even this is too little in your
sight, Lord GOD! For you have made a
promise regarding your servant's house
reaching into the future, and giving guidance
to the people, Lord GOD! 20What more can
David say to you? You know* your servant,
Lord GOD! 21For your servant's sake and as
you have had at heart, you have brought
about this whole magnificent disclosure to
your servant. 22Therefore, great are you,
Lord GOD! There is no one like you, no God
but you, as we have always heard.[r] 23What
other nation on earth is there like your people Israel? What god has ever led a nation,
redeeming it as his people and making a
name by great and awesome deeds, as you
drove out the nations and their gods before
your people, whom you redeemed for yourself from Egypt?[s] 24[t] You have established
for yourself your people Israel as your people forever, and you, LORD, have become
their God. 25Now, LORD God, confirm the
promise that you have spoken concerning

**7:8–16** The message Nathan delivers to David, called the Dynastic Oracle, is prompted by David's intention to build a house (i.e., a temple) for the Lord, like David's own house (i.e., palace) of cedar. David is told, in effect, not to bother building a house for the Lord; rather, the Lord will make a house for him—a dynasty, the House of David. Not only will he have descendants (v. 12) who will sit upon the throne of Israel (v. 13), their rule will last forever (vv. 13, 16); and even if they transgress the Lord's commands, the line of David will never be removed from kingship as Saul was (cf. 1 Sm 13; 15). The oracle establishes the Davidic king as standing in relationship to the Lord as a son to a father (v. 14; cf. Ps 2:7; 89:27). The Dynastic Oracle, with cognate texts in the Scriptures, is the basis for Jewish expectations of an anointed king (1 Sm 12:3, 5), son of David (Mt 21:9); cf. Acts 2:30; Heb 1:5.

**7:13 He it is**: Solomon, in the event.

**7:16** The unconditional promise made here, and reflected in Ps 89:34–35, stands in contrast to the tradition in Ps 132:12, where the continuation of the line of David depends on their fidelity to the Lord; cf. also 1 Kgs 2:4; 6:12; 8:25.

**7:20 Know**: give recognition, choose, single out: cf. Gn 18:19; Ex 33:12; Am 3:2.

*j:* 1 Sm 16:13; 17:15–20; Ps 78:70–71; Am 7:14–15. *k:* Ps 89:27. *l:* 2 Sm 23:5; 1 Kgs 2:4–24. *m:* 1 Kgs 5:19; 8:19; 1 Chr 22:10; 2 Chr 7:18; Ps 89:4, 26–29, 36–37; Lk 1:32; Heb 1:5. *n:* Ps 2:7; 89:26; Prv 3:12. *o:* 2 Sm 23:5; 1 Sm 13:14; 15:26, 28; 2 Kgs 19:34; 1 Chr 17:11–14; Ps 89:33–34. *p:* 2 Sm 23:5; Dn 2:44; 1 Mc 2:57; Mk 11:10; Lk 1:32–33; Heb 1:8. *q:* 1 Chr 17:16. *r:* Ex 15:11; Is 45:5. *s:* Dt 4:7, 34. *t:* Ex 6:7; Dt 7:6; 26:17; 29:13.

your servant and his house forever. Bring about what you have promised [26]so that your name may be forever great. People will say: 'The LORD of hosts is God over Israel,' when the house of your servant David is established in your presence. [27]Because you, LORD of hosts, God of Israel, have revealed to your servant, 'I will build you a house,' your servant now finds the courage to make this prayer before you. [28]Since you, Lord GOD, are truly God and your words are truth and you have made this generous promise to your servant,[u] [29]do, then, bless the house of your servant, that it may be in your presence forever—since you, Lord GOD, have promised, and by your blessing the house of your servant shall be blessed forever."

## CHAPTER 8

See RG 120

*Summary of David's Wars.* [1][v] After this, David defeated the Philistines and subdued them; and David took . . .* from the Philistines. [2]He also defeated Moab and measured them with a line. Making them lie down on the ground, he measured two lengths of line for death, and a full length for life.* Thus the Moabites became subject to David, paying tribute. [3][w] David then defeated Hadadezer, son of Rehob, king of Zobah, when he went to re-establish his dominion at the River.[x] [4]David captured from him one thousand seven hundred horsemen and twenty thousand foot soldiers. David hamstrung all the chariot horses, but left one hundred for his chariots.[y] [5]The Arameans of Damascus came to help Hadadezer, king of Zobah, but David also defeated twenty-two thousand of them in Aram. [6]David then placed garrisons in the Damascus region of Aram, and the Arameans became David's subjects, paying tribute. The LORD brought David victory in all his undertakings. [7]David took the golden shields that were carried by Hadadezer's attendants and brought them to Jerusalem. (These Shishak, king of Egypt, took away when he came to Jerusalem in the days of Rehoboam, son of Solomon.) [8]From Tebah and Berothai, cities of Hadadezer, King David removed a very large quantity of bronze. [9]When Toi, king of Hamath, heard that David had defeated the entire army of Hadadezer, [10]Toi sent his son Hadoram to wish King David well and to congratulate him on having waged a victorious war against Hadadezer; for Hadadezer had been at war with Toi. Hadoram also brought with him articles of silver, gold, and bronze. [11]These also King David consecrated to the LORD along with the silver and gold that he had taken for this purpose from all the nations he had subdued: [12]from Edom, Moab, the Ammonites, the Philistines, and Amalek, and from the spoils of Hadadezer, son of Rehob, king of Zobah.

[13]On his return,* David made a name for himself by defeating eighteen thousand Edomites in the Valley of Salt.[z] [14]He set up garrisons in Edom, and all the Edomites became David's subjects. Thus the LORD brought David victory in all his undertakings.

***David's Officials.*** [15][a] David was king over all Israel; he dispensed justice and right to all his people. [16]Joab, son of Zeruiah, was in command of the army. Jehoshaphat, son of Ahilud, was chancellor. [17]Zadok, son of Ahitub, and Ahimelech, son of Abiathar, were priests.* Shavsha was scribe. [18]Benaiah, son

**8:1 David took . . .**: the original Hebrew seems irretrievable. The transmitted text gives "the bridle of the cubit"; 1 Chr 18:1 understood "Gath and its towns"; others implausibly read "dominion of the capital city."

**8:2 Two lengths . . . a full length for life**: usually taken to mean that two-thirds of them were executed; but it could mean that two-thirds were spared, if the line was used full length in their case but doubled on itself to make "two lines" for those to be put to death. Note the contrasting good relations in 1 Sm 22:3–4.

**8:13 On his return**: possibly to Jerusalem, after the revolt of Absalom (chaps. 15–18), which this catalogue of victories would avoid mentioning. 1 Chr 18:12 attributes the defeat of the Edomites to Abishai, while the superscription of Ps 60 attributes it to Joab.

**8:17 Zadok . . . Ahimelech, son of Abiathar, were priests**: the names of Abiathar and Ahimelech are frequently associated with David (1 Sm 22:20; 23:6; 30:7; 2 Sm 15:24, 29, 35; 17:15; 19:12; 20:25), but they show Abiathar acting as priest, not Ahimelech: Abiathar shared the priestly office with Zadok in David's reign and even during Solomon's early years (1 Kgs 2:26; 4:4). Ahimelech was the name of Abiathar's father. This

*u:* Nm 23:19; Jn 17:17. *v:* 1 Chr 18:1–17. *w:* 2 Sm 10:15–19. *x:* 2 Sm 10:6; 1 Kgs 11:23. *y:* Jos 11:6, 9. *z:* 2 Kgs 14:7. *a:* 2 Sm 20:23–26; 1 Kgs 4:1–6; 1 Chr 18:14–17.

of Jehoiada, was in command of the Cherethites and the Pelethites; and David's sons were priests.[b]

## CHAPTER 9

See RG 120

*David and Meribbaal.* 1David asked, "Is there any survivor of Saul's house to whom I may show kindness for the sake of Jonathan?"[c] 2Now there was an official of the house of Saul named Ziba. He was summoned to David, and the king asked him, "Are you Ziba?" He replied, "Your servant."[d] 3Then the king asked, "Is there any survivor of Saul's house to whom I may show God's kindness?" Ziba answered the king, "There is still Jonathan's son, the one whose feet are crippled."[e] 4The king asked him, "Where is he?" and Ziba answered the king, "He is in the house of Machir, son of Ammiel, in Lodebar."[f] 5So King David sent for him and had him brought from the house of Machir, son of Ammiel, from Lodebar. 6When Meribbaal, son of Jonathan, son of Saul, came to David, he fell face down in homage. David said, "Meribbaal," and he answered, "Your servant." 7"Do not be afraid," David said to him, "I will surely be kind to you for the sake of Jonathan your father. I will restore to you all the lands of Saul your grandfather, and you shall eat at my table always." 8Bowing low, he answered, "What am I, your servant, that you should pay attention to a dead dog like me?"[g] 9The king then called Ziba, Saul's attendant, and said to him: "All that belonged to Saul and to his entire house, I am giving to your lord's son. 10You and your sons and servants must till the land for him. You shall bring in the produce, which shall be food for your lord's household to eat. But Meribbaal, your lord's son, shall always eat at my table." Now Ziba had fifteen sons and twenty servants. 11Ziba answered the king, "Whatever my lord the king commands his servant, so shall your servant do." And so Meribbaal ate at David's table like one of the king's sons.[h] 12Meribbaal had a young son whose name was Mica; and all the tenants of Ziba's household worked for Meribbaal.[i] 13But Meribbaal lived in Jerusalem, because he always ate at the king's table. He was lame in both feet.[j]

## CHAPTER 10

See RG 120

*Campaigns Against Ammon.* 1[k] After this,* the king of the Ammonites died, and Hanun his son succeeded him as king. 2David said, "I will show kindness to Hanun, the son of Nahash, as his father showed kindness to me." Therefore David sent his servants to Hanun to console him concerning his father. But when David's servants had entered the land of the Ammonites, 3the Ammonite princes said to their lord Hanun, "Do you think David is doing this—sending you these consolers—to honor your father? Is it not rather to explore the city, to spy on it, and to overthrow it, that David has sent his servants to you?" 4So Hanun seized David's servants, shaved off half their beards, cut away the lower halves of their garments at the buttocks, and sent them away.[l] 5David was told of it and he sent word for them to be intercepted, for the men had been greatly disgraced. "Remain at Jericho," the king told them, "until your beards have grown again; then come back here."

6* When the Ammonites realized that they were in bad odor with David, they sent for and hired twenty thousand Aramean foot soldiers from Beth-rehob and Zobah, as well as the king of Maacah with one thousand men, and twelve thousand men from Tob.[m]

7When David heard of this, he sent Joab and his whole army of warriors against them.[n] 8The Ammonites marched out and lined up for battle at the entrance of their city

verse and 1 Chr 18:16 may indicate that Abiathar had a son named Ahimelech who also acted as a priest, like his father and his namesake grandfather, in the last years of David.

**10:1 After this**: early in the reign of David, since Hanun's father Nahash (1 Chr 19:1) had been ruling in Ammon at the beginning of Saul's reign (1 Sm 11) and Solomon was not yet born (2 Sm 11:1; 12:24).

**10:6–9** A Hebrew text from Qumran (4QSam$^{a}$) comes closer in these verses to what is given in 1 Chr 19:6–9. The scene of the conflict is more likely the Ammonite capital, Rabbath-Ammon (v. 8; cf. Josephus *Antiquities*, 7:123), than Medeba (1 Chr 19:7).

*b:* 2 Sm 15:18; 20:7, 23; 23:20. *c:* 2 Sm 21:7; 1 Sm 18:1–4; 20:8–10, 15–17, 42. *d:* 2 Sm 16:1–4; 19:27. *e:* 2 Sm 4:4. *f:* 2 Sm 17:27. *g:* 1 Sm 24:15. *h:* 2 Sm 19:29. *i:* 1 Chr 8:34. *j:* 2 Sm 21:7. *k:* 1 Chr 19:1–19. *l:* Is 20:4. *m:* 2 Sm 8:3; 1 Sm 14:47. *n:* 2 Sm 11:1.

**Adultery and Murder**

IT IS HIGHLY unusual for ancient literature to criticize powerful and successful kings. The way David's behavior is depicted and condemned in the Bible (cf. 2 Sm 11:1–12:25) shows the overriding importance it assigns to moral values.

gate, while the Arameans of Zobah and Rehob and the men of Tob and Maacah remained apart in the open field. 9When Joab saw that there was a battle line both in front of and behind him, he chose some of the best fighters of Israel and lined them up against the Arameans; 10the rest of the army he placed under the command of his brother Abishai and lined up to oppose the Ammonites. 11And he said, "If the Arameans prove too strong for me, you must come and save me; and if the Ammonites prove too strong for you, I will come to save you. 12Hold firm and let us show ourselves courageous for the sake of our people and the cities of our God; and may the LORD do what is good in his sight." 13Joab therefore advanced with his men for battle with the Arameans, but they fled before him. 14And when the Ammonites saw that the Arameans had fled, they too fled before Abishai, and reentered their city. Joab then ceased his attack on the Ammonites and came to Jerusalem. 15[o] Seeing themselves vanquished by Israel, the Arameans held a full muster of troops. 16Hadadezer sent for and brought Arameans from beyond the River. They came to Helam, with Shobach, the captain of Hadadezer's army, at their head. 17When this was reported to David, he gathered all Israel together, crossed the Jordan, and went to Helam. The Arameans drew up in formation against David and gave battle. 18But the Arameans fled before Israel, and David killed seven hundred of their chariot fighters and forty thousand of their foot soldiers. He struck down Shobach, commander of the army, and he died on the field. 19When Hadadezer's vassal kings saw themselves vanquished by Israel, they made peace with the Israelites and became their subjects. After this, the Arameans were afraid to give further aid to the Ammonites.

## CHAPTER 11

See RG 120

***David's Sin.*** 1At the turn of the year,* the time when kings go to war, David sent out Joab along with his officers and all Israel, and they laid waste the Ammonites and besieged Rabbah. David himself remained in Jerusalem.[p] 2One evening David rose from his bed and strolled about on the roof of the king's house. From the roof he saw a woman bathing; she was very beautiful. 3David sent people to inquire about the woman and was told, "She is Bathsheba, daughter of Eliam, and wife of Uriah the Hittite, Joab's armor-bearer."[q] 4Then David sent messengers and took her. When she came to him, he took her to bed, at a time when she was just purified after her period; and she returned to her house.[r] 5But the woman had become pregnant; she sent a message to inform David, "I am pregnant."

6So David sent a message to Joab, "Send me Uriah the Hittite." Joab sent Uriah to David. 7And when he came, David asked him how Joab was, how the army was, and how the war was going, and Uriah answered that all was well. 8David then said to Uriah, "Go down to your house and bathe your feet." Uriah left the king's house, and a portion from the king's table was sent after him. 9But Uriah slept at the entrance of the king's house with the other officers of his lord, and did not go down to his own house. 10David was told, "Uriah has not gone down to his house." So he said to Uriah, "Have you not come from a journey? Why, then, did you not go down to your house?" 11Uriah answered David, "The ark and Israel and Judah are staying in tents, and my lord Joab and my lord's servants are

**11:1 At the turn of the year**: in the spring.

*o:* 2 Sm 8:3–8; 1 Chr 9:16–19. *p:* 2 Sm 10:7; 1 Chr 20:1. *q:* 2 Sm 23:39. *r:* Lv 15:19.

encamped in the open field. Can I go home to eat and to drink and to sleep with my wife? As the LORD lives and as you live, I will do no such thing."[s] 12 Then David said to Uriah, "Stay here today also, and tomorrow I will send you back." So Uriah stayed in Jerusalem that day. On the following day, 13 David summoned him, and he ate and drank with David, who got him drunk. But in the evening he went out to sleep on his bed among his lord's servants, and did not go down to his house. 14 The next morning David wrote a letter to Joab which he sent by Uriah. 15 This is what he wrote in the letter: "Place Uriah up front, where the fighting is fierce. Then pull back and leave him to be struck down dead." 16 So while Joab was besieging the city, he assigned Uriah to a place where he knew the defenders were strong. 17 When the men of the city made a sortie against Joab, some officers of David's army fell, and Uriah the Hittite also died.

18 Then Joab sent David a report of all the details of the battle, 19 instructing the messenger, "When you have finished giving the king all the details of the battle, 20 the king may become angry and say to you: 'Why did you go near the city to fight? Did you not know that they would shoot from the wall above? 21 Who killed Abimelech, son of Jerubbaal? Was it not a woman who threw a millstone down on him from the wall above, so that he died in Thebez? Why did you go near the wall?' Then you in turn are to say, 'Your servant Uriah the Hittite is also dead.' "[t] 22 The messenger set out, and on his arrival he reported to David everything Joab had sent him to tell.* 23 He told David: "The men had the advantage over us and came out into the open against us, but we pushed them back to the entrance of the city gate. 24 Then the archers shot at your servants from the wall above, and some of the king's servants died; and your servant Uriah the Hittite is also dead." 25 David said to the messenger: "This is what you shall say to Joab: 'Do not let this be a great evil in your sight, for the sword devours now here and now there. Strengthen your attack on the city and destroy it.' Encourage him."

26 When the wife of Uriah heard that her husband had died, she mourned her lord. 27 But once the mourning was over, David sent for her and brought her into his house. She became his wife and bore him a son. But in the sight of the LORD what David had done was evil.

## CHAPTER 12

See RG 120

***Nathan's Parable.**** 1 The LORD sent Nathan to David, and when he came to him, he said: "Tell me how you judge this case: In a certain town there were two men, one rich, the other poor.[u] 2 The rich man had flocks and herds in great numbers. 3 But the poor man had nothing at all except one little ewe lamb that he had bought. He nourished her, and she grew up with him and his children. Of what little he had she ate; from his own cup she drank; in his bosom she slept; she was like a daughter to him. 4 Now, a visitor came to the rich man, but he spared his own flocks and herds to prepare a meal for the traveler who had come to him: he took the poor man's ewe lamb and prepared it for the one who had come to him." 5 David grew very angry with that man and said to Nathan: "As the LORD lives, the man who has done this deserves death! 6 He shall make fourfold restitution* for the lamb because he has done this and was unsparing."[v] 7 Then Nathan said to David: "You are the man!

**11:22–24** In these verses the Greek text has David, angry with Joab, repeat exactly the questions Joab had foreseen in vv. 20–21. In v. 24 of our oldest Greek text, the messenger specifies that about eighteen men were killed. The Greek is considerably longer than the transmitted Hebrew text, suggesting that the Hebrew may have lost some sentences.

**12:1–7** David has committed adultery with Bathsheba and arranged the death of her husband. Instead of directly indicting the king for this criminal abuse of his royal authority, the prophet Nathan tells David a story. In the story, a parable of David's own actions, a powerful man takes cruel advantage of his vulnerable neighbor. Hearing the story, David is outraged and denounces the rich man—thus unwittingly pronouncing judgment on himself ("You are the man," v. 7).

**12:6 Fourfold restitution**: David's judgment foreshadows the deaths of four of his own sons: the child born of his adulterous union with Bathsheba (v. 18); Amnon (13:28–29); Absalom (18:15; 19:1); and Adonijah (1 Kgs 2:24–25).

*s:* 1 Sm 4:3–4. *t:* Jgs 9:50–54. *u:* Sir 47:1. *v:* Ex 21:37; Lk 19:8.

***Nathan's Indictment.*** "Thus says the LORD God of Israel: I anointed you king over Israel. I delivered you from the hand of Saul.[w] [8]I gave you your lord's house and your lord's wives for your own. I gave you the house of Israel and of Judah. And if this were not enough, I could count up for you still more. [9]Why have you despised the LORD and done what is evil in his sight? You have cut down Uriah the Hittite with the sword; his wife you took as your own, and him you killed with the sword of the Ammonites. [10]Now, therefore, the sword shall never depart from your house, because you have despised me and have taken the wife of Uriah the Hittite to be your wife.[x] [11]Thus says the LORD: I will bring evil upon you out of your own house. I will take your wives before your very eyes, and will give them to your neighbor: he shall lie with your wives in broad daylight.[*] [y] [12]You have acted in secret, but I will do this in the presence of all Israel, in the presence of the sun itself."

***David's Repentance.*** [13]Then David said to Nathan, "I have sinned against the LORD." Nathan answered David: "For his part, the LORD has removed your sin. You shall not die,[z] [14]but since you have utterly spurned the LORD by this deed, the child born to you will surely die." [15]Then Nathan returned to his house.

The LORD struck the child that the wife of Uriah had borne to David, and it became desperately ill. [16]David pleaded with God on behalf of the child. He kept a total fast, and spent the night lying on the ground clothed in sackcloth. [17]The elders of his house stood beside him to get him to rise from the ground; but he would not, nor would he take food with them. [18]On the seventh day, the child died. David's servants were afraid to tell him that the child was dead, for they said: "When the child was alive, we spoke to him, but he would not listen to what we said. How can we tell him the child is dead? He may do some harm!" [19]But David noticed his servants whispering among themselves and realized that the child was dead. He asked his servants, "Is the child dead?" They said, "Yes." [20]Rising from the ground, David washed and anointed himself, and changed his clothes. Then he went to the house of the LORD and worshiped. He returned to his own house and asked for food; they set it before him, and he ate. [21]His servants said to him: "What is this you are doing? While the child was living, you fasted and wept and kept vigil; now that the child is dead, you rise and take food." [22]He replied: "While the child was living, I fasted and wept, thinking, 'Who knows? The LORD may grant me the child's life.' [23]But now he is dead. Why should I fast? Can I bring him back again? I shall go to him, but he will not return to me."[a] [24]Then David consoled Bathsheba his wife. He went and slept with her; and she conceived and bore him a son, who was named Solomon. The LORD loved him [25]and sent the prophet Nathan to name him Jedidiah,[*] on behalf of the LORD.

***End of the Ammonite War.*** [26][b] Joab fought against Rabbah of the Ammonites and captured that royal city. [27]He sent messengers to David to say: "I have fought against Rabbah and have taken the water-city. [28]Therefore, assemble the rest of the soldiers, join the siege against the city, and capture it, lest I be the one to capture the city and mine be the name people mention, not yours." [29]So David assembled the rest of the soldiers, went to Rabbah, fought against it, and captured it. [30]He took the crown of Milcom from the idol's head, a talent[*] of gold in weight, with precious stones; this crown David wore on his own head. He also brought out a great amount of spoil from the city. [31]He deported the people of the city and set them to work with saws, iron picks, and iron axes, or put them to work at the brickmold. He dealt thus with all the cities of the Ammonites. Then David and his whole army returned to Jerusalem.

**12:11 In broad daylight**: lit., "before the eyes of the sun"; the phrase echoes "before your very eyes" and anticipates "in the presence of the sun itself" (v. 12). The reference is to Absalom's action in appropriating his father's harem (16:22).

**12:25 Jedidiah**: the name means "beloved of Yhwh."

**12:30 A talent**: since this would normally be more than seventy-five pounds, the report may have been embellished.

*w:* 1 Sm 16:13. *x:* 2 Sm 13:28–29; 18:14. *y:* 2 Sm 16:21–22. *z:* 1 Kgs 21:29; Ps 32:5; 51:4; Sir 47:11. *a:* Jb 7:9–10. *b:* 1 Chr 20:1–3.

## CHAPTER 13

See RG 120

***Amnon's Rape of Tamar.*** 1 After this, the following occurred. David's son Absalom had a beautiful sister named Tamar, and David's son Amnon loved her.[c] 2 He was in such anguish over his sister Tamar that he became sick; she was a virgin, and Amnon thought it impossible to do anything to her. 3 Now Amnon had a friend named Jonadab, son of David's brother Shimeah, who was very clever.* [d] 4 He asked him, "Prince, why are you so dejected morning after morning? Why not tell me?" So Amnon said to him, "I am in love with Tamar, my brother Absalom's sister." 5 Then Jonadab replied, "Lie down on your bed and pretend to be sick. When your father comes to visit you, say to him, 'Please let my sister Tamar come and encourage me to take food. If she prepares something in my presence, for me to see, I will eat it from her hand.' " 6 So Amnon lay down and pretended to be sick. When the king came to visit him, Amnon said to the king, "Please let my sister Tamar come and prepare some fried cakes before my eyes, that I may take food from her hand."

7 David then sent home a message to Tamar, "Please go to the house of your brother Amnon and prepare some food for him." 8 Tamar went to the house of her brother Amnon, who was in bed. Taking dough and kneading it, she twisted it into cakes before his eyes and fried the cakes. 9 Then she took the pan and set out the cakes before him. But Amnon would not eat; he said, "Have everyone leave me." When they had all left him, 10 Amnon said to Tamar, "Bring the food into the bedroom, that I may have it from your hand." So Tamar picked up the cakes she had prepared and brought them to her brother Amnon in the bedroom. 11 But when she brought them close to him so he could eat, he seized her and said to her, "Come! Lie with me, my sister!" 12 But she answered him, "No, my brother! Do not force me! This is not done in Israel. Do not commit this terrible crime.[e] 13 Where would I take my shame? And you would be labeled a fool in Israel.* So please, speak to the king; he will not keep me from you."[f] 14 But he would not listen to her; he was too strong for her: he forced her down and raped her. 15 Then Amnon felt intense hatred for her; the hatred he felt for her far surpassed the love he had had for her. Amnon said to her, "Get up, leave." 16 She replied, "No, brother, because sending me away would be far worse than this evil thing you have done to me." He would not listen to her, 17 but called the youth who was his attendant and said, "Send this girl outside, away from me, and bar the door after her." 18 Now she had on a long tunic, for that is how virgin princesses dressed in olden days. When his attendant put her out and barred the door after her, 19 Tamar put ashes on her head and tore the long tunic in which she was clothed. Then, putting her hands to her head, she went away crying loudly. 20 Her brother Absalom said to her: "Has your brother Amnon been with you? Keep still now, my sister; he is your brother. Do not take this so to heart." So Tamar remained, devastated, in the house of her brother Absalom. 21 King David, when he heard of the whole affair, became very angry. He would not, however, antagonize Amnon, his high-spirited son; he loved him, because he was his firstborn. 22 And Absalom said nothing, good or bad, to Amnon; but Absalom hated Amnon for having humiliated his sister Tamar.

***Absalom's Plot.*** 23 Two years went by. It was sheep-shearing time for Absalom in Baal-hazor near Ephraim, and Absalom invited all the king's sons. 24 Absalom went to the king and said: "Your servant has hired the shearers. Please, may the king come with all his servants to your servant." 25 But the king said to Absalom, "No, my son, all of us should not go lest we be a burden to you." And though Absalom urged him, he would not go but began to bid him good-bye. 26 Ab-

**13:3 Clever**: lit., "wise." Jonadab's "wisdom" extends only to sly cleverness in getting things done; he devises the plan that will enable Amnon to pursue his infatuation. In the categories of the Old Testament wisdom tradition, Jonadab is a fool.

**13:13 A fool in Israel**: a play on *nebala* (v. 12), "terrible crime," lit., "folly."

*c:* 2 Sm 3:2–3; 1 Chr 3:9. *d:* 2 Sm 21:21. *e:* Lv 18:9; 20:17; Dt 22:21; 27:22. *f:* Gn 34:7–8.

salom then said, "If not you, then please let my brother Amnon come with us." The king asked him, "Why should he go with you?" 27But at Absalom's urging, the king sent Amnon and with him all his other sons. Absalom prepared a banquet fit for a king. 28[g] But Absalom had instructed his attendants: "Now watch! When Amnon is merry with wine and I say to you, 'Kill Amnon,' put him to death. Do not be afraid, for it is I who order you to do it. Be strong and act like warriors."

***Death of Amnon.*** 29When the attendants did to Amnon as Absalom had commanded, all the king's other sons rose up, mounted their mules, and fled. 30While they were still on the road, a report reached David: "Absalom has killed all the king's sons and not one of them is left." 31The king stood up, tore his garments, and lay on the ground. All his servants standing by him also tore their garments.[h] 32But Jonadab, son of David's brother Shimeah, spoke up: "Let not my lord think that all the young men, the king's sons, have been killed! Amnon alone is dead, for Absalom was set on this ever since Amnon humiliated his sister Tamar. 33Now let my lord the king not take so to heart that report, 'All the king's sons are dead.' Amnon alone is dead." 34Meanwhile, Absalom had taken flight. Then the servant on watch looked out and saw a large group coming down the slope from the direction of Bahurim. He came in and reported this to the king: "I saw some men coming down the mountainside from the direction of Bahurim." 35So Jonadab said to the king: "There! The king's sons have come. It is as your servant said." 36No sooner had he finished speaking than the king's sons came in, weeping aloud. The king, too, and all his servants wept very bitterly. 37But Absalom, who had taken flight, went to Talmai, son of Ammihud, king of Geshur,[i] 38and stayed in Geshur for three years. 39All that time the king continued to mourn his son; but his intention of going out against Absalom abated as he was consoled over the death of Amnon.

## CHAPTER 14

See RG 120

***The Wise Woman of Tekoa.*** 1Now Joab, son of Zeruiah, knew how the king felt toward Absalom. 2Joab sent to Tekoa and brought from there a wise woman, to whom he said: "Pretend to be in mourning. Put on mourning apparel and do not anoint yourself with oil, that you may appear to be a woman who has long been mourning someone dead. 3Then go to the king and speak to him in this manner." And Joab told her what to say.

4So the woman of Tekoa went to the king and fell to the ground in homage, saying, "Help, O king!" 5[j] The king said to her, "What do you want?" She replied: "Alas, I am a widow; my husband is dead. 6Your servant had two sons, who quarreled in the field, with no one to part them, and one of them struck his brother and killed him. 7Then the whole clan confronted your servant and demanded: 'Give up the one who struck down his brother. We must put him to death for the life of his brother whom he has killed; we must do away with the heir also.' Thus they will quench my remaining hope* and leave my husband neither name nor posterity upon the earth."[k] 8The king then said to the woman: "Go home. I will issue a command on your behalf." 9The woman of Tekoa answered him, "Upon me and my family be the blame, my lord king; the king and his throne are innocent." 10Then the king said, "If anyone says a word to you, have him brought to me, and he shall not touch you again." 11But she said, "Please, let the king remember the LORD your God, that the avenger of blood may not go too far in destruction and that my son may not be done away with." He replied, "As the LORD lives, not a hair of your son shall fall to the ground."

12But the woman continued, "Please let your servant say still another word to my lord the king." He replied, "Speak." 13So the woman said: "Why, then, do you think the way you do against the people of God? In pronouncing as he has, the king shows him-

**14:7 Hope**: lit., "glowing coal." The image is similar to that of a lighted lamp, e.g., Ps 132:17, or small hearth fire, to keep alive the ancestral name.

*g:* 2 Sm 12:10. *h:* 2 Sm 1:11. *i:* 2 Sm 3:3; 15:8. *j:* 2 Kgs 6:26–28. *k:* Nm 35:19.

self guilty, in not bringing back his own banished son. 14We must indeed die; we are then like water that is poured out on the ground and cannot be gathered up. Yet, though God does not bring back to life, he does devise means so as not to banish* anyone from him.[l] 15And now, if I have presumed to speak to the king of this matter, it is because the people have given me cause to fear. And so your servant thought: 'Let me speak to the king. Perhaps he will grant the petition of his servant. 16For the king must surely listen and rescue his servant from the grasp of one who would destroy both me and my son from the heritage of God.' 17And your servant says, 'Let the word of my lord the king lead to rest;* indeed, my lord the king is like an angel of God, discerning good and evil. The LORD your God be with you.' "[m]

18The king answered the woman, "Now do not conceal from me anything I may ask you!" The woman said, "Let my lord the king speak." 19So the king asked, "Is the hand of Joab with you in all this?" And the woman answered: "As you live, my lord the king, it is just as my lord has said, and not otherwise. It was your servant Joab who instructed me and told your servant all these things she was to say. 20Your servant Joab did this in order to approach the matter in a roundabout way. But my lord is wise with the wisdom of an angel of God, knowing all things on earth."

***Absalom's Return.*** 21Then the king said to Joab: "I am granting this request. Go and bring back young Absalom." 22Falling to the ground in homage and blessing the king, Joab said, "This day your servant knows that I am in good favor with you, my lord king, since the king has granted the request of your servant." 23Joab then went off to Geshur and brought Absalom to Jerusalem. 24But the king said, "Let him go off to his own house; he shall not appear before* me." So Absalom went off to his house and did not appear before the king.

25In all Israel there was no man more praised for his beauty than Absalom, flawless from the sole of his foot to the crown of his head. 26When he shaved his head—as he used to do at the end of every year, because his hair became too heavy for him—the hair weighed two hundred shekels according to the royal standard. 27Absalom had three sons born to him, besides a daughter named Tamar, who was a beautiful woman.[n]

***Absalom Is Pardoned.*** 28Absalom lived in Jerusalem for two years without appearing before the king. 29Then he sent a message asking Joab to send him to the king, but Joab would not come to him. Although he asked him a second time, Joab would not come. 30He therefore instructed his servants: "You see Joab's field that borders mine, where he has barley. Go, set it on fire." And so Absalom's servants set the field on fire.[o] Joab's farmhands came to him with torn garments and told him, "Absalom's servants set your field on fire." 31Joab went to Absalom in his house and asked him, "Why have your servants set my field on fire?" 32Absalom answered Joab: "I sent you a message: Come here, that I may send you to the king to say: 'Why did I come back from Geshur? I would be better off if I were still there!' Now, let me appear before the king. If I am guilty, let him put me to death." 33Joab went to the king and reported this. The king then called Absalom; he came to him and in homage fell on his face to the ground before the king. Then the king kissed Absalom.

## CHAPTER 15

See RG 121

***Absalom's Ambition.*** 1After this, Absalom provided himself with chariots, horses, and a retinue of fifty.[p] 2Moreover, Absalom used to rise early and stand alongside the road leading to the gate. If someone had a lawsuit to be decided by the king, Absalom would call to him and say, "From what city are you?" And when he replied, "Your servant is of such and such a tribe of Israel,"

**14:14 Not to banish**: a possible allusion to the religious institution of cities of refuge for involuntary murderers; see Nm 35:9–15.

**14:17 Rest**: cf. Ru 1:9; Ps 95:11; Mi 2:10. The reference here is to a return home for Absalom.

**14:24 Appear before**: lit., "see the face of," a term from court etiquette; so also in vv. 28, 32.

*l:* Jb 7:9; 14:7–12; Ps 88:4, 10–12. *m:* 1 Sm 29:9. *n:* 2 Sm 18:18. *o:* Jgs 15:4–5. *p:* 1 Sm 8:11; 1 Kgs 1:5.

### Hebron and Absalom's Rebellion

HEBRON WAS THE capital of Judah, where David had been made king of both Judah and Israel and had ruled Judah for seven years. Absalom mirrored his father's rise by declaring himself king in Hebron (15:7–12). His revolt, however, was not limited to Judah but spread throughout all the tribes of Israel (v. 10). Absalom would have become king on David's death. He either became too impatient or was embittered by the circumstances of the preceding years. Absalom's chariots, horses, and a retinue of fifty (15:1) gave him the airs of a king-to-be.

3 Absalom would say to him, "Your case is good and just, but there is no one to hear you in the king's name." 4 And he would continue: "If only I could be appointed judge in the land! Then everyone who has a lawsuit to be decided might come to me and I would render him justice." 5 Whenever a man approached him to show homage, he would extend his hand, hold him, and kiss him. 6 By behaving in this way toward all the Israelites who came to the king for judgment, Absalom was stealing the heart of Israel.

***Conspiracy in Hebron.*** 7 After a period of four years, Absalom said to the king: "Please let me go to Hebron and fulfill a vow I made to the LORD. 8 For while living in Geshur in Aram, your servant made this vow: 'If the LORD ever brings me back to Jerusalem, I will worship him in Hebron.' "[q] 9 The king said to him, "Go in peace," and he went off to Hebron. 10 Then Absalom sent agents throughout the tribes of Israel to say, "When you hear the sound of the horn, say, 'Absalom is king in Hebron!' " 11 Two hundred men had accompanied Absalom from Jerusalem. They had been invited and went in all innocence, knowing nothing. 12 Absalom also sent to Ahithophel the Gilonite, David's counselor, an invitation to come from his town, Giloh, for the sacrifices he was about to offer. So the conspiracy gained strength, and the people with Absalom increased in numbers.[r]

***David Flees Jerusalem.*** 13 An informant came to David with the report, "The Israelites have given their hearts to Absalom,[s] and they are following him." 14 At this, David said to all his servants who were with him in Jerusalem: "Get up, let us flee, or none of us will escape from Absalom. Leave at once, or he will quickly overtake us, and then bring disaster upon us, and put the city to the sword." 15 The king's servants answered him, "Whatever our lord the king chooses to do, we are your servants." 16 Then the king set out, accompanied by his entire household, except for ten concubines whom he left behind to care for the palace.[t] 17 As the king left the city, with all his officers accompanying him, they halted opposite the ascent of the Mount of Olives, at a distance, 18 while the whole army marched past him.

***David and Ittai.*** As all the Cherethites and Pelethites, and the six hundred Gittites who had entered his service from that city, were passing in review before the king,[u] 19 the king said to Ittai the Gittite: "Why should you also go with us? Go back and stay with the king, for you are a foreigner and you, too, are an exile from your own country. 20 You came only yesterday, and today shall I have you wander off with us wherever I have to go? Return and take your brothers with you, and may the LORD show you kindness and fidelity." 21 But Ittai answered the king, "As the LORD lives, and as my lord the king lives, your servant shall be wherever my lord the king is, whether for death or for life."[v] 22 So the king said to Ittai, "Go, then, march on." And Ittai the Gittite, with all his men and all the dependents that were with him, marched on. 23 The whole land wept aloud as the last of the soldiers went by, and the king crossed the Wadi Kidron with all the soldiers moving on ahead of him by way of the ascent of the Mount of Olives, toward the wilderness.

***David and the Priests.*** 24 Zadok, too, and all the Levites bearing the ark of the covenant of

*q:* 2 Sm 3:3; 13:37. *r:* 2 Sm 16:23. *s:* Ps 3. *t:* 2 Sm 16:21–22; 20:3. *u:* 2 Sm 8:18. *v:* Ru 1:16–17.

God set down the ark of God until the whole army had finished marching out of the city; and Abiathar came up. [25]Then the king said to Zadok: “Take the ark of God back to the city. If I find favor with the LORD, he will bring me back and permit me to see it and its lodging place. [26]But if he should say, ‘I am not pleased with you,’ I am ready; let him do to me as he sees fit.”[w] [27]The king also said to Zadok the priest: “Look, you and Abiathar return to the city in peace, and both your sons with you, your own son Ahimaaz, and Abiathar’s son Jonathan. [28]Remember, I shall be waiting at the fords near the wilderness until a report from you comes to me.” [29]So Zadok and Abiathar took the ark of God back to Jerusalem and remained there.

[30]As David went up the ascent of the Mount of Olives, he wept without ceasing. His head was covered, and he was walking barefoot. All those who were with him also had their heads covered and were weeping as they went.[x] [31]When David was told, “Ahithophel is among the conspirators with Absalom,” he said, “O LORD, turn the counsel of Ahithophel to folly!”[y]

***David and Hushai.*** [32]When David reached the top, where God was worshiped, Hushai the Archite was there to meet him, with garments torn and dirt upon his head.[z] [33]David said to him: “If you come with me, you will be a burden to me; [34]but if you return to the city and say to Absalom, ‘Let me be your servant, O king; I was formerly your father’s servant, but now I will be yours,’ you will thwart for me the counsel of Ahithophel.[a] [35]You will have the priests Zadok and Abiathar there with you. If you hear anything from the king’s house, you shall report it to the priests Zadok and Abiathar, [36]who have there with them their two sons, Zadok’s son Ahimaaz and Abiathar’s son Jonathan. Through them you shall send on to me whatever you hear.” [37]So David’s friend Hushai went into the city, Jerusalem, as Absalom was about to enter it.

## CHAPTER 16

See RG 121

***David and Ziba.*** [1]David went a little beyond the top and Ziba, the servant of Meribbaal, was there to meet him with saddled donkeys laden with two hundred loaves of bread, an ephah of cakes of pressed raisins, an ephah of summer fruits, and a skin of wine.[b] [2]The king said to Ziba, “What are you doing with all this?” Ziba replied: “The donkeys are for the king’s household to ride on. The bread and summer fruits are for your servants to eat, and the wine to drink when they grow weary in the wilderness.” [3]Then the king said, “And where is your lord’s son?” Ziba answered the king, “He is staying in Jerusalem, for he said, ‘Today the house of Israel will restore to me my father’s kingdom.’ ”[c] [4]The king therefore said to Ziba, “So! Everything Meribbaal had is yours.” Then Ziba said: “I pay you homage, my lord the king. May I find favor with you!”[d]

***David and Shimei.*** [5]As King David was approaching Bahurim, there was a man coming out; he was of the same clan as the house of Saul, and his name was Shimei, son of Gera. He kept cursing as he came out,[e] [6]and throwing stones at David and at all King David’s officers, even though all the soldiers, including the royal guard, were on David’s right and on his left. [7]Shimei was saying as he cursed: “Get out! Get out! You man of blood, you scoundrel! [8]The LORD has paid you back for all the blood shed from the family of Saul,* whom you replaced as king, and the LORD has handed over the kingdom to your son Absalom. And now look at you: you suffer ruin because you are a man of blood.” [9]Abishai, son of Zeruiah, said to the king: “Why should this dead dog curse my lord the king? Let me go over and take off his head.”[f] [10]But the king replied: “What business is it of mine or of yours, sons of Zeruiah, that he curses? Suppose the LORD has told him to curse David; who then will dare to say, ‘Why are you doing this?’ ”[g]

**16:8 Blood shed . . . Saul**: probably refers to the episode recounted in 21:1–14.

*w:* 2 Sm 16:10. *x:* 2 Sm 19:5; Mi 1:8. *y:* 2 Sm 16:23; 17:14, 23. *z:* 2 Sm 16:16. *a:* 2 Sm 16:19. *b:* 2 Sm 4:4; 9:1–13; 19:18, 25. *c:* 2 Sm 19:26–27. *d:* 2 Sm 19:30. *e:* 2 Sm 3:16; 19:17, 22–23; 1 Kgs 2:8. *f:* 2 Sm 19:22; 1 Sm 24:15; 26:6. *g:* 2 Sm 15:25–26; 19:23.

11Then David said to Abishai and to all his
servants: “If my own son, who came forth
from my loins, is seeking my life, how much
more might this Benjaminite do so! Let him
alone and let him curse, for the LORD has
told him to.[h] 12Perhaps the LORD will look
upon my affliction and repay me with good
for the curses he is uttering this day.” 13Da-
vid and his men continued on the road, while
Shimei kept up with them on the hillside, all
the while cursing and throwing stones and
dirt as he went.[i] 14The king and all the soldiers with him arrived at the Jordan tired out,
and stopped there to rest.

***Absalom's Counselors.*** 15In the meantime
Absalom, with all the Israelites, entered
Jerusalem, and Ahithophel was with him.
16When David's friend Hushai the Archite
came to Absalom, he said to him: “Long live
the king! Long live the king!”[j] 17But Absalom asked Hushai: “Is this your devotion to
your friend? Why did you not go with your
friend?” 18Hushai replied to Absalom: “On
the contrary, I am his whom the LORD and all
this people and all Israel have chosen, and
with him I will stay. 19Furthermore, as I was
in attendance upon your father, so will I be
before you. Whom should I serve, if not his
son?”[k]

20Then Absalom said to Ahithophel, “Offer your counsel on what we should do.”
21Ahithophel replied to Absalom: “Go to
your father's concubines, whom he left behind to take care of the palace. When all Israel hears how odious you have made yourself to your father, all those on your side will
take courage.”[l] 22So a tent was pitched on
the roof for Absalom, and Absalom went to
his father's concubines in view of all Israel.[m]

***Counsel of Ahithophel.*** 23Now the counsel given by Ahithophel at that time was as
though one sought the word of God. Such
was all the counsel of Ahithophel both to
David and to Absalom.[n]

## CHAPTER 17

See RG 121

1Ahithophel went on to say to Absalom: “Let me choose twelve thousand men
and be off in pursuit of David tonight. 2If I
come upon him when he is weary and discouraged, I shall cause him panic, and all the
people with him will flee, and I shall strike
down the king alone. 3Then I can bring back
the rest of the people to you, as a bride returns to her husband. It is the death of only
one man you are seeking; then all the people
will be at peace.” 4This plan sounded good
to Absalom and to all the elders of Israel.

***Counsel of Hushai.*** 5Then Absalom said,
“Now call Hushai the Archite also; let us
hear what he too has to say.” 6When Hushai
came to Absalom, Absalom said to him:
“This is Ahithophel's plan. Shall we follow
his plan? If not, give your own.” 7Hushai
replied to Absalom, “This time Ahithophel
has not given good counsel.” 8And he went
on to say: “You know that your father and
his men are warriors, and that they are as
fierce as a bear in the wild robbed of her
cubs. Moreover, since your father is a skilled
fighter, he will not spend the night with the
army.[o] 9Even now he lies hidden in one of
the caves or in one of his other places. And
if some of our soldiers should fall at the first
attack, whoever hears of it will say, ‘Absalom's followers have been slaughtered.’
10Then even the brave man with the heart of
a lion—his heart will melt. For all Israel
knows that your father is a fighter and those
who are with him are brave. 11This is what I
counsel: Let all Israel be assembled, from
Dan to Beer-sheba, as numerous as the sands
by the sea, and you yourself go with them.
12We can then attack him wherever we find
him, settling down upon him as dew alights
on the ground. None shall survive—neither
he nor any of his followers. 13And if he re-
tires into a city, all Israel shall bring ropes to
that city and we can drag it into the gorge, so
that not even a pebble of it can be found.”
14Then Absalom and all the Israelites said,
“The counsel of Hushai the Archite is better
than the counsel of Ahithophel.” For the
LORD had commanded that Ahithophel's
good counsel should be thwarted, so that he
might bring Absalom to ruin.[p]

*h:* 2 Sm 12:11. *i:* 2 Sm 19:19–24. *j:* 2 Sm 15:32–37. *k:* 2 Sm 15:34. *l:* 2 Sm 15:16; 20:3. *m:* 2 Sm 12:11–12. *n:* 2 Sm 15:12, 31; 17:23. *o:* Hos 13:8. *p:* 2 Sm 15:31, 34.

*David Told of the Plan.* [15]Then Hushai said to the priests Zadok and Abiathar: "This is the counsel Ahithophel gave Absalom and the elders of Israel, and this is what I counseled. [16]So send a warning to David immediately: 'Do not spend the night at the fords near the wilderness, but cross over without fail. Otherwise the king and all the people with him will be destroyed.' " [17]Now Jonathan and Ahimaaz were staying at En-rogel. A maidservant was to come with information for them, and they in turn were to go and report to King David. They could not risk being seen entering the city, [18]but an attendant did see them and informed Absalom. They hurried on their way and reached the house of a man in Bahurim who had a cistern in his courtyard. They let themselves down into it, [19]and the woman took the cover and spread it over the mouth of the cistern, strewing crushed grain on the cover so that nothing could be noticed. [20]When Absalom's servants came to the woman at the house, they asked, "Where are Ahimaaz and Jonathan?" The woman replied, "They went by a short while ago toward the water." They searched, but found no one, and so returned to Jerusalem. [21]As soon as they left, Ahimaaz and Jonathan came up out of the cistern and went on to report to King David. They said to him: "Leave! Cross the water at once, for Ahithophel has given such and such counsel in regard to you." [22]So David and all his people moved on and crossed the Jordan. By daybreak, there was no one left who had not crossed.

[23]When Ahithophel saw that his counsel was not acted upon, he saddled his donkey and departed, going to his home in his own city. Then, having left orders concerning his household, he hanged himself. And so he died and was buried in his father's tomb.[q]

[24]Now David had arrived at Mahanaim while Absalom crossed the Jordan accompanied by all the Israelites. [25]Absalom had put Amasa in command of the army in Joab's place. Amasa was the son of an Ishmaelite named Ithra, who had married Abigail, daughter of Jesse and sister of Joab's mother Zeruiah.[r] [26]Israel and Absalom encamped in the land of Gilead.

[27]When David came to Mahanaim, Shobi, son of Nahash from Rabbah of the Ammonites, Machir, son of Ammiel from Lodebar, and Barzillai, the Gileadite from Rogelim,[s] [28]brought beds and covers, basins and pottery, as well as wheat, barley, flour, roasted grain, beans, lentils, [29]honey, and butter and cheese from the flocks and herds, for David and those who were with him to eat; for they said, "The people will be hungry and tired and thirsty in the wilderness."

## CHAPTER 18

See RG 121

*Preparation for Battle.* [1]After mustering the troops he had with him, David placed officers in command of units of a thousand and units of a hundred. [2]David then divided the troops three ways, a third under Joab, a third under Abishai, son of Zeruiah and brother of Joab, and a third under Ittai the Gittite. The king said to the troops, "I intend to go out with you myself." [3]But they replied: "You must not come out with us. For if we flee, no one will care; even if half of us die, no one will care. But you are worth ten thousand of us. Therefore it is better that we have you to help us from the city." [4]The king said to them, "I will do what you think best." So the king stood by the gate as all the soldiers marched out in units of a hundred and a thousand. [5]But the king gave this command to Joab, Abishai, and Ittai: "Be gentle with young Absalom for my sake." All the soldiers heard as the king gave commands to the various leaders with regard to Absalom.

*Defeat of Absalom's Forces.* [6]David's army then took the field against Israel, and a battle was fought in the forest near Mahanaim. [7]The forces of Israel were defeated by David's servants, and the casualties there that day were heavy—twenty thousand men. [8]The battle spread out over that entire region, and the forest consumed more combatants that day than did the sword.

*Death of Absalom.* [9]Absalom unexpectedly came up against David's servants. He was mounted on a mule, and, as the mule

*q:* 2 Sm 15:31; 16:23. *r:* 2 Sm 19:14; 20:4–13. *s:* 2 Sm 9:4; 19:32; 1 Kgs 2:7; Ezr 2:61.

passed under the branches of a large oak tree, his hair caught fast in the tree. He hung between heaven and earth while the mule under him kept going. [10]Someone saw this and reported to Joab, "I saw Absalom hanging from an oak tree." [11]Joab said to the man who told him this: "If you saw him, why did you not strike him to the ground on the spot? Then it would have been my duty to give you fifty pieces of silver and a belt." [12]But the man replied to Joab: "Even if I already held a thousand pieces of silver in my two hands, I would not lay a hand on the king's son, for in our hearing the king gave you and Abishai and Ittai a command: 'Protect the youth Absalom for my sake.' [13]Had I been disloyal and killed him, it would all have come out before the king, and you would stand aloof." [14]Joab replied, "I will not waste time with you in this way." And taking three pikes in hand, he thrust for the heart of Absalom. He was still alive in the tree.[t] [15]When ten of Joab's young armor-bearers closed in on Absalom, and killed him with further blows, [16]Joab then sounded the horn, and the soldiers turned back from the pursuit of the Israelites, because Joab called them to halt. [17]They took Absalom and cast him into a deep pit in the forest, and built up a very large mound of stones over him. And all the Israelites fled to their own tents.[u]

[18]During his lifetime Absalom had taken a pillar and set it up for himself in the King's Valley, for he said, "I have no son to perpetuate my name." The pillar which he named for himself is called Absalom's Monument to the present day.[v]

***David Told of Absalom's Death.*** [19]Then Ahimaaz, son of Zadok, said, "Let me run to take the good news to the king that the LORD has set him free from the power of his enemies." [20]But Joab said to him: "You are not the man to bring the news today. On some other day you may take the good news, but today you would not be bringing good news, for in fact the king's son is dead." [21]Then Joab said to a Cushite, "Go, tell the king what you have seen." The Cushite bowed to Joab and ran off. [22]But Ahimaaz, son of Zadok, said to Joab again, "Come what may, permit me also to run after the Cushite." Joab replied: "Why do you want to run, my son? You will receive no reward." [23]But he insisted, "Come what may, I want to run." Joab said to him, "Run." Ahimaaz took the way of the Jordan plain and outran the Cushite.

[24]Now David was sitting between the two gates, and a lookout mounted to the roof of the gate above the city wall, where he looked out and saw a man running all alone. [25]The lookout shouted to inform the king, who said, "If he is alone, he has good news to report." As he kept coming nearer, [26]the lookout spied another runner. From his place atop the gate he cried out, "There is another man running by himself." And the king responded, "He, too, is bringing good news." [27]Then the lookout said, "I notice that the first one runs like Ahimaaz, son of Zadok." The king replied, "He is a good man; he comes with good news."[w] [28]Then Ahimaaz called out and greeted the king. With face to the ground he paid homage to the king and said, "Blessed be the LORD your God, who has delivered up the men who rebelled against my lord the king." [29]But the king asked, "Is young Absalom safe?" And Ahimaaz replied, "I saw a great disturbance when the king's servant Joab sent your servant on, but I do not know what it was." [30]The king said, "Step aside and remain in attendance here." So he stepped aside and remained there. [31]When the Cushite came in, he said, "Let my lord the king receive the good news that this day the LORD has freed you from the power of all who rose up against you." [32]But the king asked the Cushite, "Is young Absalom all right?" The Cushite replied, "May the enemies of my lord the king and all who rebel against you with evil intent be as that young man!"

## CHAPTER 19

See RG 121

[1]The king was shaken, and went up to the room over the city gate and wept. He said as he wept, "My son Absalom! My son, my son Absalom! If only I had died instead of you, Absalom, my son, my son!"

***Joab Reproves David.*** [2]Joab was told,

*t:* 2 Sm 12:10; 13:28–29. *u:* Jos 7:26; 8:29; 10:27. *v:* 2 Sm 14:27. *w:* 2 Kgs 9:20.

"The king is weeping and mourning for Absalom," 3and that day's victory was turned
into mourning for the whole army when they
heard, "The king is grieving for his son."
4The soldiers stole into the city that day like
men shamed by flight in battle. 5Meanwhile
the king covered his face and cried out in a
loud voice, "My son Absalom! Absalom!
My son, my son!"[x] 6So Joab went to the
king's residence and said: "Though they
saved your life and your sons' and daughters' lives, and the lives of your wives and
your concubines, you have put all your servants to shame today 7by loving those who
hate you and hating those who love you. For
you have announced today that officers and
servants are nothing to you. Indeed I am now
certain that if Absalom were alive today and
all of us dead, that would be fine with you.
8Now then, get up! Go out and speak kindly
to your servants. I swear by the LORD that if
you do not go out, not a single man will remain with you overnight, and this will be a
far greater disaster for you than any that has
come upon you from your youth until now."
9So the king got up and sat at the gate. When
all the people were told, "The king is sitting
at the gate," they came into his presence.

*The Reconciliation.* Now the Israelites
had fled to their separate tents, 10but
throughout the tribes of Israel all the people
were arguing among themselves, saying to
one another: "The king delivered us from the
grasp of our enemies, and it was he who rescued us from the grasp of the Philistines.
Now, he has fled the country before Absalom, 11but Absalom, whom we anointed over
us, has died in battle. Why, then, should you
remain silent about restoring the king to his
palace?" When the talk of all Israel reached
the king, 12David sent word to the priests Zadok and Abiathar: "Say to the elders of Judah: 'Why should you be last to restore the
king to his palace? 13You are my brothers,
you are my bone and flesh. Why should you
be last to restore the king?' 14Also say to
Amasa: 'Are you not my bone and flesh?
May God do thus to me, and more, if you do
not become commander of my army permanently in place of Joab.' "[y] 15He won the
hearts of the Judahites all together, and so
they sent a message to the king: "Return,
with all your servants."

*David and Shimei.* 16So the king returned,
and when he reached the Jordan, Judah had
come to Gilgal to meet him and to bring him
across the Jordan. 17Shimei, son of Gera, the
Benjaminite from Bahurim, hurried down
with the Judahites to meet King David,[z]
18accompanied by a thousand men from
Benjamin. Ziba, too, the servant of the house
of Saul, accompanied by his fifteen sons and
twenty servants, hastened to the Jordan before the king.[a] 19[b] They crossed over the ford
to bring the king's household over and to do
whatever he wished. When Shimei, son of
Gera, crossed the Jordan, he fell down before the king 20and said to him: "May my
lord not hold me guilty; do not remember or
take to heart the wrong that your servant did
the day my lord the king left Jerusalem.
21For your servant knows that I have done
wrong. But I now am the first of the whole
house of Joseph to come down today to meet
my lord the king." 22But Abishai, son of Zeruiah, countered: "Shimei must be put to
death for this. He cursed the anointed of the
LORD." 23David replied: "What has come
between you and me, sons of Zeruiah, that
you would become my adversaries this day?
Should anyone die today in Israel? Am I not
aware that today I am king over Israel?"[c]
24Then the king said to Shimei, "You shall
not die." And the king gave him his oath.

*David and Meribbaal.* 25Meribbaal, son of
Saul, also went down to meet the king. He
had not cared for his feet nor trimmed his
mustache nor washed his clothes from the
day the king left until he returned safely.
26When he came from Jerusalem to meet the
king, the king asked him, "Why did you not
go with me, Meribbaal?"[d] 27He replied: "My
lord king, my servant deceived me. For your
servant said to him, 'Saddle the donkey for
me, that I may ride on it and go with the
king'; your servant is lame.[e] 28But he slan-

*x:* 2 Sm 15:30. *y:* 2 Sm 17:25; 20:4. *z:* 2 Sm 16:5–13. *a:* 2 Sm 16:1–4; 19:25–31. *b:* 2 Sm 16:13; Ex 22:27; 1 Kgs 2:8–9. *c:* 2 Sm 16:9–10; 1 Sm 11:13; 1 Kgs 2:8–9, 36–46. *d:* 2 Sm 16:3. *e:* 2 Sm 9:2–13.

dered your servant before my lord the king. But my lord the king is like an angel of God. Do whatever seems good to you. [29]For though my father's entire house deserved only death from my lord the king, yet you placed your servant among those who eat at your table. What right do I still have to make further appeal to the king?"[f] [30]But the king said to him: "Why do you go on talking? I say, 'You and Ziba shall divide the property.' "[g] [31]Meribbaal answered the king, "Indeed let him take it all, now that my lord the king has returned safely to his house."

***David and Barzillai.*** [32]Barzillai the Gileadite also came down from Rogelim and escorted the king to the Jordan for his crossing, taking leave of him at the Jordan.[h] [33]It was Barzillai, a very old man of eighty, who had provided for the king during his stay in Mahanaim; he was a very great man. [34]The king said to Barzillai, "Cross over with me, and I will provide for your old age as my guest in Jerusalem." [35]But Barzillai answered the king: "How much longer have I to live, that I should go up to Jerusalem with the king? [36]I am now eighty years old. Can I distinguish between good and evil? Can your servant taste what he eats and drinks, or still hear the voices of men and women singers? Why should your servant be any further burden to my lord the king? [37]In escorting the king across the Jordan, your servant is doing little enough! Why should the king give me this reward? [38]Please let your servant go back to die in my own city by the tomb of my father and mother. Here is your servant Chimham. Let him cross over with my lord the king. Do for him whatever seems good to you." [39]Then the king said to him, "Chimham shall cross over with me, and for him I will do whatever seems good to you. And anything else you would like me to do for you, I will do." [40]Then all the people crossed over the Jordan but the king remained; he kissed Barzillai and bade him farewell as he returned to his own place. [41]Finally the king crossed over to Gilgal, accompanied by Chimham.

***Israel and Judah Quarrel.*** All of the people of Judah and half of the people of Israel had escorted the king across. [42]But then all these Israelites began coming to the king and saying, "Why did our brothers the Judahites steal you away and bring the king and his household across the Jordan, along with all David's men?" [43]All the Judahites replied to the men of Israel: "Because the king is our relative. Why are you angry over this? Have we had anything to eat at the king's expense? Or have portions from his table been given to us?" [44]The Israelites answered the Judahites: "We have ten shares in the king. Also, we are the firstborn* rather than you. Why do you slight us? Were we not first to speak of restoring our king?" Then the Judahites in turn spoke even more fiercely than the Israelites.[i]

## CHAPTER 20

See RG 121

***Sheba's Rebellion.*** [1]Now a scoundrel named Sheba, the son of Bichri, a Benjaminite, happened to be there. He sounded the horn and cried out,

> "We have no share in David,
> nor any heritage in the son of Jesse.
> Everyone to your tents, O Israel!"[j]

[2]So all the Israelites left David to follow Sheba, son of Bichri. But the Judahites, from the Jordan to Jerusalem, remained loyal to their king. [3]David came to his house in Jerusalem, and the king took the ten concubines whom he had left behind to care for the palace and placed them under guard. He provided for them, but never again saw them. And so they remained shut away to the day of their death, lifelong widows.[k]

***Amasa's Death.*** [4]Then the king said to Amasa: "Summon the Judahites for me within three days. Then present yourself here."[l] [5]Accordingly Amasa set out to summon Judah, but delayed beyond the time set for him. [6]Then David said to Abishai: "Sheba, son of Bichri, may now do us more harm than Absalom did. Take your lord's

**19:44** The firstborn had special rights over the other siblings.

---

*f:* 2 Sm 9:9–11. *g:* 2 Sm 16:4. *h:* 2 Sm 17:27–29; 1 Kgs 2:7; Ezr 2:61. *i:* 1 Kgs 11:31. *j:* 1 Kgs 12:16. *k:* 2 Sm 15:16; 16:20–22. *l:* 2 Sm 17:25; 19:14.

servants and pursue him, lest he find fortified cities and take shelter while we look on.” 7 So Joab and the Cherethites and Pelethites and all the warriors marched out behind Abishai from Jerusalem to campaign in pursuit of Sheba, son of Bichri.[m] 8* They were at the great stone in Gibeon when Amasa met them. Now Joab had a belt over his tunic, from which was slung a sword in its sheath at his thigh; the sword would slide out downwards.[n] 9 Joab asked Amasa, “Is everything all right, my brother?” and with his right hand held Amasa’s beard as if to kiss him. 10 And since Amasa was not on his guard against the sword in Joab’s other hand, Joab stabbed him in the abdomen with it, so that his entrails burst forth to the ground, and he died; there was no second thrust. Then Joab and Abishai his brother pursued Sheba, son of Bichri.[o] 11 One of Joab’s attendants stood by Amasa and said, “Let him who favors Joab and is for David follow Joab.” 12 Amasa lay covered with blood in the middle of the highroad, and the man noticed that all the soldiers were stopping. So he rolled Amasa away from the road to the field and spread a garment over him, because he saw how all who came upon him were stopping. 13 When he had been removed from the road, everyone went on after Joab in pursuit of Sheba, son of Bichri.

***Joab Pursues Sheba.*** 14 Sheba had passed through all the tribes of Israel to Abel Beth-maacah. Then all the Bichrites assembled and they too entered the city after him. 15 So all Joab’s troops came and besieged him in Abel Beth-maacah. They built up a mound against the city, so that it stood against the rampart, and were battering the wall to knock it down. 16 Then a wise woman from the city called out, “Listen, listen! Tell Joab, ‘Come here, so I can speak with you.’ ” 17 When Joab had come near her, the woman said, “Are you Joab?” And he replied, “Yes.” She said to him, “Listen to what your servant has to say.” He replied, “I am listening.” 18 Then she went on to say: “There is a saying from long ago,* ‘Let them ask if they will in Abel or in Dan whether loyalty is finished 19 or ended in Israel.’ You are seeking to batter down a city that is a mother in Israel. Why do you wish to swallow up the heritage of the LORD?”[p] 20 Joab answered, “Not at all, not at all! I do not wish to swallow or batter anything. 21 That is not the case at all. A man from the hill country of Ephraim, whose name is Sheba, son of Bichri, has rebelled against King David. Give him up, just him, and I will withdraw from the city.” Then the woman said to Joab, “His head shall be thrown to you across the wall.” 22 In her wisdom, the woman went to all the people, and they cut off the head of Sheba, son of Bichri, and threw it out to Joab. He then sounded the horn, and they scattered from the city to their own tents, while Joab returned to Jerusalem to the king.

***David’s Officials.*** 23 Joab was in command of the whole army of Israel. Benaiah, son of Jehoiada, was in command of the Cherethites and Pelethites.[q] 24 Adoram was in charge of the forced labor. Jehoshaphat, son of Ahilud, was the chancellor. 25 Shawsha was the scribe. Zadok and Abiathar were priests.[r] 26 Ira the Jairite was also David’s priest.

# V. Appendixes

## CHAPTER 21

See RG 121

***Gibeonite Vengeance.*** 1 In David’s time there was a famine for three years, year after year. David sought the presence of the LORD, who said: There is bloodguilt on Saul and his family because he put the Gibeonites to death.[s] 2 So the king called the Gibeonites and spoke to them. (Now the Gibeonites were not Israelites, but survivors of the Amorites; and although the Israelites had given them their oath, Saul had sought to kill them off in his zeal for the Israelites and for Judah.)[t] 3 David said to the Gibeonites, “What must I do for you and how must I make atonement, that

**20:8** The text of this verse is quite uncertain.

**20:18–19** This proverbial expression is obscure but seems to reflect a tradition that this Danite town was associated with oracles or other sorts of revelation. Cf. Mt 16:13–17; and the intertestamental *Testament of Levi* 2:3.

*m:* 2 Sm 8:18. *n:* 2 Sm 2:13. *o:* 1 Kgs 2:5. *p:* Gn 49:16. *q:* 2 Sm 8:16–18; 23:20. *r:* 2 Sm 8:17–18. *s:* 2 Sm 24:13. *t:* Jos 9:3–27.

you may bless the heritage of the LORD?" [4]The Gibeonites answered him, "We have no claim against Saul and his house for silver or gold, nor is it our place to put anyone to death in Israel." Then he said, "I will do for you whatever you propose." [5]They said to the king, "As for the man who was exterminating us and who intended to destroy us that we might have no place in all the territory of Israel, [6]let seven men from among his descendants be given to us, that we may execute them before the LORD in Gibeon, on the LORD's mountain." The king replied, "I will give them up." [7]The king, however, spared Meribbaal, son of Jonathan, son of Saul, because of the LORD's oath that formed a bond between David and Saul's son Jonathan.[u] [8]But the king took Armoni and Meribbaal, the two sons that Aiah's daughter Rizpah had borne to Saul, and the five sons of Saul's daughter Merob that she had borne to Adriel, son of Barzillai the Meholathite,[v] [9]and delivered them into the power of the Gibeonites, who then executed them on the mountain before the LORD. The seven fell at the one time; they were put to death during the first days of the harvest—that is, at the beginning of the barley harvest.

[10]Then Rizpah, Aiah's daughter, took sackcloth and spread it out for herself on the rock from the beginning of the harvest until rain came down on them from the heavens, fending off the birds of the heavens from settling on them by day, and the wild animals by night.[w] [11]When David was informed of what Rizpah, Aiah's daughter, the concubine of Saul, had done, [12]he went and obtained the bones of Saul and of his son Jonathan from the citizens of Jabesh-gilead, who had stolen them away secretly from the public square of Beth-shan, where the Philistines had hanged them at the time they defeated Saul on Gilboa.[x] [13]When he had brought up from there the bones of Saul and of his son Jonathan, the bones of those who had been executed were also gathered up. [14]Then the bones of Saul and of his son Jonathan were buried in the land of Benjamin, at Zela, in the tomb of his father Kish. After all that the king commanded had been carried out, God granted relief to the land.[y]

***Exploits in Philistine Wars.*** [15]There was another battle between the Philistines and Israel. David went down with his servants and fought the Philistines, but David grew tired. [16]Dadu, a descendant of the Rephaim, whose bronze spear weighed three hundred shekels, was about to take him captive. Dadu was girt with a new sword and thought he would kill David, [17]but Abishai, son of Zeruiah, came to help him, and struck and killed the Philistine. Then David's men swore to him, "You must not go out to battle with us again, lest you quench the lamp of Israel."[z]

[18a] After this, there was another battle with the Philistines, in Gob. On that occasion Sibbecai the Hushathite struck down Saph, a descendant of the Rephaim.[b] [19c] There was another battle with the Philistines, in Gob, and Elhanan, son of Jair from Bethlehem, killed Goliath of Gath, whose spear shaft was like a weaver's beam. [20]There was another battle, at Gath, and there was a giant, who had six fingers on each hand and six toes on each foot—twenty-four in all. He too was descended from the Rephaim. [21]And when he insulted Israel, Jonathan, son of David's brother Shimei, struck him down.[d] [22]These four were descended from the Rephaim in Gath, and they fell at the hands of David and his servants.

## CHAPTER 22

See RG 121

***Song of Thanksgiving.**** [1]David proclaimed the words of this song to the LORD when the LORD had rescued him from the

**22:1–51** This psalm of thanksgiving also appears in the Psalter, with a few small variants, as Ps 18. In both places it is attributed to David. Two main sections can be distinguished. In the first part, after an introductory stanza of praise to God (vv. 2–4), the writer describes the peril he was in (vv. 5–7), and then poetically depicts, under the form of a theophany, God's intervention in his behalf (vv. 8–20), concluding with an acknowledgment of God's justice (vv. 21–31). In the second part, God is praised for having prepared the psalmist for war (vv. 32–35), given him victory over his enemies (vv. 36–39), whom he put to flight (vv. 40–43), and bestowed on him dominion over many peoples (vv. 44–46). The entire song ends with an expression of grateful praise (vv. 47–51).

*u:* 2 Sm 9:13; 1 Sm 18:3; 20:8–10, 15–16, 42. *v:* 2 Sm 3:7. *w:* 2 Sm 3:31; 12:16. *x:* 1 Sm 31:10–13. *y:* 2 Sm 24:25. *z:* 1 Kgs 11:36; 15:4; 2 Kgs 8:19. *a:* 1 Chr 20:4–8. *b:* 2 Sm 23:27. *c:* 1 Sm 17:4, 7. *d:* 2 Sm 13:3.

grasp of all his enemies and from the grasp of Saul.[e] 2 He said:[f]

O LORD, my rock, my fortress, my
deliverer,
3 my God, my rock of refuge!
My shield, my saving horn,*
my stronghold, my refuge,
my savior, from violence you keep me
safe.[g]
4 Praised be the LORD, I exclaim!
I have been delivered from my
enemies.
5 The breakers of death surged round
about me,
the menacing floods* terrified me;
6 The cords of Sheol tightened;
the snares of death lay in wait for me.
7 In my distress I called out: LORD!
I cried out to my God;
From his temple* he heard my voice,
my cry reached his ears.

8 The earth rocked and shook;*
the foundations of the heavens
trembled;
they shook as his wrath flared up.
9 Smoke rose in his nostrils,
a devouring fire from his mouth;
it kindled coals into flame.
10 He parted the heavens and came down,
a dark cloud under his feet.[h]
11 Mounted on a cherub* he flew,
borne along on the wings of the wind.[i]
12 He made darkness the cover about him,
a mass of water, heavy thunderheads.
13 From the brightness of his presence
coals were kindled to flame.
14 The LORD thundered from heaven;
the Most High made his voice resound.
15 He let fly arrows and scattered them;
lightning, and dispersed them.[j]
16 Then the bed of the sea appeared;
the world's foundations lay bare,
At the roar of the LORD,
at the storming breath of his nostrils.[k]
17 He reached down from on high and
seized me,
drew me out of the deep waters.[l]
18 He rescued me from my mighty enemy,
from foes too powerful for me.
19 They attacked me on a day of distress,
but the LORD came to my support.
20 He set me free in the open;
he rescued me because he loves me.

21 The LORD acknowledged my
righteousness;
rewarded my clean hands.
22 For I kept the ways of the LORD;
I was not disloyal to my God.
23 His laws were all before me,
his decrees I did not cast aside.
24 I was honest toward him;
I was on guard against sin.
25 So the LORD rewarded my righteousness,
the cleanness of my hands in his sight.
26 [m] Toward the faithful you are faithful;*
to the honest you are honest;
27 Toward the sincere you are sincere;
but to the perverse you are devious.
28 Humble people you save,
though on the haughty your eyes look
down.
29 You are my lamp, O LORD!
My God brightens the darkness about
me.
30 With you I can rush an armed band,
with my God to help I can leap a wall.
31 God's way is unerring;

**22:3 My saving horn**: my strong savior. The horn, such as that of an enraged bull, was a symbol of strength; cf. Lk 1:69.

**22:5–6 Breakers . . . floods**: traditional Old Testament imagery for lethal danger, from which the Lord is uniquely able to rescue; cf. Ps 69:2, 15–16; 89:10–11; Jon 2:3–6.

**22:7 His temple**: his heavenly abode.

**22:8–10** The Lord's coming is depicted by means of a storm theophany, including earthquake (vv. 8, 16) and thunderstorm (vv. 9–15); cf. Jgs 5:4–5; Ps 29; 97:2–6; Hb 3.

**22:11 Mounted on a cherub**: in the traditional storm theophany, as here, the Lord appears with thunder, lightning, earthquake, rain, darkness, cloud, and wind. Sometimes these are represented as his retinue; sometimes he is said to ride upon the clouds or "the wings of the wind" (Ps 104:3). The parallelism in v. 11 suggests that the winged creatures called cherubim are imagined as bearing the Lord aloft. In the iconography of the ark of the covenant, the Lord was "enthroned upon the cherubim"; cf. Ex 37:7–9; 1 Sm 4:4; 2 Sm 6:2; 2 Kgs 19:15; Ps 80:2; 99:1.

**22:26–27** People are treated by God in the same way they treat him and other people.

*e:* Ps 18:1. *f:* Ps 18:3–51. *g:* 1 Sm 2:1–2. *h:* Ps 144:5. *i:* Ex 25:18–22. *j:* Ps 144:6. *k:* Ex 15:8. *l:* Ps 144:7. *m:* 1 Sm 2:30.

## Words of David

THERE MAY HAVE been a literary tradition in the Bible of ascribing poems to leading characters as their "last words" (see ch 23:1–7). Compare the poems attributed to Jacob in Genesis 49 and to Moses in Deuteronomy 32–33. David's last words, though, do not consist of a benediction of Israel. Like Moses, David is portrayed as a prophet pronouncing an oracle (23:1–2). The actual date of David's "last words" is uncertain. In contrast to ch 22, the poem in 23, 1–7 has no parallel in the Psalms. "Anointed" (v. 1) is a royal title, here referring to David, echoing the end of ch 22. "Mighty One of Israel" (v. 1) is an epithet for the LORD. The image of king as the sun (v. 4) was common in the ancient Near East, especially in Egypt, although less so in Israel. The "eternal covenant" (v. 5) was the LORD's promise of a dynasty for David in 7:16 (cf. Ps 89:28–29). The wicked are like thorns (v. 6) consumed by the sun's heat.

the LORD's promise is tried and true;
he is a shield for all who trust in him.[n]
32 Truly, who is God except the LORD?
Who but our God is the rock?
33 This God who girded me with might,
kept my way unerring,
34 Who made my feet swift as a deer's,
set me safe on the heights,[o]
35 Who trained my hands for war,
my arms to bend even a bow of bronze.

36 You have given me your protecting shield,
and your help has made me great.
37 You gave me room to stride;
my feet never stumbled.
38 I pursued my enemies and overtook them;
I did not turn back till I destroyed them.
39 I struck them down, and they did not rise;
they fell dead at my feet.
40 You girded me with strength for war;
subdued adversaries at my feet.
41 My foes you put to flight before me;
those who hated me I destroyed.
42 They cried for help, but no one saved them,
cried to the LORD but got no answer.
43 I ground them fine as the dust of the earth;
like mud in the streets I trod them down.
44 You rescued me from the strife of my people;
you made me head over nations.
A people I had not known became my slaves;
45 Foreigners cringed before me;
as soon as they heard of me they obeyed.
46 Their courage failed;
they came trembling from their fortresses.
47 The LORD lives! Blessed be my rock!
Exalted be God, the rock of my salvation.
48 O God who granted me vindication,
subdued peoples under me,
49 and helped me escape from my enemies,
Truly you have exalted me above my adversaries,
from the violent you have rescued me.
50 Thus I will proclaim you, LORD, among the nations;
I will sing the praises of your name.[p]
51 You have given great victories to your king,
and shown kindness to your anointed,
to David and his posterity forever.

### CHAPTER 23

See RG 121

*The Last Words of David.** 1 These are the last words of David:

The oracle of David, son of Jesse;
the oracle of the man God raised up,

**23:1–7 The last words of David**: the text of this short composition is difficult in places; it views David's career in retrospect.

*n:* Prv 30:5. *o:* Ps 62:3; Hb 3:19. *p:* Ps 22:23; Rom 15:9.

Anointed of the God of Jacob,
favorite of the Mighty One of Israel.[q]
2 The spirit of the LORD spoke through me;
his word was on my tongue.[r]
3 The God of Israel spoke;
of me the Rock of Israel said,
"One who rules over humankind with
justice,
who rules in the fear of God,[s]
4 Is like the light at sunrise
on a cloudless morning,
making the land's vegetation glisten
after rain."[t]
5 Is not my house firm before God?
He has made an eternal covenant
with me,
set forth in detail and secured.[u]
Will he not bring to fruition
all my salvation and my every desire?
6 But the wicked are all like thorns to be
cast away;
they cannot be taken up by hand.[v]
7 One wishing to touch them
must be armed with iron or the shaft of
a spear.
They must be utterly consumed by fire.

***David's Warriors.*** 8These are the names of
David's warriors.* Ishbaal, the son of
Hachamoni, chief of the Three. He brandished his spear over eight hundred whom
he had slain in a single encounter.[w] 9Next to
him was Eleazar, the son of Dodo the Ahohite, one of the Three warriors with David at
Ephes-dammim, when they insulted the Philistines who had massed there for battle. The
Israelites had retreated,[x] 10but he stood there
and struck down the Philistines until his
hand grew tired from clutching the sword.
The LORD brought about a great victory on
that day; the army turned back to rejoin Eleazar, but only to strip the slain. 11Next to him
was Shammah, son of Agee the Hararite.
The Philistines had assembled at Lehi,
where there was a plot of land full of lentils.
The people were fleeing before the Philistines,[y] 12but he took his stand in the middle
of the plot, kept it safe, and cut down the
Philistines. Thus the LORD brought about a
great victory. Such deeds as these the Three
warriors performed.

13Three of the Thirty chiefs went down to
David in the cave of Adullam during the harvest, while a Philistine clan was encamped
in the Valley of Rephaim.[z] 14David was then
in the stronghold, and there was a garrison of
Philistines in Bethlehem. 15Now David had
a craving and said, "If only someone would
give me a drink of water from the cistern by
the gate of Bethlehem!" 16Thereupon the
three warriors broke through the encampment of the Philistines, drew water from the
cistern by the gate of Bethlehem, and carried
it back to David. But he refused to drink it,
and instead poured it out* to the LORD, 17say-
ing: "The LORD forbid that I do such a thing!
Could I drink the blood of these men who
went at the risk of their lives?" So he refused
to drink it.

18Abishai, the brother of Joab, son of Zeruiah, was the chief of the Thirty; he brandished his spear over three hundred whom
he had slain. He made a name among the
Thirty, 19but was more famous than any of
the Thirty, becoming their leader. However,
he did not attain to the Three.

20Benaiah, son of Jehoiada, a valiant man
of mighty deeds, from Kabzeel, killed the
two sons of Ariel of Moab. Also, he went
down and killed the lion in the cistern on a
snowy day.[a] 21He likewise slew an Egyptian,
a huge man. The Egyptian carried a spear,
but Benaiah came against him with a staff;
he wrested the spear from the Egyptian's
hand, and killed him with that spear. 22Such
deeds as these Benaiah, the son of Jehoiada,
performed; and he made a name among the
Thirty warriors 23but was more famous than

**23:8–39** There are thirty-seven warriors in all named in this list. First there are the Three warriors most noted for single-handed exploits (vv. 8–12). Then comes the story of a daring adventure by three unnamed members of the larger group of the Thirty (vv. 13–17). Next come the commanders of the king's bodyguard, Abishai (vv. 18–19) and Benaiah (vv. 20–23), with whom must be counted Asahel (v. 24) and Joab (vv. 18, 24, 37), and finally the group of the Thirty (vv. 24–39).

**23:16 Poured it out:** as a libation.

*q:* 1 Kgs 2:1–9; Sir 47:8. *r:* Is 59:21; Jer 1:9. *s:* Ps 72:1–4. *t:* Jgs 5:31; Ps 72:6. *u:* 2 Sm 7:11, 15–16; Ps 89:30; Is 55:3. *v:* Dt 13:14. *w:* 1 Chr 11:11–41; 27:1–15. *x:* 1 Sm 17:1. *y:* Jgs 15:9. *z:* 1 Sm 22:1; Mi 1:15. *a:* 2 Sm 8:18; 20:23; Jgs 14:6; 1 Kgs 2:29–30.

any of the Thirty. However, he did not attain
to the Three. David put him in charge of his
bodyguard.[b] 24 Asahel,[c] brother of Joab, was
among the Thirty; Elhanan, son of Dodo,
from Bethlehem; 25 Shammah, from En-harod; Elika, from En-harod; 26 Helez, from
Beth-pelet; Ira, son of Ikkesh, from Tekoa;
27 Abiezer, from Anathoth; Sibbecai, from
Husha;[d] 28 Zalmon, from Ahoh; Maharai,
from Netophah; 29 Heled, son of Baanah,
from Netophah; Ittai, son of Ribai, from
Gibeah of Benjamin; 30 Benaiah, from Pirathon; Hiddai, from the valley of Gaash;
31 Abibaal, from Beth-arabah; Azmaveth,
from Bahurim; 32 Eliahba, from Shaalbon;
Jashen the Gunite; Jonathan, 33 son of Shammah the Hararite; Ahiam, son of Sharar the
Hararite; 34 Eliphelet, son of Ahasbai, from
Beth-maacah; Eliam, son of Ahithophel,
from Gilo; 35 Hezrai, from Carmel; Paarai
the Arbite; 36 Igal, son of Nathan, from Zobah; Bani the Gadite; 37 Zelek the Ammonite;
Naharai, from Beeroth, the armor-bearer of
Joab, son of Zeruiah; 38 Ira, from Jattir; Gareb, from Jattir; 39 Uriah the Hittite—thirty-
seven in all.[e]

## CHAPTER 24

See RG 121

***David's Census; the Plague.*** 1 The
LORD's anger against Israel flared again,[f]
and he incited David against them: "Go, take
a census of Israel and Judah." 2 The king
therefore said to Joab and the leaders of the
army who were with him, "Tour all the tribes
of Israel from Dan to Beer-sheba and register the people, that I may know their number." 3 But Joab replied to the king: "May the
LORD your God increase the number of people a hundredfold for my lord the king to see
it with his own eyes. But why does it please
my lord to do a thing of this kind?" 4 However, the king's command prevailed over
Joab and the leaders of the army, so they left
the king's presence in order to register the
people of Israel. 5 Crossing the Jordan, they
began near Aroer, south of the city in the
wadi, and turned in the direction of Gad toward Jazer. 6 They continued on to Gilead
and to the district below Mount Hermon.
Then they proceeded to Dan; from there they
turned toward Sidon, 7 going to the fortress
of Tyre and to all the cities of the Hivites and
Canaanites, and ending up in the Negeb of
Judah, at Beer-sheba. 8 Thus they toured the
whole land, reaching Jerusalem again after
nine months and twenty days. 9 Joab then reported the census figures to the king: of men
capable of wielding a sword, there were in
Israel eight hundred thousand, and in Judah
five hundred thousand.

10 Afterward, however, David regretted
having numbered the people. David said to
the LORD: "I have sinned grievously in what
I have done.[g] Take away, LORD, your servant's guilt, for I have acted very foolishly."*
11 When David rose in the morning, the word
of the LORD came to the prophet Gad, David's seer, saying: 12 Go, tell David: Thus
says the LORD: I am offering you three options; choose one of them, and I will give
you that. 13 Gad then went to David to inform
him. He asked: "Should three years of
famine come upon your land; or three
months of fleeing from your enemy while he
pursues you; or is it to be three days of
plague in your land? Now consider well:
what answer am I to give to him who sent
me?"[h] 14 David answered Gad: "I am greatly
distressed. But let us fall into the hand of
God, whose mercy is great, rather than into
human hands." 15 Thus David chose the
plague. At the time of the wheat harvest it
broke out among the people. The LORD sent
plague over Israel from morning until the
time appointed, and from Dan to Beer-sheba
seventy thousand of the people died. 16 But
when the angel stretched forth his hand toward Jerusalem to destroy it, the LORD
changed his mind about the calamity, and
said to the angel causing the destruction

**24:10** The narrative supposes that since the people belonged to the Lord rather than to the king, only the Lord should know their exact number. Further, since such an exact numbering of the people would make it possible for the king to exercise centralized power, imposing taxation, conscription, and expropriation upon Israel, the story shares the view of monarchy found in 1 Sm 8:4–18. See also Nm 3:44–51, where census taking requires an apotropaic offering.

*b:* 1 Sm 22:14. *c:* 2 Sm 2:18–23. *d:* 2 Sm 21:18. *e:* 2 Sm 11:3. *f:* 1 Chr 21:1–27. *g:* 1 Sm 24:6; 1 Chr 21:7–8. *h:* 2 Sm 21:1.

among the people: Enough now! Stay your
hand.[i] The angel of the LORD was then standing at the threshing floor of Araunah the Jebusite.[j] 17 When David saw the angel who was
striking the people, he said to the LORD: "It
is I who have sinned; it is I, the shepherd,
who have done wrong. But these sheep,
what have they done? Strike me and my father's family!"

*David Offers Sacrifices.* 18 On the same
day Gad went to David and said to him, "Go
and set up an altar to the LORD on the threshing floor of Araunah the Jebusite." 19 According to Gad's word, David went up as the
LORD had commanded. 20 Now Araunah
looked down and saw the king and his servants coming toward him while he was
threshing wheat. So he went out and bowed
down before the king, his face to the ground.
21 Then Araunah asked, "Why does my lord
the king come to his servant?" David
replied, "To buy the threshing floor from
you, to build an altar to the LORD, that the
plague may be withdrawn from the people."
22[k] But Araunah said to David: "Let my lord
the king take it and offer up what is good in
his sight. See, here are the oxen for burnt offerings, and the threshing sledges and the
yokes of oxen for wood. 23 All this does
Araunah give to the king." Araunah then
said to the king, "May the LORD your God
accept your offering." 24 The king, however,
replied to Araunah, "No, I will buy it from
you at the proper price, for I cannot sacrifice
to the LORD my God burnt offerings that cost
me nothing." So David bought the threshing
floor and the oxen for fifty silver shekels.
25 Then David built an altar to the LORD
there, and sacrificed burnt offerings and
communion offerings. The LORD granted relief to the land, and the plague was withdrawn from Israel.

*i:* Gn 6:6; Ex 32:14; 1 Chr 21:15; Jon 3:10. *j:* Ex 12:23; 2 Kgs 19:35. *k:* 1 Sm 6:14; 1 Kgs 19:21.

See RG 122–36

# The Books of Kings

The two Books of Kings are regarded by many as the last part of a work commonly known as the Deuteronomistic History. The latter tells the story of Israel from its settlement in the land (Joshua and Judges) through the transition from judgeship to monarchy under Samuel, Saul, and David (1 and 2 Samuel) to the reign of Solomon, the disintegration of the united kingdom into the kingdoms of Israel and Judah and the eventual downfall of both kingdoms (1 and 2 Kings). The Deuteronomistic History along with the Pentateuch forms a single historical narrative stretching from creation to exile.

The Books of Kings can be approached in several ways. They contain history and are an important source of information about the Israelite kingdoms. They are also narrative that calls for careful reading; historical accuracy is sometimes sacrificed to the demands of compelling characterization and dramatic tension. Most importantly, both historical presentation and narrative creativity are shaped by a particular religious worldview.

The multifaceted character of the work means that it has a variety of focal points. The historical events themselves, of course, are important, but the patterns according to which the author organizes those events give a unity to the author's historical reconstruction. The northern kings are condemned without exception, and the royal line degenerates from the divine election of Jeroboam I through a succession of short-lived dynasties to the bloodbath of Jehu's coup d'état, and finally dies out in a series of assassinations. (It must be admitted that the author at times skews the story to preserve the pattern: the relatively prosperous forty-one-year reign of Jeroboam II is dismissed in seven verses!) Judah's kings, on the other hand, follow a cyclic pattern of infidelity followed by reform, with each reformer king (Asa, Joash, Hezekiah, Josiah) greater than the last. Unfortunately the apostate kings also progress in wickedness, until the evil of Manasseh is so great that even Josiah's fidelity cannot turn away the Lord's wrath (2 Kgs 23:26).

As a literary work, the Books of Kings are admirable. Some of the brilliance is accessible only in Hebrew: wordplays, the sounds and rhythms of poetic passages, verbal allusions to other passages of the Hebrew Bible. Scenes are drawn with a vibrancy and immediacy that English cannot reproduce without sounding overdone. But other literary techniques survive translation: symmetrical structures for narrative units (and the disruptions of symmetry at significant points), rich ambiguities (see 1 Kgs 3:26), foreshadowings (such as the way the prophet of Bethel and the man of God of Judah in 1 Kgs 13 portend the destinies of their respective kingdoms). Characterization is rich and complex (Solomon, Jeroboam, Elijah, Ahab, Elisha, Jehu, etc.), revealing deep insight into human nature.

In offering a theological interpretation of history, 1–2 Kings upholds a double principle: the justification of the political disintegration of the Davidic empire, and the necessity of the religious unity of the Lord's people. This double principle is, practically speaking, unrealistic; see Jeroboam I's reasonable assessment in 1 Kgs 12:26–27. But for the Deuteronomistic historian, that is irrelevant. Just as the separation of the kingdoms is the Lord's will (1 Kgs 12:22–24), so too is the centralization of worship at the Temple in Jerusalem (1 Kgs 9:3; see Dt 12). 1–2 Kings reflects that double principle in its organization. The story of each king is told integrally, whether the king is of Israel or Judah: both lines of kings are legitimate. But the stories of the two lines are recounted in the order in which each king came to the throne, irrespective of which kingdom he ruled: there is only one people of God, though they are under two different royal jurisdictions. Moreover, each king is evaluated on theological grounds, with no allowance made for political or economic successes or failures. All Israelite kings are condemned because they did not reverse Jeroboam I's sin of setting up sanctuaries outside Jerusalem. Judahite kings are condemned for apostasy or praised for reform, as the case may be; but a continuing source of irritation to the Deuteronomistic historian is the failure of even the praiseworthy kings to do anything about local shrines outside Jerusalem (the "high places").

Into the stories of the kings, almost as a counterpoint, are woven numerous stories of prophets, named and great (Elijah, Elisha, Isaiah), and less known or anonymous (1 Kgs 13; 22). Many of the stories are anecdotal, reflecting the everyday life of prophets and prophetic guilds (1 Kgs 17; 2 Kgs 4). But the volatile dynamics of prophetic involvement in the political realm are prominent: prophets in opposition to kings (1 Kgs 14; 21; 2 Kgs 9), prophets in support of kings (1 Kgs 20:1–34; 2 Kgs 19–20; 22:14–20). This too is part of the theological worldview of the Deuteronomistic historian. The destiny of Israel is in God's hand. Through prophets, the divine will is made known on earth to kings and people and the future consequences of their response to God's will are spelled out. It is perhaps indicative of the importance prophets have in 1 and 2 Kings that the structural center of the two books is the story of Elisha's succession to Elijah's prophetic ministry (2 Kgs 2), and that this is one of the few passages in Kings that occurs outside the account of any king's reign. Behind the temporal realm of kings and reigns lies the continuing realm of the divine word and its servants, the prophets.

1–2 Kings draws on older sources (perhaps on archival records, certainly on works called "The Book of the Chronicles of the Kings"; see, for example, 1 Kgs 14:19, 29), which it uses for its own theological purpose. The so-called Deuteronomistic History itself underwent a complex process of editorial revision whose stages are disputed by scholars. There may have been an edition sometime late in the reign of Josiah (640–609 B.C.), but in the form we have it the work comes from the time of the exile (see 2 Kgs 25:27–30). In its turn the Deuteronomistic History was one of the sources used by the Chronicler in postexilic times to compile the history presented in 1 and 2 Chronicles. Though Chronicles has little interest in the Northern Kingdom, much of the material in Kings about the kingdom of Judah reappears, sometimes in altered form, in Chronicles.

The Books of Kings may be divided as follows:

See RG 126–29

# The First Book of Kings

## I. The Reign of Solomon*

### CHAPTER 1

See RG 126

*David's Old Age.* 1* When King David
was old and advanced in years, though they
covered him with blankets he could not get
warm. 2 His servants therefore said to him,
"Let a young virgin be sought to attend my
lord the king,* and to nurse him. If she sleeps
with you, my lord the king will be warm."
3 So they sought for a beautiful girl throughout the territory of Israel, and found Abishag
the Shunamite. So they brought her to the
king. 4 The girl was very beautiful indeed,
and she nursed the king and took care of him.
But the king did not have relations with her.
*Adonijah's Ambition.* 5 Adonijah, son of
Haggith, boasted, "I shall be king!" and he
provided himself with chariots, horses, and a
retinue of fifty to go before him.[a] 6 Yet his father would never antagonize him by asking,
"Why are you doing this?" Adonijah was
also very handsome, and next in age to Absalom by the same mother. 7 He consulted
with Joab, son of Zeruiah, and with Abiathar
the priest, and they became Adonijah's supporters. 8 However, Zadok the priest, Benaiah, son of Jehoiada, Nathan the prophet,
Shimei and Rei, and David's warriors did
not support Adonijah.
9 Adonijah slaughtered sheep, oxen, and
fatlings at the stone Zoheleth near En-rogel*
and invited all his brothers, the king's sons,
and all the royal officials of Judah; 10 but he
did not invite Nathan the prophet, or Benaiah, or the warriors, or Solomon his brother.
*Solomon Proclaimed King.* 11 Then Nathan
said to Bathsheba, Solomon's mother:
"Have you not heard that Adonijah, son of
Haggith, has become king, and our lord David does not know? 12 Come now, let me advise you so that you may save your life and
the life of your son Solomon. 13 Go, visit
King David, and say to him, 'Did you not,
my lord king, swear to your handmaid: Your
son Solomon shall be king after me; it is he
who shall sit upon my throne? Why, then,
has Adonijah become king?' 14 And while
you are still there speaking to the king, I will
come in after you and confirm your words."
15 So Bathsheba visited the king in his
room. The king was very old, and Abishag
the Shunamite was caring for the king.*
16 Bathsheba bowed in homage to the king.
The king said to her, "What do you wish?"*
17 She answered him: "My lord, you swore to
your servant by the LORD, your God, 'Solomon your son will be king after me; it is he
who shall sit upon my throne.' 18 But now
Adonijah has become king, and you, my lord
king, do not know it.* 19 He has sacrificed

**1:1–11:43** The story of the reign of Solomon comprises twelve major units, organized concentrically. That is, the first unit (1:1–2:12a) balances the last (11:26–43), the second (2:12b–46) balances the second last (11:14–25), and so forth. (See the structural notes at the beginning of each major unit.) The center of the whole story is a diptych that narrates the construction of the Temple (6:1–7:51) and its dedication (8:1–9:10).

**1:1–2:12a** The first major unit of the Solomon story concludes the so-called Succession Narrative (2 Sm 9–20; 1 Kgs 1–2). This unit tells how Solomon, a younger son, came to succeed David on the throne of Israel through the intervention of the prophet Nathan. Compare the last unit of the Solomon story, 11:26–43, where the prophet Ahijah begins the process whereby Jeroboam becomes king of the northern tribes after Solomon's death. The story of Solomon's accession is itself concentrically arranged: David's decline, Adonijah's rise, Solomon's supporters, David's decision, Solomon's inauguration, Adonijah's fall, David's death. Chronicles has no developed parallel to this story (see 1 Chr 23:1).

**1:2** The fulsome use of royal titles and the elaborate etiquette in the Succession Narrative suggest the raw ambition of the contending parties and the oppressive atmosphere of the court.

**1:9 En-rogel**: the modern Job's Well just southeast of Jerusalem. It marked the ancient boundary between the tribes of Benjamin and Judah (Jos 15:7; 18:16).

**1:15** Entering the king's chambers, Bathsheba confronts two realities: he is very old; and she herself, the woman for whom David once committed adultery and murder, has been replaced at the king's side and in his bed.

**1:16** Throughout 1 Kgs 1 the key question is "Who shall be king (*malak*)?" David's feeble, two-syllable question to Bathsheba is an ironic echo of that key word: "What do you wish?" renders the Heb. *mahlak?*

**1:18** Bathsheba uses a clever wordplay to conceal the rivalry between Solomon and Adonijah and imply that the real

*a:* 2 Sm 15:1.

**Nathan and Bathsheba**

IT IS SURPRISING to find Nathan and Bathsheba in alliance with each other (1:11ff). When they were mentioned together previously (2 Sm 11–12), Nathan was condemning David for his adultery with Bathsheba and the murder of her husband. Nathan advises Bathsheba on how to save her life and that of her son, Solomon. The lives of Bathsheba and Solomon were in danger if Adonijah became king, because new kings customarily killed off their potential rivals.

bulls, fatlings, and sheep in great numbers; he has invited all the king's sons, Abiathar the priest, and Joab, the commander of the army, but not your servant Solomon. [20*] Now, my lord king, all Israel is looking to you to declare to them who is to sit upon the throne of my lord the king after him. [21] If this is not done, when my lord the king rests with his ancestors, I and my son Solomon will be considered criminals."

[22] While she was still speaking to the king, Nathan the prophet came in. [23] They told the king, "Nathan the prophet is here." He entered the king's presence and did him homage, bowing to the floor. [24] Then Nathan said: "My lord king, did you say, 'Adonijah shall be king after me and shall sit upon my throne'? [25] For today he went down and sacrificed bulls, fatlings, and sheep in great numbers; he invited all the king's sons, the commanders of the army, and Abiathar the priest, and even now they are eating and drinking in his company and saying, 'Long live King Adonijah!' [26] But me, your servant, he did not invite; nor Zadok the priest, nor Benaiah, son of Jehoiada, nor your servant Solomon. [27] If this was done by order of my lord the king, you did not tell me, your servant, who is to sit upon the throne of my lord the king after him."

[28] King David answered, "Call Bathsheba here." When she entered the king's presence and stood before him, [29] the king swore, "As the LORD lives, who has redeemed my life from all distress, [30] this very day I will fulfill the oath I swore to you by the LORD, the God of Israel, 'Your son Solomon shall be king after me and shall sit upon my throne in my place.' " [31] Bowing to the floor in homage to the king, Bathsheba said, "May my lord, King David, live forever!"

[32] Then King David said, "Call Zadok the priest, Nathan the prophet, and Benaiah, son of Jehoiada." When they had entered the king's presence, [33] he said to them: "Take with you the royal officials. Mount my son Solomon upon my own mule and escort him down to Gihon. [34] There Zadok the priest and Nathan the prophet shall anoint him king over Israel, and you shall blow the ram's horn and cry, 'Long live King Solomon!' [35] When you come back up with him, he is to go in and sit upon my throne. It is he that shall be king in my place: him I designate ruler of Israel and of Judah." [36] Benaiah, son of Jehoiada, answered the king: "So be it! May the LORD, the God of my lord the king, so decree! [37] As the LORD has been with my lord the king, so may he be with Solomon, and make his throne even greater than that of my lord, King David!"

[38] So Zadok the priest, Nathan the prophet, Benaiah, son of Jehoiada, and the Cherethites and Pelethites* went down, and mounting Solomon on King David's mule, escorted him to Gihon. [39] Then Zadok the priest took the horn of oil from the tent and anointed Solomon. They blew the ram's horn and all the people shouted, "Long live King Solomon!" [40] Then all the people went

rivalry is between David and Adonijah. She repeatedly addresses David as "my lord king" (*'adoni hammelek*), but claims that "Adonijah has become king" (*'adoniya malak*). **Know**: the term means both "be aware of" and "recognize, acknowledge, ratify."

**1:20** There was no precedent for determining succession to the throne of Israel. Adonijah and his supporters assumed that primogeniture would assure the succession as it did in the monarchies of the surrounding nations. But Bathsheba persuades David that he is free to name anyone he chooses.

**1:38 Cherethites and Pelethites**: mercenaries in David's bodyguard. They became part of his retinue after he defeated the Philistines and established himself in Jerusalem; cf. 2 Sm 8:18; 15:18; 20:23.

up after him, playing flutes and rejoicing so much the earth split with their shouting.

***Adonijah Submits to Solomon.*** 41 Adonijah and all the guests who were with him heard it, just as they ended their banquet. When Joab heard the sound of the ram's horn, he asked, "Why this uproar in the city?" 42 As he was speaking, Jonathan, son of Abiathar the priest, arrived. Adonijah said, "Come, you are a man of worth and must bring good news." 43 Jonathan answered Adonijah, "Hardly!* Our lord, King David, has made Solomon king. 44 The king sent with him Zadok the priest, Nathan the prophet, Benaiah, son of Jehoiada, and the Cherethites and Pelethites, and they mounted him upon the king's own mule. 45 Zadok the priest and Nathan the prophet anointed him king at Gihon, and they went up from there rejoicing, so that the city is in an uproar. That is the noise you hear. 46 Moreover, Solomon has taken his seat on the royal throne, 47 and moreover the king's servants have come to pay their respects to our lord, King David, saying, 'May your God make Solomon's name more famous than your name, his throne greater than your throne!' And the king in his bed did homage. 48 This is what the king said: 'Blessed be the LORD, the God of Israel, who has this day provided one to sit upon my throne, so that I see it with my own eyes.' " 49 All the guests of Adonijah got up trembling, and went each their way, 50 but Adonijah, in fear of Solomon, got up and went to grasp the horns of the altar.*

51 It was reported to Solomon: "Adonijah, in fear of King Solomon, is clinging to the horns of the altar and saying, 'Let King Solomon first swear that he will not kill me, his servant, with the sword.' " 52 Solomon answered, "If he proves worthy, not a hair of his shall fall to the ground. But if evil is found in him, he shall die." 53 King Solomon sent to have him brought down from the altar, and he came and paid homage to King Solomon. Solomon then said to him, "Go to your house."

## CHAPTER 2

See RG 126

***David's Last Instructions and Death.*** 1 When the time of David's death drew near, he gave these instructions to Solomon his son: 2 "I am going the way of all the earth. Be strong and be a man! 3[b] Keep the mandate of the LORD, your God, walking in his ways and keeping his statutes, commands, ordinances, and decrees as they are written in the law of Moses, that you may succeed in whatever you do, and wherever you turn, 4[c] and that the LORD may fulfill the word he spoke concerning me: If your sons so conduct themselves that they walk before me in faithfulness with their whole heart and soul, there shall never be wanting someone of your line on the throne of Israel.

5*[d] "You yourself know what Joab, son of Zeruiah, did to me—what he did to the two commanders of Israel's armies, Abner, son of Ner, and Amasa, son of Jether: he killed them and brought the blood of war into a time of peace, and put the blood of war on the belt about his waist and the sandal on his foot. 6 Act with all the wisdom you possess; do not let his gray head go down to Sheol in peace. 7[e] But be true to the sons of Barzillai the Gileadite, and have them among those who eat at your table. For they were loyal to me when I was fleeing from your brother Absalom. 8[f] You also have with you Shimei,

**1:43 Hardly**: Jonathan's first word, *'abal*, whose meaning (such as "indeed," "on the contrary") must be discerned from the context, may be ironic. This irony is deepened by an untranslatable wordplay in Hebrew: a very similar word means "to mourn," which is an appropriate comment about the death of Adonijah's hopes for the throne.

**1:50 Horns of the altar**: the protuberances on each of the four corners of the altar (Ex 27:2; 29:12). By grasping the horns of the altar Adonijah is claiming asylum (Ex 21:13–14; 1 Kgs 2:28).

**2:5–9** David urges Solomon to purge Joab and Shimei and supplies him with justification for doing so. Joab had killed Abner (2 Sm 3:22–30) and Amasa (2 Sm 20:4–12), thereby bringing blood guilt upon himself and perhaps upon his master David. Shimei had cursed David (2 Sm 16:5–8), though David pledged that Shimei would not be killed for it (2 Sm 19:16–24). David's motives, however, may have been more personal. Joab also killed David's son Absalom and chided David for his untimely public display of grief (2 Sm 18:9–19:8), and David may have felt himself free of the promise he made to Shimei because that promise was coerced by the presence of Shimei's thousand partisans backing him at the time.

*b:* Dt 17:18–19. *c:* 2 Sm 7:11–16; Ps 132:11–12. *d:* 2 Sm 3:22–30; 20:8–10. *e:* 2 Sm 17:27–29; 19:32–41. *f:* 2 Sm 16:5–13; 19:17–24.

son of Gera, the Benjaminite of Bahurim, who cursed me bitterly the day I was going to Mahanaim. When he came down to meet me at the Jordan, I swore to him by the LORD: 'I will not kill you by the sword.' [9]But you must not let him go unpunished. You are wise; you will know what to do to send his gray head down to Sheol in blood."

[10g] David rested with his ancestors and was buried in the City of David. [11h] David was king over Israel for forty years: he was king seven years in Hebron and thirty-three years in Jerusalem.

***The Kingdom Made Secure.**** [12]Then Solomon sat on the throne of David his father, and his kingship was established.

[13]Adonijah, son of Haggith, came to Bathsheba, the mother of Solomon. "Do you come in peace?" she asked. "In peace," he answered, [14]and he added, "I have something to say to you." She replied, "Speak." [15]So he said: "You know that the kingship was mine, and all Israel expected me to be king. But the kingship passed me by and went to my brother; by the LORD's will it went to him. [16]But now there is one favor I would ask of you. Do not refuse me." And she said, "Speak on." [17*] He said, "Please ask King Solomon, who will not refuse you, to give me Abishag the Shunamite to be my wife." [18]Bathsheba replied, "Very well, I will speak to the king for you."

[19]Then Bathsheba went to King Solomon to speak to him for Adonijah, and the king stood up to meet her and paid her homage. Then he sat down upon his throne, and a throne was provided for the king's mother, who sat at his right. [20]She said, "There is one small favor I would ask of you. Do not refuse me." The king said to her, "Ask it, my mother, for I will not refuse you." [21]So she said, "Let Abishag the Shunamite be given to your brother Adonijah to be his wife." [22]King Solomon answered his mother, "And why do you ask that Abishag the Shunamite be given to Adonijah? Ask the kingship for him as well, for he is my older brother! Ask for him, for Abiathar the priest, for Joab, son of Zeruiah!" [23]And King Solomon swore by the LORD: "May God do thus to me and more, if Adonijah has not spoken this word at the cost of his life. [24i] And now, as the LORD lives, who has established me and set me on the throne of David my father and made for me a house as he promised, this day shall Adonijah be put to death." [25]Then King Solomon sent Benaiah, son of Jehoiada, who struck him dead.

[26j] The king said to Abiathar the priest: "Go to your estate in Anathoth. Though you deserve to die, I will not put you to death at this time, because you carried the ark of the Lord GOD before David my father and shared in all the hardships my father endured."* [27k] So Solomon dismissed Abiathar from the office of priest of the LORD, thus fulfilling the word the LORD had spoken in Shiloh against the house of Eli.

[28]When the news came to Joab, since he had sided with Adonijah, though not with Absalom, he fled to the tent of the LORD and clung to the horns of the altar. [29]King Solomon was told, "Joab has fled to the tent of the LORD and is by the altar." He sent Benaiah, son of Jehoiada, with the order, "Go, strike him down." [30]Benaiah went to the tent of the LORD and said to him, "The king says, 'Come out.' " But he answered, "No! I will die here." Benaiah reported to the king, "This is what Joab said to me in reply." [31]The king answered him: "Do as he has said. Strike him down and bury him, and remove from me and from my father's house the blood which Joab shed without provocation. [32l] The LORD will bring blood upon his own head, because he struck down two men

**2:12–46** The second major unit of the Solomon story shows how Solomon eliminated people he considered threats to the security of his throne. It is marked by a device called "inclusion," where the text repeats a word, phrase, or idea at the beginning and end of a literary unit (see vv. 12b, 46b). Compare 11:14–25, where Solomon is unable to eliminate other threats to his security.

**2:17–25** Abishag had belonged to David's harem (1:3–4), which Solomon inherited. Adonijah's request could imply a challenge to Solomon's accession and so exposes Adonijah to the suspicion of insurrection that will cost him his life; cf. 2 Sm 3:6–11; 16:21–22.

**2:26** The narrator indulges in a subtle wordplay: Abiathar's exile to Anathoth (*'anatot*) continues the series of hardships he has endured (*hit'annita*).

*g:* Acts 2:29. *h:* 2 Sm 2:1–4; 5:1–5. *i:* 2 Sm 7:11–16. *j:* 1 Sm 22:20–23. *k:* 1 Sm 2:27–33. *l:* 2 Sm 3:22–30; 20:8–10.

better and more just than himself, and slew
them with the sword without my father David's knowledge: Abner, son of Ner, commander of Israel's army, and Amasa, son of
Jether, commander of Judah's army. [33]Their
blood will be upon the head of Joab and his
descendants. But upon David and his descendants, upon his house and his throne,
there shall be peace forever from the LORD."
[34]Benaiah, son of Jehoiada, went back,
struck him down and killed him; he was
buried in his house in the wilderness. [35]The
king appointed Benaiah, son of Jehoiada,
over the army in his place; Zadok the priest
the king put in place of Abiathar.

[36]Then the king summoned Shimei and
said to him: "Build yourself a house in Jerusalem and stay there. Do not go anywhere
else. [37]For the day you leave, and cross the
Wadi Kidron, be certain you shall surely die.
Your blood shall be upon your own head."
[38]Shimei answered the king: "I accept. Your
servant will do just as my lord the king has
said." So Shimei stayed in Jerusalem for a
long time. [39]But three years later, two of
Shimei's servants ran away to Achish, son of
Maacah, king of Gath, and Shimei was told,
"Your servants are in Gath." [40]So Shimei
rose, saddled his donkey, and went to Achish
in Gath in search of his servants; and Shimei
returned from Gath with his servants.
[41]When Solomon was told that Shimei had
gone from Jerusalem to Gath, and had returned, [42]the king summoned Shimei and
said to him: "Did I not have you swear by the
LORD and warn you clearly, 'The day you
leave and go anywhere else, be certain you
shall surely die'? And you answered, 'I accept and obey.'* [43]Why, then, have you not
kept the oath of the LORD and the command
that I gave you?" [44m] And the king said to
Shimei: "In your heart you know very well
the evil that you did to David my father.
Now the LORD is bringing your own evil
upon your head. [45]But King Solomon shall
be blessed, and David's throne shall be established before the LORD forever." [46]The
king then gave the order to Benaiah, son of
Jehoiada, who went out and struck him dead.

And the royal power was established in
Solomon's hand.

## CHAPTER 3

See RG 126–29

### *Early Promise of Solomon's Reign.**

[1n] Solomon allied himself by marriage with
Pharaoh, king of Egypt. He married the
daughter of Pharaoh and brought her to the
City of David, until he should finish building his own house, and the house of the
LORD, and the wall around Jerusalem. [2]The
people were sacrificing on the high places,
however, for up to that time no house had
been built for the name of the LORD. [3]Al-
though Solomon loved the LORD, walking in
the statutes of David his father, he offered
sacrifice and burned incense on the high
places.

[4]The king went to Gibeon to sacrifice
there, because that was the great high place.
Upon its altar Solomon sacrificed a thousand burnt offerings. [5]In Gibeon the LORD
appeared to Solomon in a dream at night.
God said: Whatever you ask I shall give you.
[6]Solomon answered: "You have shown great
kindness to your servant, David my father,
because he walked before you with fidelity,
justice, and an upright heart; and you have
continued this great kindness toward him today, giving him a son to sit upon his throne.
[7]Now, LORD, my God, you have made me,
your servant, king to succeed David my father; but I am a mere youth, not knowing at
all how to act— [8]I, your servant, among the
people you have chosen, a people so vast
that it cannot be numbered or counted. [9]Give
your servant, therefore, a listening heart to

**2:42–44** In his charge against Shimei, Solomon misrepresents the truth in two ways. He did not make Shimei take an oath. And he imposed capital punishment only on crossing the Wadi Kidron, to the east of Jerusalem. This was presumably to prevent Shimei from returning to his home, Bahurim, which lay in that direction; Gath, however, is southwest of Jerusalem. Solomon's next words to Shimei reveal that he is really being punished for cursing David, not for violating Solomon's command.

**3:1–15** The third major unit of the Solomon story depicts the bright beginning of his reign. It includes the narrator's remarks about Solomon's marriage and his building projects, and a divine appearance to Solomon. Compare 11:1–13, where the same themes recur, but in negative fashion. The story of the divine appearance is told also in 2 Chr 1:1–13.

*m:* 2 Sm 16:5–13; 19:17–24. *n:* 1 Kgs 7:8; 9:24.

judge your people and to distinguish between good and evil. For who is able to give
judgment for this vast people of yours?"
[10]The Lord was pleased by Solomon's request. [11]So God said to him: Because you
asked for this—you did not ask for a long
life for yourself, nor for riches, nor for the
life of your enemies—but you asked for discernment to know what is right— [12]I now do
as you request. I give you a heart so wise and
discerning that there has never been anyone
like you until now, nor after you will there be
anyone to equal you. [13o] In addition, I give
you what you have not asked for: I give you
such riches and glory that among kings there
will be no one like you all your days. [14]And
if you walk in my ways, keeping my statutes
and commandments, as David your father
did, I will give you a long life. [15]Solomon
awoke; it was a dream! He went to Jerusalem, stood before the ark of the covenant of
the Lord, sacrificed burnt offerings and
communion offerings, and gave a feast for
all his servants.

*Solomon's Listening Heart.** [16]Later, two
prostitutes came to the king and stood before
him. [17]One woman said: "By your leave, my
lord, this woman and I live in the same
house, and I gave birth in the house while she
was present. [18]On the third day after I gave
birth, this woman also gave birth. We were
alone; no one else was in the house with us;
only the two of us were in the house. [19]This
woman's son died during the night when she
lay on top of him. [20]So in the middle of the
night she got up and took my son from my
side, as your servant was sleeping. Then she
laid him in her bosom and laid her dead son
in my bosom. [21]I rose in the morning to nurse
my son, and he was dead! But when I examined him in the morning light, I saw it was
not the son I had borne." [22]The other woman
answered, "No! The living one is my son, the
dead one is yours." But the first kept saying,
"No! the dead one is your son, the living one
is mine!" Thus they argued before the king.
[23]Then the king said: "One woman claims,
'This, the living one, is my son, the dead one
is yours.' The other answers, 'No! The dead
one is your son, the living one is mine.' "
[24]The king continued, "Get me a sword."
When they brought the sword before the
king, [25]he said, "Cut the living child in two,
and give half to one woman and half to the
other." [26*] The woman whose son was alive,
because she was stirred with compassion for
her son, said to the king, "Please, my lord,
give her the living baby—do not kill it!" But
the other said, "It shall be neither mine nor
yours. Cut it in two!" [27]The king then answered, "Give her the living baby! Do not
kill it! She is the mother." [28]When all Israel
heard the judgment the king had given, they
were in awe of him, because they saw that the
king had in him the wisdom of God for giving right judgment.

## CHAPTER 4

See RG 126–29

*Solomon's Riches: Domestic Affairs.**
[1]Solomon was king over all Israel, [2]and
these were the officials he had in his service:

Azariah, son of Zadok, the priest;
[3] Elihoreph and Ahijah, sons of Shisha, scribes;
Jehoshaphat, son of Ahilud, the chancellor;
[4] Benaiah, son of Jehoiada, in charge of the army;
Zadok and Abiathar, priests;
[5] Azariah, son of Nathan, in charge of the governors;
Zabud, son of Nathan, priest and companion to the king;
[6] Ahishar, master of the palace; and

**3:16–5:14** The fourth major unit of the Solomon story shows how Solomon used the three gifts that the Lord gave him in 3:12–13: a listening heart (3:16–28), riches (4:1–5:8), universal renown (5:9–14). In each case his gifts benefited the populace, from the lowest classes (3:16–28) to his whole people (4:20; 5:5) to the whole world (5:9–14). Compare 9:26–10:29, where the same three gifts all redound to the benefit of Solomon himself.

**3:26–27** The true mother reveals herself by an uncommon and tender word for the child, "baby." With this, and the woman's willingness to give up her child, Solomon realizes that she is the true mother, and quotes her words exactly in rendering his judgment.

**4:1–5:8** The sub-unit on Solomon's riches is organized around domestic affairs (4:1–20) and international affairs (5:1–5), with a short appendix on Solomon's horses and chariots (5:6–8). Compare 9:26–10:29, where comparable elements reappear.

*o:* Eccl 1:12–13; Wis 7:7–11; Mt 6:29.

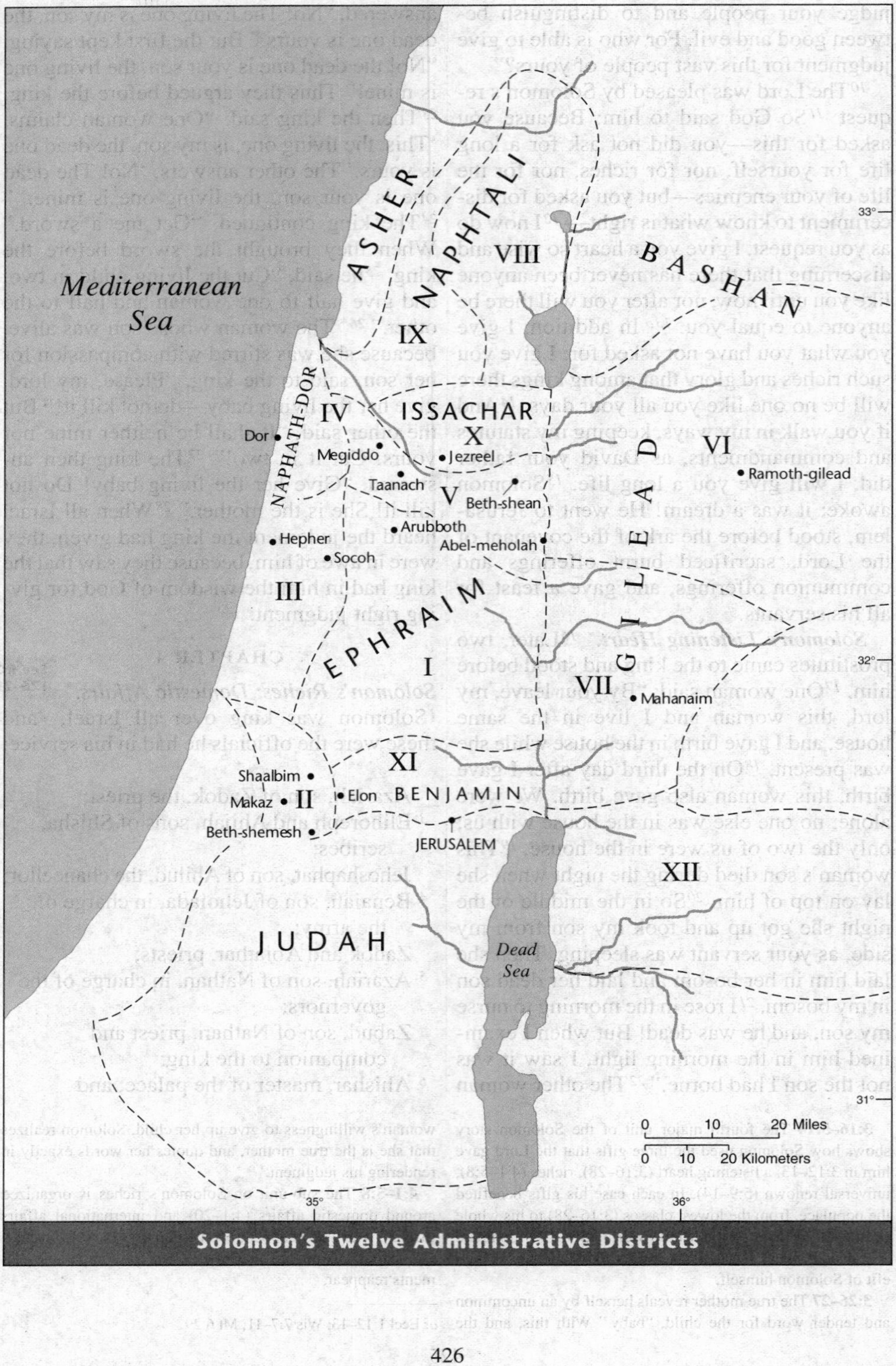


**Solomon's Twelve Administrative Districts**

Adoniram, son of Abda, in charge of the
forced labor.

7* Solomon had twelve governors over all
Israel who supplied food for the king and his
household, each having to provide for one
month in the year. 8 Their names were:*

the son of Hur in the hill country of
Ephraim;
9 the son of Deker in Makaz, Shaalbim,
Beth-shemesh, and Elon Beth-hanan;
10 the son of Hesed in Arubboth, as well as in
Socoh and the whole region of Hepher;
11 the son of Abinadab, in all Naphath-dor;
he was married to Taphath, Solomon's
daughter;
12 Baana, son of Ahilud, in Taanach and
Megiddo and all Beth-shean near
Zarethan below Jezreel, from Beth-
shean to Abel-meholah to beyond
Jokmeam;
13 the son of Geber in Ramoth-gilead,
having charge of the villages of Jair,
son of Manasseh, in Gilead; and of the
district of Argob in Bashan—sixty
large walled cities with gates barred
with bronze;
14 Ahinadab, son of Iddo, in Mahanaim;
15 Ahimaaz, in Naphtali; he was married
to Basemath, another daughter of
Solomon;
16 Baana, son of Hushai, in Asher and Aloth;
17 Jehoshaphat, son of Paruah, in Issachar;
18 Shimei, son of Ela, in Benjamin;
19 Geber, son of Uri, in the land of Gilead,
the land of Sihon, king of the
Amorites, and of Og, king of Bashan.

There was one governor besides, in the
land of Judah.* 20p Judah and Israel were as
numerous as the sands by the sea; they ate
and drank and rejoiced.

## CHAPTER 5

See RG 126–29

***Solomon's Riches: International Af-***
***fairs.*** 1* Solomon ruled over all the kingdoms from the River* to the land of the Philistines, down to the border of Egypt; they
paid Solomon tribute and served him as long
as he lived. 2* Solomon's provisions for each
day were thirty kors of fine flour, sixty kors
of meal, 3 ten fatted oxen, twenty pasture-fed
oxen, and a hundred sheep, not counting
harts, gazelles, roebucks, and fatted fowl.
4 He had dominion over all the land west of
the River, from Tiphsah to Gaza, and all its
kings, and he had peace on all his borders
round about. 5q Thus Judah and Israel lived
in security, everyone under their own vine
and fig tree from Dan to Beer-sheba, as long
as Solomon lived.

***Solomon's Riches: Chariots and Horses.***
6r Solomon had forty thousand stalls for
horses for chariots and twelve thousand
horsemen. 7* The governors, one for each
month, provided food for King Solomon and
for all the guests at King Solomon's table.
They left nothing unprovided. 8 For the chariot horses and draft animals also, each
brought his quota of barley and straw to the
required place.

***Solomon's Renown.*** 9s Moreover, God
gave Solomon wisdom, exceptional understanding, and knowledge, as vast as the sand
on the seashore. 10 Solomon's wisdom sur-

**4:7–19** The administration of the kingdom thus initiated by Solomon continued in its main features for the duration of the monarchy in Israel and Judah. Note the use of "all Israel" to mean only the northern tribes (see also 5:27). Solomon's exactions did not fall evenly on the whole people, but favored his own southern tribe of Judah. Eventually this inequity would lead to the dissolution of the union of Israel and Judah (12:1–19).

**4:8–19** Several of the governors are identified only by their fathers' names.

**4:19 One governor . . . land of Judah**: the royal territory of Judah had its own peculiar administration different from that of the twelve northern districts, each of which had to supply the king and his household with a month's provisions of food each year (v. 7).

**5:1–32** This translation follows the numeration of the Hebrew Bible, rather than the Vulgate; in many English translations, 5:1–14 is 4:21–34, and 5:15 is 5:1.

**5:1 The River**: that is, the Euphrates. This claim may be exaggerated, but "from the Euphrates to the border of Egypt" was the traditional description of the extent of the Davidic holdings.

**5:2** The list of Solomon's supplies may have originally belonged with the list of governors in 4:7–19, but the author has placed it here to imply that Solomon's vassal kingdoms, not his own citizenry, supplied his vast daily needs. The daily provisions listed could have supported several thousand people. **Kors**: see note on Ez 45:14.

**5:7** This verse suggests that the governors also saw to the provender for Solomon's animals (v. 8).

*p:* Gn 22:17; 32:13; Dn 3:36; Hos 1:10; Heb 11:12. *q:* Sir 47:13. *r:* 1 Kgs 10:26; Dt 17:16; 2 Chr 1:14; 9:25. *s:* Sir 47:15–17.

passed that of all the peoples of the East and
all the wisdom of Egypt. [11]He was wiser
than anyone else—wiser than Ethan the Ezrahite, or Heman, Chalcol, and Darda, the
musicians—and his fame spread throughout
the neighboring peoples. [12]Solomon also uttered three thousand proverbs, and his songs
numbered a thousand and five. [13]He spoke
of plants, from the cedar on Lebanon to the
hyssop growing out of the wall, and he
spoke about beasts, birds, reptiles, and
fishes. [14t] People from all nations came to
hear Solomon's wisdom, sent by all the
kings of the earth who had heard of his wisdom.

*Preparations for the Temple.** [15]When Hiram, king of Tyre, heard that Solomon had
been anointed king in place of his father, he
sent an embassy to him; for Hiram had always been David's friend.* [16]Solomon sent
back this message to Hiram: [17u] "You know
that David my father, because of the wars
that beset him, could not build a house for
the name of the LORD his God until such
time as the LORD should put his enemies under the soles of his feet. [18]But now the LORD,
my God, has given me rest on all sides, without adversary or misfortune. [19v] So I intend
to build a house for the name of the LORD,
my God, as the LORD said to David my father: Your son whom I will put upon your
throne in your place shall build the house for
my name. [20]Give orders, then, to have cedars
from the Lebanon cut down for me. My servants shall accompany yours, and I will pay
you whatever you say for your servants'
wages. For you know that there is no one
among us who is skilled in cutting timber
like the Sidonians." [21]When Hiram had
heard the words of Solomon, he was overjoyed, and said, "Blessed be the LORD this
day, who has given David a wise son over
this numerous people." [22*] Hiram then sent
word to Solomon, "I have heard the proposal
you sent me, and I will provide all the cedars
and fir trees you desire. [23]My servants shall
bring them down from the Lebanon to the
sea, and I will arrange them into rafts in the
sea and bring them wherever you say. There
I will break up the rafts, and you shall take
the lumber. You, for your part, shall furnish
the provisions I desire for my household."
[24]So Hiram continued to provide Solomon
with all the cedars and fir trees he desired,
[25]while Solomon gave Hiram twenty thousand kors of wheat to provide for his household, and twenty kors* of hand-pressed oil.
Solomon gave Hiram all this every year.
[26]The LORD gave Solomon wisdom as he
promised him. So there was peace between
Hiram and Solomon, and the two of them
made* a covenant.

[27]King Solomon raised thirty thousand
forced laborers from all Israel.* [28]He sent
them to the Lebanon for a month in relays of
ten thousand, so that they spent one month in
the Lebanon and two months at home. Adoniram was in charge of the forced labor.
[29]Solomon had seventy thousand carriers
and eighty thousand stonecutters in the
mountain, [30]in addition to three thousand
three hundred overseers answerable to Solo-

**5:15–32** The fifth major unit of the Solomon story explains the preparations Solomon made for the construction of the Temple. He negotiates with Hiram of Tyre for materiel (5:15–26), and conscripts a labor force for personnel (5:27–32). Compare 9:11–23, which returns to the same two themes after the Temple has been built and dedicated. 2 Chr 2:1–17 presents another version of the same material.

**5:15 David's friend**: the term "to be a friend," lit., "to love," is political, and means that David and Hiram had been allies. The purpose of Hiram's embassy is to determine whether Solomon is willing to continue the alliance. This unspoken agenda lies behind the negotiations about materials for the Temple, as the concluding v. 26 makes clear.

**5:22–23** Although his reply is couched in polite, diplomatic language, Hiram renegotiates Solomon's terms in his own favor. No Israelites are to enter Tyrian territory, and Solomon is not to pay the salary of Hiram's laborers but rather to furnish "provisions" for his household—the same language used of the tribute Solomon received from his own vassals in v. 2.

**5:25 Twenty kors**: this means about two thousand gallons of the finest olive oil available, hand-pressed rather than produced in large olive presses, so that no debris (such as crushed olive pits, powder from the grinding stones) would contaminate the oil. Also see note on 2 Chr 2:9.

**5:26 Made**: lit., "cut." The story of Solomon's arrangements with Hiram is framed by references to political alliance between Israel and Tyre (vv. 15, 26). Since, in Hebrew idiom, Hiram and Solomon "cut" a covenant, this suggests that the agreement they reach for "cutting" wood (which clearly favors Hiram) reflects the terms of the larger treaty.

**5:27 All Israel**: see note on 4:7–19.

---

*t:* 1 Kgs 10:1. *u:* 2 Sm 7:5–7; 1 Chr 22:7–8. *v:* 2 Sm 7:12–13.

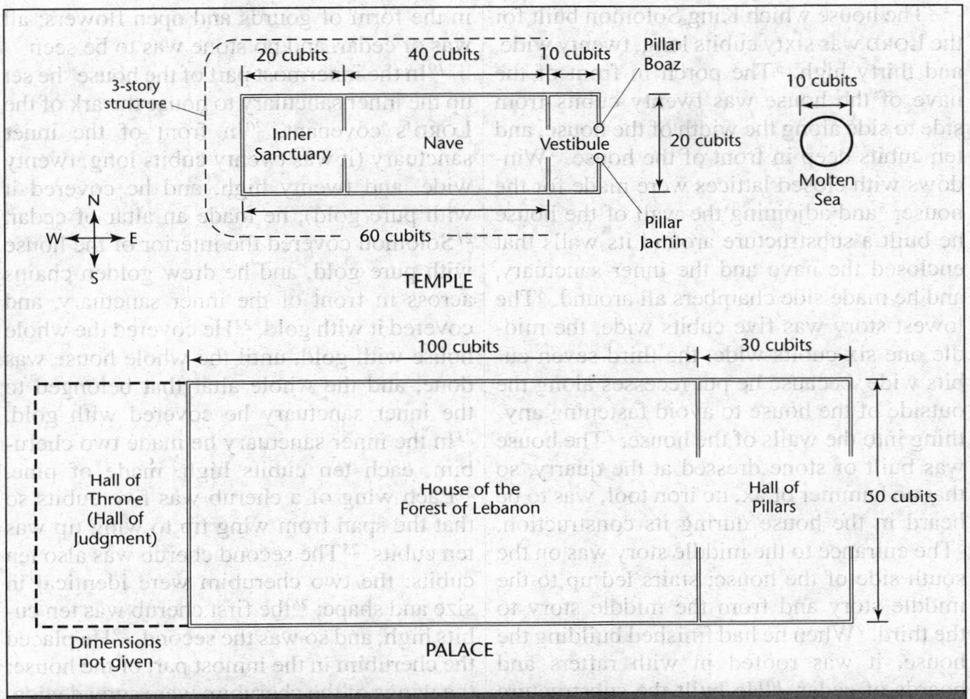


**The Temple and Palace of Solomon**

mon, who were in charge of the work and directed the people engaged in the work. 31 By
order of the king, fine, large blocks of stone
were quarried to give the house a foundation
of hewn stone. 32 Solomon's and Hiram's
builders, along with others from Gebal,*
shaped them, and prepared the wood and
stones for building the house.

## CHAPTER 6

See RG 126–29

*Building of the Temple.** 1 In the four
hundred and eightieth year after the Israelites went forth from the land of Egypt, in the
fourth year of Solomon's reign over Israel,
in the month of Ziv (the second month), he
began to build the house of the LORD.*

**5:32 Gebal**: Byblos.

**6:1–7:51** The central units of the Solomon story describe the building of the Temple (6:1–7:51) and its dedication ceremony (8:1–9:10). The account of the construction of the Temple ("the house") is organized to give the reader a guided tour. Approaching from a distance, we see ground plans (6:2–3) and structural work in stone (6:4–8) and wood (6:9–10). After a brief interruption that recounts a divine word to Solomon (6:11–13), we enter the Temple to view the paneling and ornamentation of the nave (6:14–18), the gilded walls and golden entrance of the inner sanctuary or holy of holies (6:19–22), with its priceless interior decoration and furnishings (6:23–28). As we leave, we admire the interior carvings and gilded floor of the inner sanctuary (6:29–30), return to the nave through carved and gilded doors (6:31–32), and exit from the nave through another set of carved and gilded doors (6:33–35) to the courtyard (6:36). Our guide briefly points out the nearby palace complex (7:1–12); then we walk around the courtyard to marvel at Hiram's heroic works in bronze: the two columns (7:15–22), the "sea" (7:23–26), and the ten stands and basins set along either side of the Temple buildings (7:27–39). The account ends with the smaller bronze vessels Hiram made for the Temple services (7:40–47) and the gold vessels that Solomon made (7:48–50). Unfortunately, several factors make it impossible to use the account to produce a satisfactory model of Solomon's Temple. Throughout the account there are numerous technical architectural terms whose meaning is lost to us; and it is moreover likely that the author is describing the Temple as it stood in his own time, centuries after Solomon's day. The Chronicler also describes the construction of the Temple in 2 Chr 3:1–4:22 and its dedication in 2 Chr 5:1–7:22.

**6:1** Construction of the Temple is here dated in relation to the traditional date of the exodus from Egypt, rounded off to a conventional twelve generations of forty years each. This chronology means that the Temple was built approximately midway between Israel's two foundational deliverances, the exodus and the return from the Babylonian exile. The

[2]The house which King Solomon built for the LORD was sixty cubits long, twenty wide, and thirty high. [3]The porch in front of the nave of the house was twenty cubits from side to side along the width of the house, and ten cubits deep in front of the house. [4]Windows with closed lattices were made for the house, [5]and adjoining the wall of the house he built a substructure around its walls that enclosed the nave and the inner sanctuary, and he made side chambers all around. [6]The lowest story was five cubits wide, the middle one six cubits wide, the third seven cubits wide, because he put recesses along the outside of the house to avoid fastening anything into the walls of the house. [7]The house was built of stone dressed at the quarry, so that no hammer or ax, no iron tool, was to be heard in the house during its construction. [8]The entrance to the middle story was on the south side of the house; stairs led up to the middle story and from the middle story to the third. [9]When he had finished building the house, it was roofed in with rafters and boards of cedar. [10]He built the substructure five cubits high all along the outside of the house, to which it was joined by cedar beams.

[11]The word of the LORD came to Solomon: [12w] As to this house you are building—if you walk in my statutes, carry out my ordinances, and observe all my commands, walking in them, I will fulfill toward you my word which I spoke to David your father. [13]I will dwell in the midst of the Israelites and will not forsake my people Israel.

[14]When Solomon finished building the house, [15]its inside walls were lined with cedar paneling: he covered the interior with wood from floor to ceiling, and he covered its floor with fir planking. [16]At the rear of the house a space of twenty cubits was set off by cedar panels from the floor to the ceiling, enclosing the inner sanctuary, the holy of holies. [17]The house was forty cubits long, that is, the nave, the part in front. [18]The cedar in the interior of the house was carved in the form of gourds and open flowers; all was of cedar, and no stone was to be seen.

[19]In the innermost part of the house* he set up the inner sanctuary to house the ark of the LORD's covenant. [20]In front of the inner sanctuary (it was twenty cubits long, twenty wide, and twenty high, and he covered it with pure gold), he made an altar of cedar. [21]Solomon covered the interior of the house with pure gold, and he drew golden chains across in front of the inner sanctuary, and covered it with gold. [22]He covered the whole house with gold, until the whole house was done, and the whole altar that belonged to the inner sanctuary he covered with gold. [23]In the inner sanctuary he made two cherubim, each ten cubits high, made of pine. [24]Each wing of a cherub was five cubits so that the span from wing tip to wing tip was ten cubits. [25]The second cherub was also ten cubits: the two cherubim were identical in size and shape; [26]the first cherub was ten cubits high, and so was the second. [27]He placed the cherubim in the inmost part of the house; the wings of the cherubim were spread wide, so that one wing of the first touched the side wall and the wing of the second touched the other wall; the wings pointing to the middle of the room touched each other. [28]He overlaid the cherubim with gold.

[29]The walls of the house on all sides of both the inner and the outer rooms had carved figures of cherubim, palm trees, and open flowers. [30]The floor of the house of both the inner and the outer rooms was overlaid with gold. [31]At the entrance of the inner sanctuary, doors of pine were made; the doorframes had five-sided posts. [32]The two doors were of pine, with carved figures of cherubim, palm trees, and open flowers. The doors were overlaid with gold, and the cherubim and the palm trees were also covered with beaten gold. [33]He did the same at the entrance to the nave, where the doorposts were of pine and were four-sided. [34]The two doors were of fir wood, each door consisting of two panels hinged together; [35]and he

schematization of history implied in these figures recommends caution in using them for historical reconstruction.

**6:19 The innermost part of the house**: the inner sanctuary or holy of holies reserved exclusively for the Lord, enthroned upon the cherubim over the ark of the covenant (2 Chr 3:10–13). See note on Ex 25:18–20.

*w*: 2 Sm 7:13–16.

carved cherubim, palm trees, and open flowers, and plated them with gold. 36He walled off the inner court with three courses of hewn stones and one course of cedar beams.

37The foundations of the LORD's house were laid in the month of Ziv in the fourth year, 38and it was finished, in all particulars, exactly according to plan, in the month of Bul, the eighth month, in the eleventh year. Thus Solomon built it in seven years.

See RG 126–29

## CHAPTER 7

1*[x] To finish the building of his own house Solomon took thirteen years. 2He built the House of the Forest of Lebanon one hundred cubits long, fifty wide, and thirty high; it was supported by four rows of cedar columns, with cedar beams upon the columns. 3Moreover, it had a ceiling of cedar above the rafters resting on the columns; these rafters numbered forty-five, fifteen to a row. 4There were lattices in three rows, each row facing the next, 5and all the openings and doorposts were squared with lintels, each facing across from the next. 6He also made the Porch of Columns, fifty cubits long and thirty wide. The porch extended across the front, and there were columns with a canopy in front of them. 7He also made the Porch of the Throne where he gave judgment—that is, the Porch of Judgment; it was paneled with cedar from floor to ceiling beams. 8[y] The house in which he lived was in another court, set in deeper than the Porch and of the same construction. (Solomon made a house like this Porch for Pharaoh's daughter, whom he had married.)* 9All these buildings were of fine stones, hewn to size and trimmed front and back with a saw, from the foundation to the bonding course and outside as far as the great court. 10The foundation was made of fine, large blocks, some ten cubits and some eight cubits. 11Above were fine stones hewn to size, and cedar wood. 12The great court had three courses of hewn stones all around and a course of cedar beams. So also were the inner court of the house of the LORD and its porch.

13King Solomon brought Hiram* from Tyre. 14He was a bronze worker, the son of a widow from the tribe of Naphtali; his father had been from Tyre. He was endowed with wisdom, understanding, and knowledge for doing any work in bronze. He came to King Solomon and did all his metal work.

15*[z] He fashioned two bronze columns, each eighteen cubits high and twelve cubits in circumference. 16He also made two capitals cast in bronze, to be placed on top of the columns, each of them five cubits high. 17There were meshes made like netting and braid made like chains for the capitals on top of the columns, seven for each capital. 18* He also cast pomegranates, two rows around each netting to cover the capital on top of the columns. 19The capitals on top of the columns (in the porch) were made like lilies, four cubits high. 20And the capitals on the two columns, both above and adjoining the bulge where it crossed out of the netting, had two hundred pomegranates in rows around each capital. 21He set up the columns

**7:1–12** The account of Solomon's building of the Temple (the Lord's "house") is interrupted by an account of his building of the palace (Solomon's "house"), which contained also the main buildings of public administration. The passage is anachronistic, since 6:38–7:1 and 9:10 imply that the palace was not begun until the Temple was completed. By placing the account here, the narrator highlights the fact that Solomon spent almost twice as long on his own "house" as on the Lord's.

**7:8** Solomon did not build the house for Pharaoh's daughter until Temple and palace were finished (3:1). By mentioning this marriage, the narrator keeps before the reader a developing theme in the Solomon story: the king's building activities for his foreign wives, which eventually implicate him in idolatry (3:1; 7:8; 9:24; 11:1–8).

**7:13 Hiram**: a craftsman, not the king of Tyre (5:15–26).

**7:15** The two bronze columns were called Jachin and Boaz (v. 21; also 2 Chr 3:17); the significance of the names is unclear. The columns stood to the right and left of the Temple porch, and may have been intended to mark the entrance to the building as the entrance to God's private dwelling. Their extraordinary size and elaborate decoration would have made them the most impressive parts of the Temple visible to the ordinary viewer, who was not permitted into the nave, let alone into the innermost sanctuary. According to Jer 52:21, the columns were hollow, the bronze exterior being "four fingers thick."

**7:18–20** The Hebrew text is corrupt in many places here, and alternative readings attested in the ancient versions are secondary attempts to make sense of the text. A clearer description of the columns and their decoration is found in vv. 41–42.

*x:* 1 Kgs 9:10. *y:* 1 Kgs 3:1; 9:24. *z:* Jer 52:21–23.

at the temple porch; one he set up to the south, and called it Jachin, and the other to the north, and called it Boaz.* [22]The top of the columns was made like a lily. Thus the work on the columns was completed.

[23]Then he made the molten sea;* it was made with a circular rim, and measured ten cubits across, five in height, and thirty in circumference. [24]Under the brim, gourds encircled it for ten cubits around the compass of the sea; the gourds were in two rows and were cast in one mold with the sea. [25]This rested on twelve oxen, three facing north, three facing west, three facing south, and three facing east, with their haunches all toward the center; upon them was set the sea. [26]It was a handbreadth thick, and its brim resembled that of a cup, being lily-shaped. Its capacity was two thousand baths.*

[27]He also made ten stands of bronze, each four cubits long, four wide, and three high. [28]When these stands were constructed, panels were set within the framework. [29]On the panels within the frames there were lions, oxen, and cherubim; and on the frames likewise, above and below the lions and oxen, there were wreaths in hammered relief. [30]Each stand had four bronze wheels and bronze axles. The four legs of each stand had cast braces, which were under the basin; they had wreaths on each side. [31]The mouth of the basin was inside, and a cubit above, the crown, whose opening was round, made like a receptacle, a cubit and a half in depth. There was carved work at the opening, on panels that were square, not circular. [32]The four wheels were below the paneling, and the axletrees of the wheels and the stand were of one piece. Each wheel was a cubit and a half high. [33]The wheels were constructed like chariot wheels; their axletrees, rims, spokes, and hubs were all cast. [34]The four braces reached the four corners of each stand, and formed part of the stand. [35]At the top of the stand there was a raised collar half a cubit high, and the handles and panels on top of the stand formed part of it. [36]On the flat ends of the handles and on the panels, wherever there was a bare space, cherubim, lions, and palm trees were carved, as well as wreaths all around. [37]This was how he made the ten stands, all of the same casting, the same size, the same shape. [38]He made ten bronze basins, each four cubits in diameter with a capacity of forty baths, one basin atop each of the ten stands.

[39]He placed the stands, five on the south side of the house and five on the north. The sea he placed off to the southeast from the south side of the house.

[40]When Hiram had made the pots, shovels, and bowls, he finished all his work for King Solomon in the house of the LORD: [41]two columns; two nodes for the capitals on top of the columns; two pieces of netting covering the two nodes for the capitals on top of the columns; [42]four hundred pomegranates in double rows on both pieces of netting that covered the two nodes of the capitals on top of the columns; [43]ten stands; ten basins on the stands; [44]one sea; twelve oxen supporting the sea; [45]pots, shovels, and bowls. All these articles which Hiram made for King Solomon in the house of the LORD were of burnished bronze. [46]The king had them cast in the neighborhood of the Jordan, between Succoth and Zarethan, in thick clay molds. [47]Solomon did not weigh all the articles because they were so numerous; the weight of the bronze, therefore, was not determined.

[48]Solomon made all the articles that were for the house of the LORD: the golden altar; the table on which the showbread lay; [49]the lampstands of pure gold, five to the right and five to the left before the inner sanctuary; their flowers, lamps, and tongs of gold; [50]basins, snuffers, bowls, cups, and firepans of pure gold; hinges of gold for the doors of the innermost part of the house, or holy of holies, and for the doors of the outer room, the nave. [51][a] When all the work undertaken by King Solomon in the house of the LORD was completed,* he brought in the votive of-

**7:21 Jachin . . . Boaz**: see note on 7:15.

**7:23–26 The molten sea**: this was a large circular tank containing about twelve thousand gallons of water.

**7:26 Baths**: see note on Is 5:10.

**7:51** The account of the Temple's construction has been punctuated by references to "building" (*banah*) or "finishing"

*a*: 2 Sm 8:9–12.

## The Dedication of the Temple

THE DEDICATION OF the temple occurred nearly a year after its completion, to coincide with the autumn new year celebration. The ark was carried by poles inside of rings on either side of the box that was the ark proper. The "glory of the LORD" (8:11) was the thick cloud that symbolized the LORD's presence. Solomon's speech (vv. 15–21) is a deuteronomistic composition. It links the promise to David of a dynasty (2 Sm 7) with that of rest for Israel (Dt 12:10–12).

ferings of his father David, and put the silver, gold, and other articles in the treasuries of the house of the LORD.

### CHAPTER 8

See RG 126–29

*Dedication of the Temple.** 1 Then Solomon assembled the elders of Israel and all the heads of the tribes, the princes in the ancestral houses of the Israelites. They came to King Solomon in Jerusalem, to bring up the ark of the LORD's covenant from the city of David (which is Zion). 2 All the people of Israel assembled before King Solomon during the festival in the month of Ethanim (the seventh month).* 3 When all the elders of Israel had arrived, the priests took up the ark; 4 and they brought up the ark of the LORD and the tent of meeting with all the sacred vessels that were in the tent. The priests and Levites brought them up. 5 King Solomon and the entire community of Israel, gathered for the occasion before the ark, sacrificed sheep and oxen too many to number or count. 6* The priests brought the ark of the covenant of the LORD to its place, the inner sanctuary of the house, the holy of holies, beneath the wings of the cherubim. 7 The cherubim had their wings spread out over the place of the ark, sheltering the ark and its poles from above. 8b The poles were so long that their ends could be seen from the holy place in front of the inner sanctuary. They cannot be seen from outside, but they remain there to this day. 9c There was nothing in the ark but the two stone tablets which Moses had put there at Horeb, when the LORD made a covenant with the Israelites after they went forth from the land of Egypt. 10d When the priests left the holy place, the cloud filled the house of the LORD 11 so that the priests could no longer minister because of the cloud, since the glory of the LORD had filled the house of the LORD. 12* e Then Solomon said,

(*killah*) it (6:1b, 9a, 14, 38; 7:40). Here, at the end of the account, the narrator uses a different verb for its "completion," *shillem*, which allows him to play on the name of Solomon (*shelomo*).

**8:1–66** The account of the Temple's dedication ceremony is organized concentrically: Solomon gathers the assembly (vv. 1–13), blesses it (vv. 14–21), utters a long dedicatory prayer (vv. 22–53), blesses the assembly again (vv. 54–61), and dismisses it (vv. 62–66). To this account is appended an appearance of the Lord to Solomon (9:2–9) that balances the divine word to Solomon in the account of the Temple's construction (6:11–13).

**8:2** "The seventh month" ("Ethanim" in the Canaanite calendar) corresponded to late September/early October. The great festival at that time of year is the feast of Booths, or Succoth/Sukkoth (see Lv 23:33–43; Dt 16:13–15). The feast was important enough to warrant holding the dedication ceremony either a month before or eleven months after the Temple was completed in the eighth month (6:38).

**8:6–9** The transfer of the ark of the covenant into the newly constructed Temple building, God's act of possession (8:10–13), and Solomon's dedicatory prayer and sacrifices constituted the Temple's solemn dedication and made of it the place of God's presence in the midst of Israel for which David had hoped (2 Sm 6:12–15; 7:1–3). Later God expresses approval of the Temple with an oracle (1 Kgs 9:3–9).

**8:12–13** This brief poem is rich in layered meanings. The "dark cloud" in which the Lord intends to dwell refers not only to the cloud that filled the Temple (v. 10) but to the darkness of the windowless holy of holies and to the mystery of the God enthroned invisibly upon the cherubim as well. Solomon calls the Temple he offers God a firm base, using terminology similar to that used for God's firm establishment of Solomon's own kingdom (2:12, 46). Finally, Solomon intends this as a place for God to *yashab*, but the Hebrew word *yashab* can mean "to dwell" or "to sit." In other words, the Temple can be understood both as a place where God resides and as the earthly foundation of God's heavenly throne. The double meaning allows an understanding of the divine presence as both transcendent and graciously immanent. See Solomon's sentiments in 8:27, and the frequent reference in 8:30–52 to God's hearing in heaven prayers that were offered in or toward the Temple.

---

*b:* Ex 25:13–15. *c:* Ex 25:16; 34:27–28; Dt 10:5; Heb 9:4. *d:* Ex 13:21; 40:34–38. *e:* Ex 20:21; Dt 4:11; 5:22; Ps 97:2.

SOLOMON'S PRAYER (8:22–53) CONTAINS seven petitions, which address future problems and ask the LORD to heed prayers made in and toward the temple. This prayer may have been written after the exile. The idea behind the word "heritage" (8:53) is that each nation has its own god, and each god has his own people; the LORD's heritage is Israel.

"The LORD intends to dwell in the dark
cloud;
13 I have indeed built you a princely
house,
the base for your enthronement
forever."

[14]The king turned and blessed the whole assembly of Israel, while the whole assembly of Israel stood. [15]He said: "Blessed be the LORD, the God of Israel, who with his own mouth spoke a promise to David my father and by his hand fulfilled it, saying: [16f]Since the day I brought my people Israel out of Egypt, I have not chosen a city out of any tribe of Israel for the building of a house, that my name might be there; but I have chosen David to rule my people Israel. [17]When David my father wished to build a house for the name of the LORD, the God of Israel, [18]the LORD said to him: In wishing to build a house for my name, you did well. [19]But it is not you who will build the house, but your son, who comes from your loins; he shall build the house for my name. [20]Now the LORD has fulfilled the word he spoke: I have succeeded David my father, and I sit on the throne of Israel, as the LORD has spoken, and I have built this house for the name of the LORD, the God of Israel. [21]I have provided there a place for the ark in which is the covenant of the LORD that he made with our ancestors when he brought them out of the land of Egypt."

***Solomon's Prayer.*** [22]Solomon stood before the altar of the LORD in the presence of the whole assembly of Israel, and stretching forth his hands toward heaven, [23]he said, "LORD, God of Israel, there is no God like you in heaven above or on earth below; you keep covenant and love toward your servants who walk before you with their whole heart, [24]the covenant that you kept toward your servant, David my father, what you promised him; your mouth has spoken and your hand has fulfilled this very day. [25g]And now, LORD, God of Israel, keep toward your servant, David my father, what you promised: There shall never be wanting someone from your line to sit before me on the throne of Israel, provided that your descendants keep to their way, walking before me as you have. [26]Now, God of Israel, may the words you spoke to your servant, David my father, be confirmed.

[27]"Is God indeed to dwell on earth? If the heavens and the highest heavens cannot contain you, how much less this house which I have built! [28]Regard kindly the prayer and petition of your servant, LORD, my God, and listen to the cry of supplication which I, your servant, utter before you this day. [29]May your eyes be open night and day toward this house, the place of which you said, My name shall be there; listen to the prayer your servant makes toward this place. [30]Listen to the petition of your servant and of your people Israel which they offer toward this place. Listen, from the place of your enthronement, heaven, listen and forgive.

[31h] "If someone sins in some way against a neighbor and is required to take an oath sanctioned by a curse, and comes and takes the oath before your altar in this house, [32]listen in heaven; act and judge your servants. Condemn the wicked, requiting their ways; acquit the just, rewarding their justice.

[33]"When your people Israel are defeated by an enemy because they sinned against you, and then they return to you, praise your name, pray to you, and entreat you in this house, [34]listen in heaven and forgive the sin of your people Israel, and bring them back to the land you gave their ancestors.

*f:* 2 Sm 7:5–8, 12–13. *g:* 1 Kgs 2:4; 9:5; 2 Sm 7:14–16; Jer 33:17. *h:* Ex 22:6–10.

[35]"When the heavens are closed, so that
there is no rain, because they have sinned
against you, but they pray toward this place
and praise your name, and turn from their sin
because you have afflicted them, [36]listen in
heaven and forgive the sin of your servants,
your people Israel (for you teach them the
good way in which they should walk). Give
rain to this land of yours which you have
given to your people as their heritage.
[37]"If there is famine in the land or pestilence; or if blight comes, or mildew, or locusts, or caterpillars; if an enemy of your
people presses upon them in the land and at
their gates; whatever plague or sickness
there may be; [38]whatever prayer or petition
any may make, any of your people Israel,
who know heartfelt remorse and stretch out
their hands toward this house, [39]listen in
heaven, the place of your enthronement; forgive and take action. Render to each and all
according to their ways, you who know
every heart; for it is you alone who know the
heart of every human being. [40]So may they
revere you as long as they live on the land
you gave our ancestors.
[41]"To the foreigners, likewise, who are
not of your people Israel, but who come
from a distant land for the sake of your name
[42](since people will hear of your great name
and your mighty hand and your outstretched
arm), when they come and pray toward this
house, [43]listen in heaven, the place of your
enthronement. Do all that the foreigner asks
of you, that all the peoples of the earth may
know your name, may revere you as do your
people Israel, and may know that your name
has been invoked upon this house that I have
built.
[44]"When your people go out to war against
their enemies, by whatever way you send
them, and they pray to the LORD toward the
city you have chosen and the house I have
built for your name, [45]listen in heaven to their
prayer and petition, and uphold their cause.
[46][i] "When they sin against you (for there
is no one who does not sin), and in your
anger against them you deliver them to an
enemy, so that their captors carry them off to
the land of the enemy, far or near, [47]and they
have a change of heart in the land of their
captivity and they turn and entreat you in the
land of their captors and say, 'We have
sinned and done wrong; we have been
wicked'; [48]if with their whole heart and soul
they turn back to you in the land of their enemies who took them captive, and pray to
you toward the land you gave their ancestors, the city you have chosen, and the house
I have built for your name, [49]listen in
heaven, your dwelling place, to their prayer
and petition, and uphold their cause. [50]For-
give your people who have sinned against
you and all the offenses they have committed against you, and grant them mercy in the
sight of their captors, so that these will be
merciful to them. [51]For they are your people
and your heritage, whom you brought out of
Egypt, from the midst of the iron furnace.
[52]"Thus may your eyes be open to the petition of your servant and to the petition of
your people Israel; thus may you listen to
them whenever they call upon you. [53]For
you have set them apart from all the peoples
of the earth to be your heritage, as you declared through Moses your servant when
you brought our ancestors out of Egypt,
Lord my GOD."
[54]After Solomon finished offering this entire prayer and petition to the LORD, he rose
from before the altar of the LORD, where he
had been kneeling, hands outstretched toward heaven. [55]He stood and blessed the
whole assembly of Israel, saying in a loud
voice: [56]"Blessed be the LORD who has
given rest to his people Israel, just as he
promised. Not a single word has gone unfulfilled of the entire gracious promise he made
through Moses his servant. [57]May the LORD,
our God, be with us as he was with our ancestors and may he not forsake us nor cast us
off. [58]May he draw our hearts to himself,
that we may walk in his ways and keep the
commands, statutes, and ordinances that he
enjoined on our ancestors. [59]May these
words of mine, the petition I have offered
before the LORD, our God, be present to the
LORD our God day and night, that he may

*i:* Eccl 7:20; 1 Jn 1:8.

uphold the cause of his servant and the cause
of his people Israel as each day requires, 60 so
that all the peoples of the earth may know
that the LORD is God and there is no other.
61* Your heart must be wholly devoted to the
LORD, our God, observing his statutes and
keeping his commandments, as on this day."
62 The king and all Israel with him offered
sacrifices before the LORD. 63* Solomon offered as communion offerings to the LORD
twenty-two thousand oxen and one hundred
twenty thousand sheep. Thus the king and all
the Israelites dedicated the house of the
LORD. 64 On that day the king consecrated the
middle of the court facing the house of the
LORD; he offered there the burnt offerings,
the grain offerings, and the fat of the communion offerings, because the bronze altar
before the LORD was too small to hold the
burnt offering, the grain offering, and the fat
of the communion offering. 65 On this occasion Solomon and all Israel with him, a great
assembly from Lebo-hamath to the Wadi of
Egypt, celebrated the festival before the
LORD, our God, for seven days. 66 On the
eighth day he dismissed the people, who
blessed the king and went to their tents, rejoicing and glad of heart because of all the
blessings the LORD had given to David his
servant and to his people Israel.

See RG 126–29

## CHAPTER 9

### *Promise and Warning to Solomon.*

1 After Solomon finished building the house
of the LORD, the house of the king, and
everything else that he wanted to do, 2[j] the
LORD appeared to Solomon a second time,
as he had appeared to him in Gibeon. 3 The
LORD said to him: I have heard the prayer of
petition which you offered in my presence. I
have consecrated this house which you have
built and I set my name there forever; my
eyes and my heart shall be there always. 4 As
for you, if you walk before me as David your
father did, wholeheartedly and uprightly, doing all that I have commanded you, keeping
my statutes and ordinances, 5[k] I will establish your royal throne over Israel forever, as
I promised David your father: There shall
never be wanting someone from your line on
the throne of Israel. 6 But if ever you and
your descendants turn from following me,
fail to keep my commandments and statutes
which I set before you, and proceed to serve
other gods and bow down to them, 7 I will cut
off Israel from the land I gave them and repudiate the house I have consecrated for my
name. Israel shall become a proverb and a
byword among all nations, 8[l] and this house
shall become a heap of ruins. Every
passerby shall gasp in horror and ask, "Why
has the LORD done such things to this land
and to this house?" 9 And the answer will
come: "Because they abandoned the LORD,
their God, who brought their ancestors out
of the land of Egypt, and they embraced
other gods, bowing down to them and serving them. That is why the LORD has brought
upon them all this evil."

*After Building the Temple.** 10[m] After the
twenty years during which Solomon built
the two houses, the house of the LORD and
the house of the king— 11 Hiram, king of
Tyre, supplying Solomon with all the cedar
wood, fir wood, and gold he wished, and
King Solomon giving Hiram in return
twenty cities in the land of Galilee— 12 Hiram left Tyre to see the cities Solomon had
given him, but he was not satisfied with
them. 13 So he said, "What are these cities
you have given me, my brother?"* And he
called them the land of Cabul, as they are
called to this day. 14 Hiram, however, had
sent King Solomon one hundred and twenty
talents of gold.*
15 This is an account of the conscript labor

**8:61** In urging the people to be "wholly devoted" (*shalem*), Solomon plays on his own name (*shelomo*), as if to imply that he himself exemplifies perfect fidelity to God.

**8:63** "Communion offerings" (*shelamim*) is another wordplay on the name of Solomon.

**9:10–25** This unit of the Solomon story corresponds to 5:15–32. It comprises the same two themes, negotiations with Hiram of Tyre (vv. 10–14) and use of conscripted labor (vv. 15–23); the last two verses mark the end of the account of Solomon's building projects (vv. 24–25). Chronicles has an incomplete parallel in 2 Chr 8:1–13.

**9:13 Brother**: a term for a treaty partner; cf. 20:32–33. **Cabul**: the meaning is uncertain; perhaps "of no value."

**9:14** The talent was a measure of weight that varied in the course of ancient Israel's history from forty-five to one hun-

*j:* 1 Kgs 3:4–15; 6:11–13; 11:9–13. *k:* 2 Sm 7:16. *l:* Dt 29:23; Jer 22:8. *m:* 1 Kgs 6:38–7:1.

force King Solomon raised in order to build
the house of the LORD, his own house,
Millo,* the wall of Jerusalem, Hazor, Megiddo, Gezer 16(Pharaoh, king of Egypt, had
come up and taken Gezer and, after destroying it by fire and slaying all the Canaanites
living in the city, had given it as a farewell
gift to his daughter, Solomon's wife; 17Solo-
mon then rebuilt Gezer), Lower Beth-horon,
18Baalath, Tamar in the desert of Judah, 19all
his cities for supplies, cities for chariots and
cities for cavalry, and whatever Solomon desired to build in Jerusalem, in Lebanon, and
in the entire land under his dominion. 20All
the people who were left of the Amorites,
Hittites, Perizzites, Hivites, and Jebusites,
who were not Israelites— 21those of their
descendants who were left in the land and
whom the Israelites had not been able to destroy under the ban—these Solomon conscripted as forced laborers, as they are to this
day. 22But Solomon made none of the Israelites forced laborers, for they were his fighting force, his ministers, commanders, adjutants, chariot officers, and cavalry. 23There
were five hundred fifty overseers answerable to Solomon's governors for the work,
directing the people engaged in the work.
24[n] As soon as Pharaoh's daughter went
up from the City of David to her house,
which he had built for her, Solomon built
Millo. 25Three times a year Solomon used to
offer burnt offerings and communion offerings on the altar which he had built to the
LORD, and to burn incense before the LORD.
Thus he completed the temple.*

***Solomon's Gifts.**** 26King Solomon also
built a fleet at Ezion-geber, which is near
Elath on the shore of the Red Sea in the land
of Edom.* 27To this fleet Hiram sent his own
servants, expert sailors, with the servants of
Solomon. 28They went to Ophir, and obtained four hundred and twenty talents of
gold and brought it to King Solomon.

## CHAPTER 10

See RG 126–29

***Solomon's Listening Heart: the Queen
of Sheba.**** 1[o] The queen of Sheba,* having
heard a report of Solomon's fame, came to
test him with subtle questions. 2She arrived
in Jerusalem with a very numerous retinue,
and with camels bearing spices, a large
amount of gold, and precious stones. She
came to Solomon and spoke to him about
everything that she had on her mind. 3King
Solomon explained everything she asked
about, and there was nothing so obscure that
the king could not explain it to her. 4When
the queen of Sheba witnessed Solomon's
great wisdom, the house he had built, 5the
food at his table, the seating of his ministers,
the attendance and dress of his waiters, his
servers, and the burnt offerings he offered in
the house of the LORD, it took her breath
away. 6"The report I heard in my country
about your deeds and your wisdom is true,"

dred thirty pounds. This would mean that, at the least, Hiram sent five thousand pounds of gold to Solomon, and the figure may be as much as three times that amount.

**9:15 Millo**: probably means ground fill, and may refer to an artificial earthwork or platform of stamped ground south of the Temple area. It was begun by David (2 Sm 5:9); cf. 1 Kgs 9:24; 11:27.

**9:25** With these words the account of the construction and dedication of the Temple, which began in 6:1, comes to a close. The verb "complete" (*shillem*) is a play on Solomon's name (*shelomo*); see also the note on 7:51.

**9:26–10:29** The next major unit of the Solomon story returns to the theme of the three gifts the Lord gave Solomon in 3:12–13: a listening heart (10:1–13), riches (9:26–27; 10:14–22, 26–29), universal renown (10:23–25). In 3:16–5:14, where the same three themes structure the passage, the emphasis was on the benefits these gifts brought to the whole nation; here it is on the luxury they afford to Solomon's own court. The material in 9:26–28; 10:11–12, 22 dealing with Solomon's commercial fleet corresponds to the material on Solomon's international affairs in 5:1–5. Chronicles has a partial parallel to this material in 2 Chr 9:17–28; see also 2 Chr 1:14–17.

**9:26 Ezion-geber . . . Edom**: the first mention of maritime commerce in the Israelite kingdom; Edom was subject after David conquered it; cf. 2 Sm 8:13–14.

**10:1–13** The sub-unit on Solomon's wisdom contrasts with 3:16–28. There Solomon's gifts led him to listen to the humblest of his subjects; he accomplished justice and was revered by all his people. Here the emphasis is on his clever speech to a foreign monarch. She is duly impressed by the glory of his court, but it is she, not Solomon, who recalls the monarch's duty of establishing justice (v. 9). The unit is interrupted briefly by a remark about Solomon's maritime commerce (10:11–12).

**10:1 Queen of Sheba**: women rulers among the Arabs are recorded in eighth-century B.C. Assyrian inscriptions. Sheba was for centuries the leading principality in what is now Yemen.

*n:* 1 Kgs 3:1; 7:8. *o:* Mt 12:42; Lk 11:31.

## Solomon's Apostasy

SOLOMON LOVED THE LORD (3:3); yet he also loved the daughter of Pharaoh (3:1; 9:16, 24) and many other women besides. Deuteronomy 6:5; 10:12, 20; and 11:1, 22, however, speak of loving God as unswerving loyalty and obedience to God—the God who had forbidden intermarriage with foreign women (Dt 7:3–4). A divided heart led Solomon in the end after other gods, including Astarte, a leading Canaanite goddess, and Milcom, the national god of the Ammonites. Solomon built sanctuaries on the Mount of Olives and elsewhere rivaling the temple.

she told the king. [7]"I did not believe the report until I came and saw with my own eyes that not even the half had been told me. Your wisdom and prosperity surpass the report I heard. [8]Happy are your servants, happy these ministers of yours, who stand before you always and listen to your wisdom. [9]Blessed be the LORD, your God, who has been pleased to place you on the throne of Israel. In his enduring love for Israel, the LORD has made you king to carry out judgment and justice." [10]Then she gave the king one hundred and twenty gold talents, a very large quantity of spices, and precious stones. Never again did anyone bring such an abundance of spices as the queen of Sheba gave to King Solomon.

[11]Hiram's fleet, which used to bring gold from Ophir, also brought from there a very large quantity of almug* wood and precious stones. [12]With this wood the king made supports for the house of the LORD and for the house of the king, and harps and lyres for the singers. Never again was any such almug wood brought or seen to the present day.

[13]King Solomon gave the queen of Sheba everything she desired and asked for, besides what King Solomon gave her from Solomon's royal bounty. Then she returned with her servants to her own country.

***Solomon's Riches: Domestic Affairs.**** [14][p]The gold that came to Solomon in one year weighed six hundred and sixty-six gold talents, [15]in addition to what came from the tolls on travelers, from the traffic of merchants, and from all the kings of Arabia and the governors of the country. [16][q]King Solomon made two hundred shields of beaten gold (six hundred shekels of gold went into each shield) [17]and three hundred bucklers of beaten gold (three minas of gold went into each buckler); and the king put them in the house of the Forest of Lebanon. [18]The king made a large ivory throne, and overlaid it with refined gold. [19]The throne had six steps, a back with a round top, and an arm on each side of the seat, with two lions standing next to the arms, [20]and twelve other lions standing there on the steps, two to a step, one on either side of each step. Nothing like this was made in any other kingdom. [21]All King Solomon's drinking vessels were gold, and all the utensils in the house of the Forest of Lebanon were pure gold. There was no silver, for in Solomon's time silver was reckoned as nothing. [22]For the king had a fleet of Tarshish ships* at sea with Hiram's fleet. Once every three years the fleet of Tarshish ships would come with a cargo of gold, silver, ivory, apes, and peacocks.

***Solomon's Renown.*** [23]Thus King Solomon surpassed all the kings of the earth in

**10:11–12 Almug**: the identification of this wood is unknown.

**10:14–29** The material on Solomon's riches, like that in 4:1–5:8, is organized around domestic affairs, international affairs, and chariots and horses (see note on 4:1–5:8), but contrasts with that earlier passage. There, Solomon's domestic administration produced prosperity for all Judah and Israel (4:20); here the focus is on the wealth and luxury of Solomon's own palace (10:14–21). There his international hegemony assured peace for all Judah and Israel (5:5); here his maritime ventures simply bring him more and more wealth (9:26–28; 10:11–12, 22). There even his livestock benefited from his prudent administration; here chariotry and horses are just another commodity to be traded (10:26–29).

**10:22 Tarshish ships**: large, strong vessels for long voyages. Tarshish was probably the ancient Tartessus, a Phoenician colony in southern Spain. **Ivory, apes, and peacocks**: the

*p:* Dt 17:17; Sir 47:18. *q:* 1 Kgs 14:26–28; 2 Sm 8:7.

riches and wisdom. [24]And the whole world
sought audience with Solomon, to hear the
wisdom God had put into his heart. [25]They
all brought their yearly tribute: vessels of silver and gold, garments, weapons, spices,
horses and mules—what was due each year.

*Solomon's Riches: Chariots and Horses.*
[26r] Solomon amassed chariots and horses; he
had one thousand four hundred chariots and
twelve thousand horses; these he allocated
among the chariot cities and to the king's service in Jerusalem. [27s] The king made silver as
common in Jerusalem as stones, and cedars
as numerous as the sycamores of the Shephelah. [28]Solomon's horses were imported
from Egypt and from Cilicia, where the
king's merchants purchased them. [29]A chariot imported from Egypt cost six hundred
shekels of silver, a horse one hundred and
fifty shekels; they were exported at these
rates to all the Hittite and Aramean kings.

## CHAPTER 11

See RG 126–29

*The End of Solomon's Reign.** [1t] King
Solomon loved many foreign women besides
the daughter of Pharaoh—Moabites, Ammonites, Edomites, Sidonians, Hittites—
[2u] from nations of which the LORD had said
to the Israelites: You shall not join with them
and they shall not join with you, lest they turn
your hearts to their gods. But Solomon held
them* close in love. [3]He had as wives seven
hundred princesses and three hundred concubines, and they turned his heart.

[4]When Solomon was old his wives had
turned his heart to follow other gods, and his
heart was not entirely with the LORD, his
God, as the heart of David his father had
been. [5]Solomon followed Astarte, the goddess of the Sidonians, and Milcom, the
abomination of the Ammonites. [6]Solomon
did what was evil in the sight of the LORD,
and he did not follow the LORD unreservedly
as David his father had done. [7]Solomon then
built a high place to Chemosh, the abomination of Moab, and to Molech, the abomination of the Ammonites, on the mountain opposite Jerusalem. [8]He did the same for all his
foreign wives who burned incense and sacrificed to their gods.

[9v] The LORD became angry with Solomon,
because his heart turned away from the
LORD, the God of Israel, who had appeared
to him twice [10]and commanded him not to
do this very thing, not to follow other gods.
But he did not observe what the LORD commanded. [11]So the LORD said to Solomon:
Since this is what you want, and you have
not kept my covenant and the statutes which
I enjoined on you, I will surely tear the kingdom away from you and give it to your servant. [12w] But I will not do this during your
lifetime, for the sake of David your father; I
will tear it away from your son's hand. [13]Nor
will I tear away the whole kingdom. I will
give your son one tribe for the sake of David
my servant and for the sake of Jerusalem,
which I have chosen.

*Threats to Solomon's Kingdom.** [14]The
LORD then raised up an adversary* against
Solomon: Hadad the Edomite, who was of
the royal line in Edom. [15x] Earlier, when David had conquered Edom, Joab, the commander of the army, while going to bury the
slain, killed every male in Edom. [16]Joab and
all Israel remained there six months until
they had killed off every male in Edom. [17]But
Hadad, with some Edomite servants of his

Hebrew words are obscure and the translations conjectural; however, the reference is certainly to exotic luxury items.

**11:1–13** The next major unit of the Solomon story corresponds to 3:1–15. Like the earlier passage it includes the narrator's remarks about Solomon's foreign wives and his building projects, and a divine word commenting on Solomon's conduct. However, where 3:1–15 is generally positive toward Solomon, the present passage is unrelievedly negative. Chronicles has no parallel to this material.

**11:2 Them**: both the nations and their gods.

**11:14–25** This unit of the Solomon story corresponds to 2:12b–46, where Solomon secured his kingdom by eliminating three men he perceived as threats. In this passage, we learn of two foreigners the Lord raised up as "adversaries" to Solomon as early as the beginning of his reign (despite Solomon's complacent claim to Hiram in 5:18 that he had no adversary). In the next section we will learn of a third opponent, Israelite rather than foreign, who turns out to be the "servant of Solomon" announced by the Lord in 11:11. Chronicles has no parallel to this material.

**11:14 Adversary**: Hebrew *Satan*, one who stands in opposition; in this context a political opponent.

*r:* 1 Kgs 5:6; Dt 17:16; 2 Chr 1:14; 9:25. *s:* Dt 17:17; Sir 47:18. *t:* Dt 17:17; Sir 47:19–20. *u:* Ex 34:16. *v:* 1 Kgs 3:4–15; 6:11–13; 9:2–9. *w:* 1 Kgs 11:34–36. *x:* 2 Sm 8:13–14.

father, fled toward Egypt. Hadad was then a
young boy. [18]They left Midian and came to
Paran; they gathered men from Paran and
came to Egypt, to Pharaoh, king of Egypt; he
gave Hadad a house, appointed him rations,
and assigned him land. [19]Hadad won great
favor with Pharaoh, so that he gave him in
marriage his sister-in-law, the sister of Queen
Tahpenes, his own wife. [20]Tahpenes' sister
bore Hadad a son, Genubath. Tahpenes
weaned him in Pharaoh's palace. And Genubath lived in Pharaoh's house, with Pharaoh's own sons. [21]When Hadad in Egypt
heard that David rested with his ancestors
and that Joab, the commander of the army,
was dead, he said to Pharaoh, "Give me leave
to return to my own land." [22]Pharaoh said to
him, "What do you lack with me, that you are
seeking to return to your own land?" He answered, "Nothing, but please let me go!"

[23]God raised up against Solomon another
adversary, Rezon, the son of Eliada, who
had fled from his lord, Hadadezer, king of
Zobah, [24][y] when David was slaughtering
them. Rezon gathered men about him and
became leader of a marauding band. They
went to Damascus, settled there, and made
him king in Damascus. [25]Rezon was an adversary of Israel as long as Solomon lived, in
addition to the harm done by Hadad, and he
felt contempt for Israel. He became king
over Aram.

***Ahijah Announces Jeroboam's Kingship.****

[26]Solomon had a servant, Jeroboam, son of
Nebat, an Ephraimite from Zeredah with a
widowed mother named Zeruah. He rebelled
against the king. [27]This is how he came to
rebel. King Solomon was building Millo,
closing up the breach of the City of David,
his father. [28]Jeroboam was a very able man,
and when Solomon saw that the young man
was also a good worker, he put him in charge
of all the carriers conscripted from the house
of Joseph.

[29]At that time Jeroboam left Jerusalem,
and the prophet Ahijah the Shilonite met him
on the road. The prophet was wearing a new
cloak,* and when the two were alone in the
open country, [30][z] Ahijah took off his new
cloak, tore it into twelve pieces, [31][a] and said
to Jeroboam: "Take ten pieces for yourself.
Thus says the LORD, the God of Israel: I am
about to tear the kingdom out of Solomon's
hand and will give you ten of the tribes. [32]He
shall have one tribe for the sake of my servant David, and for the sake of Jerusalem,
the city I have chosen out of all the tribes of
Israel. [33]For they have forsaken me and have
bowed down to Astarte, goddess of the Sidonians, Chemosh, god of Moab, and Milcom,
god of the Ammonites. They have not
walked in my ways or done what is right in
my eyes, according to my statutes and my
ordinances, as David his father did. [34]Yet I
will not take any of the kingdom from Solomon himself, but will keep him a prince as
long as he lives, for the sake of David my
servant, whom I have chosen, who kept my
commandments and statutes.

[35]But I will take the kingdom from his
son's hand and give it to you—that is, the ten
tribes. [36]I will give his son one tribe, that David my servant may always have a holding
before me in Jerusalem, the city I have chosen, to set my name there. [37]You I will take
and you shall reign over all that you desire
and shall become king of Israel. [38]If, then,
you heed all that I command you, walking in
my ways, and do what is right in my eyes by
keeping my statutes and my commandments
like David my servant, I will be with you. I
will build a lasting house for you, just as I did
for David; I will give Israel to you. [39]I will
humble David's line for this, but not forever."

**11:26–43** The last major unit of the Solomon story tells how the prophet Ahijah announces the divine intention to take the larger part of Solomon's kingdom from his control and give it to Jeroboam, Solomon's servant. This counterbalances the first unit of the story, 1:1–2:12a, where another prophet, Nathan, managed to influence the royal succession and obtain the throne for Solomon. The unit is also the first part of the story of Jeroboam (11:26–14:20). It thus acts as a literary hinge connecting the two stories. Chronicles contains a death notice for Solomon in 2 Chr 9:29–31.

**11:29** The narrator uses a powerful wordplay here. In the Hebrew consonantal text, Ahijah's cloak (*slmh*) is indistinguishable from Solomon's name (*slmh*). Since a prophetic gesture such as Ahijah's was understood as effecting the event it announced, Ahijah's tearing of his cloak embodies the divine action that will tear Solomon's kingdom apart (cf. vv. 11–13).

*y:* 2 Sm 8:3–6. *z:* 1 Sm 15:27–28. *a:* 1 Kgs 12:20.

[40]When Solomon tried to have Jeroboam killed, Jeroboam fled to Shishak, king of Egypt. He remained in Egypt until Solomon's death.

[41]The rest of the acts of Solomon, with all that he did and his wisdom, are recorded in the book of the acts of Solomon. [42]Solomon was king in Jerusalem over all Israel for forty years. [43]Solomon rested with his ancestors and was buried in the City of David, his father, and Rehoboam his son succeeded him as king.

## II. The Reign of Jeroboam*

### CHAPTER 12

See RG 129–34

*Political Disunity.** [1]Rehoboam went to Shechem,* where all Israel had come to make him king. [2]When Jeroboam, son of Nebat, heard about it, he was still in Egypt. He had fled from King Solomon and remained in Egypt, [3]and they sent for him.

Then Jeroboam and the whole assembly of Israel came and they said to Rehoboam, [4]"Your father put a heavy yoke on us. If you now lighten the harsh servitude and the heavy yoke your father imposed on us, we will be your servants." [5]He answered them, "Come back to me in three days," and the people went away.

[6]King Rehoboam asked advice of the elders who had been in his father Solomon's service while he was alive, and asked, "How do you advise me to answer this people?" [7]They replied, "If today you become the servant of this people and serve them, and give them a favorable answer, they will be your servants forever." [8]But he ignored the advice the elders had given him, and asked advice of the young men who had grown up with him and were in his service. [9]He said to them, "What answer do you advise that we should give this people, who have told me, 'Lighten the yoke your father imposed on us'?" [10]The young men who had grown up with him replied, "This is what you must say to this people who have told you, 'Your father made our yoke heavy; you lighten it for us.' You must say, 'My little finger is thicker than my father's loins. [11]My father put a heavy yoke on you, but I will make it heavier. My father beat you with whips, but I will beat you with scorpions.' " [12]Jeroboam and the whole people came back to King Rehoboam on the third day, as the king had instructed them: "Come back to me in three days." [13]Ignoring the advice the elders had given him, the king gave the people a harsh answer. [14]He spoke to them as the young men had advised: "My father made your yoke heavy, but I will make it heavier. My father beat you with whips, but I will beat you with scorpions." [15b] The king did not listen to the people, for this turn of events was from the LORD: he fulfilled the word the LORD had spoken through Ahijah the Shilonite to Jeroboam, son of Nebat. [16c] When all Israel saw that the king did not listen to them, the people answered the king:

"What share have we in David?*  
  We have no heritage in the son of  
    Jesse.  
To your tents, Israel!  
  Now look to your own house, David."

**12:1–14:20** Like the story of the reign of Solomon, the story of the reign of Jeroboam is concentrically organized. Ahijah's oracle of promise to Jeroboam (11:26–43) belongs to both stories, ending that of Solomon (see note on 1:1–11:43) and beginning that of Jeroboam; it corresponds to Ahijah's oracle of condemnation in 14:1–20. Within those literary boundaries are accounts of political (12:1–20) and religious (13:11–34) disunity between Israel and Judah. The center of the story is the account of Jeroboam's heterodox cultic innovations (12:26–31).

**12:1–20** The first major unit of the Jeroboam story was Ahijah's oracle (11:26–40), followed by the notice of Solomon's death (11:41–43). This is the second major unit. It tells how Jeroboam came to the throne of Israel after the intransigence of Solomon's son Rehoboam provoked the northern tribes to secede from Jerusalem. The political disunity of the two kingdoms fulfills the word spoken by Ahijah. Compare 13:11–32, where Jeroboam's improper cultic innovations produce religious disunity as well. The scene is concentrically arranged: narrative introduction, first interview, first consultation, second consultation, second interview, narrative conclusion. Chronicles has a parallel version of this story in 2 Chr 10:1–19.

**12:1 Shechem**: chief city of the northern tribes, where a covenant had previously been made between the Lord and his people and a stone of witness had been erected in memory of the event (Jos 24:25–27). **All Israel**: see note on 4:7–19.

**12:16 What share have we in David?**: even in David's time the northern tribes seemed ready to withdraw from the union with Judah (2 Sm 20:1). The unreasonable attitude of

*b:* 1 Kgs 11:26–39. *c:* 2 Sm 20:1.

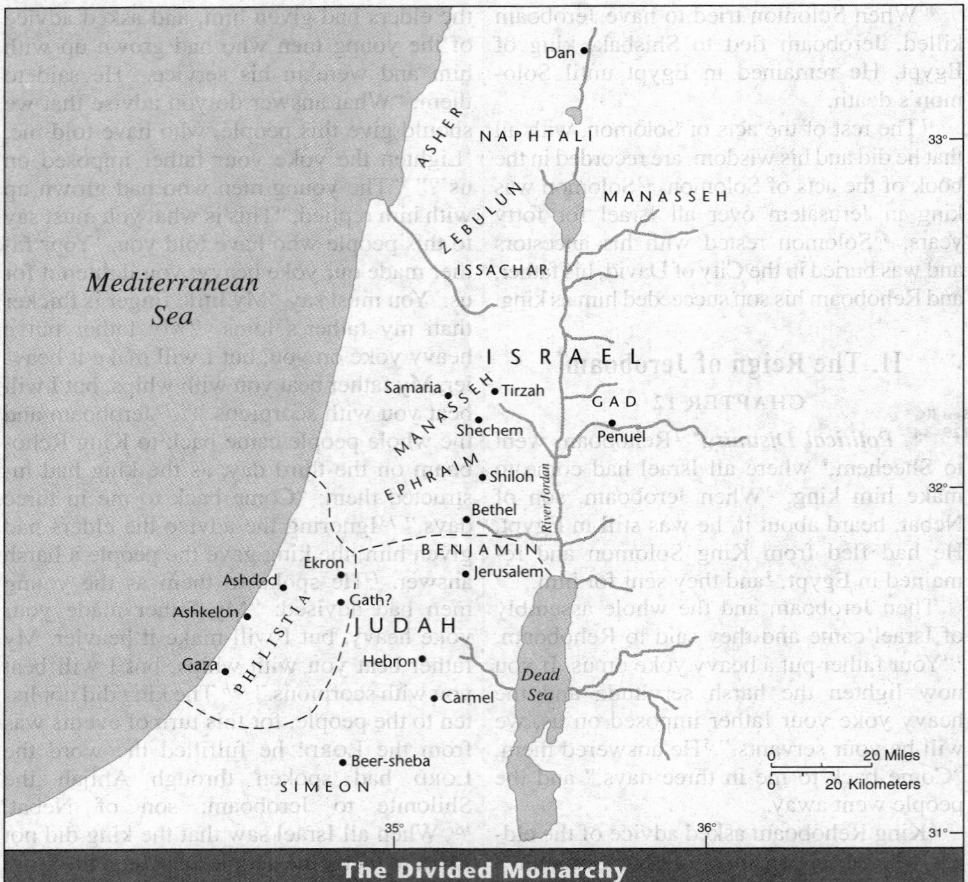

**The Divided Monarchy**

So Israel went off to their tents. 17But Rehoboam continued to reign over the Israelites
who lived in the cities of Judah.
18King Rehoboam then sent out Adoram,*
who was in charge of the forced labor, but all
Israel stoned him to death. King Rehoboam
then managed to mount his chariot and flee
to Jerusalem. 19And so Israel has been in rebellion against the house of David to this
day. 20When all Israel heard that Jeroboam
had returned, they summoned him to an assembly and made him king over all Israel.
None remained loyal to the house of David
except the tribe of Judah alone.

***Divine Approval.**** 21On his arrival in
Jerusalem, Rehoboam assembled all the
house of Judah and the tribe of Benjamin—
one hundred and eighty thousand elite warriors—to wage war against the house of Israel, to restore the kingdom to Rehoboam,

Rehoboam toward them intensified the discontent caused by the oppression of Solomon (v. 4) and thus precipitated the political separation of the two kingdoms. In the view of the Deuteronomistic historian (1 Kgs 11:35–36; 12:24), this was by the Lord's decree.

**12:18 Adoram**: the name is a shortened form of "Adoniram" (see 4:6; 5:28). If this is the same Adoram who held the position in David's day (2 Sm 20:24), he would have been a very old man.

**12:21–25** The center of this unit is a divine oracle delivered by a man of God of the Southern Kingdom in which the Lord affirms his approval of the secession of the northern tribes. Compare 13:1–10, where another man of God from Judah proclaims the Lord's condemnation of Jeroboam's religious separatism. Chronicles has a very similar version of Shemaiah's oracle in 2 Chr 11:1–4.

## The Sins of Jeroboam

JEROBOAM MADE TWO "calves of gold" (12:28) and offered them to the people to worship. Images of calves and bulls were commonly used in the ancient Near East to represent deities, especially fertility gods like Baal.

Jeroboam also built "temples on the high places" (v. 31), which were probably shrines to the LORD. However, they and the calves were in Bethel and Dan, and the writer regards Jerusalem as the only legitimate place to worship the LORD. Another aspect of Jeroboam's apostasy was the appointment of non-Levites as priests (v. 31).

son of Solomon. [22]However, the word of
God came to Shemaiah, a man of God:
[23]Say to Rehoboam, son of Solomon, king
of Judah, and to all the house of Judah and
to Benjamin, and to the rest of the people:
[24]Thus says the LORD: You must not go out
to war against your fellow Israelites. Return
home, each of you, for it is I who have
brought this about. They obeyed the word of
the LORD and turned back, according to the
word of the LORD.

[25]Jeroboam built up Shechem in the hill
country of Ephraim and lived there. Then he
left it and built up Penuel.

***Jeroboam's Cultic Innovations.**** [26]Jero-
boam thought to himself: "Now the kingdom will return to the house of David. [27]If
this people go up to offer sacrifices in the
house of the LORD in Jerusalem, the hearts
of this people will return to their master,
Rehoboam, king of Judah, and they will kill
me and return to Rehoboam, king of Judah."
[28d] The king took counsel, made two calves
of gold, and said to the people: "You have
been going up to Jerusalem long enough.
Here are your gods, O Israel, who brought
you up from the land of Egypt." [29e] And he
put one in Bethel, the other in Dan.* [30]This
led to sin, because the people frequented
these calves in Bethel and in Dan. [31]He also
built temples on the high places and made
priests from among the common people
who were not Levites.

***Divine Disapproval.**** [32]Jeroboam established a feast in the eighth month on the fifteenth day of the month like the pilgrimage
feast in Judah, and he went up to the altar.
He did this in Bethel, sacrificing to the
calves he had made. He stationed in Bethel
the priests of the high places he had built.
[33]Jeroboam went up to the altar he built in
Bethel on the fifteenth day of the eighth
month, the month he arbitrarily chose. He
established a feast for the Israelites, and he
went up to the altar to burn incense.

### CHAPTER 13

See RG 129–34

[1]A man of God came from Judah to
Bethel by the word of the LORD, while Jeroboam was standing at the altar to burn incense. [2f] He cried out against the altar by the
word of the LORD: "Altar, altar, thus says

**12:26–31** At the center of the story of Jeroboam the narrator describes how the king went beyond the political separation of Israel from Judah to create a separatist religious system as well. Jeroboam feared that continued worship in the single Temple in Jerusalem would threaten the political independence of his kingdom. To prevent this he established sanctuaries with non-levitical clergy in his own territory. At two of the sanctuaries he set up golden calves, which the narrator depicts as idols. Thus begins what will later be called "the sin of Jeroboam" (13:34), a theme that will be echoed throughout 1–2 Kings in the condemnations of almost every king of the Northern Kingdom. Historically, Jeroboam's innovations were not as heterodox as our narrative portrays them. Bethel was an ancient and traditional site for worship of the Lord; and the calves were probably intended to be a dais for the deity invisibly enthroned upon them, rather like the cherubim atop the ark of the covenant.

**12:29 Bethel . . . Dan**: at the southern and northern boundaries of the separate kingdom of Israel, where sanctuaries had existed in the past (Gn 12:8; 13:3–4; 28:10–22; 35:1–15; Jgs 18:1–31).

**12:32–13:10** This unit of the Jeroboam story corresponds to 12:21–25. Before Jeroboam's cultic innovations, a man of God from Judah proclaimed the Lord's approval of the political separation of the kingdoms. After Jeroboam's cultic innovations, a man of God from Judah proclaims the Lord's disapproval of Israel's religious separatism. The unit begins with a long, detailed introduction about the dedication festival Jeroboam holds at Bethel (12:32–33); then follows the scene of the ceremony disrupted by the oracle of the man of God (13:1–10).

*d:* Ex 32:1–10. *e:* Tb 1:5. *f:* 2 Kgs 23:16.

the LORD: A child shall be born to the house of David, Josiah by name, who shall slaughter upon you the priests of the high places who burn incense upon you, and they shall burn human bones upon you." [3][g] He also gave a sign that same day and said: "This is the sign that the LORD has spoken: The altar shall be torn apart and the ashes on it shall be scattered." [4]When the king heard the word of the man of God which he was crying out against the altar in Bethel, Jeroboam stretched forth his hand from the altar and said, "Seize him!" But the hand he stretched forth against him withered, so that he could not draw it back. [5](The altar was torn apart and the ashes from the altar were scattered, in accordance with the sign the man of God gave by the word of the LORD.)

[6]Then the king said to the man of God, "Entreat the LORD, your God, and intercede for me that my hand may be restored." So the man of God entreated the LORD, and the king's hand was restored as it was before. [7]The king told the man of God, "Come with me to the house for some refreshment so that I may give you a present." [8]The man of God said to the king, "If you gave me half your palace, I would not go with you, nor eat bread or drink water in this place. [9]For I was instructed by the word of the LORD: Do not eat bread or drink water, and do not return by the way you came." [10]So he departed by another road and did not go back the way he had come to Bethel.

***Prophetic Disunity.**** [11]There was an old prophet living in Bethel, whose son came and told him all that the man of God had done that day in Bethel. When his sons repeated to their father the words the man of God had spoken to the king, [12]the father asked them, "Which way did he go?" So his sons pointed out to him the road taken by the man of God who had come from Judah. [13]Then he said to his sons, "Saddle the donkey for me." When they had saddled it, he mounted [14]and followed the man of God, whom he found seated under a terebinth. When he asked him, "Are you the man of God who came from Judah?" he answered, "Yes." [15]Then he said, "Come home with me and have some bread." [16]"I cannot return with you or go with you, and I cannot eat bread or drink water with you in this place," he answered, [17]"for I was told by the word of the LORD: You shall not eat bread or drink water there, and do not go back the way you came." [18]But he said to him, "I, too, am a prophet like you, and an angel told me by the word of the LORD: Bring him back with you to your house to eat bread and drink water." But he was lying to him. [19]So he went back with him, and ate bread and drank water in his house. [20]But while they were sitting at table, the word of the LORD came to the prophet who had brought him back, [21]and he cried out to the man of God who had come from Judah: "Thus says the LORD: Because you rebelled against the charge of the LORD and did not keep the command which the LORD, your God, gave you, [22]but returned and ate bread and drank water in the place where he told you, Do not eat bread or drink water, your corpse shall not be brought to the grave of your ancestors." [23]After he had eaten bread and drunk, they saddled for him the donkey that belonged to the prophet who had brought him back, [24]and he set out. But a lion met him on the road, and killed him. His body lay sprawled on the road, and the donkey remained standing by it, and so did the lion.

[25]Some passersby saw the body lying in the road, with the lion standing beside it, and carried the news to the city where the old prophet lived. [26]On hearing it, the prophet who had brought him back from his journey said: "It is the man of God who rebelled against the charge of the LORD. The LORD has delivered him to a lion, which mangled and killed him, according to the word which

**13:11–34** The next major unit illustrates how Jeroboam's cultic innovations begin to alienate prophetic figures of the two kingdoms. Nevertheless, the Lord's word is stronger than any human attempt to thwart it. The two prophets also foreshadow the destinies of their respective kingdoms. Israel's experiment with idolatry can tempt Judah to abandon its faithfulness to the Lord. If Judah succumbs, and no longer speaks the word that can call Israel back to the true God, then the only hope for reuniting the two kingdoms will be when they have both died the death of exile.

*g:* 2 Kgs 23:15.

the LORD had spoken to him." [27]Then he said to his sons, "Saddle the donkey for me," and they saddled it. [28]He went off and found the body sprawled on the road with the donkey and the lion standing beside it. The lion had not eaten the body nor had it harmed the donkey. [29]The prophet lifted up the body of the man of God and put it on the donkey, and brought him back to the city to mourn and to bury him. [30]He laid the man's body in his own grave, and they mourned over it: "Alas, my brother!" [31h] After he had buried him, he said to his sons, "When I die, bury me in the grave where the man of God is buried. Lay my bones beside his. [32i] For the word which he proclaimed by the word of the LORD against the altar in Bethel and against all the temples on the high places in the cities of Samaria shall certainly come to pass."

[33]Even after this, Jeroboam did not turn from his evil way, but again made priests for the high places from among the common people. Whoever desired it was installed as a priest of the high places. [34]This is the account of the sin of the house of Jeroboam for which it was to be cut off and destroyed from the face of the earth.

See RG 129–34

## CHAPTER 14

***Ahijah Announces Jeroboam's Downfall.**** [1]At that time Abijah, son of Jeroboam, took sick. [2j] So Jeroboam said to his wife, "Go and disguise yourself so that no one will recognize you as Jeroboam's wife. Then go to Shiloh, where you will find Ahijah the prophet. It was he who spoke the word that made me king over this people. [3]Take along ten loaves, some cakes, and a jar of honey, and go to him. He will tell you what will happen to the child." [4]The wife of Jeroboam did so. She left and went to Shiloh and came to the house of Ahijah.

Now Ahijah could not see because age had dimmed his sight. [5]But the LORD said to Ahijah: Jeroboam's wife is coming to consult you about her son, for he is sick. Thus and so you must tell her. When she comes, she will be in disguise. [6]So Ahijah, hearing the sound of her footsteps as she entered the door, said, "Come in, wife of Jeroboam. Why are you in disguise? For my part, I have been commissioned to give you bitter news. [7]Go, tell Jeroboam, 'Thus says the LORD, the God of Israel: I exalted you from among the people and made you ruler of my people Israel. [8]I tore the kingdom away from the house of David and gave it to you. Yet you have not been like my servant David, who kept my commandments and followed me with his whole heart, doing only what is right in my sight. [9]You have done more evil than all who were before you: you have gone and made for yourself other gods and molten images to provoke me; but me you have cast behind your back. [10k] Therefore, I am bringing evil upon the house of Jeroboam:

> I will cut off from Jeroboam's line every male
> —bond or free—in Israel;
> I will burn up what is left of the house of Jeroboam
> as dung is burned, completely.
> [11 l] Anyone of Jeroboam's line who dies in the city,
> dogs will devour;
> anyone who dies in the field,
> the birds of the sky will devour.

For the LORD has spoken!' [12]As for you, leave, and go home! As you step inside the city, the child will die, [13]and all Israel will mourn him and bury him, for he alone of Jeroboam's line will be laid in the grave, since in him alone of Jeroboam's house has something pleasing to the LORD, the God of Israel, been found. [14]The LORD will raise up for himself a king over Israel who will cut off the house of Jeroboam—today, at this very moment! [15]The LORD will strike Israel like a reed tossed about in the water and will pluck out Israel from this good land which he gave their ancestors, and will scatter them

**14:1–20** The last major unit of the Jeroboam story recounts the story of Ahijah of Shiloh's oracle condemning the entire house of Jeroboam; this is followed by a formulaic notice of Jeroboam's death and the succession of his son. Compare the first unit of the Jeroboam story, 11:26–43, which recounted Ahijah's oracle proclaiming Jeroboam's kingship, followed by the formulaic notice of the death of Solomon.

*h:* 2 Kgs 23:17–18. *i:* 2 Kgs 23:19–20. *j:* 1 Kgs 11:29–39. *k:* 1 Kgs 15:29–30. *l:* 1 Kgs 16:4; 21:22.

beyond the River,* because they made asherahs for themselves, provoking the LORD.
16He will give up Israel because of the sins
Jeroboam has committed and caused Israel
to commit." 17So Jeroboam's wife left and
went back; when she came to Tirzah and
crossed the threshold of her house, the child
died. 18He was buried and all Israel mourned
him, according to the word of the LORD spoken through his servant Ahijah the prophet.
19The rest of the acts of Jeroboam, how he
fought and how he reigned, these are
recorded in the book of the chronicles of the
kings of Israel. 20The length of Jeroboam's
reign was twenty-two years. He rested with
his ancestors, and Nadab his son succeeded
him as king.

## III. Kings of Judah and Israel*

***Reign of Rehoboam.*** 21* Rehoboam, son of
Solomon, became king in Judah. Rehoboam
was forty-one years old when he became
king, and he reigned seventeen years in
Jerusalem, the city in which, out of all the
tribes of Israel, the LORD chose to set his
name. His mother's name was Naamah the
Ammonite.
22Judah did evil in the LORD's sight and
they angered him even more than their ancestors had done. 23They, too, built for themselves high places, sacred pillars, and asherahs,* upon every high hill and under every
green tree. 24There were also pagan priests
in the land. Judah imitated all the abominable practices of the nations whom the
LORD had driven out of the Israelites' way.
25* In the fifth year of King Rehoboam, Shishak, king of Egypt, attacked Jerusalem.
26[m] He took everything, including the treasures of the house of the LORD and the treasures of the house of the king, even the gold
shields Solomon had made. 27To replace
them, King Rehoboam made bronze shields,
which he entrusted to the officers of the
guard on duty at the entrance of the royal
house. 28Whenever the king visited the
house of the LORD, those on duty would
carry the shields, and then return them to the
guardroom.
29The rest of the acts of Rehoboam, with
all that he did, are recorded in the book of
the chronicles of the kings of Judah. 30There
was war between Rehoboam and Jeroboam
all their days. 31Rehoboam rested with his
ancestors; he was buried with his ancestors
in the City of David. His mother's name was
Naamah the Ammonite. His son Abijam succeeded him as king.

### CHAPTER 15

See RG 129–34

***Reign of Abijam.*** 1In the eighteenth
year of King Jeroboam, son of Nebat, Abijam became king of Judah; 2he reigned three
years in Jerusalem. His mother's name was
Maacah, daughter of Abishalom.
3He followed all the sins his father had
committed before him, and his heart was not
entirely with the LORD, his God, as was the
heart of David his father. 4Yet for David's
sake the LORD, his God, gave him a holding
in Jerusalem, raising up his son after him
and permitting Jerusalem to endure, 5[n] because David had done what was right in the
sight of the LORD and did not disobey any of
his commands as long as he lived, except in
the case of Uriah the Hittite.
6There was war between Rehoboam and
Jeroboam all their days. 7The rest of the acts

**14:15 The River**: the Euphrates; see note on 5:1.

**14:21–16:34** The treatment of the events of Jeroboam's reign shows that the author believes that the political division of the kingdoms embodies the Lord's will, but that their religious separation is undesirable. The Israelites are, in effect, one people of God under two royal administrations. This complex arrangement is reflected in the way 1–2 Kings organizes the history of the divided kingdoms. Each reign is treated as a unity: the kings, whether of Israel or Judah, are legitimate rulers. But the accounts of northern and southern kings are interwoven in the order in which each came to the throne, without regard to which kingdom they ruled: the people of God is one.

**14:21** The account of each king's reign follows the same basic pattern: a formulaic introduction, a theological evaluation based on religious fidelity, a brief account of an event from the king's reign, and a formulaic conclusion.

**14:23 Asherahs**: see note on Ex 34:13.

**14:25–28, 30** The narrator recounts Shishak's campaign here to imply that it was punishment for Judah's evil, and perhaps to cast him as supporting Jeroboam in his constant warfare with Rehoboam. (Shishak was named as Jeroboam's protector and patron in 11:40.) Egyptian records of the campaign list one hundred fifty cities conquered in Israel as well as Judah, but Jerusalem is not one of them. Chronicles has a parallel version of this account in 2 Chr 12:9–11.

*m:* 1 Kgs 10:16–17. *n:* 2 Sm 11:1–27.

of Abijam, with all that he did, are recorded
in the book of the chronicles of the kings of
Judah. There was war between Abijam and
Jeroboam. [8]Abijam rested with his ancestors; they buried him in the City of David,
and his son Asa succeeded him as king.

***Reign of Asa.*** [9]In the twentieth year of Jeroboam, king of Israel, Asa, king of Judah,
became king; [10]he reigned forty-one years in
Jerusalem. His mother's* name was Maacah,
daughter of Abishalom. [11]Asa did what was
right in the sight of the LORD like David his
father, [12]banishing the pagan priests from
the land and removing all the idols his ancestors had made. [13]He also deposed his
grandmother Maacah from her position as
queen mother, because she had made an outrageous object for Asherah. Asa cut down
this object and burned it in the Wadi Kidron.
[14]The high places did not disappear; yet
Asa's heart was entirely with the LORD as
long as he lived. [15]He brought into the house
of the LORD his father's and his own votive
offerings of silver and gold and various vessels. [16]There was war between Asa and Baasha, king of Israel, all their days. [17]Baasha,
king of Israel, attacked Judah and fortified
Ramah to blockade Asa, king of Judah.
[18]Asa then took all the silver and gold remaining in the treasuries of the house of the
LORD and the house of the king. Entrusting
them to his ministers, King Asa sent them to
Ben-hadad, son of Tabrimmon, son of He-
zion, king of Aram,* who ruled in Damascus. He said: [19]"There is a treaty between
you and me, as there was between your father and my father. I am sending you a present of silver and gold. Go, break your treaty
with Baasha, king of Israel, that he may
withdraw from me." [20]Ben-hadad agreed
with King Asa and sent the leaders of his
troops against the cities of Israel. They attacked Ijon, Dan, Abel-beth-maacah, and all
Chinnereth, besides all the land of Naphtali.
[21]When Baasha heard of it, he left off fortifying Ramah, and stayed in Tirzah. [22]Then
King Asa summoned all Judah without exception, and they carried away the stones
and beams with which Baasha was fortifying Ramah. With them King Asa built Geba
of Benjamin and Mizpah. [23]All the rest of
the acts of Asa, with all his valor and all that
he did, and the cities he built, are recorded in
the book of the chronicles of the kings of Judah. But in his old age, Asa had an infirmity
in his feet. [24]Asa rested with his ancestors;
he was buried with his ancestors in the City
of David his father, and his son Jehoshaphat
succeeded him as king.

***Reign of Nadab.*** [25]Nadab, son of Jeroboam, became king of Israel in the second
year of Asa, king of Judah. For two years he
reigned over Israel.

[26]He did what was evil in the LORD's sight,
walking in the way of his father and the sin he
had caused Israel to commit. [27]Baasha, son of
Ahijah, of the house of Issachar, plotted
against him and struck him down at Gibbethon of the Philistines, which Nadab and all
Israel were besieging. [28]Baasha killed him in
the third year of Asa, king of Judah, and succeeded him as king. [29][o] Once he was king, he
killed the entire house of Jeroboam, not leaving a single soul but destroying Jeroboam utterly, according to the word of the LORD spoken through his servant, Ahijah the Shilonite,
[30]because of the sins Jeroboam committed
and caused Israel to commit, by which he provoked the LORD, the God of Israel, to anger.

[31]The rest of the acts of Nadab, with all
that he did, are recorded in the book of the
chronicles of the kings of Israel. [32]There was
war between Asa and Baasha, king of Israel,
all their days.

***Reign of Baasha.*** [33]In the third year of
Asa, king of Judah, Baasha, son of Ahijah,
became king of all Israel in Tirzah for
twenty-four years.

**15:10** Maacah was in fact Asa's grandmother (see v. 2), but "king's mother" was perhaps a title for the *gebira*, the "Great Lady" or "queen mother" (see, for instance, 2:19). This influential position was usually held by the king's biological mother, but Maacah may have retained it after the early death of her son Abijam.

**15:18 Ben-hadad . . . king of Aram**: Ben-hadad I, third successor of Rezon, who had thrown off the yoke of the Israelites during the reign of Solomon and become king of Aram (11:23–24). Chronicles has a parallel version of this account in 2 Chr 16:1–6. **Who ruled**: lit., "sitting," i.e., enthroned, possibly also meaning "resident" or "residing."

*o:* 1 Kgs 14:10–11.

[34]He did what was evil in the LORD's
sight, walking in the way of Jeroboam and
the sin he had caused Israel to commit.

## CHAPTER 16

See RG 129–34

[1]The word of the LORD came to Jehu,
son of Hanani, against Baasha: [2]Inasmuch as
I exalted you from the dust and made you
ruler of my people Israel, but you have
walked in the way of Jeroboam and have
caused my people Israel to sin, provoking
me to anger by their sins, [3p]I will burn up
what is left of Baasha and his house; I will
make your house like that of Jeroboam, son
of Nebat:

[4 q] One of Baasha's line who dies in the
city,
dogs will devour;
One who dies in the field,
the birds of the sky will devour.

[5]The rest of the acts of Baasha, what he
did and his valor, are recorded in the book of
the chronicles of the kings of Israel. [6]Baasha
rested with his ancestors; he was buried in
Tirzah, and his son Elah succeeded him as
king. [7](Through the prophet Jehu, son of Hanani, the word of the LORD came against Baasha and his house, because of all the evil
Baasha did in the sight of the LORD, provoking him to anger by his deeds so that he became like the house of Jeroboam, and because of what he destroyed.)

***Reign of Elah.*** [8]In the twenty-sixth year of
Asa, king of Judah, Elah, son of Baasha, became king of Israel in Tirzah for two years.
[9]His servant Zimri, commander of half his
chariots, plotted against him. As he was in
Tirzah, drinking to excess in the house of
Arza, master of his palace in Tirzah,
[10r] Zimri entered; he struck and killed him in
the twenty-seventh year of Asa, king of Judah, and succeeded him as king. [11]Once he
was king, seated on the throne, he killed the
whole house of Baasha, not sparing a single
male relative or friend of his. [12s] Zimri destroyed the entire house of Baasha, according to the word the LORD spoke against Baasha through Jehu the prophet, [13]because of
all the sins which Baasha and his son Elah
committed and caused Israel to commit, provoking the LORD, the God of Israel, to anger
by their idols.
[14]The rest of the acts of Elah, with all that
he did, are recorded in the book of the chronicles of the kings of Israel.

***Reign of Zimri.*** [15]In the twenty-seventh
year of Asa, king of Judah, Zimri became
king for seven days in Tirzah.

The army was encamped at Gibbethon of
the Philistines [16]when they heard, "Zimri
has formed a conspiracy and has killed the
king." So that day in the camp all Israel
made Omri, commander of the army, king of
Israel. [17]Omri and all Israel with him
marched up from Gibbethon and besieged
Tirzah. [18]When Zimri saw that the city was
captured, he entered the citadel of the king's
house and burned it down over him. He died
[19]because of the sins he had committed, doing what was evil in the LORD's sight by
walking in the way of Jeroboam and the sin
he had caused Israel to commit.
[20]The rest of the acts of Zimri, with the
conspiracy he carried out, are recorded in
the book of the chronicles of the kings of Israel.

***Civil War.*** [21]At that time the people of Israel were divided in two, half following
Tibni, son of Ginath, to make him king, and
half for Omri. [22]The partisans of Omri prevailed over those of Tibni, son of Ginath.
Tibni died and Omri became king.

***Reign of Omri.*** [23]In the thirty-first year of
Asa, king of Judah, Omri became king of Israel for twelve years; the first six of them he
reigned in Tirzah.
[24]He then bought the mountain of Samaria
from Shemer for two silver talents and built
upon the mountain the city he named
Samaria, after Shemer, the former owner.
[25]But Omri did what was evil in the LORD's
sight, more than any of his predecessors.
[26]In every way he imitated the sinful conduct of Jeroboam, son of Nebat, and the sin
he had caused Israel to commit, thus provoking the LORD, the God of Israel, to anger
by their idols.

---

*p:* 1 Kgs 16:11; 21:22. *q:* 1 Kgs 14:11. *r:* 2 Kgs 9:31. *s:* 1 Kgs 16:2–4.

**Elijah and the Drought**

THE MAJOR THEME of chs 12–16 has been that God is in control of history, rather than kings or other gods whom the kings worship. Everything comes to pass just as the prophets say. The Elijah and Elisha cycles, placed at the center of 1–2 Kings, further establish this perspective. In chs 17–18, in particular, the most sinful of Israel's kings, Ahab, is forced to reckon with the most powerful of prophetic interventions in the person of Elijah.

The name Elijah means "Yahweh is my God," and it sets the theme for the following chapters. These chapters make clear that Baal is no more a god in any real sense than are Jeroboam's calves. The divinely ordained drought (17:1) provides the context for showing that it is the LORD and not Baal who controls both life and death, both fertility and infertility.

[27]The rest of the acts of Omri, what he did
and his valor, are recorded in the book of the
chronicles of the kings of Israel. [28]Omri
rested with his ancestors; he was buried in
Samaria, and Ahab his son succeeded him as
king.

*Reign of Ahab.* [29]Ahab, son of Omri, became king of Israel in the thirty-eighth year
of Asa, king of Judah. Ahab, son of Omri,
reigned over Israel in Samaria for twenty-
two years.

[30]Ahab, son of Omri, did what was evil in
the LORD's sight more than any of his predecessors. [31]It was not enough for him to follow the sins of Jeroboam, son of Nebat. He
even married Jezebel, daughter of Ethbaal,
king of the Sidonians, and began to serve
Baal, and worship him. [32]Ahab set up an altar to Baal in the house of Baal which he
built in Samaria, [33]and also made an asherah. Ahab did more to provoke the LORD, the
God of Israel, to anger than any of the kings
of Israel before him. [34][t] During his reign,
Hiel from Bethel rebuilt Jericho. At the cost
of Abiram, his firstborn son, he laid the
foundation, and at the cost of Segub, his
youngest son, he set up the gates, according
to the word of the LORD spoken through
Joshua, son of Nun.*

## IV. The Story of Elijah*

### CHAPTER 17

See RG 129–34

*Elijah Proclaims a Drought.** [1]Elijah
the Tishbite,*[u] from Tishbe in Gilead, said to
Ahab: "As the LORD, the God of Israel, lives,
whom I serve, during these years there shall
be no dew or rain except at my word." [2]The

**16:34** See note on Jos 6:26.

**17:1–19:21** The central section of 1–2 Kings tells the story of the dynasty of Omri. That dynasty begins and ends in civil war (1 Kgs 16:21–22; 2 Kgs 9–11). Most of the story is set during the reigns of Ahab of Israel (1 Kgs 16:29–22:40) and his son Joram (2 Kgs 3:1–9:26) and focuses particularly on the interaction of the king with various prophets, especially Ahab with Elijah and Joram with Elisha. The story of Ahab itself contains two large complexes, a series of narratives about Elijah (1 Kgs 17:1–19:21) and a series about hostility between Ahab and the prophets (1 Kgs 20:1–22:38).

**17:1–24** The story of Elijah is in three parts. The first (chap. 17) describes how Elijah proclaimed a drought on God's authority and how he survived during the drought. The second (chap. 18) describes how he ends the drought by bringing the populace back to exclusive worship of the Lord. The third (chap. 19) describes Elijah's despair at the failure of his prophetic mission and his consequent attempt to resign from the prophetic office.

**17:1** This verse introduces the enigmatic figure of Elijah the Tishbite. (The name "Elijah" means "the Lord is my God." The meaning of "Tishbite" is unknown; it may refer to a place or to a social class.) His appearance before Ahab is abrupt and involves several matters that will unify the whole Elijah story. His claim to "serve the Lord" (lit., to "stand before the Lord") points forward to 19:13, where he refuses to do so; the center of narrative tension on this level is the question of the prophet's autonomy in God's service. His proclamation of a drought points forward to 18:41–45 where he announces the drought's end; the center of narrative tension on this level is the struggle between the Lord and the Canaanite fertility god Baal for the loyalties of Israel. His claim that the drought is due to his own word of power ("except at my word") points forward to 17:24 where the widow acknowledges the divine source of the word Elijah speaks; the center of narrative tension on this level is the gradual characterization of the prophet as one who receives a divine word (vv. 2, 8), obeys it (v. 5), conveys an effective divine word of threat (v. 1) or promise (vv. 14, 16), and even speaks an effective human word of entreaty to God (vv. 20, 22).

*t:* Jos 6:26. *u:* Sir 48:1–12; Jas 5:17–18.

word of the LORD came to Elijah: 3Leave
here, go east and hide in the Wadi Cherith,
east of the Jordan. 4You shall drink of the
wadi, and I have commanded ravens to feed
you there. 5So he left and did as the LORD
had commanded. He left and remained by
the Wadi Cherith, east of the Jordan.
6[v] Ravens brought him bread and meat in the
morning, and bread and meat in the evening,
and he drank from the wadi.

7After some time, however, the wadi ran
dry, because no rain had fallen in the land.
8[w] So the word of the LORD came to him:
9Arise, go to Zarephath of Sidon and stay
there. I have commanded a widow there to
feed you. 10He arose and went to Zarephath.
When he arrived at the entrance of the city, a
widow was there gathering sticks; he called
out to her, "Please bring me a small cupful of
water to drink." 11She left to get it, and he
called out after her, "Please bring along a
crust of bread." 12She said, "As the LORD,
your God, lives, I have nothing baked; there
is only a handful of flour in my jar and a little
oil in my jug. Just now I was collecting a few
sticks, to go in and prepare something for myself and my son; when we have eaten it, we
shall die." 13Elijah said to her, "Do not be
afraid. Go and do as you have said. But first
make me a little cake and bring it to me. Afterwards you can prepare something for yourself and your son. 14For the LORD, the God of
Israel, says: The jar of flour shall not go
empty, nor the jug of oil run dry, until the day
when the LORD sends rain upon the earth."
15She left and did as Elijah had said. She had
enough to eat for a long time—he and she and
her household. 16The jar of flour did not go
empty, nor the jug of oil run dry, according to
the word of the LORD spoken through Elijah.

17[x] Some time later the son of the woman,
the owner of the house, fell sick, and his sickness grew more severe until he stopped
breathing. 18So she said to Elijah, "Why have
you done this to me, man of God? Have you
come to me to call attention to my guilt and
to kill my son?" 19Elijah said to her, "Give
me your son." Taking him from her lap, he
carried him to the upper room where he was
staying, and laid him on his own bed. 20He
called out to the LORD: "LORD, my God, will
you afflict even the widow with whom I am
staying by killing her son?" 21Then he
stretched himself out upon the child three
times and he called out to the LORD: "LORD,
my God, let the life breath return to the body
of this child." 22The LORD heard the prayer of
Elijah; the life breath returned to the child's
body and he lived. 23Taking the child, Elijah
carried him down into the house from the upper room and gave him to his mother. Elijah
said, "See! Your son is alive." 24The woman
said to Elijah, "Now indeed I know that you
are a man of God, and it is truly the word of
the LORD that you speak."

## CHAPTER 18

See RG 129–34

***Elijah Ends the Drought.**** 1Long afterward, in the third year, the word of the
LORD came to Elijah: Go, present yourself to
Ahab, that I may send rain upon the earth.
2So Elijah went to present himself to Ahab.

Now the famine in Samaria was severe,
3and Ahab had summoned Obadiah, master
of his palace, who greatly revered the LORD.
4When Jezebel was slaughtering the prophets of the LORD, Obadiah took a hundred
prophets, hid them away by fifties in caves,
and supplied them with food and water.
5Ahab said to Obadiah, "Go through the land
to all sources of water and to all the wadis.
We may find grass and keep the horses and
mules alive, so that we shall not have to
slaughter any of the beasts." 6Dividing the

**18:1–45** The story of the conflict with the prophets of Baal (vv. 21–40) is embedded in the story of the drought and its ending (vv. 1–20, 41–45). The connection between the two stories is found in Canaanite theology, in whose pantheon Baal, "the Cloud Rider," the god of rain and storm, was recognized as the one who brings fertility. Worship of many gods was virtually universal in the ancient world; the Israelite requirement of exclusive worship of the Lord (Ex 20:3) was unique. The people of Israel had apparently become comfortable worshiping both Baal and the Lord, perhaps assigning mutually exclusive spheres of influence to each. By claiming authority over the rain (17:1; 18:1), the Lord was challenging Baal's power in Baal's own domain. The entire drought story in chaps. 17–18 implies what becomes explicit in 18:21–40: this is a struggle between the Lord and Baal for the loyalties of the people of Israel.

---

*v:* Ex 16:8, 12. *w:* 2 Kgs 4:1–7; Lk 4:25–26. *x:* 2 Kgs 4:18–37; Lk 7:11–16.

land to explore between them, Ahab went
one way by himself, Obadiah another way
by himself. 7As Obadiah was on his way,
Elijah met him. Recognizing him, Obadiah
fell prostrate and asked, "Is it you, my lord
Elijah?" 8He said to him, "Yes. Go tell your
lord, 'Elijah is here!' "* 9But Obadiah said,
"What sin has your servant committed, that
you are handing me over to Ahab to be
killed? 10As the LORD, your God, lives, there
is no nation or kingdom where my lord has
not sent in search of you. When they replied,
'He is not here,' he made each kingdom and
nation swear they could not find you. 11And
now you say, 'Go tell your lord: Elijah is
here!' 12After I leave you, the spirit of the
LORD will carry you to some place I do not
know, and when I go to inform Ahab and he
does not find you, he will kill me—though
your servant has revered the LORD from his
youth! 13Have you not been told, my lord,
what I did when Jezebel was murdering the
prophets of the LORD—that I hid a hundred
of the prophets of the LORD, fifty each in
caves, and supplied them with food and water? 14And now you say, 'Go tell your lord:
Elijah is here!' He will kill me!" 15Elijah answered, "As the LORD of hosts lives, whom
I serve, I will present myself to him today."

16So Obadiah went to meet Ahab and informed him, and Ahab came to meet Elijah.
17When Ahab saw Elijah, he said to him, "Is
it you, you disturber of Israel?" 18He answered, "It is not I who disturb Israel, but
you and your father's house, by forsaking
the commands of the LORD and you by following the Baals. 19Now summon all Israel
to me on Mount Carmel, as well as the four
hundred and fifty prophets of Baal and the
four hundred prophets of Asherah who eat at
Jezebel's table." 20So Ahab summoned all
the Israelites and had the prophets gather on
Mount Carmel.

21Elijah approached all the people and
said, "How long will you straddle the issue?
If the LORD is God, follow him; if Baal, follow him." But the people did not answer
him. 22So Elijah said to the people, "I am the
only remaining prophet of the LORD, and
there are four hundred and fifty prophets of
Baal. 23Give us two young bulls. Let them
choose one, cut it into pieces, and place it on
the wood, but start no fire. I shall prepare the
other and place it on the wood, but shall start
no fire. 24You shall call upon the name of
your gods, and I will call upon the name of
the LORD. The God who answers with fire is
God." All the people answered, "We agree!"

25Elijah then said to the prophets of Baal,
"Choose one young bull and prepare it first,
for there are more of you. Call upon your
gods, but do not start the fire." 26Taking the
young bull that was turned over to them,
they prepared it and called upon Baal from
morning to noon, saying, "Baal, answer us!"
But there was no sound, and no one answering. And they hopped around the altar they
had prepared. 27When it was noon, Elijah
taunted them: "Call louder, for he is a god;
he may be busy doing his business, or may
be on a journey. Perhaps he is asleep and
must be awakened." 28They called out
louder and slashed themselves with swords
and spears according to their ritual until
blood gushed over them. 29Noon passed and
they remained in a prophetic state until the
time for offering sacrifice. But there was no
sound, no one answering, no one listening.

30Then Elijah said to all the people,
"Come here to me." When they drew near to
him, he repaired the altar of the LORD which
had been destroyed. 31He took twelve
stones, for the number of tribes of the sons of
Jacob, to whom the LORD had said: Israel
shall be your name. 32He built the stones into
an altar to the name of the LORD, and made
a trench around the altar large enough for
two measures of grain. 33When he had
arranged the wood, he cut up the young bull
and laid it on the wood. 34He said, "Fill four
jars with water and pour it over the burnt offering and over the wood." "Do it again," he
said, and they did it again. "Do it a third
time," he said, and they did it a third time.
35The water flowed around the altar; even
the trench was filled with the water. 36At the

**18:8 Elijah is here**: the Hebrew *hinneh 'eliyahu* involves a pun. The sentence means both "Elijah is here," informing Ahab that the prophet has been found, and "Behold, Yhwh is my God" (the meaning of the name "Elijah").

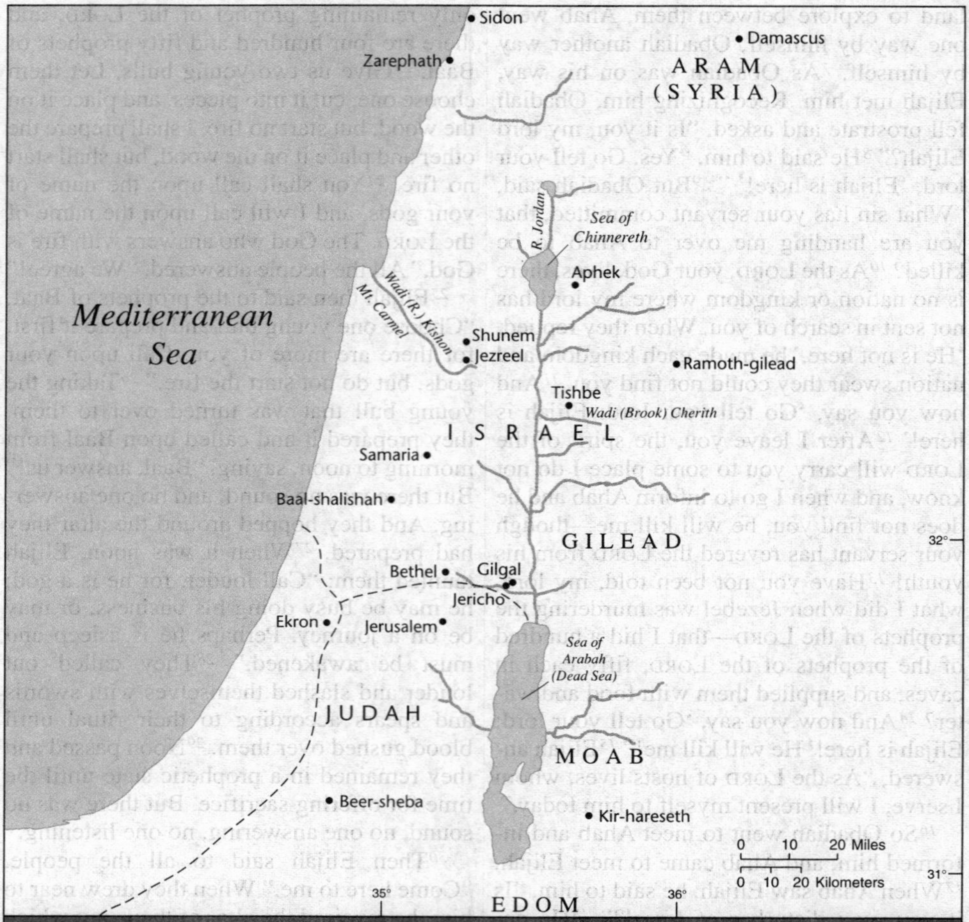


**Places Associated with Elijah**

time for offering sacrifice, Elijah the prophet
came forward and said, "LORD, God of
Abraham, Isaac, and Israel, let it be known
this day that you are God in Israel and that I
am your servant and have done all these
things at your command. [37y] Answer me,
LORD! Answer me, that this people may
know that you, LORD, are God and that you
have turned their hearts back to you." [38]The
LORD's fire came down and devoured the
burnt offering, wood, stones, and dust, and
lapped up the water in the trench. [39]Seeing
this, all the people fell prostrate and said,
"The LORD is God! The LORD is God!"
[40z] Then Elijah said to them, "Seize the
prophets of Baal. Let none of them escape!"
They seized them, and Elijah brought them
down to the Wadi Kishon and there he
slaughtered them. [41]Elijah then said to Ahab,
"Go up, eat and drink, for there is the sound
of a heavy rain." [42]So Ahab went up to eat
and drink, while Elijah went up to the top of
Carmel, crouched down to the earth, and put
his head between his knees. [43]He said to his
servant, "Go up and look out to sea." He
went up and looked, but reported, "There is
nothing." Seven times he said, "Go look
again!" [44]And the seventh time the youth re-

*y:* Ex 32:13. *z:* Ex 32:26–28.

**Elijah on Mount Horeb**

LIKE MOSES, ELIJAH fasts forty days and nights (19:8), and he goes to Mount Horeb, the place where Moses received the law. Here the LORD appears to him. There is a strong wind, then an earthquake, then a fire. But the LORD does not appear in any of these violent forms, which might be associated with the storm god, Baal. Rather, the LORD appears quietly, in a "light silent sound" (v. 12).

ported, "There is a cloud as small as a man's
hand rising from the sea." Elijah said, "Go
and say to Ahab, 'Harness up and go down
the mountain before the rain stops you.' "
45All at once the sky grew dark with clouds
and wind, and a heavy rain fell. Ahab
mounted his chariot and headed for Jezreel.
46But the hand of the LORD was on Elijah.
He girded up his clothing and ran before
Ahab as far as the approaches to Jezreel.

See RG 129–34

## CHAPTER 19

*Flight to Horeb.** 1Ahab told Jezebel
all that Elijah had done—that he had murdered all the prophets by the sword. 2Jezebel
then sent a messenger to Elijah and said,
"May the gods do thus to me and more, if by
this time tomorrow I have not done with
your life what was done to each of them."
3Elijah was afraid and fled for his life, going
to Beer-sheba of Judah. He left his servant
there 4[a] and went a day's journey into the
wilderness, until he came to a solitary broom
tree and sat beneath it. He prayed for death:
"Enough, LORD! Take my life, for I am no
better than my ancestors." 5He lay down and
fell asleep under the solitary broom tree, but
suddenly a messenger* touched him and
said, "Get up and eat!" 6He looked and there
at his head was a hearth cake and a jug of
water. After he ate and drank, he lay down
again, 7but the angel of the LORD came back
a second time, touched him, and said, "Get
up and eat or the journey will be too much
for you!" 8[b] He got up, ate, and drank; then
strengthened by that food, he walked forty
days and forty nights to the mountain of
God, Horeb.

9There he came to a cave, where he took
shelter. But the word of the LORD came to
him: Why are you here, Elijah? 10He answered: "I have been most zealous for the
LORD, the God of hosts, but the Israelites
have forsaken your covenant. They have destroyed your altars and murdered your
prophets by the sword. I alone remain, and
they seek to take my life." 11[c] Then the LORD
said: Go out and stand on the mountain before the LORD;* the LORD will pass by. There
was a strong and violent wind rending the
mountains and crushing rocks before the
LORD—but the LORD was not in the wind;
after the wind, an earthquake—but the LORD
was not in the earthquake; 12after the earthquake, fire—but the LORD was not in the
fire; after the fire, a light silent sound.*

13When he heard this, Elijah hid his face
in his cloak and went out and stood at the en-

**19:1–21** The story of Elijah's journey to Mount Horeb begins as a flight from danger, but takes a surprising turn. The prophet makes his solitary way to the mountain where the Lord had appeared to Moses and the Israelites ("Horeb" is an alternate name for "Sinai"). Like Moses on the holy mountain, Elijah experiences a theophany and receives a commission.

**19:5–7** Sound asleep, Elijah is startled awake by an unspecified "messenger." Only in v. 7 is the figure identified as a messenger (or "angel") of the Lord.

**19:11–13** To "stand before the Lord" is a literal translation of a Hebrew idiom meaning "to serve the Lord"; Elijah has used this idiom twice before to describe himself as the Lord's servant (17:1; 18:15). The Lord's command, then, means that Elijah is to take up once again the prophetic service to which he has been appointed. The Lord's question, "Why are you here?" (v. 9, repeated in v. 13), could imply an accusation that he is abandoning his prophetic office. In v. 15, the Lord tells him to go back.

**19:12** Compare these divine manifestations to Elijah with those to Moses on the same mountain (Ex 19:16–19; 33:18–23; 34:5–6; Dt 4:10–15). Though various phenomena, such as wind, storms, earthquakes, fire, accompany the divine presence, they do not constitute the presence itself which, like the "silent sound," is mysterious and ultimately ungraspable. Moses and Elijah, the two figures who experienced God's theophany on this mountain, reappear with Jesus on another mountain at his transfiguration (Mt 17:1–9; Mk 9:2–9; Lk 9:28–36).

*a:* Jon 4:6–9. *b:* Ex 34:28. *c:* Ex 33:18–23; 34:5–6.

trance of the cave. A voice said to him, Why are you here, Elijah? [14d] He replied, "I have been most zealous for the LORD, the God of hosts, but the Israelites have forsaken your covenant. They have destroyed your altars and murdered your prophets by the sword. I alone remain, and they seek to take my life." [15*e] The LORD said to him: Go back! Take the desert road to Damascus. When you arrive, you shall anoint Hazael as king of Aram. [16f] You shall also anoint Jehu, son of Nimshi, as king of Israel, and Elisha, son of Shaphat of Abel-meholah, as prophet to succeed you. [17] Anyone who escapes the sword of Hazael, Jehu will kill. Anyone who escapes the sword of Jehu, Elisha will kill. [18g] But I will spare seven thousand in Israel—every knee that has not bent to Baal, every mouth that has not kissed him.

[19*] Elijah set out, and came upon Elisha, son of Shaphat, as he was plowing with twelve yoke of oxen; he was following the twelfth. Elijah went over to him and threw his cloak on him. [20h] Elisha left the oxen, ran after Elijah, and said, "Please, let me kiss my father and mother good-bye, and I will follow you." Elijah answered, "Go back! What have I done to you?" [21] Elisha left him and, taking the yoke of oxen, slaughtered them; he used the plowing equipment for fuel to boil their flesh, and gave it to the people to eat. Then he left and followed Elijah to serve him.

## V. The Story of Ahab*

### CHAPTER 20

See RG 129–34

***Ahab's Victories over Aram.**** [1] Ben-hadad, king of Aram, gathered all his forces and, accompanied by thirty-two kings with horses and chariotry, set out to besiege and attack Samaria. [2] He sent messengers to Ahab, king of Israel, within the city, [3] and said to him, "This is Ben-hadad's message: 'Your silver and gold are mine, and your wives and your fine children are mine.' " [4] The king of Israel answered, "Just as you say, my lord king, I and all I have are yours." [5] But the messengers came again and said, "This is Ben-hadad's message: 'I sent you word: Give me your silver and gold, your wives and your children. [6] But now I say: At this time tomorrow I will send my servants to you, and they shall ransack your house and the houses of your servants. They shall seize and take away whatever you consider valuable.' " [7] The king of Israel then summoned all the elders of the land and said: "Understand clearly that this man is intent on evil. When he sent to me for my wives and children, my silver and my gold, I did not refuse him." [8] All the elders and all the people said to him, "Do not listen. Do not give in." [9] Accordingly he directed the messengers of Ben-hadad, "Say this: 'To my lord the king: I will do all that you demanded of your servant the first time. But this I cannot do.' " The messengers left and reported this. [10] Ben-hadad then responded, "May the gods do thus to me and more, if there will remain enough dust in Samaria to make handfuls for all my followers." [11] The king of Israel replied, "Tell him, 'Let not one who puts on armor boast like one who takes it off.' " [12] Ben-hadad was drinking in the pavilions with the kings when he heard this reply. He commanded his servants, "Get ready!"; and they got ready to storm the city.

**19:15–17** Elijah himself carried out only the last of the three commissions entrusted to him (vv. 19–21); Elisha performed the first himself (2 Kgs 8:7–19), and the second, the anointing of Jehu, through one of his followers (2 Kgs 9:1–10).

**19:19–21** Elijah's act of throwing his mantle over the shoulders of Elisha associates him with Elijah as a servant (v. 21). Elisha will later succeed to Elijah's position and prophetic power (2 Kgs 2:1–15). Elisha's prompt response, destroying his plow and oxen, signifies a radical change from his former manner of living.

**20:1–22:54** Although coverage of Ahab's reign began in 16:29, he was only a secondary character in the chapters about Elijah. Now attention focuses on Ahab. Each of these chapters tells a story of the king (20:1–34; 21:1–16; 22:1–4, 29–38), to which is attached a scene of prophetic condemnation (20:30–42; 21:17–29; 22:5–28). As relations between Ahab and the prophets of the Lord deteriorate, the scenes of prophetic condemnation get longer and the condemnations themselves become more pointed. Some historians doubt that the stories of hostility between Israel and Aram (chaps. 20 and 22) originally pertained to the reign of Ahab. If this is correct, their original setting may have been several decades later.

**20:1–34** This story recounts two battles through which Ahab won freedom for Israel from vassalage to Ben-hadad of Syria. The story is chiastically arranged: negotiations (vv. 1–12), battle (vv. 13–21), battle (vv. 22–30), negotiations (vv. 31–34). The ensuing prophetic condemnation is surprising, since the

*d:* Rom 11:3. *e:* 2 Kgs 8:7–15. *f:* 2 Kgs 2:1–15; 9:1–10. *g:* Rom 11:4. *h:* Lk 9:61–62.

13 Then a prophet came up to Ahab, king of
Israel, and said: "The LORD says, Do you see
all this vast army? Today I am giving it into
your power, that you may know that I am the
LORD." 14 But Ahab asked, "Through whom
will it be given over?" He answered, "The
LORD says, Through the aides of the provincial governors." Then Ahab asked, "Who is
to attack?" He replied, "You are." 15 So Ahab
mustered the aides of the provincial governors, two hundred thirty-two of them. Behind them he mustered all the Israelite sol-
diery, who numbered seven thousand in all.
16* They marched out at noon, while Ben-hadad was drinking heavily in the pavilions
with the thirty-two kings who were his allies.
17 When the aides of the provincial governors
marched out first, Ben-hadad received word,
"Some men have marched out of Samaria."
18 He answered, "Whether they have come
out for peace or for war, take them alive."
19 But when these had come out of the city—
the aides of the provincial governors with the
army following them— 20 each of them
struck down his man. The Arameans fled
with Israel pursuing them, while Ben-hadad,
king of Aram, escaped on a chariot horse.
21 Then the king of Israel went out and destroyed the horses and chariots. Thus he inflicted a severe defeat on Aram.

22 Then the prophet approached the king of
Israel and said to him: "Go, regroup your
forces. Understand clearly what you must
do, for at the turning of the year* the king of
Aram will attack you." 23 Meanwhile the servants of the king of Aram said to him: "Their
gods are mountain gods. That is why they
defeated us. But if we fight them on level
ground, we shall be sure to defeat them.
24 This is what you must do: Take the kings
from their posts and put prefects in their
places. 25 Raise an army as large as the army
you have lost, horse for horse, chariot for
chariot. Let us fight them on level ground,
and we shall surely defeat them." He took
their advice and did this. 26 At the turning of
the year, Ben-hadad mustered Aram and
went up to Aphek to fight against Israel.
27 The Israelites, too, were mustered and supplied with provisions; then they went out to
meet the enemy. The Israelites, encamped
opposite, looked like little flocks of goats,
while Aram covered the land. 28 A man of
God approached and said to the king of Israel: "The LORD says, Because Aram has
said the LORD is a god of mountains, not a
god of plains, I will give all this vast army
into your power that you may know I am the
LORD." 29 They were encamped opposite
each other for seven days. On the seventh
day battle was joined, and the Israelites
struck down one hundred thousand foot soldiers of Aram in one day. 30 The survivors
fled into the city of Aphek, where the wall
collapsed on twenty-seven thousand of
them. Ben-hadad, too, fled, and took refuge
within the city, in an inner room.

31 His servants said to him: "We have
heard that the kings of the house of Israel are
merciful kings. Allow us, therefore, to garb
ourselves in sackcloth, with cords around
our heads, and go out to the king of Israel.
Perhaps he will spare your life." 32 Dressed
in sackcloth girded at the waist and wearing
cords around their heads, they went to the
king of Israel and said, "Your servant Ben-
hadad says, 'Spare my life!' " He asked, "Is
he still alive? He is my brother."* 33 Hearing
this as a good omen, the men quickly took
him at his word and said, "Ben-hadad is your
brother." He answered, "Go and get him."
When Ben-hadad came out to him, the king
had him mount his chariot. 34 Ben-hadad said
to him, "The cities my father took from your
father I will restore, and you may set up
bazaars for yourself in Damascus, as my father did in Samaria." Ahab replied, "For my
part, I will set you free on those terms." So
he made a covenant with him and then set
him free.

portrait of Ahab in vv. 1–34 is apparently quite positive.

**20:16–19** The narrator uses a sort of verbal split-screen technique to show us two separate and simultaneous scenes. At the gates of Samaria, the Israelite forces are coming out to battle (v. 16a): first the aides (lit., "young men"; v. 17a), then the whole army (v. 19). Meanwhile in the Aramean camp Ben-hadad is getting drunk (v. 16b), receiving reports (v. 17b) and issuing commands (v. 18).

**20:22 At the turning of the year**: the idiom may mean "next year about this time" or "at the beginning of the year," i.e., the spring (cf. 2 Sm 11:1).

**20:32 He is my brother**: cf. note on 9:13.

***Prophetic Condemnation.*** 35 Acting on the word of the LORD, one of the guild prophets said to his companion, "Strike me." But he refused to strike him. 36 Then he said to him, "Since you did not obey the voice of the LORD, a lion will attack you when you leave me." When he left him, a lion came upon him and attacked him.[i] 37 Then the prophet met another man and said, "Strike me." The man struck him a blow and wounded him. 38 The prophet went on and waited for the king on the road, disguising himself with a bandage over his eyes. 39 As the king was passing, he called out to the king and said: "Your servant went into the thick of the battle, and suddenly someone turned and brought me a man and said, 'Guard this man. If he is missing, you shall have to pay for his life with your life or pay out a talent of silver.'* 40 But while your servant was occupied here and there, the man disappeared." The king of Israel said to him, "That is your sentence. You have decided it yourself." 41 He quickly removed the bandage from his eyes, and the king of Israel recognized him as one of the prophets. 42[j] He said to him: "The LORD says, Because you have set free the man I put under the ban,* your life shall pay for his life, your people for his people." 43[k] Disturbed and angry, the king of Israel set off for home and entered Samaria.

## CHAPTER 21

See RG 129–34

***Seizure of Naboth's Vineyard.**** 1 Naboth the Jezreelite had a vineyard in Jezreel next to the palace of Ahab, king of Samaria. Some time later, 2 Ahab said to Naboth, "Give me your vineyard to be my vegetable garden, since it is close by, next to my house. I will give you a better vineyard in exchange, or, if you prefer, I will give you its value in money." 3 Naboth said to Ahab, "The LORD forbid that I should give you my ancestral heritage."* 4 Ahab went home disturbed and angry at the answer Naboth the Jezreelite had given him: "I will not give you my ancestral heritage." Lying down on his bed, he turned away and would not eat. 5 His wife Jezebel came to him and said to him, "Why are you so sullen that you will not eat?" 6 He answered her, "Because I spoke to Naboth the Jezreelite and said to him, 'Sell me your vineyard, or, if you prefer, I will give you a vineyard in exchange.' But he said, 'I will not give you my vineyard.' " 7 Jezebel his wife said to him, "What a king of Israel you are! Get up! Eat and be cheerful. I will give you the vineyard of Naboth the Jezreelite."

8 So she wrote letters in Ahab's name and, having sealed them with his seal, sent them to the elders and to the nobles who lived in the same city with Naboth. 9 This is what she wrote in the letters: "Proclaim a fast and set Naboth at the head of the people. 10 Next, set two scoundrels opposite him to accuse him: 'You have cursed God and king.' Then take him out and stone him to death."

11 His fellow citizens—the elders and the nobles who dwelt in his city—did as Jezebel had ordered in the letters she sent them. 12 They proclaimed a fast and set Naboth at the head of the people. 13 Two scoundrels came in and sat opposite Naboth, and the scoundrels accused him in the presence of the people, "Naboth has cursed God and king." And they led him out of the city and stoned him to death. 14 Then they sent word to Jezebel: "Naboth has been stoned to death."

**20:39** The "man" is ostensibly a prisoner of war, to be kept or sold as a slave. In the event he escapes, the one charged with guarding him would be obliged either to pay a fine or to take his place as a slave. The fine, however, is exorbitant: a talent of silver is roughly one hundred times the price of an ordinary slave (see Ex 21:32). This is the only clue Ahab will get that he is being set up and that the story is really about himself in his dealings with Ben-hadad. In 2 Sm 14:1–20, the wise woman of Tekoa uses the same technique with King David: she tells a story that elicits a reaction from the king; David is tricked into pronouncing judgment on himself, as the story parallels his own situation. The prophet Nathan (2 Sm 12:1–7) likewise uses a story that leads David to see his sin for what it is.

**20:42 Under the ban**: cf. note on Dt 2:34.

**21:1–16** The story tells how Jezebel manipulates important structures of Israelite social order, law, and religious observance to eliminate a faithful Israelite landowner who frustrates Ahab's will.

**21:3 Heritage**: Hebrew *nahalah*. Naboth is unwilling to sell or exchange his vineyard. According to the Israelite system of land tenure and distribution, land was held in common within a social unit. The ancestral *nahalah* was not private property, to be alienated at will.

*i:* 1 Kgs 13:24. *j:* 1 Kgs 22:35. *k:* 1 Kgs 21:4.

15 When Jezebel learned that Naboth had
been stoned to death, she said to Ahab, "Go,
take possession of the vineyard of Naboth the
Jezreelite which he refused to sell you, because Naboth is not alive, but dead." 16 When
Ahab heard that Naboth was dead, he started
on his way down to the vineyard of Naboth
the Jezreelite, to take possession of it.

***Prophetic Condemnation.*** 17 Then the word
of the LORD came to Elijah the Tishbite: 18 Go
down to meet Ahab, king of Israel, who is in
Samaria. He will be in the vineyard of Naboth, where he has gone to take possession.
19[l] Tell him: "Thus says the LORD: After murdering, do you also take possession?" And
tell him, "Thus says the LORD: In the place
where the dogs licked up the blood of Naboth, the dogs shall lick up your blood, too."

20* Ahab said to Elijah, "Have you found
me out, my enemy?" He said, "I have found
you. Because you have given yourself up to
doing evil in the LORD's sight, 21[m] I am
bringing evil upon you: I will consume you
and will cut off every male belonging to
Ahab, whether bond or free, in Israel. 22 I
will make your house like that of Jeroboam,
son of Nebat, and like the house of Baasha,
son of Ahijah, because you have provoked
me by leading Israel into sin."

23 Against Jezebel, too, the LORD declared:
The dogs shall devour Jezebel in the confines of Jezreel.

24 Anyone of Ahab's line who dies in the city,
dogs will devour;
Anyone who dies in the field,
the birds of the sky will devour.

25 Indeed, no one gave himself up to the
doing of evil in the sight of the LORD as did
Ahab, urged on by his wife Jezebel. 26 He became completely abominable by going after
idols, just as the Amorites had done, whom
the LORD drove out of the Israelites' way.

27 When Ahab heard these words, he tore
his garments and put on sackcloth over his
bare flesh. He fasted, slept in the sackcloth,
and went about subdued. 28 Then the word of
the LORD came to Elijah the Tishbite,
29[n] Have you seen how Ahab has humbled
himself before me? Since he has humbled
himself before me, I will not bring the evil in
his time. I will bring the evil upon his house
in his son's time.

## CHAPTER 22

See RG 129–34

***Ahab's Defeat by Aram.**** 1 Three years
passed without war between Aram and Israel. 2 In the third year, however, King Jehoshaphat of Judah came down to the king
of Israel. 3 The king of Israel said to his servants, "Do you not know that Ramoth-gilead
is ours and we are doing nothing to take it
from the king of Aram?" 4 He asked Jehoshaphat, "Will you come with me to fight
against Ramoth-gilead?" Jehoshaphat answered the king of Israel, "You and I are as
one, and your people and my people, your
horses and my horses as well."

***Prophetic Condemnation.*** 5 Jehoshaphat
also said to the king of Israel, "Seek the
word of the LORD at once." 6 The king of Israel assembled the prophets, about four hundred of them, and asked, "Shall I go to fight
against Ramoth-gilead or shall I refrain?"
They said, "Attack. The Lord will give it
into the power of the king."* 7 But Jehoshaphat said, "Is there no other prophet of the
LORD here we might consult?" 8 The king of

**21:20–26** In these verses the narrator uses against the third Israelite dynasty the same condemnation formula that was uttered against the first two dynasties, those of Jeroboam (14:9–11) and Baasha (16:2–4). Part of the formula is put in Elijah's mouth, in an oracle against Ahab and his descendants (vv. 21–22), and part of it in an aside to the reader that extends the condemnation to Ahab's wife, Jezebel, and his whole household (vv. 23–24). The oracle against Jezebel will be fulfilled in 2 Kgs 9:36; the obliteration of the dynasty will be recounted in the bloody stories of 2 Kgs 9–11.

**22:1–40** This chapter presents a contrasting parallel to chap. 20, where Ahab enjoyed victories over Aram's aggression. Here Ahab is the aggressor, but falls in battle against Aram. Like the preceding chapters, it contains a story of Ahab plus an episode of prophetic condemnation. The story ends with the formulaic conclusion to Ahab's reign (vv. 39–40). Chronicles has a parallel version of this account in 2 Chr 18:1–34. After the story of Ahab's death come accounts of the reign of Jehoshaphat (paralleled in 2 Chr 20:31–37) and of the beginning of the reign of Ahaziah.

**22:6** Though Ahab is clearly intended to understand the oracle as prophesying his success, the prophets' words are ambiguous. "The lord" (not "the LORD," i.e., the proper name of Israel's God) who will give victory is unidentified, as is the king to whom it will be given.

*l:* 1 Kgs 22:38; 2 Kgs 9:26. *m:* 1 Kgs 14:10–11; 15:29; 16:3–4, 11; 2 Kgs 9:8–10, 36. *n:* 2 Kgs 9:25–26.

Israel answered, "There is one other man
through whom we might consult the LORD;
but I hate him because he prophesies not
good but evil about me. He is Micaiah, son
of Imlah." Jehoshaphat said, "Let not the
king say that." 9So the king of Israel called
an official and said to him, "Get Micaiah,
son of Imlah, at once."

10The king of Israel and Jehoshaphat, king
of Judah, were seated, each on his throne,
clothed in their robes of state in the square at
the entrance of the gate of Samaria, and all
the prophets were prophesying before them.
11[o] Zedekiah, son of Chenaanah, made himself two horns of iron* and said, "The LORD
says, With these you shall gore Aram until
you have destroyed them." 12The other
prophets prophesied in a similar vein, saying: "Attack Ramoth-gilead and conquer!
The LORD will give it into the power of the
king."

13Meanwhile, the messenger who had
gone to call Micaiah said to him, "Look now,
the prophets are unanimously predicting
good for the king. Let your word be the same
as any of theirs; speak a good word." 14Mi-
caiah said, "As the LORD lives, I shall speak
whatever the LORD tells me."

15When he came to the king, the king said
to him, "Micaiah, shall we go to fight at Ramoth-gilead, or shall we refrain?" He said,
"Attack and conquer! The LORD will give it
into the power of the king." 16But the king
answered him, "How many times must I adjure you to tell me nothing but the truth in
the name of the LORD?" 17* So Micaiah said:

"I see all Israel
scattered on the mountains,
like sheep without a shepherd,
And the LORD saying,
These have no master!
Let each of them go back home in
peace."

18The king of Israel said to Jehoshaphat,
"Did I not tell you, he does not prophesy
good about me, but only evil?" 19* Micaiah
continued: "Therefore hear the word of the
LORD: I saw the LORD seated on his throne,
with the whole host of heaven standing to
his right and to his left. 20The LORD asked:
Who will deceive Ahab, so that he will go up
and fall on Ramoth-gilead?* And one said
this, another that, 21until this spirit came
forth and stood before the LORD, saying, 'I
will deceive him.' The LORD asked: How?
22He answered, 'I will go forth and become
a lying spirit in the mouths of all his prophets.' The LORD replied: You shall succeed in
deceiving him. Go forth and do this. 23So
now, the LORD has put a lying spirit in the
mouths of all these prophets of yours; the
LORD himself has decreed evil against you."

24Thereupon Zedekiah, son of
Chenaanah, came up and struck Micaiah on
the cheek, saying, "Has the spirit of the
LORD, then, left me to speak with you?"
25Micaiah said, "You shall find out on the
day you go into an inner room to hide."
26The king of Israel then said, "Seize Micaiah and take him back to Amon, prefect of
the city, and to Joash, the king's son, 27and
say, 'This is the king's order: Put this man in
prison and feed him scanty rations of bread
and water until I come back in safety.' "
28[p] But Micaiah said, "If you return in safety,
the LORD has not spoken through me." (He
also said, "Hear, O peoples, all of you.")*

***Ahab at Ramoth-gilead.*** 29The king of Is-

**22:11** The "two" horns probably symbolize the coalition of two kings, Ahab and Jehoshaphat.

**22:17** Micaiah's oracle uses the common ancient metaphor of "shepherd" for the king. It means that the Israelite forces will be left leaderless because the king (or perhaps both kings: the word "master" could be singular or plural in Hebrew) will die in battle.

**22:19–23** Since Ahab's intention to attack Ramoth-gilead is unshaken, Micaiah reveals God's plan to trick Ahab to his death, and thus virtually dares Ahab to walk into the trap with his eyes open. The work of the "lying spirit" explains the ambiguities of the prophets' original oracle in v. 6. Prophets "stand in the council of the Lord" and are privy to its deliberations; cf. Jer 23:22.

**22:20 Fall on Ramoth-gilead**: lit., "heights of Gilead"; even the Lord's words are double-meaning. God wants Ahab to "fall on" (that is, attack) Ramoth-gilead so that he will "fall on" (that is, die on) Ramoth-gilead.

**22:28** The last words of the verse are a scribal gloss attributing to Micaiah, son of Imlah, the opening words of the book of a different Micaiah (Micah), the prophet of Moresheth, the sixth of the twelve minor prophets of the Old Testament canon.

*o:* Dt 33:17. *p:* Mi 1:2.

rael and Jehoshaphat, king of Judah, went up
to Ramoth-gilead, 30 and the king of Israel
said to Jehoshaphat, “I will disguise myself
and go into battle, but you put on your own
robes.” So the king of Israel disguised himself and entered the battle. 31 In the meantime
the king of Aram had given his thirty-two
chariot commanders the order, “Do not fight
with anyone, great or small, except the king
of Israel alone.”

32 When the chariot commanders saw Jehoshaphat, they cried out, “There is the king
of Israel!” and wheeled to fight him. But Jehoshaphat cried out, 33 and the chariot commanders, seeing that he was not the king of
Israel, turned away from him. 34 But someone drew his bow at random, and hit the king
of Israel between the joints of his breastplate. He ordered his charioteer, “Rein about
and take me out of the ranks, for I am
wounded.”

35[q] The battle grew fierce during the day,
and the king, who was propped up in his
chariot facing the Arameans, died in the
evening. The blood from his wound flowed
to the bottom of the chariot. 36 At sunset a cry
went through the army, “Every man to his
city, every man to his land!”

37 And so the king died, and came back to
Samaria, and they buried him there.
38[r] When they washed out the chariot at the
pool of Samaria, the dogs licked up his
blood and prostitutes bathed there, as the
LORD had prophesied.

39 The rest of the acts of Ahab, with all that
he did, including the ivory house he built
and all the cities he built, are recorded in the
book of the chronicles of the kings of Israel.
40 Ahab rested with his ancestors, and his son
Ahaziah succeeded him as king.

***Reign of Jehoshaphat.*** 41 Jehoshaphat, son
of Asa, became king of Judah in the fourth
year of Ahab, king of Israel. 42 Jehoshaphat
was thirty-five years old when he became
king, and he reigned twenty-five years in
Jerusalem. His mother’s name was Azubah,
daughter of Shilhi.

43 He walked in the way of Asa his father
unceasingly, doing what was right in the
LORD’s sight. 44 Nevertheless, the high
places did not disappear, and the people still
sacrificed on the high places and burned incense there. 45 Jehoshaphat also made peace
with the king of Israel.

46 The rest of the acts of Jehoshaphat, with
his valor, what he did and how he fought, are
recorded in the book of the chronicles of the
kings of Judah. 47 He removed from the land
the rest of the pagan priests who had remained in the reign of Asa his father. 48 There
was no king in Edom, but an appointed regent. 49 Jehoshaphat made Tarshish ships to
go to Ophir for gold; but in fact the ships did
not go, because they were wrecked at Ezion-
geber. 50 That was the time when Ahaziah,
son of Ahab, had said to Jehoshaphat, “Let
my servants accompany your servants in the
ships.” But Jehoshaphat would not agree.
51 Jehoshaphat rested with his ancestors; he
was buried with his ancestors in the City of
David his father, and his son Jehoram succeeded him as king.

***Reign of Ahaziah.**** 52 Ahaziah, son of
Ahab, became king over Israel in Samaria in
the seventeenth year* of Jehoshaphat, king
of Judah; he reigned two years over Israel.

53 He did what was evil in the sight of the
LORD, walking in the way of his father, his
mother, and Jeroboam, son of Nebat, who
caused Israel to sin. 54 He served Baal and
worshiped him, thus provoking the LORD,
the God of Israel, just as his father had done.

**22:52–54** The account of Ahaziah’s reign continues in 2 Kings.

**22:52 Seventeenth year**: so the present Hebrew text. This is consistent with the figures in 2 Kgs 3:1, but together those figures conflict with information in 1 Kgs 22:42 and 2 Kgs 1:17. The problem of the chronology of the kings of Israel and Judah has never been convincingly resolved; it is complicated by the fact that the ancient Greek translation sometimes has different lengths of reign and different accession dates. See further note on 2 Kgs 3:1.

*q:* 1 Kgs 20:42. *r:* 1 Kgs 21:19.

See RG 122–36

# The Second Book of Kings

See RG 129–34

## CHAPTER 1

***Reign of Ahaziah, Continued.*** 1After Ahab's death, Moab rebelled against Israel.[a]

2Ahaziah fell through the lattice of his roof terrace at Samaria and was injured. So he sent out messengers with the instructions: "Go and inquire of Baalzebub,* the god of Ekron, whether I shall recover from this injury."

3Meanwhile, the messenger of the LORD said to Elijah the Tishbite: Go and meet the messengers of Samaria's king, and tell them: "Is it because there is no God in Israel that you are going to inquire of Baalzebub, the god of Ekron?" 4For this, the LORD says: You shall not leave the bed upon which you lie; instead, you shall die. And Elijah departed. 5The messengers then returned to Ahaziah, who asked them, "Why have you returned?" 6They answered, "A man met us and said to us, 'Go back to the king who sent you and tell him: The LORD says: Is it because there is no God in Israel that you are sending to inquire of Baalzebub, the god of Ekron? For this you shall not leave the bed upon which you lie; instead, you shall die.' " 7The king asked them, "What was the man like who met you and said these things to you?" 8They replied, "He wore a hairy garment* with a leather belt around his waist." "It is Elijah the Tishbite!" he exclaimed.

9Then the king sent a captain with his company of fifty men after Elijah. The prophet was seated on a hilltop when he found him. He said, "Man of God, the king commands you, 'Come down.' " 10Elijah answered the captain, "Well, if I am a man of God, may fire come down from heaven and consume you and your fifty men." And fire came down from heaven and consumed him and his fifty men.[b] 11The king sent another captain with his company of fifty men after Elijah. He shouted up and said, "Man of God, the king says, 'Come down immediately!' " 12Elijah answered them, "If I am a man of God, may fire come down from heaven and consume you and your fifty men." And divine fire* came down from heaven and consumed him and his fifty men. 13The king sent a third captain with his company of fifty men. When the third captain had climbed the hill, he fell to his knees before Elijah, pleading with him. He said, "Man of God, let my life and the lives of these fifty men, your servants, count for something in your sight! 14Already fire has come down from heaven, consuming the first two captains with their companies of fifty men. But now, let my life count for something in your sight!" 15Then the messenger of the LORD said to Elijah: Go down with him; you need not be afraid of him. So Elijah left and went down with him to the king. 16He declared to the king: "Thus says the LORD: Because you sent messengers to inquire of Baalzebub, the god of Ekron—do you think there is no God in Israel to inquire of?—you shall not leave the bed upon which you lie; instead you shall die."[c]

17Ahaziah died according to the word of the LORD spoken by Elijah. Since he had no son, Joram* succeeded him as king, in the second year of Joram, son of Jehoshaphat, king of Judah.

**1:2 Baalzebub**: in this form, "Baal of flies." The name in the Hebrew text is a derisive alteration of Baalzebul, "Prince Baal." The best New Testament evidence supports the latter form in Mt 10:25; Lk 11:15.

**1:8 Hairy garment**: a sign of prophetic calling; see Zec 13:4. John the Baptizer wore a similarly distinctive mantle; see Mt 3:4; Mk 1:6.

**1:12 Divine fire**: lit., "fire of God," which in Hebrew sounds quite like "man of God." The play on words is the basis for Elijah's retort. This story was told among the people to enhance the dignity of the prophet and to reflect the power of God whom he served. A similar phrase, "the LORD's fire," described the miraculous divine fire that fell from a cloudless sky to consume Elijah's offering in 1 Kgs 18:38.

**1:17 Joram**: in 2 Kings the name "Joram" (*yoram*) and its variant "Jehoram" (*yehoram*) are used interchangeably. To avoid the impression that they are different names and designate different people, both forms are rendered "Joram" in this translation. Confusion arises, however, because the king of

*a:* 2 Kgs 3:4–27. *b:* Lv 10:1–2; Sir 48:3; Lk 9:51–55. *c:* Sir 48:6.

18The rest of the acts of Ahaziah, which he
did, are recorded in the book of chronicles of
the kings of Israel.

## VI. Elisha Succeeds Elijah*

### CHAPTER 2

See RG 129–34

*Elijah's Journey.* 1When the LORD
was about to take Elijah up to heaven in a
whirlwind, he and Elisha were on their way
from Gilgal.*
2Elijah said to Elisha, "Stay here, please.
The LORD has sent me on to Bethel." Elisha
replied, "As the LORD lives, and as you
yourself live, I will not leave you." So they
went down to Bethel. 3The guild prophets
who were in Bethel went out to Elisha and
asked him, "Do you know that today the
LORD will take your master from you?" He
replied, "Yes, I know that. Be still."
4Elijah said to him, "Elisha, stay here,
please. The LORD has sent me on to Jericho."
Elisha replied, "As the LORD lives, and as
you yourself live, I will not leave you." So
they came to Jericho. 5The guild prophets
who were in Jericho approached Elisha and
asked him, "Do you know that today the
LORD will take your master from you?" He
replied, "Yes, I know that. Be still."
6Elijah said to him, "Stay here, please.
The LORD has sent me on to the Jordan." Elisha replied, "As the LORD lives, and as you
yourself live, I will not leave you." So the
two went on together. 7Fifty of the guild
prophets followed and stood facing them at
a distance, while the two of them stood next
to the Jordan.
*Elisha Succeeds Elijah.* 8Elijah took his
mantle, rolled it up and struck the water: it
divided, and the two of them crossed over on
dry ground.[d]
9[e] When they had crossed over, Elijah said
to Elisha, "Request whatever I might do for
you, before I am taken from you." Elisha answered, "May I receive a double portion of
your spirit."* 10He replied, "You have asked
something that is not easy. Still, if you see
me taken up from you, your wish will be
granted; otherwise not." 11As they walked
on still conversing, a fiery chariot and fiery
horses came between the two of them, and
Elijah went up to heaven in a whirlwind,[f]
12and Elisha saw it happen. He cried out,
"My father! my father!* Israel's chariot and
steeds!" Then he saw him no longer.
He gripped his own garment, tore it into
two pieces, 13and picked up the mantle which
had fallen from Elijah. Then he went back
and stood at the bank of the Jordan. 14Wield-
ing the mantle which had fallen from Elijah,
he struck the water and said, "The LORD, the
God of Elijah—where is he now?"* He struck
the water: it divided, and he crossed over.
*Elisha's Journey.* 15The guild prophets in
Jericho, who were on the other side, saw him
and said, "The spirit of Elijah rests on Elisha."

Israel whose reign is recounted beginning in 3:1 and the contemporary king of Judah whose reign is recounted beginning in 8:16 share this name. On the relationship of Joram of Israel to Joram of Judah, see note on 3:1.

**2:1–25** The story of Elisha's succession to Elijah's prophetic office is oddly set between the death of Ahaziah (1:17) and the accession of his successor (3:1). The effect is to place this scene, which is the central scene in the whole of 1–2 Kings, outside of time. It thereby becomes almost mythic in its import and reminds us that, behind the transitory flow of kings and kingdoms, stand the eternal word of God and the prophets who give it voice. Just as 1–2 Kings pivots on this chapter, so this scene too is concentrically constructed. Together Elijah and Elisha journey to Bethel, thence to Jericho, and thence across the Jordan. There Elijah is taken up in the whirlwind and Elijah's mantle of power comes to Elisha. Now alone, Elisha crosses the Jordan again, returns to Jericho and thence back to Bethel.

**2:1 Gilgal**: there are several places in the Hebrew Bible named Gilgal; the word probably means "circle," viz. of stones. Here the route of the prophets' journey rules out the most famous Gilgal (Jos 4–5), the one near Jericho. This Gilgal may have been located in the area of modern Jiljulieh, approximately seven miles north of Bethel, which seems to preserve the ancient name.

**2:9 Double portion of your spirit**: as the firstborn son inherited a double portion of his father's property (Dt 21:17), so Elisha asks to inherit from Elijah his spirit of prophecy in the degree befitting his principal disciple. In Nm 11:17–25, God bestows some of the spirit of Moses on others.

**2:12 My father**: a religious title accorded prophetic leaders; cf. 6:21; 8:9; and 13:14, where King Joash of Israel reacts to Elisha's own impending death with the same words Elisha uses here.

**2:14 The LORD, the God of Elijah—where is he now?**: the words in Hebrew have an incantatory quality, as if Elisha is invoking both the divine name and the name of his departed master in an attempt to duplicate Elijah's miracle.

*d:* Ex 14:15–22; Jos 3:14–17. *e:* Nm 11:16–17, 24–29. *f:* Gn 5:24; 1 Mc 2:58; Sir 48:9–12; Acts 1:9.

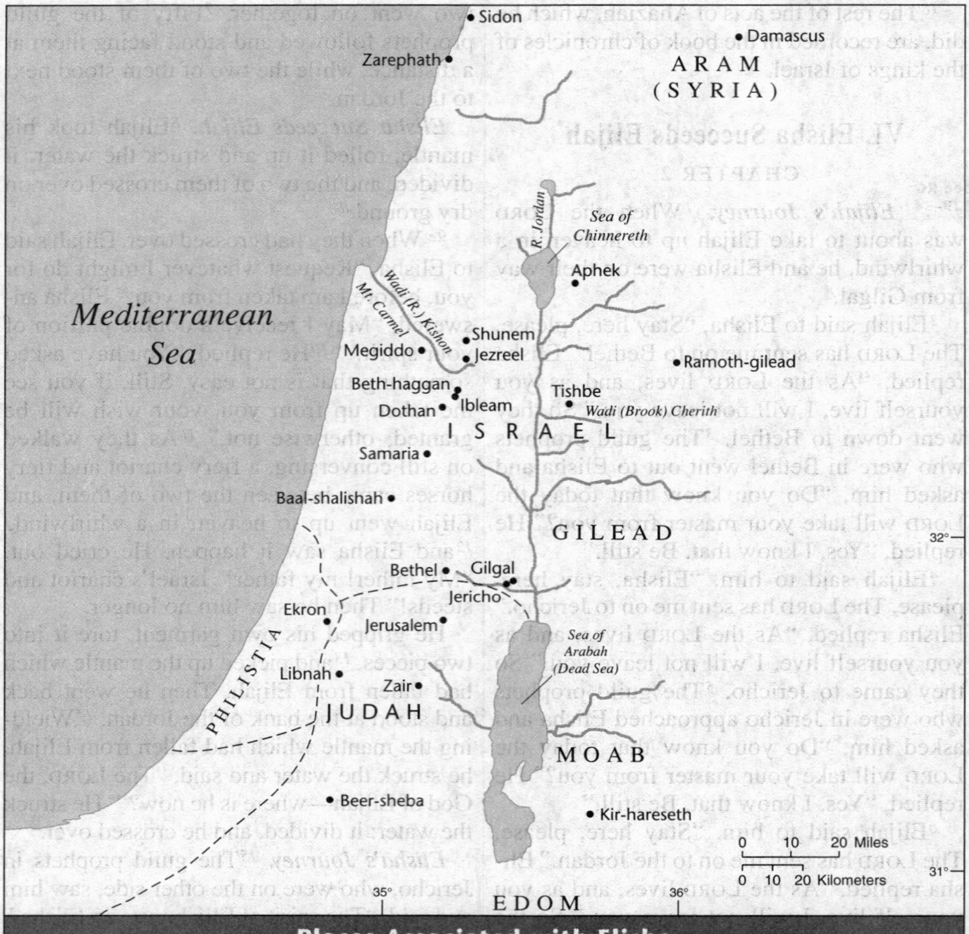


**Places Associated with Elisha**

They went to meet him, bowing to the ground before him.[g] 16They said, "Among your servants are fifty brave men. Let them go in search of your master. Perhaps the spirit of the LORD has lifted him up and left him on some mountain or in some valley." He answered, "Do not send them."[h] 17But they kept urging him, until he was embarrassed and said, "Send them." So they sent the fifty men, who searched for three days without finding him.[i] 18When they returned to Elisha in Jericho, where he was staying, he said to them, "Did I not tell you not to go?"

19[j] The inhabitants of the city complained to Elisha, "The site of the city is fine indeed, as my lord can see, but the water is bad and the land sterile." 20Elisha said, "Bring me a new bowl and put salt into it." When they had brought it to him, 21he went out to the spring and threw salt into it, saying, "Thus says the LORD: I have purified this water. Never again shall death or sterility come from it." 22And the water has stayed pure even to this day, according to the word Elisha had spoken.

23* From there Elisha went up to Bethel. While he was on the way, some little boys

**2:23–24** This story probably was told to warn children of the importance of respect for prophets.

*g:* 1 Kgs 19:19; Sir 48:12. *h:* 1 Kgs 18:12. *i:* 1 Kgs 17:2; 18:10. *j:* 2 Kgs 4:38–41.

### Elisha as Elijah's Successor

THE STORIES IN 2 Kgs 2:13–25 show that Elisha has inherited Elijah's power as a man of God. Elisha picked up the mantle of Elijah, which was the symbol of his prophetic power. He then struck the water of the Jordan with it and parted it just as Elijah had done (v. 8), and much as Joshua did when he succeeded Moses (Jos 3:13–17). By this the guild prophets recognized Elisha as Elijah's successor (v. 15).

The Elisha stories in chs 2–13 are presented in cycles and interspersed between historical and prophetic narratives, citations from chronicles and remarks of the author. In contrast to the four major Elijah stories and the story of his death, there are fifteen Elisha stories of varying length. Though many of their activities are similar, Elisha is generally much more sympathetic to the Israelite king than his mentor, Elijah.

came out of the city and jeered at him: "Go
away, baldy; go away, baldy!" 24 The prophet
turned and saw them, and he cursed them in
the name of the LORD. Then two she-bears
came out of the woods and tore forty-two of
the children to pieces.
25 From there he went to Mount Carmel,
and returned to Samaria from there.

## VII. Stories of Elisha and Joram*

See RG 129–34

### CHAPTER 3

*Reign of Joram of Israel.* 1 Joram, son
of Ahab, became king over Israel in Samaria
in the eighteenth year of Jehoshaphat, king
of Judah, and he reigned twelve years.*
2k He did what was evil in the LORD's
sight, though not like his father and mother.
He did away with the pillar of Baal that his
father had made, 3 but he still held fast unceasingly to the sins which Jeroboam, son of
Nebat, caused Israel to commit.

*War Against Moab: Drought.* 4* Now Mesha, king of Moab, who raised sheep, used to
pay the king of Israel as tribute a hundred
thousand lambs and the wool of a hundred
thousand rams. 5 But when Ahab died, the
king of Moab rebelled against the king of Israel. 6 King Joram set out from Samaria and
mustered all Israel. 7l Then he sent Jehoshaphat, the king of Judah, the message: "The
king of Moab has rebelled against me. Will

**3:1–9:13** After the formulaic introduction to the reign of Joram of Israel, this section falls into two parts. The first contains several stories about the prophet Elisha, both in private and in public life. There are four longer stories, arranged in an ABBA pattern: drought during war with Moab (vv. 4–27), restoration of the Shunammite's son (4:8–37), healing of Naaman (5:1–27), famine during war with Aram (6:24–7:20). The last three of these stories are each preceded and followed by short anecdotal tales about Elisha. The second part of this section turns to the political realm. Elisha carries out the Lord's commissions to Elijah (1 Kgs 19:15–17) to anoint Hazael king of Aram (2 Kgs 8:7–15) and Jehu king of Israel (9:1–13). To prepare for the story of Jehu's insurrection (9:14–11:20), the narrator places between those two narratives notices about the royal succession in Judah (8:16–24, 25–29). The formulaic conclusions to the reigns of Joram of Israel and Ahaziah of Judah (8:25–29) are missing, since the deaths of both will be recounted in the story of Jehu's insurrection.

**3:1** The contradiction between 1:17 and v. 1 regarding the year when Joram succeeded Ahaziah of Israel makes any reconstruction of the chronology of Israel's and Judah's kings uncertain. Some scholars think that one or the other notice is simply incorrect. Others propose to explain the discrepancy by a co-regency: Jehoshaphat of Judah would have shared the throne with his son Joram from Jehoshaphat's seventeenth year until he died in the twenty-fifth year of his reign (1 Kgs 22:42; see also 2 Kgs 8:16). The issue is further complicated by the speculation of some historians that "Joram of Israel" ("son" of Ahab of Israel: v. 1) and "Joram of Judah" ("son-in-law" of Ahab of Israel: 8:18) were in fact the same person, in whom the royal houses and separate realms of Israel and Judah were briefly reunited.

**3:4** In the period of oral tradition, it seems that stories of kings were often told without identifying the kings by name. (Vestiges of this anonymity are still visible in 1 Kgs 3:16–28; 20:4–43; 22:1–38; 2 Kgs 6:8–7:20.) Names (such as "Ahab" in 1 Kgs 20:13–14; 22:20) were added later. As a consequence, the historical attachment of such stories to the kings about whom they are told is open to question. (See note on 1 Kgs 20:1–22:54.) The present story about a campaign against Moab by Joram and Jehoshaphat has several striking similarities to the campaign against Ramoth-gilead by Ahab and Jehoshaphat in 1 Kgs 22:1–38. There exists a Moabite inscription that contains Mesha's self-aggrandizing account of his successful rebellion against Israel, but the times and places it mentions are different from those implied in vv. 4–27.

*k:* 1 Kgs 16:32. *l:* 1 Kgs 22:3–8.

you come with me to Moab to fight?" He replied, "I will. You and I are as one, your people and my people, and your horses and my horses as well." [8]He said, "By what route shall we attack?" and the other said, "By way of the wilderness of Edom."

[9]So the king of Israel set out, accompanied by the king of Judah and the king of Edom. After a roundabout journey of seven days the water gave out for the army and for the animals with them. [10]The king of Israel exclaimed, "Alas! The LORD has called three kings together only to deliver us into the power of Moab." [11]But Jehoshaphat asked, "Is there no prophet of the LORD here through whom we may inquire of the LORD?" One of the servants of the king of Israel replied, "Elisha, son of Shaphat, who poured water on the hands of Elijah,* is here." [12]Jehoshaphat agreed, "He has the word of the LORD." So the king of Israel, along with Jehoshaphat and the king of Edom, went down to Elisha. [13]Elisha asked the king of Israel, "What do you want with me? Go to the prophets of your father and to the prophets of your mother." The king of Israel replied, "No, the LORD has called these three kings together only to deliver us into the power of Moab." [14]Then Elisha said, "As the LORD of hosts lives, whom I serve, were it not that I respect Jehoshaphat, the king of Judah, I should neither look at you nor notice you at all. [15]Now get me a minstrel." When the minstrel played, the hand of the LORD came upon Elisha, [16]and he announced: "Thus says the LORD: Provide many catch basins in this wadi. [17]For the LORD says: Though you will see neither wind nor rain, yet this wadi will be filled with water for you to drink, and for your livestock and pack animals. [18]And since the LORD does not consider this enough, he will also deliver Moab into your power. [19]You shall destroy every fortified city and every choice city, fell every fruit tree, stop up all the springs, and ruin every fertile field with stones."[m]

[20]In the morning, at the time of the sacrifice, water came from the direction of Edom and filled the land.

[21]Meanwhile, all Moab had heard that the kings had come to war against them; troops from the youngest on up were mobilized and stationed at the border. [22]When they rose early that morning, the sun was shining across the water. The Moabites saw the water as red as blood, [23]and said, "This is blood! The kings have fought among themselves and killed one another. Quick! To the spoils, Moab!" [24]But when they reached the camp of Israel, the Israelites rose up and attacked the Moabites, who fled from them. They ranged through the countryside destroying Moab— [25]leveling the cities, each one casting the stones onto every fertile field and filling it, stopping up every spring, felling every fruit tree, until only the stones of Kir-hareseth* remained. Then the slingers surrounded and attacked it. [26]When he saw that the battle was going against him, the king of Moab took seven hundred swordsmen to break through to the king of Edom, but he failed. [27]So he took his firstborn, who was to succeed him as king, and offered him as a burnt offering upon the wall. The wrath against Israel* was so great that they gave up the siege and returned to their own land.[n]

### CHAPTER 4

See RG 129–34

*The Widow's Oil.* [1][o] A certain woman, the widow of one of the guild prophets, cried out to Elisha: "My husband, your servant, is dead. You know that he revered the LORD, yet now his creditor has come to take my two children into servitude."* [2]Elisha answered her, "What am I to do for you? Tell me what you have in the house." She replied, "This servant of yours has nothing

**3:11 Poured water on the hands of Elijah**: possibly a metaphor for "was Elijah's servant." But the phrase occurs nowhere else in the Old Testament and its meaning is not certain.

**3:25 Kir-hareseth**: a major city of Moab, identified with modern Kerak, east of the Dead Sea; cf. Is 16:7, 11; Jer 48:31, 36.

**3:27 The wrath against Israel**: probably the wrath of Chemosh, the Moabite god to whom the child was offered. The Israelites, intimidated by this wrath, retreat.

**4:1 His creditor . . . into servitude**: Israelite law permitted the selling of wife and children into slavery for debt; cf. Ex 21:7; Am 2:6; 8:6; Is 50:1.

*m:* Dt 20:19. *n:* Jgs 11:30–31. *o:* 1 Kgs 17:8–16.

in the house but a jug of oil." 3He said, "Go
out, borrow vessels from all your neighbors—as many empty vessels as you can.
4Then come back and close the door on
yourself and your children; pour the oil into
all the vessels, and as each is filled, set it
aside." 5So she went out. She closed the door
on herself and her children and, as they
handed her the vessels, she would pour in
oil. 6When all the vessels were filled, she
said to her son, "Bring me another vessel."
He answered, "There is none left." And then
the oil stopped. 7She went and told the man
of God, who said, "Go sell the oil to pay off
your creditor; with what remains, you and
your children can live."

***Elisha Raises the Shunammite's Son.***
8One day Elisha came to Shunem, where
there was a woman of influence, who
pressed him to dine with her. Afterward,
whenever he passed by, he would stop there
to dine. 9So she said to her husband, "I know
that he is a holy man of God. Since he visits
us often, 10let us arrange a little room on the
roof and furnish it for him with a bed, table,
chair, and lamp, so that when he comes to us
he can stay there."[p]

11One day Elisha arrived and stayed in the
room overnight. 12Then he said to his servant Gehazi, "Call this Shunammite
woman." He did so, and when she stood before Elisha, 13he told Gehazi, "Say to her,
'You have troubled yourself greatly for us;
what can we do for you? Can we say a good
word for you to the king or to the commander of the army?' " She replied, "I am living
among my own people."* 14Later Elisha
asked, "What can we do for her?" Gehazi
answered, "She has no son, and her husband
is old." 15Elisha said, "Call her." He did so,
and when she stood at the door, 16Elisha
promised, "This time next year you will be
cradling a baby son." She said, "My lord,
you are a man of God; do not deceive your
servant."[q] 17Yet the woman conceived, and
by the same time the following year she had
given birth to a son, as Elisha had promised;
18and the child grew up healthy.[r]

One day the boy went out to his father
among the reapers. 19He said to his father,
"My head! My head!" And his father said to
the servant, "Carry him to his mother."
20The servant picked him up and carried him
to his mother; he sat in her lap until noon,
and then died. 21She went upstairs and laid
him on the bed of the man of God. Closing
the door on him, she went out 22and called to
her husband, "Let me have one of the servants and a donkey. I must go quickly to the
man of God, and I will be back." 23He asked,
"Why are you going to him today? It is neither the new moon nor the sabbath." But she
said, "It is all right." 24When the donkey was
saddled, she said to her servant, "Lead on!
Do not stop my donkey unless I tell you."
25She kept going till she reached the man of
God on Mount Carmel. When he saw her at
a distance, the man of God said to his servant
Gehazi: "There is the Shunammite! 26Hurry
to meet her, and ask if everything is all right
with her, with her husband, and with the
boy." "Everything is all right," she replied.
27But when she reached the man of God on
the mountain, she clasped his feet. Gehazi
came near to push her away, but the man of
God said: "Let her alone, she is in bitter anguish; the LORD hid it from me and did not
let me know." 28She said, "Did I ask my lord
for a son? Did I not say, 'Do not mislead
me'?" 29He said to Gehazi, "Get ready for a
journey. Take my staff with you and be off;
if you meet anyone, give no greeting,* and if
anyone greets you, do not answer. Lay my
staff upon the boy." 30But the boy's mother
cried out: "As the LORD lives and as you
yourself live, I will not release you." So he
started back with her.

31Meanwhile, Gehazi had gone on ahead
and had laid the staff upon the boy, but there
was no sound, no response. He returned to

**4:13 I am living among my own people**: the Shunammite woman declines Elisha's offer. Surrounded by the support of her family and her clan, she is secure. Ironically, at some point in the future Elisha's advice will send her to live among foreigners (see 8:1–2).

**4:29 Give no greeting**: a profuse exchange of greetings and compliments would normally surround the chance encounter of acquaintances on the road. This would, however, take time, and Gehazi's mission was urgent. Compare Lk 10:4.

*p:* 1 Kgs 17:9. *q:* Gn 18:9–15. *r:* 1 Kgs 17:17–24; Lk 7:11–16; Acts 20:10–12.

**Feeding the Hungry**

A LIMITED AMOUNT of food is once again multiplied (4:42–44; see 4:1–7). Compare the New Testament stories of Jesus' multiplication of the loaves (Mt 14:13–21; 15:32–38).

meet Elisha and told him, "The boy has not awakened." [32]When Elisha reached the house, he found the boy dead, lying on the bed. [33]He went in, closed the door on them both, and prayed to the LORD. [34]Then he lay upon the child on the bed, placing his mouth upon the child's mouth, his eyes upon the eyes, and his hands upon the hands. As Elisha stretched himself over the child, the boy's flesh became warm.[s] [35]He arose, paced up and down the room, and then once more stretched himself over him, and the boy sneezed seven times and opened his eyes.[t] [36]Elisha summoned Gehazi and said, "Call the Shunammite." He called her, and she came to him, and Elisha said to her, "Take your son." [37]She came in and fell at his feet in homage; then she took her son and left.

***The Poisoned Stew.*** [38][u] When Elisha returned to Gilgal, there was a famine in the land. Once, when the guild prophets were seated before him, he said to his servant, "Put the large pot on, and make some vegetable stew for the guild prophets." [39]Someone went out into the field to gather herbs and found a wild vine, from which he picked a sackful of poisonous wild gourds. On his return he cut them up into the pot of vegetable stew without anybody's knowing it. [40]The stew was served, but when they began to eat it, they cried, "Man of God, there is death in the pot!" And they could not eat it. [41]He said, "Bring some meal." He threw it into the pot and said, "Serve it to the people to eat." And there was no longer anything harmful in the pot.

***The Barley Loaves.*** [42][v] A man came from Baal-shalishah bringing the man of God twenty barley loaves made from the first fruits, and fresh grain in the ear. Elisha said, "Give it to the people to eat." [43]But his servant objected, "How can I set this before a hundred?" Elisha again said, "Give it to the people to eat, for thus says the LORD: You will eat and have some left over." [44]He set it before them, and when they had eaten, they had some left over, according to the word of the LORD.

## CHAPTER 5

See RG 129–34

***Elisha Cures Naaman's Leprosy.*** [1]Naaman, the army commander of the king of Aram, was highly esteemed and respected by his master, for through him the LORD had brought victory to Aram. But valiant as he was, the man was a leper.* [2]Now the Arameans had captured from the land of Israel in a raid a little girl, who became the servant of Naaman's wife. [3]She said to her mistress, "If only my master would present himself to the prophet in Samaria! He would cure him of his leprosy."

[4]Naaman went and told his master, "This is what the girl from the land of Israel said." [5]The king of Aram said, "Go. I will send along a letter to the king of Israel." So Naaman set out, taking along ten silver talents, six thousand gold pieces, and ten festal garments. [6]He brought the king of Israel the letter, which read: "With this letter I am sending my servant Naaman to you, that you may cure him of his leprosy." [7]When he read the letter, the king of Israel tore his garments and exclaimed: "Am I a god with power over life and death, that this man should send someone for me to cure him of leprosy? Take note! You can see he is only looking for a quarrel with me!"[w] [8]When Elisha, the man

**5:1 Leper:** the terms traditionally translated "leper" and "leprosy" covered a wide variety of skin disorders like psoriasis, eczema, and seborrhea, but probably not Hansen's disease (modern "leprosy"); there is no clear evidence of its existence in biblical times.

*s:* Sir 48:13. *t:* Heb 11:35. *u:* 2 Kgs 2:19–22. *v:* Mt 14:13–21; 15:32–38; Mk 6:34–44; 8:1–9; Lk 9:10–17; Jn 6:1–13. *w:* 1 Sm 2:6; Jn 5:21.

of God, heard that the king of Israel had torn
his garments, he sent word to the king:
"Why have you torn your garments? Let him
come to me and find out that there is a
prophet in Israel."
9Naaman came with his horses and chariot and stopped at the door of Elisha's house.
10Elisha sent him the message: "Go and
wash seven times in the Jordan, and your
flesh will heal, and you will be clean."[x] 11But
Naaman went away angry, saying, "I
thought that he would surely come out to me
and stand there to call on the name of the
LORD his God, and would move his hand
over the place, and thus cure the leprous
spot. 12Are not the rivers of Damascus, the
Abana and the Pharpar, better than all the
waters of Israel? Could I not wash in them
and be cleansed?"* With this, he turned
about in anger and left.
13But his servants came up and reasoned
with him: "My father, if the prophet told you
to do something extraordinary, would you
not do it? All the more since he told you,
'Wash, and be clean'?" 14So Naaman went
down and plunged into the Jordan seven
times, according to the word of the man of
God. His flesh became again like the flesh of
a little child, and he was clean.[y]
15He returned with his whole retinue to
the man of God. On his arrival he stood before him and said, "Now I know that there is
no God in all the earth, except in Israel.
Please accept a gift from your servant."[z]
16Elisha replied, "As the LORD lives whom I
serve, I will not take it." And despite Naaman's urging, he still refused. 17Naaman
said: "If you will not accept, please let me,
your servant, have two mule-loads of earth,*
for your servant will no longer make burnt
offerings or sacrifices to any other god except the LORD. 18But may the LORD forgive
your servant this: when my master enters the
temple of Rimmon to bow down there, as he
leans upon my arm, I too must bow down in
the temple of Rimmon. When I bow down in
the temple of Rimmon, may the LORD please
forgive your servant this." 19Elisha said to
him, "Go in peace."*
Naaman had gone some distance 20when
Gehazi, the servant of Elisha, the man of
God, thought to himself: "My master was
too easy on this Aramean Naaman, not accepting what he brought. As the LORD lives,
I will run after him and get something out of
him." 21So Gehazi hurried after Naaman.
Seeing that someone was running after him,
Naaman alighted from his chariot to wait for
him. He asked, "Is everything all right?"
22Gehazi replied, "Yes, but my master sent
me to say, 'Two young men have just come
to me, guild prophets from the hill country
of Ephraim. Please give them a talent of silver and two festal garments.' " 23Naaman
said, "I insist! Take two talents," and he
pressed him. He tied up two silver talents in
bags and gave them, with two festal garments, to two of his servants, who carried
them before Gehazi. 24When he reached the
hill, Gehazi received these things, appropriated them for his house, and sent the men on
their way.
25He went in and stood by Elisha his master, who asked him, "Where have you been,
Gehazi?" He answered, "Your servant has
not gone anywhere." 26But Elisha said to
him: "Was I not present in spirit when someone got down from his chariot to wait for
you? Is this a time to take money or to take
garments, olive orchards or vineyards, sheep
or cattle, male or female servants? 27The leprosy of Naaman shall cling to you and your
descendants forever." And Gehazi went out,
a leper with skin like snow.*

**5:12 Wash in them and be cleansed**: typical of the ambiguity in ritual healing or cleanliness. The muddy waters of the Jordan are no match hygienically for the mountain spring waters of Damascus; ritually, it is the other way around.

**5:17 Two mule-loads of earth**: worship of the Lord is associated with the soil of the Holy Land, where he is present.

**5:19 Go in peace**: Elisha understands and approves the situation of Naaman who, though now a worshiper of the God of Israel, is required by his courtly office to assist his master, the king ("leans upon my arm," v. 18), worshiping in the temple of the Canaanite god Baal-Rimmon.

**5:27 With skin like snow**: "snow" is often used to describe the skin conditions covered by the term "leprosy" (Ex 4:6; Nm 12:10; see note on 5:1). It is unclear whether the comparison is with the white color, dry flakes, or moist shine, any of which can occur in the relevant skin diseases.

*x:* Jn 9:7. *y:* Lk 4:27. *z:* Lk 17:17–19.

## CHAPTER 6

See RG 129–34

***The Lost Ax.*** [1]The guild prophets once said to Elisha: "This place where we live with you is too cramped for us. [2]Let us go to the Jordan, where by getting one beam apiece we can build ourselves a place to live." Elisha said, "Go." [3]One of them requested, "Please agree to accompany your servants." He replied, "Yes, I will come."

[4]So he went with them, and when they arrived at the Jordan they began to cut down trees. [5]While one of them was felling a tree trunk, the iron ax blade slipped into the water. He cried out, "Oh, no, master! It was borrowed!" [6]"Where did it fall?" asked the man of God. When he pointed out the spot, Elisha cut off a stick, threw it into the water, and brought the iron to the surface. [7]He said, "Pick it up." And the man stretched out his hand and grasped it.

***The Aramean Ambush.*** [8]When the king of Aram was waging war on Israel, he would make plans with his servants: "I will bivouac at such and such a place." [9]But the man of God would send word to the king of Israel, "Be careful! Do not pass by this place, for Aram will attack there." [10]So the king of Israel would send word to the place which the man of God had indicated, and alert it; then they would be on guard. This happened several times.

[11]Greatly disturbed over this, the king of Aram called together his officers and asked them, "Will you not tell me who among us is for the king of Israel?" [12]"No one, my lord king," answered one of the officers. "The Israelite prophet Elisha can tell the king of Israel the very words you speak in your bedroom." [13]He said, "Go, find out where he is, so that I may take him captive."

Informed that Elisha was in Dothan, [14]he sent there a strong force with horses and chariots. They arrived by night and encircled the city. [15]Early the next morning, when the servant of the man of God arose and went out, he saw the force with its horses and chariots surrounding the city. "Alas!" he said to Elisha. "What shall we do, my lord?" [16]Elisha answered, "Do not be afraid. Our side outnumbers theirs." [17]Then he prayed, "O LORD, open his eyes, that he may see." And the LORD opened the eyes of the servant, and he saw that the mountainside was filled with fiery chariots and horses around Elisha.[a]

[18]When the Arameans came down to get him, Elisha prayed to the LORD, "Strike this people blind, I pray you." And the LORD struck them blind, according to Elisha's word. [19]Then Elisha said to them: "This is the wrong road, and this is the wrong city. Follow me! I will take you to the man you want." And he led them to Samaria. [20]When they entered Samaria, Elisha prayed, "O LORD, open their eyes that they may see." The LORD opened their eyes, and they saw that they were inside Samaria. [21]When the king of Israel saw them, he asked, "Shall I kill them, my father? Shall I kill them?" [22]Elisha replied, "You must not kill them. Do you slay those whom you have taken captive with your sword or bow?* Serve them a meal. Let them eat and drink, and then go back to their master." [23]The king spread a great feast for them. When they had eaten and drunk he sent them away, and they went back to their master. No more Aramean raiders came into the land of Israel.

***War Against Aram: Famine.*** [24]After this, Ben-hadad, king of Aram, mustered his whole army and laid siege to Samaria. [25]Because of the siege the famine in Samaria was so severe that a donkey's head sold for eighty pieces of silver, and a fourth of a kab of "dove droppings"* for five pieces of silver.

[26b] One day, as the king of Israel was walking on the city wall, a woman cried out to him, "Save us, my lord king!" [27]He replied, "If the LORD does not save you, where could I find means to save you? On

**6:22 With your sword or bow**: since the king would not slay prisoners who had surrendered to his power, much less should he slay prisoners captured by God's power. This wartime practice stands in contrast to that of holy war, where prisoners were placed under the ban and so devoted to destruction (see 1 Kgs 20:35–43).

**6:25 "Dove droppings"**: it is unclear whether this phrase is to be read literally (e.g., dung used as fuel) or as the nickname of a type of edible plant, as attested in Arabic. A kab was probably around a quart.

*a:* 2 Kgs 2:11; 7:6; Ps 68:18. *b:* Dt 28:53–57.

the threshing floor? In the wine press?”
28Then the king asked her, “What is your
trouble?” She replied: “This woman said to
me, ‘Give up your son that we may eat him
today; then tomorrow we will eat my son.’
29So we boiled my son and ate him. The next
day I said to her, ‘Now give up your son that
we may eat him.’ But she hid her son.”
30When the king heard the woman’s words,
he tore his garments. And as he was walking
on the wall, the people saw that he was wearing sackcloth underneath, next to his skin.
31The king exclaimed, “May God do thus
to me, and more, if the head of Elisha, son of
Shaphat, stays on him today!”

32Meanwhile, Elisha was sitting in his
house in conference with the elders. The
king had sent one of his courtiers; but before
the messenger reached him, Elisha said to
the elders: “Do you know that this murderer
is sending someone to cut off my head?
When the messenger comes, see that you
close the door and hold it fast against him.
His master’s footsteps are echoing behind
him.” 33While Elisha was still speaking, the
messenger came down to him and said,
“This evil is from the LORD. Why should I
trust in the LORD any longer?”*

## CHAPTER 7

See RG 129–34

1Elisha replied: “Hear the word of the
LORD! Thus says the LORD: At this time tomorrow a seah of fine flour will sell for a
shekel, and two seahs of barley for a shekel,
in the market* of Samaria.” 2But the adjutant,
upon whose arm the king leaned, answered
the man of God, “Even if the LORD were to
make windows in heaven, how could this
happen?” Elisha said, “You shall see it with
your own eyes, but you shall not eat of it.”

3At the city gate four lepers were asking
one another, “Why should we sit here until
we die?[c] 4If we decide to go into the city, we
shall die there, for there is famine in the city.
If we remain here, we shall die too. So come,
let us desert to the camp of the Arameans. If
they let us live, we live; if they kill us, we
die.” 5At twilight they left for the Arameans;
but when they reached the edge of the camp,
no one was there. 6[d] The Lord had caused the
army of the Arameans to hear the sound of
chariots and horses, the sound of a large
army, and they had reasoned among themselves, “The king of Israel has hired the
kings of the Hittites and the kings of Egypt
to fight us.” 7Then in the twilight they had
fled, abandoning their tents, their horses,
and their donkeys, the whole camp just as it
was, and fleeing for their lives.

8After the lepers reached the edge of the
camp, they went first into one tent, ate and
drank, and took silver, gold, and clothing
from it, and went out and hid them. Back
they came into another tent, took things
from it, and again went out and hid them.
9Then they said to one another: “We are not
doing right. This is a day of good news, and
we are keeping silent. If we wait until morning breaks, we will be blamed. So come, let
us go and inform the palace.” 10They came
and summoned the city gatekeepers. They
said, “We went to the camp of the Arameans,
but no one was there—not a human voice,
only the horses and donkeys tethered, and
the tents just as they were left.” 11The gatekeepers announced this and it was reported
within the palace.

12Though it was night, the king got up; he
said to his servants, “Let me tell you what the
Arameans have done to us. Knowing that we
are starving, they have left their camp to hide
in the field. They are thinking, ‘The Israelites
will leave the city and we will take them
alive and enter it.’ ” 13* One of his servants,
however, suggested: “Let some of us take
five of the horses remaining in the city—they
are just like the whole throng of Israel that
has reached its limit—and let us send scouts
to investigate.” 14They took two chariots, and
horses, and the king sent them to reconnoiter
the Aramean army with the order, “Go and
find out.” 15They followed the Arameans as

**6:33** The messenger speaks in the king’s name. Similarly, Elisha’s response in the next verse can be spoken of as delivered to the king (7:18).

**7:1 Market**: lit., “gate,” the principal place of trading in ancient walled cities in time of peace.

**7:13** The Hebrew of this verse is difficult and its meaning is uncertain.

*c:* Lv 13:46. *d:* 2 Kgs 6:17; 2 Sm 5:24.

**Elisha and the Shunammite**

THE WOMAN WHO had helped Elisha (4:8–13) now needs the help that Elisha had offered her in return. Chapter 8:1–6 tells that she has followed his advice by leaving her homeland to avoid a famine, and while she was away, someone took her land. Just as she arrives at the royal court to appeal for her house and her land, Elisha's servant Gehazi is telling the king all about her. His words serve as the advocacy on her behalf that Elisha earlier had in mind (4:13). God looks after those who look after his prophets.

far as the Jordan, and the whole route was strewn with garments and other objects that the Arameans had thrown away in their haste. The messengers returned and told the king. [16]The people went out and plundered the camp of the Arameans.

Then a seah of fine flour sold for a shekel and two seahs of barley for a shekel, according to the word of the LORD. [17]The king had put in charge of the gate the officer upon whose arm he leaned; but the people trampled him to death at the gate, just as the man of God had predicted when the messenger came down to him. [18]This was in accordance with the word the man of God spoke to the king: "Two seahs of barley will sell for a shekel, and a seah of fine flour for a shekel at this time tomorrow in the market of Samaria." [19]The adjutant had answered the man of God, "Even if the LORD were to make windows in heaven, how could this happen?" And Elisha had replied, "You shall see it with your own eyes, but you shall not eat of it." [20]And that is what happened to him, for the people trampled him to death at the gate.

### CHAPTER 8

See RG 129–34

*The Shunammite's Return.* [1]Elisha once said to the woman whose son he had restored to life: "Get ready! Leave with your household and live wherever you can, because the LORD has decreed a seven-year famine which is coming upon the land."[e] [2]The woman got ready and did as the man of God said, setting out with her household, and living in the land of the Philistines for seven years.

[3]At the end of the seven years, the woman returned from the land of the Philistines and went out to the king to appeal for her house and her field. [4]The king was talking with Gehazi, the servant of the man of God: "Tell me all the great things that Elisha has done." [5]Just as he was telling the king how his master had restored a dead person to life, the very woman whose son Elisha had restored to life came to the king appealing for her house and field. Gehazi said, "My lord king, this is the woman, and this is that son of hers whom Elisha restored to life." [6]The king questioned the woman, and she told him her story. With that the king placed an official* at her disposal, saying, "Restore all her property to her, with all that the field produced from the day she left the land until now."

*Elisha and Hazael of Aram.** [7][f] Elisha came to Damascus at a time when Ben-hadad, king of Aram, lay sick. When he was told, "The man of God has come here," [8]the king said to Hazael, "Take a gift with you and go call on the man of God. Consult the LORD through him, 'Will I recover from this sickness?' "[g] [9]Hazael went to visit him, carrying a present, and with forty camel loads of the best goods of Damascus. On his arrival, he stood before Elisha and said, "Your son Ben-hadad, king of Aram, has sent me to you to ask, 'Will I recover from my sickness?' " [10]Elisha answered, "Go and tell him, 'You will surely recover.' But the LORD has showed me that he will surely die." [11]Then he stared him down until he became ill at ease. The man of God wept, [12]and Hazael asked, "Why are you weeping, my lord?" Elisha

**8:6 An official**: lit., "eunuch," and perhaps actually so in this instance.

**8:7–15** Elisha carries out the commission the Lord gave Elijah in 1 Kgs 19:15. See note on 2 Kgs 3:1–9:13.

*e:* 2 Kgs 4:18–37. *f:* 1 Kgs 19:15. *g:* 1 Kgs 14:1–3.

replied, "Because I know the evil that you will inflict upon the Israelites. You will burn their fortresses, you will slay their youth with the sword, you will dash their little children to pieces, you will rip open their pregnant women."[h] [13]Hazael exclaimed, "How can your servant, a dog* like me, do anything so important?" Elisha replied, "The LORD has showed you to me as king over Aram."

[14]Hazael left Elisha and returned to his master, who asked, "What did Elisha tell you?" Hazael replied, "He said, 'You will surely recover.' " [15]The next day, however, Hazael took a cloth, dipped it in water, and spread it over the king's face, so that he died. And Hazael succeeded him as king.

***Reign of Joram of Judah.*** [16]* In the fifth year of Joram, son of Ahab, king of Israel, Joram, son of Jehoshaphat, king of Judah, became king. [17]He was thirty-two years old when he became king, and he reigned eight years in Jerusalem.

[18]He walked in the way of the kings of Israel as the house of Ahab had done, since the daughter of Ahab was his wife; and he did what was evil in the LORD's sight. [19]Even so, the LORD was unwilling to destroy Judah, for the sake of his servant David. For he had promised David that he would leave him a holding in the LORD's presence for all time.[i] [20]During Joram's reign, Edom revolted against the rule of Judah and installed a king of its own. [21]Thereupon Joram with all his chariots crossed over to Zair. He arose by night and broke through the Edomites when they had surrounded him and the commanders of his chariots. Then his army fled homeward. [22]To this day Edom has been in revolt against the rule of Judah. Libnah also revolted at that time.[j]

[23]The rest of the acts of Joram, with all that he did, are recorded in the book of the chronicles of the kings of Judah. [24]Joram rested with his ancestors; he was buried with his ancestors in the City of David, and his son Ahaziah succeeded him as king.

***Reign of Ahaziah of Judah.**** [25]In the twelfth year of Joram, son of Ahab, king of Israel, Ahaziah, son of Joram, king of Judah, became king. [26]Ahaziah was twenty-two years old when he became king, and he reigned one year in Jerusalem. His mother's name was Athaliah, daughter of Omri, king of Israel.*

[27]He walked in the way of the house of Ahab and did what was evil in the LORD's sight like the house of Ahab, since he was related to them by marriage. [28]He joined Joram, son of Ahab, in battle against Hazael, king of Aram, at Ramoth-gilead, where the Arameans wounded Joram.[k] [29]King Joram returned to Jezreel to be healed of the wounds which the Arameans had inflicted on him at Ramah in his battle against Hazael, king of Aram. Then Ahaziah, son of Joram, king of Judah, went down to Jezreel to visit Joram, son of Ahab, for he was sick.

## CHAPTER 9

See RG 129–34

***Elisha and Jehu of Israel.**** [1][l] Elisha the prophet called one of the guild prophets and said to him: "Get ready for a journey. Take this flask of oil with you, and go to Ramoth-gilead. [2]When you get there, look for Jehu, son of Jehoshaphat, son of Nimshi. Enter and take him away from his companions and bring him into an inner chamber. [3]From the flask you have, pour oil on his head, and say, 'Thus says the LORD: I anoint you king over Israel.' Then open the door and flee without delay."

[4]The aide (the prophet's aide) went to Ramoth-gilead. [5]When he arrived, the commanders of the army were in session. He

**8:13** To call oneself a "dog" is to admit one's insignificance (1 Sm 24:15; 2 Sm 9:8); it is not necessarily a term of contempt, as in English. Hazael focuses on the question of his power, making no comment on the atrocities Elisha predicts he will commit.

**8:16** On the apparent contradictions among 1:17, 3:1, and this verse, see note on 3:1.

**8:25–29** The narrative of Ahaziah's reign, like that of Joram of Israel, lacks the standard formulaic conclusion. The deaths of both kings, and indeed the obliteration of the whole house of Omri, will be recounted in the story of Jehu's insurrection.

**8:26** It is unclear whether Athaliah was Omri's daughter (v. 26) or his granddaughter (v. 18). Perhaps "daughter" here is being used loosely for "female descendant."

**9:1–13** Elisha carries out the commission the Lord gave Elijah in 1 Kgs 19:16. See note on 2 Kgs 3:1–9:13.

*h:* 2 Kgs 13:3–7. *i:* 2 Sm 7:12–16; 1 Kgs 11:36; 15:4. *j:* Gn 27:40. *k:* 2 Kgs 9:14–15. *l:* 1 Kgs 19:16.

said, "I have a message for you, commander." Jehu asked, "For which one of us?" "For
you, commander," he answered. [6]Jehu got
up and went into the house. Then the
prophet's aide poured the oil on his head and
said, "Thus says the LORD, the God of Israel:
I anoint you king over the people of the
LORD, over Israel. [7*] You shall destroy the
house of Ahab your master; thus will I
avenge the blood of my servants the prophets, and the blood of all the other servants of
the LORD shed by Jezebel. [8m] The whole
house of Ahab shall perish:

I will cut off from Ahab's line every male,
whether bond or free in Israel.

[9]I will make the house of Ahab like that of
Jeroboam, son of Nebat, and like that of Baasha, son of Ahijah. [10]In the confines of Jezreel, the dogs shall devour Jezebel so that no
one can bury her." Then he opened the door
and fled.

[11]When Jehu rejoined his master's servants, they asked him, "Is all well? Why did
that madman come to you?" He replied,
"You know that kind of man and his talk."
[12]But they said, "Tell us another lie!" So he
told them, "This is what the prophet's aide
said to me, 'Thus says the LORD: I anoint
you king over Israel.' " [13]At once each took
his garment, spread it under Jehu on the bare
steps, blew the horn, and cried out, "Jehu is
king!"

## VIII. The End of the Omrid Dynasty*

***Death of Joram of Israel.*** [14n] Jehu, son of Jehoshaphat, son of Nimshi, formed a conspiracy against Joram. (Joram, with all Israel,
had been besieging Ramoth-gilead against
Hazael, king of Aram, [15]but had returned to
Jezreel to be healed of the wounds the Arameans had inflicted on him in the battle
against Hazael, king of Aram.)

Jehu said to them, "If this is what you really want, see that no one escapes from the
city to report in Jezreel."

[16]Then Jehu mounted his chariot and
drove to Jezreel, where Joram lay ill and
Ahaziah, king of Judah, had come to visit
him. [17]The watchman standing on the tower
in Jezreel saw the troop of Jehu coming and
reported, "I see chariots." Joram said, "Get a
driver and send him to meet them and to ask
whether all is well." [18]So a horseman went
out to meet him and said, "The king asks, 'Is
everything all right?' " Jehu said, "What
does it matter to you how things are? Get behind me." The watchman reported to the
king, "The messenger has reached them, but
is not returning." [19]Joram sent a second
horseman, who went to them and said, "The
king asks, 'Is everything all right?' " "What
does it matter to you how things are?" Jehu
replied. "Get behind me." [20]The watchman
reported, "He has reached them, but is not
returning. The driving is like that of Jehu,
son of Nimshi; he drives like a madman."
[21o] "Hitch up my chariot," said Joram, and
they hitched up his chariot. Then Joram,
king of Israel, and Ahaziah, king of Judah,
set out, each in his own chariot, to meet
Jehu. They reached him near the plot of
ground of Naboth the Jezreelite.

[22]When Joram recognized Jehu, he asked,
"Is everything all right, Jehu?" Jehu replied,
"How could everything be all right as long
as all the harlotry and sorcery* of your
mother Jezebel continues?" [23]Joram reined
about and fled, crying to Ahaziah, "Treason,
Ahaziah!" [24]But Jehu had drawn his bow

**9:7–10** The author has Elisha's emissary expand considerably the speech Elisha told him to deliver by adding the same type of prophetic indictments and sanctions as were invoked on previous occasions against the dynasties of Jeroboam (1 Kgs 14:10–11), of Baasha (1 Kgs 16:3–4), and of Ahab himself (1 Kgs 21:21–24).

**9:14–11:20** Death pervades this section. The dynasty founded by Omri (1 Kgs 16:23) drowns in a bloodbath, taking numberless others along with it. The scenes are in three parallel sets of three: death comes (1) to Joram of Israel, Ahab's son; to Ahaziah of Judah, his son-in-law; and to Jezebel, the Baalist queen mother of Israel; (2) then to seventy descendants of Ahab; to forty-two relatives of Ahaziah of Judah; and to numerous Baal worshipers; (3) finally to Jehu of Israel; to the blood royal of Judah; and to Athaliah, the Baalist queen mother of Judah and last of the Omrids.

**9:22 Harlotry and sorcery**: both terms are metaphors referring to Jezebel's worship of the foreign god Baal.

*m:* 1 Kgs 14:10–11; 16:3–4; 21:21–24. *n:* 2 Kgs 8:28–29.
*o:* 1 Kgs 21:1–24.

and he shot Joram between the shoulders, so
that the arrow went through his heart and he
collapsed in his chariot. [25]Then Jehu said to
his adjutant Bidkar, "Take him and throw
him into the plot of ground in the field of
Naboth the Jezreelite. For remember when
you and I were driving teams behind Ahab
his father, the LORD delivered this oracle
against him: [26]As surely as I saw yesterday
the blood of Naboth and the blood of his
sons—oracle of the LORD—I will repay you
for it in that very plot of ground—oracle of
the LORD. So now take him and throw him
into this plot of ground, in keeping with the
word of the LORD."

*Death of Ahaziah of Judah.* [27][p] Seeing
what was happening, Ahaziah, king of Judah, fled toward Beth-haggan. Jehu pursued
him, shouting, "Him too!" They struck him
as he rode through the pass of Gur near Ibleam, but he continued his flight as far as
Megiddo and died there. [28]His servants
brought him in a chariot to Jerusalem and
they buried him in his grave with his ancestors in the City of David. [29]In the eleventh
year of Joram, son of Ahab, Ahaziah became
king over Judah.

*Death of Jezebel.* [30]Jehu came to Jezreel,
and when Jezebel heard of it, she shadowed
her eyes, adorned her hair, and looked down
from her window. [31]As Jehu came through
the gate, she cried out, "Is all well, you
Zimri, murderer of your master?"[q] [32]Jehu
looked up to the window and shouted, "Who
is on my side? Who?" At this, two or three
eunuchs looked down toward him. [33]"Throw
her down," he ordered. They threw her
down, and some of her blood spurted against
the wall and against the horses. Jehu trod
over her body [34]and, after eating and drinking, he said: "Attend to that accursed woman
and bury her; for she was the daughter of a
king." [35]But when they went to bury her,
they found nothing of her but the skull, the
feet, and the hands. [36]They returned to Jehu,
and when they told him, he said, "This is the
word the LORD spoke through his servant
Elijah the Tishbite: In the confines of Jezreel
the dogs shall devour the flesh of Jezebel.[r]
[37]The corpse of Jezebel shall be like dung in
the field in the confines of Jezreel, so that no
one can say: This was Jezebel."

## CHAPTER 10

See RG 129–34

### *Death of the Sons of Ahab of Israel.*

[1][s] Ahab had seventy sons in Samaria. Jehu
wrote letters and sent them to Samaria, to the
elders who were rulers of Jezreel and to
Ahab's guardians. Jehu wrote: [2]"Since your
master's sons are with you, as well as his
chariots, horses, fortified city, and
weaponry, when this letter reaches you [3]de-
cide which is the best and the fittest of your
master's sons, place him on his father's
throne, and fight for your master's house."
[4]They were overcome with fright and said,
"If the two kings could not withstand him,
how can we?" [5]So the master of the palace
and the chief of the city, along with the elders and the guardians, sent this message to
Jehu: "We are your servants, and we will do
everything you tell us. We will proclaim no
one king; do whatever you think best." [6]So
Jehu wrote them a second letter: "If you are
on my side and will obey me, bring along the
heads of your master's sons* and come to me
in Jezreel at this time tomorrow." (The seventy princes were in the care of prominent
men of the city, who were rearing them.)

[7]When the letter arrived, they took the
princes and slew all seventy of them, put
their heads in baskets, and sent them to Jehu
in Jezreel. [8]A messenger came in and told
him, "They have brought the heads of the
princes." He said, "Pile them in two heaps at
the gate of the city until morning."

[9]In the morning he came outside, stood
there, and said to all the people: "You are
guiltless, for it was I who conspired against
my lord and slew him. But who killed all
these? [10]Know that not a single word which
the LORD has spoken against the house of

**10:6 Heads of your master's sons**: Jehu's command is cleverly ambiguous. He allows the Samarian leaders to understand "heads" either literally or metaphorically as "most important individuals." Then, when the leaders decapitate Ahab's potential successors, Jehu can claim to be innocent of their blood (v. 9).

*p:* 2 Chr 22:7–9. *q:* 1 Kgs 16:8–13. *r:* 1 Kgs 21:23. *s:* Jgs 9:5; 1 Kgs 15:29; 16:11–12; 21:8.

Ahab shall fail. The LORD has accomplished
what he decreed through his servant Elijah."[t]
11 (And so Jehu slew all who were left of the
house of Ahab in Jezreel, as well as all his
powerful supporters, intimates, and priests,
leaving him no survivor.)[u] 12 Then he went
back inside.

***Death of the Relatives of Ahaziah of Judah.*** He set out for Samaria and, at Beth-
eked-haroim on the way, 13 Jehu came across
relatives of Ahaziah, king of Judah. "Who
are you?" he asked, and they said, "We are
relatives of Ahaziah. We are going down to
visit the princes and the family of the queen
mother."* 14 "Take them alive," Jehu ordered.
They were taken alive, forty-two in number,
then slain at the pit of Beth-eked. Not one of
them survived.

15 When he set out from there, Jehu met
Jehonadab, son of Rechab, on the road. He
greeted him and asked, "Are you with me
wholeheartedly, as I am with you?" "Yes,"
he replied. "If you are, give me your hand."
He gave him his hand, and he had him
mount his chariot,[v] 16 and said, "Come with
me and see my zeal for the LORD." And they
took him along in his chariot.

***Slaughter of the Worshipers of Baal.***
17 When he arrived in Samaria, Jehu slew all
who were left of Ahab's line in Samaria, doing away with them completely, according
to the word the LORD spoke to Elijah.

18 Jehu gathered all the people together
and said to them: "Ahab served Baal to some
extent, but Jehu will serve him yet more.[w]
19 Now summon for me all Baal's prophets,
all his servants, and all his priests. See that
no one is absent, for I have a great sacrifice
for Baal. Whoever is absent shall not live."
This Jehu did as a ruse, so that he might destroy the servants of Baal.[x]

20 Jehu said further, "Proclaim a solemn
assembly in honor of Baal." They did so,
21 and Jehu sent word of it throughout all Israel. All the servants of Baal came; there was
no one who did not come; they came to the
temple of Baal, and it was filled from wall to
wall. 22 Then Jehu said to the custodian of the
wardrobe, "Bring out garments for all the
servants of Baal." When he had brought out
the garments for them, 23 Jehu, with Jehonadab, son of Rechab, entered the temple
of Baal and said to the servants of Baal,
"Search and be sure that there is no one who
serves the LORD here with you, but only servants of Baal." 24 Then they proceeded to offer sacrifices and burnt offerings. Now Jehu
had stationed eighty troops outside with this
warning, "Any of you who lets someone escape of those whom I shall deliver into your
hands shall pay life for life."

25 As soon as he finished offering the burnt
offering, Jehu said to the guards and aides,
"Go in and slay them. Let no one escape."
So the guards and aides put them to the
sword and cast them out. Afterward they
went into the inner shrine of the temple of
Baal, 26 and took out the pillars of the temple
of Baal. They burned the shrine, 27 tore down
the pillar of Baal, tore down the temple of
Baal, and turned it into a latrine, as it remains today.

28 Thus Jehu destroyed Baal in Israel.

***Death of Jehu of Israel.*** 29 However, Jehu
did not desist from the sins which Jeroboam,
son of Nebat, had caused Israel to commit,
the golden calves at Bethel and at Dan.[y]

30 The LORD said to Jehu: Because you
have done well what is right in my eyes, and
have done to the house of Ahab all that was
in my heart, your sons to the fourth generation shall sit upon the throne of Israel.[z] 31 But
Jehu was not careful to walk in the law of the
LORD, the God of Israel, with all his heart,
since he did not desist from the sins which
Jeroboam had caused Israel to commit.
32[a] At that time the LORD began to dismember Israel. Hazael defeated the Israelites

**10:13** Since Athaliah, the queen mother in Judah, was of the Israelite royal house (8:18, 26), both the "princes" (lit., the "king's sons") and the queen mother's "family" (lit., her "sons") would belong to the royal houses of both kingdoms. They may thus be numbered among the seventy "sons of Ahab" killed in vv. 1–7. Because "sons" can refer to more remote offspring, the queen mother's "sons" may include Ahaziah's brothers, sons, nephews, as well as the "relatives" (lit., the "brothers") of Ahaziah who are speaking in this scene.

*t:* 1 Kgs 21:17–29. *u:* Hos 1:4. *v:* 1 Kgs 20:33; 1 Chr 2:55; Jer 35:1–19. *w:* 1 Kgs 16:30–33. *x:* 1 Kgs 18:19, 40. *y:* 1 Kgs 12:28–30. *z:* 2 Kgs 15:12. *a:* 2 Kgs 8:12; Am 1:3.

throughout their territory 33 east of the Jordan (all the land of Gilead, of the Gadites, Reubenites, and Manassites), from Aroer on the wadi Arnon up through Gilead and Bashan.

34 The rest of the acts of Jehu, with all that he did and all his valor, are recorded in the book of the chronicles of the kings of Israel. 35 Jehu rested with his ancestors and was buried in Samaria, and his son Jehoahaz succeeded him as king. 36 The length of Jehu's reign over Israel was twenty-eight years in Samaria.

## CHAPTER 11

See RG 129–34

***Death of the Heirs of Ahaziah of Judah.*** 1[b] When Athaliah, the mother of Ahaziah, saw that her son was dead, she began to kill off the whole royal family. 2 But Jehosheba,* daughter of King Joram and sister of Ahaziah, took Joash, Ahaziah's son, and spirited him away, along with his nurse, from the bedroom where the princes were about to be slain. He was concealed from Athaliah, and so he did not die. 3 For six years he remained hidden with her in the house of the LORD, while Athaliah ruled as queen over the land.

***Death of Athaliah.*** 4 But in the seventh year, Jehoiada summoned the captains of the Carians* and of the guards. He had them come to him in the house of the LORD, made a covenant with them, exacted an oath from them in the house of the LORD, and then showed them the king's son. 5 He gave them these orders: "This is what you must do: one third of you who come on duty on the sabbath shall guard the king's house; 6 another third shall be at the gate Sur; and the last third shall be at the gate behind the guards. You shall guard the palace on all sides, 7 while the two of your divisions who are going off duty that week shall keep guard over the house of the LORD for the king. 8 You shall surround the king, each with drawn weapons, and anyone who tries to approach the guard detail is to be killed; stay with the king, wherever he goes."

9 The captains did just as Jehoiada the priest commanded. Each took his troops, both those going on duty for the week and those going off duty that week, and came to Jehoiada the priest. 10[c] He gave the captains King David's spear and quivers, which were in the house of the LORD. 11 And the guards, with drawn weapons, lined up from the southern to the northern limit of the enclosure, surrounding the altar and the temple on the king's behalf. 12 Then Jehoiada brought out the king's son and put the crown and the testimony* upon him. They proclaimed him king and anointed him, clapping their hands and shouting, "Long live the king!"

13 When Athaliah heard the noise made by the people, she came before them in the house of the LORD. 14 When she saw the king standing by the column,* as was the custom, and the captains and trumpeters near the king, and all the people of the land rejoicing and blowing trumpets, Athaliah tore her garments and cried out, "Treason, treason!" 15 Then Jehoiada the priest instructed the captains in command of the force: "Escort her with a guard detail. If anyone follows her, let him die by the sword." For the priest had said, "She must not die in the house of the LORD." 16 So they seized her, and when she reached the Horse Gate of the king's house, she was put to death.

17[d] Then Jehoiada made a covenant between the LORD and the king and the people,*

**11:2** According to 2 Chr 22:11, Jehosheba was the wife of Jehoiada, the high priest. If this is historical, it would explain her access to the Temple's residential precincts.

**11:4 Carians**: foreign mercenaries serving as the royal bodyguard. Compare "Cherethites and Pelethites" in 1 Kgs 1:38.

**11:12 Testimony**: that is, the two tablets of the law preserved in the ark in the Temple. Presumably they were placed upon the king during his installation ceremony as a reminder of the law he was to uphold.

**11:14 By the column**: the king's special place in the Temple court; cf. 23:3; 2 Chr 23:13. **People of the land**: in this period, the phrase referred to the important citizenry, whose influence sometimes extended to the selection of royal successors (cf. 2 Kgs 11:14–20; 15:5; 16:15; 21:24; 23:6, 30–35; 24:14; 25:3, 19). In postexilic times, by contrast, the phrase was used of the poor.

**11:17** There are two covenants. One is between the Lord as one party and the people, headed by the king, as the other. The second covenant, between king and people, is comparable to that made between David and the elders of Israel at Hebron (2 Sm 5:3).

*b*: Jgs 9:5. *c*: 2 Sm 8:7. *d*: 2 Kgs 23:3.

by which they would be the LORD's people; and another between the king and the people. [18]Thereupon all the people of the land went to the temple of Baal and demolished it. They shattered its altars and images completely, and slew Mattan, the priest of Baal, before the altars. Jehoiada the priest appointed a detachment for the house of the LORD, [19]and took the captains, the Carians, the guards, and all the people of the land, and they led the king down from the house of the LORD; they came through the guards' gate to the king's house, and Joash took his seat on the royal throne. [20]All the people of the land rejoiced and the city was quiet, now that Athaliah had been slain with the sword at the king's house.

## IX. Kings of Judah and Israel*

### CHAPTER 12

See RG 129–34

***Reign of Joash of Judah.*** [1]Joash was seven years old when he became king. [2]In the seventh year of Jehu, Joash became king, and he reigned forty years in Jerusalem. His mother's name was Zibiah, from Beersheba.

[3]Joash did what was right in the LORD's sight as long as he lived, because Jehoiada the priest guided him, [4]though the high places did not disappear; the people continued to sacrifice and to burn incense on the high places.

[5]Joash said to the priests: "All the funds for sacred purposes that are brought to the house of the LORD—the census tax, personal redemption money—and all funds that are freely brought to the house of the LORD, [6]the priests may take for themselves, each from his own vendor. However, they must make whatever repairs on the temple may prove necessary." [7]Nevertheless, as late as the twenty-third year of the reign of King Joash, the priests had not made needed repairs on the temple. [8]Accordingly, King Joash summoned the priest Jehoiada and the other priests. He asked, "Why do you not repair the temple? You must no longer take funds from your vendors, but you shall turn them over for the repairs." [9]So the priests agreed that they would neither take funds from the people nor make the repairs on the temple.

[10]Jehoiada the priest then took a chest, bored a hole in its lid, and set it beside the altar, on the right as one entered the house of the LORD. The priests who kept the doors would put into it all the silver that was brought to the house of the LORD. [11][e] When they noticed that there was a large amount of silver in the chest, the royal scribe would come up with the high priest, and they would gather up and weigh all the silver that was in the house of the LORD. [12]The amount thus realized they turned over to the workers assigned to the house of the LORD. They in turn would pay it to the carpenters and builders working in the house of the LORD, [13]and to the masons and stone cutters, and for the purchase of the wood and hewn stone used in repairing the breaches, and for any other expenses that were necessary to repair the house of the LORD. [14]None of the valuables brought to the house of the LORD were used there to make silver basins, snuffers, bowls, trumpets, or any gold or silver article. [15]Instead, they were given to the workers, and with them they repaired the house of the LORD. [16]Moreover, no reckoning was asked of those who were provided with the funds to give to the workers, because they held positions of trust. [17]The funds from reparation offerings and from purification offerings, however, were not brought to the house of the LORD; they belonged to the priests.

[18]Then Hazael, king of Aram, came up and attacked Gath. When he had taken it, Hazael resolved to go on to attack Jerusalem. [19]Joash,* king of Judah, took all the sa-

**12:1–17:5** This section recounts briefly the reigns of the last several kings of Israel and the kings of Judah contemporary with them. As always, the accounts of the kings are given in the order in which each came to the throne, without regard to which kingdom they ruled. See note on the similar section that begins in 1 Kgs 14:21.

**12:19 Joash**: in 2 Kings the name "Joash" and its variant "Jehoash" are interchangeable (see note on "Joram" and "Jehoram" at 1:17), whether in reference to the king of Judah (vv. 1–22) or his slightly later contemporary, Joash of Israel (13:10–25). Both forms are rendered "Joash" in this translation.

*e*: 2 Kgs 22:3–7.

cred offerings presented by his forebears, Jehoshaphat, Jehoram, and Ahaziah, kings of Judah, as well as his own, and all the gold there was in the treasuries of the house of the LORD and the king's house, and sent them to King Hazael of Aram, who then turned away from Jerusalem.

[20]The rest of the acts of Joash, with all that he did, are recorded in the book of the chronicles of the kings of Judah. [21]Certain of his officials* entered into a conspiracy and struck Joash down at Beth-millo. [22]Jozacar, son of Shimeath, and Jehozabad, son of Shomer, were the officials who struck and killed him. He was buried with his ancestors in the City of David, and his son Amaziah succeeded him as king.

## CHAPTER 13

See RG 129–34

***Reign of Jehoahaz of Israel.*** [1]In the twenty-third year of Joash, son of Ahaziah, king of Judah, Jehoahaz, son of Jehu, became king over Israel in Samaria for seventeen years.

[2]He did what was evil in the LORD's sight: he did not depart from following the sins that Jeroboam, son of Nebat, had caused Israel to commit. [3]The LORD was angry with Israel and for a long time gave them into the power of Hazael, king of Aram, and of Ben-hadad, son of Hazael. [4]Then Jehoahaz entreated the LORD, who heard him, since he saw the oppression to which the king of Aram had subjected Israel.[f] [5]So the LORD gave Israel a savior,* and the Israelites, freed from the power of Aram, dwelt in their own tents as formerly. [6]Nevertheless, they did not desist from the sins the house of Jeroboam had caused Israel to commit, but persisted in them. The Asherah* remained even in Samaria.[g] [7]No army was left to Jehoahaz, except fifty horses with ten chariots and ten thousand foot soldiers, since the king of Aram had destroyed them and trampled them like dust.

[8]The rest of the acts of Jehoahaz, with all that he did and his valor, are recorded in the book of the chronicles of the kings of Israel. [9]Jehoahaz rested with his ancestors; he was buried in Samaria and his son Joash succeeded him as king.

***Reign of Joash of Israel.*** [10]In the thirty-seventh year of Joash, king of Judah, Joash, son of Jehoahaz, became king over Israel in Samaria sixteen years.

[11]He did what was evil in the LORD's sight; he did not desist from any of the sins Jeroboam, son of Nebat, had caused Israel to commit, but persisted in them.

[12]* The rest of the acts of Joash, with all that he did and his valor, and how he fought with Amaziah, king of Judah, are recorded in the book of the chronicles of the kings of Israel. [13]Joash rested with his ancestors. Then Jeroboam sat on his throne. Joash was buried in Samaria with the kings of Israel.

***Elisha's Deathbed Prophecy.*** [14]When Elisha was suffering from the sickness of which he was to die, Joash, king of Israel, went down to weep over him. "My father, my father!"* he exclaimed, "Israel's chariot and steeds!"[h] [15]Elisha said to him, "Take bow and arrows," and he took bow and arrows. [16]* Elisha said to the king of Israel, "Rest your hand on the bow," and he rested his hand on it. Elisha placed his hands over the king's hands [17]and said, "Open the window toward the east." He opened it. Elisha said, "Shoot," and he shot. He said,

**12:21 Officials**: lit., "servants." The Hebrew *ebed* ("servant") has a wide range of meanings, always including service to another.

**13:5 A savior**: i.e., a military leader (cf. Jgs 3:9, 15). Here the identity of the savior is unclear, but the reappearance of a militant Elisha in this chapter after an absence of several chapters and nearly thirty years suggests the narrator may have had him in mind. Two generations later Joash's grandson, Jeroboam II, will also "save" Israel (14:27).

**13:6 Asherah**: see note on Ex 34:13.

**13:12–13** The conclusion to the reign of Joash is given again in 14:15–16. In both places it disrupts the standard pattern followed in the Books of Kings. The account of Joash's reign ends in vv. 12–13; this leaves the story of Elisha's last illness (in which Joash figures prominently) suspended between regnal accounts, much as the story of Elisha's succession to Elijah's prophetic office (chap. 2) was suspended between the accounts of Ahaziah and Joram. In 14:15–16 the concluding formula for Joash's reign interrupts the account of the reign of Amaziah of Judah (14:1–22), much as Joash himself invaded Amaziah's kingdom (14:11–14).

**13:14 My father, my father**: the way the king addresses the dying Elisha echoes Elisha's address to Elijah in 2:12.

**13:16–19** Symbolic acts, like prophetic oracles, were understood to unleash the power they expressed. Similar symbolic acts are seen in Ex 17:8–13; Jos 8:18–20; Ez 4:1–3.

*f:* 2 Kgs 14:26–27. *g:* Ex 34:13; 1 Kgs 16:33. *h:* 2 Kgs 2:12.

"An arrow of victory for the LORD!
An arrow of victory over Aram!
You will beat Aram at Aphek and finish
him!"

18Then he said to the king of Israel, "Take the
arrows," which he did. Elisha said to the king
of Israel, "Beat the ground!" He beat the
ground three times and stopped. 19The man
of God became angry with him and said,
"You should have beat five or six times. You
would have beaten Aram and finished him.
Now you will beat Aram only three times."
20And so Elisha died and was buried.

At that time of year, bands of Moabites
used to raid the land. 21Once some people
were burying a man, when suddenly they
saw such a raiding band. So they cast the
man into the grave of Elisha, and everyone
went off. But when the man came in contact
with the bones of Elisha, he came back to
life and got to his feet.[i]

22King Hazael of Aram oppressed Israel
all the days of Jehoahaz. 23But the LORD was
gracious with Israel and looked on them with
compassion because of his covenant with
Abraham, Isaac, and Jacob. He was unwilling to destroy them or to cast them out from
his presence even up to now. 24So when King
Hazael of Aram died and his son Ben-hadad
succeeded him as king, 25Joash, son of Jehoahaz, took back from Ben-hadad, son of Hazael, the cities Hazael had taken in battle from
Jehoahaz, his father. Three times Joash beat
him, and thus recovered the cities of Israel.

## CHAPTER 14

See RG 129-34

*Reign of Amaziah of Judah.* 1In the
second year* of Joash, son of Jehoahaz, king
of Israel, Amaziah, son of Joash, king of Judah, became king. 2He was twenty-five years
old when he became king, and he reigned
twenty-nine years in Jerusalem. His mother's
name was Jehoaddin, from Jerusalem.

3He did what was right in the LORD's
eyes, though not like David his father. He
did just as his father Joash had done, 4though
the high places did not disappear, and the
people continued to sacrifice and to burn incense on the high places.

5When Amaziah had the kingdom firmly
in hand, he struck down the officials who
had struck down the king, his father. 6But
their children he did not put to death, according to what is written in the book of the
law of Moses, which the LORD commanded:
"Parents shall not be put to death for their
children, nor shall children be put to death
for their parents; only for one's own crimes
shall a person be put to death."[j]

7Amaziah struck down ten thousand
Edomites in the Salt Valley. He took Sela in
battle and renamed it Joktheel, the name it
has to this day.[k]

8Then Amaziah sent messengers to Joash,
son of Jehoahaz, son of Jehu, king of Israel,
with this message: "Come, let us meet face
to face." 9Joash, king of Israel, sent this reply to Amaziah, king of Judah: "A thistle of
Lebanon sent word to a cedar of Lebanon,
'Give your daughter to my son in marriage,'
but an animal of Lebanon passed by and
trampled the thistle underfoot.[l] 10You have
indeed struck down Edom, and your heart is
lifted up; enjoy your glory, but stay home!
Why bring misfortune and failure on yourself and on Judah with you?" 11But Amaziah
did not listen. So Joash, king of Israel, advanced, and he and Amaziah, king of Judah,
met face to face at Beth-shemesh of Judah,
12and Judah was defeated by Israel, and all
fled to their tents. 13But Amaziah, king of Judah, son of Joash, son of Ahaziah, was captured by Joash, king of Israel, at Beth-shemesh. When they came to Jerusalem Joash
tore down the wall of Jerusalem, from the
Gate of Ephraim to the Corner Gate, four
hundred cubits. 14He took all the gold and
silver and all the vessels found in the house
of the LORD and in the treasuries of the

**14:1–2 In the second year . . . twenty-nine years in Jerusalem**: as they stand, the chronological data in the introductions to the reigns of the kings of Judah and Israel are incompatible with one another. The kings of Judah between Athaliah and Ahaz are assigned too many years in all to correspond to the reigns in Israel from Jehu to the fall of Samaria. Various theories have been proposed in an attempt to explain the discrepancy, such as co-regencies, or textual corruption in the process of transmission.

*i:* Sir 48:14. *j:* Dt 24:16; Ez 18:20. *k:* 2 Sm 8:13–14. *l:* Jgs 9:8–15.

king's house, and hostages as well. Then he returned to Samaria.

15* The rest of the acts of Joash, what he did and his valor, and how he made war against Amaziah, king of Judah, are recorded in the book of the chronicles of the kings of Israel. 16 Joash rested with his ancestors; he was buried in Samaria with the kings of Israel, and his son Jeroboam succeeded him as king.

17* Amaziah, son of Joash, king of Judah, survived Joash, son of Jehoahaz, king of Israel, by fifteen years. 18 The rest of the acts of Amaziah are recorded in the book of the chronicles of the kings of Judah. 19 When a conspiracy was formed against him in Jerusalem, he fled to Lachish. But he was pursued to Lachish and killed there. 20 He was brought back on horses and was buried in Jerusalem with his ancestors in the City of David. 21 Thereupon all the people of Judah* took Azariah, who was only sixteen years old, and made him king to succeed Amaziah, his father. 22 It was he who rebuilt Elath and restored it to Judah, after the king rested with his ancestors.

***Reign of Jeroboam II of Israel.*** 23 In the fifteenth year of Amaziah, son of Joash, king of Judah, Jeroboam, son of Joash, king of Israel, became king in Samaria for forty-one years.

24 He did evil in the LORD's sight; he did not desist from any of the sins that Jeroboam, son of Nebat, had caused Israel to commit. 25 He restored the boundaries of Israel from Lebo-hamath to the sea of the Arabah,* as the LORD, the God of Israel, had foretold through his servant, the prophet Jonah, son of Amittai, from Gath-hepher. 26 For the LORD saw the very bitter affliction of Israel, where there was neither bond nor free, no one at all to help Israel. 27 Since the LORD had not resolved to wipe out the name of Israel from under the heavens, he saved them through Jeroboam, son of Joash.

28 The rest of the acts of Jeroboam, with all that he did and his valor, how he fought, and how he regained Damascus and Hamath for Israel, are recorded in the book of the chronicles of the kings of Israel. 29 Jeroboam rested with his ancestors, the kings of Israel, and his son Zechariah succeeded him as king.

## CHAPTER 15

See RG 129–34

***Reign of Azariah of Judah.*** 1 In the twenty-seventh year* of Jeroboam, king of Israel, Azariah, son of Amaziah, king of Judah, became king. 2 He was sixteen years old when he became king, and he reigned fifty-two years in Jerusalem. His mother's name was Jecholiah, from Jerusalem.

3 He did what was right in the LORD's sight, just as his father Amaziah had done, 4 though the high places did not disappear, and the people continued to sacrifice and to burn incense on the high places. 5 The LORD afflicted the king, and he was a leper until the day he died. He lived in a house apart, while Jotham, the king's son, was master of the palace and ruled the people of the land.*

6 The rest of the acts of Azariah, and all that he did, are recorded in the book of the chronicles of the kings of Judah. 7 Azariah rested with his ancestors, and was buried with them in the City of David, and his son Jotham succeeded him as king.

***Reign of Zechariah of Israel.*** 8 In the thirty-eighth year of Azariah, king of Judah, Zechariah, son of Jeroboam, became king over Israel in Samaria for six months.

9 He did what was evil in the LORD's sight, as his ancestors had done, and did not desist from the sins that Jeroboam, son of Nebat, had caused Israel to commit. 10 Shallum, son of Jabesh, plotted against him and struck him down at Ibleam. He killed him and reigned in his place.

11 As for the rest of the acts of Zechariah, these are recorded in the book of the chronicles of the kings of Israel. 12 This was the

**14:15–16** See note on 13:12–13.

**14:17** See note on vv. 1–2.

**14:21 All the people of Judah**: this phrase may refer to the army (compare, for example, "all Israel" in 1 Kgs 16:16–17). If this is its meaning here, then Amaziah's assassination and Azariah's succession are owing to a military coup. **Azariah**: also called Uzziah in many texts.

**14:25 Sea of the Arabah**: the Dead Sea. **Jonah, son of Amittai**: see note on Jon 1:1.

**15:1 Twenty-seventh year**: see note on 14:1–2.

**15:5 People of the land**: see note on 11:14.

word the LORD had spoken to Jehu: Sons of
your line to the fourth generation shall sit
upon the throne of Israel; and so it was.[m]

***Reign of Shallum of Israel.*** [13]Shallum, son
of Jabesh, became king in the thirty-ninth
year of Uzziah, king of Judah; he reigned
one month in Samaria.

[14]Menahem, son of Gadi, came up from
Tirzah to Samaria, and struck down Shallum, son of Jabesh, in Samaria. He killed
him and reigned in his place.

[15]As for the rest of the acts of Shallum,
with the conspiracy he carried out, these are
recorded in the book of the chronicles of the
kings of Israel. [16]At that time, Menahem attacked Tappuah, all its inhabitants, and its
whole district as far as Tirzah, because they
did not let him in. He attacked them; he even
ripped open all their pregnant women.

***Reign of Menahem of Israel.*** [17]In the thirty-
ninth year of Azariah, king of Judah, Menahem, son of Gadi, became king over Israel for
ten years in Samaria. [18]He did what was evil
in the LORD's sight as long as he lived, not desisting from the sins that Jeroboam, son of
Nebat, had caused Israel to commit. [19]Pul,*
king of Assyria, came against the land. But
Menahem gave Pul a thousand talents of silver to have his help in holding onto his kingdom. [20]Menahem paid out silver on behalf of
Israel, that is, for all the people of substance,
by giving the king of Assyria fifty shekels of
silver for each one. So the king of Assyria
went home and did not stay in the land.

[21]The rest of the acts of Menahem, with
all that he did, are recorded in the book of
the chronicles of the kings of Israel. [22]Men-
ahem rested with his ancestors, and his son
Pekahiah succeeded him as king.

***Reign of Pekahiah of Israel.*** [23]In the fiftieth year of Azariah, king of Judah, Pekahiah,
son of Menahem, became king over Israel in
Samaria for two years.

[24]He did what was evil in the LORD's
sight, not desisting from the sins that Jeroboam, son of Nebat, had caused Israel to
commit. [25]His adjutant Pekah, son of Remaliah, conspired against him, and struck him
down at Samaria within the palace stronghold; he had with him fifty men from Gilead.
He killed him and reigned in his place. [26]As
for the rest of the acts of Pekahiah, with all
that he did, these are recorded in the book of
the chronicles of the kings of Israel.

***Reign of Pekah of Israel.*** [27*] In the fifty-
second year of Azariah, king of Judah, Pekah, son of Remaliah, became king over Israel in Samaria for twenty years.

[28]He did what was evil in the LORD's
sight, not desisting from the sins that Jeroboam, son of Nebat, had caused Israel to
commit. [29]In the days of Pekah, king of Israel, Tiglath-pileser, king of Assyria, came
and took Ijon, Abel-beth-maacah, Janoah,
Kedesh, Hazor, Gilead, and Galilee—all the
land of Naphtali—deporting the inhabitants
to Assyria. [30*] Hoshea, son of Elah, carried
out a conspiracy against Pekah, son of Remaliah; he struck and killed him, and succeeded him as king in the twentieth year of
Jotham, son of Uzziah.

[31]As for the rest of the acts of Pekah, with
all that he did, these are recorded in the book
of the chronicles of the kings of Israel.

***Reign of Jotham of Judah.*** [32]In the second
year of Pekah, son of Remaliah, king of Israel, Jotham, son of Uzziah, king of Judah,
became king. [33]He was twenty-five years
old when he became king, and he reigned
sixteen years in Jerusalem. His mother's
name was Jerusha, daughter of Zadok.

[34]He did what was right in the LORD's
sight, just as his father Uzziah had done,
[35]though the high places did not disappear,
and the people continued to sacrifice and to
burn incense on the high places. It was he

**15:19 Pul**: the Babylonian throne name of the Assyrian Tiglath-pileser III; cf. v. 29.

**15:27** The twenty years here ascribed to Pekah are difficult to reconcile with other chronological notices about the kings. One theory would see Pekah and Menahem as rival kings over parts of a divided Israelite territory; this could explain Menahem's concern for Assyrian support (vv. 19–20) and Assyria's attack on Pekah (v. 29). See 16:1 and note on 14:1–2.

**15:30** The twenty years here reckoned to Jotham of Judah may include his co-regency with Azariah (v. 5); otherwise they are impossible to reconcile with v. 33, which ascribes him only sixteen years. The verse also appears to contradict 16:1, which has Jotham's son and successor, Ahaz, coming to the throne while Pekah still reigns in Israel, and 17:1, which dates Hoshea's accession to the throne to the twelfth year of Ahaz.

*m:* 2 Kgs 10:30.

who built the Upper Gate* of the LORD's house.

[36]The rest of the acts of Jotham, with what he did, are recorded in the book of the chronicles of the kings of Judah. [37]It was at that time that the LORD began to unleash Rezin, king of Aram, and Pekah, son of Remaliah, against Judah.[n] [38]Jotham rested with his ancestors; he was buried with his ancestors in the City of David his father, and his son Ahaz succeeded him as king.

## CHAPTER 16

See RG 129-34

***Reign of Ahaz of Judah.**** [1]In the seventeenth year of Pekah, son of Remaliah, Ahaz, son of Jotham, king of Judah, became king. [2]Ahaz was twenty years old when he became king, and he reigned sixteen years in Jerusalem.

He did not do what was right in the sight of the LORD his God, as David his father had done. [3]He walked in the way of the kings of Israel; he even immolated his child by fire, in accordance with the abominable practices of the nations whom the LORD had dispossessed before the Israelites.[o] [4]Further, he sacrificed and burned incense on the high places, on hills, and under every green tree.[p]

[5]Then Rezin, king of Aram, and Pekah, son of Remaliah, king of Israel, came up to Jerusalem to attack it. Although they besieged Ahaz, they were unable to do battle. [6](In those days Rezin, king of Aram, recovered Elath for Aram, and drove the Judahites out of it. The Edomites then entered Elath, which they have occupied until the present.)

[7]Meanwhile, Ahaz sent messengers to Tiglath-pileser, king of Assyria, with the plea: "I am your servant and your son. Come up and rescue me from the power of the king of Aram and the king of Israel, who are attacking me." [8]Ahaz took the silver and gold that were in the house of the LORD and in the treasuries of the king's house and sent them as a present to the king of Assyria. [9]The king of Assyria listened to him and moved against Damascus, captured it, deported its inhabitants to Kir, and put Rezin to death.

[10]King Ahaz went to Damascus to meet Tiglath-pileser, king of Assyria. When he saw the altar in Damascus, King Ahaz sent to Uriah the priest a model of the altar and a detailed design of its construction. [11]Uriah the priest built an altar according to the plans which King Ahaz sent him from Damascus, and had it completed by the time King Ahaz returned from Damascus. [12]On his arrival from Damascus, the king inspected the altar; the king approached the altar, went up [13]and sacrificed his burnt offering and grain offering, pouring out his libation, and sprinkling the blood of his communion offerings on the altar. [14]The bronze altar that stood before the LORD he brought from the front of the temple—that is, from the space between the new altar and the house of the LORD—and set it on the north side of his altar. [15][q] King Ahaz commanded Uriah the priest, "Upon the large altar sacrifice the morning burnt offering and the evening grain offering, the king's burnt offering and grain offering, and the burnt offering and grain offering of the people of the land.* Their libations you must sprinkle on it along with all the blood of burnt offerings and sacrifices. But the old bronze altar shall be mine for consultation." [16]Uriah the priest did just as King Ahaz had commanded. [17]King Ahaz detached the panels from the stands and removed the basins from them; he also took down the bronze sea from the bronze oxen that supported it, and set it on a stone pavement. [18]In deference to the king of Assyria he removed the sabbath

**15:35 The Upper Gate**: also called the Gate of Benjamin; cf. Jer 20:2; Ez 9:2.

**16:1–20** Firmly dated events bearing on chaps. 16–20 are: the fall of Damascus (16:9) in 732 B.C., the fall of Samaria (18:9–11) in 722/721 B.C., and Sennacherib's invasion of Judah (18:13) in 701 B.C., which both in Kings and in Is 36:1 occurs in the fourteenth year of Hezekiah. These data make it possible to connect the chronology of Israel and Judah to the larger chronology of ancient Near Eastern history, but they also complicate further the already vexed problem of inconsistencies in the biblical data about accession years and lengths of reign.

**16:15 People of the land**: see note on 11:14. **For consultation**: perhaps the introduction into Judah of the Babylonian practice of reading omens from animal sacrifices; cf. Ez 21:26.

*n:* Is 7:1–16. *o:* Lv 18:21; Dt 18:10. *p:* Dt 12:2. *q:* Ex 29:38–41; Nm 28:3–8.

canopy that had been set up in the house of
the LORD and the king's outside entrance* to
the temple.
19 The rest of the acts of Ahaz, with what
he did, are recorded in the book of the chronicles of the kings of Judah. 20 Ahaz rested
with his ancestors; he was buried with his
ancestors in the City of David, and his son
Hezekiah succeeded him as king.

## CHAPTER 17

See RG 129–34

***Reign of Hoshea of Israel.*** 1 In the
twelfth year of Ahaz, king of Judah, Hoshea,
son of Elah, became king in Samaria over Israel for nine years.
2 He did what was evil in the LORD's sight,
yet not to the extent of the kings of Israel before him. 3 Shalmaneser,* king of Assyria,
advanced against him, and Hoshea became
his vassal and paid him tribute.[r] 4 But the
king of Assyria found Hoshea guilty of conspiracy for sending messengers to the king
of Egypt at Sais, and for failure to pay the
annual tribute to the king of Assyria. So the
king of Assyria arrested and imprisoned
him. 5 Then the king of Assyria* occupied the
whole land and attacked Samaria, which he
besieged for three years.

## X. The End of Israel*

***Israelites Deported.*** 6 In Hoshea's ninth year,
the king of Assyria took Samaria, deported
the Israelites to Assyria, and settled them in
Halah, and at the Habor, a river of Gozan,
and in the cities of the Medes.[s] 7 This came
about because the Israelites sinned against
the LORD, their God, who had brought them
up from the land of Egypt, from under the
hand of Pharaoh, king of Egypt. They venerated other gods, 8[t] they followed the rites of
the nations whom the LORD had dispossessed before the Israelites and those that the
kings of Israel had practiced. 9 They adopted
unlawful practices toward the LORD, their
God. They built high places in all their cities,
from guard post to garrisoned town. 10 They
set up pillars and asherahs* for themselves
on every high hill and under every green
tree. 11 They burned incense there, on all the
high places, like the nations whom the LORD
had sent into exile at their coming. They did
evil things that provoked the LORD, 12 and
served idols, although the LORD had told
them: You must not do this.
13[u] The LORD warned Israel and Judah by
every prophet and seer: Give up your evil
ways and keep my commandments and statutes, in accordance with the entire law
which I enjoined on your ancestors and
which I sent you by my servants the prophets. 14 But they did not listen. They grew as
stiff-necked as their ancestors, who had not
believed in the LORD, their God.[v] 15 They rejected his statutes, the covenant he had made
with their ancestors, and the warnings he
had given them. They followed emptiness
and became empty; they followed the surrounding nations whom the LORD had commanded them not to imitate.[w] 16 They abandoned all the commandments of the LORD,
their God: they made for themselves two
molten calves; they made an asherah; they
bowed down to all the host of heaven; they
served Baal.[x] 17[y] They immolated their sons
and daughters by fire. They practiced augury
and divination. They surrendered themselves to doing what was evil in the LORD's
sight, and provoked him.

**16:18 Sabbath canopy . . . outside entrance**: the Hebrew is obscure, but as a vassal Ahaz must have had to divest himself of signs of sovereignty.

**17:3 Shalmaneser**: son and successor of the Assyrian king Tiglath-pileser III. **Vassal**: lit., "servant"; cf. 16:7; so also in 24:1.

**17:5 The king of Assyria**: Shalmaneser was succeeded by Sargon II, who usurped the Assyrian throne in 722/721 B.C. In his inscriptions, Sargon claims to have captured Samaria during the first year of his reign.

**17:6–41** This brief section is the Deuteronomistic historian's theological reflection on the causes and aftermath of Assyria's conquest of the Northern Kingdom. The text contrasts the Israelites, who were deported (v. 6) because they abandoned the worship of the Lord (vv. 7–23), with the foreigners who were brought into the land (v. 24) and undertook, however imperfectly, to worship the Lord alongside their own traditional deities (vv. 25–34a). The last verses recapitulate the apostasy of the Israelites (vv. 34b–40) and the syncretism of the foreigners (v. 41). This is a deliberately disparaging, and not wholly accurate, account of the origin of the Samaritans; it reflects the hostility the Judahites continued to hold toward the inhabitants of the northern territories.

**17:10 Asherahs**: see note on Ex 34:13.

*r*: 2 Kgs 18:9. *s*: 2 Kgs 18:10–11; Tb 1:2. *t*: Ex 23:24; 34:13; Dt 12:2. *u*: Jer 25:5. *v*: Dt 9:13. *w*: Jer 2:5. *x*: Ex 34:13; Dt 4:19; 17:2–3; 1 Kgs 12:28; 16:33. *y*: Lv 18:21; Dt 18:10.

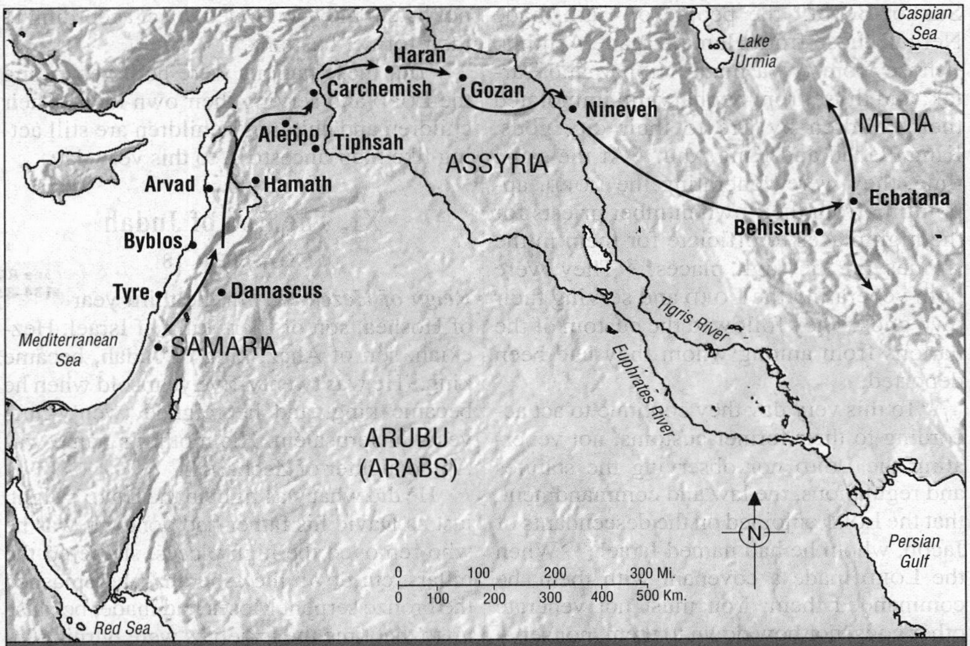


**Exile of Northern Kingdom**

18[z] The LORD became enraged, and removed them from his presence. Only the
tribe of Judah was left. 19 Even the people of
Judah did not keep the commandments of
the LORD, their God, but followed the rites
practiced by Israel. 20 So the LORD rejected
the entire people of Israel: he afflicted them
and delivered them over to plunderers, finally casting them from his presence.[a]
21 When he tore Israel away from the house
of David, they made Jeroboam, son of Nebat, king; but Jeroboam lured the Israelites
away from the LORD, causing them to commit a great sin.[b] 22 The Israelites imitated Jeroboam in all the sins he committed; they
would not depart from them.

23 Finally, the LORD removed Israel from
his presence, just as he had declared through
all his servants, the prophets. Thus Israel
went into exile from their native soil to Assyria until this very day.

***Foreigners Deported to Israel.*** 24 The king
of Assyria brought people from Babylon,
Cuthah, Avva, Hamath, and Sepharvaim,
and settled them in the cities of Samaria in
place of the Israelites. They took possession
of Samaria and dwelt in its cities. 25 When
they first settled there, they did not venerate
the LORD, so he sent lions among them that
killed some of them. 26 A report reached the
king of Assyria: "The nations you deported
and settled in the cities of Samaria do not
know the proper worship of the god of the
land, so he has sent lions among them that
are killing them, since they do not know the
law of the god of the land." 27 The king of Assyria gave the order, "Send back some of the
priests you deported, to go there and settle,
to teach them the proper worship of the god
of the land." 28 So one of the priests who had
been deported from Samaria returned and
settled in Bethel, and began to teach them
how to venerate the LORD.

29 Thus each of these nations continued
to make its own gods, setting them up in
the shrines of the high places the Samari-
ans had made: each nation in the cities in
which they dwelt. 30 The Babylonians made

*z:* Sir 48:15. *a:* Jer 25:9. *b:* 1 Kgs 12:20, 26–33; 13:34.

Sukkot-Benot;* the people of Cuth made Nergal; those from Hamath made Ashima; [31]those from Avva made Nibhaz and Tartak; and those from Sepharvaim immolated their children by fire to their city gods, King Hadad and King Anu. [32]At the same time, they were venerating the LORD, appointing from their own number priests for the high places to officiate for them in the shrines on the high places. [33]They were both venerating the LORD and serving their own gods. They followed the custom of the nations from among whom they had been deported.

[34]To this very day they continue to act according to their former customs, not venerating the LORD nor observing the statutes and regulations, the law and commandment, that the LORD enjoined on the descendants of Jacob, whom he had named Israel.[c] [35]When the LORD made a covenant with them, he commanded them: You must not venerate other gods, nor bow down to them, nor serve them, nor offer sacrifice to them,[d] [36]but only to the LORD, who brought you up from the land of Egypt with great power and outstretched arm. Him shall you venerate, to him shall you bow down, and to him shall you offer sacrifice. [37]You must be careful always to observe the statutes and ordinances, the law and commandment, which he wrote for you; you must not venerate other gods. [38]The covenant I made with you, you must not forget; you must not venerate other gods. [39]You must venerate only the LORD, your God; it is he who will deliver you from the power of all your enemies. [40]But they did not listen; they continued to act according to their former customs.

[41]But these nations were both venerating the LORD and serving their own idols. Their children and children's children are still acting like their ancestors, to this very day.

## XI. The End of Judah*

### CHAPTER 18

See RG 134–35

***Reign of Hezekiah.*** [1]In the third year of Hoshea, son of Elah, king of Israel, Hezekiah, son of Ahaz, king of Judah, became king. [2]He was twenty-five years old when he became king, and he reigned twenty-nine years in Jerusalem. His mother's name was Abi, daughter of Zechariah.

[3]He did what was right in the LORD's sight, just as David his father had done. [4]It was he who removed the high places, shattered the pillars, cut down the asherah,* and smashed the bronze serpent Moses had made, because up to that time the Israelites were burning incense to it. (It was called Nehushtan.)[e] [5]He put his trust in the LORD, the God of Israel; and neither before nor after him was there anyone like him among all the kings of Judah. [6]Hezekiah held fast to the LORD and never turned away from following him, but observed the commandments the LORD had given Moses. [7]The LORD was with him, and he succeeded in all he set out to do. He rebelled against the king of Assyria and did not serve him. [8]It was he who struck the Philistines as far as Gaza, and all its territory from guard post to garrisoned town.

[9]* In the fourth year of King Hezekiah,

**17:30 Sukkot-Benot**: several of the divine names in vv. 30–31 are problematic or conjectural. Sukkot-Benot is unknown, but the name may have been corrupted from that of Sarpanitu, the consort of the Babylonian god Marduk.

**18:1–25:30** The Books of Kings end, as they began, with the people of the Lord in a single kingdom, Judah, centered on the capital, Jerusalem, and the Solomonic Temple. The reigns of two reformer kings, both praised, are recounted at length: Hezekiah (chaps. 18–20) and Josiah (22:1–23:30). Each is followed by shorter accounts of two kings who are condemned: Manasseh and Amon (chap. 21) and Jehoahaz and Jehoiakim (23:31–24:7). The book ends with the last days of Judah under Jehoiachin and Zedekiah and the beginning of the Babylonian exile.

**18:4 Asherah**: see note on Ex 34:13. **Nehushtan**: the name *nehushtan* contains several wordplays in Hebrew. It recalls the word "serpent" (*nahash*), the word "bronze" (*nehoshet*), and the word "to read omens" (*nihesh*). The sentence is also unclear about who named the bronze serpent "Nehushtan"—whether Moses when he made it, or the people when they venerated it, or Hezekiah when he destroyed it.

**18:9** The correlations between the reigns of Hezekiah and Hoshea in vv. 9–10 conflict with other biblical data and with the date for the fall of Samaria, 722/721 B.C. (see note on 16:1–20). Since Sennacherib's invasion in the fourteenth year of Hezekiah (v. 13) took place in 701, Hezekiah cannot have been on the throne twenty years earlier. Various solutions have been proposed: scribal errors in writing the numbers; a Hezekian co-regency with his father Ahaz beginning

*c:* Gn 32:29; 35:10. *d:* Ex 20:3–6. *e:* Ex 23:24; 34:13; Nm 21:4–9; Dt 12:2; Wis 16:5–7; Jn 3:14.

which was the seventh year of Hoshea, son of Elah, king of Israel, Shalmaneser, king of Assyria, attacked Samaria and laid siege to it, 10[f] and after three years they captured it. In the sixth year of Hezekiah, the ninth year of Hoshea, king of Israel, Samaria was taken. 11 The king of Assyria then deported the Israelites to Assyria and led them off to Halah, and the Habor, a river of Gozan, and the cities of the Medes. 12 This happened because they did not obey the LORD, their God, but violated his covenant; they did not obey nor do all that Moses, the servant of the LORD, commanded.[g]

***Sennacherib and Hezekiah.*** 13* In the fourteenth year of King Hezekiah, Sennacherib, king of Assyria,* attacked all the fortified cities of Judah and captured them.[h] 14 Hezekiah, king of Judah, sent this message to the king of Assyria at Lachish: "I have done wrong. Leave me, and whatever you impose on me I will bear." The king of Assyria exacted three hundred talents of silver and thirty talents of gold from Hezekiah, king of Judah. 15 Hezekiah gave him all the funds there were in the house of the LORD and in the treasuries of the king's house. 16 At the same time, Hezekiah removed the nave doors and the uprights of the house of the LORD, which the king of Judah had ordered to be overlaid with gold, and gave them to the king of Assyria.[i]

17 The king of Assyria sent the general, the lord chamberlain, and the commander* from Lachish with a great army to King Hezekiah at Jerusalem. They went up and came to Jerusalem, to the conduit of the upper pool on the highway of the fuller's field, where they took their stand. 18 They called for the king, but Eliakim, son of Hilkiah, the master of the palace, came out, along with Shebnah the scribe and the chancellor Joah, son of Asaph.[j]

19 The commander said to them, "Tell Hezekiah, 'Thus says the great king, the king of

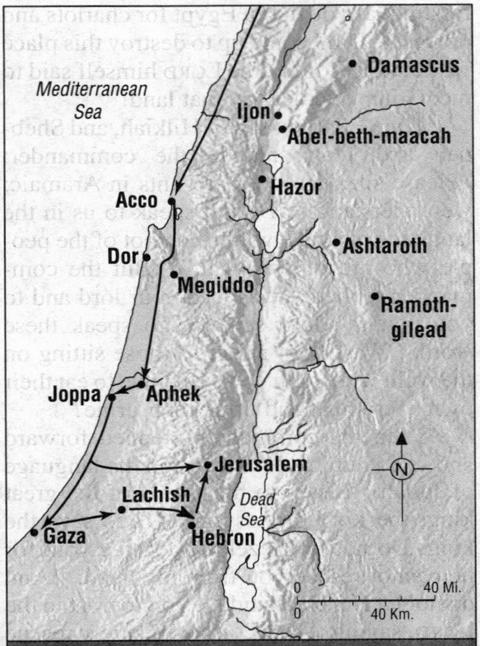

Campaign of Sennacherib

Assyria: On what do you base this trust of yours? 20 Do you think mere words substitute for strategy and might in war? In whom, then, do you place your trust, that you rebel against me? 21 Do you trust in Egypt, that broken reed of a staff, which pierces the hand of anyone who leans on it? That is what Pharaoh, king of Egypt, is to all who trust in him.[k] 22 Or do you people say to me, "It is in the LORD our God we trust!"? Is it not he whose high places and altars Hezekiah has removed, commanding Judah and Jerusalem, "Worship before this altar in Jerusalem"?'

23 "Now, make a wager with my lord, the king of Assyria: I will give you two thousand horses if you are able to put riders on them. 24 How then can you turn back even a captain, one of the least servants of my lord,

in 729; etc. None of the solutions has won a consensus among historians.

**18:13–20:19** This material is found also in Is 36–39, with one long addition (Is 38:9–20) and only a few other changes.

**18:13** Sennacherib succeeded Sargon II as king of Assyria. His Judean campaign was waged in 701 B.C. See notes on 16:1–20 and 18:9.

**18:17 General, the lord chamberlain . . . commander**: the text lists three major functionaries by their Assyrian titles, of which only the first, more nearly "lord lieutenant," is military in origin; the commander was technically the king's chief butler.

*f:* 2 Kgs 17:5–6; Tb 1:2. *g:* 2 Kgs 17:6–23; Ex 24:7. *h:* Sir 48:18–21. *i:* 1 Kgs 6:31–35. *j:* Is 22:15–25. *k:* Is 30:1–7; 31:1–3; Ez 29:6–7.

trusting, as you do, in Egypt for chariots and horses? [25]Did I come up to destroy this place without the LORD? The LORD himself said to me: Go up and destroy that land!"

[26]Then Eliakim, son of Hilkiah, and Shebnah and Joah said to the commander: "Please speak to your servants in Aramaic; we understand it. Do not speak to us in the language of Judah within earshot of the people who are on the wall." [27]But the commander replied: "Was it to your lord and to you that my lord sent me to speak these words? Was it not rather to those sitting on the wall, who, with you, will have to eat their own excrement and drink their urine?"*

[28]Then the commander stepped forward and cried out in a loud voice in the language of Judah, "Listen to the words of the great king, the king of Assyria. [29]Thus says the king: Do not let Hezekiah deceive you, for he cannot rescue you from my hand. [30]And do not let Hezekiah induce you to trust in the LORD, saying, 'The LORD will surely rescue us, and this city will not be handed over to the king of Assyria.' [31]Do not listen to Hezekiah, for thus says the king of Assyria: Make peace with me, and surrender to me! Eat, each of you, from your vine, each from your own fig tree. Drink water, each from your own well, [32]until I arrive and take you to a land like your own, a land of grain and wine, a land of bread and vineyards, a land of rich olives and honey. Live, and do not die! And do not listen to Hezekiah when he would incite you by saying, 'The LORD will rescue us.' [33]Has any of the gods of the nations ever rescued his land from the power of the king of Assyria? [34]Where are the gods of Hamath and Arpad? Where are the gods of Sepharvaim, Hena, and Ivvah? Did they indeed rescue Samaria from my power?* [35]Which of the gods for all these lands ever rescued his land from my power? Will the LORD then rescue Jerusalem from my power?" [36]But the people remained silent and did not answer at all, for the king's command was, "Do not answer him."

[37]Then the master of the palace, Eliakim, son of Hilkiah, Shebnah the scribe, and the chancellor Joah, son of Asaph, came to Hezekiah with their garments torn, and reported to him the words of the commander.

## CHAPTER 19

See RG 134-35

***Hezekiah and Isaiah.*** [1]When King Hezekiah heard this, he tore his garments, covered himself with sackcloth, and went into the house of the LORD. [2]He sent Eliakim, the master of the palace, Shebnah the scribe, and the elders of the priests, covered with sackcloth, to tell the prophet Isaiah, son of Amoz, [3]"Thus says Hezekiah:

A day of distress and rebuke,
  a day of disgrace is this day!
Children are due to come forth,
  but the strength to give birth is lacking.*

[4]Perhaps the LORD, your God, will hear all the words of the commander, whom his lord, the king of Assyria, sent to taunt the living God, and will rebuke him for the words which the LORD, your God, has heard. So lift up a prayer for the remnant that is here." [5]When the servants of King Hezekiah had come to Isaiah, [6]he said to them, "Tell this to your lord: Thus says the LORD: Do not be frightened by the words you have heard, by which the deputies of the king of Assyria have blasphemed me.[l] [7]I am putting in him such a spirit that when he hears a report he will return to his land. I will make him fall by the sword in his land."

[8]When the commander, on his return, heard that the king of Assyria had withdrawn from Lachish, he found him besieging Libnah.

***Sennacherib, Hezekiah, and Isaiah.*** [9]The

**18:27 Excrement . . . urine**: the reference is to the famine that results from a prolonged siege (compare 6:24–25; Dt 28:53–57). For public reading, ancient tradition (e.g., the Qere reading of the Masoretic text) softened the terms to "eat their own waste and drink their own bodies' water."

**18:34 Did they indeed . . . power?**: some time after the fall of Samaria in 722/721 B.C., Hamath, Arpad, and other small states in the region formed an anti-Assyrian coalition. If the coalition had succeeded, it could have broken Assyrian control over the whole region, including Samaria, and allowed the kingdom of Israel to free itself. When Assyria crushed the coalition, it also crushed Israel's hopes for liberation.

**19:3** See note on Is 37:3.

*l:* Is 10:5–14.

king of Assyria heard a report: “Tirhakah,
king of Ethiopia, has come out to fight
against you.” Again he sent messengers to
Hezekiah to say: 10 “Thus shall you say to
Hezekiah, king of Judah: Do not let your
God in whom you trust deceive you by saying, ‘Jerusalem will not be handed over to
the king of Assyria.’ 11 You, certainly, have
heard what the kings of Assyria have done to
all the lands: they put them under the ban!
And are you to be rescued? 12[m] Did the gods
of the nations whom my fathers destroyed
deliver them—Gozan, Haran, Rezeph, or the
Edenites in Telassar? 13 Where are the king
of Hamath, the king of Arpad, or the kings of
the cities Sepharvaim, Hena and Ivvah?”

14 Hezekiah took the letter from the hand
of the messengers and read it; then he went
up to the house of the LORD, and spreading it
out before the LORD, 15 Hezekiah prayed in
the LORD’s presence: “LORD, God of Israel,
enthroned on the cherubim! You alone are
God over all the kingdoms of the earth. It is
you who made the heavens and the earth.[n]
16 Incline your ear, LORD, and listen! Open
your eyes, LORD, and see! Hear the words
Sennacherib has sent to taunt the living God.
17 Truly, O LORD, the kings of Assyria have
laid waste the nations and their lands. 18 They
gave their gods to the fire—they were not
gods at all, but the work of human hands—
wood and stone, they destroyed them.
19 Therefore, LORD, our God, save us from
this man’s power, that all the kingdoms of
the earth may know that you alone, LORD,
are God.”[o]

20 Then Isaiah, son of Amoz, sent this message to Hezekiah: “Thus says the LORD, the
God of Israel, to whom you have prayed
concerning Sennacherib, king of Assyria: I
have listened! 21* This is the word the LORD
has spoken concerning him:

She despises you, laughs you to scorn,
  the virgin daughter Zion!
Behind you she wags her head,
  daughter Jerusalem.
22 Whom have you insulted and blasphemed,
  at whom have you raised your voice
And lifted up your eyes on high?
  At the Holy One of Israel!
23 Through the mouths of your messengers
  you insulted the Lord when you said,
‘With my many chariots I went up
  to the tops of the peaks,
  to the recesses of Lebanon,
To cut down its lofty cedars,
  its choice cypresses;
I reached to the farthest shelter,
  the forest ranges.
24 I myself dug wells
  and drank foreign waters,
Drying up all the rivers of Egypt
  beneath the soles of my feet.’

25 “Have you not heard?
  A long time ago I prepared it,
  from days of old I planned it.
Now I have brought it about:
You are here to reduce
  fortified cities to heaps of ruins,
26 Their people powerless,
  dismayed and distraught.
They are plants of the field,
  green growth,
  thatch on the rooftops,
Grain scorched by the east wind.
27 I know when you stand or sit,
  when you come or go[p]
  and how you rage against me.

28 Because you rage against me,
  and your smugness has reached my
    ears,
I will put my hook in your nose
  and my bit in your mouth,
And make you leave by the way you
    came.
29 “This shall be a sign for you:
This year you shall eat the aftergrowth,
  next year, what grows of itself;
But in the third year, sow and reap,
  plant vineyards and eat their fruit!
30 The remaining survivors of the house of
    Judah
  shall again strike root below
  and bear fruit above.

**19:21–31** Verses 21–28 are addressed to Sennacherib, vv. 29–31 to Judah.

*m:* 2 Kgs 17:6, 24; 18:34. *n:* Ex 25:17–22; 1 Kgs 6:23–28; 8:6–7. *o:* 1 Kgs 18:36. *p:* Ps 139:2–3.

31 For out of Jerusalem shall come a
remnant,
and from Mount Zion, survivors.
The zeal of the LORD of hosts shall do this.

32 "Therefore, thus says the LORD about
the king:

He shall not come as far as this city,
nor shoot there an arrow,
nor confront it with a shield,
Nor cast up a siege-work against it.
33 By the way he came he shall leave,
never coming as far as this city,
oracle of the LORD.
34 I will shield and save this city
for my own sake and the sake of David
my servant."[q]

35 That night the angel of the LORD went
forth and struck down one hundred and
eighty-five thousand men in the Assyrian
camp. Early the next morning, there they
were, dead, all those corpses![r] 36 So Sennacherib, the king of Assyria, broke camp, departed, returned home, and stayed in Nineveh.
37 When he was worshiping in the temple
of his god Nisroch, his sons Adrammelech
and Sharezer struck him down with the
sword and fled into the land of Ararat. His
son Esarhaddon reigned in his place.

## CHAPTER 20

See RG 134–35

*End of Hezekiah's Reign.* 1[s] In those
days, when Hezekiah was mortally ill, the
prophet Isaiah, son of Amoz, came and said
to him: "Thus says the LORD: Put your house
in order, for you are about to die; you shall
not recover." 2 He turned his face to the wall
and prayed to the LORD: 3 "Ah, LORD, remember how faithfully and wholeheartedly I
conducted myself in your presence, doing
what was good in your sight!" And Hezekiah
wept bitterly. 4 Before Isaiah had left the central courtyard, the word of the LORD came to
him: 5 Go back and tell Hezekiah, the leader
of my people: "Thus says the LORD, the God
of David your father:

I have heard your prayer;
I have seen your tears.
Now I am healing you.
On the third day you shall go up
to the house of the LORD.
6 I will add to your life fifteen years.
I will rescue you and this city
from the hand of the king of Assyria;
I will be a shield to this city
for my own sake and the sake of David
my servant."

7 Then Isaiah said, "Bring a poultice of figs
and apply it to the boil for his recovery."
8 Hezekiah asked Isaiah, "What is the sign
that the LORD will heal me and that I shall go
up to the house of the LORD on the third
day?" 9 Isaiah replied, "This will be the sign
for you from the LORD that he will carry out
the word he has spoken: Shall the shadow go
forward or back ten steps?" 10 "It is easy for
the shadow to advance ten steps," Hezekiah
answered. "Rather, let it go back ten steps."
11 So Isaiah the prophet invoked the LORD.
He made the shadow go back the ten steps it
had descended on the staircase to the terrace
of Ahaz.
12 At that time, Berodach-baladan,[*] son of
Baladan, king of Babylon, sent letters and
gifts to Hezekiah when he heard that he had
been ill. 13 Hezekiah listened to the envoys
and then showed off his whole treasury: his
silver, gold, spices and perfumed oil, his armory, and everything in his storerooms;
there was nothing in his house or in all his
realm that Hezekiah did not show them.
14 Then Isaiah the prophet came to King Hezekiah and asked him: "What did these men
say to you? Where did they come from?"
Hezekiah replied, "They came from a distant
land, from Babylon." 15 He asked, "What did
they see in your house?" Hezekiah answered, "They saw everything in my house.
There is nothing in my storerooms that I did
not show them." 16 Then Isaiah said to Hezekiah: "Hear the word of the LORD: 17 The
time is coming when all that is in your

**20:12 Berodach-baladan**: this famous king's name is more correctly recorded in Is 39:1 as "Merodach-baladan." The Babylonian form, Marduk-apal-idinna, means "Marduk has granted a son." Historically, any embassy from him to Hezekiah must have been aimed at establishing an anti-Assyrian strategy of cooperation.

*q:* 2 Sm 7:12. *r:* 1 Mc 7:41; 2 Mc 8:19. *s:* Sir 48:23.

### Manasseh

MANASSEH IS CREDITED with the longest reign, fifty-five years, of any king of Israel or Judah but he "did what was evil in the LORD's sight" (21:2). He set up a sacred pole, which was an important part of the worship of the Canaanite goddess Asherah. The host of heaven that he worshiped (v. 3) refers to the astral gods—sun, moon, and stars. He practiced child sacrifice and consulted ghosts and spirits. All such practices are condemned by the law (Dt 12:29–31; 17:3; 18:10–12).

house, everything that your ancestors have
stored up until this day, shall be carried off to
Babylon; nothing shall be left, says the
LORD. [18]Some of your own descendants,
your offspring, your progeny, shall be taken
and made attendants in the palace of the king
of Babylon." [19]Hezekiah replied to Isaiah,
"The word of the LORD which you have spoken is good." For he thought, "There will be
peace and stability in my lifetime."
[20]The rest of the acts of Hezekiah, with all
his valor, and how he constructed the pool
and conduit* and brought water into the city,
are recorded in the book of the chronicles of
the kings of Judah.[t] [21]Hezekiah rested with
his ancestors, and his son Manasseh succeeded him as king.

## CHAPTER 21

See RG 134–35

*Reign of Manasseh.* [1]Manasseh was
twelve years old when he became king, and
he reigned fifty-five years in Jerusalem. His
mother's name was Hephzibah.
[2]He did what was evil in the LORD's sight,
following the abominable practices of the
nations whom the LORD had dispossessed
before the Israelites. [3]He rebuilt the high
places which Hezekiah his father had destroyed. He set up altars to Baal and also
made an asherah, as Ahab, king of Israel,
had done. He bowed down to the whole host
of heaven and served them.[u] [4]He built altars
in the house of the LORD, of which the LORD
had said: In Jerusalem I will set my name.
[5]And he built altars for the whole host of
heaven in the two courts of the house of the
LORD. [6]He immolated his child by fire. He
practiced soothsaying and divination, and
reintroduced the consulting of ghosts and
spirits.

He did much evil in the LORD's sight and
provoked him to anger.[v] [7]The Asherah idol
he had made, he placed in the LORD's house,
of which the LORD had said to David and to
his son Solomon: In this house and in Jerusalem, which I have chosen out of all the
tribes of Israel, I shall set my name forever.[w]
[8]I will no longer make Israel step out of the
land I gave their ancestors, provided that
they are careful to observe all I have commanded them and the entire law which Moses my servant enjoined upon them. [9]But
they did not listen.

Manasseh misled them into doing even
greater evil than the nations the LORD had destroyed at the coming of the Israelites.
[10]Then the LORD spoke through his servants
the prophets: [11]"Because Manasseh, king of
Judah, has practiced these abominations, and
has done greater evil than all that was done
by the Amorites before him, and has led Judah into sin by his idols,[x] [12]therefore, thus
says the LORD, the God of Israel: I am about
to bring such evil on Jerusalem and Judah
that, when any hear of it, their ears shall ring:
[13]I will measure Jerusalem with the same
cord as I did Samaria, and with the plummet
I used for the house of Ahab. I will wipe Jerusalem clean as one wipes a dish, wiping it
inside and out.[y] [14]I will cast off the survivors
of my inheritance. I will deliver them into enemy hands, to become prey and booty for all
their enemies, [15]because they have done
what is evil in my sight and provoked me
from the day their ancestors came forth from
Egypt until this very day." [16]Manasseh shed

**20:20 Pool and conduit**: Hezekiah's tunnel is described in more detail in 2 Chr 32:30.

---

*t:* Sir 48:17. *u:* 2 Kgs 17:16; 1 Kgs 16:31–33. *v:* Lv 18:21; 19:26; Dt 18:10–14; 1 Sm 28:3. *w:* 2 Sm 7:13; 1 Kgs 8:16; 9:3. *x:* Jer 15:4. *y:* Is 34:11; Lam 2:8; Am 7:7–9.

so much innocent blood that it filled the length and breadth of Jerusalem, in addition to the sin he caused Judah to commit by doing what was evil in the LORD's sight.

[17]The rest of the acts of Manasseh, with all that he did and the sin he committed, are recorded in the book of the chronicles of the kings of Judah. [18]Manasseh rested with his ancestors; he was buried in his palace garden, the garden of Uzza, and his son Amon succeeded him as king.

***Reign of Amon.*** [19]Amon was twenty-two years old when he became king, and he reigned two years in Jerusalem. His mother's name was Meshullemeth, daughter of Haruz, from Jotbah.

[20]He did what was evil in the LORD's sight, as his father Manasseh had done. [21]He walked in all the ways of his father; he served the idols his father had served, and bowed down to them. [22]He abandoned the LORD, the God of his ancestors, and did not walk in the way of the LORD.

[23]Officials of Amon plotted against him and killed the king in his palace, [24]but the people of the land* then slew all who had plotted against King Amon, and the people of the land made his son Josiah king in his stead. [25]The rest of the acts of Amon, which he did, are recorded in the book of the chronicles of the kings of Judah. [26]He was buried in his own grave in the garden of Uzza, and his son Josiah succeeded him as king.

## CHAPTER 22

See RG 134–35

***Reign of Josiah.*** [1]Josiah was eight years old when he became king, and he reigned thirty-one years in Jerusalem. His mother's name was Jedidah, daughter of Adaiah, from Bozkath.

[2]He did what was right in the LORD's sight, walking in the way of David his father, not turning right or left.

***The Book of the Law.*** [3][z] In his eighteenth year, King Josiah sent the scribe Shaphan,* son of Azaliah, son of Meshullam, to the house of the LORD with these orders: [4]"Go to the high priest Hilkiah and have him calculate the valuables that have been brought to the house of the LORD, which the doorkeepers have collected from the people. [5]Then have him turn them over to the master workers in the house of the LORD, and have them give them to the ordinary workers who are in the house of the LORD to repair its breaches: [6]to the carpenters, the builders, and the masons, and to purchase wood and hewn stone. [7]No reckoning shall be asked of them regarding the funds provided to them, because they hold positions of trust."

[8]The high priest Hilkiah informed the scribe Shaphan, "I have found the book of the law* in the temple of the LORD." Hilkiah gave the book to Shaphan, who read it. [9]Then the scribe Shaphan went to the king and reported, "Your servants have smelted down the silver deposited in the temple and have turned it over to the master workers in the house of the LORD." [10]The scribe Shaphan also informed the king, "Hilkiah the priest has given me a book," and then Shaphan read it in the presence of the king. [11]When the king heard the words of the book of the law, he tore his garments.

[12]The king then issued this command to Hilkiah the priest, Ahikam, son of Shaphan, Achbor, son of Micaiah, Shaphan the scribe, and Asaiah the king's servant: [13]"Go, consult the LORD for me, for the people, and for all Judah, about the words of this book that has been found, for the rage of the LORD has been set furiously ablaze against us, because our ancestors did not obey the words of this book, nor do what is written for us." [14]So Hilkiah the priest, Ahikam, Achbor, Shaphan, and Asaiah went to Huldah the prophet, wife of Shallum, son of Tikvah, son of Harhas, keeper of the wardrobe; she lived in Jerusalem, in the Second Quarter. When they had spoken to her, [15]she said to them, "Thus says the LORD, the God of Israel: Say to the man who sent you to me, [16]Thus says

**21:24 People of the land**: see note on 11:14.

**22:3 Shaphan**: head of a prominent family in the reign of Josiah, secretary to the king, bearer and reader of the newly found book of the law (vv. 3–13; 25:22). He and his sons favored the reform of King Josiah and supported the prophet Jeremiah; cf. Jer 26:24; 29:1–3; 36:10–12; 39:14.

**22:8 Book of the law**: probably an early edition of material now found in the Book of Deuteronomy.

*z:* 2 Kgs 12:11–16.

TOPHETH (23:10) WAS A valley that marked Jerusalem's western border. Also known as the valley of Hinnom, it became Jerusalem's trash dump and was used by Jesus as the image for hell (Gehenna, see Mt 10:28). It was despised because it had served as a place of child sacrifice to the Ammonite god Molech.

the LORD: I am about to bring evil upon this place and upon its inhabitants—all the words of the book which the king of Judah has read. [17]Because they have abandoned me and have burned incense to other gods, provoking me by all the works of their hands, my rage is ablaze against this place and it cannot be extinguished.

[18]"But to the king of Judah who sent you to consult the LORD, give this response: Thus says the LORD, the God of Israel: As for the words you have heard, [19]because you were heartsick and have humbled yourself before the LORD when you heard what I have spoken concerning this place and its inhabitants, that they would become a desolation and a curse; and because you tore your garments and wept before me, I in turn have heard, oracle of the LORD. [20]I will therefore gather you to your ancestors; you shall go to your grave in peace, and your eyes shall not see all the evil I am about to bring upon this place." This they reported to the king.

## CHAPTER 23

See RG 134–35

[1]The king then had all the elders of Judah and of Jerusalem summoned before him. [2]The king went up to the house of the LORD with all the people of Judah and all the inhabitants of Jerusalem: priests, prophets, and all the people, great and small. He read aloud to them all the words of the book of the covenant that had been found in the house of the LORD.[a] [3]The king stood by the column and made a covenant in the presence of the LORD to follow the LORD and to observe his commandments, statutes, and decrees with his whole heart and soul, and to re-establish the words of the covenant written in this book. And all the people stood by the covenant.

***Josiah's Religious Reform.*** [4]Then the king commanded the high priest Hilkiah, his assistant priests, and the doorkeepers to remove from the temple of the LORD all the objects that had been made for Baal, Asherah, and the whole host of heaven. These he burned outside Jerusalem on the slopes of the Kidron; their ashes were carried to Bethel.[b] [5]He also put an end to the idolatrous priests whom the kings of Judah had appointed to burn incense on the high places in the cities of Judah and in the vicinity of Jerusalem, as well as those who burned incense to Baal, to the sun, moon, and signs of the zodiac, and to the whole host of heaven.[c] [6]From the house of the LORD he also removed the Asherah to the Wadi Kidron, outside Jerusalem; he burned it and beat it to dust, in the Wadi Kidron, and scattered its dust over the graveyard of the people of the land.* [d] [7]He tore down the apartments of the cult prostitutes in the house of the LORD, where the women wove garments for the Asherah.[e] [8]He brought in all the priests from the cities of Judah, and then defiled, from Geba to Beer-sheba, the high places where they had offered incense. He also tore down the high places of the gates, which were at the entrance of the Gate of Joshua, governor of the city, north of the city gate. [9](The priests of the high places could not function at the altar of the LORD in Jerusalem; but they, along with their relatives, ate the unleavened bread.)

[10]The king also defiled Topheth in the Valley of Ben-hinnom, so that there would no longer be any immolation of sons or daughters by fire* in honor of Molech.[f] [11]He

**23:6 People of the land**: see note on 11:14.

**23:10 Topheth . . . by fire**: Topheth was a cultic site probably in the Hinnom Valley just west of Jerusalem where, apparently, children were immolated to the deity Molech (Hebrew *melek*, "king," deformed in the biblical tradition to "Molech"). The practice was condemned by Deuteronomic law and denounced by Jeremiah (Dt 12:31; Jer 7:29–31). In

*a:* Dt 17:18–19. *b:* Sir 49:3. *c:* Dt 4:19; 17:2–7. *d:* Dt 16:21. *e:* Dt 23:18–19. *f:* Lv 18:21; Dt 18:10–12.

**The Reign and Reform of Josiah**

JOSIAH, ALONG WITH Hezekiah, is one of the good kings of Judah and one of the heroes of the deuteronomistic history. The temple repairs made by Josiah led to the discovery of a copy of the book of the law, which has long been identified as a form of the book of Deuteronomy. He is renowned for his obedience (22:2; 23:25) to the law book found in his reign.

did away with the horses which the kings of
Judah had dedicated to the sun; these were at
the entrance of the house of the LORD, near
the chamber of Nathan-melech the official,
which was in the large building. The chariots
of the sun he destroyed by fire. [12]He also demolished the altars made by the kings of Judah on the roof (the roof terrace of Ahaz),
and the altars made by Manasseh in the two
courts of the LORD's house. He pulverized
them and threw the dust into the Wadi Kidron.[g] [13]The king defiled the high places east
of Jerusalem, south of the Mount of the Destroyer,* which Solomon, king of Israel, had
built in honor of Astarte, the Sidonian horror, of Chemosh, the Moabite horror, and of
Milcom, the Ammonites' abomination.[h]
[14]He broke to pieces the pillars, cut down the
asherahs, and filled the places where they
had been with human bones.[i]
[15]Likewise the altar which was at Bethel,
the high place built by Jeroboam, son of Nebat, who caused Israel to sin—this same altar and high place he tore down and burned,
grinding the high place to powder and burning the asherah.[j] [16]When Josiah turned and
saw the graves there on the mountainside, he
ordered the bones taken from the graves and
burned on the altar, and thus defiled it, according to the LORD's word proclaimed by
the man of God as Jeroboam stood by the altar on the feast day. When the king looked up
and saw the grave of the man of God who
had proclaimed these words, [17]he asked,
"What is that marker I see?" The people of
the city replied, "The grave of the man of
God who came from Judah and proclaimed
the very things you have done to the altar in
Bethel." [18]"Let him be," he said, "let no one
move his bones." So they left his bones
undisturbed together with the bones of the
prophet who had come from Samaria.* [19]Jo-
siah also removed all the temples on the high
places in the cities of Samaria which the
kings of Israel had built, provoking the
LORD; he did the very same to them as he
had done in Bethel. [20]He slaughtered upon
the altars all the priests of the high places
that were there, and burned human bones
upon them. Then he returned to Jerusalem.
[21]The king issued a command to all the
people: "Observe the Passover of the LORD,
your God, as it is written in this book of the
covenant."[k] [22]No Passover such as this had
been observed during the period when the
judges ruled Israel, or during the entire period of the kings of Israel and the kings of
Judah, [23]until the eighteenth year of King Josiah, when this Passover of the LORD was
kept in Jerusalem.
[24]Further, Josiah purged the consultation
of ghosts and spirits, with the household
gods, idols,* and all the other horrors to be
seen in the land of Judah and in Jerusalem,
so that he might carry out the words of the
law that were written in the book that Hil-

Jer 19 the deity is identified as the Canaanite god Baal.

**23:13 Mount of the Destroyer**: the name of the mountain in Hebrew is a wordplay. "The Mount of the *mashchit*" means "the Mount of the Destroyer" or perhaps "the Mount of Destruction." The word plays on *mishchah*, "anointment," and on *mashiach*, "anointed one," both of which are references to the ceremony that consecrated the king. The mountain in question was the Mount of Olives, whose trees produced oil for the royal anointing. In the present context, both sides of the wordplay allude to Solomon, the anointed king (*mashiach*), whose building of non-Yahwistic shrines on this very mountain resulted in the destruction (*mashchit*) of the Davidic realm (see 1 Kgs 11:4–13). **Horror . . . abomination**: all three idols are described with pejorative terms.

**23:18 From Samaria**: an anachronistic use of the name of the later capital city for the whole region. The prophet was from Bethel; cf. 1 Kgs 13:11.

**23:24 Household gods, idols**: teraphim. See note on Gn 31:19.

*g:* 2 Kgs 20:11; 21:5. *h:* 1 Kgs 11:4–8. *i:* Dt 16:21; 1 Kgs 14:23. *j:* 1 Kgs 12:26–13:34. *k:* Dt 16:1–8.

kiah the priest had found in the house of the
LORD.[l]
25 Before him there had been no king who
turned to the LORD as he did, with his whole
heart, his whole being, and his whole
strength, in accord with the entire law of
Moses; nor did any king like him arise after
him.[m] 26 Yet the LORD did not turn from his
fiercely burning anger against Judah, because of all the provocations that Manasseh
had given. 27 The LORD said: Even Judah will
I put out of my sight as I did Israel. I will reject this city, Jerusalem, which I chose, and
the house of which I said: There shall my
name be.
28 The rest of the acts of Josiah, with all
that he did, are recorded in the book of the
chronicles of the kings of Judah. 29 In his
time Pharaoh Neco, king of Egypt, went up
toward the Euphrates River against the king
of Assyria.* King Josiah set out to meet him,
but was slain at Megiddo at the first encounter. 30 His servants brought his body on
a chariot from Megiddo to Jerusalem, where
they buried him in his own grave. Then the
people of the land took Jehoahaz, son of Josiah, anointed him, and proclaimed him king
to succeed his father.

***Reign of Jehoahaz.*** 31 Jehoahaz was
twenty-three years old when he became
king, and he reigned three months in
Jerusalem. His mother's name was Hamutal,
daughter of Jeremiah, from Libnah.[n]
32 He did what was evil in the LORD's
sight, just as his ancestors had done. 33 Pharaoh Neco took him prisoner at Riblah in the
land of Hamath, thus ending his reign in Jerusalem. He imposed a fine upon the land of
a hundred talents of silver and a talent of
gold.* 34 Pharaoh Neco then made Eliakim,
son of Josiah, king in place of Josiah his father; he changed his name to Jehoiakim. Jehoahaz he took away with him to Egypt,
where he died. 35 Jehoiakim gave the silver

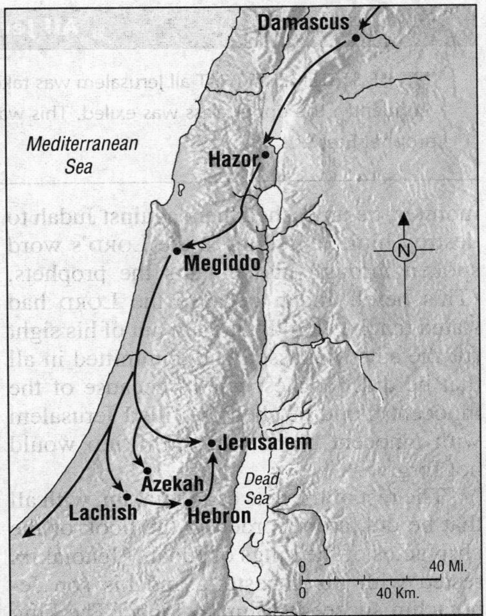

**Nebuchadnezzar's Campaign**

and gold to Pharaoh, but taxed the land to
raise the amount Pharaoh demanded. He exacted the silver and gold from the people of
the land, from each proportionately, to pay
Pharaoh Neco.

***Reign of Jehoiakim.*** 36 Jehoiakim was
twenty-five years old when he became king,
and he reigned eleven years in Jerusalem.
His mother's name was Zebidah, daughter
of Pedaiah, from Rumah.
37 He did what was evil in the LORD's
sight, just as his ancestors had done.

## CHAPTER 24

See RG 134–35

1 During Jehoiakim's reign Nebuchadnezzar, king of Babylon, attacked, and Jehoiakim became his vassal for three years.
Then Jehoiakim turned and rebelled against
him. 2 The LORD loosed against him bands of
Chaldeans, Arameans, Moabites, and Am-

**23:29 Against the king of Assyria**: the narrator depicts Neco's advance as an attack on Assyrian forces. The Babylonian record of the event, however, implies that Neco intended to support the remnant of Assyrian forces against a Babylonian onslaught in order to prop up a buffer state between Egypt and Babylon and assure Egyptian control of the Syro-Palestinian region.

**23:33 A talent of gold**: unless the fine imposed was a mere token, this figure seems too low; cf. 18:14. A number may have dropped from the Hebrew text; various ancient translations read "ten" or "one hundred" here.

*l:* 2 Kgs 21:6; Gn 31:19; Dt 18:10–14; Jgs 18:14. *m:* Dt 6:5; Sir 49:1–3. *n:* 2 Kgs 24:18.

**All Jerusalem**

THE STATEMENT THAT all Jerusalem was taken captive (v. 14) is an obvious exaggeration. Evidently, the upper class was exiled. This wave of captives included King Jehoiachin and the prophet Ezekiel.

monites; he unleashed them against Judah to destroy him, according to the LORD's word spoken through his servants the prophets. [3]This befell Judah because the LORD had stated that he would put them out of his sight for the sins Manasseh had committed in all that he did, [4]and especially because of the innocent blood he shed; he filled Jerusalem with innocent blood, and the LORD would not forgive.[o]

[5]The rest of the acts of Jehoiakim, with all that he did, are recorded in the book of the chronicles of the kings of Judah. [6]Jehoiakim rested with his ancestors, and his son Jehoiachin succeeded him as king. [7]The king of Egypt did not again leave his own land, for the king of Babylon had taken all that belonged to the king of Egypt from the wadi of Egypt to the Euphrates River.

*Reign of Jehoiachin.* [8]Jehoiachin was eighteen years old when he became king, and he reigned three months in Jerusalem. His mother's name was Nehushta, daughter of Elnathan, from Jerusalem.

[9]He did what was evil in the LORD's sight, just as his father had done.

[10p] At that time officers of Nebuchadnezzar, king of Babylon, attacked Jerusalem, and the city came under siege. [11]Nebuchadnezzar, king of Babylon, himself arrived at the city while his officers were besieging it. [12]Then Jehoiachin, king of Judah, together with his mother, his ministers, officers, and functionaries, surrendered to the king of Babylon, who, in the eighth year of his reign,* took him captive. [13]He carried off all the treasures of the house of the LORD and the treasures of the king's house, and broke up all the gold utensils that Solomon, king of Israel, had provided in the house of the LORD, as the LORD had decreed.[q] [14]He deported all Jerusalem: all the officers and warriors of the army, ten thousand in number, and all the artisans and smiths. Only the lowliest of the people of the land* were left. [15]He deported Jehoiachin to Babylon, and the king's mother, his wives, his functionaries, and the chiefs of the land he led captive from Jerusalem to Babylon.[r] [16]All seven thousand soldiers of the army, and a thousand artisans and smiths, all of them trained warriors, these too the king of Babylon brought captive to Babylon. [17]In place of Jehoiachin the king of Babylon made Mattaniah, Jehoiachin's uncle, king; he changed his name to Zedekiah.[s]

*Reign of Zedekiah.* [18*] Zedekiah was twenty-one years old when he became king, and he reigned eleven years in Jerusalem. His mother's name was Hamutal, daughter of Jeremiah, from Libnah.[t]

[19]He did what was evil in the sight of the LORD, just as Jehoiakim had done. [20]This befell Jerusalem and Judah because the LORD was so angry that he cast them out of his sight.

Zedekiah rebelled against the king of Babylon.

## CHAPTER 25

See RG 134–35

[1]In the tenth month of the ninth year of Zedekiah's reign, on the tenth day of the month, Nebuchadnezzar, king of Babylon, and his whole army advanced against Jerusalem, encamped around it, and built siege walls on every side. [2]The siege of the city continued until the eleventh year of Zedekiah. [3]On the ninth day of the month,* when

**24:12 The eighth year of his reign**: that is, of Nebuchadnezzar's reign, not Jehoiachin's. The year was 597 B.C.

**24:14 People of the land**: see note on 11:14.

**24:18–25:30** Much of this material closely parallels Jer 52; some of the events are also recounted in Jer 39.

**25:3 Ninth day of the month**: the text does not say which month, but Jer 39:2 and 52:6 set the breaching of the city

*o:* 2 Kgs 21:16. *p:* Dn 1:1–2. *q:* 2 Kgs 20:17. *r:* Est A:3; 2:6. *s:* Jer 37:1. *t:* 2 Kgs 23:31.

## The Reign of Zedekiah and the Fall of Jerusalem

THIS SECTION ON Zedekiah (24:18–25:21) is very similar to Jer 52 and the first part of it to Jer 39:1–10. Here the exile is blamed mostly on Zedekiah and his generation. Jerusalem fell to the Babylonians in 587 or 586 B.C. Jeremiah 52:29 gives the number of captives from this deportation as 832.

famine had gripped the city, and the people of the land had no more food, [4]the city walls were breached. That night, all the soldiers came to the gate between the two walls near the king's garden (the Chaldeans had the city surrounded), while the king went toward the Arabah.* [5]But the Chaldean army pursued the king and overtook him in the desert near Jericho, abandoned by his whole army. [6]The king was therefore arrested and brought to Riblah to the king of Babylon, who pronounced sentence on him. [7]They slew Zedekiah's sons before his eyes; then they put out his eyes, bound him with fetters, and brought him to Babylon.

[8]On the seventh day of the fifth month (this was in the nineteenth year of Nebuchadnezzar, king of Babylon), Nebuzaradan, captain of the bodyguard, came to Jerusalem as the agent of the king of Babylon. [9]He burned the house of the LORD, the house of the king, and all the houses of Jerusalem (every noble house); he destroyed them by fire.[u] [10]The Chaldean troops who were with the captain of the guard tore down the walls that surrounded Jerusalem, [11]and Nebuzaradan, captain of the guard, led into exile the last of the army remaining in the city, and those who had deserted* to the king of Babylon, and the last of the commoners. [12]But some of the country's poor the captain of the guard left behind as vinedressers and farmers.

[13]The bronze columns that belonged to the house of the LORD, and the stands and the bronze sea in the house of the LORD, the Chaldeans broke into pieces; they carried away the bronze to Babylon.[v] [14]They took also the pots, the shovels, the snuffers, the cups and all the bronze articles used for service.[w] [15]The fire pans and the bowls that were of solid gold or silver the captain of the guard also carried off.[x] [16]The two columns, the one bronze sea, and the stands, which Solomon had made for the house of the LORD—the weight in bronze of all these articles was never calculated.[y] [17]Each of the columns was eighteen cubits high; a bronze capital three cubits high surmounted each column, and a netting with pomegranates encircled the capital, all of bronze; and they were duplicated on the other column, on the netting.[z]

[18]The captain of the guard also took Seraiah, the chief priest, Zephaniah, an assistant priest, and the three doorkeepers. [19]And from the city he took one officer who was a commander of soldiers, five courtiers in the personal service of the king who were still in the city, the scribe in charge of the army who mustered the people of the land,* and sixty of the people of the land still remaining in the city. [20]The captain of the guard, Nebuzaradan, arrested these and brought them to the king of Babylon at Riblah, and [21]the king of Babylon struck them down and put them to death in Riblah, in the land of Hamath. And thus Judah went into exile from their native soil.

***Governorship of Gedaliah.*** [22a]As for the people whom he had allowed to remain in the land of Judah, Nebuchadnezzar, king of Babylon, appointed Gedaliah, son of Ahikam,

walls in the fourth month; in later times that was the date of a fast commemorating the event (cf. Zec 8:19). **People of the land**: the influential citizens (see note on 11:14); even they, whose resources went beyond those of the ordinary people, were starving.

**25:4** The Hebrew text of this verse is missing some words. The present translation is based on a likely reconstruction.

**25:11 Those who had deserted**: perhaps on the advice of Jeremiah; cf. Jer 38:2–3.

**25:19 People of the land**: see note on 11:14.

*u:* Ps 74:2–7. *v:* 2 Kgs 16:17; 1 Kgs 7:15–39; Jer 27:19–23. *w:* 1 Kgs 7:40–45. *x:* 1 Kgs 7:50. *y:* 1 Kgs 7:47. *z:* 1 Kgs 7:15–20; Jer 52:21–23. *a:* Jer 40:7–41:18.

son of Shaphan, over them. [23]Hearing that
the king of Babylon had appointed Gedaliah
over them, all the army commanders and the
troops came to him at Mizpah: Ishmael, son
of Nethaniah, Johanan, son of Kareah, Seraiah, son of Tanhumeth the Netophathite, and
Jaazaniah, son of the Maakite, each with his
troops. [24]Gedaliah gave the commanders and
their troops his oath. He said to them, "Do
not be afraid of the Chaldean officials. Remain in the country and serve the king of
Babylon, so that all will be well with you."
[25]But in the seventh month Ishmael, son
of Nethaniah, son of Elishama, of royal descent, came with ten others, attacked Gedaliah and killed him, along with the Judahites
and Chaldeans who were in Mizpah with
him. [26]Then all the people, great and small,
left with the army commanders and went to
Egypt for fear of the Chaldeans.
*Release of Jehoiachin.* [27]In the thirty-seventh year of the exile of Jehoiachin, king of
Judah, on the twenty-seventh day of the
twelfth month, Evil-merodach, king of Babylon, in the inaugural year of his own reign,
raised up Jehoiachin, king of Judah, from
prison. [28]He spoke kindly to him and gave
him a throne higher than that of the other
kings who were with him in Babylon. [29]Je-
hoiachin took off his prison garb; he ate regularly in the king's presence as long as he
lived; [30]and for his allowance the king
granted him a regular allowance, in fixed
daily amounts, for as long as he lived.

See RG 137–44

# The First Book of Chronicles

The Greek title, *paraleipomena*, means "things omitted," or "passed over" (i.e., in the accounts found in Samuel and Kings). The Books of Chronicles, however, are much more than a supplement to Samuel and Kings; a comparison of the two histories discloses striking differences of scope and purpose. The Books of Chronicles record in some detail the lengthy span (some five hundred fifty years) from the death of King Saul to the return from the exile. Unlike today's history writing, wherein factual accuracy and impartiality of judgment are the norm, biblical history, with rare exceptions, was less concerned with reporting in precise detail all the facts of a situation than with drawing out the meaning of those facts. Biblical history was thus primarily interpretative, and its purpose was to disclose the action of the living God in human affairs. For this reason we speak of it as "sacred history."

These characteristics are apparent when we examine the primary objective of the Chronicler (the conventional designation for the anonymous author) in compiling his work. Given the situation which confronted the Jewish people at this time (the end of the fifth century B.C.), the Chronicler realized that Israel's political greatness was a thing of the past. Yet, for the Chronicler, Israel's past held the key to the people's future. In particular, the Chronicler aimed to establish and defend the legitimate claims of the Davidic monarchy in Israel's history, and to underscore the status of Jerusalem and its divinely established Temple worship as the center of religious life for the Jewish people. If Judaism was to survive and prosper, it would have to heed the lessons of the past and devoutly serve its God in the place where he had chosen to dwell, the Temple in Jerusalem. From the Chronicler's point of view, the reigns of David and Solomon were the ideal to which all subsequent rule in Judah must aspire. The Chronicler was much more interested in David's religious and cultic influence than in his political power, however. He saw David's (and Solomon's) primary importance as deriving rather from their roles in the establishment of Jerusalem and its Temple as the center of the true worship of the Lord. Furthermore, he presents David as the one who prescribed the Temple's elaborate ritual (which, in point of fact, only gradually evolved in the Second Temple period) and who appointed the Levites to supervise the liturgical services there.

The Chronicler used a variety of sources in writing his history. Besides the canonical Books of Genesis, Exodus, Numbers, Joshua, and Ruth, and especially the Books of Samuel and Kings (specifically 1 Sm 31–2 Kings 25), he cites the titles of many other works which have not come down to us, e.g., "The Books of the Kings of Israel," or "The Books of the Kings of Israel and Judah," and "The History of Gad the Seer." In addition, the Chronicler's work contains early preexilic material not found in the Books of Kings.

The principal divisions of 1 Chronicles are as follows:

I. Genealogical Tables (1:1–9:34)

II. The History of David (9:35–29:30)

---

## I. Genealogical Tables*

### CHAPTER 1

See RG 138

***From Adam to Abraham.*** [1]Adam,
Seth, Enosh,[a] [2]Kenan, Mahalalel, Jared,[b]
[3]Enoch, Methuselah, Lamech,[c] [4]Noah,
Shem, Ham, and Japheth.[d] [5]The sons of Japheth were Gomer, Magog, Madai, Javan,
Tubal, Meshech, and Tiras.[e] [6]The sons of
Gomer were Ashkenaz, Riphath, and Togarmah. [7]The sons of Javan were Elishah, Tarshish, the Kittim, and the Rodanim.

[8]The sons of Ham were Cush, Mizraim,
Put, and Canaan. [9]The sons of Cush were
Seba, Havilah, Sabta, Raama, and Sabteca.
The sons of Raama were Sheba and Dedan.
[10]Cush became the father of Nimrod, who
was the first to be a warrior on the earth.[f]
[11][g] Mizraim became the father of the Ludim,
Anamim, Lehabim, Naphtuhim, [12]Pathru-
sim, Casluhim, and Caphtorim, from whom
the Philistines sprang. [13]Canaan became the
father of Sidon, his firstborn, and Heth,
[14]and the Jebusites, the Amorites, the Girgashites, [15]the Hivites, the Arkites, the Sinites,
[16]the Arvadites, the Zemarites, and the
Hamathites.

[17][h] The sons of Shem were Elam, Asshur,
Arpachshad, Lud, and Aram. The sons of
Aram were Uz, Hul, Gether, and Mash.
[18]Arpachshad became the father of Shelah,
and Shelah became the father of Eber. [19]Two
sons were born to Eber; the first was named
Peleg (for in his time the world was divided),* and his brother was named Joktan.
[20]Joktan became the father of Almodad,
Sheleph, Hazarmaveth, Jerah, [21]Hadoram,
Uzal, Diklah, [22]Ebal, Abimael, Sheba,
[23]Ophir, Havilah, and Jobab; all these were
the sons of Joktan.

[24][i] Shem, Arpachshad, Shelah, [25]Eber, Peleg, Reu, [26]Serug, Nahor, Terah, [27]Abram,
that is, Abraham.[j]

***From Abraham to Jacob.*** [28]The sons of
Abraham were Isaac and Ishmael.[k] [29]These
were their generations:

Nebaioth, the firstborn of Ishmael, then
Kedar, Adbeel, Mibsam, [30]Mishma, Dumah,
Massa, Hadad, Tema, [31]Jetur, Naphish, and
Kedemah. These were the sons of Ishmael.[l]
[32]The sons of Keturah, Abraham's concubine: she bore Zimran, Jokshan, Medan,
Midian, Ishbak, and Shuah. The sons of Jokshan were Sheba and Dedan. [33]The sons of
Midian were Ephah, Epher, Hanoch, Abida,
and Eldaah. All these were the sons of Keturah.[m]

[34]Abraham begot Isaac. The sons of Isaac
were Esau and Israel.[n]

[35]The descendants of Esau were Eliphaz,
Reuel, Jeush, Jalam, and Korah. [36]The de-
scendants of Eliphaz were Teman, Omar,
Zephi, Gatam, Kenaz, Timna, and Amalek.
[37]The descendants of Reuel were Nahath,
Zerah, Shammah, and Mizzah.[o]

[38]The sons of Seir* were Lotan, Shobal,
Zibeon, Anah, Dishon, Ezer, and Dishan.
[39]The sons of Lotan were Hori and Homam;
Timna was the sister of Lotan. [40]The sons of
Shobal were Alian, Manahath, Ebal, Shephi,
and Onam. The sons of Zibeon were Aiah
and Anah. [41]The sons of Anah: Dishon. The

**1:1–9:34** The Chronicler's intention seems to have been to retell, from his particular viewpoint, the story of God's people from creation down to his own day. Since his primary interest was the history of David and the Davidic dynasty of Judah, he hurries through everything that preceded the death of Saul, David's predecessor as king, by the use of genealogical lists. The sources for these genealogies are mostly the books, already largely in their present form in the Chronicler's time, that eventually formed the Hebrew canon. For any given portion of these chapters, see the cross-references to their scriptural sources.

**1:19 Divided**: see note on Gn 10:25.

**1:38 Seir**: another name for Esau (v. 35) or Edom (v. 43).

*a:* Gn 5:3, 6, 9. *b:* Gn 5:9–32; 10:2–32. *c:* Gn 4:24. *d:* Gn 5:32; 6:10; 9:18. *e:* Gn 10:2–4. *f:* Gn 10:8. *g:* Gn 10:13–18. *h:* Gn 10:22–29; 11:10–18. *i:* Gn 11:10–26; Lk 3:34–36. *j:* Gn 17:5; Neh 9:7. *k:* Gn 16:11, 15; 21:2–3; Gal 4:22–23; Heb 11:11. *l:* Gn 25:13–16. *m:* Gn 25:1–4. *n:* Gn 21:2–3; 25:19, 25–26; 32:28–29; Mt 1:2; Lk 3:34. *o:* Gn 36:4–5, 10–13, 15–19.

THE CHRONICLER BEGINS his history in a way similar to a number of ancient Greek histories by trying to show the internal connectedness of the nation. After tracing the nation's descent from a common stock of ancestors, the historian focuses on the tribe of Judah and the family line of David, which is of central importance to the destiny of Jerusalem.

sons of Dishon were Hemdan, Eshban, Ithran, and Cheran. [42]The sons of Ezer were Bilhan, Zaavan, and Jaakan. The sons of Dishan were Uz and Aran.[p]

[43q]The kings who reigned in the land of Edom before the Israelites had kings were the following: Bela, son of Beor, the name of whose city was Dinhabah. [44]When Bela died, Jobab, son of Zerah, from Bozrah, succeeded him as king.[r] [45]When Jobab died, Husham, from the land of the Temanites, succeeded him as king.[s] [46]Husham died and Hadad, son of Bedad, succeeded him as king. He overthrew the Midianites on the Moabite plateau, and the name of his city was Avith. [47]Hadad died and Samlah of Masrekah succeeded him as king. [48]Samlah died and Shaul from Rehoboth on the Euphrates succeeded him as king. [49]When Shaul died, Baalhanan, son of Achbor, succeeded him as king. [50]Baalhanan died and Hadad succeeded him as king. The name of his city was Pai, and his wife's name was Mehetabel. She was the daughter of Matred, who was the daughter of Mezahab. [51t]After Hadad died, there were chiefs in Edom: the chiefs of Timna, Aliah, Jetheth, [52]Oholibamah, Elah, Pinon, [53]Kenaz, Teman, Mibzar, [54]Magdiel, and Iram were the chiefs of Edom.

## CHAPTER 2

See RG 138

[1]These were the sons of Israel: Reuben, Simeon, Levi, Judah, Issachar, Zebulun,[u] [2]Dan, Joseph, Benjamin, Naphtali, Gad, and Asher.[v]

***Judah.*** [3]The sons of Judah* were: Er, Onan, and Shelah; these three Bathshua, a Canaanite woman, bore to him. But Judah's firstborn, Er, was wicked in the sight of the LORD, so he took his life.[w] [4]Judah's daughter-in-law Tamar bore him Perez and Zerah, so that he had five sons in all.[x]

[5]The sons of Perez were Hezron and Hamul.[y] [6]The sons of Zerah were Zimri, Ethan, Heman, Calcol, and Darda—five in all.[z] [7]The sons of Zimri: Carmi. The sons of Carmi: Achar, who brought trouble upon Israel by violating the ban.[a] [8]The sons of Ethan: Azariah. [9]The sons born to Hezron were Jerahmeel, Ram, and Chelubai.*[b]

[10*]Ram became the father of Amminadab, and Amminadab became the father of Nahshon, a prince of the Judahites.[c] [11d]Nahshon became the father of Salmah. Salmah became the father of Boaz. [12]Boaz became the father of Obed. Obed became the father of Jesse. [13e]Jesse became the father of Eliab, his firstborn, of Abinadab, the second son, Shimea, the third,[f] [14]Nethanel, the fourth, Raddai, the fifth, [15]Ozem, the sixth, and David, the seventh. [16]Their sisters were Zeruiah and Abigail. Zeruiah had three sons: Abishai, Joab, and Asahel.[g] [17]Abigail bore Amasa, whose father was Jether the Ishmaelite.[h]

[18*]By his wife Azubah, Caleb, son of Hezron, became the father of a daughter, Jer-

**2:3–4:23** The Chronicler had two reasons for placing his genealogy of the tribe of Judah before those of the other tribes, and for making it longer than all the others: his interest in David, who was of the tribe of Judah; and the prominence of descendants of that tribe among the Jews of the Chronicler's time.

**2:9 Chelubai**: a variant form of the name Caleb (vv. 18, 42), a different person from the Chelub mentioned in 4:11.

**2:10–17** These verses list the immediate ancestors of David. A similar list appears in Ru 4:18–22.

**2:18–24** These verses record the descendants of Caleb. In 4:15 as well as frequently in the Pentateuch (see Nm 13:6; 14:6, 30; 26:65; etc.), Caleb is called the son of Jephunneh. Here his father is called Hezron, perhaps because the Calebites were reckoned as part of the clan of the Hezronites.

*p:* Gn 36:20–28. *q:* Gn 36:31–43. *r:* Is 34:6; 63:1; Jer 49:13, 22. *s:* Gn 36:11; Jb 2:11; Jer 49:7, 20. *t:* Gn 36:40–43. *u:* Gn 29:32–35; 30:18, 20; 35:23. *v:* Gn 30:6, 8, 11, 13, 24; 35:18, 24–26. *w:* 1 Chr 4:21; Gn 38:1–5; 46:12. *x:* Gn 38:7, 13–30; 46:12; Mt 1:3. *y:* Gn 46:12. *z:* 1 Kgs 5:11. *a:* Jos 7:1, 18–21, 24–25; 22:20. *b:* Mt 1:3. *c:* Mt 1:4. *d:* Nm 1:7; Mt 1:4–5. *e:* 1 Sm 16:6–13; 17:13–14. *f:* 2 Chr 11:18. *g:* 2 Sm 2:18. *h:* 2 Sm 17:25; 19:14; 20:4–13.

THE TERM FOR "prince" (2:10) had a variety of meanings in antiquity. Nahshon (Hebrew, nasi, meaning "prince") may be described in this way to highlight the line of David, because Nahshon's sister married Moses' brother Aaron (Ex 6:23) and thus helped form the primary line of Israel's priesthood. Such a connection would tie the royal and priestly families together.

ioth. Her sons were Jesher, Shobab, and Ardon.[i] 19When Azubah died, Caleb married Ephrath, who bore him Hur.[j] 20Hur became the father of Uri, and Uri became the father of Bezalel.[k] 21Then Hezron had relations with the daughter of Machir, the father of Gilead, whom he married when he was sixty years old. She bore him Segub.[l] 22Segub became the father of Jair, who possessed twenty-three cities in the land of Gilead.[m] 23Geshur and Aram took from them the villages of Jair, that is, Kenath and its towns, sixty cities in all, which had belonged to the sons of Machir, the father of Gilead.[n] 24After the death of Hezron, Caleb had relations with Ephrathah, the widow of his father Hezron, and she bore him Ashhur, the father of Tekoa.[o]

25The sons of Jerahmeel,* the firstborn of Hezron, were Ram, the firstborn, then Bunah, Oren, and Ozem, his brothers.[p] 26Jerahmeel also had another wife, named Atarah, who was the mother of Onam. 27The sons of Ram, the firstborn of Jerahmeel, were Maaz, Jamin, and Eker. 28The sons of Onam were Shammai and Jada. The sons of Shammai were Nadab and Abishur. 29Abishur's wife, who was named Abihail, bore him Ahban and Molid. 30The sons of Nadab were Seled and Appaim. Seled died childless. 31The sons of Appaim: Ishi. The sons of Ishi: Sheshan. The sons of Sheshan: Ahlai.[q] 32The sons of Jada, the brother of Shammai, were Jether and Jonathan. Jether died childless. 33The sons of Jonathan were Peleth and Zaza. These were the sons of Jerahmeel. 34Sheshan had no sons, only daughters; he had an Egyptian slave named Jarha. 35Sheshan gave his daughter in marriage to his slave Jarha, and she bore him Attai. 36Attai became the father of Nathan. Nathan became the father of Zabad. 37Zabad became the father of Ephlal. Ephlal became the father of Obed. 38Obed became the father of Jehu. Jehu became the father of Azariah. 39Azariah became the father of Helez. Helez became the father of Eleasah. 40Eleasah became the father of Sismai. Sismai became the father of Shallum. 41Shallum became the father of Jekamiah. Jekamiah became the father of Elishama.

42The sons of Caleb,* the brother of Jerahmeel: Mesha his firstborn, who was the father of Ziph. Then the sons of Mareshah, who was the father of Hebron. 43The sons of Hebron were Korah, Tappuah, Rekem, and Shema. 44Shema became the father of Raham, who was the father of Jorkeam. Rekem became the father of Shammai. 45The son of Shammai: Maon, who was the father of Beth-zur. 46Ephah, Caleb's concubine, bore Haran, Moza, and Gazez. Haran became the father of Gazez. 47The sons of Jahdai were Regem, Jotham, Geshan, Pelet, Ephah, and Shaaph. 48Maacah, Caleb's concubine, bore Sheber and Tirhanah. 49She also bore Shaaph, the father of Madmannah, Sheva, the father of Machbenah, and the father of Gibea. Achsah was Caleb's daughter.[r]

50These were sons of Caleb, sons of Hur,* the firstborn of Ephrathah: Shobal, the father of Kiriath-jearim, 51Salma, the father of Bethlehem, and Hareph, the father of Bethgader. 52The sons of Shobal, the father of

**2:25–41** The Jerahmeelites were a clan living in the Negeb of Judah.

**2:42–49** Another list (see vv. 18–24) of the Calebites, a clan inhabiting the south of Judah.

**2:50–55** The Hurites were a clan dwelling to the south and west of Jerusalem and related to the Calebites.

*i:* 1 Chr 2:24. *j:* 1 Chr 2:24. *k:* Ex 24:14; 31:2; 35:30; 2 Chr 1:5. *l:* Nm 26:29; 27:1; 32:39; Jos 13:31; Jgs 5:14. *m:* Nm 32:41; 1 Kgs 4:13. *n:* Dt 3:14; Jos 13:30. *o:* 1 Chr 2:19; 2 Sm 14:2; 2 Chr 11:6. *p:* 1 Sm 27:10; 30:29; Jb 32:2. *q:* 1 Chr 4:20. *r:* Jos 15:16; Jgs 1:12.

Kiriath-jearim, were Reaiah, half of the
Manahathites, [53]and the clans of Kiriath-jearim: the Ithrites, the Puthites, the Shumath-
ites, and the Mishraites. From these the Zo-
rahites and the Eshtaolites derived.[s] [54]The
sons of Salma were Bethlehem, the Netophathites, Atroth-beth-Joab, half of the Manahathites, and the Zorites. [55]The clans of the
Sopherim dwelling in Jabez were the Tirath-
ites, the Shimeathites, and the Sucathites.
They were the Kenites, who descended from
Hammath, the ancestor of the Rechabites.[t]

## CHAPTER 3

See RG 138

[1*] [u] These were the sons of David
born to him in Hebron: the firstborn, Amnon, by Ahinoam of Jezreel; the second,
Daniel,* by Abigail of Carmel; [2]the third,
Absalom, son of Maacah, who was the
daughter of Talmai, king of Geshur; the
fourth, Adonijah, son of Haggith; [3]the fifth,
Shephatiah, by Abital; the sixth, Ithream, by
his wife Eglah. [4]Six in all were born to him
in Hebron, where he reigned seven years and
six months. Then he reigned thirty-three
years in Jerusalem.[v] [5][w] In Jerusalem the following were born to him: Shimea,* Shobab,
Nathan, Solomon—four by Bathsheba, the
daughter of Ammiel;[x] [6]Ibhar, Elishua,
Eliphelet, [7]Nogah, Nepheg, Japhia, [8]Elish-
ama, Eliada, and Eliphelet—nine. [9]All these
were sons of David, in addition to other sons
by concubines; and Tamar was their sister.[y]
[10*] [z] The son of Solomon was Rehoboam,
whose son was Abijah, whose son was Asa,
whose son was Jehoshaphat,[a] [11]whose son
was Joram, whose son was Ahaziah, whose
son was Joash,[b] [12]whose son was Amaziah,
whose son was Azariah, whose son was Jotham,[c] [13]whose son was Ahaz, whose son
was Hezekiah, whose son was Manasseh,[d]
[14]whose son was Amon, whose son was Josiah.[e] [15]The sons of Josiah were: the firstborn Johanan; the second, Jehoiakim; the
third, Zedekiah; the fourth, Shallum.*[f] [16]The
sons of Jehoiakim were: Jeconiah, his son;
Zedekiah, his son.[g]
[17]The sons of Jeconiah* the captive were:
Shealtiel,[h] [18]Malchiram, Pedaiah, Shenazzar,* Jekamiah, Hoshama, and Nedabiah.
[19]The sons of Pedaiah were Zerubbabel* and
Shimei. The sons of Zerubbabel were Meshullam and Hananiah; Shelomith was their
sister. [20]The sons of Meshullam were Ha-
shubah, Ohel, Berechiah, Hasadiah, Jushab-
hesed—five. [21]The sons of Hananiah were
Pelatiah, Jeshaiah, Rephaiah, Arnan, Obadiah, and Shecaniah. [22]The sons of Shecaniah were Shemaiah, Hattush, Igal, Bariah,
Neariah, Shaphat—six.[i] [23]The sons of Neariah were Elioenai, Hizkiah, and Azrikam—
three. [24]The sons of Elioenai were Hodaviah, Eliashib, Pelaiah, Akkub, Johanan,
Delaiah, and Anani—seven.

## CHAPTER 4

See RG 138

[1*] The sons of Judah were: Perez,
Hezron, Carmi, Hur, and Shobal.[j] [2]Reaiah,
the son of Shobal, became the father of Jahath, and Jahath became the father of Ahu-

**3:1–9** A list of David's sons.

**3:1 Daniel**: he is called Chileab in 2 Sm 3:3.

**3:5 Shimea**: he bears the name Shammua in 2 Sm 5:14. **Ammiel**: Bathsheba's father is called Eliam in 2 Sm 11:3.

**3:10–16** The kings of Judah from Solomon down to the destruction of Jerusalem by the Babylonians.

**3:15 Shallum**: another name for Jehoahaz, Josiah's immediate successor; cf. Jer 22:11.

**3:17–24** The descendants of King Jeconiah down to the time of the Chronicler. If twenty-five years are allowed for each generation, the ten generations between Jeconiah and Anani (the last name on the list) would put the birth of the latter at about 405 B.C.—an important item in establishing the approximate date of the Chronicler's work in its final form.

**3:18 Shenazzar**: presumably he is the same as Sheshbazzar (Ezr 1:8, 11; 5:14–16), the prince of Judah who was the first Jewish governor of Judah after the exile. Both forms of the name probably go back to the Babylonian name Sin-abussar, meaning "O [god] Sin, protect [our] father!"

**3:19 Zerubbabel**: here called the son of Pedaiah, though elsewhere (Hg 1:12, 14; 2:2, 23; Ezr 3:2, 8; 5:2; Neh 12:1) his father's name is given as Shealtiel. The latter indication may merely point to the fact that Zerubbabel succeeded Shealtiel as head of the house of David.

**4:1–43** Genealogies of the southern tribes, Judah and Simeon.

*s:* Jgs 18:2. *t:* Nm 24:21; Jgs 1:16; 4:11; 1 Sm 15:6; Jer 35. *u:* 2 Sm 3:2–5. *v:* 2 Sm 2:11; 5:5. *w:* 2 Sm 5:14–16. *x:* 2 Sm 11:3. *y:* 2 Sm 13:1–2. *z:* Mt 1:7–12. *a:* 1 Kgs 11:43; 14:31; 15:1, 8, 24; 2 Chr 9:31; 12:16; 13:23; 17:1. *b:* 1 Kgs 22:51; 2 Chr 21:1; 22:1; 24:1, 27. *c:* 2 Kgs 12:21; 14:21; 15:7; 2 Chr 25:1; 26:1, 23; 27:1. *d:* 2 Kgs 15:38; 16:20; 20:21; 2 Chr 28:1, 27; 32:33. *e:* 2 Kgs 21:18, 26; 2 Chr 33:20, 25. *f:* 2 Kgs 23:34; 24:17; 2 Chr 36:4, 10. *g:* 2 Kgs 24:6, 17; 2 Chr 36:8, 10. *h:* Ezr 2:2; 3:2, 8; 5:2; Sir 49:11; Hg 1:1, 12, 14; Mt 1:12–13; Lk 3:27. *i:* Neh 3:29. *j:* 1 Chr 2:4–5, 7, 9, 50; Gn 38:29; 46:12; Mt 1:3.

### The Tribe of Simeon

BECAUSE THE AUTHOR has begun with Judah (2:3), it makes some sense to continue the examination of Israel by turning to the family group of Simeon (4:24), a tribe connected with Judah both by birth (Judah and Simeon were Jacob's sons by the same mother) and by proximity.

mai and Lahad. These were the clans of the Zorathites.

3 These were the sons of Hareph, the father of Etam: Jezreel, Ishma, and Idbash; their sister was named Hazzelelponi. 4 Penuel was the father of Gedor, and Ezer the father of Hushah. These were the sons of Hur, the firstborn of Ephrathah, the father of Bethlehem.

5 Ashhur, the father of Tekoa, had two wives, Helah and Naarah.[k] 6 Naarah bore him Ahuzzam, Hepher, the Temenites, and the Ahashtarites. These were the sons of Naarah. 7 The sons of Helah were Zereth, Izhar, Ethnan, and Koz. 8 Koz became the father of Anub and Zobebah, as well as of the clans of Aharhel, son of Harum. 9 Jabez was the most distinguished of his brothers. His mother had named him Jabez, saying, "I bore him with pain." 10 Jabez prayed to the God of Israel: "Oh, that you may truly bless me and extend my boundaries! May your hand be with me and make me free of misfortune, without pain!" And God granted his prayer.

11 Chelub, the brother of Shuhah, became the father of Mehir, who was the father of Eshton. 12 Eshton became the father of Bethrapha, Paseah, and Tehinnah, the father of the city of Nahash. These were the men of Recah.

13 The sons of Kenaz were Othniel and Seraiah. The sons of Othniel were Hathath and Meonothai;[l] 14 Meonothai became the father of Ophrah. Seraiah became the father of Joab, the father of Geharashim, so called because they were artisans. 15 The sons of Caleb, son of Jephunneh, were Ir, Elah, and Naam. The sons of Elah: Kenaz.[m] 16 The sons of Jehallelel were Ziph, Ziphah, Tiria, and Asarel. 17 The sons of Ezrah were Jether, Mered, Epher, and Jalon. Jether became the father of Miriam, Shammai, and Ishbah, the father of Eshtemoa.[n] 18 Mered's Egyptian wife bore Jered, the father of Gedor, Heber, the father of Soco, and Jekuthiel, the father of Zanoah. These were the sons of Bithiah, the daughter of Pharaoh, whom Mered married. 19 The sons of his Jewish wife, the sister of Naham, the father of Keilah, were Shimon the Garmite and Ishi the Maacathite. 20 The sons of Shimon were Amnon, Rinnah, Benhanan, and Tilon. The son of Ishi was Zoheth and the son of Zoheth. . . .

21 The sons of Shelah, son of Judah, were: Er, the father of Lecah; Laadah, the father of Mareshah; the clans of the linen weavers' guild in Bethashbea;[o] 22 Jokim; the people of Cozeba; and Joash and Saraph, who held property in Moab, but returned to Bethlehem. (These are events of old.) 23 They were potters and inhabitants of Netaim and Gederah, where they lived in the king's service.

*Simeon.* 24 The sons of Simeon were Nemuel, Jamin, Jachin, Zerah, and Shaul,[p] 25 whose son was Shallum, whose son was Mibsam, whose son was Mishma. 26 The sons of Mishma were his son Hammuel, whose son was Zaccur, whose son was Shimei. 27 Shimei had sixteen sons and six daughters. His brothers, however, did not have many sons, and as a result all their clans did not equal the number of the Judahites.

28 They dwelt in Beer-sheba, Moladah, Hazar-shual, 29 Bilhah, Ezem, Tolad, 30 Bethuel, Hormah, Ziklag, 31 Beth-marcaboth, Hazar-susim, Bethbiri, and Shaaraim. Until the reign of David, these were their cities 32 and their villages. Etam, also, and Ain, Rimmon, Tochen, and Ashan—five cities,[q] 33 together with all their outlying villages as far as Baal. Here is where they dwelt, and so

*k:* 1 Chr 2:24. *l:* Jos 15:17; Jgs 1:13; 3:9, 11. *m:* Nm 13:6; 14:6; 32:12; Jos 14:6, 14. *n:* 1 Sm 30:28. *o:* 1 Chr 2:3; Gn 38:5; 46:12; Nm 26:20. *p:* Gn 46:10; Ex 6:15; Nm 26:12–13. *q:* Jos 19:2–8.

it was inscribed of them in their family records.

34 Meshobab, Jamlech, Joshah, son of Amaziah, 35 Joel, Jehu, son of Joshibiah, son of Seraiah, son of Asiel, 36 Elioenai, Jaakobah, Jeshohaiah, Asaiah, Adiel, Jesimiel, Benaiah, 37 Ziza, son of Shiphi, son of Allon, son of Jedaiah, son of Shimri, son of Shemaiah— 38 these just named were princes in their clans, and their ancestral houses spread out to such an extent[r] 39 that they went to the approaches of Gedor,* east of the valley, seeking pasture for their flocks. 40 They found abundant and good pastures, and the land was spacious, quiet, and peaceful—for the Hamites dwelt there formerly. 41 They who have just been listed by name set out during the reign of Hezekiah, king of Judah, and attacked their tents and also the Meunites who were there. They put them under the ban that is still in force to this day and dwelt in their place because they found pasture there for their flocks.[s]

42 Five hundred of them (the Simeonites) went to Mount Seir, with Pelatiah, Neariah, Rephaiah, and Uzziel, sons of Ishi, at their head. 43 They attacked the surviving Amalekites who had escaped, and have lived there to the present day.[t]

See RG 138

## CHAPTER 5

***Reuben.*** 1* The sons of Reuben, the firstborn of Israel. (He was indeed the firstborn, but because he defiled the couch of his father his birthright was given to the sons of Joseph, son of Israel, so that he is not listed in the family records according to his birthright.[u] 2 Judah, in fact, became powerful among his brothers, so that the ruler came from him, though the birthright had been Joseph's.)[v] 3 The sons of Reuben, the firstborn of Israel, were Hanoch, Pallu, Hezron, and Carmi.[w] 4 His son was Joel, whose son was Shemaiah, whose son was Gog, whose son was Shimei, 5 whose son was Micah, whose son was Reaiah, whose son was Baal, 6 whose son was Beerah, whom Tilgath-pileser, the king of Assyria, took into exile; he was a prince of the Reubenites.[x] 7 His brothers who belonged to his clans, when they were listed in the family records according to their descendants, were: Jeiel, the chief, and Zechariah, 8 and Bela, son of Azaz, son of Shema, son of Joel. The Reubenites lived in Aroer and as far as Nebo and Baal-meon;[y] 9 toward the east they dwelt as far as the wilderness which extends from the Euphrates River, for they had much livestock in the land of Gilead.[z] 10 In Saul's time they waged war with the Hagrites, and when they had defeated them they dwelt in their tents throughout the region east of Gilead.[a]

*Gad.* 11 The Gadites lived alongside them in the land of Bashan as far as Salecah.[b] 12 Joel was chief, Shapham was second in command, and Janai was judge in Bashan.[c] 13 Their brothers, according to their ancestral houses, were: Michael, Meshullam, Sheba, Jorai, Jacan, Zia, and Eber—seven. 14 These were the sons of Abihail, son of Huri, son of Jaroah, son of Gilead, son of Michael, son of Jeshishai, son of Jahdo, son of Buz. 15 Ahi, son of Abdiel, son of Guni, was the head of their ancestral houses. 16 They dwelt in Gilead, in Bashan and its towns, and in all the pasture lands of Sirion to the borders. 17 All were listed in the family records in the time of Jotham, king of Judah, and of Jeroboam, king of Israel.

18 The Reubenites, Gadites, and the half-tribe of Manasseh were warriors, men who bore shield and sword and who drew the bow, trained in warfare—forty-four thousand seven hundred and sixty men fit for military service. 19 When they waged war against the Hagrites and against Jetur, Naphish, and Nodab,[d] 20 they received help so that the Hagrites and all who were with them were delivered into their power. For during the battle they cried out to God, and he heard

**4:39 Gedor**: the Greek reads Gerar, probably correctly.

**5:1–26** Genealogies of the Transjordanian tribes, Reuben, Gad, and the half-tribe of Manasseh.

---

*r:* Nm 1:2. *s:* 2 Kgs 18:1–2; 2 Chr 29:1. *t:* Ex 17:8, 14; Dt 25:17–19; 1 Sm 14:48; 15:3, 7–8; 2 Sm 8:12. *u:* Gn 35:22; 48:5, 15–22; 49:3–4; Dt 33:6. *v:* 1 Chr 28:4; Gn 49:8–12. *w:* Gn 46:9; Ex 6:14; Nm 26:5–6. *x:* 2 Kgs 15:29. *y:* Jos 13:9, 16–17; Nm 32:3, 38. *z:* Jos 22:9. *a:* Ps 83:6–7. *b:* Jos 13:11, 24–28. *c:* Gn 46:16. *d:* 1 Chr 1:31; 5:10; Gn 25:15; Ps 83:6–7.

them because they had put their trust in him.[e]
21 Along with one hundred thousand persons
they also captured their livestock: fifty thousand camels, two hundred fifty thousand
sheep, and two thousand donkeys. 22 Many
were slain and fell; for "From God the victory." They dwelt in their place until the time
of the exile.[f]

***The Half-tribe of Manasseh.*** 23 The half-
tribe of Manasseh lived in the land of Bashan as far as Baal-hermon, Senir, and
Mount Hermon; they were numerous. 24 The
following were the heads of their ancestral
houses: Epher, Ishi, Eliel, Azriel, Jeremiah,
Hodaviah, and Jahdiel—men who were warriors, famous men, and heads over their ancestral houses.

25 However, they acted treacherously toward the God of their ancestors by prostituting themselves to follow the gods of the peoples of the land, whom God had destroyed
before them.[g] 26 Therefore the God of Israel
stirred up against them the anger of Pul,*
king of Assyria, and the anger of Tilgath-pil-
neser [*sic*], king of Assyria, who deported
the Reubenites, the Gadites, and the half-
tribe of Manasseh and brought them to Halah, Habor, and Hara, and to the river Gozan,
where they have remained to this day.[h]

***Levi.**** 27 The sons of Levi were Gershon,
Kohath, and Merari.[i] 28 The sons of Kohath
were Amram, Izhar, Hebron, and Uzziel.[j]
29 The children of Amram were Aaron, Moses, and Miriam. The sons of Aaron were
Nadab, Abihu, Eleazar, and Ithamar.[k] 30* Eleazar became the father of Phinehas. Phinehas became the father of Abishua. 31 Abishua
became the father of Bukki. Bukki became
the father of Uzzi. 32 Uzzi became the father
of Zerahiah. Zerahiah became the father of
Meraioth. 33 Meraioth became the father of
Amariah. Amariah became the father of Ahitub. 34 Ahitub became the father of Zadok.
Zadok became the father of Ahimaaz.
35 Ahimaaz became the father of Azariah.
Azariah became the father of Johanan. 36 Johanan became the father of Azariah, who
served as priest in the temple Solomon built
in Jerusalem. 37 Azariah became the father of
Amariah. Amariah became the father of Ahitub. 38 Ahitub became the father of Zadok.
Zadok became the father of Shallum. 39 Shallum became the father of Hilkiah. Hilkiah
became the father of Azariah. 40 Azariah became the father of Seraiah. Seraiah became
the father of Jehozadak. 41 Jehozadak was
one of those who went into the exile which
the LORD inflicted on Judah and Jerusalem
through Nebuchadnezzar.

## CHAPTER 6

See RG 138

1 The sons of Levi were Gershon, Kohath, and Merari.[l] 2 The sons of Gershon were
named Libni and Shimei.[m] 3 The sons of Kohath were Amram, Izhar, Hebron, and Uzziel.[n]
4 The sons of Merari were Mahli and Mushi.[o]

These were the clans of Levi, according to
their ancestors. 5 Of Gershon: his son Libni,
whose son was Jahath, whose son was Zimmah, 6 whose son was Joah, whose son was
Iddo, whose son was Zerah, whose son was
Jetherai.

7 The sons of Kohath: his son Amminadab,
whose son was Korah, whose son was Assir,
8 whose son was Elkanah, whose son was
Ebiasaph, whose son was Assir, 9 whose son
was Tahath, whose son was Uriel, whose son
was Uzziah, whose son was Shaul. 10 The
sons of Elkanah were Amasai and Ahimoth,
11 whose son was Elkanah, whose son was
Zophai, whose son was Nahath, 12 whose son
was Eliab, whose son was Jeroham, whose
son was Elkanah, whose son was Samuel.
13 The sons of Samuel were Joel, the firstborn, and Abijah, the second.

14 The sons of Merari: Mahli, whose son

**5:26 Pul**: the Chronicler seems to speak of two different kings here, but Pul was the name which the Assyrian king Tilgath-pileser III (745–727 B.C.) adopted as king of Babylon.

**5:27–6:66** The tribe of Levi. The Chronicler's list gives special prominence to Levi's son Kohath, from whom were descended both the Aaronite priests (vv. 28–41) and the leading group of Temple singers (6:18–23).

**5:30–41** The line of preexilic high priests. The list seems to become confused in vv. 36–38, which repeat the same names, mostly in inverse order, that occur in vv. 34–36. A similar but shorter list occurs, with variations, in Ezr 7:1–5.

*e:* Dt 33:20–21. *f:* Nm 32:39; Dt 3:8–10; Jgs 3:3. *g:* Ex 34:14–16; 2 Kgs 17:7. *h:* 2 Kgs 15:9, 29; 17:6. *i:* 1 Chr 6:1; 23:6; Gn 46:11; Ex 6:16; Nm 26:57. *j:* 1 Chr 6:3; Ex 6:18. *k:* Ex 6:20; Nm 26:59–60. *l:* 1 Chr 5:27; 23:6; Gn 46:11; Ex 6:16; Nm 26:57. *m:* Ex 6:17. *n:* Ex 6:18; Nm 3:19; 26:59. *o:* 1 Chr 6:14; Ex 6:19; Nm 3:20; 26:58.

ALTHOUGH DAVID'S SON Solomon is the one who built the temple, the Chronicler asserts that all the main elements of temple worship, such as those entrusted with the choir services (6:16), were put in place by David. He justifies this perspective by noting that such worship was instigated after the ark had "a resting place," assuming that once the ark had been brought into Jerusalem, regular forms of worship would be required. While it is certainly possible that David authorized the formation of dedicated musicians prior to the foundation of the temple, this elaborate form of the organization suggests the Chronicler is referring to the temple music professionals of his own day.

was Libni, whose son was Shimei, whose son was Uzzah,[p] 15 whose son was Shimea, whose son was Haggiah, whose son was Asaiah.

16 The following were established by David for the service of song* in the LORD's house at the time when the ark had a resting place. 17 They served as singers before the tabernacle of the tent of meeting until Solomon built the house of the LORD in Jerusalem, and they performed their services according to the order prescribed for them. 18 Those who so performed are the following, together with their sons.

Among the Kohathites: Heman, the chanter, son of Joel, son of Samuel, 19 son of Elkanah, son of Jeroham, son of Eliel, son of Toah, 20 son of Zuph, son of Elkanah, son of Mahath, son of Amasi, 21 son of Elkanah, son of Joel, son of Azariah, son of Zephaniah, 22 son of Tahath, son of Assir, son of Ebiasaph, son of Korah,[q] 23 son of Izhar, son of Kohath, son of Levi, son of Israel.

24 His brother Asaph stood at his right hand. Asaph was the son of Berechiah, son of Shimea, 25 son of Michael, son of Baaseiah, son of Malchijah, 26 son of Ethni, son of Zerah, son of Adaiah, 27 son of Ethan, son of Zimmah,[r] son of Shimei, 28 son of Jahath, son of Gershon, son of Levi.

29 Their brothers, the Merarites, stood at the left: Ethan, son of Kishi, son of Abdi, son of Malluch, 30 son of Hashabiah, son of Amaziah, son of Hilkiah, 31 son of Amzi, son of Bani, son of Shemer, 32 son of Mahli, son of Mushi, son of Merari, son of Levi.[s]

33 Their brother Levites were appointed to all the other services of the tabernacle of the house of God.[t] 34 However, it was Aaron and his sons who made the sacrifice on the altar for burnt offerings and on the altar of incense; they alone had charge of the holy of holies and of making atonement for Israel, as Moses, the servant of God, had commanded.[u]

35 These were the sons of Aaron: his son Eleazar, whose son was Phinehas, whose son was Abishua, 36 whose son was Bukki, whose son was Uzzi, whose son was Zerahiah, 37 whose son was Meraioth, whose son was Amariah, whose son was Ahitub, 38 whose son was Zadok, whose son was Ahimaaz.

39* The following were their dwelling places, by encampments in their territories. To the sons of Aaron who belonged to the clan of the Kohathites, since the lot fell to them, 40 was assigned Hebron in the land of Judah, with its adjacent pasture lands. 41 However, the open country and the villages belonging to the city had been given to Caleb, the son of Jephunneh. 42 There were assigned to the sons of Aaron: Hebron a city of refuge, Libnah with its pasture lands, Jattir with its pasture lands, Eshtemoa with its pasture lands, 43 Holon with its pasture lands, Debir with its pasture lands, 44 Ashan with its pasture lands, Jetta with its pasture lands, and Beth-shemesh with its pasture lands. 45 Also from the tribe of Benjamin: Gibeon with its pasture lands, Geba with its pasture lands, Almon with its pasture lands, Ana-

**6:16–32** The cultic functions performed by the levitical families in the postexilic Temple at the time of the Chronicler are here traced back to David, in a way analogous to that in which all the laws in the Pentateuch are attributed to Moses.

**6:39–66** For the rights of the Levites in the cities assigned to them, see note on Jos 21:1.

*p:* 1 Chr 6:4; Ex 6:19; Nm 3:20; 26:58. *q:* Ex 6:24. *r:* 1 Chr 6:2, 5. *s:* Ex 6:19; Nm 26:58. *t:* 1 Chr 15:17, 19; 16:41–42; 2 Chr 5:12. *u:* 1 Chr 16:39–40.

## Priests—Levite and Aaronides

THE GENEALOGY OF Levi (6:1–66), along with that of the tribe of Judah (2:3–4:23), represents the most elaborate portion of the genealogy. From the Chronicler's viewpoint, the tribe of Levi and the formal temple service responsibilities that only this family can undertake for Israel are of critical importance for Israel's destiny. By the time of the Chronicler's history, the priesthood of Israel had been segmented into various family lines with different responsibilities and social standings. Those who belonged to the sons of Aaron were eligible for the high priesthood, the chief administrative office of the temple. Those who belonged to the various lines of the Levites other than Aaron's had lesser roles in the temple.

One of the prime distinctions between the line of Aaron and the other members of the tribe of Levi is that it was the descendants of Aaron alone who could offer the sacrifice to atone for sin and purify the worshiper (v. 34).

thoth with its pasture lands. In all, they had thirteen cities with their pasture lands. [49]The Israelites assigned these cities with their pasture lands to the Levites, [50]designating them by name and assigning them by lot from the tribes of the Judahites, Simeonites, and Benjaminites.

[46]The other Kohathites obtained ten cities by lot for their clans from the tribe of Ephraim, from the tribe of Dan, and from the half-tribe of Manasseh. [47]The clans of the Gershonites obtained thirteen cities from the tribes of Issachar, Asher, and Naphtali, and from the half-tribe of Manasseh in Bashan. [48]The clans of the Merarites obtained twelve cities by lot from the tribes of Reuben, Gad, and Zebulun.

[51]The clans of the Kohathites obtained cities by lot from the tribe of Ephraim. [52]They were assigned cities of refuge: Shechem in the mountain region of Ephraim, with its pasture lands, Gezer with its pasture lands, [53]Kibzaim with its pasture lands, and Beth-horon with its pasture lands. [54]From the tribe of Dan: Elteke with its pasture lands, Gibbethon with its pasture lands, Aijalon with its pasture lands, and Gath-rimmon with its pasture lands. [55]From the half-tribe of Manasseh: Taanach with its pasture lands and Ibleam with its pasture lands. These belonged to the rest of the Kohathite clan.

[56]The clans of the Gershonites received from the half-tribe of Manasseh: Golan in Bashan with its pasture lands and Ashtaroth with its pasture lands. [57]From the tribe of Issachar: Kedesh with its pasture lands, Daberath with its pasture lands, [58]Ramoth with its pasture lands, and Engannim with its pasture lands. [59]From the tribe of Asher: Mashal with its pasture lands, Abdon with its pasture lands, [60]Hilkath with its pasture lands, and Rehob with its pasture lands. [61]From the tribe of Naphtali: Kedesh in Galilee with its pasture lands, Hammon with its pasture lands, and Kiriathaim with its pasture lands.

[62]The rest of the Merarites received from the tribe of Zebulun: Jokneam with its pasture lands, Kartah with its pasture lands, Rimmon with its pasture lands, and Tabor with its pasture lands. [63]Across the Jordan at Jericho (that is, east of the Jordan) they received from the tribe of Reuben: Bezer in the desert with its pasture lands, Jahzah with its pasture lands, [64]Kedemoth with its pasture lands, and Mephaath with its pasture lands. [65]From the tribe of Gad: Ramoth in Gilead with its pasture lands, Mahanaim with its pasture lands, [66]Heshbon with its pasture lands, and Jazer with its pasture lands.

### CHAPTER 7

See RG 138

*Issachar.* [1*] The sons of Issachar were Tola, Puah, Jashub, and Shimron: four.[v]

**7:1–40** The seven northern tribes.

*v:* Gn 46:13.

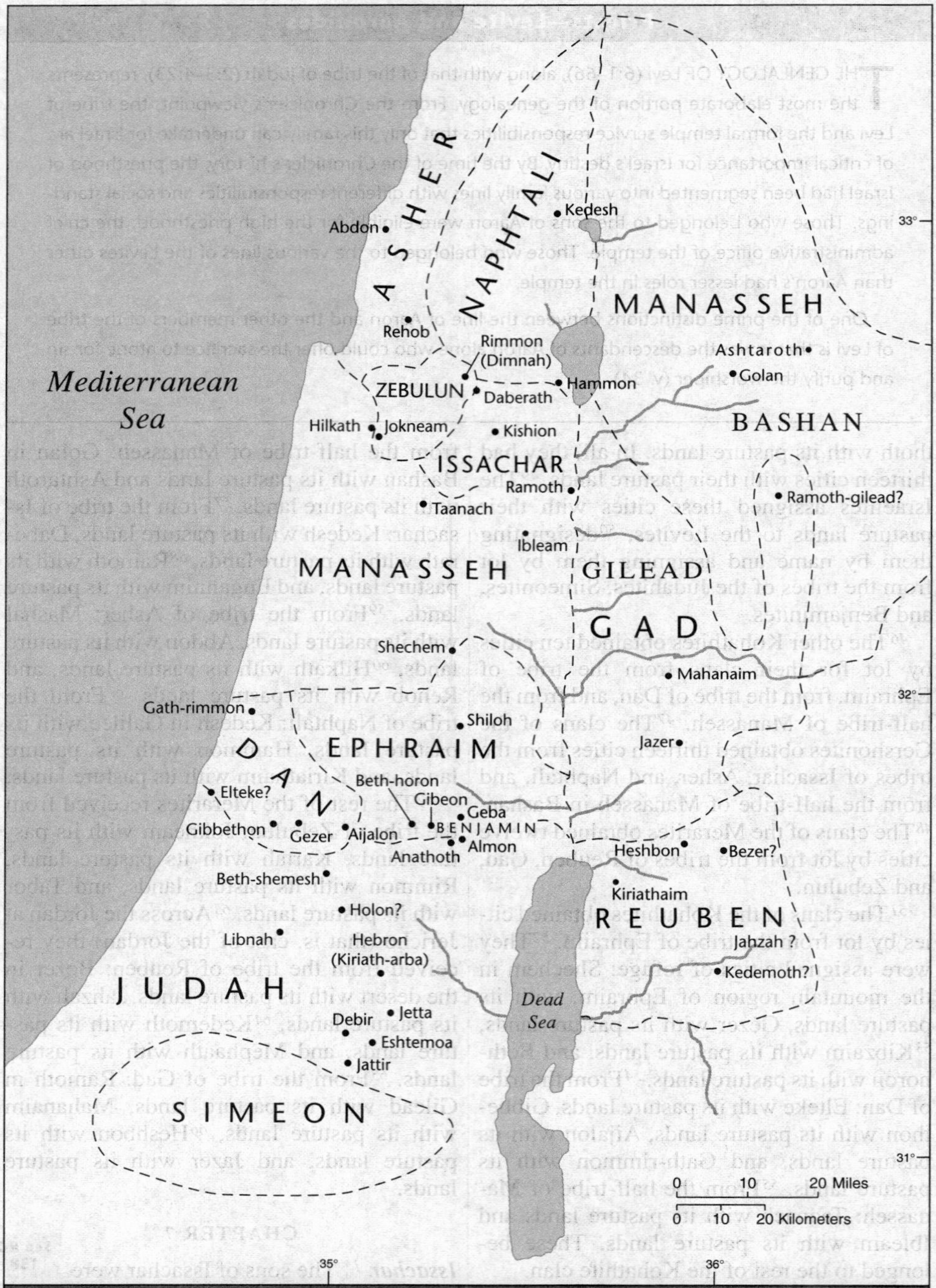


**The Levitical Cities according to 1 Chronicles**

2The sons of Tola were Uzzi, Rephaiah, Jeriel, Jahmai, Ibsam, and Shemuel, heads of the ancestral houses of Tola, mighty warriors in their generations. In the time of David they numbered twenty-two thousand six hundred.[w] 3The sons of Uzzi: Izarahiah. The sons of Izarahiah were Michael, Obadiah, Joel, and Isshiah. All five of these were chiefs. 4Along with them, in their generations, according to ancestral houses, were thirty-six thousand men in organized military troops, since they had more wives and children 5than their fellow tribesmen. In all the clans of Issachar there was a total of eighty-seven thousand warriors listed in their family records.

***Benjamin.*** 6The sons of Benjamin were Bela, Becher, and Jediael—three.[x] 7The sons of Bela were Ezbon, Uzzi, Uzziel, Jerimoth, and Iri—five. They were heads of their ancestral houses and warriors. Their family records listed twenty-two thousand and thirty-four. 8The sons of Becher were Zemirah, Joash, Eliezer, Elioenai, Omri, Jeremoth, Abijah, Anathoth, and Alemeth—all these were sons of Becher.[y] 9Their family records listed twenty thousand two hundred of their kindred who were heads of their ancestral houses and warriors. 10The sons of Jediael: Bilhan. The sons of Bilhan were Jeush, Benjamin, Ehud, Chenaanah, Zethan, Tarshish, and Ahishahar. 11All these were sons of Jediael, heads of ancestral houses and warriors. They numbered seventeen thousand two hundred men fit for military service . . .* 12Shupham and Hupham.[z]

***Dan, Naphtali and Manasseh.*** The sons of Dan: Hushim. 13The sons of Naphtali were Jahziel, Guni, Jezer, and Shallum. These were sons of Bilhah.[a] 14The sons of Manasseh, whom his Aramean concubine bore:[b] she bore Machir, the father of Gilead.[c] 15Machir took a wife whose name was Maacah; his sister's name was Molecheth. Manasseh's second son was named Zelophehad, who had only daughters.[d] 16Maacah, Machir's wife, bore a son whom she named Peresh. He had a brother named Sheresh, whose sons were Ulam and Rakem. 17The sons of Ulam: Bedan. These were the sons of Gilead, the son of Machir, the son of Manasseh. 18His sister Molecheth bore Ishhod, Abiezer, and Mahlah. 19The sons of Shemida were Ahian, Shechem, Likhi, and Aniam.

***Ephraim.*** 20[e] The sons of Ephraim: Shuthelah, whose son was Bered, whose son was Tahath, whose son was Eleadah, whose son was Tahath, 21whose son was Zabad. Ephraim's son Shuthelah, and Ezer and Elead, who were born in the land, were killed by the inhabitants of Gath because they had gone down to take away their livestock. 22Their father Ephraim mourned a long time, but after his relatives had come and comforted him, 23he had relations with his wife, who conceived and bore a son whom he named Beriah, since evil* had befallen his house.[f] 24He had a daughter, Sheerah, who built Lower and Upper Beth-horon and Uzzen-sheerah. 25Zabad's son was Rephah, whose son was Resheph, whose son was Telah, whose son was Tahan, 26whose son was Ladan, whose son was Ammihud, whose son was Elishama,[g] 27whose son was Nun, whose son was Joshua.

28Their property and their dwellings were in Bethel and its towns, Naaran to the east, Gezer and its towns to the west, and also Shechem and its towns as far as Ayyah and its towns.[h] 29Manasseh, however, had possession of Beth-shean and its towns, Taanach and its towns, Megiddo and its towns, and Dor and its towns. In these dwelt the sons of Joseph, the son of Israel.[i]

***Asher.*** 30The sons of Asher were Imnah, Ishvah, Ishvi, and Beriah; their sister was Serah.[j] 31Beriah's sons were Heber and Malchiel, who was the father of Birzaith. 32Heber became the father of Japhlet, Shomer, Hotham, and their sister Shua. 33The

**7:11** The Hebrew text appears to be defective.

**7:23 Beriah . . . evil**: the name sounds like the Hebrew word for "evil," with the preposition *be*.

*w:* Nm 26:23–24; Jgs 10:1. *x:* Gn 46:21; Nm 26:38. *y:* Gn 46:21. *z:* Nm 26:39. *a:* Gn 46:24; Nm 26:48–49. *b:* Nm 26:29–32. *c:* Nm 26:29; Jos 17:1. *d:* Nm 26:33; Jos 17:3. *e:* Nm 26:35. *f:* 1 Chr 8:13. *g:* Nm 1:10; 2:18; 7:48; 10:22. *h:* Gn 12:8; 1 Kgs 9:16. *i:* Jos 17:11. *j:* Gn 46:17; Nm 26:44–46.

sons of Japhlet were Pasach, Bimhal, and Ashvath; these were the sons of Japhlet. 34 The sons of Shomer were Ahi, Rohgah, Jehubbah, and Aram. 35 The sons of his brother Hotham were Zophah, Imna, Shelesh, and Amal. 36 The sons of Zophah were Suah, Harnepher, Shual, Beri, Imrah, 37 Bezer, Hod, Shamma, Shilshah, Ithran, and Beera. 38 The sons of Jether were Jephunneh, Pispa, and Ara. 39 The sons of Ulla were Arah, Hanniel, and Rizia. 40 All these were sons of Asher, heads of ancestral houses, distinguished men, warriors, and chiefs among the princes. Their family records numbered twenty-six thousand men fit for military service.

## CHAPTER 8

See RG 138

***Benjamin.*** 1* Benjamin became the father of Bela, his firstborn, Ashbel, the second son, Aharah, the third,[k] 2 Nohah, the fourth, and Rapha, the fifth. 3 The sons of Bela were Addar and Gera, the father of Ehud. 4 The sons of Ehud were Abishua, Naaman, Ahoah,[l] 5 Gera, Shephuphan, and Huram. 6 These were the sons of Ehud, family heads over those who dwelt in Geba and were deported to Manahath. 7 Also Naaman, Ahijah, and Gera. The last, who led them into exile, became the father of Uzza and Ahihud. 8 Shaharaim became a father on the Moabite plateau after he had put away his wives Hushim and Baara. 9 By his wife Hodesh he begot Jobab, Zibia, Mesha, Malcam, 10 Jeuz, Sachia, and Mirmah. These were his sons, family heads. 11 By Hushim he begot Abitub and Elpaal. 12 The sons of Elpaal were Eber, Misham, Shemed (who built Ono and Lod with its nearby towns),[m] 13 and Beriah, and Shema. They were family heads of those who dwelt in Aijalon, and they put the inhabitants of Gath to flight. 14 Their relatives were Elpaal, Shashak, and Jeremoth. 15 Zebadiah, Arad, Eder, 16 Michael, Ishpah, and Joha were the sons of Beriah. 17 Zebadiah, Meshullam, Hizki, Heber, 18 Ishmerai, Izliah, and Jobab were the sons of Elpaal. 19 Jakim, Zichri, Zabdi, 20 Elienai, Zillethai, Eliel, 21 Adaiah, Beraiah, and Shimrath were the sons of Shimei. 22 Ishpan, Eber, Eliel, 23 Abdon, Zichri, Hanan, 24 Hananiah, Elam, Anthothijah, 25 Iphdeiah, and Penuel were the sons of Shashak. 26 Shamsherai, Shehariah, Athaliah, 27 Jaareshiah, Elijah, and Zichri were the sons of Jeroham. 28 These were family heads in their generations, chiefs who dwelt in Jerusalem.

29[n] In Gibeon dwelt Jeiel, the founder of Gibeon, whose wife's name was Maacah; 30 also his firstborn son, Abdon, and Zur, Kish, Baal, Ner, Nadab, 31 Gedor, Ahio, Zecher, and Mikloth. 32 Mikloth became the father of Shimeah. These, too, dwelt with their relatives in Jerusalem, opposite their fellow tribesmen. 33[o] Ner became the father of Kish, and Kish became the father of Saul. Saul became the father of Jonathan, Malchishua, Abinadab, and Eshbaal.[p] 34 The son of Jonathan was Meribbaal, and Meribbaal became the father of Micah.[q] 35 The sons of Micah were Pithon, Melech, Tarea, and Ahaz. 36 Ahaz became the father of Jehoaddah, and Jehoaddah became the father of Alemeth, Azmaveth, and Zimri. Zimri became the father of Moza.[r] 37 Moza became the father of Binea, whose son was Raphah, whose son was Eleasah, whose son was Azel. 38 Azel had six sons, whose names were Azrikam, his firstborn, Ishmael, Sheariah, Azariah, Obadiah, and Hanan; all these were the sons of Azel.[s] 39 The sons of Eshek, his brother, were Ulam, his firstborn, Jeush, the second son, and Eliphelet, the third. 40 The sons of Ulam were warriors, skilled with the bow, and they had many sons and grandsons: one hundred and fifty. All these were the sons of Benjamin.

## CHAPTER 9

See RG 138

1 Thus all Israel was listed in family lists, and these are recorded in the book of the kings of Israel.[t]

Now Judah had been exiled to Babylon because of its treachery. 2* [u] The first to set-

**8:1–40** A second, variant list (cf. 7:6–11) of the Benjaminites, highlighting the family of Saul (vv. 33–40).

**9:2–34** The inhabitants of Jerusalem after the exile. A similar list, though with many variants in the names, occurs in Neh 11:3–24.

*k:* 1 Chr 7:6; Gn 46:21; Nm 26:38–44. *l:* Jgs 3:15. *m:* Neh 11:35. *n:* 1 Chr 9:35–38. *o:* 1 Chr 9:39–44. *p:* 1 Chr 10:2; 1 Sm 9:1; 14:49, 51; 31:2. *q:* 2 Sm 4:4; 9:6; 10:12. *r:* 1 Chr 9:42. *s:* 1 Chr 9:43. *t:* 2 Chr 16:11; 20:34; 25:26; 27:7; 33:18; 36:8. *u:* Neh 11:3–24.

## The Organization of the Postexilic Community

CHAPTER 9 OPENS with a summary of what has gone before (vv. 1–2) and moves on to a detailed listing of those responsible for Jerusalem after the return from exile. The Chronicler places characteristic emphasis on the role of the Levites in maintaining proper worship in postexilic Yehud (the name for the Persian province of Judah). In v. 2, the Israelites are all those in the population with no formal temple function; the priests are the sons of Aaron, those entitled to offer the sacrifices on behalf of the worshipers; the Levites are those with nonsacrificial responsibilities in the temple; and the temple servants are a class of persons assigned to assist in the mundane functions of the temple. The Chronicler spends a large portion of this section on those with a connection to the temple to underscore its importance.

tle again in their cities and dwell there were certain Israelites, the priests, the Levites, and the temple servants.[v]

***Jerusalemites.*** 3In Jerusalem lived Judahites and Benjaminites; also Ephraimites and Manassites. 4Among the Judahites was Uthai, son of Ammihud, son of Omri, son of Imri, son of Bani, one of the sons of Perez, son of Judah. 5Among the Shelanites were Asaiah, the firstborn, and his sons. 6Among the Zerahites were Jeuel and six hundred and ninety of their relatives. 7Among the Benjaminites were Sallu, son of Meshullam, son of Hodaviah, son of Hassenuah, 8as well as Ibneiah, son of Jeroham; Elah, son of Uzzi, son of Michri; Meshullam, son of Shephatiah, son of Reuel, son of Ibnijah. 9Their kindred of various families were nine hundred and fifty-six. All those named were heads of their ancestral houses.

10Among the priests were Jedaiah; Jehoiarib; Jachin; 11Azariah, son of Hilkiah, son of Meshullam, son of Zadok, son of Meraioth, son of Ahitub, the ruler of the house of God; 12Adaiah, son of Jeroham, son of Pashhur, son of Malchijah; Maasai, son of Adiel, son of Jahzerah, son of Meshullam, son of Meshillemith, son of Immer. 13Their brothers, heads of their ancestral houses, were one thousand seven hundred and sixty, valiant in the work of the service of the house of God.

14Among the Levites were Shemaiah, son of Hasshub, son of Azrikam, son of Hashabiah, one of the sons of Merari; 15Bakbakkar; Heresh; Galal; Mattaniah, son of Mica, son of Zichri, a descendant of Asaph; 16Obadiah, son of Shemaiah, son of Galal, a descendant of Jeduthun; and Berechiah, son of Asa, son of Elkanah, whose family lived in the villages of the Netophathites.

17The gatekeepers were Shallum, Akkub, Talmon, Ahiman, and their brothers; Shallum was the chief. 18Previously they had stood guard at the king's gate on the east side; now they became gatekeepers for the encampments of the Levites. 19Shallum, son of Kore, son of Ebiasaph, a descendant of Korah, and his brothers of the same ancestral house of the Korahites had as their assigned task the guarding of the threshold of the tent, just as their fathers had guarded the entrance to the encampment of the LORD. 20Phinehas, son of Eleazar, had been their chief in times past; the LORD was with him.[w] 21Zechariah, son of Meshelemiah, guarded the gate of the tent of meeting.[x] 22In all, those who were chosen for gatekeepers at the threshold were two hundred and twelve. They were inscribed in the family records of their villages. David and Samuel the seer had established them in their position of trust. 23Thus they and their sons kept guard over the gates of the house of the LORD, the house which was then a tent. 24The gatekeepers were stationed at the four sides, to the east, the west, the north, and the south.[y] 25Their brothers who lived in their own villages took turns in assisting them for seven-day periods,[z] 26while the four chief gate-

*v:* Ezr 2:70; 7:7; Neh 11:3. *w:* Ex 6:25; Nm 25:7, 11; Jgs 20:28. *x:* 1 Chr 26:2, 14. *y:* 1 Chr 26:13. *z:* 2 Chr 23:4–5.

**Account of David's Reign**

CHAPTERS 10–20 SOMETIMES repeat, and on occasion summarize, portions of the narratives of David's reign (2 Sm 5 through 1 Kgs 2). Many of these earlier accounts are completely left out by the Chronicler, and others are rewritten so thoroughly as to bear little resemblance to the earlier account. In these narratives, the Chronicler highlights David's success as king and his role in selecting Jerusalem as the capital, along with preparing for the construction and staffing of the temple.

keepers were on permanent duty. These were the Levites who also had charge of the chambers and treasures of the house of God. [27]They would spend the night near the house of God, for it was in their charge and they had the duty of opening it each morning.

[28]Some of them had charge of the vessels used there, tallying them as they were brought in and taken out. [29]Others were appointed to take care of the utensils and all the sacred vessels, as well as the fine flour, the wine, the oil, the frankincense, and the spices. [30]It was the sons of priests, however, who mixed the spiced ointments.[a] [31][b] Mattithiah, one of the Levites, the firstborn of Shallum the Korahite, was entrusted with preparing the cakes. [32]Benaiah the Kohathite, one of their brothers, was in charge of setting out the showbread each sabbath.[c]

[33]These were the singers and the gatekeepers, family heads over the Levites. They stayed in the chambers when free of duty, for day and night they had to be ready for service. [34]These were the levitical family heads by their generations, chiefs who dwelt in Jerusalem.

## II. The History of David

***Genealogy of Saul.*** [35][d] Jeiel, the founder of Gibeon, dwelt in Gibeon; his wife's name was Maacah. [36]His firstborn son was Abdon; then came Zur, Kish, Baal, Ner, Nadab, [37]Gedor, Ahio, Zechariah, and Mikloth. [38]Mikloth became the father of Shimeam. These, too, with their relatives, dwelt opposite their relatives in Jerusalem. [39]Ner became the father of Kish, and Kish became the father of Saul. Saul became the father of Jonathan, Malchishua, Abinadab, and Eshbaal. [40]The son of Jonathan was Meribbaal, and Meribbaal became the father of Micah. [41]The sons of Micah were Pithon, Melech, Tahrea, and Ahaz. [42]Ahaz became the father of Jehoaddah, and Jehoaddah became the father of Alemeth, Azmaveth, and Zimri. Zimri became the father of Moza. [43]Moza became the father of Binea, whose son was Rephaiah, whose son was Eleasah, whose son was Azel. [44]Azel had six sons, whose names were Azrikam, his firstborn, Ishmael, Sheariah, Azariah, Obadiah, and Hanan; these were the sons of Azel.

### CHAPTER 10

See RG 138–40

***Death of Saul and His Sons.*** [1][e] Now the Philistines went to war against Israel, and Israel fled before them, and they fell, slain on Mount Gilboa. [2]The Philistines pressed hard after Saul and his sons. When the Philistines had struck down Jonathan, Abinadab, and Malchishua, sons of Saul, [3]the fury of the battle converged on Saul. Then the archers hit him, and he was severely wounded.

[4]Saul said to his armor-bearer, "Draw your sword and run me through; otherwise these uncircumcised will come and abuse me." But the armor-bearer, badly frightened, refused, so Saul took his own sword and fell upon it. [5]When the armor-bearer saw that Saul was dead, he too fell upon his sword and died. [6]Thus Saul, and his three sons, his whole house, died together. [7]When all the Israelites in the valley saw that Saul and his sons had fled and that they had died, they abandoned their cities and fled. Then the Philistines came and lived in those cities.

[8]On the following day, when the Philistines came to strip the slain, they found Saul and his sons fallen on Mount Gilboa. [9]They

*a:* Ex 30:20–33. *b:* 1 Chr 23:29; Lv 2:1–15; 6:13–16; 7:11. *c:* Ex 25:30; Lv 24:5–8. *d:* 1 Chr 8:29–38. *e:* 1 Sm 31:1–13.

stripped him, and took his head and his armor; these they sent throughout the land of the Philistines to bring the good news to their idols and to the people. 10 They put his armor in the temple of their gods, but his skull they impaled at the temple of Dagon.

***Burial of Saul.*** 11 When all the inhabitants of Jabesh-gilead heard all that the Philistines had done to Saul, 12 all their warriors set out, recovered the corpses of Saul and his sons, and brought them to Jabesh. They buried their bones under the oak of Jabesh, and fasted for seven days.[f]

13* Thus Saul died because of his treason against the LORD in disobeying his word, and also because he had sought counsel from a ghost,[g] 14 rather than from the LORD. Therefore the LORD took his life, and turned his kingdom over to David, the son of Jesse.[h]

## CHAPTER 11

See RG 138–40

***David Is Made King.*** 1[i] Then all Israel gathered around David in Hebron, and they said: "Look! We are your bone and your flesh. 2 In days past, when Saul was still the king, it was you who led Israel in all its battles. And now the LORD, your God, has said to you: You shall shepherd my people Israel; you shall be ruler over my people Israel."[j] 3 Then all the elders of Israel came to the king at Hebron, and at Hebron David made a covenant with them in the presence of the LORD; and they anointed David king over Israel, in accordance with the word of the LORD given through Samuel.[k]

***Jerusalem Captured.*** 4 Then David and all Israel went to Jerusalem, that is, Jebus, where the inhabitants of the land were called Jebusites.[l] 5 The inhabitants of Jebus said to David, "You shall not enter here." David nevertheless captured the fortress of Zion, which is the City of David. 6 David said, "Whoever strikes the Jebusites first shall be made chief and captain." Joab, the son of Zeruiah, was the first to attack; and so he became chief.[m] 7 David took up residence in the fortress, which therefore was called the City of David. 8 He built up the city on all sides, from the Millo all the way around, while Joab restored the rest of the city.[n] 9 David became ever more powerful, for the LORD of hosts was with him.

***David's Warriors.*** 10[o] These were David's chief warriors who, together with all Israel, supported him in his reign in order to make him king, according to the LORD's word concerning Israel.

11 Here is the list of David's warriors:

Ishbaal, the son of Hachamoni, chief of the Three.* He brandished his spear over three hundred, whom he had slain in a single encounter.

12 Next to him was Eleazar, the son of Dodo the Ahohite, one of the Three warriors.[p] 13 He was with David at Pas-dammim, where the Philistines had massed for battle. There was a plot of land full of barley. The people were fleeing before the Philistines,[q] 14 but he took his stand in the middle of the plot, kept it safe, and cut down the Philistines. Thus the LORD brought about a great victory.

15 Three of the Thirty chiefs went down to the rock, to David, who was in the cave of Adullam while the Philistines were encamped in the valley of Rephaim.[r] 16 David was then in the stronghold, and a Philistine garrison was at Bethlehem. 17 David had a strong craving, and said, "If only someone would give me a drink of water from the cistern by the gate of Bethlehem!" 18 Thereupon the Three broke through the encampment of the Philistines, drew water from the cistern by the gate of Bethlehem, and carried it back to David. But David refused to drink it. Instead, he poured it out* to the LORD, 19 say-

**10:13–14** The Chronicler explains why Saul met his tragic end: he had disobeyed the Lord's command given through the prophet Samuel (1 Sm 15:3–9), and had consulted a necromancer (1 Sm 28:6–19), contrary to the Mosaic law (Dt 18:10–11).

**11:11 The Three**: the Chronicler actually names only two of these figures, Ishbaal and Eleazar. According to 2 Sm 23:11, the third member of the Three was Shammah.

**11:18 Poured it out**: as a libation.

*f:* 2 Sm 2:5. *g:* Dt 18:10–14; 1 Sm 13:13–14; 15:3, 11, 26. *h:* 1 Sm 15:28; 2 Sm 3:9–10. *i:* 2 Sm 5:1–10. *j:* 1 Sm 18:5, 13–16, 30; 19:8. *k:* 1 Sm 16:1, 13; 2 Sm 2:4. *l:* Jos 15:8; Jgs 1:21; 19:10–11. *m:* 2 Sm 8:16. *n:* 1 Kgs 9:15, 24; 11:27; 2 Chr 32:5. *o:* 2 Sm 23:8–39. *p:* 1 Chr 27:4. *q:* 1 Sm 17:1. *r:* 1 Chr 14:9; 2 Sm 5:18, 22.

ing, "God forbid that I should do such a
thing! Could I drink the blood of these men
who risked their lives? For at the risk of their
lives they brought it." So he refused to drink
it. Such deeds as these the Three warriors
performed.
20[s] Abishai, the brother of Joab, was the
chief of the Thirty;* he brandished his spear
over three hundred, whom he had slain. He
made a name beside the Three,[t] 21 but was
twice as famous as any of the Thirty, becoming their leader. However, he did not attain to the Three.
22 Benaiah, son of Jehoiada, a valiant man
of mighty deeds, from Kabzeel, killed the
two sons of Ariel of Moab. Also, he went
down and killed the lion in the cistern on a
snowy day. 23 He likewise slew the Egyptian,
a huge man five cubits tall. The Egyptian
carried a spear that was like a weaver's
beam, but Benaiah came against him with a
staff; he wrested the spear from the Egyptian's hand, and killed him with that spear.
24 Such deeds as these Benaiah, the son of Jehoiada, performed, and he made a name beside the Three warriors, 25 but was more famous than any of the Thirty. However, he
did not attain to the Three. David put him in
charge of his bodyguard.[u]
26 Also these warriors: Asahel, the brother
of Joab; Elhanan, son of Dodo, from Bethlehem;[v] 27 Shammoth, from En-harod; Helez,
from Beth-pelet; 28 Ira, son of Ikkesh, from
Tekoa; Abiezer, from Anathoth; 29 Sibbecai,
from Husha; Ilai, from Ahoh;[w] 30 Maharai,
from Netophah; Heled, son of Baanah, from
Netophah;[x] 31 Ithai, son of Ribai, from Gibeah
of Benjamin; Benaiah, from Pirathon;[y] 32 Hu-
rai, from Nahale-gaash; Abiel, from Beth-arabah; 33 Azmaveth, from Bahurim; Eliahba,
from Shaalbon; 34 Jashen the Gunite; Jonathan, son of Shagee the Hararite; 35 Ahiam,
son of Sachar the Hararite; Elipheleth, son of
36 Ahasbai, from Beth-maacah; Ahijah, from
Gilo; 37 Hezro, from Carmel; Naarai, the son
of Ezbai; 38 Joel, brother of Nathan, from Rehob, the Gadite; 39 Zelek the Ammonite; Naharai, from Beeroth, the armor-bearer of
Joab, son of Zeruiah; 40 Ira, from Jattir; Gareb,
from Jattir; 41 Uriah the Hittite; Zabad, son of
Ahlai, 42 and, in addition to the Thirty, Adina,
son of Shiza, the Reubenite, chief of the tribe
of Reuben; 43 Hanan, son of Maacah;
Joshaphat the Mithnite; 44 Uzzia, the Ash-
terathite; Shama and Jeiel, sons of Hotham,
from Aroer; 45 Jediael, son of Shimri, and
Joha, his brother, the Tizite; 46 Eliel the Maha-
vite; Jeribai and Joshaviah, sons of Elnaam;
Ithmah, from Moab; 47 Eliel, Obed, and Jaasiel the Mezobian.

## CHAPTER 12

See RG 138–40

***David's Early Followers.*** 1 The following men came to David in Ziklag while he
was still under banishment from Saul, son of
Kish; they, too, were among the warriors
who helped him in his battles.[z] 2 They were
archers who could use either the right or the
left hand, both in slinging stones and in
shooting arrows with the bow. They were
some of Saul's kinsmen, from Benjamin.
3 Ahiezer was their chief, along with Joash,
both sons of Shemaah of Gibeah; also Jeziel
and Pelet, sons of Azmaveth; Beracah; Jehu,
from Anathoth;[a] 4 Ishmaiah the Gibeonite, a
warrior among the Thirty, and over the
Thirty; 5 Jeremiah; Jahaziel; Johanan; Jozabad from Gederah; 6 Eluzai; Jerimoth; Bea-
liah; Shemariah; Shephatiah the Haruphite;
7 Elkanah, Isshiah, Azarel, Joezer, and
Jashobeam, who were Korahites; 8 Joelah
and Zebadiah, sons of Jeroham, from Gedor.
9 Some of the Gadites also went over to
David when he was at the stronghold in the
wilderness. They were valiant warriors, experienced soldiers equipped with shield and
spear, fearsome as lions, swift as gazelles on
the mountains.[b] 10 Ezer was their chief, Obadiah was second, Eliab third, 11 Mishmannah
fourth, Jeremiah fifth, 12 Attai sixth, Eliel
seventh, 13 Johanan eighth, Elzabad ninth,
14 Jeremiah tenth, and Machbannai eleventh.

**11:20 The Thirty**: they are listed by name in vv. 26–47. The parallel list in 2 Sm 23:8–39 often differs in names and spellings; for the numbers, see note on 2 Sm 23:8–39.

*s:* 2 Sm 23:18–19. *t:* 1 Chr 18:12; 1 Sm 26:6–10; 2 Sm 16:9; 18:2; 21:17. *u:* 2 Sm 8:18; 20:23. *v:* 1 Chr 2:16; 27:7. *w:* 1 Chr 27:11. *x:* 1 Chr 27:13. *y:* 1 Chr 27:14. *z:* 1 Sm 27:1–7. *a:* 1 Chr 27:12. *b:* Dt 33:20.

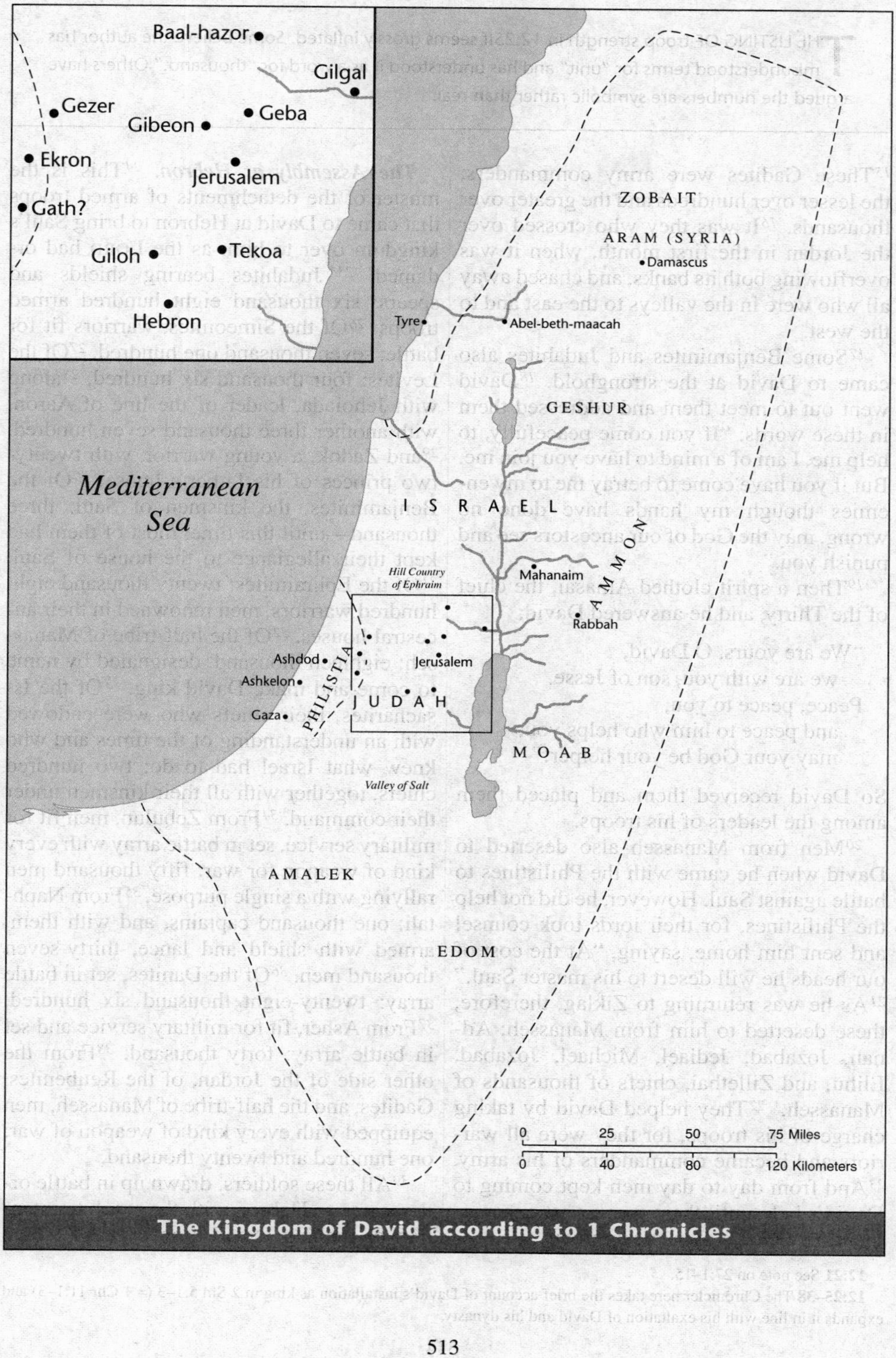


**The Kingdom of David according to 1 Chronicles**

THE LISTING OF troop strength in 12:25ff seems grossly inflated. Some believe the author has misunderstood terms for "unit" and has understood it as a word for "thousand." Others have argued the numbers are symbolic rather than real.

[15]These Gadites were army commanders, the lesser over hundreds and the greater over thousands. [16]It was they who crossed over the Jordan in the first month, when it was overflowing both its banks, and chased away all who were in the valleys to the east and to the west.

[17]Some Benjaminites and Judahites also came to David at the stronghold. [18]David went out to meet them and addressed them in these words: "If you come peacefully, to help me, I am of a mind to have you join me. But if you have come to betray me to my enemies though my hands have done no wrong, may the God of our ancestors see and punish you."

[19]Then a spirit clothed Amasai, the chief of the Thirty, and he answered David:

"We are yours, O David,
  we are with you, son of Jesse.
Peace, peace to you,
  and peace to him who helps you;
  may your God be your helper!"

So David received them and placed them among the leaders of his troops.

[20]Men from Manasseh also deserted to David when he came with the Philistines to battle against Saul. However, he did not help the Philistines, for their lords took counsel and sent him home, saying, "At the cost of our heads he will desert to his master Saul." [21]As he was returning to Ziklag, therefore, these deserted to him from Manasseh: Adnah, Jozabad, Jediael, Michael, Jozabad, Elihu, and Zillethai, chiefs of thousands of Manasseh.* [22]They helped David by taking charge of his troops, for they were all warriors and became commanders of his army. [23]And from day to day men kept coming to David's help until there was a vast encampment, like God's own encampment.

***The Assembly at Hebron.*** [24]This is the muster of the detachments of armed troops that came to David at Hebron to bring Saul's kingdom over to him, as the LORD had ordained. [25*] Judahites bearing shields and spears: six thousand eight hundred armed troops. [26]Of the Simeonites, warriors fit for battle: seven thousand one hundred. [27]Of the Levites: four thousand six hundred, [28]along with Jehoiada, leader of the line of Aaron, with another three thousand seven hundred, [29]and Zadok, a young warrior, with twenty-two princes of his father's house. [30]Of the Benjaminites, the kinsmen of Saul: three thousand—until this time, most of them had kept their allegiance to the house of Saul. [31]Of the Ephraimites: twenty thousand eight hundred warriors, men renowned in their ancestral houses. [32]Of the half-tribe of Manasseh: eighteen thousand, designated by name to come and make David king. [33]Of the Issacharites, their chiefs who were endowed with an understanding of the times and who knew what Israel had to do: two hundred chiefs, together with all their kinsmen under their command. [34]From Zebulun, men fit for military service, set in battle array with every kind of weapon for war: fifty thousand men rallying with a single purpose. [35]From Naphtali: one thousand captains, and with them, armed with shield and lance, thirty-seven thousand men. [36]Of the Danites, set in battle array: twenty-eight thousand six hundred. [37]From Asher, fit for military service and set in battle array: forty thousand. [38]From the other side of the Jordan, of the Reubenites, Gadites, and the half-tribe of Manasseh, men equipped with every kind of weapon of war: one hundred and twenty thousand.

[39]All these soldiers, drawn up in battle order, came to Hebron with the resolute intention of making David king over all Israel.

**12:21** See note on 27:1–15.

**12:25–38** The Chronicler here takes the brief account of David's installation as king in 2 Sm 5:1–3 (= 1 Chr 11:1–3) and expands it in line with his exaltation of David and his dynasty.

### Moving the Ark into Jerusalem

AN IMPORTANT PRELUDE to David's effectual rule from Jerusalem was bringing the ark of God into what will be the "chosen city" of Jerusalem (ch 13). Rearranging the order of his source (2 Sm 6:1–11), the Chronicler has David acting to bring the divine presence as symbolized by the ark (Nm 10:33–36) into the capital city even before beginning his own palace. The Chronicler's deliberate reformatting of the sequence of events highlights the importance the narrative will give to honoring God's presence in Jerusalem.

The rest of Israel was likewise of one mind
to make David king. [40]They remained with
David for three days, eating and drinking,
for their relatives had prepared for them.
[41]Moreover, their neighbors from as far as
Issachar, Zebulun, and Naphtali came bringing food on donkeys, camels, mules, and
oxen—provisions in great quantity of meal,
pressed figs, raisins, wine, oil, oxen, and
sheep. For there was rejoicing in Israel.

## CHAPTER 13

See RG 138–40

*Transfer of the Ark.* [1][c] After David
had taken counsel with his commanders of
thousands and of hundreds, that is, with
every leader, [2]he said to the whole assembly
of Israel: "If it seems good to you, and is so
decreed by the LORD our God, let us send to
the rest of our kindred from all the districts
of Israel, and also the priests and the Levites
from their cities with pasture lands, that they
may join us;[d] [3]and let us bring the ark of our
God here among us, for in the days of Saul
we did not consult it." [4]And the whole assembly agreed to do it, for it seemed right in
the eyes of all the people.
[5]Then David assembled all Israel, from
Shihor of Egypt* to Lebo-hamath, to bring
the ark of God from Kiriath-jearim.[e] [6]David
and all Israel went up to Baalah, that is, to
Kiriath-jearim, of Judah, to bring up from
there the ark of God, which was known by
the name "LORD enthroned upon the cherubim."[f] [7]They transported the ark of God on a
new cart from the house of Abinadab; Uzzah
and Ahio were guiding the cart, [8]while David and all Israel danced before God with all
their might, with singing, and with lyres,
harps, tambourines, cymbals, and trumpets.
[9]As they reached the threshing floor of
Chidon,* Uzzah stretched out his hand to
steady the ark, for the oxen were tipping it.
[10]Then the LORD became angry with Uzzah
and struck him, because he had laid his hand
on the ark; he died there in God's presence.
[11]David was angry because the LORD's anger
had broken out against Uzzah. Therefore
that place has been called Perez-uzzah* even
to this day.
[12]David was afraid of God that day, and
he said, "How can I bring in the ark of God
to me?" [13]Therefore he did not take the ark
with him into the City of David, but deposited it instead at the house of Obed-edom
the Gittite. [14]The ark of God remained in the
house of Obed-edom with his family for
three months, and the LORD blessed Obed-
edom's household and all that he possessed.[g]

## CHAPTER 14

See RG 138–40

*David in Jerusalem.* [1][h] Hiram, king of
Tyre, sent envoys to David along with cedar
wood, and masons and carpenters to build
him a house.* [i] [2]David now knew* that the
LORD had truly established him as king over
Israel, for his kingdom was greatly exalted
for the sake of his people Israel. [3]David took
other wives in Jerusalem and became the fa-

**13:5 Shihor of Egypt**: the eastern branch of the Nile delta. **Lebo-hamath**: in southern Syria.

**13:9 Chidon**: in 2 Sm 6:6 the name is Nodan (variant: Nacon).

**13:11 Perez-uzzah**: this Hebrew phrase means "the breaking out against Uzza."

**14:1** The Chronicler's account of David's establishment as king and his victories over the Philistines follows 2 Sm 5:11–25, but makes David's rule even more prominent.

**14:2 David now knew**: see note on 2 Sm 5:12.

*c:* 2 Sm 6:1–11. *d:* Nm 35:1–8; Jos 14:4; 21:2–42. *e:* 1 Chr 15:3; Jos 13:3, 5; 1 Sm 6:21; 7:1–2; 2 Sm 6:1–11. *f:* Jos 15:9; 18:14; 1 Sm 4:4; 7:1. *g:* 1 Chr 26:4–5. *h:* 2 Sm 5:11–25. *i:* 2 Sm 5:11; 2 Chr 2:4.

ther of more sons and daughters. [4]These are the names of those who were born to him in Jerusalem: Shammua, Shobab, Nathan, Solomon, [5]Ibhar, Elishua, Elpelet, [6]Nogah, Nepheg, Japhia, [7]Elishama, Beeliada, and Eliphelet.[j]

***The Philistine Wars.*** [8]When the Philistines had heard that David was anointed king over all Israel, they marched out in force looking for him. But when David heard of this, he went out against them. [9]Meanwhile the Philistines had come and raided the valley of Rephaim.[k] [10]David inquired of God, "Shall I attack the Philistines, and will you deliver them into my power?" The LORD answered him, "Attack, for I have delivered them into your power." [11]So they attacked, at Baal-perazim, and David defeated them there. Then David said, "By my hand God has broken through my enemies just as water breaks through a dam." Therefore that place was called Baal-perazim.* [12]The Philistines abandoned their gods there, and David ordered them to be burnt.[l]

[13]Once again the Philistines raided the valley, [14]and again David inquired of God. But God answered him: Do not try to pursue them, but go around them and come against them near the balsam trees. [15]When you hear the sound of marching in the tops of the balsam trees, then go forth to battle, for God has already gone before you to strike the army of the Philistines. [16]David did as God commanded him, and they routed the Philistine army from Gibeon to Gezer.

[17]Thus David's fame was spread abroad through every land, and the LORD put the fear of him on all the nations.

## CHAPTER 15

See RG 138–40

***Preparations for Moving the Ark.*** [1]David built houses for himself in the City of David and prepared a place for the ark of God, pitching a tent for it there. [2]At that time he said, "No one may carry the ark of God except the Levites, for the LORD chose them to carry the ark of the LORD and to minister to him forever."[m] [3]Then David assembled all Israel to Jerusalem to bring up the ark of the LORD to its place, which he had prepared for it.[n] [4]David also convened the sons of Aaron and the Levites: [5]of the sons of Kohath, Uriel, their chief, and one hundred and twenty of his brothers; [6]of the sons of Merari, Asaiah, their chief, and two hundred and twenty of his brothers; [7]of the sons of Gershon, Joel, their chief, and one hundred and thirty of his brothers; [8]of the sons of Elizaphan, Shemaiah, their chief, and two hundred of his brothers; [9]of the sons of Hebron, Eliel, their chief, and eighty of his brothers; [10]of the sons of Uzziel, Amminadab, their chief, and one hundred and twelve of his brothers.

[11]David summoned the priests Zadok and Abiathar, and the Levites Uriel, Asaiah, Joel, Shemaiah, Eliel, and Amminadab,[o] [12]and said to them: "You heads of the levitical houses, sanctify yourselves along with your brothers to bring up the ark of the LORD, the God of Israel, to the place which I have prepared for it.[p] [13]Because you were not with us the first time, the LORD our God broke out against us, for we did not seek him aright."[q] [14]Accordingly, the priests and the Levites sanctified themselves to bring up the ark of the LORD, the God of Israel. [15]The Levites carried the ark of God on their shoulders with poles, as Moses had commanded according to the word of the LORD.[r]

[16]David commanded the commanders of the Levites to appoint their brothers as singers and to play on musical instruments, harps, lyres, and cymbals, to make a loud sound of rejoicing.[s] [17]Therefore the Levites appointed Heman, son of Joel, and, among his brothers, Asaph, son of Berechiah; and among the sons of Merari, their brothers, Ethan, son of Kushaiah;[t] [18]and, together with these, their brothers of the second rank: the gatekeepers Zechariah, Uzziel, Shemiramoth, Jehiel, Unni, Eliab, Benaiah, Maaseiah, Mattithiah, Eliphelehu, Mikneiah,

**14:11** See note on 2 Sm 5:20.

*j:* 1 Chr 3:5–8; 2 Sm 5:13–16. *k:* 1 Chr 11:15. *l:* Dt 7:5, 25. *m:* Nm 1:50; 7:9; Dt 10:8; 31:25; 1 Sm 6:15; Jos 3:8. *n:* 1 Chr 13:5; 2 Sm 6:15, 17. *o:* 1 Chr 16:39; 2 Sm 8:17; 15:29, 35. *p:* 2 Chr 29:5, 15, 34; 30:3, 15, 24. *q:* 1 Chr 13:3. *r:* Ex 25:10–22; Nm 1:50; 7:9; 2 Chr 35:3. *s:* 1 Chr 13:8; 16:5; 2 Chr 5:12; 29:25; Neh 12:27. *t:* 1 Chr 6:31–47; 25:1–8.

CHAPTER 15, V. 29 IS an abridged version of 2 Samuel 6:16–23, but without the observation that David's nakedness disturbed Michal. The Chronicler may be trying to draw another contrast between Saul and David by portraying Michal's displeasure at David's joy in bringing the ark to Jerusalem.

Obed-edom, and Jeiel. 19 The singers, Heman, Asaph, and Ethan, sounded brass cymbals. 20 Zechariah, Uzziel, Shemiramoth, Jehiel, Unni, Eliab, Maaseiah, and Benaiah
played on harps set to "Alamoth."* 21 But
Mattithiah, Eliphelehu, Mikneiah, Obed-
edom, and Jeiel led the song on lyres set to
"sheminith." 22 Chenaniah was the chief of
the Levites in the singing; he directed the
singing, for he was skillful.[u] 23 Berechiah and
Elkanah were gatekeepers before the ark.
24 The priests, Shebaniah, Joshaphat, Nethanel, Amasai, Zechariah, Benaiah, and Eliezer, sounded the trumpets before the ark of
God.[v] Obed-edom and Jeiel were also gatekeepers before the ark.

***The Ark Comes to Jerusalem.*** 25[w] Thus
David, the elders of Israel, and the commanders of thousands went to bring up the
ark of the covenant of the LORD with joy
from the house of Obed-edom. 26 While God
helped the Levites to carry the ark of the
covenant of the LORD, they sacrificed seven
bulls and seven rams.[x] 27 David was vested in
a robe of fine linen, as were all the Levites
who carried the ark, the singers, and
Chenaniah, the leader of song; David was
also wearing a linen ephod.[y] 28 Thus all Israel
brought up the ark of the covenant of the
LORD with joyful shouting, to the sound of
horns, trumpets, and cymbals, and the music
of harps and lyres. 29 But as the ark of the
covenant of the LORD was entering the City
of David, Michal, daughter of Saul, looked
down from her window, and when she saw
King David leaping and dancing, she despised him in her heart.[z]

## CHAPTER 16

See RG 138–40

1[a] They brought in the ark of God and
set it within the tent which David had
pitched for it.[b] Then they sacrificed burnt offerings and communion offerings to God.
2 When David had finished sacrificing the
burnt offerings and communion offerings,
he blessed the people in the name of the
LORD, 3 and distributed to every Israelite, to
every man and every woman, a loaf of
bread, a piece of meat, and a raisin cake.

***David's Directives for the Levites.*** 4 He
then appointed certain Levites to minister
before the ark of the LORD, to celebrate,
thank, and praise the LORD, the God of Israel.[c] 5 Asaph was their chief, and second to
him were Zechariah, Uzziel, Shemiramoth,
Jehiel, Mattithiah, Eliab, Benaiah, Obed-
edom, and Jeiel. These were to play on harps
and lyres, while Asaph was to sound the
cymbals, 6 and the priests Benaiah and Jahaziel were to be the regular trumpeters before
the ark of the covenant of God.

7 On that same day, David appointed
Asaph and his brothers to sing for the first
time these praises of the LORD:

8 * Give thanks to the LORD, invoke his
  name;[d]
 make known among the peoples his
  deeds.
9 Sing praise, play music;
 proclaim all his wondrous deeds.
10 Glory in his holy name;
 rejoice, O hearts that seek the LORD!
11 Rely on the mighty LORD;

**15:20–21 Alamoth . . . sheminith**: musical terms of uncertain meaning. *Alamoth*, lit., "young women," occurs in the superscription to Ps 46. The term *sheminith*, in v. 21, might mean "bass" or "octave"; cf. Ps 6:1; 12:1.

**16:8–36** A hymn composed of parts of several psalms: vv. 8–22 = Ps 105:1–15; vv. 23–33 = Ps 96:1–13; vv. 34–36 = Ps 106:1, 47–48. There are minor textual variants between this hymn and the psalms it is drawn from.

*u:* 1 Chr 26:29. *v:* Nm 10:8; Jos 6:4–8. *w:* 2 Sm 6:12–16. *x:* 2 Sm 6:17; 2 Chr 29:21. *y:* 1 Sm 2:18; 2 Sm 6:14. *z:* 2 Sm 6:20–23. *a:* 2 Sm 6:17–19. *b:* 1 Chr 15:1. *c:* Sir 47:9. *d:* Ps 105:1–15.

constantly seek his face.
12 Recall the wondrous deeds he has done,
his signs, and his words of judgment,
13 You sons of Israel, his servants,
offspring of Jacob, the chosen ones!
14 The LORD is our God;
who rules the whole earth.
15 He remembers forever his covenant
the pact imposed for a thousand generations—
16 Which was made with Abraham,
confirmed by oath to Isaac,
17 And ratified as binding for Jacob,
an everlasting covenant for Israel:
18 "To you will I give the land of Canaan,
your own allotted heritage."
19 When they were few in number,
a handful, and strangers there,
20 Wandering from nation to nation,
from one kingdom to another,
21 He let no one oppress them;
for their sake he rebuked kings:
22 "Do not touch my anointed,
to my prophets do no harm."
23 [e] Sing to the LORD, all the earth,
announce his salvation, day after day.
24 Tell his glory among the nations;
among all peoples, his wondrous deeds.
25 For great is the LORD and highly to be praised;
to be feared above all gods.
26 For the gods of the nations all do nothing,
but the LORD made the heavens.
27 Splendor and majesty go before him;
power and rejoicing are in his holy place.
28 Give to the LORD, you families of nations,
give to the LORD glory and might;
29 Give to the LORD the glory due his name!
Bring gifts, and come before him;
bow down to the LORD, splendid in holiness.
30 Tremble before him, all the earth;
the world will surely stand fast, never to be moved.
31 Let the heavens be glad and the earth rejoice;
let them say among the nations: The LORD is king.
32 Let the sea and what fills it resound;
let the plains be joyful and all that is in them!
33 Then let all the trees of the forest exult
before the LORD, who comes,
who comes to rule the earth.
34 [f] Give thanks to the LORD, who is good,
whose love endures forever;
35 And say, "Save us, O God, our savior,
gather us and deliver us from among the nations,
That we may give thanks to your holy name
and glory in praising you."
36 Blessed be the LORD, the God of Israel,
from everlasting to everlasting!
Let all the people say, Amen! Hallelujah.

37 Then David left Asaph and his brothers
there before the ark of the covenant of the
LORD to minister before the ark regularly according to the daily ritual; 38 he also left there
Obed-edom and sixty-eight of his brothers,
including Obed-edom, son of Jeduthun, and
Hosah, to be gatekeepers.[g]
39 But the priest Zadok and his priestly
brothers he left before the tabernacle of the
LORD on the high place at Gibeon,[h]
40 to
make burnt offerings to the LORD on the altar for burnt offerings regularly, morning
and evening, and to do all that is written in
the law of the LORD which he commanded
Israel.[i]
41 With them were Heman and Jeduthun and the others who were chosen and
designated by name to give thanks to the
LORD, "whose love endures forever,"[j]
42 with
trumpets and cymbals for accompaniment,
and instruments for sacred song. The sons of
Jeduthun kept the gate.[k]
43 Then all the people departed, each to
their own homes, and David returned to
bless his household.[l]

## CHAPTER 17

See RG 138–40

***The Oracle of Nathan.*** 1 [m] After David
had taken up residence in his house, he said

e: Ps 96:1–13. f: Ps 106:1, 47–48. g: 1 Chr 15:24. h: 1 Kgs 3:4. i: Ex 29:38–42; Lv 6:9; Nm 28:3, 6; 2 Chr 13:11. j: 2 Chr 5:12; 7:3, 6; 20:21; Ezr 3:11. k: 2 Chr 29:27. l: 2 Sm 6:19–20. m: 2 Sm 7:1–29.

to Nathan the prophet, "See, I am living in a
house of cedar, but the ark of the covenant of
the LORD is under tentcloth."[n] [2]Nathan
replied to David, "Whatever is in your heart,
go and do, for God is with you."
[3]But that same night the word of God
came to Nathan: [4]Go and tell David my servant, Thus says the LORD: It is not you who
are to build the house for me to dwell in.[o]
[5]For I have never dwelt in a house, from the
day I brought Israel up, even to this day, but
I have been lodging in tent or tabernacle. [6]As
long as I have wandered about with all Israel,
did I ever say a word to any of the judges of
Israel whom I commanded to shepherd my
people, Why have you not built me a house
of cedar? [7]Now then, speak thus to my servant David, Thus says the LORD of hosts: I
took you from the pasture, from following
the flock, to become ruler over my people Israel.[p] [8]I was with you wherever you went,
and I cut down all your enemies before you.
I will make your name like that of the greatest on the earth. [9]I will assign a place for my
people Israel and I will plant them in it to
dwell there; they will never again be disturbed, nor shall the wicked ever again oppress them, as they did at the beginning,
[10]and during all the time when I appointed
judges over my people Israel. And I will subdue all your enemies. Moreover, I declare to
you that the LORD will build you a house:
[11]when your days have been completed and
you must join your ancestors, I will raise up
your offspring after you who will be one of
your own sons, and I will establish his kingdom.[q] [12]He it is who shall build me a house,
and I will establish his throne forever.[r] [13]I
will be a father to him, and he shall be a son
to me, and I will not withdraw my favor from
him as I withdrew it from the one who was
before you;[s] [14]but I will maintain him in my
house and in my kingdom forever, and his
throne shall be firmly established forever.
[15]In accordance with all these words and
this whole vision Nathan spoke to David.
***David's Thanksgiving.*** [16]Then King David
came in and sat in the LORD's presence, and
said: "Who am I, LORD God, and what is my
house, that you should have brought me so
far? [17]And yet, even this is too little in your
sight, O God! For you have made a promise
regarding your servant's house reaching into
the future, and you have looked on me as
henceforth the most notable of men, LORD
God.[t] [18]What more can David say to you?
You have known* your servant. [19]LORD, for
your servant's sake and in keeping with your
purpose, you have done this great thing.
[20]LORD, there is no one like you, no God but
you, just as we have always heard.[u]
[21]"Is there, like your people Israel, whom
you redeemed from Egypt, another nation on
earth whom a god went to redeem as his people? You won for yourself a name for great
and awesome deeds by driving out the nations before your people.[v] [22]You made your
people Israel your own forever, and you,
LORD, became their God. [23]Now, LORD, may
the promise that you have spoken concerning your servant and his house remain firm
forever. Bring about what you have promised, [24]that your name, LORD of hosts, God
of Israel, may be great and abide forever,
while the house of your servant is established in your presence.
[25]"Because you, my God, have revealed
to your servant that you will build him a
house, your servant dares to pray before
you.[w] [26]Since you, LORD, are truly God and
have made this generous promise to your
servant, [27]do, then, bless the house of your
servant, that it may be in your presence forever—since it is you, LORD, who blessed it,
it is blessed forever."[x]

## CHAPTER 18

See RG 138–40

***David's Victories.*** [1y]After this, David
defeated the Philistines and subdued them;
and he took Gath and its towns away from
the Philistines. [2]He also defeated Moab, and
the Moabites became David's subjects, paying tribute.
[3]David then defeated Hadadezer, king of

**17:18 Known**: given David recognition, chosen him, singled him out; cf. Gn 18:19; Ex 33:12; Am 3:2.

*n:* 1 Chr 15:1; 2 Sm 5:11. *o:* 1 Chr 28:3; 1 Kgs 8:19. *p:* 1 Sm 16:11. *q:* 2 Sm 7:12–13. *r:* 1 Chr 22:10; 28:6, 10. *s:* 2 Sm 7:14. *t:* 2 Sm 7:19. *u:* Sir 36:4. *v:* Dt 4:7; 2 Sm 7:23. *w:* 2 Sm 7:27. *x:* Nm 22:6. *y:* 2 Sm 8:1–14.

Zobah, toward Hamath, who was on his way
to set up his victory stele at the river Euphrates. [4]David captured from him one
thousand chariots, seven thousand horsemen, and twenty thousand foot soldiers. David hamstrung all the chariot horses, but left
one hundred for his chariots.[z] [5]The Arameans of Damascus came to help Hadadezer,
king of Zobah, but David also defeated
twenty-two thousand of their men in Aram.
[6]Then David set up garrisons in the Damascus region of Aram, and the Arameans became David's subjects, paying tribute. Thus
the LORD made David victorious in all his
campaigns.
[7]David took the golden shields that were
carried by Hadadezer's attendants and
brought them to Jerusalem. [8]David likewise
took away from Tibhath and Cun, cities of
Hadadezer, large quantities of bronze; Solomon later used it to make the bronze sea and
the pillars and the vessels of bronze.[a]
[9]When Tou, king of Hamath, heard that
David had defeated the entire army of
Hadadezer, king of Zobah, [10]he sent his son
Hadoram to wish King David well and to
congratulate him on having waged a victorious war against Hadadezer; for Hadadezer
had been at war with Tou. He also brought
gold, silver and bronze articles of every
sort.[b] [11]These also King David consecrated
to the LORD along with all the silver and gold
that he had taken from the nations: from
Edom, Moab, the Ammonites, the Philistines, and Amalek.
[12]Abishai, the son of Zeruiah, also defeated eighteen thousand Edomites in the
Valley of Salt.[c] [13]He set up garrisons in
Edom, and all the Edomites became David's
subjects. Thus the LORD brought David victory in all his undertakings.
***David's Officials.*** [14d] David was king over
all Israel; he dispensed justice and right to
all his people. [15]Joab, son of Zeruiah, was in
command of the army; Jehoshaphat, son of
Ahilud, was chancellor;[e] [16]Zadok, son of
Ahitub, and Ahimelech, son of Abiathar,
were priests;* Shavsha was scribe;[f] [17]Bena-
iah, son of Jehoiada, was in command of the
Cherethites and the Pelethites; and David's
sons were the chief assistants to the king.* [g]

## CHAPTER 19

See RG 138-40

***Campaigns Against Ammon.*** [1h] Afterward Nahash, king of the Ammonites, died
and his son succeeded him as king. [2]David
said, "I will show kindness to Hanun, the
son of Nahash, for his father showed kindness to me." Therefore he sent envoys to
console him over his father. But when David's servants had entered the land of the
Ammonites to console Hanun, [3]the Ammonite princes said to Hanun, "Do you think David is doing this—sending you these consolers—to honor your father? Have not his
servants rather come to you to explore the
land, spying it out for its overthrow?" [4]So
Hanun seized David's servants and had them
shaved and their garments cut off halfway at
the hips. Then he sent them away. [5]David
was told about the men, and he sent word for
them to be intercepted, for the men had been
greatly disgraced. "Remain at Jericho," the
king told them, "until your beards have
grown again; then come back here."
[6]When the Ammonites realized that they
had put themselves in bad odor with David,
Hanun and the Ammonites sent a thousand
talents of silver to hire chariots and horsemen
from Aram Naharaim, from Aram-maacah,
and from Zobah. [7]They hired thirty-two
thousand chariots along with the king of Maacah and his army, who came and encamped
before Medeba. The Ammonites also assembled from their cities and came out for war.
[8]When David heard of this, he sent Joab
and his whole army of warriors against
them. [9]The Ammonites marched out and

**18:16 Zadok . . . and Ahimelech, son of Abiathar, were priests**: emendation—the Masoretic text here reads "Abimelech," not "Ahimelech"; but 2 Sm 8:17, the Chronicler's source, has "Ahimelech." See note there.

**18:17 Chief assistants to the king**: according to 2 Sm 8:18, the Chronicler's source here, David's sons were priests. The Chronicler's modification reflects his conviction that only Aaron's descendants could be priests.

*z:* 2 Sm 8:14; Jos 11:6, 9. *a:* 2 Sm 8:8; 1 Kgs 7:15, 23, 27. *b:* 2 Sm 8:10. *c:* 2 Sm 8:13; 2 Kgs 14:7. *d:* 2 Sm 8:15–18. *e:* 1 Chr 11:6; 2 Sm 8:16; 1 Kgs 4:3. *f:* 1 Chr 24:3, 6, 31; 2 Sm 8:17. *g:* 1 Chr 11:22; 2 Sm 8:18; 1 Kgs 1:38, 44. *h:* 2 Sm 10:1–19.

lined up for battle at the entrance of the city,
while the kings who had come to their help
remained apart in the open field. [10]When
Joab saw that there was a battle line both in
front of and behind him, he chose some of
the best fighters among the Israelites and
lined them up against the Arameans; [11]the
rest of the army, which he placed under the
command of his brother Abishai, then lined
up to oppose the Ammonites. [12]And he said:
"If the Arameans prove too strong for me,
you must come and save me; and if the Ammonites prove too strong for you, I will save
you. [13]Hold firm and let us show ourselves
courageous for the sake of our people and
the cities of our God; and may the LORD do
what is good in his sight." [14]Joab therefore
advanced with his men to engage the Arameans in battle; but they fled before him.
[15]And when the Ammonites saw that the Arameans had fled, they too fled before his
brother Abishai, and entered their city. Joab
then came to Jerusalem.

[16]Seeing themselves vanquished by Israel, the Arameans sent messengers to bring
out the Arameans from beyond the Euphrates, with Shophach, the commander of
Hadadezer's army, at their head. [17]When this
was reported to David, he gathered all Israel
together, crossed the Jordan, and met them.
With the army of David drawn up to fight the
Arameans, they gave battle. [18]But the Arameans fled before Israel, and David killed
seven thousand of their chariot fighters and
forty thousand of their foot soldiers; he also
put to death Shophach, the commander of
the army. [19]When the vassals of Hadadezer
saw themselves vanquished by Israel, they
made peace with David and became his subjects. After this, the Arameans refused to
come to the aid of the Ammonites.

## CHAPTER 20

See RG 138–40

[1]At the turn of the year,* the time
when kings go to war, Joab led the army out
in force, laid waste the land of the Ammonites, and went on to besiege Rabbah;
David himself remained in Jerusalem. When
Joab had attacked Rabbah and destroyed it,
[2]David took the crown of Milcom from the
idol's head. It was found to weigh a talent of
gold, with precious stones on it; this crown
David wore on his own head. He also
brought out a great amount of spoil from the
city. [3]He deported the people of the city and
set them to work with saws, iron picks, and
axes. David dealt thus with all the cities of
the Ammonites. Then David and his whole
army returned to Jerusalem.[i]

*Victories over the Philistines.* [4][j] Afterward
there was another battle with the Philistines,
at Gezer. At that time, Sibbecai the Hushathite struck down Sippai, one of the descendants of the Rephaim, and the Philistines
were subdued.[k]

[5]There was another battle with the Philistines, and Elhanan, the son of Jair, slew
Lahmi, the brother of Goliath* of Gath,
whose spear shaft was like a weaver's beam.[l]

[6]There was another battle, at Gath, and
there was a giant, who had six fingers to
each hand and six toes to each foot; twenty-
four in all. He too was descended from the
Rephaim. [7]He defied Israel, and Jonathan,
the son of Shimea, David's brother, slew
him. [8]These were the descendants of the
Rephaim of Gath who died at the hands of
David and his servants.

## CHAPTER 21

See RG 138–40

*David's Census; the Plague.* [1][m] A satan* rose up against Israel, and he incited Da-

**20:1 At the turn of the year:** thus in 2 Sm 11 begins the story of David's adultery with Bathsheba and his murder of her husband Uriah, but the Chronicler omits it.

**20:5 Elhanan . . . slew Lahmi, the brother of Goliath**: with this notice the Chronicler solves the difficulty of the apparent contradiction between 1 Sm 17:49, 51 (David killed Goliath) and 2 Sm 21:19 (Elhanan killed Goliath).

**21:1 A satan**: in the parallel passage (2 Sm 24:1) David is led astray because of the Lord's anger. The Chronicler's modification reflects the changed theological outlook of postexilic Israel, when evil was no longer attributed directly to God. At an earlier period the Hebrew word *satan* ("adversary," or, especially in a court of law, "accuser") designated both human beings (1 Kgs 11:14) and a "son of God" who accused people before God (Jb 1:6–12; 2:1–7; Zec 3:1–2). In later Judaism (cf. Wis 2:24) and in the New Testament, *satan*, or the "devil" (from *diablos*, the Greek translation of the Hebrew word), designates an evil spirit who tempts people to do wrong.

*i:* 2 Sm 12:30–31. *j:* 2 Sm 21:18–22. *k:* 1 Chr 11:29; 27:11. *l:* 1 Chr 11:26; 1 Sm 17:4, 23. *m:* 2 Sm 24:1–25.

## Transition in Reigns

WHILE DAVID IS still clearly on the throne, chs 21–29 provide a number of points of continuity between David's reign, which is ending, and Solomon's, which is beginning. Along the way, David makes all the necessary provisions to ensure the successful completion of the temple and the continuing growth of Jerusalem. The Chronicler's version is in marked contrast to the opening chapters of 1 Kings, where Solomon apparently gains the throne at the last minute thanks to the resourceful intervention of the prophet Nathan and Solomon's mother Bathsheba.

vid to take a census of Israel.[n] 2 David therefore said to Joab and to the other generals of the army, "Go, number the Israelites from Beer-sheba to Dan, and report back to me that I may know their number." 3 But Joab replied: "May the LORD increase his people a hundredfold! My lord king, are not all of them my lord's subjects? Why does my lord seek to do this thing? Why should he bring guilt upon Israel?" 4 However, the king's command prevailed over Joab, who departed and traversed all of Israel, and then returned to Jerusalem. 5 Joab reported the census figures to David: of men capable of wielding a sword, there were in all Israel one million one hundred thousand, and in Judah four hundred and seventy thousand. 6 Levi and Benjamin, however, he did not include in the census, for the king's command was repugnant to Joab.[o] 7 This command was evil in the sight of God, and he struck Israel. 8 Then David said to God, "I have sinned greatly in doing this thing. Take away your servant's guilt, for I have acted very foolishly."

9 Then the LORD spoke to Gad, David's seer, in these words:[p] 10 Go, tell David: Thus says the LORD: I am laying out three options; choose one of them, and I will inflict it on you. 11 Accordingly, Gad went to David and said to him: "Thus says the LORD: Decide now— 12 will it be three years of famine; or three months of fleeing your enemies, with the sword of your foes ever at your back; or three days of the LORD's own sword, a plague in the land, with the LORD's destroying angel in every part of Israel? Now consider: What answer am I to give him who sent me?" 13 Then David said to Gad: "I am in serious trouble. But let me fall into the hand of the LORD, whose mercy is very great, rather than into hands of men."

14 Therefore the LORD sent a plague upon Israel, and seventy thousand Israelites died. 15 God also sent an angel to Jerusalem to destroy it; but as the angel was on the point of destroying it, the LORD saw and changed his mind about the calamity, and said to the destroying angel, "Enough now! Stay your hand!"[q]

***Ornan's Threshing Floor.*** The angel of the LORD was then standing by the threshing floor of Ornan the Jebusite. 16 When David raised his eyes, he saw the angel of the LORD standing between earth and heaven, drawn sword in hand stretched out against Jerusalem.[r] David and the elders, clothed in sackcloth, fell face down, 17 and David prayed to God: "Was it not I who ordered the census of the people? I am the one who sinned, I did this wicked thing. But these sheep, what have they done? O LORD, my God, strike me and my father's family, but do not afflict your people with this plague!"

18 Then the angel of the LORD commanded Gad to tell David to go up and set up an altar to the LORD on the threshing floor of Ornan the Jebusite.[s] 19 David went up at the word of Gad, which he spoke in the name of the LORD. 20 Ornan turned around and saw the king; his four sons who were with him hid themselves, but Ornan kept on threshing wheat. 21 But as David came toward Ornan, he looked up and saw that it was David, and left the threshing floor and bowed down before David, his face

*n:* Zec 3:1–2. *o:* 1 Chr 27:24; Nm 1:49. *p:* 1 Chr 29:29; 1 Sm 9:9; 2 Chr 29:25. *q:* Gn 6:6; Ex 32:14; 2 Sm 24:16; Jon 3:10. *r:* Jos 5:13. *s:* 2 Chr 3:1.

CHAPTER 22:12 IS a reflection of 1 Kings 3, where God grants Solomon an understanding mind and the ability to discern between good and evil. The Chronicler's version narrows the scope of Solomon's fabled wisdom by defining its purpose as directing him in the law.

to the ground. 22 David said to Ornan: "Sell me the site of this threshing floor, that I may build on it an altar to the LORD. Sell it to me at its full price, that the plague may be withdrawn from the people." 23 But Ornan said to David: "Take it as your own, and let my lord the king do what is good in his sight. See, I also give you the oxen for the burnt offerings, the threshing sledges for the wood, and the wheat for the grain offering. I give it all to you." 24 But King David replied to Ornan: "No! I will buy it from you properly, at its full price. I will not take what is yours for the LORD, nor bring burnt offerings that cost me nothing." 25 So David paid Ornan six hundred shekels of gold* for the place.

***Altar for Burnt Offerings.*** 26 David then built an altar there to the LORD, and sacrificed burnt offerings and communion offerings. He called upon the LORD, who answered him by sending down fire from heaven upon the altar for burnt offerings.[t] 27 Then the LORD gave orders to the angel to return his sword to its sheath.

28 Once David saw that the LORD had answered him at the threshing floor of Ornan the Jebusite, he continued to offer sacrifices there. 29 The tabernacle of the LORD, which Moses had made in the wilderness, and the altar for burnt offerings were at that time on the high place at Gibeon.[u] 30 But David could not go into his presence to inquire of God, for he was fearful of the sword of the angel of the LORD.

## CHAPTER 22

See RG 138–40

1 Thus David said, "This is the house of the LORD God, and this is the altar for burnt offerings for Israel."[v] 2* David then ordered that the resident aliens in the land of Israel should be brought together, and he appointed them stonecutters to hew out stone blocks for building the house of God.[w] 3 David also laid up large stores of iron to make nails for the doors of the gates, and clamps, together with so much bronze that it could not be weighed,[x] 4 and cedar trees without number. The Sidonians and Tyrians brought great stores of cedar logs to David.[y] 5 David said: "My son Solomon is young and inexperienced; but the house that is to be built for the LORD must be made so magnificent that it will be renowned and glorious in all lands. Therefore I will make preparations for it." Thus before his death David laid up materials in abundance.[z]

***Charge to Solomon.*** 6 Then he summoned his son Solomon and commanded him to build a house for the LORD, the God of Israel. 7a David said to Solomon: "My son, it was my purpose to build a house myself for the name of the LORD, my God. 8 But this word of the LORD came to me: You have shed much blood, and you have waged great wars. You may not build a house for my name, because you have shed too much blood upon the earth in my sight. 9 However, a son will be born to you. He will be a peaceful man, and I will give him rest from all his enemies on every side. For Solomon shall be his name, and in his time I will bestow peace* and tranquility on Israel.[b] 10 It is he who shall build a house for my name; he shall be a son to me, and I will be a father to him,[c] and I will establish the throne of his kingship over Israel forever.

**21:25 Six hundred shekels of gold**: according to 2 Sm 24:24, David paid only fifty shekels of silver for Ornan's threshing floor; the Chronicler's higher figure reflects the value the site of the future Temple had in his eyes.

**22:2–4** According to 1 Kgs 5:15–32, Solomon himself made the material preparations for building the Temple, even though David had wished to do so (1 Kgs 5:17–19). The Chronicler, however, seeks to enhance David's role in the building of the Temple.

**22:9** The Hebrew word for peace, *shalom*, is reflected in the name Solomon, in Hebrew, *Shelomo*. The Chronicler

*t:* Lv 9:24; Jgs 6:21; 1 Kgs 18:38; 2 Chr 7:1; 2 Mc 2:10–12. *u:* 1 Chr 16:39; 1 Kgs 8:4; 2 Chr 1:3. *v:* 1 Chr 21:18, 26, 28; 2 Chr 3:1. *w:* 1 Kgs 5:31–32; 9:20–21; 2 Chr 2:16–17. *x:* 1 Chr 18:8; 1 Kgs 7:47. *y:* Ezr 3:7; 2 Chr 2:9. *z:* 1 Chr 29:1. *a:* 1 Chr 17:1–14; 28:2–7; 2 Sm 7:1–16; 1 Kgs 5:17–19; 8:17–21. *b:* 2 Sm 12:24. *c:* Heb 1:5.

11“Now, my son, the LORD be with you,
and may you succeed in building the house
of the LORD your God, as he has said you
shall. 12But may the LORD give you prudence and discernment when he gives you
command over Israel, so that you keep the
law of the LORD, your God. 13Only then shall
you succeed, if you are careful to observe
the statutes and ordinances which the LORD
commanded Moses for Israel. Be strong and
steadfast; do not fear or be dismayed.[d] 14See,
with great effort I have laid up for the house
of the LORD a hundred thousand talents of
gold,* a million talents of silver, and bronze
and iron in such great quantities that they
cannot be weighed. I have also laid up wood
and stones, to which you must add.[e] 15More-
over, you have available workers, stonecutters, masons, carpenters, and experts in
every craft, 16without number, skilled with
gold, silver, bronze, and iron. Set to work,
therefore, and the LORD be with you!”

*Charge to the Officials.* 17David also commanded all of the officials of Israel to help
his son Solomon: 18“Is not the LORD your
God with you? Has he not given you rest on
every side? Indeed, he has delivered the
inhabitants of the land into my power, and
the land is subdued before the LORD and his
people.[f] 19Therefore, devote your hearts and
souls to seeking the LORD your God. Proceed to build the sanctuary of the LORD God,
that the ark of the covenant of the LORD and
God’s sacred vessels may be brought into
the house built for the name of the LORD.”[g]

## CHAPTER 23

See RG 138–40

***The Levitical Divisions.*** 1When David
had grown old and was near the end of his
days, he made his son Solomon king over Israel.[h] 2He then gathered together all the officials of Israel, along with the priests and the
Levites.

3The Levites thirty years old and above
were counted, and their total number was
found to be thirty-eight thousand.[i] 4Of these,
twenty-four thousand were to direct the service of the house of the LORD, six thousand
were to be officials and judges, 5four thousand were to be gatekeepers,[j] and four thousand were to praise the LORD with the instruments which [David] had devised for
praise. 6David apportioned them into divisions according to the sons of Levi: Gershon, Kohath, and Merari.[k]

7To the Gershonites belonged Ladan and
Shimei. 8The sons of Ladan: Jehiel the chief,
then Zetham and Joel; three in all.[l] 9The sons
of Shimei were Shelomoth, Haziel, and Haran; three. These were the heads of the families of Ladan. 10The sons of Shimei were Jahath, Zizah, Jeush, and Beriah; these were
the sons of Shimei, four in all. 11Jahath was
the chief and Zizah was second to him; but
Jeush and Beriah had few sons, and therefore they were classed as a single family, exercising a single office.

12The sons of Kohath: Amram, Izhar, Hebron, and Uzziel; four in all.[m] 13The sons of
Amram were Aaron and Moses. Aaron was
set apart to be consecrated as most holy, he
and his sons forever, to offer sacrifice before
the LORD, to minister to him, and to bless in
his name forever.[n] 14As for Moses, however,
the man of God, his sons were counted as
part of the tribe of Levi. 15The sons of Moses were Gershom and Eliezer.[o] 16The sons
of Gershom: Shubael the chief.[p] 17The sons
of Eliezer were Rehabiah the chief—Eliezer
had no other sons, but the sons of Rehabiah
were very numerous. 18The sons of Izhar:
Shelomith the chief. 19The sons of Hebron:

draws a contrast here between Solomon, the “peaceful man,” and David, who “waged great wars” (v. 8). David was prevented from building the Temple, not only because his time was taken up in waging war (1 Kgs 5:17), but also because he shed much blood (1 Chr 22:8), thereby making himself, in the Chronicler’s view, ritually unfit for the task.

**22:14 A hundred thousand talents of gold**: about 3,775 tons of gold. **A million talents of silver**: about 37,750 tons of silver. These highly exaggerated figures are intended to stress the inestimable value of the Temple as the center of Israelite worship. More modest figures are given in 1 Kgs 9:14, 28; 10:10, 14.

*d:* 1 Chr 28:7, 20; Dt 31:6, 23; Jos 1:6–7, 9; 1 Kgs 2:2–3. *e:* 1 Chr 29:2–5. *f:* 1 Chr 23:25; Jos 21:44; 23:1; 2 Sm 7:1. *g:* 1 Kgs 8:6, 21; 2 Chr 5:7; 6:11. *h:* 1 Chr 28:5; 1 Kgs 1:30. *i:* Nm 4:3, 23, 30, 35, 39, 43, 47; 8:23–26; 2 Chr 31:17. *j:* 1 Chr 9:22. *k:* 1 Chr 6:1, 16–30; 26:1–19; Ex 6:16; Nm 3:17; 26:57. *l:* 1 Chr 26:21–22; 29:8. *m:* 1 Chr 26:23; Ex 6:18; Nm 3:19; 26:58–61. *n:* 1 Chr 6:49; Ex 6:20; 28:1; Nm 6:23. *o:* Ex 2:22; 18:3–4. *p:* 1 Chr 26:24.

Jeriah, the chief, Amariah, the second, Jahaziel, the third, and Jekameam, the fourth.[q] [20]The sons of Uzziel: Micah, the chief, and Isshiah, the second.[r]

[21]The sons of Merari: Mahli and Mushi. The sons of Mahli: Eleazar and Kish.[s] [22]Eleazar died leaving no sons, only daughters; the sons of Kish, their kinsmen, married them.[t] [23]The sons of Mushi: Mahli, Eder, and Jeremoth; three in all.[u]

[24]These were the sons of Levi according to their ancestral houses, the family heads as they were enrolled one by one according to their names. They performed the work of the service of the house of the LORD beginning at twenty years of age.[v]

[25]David said: "The LORD, the God of Israel, has given rest to his people, and has taken up his dwelling in Jerusalem forever.[w] [26]Henceforth the Levites need not carry the tabernacle or any of the equipment for its service."[x] [27]For by David's last words the Levites were enlisted from the time they were twenty years old. [28]Their duty is to assist the sons of Aaron in the service of the house of the LORD, having charge of the courts, the chambers, and the preservation of everything holy: they take part in the service of the house of God. [29]They also have charge of the showbread, of the fine flour for the grain offering, of the wafers of unleavened bread, and of the baking and mixing, and of all measures of quantity and size.[y] [30]They are to be present every morning to offer thanks and to praise the LORD, and likewise in the evening;[z] [31]and at every sacrifice of burnt offerings to the LORD on sabbaths, new moons, and feast days, in such numbers as are prescribed, they must always be present before the LORD[a] [32]and observe what is prescribed for them concerning the tent of meeting, the sanctuary, and the sons of Aaron, their kinsmen, in the service of the house of the LORD.[b]

## CHAPTER 24

See RG 138–40

***The Priestly Divisions.*** [1]There were also divisions for the sons of Aaron. The sons of Aaron were Nadab, Abihu, Eleazar, and Ithamar.[c] [2]Nadab and Abihu died before their father, leaving no sons; therefore only Eleazar and Ithamar served as priests.[d] [3]David, with Zadok, a descendant of Eleazar, and Ahimelech, a descendant of Ithamar, apportioned them their offices in the priestly service.[e] [4]But since the sons of Eleazar were found to be more numerous by male heads than those of Ithamar, the former were divided into sixteen groups, and the latter into eight groups, each under its family heads. [5]Their functions were assigned impartially by lot, for there were officers of the holy place, and officers of God, descended both from Eleazar and from Ithamar. [6]The scribe Shemaiah, son of Nethanel, a Levite, recorded them in the presence of the king, and of the officials, of Zadok the priest, and of Ahimelech, son of Abiathar,* and of the heads of the ancestral houses of the priests and of the Levites, listing two successive family groups from Eleazar before each one from Ithamar.[f]

[7][g] The first lot fell to Jehoiarib, the second to Jedaiah, [8]the third to Harim, the fourth to Seorim, [9]the fifth to Malchijah, the sixth to Mijamin, [10]the seventh to Hakkoz, the eighth to Abijah,[h] [11]the ninth to Jeshua, the tenth to Shecaniah, [12]the eleventh to Eliashib, the twelfth to Jakim, [13]the thirteenth to Huppah, the fourteenth to Ishbaal, [14]the fifteenth to Bilgah, the sixteenth to Immer, [15]the seventeenth to Hezir, the eighteenth to Happizzez, [16]the nineteenth to Pethahiah, the twentieth to Jehezkel, [17]the twenty-first to Jachin, the twenty-second to Gamul, [18]the twenty-third to Delaiah, the twenty-fourth to Maaziah. [19]This was the appointed order of their service when they functioned in the house of the

**24:6 Ahimelech, son of Abiathar**: see note on 18:16.

*q:* 1 Chr 24:23. *r:* 1 Chr 24:24–25. *s:* 1 Chr 6:29; 24:26, 28–29; Ex 6:19; Nm 3:20, 33. *t:* 1 Chr 24:28–29. *u:* 1 Chr 6:47; 24:30. *v:* 2 Chr 31:17; Ezr 3:8. *w:* 1 Chr 22:18; Ps 132:13. *x:* 1 Chr 15:15; 2 Chr 35:3. *y:* 1 Chr 9:29, 31–32; Lv 2:1, 4–5; 24:5–8. *z:* Nm 28:3–8. *a:* Nm 28:2–29:39. *b:* Nm 3:6–9; 18:2–5. *c:* Ex 6:23; Nm 3:2–4; 26:60. *d:* Lv 10:1–7, 12; Nm 3:2, 4. *e:* 1 Chr 18:16; 2 Sm 8:17; 2 Chr 8:14. *f:* 1 Chr 18:16; 2 Sm 8:17. *g:* 1 Chr 9:10–13; Ezr 2:36–38; Neh 7:39–42; 11:10–14. *h:* Lk 1:5.

LORD according to the precepts given them by Aaron, their father, as the LORD, the God of Israel, had commanded him.[i]

***Other Levites.*** 20[j] Of the remaining Levites, there were Shubael, of the sons of Amram, and Jehdeiah, of the sons of Shubael; 21 Isshiah, the chief, of the sons of Rehabiah; 22 Shelomith of the Izharites, and Jahath of the sons of Shelomith. 23 The sons of Hebron were Jeriah, the chief, Amariah, the second, Jahaziel, the third, Jekameam, the fourth. 24 The sons of Uzziel were Micah; Shamir, of the sons of Micah; 25 Isshiah, the brother of Micah; and Zechariah, a descendant of Isshiah. 26 The sons of Merari were Mahli, Mushi, and the sons of his son Uzziah. 27 The sons of Merari through his son Uzziah: Shoham, Zaccur, and Ibri. 28 The sons of Mahli were Eleazar, who had no sons, 29 and Jerahmeel, of the sons of Kish. 30 The sons of Mushi were Mahli, Eder, and Jerimoth.

These were the sons of the Levites according to their ancestral houses. 31 They too, in the same manner as their kinsmen, the sons of Aaron, cast lots in the presence of King David, Zadok, Ahimelech, and the heads of the priestly and levitical families; the more important family did so in the same way as the less important one.[k]

## CHAPTER 25

See RG 138–40

***The Singers.*** 1 David and the leaders of the liturgy set apart for the service the sons of Asaph, Heman, and Jeduthun, who prophesied* to the accompaniment of lyres and harps and cymbals.[l]

This is the list of those who performed this service: 2 Of the sons of Asaph: Zaccur, Joseph, Nethaniah, and Asharelah, sons of Asaph, under the direction of Asaph, who prophesied under the guidance of the king. 3 Of Jeduthun, these sons of Jeduthun: Gedaliah, Zeri, Jeshaiah, Shimei, Hashabiah, and Mattithiah; six, under the direction of their father Jeduthun, who prophesied to the accompaniment of a lyre, to give thanks and praise to the LORD. 4 Of Heman, these sons of Heman: Bukkiah, Mattaniah, Uzziel, Shubael, and Jerimoth; Hananiah, Hanani, Eliathah, Giddalti, Romamti-ezer, Joshbekashah, Mallothi, Hothir, and Mahazioth. 5 All these were the sons of Heman, the king's seer for divine matters; to exalt him God gave Heman fourteen sons and three daughters.[m] 6 All these, whether of Asaph, Jeduthun, or Heman, were under their fathers' direction in the singing in the house of the LORD to the accompaniment of cymbals, harps and lyres, serving in the house of God, under the guidance of the king.[n] 7 Their number, together with that of their kinsmen who were trained in singing to the LORD, all of them skilled men, was two hundred and eighty-eight. 8 They cast lots for their functions equally, young and old, master and pupil alike.[o]

9 The first lot fell to Asaph, to the family of Joseph; he and his sons and his kinsmen were twelve. Gedaliah was the second; he and his kinsmen and his sons were twelve. 10 The third was Zaccur, his sons, and his kinsmen: twelve. 11 The fourth fell to Izri, his sons, and his kinsmen: twelve. 12 The fifth was Nethaniah, his sons, and his kinsmen: twelve. 13 The sixth was Bukkiah, his sons, and his kinsmen: twelve. 14 The seventh was Jesarelah, his sons, and his kinsmen: twelve. 15 The eighth was Jeshaiah, his sons, and his kinsmen: twelve. 16 The ninth was Mattaniah, his sons, and his kinsmen: twelve. 17 The tenth was Shimei, his sons, and his kinsmen: twelve. 18 The eleventh was Uzziel, his sons, and his kinsmen: twelve. 19 The twelfth fell to Hashabiah, his sons, and his kinsmen: twelve. 20 The thirteenth was Shubael, his sons, and his kinsmen: twelve. 21 The fourteenth was Mattithiah, his sons, and his kinsmen: twelve. 22 The fifteenth fell

**25:1** This list of twenty-four classes of Temple singers balances the list of the twenty-four classes of priests (24:4–19). The last nine names in v. 4, which seem to form a special group, were perhaps originally fragments or incipits (the opening words) of hymns. With some slight changes in the vocalization, these names would mean: "Have mercy on me, O LORD," "Have mercy on me," "You are my God," "I magnify," "I extol the help of . . . ," "Sitting in adversity," "I have fulfilled," "He made abundant," and "Visions."

*i:* 2 Chr 23:8. *j:* 1 Chr 23:7–23. *k:* 1 Chr 25:8; 26:13. *l:* 1 Chr 6:16–32; 15:16–17, 19; 16:37; 2 Chr 5:12; 35:15; Neh 12:27, 45. *m:* 2 Chr 35:15. *n:* 1 Chr 15:16. *o:* 1 Chr 24:31.

to Jeremoth, his sons, and his kinsmen: twelve. [23]The sixteenth fell to Hananiah, his sons, and his kinsmen: twelve. [24]The seventeenth fell to Joshbekashah, his sons, and his kinsmen: twelve. [25]The eighteenth fell to Hanani, his sons, and his kinsmen: twelve. [26]The nineteenth fell to Mallothi, his sons, and his kinsmen: twelve. [27]The twentieth fell to Eliathah, his sons, and his kinsmen: twelve. [28]The twenty-first fell to Hothir, his sons, and his kinsmen: twelve. [29]The twenty-second fell to Giddalti, his sons, and his kinsmen: twelve. [30]The twenty-third fell to Mahazioth, his sons, and his kinsmen: twelve. [31]The twenty-fourth fell to Romamti-ezer, his sons, and his kinsmen: twelve.

## CHAPTER 26

See RG 138–40

***Divisions of Gatekeepers.*** [1][p] As for the divisions of gatekeepers: Of the Korahites was Meshelemiah, the son of Kore, one of the sons of Abiasaph. [2]Meshelemiah's sons: Zechariah, the firstborn, Jediael, the second son, Zebadiah, the third, Jathniel, the fourth, [3]Elam, the fifth, Jehohanan, the sixth, Eliehoenai, the seventh. [4]Obed-edom's sons: Shemaiah, the firstborn, Jehozabad, a second son, Joah, the third, Sachar, the fourth, Nethanel, the fifth, [5]Ammiel, the sixth, Issachar, the seventh, Peullethai, the eighth, for God blessed him. [6]To his son Shemaiah were born sons who ruled over their family, for they were warriors. [7]The sons of Shemaiah were Othni, Rephael, Obed, and Elzabad; also his kinsmen who were men of substance, Elihu and Semachiah. [8]All these were the sons of Obed-edom, who, together with their sons and their kinsmen, were men of substance, fit for the service. Of Obed-edom, sixty-two. [9]Of Meshelemiah, eighteen sons and kinsmen, men of substance.

[10]Hosah, a descendant of Merari, had these sons: Shimri, the chief (for though he was not the firstborn, his father made him chief),[q] [11]Hilkiah, the second son, Tebaliah, the third, Zechariah, the fourth. All the sons and kinsmen of Hosah were thirteen.

[12]To these divisions of the gatekeepers, by their chief men, were assigned watches for them to minister in the house of the LORD, for each group in the same way. [13]They cast lots for each gate, small and large families alike. [14]When the lot was cast for the east side, it fell to Meshelemiah. Then they cast lots for his son Zechariah, a prudent counselor, and the north side fell to his lot.[r] [15]To Obed-edom fell the south side, and to his sons the storehouse. [16]To Hosah fell the west side with the Shallecheth gate at the ascending highway. For each family, watches were established. [17]On the east, six watched each day, on the north, four each day, on the south, four each day, and at the storehouse they were two and two; [18]as for the large building* on the west, there were four at the highway and two at the large building. [19]These were the classes of the gatekeepers, sons of Korah and Merari.

***Treasurers.*** [20]Their brother Levites had oversight of the treasuries of the house of God and the treasuries of votive offerings.[s] [21]Among the sons of Ladan the Gershonite, the family heads were sons of Jehiel:[t] [22][u] the sons of Jehiel, Zetham and his brother Joel, who oversaw the treasures of the house of the LORD. [23]Of the Amramites, Izharites, Hebronites, and Uzzielites, [24]Shubael, son of Gershom, son of Moses, was principal overseer of the treasures. [25][v] His associate was of the line of Eliezer, whose son was Rehabiah, whose son was Jeshaiah, whose son was Joram, whose son was Zichri, whose son was Shelomith. [26]This Shelomith and his kinsmen oversaw all the treasures of the votive offerings dedicated by King David, the heads of the families, the commanders of thousands and of hundreds, and the commanders of the army;[w] [27]what came from wars and from spoils, they dedicated for the support of the house of the LORD. [28]Also, whatever Samuel the seer, Saul, son of Kish, Abner, son of Ner, Joab, son of Zer-

**26:18 The large building**: *parbar*, mentioned also in 2 Kgs 23:11; the meaning of the word is unclear.

*p:* 1 Chr 9:19; 2 Chr 8:14; 23:19; 35:15; Neh 12:45. *q:* 1 Chr 16:38. *r:* 1 Chr 9:21. *s:* 1 Chr 28:12; 1 Kgs 7:51. *t:* 1 Chr 23:7–8; 29:8. *u:* 1 Chr 23:8, 12, 16. *v:* 1 Chr 23:17–18; 24:21. *w:* 2 Sm 8:11.

uiah, and all others had consecrated, was under the charge of Shelomith and his kinsmen.

***Magistrates.*** 29 Among the Izharites, Chenaniah and his sons were in charge of Israel's civil affairs* as officials and judges.[x] 30 Among the Hebronites, Hashabiah[y] and his kinsmen, one thousand seven hundred men of substance, had the administration of Israel on the western side of the Jordan for all the work of the LORD and the service of the king. 31 Among the Hebronites, Jerijah was their chief according to their family records. In the fortieth year of David's reign search was made, and there were found among them warriors at Jazer of Gilead.[z] 32 His kinsmen were also men of substance, two thousand seven hundred heads of families. King David appointed them to the administration of the Reubenites, the Gadites, and the half-tribe of Manasseh for everything pertaining to God and to the king.

## CHAPTER 27

See RG 138–40

***Army Commanders.**** 1 This is the list of the Israelite family heads, commanders of thousands and of hundreds, and other officers who served the king in all that pertained to the divisions, of twenty-four thousand men each, that came and went month by month throughout the year.

2 Over the first division for the first month was Ishbaal, son of Zabdiel, and in his division were twenty-four thousand men; 3 a descendant of Perez, he was chief over all the commanders of the army for the first month. 4 Over the division of the second month was Eleazar, son of Dodo, from Ahoh, and in his division were twenty-four thousand men.[a] 5[b] The third army commander, for the third month, was Benaiah, son of Jehoiada the chief priest, and in his division were twenty-four thousand men. 6 This Benaiah was a warrior among the Thirty and over the Thirty. His son Ammizabad was over his division. 7 Fourth, for the fourth month, was Asahel, brother of Joab, and after him his son Zebadiah, and in his division were twenty-four thousand men.[c] 8 Fifth, for the fifth month, was the commander Shamhuth, a descendant of Zerah, and in his division were twenty-four thousand men. 9 Sixth, for the sixth month, was Ira, son of Ikkesh, from Tekoa, and in his division were twenty-four thousand men. 10 Seventh, for the seventh month, was Hellez, from Beth-pelet, of the Ephraimites, and in his division were twenty-four thousand men. 11 Eighth, for the eighth month, was Sibbecai the Hushathite, a descendant of Zerah, and in his division were twenty-four thousand men.[d] 12 Ninth, for the ninth month, was Abiezer from Anathoth, of Benjamin, and in his division were twenty-four thousand men. 13 Tenth, for the tenth month, was Maharai from Netophah, a descendant of Zerah, and in his division were twenty-four thousand men. 14 Eleventh, for the eleventh month, was Benaiah the Pirathonite, of the Ephraimites, and in his division were twenty-four thousand men. 15 Twelfth, for the twelfth month, was Heldai the Netophathite, of the family of Othniel, and in his division were twenty-four thousand men.

***Tribal Leaders.*** 16 Over the tribes of Israel, for the Reubenites the leader was Eliezer, son of Zichri; for the Simeonites, Shephatiah, son of Maacah; 17 for Levi, Hashabiah, son of Kemuel; for Aaron, Zadok; 18 for Judah, Eliab,[e] one of David's brothers; for Issachar, Omri, son of Michael; 19 for Zebulun, Ishmaiah, son of Obadiah; for Naphtali, Jeremoth, son of Azriel; 20 for the Ephraimites, Hoshea, son of Azaziah; for the half-tribe of Manasseh, Joel, son of Pedaiah; 21 for the half-tribe of Manasseh in Gilead, Iddo, son of Zechariah; for Benjamin, Jaasiel, son of Abner; 22 for Dan, Azarel, son of Jeroham.

**26:29 Civil affairs**: lit., "external work," i.e., conduct of affairs external to the Temple.

**27:1–15** This list of army commanders is similar to, but distinct from, the list of David's warriors given in 11:10–47. The schematic enumeration of the soldiers presented here appears artificial and exaggerated (12 x 24,000 = 288,000 men!). However, the Hebrew word (*'eleph*) translated "thousand" might also designate a military unit of much smaller size.

*x:* 1 Chr 23:4. *y:* 1 Chr 27:17; Neh 11:15–16. *z:* 1 Chr 23:19; 29:27; Jos 13:25. *a:* 1 Chr 11:12; 2 Sm 23:9. *b:* 1 Chr 11:22–25; 18:17; 2 Sm 23:20–23. *c:* 2 Sm 2:18; 23:24. *d:* 1 Chr 11:29; 20:4; 2 Sm 21:18. *e:* 1 Chr 2:13.

## David's Charge to Solomon

EMPLOYING THE ROYAL speech as a means of giving voice to his own concerns, the Chronicler has David offer the charge in ch 28 at the conclusion of organizing the community for the future. The end of v. 9 is the Chronicler's primary theology: "If you search for him, he will be found; but if you abandon him, he will cast you off forever."

These were the commanders of the tribes of Israel.

[23]David did not count those who were twenty years of age or younger, for the LORD had promised to multiply Israel like the stars of the heavens.[f] [24]Joab, son of Zeruiah, began to take the census, but he did not complete it, for because of it wrath fell upon Israel. Therefore the number was not recorded in the book of chronicles of King David.[g]

***Overseers.*** [25]Over the treasuries of the king was Azmaveth,[h] the son of Adiel. Over the treasuries in the country, the cities, the villages, and the towers was Jonathan, son of Uzziah. [26]Over the farm workers who tilled the soil was Ezri, son of Chelub. [27]Over the vineyards was Shimei from Ramah, and over their produce for the wine cellars was Zabdi the Shiphmite. [28]Over the olive trees and sycamores of the Shephelah was Baal-hanan the Gederite, and over the stores of oil was Joash. [29]Over the cattle that grazed in Sharon was Shitrai the Sharonite, and over the cattle in the valleys was Shaphat, the son of Adlai; [30]over the camels was Obil the Ishmaelite; over the donkeys was Jehdeiah the Meronothite; [31]and over the flocks was Jaziz the Hagrite. All these were the overseers of King David's possessions.

***David's Court.*** [32]Jonathan, David's uncle and a man of intelligence, was counselor and scribe; he and Jehiel, the son of Hachmoni, attended the king's sons. [33]Ahithophel was also the king's counselor, and Hushai the Archite was the king's friend.[i] [34]After Ahithophel* came Jehoiada, the son of Benaiah, and Abiathar. The commander of the king's army was Joab.

### CHAPTER 28

See RG 138–40

***The Assembly at Jerusalem.*** [1]David assembled at Jerusalem all the commanders of Israel, the tribal commanders, the commanders of the divisions who were in the service of the king, the commanders of thousands and of hundreds, those in command of all the king's estates and possessions, and his sons, together with the courtiers, the warriors, and every person of substance.[j] [2][k] King David rose to his feet and said: "Hear me, my kinsmen and my people. It was my purpose to build a house of repose myself for the ark of the covenant of the LORD, the footstool for the feet of our God;* and I was preparing to build it. [3]But God said to me, You may not build a house for my name, for you are a man who waged wars and shed blood. [4]However, the LORD, the God of Israel, chose me from all my father's family to be king over Israel forever. For he chose Judah as leader, then one family of Judah, that of my father; and finally, among all the sons of my father, it pleased him to make me king over all Israel.[l] [5]And of all my sons—for the LORD has given me many sons—he has chosen my son Solomon to sit on the throne of the LORD's kingship over Israel.[m] [6]For he said to me: It is your son Solomon who shall build my house and my courts, for I have chosen him for my son, and I will be a father to him.[n] [7]I will establish his kingdom forever, if he perseveres in

**27:34 After Ahithophel**: after Ahithophel's suicide (2 Sm 17:23), Jehoiada succeeded him as the king's counselor. **Abiathar**: David's priest, along with Zadok. See note on 18:16.

**28:2 The ark . . . the footstool . . . of our God**: the Lord, who was invisibly enthroned upon the cherubim associated with the ark of the covenant at Shiloh and later in the Jerusalem Temple, had the ark as his footstool; cf. Ps 99:5; 132:7. There was no ark in the postexilic Temple. Cf. note on 2 Chr 5:9.

*f:* Gn 22:17. *g:* 2 Sm 24:10. *h:* 2 Sm 23:31. *i:* 2 Sm 15:12, 32–37; 16:16–19, 23; 17:5–16, 23. *j:* 1 Chr 27:2–22, 25–31; 11:10–47. *k:* 1 Chr 17:4; 22:7–10; 2 Sm 7:5; 1 Kgs 5:3; Ps 132:3–7. *l:* 1 Chr 17:23; Gn 49:8–12; 1 Sm 16:6–13. *m:* 1 Chr 3:1–9; 14:3–7; 22:9; 23:1; Wis 9:7. *n:* 1 Chr 17:11–14; 22:9–10; 2 Sm 7:12–13.

carrying out my commandments and ordinances as he does now. [8]Therefore, in the sight of all Israel, the assembly of the LORD, and in the hearing of our God: keep and carry out all the commandments of the LORD, your God, that you may continue to possess this good land and afterward leave it as an inheritance to your children forever.[o]

[9]"As for you, Solomon, my son, know the God of your father and serve him with a whole heart and a willing soul, for the LORD searches all hearts and understands all the mind's thoughts. If you search for him, he will be found; but if you abandon him, he will cast you off forever.[p] [10]See, then! The LORD has chosen you to build a house as his sanctuary. Be strong and set to work."

***Temple Plans Given to Solomon.*** [11]Then David gave to his son Solomon the design of the portico and of the house itself, with its storerooms, its upper rooms and inner chambers, and the shrine containing the cover of the ark.[q] [12]He provided also the design for all else that he had in mind by way of courts for the house of the LORD, with the surrounding compartments for the treasuries of the house of God and the treasuries for the votive offerings, [13]as well as for the divisions of the priests and Levites, for all the work of the service of the house of the LORD, and for all the liturgical vessels of the house of the LORD. [14]He specified the weight of gold to be used in the golden vessels for the various services and the weight of silver to be used in the silver vessels for the various services; [15]likewise for the golden menorahs and their lamps he specified the weight of gold for each menorah and its lamps, and for the silver menorahs he specified the weight of silver for each menorah and its lamps, depending on the use to which each menorah was to be put.[r] [16]He specified the weight of gold for each table that was to hold the showbread, and the silver for the silver tables; [17]the pure gold for the forks, basins, and pitchers; the weight of gold for each golden bowl and the weight of silver for each silver bowl; [18]the refined gold, and its weight, to be used for the altar of incense; and, finally, gold to fashion the chariot:* the cherubim spreading their wings and covering the ark of the covenant of the LORD.[s] [19]All this he wrote down, by the hand of the LORD, to make him understand it—the working out of the whole design.

[20]Then David said to his son Solomon: "Be strong and steadfast, and go to work; do not fear or be dismayed, for the LORD God, my God, is with you. He will not fail you or abandon you before you have completed all the work for the service of the house of the LORD.[t] [21]The divisions of the priests and Levites are ready for all the service of the house of God; they will be with you in all the work with all those who are eager to show their skill in every kind of craftsmanship. Also the commanders and all the people will do everything that you command."[u]

## CHAPTER 29

See RG 138–40

***Offerings for the Temple.*** [1]King David then said to the whole assembly: "My son Solomon, whom alone God has chosen, is still young and inexperienced; the work, however, is great, for this palace is not meant for human beings, but for the LORD God.[v] [2]For this reason I have stored up for the house of my God, as far as I was able, gold for what will be made of gold, silver for what will be made of silver, bronze for what will be made of bronze, iron for what will be made of iron, wood for what will be made of wood, onyx stones and settings for them, carnelian and mosaic stones, every other kind of precious stone, and great quantities of marble.[w] [3]But now, because of the delight I take in the house of my God, in addition to all that I stored up for the holy house, I give to the house of my God my personal fortune in gold and silver: [4]three thousand talents of Ophir gold, and seven thousand talents of refined silver, for overlaying the walls of the rooms,[x] [5]for the various utensils to be made of gold and silver, and for every work that is

**28:18 Chariot**: this reference is probably inspired by the vision account in Ez 1:4–24; 10:1–22.

*o:* Dt 4:5. *p:* 1 Chr 29:17; 2 Chr 15:2; 1 Kgs 8:61. *q:* Ex 25:9, 40; 26:30. *r:* Ex 25:31–37. *s:* Ex 25:18–22; 30:1–10; 1 Kgs 6:23–28. *t:* 1 Chr 22:13; Jos 1:5. *u:* Ex 36:1–5. *v:* 1 Chr 22:5; 28:5. *w:* 1 Chr 22:14. *x:* 2 Chr 9:10; 1 Kgs 9:28; 10:11.

to be done by artisans. Now, who else will contribute generously and consecrate themselves this day to the LORD?"[y]

6 Then the heads of the families, the tribal commanders of Israel, the commanders of thousands and of hundreds, and those who had command of the king's affairs came forward willingly[z] 7 and contributed for the service of the house of God five thousand talents and ten thousand darics of gold, ten thousand talents of silver, eighteen thousand talents of bronze, and one hundred thousand talents of iron.[a] 8 Those who had precious stones gave them into the keeping of Jehiel the Gershonite for the treasury of the house of the LORD.[b] 9 The people rejoiced over these free-will offerings, for they had been contributed to the LORD wholeheartedly. King David also rejoiced greatly.[c]

***David's Prayer.*** 10 Then David blessed the LORD in the sight of the whole assembly. David said:

"Blessed are you, LORD,
God of Israel our father,
from eternity to eternity.
11 Yours, LORD, are greatness and might,
majesty, victory, and splendor.
For all in heaven and on earth is yours;
yours, LORD, is kingship;
you are exalted as head over all.
12 Riches and glory are from you,
and you have dominion over all.
In your hand are power and might;
it is yours to give greatness and
strength to all.[d]
13 Therefore, our God, we give you thanks
and we praise the majesty of your
name.

14 "But who am I, and who are my people, that we should have the means to contribute so freely? For everything is from you, and what we give is what we have from you. 15 For before you we are strangers and travelers, like all our ancestors. Our days on earth are like a shadow, without a future.[e] 16 LORD our God, all this wealth that we have brought together to build you a house for your holy name comes from you and is entirely yours. 17 I know, my God, that you put hearts to the test and that you take pleasure in integrity. With a whole heart I have willingly given all these things, and now with joy I have seen your people here present also giving to you generously. 18 LORD, God of our ancestors Abraham, Isaac, and Israel,[f] keep such thoughts in the hearts and minds of your people forever, and direct their hearts toward you. 19 Give to my son Solomon a wholehearted desire to keep your commandments, precepts, and statutes, that he may carry out all these plans and build the palace for which I have made preparation."

20 Then David told the whole assembly, "Now bless the LORD your God!" And the whole assembly blessed the LORD, the God of their ancestors, bowing down in homage before the LORD and before the king. 21 On the following day they brought sacrifices and burnt offerings to the LORD, a thousand bulls, a thousand rams, and a thousand lambs, together with their libations and many other sacrifices for all Israel; 22 and on that day they ate and drank in the LORD's presence with great rejoicing.

***Solomon Anointed.*** Then for a second time* they proclaimed David's son Solomon king, and they anointed him for the LORD as ruler, and Zadok as priest. 23 Thereafter Solomon sat on the throne of the LORD as king succeeding his father David; he prospered, and all Israel obeyed him.[g] 24 All the commanders and warriors, and also all the other sons of King David, swore allegiance to King Solomon. 25 And the LORD exalted Solomon greatly in the eyes of all Israel, giving him a glorious reign such as had not been enjoyed by any king over Israel before him.[h]

***David's Death.*** 26 Thus David, the son of Jesse, had reigned over all Israel. 27 He was

**29:22 For a second time**: the first time is in 23:1 where David appoints Solomon his successor. Now there is a solemn public ratification of that appointment.

*y:* Ex 25:2; 35:5–6. *z:* 1 Chr 27:1, 25–31; 28:1. *a:* Ezr 2:69; 8:27; Neh 7:70–71. *b:* 1 Chr 23:8; 26:21. *c:* 2 Kgs 12:4. *d:* 2 Chr 20:6; Wis 6:3. *e:* Lv 25:23; Wis 2:5; 5:9. *f:* Ex 3:6, 15; 4:5; 1 Kgs 18:36. *g:* 1 Chr 28:5; 2 Chr 9:8; 1 Kgs 2:12. *h:* 2 Chr 1:12; 1 Kgs 3:13.

king over Israel for forty years: he was king seven years in Hebron and thirty-three years in Jerusalem.[i] [28]He died at a ripe old age, rich in years and wealth and glory, and his son Solomon succeeded him as king.[j]
[29]Now the deeds of King David, first and last, are recorded in the history of Samuel the seer, the history of Nathan the prophet, and the history of Gad the seer,[k] [30]together with the particulars of his reign and valor, and of the events that affected him and all Israel and all the kingdoms of the earth.

*i:* 2 Sm 5:5; 1 Kgs 2:11. *j:* 1 Chr 23:1. *k:* 1 Chr 21:9; 1 Sm 22:5.

See RG 137–44

# The Second Book of Chronicles

The Second Book of Chronicles takes up the history of the monarchy where the First Book leaves off. It begins with the account of the reign of Solomon (chaps. 1–9) from the special viewpoint of the Chronicler. The portrait of Solomon is an idealized one; he appears as second only to David. Solomon's building of the Temple and the magnificence of his court are described in detail while the serious defects of his reign as cited in 1 Kings are simply not mentioned. This procedure is in keeping with the Chronicler's purpose of stressing the supreme importance of the Temple and its worship. He wishes to impress on his readers the splendor of God's dwelling and the magnificence of the liturgy of sacrifice, prayer, and praise offered there. Judah's kings are judged by their attitude toward the Temple and its cult. To this ideal of one people, united in the worship of the one true God at the Temple of Jerusalem founded by David and Solomon, the restored community is to conform.

In treating the period of divided monarchy (chaps. 10–36), the Chronicler gives practically all his attention to the kingdom of Judah. His virtual omission of the northern Israelite kings is significant. In his view, the northern tribes of Israel were guilty of religious schism as long as they worshiped the Lord in a place other than the Temple of Jerusalem. The Chronicler makes no mention of the important sanctuaries of Yhwh at Dan and Bethel—as though they had never existed. Nevertheless, he retains the ancient ideal of "all Israel" (a phrase occurring forty-one times in Chronicles) as the people of God. This unity, however, can exist only if the worship of "the whole congregation of Israel" takes place exclusively in the Jerusalem Temple. This requirement explains the Chronicler's praise of Kings Hezekiah and Josiah for striving, after the fall of Samaria, to unite the remnants of the northern tribes of Israel with the kingdom of Judah. Nevertheless, after Josiah's death, Judah quickly careens toward its demise at the hands of the Babylonians. That catastrophe is reversed by the edict of Cyrus allowing a return to Jerusalem and rebuilding of the Temple. Thus 2 Chronicles ends.

The Second Book of Chronicles can be divided into two major segments as follows:

I. The Reign of Solomon (1:1–9:31)
II. The Post-Solomonic Monarchy of Judah (10:1–36:23)

## I. The Reign of Solomon

### CHAPTER 1

See RG 141

***Solomon at Gibeon.*** [1]Solomon, son of David, strengthened his hold on the kingdom, for the LORD, his God, was with him, making him ever greater. [2]Solomon summoned all Israel, the commanders of thousands and of hundreds, the judges, the princes of all Israel, and the family heads; [3a]and, accompanied by the whole assembly, Solomon went to the high place at Gibeon, because the tent of meeting of God, made in the wilderness by Moses, the LORD's servant, was there. [4]David had, however, brought up the ark of God from Kiriath-jearim to Jerusalem, where he had provided a place and pitched a tent for it;

*a:* 1 Kgs 3:4–15; 1 Chr 21:29.

[5]the bronze altar made by Bezalel, son of
Uri, son of Hur, he put in front of the tabernacle of the LORD.* There Solomon and the
assembly sought out the LORD,[b] [6]and Solomon offered sacrifice in the LORD's presence
on the bronze altar at the tent of meeting; he
sacrificed a thousand burnt offerings upon it.
[7]That night God appeared to Solomon and
said to him: Whatever you ask, I will give
you. [8]Solomon answered God: "You have
shown great favor to David my father, and
you have made me king to succeed him.
[9]Now, LORD God, may your word to David
my father be confirmed, for you have made
me king over a people as numerous as the
dust of the earth.[c] [10]Give me, therefore, wisdom and knowledge to govern this people,
for otherwise who could rule this vast people
of yours?" [11]God then replied to Solomon:
Because this has been your wish—you did
not ask for riches, treasures, and glory, or the
life of those who hate you, or even for a long
life for yourself, but you have asked for wisdom and knowledge in order to rule my people over whom I have made you king—
[12]wisdom and knowledge are given you. I
will also give you riches, treasures, and
glory, such as kings before you never had,
nor will those who come after you.

***Solomon's Wealth.*** [13]Solomon returned to
Jerusalem from the high place at Gibeon,
from before the tent of meeting, and became
king over Israel. [14]Solomon amassed chariots and horses: he had one thousand four
hundred chariots and twelve thousand
horses; these he allocated among the chariot
cities and to the king's service in Jerusalem.[d]
[15]The king made silver and gold as common
in Jerusalem as stones, and cedars as numerous as the sycamores of the Shephelah.[e]
[16]Solomon's horses were imported from
Egypt and Cilicia,* where the king's agents
purchased them at the prevailing price.[f] [17]A
chariot imported from Egypt cost six hundred shekels of silver, a horse one hundred
and fifty shekels; so they were exported to
all the Hittite and Aramean kings.[g]

***Preparations for the Temple.*** [18]Solomon
gave orders for the building of a house for
the name of the LORD and also a king's
house for himself.

## CHAPTER 2

See RG 141

[1]Solomon conscripted seventy thousand men to carry stones and eighty thousand
to cut the stones in the mountains, and over
these he placed three thousand six hundred
overseers.[h] [2][i] Moreover, Solomon sent this
message to Huram, king of Tyre: "As you
dealt with David my father, and sent him
cedars to build a house for his dwelling—
[3]now I am going to build a house for the
name of the LORD, my God, and to consecrate it to him, for the burning of fragrant incense in his presence, for the perpetual display of the showbread, for burnt offerings
morning and evening, and for the sabbaths,
new moons, and festivals of the LORD, our
God: such is Israel's perpetual obligation.[j]
[4]And the house I am going to build must be
great, for our God is greater than all other
gods. [5]Yet who is really able to build him a
house, since the heavens and even the highest heavens cannot contain him? And who
am I that I should build him a house,[k] unless
it be to offer incense in his presence? [6]Now,
send me men skilled at work in gold, silver,
bronze, and iron, in purple, crimson, and violet fabrics, and who know how to do engraved work, to join the skilled craftsmen
who are with me in Judah and Jerusalem,
whom David my father appointed. [7]Also
send me boards of cedar, cypress and cabinet
wood from Lebanon, for I realize that your

**1:5 The bronze altar . . . the tabernacle of the LORD**: by this notice, the Chronicler justifies Solomon's worship at the high place of Gibeon. He pictures the tabernacle, i.e., the Mosaic meeting tent, and the bronze altar made at Moses' command (Ex 31:1–9) as remaining at Gibeon after David had installed the ark of the covenant in another tent in Jerusalem (1 Chr 15:1, 25; 16:1). Bezalel's altar was made of acacia wood plated with bronze (Ex 27:1–2). Later, Solomon made an all-bronze altar for the Temple in Jerusalem (2 Chr 4:1).

**1:16–17 Egypt and Cilicia**: it seems likely that the horses came from Cilicia and the chariots from Egypt. Some scholars find a reference to Musur, a mountain district north of Cilicia, rather than to Egypt (Misrayim) in 1 Kgs 10:28–29, the Chronicler's source for this notice. The Chronicler himself probably understood the source to be speaking of Egypt; cf. 2 Chr 9:28.

*b:* Ex 27:1–2; 31:2; 1 Chr 2:20. *c:* Gn 13:16; 28:14. *d:* 2 Chr 9:25; 1 Kgs 10:26–29. *e:* 1 Kgs 10:27. *f:* 1 Kgs 10:28. *g:* 1 Kgs 10:29. *h:* 2 Chr 2:17; 5:29–30. *i:* 1 Kgs 5:15–20; 1 Chr 14:1. *j:* Lv 24:5–8; Nm 28–29. *k:* 2 Chr 6:18.

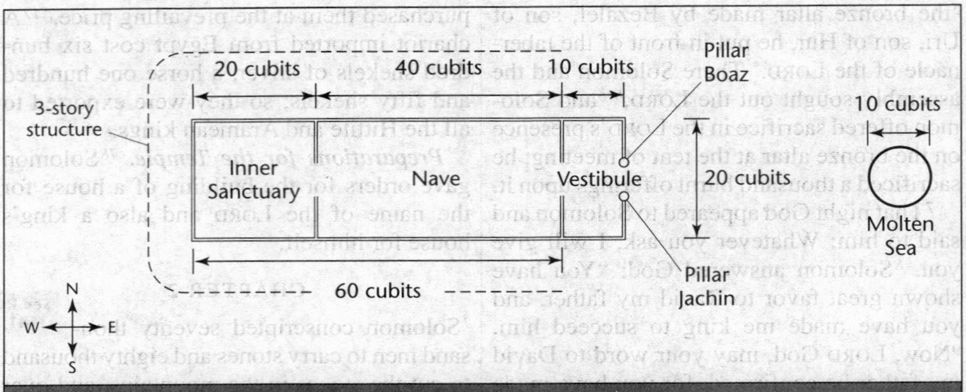


**The Temple of Solomon according to 2 Chronicles**

servants know how to cut the wood of Lebanon. My servants will work with yours 8in
order to prepare for me a great quantity of
wood, since the house I intend to build must
be great and wonderful. 9I will furnish as
food for your servants, the woodcutters,
twenty thousand kors of wheat, twenty thousand kors of barley, twenty thousand baths of
wine, and twenty thousand baths of oil."* [l]
10Huram, king of Tyre, wrote an answer
which he sent to Solomon: "Because the
LORD loves his people, he has placed you
over them as king." 11He added: "Blessed be
the LORD, the God of Israel, who made
heaven and earth, for having given King David a wise son of intelligence and understanding, who will build a house for the
LORD and also his own royal house.[m] 12[n]I
am now sending you a craftsman of great
skill, Huram-abi, 13son of a Danite woman*
and of a father from Tyre; he knows how to
work with gold, silver, bronze, and iron,
with stone and wood, with purple, violet,
fine linen, and crimson, and also how to do
all kinds of engraved work and to devise
every type of design that may be given him
and your craftsmen and the craftsmen of my
lord David your father. 14[o] And now, let my
lord send to his servants the wheat, barley,
oil, and wine which he has promised. 15For
our part, we will cut trees on Lebanon, as
many as you need, and send them down to
you in rafts to the port of Joppa, whence you
may take them up to Jerusalem."[p]
16[q] Thereupon Solomon took a census of
all the alien men resident in the land of Israel
(following the census David his father had
taken of them); they were found to number
one hundred fifty-three thousand six hundred. 17Of these he made seventy thousand
carriers and eighty thousand cutters in the
mountains, and three thousand six hundred
overseers to keep the people working.[r]

## CHAPTER 3

See RG 141

*Building of the Temple.* 1[s] Then Solomon began to build the house of the LORD in
Jerusalem on Mount Moriah,* which had
been shown to David his father, in the place
David had prepared, the threshing floor of
Ornan the Jebusite. 2He began to build in the
second month of the fourth year of his reign.

**2:9** There is probably some exaggeration here. The parallel passage in 1 Kgs 5:25 does not list the barley or the wine, and mentions only twenty kors of olive oil. **Kors**: see note on Ez 45:14; **baths**: see note on Is 5:10. The amount given in Chronicles would be one hundred times as much (20,000 baths equals 2,000 kors).

**2:13 A Danite woman**: in 1 Kgs 7:14 she is called a widow of the tribe of Naphtali. The Danites had settled in the northern section of Naphtali's territory (Jgs 18:27–29). Bezalel, the head artisan in the time of Moses, had as his assistant a member of the tribe of Dan (Ex 31:6).

**3:1 Mount Moriah**: Gn 22:2 speaks of a "height in the land of Moriah." This is the only place in the Bible where the Temple mount is identified with the site where Abraham was to have sacrificed Isaac.

*l:* 1 Kgs 5:25; Ezr 3:7. *m:* 1 Kgs 5:21. *n:* Ex 31:1–5; 1 Kgs 7:13–14. *o:* 1 Kgs 5:22–26. *p:* Ezr 3:7. *q:* 1 Chr 22:2. *r:* 2 Chr 2:1. *s:* Gn 22:2; 1 Kgs 6:1; 1 Chr 21:22–26; 22:1.

3 These were the specifications laid down by
Solomon for building the house of God: the
length was sixty cubits according to the old
measure, and the width was twenty cubits;[t]
4 the front porch along the width of the house
was also twenty cubits, and it was twenty cubits high.* He covered its interior with pure
gold.[u] 5 The nave he overlaid with cypress
wood and overlaid that with fine gold, em-
bossing on it palms and chains.[v] 6 He also
covered the house with precious stones for
splendor; the gold was from Parvaim. 7 The
house, its beams and thresholds, as well as
its walls and its doors, he overlaid with gold,
and he engraved cherubim upon the walls.
8 He also made the room of the holy of
holies. Its length corresponded to the width
of the house, twenty cubits, and its width
was also twenty cubits. He overlaid it with
fine gold to the amount of six hundred talents.[w] 9 The weight of the nails was fifty gold
shekels. The upper chambers he likewise
overlaid with gold.

10[x] For the room of the holy of holies he
made two cherubim of carved workmanship, which were then covered with gold.
11 The wings of the cherubim spanned
twenty cubits: one wing of each cherub, five
cubits in length, extended to a wall of the
house, while the other wing, also five cubits
in length, touched the corresponding wing
of the other cherub. 12 The wing of the
cherub, five cubits, touched the wall of the
house, and the other wing, five cubits, was
joined to the wing of the other cherub. 13 The
combined wingspread of the two cherubim
was thus twenty cubits. They stood upon
their own feet, facing toward the nave. 14 He
made the veil* of violet, purple, crimson,
and fine linen, and had cherubim embroidered upon it.[y]

15[z] In front of the house he set two
columns thirty-five cubits high; the capital
of each was five cubits. 16 He devised chains
in the form of a collar with which he encircled the capitals of the columns, and he
made a hundred pomegranates which he set
on the chains. 17 He set up the columns to
correspond with the nave, one for the right
side and the other for the left, and he called
the one to the right Jachin and the one to the
left Boaz.

## CHAPTER 4

See RG 141

1 Then he made a bronze altar twenty
cubits long, twenty cubits wide and ten cubits
high.[a] 2[b] He also made the molten sea. It was
made with a circular rim, and measured ten
cubits across, five in height, and thirty in circumference. 3 Under the brim a ring of figures
of oxen* encircled it for ten cubits, all the way
around the compass of the sea; there were two
rows of oxen cast in one mold with the sea.
4 This rested on twelve oxen, three facing
north, three facing west, three facing south,
and three facing east, with their haunches all
toward the center; upon them was set the sea.
5 It was a handbreadth thick, and its brim resembled that of a cup, being lily-shaped. It
had a capacity of three thousand baths.*

6 Then he made ten basins for washing,
placing five of them to the right and five to
the left. In these the victims for the burnt offerings were washed; but the sea was for the
priests to wash in.[c]

7 He made the menorahs of gold, ten of
them as was prescribed, and placed them in
the nave, five to the right and five to the left.[d]

**3:4 The front porch . . . twenty cubits high**: this figure, not given in 1 Kgs 7, is based on a variant Greek text that may be due to a later revision. The Hebrew text itself has "one hundred and twenty cubits high." The Chronicler nearly doubles the height of the two free-standing columns adjacent to the porch in 2 Chr 3:15 as compared with the source, 1 Kgs 7:15–16.

**3:14 The veil**: this was suspended at the entrance of the holy of holies, in imitation of the veil of the Mosaic meeting tent (Ex 26:31–32). Solomon's Temple had doors at this point, according to 1 Kgs 6:31. Apparently the Temple of the Chronicler's time did have a veil, just as did Herod's Temple (Mt 27:51; Mk 15:38; Lk 23:45).

**4:3 Oxen**: in 1 Kgs 7:24 this double row of ornaments is described as consisting of gourds. The text of Kings available to the Chronicler may have been corrupt at this point since the two words sound similar in Hebrew. In 4:16 the Chronicler speaks of forks while 1 Kgs 7:40 refers to bowls.

**4:5 Three thousand baths**: two thousand baths according to 1 Kgs 7:26; see note on 1 Kgs 7:23–26.

*t:* 1 Kgs 6:2. *u:* 1 Kgs 6:3. *v:* 1 Kgs 6:15; Ez 41:1. *w:* 1 Kgs 6:16–17, 20. *x:* 1 Kgs 6:23–27. *y:* Mt 27:51. *z:* 1 Kgs 7:15–20; Ez 40:49. *a:* Ez 43:13–17. *b:* 1 Kgs 7:23–26. *c:* 1 Kgs 7:38–39; Ez 40:38. *d:* 1 Kgs 7:49.

[8]He made ten tables and had them set in the
nave, five to the right and five to the left; and
he made a hundred golden bowls.[e] [9]He made
the court of the priests and the great courtyard[f] and the gates of the courtyard; the
gates he covered with bronze. [10]The sea he
placed off to the southeast from the south
side of the house.[g]

[11][h] When Huram had made the pots, shovels, and bowls, he finished all his work for
King Solomon in the house of God: [12]two
columns; two nodes for the capitals on top of
the columns; and two pieces of netting covering the two nodes for the capitals on top of
the columns; [13]four hundred pomegranates
in double rows on both pieces of netting that
covered the two nodes of the capitals on top
of the columns. [14]He made the stands, and
the basins on the stands; [15]one sea, and the
twelve oxen under it; [16]pots, shovels, forks,
and all the articles Huram-abi made for King
Solomon for the house of the LORD; they
were of burnished bronze. [17]The king had
them cast in the neighborhood of the Jordan,
between Succoth and Zeredah, in thick clay
molds. [18]Solomon made all these vessels, so
many in number that the weight of the
bronze could not be determined.

[19]Solomon made all the articles that were
for the house of God: the golden altar, the tables on which the showbread lay, [20]the
menorahs and their lamps of pure gold
which were to burn as prescribed before the
inner sanctuary, [21]flowers, lamps, and gold
tongs (this was of purest gold), [22]snuffers,
bowls, cups, and firepans of pure gold. As
for the entrance to the house, its inner doors
to the holy of holies, as well as the doors to
the nave of the temple, were of gold.

See RG 141

## CHAPTER 5

***Dedication of the Temple.*** [1][i] When all
the work undertaken by Solomon for the
house of the LORD was completed, he
brought in the votive offerings of David his
father, putting the silver, the gold, and other
articles in the treasuries of the house of God.
[2]Then Solomon assembled the elders of Israel and all the heads of the tribes, the
princes in the ancestral houses of the Israelites, to Jerusalem to bring up the ark of the
LORD's covenant from the City of David,
which is Zion. [3]All the people of Israel assembled before the king during the festival
of the seventh month.* [4][j] When all the elders
of Israel had arrived, the Levites* took up the
ark; [5]and they brought up the ark and the tent
of meeting with all the sacred vessels that
were in the tent. The levitical priests brought
them up.

[6]King Solomon and the entire community
of Israel, gathered for the occasion before
the ark, sacrificed sheep and oxen too many
to number or count. [7]The priests brought the
ark of the covenant of the LORD to its place:
the inner sanctuary of the house, the holy of
holies, beneath the wings of the cherubim.
[8]The cherubim had their wings spread out
over the place of the ark, covering the ark
and its poles from above. [9]The poles were so
long that their ends could be seen from the
holy place in front of the inner sanctuary.
(They cannot be seen from outside, but they
remain there to this day.)* [10]There was nothing in the ark but the two tablets which Moses had put there at Horeb when the LORD
made a covenant with the Israelites after
they went forth from Egypt.

[11]When the priests left the holy place (all
the priests who were present had purified
themselves regardless of the rotation of their
various divisions), [12]the Levites who were
singers, all who belonged to Asaph, Heman,
Jeduthun, and their sons and brothers,
clothed in fine linen, with cymbals, harps,
and lyres, stood east of the altar, and with
them a hundred and twenty priests blowing
trumpets.

**5:3 Festival of the seventh month**: feast of Booths (Tabernacles); cf. notes on 7:9–10; 1 Kgs 8:2.

**5:4 The Levites**: the parallel passage in 1 Kgs 8:3 reads "the priests"; but in 2 Chr 5:5 the Deuteronomic expression "levitical priests" is used, as it is in 23:18; 30:27.

**5:9 They remain there to this day**: the Chronicler must have copied this notice from his source (1 Kgs 8:8), losing sight of the fact that there was no ark in the Temple of his own day. (According to 2 Mc 2:4–8, the ark of Solomon's Temple was concealed by Jeremiah at the time of the Babylonian destruction of Jerusalem.)

*e:* 1 Kgs 7:50; 1 Chr 28:16. *f:* 1 Kgs 7:12. *g:* 1 Kgs 7:39. *h:* 1 Kgs 7:40–51. *i:* 1 Kgs 7:51–8:13. *j:* 2 Chr 35:3.

13 When the trumpeters and singers were
heard as a single voice praising and giving
thanks to the LORD, and when they raised the
sound of the trumpets, cymbals, and other
musical instruments to "Praise the LORD,
who is so good, whose love endures forever," the cloud filled the house of the
LORD.[k] 14 The priests could no longer minister because of the cloud, since the glory of
the LORD had filled the house of God.[l]

See RG 141

## CHAPTER 6

1[m] Then Solomon said:

"The LORD intends to dwell in the dark
cloud;
2 I have built you a princely house,
the base for your enthronement
forever."

3[n] The king turned and blessed the whole assembly of Israel, while the whole assembly
of Israel stood. 4 He said: "Blessed be the
LORD, the God of Israel, who with his own
mouth spoke a promise to David my father
and by his hand fulfilled it, saying: 5 Since
the day I brought my people out of the land
of Egypt, I have not chosen a city out of any
tribe of Israel for the building of a house,
that my name might be there; nor have I chosen any man to be ruler of my people Israel;
6 but now I have chosen Jerusalem, that my
name may be there, and I have chosen David* to rule my people Israel. 7 When David
my father wished to build a house for the
name of the LORD, the God of Israel, 8 the
LORD said to him: In wishing to build a
house for my name, you did well. 9 But it is
not you who will build the house, but your
son, who comes from your loins: he shall
build the house for my name.

10 "Now the LORD has fulfilled the word he
spoke. I have succeeded David my father,
and I sit on the throne of Israel, as the LORD
has said, and I have built this house for the
name of the LORD, the God of Israel. 11 I have
placed there the ark, in which is the covenant
of the LORD that he made with the Israelites."

***Solomon's Prayer.*** 12[o] Then he stood before the altar of the LORD in the presence of
the whole assembly of Israel and stretched
forth his hands. 13* Solomon had made a
bronze platform five cubits long, five cubits
wide, and three cubits high, which he had
placed in the middle of the courtyard. Having ascended it, Solomon knelt in the presence of the whole assembly of Israel and
stretched forth his hands toward heaven.
14 He said: "LORD, God of Israel, there is no
God like you in heaven or on earth; you keep
the covenant and love toward your servants
who walk before you with their whole heart,
15 the covenant that you kept toward your
servant, David my father. That which you
promised him, your mouth has spoken and
your hand has fulfilled this very day. 16 And
now, LORD, God of Israel, keep toward your
servant, David my father, what you promised: There shall never be wanting someone
from your line to sit before me on the throne
of Israel, provided that your descendants
keep to their way, walking by my law, as you
have. 17 Now, LORD, God of Israel, may the
words which you spoke to David your servant be confirmed.

18 "Is God indeed to dwell with human beings on earth? If the heavens and the highest
heavens cannot contain you, how much less
this house which I have built! 19 Regard
kindly the prayer and petition of your servant, LORD, my God, and listen to the cry of
supplication which I, your servant, utter before you. 20 May your eyes be open day and
night toward this house, the place where you
have decreed your name shall be; listen to the
prayer your servant makes toward this place.
21 Listen to the petition of your servant and of
your people Israel which they offer toward
this place. Listen, from the place of your enthronement, heaven, and listen and forgive.

22 "If someone sins against a neighbor and

**6:6 Jerusalem . . . David**: Ps 132:11, 13 puts in parallel the Lord's choice of David and Zion, the royal house of David and the mountain in Jerusalem as the site for the Lord's house.

**6:13** This verse has no equivalent in 1 Kgs 8:22–23, the Chronicler's source. Solomon is depicted as praying on "a bronze platform . . . in the middle of the courtyard" because in the time of the Chronicler only priests were permitted to pray before the altar.

*k:* Ps 136; Jer 33:11. *l:* 2 Chr 7:2; 1 Kgs 8:10–11. *m:* 1 Kgs 8:12–13. *n:* 1 Kgs 8:14–21. *o:* 1 Kgs 8:22–53.

is required to take an oath sanctioned by a curse, and comes and takes the oath before your altar in this house, 23listen in heaven: act and judge your servants. Condemn the wicked, requiting their ways; acquit the just, rewarding their justice. 24When your people Israel are defeated by an enemy because they have sinned against you, and then they turn, praise your name, pray to you, and entreat you in this house, 25listen from heaven and forgive the sin of your people Israel, and bring them back to the land you gave them and their ancestors. 26When the heavens are closed so that there is no rain, because they have sinned against you, but they pray toward this place and praise your name, and turn from their sin because you have afflicted them, 27listen in heaven and forgive the sin of your servants, your people Israel. (For you teach them the good way in which they should walk.) Give rain upon this land of yours which you have given to your people as their heritage.

28"If there is famine in the land or pestilence; or if blight comes, or mildew, or locusts swarm, or caterpillars; when their enemies besiege them at any of their gates; whatever plague or sickness there may be; 29whatever prayer of petition any may make, any of your people Israel, who know affliction and pain and stretch out their hands toward this house, 30listen from heaven, the place of your enthronement, and forgive. Render to each and all according to their ways, you who know every heart; for it is you alone who know the heart of every human being. 31So may they revere you and walk in your ways as long as they live on the land you gave our ancestors.

32"To the foreigners, likewise, who are not of your people Israel, but who come from a distant land for the sake of your great name, your mighty hand and outstretched arm, and come in prayer to this house, 33listen from heaven, the place of your enthronement. Do all that the foreigner asks of you, that all the peoples of the earth may know your name, may revere you as do your people Israel, and may know that your name has been invoked upon this house that I have built.

34"When your people go out to war against their enemies, by whatever way you send them, and they pray to you toward the city you have chosen and the house I have built for your name, 35listen from heaven to their prayer and petition, and uphold their cause. 36When they sin against you (for there is no one who does not sin), and in your anger against them you deliver them to an enemy, so that their captors carry them off to another land, far or near, 37and they have a change of heart in the land of their captivity and they turn and entreat you in the land of their captors and say, 'We have sinned and done wrong; we have been wicked,' 38if with all their heart and soul they turn back to you in the land of those who took them captive, and pray toward their land which you gave their ancestors, the city you have chosen, and the house which I have built for your name, 39listen from heaven, the place of your enthronement, to their prayer and petitions, and uphold their cause. Forgive your people who have sinned against you. 40Now, my God, may your eyes be open and your ears be attentive to the prayer of this place. 41And now:

"Arise, LORD God, come to your resting place,
you and your majestic ark.
Your priests, LORD God, will be clothed with salvation,
your faithful ones rejoice in good things.
42 LORD God, do not reject the plea of your anointed,
remember the devotion of David, your servant."[p]

## CHAPTER 7

See RG 141

1[q] When Solomon had ended his prayer, fire came down from heaven and consumed the burnt offerings and the sacrifices, and the glory of the LORD filled the house. 2But the priests could not enter the house of the LORD, for the glory of the LORD filled the house of the LORD.[r] 3All the Israelites looked on while the fire came down and

*p:* Ps 132:8–10. *q:* Jgs 6:21; 1 Kgs 8:54–66; 1 Chr 21:26; 2 Mc 2:10. *r:* 2 Chr 5:14; Ex 24:16; 1 Kgs 8:10–11.

FOR THE CHRONICLER, the temple is important because God has consecrated the place by choosing it for himself. This interpretation by the Chronicler is related to the idea in Deuteronomy of God's choosing a place for his name to dwell (Dt 12:11, 14). The concept of a "house of sacrifice" (7:12) places emphasis on the ritual aspects of temple service and its role as a place of mediation between God and the community.

the glory of the LORD was upon the house,
and they fell down upon the pavement with
their faces to the earth and worshiped, praising the LORD, "who is so good, whose love
endures forever." 4The king and all the people offered sacrifices before the LORD.[s]
5King Solomon offered as sacrifice twenty-
two thousand oxen, and one hundred twenty
thousand sheep.[t]
*End of the Dedication.* Thus the king and
all the people dedicated the house of God.
6The priests were standing at their stations,
as were the Levites, with the musical instruments of the LORD which King David had
made to give thanks to the LORD, "whose
love endures forever," when David offered
praise through them. The priests opposite
them blew the trumpets and all Israel stood.[u]
7Then Solomon consecrated the middle of
the court facing the house of the LORD; he
offered there the burnt offerings and the fat
of the communion offerings, since the
bronze altar which Solomon had made could
not hold the burnt offering, the grain offering, and the fat.[v]
8On this occasion Solomon and with him
all Israel, a great assembly from Lebo-hamath to the Wadi of Egypt, celebrated the
festival for seven days.[w] 9[x] On the eighth day
they held a solemn assembly, for they had
celebrated the dedication of the altar for
seven days and the feast* for seven days.
10On the twenty-third day of the seventh
month he dismissed the people to their tents,
rejoicing and glad of heart because of all the
blessings the LORD had given to David, to
Solomon, and to his people Israel. 11[y] Solomon finished building the house of the
LORD, the house of the king, and everything
else he wanted to do in regard to the house of
the LORD and his own house.
***God's Promise to Solomon.*** 12The LORD
appeared to Solomon during the night and
said to him: I have heard your prayer, and I
have chosen this place for my house of sacrifice. 13If I close heaven so that there is no
rain, if I command the locust to devour the
land, if I send pestilence among my people,
14if then my people, upon whom my name
has been pronounced, humble themselves
and pray, and seek my face and turn from
their evil ways, I will hear them from heaven
and pardon their sins and heal their land.
15Now, therefore, my eyes shall be open and
my ears attentive to the prayer of this place;
16now I have chosen and consecrated this
house that my name may be there forever;
my eyes and my heart shall be there always.
17As for you, if you walk before me as David your father did, doing all that I have
commanded you and keeping my statutes
and ordinances, 18I will establish the throne
of your kingship as I covenanted with David
your father when I said, There shall never be
wanting someone from your line as ruler in
Israel. 19But if ever you turn away and forsake my commandments and statutes which
I set before you, and proceed to serve other
gods, and bow down to them, 20I will uproot
the people from the land I gave and repudi-

**7:9–10 The feast**: Booths, celebrated on the fifteenth day of the seventh month and followed by a solemn octave lasting through the twenty-second day (Lv 23:33–36; Nm 29:12–35); the people are therefore sent home on the twenty-third day of the month (v. 10). The festival (v. 8) marking the dedication of the altar and of the Temple was held during the seven days prior to the feast of Booths, i.e., from the seventh to the fourteenth day of the seventh month. According to 1 Kgs 8:3, 65–66 the dedication of the Temple was celebrated concomitantly with the seven days of the feast of Booths, after which the people were dismissed on the eighth day.

*s:* 2 Chr 5:13; 1 Kgs 8:62; Ps 136:1. *t:* 1 Kgs 8:63. *u:* Nm 10:8, 10; Ps 136:1. *v:* 1 Kgs 8:64. *w:* 1 Kgs 8:65. *x:* 1 Kgs 8:66. *y:* 1 Kgs 9:1–9.

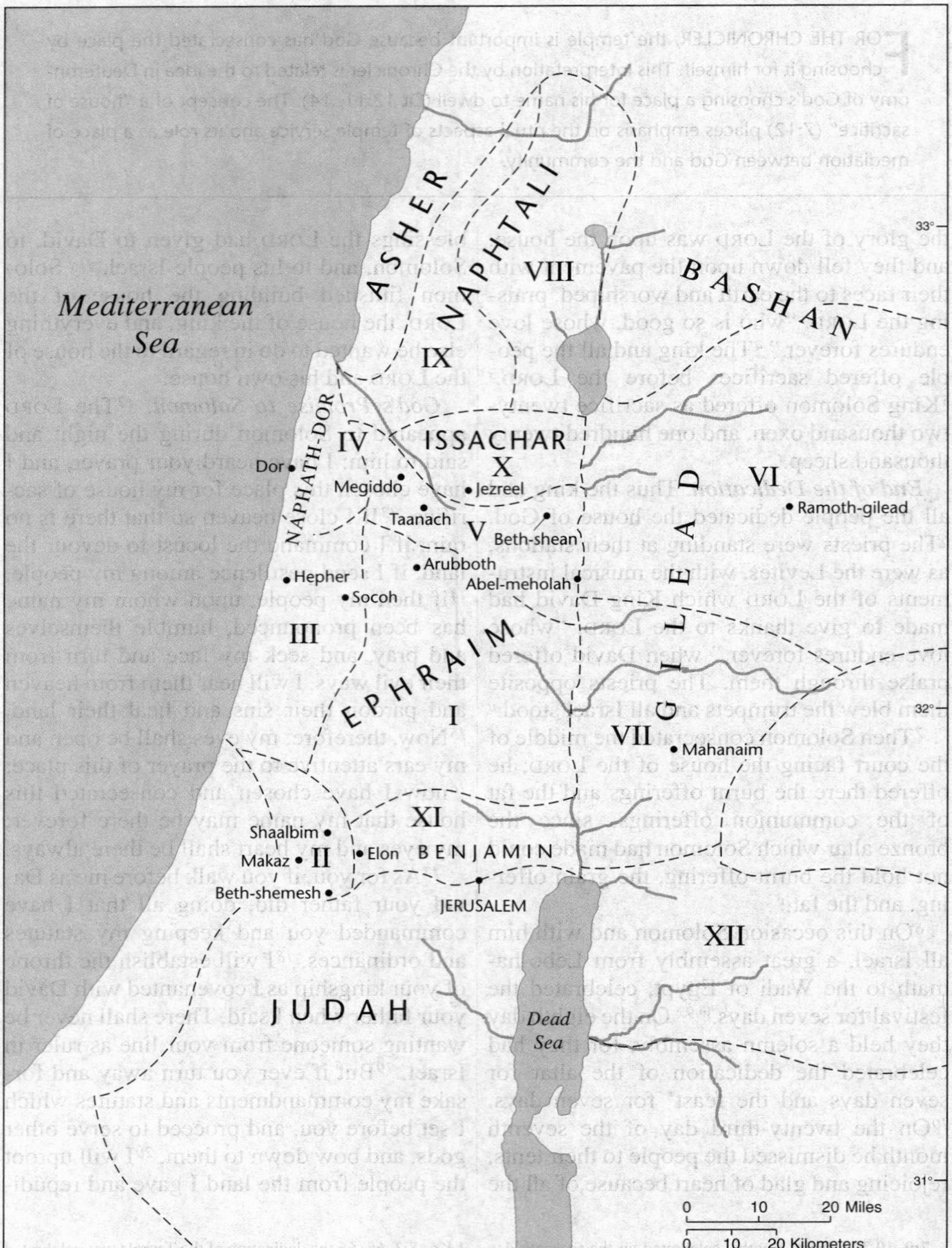


**The Kingdom of Solomon according to 2 Chronicles**

ate the house I have consecrated for my name. I will make it a proverb and a byword among all nations. [21]And this house which is so exalted—every passerby shall be horrified and ask: "Why has the LORD done such things to this land and to this house?" [22]And the answer will come: "Because they abandoned the LORD, the God of their ancestors, who brought them out of the land of Egypt, and they embraced other gods, bowing down to them and serving them. That is why he has brought upon them all this evil."

## CHAPTER 8

See RG 141

***Public Works.*** [1][z]After the twenty years during which Solomon built the house of the LORD and his own house, [2]he built up the cities which Huram had given him,* and settled Israelites there. [3]Then Solomon went to Hamath of Zoba and conquered it. [4]He built Tadmor* in the wilderness and all the supply cities, which he built in Hamath. [5][a]He built Upper Beth-horon and Lower Beth-horon, fortified cities with walls, gates, and bars; [6]also Baalath, all the supply cities belonging to Solomon, and all the cities for the chariots, the cities for horses, and whatever else Solomon desired to build in Jerusalem, in Lebanon, and in the entire land under his dominion. [7]All the people who were left of the Hittites, Amorites, Perizzites, Hivites, and Jebusites who were not Israelites—[8]those of their descendants who were left in the land and whom the Israelites had not destroyed—Solomon conscripted as forced laborers, as they are to this day. [9]But Solomon made none of the Israelites forced laborers for his works, for they were his fighting force, commanders, adjutants, chariot officers, and cavalry. [10]They were also King Solomon's two hundred and fifty overseers who directed the people.

***Solomon's Piety.*** [11]Solomon brought the daughter of Pharaoh up from the City of David to the house which he had built for her, for he said, "No wife of mine shall dwell in the house of David, king of Israel, for the places where the ark of the LORD has come are holy."

[12]In those times Solomon sacrificed burnt offerings to the LORD upon the altar of the LORD which he had built in front of the porch, [13]as was required to be done day by day according to the command of Moses, especially on the sabbaths, at the new moons, and on the fixed festivals three times a year: on the feast of the Unleavened Bread, the feast of Weeks, and the feast of Booths.[b]

[14]And according to the ordinance of David his father he appointed the various divisions of the priests for their service, and the Levites according to their functions of praise and attendance upon the priests, as the daily duty required. The gatekeepers by their divisions stood guard at each gate, since such was the command of David, the man of God.[c] [15]There was no deviation from the king's command in whatever related to the priests and Levites or the treasuries. [16]All of Solomon's work was carried out successfully from the day the foundation of the house of the LORD was laid until its completion. The house of the LORD was finished.

***Glories of the Court.*** [17]In those times Solomon went to Ezion-geber and to Elath on the seashore of the land of Edom.[d] [18]Huram had his servants send him ships and his own servants, expert seamen; they went with Solomon's servants to Ophir, and obtained there four hundred and fifty talents of gold and brought it to King Solomon.[e]

## CHAPTER 9

See RG 141

***The Queen of Sheba.*** [1][f]The queen of Sheba, having heard a report of Solomon's fame, came to Jerusalem to test him with subtle questions, accompanied by a very numerous retinue and by camels bearing spices, a

**8:2 The cities which Huram had given him**: according to 1 Kgs 9:10–14, it was Solomon who ceded the cities to the king of Tyre as payment for the timber and gold received from him. Since, however, 1 Kgs 9:12 states that Hiram was not satisfied with the cities, the Chronicler may have inferred that he gave them back to Solomon.

**8:4 Tadmor**: later known as Palmyra, an important caravan city in the Syrian desert. The parallel passage in 1 Kgs 9:18 has "Tamar," in southern Judah; cf. Ez 47:19; 48:28. But Solomon may well have fortified Tadmor against the Arameans.

*z:* 1 Kgs 9:10–11. *a:* 1 Kgs 9:17–25. *b:* Ex 23:14; Nm 28–29; 1 Kgs 9:25. *c:* 1 Chr 23–26; Neh 12:46. *d:* 1 Kgs 9:26. *e:* 1 Kgs 9:27–28. *f:* 1 Kgs 10:1–2.

large amount of gold, and precious stones.
She came to Solomon and spoke to him about
everything that she had on her mind. [2]Solo-
mon explained to her everything she asked
about, and there was nothing so obscure that
Solomon could not explain it to her.[g]

[3][h] When the queen of Sheba witnessed
Solomon's great wisdom, the house he had
built, [4]the food at his table, the seating of his
ministers, the attendance and dress of his
waiters, his cupbearers and their dress, and
the burnt offerings he sacrificed in the house
of the LORD, it took her breath away. [5]"The
report I heard in my country about your
deeds and your wisdom is true," she told the
king. [6]"I did not believe the report until I
came and saw with my own eyes that not
even the half of your great wisdom had been
told me. You have surpassed the report I
heard. [7]Happy your servants, happy these
ministers of yours, who stand before you always and listen to your wisdom. [8]Blessed be
the LORD, your God, who was pleased to set
you on his throne as king for the LORD, your
God. In the love your God has for Israel, to
establish them forever, he has made you
king over them to carry out judgment and
justice." [9]Then she gave the king one hundred and twenty gold talents, a very large
quantity of spices, and precious stones.
Never again did anyone bring such an abundance of spices as the queen of Sheba gave
to King Solomon.

[10]The servants of Huram and of Solomon
who brought gold from Ophir also brought
cabinet wood and precious stones. [11]With
the cabinet wood the king made stairs for the
house of the LORD and the house of the king,
and harps and lyres for the chanters. The like
of these had not been seen before in the land
of Judah.[i]

[12]King Solomon gave the queen of Sheba
everything she desired and asked for, more
than she had brought to the king. Then she returned with her servants to her own country.[j]

[13][k] The gold that came to Solomon in one
year weighed six hundred and sixty-six gold
talents, [14]in addition to what came from the
tolls on travelers and what the merchants
brought. All the kings of Arabia also, and the
governors of the country, brought gold and
silver to Solomon.

[15]King Solomon made two hundred large
shields of beaten gold (six hundred shekels
of gold went into each shield) [16]and three
hundred bucklers of beaten gold (three hundred shekels of gold went into each buckler);
and the king put them in the house of the
Forest of Lebanon.

[17]The king made a large ivory throne, and
overlaid it with fine gold. [18]The throne had
six steps; a footstool of gold was fastened to
the throne, and there was an arm on each
side of the seat, with two lions standing next
to the arms, [19]and twelve other lions standing there on the steps, two to a step. Nothing
like this was made in any other kingdom.
[20]All King Solomon's drinking vessels were
gold, and all the utensils in the house of the
Forest of Lebanon were pure gold. There
was no silver, for in Solomon's time silver
was reckoned as nothing. [21]For the king had
ships that went to Tarshish with the servants
of Huram. Once every three years the fleet
of Tarshish ships would come with a cargo
of gold, silver, ivory, apes, and monkeys.

***Solomon's Renown.*** [22]Thus King Solomon surpassed all the kings of the earth in
riches and wisdom.

[23]All the kings of the earth sought audience with Solomon, to hear the wisdom God
had put into his heart. [24]They all brought
their tribute: vessels of silver and gold, garments, weapons, spices, horses, and
mules—what was due each year. [25]Solomon
had four thousand stalls for horses, chariots,
and twelve thousand horses; these he allocated among the chariot cities and to the
king's service in Jerusalem. [26]He was ruler
over all the kings from the River to the land
of the Philistines and down to the border of
Egypt. [27]The king made silver as common in
Jerusalem as stones, and cedars as numerous
as the sycamores of the Shephelah. [28]* Solomon's horses were imported from Egypt and
from all the lands.

***The Death of Solomon.*** [29][l] The remainder
of the acts of Solomon, first and last, are

g: 1 Kgs 10:3. h: 1 Kgs 10:4–9. i: 1 Kgs 10:11–12. j: 1 Kgs 10:13. k: 1 Kgs 10:14–28. l: 1 Kgs 11:41–43.

**The Dissolution of Judah**

HAVING DESCRIBED THE high point of Israel under David and Solomon, the Chronicler turns his attention in chs 10 through 36 to the flow of Israel's history after the division of the kingdom into two parts. Writing in Jerusalem during the postexilic period, the Chronicler wants to present positive models for his own readership from Israel's past. These models share with David and Solomon a desire to ensure the proper worship of God in the temple and to instill in the community the idea of seeking God. Focused on the temple in Jerusalem, the Chronicler recounts the historical ebb and flow of the Davidic line that ruled Judah, only rarely incorporating any of the northern kingdom's history into his narrative.

recorded in the acts of Nathan the prophet, in
the prophecy of Ahijah the Shilonite, and in
the visions of Iddo the seer concerning Jeroboam, son of Nebat. [30]Solomon was king in
Jerusalem over all Israel for forty years.
[31]Solomon rested with his ancestors and was
buried in the City of David, his father, and
Rehoboam his son succeeded him as king.

## II. The Post-Solomonic Monarchy of Judah

### CHAPTER 10

See RG 141–42

*Division of the Kingdom.* [1m]Reho-
boam went to Shechem, where all Israel*
had come to make him king. [2]When Jeroboam, son of Nebat, heard about it, he was in
Egypt where he had fled from King
Solomon; and he returned from Egypt.
[3]They sent for him; Jeroboam and all Israel
came and said to Rehoboam: [4]"Your father
put on us a heavy yoke. If you now lighten
the harsh servitude and the heavy yoke your
father imposed on us, we will be your servants." [5]He answered them, "Come back to
me in three days," and the people went away.
[6]King Rehoboam asked advice of the elders who had been in his father Solomon's
service while he was still alive, and asked,
"How do you advise me to answer this people?" [7]They replied, "If you will deal kindly
with this people and please them, giving
them a favorable reply, they will be your
servants forever." [8]But he ignored the advice
the elders had given him and asked advice of
the young men who had grown up with him
and were in his service. [9]He said to them,
"What answer do you advise us to give this
people, who have told me, 'Lighten the yoke
your father imposed on us'?" [10]The young
men who had grown up with him replied:
"This is what you must say to this people
who have told you, 'Your father laid a heavy
yoke on us; lighten it for us.' You must say,
'My little finger is thicker than my father's
loins. [11]My father put a heavy yoke on you;
I will make it heavier. My father beat you
with whips; I will use scorpions!' "
[12]On the third day, Jeroboam and the
whole people came back to King Rehoboam
as the king had instructed them: "Come back
to me in three days." [13]Ignoring the advice
the elders had given him, King Rehoboam
gave the people a harsh answer. [14]He spoke
to them as the young men had advised: "My
father laid a heavy yoke on you; I will make
it heavier. My father beat you with whips; I
will use scorpions." [15]The king did not listen
to the people, for this turn of events was
from God: the LORD fulfilled the word he
had spoken through Ahijah the Shilonite to
Jeroboam, the son of Nebat.[n]
[16o]When all Israel saw that the king did
not listen to them, the people answered the
king:

**9:28** See note on 1:16–17.

**10:1 All Israel**: as in the source (1 Kgs 12:1), this term designates the northern tribes, as distinct from Judah and Benjamin. Elsewhere the Chronicler, writing on his own, speaks comprehensively of "those Israelites who lived in the cities of Judah" (10:17), and "all the Israelites [lit., all Israel] in Judah and Benjamin" (11:3).

*m:* 1 Kgs 12:1–14. *n:* 1 Kgs 11:29–39; 12:15. *o:* 1 Kgs 12:16–19.

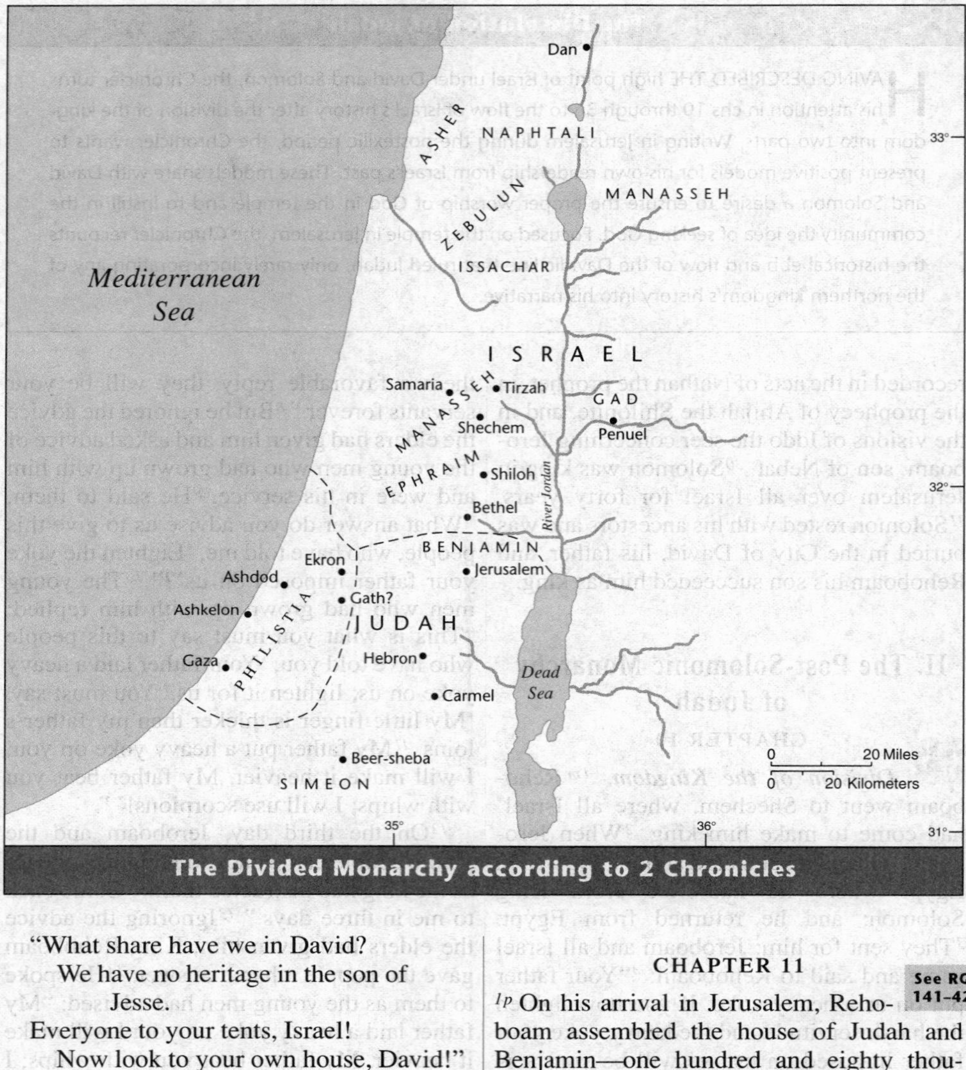


**The Divided Monarchy according to 2 Chronicles**

"What share have we in David?
We have no heritage in the son of Jesse.
Everyone to your tents, Israel!
Now look to your own house, David!"

So all Israel went off to their tents, 17 but the Israelites who lived in the cities of Judah had Rehoboam as their king. 18 King Rehoboam then sent out Hadoram, who was in charge of the forced labor, but the Israelites stoned him to death. King Rehoboam, however, managed to mount his chariot and flee to Jerusalem. 19 And so Israel has been in rebellion against the house of David to this day.

## CHAPTER 11

See RG 141–42

1p On his arrival in Jerusalem, Rehoboam assembled the house of Judah and Benjamin—one hundred and eighty thousand elite warriors—to wage war against Israel and restore the kingdom to Rehoboam. 2 However, the word of the LORD came to Shemaiah, a man of God: 3 Say to Rehoboam, son of Solomon, king of Judah, and to all the Israelites in Judah and Benjamin: 4 "Thus says the LORD: You must not go out to war against your kinsmen. Return home, each of you, for it is I who have brought this about." They obeyed the word of the LORD and turned back from going against Jeroboam.

*p:* 1 Kgs 12:21–24.

*Rehoboam's Works.** 5 Rehoboam took up residence in Jerusalem and built fortified cities in Judah. 6 He built up Bethlehem, Etam, Tekoa, 7 Beth-zur, Soco, Adullam, 8 Gath, Mareshah, Ziph, 9 Adoraim, Lachish, Azekah, 10 Zorah, Aijalon, and Hebron; these were fortified cities in Judah and Benjamin. 11 Then he strengthened the fortifications and put commanders in them, along with supplies of food, oil, and wine. 12 In every city were shields and spears, and he made them very strong. Thus Judah and Benjamin remained his.

*Refugees from the North.* 13 Now the priests and Levites throughout Israel presented themselves to him from all parts of their land, 14 for the Levites left their assigned pasture lands and their holdings and came to Judah and Jerusalem, because Jeroboam and his sons rejected them as priests of the LORD.[q] 15 In their place, he himself appointed priests for the high places as well as for the satyrs and calves he had made.[r] 16 After them, all those, of every tribe of Israel, who set their hearts to seek the LORD, the God of Israel, came to Jerusalem to sacrifice to the LORD, the God of their ancestors. 17 Thus they strengthened the kingdom of Judah and made Rehoboam, son of Solomon, prevail for three years; for they walked in the way of David and Solomon three years.

*Rehoboam's Family.* 18 Rehoboam married Mahalath, daughter of Jerimoth, son of David and of Abihail, daughter of Eliab, son of Jesse. 19 She bore him sons: Jehush, Shemariah, and Zaham. 20 After her, he married Maacah, daughter of Absalom, who bore him Abijah,[s] Attai, Ziza, and Shelomith. 21 Rehoboam loved Maacah, daughter of Absalom, more than all his other wives and concubines; he had taken eighteen wives and sixty concubines, and he fathered twenty-eight sons and sixty daughters. 22 Rehoboam put Abijah, son of Maacah, first among his brothers, as leader, for he intended to make him king. 23 He acted prudently, distributing his various sons throughout all the districts of Judah and Benjamin, in all the fortified cities; and he gave them generous provisions and sought an abundance of wives for them.

## CHAPTER 12

See RG 141–42

*Rehoboam's Apostasy.* 1 Once Rehoboam had established himself as king and was firmly in charge, he abandoned the law of the LORD, and so did all Israel with him.[t] 2 So in the fifth year of King Rehoboam, Shishak, king of Egypt, attacked Jerusalem, for they had acted treacherously toward the LORD.[u] 3 He had twelve hundred chariots and sixty thousand horsemen, and there was no counting the army that came with him from Egypt—Libyans, Sukkites,* and Ethiopians. 4 They captured the fortified cities of Judah and came as far as Jerusalem. 5 Then Shemaiah[v] the prophet came to Rehoboam and the commanders of Judah who had gathered at Jerusalem because of Shishak, and said to them: "Thus says the LORD: You have abandoned me, and so I have abandoned you to the power of Shishak."

6 Then the commanders of Israel and the king humbled themselves saying, "The LORD is in the right." 7 When the LORD saw that they had humbled themselves, the word of the LORD came to Shemaiah: Because they have humbled themselves, I will not destroy them; I will give them some deliverance, and my wrath shall not be poured out upon Jerusalem through Shishak. 8 But they shall be his servants. Then they will know what it is to serve me and what it is to serve the kingdoms of the earth. 9[w] Thereupon Shishak, king of Egypt, attacked Jerusalem and took away the treasures of the house of the LORD and the treasures of the house of the king. He took everything, including the gold shields that Solomon had made. 10 To replace them, King Rehoboam made bronze shields, which he entrusted to the officers of the attendants on duty at the entrance of the king's house. 11 Whenever the king visited the house of the LORD, the attendants would

**11:5–12** These verses have no parallel in 1 Kings; they are apparently based on a separate source.
**12:3 Sukkites**: foreign mercenaries in the Egyptian army.

*q:* 1 Kgs 12:32. *r:* Lv 17:7; 1 Kgs 12:32. *s:* 1 Kgs 15:2. *t:* 1 Kgs 11:4; 14:22. *u:* 1 Kgs 14:25. *v:* 2 Chr 11:2. *w:* 1 Kgs 14:25–28.

carry them, and then return them to the
guardroom. 12 Because he had humbled himself, the anger of the LORD turned from him
so as not to destroy him completely; in Judah, moreover, there was some good.
13 King Rehoboam was firmly in power in
Jerusalem and continued to rule. Rehoboam
was forty-one years old when he became
king, and he reigned seventeen years in Jerusalem, the city in which, out of all the tribes
of Israel, the LORD chose to set his name. His
mother's name was Naamah, the Ammon-
ite.[x] 14 He did evil, for he had not set his heart
to seek the LORD. 15[y] The acts of Rehoboam,
first and last, are recorded in the history of
Shemaiah the prophet and of Iddo the seer
(his family record). There were wars between Rehoboam and Jeroboam all their
days. 16 Rehoboam rested with his ancestors;
he was buried in the City of David. His son
Abijah* succeeded him as king.

See RG 141–42

## CHAPTER 13

### *War Between Abijah and Jeroboam.*

1[z] In the eighteenth year of King Jeroboam,
Abijah became king of Judah; 2 he reigned
three years in Jerusalem. His mother was
named Micaiah, daughter of Uriel of Gibeah. There was war between Abijah and Jeroboam.
3* Abijah joined battle with a force of four
hundred thousand picked warriors, while
Jeroboam lined up against him in battle with
eight hundred thousand picked and valiant
warriors. 4 Abijah stood on Mount Zemaraim, which is in the highlands of Ephraim,
and said: "Listen to me, Jeroboam and all Israel! 5 Do you not know that the LORD, the
God of Israel, has given David kingship over
Israel forever, to him and to his sons, by a
covenant of salt?* 6 Yet Jeroboam, son of Nebat, the servant of Solomon, son of David,
arose and rebelled against his lord![a] 7 Worthless men, scoundrels, joined him and overcame Rehoboam, son of Solomon, when Rehoboam was young and inexperienced, and
no match for them. 8 But now, do you think
you are a match for the kingdom of the LORD
led by the descendants of David, simply because you are a huge multitude and have
with you the golden calves which Jeroboam
made you for gods? 9 Have you not expelled
the priests of the LORD, the sons of Aaron,
and the Levites, and made for yourselves
priests like the peoples of other lands?
Everyone who comes to consecrate himself
with a young bull and seven rams becomes a
priest of no-gods. 10 But as for us, the LORD
is our God, and we have not abandoned him.
The priests ministering to the LORD are sons
of Aaron, and the Levites also have their offices. 11 They sacrifice burnt offerings to the
LORD and fragrant incense morning after
morning and evening after evening; they set
out the showbread on the pure table, and the
lamps of the golden menorah burn evening
after evening; for we observe our duties to
the LORD, our God, but you have abandoned
him. 12 See, God is with us, at our head, and
his priests are here with trumpets to sound
the attack against you. Israelites, do not fight
against the LORD, the God of your ancestors,
for you will not succeed!"
13 But Jeroboam had an ambush go around
them to come at them from the rear; so that
while his army faced Judah, his ambush lay
behind them. 14 When Judah turned and saw
that they had to battle on both fronts, they
cried out to the LORD and the priests
sounded the trumpets. 15 Then the Judahites
shouted; and when they shouted, God struck
down Jeroboam and all Israel before Abijah
and Judah. 16 The Israelites fled before Judah, and God delivered them into their
power. 17 Abijah and his people inflicted a
severe defeat upon them; five hundred thousand picked men of Israel fell slain. 18 The Israelites were humbled on that occasion,
while the Judahites were victorious because
they relied on the LORD, the God of their ancestors. 19 Abijah pursued Jeroboam and
seized cities from him: Bethel and its de-

**12:16 Abijah**: in 1 Kgs 14:31–15:8 this king is called Abijam.

**13:3–21** This passage is a free composition of the Chronicler based on the reference in 1 Kgs 15:6 to the war between Abijam (so in Kings, "Abijah" in Chronicles) and Jeroboam.

**13:5 Covenant of salt**: see note on Nm 18:19.

*x:* 1 Kgs 14:21. *y:* 1 Kgs 14:29–31. *z:* 1 Kgs 15:1–2. *a:* 1 Kgs 11:26.

## The Reign of Asa

IN THIS CLASSIC expansion of his source in 1 Kings, the Chronicler takes a mere seven verses on the reign of Asa and develops three chapters (14–16) with complex plots and a rich theological content. The Chronicler portrays Asa as a model ruler who succeeds in bringing the community into peace, security, and joy by his devotion to God.

pendencies, Jeshanah and its dependencies,
and Ephron and its dependencies. [20]Jero-
boam did not regain power during Abijah's
time; the LORD struck him down and he died,
[21]while Abijah continued to grow stronger.
He married fourteen wives and fathered
twenty-two sons and sixteen daughters.
***Death of Abijah.*** [22][b]The rest of the acts of
Abijah, his deeds and his words, are
recorded in the midrash of the prophet Iddo.
[23]Abijah rested with his ancestors; they
buried him in the City of David and his son
Asa succeeded him as king. During his time,
the land had ten years of peace.

### CHAPTER 14

See RG 141–42

***Asa's Initial Reforms.*** [1][c]Asa did what
was good and right in the sight of the LORD,
his God. [2]He removed the illicit altars and
the high places, smashed the sacred pillars,
and cut down the asherahs. [3]He told Judah to
seek the LORD, the God of their ancestors,
and to observe the law and the commandment. [4]He removed the high places and incense stands from all the cities of Judah, and
under him the kingdom had peace. [5]He built
fortified cities in Judah, for the land had
peace and no war was waged against him
during these years, because the LORD had
given him rest. [6]He said to Judah: "Let us
build these cities and surround them with
walls, towers, gates and bars. The land is
still ours, for we have sought the LORD, our
God; we sought him, and he has given us rest
on every side." So they built and prospered.
***The Ethiopian Invasion.**** [7]Asa had an
army of three hundred thousand shield- and
lance-bearers from Judah, and from Benjamin two hundred and eighty thousand who
carried bucklers and were archers, all of
them valiant warriors. [8]Zerah the Ethiopian
advanced against them with a force of one
million men and three hundred chariots, and
he came as far as Mareshah.[d] [9]Asa went out
to meet him and they drew up for battle in
the valley of Zephathah, near Mareshah.
[10]Asa called upon the LORD, his God:
"LORD, there is none like you to help the
powerless against the strong. Help us, LORD,
our God, for we rely on you, and in your
name we have come against this multitude.
You are the LORD, our God; do not let men
prevail against you."[e] [11]And so the LORD defeated the Ethiopians before Asa and Judah,
and the Ethiopians fled. [12]Asa and those
with him pursued them as far as Gerar, and
the Ethiopians fell until there were no survivors, for they were crushed before the
LORD and his army, which carried away
enormous spoils. [13]Then the Judahites conquered all the cities around Gerar, for the
fear of the LORD was upon them; they plundered all the cities, for there was much plunder in them. [14]They also attacked the tents of
the cattle-herders and carried off a great
number of sheep and camels. Then they returned to Jerusalem.

### CHAPTER 15

See RG 141–42

***Further Reforms.*** [1]The spirit of God
came upon Azariah, son of Oded. [2]He went
forth to meet Asa and said to him: "Hear me,
Asa and all Judah and Benjamin! The LORD
is with you when you are with him, and if

**14:7–14** This Ethiopian invasion of Judah is not mentioned in 1 Kings. The account is likely a legend intended to show the pious King Asa being rewarded with divine assistance. It could, however, reflect an incursion by nomads from the Negeb in Asa's time.

*b:* 2 Chr 12:15–16; 1 Kgs 15:7–8. *c:* 2 Chr 33:15; Ex 23:24; 34:13; 1 Kgs 15:11–12. *d:* 2 Chr 16:8. *e:* 2 Chr 32:8.

you seek him he will be found; but if you
abandon him, he will abandon you.[f] 3For a
long time Israel was without a true God,
without a priest-teacher, without instruction,
4but when in their distress they turned to the
LORD, the God of Israel, and sought him, he
was found by them.[g] 5At that time there was
no peace for anyone to go or come; rather,
there were many terrors upon the inhabitants
of the lands. 6Nation crushed nation and city
crushed city,[h] for God overwhelmed them
with every kind of distress. 7But as for you,
be strong and do not slack off, for there shall
be a reward for what you do."[i]
8When Asa heard these words and the
prophecy (Oded the prophet), he was encouraged to remove the detestable idols from the
whole land of Judah and Benjamin and from
the cities he had taken in the highlands of
Ephraim, and to restore the altar of the LORD
which was before the vestibule of the LORD.
9Then he gathered all Judah and Benjamin,
together with those of Ephraim, Manasseh,
and Simeon who were resident with them;
for many had defected to him from Israel
when they saw that the LORD, his God, was
with him. 10They gathered at Jerusalem in the
third month* of the fifteenth year of Asa's
reign, 11and sacrificed to the LORD on that
day seven hundred oxen and seven thousand
sheep from the spoils they had brought.
12[j] They entered into a covenant to seek the
LORD, the God of their ancestors, with all
their heart and soul; 13and everyone who
would not seek the LORD, the God of Israel,
was to be put to death, from least to greatest,
man or woman. 14They swore an oath to the
LORD with a loud voice, with shouting and
with trumpets and horns. 15All Judah rejoiced over the oath, for they had sworn it
with their whole heart and sought him with
complete desire. The LORD was found by
them,[k] and gave them rest on every side.
16[l] He also deposed Maacah, the mother*
of King Asa, from her position as queen
mother because she had made an obscene object for Asherah; Asa cut down this object,
smashed it, and burnt it in the Wadi Kidron.
17The high places did not disappear from Israel, yet Asa's heart was undivided as long as
he lived. 18He brought into the house of God
his father's and his own votive offerings: silver, gold, and vessels. 19There was no war
until the thirty-fifth year of Asa's reign.

## CHAPTER 16

See RG 141–42

***Asa's Infidelity.*** 1[m] In the thirty-sixth
year of Asa's reign, Baasha, king of Israel,
attacked Judah and fortified Ramah to block
all movement for Asa, king of Judah. 2Asa
then brought out silver and gold from the
treasuries of the house of the LORD and the
house of the king and sent them to Ben-hadad, king of Aram, who ruled in Damascus.
He said: 3"There is a treaty between you and
me, as there was between your father and my
father. I am sending you silver and gold. Go,
break your treaty with Baasha, king of Israel, that he may withdraw from me." 4Ben-
hadad agreed with King Asa and sent the
leaders of his troops against the cities of Israel. They attacked Ijon, Dan, Abel-maim,
besides all the store cities of Naphtali.
5When Baasha heard of it, he left off fortifying Ramah, putting an end to his work.
6Then King Asa commandeered all Judah
and they carried away the stones and beams
with which Baasha was fortifying Ramah.
With them he fortified Geba and Mizpah.
7At that time Hanani the seer came to Asa,
king of Judah, and said to him: "Because
you relied on the king of Aram and did not
rely on the LORD, your God, the army of the
king of Aram has escaped* your power.
8[n] Were not the Ethiopians and Libyans a
vast army, with great numbers of chariots

**15:10–12** With this description of a covenant ceremony in "the third month" of a year beginning in the spring, the Chronicler provides a basis for the later understanding of the ancient Jewish spring feast of Weeks as a commemoration of the covenant on Mount Sinai; see Ex 19:1–3; Lv 23:16 and note on Lv 23:16–21. In the Greek period the feast came to be called Pentecost, from the Greek word for "fifty," i.e., fifty days or seven weeks after Passover. The Chronicler's presentation here has also influenced the celebration of Christian Pentecost as the "birthday of the Church"; cf. Acts 2.

**15:16 Mother**: see note on 1 Kgs 15:10.

**16:7 The king of Aram has escaped**: the Lucianic recension of the Septuagint reads, "the king of Israel escaped." This may well be the original reading, since according to the

*f:* Jer 29:13–14; Hos 3:4–5. *g:* Dt 4:29–30. *h:* Is 19:2. *i:* Is 7:4; Jer 31:16. *j:* Neh 10:29–30. *k:* Dt 4:29. *l:* 1 Kgs 15:13–15. *m:* 1 Kgs 15:16–21. *n:* 2 Chr 14:8–14.

**The Reign of Jehoshaphat**

CHAPTERS 17 TO 20 are another example of the Chronicler's expansions of limited material in the narratives of 1 and 2 Kings. The Chronicler takes an initially positive assessment of Jehoshaphat and expands his role into a model of bringing the community into accord with God.

and horses? And yet, because you relied on
the LORD, he delivered them into your
power. 9The eyes of the LORD roam over the
whole earth,[o] to encourage those who are devoted to him wholeheartedly. You have
acted foolishly in this matter, for from now
on you will have wars." 10But Asa became
angry with the seer and imprisoned him in
the stocks, so greatly was he enraged at him
over this. Asa also oppressed some of his
people at this time.

11[p] Now the acts of Asa, first and last, are
recorded in the book of the kings of Judah
and Israel. 12In the thirty-ninth year of his
reign, Asa contracted disease in his feet; it
became worse, but even with this disease he
did not seek the LORD, only physicians.
13Asa rested with his ancestors; he died in the
forty-first year of his reign. 14They buried
him in the tomb he had hewn for himself in
the City of David, after laying him on a
couch that was filled with spices and various
kinds of aromatics compounded into an ointment; and they kindled a huge fire for him.

CHAPTER 17

See RG 141–42

***Jehoshaphat's Zeal for the Law.*** 1His
son Jehoshaphat succeeded him as king and
strengthened his position against Israel.[q]
2He placed armed forces in all the fortified
cities of Judah, and set garrisons in the land
of Judah and in the cities of Ephraim which
Asa his father had taken. 3The LORD was
with Jehoshaphat,* for he walked in the earlier ways of David his father, and did not
seek the Baals. 4Rather, he sought the God
of his father and walked in his commands,
and not the practices of Israel. 5Through
him, the LORD made the kingdom secure,
and all Judah gave Jehoshaphat gifts, so that
great wealth and glory was his. 6Thus he was
encouraged* to follow the LORD's ways, and
once again he removed the high places and
the asherahs from Judah.[r]

7In the third year of his reign he sent his
officials, Ben-hail, Obadiah, Zechariah, Nethanel, and Micaiah, to teach in the cities
of Judah. 8With them he sent the Levites
Shemaiah, Nethaniah, Zebadiah, Asahel,
Shemiramoth, Jehonathan, Adonijah, and
Tobijah, together with Elishama and Jehoram the priests.[s] 9They taught in Judah, having with them the book of the law of the
LORD; they traveled through all the cities of
Judah and taught among the people.[t]

***His Power.*** 10Now the fear of the LORD
was upon all the kingdoms of the countries
surrounding Judah, so that they did not war
against Jehoshaphat. 11Some of the Philistines brought Jehoshaphat gifts and a tribute
of silver; the Arabians also brought him a
flock of seven thousand seven hundred rams
and seven thousand seven hundred he-goats.
12Jehoshaphat grew ever greater. He built
strongholds and store cities in Judah. 13He
carried out many works in the cities of Judah,
and he had soldiers, valiant warriors, in Jerusalem. 14This was their mustering according
to their ancestral houses. From Judah, the
commanders of thousands: Adnah the commander, and with him three hundred thousand valiant warriors. 15Next to him, Jehohanan the commander, and with him two
hundred eighty thousand. 16Next to him, Am-
asiah, son of Zichri, who offered himself to
the LORD, and with him two hundred thou-

story Asa hired the king of Aram as an ally against Israel.

**17:3 The LORD was with Jehoshaphat**: along with his successors Hezekiah and Josiah, Jehoshaphat is one of the Chronicler's exemplary kings.

**17:6 Thus he was encouraged**: lit., "his heart was high," a phrase that ordinarily describes arrogance and rebelliousness; in this case, however, it introduces a notice of Jehoshaphat's fidelity to the Lord.

*o:* Ps 33:13–15. *p:* 1 Kgs 15:23–24. *q:* 1 Kgs 15:24. *r:* 2 Chr 20:33; Ex 34:13. *s:* 2 Chr 19:8. *t:* Ezr 7:25.

sand valiant warriors. 17 From Benjamin: Eliada, a valiant warrior, and with him two hundred thousand armed with bow and buckler. 18 Next to him, Jehozabad, and with him one hundred and eighty thousand equipped for war. 19 These attended the king; in addition to those whom the king had stationed in the fortified cities throughout all Judah.

## CHAPTER 18

See RG 141–42

***Alliance with Israel.*** 1[u] Jehoshaphat therefore had wealth and glory in abundance; but he became related to Ahab by marriage. 2 After some years he went down to Ahab at Samaria; Ahab slaughtered numerous sheep and oxen for him and for the people with him, and incited him to go up against Ramoth-gilead. 3 Ahab, king of Israel, asked Jehoshaphat, king of Judah, "Will you come with me to Ramoth-gilead?" He answered, "You and I are as one, and your people and my people as well. We will be with you in the battle." 4 Jehoshaphat also said to the king of Israel, "Seek the word of the LORD at once."

***Prophets in Conflict.*** 5 The king of Israel assembled the prophets, four hundred of them, and asked, "Shall we go to fight against Ramoth-gilead, or shall I refrain?" They said, "Attack. God will give it into the power of the king." 6 But Jehoshaphat said, "Is there no other prophet of the LORD here we might consult?" 7 The king of Israel answered, "There is one other man through whom we may consult the LORD; but I hate him, because he prophesies not good but always evil about me. He is Micaiah, son of Imlah." Jeshoshaphat said, "Let not the king say that." 8 So the king of Israel called an official, and said to him, "Get Micaiah, son of Imlah, at once." 9 The king of Israel and Jehoshaphat, king of Judah, were seated, each on his throne, clothed in their robes of state in the square at the entrance of the gate of Samaria, and all the prophets were prophesying before them.

10 Zedekiah, son of Chenaanah, made himself two horns of iron and said: "The LORD says: With these you shall gore Aram until you have destroyed them." 11 The other prophets prophesied in the same vein, saying: "Attack Ramoth-gilead, and conquer! The LORD will give it into the power of the king." 12* Meanwhile the messenger who had gone to call Micaiah said to him: "Look now, the words of the prophets are as one in speaking good for the king. Let your word be at one with theirs; speak a good word." 13 Micaiah said, "As the LORD lives, I shall speak whatever my God says."

14 When he came to the king, the king said to him, "Micah, shall we go to fight at Ramoth-gilead, or shall I refrain?" He said, "Attack and conquer! They will be delivered into your power." 15 But the king answered him, "How many times must I adjure you to tell me nothing but the truth in the name of the LORD?" 16 So Micaiah said:

"I see all Israel
scattered on the mountains,
like sheep without a shepherd,
And the LORD saying,
These have no masters!
Let each of them go back home in
peace."

17 The king of Israel said to Jehoshaphat, "Did I not tell you, he does not prophesy good about me, but only evil?" 18 Micaiah continued: "Therefore hear the word of the LORD. I saw the LORD seated on his throne, with the whole host of heaven standing to his right and to his left. 19 The LORD asked: Who will deceive Ahab, king of Israel, so that he will go up and fall on Ramoth-gilead? And one said this, another that, 20 until this spirit came forth and stood before the LORD, saying, 'I will deceive him.' The LORD asked: How? 21 He answered, 'I will go forth and become a lying spirit in the mouths of all his prophets.' The LORD replied: You shall succeed in deceiving him. Go forth and do this. 22 So now the LORD has put a lying spirit in the mouths of these prophets of yours; but the LORD himself has decreed evil against you."

**18:12–22** See note on 1 Kgs 22:19–23.

*u:* 1 Kgs 22:1–35.

23Thereupon Zedekiah, son of Chenaanah, came up and struck Micaiah on the cheek, saying, "Has the spirit of the LORD, then, passed from me to speak with you?" 24Micaiah said, "You shall find out on the day you go into an innermost room to hide." 25The king of Israel then said: "Seize Micaiah and take him back to Amon, prefect of the city, and to Joash the king's son, 26and say, 'This is the king's order: Put this man in prison and feed him scanty rations of bread and water until I come back in safety!' " 27But Micaiah said, "If ever you return in safety, the LORD has not spoken through me." (He also said, "Hear, O peoples, all of you!")[*]

***Ahab's Death.*** 28The king of Israel and Jehoshaphat, king of Judah, went up to Ramoth-gilead, 29and the king of Israel said to Jehoshaphat, "I will disguise myself and go into battle. But you, put on your own robes." So the king of Israel disguised himself and they entered the battle. 30In the meantime, the king of Aram had given his chariot commanders the order, "Fight with no one, great or small, except the king of Israel alone." 31When the chariot commanders saw Jehoshaphat, they thought, "There is the king of Israel!" and wheeled to fight him. But Jehoshaphat cried out and the LORD helped him; God induced them to leave him alone. 32The chariot commanders, seeing that he was not the king of Israel, turned away from him. 33But someone drew his bow at random and hit the king of Israel between the joints of his breastplate. He ordered his charioteer, "Rein about and take me out of the ranks, for I am wounded."[v] 34The battle grew fierce during the day, and the king of Israel braced himself up in his chariot facing the Arameans until evening. He died as the sun was setting.

## CHAPTER 19

See RG 141–42

***Jehoshaphat Rebuked.*** 1Jehoshaphat king of Judah returned in safety to his house in Jerusalem. 2Jehu the seer, son of Hanani,[*] went out to meet King Jehoshaphat and said to him: "Should you help the wicked and love those who hate the LORD? For this reason, wrath is upon you from the LORD. 3Yet some good has been found[*] in you, since you have removed the asherahs from the land and have set your heart to seek God."

***Judges Appointed.*** 4Jehoshaphat dwelt in Jerusalem; but he went out again among the people from Beer-sheba to the highlands of Ephraim and brought them back to the LORD, the God of their ancestors. 5He appointed judges in the land, in all the fortified cities of Judah, city by city, 6and he said to them: "Take care what you do, for the judgment you give is not human but divine; for when it comes to judgment God will be with you.[w] 7And now, let the fear of the LORD be upon you. Act carefully, for with the LORD, our God, there is no injustice, no partiality, no bribe-taking."[x] 8In Jerusalem also, Jehoshaphat appointed some Levites and priests and some of the family heads of Israel for the LORD's judgment and the disputes of those who dwell in Jerusalem.[y] 9He gave them this command: "Thus you shall act: in the fear of the LORD, with fidelity and with an undivided heart. 10And in every dispute that comes to you from your kin living in their cities, whether it concerns bloodguilt or questions of law, command, statutes, or ordinances, warn them lest they incur guilt before the LORD and his wrath come upon you and your kin. Do that and you shall not incur guilt.[z] 11See now, Amariah is chief priest over you for everything that pertains to the LORD, and Zebadiah, son of Ishmael, is leader of the house of Judah in all that pertains to the king; and the Levites will be your officials. Take firm action, and the LORD will be with the good."

**18:27 "Hear, O peoples, all of you!"**: this quotation, which also appears in 1 Kgs 22:28, ascribes to the prophet Micaiah ben Imlah the opening words of the book of the prophet Micah of Moresheth (Mi 1:2), who was active a century later.

**19:2 Jehu the seer, son of Hanani**: probably not the Jehu, son of Hanani, who prophesied against Baasha of Israel almost fifty years earlier (1 Kgs 16:1).

**19:3 Has been found**: theological passive, i.e., God is the implied agent.

*v:* 2 Chr 35:23; 1 Kgs 22:34. *w:* Dt 1:16–18; 16:19–20. *x:* Dt 10:17. *y:* 2 Chr 17:8–9; Dt 17:8–13; Ps 122:3–5. *z:* Dt 17:8–13.

## CHAPTER 20

See RG 141–42

***Invasion from Edom.*** 1* After this the Moabites, the Ammonites, and with them some Meunites came to fight against Jehoshaphat. 2 Jehoshaphat was told: "A great multitude is coming against you from across the sea, from Edom; they are already in Hazazon-tamar" (which is En-gedi). 3 Frightened, Jehoshaphat resolved to consult the LORD. He proclaimed a fast throughout all Judah. 4 Then Judah gathered to seek the LORD's help; from every one of the cities of Judah they came to seek the LORD.[a]

***Jehoshaphat's Prayer.*** 5 Jehoshaphat stood up in the assembly of Judah and Jerusalem in the house of the LORD before the new court, 6 and he said: "LORD, God of our ancestors, are you not God in heaven, and do you not rule over all the kingdoms of the nations? In your hand is power and might, and no one can withstand you.[b] 7 Was it not you, our God, who dispossessed the inhabitants of this land before your people Israel and gave it forever to the descendants of Abraham, your friend? 8 They have dwelt in it and they built in it a sanctuary for your name. They have said: 9 'If evil comes upon us, the sword of judgment, or pestilence, or famine, we will stand before this house and before you, for your name is in this house, and we will cry out to you in our affliction, and you will hear and save!'[c] 10 And now, see the Ammonites, Moabites, and those of Mount Seir whom you did not allow Israel to invade when they came from the land of Egypt, but instead they passed them by and did not destroy them:[d] 11 See how they are now repaying us by coming to drive us out of the possession you have given us. 12 O our God, will you not bring judgment on them? We are powerless before this vast multitude that is coming against us. We ourselves do not know what to do, so our eyes are turned toward you."

***Victory Prophesied.*** 13 All Judah was standing before the LORD, with their little ones, their wives, and their children. 14 And the spirit of the LORD came upon Jahaziel, son of Zechariah, son of Benaiah, son of Jeiel, son of Mattaniah, a Levite of the clan of Asaph, in the midst of the assembly, 15 and he said: "Pay attention, all of Judah, inhabitants of Jerusalem, and King Jehoshaphat! The LORD says to you: Do not fear or be dismayed at the sight of this vast multitude, for the battle is not yours but God's. 16 Go down against them tomorrow. You will see them coming up by the ascent of Ziz, and you will come upon them at the end of the wadi which opens on the wilderness of Jeruel. 17 You will not have to fight in this encounter. Take your places, stand firm, and see the salvation of the LORD; he will be with you, Judah and Jerusalem. Do not fear or be dismayed. Tomorrow go out to meet them, and the LORD will be with you."[e] 18 Then Jehoshaphat knelt down with his face to the ground, and all Judah and the inhabitants of Jerusalem fell down before the LORD in worship. 19 Levites from among the Kohathites and Korahites stood up to sing the praises of the LORD, the God of Israel, their voices ever louder.

***The Invaders Destroyed.*** 20 Early in the morning they went out to the wilderness of Tekoa. As they were going out, Jehoshaphat halted and said: "Listen to me, Judah and inhabitants of Jerusalem! Let your faith in the LORD, your God, be firm, and you will be firm.[f] Have faith in his prophets and you will succeed." 21* After taking counsel with the

**20:1–30** This account seems to be a free composition of the Chronicler. However, there could well have been a raid of nomads against Judah in the reign of Jehoshaphat, similar to the one that occurred under Asa (14:8–14). The story may also be connected in some way with the campaign of Israel and Judah against Moab launched through the territory of Edom (2 Kgs 3:4–27).

**20:21** In accordance with Israelite conceptions of Holy War (cf. Ex 14:13–14), this highly stylized narrative presents the Lord as active in battle, while the people have only to sing hymns of praise; the enemy, in panic, fight among themselves to their mutual destruction (v. 23). **Splendor**: the Lord "goes before," i.e., leads, the army of Israel (cf. 2 Sm 5:24) with the heavenly hosts. Israel's God is depicted as present "enthroned upon the cherubim" atop the ark of the covenant. By postexilic times, the ark had disappeared, but the Lord was still present to his people. Here that presence is described as "holy Splendor," a phrase found in Ps 29:2; 96:9. Cf. the cognate

*a:* Jer 36:6. *b:* 2 Chr 32:7; Dt 4:39. *c:* 2 Chr 6:28–31; 7:13–14; 1 Kgs 8:37–40. *d:* Dt 2:4–5, 9–10, 18–19. *e:* Ex 14:13–14; Is 8:10. *f:* Is 7:9.

people, he appointed some to sing to the
LORD and some to praise the holy Splendor
as it went forth at the head of the army. They
sang: "Give thanks to the LORD, whose love
endures forever."[g] 22 At the moment they began their jubilant praise, the LORD laid an
ambush against the Ammonites, Moabites,
and those of Mount Seir who were coming
against Judah, so that they were defeated.
23 For the Ammonites and Moabites set upon
the inhabitants of Mount Seir and exterminated them according to the ban.[h] And when
they had finished with the inhabitants of
Seir, each helped to destroy the other.
24 When Judah came to the watchtower of
the wilderness and looked toward the
throng, there were only corpses fallen on the
ground, with no survivors. 25 Jehoshaphat
and his people came to gather the spoils, and
they found an abundance of cattle and personal property, garments and precious vessels. They took so much that they were unable to carry it all; it took them three days to
gather the spoils, there was so much of it.
26 On the fourth day they held an assembly in
the Valley of Berakah*—for there they
blessed the LORD; that is why the place is
called the Valley of Berakah to this day.
27 Then all the men of Judah and Jerusalem,
with Jehoshaphat at their head, returned to
Jerusalem with joy; for the LORD had given
them joy over their enemies. 28 They came to
Jerusalem, with harps, lyres, and trumpets,
to the house of the LORD. 29 And the fear of
God came upon all the kingdoms of the surrounding lands when they heard how the
LORD had fought against the enemies of Israel. 30 Thereafter Jehoshaphat's kingdom
had peace, for his God gave him rest on
every side.

***Jehoshaphat's Other Deeds.*** 31[i] Thus Jehoshaphat reigned over Judah. He was
thirty-five years old when he became king,
and he reigned twenty-five years in
Jerusalem. His mother's name was Azubah,
daughter of Shilhi. 32 He walked in the way
of Asa his father unceasingly, doing what
was right in the LORD's sight. 33 Nevertheless, the high places did not disappear and
the people had not yet set their hearts on the
God of their ancestors.

34 The rest of the acts of Jehoshaphat, first
and last, are recorded in the chronicle of
Jehu, son of Hanani, which was incorporated into the book of the kings of Israel.
35 After this, Jehoshaphat king of Judah
joined with Ahaziah king of Israel—he acted
wickedly. 36[j] He joined with him in building
ships to go to Tarshish; the fleet was built at
Ezion-geber. 37 But Eliezer, son of Dodavahu
from Mareshah, prophesied against Jehoshaphat. He said: "Because you have joined
with Ahaziah, the LORD will shatter your
work." And the ships were wrecked and
were unable to sail to Tarshish.

## CHAPTER 21

See RG 141–42

1 Jehoshaphat rested with his ancestors; he was buried with them in the City of
David. Jehoram, his son, succeeded him as
king.[k] 2 He had brothers, Jehoshaphat's sons:
Azariah, Jehiel, Zechariah, Azariah, Michael, and Shephatiah; all these were sons of
King Jehoshaphat of Judah. 3 Their father
gave them many gifts of silver, gold, and
precious objects, together with fortified cities in Judah, but the kingship he gave to Jehoram because he was the firstborn.

***Jehoram's Evil Deeds.*** 4 When Jehoram
had acceded to his father's kingdom and was
firmly in power, he killed all his brothers
with the sword, and also some of the princes
of Israel. 5[l] Jehoram was thirty-two years old
when he became king, and he reigned eight
years in Jerusalem. 6 He walked in the way of
the kings of Israel as the house of Ahab had
done, since the daughter of Ahab* was his
wife; and he did what was evil in the LORD's
sight. 7 Even so, the LORD was unwilling to
destroy the house of David because of the

image of cloud and fire that led Israel in the wilderness (Ex 13:21–22), or the cloud of the Lord's glory that fills the sanctuary (Ex 40:34; 1 Kgs 8:10–11).

**20:26 Berakah**: the Hebrew word for "blessing."

**21:6 The daughter of Ahab**: her name was Athaliah. In 22:2 (and its source, 2 Kgs 8:26) she is called the daughter of Ahab's father Omri, but this should probably be understood in the sense of granddaughter.

*g:* Ps 136:1. *h:* Jos 6:17. *i:* 1 Kgs 22:41–45. *j:* 1 Kgs 22:48–49. *k:* 1 Kgs 22:51. *l:* 1 Kgs 8:17–19.

covenant he had made with David and because of his promise to leave him and his sons a holding for all time.[m]

8[n] During his time Edom revolted against the rule of Judah and installed its own king. 9Thereupon Jehoram with his officers and all his chariots crossed over. He arose by night and broke through the Edomites when they had surrounded him and the commanders of his chariots. 10To this day Edom has been in revolt against the rule of Judah. Libnah also revolted at that time against his rule because he had abandoned the LORD, the God of his ancestors. 11He also set up high places in the mountains of Judah, prostituting the inhabitants of Jerusalem, leading Judah astray.

***Jehoram Punished.*** 12A letter came to him from Elijah* the prophet with this message: "Thus says the LORD, the God of David your father: Because you have not walked in the way of your father Jehoshaphat, nor of Asa, king of Judah, 13but instead have walked in the way of the kings of Israel, leading Judah and the inhabitants of Jerusalem into prostitution, like the harlotries of the house of Ahab, and because you have killed your brothers of your father's house, who were better than you, 14the LORD will strike your people, your children, your wives, and all that is yours with a great plague. 15You shall have severe pains from a disease in your bowels, which will fall out because of the disease, day after day."

16Then the LORD stirred up against Jehoram the animosity of the Philistines and of the Arabians who were neighbors of the Ethiopians. 17They came up against Judah, breached it, and carried away all the wealth found in the king's house, along with his sons and his wives. He was left with only one son, Jehoahaz, his youngest. 18After these events, the LORD afflicted him with a disease of the bowels for which there was no cure. 19Some time later, after a period of two years had elapsed, his bowels fell out because of the disease and he died in great pain. His people did not make a fire for him as they had for his ancestors.[o] 20He was thirty-two years old when he became king, and he reigned eight years in Jerusalem. He departed unloved; and they buried him in the City of David, though not in the tombs of the kings.[p]

## CHAPTER 22

See RG 141–42

***Ahaziah.*** 1[q] Then the inhabitants of Jerusalem made Ahaziah, his youngest son, king to succeed him, since all the older sons had been killed by the band that had come into the camp with the Arabians. Thus Ahaziah, son of Jehoram, reigned as the king of Judah. 2Ahaziah was twenty-two years old when he became king, and he reigned one year in Jerusalem. His mother's name was Athaliah, daughter of Omri. 3He, too, walked in the ways of the house of Ahab, because his mother was his counselor in doing evil. 4To his own destruction, he did what was evil in the sight of the LORD, like the house of Ahab, since they were his counselors after the death of his father.

5He was also following their counsel when he joined Jehoram, son of Ahab, king of Israel, in battle against Hazael, king of Aram, at Ramoth-gilead, where the Arameans wounded Jehoram. 6He returned to Jezreel to be healed of the wounds that had been inflicted on him at Ramah in his battle against Hazael, king of Aram. Then Ahaziah, son of Jehoram, king of Judah, went down to Jezreel to visit Jehoram, son of Ahab, for he was sick. 7Now from God came Ahaziah's downfall, that he should join Jehoram; for after his arrival he rode out with Jehoram to Jehu, son of Nimshi, whom the LORD had anointed to cut down the house of Ahab.[r] 8While Jehu was executing judgment on the house of Ahab, he also came upon the princes of Judah and the nephews of Ahaziah who were his attendants, and he killed them.[s] 9Then he looked for Ahaziah himself. They caught him hiding in Samaria and brought him to Jehu,

**21:12 Elijah**: this is the Chronicler's only mention of this prophet of the Northern Kingdom. It is doubtful that Elijah was still living in the reign of Jehoram of Judah; in any case, the attribution of the letter to him has a folkloristic quality.

---

*m:* 1 Kgs 11:36; 2 Kgs 8:19. *n:* Gn 27:40; 2 Kgs 8:20–22. *o:* 2 Chr 16:14. *p:* 2 Kgs 8:24. *q:* 2 Kgs 8:24–29. *r:* 2 Kgs 9:21. *s:* 2 Kgs 10:12–14.

who put him to death. They buried him, for they said, "He was the grandson of Jehoshaphat, who sought the LORD with his whole heart."[t] Now the house of Ahaziah did not retain the power of kingship.*

***Usurpation of Athaliah.*** 10[u] When Athaliah, the mother of Ahaziah, saw that her son was dead, she began to kill off the whole royal family of the house of Judah. 11 But Jehosheba, a daughter of the king, took Joash, Ahaziah's son, and spirited him away from among the king's sons who were about to be slain, and put him and his nurse in a bedroom. In this way Jehosheba, the daughter of King Jehoram, a sister of Ahaziah and wife of Jehoiada the priest, concealed the child from Athaliah, so that she did not put him to death. 12 For six years he remained hidden with them in the house of God, while Athaliah ruled as queen over the land.

## CHAPTER 23

See RG 141–42

***Athaliah Overthrown.*** 1[v] In the seventh year, Jehoiada took courage and brought into covenant with himself the captains: Azariah, son of Jehoram; Ishmael, son of Jehohanan; Azariah, son of Obed; Maaseiah, son of Adaiah; and Elishaphat, son of Zichri. 2 They journeyed about Judah, gathering the Levites from all the cities of Judah and also the heads of the Israelite families, and they came to Jerusalem. 3 The whole assembly made a covenant with the king in the house of God. Jehoiada said to them: "Here is the king's son who must reign, as the LORD promised concerning the sons of David. 4 This is what you must do: a third of your number, both priests and Levites, who come on duty on the sabbath must guard the thresholds, 5 another third must be at the king's house, and the final third at the Foundation Gate, when all the people will be in the courts of the LORD's house. 6 Let no one enter the LORD's house except the priests and those Levites who are ministering. They may enter because they are holy; but all the other people must observe the prescriptions of the LORD. 7 The Levites shall surround the king on all sides, each with drawn weapon. Whoever tries to enter the house is to be killed. Stay with the king wherever he goes."

8 The Levites and all Judah did just as Jehoiada the priest commanded. Each took his troops, both those going on duty for the week and those going off duty that week, since Jehoiada the priest had not dismissed any of the divisions.[w] 9 Jehoiada the priest gave to the captains the spears, shields, and bucklers of King David which were in the house of God. 10 He stationed all the people, each with spear in hand, from the southern to the northern limit of the enclosure, surrounding the altar and the temple on the king's behalf. 11 Then they brought out the king's son and put the crown and the testimony upon him, and proclaimed him king. Jehoiada and his sons anointed him, and they cried, "Long live the king!"

12 When Athaliah heard the noise of the people running and acclaiming the king, she came before them in the house of the LORD. 13 When she saw the king standing by his column* at the entrance, the captains and the trumpeters near the king, and all the people of the land rejoicing and blowing trumpets, while the singers with their musical instruments were leading the acclaim, Athaliah tore her garments, saying, "Treason! treason!" 14 Then Jehoiada the priest brought out the captains in command of the force: "Escort her with a guard detail. If anyone follows her, let him die by the sword." For the priest had said, "You must not put her to death in the house of the LORD." 15 So they seized her, and when she reached the Horse Gate of the royal palace, they put her to death.

16 Then Jehoiada made a covenant between himself and all the people and the king, that they should be the LORD's people. 17 Thereupon all the people went to the temple of

**22:9** This account of the death of Ahaziah of Judah does not agree with that given in 2 Kgs 9:27–28.

**23:13 By his column**: there was a special place reserved for the king in the eastern gateway of the Temple court where the altar for burnt offerings stood. The king occupied this place on feasts and sabbaths at the time of the prescribed offerings, or when he came to make voluntary offerings of his own; cf. 2 Kgs 11:14 and Ez 46:1–8.

*t*: 2 Kgs 9:27–28. *u*: 2 Kgs 11:1–3. *v*: 2 Kgs 11:4–20. *w*: 2 Kgs 11:9; 1 Chr 24:19.

Baal and demolished it. They shattered its altars and images completely, and killed Mattan, the priest of Baal, before the altars.
18 Then Jehoiada gave the charge of the
LORD's house into the hands of the levitical
priests, to whom David had assigned turns in
the LORD's house for sacrificing the burnt offerings of the LORD, as is written in the law
of Moses, with rejoicing and song, as David
had provided.[x] 19 Moreover, he stationed
guards at the gates of the LORD's house so
that no one unclean in any respect might enter. 20 Then he took the captains, the nobles,
the rulers among the people, and all the people of the land, and led the king out of the
LORD's house; they came within the upper
gate of the king's house, and seated the king
upon the royal throne. 21 All the people of the
land rejoiced and the city was quiet, now that
Athaliah had been slain with the sword.

See RG 141–42

## CHAPTER 24

*The Temple Restored.* 1[y] Joash was
seven years old when he became king, and he
reigned forty years in Jerusalem. His
mother's name was Zibiah, from Beer-sheba.
2 Joash did what was right in the LORD's sight
as long as Jehoiada the priest lived. 3 Jehoiada
provided him with two wives, and he became
the father of sons and daughters.
4 After some time, Joash decided to restore
the house of the LORD. 5 He gathered together the priests and Levites and said to
them: "Go out to all the cities of Judah and
gather money* from all Israel that you may
repair the house of your God over the years.
You must hurry this project." But the Levites
did not. 6 Then the king summoned Jehoiada,
who was in charge, and said to him: "Why
have you not required the Levites to bring in
from Judah and Jerusalem the tax levied by
Moses, the servant of the LORD, and by the
assembly of Israel, for the tent of the testimony?"[z] 7 For the wicked Athaliah and her
sons had damaged the house of God and had
even turned over to the Baals the holy things
of the LORD's house.
8 At the king's command, therefore, they
made a chest, which they put outside the gate
of the LORD's house.[a] 9 They had it proclaimed throughout Judah and Jerusalem that
the tax which Moses, the servant of God, had
imposed on Israel in the wilderness should be
brought to the LORD.[b] 10 All the princes and
the people rejoiced; they brought what was
asked and cast it into the chest until it was
filled. 11 Whenever the chest was brought to
the royal officials by the Levites and they noticed that there was a large amount of money,
the royal scribe and an overseer for the chief
priest would come up, empty the chest, and
then take it back and return it to its place.
This they did day after day until they had collected a large sum of money. 12 Then the king
and Jehoiada gave it to the workers in charge
of the labor on the LORD's house, who hired
masons and carpenters to restore the LORD's
house, and also iron- and bronze-smiths to
repair it. 13 The workers labored, and the task
of restoration progressed under their hands.
They restored the house of God according to
its original form, and reinforced it. 14 After
they had finished, they brought the rest of the
money to the king and to Jehoiada, who had
it made into utensils for the house of the
LORD, utensils for the service and the burnt
offerings, and basins and other gold and silver utensils.* They sacrificed burnt offerings
in the LORD's house continually all the days
of Jehoiada. 15 Jehoiada grew old, full of
years, and died; he was a hundred and thirty
years old. 16 They buried him in the City of
David with the kings, because of the good he
had done in Israel, especially for God and his
house.

*Joash's Apostasy.* 17 After the death of Jehoiada, the princes of Judah came and paid
homage to the king; then the king listened to
them. 18 They abandoned the house of the
LORD, the God of their ancestors, and began

**24:5 Gather money**: according to 2 Kgs 12:5 the people themselves brought the money, consisting at least in part of voluntary contributions, to the Temple. By the time of the Chronicler, a fixed head tax for the upkeep of the Temple had been introduced; see 2 Chr 34:9; Neh 10:32; Ex 30:12–16. This was still in force in New Testament times (Mt 17:24–25).

**24:14** See the parallel in 2 Kgs 12:14–15; the passages are difficult to reconcile.

*x:* 1 Chr 23:13. *y:* 2 Kgs 12:1–13. *z:* Ex 25:1–9; Neh 10:33. *a:* 2 Chr 34:9. *b:* Ex 30:13.

to serve the asherahs and the idols;[c] and because of this crime of theirs, wrath came
upon Judah and Jerusalem. [19]Although
prophets were sent to them to turn them back
to the LORD and to warn them, the people
would not listen. [20][d] Then the spirit of God
clothed Zechariah, son of Jehoiada the
priest. He took his stand above the people
and said to them: "Thus says God, Why are
you transgressing the LORD's commands, so
that you cannot prosper? Because you have
abandoned the LORD, he has abandoned
you." [21]But they conspired against him, and
at the king's command they stoned him in
the court of the house of the LORD. [22]Thus
King Joash was unmindful of the devotion
shown him by Jehoiada, Zechariah's father,
and killed the son. As he was dying, he said,
"May the LORD see and avenge."

***Joash Punished.*** [23]At the turn of the year a
force of Arameans came up against Joash.
They invaded Judah and Jerusalem, killed all
the princes of the people, and sent all their
spoil to the king of Damascus.[e] [24]Though the
Aramean force was small, the LORD handed
over a very large force into their power,[f] because Judah had abandoned the LORD, the
God of their ancestors. So judgment was
meted out to Joash. [25][g] After the Arameans
had departed from him, abandoning him to
his many injuries, his servants conspired
against him because of the murder of the son
of Jehoiada the priest. They killed him on his
sickbed. He was buried in the City of David,
but not in the tombs of the kings.

[26]Those who conspired against him were
Zabad, son of Shimeath from Ammon, and
Jehozabad, son of Shimrith from Moab.
[27]An account of his sons, the great tribute
imposed on him, and his rebuilding of the
house of God is written in the midrash of the
book of the kings. His son Amaziah succeeded him as king.[h]

See RG 141–42

## CHAPTER 25

***Amaziah's Good Start.*** [1][i] Amaziah
was twenty-five years old when he became
king, and he reigned twenty-nine years in
Jerusalem. His mother's name was Jehoad-
dan, from Jerusalem. [2]He did what was right
in the LORD's sight, though not wholeheartedly. [3]When he had the kingdom firmly in
hand, he struck down the officials who had
struck down the king, his father. [4]But their
children he did not put to death, for he acted
according to what is written in the law, in the
Book of Moses, which the LORD commanded: "Parents shall not be put to death
for their children, nor shall children be put to
death for their parents; they shall each die
for their own sin."[j]

[5]Amaziah gathered Judah and placed
them, out of all Judah and Benjamin according to their ancestral houses, under leaders
of thousands and of hundreds. When he
made a count of those twenty years old and
over, he found that there were three hundred
thousand picked men fit for war, capable of
handling lance and shield. [6]He also hired a
hundred thousand valiant warriors from Israel for a hundred talents of silver. [7]But a
man of God came to him and said: "O king,
let not the army of Israel go with you, for the
LORD is not with Israel—with any Ephraimite. [8]Instead, go on your own, strongly prepared for the battle; why should the LORD
hinder you in the face of the enemy: for with
God is power to help or to hinder." [9]Ama-
ziah answered the man of God, "But what is
to be done about the hundred talents that I
paid for the troops of Israel?" The man of
God replied, "The LORD can give you much
more than that." [10]Amaziah then disbanded
the troops that had come to him from
Ephraim, and sent them home. But they became furiously angry with Judah, and returned home blazing with anger.

[11]Amaziah now assumed command of his
army. They proceeded to the Valley of Salt,
where they killed ten thousand men of Seir.[k]
[12]The Judahites also brought back another
ten thousand alive, led them to the summit of
Sela, and then threw them down from that
rock* so that their bodies split open. [13]Mean-

**25:12 Sela . . . rock**: a pun—the name of the city, Sela, in Hebrew means "rock."

---

*c:* Ex 34:13. *d:* Jgs 6:34. *e:* 2 Kgs 12:17–18. *f:* Dt 32:30. *g:* 2 Kgs 12:21–22. *h:* 2 Kgs 12:19, 22. *i:* 2 Kgs 14:1–6. *j:* Dt 24:16; 2 Kgs 14:5–6; Ez 18:20. *k:* 2 Kgs 14:7.

while, the troops Amaziah had dismissed from going into battle with him raided the cities of Judah from Samaria to Beth-horon. They struck down three thousand of the inhabitants and carried off much plunder.

*Amaziah's Apostasy.* 14When Amaziah returned from his conquest of the Edomites he brought back with him the gods of the people of Seir. He set these up as his own gods; he bowed down before them and offered sacrifice to them. 15Then the anger of the LORD blazed out against Amaziah, and he sent a prophet to him who said: "Why have you sought this people's gods that could not deliver their own people from your power?" 16While he was still speaking, however, the king said to him: "Have you been appointed the king's counselor? Stop! Why should you have to be killed?" Therefore the prophet stopped. But he said, "I know that God's counsel is your destruction, for by doing this you have refused to listen to my counsel."

*Amaziah Punished.* 17[l] Having taken counsel, Amaziah, king of Judah, sent word to Joash, son of Jehoahaz, son of Jehu, the king of Israel, saying, "Come, let us meet face to face." 18Joash, king of Israel, sent this reply to Amaziah, king of Judah: "A thistle of Lebanon sent word to a cedar of Lebanon, 'Give your daughter to my son in marriage,' but an animal of Lebanon passed by and trampled the thistle underfoot.[m] 19You are thinking,

'See, I have struck down Edom!'
  Your heart is lifted up,
And glories in it. Stay home!
Why bring misfortune and failure
  on yourself and on Judah with you?"

20But Amaziah did not listen; for it was God's doing that they be handed over because they sought the gods of Edom.

21So Joash, king of Israel, advanced, and he and Amaziah, king of Judah, met face to face at Beth-shemesh of Judah, 22and Judah was defeated by Israel, and all fled to their tents. 23But Amaziah, king of Judah, son of Joash, son of Jehoahaz, was captured by Joash, king of Israel, at Beth-shemesh. Joash brought him to Jerusalem and tore down the wall of Jerusalem from the Gate of Ephraim to the Corner Gate, four hundred cubits. 24He took all the gold and silver and all the vessels found in the house of God with Obed-edom,* and in the treasuries of the king's house, and hostages as well. Then he returned to Samaria.

25[n] Amaziah, son of Joash, king of Judah, survived Joash, son of Jehoahaz, king of Israel, by fifteen years. 26The rest of the acts of Amaziah, first and last, are recorded in the book of the kings of Judah and Israel. 27Now from the time that Amaziah turned away from the LORD, a conspiracy was formed against him in Jerusalem, and he fled to Lachish. But he was pursued to Lachish and killed there. 28He was brought back on horses and was buried with his ancestors in the City of Judah.*

## CHAPTER 26

See RG 141–42

*Uzziah's Projects.* 1[o] All the people of Judah took Uzziah, who was only sixteen years old, and made him king to succeed Amaziah his father. 2It was he who rebuilt Elath and restored it to Judah, after the king rested with his ancestors. 3Uzziah was sixteen years old when he became king, and he reigned fifty-two years in Jerusalem. His mother's name was Jecoliah, from Jerusalem. 4He did what was right in the LORD's sight, just as his father Amaziah had done.

5He was prepared to seek God as long as Zechariah* lived,[p] who taught him to fear God; and as long as he sought the LORD, God made him prosper. 6He went out and fought the Philistines and razed the walls of Gath, Jabneh, and Ashdod, and built cities in the district of Ashdod and in Philistia.[q] 7God helped him against the Philistines, against the Arabians who dwelt in Gurbaal, and against the Meunites. 8The Ammonites paid tribute to

**25:24 With Obed-edom**: perhaps an Edomite priest (cf. v. 14), or possibly a member of a levitical family of gatekeepers; cf. 1 Chr 15:18; 26:12–15.

**25:28 The City of Judah**: i.e., Jerusalem, the capital of Judah; the parallel passage (2 Kgs 14:20) reads "the City of David."

**26:5 Zechariah**: not otherwise identified, but cf. 29:1.

*l:* 2 Kgs 14:8–14. *m:* Jgs 9:7–15; 2 Kgs 14:9. *n:* 2 Kgs 14:17–20. *o:* 2 Kgs 14:21–22; 15:1–3. *p:* 2 Chr 24:2. *q:* Am 1:8.

Uzziah and his fame spread as far as Egypt, for he grew stronger and stronger. [9]Moreover, Uzziah built towers in Jerusalem at the Corner Gate, at the Valley Gate, and at the Angle, and he fortified them. [10]He built towers in the wilderness and dug numerous cisterns, for he had many cattle. He had plowmen in the Shephelah and the plains, farmers and vinedressers in the highlands and the garden land. He was a lover of the soil.

[11]Uzziah also had a standing army of fit soldiers divided into bands according to the number in which they were mustered by Jeiel the scribe and Maaseiah the recorder, under the command of Hananiah, one of the king's officials. [12]The entire number of family heads over these valiant warriors was two thousand six hundred, [13]and at their disposal was a mighty army of three hundred seven thousand five hundred fighting men of great valor to help the king against his enemies. [14]Uzziah provided for them—for the entire army—bucklers, lances, helmets, breastplates, bows, and slingstones. [15]He also built machines in Jerusalem, devices designed to stand on the towers and at the angles of the walls to shoot arrows and cast large stones. His name spread far and wide; the help he received was wondrous, so strong did he become.

***Pride and Fall.*** [16]But after he had become strong, he became arrogant to his own destruction and acted treacherously with the LORD, his God. He entered the temple of the LORD to make an offering on the altar of incense. [17]But Azariah the priest, and with him eighty other priests of the LORD, courageous men, followed him. [18]They stood up to King Uzziah, saying to him: "It is not for you, Uzziah, to burn incense to the LORD, but for the priests, the sons of Aaron, who have been consecrated for this purpose.[r] Leave the sanctuary, for you have acted treacherously and no longer have a part in the glory that comes from the LORD God." [19]Uzziah, who was holding a censer for burning the incense, became angry. But at the very moment he showed his anger to the priests, while they were looking at him in the house of the LORD beside the altar of incense, leprosy broke out on his forehead.[s] [20]Azariah the chief priest and all the other priests examined him, and when they saw that his forehead was leprous, they rushed him out. He let himself be expelled, for the LORD had afflicted him. [21][t]King Uzziah remained a leper till the day he died. As a leper he lived in a house apart, for he was excluded from the house of the LORD. Therefore his son Jotham was master of the palace and ruled the people of the land.

[22]The rest of the acts of Uzziah, first and last, were written by Isaiah the prophet, son of Amoz. [23]Uzziah rested with his ancestors and was buried with them in the field adjoining the royal cemetery, for they said, "He was a leper." His son Jotham succeeded him as king.

## CHAPTER 27

See RG 141–42

***Jotham.*** [1][u]Jotham was twenty-five years old when he became king, and he reigned sixteen years in Jerusalem. His mother's name was Jerusha, daughter of Zadok. [2]He did what was right in the LORD's sight, just as his father Uzziah had done, though he did not enter the temple of the LORD. The people, however, continued to act corruptly.

[3]It was he who built the Upper Gate of the LORD's house and did much construction on the wall of Ophel. [4]Moreover, he built cities in the hill country of Judah, and in the wooded areas he set up fortresses and towers. [5]He fought with the king of the Ammonites and conquered them. That year the Ammonites paid him one hundred talents of silver, together with ten thousand kors of wheat and ten thousand of barley. They brought the same to him also in the second and in the third year. [6]Thus Jotham continued to grow strong because he made sure to walk before the LORD, his God. [7][v]The rest of the acts of Jotham, his wars and his activities, are recorded in the book of the kings of Israel and Judah. [8]He was twenty-five years old when he became king, and he reigned sixteen years in Jerusalem. [9]Jotham rested

*r:* Ex 30:7. *s:* Nm 12:10. *t:* 2 Kgs 15:5–7; Lv 13:46; Nm 19:20. *u:* 2 Kgs 15:32–35. *v:* 2 Kgs 15:36–38.

with his ancestors and was buried in the City of David, and his son Ahaz succeeded him as king.

## CHAPTER 28

See RG 141–42

***Ahaz's Misdeeds.*** [1][w] Ahaz was twenty years old when he became king, and he reigned sixteen years in Jerusalem. He did not do what was right in the sight of the LORD as David his father had done. [2]He walked in the ways of the kings of Israel and even made molten idols for the Baals. [3]Moreover, he offered sacrifice in the Valley of Ben-hinnom, and immolated his children by fire in accordance with the abominable practices of the nations whom the LORD had dispossessed before the Israelites.[x] [4]He sacrificed and burned incense on the high places, on hills, and under every green tree.

***Ahaz Punished.*** [5]* Therefore the LORD, his God, delivered him into the power of the king of Aram. The Arameans defeated him and carried away captive a large number of his people, whom they brought to Damascus. He was also delivered into the power of the king of Israel, who defeated him with great slaughter.[y] [6]For Pekah, son of Remaliah, killed one hundred and twenty thousand of Judah in a single day, all of them valiant men, because they had abandoned the LORD, the God of their ancestors. [7]Zichri, an Ephraimite warrior, killed Maaseiah, the king's son, and Azrikam, the master of the palace, and also Elkanah, who was second to the king. [8]The Israelites took away as captives two hundred thousand of their kinfolk's wives, sons, and daughters; they also took from them much plunder, which they brought to Samaria.

***Oded's Prophecy.*** [9]In Samaria there was a prophet of the LORD by the name of Oded. He went out to meet the army returning to Samaria and said to them: "It was because the LORD, the God of your ancestors, was angry with Judah that he delivered them into your power. You, however, have killed them with a fury that has reached up to heaven. [10]And now you are planning to subjugate the people of Judah and Jerusalem as your slaves and bondwomen. Are not you yourselves, therefore, guilty of a crime against the LORD, your God? [11]Now listen to me: send back the captives you have carried off from among your kin, for the burning anger of the LORD is upon you."

[12]At this, some of the Ephraimite leaders, Azariah, son of Johanan, Berechiah, son of Meshillemoth, Jehizkiah, son of Shallum, and Amasa, son of Hadlai, themselves stood up in opposition to those who had returned from the war. [13]They said to them: "Do not bring the captives here, for what you are planning will make us guilty before the LORD and increase our sins and our guilt. Great is our guilt, and there is burning anger upon Israel." [14]Therefore the soldiers left their captives and the plunder before the princes and the whole assembly. [15]Then the men just named proceeded to help the captives. All of them who were naked they clothed from the spoils; they clothed them, put sandals on their feet, gave them food and drink, anointed them, and all who were weak they set on donkeys. They brought them to Jericho, the City of Palms, to their kinfolk. Then they returned to Samaria.[z]

***Further Sins of Ahaz.*** [16]At that time King Ahaz sent an appeal for help to the kings of Assyria.[a] [17]The Edomites had returned, attacked Judah, and carried off captives.[b] [18]The Philistines too had raided the cities of the Shephelah and the Negeb of Judah; they captured Beth-shemesh, Aijalon, Gederoth, Soco and its dependencies, Timnah and its dependencies, and Gimzo and its dependencies, and settled there. [19]For the LORD had

**28:5–8, 16–23** The account of Ahaz's reign in 2 Kings refers to hostilities of Syria (Aram) and Israel against Judah, the revolt of the Edomites, submission to Tiglath-pileser, king of Assyria, the stripping of Temple treasures to pay him tribute, and, in deference to him, shaping the cult of the Jerusalem Temple according to patterns seen in Damascus (2 Kgs 16:5–18; cf. Is 7:1–2). The account in Kings relates all this to an attack of Syria and Israel on Judah (735 B.C.), as they attempted to force Judah into an anti-Assyrian coalition; but the Chronicler, who does not mention the attack, depicts these troubles as the result of, or examples of, Ahaz's infidelity.

*w:* 2 Kgs 16:1–4. *x:* Lv 18:21; 2 Kgs 16:3. *y:* 2 Kgs 16:5; Is 7:1–9. *z:* Lk 10:25–37. *a:* 2 Kgs 16:7. *b:* 2 Kgs 16:6.

**The Reign of Hezekiah**

ONE OF THE great narratives of the Chronicler's history is the account of Hezekiah in chs 29–32. Incorporating large portions of his source in 2 Kings 18–20, he adds considerable materials concerning Hezekiah's reforms and the great worshiping assemblies, in which the king tries to bring the community back into alignment with God.

brought Judah low because of Ahaz, king of Israel,* who let Judah go its own way and committed treachery against the LORD. 20 Tiglath-pileser, king of Assyria, did indeed come to him, but to oppress him rather than to lend strength.[c] 21 Though Ahaz plundered the LORD's house and the houses of the king and the princes to pay off the king of Assyria, it was no help to him.[d]

22 While he was already in distress, the same King Ahaz increased his treachery to the LORD. 23 He sacrificed to the gods of Damascus who had defeated him, saying, "Since it was the gods of the kings of Aram who helped them, I will sacrifice to them that they may help me also." However, they only furthered his downfall and that of all Israel.[e] 24 Ahaz gathered up the utensils of God's house and broke them in pieces. He closed the doors of the LORD's house and made altars for himself in every corner of Jerusalem.[f] 25 In every city throughout Judah he set up high places to offer sacrifice to other gods. Thus he provoked the LORD, the God of his ancestors, to anger.

26[g] The rest of his words and his deeds, first and last, are recorded in the book of the kings of Judah and Israel. 27 Ahaz rested with his ancestors and was buried in Jerusalem—in the city, for they did not bring him to the tombs of the kings of Israel. His son Hezekiah succeeded him as king.

See RG 141–42

## CHAPTER 29

***Hezekiah's Reforms.*** 1[h] Hezekiah was twenty-five years old when he became king, and he reigned twenty-nine years in Jerusalem. His mother's name was Abijah, daughter of Zechariah. 2 He did what was right in the LORD's sight, just as David his father had done. 3 In the first month of the first year of his reign, he opened the doors of the LORD's house and repaired them.[i] 4 He summoned the priests and Levites, gathering them in the open space to the east, 5 and said to them: "Listen to me, you Levites! Sanctify yourselves now and sanctify the house of the LORD, the God of your ancestors, and clean out the filth from the sanctuary. 6 Our ancestors acted treacherously and did what was evil in the eyes of the LORD, our God. They abandoned him, turned away their faces from the LORD's dwelling, and turned their backs on him. 7 They also closed the doors of the vestibule, extinguished the lamps, and failed to burn incense and sacrifice burnt offerings in the sanctuary to the God of Israel.[j] 8[k] Therefore the anger of the LORD has come upon Judah and Jerusalem; he has made them an object of terror, horror, and hissing, as you see with your own eyes. 9 For our ancestors fell by the sword, and our sons, our daughters, and our wives have been taken captive because of this. 10 Now, I intend to make a covenant with the LORD, the God of Israel, that his burning anger may turn away from us. 11 My sons, do not be negligent any longer, for it is you whom the LORD has chosen to stand before him, to minister to him, to be his ministers and to offer incense."

12 Then the Levites arose: Mahath, son of Amasai, and Joel, son of Azariah, of the Kohathites; of the descendants of Merari: Kish, son of Abdi, and Azariah, son of Jehallel; of the Gershonites: Joah, son of Zimmah, and

**28:19 Ahaz, king of Israel**: in his account of the period of the divided monarchy, the Chronicler regularly uses the term "Israel" as here to designate, not the Northern Kingdom, but the entire people. See note on 10:1.

*c:* 2 Kgs 16:10; Is 7:17–20; 8:5–8. *d:* 2 Kgs 16:8. *e:* 2 Kgs 16:12–13; Is 10:20. *f:* 2 Chr 29:3; 30:14; 2 Kgs 16:17. *g:* 2 Kgs 16:19–20. *h:* 2 Kgs 18:2–3. *i:* 2 Chr 28:24. *j:* 2 Kgs 16:15. *k:* Lv 26:32–33; Dt 28:25; Jer 25:18.

Eden, son of Joah; [13]of the sons of Elizaphan: Shimri and Jeuel; of the sons of Asaph: Zechariah and Mattaniah; [14]of the sons of Heman: Jehuel and Shimei; of the sons of Jeduthun: Shemiah and Uzziel. [15]They gathered their kinfolk together and sanctified themselves; then they came as the king had ordered, in keeping with the words of the LORD, to cleanse the LORD's house.

[16]The priests entered the interior of the LORD's house to cleanse it. Whatever they found in the LORD's temple that was unclean they brought out to the court of the LORD's house, where the Levites took it from them and carried it out to the Wadi Kidron. [17]They began the work of consecration on the first day of the first month, and on the eighth day of the month they reached the vestibule of the LORD; they consecrated the LORD's house over an eight-day period, and on the sixteenth day of the first month, they had finished.

[18]Then they went inside to King Hezekiah and said: "We have cleansed the entire house of the LORD, the altar for burnt offerings with all its utensils, and the table for the showbread with all its utensils. [19]We have restored and consecrated all the articles which King Ahaz had thrown away during his reign because of his treachery; they are now before the LORD's altar."

***The Rite of Expiation.*** [20]Then King Hezekiah hastened to convoke the princes of the city and went up to the LORD's house. [21]Seven bulls, seven rams, seven lambs, and seven he-goats were presented as a purification offering for the kingdom, for the sanctuary, and for Judah. Hezekiah ordered the sons of Aaron, the priests, to offer them on the altar of the LORD. [22]They slaughtered the bulls, and the priests collected the blood and splashed it on the altar. Then they slaughtered the rams and splashed the blood on the altar; then they slaughtered the lambs and splashed the blood on the altar. [23]Then the he-goats for the purification offering were led before the king and the assembly, who laid their hands upon them. [24]The priests then slaughtered them and offered their blood on the altar to atone for the sin of all Israel. For the king had said, "The burnt offering and the purification offering are for all Israel."

[25]He stationed the Levites in the LORD's house with cymbals, harps, and lyres, according to the command of David, of Gad the king's seer, and of Nathan the prophet; for this command was from the LORD through his prophets. [26]The Levites were stationed with the instruments of David, and the priests with the trumpets. [27]Then Hezekiah ordered the burnt offering to be sacrificed on the altar. At the very moment the burnt offering began, they also began the song of the LORD, to the accompaniment of the trumpets and the instruments of David, king of Israel. [28]The entire assembly bowed down, and the song was sung and the trumpets sounded until the burnt offering had been completed. [29]Once the burnt offering was completed, the king and all who were with him knelt and worshiped. [30]King Hezekiah and the princes then told the Levites to sing the praises of the LORD in the words of David and of Asaph the seer. They sang praises till their joy was full, then fell down and worshiped.

[31]Hezekiah then said: "You have dedicated yourselves to the LORD. Approach, and bring forward the sacrifices and thank offerings for the house of the LORD." Then the assembly brought forward the sacrifices and thank offerings and all their voluntary burnt offerings. [32]The number of burnt offerings that the assembly brought forward was seventy oxen, one hundred rams, and two hundred lambs: all of these as a burnt offering to the LORD. [33]As consecrated gifts there were six hundred oxen and three thousand sheep. [34]Since there were too few priests to skin all the victims for the burnt offerings, their fellow Levites assisted them until the task was completed and the priests had sanctified themselves. The Levites, in fact, were more careful than the priests to sanctify themselves.[l] [35]The burnt offerings were indeed many, along with the fat of the communion offerings and the libations for the burnt offerings. Thus the service of the house of the LORD was re-established. [36]Hezekiah and all the people rejoiced over what God had re-es-

*l:* 1 Chr 15:12.

tablished for the people, and at how suddenly this had been done.

## CHAPTER 30

See RG 141–42

***Invitation to Passover.*** [1]Hezekiah sent word to all Israel and Judah, and even wrote letters to Ephraim and Manasseh, saying that they should come to the house of the LORD in Jerusalem to celebrate the Passover to the LORD, the God of Israel.[m] [2][n]The king, his princes, and the entire assembly in Jerusalem had agreed to celebrate the Passover during the second month. [3]They could not celebrate it at the regular time because the priests had not sanctified themselves in sufficient numbers, and the people were not gathered at Jerusalem. [4]This seemed right to the king and the entire assembly, [5]and they issued a decree to be proclaimed throughout all Israel from Beer-sheba to Dan, that everyone should come to celebrate the Passover to the LORD, the God of Israel, in Jerusalem; for not many had kept it in the prescribed manner. [6]By the king's command, the couriers, with the letters written by the king and his princes, went through all Israel and Judah. They said: "Israelites, return to the LORD, the God of Abraham, Isaac, and Israel, that he may return to you, the remnant left from the hands of the Assyrian kings. [7]Do not be like your ancestors and your kin who acted treacherously toward the LORD, the God of their ancestors, so that he handed them over to desolation, as you yourselves now see.[o] [8]Do not be stiff-necked, as your ancestors were; stretch out your hands to the LORD and come to his sanctuary that he has consecrated forever, and serve the LORD, your God, that he may turn his burning anger from you. [9]If you return to the LORD, your kinfolk and your children will find mercy with their captors and return to this land. The LORD, your God, is gracious and merciful and he will not turn away his face from you if you return to him."[p]

[10]So the couriers passed from city to city in the land of Ephraim and Manasseh and as far as Zebulun, but they were derided and scoffed at. [11]Nevertheless, some from Asher, Manasseh, and Zebulun humbled themselves and came to Jerusalem. [12]In Judah, however, the hand of God brought it about that the people were of one heart to carry out the command of the king and the princes by the word of the LORD. [13]Thus many people gathered in Jerusalem to celebrate the feast of Unleavened Bread in the second month; it was a very great assembly.

***Passover Celebrated.*** [14]They proceeded to remove the altars that were in Jerusalem as well as all the altars of incense, and cast them into the Wadi Kidron.[q] [15]They slaughtered the Passover on the fourteenth day of the second month. The priests and Levites were shamed into sanctifying themselves and brought burnt offerings into the house of the LORD. [16]They stood in the places prescribed for them according to the law of Moses, the man of God. The priests splashed the blood given them by the Levites; [17]for many in the assembly had not sanctified themselves, and the Levites were in charge of slaughtering the Passover victims for all who were unclean so as to consecrate them to the LORD.[r] [18]The greater part of the people, in fact, chiefly from Ephraim, Manasseh, Issachar, and Zebulun, had not cleansed themselves. Nevertheless they ate the Passover, contrary to the prescription; because Hezekiah prayed for them, saying, "May the good LORD grant pardon to [19]all who have set their heart to seek God, the LORD, the God of their ancestors, even though they are not clean as holiness requires." [20]The LORD heard Hezekiah and healed the people.

[21]Thus the Israelites who were in Jerusalem celebrated the feast of Unleavened Bread with great rejoicing for seven days, and the Levites and the priests sang the praises of the LORD day after day with all their strength. [22]Hezekiah spoke encouragingly to all the Levites who had shown themselves well skilled in the service of the LORD. And when they had completed the seven days of festival, sacrificing communion offerings and singing praises to the LORD, the God of their ancestors, [23]the whole assembly agreed to celebrate another

*m:* Ex 12:1–28. *n:* Nm 9:6–13. *o:* Acts 7:51. *p:* 1 Kgs 8:50. *q:* 2 Chr 28:24–25. *r:* 2 Chr 35:6.

seven days. So with joy they celebrated seven days more. [24]King Hezekiah of Judah had contributed a thousand bulls and seven thousand sheep to the assembly, and the princes a thousand bulls and ten thousand sheep. The priests sanctified themselves in great numbers, [25]and the whole assembly of Judah rejoiced, together with the priests and Levites and the rest of the assembly that had come from Israel, as well as the resident aliens from the land of Israel and those that lived in Judah. [26]There was great rejoicing in Jerusalem, for since the days of Solomon, son of David, king of Israel, there had been nothing like it in the city. [27]Then the levitical priests rose and blessed the people; their voice was heard and their prayer reached heaven, God's holy dwelling.

## CHAPTER 31

See RG 141–42

***Liturgical Reforms.*** [1]After all this was over, those Israelites who had been present went forth to the cities of Judah and smashed the sacred pillars, cut down the asherahs, and tore down the high places and altars throughout Judah, Benjamin, Ephraim, and Manasseh, until they were all destroyed.[s] Then the Israelites returned to their cities, each to his own possession.

[2]Hezekiah re-established the divisions of the priests and the Levites according to their former divisions, assigning to each priest and Levite his proper service, whether in regard to burnt offerings or communion offerings, thanksgiving or praise, or ministering in the gates of the encampment of the LORD. [3]From his own wealth the king allotted a portion for burnt offerings, those of morning and evening and those on sabbaths, new moons, and festivals, as is written in the law of the LORD.[t] [4]He also commanded the people living in Jerusalem to provide for the support of the priests and Levites, that they might firmly adhere to the law of the LORD. [5]As soon as the order was promulgated, the Israelites brought, in great quantities, the best of their grain, wine, oil, and honey, and all the produce of the fields; they gave a generous tithe of everything.[u] [6]Israelites and Judahites living in other cities of Judah also brought in tithes of oxen, sheep, and votive offerings consecrated to the LORD, their God; these they brought in and heaped up in piles.[v] [7]It was in the third month that they began to establish these heaps, and they completed them in the seventh month.* [8]When Hezekiah and the princes had come and seen the piles, they blessed the LORD and his people Israel. [9]Then Hezekiah questioned the priests and the Levites concerning the piles, [10]and the priest Azariah, head of the house of Zadok, answered him, "Since they began to bring the offerings to the house of the LORD, we have eaten, been satisfied, and had much left over, for the LORD has blessed his people. This great supply is what was left over."[w]

[11]Hezekiah then gave orders that chambers be constructed in the house of the LORD. When this had been done, [12]they deposited the offerings, tithes, and votive offerings there for safekeeping. The overseer of these things was Conaniah the Levite, and his brother Shimei was second in command. [13]Jehiel, Azaziah, Nahath, Asahel, Jerimoth, Jozabad, Eliel, Ismachiah, Mahath, and Benaiah were supervisors subject to Conaniah the Levite and his brother Shimei by appointment of King Hezekiah and of Azariah, the prefect of the house of God. [14]Kore, the son of Imnah, a Levite and the keeper of the eastern gate, was in charge of the voluntary offerings made to God; he distributed the offerings made to the LORD and the most holy of the votive offerings. [15]Under him in the priestly cities were Eden, Miniamin, Jeshua, Shemaiah, Amariah, and Shecaniah, who faithfully made the distribution to their brothers, great and small alike, according to their divisions.

**31:7 Third month . . . seventh month**: between the late spring feast of Weeks or Pentecost and the fall feast of Booths or Tabernacles, there is seldom any rain in Palestine; at the end of this dry period the problem of storage (v. 11) would become acute.

*s:* 2 Chr 34:3–4; 2 Kgs 18:4. *t:* Nm 28–29; 1 Chr 29:3; Ez 45:17. *u:* Nm 18:18–24; Dt 14:22–23. *v:* Neh 12:44–47; 13:10–13. *w:* Lv 25:19–22.

16There was also a register by ancestral
houses of males three years of age* and over,
for all priests who were eligible to enter the
house of the LORD according to the daily
schedule to fulfill their service in the order
of their divisions.[x] 17The priests were inscribed in their family records according to
their ancestral houses, as were the Levites
twenty years of age and over according to
their various offices and divisions.[y] 18A distribution was also made to all who were inscribed in the family records, for their little
ones, wives, sons and daughters—thus for
the entire assembly, since they were to sanctify themselves by sharing faithfully in the
votive offerings. 19The sons of Aaron, the
priests who lived on the lands attached to
their cities, had in every city men designated
by name to distribute portions to every male
of the priests and to every Levite listed in the
family records.
20Hezekiah did this in all Judah. He did
what was good, upright, and faithful before
the LORD, his God. 21Everything that he undertook, for the service of the house of God
or for the law and the commandment, was to
seek his God. He did this with all his heart,
and he prospered.[z]

## CHAPTER 32

See RG 141–42

***Sennacherib's Invasion.*** 1But after all
this and all Hezekiah's fidelity, there came
Sennacherib, king of Assyria. He invaded
Judah and besieged the fortified cities, intending to breach and take them.[a] 2When
Hezekiah saw that Sennacherib was coming
with the intention of attacking Jerusalem,
3he took the advice of his princes and warriors to stop the waters of the springs outside
the city; they promised their help. 4[b] A large
force was gathered and stopped all the
springs and also the stream running nearby.
For they said, "Why should the kings of Assyria come and find an abundance of water?" 5He then looked to his defenses: he rebuilt the wall where it was broken down,
raised towers upon it, and built another wall
outside.[c] He strengthened the Millo of the
City of David and made a great number of
spears and shields. 6Then he appointed army
commanders over the people. He gathered
them together in his presence in the open
space at the gate of the city and encouraged
them with these words: 7"Be strong and
steadfast; do not be afraid or dismayed because of the king of Assyria and all the horde
coming with him, for there is more with us
than with him.[d] 8He has only an arm of flesh,
but we have the LORD, our God, to help us
and to fight our battles."[e] And the people
took confidence from the words of Hezekiah, king of Judah.

***Threat of Sennacherib.*** 9[f] After this, while
Sennacherib, king of Assyria, himself remained at Lachish with all his forces, he sent
his officials to Jerusalem with this message
for Hezekiah, king of Judah, and all the Judahites who were in Jerusalem: 10"Thus says
Sennacherib, king of Assyria: In what are
you trusting, now that you are under siege in
Jerusalem? 11Is not Hezekiah deceiving you,
delivering you over to a death of famine and
thirst, by his claim that 'the LORD, our God,
will rescue us from the grasp of the king of
Assyria'? 12Has not this same Hezekiah removed the Lord's own high places and altars
and commanded Judah and Jerusalem, 'You
shall bow down before one altar only, and on
it alone you shall offer incense'? 13Do you
not know what my fathers and I have done to
all the peoples of other lands? Were the gods
of the nations in those lands able to rescue
their lands from my hand? 14Who among all
the gods of those nations which my fathers
put under the ban was able to rescue their
people from my hand? Will your god, then,
be able to rescue you from my hand? 15Let
not Hezekiah mislead you further and deceive you in any such way. Do not believe
him! Since no other god of any other nation
or kingdom has been able to rescue his people from my hand or the hands of my fathers,

**31:16 Three years of age**: this may be a textual error for "thirty years." According to Nm 4:3, 23, 30, men of the priestly clans served from the ages of thirty to fifty.

---

*x:* 1 Chr 23:3–4. *y:* 1 Chr 23:6–24. *z:* Ps 119:2. *a:* 2 Kgs 18:13. *b:* Is 22:9, 11. *c:* Neh 2:17–18. *d:* 2 Chr 14:10; 20:6–12. *e:* Is 31:3. *f:* 2 Kgs 18:17–37; Is 36:1–22.

how much the less shall your god rescue you from my hand!”

[16]His officials said still more against the LORD God and against his servant Hezekiah, [17]for he had written letters to deride the LORD, the God of Israel, speaking of him in these terms: “As the gods of the nations in other lands have not rescued their people from my hand, neither shall Hezekiah’s god rescue his people from my hand.”[g] [18]In a loud voice they shouted in the language of Judah to the people of Jerusalem who were on the wall, to frighten and terrify them so that they might capture their city. [19]They spoke of the God of Israel as though he were one of the gods of the other peoples of the earth, a work of human hands. [20]But because of this, King Hezekiah and Isaiah the prophet, son of Amoz, prayed and cried out to heaven.[h]

***Sennacherib’s Defeat.*** [21]Then the LORD sent an angel, who destroyed every warrior, leader, and commander in the camp of the Assyrian king, so that he had to return shamefaced to his own country. And when he entered the temple of his god, some of his own offspring struck him down there with the sword.[i] [22]Thus the LORD saved Hezekiah and the inhabitants of Jerusalem from the hand of Sennacherib, king of Assyria, as from every other power; he gave them rest on every side. [23]Many brought gifts for the LORD to Jerusalem and costly objects for Hezekiah, king of Judah, who thereafter was exalted in the eyes of all the nations.[j]

***Hezekiah’s Later Reign.*** [24]In those days Hezekiah became mortally ill. He prayed to the LORD, who answered him by giving him a sign.[k] [25]Hezekiah, however, did not respond with like generosity, for he had become arrogant. Therefore wrath descended upon him and upon Judah and Jerusalem. [26][l] But then Hezekiah humbled himself for his pride—both he and the inhabitants of Jerusalem; and therefore the wrath of the LORD did not come upon them during the time of Hezekiah.

[27][m] Hezekiah possessed very great wealth and glory. He made treasuries for his silver, gold, precious stones, spices, jewels, and other precious things of all kinds; [28]also storehouses for the harvest of grain, for wine and oil, and barns for the various kinds of cattle and flocks. [29]He built cities for himself, and he acquired sheep and oxen in great numbers, for God gave him very great riches. [30]This same Hezekiah stopped the upper outlet for water from Gihon and redirected it underground westward to the City of David. Hezekiah prospered in all his works.[n] [31]Nevertheless, in respect to the ambassadors of the Babylonian officials who were sent to him to investigate the sign that had occurred in the land, God abandoned him as a test, to know all that was in his heart.

[32]The rest of Hezekiah’s acts, including his good deeds, are recorded in the vision of Isaiah the prophet, son of Amoz, and in the book of the kings of Judah and Israel. [33]Hezekiah rested with his ancestors; he was buried at the approach to the tombs* of the descendants of David. All Judah and the inhabitants of Jerusalem paid him honor at his death. His son Manasseh succeeded him as king.

## CHAPTER 33

See RG 141–42

***Manasseh’s Impiety.*** [1][o] Manasseh was twelve years old when he became king, and he reigned fifty-five years in Jerusalem. [2]He did what was evil in the LORD’s sight, following the abominable practices of the nations whom the LORD dispossessed before the Israelites. [3]He rebuilt the high places which Hezekiah his father had torn down. He set up altars to the Baals, and also made asherahs. He bowed down to the whole host of heaven and served them. [4]He built altars in the house of the LORD, of which the LORD had said: In Jerusalem shall my name be forever; [5]and he built altars to the whole host of heaven in the two courts of the house of the LORD. [6]It was he, too, who immolated his children by fire in the Valley of Ben-hinnom. He practiced soothsaying and divination,

**32:33 The approach to the tombs**: lit., “the ascent of the tombs,” perhaps “the upper section of the tombs,” i.e., their most prominent and honored place.

---

*g:* 2 Kgs 19:9–13; Is 37:9–13. *h:* 2 Kgs 19:14–19; Is 37:14–20. *i:* 2 Kgs 19:35–37; Is 37:36–38. *j:* 2 Chr 17:10–11. *k:* 2 Kgs 20:1–11; Is 38:1–8. *l:* 2 Kgs 20:12–19; Is 39:1–8. *m:* 2 Kgs 20:13; Is 39:2. *n:* 2 Kgs 20:20–21. *o:* 2 Kgs 21:1–9.

and reintroduced the consulting of ghosts
and spirits.
He did much evil in the LORD's sight and
provoked him to anger. 7An idol he had
made he placed in the house of God, of
which God had said to David and to his son
Solomon: In this house and in Jerusalem,
which I have chosen out of all the tribes of
Israel, I shall set my name forever. 8I will no
longer make Israel step out of the land I assigned to your ancestors, provided that they
are careful to observe all I commanded
them, the entire law, the statutes, and the ordinances given by Moses.
9Manasseh misled Judah and the inhabitants of Jerusalem into doing even greater
evil than the nations the LORD had destroyed
at the coming of the Israelites. 10The LORD
spoke to Manasseh and his people, but they
paid no attention.
*Manasseh's Conversion.* 11[p] Therefore the
LORD brought against them the army commanders of the Assyrian king; they captured
Manasseh with hooks, shackled him with
chains, and transported him to Babylon.*
12In his distress, he began to appease the
LORD, his God. He humbled himself abjectly
before the God of his ancestors, 13and
prayed to him.* The LORD let himself be won
over: he heard his prayer and restored him to
his kingdom in Jerusalem. Then Manasseh
knew that the LORD is indeed God.
14Afterward he built an outer wall for the
City of David to the west of Gihon in the valley, extending to the Fish Gate and encircling Ophel; he built it very high. He stationed army officers in all the fortified cities
of Judah. 15He removed the foreign gods and
the idol from the LORD's house and all the altars he had built on the mount of the LORD's
house and in Jerusalem, and cast them outside the city.[q] 16He restored the altar of the
LORD, and sacrificed on it communion offerings and thank offerings, and commanded
Judah to serve the LORD, the God of Israel.
17Though the people continued to sacrifice
on the high places, they now did so to the
LORD, their God.
18[r] The rest of the acts of Manasseh, his
prayer to his God, and the words of the seers
who spoke to him in the name of the LORD,
the God of Israel, are written in the chronicles of the kings of Israel. 19His prayer and
how his supplication was heard, all his sins
and his treachery, the sites where he built
high places and set up asherahs and carved
images before he humbled himself, all this is
recorded in the chronicles of his seers. 20Ma-
nasseh rested with his ancestors and was
buried in his own palace. His son Amon succeeded him as king.
*Reign of Amon.* 21[s] Amon was twenty-two
years old when he became king, and he
reigned two years in Jerusalem. 22He did
what was evil in the LORD's sight, as his father Manasseh had done. Amon offered sacrifice to all the idols his father Manasseh had
made, and served them. 23Moreover, he did
not humble himself before the LORD as his
father Manasseh had humbled himself; on
the contrary, Amon only increased his guilt.
24His officials plotted against him and put
him to death in his palace, 25but the people
of the land then slew all who had plotted
against King Amon, and the people of the
land made his son Josiah king in his stead.

## CHAPTER 34

See RG 141–42

*Josiah's Reforms.* 1[t] Josiah was eight
years old when he became king, and he
reigned thirty-one years in Jerusalem. 2He
did what was right in the LORD's sight, walking in the way of David his father, not turning right or left. 3[u] In the eighth year of his
reign, while he was still a youth, he began to
seek after the God of David his father. Then

**33:11** There is no evidence elsewhere for such an imprisonment of King Manasseh in Babylon. According to the Assyrian inscriptions, however, Manasseh did pay tribute to the Assyrian kings Esarhaddon (680–669 B.C.) and Asshurbanipal (668–627 B.C.). He may well then have been obliged to go to Nineveh, Assyria's capital (rather than to Babylon as the Chronicler has it), to take his oath of allegiance as vassal to the king of Assyria.

**33:13 And prayed to him**: these words inspired an unknown writer to compose the apocryphal "Prayer of Manasseh," which since the Council of Trent appears as an appendix to many editions of the Vulgate Bible and is used in the Church's liturgy.

*p:* Jb 36:8; Ez 19:9. *q:* 2 Chr 14:2. *r:* 2 Kgs 21:17–18. *s:* 2 Kgs 21:19–26. *t:* 2 Kgs 22:1–2. *u:* 2 Chr 14:1–4; 31:1; 2 Kgs 23:4–20.

in his twelfth year* he began to purify Judah and Jerusalem of the high places, the asherahs, and the carved and molten images. [4]In his presence, the altars of the Baals were torn down; the incense stands erected above them he broke down; the asherahs and the carved and molten images he smashed and beat into dust, which he scattered over the tombs of those who had sacrificed to them; [5]and the bones of the priests he burned upon their altars. Thus he purified Judah and Jerusalem. [6]He did likewise in the cities of Manasseh, Ephraim, Simeon, and in the ruined villages of the surrounding country as far as Naphtali; [7]he tore down the altars and asherahs, and the carved images he beat into dust, and broke down the incense stands throughout the land of Israel. Then he returned to Jerusalem.

*The Temple Restored.* [8][v] In the eighteenth year of his reign, in order to purify the land and the temple, he sent Shaphan, son of Azaliah, Maaseiah, the ruler of the city, and Joah, son of Joahaz, the chancellor, to restore the house of the LORD, his God. [9]They came to Hilkiah the high priest and turned over the money brought to the house of God which the Levites, the guardians of the threshold, had collected from Manasseh, Ephraim, and all the remnant of Israel, as well as from all of Judah, Benjamin, and the inhabitants of Jerusalem.[w] [10]They turned it over to the master workers in the house of the LORD, and these in turn used it to pay the workers in the LORD's house who were restoring and repairing it. [11]They also gave it to the carpenters and the masons to buy hewn stone and timber for the tie beams and rafters of the buildings which the kings of Judah had allowed to fall into ruin. [12]The men worked faithfully at their task; their overseers were Jahath and Obadiah, Levites of the line of Merari, and Zechariah and Meshullam, of the Kohathites, who directed them. All those Levites who were skillful with musical instruments [13]were in charge of the men who carried the burdens, and they directed all the workers in every kind of labor. Some of the other Levites were scribes, officials, and gatekeepers.

*The Finding of the Law.* [14][x] When they brought out the money that had been deposited in the house of the LORD, Hilkiah the priest found the book of the law of the LORD given through Moses. [15]He reported this to Shaphan the scribe, saying, "I have found the book of the law in the house of the LORD." Hilkiah gave the book to Shaphan, [16]who brought it to the king at the same time that he made his report to him. He said, "Your servants are doing everything that has been entrusted to them; [17]they have smelted down the silver deposited in the LORD's house and have turned it over to the overseers and the workers." [18]Then Shaphan the scribe also informed the king, "Hilkiah the priest has given me a book," and then Shaphan read it in the presence of the king.

[19]When the king heard the words of the law, he tore his garments. [20]The king then issued this command to Hilkiah, to Ahikam, son of Shaphan, to Abdon, son of Michah, to Shaphan the scribe, and to Asaiah, the king's servant: [21]"Go, consult the LORD for me and for those who are left in Israel and Judah, about the words of the book that has been found, for the anger of the LORD burns furiously against us, because our ancestors did not keep the word of the LORD and have not done all that is written in this book." [22]Then Hilkiah and others from the king went to Huldah the prophet, wife of Shallum, son of Tokhath, son of Hasrah, keeper of the wardrobe; she lived in Jerusalem, in the Second Quarter. They spoke to her as they had been instructed, [23]and she said to them: "Thus says the LORD, the God of Israel: Say to the man who sent you to me, [24]Thus says

**34:3 In his twelfth year**: ca. 628 B.C., i.e., around the time of the Assyrian emperor Asshurbanipal's death, which enabled Judah to free itself from Assyrian domination. On the basis of 2 Kgs 22:1–23:25 alone, one might suppose that Josiah's reform began only after and as a result of the discovery of the book of the law in the Temple, in the eighteenth year of his reign (622 B.C.). But the Chronicler is no doubt right in placing the beginning of the reform at an earlier period. The repair of the Temple itself, which led to the finding of the book of the law, was likely part of a cultic reform initiated by Josiah.

*v:* 2 Kgs 22:3–7. *w:* 2 Chr 24:8–9. *x:* 2 Kgs 22:8–20.

the LORD: I am about to bring evil upon this
place and upon its inhabitants, all the curses
written in the book that was read before the
king of Judah. 25 Because they have abandoned me and have burned incense to other
gods, provoking me by all the works of their
hands, my anger burns against this place and
it cannot be extinguished.

26 "But to the king of Judah who sent you
to consult the LORD, give this response: Thus
says the LORD, the God of Israel: As for the
words you have heard, 27 because you were
heartsick and have humbled yourself before
God when you heard his words concerning
this place and its inhabitants; because you
humbled yourself before me, tore your garments, and wept before me, I in turn have
heard—oracle of the LORD. 28 I will gather
you to your ancestors and you shall go to
your grave in peace, and your eyes shall not
see all the evil I am about to bring upon this
place and upon its inhabitants."

This they reported to the king.

***Covenant Renewal.*** 29 [y] The king then had
all the elders of Judah and of Jerusalem summoned before him. 30 The king went up to the
house of the LORD with all the people of Judah and the inhabitants of Jerusalem: priests,
Levites, and all the people, great and small.
He read aloud to them all the words of the
book of the covenant that had been found in
the house of the LORD. 31 The king stood by
the column* and made a covenant in the
presence of the LORD to follow the LORD and
to observe his commandments, statutes, and
decrees with his whole heart and soul, carrying out the words of the covenant written in
this book. 32 He thereby committed all who
were in Jerusalem and Benjamin, and the inhabitants of Jerusalem acted according to
the covenant of God, the God of their ancestors. 33 Josiah removed every abomination
from all the territories belonging to the Israelites, and he obliged all who were in Israel
to serve the LORD, their God. During his lifetime they did not turn away from following
the LORD, the God of their ancestors.[z]

## CHAPTER 35

See RG 141–42

***The Passover.*** 1 [a] Josiah celebrated in
Jerusalem a Passover to honor the LORD; the
Passover sacrifice was slaughtered on the
fourteenth day of the first month.[b] 2 He reap-
pointed the priests to their duties and confirmed them in the service of the LORD's
house. 3 He said to the Levites who were to
instruct all Israel, and who were consecrated
to the LORD: "Put the holy ark in the house
built by Solomon, son of David, king of Israel. It shall no longer be a burden on your
shoulders. Serve now the LORD, your God,
and his people Israel.[c] 4 Prepare yourselves
by your ancestral houses and your divisions
according to the prescriptions of David, king
of Israel, and the prescriptions of his son
Solomon. 5 Stand in the sanctuary according
to the branches of the ancestral houses of
your kin, the common people, so that the
distribution of the Levites and the families
may be the same.[d] 6 Slaughter the Passover
sacrifice, sanctify yourselves, and be at the
disposition of your kin, that all may be done
according to the word of the LORD given
through Moses."[e]

7 Josiah contributed to the common people
a flock of lambs and young goats,[f] thirty
thousand in number, each to serve as a
Passover victim for all who were present,
and also three thousand oxen; these were
from the king's property. 8 His princes also
gave a voluntary offering to the people, the
priests, and the Levites. Hilkiah, Zechariah,
and Jehiel, prefects of the house of God,
gave to the priests two thousand six hundred
Passover victims along with three hundred
oxen.[g] 9 Conaniah and his brothers Shemaiah, Nethanel, Hashabiah, Jehiel, and Jozabad, the rulers of the Levites, contributed to
the Levites five thousand Passover victims,
together with five hundred oxen.

10 When the service had been arranged, the
priests took their places, as did the Levites in
their divisions according to the king's command. 11 The Passover sacrifice was slaugh-

**34:31 The column**: see note on 23:13.

*y:* 2 Kgs 23:1–3. *z:* 2 Kgs 23:4–20. *a:* 2 Kgs 23:21–23. *b:* Ex 12:1–28; 2 Kgs 23:21. *c:* 2 Chr 5:4; 1 Chr 15:12, 15. *d:* 1 Chr 24–26. *e:* 2 Chr 30:17. *f:* Ex 12:5. *g:* Nm 7:1–83.

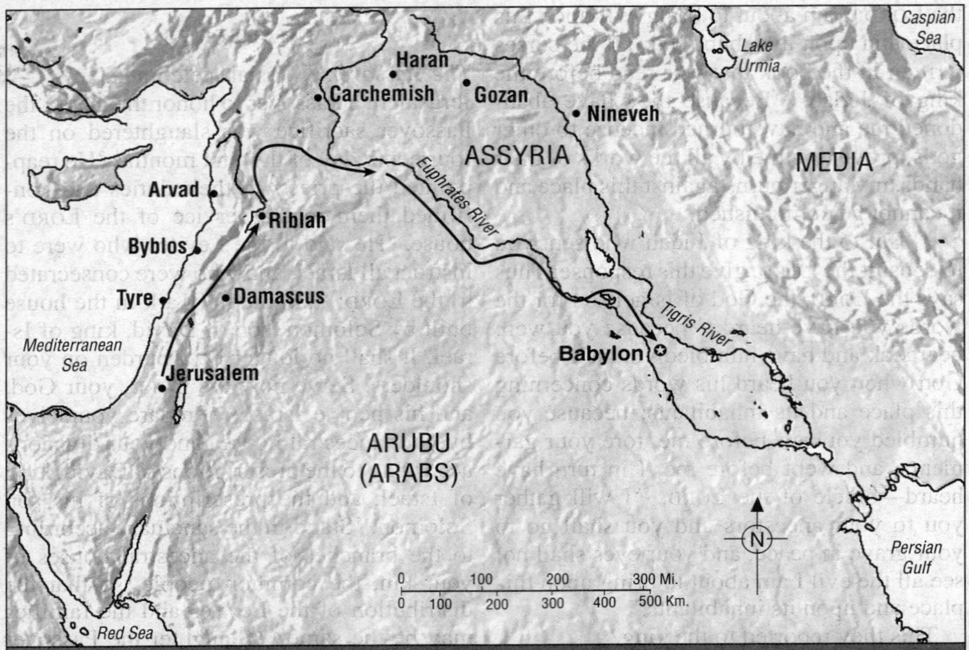


Exile of Southern Kingdom

tered, whereupon the priests splashed some of the blood and the Levites proceeded with the skinning. [12]They separated out what was destined for the burnt offering and gave it to various groups of the ancestral houses of the common people to offer to the LORD, as is written in the book of Moses. They did the same with the oxen. [13]They cooked the Passover on the fire as prescribed, and also cooked the sacred portions in pots, caldrons, and pans, then brought them quickly to all the common people.[h] [14]Afterward they prepared the Passover for themselves and for the priests. Indeed the priests, the sons of Aaron, were busy sacrificing burnt offerings and the fatty portions until night; therefore the Levites prepared for themselves and for the priests, the sons of Aaron. [15]The singers, the sons of Asaph, were at their posts as commanded by David and by Asaph, Heman, and Jeduthun, the king's seer. The gatekeepers were at every gate; there was no need for them to leave their stations, for their fellow Levites prepared for them. [16]Thus the entire service of the LORD was arranged that day so that the Passover could be celebrated and the burnt offerings sacrificed on the altar of the LORD, as King Josiah had commanded. [17]The Israelites who were present on that occasion kept the Passover and the feast of the Unleavened Bread for seven days. [18][i] No such Passover had been observed in Israel since the time of Samuel the prophet; no king of Israel had observed a Passover like that celebrated by Josiah, the priests, and Levites, all of Judah and Israel that were present, and the inhabitants of Jerusalem. [19]It was in the eighteenth year of Josiah's reign that this Passover was observed.

***Josiah's End.*** [20]After Josiah had done all this to restore the temple, Neco, king of Egypt, came up to fight at Carchemish on the Euphrates, and Josiah went out to meet him. [21]Neco sent messengers to him, saying: "What quarrel is between us, king of Judah?

*h:* Ex 12:8–9. *i:* 2 Kgs 23:22–23.

I have not come against you this day, for my war is with another kingdom, and God has told me to hasten. Do not interfere with God who is with me; let him not destroy you." 22 But Josiah would not withdraw from him, for he was seeking a pretext to fight with him. Therefore he would not listen to the words of Neco that came from the mouth of God, but went out to fight in the plain of Megiddo. 23 Then the archers shot King Josiah, who said to his servants, "Take me away, I am seriously wounded."[j] 24 His servants took him from his own chariot, placed him in the one he had in reserve, and brought him to Jerusalem, where he died. He was buried in the tombs of his ancestors, and all Judah and Jerusalem mourned him. 25 Jeremiah also composed a lamentation for Josiah, which is recited to this day by all the male and female singers in their lamentations for Josiah. These have been made an ordinance for Israel, and can be found written in the Lamentations.*

26[k] The rest of the acts of Josiah, his good deeds in accord with what is written in the law of the LORD, 27 and his words, first and last, are recorded in the book of the kings of Israel and Judah.

## CHAPTER 36

See RG 141–42

*Jehoahaz.* 1 The people of the land took Jehoahaz, son of Josiah, and made him king in Jerusalem to succeed his father. 2 Jehoahaz was twenty-three years old when he became king, and he reigned three months in Jerusalem. 3 The king of Egypt deposed him in Jerusalem and fined the land one hundred talents of silver and a talent of gold. 4 Then the king of Egypt made Eliakim, the brother of Jehoahaz, king over Judah and Jerusalem, changing his name to Jehoiakim. Neco took Jehoahaz his brother away and brought him to Egypt.

*Jehoiakim.* 5 Jehoiakim was twenty-five years old when he became king, and he reigned eleven years in Jerusalem. He did what was evil in the sight of the LORD, his God.[m] 6[n] Nebuchadnezzar, king of Babylon, attacked and bound him in chains to take him to Babylon.* 7 Nebuchadnezzar also carried away to Babylon some of the vessels of the house of the LORD and put them in his palace in Babylon. 8 The rest of the acts of Jehoiakim, the abominable things that he did, and what therefore happened to him, are recorded in the book of the kings of Israel and Judah. His son Jehoiachin succeeded him as king.[o]

*Jehoiachin.* 9 Jehoiachin was eighteen years old when he became king, and he reigned three months and ten days in Jerusalem. He did what was evil in the LORD's sight.[p] 10 At the turn of the year, King Nebuchadnezzar sent for him and had him brought to Babylon, along with precious vessels from the house of the LORD. He made his brother Zedekiah* king over Judah and Jerusalem.[q]

*Zedekiah.* 11 Zedekiah was twenty-one years old when he became king, and he reigned eleven years in Jerusalem.[r] 12 He did what was evil in the sight of the LORD, his God, and he did not humble himself before Jeremiah the prophet, who spoke for the LORD.[s] 13 He also rebelled against King Nebuchadnezzar, who had made him swear by God. He became stiff-necked and hardened his heart rather than return to the LORD, the God of Israel.[t] 14 Likewise all the princes of Judah, the priests, and the people added treachery to treachery, practicing all the abominations of the nations and defiling the

**35:25** There is no mention of such a lamentation for Josiah composed by Jeremiah in either 2 Kings or Jeremiah; but see note on Zec 12:11. **Lamentations**: probably a reference to the Book of Lamentations.

**36:6 Nebuchadnezzar . . . bound him in chains to take him to Babylon**: the Chronicler does not state that Jehoiakim was actually taken to Babylon. According to 2 Kgs 24:1–6, Jehoiakim revolted after being Nebuchadnezzar's vassal for three years; he died in Jerusalem before the city surrendered to the Babylonians. Dn 1:1–2, apparently based on 2 Chr 36:6–7, does speak of Jehoiakim's deportation to Babylon.

**36:10 His brother Zedekiah**: Zedekiah was actually the brother of Jehoiakim and the uncle of Jehoiachin (2 Kgs 24:17; Jer 37:1), though scarcely older than his nephew (2 Kgs 24:8, 18; 2 Chr 36:9, 11).

*j:* 2 Chr 18:33–34. *k:* 2 Kgs 23:28. *l:* 2 Kgs 23:30–34; 1 Chr 3:15–16. *m:* 2 Kgs 23:36–37; Jer 22:18–19. *n:* 2 Kgs 24:1–2. *o:* 2 Kgs 24:5. *p:* 2 Kgs 24:8–9. *q:* 2 Kgs 24:10–17. *r:* 2 Kgs 24:18–19; Jer 52:1. *s:* Jer 37:1–2. *t:* 2 Kgs 24:20; Jer 52:4; Ez 17:13–16.

LORD's house which he had consecrated in Jerusalem.

*The Fall of Judah.* [15]Early and often the LORD, the God of their ancestors, sent his messengers to them, for he had compassion on his people and his dwelling place.[u] [16]But they mocked God's messengers, despised his words, and scoffed at his prophets, until the LORD's anger against his people blazed up beyond remedy.[v] [17]Then he brought up against them the king of the Chaldeans, who killed their young men with the sword in their own sanctuary, with compassion for neither young men nor young women, neither the old nor the infirm; all of them he delivered into his power.[w] [18]All the utensils of the house of God, large and small, the treasures of the LORD's house, and the treasures of the king and his princes, all these he brought to Babylon.[x] [19]They burnt the house of God, tore down the walls of Jerusalem, burnt down all its palaces, and destroyed all its precious objects.[y] [20]Those who escaped the sword he carried captive to Babylon, where they became servants to him and his sons until the Persian kingdom came to power. [21]All this was to fulfill the word of the LORD spoken by Jeremiah: Until the land has retrieved its lost sabbaths, during all the time it lies waste it shall have rest while seventy years are fulfilled.

*Decree of Cyrus.* [22*] In the first year of Cyrus, king of Persia, in order to realize the word of the LORD spoken by Jeremiah, the LORD roused the spirit of Cyrus, King of Persia, to spread this proclamation throughout his kingdom, both by word of mouth and in writing:[z] [23]"Thus says Cyrus, king of Persia: The LORD, the God of heaven, has given to me all the kingdoms of the earth. He has also charged me to build him a house in Jerusalem, which is in Judah. All among you, therefore, who belong to his people, may their God be with them; let them go up."

**36:22–23** These verses are identical with those of Ezr 1:1–3a and were to prevent the work from ending on a note of doom.

*u:* Jer 7:25; Heb 1:1. *v:* Mt 23:34–37. *w:* Lam 1:15; 5:11–14. *x:* 2 Kgs 25:14–15. *y:* 2 Kgs 25:9–10; Lam 2:8. *z:* Ezr 1:1–4.

See RG 144–50

# The Book of Ezra

The last four books of the Hebrew canon are Ezra, Nehemiah, and 1 and 2 Chronicles, in that order. At one time, however, Ezra and Nehemiah followed 1 and 2 Chronicles and were generally considered to be the work of one and the same author known as "the Chronicler." In recent years, however, the question of the authorship of Ezra and Nehemiah is seen to be more complex. While some scholars still maintain unity of authorship, others prefer to speak of the influence of a "Chronistic school" on the formation of Ezra-Nehemiah as a single book. The treatment of Ezra-Nehemiah as a single book by the earliest editors was undoubtedly due to the fact that in ancient times the two books were put under the one name, Ezra. The combined work Ezra-Nehemiah is our most important literary source for the formation of the Jewish religious community in the province of Judah after the Babylonian exile. This is known as the period of the Restoration, and the two men most responsible for the reorganization of Jewish life at this time were Ezra and Nehemiah.

In the present state of the Ezra-Nehemiah text, there are several dislocations of large sections so that the chronological or logical sequence is disrupted. The major instance is Ezra's public reading of the law in Neh 8; others will be pointed out in the footnotes. Since arguments in favor of the chronological priority of Nehemiah to Ezra are indecisive, we accept the order in the text according to which Ezra's activity preceded that of Nehemiah.

What is known of Ezra and his work is derived almost exclusively from Ezr 7–10 (the "Ezra Memoirs") and Neh 8–9. Strictly speaking, the term "Ezra Memoirs" should be used only of that section in which Ezra speaks in the first person, i.e., Ezr 7:27–9:15. Compare the "Nehemiah Memoirs" in Neh 1:1–7:72a; 11:1, 2; 12:27–43; 13:4–31. The author combined this material with other sources at his disposal. The personality of

Ezra is not so well-known as that of Nehemiah. Ben Sira, in his praise of the fathers (Sir 44–49), omits mention of Ezra, perhaps for polemical reasons. The genealogy of Ezra (7:1–5) traces his priesthood back to Aaron, brother of Moses. This was the accepted way of establishing the legality of one's priestly office. He is also called a scribe, well-versed in the law of Moses (7:6), indicating Ezra's dedication to the study of the Torah, which he sought to make the basic rule of life in the restored community. It was in religious and cultic reform rather than in political affairs that Ezra made his mark as a postexilic leader. Jewish tradition holds him in great esteem. The apocryphal 2 Esdras, sometimes included as an appendix to the Vulgate, where it is known as 4 Esdras, transforms him into a prophet and visionary. The Talmud regards him as a second Moses, claiming that the Torah would have been given to Israel through Ezra had not Moses preceded him.

Ezra is sometimes accused of having been a legalist who gave excessive attention to the letter of the law. His work, however, should be seen and judged within a specific historical context. He gave to his people a cohesion and spiritual unity which helped to prevent the disintegration of the small Jewish community settled in the province of Judah. Had it not been for the intransigence of Ezra and of those who adopted his ideal, it is doubtful that Judaism would have so effectively resisted Hellenism in later centuries. Ezra set the tone of the postexilic community, and it was characterized by fidelity to the Torah, Judaism's authentic way of life. It is in this light that we can judge most fairly the work of Ezra during the Restoration.

The Book of Ezra is divided as follows:

I. The Return from Exile (1:1–6:22)

II. The Work of Ezra (7:1–10:44)

The following list of the kings of Persia, with the dates of their reigns, will be useful for dating the events mentioned in Ezra-Nehemiah:

| | |
|---|---|
| Cyrus | 539–530 B.C. |
| Cambyses | 530–522 B.C. |
| Darius I | 522–486 B.C. |
| Xerxes I | 486–465 B.C. |
| Artaxerxes I | 465–424 B.C. |
| Darius II | 423–404 B.C. |
| Artaxerxes II | 404–358 B.C. |
| Artaxerxes III | 358–337 B.C. |
| End of the Persian Empire (Defeat of Darius III) | 331 B.C. |

# I. The Return from Exile

## CHAPTER 1

See RG 145

*The Decree of Cyrus.* 1a In the first
year of Cyrus,* king of Persia, in order to
fulfill the word of the LORD spoken by Jeremiah, the LORD stirred up the spirit of Cyrus
king of Persia to issue a proclamation
throughout his entire kingdom, both by word
of mouth and in writing: 2"Thus says Cyrus,
king of Persia: 'All the kingdoms of the
earth the LORD, the God of heaven,* has
given to me, and he has charged me to build
him a house in Jerusalem, which is in Judah.
3Those among you who belong to any part of
his people, may their God be with them! Let
them go up to Jerusalem in Judah to build
the house of the LORD the God of Israel, that
is, the God who is in Jerusalem. 4Let all
those who have survived, in whatever place
they may have lived, be assisted by the people of that place with silver, gold, goods, and
livestock, together with voluntary offerings
for the house of God in Jerusalem.' "
5Then the heads of ancestral houses* of
Judah and Benjamin and the priests and Levites—everyone, that is, whose spirit had
been stirred up by God—prepared to go up
to build the house of the LORD in Jerusalem.
6b All their neighbors gave them help in
every way, with silver, gold, goods, livestock, and many precious gifts, besides all

**1:1 In the first year of Cyrus**: the first regnal year of Cyrus was 539 B.C., but his first year as ruler of Babylon, after the conquest of that city, was 538 B.C., the year in which he issued an edict, replicated on the famous Cyrus cylinder, permitting the repatriation of peoples deported by the Babylonians.

**1:2 The God of heaven**: this title, used as in 7:12, 21, 23, corresponds to a title of the Zoroastrian supreme deity Ahura Mazda, though it is not certain that Cyrus was a Zoroastrian.

**1:5 Heads of ancestral houses**: the ancestral house was the basic organizational unit of the postexilic community, consisting of an extended kinship group claiming descent from a common ancestor. The patriarchs of these units played an important role in civic government.

*a:* Ezr 6:3–5; 2 Chr 36:22–23; Jer 25:11–12; 29:10; Zec 1:12.
*b:* Ex 3:21–22; 11:2; 12:35.

**Utensils from the Temple**

THE RETURN OF these utensils from the temple of Solomon that had been destroyed by the Babylonians (v. 7) links that temple with the temple that will be built after the Exile.

their voluntary offerings. [7][c] King Cyrus, too, had the vessels of the house of the LORD brought forth that Nebuchadnezzar had taken from Jerusalem and placed in the house of his god. [8]Cyrus, king of Persia, had them brought forth by the treasurer Mithredath, who counted them out to Sheshbazzar, prince of Judah.* [9]This was the inventory: baskets of goldware, thirty; baskets of silverware, one thousand and twenty-nine; [10]golden bowls, thirty; silver bowls, four hundred and ten; other vessels, one thousand. [11]Total of the gold and silver vessels: five thousand four hundred.* All these Sheshbazzar took with him when the exiles were brought up from Babylon to Jerusalem.

## CHAPTER 2

See RG 145

### *A Census of the Returned Exiles.*

[1]* [d] These are the inhabitants of the province who returned from the captivity of the exiles, whom Nebuchadnezzar, king of Babylon, had carried away to Babylon, and who came back to Jerusalem and Judah, to their various cities [2](those who returned with Zerubbabel, Jeshua, Nehemiah, Seraiah, Reelaiah, Mordecai, Bilshan, Mispar, Bigvai, Rehum, and Baanah):

The census of the people of Israel: [3]descendants of Parosh, two thousand one hundred and seventy-two; [4]descendants of Shephatiah, three hundred and seventy-two; [5]descendants of Arah, seven hundred and seventy-five; [6]descendants of Pahath-moab, who were descendants of Jeshua and Joab, two thousand eight hundred and twelve; [7]descendants of Elam, one thousand two hundred and fifty-four; [8]descendants of Zattu, nine hundred and forty-five; [9]descendants of Zaccai, seven hundred and sixty; [10]descendants of Bani, six hundred and forty-two; [11]descendants of Bebai, six hundred and twenty-three; [12]descendants of Azgad, one thousand two hundred and twenty-two; [13]descendants of Adonikam, six hundred and sixty-six; [14]descendants of Bigvai, two thousand and fifty-six; [15]descendants of Adin, four hundred and fifty-four; [16]descendants of Ater, who were descendants of Hezekiah, ninety-eight; [17]descendants of Bezai, three hundred and twenty-three; [18]descendants of Jorah, one hundred and twelve; [19]descendants of Hashum, two hundred and twenty-three; [20]descendants of Gibeon, ninety-five; [21]descendants of Bethlehem, one hundred and twenty-three; [22]people of Netophah, fifty-six; [23]people of Anathoth, one hundred and twenty-eight; [24]people of Beth-azmaveth, forty-two; [25]people of Kiriath-jearim, Chephirah, and Beeroth, seven hundred and forty-three; [26]people of Ramah and Geba, six hundred and twenty-one; [27]people of Michmas, one hundred and twenty-two; [28]people of Bethel and Ai, two hundred and twenty-three; [29]descendants of Nebo, fifty-two; [30]descendants of Magbish, one hundred and fifty-six; [31]descendants of the other Elam, one thousand two hundred and fifty-four; [32]descendants of Harim, three hundred and twenty; [33]descendants of Lod, Hadid, and Ono, seven hundred and twenty-five; [34]descendants of Jericho, three hundred and forty-five; [35]descendants of Senaah, three thousand six hundred and thirty.

[36]The priests: descendants of Jedaiah, of the house of Jeshua, nine hundred and seventy-three; [37]descendants of Immer, one thousand and fifty-two; [38]descendants of

**1:8 Sheshbazzar, prince of Judah**: often identified with Shenassar, fourth son of Jehoiachin, king of Judah, exiled in 598 B.C. (see 1 Chr 3:17–18), and therefore the uncle of Zerubbabel (Ezr 3:2–4). This identification is uncertain.

**1:11 Five thousand four hundred**: either this figure or the figures given for one or more of the items listed have been corrupted in the transmission of the text.

**2:1–67** As it now stands, this list, which also appears at Neh 7:6–72, is an expanded form of lists of Babylonian repatriates from the sixth century B.C. It served to establish membership in the reconstituted Temple community; civic status and perhaps also title to property depended on this membership.

*c*: 2 Kgs 25:14–15. *d*: Neh 7:6–72.

THE BEGINNING OF Ezra-Nehemiah seeks to establish the legitimacy of rebuilding the house of God, the temple. This is expressed by opening ch 1 with the imperial order to return to Jerusalem and rebuild the temple.

Pashhur, one thousand two hundred and forty-seven; 39 descendants of Harim, one thousand and seventeen.

40e The Levites: descendants of Jeshua and Kadmiel, of the descendants of Hodaviah, seventy-four.

41 The singers:* descendants of Asaph, one hundred and twenty-eight.

42 The gatekeepers:* descendants of Shallum, descendants of Ater, descendants of Talmon, descendants of Akkub, descendants of Hatita, descendants of Shobai, one hundred and thirty-nine in all.

43 The temple servants: descendants of Ziha, descendants of Hasupha, descendants of Tabbaoth, 44 descendants of Keros, descendants of Siaha, descendants of Padon, 45 descendants of Lebanah, descendants of Hagabah, descendants of Akkub, 46 descendants of Hagab, descendants of Shamlai, descendants of Hanan, 47 descendants of Giddel, descendants of Gahar, descendants of Reaiah, 48 descendants of Rezin, descendants of Nekoda, descendants of Gazzam, 49 descendants of Uzza, descendants of Paseah, descendants of Besai, 50 descendants of Asnah, descendants of the Meunites, descendants of the Nephusites, 51 descendants of Bakbuk, descendants of Hakupha, descendants of Harhur, 52 descendants of Bazluth, descendants of Mehida, descendants of Harsha, 53 descendants of Barkos, descendants of Sisera, descendants of Temah, 54 descendants of Neziah, descendants of Hatipha.

55 Descendants of Solomon's servants: descendants of Sotai, descendants of Hassophereth, descendants of Peruda, 56 descendants of Jaalah, descendants of Darkon, descendants of Giddel, 57 descendants of Shephatiah, descendants of Hattil, descendants of Pochereth-hazzebaim, descendants of Ami. 58 The total of the temple servants together with the descendants of Solomon's servants was three hundred and ninety-two.

59 The following who returned from Tel-melah, Tel-harsha, Cherub, Addan, and Immer were unable to prove that their ancestral houses and their descent were Israelite: 60 descendants of Delaiah, descendants of Tobiah, descendants of Nekoda, six hundred and fifty-two. 61f Also, of the priests: descendants of Habaiah, descendants of Hakkoz, descendants of Barzillai (he had married one of the daughters of Barzillai the Gileadite and was named after him). 62 These searched their family records, but their names could not be found there, and they were excluded from the priesthood. 63g The governor* ordered them not to partake of the most holy foods until there should be a priest to consult the Urim and Thummim.

64 The entire assembly taken together came to forty-two thousand three hundred and sixty, 65 not counting their male and female servants, who numbered seven thousand three hundred and thirty-seven. They also had two hundred male and female singers. 66 Their horses numbered seven hundred and thirty-six, their mules two hundred and forty-five, 67 their camels four hundred and thirty-five, their donkeys six thousand seven hundred and twenty.

**2:41 The singers**: the term covers the composition as well as the rendition of liturgical music. Since they are listed as distinct from Levites (2:40), they had not yet attained levitical status, as in Chronicles (e.g., 1 Chr 9:33–34; 23:3–6).

**2:42 The gatekeepers**: their principal task was to protect the ritual purity of the temple area (e.g., 2 Chr 23:19). The author assumes that they were established by David as a distinct levitical category (1 Chr 15:18; 26:1–19).

**2:63 The governor**: the honorific title was also held by Nehemiah (Neh 8:9; 10:2). The identity of the governor is unknown; both Sheshbazzar (Ezr 5:14) and Zerubbabel (Hg 1:1, 14; 2:2, 21) are identified as governors of Judah in the early Persian period. Mal 1:8 refers to an unnamed governor, and the names of other occupants of the office (Yehoezer, Ahzai, Elnathan) occur on seal impressions, though their date is uncertain. **Urim and Thummim**: cf. Ex 28:30.

*e:* Neh 12:23. *f:* 2 Sm 17:27; 19:32–33; 1 Kgs 2:7. *g:* Nm 27:21; Dt 33:8; 1 Sm 14:41–42; 28:6.

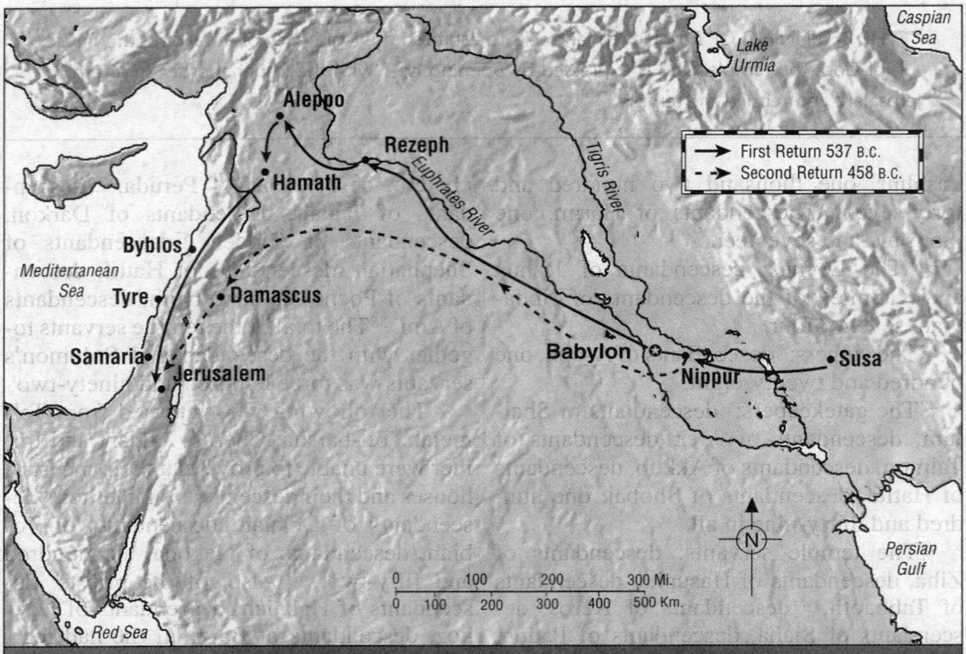


The Return from Exile

[68]When they arrived at the house of the
LORD in Jerusalem, some of the heads of ancestral houses made voluntary offerings for
the house of God, to rebuild it in its place.
[69]According to their means they contributed
to the treasury for the temple service: sixty-
one thousand drachmas of gold, five thousand minas of silver, and one hundred
priestly robes. [70]The priests, the Levites, and
some of the people took up residence in Jerusalem; the singers, the gatekeepers, and
the temple servants settled in their cities.
Thus all the Israelites settled in their cities.

## CHAPTER 3

See RG 145

*Restoration of Worship.* [1h] Now when
the seventh month* came, after the Israelites
had settled in their cities, the people gathered as one in Jerusalem. [2]Then Jeshua, son
of Jozadak, together with his kinsmen the
priests, and Zerubbabel, son of Shealtiel, together with his kinsmen, began building the
altar of the God of Israel in order to offer on
it the burnt offerings prescribed in the law of
Moses, the man of God. [3i] They set the altar
on its foundations, for they lived in fear of
the peoples of the lands,* and offered burnt
offerings to the LORD on it, both morning
and evening. [4j] They also kept the feast of
Booths in the manner prescribed, and they
offered the daily burnt offerings in the
proper number required for each day.
[5]Thereafter they offered regular burnt offerings, the sacrifices prescribed for the new

**3:1–2 The seventh month**: Tishri (September–October), apparently of the first year of the return (538 B.C.), followed by events in the second year (v. 8). In that case it was Sheshbazzar who laid the foundations of the Temple (5:16), and it was in the second year of Darius I (520 B.C.) that Jeshua and Zerubbabel resumed work on the Temple that had been temporarily interrupted (Ezr 4:24–5:1; Hg 1:1; 2:1). The author, or a later editor, has set the construction and dedication of the Temple under Darius I back into the earliest period of the return. Shealtiel was the oldest son of King Jehoiachin (1 Chr 3:17–19); Zerubbabel was therefore Jehoiachin's grandson; see note on Ezr 1:8.

**3:3 Peoples of the lands**: referring either to those who had never left Judah or to neighboring peoples—Edomites, Arabs, inhabitants of Samaria—who opposed those who returned.

*h:* Neh 7:7–78. *i:* Dt 9:25; 1 Kgs 8:64. *j:* Ex 23:16; Nm 28:3–8; Dt 16:13–15.

## The Reinstitution of Worship

THE RESUMPTION OF worship at the site of the ruined temple is described in 3:1–7 as a prelude to building the temple according to rules on the composition of the altar found in Exodus 20:25.

moons and all the festivals sacred to the LORD, and those which anyone might bring as a voluntary offering to the LORD.

*Laying the Foundations of the Temple.* [6]From the first day of the seventh month they reinstituted the burnt offering to the LORD, though the foundation of the LORD's temple had not yet been laid. [7k] Then they hired stonecutters and carpenters, and sent food and drink and oil to the Sidonians and Tyrians that they might ship cedar trees from the Lebanon to the port of Joppa, as Cyrus, king of Persia, had authorized. [8]In the year after their coming to the house of God in Jerusalem, in the second month, Zerubbabel, son of Shealtiel, and Jeshua, son of Jozadak, together with the rest of their kinsmen, the priests and Levites and all who had come from the captivity to Jerusalem, began by appointing the Levites twenty years of age and over to supervise the work on the house of the LORD. [9]Jeshua and his sons and kinsmen, with Kadmiel and Binnui, son of Hodaviah, and their sons and their kindred, the Levites, together undertook to supervise those who were engaged in the work on the house of God. [10l] While the builders were laying the foundation of the LORD's temple, the priests in their vestments were stationed with trumpets and the Levites, sons of Asaph, with cymbals to praise the LORD in the manner laid down by David, king of Israel. [11m] They alternated in songs of praise and thanksgiving to the LORD, "for he is good, for his love for Israel endures forever";* and all the people raised a great shout of joy, praising the LORD because the foundation of the LORD's house had been laid. [12n] Many of the priests, Levites, and heads of ancestral houses, who were old enough to have seen the former house, cried out in sorrow as they watched the foundation of the present house being laid. Many others, however, lifted up their voices in shouts of joy. [13]No one could distinguish the sound of the joyful shouting from the sound of those who were weeping; for the people raised a mighty clamor which was heard far away.

### CHAPTER 4

See RG 145

*Outside Interference.* [1]When the enemies of Judah and Benjamin heard that the exiles were building a temple for the LORD, the God of Israel, [2o] they approached Zerubbabel and the heads of ancestral houses and said to them, "Let us build with you, for we seek your God just as you do, and we have sacrificed to him since the days of Esarhaddon, king of Assyria,* who brought us here." [3]But Zerubbabel, Jeshua, and the rest of the heads of ancestral houses of Israel answered them, "It is not your responsibility to build with us a house for our God, but we alone must build it for the LORD, the God of Israel, as Cyrus king of Persia has commanded us." [4]Thereupon the local inhabitants* discouraged the people of Judah and frightened them off from building. [5]They also bribed counselors to work against them and to frustrate their plans during all the years of Cyrus, king of Persia, and even into the reign of Darius,* king of Persia.

**3:11 "For he is good . . . forever"**: a refrain occurring frequently in liturgies of ancient Israel (cf. Ps 136).

**4:2 Esarhaddon, king of Assyria**: the enemies represent themselves as descendants of foreigners forcibly resettled in the Samaria region after the incorporation of the Northern Kingdom into the Assyrian empire (722 B.C.; cf. 2 Kgs 17:24). We have no record of a settlement under Esarhaddon (681–669 B.C.); the Aramaic source (Ezr 4:10) refers to a different resettlement under Osnappar/Ashurbanipal (668–627 B.C.).

**4:4 Local inhabitants**: lit., "the people of the land."

**4:5 Darius**: Darius I (522–486 B.C.). The Temple-building narrative continues in v. 24. In between (vv. 6–23) is a series of notices about opposition to the returned exiles voiced at the

*k:* 1 Chr 22:4; 2 Chr 2:9. *l:* Ezr 2:41. *m:* 1 Chr 16:34; 2 Chr 5:13; 7:3; Ps 106:1; 136:1; Jer 33:11. *n:* Hg 2:3. *o:* Ezr 4:10.

## Opposition during the Reign of Artaxerxes

THE CORRESPONDENCE IN 4:8 to 6:18, mostly in Aramaic, is out of chronological order. In 4:7–24 it serves thematic functions, documenting how adversaries successfully sabotaged Jewish activities and identifying the opponents as foreigners who displaced the legitimate inhabitants (v. 10).

*Later Hostility.* 6In the reign of Ahasuerus,* at the beginning of his reign, they prepared a written accusation against the inhabitants of Judah and Jerusalem.

7* Again, in the time of Artaxerxes, Tabeel and the rest of his fellow officials, in concert with Mithredath, wrote to Artaxerxes, king of Persia. The document was written in Aramaic and was accompanied by a translation.

8* Then Rehum, the governor, and Shimshai, the scribe, wrote the following letter against Jerusalem to King Artaxerxes: 9"Rehum, the governor, Shimshai, the scribe, and their fellow officials, judges, legates, and agents from among the Persians, Urukians, Babylonians, Susians (that is, Elamites), 10and the other peoples whom the great and illustrious Osnappar* transported and settled in the city of Samaria and elsewhere in the province West-of-Euphrates, as follows . . . ." 11This is a copy of the letter that they sent to him:

"To King Artaxerxes, your servants, the men of West-of-Euphrates, as follows: 12Let it be known to the king that the Jews who came up from you to us have arrived at Jerusalem and are now rebuilding this rebellious and evil city. They are completing its walls, and the foundations have already been laid. 13Now let it be known to the king that if this city is rebuilt and its walls completed, they will no longer pay taxes, tributes, or tolls; eventually the throne will be harmed. 14Now, since we eat the salt of the palace* and it is not fitting for us to look on while the king is being dishonored, we have sent this message to inform the king, 15so that inquiry may be made in the historical records of your fathers. In the historical records you will discover and verify that this is a rebellious city, harmful to kings and provinces; its people have been acting seditiously there since ancient times. That is why this city was destroyed. 16We therefore inform the king, that if this city is rebuilt and its walls completed again, you will thereupon not have a portion in the province West-of-Euphrates."

17The king sent this answer: "To Rehum, the governor, Shimshai, the scribe, and their fellow officials living in Samaria and elsewhere in the province West-of-Euphrates, greetings: 18The communication which you sent us has been read in translation in my presence. 19When at my command inquiry was made, it was verified that from ancient times this city has risen up against kings and that rebellion and sedition have been fostered there. 20Powerful kings once ruled in Jerusalem who controlled all West-of-Euphrates, and taxes, tributes, and tolls were paid to them. 21Give orders, therefore, to stop these men. This city may not be rebuilt until a further decree has been issued by me. 22Take care that you do not neglect this matter. Why should evil increase to harm the throne?"

23p As soon as a copy of King Artaxerxes' letter had been read before Rehum, the governor, Shimshai, the scribe, and their fellow officials, they immediately went to the Jews in Jerusalem and stopped their work by force of arms. 24As a result, work on the house of

Persian court in the early fifth century B.C., after the Temple had been built.

**4:6 Ahasuerus**: Xerxes (486–465 B.C.); the early years of his reign were occupied with revolts in several parts of the empire.

**4:7** There is a note placed in the original text to indicate a change from Hebrew to Aramaic. The Aramaic section beginning here ends with 6:18; in 7:12–26 a royal letter is cited in Aramaic.

**4:8–23** The letter to Artaxerxes I (465–424 B.C.) deals with the building of the fortification walls of Jerusalem, not the building of the Temple. The interruption of the work on the city wall some time before 445 B.C. was the occasion for the arrival of Nehemiah in the province (Neh 1:1–4; 2:1–5).

**4:10 Osnappar**: probably Ashurbanipal; see note on 4:2.

**4:14 Eat the salt of the palace**: the idiom signifies sharing in the benefits of the palace.

p: Neh 1:3.

God in Jerusalem ceased. This interruption lasted until the second year of the reign of Darius,* king of Persia.

See RG 145

## CHAPTER 5

***The Work Resumed Under Darius; Further Problems.*** 1[q] Then the prophets Haggai and Zechariah,* son of Iddo, began to prophesy to the Jews in Judah and Jerusalem in the name of the God of Israel. 2 Thereupon Zerubbabel, son of Shealtiel, and Jeshua, son of Jozadak, began again to build the house of God in Jerusalem, with the prophets of God giving them support. 3 At that time Tattenai, governor of West-of-Euphrates, came to them, along with Shethar-bozenai, and their fellow officials, and asked of them: "Who issued the decree for you to build this house and complete this edifice? 4 What are the names of the men who are building this structure?" 5 But the eye of their God was upon the elders of the Jews, and they were not delayed during the time a report went to Darius and a written order came back concerning this matter.

6 A copy of the letter which Tattenai, governor of West-of-Euphrates, along with Shethar-bozenai and their fellow officials from West-of-Euphrates, sent to King Darius; 7 they sent him a report in which was written the following:

"To King Darius, all good wishes! 8 Let it be known to the king that we have visited the province of Judah and the house of the great God: it is being rebuilt of cut stone and the walls are being reinforced with timber; the work is being carried out diligently, prospering under their hands. 9 We then questioned the elders, addressing to them the following words: 'Who issued the decree for you to build this house and complete this edifice?' 10 We also asked them their names, in order to give you a list of the men who are their leaders. 11 This was their answer to us: 'We are the servants of the God of heaven and earth, and we are rebuilding the house built here many years ago, which a great king of Israel built and completed. 12 But because our ancestors provoked the wrath of the God of heaven, he delivered them into the power of the Chaldean, Nebuchadnezzar, king of Babylon, who destroyed this house and exiled the people to Babylon. 13[r] However, in the first year of Cyrus, king of Babylon, King Cyrus issued a decree for the rebuilding of this house of God. 14 Moreover, the gold and silver vessels of the house of God, which Nebuchadnezzar had taken from the temple in Jerusalem and carried off to the temple in Babylon, King Cyrus ordered to be removed from the temple in Babylon, and they were given to a certain Sheshbazzar, whom he named governor. 15 He commanded him: Take these vessels and deposit them in the temple of Jerusalem, and let the house of God be rebuilt on its former site. 16 Then this same Sheshbazzar came and laid the foundations of the house of God in Jerusalem. Since that time to the present the building has been going on, and is not yet completed.' 17 Now, if it please the king, let a search be made in the royal archives of Babylon to discover whether a decree really was issued by King Cyrus for the rebuilding of this house of God in Jerusalem. And may the king's decision in this matter be communicated to us."

## CHAPTER 6

See RG 145

***The Decree of Darius.*** 1* Thereupon King Darius issued an order to search the archives in which the treasures were stored in Babylon. 2[s] However, a scroll was found in Ecbatana, the stronghold in the province of Media, containing the following text: "Memorandum. 3 In the first year of his

**4:24 The second year . . . of Darius**: that is, 520 B.C.; it marks the beginning of the successful restoration of the Temple, completed within the five years following (5:1–6:18).

**5:1 The prophets Haggai and Zechariah**: Haggai and Zechariah were active during the early years of Darius I. They document the rebuilding of the Temple and the messianic expectations associated with the Davidic descendant Zerubbabel.

**6:1–2** Babylon was the capital city of the satrapy to which Judah belonged; it was therefore the natural place to look. The decree was discovered eventually, however, in Ecbatana (Hamadan), the former capital of the Medes and summer residence of the Persian kings. Cf. the Hebrew version of the decree (1:2–4).

*q:* Hg 1:14–2:9; Zec 4:9. *r:* Ezr 1:1–5. *s:* Ezr 1:4–11.

THE SCROLL WITH Cyrus' decree is found in Ecbatana, the summer residence of Persian kings, now Hamadan in Iran. This archival version of Cyrus' decree (6:2–5) emphasizes building size and funding and is more generous than the public version (1:1–4) in explicitly offering royal financial support. Darius' subsequent decree also provides funds from the royal treasury and gives extremely generous support (vv. 8–9).

reign, King Cyrus issued a decree: With regard to the house of God in Jerusalem: the house is to be rebuilt as a place for offering sacrifices and bringing burnt offerings. Its height is to be sixty cubits and its width sixty cubits. [4]It shall have three courses of cut stone for each one of timber. The costs are to be borne by the royal house. [5]Also, let the gold and silver vessels of the house of God which Nebuchadnezzar took from the temple of Jerusalem and brought to Babylon be sent back; let them be returned to their place in the temple of Jerusalem and deposited in the house of God."

[6]"Now, therefore, Tattenai, governor of West-of-Euphrates, and Shethar-bozenai, and you, their fellow officials in West-of-Euphrates, stay away from there. [7]Let the governor and the elders of the Jews continue the work on that house of God; they are to rebuild it on its former site. [8]I also issue this decree concerning your dealing with these elders of the Jews in the rebuilding of that house of God: Let these men be repaid for their expenses, in full and without delay from the royal revenue, deriving from the taxes of West-of-Euphrates, so that the work not be interrupted. [9]Whatever else is required—young bulls, rams, and lambs for burnt offerings to the God of heaven, wheat, salt, wine, and oil, according to the requirements of the priests who are in Jerusalem—let that be delivered to them day by day without fail, [10]that they may continue to offer sacrifices of pleasing odor to the God of heaven and pray for the life of the king and his sons. [11]I also issue this decree: if any man alters this edict, a beam is to be taken from his house, and he is to be lifted up and impaled on it; and his house is to be reduced to rubble for this offense. [12]And may the God who causes his name to dwell there overthrow every king or people who may undertake to alter this decree or to destroy this house of God in Jerusalem. I, Darius, have issued this decree; let it be diligently executed."

***The Task Finally Completed.*** [13]Then Tattenai, the governor of West-of-Euphrates, and Shethar-bozenai, and their fellow officials carried out with all diligence the instructions King Darius had sent them. [14]The elders of the Jews continued to make progress in the building, supported by the message of the prophets, Haggai and Zechariah, son of Iddo. They finished the building according to the command of the God of Israel and the decrees of Cyrus and Darius, and of Artaxerxes, king of Persia. [15]They completed this house on the third day of the month Adar, in the sixth year of the reign of King Darius. [16]The Israelites—priests, Levites, and the other returned exiles—celebrated the dedication of this house of God with joy. [17]For the dedication of this house of God, they offered one hundred bulls, two hundred rams, and four hundred lambs, together with twelve he-goats as a sin offering for all Israel, in keeping with the number of the tribes of Israel. [18]Finally, they set up the priests in their classes and the Levites in their divisions for the service of God in Jerusalem, as is prescribed in the book of Moses.

***The Passover.*** [19][t] The returned exiles kept the Passover on the fourteenth day of the first month. [20]The Levites, every one of whom had purified himself for the occasion, sacrificed the Passover for all the exiles, for their colleagues the priests, and for themselves. [21]The Israelites who had returned from the exile and all those who had separated themselves from the uncleanness of the Gentiles in the land shared in it, seeking the LORD, the

---

*t:* Ex 12:1–20; 2 Chr 30:14–27; 35:1–19.

**The First Passover in the Rebuilt Temple**

AS A CELEBRATION of God's miraculous deliverance and the formation of the people into a nation, Passover was a powerful symbol of identity. Since some viewed the return as a second Exodus, those who had been exiled and returned clearly would be recognized as part of Israel. The population that remained behind joined the exiled community by separating from the surrounding peoples (6:21).

God of Israel. [22u] They joyfully kept the feast
of Unleavened Bread for seven days, for the
LORD had filled them with joy by making the
king of Assyria* favorable to them, so that he
gave them help in their work on the house of
God, the God of Israel.

## II. The Work of Ezra

### CHAPTER 7

See RG 145–47

*Ezra, Priest and Scribe.* [1*v] After
these events, during the reign of Artaxerxes,
king of Persia, Ezra, son of Seraiah, son of
Azariah, son of Hilkiah, [2]son of Shallum,
son of Zadok, son of Ahitub, [3]son of Amariah, son of Azariah, son of Meraioth, [4]son
of Zerahiah, son of Uzzi, son of Bukki, [5]son
of Abishua, son of Phinehas, son of Eleazar,
son of Aaron, the high priest— [6w] this Ezra
came up from Babylon. He was a scribe,
well-versed in the law of Moses given by the
LORD, the God of Israel. The king granted
him all that he requested, because the hand
of the LORD, his God, was over him.

[7]Some of the Israelites and some priests,
Levites, singers, gatekeepers, and temple
servants also came up to Jerusalem in the
seventh year of King Artaxerxes. [8]Ezra
came to Jerusalem in the fifth month of that
seventh year of the king. [9]On the first day of
the first month he began the journey up from
Babylon, and on the first day of the fifth
month he arrived at Jerusalem, for the favoring hand of his God was over him. [10x] Ezra
had set his heart on the study and practice of
the law of the LORD and on teaching statutes
and ordinances in Israel.

*The Decree of Artaxerxes.* [11]This is a copy
of the rescript which King Artaxerxes gave
to Ezra the priest-scribe, the scribe versed in
matters concerning the LORD's commandments and statutes for Israel:

[12y] "Artaxerxes, king of kings, to Ezra the
priest, scribe of the law of the God of heaven,
greetings! And now, [13]I have issued this decree, that anyone in my kingdom belonging
to the people of Israel, its priests or Levites,
who is willing to go up to Jerusalem with
you, may go, [14]for you are the one sent by the
king and his seven counselors to supervise
Judah and Jerusalem with regard to the law
of your God which is in your possession,
[15]and to bring the silver and gold which the
king and his counselors have freely contributed to the God of Israel, whose dwelling
is in Jerusalem, [16]as well as all the silver and
gold which you may receive throughout the
province of Babylon, together with the voluntary offerings the people and priests freely
contribute for the house of their God in Jerusalem. [17]Therefore, you must use this money
with all diligence to buy bulls, rams, lambs,
and the grain offerings and libations proper
to these, and offer them on the altar of the
house of your God in Jerusalem. [18]You and
your kinsmen may do whatever seems best to
you with the remainder of the silver and gold,
as your God wills. [19]The vessels given to you

**6:22 The king of Assyria**: "Assyria" is perhaps used in a broad sense for the Persian empire; or the editor may have in mind the account of Hezekiah's Passover which refers to those who had escaped the hand of the king of Assyria (2 Chr 30:6).

**7:1–10** The editor's introduction to Ezra's autobiographical narrative. The context suggests the seventh year of Artaxerxes I, therefore, 458 B.C., as the date of Ezra's arrival in Jerusalem. The arguments often advanced for 398 B.C., the seventh year of Artaxerxes II, or less often for the thirty-seventh year of Artaxerxes I, that is, 428 B.C., are inconclusive. For Ezra's descent from Aaron, the editor has drawn selectively on 1 Chr 5:27–41. Seraiah, the chief priest executed by the Babylonians after the fall of Jerusalem (2 Kgs 25:18–21), cannot be Ezra's father in a literal sense, and Ezra was not himself high priest.

*u:* 2 Chr 30:6. *v:* 1 Chr 5:27–41. *w:* Ezr 7:28; 8:18; Neh 2:8, 18. *x:* Ps 119:45. *y:* Ezr 1:2–4.

**The Narrator's Introduction of Ezra**

EZRA'S LONG PEDIGREE (7:1–6) establishes his credentials as priest of the most distinguished line and scribe—two roles that will account for his stature and acceptance within the Jewish community. Ezra's goals of studying, teaching, and implementing the Torah (v. 10) account for his subsequent actions.

for the service of the house of your God you
are to deposit before the God of Jerusalem.
[20]Whatever else you may be required to supply for the needs of the house of your God,
you may draw from the royal treasury. [21]I,
Artaxerxes the king, issue this decree to all
the treasurers of West-of-Euphrates: Whatever Ezra the priest, scribe of the law of the
God of heaven, requests of you, let it be done
with all diligence, [22]within these limits: silver, one hundred talents; wheat, one hundred
kors;* wine, one hundred baths; oil, one hundred baths; salt, without limit. [23]Let everything that is decreed by the God of heaven be
carried out exactly for the house of the God
of heaven, that wrath may not come upon the
realm of the king and his sons. [24]We also inform you that it is not permitted to impose
taxes, tributes, or tolls on any priest, Levite,
singer, gatekeeper, temple servant, or any
other servant of that house of God.

[25][z]"As for you, Ezra, in accordance with
the wisdom of your God* which is in your
possession, appoint magistrates and judges
to administer justice to all the people in
West-of-Euphrates, to all, that is, who know
the laws of your God. Instruct those who do
not know these laws. [26]All who will not
obey the law of your God and the law of the
king, let judgment be executed upon them
with all diligence, whether death, or corporal punishment, or confiscation of goods, or
imprisonment."

***Ezra Prepares for the Journey.*** [27]Blessed
be the LORD, the God of our ancestors, who
put it into the heart of the king thus to glorify
the house of the LORD in Jerusalem, [28][a]and
who let me find favor with the king, with his
counselors, and with all the most influential
royal officials. I therefore took courage and,
with the hand of the LORD, my God, over
me, I gathered together Israelite leaders to
make the return journey with me.

## CHAPTER 8

See RG 145–47

***Ezra's Caravan.*** [1]These are the heads
of the ancestral houses and the genealogies
of those who returned with me from Babylon during the reign of King Artaxerxes:

[2]Of the descendants of Phinehas, Gershon;
of the descendants of Ithamar, Daniel; of the
descendants of David, Hattush, [3]son of Shecaniah; of the descendants of Parosh, Zechariah,
and with him one hundred and fifty males
were enrolled; [4]of the descendants of Pahath-
moab, Eliehoenai, son of Zerahiah, and with
him two hundred males; [5]of the descendants
of Zattu, Shecaniah, son of Jahaziel, and with
him three hundred males; [6]of the descendants
of Adin, Ebed, son of Jonathan, and with him
fifty males; [7]of the descendants of Elam, Jeshaiah, son of Athaliah, and with him seventy
males; [8]of the descendants of Shephatiah,
Zebadiah, son of Michael, and with him
eighty males; [9]of the descendants of Joab,
Obadiah, son of Jehiel, and with him two hundred and eighteen males; [10]of the descendants
of Bani, Shelomoth, son of Josiphiah, and
with him one hundred and sixty males; [11]of the
descendants of Bebai, Zechariah, son of Bebai, and with him twenty-eight males; [12]of the
descendants of Azgad, Johanan, son of Hak-
katan, and with him one hundred and ten
males; [13]of the descendants of Adonikam,
younger sons, whose names were Eliphelet,
Jeiel, and Shemaiah, and with them sixty
males; [14]of the descendants of Bigvai, Uthai,
son of Zakkur, and with him seventy males.

**7:22 Kors**: see note on Ez 45:14; **baths**: see note on Is 5:10.

**7:25 The wisdom of your God**: with reference to the law (cf. Dt 4:6). The law in question was certainly not new, since it was assumed to be known by Jews in Judah and elsewhere. It corresponded to Pentateuchal law, though perhaps this had not yet been given its final form.

*z:* Dt 4:6; 2 Chr 17:7–9; Ps 37:30–31; 119:98. *a:* Ezr 7:6.

AT FIRST READING the statement in 6:14 that the Israelites finished their building under the decrees of Kings Cyrus, Darius, and Artaxerxes seems incorrect; the physical temple was completed in the reign of Darius and Artaxerxes had nothing to do with it. However, the formation of the "house of God" (6:16) involved not only rebuilding the temple, but also rebuilding the city and separating the community from the surrounding peoples by prohibiting intermarriages. These later steps, under reformers Ezra and Nehemiah, occurred in the time of Artaxerxes.

***Final Preparations for the Journey.*** [15]I assembled them by the river that flows toward Ahava,* where we camped for three days. There I perceived that both laymen and priests were present, but I could not discover a single Levite. [16]So I sent for discerning leaders, Eliezer, Ariel, Shemaiah, Jarib, Elnathan, Nathan, Zechariah, and Meshullam, [17]with a command for Iddo, the leader in the place Casiphia, instructing them what to say to Iddo and his kinsmen, and to the temple servants in Casiphia, in order to procure for us ministers for the house of our God. [18b] Since the favoring hand of our God was over us, they sent to us a well-instructed man, one of the descendants of Mahli, son of Levi, son of Israel, namely Sherebiah, with his sons and kinsmen, eighteen men. [19]They also sent us Hashabiah, and with him Jeshaiah, descendants of Merari, and their kinsmen and their sons, twenty men. [20c] Of the temple servants, those whom David and the princes appointed to serve the Levites, there were two hundred and twenty. All these were enrolled by name.

[21]Then I proclaimed a fast, there by the river of Ahava, that we might humble ourselves before our God to seek from him a safe journey for ourselves, our children, and all our possessions. [22d] For I was ashamed to ask the king for troops and horsemen to protect us against enemies along the way, since we had said to the king, "The favoring hand of our God is over all who seek him, but his fierce anger is against all who forsake him." [23]So we fasted, seeking this from our God, and it was granted. [24]Next I selected twelve of the priestly leaders along with Sherebiah, Hashabiah, and ten of their kinsmen, [25]and I weighed out before them the silver and the gold and the vessels offered for the house of our God by the king, his counselors, his officials, and all the Israelites of that region. [26]I weighed out into their hands these amounts: silver, six hundred and fifty talents; silver vessels, one hundred; gold, one hundred talents; [27]twenty golden bowls valued at a thousand darics; two vases of excellent polished bronze, as precious as gold. [28]I addressed them in these words: "You are consecrated to the LORD, and the vessels are also consecrated; the silver and the gold are a voluntary offering to the LORD, the God of your ancestors. [29]Watch over them carefully until you weigh them out in Jerusalem in the presence of the chief priests and Levites and the leaders of ancestral houses of Israel, in the chambers of the house of the LORD." [30]The priests and the Levites then took over the silver, the gold, and the vessels that had been weighed out, to bring them to Jerusalem, to the house of our God.

***Arrival in Jerusalem.*** [31]We set out from the river of Ahava on the twelfth day of the first month to go to Jerusalem. The hand of our God remained over us, and he protected us from enemies and robbers along the way. [32]We arrived in Jerusalem, where we rested for three days. [33]On the fourth day, the silver, the gold, and the vessels were weighed out in the house of our God and given to the priest Meremoth, son of Uriah, with whom was Eleazar, son of Phinehas; they were assisted by the Levites Jozabad, son of Jeshua, and Noadiah, son of Binnui. [34]Everything was in order as to number and weight, and

**8:15 Ahava**: an unidentified location near Babylon; also the name of the river or canal on which it stood (vv. 21, 31). A location near water was dictated by ritual as well as practical reasons (cf. Ps 137:1; Ez 1:1, 3; 3:15).

*b:* Ezr 7:6. *c:* Ezr 2:43. *d:* Neh 2:9.

**The Crisis of Mixed Marriages**

THE CRISIS IN this second stage of reconstruction comes when men, including Jewish leaders, marry foreign women (9:1–2). To ensure survival as a small minority in the midst of surrounding cultures, Ezra advocates this not be allowed.

the total weight was registered. At that same time, [35]those who had returned from the captivity, the exiles, offered as burnt offerings to the God of Israel twelve bulls for all Israel, ninety-six rams, seventy-seven lambs, and twelve goats as sin offerings: all these as a burnt offering to the LORD. [36*] Finally, the orders of the king were presented to the king's satraps and to the governors in West-of-Euphrates, who gave their support to the people and to the house of God.

## CHAPTER 9

See RG 145–47

*The Crisis of Mixed Marriages.* [1e] When these matters had been concluded, the leaders approached me with this report: "Neither the Israelite laymen nor the priests nor the Levites have kept themselves separate from the peoples of the lands and their abominations—Canaanites, Hittites, Perizzites, Jebusites, Ammonites, Moabites, Egyptians, and Amorites—[2]for they have taken some of their daughters as wives for themselves and their sons, thus intermingling the holy seed with the peoples of the lands. Furthermore, the leaders and rulers have taken a prominent part in this apostasy!"

*Ezra's Reaction.* [3f] When I had heard this, I tore my cloak and my mantle, plucked hair from my head and beard, and sat there devastated. [4g] Around me gathered all who were in dread of the sentence of the God of Israel* on the apostasy of the exiles, while I remained devastated until the evening sacrifice. [5]Then, at the time of the evening sacrifice, I rose in my wretchedness, and with cloak and mantle torn I fell on my knees, stretching out my hands to the LORD, my God.

*A Penitential Prayer.* [6*] [h] I said: "My God, I am too ashamed and humiliated to raise my face to you, my God, for our wicked deeds are heaped up above our heads and our guilt reaches up to heaven. [7]From the time of our ancestors even to this day our guilt has been great, and for our wicked deeds we have been delivered, we and our kings and our priests, into the hands of the kings of foreign lands, to the sword, to captivity, to pillage, and to disgrace, as is the case today.

[8i] "And now, only a short time ago, mercy came to us from the LORD, our God, who left us a remnant and gave us a stake in his holy place; thus our God has brightened our eyes and given us relief in our slavery. [9j] For slaves we are, but in our slavery our God has not abandoned us; rather, he has turned the good will of the kings of Persia toward us. Thus he has given us new life to raise again the house of our God and restore its ruins, and has granted us a protective wall in Judah and Jerusalem. [10]But now, our God, what can we say after all this? For we have abandoned your commandments, [11k] which you gave through your servants the prophets: The land which you are entering to take as your possession is a land unclean with the filth of the peoples of the lands, with the abominations with which they have filled it from one end to the other by their uncleanness. [12l] Do not, then, give your daughters to their sons in marriage, and do not take their daughters for your sons. Never promote their welfare and prosperity; thus you will grow strong, enjoy the produce of the land, and leave it as an inheritance to your children forever.

**8:36** The story of Ezra's mission is apparently continued from this point by Neh 7:72b–8:18, which may be read before Ezr 9:1.

**9:4 All who were in dread . . . God of Israel**: lit., "all who trembled"; these people are also mentioned at 10:3, and a similar designation occurs at Is 66:2, 5, a text more or less contemporary with this passage. The allusion may be to a distinct social group of rigorist tendencies who supported Ezra's marriage reform.

**9:6–15** The prayer attributed to Ezra is a communal confession of sin, of a kind characteristic of the Second Temple period (cf. Neh 9:6–37; Dn 9:4–19; 1QS 1:4–2:1), but adapted to the present situation.

*e:* Dt 7:1; Neh 9:2. *f:* Ps 119:136. *g:* Ezr 10:3; Is 66:2, 5. *h:* Neh 9:6–37; Ps 38:4; Dn 9:4–19. *i:* Is 4:3. *j:* Ps 106:46. *k:* Lv 18:24–25; Ez 36:17. *l:* Dt 7:3.

**Ezra's Prayer**

MORE A SERMON than a confession, the prayer in 9:5–15 teaches values and history to alter community behavior. Like the prophets and the deuteronomistic history, Ezra interprets Israel's political devastation as the consequence of religious and moral failings by Israel and uses the fear of a recurrence to motivate the community.

13"After all that has come upon us for our
evil deeds and our great guilt—though you,
our God, have made less of our sinfulness
than it deserved and have allowed us to survive as we do— 14shall we again violate your
commandments by intermarrying with these
abominable peoples? Would you not become
so angered with us as to destroy us without
remnant or survivor? 15LORD, God of Israel,
you are just; yet we have been spared, the
remnant we are today. Here we are before
you in our sins. Because of all this, we can no
longer stand in your presence."

## CHAPTER 10

See RG 145–47

*Response to the Crisis.* 1While Ezra
prayed and acknowledged their guilt, weeping and prostrate before the house of God, a
very large assembly of Israelites gathered
about him, men, women, and children; and
the people wept profusely. 2Then Shecaniah,
the son of Jehiel, one of the descendants of
Elam, made this appeal to Ezra: "We have
indeed betrayed our God by taking as wives
foreign women of the peoples of the land.
Yet in spite of this there still remains a hope
for Israel. 3Let us therefore enter into a covenant before our God to dismiss all our foreign wives and the children born of them, in
keeping with what you, my lord, advise, and
those who are in dread of the commandments of our God. Let it be done according
to the law! 4Rise, then, for this is your duty!
We are with you, so have courage and act!"

5Ezra stood and demanded an oath from
the leaders of the priests, from the Levites
and from all Israel that they would do as had
been proposed; and they swore it. 6Then
Ezra left his place before the house of God
and entered the chamber of Johanan, son of
Eliashib,* where he spent the night neither
eating food nor drinking water, for he was in
mourning over the apostasy of the exiles. 7A
proclamation was made throughout Judah
and Jerusalem that all the exiles should
gather together in Jerusalem, 8and that whoever failed to appear within three days
would, according to the judgment of the
leaders and elders, suffer the confiscation of
all his possessions, and would be excluded
from the assembly of the exiles.

9All the men of Judah and Benjamin gathered together in Jerusalem within the three-
day period: it was in the ninth month,* on the
twentieth day of the month. All the people,
sitting in the open place before the house of
God, were trembling both over the matter at
hand and because it was raining. 10m Then
Ezra, the priest, stood up and said to them:
"Your apostasy in taking foreign women as
wives has added to Israel's guilt. 11But now,
give praise to the LORD, the God of your ancestors, and do his will: separate yourselves
from the peoples of the land and from the
foreign women." 12In answer, the whole assembly cried out with a loud voice: "Yes, it
is our duty to do as you say! 13But the people are numerous and it is the rainy season,
so that we cannot remain outside; besides,
this is not a task that can be performed in a
single day or even two, for those of us who
have sinned in this regard are many. 14Let
our leaders represent the whole assembly;
then let all those in our cities who have taken

**10:6 Johanan, son of Eliashib**: if this Eliashib is identical with the high priest of that name during Nehemiah's mission (Neh 3:1), it would be difficult to avoid the conclusion that Ezra followed Nehemiah. But Eliashib is a common name, and, on the hypothesis of Nehemiah's chronological priority, it would be unlikely that Ezra would consort with a family which had "defiled the priesthood" (Neh 13:28–29).

**10:9 The ninth month**: Kislev (November–December), during the first of two rainy seasons in Palestine.

*m*: Neh 9:2.

**Results: Compliance with Communal Decision**

THE ISSUE OF mixed marriages constitutes the first test of the new, legal status of the Torah, illustrating how an ancient book may shape the present and future through communal interpretive process. Verses 18–19 give an explicit report that the high priest's most powerful family fully complied with the communal decision. Given the power of that family over the community, its cooperation and compliance signal a crucial victory for this process.

foreign women for wives appear at appointed times, accompanied by the elders
and magistrates of each city in question, till
we have turned away from us our God's
burning anger over this affair." 15 Only Jonathan, son of Asahel, and Jahzeiah, son of
Tikvah, were against this proposal, with Meshullam and Shabbethai the Levite supporting them.
16* The exiles did as agreed. Ezra the priest
appointed as his assistants men who were
heads of ancestral houses, one for each ancestral house, all of them designated by name.
They held sessions to examine the matter, beginning with the first day of the tenth month.
17 By the first day of the first month they had
finished dealing with all the men who had
taken foreign women for wives.
***The List of Transgressors.*** 18 Among the
priests, the following were found to have
taken foreign women for wives: Of the descendants of Jeshua, son of Jozadak, and his
kinsmen: Maaseiah, Eliezer, Jarib, and Gedaliah. 19 They pledged themselves to dismiss
their wives, and as a guilt offering for their
guilt they gave a ram from the flock. 20 Of the
descendants of Immer: Hanani and Zebadiah;
21 of the descendants of Harim: Maaseiah, Elijah, Shemaiah, Jehiel, and Uzziah; 22 of the
descendants of Pashhur: Elioenai, Maaseiah,
Ishmael, Nethanel, Jozabad, and Elasah.
23[n] Of the Levites: Jozabad, Shimei, Kela-
iah (also called Kelita), Pethahiah, Judah,
and Eliezer.
24 Of the singers: Eliashib; of the gatekeepers: Shallum, Telem, and Uri.
25 Of the people of Israel: Of the descendants of Parosh: Ramiah, Izziah, Malchijah,
Mijamin, Eleazar, Malchijah, and Benaiah;
26 of the descendants of Elam: Mattaniah,
Zechariah, Jehiel, Abdi, Jeremoth, and Elijah; 27 of the descendants of Zattu: Elioenai,
Eliashib, Mattaniah, Jeremoth, Zabad, and
Aziza; 28 of the descendants of Bebai: Jehohanan, Hananiah, Zabbai, and Athlai; 29 of
the descendants of Bani: Meshullam, Malluch, Adaiah, Jashub, Sheal, and Jeremoth;
30 of the descendants of Pahath-moab: Adna,
Chelal, Benaiah, Maaseiah, Mattaniah, Bezalel, Binnui, and Manasseh; 31 of the descendants of Harim: Eliezer, Isshijah, Malchijah,
Shemaiah, Shimeon, 32 Benjamin, Malluch,
Shemariah; 33 of the descendants of Hashum:
Mattenai, Mattattah, Zabad, Eliphelet, Jere-
mai, Manasseh, Shimei; 34 of the descendants of Begui: Maadai, Amram, Uel, 35 Benaiah, Bedeiah, Cheluhi, 36 Vaniah,
Meremoth, Eliashib, 37 Mattaniah, Mattenai,
and Jaasu; 38 of the descendants of Binnui:
Shimei, 39 Shelemiah, Nathan, and Adaiah;
40 of the descendants of Zachai: Shashai,
Sharai, 41 Azarel, Shelemiah, Shemariah,
42 Shallum, Amariah, Joseph; 43 of the descendants of Nebo: Jeiel, Mattithiah, Zabad,
Zebina, Jaddai, Joel, Benaiah.
44* All these had taken foreign wives; but
they sent them away, both the women and
their children.

**10:16–17** The work of the committee lasted three months, from the first day of the tenth month, Tebeth (December–January), to the first day of the first month, Nisan (March–April), of the following year.

**10:44** Some scholars find the continuation of the account of the marriage reform in Neh 9:1–5, though the date given at Neh 9:1 would fit better after Ezr 10:15; cf. Hg 2:10–14. The abrupt conclusion to Ezr 9–10 suggests that the policy of forced separation from foreign wives, not mandated by any law known to us, did not succeed. Assuming the chronological priority of Ezra, marriage outside the community was still prevalent during Nehemiah's administration, and the remarkable demographic expansion of Judaism in the following centuries would be difficult to explain if Ezra's measures had been put into effect.

*n:* Neh 8:7; 10:11.

See RG 144–50

# The Book of Nehemiah

Problems common to the combined books Ezra-Nehemiah have been pointed out in the Introduction to the Book of Ezra. The achievements of the two men were complementary; each helped to make it possible for Judaism to maintain its identity during the difficult days of the Restoration. Ezra was the great religious reformer who succeeded in establishing the Torah as the constitution of the returned community. Nehemiah, governor of the province of Judah, was the man of action who rebuilt the walls of Jerusalem and introduced necessary administrative reforms.

The biblical sources for Nehemiah's life and work are the autobiographical portions scattered through the book. They are called the "Memoirs of Nehemiah," and have been used more effectively by the editor than the "Memoirs of Ezra." The substantial authenticity of Nehemiah's memoirs is widely accepted. From these and other sources, the picture emerges of a man dedicated to the single purpose of the welfare of his people. While serving as cupbearer to the king at the Persian court in Susa, Nehemiah received permission from Artaxerxes I to fortify Jerusalem, and served as governor of Judah for two terms, the first lasting twelve years (445–432 B.C.), the second of unknown length (Neh 5:14; 13:6). Despite temperamental shortcomings, Nehemiah was a man of good practical sense combined with deep faith in God. He used his influence as governor of Judah to serve God and the fledgling Jewish community in Jerusalem.

The Book of Nehemiah is divided as follows:

I. The Deeds of Nehemiah (1:1–7:72)
II. Promulgation of the Law (8:1–10:40)
III. Dedication of the Wall; Other Reforms (11:1–13:31)

## I. The Deeds of Nehemiah

### CHAPTER 1

See RG 148

*Nehemiah Hears Bad News.* [1*] The words of Nehemiah, son of Hacaliah.

In the month Kislev of the twentieth year, I was in the citadel of Susa [2] when Hanani, one of my brothers, came with other men from Judah. I asked them about the Jews, the remnant preserved after the captivity, and about Jerusalem. [3] They answered me: "The survivors of the captivity there in the province are in great distress and under reproach. The wall of Jerusalem has been breached, its gates gutted by fire." [4] When I heard this report, I began to weep and continued mourning for several days, fasting and praying before the God of heaven.

[5*] [a] I prayed: "LORD, God of heaven, great and awesome God, you preserve your covenant of mercy with those who love you and keep your commandments. [6] [b] May your ears be attentive, and your eyes open, to hear the prayer that I, your servant, now offer in your presence day and night for your servants the Israelites, confessing the sins we have committed against you, I and my ancestral house included. [7] [c] We have greatly offended you, not keeping the commandments, the statutes, and the ordinances you entrusted to your servant Moses. [8] [d] But remember the admonition which you addressed to Moses, your servant, when you said: If you prove faithless, I will scatter you among the peoples; [9] but if you return to me and carefully keep my commandments, even though your outcasts have been driven to the farthest corner of the world, I will gather them from there, and bring them back to the place I

**1:1** The first mission of Nehemiah, from the twentieth year of Artaxerxes I, lasted from the spring (2:1) of 445 B.C. until 433 B.C. (5:14). It is recounted in 1:1–6:15; 12:27–43; 6:16–7:5; 11:1–21; in terms of chronology, these texts may usefully be read in that order. **Kislev**: the ninth month (November–December). **Susa**: the winter residence of the Persian kings, in southwest Iran.

**1:5** Nehemiah's prayer is a communal confession of sin, characteristic of Second Temple piety; cf. Ezr 9:6–15; Neh 9:6–37; Dn 9:4–19.

*a:* Dt 7:9, 12; Dn 9:4. *b:* 2 Chr 6:40. *c:* Dn 3:29–30. *d:* Dt 30:1–5.

NEHEMIAH OPENS WITH a first-person narrative relating his concerns over Jerusalem and the Persian monarch's appointment of him as governor over the province. The bulk of the account covers the various incidents of Nehemiah's rule as governor as he attempted to rebuild the walls of Jerusalem.

have chosen as the dwelling place for my
name. 10e They are your servants, your people, whom you freed by your great might
and strong hand. 11f LORD, may your ears be
attentive to the prayer of your servant and
that of all your servants who willingly revere
your name. Grant success to your servant
this day, and let him find favor with this
man"—for I was cupbearer to the king.*

## CHAPTER 2

See RG 148

*Appointment by the King.* 1In the
month Nisan of the twentieth year of King
Artaxerxes, when the wine was in my
charge, I took some and offered it to the
king. Because I had never before been sad in
his presence, 2the king asked me, "Why do
you look sad? If you are not sick, you must
be sad at heart." Though I was seized with
great fear, 3I answered the king: "May the
king live forever! How could I not look sad
when the city where my ancestors are buried
lies in ruins, and its gates consumed by
fire?" 4The king asked me, "What is it, then,
that you wish?" I prayed to the God of
heaven 5and then answered the king: "If it
please the king, and if your servant is deserving of your favor, send me to Judah, to
the city where my ancestors are buried, that
I may rebuild it." 6Then the king, with the
queen seated beside him, asked me, "How
long will your journey take and when will
you return?" My answer was acceptable to
the king and he agreed to let me go; I set a
date for my return.
7I asked the king further: "If it please the
king, let letters be given to me for the governors of West-of-Euphrates, that they may
give me safe-conduct till I arrive in Judah;
8g also a letter for Asaph, the keeper of the
royal woods, that he may give me timber to
make beams for the gates of the temple
citadel, for the city wall and the house that I
will occupy." Since I enjoyed the good favor
of my God, the king granted my requests.
9h Thus I proceeded to the governors of
West-of-Euphrates and presented the king's
letters to them. The king also sent with me
army officers and cavalry.
10When Sanballat the Horonite* and Tobiah the Ammonite official had heard of this,
they were very much displeased that someone
had come to improve the lot of the Israelites.
*Circuit of the City.* 11i When I arrived in
Jerusalem, and had been there three days, 12I
set out by night with only a few other men
and with no other animals but my own
mount (for I had not told anyone what my
God had inspired me to do for Jerusalem).
13* I rode out at night by the Valley Gate,
passed by the Dragon Spring, and came to
the Dung Gate, observing how the walls of

**1:11 Cupbearer to the king**: an important official in the royal household.

**2:10 Sanballat the Horonite**: the governor of the province of Samaria (3:33–34), apparently a native of one of the Beth-horons. A letter from the Jews living at Elephantine in southern Egypt, dated 408–407 B.C., mentions "Delayah and Shelemyah, the sons of Sanballat, the governor of Samaria," and papyri discovered in the Wadi ed-Dâliyeh in the Jordan Valley refer to a Sanballat, governor of Samaria, during the last years of Persian rule. Although his own name was Babylonian—Sin-uballit, i.e., "Sin (the moon god) has given life"—his two sons had names based on the divine name Yhwh. **Tobiah the Ammonite official**: the governor of the province of Ammon in Transjordan. His title, "official," lit., "servant" (in Hebrew, *'ebed*), could also be understood as "slave," and Nehemiah perhaps meant it in this derogatory sense. The Tobiads remained a powerful family even in Maccabean times, and something of their history is known from 2 Maccabees (3:11; 12:17), Josephus (*Antiquities* 12:160–236), the Zeno papyri of the third century B.C., and excavation at ʿAraq el-ʿEmir in Jordan. Sanballat and Tobiah, together with Geshem the Arab (Neh 2:19; 6:1–2), who was probably in charge of Edom and the regions to the south and southeast of Judah, opposed the rebuilding of Jerusalem's walls on political grounds; the city was the capital of a rival province.

**2:13–15** Nehemiah left Jerusalem by the Valley Gate near the northwestern end of the old City of David and went south

*e:* Dt 9:29. *f:* Ps 118:25. *g:* Ezr 7:6. *h:* Ezr 8:22. *i:* Ezr 8:32.

Jerusalem were breached and its gates consumed by fire. [14]Then I passed over to the
Fountain Gate and to the King's Pool. Since
there was no room here for my mount to pass
with me astride, [15]I continued on foot up the
wadi by night, inspecting the wall all the
while, until I once more reached the Valley
Gate, by which I went back in. [16]The magistrates knew nothing of where I had gone or
what I was doing, for as yet I had disclosed
nothing to the Jews, neither to the priests,
nor to the nobles, nor to the magistrates, nor
to the others who were to do the work.
***Decision to Rebuild the City Wall.*** [17]After-
ward I said to them: "You see the trouble we
are in: how Jerusalem lies in ruins and its
gates have been gutted by fire. Come, let us
rebuild the wall of Jerusalem, so that we may
no longer be a reproach!" [18j]Then I explained to them how God had shown his gracious favor to me, and what the king had said
to me. They replied, "Let us begin building!"
And they undertook the work with vigor.
[19]When they heard about this, Sanballat
the Horonite, Tobiah the Ammonite official,
and Geshem the Arab* mocked and ridiculed
us. "What are you doing?" they asked. "Are
you rebelling against the king?" [20]My answer to them was this: "It is the God of
heaven who will grant us success. We, his
servants, shall set about the rebuilding; but
you have neither share nor claim nor memorial* in Jerusalem."

## CHAPTER 3

See RG 148

***List of Workers.*** [1*k]Eliashib the high
priest and his priestly kinsmen took up the
task of rebuilding the Sheep Gate. They consecrated it and set up its doors, its bolts, and
its bars, then continued the rebuilding to the
Tower of the Hundred, the Tower of Hananel. [2]At their side the men of Jericho were rebuilding, and next to them was Zaccur, son of
Imri. [3l]The Fish Gate was rebuilt by the people of Hassenaah; they timbered it and set up
its doors, its bolts, and its bars. [4]At their side
Meremoth, son of Uriah, son of Hakkoz,
carried out the work of repair; next to him
was Meshullam, son of Berechiah, son of
Meshezabel; and next to him was Zadok, son
of Baana. [5]Next to him the Tekoites carried
out the work of repair; however, some of
their most powerful men would not submit to
the labor asked by their masters. [6]The Mishneh Gate* was repaired by Joiada, son of Paseah; and Meshullam, son of Besodeiah; they
timbered it and set up its doors, its bolts, and
its bars. [7]At their side Melatiah the Gibeonite
did the repairing, together with Jadon the
Meronothite, and the men of Gibeon and of
Mizpah, who were under the jurisdiction of
the governor of West-of-Euphrates. [8]Next to
them the work of repair was carried out by
Uzziel, son of Harhaiah, a member of the
goldsmiths' guild, and at his side was Hananiah, one of the perfumers' guild. They restored Jerusalem as far as the Broad Wall.*
[9]Next to them the work of repair was carried
out by Rephaiah, son of Hur, administrator of
half the district of Jerusalem, [10]and at his side
was Jedaiah, son of Harumaph, who repaired
opposite his own house. Next to him Hattush,
son of Hashabneiah, carried out the work of
repair. [11]The adjoining sector, as far as the
Oven Tower, was repaired by Malchijah, son
of Harim, and Hasshub, son of Pahath-moab.

down the Tyropoean Valley toward the Dragon Spring (or the En-rogel [Jos 15:7; 18:16; 2 Sm 17:17; 1 Kgs 1:9], now known as Job's Well) at the juncture of the Valley of Hinnom and the Kidron Valley. He then turned north at the Dung Gate (or the Potsherd Gate of Jer 19:2) at the southern end of the city and proceeded up the wadi, that is, the Kidron Valley, passing the Fountain Gate (at the Spring of Gihon) and the King's Pool (unidentified); finally he turned west and then south to his starting point.

**2:19 Geshem the Arab**: see also 6:1–2; in 6:6 the name occurs as Gashmu. He is known from a contemporary inscription as ruler of the Kedarite Arabs, who were threatening Judah from the south and east.

**2:20 Neither share nor claim nor memorial**: although Sanballat and Tobiah worshiped Yhwh, Nehemiah would not let them participate in any of the activities of the religious community in Jerusalem.

**3:1–32** The construction work on the gates and walls of the city is described in counterclockwise direction, beginning and ending at the Sheep Gate (to the north of the Temple). The exact locations of many of the topographical points mentioned are uncertain.

**3:6 The Mishneh Gate**: the gate leading into the second, expanded quarter of the city; cf. 2 Kgs 22:14; Zep 1:10.

**3:8 The Broad Wall**: perhaps identical with the wall, seven meters thick, discovered in the Jewish quarter of the Old City.

*j:* Ezr 7:6. *k:* Jer 31:38. *l:* Ezr 2:35; Zep 1:10.

**The Community Organizes to Rebuild**

CHAPTER 3 MARKS the center point of the combined work Ezra-Nehemiah and places the emphasis squarely on the community's efforts. While having "the good favor of my God" (2:8) on them marks Ezra and Nehemiah, the heroes of the narrative are the community members, elaborated in various lists, who willingly undertake the formation of the "house of God."

12 At their side the work of repair was carried
out by Shallum, son of Hallohesh, administrator of half the district of Jerusalem, together with his daughters. 13 The Valley Gate
was repaired by Hanun and the inhabitants of
Zanoah; they rebuilt it and set up its doors, its
bolts, and its bars. They also repaired a thousand cubits of the wall up to the Dung Gate.
14 The Dung Gate was repaired by Malchijah,
son of Rechab, administrator of the district of
Beth-haccherem; he rebuilt it and set up its
doors, its bolts, and its bars. 15 The Fountain
Gate was repaired by Shallum, son of Colhozeh, administrator of the district of Mizpah; he rebuilt it, roofed it, and set up its
doors, its bolts, and its bars. He also repaired
the wall of the Aqueduct Pool near the King's
Garden as far as the steps that lead down
from the City of David. 16 After him, the work
of repair was carried out by Nehemiah, son
of Azbuk, administrator of half the district of
Beth-zur, to a place opposite the tombs of
David, as far as the Artificial Pool and the
barracks.

17 After him, these Levites carried out the
work of repair: Rehum, son of Bani, and
next to him, for his own district, was
Hashabiah, administrator of half the district
of Keilah. 18 After him, their kinsmen carried
out the work of repair: Binnui, son of Henadad, administrator of half the district of Keilah; 19 next to him Ezer, son of Jeshua, administrator of Mizpah, who repaired the
adjoining sector, the Corner, opposite the ascent to the arsenal. 20 After him, Baruch, son
of Zabbai, repaired the adjoining sector from
the Corner to the entrance of the house of
Eliashib, the high priest. 21 After him, Meremoth, son of Uriah, son of Hakkoz, repaired
the adjoining sector from the entrance of Eliashib's house to its end.

22 After him, the work of repair was carried out by the priests, men of the surrounding country. 23 After them, Benjamin and
Hasshub carried out the repair in front of
their houses; after them, Azariah, son of Maaseiah, son of Ananiah, made the repairs
alongside his house. 24 After him, Binnui,
son of Henadad, repaired the adjoining sector from the house of Azariah to the Corner
(that is, to the Angle). 25 After him, Palal, son
of Uzai, carried out the work of repair opposite the Corner and the tower projecting
from the Upper Palace at the quarters of the
guard. After him, Pedaiah, son of Parosh,
carried out the work of repair 26 to a point opposite the Water Gate on the east, and the
projecting tower. 27 After him, the Tekoites
repaired the adjoining sector opposite the
great projecting tower, to the wall of Ophel.

28 Above the Horse Gate the priests carried
out the work of repair, each opposite his own
house. 29 [m] After them Zadok, son of Immer,
carried out the repair opposite his house, and
after him the repair was carried out by Shemaiah, son of Shecaniah, keeper of the East
Gate. 30 After him, Hananiah, son of
Shelemiah, and Hanun, the sixth son of Za-
laph, repaired the adjoining sector; after
them, Meshullam, son of Berechiah, repaired
the place opposite his own lodging. 31 After
him, Malchijah, a member of the goldsmiths'
guild, carried out the work of repair as far as
the quarters of the temple servants and the
merchants, in front of the Gate of Inspection
and as far as the upper chamber of the Angle.
32 Between the upper chamber of the Angle
and the Sheep Gate, the goldsmiths and the
merchants carried out the work of repair.

*Opposition from Judah's Enemies.*
33 When Sanballat heard that we were rebuilding the wall, he became angry and very

*m:* Ez 40:6.

much incensed. He ridiculed the Jews, [34]saying in the presence of his associates and the troops of Samaria: "What are these miserable Jews trying to do? Will they complete their restoration in a single day? Will they recover these stones, burnt as they are, from the heaps of dust?" [35]Tobiah the Ammonite was beside him, and he said: "Whatever they are building—if a fox attacks it, it will breach their wall of stones!" [36]Hear, our God, how we were mocked! Turn back their reproach upon their own heads and deliver them up as plunder in a land of captivity! [37][n] Do not hide their crime and do not let their sin be blotted out in your sight, for they insulted the builders to their faces! [38]We, however, continued to build the wall, and soon it was completed up to half its height. The people worked enthusiastically.

## CHAPTER 4

See RG 148

[1]When Sanballat, Tobiah, the Arabs, the Ammonites, and the Ashdodites heard that the restoration of the walls of Jerusalem was progressing—for the gaps were beginning to be closed up—they became extremely angry. [2]They all plotted together to come and fight against Jerusalem and to throw us into confusion. [3]We prayed to our God and posted a watch against them day and night for fear of what they might do. [4]Meanwhile the Judahites were saying:

"Slackened is the bearers' strength,
 there is no end to the rubbish;
Never will we be able
 to rebuild the wall."

[5]Our enemies thought, "Before they are aware of it or see us, we will come into their midst, kill them, and put an end to the work."

[6]When the Jews who lived near them had come to us from one place after another, and had told us ten times over that they were about to attack us, [7]I stationed guards down below, behind the wall, near the exposed points, assigning them by family groups with their swords, spears, and bows. [8]I made an inspection, then addressed these words to the nobles, the magistrates, and the rest of the people: "Do not fear them! Keep in mind the LORD, who is great and to be feared, and fight for your kindred, your sons and daughters, your wives and your homes." [9]When our enemies realized that we had been warned and that God had upset their plan, we all went back, each to our own task at the wall.

[10][o] From that time on, however, only half my work force took a hand in the work, while the other half, armed with spears, bucklers, bows, and breastplates, stood guard behind the whole house of Judah [11]as they rebuilt the wall. The load carriers, too, were armed; each worked with one hand and held a weapon with the other. [12]Every builder, while working, had a sword tied at his side. A trumpeter stood beside me, [13]for I had said to the nobles, the magistrates, and the rest of the people: "Our work is scattered and extensive, and we are widely separated from one another along the wall; [14]wherever you hear the trumpet sound, join us there; our God will fight with us." [15]Thus we went on with the work, half with spears in hand, from daybreak till the stars came out.

[16]At the same time I told the people to spend the nights inside Jerusalem, each with an attendant, so that they might serve as a guard by night and a working force by day. [17]Neither I, nor my kindred, nor any of my attendants, nor any of the bodyguard that accompanied me took off our clothes; everyone kept a weapon at hand.

## CHAPTER 5

See RG 148

### *Social and Economic Problems.*

[1][p] Then there rose a great outcry of the people and their wives against certain of their Jewish kindred.* [2]Some said: "We are forced to pawn our sons and daughters in order to get grain to eat that we may live." [3]Others said: "We are forced to pawn our fields, our vineyards, and our houses, that we may have grain during the famine." [4]Still others said: "To pay the king's tax we

**5:1 Certain of their Jewish kindred**: probably Jews who had returned from Babylonia who formed the social and economic elite in the province.

*n:* Neh 6:14; 13:29; Jer 18:23. *o:* Ps 149:6. *p:* Jer 34:8–22.

ECONOMIC HARDSHIPS, INCLUDING the payment of heavy taxes to the Persian king (5:4), are made worse by the actions of wealthier members of society who exploit the situation to their own profit. In response, Nehemiah initiates economic reforms. He reforms practices of the wealthy and contributes personally to the economy from his own funds (vv. 11–19).

have borrowed money on our fields and
vineyards. 5[q] And though these are our own
kindred, and our children are as good as
theirs, we have had to reduce our sons and
daughters to slavery, and violence has been
done to some of our daughters! Yet we can
do nothing about it, for our fields and vineyards belong to others."
6I was extremely angry when I heard the
reasons for their complaint. 7[r] After some
deliberation, I called the nobles and magistrates to account, saying to them, "You are
exacting interest from your own kindred!"* I
then rebuked them severely, 8[s] saying to
them: "As far as we were able, we bought
back our Jewish kindred who had been sold
to Gentiles; you, however, are selling your
own kindred, to have them bought back by
us." They remained silent, for they could
find no answer. 9I continued: "What you are
doing is not good. Should you not conduct
yourselves out of fear of our God rather than
fear of the reproach of our Gentile enemies?
10I myself, my kindred, and my attendants
have lent the people money and grain without charge. Let us put an end to this usury!
11Return to them this very day their fields,
vineyards, olive groves, and houses, together with the interest on the money, the
grain, the wine, and the oil that you have lent
them." 12They answered: "We will return
everything and exact nothing further from
them. We will do just what you ask." Then I
called for the priests to administer an oath to
them that they would do as they had promised. 13I shook out the folds of my garment,
saying, "Thus may God shake from home
and fortune every man who fails to keep this
promise, and may he thus be shaken out and
emptied!" And the whole assembly answered, "Amen," and praised the LORD.
Then the people did as they had promised.

***Nehemiah's Record.*** 14Moreover, from the
time that King Artaxerxes appointed me governor in the land of Judah, from his twentieth
to his thirty-second year—during these
twelve years neither I nor my kindred lived
off the governor's food allowance. 15The earlier governors,* my predecessors, had laid a
heavy burden on the people, taking from
them each day forty silver shekels for their
food; then, too, their attendants oppressed
the people. But I, because I feared God, did
not do this. 16In addition, though I had acquired no land of my own, I did my part in
this work on the wall, and all my attendants
were gathered there for the work. 17Though I
set my table for a hundred and fifty persons,
Jews and magistrates, as well as the neighboring Gentiles who came to us, 18and
though the daily preparations were made at
my expense—one ox, six choice sheep, poul-
try—besides all kinds of wine in abundance
every ten days, despite this I did not claim the
governor's allowance, for the labor lay heavy
upon this people. 19Keep in mind, my God, to
my credit all that I did for this people.

## CHAPTER 6

See RG 148

***Plots Against Nehemiah.*** 1When it had
been reported to Sanballat, Tobiah, Geshem
the Arab, and our other enemies that I had rebuilt the wall and that there was no breach
left in it (though up to that time I had not yet
set up the doors in the gates), 2Sanballat and
Geshem sent me this message: "Come, let us
hold council together at Chephirim in the
plain of Ono." They were planning to do me
harm. 3I sent messengers to them with this
reply: "I am engaged in a great enterprise and

**5:7 You are exacting interest from your own kindred!**: contrary to the Mosaic law (Dt 23:20).

**5:15 The earlier governors**: both Sheshbazzar (Ezr 5:14) and Zerubbabel (Hg 1:1, 14; 2:2, 21) are said to be governors, and Mal 1:8 mentions a governor but does not name him. Other names are known from seal impressions of uncertain date.

*q:* Ex 21:7; Lv 25:39. *r:* Dt 23:20. *s:* Lv 25:48.

am unable to come down. Why should the work stop, while I leave it to come down to you?" 4 Four times they sent me this same proposal, and each time I gave the same reply. 5 Then, the fifth time, Sanballat sent me the same message by one of his servants, who bore an unsealed letter 6 containing this text: "Among the nations it has been reported—Gashmu* is witness to this—that you and the Jews are planning a rebellion; that for this reason you are rebuilding the wall; and that you are to be their king. 7 Also, that you have set up prophets in Jerusalem to proclaim you king of Judah. Now, since matters like these will reach the ear of the king, come, let us hold council together." 8 I sent him this answer: "Nothing of what you report is happening; rather, it is the invention of your own mind." 9 They were all trying to intimidate us, thinking, "They will be discouraged from continuing with the work, and it will never be completed." But instead, I then redoubled my efforts.

10 I went to the house of Shemaiah, son of Delaiah, son of Mehetabel, who was confined to his house, and he said: "Let us meet in the house of God, inside the temple building; let us lock the doors of the temple. For they are coming to kill you—by night they are coming to kill you." 11 My answer was: "A man like me take flight? Should a man like me enter the temple to save his life? I will not go!" 12 For on consideration, it was plain to me that God had not sent him; rather, because Tobiah and Sanballat had bribed him, he voiced this prophecy concerning me, 13 that I might act on it out of fear and commit this sin. Then they would have had a shameful story with which to discredit me. 14[t] Keep in mind Tobiah and Sanballat, my God, because of these things they did; keep in mind as well Noadiah the woman prophet and the other prophets who were trying to intimidate me.

*Completion of the Work.* 15 The wall was finished on the twenty-fifth day of Elul;* the work had taken fifty-two days. 16[u] When all our enemies had heard of this, and all the neighboring Gentiles round about had taken note of it, they were very discouraged, for they knew that it was with our God's help that this work had been completed. 17 At that same time, however, many letters were going to Tobiah from the nobles of Judah, and Tobiah's letters were reaching them, 18 for many in Judah were in league with him, since he was the son-in-law of Shecaniah, son of Arah, and his son Jehohanan had married the daughter of Meshullam, son of Berechiah. 19 They would praise his good deeds in my presence and relate to him whatever I said; and Tobiah sent letters trying to intimidate me.

## CHAPTER 7

See RG 148

1 Now that the wall had been rebuilt, I had the doors set up, and the gatekeepers, the singers, and the Levites were put in charge of them. 2 Over Jerusalem I placed Hanani, my brother, and Hananiah, the commander of the citadel, who was more trustworthy and God-fearing than most. 3 I said to them: "The gates of Jerusalem are not to be opened until the sun is hot, and while the sun is still shining they shall shut and bar the doors. Appoint as sentinels the inhabitants of Jerusalem, some at their watch posts, and others in front of their own houses."

*Census of the Province.* 4 Now, the city was quite wide and spacious, but its population was small, and none of the houses had been rebuilt. 5 When my God had inspired me to gather together the nobles, the magistrates, and the people, and to examine their family records, I came upon the family list of those who had returned in the earliest period. There I found the following written:

6*[v] These are the inhabitants of the province who returned from the captivity of the exiles whom Nebuchadnezzar, king of Babylon, had carried away, and who came back to Jerusalem and Judah, to their own cities:

**6:6 Gashmu**: elsewhere (vv. 1–2; 2:19) the name is given as Geshem.

**6:15 Elul**: the sixth month (August–September). **Fifty-two days**: according to Josephus (*Ant.* 11:174–183), the rebuilding of the walls of Jerusalem by Nehemiah took two years and four months.

**7:6–72** See note on Ezr 2:1–67.

*t:* Jer 23:9–40; Zec 13:3. *u:* Ps 118:22–23; 127:1. *v:* Ezr 2:1–70.

7They returned with Zerubbabel, Jeshua,
Nehemiah, Azariah, Raamiah, Nahamani,
Mordecai, Bilshan, Mispereth, Bigvai, Ne-
hum, and Baanah.

The census of the people of Israel: 8de-
scendants of Parosh, two thousand one hundred and seventy-two; 9descendants of
Shephatiah, three hundred and seventy-two;
10descendants of Arah, six hundred and
fifty-two; 11descendants of Pahath-moab
who were descendants of Jeshua and Joab,
two thousand eight hundred and eighteen;
12descendants of Elam, one thousand two
hundred and fifty-four; 13descendants of
Zattu, eight hundred and forty-five; 14de-
scendants of Zaccai, seven hundred and
sixty; 15descendants of Binnui, six hundred
and forty-eight; 16descendants of Bebai, six
hundred and twenty-eight; 17descendants of
Azgad, two thousand three hundred and
twenty-two; 18descendants of Adonikam, six
hundred and sixty-seven; 19descendants of
Bigvai, two thousand and sixty-seven; 20de-
scendants of Adin, six hundred and fifty-
five; 21descendants of Ater who were descendants of Hezekiah, ninety-eight;
22descendants of Hashum, three hundred
and twenty-eight; 23descendants of Bezai,
three hundred and twenty-four; 24descen-
dants of Hariph, one hundred and twelve;
25descendants of Gibeon, ninety-five; 26peo-
ple of Bethlehem and Netophah, one hundred and eighty-eight; 27people of Anathoth,
one hundred and twenty-eight; 28people of
Beth-azmaveth, forty-two; 29people of Kiriath-jearim, Chephirah, and Beeroth, seven
hundred and forty-three; 30people of Ramah
and Geba, six hundred and twenty-one;
31people of Michmas, one hundred and
twenty-two; 32people of Bethel and Ai, one
hundred and twenty-three; 33people of
Nebo, fifty-two; 34descendants of the other
Elam, one thousand two hundred and fifty-
four; 35descendants of Harim, three hundred
and twenty; 36descendants of Jericho, three
hundred and forty-five; 37descendants of
Lod, Hadid, and Ono, seven hundred and
twenty-one; 38descendants of Senaah, three
thousand nine hundred and thirty.

39The priests: descendants of Jedaiah of
the house of Jeshua, nine hundred and seventy-three; 40descendants of Immer, one
thousand and fifty-two; 41descendants of
Pashhur, one thousand two hundred and
forty-seven; 42descendants of Harim, one
thousand and seventeen.

43The Levites: descendants of Jeshua,
Kadmiel of the descendants of Hodeviah,
seventy-four.

44The singers: descendants of Asaph, one
hundred and forty-eight.

45The gatekeepers: descendants of Shallum, descendants of Ater, descendants of
Talmon, descendants of Akkub, descendants
of Hatita, descendants of Shobai, one hundred and thirty-eight.

46The temple servants: descendants of
Ziha, descendants of Hasupha, descendants
of Tabbaoth, 47descendants of Keros, descendants of Sia, descendants of Padon,
48descendants of Lebana, descendants of
Hagaba, descendants of Shalmai, 49descen-
dants of Hanan, descendants of Giddel, de-
scendants of Gahar, 50descendants of Reaiah, descendants of Rezin, descendants of
Nekoda, 51descendants of Gazzam, descendants of Uzza, descendants of Paseah, 52de-
scendants of Besai, descendants of the Meunites, descendants of the Nephusites,
53descendants of Bakbuk, descendants of
Hakupha, descendants of Harhur, 54descen-
dants of Bazlith, descendants of Mehida, de-
scendants of Harsha, 55descendants of Barkos, descendants of Sisera, descendants of
Temah, 56descendants of Neziah, descendants of Hatipha.

57Descendants of Solomon's servants: descendants of Sotai, descendants of So-
phereth, descendants of Perida, 58descen-
dants of Jaala, descendants of Darkon,
descendants of Giddel, 59descendants of
Shephatiah, descendants of Hattil, descendants of Pochereth-hazzebaim, descendants
of Amon. 60The total of the temple servants
and the descendants of Solomon's servants
was three hundred and ninety-two.

61The following who returned from Tel-
melah, Tel-harsha, Cherub, Addon, and Immer were unable to prove that their ancestral
houses and their descent were Israelite: 62de-
scendants of Delaiah, descendants of Tobiah,
descendants of Nekoda, six hundred and

forty-two. [63]Also, of the priests: descendants of Hobaiah, descendants of Hakkoz, descendants of Barzillai (he had married one of the daughters of Barzillai the Gileadite and was named after him). [64]These men searched their family records, but their names could not be found written there; hence they were disqualified from the priesthood, [65]and the governor[*] ordered them not to partake of the most holy foods until there should be a priest to consult the Urim and Thummim.

[66]The entire assembly taken together came to forty-two thousand three hundred and sixty, [67]not counting their male and female servants, who were seven thousand three hundred and thirty-seven. They also had two hundred male and female singers. Their horses were seven hundred and thirty-six, their mules two hundred and forty-five, [68]their camels four hundred and thirty-five, their donkeys six thousand seven hundred and twenty.

[69]Certain of the heads of ancestral houses contributed to the temple service. The governor put into the treasury one thousand drachmas of gold, fifty basins, thirty vestments for priests, and five hundred minas of silver. [70]Some of the heads of ancestral houses contributed to the treasury for the temple service: twenty thousand drachmas of gold and two thousand two hundred minas of silver. [71]The contributions of the rest of the people amounted to twenty thousand drachmas of gold, two thousand minas of silver, and sixty-seven vestments for priests.

[72]The priests, the Levites, the gatekeepers, the singers, the temple servants, and all Israel took up residence in their cities.

## II. Promulgation of the Law

### CHAPTER 8

See RG 149

*Ezra Reads the Law.* [1][*][w] Now when the seventh month came, the whole people gathered as one in the square in front of the Water Gate, and they called upon Ezra the scribe to bring forth the book of the law of Moses which the LORD had commanded for Israel. [2][x] On the first day of the seventh month, therefore, Ezra the priest brought the law before the assembly, which consisted of men, women, and those children old enough to understand. [3]In the square in front of the Water Gate, Ezra read out of the book from daybreak till midday, in the presence of the men, the women, and those children old enough to understand; and all the people listened attentively to the book of the law. [4]Ezra the scribe stood on a wooden platform that had been made for the occasion; at his right side stood Mattithiah, Shema, Anaiah, Uriah, Hilkiah, and Maaseiah, and on his left Pedaiah, Mishael, Malchijah, Hashum, Hashbaddanah, Zechariah, Meshullam. [5]Ezra opened the scroll so that all the people might see it, for he was standing higher than any of the people. When he opened it, all the people stood. [6]Ezra blessed the LORD, the great God, and all the people, their hands raised high, answered, "Amen, amen!" Then they knelt down and bowed before the LORD, their faces to the ground. [7][y] The Levites Jeshua, Bani, Sherebiah, Jamin, Akkub, Shabbethai, Hodiah, Maaseiah, Kelita, Azariah, Jozabad, Hanan, and Pelaiah explained the law to the people, who remained in their places. [8][z] Ezra read clearly from the book of the law of God, interpreting it so that all could understand what was read. [9]Then Nehemiah, that is, the governor, and Ezra the priest-scribe, and the Levites who were instructing the people said to all the people: "Today is holy to the LORD your God. Do not lament, do not weep!"—for all the people were weeping as they heard the words of the law. [10][a] He continued: "Go, eat rich foods and drink sweet drinks, and allot portions to those who had nothing prepared; for today is holy to our LORD. Do not be saddened this day, for rejoicing in the LORD is your strength!" [11]And the Levites quieted all the people, saying, "Silence! Today is holy, do

**7:65, 69 The governor**: see note on Ezr 2:63.

**8:1–18** Chronologically this belongs after Ezr 8:36. The gloss mentioning Nehemiah in Neh 8:9 was inserted in this Ezra section after the dislocation of several parts of Ezra-Nehemiah had occurred. There is no clear evidence of a simultaneous presence of Nehemiah and Ezra in Jerusalem; Neh 12:26, 36 are also scribal glosses.

*w:* Ezr 3:1. *x:* Lv 23:23–25; Nm 29:1–6. *y:* Neh 10:10–13. *z:* Ezr 7:6. *a:* Est 9:19.

## Celebration of Renewal and Reconstruction

THE GREAT CELEBRATION that inaugurates the reconstructed community extends over several weeks, at least from the first day of the seventh month (8:2) to the twenty-fourth (9:1), longer than any other celebration in the Bible. The narrative depicts four steps and a coda.

**First step: reading and implementing the Torah** (8:1–18). The reconstruction culminates in this momentous event, as the community summons Ezra to bring the book of the law of Moses, the Torah. Chapter 8 signals the historical moment when the Pentateuch is publicly reintroduced and received communal sanction. This parallels the events at Mount Sinai in its impact as the receiving of God's teachings by the entire people, transforming them into "the people of the Book."

**Second step: confession and commitment** (9:1–10:39). The great communal confession rehearses Israel's shared history and leads to a renewed formal commitment to God's teaching. The community recalls the cycles of God's forbearance despite Israel's earlier infidelities and hopes to be worthy of it in the present dire circumstances.

**Third step: repopulation and review** (11:1–12:26). The restored community repopulates the rebuilt city. The lists of chs. 11–12 are compiled from different sources.

**Fourth step: a service of dedication** (12:27–13:3). Celebration, purification, procession, and separation are part of the service. The initiative for the grand finale again comes from the community (12:27; cf 8:1). Unique in the Hebrew Bible, the purification in 12:30 signals that Israel is holy, and Jerusalem is a "holy city."

**Coda** (13:4–31). Nehemiah's memoirs resume with a retrospective from a time after 433 B.C., after completing twelve years as governor. At some point after returning to King Artaxerxes, Nehemiah came back to Jerusalem, discovered violations of the communal pledge of ch 10, and took steps to restore order.

not be saddened." [12]Then all the people began to eat and drink, to distribute portions, and to celebrate with great joy, for they understood the words that had been explained to them.

*The Feast of Booths.* [13]On the second day, the heads of ancestral houses of the whole people, and also the priests and the Levites, gathered around Ezra the scribe to study the words of the law. [14b] They found it written in the law commanded by the LORD through Moses that the Israelites should dwell in booths during the feast of the seventh month; [15c] and that they should have this proclamation made throughout their cities and in Jerusalem: "Go out into the hill country and bring in branches of olive, oleaster, myrtle, palm, and other trees in leaf, to make booths, as it is written." [16]The people went out and brought in branches with which they made booths for themselves, on the roof of their houses, in their courtyards, in the courts of the house of God, and in the squares of the Water Gate and the Gate of Ephraim. [17d] So the entire assembly of the returned exiles made booths and dwelt in them. Now the Israelites had done nothing of this sort from the days of Jeshua, son of Nun, until this occasion; therefore there was very great joy. [18]Ezra read from the book of the law of God day after day, from the first day to the last. They kept the feast for seven days, and the solemn assembly on the eighth day, as was required.

*b:* Ex 23:14–16; Lv 23:33–36; Nm 29:1–38; Ez 45:25. *c:* Ps 118:27. *d:* 2 Chr 30:26; 35:18.

See RG 149

## CHAPTER 9

***Public Confession of Sin.*** 1* [e] On the
twenty-fourth day of this month, the Israelites
gathered together while fasting and wearing
sackcloth, their heads covered with dust.
2 [f] Those of Israelite descent separated themselves from all who were of foreign extraction,
then stood forward and confessed their sins
and the guilty deeds of their ancestors. 3 When
they had taken their places, they read from the
book of the law of the LORD their God, for a
fourth of the day, and during another fourth
they made their confession and bowed down
before the LORD their God. 4 Standing on the
platform of the Levites were Jeshua, Binnui,
Kadmiel, Shebaniah, Bunni, Sherebiah, Bani,
and Chenani, who cried out to the LORD their
God, with a loud voice. 5 [g] The Levites Jeshua,
Kadmiel, Bani, Hashabneiah, Sherebiah, Hodiah, Shebaniah, and Pethahiah said,

"Arise, bless the LORD, your God,
from eternity to eternity!"
"And may they bless your glorious name,
which is exalted above all blessing and praise."
6 * "You are the LORD, you alone;
You made the heavens,
the highest heavens and all their host,
The earth and all that is upon it,
the seas and all that is in them.
To all of them you give life,
the heavenly hosts bow down before you.
7 [h] You are the LORD God
who chose Abram,
Who brought him from Ur of the Chaldees,
who named him Abraham.
8 [i] You found his heart faithful in your sight,
you made the covenant with him
To give the land of the Canaanites,
Hittites, Amorites,
Perizzites, Jebusites, and Girgashites
to him and his descendants.
You fulfilled your promises,
for you are just.
9 [j] You saw the affliction of our ancestors
in Egypt,
you heard their cry by the Red Sea;
10 [k] You worked signs and wonders against
Pharaoh,
against all his servants and the people
of his land,
Because you knew of their insolence
toward them;
thus you made for yourself a name
even to this day.
11 [l] The sea you divided before them,
on dry ground they passed through the
midst of the sea;
Their pursuers you hurled into the depths,
like a stone into the mighty waters.
12 [m] With a column of cloud you led them
by day,
and by night with a column of fire,
To light the way of their journey,
the way in which they must travel.
13 [n] On Mount Sinai you came down,
you spoke with them from heaven;
You gave them just ordinances, true laws,
good statutes and commandments;
14 [o] Your holy sabbath you made known to
them,
commandments, statutes, and law you
prescribed for them,
by the hand of Moses your servant.
15 [p] Food from heaven you gave them in
their hunger,
water from a rock you sent them in
their thirst.
You told them to enter and occupy the land
which you had sworn to give them.
16 But they, our ancestors, proved to be
insolent;
they were obdurate* and did not obey
your commandments.

**9:1–5** The feast of Booths is followed by a penitential liturgy. Since it includes separation from foreigners, some read it as a sequel to Ezr 9–10.

**9:6–37** The Septuagint attributes the prayer to Ezra; cf. Ezr 9:6–15.

**9:16 They were obdurate**: lit., "they stiffened their necks."

*e:* Dn 9:3. *f:* Ezr 9:1–2; 10:11. *g:* Ps 41:14; 106:48; Dn 2:20; 3:52. *h:* Gn 12:1; 17:5. *i:* Gn 15:18–19. *j:* Ex 2:23–24. *k:* Ex 7–11; 14. *l:* Ex 15:5, 10. *m:* Ex 13:21–22. *n:* Ex 19–24. *o:* Ex 20:8. *p:* Ex 16:4; 17:1–2.

17 q They refused to obey and no longer remembered
the wonders you had worked for them.
They were obdurate and appointed a leader
in order to return to their slavery in Egypt.
But you are a forgiving God, gracious and merciful,
slow to anger and rich in mercy;
you did not forsake them.
18 r Though they made for themselves a molten calf,
and proclaimed, 'Here is your God who brought you up from Egypt,'
and were guilty of great insults,
19 Yet in your great mercy
you did not forsake them in the desert.
By day the column of cloud did not cease to lead them on their journey,
by night the column of fire did not cease to light the way they were to travel.
20 s Your good spirit you bestowed on them,
to give them understanding;
Your manna you did not withhold from their mouths,
and you gave them water in their thirst.
21 t Forty years in the desert you sustained them:
they did not want;
Their garments did not become worn,
and their feet did not swell.
22 u You gave them kingdoms and peoples,
which you divided among them as border lands.
They possessed the land of Sihon, king of Heshbon,
and the land of Og, king of Bashan.
23 v You made their children as numerous as the stars of the heavens,
and you brought them into the land
which you had commanded their ancestors to enter and possess.
24 The children went in to possess the land;
you humbled before them the Canaanite inhabitants
and gave them into their power,
Their kings and the peoples of the land,
to do with them as they wished.
25 w They captured fortified cities and fertile land;
they took possession of houses filled with all good things,
Cisterns already dug, vineyards, olive groves,
and fruit trees in abundance.
They ate and had their fill,
fattened and feasted on your great goodness.
26 x But they were contemptuous and rebelled against you:
they cast your law behind their backs.
They murdered your prophets
who bore witness against them to bring them back to you:
they were guilty of great insults.
27 y Therefore you gave them into the power of their enemies,
who oppressed them.
But in the time of their oppression they would cry out to you,
and you would hear them from heaven,
And according to your great mercy give them saviors
to deliver them from the power of their enemies.
28 As soon as they had relief,
they would go back to doing evil in your sight.
Again you abandoned them to the power of their enemies,
who crushed them.
Once again they cried out to you, and you heard them from heaven
and delivered them according to your mercy, many times over.
29 z You bore witness against them,
to bring them back to your law.
But they were insolent
and would not obey your commandments;
They sinned against your ordinances,
which give life to those who keep them.

---

*q:* Ex 34:6; Nm 14:1–4; Dt 9:9. *r:* Ex 32:4, 8. *s:* Dt 2:7. *t:* Dt 8:4. *u:* Nm 21:21–35; Dt 1:4; 2:26–3:11. *v:* Dt 1:10. *w:* Dt 3:5; 6:10–11; 11:11; 32:15. *x:* Wis 2:10–20. *y:* Dn 9:19. *z:* Lv 18:5; Dt 30:16; 32:47.

They turned stubborn backs, stiffened
their necks,
and would not obey.
30 You were patient with them for many
years,
bearing witness against them through
your spirit, by means of your
prophets;
Still they would not listen.
Therefore you delivered them into the
power of the peoples of the lands.
31 Yet in your great mercy you did not
completely destroy them
and did not forsake them, for you are a
gracious and merciful God.
32 [a] Now, our God, great, mighty, and
awesome God,
who preserves the covenant of mercy,
do not discount all the hardship that
has befallen us,
Our kings, our princes, our priests,
our prophets, our ancestors, and your
entire people,
from the time of the kings of Assyria
until this day!
33 [b] In all that has come upon us you have
been just,
for you kept faith while we have done
evil.
34 Yes, our kings, our princes, our priests,
and our ancestors
have not kept your law;
They paid no attention to your
commandments
and the warnings which you gave them.
35 While they were still in their kingdom,
in the midst of the many good things
that you had given them
And in the wide, fertile land
that you had spread out before them,
They did not serve you
nor turn away from their evil deeds.
36 Today we are slaves!
As for the land which you gave our
ancestors
That they might eat its fruits and good
things—
see, we have become slaves upon it!
37 Its rich produce goes to the kings
you set over us because of our sins,
Who rule over our bodies and our cattle
as they please.
We are in great distress!"

### CHAPTER 10

See RG 149

***Signatories to the Pact.*** 1* In view of
all this, we are entering into a firm pact,
which we are putting into writing. On the
sealed document appear the names of our
princes, our Levites, and our priests.
2 On the sealed document: the governor
Nehemiah, son of Hacaliah, and Zedekiah.
3 [c] Seraiah, Azariah, Jeremiah, 4 Pashhur,
Amariah, Malchijah, 5 Hattush, Shebaniah,
Malluch, 6 Harim, Meremoth, Obadiah,
7 Daniel, Ginnethon, Baruch, 8 Meshullam,
Abijah, Mijamin, 9 Maaziah, Bilgai, Shemaiah: these are the priests.
10 The Levites: Jeshua, son of Azaniah;
Binnui, of the descendants of Henadad;
Kadmiel; 11 [d] and their kinsmen Shebaniah,
Hodiah, Kelita, Pelaiah, Hanan, 12 Mica, Rehob, Hashabiah, 13 Zaccur, Sherebiah, Shebaniah, 14 Hodiah, Bani, Beninu.
15 The leaders of the people: Parosh, Pahath-moab, Elam, Zattu, Bani, 16 Bunni, Azgad, Bebai, 17 Adonijah, Bigvai, Adin,
18 Ater, Hezekiah, Azzur, 19 Hodiah, Hashum,
Bezai, 20 Hariph, Anathoth, Nebai, 21 Magpi-
ash, Meshullam, Hezir, 22 Meshezabel, Zadok, Jaddua, 23 Pelatiah, Hanan, Anaiah,
24 Hoshea, Hananiah, Hasshub, 25 Hallho-
hesh, Pilha, Shobek, 26 Rehum, Hashabnah,
Maaseiah, 27 Ahiah, Hanan, Anan, 28 Malluch, Harim, Baanah.
***Provisions of the Pact.*** 29 The rest of the
people, priests, Levites, gatekeepers,
singers, temple servants, and all others who
have separated themselves from the local inhabitants in favor of the law of God, with
their wives, their sons, their daughters, all
who are of the age of discretion, 30 [e] join their
influential kindred, and with the sanction of
a curse take this oath to follow the law of

**10:1–39** This section belongs to the Nehemiah narrative rather than to that of Ezra. It is best read after Neh 13:31, since the stipulations of the pact seem to presuppose Nehemiah's measures recorded in Neh 13. **In view of all this:** considering the situation described in Neh 13:4–31.

*a:* Lam 5. *b:* Dn 3:27; 9:14. *c:* Neh 12:1–7, 12–26. *d:* Ezr 10:23. *e:* Neh 13:23–27.

God given through Moses, the servant of God, and to observe carefully all the commandments of the LORD, our Lord, his ordinances and his statutes.

31f We will not marry our daughters to the local inhabitants, and we will not accept their daughters for our sons.

32g When the local inhabitants bring in merchandise or any kind of grain for sale on the sabbath day, we will not buy from them on the sabbath or on any other holy day. In the seventh year we will forgo the produce, and forgive every kind of debt.

33h We impose these commandments on ourselves: to give a third of a shekel each year for the service of the house of our God, 34for the showbread, the daily grain offering, the daily burnt offering, for the sabbaths, new moons, and festivals, for the holy offerings and sin offerings to make atonement for Israel, for every service of the house of our God. 35i We, priests, Levites, and people, have determined by lot concerning the procurement of wood: it is to be brought to the house of our God by each of our ancestral houses at stated times each year, to be burnt on the altar of the LORD, our God, as the law prescribes. 36j We have agreed to bring each year to the house of the LORD the first fruits of our fields and of our fruit trees, of every kind; 37also, as is prescribed in the law, to bring to the house of our God, to the priests who serve in the house of our God, the firstborn of our children and our animals, including the firstborn of our flocks and herds. 38k The first batch of our dough, and our offerings of the fruit of every tree, of wine and oil, we will bring to the priests, to the chambers of the house of our God. The tithe of our fields we will bring to the Levites; they, the Levites, shall take the tithe in all the cities of our service. 39An Aaronite priest shall be with the Levites when they take the tithe, and the Levites shall bring the tithe of the tithes to the house of our God, to the chambers of the treasury. 40For to these chambers the Israelites and Levites bring the offerings of grain, wine, and oil; there also are housed the vessels of the sanctuary, and the ministering priests, the gatekeepers, and the singers. We will not neglect the house of our God.

## III. Dedication of the Wall; Other Reforms

### CHAPTER 11

See RG 149

*Resettlement of Jerusalem.* 1* l The administrators took up residence in Jerusalem, and the rest of the people cast lots to bring one man in ten to reside in Jerusalem, the holy city, while the other nine would remain in the other cities. 2The people blessed all those who willingly agreed to take up residence in Jerusalem.

3m These are the heads of the province who took up residence in Jerusalem. In the cities of Judah dwelt Israelites, priests, Levites, temple servants, and the descendants of Solomon's servants, each on the property they owned in their own cities.

4In Jerusalem dwelt both Judahites and Benjaminites. Of the Judahites: Athaiah, son of Uzziah, son of Zechariah, son of Amariah, son of Shephatiah, son of Mehallalel, of the sons of Perez; 5Maaseiah, son of Baruch, son of Colhozeh, son of Hazaiah, son of Adaiah, son of Joiarib, son of Zechariah, a son of the Shelanites. 6The total of the descendants of Perez who dwelt in Jerusalem was four hundred and sixty-eight people of substance.

7These were the Benjaminites: Sallu, son of Meshullam, son of Joed, son of Pedaiah, son of Kolaiah, son of Maaseiah, son of Ithiel, son of Jeshaiah, 8and his kinsmen, warriors, nine hundred and twenty-eight in number. 9Joel, son of Zichri, was their commander, and Judah, son of Hassenuah, was second in command of the city.

10Among the priests were: Jedaiah; Joiarib; Jachin; 11Seraiah, son of Hilkiah, son of

**11:1–19** This list of the family heads who lived in Jerusalem at the time of Nehemiah is best read after Neh 7:72. It parallels at many points the list of early settlers in 1 Chr 9:2–17.

---

*f:* Dt 7:2–4; Ezr 9:2, 12; Neh 13:15–22. *g:* Neh 5:1–13; 13:15–22; Ex 20:8; Lv 25:2–7. *h:* Lv 24:5–9; 2 Chr 24:6, 9–10. *i:* Neh 13:31. *j:* Ex 13:1, 11–16; Dt 26:1. *k:* Neh 13:10–14; Nm 18:21–32. *l:* Neh 7:4. *m:* 1 Chr 9:2–34.

Meshullam, son of Zadok, son of Meraioth,
son of Ahitub, the ruler of the house of God,
[12]and their kinsmen who carried out the temple service, eight hundred and twenty-two;
Adaiah, son of Jeroham, son of Pelaliah, son
of Amzi, son of Zechariah, son of Pashhur,
son of Malchijah, [13]and his kinsmen, heads
of ancestral houses, two hundred and forty-
two; and Amasai, son of Azarel, son of Ahzai, son of Meshillemoth, son of Immer,
[14]and his kinsmen, warriors, one hundred
and twenty-eight. Their commander was
Zabdiel, son of Haggadol.
[15]Among the Levites were Shemaiah, son
of Hasshub, son of Azrikam, son of
Hashabiah, son of Bunni; [16]Shabbethai and
Jozabad, levitical chiefs who were placed
over the external affairs of the house of God;
[17]Mattaniah, son of Micah, son of Zabdi, son
of Asaph, director of the psalms, who led the
thanksgiving at prayer; Bakbukiah, second
in rank among his kinsmen; and Abda, son
of Shammua, son of Galal, son of Jeduthun.
[18]The total of the Levites in the holy city was
two hundred and eighty-four.
[19]The gatekeepers were Akkub, Talmon,
and their kinsmen, who kept watch over the
gates; one hundred and seventy-two in number.
[20]The rest of Israel, including priests and
Levites, were in all the other cities of Judah
in their own inheritances.
[21]The temple servants lived on Ophel.
Ziha and Gishpa were in charge of the temple servants.
[22][n] The prefect of the Levites in Jerusalem
was Uzzi, son of Bani, son of Hashabiah,
son of Mattaniah, son of Micah; he was one
of the descendants of Asaph, the singers appointed to the service of the house of God—
[23]for they had been appointed by royal decree, and there was a fixed schedule for the
singers assigning them their daily duties.
[24]Pethahiah, son of Meshezabel, a descendant of Zerah, son of Judah, was royal deputy
in all affairs that concerned the people.
*Other Settlements.* [25]As concerns their
villages with their fields: Judahites lived in
Kiriath-arba and its dependencies, in Dibon
and its dependencies, in Jekabzeel and its
villages, [26]in Jeshua, Moladah, Beth-pelet,
[27]in Hazarshual, in Beer-sheba and its dependencies, [28]in Ziklag, in Meconah and its
dependencies, [29]in En-rimmon, Zorah, Jarmuth, [30]Zanoah, Adullam, and their villages,
Lachish and its fields, Azekah and its dependencies. They were settled from Beer-
sheba to Ge-hinnom.
[31]Benjaminites were in Geba, Michmash,
Aija, Bethel and its dependencies, [32]Ana-
thoth, Nob, Ananiah, [33]Hazor, Ramah, Gittaim, [34]Hadid, Zeboim, Neballat, [35]Lod,
Ono, and the Valley of the Artisans.
[36]Some divisions of the Levites from Judah were attached to Benjamin.

## CHAPTER 12

See RG 149

***Priests and Levites at the Time of Ze-
rubbabel.*** [1][o] The following are the priests and
Levites who returned with Zerubbabel, son of
Shealtiel, and Jeshua: Seraiah, Jeremiah,
Ezra, [2]Amariah, Malluch, Hattush, [3]Sheca-
niah, Rehum, Meremoth, [4]Iddo, Ginnethon,
Abijah, [5]Mijamin, Maadiah, Bilgah, [6]Shema-
iah, and Joiarib, Jedaiah, [7]Sallu, Amok, Hilkiah, Jedaiah. These were the priestly heads
and their kinsmen in the days of Jeshua.
[8]The Levites were Jeshua, Binnui, Kadmiel, Sherebiah, Judah, Mattaniah, who, together with his kinsmen, was in charge of
the thanksgiving hymns, [9]while Bakbukiah
and Unno and their kinsmen ministered opposite them by turns.
***High Priests.*** [10][*] Jeshua became the father
of Joiakim, Joiakim the father of Eliashib,
and Eliashib the father of Joiada; [11]Joiada
the father of Johanan, and Johanan the father
of Jaddua.

**12:10–11** Jeshua was the high priest when Zerubbabel was governor, in the last decades of the sixth century B.C. (Hg 1:1, 12, 14; 2:2, 4). He was the grandfather of Eliashib, the high priest early in Nehemiah's governorship (445–433 B.C.; Neh 3:1, 20, 21) and perhaps later. Eliashib, the grandfather of Johanan, was a grown man, if not yet a high priest, at the time of Ezra, ca. 400 B.C. (Ezr 10:6; and note). According to Josephus (*Ant.* 11:120–183), whose testimony here is doubtful, Jaddua, son of Johanan, died as an old man about the time that Alexander the Great died, 323 B.C. If, as seems probable, this list of the postexilic high priests, at least as far as Johanan, comes from the author himself (cf. Neh 12:23) and not from a later scribe, it is of prime importance for dating the author's work in the first decades of the fourth century B.C.

*n:* 2 Chr 20:14. *o:* Neh 12:12–22.

***Priests and Levites Under Joiakim.*** [12][p] In
the days of Joiakim these were the priestly
family heads: for Seraiah, Meraiah; for Jeremiah, Hananiah; [13]for Ezra, Meshullam; for
Amariah, Jehohanan; [14]for Malluchi, Jonathan; for Shebaniah, Joseph; [15]for Harim,
Adna; for Meremoth, Helkai; [16]for Iddo,
Zechariah; for Ginnethon, Meshullam; [17]for
Abijah, Zichri; for Miamin, . . . ; for Moa-
diah, Piltai; [18]for Bilgah, Shammua; for Shemaiah, Jehonathan; [19]and for Joiarib, Mattenai; for Jedaiah, Uzzi; [20]for Sallu, Kallai; for
Amok, Eber; [21]for Hilkiah, Hashabiah; for
Jedaiah, Nethanel.

[22]In the time of Eliashib, Joiada, Johanan,
and Jaddua, the heads of ancestral houses of
the priests were written down in the Book of
Chronicles, up until the reign of Darius the
Persian. [23]The sons of Levi: the family heads
were written down in the Book of Chronicles, up until the time of Johanan, the son of
Eliashib.

[24][q] The heads of the Levites were
Hashabiah, Sherebiah, Jeshua, Binnui, Kadmiel. Their kinsmen who stood opposite
them to sing praises and thanksgiving in fulfillment of the command of David, the man
of God, one section opposite the other,
[25][r] were Mattaniah, Bakbukiah, Obadiah.

Meshullam, Talmon, and Akkub were
gatekeepers. They guarded the storerooms at
the gates.

[26]All these lived in the time of Joiakim,
son of Jeshua, son of Jozadak (and in the
time of Nehemiah the governor and of Ezra
the priest-scribe).

***Dedication of the Wall.*** [27]* At the dedication of the wall of Jerusalem, the Levites
were sought out wherever they lived and
were brought to Jerusalem to celebrate a joyful dedication with thanksgiving hymns and
the music of cymbals, harps, and lyres. [28]The
levitical singers gathered together from the
region about Jerusalem, from the villages of
the Netophathites, [29]from Beth-gilgal, and
from the plains of Geba and Azmaveth (for
the singers had built themselves settlements
about Jerusalem). [30]The priests and Levites
first purified themselves, then they purified
the people, the gates, and the wall.

[31]I had the administrators of Judah go up
on the wall, and I arranged two great choirs.
The first of these proceeded to the right,
along the top of the wall, in the direction of
the Dung Gate, [32]followed by Hoshaiah and
half the administrators of Judah, [33]along with
Azariah, Ezra, Meshullam, [34]Judah, Benjamin, Shemaiah, and Jeremiah, [35]priests with
the trumpets, and also Zechariah, son of Jonathan, son of Shemaiah, son of Mattaniah,
son of Micaiah, son of Zaccur, son of Asaph,
[36]and his kinsmen Shemaiah, Azarel, Mila-
lai, Gilalai, Maai, Nethanel, Judah, and Hanani, with the musical instruments of David,
the man of God. Ezra the scribe was at their
head. [37]At the Fountain Gate they went
straight up by the steps of the City of David
and continued along the top of the wall above
the house of David until they came to the Water Gate on the east.

[38]The second choir proceeded to the left,
followed by myself and the other half of the
administrators, along the top of the wall past
the Oven Tower as far as the Broad Wall,
[39]then past the Ephraim Gate to the Mishneh
Gate, the Fish Gate, the Tower of Hananel,
and the Hundred Tower, as far as the Sheep
Gate. They came to a halt at the Prison Gate.
[40]Both choirs took up a position in the
house of God; I, too, and half the magistrates
with me, [41]together with the priests Eliakim,
Maaseiah, Minjamin, Micaiah, Elioenai,
Zechariah, Hananiah, with the trumpets,
[42]and Maaseiah, Shemaiah, Eleazar, Uzzi,
Jehohanan, Malchijah, Elam, and Ezer. The
singers were heard under the leadership of
Jezrahiah. [43]Great sacrifices were offered on
that day, and they rejoiced, for God had given
them cause for great rejoicing. The women
and the children joined in, and the rejoicing
at Jerusalem could be heard from far off.

[44]* [s] At that time men were appointed over

**12:27–43** The dedication of the wall of Jerusalem took place, no doubt, soon after the restoration of the wall and its gates had been completed. This section, therefore, is best read after Neh 6:15.

**12:44–47** This account of the provisions made for the Temple services is a composition either of the author or of a later scribe. The gloss mentioning Nehemiah is not in the Septuagint.

*p:* Neh 10:3–9; 12:1–6. *q:* Ezr 2:40. *r:* Neh 11:17. *s:* 1 Chr 23–26; 2 Chr 8:14.

the chambers set aside for stores, offerings, first fruits, and tithes; in them they were to collect from the fields of the various cities the portions legally assigned to the priests and Levites. For Judah rejoiced in its appointed priests and Levites [45]who carried out the ministry of their God and the ministry of purification (as did the singers and the gatekeepers) in accordance with the prescriptions of David and Solomon, his son. [46][t] For in the days of David and Asaph, long ago, there were leaders of singers for songs of praise and thanksgiving to God. [47][u] All Israel, in the days of Zerubbabel and in the days of Nehemiah, gave the singers and the gatekeepers their portions, according to their daily needs. They made their consecrated offering to the Levites, and the Levites made theirs to the descendants of Aaron.

### CHAPTER 13

See RG 149

[1*][v] At that time, when the book of Moses was being read in the hearing of the people, it was found written there: "No Ammonite or Moabite may ever be admitted into the assembly of God; [2][w] for they did not meet the Israelites with food and water, but they hired Balaam to curse them, though our God turned the curse into a blessing." [3][x] When they had heard the law, they separated all those of mixed descent from Israel.

***Reform in the Temple.*** [4*] Before this, the priest Eliashib, who had been placed in charge of the chambers of the house of our God and who was an associate of Tobiah, [5][y] had set aside for the latter's use a large chamber in which had previously been stored the grain offerings, incense and vessels, the tithes in grain, wine, and oil allotted to the Levites, singers, and gatekeepers, and the offerings due the priests. [6]During all this time I had not been in Jerusalem, for in the thirty-second year of Artaxerxes,* king of Babylon, I had gone back to the king. After a suitable period of time, however, I asked leave of the king [7]and returned to Jerusalem, where I discovered the evil thing that Eliashib had done for Tobiah, in setting aside for him a chamber in the courts of the house of God. [8]This displeased me very much, so I had all of Tobiah's household goods thrown outside the chamber. [9]Then I gave orders to purify the chambers, and I brought back the vessels of the house of God, the grain offerings, and the incense.

[10]I learned, too, that the portions due the Levites were no longer being given, so that the Levites and the singers who should have been carrying out the services had deserted to their own fields. [11]I reprimanded the magistrates, demanding, "Why is the house of God neglected?" Then I brought the Levites together and had them resume their stations. [12][z] All Judah once more brought in the tithes of grain, wine, and oil to the storerooms. [13]In charge of the storerooms I appointed Shelemiah the priest, Zadok the scribe, and Pedaiah, one of the Levites, together with Hanan, son of Zaccur, son of Mattaniah, as their assistant; for they were considered trustworthy. It was their duty to make the distribution to their kinsmen. [14]Remember this to my credit, my God! Do not forget the good deeds I have done for the house of my God and its services!

***Sabbath Observance.*** [15][a] In those days I perceived that people in Judah were treading the wine presses on the sabbath; that they were bringing in sheaves of grain, loading them on their donkeys, together with wine, grapes, figs, and every other kind of load, and bringing them to Jerusalem on the sabbath day. I warned them to sell none of these provisions. [16]In Jerusalem itself the Tyrians residing there were importing fish and every other kind of merchandise and selling it to the Judahites on the sabbath. [17]I reprimanded the nobles of Judah, demanding:

**13:1–3** These verses serve as an introduction to the reforms Nehemiah instituted during his second mission in Jerusalem (vv. 4–31). The part of the Book of Moses read to the people is freely quoted here from Dt 23:3–6.

**13:4–31** This is part of the "Memoirs of Nehemiah"; it is continued in 10:1–40.

**13:6 In the thirty-second year of Artaxerxes**: Artaxerxes I, therefore 433 B.C. **After . . . time**: it is not known when Nehemiah returned to Jerusalem or how long his second period of activity there lasted.

*t:* 2 Chr 29:30; 35:15. *u:* Neh 10:39; 13:10–11; Nm 18:26. *v:* Dt 23:3–6. *w:* Nm 22–24. *x:* Neh 13:23–28. *y:* Neh 12:44. *z:* Neh 10:38–39; 12:44–45, 47; 2 Chr 31:6. *a:* Neh 10:32; Ex 20:8.

"What is this evil thing you are doing, profaning the sabbath day? [18]Did not your ancestors act in this same way, with the result that our God has brought all this evil upon us and upon this city? Would you add to the wrath against Israel by once more profaning the sabbath?"

[19]When the shadows were falling on the gates of Jerusalem before the sabbath, I ordered the doors to be closed and prohibited their reopening until after the sabbath. I posted some of my own people at the gates so that no load might enter on the sabbath day. [20]The merchants and sellers of various kinds of merchandise spent the night once or twice outside Jerusalem, [21]but then I warned them: "Why do you spend the night alongside the wall? If you keep this up, I will beat you!" From that time on, they did not return on the sabbath. [22]Then I ordered the Levites to purify themselves and to watch the gates, so that the sabbath day might be kept holy. This, too, remember in my favor, my God, and have mercy on me in accordance with your great mercy!

***Mixed Marriages.*** [23b] Also in those days I saw Jews who had married women of Ashdod, Ammon, or Moab. [24]Of their children, half spoke the language of Ashdod,* or of one of the other peoples, and none of them knew how to speak the language of Judah. [25]So I reprimanded and cursed them; I beat some of their men and pulled out their hair; and I adjured them by God: "You shall not marry your daughters to their sons nor accept any of their daughters for your sons or for yourselves! [26c] Did not Solomon, the king of Israel, sin because of them? Though among the many nations there was no king like him, and though he was beloved of his God and God had made him king over all Israel, yet even he was led into sin by foreign women. [27]Must it also be heard of you that you have done this same terrible evil, betraying our God by marrying foreign women?"

[28d] One of the sons of Joiada, son of Eliashib the high priest, was the son-in-law of Sanballat the Horonite! I drove him from my presence. [29]Remember against them, my God, how they defiled the priesthood and the covenant of the priesthood and the Levites!

[30]So I cleansed them of all foreign contamination. I established the various functions for the priests and Levites, so that each had an appointed task. [31e] I also provided for the procurement of wood at stated times and for the first fruits. Remember this in my favor, my God!

**13:24 Language of Ashdod**: more likely an Aramaic rather than a Philistine dialect. **The language of Judah**: probably Hebrew.

*b:* Neh 10:31; 13:1–3; Dt 23:3; Ezr 9–10. *c:* 1 Kgs 11:1–13. *d:* Neh 2:10; 13:4–5, 7–9. *e:* Neh 10:35–36.

# BIBLICAL NOVELLAS

See RG 34–47

The Bible conveys the Word of God in many literary forms: historical narrative, poetry, prophetic exhortation, wisdom sayings, and novellas (edifying stories). In the Constitution on Divine Revelation from Vatican II (*Dei Verbum*), the council fathers give instruction on how to approach this variety: "Attention must be paid to literary forms, for the fact is that truth is differently presented and expressed in the various types of historical writing, in prophetical and poetical texts, and in other forms of literary expression. Hence the interpreter must look for that meaning which the sacred writer intended to express and did in fact express through the medium of a contemporary literary form" (DV 12).

The Books of Tobit, Judith, and Esther are often grouped together. They are stories told to instruct the people concerning the ways of God, to encourage them in critical times, and to entertain. They are aids to the imagination. While they may contain kernels of historical fact, these stories are told primarily to illustrate truths that transcend history.

The author of the Book of Tobit, writing in the second century B.C., tells a story about the life of a devout family in seventh-century Assyria. He gives the people of his own time an example to follow as they struggle with the tensions of living a faithful Jewish life in the midst of a non-Jewish civilization. Tobit, suffering from the affliction of blindness, perseveres in good works and prayer, as do the other characters in the story. God sends an angel who, while hidden from them, leads them to health and happiness. The conclusion demonstrates that God does answer prayer and that perseverance in good works does not go unrewarded.

The author of the Book of Judith gives many clues that this story is beyond history. All the worst enemies of the people—the Assyrians of the eighth and seventh centuries, the sixth-century Babylonian king Nebuchadnezzar—are rolled into one terror. The hero, Judith, is modeled on the heroes of the Book of Judges, yet her story is also reminiscent of a second-century hero, Judas Maccabeus (1–2 Maccabees). Even the conflation of time indications—the eighteenth year of Nebuchadnezzar (2:1; the year 587 B.C., when he destroyed Jerusalem and took the Jews into exile) with the return from exile and rededication of the Temple (4:3; the events of 538 and 515 respectively)—suggests God's deliverance from the most terrible circumstances. The story may be set in a time long past, but it is meant to encourage the people of the late second century to trust in God when their way of life is threatened. God can use even the most unlikely means, such as a widow, a biblical figure of powerlessness and vulnerability, to deliver them from their enemies.

The Book of Esther includes several historical elements. The Persian king Xerxes (486–465 B.C.), the city of Susa, a court official named Marduka, are all known from other sources. But further investigation shows this is not meant to be a historical account. There is no record of Xerxes having any other queen than Amestris and no mention of such a massacre during his reign. The book has a different purpose: to suggest a historical basis to the festival of Purim, perhaps originally a Persian feast. Through the story of Esther, Purim becomes a celebration of God's rescue of the people from persecution and certain death.

The message conveyed in these stories is not confined to one geographic place or historical period. It remains a valid expression of God's care for faithful people in every time and place.

See RG 151–53

# The Book of Tobit

The Book of Tobit, named after its principal character, combines Jewish piety and morality with folklore in a fascinating story that has enjoyed wide popularity in both Jewish and Christian circles. Prayers, psalms, and words of wisdom, as well as the skillfully constructed story itself, provide valuable insights into the faith and the religious milieu of its unknown author. The book was probably written early in the second century B.C.; it is not known where.

Tobit, a devout and wealthy Israelite living among the captives deported to Nineveh from the Northern Kingdom of Israel in 722/721 B.C., suffers severe reverses and is finally blinded. Because of his misfortunes he begs the Lord to let him die. But recalling the large sum he had formerly deposited in far-off Media, he sends his son Tobiah there to bring back the money. In Media, at this same time, a young woman, Sarah, also prays for death, because she has lost seven husbands, each killed in turn on his wedding night by the demon Asmodeus. God hears the prayers of Tobit and Sarah and sends the angel Raphael in human form to aid them both.

Raphael makes the trip to Media with Tobiah. When Tobiah is attacked by a large fish as he bathes in the Tigris River, Raphael orders him to seize it and to remove its gall, heart, and liver because they are useful for medicine. Later, at Raphael's urging, Tobiah marries Sarah, and uses the fish's heart and liver to drive Asmodeus from the bridal chamber. Returning to Nineveh with his wife and his father's money, Tobiah rubs the fish's gall into his father's eyes and cures him. Finally, Raphael reveals his true identity and returns to heaven. Tobit then utters his beautiful hymn of praise. Before dying, Tobit tells his son to leave Nineveh because God will destroy that wicked city. After Tobiah buries his father and mother, he and his family depart for Media, where he later learns that the destruction of Nineveh has taken place.

The inspired author of the book used the literary form of religious novel (as in Esther and Judith) for the purpose of instruction and edification. The seemingly historical data, names of kings, cities, etc., are used as vivid details not only to create interest and charm, but also to illustrate the negative side of the theory of retribution: the wicked are indeed punished.

Although the Book of Tobit is usually listed with the historical books, it more correctly stands midway between them and the wisdom literature. It contains numerous maxims like those found in the wisdom books (cf. 4:3–19, 21; 12:6–10; 14:7, 9) as well as standard wisdom themes: fidelity to the law, intercessory function of angels, piety toward parents, purity of marriage, reverence for the dead, and the value of almsgiving, prayer, and fasting. The book makes Tobit a relative of Ahiqar, a noted hero of ancient Near Eastern wisdom literature and folklore.

Written most likely in Aramaic, the original of the book was lost for centuries. Fragments of four Aramaic texts and of one Hebrew text were discovered in Qumran Cave 4 in 1952 and have only recently been published. These Semitic forms of the book are in substantial agreement with the long Greek recension of Tobit found in Codex Sinaiticus, which had been recovered from St. Catherine's Monastery (Mount Sinai) only in 1844, and in mss. 319 and 910. Two other Greek forms of Tobit have long been known: the short recension, found mainly in the mss. Alexandrinus, Vaticanus, Venetus, and numerous cursive mss.; and an intermediate Greek recension, found in mss. 44, 106, 107. The Book of Tobit has also been known from two Latin versions: the long recension in the Vetus Latina, which is closely related to the long Greek recension and sometimes is even closer to the Aramaic and Hebrew texts than the Greek is; and the short recension in the Vulgate, related to the short Greek recension. The present English translation has been based mainly on Sinaiticus, which is the most complete form of the long Greek recension, despite two lacunae (4:7–19b and 13:6i–10b) and some missing phrases, which make succeeding verses difficult to understand and make it necessary to supplement Sinaiticus from the Vetus Latina or from the short Greek recension. Occasionally, phrases or words have been introduced from the Aramaic or Hebrew texts, when they are significantly different. Forms of the Book of Tobit are also extant in ancient Arabic, Armenian, Coptic (Sahidic), Ethiopic, and Syriac, but these are almost all secondarily derived from the short Greek recension.

The divisions of the Book of Tobit are:

I. Tobit's Ordeals (1:3–3:6)
II. Sarah's Plight (3:7–17)
III. Preparation for the Journey (4:1–6:1)
IV. Tobiah's Journey to Media (6:2–18)
V. Marriage and Healing of Sarah (7:1–9:6)
VI. Tobiah's Return Journey to Nineveh and the Healing of Tobit (10:1–11:18)
VII. Raphael Reveals His Identity (12:1–22)
VIII. Tobit's Song of Praise (13:1–18)
IX. Epilogue (14:1–15)

See RG 152

## CHAPTER 1

*Tobit.* [1]This book tells the story of Tobit,* son of Tobiel, son of Hananiel, son of Aduel, son of Gabael, son of Raphael, son of Raguel, of the family of Asiel and the tribe of Naphtali. [2]During the days of Shalmaneser,* king of the Assyrians, he was taken captive from Thisbe, which is south of Kedesh Naphtali in upper Galilee, above and to the west of Asher, north of Phogor.[a]

## I. Tobit's Ordeals

***His Virtue.*** [3]I, Tobit, have walked all the days of my life on paths of fidelity and righteousness. I performed many charitable deeds for my kindred and my people who had been taken captive with me to Nineveh, in the land of the Assyrians. [4]When I lived as a young man in my own country, in the land of Israel, the entire tribe of my ancestor Naphtali broke away from the house of David, my ancestor, and from Jerusalem, the city that had been singled out of all Israel's tribes that all Israel might offer sacrifice there. It was the place where the temple, God's dwelling, had been built and consecrated for all generations to come. [5b] All my kindred, as well as the house of Naphtali, my ancestor, used to offer sacrifice on every hilltop in Galilee to the calf that Jeroboam, king of Israel, had made in Dan.*

[6c] But I alone used to go often to Jerusalem for the festivals, as was prescribed for all Israel by longstanding decree.* Bringing with me the first fruits of crops, the firstlings of the flock, the tithes of livestock, and the first shearings of sheep,[d] I used to hasten to Jerusalem [7e] and present them to the priests, Aaron's sons, at the altar. To the Levites ministering in Jerusalem I used to give the tithe of grain, wine, olive oil, pomegranates, figs, and other fruits. Six years in a row, I used to give a second tithe in money, which each year I would go to pay in Jerusalem. [8]The third-year tithe I gave to orphans, widows, and converts who had joined the Israelites. Every third year I would bring them this offering, and we ate it in keeping with the decree laid down in the Mosaic law concerning it, and according to the commands of Deborah, the mother of my father Tobiel; for my father had died and left me an orphan.

[9]When I reached manhood, I married Anna, a woman of our ancestral family. By her I had a son whom I named Tobiah. [10]Now, after I had been deported to the Assyrians and came as a captive to Nineveh, all my kindred and my people used to eat the food of the Gentiles,[f] [11]but I refrained from eating that Gentile food. [12]Because I was

**1:1 Tobit**: in the Aramaic text the name is given as Tobi, an abbreviated form of Tobiyah (Ezr 2:60) or of Tobiyahu (2 Chr 17:8), a name that means "Yhwh is my welfare." **Tobiel**: "El [God] is my welfare." **Hananiel**: "El [God] has shown mercy." The book abounds in theophoric names.

**1:2 Shalmaneser** (V) (727–722 B.C.): began the siege of Samaria; the inhabitants of the Northern Kingdom were taken into captivity by his successor, Sargon II (722–705); cf. 2 Kgs 17:1–6. **Thisbe** and **Phogor**: unidentified towns of Galilee. **Kedesh Naphtali**: cf. Jos 20:7; 2 Kgs 15:29. **Asher**: probably Hazor (Jos 11:1).

**1:5** Jeroboam established sanctuaries in Dan and Bethel so that the people would no longer have to go to Jerusalem for the festivals. The gold statues of calves that he placed in the sanctuaries were considered the throne of Yhwh; but the people may have tended to worship the images themselves. Jeroboam also encouraged high places or hilltop shrines (1 Kgs 12:26–33).

**1:6–8 Longstanding decree**: Dt 12:11, 13–14. Refusing to worship at Jeroboam's shrines, the faithful Tobit continued to bring his offerings to Jerusalem; see 2 Chr 11:16. For the various tithes, cf. Lv 27:30–33; Nm 18:20–32; 2 Chr 31:4–6; Dt 14:22–29; 26:12–13.

*a:* 2 Kgs 17:3; 18:9–12. *b:* 1 Kgs 12:26–32. *c:* Ex 23:14–15, 17; 34:23. *d:* Dt 16:16. *e:* Nm 18:12–13, 24; Dt 14:22–29; 18:4–5. *f:* Lv 11; Dt 14:3–21; Acts 15:29; 1 Cor 8:7–13.

A DEAD BODY left unburied (1:18) was considered a curse, a punishment for an evil life, which somehow affected the peace of the deceased. See 2 Kings 19:35–36; Jeremiah 8:2; Ecclesiasticus 44:14.

mindful of God with all my heart, [13]the Most High granted me favor and status with Shalmaneser, so that I became purchasing agent for all his needs.[g] [14]Until he died, I would go to Media to buy goods for him there. I also deposited pouches of silver worth ten talents* in trust with my kinsman Gabael, son of Gabri, who lived at Rages, in the land of Media. [15]When Shalmaneser died and his son Sennacherib* came to rule in his stead, the roads to Media became unsafe, so I could no longer go to Media.

***Courage in Burying the Dead.*** [16]In the days of Shalmaneser I had performed many charitable deeds for my kindred, members of my people. [17][h] I would give my bread to the hungry and clothing to the naked. If I saw one of my people who had died and been thrown behind the wall of Nineveh, I used to bury him.* [18]Sennacherib returned from Judea, having fled during the days of the judgment enacted against him by the King of Heaven because of the blasphemies he had uttered; whomever he killed I buried. For in his rage he killed many Israelites, but I used to take their bodies away by stealth and bury them. So when Sennacherib looked for them, he could not find them. [19]But a certain Ninevite went and informed the king about me, that I was burying them, and I went into hiding. When I realized that the king knew about me and that I was being hunted to be put to death, I became afraid and took flight. [20]All my property was confiscated; I was left with nothing. All that I had was taken to the king's palace, except for my wife Anna and my son Tobiah.*

[21]But forty days did not pass before two of the king's sons assassinated him and fled to the mountains of Ararat. A son of his, Esarhaddon,* succeeded him as king. He put Ahiqar, my kinsman Anael's son, in charge of all the credit accounts of his kingdom, and he took control over the entire administration.[i] [22]Then Ahiqar interceded on my behalf, and I returned to Nineveh. Ahiqar had been chief cupbearer, keeper of the signet ring, treasury accountant, and credit accountant under Sennacherib, king of the Assyrians; and Esarhaddon appointed him as Second to himself. He was, in fact, my nephew, of my father's house, and of my own family.

## CHAPTER 2

See RG 152

[1]Thus under King Esarhaddon I returned to my home, and my wife Anna and my son Tobiah were restored to me. Then on our festival of Pentecost, the holy feast of Weeks,* a fine dinner was prepared for me, and I reclined to eat.[j] [2]The table was set for me, and the dishes placed before me were many. So I said to my son Tobiah: "Son, go out and bring in whatever poor person you find among our kindred exiled here in Nineveh who may be a sincere worshiper of

**1:14 Silver worth ten talents**: a great sum of money; about ten thousand dollars, at least. **Rages**: modern Rai, about five miles southeast of Tehran. **Media**: the northwestern part of modern Iran.

**1:15 Sennacherib** (705–681 B.C.): the son of Sargon II; neither was descended from Shalmaneser. On such historical inconsistencies, see Introduction; also notes on 5:6; 6:2; 9:2; 14:15.

**1:17–18** Tobit risked his own life to bury the dead. Deprivation of burial was viewed with horror by the Jews. Cf. 4:3–4; 6:15; 14:12–13.

**1:20 Tobiah**: the son bears the fuller form of his father's name; see note on 1:1.

**1:21 Esarhaddon**: 681–669 B.C. **Ahiqar**: a hero of ancient folklore, known for his outstanding wisdom. *The Story (or Wisdom) of Ahiqar* was very popular in antiquity and is extant in many different forms: Aramaic, Syriac, Armenian, Arabic (*Arabian Nights*), Greek (*Aesop's Fables*), Slavonic, Ethiopic, and Romanian. The sacred author makes Tobit the uncle of the famous Ahiqar in order to enhance Tobit's own prestige. See note on 14:10.

**2:1 Feast of Weeks**: also called by its Greek name, Pentecost, was celebrated fifty days after the Passover. Cf. Lv 23:15–21; Dt 16:9–12.

*g:* Dn 2:48–49. *h:* Jb 31:16–20. *i:* 2 Kgs 19:37; 2 Chr 32:21; 2 Mc 8:19; Sir 48:21; Is 37:38. *j:* Lv 23:15–21; Nm 28:26–31; Dt 16:9–12.

**Tobit's Misfortunes**

TOBIT'S CHARITABLE ACTS land him in trouble (1:16–22). His zealous efforts to obey the law earn him the persecution of the pagans and the jeers of the other Jews (2:8).

God to share this meal with me. Indeed, son, I shall wait for you to come back."'*
3Tobiah went out to look for some poor person among our kindred, but he came back and cried, "Father!" I said to him, "Here I am, son." He answered, "Father, one of our people has been murdered! He has been thrown out into the market place, and there he lies strangled." 4I sprang to my feet, leaving the dinner untouched, carried the dead man from the square, and put him in one of the rooms until sundown, so that I might bury him. 5I returned and washed* and in sorrow ate my food.[k] 6I remembered the oracle pronounced by the prophet Amos against Bethel:[l]

"I will turn your feasts into mourning,
and all your songs into dirges."

7Then I wept. At sunset I went out, dug a grave, and buried him.

8My neighbors mocked me, saying: "Does he have no fear? Once before he was hunted, to be executed for this sort of deed, and he ran away; yet here he is again burying the dead!"

***Tobit's Blindness.*** 9That same night I washed and went into my courtyard, where I lay down to sleep beside the wall. Because of the heat I left my face uncovered. 10I did not know that sparrows were perched on the wall above me; their warm droppings settled in my eyes, causing white scales* on them. I went to doctors for a cure, but the more they applied ointments, the more my vision was obscured by the white scales, until I was totally blind. For four years I was unable to see, and all my kindred were distressed at my condition. Ahiqar, however, took care of me for two years, until he left for Elam.

11At that time my wife Anna worked for hire at weaving cloth, doing the kind of work women do. 12When she delivered the material to her employers, they would pay her a wage. On the seventh day of the month of Dystrus,* she finished the woven cloth and delivered it to her employers. They paid her the full salary and also gave her a young goat for a meal. 13On entering my house, the goat began to bleat. So I called to my wife and said: "Where did this goat come from? It was not stolen, was it? Give it back to its owners; we have no right to eat anything stolen!" 14[m] But she said to me, "It was given to me as a bonus over and above my wages." Yet I would not believe her and told her to give it back to its owners. I flushed with anger at her over this. So she retorted: "Where are your charitable deeds now? Where are your righteous acts? Look! All that has happened to you is well known!"'*

## CHAPTER 3

See RG 152

1Then sad at heart, I groaned and wept aloud. With sobs I began to pray:*

### Tobit's Prayer for Death

2 "You are righteous, Lord,
and all your deeds are just;
All your ways are mercy and fidelity;

**2:2** Almsgiving and charity to the poor are important virtues taught by the book (4:7–11, 16–17; 12:8–9; 14:10–11). **A sincere worshiper of God**: lit., "who is mindful of God with the whole heart."

**2:5 Washed**: because of ritual defilement from touching a corpse (Nm 19:11–13).

**2:10 White scales**: or white films. A primitive way of describing an eye ailment that results in blindness. **Elam**: or in Greek, *Elymais*, an ancient district northeast of the head of the Persian Gulf.

**2:12 Seventh day of the month of Dystrus**: late in winter. The Macedonian month Dystros corresponds to the Jewish month of Shebat (January–February). **A meal**: lit., "for the hearth"; the gift had probably been made in view of some springtime festival like the Jewish Purim.

**2:14** Anna's sharp rebuke calls to mind the words of Job's wife (Jb 2:9).

**3:1 Pray**: prayer is a significant theme, occurring at six major turning points in the story (3:2–6, 11–15; 8:5–8, 15–17; 11:14–15; 13:1–18).

*k*: Nm 19:11–22. *l*: 1 Mc 1:39; Am 8:10. *m*: Jb 2:9.

you are judge of the world.[n]
3 And now, Lord, be mindful of me
and look with favor upon me.
Do not punish me for my sins,
or for my inadvertent offenses,
or for those of my ancestors.[o]

"They sinned against you,
4 and disobeyed your commandments.
So you handed us over to plunder,
captivity, and death,
to become an object lesson, a byword,
and a reproach
in all the nations among whom you
scattered us.[p]

5 "Yes, your many judgments are right
in dealing with me as my sins,
and those of my ancestors, deserve.
For we have neither kept your
commandments,
nor walked in fidelity before you.

6 "So now, deal with me as you please;
command my life breath to be taken
from me,
that I may depart from the face of the
earth and become dust.
It is better for me to die than to live,*
because I have listened to undeserved
reproaches,
and great is the grief within me.[q]

"Lord, command that I be released from
such anguish;
let me go to my everlasting abode;
Do not turn your face away from me,
Lord.
For it is better for me to die
than to endure so much misery in life,
and to listen to such reproaches!"

## II. Sarah's Plight

***Sarah Falsely Accused.*** 7* On that very day,
at Ecbatana in Media, it so happened that
Raguel's daughter Sarah also had to listen to
reproaches from one of her father's maids.
8 For she had been given in marriage to seven
husbands, but the wicked demon Asmodeus*
kept killing them off before they could have
intercourse with her, as is prescribed for
wives. The maid said to her: "You are the
one who kills your husbands! Look! You
have already been given in marriage to
seven husbands, but you do not bear the
name of a single one of them. 9 Why do you
beat us? Because your husbands are dead?
Go, join them! May we never see son or
daughter of yours!"
10 That day Sarah was sad at heart. She
went in tears to an upstairs room in her father's house and wanted to hang herself. But
she reconsidered, saying to herself: "No!
May people never reproach my father and
say to him, 'You had only one beloved
daughter, but she hanged herself because of
her misfortune.' And thus would I bring my
father laden with sorrow in his old age to
Hades. It is far better for me not to hang myself, but to beg the Lord that I might die, and
no longer have to listen to such reproaches
in my lifetime."[r]
11 At that same time, with hands outstretched toward the window,* she implored
favor:

## Sarah's Prayer for Death

"Blessed are you, merciful God!
Blessed be your holy and honorable
name forever!

**3:6 It is better for me to die than to live**: in his distress Tobit uses the words of the petulant Jonah (Jon 4:3, 8), who wished to die because God did not destroy the hated Ninevites. In similar circumstances, Moses (Nm 11:15), Elijah (1 Kgs 19:4), and Job (Jb 7:15) also prayed for death. **Everlasting abode**: a reference to Sheol, the dismal abode of the dead from which no one returns (Jb 7:9–10; 14:12; Is 26:14). See note on Tb 4:6.

**3:7** From here on, the story is told in the third person. Verse 7 relates one of the several marvelous coincidences that the storyteller uses to suggest divine providence; see also vv. 16–17; 4:1; 5:4. **Ecbatana**: Hamadan in modern Iran; this was the capital of ancient Media. **Raguel**: the Greek form of the Hebrew name *Re'u'el*, "friend of God."

**3:8 Asmodeus**: in Persian *aeshma daeva*, "demon of wrath," adopted into Aramaic with the sense of "the Destroyer." It will be subdued (8:3) by Raphael (v. 17), whose name means "God has healed."

**3:11 Toward the window**: that is, looking in prayer toward Jerusalem; cf. Dn 6:11. "Blessed are you" and "Blessed be God" are traditional openings of Jewish prayers (Tb 8:5, 15; 11:14; 13:1).

*n:* Ps 25:10; 119:137; Dn 3:27. *o:* Ex 34:7. *p:* Dt 28:15; Bar 1:16–22; 2:4–5; 3:8; Dn 9:5–6. *q:* Nm 11:15; 1 Kgs 19:4; Jb 7:15; Jon 4:3, 8. *r:* Tb 6:15; Gn 37:35; 42:38; 44:29, 31.

May all your works forever bless you.[s]
12 Now to you, Lord, I have turned my face
and have lifted up my eyes.
13 Bid me to depart from the earth,
never again to listen to such reproaches.
14 "You know, Master, that I am clean
of any defilement with a man.
15 I have never sullied my own name
or my father's name in the land of my captivity.
"I am my father's only daughter,
and he has no other child to be his heir,
Nor does he have a kinsman or close relative
whose wife I should wait to become.
Seven husbands of mine have already died.
Why then should I live any longer?
But if it does not please you, Lord, to take my life,
look favorably upon me and have pity on me,
that I may never again listen to such reproaches!"

*An Answer to Prayer.* 16 At that very time, the prayer of both of them was heard in the glorious presence of God. 17[t] So Raphael was sent to heal them both: to remove the white scales from Tobit's eyes, so that he might again see with his own eyes God's light; and to give Sarah, the daughter of Raguel, as a wife to Tobiah, the son of Tobit, and to rid her of the wicked demon Asmodeus. For it fell to Tobiah's lot* to claim her before any others who might wish to marry her.

At that very moment Tobit turned from the courtyard to his house, and Raguel's daughter Sarah came down from the upstairs room.

## III. Preparation for the Journey

### CHAPTER 4

See RG 152

*A Father's Instruction.* 1 That same day Tobit remembered the money he had deposited in trust with Gabael at Rages in Media. 2 He thought to himself, "Now that I have asked for death, why should I not call my son Tobiah and let him know about this money before I die?" 3 So he called his son Tobiah; and when he came, he said to him:* "Son, when I die, give me a decent burial. Honor your mother, and do not abandon her as long as she lives. Do whatever pleases her, and do not grieve her spirit in any way.[u] 4 Remember, son, how she went through many dangers for you while you were in her womb. When she dies, bury her in the same grave with me.

5 "Through all your days, son, keep the Lord in mind, and do not seek to sin or to transgress the commandments. Perform righteous deeds all the days of your life, and do not tread the paths of wickedness. 6[v] For those who act with fidelity, all who practice righteousness, will prosper in their affairs.*

7 "Give alms from your possessions. Do not turn your face away from any of the poor, so that God's face will not be turned away from you.[w] 8 Give in proportion to what you own. If you have great wealth, give alms out of your abundance; if you have but little, do not be afraid to give alms even of that little. 9 You will be storing up a goodly treasure for yourself against the day of adversity.[x] 10 For almsgiving delivers from death and keeps one from entering into Darkness. 11 Almsgiving is a worthy offering in the sight of the Most High for all who practice it.[y]

12 "Be on your guard, son, against every

**3:17 It fell to Tobiah's lot**: according to the patriarchal custom of marriage within the family group. Tobiah was Sarah's closest eligible relative (6:12). Cf. 4:12–13; Gn 24:4; 28:2; Ru 3:9–12; 4:1–12.

**4:3–19** A collection of maxims that parallel those in the wisdom literature, especially Proverbs and Sirach (see Introduction): duties toward parents (vv. 3–4; cf. also 14:13); perseverance in virtue and avoidance of evil (vv. 5–6, 14b); necessity and value of almsgiving and charity (vv. 7–11, 16–17); marriage within the clan (vv. 12–13a); industry (v. 13b); prompt payment of wages (v. 14a); the golden rule (v. 15a); temperance (v. 15b); docility (v. 18); prayer (v. 19).

**4:6** It was commonly thought in the Old Testament that virtue guaranteed earthly prosperity, and sin earthly disaster (Prv 10:2; cf. Dt 28).

*s:* 1 Kgs 8:44, 48; Ps 28:2; 134:2; Dn 6:11. *t:* Tb 4:12–13; 6:12–13; Gn 24:3–4. *u:* Ex 20:12; Prv 23:22; Sir 7:27. *v:* Tb 13:6; Jn 3:21; Eph 4:15. *w:* Tb 12:8–10; Dt 15:7–8, 11; Prv 19:17; Sir 4:1–6; 14:13; Lk 14:13; 1 Jn 3:17. *x:* Mt 6:20–21. *y:* Sir 3:30; 29:12.

## Tobit Sends for His Son

TOBIT'S SAGE ADVICE to Tobiah (4:3–21) reflects the morals of Judaism of the Hellenistic period. Indeed, Tobit is the picture of virtue, speaking wisely, offering "Azariah" (5:13) generous compensation, and keeping faith with God. Tobiah follows his example, and under the inspiration of the angel Raphael, saves himself from danger and brings healing to others.

kind of fornication, and above all, marry a woman of your own ancestral family. Do not marry a foreign woman, one who is not of your father's tribe, because we are descendants of the prophets, who were the first to speak the truth. Noah prophesied first, then Abraham, Isaac, and Jacob, our ancestors from the beginning of time. Son, remember that all of them took wives from among their own kindred and were blessed in their children, and that their posterity would inherit the land.[z] [13]Therefore, son, love your kindred. Do not act arrogantly toward any of them, the sons and daughters of your people, by refusing to take a wife for yourself from among them. For in arrogance there is ruin and great instability. In idleness there is loss and dire poverty, for idleness is the mother of famine.

[14]"Do not keep with you overnight the wages of those who have worked for you, but pay them at once. If you serve God thus, you will receive your reward. Be on your guard, son, in everything you do; be wise in all that you say and discipline yourself in all your conduct.[a] [15]Do to no one what you yourself hate. Do not drink wine till you become drunk or let drunkenness accompany you on your way.[b]

[16][c]"Give to the hungry some of your food, and to the naked some of your clothing. Whatever you have left over, give away as alms; and do not let your eye begrudge the alms that you give. [17][d] Pour out your wine and your bread on the grave of the righteous, but do not share them with sinners.*

[18]"Seek counsel from every wise person, and do not think lightly of any useful advice. [19][e] At all times bless the Lord, your God, and ask him that all your paths may be straight and all your endeavors and plans may prosper. For no other nation possesses good counsel, but it is the Lord who gives all good things. Whomever the Lord chooses to raise is raised; and whomever the Lord chooses to cast down is cast down to the recesses of Hades. So now, son, keep in mind these my commandments, and never let them be erased from your heart.

[20]"Now, I must tell you, son, that I have deposited in trust ten talents of silver with Gabael, the son of Gabri, at Rages in Media. [21]Do not fear, son, that we have lived in poverty. You will have great wealth, if you fear God, avoid all sin, and do what is good before the Lord your God."[f]

### CHAPTER 5

See RG 152

***The Angel Raphael.*** [1]Then Tobiah replied to his father Tobit: "Everything that you have commanded me, father, I shall do. [2]But how will I be able to get that money from him, since he does not know me, and I do not know him? What sign can I give him so that he will recognize and trust me, and give me the money? I do not even know the roads to Media, in order to go there." [3]Tobit answered his son Tobiah: "He gave me his bond,* and I gave him mine; I divided his into two parts, and each of us took one part; I put one part with the money. It is twenty years

**4:17** Tobit counsels his son to give alms in honor of the dead or, more probably, to give the "bread of consolation" to the family of the deceased. Cf. Jer 16:7; Ez 24:17.

**5:3 Bond**: a document called in Greek *cheirographon*. In the Middle Ages, notably in England, a deed and its duplicate were written on one piece of parchment, with the Latin word *chirographum* inscribed across the top of the sheet or between the two copies of the text. The document was then cut in two in either a straight or a wavy line, the parts being given to the persons concerned. Perhaps this procedure was derived from the present verse of Tobit. Duplicate documents, usually one part open and the other sealed, are well known from the ancient Near East.

*z:* Tb 3:15, 17; 6:12; Gn 11:29, 31; 25:20; 28:1–4; 29:15–30; Ex 34:16; Dt 7:3; Jgs 14:3. *a:* Lv 19:3; Dt 24:15. *b:* Mt 7:12; Lk 6:31. *c:* Dt 15:10; Is 58:7; Mt 25:35–36; 2 Cor 9:7. *d:* Jer 16:7; Lk 14:13. *e:* Dt 4:6; Ps 119:10. *f:* 1 Tm 6:6–10.

since I deposited that money! So, son, find yourself a trustworthy person who will make the journey with you, and we will give him wages when you return; but bring back that money from Gabael while I am still alive."

4 Tobiah went out to look for someone who would travel with him to Media, someone who knew the way. He went out and found the angel Raphael standing before him (though he did not know* that this was an angel of God).[g] 5 Tobiah said to him, "Where do you come from, young man?" He replied, "I am an Israelite, one of your kindred. I have come here to work." Tobiah said to him, "Do you know the way to Media?" 6 "Yes," he replied, "I have been there many times. I know the place well and am acquainted with all the routes. I have often traveled to Media; I used to stay with our kinsman Gabael, who lives at Rages in Media. It is a good two days' journey from Ecbatana to Rages,* for Rages is situated in the mountains, but Ecbatana is in the middle of the plain." 7 Tobiah said to him, "Wait for me, young man, till I go in and tell my father; for I need you to make the journey with me. I will pay you your wages."[h] 8 He replied, "Very well, I will wait; but do not be long."

9 Tobiah went in and informed his father Tobit: "I have found someone of our own Israelite kindred who will go with me!" Tobit said, "Call the man in, so that I may find out from what family and tribe he comes, and whether he is trustworthy enough to travel with you, son."

10 Tobiah went out to summon him, saying, "Young man, my father is calling for you." When Raphael entered the house, Tobit greeted him first. He replied, "Joyful greetings to you!" Tobit answered, "What joy is left for me? Here I am, a blind man who cannot see the light of heaven, but must remain in darkness, like the dead who no longer see the light! Though alive, I am among the dead. I can hear people's voices, but I do not see them." The young man said, "Take courage! God's healing is near; so take courage!" Tobit then said: "My son Tobiah wants to go to Media. Can you go with him to show him the way? I will pay you your wages, brother." He answered: "Yes, I will go with him, and I know all the routes. I have often traveled to Media and crossed all its plains so I know well the mountains and all its roads." 11 Tobit asked him, "Brother, tell me, please, from what family and tribe are you?" 12 He replied, "Why? What need do you have for a tribe? Aren't you looking for a hired man?" Tobit replied, "I only want to know, brother, whose son you truly are and what your name is."[i]

13 He answered, "I am Azariah,* son of the great Hananiah, one of your own kindred." 14 Tobit exclaimed: "Welcome! God save you, brother! Do not be provoked with me, brother, for wanting to learn the truth about your family. It turns out that you are a kinsman, from a noble and good line! I knew Hananiah and Nathan, the two sons of the great Shemeliah. They used to go to Jerusalem with me, where we would worship together. They were not led astray; your kindred are good people. You are certainly of good lineage. So welcome!"

15 Then he added: "For each day I will give you a drachma as wages,* as well as expenses for you and for my son. So go with my son, and 16 I will even add a bonus to your wages!" The young man replied: "I will go with him. Do not fear. In good health we will leave you, and in good health we will return to you, for the way is safe." 17 Tobit said, "Blessing be upon you, brother." Then he called his son and said to him: "Son, prepare whatever you need for the journey, and set out with your kinsman. May God in heaven protect you on the way and bring you back to me safe and sound; may his angel accompany you for your safety, son."

**5:4 He did not know**: the theme of an angel in disguise occurs frequently in folklore as well as in the Old Testament (Gn 18; cf. Heb 13:2).

**5:6 It is a good two days' journey from Ecbatana to Rages**: Alexander's army took eleven days in forced marches to cover this distance, about 180 miles. (See notes on 1:15; 3:7 and Introduction.)

**5:13–14** Azariah, "Yhwh has helped"; Hananiah, "Yhwh has shown mercy"; Nathan is a shortened form of Nathaniah, "Yhwh has given"; Shemeliah may be a Greek corruption of the Hebrew name, Shemaiah, "Yhwh has heard."

**5:15 A drachma as wages**: the normal wages, about seventeen cents, a day's wage for a laborer.

*g:* Heb 13:2. *h:* Tb 12:2. *i:* Jgs 13:17–18.

Tobiah left to set out on his journey, and
he kissed his father and mother. Tobit said to
him, "Have a safe journey." 18But his mother
began to weep and she said to Tobit: "Why
have you sent my child away? Is he not the
staff of our hands, as he goes in and out before us? 19Do not heap money upon money!
Rather relinquish it in exchange for our
child! 20What the Lord has given us to live
on is certainly enough for us." 21Tobit reassured her: "Do not worry! Our son will leave
in good health and come back to us in good
health. Your own eyes will see the day when
he returns to you safe and sound. So, do not
worry; do not fear for them, my sister.* 22For
a good angel* will go with him, his journey
will be successful, and he will return in good
health." 1Then she stopped weeping.

## IV. Tobiah's Journey to Media

### CHAPTER 6

See RG 152

*On the Way to Rages.* 2When the
young man left home, accompanied by the
angel, the dog followed Tobiah out and went
along with them. Both journeyed along, and
when the first night came, they camped beside the Tigris River.* 3When the young man
went down to wash his feet in the Tigris
River, a large fish leaped out of the water
and tried to swallow his foot. He shouted in
alarm. 4But the angel said to the young man,
"Grab the fish and hold on to it!" He seized
the fish and hauled it up on dry land. 5The
angel then told him: "Slit the fish open and
take out its gall, heart, and liver, and keep
them with you; but throw away the other entrails. Its gall, heart, and liver are useful for
medicine."* 6After Tobiah had slit the fish
open, he put aside the gall, heart, and liver.
Then he roasted and ate part of the fish; the
rest he salted and kept for the journey.

*Raphael's Instructions.* Afterward the two
of them traveled on together till they drew
near to Media. 7Then the young man asked
the angel this question: "Brother Azariah,
what medicine is in the fish's heart, liver,
and gall?" 8He answered: "As for the fish's
heart and liver, if you burn them to make
smoke in the presence of a man or a woman
who is afflicted by a demon or evil spirit,
any affliction will flee and never return. 9As
for the gall, if you apply it to the eyes of one
who has white scales, blowing right into
them, sight will be restored."

10When they had entered Media and were
getting close to Ecbatana, 11Raphael said to
the young man, "Brother Tobiah!" He answered, "Here I am!" Raphael continued,
"Tonight we must stay in the house of
Raguel, who is a relative of yours. He has a
beautiful daughter named Sarah, 12but no
other son or daughter apart from Sarah.
Since you are Sarah's closest relative, you
more than any other have the right to marry
her. Moreover, her father's estate is rightfully yours to inherit. The girl is wise, courageous, and very beautiful; and her father is a
good man who loves her dearly."[j] 13He continued: "You have the right to marry her. So
listen to me, brother. Tonight I will speak to
her father about the girl so that we may take
her as your bride. When we return from
Rages, we will have the wedding feast for
her. I know that Raguel cannot keep her
from you or promise her to another man; he
would incur the death penalty as decreed in
the Book of Moses.* For he knows that you,
more than anyone else, have the right to
marry his daughter. Now listen to me,
brother; we will speak about this girl
tonight, so that we may arrange her engagement to you. Then when we return from
Rages, we will take her and bring her back
with us to your house."

14But Tobiah said to Raphael in reply,

**5:21 My sister**: "sister" was a term of endearment used in antiquity even for one's wife; similarly "brother" for one's husband. Cf. 7:11, 15; 8:4, 21; 10:6, 13; Sg 4:9–10, 12; 5:1–2.

**5:22 A good angel**: a reference to a guardian angel, though Tobit does not know, of course, that Raphael himself, disguised as Azariah, is the good angel in this case.

**6:2 Tigris River**: this river is actually west of Nineveh, so they would not have come to it on their way to Media. See note on 1:15 and the Introduction.

**6:5 Its gall . . . medicine**: belief in the healing power of these organs was common among the physicians of antiquity.

**6:13 Raguel . . . Book of Moses**: Nm 36:6–8 prescribed marriage within the ancestral tribe for daughters who had no brothers who might inherit the ancestral property, but no death penalty is mentioned.

*j*: Tb 4:12–13; Nm 36:8.

**Tobiah and Sarah Are Married**

SIMILAR MARRIAGE ARRANGEMENTS are related in Genesis 24:14; 29:9–12; Exodus 2:16–21. The author strongly favors arranged marriages (see also Tb 6:16), probably because in a foreign society romantic marriages were likely to involve non-Israelites or members of other tribes, thus weakening religious unity or tribal integrity.

"Brother Azariah, I have heard that she has already been given in marriage to seven husbands, and that they have died in the bridal chamber. On the very night they approached her, they would die. I have also heard it said that it was a demon that killed them. [15]So now I too am afraid of this demon, because it is in love with her and does not harm her; but it kills any man who wishes to come close to her. I am my father's only child. If I should die, I would bring the life of my father and mother down to their grave in sorrow over me; they have no other son to bury them!"[k]

[16]Raphael said to him: "Do you not remember your father's commands? He ordered you to marry a woman from your own ancestral family. Now listen to me, brother; do not worry about that demon. Take Sarah. I know that tonight she will be given to you as your wife! [17]When you go into the bridal chamber, take some of the fish's liver and the heart, and place them on the embers intended for incense, and an odor will be given off. [18]As soon as the demon smells the odor, it will flee and never again show itself near her. Then when you are about to have intercourse with her, both of you must first get up to pray.* Beg the Lord of heaven that mercy and protection be granted you. Do not be afraid, for she was set apart for you before the world existed. You will save her, and she will go with you. And I assume that you will have children by her, and they will be like brothers for you. So do not worry."

When Tobiah heard Raphael's words that she was his kinswoman, and of the lineage of his ancestral house, he loved her deeply, and his heart was truly set on her.

## V. Marriage and Healing of Sarah

### CHAPTER 7

See RG 152

***At the House of Raguel.*** [1]When they entered Ecbatana, Tobiah said, "Brother Azariah, bring me straight to the house of our kinsman Raguel." So he did, and they came to the house of Raguel, whom they found seated by his courtyard gate. They greeted him first, and he answered, "Many greetings to you, brothers! Welcome! You have come in peace! Now enter in peace!" And he brought them into his house. [2]He said to his wife Edna, "How this young man resembles Tobit, the son of my uncle!" [3]So Edna asked them, saying, "Where are you from, brothers?" They answered, "We are descendants of Naphtali, now captives in Nineveh." [4]She said to them, "Do you know our kinsman Tobit?" They answered her, "Indeed, we do know him!" She asked, "Is he well?" [5]They answered, "Yes, he is alive and well." Then Tobiah said, "He is my father!" [6]Raguel jumped up, kissed him, and broke into tears. [7]Then, finding words, he said, "A blessing upon you, son! You are the son of a good and noble father. What a terrible misfortune that a man so righteous and charitable has been afflicted with blindness!" He embraced his kinsman Tobiah and continued to weep. [8]His wife Edna also wept for Tobit; and their daughter Sarah also began to weep.

***Marriage of Tobiah and Sarah.*** [9]Afterward, Raguel slaughtered a ram from the flock and gave them a warm reception. When they had washed, bathed, and reclined to eat and drink, Tobiah said to Raphael, "Brother Azariah, ask Raguel to give me my

**6:18 Get up to pray**: prayer, combined with ritual action, drives out the demon.

*k:* Tb 3:10.

kinswoman Sarah." [10]Raguel overheard the words; so he said to the young man: "Eat and drink and be merry tonight, for no man has a greater right to marry my daughter Sarah than you, brother. Besides, not even I have the right to give her to anyone but you, because you are my closest relative. However, son, I must frankly tell you the truth. [11]I have given her in marriage to seven husbands who were kinsmen of ours, and all died on the very night they approached her. But now, son, eat and drink. The Lord will look after you both." Tobiah answered, "I will neither eat nor drink anything here until you settle what concerns me."

Raguel said to him: "I will do it. She is yours as decreed by the Book of Moses. It has been decided in heaven that she be given to you! Take your kinswoman; from now on you are her brother, and she is your sister.* She is given to you today and here ever after. May the Lord of heaven prosper you both tonight, son, and grant you mercy and peace." [12]Then Raguel called his daughter Sarah, and she came to him. He took her by the hand and gave her to Tobiah with these words: "Take her according to the law. According to the decree written in the Book of Moses I give her to be your wife. Take her and bring her safely to your father. And may the God of heaven grant both of you a safe journey in peace!"[l] [13]He then called her mother and told her to bring writing materials. He wrote out a copy of a marriage contract stating that he gave Sarah to Tobiah as his wife as decreed by the law of Moses. Her mother brought the material, and he drew up the contract, to which he affixed his seal.[m]

[14]Afterward they began to eat and drink. [15]Later Raguel called his wife Edna and said, "My sister, prepare the other bedroom and bring Sarah there." [16]She went, made the bed in the room, as he had told her, and brought Sarah there. After she had cried over her, she wiped away her tears and said, [17]"Take courage, my daughter! May the Lord of heaven grant you joy in place of your grief! Courage, my daughter!" Then she left.

## CHAPTER 8

See RG 152

*Expulsion of the Demon.* [1]When they had finished eating and drinking, they wanted to retire. So they brought the young man out and led him to the bedroom. [2]Tobiah, mindful of Raphael's instructions, took the fish's liver and heart from the bag where he had them, and put them on the embers intended for incense.* [3]The odor of the fish repulsed the demon, and it fled to the upper regions of Egypt;* Raphael went in pursuit of it and there bound it hand and foot. Then Raphael returned immediately.

[4]When Sarah's parents left the bedroom and closed the door behind them, Tobiah rose from bed and said to his wife, "My sister, come, let us pray and beg our Lord to grant us mercy and protection." [5]She got up, and they started to pray and beg that they might be protected. He began with these words:

"Blessed are you, O God of our ancestors;
blessed be your name forever and ever!
Let the heavens and all your creation
bless you forever.[n]
[6] You made Adam, and you made his wife Eve
to be his helper and support;
and from these two the human race has come.
You said, 'It is not good for the man to be alone;
let us make him a helper like himself.'[o]
[7] Now, not with lust,
but with fidelity I take this kinswoman
as my wife.

**7:11 You are her brother, and she is your sister**: the marriage formula is similar to a marriage contract from the fifth century B.C. found at Elephantine in Egypt: "She is my wife and I am her husband from this day forever."

**8:2–3** The manner of coping with demonic influences among the ancients seems strange to us. However, the fish here is a folktale element, suggesting the hero's fight with a dragon, and not a recipe for exorcism. It is clear that the author places primary emphasis on the value of prayer to God (6:18; 8:4–8), on the role of the angel as God's agent, and on the pious disposition of Tobiah.

**8:3** The desert was considered the dwelling place of demons. Cf. Is 13:21; 34:14; Mt 4:1; 12:43.

*l:* Gn 24:50–51. *m:* Tb 6:12. *n:* Dn 3:26. *o:* Gn 2:18–23.

Send down your mercy on me and on
her,
and grant that we may grow old
together.
Bless us with children."

8They said together, "Amen, amen!" 9Then they went to bed for the night.

But Raguel got up and summoned his servants. They went out with him and dug a grave, 10for he said, "Perhaps Tobiah will die; then we would be a laughingstock and an object of mockery." 11When they had finished digging the grave, Raguel went back into the house and called his wife, 12saying, "Send one of the maids in to see whether he is alive. If he has died, let us bury him without anyone knowing about it." 13They sent the maid, lit a lamp, and opened the bedroom door; she went in and found them sleeping together. 14The maid came out and told them that Tobiah was alive, and that nothing was wrong. 15Then they praised the God of heaven in these words:

"Blessed are you, God, with every pure
blessing!
Let all your chosen ones bless you
forever!
16 Blessed are you, for you have made me
happy;
what I feared did not happen.
Rather you have dealt with us
according to your abundant mercy.
17 Blessed are you, for you have shown
mercy
toward two only children.
Grant them, Master, mercy and
protection,
and bring their lives to fulfillment
with happiness and mercy."

18Then Raguel told his servants to fill in the grave before dawn.

***Wedding Feast.*** 19He asked his wife to bake many loaves of bread; he himself went out to the herd and brought two steers and four rams, which he ordered to be slaughtered. So they began to prepare the feast. 20He summoned Tobiah and said to him, "For fourteen days* you shall not stir from here, but shall remain here eating and drinking with me; you shall bring joy to my daughter's afflicted spirit. 21Now take half of what I own here; go back in good health to your father. The other half will be yours when I and my wife die. Take courage, son! I am your father, and Edna is your mother; we belong to you and to your sister both now and forever. So take courage, son!"

## CHAPTER 9

See RG 152

***The Money Recovered.*** 1Then Tobiah called Raphael and said to him: 2"Brother Azariah, take along with you from here four servants and two camels and travel to Rages.* Go to Gabael's house and give him this bond. Get the money and then bring him along with you to the wedding celebration. 3For you know that my father will be counting the days. If I should delay even by a single day, I would cause him intense grief. 4You have witnessed the oath that Raguel has sworn; I cannot violate his oath." 5So Raphael, together with the four servants and two camels, traveled to Rages in Media, where they stayed at Gabael's house. Raphael gave Gabael his bond and told him about Tobit's son Tobiah, that he had married and was inviting him to the wedding celebration. Gabael got up and counted out for him the moneybags with their seals, and they packed them on the camels.

6The following morning they both got an early start and traveled to the wedding celebration. When they entered Raguel's house, they found Tobiah reclining at table. He jumped up and greeted Gabael, who wept and blessed him, exclaiming: "Good and noble child, son of a good and noble, righteous and charitable man, may the Lord bestow a heavenly blessing on you and on your wife, and on your wife's father and mother. Blessed be God, because I have seen the very image of my cousin Tobit!"

**8:20 For fourteen days**: because of the happy, and unexpected, turn of events, Raguel doubles the time of the wedding feast. When Tobiah returns home, the usual seven-day feast is held (11:18). Cf. Jgs 14:12.

**9:2 To Rages**: see note on 5:6.

**Tobiah and Sarah Leave Ecbatana**

WHEN ANNA CALLS Tobiah the "light of my eyes" (10:5), she is expressing the symbolic sight-blindness motif: Israel is blind to the meaning of history, but light will come at the end. See Tobit 11:15. Tobiah's pleas to be allowed to go home are meant to be a model for all exiled Israelites who should yearn constantly for home.

# VI. Tobiah's Return Journey to Nineveh and the Healing of Tobit

## CHAPTER 10

See RG 152

***Anxiety of the Parents.*** 1Meanwhile, day by day, Tobit was keeping track of the time Tobiah would need to go and to return. When the number of days was reached and his son did not appear, 2he said, "Could it be that he has been detained there? Or perhaps Gabael has died, and there is no one to give him the money?" 3And he began to grieve. 4His wife Anna said, "My son has perished and is no longer among the living!" And she began to weep aloud and to wail over her son: 5"Alas, child, light of my eyes, that I have let you make this journey!" 6But Tobit kept telling her: "Be still, do not worry, my sister; he is safe! Probably they have to take care of some unexpected business there. The man who is traveling with him is trustworthy and one of our kindred. So do not grieve over him, my sister. He will be here soon." 7But she retorted, "You be still, and do not try to deceive me! My son has perished!" She would rush out and keep watch every day at the road her son had taken. She ate nothing. After the sun had set, she would go back home to wail and cry the whole night through, getting no sleep at all.[p]

***Departure from Ecbatana.*** Now when the fourteen days of the wedding celebration, which Raguel had sworn to hold for his daughter, had come to an end, Tobiah went to him and said: "Send me off, now, since I know that my father and mother do not believe they will ever see me again. So I beg you, father, let me depart and go back to my own father. I have already told you how I left him." 8Raguel said to Tobiah: "Stay, son, stay with me. I am sending messengers to your father Tobit, and they will give him news of you." 9But Tobiah insisted, "No, I beg you to send me back to my father."

10Raguel then promptly handed over to Tobiah his wife Sarah, together with half of all his property: male and female slaves, oxen and sheep, donkeys and camels, clothing, money, and household goods. 11He saw them safely off. Embracing Tobiah, he said to him: "Farewell, son. Have a safe journey. May the Lord of heaven grant prosperity to you and to your wife Sarah. And may I see children of yours before I die!" 12Then he said to his daughter Sarah, "My daughter, honor your father-in-law and your mother-in-law, because from now on they are as much your parents as the ones who brought you into the world. Go in peace, daughter; let me hear a good report about you as long as I live." Finally he said good-bye to them and let them go.

Edna also said to Tobiah: "My child and beloved kinsman, may the Lord bring you back safely, and may I live long enough to see children of you and of my daughter Sarah before I die. Before the Lord, I entrust my daughter to your care. Never cause her grief all the days of your life. Go in peace, son. From now on I am your mother, and Sarah is your sister. Together may we all prosper throughout the days of our lives." She kissed them both and saw them safely off.

13Tobiah left Raguel, full of happiness and joy, and he blessed the Lord of heaven and earth, the King of all, for making his journey so successful. Finally he blessed Raguel and his wife Edna, and added, "I have been commanded by the Lord to honor you all the days of your life!"

*p:* Gn 45:26.

## CHAPTER 11

See RG 152

*Homeward Journey.* 1As they drew
near to Kaserin, which is opposite Nineveh,
2Raphael said: "You know how we left your
father. 3Let us hurry on ahead of your wife to
prepare the house while they are still on the
way." 4So both went on ahead together, and
Raphael said to him, "Take the gall in your
hand!" And the dog ran along behind them.
5Meanwhile, Anna sat watching the road
by which her son was to come. 6When she
saw him coming, she called to his father,
"Look, your son is coming, and the man who
traveled with him!"
7Raphael said to Tobiah before he came
near to his father: "I know that his eyes will
be opened. 8Apply the fish gall to his eyes,
and the medicine will make the white scales
shrink and peel off from his eyes; then your
father will have sight again and will see the
light of day."

*Sight Restored.* 9Then Anna ran up to her
son, embraced him, and said to him, "Now
that I have seen you again, son, I am ready to
die!" And she sobbed aloud.[q] 10Tobit got up
and stumbled out through the courtyard gate
to meet his son. Tobiah went up to him
11with the fish gall in his hand and blew into
his eyes. Holding him firmly, he said,
"Courage, father." Then he applied the medicine to his eyes, and it made them sting.
12,13Tobiah used both hands to peel the white
scales from the corners of his eyes. Tobit
saw his son and threw his arms around him.
14Weeping, he exclaimed, "I can see you,
son, the light of my eyes!" Then he prayed,

"Blessed be God,
blessed be his great name,
and blessed be all his holy angels.
May his great name be with us,
and blessed be all the angels
throughout all the ages.
15 God it was who afflicted me,
and God who has had mercy on me.
Now I see my son Tobiah!"

Then Tobit went back in, rejoicing and praising God with full voice. Tobiah related to his
father how his journey had been a success;
that he had brought back the money; and that
he had married Raguel's daughter Sarah,
who was about to arrive, for she was near the
gate of Nineveh.[r]
16Rejoicing and blessing God, Tobit went
out to the gate of Nineveh to meet his daughter-in-law. When the people of Nineveh saw
him coming, walking along briskly, with no
one leading him by the hand, they were
amazed. 17Before them all Tobit proclaimed
how God had shown mercy to him and
opened his eyes. When Tobit came up to
Sarah, the wife of his son Tobiah, he blessed
her and said: "Welcome, my daughter!
Blessed be your God for bringing you to us,
daughter! Blessed are your father and your
mother. Blessed be my son Tobiah, and
blessed be you, daughter! Welcome to your
home with blessing and joy. Come in,
daughter!" That day there was joy for all the
Jews who lived in Nineveh. 18Ahiqar and his
nephew Nadin* were also on hand to rejoice
with Tobit. Tobiah's wedding feast was celebrated with joy for seven days, and many
gifts were given to him.

# VII. Raphael Reveals His Identity

## CHAPTER 12

See RG 152

*Raphael's Wages.** 1When the wedding celebration came to an end, Tobit called
his son Tobiah and said to him, "Son, see to
it that you pay his wages to the man who
made the journey with you and give him a
bonus too." 2Tobiah said: "Father, how
much shall I pay him? It would not hurt to
give him half the wealth he brought back
with me.[s] 3He led me back safe and sound,
healed my wife, brought the money back
with me, and healed you. How much should
I pay him?" 4Tobit answered, "It is only fair,
son, that he should receive half of all that he
brought back." 5So Tobiah called Raphael

**11:18 Nadin**: see note on 14:10.
**12:1–5** Tobit and his son generously agree to give Raphael far more than the wages agreed upon in 5:15–16.

*q:* Gn 33:4; 45:14; 46:29–30; Lk 15:20. *r:* Tb 13:2; Dt 32:39; 1 Sm 2:6. *s:* Tb 5:3, 7, 15–16.

> **THE "WHOLE TRUTH"** (12:11) is that God's Providence works through human misfortune to test human beings, a theme that pervades Wisdom literature; see Wis 3:6; Prv 17:3.

and said, "Take as your wages half of all that you have brought back, and farewell!"

***Exhortation.**** [6]Raphael called the two of them aside privately and said to them: "Bless God and give him thanks before all the living for the good things he has done for you, by blessing and extolling his name in song. Proclaim before all with due honor the deeds of God, and do not be slack in thanking him.* [7]A king's secret should be kept secret, but one must declare the works of God and give thanks with due honor. Do good, and evil will not overtake you. [8]Prayer with fasting is good. Almsgiving with righteousness is better than wealth with wickedness. It is better to give alms than to store up gold,[t] [9]for almsgiving saves from death, and purges all sin. Those who give alms will enjoy a full life,[u] [10]but those who commit sin and do evil are their own worst enemies.

***Raphael's Identity.*** [11]"I shall now tell you the whole truth and conceal nothing at all from you. I have already said to you, 'A king's secret should be kept secret, but one must declare the works of God with due honor.' [12][v] Now when you, Tobit, and Sarah prayed, it was I who presented the record of your prayer before the Glory of the Lord; and likewise whenever you used to bury the dead.* [13]When you did not hesitate to get up and leave your dinner in order to go and bury that dead man, [14]I was sent to put you to the test. At the same time, however, God sent me to heal you and your daughter-in-law Sarah. [15]I am Raphael, one of the seven angels who stand and serve before the Glory of the Lord."[w]

[16]Greatly shaken, the two of them fell prostrate in fear. [17]But Raphael said to them: "Do not fear; peace be with you! Bless God now and forever. [18]As for me, when I was with you, I was not acting out of any favor on my part, but by God's will. So bless God every day; give praise with song. [19]Even though you saw me eat and drink, I did not eat or drink anything; what you were seeing was a vision. [20]So now bless the Lord on earth and give thanks to God. Look, I am ascending to the one who sent me. Write down all that has happened to you."[x] And he ascended. [21]They stood up but were no longer able to see him. [22]They kept blessing God and singing his praises, and they continued to give thanks for these marvelous works that God had done, because an angel of God appeared to them.

## VIII. Tobit's Song of Praise

### CHAPTER 13

See RG 152

[1]* Then Tobit spoke and composed a song of joyful praise; he said:

Blessed be God who lives forever,
  because his kingship lasts for all ages.[y]
[2] For he afflicts and shows mercy,
  casts down to the depths of Hades,
  brings up from the great abyss.
What is there that can snatch from his
  hand?[z]

**12:6–10** In the fashion of a wisdom teacher, Raphael gives the two men a short exhortation similar to the one Tobit gave his son in 4:3–19.

**12:6–7** The faithful considered the praise of God their most esteemed privilege. Without it, life was meaningless; cf. Is 38:16–20.

**12:12** Raphael is one of the seven Angels of the Presence, specially designated intercessors who present prayers to God. Angelology was developing in this period. The names of two other of these seven angels are given in the Bible: Gabriel (Dn 8:16; 9:21; Lk 1:19, 26) and Michael (Dn 10:13, 21; 12:1; Jude 9; Rev 12:7). See 1 Enoch for the names of the rest.

**13:1–18** Tobit's hymn of praise is divided into two parts. The first part (vv. 1–8) is a song of praise that echoes themes from the psalms; the second (vv. 9–18) is addressed to Jerusalem in the style of those prophets who spoke of a new and ideal Jerusalem (Is 60; cf. Rev 21). **Joyful praise**: words for joy and gladness occur throughout this prayer (vv. 1, 7, 10, 11, 13, 14, 16, 18).

*t:* Tb 4:7–11; Sir 29:8–13. *u:* Dn 4:24. *v:* Jb 33:23–24; Acts 10:4; Rev 8:3–4. *w:* Lk 1:19; Rev 8:2. *x:* Jgs 13:20. *y:* Tb 3:11; 8:5, 15; 1 Chr 29:10; Dn 3:26. *z:* Tb 11:15; 13:9; Dt 32:39; 1 Sm 2:6; Wis 16:13.

to see your glory and to give thanks to
the King of heaven!
The gates of Jerusalem will be built with
sapphire and emerald,
and all your walls with precious
stones.
The towers of Jerusalem will be built
with gold,
and their battlements with purest
gold.[h]
17 The streets of Jerusalem will be paved
with rubies and stones of Ophir;
18 The gates of Jerusalem will sing hymns
of gladness,
and all its houses will cry out,
Hallelujah!
Blessed be the God of Israel for all ages!
For in you the blessed will bless the holy
name forever and ever.

## IX. Epilogue

### CHAPTER 14

See RG 152

*Parting Advice.* 1 So the words of Tobit's hymn of praise came to an end. Tobit
died in peace at the age of a hundred and
twelve and was buried with honor in Nineveh. 2 He was fifty-eight years old when he
lost his eyesight, and after he recovered it he
lived in prosperity, giving alms; he continued to fear God and give thanks to the divine
Majesty.
3 As he was dying, he summoned his son
Tobiah and Tobiah's seven sons, and commanded him, "Son, take your children[l] 4 and
flee into Media, for I believe God's word
that Nahum* spoke against Nineveh. It will
all happen and will overtake Assyria and
Nineveh; indeed all that was said by Israel's
prophets whom God sent will come to pass.
Not one of all their words will remain unfulfilled, but everything will take place in the
time appointed for it. So it will be safer in
Media than in Assyria or Babylon. For I
know and believe that whatever God has
said will be accomplished. It will happen,
and not a single word of the prophecies will
fail.
As for our kindred who dwell in the land
of Israel, they will all be scattered and taken
into captivity from the good land. All the
land of Israel will become a wilderness;
even Samaria and Jerusalem will be a wilderness! For a time, the house of God will be
desolate and will be burned.[j] 5 But God will
again have mercy on them and bring them
back to the land of Israel. They will build the
house again, but it will not be like the first
until the era when the appointed times will
be completed.* Afterward all of them will return from their captivity, and they will rebuild Jerusalem with due honor. In it the
house of God will also be rebuilt, just as the
prophets of Israel said of it.[k] 6 All the nations of the world will turn and reverence
God in truth; all will cast away their idols,
which have deceitfully led them into error.*
7 They will bless the God of the ages in righteousness. All the Israelites truly mindful of
God, who are to be saved in those days, will
be gathered together and will come to Jerusalem; in security will they dwell forever in
the land of Abraham, which will be given to
them. Those who love God sincerely will rejoice, but those who commit sin and wickedness will disappear completely from the
land.[m]
8,9 "Now, my children, I give you this command: serve God sincerely and do what is
pleasing in his sight; you must instruct your
children to do what is right and to give alms,
to be mindful of God and at all times to bless
his name sincerely and with all their strength.
Now, as for you, son, leave Nineveh; do not
stay here. 10 The day you bury your mother

**14:4–5 Nahum**: one of the minor prophets, whose book contains oracles of doom against Nineveh. Here, in keeping with the period in which the story is set, the author makes Tobit speak as if the punishment of Nineveh, the destruction of Jerusalem (587 B.C.), the exile from Judah and the return, would all take place in the future. The technique of using the facts of past history as seemingly future predictions is a frequent device of apocalyptic writers. **The good land**: a favorite name for the promised land. Cf. Dt 1:35; 3:25; 4:21–22.

**14:5 Until the era . . . completed**: a reference to the coming of the day of the Lord, when a new, more perfect temple was to be expected. Cf. Heb 9:1–14.

**14:6** Conversion of the nations is also to come with the day of the Lord.

*h:* Tb 14:5; Is 54:11–13; 62:2; Rev 21:10–21. *i:* Gn 47:29–30. *j:* Na 2:2–3:19. *k:* Neh 12:27; Jer 31:38. *l:* Is 60:1–4. *m:* Is 60:21; Jer 32:37; Ez 34:28; 37:25; 39:26.

3 Give thanks to him, you Israelites, in the presence of the nations,
for though he has scattered you among them,
4 even there recount his greatness.
Exalt him before every living being,
because he is your Lord, and he is your God,
our Father and God forever and ever!
5 He will afflict you for your iniquities,
but will have mercy on all of you.
He will gather you from all the nations
among whom you have been scattered.[a]

6 When you turn back to him with all your heart,
and with all your soul do what is right before him,
Then he will turn to you,
and will hide his face from you no longer.[b]
Now consider what he has done for you,
and give thanks with full voice.
Bless the Lord of righteousness,
and exalt the King of the ages.

In the land of my captivity I give thanks,
and declare his power and majesty to a sinful nation.
According to your heart do what is right before him:
perhaps there will be pardon for you.
7 As for me, I exalt my God,
my soul exalts the King of heaven,
and rejoices all the days of my life.
Let all sing praise to his greatness,
8 let all speak and give thanks in Jerusalem.

9 Jerusalem, holy city,
he will afflict you for the works of your hands,*
but will again pity the children of the righteous.[c]
10 Give thanks to the Lord with righteousness,
and bless the King of the ages,
so that your tabernacle may be rebuilt in you with joy.
May he gladden within you all who are captives;
may he cherish within you all who are distressed
for all generations to come.[d]

11 A bright light will shine to the limits of the earth.
Many nations will come to you from afar,
And inhabitants of all the ends of the earth
to your holy name,
Bearing in their hands gifts for the King of heaven.
Generation after generation will offer
joyful worship in you;
your name will be great forever and ever.[e]

12 Cursed be all who despise you and revile you;
cursed be all who hate you and speak a harsh word against you;
cursed be all who destroy you
and pull down your walls,
And all who overthrow your towers
and set fire to your homes.
But blessed forever be all those who respect you.[f]
13 Go, then, rejoice and exult over the children of the righteous,
for they will all be gathered together
and will bless the Lord of the ages.
14 Happy are those who love you,
and happy are those who rejoice in your peace.
Happy too are all who grieve
over all your afflictions,
For they will rejoice over you
and behold all your joy forever.[g]
15 My soul, bless the Lord, the great King;
16 for Jerusalem will be rebuilt as his house forever.
Happy too will I be if a remnant of my offspring survives

**13:9 Works of your hands**: idols.

*a:* Dt 30:3; Neh 1:9. *b:* Dt 30:2. *c:* Tb 11:15; Mi 7:19; Rev 21. Mi 4:2; Zec 8:22. *f:* Bar 4:31–32. *g:* Ps 122:6; Is 66:10. *d:* Is 44:26, 28; Am 9:11; Zec 1:16. *e:* Is 2:3–4; 9:1; 49:6; 60:1;

next to me, do not even stay overnight within the confines of the city. For I see that there is much wickedness in it, and much treachery is practiced in it, and people are not ashamed. See, my son, all that Nadin* did to Ahiqar, the very one who reared him. Was not Ahiqar brought down alive into the earth? Yet God made Nadin's disgraceful crime rebound against him. Ahiqar came out again into the light, but Nadin went into the everlasting darkness, for he had tried to kill Ahiqar. Because Ahiqar had given alms he escaped from the deadly trap Nadin had set for him. But Nadin fell into the deadly trap himself, and it destroyed him.[n] [11]So, my children, see what almsgiving does, and also what wickedness does—it kills! But now my spirit is about to leave me."

***Death of Tobit and Tobiah.*** They laid him on his bed, and he died; and he was buried with honor. [12]When Tobiah's mother died, he buried her next to his father. He then departed with his wife and children for Media, where he settled in Ecbatana with his father-in-law Raguel.[o] [13]He took respectful care of his aging father-in-law and mother-in-law; and he buried them at Ecbatana in Media. Then he inherited Raguel's estate as well as that of his father Tobit. [14]He died highly respected at the age of one hundred seventeen. [15]But before he died, he saw and heard of the destruction of Nineveh. He saw the inhabitants of the city being led captive into Media by Cyaxares,* the king of Media. Tobiah blessed God for all that he had done against the Ninevites and Assyrians. Before dying he rejoiced over Nineveh, and he blessed the Lord God forever and ever.

**14:10 Nadin**: in the *Story of Ahiqar*, the hero Ahiqar, chancellor under the Assyrian kings Sennacherib and Esarhaddon, adopts his nephew Nadin and prepares him to become his successor. But Nadin treacherously plots to have his uncle put to death. Ahiqar hides in a friend's house and is finally vindicated when Nadin's scheme is discovered. Thereupon Nadin is thrown into a dungeon where he dies. It was Ahiqar's almsgiving that delivered him from death; see note on 2:2. The Greek and Latin versions of the Book of Tobit read the name as Nadab, but the Aramaic form has the ancient name Nadin, which is also found in the fifth-century B.C. Aramaic *Story of Ahiqar*.

**14:15 Cyaxares**: Nabopolassar, king of Babylon, and Cyaxares conquered and destroyed Nineveh in 612 B.C.; see note on 1:15.

*n:* Tb 1:21–22. *o:* Tb 4:4.

See RG 153–55

# The Book of Judith

The Book of Judith relates the story of God's deliverance of the Jewish people. This was accomplished "by the hand of a female"—a constant motif (cf. 8:33; 9:9, 10; 12:4; 13:4, 14, 15; 15:10; 16:5) meant to recall the "hand" of God in the Exodus narrative (cf. Ex 15:6). The work may have been written around 100 B.C., but its historical range is extraordinary. Within the reign of Nebuchadnezzar (1:1; 2:1), it telescopes five centuries of historical and geographical information with imaginary details. There are references to Nineveh, the Assyrian capital destroyed in 612 B.C., to Nebuchadnezzar, the ruler not of Assyria but of Babylon (605/604–562), and to the second Temple, built around 515. The postexilic period is presumed (e.g., governance by the High Priest). The Persian period is represented by two characters, Holofernes and Bagoas, who appear together in the military campaigns of Artaxerxes III Ochus (358–338); there seem to be allusions to the second-century Seleucid ruler Antiochus IV Epiphanes. Several mysteries remain: Judith herself, Arphaxad, and others are otherwise unknown. The geographical details, such as the narrow defile into Bethulia (an unidentified town which gives access to the heart of the land), are fanciful. The simple conclusion from these and other details is that the work is historical fiction, written to exalt God as Israel's deliverer from foreign might, not by an army, but by means of a simple widow.

There are four Greek recensions of Judith (Septuagint codices Vaticanus, Sinaiticus, Alexandrinus, and Basiliano-Vaticanus), four ancient translations (Old Latin, Syriac, Sahidic, and Ethiopic), and some late Hebrew versions, apparently translated from the Vulgate. Despite Jerome's claim to have translated an Aramaic

## Nebuchadnezzar Wages War on Arphaxad

NEBUCHADNEZZAR, KING OF the Babylonians from 605 to 561 B.C., directed the destruction of Jerusalem in 587 B.C. His father had conquered the Assyrians and destroyed Nineveh in 612 B.C. The historically impossible combination of Nebuchadnezzar and the Assyrians suggests that the author wished to combine Israel's traditional enemies to create a literary confrontation between faith and secular power.

text, no ancient Aramaic or Hebrew manuscripts have been found. The oldest extant text of Judith is the preservation of 15:1–7 inscribed on a third-century A.D. potsherd. Whatever the reasons, the rabbis did not count Judith among their scriptures, and the Reformation adopted that position. The early Church, however, held this book in high honor. The first-century Pope, St. Clement of Rome, proposes Judith as an example of courageous love (1 Corinthians 55). St. Jerome holds her up as an example of a holy widow and a type of the Church (To Salvina: Letter 79, par. 10; see also To Furia: Letter 54, par. 16) and, in another place, describes Mary as a new Judith (To Eustochium: Letter 22, par. 21). The Council of Trent (1546) included Judith in the canon; thus it is one of the seven deuterocanonical books.

Inner-biblical references are noteworthy: as God acted through Moses' hand (Ex 10:21–22; 14:27–30), so God delivers "by the hand of a female," Judith. Like Jael, who drove a tent peg through the head of Sisera (Jgs 4), Judith kills an enemy general. Like Deborah (Jgs 4–5), Judith "judges" Israel in the time of military crisis. Like Sarah, the mother of Israel's future (Gn 17:6), Judith's beauty deceives foreigners, with the result that blessings redound to Israel (Gn 12:11–20). Her Hebrew name means "Jewish woman." Her exploits captured the imagination of liturgists, artists, and writers through the centuries. The book is filled with double entendres and ironic situations, e.g., Judith's conversation with Holofernes in 11:5–8, 19, where "my lord" is ambiguous, and her declaration to Holofernes that she will lead him through Judea to Jerusalem (his head goes on such a journey).

The book can be divided into five parts:

I. Assyrian Threat (1:1–3:10)
II. Siege of Bethulia (4:1–7:32)
III. Judith, Instrument of the Lord (8:1–10:10)
IV. Judith Goes Out to War (10:11–13:20)
V. Victory and Thanksgiving (14:1–16:25)

# I. Assyrian Threat*

## CHAPTER 1

See RG 154-56

### *Nebuchadnezzar Against Arphaxad.**

1 It was the twelfth year* of the reign of Nebuchadnezzar, who ruled over the Assyrians
in the great city of Nineveh. At that time Arphaxad was ruling over the Medes in Ecbatana.[a] 2* Around Ecbatana he built a wall of
hewn stones, three cubits thick and six cubits long. He made the walls seventy cubits
high and fifty cubits wide. 3 At its gates he
raised towers one hundred cubits high with
foundations sixty cubits wide. 4 He made its
gates seventy cubits high and forty cubits
wide to allow passage of his mighty forces,
with his infantry in formation. 5 At that time
King Nebuchadnezzar waged war against
King Arphaxad in the vast plain that borders
Ragau.* 6 Rallying to him were all who lived
in the hill country, all who lived along the

**1:1–3:10** This section consists of an introduction to Nebuchadnezzar (1:1–16), his commissioning of Holofernes (2:1–13), and a description of the campaigns Holofernes leads against the disobedient vassal nations of the west (2:14–3:10).

**1:1–16** Introduction to Nebuchadnezzar and his campaign against Arphaxad. Nebuchadnezzar (605/4–562 B.C.), the most famous Neo-Babylonian king, destroyed Jerusalem in 587 B.C., the eighteenth year of his reign (see Jer 32:1). His depiction here as an Assyrian is an invention of the author, as is the description of Arphaxad, an otherwise unknown king of the Medes, in Ecbatana.

**1:1 Twelfth year**: in the twelfth year of Nebuchadnezzar (593 B.C.) Zedekiah, king of Judah, refused to join a revolt against him (see Jer 27:3; 28:1). **Nineveh**: capital of Assyria, destroyed in 612 B.C.

**1:2–4** Since a cubit was the distance from the elbow to the

*a*: Gn 10:22; Ezr 6:2; Tb 3:7; 5:6; 6:10; 7:1; 14:12–13; 2 Mc 9:3; Jon 1:2; 3:2–3.

NEBUCHADNEZZAR'S DESIGNATION OF himself as "lord" without references to the rights of God (2:5) makes this a battle between the ungodly and the God-fearing. The offering of earth and water (v. 7) was a Persian expression for the provisioning of an invading and conquering army by the occupied country.

Euphrates, the Tigris, and the Hydaspes, as
well as Arioch, king of the Elamites, in the
plains. Thus many nations joined the ranks
of the Chelodites.* [b]
7Then Nebuchadnezzar, king of the Assyrians, contacted all the inhabitants of Persia* and all who lived in the west, the inhabitants of Cilicia and Damascus, Lebanon and
Antilebanon, and all who lived along the
seacoast, 8the peoples of Carmel, Gilead,
Upper Galilee, and the vast plain of Esdraelon, 9and all in Samaria and its cities,
and west of the Jordan as far as Jerusalem,
Bethany, Chelous, Kadesh,[c] and the river of
Egypt; Tahpanhes,[d] Raamses, all the land of
Goshen, 10Tanis, Memphis[e] and beyond, and
all the inhabitants of Egypt as far as the borders of Ethiopia.
11But all the inhabitants of the whole land*
made light of the summons of Nebuchadnezzar, king of the Assyrians, and would not join
him in the war. They were not afraid of him,
since he was only a single opponent. So they
sent back his envoys empty-handed and disgraced.[f] 12Then Nebuchadnezzar fell into a
violent rage against all the land, and swore by
his throne and his kingdom that he would take
revenge on all the territories of Cilicia, Damascus, and Syria, and would destroy with
his sword all the inhabitants of Moab, Ammon, the whole of Judea, and all those living
in Egypt as far as the coasts of the two seas.*
***Defeat of Arphaxad.*** 13In the seventeenth
year* he mustered his forces against King
Arphaxad and was victorious in his campaign. He routed the whole force of Arphaxad, his entire cavalry, and all his chariots, 14and took possession of his cities. He
pressed on to Ecbatana, took its towers,
sacked its marketplaces, and turned its glory
into shame. 15He captured Arphaxad in the
mountains of Ragau, ran him through with
spears, and utterly destroyed him once and
for all. 16Then he returned to Nineveh with
all his consolidated forces, a very great multitude of warriors; and there he and his
forces relaxed and feasted for one hundred
and twenty days.[g]

## CHAPTER 2

See RG 154–56

***Revenge Planned Against the Western Nations.**** 1In the eighteenth year,* on the

fingertip (approximately eighteen inches), these dimensions are prodigious. The massive wall around Ecbatana is described as 105 feet high and 75 feet thick, with each stone measuring four and a half feet thick and nine feet long. The tower gates are 150 feet high and 60 feet wide. Such unlikely massive structures have never been found at Ecbatana, which lies beneath the modern city of Hamadan, located in the Zagros mountains of northwest Iran. Ecbatana is mentioned in vv. 1, 2, 14 as Arphaxad's headquarters. Tradition claims Esther and Mordecai are buried there.

**1:5** Ragau, the place where Arphaxad is slain (v. 15), one of the oldest settlements in Iran, is located on a plain one hundred miles northeast of Ecbatana. In the Book of Tobit it is the home of Gabael (Tb 1:14; 4:1, 20; 5:6; 6:13; 9:2, 5).

**1:6 Chelodites**: Greek *Cheleoud*, probably a corruption of "Chaldeans," i.e., the Neo-Babylonians.

**1:7** Mention of Persia suggests a postexilic setting for the book, since this area would have been designated Media before the middle of the fifth century B.C.

**1:11** References to "the whole land," "all the land" are used ten times in the first two chapters (vv. 11, 12; 2:1, 2, 5, 6, 7, 9, 10, 19). This signifies all the nations west of Persia as far as Egypt that were subject to Nebuchadnezzar, i.e., the whole earth or world (esp. 2:9). These and similar formulations throughout the book build the case that the "God of heaven" (5:8; 6:19; 11:17) is the true "Master of heaven and earth" (9:12).

**1:12 The two seas**: probably the Mediterranean to the Persian Gulf, though possibly the Red Sea and Mediterranean.

**1:13 Seventeenth year**: 588 B.C. Without help from the vassal nations, Nebuchadnezzar defeats Arphaxad.

**2:1–13** Nebuchadnezzar commissions Holofernes to take vengeance on the vassal nations that refused him auxiliary military support (see 1:7–12).

**2:1 Eighteenth year**: 587 B.C. Most of the story is set in the catastrophic year when the historical Nebuchadnezzar, king of Babylon, destroyed Jerusalem.

*b:* Gn 14:1, 9. *c:* Nm 34:4; Dt 32:51; Jos 15:23. *d:* Jer 2:16; 43:7–9; 44:1; 46:14. *e:* Is 19:13; Jer 2:16; 44:1; 46:14, 19; Ez 30:13, 15; Hos 9:6. *f:* 2 Sm 17:3; Ez 33:24. *g:* Est 1:3–4.

twenty-second day of the first month, there was a discussion in the palace of Nebuchadnezzar, king of the Assyrians, about taking revenge on all the land, as he had threatened.[h] 2He summoned all his attendants and officers, laid before them his secret plan, and with his own lips recounted in full detail the wickedness of all the land. 3They decided to destroy all who had refused to obey the order he had issued.

4When he had fully recounted his plan, Nebuchadnezzar, king of the Assyrians, summoned Holofernes, the ranking general* of his forces, second only to himself in command, and said to him: 5"Thus says the great king, the lord of all the earth: Go forth from my presence, take with you men of proven valor, one hundred and twenty thousand infantry and twelve thousand cavalry,[i] 6and proceed against all the land of the west, because they disobeyed the order I issued. 7Tell them to have earth and water* ready, for I will come against them in my wrath; I will cover all the land with the feet of my soldiers, to whom I will deliver them as spoils. 8Their wounded will fill their ravines and wadies, the swelling river will be choked with their dead; 9and I will deport them as exiles to the very ends of the earth.

10"Go before me and take possession of all their territories for me. If they surrender to you, guard them for me until the day of their sentencing. 11As for those who disobey, show them no mercy, but deliver them up to slaughter and plunder in all the land you occupy.[j] 12For as I live,* and by the strength of my kingdom, what I have spoken I will accomplish by my own hand.[k] 13Do not disobey a single one of the orders of your lord; fulfill them exactly as I have commanded you, and do it without delay."

***Campaigns of Holofernes.**** 14So Holofernes left the presence of his lord, and summoned all the commanders, generals, and officers of the Assyrian forces. 15He mustered one hundred and twenty thousand picked troops, as his lord had commanded, and twelve thousand mounted archers, 16and drew them up as a vast force organized for battle. 17He took along a very large number of camels, donkeys, and mules for carrying their supplies; innumerable sheep, cattle, and goats for their food;[l] 18abundant provisions for each man, and much gold and silver from the royal palace.

19Then he and all his forces set out on their expedition in advance of King Nebuchadnezzar, to overrun all the lands of the western region with their chariots, cavalry, and picked infantry. 20A huge, irregular force, too many to count, like locusts, like the dust of the earth, went along with them.[m]

21After a three-day march* from Nineveh, they reached the plain of Bectileth, and camped opposite Bectileth near the mountains to the north of Upper Cilicia. 22From there Holofernes took all his forces, the infantry, cavalry, and chariots, and marched into the hill country. 23He devastated Put and Lud,* and plundered all the Rassisites and the Ishmaelites on the border of the wilderness toward the south of the Chelleans.[n]

24Then, following the Euphrates, he went through Mesopotamia, and battered down

**2:4 The ranking general**: Holofernes is so identified six times in Judith. See also 4:1; 5:1; 6:1; 10:13; 13:15. Holofernes and Bagoas (12:11) are Persian names; two officers of Artaxerxes III Ochos (358–338 B.C.) were so named.

**2:7 Earth and water**: in the Persian period, offering these to a conqueror was a symbolic gesture signifying humble submission of one asking for a treaty.

**2:12 As I live**: an oath proper to God; see the promissory oath of God the divine warrior in Dt 32:39–42; cf. Is 49:18; Jer 22:24; Ez 5:11. **By my own hand**: in his pride, Nebuchadnezzar claims to do this by his own hand (cf. Is 10:13). In contrast, Judith claims that God will deliver Israel "by my hand" (8:33; 12:4).

**2:14–3:10** As Holofernes attacks the western nations, terror sweeps across the empire at large (2:28), then Judea (4:1–2), and finally Bethulia (7:1). In these verses, the line of advance is from Nineveh to Damascus and all who submit are nonetheless devastated and forced to worship Nebuchadnezzar.

**2:21 A three-day march**: no ancient army could have traveled three hundred miles from Nineveh to Cilicia in three days.

**2:23 Put and Lud**: mentioned together in Jer 46:9; Ez 27:10; 30:5. Put is thought to be in Libya in Africa; Lud is usually identified with Lydia in Asia Minor. Rather than indicating definite localities here, Put and Lud add assonance and prophetic overtones to the narrative.

*h:* Jer 32:1; 52:29. *i:* 2 Kgs 18:19, 28; 1 Mc 15:13; Is 36:4, 13; Hos 5:13; 10:6. *j:* Dt 7:2; Jos 11:20; Is 13:18. *k:* Dt 32:39–41. *l:* Gn 41:49. *m:* Ex 10:4, 13, 14; Jgs 6:5; 7:12; Ps 105:34; Jl 1:4. *n:* Gn 2:2; 10:6, 22; Is 66:19; Ez 30:5.

every fortified city along the Wadi Abron, until he reached the sea. [25]He seized the territory of Cilicia, and cut down everyone who resisted him. Then he proceeded to the southern borders of Japheth, toward Arabia. [26]He surrounded all the Midianites, burned their tents, and sacked their encampments.[o] [27]Descending to the plain of Damascus at the time of the wheat harvest, he set fire to all their fields, destroyed their flocks and herds, looted their cities, devastated their plains, and put all their young men to the sword.[p]

[28][q] Fear and dread of him fell upon all the inhabitants of the coastland, upon those in Sidon and Tyre,[r] and those who dwelt in Sur and Ocina, and the inhabitants of Jamnia. Those in Azotus and Ascalon also feared him greatly.*

See RG 154–56

### CHAPTER 3

***Submission of the Vassal Nations.*** [1]So they sent messengers to him to sue for peace in these words: [2]"We, the servants of Nebuchadnezzar the great king, lie prostrate before you; do with us as you will. [3]See, our dwellings and all our land and every wheat field, our flocks and herds, and all our encampments are at your disposal; make use of them as you please. [4]Our cities and their inhabitants are also at your service; come and deal with them as you see fit."

[5]After the spokesmen had reached Holofernes and given him this message, [6]he went down with his forces to the seacoast, stationed garrisons in the fortified cities, and took selected men from them as auxiliaries. [7]The people of these cities and all the inhabitants of the countryside received him with garlands and dancing to the sound of timbrels. [8]But he devastated their whole territory and cut down their sacred groves, for he was allowed to destroy all the gods of the land, so that every nation might worship only Nebuchadnezzar, and all their tongues and tribes should invoke him as a god.*[s] [9]At length Holofernes reached Esdraelon in the neighborhood of Dothan,* the approach to the main ridge of the Judean mountains; [10]he set up his camp between Geba* and Scythopolis, and stayed there a whole month to replenish all the supplies of his forces.

## II. Siege of Bethulia*

### CHAPTER 4

See RG 154–56

***Israel Prepares for War.**** [1]When the Israelites who lived in Judea heard of all that Holofernes, the ranking general of Nebuchadnezzar king of the Assyrians, had done to the nations, and how he had looted all their shrines* and utterly destroyed them, [2]they were in very great fear of him, and greatly alarmed for Jerusalem and the temple of the Lord, their God. [3]Now, they had only recently returned from exile, and all the people of Judea were just now reunited, and the vessels, the altar, and the temple had been purified from profanation.*[t] [4]So they sent word

**2:28** Symbolic of the completeness of the terror that descended on the area, seven towns are listed: Tyre, Sidon, Sur, Ocina, Jamnia, Ashdod, and Ashkelon.

**3:8 Invoke him as a god**: Holofernes violates Nebuchadnezzar's instructions (see 2:5–13). No Assyrian, Neo-Babylonian, or Persian king is known to have claimed divinity. During Hellenistic times, Ptolemy V (203–181 B.C.) and the Seleucid Antiochus IV made claims to divinity. In Dn 3 and 6, divinity is ascribed to Nebuchadnezzar and Darius, respectively.

**3:9 Dothan**: a town in Ephraimite territory fourteen miles north of Shechem, mentioned elsewhere only twice (Gn 37:17 and 2 Kgs 6:13), but five times in Judith (3:9; 4:6; 7:3, 18; 8:3). Destroyed in 810 B.C. by Aramean invasions, Dothan was deserted until the Hellenistic period when a small settlement was constructed. Because it is mentioned so often, Dothan is sometimes thought to be the author's home.

**3:10 Geba**: location uncertain. Scythopolis, the Greek name for ancient Beth-shean (Jos 17:11), the only city in Judith given its Greek name, strategically guarded the eastern end of the Valley of Jezreel.

**4:1–7:32** In this section the focus narrows to Judea and specifically the little town of Bethulia. The scenes alternate between the Assyrian camp (5:1–6:13; 7:1–3, 6–18) and Judea/Bethulia (4:1–15; 6:14–21; 7:4–5, 19–32).

**4:1–15** Here the scene shifts to Judea where Israel hears and is greatly terrified about Holofernes' destruction of the neighboring places of worship. At Joakim's instruction they take defensive measures and then pray fervently that God will not allow their sanctuary to be destroyed.

**4:1 Shrines**: the Greek word *hiera* is used only here and may mean holy places or things. By contrast, the sanctuary in Jerusalem is *naos*, "temple" (v. 2); *oikos*, "house" (v. 3); and *hagia*, lit., "holy things" (v. 12).

**4:3 Returned from exile . . . purified from profanation**: conflated historical references associated with events in 538 B.C.

*o:* Gn 37:36; Ex 2:15; Jgs 6–8. *p:* Gn 34:26; Jos 6:21; 1 Sm 15:8. *q:* Ex 15:16; Ps 55:6. *r:* Ez 26:7–14; 29:17–20. *s:* Ex 34:13; 2 Kgs 18:4; 23:14–15; 2 Chr 14:2; 17:6; 31:1; 34:4. *t:* 1 Mc 4:36–61; 2 Mc 10:3–5.

**B**ETHULIA (4:6), MENTIONED FREQUENTLY in Judith, is not mentioned elsewhere in the Bible; this would be unthinkable if the story were historical. Betomesthaim is unknown.

to the whole region of Samaria, to Kona,
Beth-horon, Belmain, and Jericho, to Choba
and Aesora, and to the valley of Salem.* 5The
people there secured all the high hilltops, fortified the villages on them, and since their
fields had recently been harvested, stored up
provisions in preparation for war.
6Joakim, who was high priest* in Jerusalem in those days, wrote to the inhabitants of
Bethulia and Betomesthaim, which is opposite Esdraelon, facing the plain near Dothan,[u]
7and instructed them to keep firm hold of the
mountain passes, since these offered access
to Judea. It would be easy to stop those advancing, as the approach was only wide
enough for two at a time.* 8The Israelites carried out the orders given them by Joakim, the
high priest, and the senate of the whole people of Israel, in session in Jerusalem.[v]
*Israel at Prayer.* 9All the men of Israel
cried to God with great fervor and humbled
themselves. 10They, along with their wives,
and children, and domestic animals, every
resident alien, hired worker, and purchased
slave, girded themselves with sackcloth.* [w]
11And all the Israelite men, women, and children who lived in Jerusalem fell prostrate in
front of the temple* [x] and sprinkled ashes on
their heads, spreading out their sackcloth before the Lord.[y] 12The altar, too, they draped in
sackcloth;* and with one accord they cried
out fervently to the God of Israel not to allow
their children to be seized, their wives to be
taken captive, the cities of their inheritance to
be ruined, or the sanctuary to be profaned
and mocked for the nations to gloat over.
13The Lord heard their cry* and saw their
distress. The people continued fasting for
many days throughout Judea and before the
sanctuary of the Lord Almighty in Jerusalem.[z] 14Also girded with sackcloth, Joakim,
the high priest, and all the priests in attendance before the Lord, and those who ministered to the Lord offered the daily burnt offering, the votive offerings, and the
voluntary offerings of the people.[a] 15With
ashes upon their turbans, they cried to the
Lord with all their strength to look with favor on the whole house of Israel.[b]

## CHAPTER 5

See RG 154–56

### *Achior in the Assyrian War Council.**

1It was reported to Holofernes, the ranking
general of the Assyrian forces, that the Israelites were ready for battle, had blocked the
mountain passes, fortified the high hilltops,
and placed roadblocks in the plains. 2In great
anger he summoned all the rulers of Moab,
the governors of Ammon, and all the satraps
of the coastland[c] 3and said to them: "Now
tell me, you Canaanites, what sort of people
is this that lives in the hill country? Which

(return from exile) and 515 B.C. (dedication of the Second Temple) or perhaps even 164 B.C. (the rededication of the Second Temple in the Maccabean period).

**4:4** Of the eight cities listed, only the locations of Beth-horon, Jericho, and Samaria are known. Salem, mentioned in Gn 17:17, is thought to be an ancient name of Jerusalem.

**4:6 Joakim, who was high priest**: see also vv. 8, 14; 15:8. Joakim exercises religious and military authority comparable to that of Jonathan in Maccabean times (cf. 1 Mc 10:18–21). **Bethulia and Betomesthaim**: unknown locations mentioned only in Judith. Bethulia may mean "House of God" (*byt 'l/yh*) or "House of Ascent" (*byt 'lyh*), perhaps a reference to either Bethel or Shechem.

**4:7 Only wide enough for two at a time**: such a narrow pass near Esdraelon cannot be identified.

**4:10 Sackcloth**: traditional sign of penitence and supplication is here taken to the extreme. Cf. Jon 3:8.

**4:11 Fell prostrate in front of the temple**: for a parallel to this ceremony of entreaty see Jl 1:13, 14; 2:15–17.

**4:12 The altar . . . draped in sackcloth**: attested nowhere else in the Bible.

**4:13 The Lord heard their cry**: this anticipates the role of Judith, the instrument of deliverance (chap. 16), though the people believe God has abandoned them (7:25).

**5:1–6:13** The scene shifts to the Assyrian camp below Bethulia where Holofernes talks with Achior and then expels him to the foot of the hill below the little town.

*u:* Dn 13:1, 4, 28, 29, 63. *v:* 2 Mc 11:27. *w:* Neh 9:1; Est 4:1–4; Jl 1:13, 14; Jon 3:5, 6, 8. *x:* 1 Chr 29:20; 2 Mc 3:15. *y:* 2 Sm 21:10. *z:* Est 4:16; Jl 2:15. *a:* Ex 29:38–46; Nm 28:1–8; Ezr 3:4. *b:* Lv 16:4; Ez 24:23; 44:18; Zec 3:5. *c:* Dt 2:21; 2 Kgs 24:2.

cities do they inhabit? How large is their
force? In what does their power and strength
consist? Who has set himself up as their king
and the leader of their army? [4]Why have
they alone of all the inhabitants of the west
refused to come out to meet me?"
[5]* Then Achior, the leader of all the Ammonites, said to him: "My lord, please listen
to a report from your servant. I will tell you
the truth about this people that lives in the
hill country near here. No lie shall escape
your servant's lips.
[6]"These people are descendants of the
Chaldeans. [7]They formerly lived in Mesopotamia, for they did not wish to follow the
gods of their ancestors who were in the land
of the Chaldeans.[d] [8]Since they abandoned
the way of their ancestors, and worshiped
the God of heaven,* the God whom they had
come to know, their ancestors expelled them
from the presence of their gods. So they fled
to Mesopotamia and lived there a long time.
[9]Their God told them to leave the place
where they were living and go to the land of
Canaan. Here they settled, and grew very
rich in gold, silver, and a great abundance of
livestock.[e] [10]Later, when famine had gripped
the land of Canaan, they went down into
Egypt. They stayed there as long as they
found sustenance and there they grew into
such a great multitude that the number of
their people could not be counted.[f] [11][g] The
king of Egypt, however, rose up against
them, and shrewdly forced them to labor at
brickmaking; they were oppressed and made
into slaves. [12]But they cried to their God,
and he struck the whole land of Egypt with
plagues for which there was no remedy. So
the Egyptians drove them out. [13]Then God
dried up the Red Sea before them[h] [14]and led
them along the route to Sinai and Kadesh-
barnea. They drove out all the inhabitants of
the wilderness [15]and settled in the land of the
Amorites. By their strength they destroyed
all the Heshbonites,[i] crossed the Jordan, and
took possession of all the hill country.[j]
[16]They drove out before them the Canaanites, the Perizzites, the Jebusites, the Shechemites,* and all the Gergesites,[k] and they
lived there a long time.
[17][l] "As long as the Israelites did not sin in
the sight of their God, they prospered, for
their God, who hates wickedness, was with
them. [18]* But when they abandoned the way
he had prescribed for them, they were utterly
destroyed by frequent wars, and finally
taken as captives into foreign lands. The
temple of their God was razed to the ground,
and their cities were occupied by their enemies.[m] [19]But now they have returned to their
God, and they have come back from the Diaspora where they were scattered. They have
reclaimed Jerusalem, where their sanctuary
is, and have settled again in the hill country,
because it was unoccupied.
[20][n] "So now, my master* and lord, if these
people are inadvertently at fault, or if they
are sinning against their God, and if we verify this offense of theirs, then we will be able
to go up and conquer them. [21]But if they are
not a guilty nation, then let my lord keep his
distance; otherwise their Lord and God will
shield them, and we will be mocked in the
eyes of all the earth."
[22]Now when Achior had finished saying
these things, all the people standing round
about the tent murmured; and the officers of
Holofernes and all the inhabitants of the sea-

**5:5–21** Achior (Heb. "brother of light") traces the covenant of Israel from Abraham to the exile and defends the inviolability of the people because their powerful God will defend them if they do not sin. He later identifies the head Judith displays as that of Holofernes (14:6–10). He may be modeled on the famous sage, Ahiqar (see note on Tb 1:21). Achior is wise, but the wisdom granted Judith by God is more effective than his.

**5:8 God of heaven**: a common expression in Persian times; see also 6:19; 11:17 (cf. 7:28; 9:12; 13:18).

**5:16 Shechemites**: perhaps anticipates the allusion in Judith's prayer (9:2) to Simeon's revenge on these people.

**5:18–19** Knowledge of the Babylonian exile is presupposed; cf. also 4:3.

**5:20 Master**: the Greek word *despota*, usually applied to God in the Septuagint, is applied to Holofernes five times in the Book of Judith (vv. 20, 24; 7:9, 11; 11:10), and only once to God (9:12).

*d:* Gn 11:31. *e:* Gn 11:31–12:5; 13:2. *f:* Gn 42:1–5; 46:1–7; Ex 1:7. *g:* Ex 1:10–14; 5:1–21; 7:1–11:10. *h:* Ex 14:21; Jos 2:10; 4:23; Ps 106:9; Wis 19:7; Heb 11:29. *i:* Nm 21:25–28, 30, 34; Dt 1:4; 2:24, 26, 30; 3:2, 6; 4:46. *j:* Jos 3. *k:* Gn 10:16; 15:20; Dt 7:1; Jos 3:10; 24:12; 1 Chr 1:14. *l:* Dt 28–30; Jgs 2:11–15; Ps 106:40–46. *m:* 2 Kgs 25. *n:* Jdt 8:18–23; 11:10; Tb 3:3.

coast and of Moab alike said he should be cut to pieces. 23[o] "We are not afraid of the Israelites," they said, "for they are a powerless people, incapable of a strong defense. 24Therefore let us attack, master Holofernes. They will become fodder for your great army."

## CHAPTER 6

See RG 154–56

1When the noise of the crowd surrounding the council had subsided, Holofernes, the ranking general of the Assyrian forces, said to Achior, in the presence of the whole throng of foreigners, of the Moabites, and of the Ammonite mercenaries: 2"Who are you,* Achior and the mercenaries of Ephraim, to prophesy among us as you have done today, and to tell us not to fight against the people of Israel because their God shields them? Who is God beside Nebuchadnezzar? He will send his force and destroy them from the face of the earth. Their God will not save them;[p] 3but we, the servants of Nebuchadnezzar, will strike them down with one blow, for they will be unable to withstand the force of our cavalry. 4We will overwhelm them with it, and their mountains shall be drunk with their blood, and their plains filled with their corpses. Not a trace of them shall survive our attack; they will utterly perish. So says King Nebuchadnezzar, lord of all the earth. For he has spoken, and his words will not be in vain. 5As for you, Achior, you Ammonite mercenary, for saying these things in a moment of perversity, you will not see my face after today, until I have taken revenge on this people that came out of Egypt. 6Then at my return, the sword of my army or the spear of my attendants will pierce your sides, and you will fall among their wounded. 7My servants will now conduct you to the hill country, and leave you at one of the cities beside the passes. 8You will not die until you are destroyed together with them. 9If you still harbor the hope that they will not be taken, then there is no need for you to be downcast.[q] I have spoken, and not one of my words will fail to be fulfilled."

10Then Holofernes ordered the servants who were standing by in his tent to seize Achior, conduct him to Bethulia, and hand him over to the Israelites. 11So the servants seized him and took him out of the camp into the plain. From the plain they led him up into the hill country until they reached the springs below Bethulia.

12When the men of the city saw them, they seized their weapons and ran out of the city to the top of the hill, and all the slingers kept them from coming up by hurling stones at them. 13So, taking cover below the hill, they bound Achior and left him lying at the foot of the hill; then they returned to their lord.

***Achior in Bethulia.**** 14The Israelites came down from their city and found him, untied him, and brought him into Bethulia. They placed him before the rulers of the city, 15who in those days were Uzziah,* son of Micah of the tribe of Simeon, and Chabris, son of Gothoniel, and Charmis, son of Melchiel.[r] 16They then convened all the elders of the city, and all their young men, as well as the women, gathered in haste at the place of assembly. They placed Achior in the center of the people, and Uzziah questioned him about what had happened. 17He replied by giving them an account of what was said in the council of Holofernes, and of all his own words among the Assyrian rulers, and of all the boasting threats of Holofernes against the house of Israel.

18At this the people fell prostrate and worshiped God,* and they cried out: 19"Lord, God of heaven, look at their arrogance! Have

**6:2 Who are you**: repeated by Judith in 8:12 to the officials of Bethulia and modified in 12:14 in her response to Bagoas' invitation on Holofernes' behalf. The question, "Who is God?" motivates the entire narrative. Holofernes defends Nebuchadnezzar; Judith defends the Lord.

**6:14–21** The scene shifts back to Bethulia where Achior tells the town leaders and citizens all that Holofernes has planned against them. The people cry out to God for help.

**6:15 Uzziah**: *Ozeias* is the Greek equivalent of the Hebrew *'uzziyyah*, "Yah-is-my-strength." His compromise in 7:30 highlights the irony of his name. **Chabris . . . Charmis**: unknown outside Judith.

**6:18 The people fell prostrate and worshiped God**: here in response to Achior's report, the people properly turn to God in their distress. See 4:12.

*o:* Jdt 6:2; 9:7–8; 16:2. *p:* Jdt 3:8; 9:7–8; 1 Kgs 22:15–17; 2 Kgs 18:32–35; Is 36:18–20; Dn 3:14–18. *q:* Gn 4:5; 40:7. *r:* Gn 29:33; 34:25, 30; 35:23.

mercy on our people in their abject state, and look with favor this day on the faces of those who are consecrated to you." 20Then they reassured Achior and praised him highly. 21Uzziah brought him from the place of assembly to his home, where he gave a banquet for the elders. That whole night they called upon the God of Israel for help.

### CHAPTER 7

See RG 154–56

*The Campaign Against Israel.** 1The following day Holofernes ordered his whole army, and all the troops who had come to join him, to break camp and move against Bethulia, seize the passes into the hills, and make war on the Israelites. 2That same day all their fighting men went into action. Their forces numbered a hundred and seventy thousand infantry and twelve thousand cavalry, not counting the baggage train or the men who accompanied it on foot, a very great army. 3They encamped at the spring in the valley near Bethulia, and spread crosswise toward Dothan as far as Balbaim, and lengthwise from Bethulia to Cyamon, which faces Esdraelon.

4When the Israelites saw how many there were, they were greatly distressed and said to one another, "Soon they will strip the whole land bare. Neither the high mountains nor the valleys nor the hills will bear their weight." 5Yet they all seized their weapons, lighted fires on their towers, and kept watch throughout the night.[s]

***The Siege of Bethulia.**** 6On the second day Holofernes led out all his cavalry in the sight of the Israelites who were in Bethulia. 7He reconnoitered the ascents to their city and located their springs of water; these he seized, stationing armed detachments around them, while he himself returned to his troops.

8All the rulers of the Edomites, all the leaders of the Moabites, together with the generals of the coastal region, came to Holofernes and said:[t] 9"Master, please listen to what we have to say, that there may be no losses among your forces. 10These Israelite troops do not rely on their spears, but on the height of the mountains where they dwell, for it is not easy to reach the summit of their mountains.[u] 11Therefore, master, do not attack them in regular formation, and not a single one of your troops will fall. 12Stay in your camp, and spare every man of your force. Have some of your servants keep control of the spring of water that flows out at the base of the mountain, 13for that is where the inhabitants of Bethulia get their water. Then thirst will destroy them, and they will surrender their city. Meanwhile, we and our troops will go up to the nearby hilltops and encamp there to guard against anyone's leaving the city. 14They and their wives and children will languish with hunger, and even before the sword strikes them they will be laid low in the streets where they live. 15Thus you will render them dire punishment for their rebellion and their refusal to meet you peacefully."

16Their words pleased Holofernes and all his attendants, and he ordered their proposal to be carried out. 17So the Ammonites moved camp, together with five thousand Assyrians. They encamped in the valley and held the water supply and the springs of the Israelites. 18The Edomites and the Ammonites went up and encamped in the hill country opposite Dothan; and they sent some of their men to the southeast opposite Egrebel, near Chusi, which is on Wadi Mochmur. The rest of the Assyrian army was encamped in the plain, covering all the land. Their tents and equipment were spread out in profusion everywhere, and they formed a vast multitude.

***The Distress of the Israelites.*** 19The Israelites cried to the Lord, their God, for they were disheartened, since all their enemies had them surrounded, and there was no way of escaping from them.* 20The whole Assyr-

**7:1–5** The scene returns to the Assyrian camp (vv. 1–3) and then shifts back to Bethulia (vv. 4–5). Holofernes orders war preparations; Israel sees and is greatly terrified.

**7:6–32** The scene is set first in the Assyrian camp where Holofernes moves against Bethulia (vv. 6–18), and then in Bethulia where the people cry out to God and, when their courage fails, determine it is time to surrender (vv. 19–32).

**7:19** The prayers of the Israelites shift focus from concern for the Temple and Jerusalem (4:12), to concern that God see

*s:* 1 Mc 12:28–29; 2 Mc 10:36. *t:* Gn 36:1; 1 Mc 5:3. *u:* 1 Kgs 20:23, 28; 2 Kgs 19:23; Ps 95:4; Is 37:24.

ian army, infantry, chariots, and cavalry, kept them thus surrounded for thirty-four days.* All the reservoirs of water failed the inhabitants of Bethulia, [21]and the cisterns ran dry, so that on no day did they have enough water to drink, for their drinking water was rationed. [22]Their children were listless, and the women and youths were fainting from thirst and were collapsing in the streets and gateways of the city, with no strength left in them.

[23]So all the people, including youths, women, and children, went in a crowd to Uzziah and the rulers of the city. They cried out loudly and said before all the elders: [24]"May God judge between you and us! You have done us grave injustice in not making peace with the Assyrians.[v] [25]There is no one to help us now! God has sold us into their hands by laying us prostrate before them in thirst and utter exhaustion.[w] [26]So now, summon them and deliver the whole city as plunder to the troops of Holofernes and to all his forces; [27]we would be better off to become their prey. Although we would be made slaves, at least we would live, and not have to see our little ones dying before our eyes, and our wives and children breathing their last.[x] [28]We adjure you by heaven and earth and by our God, the Lord of our ancestors, who is punishing us for our sins and the sins of our ancestors,* that this very day you do as we have proposed."[y]

[29]All in the assembly with one accord broke into shrill wailing and cried loudly to the Lord their God. [30]But Uzziah said to them, "Courage, my brothers and sisters! Let us endure patiently five days more for the Lord our God to show mercy toward us; for God will not utterly forsake us. [31]But if these days pass and help does not come to us, I will do as you say." [32]Then he dismissed the people. The men returned to their posts on the walls and towers of the city, the women and children went back to their homes. Throughout the city they were in great misery.

## III. Judith, Instrument of the Lord*

### CHAPTER 8

See RG 154–56

***Description of Judith.*** [1*] [z] Now in those days Judith, daughter of Merari,[a] son of Ox, son of Joseph, son of Oziel, son of Elkiah, son of Ananias, son of Gideon, son of Raphain, son of Ahitub, son of Elijah, son of Hilkiah, son of Eliab, son of Nathanael, son of Salamiel, son of Sarasadai, son of Simeon, son of Israel, heard of this. [2]Her husband, Manasseh,* of her own tribe and clan, had died at the time of the barley harvest. [3]While he was supervising those who bound the sheaves in the field, he was overcome by the heat; and he collapsed on his bed and died in Bethulia, his native city. He was buried with his ancestors in the field between Dothan and Balamon. [4b] Judith was living as a widow* in her home for three years and four months. [5]She set up a tent for herself on the roof of her house, put sackcloth about her waist, and wore widow's clothing.[c] [6]She fasted all the days of her widowhood, except sabbath eves and sabbaths, new moon eves and new moons, feastdays and holidays of the house of Israel.[d] [7]She was beautiful in appearance and very lovely to behold.[e] Her husband, Manas-

the arrogance of the enemy and show pity on the covenant people (6:18), to expression of fear and loss of courage regarding their own safety (7:19).

**7:20 Thirty-four days**: the Bethulians lose heart after being without water; Judith will spend four days in the enemy camp (12:10) and the Israelites will plunder the enemy camp for thirty days (15:11).

**7:28** In keeping with the deuteronomic theme of retribution, the Bethulians interpret their persecution as punishment for their sins and the sins of their ancestors (see Ex 20:5; 34:7; Ez 18). In 8:18–27, Judith argues that they are being tested.

**8:1–10:10** In this section the hero is introduced (8:1–8) and prepares to deliver Israel (8:9–10:10).

**8:1** Judith has the longest genealogy accorded any biblical woman, with family ties back to Israel/Jacob.

**8:2 Manasseh**: Judith's marriage was endogamous, within her own tribe. The tribe and clan are identified as hers, though usually it is the husband's tribe and clan that are noted.

**8:4 Widow**: in a reversal of traditional property law, Judith holds title to her husband's estate (see v. 7). However, she will give a part of her inheritance to her late husband's family before her death (16:24); she chooses not to remarry (16:22).

*v:* Ex 5:21. *w:* Est 7:4. *x:* Ex 14:12; 16:3; 1 Mc 1:62–63. *y:* Ps 106:6; Lam 5:7. *z:* Gn 26:34; Jer 36:14, 21, 23. *a:* Gn 46:11; Ex 6:16; Nm 3:17. *b:* 1 Sm 25:39–42; 2 Sm 11:27; Is 54:4; Lam 1:1; 5:3. *c:* Jos 2:6, 8; Jgs 3:20–25; 1 Sm 9:25–26; 2 Sm 11:2; 16:22; 2 Kgs 4:10; 23:12; Ps 102:8; Acts 10:9. *d:* Lk 2:37. *e:* Gn 12:11; 29:17; Est 2:7.

seh, had left her gold and silver, male and female servants, livestock and fields, which she was maintaining. 8No one had a bad word to say about her, for she feared God greatly.

***Judith and the Elders.**** 9So when Judith heard of the harsh words that the people, discouraged by their lack of water, had spoken against their ruler, and of all that Uzziah had said to them in reply, swearing that he would hand over the city to the Assyrians at the end of five days, 10she sent her maid who was in charge of all her things* to summon Uzziah, Chabris, and Charmis, the elders of her city. 11When they came, she said to them: "Listen to me, you rulers of the people of Bethulia. What you said to the people today is not right. You pronounced this oath, made between God and yourselves, and promised to hand over the city to our enemies unless within a certain time the Lord comes to our aid. 12Who are you to put God to the test today, setting yourselves in the place of God in human affairs?*[f] 13And now it is the Lord Almighty you are putting to the test, but you will never understand anything! 14You cannot plumb the depths of the human heart or grasp the workings of the human mind; how then can you fathom God, who has made all these things, or discern his mind, or understand his plan?[g]

"No, my brothers, do not anger the Lord our God. 15* For if he does not plan to come to our aid within the five days, he has it equally within his power to protect us at such time as he pleases, or to destroy us in the sight of our enemies. 16Do not impose conditions on the plans of the Lord our God. God is not like a human being to be moved by threats, nor like a mortal to be cajoled.

17"So while we wait for the salvation that comes from him, let us call upon him to help us, and he will hear our cry if it pleases him. 18For there has not risen among us in recent generations, nor does there exist today, any tribe, or clan, or district, or city of ours that worships gods made by hands, as happened in former days.[h] 19It was for such conduct that our ancestors were handed over to the sword and to pillage, and fell with great destruction before our enemies.[i] 20But since we acknowledge no other god but the Lord, we hope that he will not disdain us or any of our people. 21If we are taken, then all Judea will fall, our sanctuary will be plundered, and God will demand an account from us for their profanation. 22For the slaughter of our kindred, for the taking of exiles from the land, and for the devastation of our inheritance, he will hold us responsible among the nations. Wherever we are enslaved, we will be a scandal and a reproach in the eyes of our masters. 23Our servitude will not work to our advantage, but the Lord our God will turn it to disgrace.

24"Therefore, my brothers, let us set an example* for our kindred. Their lives depend on us, and the defense of the sanctuary, the temple, and the altar rests with us. 25[j] Besides all this, let us give thanks to the Lord our God for putting us to the test as he did our ancestors.[k] 26Recall how he dealt with

**8:9–10:10** This section opens with a repetition of the information that Judith heard about the discouragement of the people and about Uzziah's vow (cf. v. 1). Judith's plan to save Israel then takes shape. In her own home, she meets with the elders of Bethulia (vv. 9–36), prays (9:1–14), prepares herself and the food she will need in the Assyrian camp (10:1–5), goes out to meet the elders again at the gate of Bethulia (10:6–8), and sets out with her maid for the Assyrian camp (10:9–10).

**8:10 Her maid who was in charge of all her things**: cf. Gn 15:2; 24:2; 39:4. Judith's first act in the story is to send this unnamed maid (*habra*, lit., "graceful one" or "favorite slave," v. 33; 10:2, 5, 17; 13:9; 16:23) to summon the town officials (see also other terms for female servants, *paidiske* in 10:10 and *doule* in 12:15; 13:3). Her last act in the story will be to give this woman her freedom (16:23).

**8:12** Judith reprimands the leaders for putting God to the test (cf. Dt 6:16). She will argue that the right to test belongs to God (vv. 25–27).

**8:15–16** God's plans are in opposition to Nebuchadnezzar's plans (2:2, 4). **To protect . . . or to destroy**: Judith defends God's freedom (cf. Jb 1:21; 2:10).

**8:24 Let us set an example**: when Judith says "us," she includes herself. She proposes that she together with Uzziah, Chabris, and Charmis model a faithful response to God's test for the wavering people. "Let us give thanks to the Lord our God for putting us to the test" (v. 25) repeats her intention. "Us" for Uzziah does not include her (see vv. 30, 31).

*f:* Dt 6:16; Jb 38:2; 40:2, 7–8; Ps 106:14; Mal 3:15. *g:* Ps 139:17–18; Wis 9:13; Is 40:13; Rom 11:33–34; 1 Cor 2:11. *h:* Jdt 5:20–21; 11:10. *i:* Ps 78:56–57; 106:13–14; Jer 7:16–20. *j:* Dt 8:5; Tb 12:14; Ps 94:12; Prv 3:11–12; Wis 3:4–6; Sir 2:1–6; Heb 12:5–6. *k:* Gn 22:1–19; 32:22–32; Ex 20:20; Dt 8:16.

## Judith Upbraids the Magistrates

JUDITH'S ELOQUENT EXHORTATION (8:32–34) is an expression of what faith requires of Israel in the postexilic period of apparent abandonment by God. God puts Israel to the test by awaiting a response of fidelity. When faith interprets history, it tends to see suffering as a warning.

Abraham, and how he tested Isaac, and all that happened to Jacob in Syrian Mesopotamia while he was tending the flocks of Laban, his mother's brother. 27He has not tested us with fire, as he did them, to try their hearts, nor is he taking vengeance on us. But the Lord chastises those who are close to him in order to admonish them."

28Then Uzziah said to her: "All that you have said you have spoken truthfully, and no one can deny your words. 29For today is not the first time your wisdom has been evident, but from your earliest days all the people have recognized your understanding, for your heart's disposition is right. 30The people, however, were so thirsty that they forced us to do for them as we have promised, and to bind ourselves by an oath that we cannot break.* [l] 31But now, since you are a devout woman, pray for us that the Lord may send rain to fill up our cisterns. Then we will no longer be fainting from thirst."

32Then Judith said to them: "Listen to me! I will perform a deed that will go down from generation to generation among our descendants. 33Stand at the city gate tonight to let me pass through with my maid; and within the days you have specified before you will surrender the city to our enemies, the Lord will deliver Israel by my hand. 34You must not inquire into the affair, for I will not tell you what I am doing until it has been accomplished." 35Uzziah and the rulers said to her, "Go in peace, and may the Lord God go before you to take vengeance upon our enemies!" 36Then they withdrew from the tent and returned to their posts.

### CHAPTER 9

See RG 154–56

*The Prayer of Judith.** 1Judith fell prostrate, put ashes upon her head, and uncovered the sackcloth she was wearing. Just as the evening incense was being offered in the temple of God in Jerusalem, Judith cried loudly to the Lord:[m] 2"Lord, God of my father Simeon, into whose hand you put a sword to take revenge upon the foreigners* who had defiled a virgin by violating her, shaming her by uncovering her thighs, and dishonoring her by polluting her womb. You said, 'This shall not be done!' Yet they did it. 3Therefore you handed over their rulers to slaughter; and you handed over to bloodshed the bed in which they lay deceived, the same bed that had felt the shame of their own deceiving. You struck down the slaves together with their masters, and the masters upon their thrones.* 4Their wives you handed over to plunder, and their daughters to captivity, and all the spoils you divided among your favored children, who burned with zeal for you and in their abhorrence of the defilement of their blood called on you for help. O God, my God, hear me also, a widow.

5"It is you who were the author of those events and of what preceded and followed them. The present and the future you have also planned.[n] Whatever you devise comes

**8:30–31 An oath that we cannot break**: Uzziah's request that Judith pray for rain underscores his lack of imagination concerning how God's deliverance might come.

**9:1–14** Judith prepares to confront the enemy by turning to God, the source of her strength. Her prayer, an individual lament, moves from a remembrance of God's saving deeds of the past to an appeal to God to exercise the same power in the present. Judith contrasts the empty pride of the Assyrians with God's surpassing might, powerful enough to be exercised in unlikely ways, even through the hand of a woman.

**9:2 The foreigners**: Shechem, the Hivite, violated Dinah, Jacob and Leah's daughter (Gn 34:2). **Defiled a virgin by violating her**: meaning of the Greek is unclear; lit., "who loosened the virgin's womb (*metran*) to defilement." Some read "headdress" or "girdle" (*mitran*) instead of "womb" (*metran*).

**9:3** Because Shechem had deceived and violated Dinah, her brothers, Simeon and Levi, tricked Shechem and the men of his city into being circumcised, and then killed them while they were recovering from the circumcision (Gn 34:13–29).

*l:* Ex 32:22; 1 Sm 15:20–24. *m:* Ex 30:7–8; 1 Chr 28:18; Ezr 9:5; Ps 141:2; Dn 9:21. *n:* Is 41:22–23; 42:9; 43:9; 44:7; 46:10.

into being. [6]The things you decide come forward and say, 'Here we are!' All your ways are in readiness, and your judgment is made with foreknowledge.[o]

[7]"Here are the Assyrians, a vast force, priding themselves on horse and chariot, boasting of the power of their infantry, trusting in shield and spear, bow and sling.[p] They do not know that you are the Lord who crushes wars;* [8]Lord is your name. Shatter their strength in your might, and crush their force in your wrath.[q] For they have resolved to profane your sanctuary, to defile the tent where your glorious name resides, and to break off the horns of your altar with the sword. [9]* See their pride, and send forth your fury upon their heads.[r] Give me, a widow, a strong hand to execute my plan.[s] [10]By the deceit of my lips, strike down slave together with ruler, and ruler together with attendant. Crush their arrogance by the hand of a female.[t]

[11]* [u] "Your strength is not in numbers, nor does your might depend upon the powerful.[v] You are God of the lowly, helper of those of little account, supporter of the weak, protector of those in despair, savior of those without hope.

[12]"Please, please, God of my father, God of the heritage of Israel, Master of heaven and earth, Creator of the waters, King of all you have created, hear my prayer! [13]Let my deceitful words* [w] wound and bruise those who have planned dire things against your covenant, your holy temple, Mount Zion, and the house your children possess.[x] [14]Make every nation and every tribe know clearly that you are God, the God of all power and might, and that there is no other who shields the people of Israel but you alone."

## CHAPTER 10

See RG 154-56

***Judith Prepares to Depart.*** [1]As soon as Judith had ceased her prayer to the God of Israel and finished all these words, [2]she rose from the ground. She called her maid and they went down into the house, which she used only on sabbaths and feast days. [3]She took off the sackcloth she had on, laid aside the garments of her widowhood, washed her body with water, and anointed herself with rich ointment. She arranged her hair, put on a diadem, and dressed in the festive attire she had worn while her husband, Manasseh, was living.[y] [4]She chose sandals for her feet, and put on her anklets, bracelets, rings, earrings, and all her other jewelry.[z] Thus she made herself very beautiful, to entice the eyes of all the men who should see her.*

[5]She gave her maid a skin of wine and a jug of oil. She filled a bag with roasted grain, dried fig cakes, and pure bread.* [a] She wrapped all her dishes and gave them to the maid to carry.[b]

[6]Then they went out to the gate of the city of Bethulia and found Uzziah and the elders of the city, Chabris and Charmis, standing there. [7]When they saw Judith transformed in looks and differently dressed, they were very much astounded at her beauty and said to her, [8]"May the God of our ancestors grant

**9:7–8 You are the Lord who crushes wars; Lord is your name**: cf. Ex 15:3, "The Lord is a warrior; Lord is his name" and Jdt 16:2, "The Lord is a God who crushes wars."

**9:9–10** In a five-fold petition, Judith asks that God see their pride, send fury on their heads, give her a strong hand, strike down the enemy through her deceit, and crush their pride by the hand of a female (*theleia*, see also 13:15 and 16:5, rather than the more usual *gyne, woman*). In an androcentric society, there was no greater dishonor for a male than that he die at the hand of a female (see Jgs 9:53–54). Nine verses emphasize that by her hand God's deliverance is accomplished: 8:33; 9:9, 10; 12:4; 13:4, 14, 15; 15:10; and 16:5.

**9:11–12** Ten titles for God are arranged in two groups of five on either side of the repeated Greek particle, *nai nai* ("verily" or "please"). The title "Master of heaven and earth" (v. 12; see notes on 1:11 and 5:20) is unique to Judith in the Septuagint, as are also "God of the heritage of Israel" and "Creator of the waters."

**9:13 Deceitful words**: twice Judith asks God to make her a successful liar in order to preserve her people (vv. 10, 13).

**10:4** Judith's beauty overcomes all who meet her (8:7; 10:7, 14, 19, 23; 11:21, 23; 12:13).

**10:5** Concern for Israel's dietary laws, reflected in her selection of wine, roasted grain, and bread, emphasizes Judith's religious fidelity (cf. 1 Sm 25:18 and Dn 1:8–16).

*o:* Jb 38:35; Is 46:9–13; Bar 3:35. *p:* Ex 15:1, 21. *q:* Ex 15:3; Ps 46:9–10; 76:4–5. *r:* Ex 15:7. *s:* Ex 3:19–20; 4:2, 4, 6, 7, 17, 20; 5:21; 6:1; 7:4, 5, 15, 17, 19; 8:1, 2, 12, 13; 9:3, 22; 10:12, 21, 22; 12:11; 13:3, 9, 14, 16; 14:16, 21, 26, 27; 15:6, 9, 12, 20; Jgs 5:26. *t:* Jgs 4:9. *u:* Ps 33:16–17. *v:* Ex 15:2; Jgs 7:2; 1 Sm 17:45–47; 2 Chr 16:8–9. *w:* Jdt 10:4; 11:20, 23; 16:6, 9; Est C:24. *x:* Dn 11:28. *y:* Gn 43:24; Lv 8:6; 22:6; Tb 6:3; Ez 16:4, 9. *z:* Gn 24:47, 53; 35:4; Ex 3:22; 12:35; 32:3; 35:22; Nm 31:50; Is 3:18, 21; Hos 2:15. *a:* 1 Sm 25:18. *b:* Jdt 12:2; Est C:28.

**Fatal Error**

HOLOFERNES GUARANTEES FREEDOM from danger to his prospective executioner (11:1–4). The Bible delights in showing how God uses evil people to bring about positive results. "God will successfully perform a deed through you" (v. 6) has an altogether different meaning for Judith than for Holofernes. Judith's conversation is full of such delightful ambiguities.

you favor and make your design successful,
for the glory of the Israelites and the exaltation of Jerusalem." 9Judith bowed down to
God.

*Judith and Her Maid Leave Bethulia.*
Then she said to them, "Order the gate of the
city opened for me, that I may go to accomplish the matters we discussed." So they ordered the young men to open the gate for
her, as she had requested, 10and they did so.
Then Judith and her maidservant went out.
The men of the city kept her in view as she
went down the mountain and crossed the
valley; then they lost sight of her.

## IV. Judith Goes Out to War*

11As Judith and her maid walked directly
across the valley, they encountered the Assyrian patrol. 12The men took her in custody
and asked her, "To what people do you belong? Where do you come from, and where
are you going?"[c] She replied: "I am a daughter of the Hebrews, and I am fleeing from
them, because they are about to be delivered
up to you as prey. 13I have come to see
Holofernes, the ranking general of your
forces, to give him a trustworthy report; in
his presence I will show him the way by
which he can ascend and take possession of
the whole hill country without a single one
of his men suffering injury or loss of life."[d]

14When the men heard her words and
gazed upon her face, which appeared marvelously beautiful to them, they said to her,
15"By hastening down to see our master, you
have saved your life. Now go to his tent;
some of us will accompany you to hand you
over to him. 16When you stand before him,
have no fear in your heart; give him the report you have given us, and he will treat you
well." 17So they selected a hundred of their
men as an escort for her and her maid, and
these conducted them to the tent of Holofernes.

18As the news of her arrival spread among
the tents, a crowd gathered in the camp.
They came and stood around her as she
waited outside the tent of Holofernes, while
he was being informed about her. 19They
marveled at her beauty, regarding the Israelites with wonder because of her, and they
said to one another, "Who can despise this
people who have such women among them?
It is not good to leave one of their men alive,
for if any were to be spared they could beguile the whole earth."

*Judith Meets Holofernes.* 20Then the
guards of Holofernes and all his attendants
came out and ushered her into the tent.
21Holofernes was reclining on his bed under
a canopy* woven of purple, gold, emeralds,
and other precious stones. 22When they announced her to him, he came out to the front
part of the tent, preceded by silver lamps.
23When Judith came before Holofernes and
his attendants, they all marveled at the
beauty of her face. She fell prostrate and
paid homage to him, but his servants raised
her up.[e]

### CHAPTER 11

See RG 154–56

1Then Holofernes said to her: "Take
courage, woman! Have no fear in your
heart! I have never harmed anyone who
chose to serve Nebuchadnezzar, king of all
the earth. 2As for your people who live in the

**10:11–13:20** In this section Judith and her maid arrive in the Assyrian camp (10:11–19), where Judith meets (10:20–12:9) and triumphs over Holofernes (12:10–13:10a). Then she and her maid return to Bethulia and announce the victory (13:10b–20).

**10:21 Canopy**: netting for protection against insects. A prized possession in this story (cf. 13:15; 16:19).

*c:* Gn 16:8. *d:* Jdt 11:5–6. *e:* Ru 2:10; 1 Sm 25:41; 2 Sm 14:4.

hill country, I would never have raised my
spear against them, had they not insulted me.
They have brought this upon themselves.
3 But now tell me why you have fled from
them and come to us? In any case, you have
come to safety. Take courage! Your life is
spared tonight and for the future.[f] 4 No one at
all will harm you. Rather, you will be well
treated, as are the servants of my lord, King
Nebuchadnezzar."

5 Judith answered him: "Listen to the
words of your servant, and let your maidservant speak in your presence! I will say nothing false to my lord* this night. 6 If you follow
the words of your maidservant, God will successfully perform a deed through you, and
my lord will not fail to achieve his designs.*
7 I swear by the life of Nebuchadnezzar, king
of all the earth, and by the power of him who
has sent you to guide all living things, that
not only do human beings serve him through
you; but even the wild animals, and the cattle, and the birds of the air, because of your
strength, will live for Nebuchadnezzar and
his whole house.[g] 8 Indeed, we have heard of
your wisdom and cleverness.[h] The whole
earth is aware that you above all others in the
kingdom are able, rich in experience, and
distinguished in military strategy.

9[i] "As for Achior's speech in your council, we have heard it. When the men of
Bethulia rescued him, he told them all he
had said to you. 10 So then, my lord and master, do not disregard his word, but bear it in
mind, for it is true. Indeed our people are not
punished, nor does the sword prevail against
them, except when they sin against their
God.[j] 11 But now their sin* has caught up with
them, by which they will bring the wrath of
their God upon them when they do wrong;
so that my lord will not be repulsed and fail,
but death will overtake them. 12 Because
their food has given out and all their water is
running low, they have decided to kill their
animals, and are determined to consume all
the things which God in his laws has forbidden them to eat. 13 They have decided that
they would use the first fruits of grain and
the tithes of wine and oil, which they had
consecrated and reserved for the priests who
minister in the presence of our God in Jerusalem—things which the people should not
so much as touch with their hands.[k] 14 They
have sent messengers to Jerusalem to bring
back permission from the senate, for even
there people have done these things.[l] 15 On
the very day when the response reaches
them and they act upon it, they will be
handed over to you for destruction.

16 "As soon as I, your servant, learned all
this, I fled from them. God has sent me to
perform with you such deeds as will astonish people throughout the whole earth who
hear of them. 17 Your servant is, indeed, a
God-fearing woman, serving the God of
heaven night and day. Now I will remain
with you, my lord; but each night your servant will go out into the valley and pray to
God. He will tell me when they have committed their offenses. 18 Then I will come and
let you know, so that you may march out
with all your forces, and not one of them will
be able to withstand you. 19 I will lead you
through the heart of Judea until you come to
Jerusalem, and there in its center I will set up
your throne. You will drive them like sheep
that have no shepherd, and not even a dog
will growl at you.[m] This was told to me in
advance and announced to me, and I have
been sent to tell you."

20 Her words pleased Holofernes and all
his attendants. They marveled at her wisdom
and exclaimed, 21 "No other woman from
one end of the earth to the other looks so
beautiful and speaks so wisely!" 22 Then
Holofernes said to her: "God has done well
in sending you ahead of your people, to
bring victory to our hands, and destruction

**11:5–6** Here the word "lord" has a double meaning, indicating both Holofernes and God. Much irony is evident in Judith's conversation with Holofernes (e.g., 12:4).

**11:6 Designs**: cf. 10:8; 11:6; 13:5 where this word is used as a synonym for Judith's "affair" (8:34), which she kept secret as she carried out the plan of her God (8:15, 16), unlike her counterpart Nebuchadnezzar, who told all the details of his plan (2:2, 4).

**11:11 Sin**: but in 8:18–20 Judith asserts that the people have not committed idolatry in recent generations.

*f:* 2 Mc 11:19. *g:* Jgs 8:19; 1 Sm 14:45; 25:26; 28:10; 2 Sm 11:11; Ez 17:16; Dn 2:38. *h:* Sir 1:6; 42:18. *i:* Jdt 5:5. *j:* Jdt 5:21; 8:18. *k:* Nm 18:8–9. *l:* 1 Mc 2:31–41. *m:* Ex 11:7.

to those who have despised my lord. 23 You are not only beautiful in appearance, but you are also eloquent. If you do as you have said, your God will be my God;* you will live in the palace of King Nebuchadnezzar and be renowned throughout the whole earth."

## CHAPTER 12

See RG 154–56

1 Then he ordered them to lead her into the room where his silver dinnerware was kept, and ordered them to set a table for her with his own delicacies to eat and his own wine to drink. 2 But Judith said, "I cannot eat any* of them, because it would be a scandal.[n] Besides, I will have enough with the things I brought with me." 3 Holofernes asked her, "But if your provisions give out, where can we get more of the same to provide for you? None of your people are with us." 4 Judith answered him, "As surely as you live, my lord, your servant will not use up her supplies before the Lord accomplishes by my hand what he has determined."

5 Then the attendants of Holofernes led her to her tent, where she slept until the middle of the night. Toward the early morning watch, she rose[o] 6 and sent this message to Holofernes, "Give orders, my lord, to let your servant go out for prayer." 7 So Holofernes ordered his guards not to hinder her. Thus she stayed in the camp three days. Each night she went out to the valley of Bethulia, where she bathed herself* at the spring of the camp.[p] 8 After bathing, she prayed to the Lord, the God of Israel, to direct her way for the triumph of her people. 9 Then she returned purified to the tent and remained there until her food was brought to her toward evening.[q]

***Judith at the Banquet of Holofernes.*** 10 On the fourth day Holofernes gave a banquet for his servants alone, to which he did not invite any of the officers. 11 And he said to Bagoas, the eunuch in charge of his personal affairs, "Go and persuade the Hebrew woman in your care to come and to eat and drink with us. 12 It would bring shame on us to be with such a woman without enjoying her. If we do not seduce her, she will laugh at us."[r]

13 So Bagoas left the presence of Holofernes, and came to Judith and said, "So lovely a maidservant should not be reluctant to come to my lord to be honored by him, to enjoy drinking wine with us, and to act today like one of the Assyrian women who serve in the palace of Nebuchadnezzar." 14 Judith replied, "Who am I to refuse my lord? Whatever is pleasing to him I will promptly do. This will be a joy* for me until the day of my death."

15 So she proceeded to put on her festive garments and all her finery. Meanwhile her servant went ahead and spread out on the ground opposite Holofernes the fleece Bagoas had furnished for her daily use in reclining while eating.[s] 16 Then Judith came in and reclined. The heart of Holofernes was in rapture over her and his passion was aroused. He was burning with the desire to possess her, for he had been biding his time to seduce her from the day he saw her.[t] 17 Holofernes said to her, "Drink and be happy with us!" 18 Judith replied, "I will gladly drink, my lord, for today is the greatest day of my whole life." 19 She then took the things her servant had prepared and ate and drank in his presence. 20 Holofernes, charmed by her, drank a great quantity of wine, more than he had ever drunk on any day since he was born.

## CHAPTER 13

See RG 154–56

***Judith Beheads Holofernes.*** 1 When it grew late, his servants quickly withdrew. Bagoas closed the tent from the outside and dismissed the attendants from their master's

**11:23 Your God will be my God**: in 3:8, Holofernes insisted that Nebuchadnezzar alone is god.

**12:2 Cannot eat any**: the food of Gentiles was avoided by pious Jews (see Dn 1:8, 13, 15; Tb 1:10–11) because it might have been prohibited as unclean (see Lv 11:13–44), sacrificed to idols (see Ex 34:15; Dt 32:37–38), or contaminated with blood (see Lv 7:26–27). In addition, eating together symbolized the sharing of life.

**12:7 Bathed herself**: she bathes to purify herself after contact with the Gentiles. Her nightly departure from the camp provides for her escape (cf. 13:10).

**12:14 Joy**: the irony of this response is obvious; see also the joy of 14:9 and Judith's "new song" in chap. 16.

*n:* Tb 1:10–11; Est C:28; 1 Mc 1:62–63; 2 Mc 5:27; 6:18–7:2; Dn 1:8. *o:* Ex 14:24; 1 Sm 11:11. *p:* Tb 7:9. *q:* 2 Sm 3:35. *r:* Dn 13:37, 54, 57–58. *s:* Tb 9:6; Ez 23:41. *t:* Dn 13:20, 39.

> JUDITH'S VICTORY IS proof that power and violence can be conquered by faith and wisdom. The weak, oppressed, and demoralized postexilic Israel needs this reminder.

presence. They went off to their beds, for they were all tired because the banquet had lasted so long. 2 Judith was left alone in the tent with Holofernes, who lay sprawled on his bed, for he was drunk with wine. 3 Judith had ordered her maidservant to stand outside the bedchamber and to wait, as on the other days, for her to come out; she had said she would be going out for her prayer. She had also said this same thing to Bagoas.

4 When all had departed, and no one, small or great, was left in the bedchamber, Judith stood by Holofernes' bed and prayed silently, "O Lord, God of all might, in this hour look graciously on the work of my hands for the exaltation of Jerusalem. 5 Now is the time for aiding your heritage and for carrying out my design to shatter the enemies who have risen against us."[u] 6 She went to the bedpost near the head of Holofernes, and taking his sword from it, 7 she drew close to the bed, grasped the hair of his head, and said, "Strengthen me this day, Lord, God of Israel!" 8 Then with all her might she struck his neck twice and cut off his head.[v] 9 She rolled his body off the bed and took the canopy from its posts. Soon afterward, she came out and handed over the head of Holofernes to her maid, 10 who put it into her food bag. Then the two went out together for prayer as they were accustomed to do.

***Judith and Her Maid Return to Bethulia.*** They passed through the camp, and skirting that valley, went up the mountain to Bethulia, and approached its gates. 11 From a distance, Judith shouted to the guards at the gates: "Open! Open the gate! God, our God, is with us. Once more he has shown his strength in Israel and his power against the enemy, as he has today!"

***Judith Displays the Head of Holofernes.*** 12* When the citizens heard her voice, they hurried down to their city gate and summoned the elders of the city. 13 All the people, from the least to the greatest, hurriedly assembled, for her return seemed unbelievable. They opened the gate and welcomed the two women. They made a fire for light and gathered around the two. 14 Judith urged them with a loud voice: "Praise God, give praise! Praise God, who has not withdrawn his mercy from the house of Israel, but has shattered our enemies by my hand this very night!" 15 Then she took the head out of the bag, showed it to them, and said: "Here is the head of Holofernes, the ranking general of the Assyrian forces, and here is the canopy under which he lay in his drunkenness. The Lord struck him down by the hand of a female!* 16 Yet I swear by the Lord, who has protected me in the way I have walked, that it was my face that seduced Holofernes to his ruin, and that he did not defile me with sin or shame."

17 All the people were greatly astonished. They bowed down and worshiped God, saying with one accord, "Blessed are you, our God, who today have humiliated the enemies of your people." 18 Then Uzziah said to her, "Blessed are you, daughter, by the Most High God, above all the women on earth; and blessed be the Lord God, the creator of heaven and earth, who guided your blow at the head of the leader of our enemies.[w] 19 Your deed of hope will never be forgotten by those who recall the might of God.[x] 20 May God make this redound to your everlasting honor, rewarding you with blessings, because you risked your life when our people were being oppressed, and you averted our disaster, walking in the straight path before our God." And all the people answered, "Amen! Amen!"[y]

**13:12–20** Elements from chaps. 8–9 are echoed here. The assembly of the people at Judith's return parallels the meeting of the town officials summoned by Judith in 8:10. Uzziah blesses Judith in 8:5 and again in 13:18–20.

**13:15 By the hand of a female**: cf. 16:5 and note on 9:9–10.

*u:* Gn 24:45; 1 Sm 1:13. *v:* Jgs 4:21; 1 Sm 17:51; 31:9. *w:* Jgs 5:24; Lk 1:42. *x:* Sir 35:9. *y:* Dt 27:15–26; Ps 41:14; 72:19; 89:53.

## V. Victory and Thanksgiving*

### CHAPTER 14

See RG 154–56

*Judith's Plan of Attack.* 1Then Judith
said to them: "Listen to me,* my brothers and
sisters. Take this head and hang it on the parapet of your wall.[z] 2At daybreak, when the sun
rises on the earth, each of you seize your
weapons, and let all the able-bodied men rush
out of the city under command of a captain, as
if about to go down into the valley against the
Assyrian patrol, but without going down.
3The Assyrians will seize their weapons and
hurry to their camp to awaken the generals of
the army. When they run to the tent of
Holofernes and do not find him, panic will
seize them, and they will flee before you.[a]
4Then you and all the other inhabitants of the
whole territory of Israel will pursue them and
strike them down in their tracks. 5But before
doing this, summon for me Achior the Ammonite, that he may see and recognize the one
who despised the house of Israel and sent him
here to meet his death."

*Achior's Conversion.** 6So they called
Achior from the house of Uzziah. When he
came and saw the head of Holofernes in the
hand of one of the men in the assembly of
the people, he collapsed in a faint. 7Then, after they lifted him up, he threw himself at the
feet of Judith in homage, saying: "Blessed
are you in every tent of Judah! In every nation, all who hear your name will be struck
with terror.[b] 8But now, tell me all that you
did during these days." So Judith told him,
in the midst of the people, all that she had
done, from the day she left until the time she
began speaking to them. 9When she had finished her account, the people cheered
loudly, so that the city resounded with
shouts of joy. 10Now Achior, seeing all that
the God of Israel had done, believed firmly
in God. He circumcised the flesh of his foreskin and he has been united with the house
of Israel to the present day.[c]

*Panic in the Assyrian Camp.* 11At daybreak they hung the head of Holofernes on
the wall. Then all the Israelite men took up
their weapons and went out by groups to the
mountain passes.[d] 12When the Assyrians saw
them, they notified their commanders, who,
in turn, went to their generals, their division
leaders, and all their other leaders. 13They
came to the tent of Holofernes and said to
the one in charge of all his things, "Awaken
our lord, for the slaves have dared come
down against us in battle, to their utter destruction." 14So Bagoas went in and knocked
at the entry of the tent, presuming that
Holofernes was sleeping with Judith.
15When no one answered, he parted the curtains, entered the bedchamber, and found
him thrown on the floor dead, with his head
gone! 16He cried out loudly, weeping, groaning, and howling, and tore his garments.
17Then he entered the tent where Judith had
her quarters; and, not finding her, he rushed
out to the troops and cried: 18"The slaves
have duped us! One Hebrew woman has
brought shame on the house of King Nebuchadnezzar. Look! Holofernes on the
ground—without a head!"[e]

19When the leaders of the Assyrian forces
heard these words, they tore their tunics and
were overcome with great distress. Their

**14:1–16:25** This section describes Judith's plan to attack the Assyrian camp (14:1–5) and its execution (14:11–15:7). Between the plan and its execution, Achior identifies the head of Holofernes and is converted to Judaism. The book concludes with the victory celebration (15:8–14), hymn of thanksgiving (16:1–20), and a description of Judith's final days (16:21–25). Elements from chaps. 8–9 recur here: Judith, widow of Manasseh (8:2; 16:22), lived alone in Bethulia on her estate (8:4; 16:22), with servants and property (8:7; 16:21). Judith's instructions begin with the words "listen to me" (8:11; 14:1). Her prayer for success (9:1–14) is balanced by a prayer and display of success in 14:14–16.

**14:1–5 Listen to me**: an imperative (used also in 8:11, 32) opens Judith's instruction that the people display the head of Holofernes on the parapet and themselves in ranks before the enemy at daybreak. The strategy is to throw the Assyrians into panic and strike them down in their confusion; cf. 15:1–3.

**14:6–10** Recognizing the head of Holofernes, Achior faints. Then he throws himself down before Judith, acclaiming her blessed in Judah and every nation. After listening to all she had done, Achior is circumcised and joins the house of Israel. Since this violates the prohibition of Dt 23:4 that no Ammonite or Moabite shall enter the assembly, even to the tenth generation, some suggest that the book was not included in the Hebrew scriptures for this reason. However, see Is 56:3–6.

*z:* 1 Sm 17:54; 31:9–10; 2 Sm 20:21; 2 Kgs 10:7–8; 1 Mc 7:47; 2 Mc 15:30; Mt 14:8. *a:* 1 Mc 7:44. *b:* Jgs 5:24. *c:* Dt 23:4. *d:* 2 Mc 8:23; 12:20. *e:* Jgs 9:54.

loud cries and shouts were heard throughout
the camp.

## CHAPTER 15

See RG 154–56

1 On hearing what had happened,
those still in their tents were horrified.
2 Overcome with fear and dread, no one kept
ranks any longer. They scattered in all directions, and fled along every path, both
through the valley and in the hill country.[f]
3 Those who were stationed in the hill country around Bethulia also took to flight. Then
the Israelites, every warrior among them,
came charging down upon them.
4 Uzziah sent messengers to Betomas-
thaim, to Choba and Kona, and to the whole
territory of Israel to report what had happened and to urge them all to attack the enemy and destroy them. 5 On hearing this, all
the Israelites, with one accord, attacked
them and cut them down as far as Choba.
Even those from Jerusalem and the rest of
the hill country took part in this, for they too
had been notified of the happenings in the
camp of their enemy. The Gileadites and the
Galileans struck the enemy's flanks with
great slaughter, even beyond Damascus and
its borders. 6 The remaining people of Bethulia swept down on the camp of the Assyrians, plundered it, and acquired great riches.
7 The Israelites, when they returned from the
slaughter, took possession of what was left.
Even the towns and villages in the hill country and on the plain got an enormous quantity of spoils, for there was a tremendous
amount of it.

***Israel Celebrates Judith's Victory.*** 8 Then
the high priest Joakim and the senate of the
Israelites who lived in Jerusalem came to
see for themselves the good things that the
Lord had done for Israel, and to meet and
congratulate Judith. 9 When they came to
her, all with one accord blessed her, saying:

"You are the glory of Jerusalem!*
You are the great pride of Israel!
You are the great boast of our nation!
10 By your own hand you have done all this.
You have done good things for Israel,
and God is pleased with them.
May the Almighty Lord bless you
forever!"

And all the people said, "Amen!"
11 For thirty days* all the people plundered
the camp, giving Judith the tent of
Holofernes, with all his silver, his beds, his
dishes, and all his furniture. She took them
and loaded her mule, hitched her carts, and
loaded these things on them.
12 All the women of Israel gathered to see
her, and they blessed her and performed a
dance in her honor.[g] She took branches in
her hands and distributed them to the women
around her, 13 and she and the other women
crowned themselves with olive leaves.
Then, at the head of all the people, she led
the women in the dance, while the men of Israel followed, bearing their weapons, wearing garlands and singing songs of praise.
14* Judith led all Israel in this song of thanksgiving, and the people loudly sang this hymn
of praise:

## CHAPTER 16

### Judith's Hymn of Deliverance

See RG 154–56

1 And Judith sang:

"Strike up a song to my God with
tambourines,[h]
sing to the Lord with cymbals;
Improvise for him a new song,
exalt and acclaim his name.
2 For the Lord is a God who crushes wars;[i]
he sets his encampment among his
people;

**15:9** In the Lectionary of the Catholic Church, this passage is one of several choices for feasts of Mary (e.g., the Presentation of Mary). These words of praise are also echoed in antiphons for the Liturgy of the Hours on Marian feasts.

**15:11 Thirty days**: the central actions in each half of the book are accomplished in a total of thirty-four days. Bethulia was without water for thirty-four days (7:20). Judith spent four days in the enemy camp and the Israelites plunder the Assyrian camp for thirty days.

**15:14–16:17** Judith's hymn of deliverance is patterned on the Song of Miriam (Ex 15:20–21).

*f:* Gn 9:2; Dt 11:25; 1 Mc 7:18; Sir 4:17. *g:* Ex 15:20; Jgs 11:34; 1 Sm 18:6; Jer 31:4. *h:* Gn 31:27; Ex 15:20; 1 Sm 18:6; 2 Sm 6:5; 1 Chr 13:8; Ps 68:26; 81:3; 149:3; Jer 31:4. *i:* Ex 15:3; Ps 46:10.

he delivered me from the hands of my
pursuers.
3 "The Assyrian came from the mountains
of the north,
with myriads of his forces he came;
Their numbers blocked the wadis,
their cavalry covered the hills.
4 He threatened to burn my territory,
put my youths to the sword,
Dash my infants to the ground,
seize my children as plunder.
And carry off my virgins as spoil.

5 "But the Lord Almighty thwarted them,
by the hand of a female!
6 Not by youths was their champion struck
down,[j]
nor did Titans bring him low,
nor did tall giants attack him;[k]
But Judith, the daughter of Merari,
by the beauty of her face brought him
down.
7 She took off her widow's garb
to raise up the afflicted in Israel.
She anointed her face with fragrant oil;
8 fixed her hair with a diadem,
and put on a linen robe to beguile him.
9 Her sandals ravished his eyes,[l]
her beauty captivated his mind,
the sword cut through his neck![m]

10 "The Persians trembled at her boldness,
the Medes were daunted at her daring.
11 When my lowly ones shouted,
and my weak ones cried out,
The enemy was terrified,
screamed and took to flight.
12 Sons of maidservants pierced them
through;
wounded them like deserters' children.
They perished before the ranks of my
Lord.

13 "I will sing a new song to my God.[n]
O Lord, great are you and glorious,
marvelous in power and
unsurpassable.
14 Let your every creature serve you;
for you spoke, and they were made.
You sent forth your spirit, and it created
them;[o]
no one can resist your voice.[p]
15 For the mountains to their bases
are tossed with the waters;
the rocks, like wax, melt before your
glance.[q]

"But to those who fear you,
you will show mercy.
16 Though the sweet fragrance of every
sacrifice is a trifle,
and the fat of all burnt offerings but
little in your sight,
one who fears the Lord is forever
great.

17 "Woe to the nations that rise against my
people!
the Lord Almighty will requite them;
in the day of judgment he will punish
them:
He will send fire and worms into their
flesh,[r]
and they will weep and suffer forever."

18 When they arrived at Jerusalem, they
worshiped God. As soon as the people were
purified, they offered their burnt offerings,
voluntary offerings, and donations.[s] 19 Judith
dedicated to God all the things of Holofernes
that the people had given her, putting under
the ban the canopy that she herself had taken
from his bedchamber.[t] 20 For three months
the people continued their celebration in Jerusalem before the sanctuary, and Judith remained with them.

***The Renown and Death of Judith.*** 21 When
those days were over, all of them returned to
their inheritance. Judith went back to Bethulia
and remained on her estate. For the rest of her
life she was renowned throughout the land.
22 Many wished to marry her, but she gave herself to no man all the days of her life from the
time her husband, Manasseh, died and was
gathered to his people. 23 Her fame continued
to increase, and she lived in the house of her
husband, reaching the advanced age of one

*j:* 1 Sm 17:4, 51. *k:* Gn 6:1–4; Dt 2:10, 21; 2 Sm 21:16–22; 1 Chr 20:4–8. *l:* Sg 7:2; Ez 16:10. *m:* Jgs 5:26. *n:* Ps 33:3; 40:4; 96:1; 98:1; 144:9; 149:1; Is 42:10. *o:* Gn 1; Ps 104:30; 148:5. *p:* Est C:3–4; Ps 33:9; Is 55:11. *q:* Ps 97:5; Mi 1:4; Na 1:5. *r:* Sir 7:17; Is 66:24; Mk 9:48. *s:* Nm 19:11–22; 31:19. *t:* Lv 7:16. *u:* Jb 42:16; Prv 16:31; 20:29; Sir 18:9; Lk 2:36.

hundred and five.* [u] She set her maid free. And
when she died in Bethulia, they buried her in
the cave of her husband, Manasseh;[v]
24 and the
house of Israel mourned her for seven days.* [w]
Before she died, she distributed her property
to the relatives of her husband, Manasseh, and
to her own relatives.[x]
25 [y] During the lifetime of Judith and for a
long time after her death, no one ever again
spread terror* among the Israelites.

**16:23 One hundred and five**: long life was a sign of blessing (see Jb 42:16; Prv 16:31; 20:29). The fact that the Maccabean period was one hundred and five years long (168–63 B.C.) may account for assigning this age to Judith.

**16:24 Seven days**: the customary period for mourning the dead (1 Sm 31:13).

**16:25 Spread terror**: Judith is compared to the heroes of the Book of Judges (cf. Jgs 3:11, 30).

*v:* Gn 23:19; 25:9; 49:29–32; 50:13. *w:* Gn 50:3; 1 Sm 31:13; 1 Chr 10:12; Sir 22:12. *x:* Nm 27:6–11. *y:* Jgs 3:11, 30; 5:31; 8:28.

See RG 156–59

# The Book of Esther

The Book of Esther tells a story of the deliverance of the Jewish people. We are shown a Persian emperor, Ahasuerus (loosely based on Xerxes, 485–464 B.C.), who makes momentous decisions for trivial reasons, and his wicked minister, Haman, who takes advantage of the king's compliance to pursue a personal vendetta against the Jews by having a royal decree issued ordering their destruction. The threat is averted by two Jews, Esther and Mordecai. Their influence and intervention allow the Jews to turn the tables on their enemies and rout their attackers. This deliverance is commemorated by the inauguration of the Jewish festival of Purim on the fourteenth and fifteenth of Adar (mid-February through mid-March). The book confronts the modern reader with important themes, the evils of genocide and racism.

Esther's character matures over the course of the narrative. As a girl she is recruited for the king's harem because of her physical beauty. But at a key moment in the book (chap. 4), she rises to the challenge to risk her life for the salvation of her people. At that point, she transforms her status as queen from a position of personal privilege to one of power and public responsibility.

Esther's uncle, Mordecai, appears first as an adoptive father, whose solicitude for Esther leads him to the king's gate, where he foils a plot to assassinate the king. When he learns of the edict against the Jews, he encourages Esther to confront the king. The book ends with Mordecai as the king's chief minister.

The book is a free composition, not a historical document. Its fictional character can be illustrated by many examples of literary motifs: the use of extensive conversation to move the plot along; the motif of concealment (Esther is a Jew, related to Mordecai, but Haman does not know it, even as he comes to her banquet in chap. 7). A whole series of banquets structure the work: two by the king, one by Vashti, three by Esther, and the joyful banqueting that ends the book. Further artificialities are clear in the way characters are paired (e.g., Mordecai and Esther) and in the delays and the speed of the action (Esther delays the banquet in 5:3–8, but the tempo of chaps. 5–6 is particularly fast); Mordecai passes from the threat of death (5:9–14) to royal honors (6:10–11) within twenty-four hours. There are many exaggerations, and even sarcastic implausibilities (cf. the effect of Vashti's disobedience in 1:17–18), and huge ironies (e.g., Haman in 6:6, 10). The work is a composite of reversals (cf. 9:1) in the lives of individuals and communities.

The book was probably written in the third or second century B.C. It has come down to us in two versions: an older Hebrew version, and a Greek version based on a text similar to the Hebrew, but with additions and alterations as described below.

One striking feature of the Hebrew version of the Book of Esther is that no divine names or titles are employed here; God is not mentioned at all. This would not be unusual in a book whose subject matter or outlook was more secular, but Esther is a book in which the religious element is prominent: the Jews fast in order to be delivered from imminent peril, experience deliverance at the eleventh hour, and commemorate their deliverance with an annual festival. Moreover, there are indirect references to divine activity (for example, in 4:14).

The Greek additions to Esther have many explicit references to God, as well as explicit descriptions of the beliefs and emotional states of Esther and Mordecai. They also elaborate on the content of the edicts from Ahasuerus as illustrations of Gentile attitudes toward Jews. While there are only a few contradictions between these Greek additions and the older Hebrew text, reading the book with these additions is a very different experience from reading the book without them. The additions to Esther are an excellent example of a process that occurs throughout the Bible: further reflections on the story become part of the story itself. Although the Book of Esther was questioned by some early Christians, even St. Jerome, the whole book, including the Greek additions, was included in the canon of Scripture by the Council of Trent.

The Greek version of the book dates from ca. 116 to 48 B.C. (see note on F:11). In the present translation, the Greek additions are indicated by the letters A through F. The regular chapter numbers apply to the Hebrew text.

The book may be divided as follows:

I. Prologue (A:1–17)
II. Esther Becomes Queen (1:1–2:23)
III. Haman's Plot Against the Jews (3:1–13; B:1–7; 3:14–15)
IV. Esther and Mordecai Plead for Help (4:1–17; C:1–D:16; 5:1–5)
V. Haman's Downfall (5:6–8:2)
VI. The Jewish Victory and the Feast of Purim (8:3–12; E:1–24; 8:13–9:23)
VII. Epilogue: The Rise of Mordecai (9:24–10:3; F:1–11)

The order of the Vulgate text in relation to the order of the Greek text is as follows:

| | | |
|---|---|---|
| Vulg. 11:2–12:6 | = | A:1–17 at the beginning of the book. |
| 13:1–7 | = | B:1–7 after 3:13. |
| 13:8—15:3–19 | = | C:1–D:16 after 4:17. |
| 15:1–2 | = | B:8, 9 after 4:8. |
| 16:1–24 | = | E:1–24 after 8:12. |
| 10:4–13 | = | F:1–10 after 10:3. |

# I. Prologue

## CHAPTER A

See RG 157–59

***Dream of Mordecai.*** 1 In the second
year of the reign of Ahasuerus the great, on
the first day of Nisan, Mordecai, son of Jair,
son of Shimei, son of Kish, of the tribe of
Benjamin, had a dream.* [a] 2* He was a Jew
residing in the city of Susa, a prominent man
who served at the king's court, 3 and one of
the captives whom Nebuchadnezzar, king of
Babylon, had taken from Jerusalem with
Jeconiah, king of Judah.[b]
4[c] This was his dream.* There was noise
and tumult, thunder and earthquake—confusion upon the earth. 5 Two great dragons advanced, both poised for combat. They uttered
a mighty cry, 6 and at their cry every nation
prepared for war, to fight against the nation
of the just. 7 It was a dark and gloomy day.
Tribulation and distress, evil and great confusion, lay upon the earth. 8 The whole nation
of the just was shaken with fear at the evils to
come upon them, and they expected to perish. 9[d] Then they cried out to God, and from
their crying there arose, as though from a tiny
spring, a mighty river, a flood of water. 10 The
light of the sun broke forth; the lowly were
exalted and they devoured the boastful.
11 Having seen this dream and what God
intended to do, Mordecai awoke. He kept it
in mind, and tried in every way, until night,
to understand its meaning.

***Mordecai Thwarts an Assassination.****
12[e] Mordecai lodged in the courtyard with

**A:1** The genealogy of Mordecai is designed to reflect opposition to Israel's enemy Haman, an Agagite (v. 17). In 1 Sm 15:1–9, Saul (whose father's name was Kish, of the tribe of Benjamin) conquered Agag the Amalekite.

**A:2–3** Repeats information from 2:5–6, on which see note, but states that Mordecai is already a court official. In the Hebrew text, Mordecai is not given this rank until 7:10–8:2.

**A:4** An interpretation of the dream that relates its features to the plot of the book is given in F:1–6.

**A:12–17** Retells the story in 2:21–23, but with several differences. Addition A has Mordecai inform the king directly, whereas in 2:22 Mordecai informs the king through Esther after she has become queen. A:16 has Mordecai rewarded immediately after his service, whereas the Hebrew text defers the reward of Mordecai to 6:3–13. In A:17, the failure of the eunuchs' plot becomes Haman's reason for seeking the destruction of Mordecai and his people, something which the Hebrew text attributes to Mordecai's refusal to bow to Haman (see note on 3:2).

*a:* Est 2:5. *b:* Est 2:6; 2 Kgs 24:15; 2 Chr 36:9–10; Jer 22:24–30; 24:1; 29:1–2. *c:* Est F:2, 4–6. *d:* Est F:3. *e:* Est 2:21–23; 6:1–3.

Bigthan and Teresh, two eunuchs of the king who guarded the courtyard. [13]He overheard them plotting, investigated their plans, and discovered that they were preparing to assassinate King Ahasuerus. So he informed the king about them. [14]The king had the two eunuchs questioned and, upon their confession, put to death. [15]Then the king had these things recorded; Mordecai, too, put them into writing. [16]The king also appointed Mordecai to serve at the court, and rewarded him for his actions.[f]

[17]Haman, however, son of Hammedatha, a Bougean,* who was held in high honor by the king, sought to harm Mordecai and his people because of the two eunuchs of the king.[g]

## II. Esther Becomes Queen

### CHAPTER 1

See RG 157–59

***The Banquet of Ahasuerus.*** [1]* During the reign of Ahasuerus—the same Ahasuerus who ruled over a hundred and twenty-seven provinces from India to Ethiopia—[2]while he was occupying the royal throne in the royal precinct of Susa,* [3]in the third year of his reign, he gave a feast for all his officials and ministers: the Persian and Median army officers, the nobles, and the governors of the provinces.[h] [4]For as many as a hundred and eighty days, he displayed the glorious riches of his kingdom and the resplendent wealth of his royal estate.

[5]At the end of this time the king gave a feast of seven days in the garden court of the royal palace for all the people, great and small, who were in the royal precinct of Susa. [6]There were white cotton draperies and violet hangings, held by cords of fine crimson linen from silver rings on marble pillars. Gold and silver couches were on a mosaic pavement, which was of porphyry, marble, mother-of-pearl, and colored stones. [7]Drinks were served in a variety of golden cups, and the royal wine flowed freely, as befitted the king's liberality. [8]By ordinance of the king the drinking was unstinted, for he had instructed all the stewards of his household to comply with the good pleasure of everyone. [9]Queen Vashti also gave a feast for the women in the royal palace of King Ahasuerus.

***Refusal of Vashti.*** [10]On the seventh day, when the king was merry with wine, he instructed Mehuman, Biztha, Harbona, Bigtha, Abagtha, Zethar, and Carkas, the seven eunuchs who attended King Ahasuerus,[i] [11]to bring Queen Vashti into his presence wearing the royal crown, that he might display her beauty to the populace and the officials, for she was lovely to behold. [12]But Queen Vashti refused to come at the royal order issued through the eunuchs. At this the king's wrath flared up, and he burned with fury. [13]He conferred with the sages who understood the times, because the king's business was conducted in general consultation with lawyers and jurists. [14]He summoned Carshena, Shethar, Admatha, Tarshish, Meres, Marsena, and Memucan, the seven Persian and Median officials who were in the king's personal service and held first rank in the realm,[j] [15]and asked them, "What is to be done by law with Queen Vashti for disobeying the order of King Ahasuerus issued through the eunuchs?"

[16]In the presence of the king and of the officials, Memucan answered: "Queen Vashti has not wronged the king alone, but all the officials and the populace throughout the provinces of King Ahasuerus. [17]For the queen's conduct will become known to all the women, and they will look with disdain upon their husbands when it is reported, 'King Ahasuerus commanded that Queen Vashti be ushered into his presence, but she would not come.' [18]This very day the Persian

**A:17 A Bougean**: the origin of this term is unknown; it may represent a garbled attempt to render the Hebrew "Agagite" (3:1). In the Greek additions Haman not only knows the plot to assassinate the king, but is apparently a co-conspirator.

**1:1** The Hebrew text opens with a portrait of the power and luxury of the Persian king Ahasuerus (Xerxes I, whose empire consisted of only about thirty provinces).

**1:2** Susa was the winter capital of the Persian empire. The "royal precinct" (sometimes translated "stronghold" or "citadel") was a well-fortified section of the city that included the king's residence. The Book of Esther depicts other citizens living in this section as well.

*f:* Est 6:3. *g:* Est 3:1–15; B:1–7; E:13. *h:* Jdt 1:16. *i:* Dn 5:1. *j:* 1 Chr 12:32; Ezr 7:14.

### Vashti Deposed

THE WISE MEN (1:13) are possibly the king's seven counselors (Ezr 7:14). Reference to irrevocable laws (Est 1:19) is also made in Est 8:8 and in Dn 6:9. There may be some irony in the allusion that in both Esther and Daniel the irrevocable decrees against the Jews are ineffective.

and Median noblewomen who hear of the
queen's conduct will recount it to all the
royal officials, and disdain and rancor will
abound. 19If it please the king, let an irrevocable royal decree* be issued by him and inscribed among the laws of the Persians and
Medes, forbidding Vashti to come into the
presence of King Ahasuerus and authorizing
the king to give her royal dignity to one more
worthy than she.[k] 20Thus, when the decree
that the king will issue is published throughout his realm, vast as it is, all wives will
honor their husbands, from the greatest to the
least."

21This proposal pleased the king and the
officials, and the king acted on the advice of
Memucan. 22He sent letters to all the royal
provinces, to each province in its own script
and to each people in its own language, to
the effect that every man should be lord in
his own home.

## CHAPTER 2

See RG 157–59

*The Search for a New Queen.* 1After
this, when King Ahasuerus' wrath had
cooled, he thought over what Vashti had
done and what had been decreed against her.
2Then the king's personal attendants suggested: "Let beautiful young virgins be
sought for the king. 3Let the king appoint
emissaries in all the provinces of his realm
to gather all beautiful young virgins into the
harem in the royal precinct of Susa. Under
the care of the royal eunuch Hegai, guardian
of the women, let cosmetics be given them.
4Then the young woman who pleases the
king shall reign in place of Vashti." This
suggestion pleased the king, and he acted accordingly.

5There was in the royal precinct of Susa a
certain Jew named Mordecai,* son of Jair,
son of Shimei, son of Kish, a Benjaminite,
6who had been exiled from Jerusalem with
the captives taken with Jeconiah, king of Judah, whom Nebuchadnezzar, king of Babylon, had deported.[l] 7He became foster father to his cousin Hadassah, that is, Esther,*
when she lost both father and mother. The
young woman was beautifully formed and
lovely to behold. On the death of her father
and mother, Mordecai adopted her as his
own daughter.[m]

8When the king's order and decree had
been proclaimed and many young women
brought together to the royal precinct of
Susa under the care of Hegai, Esther also
was brought in to the royal palace under the
care of Hegai, guardian of the women. 9The
young woman pleased him and won his favor. So he promptly furnished her with cosmetics and provisions. Then choosing seven
maids for her from the royal palace, he transferred both her and her maids to the best
place in the harem. 10Esther did not reveal
her nationality or family, for Mordecai had
commanded her not to do so.

11Day by day Mordecai would walk about
in front of the court of the harem to learn
how Esther was faring and what was to become of her.

12After the twelve months' preparation decreed for the women, each one went in turn

**1:19 An irrevocable royal decree**: the first of several in the book. In a satiric portrayal, even a minor domestic disagreement is resolved through a sweeping international edict. The irrevocable nature of the decree is intended to increase its force, but creates problems if the king needs to adapt to new information or conditions. See note on 8:8.

**2:5 Mordecai**: a Babylonian name, deriving from the god Marduk. Like Esther, Mordecai may have had a Jewish name as well, although in his case we do not know what it is. The chronology of the book makes him well over one hundred years old, since he was deported with Jehoiachin about 598 B.C.; cf. A:1.

**2:7 Esther**: a Babylonian name, deriving from the goddess Ishtar. She is given a Hebrew name as well, "Hadassah," which means "myrtle."

*k:* Est 8:5, 8; Dn 6:8–9. *l:* Est A:3; 2 Kgs 24:15; 2 Chr 36:9–10; Jer 22:24–30; 24:1; 29:1–2. *m:* Est 2:15.

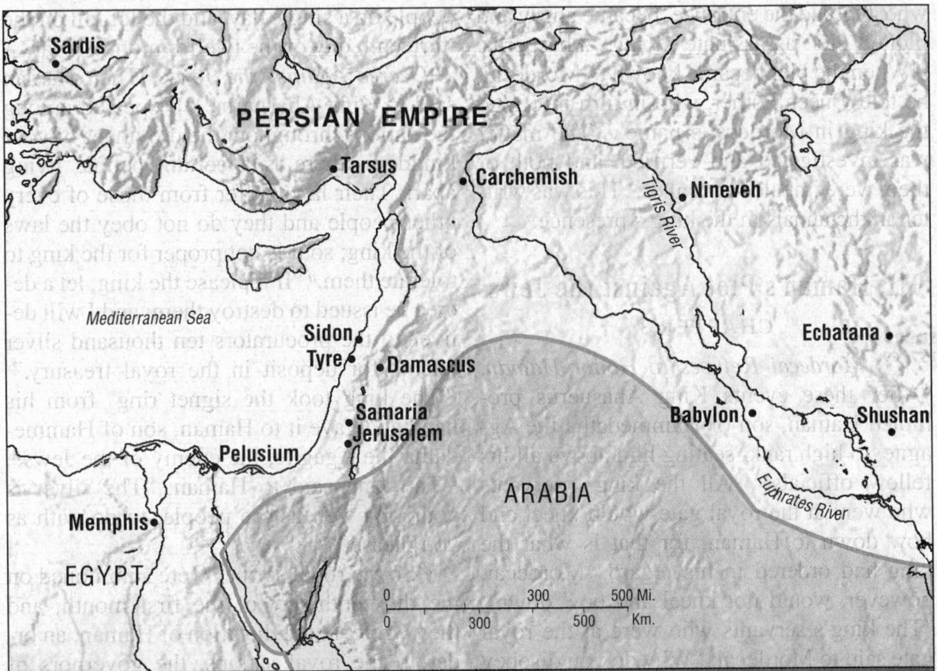


The Persian Empire

to visit King Ahasuerus. During this period of beautifying treatment, six months were spent with oil of myrrh, and the other six months with perfumes and cosmetics. [13]Then, when each one was to visit the king, she was allowed to take with her from the harem to the royal palace whatever she chose. [14]She would go in the evening and return in the morning to a second harem under the care of the royal eunuch Shaashgaz, guardian of the concubines. She could not return to the king unless he was pleased with her and had her summoned by name.[n] [15]As for Esther, daughter of Abihail and adopted daughter of his nephew Mordecai, when her turn came to visit the king, she did not ask for anything but what the royal eunuch Hegai, guardian of the women, suggested. And she won the admiration of all who saw her.

*Ahasuerus Chooses Esther.* [16]Esther was led to King Ahasuerus in his palace in the tenth month, Tebeth, in the seventh year of his reign. [17]The king loved Esther more than all other women, and of all the virgins she won his favor and good will. So he placed the royal crown on her head and made her queen in place of Vashti. [18]Then the king gave a great feast in honor of Esther to all his officials and servants, granting a holiday to the provinces and bestowing gifts with royal generosity.

*Mordecai Thwarts an Assassination.**
[19][o] As was said, from the time the virgins had been brought together, and while Mordecai was passing his time at the king's gate, [20]Esther had not revealed her family or nationality, because Mordecai had told her not to; and Esther continued to follow Mordecai's instructions, just as she had when she was being brought up by him. [21][p] During the time that Mordecai spent at the king's gate, Bigthan and Teresh, two of the royal eunuchs

**2:19–23** This story is retold and placed at the beginning of the book in Greek addition A:12–17, with significant differences (see note). The Greek also has a translation of the account in 2:19–23 at this point in the narrative.

*n:* Est 2:19–20; 4:11, 16. *o:* Est 2:14. *p:* Est A:12–15; 6:1–3.

who guarded the entrance, became angry and plotted to assassinate King Ahasuerus.
22When the plot became known to Mordecai, he told Queen Esther, who in turn informed the king in Mordecai's name. 23The matter was investigated and verified, and both of them were impaled on stakes.* This was written in the annals in the king's presence.

## III. Haman's Plot Against the Jews

### CHAPTER 3

See RG 157–59

***Mordecai Refuses to Honor Haman.***
1After these events King Ahasuerus promoted Haman, son of Hammedatha the Agagite, to high rank, seating him above all his fellow officials.[q] 2All the king's servants who were at the royal gate would kneel and bow down to Haman, for that is what the king had ordered in his regard.[r] Mordecai, however, would not kneel and bow down.*
3The king's servants who were at the royal gate said to Mordecai, "Why do you disobey the king's order?"[s] 4When they had reminded him day after day and he would not listen to them, they informed Haman, to see whether Mordecai's explanation would prevail, since he had told them that he was a Jew.

***Haman's Reprisal.*** 5When Haman observed that Mordecai would not kneel and bow down to him, he was filled with anger.
6But he thought it was beneath him to attack only Mordecai. Since they had told Haman of Mordecai's nationality, he sought to destroy all the Jews, Mordecai's people, throughout the realm of King Ahasuerus. 7In the first month, Nisan, in the twelfth year of King Ahasuerus, the *pur*, or lot,* was cast in Haman's presence to determine the day and the month for the destruction of Mordecai's people on a single day, and the lot fell on the thirteenth day of the twelfth month, Adar.[t]

***Decree Against the Jews.*** 8Then Haman said to King Ahasuerus: "Dispersed among the nations throughout the provinces of your kingdom, there is a certain people living apart. Their laws differ from those of every other people and they do not obey the laws of the king; so it is not proper for the king to tolerate them.[u] 9If it please the king, let a decree be issued to destroy them; and I will deliver to the procurators ten thousand silver talents for deposit in the royal treasury."[v]
10The king took the signet ring* from his hand and gave it to Haman, son of Hammedatha the Agagite, the enemy of the Jews.[w]
11The king said to Haman, "The silver is yours, as well as the people, to do with as you please."*

12So the royal scribes were summoned on the thirteenth day of the first month, and they wrote, at the dictation of Haman, an order to the royal satraps, the governors of every province, and the officials of every people, to each province in its own script and to each people in its own language. It was written in the name of King Ahasuerus and sealed with the royal signet ring. 13Letters were sent by couriers to all the royal provinces, to destroy, kill and annihilate all the Jews, young and old, including women and children in one day, the thirteenth day of the twelfth month, Adar, and to seize their goods as spoil.[x]

### CHAPTER B

See RG 157–59

1This is a copy of the letter:
"The great King Ahasuerus writes to the satraps of the hundred and twenty-seven provinces from India to Ethiopia, and the

**2:23 Impaled on stakes**: a method of execution used by the Persians, known from ancient records and reliefs.

**3:2** We are not told the reasons for Mordecai's refusal to bow. It may be the result of a form of Jewish piety that refuses to offer such homage to any mortal; see also Greek addition C:5–7.

**3:7 The pur, or lot**: the Hebrew text preserves the Akkadian word *pur* because its plural, *purim*, became the name of the feast of Purim commemorating the deliverance of the Jews; cf. 9:24, 26. The lot functions as a kind of horoscope to determine the most favorable day for the pogrom.

**3:10 Signet ring**: a ring containing a seal that was impressed on documents to authenticate them. With this ring, Haman can issue decrees in the king's name.

**3:11** Although Ahasuerus seems to refuse the bribe, this is probably a polite way of accepting it that makes him appear munificent (compare Gn 23:11–15, where Ephron tells Abraham that he "gives" him the field and, after a few more pleasantries, sets a very high price for it). Both 4:7 and 7:4 seem to assume Ahasuerus has accepted the money.

*q:* Est B:3; 5:11; E:11. *r:* Est C:5; 5:9, 13; 6:10, 12. *s:* Est 4:16. *t:* Est 9:24–32; F:10. *u:* Est 3:13; B:4; E:24; Wis 2:14–15; Dn 3:8–12. *v:* Est 7:4. *w:* Gn 41:42. *x:* Est B:6; 7:4.

governors subordinate to them, as follows: 2When I came to rule many peoples and to hold sway over the whole world, not being carried away by a sense of my own authority but always acting fairly and with mildness, I determined to provide for my subjects a life of lasting tranquility; and, by making my kingdom civilized and safe for travel to its farthest borders, to restore the peace desired by all people.[y] 3When I consulted my counselors as to how this might be accomplished, Haman, who excels among us in discretion, who is outstanding for constant good will and steadfast loyalty, and who has gained a place in the kingdom second only to me,[z] 4brought it to our attention that, mixed among all the nations throughout the world, there is one people of ill will, which by its laws is opposed to every other people and continually disregards the decrees of kings, so that the unity of empire blamelessly designed by us cannot be established.[a]

5"Having noted, therefore, that this nation, and it alone, is continually at variance with all people, lives by divergent and alien laws, is inimical to our government, and does all the harm it can to undermine the stability of the kingdom, 6we hereby decree that all those who are indicated to you in the letters of Haman, who is in charge of the administration and is a second father to us, shall, together with their wives and children, be utterly destroyed by the swords of their enemies, without any pity or mercy, on the fourteenth day* of the twelfth month, Adar, of the current year;[b] 7so that when these people, whose present ill will is of long standing, have gone down into Hades by a violent death on a single day, they may leave our government completely stable and undisturbed for the future."

### (CHAPTER 3)

See RG 157-59

14A copy of the decree to be promulgated as law in every province was published to all the peoples, that they might be prepared for that day. 15The couriers set out in haste at the king's command; meanwhile, the decree was promulgated in the royal precinct of Susa. The king and Haman then sat down to drink, but the city of Susa was thrown into confusion.

## IV. Esther and Mordecai Plead for Help

### CHAPTER 4

See RG 157-59

*Mordecai Exhorts Esther.* 1When Mordecai learned all that was happening, he tore his garments, put on sackcloth and ashes, and went through the city crying out loudly and bitterly,[c] 2till he came before the royal gate, which no one clothed in sackcloth might enter. 3Likewise in each of the provinces, wherever the king's decree and law reached, the Jews went into deep mourning, with fasting, weeping, and lament; most of them lay on sackcloth and ashes.

4Esther's maids and eunuchs came and told her. Overwhelmed with anguish, the queen sent garments for Mordecai to put on, so that he might take off his sackcloth; but he refused. 5Esther then summoned Hathach, one of the king's eunuchs whom he had placed at her service, and commanded him to find out what this action of Mordecai meant and the reason for it. 6So Hathach went out to Mordecai in the public square in front of the royal gate, 7and Mordecai recounted all that had happened to him, as well as the exact amount of silver Haman had promised to pay to the royal treasury for the slaughter of the Jews. 8He also gave him a copy of the written decree for their destruction that had been promulgated in Susa, to show and explain to Esther. Hathach was to instruct her to go to the king and to plead and intercede with him on behalf of her people.*

**B:6 Fourteenth day**: only the Greek text here names the fourteenth of Adar as the day set aside for the destruction of the Jews. The Hebrew text consistently gives the date as the thirteenth of Adar (e.g., 3:13) as does Greek addition E:20; see note on 9:17–19.

**4:8** The Greek text adds the following to Mordecai's message to Esther: "Remember the days of your lowly estate, when you were brought up in my charge; for Haman, who is second to the king, has asked for our death. Invoke the Lord and speak to the king for us: save us from death."

*y:* Est E:8–9. *z:* Est 3:1; 5:11; E:11. *a:* Est 3:8; E:24. *b:* Est 3:13; 7:4; E:11. *c:* Jdt 4:12.

9Hathach returned to Esther and told her what Mordecai had said. 10Then Esther replied to Hathach and gave him this message for Mordecai: 11"All the servants of the king and the people of his provinces know that any man or woman who goes to the king in the inner court without being summoned is subject to the same law—death. Only if the king extends the golden scepter will such a person live. Now as for me, I have not been summoned to the king for thirty days."[d]

12When Esther's words were reported to Mordecai, 13he had this reply brought to her: "Do not imagine that you are safe in the king's palace, you alone of all the Jews. 14Even if you now remain silent, relief and deliverance will come to the Jews from another source;* but you and your father's house will perish. Who knows—perhaps it was for a time like this that you became queen?"

15Esther sent back to Mordecai the response: 16"Go and assemble all the Jews who are in Susa; fast on my behalf, all of you, not eating or drinking night or day for three days. I and my maids will also fast in the same way. Thus prepared, I will go to the king, contrary to the law. If I perish, I perish!"[e] 17Mordecai went away and did exactly as Esther had commanded.

## CHAPTER C

See RG 157–59

***Prayer of Mordecai.*** 1Recalling all that the Lord had done, Mordecai prayed to the Lord 2and said: "Lord, Lord, King and Ruler of all, everything is in your power, and there is no one to oppose you when it is your will to save Israel. 3You made heaven and earth and every wonderful thing under heaven. 4You are Lord of all, and there is no one who can resist you, the Lord. 5[f] You know all things. You know, Lord, that it was not out of insolence or arrogance or desire for glory that I acted thus in not bowing down to the arrogant Haman. 6I would have gladly kissed the soles of his feet for the salvation of Israel. 7But I acted as I did so as not to place the honor of a mortal above that of God. I will not bow down to anyone but you, my Lord. It is not out of arrogance that I am acting thus. 8And now, Lord God, King, God of Abraham, spare your people, for our enemies regard us with deadly envy and are bent upon destroying the inheritance that was yours from the beginning. 9Do not spurn your portion, which you redeemed for yourself out of the land of Egypt. 10Hear my prayer; have pity on your inheritance and turn our mourning into feasting, that we may live to sing praise to your name, Lord. Do not silence the mouths of those who praise you."

11All Israel, too, cried out with all their strength, for death was staring them in the face.

***Prayer of Esther.*** 12[g] Queen Esther, seized with mortal anguish, fled to the Lord for refuge. 13Taking off her splendid garments, she put on garments of distress and mourning. In place of her precious ointments she covered her head with dung and ashes. She afflicted her body severely and in place of her festive adornments, her tangled hair covered her.

14Then she prayed to the Lord, the God of Israel, saying: "My Lord, you alone are our King. Help me, who am alone and have no help but you, 15for I am taking my life in my hand.[h] 16From birth, I have heard among my people that you, Lord, chose Israel from among all nations, and our ancestors from among all their forebears, as a lasting inheritance, and that you fulfilled all your promises to them.[i] 17But now we have sinned in your sight, and you have delivered us into the hands of our enemies, 18because we worshiped their gods. You are just, O Lord. 19But now they are not satisfied with our bitter servitude, but have sworn an oath to their idols 20to do away with the decree you have pronounced, to destroy your inheritance, to close the mouths of those who praise you, to extinguish the glory of your house and your altar, 21to open the mouths of the nations to acclaim their worthless gods, and to extol a mortal king forever.

22"Lord, do not relinquish your scepter to those who are nothing. Do not let our foes

**4:14 From another source**: probably Mordecai refers to divine aid; the Greek additions (C) are explicit about this.

*d:* Est 2:14; 4:12; D:12. *e:* Est C:12–13. *f:* Est 3:2; 5:9. *g:* Est 4:16. *h:* Est 4:16. *i:* Dt 4:20; 7:6; 9:29; 14:2; 26:18; 32:9.

gloat over our ruin, but turn their own counsel against them and make an example of the one who began this against us. 23Be mindful of us, Lord. Make yourself known in the time of our distress and give me courage, King of gods and Ruler of every power. 24Put in my mouth persuasive words in the presence of the lion, and turn his heart to hatred for our enemy, so that he and his co-conspirators may perish. 25Save us by your power, and help me, who am alone and have no one but you, Lord.

26"You know all things. You know that I hate the pomp of the lawless, and abhor the bed of the uncircumcised or of any foreigner. 27You know that I am under constraint, that I abhor the sign of grandeur that rests on my head when I appear in public. I abhor it like a polluted rag, and do not wear it in private. 28I, your servant, have never eaten at the table of Haman, nor have I graced the banquet of the king or drunk the wine of libations.* 29From the day I was brought here till now, your servant has had no joy except in you, Lord, God of Abraham. 30O God, whose power is over all, hear the voice of those in despair. Save us from the power of the wicked, and deliver me from my fear."

### CHAPTER D

See RG 157–59

***Esther Goes to Ahasuerus.**** 1On the third day, ending her prayers, she took off her prayer garments and arrayed herself in her splendid attire. 2In making her appearance, after invoking the all-seeing God and savior, she took with her two maids; 3on the one she leaned gently for support, 4while the other followed her, bearing her train. 5She glowed with perfect beauty and her face was as joyous as it was lovely, though her heart was pounding with fear. 6She passed through all the portals till she stood before the king, who was seated on his royal throne, clothed in full robes of state, and covered with gold and precious stones, so that he inspired great awe. 7As he looked up in extreme anger, his features fiery and majestic, the queen staggered, turned pale and fainted, collapsing against the maid in front of her. 8But God changed the king's anger to gentleness. In great anxiety he sprang from his throne, held her in his arms until she recovered, and comforted her with reassuring words. 9"What is it, Esther?" he said to her. "I am your brother.* Take courage! 10You shall not die; this order of ours applies only to our subjects. 11Come near!" 12Raising the golden scepter, he touched her neck with it, embraced her, and said, "Speak to me."[j]

13She replied: "I saw you, my lord, as an angel of God, and my heart was shaken by fear of your majesty. 14For you are awesome, my lord, though your countenance is full of mercy." 15As she said this, she fainted. 16The king was shaken and all his attendants tried to revive her.

### CHAPTER 5

See RG 157–59

1* [Now on the third day, Esther put on her royal garments and stood in the inner courtyard, looking toward the royal palace, while the king was seated on his royal throne in the audience chamber, facing the palace doorway. 2When he saw Queen Esther standing in the courtyard, she won his favor and he extended toward her the golden scepter he held. She came up to him, and touched the top of the scepter.]

3Then the king said to her, "What is it, Queen Esther? What is your request? Even if it is half of my kingdom, it shall be granted you."[k] 4Esther replied, "If it please your majesty, come today with Haman to a banquet I have prepared." 5The king ordered, "Have Haman make haste to fulfill the wish of Esther."

## V. Haman's Downfall

***First Banquet of Esther.*** So the king went with Haman to the banquet Esther had prepared. 6During the drinking of the wine, the

**C:28 Wine of libations**: offered in sacrifice to the gods.

**D:1–16** Addition D expands on and replaces 5:1–2 of the Hebrew text.

**D:9 Brother**: along with "sister," a common term of affection between lovers or husband and wife. See, e.g., Sg 4:9–12; 8:1; Tb 5:22; 7:11.

**5:1–2** The Hebrew text translated here is a short form of the account which is in Greek addition D.

*j:* Est 4:11. *k:* Est 5:6; 7:2; 9:12.

## Royal Gifts

THE BESTOWAL OF the royal robe (6:8) was common in ancient times (cf Gn 41:42). Horses wearing royal crowns are pictured on Persian monuments.

king said to Esther, "Whatever you ask for shall be granted, and whatever request you make shall be honored, even if it is for half my kingdom."[l] 7 Esther replied: "This is my petition and request: 8 if I have found favor with the king and if it pleases your majesty to grant my petition and honor my request, let the king come with Haman tomorrow to a banquet I will prepare; and tomorrow I will do as the king asks."

***Haman's Plot Against Mordecai.*** 9 That day Haman left happy and in good spirits. But when he saw that Mordecai at the royal gate did not rise, and showed no fear of him, he was filled with anger toward him.[m] 10 Haman restrained himself, however, and went home, where he summoned his friends and his wife Zeresh. 11 He recounted the greatness of his riches, the large number of his sons, and how the king had promoted him and placed him above the officials and royal servants.[n] 12 "Moreover," Haman added, "Queen Esther invited no one but me to come with the king to the banquet she prepared; again tomorrow I am to be her guest with the king. 13 Yet none of this satisfies me as long as I continue to see the Jew Mordecai sitting at the royal gate."[o] 14 His wife Zeresh and all his friends said to him, "Have a stake set up, fifty cubits in height, and in the morning ask the king to have Mordecai impaled on it. Then go to the banquet with the king in good spirits." This suggestion pleased Haman, and he had the stake erected.[p]

### CHAPTER 6

See RG 157–59

***Mordecai's Reward from the King.*** 1 That night the king, unable to sleep, asked that the chronicle of notable events be brought in. While this was being read to him, 2 the passage occurred in which Mordecai reported Bigthan and Teresh, two of the royal eunuchs who guarded the entrance, for seeking to assassinate King Ahasuerus.[q] 3 The king asked, "What was done to honor and exalt Mordecai for this?" The king's attendants replied, "Nothing was done for him."[r]

4* "Who is in the court?" the king asked. Now Haman had entered the outer court of the king's palace to suggest to the king that Mordecai should be impaled on the stake he had raised for him.[s] 5 The king's attendants answered him, "Haman is waiting in the court." The king said, "Let him come in." 6 When Haman entered, the king said to him, "What should be done for the man whom the king wishes to reward?" Now Haman thought to himself, "Whom would the king wish to honor more than me?" 7 So he replied to the king: "For the man whom the king wishes to honor 8 there should be brought the royal robe the king wore and the horse the king rode with the royal crest placed on its head. 9 The robe and the horse should be given to one of the noblest of the king's officials, who must clothe the man the king wishes to reward, have him ride on the horse in the public square of the city, and cry out before him, 'This is what is done for the man whom the king wishes to honor!' "[t] 10 Then the king said to Haman: "Hurry! Take the robe and horse as you have proposed, and do this for the Jew Mordecai, who is sitting at the royal gate. Do not omit anything you proposed."[u] 11 So Haman took the robe and horse, clothed Mordecai, had him ride in the public square of the city, and cried out be-

**6:4–13** Haman's presumption that the king wants to honor him creates the irony that Haman himself prescribes and fulfills the elaborate terms of Mordecai's reward. This comic reversal mirrors the fatal reversal to come: Haman and those who hate the Jews find that their plot to destroy them recoils on their own head.

---

*l:* Est 5:3. *m:* Est 3:2–3; C:5–7; 6:10, 12. *n:* Est 3:1; B:3; E:11; 9:6–10. *o:* Est 3:2–3; 6:10, 12. *p:* Est 6:4; 7:9–10. *q:* Est A:12–14; 2:21–23. *r:* Est A:16. *s:* Est 5:14; 7:9–10. *t:* Gn 41:42–43; 1 Kgs 1:33; Dn 5:29. *u:* Est 2:21; 3:2–3; 5:9, 13.

fore him, “This is what is done for the man whom the king wishes to honor!”

[12]Mordecai then returned to the royal gate, while Haman hurried home grieving, with his head covered.[v] [13]When he told his wife Zeresh and all his friends everything that had happened to him, his advisers and his wife Zeresh said to him, “If Mordecai, before whom you are beginning to fall, is of Jewish ancestry, you will not prevail against him, but will surely be defeated by him.”

***Esther's Second Banquet.*** [14]While they were speaking with him, the king's eunuchs arrived and hurried Haman off to the banquet Esther had prepared.

### CHAPTER 7

See RG 157–59

[1]So the king and Haman went to the banquet with Queen Esther. [2]Again, on this second day, as they were drinking wine, the king said to Esther, “Whatever you ask, Queen Esther, shall be granted you. Whatever request you make, even for half the kingdom, shall be honored.”[w] [3]Queen Esther replied: “If I have found favor with you, O king, and if it pleases your majesty, I ask that my life be spared, and I beg that you spare the lives of my people. [4]For we have been sold, I and my people, to be destroyed, killed, and annihilated. If we were only to be sold into slavery I would remain silent, for then our distress would not have been worth troubling the king.”[x] [5]King Ahasuerus said to Queen Esther, “Who and where is the man who has dared to do this?”[y] [6]Esther replied, “The enemy oppressing us is this wicked Haman.” At this, Haman was seized with dread of the king and queen.

[7]The king left the banquet in anger and went into the garden of the palace, but Haman stayed to beg Queen Esther for his life, since he saw that the king had decided on his doom. [8]When the king returned from the palace garden to the banquet hall, Haman had thrown himself on the couch on which Esther was reclining; and the king exclaimed, “Will he also violate the queen while she is with me in my own house!” Scarcely had the king spoken when the face of Haman was covered over.

***Punishment of Haman.*** [9][z] Harbona, one of the eunuchs who attended the king, said, “At the house of Haman stands a stake fifty cubits high. Haman made it for Mordecai, who gave the report that benefited the king.” The king answered, “Impale him on it.” [10]So they impaled Haman on the stake he had set up for Mordecai, and the anger of the king abated.

### CHAPTER 8

See RG 157–59

[1]That day King Ahasuerus gave the house of Haman, enemy of the Jews, to Queen Esther; and Mordecai was admitted to the king's presence, for Esther had revealed his relationship to her.[a] [2]The king removed his signet ring that he had taken away from Haman, and gave it to Mordecai; and Esther put Mordecai in charge of the house of Haman.[b]

## VI. The Jewish Victory and the Feast of Purim

***The Second Royal Decree.*** [3]Esther again spoke to the king. She fell at his feet and tearfully implored him to revoke the harm done by Haman the Agagite and the plan he had devised against the Jews. [4]The king stretched forth the golden scepter to Esther. So she rose and, standing before him, [5]said: “If it seems good to the king and if I have found favor with him, if the thing seems right to the king and I am pleasing in his eyes, let a document be issued to revoke the letters that the schemer Haman, son of Hammedatha the Agagite, wrote for the destruction of the Jews in all the royal provinces.[c] [6]For how can I witness the evil that is to befall my people, and how can I behold the destruction of my kindred?”

[7]King Ahasuerus then said to Queen Esther and to the Jew Mordecai: “Now that I have given Esther the house of Haman, and they have impaled him on the stake because he was going to attack the Jews, [8][d] you in

*v:* Est 2:21; 3:2–3; 5:9, 13. *w:* Est 5:3. *x:* Est 3:13; B:6. *y:* Est 3:8–9. *z:* Est 5:14; 6:4. *a:* Est 9:1; Prv 11:8; 26:27; Mt 7:2. *b:* Prv 13:22; Dn 2:48–49. *c:* Est 1:19. *d:* Est 1:19.

A PERSIAN KING would hardly have allowed a slaughter of his people, as told in Esther 8:9–12; this section is not history, but theology, emphasizing retributive justice.

turn may write in the king's name what you see fit concerning the Jews and seal the letter with the royal signet ring." For a decree written in the name of the king and sealed with the royal signet ring cannot be revoked.*

[9]At that time, on the twenty-third day of the third month, Sivan, the royal scribes were summoned. Exactly as Mordecai dictated, they wrote to the Jews and to the satraps, governors, and officials of the hundred and twenty-seven provinces from India to Ethiopia: to each province in its own script and to each people in its own language, and to the Jews in their own script and language. [10]These letters, which he wrote in the name of King Ahasuerus and sealed with the royal signet ring, he sent by mounted couriers riding thoroughbred royal steeds. [11][e] In these letters the king authorized the Jews in each and every city to gather and defend their lives, to destroy, kill, and annihilate every armed group of any nation or province that might attack them, along with their wives and children, and to seize their goods as spoil [12]on a single day throughout the provinces of King Ahasuerus, the thirteenth day of the twelfth month, Adar.

See RG 157–59

## CHAPTER E

[1]The following is a copy of the letter:

"The great King Ahasuerus to the governors of the provinces in the hundred and twenty-seven satrapies from India to Ethiopia, and to those who are loyal to our government: Greetings!

[2]"Many have become more ambitious the more they were showered with honors through the bountiful generosity of their patrons. [3]Not only do they seek to do harm to our subjects but, incapable of dealing with such greatness, they even begin plotting against their own benefactors. [4]Not only do they drive out gratitude from among humankind but, with the arrogant boastfulness of those to whom goodness has no meaning, they suppose they will escape the stern judgment of the all-seeing God.

[5]"Often, too, the fair speech of friends entrusted with the administration of affairs has induced many placed in authority to become accomplices in the shedding of innocent blood, and has involved them in irreparable calamities [6]by deceiving with malicious slander the sincere good will of rulers. [7]This can be verified in the ancient stories that have been handed down to us, but more fully when you consider the wicked deeds perpetrated in your midst by the pestilential influence of those undeserving of authority. [8][f] We must provide for the future, so as to render the kingdom undisturbed and peaceful for all people, [9]taking advantage of changing conditions and always deciding matters coming to our attention with equitable treatment.

[10]"For instance, Haman, son of Hammedatha, a Macedonian,* certainly not of Persian blood, and very different from us in generosity, was hospitably received by us. [11]He benefited so much from the good will we have toward all peoples that he was proclaimed 'our father,' before whom everyone was to bow down; and he attained a position second only to the royal throne.[g] [12]But, un-

**8:8 A decree written . . . cannot be revoked**: the king cannot directly grant Esther's request (v. 5) to revoke the previous decree against the Jews because of the irrevocable character of the laws of the Medes and Persians (see 1:19 and note). He can, however, empower Esther to issue another decree in his name to counteract the earlier one. The second decree authorizes the Jews to defend themselves against those who would kill them, which is what they do in 9:2. This is why the outcome of the two decrees is that the attackers are killed instead of the Jews, rather than a simple cancellation of all hostilities.

**E:10 Macedonian**: throughout the book Haman is identified with terms of contempt—in the Hebrew text as an Agagite (3:1, 10; 8:3, 5; 9:24; cf. note on A:17), thus making him a descendant of Agag, king of the Amalekites, a group hated by the Israelites; in the Greek additions Haman is identified as a Macedonian, reflecting the enmity between the Persians and the Macedonians after Macedonia's conquest of Persia in the fourth century B.C.

*e:* Est 9:1–4. *f:* Est B:2. *g:* Est B:3, 6.

able to control his arrogance, he strove to deprive us of kingdom and of life, 13 and by weaving intricate webs of deceit he demanded the destruction of Mordecai, our savior and constant benefactor, and of Esther, our blameless royal consort, together with their whole nation.[h] 14 For by such measures he hoped to catch us defenseless and to transfer the rule of the Persians to the Macedonians. 15 But we find that the Jews, who were doomed to extinction by this archcriminal, are not evildoers, but rather are governed by very just laws 16 and are the children of the Most High, the living God of majesty, who has maintained the kingdom in a flourishing condition for us and for our forebears.

17 "You will do well, then, to ignore the letter sent by Haman, son of Hammedatha, 18 for he who composed it has been impaled, together with his entire household, before the gates of Susa. Thus swiftly has God, who governs all, brought just punishment upon him.[i]

19 "You shall exhibit a copy of this letter publicly in every place to certify that the Jews may follow their own laws 20 and that you may help them on the day set for their ruin, the thirteenth day of the twelfth month, Adar, to defend themselves against those who attack them. 21 For God, the ruler of all, has turned that day from one of destruction of the chosen people into one of joy for them. 22 Therefore, you too must celebrate this memorable day among your designated feasts with all rejoicing, 23 so that both now and in the future it may be a celebration of deliverance for us and for Persians of good will, but for those who plot against us a reminder of destruction.

24 "Every city and province without exception that does not observe this decree shall be ruthlessly destroyed with fire and sword, so that it will be left not merely untrodden by people, but even shunned by wild beasts and birds forever."[j]

### (CHAPTER 8)

See RG 157–59

13 A copy of the letter to be promulgated as law in each and every province was published among all the peoples, so that the Jews might be prepared on that day to avenge themselves on their enemies. 14 Couriers mounted on royal steeds sped forth in haste at the king's order, and the decree was promulgated in the royal precinct of Susa.

15 Mordecai left the king's presence clothed in a royal robe of violet and of white cotton, with a large crown of gold and a mantle of fine crimson linen. The city of Susa shouted with joy,[k] 16 and for the Jews there was splendor and gladness, joy and triumph. 17 In each and every province and in each and every city, wherever the king's order arrived, there was merriment and joy, banqueting and feasting for the Jews. And many of the peoples of the land identified themselves as Jews, for fear of the Jews fell upon them.[l]

### CHAPTER 9

See RG 157–59

*The Massacre Reversed.* 1[m] When the day arrived on which the order decreed by the king was to be carried out, the thirteenth day of the twelfth month, Adar, on which the enemies of the Jews had expected to overpower them, the situation was reversed: the Jews overpowered those who hated them. 2 The Jews mustered in their cities throughout the provinces of King Ahasuerus to attack those who sought to do them harm, and no one could withstand them, for fear of them fell upon all the peoples. 3 Moreover, all the officials of the provinces, the satraps, governors, and royal procurators supported the Jews out of fear of Mordecai; 4 for Mordecai was powerful in the royal palace, and the report was spreading through all the provinces that he was continually growing in power.

5 The Jews struck down all their enemies with the sword, killing and destroying them; they did to those who hated them as they pleased.[n] 6[o] In the royal precinct of Susa, the Jews killed and destroyed five hundred people. 7 They also killed Parshandatha, Dalphon, Aspatha, 8 Poratha, Adalia, Aridatha, 9 Parmashta, Arisai, Aridai, and Vaizatha, 10[p] the ten sons of Haman, son of Hamme-

*h:* Est A:17. *i:* Est 7:10; 9:14. *j:* Est 3:8–9; B:4. *k:* Dn 5:7. *l:* Est 9:27. *m:* Est 8:11–12. *n:* Jdt 15:6. *o:* Est 5:11; B:3; E:11. *p:* Est 9:15; Jdt 15:7, 11.

**Purim Celebrations**

IN KEEPING WITH the book's strong emphasis on banqueting, both ancient and modern Purim observances include gifts of food (9:19) to friends and charities. Because Purim is not found in the Torah, its acceptance would have needed explanation and support.

datha, the foe of the Jews. However, they did not engage in plundering.

[11]On the same day, when the number of those killed in the royal precinct of Susa was reported to the king, [12]he said to Queen Esther: "In the royal precinct of Susa the Jews have killed and destroyed five hundred people, as well as the ten sons of Haman. What must they have done in the other royal provinces! You shall again be granted whatever you ask, and whatever you request shall be honored." [13]So Esther said, "If it pleases your majesty, let the Jews in Susa be permitted again tomorrow to act according to today's decree, and let the ten sons of Haman be impaled on stakes." [14]The king then gave an order that this be done, and the decree was published in Susa. So the ten sons of Haman were impaled,[q] [15]and the Jews in Susa mustered again on the fourteenth of the month of Adar and killed three hundred people in Susa. However, they did not engage in plundering.[r]

[16]The other Jews, who dwelt in the royal provinces, also mustered and defended themselves, and obtained rest from their enemies. They killed seventy-five thousand of those who hated them, but they did not engage in plunder.[s] [17]This happened on the thirteenth day of the month of Adar.

***The Feast of Purim.**** On the fourteenth of the month they rested, and made it a day of feasting and rejoicing.

[18]The Jews in Susa, however, mustered on the thirteenth and fourteenth of the month. But on the fifteenth they rested, and made it a day of joyful banqueting. [19]That is why the rural Jews, who dwell in villages, celebrate the fourteenth of the month of Adar as a day of joyful banqueting, a holiday on which they send food to one another.

[20]Mordecai recorded these events and sent letters to all the Jews, both near and far, in all the provinces of King Ahasuerus. [21]* He ordered them to celebrate every year both the fourteenth and the fifteenth of the month of Adar [22]as the days on which the Jews obtained rest from their enemies and as the month which was turned for them from sorrow into joy, from mourning into celebration. They were to observe these days with joyful banqueting, sending food to one another and gifts to the poor. [23]* The Jews adopted as a custom what they had begun doing and what Mordecai had written to them.[t]

## VII. Epilogue: The Rise of Mordecai

***Summary of the Story.*** [24][u] Haman, son of Hammedatha the Agagite, the foe of all the Jews, had planned to destroy them and had cast the *pur*, or lot, for the time of their defeat and destruction. [25]Yet, when the plot became known to the king, the king ordered in writing that the wicked plan Haman had devised against the Jews should instead be turned against Haman and that he and his sons should be impaled on stakes.[v] [26]And so these days have been named Purim after the word *pur*.

Thus, because of all that was contained in this letter, and because of what they had wit-

**9:17–19** According to Esther, Jewish feasting on the day after the defeat of their enemies establishes the date of the holiday. Since in Susa the fighting lasts for two days, the Jews of that community initially celebrate Purim a day later than Jews elsewhere.

**9:21** Mordecai creates a compromise among the Jews by making Purim a two-day festival.

**9:23** According to the story, the two-day celebration has its roots in popular observance, which Mordecai's leadership reinforces and regularizes.

*q:* Est 7:10; E:18. *r:* Est 9:10. *s:* Jdt 15:6. *t:* Est 9:29. *u:* Est 3:7; F:10. *v:* Est 6:5–13.

nessed and experienced in this event, [27]the Jews established and adopted as a custom for themselves, their descendants, and all who should join them, the perpetual obligation of celebrating these two days every year in the manner prescribed by this letter, and at the time appointed.[w] [28]These days were to be commemorated and kept in every generation, by every clan, in every province, and in every city. These days of Purim were never to be neglected among the Jews, nor forgotten by their descendants.

***Esther and Mordecai Act in Concert.**** [29]Queen Esther, daughter of Abihail, and Mordecai the Jew, wrote to confirm with full authority this second letter about Purim, [30]and Mordecai sent documents concerning peace and security to all the Jews in the hundred and twenty-seven provinces of Ahasuerus' kingdom.[x] [31]Thus were established, for their appointed time, these days of Purim which Mordecai the Jew and Queen Esther had designated for the Jews, just as they had previously enjoined upon themselves and upon their descendants the duty of fasting and supplication. [32]The command of Esther confirmed these prescriptions for Purim and was recorded in the book.

## CHAPTER 10

See RG 157–59

***The Rise of Mordecai Completed.*** [1]King Ahasuerus levied a tax on the land and on the islands of the sea. [2]All the acts of his power and valor, as well as a detailed account of the greatness of Mordecai, whom the king promoted, are recorded in the chronicles of the kings of Media and Persia. [3]The Jew Mordecai was next in rank to King Ahasuerus, in high standing among the Jews, popular with many of his kindred, seeking the good of his people and speaking out on behalf of the welfare of all its descendants.[y]

## CHAPTER F

See RG 157–59

***Mordecai's Dream Fulfilled.*** [1z]Then Mordecai said: "This is the work of God. [2]I recall the dream I had about these very things, and not a single detail has been left unfulfilled— [3]the tiny spring that grew into a river, and there was light, and sun, and many waters. The river is Esther, whom the king married and made queen. [4]The two dragons are myself and Haman. [5]The nations are those who assembled to destroy the name of the Jews, [6]but my people is Israel, who cried to God and was saved.

"The Lord saved his people and delivered us from all these evils. God worked signs and great wonders, such as have not occurred among the nations. [7]For this purpose he arranged two lots:* one for the people of God, the second for all the other nations. [8]These two lots were fulfilled in the hour, the time, and the day of judgment before God and among all the nations. [9]God remembered his people and rendered justice to his inheritance.

[10a] "Gathering together with joy and happiness before God, they shall celebrate these days on the fourteenth and fifteenth of the month Adar throughout all future generations of his people Israel."

***Colophon.**** [11]In the fourth year of the reign of Ptolemy and Cleopatra, Dositheus, who said he was a priest and Levite, and his son Ptolemy brought the present letter of Purim, saying that it was genuine and that Lysimachus, son of Ptolemy, of the community of Jerusalem, had translated it.

**9:29–32** In attempting to give the impression of concerted action between Esther and Mordecai, the Hebrew text here presents several unresolved difficulties. Verse 29 makes Mordecai and Esther joint authors of a letter that is ascribed in v. 32 to Esther alone. Verse 31 makes Mordecai and Esther joint authors of a letter that is ascribed in vv. 20–22 to Mordecai alone. Finally, it is difficult to see the purpose of confirming a second letter in the second letter itself.

**F:7 Two lots**: this passage of the Greek text gives an additional interpretation of the feast. The two lots are drawn by God to determine, respectively, the destiny of Israel and that of the nations; contrast with 3:7 of the Hebrew text.

**F:11** Several "Ptolemies" (Greek kings reigning in Egypt) had wives named Cleopatra. This postscript dates the Greek version somewhere between 116 B.C. and 48 B.C.

*w:* Est 8:12, 17. *x:* Est 9:23–26. *y:* 2 Mc 15:14. *z:* Est A:4–10. *a:* Est 3:7; 9:17–18, 21, 24–28.

See RG 160–64

# The First Book of Maccabees

The name Maccabee, probably meaning "hammer," is actually applied in the Books of Maccabees to only one man, Judas, third son of the priest Mattathias and first leader of the revolt against the Seleucid kings who persecuted the Jews (1 Mc 2:4, 66; 2 Mc 8:5, 16; 10:1, 16). Traditionally the name has come to be extended to the brothers of Judas, his supporters, and even to other Jewish heroes of the period, such as the seven brothers (2 Mc 7).

The two Books of Maccabees contain independent accounts of events (in part identical) that accompanied the attempted suppression of Judaism in Palestine in the second century B.C. The vigorous reaction to this attempt established for a time the religious and political independence of the Jews.

First Maccabees was written about 100 B.C., in Hebrew, but the original has not come down to us. Instead, we have an early, pre-Christian, Greek translation full of Hebrew idioms. The author, probably a Palestinian Jew, is unknown. He was familiar with the traditions and sacred books of his people and had access to much reliable information on their recent history (from 175 to 134 B.C.). He may well have played some part in it himself in his youth. His purpose in writing is to record the deliverance of Israel that God worked through the family of Mattathias (5:62)—especially through his three sons, Judas, Jonathan, and Simon, and his grandson, John Hyrcanus. The writer compares their virtues and their exploits with those of Israel's ancient heroes, the Judges, Samuel, and David.

There are seven poetic sections in the book that imitate the style of classical Hebrew poetry: four laments (1:25–28, 36–40; 2:7–13; 3:45), and three hymns of praise of "our fathers" (2:51–64), of Judas (3:3–9), and of Simon (14:4–15). The doctrine expressed in the book is the customary belief of Israel, without the new developments which appear in 2 Maccabees and Daniel. The people of Israel have been specially chosen by the one true God as covenant-partner, and they alone are privileged to know and worship God, their eternal benefactor and unfailing source of help. The people, in turn, must worship the Lord alone and observe exactly the precepts of the law given to them. The rededication of the Jerusalem Temple described in 4:36–59 (see 2 Mc 10:1–8) is the origin of the Jewish feast of Hanukkah.

Unlike the Second Book of Maccabees, there is no doctrine of individual immortality except in the survival of one's name and fame, nor does the book express any messianic expectation, though messianic images are applied historically to "the days of Simon" (1 Mc 14:4–17). In true Deuteronomic tradition, the author insists on fidelity to the law as the expression of Israel's love for God. The contest which he describes is a struggle, not simply between Jew and Gentile, but between those who would uphold the law and those, Jews or Gentiles, who would destroy it. His severest condemnation goes, not to the Seleucid politicians, but to the lawless apostates among his own people, adversaries of Judas and his brothers, who are models of faith and loyalty.

The first and second Books of Maccabees, though regarded by Jews and Protestants as apocryphal, i.e., not inspired Scripture, because not contained in the Jewish list of books drawn up at the end of the first century A.D., have always been accepted by the Catholic Church as inspired and are called "deuterocanonical" to indicate that they are canonical even though disputed by some.

First Maccabees can be divided as follows:

I. Crisis and Response (1:1–2:70)
II. Leadership of Judas Maccabeus (3:1–9:22)
III. Leadership of Jonathan (9:23–12:53)
IV. Leadership of Simon (13:1–16:24)

## I. Crisis and Response

### CHAPTER 1

See RG 162–63

*From Alexander to Antiochus.* 1[a] After
Alexander the Macedonian, Philip's son, who

a: Dn 8:20–22; 11:3–4, 21.

## Alexander the Great

VERSES 1 TO 10 summarize the history from Alexander to Antiochus IV. Alexander planned a universal empire dominated by Greek culture.

came from the land of Kittim,* had defeated Darius, king of the Persians and Medes, he became king in his place, having first ruled in Greece. 2He fought many battles, captured fortresses, and put the kings of the earth to death. 3He advanced to the ends of the earth, gathering plunder from many nations; the earth fell silent before him, and his heart became proud and arrogant. 4He collected a very strong army and won dominion over provinces, nations, and rulers, and they paid him tribute.

5But after all this he took to his bed, realizing that he was going to die. 6So he summoned his noblest officers, who had been brought up with him from his youth, and divided his kingdom among them while he was still alive. 7Alexander had reigned twelve years* when he died.

8So his officers took over his kingdom, each in his own territory, 9and after his death they all put on diadems,* and so did their sons after them for many years, multiplying evils on the earth.

10There sprang from these a sinful offshoot, Antiochus Epiphanes, son of King Antiochus, once a hostage at Rome. He became king in the one hundred and thirty-seventh year* of the kingdom of the Greeks.

***Lawless Jews.*** 11bIn those days there appeared in Israel transgressors of the law who seduced many, saying: "Let us go and make a covenant with the Gentiles all around us; since we separated from them, many evils have come upon us." 12The proposal was agreeable; 13some from among the people promptly went to the king, and he authorized them to introduce the ordinances of the Gentiles. 14Thereupon they built a gymnasium* in Jerusalem according to the Gentile custom. 15They disguised their circumcision and abandoned the holy covenant; they allied themselves with the Gentiles and sold themselves to wrongdoing.

***Antiochus in Egypt.*** 16c When his kingdom seemed secure, Antiochus undertook to become king of the land of Egypt and to rule over both kingdoms. 17He invaded Egypt with a strong force, with chariots, elephants* and cavalry, and with a large fleet, 18to make war on Ptolemy,* king of Egypt. Ptolemy was frightened at his presence and fled, and many were wounded and fell dead. 19The fortified cities in the land of Egypt were captured, and Antiochus plundered the land of Egypt.

***Robbery of the Temple.*** 20d After Antiochus had defeated Egypt in the one hundred

**1:1 Land of Kittim**: Greece. The name referred originally to inhabitants of Kiti, capital of the isle of Cyprus, then to any Cypriots (Is 23:1; Jer 2:10), later to Greeks in general, and finally even to Romans. See note on Dn 11:30. **Darius**: Darius III, Codoman (336–331 B.C.).

**1:7 Twelve years**: 336–323 B.C. The division of the empire was not fully settled until 305 B.C.

**1:9 Diadems**: decorated bands of white cloth worn around the head, symbolizing kingship. The Ptolemies, based in Egypt, controlled Judea until 198 B.C., when they were replaced by the Seleucids, based in Syria.

**1:10 The one hundred and thirty-seventh year**: Antiochus IV seized the throne in September, 175 B.C. Dates are given in this book according to the beginning of the Seleucid era, which however was reckoned in two different ways. Antiochians considered this date to be October, 312 B.C. (Syrian calendar), while Babylonians and Jewish priests accepted April, 311 B.C. as the commencement of the era (Temple calendar). The author of 1 Maccabees dates political events by the Syrian calendar but religious events by the Temple calendar. Accordingly, the civil New Year occurred variously in September or October, the religious New Year in March or April.

**1:14 Gymnasium**: symbol and center of Greek athletic and intellectual life, it was the chief instrument of Hellenistic culture. Jewish youth were attracted by sports and encouraged to join youth clubs. They received training in military skills and in the duties of citizens. Many were won over to paganism, and some even sought surgical correction of their circumcision (since physical exercise was carried out in nudity).

**1:17 Elephants**: an important part of Seleucid armament (cf. 6:34–37).

**1:18** Ptolemy VI Philometer, a nephew of Antiochus.

---

*b:* 2 Mc 4:12–17. *c:* 2 Mc 5:1–10; Dn 11:25–30. *d:* 2 Mc 5:11–21.

**Antiochus Epiphanes**

AFTER HIS SUCCESSFUL invasion of Egypt, Epiphanes plundered the temple of Jerusalem (a sacrilegious act), simply to replenish his funds (1:20–24). (This is also reported by Josephus, *Against Apion* 2, 83–84.)

and forty-third year,* he returned and went
up against Israel and against Jerusalem with
a strong force. 21 He insolently entered the
sanctuary* and took away the golden altar,
the lampstand for the light with all its utensils, 22 the offering table, the cups and bowls,
the golden censers, and the curtain. The cor-
nices and the golden ornament on the facade
of the temple—he stripped it all off. 23 And
he took away the silver and gold and the precious vessels; he also took all the hidden
treasures he could find. 24 Taking all this, he
went back to his own country. He shed much
blood and spoke with great arrogance.

25 And there was great mourning
 throughout all Israel,
26 and the rulers and the elders groaned.
Young women and men languished,
 and the beauty of the women faded.
27 Every bridegroom took up lamentation,
 while the bride sitting in her chamber
 mourned,
28 And the land quaked on account of its
 inhabitants,
 and all the house of Jacob was clothed
 with shame.

***Attack and Occupation.*** 29 e Two years
later, the king sent the Mysian commander*
to the cities of Judah, and he came to Jerusalem with a strong force. 30 He spoke to them
deceitfully in peaceful terms, and they believed him. Then he attacked the city suddenly, in a great onslaught, and destroyed
many of the people in Israel. 31 He plundered
the city and set fire to it, demolished its
houses and its surrounding walls. 32 And they
took captive the women and children, and
seized the animals. 33 Then they built up the
City of David with a high, strong wall and
strong towers, and it became their citadel.*
34 There they installed a sinful race, transgressors of the law, who fortified themselves
inside it. 35 They stored up weapons and provisions, depositing there the plunder they
had collected from Jerusalem, and they became a great snare.

36 The citadel became an ambush against
 the sanctuary,
 and a wicked adversary to Israel at all
 times.
37 They shed innocent blood around the
 sanctuary;
 they defiled the sanctuary.
38 Because of them the inhabitants of
 Jerusalem fled away,
 she became the abode of strangers.
She became a stranger to her own
 offspring,
 and her children forsook her.
39 f Her sanctuary became desolate as a
 wilderness;
 her feasts were turned into mourning,
Her sabbaths to shame,
 her honor to contempt.
40 As her glory had been, so great was her
 dishonor:
 her exaltation was turned into
 mourning.

***Religious Persecution.*** 41 g Then the king
wrote to his whole kingdom that all should

**1:20 Defeated Egypt in the one hundred and forty-third year**: 169 B.C. No mention is made in 1 Maccabees of the second expedition to Egypt a year later, described in 2 Mc 5:1, 11; Dn 11:25, 29 records both.

**1:21 Entered the sanctuary**: to pay his soldiers, Antiochus seized the sacred vessels and the money deposited at the Temple (see 2 Mc 3:10–11).

**1:29 Mysian commander**: in 2 Mc 5:24 he is identified as "Apollonius, commander of the Mysians" (mercenaries from Asia Minor). The Greek text of 1 Mc 1:29 ("chief collector of tribute") reflects a misreading of the Hebrew original.

**1:33 Citadel**: literally, *akra* means fortress. This was a garrison for foreign troops and renegade Jews that was established near the Temple area and fell to Simon only in 141 B.C. (13:49–50).

*e*: 2 Mc 5:24–26. *f*: Am 8:10; Tb 2:6. *g*: 2 Mc 6:1–11.

**Mattathias**

MATTATHIAS IS NOT mentioned in 2 Maccabees. His prominence in 1 Maccabees 2 has the effect of exalting the whole family, not just Judas.

be one people, [42]and abandon their particular customs. All the Gentiles conformed to the command of the king, [43]and many Israelites delighted in his religion; they sacrificed to idols and profaned the sabbath.

[44]The king sent letters by messenger to Jerusalem and to the cities of Judah, ordering them to follow customs foreign to their land; [45]to prohibit burnt offerings, sacrifices, and libations in the sanctuary, to profane the sabbaths and feast days, [46]to desecrate the sanctuary and the sacred ministers, [47]to build pagan altars and temples and shrines, to sacrifice swine and unclean animals, [48]to leave their sons uncircumcised, and to defile themselves with every kind of impurity and abomination; [49]so that they might forget the law and change all its ordinances. [50]Whoever refused to act according to the command of the king was to be put to death.[h]

[51]In words such as these he wrote to his whole kingdom. He appointed inspectors over all the people, and he ordered the cities of Judah to offer sacrifices, each city in turn. [52]Many of the people, those who abandoned the law, joined them and committed evil in the land. [53]They drove Israel into hiding, wherever places of refuge could be found.

[54]On the fifteenth day of the month Kislev, in the year one hundred and forty-five,* the king erected the desolating abomination upon the altar of burnt offerings, and in the surrounding cities of Judah they built pagan altars.[i] [55]They also burned incense at the doors of houses and in the streets. [56]Any scrolls of the law* that they found they tore up and burned. [57]Whoever was found with a scroll of the covenant, and whoever observed the law, was condemned to death by royal decree. [58]So they used their power against Israel, against those who were caught, each month, in the cities. [59]On the twenty-fifth day of each month they sacrificed on the pagan altar that was over the altar of burnt offerings. [60]In keeping with the decree, they put to death women who had their children circumcised, [61]and they hung their babies from their necks; their families also and those who had circumcised them were killed.

[62]But many in Israel were determined and resolved in their hearts not to eat anything unclean; [63]they preferred to die rather than to be defiled with food or to profane the holy covenant; and they did die. [64]And very great wrath came upon Israel.

## CHAPTER 2

See RG 162–63

*Mattathias and His Sons.* [1]In those days Mattathias, son of John, son of Simeon, a priest of the family of Joarib,[j] left Jerusalem and settled in Modein.* [2]He had five sons: John, who was called Gaddi; [3]Simon, who was called Thassi; [4]Judas, who was called Maccabeus; [5]Eleazar, who was called Avaran; and Jonathan, who was called Apphus. [6]When he saw the sacrileges that were being committed in Judah and in Jerusalem, [7]he said:

"Woe is me! Why was I born
to see the ruin of my people,
the ruin of the holy city—
To dwell there
as it was given into the hands of enemies,
the sanctuary into the hands of strangers?

**1:54 Fifteenth day of the month Kislev, in the year one hundred and forty-five**: December 6, 167 B.C. **Desolating abomination**: in the original Hebrew, a contemptuous pun on the title "Lord of heaven" given to the god to whom an image or perhaps an altar was erected upon the altar of burnt offerings in the Temple of Jerusalem; cf. Dn 9:27; 11:31.

**1:56 Scrolls of the law**: one or more of the first five books of the Old Testament, the traditional law of Israel.

**2:1 Modein**: a village about twenty miles northwest of Jerusalem, the family's ancestral home (see 2:70; 9:19).

*h:* 1 Mc 2:29–38; 2 Mc 6:18–7:42. *i:* Dn 9:27; 11:31; Mk 13:14. *j:* 1 Chr 9:10; 24:7.

**Zeal for the Law**

WHEN THE SYRIANS had first conquered Jerusalem, the Jews had been given the right to follow their ancestral laws (2:21). This right was very widely recognized in the Hellenistic and Roman worlds. In Numbers 25, Phinehas shows his zeal for the law by driving his spear through an Israelite man and Midianite woman in the act of intercourse. For this God gave him a covenant of perpetual priesthood. He became the prototypical zealot whose example legitimized religious violence. The fate of the zealots in the wilderness (2:31–38) highlights the dilemma of the observant Jew. Strict observance of the law forbids fighting on the sabbath. The Maccabees resolved this dilemma by making an exception in the case of this commandment.

8 Her temple has become like a man
disgraced,
9 her glorious vessels carried off as spoils,
Her infants murdered in her streets,
her youths by the sword of the enemy.[k]
10 What nation has not taken its share of her
realm,
and laid its hand on her spoils?
11 All her adornment has been taken away.
Once free, she has become a slave.
12 We see our sanctuary laid waste,
our beauty, our glory.
The Gentiles have defiled them!
13 Why are we still alive?"

14 Then Mattathias and his sons tore their
garments, put on sackcloth, and mourned
bitterly.

*Pagan Worship Refused and Resisted.*
15 The officers of the king in charge of enforcing the apostasy came to the city of
Modein to make them sacrifice. 16 Many of
Israel joined them, but Mattathias and his
sons drew together. 17 Then the officers of
the king addressed Mattathias: "You are a
leader, an honorable and great man in this
city, supported by sons and kindred. 18 Come
now, be the first to obey the king's command, as all the Gentiles and Judeans and
those who are left in Jerusalem have done.
Then you and your sons shall be numbered
among the King's Friends,* and you and
your sons shall be honored with silver and
gold and many gifts."

19 But Mattathias answered in a loud voice:
"Although all the Gentiles in the king's realm
obey him, so that they forsake the religion of
their ancestors and consent to the king's orders, 20 yet I and my sons and my kindred will
keep to the covenant of our ancestors.
21 Heaven forbid that we should forsake the
law and the commandments. 22 We will not
obey the words of the king by departing from
our religion in the slightest degree."

23 As he finished saying these words, a certain Jew came forward in the sight of all to
offer sacrifice on the altar in Modein according to the king's order. 24 When Mattathias
saw him, he was filled with zeal; his heart
was moved and his just fury was aroused; he
sprang forward and killed him upon the altar.
25 At the same time, he also killed the messenger of the king who was forcing them to
sacrifice, and he tore down the altar. 26 Thus
he showed his zeal for the law, just as Phinehas did with Zimri, son of Salu.[l]

27 Then Mattathias cried out in the city,
"Let everyone who is zealous for the law
and who stands by the covenant follow me!"
28 Then he and his sons fled to the mountains,
leaving behind in the city all their possessions.[m]

29 At that time many who sought righteousness and justice went out into the wilderness* to settle there, 30 they and their children, their wives and their animals, because
misfortunes pressed so hard on them. 31 It
was reported to the officers and soldiers of

**2:18 The King's Friends**: a regular order of nobility at Hellenistic courts (see 10:65; 11:27).

**2:29 The wilderness**: the sparsely inhabited mountain country southward from Jerusalem and west of the Dead Sea, in the region where the Dead Sea Scrolls were found.

*k*: Lam 2:11, 21. *l*: Nm 25:6–15; Ps 106:28–31; Sir 45:23–24; 1 Mc 2:54. *m*: 2 Mc 5:27.

the king who were in the City of David, in Jerusalem, that those who had flouted the king's order had gone out to secret refuges in the wilderness. 32[n] Many hurried out after them, and having caught up with them, camped opposite and prepared to attack them on the sabbath. 33 The pursuers said to them, "Enough of this! Come out and obey the king's command, and you will live." 34 But they replied, "We will not come out, nor will we obey the king's command to profane the sabbath." 35 Then the enemy attacked them at once. 36 But they did not retaliate; they neither threw stones, nor blocked up their secret refuges. 37 They said, "Let us all die in innocence; heaven and earth are our witnesses that you destroy us unjustly." 38 So the officers and soldiers attacked them on the sabbath, and they died with their wives, their children and their animals, to the number of a thousand persons.

39 When Mattathias and his friends heard of it, they mourned deeply for them. 40 They said to one another, "If we all do as our kindred have done, and do not fight against the Gentiles for our lives and our laws, they will soon destroy us from the earth." 41 So on that day they came to this decision: "Let us fight against anyone who attacks us on the sabbath, so that we may not all die as our kindred died in their secret refuges."

42 Then they were joined by a group of Hasideans,* mighty warriors of Israel, all of them devoted to the law. 43 And all those who were fleeing from the persecutions joined them and supported them. 44 They gathered an army and struck down sinners in their wrath and the lawless in their anger, and the survivors fled to the Gentiles for safety. 45 Mattathias and his friends went about and tore down the pagan altars; 46 they also forcibly circumcised any uncircumcised boys whom they found in the territory of Israel. 47 They put to flight the arrogant, and the work prospered in their hands. 48 They saved the law from the hands of the Gentiles and of the kings and did not let the sinner triumph.

*Farewell of Mattathias.* 49 When the time came for Mattathias to die, he said to his sons: "Arrogance and scorn have now grown strong; it is a time of disaster and violent wrath. 50 Therefore, my children, be zealous for the law and give your lives for the covenant of our ancestors.

51 "Remember the deeds that our ancestors
did in their times,
and you shall win great honor and an
everlasting name.
52 Was not Abraham found faithful in trial,
and it was credited to him as
righteousness?[o]
53 Joseph, when in distress, kept the
commandment,
and he became master of Egypt.[p]
54 Phinehas our ancestor, for his burning zeal,
received the covenant of an everlasting
priesthood.[q]
55 Joshua, for executing his commission,
became a judge in Israel.[r]
56 Caleb, for bearing witness before the
assembly,
received an inheritance in the land.[s]
57 David, for his loyalty,
received as a heritage a throne of
eternal kingship.[t]
58 Elijah, for his burning zeal for the law,
was taken up to heaven.[u]
59 Hananiah, Azariah and Mishael, for their
faith,
were saved from the fire.[v]
60 Daniel, for his innocence,
was delivered from the mouths of
lions.[w]
61 And so, consider this from generation to
generation,
that none who hope in Heaven shall
fail in strength.
62 Do not fear the words of sinners,
for their glory ends in corruption and
worms.[x]

**2:42 Hasideans**: in Hebrew *hasidim*, "pious ones," a militant religious group devoted to the strict observance of the law. They first supported the Maccabean movement, but subsequently opposed it, regarding it as too political (see 7:12–18).

*n:* 2 Mc 6:11. *o:* Gn 15:6; 22:1–18. *p:* Gn 39:7–10; 41:39–43. *q:* Nm 25:6–15. *r:* Jos 1, 2, 5. *s:* Nm 13:30; 14:6–9, 24; Jos 14:14. *t:* 2 Sm 2:4; 7:16. *u:* 1 Kgs 19:10, 14; 2 Kgs 2:11. *v:* Dn 3:26. *w:* Dn 6:23. *x:* 2 Mc 9:5–10, 28.

63 Today exalted, tomorrow not to be found,
they have returned to dust,
their schemes have perished.
64 Children! be courageous and strong in keeping the law,
for by it you shall be honored.

65“Here is your brother Simeon who I know is a wise counselor; listen to him always, and he will be a father to you. 66And Judas Maccabeus, a mighty warrior from his youth, shall be the leader of your army and wage the war against the nations. 67Gather about you all who observe the law, and avenge your people. 68Pay back the Gentiles what they deserve, and observe the precepts of the law.”

69Then he blessed them, and he was gathered to his ancestors. 70He died in the year one hundred and forty-six,* and was buried in the tombs of his ancestors in Modein, and all Israel mourned him greatly.

## II. Leadership of Judas Maccabeus

### CHAPTER 3

See RG 163

***Judas and His Early Victories.*** 1Then his son Judas, who was called Maccabeus, took his place. 2All his brothers and all who had joined his father supported him, and they gladly carried on Israel's war.

3 He spread abroad the glory of his people,
and put on his breastplate like a giant.
He armed himself with weapons of war;
he fought battles and protected the camp with his sword.
4 In his deeds he was like a lion,
like a young lion roaring for prey.
5 He pursued the lawless, hunting them out,
and those who troubled his people he destroyed by fire.
6 The lawless were cowed by fear of him,
and all evildoers were dismayed.
By his hand deliverance was happily achieved,
7 and he afflicted many kings.
He gave joy to Jacob by his deeds,
and his memory is blessed forever.
8 He went about the cities of Judah
destroying the renegades there.
He turned away wrath from Israel,
9 was renowned to the ends of the earth;
and gathered together those who were perishing.

10Then Apollonius* gathered together the Gentiles, along with a large army from Samaria, to fight against Israel. 11When Judas learned of it, he went out to meet him and struck and killed him. Many fell wounded, and the rest fled. 12They took their spoils, and Judas took the sword of Apollonius and fought with it the rest of his life.

13But Seron, commander of the Syrian army, heard that Judas had mustered an assembly of faithful men ready for war. 14So he said, “I will make a name for myself and win honor in the kingdom. I will wage war against Judas and his followers, who have despised the king's command.” 15And again a large company of renegades advanced with him to help him take revenge on the Israelites.

16When he reached the ascent of Beth-horon,* Judas went out to meet him with a few men. 17But when they saw the army coming against them, they said to Judas: “How can we, few as we are, fight such a strong host as this? Besides, we are weak since we have not eaten today.” 18But Judas said: “Many are easily hemmed in by a few; in the sight of Heaven there is no difference between deliverance by many or by few; 19for victory in war does not depend upon the size of the army, but on strength that comes from Heaven.[y] 20With great presumption and lawlessness they come against us to destroy us and our wives and children and to despoil us; 21but we are fighting for our lives and our laws. 22He* will crush them before us; so do not fear them.” 23When he finished speaking, he rushed suddenly upon Seron and his

**2:70 In the year one hundred and forty-six**: 166 B.C.

**3:10 Apollonius**: the Mysian commander mentioned in 1 Mc 1:29; 2 Mc 5:24.

**3:16 Beth-horon**: the famous pass leading up from the coastal plain to the Judean hill country. Here Joshua won an important battle (Jos 10:10–11), and in A.D. 66 a Roman force under Cestius was trapped and massacred.

**3:22 He**: out of reverence for God, the author of 1 Maccabees prefers to use the pronoun and other expressions, such as “Heaven,” instead of the divine name. Cf. v. 50.

*y*: 1 Sm 14:6.

**The Early Victories of Judas**

THE IDEA THAT God can give victory to the few over the many (3:18–19) is a popular biblical motif. Compare the story of Gideon in Judges 7 or Jonathan's statement in 1 Samuel 14:6: ". . . it is no more difficult for the LORD to grant victory by means of a few than it is by means of many." Judas is careful to observe ritual as well as military preparation for battle. The victory is not attributed to superior tactics, but to the miraculous power of God.

army, who were crushed before him. 24He
pursued Seron down the descent of Beth-horon into the plain. About eight hundred* of
their men fell, and the rest fled to the land of
the Philistines. 25Then Judas and his brothers began to be feared, and dread fell upon
the Gentiles about them. 26His fame reached
the king, and the Gentiles talked about the
battles of Judas.

*The King's Strategy.* 27When King Antiochus heard these reports, he was filled with
rage; so he ordered that all the forces of his
kingdom be gathered, a very strong army.
28He opened his treasury, gave his soldiers a
year's pay, and commanded them to be prepared for anything. 29But then he saw that this
exhausted the money in his treasury; moreover the tribute from the province was small
because of the dissension and distress he had
brought upon the land by abolishing the laws
which had been in effect from of old. 30He
feared that, as had happened once or twice, he
would not have enough for his expenses and
for the gifts that he was accustomed to give
with a lavish hand—more so than all previous
kings. 31Greatly perplexed, he decided to go
to Persia and levy tribute on those provinces,
and so raise a large sum of money.

32He left Lysias, a noble of royal descent,
in charge of the king's affairs from the Euphrates River to the frontier of Egypt, 33and
commissioned him to take care of his son
Antiochus until his return. 34He entrusted to
him half of his forces, and the elephants, and
gave him instructions concerning everything
he wanted done. As for the inhabitants of Judea and Jerusalem, 35Lysias was to send an
army against them to crush and destroy the
power of Israel and the remnant of Jerusalem and efface their memory from the place.
36He was to settle foreigners in all their territory and distribute their land by lot. 37* The
king took the remaining half of the army and
set out from Antioch, his capital, in the year
one hundred and forty-seven; he crossed the
Euphrates River and went through the
provinces beyond.

***Preparations for Battle.*** 38z Lysias chose
Ptolemy, son of Dorymenes, and Nicanor*
and Gorgias, powerful men among the
King's Friends, 39and with them he sent
forty thousand foot soldiers and seven thousand cavalry to invade and ravage the land
of Judah according to the king's orders.
40Setting out with their whole force, they
came and pitched their camp near Emmaus*
in the plain. 41When the merchants of the region heard of their prowess, they came to the
camp, bringing a huge sum of silver and
gold, along with fetters, to buy the Israelites
as slaves. A force from Edom and from
Philistia joined with them.

42Judas and his brothers saw that evils had
multiplied and that armies were encamped
within their territory. They learned of the orders which the king had given to destroy and
utterly wipe out the people. 43So they said to
one another, "Let us raise our people from
their ruin and fight for them and for our
sanctuary!"

**3:24 About eight hundred**: the figures given in this book for strength of armies and number of casualties are not always to be taken literally. In accordance with biblical usage, they indicate rather the importance of the battle described or the greatness of the victory.

**3:37** This expedition, in the spring of 165 B.C., resulted in failure; cf. chap. 6.

**3:38 Nicanor**: perhaps the leader of another attack against the Jews four years later; he was finally killed by Judas; cf. 7:26–46.

**3:40 Emmaus**: probably not the village mentioned in Lk 24:13 but a settlement about twenty miles west of Jerusalem at the edge of the hill country.

*z:* 2 Mc 8:9–23.

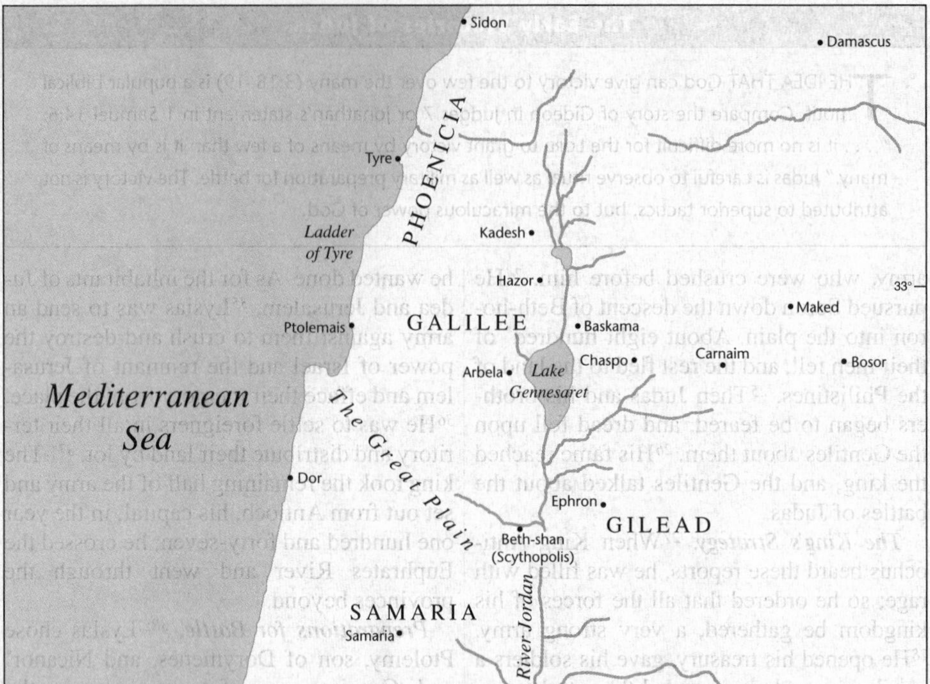

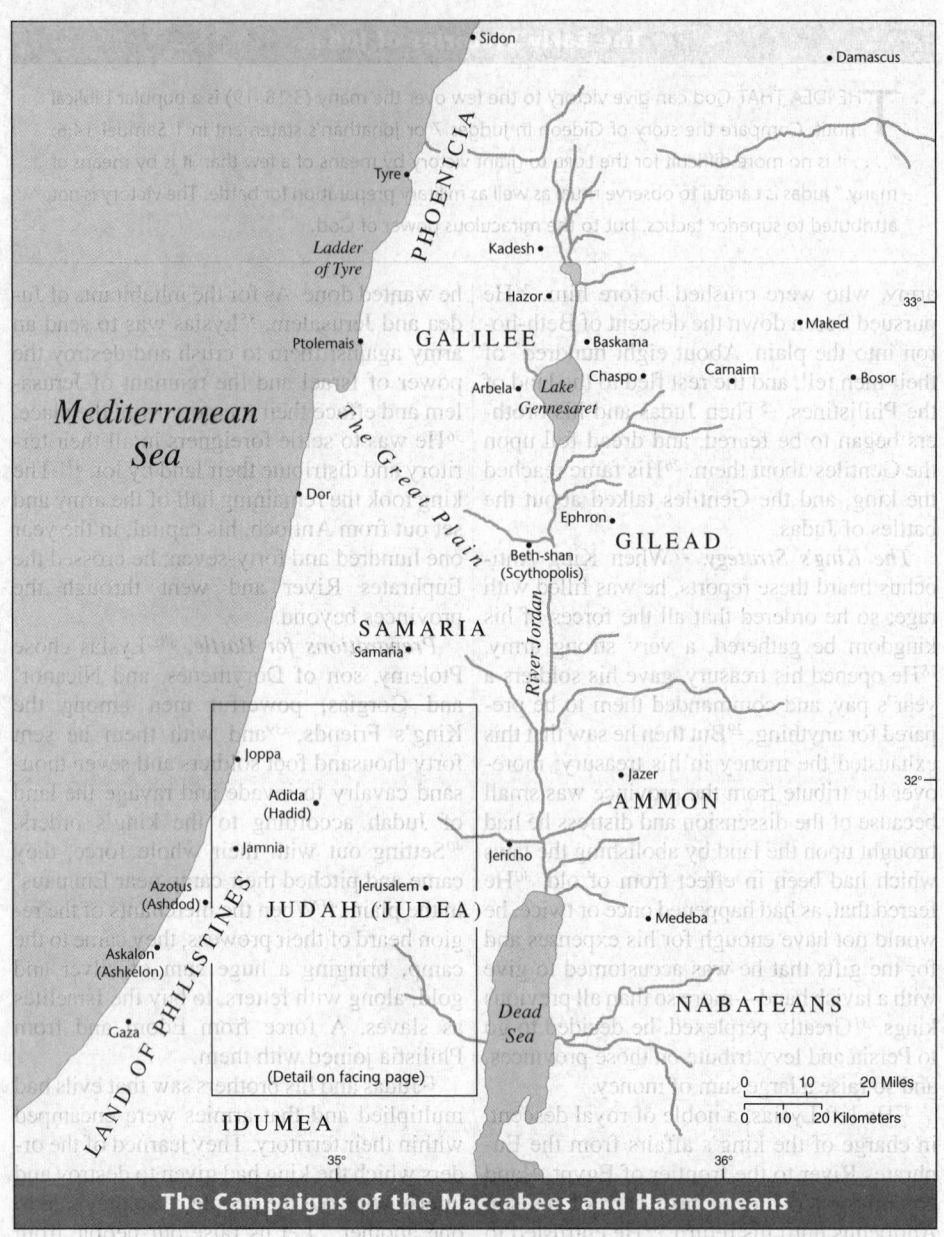

The Campaigns of the Maccabees and Hasmoneans

44 The assembly gathered together to prepare for battle and to pray and ask for mercy and compassion.

45 Jerusalem was uninhabited, like a
wilderness;
not one of her children came in or
went out.
The sanctuary was trampled on,
and foreigners were in the citadel;
it was a habitation for Gentiles.
Joy had disappeared from Jacob,
and the flute and the harp were
silent.

46 *Thus they assembled and went to Mizpah near Jerusalem, because formerly at Mizpah there was a place of prayer for Is-

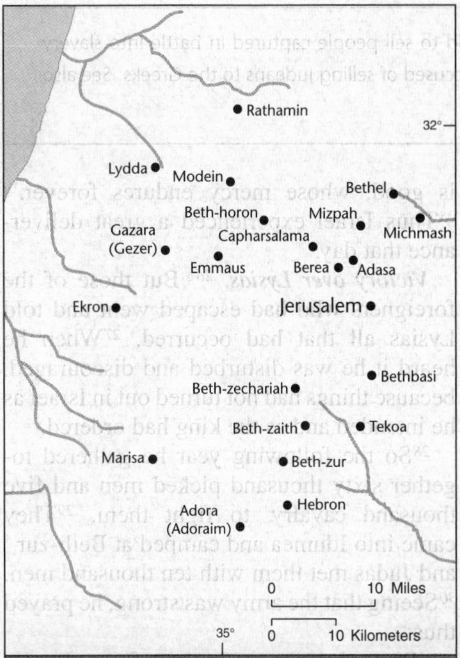

The Jerusalem Vicinity

rael.[a] 47 That day they fasted and wore sackcloth; they sprinkled ashes on their heads and tore their garments. 48 They unrolled the scroll of the law, to learn about the things for which the Gentiles consulted the images of their idols.* 49 They brought with them the priestly garments, the first fruits, and the tithes; and they brought forward the nazirites* [b] who had completed the time of their vows. 50 And they cried aloud to Heaven: "What shall we do with these, and where shall we take them? 51 For your sanctuary has been trampled on and profaned, and your priests are in mourning and humbled. 52 Now the Gentiles are gathered together against us to destroy us. You know what they plot against us. 53 How shall we be able to resist them unless you help us?" 54 Then they blew the trumpets and cried out loudly.

55 After this Judas appointed officers for the people, over thousands, over hundreds, over fifties, and over tens. 56 He proclaimed that those who were building houses, or were just married, or were planting vineyards, and those who were afraid, could each return home, according to the law.[c] 57 Then the army moved off, and they camped to the south of Emmaus. 58 Judas said: "Arm yourselves and be brave; in the morning be ready to fight these Gentiles who have assembled against us to destroy us and our sanctuary. 59 It is better for us to die in battle than to witness the evils befalling our nation and our sanctuary. 60 Whatever is willed in heaven will be done."

## CHAPTER 4

See RG 163

*Victory over Gorgias.* 1 Now Gorgias took five thousand infantry and a thousand picked cavalry, and this detachment set out at night 2 in order to fall upon the camp of the Jews in a surprise attack. Some from the citadel were his guides. 3 Judas heard of it and himself set out with his soldiers to attack the king's army at Emmaus 4 while these forces were still scattered away from the camp. 5 During the night Gorgias came into the camp of Judas, and found no one there; so he sought them in the mountains, saying, "They are fleeing from us."

6 But at daybreak Judas appeared in the plain with three thousand men; furthermore they lacked the helmets and swords they wanted. 7 They saw the army of the Gentiles,* strong, breastplated, and flanked with cavalry, and made up of experienced soldiers. 8[d] Judas said to the men with him: "Do not fear their numbers or dread their attack. 9 Remember how our ancestors were saved in the Red Sea, when Pharaoh pursued them with an army.[e] 10 So now let us cry to Heaven

**3:46 Mizpah . . . a place of prayer for Israel**: a holy place of great antiquity eight miles north and slightly west of Jerusalem. It was here that Samuel began to judge the Israelites (1 Sm 7:5–11; 10:17).

**3:48 To learn . . . idols**: favorable omens for the coming battle. A contrast is intended between the idol worship of the pagans and the consultation of the word of God by the Jews; cf. 2 Mc 8:23.

**3:49 Nazirites**: see note on Nm 6:2–21.

**4:7 Army of the Gentiles**: the main force; cf. 3:39–40; 4:1–2.

*a:* Jgs 20:1; 1 Sm 7:5–9; 10:17. *b:* Nm 6:1–21. *c:* Dt 20:5–8. *d:* Dt 20:3–4; Jgs 7:2–3. *e:* Ex 14:21–31.

IT WAS COMMON practice in the ancient world to sell people captured in battle into slavery (3:41). See Joel 4:6 where Tyre and Sidon are accused of selling Judeans to the Greeks. See also 2 Maccabees 8:10.

in the hope that he will favor us, remember
the covenant with our ancestors, and destroy
this army before us today. 11 All the Gentiles
shall know that there is One who redeems
and delivers Israel."
12 When the foreigners looked up and saw
them marching toward them, 13 they came
out of their camp for battle. The men with
Judas blew the trumpet, and 14 joined the battle. They crushed the Gentiles, who fled toward the plain. 15 Their whole rear guard fell
by the sword, and they were pursued as far
as Gazara* and the plains of Idumaea, to
Azotus and Jamnia. About three thousand of
their men fell.
16 When Judas and the army returned from
the pursuit, 17 he said to the people: "Do not
be greedy for plunder; for there is a fight
ahead of us, 18 and Gorgias and his army are
near us on the mountain. But now stand firm
against our enemies and fight them. Afterward you can freely take the plunder."
19 As Judas was finishing this speech, a detachment* appeared, looking down from the
mountain. 20 They saw that their army had
been put to flight and their camp was burning. The smoke they saw revealed what had
happened. 21 When they realized this, they
completely lost heart; and when they also
saw the army of Judas in the plain ready to
attack, 22 they all fled to the land of the foreigners.*
23 Then Judas went back to plunder the
camp, and they took much gold and silver,
cloth dyed blue and marine purple, and great
treasure. 24 As they returned, they were
singing hymns and glorifying Heaven, "who
is good, whose mercy endures forever."[f]
25 Thus Israel experienced a great deliverance that day.

*Victory over Lysias.* 26[g] But those of the
foreigners who had escaped went and told
Lysias all that had occurred. 27 When he
heard it he was disturbed and discouraged,
because things had not turned out in Israel as
he intended and as the king had ordered.
28 So the following year he gathered together sixty thousand picked men and five
thousand cavalry, to fight them. 29 They
came into Idumea and camped at Beth-zur,*
and Judas met them with ten thousand men.
30 Seeing that the army was strong, he prayed
thus:

"Blessed are you, Savior of Israel, who
crushed the attack of the mighty one by the
hand of your servant David and delivered
the foreign camp into the hand of Jonathan,
the son of Saul, and his armor-bearer.[h]
31 Give this army into the hands of your people Israel; make them ashamed of their
troops and their cavalry. 32 Strike them with
cowardice, weaken the boldness of their
strength, and let them tremble at their own
destruction. 33 Strike them down by the
sword of those who love you, that all who
know your name may sing your praise."
34 Then they engaged in battle, and about
five thousand of Lysias' army fell in hand-
to-hand fighting. 35* When Lysias saw the
tide of the battle turning, and the increased
boldness of Judas, whose men were ready
either to live or to die nobly, he withdrew to
Antioch and began to recruit mercenaries so
as to return to Judea with greater numbers.[i]

**4:15 Gazara**: Gezer of the Hebrew Bible, five miles northwest of Emmaus; **Azotus**, Hebrew Ashdod, lay to the southwest; **and Jamnia**, Hebrew Jabneel (Jos 15:11) or Jabneh (2 Chr 26:6), to the west of Gazara.

**4:19 A detachment**: i.e., Gorgias' force; cf. vv. 1–5.

**4:22 The land of the foreigners**: i.e., territory controlled by the Syrians. The Greek term used here is the same as that used throughout 1–2 Samuel in Greek for Philistine territory and intends to compare Maccabean victories to those of Saul and David.

**4:29 Beth-zur**: an important frontier city (between Judea and Idumea) in the mountain area, fifteen miles south of Jerusalem.

**4:35** According to 2 Mc 11:13–15, peace negotiations followed between Lysias and Judas.

*f:* Ps 118:1–4, 29; 136. *g:* 2 Mc 11:1–15. *h:* 1 Sm 17:48–58. *i:* 1 Mc 6:28–31.

See RG 163

## CHAPTER 5

***Victories over Hostile Neighbors.****

1[r] When the nations round about heard that the altar had been rebuilt and the sanctuary restored as before, they were enraged. 2 So they decided to destroy the descendants of Jacob who were among them, and they began to kill and eradicate the people. 3[s] Then Judas attacked the Edomites* at Akrabattene in Idumea, because they were blockading Israel; he dealt them a heavy blow, humbled and despoiled them. 4 He also remembered the malice of the Baeanites,* who had become a snare and a stumbling block to the people by ambushing them along the roads. 5 He forced them to take refuge in towers, which he besieged; he put them under the ban and burned down their towers along with all who were in them. 6*[t] Then he crossed over to the Ammonites, where he found a strong army and a large body of people with Timothy as their leader. 7 He fought many battles with them, routed them, and struck them down. 8 After seizing Jazer and its villages, he returned to Judea.

***Liberation of Jews in Galilee and Gilead.*** 9 The Gentiles in Gilead assembled to destroy the Israelites who were in their territory; these then fled to the stronghold of Dathema.* 10 They sent a letter to Judas and his brothers saying: "The Gentiles around us have assembled against us to destroy us, 11 and they are preparing to come and seize this stronghold to which we have fled. Timothy is the leader of their army. 12 Come at once to rescue us from them, for many of us have fallen. 13 All our kindred who were in the territory of the Tobiads* have been killed; the Gentiles have captured their wives, their children and their goods, and they have slain there about a thousand men."[u]

14 While they were reading this letter, suddenly other messengers, with garments torn, arrived from Galilee to deliver a similar message: 15 that "the inhabitants of Ptolemais,* Tyre, and Sidon, and the whole of Gentile Galilee have joined forces to destroy us." 16 When Judas and the people heard this, a great assembly convened to consider what they should do for their kindred who were in distress and being attacked by enemies.

17 Judas said to his brother Simon: "Choose men for yourself, and go, rescue your kindred in Galilee; my brother Jonathan and I will go to Gilead."

18 He left Joseph, son of Zechariah, and Azariah, leader of the people, with the rest of the army in Judea to guard it. 19 He commanded them, "Take charge of these people, but do not join battle against the Gentiles until we return." 20 Three thousand men were allotted to Simon to go into Galilee, and eight thousand men to Judas, for Gilead.

21 Simon went into Galilee and fought many battles with the Gentiles. They were crushed before him, 22 and he pursued them to the very gate of Ptolemais. About three thousand of the Gentiles fell, and he gathered their spoils. 23 He took with him the Jews who were in Galilee and in Arbatta,* with their wives and children and all that they had, and brought them to Judea with great rejoicing.

24[v] Judas Maccabeus and his brother Jonathan crossed the Jordan and marched for three days through the wilderness. 25 There

**5:1** The events of this chapter occurred within the year 163 B.C.

**5:3 Edomites**: lit., "sons of Esau"; here a pejorative term for the Idumeans. Cf. also 5:65. **Akrabattene**: either a district southwest of the Dead Sea or on the eastern border of Judea and Samaria.

**5:4 Baeanites**: 2 Mc 10:15–23 calls them simply Idumeans.

**5:6–8** This summary anticipates the order of events and would fit better between vv. 36 and 37. It corresponds to 2 Mc 12:17–23. The action was probably a reprisal for the massacre referred to in 1 Mc 5:13. Timothy may have been a local ruler, or the Seleucid governor of Transjordan. **Jazer**: a town on the road from the Jordan to Amman.

**5:9 Dathema**: the exact location is uncertain; it was east of the Jordan (in Gilead) and a night's journey from Bozrah (v. 29).

**5:13 Tobiads**: a prominent Jewish family that settled east of the Jordan.

**5:15 Ptolemais**: Hebrew *Acco* (Jgs 1:31), modern Acre, on the coast north of Haifa.

**5:23 Arbatta**: (or, Narbatta), probably south of Mount Carmel.

*r:* 1 Mc 13:6. *s:* 2 Mc 10:15–23. *t:* 2 Mc 8:30–33. *u:* 2 Mc 12:17. *v:* 2 Mc 12:10–16.

THE HIGH POINT of Judas's career is the purification of the temple. This is the event commemorated in the Jewish festival of Hanukkah (Hebrew for "dedication"; see 4:59).

***Purification and Rededication of the Temple.*** 36[j] Then Judas and his brothers said, "Now that our enemies have been crushed, let us go up to purify the sanctuary* and rededicate it." 37 So the whole army assembled, and went up to Mount Zion. 38 They found the sanctuary desolate, the altar desecrated, the gates burnt, weeds growing in the courts as in a thicket or on some mountain, and the priests' chambers demolished.[k] 39 Then they tore their garments and made great lamentation; they sprinkled their heads with ashes 40 and prostrated themselves. And when the signal was given with trumpets, they cried out to Heaven.

41 Judas appointed men to attack those in the citadel, while he purified the sanctuary. 42 He chose blameless priests, devoted to the law; 43 these purified the sanctuary and carried away the stones of the defilement to an unclean place. 44 They deliberated what ought to be done with the altar for burnt offerings that had been desecrated.[l] 45 They decided it best to tear it down, lest it be a lasting shame to them that the Gentiles had defiled it; so they tore down the altar. 46 They stored the stones in a suitable place on the temple mount, until the coming of a prophet who could determine what to do with them.[m] 47 Then they took uncut stones, according to the law, and built a new altar like the former one.[n] 48 They also repaired the sanctuary and the interior of the temple and consecrated the courts. 49 They made new sacred vessels and brought the lampstand, the altar of incense, and the table into the temple.[o] 50 Then they burned incense on the altar and lighted the lamps on the lampstand, and these illuminated the temple. 51 They also put loaves on the table and hung up the curtains. Thus they finished all the work they had undertaken.

52 They rose early on the morning of the twenty-fifth day of the ninth month, that is, the month of Kislev, in the year one hundred and forty-eight,* 53 and offered sacrifice according to the law on the new altar for burnt offerings that they had made.[p] 54 On the anniversary of the day on which the Gentiles had desecrated it, on that very day it was rededicated with songs, harps, lyres, and cymbals. 55 All the people prostrated themselves and adored and praised Heaven, who had given them success.

56 For eight days they celebrated the dedication of the altar and joyfully offered burnt offerings and sacrifices of deliverance and praise. 57 They ornamented the facade of the temple with gold crowns and shields; they repaired the gates and the priests' chambers and furnished them with doors. 58 There was great joy among the people now that the disgrace brought by the Gentiles was removed. 59 Then Judas and his brothers and the entire assembly of Israel decreed that every year for eight days, from the twenty-fifth day of the month Kislev,[q] the days of the dedication* of the altar should be observed with joy and gladness on the anniversary.

60 At that time they built high walls and strong towers around Mount Zion, to prevent the Gentiles from coming and trampling it as they had done before. 61 Judas also placed a garrison there to protect it, and likewise fortified Beth-zur, that the people might have a stronghold facing Idumea.

**4:36 The sanctuary**: the whole Temple area with its walls, courts and outbuildings, to be distinguished from the Temple proper, the oblong edifice with porch, main room and inner shrine.

**4:52 Twenty-fifth day of the ninth month . . . in the year one hundred and forty-eight**: December 14, 164 B.C.

**4:59 Days of the dedication**: institution of the feast of Hanukkah, also called the feast of Dedication (Jn 10:22). Josephus calls it the feast of Lights (*Antiquities* 12:325).

*j*: 2 Mc 10:1–8. *k*: Ps 74:2–7. *l*: 1 Kgs 8:64. *m*: 1 Mc 14:41; Dt 18:15. *n*: Ex 20:25. *o*: Ex 25:23–39; 30:1–6. *p*: Ex 30:10; Ez 43:18–27. *q*: Jn 10:22.

leveled the city, took spoils and passed through it over the slain.

[52]Then they crossed the Jordan to the great plain in front of Beth-shan; [53]and Judas kept gathering the stragglers and encouraging the people the whole way, until he reached the land of Judah. [54]They ascended Mount Zion in joy and gladness and sacrificed burnt offerings, because not one of them had fallen; they had returned in safety.

***Joseph and Azariah Defeated.*** [55]In those days when Judas and Jonathan were in the land of Gilead, and Simon his brother was in Galilee opposite Ptolemais, [56]Joseph, son of Zechariah, and Azariah, the leaders of the army, heard about the brave deeds and the fighting that they were doing. [57]They said, "Let us also make a name for ourselves by going out and fighting against the Gentiles around us." [58]They gave orders to those of their army who were with them, and marched against Jamnia.* [59]But Gorgias and his men came out of the city to meet them in battle. [60]Joseph and Azariah were routed and were pursued to the frontiers of Judea, and about two thousand Israelites fell that day. [61]It was a great setback for the people, because they had not obeyed Judas and his brothers, thinking that they would do brave deeds. [62]But they were not of the family through whom Israel's deliverance was given.

***Victories at Hebron and Azotus.*** [63]The valiant Judas and his brothers were greatly honored in all Israel and among all the Gentiles, wherever their name was heard; [64]and people gathered about them and praised them.

[65][a] Then Judas and his brothers went out and attacked the Edomites in the land toward the south; he took Hebron and its villages, and he destroyed its strongholds and burned the towers around it. [66]He then set out for the land of the foreigners and passed through Marisa. [67]On that day some priests fell in battle who had gone out rashly to fight in their desire to do brave deeds. [68]Judas then turned toward Azotus in the land of the foreigners. He destroyed their altars and burned the carved images of their gods; and after plundering their cities he returned to the land of Judah.

## CHAPTER 6

See RG 163

[1][b] As King Antiochus passed through the eastern provinces, he heard that in Persia there was a city, Elam,* famous for its wealth in silver and gold, [2]and that its temple was very rich, containing gold helmets, breastplates, and weapons left there by the first king of the Greeks, Alexander, son of Philip, king of Macedon. [3]He went therefore and tried to capture and loot the city. But he could not do so, because his plan became known to the people of the city [4]who rose up in battle against him. So he fled and in great dismay withdrew from there to return to Babylon.

[5]While he was in Persia, a messenger brought him news that the armies that had gone into the land of Judah had been routed; [6]that Lysias had gone at first with a strong army and been driven back; that the people of Judah had grown strong by reason of the arms, wealth, and abundant spoils taken from the armies they had cut down; [7]that they had pulled down the abomination which he had built upon the altar in Jerusalem; and that they had surrounded with high walls both the sanctuary, as it had been before, and his city of Beth-zur.[c]

[8]When the king heard this news, he was astonished and very much shaken. Sick with grief because his designs had failed, he took to his bed. [9]There he remained many days, assailed by waves of grief, for he thought he was going to die. [10]So he called in all his Friends and said to them: "Sleep has departed from my eyes, and my heart sinks from anxiety. [11]I said to myself: 'Into what tribulation have I come, and in what floods of sorrow am I now! Yet I was kindly and beloved in my rule.' [12]But I now recall the

**5:58 Jamnia**: Yavneh (see 10:69), the capital of the province of Azotus (Ashdod).

**6:1 Elam**: in fact, the mountainous region north of the Persian Gulf, rather than a city. The city may have been Persepolis. This section continues the story from 3:37 and pertains to events preceding those in 4:37–39.

*a:* 2 Mc 12:36–46. *b:* 2 Mc 1:13–17; 9:1–29; Dn 11:40–45. *c:* 1 Mc 1:54; 4:41–61.

they met some Nabateans,* who received
them peaceably and told them all that had
happened to their kindred in Gilead:
26“Many of them are shut up in Bozrah, in
Bosor near Alema, in Chaspho, Maked, and
Carnaim”—all of these are large, fortified
cities— 27“and some are shut up in other cities of Gilead. Tomorrow their enemies plan
to attack the strongholds and to seize and destroy all these people in one day.”
28Thereupon Judas suddenly changed direction with his army, marched across the
wilderness to Bozrah, and captured the city.
He put every male to the sword, took all their
spoils, and set fire to the city. 29* He led his
army from that place by night, and they
marched toward the stronghold. 30When
morning came, they looked ahead and saw a
countless multitude, with ladders and machines for capturing the stronghold, beginning to attack. 31When Judas perceived that
the struggle had begun and that the noise of
the battle was resounding to heaven with
trumpet blasts and loud shouting, 32he said
to the men of his army, “Fight for our kindred today.” 33He came up behind them with
three columns blowing their trumpets and
crying out in prayer. 34When the army of
Timothy realized that it was Maccabeus,
they fled before him, and he inflicted on
them a great defeat. About eight thousand of
their men fell that day.
35Then he turned toward Alema* and attacked and captured it; he killed every male,
took spoils, and burned it down. 36From
there he moved on and took Chaspho,
Maked, Bosor, and the other cities of Gilead.
37[w] After these events Timothy assembled
another army and camped opposite Raphon,
on the other side of the wadi. 38Judas sent
men to spy on the camp, and they reported to
him: “All the Gentiles around us have rallied
to him, making a very large force; 39they have
also hired Arabians to help them, and have
camped beyond the wadi, ready to attack
you.” So Judas went forward to meet them.
40As Judas and his army were approaching the flowing wadi, Timothy said to the officers of his army: “If he crosses over to us
first, we shall not be able to resist him; he
will certainly defeat us.[x] 41But if he is hesi-
tant and camps on the other side of the river,
we will cross over to him and defeat him.”
42But when Judas reached the flowing wadi,
he stationed the officers of the people beside
it and gave them this order: “Do not allow
anyone to encamp; all must go into battle.”
43He was the first to cross to the attack, with
all the people behind him, and all the Gentiles were crushed before them. They threw
away their arms and fled to the temple enclosure at Carnaim. 44But Judas’ troops captured the city and burnt the temple enclosure
with all who were in it. So Carnaim was subdued, and Judas met with no more resistance.

***Return to Jerusalem.*** 45[y] Then Judas assembled all the Israelites, great and small,
who were in Gilead, with their wives and
children and their goods, a very large company, to go into the land of Judah. 46When
they reached Ephron,* a large and strongly
fortified city along the way, they found it
impossible to go around it on either the right
or the left; they would have to march right
through it.[z] 47But the people in the city shut
them out and blocked up the gates with
stones. 48Then Judas sent them this peaceful
message: “Let us cross your territory in order to reach our own; no one will harm you;
we will only march through.” But they
would not open to him. 49So Judas ordered a
proclamation to be made in the camp that
everyone should take up positions where
they were. 50When the men of the army took
up their positions, he assaulted the city all
that day and night, and it was delivered into
his hand. 51He put every male to the sword,

**5:25 Nabateans**: an Arab people who acquired wealth and power as caravan merchants in the final two centuries B.C. They established Petra as their capital and for a time controlled all of Transjordan, even as far as Damascus. It was from a Nabatean governor of Damascus that Paul escaped (2 Cor 11:32–33).

**5:29** Cf. v. 9.

**5:35 Alema**: see v. 26; other manuscripts read Maapha, which may be Mizpah of Gilead (Jgs 11:29).

**5:46 Ephron**: a city in Transjordan opposite Beth-shan (v. 52), about nine miles east of the Jordan River. Situated on a height, it dominated the valleys of the two tributaries of the Jordan.

*w:* 2 Mc 12:17–25. *x:* 1 Sm 14:9–10. *y:* 2 Mc 12:26–31. *z:* Nm 20:17–21; 21:21–25.

made the elephants drunk on the juice of grapes and mulberries to get them ready to fight. [35]The beasts were distributed along the phalanxes, each elephant having assigned to it a thousand men in coats of mail, with bronze helmets on their heads, and five hundred picked cavalry. [36]These accompanied the beast wherever it was; wherever it moved, they moved too and never left it. [37]Each elephant was outfitted with a strong wooden tower, fastened to it by a harness; each tower held three soldiers who fought from it, besides the Indian driver. [38]The remaining cavalry were stationed on one or the other of the two flanks of the army, to harass the enemy and to be protected by the phalanxes. [39]When the sun shone on the gold and bronze shields, the mountains gleamed with their brightness and blazed like flaming torches. [40]Part of the king's army spread out along the heights, while some were on low ground, and they marched forward steadily in good order. [41]All who heard the noise of their numbers, the tramp of their marching, and the clanging of the arms, trembled; for the army was very great and strong.

[42]Judas with his army advanced to fight, and six hundred men of the king's army fell. [43]Eleazar, called Avaran, saw one of the beasts covered with royal armor and bigger than any of the others, and so he thought the king was on it.[g] [44]He gave up his life to save his people and win an everlasting name for himself. [45]He dashed courageously up to it in the middle of the phalanx, killing men right and left, so that they parted before him. [46]He ran under the elephant, stabbed it and killed it. The beast fell to the ground on top of him, and he died there. [47]But when Judas' troops saw the strength of the royal army and the ardor of its forces, they retreated from them.

*The Siege of Jerusalem.* [48]Some of the king's army went up to Jerusalem to attack them, and the king established camps in Judea and at Mount Zion. [49]He made peace with the people of Beth-zur, and they evacuated the city, because they had no food there to enable them to withstand a siege, for that was a sabbath year in the land.* [h] [50]The king took Beth-zur and stationed a garrison there to hold it. [51]For many days he besieged the sanctuary, setting up platforms and siege engines, fire-throwers, catapults and mechanical bows for shooting arrows and projectiles. [52]The defenders countered by setting up siege engines of their own, and kept up the fight a long time. [53]But there were no provisions in the storerooms, because it was the seventh year, and the reserves had been eaten up by those who had been rescued from the Gentiles and brought to Judea. [54]Few men remained in the sanctuary because the famine was too much for them; the rest scattered, each to his own home.

*Peace Treaty.* [55][i] Lysias heard that Philip, whom King Antiochus, before his death, had appointed to train his son Antiochus to be king, [56]had returned from Persia and Media with the army that accompanied the king, and that he was seeking to take over the government. [57]So he hastily decided to withdraw. He said to the king, the leaders of the army, and the soldiers: "We are growing weaker every day, our provisions are scanty, the place we are besieging is strong, and it is our duty to take care of the affairs of the kingdom.[j] [58]Therefore let us now come to terms with these people and make peace with them and all their nation. [59]Let us grant them freedom to live according to their own laws as formerly; it was on account of their laws, which we abolished, that they became enraged and did all these things."

[60]The proposal pleased the king and the leaders; he sent peace terms to the Jews, and they accepted. [61]So the king and the leaders swore an oath to them, and on these terms the Jews evacuated the fortification. [62]But when the king entered Mount Zion and saw how the place was fortified, he broke the oath he had sworn and gave orders to tear down the encircling wall. [63]Then he departed in haste and returned to Antioch, where he found

**6:49 A sabbath year in the land**: when sowing and reaping were prohibited (Ex 23:10–11; Lv 25:2–7). The year without a harvest (autumn of 164 to autumn of 163) was followed by a food shortage.

*g:* 2 Mc 13:15. *h:* Lv 25:1–7. *i:* 2 Mc 13:23–26. *j:* 2 Mc 11:13–15.

**The Death of Epiphanes**

THERE ARE THREE distinct accounts of the death of Antiochus Epiphanes in the Maccabean books: 1 Mc 6:1–17; 2 Mc 1:11–17; and 9:1–29. The first two agree that Epiphanes was trying to rob a temple but differ in attributing his death to remorse over what he had done in Jerusalem. Second Maccabees 9 goes further in claiming that Epiphanes repented on his deathbed and wanted to become a Jew. First Maccabees assumes that the death of the king is divine punishment for what he did in Jerusalem.

evils I did in Jerusalem, when I carried away
all the vessels of silver and gold that were in
it, and for no cause gave orders that the inhabitants of Judah be destroyed. 13I know
that this is why these evils have overtaken
me; and now I am dying, in bitter grief, in a
foreign land."
14Then he summoned Philip, one of his
Friends, and put him in charge of his whole
kingdom. 15He gave him his diadem, his
robe, and his signet ring, so that he might
guide the king's son Antiochus and bring
him up to be king. 16So King Antiochus died
there in the one hundred and forty-ninth
year.* 17When Lysias learned that the king
was dead, he set up the king's son Antiochus,* whom he had reared as a child, to be
king in his place; and he gave him the title
Eupator.[d]

*Siege of the Citadel.* 18Those in the citadel
were hemming Israel in around the sanctuary, continually trying to harm them and to
strengthen the Gentiles.[e] 19And so Judas
planned to destroy them, and assembled the
people to besiege them. 20So in the one hundred and fiftieth year* they assembled and
besieged the citadel, for which purpose he
constructed platforms and siege engines.
21But some of the besieged escaped, and
some renegade Israelites joined them.
22They went to the king and said: "How long
will you fail to do justice and to avenge our
kindred? 23We agreed to serve your father
and to follow his orders and obey his edicts.
24And for this our own people have become
our enemies; they have put to death as many
of us as they could find and have seized our
inheritances. 25They have acted aggressively
not only against us, but throughout their
whole territory. 26Look! Today they have besieged the citadel in Jerusalem in order to
capture it, and they have fortified the sanctuary and Beth-zur. 27Unless you act quickly
to prevent them, they will do even worse
things than these, and you will not be able to
stop them."
28[f] When the king heard this he was enraged, and he called together all his Friends,
the officers of his army, and the commanders of the cavalry. 29Mercenary forces also
came to him from other kingdoms and from
the islands of the seas. 30His army numbered
a hundred thousand footsoldiers, twenty
thousand cavalry, and thirty-two elephants
trained for war. 31They passed through Idumea and camped before Beth-zur. For many
days they attacked it; they constructed siege
engines, but the besieged made a sortie and
burned these, and they fought bravely.

*Battle of Beth-zechariah.* 32Then Judas
marched away from the citadel and moved
his camp to Beth-zechariah,* opposite the
king's camp. 33The king, rising before dawn,
moved his force hastily along the road to
Beth-zechariah; and the troops prepared for
battle and sounded the trumpet. 34They

**6:16 The one hundred and forty-ninth year**: September 22, 164, to October 9, 163 B.C. A Babylonian list of the Seleucid kings indicates that Antiochus died in November or early December of 164, about the same time as the rededication of the Temple.

**6:17 The king's son Antiochus**: Antiochus V Eupator ("of a good father"), then about nine years old. He was in Antioch, still in the charge of Lysias, who proceeded to govern and wage wars in his name. Both were put to death two years later, when Demetrius, brother of Antiochus IV, arrived to claim the kingship; cf. 7:1–3.

**6:20 The one hundred and fiftieth year**: October, 163, to September, 162 B.C.

**6:32 Beth-zechariah**: south of Jerusalem, and six miles north of Beth-zur.

*d:* 2 Mc 10:10–11. *e:* 1 Mc 1:33–36. *f:* 2 Mc 13:1–26.

Philip in control of the city. He fought against him and took the city by force.

See RG 163

## CHAPTER 7

### *Expedition of Bacchides and Alcimus.*

1[k] In the one hundred and fifty-first year,* Demetrius, son of Seleucus, set out from Rome, arrived with a few men at a coastal city, and began to rule there. 2 As he was entering the royal palace of his ancestors, the soldiers seized Antiochus and Lysias to bring them to him. 3 When he was informed of this, he said, "Do not show me their faces." 4 So the soldiers killed them, and Demetrius assumed the royal throne.

5 Then all the lawless men and renegades of Israel came to him. They were led by Alcimus,* who desired to be high priest. 6 They made this accusation to the king against the people: "Judas and his brothers have destroyed all your friends and have driven us out of our land. 7 So now, send a man whom you trust to go and see all the destruction Judas has wrought on us and on the king's territory, and let him punish them and all their supporters."

8 So the king chose Bacchides, one of the King's Friends, who ruled the province of West-of-Euphrates, a great man in the kingdom, and faithful to the king. 9 He sent him and the renegade Alcimus, to whom he granted the high priesthood, with orders to take revenge on the Israelites. 10 They set out and, on arriving in the land of Judah with a great army, sent messengers who spoke deceitfully to Judas and his brothers in peaceful terms. 11 But these paid no attention to their words, seeing that they had come with a great army.

12 A group of scribes, however, gathered about Alcimus and Bacchides to ask for a just agreement. 13[l] The Hasideans were the first among the Israelites to seek peace with them, 14 for they said, "A priest of the line of Aaron has come with the army, and he will not do us any wrong." 15 He spoke with them peacefully and swore to them, "We will not seek to injure you or your friends." 16 So they trusted him. But he arrested sixty of them and killed them in one day, according to the words that he wrote:*

17 "The flesh of your faithful,
and their blood they have spilled all around about Jerusalem,
and no one was left to bury them."[m]

18 Then fear and dread of them came upon all the people, who said: "There is no truth or justice among them; they violated the agreement and the oath that they swore."

19 Bacchides withdrew from Jerusalem and camped in Beth-zaith.* He had many of the men who deserted to him arrested and some of the people. He killed them and threw them into a great cistern. 20 He handed the province over to Alcimus, leaving troops to help him, while he himself returned to the king.

21 Alcimus struggled to maintain his high priesthood, 22 and all those who were troubling the people gathered about him. They took possession of the land of Judah and caused great distress in Israel. 23 When Judas saw all the evils that Alcimus and those with him were bringing upon the Israelites, even more than the Gentiles had, 24 he went about all the borders of Judea and took revenge on the men who had deserted, preventing them from going out into the country. 25 But when Alcimus saw that Judas and his followers were gaining strength and realized that he could not resist them, he returned to the king and accused them of grave crimes.

***Defeat of Nicanor.*** 26[n] Then the king sent Nicanor, one of his honored officers, who

**7:1–3 The one hundred and fifty-first year**: the spring of 161 B.C. Demetrius, son of Seleucus, was the lawful heir to the kingdom; but when only nine years old, he was taken as a hostage to Rome in place of his uncle, who ruled as Antiochus IV Epiphanes. At the age of twenty-five Demetrius fled secretly from Rome and, with the support of the Syrians, overcame his rival Antiochus V and put him to death. **The royal palace**: at Antioch.

**7:5–6 Alcimus**: a Jew hostile to the Maccabees, who became high priest after the death of Menelaus (2 Mc 14:3). He received confirmation in his office from the new king Demetrius (1 Mc 7:9), and brought malicious charges against Judas and his brothers and the people (1 Mc 7:6).

**7:16 The words that he wrote**: based on Ps 79:2–3. But who is "he"—David, Alcimus, Judas, or someone else?

**7:19 Beth-zaith**: about three miles north of Beth-zur and twelve miles south of Jerusalem.

*k*: 2 Mc 14:1–11. *l*: 1 Mc 2:42. *m*: Ps 79:2–3. *n*: 1 Mc 3:38; 2 Mc 8:9; 14:12–13.

### The Defeat of Nicanor

THE DISPLAY OF Nicanor's head (7:47) is shocking to modern sensibilities. However, it is a practice that has continued intermittently down to modern times, designed to terrorize the enemy and bolster the morale of one's own troops.

was a bitter enemy of Israel, with orders to
destroy the people. [27]Nicanor came to
Jerusalem with a large force and deceitfully
sent to Judas* and his brothers this peaceable
message: [28]"Let there be no fight between
me and you. I will come with a few men to
meet you face to face in peace."
[29]So he came to Judas, and they greeted
one another peaceably. But Judas' enemies
were prepared to seize him. [30]When he became aware that Nicanor had come to him
with deceit in mind, Judas was afraid of him
and would not meet him again.[o] [31]When Nicanor saw that his plan had been discovered,
he went out to fight Judas near Capharsalama.* [32]About five hundred men of Nicanor's army fell; the rest fled to the City of
David.*
[33][p] After this, Nicanor went up to Mount
Zion. Some of the priests from the sanctuary
and some of the elders of the people came
out to greet him peaceably and to show him
the burnt offering that was being sacrificed
for the king. [34]But he mocked and ridiculed
them, defiled them,* and spoke arrogantly.
[35]In a rage he swore: "If Judas and his army
are not delivered to me at once, when I return victorious I will burn this temple
down." He went away in great anger. [36][q] The
priests, however, went in and stood before
the altar and the sanctuary. They wept and
said: [37]"You have chosen this house to bear
your name, to be a house of prayer and supplication for your people. [38]Take revenge on
this man and his army, and let them fall by
the sword. Remember their blasphemies,
and do not let them continue."
[39]Nicanor left Jerusalem and camped at
Beth-horon, where the Syrian army joined
him. [40]But Judas camped in Adasa* with
three thousand men. Here Judas uttered this
prayer: [41][r] "When they who were sent by the
king* blasphemed, your angel went out and
killed a hundred and eighty-five thousand of
them.[s] [42]In the same way, crush this army before us today, and let the rest know that Nicanor spoke wickedly against your sanctuary; judge him according to his wickedness."
[43]The armies met in battle on the thirteenth day of the month Adar. Nicanor's
army was crushed, and he himself was the
first to fall in the battle.[t] [44]When his army
saw that Nicanor had fallen, they threw
down their weapons and fled. [45]The Jews
pursued them a day's journey from Adasa to
near Gazara, blowing the trumpets behind
them as signals. [46]From all the surrounding
villages of Judea people came out and out-
flanked them. They turned them back, and
all the enemies fell by the sword; not a single one escaped.
[47]Then the Jews collected the spoils and
the plunder; they cut off Nicanor's head and
his right arm, which he had lifted up so arrogantly. These they brought and displayed in
the sight of Jerusalem. [48]The people rejoiced
greatly, and observed that day as a day of
much joy. [49]They decreed that it should be

**7:27 Nicanor . . . deceitfully sent to Judas**: a more favorable picture of Nicanor, as an honest man who became a personal friend of Judas, is given in 2 Mc 14:17–25. Their friendship was broken by the intrigues of Alcimus (2 Mc 14:26–30).

**7:31 Capharsalama**: a village north of Jerusalem whose precise location is disputed.

**7:32 City of David**: the citadel occupied by the Seleucid garrison in Jerusalem.

**7:34 Defiled them**: spitting on the priests caused them to become legally defiled.

**7:40 Adasa**: a village between Jerusalem and Beth-horon.

**7:41 They who were sent by the king**: 2 Kgs 18:19–25, 29–35; 19:10–13 recount in detail the boastful threats made by Sennacherib, the Assyrian king, through his emissaries. **Your angel**: a reference to 2 Kgs 19:35, which describes the fate of the Assyrian army which besieged Jerusalem in the days of Hezekiah, king of Judah.

*o:* 2 Mc 14:30. *p:* 2 Mc 14:31–36. *q:* 1 Kgs 8:29–30, 33–34, 43. *r:* 2 Mc 8:19; 15:22–24. *s:* 2 Kgs 19:35–36; Is 37:36–37. *t:* 2 Mc 15:25–36.

observed every year on the thirteenth of
Adar.* 50And so for a few days* the land of
Judah was at rest.

## CHAPTER 8

See RG 163

*Eulogy of the Romans.* 1* Judas had
heard of the reputation of the Romans. They
were valiant fighters and acted amiably to all
who took their side. They established a
friendly alliance with all who applied to
them. 2He was also told of their battles and
the brave deeds that they performed against
the Gauls,* conquering them and forcing
them to pay tribute; 3and what they did in
Spain to get possession of the silver and gold
mines there. 4By planning and persistence
they subjugated the whole region, although
it was very remote from their own. They also
subjugated the kings who had come against
them from the far corners of the earth until
they crushed them and inflicted on them severe defeat. The rest paid tribute to them
every year. 5Philip* and Perseus, king of the
Macedonians, and the others who opposed
them in battle they overwhelmed and subjugated. 6Antiochus* the Great, king of Asia,
who fought against them with a hundred and
twenty elephants and with cavalry and chariots and a very great army, was defeated by
them. 7They took him alive and obliged him
and the kings who succeeded him to pay a
heavy tribute, to give hostages and to cede
8Lycia, Mysia, and Lydia* from among their
best provinces. The Romans took these from
him and gave them to King Eumenes.
9* When the Greeks planned to come and destroy them, 10the Romans discovered it, and
sent against the Greeks a single general who
made war on them. Many were wounded
and fell, and the Romans took their wives
and children captive. They plundered them,
took possession of their land, tore down
their strongholds and reduced them to slavery even to this day. 11All the other kingdoms and islands that had ever opposed
them they destroyed and enslaved; with their
friends, however, and those who relied on
them, they maintained friendship. 12They
subjugated kings both near and far, and all
who heard of their fame were afraid of them.
13Those whom they wish to help and to
make kings, they make kings; and those
whom they wish, they depose; and they were
greatly exalted. 14Yet with all this, none of
them put on a diadem or wore purple as a
display of grandeur. 15But they made for
themselves a senate chamber, and every day
three hundred and twenty men took counsel,
deliberating on all that concerned the people
and their well-being. 16They entrust their

**7:49 The thirteenth of Adar**: March 27, 160 B.C. This day in the Jewish calendar was called the "Day of Nicanor" (2 Mc 15:36), but it was not long celebrated by the Jews.

**7:50 For a few days**: about one month following the death of Nicanor. After that began the attack of Bacchides resulting in the death of Judas (9:1–18).

**8:1** This chapter contains the account of the embassy which Judas sent to Rome, probably before the death of Nicanor, to conclude a treaty of alliance between Rome and the Jewish nation. Without precise chronology, the pertinent data are gathered into a unified theme.

The image of the Roman Republic greatly impressed the smaller Eastern peoples seeking support against their overlords (vv. 1–16), because of Roman success in war (vv. 2–11) and effective aid to their allies (vv. 12–13). Numerous interventions by Rome in the politics of the Near East bear witness to its power and prestige in the second century B.C. See 1:10; 7:2; 12:3; 15:15–24; 2 Mc 11:34. With the increased Roman control of Palestine after 63 B.C., the Republic and later the Empire became heartily detested. The eulogy of Rome in this chapter is one of the reasons why 1 Maccabees was not preserved by the Palestinian Jews of the century that followed.

**8:2 Gauls**: probably the Celts of northern Italy and southern France, subdued by the Romans in 222 B.C., and again in 200–191 B.C.; but also those in Asia Minor (the Galatians), whom the Romans defeated in 189 B.C.

**8:5 Philip**: Philip V of Macedonia, defeated by a Graeco-Roman alliance at Cynoscephalae in 197 B.C. Perseus, his son, was defeated at Pydna in 168 B.C., and died a prisoner. With this, the kingdom of Macedonia came to an end.

**8:6 Antiochus**: Antiochus III, greatest of the Seleucid kings. He was defeated at Magnesia in 190 B.C. By the Treaty of Apamea in 189 B.C., he was obliged to pay Rome a crushing indemnity of 15,000 talents. The weakening of Antiochene power and the growing military and economic influence of Rome may have led Antiochus IV to adopt the policy of political, religious, and cultural unification of Syria and Palestine.

**8:8 Lycia, Mysia, and Lydia**: regions in western Asia Minor. "Lycia" and "Mysia" are restored here by conjectural emendation; the Greek text has "India, Media," most likely through scribal error. **Eumenes**: Eumenes II (197–158 B.C.), king of Pergamum, an ally of Rome who benefited greatly from Antiochus' losses.

**8:9–10** The revolt of the Achaean League, inserted here, occurred in 146 B.C., after Judas' time. It was crushed by the Roman consul Lucius Mummius and marked the end of Greek independence.

**The Treaty with Rome**

ROME IS ADMIRED for its might and organization, despite the general hostility of 1 Maccabees toward the Gentiles. The authenticity of the letter in 8:23–32 is sometimes disputed, but it is probably genuine. The Romans promised little and made no effort to intervene on behalf of the Jews, but they were gaining a potential foothold in the Near East. Judas gained some international recognition and moral support. The short-term results were harmless. When the Romans actually intervened in Judea a century later, the results were disastrous for the Jews.

government to one man* every year, to rule over their entire land, and they all obey that one, and there is no envy or jealousy among them.

*Treaty with the Romans.* [17]So Judas chose Eupolemus, son of John, son of Accos, and Jason, son of Eleazar, and sent them to Rome to establish friendship and alliance with them.[u] [18]He did this to lift the yoke from Israel, for it was obvious that the kingdom of the Greeks was subjecting them to slavery. [19]After making a very long journey to Rome, the envoys entered the senate chamber and spoke as follows: [20]"Judas, called Maccabeus, and his brothers, with the Jewish people, have sent us to you to establish alliance and peace with you, and to be enrolled among your allies and friends." [21]The proposal pleased the Romans, [22]and this is a copy of the reply they inscribed on bronze tablets and sent to Jerusalem,* to remain there with the Jews as a record of peace and alliance:[v]

[23]"May it be well with the Romans and the Jewish nation at sea and on land forever; may sword and enemy be far from them. [24]But if war is first made on Rome, or any of its allies in any of their dominions, [25]the Jewish nation will fight along with them wholeheartedly, as the occasion shall demand; [26]and to those who wage war they shall not give or provide grain, weapons, money, or ships, as seems best to Rome. They shall fulfill their obligations without receiving any recompense. [27]In the same way, if war is made first on the Jewish nation, the Romans will fight along with them willingly, as the occasion shall demand, [28]and to those who attack them there shall not be given grain, weapons, money, or ships, as seems best to Rome. They shall fulfill their obligations without deception. [29]On these terms the Romans have made an agreement with the Jewish people. [30]But if both parties hereafter agree to add or take away anything, they shall do as they choose, and whatever they shall add or take away shall be valid.

[31]"Moreover, concerning the wrongs that King Demetrius is doing to them, we have written to him thus: 'Why have you made your yoke heavy upon our friends and allies the Jews? [32]If they petition against you again, we will enforce justice and make war on you by sea and land.' "

## CHAPTER 9

See RG 163

*Death of Judas.* [1]When Demetrius heard that Nicanor and his army had fallen in battle, he again sent Bacchides and Alcimus into the land of Judah, along with the right wing of his army. [2]They took the road to Galilee, and camping opposite the ascent at Arbela, they captured it* and killed many people. [3]In the first month of the one hundred and fifty-second year,* they encamped

**8:16 They entrust their government to one man**: actually the Roman Republic had two consuls chosen yearly as joint heads of the government.

**8:22 The reply . . . on bronze tablets and sent to Jerusalem**: the decree of the Senate would be inscribed on bronze and kept in the Roman Capitol, with only a copy in letter form sent to Jerusalem.

**9:2 They took the road . . . Arbela, they captured it**: this passage is restored, in part, by conjectural emendation. The present Greek text could be translated, "They took the road to Gilgal, and camping opposite Mesaloth at Arbela, they captured it." But Arbela (modern Khirbet Irbid) was in Galilee, on a high hill overlooking the western shore of the Sea of Galilee. Gilgal, on the contrary, was in the Jordan valley near Jericho. "Mesaloth" is probably a corrupt form of a Hebrew word meaning "steps, ascent." It is possible, however, that all these terms referred to places in the Judean hills.

**9:3 The first month of the one hundred and fifty-second**

*u*: 1 Mc 12:1–4; 15:15–22. *v*: 1 Mc 14:17–18.

against Jerusalem. [4]Then they set out for Berea with twenty thousand men and two thousand cavalry. [5]Judas, with three thousand picked men, had camped at Elasa. [6]When they saw the great number of the troops, they were very much afraid, and many slipped away from the camp, until only eight hundred of them remained.

[7]When Judas saw that his army was melting away just as the battle was imminent, he was brokenhearted, because he had no time to gather them together. [8]In spite of his discouragement he said to those who remained: "Let us go forward to meet our enemies; perhaps we can put up a good fight against them." [9]They tried to dissuade him, saying: "We certainly cannot. Let us save our own lives now, and come back with our kindred, and then fight against them. Now we are too few." [10]But Judas said: "Far be it from me to do such a thing as to flee from them! If our time has come, let us die bravely for our kindred and not leave a stain upon our honor!"

[11]Then the army of Bacchides moved out of camp and took its position for combat. The cavalry were divided into two squadrons, and the slingers and the archers came on ahead of the army, and in the front line were all the best warriors. Bacchides was on the right wing. [12]Flanked by the two squadrons, the phalanx attacked as they blew their trumpets. Those who were on Judas' side also blew their trumpets. [13]The earth shook with the noise of the armies, and the battle raged from morning until evening.

[14]When Judas saw that Bacchides was on the right, with the main force of his army, all the most stouthearted rallied to him, [15]and the right wing was crushed; Judas pursued them as far as the mountain slopes.* [16]But when those on the left wing saw that the right wing was crushed, they closed in behind Judas and those with him. [17]The battle became intense, and many on both sides fell wounded. [18]Then Judas fell, and the rest fled.

[19]Jonathan and Simon took their brother Judas and buried him in the tomb of their ancestors at Modein. [20]All Israel wept for him with great lamentation. They mourned for him many days, and they said, [21]"How the mighty one has fallen, the savior of Israel!"[w] [22]The other acts of Judas, his battles, the brave deeds he performed, and his greatness have not been recorded; but they were very many.

## III. Leadership of Jonathan

***Jonathan Succeeds Judas.*** [23]After the death of Judas, the lawless raised their heads in every part of Israel, and all kinds of evildoers appeared. [24]In those days there was a very great famine, and the country deserted to them. [25]Bacchides chose renegades and made them masters of the country. [26]These sought out and hunted down the friends of Judas and brought them to Bacchides, who punished and derided them. [27]There was great tribulation in Israel, the like of which had not been since the time prophets ceased to appear among them.

[28]Then all the friends of Judas came together and said to Jonathan: [29]"Ever since your brother Judas died, there has been no one like him to lead us against our enemies, both Bacchides and those of our nation who are hostile to us. [30]Now therefore we have chosen you today to be our ruler and leader in his place, to fight our battle." [31]From that moment Jonathan accepted the leadership, and took the place of Judas his brother.

***Bacchides Pursues Jonathan.*** [32]When Bacchides learned of it, he sought to kill him. [33]But Jonathan and his brother Simon and all who were with him discovered this, and they fled to the wilderness of Tekoa* and camped by the waters of the pool of Asphar. [34]*

[35]Jonathan sent his brother* as leader of the convoy to implore his friends, the Nabateans, to let them deposit with them their great quantity of baggage.[x] [36]But the

**year**: April/May 160 B.C., by the Temple calendar.

**9:15 As far as the mountain slopes**: conjectural emendation. The Greek text has "as far as Mount Azotus"; this is most unlikely. Apparently the Greek translator mistook the Hebrew word *ashdot*, "slopes," for *ashdod*, "Azotus."

**9:33 Tekoa**: home of the prophet Amos in the wild country above the Dead Sea, southeast of Jerusalem.

**9:34** Omitted, it is a dittography of v. 43.

**9:35 Jonathan sent his brother**: this was John who was called Gaddi (2:2; cf. 9:36, 38).

*w*: 2 Sm 1:19, 25, 27; Jgs 3:9. *x*: 1 Mc 5:25.

tribe of Jambri from Medaba* made a raid
and seized and carried off John and everything he had.
[37]After this, word was brought to Jonathan and his brother Simon: "The tribe of
Jambri are celebrating a great wedding, and
with a large escort they are bringing the
bride, the daughter of one of the great
princes of Canaan, from Nadabath." [38]Re-
membering the blood of John their brother,
they went up and hid themselves under
cover of the mountain. [39]As they watched
there appeared a noisy throng with much
baggage; then the bridegroom and his
friends and kinsmen had come out to meet
them with tambourines and musicians with
their instruments. [40]Jonathan and his party
rose up against them from their ambush and
killed them. Many fell wounded; the rest
fled toward the mountain; all their spoils
were taken. [41]Thus the wedding was turned
into mourning, and the sound of their music
into lamentation. [42]Having taken their revenge for the blood of their brother, they returned to the marshes of the Jordan.
[43]When Bacchides heard of it, he came on
the sabbath to the banks of the Jordan with a
large force. [44]Then Jonathan said to his companions, "Let us rise up now and fight for
our lives, for today is not like yesterday and
the day before. [45]The battle is before us, behind us are the waters of the Jordan, on either side of us, marsh and thickets; there is
no way of escape.* [46]Cry out now to Heaven
so that you may be delivered from the hand
of our enemies." [47]When they joined battle,
Jonathan raised his hand to strike Bacchides,
but Bacchides backed away from him.
[48]Jonathan and those with him jumped into
the Jordan and swam across to the other side,
but the enemy did not pursue them across
the Jordan. [49]About a thousand men on Bacchides' side fell that day.
[50]On returning to Jerusalem, Bacchides
built strongholds in Judea: the Jericho
fortress, as well as Emmaus, Beth-horon,
Bethel, Timnath, Pharathon, and Tephon,
with high walls and gates and bars.* [51]In
each he put a garrison to harass Israel. [52]He
fortified the city of Beth-zur, Gazara and the
citadel, and put troops in them and stores of
provisions. [53]He took as hostages the sons of
the leading people of the country and put
them in custody in the citadel at Jerusalem.[y]
[54]In the one hundred and fifty-third year, in
the second month,* Alcimus ordered the wall
of the inner court of the sanctuary to be torn
down, thus destroying the work of the prophets. But he only began to tear it down. [55]Just
at that time Alcimus was stricken, and his
work was interrupted; his mouth was closed
and he was paralyzed, so that he could no
longer utter a word or give orders concerning
his household. [56]Alcimus died in great agony
at that time. [57]Seeing that Alcimus was dead,
Bacchides returned to the king, and the land
of Judah was at rest for two years.
[58]Then all the lawless took counsel and
said: "Jonathan and those with him are living in peace and security. Now then, let us
have Bacchides return, and he will capture
all of them in a single night." [59]So they went
and took counsel with him. [60]When Bacchides was setting out with a large force, he
sent letters secretly to all his allies in Judea,
telling them to seize Jonathan and his companions. They were not able to do this, however, because their plan became known. [61]In
fact, Jonathan's men seized about fifty of the
men of the country who were leaders in the
conspiracy and put them to death.
[62]Then Jonathan and those with him,
along with Simon, withdrew to Bethbasi* in
the wilderness; he rebuilt its ruins and fortified it. [63]When Bacchides learned of this, he
gathered together his whole force and sent
word to those who were in Judea. [64]He came
and camped before Bethbasi, and construct-

**9:36 Medaba**: northeast of the Dead Sea.

**9:45** Jonathan's force may have been trapped in one of the many oxbows of the lower Jordan. Bacchides had crossed and caught them still on the east bank.

**9:50** These sites constitute a ring on the edges of the province of Judea.

**9:54 In the one hundred and fifty-third year, in the second month**: May, 159 B.C. **The work of the prophets**: probably Haggai and Zechariah, who were instrumental in building the Second Temple after the Babylonian exile; cf. Hg 1:12–14; Zec 4:8–10; Ezr 5:1–2.

**9:62 Bethbasi**: two miles east of Bethlehem and six miles north of Tekoa.

y: 1 Mc 10:9.

**Jonathan and the Syrian Pretenders**

JONATHAN ACKNOWLEDGED THE authority of the Syrian king when it worked to his advantage (10:6). Then Alexander made Jonathan a better offer: He appointed him high priest (10:20). Jonathan was not a legitimate high priest any more than Menelaus had been, but he accepted the office from a king whose own legitimacy was questionable. Many scholars think that Jonathan's acceptance of the high priesthood caused the Dead Sea sect to break away from the Jerusalem temple and its cult, and that he is the figure who is called "The Wicked Priest" in the Pesher (commentary) on Habakkuk from the Dead Sea Scrolls. The destruction of the temple of Dagon and those who had sought asylum there (v. 84) was in violation of all law and custom in the ancient world. Presumably 1 Maccabees regards the action as justifiable because the temple was pagan. Even while Jonathan fraternizes with the Gentile kings, he is still represented as hostile to pagan religion.

ing siege engines, he fought against it for many days.
65Leaving his brother Simon in the city, Jonathan, accompanied by a small group of men, went out into the countryside. 66He struck down Odomera and his kindred and the tribe of Phasiron in their encampment; these men had begun to attack and they were going up with their forces. 67Simon and those with him then sallied forth from the city and set fire to the siege engines. 68They fought against Bacchides, and he was crushed. They caused him great distress, because the enterprise he had planned was in vain. 69He was enraged with the lawless men who had advised him to invade the province. He killed many of them and resolved to return to his own country.
70Jonathan learned of this and sent ambassadors to agree on peace with him and to obtain the release of the prisoners. 71He agreed to do as Jonathan asked. He swore an oath to him that he would never try to do him any harm for the rest of his life; 72and he released to him the prisoners he had previously taken from the land of Judah. Thereupon he returned to his own land and never came into their territory again. 73Then the sword ceased from Israel. Jonathan settled in Michmash;* he began to judge the people and he eliminated the renegades from Israel.

## CHAPTER 10

See RG 163

*Jonathan Becomes High Priest.* 1In the one hundred and sixtieth year,* Alexander Epiphanes, son of Antiochus, came up and took Ptolemais. They accepted him as king and he began to reign there. 2When King Demetrius heard of it, he mustered a very large army and marched out to engage him in battle. 3Demetrius sent a letter to Jonathan written in peaceful terms, to exalt him; 4for he said: "Let us be the first to make peace with him, before he makes peace with Alexander against us, 5since he will remember all the wrongs we have done to him, his brothers, and his nation."
6So Demetrius authorized him to gather an army and procure arms as his ally; and he ordered that the hostages in the citadel be released to him. 7Accordingly Jonathan went to Jerusalem and read the letter to all the people and to those who were in the citadel. 8They were struck with fear when they heard that the king had given him authority to gather an army. 9Those in the citadel released the hostages to Jonathan, and he gave them back to their parents.[z] 10Thereafter Jon-

**9:73 Michmash**, southeast of Bethel, famous for the exploits of Jonathan, son of Saul; see 1 Sm 14. It was Jonathan's base from 157 to 152 B.C. **Began to judge**: exercise the governing authority as in the Book of Judges. With Jerusalem and the garrison towns (v. 50) firmly in Seleucid hands, Jonathan's freedom of action was greatly restricted.

**10:1 The one hundred and sixtieth year**: 152 B.C. **Alexander . . . Antiochus**: Alexander Balas claimed to be a son of Antiochus IV. He had the backing of the Romans, who had never forgiven Demetrius for becoming king without their permission. The latter meanwhile had become unpopular with his own people as well as with the Jews.

*z*: 1 Mc 9:53.

athan dwelt in Jerusalem, and began to build and restore the city. [11]He ordered those doing the work to build the walls and to encircle Mount Zion with square stones for its fortification, and they did so. [12]The foreigners in the strongholds that Bacchides had built took flight; [13]all of them left their places and returned to their own lands. [14]Only in Beth-zur did some remain of those who had abandoned the law and the commandments, for it was a place of refuge.

[15]King Alexander heard of the promises that Demetrius had made to Jonathan; he was also told of the battles and brave deeds of Jonathan and his brothers and of the troubles that they had endured. [16]He said, "Shall we ever find another man like him? Let us now make him our friend and ally." [17]So he sent Jonathan a letter written in these terms: [18]"King Alexander sends greetings to his brother Jonathan. [19]We have heard of you, that you are a mighty warrior and worthy to be our friend. [20]We have therefore appointed you today to be high priest of your nation; you are to be called the King's Friend, and you are to look after our interests and preserve friendship with us." He also sent him a purple robe and a crown of gold.[a] [21]Jonathan put on the sacred vestments in the seventh month of the one hundred and sixtieth year at the feast of Booths,* and he gathered an army and procured many weapons.

***A Letter from Demetrius to Jonathan.*** [22]When Demetrius heard of these things, he was distressed and said: [23]"Why have we allowed Alexander to get ahead of us by gaining the friendship of the Jews and thus strengthening himself? [24]I too will write them encouraging words and offer honors and gifts, so that they may support me." [25]So he sent them this message: "King Demetrius sends greetings to the Jewish nation. [26]We have heard how you have kept the treaty with us and continued in our friendship and not gone over to our enemies, and we are glad. [27]Continue, therefore, to keep faith with us, and we will reward you with favors in return for what you do in our behalf. [28]We will grant you many exemptions and will bestow gifts on you.

[29][b]"I now free you and exempt all the Jews from the tribute, the salt tax, and the crown levies. [30]Instead of collecting the third of the grain and the half of the fruit of the trees that should be my share, I renounce the right from this day forward. Neither now nor in the future will I collect them from the land of Judah or from the three districts annexed from Samaria.* [31]Let Jerusalem and her territory, her tithes and her tolls, be sacred and free from tax. [32]I also yield my authority over the citadel in Jerusalem, and I transfer it to the high priest, that he may put in it such men as he shall choose to guard it. [33]Every Jew who has been carried into captivity from the land of Judah into any part of my kingdom I set at liberty without ransom; and let all their taxes, even those on their cattle, be canceled.

[34]Let all feast days, sabbaths, new moon festivals, appointed days, and the three days that precede each feast day, and the three days that follow, be days of immunity and exemption for all Jews in my kingdom. [35]No one will have authority to exact payment from them or to harass any of them in any matter.

[36]"Let thirty thousand Jews be enrolled in the king's army and allowances be given them, as is due to all the king's soldiers. [37]Let some of them be stationed in the king's principal strongholds, and of these let some be given positions of trust in the affairs of the kingdom. Let their superiors and their rulers be chosen from among them, and let them follow their own laws, as the king has commanded in the land of Judah.

[38]"Let the three districts that have been added to Judea from the province of Samaria

**10:21 Jonathan . . . feast of Booths**: Jonathan began to discharge the office of high priest in October 152 B.C. For seven years after the death of Alcimus there had been no high priest in Jerusalem. It was taken for granted that the king, though a Gentile, had the power to appoint one (2 Mc 4:7, 23–24). The Maccabees, though a priestly family (1 Mc 2:1), were not of the line of Zadok, and some in Israel (perhaps the Qumran community) regarded Jonathan's tenure as a usurpation.

**10:30 The three districts annexed from Samaria**: mentioned by name in 11:34. The present Greek text, by a scribal error, has added "and Galilee" after "Samaria."

*a:* 1 Mc 2:18. *b:* 1 Mc 11:28, 34.

be annexed to Judea so that they may be under one rule and obey no other authority than the high priest. 39Ptolemais and its confines I give as a present to the sanctuary in Jerusalem for the necessary expenses of the sanctuary. 40I make a yearly personal grant of fifteen thousand silver shekels out of the royal revenues, taken from appropriate places. 41All the additional funds that the officials did not hand over as they had done in the first years shall henceforth be handed over for the services of the temple. 42Moreover, the dues of five thousand silver shekels that used to be taken from the revenue of the sanctuary every year shall be canceled, since these funds belong to the priests who perform the services. 43All who take refuge in the temple of Jerusalem or in any of its precincts, because of money they owe the king, or because of any other debt, shall be released, together with all the goods they possess in my kingdom. 44The cost of rebuilding and restoring the structures of the sanctuary shall be covered out of the royal revenue. 45Likewise the cost of building the walls of Jerusalem and fortifying it all around, and of building walls in Judea, shall be donated from the royal revenue."

46When Jonathan and the people heard these words, they neither believed nor accepted them, for they remembered the great evil that Demetrius had done in Israel, and the great tribulation he had brought upon them. 47They therefore decided in favor of Alexander, for he had been the first to address them peaceably, and they remained his allies for the rest of his life.

48Then King Alexander gathered together a large army and encamped opposite Demetrius. 49The two kings joined battle, and when the army of Demetrius fled, Alexander pursued him, and overpowered his soldiers. 50He pressed the battle hard until sunset, and Demetrius fell that day.

***Treaty of Ptolemy and Alexander.*** 51Alexander sent ambassadors to Ptolemy, king of Egypt, with this message: 52"Now that I have returned to my realm, taken my seat on the throne of my ancestors, and established my rule by crushing Demetrius and gaining control of my country— 53for I engaged him in battle, he and his army were crushed by us, and we assumed his royal throne— 54let us now establish friendship with each other. Give me now your daughter for my wife; and as your son-in-law, I will give to you and to her gifts worthy of you."

55King Ptolemy answered in these words: "Happy the day on which you returned to the land of your ancestors and took your seat on their royal throne! 56I will do for you what you have written; but meet me in Ptolemais, so that we may see each other, and I will become your father-in-law as you have proposed."

57So Ptolemy with his daughter Cleopatra* set out from Egypt and came to Ptolemais in the one hundred and sixty-second year. 58There King Alexander met him, and Ptolemy gave him his daughter Cleopatra in marriage. Their wedding was celebrated at Ptolemais with great splendor according to the custom of kings.

59King Alexander also wrote to Jonathan to come and meet him. 60So he went with pomp to Ptolemais, where he met the two kings and gave them and their friends silver and gold and many gifts and thus won their favor.[c] 61Some villainous men of Israel, transgressors of the law, united against him to accuse him, but the king paid no heed to them. 62The king ordered Jonathan to be divested of his garments and to be clothed in royal purple; and so it was done. 63The king also had him seated at his side. He said to his magistrates: "Go with him to the center of the city and make a proclamation that no one is to bring charges against him on any grounds or be troublesome to him for any reason." 64[d] When his accusers saw the honor paid to him according to the king's proclamation, and him clothed in purple, they all fled. 65And so the king honored him, enrolling him among his Chief Friends, and

**10:57 Cleopatra:** Cleopatra Thea, then about fifteen years old. She later married Demetrius II, and later still, his brother Antiochus VII. Ptolemais (Acco) on the coast of Palestine was a neutral site. **The one hundred and sixty-second year**: 151/150 B.C.

*c:* 1 Mc 2:18. *d:* 1 Mc 2:18; 11:27.

he made him governor and chief of the province. 66So Jonathan returned in peace and happiness to Jerusalem.

***Jonathan Defeats Apollonius.*** 67In the one hundred and sixty-fifth year,* Demetrius, son of Demetrius, came from Crete to the land of his ancestors. 68When King Alexander heard of it he was greatly troubled, and returned to Antioch. 69Demetrius set Apollonius over Coelesyria.* Having gathered a large army, Apollonius encamped at Jamnia. From there he sent this message to Jonathan the high priest:

70"You are the only one who resists us. I am laughed at and put to shame on your account. Why are you exercising authority against us in the mountains? 71If you have confidence in your forces, come down now to us in the plain, and let us test each other's strength there; for the forces of the cities are on my side. 72Inquire and find out who I am and who the others are who are helping me. People are saying that you cannot make a stand against us because your ancestors were twice put to flight* in their own land. 73Now you too will be unable to withstand our cavalry and such a force as this in the plain, where there is not a stone or a pebble or a place to flee."

74When Jonathan heard the message of Apollonius, he was provoked. Choosing ten thousand men, he set out from Jerusalem, and Simon his brother joined him to help him. 75He encamped near Joppa, but the people of the city shut him out because Apollonius had a garrison in Joppa. When they attacked it, 76the people of the city became afraid and opened the gates, and so Jonathan took possession of Joppa.*

77When Apollonius heard of it, he drew up three thousand cavalry and a large force of infantry. He marched toward Azotus as though he were going on through, but at the same time he was advancing into the plain, because he had such a large number of cavalry to rely on. 78Jonathan pursued him toward Azotus, and the armies engaged in battle. 79Apollonius, however, had left a thousand cavalry in hiding behind them. 80Jonathan discovered that there was an ambush behind him; his army was surrounded. From morning until evening they showered his troops with arrows. 81But his troops held their ground, as Jonathan had commanded, while the enemy's horses became tired out.

82Then Simon brought forward his force, and engaged the phalanx in battle. Since the cavalry were exhausted, the phalanx was crushed by him and fled, 83while the cavalry too were scattered over the plain. They fled to Azotus and entered Beth-dagon, the temple of their idol, to save themselves. 84But Jonathan burned and plundered Azotus with its neighboring towns, and destroyed by fire both the temple of Dagon and those who had taken refuge in it.[e] 85Those who fell by the sword, together with those who were burned alive, came to about eight thousand.

86Then Jonathan left there and encamped at Askalon, and the people of that city came out to meet him with great pomp. 87Jonathan and those with him then returned to Jerusalem, with much spoil. 88When King Alexander heard of these events, he accorded new honors to Jonathan. 89He sent him a gold buckle, such as is usually given to King's Kinsmen;* he also gave him Ekron and all its territory as a possession.

## CHAPTER 11

See RG 163

***Alliance of Ptolemy and Demetrius II.*** 1Then the king of Egypt gathered forces as numerous as the sands of the seashore, and many ships; and he sought by deceit to take Alexander's kingdom and add it to his own. 2He set out for Syria with peaceful words, and the people in the cities opened their gates to welcome him, as King Alexander had ordered them to do, since Ptolemy was his father-in-law. 3But when Ptolemy en-

**10:67 The one hundred and sixty-fifth year**: 147 B.C. **Demetrius**: Demetrius II Nicator.

**10:69 Coelesyria**: originally the region between the Lebanon and anti-Lebanon mountains, it came later to refer to Palestine also. **Jamnia**: on the coast, also known as Yavneh (5:58).

**10:72 Twice put to flight**: the reference is unclear.

**10:76 Joppa**: about forty miles northwest of Jerusalem. For the first time the Maccabees took possession of a seaport, though nominally it was on behalf of King Alexander.

**10:89 Kinsmen**: a rank higher than Chief Friends.

*e*: 1 Mc 11:4; 1 Sm 5:2–5.

**Dynastic Struggles**

IN CH 11, the king of Egypt was Ptolemy VI Philometor, who was known for his sympathy to the Jews, and who allowed the exiled High Priest Onias IV to build a temple at Leontopolis in Egypt. His campaign in Asia is of interest to 1 Maccabees, because it led to the death of Alexander Epiphanes, who had been Jonathan's patron.

tered the cities, he stationed a garrison of
troops in each one.
[4]As they neared Azotus, they showed him
the temple of Dagon destroyed by fire, Azotus and its suburbs demolished, corpses lying about, and the charred bodies of those
burned in the war, for they had heaped them
up along his route.[f] [5]They told the king what
Jonathan had done in order to denigrate him;
but the king said nothing. [6]Jonathan met the
king with pomp at Joppa, and they greeted
each other and spent the night there. [7]Jona-
than accompanied the king as far as the river
called Eleutherus* and then returned to Jerusalem.
[8]And so King Ptolemy took possession of
the cities along the seacoast as far as Seleucia by the sea,* plotting evil schemes against
Alexander all the while. [9]He sent ambassadors to King Demetrius, saying: "Come, let
us make a covenant with each other; I will
give you my daughter whom Alexander has
married, and you shall reign over your father's kingdom. [10]I regret that I gave him my
daughter, for he has sought to kill me."* [11]He
was criticizing Alexander, however, because
he coveted his kingdom. [12]After taking his
daughter away, Ptolemy gave her to
Demetrius and broke with Alexander; the
enmity between them was now evident.
[13]Then Ptolemy entered Antioch and assumed the crown* of Asia; thus he set upon
his head two crowns, that of Egypt and that
of Asia.
[14]Now King Alexander was in Cilicia at
that time, because the people of that region
had revolted. [15]When Alexander heard the
news, he came against Ptolemy in battle.
Ptolemy marched out and met him with a
strong force and routed him. [16]When
Alexander fled to Arabia to seek protection,
King Ptolemy was triumphant. [17]Zabdiel the
Arabian cut off Alexander's head and sent it
to Ptolemy. [18]But three days later King
Ptolemy himself died, and his troops in the
strongholds were killed by the inhabitants of
the strongholds. [19]Thus Demetrius became
king in the one hundred and sixty-seventh
year.*

***Alliance of Jonathan and Demetrius II.***
[20]In those days Jonathan gathered together
the people of Judea to attack the citadel in
Jerusalem, and they set up many siege engines against it. [21]But some transgressors of
the law, enemies of their own nation, went to
the king and informed him that Jonathan was
besieging the citadel. [22]When Demetrius
heard this, he was enraged; and as soon as he
heard it, he set out and came to Ptolemais.
He wrote to Jonathan to discontinue the
siege and to meet him for a conference at
Ptolemais as soon as possible.
[23]On hearing this, Jonathan ordered the
siege to continue. He selected some elders
and priests of Israel and put himself at risk.
[24]Taking with him silver, gold and apparel,
and many other presents, he went to the king
at Ptolemais, and found favor with him.
[25]Although certain renegades of his own nation kept on bringing charges against him,
[26]the king treated him just as his predecessors had done and exalted him in the pres-

**11:7 Eleutherus**: two hundred miles north of Joppa, in the second century B.C. the northern limit of Coelesyria.

**11:8 Seleucia by the sea**: at the mouth of the Orontes, the port city of Antioch.

**11:10 I regret . . . to kill me**: according to Josephus, Ammonius, a friend of Alexander, had tried to assassinate Ptolemy, and the latter claimed that Alexander was the instigator, thus calumniating him to gain his kingdom (v. 11).

**11:13 Crown**: lit., diadem.

**11:19 The one hundred and sixty-seventh year**: 146/145 B.C. The two deaths (vv. 17–18) occurred in the summer of 145 B.C.

*f*: 1 Mc 10:84.

ence of all his Friends. [27]He confirmed him in the high priesthood and in the other honors he had previously held, and had him enrolled among his Chief Friends.

[28]Jonathan asked the king to exempt Judea and the three districts of Samaria from tribute, promising him in return three hundred talents.[g] [29]The king agreed and wrote a letter to Jonathan about all these matters as follows:

[30h] "King Demetrius sends greetings to his brother* Jonathan and to the Jewish nation. [31]We are sending you, for your information, a copy of the letter that we wrote to Lasthenes* our Kinsman concerning you. [32]'King Demetrius sends greetings to his father Lasthenes. [33]Upon the Jewish nation, who are our friends and observe their obligations to us, we have decided to bestow benefits because of the good will they show us. [34i] Therefore we confirm their possession, not only of the territory of Judea, but also of the three districts of Aphairema,* Lydda, and Ramathaim. These districts, together with all their dependencies, are hereby transferred from Samaria to Judea for those who offer sacrifices in Jerusalem in lieu of the royal taxes the king used to receive yearly from the produce of earth and trees. [35]From payment of the other things that would henceforth be due to us, namely, the tithes and taxes, as well as the salt tax, and the crown tax—from all these we grant them release. [36]Henceforth and forever not one of these provisions shall ever be revoked. [37]See to it, therefore, that a copy of these instructions be made and given to Jonathan. Let it be displayed on the holy mountain in a conspicuous place.' "

***The Intrigue of Trypho.*** [38]When King Demetrius saw that the land was peaceful under his rule and that he had no opposition, he dismissed his entire army, each to his own home, except the foreign troops which he had hired from the islands of the nations. So all the soldiers who had served under his predecessors became hostile to him. [39]When a certain Trypho, who had previously supported Alexander, saw that all the troops were grumbling against Demetrius, he went to Imalkue the Arabian, who was raising Alexander's young son Antiochus.[j] [40]Trypho kept urging Imalkue to hand over the boy to him, so that he might succeed his father as king. He told him of all that Demetrius had done and of the hostility his soldiers had for him; and he remained there for many days.

***Jonathan Aids Demetrius II.*** [41]Meanwhile Jonathan sent the request to King Demetrius to withdraw the troops in the citadel from Jerusalem and from the other strongholds, for they were constantly waging war on Israel. [42]Demetrius, in turn, sent this word to Jonathan: "I will do not only this for you and your nation, but I will greatly honor you and your nation when I find the opportunity. [43]Now, therefore, you will do well to send men to fight for me, because all my troops have revolted."

[44]So Jonathan sent three thousand good fighting men to him at Antioch. When they came to the king, he was delighted over their arrival. [45]The populace, one hundred and twenty thousand strong, massed in the center of the city in an attempt to kill the king. [46]So the king took refuge in the palace, while the populace gained control of the main streets of the city and prepared for battle. [47]Then the king called the Jewish force to his aid. They all rallied around him and spread out through the city. On that day they killed about a hundred thousand in the city. [48]At the same time, they set the city on fire and took much spoil. Thus they saved the king. [49]When the populace saw that the Jew-

**11:30 Brother**: this term and "father" in v. 32 are honorific expressions used of the Kinsmen.

**11:31 Lasthenes**: leader of the mercenary troops who had come with Demetrius from Crete. He was now the young king's chief minister and was apparently responsible for the disastrous policy (v. 38) of disbanding the national army.

**11:34 Aphairema**: the Ophrah of Jos 18:23; 1 Sm 13:17; the Ephron of 2 Chr 13:19; and the Ephraim of Jn 11:54—modern et-Taiyibeh, five miles northeast of Bethel. **Lydda**: the Lod of the postexilic Jews (Ezr 2:33; Neh 11:35) and the hometown of Aeneas, who was cured by Peter (Acts 9:32–34). It is ten miles southeast of Joppa. **Ramathaim**: the Ramathaim-zophim of 1 Sm 1:1, and the Arimathea of Mt 27:57, modern Rentis, nine miles northeast of Lydda.

*g*: 1 Mc 10:29; 11:34–35. *h*: 1 Mc 10:25–45. *i*: 1 Mc 10:29; 11:28. *j*: 1 Mc 12:39.

JONATHAN SENT TROOPS to suppress a revolt against Demetrius in Antioch (11:47). Jewish soldiers often acted as mercenaries in the service of foreign kings. This action in turn often led to anti-Jewish sentiment on the part of the opponents of those kings.

ish force controlled the city, they lost courage and cried out to the king in supplication, 50“Extend the hand of friendship to us, and make the Jews stop attacking us and the city.” 51So they threw down their weapons and made peace. The Jews thus gained honor in the eyes of the king and all his subjects, and they became renowned throughout his kingdom. Finally they returned to Jerusalem with much plunder.

52But when King Demetrius was sure of his royal throne, and the land was peaceful under his rule, 53he broke all his promises and became estranged from Jonathan. Instead of repaying Jonathan for all the favors he had received from him, he caused him much distress.

***Alliance of Jonathan and Antiochus VI.*** 54After this, Trypho returned and brought with him the young boy Antiochus, who became king and put on the diadem.[k] 55All the soldiers whom Demetrius had discharged rallied around Antiochus and fought against Demetrius, who was routed and fled. 56Trypho captured the elephants and occupied Antioch. 57Then young Antiochus wrote to Jonathan: “I confirm you in the high priesthood and appoint you ruler over the four districts, and to be one of the King’s Friends.” 58He also sent him gold dishes and a table service, gave him the right to drink from gold cups, to dress in royal purple, and to wear a gold buckle.[l] 59Likewise, he made Jonathan’s brother Simon governor of the region from the Ladder of Tyre* to the borders of Egypt.

***Campaigns of Jonathan and Simon.*** 60Jonathan set out and traveled through the province of West-of-Euphrates* and its cities, and all the forces of Syria espoused his cause as allies. When he arrived at Askalon, the citizens welcomed him with pomp. 61But when he set out for Gaza, the people of Gaza shut him out. So he besieged it, and burned and plundered its suburbs. 62Then the people of Gaza appealed to Jonathan, and he granted them terms of peace. He took the sons of their leaders as hostages and sent them to Jerusalem. He then traveled on through the province as far as Damascus.

63Jonathan heard that the generals of Demetrius had come with a strong force to Kadesh in Galilee, intending to remove him from office. 64So he went to meet them, leaving his brother Simon in the province. 65[m]Simon encamped against Beth-zur, attacked it for many days, and shut in the inhabitants. 66They appealed to him, and he granted them terms of peace. He expelled them from the city, took possession of it, and put a garrison there.

67Meanwhile, Jonathan and his army pitched their camp near the waters of Gennesaret, and at daybreak they went to the plain of Hazor.* 68There the army of the foreigners met him on the plain. Having first detached an ambush in the mountains, this army mounted a frontal attack. 69Then those in ambush rose out of their places and joined in the battle. 70All of Jonathan’s men fled; no one stayed except the army commanders Mattathias, son of Absalom, and Judas, son of Chalphi. 71Jonathan tore his clothes, threw dust on his head, and prayed. 72Then he went back to the battle and routed them, and they fled. 73Those of his men who were running away saw it and returned to him; and with him they pursued the enemy as far

**11:59 Ladder of Tyre**: modern Ras en-Naqurah, where the mountains reach the sea, so that the coastal road must ascend in a series of steps. Thus the Maccabees controlled the coastal area from Syria to Egypt.

**11:60 The province of West-of-Euphrates**: refers here to the territory of Palestine and Coelesyria, but not Upper Syria; cf. 7:8.

**11:67 Plain of Hazor**: the site of the ancient Canaanite city (Jos 11:10), ten miles north of the Lake of Gennesaret.

*k:* 1 Mc 11:39; 12:39. *l:* 1 Mc 2:18. *m:* 1 Mc 9:52; 10:14.

as their camp in Kadesh, and there they encamped. [74]About three thousand of the foreign troops fell on that day. Then Jonathan returned to Jerusalem.

See RG 163

## CHAPTER 12

***Alliances with Rome and Sparta.*** [1]When Jonathan saw that the time was right, he chose men and sent them to Rome to confirm and renew the friendship with the Romans.[n] [2]He also sent letters to the Spartans and other places to the same effect.

[3]After reaching Rome, the men entered the senate chamber and said, "The high priest Jonathan and the Jewish people have sent us to renew the friendship and alliance of earlier times with them." [4]The Romans gave them letters addressed to authorities in various places, with the request to provide them with safe conduct to the land of Judah.

[5]This is a copy of the letter that Jonathan wrote to the Spartans: [6]"Jonathan the high priest, the senate of the nation, the priests, and the rest of the Jewish people send greetings to their brothers the Spartans. [7]Long ago a letter was sent* to the high priest Onias from Arius, who then reigned over you, stating that you are our brothers, as the attached copy shows.[o] [8]Onias welcomed the envoy with honor and received the letter, which spoke clearly of alliance and friendship. [9]Though we have no need of these things, since we have for our encouragement the holy books that are in our possession,*[p] [10]we have ventured to send word to you for the renewal of brotherhood and friendship, lest we become strangers to you; a long time has passed since you sent your message to us. [11]We, on our part, have unceasingly remembered you in the sacrifices and prayers that we offer on our feasts and other appropriate days, as it is right and proper to remember brothers. [12]We likewise rejoice in your renown. [13]But many tribulations and many wars have beset us, and the kings around us have attacked us. [14]We did not wish to be troublesome to you and to the rest of our allies and friends in these wars. [15]For we have the help of Heaven for our support, and we have been saved from our enemies, and our enemies have been humbled. [16]So we have chosen Numenius, son of Antiochus, and Antipater, son of Jason, and we have sent them to the Romans to renew with them the friendship and alliance of earlier times.[q] [17]We have also ordered them to come to you and greet you, and to deliver to you our letter concerning the renewal of our brotherhood. [18]Therefore kindly send us an answer on this matter."

[19]This is a copy of the letter that they sent to Onias: [20][r] "Arius, king of the Spartans, sends greetings to Onias the high priest. [21]A document has been found stating that the Spartans and the Jews are brothers and that they are of the family of Abraham. [22]Now that we have learned this, kindly write to us about your welfare. [23]We, for our part, declare to you that your animals and your possessions are ours, and ours are yours. We have, therefore, given orders that you should be told of this."

***More Campaigns of Jonathan and Simon.*** [24]Then Jonathan heard that the officers of Demetrius had returned to attack him with a stronger army than before. [25]So he set out from Jerusalem and met them in the territory of Hamath,* giving them no opportunity to enter his province. [26]The spies he had sent into their camp came back and reported to him that the enemy were preparing to attack them that night. [27]Therefore, when the sun set, Jonathan ordered his men to keep watch, with their weapons at the ready for battle, throughout the night; and he set outposts around the camp. [28]When the enemy heard that Jonathan and his men were ready for battle, their hearts sank with fear and dread.

**12:7 Long ago a letter was sent**: i.e., a century and a half before. **Onias**: Onias I, high priest from 323 to 300 or 290 B.C. **Arius**: Arius I, king from 309 to 265 B.C.

**12:9 The holy books . . . in our possession**: a reference to "the law, the prophets and other books," as mentioned in the Prologue to Sirach.

**12:25 Territory of Hamath**: the Seleucid territory of Upper Syria northeast of Coelesyria and separated from it by the Eleutherus River. The latter territory was under the command of Jonathan (11:59–60).

*n:* 1 Mc 8:17. *o:* 1 Mc 12:20–23. *p:* 2 Mc 2:14. *q:* 1 Mc 14:22; 15:15. *r:* 1 Mc 12:7.

**The Capture of Jonathan**

JONATHAN'S REMARKABLE SUCCESS in the world of Hellenistic politics ultimately led to his downfall (12:39–53). He was too powerful to be ignored by an ambitious climber like Trypho. His fatal mistake was unwarranted trust. The Pesher (commentary) on Habakkuk from the Dead Sea Scrolls says that God delivered the Wicked Priest into the hands of his enemies to destroy him. Many scholars think the reference is to Jonathan. If this is indeed the case, it gives an evaluation of Jonathan that is very different from that of 1 Maccabees.

They lighted fires in their camp and then
withdrew. [29]But because Jonathan and his
men were watching the campfires burning,
they did not know until the morning what
had happened. [30]Then Jonathan pursued
them, but he could not overtake them, for
they had crossed the river Eleutherus. [31]So
Jonathan turned aside against the Arabians
who are called Zabadeans, and he struck
them down and plundered them. [32]Then he
broke camp, marched on toward Damascus
and traveled through the whole region.
[33]Simon also set out and traveled as far as
Askalon and its neighboring strongholds. He
then turned to Joppa and took it by surprise,
[34]for he heard that its people intended to hand
over the stronghold to the supporters of
Demetrius. He left a garrison there to guard it.
[35]When Jonathan returned, he assembled
the elders of the people, and with them he
made plans for building strongholds in Judea, [36]for making the walls of Jerusalem still
higher, and for erecting a high barrier between the citadel and the city, to separate it
from the city and isolate it, so that its garrison could neither buy nor sell. [37]The people
therefore gathered together to build up the
city, for part of the wall of the eastern valley
had collapsed. And Jonathan repaired the
quarter called Chaphenatha. [38]Simon likewise built up Adida in the Shephelah, and
fortified it by installing gates and bars.
*Capture of Jonathan.* [39]Then Trypho
sought to become king of Asia, assume the
diadem, and do violence to King Antiochus.[s]
[40]But he was afraid that Jonathan would not
permit him, but would fight against him.
Looking for a way to seize and kill him, he
set out and came to Beth-shan. [41]Jonathan
marched out to meet him with forty thousand picked fighting men and came to Beth-
shan. [42]But when Trypho saw that Jonathan
had arrived with a large army he was afraid
to do him violence. [43]Instead, he received
him with honor, introduced him to all his
friends, and gave him presents. He also ordered his friends and soldiers to obey him as
they would himself. [44]Then he said to Jonathan: "Why have you put all these people to
so much trouble when we are not at war?
[45]Now pick out a few men to stay with you,
send the rest to their homes, and then come
with me to Ptolemais. I will hand it over to
you together with other strongholds and the
remaining troops, as well as all the officials;
then I will turn back and go home. That is
why I came here."
[46]Jonathan trusted him and did as he said.
He dismissed his troops, and they returned to
the land of Judah. [47]But he kept with him
three thousand men, of whom he left two
thousand in Galilee while one thousand accompanied him. [48]Then as soon as Jonathan
entered Ptolemais, the people of Ptolemais
closed the gates and seized him; all who had
entered with him, they killed with the sword.[t]
[49]Then Trypho sent soldiers and cavalry
to Galilee and the Great Plain* to destroy all
Jonathan's men. [50]These, upon learning that
Jonathan had been captured and killed along
with his companions, encouraged one another and went out in close formation, ready
to fight. [51]As their pursuers saw that they
were ready to fight for their lives, they

**12:49 The Great Plain**: of Beth-shan (v. 41), where Jonathan's disbanded troops remained.

*s:* 1 Mc 11:39–40, 54–55. *t:* 1 Mc 5:15, 22, 55.

turned back. [52]Thus all Jonathan's men came
safely into the land of Judah. They mourned
Jonathan and those who were with him.
They were in great fear, and all Israel fell
into deep mourning. [53]All the nations round
about sought to crush them. They said,
"Now that they have no leader or helper, let
us make war on them and wipe out their
memory from the earth."[u]

## IV. Leadership of Simon

### CHAPTER 13

See RG 163

*Simon as Leader.* [1]When Simon heard
that Trypho was gathering a large army to invade and ravage the land of Judah, [2]and saw
that the people were trembling with terror, he
went up to Jerusalem. There he assembled
the people [3]and exhorted them in these
words: "You know what I, my brothers, and
my father's house have done for the laws and
the sanctuary; what battles and hardships we
have seen. [4]For the sake of this, for the sake
of Israel, all my brothers have perished, and
I alone am left. [5]Far be it from me, then, to
save my own life in any time of distress, for
I am not better than my brothers. [6]But I will
avenge my nation and the sanctuary, as well
as your wives and children, for out of hatred
all the Gentiles have united to crush us."[v]

[7]As the people heard these words, their
spirit was rekindled. [8]They shouted in reply:
"You are our leader in place of your brothers
Judas and Jonathan. [9]Fight our battles, and
we will do everything that you tell us." [10]So
Simon mustered all the men able to fight,
and hastening to complete the walls of Jerusalem, fortified it on every side. [11]He sent
Jonathan, son of Absalom, to Joppa with a
strong force; Jonathan drove out the occupants and remained there.

*Trypho's Deceit.* [12]Then Trypho moved
from Ptolemais with a large army to invade
the land of Judah, bringing Jonathan with him
as a prisoner. [13]Simon encamped at Adida,
facing the plain. [14]When Trypho learned that
Simon had succeeded his brother Jonathan,
and that he intended to fight him, he sent ambassadors to him with this message: [15]"It was
on account of the money your brother Jonathan owed the royal treasury in connection
with the offices that he held, that we have detained him. [16]Now send a hundred talents of
silver, and two of his sons as hostages to guarantee that when he is set free he will not revolt
against us, and we will release him."

[17]Simon knew that they were speaking
deceitfully to him. Nevertheless, for fear of
provoking much hostility among the people,
he sent for the money and the boys, [18]lest the
people say "Jonathan perished because I
would not send Trypho the money and the
boys." [19]So he sent the boys and the hundred
talents; but Trypho broke his promise and
would not release Jonathan.

[20]* Next Trypho moved to invade and ravage the country. His troops went around by
the road that leads to Adora, but Simon and
his army moved along opposite him everywhere he went. [21]The people in the citadel
kept sending emissaries to Trypho, pressing
him to come to them by way of the wilderness, and to send them provisions. [22]Al-
though Trypho got all his cavalry ready to
go, there was a very heavy snowfall that
night, and he could not go on account of the
snow. So he left for Gilead. [23]When he was
approaching Baskama,* he had Jonathan
killed and buried him there. [24]Then Trypho
returned to his own land.

*Jonathan's Tomb.* [25]Simon sent for the remains of his brother Jonathan, and buried him
in Modein, the city of his ancestors. [26]All Israel bewailed him with solemn lamentation,
mourning over him for many days. [27]Then Simon erected over the tomb of his father and
his brothers a monument of stones, polished
front and back, and raised high enough to be
seen at a distance. [28]He set up seven pyramids
facing one another for his father and his
mother and his four brothers.[w] [29]For the pyramids he devised a setting of massive
columns, which he adorned with suits of armor as a perpetual memorial, and next to the

**13:20–21** The invaders made a wide flanking movement to invade Judea from the south (see 4:29; 6:31). Adora was a few miles southwest of Beth-zur. They would avoid Beth-zur itself and other strongholds of the Maccabees by following the way of the wilderness.

**13:23 Baskama**: perhaps northeast of the Sea of Galilee.

*u:* 1 Mc 5:2; 13:6. *v:* 1 Mc 5:2; 12:53. *w:* 2 Sm 18:18.

armor carved ships, which could be seen by all who sailed the sea. 30 This tomb which he built at Modein is there to the present day.

***Alliance of Simon and Demetrius II.*** 31 Trypho dealt treacherously with the young King Antiochus. He killed him 32 and became king in his place, putting on the crown of Asia. Thus he brought much evil on the land.[x] 33 Simon, for his part, built up the strongholds of Judea, fortifying them all around with high towers, thick walls, and gates with bars, and he stored up provisions in the strongholds. 34 Simon also chose men and sent them to King Demetrius to obtain for the land an exemption from taxation, since Trypho did nothing but plunder. 35 King Demetrius replied favorably and sent him the following letter:

36 "King Demetrius sends greetings to Simon, high priest and friend of kings, and to the elders and the Jewish people. 37 We have received the gold crown and the palm branch that you sent. We are ready to make a lasting peace with you and to write to our officials to grant you exemption. 38 Whatever decrees we have made in your regard remain in force, and the strongholds that you have built you may keep. 39 We pardon any oversights and offenses committed up to now, as well as the crown tax that you owe. Any other tax that used to be collected in Jerusalem shall no longer be collected there. 40 Any of you qualified for enrollment in our service may be enrolled. Let there be peace between us."

41 Thus in the one hundred and seventieth year,* the yoke of the Gentiles was removed from Israel, 42 and the people began to write in their records and contracts, "In the first year of Simon, great high priest, governor, and leader of the Jews."

***Simon Captures Gazara.*** 43[y] In those days Simon besieged Gazara* and surrounded it with troops. He made a siege machine, brought it up against the city, and attacked and captured one of the towers. 44 Those in the siege machine leaped down into the city and a great tumult arose there. 45 Those in the city, together with their wives and children, went up on the wall, with their garments rent, and cried out in loud voices, begging Simon to grant them terms of peace. 46 They said, "Treat us not according to our evil deeds but according to your mercy." 47 So Simon came to terms with them and did not attack them. He expelled them from the city, however, and he purified the houses in which there were idols. Then he entered the city with hymns and songs of praise. 48 After removing from it everything that was impure, he settled there people who observed the law. He improved its fortifications and built himself a residence.

***Simon Captures the Citadel.*** 49 The people in the citadel in Jerusalem were prevented from going out into the country and back to buy or sell; they suffered greatly from hunger, and many of them died of starvation. 50 They finally cried out to Simon, and he gave them terms of peace. He expelled them from the citadel and cleansed it of impurities. 51 On the twenty-third day of the second month,* in the one hundred and seventy-first year, the Jews entered the citadel with shouts of praise, the waving of palm branches, the playing of harps and cymbals and lyres, and the singing of hymns and canticles, because a great enemy of Israel had been crushed.[z] 52 Simon decreed that this day should be celebrated every year with rejoicing. He also strengthened the fortifications of the temple mount alongside the citadel, and he and his people dwelt there. 53 Seeing that his son John* was now a grown man, Simon made him commander of all his soldiers, and he dwelt in Gazara.

## CHAPTER 14

See RG 163

***Capture of Demetrius II.*** 1 In the one hundred and seventy-second year,* King

**13:41 The one hundred and seventieth year**: March, 142, to April, 141 B.C., by the Temple calendar.

**13:43 Gazara**: ancient Gezer, a key position in the Shephelah, fortified by Bacchides in 160 B.C.; cf. 9:52.

**13:51 The twenty-third day of the second month**: June 3, 141 B.C.

**13:53 John**: John Hyrcanus, who was to succeed his father as ruler and high priest; cf. 16:23–24.

**14:1 The one hundred and seventy-second year**: 141/140 B.C. The expedition began most probably in the spring of 140.

*x*: 1 Mc 8:6. *y*: 2 Mc 10:32–38. *z*: 1 Mc 1:36.

Demetrius assembled his army and marched into Media to obtain help so that he could fight Trypho. [2]When Arsaces,* king of Persia and Media, heard that Demetrius had entered his territory, he sent one of his generals to take him alive. [3]The general went forth and attacked the army of Demetrius; he captured him and brought him to Arsaces, who put him under guard.

## Praise of Simon

[4] The land was at rest all the days of
Simon,
who sought the good of his nation.
His rule delighted his people
and his glory all his days.[a]
[5] As his crowning glory he took Joppa for
a port
and made it a gateway to the isles of
the sea.[b]
[6] He enlarged the borders of his nation
and gained control of the country.
[7] He took many prisoners of war
and made himself master of Gazara,
Beth-zur, and the citadel.
He cleansed the citadel of its impurities;
there was no one to withstand him.
[8] The people cultivated their land in peace;
the land yielded its produce,
the trees of the field their fruit.[c]
[9] Old men sat in the squares,
all talking about the good times,
while the young men put on the
glorious raiment of war.[d]
[10] He supplied the cities with food
and equipped them with means of
defense,
till his glorious name reached the ends
of the earth.
[11] He brought peace to the land,
and Israel was filled with great joy.[e]
[12] Every one sat under his vine and fig tree,
with no one to disturb them.[f]
[13] No attacker was left in the land;
the kings in those days were crushed.
[14] He strengthened all the lowly among his
people
and was zealous for the law;
he destroyed the lawless and the
wicked.
[15] The sanctuary he made splendid
and multiplied its furnishings.

***Alliance with Rome and Sparta.*** [16]When people in Rome and even in Sparta heard that Jonathan had died, they were deeply grieved.* [17]But when they heard that his brother Simon had become high priest in his place and was master of the territory and its cities, [18]they sent him inscribed tablets of bronze to renew with him the friendship and alliance that they had established with his brothers Judas and Jonathan.[g] [19]These were read before the assembly in Jerusalem.

[20]This is a copy of the letter that the Spartans sent: "The rulers and the city of the Spartans send greetings to Simon the high priest, the elders, the priests, and the rest of the Jewish people, our brothers. [21]The ambassadors sent to our people have informed us of your glory and renown, and we rejoiced at their coming. [22]In accordance with what they said we have recorded the following in the public decrees: Numenius, son of Antiochus, and Antipater, son of Jason, ambassadors of the Jews, have come to us to renew their friendship with us.[h] [23]The people have resolved to receive these men with honor, and to deposit a copy of their words in the public archives, so that the people of Sparta may have a record of them. A copy of this decree has been made for Simon the high priest."

[24]After this, Simon sent Numenius to Rome with a large gold shield weighing a thousand minas, to confirm the alliance with the Romans.

***Official Honors for Simon.*** [25]When the people heard of these things, they said, "How shall we thank Simon and his sons?

**14:2 Arsaces:** Arsaces VI, also called Mithridates I, the Parthian king (171–138 B.C.). Parthians had overrun Persia and now held Babylonia, both of which had hitherto belonged to the Seleucid empire. The Greeks and Macedonians in these countries had appealed to Demetrius for help.

**14:16** The embassy to Rome and Sparta was sent soon after Simon's accession to power, and the replies were received before Demetrius' expedition (vv. 1–3), probably in 142 B.C.

*a:* 1 Mc 3:3–9. *b:* 1 Mc 12:33; 13:11. *c:* Lv 26:3–4; Zec 8:12. *d:* Zec 8:4–5. *e:* Lv 26:6. *f:* Mi 4:4; Zec 3:10. *g:* 1 Mc 8:22. *h:* 1 Mc 12:16; 15:15.

THE GIFT SENT to Rome (14:25) was very substantial for a small nation, indicating a strong desire on the part of Simon for friendship with Rome.

[26]He and his brothers and his father's house
have stood firm and repulsed Israel's enemies, and so have established its freedom."
So they made an inscription on bronze
tablets, which they affixed to pillars on
Mount Zion.
[27]The following is a copy of the inscription: "On the eighteenth day of Elul,* in the
one hundred and seventy-second year, that
is, the third year under Simon the great high
priest in Asaramel, [28]in a great assembly of
priests, people, rulers of the nation, and elders of the region, the following proclamation
was made to us:
[29]" 'Since there have often been wars in
our country, Simon, son of the priest Mattathias, descendant of Joarib, and his brothers have put themselves in danger and resisted the enemies of their nation, so that their
sanctuary and law might be maintained, and
they have thus brought great glory to their
nation. [30]Jonathan rallied the nation, became
their high priest, and was gathered to his
people. [31]When their enemies sought to invade and ravage their country and to violate
their sanctuary, [32]Simon rose up and fought
for his nation, spending large sums of his
own money to equip his nation's forces and
give them their pay. [33]He fortified the cities
of Judea, especially the border city of Beth-
zur, formerly the site of the enemy's
weaponry, and he stationed there a garrison
of Jewish soldiers. [34]He also fortified Joppa
by the sea and Gazara on the border of Azotus, a place previously occupied by the enemy; these cities he settled with Jews and
furnished them with all that was necessary
for their restoration. [35]When the people saw
Simon's fidelity and the glory he planned to
bring to his nation, they made him their
leader and high priest because of all he had
accomplished and the justice and fidelity he
had shown his nation. In every way he
sought to exalt his people.
[36]" 'In his time and under his guidance
they succeeded in driving the Gentiles out of
their country and those in the City of David
in Jerusalem, who had built for themselves a
citadel from which they used to sally forth to
defile the environs of the sanctuary and inflict grave injury on its purity. [37]In this
citadel he stationed Jewish soldiers, and he
strengthened its fortifications for the security of the land and the city, while he also
built up the wall of Jerusalem to a greater
height. [38]Consequently, King Demetrius
confirmed him in the high priesthood,
[39]made him one of his Friends, and conferred great honor on him.[i] [40]This was because he had heard that the Romans had addressed the Jews as friends, allies, and
brothers, that they had received Simon's envoys with honor, [41]and that the Jewish people and their priests had decided the following: Simon shall be their leader and high
priest forever until a trustworthy prophet
arises.[j] [42]He shall act as governor over them,
and shall have charge of the sanctuary, to
make regulations concerning its functions
and concerning the country, its weapons and
strongholds. [43]He shall be obeyed by all. All
contracts in the country shall be written in
his name, and he shall be clothed in purple
and gold.[k] [44]It shall not be lawful for any of
the people or priests to nullify any of these
decisions, or to contradict the orders given
by him, or to convene an assembly in the
country without his consent, to be clothed in
purple or wear a gold buckle. [45]Whoever
acts otherwise or violates any of these prescriptions shall be liable to punishment.
[46]" 'Thus all the people approved of
granting Simon the right to act in accord
with these decisions, [47]and Simon accepted

**14:27 Eighteenth day of Elul**: September 13, 140 B.C. **Asaramel**: perhaps a Hebrew name meaning "court of the people of God."

*i:* 1 Mc 2:18. *j:* 1 Mc 4:46; 9:27. *k:* 1 Mc 10:20, 89.

and agreed to be high priest, governor, and
ethnarch* of the Jewish people and priests,
and to have authority over all.' "
48It was decreed that this inscription
should be engraved on bronze tablets, to be
set up in a conspicuous place in the precincts
of the sanctuary, 49and that copies of it should
be deposited in the treasury, where they
would be available to Simon and his sons.

## CHAPTER 15

See RG 163

*Letter of Antiochus VII.* 1Antiochus,*
son of King Demetrius, sent a letter from the
islands of the sea to Simon, the priest and
ethnarch of the Jews, and to all the nation,
2which read as follows:
"King Antiochus sends greetings to Simon, the high priest and ethnarch, and to the
Jewish nation. 3Whereas certain villains
have gained control of the kingdom of our
ancestors, I intend to reclaim it, that I may
restore it to its former state. I have recruited
a large number of mercenary troops and
equipped warships. 4I intend to make a landing in the country so that I may take revenge
on those who have ruined our country and
laid waste many cities in my kingdom.
5"Now, therefore, I confirm to you all the
tax exemptions that the kings before me
granted you and whatever other privileges
they conceded to you. 6I authorize you to
coin your own money, as legal tender in your
country. 7Jerusalem and its sanctuary shall
be free. All the weapons you have prepared
and all the strongholds you have built and
now occupy shall remain in your possession.
8All debts, present or future, due to the royal
treasury shall be canceled for you, now and
for all time. 9When we establish our kingdom, we will greatly honor you and your nation and the temple, so that your glory will
be manifest in all the earth."

10In the one hundred and seventy-fourth
year* Antiochus invaded the land of his ancestors, and all the troops rallied to him, so
that few were left with Trypho. 11Pursued by
Antiochus, Trypho fled to Dor, by the sea,*
12realizing what troubles had come upon
him now that his soldiers had deserted him.
13Antiochus encamped before Dor with a
hundred and twenty thousand infantry and
eight thousand cavalry. 14While he surrounded the city, his ships closed from the
sea, so that he pressed it hard by land and sea
and let no one go in or out.
***Roman Alliance Renewed.*** 15Meanwhile,
Numenius and his companions came from
Rome with letters containing this message to
various kings and countries:[l] 16"Lucius,*
Consul of the Romans, sends greetings to
King Ptolemy. 17Ambassadors of the Jews,
our friends and allies, have come to us to renew their earlier friendship and alliance.
They had been sent by Simon the high priest
and the Jewish people, 18and they brought
with them a gold shield of a thousand minas.[m] 19Therefore we have decided to write
to various kings and countries, that they are
not to venture to harm them, or wage war
against them or their cities or their country,
and are not to assist those who fight against
them. 20We have also decided to accept the
shield from them. 21If, then, any troublemakers from their country take refuge with
you, hand them over to Simon the high
priest, so that he may punish them according
to their law."
22The consul sent identical letters to
Kings Demetrius, Attalus,* Ariarthes and Arsaces; 23to all the countries—Sampsames,
the Spartans, Delos, Myndos, Sicyon, Caria,
Samos, Pamphylia, Lycia, Halicarnassus,
Rhodes, Phaselis, Cos, Side, Aradus,
Gortyna, Cnidus, Cyprus, and Cyrene. 24A

**14:47 Ethnarch**: a subordinate ruler over an ethnic group whose office needed confirmation by a higher authority within the empire.

**15:1 Antiochus**: Antiochus VII Sidetes, son of Demetrius I, and younger brother of Demetrius II (now a prisoner of the Parthians). At the age of twenty he set out from the island of Rhodes to take his brother's place and drive out the usurper Trypho.

**15:10 The one hundred and seventy-fourth year**: 138 B.C.

**15:11 Dor, by the sea**: a fortress on the Palestinian coast, fifteen miles south of Carmel.

**15:16 Lucius**: perhaps Lucius Caecilius Metellus, consul in 142 B.C., or Lucius Calpurnicus Piso, consul in 140–139 B.C. This document pertains to Simon's first years as leader.

**15:22 Attalus**: Attalus II of Pergamum, reigned 159–138 B.C. **Ariarthes**: Ariarthes V of Cappadocia, reigned 162–130 B.C. **Arsaces**: see note on 14:2.

*l:* 1 Mc 8:17; 12:16; 14:22, 24. *m:* 1 Mc 14:24.

copy of the letter was also sent to Simon the high priest.

***Hostility from Antiochus VII.*** [25]When King Antiochus encamped before Dor, he assaulted it continuously both with troops and with the siege engines he had made. He blockaded Trypho by preventing anyone from going in or out. [26]Simon sent to Antiochus' support two thousand elite troops, together with silver and gold and much equipment. [27]But he refused to accept the aid; in fact, he broke all the agreements he had previously made with Simon and became hostile toward him.[n]

[28]He sent Athenobius, one of his Friends, to confer with Simon and say: "You are occupying Joppa and Gazara and the citadel of Jerusalem; these are cities of my kingdom. [29]You have laid waste their territories, done great harm to the land, and taken possession of many districts in my kingdom. [30]Now, therefore, give up the cities you have seized and the tribute money of the districts you control outside the territory of Judea; [31]or instead, pay me five hundred talents of silver for the devastation you have caused and five hundred talents more for the tribute money of the cities. If you do not do this, we will come and make war on you."

[32]So Athenobius, the king's Friend, came to Jerusalem and on seeing the splendor of Simon's court, the gold and silver plate on the sideboard, and his rich display, he was amazed. When he gave him the king's message, [33]Simon said to him in reply: "It is not foreign land we have taken nor have we seized the property of others, but only our ancestral heritage which for a time had been unjustly held by our enemies. [34]Now that we have the opportunity, we are holding on to the heritage of our ancestors. [35]As for Joppa and Gazara, which you demand, those cities were doing great harm to our people and our country. For these we will give you a hundred talents." Athenobius made no reply, [36]but returned to the king in anger. When he told him of Simon's words, of his splendor, and of all he had seen, the king fell into a violent rage.

***Victory over Cendebeus.*** [37]Trypho had boarded a ship and escaped to Orthosia.* [38]Then the king appointed Cendebeus commander-in-chief of the seacoast, and gave him infantry and cavalry forces. [39]He ordered him to encamp against Judea and to fortify Kedron* and strengthen its gates, so that he could wage war on the people. Meanwhile the king went in pursuit of Trypho. [40]When Cendebeus came to Jamnia, he began to harass the people and to make incursions into Judea, where he took people captive and massacred them. [41]As the king ordered, he fortified Kedron and stationed cavalry and infantry there, so that they could go out and patrol the roads of Judea.

## CHAPTER 16

See RG 163

[1]John then went up from Gazara and told his father Simon what Cendebeus was doing.[o] [2]Simon called his two oldest sons, Judas and John, and said to them: "I and my brothers and my father's house have fought the wars of Israel from our youth until today, and many times we succeeded in saving Israel. [3]I have now grown old, but you, by the mercy of Heaven, have come to maturity. Take my place and my brother's, and go out and fight for our nation; and may the help of Heaven be with you!"

[4]John then mustered in the land twenty thousand warriors and cavalry. Setting out against Cendebeus, they spent the night at Modein, [5]rose early, and marched into the plain. There, facing them, was an immense army of foot soldiers and cavalry, and between the two armies was a wadi. [6]John and his people took their position against the enemy. Seeing that his people were afraid to cross the wadi, John crossed first. When his men saw this, they crossed over after him.[p] [7]Then he divided his infantry and put his cavalry in the center, for the enemy's cavalry were very numerous. [8]They blew the trumpets, and Cendebeus and his army were routed; many of them fell wounded, and the rest fled toward the stronghold. [9]It was then that John's brother Judas fell wounded; but

**15:37 Orthosia**: a port between Tripoli and the Eleutherus River.

**15:39 Kedron**: a few miles southeast of Jamnia and facing the fortress of Gazara held by John Hyrcanus (13:53; 16:1).

*n:* 1 Mc 15:5–9. *o:* 1 Mc 13:53. *p:* 1 Mc 5:40–43.

**The Death of Simon**

LIKE ALL HIS brothers, Simon met a violent death, treacherously murdered by his own son-in-law (16:11–24). His death was also ignominious, because he was drunk. This episode also recalls a statement about the Wicked Priest in the Pesher on Habakkuk from the Dead Sea Scrolls (column 11): "Its interpretation concerns the Priest whose shame has exceeded his glory because he . . . walked on paths of drunkenness to slake his thirst; but the cup of God's anger will engulf him." The death of Simon is a somber conclusion to 1 Maccabees, but the survival of John Hyrcanus provides a note of hope for the future.

John pursued them until Cendebeus reached
Kedron, which he had fortified. [10]Some took
refuge in the towers on the plain of Azotus,
but John set fire to these, and about two
thousand of the enemy perished. He then returned to Judea in peace.[q]

*Murder of Simon and His Sons.* [11]Ptolemy,
son of Abubus, had been appointed governor
of the plain of Jericho, and he had much silver and gold, [12]being the son-in-law of the
high priest. [13]But his heart became proud
and he was determined to get control of the
country. So he made treacherous plans to do
away with Simon and his sons. [14]As Simon
was inspecting the cities of the country and
providing for their needs, he and his sons
Mattathias and Judas went down to Jericho
in the one hundred and seventy-seventh
year, in the eleventh month* (that is, the
month Shebat). [15]The son of Abubus gave
them a deceitful welcome in the little stronghold called Dok* which he had built. He
served them a sumptuous banquet, but he
had his men hidden there. [16]Then, when Simon and his sons were drunk, Ptolemy and
his men sprang up, weapons in hand, rushed
upon Simon in the banquet hall, and killed
him, his two sons, and some of his servants.
[17]By this vicious act of treachery he repaid
good with evil.

[18]Then Ptolemy wrote a report and sent it
to the king, asking him to send troops to help
him and to turn over to him their country and
its cities. [19]He sent other men to Gazara to
do away with John. To the army officers he
sent letters inviting them to come to him so
that he might present them with silver, gold,
and gifts. [20]He also sent others to seize Jerusalem and the temple mount. [21]But someone
ran ahead and brought word to John at
Gazara that his father and his brothers had
perished, and "Ptolemy has sent men to kill
you also." [22]On hearing this, John was utterly astounded. When the men came to kill
him, he seized them and put them to death,
for he knew that they sought to kill him.

[23]* Now the rest of the acts of John, his
wars and the brave deeds he performed, his
rebuilding of the walls, and all his achievements—[r] [24]these are recorded in the chronicle of his high priesthood, from the time that
he succeeded his father as high priest.

**16:14 In the one hundred and seventy-seventh year, in the eleventh month**: January–February, 134 B.C., by the Temple calendar.

**16:15 Dok**: a fortress built on a cliff three miles northwest of Jericho, near modern Ain Duq.

**16:23–24** John Hyrcanus was ruler and high priest from 134 B.C. till his death in 104 B.C. These verses suggest that the book was written, or at least completed, only after he died.

*q:* 1 Mc 10:84. *r:* 1 Mc 9:22.

See RG 164–67

# The Second Book of Maccabees

Although this book, like the preceding one, receives its title from its protagonist, Judas Maccabee (or Maccabeus), it is not a sequel to 1 Maccabees. The two differ in many respects. Whereas the first covers the period from the beginning of the reign of Antiochus IV (175 B.C.) to the accession of John Hyrcanus I (134 B.C.), this book treats of the events in Jewish history from the time of the high priest Onias III and King Seleucus IV (ca. 180 B.C.) to the defeat of Nicanor's army (161 B.C.).

The author of 2 Maccabees states (2:23) that this one-volume work is an abridgment of a five-volume work by Jason of Cyrene; but since this latter has not survived, it is difficult to determine its relationship to the present epitome. One does not know how freely the anonymous epitomizer may have rewritten the original composition or how closely the abridgment follows the wording of the original. Some parts of the text here clearly not derived from Jason's work are the preface (2:19–32), the epilogue (15:37–39), and probably also certain moralizing reflections (e.g., 5:17–20; 6:12–17). It is certain, however, that both works were written in Greek, which explains in part why 2 Maccabees was not included in the canon of the Hebrew Bible.

The book is not without genuine historical value in supplementing 1 Maccabees, and it contains some apparently authentic official documents (11:16–38). Its purpose, whether intended by Jason himself or read into it by the compiler, is to give a theological interpretation to the history of the period. The major concern is the Jerusalem Temple, whose defender is the God of Israel. There is less interest, therefore, in the military exploits of Judas Maccabeus and more in God's marvelous interventions on behalf of the Jews and their Temple. These divine actions direct the course of events, both to punish the sacrilegious and blasphemous pagans and to purify and restore the Temple. The author sometimes effects this purpose by transferring events from their proper chronological order, by giving exaggerated figures for the size of armies and the numbers killed in battle, by placing long, edifying discourses and prayers in the mouths of heroes, and by describing elaborate celestial apparitions (3:24–34; 5:2–4; 10:29–30; 15:11–16). The book is the earliest known source of stories that glorify God's holy martyrs (6:18–7:42; 14:37–46).

Of theological importance are the author's teachings on Israel's sufferings (5:17–20; 6:12–17), the resurrection of the just on the last day (7:9, 11, 14, 23; 14:46), the intercession of the saints in heaven for people living on earth (15:11–16), and the power of the living to offer prayers and sacrifices for the dead (12:39–46).

The beginning of 2 Maccabees consists of two letters sent by the Jews of Jerusalem to their coreligionists in Egypt. They deal with the observance of the feast commemorating the central event of the book, the purification of the Temple (Hanukkah). It is uncertain whether the author or a later scribe prefixed these letters to the narrative proper. If the author is responsible for their insertion, the book must have been written some time after 124 B.C., the date of the more recent of the two letters. A date of composition in the late second century B.C. is likely.

The main divisions of 2 Maccabees are:

I. Letters to the Jews in Egypt (1:1–2:18)
II. Compiler's Preface (2:19–32)
III. Heliodorus' Attempt to Profane the Temple (3:1–40)
IV. Profanation and Persecution (4:1–7:42)
V. Victories of Judas and Purification of the Temple (8:1–10:9)
VI. Renewed Persecution (10:10–15:36)
VII. Epilogue (15:37–39)

# I. Letters to the Jews in Egypt

## CHAPTER 1

See RG 165

*Letter 1: 124 B.C.* 1The Jews in
Jerusalem and in the land of Judea send
greetings to their kindred, the Jews in Egypt,
and wish them true peace! 2May God do
good to you and remember his covenant with
his faithful servants, Abraham, Isaac and Jacob, 3give to all of you a heart to worship him
and to do his will wholeheartedly and with a
willing spirit, 4open your heart to his law and
commandments and grant you peace, 5hear
your prayers, and be reconciled to you, and
never forsake you in time of adversity. 6Even
now we are praying for you here.
7In the reign of Demetrius,* the one hundred and sixty-ninth year, we Jews wrote to
you during the height of the distress that
overtook us in those years after Jason and
his followers revolted against the holy land
and the kingdom,[a] 8set fire to the gatehouse

**1:7 Demetrius**: Demetrius II, king of Syria (145–139, 129–125 B.C.). **The one hundred and sixty-ninth year**: i.e., of the Seleucid era, 143 B.C. Regarding the dates in 1 and 2 Maccabees, see note on 1 Mc 1:10. On the troubles caused by Jason and his revolt against the kingdom, i.e., the rule of the legitimate high priest, see 2 Mc 4:7–22.

*a*: 2 Mc 4:7–20.

> **The First Letter**
>
> THE PURPOSE OF the letter in 1:1–10 is to urge the Jews of Egypt to celebrate the festival of Hanukkah, to commemorate the rededication of the temple by Judas. The covenant with Abraham, Isaac, and Jacob (v. 2) is the basis for unity between the different branches of Judaism. This should not be set over against the covenant with Moses, because the latter entails observance of the law and commandments (v. 4).

and shed innocent blood. But we prayed to the Lord, and our prayer was heard;* we offered sacrifices and fine flour; we lighted the lamps and set out the loaves of bread.[b] 9 We are now reminding you to celebrate the feast of Booths in the month of Kislev.* 10 Dated in the one hundred and eighty-eighth year.*

*Letter 2: 164 B.C.* The people of Jerusalem and Judea, the senate, and Judas send greetings and good wishes to Aristobulus, teacher of King Ptolemy and member of the family of the anointed priests, and to the Jews in Egypt. 11 Since we have been saved by God from grave dangers, we give him great thanks as befits those who fought against the king;* 12[c] for it was God who drove out those who fought against the holy city. 13 When their leader arrived in Persia with his seemingly irresistible army, they were cut to pieces in the temple of the goddess Nanea* through a deceitful stratagem employed by Nanea's priests. 14* On the pretext of marrying the goddess, Antiochus with his Friends had come to the place to get its great treasures as a dowry. 15 When the priests of Nanea's temple had displayed the treasures and Antiochus with a few attendants had come inside the wall of the temple precincts, the priests locked the temple as soon as he entered. 16 Then they opened a hidden trapdoor in the ceiling, and hurling stones at the leader and his companions, struck them down. They dismembered the bodies, cut off their heads and tossed them to the people outside. 17 Forever blessed be our God, who has thus punished the impious!

18* Since we shall be celebrating the purification of the temple on the twenty-fifth day of the month Kislev,[d] we thought it right to inform you, that you too may celebrate the feast of Booths and of the fire that appeared when Nehemiah, the rebuilder of the temple* and the altar, offered sacrifices. 19 For when our ancestors were being led into captivity in Persia,* devout priests at the time took some of the fire from the altar and hid it secretly in the hollow of a dry cistern, making sure that the place would be unknown to anyone. 20 Many years later, when it so pleased God, Nehemiah, commissioned by the king of Persia, sent the descendants of the priests who had hidden the fire to look for it.

**1:8 Our prayer was heard**: in the victory of the Maccabees.

**1:9 Feast of Booths in the month of Kislev**: really the feast of the Dedication of the Temple, Hanukkah (2 Mc 10:1–8), celebrated on the twenty-fifth of Kislev (Nov.–Dec.). Its solemnity resembles that of the actual feast of Booths (Lv 23:33–43), celebrated on the fifteenth of Tishri (Sept.–Oct.); cf. 2 Mc 1:18.

**1:10 The one hundred and eighty-eighth year**: 124 B.C. The date pertains to the preceding, not the following letter. **Senate**: the council of Jewish elders of Jerusalem; cf. 1 Mc 12:6. **King Ptolemy**: Ptolemy VI Philometor, ruler of Egypt from 180 to 145 B.C.; he is mentioned also in 1 Mc 1:18; 10:51–59.

**1:11–12 The king**: Antiochus IV of Syria, the bitter persecutor of the Jews, who, as leader of the Syrian army that invaded Persia, perished there in 164 B.C.

**1:13 Nanea**: an oriental goddess comparable to Artemis of the Greeks.

**1:14–17** Differing accounts of the death of Antiochus IV are found in 2 Mc 9:1–29 and in 1 Mc 6:1–16 (see also Dn 11:40–45). The writer of this letter had probably heard a distorted rumor of the king's death. This and other indications suggest that the letter was written very soon after Antiochus IV died, perhaps in 164 B.C.

**1:18–36** This legendary account of Nehemiah's miraculous fire is incorporated in the letter because of its connection with the Temple and its rededication. **Booths**: see note on v. 9.

**1:18 Nehemiah, the rebuilder of the temple**: he rebuilt the walls of Jerusalem, but the Temple had been rebuilt by Zerubbabel almost a century before.

**1:19 Persia**: actually Babylonia, which later became part of the Persian empire.

*b:* 1 Mc 4:50–51. *c:* 2 Mc 9:1–29; 1 Mc 6:1–13; Dn 11:40–45. *d:* 2 Mc 6:7; 10:5; 1 Mc 1:59; 4:59.

## The Second Letter

THE LETTER IN 1:10–2:18 presents itself as having been sent in the time of Judas, but it was probably inserted in the first century B.C. It is filled with legendary details and has no historical value, but it attempts to reinforce the importance of Hanukkah by associating the festival not only with Judas, but also with traditions about Nehemiah and even Solomon.

21 When they informed us that they could not find any fire, but only a thick liquid, he ordered them to scoop some out and bring it. After the material for the sacrifices had been prepared, Nehemiah ordered the priests to sprinkle the wood and what lay on it with the liquid. 22 This was done, and when at length the sun, which had been clouded over, began to shine, a great fire blazed up, so that everyone marveled. 23 While the sacrifice was being burned, the priests recited a prayer, and all present joined in with them. Jonathan led and the rest responded with Nehemiah.

24 The prayer was as follows: "Lord, Lord God, creator of all things, awesome and strong, just and merciful, the only king and benefactor, 25 who alone are gracious, just, almighty, and eternal, Israel's savior from all evil, who chose our ancestors and sanctified them: 26 accept this sacrifice on behalf of all your people Israel and guard and sanctify your portion. 27 Gather together our scattered people, free those who are slaves among the Gentiles, look kindly on those who are despised and detested, and let the Gentiles know that you are our God. 28 Punish those who lord it over us and in their arrogance oppress us. 29 Plant your people in your holy place, as Moses said."[e]

30 Then the priests sang hymns. 31 After the sacrifice was consumed, Nehemiah ordered the rest of the liquid to be poured upon large stones. 32 As soon as this was done, a flame blazed up, but its light was lost in the brilliance coming from the altar. 33 When the event became known and the king of the Persians was told that, in the very place where the exiled priests had hidden the fire, a liquid was found with which Nehemiah and his people had burned the sacrifices, 34 the king, after verifying the fact, fenced the place off and declared it sacred. 35 To those whom the king favored, he distributed many benefits he received. 36 Nehemiah and his companions called the liquid nephthar, meaning purification, but most people named it naphtha.* [f]

### CHAPTER 2

See RG 165

1 In the records it will be found that Jeremiah the prophet ordered the deportees to take some of the fire with them as indicated, 2 and that the prophet, in giving them the law, directed the deportees not to forget the commandments of the Lord or be led astray in their thoughts, when seeing the gold and silver idols and their adornments.[g] 3 With other similar words he exhorted them that the law should not depart from their hearts.

4* The same document also tells how the prophet, in virtue of an oracle, ordered that the tent and the ark should accompany him, and how he went to the very mountain that Moses climbed to behold God's inheritance.[h] 5 When Jeremiah arrived there, he found a chamber in a cave in which he put the tent, the ark, and the altar of incense; then he sealed the entrance. 6 Some of those who followed him came up intending to mark the path, but they could not find it. 7 When Jeremiah heard of this, he reproved them: "The place is to remain unknown until God gathers his people together again and shows them mercy. 8 Then the Lord will disclose these things, and the glory of the Lord and the cloud will be seen, just as they appeared in the time of Moses and of Solomon

**1:36** By a play on words, the Greek term *naphtha* (petroleum) is assimilated to some Semitic word, perhaps *nephthar*, meaning "loosened."

**2:4–5** This legendary account is given for the purpose of explaining why the postexilic Temple was the legitimate place of worship even without these sacred objects. **The very mountain**: Nebo; cf. Dt 32:49; 34:1.

*e:* 2 Mc 2:18; Ex 15:17; Dt 30:3–5. *f:* 2 Mc 2:18; 10:3; 14:36. *g:* Bar 6:1–72. *h:* Dt 32:49; 34:1; Rev 11:19.

VERSES 13 AND 14 mention collections of books by Nehemiah and Judas. There is no other evidence that Nehemiah founded a library or established a canon. Some scholars credit Judas with forming the canon of Hebrew Scriptures. He does not appear, however, to have made judgments about the authority of texts, but simply to have collected books that were in danger of being lost.

when he prayed that the place* might be greatly sanctified."[i]

9 It is also related how Solomon in his wisdom offered a sacrifice for the dedication and the completion of the temple. 10 Just as Moses prayed to the Lord and fire descended from the sky and consumed the sacrifices, so also Solomon prayed and fire came down and consumed the burnt offerings.[j] 11* Moses had said, "Because it had not been eaten, the purification offering was consumed."[k] 12 Solomon also celebrated the feast in the same way for eight days.

13 These same things are also told in the records and in Nehemiah's memoirs,* as well as how he founded a library and collected the books about the kings and the prophets, the books of David, and the royal letters about votive offerings. 14 In like manner Judas also collected for us all the books that had been scattered because of the war, and we now have them in our possession.[l] 15 If you need them, send messengers to get them for you.

16 As we are about to celebrate the purification, we are writing: you should celebrate the feast days. 17 It is God who has saved all his people and has restored to all of them their inheritance, the kingdom, the priesthood, and the sacred rites, 18 as he promised through the law. For we hope in God, that he will soon have mercy on us and gather us together from everywhere under the heavens to his holy place, for he has rescued us from great perils and has purified the place.[m]

## II. Compiler's Preface

19 This is the story of Judas Maccabeus and his brothers, of the purification of the great temple, the dedication of the altar, 20 the campaigns against Antiochus Epiphanes and his son Eupator,* 21 and of the heavenly manifestations accorded to the heroes who fought bravely for the Jewish people. Few as they were, they plundered the whole land, put to flight the barbarian hordes, 22 regained possession of the temple renowned throughout the world, and liberated the city. They reestablished the laws that were in danger of being abolished, while the Lord favored them with every kindness. 23 All this, detailed by Jason of Cyrene in five volumes, we will try to condense into a single book.

24 For in view of the flood of data, and the difficulties encountered, given such abundant material, by those who wish to plunge into accounts of the history, 25 we have aimed to please those who prefer simply to read, to make it easy for the studious who wish to commit things to memory, and to be helpful to all. 26 For us who have undertaken the labor of making this digest, the task, far from being easy, is one of sweat and of sleepless nights. 27 Just so, the preparation of a festive banquet is no light matter for one who seeks to give enjoyment to others. Similarly, to win the gratitude of many we will gladly endure this labor, 28 leaving the responsibility for exact details to the historian, and confining our efforts to presenting only a summary outline. 29 As the architect of a new house must pay attention to the whole structure, while the one who undertakes the decoration and the frescoes has to be concerned only with what is needed for ornamentation, so I think it is with us.[n] 30 To enter into questions and examine them from all sides and to be

**2:8 The place**: the Temple of Jerusalem.

**2:11** The statement attributed here to Moses seems to be based on Lv 10:16–20.

**2:13 Nehemiah's memoirs**: a lost apocryphal work, or perhaps Neh 1–7, 11–13.

**2:20** For the account of the campaigns against Antiochus IV Epiphanes, see 4:7–10:9; and for the account of those against his son Antiochus V Eupator, see 10:10–13:26.

*i:* Ex 40:34–35; 1 Kgs 8:11. *j:* Lv 9:23–24; 2 Chr 7:1. *k:* Lv 10:16–20. *l:* 1 Mc 1:57. *m:* Dt 30:3–5. *n:* 2 Mc 15:38–39.

busy about details is the task of the historian; [31]but one who is making an adaptation should be allowed to aim at brevity of expression and to forgo complete treatment of the matter. [32]Here, then, let us begin our account without adding to what has already been said; it would be silly to lengthen the preface to the history and then cut short the history itself.

## III. Heliodorus' Attempt to Profane the Temple*

### CHAPTER 3

See RG 165–67

*Heliodorus' Arrival in Jerusalem.* [1]While the holy city lived in perfect peace and the laws were strictly observed because of the piety of the high priest Onias* and his hatred of evil,[o] [2]the kings themselves honored the place and glorified the temple with the most magnificent gifts. [3]Thus Seleucus,* king of Asia, defrayed from his own revenues all the expenses necessary for the liturgy of sacrifice.

[4]But a certain Simon, of the priestly clan of Bilgah,* who had been appointed superintendent of the temple, had a quarrel with the high priest about the administration of the city market.[p] [5]Since he could not prevail against Onias, he went to Apollonius of Tarsus, who at that time was governor of Coelesyria and Phoenicia, [6]and reported to him that the treasury in Jerusalem was full of such untold riches that the sum total of the assets was past counting and that since they did not belong to the account of the sacrifices, it would be possible for them to fall under the authority of the king.

[7]When Apollonius had an audience with the king, he informed him about the riches that had been reported to him. The king chose his chief minister Heliodorus and sent him with instructions to seize those riches. [8]So Heliodorus immediately set out on his journey, ostensibly to visit the cities of Coelesyria and Phoenicia, but in reality to carry out the king's purpose.

[9]When he arrived in Jerusalem and had been graciously received by the high priest of the city, he told him about the information that had been given, and explained the reason for his presence, and he inquired if these things were really true. [10]The high priest explained that there were deposits for widows and orphans,[q] [11]and some was the property of Hyrcanus, son of Tobias,* a man who occupied a very high position. Contrary to the misrepresentations of the impious Simon, the total amounted only to four hundred talents of silver and two hundred of gold. [12]It was utterly unthinkable to defraud those who had placed their trust in the sanctity of the place and in the sacred inviolability of a temple venerated all over the world.

*Heliodorus' Plan To Rob the Temple.* [13]But Heliodorus, because of the orders he had from the king, said that in any case this money must be confiscated for the royal treasury. [14]So on the day he had set he went in to take an inventory of the funds. There was no little anguish throughout the city. [15]Priests prostrated themselves before the altar in their priestly robes, and called toward heaven for the one who had given the law about deposits to keep the deposits safe for those who had made them.[r] [16]Whoever saw the appearance of the high priest was pierced to the heart, for the changed complexion of his face revealed his mental anguish. [17]The terror and bodily trembling that had come over the man clearly showed those who saw him the pain that lodged in his heart. [18]People rushed out of their houses and crowded together making common supplication, because the place was in danger of being pro-

**3:1–40** This legendary episode about Heliodorus is recounted here for the purpose of stressing the inviolability of the Temple of Jerusalem; its later profanation was interpreted as owing to the sins of the people; cf. 5:17–18.

**3:1 Onias**: Onias III was high priest from 196 to 175 B.C. and died in 171 B.C. He was the son of Simon, whose praises are sung in Sir 50:1–21.

**3:3 Seleucus**: Seleucus IV Philopator, who reigned from 187 to 175 B.C.

**3:4 Bilgah**: a priestly family mentioned in 1 Chr 24:14; Neh 12:5, 18.

**3:11 Hyrcanus, son of Tobias**: a member of the Tobiad family of Transjordan (Neh 2:10; 6:17–19; 13:4–8). Hyrcanus' father was Joseph, whose mother was the sister of the high priest Onias II.

*o*: 2 Mc 5:19–20; 15:12. *p*: 2 Mc 4:23. *q*: Dt 14:29; 26:12. *r*: Ex 22:6–14.

faned. 19 Women, girded with sackcloth below their breasts, filled the streets. Young women secluded indoors all ran, some to the gates, some to the walls, others peered through the windows— 20 all of them with hands raised toward heaven, making supplication. 21 It was pitiful to see the populace prostrate everywhere and the high priest full of dread and anguish. 22 While they were imploring the almighty Lord to keep the deposits safe and secure for those who had placed them in trust, 23 Heliodorus went on with his plan.

*God Protects the Temple.* 24 But just as Heliodorus was arriving at the treasury with his bodyguards, the Lord of spirits and all authority produced an apparition so great that those who had been bold enough to accompany Heliodorus were panic-stricken at God's power and fainted away in terror. 25 There appeared to them a richly caparisoned horse, mounted by a fearsome rider. Charging furiously, the horse attacked Heliodorus with its front hooves. The rider was seen wearing golden armor. 26 Then two other young men, remarkably strong, strikingly handsome, and splendidly attired, appeared before him. Standing on each side of him, they flogged him unceasingly, inflicting innumerable blows. 27 Suddenly he fell to the ground, enveloped in great darkness. His men picked him up and laid him on a stretcher. 28 They carried away helpless the man who a moment before had entered that treasury under arms with a great retinue and his whole bodyguard. They clearly recognized the sovereign power of God.

*The Restoration and Testimony of Heliodorus.* 29 As Heliodorus lay speechless because of God's action and deprived of any hope of recovery, 30 the people praised the Lord who had marvelously glorified his own place; and the temple, charged so shortly before with fear and commotion, was filled with joy and gladness, now that the almighty Lord had appeared. 31 Quickly some of the companions of Heliodorus begged Onias to call upon the Most High to spare the life of one who was about to breathe his last. 32 The high priest, suspecting that the king might think that Heliodorus had suffered some foul play at the hands of the Jews, offered a sacrifice for the man's recovery. 33 While the high priest was offering the sacrifice of atonement, the same young men dressed in the same clothing again appeared and stood before Heliodorus. "Be very grateful to the high priest Onias," they told him. "It is for his sake that the Lord has spared your life. 34 Since you have been scourged by Heaven, proclaim to all God's great power." When they had said this, they disappeared.

35 After Heliodorus had offered a sacrifice to the Lord and made most solemn vows to the one who had spared his life, he bade Onias farewell, and returned with his soldiers to the king. 36 Before all he gave witness to the deeds of the most high God that he had seen with his own eyes. 37 When the king asked Heliodorus what sort of person would be suitable to be sent to Jerusalem next, he answered: 38 "If you have an enemy or one who is plotting against the government, send him there, and you will get him back with a flogging, if indeed he survives at all; for there is certainly some divine power about the place. 39 The one whose dwelling is in heaven watches over that place and protects it, and strikes down and destroys those who come to harm it." 40 This was how the matter concerning Heliodorus and the preservation of the treasury turned out.

## IV. Profanation and Persecution

### CHAPTER 4

See RG 165-67

*Simon Accuses Onias.* 1 The Simon mentioned above as the informer about the funds against his own country slandered Onias as the one who incited Heliodorus and instigated the whole miserable affair. 2 He dared to brand as a schemer against the government the man who was the benefactor of the city, the protector of his compatriots, and a zealous defender of the laws. 3 When Simon's hostility reached such a pitch that murders were being committed by one of his henchmen, 4 Onias saw that the opposition was serious and that Apollonius, son of Menestheus, the governor of Coelesyria and Phoenicia, was abetting Simon's wickedness. 5 So he had recourse to the king, not as

## The Hellenistic Reform

IT IS POSSIBLE that Jason had a genuine desire to improve the lot of his people by adopting the Greek way of life (v. 10) but would hardly have paid such substantial sums of money if he did not stand to gain in return. The existing royal concessions that he did away with (v. 11) had been granted by Antiochus III when he gained control of Jerusalem in 198 B.C. They guaranteed the Jews the right to live according to their ancestral laws.

an accuser of his compatriots, but as one
looking to the general and particular good of
all the people. 6He saw that without royal attention it would be impossible to have a
peaceful government, and that Simon would
not desist from his folly.
***Jason as High Priest.*** 7But Seleucus died,*
and when Antiochus surnamed Epiphanes
succeeded him on the throne, Onias' brother
Jason obtained the high priesthood by corrupt means:[s] 8in an interview, he promised
the king three hundred and sixty talents of
silver, as well as eighty talents from another
source of income. 9Besides this he would
undertake to pay a hundred and fifty more, if
he was given authority to establish a gymnasium and a youth center* for it and to enroll
Jerusalemites as citizens of Antioch.
10When Jason received the king's approval and came into office, he immediately
initiated his compatriots into the Greek way
of life. 11He set aside the royal concessions
granted to the Jews through the mediation of
John, father of Eupolemus* (that Eupolemus
who would later go on an embassy to the Romans to establish friendship and alliance
with them); he set aside the lawful practices
and introduced customs contrary to the law.[t]
12[u] With perverse delight he established a
gymnasium* at the very foot of the citadel,
where he induced the noblest young men to
wear the Greek hat. 13The craze for Hellenism and the adoption of foreign customs
reached such a pitch, through the outrageous
wickedness of Jason, the renegade and
would-be high priest, 14that the priests no
longer cared about the service of the altar.
Disdaining the temple and neglecting the
sacrifices, they hastened, at the signal for the
games, to take part in the unlawful exercises
at the arena. 15What their ancestors had regarded as honors they despised; what the
Greeks esteemed as glory they prized highly.
16For this reason they found themselves in
serious trouble: the very people whose manner of life they emulated, and whom they desired to imitate in everything, became their
enemies and oppressors. 17It is no light matter to flout the laws of God, as subsequent
events will show.
18When the quinquennial games were
held at Tyre in the presence of the king, 19the
vile Jason sent representatives of the Antiochians of Jerusalem, to bring three hundred
silver drachmas for the sacrifice to Hercules.
But the bearers themselves decided that the
money should not be spent on a sacrifice, as
that was not right, but should be used for
some other purpose. 20So the contribution
meant for the sacrifice to Hercules by the
sender, was in fact applied to the construction of triremes* by those who brought it.

**4:7 Seleucus died**: he was murdered by Heliodorus. Antiochus Epiphanes was his younger brother. Onias' brother showed his enthusiasm for the Greek way of life (v. 10) by changing his Hebrew name Joshua, or Jesus, to the Greek name Jason.

**4:9 Youth center**: an educational institution in which young men were trained both in Greek intellectual culture and in physical fitness. **Citizens of Antioch**: honorary citizens of Antioch, a Hellenistic city of the Seleucid Kingdom that had a corporation of such Antiochians, who enjoyed certain political and commercial privileges.

**4:11 Eupolemus**: one of the two envoys sent to Rome by Judas Maccabeus (1 Mc 8:17).

**4:12** Since the **gymnasium**, where the youth exercised naked (Greek *gymnos*), lay in the Tyropoeon Valley to the east of the citadel, it was directly next to the Temple on its eastern side. **The Greek hat**: a wide-brimmed hat, traditional headgear of Hermes, the patron god of athletic contests; it formed part of the distinctive costume of the members of the "youth center."

**4:20 Triremes**: war vessels with three banks of oars.

*s:* 2 Mc 1:7; 1 Mc 1:10. *t:* 1 Mc 8:17. *u:* 1 Mc 1:11–15.

### Corruption of the High Priesthood

THE YEARS OF persecution under Antiochus were precipitated by the strife over the high priesthood recorded in chs 4 and 5. Jason "obtained the priesthood by corrupt means" (4:7) and then Menelaus "secured the high priesthood for himself, outbidding Jason by three hundred talents of silver" (v. 24).

[21]When Apollonius, son of Menestheus, was sent to Egypt for the coronation of King Philometor,* Antiochus learned from him that the king was opposed to his policies. He took measures for his own security; so after going to Joppa, he proceeded to Jerusalem. [22]There he was received with great pomp by Jason and the people of the city, who escorted him with torchlights and acclamations; following this, he led his army into Phoenicia.

*Menelaus as High Priest.* [23]Three years later Jason sent Menelaus,* brother of the aforementioned Simon, to deliver the money to the king, and to complete negotiations on urgent matters. [24]But after his introduction to the king, he flattered him with such an air of authority that he secured the high priesthood for himself, outbidding Jason by three hundred talents of silver. [25]He returned with the royal commission, but with nothing that made him worthy of the high priesthood; he had the temper of a cruel tyrant and the rage of a wild beast. [26]So Jason, who had cheated his own brother and now saw himself cheated by another man, was driven out as a fugitive to the country of the Ammonites. [27]But Menelaus, who obtained the office, paid nothing of the money he had promised to the king, [28]in spite of the demand of Sostratus, the commandant of the citadel, whose duty it was to collect the taxes. For this reason, both were summoned before the king. [29]Menelaus left his brother Lysimachus as his deputy in the high priesthood, while Sostratus left Crates, commander of the Cypriots.[v]

*Murder of Onias.* [30]While these things were taking place, the people of Tarsus and Mallus* rose in revolt, because their cities had been given as a gift to Antiochis, the king's concubine. [31]So the king hastened off to settle the affair, leaving Andronicus, one of his nobles, as his deputy. [32]Menelaus, for his part, thinking this a good opportunity, stole some gold vessels from the temple and presented them to Andronicus; he had already sold other vessels in Tyre and in the neighboring cities. [33]When Onias had clear evidence, he accused Menelaus publicly, after withdrawing to the inviolable sanctuary at Daphne, near Antioch. [34]Thereupon Menelaus approached Andronicus privately and urged him to seize Onias. So Andronicus went to Onias, treacherously reassuring him by offering his right hand in oath, and persuaded him, in spite of his suspicions, to leave the sanctuary. Then, with no regard for justice, he immediately put him to death.

[35]As a result, not only the Jews, but many people of other nations as well, were indignant and angry over the unjust murder of the man. [36]When the king returned from the region of Cilicia, the Jews of the city,* together with the Greeks who detested the crime, went to see him about the murder of Onias. [37]Antiochus was deeply grieved and full of pity; he wept as he recalled the prudence and noble conduct of the deceased. [38]Inflamed with anger, he immediately stripped Andronicus of his purple robe, tore off his garments, and had him led through the whole city to the very place where he had committed the outrage against Onias; and there he put the murderer to death. Thus the Lord rendered him the punishment he deserved.

**4:21 Philometor**: Ptolemy VI, king of Egypt, ca. 172 to ca. 145 B.C.

**4:23 Menelaus**: Jewish high priest from ca. 172 to his execution in 162 B.C. (13:3–8).

**4:30 Mallus**: a city of Cilicia (v. 36) in southeastern Asia Minor, about thirty miles east of Tarsus.

**4:36 The city**: Antioch. But some understand the Greek to mean "each city."

*v:* 2 Mc 4:39–42.

**The Intervention of Antiochus**

JASON'S ATTEMPT TO recover the high priesthood resulted in the wholesale massacre of Jewish citizens (5:6). That Antiochus took this to mean that Judea was in revolt is perhaps the most plausible explanation of his violent intervention in Jerusalem. His rage was also stirred up because he had been humiliated in Egypt; see 1 Mc 1:20.

***More Outrages.*** 39 Many acts of sacrilege had been committed by Lysimachus in the city* with the connivance of Menelaus. When word spread, the people assembled in protest against Lysimachus, because a large number of gold vessels had been stolen. 40 As the crowds, now thoroughly enraged, began to riot, Lysimachus launched an unjustified attack against them with about three thousand armed men under the leadership of a certain Auranus, a man as advanced in folly as he was in years. 41 Seeing Lysimachus' attack, people picked up stones, pieces of wood or handfuls of the ashes lying there and threw them in wild confusion at Lysimachus and his men. 42 As a result, they wounded many of them and even killed a few, while they put all to flight. The temple robber himself they killed near the treasury.

43 Charges about this affair were brought against Menelaus. 44 When the king came to Tyre, three men sent by the senate pleaded the case before him. 45 But Menelaus, seeing himself on the losing side, promised Ptolemy, son of Dorymenes, a substantial sum of money if he would win the king over.[w] 46 So Ptolemy took the king aside into a colonnade, as if to get some fresh air, and persuaded him to change his mind. 47 Menelaus, who was the cause of all the trouble, the king acquitted of the charges, while he condemned to death those poor men who would have been declared innocent even if they had pleaded their case before Scythians. 48 Thus, those who had prosecuted the case on behalf of the city, the people, and the sacred vessels, quickly suffered unjust punishment. 49 For this reason, even Tyrians, detesting the crime, provided sumptuously for their burial. 50 But Menelaus, thanks to the greed of those in power, remained in office, where he grew in wickedness, scheming greatly against his fellow citizens.

## CHAPTER 5

See RG 165–67

***Jason's Revolt.*** 1 About this time Antiochus sent his second expedition* into Egypt.[x] 2[y] It then happened that all over the city, for nearly forty days, there appeared horsemen, clothed in garments of a golden weave, charging in midair—companies fully armed with lances and drawn swords; 3 squadrons of cavalry in battle array, charges and countercharges on this side and that, with brandished shields and bristling spears, flights of arrows and flashes of gold ornaments, together with armor of every sort. 4 Therefore all prayed that this vision might be a good omen.

5 But when a false rumor circulated that Antiochus was dead, Jason* gathered at least a thousand men and suddenly attacked the city. As the defenders on the walls were forced back and the city was finally being taken, Menelaus took refuge in the citadel. 6 For his part, Jason continued the merciless slaughter of his fellow citizens, not realizing that triumph over one's own kindred is the greatest calamity; he thought he was winning a victory over his enemies, not over his own people. 7 Even so, he did not gain con-

**4:39 The city**: Jerusalem. Menelaus was still in Syria.

**5:1 Second expedition**: the first invasion of Egypt by Antiochus IV in 169 B.C. (1 Mc 1:16–20) is not mentioned in 2 Maccabees, unless the coming of the Syrian army to Palestine (2 Mc 4:21–22) is regarded as the first invasion. The author of 2 Maccabees apparently combines the first pillage of Jerusalem in 169 B.C. after Antiochus' first invasion of Egypt (1 Mc 1:20–28; cf. 2 Mc 5:5–7) with the second pillage of the city two years later (167 B.C.), following the king's second invasion of Egypt in 168 B.C. (1 Mc 1:29–35; cf. 2 Mc 5:24–26).

**5:5 Jason**: brother of Onias III, claimant of the high priesthood (4:7–10). Later he was supplanted by Menelaus, who drove him into Transjordan (4:26).

*w:* 2 Mc 8:8; 1 Mc 3:38. *x:* 1 Mc 1:16–19; Dn 11:25–30. *y:* 2 Mc 3:24–26; 10:29–30; 11:8.

trol of the government, but in the end received only disgrace for his treachery, and once again took refuge in the country of the Ammonites. [8]At length he met a miserable end. Called to account before Aretas,* ruler of the Arabians, he fled from city to city, hunted by all, hated as an apostate from the laws, abhorred as the executioner of his country and his compatriots. Driven into Egypt, [9]he set out by sea for the Lacedaemonians, among whom he hoped to find protection because of his relations with them. He who had exiled so many from their country perished in exile; [10]and he who had cast out so many to lie unburied went unmourned and without a funeral of any kind, nor any place in the tomb of his ancestors.

***Revenge by Antiochus.*** [11][z]When these happenings were reported to the king, he thought that Judea was in revolt. Raging like a wild animal, he set out from Egypt and took Jerusalem by storm. [12]He ordered his soldiers to cut down without mercy those whom they met and to slay those who took refuge in their houses. [13]There was a massacre of young and old, a killing of women and children, a slaughter of young women and infants. [14]In the space of three days, eighty thousand were lost, forty thousand meeting a violent death, and the same number being sold into slavery.

[15]Not satisfied with this, the king dared to enter the holiest temple in the world; Menelaus, that traitor both to the laws and to his country, served as guide. [16]He laid his impure hands on the sacred vessels and swept up with profane hands the votive offerings made by other kings for the advancement, the glory, and the honor of the place. [17]Antiochus became puffed up in spirit, not realizing that it was because of the sins of the city's inhabitants that the Sovereign Lord was angry for a little while: hence the disregard of the place.[a] [18]If they had not become entangled in so many sins, this man, like that Heliodorus sent by King Seleucus to inspect the treasury, would have been flogged and turned back from his presumptuous act as soon as he approached. [19]The Lord, however, had not chosen the nation for the sake of the place, but the place for the sake of the nation. [20]Therefore, the place itself, having shared in the nation's misfortunes, afterward participated in their good fortune; and what the Almighty had forsaken in wrath was restored in all its glory, once the great Sovereign Lord became reconciled.

[21][b] Antiochus carried off eighteen hundred talents from the temple and hurried back to Antioch, thinking in his arrogance that he could make the land navigable and the sea passable on foot, so carried away was he with pride. [22]He left governors to harass the nation: at Jerusalem, Philip, a Phrygian by birth,* and in character more barbarous than the man who appointed him;[c] [23]at Mount Gerizim,* Andronicus; and besides these, Menelaus, who lorded it over his fellow citizens more than the others. Out of hatred for the Jewish citizens, [24][d] the king sent Apollonius,* commander of the Mysians, at the head of an army of twenty-two thousand, with orders to kill all the grown men and sell the women and children into slavery. [25]When this man arrived in Jerusalem, he pretended to be peacefully disposed and waited until the holy day of the sabbath; then, finding the Jews refraining from work, he ordered his men to parade fully armed. [26]All those who came out to watch, he massacred, and running through the city with armed men, he cut down a large number of people.

[27]But Judas Maccabeus and about nine others withdrew to the wilderness to avoid sharing in defilement; there he and his companions lived like the animals in the hills, eating what grew wild.[e]

**5:8 Aretas**: King Aretas I of the Nabateans; cf. 1 Mc 5:25.

**5:22 Philip, a Phrygian by birth**: the Philip of 2 Mc 6:11 and 8:8, but probably not the same as Philip the regent of 2 Mc 9:29 and 1 Mc 6:14.

**5:23 Mount Gerizim**: the sacred mountain of the Samaritans at Shechem; cf. 2 Mc 6:2.

**5:24 Apollonius**: the Mysian commander of 1 Mc 1:29; mentioned also in 2 Mc 3:5; 4:4.

*z*: 1 Mc 1:20–24. *a*: 2 Mc 6:12–16; 7:16–19, 32–38. *b*: 1 Mc 1:23–24. *c*: 2 Mc 6:11; 8:8. *d*: 1 Mc 1:29–40. *e*: 2 Mc 8:1; 1 Mc 2:28.

**The Religious Persecution**

IT WAS COMMON in the Hellenistic world to identify the deities of one culture with those of another (6:2). Olympian Zeus was presumably regarded as equivalent to "God Most High." The Letter of Aristeas, a Jewish document written in Greek in the second century B.C., says that the Jews worship the same God, Zeus, as the Greeks, but by a different name. What is at issue here is not the suppression of all Jewish religion, but its translation and adaptation to Hellenistic categories. Gentiles sometimes thought that Jewish worship was related to that of Dionysus (v. 7), god of wine, because Jews drank wine in ritual celebration.

See RG 165–67

## CHAPTER 6

***Abolition of Judaism.*** 1[f] Not long after this the king sent an Athenian senator* to force the Jews to abandon the laws of their ancestors and live no longer by the laws of God, 2 also to profane the temple in Jerusalem and dedicate it to Olympian Zeus,* and the one on Mount Gerizim to Zeus the Host to Strangers, as the local inhabitants were wont to be.[g] 3 This was a harsh and utterly intolerable evil. 4 The Gentiles filled the temple with debauchery and revelry; they amused themselves with prostitutes and had intercourse with women even in the sacred courts. They also brought forbidden things into the temple,[h] 5 so that the altar was covered with abominable offerings prohibited by the laws.

6 No one could keep the sabbath or celebrate the traditional feasts, nor even admit to being a Jew. 7 Moreover, at the monthly celebration of the king's birthday the Jews, from bitter necessity, had to partake of the sacrifices, and when the festival of Dionysus* was celebrated, they were compelled to march in his procession, wearing wreaths of ivy.[i]

8 Following upon a vote of the citizens of Ptolemais, a decree was issued ordering the neighboring Greek cities to adopt the same measures, obliging the Jews to partake of the sacrifices 9 and putting to death those who would not consent to adopt the customs of the Greeks. It was obvious, therefore, that disaster had come upon them. 10 Thus, two women who were arrested for having circumcised their children were publicly paraded about the city with their babies hanging at their breasts and then thrown down from the top of the city wall.[j] 11 Others, who had assembled in nearby caves to observe the seventh day in secret, were betrayed to Philip and all burned to death. In their respect for the holiness of that day, they refrained from defending themselves.[k]

***God's Purpose.*** 12[l] Now I urge those who read this book not to be disheartened by these misfortunes, but to consider that these punishments were meant not for the ruin but for the correction of our nation. 13 It is, in fact, a sign of great kindness to punish the impious promptly instead of letting them go for long. 14[m] Thus, in dealing with other nations, the Sovereign Lord patiently waits until they reach the full measure of their sins before punishing them; but with us he has decided to deal differently, 15 in order that he may not have to punish us later, when our sins have reached their fullness. 16 Therefore he never withdraws his mercy from us. Although he disciplines us with misfortunes, he does not abandon his own people. 17 Let these words suffice for recalling this truth. Without further ado we must go on with our story.

***Martyrdom of Eleazar.*** 18* Eleazar, one of

**6:1 Athenian senator**: or, Geron the Athenian, since *geron* can also be a proper name.

**6:2 Olympian Zeus**: equated with the Syrian Baal Shamen ("the lord of the heavens"), a term which the Jews mockingly rendered as *shiqqus shomem*, "desolating abomination" (Dn 9:27; 11:31; 12:11; 1 Mc 1:54).

**6:7 Dionysus**: also called Bacchus, the god of the grape harvest and of wine; ivy was one of his symbols.

**6:18–7:42** The stories of Eleazar and of the mother and her seven sons, among the earliest models of "martyrology," were understandably popular. Written to encourage God's

*f:* 1 Mc 1:41–63. *g:* 1 Mc 1:46, 54; Dn 9:27; 11:31; 12:11. *h:* Ez 23:36–49; Dn 11:31; Am 2:7. *i:* 1 Mc 1:58–59. *j:* 1 Mc 1:60–61. *k:* 1 Mc 2:32–38. *l:* 2 Mc 5:17; 7:16–19, 32–38. *m:* Wis 11:9–10; 12:2, 22.

## The Martyrdom of Eleazar

DEATH WITH HONOR, rather than life without it (6:19), was an ideal of Greek culture, beginning with Achilles in the Trojan War. Compare the decision of Judas Maccabee that led to his death in 1 Maccabees 9:10. Eleazar refuses any subterfuge that might save his life (6:23), partly for reasons of honor, and partly because of the example he would set.

the foremost scribes, a man advanced in age
and of noble appearance, was being forced to
open his mouth to eat pork.[n] 19But preferring
a glorious death to a life of defilement, he
went forward of his own accord to the instrument of torture, 20spitting out the meat as they
should do who have the courage to reject food
unlawful to taste even for love of life.
21Those in charge of that unlawful sacrifice took the man aside, because of their
long acquaintance with him, and privately
urged him to bring his own provisions that
he could legitimately eat, and only to pretend to eat the sacrificial meat prescribed by
the king. 22Thus he would escape death, and
be treated kindly because of his old friendship with them. 23But he made up his mind
in a noble manner, worthy of his years, the
dignity of his advanced age, the merited distinction of his gray hair, and of the admirable
life he had lived from childhood. Above all
loyal to the holy laws given by God, he
swiftly declared, "Send me to Hades!"
24"At our age it would be unbecoming to
make such a pretense; many of the young
would think the ninety-year-old Eleazar had
gone over to an alien religion. 25If I dissem-
ble to gain a brief moment of life, they
would be led astray by me, while I would
bring defilement and dishonor on my old
age. 26Even if, for the time being, I avoid human punishment, I shall never, whether alive
or dead, escape the hand of the Almighty.
27Therefore, by bravely giving up life now, I
will prove myself worthy of my old age,
28and I will leave to the young a noble example of how to die willingly and nobly for
the revered and holy laws."
He spoke thus, and went immediately to
the instrument of torture. 29Those who
shortly before had been kindly disposed,
now became hostile toward him because
what he had said seemed to them utter madness.[o] 30When he was about to die under the
blows, he groaned, saying: "The Lord in his
holy knowledge knows full well that, although I could have escaped death, I am not
only enduring terrible pain in my body from
this scourging, but also suffering it with joy
in my soul because of my devotion to him."
31This is how he died, leaving in his death a
model of nobility and an unforgettable example of virtue not only for the young but
for the whole nation.

### CHAPTER 7

*Martyrdom of a Mother and Her Seven*
*Sons.* 1It also happened that seven
brothers with their mother were arrested and
tortured with whips and scourges by the king
to force them to eat pork in violation of
God's law.[p] 2One of the brothers, speaking
for the others, said: "What do you expect to
learn by questioning us? We are ready to die
rather than transgress the laws of our ancestors."

See RG 165–67

3At that the king, in a fury, gave orders to
have pans and caldrons heated. 4These were
quickly heated, and he gave the order to cut
out the tongue of the one who had spoken for
the others, to scalp him and cut off his hands
and feet, while the rest of his brothers and
his mother looked on. 5When he was completely maimed but still breathing, the king
ordered them to carry him to the fire and fry
him. As a cloud of smoke spread from the
pan, the brothers and their mother encouraged one another to die nobly, with these

people in times of persecution, they add gruesome details to the record of tortures, and place long speeches in the mouths of the martyrs.

*n:* Lv 11:6–8. *o:* Wis 3:1–4; 5:4. *p:* Jer 15:9.

## The Seven Brothers

VARIANTS OF THE story of the mother with seven sons (ch 7) are found in rabbinic literature, set in Roman times. The story is a legend. The quotation from the Song of Moses (Dt 32) sheds light on the motivation of the martyrs, where it is said that God "will avenge the blood of his servants, . . . and purge his people's land" (v. 43). The second brother introduces another consideration: the hope of resurrection (2 Mc 7:9). The third brother gives the resurrection a very physical character: He hopes to get his limbs back (v. 11). Such a physical view of resurrection is exceptional in Jewish texts of the second century B.C. (Daniel, 1 Enoch), most of which envisage a resurrection of the spirit. The mother grounds the hope for resurrection in the doctrine of creation. If God gave life once, he can do so again (v. 23).

words: 6"The Lord God is looking on and truly has compassion on us, as Moses declared in his song, when he openly bore witness, saying, 'And God will have compassion on his servants.' "[q]

7After the first brother had died in this manner, they brought the second to be made sport of. After tearing off the skin and hair of his head, they asked him, "Will you eat the pork rather than have your body tortured limb by limb?" 8Answering in the language of his ancestors, he said, "Never!" So he in turn suffered the same tortures as the first. 9With his last breath he said: "You accursed fiend, you are depriving us of this present life, but the King of the universe will raise us up* to live again forever, because we are dying for his laws."[r]

10After him the third suffered their cruel sport. He put forth his tongue at once when told to do so, and bravely stretched out his hands, 11as he spoke these noble words: "It was from Heaven that I received these; for the sake of his laws I disregard them; from him I hope to receive them again." 12Even the king and his attendants marveled at the young man's spirit, because he regarded his sufferings as nothing.

13After he had died, they tortured and maltreated the fourth brother in the same way. 14When he was near death, he said, "It is my choice to die at the hands of mortals with the hope that God will restore me to life; but for you, there will be no resurrection to life."

15They next brought forward the fifth brother and maltreated him. 16Looking at the king, he said:[s] "Mortal though you are, you have power over human beings, so you do what you please. But do not think that our nation is forsaken by God. 17Only wait, and you will see how his great power will torment you and your descendants."

18After him they brought the sixth brother. When he was about to die, he said: "Have no vain illusions. We suffer these things on our own account, because we have sinned against our God; that is why such shocking things have happened. 19Do not think, then, that you will go unpunished for having dared to fight against God."

20Most admirable and worthy of everlasting remembrance was the mother who, seeing her seven sons perish in a single day, bore it courageously because of her hope in the Lord. 21Filled with a noble spirit that stirred her womanly reason with manly emotion, she exhorted each of them in the language of their ancestors with these words: 22[t] "I do not know how you came to be in my womb; it was not I who gave you breath and life, nor was it I who arranged the elements you are made of. 23Therefore, since it is the Creator of the universe who shaped the beginning of humankind and brought about the origin of everything, he, in his

**7:9 The King of the universe will raise us up**: here, and in vv. 11, 14, 23, 29, 36, belief in the future resurrection of the body, at least for the just, is clearly stated; cf. also 12:44; 14:46; Dn 12:2.

*q:* Dt 32:36–38. *r:* 2 Mc 12:44; 14:46; Dn 12:1–3. *s:* 2 Mc 5:17; 6:12–16; 7:32. *t:* 2 Mc 7:11, 28; Jb 1:10–12; Ps 139:13–16; Eccl 11:5.

mercy, will give you back both breath and life, because you now disregard yourselves for the sake of his law."

[24]Antiochus, suspecting insult in her words, thought he was being ridiculed. As the youngest brother was still alive, the king appealed to him, not with mere words, but with promises on oath, to make him rich and happy if he would abandon his ancestral customs: he would make him his Friend and entrust him with high office. [25]When the youth paid no attention to him at all, the king appealed to the mother, urging her to advise her boy to save his life. [26]After he had urged her for a long time, she agreed to persuade her son. [27]She leaned over close to him and, in derision of the cruel tyrant, said in their native language: "Son, have pity on me, who carried you in my womb for nine months, nursed you for three years, brought you up, educated and supported you to your present age. [28]I beg you, child, to look at the heavens and the earth and see all that is in them; then you will know that God did not make them out of existing things.* In the same way humankind came into existence. [29]Do not be afraid of this executioner, but be worthy of your brothers and accept death, so that in the time of mercy I may receive you again with your brothers."

[30]She had scarcely finished speaking when the youth said: "What is the delay? I will not obey the king's command. I obey the command of the law given to our ancestors through Moses. [31]But you, who have contrived every kind of evil for the Hebrews, will not escape the hands of God. [32]We, indeed, are suffering because of our sins.[u] [33]Though for a little while our living Lord has been angry, correcting and chastising us, he will again be reconciled with his servants. [34]But you, wretch, most vile of mortals, do not, in your insolence, buoy yourself up with unfounded hopes, as you raise your hand against the children of heaven. [35]You have not yet escaped the judgment of the almighty and all-seeing God. [36]Our brothers, after enduring brief pain, have drunk of never-failing life, under God's covenant. But you, by the judgment of God, shall receive just punishments for your arrogance. [37]Like my brothers, I offer up my body and my life for our ancestral laws, imploring God to show mercy soon to our nation, and by afflictions and blows to make you confess that he alone is God. [38]Through me and my brothers, may there be an end to the wrath of the Almighty that has justly fallen on our whole nation."

[39]At that, the king became enraged and treated him even worse than the others, since he bitterly resented the boy's contempt. [40]Thus he too died undefiled, putting all his trust in the Lord. [41]Last of all, after her sons, the mother was put to death. [42]Enough has been said about the sacrificial meals and the excessive cruelties.

## V. Victories of Judas and Purification of the Temple

### CHAPTER 8

See RG 165–67

***Resistance from Judas Maccabeus.***

[1][v] Judas Maccabeus and his companions entered the villages secretly, summoned their kindred, and enlisted others who had remained faithful to Judaism. Thus they assembled about six thousand men. [2]They implored the Lord to look kindly upon this people, who were being oppressed by all; to have pity on the sanctuary, which was profaned by renegades; [3]to have mercy on the city, which was being destroyed and was about to be leveled to the ground; to listen to the blood that cried out to him; [4]to remember the criminal slaughter of innocent children and the blasphemies uttered against his name; and to manifest his hatred of evil.

[5][w] Once Maccabeus got his men organized, the Gentiles could not withstand him, for the Lord's wrath had now changed to mercy. [6]Coming by surprise upon towns and villages, he set them on fire. He captured

**7:28 God did not make them out of existing things**: that is, all things were made solely by God's omnipotent will and creative word; cf. Heb 11:3. This statement has often been taken as a basis for "creation out of nothing" (Latin *creatio ex nihilo*).

*u:* 2 Mc 5:17; 6:12–16; 7:16–19. *v:* 2 Mc 5:27; 1 Mc 3:10–26. *w:* 1 Mc 3:3–9.

strategic positions, and put to flight not a few of the enemy. [7]He preferred the nights as being especially favorable for such attacks. Soon talk of his valor spread everywhere.

*First Victory over Nicanor.** [8]When Philip saw that Judas was gaining ground little by little and that his successful advances were becoming more frequent, he wrote to Ptolemy, governor of Coelesyria and Phoenicia, to come to the aid of the king's interests.[x] [9y] Ptolemy promptly selected Nicanor, son of Patroclus, one of the Chief Friends, and sent him at the head of at least twenty thousand armed men of various nations to wipe out the entire Jewish nation. With him he associated Gorgias, a general, experienced in the art of war.[z] [10]Nicanor planned to raise the two thousand talents of tribute owed by the king to the Romans* by selling captured Jews into slavery. [11]So he immediately sent word to the coastal cities, inviting them to buy Jewish slaves and promising to deliver ninety slaves for a talent*—little anticipating the punishment that was to fall upon him from the Almighty.

[12]When Judas learned of Nicanor's advance and informed his companions about the approach of the army, [13]those who were fearful and those who lacked faith in God's justice deserted and got away. [14]But the others sold everything they had left, and at the same time entreated the Lord to deliver those whom the ungodly Nicanor had sold before even capturing them. [15]They entreated the Lord to do this, if not for their sake, at least for the sake of the covenants made with their ancestors, and because they themselves invoked his holy and glorious name. [16]Maccabeus assembled his forces, six thousand strong, and exhorted them not to be panic-stricken before the enemy, nor to fear the very large number of Gentiles unjustly attacking them, but to fight nobly. [17]They were to keep before their eyes the lawless outrage perpetrated by the Gentiles against the holy place and the affliction of the humiliated city, as well as the subversion of their ancestral way of life. [18]He said, "They trust in weapons and acts of daring, but we trust in almighty God, who can by a mere nod destroy not only those who attack us but even the whole world." [19]He went on to tell them of the times when help had been given their ancestors: both the time of Sennacherib, when a hundred and eighty-five thousand of his men perished,[a] [20]and the time of the battle in Babylonia against the Galatians,* when only eight thousand Jews fought along with four thousand Macedonians; yet when the Macedonians were hard pressed, the eight thousand, by the help they received from Heaven, destroyed one hundred and twenty thousand and took a great quantity of spoils. [21b] With these words he encouraged them and made them ready to die for their laws and their country.

Then Judas divided his army into four, [22]placing his brothers, Simon, Joseph,* and Jonathan, each over a division, assigning them fifteen hundred men apiece.[c] [23]There was also Eleazar.* After reading to them from the holy book and giving them the watchword, "The help of God," Judas himself took charge of the first division and joined in battle with Nicanor.[d] [24]With the Almighty as their ally, they killed more than nine thousand of the enemy, wounded and disabled the greater part of Nicanor's army, and put all of them to flight. [25]They also seized the money of those who had come to buy them as slaves. When they had pursued

**8:8–29, 34–35** This account of the campaign of Nicanor and Gorgias against Judas is paralleled, with certain differences, in 1 Mc 3:38–4:24.

**8:10 Tribute owed by the king to the Romans**: the payment imposed on Antiochus III in 188 B.C. by the treaty of Apamea.

**8:11 Ninety slaves for a talent**: a low price for so many slaves, thus expressing the opponents' contempt for the Jews.

**8:20 Galatians**: a mercenary force, defeated by Jews and Macedonians in Babylon. Nothing else is known about this battle.

**8:22 Joseph**: called John in 1 Mc 2:2; 9:36, 38. This paragraph interrupts the story of Nicanor's defeat, which is resumed in v. 34. The purpose of the author apparently is to group together the defeats suffered by the Syrians on various occasions. Battles against Timothy are recounted in 1 Mc 5:37–44 and 2 Mc 12:10–25; against Bacchides, in 1 Mc 7:8–20.

**8:23 Eleazar**: this parenthetical reference notes the existence of a fifth brother; cf. 1 Mc 2:5.

*x:* 2 Mc 4:45; 1 Mc 3:38. *y:* 1 Mc 3:38–59. *z:* 1 Mc 7:26. *a:* 2 Mc 15:22; 2 Kgs 19:35–36; 1 Mc 7:41–42; Is 37:36–37. *b:* 1 Mc 4:1–25. *c:* 1 Mc 2:2–5; 5:18, 55–62. *d:* 1 Mc 3:48.

the enemy for some time, they were obliged to return by reason of the late hour. [26]It was the day before the sabbath, and for that reason they could not continue the pursuit. [27]They collected the enemy's weapons and stripped them of their spoils, and then observed the sabbath with fervent praise and thanks to the Lord who kept them safe for that day on which he allotted them the beginning of his mercy. [28]After the sabbath, they gave a share of the spoils to those who were tortured and to widows and orphans; the rest they divided among themselves and their children.[e] [29]When this was done, they made supplication in common, imploring the merciful Lord to be completely reconciled with his servants.

*Other Victories.* [30]They also challenged the forces of Timothy and Bacchides, killed more than twenty thousand of them, and captured some very high fortresses. They divided the considerable plunder, allotting half to themselves and the rest to victims of torture, orphans, widows, and the aged. [31]They collected the enemies' weapons and carefully stored them in strategic places; the rest of the spoils they carried to Jerusalem. [32]They also killed the commander of Timothy's forces, a most wicked man, who had done great harm to the Jews. [33]While celebrating the victory in their ancestral city, they burned both those who had set fire to the sacred gates and Callisthenes, who had taken refuge in a little house; so he received the reward his wicked deeds deserved.

[34f]The thrice-accursed Nicanor, who had brought the thousand slave dealers to buy the Jews, [35]after being humbled through the Lord's help by those whom he had thought of no account, laid aside his fine clothes and fled alone across country like a runaway slave, until he reached Antioch. He was eminently successful in destroying his own army. [36]So he who had promised to provide tribute for the Romans by the capture of the people of Jerusalem proclaimed that the Jews had a champion, and that because they followed the laws laid down by him, they were unharmed.

## CHAPTER 9

See RG 165–67

***Punishment and Death of Antiochus IV.**** [1g]About that time Antiochus retreated in disgrace from the region of Persia. [2]He had entered the city called Persepolis and attempted to rob the temples and gain control of the city. Thereupon the people had swift recourse to arms, and Antiochus' forces were routed, so that in the end Antiochus was put to flight by the people of that region and forced to beat a shameful retreat. [3]On his arrival in Ecbatana, he learned what had happened to Nicanor and to Timothy's forces. [4]Overcome with anger, he planned to make the Jews suffer for the injury done by those who had put him to flight. Therefore he ordered his charioteer to drive without stopping until he finished the journey. Yet the condemnation of Heaven rode with him, because he said in his arrogance, "I will make Jerusalem the common graveyard of Jews as soon as I arrive there."

[5]So the all-seeing Lord, the God of Israel, struck him down with an incurable and invisible blow; for scarcely had he uttered those words when he was seized with excruciating pains in his bowels and sharp internal torment,[h] [6]a fit punishment for him who had tortured the bowels of others with many barbarous torments. [7]Far from giving up his insolence, he was all the more filled with arrogance. Breathing fire in his rage against the Jews, he gave orders to drive even faster. As a result he hurtled from the speeding chariot, and every part of his body was racked by the violent fall. [8]Thus he who previously, in his superhuman presumption, thought he could command the waves of the sea, and imagined he could weigh the mountaintops in his scales, was now thrown to the ground and

**9:1–29** In order to keep together the various accounts of God's punishment of the persecutors of his people, the author places here the stories of Antiochus' illness and death (in actuality the king died about the same time as the purification of the Temple, i.e., 164 B.C.; cf. 1 Mc 4:36–59; 6:1–16; 2 Mc 10:1–8); of Judas' campaigns in Idumea and Transjordan; cf. 1 Mc 5:1–51; 2 Mc 10:14–38; and of the first expedition of Lysias (1 Mc 4:26–35; 2 Mc 11:1–15).

*e:* Nm 31:25–47; Dt 26:12–13; 1 Sm 30:21–25. *f:* 2 Mc 8:23–24; 1 Mc 7:26. *g:* 2 Mc 1:12–17; 1 Mc 6:1–13; Dn 11:40–45. *h:* Acts 12:20–23.

**The Death of Antiochus Epiphanes**

THE ATTEMPT TO "command the waves of the sea" (9:8) was a classic instance act of hubris or wildly excessive pride, associated with the Persian king Xerxes by the fifth-century tragedian Aeschylus. Only God could "weigh the mountains in scales" (see Is 40:12). Later Jewish tradition preserved a similar account of the death of Herod the Great.

The most fantastic part of Epiphanes' (fictitious) deathbed conversion (v. 17) is the promise that he would become a Jew. There was one notable case of conversion in the first century A.D., involving the royal house of Adiabene, but the fantasy of royal conversion is often found in Jewish writings. Usually, however, the king in question stops short of becoming a Jew (compare Nebuchadnezzar in Dn 4).

had to be carried on a litter, clearly manifesting to all the power of God.[i] [9]The body
of this impious man swarmed with worms,
and while he was still alive in hideous torments, his flesh rotted off, so that the entire
army was sickened by the stench of his corruption.[j] [10]Shortly before, he had thought
that he could reach the stars of heaven, and
now, no one could endure to transport the
man because of this intolerable stench.
[11]At last, broken in spirit, he began to give
up his excessive arrogance, and to gain some
understanding, under the scourge of God,
for he was racked with pain unceasingly.
[12]When he could no longer bear his own
stench, he said, "It is right to be subject to
God, and not to think one's mortal self equal
to God."[k] [13]Then this vile man vowed to him
who would never again show him mercy, the
Sovereign Lord, [14]that the holy city, toward
which he had been hurrying with the intention of leveling it to the ground and making
it a common graveyard, he would now set
free; [15]that the Jews, whom he had judged
not even worthy of burial, but fit only to be
thrown out with their children to be eaten by
vultures and wild animals—all of them he
would make equal to the Athenians; [16]that he
would adorn with the finest offerings the
holy temple which he had previously despoiled, restore all the sacred vessels many
times over, and provide from his own revenues the expenses required for the sacrifices.
[17]Besides all this, he would become a Jew
himself and visit every inhabited place to
proclaim there the power of God. [18]But since
his sufferings were not lessened, for God's
just judgment had come upon him, he lost
hope for himself and wrote the following letter to the Jews in the form of a supplication.
It read thus:
[19]* "To the worthy Jewish citizens, Antiochus, king and general, sends hearty greetings and best wishes for their health and
prosperity. [20]If you and your children are
well and your affairs are going as you wish,
I thank God very much, for my hopes are in
heaven. [21]Now that I am ill, I recall with affection your esteem and goodwill. On returning from the regions of Persia, I fell victim to a troublesome illness; so I thought it
necessary to form plans for the general security of all. [22]I do not despair about my health,
since I have much hope of recovering from
my illness. [23]Nevertheless, I know that my
father, whenever he went on campaigns in
the hinterland, would name his successor,
[24]so that, if anything unexpected happened
or any unwelcome news came, the people
throughout the realm would know to whom
the government had been entrusted, and so
not be disturbed. [25]I am also bearing in mind
that the neighboring rulers, especially those
on the borders of our kingdom, are on the

**9:19–27** Despite the statement in v. 18 this letter is not really a supplication. It is rather a notification to all the king's subjects of the appointment of his son as his successor and a request that they be loyal to the new king. Apparently the same letter, which has every appearance of being authentic, was sent to the various peoples throughout the kingdom, with only a few words of address changed for each group.

---

*i:* Jb 38:8–11; Ps 65:6–7; Is 40:12. *j:* Jdt 16:17; Sir 7:17; Is 14:11; 66:24; Acts 12:23. *k:* Dn 4:31–34.

watch for opportunities and waiting to see what will happen. I have therefore appointed as king my son Antiochus, whom I have often before entrusted and commended to most of you, when I made hurried visits to the outlying provinces. I have written to him what is written here. [26]Therefore I beg and entreat each of you to remember the general and individual benefits you have received, and to continue to show goodwill toward me and my son. [27]I am confident that, following my policy, he will treat you with equity and kindness in his relations with you."

[28]So this murderer and blasphemer, after extreme sufferings, such as he had inflicted on others, died a miserable death in the mountains of a foreign land. [29]His foster brother* Philip brought the body home; but fearing Antiochus' son, he later withdrew into Egypt, to Ptolemy Philometor.[l]

See RG 165-67

### CHAPTER 10

*Purification of the Temple.* [1][m]When Maccabeus and his companions, under the Lord's leadership, had recovered the temple and the city, [2]they destroyed the altars erected by the foreigners in the marketplace and the sacred shrines. [3]After purifying the temple, they made another altar. Then, with fire struck from flint, they offered sacrifice for the first time in two years,* burned incense, and lighted lamps. They also set out the showbread. [4]When they had done this, they prostrated themselves and begged the Lord that they might never again fall into such misfortunes, and that if they should sin at any time, he might chastise them with moderation and not hand them over to blasphemous and barbarous Gentiles. [5]On the anniversary of the day on which the temple had been profaned by the foreigners, that is, the twenty-fifth of the same month Kislev, the purification of the temple took place. [6]The Jews celebrated joyfully for eight days as on the feast of Booths, remembering how, a little while before, they had spent the feast of Booths living like wild animals in the mountains and in caves. [7]Carrying rods entwined with leaves,* beautiful branches and palms, they sang hymns of grateful praise to him who had successfully brought about the purification of his own place. [8]By public decree and vote they prescribed that the whole Jewish nation should celebrate these days every year. [9]Such was the end of Antiochus surnamed Epiphanes.

## VI. Renewed Persecution

***Accession of Antiochus V.*** [10]Now we shall relate what happened under Antiochus Eupator, the son of that godless man, and shall give a summary of the chief evils caused by the wars. [11]When Eupator succeeded to the kingdom, he put a certain Lysias in charge of the government as commander-in-chief of Coelesyria and Phoenicia. [12]Ptolemy, called Macron,* had taken the lead in treating the Jews fairly because of the previous injustice that had been done them, and he endeavored to have peaceful relations with them. [13]As a result, he was accused before Eupator by the King's Friends. In fact, on all sides he heard himself called a traitor for having abandoned Cyprus, which Philometor had entrusted to him, and for having gone over to Antiochus Epiphanes. Since he could not command the respect due to his high office, he ended his life by taking poison.

***Victory over the Idumeans.**** [14][n]When Gorgias became governor of the region, he employed foreign troops and used every opportunity to attack the Jews. [15]At the same time the Idumeans, who held some strategic strongholds, were harassing the Jews; they welcomed fugitives from Jerusalem and endeavored to continue the war. [16]Maccabeus

**9:29 Foster brother**: an honorary title conferred by the king on prominent courtiers, whether or not they had been raised with him. Philip tried to seize control of Antioch from the young Antiochus V (1 Mc 6:55–56, 63) and fled to Egypt when he failed.

**10:3 Two years**: three years according to 1 Mc 1:54 and 4:52.

**10:7 Rods entwined with leaves**: the wreathed wands (*thyrsoi*) carried in processions honoring Dionysus (6:7) were apparently not regarded as distinctively pagan.

**10:12 Ptolemy, called Macron**: son of Dorymenes (4:45); he supported Antiochus IV in 168 B.C. during his invasion of Cyprus.

**10:14–23** Probably the same campaign of Judas against the Idumeans that is mentioned in 1 Mc 5:1–3.

*l:* 1 Mc 6:55–56, 63. *m:* 1 Mc 4:36–61. *n:* 1 Mc 5:3–5.

and his companions, after public prayers
asking God to be their ally, moved quickly
against the strongholds of the Idumeans.
17Attacking vigorously, they gained control
of the places, drove back all who were fighting on the walls, and cut down those who
opposed them, killing no fewer than twenty
thousand. 18When at least nine thousand
took refuge in two very strong towers, well
equipped to sustain a siege, 19Maccabeus
left Simon and Joseph, along with Zacchaeus and his forces, in sufficient numbers to
besiege them, while he himself went off to
places where he was more urgently needed.
20But some of those in Simon's force who
were lovers of money let themselves be
bribed by some of those in the towers; on receiving seventy thousand drachmas, they allowed a number of them to escape. 21When
Maccabeus was told what had happened, he
assembled the rulers of the people and accused those men of having sold their kindred
for money by setting their enemies free to
fight against them. 22So he put them to death
as traitors, and without delay captured the
two towers. 23As he was successful at arms
in all his undertakings, he destroyed more
than twenty thousand in the two strongholds.

***Victory over Timothy.*** 24Timothy, who had
previously been defeated by the Jews,* gathered a tremendous force of foreign troops
and collected a large number of cavalry from
Asia; then he appeared in Judea, ready to
conquer it by force. 25At his approach, Maccabeus and his companions made supplication to God, sprinkling earth upon their
heads and girding their loins in sackcloth.
26Lying prostrate at the foot of the altar, they
begged him to be gracious to them, and to be
an enemy to their enemies, and a foe to their
foes, as the law declares.[o] 27After the prayer,
they took up their weapons and advanced a
considerable distance from the city, halting
when they were close to the enemy. 28As
soon as dawn broke,* the armies joined battle, the one having as pledge of success and
victory not only their valor but also their reliance on the Lord, and the other taking fury
as their leader in the fight.
29[p] In the midst of the fierce battle, there
appeared to the enemy five majestic men
from the heavens riding on golden-bridled
horses, leading the Jews. 30They surrounded
Maccabeus, and shielding him with their
own armor, kept him from being wounded.
They shot arrows and hurled thunderbolts at
the enemy, who were bewildered and
blinded, routed in utter confusion. 31Twenty
thousand five hundred of their foot soldiers
and six hundred cavalry were slain.
32Timothy, however, fled to a well-fortified stronghold called Gazara, where
Chaereas was in command.[q] 33For four days
Maccabeus and his forces eagerly besieged
the fortress. 34Those inside, relying on the
strength of the place, kept repeating outrageous blasphemies and uttering abominable
words. 35When the fifth day dawned, twenty
young men in the army of Maccabeus, angered over such blasphemies, bravely
stormed the wall and with savage fury cut
down everyone they encountered. 36Simi-
larly, others climbed up and swung around
on the defenders; they put the towers to the
torch, spread the fire and burned the blasphemers alive. Still others broke down the
gates and let in the rest of the troops, who
took possession of the city. 37Timothy had
hidden in a cistern, but they killed* him,
along with his brother Chaereas, and Apol-
lophanes. 38On completing these exploits,
they blessed, with hymns of grateful praise,
the Lord who shows great kindness to Israel
and grants them victory.

## CHAPTER 11

See RG 165–67

***Defeat of Lysias.**** 1[r] Very soon afterward, Lysias, guardian and kinsman of the

**10:24 Timothy, who had previously been defeated by the Jews**: as recounted in 8:30–33.

**10:28 As soon as dawn broke**: the same battle at dawn as in 1 Mc 5:30–34.

**10:37 Timothy . . . they killed**: apparently Timothy is still alive in 12:2, 18–25. Perhaps there was more than one Timothy. Or the present passage is not in chronological order. Gazara, v. 32 (Gezer), was not captured by the Jews until much later (cf. 1 Mc 9:50–52; 13:53). See 1 Mc 5:8 for the capture of Jazer.

**11:1–12** The defeat of Lysias at Beth-zur probably oc-

*o:* Ex 23:22. *p:* 2 Mc 3:24–26; 5:2–3; 11:8. *q:* 1 Mc 13:43–48. *r:* 1 Mc 4:26–35.

**Peace with the Syrians**

FIRST MACCABEES GIVES no indication that Lysias thought the Hebrews were invincible (11:13). He returns undaunted in 2 Mc 13. Second Maccabees never acknowledges the defeats of the Maccabees at Bethzechariah (1 Mc 6:32–47) or at Mount Azotus where Judas was killed (1 Mc 9:11–22).

king and head of the government, being
greatly displeased at what had happened,
2 mustered about eighty thousand infantry
and all his cavalry and marched against the
Jews. His plan was to make their city a
Greek settlement; 3 to levy tribute on the
temple, as he did on the shrines of the other
nations; and to put the high priesthood up for
sale every year.[s] 4 He did not take God's
power into account at all, but felt exultant
confidence in his myriads of foot soldiers,
his thousands of cavalry, and his eighty elephants.[t] 5 So he invaded Judea, and when he
reached Beth-zur, a fortified place about five
stadia* from Jerusalem, launched a strong attack against it.
6 When Maccabeus and his companions
learned that Lysias was besieging the strongholds, they and all the people begged the
Lord with lamentations and tears to send a
good angel to save Israel.[u] 7 Maccabeus himself was the first to take up arms, and he exhorted the others to join him in risking their
lives to help their kindred. Then they resolutely set out together. 8 Suddenly, while
they were still near Jerusalem, a horseman
appeared at their head, clothed in white garments and brandishing gold weapons.[v]
9 Then all of them together thanked the merciful God, and their hearts were filled with
such courage that they were ready to assault
not only human beings but even the most
savage beasts, or even walls of iron. 10 Now
that the Lord had shown mercy toward them,
they advanced in battle order with the aid of
their heavenly ally. 11 Hurling themselves
upon the enemy like lions, they laid low
eleven thousand foot soldiers and sixteen
hundred cavalry, and put all the rest to flight.
12 Most of those who survived were wounded
and disarmed, while Lysias himself escaped
only by shameful flight.
*Peace Negotiations.* 13[w] But Lysias was
not a stupid man. He reflected on the defeat
he had suffered, and came to realize that the
Hebrews were invincible because the
mighty God was their ally. He therefore sent
a message 14 persuading them to settle everything on just terms, and promising to persuade the king also, and to induce him to become their friend. 15 Maccabeus, solicitous
for the common good, agreed to all that Lysias proposed; and the king granted on behalf
of the Jews all the written requests of Maccabeus to Lysias.
16 These are the terms of the letter which
Lysias wrote to the Jews: "Lysias sends
greetings to the Jewish people. 17 John and
Absalom, your envoys, have presented your
signed communication and asked about the
matters contained in it. 18 Whatever had to be
referred to the king I called to his attention,
and the things that were acceptable he has
granted. 19 If you maintain your loyalty to the
government, I will endeavor to further your
interests in the future. 20 On the details of
these matters I have authorized my representatives, as well as your envoys, to confer
with you. 21 Farewell." The one hundred and
forty-eighth year,* the twenty-fourth of
Dioscorinthius.
22 The king's letter read thus: "King Antiochus sends greetings to his brother Lysias.
23 Now that our father has taken his place

curred before the purification of the Temple; cf. 1 Mc 4:26–35.

**11:5 Five stadia**: one stadium is equal to about six hundred six feet. The actual distance to Beth-zur is about twenty miles.

**11:21 The one hundred and forty-eighth year**: 164 B.C. The reading of the name of the month and its position in the calendar are uncertain. The most likely chronological sequence of the four letters is vv. 16–21; vv. 34–38; vv. 27–33; vv. 22–26.

*s:* 2 Mc 4:7–8, 23–24. *t:* 1 Mc 3:34. *u:* Ex 23:20. *v:* 2 Mc 3:24–26; 5:2–3; 10:29–30. *w:* 1 Mc 6:57–61.

## Four Letters

THE DOCUMENTS INSERTED in vv. 16–38 are authentic letters, but the chronology is confused. The first, third, and fourth letters are dated to the year 148 of the Seleucid era, or 165–164 B.C., at the beginning of the revolt against Epiphanes. The second letter is authored by Antiochus V Eupator after the death of Epiphanes. The letter of Eupator formally abandons the attempt to compel the Jews to follow a Greek way of life. The third letter documents an earlier attempt by Epiphanes to put an end to the persecution and war, at the urging of Menelaus. This letter may represent the first contact between the Romans and the Jews. It implies recognition of the Jews as a people and sets the stage for their later treaty with Rome (1 Mc 8).

among the gods, we wish the subjects of our
kingdom to be undisturbed in conducting
their own affairs. 24We have heard that the
Jews do not agree with our father's change
to Greek customs but prefer their own way
of life. They are petitioning us to let them retain their own customs. 25Since we desire
that this people too should be undisturbed,
our decision is that their temple be restored
to them and that they live in keeping with the
customs of their ancestors. 26Accordingly,
please send them messengers to give them
our assurances of friendship, so that, when
they learn of our decision, they may have
nothing to worry about but may contentedly
go about their own business."
27The king's letter to the people was as
follows: "King Antiochus sends greetings to
the Jewish senate and to the rest of the Jews.
28If you are well, it is what we desire. We too
are in good health. 29Menelaus has told us of
your wish to return home and attend to your
own affairs. 30Therefore, those who return
by the thirtieth of Xanthicus will have our
assurance of full permission 31to observe
their dietary and other laws, just as before,
and none of the Jews shall be molested in
any way for faults committed through ignorance. 32I have also sent Menelaus to reassure you. 33Farewell." In the one hundred
and forty-eighth year, the fifteenth of Xanthicus.*
34The Romans also sent them a letter as
follows: "Quintus Memmius and Titus
Manius, legates of the Romans, send greetings to the Jewish people. 35What Lysias,
kinsman of the king, has granted you, we
also approve. 36But for the matters that he
decided should be submitted to the king,
send someone to us immediately with your
decisions so that we may present them to
your advantage, for we are on our way to
Antioch. 37Make haste, then, to send us
those who can inform us of your preference.
38Farewell." In the one hundred and forty-
eighth year, the fifteenth of Xanthicus.*

## CHAPTER 12

See RG 165–67

*Incidents at Joppa and Jamnia.* 1After
these agreements were made, Lysias returned to the king, and the Jews went about
their farming. 2But some of the local governors, Timothy and Apollonius, son of Gennaeus,* as also Hieronymus and Demophon,
to say nothing of Nicanor, the commander of
the Cyprians, would not allow them to live
in peace and quiet.
3Some people of Joppa also committed
this outrage: they invited the Jews who lived
among them, together with their wives and
children, to embark on boats which they had
provided. There was no hint of enmity toward them. 4This was done by public vote of
the city. When the Jews, wishing to live on
friendly terms and not suspecting anything,
accepted the invitation, the people of Joppa

**11:33** The date, which is the same as the date of the Romans' letter (v. 38), cannot be correct. The king's letter must be connected with the peace treaty of the one hundred forty-ninth year of the Seleucid era, i.e., 163 B.C. Perhaps the mention of the month of Xanthicus in the body of the letter (v. 30) caused the date of the Romans' letter to be transferred to this one.

**11:38** The date is March 12, 164 B.C.

**12:2 Apollonius, son of Gennaeus**: not the Apollonius who was the son of Menestheus (4:21). **Nicanor**: probably distinct from the Nicanor of 14:2.

**The Massacre at Joppa**

SECOND MACCABEES IS careful to point out that the Jews were willing to live quietly and at peace. The incident in ch 12 at Joppa, modern Tel Aviv, is one of the earliest outright attacks on a Jewish community in a Greek city.

took them out to sea and drowned at least two hundred of them.

5 As soon as Judas heard of the barbarous deed perpetrated against his compatriots, he summoned his men; 6 and after calling upon God, the just judge, he marched against the murderers of his kindred. In a night attack he set the harbor on fire, burned the boats, and put to the sword those who had taken refuge there. 7 Because the gates of the town were shut, he withdrew, intending to come back later and wipe out the entire population of Joppa.

8 On hearing that the people of Jamnia planned in the same way to wipe out the Jews who lived among them, 9 he attacked the Jamnians by night, setting fire to the harbor and the fleet, so that the glow of the flames was visible as far as Jerusalem, thirty miles away.

*More Victories by Judas.* 10[x] When the Jews had gone about a mile from there* in the march against Timothy, they were attacked by Arabians numbering at least five thousand foot soldiers and five hundred cavalry. 11 After a hard fight, Judas and his companions, with God's help, were victorious. The defeated nomads begged Judas to give pledges of friendship, and they promised to supply the Jews with livestock and to be of service to them in any other way. 12 Realizing that they could indeed be useful in many respects, Judas agreed to make peace with them. After the pledges of friendship had been exchanged, the Arabians withdrew to their tents.

13 He also attacked a certain city called Caspin, fortified with earthworks and walls and inhabited by a mixed population of Gentiles. 14 Relying on the strength of their walls and their supply of provisions, the besieged treated Judas and his men with contempt, insulting them and even uttering blasphemies and profanity. 15 But Judas and his men invoked the aid of the great Sovereign of the world, who, in the days of Joshua, overthrew Jericho without battering rams or siege engines; then they furiously stormed the walls.[y] 16 Capturing the city by the will of God, they inflicted such indescribable slaughter on it that the adjacent pool, which was about a quarter of a mile wide, seemed to be filled with the blood that flowed into it.

17[z] When they had gone on some ninety miles, they reached Charax, where there were certain Jews known as Toubians.*[a] 18 But they did not find Timothy in that region, for he had already departed from there without having done anything except to leave behind in one place a very strong garrison. 19 But Dositheus and Sosipater, two of Maccabeus' captains, marched out and destroyed the force of more than ten thousand men that Timothy had left in the stronghold. 20 Meanwhile, Maccabeus divided his army into cohorts, with a commander over each cohort, and went in pursuit of Timothy, who had a force of a hundred and twenty thousand foot soldiers and twenty-five hundred cavalry. 21 When Timothy learned of the approach of Judas, he sent on ahead of him the women and children, as well as the baggage, to a place called Karnion, which was hard to besiege and even hard to reach because of the difficult terrain of that region. 22 But when Judas' first cohort appeared, the enemy was overwhelmed with fear and terror at the manifestation of the all-seeing One.

**12:10 From there**: not from Jamnia (vv. 8–9) or Joppa (vv. 3–7), but from a place in Transjordan; vv. 10–26 parallel the account given in 1 Mc 5:9–13, 24–54 of Judas' campaign in northern Transjordan.

**12:17 Certain Jews known as Toubians**: because they lived "in the land of Tob" (1 Mc 5:13).

*x:* 1 Mc 5:24–36. *y:* Jos 6:1–21. *z:* 1 Mc 5:37–44. *a:* 1 Mc 5:13.

Scattering in every direction, they rushed away in such headlong flight that in many cases they wounded one another, pierced by the points of their own swords. 23Judas pressed the pursuit vigorously, putting the sinners to the sword and destroying as many as thirty thousand men.

24Timothy himself fell into the hands of those under Dositheus and Sosipater; but with great cunning, he begged them to spare his life and let him go, because he had in his power the parents and relatives of many of them, and would show them no consideration. 25When he had fully confirmed his solemn pledge to restore them unharmed, they let him go for the sake of saving their relatives.

26[b] Judas then marched to Karnion and the shrine of Atargatis,* where he killed twenty-five thousand people. 27After the defeat and destruction of these, he moved his army to Ephron, a fortified city inhabited by Lysias and people of many nationalities. Robust young men took up their posts in defense of the walls, from which they fought valiantly; inside were large supplies of war machines and missiles. 28But the Jews, invoking the Sovereign who powerfully shatters the might of enemies, got possession of the city and slaughtered twenty-five thousand of the people in it.

29Then they set out from there and hastened on to Scythopolis,* seventy-five miles from Jerusalem. 30But when the Jews who lived there testified to the goodwill shown by the Scythopolitans and to their kind treatment even in times of adversity, 31Judas and his men thanked them and exhorted them to be well disposed to their nation in the future also. Finally they arrived in Jerusalem, shortly before the feast of Weeks.

32After this feast, also called Pentecost, they lost no time in marching against Gorgias, governor of Idumea, 33who opposed them with three thousand foot soldiers and four hundred cavalry. 34In the ensuing battle, a few of the Jews were slain. 35A man called Dositheus, a powerful horseman and one of Bacenor's men,* caught hold of Gorgias, grasped his military cloak and dragged him along by brute strength, intending to capture the vile wretch alive, when a Thracian horseman attacked Dositheus and cut off his arm at the shoulder. Then Gorgias fled to Marisa.

36After Esdris and his men had been fighting for a long time and were weary, Judas called upon the Lord to show himself their ally and leader in the battle. 37Then, raising a battle cry in his ancestral language, and with hymns, he charged Gorgias' men when they were not expecting it and put them to flight.

***Expiation for the Dead.*** 38Judas rallied his army and went to the city of Adullam. As the seventh day was approaching, they purified themselves according to custom and kept the sabbath there. 39On the following day, since the task had now become urgent, Judas and his companions went to gather up the bodies of the fallen and bury them with their kindred in their ancestral tombs. 40But under the tunic of each of the dead they found amulets sacred to the idols of Jamnia, which the law forbids the Jews to wear. So it was clear to all that this was why these men had fallen.[c] 41They all therefore praised the ways of the Lord, the just judge who brings to light the things that are hidden. 42* Turning to supplication, they prayed that the sinful deed might be fully blotted out. The noble Judas exhorted the people to keep themselves free from sin, for they had seen with their own eyes what had happened because of the sin of those who had fallen.[d] 43He then took up a collection among all his soldiers, amounting to two thousand silver drachmas, which

**12:26 Atargatis**: a Syrian goddess, represented by the body of a fish, who in Hellenistic times was identified with Astarte and Artemis.

**12:29 Scythopolis**: the Greek name of the city of Beth-shan; cf. 1 Mc 5:52.

**12:35 One of Bacenor's men**: certain ancient witnesses to the text have "one of the Toubians"; cf. v. 17.

**12:42–45** This is the earliest statement of the doctrine that prayers (v. 42) and sacrifices (v. 43) for the dead are efficacious. Judas probably intended his purification offering to ward off punishment from the living. The author, however, uses the story to demonstrate belief in the resurrection of the just (7:9, 14, 23, 36), and in the possibility of expiation for the sins of otherwise good people who have died. This belief is similar to, but not quite the same as, the Catholic doctrine of purgatory.

*b:* 1 Mc 5:45–54. *c:* Dt 7:25–26. *d:* Jos 7:1–26.

he sent to Jerusalem to provide for an expiatory sacrifice. In doing this he acted in a very excellent and noble way, inasmuch as he had the resurrection in mind; [44]for if he were not expecting the fallen to rise again, it would have been superfluous and foolish to pray for the dead. [45]But if he did this with a view to the splendid reward that awaits those who had gone to rest in godliness, it was a holy and pious thought. [46]Thus he made atonement for the dead that they might be absolved from their sin.

See RG 165–67

## CHAPTER 13

*Death of Menelaus.* [1][e] In the one hundred and forty-ninth year,* Judas and his men learned that Antiochus Eupator was invading Judea with a large force, [2]and that with him was Lysias, his guardian, who was in charge of the government. They led* a Greek army of one hundred and ten thousand foot soldiers, fifty-three hundred cavalry, twenty-two elephants, and three hundred chariots armed with scythes.

[3]Menelaus also joined them, and with great duplicity kept urging Antiochus on, not for the welfare of his country, but in the hope of being established in office. [4]But the King of kings[f] aroused the anger of Antiochus against the scoundrel. When the king was shown by Lysias that Menelaus was to blame for all the trouble, he ordered him to be taken to Beroea* and executed there in the customary local method. [5]There is at that place a tower seventy-five feet high, full of ashes,* with a circular rim sloping down steeply on all sides toward the ashes. [6]Anyone guilty of sacrilege or notorious for certain other crimes is brought up there and then hurled down to destruction. [7]In such a manner was Menelaus, that transgressor of the law, fated to die, deprived even of burial. [8]It was altogether just that he who had committed so many sins against the altar with its pure fire and ashes, in ashes should meet his death.

*Battle near Modein.* [9]The king was advancing, his mind full of savage plans for inflicting on the Jews things worse than those they suffered in his father's time. [10]When Judas learned of this, he urged the people to call upon the Lord day and night, now more than ever, to help them when they were about to be deprived of their law, their country, and their holy temple; [11]and not to allow this people, which had just begun to revive, to be subjected again to blasphemous Gentiles. [12]When they had all joined in doing this, and had implored the merciful Lord continuously with weeping and fasting and prostrations for three days, Judas encouraged them and told them to stand ready.

[13]After a private meeting with the elders, he decided that, before the king's army could invade Judea and take possession of the city, the Jews should march out and settle the matter with God's help. [14]Leaving the outcome to the Creator of the world, and exhorting his followers to fight nobly to death for the laws, the temple, the city, the country, and the government, he encamped near Modein. [15]Giving his troops the battle cry "God's Victory," he made a night attack on the king's pavilion with a picked force of the bravest young men and killed about two thousand in the camp. He also stabbed the lead elephant and its rider.[g] [16]Finally they withdrew in triumph,* having filled the camp with terror and confusion. [17]Day was just breaking when this was accomplished with the help and protection of the Lord.

*Treaty with Antiochus V.* [18][h] The king, having had a taste of the Jews' boldness, tried to take their positions by a stratagem. [19]So he marched against Beth-zur, a strong fortress of the Jews; but he was driven back, checked, and defeated. [20]Judas sent supplies to the men inside, [21]but Rhodocus, of the

**13:1 In the one hundred and forty-ninth year**: 163/162 B.C.

**13:2 They led**: the Greek means literally "each (of them) led," but it is unlikely that the author meant the already immense numbers to be doubled; the numbers are similar to those in 1 Mc 6:30.

**13:4 Beroea**: the Greek name of Aleppo in Syria.

**13:5 Ashes**: probably smoldering ashes; the tower resembles the ancient Persian fire towers.

**13:16 They withdrew in triumph**: according to 1 Mc 6:47 they fled.

**13:21 Military secrets**: probably about the lack of provisions in the besieged city; cf. 1 Mc 6:49.

---

*e:* 1 Mc 6:28–54. *f:* 1 Tm 6:15; Rev 17:14; 19:16. *g:* 1 Mc 6:43–46. *h:* 1 Mc 6:48–53.

**Alcimus and Nicanor**

SECOND MACCABEES IGNORES the slaughter of the Hasidim, perhaps because it was a setback for the Jews. Chapter 14 identifies the Hasidim closely with Judas (v. 6) and ignores that they were the first to make peace. A Hellenizer like Alcimus may well have overlooked differences within the resistance movement.

Jewish army, betrayed military secrets* to
the enemy. He was found out, arrested, and
imprisoned. [22]The king made a second attempt by negotiating with the people of
Beth-zur. After giving them his pledge and
receiving theirs, he withdrew [23]and attacked
Judas' men. But he was defeated. Next he
heard that Philip, who was left in charge of
the government in Antioch, had rebelled.
Dismayed, he negotiated with the Jews, submitted to their terms, and swore to observe
all their rights. Having come to this agreement, he offered a sacrifice, and honored the
sanctuary and the place with a generous donation. [24]He received Maccabeus, and left
Hegemonides as governor of the territory
from Ptolemais to the region of the Gerrhenes.* [25]When he came to Ptolemais, the
people of Ptolemais were angered by the
peace treaty; in fact they were so indignant
that they wanted to annul its provisions.
[26]But Lysias took the platform, defended the
treaty as well as he could and won them over
by persuasion. After calming them and gaining their goodwill, he returned to Antioch.
That is the story of the king's attack and
withdrawal.

## CHAPTER 14

See RG 165–67

[1][i]Three years later,* Judas and his
companions learned that Demetrius, son of
Seleucus, had sailed into the port of Tripolis
with a powerful army and a fleet, [2]and that he
had occupied the country, after doing away
with Antiochus and his guardian Lysias.
[3]A certain Alcimus, a former high priest,*
who had willfully incurred defilement before the time of the revolt, realized that there
was no way for him to be safe and regain access to the holy altar. [4]So he went to King
Demetrius around the one hundred and fifty-
first year and presented him with a gold
crown and a palm branch, as well as some of
the customary olive branches from the temple. On that day he kept quiet.[j] [5]But he found
an opportunity to further his mad scheme
when he was invited to the council by
Demetrius and questioned about the dispositions and intentions of the Jews. He replied:
[6]"Those Jews called Hasideans, led by Judas
Maccabeus,* are warmongers, who stir up
sedition and keep the kingdom from enjoying peace.[k] [7]For this reason, now that I am
deprived of my ancestral dignity, that is to
say, the high priesthood, I have come here,
[8]first, out of my genuine concern for the
king's interests, and second, out of consideration for my own compatriots, since our entire nation is suffering no little affliction
from the rash conduct of the people just
mentioned. [9]When you have informed yourself in detail on these matters, O king, provide for our country and its hard-pressed
people with the same gracious consideration
that you show toward all. [10]As long as Judas
is around, it is impossible for the government to enjoy peace." [11]When he had said
this, the other Friends who were hostile to
Judas quickly added fuel to Demetrius' indignation.

***Dealings with Nicanor.*** [12][l]The king immediately chose Nicanor, who had been in

**13:24 Gerrhenes**: probably the inhabitants of Gerar, southeast of Gaza.

**14:1 Three years later**: actually, Demetrius (I Soter), son of Seleucus (IV), landed at Tripolis in the year 151 of the Seleucid era (1 Mc 14:4), i.e., 162/161 B.C.; cf. 1 Mc 7:1–7.

**14:3 Alcimus, a former high priest**: he was apparently appointed high priest by Antiochus V after Menelaus was executed, and then deposed for collaborating with the Seleucids.

**14:6 Hasideans, led by Judas Maccabeus**: according to 1 Mc 2:42 and 7:12–17, the Hasideans were a party separate from the Maccabees.

*i*: 1 Mc 7:1–7. *j*: 1 Mc 7:5–7, 25. *k*: 1 Mc 2:42; 7:12–17. *l*: 2 Mc 8:9; 1 Mc 3:38; 7:26–27.

command of the elephants, and appointed
him governor of Judea. He sent him off
[13]with orders to put Judas to death, to disperse his followers, and to set up Alcimus as
high priest of the great temple. [14]The Gentiles from Judea, who had fled before Judas,
flocked to Nicanor, thinking that the misfortunes and calamities of the Jews would mean
prosperity for themselves.
[15][m] When the Jews heard of Nicanor's
coming, and that the Gentiles were rallying
to him, they sprinkled themselves with earth
and prayed to him who established his people forever, and who always comes to the aid
of his heritage by manifesting himself. [16]At
their leader's command, they set out at once
from there and came upon the enemy at the
village of Adasa. [17]Judas' brother Simon had
engaged Nicanor, but he suffered a slight
setback because of the sudden appearance of
the enemy.
[18]However, when Nicanor heard of the
valor of Judas and his companions, and the
great courage with which they fought for
their country, he shrank from deciding the
issue by bloodshed. [19]So he sent Posidonius,
Theodotus and Mattathias to exchange
pledges of friendship. [20]After a long discussion of the terms, each leader communicated
them to his troops; and when general agreement was expressed, they assented to the
treaty. [21]A day was set on which the leaders
would meet by themselves. From each side a
chariot came forward, and thrones were set
in place. [22]Judas had posted armed men in
readiness at strategic points for fear that the
enemy might suddenly commit some treachery. But the conference was held in the
proper way.
[23]Nicanor stayed on in Jerusalem, where
he did nothing out of place. He disbanded
the throngs of people who gathered around
him; [24]and he always kept Judas in his company, for he felt affection* for the man. [25]He
urged him to marry and have children; so Judas married and settled into an ordinary life.
***Nicanor's Threat Against Judas.*** [26]When
Alcimus saw their mutual goodwill, he took
the treaty that had been made, went to
Demetrius, and said that Nicanor was plotting against the government, for he had appointed Judas, that conspirator against the
kingdom, as his successor. [27]Stirred up by
the villain's slander, the king became enraged. He wrote to Nicanor, stating that he
was displeased with the treaty, and ordering
him to send Maccabeus at once as a prisoner
to Antioch. [28]When this message reached
Nicanor he was dismayed and troubled at the
thought of annulling his agreement with a
man who had done no wrong. [29]However,
there was no way of opposing the king, so he
watched for an opportunity to carry out this
order by a stratagem. [30]But Maccabeus,
noticing that Nicanor was more harsh in his
dealings with him, and acting with unaccus-
tomed rudeness when they met, concluded
that this harshness was not a good sign. So
he gathered together not a few of his men,
and went into hiding from Nicanor.
[31][n] When Nicanor realized that he had
been cleverly outwitted by the man, he went
to the great and holy temple, at a time when
the priests were offering the customary sacrifices, and ordered them to surrender Judas.
[32]As they declared under oath that they did
not know where the man they sought was,
[33]he stretched out his right arm toward the
temple and swore this oath: "If you do not
hand Judas over to me as prisoner, I will
level this shrine of God to the ground; I will
tear down the altar, and erect here a splendid
temple to Dionysus."
[34]With these words he went away. The
priests stretched out their hands toward
heaven, calling upon the unfailing defender
of our nation in these words: [35]"Lord of all,
though you are in need of nothing, you were
pleased to have a temple for your dwelling
place among us. [36]Therefore, Holy One,
Lord of all holiness, preserve forever undefiled this house, which has been so recently
purified."[o]
***Martyrdom of Razis.**** [37]A certain Razis,
one of the elders of Jerusalem, was denounced to Nicanor as a patriot. A man

**14:24 Affection**: compare 1 Mc 7:26–32, where there is no hint of this cordial relationship between Nicanor and Judas.

**14:37–46** The story of Razis belongs to the "martyrology" class of literature; it is similar to the stories in 6:18–7:42.

*m:* 1 Mc 7:26–32. *n:* 1 Mc 7:30–38. *o:* 2 Mc 15:34.

**Fresh Hope**

JUDAS'S TRUST IN the LORD is contrasted with the hubris of Nicanor (15:6–7). Onias III, the murdered high priest, was glorified in the early chapters of 2 Maccabees. By the time the book was written, however, the high priesthood had been usurped by the Maccabees; 2 Maccabees nonetheless claims the support of the dead high priest. Jeremiah is included because of his association with the temple at the time of the Babylonian attack, and because the sword is the dominant image in an oracle attributed to him in Jeremiah 50:35–38. Ironically, Jeremiah, noted for his opposition to militant resistance, said that God would turn the swords of the defenders against themselves (Jer 2: 4).

highly regarded, he was called a father of the Jews because of his goodwill toward them. [38]In the days before the revolt, he had been convicted of being a Jew, and had risked body and soul in his ardent zeal for Judaism. [39]Nicanor, to show his disdain for the Jews, sent more than five hundred soldiers to arrest him. [40]He thought that by arresting that man he would deal the Jews a hard blow.

[41]But when the troops, on the point of capturing the tower, were forcing the outer gate and calling for fire to set the door ablaze, Razis, now caught on all sides, turned his sword against himself, [42]preferring to die nobly* rather than fall into the hands of vile men and suffer outrages unworthy of his noble birth. [43]In the excitement of the struggle he failed to strike exactly. So while the troops rushed in through the doors, he gallantly ran up to the top of the wall and courageously threw himself down into the crowd. [44]But as they quickly drew back and left an opening, he fell into the middle of the empty space. [45]Still breathing, and inflamed with anger, he got up and ran through the crowd, with blood gushing from his frightful wounds. Then, standing on a steep rock, [46]as he lost the last of his blood, he tore out his entrails and flung them with both hands into the crowd, calling upon the Lord of life and of spirit to give these back to him again. Such was the manner of his death.[p]

## CHAPTER 15

See RG 165–67

*Nicanor's Arrogance.* [1]When Nicanor learned that Judas and his companions were in the territory of Samaria, he decided he could attack them in complete safety on the day of rest. [2]The Jews who were forced to accompany him pleaded, "Do not massacre them so savagely and barbarously, but show respect for the day which the All-seeing has exalted with holiness above all other days." [3]At this the thrice-accursed wretch asked if there was a ruler in heaven who prescribed the keeping of the sabbath day.[q] [4]They replied, "It is the living Lord, the ruler in heaven, who commands the observance of the sabbath day." [5]Then he said, "I, the ruler on earth, command you to take up arms and carry out the king's business." Nevertheless he did not succeed in carrying out his cruel plan.

[6]In his utter boastfulness and arrogance Nicanor had determined to erect a public victory monument* over Judas and his companions. [7]But Maccabeus remained confident, fully convinced that he would receive help from the Lord. [8]He urged his men not to fear the attack of the Gentiles, but mindful of the help they had received in the past from Heaven, to expect now the victory that would be given them by the Almighty. [9]By encouraging them with words from the law and the prophets,* and by reminding them of

**14:42 Die nobly**: Razis's willingness to die nobly rather than to fall into enemy hands had a precedent in Saul (1 Sm 31:4). Razis took his life because he was convinced that God would restore his body in the resurrection of the dead (see 7:11, 22–23; 14:46).

**15:6 Public victory monument**: a heap of stones covered with the arms and armor of the fallen enemy.

**15:9 The law and the prophets**: the first of the three parts

*p:* 2 Mc 7:9–11. *q:* 1 Mc 7:34.

the battles they had already won, he filled them with fresh enthusiasm. [10]Having stirred up their courage, he gave his orders and pointed out at the same time the perfidy of the Gentiles and their violation of oaths. [11]When he had armed each of them, not so much with the security of shield and spear as with the encouragement of noble words, he cheered them all by relating a dream, a kind of waking vision, worthy of belief.

[12]What he saw was this: Onias, the former high priest,* a noble and good man, modest in bearing, gentle in manner, distinguished in speech, and trained from childhood in all that belongs to excellence, was praying with outstretched arms for the whole Jewish community.[r] [13]Then in the same way another man appeared, distinguished by his white hair and dignity, and with an air of wondrous and majestic authority. [14]Onias then said of him, "This is a man* who loves his fellow Jews and fervently prays for the people and the holy city—the prophet of God, Jeremiah." [15]Stretching out his right hand, Jeremiah presented a gold sword to Judas. As he gave it to him he said, [16]"Accept this holy sword as a gift from God; with it you shall shatter your adversaries."

[17]Encouraged by Judas' words, so noble and capable of instilling valor and stirring young hearts to courage, they determined not merely to march, but to charge gallantly and decide the issue by hand-to-hand combat with the utmost courage, since city, sanctuary and temple were in danger. [18]They were not so much concerned about wives and children, or family and relations; their first and foremost fear was for the consecrated sanctuary.[s] [19]Those who were left in the city suffered no less an agony, anxious as they were about the battle in the open country. [20]Everyone now awaited the decisive moment. The enemy were already drawing near with their troops drawn up in battle line, their beasts placed in strategic positions, and their cavalry stationed on the flanks.

*Defeat of Nicanor.* [21]Maccabeus, surveying the hosts before him, the variety of weaponry, and the fierceness of their beasts, stretched out his hands toward heaven and called upon the Lord who works wonders; for he knew that it is not weapons but the Lord's decision that brings victory to those who deserve it. [22]Calling upon God, he spoke in this manner: "You, master, sent your angel in the days of King Hezekiah of Judea, and he slew a hundred and eighty-five thousand men of Sennacherib's camp.[t] [23]And now, Sovereign of the heavens, send a good angel to spread fear and trembling ahead of us. [24]By the might of your arm may those be struck down who have blasphemously come against your holy people!" With these words he ended his prayer.

[25][u]Nicanor and his troops advanced to the sound of trumpets and battle songs. [26]But Judas and his troops met the enemy with supplication and prayers. [27]Fighting with their hands and praying to God with their hearts, they laid low at least thirty-five thousand, and rejoiced greatly over this manifestation of God's power. [28]When the battle was over and they were joyfully departing, they discovered Nicanor fallen there in all his armor; [29]so they raised tumultuous shouts in their ancestral language in praise of the divine Sovereign.

[30]Then Judas, that man who was ever in body and soul the chief defender of his fellow citizens, and had maintained from youth his affection for his compatriots, ordered Nicanor's head and right arm up to the shoulder to be cut off and taken to Jerusalem. [31]When he arrived there, he assembled his compatriots, stationed the priests before the altar, and sent for those in the citadel.* [32]He showed them the vile Nicanor's head and the wretched blasphemer's arm that had been boastfully stretched out against the holy

of the Hebrew Scriptures, called the sacred books (1 Mc 12:9; 2 Mc 2:14).

**15:12 Onias, the former high priest**: Onias III (3:1–40). Evidently the author believed that departed just persons were in some way alive even before their resurrection.

**15:14 A man**: regarded by the postexilic Jews as one of the greatest figures in their history; cf. 2:1; Mt 16:14. **Who . . . prays for the people**: Jeremiah's prayer in heaven has been taken in the Roman Catholic tradition as a biblical witness to the intercession of the saints.

**15:31 Those in the citadel**: presumably Jewish soldiers; actually, the citadel was still in the possession of the Syrians (1 Mc 13:50).

*r:* 2 Mc 3:1–40. *s:* 1 Mc 4:36. *t:* 2 Mc 8:19; 2 Kgs 19:35–36; 1 Mc 7:41–42; Is 37:36–37. *u:* 1 Mc 7:43.

dwelling of the Almighty. [33]He cut out the
tongue of the godless Nicanor, saying he
would feed it piecemeal to the birds and
would hang up the other wages of his folly
opposite the temple. [34]At this, everyone
looked toward heaven and praised the Lord
who manifests himself: “Blessed be the one
who has preserved undefiled his own place!”
[35]Judas hung Nicanor’s head and arm on the
wall of the citadel, a clear and evident sign to
all of the Lord’s help.[v] [36]By public vote it was
unanimously decreed never to let this day
pass unobserved, but to celebrate the thirteenth day of the twelfth month, called Adar
in Aramaic, the eve of Mordecai’s Day.* [w]

## VII. Epilogue

***Compiler’s Apology.*** [37]Since Nicanor’s doings ended in this way, with the city remaining in the possession of the Hebrews from
that time on, I will bring my story to an end
here too. [38][x] If it is well written and to the
point, that is what I wanted; if it is poorly
done and mediocre, that is the best I could
do. [39]Just as it is unpleasant to drink wine by
itself or just water, whereas wine mixed with
water makes a delightful and pleasing drink,
so a skillfully composed story delights the
ears of those who read the work. Let this,
then, be the end.

**15:36 Mordecai’s Day**: the feast of Purim, celebrated on the fourteenth and fifteenth days of Adar (Est 3:7; 9:20–23; F:10).

*v:* 1 Sm 31:9–10. *w:* 1 Mc 7:49. *x:* 2 Mc 2:19–32.

See RG 168–69

# THE WISDOM BOOKS

"Wisdom" is a convenient umbrella term to designate the Books of Job, Proverbs, Ecclesiastes (Qoheleth), Wisdom, and Sirach (Ecclesiasticus). Two other books are often associated with them: Psalms, a collection of mostly devotional lyrics, and the Song of Songs, a collection of love poems. All are marked by a skillful use of parallelism, or verses of balanced and symmetrical phrases. These works have been classified as wisdom or didactic literature, so called because their general purpose is instruction.

A striking feature of the wisdom books is the absence of references to the promises made to the patriarchs or to Moses, or to Sinai or typical items in Israelite tradition; Sirach (chaps. 44–50) and Wisdom (chaps. 10–19) are the exception. Biblical wisdom literature concentrates on daily human experience: how is life to be lived? In this respect it is comparable to other ancient Near Eastern compositions from Mesopotamia and Egypt that also reflect on the problems of everyday life. The literary style is wide-ranging: aphorisms, numerical sayings, paradoxes, instructions, alphabetical and acrostic poems, lively speeches, and so forth. Wisdom itself is an art: how to deal with various situations and achieve a good life. And it is also a teaching: the lessons garnered from experience were transmitted at various levels, from education in the home all the way to training in the court. Belief in the Lord and acceptance of the prevailing codes of conduct were presupposed; they fed into the training of youths. The task of wisdom is character formation: what is the wise path to follow? The lessons are conveyed by observations that challenge as well as by admonitions that warn. Although the need of discipline is underlined, the general approach is persuasion. The pursuit of wisdom demands more than human industry. Paradoxically, it remains also the gift of God (Prv 2:6). Its religious character is indicated by the steady identification of wisdom and virtue (e.g., Prv 10–15).

But wisdom is far more than a practical guide. The strongest personification in the Bible is Woman Wisdom, and she speaks somewhat mysteriously in divine accents about her origins and identity. Her appeal to humanity is sounded in several books: Prv 8; Sir 24; Wis 7–9; Bar 3:9–4:4. She offers "life" to her followers (Prv 8:35, "whoever finds me finds life"). This image of personified Wisdom is reflected in the Logos poem of Jn 1:1–18 and in Paul's reference to Jesus as "the wisdom of God" (1 Cor 1:24, 30). The bearing of wisdom literature on the New Testament is also exemplified in the sayings and parables of Jesus and in the practical admonitions in the Letter of James.

Each book has a distinctive character. Proverbs consists of long poems dealing with moral conduct (chaps. 1–9), which introduce collections of aphorisms (chaps. 10–29) reflecting on the experiences of life. The Book of Job is a literary presentation of the problem of the suffering of the innocent and god-fearing Job. Psalms, the book of prayer par excellence, derives from varied origins, especially liturgical celebrations; it contains personal cries of agony as well as of praise and thanksgiving. Some betray a wisdom influence (e.g., Ps 37), and the very first Psalm serves as an invitation to learn about the ways of the just and wicked in the rest of the psalter. Ecclesiastes examines the hard questions of life, and has become famous for the expressive phrase "vanity of vanities." The Song of Songs is a collection of poems that give meaning to human and divine love (Sg 8:6; Prv 30:18–19). Ben Sira is the only author who identifies himself (Sir 50:27), and circa 200 B.C. he writes a compendium of Jewish wisdom and creation theology. The Wisdom of Solomon was written in Greek against a Hellenistic background, affirming human immortality in terms of a continuing relationship with God. Except for Psalms (of which almost half are attributed to David), Job, and Sirach, the books are attributed to Solomon, but he is not the author. The Solomonic claim is doubtless due to his fame as a wise man, according to 1 Kgs 5:9–14; 10:1–10. Who were the sages? Some were found in ordinary families (father, mother, Prv 1:8; 10:1); others were scribes at court. All contributed, both men (the counselors of Absalom, 2 Sm 16–17; the men of King Hezekiah, Prv 25:1) and also women (the "wise woman" of Abel Beth-maacah, 2 Sm 20:16). The wisdom literature is predominantly a postexilic composition, but the dating is only approximate.

In Jewish tradition, *Megillot* (Scrolls) came to be the accepted term for the five books of Ruth, Song of Songs, Ecclesiastes, Lamentations, and Esther. In the Protestant tradition, Sirach and Wisdom are classified as apocrypha and not printed as a part of Scripture. The Orthodox tradition does accept them, along with other works, such as 3–4 Maccabees and the Prayer of Manasseh.

See RG 169–73

# The Book of Job

The Book of Job, named after its protagonist (apparently not an Israelite; cf. Ez 14:14, 20), is an exquisite dramatic treatment of the problem of the suffering of the innocent. The contents of the book, together with its artistic structure and elegant style, place it among the literary masterpieces of all time. This is a literary composition, and not a transcript of historical events and conversations.

The prologue (chaps. 1–2) provides the setting for Job's testing. When challenged by the satan's questioning of Job's sincerity, the Lord gives leave for a series of catastrophes to afflict Job. Three friends come to console him. Job breaks out in complaint (chap. 3), and a cycle of speeches begins. Job's friends insist that his plight can only be a punishment for personal wrongdoing and an invitation from God to repent. Job rejects their inadequate explanation and challenges God to respond (chaps. 3–31). A young bystander, Elihu, now delivers four speeches in support of the views of the three friends (chaps. 32–37). In response to Job's plea that he be allowed to see God and hear directly the reason for his suffering, the Lord answers (38:1–42:6), not by explaining divine justice, but by cataloguing the wonders of creation. Job is apparently content with this, and, in an epilogue (42:7–17), the Lord restores Job's fortune.

The author or authors of the book are unknown; it was probably composed some time between the seventh and fifth centuries B.C. Its literary pattern, with speeches, prologue and epilogue disposed according to a studied plan, indicates that the purpose of the writing is didactic. But the lessons that the book teaches are not transparent, and different interpretations of the divine speeches and of the final chapter are possible. The Book of Job does not definitively answer the problem of the suffering of the innocent, but challenges readers to come to their own understanding.

The Book of Job can be divided as follows:

I. Prologue (1:1–2:13)
II. First Cycle of Speeches (3:1–14:22)
III. Second Cycle of Speeches (15:1–21:34)
IV. Third Cycle of Speeches (22:1–27:21)
V. The Poem on Wisdom (28:1–28)
VI. Job's Final Summary of His Cause (29:1–31:37)
VII. Elihu's Speeches (32:1–37:24)
VIII. The Lord and Job Meet (38:1–42:6)
IX. Epilogue (42:7–17)

**Who Is Job the Just?**

JOB IS A venerable hero, well known beyond the confines of Israel. His homeland, Uz, is outside the holy land, located to the east, probably in Edom, an area south of the Dead Sea. Job was "blameless and upright," meaning that Job "feared God" and "avoided evil" (1:1).

## I. Prologue

### CHAPTER 1

See RG 169–73

***Job's Piety.*** [1]In the land of Uz* there was a blameless and upright man named Job,[a] who feared God and avoided evil. [2]Seven sons and three daughters were born to him; [3]and he had seven thousand sheep, three thousand camels, five hundred yoke of oxen, five hundred she-donkeys, and a very large household, so that he was greater than anyone in the East.* [4]His sons used to take turns giving feasts, sending invitations to their three sisters to eat and drink with them. [5]And when each feast had run its course, Job would send for them and sanctify them, rising early and offering sacrifices for every one of them. For Job said, "It may be that my children have sinned and cursed* God in their hearts." Job did this habitually.

***The Interview Between the Lord and the Satan.*** [6][b] One day, when the sons of God* came to present themselves before the LORD, the satan also came among them.[c] [7]The LORD said to the satan, "Where have you been?" Then the satan answered the LORD and said,[d] "Roaming the earth and patrolling it." [8]The LORD said to the satan, "Have you noticed my servant Job? There is no one on earth like him, blameless and upright, fearing God and avoiding evil." [9]The satan answered the LORD and said, "Is it for nothing that Job is God-fearing? [10]Have you not surrounded him and his family and all that he has with your protection? You have blessed the work of his hands, and his livestock are spread over the land. [11][e] But now put forth your hand and touch all that he has, and surely he will curse you to your face." [12]The LORD said to the satan, "Very well, all that he has is in your power; only do not lay a hand on him." So the satan went forth from the presence of the LORD.

***The First Trial.*** [13]One day, while his sons and daughters were eating and drinking wine in the house of their eldest brother, [14]a messenger came to Job and said, "The oxen were plowing and the donkeys grazing beside them, [15]and the Sabeans* carried them off in a raid. They put the servants to the sword, and I alone have escaped to tell you." [16]He was still speaking when another came and said, "God's fire has fallen from heaven and struck the sheep and the servants and consumed them; I alone have escaped to tell you." [17]He was still speaking when another came and said, "The Chaldeans* formed three columns, seized the camels, carried them off, and put the servants to the sword; I alone have escaped to tell you." [18]He was still speaking when another came and said, "Your sons and daughters were eating and drinking wine in the house of their eldest brother, [19]and suddenly a great wind came from across the desert and smashed the four corners of the house. It fell upon the young people and they are dead; I alone have escaped to tell you."

***Job's Reaction.*** [20]Then Job arose and tore

**1:1 Uz**: somewhere in Edom or Arabia; see Lam 4:21. **Job**: the name probably means "Where is the (divine) father?" In Hebrew it is almost a homonym with the word for "enemy" (see note on 13:24; cf. 33:10).

**1:3 The East**: that is, east of Palestine.

**1:5 Cursed**: lit., "blessed." So also in v. 11; 2:5, 9.

**1:6 Sons of God**: members of the divine council; see Gn 6:1–4; Dt 32:8; Ps 82:1. **The satan**: lit., "adversary" (as in 1 Kgs 11:14). Here a member of the heavenly court, "the accuser" (Zec 3:1). In later biblical traditions this character will be developed as the devil (Gk. *diabolos*, "adversary").

**1:15 Sabeans**: from southern Arabia.

**1:17 Chaldeans**: from southern Mesopotamia; in the mid-first millennium B.C., synonymous with "Babylonians."

*a:* Jb 2:3. *b:* Jb 2:1–3. *c:* Gn 6:2, 4; Zec 3:1; Lk 22:31; Rev 12:9. *d:* 1 Pt 5:8. *e:* Jb 2:5.

**God Tests Job**

PEOPLE IMAGINED THE heavenly court on the model of an earthly one: Courtiers present themselves before the king and officials report to the LORD (1:6–12). Satan, literally, "the satan" or adversary, is not the enemy of God as in later biblical books, but a member of the court whose particular task it is to watch the actions of humans and report back to the LORD. God is pleased by the utterly just actions of Job, but Satan cynically intimates that Job is doing them only for the abundant blessings he receives in return. God allows Satan to test Job to see whether he, when "touched" (v. 11), will curse God. The reader knows two things that the friends of Job do not: Job is genuinely just, and God is testing him.

his cloak and cut off his hair. He fell to the
ground and worshiped. 21 He said,

"Naked I came forth from my mother's
 womb,[f]
 and naked shall I go back there.*
The LORD gave and the LORD has taken
 away;
 blessed be the name of the LORD!"

22 In all this Job did not sin,[g] nor did he
charge God with wrong.

## CHAPTER 2

See RG 169–73

*The Second Interview.* 1 One day, when
the sons of God[h] came to present themselves
before the LORD, the satan also came with
them. 2 The LORD said to the satan, "Where
have you been?" Then the satan answered the
LORD and said, "Roaming the earth and patrolling it." 3 The LORD said to the satan,
"Have you noticed my servant Job? There is
no one on earth like him, blameless and upright, fearing God and avoiding evil.[i] He still
holds fast to his innocence although you incited me against him to ruin him for nothing." 4 The satan answered the LORD and said,
"Skin for skin!* All that a man has he will
give for his life. 5[j] But put forth your hand
and touch his bone and his flesh. Then surely
he will curse you to your face." 6 And the
LORD said to the satan, "He is in your power;
only spare his life."

*The Second Trial.* 7 So the satan went forth
from the presence of the LORD and struck
Job with severe boils from the soles of his
feet to the crown of his head.

*Job's Reaction.* 8 He took a potsherd to
scrape himself, as he sat among the ashes.
9 Then his wife said to him,[k] "Are you still
holding to your innocence? Curse God and
die!"* 10 But he said to her, "You speak as foolish women do. We accept good things from
God; should we not accept evil?" Through all
this, Job did not sin in what he said.[l]

*Job's Three Friends.* 11 Now when three of
Job's friends heard of all the misfortune that
had come upon him, they set out each one
from his own place: Eliphaz from Teman,*
Bildad from Shuh, and Zophar from Naamath. They met and journeyed together to
give him sympathy and comfort. 12 But
when, at a distance, they lifted up their eyes
and did not recognize him, they began to
weep aloud; they tore their cloaks and threw
dust into the air over their heads. 13 Then
they sat down upon the ground with him
seven days and seven nights, but none of
them spoke a word to him; for they saw how
great was his suffering.

# II. First Cycle of Speeches

## CHAPTER 3

See RG 169–73

*Job's Complaint.* 1 After this, Job
opened his mouth and cursed his day.* 2 Job
spoke out and said:

**1:21 Go back there**: to the earth; cf. Gn 2:7; see note on Sir 40:1.

**2:4 Skin for skin**: a proverbial expression derived perhaps from bartering; the precise meaning is unclear.

**2:9 Curse God and die**: the presupposition is that such blasphemy would be met with immediate death.

**2:11 Teman**: in Edom (see Gn 36:9–11). The Temanites (Jer 49:7; cf. Ob 8) enjoyed a reputation for wisdom. **Shuh** and **Naamath**: locations unknown.

**3:1 His day**: that is, the day of his birth.

*f:* Eccl 5:14; 1 Tm 6:7. *g:* Jb 2:10; Jas 5:11. *h:* Jb 1:6. *i:* Jb 1:1. *j:* Jb 1:11. *k:* Jb 19:17. *l:* Jb 1:22; Sir 2:4.

[3] Perish the day on which I was born,[m]
the night when they said, "The child is a boy!"
[4] May that day be darkness:
may God* above not care for it,
may light not shine upon it!
[5] May darkness and gloom claim it,
clouds settle upon it,
blackness of day* affright it!
[6] May obscurity seize that night;
may it not be counted among the days of the year,
nor enter into the number of the months!
[7] May that night be barren;
let no joyful outcry greet it!
[8] Let them curse it who curse the Sea,
those skilled at disturbing Leviathan!*
[9] May the stars of its twilight be darkened;
may it look for daylight, but have none,
nor gaze on the eyes of the dawn,
[10] Because it did not keep shut the doors of the womb
to shield my eyes from trouble!
[11] Why did I not die at birth,[n]
come forth from the womb and expire?
[12] Why did knees receive me,
or breasts nurse me?
[13] For then I should have lain down and been tranquil;
had I slept, I should then have been at rest
[14] With kings and counselors of the earth
who rebuilt what were ruins
[15] Or with princes who had gold
and filled their houses with silver.
[16] Or why was I not buried away like a stillborn child,
like babies that have never seen the light?
[17] There* the wicked cease from troubling,
there the weary are at rest.
[18] The captives are at ease together,
and hear no overseer's voice.
[19] Small and great are there;
the servant is free from the master.
[20] Why is light given to the toilers,
life to the bitter in spirit?
[21] They wait for death and it does not come;
they search for it more than for hidden treasures.
[22] They rejoice in it exultingly,
and are glad when they find the grave:
[23] A man whose path is hidden from him,
one whom God has hemmed in!*
[24] For to me sighing comes more readily than food;
my groans well forth like water.
[25] For what I feared overtakes me;
what I dreaded comes upon me.
[26] I have no peace nor ease;
I have no rest, for trouble has come!

## CHAPTER 4

See RG 169–73

*Eliphaz's First Speech.* [1] Then Eliphaz the Temanite answered and said:

[2] If someone attempts a word with you,
would you mind?
How can anyone refrain from speaking?
[3] Look, you have instructed many,
and made firm their feeble hands.
[4] Your words have upheld the stumbler;
you have strengthened faltering knees.
[5] But now that it comes to you, you are impatient;
when it touches you, you are dismayed.
[6] Is not your piety a source of confidence,
and your integrity of life your hope?
[7] Reflect now, what innocent person perishes?[o]
Where are the upright destroyed?
[8] As I see it, those who plow mischief
and sow trouble will reap them.
[9] By the breath of God they perish,[p]

**3:4 God**: in Heb. *'Eloah*, another name for the divinity, used frequently in Job.

**3:5 Blackness of day**: that is, an eclipse.

**3:8 Leviathan**: a mythological sea monster symbolizing primeval chaos. It is parallel to Sea, which was the opponent of Baal in the Ugaritic legends. Cf. 9:13; 26:13; 40:25–41:26; Ps 74:13–14; 104:26; Is 27:1.

**3:17 There**: in death.

**3:23 Hemmed in**: contrast the same verb as used in 1:10.

*m:* Jer 20:14. *n:* Jb 10:18–19. *o:* Ps 37:25. *p:* Ps 18:16; Is 11:4; 2 Thes 2:8.

ELIPHAZ BEGINS WITH an attack on Job's motives without bothering to listen to his words. The deterioration of Job's relationship to his friends increases his interest in exploring his relationship to God.

and by the blast of his wrath they are
consumed.
10 Though the lion* roars, though the king
of beasts cries out,
yet the teeth of the young lions are
broken;
11 The old lion perishes for lack of prey,
and the cubs of the lioness are
scattered.
12 A word was stealthily brought to me,*
my ear caught a whisper of it.
13 In my thoughts during visions of the
night,[q]
when deep sleep falls on mortals,
14 Fear came upon me, and shuddering,
that terrified me to the bone.
15 Then a spirit passed before me,
and the hair of my body stood on end.
16 It paused, but its likeness I could not
recognize;
a figure was before my eyes,
in silence I heard a voice:[r]
17 "Can anyone be more in the right than
God?[s]
Can mortals be more blameless than
their Maker?
18 Look, he puts no trust in his servants,[t]
and even with his messengers he finds
fault.
19 How much more with those who dwell in
houses of clay,
whose foundation is in the dust,
who are crushed more easily than a
moth!
20 Morning or evening they may be
shattered;
unnoticed, they perish forever.
21 The pegs of their tent are plucked up;
they die without knowing wisdom."

## CHAPTER 5

See RG 169–73

1 Call now! Will anyone respond to
you?
To which of the holy ones* will you
turn?
2 Surely impatience kills the fool
and indignation slays the simpleton.
3 I have seen a fool spreading his roots,[u]
but I cursed his household suddenly:
4 May his children be far from safety;
may they be crushed at the gate*
without a rescuer.
5 What they have reaped may the hungry
eat up,
or God take away by blight,
or the thirsty swallow their substance.
6 For not from dust does mischief come,
nor from the soil does trouble sprout.
7 Human beings beget mischief
as sparks* fly upward.
8 In your place, I would appeal to God,
and to God I would state my plea.
9 * He does things great and unsearchable,
things marvelous and innumerable.
10 He gives rain upon the earth
and sends water upon the fields;
11 [v] He sets up the lowly on high,
and those who mourn are raised to
safety.
12 He frustrates the plans of the cunning,
so that their hands achieve no success;
13 He catches the wise in their own ruses,[w]

**4:10 The lion**: used figuratively here for the violent, rapacious sinner who cannot prevail against God.

**4:12–21** A dramatic presentation of the idea of human nothingness in contrast to God's greatness (v. 17). The message of the "private revelation" that stirs Eliphaz so deeply is in reality expressed countless times in the Bible. The statements of the friends are often "truths" that are insensitive or irrelevant to Job's questioning.

**5:1 Holy ones**: members of the heavenly court; cf. 1:6 and note. They were viewed as heavenly intercessors.

**5:4 At the gate**: of the city, where justice was administered.

**5:7 Sparks**: in Hebrew, "sons of resheph," which the ancient versions took as the name of a bird. Resheph was an underworld deity of plague, but the word also means "flames" in Sg 8:6.

**5:9** Perhaps to be omitted here; it is a duplicate of 9:10.

*q:* Jb 33:15. *r:* 1 Kgs 19:12. *s:* Jb 9:2; 15:14–16; 25:4; Ps 130:3; 143:2. *t:* Jb 15:15; 2 Pt 2:4; Jude 6. *u:* Ps 37:35–36. *v:* 1 Sm 2:7–8; Ps 113:7; Lk 1:52. *w:* 1 Cor 3:19.

and the designs of the crafty are routed.
14 They meet with darkness in the daytime,
at noonday they grope as though it were night.
15 But he saves the poor from the sword of their mouth,*
from the hand of the mighty.
16 Thus the needy have hope,
and iniquity closes its mouth.
17 Happy the one whom God reproves!
The Almighty's* discipline do not reject.
18 For he wounds, but he binds up;[x]
he strikes, but his hands give healing.
19 Out of six troubles he will deliver you,
and at the seventh* no evil shall touch you.
20 In famine he will deliver you from death,
and in war from the power of the sword;
21 From the scourge of the tongue you shall be hidden,
and you shall not fear approaching ruin.
22 At ruin and want you shall laugh;
the beasts of the earth, do not fear.
23 With the stones of the field shall your covenant be,
and the wild beasts shall be at peace with you.
24 And you shall know that your tent is secure;
taking stock of your household, you shall miss nothing.
25 You shall know that your descendants are many,
and your offspring like the grass of the earth.
26 You shall approach the grave in full vigor,
as a shock of grain comes in at its season.
27 See, this we have searched out; so it is!
This we have heard, and you should know.

## CHAPTER 6

See RG 169–73

***Job's First Reply.*** 1 Then Job answered and said:

2 Ah, could my anguish but be measured
and my calamity laid with it in the scales,
3 They would now outweigh the sands of the sea!
Because of this I speak without restraint.
4 For the arrows of the Almighty are in me,[y]
and my spirit drinks in their poison;
the terrors of God are arrayed against me.
5 Does the wild donkey bray when it has grass?*
Does the ox low over its fodder?
6 Can anything insipid be eaten without salt?
Is there flavor in the white of an egg?
7 I refuse to touch them;
they are like loathsome food to me.
8 Oh, that I might have my request,
and that God would grant what I long for:
9 Even that God would decide to crush me,
that he would put forth his hand and cut me off!
10 Then I should still have consolation
and could exult through unremitting pain,
because I have not transgressed the commands of the Holy One.
11 What strength have I that I should endure,
and what is my limit that I should be patient?
12 Have I the strength of stones,
or is my flesh of bronze?
13 Have I no helper,[z]
and has my good sense deserted me?
14 A friend owes kindness to one in despair,

**5:15 From the sword of their mouth**: the Hebrew is obscure.

**5:17 Almighty**: standard translation of Heb. *Shaddai*.

**5:19 Six . . . the seventh**: proverbial expression for any large number; cf. Prv 24:16; Lk 17:4.

**6:5–6** Job would not complain if his life were as pleasant to him as fodder to a hungry animal; but his life is as disagreeable as insipid food. **White of an egg**: thus the obscure Hebrew has been understood in Jewish tradition; some render it "mallow juice."

*x*: Hos 6:1–2. *y*: Ps 88:17. *z*: Jb 19:14–15.

though he has forsaken the fear of the
Almighty.
15 My companions are undependable as a
wadi,
as watercourses that run dry in the
wadies;
16 Though they may be black with ice,
and with snow heaped upon them,
17 Yet once they flow, they cease to be;
in the heat, they disappear from their
place.
18 Caravans wander from their routes;
they go into the wasteland and perish.
19 The caravans of Tema* search,
the companies of Sheba have hopes;
20 They are disappointed, though they were
confident;
they come there and are frustrated.
21 It is thus that you have now become
for me;*
you see a terrifying thing and are afraid.
22 Have I said, "Give me something,
make a bribe on my behalf from your
possessions"?
23 Or "Deliver me from the hand of the
enemy,
redeem me from oppressors"?
24 Teach me, and I will be silent;
make me understand how I have erred.
25 How painful honest words can be;
yet how unconvincing is your
argument!
26 Do you consider your words as proof,
but the sayings of a desperate man as
wind?
27 You would even cast lots for the orphan,
and would barter over your friend!
28 Come, now, give me your attention;
surely I will not lie to your face.
29 Think it over; let there be no injustice.
Think it over; I still am right.
30 Is there insincerity on my tongue,
or cannot my taste discern falsehood?

## CHAPTER 7

See RG 169–73

1 [a] Is not life on earth a drudgery,*
its days like those of a hireling?
2 Like a slave who longs for the shade,
a hireling who waits for wages,
3 So I have been assigned months of
futility,
and troubled nights have been counted
off for me.
4 When I lie down I say, "When shall I
arise?"
then the night drags on;
I am filled with restlessness until the
dawn.
5 My flesh is clothed with worms and
scabs;[b]
my skin cracks and festers;
6 My days are swifter than a weaver's
shuttle;
they come to an end without hope.
7 Remember that my life is like the wind;[c]
my eye will not see happiness again.
8 The eye that now sees me shall no more
behold me;
when your eye is on me, I shall be
gone.
9 As a cloud dissolves and vanishes,[d]
so whoever goes down to Sheol shall
not come up.
10 They shall not return home again;
their place shall know them no more.
11 My own utterance I will not restrain;
I will speak in the anguish of my
spirit;
I will complain in the bitterness of my
soul.
12 * Am I the Sea, or the dragon,
that you place a watch over me?*
13 When I say, "My bed shall comfort me,
my couch shall ease my complaint,"
14 Then you frighten me with dreams
and terrify me with visions,

**6:19 Tema**: in northwest Arabia. **Sheba**: home of the Sabeans; see note on 1:15.

**6:21** It is only at this point that the previous lines (vv. 1–20) are clearly directed to the three friends. The style of replying in these chapters (3–31) is often indirect. Job and the friends become mouthpieces through which the author presents current views on divine retribution in dramatic fashion. In chap. 7, Job will not even speak directly to the friends.

**7:1 Drudgery**: taken by some to refer to military service; cf. also 14:14.

**7:12–21** Job now speaks not to his friends (who never speak to God), but to God. He does this frequently; cf. 9:28; 10:2–22; 13:20–28; 14:13–22.

**7:12** An allusion to the personification of primeval chaos as a monstrous ocean vanquished by God; see note on 3:8.

*a:* Jb 14:14. *b:* Jb 2:7–8. *c:* Ps 144:4. *d:* Jb 10:21; 14:10–12; 2 Sm 12:23; 14:14; Wis 2:1.

[15] So that I should prefer strangulation
and death rather than my existence.*
[16] I waste away: I will not live forever;[e]
let me alone, for my days are but a
breath.
[17] * What are human beings, that you make
much of them,
or pay them any heed?
[18] You observe them every morning[f]
and try them at every moment!
[19] How long before you look away from
me,
and let me alone till I swallow my
spit?
[20] If I sin, what do I do to you,
O watcher of mortals?
Why have you made me your target?
Why should I be a burden for you?
[21] Why do you not pardon my offense,
or take away my guilt?
For soon I shall lie down in the dust;
and should you seek me I shall be
gone.

## CHAPTER 8

See RG 169–73

***Bildad's First Speech.*** [1]Bildad the Shuhite answered and said:

[2] How long will you utter such things?
The words from your mouth are a
mighty wind!
[3] Does God pervert judgment,[g]
does the Almighty pervert justice?
[4] If your children have sinned against him
and he has left them in the grip of their
guilt,
[5] Still, if you yourself have recourse to
God
and make supplication to the
Almighty,
[6] Should you be blameless and upright,
surely now he will rouse himself for
you
and restore your rightful home.
[7] Though your beginning was small,
your future will flourish indeed.
[8] Inquire of the former generations,
pay attention to the experience of their
ancestors—[h]
[9] As we are but of yesterday and have no
knowledge,
because our days on earth are but a
shadow—[i]
[10] Will they not teach you and tell you
and utter their words of
understanding?
[11] * Can the papyrus grow up without mire?
Can the reed grass flourish without
water?
[12] While it is yet green and uncut,
it withers quicker than any grass.
[13] So is the end of everyone who forgets
God,
and so shall the hope of the godless
perish.
[14] His confidence is but a gossamer thread,
his trust is a spider's house.
[15] He shall lean upon his house, but it shall
not stand;
he shall cling to it, but it shall not
endure.
[16] He thrives in full sun,
and over his garden his shoots go forth;
[17] About a heap of stones his roots are
entwined;
among the rocks he takes hold.
[18] Yet if one tears him from his place,
it will disown him: "I have never seen
you!"
[19] There he lies rotting beside the road,
and out of the soil another sprouts.
[20] Behold, God will not cast away the
upright;
neither will he take the hand of the
wicked.
[21] Once more will he fill your mouth with
laughter
and your lips with rejoicing.
[22] Those who hate you shall be clothed with
shame,
and the tent of the wicked shall be no
more.

**7:15 Existence**: lit., bones; the Hebrew is unclear.

**7:17–18** An ironic allusion to Ps 8:5.

**8:11–13** As marsh plants need water, so human beings need God. These verses may be a quotation from the teaching of the ancestors; cf. v. 10.

*e:* Jb 14:1–2, 5. *f:* Ps 17:3. *g:* Jb 34:10–12. *h:* Dt 4:32; 32:7. *i:* Jb 14:2; Ps 102:12; 109:23; 144:4; Wis 2:5.

## CHAPTER 9

See RG 169–73

*Job's Second Reply.* [1]Then Job answered and said:

2 I know well that it is so;
but how can anyone be in the right before God?
3 Should one wish to contend with him,*
he could not answer him once in a thousand times.
4 God is wise in heart and mighty in strength;
who has withstood him and remained whole?
5 He removes the mountains before they know it;
he overturns them in his anger.
6 He shakes the earth out of its place,[j]
and the pillars beneath it tremble.
7 He commands the sun, and it does not rise;
he seals up the stars.
8 He alone stretches out the heavens[k]
and treads upon the back of the sea.
9 He made the Bear and Orion,
the Pleiades and the constellations of the south;
10 He does things great and unsearchable,
things marvelous and innumerable.
11 Should he come near me, I do not see him;
should he pass by, I am not aware of him;
12 Should he seize me forcibly, who can resist?
Who can say to him, "What are you doing?"
13 He is God and he does not relent;
the helpers of Rahab* bow beneath him.
14 How then could I give him any answer,
or choose out arguments against him!
15 Even though I were right, I could not answer,[l]
but should rather beg for what was due me.
16 If I appealed to him and he answered me,
I could not believe that he would listen to me;
17 With a storm he might overwhelm me,
and multiply my wounds for nothing;
18 He would not allow me to draw breath,
but might fill me with bitter griefs.
19 If it be a question of strength, he is mighty;
or of judgment, who will call him to account?
20 Though I were right, my own mouth might condemn me;[m]
were I innocent, it might put me in the wrong.
21 I am innocent, but I cannot know it;
I despise my life.
22 It is all one! therefore I say:
Both the innocent and the wicked he destroys.[n]
23 When the scourge slays suddenly,
he scoffs at the despair of the innocent.
24 The earth is given into the hands of the wicked;
he covers the faces of its judges.
If it is not he, who then is it?
25 My days are swifter than a runner,
they flee away; they see no happiness;[o]
26 They shoot by like skiffs of reed,
like an eagle swooping upon its prey.
27 If I say: I will forget my complaining,
I will lay aside my sadness and be of good cheer,
28 Then I am in dread of all my pains;
I know that you* will not hold me innocent.
29 It is I who will be accounted guilty;
why then should I strive in vain?
30 If I should wash myself with soap
and cleanse my hands with lye,
31 Yet you would plunge me in the ditch,
so that my garments would abhor me.
32 For he is not a man like myself, that I should answer him,
that we should come together in judgment.

**9:3** Job begins to explore the possibility of challenging God in a lawsuit, a theme that will recur (10:2), but he knows the odds are against him (vv. 12–20).

**9:13 Rahab**: another name for the primeval sea-monster; see notes on 3:8 and Ps 89:11; cf. Jb 7:12; 26:12.

**9:28–31 You**: refers to God.

*j:* Jb 26:11. *k:* Ps 104:2; Is 40:22. *l:* Jb 10:15. *m:* Jb 15:6. *n:* Eccl 9:2. *o:* Jb 7:6.

33 Would that there were an arbiter
between us,
who could lay his hand upon us both
34 and withdraw his rod from me,
So that his terrors did not frighten me;
35 that I might speak without being afraid
of him.
Since this is not the case with me,
10:1 * I loathe my life.[p]

See RG 169–73

## CHAPTER 10

I will give myself up to complaint;
I will speak from the bitterness of my
soul.
2 I will say to God: Do not put me in the
wrong!
Let me know why you oppose me.
3 * Is it a pleasure for you to oppress,
to spurn the work of your hands,
and shine on the plan of the wicked?
4 Have you eyes of flesh?
Do you see as mortals see?
5 Are your days like the days of a mortal,[q]
and are your years like a human
lifetime,
6 That you seek for guilt in me
and search after my sins,
7 Even though you know that I am not
wicked,[r]
and that none can deliver me out of
your hand?
8 Your hands have formed me and
fashioned me;
will you then turn and destroy me?
9 Oh, remember that you fashioned me
from clay![s]
Will you then bring me down to dust
again?
10 Did you not pour me out like milk,
and thicken me like cheese?
11 With skin and flesh you clothed me,
with bones and sinews knit me together.
12 Life and love you granted me,
and your providence has preserved my
spirit.
13 Yet these things you have hidden in your
heart;
I know they are your purpose:
14 If I should sin, you would keep a watch
on me,
and from my guilt you would not
absolve me.
15 If I should be wicked, alas for me!
even if righteous, I dare not hold up
my head,
sated with shame, drenched in
affliction!
16 Should it lift up, you hunt me like a lion:
repeatedly you show your wondrous
power against me,
17 You renew your attack* upon me
and multiply your harassment of me;
in waves your troops come against me.
18 Why then did you bring me forth from
the womb?[t]
I should have died and no eye have
seen me.
19 I should be as though I had never lived;
I should have been taken from the
womb to the grave.
20 Are not my days few? Stop!
Let me alone, that I may recover a little
21 Before I go whence I shall not return,[u]
to the land of darkness and of gloom,
22 The dark, disordered land
where darkness is the only light.

## CHAPTER 11

See RG 169–73

***Zophar's First Speech.*** 1 And Zophar
the Naamathite answered and said:

2 Should not many words be answered,
or must the garrulous man necessarily
be right?
3 Shall your babblings keep others silent,
and shall you deride and no one give
rebuke?
4 Shall you say: "My teaching is pure,
and I am clean in your sight"?
5 But oh, that God would speak,*
and open his lips against you,

**10:1 I loathe my life**: these words complete the thought of 9:35.

**10:3–12** These lines are a delicate mixture of sarcasm and prayer; Job "reminds" God, challenging the divine providence. Note the piteous tone of the final request in vv. 20–22.

**10:17 Attack**: or "witnesses," continuing the metaphor of lawsuit used in these chapters.

**11:5** This is another of many ironies (e.g., cf. 11:16–19)

*p:* Jb 9:21. *q:* Jb 36:26. *r:* Jb 2:3, 9; Dt 32:39; Wis 16:15. *s:* Jb 4:19; 33:6; Gn 2:7; 3:19; Ps 146:4. *t:* Jb 3:3, 11. *u:* Jb 7:9–10; 16:22.

6 And tell you the secrets of wisdom,
for good sense has two sides;
So you might learn that God
overlooks some of your sinfulness.
7 Can you find out the depths of God?[v]
or find out the perfection of the
Almighty?
8 It is higher than the heavens; what can
you do?
It is deeper than Sheol; what can you
know?
9 It is longer than the earth in measure,
and broader than the sea.
10 If he should seize and imprison
or call to judgment, who then could
turn him back?
11 For he knows the worthless
and sees iniquity; will he then
ignore it?
12 An empty head will gain understanding,
when a colt of a wild jackass[w] is born
human.*
13 If you set your heart aright
and stretch out your hands toward him,
14 If iniquity is in your hand, remove it,
and do not let injustice dwell in your
tent,
15 Surely then you may lift up your face in
innocence;
you may stand firm and unafraid.
16 For then you shall forget your misery,
like water that has ebbed away you
shall regard it.
17 Then your life shall be brighter than the
noonday;
its gloom shall become like the morning,
18 And you shall be secure, because there is
hope;
you shall look round you and lie down
in safety;[x]
19 you shall lie down and no one will
disturb you.
Many shall entreat your favor,
20 but the wicked, looking on, shall be
consumed with envy.
Escape shall be cut off from them,
their only hope their last breath.

## CHAPTER 12

See RG 169–73

***Job's Third Reply.*** 1* Then Job answered and said:

2 No doubt you are the people
with whom wisdom shall die!
3 But I have intelligence as well as you;[y]
I do not fall short of you;
for who does not know such things as
these?
4 I have become the sport of my
neighbors:*
"The one whom God answers when he
calls upon him,
The just, the perfect man," is a
laughingstock;[z]
5 The undisturbed esteem my downfall a
disgrace
such as awaits unsteady feet;
6 Yet the tents of robbers are prosperous,
and those who provoke God are
secure,
whom God has in his power.*
7 But now ask the beasts to teach you,
the birds of the air to tell you;
8 Or speak to the earth to instruct you,
and the fish of the sea to inform you.
9 Which of all these does not know
that the hand of God has done this?
10 In his hand is the soul of every living
thing,[a]
and the life breath of all mortal flesh.
11 Does not the ear judge words
as the mouth tastes food?[b]
12 So with old age is wisdom,[c]
and with length of days understanding.

that occur throughout the book. Zophar does not know that God will speak (chaps. 38–42), but contrary to what he thinks.

**11:12 A colt . . . is born human**: the Hebrew is obscure. As translated, it seems to be a proverb referring to an impossible event.

**12:1** Job begins his third and longest speech to the friends with sarcasm, and eventually he accuses them of falsehood (13:4–11). The dialogue between them becomes increasingly sharp. With the appeal to learning from beasts and birds (12:7), Job launches into what seems to be a bitter parody of the power of God.

**12:4–5** The Hebrew is somewhat obscure, but the general sense is that the wicked mock the pious when the latter appear to be abandoned by God; cf. Ps 22:7–9; Mt 27:39–43.

**12:6 Whom God has in his power**: the Hebrew is obscure. The line may be a scribal error; some of the phrases occur in vv. 9, 10.

*v:* Rom 11:33. *w:* Jb 39:5–8. *x:* Lv 26:6; Ps 4:9. *y:* Jb 13:2; 15:9. *z:* Jb 21:3; 30:1. *a:* Acts 17:28. *b:* Jb 34:3. *c:* Jb 32:7.

13 With him are wisdom and might;
his are counsel and understanding.
14 If he knocks a thing down, there is no rebuilding;[d]
if he imprisons, there is no release.
15 He holds back the waters and there is drought;[e]
he sends them forth and they overwhelm the land.
16 With him are strength and prudence;
the misled and the misleaders are his.
17 He sends counselors away barefoot,
makes fools of judges.
18 He loosens the belt of kings,
ties a waistcloth on their loins.*
19 He sends priests away barefoot,
leads the powerful astray.
20 He silences the trusted adviser,
takes discretion from the elders.
21 He pours shame on nobles,[f]
the waistband of the strong he loosens.
22 He uncovers deep things from the darkness,
brings the gloom into the light.
23 He makes nations great and destroys them,
spreads peoples abroad and abandons them.
24 He takes understanding from the leaders of the land,
makes them wander in a pathless desert.
25 They grope in the darkness without light;
he makes them wander like drunkards.

## CHAPTER 13

See RG 169–73

1 All this my eye has seen;
my ear has heard and perceived it.
2 What you know, I also know;[g]
I do not fall short of you.
3 But I would speak with the Almighty;[h]
I want to argue with God.
4 But you gloss over falsehoods,
you are worthless physicians, every one of you!
5 Oh, that you would be altogether silent;
that for you would be wisdom!
6 Hear now my argument
and listen to the accusations from my lips.
7 Is it for God that you speak falsehood?
Is it for him that you utter deceit?
8 Is it for him that you show partiality?
Do you make accusations on behalf of God?
9 Will it be well when he shall search you out?
Can you deceive him as you do a mere human being?
10 He will openly rebuke you
if in secret you show partiality.
11 Surely his majesty will frighten you
and dread of him fall upon you.
12 Your reminders are ashy maxims,
your fabrications mounds of clay.
13 Be silent! Let me alone that I may speak,
no matter what happens to me.
14 I will carry my flesh between my teeth,
and take my life in my hand.*
15 Slay me though he might,[i] I will wait for him;*
I will defend my conduct before him.
16 This shall be my salvation:
no impious man can come into his presence.
17 Pay close attention to my speech,
give my statement a hearing.
18 Behold, I have prepared my case,[j]
I know that I am in the right.
19 If anyone can make a case against me,
then I shall be silent and expire.
20 Two things only do not use against me,*
then from your presence I need not hide:
21 Withdraw your hand far from me,
do not let the terror of you frighten me.
22 Then call me, and I will respond;
or let me speak first, and answer me.
23 What are my faults and my sins?

**12:18** He reduces kings to the condition of slaves, who wear only a cloth wrapped about the waist.

**13:14** The second half of the verse is a common biblical expression for risking one's life; cf. Jgs 12:3; 1 Sm 19:5; 28:21; Ps 119:109; the first half of the verse must have a similar meaning. Job is so confident of his innocence that he is willing to risk his life by going to judgment with God.

**13:15** Many translations adopt the Ketib reading, "I have no hope."

**13:20** In 13:20–14:22, Job directs his address to God; cf. 7:8–21; 9:28–10:22. His three friends never do this.

*d:* Jer 1:10; Rev 3:7. *e:* Gn 7:11–24. *f:* Ps 107:40. *g:* Jb 12:3; 15:9. *h:* Jb 23:4. *i:* Jb 27:5. *j:* Jb 33:9.

**Life Is Brief**

JUST AS PSALM 103 reminds us that our days pass by like grass and the flowers that bloom and then die, so too Job underlines the brevity of human life (14:1–2). He asks how God can possibly bring such a miserable creature into judgment (vv. 3–4). Job draws a comparison between the brief human life span and mountains worn slowly away by water. In between he entertains the impossible hope that he might escape the constraints of mortality and be enabled to speak with God beyond the grave (vv. 10–17).

My misdeed, my sin make known
to me!
24 Why do you hide your face
and consider me your enemy?* [k]
25 Will you harass a wind-driven leaf
or pursue a withered straw?
26 For you draw up bitter indictments
against me,
and punish in me the faults of my youth.
27 You put my feet in the stocks;
you watch all my paths
and trace out all my footsteps,
28 Though I wear out like a leather bottle,
like a garment the moth has consumed.

### CHAPTER 14

See RG 169–73

1 Man born of woman
is short-lived and full of trouble,* [l]
2 Like a flower that springs up and fades,[m]
swift as a shadow that does not abide.
3 Upon such a one will you set your eyes,
bringing me into judgment before
you?
4 Can anyone make the unclean clean?[n]
No one can.
5 Since his days are determined—
you know the number of his months;
you have fixed the limit which he
cannot pass—
6 Look away from him and let him be,
while, like a hireling, he completes his
day.
7 For a tree there is hope;
if it is cut down, it will sprout again,
its tender shoots will not cease.
8 Even though its root grow old in the earth
and its stump die in the dust,
9 Yet at the first whiff of water it sprouts
and puts forth branches like a young
plant.
10 But when a man dies, all vigor leaves
him;[o]
when a mortal expires, where then
is he?
11 As when the waters of a lake fail,
or a stream shrivels and dries up,
12 So mortals lie down, never to rise.
Until the heavens are no more, they
shall not awake,
nor be roused out of their sleep.[p]
13 Oh, that you would hide me in Sheol,
shelter me till your wrath is past,
fix a time to remember me!
14 If a man were to die, and live again,
all the days of my drudgery I would
wait[q]
for my relief to come.
15 You would call, and I would answer you;
you would long for the work of your
hands.
16 Surely then you would count my steps,[r]
and not keep watch for sin in me.
17 My misdeeds would be sealed up in a
pouch,*
and you would cover over my guilt.
18 Mountains fall and crumble,
rocks move from their place,
19 And water wears away stone,

**13:24** The Hebrew word for "enemy" (*'oyeb*) is very close to the Hebrew form of Job's name (*'iyyob*). The play on the word implies that God has confused the two.

**14:1** The sorrowful lament of Job is that God should relent in view of the limited life of human beings. When compared to plant life, which dies but can revive, the death of human beings is final. Job's wild and "unthinkable" wish in vv. 13–17 is a bold stroke of imagination and desire: if only in Sheol he were protected till God would remember him! Were he to live again (v. 14), things would be different, but alas, God destroys "the hope of mortals" (v. 19).

**14:17** **Sealed up in a pouch**: hidden away and forgotten.

*k:* Jb 19:11; 33:10. *l:* Jb 10:20; 15:14; Ps 39:5–6; 89:46; Wis 2:1. *m:* Jb 8:9; Ps 90:6; 102:12; 103:15; 109:23; 144:4; Is 40:6–7; Jas 1:10. *n:* Ps 51:4, 7. *o:* Jb 20:7. *p:* Jb 7:10. *q:* Jb 7:1. *r:* Jb 31:4; 34:21.

and floods wash away the soil of the land—
so you destroy the hope of mortals!
20 You prevail once for all against them and they pass on;
you dismiss them with changed appearance.
21 If their children are honored, they are not aware of it;
or if disgraced, they do not know about them.
22 Only for themselves, their pain;
only for themselves, their mourning.

## III. Second Cycle of Speeches

### CHAPTER 15

See RG 169–73

*Second Speech of Eliphaz.* 1* Then Eliphaz the Temanite answered and said:

2 Does a wise man answer with windy opinions,
or puff himself up with the east wind?
3 Does he argue in speech that does not avail,
and in words that are to no profit?
4 You in fact do away with piety,
you lessen devotion toward God,
5 Because your wickedness instructs your mouth,
and you choose to speak like the crafty.
6 Your own mouth condemns you, not I;[s]
your own lips refute you.
7 Were you the first to be born?
Were you brought forth before the hills?
8 Do you listen in on God's council[t]
and restrict wisdom to yourself?
9 What do you know that we do not know,[u]
or understand that we do not?
10 There are gray-haired old men among us,
more advanced in years than your father.
11 Are the consolations of God not enough for you,
and speech that deals gently with you?
12 Why does your heart carry you away,
and why do your eyes flash,
13 So that you turn your anger against God
and let such words escape your mouth!
14 How can any mortal be blameless,[v]
anyone born of woman be righteous?[w]
15 If in his holy ones God places no confidence,[x]
and if the heavens are not without blame in his sight,
16 How much less so is the abominable and corrupt:
people who drink in iniquity like water!
17 I will show you, if you listen to me;
what I have seen I will tell—
18 What the wise relate
and have not contradicted since the days of their ancestors,
19 To whom alone the land was given,
when no foreigner moved among them:
20 The wicked is in torment all his days,
and limited years are in store for the ruthless;
21 The sound of terrors is in his ears;
when all is prosperous, a spoiler comes upon him.
22 He despairs of escaping the darkness,
and looks ever for the sword;
23 A wanderer, food for vultures,
he knows destruction is imminent.
24 A day of darkness fills him with dread;
distress and anguish overpower him,
like a king expecting an attack.
25 Because he has stretched out his hand against God
and arrogantly challenged the Almighty,
26 Rushing defiantly against him,
with the stout bosses of his shields.
27 Although he has covered his face with his crassness,
padded his loins with blubber,
28 He shall dwell in ruined cities,
in houses that are deserted,
crumbling into rubble.
29 He shall not be rich, his possessions shall not endure;

**15:1** The tone of Eliphaz's speech is now much rougher. In vv. 7–9 he ridicules Job's knowledge with a sarcastic question about whether he was a member of the divine council before creation and thus had unique wisdom (according to Prv 8:22–31, only Woman Wisdom existed before creation). Verses 20–35 are a typical description of the fate of the wicked.

*s:* Jb 9:20. *t:* Jb 11:7; Wis 9:13; Jer 23:18; Rom 11:34; 1 Cor 2:11, 16. *u:* Jb 12:3; 13:2. *v:* Jb 25:4–6. *w:* Jb 14:4. *x:* Jb 4:18–19.

his property shall not spread over the
land.
30 A flame shall sear his early growth,
and with the wind his blossoms shall
disappear.
31 Let him not trust in his height, misled,
even though his height be like the
palm tree.*
32 He shall wither before his time,
his branches no longer green.
33 He shall be like a vine that sheds its
grapes unripened,
like an olive tree casting off its blossom.
34 For the breed of the impious shall be
sterile,[y]
and fire shall consume the tents of
extortioners.
35 They conceive malice, bring forth deceit,[z]
give birth to fraud.*

## CHAPTER 16

See RG 169–73

*Job's Fourth Reply.* 1 Then Job answered and said:

2 I have heard this sort of thing many
times.[a]
Troublesome comforters, all of you!
3 Is there no end to windy words?
What sickness makes you rattle on?
4 I also could talk as you do,
were you in my place.
I could declaim over you,
or wag my head at you;
5 I could strengthen you with talk,
with mere chatter give relief.
6 If I speak, my pain is not relieved;
if I stop speaking, nothing changes.
7 But now he has exhausted me;
you have stunned all my companions.
8 You* have shriveled me up; it is a
witness,
my gauntness rises up to testify
against me;
9 His wrath tears and assails me,
he gnashes his teeth against me;
My enemy looks daggers at me.
10 They gape at me with their mouths;
They strike me on the cheek with insults;
they are all enlisted against me.
11 God has given me over to the impious;
into the hands of the wicked he has
cast me.
12 I was in peace, but he dislodged me,
seized me by the neck, dashed me to
pieces.
He has set me up for a target;
13 his arrows strike me from all directions.
He pierces my sides without mercy,
pours out my gall upon the ground.
14 He pierces me, thrust upon thrust,
rushes at me like a warrior.
15 I have sewn sackcloth on my skin,
laid my horn low in the dust.
16 My face is inflamed with weeping,
darkness covers my eyes,
17 Although my hands are free from violence,
and my prayer sincere.
18 O earth, do not cover my blood,
nor let my outcry come to rest!*
19 Even now my witness* is in heaven,
my advocate is on high.
20 My friends it is who wrong me;
before God my eyes shed tears,
21 That justice may be done for a mortal
with God:
as for a man with his neighbor.
22 For my years are numbered,
and I go the road of no return.

## CHAPTER 17

See RG 169–73

1 My spirit is broken, my days
finished,
my burial at hand.
2 Surely mockers surround me,
at their provocation, my eyes grow dim.
3 Put up a pledge for me with you:*
who is there to give surety for me?
4 You darken their minds to knowledge;
therefore you will not exalt them.

**15:31** The translation is uncertain.

**15:35** The plans of the wicked yield nothing but futile results. Cf. Ps 7:15; Is 59:4.

**16:8 You**: God. Job then describes in vv. 9–17 the savage treatment that he has received from God.

**16:18** As the exposed blood of those who were unjustly slain cries to heaven for vengeance (Gn 4:10; Ez 24:6–9), so Job's sufferings demand redress.

**16:19 Witness**: refers perhaps to God (is Job appealing to God against God?), or to a mediator (cf. 9:33), or to a personification of Job's prayer.

**17:3** Addressed to God; v. 10 to Job's friends.

*y:* Wis 3:11, 18. *z:* Ps 7:15; Is 59:4. *a:* Jb 12:3.

[5] For a share of property he informs on friends,
while the eyes of his children grow dim.
[6] I am made a byword of the people;[b]
I am one at whom people spit.
[7] My eyes are blind with anguish,
and my whole frame is like a shadow.
[8] The upright are astonished at this,
the innocent aroused against the wicked.
[9] The righteous holds to his way,
the one with clean hands increases in strength.
[10] But turn now, and come on again;
I do not find a wise man among you!
[11] My days pass by, my plans are at an end,
the yearning of my heart.
[12] They would change the night into day;
where there is darkness they talk of approaching light.
[13] * If my only hope is dwelling in Sheol,
and spreading my couch in darkness,
[14] If I am to say to the pit, "You are my father,"
and to the worm "my mother," "my sister,"
[15] Where then is my hope,
my happiness, who can see it?
[16] Will they descend with me into Sheol?
Shall we go down together into the dust?

## CHAPTER 18

See RG 169–73

*Bildad's Second Speech.* [1]Then Bildad the Shuhite answered and said:

[2] When will you put an end to words?
Reflect, and then we can have discussion.
[3] Why are we accounted like beasts,
equal to them in your sight?
[4] You who tear yourself in your anger—
shall the earth be neglected on your account
or the rock be moved out of its place?
[5] Truly, the light of the wicked is extinguished;
the flame of his fire casts no light.
[6] In his tent light is darkness;
the lamp above him goes out.[c]
[7] His vigorous steps are hemmed in,
his own counsel casts him down.
[8] A net catches him by the feet,
he wanders into a pitfall.
[9] A trap seizes him by the heel,
a snare lays hold of him.
[10] A noose is hidden for him on the ground,
a netting for him on the path.
[11] On every side terrors frighten him;[d]
they harry him at each step.
[12] His strength is famished,
disaster is ready at his side,
[13] His skin is eaten to the limbs,
the firstborn of Death* eats his limbs.
[14] He is plucked from the security of his tent;
and marched off to the king of terrors.*
[15] Fire lodges in his tent,
over his abode brimstone is scattered.
[16] Below, his roots dry up,
and above, his branches wither.
[17] His memory perishes from the earth,[e]
and he has no name in the countryside.
[18] He is driven from light into darkness,
and banished from the world.
[19] He has neither offshoot nor offspring
among his people,
no survivor where once he dwelt.
[20] Those who come after shall be appalled at his fate;
those who went before are seized with horror.
[21] So is it then with the dwelling of the impious;
such is the place of the one who does not know God!

## CHAPTER 19

See RG 169–73

*Job's Fifth Reply.* [1]* Then Job answered and said:

[2] How long will you afflict my spirit,
grind me down with words?

**17:13–16** Job elaborates another of the vivid descriptions of "life" in Sheol; cf. 3:13–23; 10:21–22.

**18:13 Firstborn of Death**: that is, disease, plague.

**18:14 The king of terrors**: of Sheol, of Death (cf. the "terrors" in v. 11). However, the Hebrew of this verse is obscure.

**19:1** Job continues railing against his friends (vv. 2–5), and describing God's savage attack in words reminiscent of 16:9–17.

*b:* Jb 30:9. *c:* Jb 21:17; Prv 13:9; 24:20. *d:* Jb 15:20–24; 27:20. *e:* Ps 34:17; Prv 2:22; 10:7.

3 These ten times you have humiliated me,
have assailed me without shame!
4 Even if it were true that I am at fault,
my fault would remain with me;
5 If truly you exalt yourselves at my expense,
and use my shame as an argument against me,
6 Know then that it is God who has dealt unfairly with me,
and compassed me round with his net.
7 If I cry out "Violence!" I am not answered.[f]
I shout for help, but there is no justice.
8 He has barred my way and I cannot pass;
veiled my path in darkness;
9 He has stripped me of my glory,
taken the diadem from my brow.
10 He breaks me down on every side, and I am gone;
he has uprooted my hope like a tree.
11 He has kindled his wrath against me;
he counts me one of his enemies.[g]
12 His troops advance as one;
they build up their road to attack me,
encamp around my tent.
13 My family has withdrawn from me,[h]
my friends are wholly estranged.
14 My relatives and companions neglect me,
my guests have forgotten me.
15 Even my maidservants consider me a stranger;
I am a foreigner in their sight.
16 I call my servant, but he gives no answer,
though I plead aloud with him.
17 My breath is abhorrent to my wife;[i]
I am loathsome to my very children.
18 Even young children despise me;
when I appear, they speak against me.
19 All my intimate friends hold me in horror;
those whom I loved have turned against me![j]
20 My bones cling to my skin,
and I have escaped by the skin of my teeth.*
21 Pity me, pity me, you my friends,
for the hand of God has struck me!
22 Why do you pursue me like God,
and prey insatiably upon me?
23 Oh, would that my words were written down![k]
Would that they were inscribed in a record:*
24 That with an iron chisel and with lead
they were cut in the rock forever!
25 As for me, I know that my vindicator lives,*
and that he will at last stand forth upon the dust.[l]
26 This will happen when my skin has been stripped off,
and from my flesh I will see God:
27 I will see for myself,
my own eyes, not another's, will behold him:
my inmost being is consumed with longing.
28 But you who say, "How shall we persecute him,
seeing that the root of the matter is found in him?"
29 Be afraid of the sword for yourselves,
for your anger is a crime deserving the sword;
that you may know that there is a judgment.

## CHAPTER 20

See RG 169–73

***Zophar's Second Speech.*** 1 Then Zophar the Naamathite answered and said:
2 So now my thoughts provide an answer for me,
because of the feelings within me.
3 A rebuke that puts me to shame I hear,
and from my understanding a spirit gives me a reply.

**19:20 Skin of my teeth**: although the metaphor is not clear, this has become a proverbial expression for a narrow escape. It does not fit Job's situation here.

**19:23–24** What Job is about to say is so important that he wants it recorded in a permanent manner.

**19:25–27** The meaning of this passage is obscure because the original text has been poorly preserved and the ancient versions do not agree among themselves. Job asserts three times that he shall see a future vindicator (Hebrew *goel*), but he leaves the time and manner of this vindication undefined. The Vulgate translation has Job indicating a belief in resurrection after death, but the Hebrew and the other ancient versions are less specific.

*f:* Jb 30:20. *g:* Jb 13:24; 33:10. *h:* Jb 6:13. *i:* Jb 2:9. *j:* Sir 6:8. *k:* Jb 31:35. *l:* Phil 3:20; Ti 2:13.

4 Do you not know this: from of old,
since human beings were placed upon the earth,
5 The triumph of the wicked is short
and the joy of the impious but for a moment?[m]
6 Though his pride mount up to the heavens
and his head reach to the clouds,
7 Yet he perishes forever like the dung he uses for fuel,
and onlookers say, "Where is he?"[n]
8 Like a dream he takes flight and cannot be found;
he fades away like a vision of the night.
9 The eye which saw him does so no more;
nor shall his dwelling again behold him.
10 His sons will restore to the poor,
and his hands will yield up his riches.[o]
11 Though his bones are full of youthful vigor,
it shall lie with him in the dust.
12 Though wickedness is sweet in his mouth,
and he hides it under his tongue,
13 Though he retains it and will not let it go
but keeps it still within his mouth,
14 Yet in his stomach the food shall turn;
it shall be venom of asps inside him.
15 The riches he swallowed he shall vomit up;
God shall make his belly disgorge them.
16 The poison of asps he shall drink in;
the viper's fangs shall slay him.
17 He shall see no streams of oil,*
no torrents of honey or milk.
18 He shall give back his gains, never used;
like his profit from trade, never enjoyed.
19 Because he has oppressed and neglected the poor,
and stolen a house he did not build;
20 For he has known no quiet in his greed,
in his treasure he cannot save himself.[p]
21 None of his survivors will consume it,
therefore his prosperity shall not endure.
22 [q] When he has more than enough,
distress shall be his,
every sort of trouble shall come upon him.
23 When he has filled his belly,
God shall send against him the fury of his wrath
and rain down his missiles upon him.
24 Should he escape an iron weapon,
a bronze bow shall pierce him through;
25 The dart shall come out of his back,
a shining point out of his gall-bladder:
terrors fall upon him.
26 Complete darkness is in store for his treasured ones;
a fire unfanned shall consume him;[r]
any survivor in his tent shall be destroyed.
27 The heavens shall reveal his guilt,
and the earth rise up against him.
28 The flood shall sweep away his house,
torrents in the day of God's anger.
29 This is the portion of the wicked,
the heritage appointed him by God.* [s]

## CHAPTER 21

See RG 169–73

*Job's Sixth Reply.* 1 Then Job answered and said:

2 At least listen to my words,[t]
and let that be the consolation you offer.
3 Bear with me while I speak;
and after I have spoken, you can mock!
4 Is my complaint toward any human being?
Why should I not be impatient?
5 Look at me and be appalled,
put your hands over your mouths.
6 When I think of it, I am dismayed,
and shuddering seizes my flesh.
7 * Why do the wicked keep on living,
grow old, become mighty in power?[u]
8 Their progeny is secure in their sight;

**20:17 Oil:** olive oil, one of the main agricultural products of ancient Palestine, a land proverbially rich in honey and milk; see Ex 3:8; etc.

**20:29** Zophar ends his lecture in the style of Bildad (cf. 18:19) with a summary appraisal of what he has been saying about the fate of the wicked.

**21:7** In vv. 7–29 Job launches into a realistic description of

*m:* Jb 21:13; Ps 37:35–36. *n:* Jb 14:10; Ps 37:10, 36. *o:* Jb 27:14. *p:* Eccl 5:9; Lk 12:20. *q:* Jb 15:20–35. *r:* Dt 32:22. *s:* Jb 27:13. *t:* Jb 13:17. *u:* Jb 12:6; Ps 37:35; 73:3; Eccl 8:14; Jer 12:1–2; Mal 3:14–15.

their offspring are before their eyes.
9 Their homes are safe, without fear,
and the rod of God is not upon them.
10 Their bulls breed without fail;
their cows calve and do not miscarry.
11 They let their young run free like sheep,
their children skip about.
12 They sing along with drum and lyre,
and make merry to the sound of the pipe.
13 They live out their days in prosperity,
and tranquilly go down to Sheol.[v]
14 Yet they say to God, "Depart from us,[w]
for we have no desire to know your ways!
15 What is the Almighty that we should serve him?
And what do we gain by praying to him?"[x]
16 Their happiness is not in their own hands.
The designs of the wicked are far from me![y]
17 How often is the lamp of the wicked put out?
How often does destruction come upon them,
the portion God allots in his anger?
18 Let them be like straw before the wind,
like chaff the storm carries away!
19 "God is storing up the man's misery for his children"?—
let him requite the man himself so that he knows it!
20 Let his own eyes behold his calamity,
and the wrath of the Almighty let him drink!
21 For what interest has he in his family after him,
when the number of his months is finished?
22 Can anyone teach God knowledge,
seeing that he judges those on high?*
23 One dies in his full vigor,
wholly at ease and content;
24 His figure is full and nourished,
his bones are moist with marrow.
25 Another dies with a bitter spirit,
never having tasted happiness.
26 Alike they lie down in the dust,
and worms cover them both.
27 See, I know your thoughts,
and the arguments you plot against me.
28 For you say, "Where is the house of the great,
and where the dwelling place of the wicked?"
29 Have you not asked the wayfarers
and do you not acknowledge the witness they give?
30 On the day of calamity the evil man is spared,
on the day that wrath is released.
31 Who will charge him to his face about his conduct,
and for what he has done who will repay him?
32 He is carried to the grave
and at his tomb they keep watch.
33 Sweet to him are the clods of the valley.
All humankind will follow after him,
and countless others before him.
34 How empty the consolation you offer me!
Your arguments remain a fraud.

## IV. Third Cycle of Speeches*

### CHAPTER 22

See RG 169–73

*Eliphaz's Third Speech.* 1 Then Eliphaz the Temanite answered and said:

2 Can a man be profitable to God?[z]
Can a wise man be profitable to him?
3 Does it please the Almighty that you are just?[a]
Does he gain if your ways are perfect?*

the fate of the wicked, contrary to the claims made by the friends.

**21:22 Those on high**: the heavenly beings; cf. 1:6; Ps 82:1–8.

**22:1–27:23** The traditional three cycles of speeches breaks down in chaps. 22–27, because Zophar does not appear. This may be interpreted as a sign that the three friends see no point in further dialogue, or that Job's replies have reduced them to silence, or that there has been a mistake in the transmission of the text (hence various transferrals of verses have been proposed to include Zophar, but without any textual evidence).

**22:3** Another irony: God will "gain," because he will have been proved right in his claim to the satan that Job is "perfect."

*v:* Jb 34:20. *w:* Jb 22:17. *x:* Mal 3:14. *y:* Jb 22:18. *z:* Jb 9:2. *a:* Jb 35:7.

4 Is it because of your piety that he
reproves you—
that he enters into judgment with you?
5 Is not your wickedness great,
your iniquity endless?
6 You keep your relatives' goods in pledge
unjustly,*
leave them stripped naked of their
clothing.[b]
7 To the thirsty you give no water to drink,
and from the hungry you withhold
bread;
8 As if the land belonged to the powerful,
and only the privileged could dwell
in it!
9 You sent widows away empty-handed,
and the resources of orphans are
destroyed.[c]
10 Therefore snares are round about you,[d]
sudden terror makes you panic,
11 Or darkness—you cannot see!
A deluge of waters covers you.
12 Does not God, in the heights of the
heavens,[e]
behold the top of the stars, high though
they are?
13 Yet you say, "What does God know?[f]
Can he judge through the thick
darkness?
14 Clouds hide him so that he cannot see
as he walks around the circuit of the
heavens!"
15 Do you indeed keep to the ancient way
trodden by the worthless?
16 They were snatched before their time;
their foundations a river swept away.
17 They said to God, "Let us alone!"
and, "What can the Almighty do to us?"
18 Yet he had filled their houses with good
things.
The designs of the wicked are far
from me!* [g]
19 The just look on and are glad,
and the innocent deride them:* [h]
20 "Truly our enemies are destroyed,
and what was left to them, fire has
consumed!"
21 Settle with him and have peace.
That way good shall come to you:
22 Receive instruction from his mouth,
and place his words in your heart.
23 If you return to the Almighty, you will be
restored;
if you put iniquity far from your tent,
24 And treat raw gold as dust,
the fine gold of Ophir* as pebbles in
the wadi,
25 Then the Almighty himself shall be your
gold
and your sparkling silver.
26 For then you shall delight in the
Almighty,
you shall lift up your face toward God.
27 Entreat him and he will hear you,[i]
and your vows you shall fulfill.
28 What you decide shall succeed for you,
and upon your ways light shall shine.
29 For when they are brought low, you will
say, "It is pride!"
But downcast eyes he saves.[j]
30 He will deliver whoever is innocent;
you shall be delivered if your hands
are clean.[k]

## CHAPTER 23

***Job's Seventh Reply.*** 1 Then Job answered and said:

See RG 169–73

2 Today especially my complaint is bitter,
his hand is heavy upon me in my
groanings.
3 Would that I knew how to find him,
that I might come to his dwelling!
4 I would set out my case before him,
fill my mouth with arguments;
5 I would learn the words he would
answer me,
understand what he would say to me.

**22:6–9** This criticism of Job by Eliphaz is untrue (cf. 31:19), but he is driven to it by his belief that God always acts justly, even when he causes someone to suffer; suffering is due to wrongdoing (cf. v. 29).

**22:18** The second part of the verse repeats 21:16.

**22:19 Them**: the wicked. Eliphaz obviously thinks that the just can be pleased by God's punishment of the wicked. Such pleasure at the downfall of the wicked is expressed elsewhere, e.g., Ps 58:11; 63:12.

**22:24 Ophir**: see note on Ps 45:10.

*b:* Jb 24:3; Dt 24:6, 17; Ez 18:12, 16. *c:* Jb 29:12–13; Dt 24:17; 27:19. *d:* Jb 18:8–10. *e:* Jb 11:8. *f:* Ps 10:11; 73:11; 94:7; Is 29:15; Ez 8:12; 9:9. *g:* Jb 21:16. *h:* Ps 107:42. *i:* Jb 33:26. *j:* Ps 138:6; Prv 29:23; Mt 23:12; Lk 1:52; Jas 4:10; 1 Pt 5:5. *k:* Jb 17:9; Ps 18:21, 25; 24:4.

[6] Would he contend against me with his
great power?
No, he himself would heed me!
[7] There an upright man might argue with
him,
and I would once and for all be
delivered from my judge.
[8] But if I go east, he is not there;*
or west, I cannot perceive him;
[9] The north enfolds him, and I cannot
catch sight of him;
The south hides him, and I cannot see
him.
[10] Yet he knows my way;
if he tested me, I should come forth
like gold.[l]
[11] My foot has always walked in his steps;
I have kept his way and not turned
aside.
[12] From the commands of his lips I have not
departed;
the words of his mouth I have
treasured in my heart.
[13] But once he decides, who can contradict
him?
What he desires, that he does.[m]
[14] For he will carry out what is appointed
for me,
and many such things he has in store.
[15] Therefore I am terrified before him;
when I take thought, I dread him.
[16] For it is God who has made my heart
faint,
the Almighty who has terrified me.
[17] Yes, would that I had vanished in
darkness,
hidden by the thick gloom before me.

## CHAPTER 24

See RG 169–73

[1] Why are times not set by the
Almighty,
and why do his friends not see his
days?*
[2] People remove landmarks;
they steal herds and pasture them.
[3] The donkeys of orphans they drive away;
they take the widow's ox for a pledge.
[4] They force the needy off the road;
all the poor of the land are driven into
hiding.
[5] Like wild donkeys in the wilderness,
they go forth to their task of seeking
prey;
the steppe provides food for their
young;
[6] They harvest fodder in the field,
and glean in the vineyard of the wicked.
[7] They pass the night naked, without
clothing;
they have no covering against the cold;
[8] They are drenched with rain from the
mountains,
and for want of shelter they cling to
the rock.
[9] Orphans are snatched from the breast,
infants of the needy are taken in
pledge.*
[10] They go about naked, without clothing,
and famished, they carry the sheaves.*
[11] Between the rows they press out the oil;
they tread the wine presses, yet are
thirsty.
[12] In the city the dying groan,
and the souls of the wounded cry out.
Yet God does not treat it as a disgrace!
[13] They are rebels against the light:[n]
they do not recognize its ways;
they do not stay in its paths.
[14] When there is no light the murderer rises,
to kill the poor and needy;
in the night he acts like a thief.
[15] The eye of the adulterer watches for the
twilight;[o]
he says, "No eye will see me."
He puts a mask over his face;
[16] in the dark he breaks into houses;
By day they shut themselves in;
they do not know the light.

**23:8** Job's confident desire to confront God (vv. 2–7, contrary to his fears in 9:14–20 and 13:21–27) gives way to his dark night: God's absence (vv. 8–9), which also terrifies (vv. 13–17).

**24:1** After his failure to find God, Job takes up the question: Why does God not favor his friends by the speedy punishment of his enemies?

**24:9** This verse continues the description of the plight of the poor in vv. 2–4, and may belong there.

**24:10** This verse is a variant of v. 7, and may be an erroneous scribal repetition.

*l:* Ps 66:10; Prv 17:3; Mal 3:3; 1 Pt 1:7. *m:* Jb 42:2; Ps 115:3; 135:6. *n:* Jn 3:19–20. *o:* Prv 7:9–10.

[17] Indeed, for all of them morning is deep
darkness;
then they recognize the terrors of deep
darkness.
[18] He is swift on the surface of the water:*
their portion in the land is accursed,
they do not turn aside by way of the
vineyards.
[19] Drought and heat snatch away the snow
waters,
Sheol, those who have sinned.
[20] May the womb forget him,
may the worm find him sweet,
may he no longer be remembered;
And may wickedness be broken like a
tree.
[21] May his companion be barren, unable to
give birth,
may his widow not prosper!
[22] He* sustains the mighty by his strength,
to him who rises without assurance of
his life
[23] he gives safety and support,
and his eyes are on their ways.
[24] They are exalted for a while, and then are
no more;
laid low, like everyone else they are
gathered up;
like ears of grain they shrivel.
[25] If this be not so, who can make me a liar,
and reduce my words to nothing?

See RG 169–73

## CHAPTER 25

***Bildad's Third Speech.*** [1]* Then Bildad
the Shuhite answered and said:

[2] Dominion and dread are his
who brings about harmony in his
heavens.
[3] Is there any numbering of his troops?*
Yet on which of them does his light
not rise?
[4] How can anyone be in the right against
God,[p]
or how can any born of woman be
innocent?
[5] Even the moon is not bright
and the stars are not clean in his eyes.
[6] How much less a human being, who is
but a worm,
a mortal, who is only a maggot?[q]

## CHAPTER 26

See RG 169–73

***Job's Reply.*** [1] Then Job answered and
said:*

[2] What help you give to the powerless,
what strength to the feeble arm!
[3] How you give counsel to one without
wisdom;
how profuse is the advice you offer!
[4] With whose help have you uttered those
words,
whose breath comes forth from you?[r]
[5] The shades* beneath writhe in terror,[s]
the waters, and their inhabitants.
[6] Naked before him is Sheol,*
and Abaddon has no covering.[t]
[7] He stretches out Zaphon* over the void,
and suspends the earth over nothing at
all;
[8] He binds up the waters in his clouds,
yet the cloud is not split by their weight;
[9] He holds back the appearance of the full
moon
by spreading his clouds before it.
[10] He has marked out a circle* on the
surface of the deep[u]
as the boundary of light and darkness.
[11] The pillars of the heavens tremble

**24:18–24** These verses are inconsistent with Job's views elsewhere. Moreover, they are in general poorly preserved, and in some cases obscure.

**24:22 He**: God.

**25:1** At this point any structure in the dialogues disappears. Bildad's speech is very short, and there follow two speeches attributed to Job, with significantly different introductions in 27:1 and 29:1, and with no intervening third speech of Zophar.

**25:3 His troops**: the heavenly host, or army, the stars (cf. Jgs 5:20), later understood as angels.

**26:1–14** Perhaps to be read as Job's reply to Bildad's short speech.

**26:5 Shades**: the dead in Sheol, the nether world; cf. Ps 88:11; Is 26:14.

**26:6 Sheol**: cf. note on Ps 6:6. **Abaddon**: Hebrew for "(place of) destruction," a synonym for nether world; cf. Jb 28:22; Rev 9:11.

**26:7 Zaphon**: lit., "the north," used here as a synonym for the firmament, the heavens; cf. Is 14:13.

**26:10 Circle**: the horizon of the ocean which serves as the boundary for the activity of light and darkness; cf. Prv 8:27.

*p:* Jb 4:17; 9:2; 35:2. *q:* Jb 4:19; 15:16. *r:* Gn 2:7. *s:* Prv 9:18. *t:* Ps 139:7–12. *u:* Jb 38:8–11; Prv 8:29.

and are stunned at his thunderous
rebuke;[v]
12 By his power he stilled Sea,
by his skill he crushed Rahab;*
13 By his wind the heavens were made clear,
his hand pierced the fleeing serpent.* [w]
14 Lo, these are but the outlines of his ways,
and what a whisper of a word we hear
of him:
Who can comprehend the thunder of
his power?

## CHAPTER 27

See RG 169–73

***Job's Reply.***
1 Job took up his theme
again and said:

2 As God lives,* who takes away my right,[x]
the Almighty, who has made my life
bitter,
3 So long as I still have life breath in me,
the breath of God in my nostrils,
4 My lips shall not speak falsehood,
nor my tongue utter deceit!
5 Far be it from me to account you right;
till I die I will not renounce my
innocence.[y]
6 My justice I maintain and I will not
relinquish it;
my heart does not reproach me for any
of my days.
7 * Let my enemy be as the wicked
and my adversary as the unjust!
8 For what hope has the impious when he
is cut off,
when God requires his life?
9 Will God then listen to his cry
when distress comes upon him,
10 If he delights in the Almighty
and calls upon God constantly?
11 I will teach you what is in God's hand,
and the way of the Almighty I will not
conceal.
12 Look, you yourselves have all seen it;
why do you spend yourselves in empty
words!
13 This is the portion of the wicked with God,
the heritage oppressors receive from
the Almighty:[z]
14 Though his children be many, the sword
awaits them.
His descendants shall want for bread.
15 His survivors shall be buried in death;
their widows shall not weep.
16 Though he heap up silver like dust
and store away mounds of clothing,
17 What he has stored the righteous shall
wear,
and the innocent shall divide the silver.
18 He builds his house as of cobwebs,
or like a booth put up by a watchman.
19 He lies down a rich man, one last time;
he opens his eyes—nothing is there.[a]
20 Terrors flood over him like water,
at night the tempest carries him off.
21 The east wind seizes him and he is gone;
it sweeps him from his place;
22 It hurls itself at him without pity,
as he tries to flee from its power.
23 It claps its hands at him,
and whistles at him from its place.

# V. The Poem on Wisdom

## CHAPTER 28

See RG 169–73

### *Where Is Wisdom to be Found?*

1 There is indeed a mine for silver,*
and a place for refining gold.
2 Iron is taken from the earth,

**26:12 Rahab**: another name for the primeval sea-monster; see notes on Jb 3:8 and Ps 89:11; cf. also Jb 7:12; 9:13.

**26:13 The fleeing serpent**: the same term occurs in Is 27:1 in apposition to Leviathan; see note on Jb 3:8.

**27:2–6 As God lives . . . far be it**: Job affirms two oaths about his innocence by the very God whom he has accused of violating his right. Such is the paradoxical situation of a tortured person who cannot give the lie to his personal justice, but also refuses to renounce God. He dares God to be "just" as he, Job, understands this.

**27:7–23** These verses are inconsistent with Job's views elsewhere, and may be part of a missing speech of Zophar; cf. notes on 24:18–24 and 25:1. Or possibly they are an ironic description of the fate of the three friends.

**28:1–28** This chapter contains a beautifully vivid description of that Wisdom which is beyond the attainment of creatures and known only to God. The pronouns referring to Wisdom may be translated as either feminine or neuter; in view of Wisdom's role as God's companion and partner in creation (see Prv 8:22–30; Sir 24:1–21; Wis 9:9; Bar 3:9–4:4), the feminine is used here. There is no consensus about the authorship of this poem; it may originally have been an independent composition incorporated into the Book of Job.

*v*: Jb 9:6; Ps 18:16; 104:7. *w*: Is 27:1. *x*: Jb 34:5. *y*: Jb 2:3, 9; 13:15; 33:9. *z*: Jb 20:4–29. *a*: Ps 49:18; 76:6.

## Poem on Wisdom

THE ANONYMOUS POEM of ch 28 breaks the cycle of speeches of Job and his three friends that began in ch 3. Some consider it a later insertion, but it is original to the story because it heightens the drama by retarding the action and by raising important questions in the reader's mind. For example, by declaring wisdom inaccessible to human beings, the poem suggests what the reader already suspects, that the dialogue between Job and his friends cannot provide a satisfactory answer to his problem. It suggests that the answer must come from a nonhuman source, pointing toward the divine response of chs 39–42.

and copper smelted out of stone.
3 * He sets a boundary for the darkness;
the farthest confines he explores.
4 He breaks open a shaft far from habitation,
unknown to human feet;
suspended, far from people, they sway.
5 The earth, though out of it comes forth bread,
is in fiery upheaval underneath.
6 Its stones are the source of lapis lazuli,
and there is gold in its dust.
7 The path no bird of prey knows,
nor has the hawk's eye seen it.
8 The proud beasts have not trodden it,
nor has the lion gone that way.
9 He sets his hand to the flinty rock,
and overturns the mountains at their root.
10 He splits channels in the rocks;
his eyes behold all that is precious.
11 He dams up the sources of the streams,
and brings hidden things to light.
12 As for wisdom—where can she be found?
Where is the place of understanding?[b]
13 Mortals do not know her path,
nor is she to be found in the land of the living.
14 The Deep says, "She is not in me";
and the Sea says, "She is not with me."
15 Solid gold cannot purchase her,
nor can her price be paid with silver.[c]
16 She cannot be bought with gold of Ophir,*
with precious onyx or lapis lazuli,
17 Gold or crystal cannot equal her,
nor can golden vessels be exchanged for her.
18 Neither coral nor crystal should be thought of;
the value of wisdom surpasses pearls.
19 Ethiopian topaz does not equal her,
nor can she be weighed out for pure gold.
20 As for wisdom, where does she come from?
Where is the place of understanding?
21 She is hidden from the eyes of every living thing;
even from the birds of the air she is concealed.
22 Abaddon* and Death say,
"Only by rumor have we heard of her."
23 * But God understands the way to her;[d]
it is he who knows her place.[e]
24 For he beholds the ends of the earth
and sees all that is under the heavens.
25 When he weighed out the wind,
and measured out the waters;
26 When he made a rule for the rain
and a path for the thunderbolts,[f]

**28:3–4** The subject of the verbs in these verses has no clear antecedent; the context of vv. 2–6 suggests miners. The Hebrew of v. 4 is especially difficult. The general sense of vv. 1–11 is that one can find minerals in the earth; in contrast, where is Wisdom to be found (vv. 12, 20)?

**28:16 Ophir**: cf. note on Ps 45:10.

**28:22 Abaddon**: cf. note on Jb 26:6.

**28:23–27** In reply to the question of vv. 12, 20, these verses indicate that the creator (vv. 24–26) knows the "place" of wisdom and even "established" her, but the specifics are not given. For further development of this theme, cf. Sir 1:1–10 and Bar 3:9–4:4.

*b:* Eccl 7:24–25; Bar 3:14–15, 29–33. *c:* Prv 3:14; 8:10–11, 19; 16:16; Wis 7:7–11. *d:* Prv 8:22–31. *e:* Prv 2:6; Sir 1:1; Jas 1:5. *f:* Jb 38:25; Prv 3:20.

27 Then he saw wisdom and appraised her,
established her, and searched her out.
28 * And to mortals he said:
See: the fear of the Lord is wisdom;
and avoiding evil is understanding.[g]

## VI. Job's Final Summary of His Cause

### CHAPTER 29

See RG 169–73

1* Job took up his theme again and said:

2 Oh, that I were as in the months past,
as in the days when God watched over me:[h]
3 While he kept his lamp shining above my head,
and by his light I walked through darkness;
4 As I was in my flourishing days,
when God sheltered my tent;
5 When the Almighty was still with me,
and my children were round about me;
6 When my footsteps were bathed in cream,
and the rock flowed with streams of oil.*
7 Whenever I went out to the gate of the city
and took my seat in the square,
8 The young men saw me and withdrew,
and the elders rose up and stood;
9 Officials refrained from speaking
and covered their mouths with their hands;[i]
10 The voice of the princes was silenced,
and their tongues stuck to the roofs of their mouths.
11 The ear that heard blessed me;
the eye that saw acclaimed me.
12 For I rescued the poor who cried out for help,
the orphans, and the unassisted;
13 The blessing of those in extremity came upon me,
and the heart of the widow I made joyful.
14 I wore my righteousness like a garment;
justice was my robe and my turban.
15 I was eyes to the blind,
and feet to the lame was I.
16 I was a father to the poor;
the complaint of the stranger I pursued,
17 And I broke the jaws of the wicked man;
from his teeth I forced the prey.
18 I said: "In my own nest I shall grow old;
I shall multiply years like the phoenix.*
19 My root is spread out to the waters;
the dew rests by night on my branches.
20 My glory is fresh within me,
and my bow is renewed in my hand!"
21 For me they listened and waited;
they were silent for my counsel.
22 Once I spoke, they said no more,
but received my pronouncement drop by drop.
23 They waited for me as for the rain;
they drank in my words like the spring rains.
24 When I smiled on them they could not believe it;
they would not let the light of my face be dimmed.
25 I decided their course and sat at their head,
I lived like a king among the troops,
like one who comforts mourners.

### CHAPTER 30

See RG 169–73

1 But now they hold me in derision
who are younger than I,[j]
Whose fathers I should have disdained
to rank with the dogs of my flock.
2 Such strength as they had meant nothing to me;

**28:28** This verse may be a later addition expressing a commonplace of the wisdom tradition; see cross-references. The addition seems to tie the poem in with the description of Job as fearing God and avoiding evil (1:1, 8; 2:3).

**29:1** This chapter begins Job's soliloquy, which will end in 31:40. He describes in florid and exaggerated terms his former lifestyle with all its blessings, a deliberate contrast to his current plight, which will be further described in chap. 30.

**29:6** Hyperbole to express abundance; see note on 20:17.

**29:18** **Phoenix**: a legendary bird which, after several centuries of life, consumed itself in fire, then rose from its ashes in youthful freshness.

*g:* Ps 111:10; Prv 1:7; 9:10; Sir 1:13–21. *h:* Jb 1:10. *i:* Wis 8:10–12. *j:* Jb 12:4; 19:18.

their vigor had perished.
3 In want and emaciating hunger[k]
they fled to the parched lands:
to the desolate wasteland by night.
4 They plucked saltwort* and shrubs;
the roots of the broom plant were their food.
5 They were banished from the community,
with an outcry like that against a thief—
6 To dwell on the slopes of the wadies,
in caves of sand and stone;
7 Among the bushes they brayed;
under the nettles they huddled together.
8 Irresponsible, of no account,
they were driven out of the land.
9 Yet now they sing of me in mockery;
I have become a byword among them.[l]
10 They abhor me, they stand aloof,
they do not hesitate to spit in my face!
11 * Because he has loosened my bowstring
and afflicted me,
they have thrown off restraint in my presence.
12 On my right the young rabble rise up;
they trip my feet,
they build their approaches for my ruin.
13 They tear up my path,
they promote my ruin,
no helper is there against them.
14 As through a wide breach they advance;
amid the uproar they come on in waves;
15 terrors roll over me.
My dignity is driven off like the wind,
and my well-being vanishes like a cloud.
16 And now my life ebbs away from me,
days of affliction have taken hold of me.
17 * At night he pierces my bones,
my sinews have no rest.
18 With great difficulty I change my clothes,
the collar of my tunic fits around my waist.
19 He has cast me into the mire;
I have become like dust and ashes.
20 I cry to you, but you do not answer me;[m]
I stand, but you take no notice.
21 You have turned into my tormentor,
and with your strong hand you attack me.
22 You raise me up and drive me before the wind;
I am tossed about by the tempest.
23 Indeed I know that you will return me to death
to the house destined for everyone alive.[n]
24 Yet should not a hand be held out
to help a wretched person in distress?
25 Did I not weep for the hardships of others;
was not my soul grieved for the poor?[o]
26 Yet when I looked for good, evil came;
when I expected light, darkness came.
27 My inward parts seethe and will not be stilled;
days of affliction have overtaken me.
28 I go about in gloom, without the sun;
I rise in the assembly and cry for help.
29 I have become a brother to jackals,
a companion to ostriches.
30 My blackened skin falls away from me;
my very frame is scorched by the heat.
31 My lyre is tuned to mourning,
and my reed pipe to sounds of weeping.

## CHAPTER 31

See RG 169–73

1 I made a covenant with my eyes
not to gaze upon a virgin.
2 What portion comes from God above,
what heritage from the Almighty on high?
3 Is it not calamity for the unrighteous,

**30:4 Saltwort**: found in salt marshes and very sour to the taste; eaten by the extremely poor as a cooked vegetable. **Broom plant**: the juniper or brushwood; cf. Ps 120:4; a figure of bitterness and poverty, because of its bitter-tasting roots which are practically inedible.

**30:11** God is the subject of the verbs. **Loosened my bowstring**: i.e., disarmed and disabled me.

**30:17–23** Job here refers to God's harsh treatment of him. Cf. 16:9–17; 19:6–12.

*k*: Jb 24:5–6. *l*: Jb 17:6. *m*: Jb 19:7. *n*: Heb 9:27. *o*: Jb 29:12–16.

and woe for evildoers?
4 Does he not see my ways,
and number all my steps?[p]
5 If I have walked in falsehood*
and my foot has hastened to deceit,
6 Let God weigh me in the scales of justice;
thus will he know my innocence![q]
7 If my steps have turned out of the way,
and my heart has followed my eyes,
or any stain clings to my hands,
8 Then may I sow, but another eat,
and may my produce be rooted up!
9 If my heart has been enticed toward a
woman,
and I have lain in wait at my
neighbor's door;
10 Then may my wife grind for another,
and may others kneel over her!
11 For that would be heinous,
a crime to be condemned,[r]
12 A fire that would consume down to
Abaddon*
till it uprooted all my crops.[s]
13 Had I refused justice to my manservant
or to my maidservant, when they had a
complaint against me,
14 What then should I do when God rises up?
What could I answer when he
demands an account?
15 Did not he who made me in the belly
make him?
Did not the same One fashion us in the
womb?
16 If I have denied anything that the poor
desired,[t]
or allowed the eyes of the widow to
languish
17 While I ate my portion alone,
with no share in it for the fatherless,
18 Though like a father he* has reared me
from my youth,
guiding me even from my mother's
womb—
19 If I have seen a wanderer without
clothing,
or a poor man without covering,
20 Whose limbs have not blessed me
when warmed with the fleece of my
sheep;
21 If I have raised my hand against the
innocent
because I saw that I had supporters at
the gate—*
22 Then may my arm fall from the shoulder,
my forearm be broken at the elbow!
23 For I dread calamity from God,
and his majesty will overpower me.
24 Had I put my trust in gold
or called fine gold my security;
25 Or had I rejoiced that my wealth was
great,
or that my hand had acquired
abundance—
26 Had I looked upon the light* as it shone,[u]
or the moon in the splendor of its
progress,
27 And had my heart been secretly enticed
to blow them a kiss with my hand,
28 This too would be a crime for
condemnation,
for I should have denied God above.[v]
29 Had I rejoiced at the destruction of my
enemy
or exulted when evil came upon him,[w]
30 Even though I had not allowed my mouth
to sin
by invoking a curse against his life—
31 Had not the men of my tent exclaimed,
"Who has not been filled with his
meat!"*
32 No stranger lodged in the street,
for I opened my door to wayfarers—
33 * Had I, all too human, hidden my sins
and buried my guilt in my bosom
34 Because I feared the great multitude
and the scorn of the clans terrified me—

**31:5–34** In a series of purificatory oaths, Job protests his innocence.

**31:12 Abaddon**: see note on 26:6.

**31:18 He**: presumably God.

**31:21 Gate**: cf. notes on 5:4; Ru 4:1.

**31:26–28 Light**: of the sun. Job never sinned by worshiping the sun or the moon. **Blow them a kiss**: an act of idolatrous worship.

**31:31** The members of his extended family will testify to his hospitality.

**31:33–34** Job's present protest is made, not in spite of hidden sins which he had been unwilling to disclose, but out of genuine innocence. **All too human**: can also be translated "like Adam."

*p:* Jb 14:16; 34:21; Ps 139:3; Prv 5:21. *q:* Jb 23:10. *r:* Ex 20:14; Lv 20:10; Dt 22:22. *s:* Sir 9:8–9. *t:* Jb 29:12–16. *u:* Dt 4:19. *v:* Dt 17:2–7. *w:* Prv 24:17.

then I should have remained silent,
and not come out of doors!
35 * Oh, that I had one to hear my case:
here is my signature:* let the Almighty answer me!
Let my accuser write out his indictment![x]
36 Surely, I should wear it on my shoulder*
or put it on me like a diadem;
37 Of all my steps I should give him an account;
like a prince* I should present myself before him.
38 If my land has cried out against me
till its furrows wept together;
39 If I have eaten its strength without payment
and grieved the hearts of its tenants;
40 Then let the thorns grow instead of wheat
and stinkweed instead of barley!

The words of Job are ended.

## VII. Elihu's Speeches

### CHAPTER 32

See RG 169–73

1 Then the three men ceased to answer
Job, because in his own eyes he was in the
right.[y] 2[z] But the anger of Elihu,* son of
Barachel the Buzite, of the clan of Ram, was
kindled. He was angry with Job for considering himself rather than God to be in the
right. 3[a] He was angry also with the three
friends because they had not found a good
answer and had not condemned Job. 4 But
since these men were older than he, Elihu
bided his time before addressing Job.
5 When, however, Elihu saw that there was
no reply in the mouths of the three men, his
wrath was inflamed. 6 So Elihu, son of
Barachel the Buzite, answered and said:

I am young and you are very old;
therefore I held back and was afraid
to declare to you my knowledge.
7 I thought, days should speak,
and many years teach wisdom![b]
8 But there is a spirit in human beings,[c]
the breath of the Almighty, that gives them understanding.
9 It is not those of many days who are wise,
nor the aged who understand the right.
10 Therefore I say, listen to me;
I also will declare my knowledge!
11 Behold, I have waited for your words,
have given ear to your arguments,
as you searched out what to say.
12 Yes, I followed you attentively:
And look, none of you has convicted Job,
not one could refute his statements.
13 So do not say, "We have met wisdom;*
God can vanquish him but no mortal!"
14 For had he addressed his words to me,
I would not then have answered him with your words.
15 They are dismayed, they make no more reply;
words fail them.
16 Must I wait? Now that they speak no more,
and have ceased to make reply,
17 I too will speak my part;
I also will declare my knowledge!
18 For I am full of words;
the spirit within me compels me.
19 My belly is like unopened wine,
like wineskins ready to burst.
20 Let me speak and obtain relief;
let me open my lips, and reply.
21 I would not be partial to anyone,

**31:35–37** This concluding bravado fits better after v. 40a.

**31:35 My signature**: lit., "*tau*," the last letter of the Hebrew alphabet, shaped like a cross. Job issues a subpoena to God, and challenges him to follow proper legal procedure as well.

**31:36 On my shoulder**: i.e., boldly, proudly.

**31:37 Like a prince**: not as a frightened criminal.

**32:2 Elihu** means "My God is he." This speaker was from Buz, which, according to Jer 25:23, was near Tema and Dedan. A young man, he impetuously and impatiently upbraids Job for his boldness toward God, and the three friends for not successfully answering Job. He undertakes to defend God's absolute justice and to explain more clearly why there is suffering. While fundamentally his position is the same as that of the three friends, he locates the place of suffering in the divine plan. Because Elihu's four speeches (32:6–33:33; 34:2–37; 35:2–16; 36:2–37:24) repeat the substance of the earlier arguments of the three friends and also anticipate the content of the divine speeches (chaps. 39–41), many scholars consider them a later addition to the book.

**32:13 Met wisdom**: in Job's arguments.

*x:* Jb 19:23; 23:3–7. *y:* Jb 33:9. *z:* Jb 13:18; 27:6; 34:5; 35:2. *a:* Jb 22:5. *b:* Jb 12:12. *c:* Jb 33:4.

nor give flattering titles to any.
22 For I know nothing of flattery;
if I did, my Maker would soon take me away.

CHAPTER 33

See RG 169–73

1 Therefore, O Job, hear my discourse;
listen to all my words.
2 Behold, now I open my mouth;
my tongue and voice form words.
3 I will state directly what is in my mind,
my lips shall speak knowledge clearly;
4 For the spirit of God made me,
the breath of the Almighty keeps me alive.[d]
5 If you are able, refute me;
draw up your arguments and take your stand.
6 Look, I am like you before God,
I too was pinched from clay.* [e]
7 Therefore fear of me should not dismay you,
nor should I weigh heavily upon you.
8 But you have said in my hearing,
as I listened to the sound of your words:
9 "I am clean, without transgression;
I am innocent, there is no guilt in me.[f]
10 Yet he invents pretexts against me
and counts me as an enemy.* [g]
11 He puts my feet in the stocks,
watches all my paths!"[h]
12 In this you are not just, let me tell you;
for God is greater than mortals.
13 Why, then, do you make complaint against him
that he gives no reply to their words?[i]
14 For God does speak, once,
even twice, though you do not see it:*
15 In a dream, in a vision of the night,
when deep sleep falls upon mortals
as they slumber in their beds.
16 It is then he opens their ears
and with a warning, terrifies them,
17 By turning mortals from acting
and keeping pride away from a man,
18 He holds his soul from the pit,
his life from passing to the grave.
19 Or he is chastened on a bed of pain,
suffering continually in his bones,
20 So that to his appetite food is repulsive,
his throat rejects the choicest nourishment.[j]
21 His flesh is wasted, it cannot be seen;
bones, once invisible, appear;
22 His soul draws near to the pit,
his life to the place of the dead.
23 If then there be a divine messenger,*
a mediator, one out of a thousand,
to show him what is right,
24 He will take pity on him and say,
"Deliver him from going down to the pit;
I have found him a ransom."
25 Then his flesh shall become soft as a boy's;
he shall be again as in the days of his youth.
26 He shall pray and God will favor him;
he shall see God's face with rejoicing;[k]
for he restores a person's righteousness.
27 He shall sing before all and say,
"I sinned and did wrong,
yet I was not punished accordingly.
28 He delivered me from passing to the pit,
and my life sees light."
29 See, all these things God does,
two, even three times, for a man,
30 Bringing back his soul from the pit
to the light, in the light of the living.
31 Be attentive, Job, listen to me!
Be silent and I will speak.
32 If you have anything to say, then answer me.
Speak out! I should like to see you justified.
33 If not, then you listen to me;
be silent, and I will teach you wisdom.

**33:6 Pinched from clay**: a reference to the tradition that human beings were made from clay; cf. Gn 2:7; Jb 10:9; Is 64:7.

**33:10 Enemy**: see note on 1:1; cf. 13:24.

**33:14** Elihu asserts that God speaks through warning in dream and also through pain. However, his presupposition is that the restored person admits sinfulness (v. 27). This of course is not relevant to Job's situation.

**33:23 Divine messenger**: or "angel," one of the thousands who serve as mediators.

*d:* Jb 32:8. *e:* Jb 31:15. *f:* Jb 10:7; 13:18; 27:5–6; 29:14; 32:1; 34:5. *g:* Jb 13:24; 19:11. *h:* Jb 13:27; 31:4. *i:* Jb 31:35. *j:* Jb 6:7. *k:* Jb 22:26–29.

## CHAPTER 34

See RG 169–73

1 Then Elihu answered and said:*

2 Hear my discourse, you that are wise;
you that have knowledge, listen to me!
3 For the ear tests words,
as the palate tastes food.[l]
4 Let us choose what is right;
let us determine among ourselves what
is good.
5 For Job has said, "I am innocent,
but God has taken away what is my
right.[m]
6 I declare the judgment on me to be a lie;
my arrow-wound is incurable, sinless
though I am."[n]
7 What man is like Job?
He drinks in blasphemies like water,
8 Keeps company with evildoers
and goes along with the wicked,
9 When he says, "There is no profit
in pleasing God."[o]
10 Therefore, you that have understanding,
hear me:
far be it from God to do wickedness;
far from the Almighty to do wrong![p]
11 Rather, he requites mortals for their
conduct,
and brings home to them their way of
life.[q]
12 Surely, God cannot act wickedly,
the Almighty cannot pervert justice.[r]
13 Who gave him charge over the earth,
or who set all the world in its place?[s]
14 If he were to set his mind to it,
gather to himself his spirit and breath,
15 All flesh would perish together,
and mortals return to dust.[t]
16 Now you*—understand, hear this!
Listen to the words I speak!
17 Can an enemy of justice be in control,
will you condemn the supreme Just
One,
18 Who says to a king, "You are worthless!"
and to nobles, "You are wicked!"
19 Who neither favors the person of princes,
nor respects the rich more than the
poor?
For they are all the work of his hands;[u]
20 in a moment they die, even at
midnight.[v]
People are shaken, and pass away,
the powerful are removed without
lifting a hand;
21 For his eyes are upon our ways,
and all our steps he sees.
22 There is no darkness so dense
that evildoers can hide in it.
23 For no one has God set a time
to come before him in judgment.
24 Without inquiry he shatters the mighty,[w]
and appoints others in their place,
25 Thus he discerns their works;
overnight they are crushed.
26 * Where the wicked are, he strikes them,
in a place where all can see,
27 Because they turned away from him
and did not understand his ways at all:
28 And made the cry of the poor reach him,
so that he heard the cry of the afflicted.
29 If he is silent, who then can condemn?
If he hides his face, who then can
behold him,
whether nation or individual?
30 Let an impious man not rule,
nor those who ensnare their people.
31 Should anyone say to God,
"I accept my punishment; I will offend
no more;
32 What I cannot see, teach me:
if I have done wrong, I will do so no
more,"
33 Would you then say that God must
punish,
when you are disdainful?
It is you who must choose, not I;
speak, therefore, what you know.

**34:1** Elihu replies, although no one else has spoken. This connective phrase (see also 35:1 and 36:1) may indicate that these speeches of Elihu are a secondary addition to the book (see note on 32:2).

**34:16 Now you**: Elihu turns to Job and addresses him directly.

**34:26, 29–30** The extant Hebrew text of these verses is obscure.

*l:* Jb 12:11. *m:* Jb 33:9–10. *n:* Jb 9:20. *o:* Jb 9:22–23, 30–31; 21:15; 35:3. *p:* Jb 36:23. *q:* Ps 62:13; Prv 24:12; Mt 16:27; Rom 2:6; 2 Cor 5:10; Rev 22:12. *r:* Jb 8:3. *s:* Jb 38:4–7. *t:* Jb 10:9. *u:* Dt 10:17; 2 Chr 19:7; Wis 6:7; Acts 10:34; Rom 2:11; Eph 6:9; Col 3:25; 1 Pt 1:17. *v:* Jb 21:13. *w:* Ps 2:9.

34 Those who understand will say to me,
all the wise who hear my views:
35 "Job speaks without knowledge,
his words make no sense.[x]
36 Let Job be tested to the limit,
since his answers are those of the impious;
37 For he is adding rebellion to his sin
by brushing off our arguments
and addressing many words to God."

## CHAPTER 35

See RG 169–73

1* Then Elihu answered and said:

2 Do you think it right to say,
"I am in the right, not God"?[y]
3 When you ask what it profits you,
"What advantage do I have from not sinning?"[z]
4 I have words for a reply to you*
and your friends as well.
5 Look up to the skies and see;
behold the heavens high above you.
6 If you sin, what do you do to God?
Even if your offenses are many, how do you affect him?
7 If you are righteous, what do you give him,
or what does he receive from your hand?[a]
8 Your wickedness affects only someone like yourself,
and your justice, only a fellow human being.
9 In great oppression people cry out;
they call for help because of the power of the great,
10 No one says, "Where is God, my Maker,
who gives songs in the night,
11 Teaches us more than the beasts of the earth,
and makes us wiser than the birds of the heavens?"
12 Though thus they cry out, he does not answer
because of the pride of the wicked.
13 But it is idle to say God does not hear
or that the Almighty does not take notice.
14 Even though you say, "You take no notice of it,"*
the case is before him; with trembling wait upon him.
15 But now that you have done otherwise,
God's anger punishes,
nor does he show much concern over a life.
16 Yet Job to no purpose opens his mouth,
multiplying words without knowledge.[b]

## CHAPTER 36

See RG 169–73

1 Elihu continued and said:

2 Wait a little and I will instruct you,
for there are still words to be said for God.
3 I will assemble arguments from afar,
and for my maker I will establish what is right.
4 For indeed, my words are not a lie;
one perfect in knowledge is before you.
5 Look, God is great, not disdainful;
his strength of purpose is great.
He does not preserve the life of the wicked.
6 He establishes the right of the poor;[c]
he does not divert his eyes from the just
7 But he seats them upon thrones
with kings, exalted forever.[d]
8 If they are bound with fetters,
held fast by bonds of affliction,
9 He lets them know what they have done,
and how arrogant are their sins.
10 He opens their ears to correction
and tells them to turn back from evil.
11 If they listen and serve him,
they spend their days in prosperity,
their years in happiness.
12 But if they do not listen, they pass to the grave,

**35:1** See note on 34:1.

**35:4 A reply to you**: Elihu refers to Job's statement that the innocent suffer as much as the wicked, and especially to Eliphaz's words in 22:2–3.

**35:14–15** The text here is uncertain. It seems to indicate that Job should have realized God's indifference is only apparent, and that, because he has not done so, God will punish him.

*x:* Jb 35:16; 38:2; 42:3. *y:* Jb 32:2. *z:* Jb 34:9. *a:* Jb 22:3; 41:2; Lk 17:10; Rom 11:35. *b:* Jb 34:35; 38:2; 42:3. *c:* Ps 72:4, 12–13. *d:* Ps 113:7–8.

they perish for lack of knowledge.
13 The impious in heart lay up anger;
they do not cry for help when he binds
them;
14 They will die young—
their life* among the reprobate.
15 But he saves the afflicted through their
affliction,
and opens their ears through oppression.
16 * He entices you from distress,
to a broad place without constraint;
what rests on your table is rich food.
17 Though you are full of the judgment of
the wicked,
judgment and justice will be
maintained.
18 Let not anger at abundance entice you,
nor great bribery lead you astray.
19 Will your wealth equip you against
distress,
or all your exertions of strength?
20 Do not long for the night,
when peoples vanish in their place.
21 Be careful; do not turn to evil;
for this you have preferred to affliction.
22 * Look, God is exalted in his power.
What teacher is there like him?
23 Who prescribes for him his way?
Who says, "You have done wrong"?[e]
24 Remember, you should extol his work,
which people have praised in song.
25 All humankind beholds it;
everyone views it from afar.
26 See, God is great beyond our knowledge,
the number of his years past searching
out.
27 He holds in check the waterdrops
that filter in rain from his flood,
28 Till the clouds flow with them
and they rain down on all humankind.
29 * Can anyone understand the spreading
clouds,
the thunderings from his tent?
30 Look, he spreads his light over it,
it covers the roots of the sea.
31 For by these he judges the nations,
and gives food in abundance.
32 In his hands he holds the lightning,
and he commands it to strike the mark.
33 His thunder announces him
and incites the fury of the storm.

## CHAPTER 37

See RG 169–73

1 At this my heart trembles
and leaps out of its place.
2 Listen to his angry voice*
and the rumble that comes forth from
his mouth!
3 Everywhere under the heavens he sends it,
with his light, to the ends of the earth.
4 Again his voice roars,
his majestic voice thunders;
he does not restrain them when his
voice is heard.
5 God thunders forth marvels with his
voice;
he does great things beyond our
knowing.
6 He says to the snow, "Fall to the earth";
likewise to his heavy, drenching rain.
7 He shuts up all humankind indoors,
so that all people may know his work.
8 The wild beasts take to cover
and remain quiet in their dens.
9 Out of its chamber the tempest comes
forth;
from the north winds, the cold.
10 With his breath God brings the frost,
and the broad waters congeal.[f]
11 The clouds too are laden with moisture,
the storm-cloud scatters its light.
12 * He it is who changes their rounds,
according to his plans,
to do all that he commands them
across the inhabited world.
13 Whether for punishment or mercy,
he makes it happen.
14 Listen to this, Job!

**36:14 Life**: a miserable life before death or a shadowy existence in Sheol. **Reprobate**: cf. Dt 23:18–19.

**36:16–20** The Hebrew text here is obscure. Although each verse makes some sense, they do not constitute a logical sequence.

**36:22–25** These verses serve as an introduction to the hymn about the divine marvels, 36:26–37:24, which in some respects anticipates the tone and content of the Lord's speeches in chaps. 38–41.

**36:29–31** The translation of these verses is uncertain.

**37:2 Voice**: the thunder.

**37:12–13** The translation of these verses is uncertain.

*e:* Jb 34:10; Is 40:13. *f:* Ps 147:17.

Stand and consider the marvels of God!
15 Do you know how God lays his
command upon them,
and makes the light shine forth from
his clouds?
16 Do you know how the clouds are banked,
the marvels of him who is perfect in
knowledge?
17 You, who swelter in your clothes
when calm lies over the land from the
south,
18 Can you with him spread out the
firmament of the skies,
hard as a molten mirror?*
19 Teach us then what we shall say to him;
we cannot, for the darkness, make our
plea.
20 Will he be told about it when I speak?
Can anyone talk when he is being
destroyed?
21 Rather, it is as the light that cannot be
seen
while it is obscured by the clouds,
till the wind comes by and sweeps
them away.*
22 From Zaphon* the golden splendor comes,
surrounding God's awesome majesty!
23 The Almighty! We cannot find him,
preeminent in power and judgment,
abundant in justice, who never
oppresses.
24 Therefore people fear him;
none can see him, however wise their
hearts.*

## VIII. The Lord and Job Meet

### CHAPTER 38

See RG 169–73

1 Then the LORD* answered Job out of
the storm and said:
2 Who is this who darkens counsel
with words of ignorance?
3 Gird up your loins* now, like a man;
I will question you, and you tell me the
answers![g]
4 Where were you when I founded the
earth?
Tell me, if you have understanding.
5 Who determined its size? Surely you
know?
Who stretched out the measuring line
for it?
6 Into what were its pedestals sunk,
and who laid its cornerstone,
7 While the morning stars sang together
and all the sons of God* shouted for
joy?
8 Who shut within doors the sea,
when it burst forth from the womb,[h]
9 When I made the clouds its garment
and thick darkness its swaddling bands?
10 When I set limits for it
and fastened the bar of its door,
11 And said: Thus far shall you come but no
farther,
and here shall your proud waves stop?
12 Have you ever in your lifetime
commanded the morning
and shown the dawn its place
13 For taking hold of the ends of the earth,
till the wicked are shaken from it?
14 The earth is changed as clay by the seal,
and dyed like a garment;
15 But from the wicked their light is
withheld,
and the arm of pride is shattered.
16 Have you entered into the sources of the
sea,
or walked about on the bottom of the
deep?

**37:18 The firmament . . . mirror**: the ancients thought of the sky as a ceiling above which were the "upper waters" (cf. Gn 1:6–7; 7:11); when this ceiling became as hard as metal, the usual rain failed to fall on the earth (cf. Lv 26:19; Dt 28:23).

**37:21** Elihu argues that even though God seems not to know our circumstances, he does know them, just as surely as the sun shines behind the clouds.

**37:22 Zaphon**: the mythical mountain of the gods; cf. note on 26:7.

**37:24** The concluding remark of Elihu is ironic in view of the appearance of the Lord in the next chapter and Job's claim in 42:5.

**38:1** Now the Lord enters the debate and addresses two discourses (chaps. 38–39 and 40–41) to Job, speaking of divine wisdom and power. Such things are altogether beyond the capacity of Job. **Out of the storm**: frequently the background of the appearances of the Lord in the Old Testament; cf. Ps 18; 50; Na 1:3; Hb 3:2–15.

**38:3 Gird up your loins**: prepare for combat—figuratively, be ready to defend yourself in debate.

**38:7 Sons of God**: see note on 1:6.

*g:* Jb 40:2. *h:* Gn 1:9.

## God's Two Speeches to Job

THE LORD'S SUDDEN appearance in the storm never fails to astonish even though the ground has been laid for it in Job's oaths and demands of chs 27 and 29–31 and, in an ironic way, by Elihu's "appearance" and final statement. God answers Job out of the storm in two speeches (chs 38–39 and 40–41), even evoking a brief response by Job (40:3–5 and 42:1–6). The structure and the meaning of the speeches have puzzled scholars. Some believe the speeches are deliberately incoherent, irrational divine blasts showing there is no answer to Job's questions except inscrutable divine will. Others rearrange the text, but no rearrangement has won wide acceptance. Most, however, find some kind of logic, even though the speeches are also an example of the mysterious communications of creator to creature. The first speech shows that the world has a design (God is wise, is able to govern), and the second demonstrates the world is just (God upholds the righteous and puts down the wicked).

17 Have the gates of death been shown to you,
or have you seen the gates of darkness?
18 Have you comprehended the breadth of the earth?
Tell me, if you know it all.
19 What is the way to the dwelling of light,
and darkness—where is its place?
20 That you may take it to its territory
and know the paths to its home?
21 You know, because you were born then,
and the number of your days is great!*
22 Have you entered the storehouses of the snow,
and seen the storehouses of the hail
23 Which I have reserved for times of distress,
for a day of war and battle?[i]
24 What is the way to the parting of the winds,
where the east wind spreads over the earth?
25 Who has laid out a channel for the downpour
and a path for the thunderstorm
26 To bring rain to uninhabited land,
the unpeopled wilderness;
27 To drench the desolate wasteland
till the desert blooms with verdure?
28 Has the rain a father?
Who has begotten the drops of dew?
29 Out of whose womb comes the ice,
and who gives the hoarfrost its birth in the skies,
30 When the waters lie covered as though with stone
that holds captive the surface of the deep?
31 Have you tied cords to the Pleiades,*
or loosened the bonds of Orion?
32 Can you bring forth the Mazzaroth in their season,
or guide the Bear with her children?
33 Do you know the ordinances of the heavens;
can you put into effect their plan on the earth?
34 Can you raise your voice to the clouds,
for them to cover you with a deluge of waters?
35 Can you send forth the lightnings on their way,
so that they say to you, "Here we are"?
36 Who gives wisdom to the ibis,
and gives the rooster* understanding?
37 Who counts the clouds with wisdom?
Who tilts the water jars of heaven
38 So that the dust of earth is fused into a mass
and its clods stick together?
39 Do you hunt the prey for the lion

**38:21** Ironic, but not a harsh rebuke.

**38:31–32 Pleiades . . . Orion . . . Bear**: cf. 9:9. **Mazzaroth**: it is uncertain what astronomical group is meant by this Hebrew word; perhaps a southern constellation.

**38:36 Ibis . . . rooster**: the translation is uncertain.

*i*: Jos 10:11; Sir 46:5.

Let him who would instruct God give
answer![l]

3 Then Job answered the LORD and said:

4 * Look, I am of little account; what can I
answer you?
I put my hand over my mouth.
5 I have spoken once, I will not reply;
twice, but I will do so no more.

6 Then the LORD answered Job out of the
storm and said:
7 Gird up your loins now, like a man.
I will question you, and you tell me the
answers!
8 * Would you refuse to acknowledge my
right?
Would you condemn me that you may
be justified?
9 Have you an arm like that of God,
or can you thunder with a voice like
his?
10 Adorn yourself with grandeur and
majesty,
and clothe yourself with glory and
splendor.
11 Let loose the fury of your wrath;
look at everyone who is proud and
bring them down.
12 Look at everyone who is proud, and
humble them.
Tear down the wicked in their place,
13 bury them in the dust together;
in the hidden world imprison them.
14 Then will I too praise you,
for your own right hand can save you.
15 Look at Behemoth,* whom I made along
with you,
who feeds on grass like an ox.
16 See the strength in his loins,
the power in the sinews of his belly.
17 He carries his tail like a cedar;
the sinews of his thighs are like
cables.
18 His bones are like tubes of bronze;
his limbs are like iron rods.
19 He is the first of God's ways,
only his maker can approach him with
a sword.
20 For the mountains bring him produce,
and all wild animals make sport there.
21 Under lotus trees he lies,
in coverts of the reedy swamp.
22 The lotus trees cover him with their
shade;
all about him are the poplars in the
wadi.
23 If the river grows violent, he is not
disturbed;
he is tranquil though the Jordan surges
about his mouth.
24 Who can capture him by his eyes,
or pierce his nose* with a trap?
25 Can you lead Leviathan* about with a
hook,
or tie down his tongue with a rope?
26 Can you put a ring into his nose,
or pierce through his cheek with a
gaff?
27 Will he then plead with you, time after
time,
or address you with tender words?
28 Will he make a covenant with you
that you may have him as a slave
forever?
29 Can you play with him, as with a bird?
Can you tie him up for your little
girls?
30 Will the traders bargain for him?
Will the merchants* divide him up?
31 Can you fill his hide with barbs,
or his head with fish spears?
32 Once you but lay a hand upon him,
no need to recall any other conflict!

**40:4–5** Job's first reaction is humble, but also seemingly cautious.

**40:8–14** The issue is joined in these verses, and the Lord seems to challenge Job to play God and to bring down the proud and wicked.

**40:15 Behemoth**: a primeval monster of chaos; identified by some scholars as the hippopotamus, on which the description of Behemoth is partially based. The point of the Behemoth-Leviathan passages is that only the Lord, not Job, can control the cosmic evil which these forces symbolize.

**40:24 Eyes . . . nose**: the only exposed parts of the submerged beast.

**40:25 Leviathan**: although identified by some scholars as the crocodile, it is more likely another chaos monster; see note on 3:8.

**40:30 Merchants**: lit., "Canaanites," whose reputation for trading was so widespread that their name came to be used for merchants; cf. Prv 31:24.

*l:* Jb 38:3.

or appease the hunger of young lions,
40 While they crouch in their dens,
or lie in ambush in the thicket?
41 Who provides nourishment for the raven
when its young cry out to God,[j]
wandering about without food?

## CHAPTER 39

See RG 169–73

1 Do you know when mountain goats
are born,
or watch for the birth pangs of deer,
2 Number the months that they must fulfill,
or know when they give birth,
3 When they crouch down and drop their
young,
when they deliver their progeny?
4 Their offspring thrive and grow in the
open,
they leave and do not return.
5 Who has given the wild donkey his
freedom,
and who has loosed the wild ass from
bonds?
6 I have made the wilderness his home
and the salt flats his dwelling.
7 He scoffs at the uproar of the city,
hears no shouts of a driver.
8 He ranges the mountains for pasture,
and seeks out every patch of green.
9 Will the wild ox consent to serve you,
or pass the nights at your manger?
10 Will you bind the wild ox with a rope in
the furrow,
and will he plow the valleys after you?
11 Will you depend on him for his great
strength
and leave to him the fruits of your toil?
12 Can you rely on him to bring in your
grain
and gather in the yield of your
threshing floor?
13 The wings of the ostrich* flap away;
her plumage is lacking in feathers.
14 When she abandons her eggs on the
ground*
and lets them warm in the sand,
15 She forgets that a foot may crush them,
that the wild beasts may trample them;
16 She cruelly disowns her young
and her labor is useless; she has no
fear.
17 For God has withheld wisdom from her
and given her no share in
understanding.
18 Yet when she spreads her wings high,
she laughs at a horse and rider.
19 Do you give the horse his strength,*
and clothe his neck with a mane?
20 Do you make him quiver like a locust,
while his thunderous snorting spreads
terror?
21 He paws the valley, he rejoices in his
strength,
and charges into battle.
22 He laughs at fear and cannot be terrified;
he does not retreat from the sword.
23 Around him rattles the quiver,
flashes the spear and the javelin.
24 Frenzied and trembling he devours the
ground;
he does not hold back at the sound of
the trumpet;
25 at the trumpet's call he cries, "Aha!"
Even from afar he scents the battle,
the roar of the officers and the shouting.
26 Is it by your understanding that the hawk
soars,
that he spreads his wings toward the
south?
27 Does the eagle fly up at your command
to build his nest up high?
28 On a cliff he dwells and spends the night,
on the spur of cliff or fortress.
29 From there he watches for his food;
his eyes behold it afar off.
30 His young ones greedily drink blood;
where the slain are, there is he.[k]

## CHAPTER 40

See RG 169–73

1 The LORD then answered Job and
said:
2 Will one who argues with the Almighty
be corrected?

**39:13** The wings of the ostrich cannot raise her from the ground, but they help her to run swiftly.

**39:14–16** People thought that, because the ostrich laid her eggs on the sand, she was thereby cruelly abandoning them; cf. Lam 4:3.

**39:19–25** A classic description of a war horse.

*j*: Ps 147:9. *k*: Mt 24:28; Lk 17:37.

### CHAPTER 41

See RG 169–73

1 Whoever might vainly hope to do so
need only see him to be overthrown.
2 No one is fierce enough to arouse him;
who then dares stand before me?
3 Whoever has assailed me, I will pay
back—
Everything under the heavens is mine.
4 I need hardly mention his limbs,
his strength, and the fitness of his
equipment.
5 Who can strip off his outer garment,
or penetrate his double armor?
6 Who can force open the doors of his face,
close to his terrible teeth?
7 Rows of scales are on his back,
tightly sealed together;
8 They are fitted so close to each other
that no air can come between them;
9 So joined to one another
that they hold fast and cannot be parted.
10 When he sneezes, light flashes forth;
his eyes are like the eyelids of the
dawn.
11 Out of his mouth go forth torches;
sparks of fire leap forth.
12 From his nostrils comes smoke
as from a seething pot or bowl.
13 His breath sets coals afire;
a flame comes from his mouth.
14 Strength abides in his neck,
and power leaps before him.
15 The folds of his flesh stick together,
it is cast over him and immovable.
16 His heart is cast as hard as stone;
cast as the lower millstone.
17 When he rises up, the gods are afraid;
when he crashes down, they fall back.
18 Should a sword reach him, it will not
avail;
nor will spear, dart, or javelin.
19 He regards iron as chaff,
and bronze as rotten wood.
20 No arrow will put him to flight;
slingstones used against him are but
straw.
21 Clubs he regards as straw;
he laughs at the crash of the spear.
22 Under him are sharp pottery fragments,
spreading a threshing sledge upon the
mire.
23 He makes the depths boil like a pot;
he makes the sea like a perfume bottle.
24 Behind him he leaves a shining path;
you would think the deep had white
hair.
25 Upon the earth there is none like him,
he was made fearless.
26 He looks over all who are haughty,
he is king over all proud beasts.

### CHAPTER 42

See RG 169–73

1 Then Job answered the LORD and
said:

2 I know that you can do all things,*
and that no purpose of yours can be
hindered.
3 "Who is this who obscures counsel with
ignorance?"
I have spoken but did not understand;
things too marvelous for me, which I
did not know.[m]
4 "Listen, and I will speak;
I will question you, and you tell me the
answers."
5 By hearsay I had heard of you,
but now my eye has seen you.*
6 Therefore I disown what I have said,
and repent in dust and ashes.*

## IX. Epilogue

***Job's Restoration.*** 7 And after the LORD had
spoken these words to Job, the LORD said to
Eliphaz the Temanite, "My anger blazes

**42:2–4** In his final speech, Job quotes God's own words (see 38:2–3; 40:7).

**42:5** In 19:25–27 Job had affirmed a hope to "see" (three times) his vindicator. Now he has seen the Lord about whom he had heard so much.

**42:6** A difficult verse. Some doubt, in view of God's commendation in v. 7, that Job does in fact express repentance, and alternative translations are often given. Along with v. 5, it describes a change in Job, which the encounter with the Lord has brought about. **Dust and ashes:** an ambiguous phrase. It can refer to the human condition (cf. Gn 18:27; Jb 30:19) or to Job's ash heap (2:8).

**42:7** The three friends of Job (Elihu is ignored in the epilogue) are criticized by the Lord because they had "not spoken rightly" (vv. 7–8).

*m:* Jb 34:35; 35:16; 38:2; Ps 131:1; Prv 30:18.

**Telling the Truth**

JOB, WHO PROTESTED and accused God of attacking an innocent man, is declared to have told the truth about God, whereas the friends, who defended God and divine justice and wisdom without regard for truth, are judged to have acted out of folly and incur God's anger. Job is once again an effective intercessor (42:10; cf 1:5).

against you and your two friends!* You have
not spoken rightly concerning me, as has
my servant Job. [8]So now take seven bulls
and seven rams, and go to my servant Job,
and sacrifice a burnt offering for yourselves, and let my servant Job pray for you.*
To him I will show favor, and not punish
your folly, for you have not spoken rightly
concerning me, as has my servant Job."
[9]Then Eliphaz the Temanite, and Bildad the
Shuhite, and Zophar the Naamathite, went
and did as the LORD had commanded them.
The LORD showed favor to Job.

[10]The LORD also restored the prosperity
of Job, after he had prayed for his friends;
the LORD even gave to Job twice* as much
as he had before. [11]Then all his brothers and
sisters came to him, and all his former acquaintances, and they dined with him in his
house. They consoled and comforted him
for all the evil the LORD had brought upon
him, and each one gave him a piece of
money* and a gold ring.

[12][n] Thus the LORD blessed the later days
of Job more than his earlier ones. Now he
had fourteen thousand sheep, six thousand
camels, a thousand yoke of oxen, and a
thousand she-donkeys. [13]He also had seven
sons and three daughters: [14]the first daughter he called Jemimah, the second Keziah,
and the third Keren-happuch.* [15]In all the
land no other women were as beautiful as
the daughters of Job; and their father gave
them an inheritance* among their brothers.

[16]After this, Job lived a hundred and forty
years; and he saw his children, his grandchildren, and even his great-grandchildren.[o]
[17]Then Job died, old and full of years.

**42:8** An ironic touch: Job becomes the intercessor for his friends.

**42:10 Twice**: this is the fine for damage inflicted upon another; cf. Ex 22:3. The Lord pays up!

**42:11 A piece of money**: lit., *qesitah*, value unknown; also used in Gn 33:19; Jos 24:32. **Gold ring**: for the nose or ear.

**42:14** Job's daughters had names symbolic of their charms: **Jemimah**, dove; **Keziah**, precious perfume (cf. Ps 45:9); **Keren-happuch**, cosmetic jar—more precisely, a container for a black powder used like modern mascara.

**42:15** Ordinarily daughters did not inherit property unless there were no sons; cf. Nm 27:1–11.

*n:* Jb 1:3. *o:* Jb 5:25–26.

See RG 174–79

# The Book of Psalms

The Hebrew Psalter numbers 150 songs. The corresponding number in the Septuagint differs because of a different division of certain Psalms. Hence the numbering in the Greek Psalter (which was followed by the Latin Vulgate) is usually one digit behind the Hebrew. In the New American Bible the numbering of the verses follows the Hebrew numbering; many of the traditional English translations are often a verse number behind the Hebrew because they do not count the superscriptions as a verse.

The superscriptions derive from pre-Christian Jewish tradition, and they contain technical terms, many of them apparently liturgical, which are no longer known to us. Seventy-three Psalms are attributed to David, but there is no sure way of dating any Psalm. Some are preexilic (before 587), and others are postexilic (after 539), but not as late as the Maccabean period (ca. 165). The Psalms are the product of many individual collections (e.g., Songs of Ascents, Ps 120–134), which were eventually combined into the present work in which one can detect five "books," because of the doxologies which occur at 41:14; 72:18–19; 89:53; 106:48.

Two important features of the Psalms deserve

**The Structure of the Book of Psalms**

PSALMS IS DIVIDED into five "books," each of which ends with a verse or song of praise (a doxology).

| | |
|---|---|
| Book 1, Psalms 1–41 | Doxology is 41:14 |
| Book 2, Psalms 42–72 | Doxology is 72:18–19 |
| Book 3, Psalms 73–89 | Doxology is 89:53 |
| Book 4, Psalms 90–106 | Doxology is 106:48 |
| Book 5, Psalms 107–150 | Doxology is Psalm 150 |

Books 1, 4, and 5 tend to use "LORD" ("Yahweh") as the name of God; books 2 and 3 use "God" ("Elohim"). This indicates that there may have been two centers of collection for Psalms, and in one case—Psalms 14 and 53—we have a nearly identical psalm with the different names for God.

nor sit in company with scoffers.[a]
2 Rather, the law of the LORD* is his joy;
and on his law he meditates day and night.[b]
3 He is like a tree[c]
planted near streams of water,
that yields its fruit in season;
Its leaves never wither;
whatever he does prospers.

II

4 But not so are the wicked,* not so!
They are like chaff driven by the wind.[d]
5 Therefore the wicked will not arise at the judgment,
nor will sinners in the assembly of the just.
6 Because the LORD knows the way of the just,[e]
but the way of the wicked leads to ruin.

See RG 176

## PSALM 2*

### *A Psalm for a Royal Coronation*

1 Why do the nations protest
and the peoples conspire in vain?[f]
2 Kings on earth rise up
and princes plot together
against the LORD and against his anointed one:*[g]
3 "Let us break their shackles
and cast off their chains from us!"[h]
4 The one enthroned in heaven laughs;
the Lord derides them,[i]
5 Then he speaks to them in his anger,
in his wrath he terrifies them:
6 "I myself have installed my king
on Zion, my holy mountain."
7 I will proclaim the decree of the LORD,
he said to me, "You are my son;
today I have begotten you.[j]
8 Ask it of me,
and I will give you the nations as your inheritance,
and, as your possession, the ends of the earth.
9 With an iron rod you will shepherd them,
like a potter's vessel you will shatter them."[k]
10 And now, kings, give heed;
take warning, judges on earth.

**1:2 The law of the LORD**: either the Torah, the first five books of the Bible, or, more probably, divine teaching or instruction.

**1:4 The wicked**: those who by their actions distance themselves from God's life-giving presence.

**Psalm 2** A royal Psalm. To rebellious kings (Ps 2:1–3) God responds vigorously (Ps 2:4–6). A speaker proclaims the divine decree (in the legal adoption language of the day), making the Israelite king the earthly representative of God (Ps 2:7–9) and warning kings to obey (Ps 2:10–11). The Psalm has a messianic meaning for the Church; the New Testament understands it of Christ (Acts 4:25–27; 13:33; Heb 1:5).

**2:2 Anointed**: in Hebrew *mashiah*, "anointed"; in Greek *christos*, whence English Messiah and Christ. In Israel kings (Jgs 9:8; 1 Sm 9:16; 16:12–13) and high priests (Lv 8:12; Nm 3:3) received the power of their office through anointing.

*a:* Ps 26:4–5; 40:5. *b:* Jos 1:8; Ps 119; Sir 39:1. *c:* Ps 52:10; 92:13–15; Jer 17:8. *d:* Ps 35:5; 83:14–16; Jb 21:18. *e:* Ps 37:18. *f:* Rev 11:18. *g:* Ps 83:6. *h:* Ps 149:8. *i:* Ps 37:13; 59:9; Wis 4:18. *j:* Ps 89:27; 110:2–3; Is 49:1. *k:* Rev 2:27; 12:5; 19:15.

special notice. First, the majority were composed originally precisely for liturgical worship. This is shown by the frequent indication of liturgical leaders interacting with the community (e.g., Ps 118:1–4). Secondly, they follow certain distinct patterns or literary forms. Thus, the hymn is a song of praise, in which a community is urged joyfully to sing out the praise of God. Various reasons are given for this praise (often introduced by "for" or "because"): the divine work of creation and sustenance (Ps 135:1–12; 136). Some of the hymns have received a more specific classification, based on content. The "Songs of Zion" are so called because they exalt Zion, the city in which God dwells among the people (Ps 47; 96–99). Characteristic of the songs of praise is the joyful summons to get involved in the activity; Ps 104 is an exception to this, although it remains universal in its thrust.

Another type of Psalm is similar to the hymn: the thanksgiving Psalm. This too is a song of praise acknowledging the Lord as the rescuer of the psalmist from a desperate situation. Very often the psalmist will give a flashback, recounting the past distress, and the plea that was uttered (Ps 30; 116). The setting for such prayers seems to have been the offering of a *todah* (a "praise" sacrifice) with friends in the Temple.

There are more Psalms of lament than of any other type. They may be individual (e.g., Ps 3–7; 22) or communal (e.g., Ps 44). Although they usually begin with a cry for help, they develop in various ways. The description of the distress is couched in the broad imagery typical of the Bible (one is in Sheol, the Pit, or is afflicted by enemies or wild beasts, etc.)—in such a way that one cannot pinpoint the exact nature of the psalmist's plight. However, Ps 51 (cf. also Ps 130) seems to refer clearly to deliverance from sin. Several laments end on a note of certainty that the Lord has heard the prayer (cf. Ps 7, but contrast Ps 88), and the Psalter has been characterized as a movement from lament to praise. If this is somewhat of an exaggeration, it serves at least to emphasize the frequent expressions of trust which characterize the lament. In some cases it would seem as if the theme of trust has been lifted out to form a literary type all its own; cf. Ps 23, 62, 91. Among the communal laments can be counted Ps 74 and 79. They complain to the Lord about some national disaster, and try to motivate God to intervene in favor of the suffering people.

Other Psalms are clearly classified on account of content, and they may be in themselves laments or Psalms of thanksgiving. Among the "royal" Psalms that deal directly with the currently reigning king, are Ps 20, 21, and 72. Many of the royal Psalms were given a messianic interpretation by Christians. In Jewish tradition they were preserved, even after kingship had disappeared, because they were read in the light of the Davidic covenant reported in 2 Sm 7. Certain Psalms are called wisdom Psalms because they seem to betray the influence of the concerns of the ages (cf. Ps 37, 49), but there is no general agreement as to the number of these prayers. Somewhat related to the wisdom Psalms are the "torah" Psalms, in which the torah (instruction or law) of the Lord is glorified (Ps 1; 19:8–14; 119). Ps 78, 105, 106 can be considered as "historical" Psalms. Although the majority of the Psalms have a liturgical setting, there are certain prayers that may be termed "liturgies," so clearly does their structure reflect a liturgical incident (e.g., Ps 15, 24).

It is obvious that not all of the Psalms can be pigeon-holed into neat classifications, but even a brief sketch of these types help us to catch the structure and spirit of the Psalms we read. It has been rightly said that the Psalms are "a school of prayer." They not only provide us with models to follow, but inspire us to voice our own deepest feelings and aspirations.

---

## First Book—Psalms 1–41

### PSALM 1*

See RG 176

### *True Happiness in God's Law*

I

1 Blessed is the man who does not walk
in the counsel of the wicked,
Nor stand in the way* of sinners,

**Psalm 1** A preface to the whole Book of Psalms, contrasting with striking similes the destiny of the good and the wicked. The Psalm views life as activity, as choosing either the good or the bad. Each "way" brings its inevitable consequences. The wise through their good actions will experience rootedness and life, and the wicked, rootlessness and death.

**1:1 The way**: a common biblical term for manner of living or moral conduct (Ps 32:8; 101:2, 6; Prv 2:20; 1 Kgs 8:36).

PSALM 4 IS an unusual individual petition: It is unclear what the petitioner's problem might be; it highlights the psalmist's confidence in God more than his troubles; and it focuses more on others than on the psalmist.

11 Serve the LORD with fear;
exult with trembling,
Accept correction
lest he become angry and you perish
along the way
when his anger suddenly blazes up.[l]
Blessed are all who take refuge in him!

See RG 175

## PSALM 3*

### *Threatened but Trusting*

1 A psalm of David, when he fled from his son Absalom.*[m]

I

2 How many are my foes, LORD!
How many rise against me!
3 *How many say of me,
"There is no salvation for him in
God."[n] *Selah*
4 But you, LORD, are a shield around me;
my glory, you keep my head high.[o]

II

5 With my own voice I will call out to the
LORD,
and he will answer me from his holy
mountain. *Selah*
6 I lie down and I fall asleep,
[and] I will wake up, for the LORD
sustains me.[p]
7 I do not fear, then, thousands of people
arrayed against me on every side.

III

8 Arise, LORD! Save me, my God!
For you strike the cheekbone of all my
foes;
you break the teeth of the wicked.[q]
9 Salvation is from the LORD!
May your blessing be upon your
people![r] *Selah*

## PSALM 4*

See RG 175

### *Trust in God*

1 For the leader;* with stringed instruments.
A psalm of David.

I

2 Answer me when I call, my saving God.
When troubles hem me in, set me free;
take pity on me, hear my prayer.[s]

II

3 How long, O people, will you be hard of
heart?
Why do you love what is worthless,
chase after lies?*[t] *Selah*
4 Know that the LORD works wonders for
his faithful one;
the LORD hears when I call out to him.
5 Tremble* and sin no more;
weep bitterly* within your hearts,
wail upon your beds,[u]

**Psalm 3** An individual lament complaining of enemies who deny that God will come to the rescue (Ps 3:2–3). Despite such taunts the psalmist hopes for God's protection even in sleep (Ps 3:4–7). The Psalm prays for an end to the enemies' power to speak maliciously (Ps 3:8) and closes peacefully with an expression of trust (Ps 3:9).

**3:1** The superscription, added later, relates the Psalm to an incident in the life of David.

**3:3, 3:5, 3:9 Selah**: the term is generally considered a direction to the cantor or musicians but its exact meaning is not known. It occurs 71 times in 39 Psalms.

**Psalm 4** An individual lament emphasizing trust in God. The petition is based upon the psalmist's vivid experience of God as savior (Ps 4:2). That experience of God is the basis for the warning to the wicked: revere God who intervenes on the side of the faithful (Ps 4:3–6). The faithful psalmist exemplifies the blessings given to the just (Ps 4:7–8).

**4:1 For the leader**: many Psalm headings contain this rubric. Its exact meaning is unknown but may signify that such Psalms once stood together in a collection of "the choirmaster," cf. 1 Chr 15:21.

**4:3 Love what is worthless . . . lies**: these expressions probably refer to false gods worshiped by those the psalmist is addressing.

**4:5 Tremble**: be moved deeply with fear for failing to worship the true God. The Greek translation understood the emotion to be anger, and it is so cited in Eph 4:26. **Weep bitterly . . . wail**: weeping within one's heart and wailing upon one's bed denote sincere repentance because these actions are not done in public or with the community but in the privacy of one's heart and one's home. The same idiom is found in Hos 7:14.

*l:* Ps 34:9; 146:5; Prv 16:20. *m:* 2 Sm 15:13ff. *n:* Ps 71:11. *o:* Ps 7:11; 18:3; 62:7–8; Dt 33:29; Is 60:19. *p:* Ps 4:9; Prv 3:24. *q:* Ps 58:7. *r:* Ps 28:9; Jon 2:10. *s:* Ps 118:5. *t:* Ps 62:4. *u:* Eph 4:26.

[6] Offer fitting sacrifices
and trust in the LORD.[v]

III

[7] Many say, "May we see better times!
LORD, show us the light of your
face!"[w] *Selah*
[8] But you have given my heart more joy
than they have when grain and wine
abound.
[9] [x]*In peace I will lie down and fall asleep,
for you alone, LORD, make me secure.

See RG 175

### PSALM 5*

### *Prayer for Divine Help*

[1]For the leader; with wind instruments.
A psalm of David.

I

[2] Give ear to my words, O LORD;
understand my sighing.[y]
[3] Attend to the sound of my cry,
my king and my God!
For to you I will pray, LORD;
[4] in the morning you will hear my voice;
in the morning I will plead before you
and wait.[z]

II

[5] You are not a god who delights in evil;
no wicked person finds refuge with
you;
[6] the arrogant cannot stand before your
eyes.
You hate all who do evil;
[7] you destroy those who speak falsely.[a]
A bloody and fraudulent man
the LORD abhors.

III

[8] But I, through the abundance of your
mercy,*
will enter into your house.
I will bow down toward your holy
sanctuary
out of fear of you.[b]
[9] LORD, guide me in your justice because
of my foes;
make straight your way before me.[c]

IV

[10] For there is no sincerity in their mouth;
their heart is corrupt.
Their throat* is an open grave;[d]
on their tongue are subtle lies.
[11] Declare them guilty, God;
make them fall by their own devices.[e]
Drive them out for their many sins;
for they have rebelled against you.

V

[12] Then all who trust in you will be glad
and forever shout for joy.[f]
You will protect them and those will
rejoice in you
who love your name.
[13] For you, LORD, bless the just one;
you surround him with favor like a
shield.

### PSALM 6*

See RG 175

### *Prayer in Distress*

[1]For the leader; with stringed instruments,
"upon the eighth."*
A psalm of David.

I

[2] Do not reprove me in your anger, LORD,
nor punish me in your wrath.[g]
[3] Have pity on me, LORD, for I am weak;
heal me, LORD, for my bones are
shuddering.[h]
[4] My soul too is shuddering greatly—

**4:9 In peace I will . . . fall asleep**: the last verse repeats two themes in the Psalm. One is the security of one who trusts in the true God; the other is the interior peace of those who sincerely repent ("on [their] beds"), whose sleep is not disturbed by a guilty conscience.

**Psalm 5** A lament contrasting the security of the house of God (Ps 5:8–9, 12–13) with the danger of the company of evildoers (Ps 5:5–7, 10–11). The psalmist therefore prays that God will hear (Ps 5:2–4) and grant the protection and joy of the Temple.

**5:8 Mercy**: used to translate the Hebrew word, *hesed*. This term speaks to a relationship between persons. It is manifested in concrete actions to persons with some need or desire. The one who offers *hesed* has the ability to respond to that need of the other person. Other possible ways to translate *hesed* include "steadfast love" and "loving kindness."

**5:10 Their throat**: their speech brings harm to their hearers (cf. Jer 5:16). The verse mentions four parts of the body, each a source of evil to the innocent.

**Psalm 6** The first of the seven Penitential Psalms (Ps 6, 32, 38, 51, 102, 130, 143), a designation dating from the seventh century A.D. for Psalms suitable to express repentance. The psalmist does not, as in many laments, claim to be innocent but appeals to God's mercy (Ps 6:5). Sin here, as often in the

*v:* Ps 51:19. *w:* Ps 31:17; 44:4; 67:1; 80:4; Jb 13:24; Nm 6:25; Dn 9:17. *x:* Ps 3:6. *y:* Ps 86:6; 130:1–2. *z:* Wis 16:28. *a:* Ps 101:7; Wis 14:9; Heb 1:13. *b:* Ps 138:2; Jon 2:5. *c:* Ps 23:3; Prv 4:11; Is 26:7. *d:* Rom 3:13. *e:* Ps 141:10. *f:* Ps 64:11. *g:* Ps 38:2. *h:* Jer 17:14–15.

and you, LORD, how long . . . ?*[i]
5 Turn back, LORD, rescue my soul;
save me because of your mercy.
6 For in death there is no remembrance of you.
Who praises you in Sheol?*[j]

II

7 I am wearied with sighing;
all night long I drench my bed with tears;
I soak my couch with weeping.
8 My eyes are dimmed with sorrow,
worn out because of all my foes.[k]

III

9 Away from me, all who do evil![l]
The LORD has heard the sound of my weeping.
10 The LORD has heard my plea;
the LORD will receive my prayer.
11 My foes will all be disgraced and will shudder greatly;
they will turn back in sudden disgrace.[m]

## PSALM 7*

See RG 175

### *God the Vindicator*

1 A plaintive song of David, which he sang to the LORD concerning Cush, the Benjaminite.

I

2 LORD my God, in you I trusted;
save me; rescue me from all who pursue me,[n]
3 Lest someone maul me like a lion,
tear my soul apart with no one to deliver.

II

4 LORD my God, if I have done this,*
if there is guilt on my hands,
5 If I have maltreated someone treating me equitably—
or even despoiled my oppressor without cause—
6 Then let my enemy pursue and overtake my soul,
trample my life to the ground,
and lay my honor in the dust.[o] *Selah*

III

7 Rise up, LORD, in your anger;
be aroused against the outrages of my oppressors.[p]
Stir up the justice, my God, you have commanded.
8 Have the assembly of the peoples gather about you;
and return on high above them,
9 the LORD will pass judgment on the peoples.
Judge me, LORD, according to my righteousness,
and my integrity.
10 Let the malice of the wicked end.
Uphold the just one,
O just God,[q]
who tries hearts and minds.

IV

11 God is a shield above me
saving the upright of heart.[r]
12 God is a just judge, powerful and patient,*
not exercising anger every day.
13 If one does not repent,
God sharpens his sword,
strings and readies the bow,[s]
14 Prepares his deadly shafts,
makes arrows blazing thunderbolts.[t]

Bible, is both the sinful act and its injurious consequences; here it is physical sickness (Ps 6:3–4, 7–8) and the attacks of enemies (Ps 6:8, 9, 11). The psalmist prays that the effects of personal and social sin be taken away.

**6:1 Upon the eighth**: apparently a musical notation, now lost.

**6:4 How long**?: elliptical for "How long will it be before you answer my prayer?" cf. Ps 13:2–3.

**6:6** A motive for God to preserve the psalmist from death: in the shadowy world of the dead no one offers you praise. Sheol is the biblical term for the underworld where the insubstantial souls of dead human beings dwelt. It was similar to the Hades of Greek and Latin literature. In the second century B.C., biblical books begin to speak positively of life with God after death (Dn 12:1–3; Wis 3).

**Psalm 7** An individual lament. The psalmist flees to God's presence in the sanctuary for justice and protection (Ps 7:2–3) and takes an oath that only the innocent can swear (Ps 7:4–6). The innocent psalmist can thus hope for the just God's protection (Ps 7:7–14) and be confident that the actions of the wicked will come back upon their own heads (Ps 7:15–17). The justice of God leads the psalmist to praise (Ps 7:18).

**7:4 Have done this**: in the accusation the enemies have made against the psalmist.

**7:12 Powerful and patient**: the inclusion of these words is drawn from the Septuagint tradition concerning this verse.

*i:* Ps 13:2–3; 74:10; 89:47. *j:* Ps 30:10; 88:11; 115:17; Is 38:18. *k:* Ps 31:10; 38:11; 40:13. *l:* Ps 119:115; Mt 7:23; Lk 13:27. *m:* Ps 35:4, 26; 40:15; 71:13. *n:* Ps 6:5; 22:21. *o:* Ps 143:3. *p:* Ps 9:4; 19:20. *q:* Ps 17:3; 26:2; 35:24; 43:1; 139:23; Jer 17:10; 20:12. *r:* Ps 3:4. *s:* Ps 11:2. *t:* Is 50:11.

V

15 Consider how one conceives iniquity;
is pregnant with mischief,
and gives birth to deception.[u]
16 He digs a hole and bores it deep,
but he falls into the pit he has made.[v]
17 His malice turns back upon his head;
his violence falls on his own skull.

VI

18 I will thank the LORD in accordance with his justice;
I will sing the name of the LORD Most High.[w]

## PSALM 8*

See RG 175–76

### *Divine Majesty and Human Dignity*

1 For the leader; "upon the *gittith*."* A psalm of David.

2 O LORD, our Lord,
how awesome is your name through all the earth!
I will sing of your majesty above the heavens
3 with the mouths of babes[x] and infants.*
You have established a bulwark* against your foes,
to silence enemy and avenger.*
4 When I see your heavens, the work of your fingers,
the moon and stars that you set in place—
5 *What is man that you are mindful of him,[y]
and a son of man that you care for him?[z]
6 Yet you have made him little less than a god,*
crowned him with glory and honor.
7 You have given him rule over the works of your hands,[a]
put all things at his feet:
8 All sheep and oxen,
even the beasts of the field,
9 The birds of the air, the fish of the sea,
and whatever swims the paths of the seas.

10 O LORD, our Lord,
how awesome is your name through all the earth!

## PSALM 9*

See RG 175–76

### *Thanksgiving for Victory and Prayer for Justice*

1 For the leader; according to *Muth Labben.** A psalm of David.

I

2 I will praise you, LORD, with all my heart;
I will declare all your wondrous deeds.
3 I will delight and rejoice in you;

**Psalm 8** While marvelling at the limitless grandeur of God (Ps 8:2–3), the psalmist is struck first by the smallness of human beings in creation (Ps 8:4–5), and then by the royal dignity and power that God has graciously bestowed upon them (Ps 8:6–9).

**8:1 Upon the gittith**: probably the title of the melody to which the Psalm was to be sung or a musical instrument.

**8:3 With the mouths of babes and infants**: the psalmist realizes that his attempts to praise such an awesome God are hopelessly inadequate and amount to little more than the sounds made by infants. **Established a bulwark**: an allusion to lost myth telling how God built a fortress for himself in the heavens in primordial times in his battle with the powers of chaos. This "bulwark" is the firmament. **Enemy and avenger**: probably cosmic enemies. The primeval powers of watery chaos are often personified in poetic texts (Ps 74:13–14; 89:11; Jb 9:13; 26:12–13; Is 51:9).

**8:5 Man . . . a son of man**: the emphasis is on the fragility and mortality of human beings to whom God has given great dignity.

**8:6 Little less than a god**: Hebrew *'elohim*, the ordinary word for "God" or "the gods" or members of the heavenly court. The Greek version translated *'elohim* by "angel, messenger"; several ancient and modern versions so translate. The meaning seems to be that God created human beings almost at the level of the beings in the heavenly world. Heb 2:9, translating "for a little while," finds the eminent fulfillment of this verse in Jesus Christ, who was humbled before being glorified, cf. also 1 Cor 15:27 where St. Paul applies to Christ the closing words of Ps 8:7.

**Psalms 9–10** Ps 9 and Ps 10 in the Hebrew text have been transmitted as separate poems but they actually form a single acrostic poem and are so transmitted in the Greek and Latin tradition. Each verse of the two Psalms begins with a successive letter of the Hebrew alphabet (though several letters have no corresponding stanza). The Psalm states loosely connected themes: the rescue of the helpless poor from their enemies, God's worldwide judgment and rule over the nations, the psalmist's own concern for rescue (Ps 9:14–15).

**9:1 Muth Labben**: probably the melodic accompaniment of the Psalm, now lost.

*u:* Jb 15:35; Is 59:4. *v:* Ps 9:16; 35:8; 57:7; Prv 26:27; Eccl 10:8; Sir 27:26. *w:* Ps 18:50; 30:5; 135:3; 146:2. *x:* Mt 21:16; Wis 10:21. *y:* Ps 144:3; Jb 7:17. *z:* Heb 2:6ff. *a:* Gn 1:26, 28; Wis 9:2; 1 Cor 15:27.

I will sing hymns to your name, Most
High.
4 When my enemies turn back,
they stumble and perish before you.
II
5 For you upheld my right and my cause,
seated on your throne, judging justly.
6 You rebuked the nations, you destroyed
the wicked;
their name you blotted out for all time.[b]
7 The enemies have been ruined forever;
you destroyed their cities;
their memory has perished.
III
8 The LORD rules forever,
has set up his throne for judgment.
9 It is he who judges the world with justice,[c]
who judges the peoples with fairness.
10 The LORD is a stronghold for the
oppressed,
a stronghold in times of trouble.[d]
11 Those who know your name trust in you;
you never forsake those who seek you,
LORD.
IV
12 Sing hymns to the LORD enthroned on
Zion;
proclaim his deeds among the nations!
13 For the avenger of bloodshed remembers,
does not forget the cry of the afflicted.[e]
V
14 Be gracious to me, LORD;
see how my foes afflict me!
You alone can raise me from the gates
of death.[f]
15 Then I will declare all your praises,
sing joyously of your salvation
in the gates of daughter Zion.*
VI
16 The nations fall into the pit they dig;
in the snare they hide, their own foot is
caught.
17 *The LORD is revealed in making
judgments:
by the deeds they do the wicked are
trapped.[g] *Higgaion. Selah**
VII
18 To Sheol the wicked will depart,
all the nations that forget God.
19 For the needy will never be forgotten,
nor will the hope of the afflicted ever
fade.[h]
20 Arise, LORD, let no mortal prevail;
let the nations be judged in your
presence.
21 Strike them with terror, LORD;
show the nations they are only
human. *Selah*

## PSALM 10

See RG 175–76

I
1 Why, LORD, do you stand afar
and pay no heed in times of trouble?
2 Arrogant scoundrels pursue the poor;
they trap them by their cunning
schemes.[i]
II
3 The wicked even boast of their greed;
these robbers curse and scorn the
LORD.[j]
4 In their insolence the wicked boast:
"God does not care; there is no God."[k]
5 Yet their affairs always succeed;
they ignore your judgment on high;
they sneer at all who oppose them.
6 They say in their hearts, "We will never
fall;
never will we see misfortune."
7 Their mouths are full of oaths, violence,
and lies;
discord and evil are under their
tongues.[l]
8 They wait in ambush near towns;
their eyes watch for the helpless
to murder the innocent in secret.[m]
9 They lurk in ambush like lions in a
thicket,
hide there to trap the poor,

**9:15 Daughter Zion**: an ancient Near Eastern city could sometimes be personified as a woman or a queen, the spouse of the god of the city.

**9:17 The LORD is revealed in making judgments**: God has so made the universe that the wicked are punished by the very actions they perform. **Selah**: see note on Ps 3:3.

*b:* Jb 18:17. *c:* Ps 96:10; 98:9. *d:* Ps 37:39; Is 25:4. *e:* Jb 16:18. *f:* Wis 16:13. *g:* Ps 35:8; Sir 27:26. *h:* Prv 23:18. *i:* Is 32:7. *j:* Ps 36:2. *k:* Ps 14:1; Jb 22:13; Is 29:15; Jer 5:12; Zep 1:12. *l:* Is 32:7; Rom 3:14. *m:* Ps 11:2; Jb 24:14.

snare them and close the net.[n]
10 The helpless are crushed, laid low;
they fall into the power of the wicked,
11 Who say in their hearts, "God has forgotten,
shows no concern, never bothers to look."[o]

III

12 Rise up, LORD! God, lift up your hand!
Do not forget the poor!
13 Why should the wicked scorn God,
say in their hearts, "God does not care"?
14 But you do see;
you take note of misery and sorrow;[p]
you take the matter in hand.
To you the helpless can entrust their cause;
you are the defender of orphans.[q]
15 Break the arm of the wicked and depraved;
make them account for their crimes;
let none of them survive.

IV

16 The LORD is king forever;[r]
the nations have vanished from his land.
17 You listen, LORD, to the needs of the poor;
you strengthen their heart and incline your ear.
18 You win justice for the orphaned and oppressed;[s]
no one on earth will cause terror again.

## PSALM 11*

See RG 175

### *Confidence in the Presence of God*

1 For the leader. Of David.

I

In the LORD I take refuge;
how can you say to me,
"Flee like a bird to the mountains![t]
2 See how the wicked string their bows,
fit their arrows to the string
to shoot from the shadows at the upright of heart.[u]
3 *If foundations are destroyed,
what can the just one do?"

II

4 The LORD is in his holy temple;
the LORD's throne is in heaven.[v]
God's eyes keep careful watch;
they test the children of Adam.
5 The LORD tests the righteous and the wicked,
hates those who love violence,
6 And rains upon the wicked
fiery coals and brimstone,
a scorching wind their allotted cup.*[w]
7 The LORD is just and loves just deeds;
the upright will see his face.

## PSALM 12*

See RG 175

### *Prayer Against Evil Tongues*

1 For the leader; "upon the eighth." A psalm of David.

I

2 Help, LORD, for no one loyal remains;
the faithful have vanished from the children of men.[x]
3 They tell lies to one another,
speak with deceiving lips and a double heart.[y]

II

4 May the LORD cut off all deceiving lips,
and every boastful tongue,
5 Those who say, "By our tongues we prevail;
when our lips speak, who can lord it over us?"[z]

**Psalm 11** A song of trust. Though friends counsel flight to the mountain country (a traditional hideout) to escape trouble (Ps 11:1–3), the innocent psalmist reaffirms confidence in God, who protects those who seek asylum in the Temple (Ps 11:4–7).

**11:3 Foundations**: usually understood of public order, cf. Ps 82:5.

**11:6 Their allotted cup**: the cup that God gives people to drink is a common figure for their destiny, cf. Ps 16:5; 75:9; Mt 20:22; 26:39; Rev 14:10.

**Psalm 12** A lament. The psalmist, thrown into a world where lying and violent people persecute the just (Ps 12:2–3), prays that the wicked be punished (Ps 12:4–5). The prayer is not simply for vengeance but arises from a desire to see God's justice appear on earth. Ps 12:6 preserves the word of assurance spoken by the priest to the lamenter; it is not usually transmitted in such Psalms. In Ps 12:7–8 the psalmist affirms the intention to live by the word of assurance.

*n:* Ps 17:12; Prv 1:11; Jer 5:26. *o:* Ps 44:25; 64:6; 73:11; 94:7; Ez 9:9. *p:* Ps 31:8; 56:9; 2 Kgs 20:5; Is 25:8; Rev 7:17. *q:* Ex 22:21–22. *r:* Ps 145:13; Jer 10:10. *s:* Dt 10:18. *t:* Ps 55:7; 91:4. *u:* Ps 7:13; 37:14; 57:5; 64:4. *v:* Ps 14:2; 102:20; Hab 2:20; Dt 26:15; Is 66:1; Mt 5:34. *w:* Ps 120:4; 140:11; Prv 16:27; Ez 38:22; Rev 8:5; 20:10. *x:* Ps 14:3; 116:11; Is 59:15; Mi 7:2. *y:* Ps 28:3; 55:22; Is 59:3–4; Jer 9:7. *z:* Sir 5:3.

III

6 "Because they rob the weak, and the needy groan,
I will now arise," says the LORD;
"I will grant safety to whoever longs for it."[a]

IV

7 The promises of the LORD are sure,
silver refined in a crucible,*
silver purified seven times.[b]
8 You, O LORD, protect us always;
preserve us from this generation.
9 On every side the wicked roam;
the shameless are extolled by the children of men.

## PSALM 13*

See RG 175

### *Prayer for Help*

1 For the leader. A psalm of David.

I

2 How long, LORD? Will you utterly forget me?
How long will you hide your face from me?[c]
3 How long must I carry sorrow in my soul,
grief in my heart day after day?
How long will my enemy triumph over me?

II

4 Look upon me, answer me, LORD, my God!
Give light to my eyes lest I sleep in death,
5 Lest my enemy say, "I have prevailed,"
lest my foes rejoice at my downfall.[d]

III

6 But I trust in your mercy.
Grant my heart joy in your salvation,
I will sing to the LORD,
for he has dealt bountifully with me![e]

## PSALM 14*

See RG 175

### *A Lament over Widespread Corruption*

1 For the leader. Of David.

I

The fool says in his heart,
"There is no God."
Their deeds are loathsome and corrupt;
not one does what is good.[f]
2 The LORD looks down from heaven
upon the children of men,[g]
To see if even one is wise,
if even one seeks God.[h]
3 All have gone astray;
all alike are perverse.
Not one does what is good,
not even one.[i]

II

4 Will these evildoers never learn?
They devour my people as they devour bread;[j]
they do not call upon the LORD.[k]
5 They have good reason, then, to fear;
God is with the company of the just.
6 They would crush the hopes of the poor,
but the poor have the LORD as their refuge.

III

7 [l]Oh, that from Zion might come
the salvation of Israel!
Jacob would rejoice, and Israel be glad
when the LORD restores his people!*

**12:7 A crucible**: lit., "in a crucible in the ground." The crucible was placed in the ground for support.

**Psalm 13** A typical lament, in which the psalmist feels forgotten by God (Ps 13:2–3)—note the force of the repetition of "How long." The references to enemies may suggest some have wished evil on the psalmist. The heartfelt prayer (Ps 13:4–5) passes on a statement of trust (Ps 13:6a), intended to reinforce the prayer, and a vow to thank God when deliverance has come (Ps 13:6b).

**Psalm 14** The lament (duplicated in Ps 53) depicts the world as consisting of two types of people: "the fool" (equals the wicked, Ps 14:1–3) and "the company of the just" (Ps 14:4–6; also called "my people," and "the poor"). The wicked persecute the just, but the Psalm expresses the hope that God will punish the wicked and reward the good.

**14:7 Jacob . . . Israel . . . his people**: the righteous poor are identified with God's people.

---

*a:* Is 33:10. *b:* Ps 18:31; 19:8; Prv 30:5. *c:* Ps 6:4; 44:25; 77:8; 79:5; 89:47; 94:3; Lam 5:20. *d:* Ps 38:17. *e:* Ps 116:7. *f:* Ps 10:4; 36:2; Is 32:6; Jer 5:12. *g:* Rom 3:11–12. *h:* Ps 11:4; 102:20. *i:* Ps 12:1. *j:* Ps 27:2; Is 9:11. *k:* Ps 79:6. *l:* Ps 85:2.

## PSALM 15*

See RG 176

### *The Righteous Israelite*

[1m]A psalm of David.

I

LORD, who may abide in your tent?*
Who may dwell on your holy mountain?*

II

2 Whoever walks without blame,[n]
doing what is right,
speaking truth from the heart;
3 Who does not slander with his tongue,
does no harm to a friend,
never defames a neighbor;
4 Who disdains the wicked,
but honors those who fear the LORD;
Who keeps an oath despite the cost,
5 lends no money at interest,*
accepts no bribe against the innocent.[o]

III

Whoever acts like this
shall never be shaken.

## PSALM 16*

See RG 175

### *God the Supreme Good*

[1p]A *miktam** of David.

I

Keep me safe, O God;
in you I take refuge.
2 I say to the LORD,
you are my Lord,
you are my only good.
3 As for the holy ones who are in the land,
they are noble,
in whom is all my delight.
4 *They multiply their sorrows
who court other gods.
Blood libations to them I will not pour out,
nor will I take their names upon my lips.
5 LORD, my allotted portion and my cup,
you have made my destiny secure.[q]
6 *Pleasant places were measured out for me;
fair to me indeed is my inheritance.

II

7 I bless the LORD who counsels me;
even at night my heart exhorts me.
8 I keep the LORD always before me;
with him at my right hand, I shall never be shaken.[r]
9 Therefore my heart is glad, my soul rejoices;
my body also dwells secure,
10 For you will not abandon my soul to Sheol,
nor let your devout one see the pit.*[s]
11 You will show me the path to life,
abounding joy in your presence,
the delights at your right hand forever.

## PSALM 17*

See RG 175

### *Prayer for Rescue from Persecutors*

[1]A prayer of David.

I

Hear, LORD, my plea for justice;
pay heed to my cry;
Listen to my prayer

**Psalm 15** The Psalm records a liturgical scrutiny at the entrance to the Temple court (cf. Ps 24:3–6; Is 33:14b–16). The Israelite wishing to be admitted had to ask the Temple official what conduct was appropriate to God's precincts. Note the emphasis on virtues relating to one's neighbor.

**15:1 Your tent**: the Temple could be referred to as "tent" (Ps 61:5; Is 33:20), a reference to the tent of the wilderness period and the tent of David (2 Sm 6:17; 7:2), predecessors of the Temple. **Holy mountain**: a venerable designation of the divine abode (Ps 2:6; 3:5; 43:3; 48:2, etc.).

**15:5 Lends no money at interest**: lending money in the Old Testament was often seen as assistance to the poor in their distress, not as an investment; making money off the poor by charging interest was thus forbidden (Ex 22:24; Lv 25:36–37; Dt 23:20).

**Psalm 16** In the first section, the psalmist rejects the futile worship of false gods (Ps 16:2–5), preferring Israel's God (Ps 16:1), the giver of the land (Ps 16:6). The second section reflects on the wise and life-giving presence of God (Ps 16:7–11).

**16:1 Miktam**: a term occurring six times in Psalm superscriptions, always with "David." Its meaning is unknown.

**16:4 Take their names**: to use the gods' names in oaths and hence to affirm them as one's own gods.

**16:6 Pleasant places were measured out for me**: the psalmist is pleased with the plot of land measured out to the family, which was to be passed on to succeeding generations ("my inheritance").

**16:10 Nor let your devout one see the pit**: Hebrew *shahath* means here the pit, a synonym for Sheol, the underworld. The Greek translation derives the word here and elsewhere from the verb *shahath*, "to be corrupt." On the basis of the Greek, Acts 2:25–32; 13:35–37 apply the verse to Christ's resurrection, "Nor will you suffer your holy one to see corruption."

**Psalm 17** A lament of an individual unjustly attacked. Confident of being found innocent, the psalmist cries out for

*m:* Is 56:7. *n:* Ps 119:1. *o:* Ex 22:24; 23:8. *p:* Ps 25:20. *q:* Ps 23:5; 73:26; Nm 18:20; Lam 3:24. *r:* Ps 73:23; 121:5, 8–12; Acts 2:25–28. *s:* Ps 28:1; 30:4; 49:16; 86:13; Jon 2:7; Acts 13:35.

from lips without guile.
2 From you let my vindication come;
your eyes see what is right.
3 You have tested my heart,
searched it in the night.[t]
You have tried me by fire,
but find no malice in me.
My mouth has not transgressed
4 as others often do.
As your lips have instructed me,
I have kept from the way of the
lawless.
5 My steps have kept to your paths;
my feet have not faltered.[u]

II

6 I call upon you; answer me, O God.
Turn your ear to me; hear my speech.
7 Show your wonderful mercy,
you who deliver with your right arm
those who seek refuge from their foes.
8 *Keep me as the apple of your eye;
hide me in the shadow of your wings
9 from the wicked who despoil me.[v]

III

My ravenous enemies press upon me;[w]
10 *they close their hearts,
they fill their mouths with proud
roaring.
11 Their steps even now encircle me;
they watch closely, keeping low to the
ground,
12 Like lions eager for prey,
like a young lion lurking in ambush.
13 Rise, O LORD, confront and cast them
down;
rescue my soul from the wicked.
14 Slay them with your sword;
with your hand, LORD, slay them;
snatch them from the world in their
prime.
Their bellies are being filled with your
friends;
their children are satisfied too,
for they share what is left with their
young.
15 I am just—let me see your face;
when I awake, let me be filled with
your presence.[x]

## PSALM 18*

See RG 176

### *A King's Thanksgiving for Victory*

1 For the leader. Of David, the servant of the LORD, who sang to the LORD the words of this song after the LORD had rescued him from the clutches of all his enemies and from the hand of Saul. 2 He said:[y]

I

I love you, LORD, my strength,
3 LORD, my rock, my fortress, my
deliverer,
My God, my rock of refuge,
my shield, my saving horn,* my
stronghold![z]
4 Praised be the LORD, I exclaim!
I have been delivered from my enemies.

II

5 The cords of death encompassed me;
the torrents of destruction terrified me.
6 The cords* of Sheol encircled me;
the snares of death lay in wait for me.[a]
7 In my distress I called out: LORD!
I cried out to my God.[b]
From his temple he heard my voice;
my cry to him reached his ears.
8 *The earth rocked and shook;

God's just judgment (Ps 17:1–5) and requests divine help against enemies (Ps 17:6–9a). Those ravenous lions (Ps 17:9b–12) should be punished (Ps 17:13–14). The Psalm ends with a serene statement of praise (Ps 17:15). The Hebrew text of Ps 17:3–4, 14 is uncertain.

**17:8 Apple of your eye . . . shadow of your wings**: images of God's special care, cf. Dt 32:10; Prv 7:2; Is 49:2.

**17:10–12, 14** An extended metaphor: the enemies are lions.

**Psalm 18** A royal thanksgiving for a military victory, duplicated in 2 Sm 22. Thanksgiving Psalms are in essence reports of divine rescue. The Psalm has two parallel reports of rescue, the first told from a heavenly perspective (Ps 18:5–20), and the second from an earthly perspective (Ps 18:36–46). The first report adapts old mythic language of a cosmic battle between sea and rainstorm in order to depict God's rescue of the Israelite king from his enemies. Each report has a short hymnic introduction (Ps 18:2–4, 32–36) and conclusion (Ps 18:21–31, 47–50).

**18:3 My saving horn**: my strong savior. The horn referred to is the weapon of a bull and the symbol of fertility, cf. 1 Sm 2:10; Ps 132:17; Lk 1:69.

**18:6 Cords**: hunting imagery, the cords of a snare.

**18:8–16** God appears in the storm, which in Palestine comes from the west. The introduction to the theophany (Ps

*t:* Ps 26:2; 139:23. *u:* Ps 18:36; Jb 23:11–12. *v:* Ps 10:9; 22:14, 22; 35:17; 58:7; Jb 4:10–11. *w:* Ps 36:8; 57:2; 61:5; 63:8; 91:4; Dt 32:10; Ru 2:12; Zec 2:12; Mt 23:37. *x:* Ps 4:7; 31:17; 67:2; 80:4; Nm 6:25; Dn 9:17. *y:* 2 Sm 22:2–51. *z:* Ps 3:4; 31:3–4; 42:10; Gn 49:24; Dt 32:4. *a:* Ps 88:8; 93:3–4; 116:3–4. *b:* Jon 2:3.

the foundations of the mountains
trembled;
they shook as his wrath flared up.[c]
9 Smoke rose from his nostrils,
a devouring fire from his mouth;
it kindled coals into flame.
10 He parted the heavens and came down,
a dark cloud under his feet.[d]
11 Mounted on a cherub* he flew,
borne along on the wings of the wind.
12 He made darkness his cloak around him;
his canopy, water-darkened
stormclouds.
13 From the gleam before him, his clouds
passed,
hail and coals of fire.[e]
14 The LORD thundered from heaven;
the Most High made his voice resound.[f]
15 He let fly his arrows* and scattered them;
shot his lightning bolts and dispersed
them.[g]
16 Then the bed of the sea appeared;
the world's foundations lay bare,[h]
At your rebuke, O LORD,
at the storming breath of your nostrils.
17 He reached down from on high and
seized me;
drew me out of the deep waters.[i]
18 He rescued me from my mighty enemy,
from foes too powerful for me.
19 They attacked me on my day of distress,
but the LORD was my support.
20 He set me free in the open;
he rescued me because he loves me.

III

21 The LORD acknowledged my
righteousness,
rewarded my clean hands.[j]
22 For I kept the ways of the LORD;
I was not disloyal to my God.
23 For his laws were all before me,
his decrees I did not cast aside.
24 I was honest toward him;
I was on guard against sin.
25 So the LORD rewarded my righteousness,
the cleanness of my hands in his sight.
26 Toward the faithful you are faithful;
to the honest man you are honest;[k]
27 Toward the pure, you are pure;
but to the perverse you are devious.
28 For humble people you save;
haughty eyes you bring low.[l]
29 For you, LORD, give light to my lamp;
my God brightens my darkness.[m]
30 With you I can rush an armed band,
with my God to help I can leap a wall.
31 God's way is unerring;
the LORD's promise is refined;
he is a shield for all who take refuge in
him.[n]

IV

32 Truly, who is God except the LORD?
Who but our God is the rock?[o]
33 This God who girded me with might,
kept my way unerring,
34 Who made my feet like a deer's,
and set me on the heights,[p]
35 Who trained my hands for war,
my arms to string a bow of bronze.*[q]

V

36 You have given me your saving shield;
your right hand has upheld me;
your favor made me great.
37 You made room for my steps beneath me;
my ankles never twisted.[r]
38 I pursued my enemies and overtook them;
I did not turn back till I destroyed
them.
39 I decimated them; they could not rise;
they fell at my feet.
40 You girded me with valor for war,
subjugated my opponents beneath me.
41 You made my foes expose their necks
to me;

18:8–9) is probably a description of a violent, hot, and dry east-wind storm. In the fall transition period from the rainless summer to the rainy winter such storms regularly precede the rains, cf. Ex 14:21–22.

**18:11 Cherub**: a winged creature, derived from myth, in the service of the deity (Gn 3:24; Ex 25:18–20; 37:6–9). Cherubim were the throne bearers of the deity (Ps 80:2; 99:1; 1 Kgs 6:23–28; 8:6–8).

**18:15 Arrows**: lightning.

**18:35 Bow of bronze**: hyperbole for a bow difficult to bend and therefore capable of propelling an arrow with great force.

*c:* Ps 97:3–4; 99:1; Jgs 5:4–5; Is 64:1; Heb 3:9–11. *d:* Ps 104:3; 144:5; Is 63:19. *e:* Ex 13:21; 19:16. *f:* Ps 29; 77:19; Ex 19:19; Jb 37:3–4. *g:* Ps 144:6; Wis 5:21. *h:* Ps 77:17; Zec 9:14. *i:* Ps 144:7. *j:* Ps 26; 1 Sm 26:23. *k:* Ps 125:4. *l:* Jb 22:29; Prv 3:34. *m:* Ps 27:1; 36:10; 43:3; 119:105; Jb 29:3; Mi 7:8. *n:* Ps 12:6; 77:13; Prv 30:5. *o:* Is 44:8; 45:21. *p:* Heb 3:19. *q:* Ps 144:1. *r:* Ps 17:5.

those who hated me I silenced.
42 They cried for help, but no one saved them;
cried to the LORD but received no answer.
43 I ground them to dust before the wind;
I left them like mud in the streets.
44 You rescued me from the strife of peoples;
you made me head over nations.
A people I had not known served me;
45 as soon as they heard of me they obeyed.
Foreigners submitted before me;
46 foreigners cringed;
they came cowering from their dungeons.[s]

VI

47 The LORD lives! Blessed be my rock![t]
Exalted be God, my savior!
48 O God who granted me vengeance,
made peoples subject to me,[u]
49 and saved me from my enemies,
Truly you have elevated me above my opponents,
from a man of lawlessness you have rescued me.
50 Thus I will praise you, LORD, among the nations;
I will sing praises to your name.[v]
51 You have given great victories to your king,
and shown mercy to his anointed,
to David and his posterity forever.[w]

## PSALM 19*

See RG 175

### *God's Glory in the Heavens and in the Law*

1 For the leader. A psalm of David.

I

2 The heavens declare the glory of God;
the firmament proclaims the works of his hands.[x]
3 Day unto day pours forth speech;
night unto night whispers knowledge.
4 *There is no speech, no words;
their voice is not heard;
5 A report goes forth through all the earth,
their messages, to the ends of the world.
He has pitched in them a tent for the sun;*
6 it comes forth like a bridegroom from his canopy,
and like a hero joyfully runs its course.
7 From one end of the heavens it comes forth;
its course runs through to the other;
nothing escapes its heat.

II

8 The law of the LORD is perfect,
refreshing the soul.
The decree of the LORD is trustworthy,
giving wisdom to the simple.[y]
9 The precepts of the LORD are right,
rejoicing the heart.
The command of the LORD is clear,
enlightening the eye.
10 The fear of the LORD is pure,
enduring forever.
The statutes of the LORD are true,
all of them just;
11 More desirable than gold,
than a hoard of purest gold,
Sweeter also than honey
or drippings from the comb.[z]
12 By them your servant is warned;*
obeying them brings much reward.

III

13 Who can detect trespasses?
Cleanse me from my inadvertent sins.
14 Also from arrogant ones restrain your servant;
let them never control me.
Then shall I be blameless,

**Psalm 19** The heavenly elements of the world, now beautifully arranged, bespeak the power and wisdom of their creator (Ps 19:2–7). The creator's wisdom is available to human beings in the law (Ps 19:8–11), toward which the psalmist prays to be open (Ps 19:12–14). The themes of light and speech unify the poem.

**19:4 No speech, no words**: the regular functioning of the heavens and the alternation of day and night inform human beings without words of the creator's power and wisdom.

**19:5 The sun**: in other religious literature the sun is a judge and lawgiver since it sees all in its daily course; Ps 19:5b–7 form a transition to the law in Ps 19:8–11. The six synonyms for God's revelation (Ps 19:8–11) are applied to the sun in comparable literature.

**19:12 Warned**: the Hebrew verb means both to shine and to warn, cf. Dn 12:3.

*s:* Mi 7:17. *t:* Ps 144:1. *u:* Ps 144:2. *v:* Ps 7:18; 30:5; 57:9; 135:3; 146:2; Rom 15:9. *w:* Ps 89:28–37; 144:10; 1 Sm 2:10. *x:* Ps 8:1; 50:6; 97:6. *y:* Ps 12:7; 119. *z:* Sir 24:19.

innocent of grave sin.
[15] Let the words of my mouth be acceptable,
the thoughts of my heart before you,
LORD, my rock and my redeemer.

### PSALM 20*

See RG 176

## *Prayer for the King in Time of War*

[1]For the leader. A psalm of David.

I

[2] The LORD answer you in time of distress;
the name of the God of Jacob defend you!
[3] May he send you help from the sanctuary,
from Zion be your support.[a]
[4] May he remember* your every offering,
graciously accept your burnt offering, *Selah*
[5] Grant what is in your heart,
fulfill your every plan.
[6] May we shout for joy at your victory,*
raise the banners in the name of our God.
The LORD grant your every petition!

II

[7] Now I know the LORD gives victory
to his anointed.[b]
He will answer him from the holy heavens
with a strong arm that brings victory.
[8] Some rely on chariots, others on horses,
but we on the name of the LORD our God.[c]
[9] They collapse and fall,
but we stand strong and firm.[d]
[10] LORD, grant victory to the king;
answer when we call upon you.

### PSALM 21*

See RG 176

## *Thanksgiving and Assurances for the King*

[1]For the leader. A psalm of David.

I

[2] LORD, the king finds joy in your power;[e]
in your victory how greatly he rejoices!
[3] You have granted him his heart's desire;
you did not refuse the request of his lips. *Selah*
[4] For you welcomed him with goodly blessings;
you placed on his head a crown of pure gold.
[5] He asked life of you;
you gave it to him,
length of days forever.[f]
[6] Great is his glory in your victory;
majesty and splendor you confer upon him.
[7] You make him the pattern of blessings forever,
you gladden him with the joy of your face.
[8] For the king trusts in the LORD,
stands firm through the mercy of the Most High.

II

[9] Your hand will find all your enemies;
your right hand will find your foes!
[10] At the time of your coming
you will make them a fiery furnace.
Then the LORD in his anger will consume them,
devour them with fire.
[11] Even their descendants you will wipe out from the earth,
their offspring from the human race.

**Psalm 20** The people pray for the king before battle. The people ask for divine help (Ps 20:2–6) and express confidence that such help will be given (Ps 20:7–10). A solemn assurance of divine help may well have been given between the two sections in the liturgy, something like the promises of Ps 12:6; 21:9–13. The final verse (Ps 20:10) echoes the opening verse.

**20:4 Remember**: God's remembering implies readiness to act, cf. Gn 8:1; Ex 2:24.

**20:6 Victory**: the Hebrew root is often translated "salvation," "to save," but in military contexts it can have the specific meaning of "victory."

**Psalm 21** The first part of this royal Psalm is a thanksgiving (Ps 21:2–8), and the second is a promise that the king will triumph over his enemies (Ps 21:9–13). The king's confident prayer (Ps 21:3–5) and trust in God (Ps 21:8) enable him to receive the divine gifts of vitality, peace, and military success. Ps 21:14 reprises Ps 21:2. When kings ceased in Israel after the sixth century B.C., the Psalm was sung of a future Davidic king.

*a:* Ps 128:5; 134:3. *b:* Ps 18:51; 144:10; 1 Sm 2:10. *c:* Ps 147:10–11; 2 Chr 14:10; Prv 21:31; 1 Sm 17:45; Is 31:1; 36:9. *d:* Is 40:30. *e:* Ps 63:12. *f:* 1 Kgs 3:14.

PSALM 22 OPENS with a plea from a person in dire straits. When his prayers are answered, he brings the offerings he vowed and gives public acclaim to God as he promised. God is praised for his care of all people, and all people, now and in the future, should praise God. Jesus quoted the beginning of this psalm from the cross (Mt 27:46; Mk 15:34); the ending of the psalm may shed new light on the meaning of the opening words.

12 Though they intend evil against you,
devising plots, they will not succeed,
13 For you will put them to flight;
you will aim at their faces with your bow.

III

14 Arise, LORD, in your power![g]
We will sing and chant the praise of your might.

## PSALM 22*

See RG 175, 178

### *The Prayer of an Innocent Person*

1 For the leader; according to "The deer of the dawn."* A psalm of David.

I

2 My God, my God, why have you abandoned me?
Why so far from my call for help,
from my cries of anguish?[h]
3 My God, I call by day, but you do not answer;
by night, but I have no relief.[i]
4 Yet you are enthroned as the Holy One;
you are the glory of Israel.[j]
5 In you our fathers trusted;
they trusted and you rescued them.
6 To you they cried out and they escaped;
in you they trusted and were not disappointed.[k]
7 *But I am a worm, not a man,
scorned by men, despised by the people.[l]
8 All who see me mock me;
they curl their lips and jeer;
they shake their heads at me:[m]
9 "He relied on the LORD—let him deliver him;
if he loves him, let him rescue him."[n]
10 For you drew me forth from the womb,
made me safe at my mother's breasts.
11 Upon you I was thrust from the womb;
since my mother bore me you are my God.[o]
12 Do not stay far from me,
for trouble is near,
and there is no one to help.[p]

II

13 Many bulls* surround me;
fierce bulls of Bashan* encircle me.
14 They open their mouths against me,
lions that rend and roar.[q]
15 Like water my life drains away;
all my bones are disjointed.
My heart has become like wax,
it melts away within me.
16 As dry as a potsherd is my throat;
my tongue cleaves to my palate;
you lay me in the dust of death.*
17 Dogs surround me;
a pack of evildoers closes in on me.
They have pierced my hands and my feet

**Psalm 22** A lament unusual in structure and in intensity of feeling. The psalmist's present distress is contrasted with God's past mercy in Ps 22:2–12. In Ps 22:13–22 enemies surround the psalmist. The last third is an invitation to praise God (Ps 22:23–27), becoming a universal chorus of praise (Ps 22:28–31). The Psalm is important in the New Testament. Its opening words occur on the lips of the crucified Jesus (Mk 15:34; Mt 27:46), and several other verses are quoted, or at least alluded to, in the accounts of Jesus' passion (Mt 27:35, 43; Jn 19:24).

**22:1 The deer of the dawn**: apparently the title of the melody.

**22:7 I am a worm, not a man**: the psalmist's sense of isolation and dehumanization, an important motif of Ps 22, is vividly portrayed here.

**22:13–14 Bulls**: the enemies of the psalmist are also portrayed in less-than-human form, as wild animals (cf. Ps 22:17, 21–22). **Bashan**: a grazing land northeast of the Sea of Galilee, famed for its cattle, cf. Dt 32:14; Ez 39:18; Am 4:1.

**22:16 The dust of death**: the netherworld, the domain of the dead.

*g:* Nm 10:35. *h:* Is 49:14; 54:7; Mt 27:46; Mk 15:34. *i:* Sir 2:10. *j:* Is 6:3. *k:* Ps 25:3; Is 49:23; Dn 3:40. *l:* Is 53:3. *m:* Ps 109:25; Mt 27:39; Mk 15:29; Lk 23:35. *n:* Ps 71:11; Wis 2:18–20; Mt 27:43. *o:* Ps 71:6; Is 44:2; 46:3. *p:* Ps 35:22; 38:22; 71:12. *q:* Ps 17:12; Jb 4:10; 1 Pt 5:8.

18 I can count all my bones.[r]
They stare at me and gloat;
19 they divide my garments among them;
for my clothing they cast lots.[s]
20 But you, LORD, do not stay far off;
my strength, come quickly to help me.
21 Deliver my soul from the sword,
my life from the grip of the dog.
22 Save me from the lion's mouth,
my poor life from the horns of wild bulls.[t]

III

23 Then I will proclaim your name to my brethren;
in the assembly I will praise you:*[u]
24 "You who fear the LORD, give praise!
All descendants of Jacob, give honor;
show reverence, all descendants of Israel!
25 For he has not spurned or disdained
the misery of this poor wretch,
Did not turn away* from me,
but heard me when I cried out.
26 I will offer praise in the great assembly;
my vows I will fulfill before those who fear him.
27 The poor* will eat their fill;
those who seek the LORD will offer praise.
May your hearts enjoy life forever!"[v]

IV

28 All the ends of the earth
will remember and turn to the LORD;
All the families of nations
will bow low before him.[w]
29 For kingship belongs to the LORD,
the ruler over the nations.[x]
30 *All who sleep in the earth
will bow low before God;
All who have gone down into the dust
will kneel in homage.
31 And I will live for the LORD;
my descendants will serve you.
32 The generation to come will be told of the Lord,
that they may proclaim to a people yet unborn
the deliverance you have brought.[y]

## PSALM 23*

See RG 175–76

### *The Lord, Shepherd and Host*

1 A psalm of David.

I

The LORD is my shepherd;*
there is nothing I lack.[z]
2 In green pastures he makes me lie down;
to still waters he leads me;
3 [a]he restores my soul.
He guides me along right paths*
for the sake of his name.
4 Even though I walk through the valley of the shadow of death,[b]
I will fear no evil, for you are with me;
your rod and your staff comfort me.

II

5 *You set a table before me
in front of my enemies;*
You anoint my head with oil;*[c]

**22:23 In the assembly I will praise you**: the person who offered a thanksgiving sacrifice in the Temple recounted to the other worshipers the favor received from God and invited them to share in the sacrificial banquet. The final section (Ps 22:24–32) may be a summary or a citation of the psalmist's poem of praise.

**22:25 Turn away**: lit., "hides his face from me," an important metaphor for God withdrawing from someone, e.g., Mi 3:4; Is 8:17; Ps 27:9; 69:18; 88:15.

**22:27 The poor**: originally the poor, who were dependent on God; the term (*'anawim*) came to include the religious sense of "humble, pious, devout."

**22:30** Hebrew unclear. The translation assumes that all on earth (Ps 22:27–28) and under the earth (Ps 22:29) will worship God.

**Psalm 23** God's loving care for the psalmist is portrayed under the figures of a shepherd for the flock (Ps 23:1–4) and a host's generosity toward a guest (Ps 23:5–6). The imagery of both sections is drawn from traditions of the exodus (Is 40:11; 49:10; Jer 31:10).

**23:1 My shepherd**: God as good shepherd is common in both the Old Testament and the New Testament (Ez 34:11–16; Jn 10:11–18).

**23:3 Right paths**: connotes "right way" and "way of righteousness."

**23:5 You set a table before me**: this expression occurs in an exodus context in Ps 78:19. **In front of my enemies**: my enemies see that I am God's friend and guest. **Oil**: a perfumed ointment made from olive oil, used especially at banquets (Ps 104:15; Mt 26:7; Lk 7:37, 46; Jn 12:2).

*r:* Ps 109:24. *s:* Mt 27:35; Mk 15:24; Lk 23:34; Jn 19:24. *t:* Ps 7:2–3; 17:12; 35:17; 57:5; 58:7; 2 Tm 4:17. *u:* Ps 26:12; 35:18; 40:10; 109:30; 149:1; 2 Sm 22:50; Heb 2:12. *v:* Ps 23:5; 69:33. *w:* Ps 86:9; Tb 13:11; Is 45:22; 52:10; Zec 14:16. *x:* Ps 103:19; Ob 21; Zec 14:9. *y:* Ps 48:14–15; 71:18; 78:6; 102:19; Is 53:10. *z:* Ps 80:2; 95:7; 100:3; Dt 2:7. *a:* Prv 4:11. *b:* Jb 10:21–22; Is 50:10. *c:* Ps 92:11.

my cup overflows.[d]
6 Indeed, goodness and mercy* will
pursue me
all the days of my life;
I will dwell in the house of the LORD[e]
for endless days.

## PSALM 24*

See RG 176

### The Glory of God in Procession to Zion

1 A psalm of David.

I

The earth is the LORD's and all it holds,[f]
the world and those who dwell in it.
2 For he founded it on the seas,
established it over the rivers.[g]

II

3 Who may go up the mountain of the
LORD?[h]
Who can stand in his holy place?
4 *"The clean of hand and pure of heart,
who has not given his soul to useless
things,
what is vain.
5 He will receive blessings from the LORD,
and justice from his saving God.
6 Such is the generation that seeks him,
that seeks the face of the God of
Jacob." *Selah*

III

7 Lift up your heads, O gates;*
be lifted, you ancient portals,
that the king of glory may enter.[i]
8 Who is this king of glory?
The LORD, strong and mighty,
the LORD, mighty in war.
9 Lift up your heads, O gates;
rise up, you ancient portals,
that the king of glory may enter.
10 Who is this king of glory?
The LORD of hosts, he is the king of
glory. *Selah*

## PSALM 25*

See RG 175–76

### Confident Prayer for Forgiveness and Guidance

1 Of David.

I

To you, O LORD, I lift up my soul,
2 [j]my God, in you I trust;
do not let me be disgraced;[k]
do not let my enemies gloat over me.
3 No one is disgraced who waits for you,[l]
but only those who are treacherous
without cause.
4 Make known to me your ways, LORD;
teach me your paths.[m]
5 Guide me by your fidelity and teach me,
for you are God my savior,
for you I wait all the day long.
6 Remember your compassion and your
mercy, O LORD,
for they are ages old.[n]
7 Remember no more the sins of my
youth;[o]
remember me according to your mercy,
because of your goodness, LORD.

II

8 Good and upright is the LORD,
therefore he shows sinners the way,
9 He guides the humble in righteousness,
and teaches the humble his way.
10 All the paths of the LORD are mercy and
truth

**23:6 Goodness and mercy**: the blessings of God's covenant with Israel.

**Psalm 24** The Psalm apparently accompanied a ceremony of the entry of God (invisibly enthroned upon the ark), followed by the people, into the Temple. The Temple commemorated the creation of the world (Ps 24:1–2). The people had to affirm their fidelity before being admitted into the sanctuary (Ps 24:3–6; cf. Ps 15). A choir identifies the approaching God and invites the very Temple gates to bow down in obeisance (Ps 24:7–10).

**24:4–5** Lit., "the one whose hands are clean." The singular is used for the entire class of worshipers.

**24:7, 9 Lift up your heads, O gates . . . you ancient portals**: the literal meaning would involve disassembly of the gates, since the portcullis (a gate that moves up and down) was unknown in the ancient world. Extra-biblical parallels might also suggest a full personification of the circle of gate towers: they are like a council of elders, bowed down and anxious, awaiting the return of the army and the great warrior gone to battle.

**Psalm 25** A lament. Each verse begins with a successive letter of the Hebrew alphabet. Such acrostic Psalms are often a series of statements only loosely connected. The psalmist mixes ardent pleas (Ps 25:1–2, 16–22) with expressions of confidence in God who forgives and guides.

*d:* Ps 16:5. *e:* Ps 27:4. *f:* Ps 50:12; 89:12; Dt 10:14; 1 Cor 10:26. *g:* Ps 136:6; Is 42:5. *h:* Ps 15:1. *i:* Ps 118:19–20. *j:* Ps 86:4; 143:8. *k:* Ps 71:1. *l:* Ps 22:6; Is 49:23; Dn 3:40. *m:* Ps 27:11; 86:11; 119:12, 35; 143:8, 10. *n:* Sir 51:8. *o:* Jb 13:26; Is 64:8.

PSALM 25 IS an individual's petition in acrostic form: The first line begins with the first letter of the Hebrew alphabet, the second line with the second letter of the alphabet, and so on to the final letter. Two letters are missing, and two are doubled, likely reflecting changes that the psalm has undergone in its transmission. The psalm is made up of alternating petitions and expressions of trust. It resembles wisdom literature in its concern with learning and finding the right path but has the religious concerns of Psalms in its hope for forgiveness and for deliverance from distress.

toward those who honor his covenant
and decrees.
11 For the sake of your name, LORD,
pardon my guilt, though it is great.
12 Who is the one who fears the LORD?
God shows him the way he should
choose.[p]
13 He will abide in prosperity,
and his descendants will inherit the
land.[q]
14 The counsel of the LORD belongs to those
who fear him;
and his covenant instructs them.
15 My eyes are ever upon the LORD,
who frees my feet from the snare.[r]

III

16 Look upon me, have pity on me,
for I am alone and afflicted.[s]
17 Relieve the troubles of my heart;
bring me out of my distress.
18 Look upon my affliction and suffering;
take away all my sins.
19 See how many are my enemies,
see how fiercely they hate me.
20 Preserve my soul and rescue me;
do not let me be disgraced, for in you I
seek refuge.
21 Let integrity and uprightness preserve
me;
I wait for you, O LORD.
22 *Redeem Israel, O God,
from all its distress!

## PSALM 26*

See RG 175

### *Prayer of Innocence*

1 Of David.

I

Judge me, LORD!
For I have walked in my integrity.[t]
In the LORD I trust;
I do not falter.
2 Examine me, Lord, and test me;
search my heart and mind.[u]
3 Your mercy is before my eyes;
I walk guided by your faithfulness.[v]

II

4 I do not sit with worthless men,
nor with hypocrites do I mingle.
5 I hate an evil assembly;
with the wicked I do not sit.
6 I will wash my hands* in innocence[w]
so that I may process around your
altar, Lord,
7 To hear the sound of thanksgiving,
and recount all your wondrous deeds.
8 Lord, I love the refuge of your house,
the site of the dwelling-place of your
glory.[x]

III

9 Do not take me away with sinners,
nor my life with the men of blood,[y]
10 In whose hands there is a plot,
their right hands full of bribery.
11 But I walk in my integrity;[z]

**25:22** A final verse beginning with the Hebrew letter *pe* is added to the normal 22-letter alphabet. Thus the letters *aleph*, *lamed*, and *pe* open the first, middle (Ps 25:11), and last lines of the Psalm. Together, they spell *aleph*, the first letter of the alphabet, from a Hebrew root that means "to learn."

**Psalm 26** Like a priest washing before approaching the altar (Ex 30:17–21), the psalmist seeks God's protection upon entering the Temple. Ps 26:1–3, matched by Ps 26:11–12, remind God of past integrity while asking for purification; Ps 26:4–5, matched by Ps 26:9–10, pray for inclusion among the just; Ps 26:6–8, the center of the poem, express the joy in God at the heart of all ritual.

**26:6 I will wash my hands**: the washing of hands was a liturgical act (Ex 30:19, 21; 40:31–32), symbolic of inner as well as outer cleanness, cf. Is 1:16.

*p:* Prv 19:23. *q:* Ps 37:9, 29. *r:* Ps 123:1, 2; 141:8. *s:* Ps 86:16; 119:132. *t:* Ps 7:9. *u:* Ps 17:3; 139:23. *v:* Ps 86:11. *w:* Ps 73:13. *x:* Ps 29:9; 63:3; Ex 24:16; 25:8. *y:* Ps 28:3. *z:* Ps 101:6.

redeem me, be gracious to me![a]
12 My foot stands on level ground;*
in assemblies I will bless the LORD.[b]

See RG 175

PSALM 27*

***Trust in God***

1 [c]Of David.

A

I

The LORD is my light and my salvation;
whom should I fear?
The LORD is my life's refuge;
of whom should I be afraid?
2 When evildoers come at me
to devour my flesh,*[d]
These my enemies and foes
themselves stumble and fall.
3 Though an army encamp against me,
my heart does not fear;
Though war be waged against me,
even then do I trust.

II

4 One thing I ask of the LORD;
this I seek:
To dwell in the LORD's house
all the days of my life,
To gaze on the LORD's beauty,
to visit his temple.[e]
5 For God will hide me in his shelter
in time of trouble,[f]
He will conceal me in the cover of his tent;
and set me high upon a rock.
6 Even now my head is held high
above my enemies on every side!
I will offer in his tent
sacrifices with shouts of joy;
I will sing and chant praise to the LORD.

B

I

7 Hear my voice, LORD, when I call;
have mercy on me and answer me.
8 "Come," says my heart, "seek his face";*
your face, LORD, do I seek![g]
9 Do not hide your face from me;
do not repel your servant in anger.
You are my salvation; do not cast me off;
do not forsake me, God my savior!
10 Even if my father and mother forsake
me,
the LORD will take me in.[h]

II

11 LORD, show me your way;
lead me on a level path
because of my enemies.[i]
12 Do not abandon me to the desire of my
foes;
malicious and lying witnesses have
risen against me.
13 I believe I shall see the LORD's goodness
in the land of the living.*[j]
14 Wait for the LORD, take courage;
be stouthearted, wait for the LORD!

PSALM 28*

See RG 175

***Petition and Thanksgiving***

1 Of David.

I

To you, LORD, I call;
my Rock, do not be deaf to me,[k]
Do not be silent toward me,
so that I join those who go down to the
pit.[l]
2 Hear the sound of my pleading when I
cry to you for help

**26:12 On level ground**: in safety, where there is no danger of tripping and falling. **In assemblies**: at the Temple. Having walked around the altar, the symbol of God's presence, the psalmist blesses God.

**Psalm 27** Tradition has handed down the two sections of the Psalm (Ps 27:1–6; 7–14) as one Psalm, though each part could be understood as complete in itself. Asserting boundless hope that God will bring rescue (Ps 27:1–3), the psalmist longs for the presence of God in the Temple, protection from all enemies (Ps 27:4–6). In part B there is a clear shift in tone (Ps 27:7–12); the climax of the poem comes with "I believe" (Ps 27:13), echoing "I trust" (Ps 27:3).

**27:2 To devour my flesh**: the psalmist's enemies are rapacious beasts (Ps 7:3; 17:12; 22:14, 17).

**27:8 Seek his face**: to commune with God in the Temple. The idiom is derived from the practice of journeying to sacred places, cf. Hos 5:15; 2 Sm 21:1; Ps 24:6.

**27:13 In the land of the living**: or "in the land of life," an epithet of the Jerusalem Temple (Ps 52:7; 116:9; Is 38:11), where the faithful had access to the life-giving presence of God.

**Psalm 28** A lament asking that the psalmist, who has taken refuge in the Temple (Ps 28:2), not be punished with the wicked, who are headed inevitably toward destruction (Ps 28:1, 3–5). The statement of praise is exceptionally lengthy and vigorous (Ps 28:6–7). The Psalm ends with a prayer (Ps 28:8–9).

*a:* Ps 25:16. *b:* Ps 22:23; 35:18; 149:1. *c:* Ps 18:29; 36:10; 43:3; Is 10:17; Mi 7:8. *d:* Ps 14:4. *e:* Ps 23:6; 61:5. *f:* Ps 31:21. *g:* Ps 24:6; Hos 5:15. *h:* Is 49:15. *i:* Ps 25:4; 86:11. *j:* Ps 116:9; Is 38:11. *k:* Ps 18:2. *l:* Ps 30:4; 88:5; 143:7; Prv 1:12.

when I lift up my hands toward your
holy place.*[m]
3 Do not drag me off with the wicked,
with those who do wrong,[n]
Who speak peace to their neighbors
though evil is in their hearts.[o]
4 Repay them for their deeds,
for the evil that they do.
For the work of their hands repay them;
give them what they deserve.[p]
5 Because they do not understand the
LORD's works,
the work of his hands,[q]
He will tear them down,
never to rebuild them.

II

6 *Blessed be the LORD,
who has heard the sound of my pleading.
7 The LORD is my strength and my shield,
in whom my heart trusts.
I am helped, so my heart rejoices;
with my song I praise him.

III

8 * LORD, you are a strength for your people,
the saving refuge of your anointed.
9 Save your people, bless your inheritance;
pasture and carry them forever!

See RG 175

## PSALM 29*

### *The Lord of Majesty Acclaimed as King of the World*

1 A psalm of David.

I

Give to the LORD, you sons of God,*
give to the LORD glory and might;
2 Give to the LORD the glory due his
name.
Bow down before the LORD's holy
splendor![r]

II

3 The voice of the LORD* is over the
waters;
the God of glory thunders,
the LORD, over the mighty waters.
4 The voice of the LORD is power;
the voice of the LORD is splendor.[s]
5 The voice of the LORD cracks the
cedars;
the LORD splinters the cedars of
Lebanon,
6 Makes Lebanon leap like a calf,
and Sirion* like a young bull.
7 The voice of the LORD strikes with fiery
flame;
8 the voice of the LORD shakes the
desert;
the LORD shakes the desert of
Kadesh.
9 *The voice of the LORD makes the deer
dance
and strips the forests bare.
All in his Temple say, "Glory!"

III

10 The LORD sits enthroned above the
flood!*[t]
The LORD reigns as king forever!
11 May the LORD give might to his
people;*
may the LORD bless his people with
peace![u]

**28:2 Your holy place**: the innermost part of the Temple, the holy of holies, containing the ark, cf. 1 Kgs 6:16, 19–23; 8:6–8.

**28:6** The psalmist shifts to fervent thanksgiving, probably responding to a priestly or prophetic oracle in Ps 28:5cd (not usually transmitted) assuring the worshiper that the prayer has been heard.

**28:8 Your people . . . your anointed**: salvation is more than individual, affecting all the people and their God-given leader.

**Psalm 29** The hymn invites the members of the heavenly court to acknowledge God's supremacy by ascribing glory and might to God alone (Ps 29:1–2a, 9b). Divine glory and might are dramatically visible in the storm (Ps 29:3–9a). The storm apparently comes from the Mediterranean onto the coast of Syria-Palestine and then moves inland. In Ps 29:10 the divine beings acclaim God's eternal kingship. The Psalm concludes with a prayer that God will impart the power just displayed to the Israelite king and through the king to Israel.

**29:1 Sons of God**: members of the heavenly court who served Israel's God in a variety of capacities.

**29:3 The voice of the LORD**: the sevenfold repetition of the phrase imitates the sound of crashing thunder and may allude to God's primordial slaying of Leviathan, the seven-headed sea monster of Canaanite mythology.

**29:6 Sirion**: the Phoenician name for Mount Hermon, cf. Dt 3:9.

**29:9b–10** Having witnessed God's supreme power (Ps 29:3–9a), the gods acknowledge the glory that befits the king of the divine and human world.

**29:10 The flood**: God defeated the primordial waters and made them part of the universe, cf. Ps 89:10–13; 93:3–4.

**29:11 His people**: God's people, Israel.

*m:* Ps 134:2. *n:* Ps 26:9. *o:* Ps 12:2; 55:22; 62:5; Prv 26:24–28. *p:* 2 Sm 3:39. *q:* Is 5:12. *r:* Ps 68:35; 96:7–9. *s:* Ps 46:7; 77:18–19; Jb 37:4; Is 30:30. *t:* Bar 3:3. *u:* Ps 68:36.

See RG 175

## PSALM 30*

### *Thanksgiving for Deliverance*

1 A psalm. A song for the dedication of the
Temple.* Of David.

I

2 I praise you, LORD, for you raised me up
and did not let my enemies rejoice
over me.
3 O LORD, my God,
I cried out to you for help and you
healed* me.
4 LORD, you brought my soul up from
Sheol;
you let me live, from going down to
the pit.*[v]

II

5 Sing praise to the LORD, you faithful;
give thanks to his holy memory.
6 For his anger lasts but a moment;
his favor a lifetime.
At dusk weeping comes for the night;
but at dawn there is rejoicing.

III

7 Complacent,* I once said,
"I shall never be shaken."
8 LORD, you showed me favor,
established for me mountains of virtue.
But when you hid your face
I was struck with terror.[w]
9 To you, LORD, I cried out;
with the Lord I pleaded for mercy:
10 *"What gain is there from my lifeblood,
from my going down to the grave?
Does dust give you thanks
or declare your faithfulness?
11 Hear, O LORD, have mercy on me;
LORD, be my helper."

IV

12 You changed my mourning into dancing;
you took off my sackcloth
and clothed me with gladness.[x]
13 So that my glory may praise you
and not be silent.
O LORD, my God,
forever will I give you thanks.

## PSALM 31*

See RG 175

### *Prayer in Distress and Thanksgiving for Escape*

1 For the leader. A psalm of David.

I

2 In you, LORD, I take refuge;[y]
let me never be put to shame.
In your righteousness deliver me;
3 incline your ear to me;
make haste to rescue me!
Be my rock of refuge,
a stronghold to save me.
4 For you are my rock and my fortress;[z]
for your name's sake lead me and
guide me.
5 Free me from the net they have set for me,
for you are my refuge.
6 *Into your hands I commend my spirit;[a]
you will redeem me, LORD, God of
truth.
7 You hate those who serve worthless
idols,
but I trust in the LORD.
8 I will rejoice and be glad in your mercy,
once you have seen my misery,

**Psalm 30** An individual thanksgiving in four parts: praise and thanks for deliverance and restoration (Ps 30:2–4); an invitation to others to join in (Ps 30:5–6); a flashback to the time before deliverance (Ps 30:7–11); a return to praise and thanks (Ps 30:12). Two sets of images recur: 1) going down, death, silence; 2) coming up, life, praising. God has delivered the psalmist from one state to the other.

**30:1 For the dedication of the Temple**: a later adaptation of the Psalm to celebrate the purification of the Temple in 164 B.C. during the Maccabean Revolt.

**30:3 Healed**: for God as healer, see also Ps 103:3; 107:20; Hos 6:1; 7:1; 11:3; 14:5.

**30:4 Sheol . . . pit**: the shadowy underworld residence of the spirits of the dead, here a metaphor for near-death.

**30:7 Complacent**: untroubled existence is often seen as a source of temptation to forget God, cf. Dt 8:10–18; Hos 13:6; Prv 30:9.

**30:10** In the stillness of Sheol no one gives you praise; let me live and be among your worshipers, cf. Ps 6:6; 88:11–13; 115:17; Is 38:18.

**Psalm 31** A lament (Ps 31:2–19) with a strong emphasis on trust (Ps 31:4, 6, 15–16), ending with an anticipatory thanksgiving (Ps 31:20–24). As is usual in laments, the affliction is couched in general terms. The psalmist feels overwhelmed by evil people but trusts in the "God of truth" (Ps 31:6).

**31:6 Into your hands I commend my spirit**: in Lk 23:46 Jesus breathes his last with this Psalm verse. Stephen in Acts 7:59 alludes to these words as he is attacked by enemies. The verse is used as an antiphon in the Divine Office at Compline, the last prayer of the day.

*v:* Ps 28:1; Jon 2:7. *w:* Ps 104:29. *x:* Is 61:3; Jer 31:13. *y:* Ps 71:1–3. *z:* Ps 18:2. *a:* Lk 23:46; Acts 7:59.

[and] gotten to know the distress of
my soul.[b]
9 You will not abandon me into enemy
hands,
but will set my feet in a free and open
space.

II

10 Be gracious to me, LORD, for I am in
distress;
affliction is wearing down my eyes,
my throat and my insides.
11 My life is worn out by sorrow,
and my years by sighing.
My strength fails in my affliction;
my bones are wearing down.[c]
12 To all my foes I am a thing of scorn,
and especially to my neighbors
a horror to my friends.
When they see me in public,
they quickly shy away.[d]
13 I am forgotten, out of mind like the
dead;
I am like a worn-out tool.*
14 I hear the whispers of the crowd;
terrors are all around me.*
They conspire together against me;
they plot to take my life.
15 But I trust in you, LORD;
I say, "You are my God."[e]
16 My destiny is in your hands;
rescue me from my enemies,
from the hands of my pursuers.
17 Let your face shine on your servant;[f]
save me in your mercy.
18 Do not let me be put to shame,
for I have called to you, LORD.
Put the wicked to shame;
reduce them to silence in Sheol.
19 Strike dumb their lying lips,
which speak arrogantly against the
righteous
in contempt and scorn.[g]

III

20 How great is your goodness, Lord,
stored up for those who fear you.
You display it for those who trust you,
in the sight of the children of Adam.
21 You hide them in the shelter of your
presence,
safe from scheming enemies.
You conceal them in your tent,
away from the strife of tongues.[h]
22 Blessed be the LORD,
marvelously he showed to me
his mercy in a fortified city.
23 Though I had said in my alarm,
"I am cut off from your eyes."[i]
Yet you heard my voice, my cry for mercy,
when I pleaded with you for help.
24 Love the LORD, all you who are faithful
to him.
The LORD protects the loyal,
but repays the arrogant in full.
25 Be strong and take heart,
all who hope in the LORD.

## PSALM 32*

See RG 175

### *Remission of Sin*

1[j]Of David. A *maskil*.

I

Blessed is the one whose fault is
removed,
whose sin is forgiven.
2 Blessed is the man to whom the LORD
imputes no guilt,
in whose spirit is no deceit.

II

3 Because I kept silent,* my bones wasted
away;
I groaned all day long.[k]
4 For day and night your hand was heavy
upon me;
my strength withered as in dry summer
heat. *Selah*

**31:13 Like a worn-out tool**: a common comparison for something ruined and useless, cf. Is 30:14; Jer 19:11; 22:28.

**31:14 Terrors are all around me**: a cry used in inescapable danger, cf. Jer 6:25; 20:10; 46:5; 49:29.

**Psalm 32** An individual thanksgiving and the second of the seven Penitential Psalms (cf. Ps 6). The opening declaration—the forgiven are blessed (Ps 32:1–2)—arises from the psalmist's own experience. At one time the psalmist was stubborn and closed, a victim of sin's power (Ps 32:3–4), and then became open to the forgiving God (Ps 32:5–7). Sin here, as often in the Bible, is not only the personal act of rebellion against God but also the consequences of that act—frustration and waning of vitality. Having been rescued, the psalmist can teach others the joys of justice and the folly of sin (Ps 32:8–11).

**32:3 I kept silent:** did not confess the sin before God.

*b:* Ps 10:14. *c:* Ps 32:3; 38:10–11. *d:* Jb 19:13–19. *e:* Ps 140:7; Is 25:1. *f:* Ps 67:1; Nm 6:24. *g:* Ps 12:4. *h:* Ps 27:5. *i:* Jon 2:5. *j:* Is 1:18; Ps 65:3; Rom 4:7–8. *k:* Ps 31:11.

5 Then I declared my sin to you;
my guilt I did not hide.[l]
I said, "I confess my transgression to the LORD,"
and you took away the guilt of my sin. *Selah*
6 Therefore every loyal person should pray to you
in time of distress.
Though flood waters* threaten,
they will never reach him.[m]
7 You are my shelter; you guard me from distress;
with joyful shouts of deliverance you surround me. *Selah*

III

8 I will instruct you and show you the way you should walk,
give you counsel with my eye upon you.
9 Do not be like a horse or mule, without understanding;
with bit and bridle their temper is curbed,
else they will not come to you.

IV

10 Many are the sorrows of the wicked one,
but mercy surrounds the one who trusts in the LORD.
11 Be glad in the LORD and rejoice, you righteous;
exult, all you upright of heart.[n]

See RG 175

## PSALM 33*

### *Praise of God's Power and Providence*

I

1 Rejoice, you righteous, in the LORD;
praise from the upright is fitting.[o]
2 Give thanks to the LORD on the harp;
on the ten-stringed lyre offer praise.[p]
3 Sing to him a new song;
skillfully play with joyful chant.
4 For the LORD's word is upright;
all his works are trustworthy.
5 He loves justice and right.
The earth is full of the mercy of the LORD.[q]

II

6 By the LORD's word the heavens were made;
by the breath of his mouth all their host.*[r]
7 *He gathered the waters of the sea as a mound;
he sets the deep into storage vaults.[s]

III

8 Let all the earth fear the LORD;
let all who dwell in the world show him reverence.
9 For he spoke, and it came to be,
commanded, and it stood in place.[t]
10 The LORD foils the plan of nations,
frustrates the designs of peoples.
11 But the plan of the LORD stands forever,
the designs of his heart through all generations.[u]
12 Blessed is the nation whose God is the LORD,
the people chosen as his inheritance.[v]

IV

13 From heaven the LORD looks down
and observes the children of Adam,[w]
14 From his dwelling place he surveys
all who dwell on earth.
15 The One who fashioned together their hearts
is the One who knows all their works.

V

16 A king is not saved by a great army,
nor a warrior delivered by great strength.
17 Useless is the horse for safety;
despite its great strength, it cannot be saved.

**32:6 Flood waters**: the untamed waters surrounding the earth, a metaphor for danger.

**Psalm 33** A hymn in which the just are invited (Ps 33:1–3) to praise God, who by a mere word (Ps 33:4–5) created the three-tiered universe of the heavens, the cosmic waters, and the earth (Ps 33:6–9). Human words, in contrast, effect nothing (Ps 33:10–11). The greatness of human beings consists in God's choosing them as a special people and their faithful response (Ps 33:12–22).

**33:6 All their host**: the stars of the sky are commonly viewed as a vast army, e.g., Neh 9:6; Is 40:26; 45:12; Jer 33:22.

**33:7 The waters . . . as a mound**: ancients sometimes attributed the power keeping the seas from overwhelming land to a primordial victory of the storm-god over personified Sea.

*l:* Ps 38:19; 51:5. *m:* Ps 18:5. *n:* Ps 33:1. *o:* Ps 32:11; 147:1. *p:* Ps 92:4; 144:9. *q:* Ps 119:64. *r:* Gn 2:1. *s:* Ps 78:13; Gn 1:9–10; Ex 15:8; Jos 3:16. *t:* Ps 148:5; Gn 1:3f; Jdt 16:14. *u:* Prv 19:21; Is 40:8. *v:* Ps 144:15; Ex 19:6; Dt 7:6. *w:* Jb 34:21; Sir 15:19; Jer 16:17; 32:19.

[18] Behold, the eye of the LORD is upon
those who fear him,
upon those who count on his mercy,
[19] To deliver their soul from death,
and to keep them alive through
famine.

VI

[20] Our soul waits for the LORD,
he is our help and shield.[x]
[21] For in him our hearts rejoice;
in his holy name we trust.
[22] May your mercy, LORD, be upon us;
as we put our hope in you.

## PSALM 34*

See RG 176

### *Thanksgiving to God Who Delivers the Just*

[1] Of David, when he feigned madness before Abimelech,* who drove him out and he went away.

I

[2] I will bless the LORD at all times;
his praise shall be always in my mouth.[y]
[3] My soul will glory in the LORD;
let the poor hear and be glad.
[4] Magnify the LORD with me;
and let us exalt his name together.

II

[5] I sought the LORD, and he answered me,
delivered me from all my fears.
[6] Look to him and be radiant,
and your faces may not blush for shame.
[7] This poor one cried out and the LORD
heard,
and from all his distress he saved him.
[8] The angel of the LORD encamps
around those who fear him, and he
saves them.[z]
[9] Taste and see that the LORD is good;
blessed is the stalwart one who takes
refuge in him.[a]
[10] Fear the LORD, you his holy ones;
nothing is lacking to those who fear
him.[b]
[11] The rich grow poor and go hungry,
but those who seek the LORD lack no
good thing.

III

[12] Come, children,* listen to me;[c]
I will teach you fear of the LORD.
[13] Who is the man who delights in life,[d]
who loves to see the good days?
[14] Keep your tongue from evil,
your lips from speaking lies.
[15] Turn from evil and do good;[e]
seek peace and pursue it.
[16] The eyes of the LORD are directed toward
the righteous[f]
and his ears toward their cry.
[17] The LORD's face is against evildoers
to wipe out their memory from the
earth.
[18] The righteous cry out, the LORD hears
and he rescues them from all their
afflictions.
[19] The LORD is close to the brokenhearted,
saves those whose spirit is crushed.
[20] Many are the troubles of the righteous,
but the LORD delivers him from them
all.
[21] He watches over all his bones;
not one of them shall be broken.[g]
[22] Evil will slay the wicked;
those who hate the righteous are
condemned.
[23] The LORD is the redeemer of the souls of
his servants;
and none are condemned who take
refuge in him.

## PSALM 35*

See RG 175

### *Prayer for Help Against Unjust Enemies*

[1] Of David.

I

*Oppose, O LORD, those who oppose me;
war upon those who make war
upon me.

**Psalm 34** A thanksgiving in acrostic form, each line beginning with a successive letter of the Hebrew alphabet. In this Psalm one letter is missing and two are in reverse order. The psalmist, fresh from the experience of being rescued (Ps 34:5, 7), can teach the "poor," those who are defenseless, to trust in God alone (Ps 34:4, 12). God will make them powerful (Ps 34:5–11) and give them protection (Ps 34:12–22).

**34:1 Abimelech**: a scribal error for Achish. In 1 Sm 21:13–16, David feigned madness before Achish, not Abimelech.

**34:12 Children**: the customary term for students in wisdom literature.

**Psalm 35** A lament of a person betrayed by friends. The

*x:* Ps 115:9. *y:* Ps 145:2. *z:* Ex 14:19. *a:* Ps 2:12. *b:* Prv 3:7. *c:* Prv 1:8; 4:1. *d:* 1 Pt 3:10–12. *e:* Ps 37:27. *f:* Ps 33:18. *g:* Jn 19:36.

2 Take up the shield and buckler;
rise up in my defense.
3 Brandish lance and battle-ax
against my pursuers.
Say to my soul,
"I am your salvation."
4 Let those who seek my life
be put to shame and disgrace.
Let those who plot evil against me[h]
be turned back and confounded.
5 Make them like chaff before the wind,[i]
with the angel of the LORD driving
them on.
6 Make their way slippery and dark,
with the angel of the LORD pursuing
them.

II

7 Without cause they set their snare for me;
without cause they dug a pit for me.
8 Let ruin overtake them unawares;
let the snare they have set catch them;
let them fall into the pit they have
dug.[j]
9 Then I will rejoice in the LORD,
exult in God's salvation.
10 My very bones shall say,
"O LORD, who is like you,[k]
Who rescue the afflicted from the
powerful,
the afflicted and needy from the
despoiler?"

III

11 Malicious witnesses rise up,
accuse me of things I do not know.
12 They repay me evil for good;
my soul is desolate.[l]
13 *Yet I, when they were ill, put on
sackcloth,
afflicted myself with fasting,
sobbed my prayers upon my bosom.
14 I went about in grief as for my brother,
bent in mourning as for my mother.
15 Yet when I stumbled they gathered with
glee,
gathered against me and I did not
know it.
They slandered me without ceasing;
16 without respect they mocked me,
gnashed their teeth against me.

IV

17 O Lord, how long will you look on?
Restore my soul from their
destruction,
my very life from lions![m]
18 Then I will thank you in the great
assembly;
I will praise you before the mighty
throng.[n]
19 Do not let lying foes rejoice over me,
my undeserved enemies wink
knowingly.[o]
20 They speak no words of peace,
but against the quiet in the land
they fashion deceitful speech.[p]
21 They open wide their mouths against me.
They say, "Aha! Good!
Our eyes have seen it!"[q]
22 You see this, LORD; do not be silent;[r]
Lord, do not withdraw from me.
23 Awake, be vigilant in my defense,
in my cause, my God and my Lord.
24 Defend me because you are just, LORD;
my God, do not let them rejoice over
me.
25 Do not let them say in their hearts,
"Aha! Our soul!"*
Do not let them say,
"We have devoured that one!"
26 Put to shame and confound
all who relish my misfortune.

psalmist prays that the evildoers be publicly exposed as unjust (Ps 35:1–8), and gives thanks in anticipation of vindication (Ps 35:9–10). Old friends are the enemies (Ps 35:11–16). May their punishment come quickly (Ps 35:17–21)! The last part (Ps 35:22–26) echoes the opening in praying for the destruction of the psalmist's persecutors. The Psalm may appear vindictive, but one must keep in mind that the psalmist is praying for public redress now of a public injustice. There is at this time no belief in an afterlife in which justice will be redressed.

**35:1–6** The mixture of judicial, martial, and hunting images shows that the language is figurative. The actual injustice is false accusation of serious crimes (Ps 35:11, 15, 20–21). The psalmist seeks lost honor through a trial before God.

**35:13, 15–17** The Hebrew is obscure.

**35:25 Aha! Our soul!**: an ancient idiomatic expression meaning that we have attained what we wanted.

*h:* Ps 40:15; 71:13. *i:* Ps 1:4; 83:14; Jb 21:18. *j:* Ps 7:16; 9:16; 57:7; Prv 26:27; Eccl 10:8; Sir 27:26. *k:* Ps 86:8; 89:7, 9; Ex 15:11. *l:* Ps 27:12; 38:20–21; 109:5; Jer 18:20. *m:* Ps 17:12; 22:22; 58:7. *n:* Ps 22:23; 26:12; 35:18; 40:10; 149:1. *o:* Ps 38:17. *p:* Ps 120:6–7. *q:* Ps 40:16; Lam 2:16. *r:* Ps 22:12; 38:21; 109:1.

Clothe with shame and disgrace
those who lord it over me.
27 But let those who favor my just cause
shout for joy and be glad.
May they ever say, "Exalted be the LORD
who delights in the peace of his loyal servant."
28 Then my tongue shall recount your justice,
declare your praise, all the day long.[s]

See RG 175–76

## PSALM 36*

### *Human Wickedness and Divine Providence*

1 For the leader. Of David, the servant of the LORD.

I

2 Sin directs the heart of the wicked man;
his eyes are closed to the fear of God.[t]
3 For he lives with the delusion:
his guilt will not be known and hated.*
4 Empty and false are the words of his mouth;
he has ceased to be wise and do good.
5 On his bed he hatches plots;
he sets out on a wicked way;
he does not reject evil.[u]

II

6 *LORD, your mercy reaches to heaven;
your fidelity, to the clouds.[v]
7 Your justice is like the highest mountains;
your judgments, like the mighty deep;
human being and beast you sustain, LORD.
8 How precious is your mercy, O God!
The children of Adam take refuge in the shadow of your wings.*[w]
9 They feast on the rich food of your house;
from your delightful stream[x] you give them drink.
10 For with you is the fountain of life,[y]
and in your light we see light.[z]
11 Show mercy on those who know you,
your just defense to the upright of heart.
12 Do not let the foot of the proud overtake me,
nor the hand of the wicked disturb me.
13 There make the evildoers fall;
thrust them down, unable to rise.

See RG 176, 178

## PSALM 37*

### *The Fate of Sinners and the Reward of the Just*

1 Of David.

**Aleph**

Do not be provoked by evildoers;
do not envy those who do wrong.[a]
2 Like grass they wither quickly;
like green plants they wilt away.[b]

**Beth**

3 Trust in the LORD and do good
that you may dwell in the land* and live secure.[c]
4 Find your delight in the LORD
who will give you your heart's desire.[d]

**Gimel**

5 Commit your way to the LORD;
trust in him and he will act[e]

**Psalm 36** A Psalm with elements of wisdom (Ps 36:2–5), the hymn (Ps 36:6–10), and the lament (Ps 36:11–13). The rule of sin over the wicked (Ps 36:2–5) is contrasted with the rule of divine love and mercy over God's friends (Ps 36:6–10). The Psalm ends with a prayer that God's guidance never cease (Ps 36:11–12).

**36:3 Hated**: punished by God.

**36:6–7** God actively controls the entire world.

**36:8 The shadow of your wings**: metaphor for divine protection. It probably refers to the winged cherubim in the holy of holies in the Temple, cf. 1 Kgs 6:23–28, 32; 2 Chr 3:10–13; Ez 1:4–9.

**Psalm 37** The Psalm responds to the problem of evil, which the Old Testament often expresses as a question: why do the wicked prosper and the good suffer? The Psalm answers that the situation is only temporary. God will reverse things, rewarding the good and punishing the wicked here on earth. The perspective is concrete and earthbound: people's very actions place them among the ranks of the good or wicked. Each group or "way" has its own inherent dynamism—eventual frustration for the wicked, eventual reward for the just. The Psalm is an acrostic, i.e., each section begins with a successive letter of the Hebrew alphabet. Each section has its own imagery and logic.

**37:3 The land**: the promised land, Israel, which became for later interpreters a type or figure of heaven, cf. Heb 11:9–10, 13–16. The New Testament Beatitudes (Mt 5:3–12; Lk 6:20–26) have been influenced by the Psalm, especially their total reversal of the present and their interpretation of the happy future as possession of the land.

*s:* Ps 71:15–16. *t:* Rom 3:18. *u:* Mi 2:1. *v:* Ps 57:11; 71:19. *w:* Ps 17:8. *x:* Gn 2:8, 10. *y:* Is 55:1; Jn 4:14. *z:* Ps 80:4, 8, 20. *a:* Prv 3:31; 23:17; 24:1, 19. *b:* Ps 90:5–6; 102:12; 103:15–16; Jb 14:2; Is 40:7. *c:* Ps 128:2. *d:* Prv 10:24. *e:* Ps 55:23; Prv 3:5; 16:3.

6 And make your righteousness shine like
the dawn,
your justice like noonday.[f]

Daleth

7 Be still before the LORD;
wait for him.
Do not be provoked by the prosperous,
nor by malicious schemers.

He

8 Refrain from anger; abandon wrath;
do not be provoked; it brings only
harm.
9 Those who do evil will be cut off,
but those who wait for the LORD will
inherit the earth.[g]

Waw

10 Wait a little, and the wicked will be no
more;
look for them and they will not be
there.
11 But the poor will inherit the earth,[h]
will delight in great prosperity.

Zayin

12 The wicked plot against the righteous
and gnash their teeth at them;
13 But my Lord laughs at them,[i]
because he sees that their day is
coming.

Heth

14 The wicked unsheath their swords;
they string their bows
To fell the poor and oppressed,
to slaughter those whose way is
upright.[j]
15 Their swords will pierce their own
hearts;
their bows will be broken.

Teth

16 Better the meagerness of the righteous
one
than the plenty of the wicked.[k]
17 The arms of the wicked will be broken,
while the LORD will sustain the
righteous.

Yodh

18 The LORD knows the days of the
blameless;
their heritage lasts forever.
19 They will not be ashamed when times are
bad;
in days of famine they will be satisfied.

Kaph

20 The wicked perish,
enemies of the LORD;
They shall be consumed like fattened
lambs;
like smoke they disappear.[l]

Lamedh

21 The wicked one borrows but does not
repay;
the righteous one is generous and
gives.
22 For those blessed by the Lord will inherit
the earth,
but those accursed will be cut off.

Mem

23 The valiant one whose steps are guided
by the LORD,
who will delight in his way,[m]
24 May stumble, but he will never fall,
for the LORD holds his hand.

Nun

25 Neither in my youth, nor now in old age
have I seen the righteous one
abandoned[n]
or his offspring begging for bread.
26 All day long he is gracious and lends,
and his offspring become a blessing.

Samekh

27 Turn from evil and do good,
that you may be settled forever.[o]
28 For the LORD loves justice
and does not abandon the faithful.

Ayin

When the unjust are destroyed,
and the offspring of the wicked cut off,
29 The righteous will inherit the earth
and dwell in it forever.[p]

Pe

30 The mouth of the righteous utters
wisdom;[q]
his tongue speaks what is right.
31 God's teaching is in his heart;[r]
his steps do not falter.

---

*f:* Wis 5:6; Is 58:10. *g:* Ps 25:13; Prv 2:21; Is 57:13. *h:* Mt 5:4. *i:* Ps 2:4; 59:9; Wis 4:18. *j:* Ps 11:2; 57:5; 64:4. *k:* Prv 15:16; 16:8. *l:* Wis 5:14. *m:* Prv 20:24. *n:* Jb 4:7; Sir 2:10. *o:* Ps 34:14–15; Am 5:14. *p:* Ps 25:13; Prv 2:21; Is 57:13. *q:* Prv 10:31. *r:* Ps 40:9; Dt 6:6; Is 51:7; Jer 31:33.

Sadhe

32 The wicked spies on the righteous
and seeks to kill him.
33 But the LORD does not abandon him in his power,
nor let him be condemned when tried.

Qoph

34 Wait eagerly for the LORD,
and keep his way;[s]
He will raise you up to inherit the earth;
you will see when the wicked are cut off.

Resh

35 I have seen a ruthless scoundrel,
spreading out like a green cedar.[t]
36 When I passed by again, he was gone;
though I searched, he could not be found.

Shin

37 Observe the person of integrity and mark the upright;
Because there is a future for a man of peace.[u]
38 Sinners will be destroyed together;
the future of the wicked will be cut off.

Taw

39 The salvation of the righteous is from the LORD,
their refuge in a time of distress.[v]
40 The LORD helps and rescues them,
rescues and saves them from the wicked,
because they take refuge in him.

See RG 175

## PSALM 38*

### *Prayer of an Afflicted Sinner*

1 A psalm of David. For remembrance.

I

2 LORD, do not punish me in your anger;
in your wrath do not chastise me![w]
3 Your arrows have sunk deep in me;[x]
your hand has come down upon me.
4 There is no wholesomeness in my flesh
because of your anger;
there is no health in my bones because of my sin.[y]
5 My iniquities overwhelm me,
a burden too heavy for me.[z]

II

6 Foul and festering are my sores
because of my folly.
7 I am stooped and deeply bowed;[a]
every day I go about mourning.
8 My loins burn with fever;
there is no wholesomeness in my flesh.
9 I am numb and utterly crushed;
I wail with anguish of heart.[b]
10 My Lord, my deepest yearning is before you;
my groaning is not hidden from you.
11 My heart shudders, my strength forsakes me;
the very light of my eyes has failed.[c]
12 Friends and companions shun my disease;
my neighbors stand far off.
13 Those who seek my life lay snares for me;
they seek my misfortune, they speak of ruin;
they plot treachery every day.

III

14 But I am like the deaf, hearing nothing,
like the mute, I do not open my mouth,
15 I am even like someone who does not hear,
who has no answer ready.
16 LORD, it is for you that I wait;
O Lord, my God, you respond.[d]
17 For I have said that they would gloat over me,
exult over me if I stumble.

IV

18 I am very near to falling;
my wounds are with me always.
19 I acknowledge my guilt
and grieve over my sin.[e]
20 My enemies live and grow strong,
those who hate me grow numerous fraudulently,

**Psalm 38** In this lament, one of the Penitential Psalms (cf. Ps 6), the psalmist acknowledges the sin that has brought physical and mental sickness and social ostracism. There is no one to turn to for help; only God can undo the past and restore the psalmist.

*s:* Ps 31:24. *t:* Ps 92:8–9; Is 2:13; Ez 31:10–11. *u:* Prv 23:18; 24:14. *v:* Ps 9:10; Is 25:4. *w:* Ps 6:2. *x:* Jb 6:4; Lam 3:12; Ps 31:11; 64:7. *y:* Is 1:5–6. *z:* Ps 40:13; Ezr 9:6. *a:* Ps 35:14. *b:* Ps 102:4–6. *c:* Ps 6:8; 31:10. *d:* Ps 13:4. *e:* Ps 32:5; 51:5.

21 Repaying me evil for good,
accusing me for pursuing good.[f]
22 Do not forsake me, O LORD;
my God, be not far from me![g]
23 Come quickly to help me,[h]
my Lord and my salvation!

See RG 175–76

## PSALM 39*

### *The Vanity of Life*

1 For the leader, for Jeduthun.[i] A psalm of David.

I

2 I said, "I will watch my ways,
lest I sin with my tongue;
I will keep a muzzle on my mouth."
3 Mute and silent before the wicked,
I refrain from good things.
But my sorrow increases;
4 my heart smolders within me.[j]
In my sighing a fire blazes up,
and I break into speech:

II

5 LORD, let me know my end, the number of my days,
that I may learn how frail I am.
6 To be sure, you establish the expanse of my days;
indeed, my life is as nothing before you.
Every man is but a breath.[k] *Selah*

III

7 Man goes about as a mere phantom;
they hurry about, although in vain;
he heaps up stores without knowing for whom.
8 And now, LORD, for what do I wait?
You are my only hope.
9 From all my sins deliver me;
let me not be the taunt of fools.
10 I am silent and do not open my mouth
because you are the one who did this.
11 Take your plague away from me;
I am ravaged by the touch of your hand.
12 You chastise man with rebukes for sin;
like a moth you consume his treasures.
Every man is but a breath. *Selah*
13 Listen to my prayer, LORD, hear my cry;
do not be deaf to my weeping!
For I am with you like a foreigner,
a refugee, like my ancestors.[l]
14 Turn your gaze from me, that I may smile
before I depart to be no more.

## PSALM 40*

See RG 175–76

### *Gratitude and Prayer for Help*

1 For the leader. A psalm of David.

A

2 Surely, I wait for the LORD;
who bends down to me and hears my cry,[m]
3 Draws me up from the pit of destruction,
out of the muddy clay,[n]
Sets my feet upon rock,
steadies my steps,
4 And puts a new song* in my mouth,[o]
a hymn to our God.
Many shall look on in fear
and they shall trust in the LORD.
5 Blessed the man who sets
his security in the LORD,
who turns not to the arrogant
or to those who stray after falsehood.[p]
6 You, yes you, O LORD, my God,
have done many wondrous deeds!
And in your plans for us
there is none to equal you.[q]

**Psalm 39** The lament of a mortally ill person who at first had resolved to remain silently submissive (Ps 39:2–4). But the grief was too much and now the psalmist laments the brevity and vanity of life (Ps 39:5–7), yet remaining hopeful (Ps 39:8–10). The psalmist continues to express both acceptance of the illness and hope for healing in Ps 39:11–13.

**Psalm 40** A thanksgiving (Ps 40:2–13) has been combined with a lament (Ps 40:14–17) that appears also in Ps 70. The psalmist describes the rescue in spatial terms—being raised up from the swampy underworld to firm earth where one can praise God (Ps 40:2–4). All who trust God will experience like protection (Ps 40:5–6)! The Psalm stipulates the precise mode of thanksgiving: not animal sacrifice but open and enthusiastic proclamation of the salvation just experienced (Ps 40:7–11). A prayer for protection concludes (Ps 40:12–17).

**40:4 A new song**: a song in response to the new action of God (cf. Ps 33:3; 96:1; 144:9; 149:1; Is 42:10). Giving thanks is not purely a human response but is itself a divine gift.

*f:* Ps 109:5. *g:* Ps 22:2, 12, 20; 35:22. *h:* Ps 40:14. *i:* 1 Chr 16:41; Ps 62:1; 77:1. *j:* Jer 20:9. *k:* Ps 62:10; 90:9–10; 144:4; Jb 7:6, 16; 14:1, 5; Eccl 6:12; Wis 2:5. *l:* Ps 119:19; Gn 23:4; Heb 11:13; 1 Pt 2:11. *m:* Lam 3:25. *n:* Ps 28:1; 30:4; 69:3, 15–16; 88:5; Prv 1:12; Jon 2:7. *o:* Ps 33:3. *p:* Ps 1:1; Prv 16:20; Jer 17:7. *q:* Ps 35:10.

Should I wish to declare or tell them,
too many are they to recount.[r]
7 *Sacrifice and offering you do not want;[s]
you opened my ears.
Holocaust and sin-offering you do not
request;
8 so I said, "See; I come
with an inscribed scroll written upon
me.
9 I delight to do your will, my God;
your law is in my inner being!"[t]
10 When I sing of your righteousness
in a great assembly,
See, I do not restrain my lips;
as you, LORD, know.[u]
11 I do not conceal your righteousness
within my heart;
I speak of your loyalty and your
salvation.
I do not hide your mercy or
faithfulness from a great
assembly.
12 LORD, may you not withhold
your compassion from me;
May your mercy and your faithfulness
continually protect me.[v]

B

13 But evils surround me
until they cannot be counted.
My sins overtake me,
so that I can no longer see.
They are more numerous than the hairs
of my head;
my courage fails me.[w]
14 LORD, graciously rescue me![x]
Come quickly to help me, LORD!
15 May those who seek to destroy my life
be shamed and confounded.
Turn back in disgrace
those who desire my ruin.[y]
16 Let those who say to me "Aha!"[z]
Be made desolate on account of their
shame.
17 While those who seek you
rejoice and be glad in you.
May those who long for your salvation
always say, "The LORD is great."[a]
18 Though I am afflicted and poor,
my Lord keeps me in mind.
You are my help and deliverer;
my God, do not delay!

## PSALM 41*

See RG 175

### *Thanksgiving After Sickness*

1 For the leader. A psalm of David.

I

2 Blessed the one concerned for the poor;*
on a day of misfortune, the LORD
delivers him.[b]
3 The LORD keeps and preserves him,
makes him blessed in the land,
and does not betray him to his
enemies.
4 The LORD sustains him on his sickbed,
you turn down his bedding whenever
he is ill.*

II

5 Even I have said, "LORD, take note of
me;
heal me, although I have sinned
against you.
6 My enemies say bad things against me:
'When will he die and his name be
forgotten?'
7 When someone comes to visit me, he
speaks without sincerity.
His heart stores up malice;
when he leaves, he gossips.[c]
8 All those who hate me whisper together
against me;
they imagine the worst about me:
9 'He has had ruin poured over him;

**40:7–9** Obedience is better than sacrifice (cf. 1 Sm 15:22; Is 1:10–20; Hos 6:6; Am 5:22–25; Mi 6:6–8; Acts 7:42–43 [quoting Am 5:25–26]). Heb 10:5–9 quotes the somewhat different Greek version and interprets it as Christ's self-oblation.

**Psalm 41** A thanksgiving for rescue from illness (Ps 41:4, 5, 9). Many people, even friends, have interpreted the illness as a divine punishment for sin and have ostracized the psalmist (Ps 41:5–11). The healing shows the return of God's favor and rebukes the psalmist's detractors (Ps 41:12–13).

**41:2 Blessed the one concerned for the poor**: cf. Ps 32:1–2; 34:9; 40:5; 65:5. The psalmist's statement about God's love of the poor is based on the experience of being rescued (Ps 41:1–3).

**41:4 You turn down his bedding whenever he is ill**: the Hebrew is obscure. It suggests ongoing attentive care of the one who is sick.

*r:* Ps 71:15; 139:17–18. *s:* Heb 10:5–7; Ps 51:18–19; Am 5:22; Hos 6:6; Is 1:11–15. *t:* Ps 37:31. *u:* Ps 22:23; 26:12; 35:18; 149:1. *v:* Ps 89:34. *w:* Ps 38:5, 11; Ezr 9:6. *x:* Ps 70:2–6; 71:12. *y:* Ps 35:4, 26. *z:* Ps 35:21, 25. *a:* Ps 35:27. *b:* Tb 4:7–11. *c:* Ps 31:12; 38:12–13; 88:8; Jb 19:13–19; Jer 20:10.

that one lying down will never rise
again.'
10 *Even my trusted friend,
who ate my bread,
has raised his heel against me.[d]
III
11 "But you, LORD, take note of me to raise
me up
that I may repay them."*

12 By this I will know you are pleased
with me,
that my enemy no longer shouts in
triumph over me.
13 In my integrity may you support me
and let me stand in your presence
forever.
14 *Blessed be the LORD, the God of Israel,
from all eternity and forever.
Amen. Amen.[e]

## Second Book—Psalms 42–72

See RG 175

### PSALM 42*

### *Longing for God's Presence in the Temple*

1 For the leader. A *maskil* of the Korahites.*
I
2 As the deer longs for streams of water,[f]
so my soul longs for you, O God.
3 My soul thirsts for God, the living God.
When can I enter and see the face of
God?*[g]
4 My tears have been my bread day and
night,[h]
as they ask me every day, "Where is
your God?"[i]
5 Those times I recall
as I pour out my soul,[j]
When I would cross over to the shrine of
the Mighty One,*
to the house of God,
Amid loud cries of thanksgiving,
with the multitude keeping festival.[k]
6 Why are you downcast, my soul;
why do you groan within me?
Wait for God, for I shall again praise
him,
my savior and my God.
II
7 My soul is downcast within me;
therefore I remember you
From the land of the Jordan* and
Hermon,
from Mount Mizar,[l]
8 *Deep calls to deep
in the roar of your torrents,
and all your waves and breakers
sweep over me.[m]
9 By day may the LORD send his mercy,
and by night may his righteousness be
with me!
I will pray* to the God of my life,
10 I will say to God, my rock:
"Why do you forget me?[n]
Why must I go about mourning

**41:10 Even my trusted friend . . . has raised his heel against me**: Jn 13:18 cites this verse to characterize Judas as a false friend. **Raised his heel against me**: an interpretation of the unclear Hebrew, "made great the heel against me."

**41:11 That I may repay them**: the healing itself is an act of judgment through which God decides for the psalmist and against the false friends. The prayer is not necessarily for strength to punish enemies.

**41:14** The doxology, not part of the Psalm, marks the end of the first of the five books of the Psalter, cf. Ps 72:18–20; 89:53; 106:48.

**Psalms 42–43** Ps 42–43 form a single lament of three sections, each section ending in an identical refrain (Ps 42:6, 12; 43:5). The psalmist is far from Jerusalem, and longs for the divine presence that Israel experienced in the Temple liturgy. Despite sadness, the psalmist hopes once again to join the worshiping crowds.

**42:1 The Korahites**: a major guild of Temple singers (2 Chr 20:19) whose name appears in the superscriptions of Ps 42; 44–49; 84–85; 87–88.

**42:3 See the face of God**: "face" designates a personal presence (Gn 33:10; Ex 10:28–29; 2 Sm 17:11). The expressions "see God/God's face" occur elsewhere (Ps 11:7; 17:15; cf. Ex 24:10; 33:7–11; Jb 33:26) for the presence of God in the Temple.

**42:5 The shrine of the Mighty One**: this reading follows the tradition of the Septuagint and the Vulgate.

**42:7 From the land of the Jordan**: the sources of the Jordan are in the foothills of Mount Hermon in present-day southern Lebanon. Mount Mizar is presumed to be a mountain in the same range.

**42:8 Deep calls to deep**: to the psalmist, the waters arising in the north are overwhelming and far from God's presence, like the waters of chaos (Ps 18:5; 69:2–3, 15; Jon 2:3–6).

**42:9–10 I will pray . . . I will say**: in the midst of his depression the psalmist turns to prayer. Despite his situation he trusts the Lord to deliver him from his sorrow so that he may

*d:* Ps 55:14–15; Jn 13:18. *e:* Neh 9:5. *f:* Ps 63:2; 84:3; 143:6; Is 26:9. *g:* Ps 27:4. *h:* Ps 80:6; 102:10. *i:* Ps 79:10; Jl 2:17. *j:* Lam 3:20. *k:* Ps 122:5. *l:* Ps 43:3. *m:* Ps 18:5; 32:6; 69:2; 88:8; Jon 2:4. *n:* Ps 18:2; 31:3–4.

with the enemy oppressing me?"
11 It shatters my bones, when my
adversaries reproach me,
when they say to me every day:
"Where is your God?"
12 Why are you downcast, my soul,
why do you groan within me?
Wait for God, for I shall again praise
him,
my savior and my God.

### PSALM 43

See RG 175

1 Grant me justice, O God;
defend me from a faithless people;
from the deceitful and unjust rescue me.[o]
2 You, O God, are my strength.
Why then do you spurn me?
Why must I go about mourning,
with the enemy oppressing me?
3 [p]Send your light and your fidelity,*
that they may be my guide;[q]
Let them bring me to your holy
mountain,
to the place of your dwelling,
4 That I may come to the altar of God,
to God, my joy, my delight.
Then I will praise you with the harp,
O God, my God.
5 Why are you downcast, my soul?
Why do you groan within me?
Wait for God, for I shall again praise him,
my savior and my God.

### PSALM 44*

See RG 175, 177

#### *God's Past Favor and Israel's Present Need*

1 For the leader. A *maskil* of the Korahites.

I

2 O God, we have heard with our own ears;
our ancestors have told us[r]
The deeds you did in their days,
with your own hand in days of old:
3 You rooted out nations to plant them,[s]
crushed peoples and expelled them.
4 Not with their own swords did they
conquer the land,[t]
nor did their own arms bring victory;
It was your right hand, your own arm,
the light of your face for you favored
them.[u]
5 You are my king and my God,[v]
who bestows victories on Jacob.
6 Through you we batter our foes;
through your name we trample our
adversaries.
7 Not in my bow do I trust,
nor does my sword bring me victory.
8 You have brought us victory over our
enemies,
shamed those who hate us.
9 In God we have boasted all the day long;
your name we will praise forever.
*Selah*

II

10 [w]But now you have rejected and
disgraced us;
you do not march out with our armies.[x]
11 You make us retreat* before the foe;
those who hate us plunder us at will.[y]
12 You hand us over like sheep to be
slaughtered,
scatter us among the nations.[z]
13 You sell your people for nothing;
you make no profit from their sale.[a]
14 You make us the reproach of our
neighbors,[b]
the mockery and scorn of those
around us.
15 You make us a byword among the
nations;

enter the Temple precincts and praise him once again (Ps 43:3–4, 5b).

**43:3 Your light and your fidelity**: a pair of divine attributes personified as guides for the pilgrimage. As in Ps 42:9 the psalmist prays that these divine attributes lead him back to Jerusalem and ultimately to God's presence in the Temple.

**Psalm 44** In this lament the community reminds God of past favors which it has always acknowledged (Ps 44:2–9). But now God has abandoned Israel to defeat and humiliation (Ps 44:10–17), though the people are not conscious of any sin against the covenant (Ps 44:18–23). They struggle with being God's special people amid divine silence; yet they continue to pray (Ps 44:24–26).

**44:11 You make us retreat**: the corollary of Ps 44:3. Defeat, like victory, is God's doing; neither Israel nor its enemies can claim credit (Ps 44:23).

*o:* Ps 119:154. *p:* Ps 18:29; 27:1; 36:10; Mi 7:8. *q:* Ps 122:1. *r:* Ps 78:3. *s:* Ps 78:55; 80:9f. *t:* Dt 8:17f; Jos 24:12. *u:* Ps 4:7; 31:17; 67:2; 80:4; Nm 6:25; Dn 9:17. *v:* Ps 145:1. *w:* Ps 89:39–52. *x:* Ps 60:12. *y:* Lv 26:17; Dt 28:25. *z:* Lv 26:33; Dt 28:64. *a:* Dt 32:30; Is 52:3. *b:* Ps 79:4; 80:7; 123:3–4; Jb 12:4; Dn 9:16.

COVENANTS ARE MUTUAL obligations; the psalmist is saying in 44:18 that even though God has broken his side, the community continues to maintain its obligations.

the peoples shake their heads at us.
16 All day long my disgrace is before me;
shame has covered my face
17 At the sound of those who taunt and
revile,
at the sight of the enemy and avenger.

III

18 All this has come upon us,
though we have not forgotten you,
nor been disloyal to your covenant.
19 *Our hearts have not turned back,
nor have our steps strayed from your
path.
20 Yet you have left us crushed,
desolate in a place of jackals;*[c]
you have covered us with a shadow of
death.
21 If we had forgotten the name of our God,
stretched out our hands to another god,
22 Would not God have discovered this,
God who knows the secrets of the
heart?
23 For you we are slain all the day long,
considered only as sheep to be
slaughtered.[d]

IV

24 Awake! Why do you sleep, O Lord?
Rise up! Do not reject us forever![e]
25 Why do you hide your face;[f]
why forget our pain and misery?
26 For our soul has been humiliated in the
dust;[g]
our belly is pressed to the earth.
27 Rise up, help us!
Redeem us in your mercy.

## PSALM 45*

See RG 176

### *Song for a Royal Wedding*

1For the leader; according to "Lilies."
A *maskil* of the Korahites.
A love song.

I

2 My heart is stirred by a noble theme,
as I sing my ode to the king.
My tongue is the pen of a nimble
scribe.

II

3 You are the most handsome of men;
fair speech has graced your lips,
for God has blessed you forever.[h]
4 Gird your sword upon your hip, mighty
warrior!
In splendor and majesty ride on
triumphant![i]
5 In the cause of truth, meekness, and
justice
may your right hand show your
wondrous deeds.
6 Your arrows are sharp;
peoples will cower at your feet;
the king's enemies will lose heart.
7 Your throne, O God,* stands forever;[j]
your royal scepter is a scepter for
justice.
8 You love justice and hate wrongdoing;
therefore God, your God, has anointed
you
with the oil of gladness above your
fellow kings.
9 With myrrh, aloes, and cassia

**44:19 Our hearts have not turned back**: Israel's defeat was not caused by its lack of fidelity.

**44:20 A place of jackals**: following Israel's defeat and exile (Ps 44:11–12), the land lies desolate, inhabited only by jackals, cf. Is 13:22; Jer 9:10; 10:22. Others take *tannim* as "sea monster" (cf. Ez 29:3; 32:2) and render: "you crushed us as you did the sea monster."

**Psalm 45** A song for the Davidic king's marriage to a foreign princess from Tyre in Phoenicia. The court poet sings (Ps 45:2, 18) of God's choice of the king (Ps 45:3, 8), of his role in establishing divine rule (Ps 45:4–8), and of his splendor as he waits for his bride (Ps 45:9–10). The woman is to forget her own house when she becomes wife to the king (Ps 45:11–13). Her majestic beauty today is a sign of the future prosperity of the royal house (Ps 45:14–17). The Psalm was retained in the collection when there was no reigning king, and came to be applied to the king who was to come, the messiah.

**45:7 O God**: the king, in courtly language, is called "god," i.e., more than human, representing God to the people. Heb 1:8–9 applies Ps 45:7–8 to Christ.

*c:* Jer 9:10. *d:* Rom 8:36. *e:* Ps 10:1; 74:1; 77:8; 79:5; 83:2. *f:* Ps 10:11; 89:47; Jb 13:24. *g:* Ps 119:25. *h:* Sg 5:10–16. *i:* Ps 21:5. *j:* Heb 1:8–9.

your robes are fragrant.
From ivory-paneled palaces*
stringed instruments bring you joy.
10 Daughters of kings are your lovely wives;
a princess arrayed in Ophir's gold*
comes to stand at your right hand.

III

11 Listen, my daughter, and understand;
pay me careful heed.
Forget your people and your father's house,*
12 that the king might desire your beauty.
He is your lord;
13 [k]honor him, daughter of Tyre.
Then the richest of the people
will seek your favor with gifts.
14 All glorious is the king's daughter as she enters,[l]
her raiment threaded with gold;
15 In embroidered apparel she is led to the king.
The maids of her train are presented
to the king.
16 They are led in with glad and joyous acclaim;
they enter the palace of the king.

IV

17 The throne of your fathers your sons will have;
you shall make them princes through all the land.[m]
18 I will make your name renowned through all generations;
thus nations shall praise you forever.[n]

## PSALM 46*

See RG 175

### *God, the Protector of Zion*

1 For the leader. A song of the Korahites. According to *alamoth*.*

I

2 God is our refuge and our strength,
an ever-present help in distress.[o]
3 *Thus we do not fear, though earth be shaken
and mountains quake to the depths of the sea,
4 Though its waters rage and foam
and mountains totter at its surging.[p] *Selah*

II

5 *Streams of the river gladden the city of God,
the holy dwelling of the Most High.[q]
6 God is in its midst; it shall not be shaken;
God will help it at break of day.[r]
7 Though nations rage and kingdoms totter,
he utters his voice and the earth melts.[s]
8 *The LORD of hosts is with us;
our stronghold is the God of Jacob. *Selah*

III

9 Come and see the works of the LORD,
who has done fearsome deeds on earth;[t]
10 Who stops wars to the ends of the earth,
breaks the bow, splinters the spear,
and burns the shields with fire;[u]
11 [v]"Be still and know that I am God!
I am exalted among the nations,
exalted on the earth."

**45:9 Ivory-paneled palaces**: lit., "palaces of ivory." Ivory paneling and furniture decoration have been found in Samaria and other ancient Near Eastern cities, cf. Am 3:15.

**45:10 Ophir's gold**: uncertain location, possibly a region on the coast of southern Arabia or eastern Africa, famous for its gold, cf. 1 Kgs 9:28; 10:11; Jb 22:24.

**45:11 Forget your people and your father's house**: the bride should no longer consider herself a daughter of her father's house, but the wife of the king—the queen.

**Psalm 46** A song of confidence in God's protection of Zion with close parallels to Ps 48. The dominant note in Ps 46 is sounded by the refrain, The LORD of hosts is with us (Ps 46:8, 12). The first strophe (Ps 46:2–4) sings of the security of God's presence even in utter chaos; the second (Ps 46:5–8), of divine protection of the city from its enemies; the third (Ps 46:9–11), of God's imposition of imperial peace.

**46:1 Alamoth**: the melody of the Psalm, now lost.

**46:3–4** Figurative ancient Near Eastern language to describe social and political upheavals.

**46:5** Jerusalem is not situated on a river. This description derives from mythological descriptions of the divine abode and symbolizes the divine presence as the source of all life (cf. Is 33:21; Ez 47:1–12; Jl 4:18; Zec 14:8; Rev 22:1–2).

**46:8** The first line of the refrain is similar in structure and meaning to Isaiah's name for the royal child, Emmanuel, With us is God (Is 7:14; 8:8, 10).

*k:* Ps 72:10–11; Is 60:5f. *l:* Ez 16:10–13. *m:* Gn 17:6. *n:* Is 60:15. *o:* Ps 48:4; Is 33:2. *p:* Ps 93:3–4; Jb 9:5–6; Is 24:18–20; 54:10. *q:* Ps 48:2–3; 76:3. *r:* Is 7:14. *s:* Ps 2:1–5; 48:5–8; 76:7–9; Is 17:12–14. *t:* Ps 48:9–10. *u:* Ps 76:4. *v:* Ps 48:11.

12 The LORD of hosts is with us;
our stronghold is the God of Jacob.
*Selah*

## PSALM 47*

See RG 175–76

### *The Ruler of All the Nations*

1 For the leader. A psalm of the Korahites.

I

2 All you peoples, clap your hands;
shout to God with joyful cries.[w]
3 For the LORD, the Most High, is to be feared,
the great king over all the earth,[x]
4 Who made people subject to us,
nations under our feet,[y]
5 *Who chose our heritage for us,
the glory of Jacob, whom he loves.[z] *Selah*

II

6 *God has gone up with a shout;
the LORD, amid trumpet blasts.[a]
7 Sing praise to God, sing praise;
sing praise to our king, sing praise.

III

8 For God is king over all the earth;[b]
sing hymns of praise.
9 God rules over the nations;
God sits upon his holy throne.
10 The princes of the peoples assemble
with the people of the God of Abraham.
For the shields of the earth belong to God,
highly exalted.[c]

## PSALM 48*

See RG 175

### *The Splendor of the Invincible City*

1 A psalm of the Korahites.* A song.

I

2 Great is the LORD and highly praised
in the city of our God:[d]
His holy mountain,
3 fairest of heights,
the joy of all the earth,[e]
Mount Zion, the heights of Zaphon,*[f]
the city of the great king.

II

4 God is in its citadel,
renowned as a stronghold.
5 See! The kings assembled,
together they advanced.
6 *When they looked they were astounded;
terrified, they were put to flight![g]
7 Trembling seized them there,
anguish, like a woman's labor,[h]
8 As when the east wind wrecks
the ships of Tarshish!*

III

9 *What we had heard we have now seen
in the city of the LORD of hosts,
In the city of our God,
which God establishes forever. *Selah*
10 We ponder, O God, your mercy
within your temple
11 Like your name, O God,
so is your praise to the ends of the earth.[i]

**Psalm 47** A hymn calling on the nations to acknowledge the universal rule of Israel's God (Ps 47:2–5) who is enthroned as king over Israel and the nations (Ps 47:6–9).

**47:5 Our heritage . . . the glory**: the land of Israel (cf. Is 58:14), which God has given Israel in an act of sovereignty.

**47:6 God has gone up**: Christian liturgical tradition has applied the verse to the Ascension of Christ.

**Psalm 48** A Zion hymn, praising the holy city as the invincible dwelling place of God. Unconquerable, it is an apt symbol of God who has defeated all enemies. After seven epithets describing the city (Ps 48:2–3), the Psalm describes the victory by the Divine Warrior over hostile kings (Ps 48:4–8). The second half proclaims the dominion of the God of Zion over all the earth (Ps 48:9–12) and invites pilgrims to announce that God is eternally invincible like Zion itself (Ps 48:13–14).

**48:1 Korahites**: see note on Ps 42:1.

**48:3 The heights of Zaphon**: the mountain abode of the Canaanite storm-god Baal in comparable texts. To speak of Zion as if it were Zaphon was to claim for Israel's God what Canaanites claimed for Baal. Though topographically speaking Zion is only a hill, viewed religiously it towers over other mountains as the home of the supreme God (cf. Ps 68:16–17).

**48:6 When they looked**: the kings are stunned by the sight of Zion, touched by divine splendor. The language is that of holy war, in which the enemy panics and flees at the sight of divine glory.

**48:8 The ships of Tarshish**: large ships, named after the distant land or port of Tarshish, probably ancient Tartessus in southern Spain, although other identifications have been proposed, cf. Is 2:16; 60:9; Jon 1:3.

**48:9 What we had heard we have now seen**: the glorious things that new pilgrims had heard about the holy city—its beauty and awesomeness—they now see with their own eyes. The seeing here contrasts with the seeing of the hostile kings in Ps 48:6.

*w:* Ps 89:16; Zep 3:14. *x:* Ps 95:3; Ex 15:18; Is 24:23; 52:7. *y:* Ps 2:8. *z:* Is 58:14. *a:* Ps 24:8, 10; 68:18–19; 98:6. *b:* Ps 72:11; 93:1; 96:10; 97:1; 99:1; Jer 10:7. *c:* Ps 89:19; Ex 3:6; Is 2:2–4. *d:* Ps 96:4; 145:3. *e:* Ps 50:2; Lam 2:15. *f:* Is 14:13. *g:* Jgs 5:19. *h:* Ex 15:14; Jer 4:31. *i:* Mal 1:11.

Your right hand is fully victorious.
12 Mount Zion is glad!
The daughters of Judah rejoice
because of your judgments![j]
IV
13 Go about Zion, walk all around it,
note the number of its towers.
14 Consider the ramparts, examine its
citadels,
that you may tell future generations:[k]
15 That this is God,
our God for ever and ever.*
He will lead us until death.

## PSALM 49*

See RG 176, 179

### *Confidence in God Rather than in Riches*

1 For the leader. A psalm of the Korahites.*
2 Hear this, all you peoples!
Give ear, all who inhabit the world,
3 You of lowly birth or high estate,
rich and poor together.
4 My mouth shall speak words of wisdom,
my heart shall offer insights.[l]
5 I will turn my ear to a riddle,*
expound my question on a lyre.
I
6 Why should I fear in evil days,
with the iniquity of my assailants
surrounding me,
7 Of those who trust in their wealth
and boast of their abundant riches?[m]
8 *No man can ransom even a brother,
or pay to God his own ransom.[n]
9 The redemption of his soul is costly;
and he will pass away forever.
10 Will he live on forever, then,
and never see the Pit of Corruption?
11 Indeed, he will see that the wise die,
and the fool will perish together with
the senseless,[o]
and they leave their wealth to others.[p]
12 Their tombs are their homes forever,
their dwellings through all generations,
"They named countries after
themselves"
13 —but man does not abide in splendor.
He is like the beasts—they perish.[q]
II
14 This is the way of those who trust in
themselves,
and the end of those who take pleasure
in their own mouth. *Selah*
15 Like a herd of sheep they will be put into
Sheol,
and Death will shepherd them.
Straight to the grave they descend,
where their form will waste away,
Sheol will be their palace.
16 But God will redeem my life,
will take me* from the hand of
Sheol.[r] *Selah*
17 Do not fear when a man becomes rich,
when the wealth of his house grows
great.
18 At his death he will not take along
anything,
his glory will not go down after him.[s]
19 During his life his soul uttered blessings;
"They will praise you, for you do well
for yourself."
20 But he will join the company of his
fathers,
never again to see the light.[t]

**48:15 Our God for ever and ever**: Israel's God is like Zion in being eternal and invincible. The holy city is therefore a kind of "sacrament" of God.

**Psalm 49** The Psalm affirms confidence in God (cf. Ps 23; 27:1–6; 62) in the face of the apparent good fortune of the unjust rich, cf. Ps 37; 73. Reliance on wealth is misplaced (Ps 49:8–10) for it is of no avail in the face of death (Ps 49:18–20). After inviting all to listen to this axiom of faith (Ps 49:2–5), the psalmist depicts the self-delusion of the ungodly (Ps 49:6–13), whose destiny is to die like ignorant beasts (Ps 49:13, 18; cf. Prv 7:21–23). Their wealth should occasion no alarm, for they will come to nought, whereas God will save the just (Ps 49:14–20).

**49:1 Korahites**: see note on Ps 42:1.

**49:5 Riddle**: the psalmist's personal solution to the perennial biblical problem of the prosperity of the wicked. **Question**: parallel in meaning to problem; in wisdom literature it means the mysterious way of how the world works.

**49:8 No man can ransom even a brother**: an axiom. For the practice of redemption, cf. Jb 6:21–23. A play on the first Hebrew word of Ps 49:8, 16 relates the two verses.

**49:16 Will take me**: the same Hebrew verb is used of God "taking up" a favored servant: Enoch in Gn 5:24; Elijah in 2 Kgs 2:11–12; the righteous person in Ps 73:24. The verse apparently states the hope that God will rescue the faithful psalmist in the same manner.

*j:* Ps 97:8. *k:* Ps 22:31–32; 71:18. *l:* Ps 78:2; Mt 13:35. *m:* Jb 31:24. *n:* Prv 10:15; 11:4; Ez 7:19; Mt 16:26. *o:* Eccl 2:16. *p:* Ps 39:7; Sir 11:18–19. *q:* Eccl 3:18–21. *r:* Ps 16:10; 86:13; 103:4; 116:8. *s:* Sir 11:18–19; Eccl 5:15; 1 Tm 6:7. *t:* Jb 10:21–22.

21 In his prime, man does not understand.
He is like the beasts—they perish.

## PSALM 50*

See RG 175

### *The Acceptable Sacrifice*

1 A psalm of Asaph.

I

The God of gods, the LORD,
has spoken and summoned the earth
from the rising of the sun to its
setting.[u]
2 From Zion, the perfection of beauty,
God shines forth.[v]
3 Our God comes and will not be silent!
Devouring fire precedes him,
it rages strongly around him.[w]
4 He calls to the heavens above
and to the earth to judge his people:
5 "Gather my loyal ones to me,
those who made a covenant with me
by sacrifice."
6 The heavens proclaim his righteousness,
for God himself is the judge.[x] *Selah*

II

7 "Listen, my people, I will speak;
Israel, I will testify against you;
God, your God, am I.
8 Not for your sacrifices do I rebuke you,
your burnt offerings are always
before me.
9 I will not take a bullock from your house,
or he-goats from your folds.[y]
10 For every animal of the forest is mine,
beasts by the thousands on my
mountains.
11 I know every bird in the heights;
whatever moves in the wild is mine.
12 Were I hungry, I would not tell you,
for mine is the world and all that fills it.[z]
13 Do I eat the flesh of bulls
or drink the blood of he-goats?
14 Offer praise as your sacrifice to God;[a]
fulfill your vows to the Most High.
15 Then call on me on the day of distress;[b]
I will rescue you, and you shall
honor me."

III

16 But to the wicked God says:
"Why do you recite my
commandments
and profess my covenant with your
mouth?
17 You hate discipline;
you cast my words behind you!
18 If you see a thief, you run with him;
with adulterers you throw in your lot.
19 You give your mouth free rein for evil;
you yoke your tongue to deceit.
20 You sit and speak against your brother,
slandering your mother's son.
21 When you do these things should I be
silent?
Do you think that I am like you?
I accuse you, I lay out the matter
before your eyes.

IV

22 "Now understand this, you who forget
God,
lest I start ripping apart and there be
no rescuer.
23 Those who offer praise as a sacrifice
honor me;
I will let him whose way is steadfast
look upon the salvation of God."[c]

## PSALM 51*

See RG 175

### *The Miserere: Prayer of Repentance*

1 For the leader. A psalm of David, 2 when
Nathan the prophet came to him after he had
gone in to Bathsheba.[d]

I

3 Have mercy on me, God, in accord with
your merciful love;

**Psalm 50** A covenant lawsuit stating that the sacrifice God really wants is the sacrifice of praise accompanied by genuine obedience (cf. Mi 6:1–8). It begins with a theophany and the summoning of the court (Ps 50:1–6). Then in direct address God explains what is required of the faithful (Ps 50:7–15), rebukes the hypocritical worshiper (Ps 50:16–21), and concludes with a threat and a promise (Ps 50:22–23; cf. Is 1:19–20).

**Psalm 51** A lament, the most famous of the seven Penitential Psalms, prays for the removal of the personal and social disorders that sin has brought. The poem has two parts of approximately equal length: Ps 51:3–10 and Ps 51:11–19, and a conclusion in Ps 51:20–21. The two parts interlock by repetition of "blot out" in the first verse of each section (Ps 51:3, 11), of "wash (away)" just after the first verse of each section (Ps 51:4) and just before the last verse (Ps 51:9) of the first

*u:* Dt 10:17; Jos 22:22. *v:* Ps 48:2. *w:* Ps 97:3; Dn 7:10. *x:* Ps 19:2; 97:6. *y:* Ps 69:32; Am 5:21–22. *z:* Ps 24:1; 89:12; Dt 10:14; 1 Cor 10:26. *a:* Heb 13:15. *b:* Ps 77:3. *c:* Ps 91:16. *d:* 2 Sm 12.

in your abundant compassion blot out
my transgressions.
4 Thoroughly wash away my guilt;
and from my sin cleanse me.
5 For I know my transgressions;
my sin is always before me.[e]
6 Against you, you alone have I sinned;
I have done what is evil in your eyes
So that you are just in your word,
and without reproach in your
judgment.[f]
7 Behold, I was born in guilt,
in sin my mother conceived me.*[g]
8 Behold, you desire true sincerity;
and secretly you teach me wisdom.
9 Cleanse me with hyssop,* that I may be
pure;
wash me, and I will be whiter than
snow.[h]
10 You will let me hear gladness and joy;
the bones you have crushed will
rejoice.

II

11 Turn away your face from my sins;
blot out all my iniquities.
12 A clean heart create for me, God;
renew within me a steadfast spirit.[i]
13 Do not drive me from before your face,
nor take from me your holy spirit.[j]
14 Restore to me the gladness of your
salvation;
uphold me with a willing spirit.
15 I will teach the wicked your ways,
that sinners may return to you.
16 Rescue me from violent bloodshed, God,
my saving God,
and my tongue will sing joyfully of
your justice.[k]
17 Lord, you will open my lips;
and my mouth will proclaim your
praise.
18 For you do not desire sacrifice* or I
would give it;
a burnt offering you would not accept.[l]
19 My sacrifice, O God, is a contrite spirit;
a contrite, humbled heart, O God, you
will not scorn.

III

20 *Treat Zion kindly according to your
good will;
build up the walls of Jerusalem.[m]
21 Then you will desire the sacrifices of the
just,
burnt offering and whole offerings;
then they will offer up young bulls on
your altar.

## PSALM 52*

See RG 175

### *The Deceitful Tongue*

1 For the leader. A *maskil* of David, 2 when
Doeg the Edomite entered and reported to
Saul, saying to him: "David has entered the
house of Ahimelech."[n]

I

3 Why do you glory in what is evil, you
who are mighty by the mercy of
God?
All day long

section, and of "heart," "God," and "spirit" in Ps 51:12, 19. The first part (Ps 51:3–10) asks deliverance from sin, not just a past act but its emotional, physical, and social consequences. The second part (Ps 51:11–19) seeks something more profound than wiping the slate clean: nearness to God, living by the spirit of God (Ps 51:12–13), like the relation between God and people described in Jer 31:33–34. Nearness to God brings joy and the authority to teach sinners (Ps 51:15–16). Such proclamation is better than offering sacrifice (Ps 51:17–19). The last two verses express the hope that God's good will toward those who are cleansed and contrite will prompt him to look favorably on the acts of worship offered in the Jerusalem Temple (Ps 51:19 [20–21]).

**51:7 In sin my mother conceived me**: lit., "In iniquity was I conceived," an instance of hyperbole: at no time was the psalmist ever without sin, cf. Ps 88:15, "I am mortally afflicted since youth," i.e., I have always been afflicted. The verse does not imply that the sexual act of conception is sinful.

**51:9 Hyssop**: a small bush whose many woody twigs make a natural sprinkler. It was prescribed in the Mosaic law as an instrument for sprinkling sacrificial blood or lustral water for cleansing, cf. Ex 12:22; Lv 14:4; Nm 19:18.

**51:18 For you do not desire sacrifice**: the mere offering of the ritual sacrifice apart from good dispositions is not acceptable to God, cf. Ps 50.

**51:20–21** Most scholars think that these verses were added to the Psalm some time after the destruction of the Temple in 587 B.C. The verses assume that the rebuilt Temple will be an ideal site for national reconciliation.

**Psalm 52** A condemnation of the powerful and arrogant (Ps 52:3–6), who bring down upon themselves God's judgment (Ps 52:7). The just, those who trust in God alone, are gladdened and strengthened by the downfall of their traditional enemies (Ps 52:8–9).

*e*: Ps 32:5; 38:19; Is 59:12. *f*: Rom 3:4. *g*: Jb 14:4. *h*: Jb 9:30; Is 1:18; Ez 36:25. *i*: Ez 11:19. *j*: Wis 1:5; 9:17; Is 63:11; Hg 2:5; Rom 8:9. *k*: Ps 30:10. *l*: Ps 40:7; 50:8; Am 5:21–22; Hos 6:6; Is 1:11–15; Heb 10:5–7. *m*: Jer 31:4; Ez 36:33. *n*: 1 Sm 21:8; 22:6ff.

4 you are thinking up intrigues;
your tongue is like a sharpened razor,
you worker of deceit.[o]
5 You love evil more than good,
lying rather than saying what is
right.[p] *Selah*
6 You love all the words that create
confusion,
you deceitful tongue.[q]

II

7 God too will strike you down forever,
he will lay hold of you and pluck you
from your tent,
uproot you from the land of the
living.[r] *Selah*
8 The righteous will see and they will fear;
but they will laugh at him:[s]
9 "Behold the man! He did not take God as
his refuge,
but he trusted in the abundance of his
wealth,
and grew powerful through his
wickedness."[t]

III

10 But I, like an olive tree* flourishing in the
house of God,[u]
I trust in God's mercy forever and ever.
11 I will thank you forever
for what you have done.
I will put my hope in your name—for it
is good,[v]
—in the presence of those devoted to
you.

## PSALM 53*

See RG 175

### *A Lament over Widespread Corruption*

1 For the leader; according to *Mahalath*.
A *maskil* of David.

I

2 The fool says in his heart,[w]
"There is no God."[x]
They act corruptly and practice injustice;
there is none that does good.
3 God looks out from the heavens
upon the children of Adam,[y]
To see if there is a discerning person[z]
who is seeking God.
4 All have gone astray;
each one is altogether perverse.
There is not one who does what is
good, not even one.[a]

II

5 [b]Do they not know better, those who do
evil,
who feed upon my people as they feed
upon bread?[c]
Have they not called upon God?
6 They are going to fear his name with
great fear,
though they had not feared it before.
For God will scatter the bones
of those encamped against you.
They will surely be put to shame,
for God has rejected them.

III

7 Who will bring forth from Zion
the salvation of Israel?
When God reverses the captivity of his
people
Jacob will rejoice and Israel will be
glad.[d]

## PSALM 54*

See RG 175

### *Confident Prayer in Great Peril*

1 For the leader. On stringed instruments.
A *maskil* of David, 2 when the Ziphites came
and said to Saul, "David is hiding among us."[e]

I

3 O God, by your name* save me.
By your strength defend my cause.
4 O God, hear my prayer.
Listen to the words of my mouth.

**52:10 Like an olive tree**: the righteous will flourish in the house of God like a well-watered olive tree, cf. Ps 92:14; 128:3.

**Psalm 53** A lament of an individual, duplicated in Ps 14, except that "God" is used for "the LORD," and Ps 53:6 is different, cf. Ps 14.

**Psalm 54** A lament in which the person under attack calls directly upon God for help (Ps 54:3–5). Refusing to despair, the psalmist hopes in God, who is active in history and just (Ps 54:6–7). The Psalm ends with a serene promise to return thanks (Ps 54:8–9).

**54:3 By your name**: one is present in one's name, hence God as revealed to human beings.

*o:* Ps 12:3; 59:8; 120:2–3; Sir 51:3. *p:* Jer 4:22; Jn 3:19–20. *q:* Jer 9:4. *r:* Ps 27:13; 28:5; 56:14; Jb 18:14; Prv 2:22; Is 38:11. *s:* Ps 44:14; 64:9. *t:* Jb 31:24; Prv 11:28. *u:* Ps 1:3; 92:12–14; Jer 11:16; 17:8. *v:* Ps 22:23; 26:12; 35:18; 149:1. *w:* Ps 14:1–5a. *x:* Ps 10:4; 36:2; Is 32:6; Jer 5:12. *y:* Rom 3:11–12. *z:* Ps 11:4; 102:20. *a:* Ps 12:2. *b:* Ps 79:6. *c:* Ps 27:2; Is 9:11. *d:* Ps 85:2. *e:* 1 Sm 23:19; 26:1.

[5] Strangers have risen against me;
the ruthless seek my life;
they do not keep God before them.[f] *Selah*

II

[6] God is present as my helper;[g]
the Lord sustains my life.
[7] Turn back the evil upon my foes;
in your faithfulness, destroy them.[h]
[8] Then I will offer you generous sacrifice
and give thanks to your name, LORD,
for it is good.
[9] Because it has rescued me from every trouble,
and my eyes look down on my foes.[i]

See RG 175

## PSALM 55*

### *A Lament over Betrayal*

[1]For the leader. On stringed instruments.
A *maskil* of David.

I

[2] Listen, God, to my prayer;[j]
do not hide from my pleading;
[3] hear me and give answer.
I rock with grief; I groan
[4] at the uproar of the enemy,
the clamor of the wicked.
They heap trouble upon me,
savagely accuse me.
[5] My heart pounds within me;
death's terrors fall upon me.
[6] Fear and trembling overwhelm me;
shuddering sweeps over me.
[7] I say, "If only I had wings like a dove
that I might fly away and find rest.[k]
[8] Far away I would flee;
I would stay in the desert.[l] [9]I would soon find a shelter *Selah*
from the raging wind and storm."

II

[10] Lord, check and confuse their tongues.
For I see violence and strife in the city
[11] making rounds on its walls day and night.
Within are mischief and trouble;
[12] treachery is in its midst;
oppression and fraud never leave its streets.[m]
[13] For it is not an enemy that reviled me—
that I could bear—
Not a foe who viewed me with contempt,
from that I could hide.
[14] But it was you, my other self,
my comrade and friend,[n]
[15] You, whose company I enjoyed,
at whose side I walked
in the house of God.

III

[16] Let death take them;
let them go down alive to Sheol,[o]
for evil is in their homes and bellies.
[17] But I will call upon God,
and the LORD will save me.
[18] At dusk, dawn, and noon
I will grieve and complain,
and my prayer will be heard.[p]
[19] He will redeem my soul in peace
from those who war against me,
though there are many who oppose me.
[20] God, who sits enthroned forever,[q]
will hear me and afflict them. *Selah*
For they will not mend their ways;
they have no fear of God.
[21] He stretched out his hand at his friends
and broke his covenant.
[22] Softer than butter is his speech,
but war is in his heart.
Smoother than oil are his words,
but they are unsheathed swords.[r]
[23] Cast your care upon the LORD,
who will give you support.
He will never allow

**Psalm 55** The psalmist, betrayed by intimate friends (Ps 55:14–15, 20–21), prays that God punish those oath breakers and thus be acknowledged as the protector of the wronged. The sufferings of the psalmist include both ostracism (Ps 55:4) and mental turmoil (Ps 55:5–6), culminating in the wish to flee society (Ps 55:7–9). The wish for a sudden death for one's enemies (Ps 55:16) occurs elsewhere in the Psalms; an example of such a death is the earth opening under the wicked Dathan and Abiram (Nm 16:31–32). The psalmist, confident of vindication, exhorts others to a like trust in the God of justice (Ps 55:23). The Psalm is not so much for personal vengeance as for a public vindication of God's righteousness now. There was no belief in an afterlife where such vindication could take place.

*f:* Ps 86:14. *g:* Ps 118:7. *h:* Ps 143:12. *i:* Ps 59:11; 91:8; 92:12. *j:* Ps 5:2–3; 86:6; 130:1–2; Lam 3:56; Jon 2:3. *k:* Ps 11:1. *l:* Jer 9:1; Rev 12:6. *m:* Jer 5:1; 6:6; Ez 22:2; Heb 1:3; Zep 3:1. *n:* Ps 41:10; Jer 9:3; Mt 26:21–24 par. *o:* Ps 49:15; Nm 16:33; Prv 1:2; Is 5:14. *p:* Dn 6:11. *q:* Ps 29:10; 93:2; Bar 3:3. *r:* Ps 12:3; 28:3; 57:5; 62:5; 64:4; Prv 26:24–28; Jer 9:7.

the righteous to stumble.[s]
24 But you, God, will bring them down
to the pit of destruction.[t]
These bloodthirsty liars
will not live half their days,
but I put my trust in you.[u]

## PSALM 56*

See RG 175

### *Trust in God*

1 For the director. According to *Yonath elem rehoqim*.* A *miktam* of David, when the Philistines seized him at Gath.[v]

I

2 Have mercy on me, God,
for I am treated harshly;
attackers press me all the day.
3 My foes treat me harshly all the day;
yes, many are my attackers.
O Most High, 4 when I am afraid,
in you I place my trust.
5 I praise the word of God;
I trust in God, I do not fear.[w]
What can mere flesh do to me?[x]

II

6 All the day they foil my plans;
their every thought is of evil against
me.
7 They hide together in ambush;
they watch my every step;
they lie in wait for my life.[y]
8 They are evil; watch them, God!
Cast the nations down in your anger!
9 My wanderings you have noted;
are my tears not stored in your flask,*
recorded in your book?[z]
10 My foes turn back when I call on you.
This I know: God is on my side.
11 I praise the word of God,
I praise the word of the LORD.
12 In God I trust, I do not fear.
What can man do to me?

III

13 I have made vows to you, God;
with offerings I will fulfill them,[a]
14 For you have snatched me from death,
kept my feet from stumbling,
That I may walk before God
in the light of the living.

## PSALM 57*

See RG 175

### *Confident Prayer for Deliverance*

1 For the director. Do not destroy.* A *miktam* of David, when he fled from Saul into a cave.[b]

I

2 Have mercy on me, God,
have mercy on me.
In you I seek refuge.
In the shadow of your wings* I seek
refuge
till harm pass by.[c]
3 I call to God Most High,
to God who provides for me.
4 May God send help from heaven to save
me,
shame those who trample upon me.
May God send fidelity and mercy.
*Selah*
5 I must lie down in the midst of lions
hungry for human prey.[d]
Their teeth are spears and arrows;
their tongue, a sharpened sword.[e]
6 Be exalted over the heavens, God;
may your glory appear above all the
earth.[f]

**Psalm 56** Beset physically (Ps 56:2–3) and psychologically (Ps 56:6–7), the psalmist maintains a firm confidence in God (Ps 56:5, 9–10). Nothing will prevent the psalmist from keeping the vow to give thanks for God's gift of life (Ps 56:13). A refrain (Ps 56:5, 11–12) divides the Psalm in two equal parts.

**56:1 Yonath elem rehoqim**: Hebrew words probably designating the melody to which the Psalm was to be sung.

**56:9 Are my tears not stored in your flask**: a unique saying in the Old Testament. The context suggests that the tears are saved because they are precious; God puts a high value on each of the psalmist's troubles.

**Psalm 57** Each of the two equal strophes contains a prayer for rescue from enemies, accompanied by joyful trust in God (Ps 57:2–5, 7–11). The refrain prays that God be manifested as saving (Ps 57:6, 12). Ps 108 is nearly identical to part of this Psalm (cf. Ps 57:8–11, Ps 108:2–6).

**57:1 Do not destroy**: probably the title of the melody to which the Psalm was to be sung.

**57:2 The shadow of your wings**: probably refers to the wings of the cherubim (powerful winged animals) whose wings spread over the ark in the inner chamber of the Temple (1 Kgs 6:23–28).

*s:* Ps 37:5; Prv 3:5; 16:3; 1 Pt 5:7. *t:* Ps 28:1; 30:4; 40:3; 88:5; 143:7; Prv 1:12; Jon 2:7. *u:* Ps 25:2; 56:4; 130:5. *v:* 1 Sm 21:10. *w:* Ps 130:5. *x:* Ps 118:6; Heb 13:6. *y:* Ps 140:5–6. *z:* Ps 10:14; 2 Kgs 20:5; Is 25:8; Rev 7:17. *a:* Nm 30:3. *b:* 1 Sm 22:1. *c:* Ps 17:8; 36:8. *d:* Ps 17:11–12; 22:22; 58:7. *e:* Ps 11:2; 64:4. *f:* Ps 72:19; Nm 14:21.

II

7 They have set a trap for my feet;
my soul is bowed down;
They have dug a pit before me.
May they fall into it themselves![g] *Selah*
8 My heart is steadfast, God,
my heart is steadfast.
I will sing and chant praise.[h]
9 Awake, my soul;
awake, lyre and harp!
I will wake the dawn.*[i]
10 I will praise you among the peoples,
Lord;
I will chant your praise among the
nations.[j]
11 For your mercy towers to the heavens;
your faithfulness reaches to the skies.[k]
12 Exalt yourself over the heavens, God;
may your glory appear above all the
earth.

## PSALM 58*

See RG 175

### *The Dethroning of Unjust Rulers*

1 For the leader. Do not destroy.* A *miktam* of David.

I

2 Do you indeed pronounce justice, O gods;*
do you judge fairly you children of
Adam?[l]
3 No, you freely engage in crime;
your hands dispense violence to the
earth.

II

4 The wicked have been corrupt since birth;
liars from the womb, they have gone
astray.
5 *Their venom is like the venom of a
snake,
like that of a serpent stopping its ears,[m]
6 So as not to hear the voice of the charmer
or the enchanter with cunning spells.

III

7 O God, smash the teeth in their mouths;
break the fangs of these lions, LORD![n]
8 Make them vanish like water flowing
away;[o]
trodden down, let them wither like
grass.[p]
9 Let them dissolve like a snail that oozes
away,*
like an untimely birth that never sees
the sun.[q]
10 Suddenly, like brambles or thistles,
have the whirlwind snatch them away.[r]
11 Then the just shall rejoice to see the
vengeance
and bathe their feet in the blood of the
wicked.[s]
12 Then people will say:
"Truly there is a reward for the just;
there is a God who is judge on earth!"

## PSALM 59*

See RG 175

### *Complaint Against Bloodthirsty Enemies*

1 For the director. Do not destroy.* A *miktam* of David, when Saul sent people to watch his house and kill him.[t]

I

2 Rescue me from my enemies, my God;
lift me out of reach of my foes.
3 Deliver me from evildoers;
from the bloodthirsty save me.

**57:9 I will wake the dawn**: by a bold figure the psalmist imagines the sound of music and singing will waken a new day.

**Psalm 58** A lament expressing trust in God's power to dethrone all powers obstructing divine rule of the world. First condemned are "the gods," the powers that were popularly imagined to control human destinies (Ps 58:2–3), then "the wicked," the human instruments of these forces (Ps 58:4–6). The psalmist prays God to prevent them from harming the just (Ps 58:7–10). The manifestation of justice will gladden the just; they will see that their God is with them (Ps 58:11). The Psalm is less concerned with personal vengeance than with public vindication of God's justice now.

**58:1 Do not destroy**: probably the title of the melody to which the Psalm was to be sung.

**58:2 Gods**: the Bible sometimes understands pagan gods to be lesser divine beings who are assigned by Israel's God to rule the foreign nations. Here they are accused of injustice, permitting the human judges under their patronage to abuse the righteous, cf. Ps 82.

**58:5–6** The image is that of a poisonous snake that is controlled by the voice or piping of its trainer.

**58:9 A snail that oozes away**: empty shells suggested to ancients that snails melted away as they left a slimy trail.

**Psalm 59** A lament in two parts (Ps 59:2–9, 11b–17), each ending in a refrain (Ps 59:10, 18). Both parts alternate prayer

*g:* Ps 7:15; 9:16–17; 140:5–6. *h:* Ps 108:2. *i:* Jb 38:12. *j:* Ps 9:12; 18:50. *k:* Ps 36:6; 71:19. *l:* Ps 82:2; Dt 16:19. *m:* Ps 64:4; 140:3; Rom 3:13. *n:* Ps 3:7. *o:* Wis 16:29. *p:* Ps 37:2. *q:* Jb 3:16. *r:* Jb 21:18; Hos 13:3; Na 1:10. *s:* Ps 68:24; Is 63:1–6. *t:* 1 Sm 19:11.

4 They have set an ambush for my life;
the powerful conspire against me.
For no offense or misdeed of mine,
LORD,
5 for no fault they hurry to take up arms.
Come near and see my plight!
6 You, LORD God of hosts, are the God of Israel!
Awake! Punish all the nations.
Have no mercy on these worthless traitors. *Selah*
7 Each evening they return,
growling like dogs, prowling the city.[u]
8 Their mouths pour out insult;
sharp words are on their lips.
They say: "Who is there to hear?"*
9 But you, LORD, laugh at them;
you deride all the nations.[v]
10 My strength, for you I watch;
you, God, are my fortress,
11 my loving God.

II

May God go before me,
and show me my fallen foes.
12 Slay them, God,
lest they deceive my people.
Shake them by your power;
Lord, our shield, bring them down.
13 For the sinful words of their mouths and lips
let them be caught in their pride.
For the lies they have told under oath[w]
14 destroy them in anger,
destroy till they are no more.
Then people will know God rules over Jacob,
yes, even to the ends of the earth.[x] *Selah*
15 Each evening they return,
growling like dogs, prowling the city.
16 They roam about as scavengers;
if they are not filled, they howl.

III

17 But I shall sing of your strength,
extol your mercy at dawn,
For you are my fortress,
my refuge in time of trouble.
18 My strength, your praise I will sing;
you, God, are my fortress, my loving God.

## PSALM 60*

See RG 175

### *Lament After Defeat in Battle*

1 For the leader; according to "The Lily of. . . . " A *miktam* of David (for teaching), 2 when he fought against Aram-Naharaim and Aram-Zobah; and Joab, coming back, killed twelve thousand Edomites in the Valley of Salt.[y]

I

3 O God, you rejected us, broke our defenses;
you were angry but now revive us.
4 You rocked the earth, split it open;[z]
repair the cracks for it totters.
5 You made your people go through hardship,
made us stagger from the wine you gave us.[a]
6 Raise up a banner for those who revere you,
a refuge for them out of bow shot. *Selah*
7 *Help with your right hand and answer us
that your loved ones may escape.

II

8 *In the sanctuary God promised:
"I will exult, will apportion Shechem;

for vindication (Ps 59:2–3, 4b–5, 11b–14) with vivid depictions of the psalmist's enemies (Ps 59:4–5a, 7–8, 15–16). The near curse in Ps 59:12–13 is not a crude desire for revenge but a wish that God's just rule over human affairs be recognized now.

**59:1 Do not destroy**: probably the title of the melody to which the Psalm was to be sung.

**59:8 Who is there to hear?**: a sample of the enemies' godless reflection. The answer is that God hears their blasphemies.

**Psalm 60** The community complains that God has let the enemy win the battle (Ps 60:3–5) and asks for an assurance of victory (Ps 60:6–7). In the oracle God affirms ownership of the land; the invasion of other nations is not permanent and will be reversed ultimately (Ps 60:8–10). With renewed confidence, the community resolves to fight again (Ps 60:11). The opening lament is picked up again (Ps 60:12), but this time with new awareness of God's power and human limitation.

**60:7–12** These verses occur again as the second half of Ps 108.

**60:8 I will . . . apportion . . . measure out**: God lays claim

*u:* Ps 55:11. *v:* Ps 2:4; 37:13; Wis 4:18. *w:* Prv 12:13; 18:7. *x:* Ps 83:18–19; Ez 5:13. *y:* 2 Sm 8:2, 3, 13; 1 Chr 18:2, 3, 12. *z:* Ps 75:4; Is 24:19. *a:* Ps 75:9; Is 51:17, 21–22; Jer 25:15.

the valley of Succoth* I will measure
out.
9 Gilead is mine, mine is Manasseh;
Ephraim is the helmet for my head,
Judah, my own scepter.*
10 *Moab is my washbowl;
upon Edom I cast my sandal.*[b]
I will triumph over Philistia."
III
11 Who will bring me to the fortified city?*
Who will lead me into Edom?
12 Was it not you who rejected us, God?
Do you no longer march with our
armies?[c]
13 Give us aid against the foe;
worthless is human help.
14 We will triumph with the help of God,
who will trample down our foes.

## PSALM 61*

See RG 175

### *Prayer of the King in Time of Danger*

1 For the leader; with stringed instruments.
Of David.
I
2 Hear my cry, O God,
listen to my prayer!
3 From the ends of the earth* I call;
my heart grows faint.
Raise me up, set me on a rock,
4 for you are my refuge,
a tower of strength against the foe.[d]
5 Let me dwell in your tent forever,
take refuge in the shelter of your
wings.[e] *Selah*
II
6 For you, O God, have heard my
vows,
you have granted me the heritage of
those who revere your name.
7 Add days to the life of the king;
may his years be as from generation to
generation;[f]
8 [g]May he reign before God forever;
send your love and fidelity* to
preserve him—[h]
9 I will duly sing to your name forever,
fulfill my vows day after day.

## PSALM 62*

See RG 175

### *Trust in God Alone*

1 For the leader; *'al Jeduthun*.* A psalm
of David.
I
2 My soul rests in God alone,[i]
from whom comes my salvation.
3 God alone is my rock and salvation,
my fortress; I shall never fall.
4 How long will you set yourself against a
man?
You shall all be destroyed,
Like a sagging wall
or a tumbled down fence!
5 Even highly placed people
plot to overthrow him.
They delight in lies;
they bless with their mouths,
but inwardly they curse.[j] *Selah*
II
6 My soul, be at rest in God alone,
from whom comes my hope.
7 God alone is my rock and my salvation,
my fortress; I shall not fall.
8 My deliverance and honor are with God,[k]
my strong rock;
my refuge is with God.

to these places. **The valley of Succoth**: probably the lower stretch of the Jabbok valley.

**60:9 Judah, my own scepter**: an allusion to the Testament of Jacob, Gn 49:10.

**60:10 Moab is my washbowl**: Moab borders the Dead Sea, hence a metaphor for the country. **Upon Edom I cast my sandal**: an ancient legal gesture of taking possession of land.

**60:11 The fortified city**: perhaps Bozrah, the fortified capital of Edom, cf. Is 34:6; 63:1; Am 1:12.

**Psalm 61** A lament of the king who feels himself at the brink of death (Ps 61:3) and cries out for the strong and saving presence of God (Ps 61:3b–5). The king cites the prayer being made for him (Ps 61:7–8), and promises to give thanks to God.

**61:3 Ends of the earth**: "earth" being taken in its occasional meaning "the underworld," cf. Jon 2:3.

**61:8 Send your love and fidelity**: as in Ps 43:3 the psalmist asks God to send these two divine attributes like angels to protect the king.

**Psalm 62** A song of trust displaying serenity from experiencing God's power (the refrains of Ps 62:2–3 and Ps 62:6–7) and anger toward unjust enemies (Ps 62:4–5). From the experience of being rescued, the psalmist can teach others to trust in God (Ps 62:9–12).

**62:1 'Al Jeduthun**: apparently the Hebrew name for the melody.

*b:* Ru 4:7–8. *c:* Ps 44:10. *d:* Ps 46:2. *e:* Ps 17:8; 36:8; 57:2. *f:* Ps 21:5. *g:* Ps 72:5; 89:5, 30, 37. *h:* Ps 85:11; 89:15, 25; Prv 20:28. *i:* Ps 18:3; 31:3–4; 42:10; 118:8; 146:3. *j:* Ps 12:3; 28:3; 55:22; Prv 26:24–25. *k:* Ps 3:3; Is 26:4; 60:19.

[9] Trust God at all times, my people!
Pour out your hearts to God our refuge! *Selah*

III

[10] Mortals are a mere breath,
the sons of man but an illusion;[l]
On a balance they rise;*
together they weigh nothing.
[11] Do not trust in extortion;
in plunder put no empty hope.
On wealth that increases,
do not set your heart.[m]
[12] *One thing God has said;
two things I have heard:[n]
Strength belongs to God;
[13] so too, my Lord, does mercy,
For you repay each man
according to his deeds.[o]

## PSALM 63*

See RG 175

### *Ardent Longing for God*

[1] A psalm of David, when he was in the wilderness of Judah.[p]

I

[2] O God, you are my God—
it is you I seek!
For you my body yearns;
for you my soul thirsts,
In a land parched, lifeless,
and without water.[q]
[3] I look to you in the sanctuary
to see your power and glory.
[4] For your love is better than life;*
my lips shall ever praise you!

II

[5] I will bless you as long as I live;
I will lift up my hands, calling on your name.
[6] My soul shall be sated as with choice food,
with joyous lips my mouth shall praise you!
[7] I think of you upon my bed,
I remember you through the watches of the night
[8] You indeed are my savior,
and in the shadow of your wings I shout for joy.[r]
[9] My soul clings fast to you;
your right hand upholds me.

III

[10] But those who seek my life will come to ruin;
they shall go down to the depths of the netherworld!
[11] Those who would hand over my life to the sword shall
become the prey of jackals!
[12] But the king shall rejoice in God;
all who swear by the Lord* shall exult,
but the mouths of liars will be shut![s]

## PSALM 64*

See RG 175

### *Treacherous Conspirators Punished by God*

[1] For the leader. A psalm of David.

I

[2] O God, hear my anguished voice;
from a dreadful foe protect my life.
[3] Hide me from the malicious crowd,
the mob of evildoers.
[4] They sharpen their tongues like swords,
bend their bows of poison words.[t]
[5] They shoot at the innocent from ambush,
they shoot him in a moment and do not fear.

**62:10 On a balance they rise**: precious objects were weighed by balancing two pans suspended from a beam. The lighter pan rises.

**62:12 One thing . . . two things**: parallelism of numbers for the sake of variation, a common device in Semitic poetry. One should not literally add up the numbers, cf. Am 1:3; Prv 6:16–19; 30:15, 18, 21.

**Psalm 63** A Psalm expressing the intimate relationship between God and the worshiper. Separated from God (Ps 63:2), the psalmist longs for the divine life given in the Temple (Ps 63:3–6), which is based on a close relationship with God (Ps 63:7–9). May all my enemies be destroyed and God's true worshipers continue in giving praise (Ps 63:10–11)!

**63:4 For your love is better than life**: only here in the Old Testament is anything prized above life—in this case God's love.

**63:12 All who swear by the Lord**: to swear by a particular god meant that one was a worshiper of that god (Is 45:23; 48:1; Zep 1:5).

**Psalm 64** A lament of a person overwhelmed by the malice of the wicked who are depicted in the Psalms as the enemies of the righteous (Ps 64:2–7). When people see God bringing upon the wicked the evil they intended against others, they will know who is the true ruler of the world (Ps 64:8–10). The final verse is a vow of praise (Ps 64:11).

*l:* Ps 39:6–7; 144:4; Jb 7:16; Wis 2:5. *m:* Jb 31:25; Eccl 5:9; Jer 17:11; Mt 6:19–21, 24. *n:* Jb 40:5. *o:* Ps 28:4; 31:24; 2 Sm 3:39; Jb 34:11; Jer 17:10; Mt 16:27; Rom 2:6; 2 Tm 4:14. *p:* 1 Sm 24. *q:* Ps 42:2; 143:6; Is 26:9. *r:* Ps 17:8; 36:8. *s:* Ps 107:42. *t:* Ps 11:2; 37:14; 55:22; 57:5.

THE BEGINNING OF Psalm 65 celebrates God and the temple, the place where vows are paid (vv. 2–5). The psalmist is thankful for the privilege of entering the temple—that is, coming into God's presence—to pay his vow (present an offering). The payment is made possible by the generous harvest that God has provided. The vow may have been to bring a special offering for a good harvest. The body of the psalm praises God for his power over the sources of water and his beneficence in providing water for irrigation. It is possible that this psalm was sung during Sukkoth, the Feast of Tabernacles, which marks the end of the summer harvest and the beginning of the rainy season. In post-biblical times it featured prayers for rain for the coming season.

6 They resolve on their wicked plan;
they conspire to set snares;
they say: "Who will see us?"
7 They devise wicked schemes,
conceal the schemes they devise;
the designs of their hearts are hidden.[u]

II

8 God shoots an arrow at them;
in a moment they are struck down.[v]
9 They are brought down by their own tongues;
all who see them flee.[w]
10 Every person fears and proclaims God's actions,
they ponder his deeds.
11 The righteous rejoices and takes refuge in the LORD;
all the upright give praise.[x]

## PSALM 65*

See RG 176, 178

### *Thanksgiving for God's Blessings*

1 For the leader. A psalm of David. A song.

I

2 To you we owe our hymn of praise,
O God on Zion;
To you our vows* must be fulfilled,
3 *you who hear our prayers.
To you all flesh must come[y]
4 with its burden of wicked deeds.
We are overcome by our sins;
only you can pardon them.[z]
5 Blessed the one whom you will choose and bring
to dwell in your courts.
May we be filled with the good things of your house,
your holy temple!

II

6 You answer us with awesome deeds* of justice,
O God our savior,
The hope of all the ends of the earth
and of those far off across the sea.[a]
7 You are robed in power,
you set up the mountains by your might.
8 You still the roaring of the seas,[b]
the roaring of their waves,
the tumult of the peoples.[c]
9 Distant peoples stand in awe of your marvels;
the places of morning and evening you make resound with joy.
10 *You visit the earth and water it,
make it abundantly fertile.[d]
God's stream* is filled with water;
you supply their grain.
Thus do you prepare it:
11 you drench its plowed furrows,
and level its ridges.

**Psalm 65** The community, aware of its unworthiness (Ps 65:3–4), gives thanks for divine bounty (Ps 65:5), a bounty resulting from God's creation victory (Ps 65:6–9). At God's touch the earth comes alive with vegetation and flocks (Ps 65:10–13).

**65:2 Vows**: the Israelites were accustomed to promising sacrifices in the Temple if their prayers were heard.

**65:3 To you all flesh must come**: all must have recourse to God's mercy.

**65:6 Awesome deeds**: the acts of creating—installing mountains, taming seas, restraining nations (Ps 65:7–8)—that are visible worldwide (Ps 65:6, 9).

**65:10–14** Apparently a description of the agricultural year, beginning with the first fall rains that soften the hard sun-baked soil (Ps 65:9–10).

**65:10 God's stream**: the fertile waters of the earth derive from God's fertile waters in the heavenly world.

*u:* Ps 140:3; Prv 6:14. *v:* Ps 7:13–14; 38:3; Dt 32:42. *w:* Ps 5:11; 44:14; 52:6. *x:* Ps 36:8; 57:2. *y:* Is 66:23. *z:* Ps 32:1–2; 78:38; Is 1:18. *a:* Is 66:19. *b:* Ps 89:10; 107:29; Jb 38:11; Mt 8:26. *c:* Is 17:12. *d:* Lv 26:4; Is 30:23, 25; Jl 2:22–23.

With showers you keep it soft,
blessing its young sprouts.
12 You adorn the year with your bounty;
your paths* drip with fruitful rain.
13 The meadows of the wilderness also drip;
the hills are robed with joy.
14 The pastures are clothed with flocks,
the valleys blanketed with grain;
they cheer and sing for joy.[e]

See RG 176

### PSALM 66*

### *Praise of God, Israel's Deliverer*

1 For the leader. A song; a psalm.

I

2 Shout joyfully to God, all the earth;
sing of his glorious name;
give him glorious praise.[f]
3 Say to God: "How awesome your deeds!
Before your great strength your enemies cringe.
4 All the earth falls in worship before you;[g]
they sing of you, sing of your name!" *Selah*

II

5 *Come and see the works of God,
awesome in deeds before the children of Adam.
6 He changed the sea to dry land;
through the river they passed on foot.[h]
There we rejoiced in him,
7 who rules by his might forever,
His eyes are fixed upon the nations.
Let no rebel rise to challenge! *Selah*
8 Bless our God, you peoples;
loudly sound his praise,
9 Who has kept us alive
and not allowed our feet to slip.[i]
10 You tested us, O God,
tried us as silver tried by fire.[j]
11 You led us into a snare;
you bound us at the waist as captives.
12 *You let captors set foot on our neck;
we went through fire and water;
then you led us out to freedom.[k]

III

13 I will bring burnt offerings* to your house;
to you I will fulfill my vows,
14 Which my lips pronounced
and my mouth spoke in my distress.
15 Burnt offerings of fatlings I will offer you
and sacrificial smoke of rams;
I will sacrifice oxen and goats. *Selah*
16 Come and hear, all you who fear God,
while I recount what has been done for me.
17 I called to him with my mouth;
praise was upon my tongue.
18 Had I cherished evil in my heart,
the Lord would not have heard.
19 But God did hear
and listened to my voice in prayer.
20 Blessed be God, who did not reject my prayer
and refuse his mercy.

### PSALM 67*

See RG 175

### *Harvest Thanks and Petition*

1 For the leader; with stringed instruments. A psalm; a song.

I

2 May God be gracious to us* and bless us;
may his face shine upon us.[l] *Selah*

**65:12 Paths**: probably the tracks of God's storm chariot dropping rain upon earth.

**Psalm 66** In the first part (Ps 66:1–12), the community praises God for powerful acts for Israel, both in the past (the exodus from Egypt and the entry into the land [Ps 66:6]) and in the present (deliverance from a recent but unspecified calamity [Ps 66:8–12]). In the second part (Ps 66:13–20), an individual from the rescued community fulfills a vow to offer a sacrifice of thanksgiving. As often in thanksgivings, the rescued person steps forward to teach the community what God has done (Ps 66:16–20).

**66:5–6** cf. the events described in Ex 14:1–15, 21; Jos 3:11–4:24 and Ps 114.

**66:12 You let captors set foot on our neck**: lit., "you let men mount our heads." Conquerors placed their feet on the neck of their enemies as a sign of complete defeat, cf. Jos 10:24. A ceremonial footstool of the Egyptian king Tutankhamen portrays bound and prostrate bodies of enemies ready for the king's feet on their heads, and one of Tutankhamen's ceremonial chariots depicts the king as a sphinx standing with paw atop the neck of an enemy.

**66:13 Burnt offerings**: cf. Lv 1:3–13; 6:1–4; 22:17–20.

**Psalm 67** A petition for a bountiful harvest (Ps 67:7), made in the awareness that Israel's prosperity will persuade the nations to worship its God.

**67:2 May God be gracious to us**: the people's petition echoes the blessing pronounced upon them by the priests, cf. Nm 6:22–27.

*e:* Is 44:23. *f:* Ps 65:14; Is 44:23. *g:* Ps 18:45; Mi 7:17. *h:* Ps 74:15; 114:3; Ex 14:21f; Jos 3:14ff; Is 44:27; 50:2. *i:* Ps 91:12; 121:3; 1 Sm 2:9; Prv 3:23. *j:* Is 48:10. *k:* Is 43:2. *l:* Ps 4:7; 31:17; 44:4; 80:4; Dn 9:17.

3 So shall your way be known upon the
earth,
your victory among all the nations.[m]
4 May the peoples praise you, God;
may all the peoples praise you!
II
5 May the nations be glad and rejoice;
for you judge the peoples with
fairness,
you guide the nations upon the earth.[n]
*Selah*
6 May the peoples praise you, God;
may all the peoples praise you!
III
7 The earth has yielded its harvest;
God, our God, blesses us.[o]
8 May God bless us still;
that the ends of the earth may revere
him.

See RG 175–76

## PSALM 68*

### *The Exodus and Conquest, Pledge of Future Help*

1 For the leader. A psalm of David; a song.
I
2 *May God arise;
may his enemies be scattered;
may those who hate him flee before
him.[p]
3 As the smoke is dispersed, disperse
them;
as wax is melted by fire,
so may the wicked perish before God.[q]
4 Then the just will be glad;
they will rejoice before God;
they will celebrate with great joy.
II
5 Sing to God, praise his name;
exalt the rider of the clouds.*
Rejoice before him
whose name is the LORD.[r]
6 Father of the fatherless, defender of
widows[s]—
God in his holy abode,
7 God gives a home to the forsaken,
who leads prisoners out to prosperity,
while rebels live in the desert.*
III
8 God, when you went forth before your
people,[t]
when you marched through the desert,
*Selah*
9 The earth quaked, the heavens poured,
before God, the One of Sinai,
before God, the God of Israel.
10 You poured abundant rains, God,
your inheritance was weak and you
repaired it.
11 Your creatures dwelt in it;
you will establish it in your goodness
for the poor, O God.
IV
12 The Lord announced:
"Those bringing news are a great Army.
13 The kings of the armies are in
desperate flight.[u]

**Psalm 68** The Psalm is extremely difficult because the Hebrew text is badly preserved and the ceremony that it describes is uncertain. The translation assumes the Psalm accompanied the early autumn Feast of Tabernacles (Sukkoth), which included a procession of the tribes (Ps 68:25–28). Israel was being oppressed by a foreign power, perhaps Egypt (Ps 68:31–32)—unless Egypt stands for any oppressor. The Psalm may have been composed from segments of ancient poems, which would explain why the transitions are implied rather than explicitly stated. At any rate, Ps 68:2 is based on Nm 10:35–36, and Ps 68:8–9 are derived from Jgs 5:4–5. The argument develops in nine stanzas (each of three to five poetic lines): 1. confidence that God will destroy Israel's enemies (Ps 68:2–4); 2. call to praise God as savior (Ps 68:5–7); 3. God's initial rescue of Israel from Egypt (Ps 68:8), the Sinai encounter (Ps 68:9), and the settlement in Canaan (Ps 68:10–11); 4. the defeat of the Canaanite kings (Ps 68:12–15); 5. the taking of Jerusalem, where Israel's God will rule the world (Ps 68:16–19); 6. praise for God's past help and for the future interventions that will be modeled on the ancient exodus-conquest (Ps 68:20–24); 7. procession at the Feast of Tabernacles (Ps 68:25–28); 8. prayer that the defeated enemies bring tribute to the Temple (Ps 68:29–32); 9. invitation for all kingdoms to praise Israel's God (Ps 68:33–35).

**68:2** The opening line alluding to Nm 10:35 makes clear that God's assistance in the period of the exodus and conquest is the model and assurance of all future divine help.

**68:5 Exalt the rider of the clouds**: God's intervention is in the imagery of Canaanite myth in which the storm-god mounted the storm clouds to ride to battle. Such theophanies occur throughout the Psalm: Ps 68:2–3, 8–10, 12–15, 18–19, 22–24, 29–32, 34–35. See Dt 33:26; Ps 18:8–16; Is 19:1.

**68:7 While rebels live in the desert**: rebels must live in the arid desert, whereas God's people will live in the well-watered land (Ps 68:8–11).

*m:* Jer 33:9. *n:* Ps 98:9. *o:* Ps 85:13; Lv 26:4; Ez 34:27; Hos 2:23–24. *p:* Nm 10:35. *q:* Ps 97:5; Jdt 16:15; Wis 5:14; Mi 1:4. *r:* Ps 18:10; 104:3; Dt 33:26; Is 19:1. *s:* Ps 103:6; 146:7, 9; Ex 22:20–22; Bar 6:37. *t:* Ps 44:10; 114:4, 7; Jgs 5:4–5; Heb 12:26. *u:* Jgs 5:19, 22.

Every household will share the spoil,
14 though you lie down among the sheepfolds,[v]
you shall be covered with silver as the wings of a dove,
her feathers bright as fine gold."
15 When the Almighty routs the kings there,
it will be as when snow fell on Zalmon.*

V

16 You mountain of God, mountain of Bashan,
you rugged mountain, mountain of Bashan,
17 You rugged mountains, why look with envy
at the mountain* where God has chosen to dwell,
where the LORD resides forever?[w]
18 God's chariots were myriad, thousands upon thousands;
from Sinai the Lord entered the holy place.
19 You went up to its lofty height;
you took captives, received slaves as tribute,[x]
even rebels, for the LORD God to dwell.

VI

20 Blessed be the Lord day by day,
God, our salvation, who carries us.[y]
*Selah*
21 Our God is a God who saves;
escape from death is the LORD God's.
22 God will crush the heads of his enemies,
the hairy scalp of the one who walks in sin.[z]
23 The Lord has said:
"Even from Bashan I will fetch them,
fetch them even from the depths of the sea.*
24 You will wash your feet in your enemy's blood;
the tongues of your dogs will lap it up."[a]

VII

25 *Your procession comes into view, O God,
your procession into the holy place, my God and king.
26 The singers go first, the harpists follow;
in their midst girls sound the timbrels.[b]
27 In your choirs, bless God;
LORD, Israel's fountain.
28 In the lead is Benjamin, few in number;
there the princes of Judah, a large throng,
the princes of Zebulun, the princes of Naphtali, too.[c]

VIII

29 Summon again, O God, your power,
the divine power you once showed for us,
30 From your temple on behalf of Jerusalem,
that kings may bring you tribute.
31 Roar at the wild beast of the reeds,*
the herd of mighty bulls, the calves of the peoples;
trampling those who lust after silver
scatter the peoples that delight in war.
32 Let bronze be brought from Egypt,[d]
Ethiopia hurry its hands to God.[e]

IX

33 You kingdoms of the earth, sing to God;[f]
chant the praises of the Lord, *Selah*
34 Who rides the heights of the ancient heavens,
Who sends forth his voice as a mighty voice?
35 Confess the power of God,
whose majesty protects Israel,
whose power is in the sky.
36 Awesome is God in his holy place,
the God of Israel,
who gives power and strength to his people.[g]
Blessed be God!

**68:15 Zalmon**: generally taken as the name of a mountain where snow is visible in winter, perhaps to be located in the Golan Heights or in the mountains of Bashan or Hauran east of the Sea of Galilee.

**68:17 The mountain**: Mount Zion, the site of the Temple.

**68:23 Even from Bashan . . . from the depths of the sea**: the heights and the depths, the farthest places where enemies might flee.

**68:25–28 Your procession**: the procession renews God's original taking up of residence on Zion, described in Ps 68:16–19.

**68:31 The wild beast of the reeds**: probably the Nile crocodile, a symbol for Egypt; see Ps 68:32 and Ez 29:2–5.

*v:* Jgs 5:16. *w:* Ps 132:13–14; Ez 43:7. *x:* Ps 47:8; Eph 4:8–10. *y:* Ps 34:2; 145:2; Is 46:3–4; 63:9. *z:* Dt 32:42. *a:* Ps 58:11; 1 Kgs 21:19; 22:38; Is 63:1–6. *b:* Ps 81:2–3; 87:7; 149:3; 150:3–5; 2 Sm 6:5. *c:* Is 8:23. *d:* Ez 29:2ff. *e:* Is 18:7; 45:14. *f:* Ps 138:4. *g:* Ps 28:8; 29:11.

THE GATE OF a city was the main public meeting place, where business and legal transactions took place. In Psalm 69:13, those who "sit in the gate" are the leading officials of the city. At the other end of the spectrum, those who congregate publicly are the "drunkards."

## PSALM 69*

See RG 175, 178

### *A Cry of Anguish in Great Distress*

1 For the leader; according to "Lilies."*
Of David.

I

2 Save me, God,
for the waters* have reached my neck.[h]
3 I have sunk into the mire of the deep,
where there is no foothold.
I have gone down to the watery depths;
the flood overwhelms me.[i]
4 I am weary with crying out;
my throat is parched.
My eyes fail,
from looking for my God.[j]
5 More numerous than the hairs of my head
are those who hate me without cause.[k]
Those who would destroy me are mighty,
my enemies without reason.
Must I now restore
what I did not steal?*

II

6 God, you know my folly;
my faults are not hidden from you.
7 Let those who wait in hope for you,
LORD of hosts,
not be shamed because of me.
Let those who seek you, God of Israel,[l]
not be disgraced because of me.
8 For it is on your account I bear insult,
that disgrace covers my face.[m]
9 I have become an outcast to my kindred,
a stranger to my mother's children.[n]
10 Because zeal for your house has consumed me,*
I am scorned by those who scorn you.*[o]
11 When I humbled my spirit with fasting,[p]
this led only to scorn.
12 When I clothed myself in sackcloth;
I became a byword for them.
13 Those who sit in the gate gossip about me;
drunkards make me the butt of songs.

III

14 But I will pray to you, LORD,
at a favorable time.
God, in your abundant kindness,
answer me
with your sure deliverance.[q]
15 Rescue me from the mire,[r]
and do not let me sink.
Rescue me from those who hate me
and from the watery depths.
16 Do not let the flood waters overwhelm me,
nor the deep swallow me,
nor the pit close its mouth over me.
17 Answer me, LORD, in your generous love;
in your great mercy turn to me.
18 Do not hide your face from your servant;

**Psalm 69** A lament complaining of suffering in language both metaphorical (Ps 69:2–3, 15–16, the waters of chaos) and literal (Ps 69:4, 5, 9, 11–13, exhaustion, alienation from family and community, false accusation). In the second part the psalmist prays with special emphasis that the enemies be punished for all to see (Ps 69:23–29). Despite the pain, the psalmist does not lose hope that all be set right, and promises public praise (Ps 69:30–36). The Psalm, which depicts the suffering of the innocent just person vividly, is cited often by the New Testament especially in the passion accounts, e.g., Ps 69:5 in Jn 15:25; Ps 69:22 in Mk 15:23, 36 and parallels and in Jn 19:29. The Psalm prays not so much for personal vengeance as for public vindication of God's justice. There was, at this time, no belief in an afterlife where such vindication could take place. Redress had to take place now, in the sight of all.

**69:1 "Lilies"**: apparently the name of the melody.

**69:2 Waters**: the waters of chaos from which God created the world are a common metaphor for extreme distress, cf. Ps 18:5; 42:8; 88:8; Jon 2:3–6.

**69:5 What I did not steal**: the psalmist, falsely accused of theft, is being forced to make restitution.

**69:10 Zeal for your house has consumed me**: the psalmist's commitment to God's cause brings only opposition, cf. Jn 2:17. **I am scorned by those who scorn you**: Rom 15:3 uses the verse as an example of Jesus' unselfishness.

*h:* Ps 18:5; 93:3–4; Jb 22:11. *i:* Ps 40:2; 124:4–5. *j:* Ps 25:15; 119:82; 123:2; 141:8; Is 38:14. *k:* Ps 40:13; Lam 3:52; Jn 15:25. *l:* Ps 40:17. *m:* Jer 15:15. *n:* Jb 19:13–15. *o:* Ps 119:139; Jn 2:17; Rom 15:3. *p:* Ps 109:24–25; Jb 30:9; Lam 3:14. *q:* Is 49:8. *r:* Ps 28:1; 30:4; 32:6; 40:3; 88:5; Prv 1:12.

hasten to answer me, for I am in
distress.[s]
19 Come and redeem my life;
because of my enemies ransom me.
20 You know my reproach, my shame, my
disgrace;
before you stand all my foes.
21 Insult has broken my heart, and I despair;
I looked for compassion, but there was
none,[t]
for comforters, but found none.
22 Instead they gave me poison for my food;
and for my thirst they gave me
vinegar.[u]

IV

23 May their own table be a snare for them,
and their communion offerings a trap.[v]
24 Make their eyes so dim they cannot see;
keep their backs ever feeble.
25 Pour out your wrath upon them;
let the fury of your anger overtake
them.
26 Make their camp desolate,
with none to dwell in their tents.[w]
27 For they pursued the one you struck,
added to the pain of the one you
wounded.
28 Heap punishment upon their punishment;
let them gain from you no vindication.
29 May they be blotted from the book of
life;
not registered among the just![x]

V

30 But here I am miserable and in pain;
let your saving help protect me, God,
31 *That I may praise God's name in song
and glorify it with thanksgiving.
32 That will please the LORD more than
oxen,
more than bulls with horns and
hooves:[y]
33 "See, you lowly ones, and be glad;
you who seek God, take heart![z]
34 For the LORD hears the poor,
and does not spurn those in bondage.
35 Let the heaven and the earth praise him,
the seas and whatever moves in them!"

VI

36 For God will rescue Zion,
and rebuild the cities of Judah.[a]
They will dwell there and possess it;
37 the descendants of God's servants will
inherit it;
those who love God's name will dwell
in it.[b]

## PSALM 70*

See RG 175

### *Prayer for Divine Help*

1 For the leader; of David. For remembrance.

2 Graciously rescue me, God![c]
Come quickly to help me, LORD![d]
3 Let those who seek my life
be confused and put to shame.[e]
Let those who desire my ruin
turn back in disgrace.
4 Let those who say "Aha!"[f]
turn back in their shame.
5 But may all who seek you
rejoice and be glad in you,
Those who long for your help
always say, "God be glorified!"[g]
6 I am miserable and poor.
God, come to me quickly!
You are my help and deliverer.
LORD, do not delay!

## PSALM 71*

See RG 175

### *Prayer in Time of Old Age*

I

1 In you, LORD, I take refuge;[h]
let me never be put to shame.[i]

**69:31 That I may praise God's name in song**: the actual song is cited in Ps 69:33–35, the word "praise" in Ps 69:35 referring back to "praise" in Ps 69:31.

**Psalm 70** A lament of a poor and afflicted person (Ps 70:6) who has no resource except God, and who cries out to be saved from the enemy. The Psalm is almost identical to Ps 40:14–17.

**Psalm 71** A lament of an old person (Ps 71:9, 18) whose afflictions are interpreted by enemies as a divine judgment (Ps 71:11). The first part of the Psalm pleads for help (Ps 71:1–4) on the basis of a hope learned from a lifetime's experience of God; the second part describes the menace (Ps 71:9–13) yet remains buoyant (Ps 71:14–16); the third develops the theme of hope and praise.

*s:* Ps 102:3; 143:7. *t:* Lam 1:2. *u:* Lam 3:15; Mt 27:34, 48; Mk 15:23. *v:* Rom 11:9–10. *w:* Acts 1:20. *x:* Ps 139:16; Ex 32:32; Is 4:3; Dn 12:1; Mal 3:16; Rev 3:5. *y:* Ps 40:7; 50:8–9, 14; 51:18; Is 1:11–15; Hos 6:6; Am 5:21–22; Heb 10:5–8. *z:* Ps 22:27; 35:27; 70:5. *a:* Is 44:26; Ez 36:10. *b:* Ps 102:29; Is 65:9. *c:* Ps 40:14–18. *d:* Ps 71:12. *e:* Ps 35:4, 26. *f:* Ps 35:21, 25. *g:* Ps 35:27. *h:* Ps 31:2–4. *i:* Ps 25:2.

[2] In your justice rescue and deliver me;
listen to me and save me!
[3] Be my rock of refuge,
my stronghold to give me safety;
for you are my rock and fortress.[j]
[4] My God, rescue me from the hand of the wicked,
from the clutches of the evil and violent.[k]
[5] You are my hope, Lord;
my trust, GOD, from my youth.
[6] On you I have depended since birth;
from my mother's womb you are my strength;[l]
my hope in you never wavers.
[7] *I have become a portent to many,
but you are my strong refuge!
[8] My mouth shall be filled with your praise,
shall sing your glory every day.

II

[9] Do not cast me aside in my old age;
as my strength fails, do not forsake me.
[10] For my enemies speak against me;
they watch and plot against me.[m]
[11] They say, "God has abandoned him.
Pursue, and seize him!
No one will come to the rescue!"
[12] God, be not far from me;
my God, hasten to help me.[n]
[13] Bring to a shameful end
those who attack me;
Cover with contempt and scorn
those who seek my ruin.[o]
[14] I will always hope in you
and add to all your praise.
[15] My mouth shall proclaim your just deeds,
day after day your acts of deliverance,
though I cannot number them all.[p]
[16] I will speak of the mighty works of the Lord;
O GOD, I will tell of your singular justice.

III

[17] God, you have taught me from my youth;
to this day I proclaim your wondrous deeds.
[18] Now that I am old and gray,[q]
do not forsake me, God,
That I may proclaim your might
to all generations yet to come,[r]
Your power [19] and justice, God,
to the highest heaven.
You have done great things;[s]
O God, who is your equal?[t]
[20] Whatever bitter afflictions you sent me,
you would turn and revive me.
From the watery depths of the earth
once more raise me up.
[21] Restore my honor;
turn and comfort me,
[22] That I may praise you with the lyre
for your faithfulness, my God,
And sing to you with the harp,
O Holy One of Israel!
[23] My lips will shout for joy as I sing your praise;
my soul, too, which you have redeemed.
[24] Yes, my tongue shall recount
your justice day by day.
For those who sought my ruin
have been shamed and disgraced.

## PSALM 72*

See RG 176

### *A Prayer for the King*

[1] Of Solomon.

I

[2] O God, give your judgment to the king;
your justice to the king's son;*[u]
That he may govern your people with justice,
your oppressed with right judgment,[v]
[3] That the mountains may yield their bounty for the people,
and the hills great abundance,[w]
[4] That he may defend the oppressed among the people,

**71:7 A portent to many**: the afflictions of the sufferer are taken as a manifestation of God's anger, cf. Dt 28:46; Ps 31:12.

**Psalm 72** A royal Psalm in which the Israelite king, as the representative of God, is the instrument of divine justice (Ps 72:1–4, 12–14) and blessing (Ps 72:5–7, 15–17) for the whole world. The king is human, giving only what he has received from God. Hence intercession must be made for him. The extravagant language is typical of oriental royal courts.

**72:2 The king . . . the king's son**: the crown prince is the king's son; the prayer envisages the dynasty.

*j:* Ps 18:3. *k:* Ps 140:2. *l:* Ps 22:11. *m:* Ps 3:2; 22:8. *n:* Ps 22:20. *o:* Ps 35:4; 40:15; 70:3. *p:* Ps 35:28. *q:* Is 46:3–4. *r:* Ps 22:31–32; 48:14–15; 145:4. *s:* Ps 72:18. *t:* Ps 86:8. *u:* Ps 99:4; Jer 23:5. *v:* Prv 31:8–9. *w:* Is 52:7; 55:12.

save the children of the poor and crush
the oppressor.

II

5 May they fear you with the sun,
and before the moon, through all
generations.[x]
6 May he be like rain coming down upon
the fields,
like showers watering the earth,[y]
7 That abundance may flourish in his days,
great bounty, till the moon be no more.

III

8 *May he rule from sea to sea,
from the river to the ends of the earth.[z]
9 May his foes kneel before him,
his enemies lick the dust.[a]
10 May the kings of Tarshish and the
islands* bring tribute,
the kings of Sheba and Seba offer
gifts.[b]
11 May all kings bow before him,
all nations serve him.[c]
12 For he rescues the poor when they cry
out,
the oppressed who have no one to help.
13 He shows pity to the needy and the poor[d]
and saves the lives of the poor.
14 From extortion and violence he redeems
them,
for precious is their blood* in his sight.

IV

15 Long may he live, receiving gold from
Sheba,
prayed for without cease, blessed day
by day.
16 *May wheat abound in the land,
flourish even on the mountain heights.
May his fruit be like that of Lebanon,
and flourish in the city like the grasses
of the land.[e]
17 May his name be forever;
as long as the sun, may his name
endure.[f]
May the tribes of the earth give blessings
with his name;*
may all the nations regard him as
favored.[g]
18 *Blessed be the LORD God, the God of
Israel,
who alone does wonderful deeds.[h]
19 Blessed be his glorious name forever;
may he fill all the earth with his glory.[i]
Amen and amen.

20 The end of the psalms of David, son of Jesse.

# Third Book—Psalms 73–89

## PSALM 73*

See RG 176

### *The Trial of the Just*

1 A psalm of Asaph.

How good God is to the upright,
to those who are pure of heart!

I

2 But, as for me, my feet had almost
stumbled;
my steps had nearly slipped,
3 Because I was envious of the arrogant
when I saw the prosperity of the wicked.[j]

**72:8 From sea to sea . . . the ends of the earth**: the boundaries of the civilized world known at the time: from the Mediterranean Sea (the western sea) to the Persian Gulf (the eastern sea), and from the Euphrates (the river) to the islands and lands of southwestern Europe, "the ends of the earth." The words may also have a mythic nuance—the earth surrounded by cosmic waters, hence everywhere.

**72:10 Tarshish and the islands**: the far west (Ps 48:6); Arabia and Seba: the far south (1 Kgs 10:1).

**72:14 Their blood**: cf. Ps 116:15.

**72:16** The translation of the difficult Hebrew is tentative.

**72:17 May the tribes of the earth give blessings with his name**: an echo of the promise to the ancestors (Gn 12:3; 26:4; 28:14), suggesting that the monarchy in Israel fulfilled the promise to Abraham, Isaac, and Jacob.

**72:18–19** A doxology marking the end of Book II of the Psalter.

**Psalm 73** The opening verse of this probing poem (cf. Ps 37; 49) is actually the psalmist's hard-won conclusion from personal experience: God is just and good! The psalmist describes near loss of faith (Ps 73:2–3), occasioned by observing the wicked who blasphemed God with seeming impunity (Ps 73:4–12). Feeling abandoned despite personal righteousness, the psalmist could not bear the injustice until an experience of God's nearness in the Temple made clear how deluded the wicked were. Their sudden destruction shows their impermanence (Ps 73:13–20). The just can thus be confident, for, as the psalmist now knows, their security is from God (Ps 73:1, 23–28).

*x:* Ps 89:37–38; Jer 31:35. *y:* Dt 32:2; Is 45:8; Hos 6:3. *z:* Dt 11:24; Zec 9:10. *a:* Is 49:23; Mi 7:17. *b:* Ps 68:30; Is 60:5–6; 1 Kgs 10:1ff. *c:* Ps 47:8. *d:* Prv 31:9. *e:* Is 27:6; Hos 14:6–8; Am 9:13. *f:* Ps 21:7. *g:* Gn 12:3; 22:18; 26:4; Zec 8:13. *h:* Ps 41:14; 89:53; 106:48; 136:4. *i:* Ps 57:5; Nm 14:21. *j:* Ps 37:1; Jb 21:13.

4 For they suffer no pain;
their bodies are healthy and sleek.
5 They are free of the burdens of life;
they are not afflicted like others.
6 Thus pride adorns them as a necklace;
violence clothes them as a robe.
7 Out of such blindness comes sin;
evil thoughts flood their hearts.[k]
8 They scoff and spout their malice;
from on high they utter threats.[l]
9 *They set their mouths against the heavens,
their tongues roam the earth.
10 *So my people turn to them
and drink deeply of their words.
11 They say, "Does God really know?"
"Does the Most High have any
knowledge?"[m]
12 Such, then, are the wicked,
always carefree, increasing their wealth.

II

13 Is it in vain that I have kept my heart pure,
washed my hands in innocence?[n]
14 For I am afflicted day after day,
chastised every morning.
15 Had I thought, "I will speak as they do,"
I would have betrayed this generation
of your children.
16 Though I tried to understand all this,
it was too difficult for me,
17 Till I entered the sanctuary of God
and came to understand their end.*

III

18 You set them, indeed, on a slippery road;
you hurl them down to ruin.
19 How suddenly they are devastated;
utterly undone by disaster!
20 They are like a dream after waking, Lord,
dismissed like shadows when you
arise.[o]

IV

21 Since my heart was embittered
and my soul deeply wounded,
22 I was stupid and could not understand;
I was like a brute beast in your
presence.
23 Yet I am always with you;
you take hold of my right hand.[p]
24 With your counsel you guide me,
and at the end receive me with honor.*
25 Whom else have I in the heavens?
None beside you delights me on earth.
26 Though my flesh and my heart fail,
God is the rock of my heart, my
portion forever.
27 But those who are far from you perish;
you destroy those unfaithful to you.
28 As for me, to be near God is my good,
to make the Lord GOD my refuge.
I shall declare all your works
in the gates of daughter Zion.*

## PSALM 74*

See RG 175, 177

### *Prayer at the Destruction of the Temple*

1 A *maskil* of Asaph.

I

Why, God, have you cast us off
forever?*[q]
Why does your anger burn against the
sheep of your pasture?[r]

**73:9 They set their mouths against the heavens**: in an image probably derived from mythic stories of half-divine giants, the monstrous speech of the wicked is likened to enormous jaws gaping wide, devouring everything in sight.

**73:10** The Hebrew is obscure.

**73:17 And came to understand their end**: the psalmist receives a double revelation in the Temple: 1) the end of the wicked comes unexpectedly (Ps 73:18–20); 2) God is with me.

**73:24 And at the end receive me with honor**: a perhaps deliberately enigmatic verse. It is understood by some commentators as reception into heavenly glory, hence the traditional translation, "receive me into glory." The Hebrew verb can indeed refer to mysterious divine elevation of a righteous person into God's domain: Enoch in Gn 5:24; Elijah in 2 Kgs 2:11–12; the righteous psalmist in Ps 49:16. Personal resurrection in the Old Testament, however, is clearly attested only in the second century B.C. The verse is perhaps best left unspecified as a reference to God's nearness and protection.

**73:28 In the gates of daughter Zion**: this reading follows the tradition of the Septuagint and Vulgate.

**Psalm 74** A communal lament sung when the enemy invaded the Temple; it would be especially appropriate at the destruction of Jerusalem in 587 B.C. Israel's God is urged to look upon the ruined sanctuary and remember the congregation who worshiped there (Ps 74:1–11). People and sanctuary are bound together; an attack on Zion is an attack on Israel. In the second half of the poem, the community brings before God the story of their origins—their creation (Ps 74:12–17)—in order to move God to reenact that deed of creation now. Will God allow a lesser power to destroy the divine project (Ps 74:18–23)?

**74:1 Forever**: the word implies that the disaster is already of long duration, cf. Ps 74:9 and note.

---

*k:* Jb 15:27. *l:* Ps 17:10. *m:* Ps 10:11; Jb 22:13. *n:* Ps 26:6; Mal 3:14. *o:* Jb 20:8. *p:* Ps 121:5. *q:* Ps 10:1; 44:24; 77:8. *r:* Ps 80:5.

2 Remember your people, whom you
acquired of old,
the tribe you redeemed as your own
heritage,
Mount Zion where you dwell.[s]
3 Direct your steps toward the utter
destruction,
everything the enemy laid waste in the
sanctuary.
4 Your foes roared triumphantly in the
place of your assembly;
they set up their own tokens of victory.
5 They hacked away like a forester
gathering boughs,
swinging his ax in a thicket of trees.
6 They smashed all its engraved work,
struck it with ax and pick.
7 They set your sanctuary on fire,
profaned your name's abode by razing
it to the ground.[t]
8 They said in their hearts, "We will
destroy them all!
Burn all the assembly-places of God in
the land!"
9 *Even so we have seen no signs for us,
there is no prophet any more,[u]
no one among us who knows for how
long.
10 How long, O God, will the enemy jeer?[v]
Will the enemy revile your name
forever?
11 Why draw back your hand,
why hold back your right hand within
your bosom?*

II

12 *Yet you, God, are my king from of old,
winning victories throughout the
earth.
13 You stirred up the sea by your might;[w]
you smashed the heads of the dragons
on the waters.[x]
14 You crushed the heads of Leviathan,[y]
gave him as food to the sharks.
15 You opened up springs and torrents,
brought dry land out of the primeval
waters.*
16 Yours the day and yours the night too;
you set the moon and sun in place.
17 You fixed all the limits of the earth;
summer and winter you made.[z]
18 Remember how the enemy has jeered,
LORD,
how a foolish people has reviled your
name.
19 Do not surrender to wild animals those
who praise you;
do not forget forever the life of your
afflicted.
20 Look to your covenant,
for the recesses of the land
are full of the haunts of violence.
21 Let not the oppressed turn back in
shame;
may the poor and needy praise your
name.
22 Arise, God, defend your cause;
remember the constant jeering of the
fools.
23 Do not forget the clamor of your foes,
the unceasing uproar of your enemies.

## PSALM 75*

See RG 176

### *God the Judge of the World*

1 For the leader. Do not destroy! A psalm
of Asaph; a song.

I

2 We thank you, God, we give thanks;
we call upon your name,

**74:9 Even so we have seen no signs . . .** : ancients often asked prophets to say for how long a divine punishment was to last, cf. 2 Sm 24:13. Here no prophet has arisen to indicate the duration.

**74:11 Why hold back . . . within your bosom**: i.e., idle beneath your cloak.

**74:12–17** Comparable Canaanite literature describes the storm-god's victory over all-encompassing Sea and its allies (dragons and Leviathan) and the subsequent peaceful arrangement of the universe, sometimes through the placement of paired cosmic elements (day and night, sun and moon), cf. Ps 89:12–13. The Psalm apparently equates the enemies attacking the Temple with the destructive cosmic forces already tamed by God. Why then are those forces now raging untamed against your own people?

**74:15 Waters**: lit., "rivers" (cf. Ps 24:7; Isa 50:2) upon which, or from which, in primordial times the earth is created.

**Psalm 75** The psalmist gives thanks and rejoices (Ps 75:2, 10) for the direct intervention of God, which is promised in two oracles (Ps 75:3–4, 11). Expecting that divine intervention, the psalmist warns evildoers to repent (Ps 75:5–9).

*s:* Ps 68:17; 132:13; Ex 15:17; Jer 10:16; 51:19. *t:* Ps 79:1; Is 64:10. *u:* Lam 2:9. *v:* Ps 89:47. *w:* Ps 89:10. *x:* Is 51:9–10. *y:* Jb 3:8; 40:25; Is 27:1. *z:* Gn 1.

we declare your wonderful deeds.
[You said:]*
[3] "I will choose the time;
I will judge fairly.
[4] Though the earth and all its inhabitants
quake,
I make steady its pillars."[a] *Selah*

II

[5] So I say to the boastful: "Do not boast!"[b]
to the wicked: "Do not raise your
horns!*
[6] Do not raise your horns against heaven!
Do not speak with a stiff neck!"[c]
[7] For judgment comes not from east or
from west,
not from the wilderness or the
mountains,[d]
[8] But from God who decides,
who brings some low and raises others
high.[e]
[9] Yes, a cup* is in the LORD's hand,
foaming wine, fully spiced.*
When God pours it out,
they will drain it even to the dregs;
all the wicked of the earth will drink.[f]
[10] But I will rejoice forever;
I will sing praise to the God of Jacob,
[11] [g][Who has said:]
"I will cut off all the horns of the wicked,
but the horns of the righteous will be
exalted."

See RG 175–76

### PSALM 76*

### *God Defends Zion*

[1]For the leader; a psalm with stringed instruments. A song of Asaph.

I

[2] Renowned in Judah is God,[h]
whose name is great in Israel.
[3] On Salem* is God's tent, his shelter on
Zion.
[4] There the flashing arrows were
shattered,
shield, sword, and weapons of war.[i]
*Selah*

II

[5] Terrible and awesome are you,
stronger than the ancient
mountains.*
[6] Despoiled are the stouthearted;
they sank into sleep;
the hands of all the men of valor have
failed.[j]
[7] At your roar, O God of Jacob,
chariot and steed lay still.
[8] You, terrible are you;
who can stand before you and your
great anger?[k]
[9] From the heavens you pronounced
sentence;
the earth was terrified and reduced to
silence,
[10] When you arose, O God, for judgment
to save the afflicted of the land.
*Selah*
[11] Surely the wrath of man will give you
thanks;
the remnant of your furor will keep
your feast.

III

[12] Make and keep vows to the LORD your
God.[l]
May all around him bring gifts to the
one to be feared,
[13] Who checks the spirit of princes,
who is fearful to the kings of earth.

**75:2 You said**: supplied for clarity here and in Ps 75:11. The translation assumes in both places that the psalmist is citing an oracle of God.

**75:5 Do not raise your horns!**: the horn is the symbol of strength; to raise one's horn is to exalt one's own power as Ps 75:5 explains.

**75:9 A cup**: "the cup of God's wrath" is the punishment inflicted on the wicked, cf. Is 51:17; Jer 25:15–29; 49:12; Eze 23:31–33. **Spiced**: lit., "a mixed drink"; spices or drugs were added to wine, cf. Prv 9:2, 5.

**Psalm 76** A song glorifying Zion, the mountain of Jerusalem where God destroyed Israel's enemies. Zion is thus the appropriate site to celebrate the victory (Ps 76:3–4), a victory described in parallel scenes (Ps 76:5–7, 8–11). Israel is invited to worship its powerful patron deity (Ps 76:12).

**76:3 Salem**: an ancient name for Jerusalem, used here perhaps on account of its allusion to the Hebrew word for peace, *shalom*, cf. Gn 14:18; Heb 7:1–3.

**76:5 Ancient mountains**: conjectural translation of a difficult Hebrew phrase on the basis of Gn 49:26. The mountains are part of the structure of the universe (Ps 89:12–13).

*a:* Ps 46:3; 60:4; 93:1; 96:10; 104:5; 1 Sm 2:8; Is 24:19. *b:* 1 Sm 2:3; Zec 2:1–4. *c:* Jb 15:25. *d:* Mt 24:23–27. *e:* Jb 5:11; 1 Sm 2:7. *f:* Ps 60:5; Jb 21:20; Is 51:17, 21–22; Jer 25:15ff; Hab 2:16. *g:* Ps 92:11. *h:* Heb 3:2. *i:* Ps 46:10; 122:6–9. *j:* 2 Kgs 19:35; Jer 51:39; Na 3:18. *k:* Dt 7:21; 1 Sm 6:20; Na 1:6; Mal 3:2. *l:* Nm 30:3.

## PSALM 77*

See RG 175

### *Confidence in God During National Distress*

*1* For the leader; According to *Jeduthun*.
A psalm of Asaph.

I

*2* I cry aloud to God,
I cry to God to hear me.
*3* On the day of my distress I seek the Lord;
by night my hands are stretched out unceasingly;[m]
I refuse to be consoled.
*4* When I think of God, I groan;
as I meditate, my spirit grows faint.[n]
*Selah*
*5* You have kept me from closing my eyes in sleep;
I am troubled and cannot speak.
*6* I consider the days of old;
the years long past *7* I remember.[o]
At night I ponder in my heart;
and as I meditate, my spirit probes:
*8* "Will the Lord reject us forever,[p]
never again show favor?
*9* Has God's mercy ceased forever?
The promise to go unfulfilled for future ages?
*10* Has God forgotten how to show mercy,
in anger withheld his compassion?" *Selah*
*11* * I conclude: "My sorrow is this,
the right hand of the Most High has abandoned us."[q]

II

*12* *I will recall the deeds of the LORD;
yes, recall your wonders of old.[r]
*13* I will ponder all your works;
on your exploits I will meditate.
*14* Your way, God, is holy;
what god is as great as our God?[s]
*15* You are the God who does wonders;
among the peoples you have revealed your might.[t]
*16* With your mighty arm you redeemed your people,
the children of Jacob and Joseph.[u] *Selah*
*17* The waters saw you, God;
the waters saw you and lashed about,
even the deeps of the sea* trembled.[v]
*18* The clouds poured down their rains;
the thunderheads rumbled;
your arrows flashed back and forth.[w]
*19* The thunder of your chariot wheels resounded;
your lightning lit up the world;
the earth trembled and quaked.[x]
*20* Through the sea was your way;
your path, through the mighty waters,
though your footsteps were unseen.[y]
*21* You led your people like a flock
by the hand of Moses and Aaron.[z]

## PSALM 78*

See RG 176

### *A New Beginning in Zion and David*

*1* A *maskil* of Asaph.

I

Attend, my people, to my teaching;
listen to the words of my mouth.

**Psalm 77** A community lament in which the speaker ("I") describes the anguish of Israel at God's silence when its very existence is at stake (Ps 77:2–11). In response the speaker recites the story of how God brought the people into existence (Ps 77:12–20). The question is thus posed to God: Will you allow the people you created to be destroyed?

**77:11 I conclude**: lit., "I said." The psalmist, after pondering the present distress and God's promises to Israel, has decided that God has forgotten the people.

**77:12 I will recall**: the verb sometimes means to make present the great deeds of Israel's past by reciting them, cf. Ps 78:42; 105:5; 106:7.

**77:17 The deeps of the sea**: Heb. *tehom*; the same word is used in Gn 1:2, where it alludes to the primeval seas which in ancient Semitic cosmography are tamed by God in creation, cf. Ps 74:12–17; 89:12–13 and notes.

**Psalm 78** A recital of history to show that past generations did not respond to God's gracious deeds and were punished by God making the gift into a punishment. Will Israel fail to appreciate God's act—the choosing of Zion and of David? The tripartite introduction invites Israel to learn the lessons hidden in its traditions (Ps 78:1–4, 5–7, 8–11); each section ends with the mention of God's acts. There are two distinct narratives of approximately equal length: the wilderness events (Ps 78:12–39) and the movement from Egypt to Canaan (Ps 78:40–72).

*m:* Ps 50:15; 88:2. *n:* Jon 2:8. *o:* Ps 143:5; Dt 32:7. *p:* Ps 13:2; 44:24; 74:1; 80:5; 89:47; Lam 3:31. *q:* Ps 17:7; 18:36; Ex 15:6, 12. *r:* Ps 143:5. *s:* Ps 18:31; Ex 15:11. *t:* Ps 86:10; 89:6. *u:* Gn 46:26–27; Neh 1:10. *v:* Ps 18:16; 114:3; Na 1:4. *w:* Ps 18:14–15; 29; 144:6; Jb 37:3–4; Wis 5:21; Hab 3:10–11; Zec 9:14. *x:* Ps 18:8; 97:4; 99:1; Ex 19:16; Jgs 5:4–5. *y:* Neh 9:11; Wis 14:3; Is 51:10; Hab 3:15. *z:* Ps 78:52; Is 63:11–14; Hos 12:14; Mi 6:4.

2 I will open my mouth in a parable,*
unfold the puzzling events of the past.[a]
3 What we have heard and know;
things our ancestors have recounted to us.[b]
4 We do not keep them from our children;
we recount them to the next generation,
The praiseworthy deeds of the LORD and his strength,
the wonders that he performed.[c]
5 God made a decree in Jacob,
established a law in Israel:[d]
Which he commanded our ancestors,
they were to teach their children;
6 That the next generation might come to know,
children yet to be born.[e]
In turn they were to recount them to their children,
7 that they too might put their confidence in God,
And not forget God's deeds,
but keep his commandments.
8 They were not to be like their ancestors,
a rebellious and defiant generation,[f]
A generation whose heart was not constant,[g]
and whose spirit was not faithful to God.
9 The ranks of Ephraimite archers,*
retreated on the day of battle.
10 They did not keep God's covenant;
they refused to walk according to his law.
11 They forgot his deeds,
the wonders that he had shown them.

II

A

12 In the sight of their ancestors God did wonders,
in the land of Egypt, the plain of Zoan.*[h]
13 He split the sea and led them across,[i]
making the waters stand like walls.[j]
14 He led them with a cloud by day,
all night with the light of fire.[k]
15 He split rocks in the desert,
gave water to drink, abundant as the deeps of the sea.[l]
16 He made streams flow from crags,
caused rivers of water to flow down.

B

17 But they went on sinning against him,
rebelling against the Most High in the desert.[m]
18 They tested God in their hearts,
demanding the food they craved.[n]
19 They spoke against God, and said,
"Can God spread a table in the wilderness?[o]
20 True, when he struck the rock,
water gushed forth,
the wadies flooded.
But can he also give bread,
or provide meat to his people?"

C

21 The LORD heard and grew angry;[p]
fire blazed up against Jacob;
anger flared up against Israel.
22 For they did not believe in God,
did not trust in his saving power.
23 *So he commanded the clouds above;
and opened the doors of heaven.

78:40–72). The structure of both is parallel: gracious act (Ps 78:12–16, 40–55), rebellion (Ps 78:17–20, 56–58), divine punishment (Ps 78:21–31, 59–64), God's readiness to forgive and begin anew (Ps 78:32–39, 65–72). While the Psalm has been thought to reflect the reunification program of either King Hezekiah (late eighth century) or King Josiah (late seventh century) in that the Northern Kingdom (Ephraim, Joseph) is especially invited to accept Zion and the Davidic king, a postexilic setting is also possible. Notable is the inclusion of the David-Zion tradition into the history of Israel recounted in the sources of the Pentateuch.

**78:2 Parable**: Hebrew *mashal* literally refers to some sort of relationship of comparison and can signify a story whose didactic potential becomes clear in the telling, as here in the retrospective examination of the history of Israel. Mt 13:35 cites the verse to explain Jesus' use of parables.

**78:9 Ephraimite archers**: Ephraim was the most important tribe of the Northern Kingdom. Its military defeat (here unspecified) demonstrates its infidelity to God, who otherwise would have protected it.

**78:12, 43 Zoan**: a city on the arm of the Nile, a former capital of Egypt.

**78:23–31** On the manna and the quail, see Ex 16 and Nm 11. Unlike Ex 16, here both manna and quail are instruments

*a:* Ps 49:5; Mt 13:35. *b:* Ps 44:2. *c:* Ex 10:2; Dt 4:9; Jb 8:8. *d:* Ps 147:19; Dt 33:4. *e:* Ps 22:31–32; Dt 4:9; 6:7. *f:* Dt 31:27; 32:5. *g:* Ps 95:10. *h:* Ps 106:7. *i:* Ps 136:13; Ex 14–15. *j:* Ex 14:22; 15:8. *k:* Ps 105:39; Ex 13:21; Wis 18:3. *l:* Ps 105:41; 114:8; Ex 17:1–7; Nm 20:2–13; Dt 8:15; Wis 11:4; Is 48:21. *m:* Dt 9:7; Ez 20:13. *n:* Ps 106:14; Ex 16:2–36. *o:* Ps 23:5. *p:* Nm 11; Dt 32:22.

while the sea enveloped their enemies.[c]
54 And he brought them to his holy
mountain,
the hill his right hand had won.[d]
55 He drove out the nations before them,
allotted them as their inherited portion,
and settled in their tents the tribes of
Israel.

B

56 But they tested and rebelled against God
Most High,
his decrees they did not observe.
57 They turned disloyal, faithless like their
ancestors;
they proved false like a slack bow.
58 They enraged him with their high places,
and with their idols provoked him* to
jealous anger.[e]

C

59 God heard and grew angry;
he rejected Israel completely.
60 He forsook the shrine at Shiloh,*[f]
the tent he set up among human
beings.
61 He gave up his might into captivity,
his glorious ark into the hands of the
foe.[g]
62 God delivered his people to the sword;
he was enraged against his heritage.
63 Fire consumed their young men;
their young women heard no wedding
songs.[h]
64 Their priests fell by the sword;
their widows made no lamentation.

D

65 Then the Lord awoke as from sleep,
like a warrior shouting from the effects
of wine.
66 He put his foes to flight;
everlasting shame he dealt them.
67 He rejected the tent of Joseph,
chose not the tribe of Ephraim.
68 *God chose the tribe of Judah,
Mount Zion which he loved.[i]
69 He built his shrine like the heavens,
like the earth which he founded
forever.
70 He chose David his servant,
took him from the sheepfolds.[j]
71 From tending ewes God brought him,
to shepherd Jacob, his people,
Israel, his heritage.[k]
72 He shepherded them with a pure heart;
with skilled hands he guided them.

## PSALM 79*

See RG 175

### *A Prayer for Jerusalem*

1 A psalm of Asaph.

I

O God, the nations have invaded your
inheritance;
they have defiled your holy
temple;
they have laid Jerusalem in ruins.[l]
2 They have left the corpses of your
servants
as food for the birds of the sky,
the flesh of those devoted to you for
the beasts of the earth.[m]
3 They have poured out their blood like
water
all around Jerusalem,
and no one is left to do the burying.[n]
4 We have become the reproach of our
neighbors,
the scorn and derision of those
around us.[o]

II

5 How long, LORD? Will you be angry
forever?

**78:58 Provoked him**: lit., "made him jealous."

**78:60 Shiloh**: an important shrine in the north prior to Jerusalem. Despite its holy status, it was destroyed (Ps 78:60–64; cf. Jer 7:12, 14).

**78:68, 70** God's ultimate offer of mercy to the sinful, helpless people is Zion and the Davidic king.

**Psalm 79** A communal lament complaining that the nations have defiled the Temple and murdered the holy people, leaving their corpses unburied (Ps 79:1–4). The occasion is probably the destruction of Jerusalem by the Babylonian army in 587 B.C. The people ask how long the withdrawal of divine favor will last (Ps 79:5), pray for action now (Ps 79:6–7), and admit that their own sins have brought about the catastrophe (Ps 79:8–9). They seek to persuade God to act for reasons of honor: the nations who do not call upon the Name are running amok (Ps 79:6); the divine honor is compromised (Ps 79:1, 10, 12); God's own servants suffer (Ps 79:2–4, 11).

*c:* Ex 14:26–28. *d:* Ex 15:17. *e:* Dt 32:16, 21. *f:* Jos 18:1; 1 Sm 1:3; Jer 7:12; 26:6. *g:* 1 Sm 4:11, 22. *h:* Dt 32:25; Jer 7:34. *i:* Ps 48:2; 50:2; Lam 2:15. *j:* Ps 89:21; Ez 34:23; 37:24; 2 Chr 6:6. *k:* 1 Sm 16:11–13; 2 Sm 7:8. *l:* 2 Kgs 25:9–10; Lam 1:10. *m:* Jer 7:33. *n:* 1 Mc 7:17; Jer 14:16. *o:* Ps 44:14; 80:7; 123:3–4; Jb 12:4; Dn 9:16; Zep 2:8.

24 God rained manna upon them for food;
grain from heaven he gave them.[q]
25 Man ate the bread of the angels;*
food he sent in abundance.
26 He stirred up the east wind in the skies;
by his might God brought on the south wind.
27 He rained meat upon them like dust,
winged fowl like the sands of the sea,
28 They fell down in the midst of their camp,
all round their dwellings.
29 They ate and were well filled;
he gave them what they had craved.
30 But while they still wanted more,
and the food was still in their mouths,
31 God's anger flared up against them,
and he made a slaughter of their strongest,
laying low the youth of Israel.[r]
32 In spite of all this they went on sinning,
they did not believe in his wonders.

D

33 God ended their days abruptly,
their years in sudden death.
34 When he slew them, they began to seek him;
they again looked for God.[s]
35 They remembered* that God was their rock,
God Most High, their redeemer.
36 But they deceived him with their mouths,
lied to him with their tongues.
37 Their hearts were not constant toward him;
they were not faithful to his covenant.[t]
38 *But God being compassionate forgave their sin;
he did not utterly destroy them.
Time and again he turned back his anger,
unwilling to unleash all his rage.[u]
39 He remembered that they were flesh,
a breath that passes on and does not return.

III

A

40 How often they rebelled against God in the wilderness,
grieved him in the wasteland.
41 Again and again they tested God,
provoked the Holy One of Israel.
42 They did not remember his power,
the day he redeemed them from the foe,[v]
43 *When he performed his signs in Egypt,
his wonders in the plain of Zoan.[w]
44 God turned their rivers to blood;
their streams they could not drink.
45 He sent swarms of insects that devoured them,[x]
frogs that destroyed them.
46 He gave their harvest to the caterpillar,
the fruits of their labor to the locust.
47 He killed their vines with hail,[y]
their sycamores with frost.
48 He exposed their cattle to plague,
their flocks to pestilence.[z]
49 He let loose against them the heat of his anger,
wrath, fury, and distress,
a band of deadly messengers.
50 He cleared a path for his anger;
he did not spare them from death,
but delivered their animals to the plague.
51 He struck all the firstborn of Egypt,[a]
the first fruits of their vigor in the tents of Ham.
52 Then God led forth his people like sheep,
guided them like a flock through the wilderness.[b]
53 He led them on secure and unafraid,

of punishment, showing that a divine gift can become deadly because of Israel's apostasy.

**78:25 Bread of the angels**: the translation "angels" comports with the supernatural origin of the manna, though the Hebrew *lechem 'abbirim* is more literally translated as "bread of the strong ones" or "bread of the mighty." In the context of the manna event, this phrase cannot possibly mean the Israelites or any human being.

**78:35 Remembered**: invoked God publicly in worship. Their words were insincere (Ps 78:36).

**78:38** God is always ready to forgive and begin anew, as in choosing Zion and David (Ps 78:65–72).

**78:43–55** Ex 7–12 records ten plagues. Here there are six divine attacks upon Egypt; the seventh climactic act is God's bringing Israel to the holy land.

*q:* Ps 105:40; Ex 16:4, 14; Dt 8:3; Wis 16:20; Jn 6:31. *r:* Nm 14:29. *s:* Dt 32:15, 18; Is 26:16. *t:* Ps 95:10; Is 29:13. *u:* Ps 85:4; Ex 32:14; Is 48:9; Ez 20:22. *v:* Ps 106:21. *w:* Ps 105:27–36; 135:9; Ex 7:14–11:10; 12:29–36; Wis 16–18. *x:* Ex 8:17. *y:* Wis 16:16. *z:* Ex 9:3. *a:* Ps 105:36; 136:10; Ex 12:29. *b:* Ps 77:21.

Will your jealous anger keep burning
like fire?[p]
6 Pour out your wrath on nations that do
not recognize you,
on kingdoms that do not call on your
name,[q]
7 For they have devoured Jacob,
laid waste his dwelling place.
8 Do not remember against us the
iniquities of our forefathers;
let your compassion move quickly
ahead of us,
for we have been brought very low.[r]
III
9 Help us, God our savior,
on account of the glory of your name.
Deliver us, pardon our sins
for your name's sake.[s]
10 Why should the nations say,
"Where is their God?"[t]
Before our eyes make known to the nations
that you avenge the blood of your
servants which has been poured
out.[u]
IV
11 Let the groaning of the imprisoned come
in before you;
in accord with the greatness of your
arm
preserve those doomed to die.[v]
12 Turn back sevenfold into the bosom of
our neighbors
the insult with which they insulted
you, Lord.[w]
13 Then we, your people, the sheep of your
pasture,
will give thanks to you forever;
from generation to generation
we will recount your praise.

## PSALM 80*

See RG 175

### *Prayer to Restore God's Vineyard*

1 For the leader; according to "Lilies."
*Eduth*.* A psalm of Asaph.
I
2 O Shepherd of Israel, lend an ear,
you who guide Joseph like a flock!
Seated upon the cherubim, shine forth[x]
3 upon Ephraim, Benjamin, and
Manasseh.
Stir up your power, and come to save us.
4 [y]O God, restore us;
light up your face and we shall be
saved.
II
5 LORD of hosts,
how long will you smolder in anger
while your people pray?[z]
6 You have fed them the bread of tears,
made them drink tears in great
measure.*[a]
7 You have left us to be fought over by our
neighbors;
our enemies deride us.[b]
8 O God of hosts, restore us;
light up your face and we shall be
saved.
III
9 You brought a vine* out of Egypt;
you drove out nations and planted it.
10 You cleared out what was before it;
it took deep root and filled the land.
11 The mountains were covered by its
shadow,
the cedars of God by its branches.
12 It sent out its boughs as far as the sea,*
its shoots as far as the river.*

**Psalm 80** A community lament in time of military defeat. Using the familiar image of Israel as a vineyard, the people complain that God has broken down the wall protecting the once splendid vine brought from Egypt (Ps 80:9–14). They pray that God will again turn to them and use the Davidic king to lead them to victory (Ps 80:15–19).

**80:1 Lilies . . . . Eduth**: the first term is probably the title of the melody to which the Psalm was to be sung; the second is unexplained.

**80:6** Both the Septuagint and the Vulgate translate this verse in the first person, i.e., "You have fed us the bread of tears."

**80:9 A vine**: a frequent metaphor for Israel, cf. Is 5:1–7; 27:2–5; Jer 2:21; Hos 10:1; Mt 21:33.

**80:12 The sea**: the Mediterranean. **The river**: the Euphrates, cf. Gn 15:18; 1 Kgs 5:1. The terms may also have a mythic nuance—the seas that surround the earth; sea and river are sometimes paralleled in poetry.

*p:* Ps 13:2; 44:24; 89:47; Dt 4:24. *q:* Ps 14:4; Jer 10:25. *r:* Ps 142:7. *s:* Ez 20:44; 36:22. *t:* Ps 42:4; 115:2; Jl 2:17. *u:* Jl 4:21. *v:* Ps 102:21. *w:* Ps 89:51–52. *x:* Ps 23:1–3; 95:7; 100:3; Gn 48:15; Ex 25:22; 1 Sm 4:4; 2 Sm 6:2; Mi 7:14. *y:* Ps 4:7; 31:17; 67:2; 85:5; Nm 6:25; Dn 9:17. *z:* Ps 13:2; 44:24; 74:1; 79:5; 89:47; Dt 4:24. *a:* Ps 42:4; 102:10. *b:* Ps 44:14; 79:4; 123:3–4; Jb 12:4; Dn 9:16; Zep 2:8.

13 Why have you broken down its walls,
so that all who pass along the way
pluck its fruit?[c]
14 The boar from the forest strips the vine;
the beast of the field feeds upon it.[d]
15 Turn back again, God of hosts;
look down from heaven and see;
Visit this vine,
16 the stock your right hand has planted,
and the son* whom you made strong
for yourself.
17 Those who would burn or cut it down—
may they perish at your rebuke.
18 May your hand be with the man on your
right,*
with the son of man whom you made
strong for yourself.
19 Then we will not withdraw from you;
revive us, and we will call on your
name.
20 LORD God of hosts, restore us;
light up your face and we shall be
saved.

See RG 175

## PSALM 81*

### *An Admonition to Fidelity*

1 For the leader; "upon the *gittith*."*
Of Asaph.

I

2 Sing joyfully to God our strength;[e]
raise loud shouts to the God of Jacob!
3 Take up a melody, sound the timbrel,
the pleasant lyre with a harp.
4 *Blow the shofar at the new moon,
at the full moon, on our solemn feast.[f]
5 For this is a law for Israel,
an edict of the God of Jacob,[g]
6 He made it a decree for Joseph
when he came out of the land of Egypt.

II

7 *I heard a tongue I did not know:
"I removed his shoulder from the
burden;*
his hands moved away from the
basket.*[h]
8 In distress you called and I rescued you;
I answered you in secret with thunder;
At the waters of Meribah* I tested you:[i]
9 'Listen, my people, I will testify
against you *Selah*
If only you will listen to me, Israel![j]
10 There shall be no foreign god among
you;*[k]
you shall not bow down to an alien
god.
11 'I am the LORD your God,
who brought you up from the land of
Egypt.
Open wide your mouth that I may
fill it.'
12 But my people did not listen to my
words;
Israel would not submit to me.
13 So I thrust them away to the hardness of
their heart;
'Let them walk in their own
machinations.'[l]
14 O that my people would listen to me,
that Israel would walk in my ways,[m]
15 In a moment I would humble their foes,

**80:16** The Vulgate and Septuagint use "son of man."

**80:18 The man on your right**: the Davidic king who will lead the army in battle.

**Psalm 81** At a pilgrimage feast, probably harvest in the fall, the people assemble in the Temple in accord with the Sinai ordinances (Ps 81:2–6). They hear a divine word (mediated by a Temple speaker) telling how God rescued them from slavery in Egypt (Ps 81:7–9), gave them the fundamental commandment of fidelity (Ps 81:9–11), which would bring punishment if they refused to obey (Ps 81:12–13). But if Israel repents, God will be with them once again, bestowing protection and fertility (Ps 81:14–16).

**81:1 Upon the gittith**: probably the title of the melody to which the Psalm was to be sung or a musical instrument.

**81:4 New moon . . . full moon**: the pilgrimage feast of harvest began with a great assembly (Lv 23:24; Nm 29:1), used the new moon as a sign (Nm 29:6), and included trumpets (Lv 23:24).

**81:7 I heard a tongue I did not know**: a Temple official speaks the word of God (Ps 81:5b–16), which is authoritative and unlike merely human words (cf. Nm 24:4, 16).

**81:7 I removed his shoulder from the burden**: A reference to the liberation of Israel from slavery in Egypt. **The basket**: for carrying clay to make bricks, cf. Ex 1:14.

**81:8 Meribah**: place of rebellion in the wilderness; cf. Ex 17:7; Nm 20:13.

**81:10 There shall be no foreign god among you**: as in Ps 50 and 95, Israel is challenged to obey the first commandment of fidelity to God after the proclamation of the exodus.

*c:* Ps 89:41. *d:* Hos 2:14. *e:* Ps 43:4; 68:26; 149:3; 150:3–4; Jdt 16:1. *f:* Lv 23:24; Nm 29:1. *g:* Ex 23:14ff. *h:* Ex 1:14; 6:6. *i:* Ps 95:8; Ex 2:23ff; 17:7; 19:16; Nm 20:13; 27:14. *j:* Ex 1:14; 6:6. *k:* Ex 20:2–6; Dt 5:6–10. *l:* Jer 3:17; 7:24. *m:* Is 48:18.

and turn back my hand against their
oppressors.[n]
16 Those who hate the LORD will try
flattering him,
but their fate is fixed forever.
17 But Israel I will feed with the finest wheat,
I will satisfy them with honey from the
rock."[o]

## PSALM 82*

See RG 175–76

### *The Downfall of Unjust Gods*

1 A psalm of Asaph.

I

God takes a stand in the divine council,
gives judgment in the midst of the gods.[p]
2 "How long will you judge unjustly
and favor the cause of the wicked?[q]
*Selah*
3 "Defend the lowly and fatherless;
render justice to the afflicted and needy.
4 Rescue the lowly and poor;
deliver them from the hand of the
wicked."[r]

II

5 *The gods neither know nor understand,
wandering about in darkness,
and all the world's foundations shake.
6 I declare: "Gods though you be,*[s]
offspring of the Most High all of you,
7 Yet like any mortal you shall die;
like any prince you shall fall."
8 Arise, O God, judge the earth,*
for yours are all the nations.

## PSALM 83*

See RG 175–77

### *Prayer Against a Hostile Alliance*

1 A song; a psalm of Asaph.

I

2 God, do not be silent;
God, do not be deaf or remain
unmoved![t]
3 See how your enemies rage;
your foes proudly raise their heads.
4 They conspire against your people,
plot against those you protect.[u]
5 They say, "Come, let us wipe them out as
a nation;
let Israel's name be remembered no
more!"
6 They scheme with one mind,
they have entered into a covenant
against you:[v]
7 *The tents of Edom and the Ishmaelites,
of Moab and the Hagrites,[w]
8 Gebal, Ammon, and Amalek,[x]
Philistia and the inhabitants of Tyre.[y]
9 Assyria, too, in league with them,
backs the descendants of Lot. *Selah*

II

10 *Deal with them as with Midian;
as with Sisera and Jabin at the wadi
Kishon,[z]
11 Those destroyed at Endor,
who became dung for the ground.[a]
12 Make their nobles like Oreb and Zeeb,

**Psalm 82** As in Ps 58, the pagan gods are seen as subordinate divine beings to whom Israel's God had delegated oversight of the foreign countries in the beginning (Dt 32:8–9). Now God arises in the heavenly assembly (Ps 82:1) to rebuke the unjust "gods" (Ps 82:2–4), who are stripped of divine status and reduced in rank to mortals (Ps 82:5–7). They are accused of misruling the earth by not upholding the poor. A short prayer for universal justice concludes the Psalm (Ps 82:8).

**82:5** The gods are blind and unable to declare what is right. Their misrule shakes earth's foundations (cf. Ps 11:3; 75:4), which God made firm in creation (Ps 96:10).

**82:6 I declare: "Gods though you be"**: in Jn 10:34 Jesus uses the verse to prove that those to whom the word of God is addressed can fittingly be called "gods."

**82:8 Judge the earth**: according to Dt 32:8–9, Israel's God had originally assigned jurisdiction over the foreign nations to the subordinate deities, keeping Israel as a personal possession. Now God will directly take over the rulership of the whole world.

**Psalm 83** The community lament complains to God of the nations' attempts to wipe out the name of Israel (Ps 83:1–8). The psalmist sees all Israel's enemies throughout its history united in a conspiracy (Ps 83:2–8). May God destroy the current crop of enemies as the enemies of old were destroyed (Ps 83:9–12), and may they be pursued until they acknowledge the name of Israel's God (Ps 83:13–18).

**83:7–9** Apart from the Assyrians, all the nations listed here were neighbors of Israel. The Hagrites are a tribe of the desert regions east of Ammon and Moab (1 Chr 5:10, 19–22). Gebal is the Phoenician city of Byblos or perhaps a mountain region south of the Dead Sea. The descendants of Lot are Moab and Edom (Gn 19:36–38 and Dt 2:9). These nations were never united against Israel in the same period; the Psalm has lumped them all together.

**83:10–13** For the historical events, see Jgs 4–8.

*n:* Lv 26:7–8. *o:* Ps 147:14; Dt 32:13–14. *p:* Is 3:13–14. *q:* Ps 58:2. *r:* Dt 1:17. *s:* 2 Pt 1:4. *t:* Ps 10:1; 44:24; 109:1. *u:* Jer 11:9. *v:* Ps 2:2. *w:* Nm 20:23; 1 Chr 5:10, 19. *x:* Ex 17:8. *y:* Jos 13:2. *z:* Ex 2:15; Is 9:3; 10:26. *a:* Jer 8:2.

all their princes like Zebah and
Zalmunna,
13 Who made a plan together,
"Let us take for ourselves the pastures
of God."
14 My God, make them like tumbleweed,
into chaff flying before the wind.[b]
15 As a fire raging through a forest,
a flame setting mountains ablaze,[c]
16 Pursue them with your tempest;
terrify them with your storm-wind.
17 Cover their faces with shame,
till they seek your name,* LORD.
18 Let them be ashamed and terrified
forever;
let them perish in disgrace.
19 Let them know that your name is LORD,
you alone are the Most High over all
the earth.[d]

## PSALM 84*

See RG 175

### *Prayer of a Pilgrim to Jerusalem*

1 For the leader; "upon the *gittith*." A psalm
of the Korahites.

I

2 How lovely your dwelling,
O LORD of hosts![e]
3 My soul yearns and pines
for the courts of the LORD.[f]
My heart and flesh cry out
for the living God.
4 *As the sparrow finds a home
and the swallow a nest to settle her
young,
My home is by your altars,
LORD of hosts, my king and my God![g]
5 Blessed are those who dwell in your
house!
They never cease to praise you. *Selah*

II

6 Blessed the man who finds refuge in you,
in their hearts are pilgrim roads.
7 As they pass through the Baca valley,*
they find spring water to drink.
The early rain covers it with blessings.
8 They will go from strength to strength*
and see the God of gods on Zion.

III

9 LORD God of hosts, hear my prayer;
listen, God of Jacob. *Selah*
10 *O God, watch over our shield;
look upon the face of your anointed.[h]

IV

11 Better one day in your courts
than a thousand elsewhere.
Better the threshold of the house of my
God
than a home in the tents of the wicked.
12 For a sun and shield is the LORD God,
bestowing all grace and glory.
The LORD withholds no good thing
from those who walk without reproach.
13 O LORD of hosts,
blessed the man who trusts in you!

## PSALM 85*

See RG 175–76

### *Prayer for Divine Favor*

1 For the leader. A psalm of the Korahites.

I

2 You once favored, LORD, your land,
restored the captives of Jacob.[i]
3 You forgave the guilt of your people,
pardoned all their sins. *Selah*
4 You withdrew all your wrath,
turned back from your burning anger.[j]

II

5 Restore us, God of our salvation;
let go of your displeasure with us.[k]

**83:17 Seek your name**: a variant of the more typical phrase "to seek the face of God" (Ps 24:6; 27:8; 105:4). Seeking the face of God refers to the worshiper having recourse to a temple or sanctuary where in non-Jewish contexts a statue embodies the physical presence of the Deity. In Israel's aniconic tradition no visible image or statue can represent God. This understanding is conveyed here concretely by use of the term "your name" rather than the more typical "your face."

**Psalm 84** Israelites celebrated three pilgrimage feasts in Jerusalem annually. The Psalm expresses the sentiments of the pilgrims eager to enjoy the divine presence.

**84:4** The desire of a restless bird for a secure home is an image of the desire of a pilgrim for the secure house of God, cf. Ps 42:2–3, where the image for the desire of the pilgrim is the thirst of the deer for water.

**84:7 Baca valley**: Hebrew obscure; probably a valley on the way to Jerusalem.

**84:8 Strength to strength**: pass through outer and inner wall.

**84:10 Our shield . . . your anointed**: the king had a role in the liturgical celebration. For the king as shield, cf. Ps 89:19.

**Psalm 85** A national lament reminding God of past favors and forgiveness (Ps 85:2–4) and begging for forgiveness and

*b:* Ps 1:4; 35:5; 58:10; Is 5:24; 10:17; 17:13; 29:5; Ez 21:3. *c:* Ps 50:3. *d:* Ps 97:9; Dt 4:39; Dn 3:45. *e:* Ps 43:3–4; 122:1. *f:* Ps 42:2–3; 63:2–3; 143:6; Is 26:9. *g:* Ps 5:3. *h:* Ps 89:19. *i:* Ps 14:7; 126:4. *j:* Ps 78:38; Ex 32:14; Is 48:9. *k:* Ps 80:4.

6 Will you be angry with us forever,
prolong your anger for all generations?[l]
7 Certainly you will again restore our life,
that your people may rejoice in you.
8 Show us, LORD, your mercy;
grant us your salvation.

III

9 *I will listen for what God, the LORD, has to say;
surely he will speak of peace
To his people and to his faithful.
May they not turn to foolishness!
10 Near indeed is his salvation for those who fear him;
glory will dwell in our land.
11 *Love and truth will meet;
justice and peace will kiss.[m]
12 Truth will spring from the earth;
justice will look down from heaven.[n]
13 Yes, the LORD will grant his bounty;
our land will yield its produce.[o]
14 Justice will march before him,
and make a way for his footsteps.

## PSALM 86*

See RG 175–76

### *Prayer in Time of Distress*

1 A prayer of David.

I

Incline your ear, LORD, and answer me,
for I am poor and oppressed.
2 Preserve my life, for I am devoted;
save your servant who trusts in you.
You are my God; 3 be gracious to me, Lord;
to you I call all the day.
4 Gladden the soul of your servant;
to you, Lord, I lift up my soul.[p]
5 Lord, you are good and forgiving,
most merciful to all who call on you.[q]
6 LORD, hear my prayer;
listen to my cry for help.[r]
7 On the day of my distress I call to you,
for you will answer me.

II

8 None among the gods can equal you, O Lord;
nor can their deeds compare to yours.[s]
9 All the nations you have made shall come
to bow before you, Lord,
and give honor to your name.[t]
10 For you are great and do wondrous deeds;
and you alone are God.

III

11 Teach me, LORD, your way
that I may walk in your truth,[u]
single-hearted and revering your name.
12 I will praise you with all my heart,
glorify your name forever, Lord my God.
13 Your mercy to me is great;
you have rescued me from the depths of Sheol.[v]
14 O God, the arrogant have risen against me;
a ruthless band has sought my life;
to you they pay no heed.
15 But you, Lord, are a compassionate and gracious God,
slow to anger, abounding in mercy and truth.[w]
16 Turn to me, be gracious to me;
give your strength to your servant;
save the son of your handmaid.[x]
17 Give me a sign of your favor:
make my enemies see, to their confusion,
that you, LORD, help and comfort me.

grace now (Ps 85:5–8). A speaker represents the people who wait humbly with open hearts (Ps 85:9–10): God will be active on their behalf (Ps 85:11–13). The situation suggests the conditions of Judea during the early postexilic period, the fifth century B.C.; the thoughts are similar to those of postexilic prophets (Hg 1:5–11; 2:6–9).

**85:9** The prophet listens to God's revelation, cf. Heb 2:1.

**85:11–13** Divine activity is personified as pairs of virtues.

**Psalm 86** An individual lament. The psalmist, "poor and oppressed" (Ps 86:1), "devoted" (Ps 86:2), "your servant" (Ps 86:2, 4, 16), "rescued . . . from the depths of Sheol" (Ps 86:13), attacked by the ruthless (Ps 86:14), desires only God's protection (Ps 86:1–7, 11–17).

*l:* Ps 79:5; 89:47. *m:* Ps 89:15; 97:2. *n:* Is 45:8. *o:* Ps 67:7; Lv 26:4; Ez 34:27; Hos 2:23–24; Zec 8:12. *p:* Ps 25:1; 143:8. *q:* Jl 2:13. *r:* Ps 5:2; 130:1–2. *s:* Ps 35:10; 89:9; Ex 15:11; Dt 3:24; Jer 10:6. *t:* Ps 22:28; Zec 14:16; Rev 15:4. *u:* Ps 25:4; 26:3; 27:11; 119:12, 35; 143:8, 10. *v:* Ps 30:4; 40:3; Jon 2:7. *w:* Ps 103:8; 130:7; 145:8; Ex 34:6. *x:* Ps 25:16; 116:16; Wis 9:5.

PSALM 88 IS a desperate complaint by a person who is mortally ill. Perhaps the complaint can be interpreted as symbolizing the national catastrophe, the destruction and exile (Sheol may represent the exile), which could potentially sever the connection between Israel and God. Prolonged thoughts of death dominate, with many synonyms for the place of the dead: Sheol, pit, grave, abyss, darkness. In the realm of the dead, humankind is cut off from God and completely forgotten; the sense of isolation and finality is overwhelming. The psalmist tries to remind God that it is to everyone's benefit if he escapes death: the dead cannot praise God. The psalm ends without hope or resolution; there is no expectation that God will cure the psalmist and no promise to praise God upon recovery.

See RG 175

## PSALM 87*

### *Zion the True Birthplace*

1[y]A psalm of the Korahites. A song.

I

His foundation is on holy mountains,
2 The LORD loves the gates* of Zion
more than any dwelling in Jacob.
3 Glorious things are said of you,
O city of God! *Selah*

II

4 Rahab and Babylon I count
among those who know me.
See, Philistia and Tyre, with Ethiopia,
"This one was born there."
5 *And of Zion it will be said:
"Each one was born in it."[z]
The Most High will establish it;[a]
6 the LORD notes in the register of the peoples:
"This one was born there."[b] *Selah*
7 So singers and dancers:
"All my springs are in you."[c]

See RG 175

## PSALM 88*

### *A Despairing Lament*

1 A song; a psalm of the Korahites. For the leader; according to *Mahalath*. For singing; a *maskil* of Heman the Ezrahite.

I

2 LORD, the God of my salvation, I call out by day;
at night I cry aloud in your presence.[d]
3 Let my prayer come before you;
incline your ear to my cry.[e]
4 *For my soul is filled with troubles;[f]
my life draws near to Sheol.
5 I am reckoned with those who go down to the pit;
I am like a warrior without strength.
6 My couch is among the dead,
like the slain who lie in the grave.
You remember them no more;
they are cut off from your influence.
7 You plunge me into the bottom of the pit,
into the darkness of the abyss.
8 Your wrath lies heavy upon me;
all your waves crash over me.[g] *Selah*

II

9 Because of you my acquaintances shun me;
you make me loathsome to them;[h]
Caged in, I cannot escape;
10 my eyes grow dim from trouble.

All day I call on you, LORD;
I stretch out my hands to you.
11 *Do you work wonders for the dead?
Do the shades arise and praise you?[i]
*Selah*

III

12 Is your mercy proclaimed in the grave,

**Psalm 87** A song of Zion, like Ps 46; 48; 76; 132.

**87:2 The gates**: the city itself, a common Hebrew idiom.

**87:5–6** The bond between the exile and the holy city was so strong as to override the exile's citizenship of lesser cities.

**Psalm 88** A lament in which the psalmist prays for rescue from the alienation of approaching death. Each of the three stanzas begins with a call to God (Ps 88:2, 10, 14) and complains of the death that separates one from God. The tone is persistently grim.

**88:4–8** In imagination the psalmist already experiences the alienation of Sheol.

**88:11–13** The psalmist seeks to persuade God to act out of

*y:* Ps 76:2–3; 78:68–69. *z:* Gal 4:26. *a:* Ps 48:9. *b:* Is 4:3. *c:* Ps 68:26; 149:3. *d:* Ps 77:3. *e:* Ps 119:170. *f:* Ps 28:1; 30:4; 40:3; 86:13; 143:7; Nm 16:33; Jb 17:1; Jon 2:7. *g:* Ps 18:5; 32:6; 42:8; 69:2; Jon 2:4. *h:* Ps 38:12; 79:4; 80:7; 123:3–4; 142:8; Jb 12:4; 19:13; Lam 3:7; Dn 9:16. *i:* Ps 6:6; 30:10; 38:18; 115:17.

your faithfulness among those who
have perished?*
13 Are your marvels declared in the darkness,
your righteous deeds in the land of
oblivion?

IV

14 But I cry out to you, LORD;
in the morning my prayer comes
before you.
15 Why do you reject my soul, LORD,
and hide your face from me?
16 I have been mortally afflicted since youth;
I have borne your terrors and I am
made numb.
17 Your wrath has swept over me;
your terrors have destroyed me.[j]
18 All day they surge round like a flood;
from every side they encircle me.
19 Because of you friend and neighbor
shun me;[k]
my only friend is darkness.

See RG 176

## PSALM 89*

### *A Lament over God's Promise to David*

1 A *maskil* of Ethan the Ezrahite.

A

I

2 I will sing of your mercy forever, LORD[l]
proclaim your faithfulness through all
ages.
3 *For I said, "My mercy is established
forever;
my faithfulness will stand as long as
the heavens.
4 I have made a covenant with my chosen
one;
I have sworn to David my servant:
5 I will make your dynasty stand forever
and establish your throne through all
ages."[m] *Selah*

II

6 The heavens praise your marvels, LORD,
your loyalty in the assembly of the
holy ones.[n]
7 Who in the skies ranks with the LORD?
Who is like the LORD among the sons
of the gods?*[o]
8 A God dreaded in the council of the holy
ones,
greater and more awesome than all
those around him!
9 LORD, God of hosts, who is like you?
Mighty LORD, your faithfulness
surrounds you.
10 You rule the raging sea;[p]
you still its swelling waves.
11 You crush Rahab* with a mortal blow;
with your strong arm you scatter your
foes.
12 Yours are the heavens, yours the earth;
you founded the world and everything
in it.[q]
13 *Zaphon and Amanus you created;
Tabor and Hermon rejoice in your name.
14 You have a mighty arm.
Your hand is strong; your right hand is
ever exalted.
15 Justice and judgment are the foundation
of your throne;
mercy and faithfulness march before
you.[r]
16 Blessed the people who know the war
cry,

concern for divine honor: the shades give you no worship, so keep me alive to offer you praise.

**88:12 Perished**: lit., "Abaddon," the deepest part of Sheol.

**Psalm 89** The community laments the defeat of the Davidic king, to whom God promised kingship as enduring as the heavens (Ps 89:2–5). The Psalm narrates how God became king of the divine beings (Ps 89:6–9) and how the Davidic king became king of earthly kings (Ps 89:20–38). Since the defeat of the king calls into question God's promise, the community ardently prays God to be faithful to the original promise to David (Ps 89:39–52).

**89:3–5** David's dynasty is to be as long-lasting as the heavens, a statement reinforced by using the same verbs (establish, stand) both of the divine love and loyalty and of the Davidic dynasty and throne, cf. Ps 89:29–30.

**89:7 The sons of the gods**: "the holy ones" and "courtiers" of Ps 89:6, 8. These heavenly spirits are members of God's court.

**89:11 Rahab**: a mythological sea monster whose name is used in the Bible mainly as a personification of primeval chaos, cf. Jb 9:13; 26:12; Ps 74:13–14; Is 51:9.

**89:13 Zaphon and Amanus**: two sacred mountains in northern Syria which came to designate the directions of north and south. **Tabor**: a high hill in the valley of Jezreel in northern Israel. **Hermon**: a mountain in Lebanon, forming the southern spur of the Anti-Lebanon range.

---

*j:* Jb 6:4; 20:25. *k:* Jb 19:13. *l:* Is 63:7. *m:* Ps 61:7–8; 132:11; 2 Sm 7:8–16. *n:* Ps 29:1; 82:1; Jb 1:6; 5:1. *o:* Ps 35:10; 86:8; 113:5; Ex 15:11; Jer 10:6. *p:* Ps 65:8; 74:13–15; 107:29; Jb 7:12; Is 51:9–10. *q:* Ps 24:1–2; 50:12; Dt 10:14; 1 Cor 10:26. *r:* Ps 85:11–12; 97:2.

who walk in the radiance of your face,
LORD.
17 In your name they sing joyfully all the
day;
they rejoice in your righteousness.[s]
18 You are their majestic strength;
by your favor our horn* is exalted.[t]
19 Truly the LORD is our shield,
the Holy One of Israel, our king![u]

III

20 Then you spoke in vision;[v]
to your faithful ones you said:
"I have set a leader over the warriors;
I have raised up a chosen one from the
people.
21 I have chosen David, my servant;
with my holy oil I have anointed him.
22 My hand will be with him;[w]
my arm will make him strong.
23 No enemy shall outwit him,
nor shall the wicked defeat him.
24 I will crush his foes before him,
strike down those who hate him.
25 My faithfulness and mercy will be with
him;
through my name his horn will be
exalted.
26 *I will set his hand upon the sea,
his right hand upon the rivers.
27 He shall cry to me, 'You are my father,[x]
my God, the Rock of my salvation!'
28 I myself make him the firstborn,
Most High* over the kings of the earth.
29 Forever I will maintain my mercy for
him;[y]
my covenant with him stands firm.
30 I will establish his dynasty forever,
his throne as the days of the heavens.
31 If his descendants forsake my teaching,[z]
do not follow my decrees,
32 If they fail to observe my statutes,
do not keep my commandments,
33 I will punish their crime with a rod
and their guilt with blows.
34 But I will not take my mercy from him,
nor will I betray my bond of
faithfulness.[a]
35 I will not violate my covenant;
the promise of my lips I will not alter.[b]
36 By my holiness I swore once for all:[c]
I will never be false to David.
37 *His dynasty will continue forever,[d]
his throne, like the sun before me.
38 Like the moon it will stand eternal,
forever firm like the sky!" *Selah*

B

IV

39 But now you have rejected and spurned,[e]
been enraged at your anointed.
40 You renounced the covenant with your
servant,
defiled his crown in the dust.
41 You broke down all city walls,[f]
left his strongholds in ruins.
42 All who pass through seize plunder;
his neighbors deride him.
43 You have exalted the right hand of his foes,
have gladdened all his enemies.[g]
44 You turned back his sharp sword,
did not support him in battle.
45 You brought to an end his splendor,
hurled his throne to the ground.
46 You cut short the days of his youth,
covered him with shame. *Selah*

V

47 How long, LORD? Will you hide forever?
Must your wrath smolder like fire?[h]
48 Remember how brief life is,
how frail the sons of man you have
created![i]
49 What is man, that he should live and not
see death?

**89:18, 25 Horn**: a concrete noun for an abstract quality; horn is a symbol of strength.

**89:26 The sea . . . the rivers**: geographically the limits of the Davidic empire (the Mediterranean and the Euphrates); mythologically, the traditional forces of chaos. See note on Ps 89:11.

**89:28 Most High**: a divine title, which is here extended to David as God's own king, cf. Ps 2:7–9; Is 9:5. As God rules over the members of the heavenly council (Ps 89:6–9), so David, God's surrogate, rules over earthly kings.

**89:37–38 Like the sun before me . . . like the sky**: as enduring as the heavenly lights, cf. Ps 89:2–5 and Ps 72:5, 17.

*s:* Ps 47:2; Zep 3:14. *t:* Ps 112:9; 148:14. *u:* Ps 47:9; 96:10; 97:1; 99:1; Is 6:3. *v:* Ps 78:70; 132:11–12; 2 Sm 7:4, 8–16; 1 Chr 17:3, 7–14; Is 42:1; Acts 13:22. *w:* 1 Sm 2:9–10. *x:* Ps 2:7; 110:2–3; 2 Sm 7:9, 14; Col 1:15, 18; Rev 1:5. *y:* Ps 18:51; 61:8; 144:10; 2 Sm 7:11; Is 55:3. *z:* Lv 26:14–33. *a:* Ps 40:12; Sir 47:22. *b:* Jer 33:20–21. *c:* Am 4:2. *d:* Ps 61:8; 72:5; Sir 43:6. *e:* Ps 44:10–25. *f:* Ps 80:13–14. *g:* Lam 1:5. *h:* Ps 13:2; 44:25; 74:10; 79:5; Dt 4:24. *i:* Ps 39:5–6; 62:10; 90:9–10; 144:4; Jb 7:6, 16; 14:1, 5; Eccl 6:12; Wis 2:5.

Who can deliver his soul from the
power of Sheol?[j] *Selah*

VI

50 Where are your former mercies, Lord,
that you swore to David in your
faithfulness?
51 Remember, Lord, the insults to your
servants,
how I have borne in my bosom the
slander of the nations.[k]
52 Your enemies, LORD, insult;
they insult each step of your anointed.
53 *Blessed be the LORD forever! Amen and
amen![l]

## Fourth Book—Psalms 90–106

### PSALM 90*

See RG 175

### *God's Eternity and Human Frailty*

1 A prayer of Moses, the man of God.

I

Lord, you have been our refuge
through all generations.
2 Before the mountains were born,
the earth and the world brought forth,
from eternity to eternity you are God.[m]
3 You turn humanity back into dust,*
saying, "Return, you children of
Adam!"[n]
4 A thousand years in your eyes
are merely a day gone by,[o]
Before a watch passes in the night,
5 *you wash them away;[p]
They sleep,
and in the morning they sprout again
like an herb.
6 In the morning it blooms only to pass
away;
in the evening it is wilted and withered.*[q]

II

7 Truly we are consumed by your anger,
filled with terror by your wrath.
8 You have kept our faults before you,
our hidden sins in the light of your face.[r]
9 Our life ebbs away under your wrath;[s]
our years end like a sigh.
10 Seventy is the sum of our years,
or eighty, if we are strong;
Most of them are toil and sorrow;
they pass quickly, and we are gone.
11 Who comprehends the strength of your
anger?
Your wrath matches the fear it inspires.
12 Teach us to count our days aright,
that we may gain wisdom of heart.

III

13 Relent, O LORD! How long?
Have pity on your servants!
14 Fill us at daybreak with your mercy,[t]
that all our days we may sing for joy.
15 Make us glad as many days as you
humbled us,
for as many years as we have seen
trouble.[u]
16 Show your deeds to your servants,
your glory to their children.
17 May the favor of the Lord our God be
ours.[v]
Prosper the work of our hands!
Prosper the work of our hands!

### PSALM 91*

See RG 175

### *Security Under God's Protection*

I

1 You who dwell in the shelter of the Most
High,*

**89:53** The doxology at the end of the third book of the Psalms; it is not part of Ps 89.

**Psalm 90** A communal lament that describes only in general terms the cause of the community's distress. After confidently invoking God (Ps 90:1), the Psalm turns to a complaint contrasting God's eternity with the brevity of human life (Ps 90:2–6) and sees in human suffering the punishment for sin (Ps 90:7–12). The Psalm concludes with a plea for God's intervention (Ps 90:13–17).

**90:3 Dust**: one word of God is enough to return mortals to the dust from which they were created. Human beings were created from earth in Gn 2:7; 3:19.

**90:5 You wash them away**: the Hebrew of Ps 90:4–5 is unclear.

**90:6 It is wilted and withered**: the transitory nature of the grass under the scorching sun was proverbial, cf. Ps 129:6; Is 40:6–8.

**Psalm 91** A prayer of someone who has taken refuge in the Lord, possibly within the Temple (Ps 91:1–2). The psalmist is

*j:* Ps 90:3. *k:* Ps 79:12. *l:* Ps 41:14; 72:18; 106:48. *m:* Ps 48:15; 55:20; 93:2; 102:13; Heb 1:12. *n:* Ps 103:14; 104:29; 146:4; Gn 3:19; 1 Mc 2:63; Jb 34:14–15; Eccl 3:20; 12:7; Sir 40:11. *o:* 2 Pt 3:8. *p:* Ps 89:48. *q:* Ps 37:2; 102:11; 103:15–16; Jb 14:1–2; Is 40:6–8. *r:* Ps 109:14–15; Hos 7:2. *s:* Ps 39:5–7; 62:10; 102:24–25; 144:4; Gn 6:3; Jb 7:6, 16; 14:5; Prv 10:27; Eccl 6:12; Wis 2:5; Sir 18:8; Is 65:20. *t:* Ps 17:15. *u:* Nm 14:34; Jer 31:13. *v:* Ps 33:22.

who abide in the shade of the
Almighty,*
2 Say to the LORD, "My refuge and
fortress,
my God in whom I trust."[w]
3 He will rescue you from the fowler's
snare,
from the destroying plague,
4 He will shelter you with his pinions,
and under his wings you may take
refuge;[x]
his faithfulness is a protecting shield.
5 You shall not fear the terror of the night
nor the arrow that flies by day,[y]
6 Nor the pestilence that roams in darkness,
nor the plague that ravages at noon.[z]
7 Though a thousand fall at your side,
ten thousand at your right hand,
near you it shall not come.
8 You need simply watch;
the punishment of the wicked you will
see.[a]
9 Because you have the LORD for your
refuge
and have made the Most High your
stronghold,
10 No evil shall befall you,
no affliction come near your tent.[b]
11 *For he commands his angels with regard
to you,[c]
to guard you wherever you go.[d]
12 With their hands they shall support you,
lest you strike your foot against a
stone.[e]
13 You can tread upon the asp and the viper,
trample the lion and the dragon.[f]

II

14 Because he clings to me I will deliver
him;
because he knows my name I will set
him on high.[g]
15 He will call upon me and I will answer;[h]
I will be with him in distress;[i]
I will deliver him and give him honor.
16 With length of days I will satisfy him,
and fill him with my saving power.[j]

## PSALM 92*

See RG 175

### *A Hymn of Thanksgiving for God's Fidelity*

1 A psalm. A sabbath song.

I

2 It is good to give thanks to the LORD,
to sing praise to your name, Most High,[k]
3 To proclaim your love at daybreak,
your faithfulness in the night,
4 With the ten-stringed harp,
with melody upon the lyre.[l]
5 For you make me jubilant, LORD, by your
deeds;
at the works of your hands I shout for
joy.

II

6 How great are your works, LORD![m]
How profound your designs!
7 A senseless person cannot know this;
a fool cannot comprehend.
8 Though the wicked flourish like grass[n]
and all sinners thrive,
They are destined for eternal destruction;
9 but you, LORD, are forever on high.
10 Indeed your enemies, LORD,
indeed your enemies shall perish;
all sinners shall be scattered.[o]

III

11 You have given me the strength of a
wild ox;[p]
you have poured rich oil upon me.[q]

confident that God's presence will protect the people in every dangerous situation (Ps 91:3–13). The final verses are an oracle of salvation promising salvation to those who trust in God (Ps 91:14–16).

**91:1 The shelter of the Most High**: basically "hiding place" but in the Psalms a designation for the protected Temple precincts, cf. Ps 27:5; 31:21; 61:5. **The shade of the Almighty**: lit., "the shadow of the wings of the Almighty," cf. Ps 17:8; 36:8; 57:2; 63:8. Ps 91:4 makes clear that the shadow is an image of the safety afforded by the outstretched wings of the cherubim in the holy of holies.

**91:11–12** The words are cited in Lk 4:10–11; Mt 4:6, as Satan tempts Jesus in the desert.

**Psalm 92** A hymn of praise and thanks for God's faithful deeds (Ps 92:2–5). The wicked, deluded by their prosperity (Ps 92:6–9), are punished (Ps 92:10), whereas the psalmist has already experienced God's protection (Ps 92:11–15).

*w:* Ps 18:3; 31:3–4; 42:10; 142:6; 2 Sm 22:3. *x:* Ps 17:8; 36:8; 57:2; 63:8; Dt 32:11; Ru 2:12; Mt 23:37. *y:* Prv 3:25; Sg 3:8. *z:* Dt 32:24. *a:* Ps 92:12. *b:* Prv 12:21; Dt 7:15. *c:* Mt 4:6; Lk 4:10f. *d:* Heb 1:14. *e:* Ps 121:3; Prv 3:23. *f:* Is 11:8; Lk 10:19. *g:* Ps 9:11; 119:132. *h:* Jer 33:3; Zec 13:9. *i:* Is 43:2. *j:* Prv 3:2. *k:* Ps 33:1; 147:1. *l:* Ps 33:2; 144:9. *m:* Ps 131:1; 139:6, 17; Wis 13:1; 17:1. *n:* Ps 37:35. *o:* Ps 68:1–2; 125:5. *p:* Ps 75:11; Dt 33:17. *q:* Ps 23:5.

12 My eyes look with glee on my wicked
enemies;
my ears shall hear what happens to my
wicked foes.[r]
13 The just shall flourish like the palm tree,
shall grow like a cedar of Lebanon.[s]
14 *Planted in the house of the LORD,
they shall flourish in the courts of our
God.
15 They shall bear fruit even in old age,
they will stay fresh and green,
16 To proclaim: "The LORD is just;
my rock, in whom there is no
wrong."[t]

## PSALM 93*

See RG 175

### God Is a Mighty King

1 The LORD is king,* robed with majesty;
the LORD is robed, girded with might.[u]
The world will surely stand in place,
never to be moved.[v]
2 Your throne stands firm from of old;
you are from everlasting.[w]
3 *The flood has raised up, LORD;
the flood has raised up its roar;
the flood has raised its pounding
waves.
4 More powerful than the roar of many
waters,
more powerful than the breakers of the
sea,
powerful in the heavens is the LORD.
5 Your decrees are firmly established;
holiness befits your house, LORD,
for all the length of days.

## PSALM 94*

See RG 175

### A Prayer for Deliverance from the Wicked

I

1 LORD, avenging God,
avenging God, shine forth![x]
2 Rise up, O judge of the earth;
give the proud what they deserve![y]

II

3 How long, LORD, shall the wicked,
how long shall the wicked glory?[z]
4 How long will they mouth haughty
speeches,
go on boasting, all these evildoers?[a]
5 They crush your people, LORD,
torment your very own.
6 They kill the widow and alien;
the orphan they murder.[b]
7 They say, "The LORD does not see;
the God of Jacob takes no notice."[c]

III

8 Understand, you stupid people!
You fools, when will you be wise?[d]
9 Does the one who shaped the ear not
hear?
The one who formed the eye not see?[e]
10 Does the one who guides nations not
rebuke?
The one who teaches man not have
knowledge?
11 The LORD knows the plans of man;
they are like a fleeting breath.[f]

IV

12 Blessed the one whom you guide, LORD,[g]

**92:14 Planted**: the just are likened to trees growing in the sacred precincts of the Temple, which is often seen as the source of life and fertility because of God's presence, cf. Ps 36:9, 10; Ez 47:1–12.

**Psalm 93** A hymn celebrating the kingship of God, who created the world (Ps 93:1–2) by defeating the sea (Ps 93:3–4). In the ancient myth that is alluded to here, Sea completely covered the land, making it impossible for the human community to live. Sea, or Flood, roars in anger against God, who is personified in the storm. God's utterances or decrees are given authority by the victory over Sea (Ps 93:5).

**93:1 The LORD is king**: lit., "the LORD reigns." This Psalm, and Ps 47; 96–99, are sometimes called enthronement Psalms. They may have been used in a special liturgy during which God's ascent to the throne was ritually reenacted. They have also been interpreted eschatologically, pointing to the coming of God as king at the end-time.

**93:3 The flood**: the primordial sea was tamed by God in the act of creation. It is a figure of chaos and rebellion, cf. Ps 46:4.

**Psalm 94** A lament of an individual who is threatened by wicked people. The danger affects the whole community. Calling upon God as judge (Ps 94:1–2), the Psalm complains about oppression of the holy community by people within (Ps 94:3–7). Bold declarations of faith follow: denunciation of evildoers (Ps 94:8–11) and assurance to the just (Ps 94:12–15). The Psalm continues with further lament (Ps 94:16–19) and ends with strong confidence in God's response (Ps 94:20–23).

*r:* Ps 91:8. *s:* Ps 1:3; 52:10; Jer 17:8. *t:* Dt 32:4. *u:* Ps 47:8; 96:10; 97:1; 99:1. *v:* Ps 75:2–3; 104:5. *w:* Ps 55:20; 90:2; 102:13; Heb 1:12. *x:* Na 1:2. *y:* Jer 51:56; Lam 3:64. *z:* Ps 13:2; 75:5; Jer 12:1. *a:* Ps 73; Mal 2:17; 3:14. *b:* Ex 22:21–22; Dt 24:17–22. *c:* Ps 10:11; 64:6; 73:11; Jb 22:13–14; Ez 9:9. *d:* Prv 1:22; 8:5. *e:* Ex 4:11; Prv 20:12. *f:* Ps 33:15; 1 Cor 3:20. *g:* Ps 119:71; Jb 5:17.

whom you teach by your instruction,
13 To give rest from evil days,
while a pit is being dug for the wicked.
14 For the LORD will not forsake his people,
nor abandon his inheritance.[h]
15 Judgment shall again be just,
and all the upright of heart will follow it.

V

16 Who will rise up for me against the wicked?
Who will stand up for me against evildoers?
17 If the LORD were not my help,
I would long have been silent in the grave.[i]
18 When I say, "My foot is slipping,"
your mercy, LORD, holds me up.[j]
19 When cares increase within me,
your comfort gives me joy.

VI

20 Can unjust judges be your allies,
those who create burdens by decree,
21 Those who conspire against the just
and condemn the innocent to death?
22 No, the LORD is my secure height,
my God, my rock of refuge,
23 [k]Who will turn back their evil upon them[l]
and destroy them for their wickedness.
Surely the LORD our God will destroy them!

## PSALM 95*

See RG 175

### A Call to Praise and Obedience

I

1 Come, let us sing joyfully to the LORD;
cry out to the rock of our salvation.[m]
2 Let us come before him with a song of praise,
joyfully sing out our psalms.
3 For the LORD is the great God,
the great king over all gods,[n]
4 Whose hand holds the depths of the earth;
who owns the tops of the mountains.
5 The sea and dry land belong to God,
who made them, formed them by hand.[o]

II

6 Enter, let us bow down in worship;
let us kneel before the LORD who made us.
7 For he is our God,
we are the people he shepherds,
the sheep in his hands.[p]

III

Oh, that today you would hear his voice:[q]
8 Do not harden your hearts as at Meribah,
as on the day of Massah in the desert.*
9 There your ancestors tested me;
they tried me though they had seen my works.[r]
10 Forty years I loathed that generation;
I said: "This people's heart goes astray;
they do not know my ways."[s]
11 Therefore I swore in my anger:
"They shall never enter my rest."*

## PSALM 96*

See RG 176

### God of the Universe

I

1 Sing to the LORD a new song;[t]
sing to the LORD, all the earth.
2 Sing to the LORD, bless his name;
proclaim his salvation day after day.
3 Tell his glory among the nations;
among all peoples, his marvelous deeds.[u]

**Psalm 95** Twice the Psalm calls the people to praise and worship God (Ps 95:1–2, 6), the king of all creatures (Ps 95:3–5) and shepherd of the flock (Ps 95:7a, 7b). The last strophe warns the people to be more faithful than were their ancestors in the journey to the promised land (Ps 95:7c–11). This invitation to praise God regularly opens the Church's official prayer, the Liturgy of the Hours.

**95:8 Meribah**: lit., "contention"; the place where the Israelites quarreled with God. **Massah**: "testing," the place where they put God to the trial, cf. Ex 17:7; Nm 20:13.

**95:11 My rest**: the promised land as in Dt 12:9. Heb 4 applies the verse to the eternal rest of heaven.

**Psalm 96** A hymn inviting all humanity to praise the glories of Israel's God (Ps 96:1–3), who is the sole God (Ps 96:4–6). To the just ruler of all belongs worship (Ps 96:7–10); even inanimate creation is to offer praise (Ps 96:11–13). This Psalm has numerous verbal and thematic contacts with Is 40–55, as does Ps 98. Another version of the Psalm is 1 Chr 16:23–33.

*h:* 1 Sm 12:22; Sir 47:22. *i:* Ps 6:6; 115:17. *j:* Ps 145:14. *k:* Ps 7:16; 9:16; 35:8; 57:7; Prv 26:27; Eccl 10:8; Sir 27:26. *l:* Ps 107:42. *m:* Dt 32:15. *n:* Ps 47:2; 135:5. *o:* Ps 24:1–2. *p:* Ps 81:8; 106:32; Heb 3:7–11, 15; 4:3, 5, 7. *q:* Ps 23:1–3; 100:3; Mi 7:14. *r:* Nm 14:22; 20:2–13; Dt 6:16; 33:8. *s:* Ps 78:8; Nm 14:34; Dt 32:5. *t:* Ps 98:1; Is 42:10. *u:* Ps 98:4; 105:1.

II

4 *For great is the LORD and highly to be praised,
to be feared above all gods.[v]
5 For the gods of the nations are idols,
but the LORD made the heavens.[w]
6 Splendor and power go before him;
power and grandeur are in his holy place.

III

7 Give to the LORD, you families of nations,
give to the LORD glory and might;
8 give to the LORD the glory due his name![x]
Bring gifts and enter his courts;
9 bow down to the LORD, splendid in holiness.
Tremble before him, all the earth;
10 [y]declare among the nations: The LORD is king.
The world will surely stand fast, never to be shaken.
He rules the peoples with fairness.

IV

11 Let the heavens be glad and the earth rejoice;
let the sea and what fills it resound;[z]
12 let the plains be joyful and all that is in them.
Then let all the trees of the forest rejoice
13 before the LORD who comes,
who comes to govern the earth,[a]
To govern the world with justice
and the peoples with faithfulness.

## PSALM 97*

See RG 175

### *The Divine Ruler of All*

I

1 The LORD is king; let the earth rejoice;
let the many islands be glad.[b]
2 Cloud and darkness surround him;
justice and right are the foundation of his throne.[c]
3 Fire goes before him,
consuming his foes on every side.
4 His lightning illumines the world;
the earth sees and trembles.[d]
5 The mountains melt like wax before the LORD,
before the Lord of all the earth.[e]
6 The heavens proclaim his justice;
all peoples see his glory.[f]

II

7 All who serve idols are put to shame,
who glory in worthless things;
all gods* bow down before him.[g]
8 Zion hears and is glad,
and the daughters of Judah rejoice
because of your judgments, O LORD.[h]
9 For you, LORD, are the Most High over all the earth,[i]
exalted far above all gods.
10 You who love the LORD, hate evil,
he protects the souls of the faithful,[j]
rescues them from the hand of the wicked.
11 Light dawns for the just,
and gladness for the honest of heart.[k]
12 Rejoice in the LORD, you just,
and give thanks at the remembrance of his holiness.[l]

## PSALM 98*

See RG 175

### *The Coming of God*

1 A psalm.

I

Sing a new song to the LORD,
for he has done marvelous deeds.[m]
His right hand and holy arm
have won the victory. *[n]

**96:4** For references to other gods, see comments on Ps 58 and 82.

**Psalm 97** The hymn begins with God appearing in a storm, a traditional picture of some ancient Near Eastern gods (Ps 97:1–6); cf. Ps 18:8–16; Mi 1:3–4; Heb 3:3–15. Israel rejoices in the overthrowing of idol worshipers and their gods (Ps 97:7–9) and the rewarding of the faithful righteous (Ps 97:10–12).

**97:7 All gods**: divine beings thoroughly subordinate to Israel's God. The Greek translates "angels," an interpretation adopted by Heb 1:6.

**Psalm 98** A hymn, similar to Ps 96, extolling God for Israel's victory (Ps 98:1–3). All nations (Ps 98:4–6) and even inanimate nature (Ps 98:7–8) are summoned to welcome God's coming to rule over the world (Ps 98:9).

**98:1 Marvelous deeds . . . victory**: the conquest of all

*v:* Ps 48:2; 95:3; 145:3. *w:* Ps 97:7; 115:4–8; Is 40:17; 1 Cor 8:4. *x:* Ps 29:2. *y:* Ps 75:4; 93:1. *z:* Ps 98:7. *a:* Ps 98:9. *b:* Ps 75:4; 93:1; 96:10. *c:* Ps 85:11; 89:15; Ex 19:6; Dt 4:11; 5:22; 1 Kgs 8:12. *d:* Ps 18:8; 50:3; 77:18; 99:1; Jgs 5:4–5. *e:* Jdt 16:15; Mi 1:4. *f:* Ps 50:6. *g:* Ps 96:5. *h:* Ps 48:12. *i:* Ps 83:19. *j:* Ps 121:7. *k:* Ps 112:4. *l:* Ps 30:5. *m:* Ps 96:1; Is 42:10. *n:* Is 59:16; 63:5.

2 The LORD has made his victory known;
has revealed his triumph in the sight of the nations,
3 He has remembered his mercy and faithfulness
toward the house of Israel.
All the ends of the earth have seen
the victory of our God.

II

4 Shout with joy to the LORD, all the earth;
break into song; sing praise.
5 Sing praise to the LORD with the lyre,
with the lyre and melodious song.
6 With trumpets and the sound of the horn
shout with joy to the King, the LORD.[o]

III

7 Let the sea and what fills it resound,[p]
the world and those who dwell there.
8 Let the rivers clap their hands,
the mountains shout with them for joy,[q]
9 [r]Before the LORD who comes,
who comes to govern the earth,[s]
To govern the world with justice
and the peoples with fairness.

See RG 175

## PSALM 99*

### *The Holy King*

I

1 The LORD is king, the peoples tremble;
he is enthroned on the cherubim,* the earth quakes.[t]
2 Great is the LORD in Zion,
exalted above all the peoples.
3 Let them praise your great and awesome name:
Holy is he![u]

II

4 O mighty king, lover of justice,
you have established fairness;
you have created just rule in Jacob.[v]
5 Exalt the LORD, our God;
bow down before his footstool;*[w]
holy is he!

III

6 Moses and Aaron were among his priests,
Samuel among those who called on his name;
they called on the LORD, and he answered them.[x]
7 From the pillar of cloud he spoke to them;
they kept his decrees, the law he had given them.[y]
8 O LORD, our God, you answered them;
you were a forgiving God to them,
though you punished their offenses.[z]
9 Exalt the LORD, our God;
bow down before his holy mountain;
holy is the LORD, our God.

## PSALM 100*

See RG 175

### *Processional Hymn*

1 A psalm of thanksgiving.

Shout joyfully to the LORD, all you lands;
2 serve the LORD with gladness;
come before him with joyful song.
3 *Know that the LORD is God,
he made us, we belong to him,
we are his people, the flock he shepherds.[a]
4 Enter his gates with thanksgiving,
his courts with praise.
Give thanks to him, bless his name;[b]

threats to the peaceful existence of Israel, depicted in the Psalms variously as a cosmic force such as sea, or nations bent on Israel's destruction, or evildoers seemingly triumphant. **His right hand and holy arm**: God is pictured as a powerful warrior.

**Psalm 99** A hymn to God as the king whose grandeur is most clearly seen on Mount Zion (Ps 99:2) and in the laws given to Israel (Ps 99:4). Israel is special because of God's word of justice, which was mediated by the revered speakers, Moses, Aaron, and Samuel (Ps 99:6–8). The poem is structured by the threefold statement that God is holy (Ps 99:3, 5, 9) and by the twice-repeated command to praise (Ps 99:5, 9).

**99:1 Enthroned on the cherubim**: cherubim were composite beings with animal and human features, common in ancient Near Eastern art. Two cherubim were placed on the ark (or box) of the covenant in the holy of holies. Upon them God was believed to dwell invisibly, cf. Ex 25:20–22; 1 Sm 4:4; 2 Sm 6:2; Ps 80:2.

**99:5 Footstool**: a reference to the ark, cf. 1 Chr 28:2; Ps 132:7.

**Psalm 100** A hymn inviting the people to enter the Temple courts with thank offerings for the God who created them.

**100:3** Although the people call on all the nations of the world to join in their hymn, they are conscious of being the chosen people of God.

*o:* Ps 47:6–7. *p:* Ps 96:11. *q:* Is 44:23; 55:12. *r:* Ps 96:13. *s:* Ps 67:5. *t:* Ps 18:8–11; 80:2; 93:1; Ex 25:22; 1 Sm 4:4; 2 Sm 6:2. *u:* Is 6:3. *v:* Ps 72:1; Jer 23:5. *w:* Ps 132:7. *x:* Jer 15:1. *y:* Ex 33:9; Nm 12:5. *z:* Ex 32:11; Nm 20:12. *a:* Ps 23:1; 95:7; Mi 7:14; Is 64:7. *b:* Ps 106:1; 107:1; 118:1; 136:1; 138:8; Jer 33:11.

5 good indeed is the LORD,
His mercy endures forever,
his faithfulness lasts through every generation.

## PSALM 101*

See RG 176

### *Norm of Life for Rulers*

1 A psalm of David.

I

I sing of mercy and justice;
to you, LORD, I sing praise.
2 I study the way of integrity;[c]
when will you come to me?
I act with integrity of heart
within my household.*[d]
3 I do not allow into my presence anything base.
I hate wrongdoing;
I will have no part of it.[e]
4 May the devious heart keep far from me;
the wicked I will not acknowledge.
5 Whoever slanders a neighbor in secret
I will reduce to silence.[f]
Haughty eyes and arrogant hearts[g]
I cannot endure.

II

6 I look to the faithful of the land*
to sit at my side.
Whoever follows the way of integrity[h]
is the one to enter my service.
7 No one who practices deceit
can remain within my house.
No one who speaks falsely
can last in my presence.[i]
8 *Morning after morning I clear all the wicked from the land,
to rid the city of the LORD of all doers of evil.

## PSALM 102*

See RG 175

### *Prayer in Time of Distress*

1 The prayer of one afflicted and wasting away whose anguish is poured out before the LORD.

I

2 LORD, hear my prayer;
let my cry come to you.
3 Do not hide your face from me
in the day of my distress.[j]
Turn your ear to me;
when I call, answer me quickly.
4 For my days vanish like smoke;[k]
my bones burn away as in a furnace.
5 My heart is withered, dried up like grass,
too wasted to eat my food.
6 From my loud groaning
I become just skin and bones.
7 I am like a desert owl,
like an owl among the ruins.
8 I lie awake and moan,
like a lone sparrow on the roof.
9 All day long my enemies taunt me;
in their rage, they make my name a curse.*
10 I eat ashes like bread,
mingle my drink with tears.[l]
11 Because of your furious wrath,
you lifted me up just to cast me down.
12 [m]My days are like a lengthening shadow;[n]
I wither like the grass.

II

13 But you, LORD, are enthroned forever;
your renown is for all generations.[o]
14 You will again show mercy to Zion;
now is the time for pity;

**Psalm 101** The king, grateful at being God's chosen (Ps 101:1), promises to be a ruler after God's own heart (Ps 101:2–3), allowing into the royal service only the God-fearing (Ps 101:3–8).

**101:2 Within my household**: the king promises to make his own household, i.e., the royal court, a model for Israel, banning all officials who abuse their power.

**101:6 I look to the faithful of the land**: the king seeks companions only among those faithful to God.

**101:8 Morning after morning**: the morning is the normal time for the administration of justice (2 Sm 15:2; Jer 21:12) and for the arrival of divine aid (Ps 59:17; 143:8; Is 33:2). **I clear all the wicked from the land**: the king, as God's servant, is responsible for seeing that divine justice is carried out.

**Psalm 102** A lament, one of the Penitential Psalms. The psalmist, experiencing psychological and bodily disintegration (Ps 102:4–12), cries out to God (Ps 102:1–3). In the Temple precincts where God has promised to be present, the psalmist recalls God's venerable promises to save the poor (Ps 102:13–23). The final part (Ps 102:24–28) restates the original complaint and prayer, and emphasizes God's eternity.

**102:9 They make my name a curse**: enemies use the psalmist's name in phrases such as, "May you be as wretched as this person!"

*c:* Ps 26:11; Is 33:15. *d:* 1 Kgs 9:4. *e:* Prv 11:20. *f:* Prv 17:20; 30:10. *g:* Prv 21:4. *h:* Ps 26:11; Prv 20:7. *i:* Ps 5:5; Prv 25:5. *j:* Ps 69:18; 143:7. *k:* Ps 38:7–9. *l:* Ps 42:4; 80:6. *m:* Ps 109:23; 144:4; Jb 8:9; 14:2; Eccl 6:12; Wis 2:5. *n:* Ps 90:5–6. *o:* Ps 55:20; 90:2; 93:2; 135:13; 145:13; Lam 5:19; Heb 1:12.

the appointed time has come.
15 Its stones are dear to your servants;
its dust moves them to pity.
16 The nations shall fear your name, LORD,
all the kings of the earth, your glory,[p]
17 Once the LORD has rebuilt Zion
and appeared in glory,
18 Heeding the plea of the lowly,
not scorning their prayer.
19 Let this be written for the next generation,
for a people not yet born,
that they may praise the LORD:[q]
20 *"The LORD looked down from the holy heights,
viewed the earth from heaven,[r]
21 To attend to the groaning of the prisoners,
to release those doomed to die."[s]
22 Then the LORD's name will be declared on Zion,
his praise in Jerusalem,
23 When peoples and kingdoms gather
to serve the LORD.[t]

III

24 He has shattered my strength in mid-course,
has cut short my days.
25 I plead, O my God,
do not take me in the midst of my days.*[u]
Your years last through all generations.
26 Of old you laid the earth's foundations;[v]
the heavens are the work of your hands.
27 They perish, but you remain;
they all wear out like a garment;
Like clothing you change them and they are changed,
28 but you are the same, your years have no end.
29 May the children of your servants live on;
may their descendants live in your presence.[w]

## PSALM 103*

See RG 175–76

### *Praise of Divine Goodness*

1 Of David.

I

Bless the LORD, my soul;
all my being, bless his holy name!
2 Bless the LORD, my soul;
and do not forget all his gifts,
3 Who pardons all your sins,
and heals all your ills,
4 Who redeems your life from the pit,[x]
and crowns you with mercy and compassion,
5 Who fills your days with good things,
so your youth is renewed like the eagle's.*

II

6 The LORD does righteous deeds,
brings justice to all the oppressed.[y]
7 He made known his ways to Moses,
to the Israelites his deeds.
8 Merciful and gracious is the LORD,
slow to anger, abounding in mercy.[z]
9 He will not always accuse,
and nurses no lasting anger;
10 He has not dealt with us as our sins merit,
nor requited us as our wrongs deserve.

III

11 For as the heavens tower over the earth,
so his mercy towers over those who fear him.[a]
12 As far as the east is from the west,
so far has he removed our sins from us.
13 As a father has compassion on his children,
so the LORD has compassion on those who fear him.

**102:20–23** Both Ps 102:20–21 and Ps 102:22–23 depend on Ps 102:19.

**102:25 In the midst of my days**: when the normal span of life is but half completed, cf. Is 38:10; Jer 17:11.

**Psalm 103** The speaker in this hymn begins by praising God for personal benefits (Ps 103:1–5), then moves on to God's mercy toward all the people (Ps 103:6–18). Even sin cannot destroy that mercy (Ps 103:11–13), for the eternal God is well aware of the people's human fragility (Ps 103:14–18). The psalmist invites the heavenly beings to join in praise (Ps 103:19–22).

**103:5 Your youth is renewed like the eagle's**: because of the eagle's long life it was a symbol of perennial youth and vigor, cf. Is 40:31.

*p:* Is 59:19; 66:18. *q:* Ps 22:31–32. *r:* Ps 11:4; 14:2. *s:* Ps 79:11. *t:* Is 60:3–4; Zec 2:15; 8:22. *u:* Ps 39:5; 90:10; Jb 14:5. *v:* Heb 1:10–12. *w:* Ps 69:36–37. *x:* Ps 28:1; 30:4; 40:3; 69:16; 88:5; 143:7; Prv 1:12; Jon 2:7. *y:* Ps 146:6–7. *z:* Ps 86:15; 145:8; Ex 34:6–7; Nm 14:18; Jer 3:12; Jl 2:13; Jon 4:2. *a:* Is 55:9.

[14] For he knows how we are formed,
remembers that we are dust.[b]
[15] As for man, his days are like the grass;
he blossoms like a flower in the field.[c]
[16] A wind sweeps over it and it is gone;
its place knows it no more.
[17] But the LORD's mercy is from age to age,
toward those who fear him.
His salvation is for the children's
children
[18] of those who keep his covenant,
and remember to carry out his
precepts.

IV

[19] The LORD has set his throne in heaven;
his dominion extends over all.
[20] Bless the LORD, all you his angels,[d]
mighty in strength, acting at his behest,
obedient to his command.
[21] Bless the LORD, all you his hosts,
his ministers who carry out his will.
[22] Bless the LORD, all his creatures,
everywhere in his domain.
Bless the LORD, my soul!

## PSALM 104*

See RG 175, 178

### *Praise of God the Creator*

I

[1] Bless the LORD, my soul!
LORD, my God, you are great indeed!
You are clothed with majesty and
splendor,
[2] robed in light as with a cloak.
You spread out the heavens like a tent;[e]
[3] setting the beams of your chambers
upon the waters.*
You make the clouds your chariot;
traveling on the wings of the wind.
[4] You make the winds your messengers;
flaming fire, your ministers.[f]

II

[5] *You fixed the earth on its foundation,
so it can never be shaken.
[6] The deeps covered it like a garment;
above the mountains stood the waters.
[7] At your rebuke they took flight;
at the sound of your thunder they fled.[g]
[8] They rushed up the mountains, down the
valleys
to the place you had fixed for them.
[9] You set a limit they cannot pass;
never again will they cover the earth.[h]

III

[10] You made springs flow in wadies
that wind among the mountains.
[11] They give drink to every beast of the field;[i]
here wild asses quench their thirst.
[12] Beside them the birds of heaven nest;
among the branches they sing.
[13] You water the mountains from your
chambers;
from the fruit of your labor the earth
abounds.
[14] You make the grass grow for the cattle
and plants for people's work
to bring forth food from the earth,
[15] wine to gladden their hearts,
oil to make their faces shine,
and bread to sustain the human heart.
[16] *The trees of the LORD drink their fill,
the cedars of Lebanon, which you
planted.
[17] There the birds build their nests;
the stork in the junipers, its home.[j]
[18] The high mountains are for wild goats;
the rocky cliffs, a refuge for badgers.

IV

[19] You made the moon to mark the seasons,[k]
the sun that knows the hour of its
setting.

**Psalm 104** A hymn praising God who easily and skillfully made rampaging waters and primordial night into a world vibrant with life. The psalmist describes God's splendor in the heavens (Ps 104:1–4), how the chaotic waters were tamed to fertilize and feed the world (Ps 104:5–18), and how primordial night was made into a gentle time of refreshment (Ps 104:19–23). The picture is like Gn 1:1–2: a dark and watery chaos is made dry and lighted so that creatures might live. The psalmist reacts to the beauty of creation with awe (Ps 104:24–34). May sin not deface God's work (Ps 104:35)!

**104:3 Your chambers upon the waters**: God's heavenly dwelling above the upper waters of the sky, cf. Gn 1:6–7; Ps 29:10.

**104:5–9** God places the gigantic disk of the earth securely on its foundation and then, as a warrior, chases away the enveloping waters and confines them under, above, and around the earth.

**104:16–18** Even the exotic flora and fauna of the high mountains of the Lebanon range receive adequate water.

*b:* Ps 90:3. *c:* Ps 37:2; 90:5–6; Is 40:7. *d:* Ps 148:2; Dn 3:58. *e:* Prv 8:27–28; Jb 9:8; Is 40:22; Gn 1:6–7; Am 9:6. *f:* Heb 1:7. *g:* Ps 29:3. *h:* Jer 5:22; Gn 9:11–15. *i:* Ps 147:8–9. *j:* Ez 31:6. *k:* Sir 43:6.

20 You bring darkness and night falls,
then all the animals of the forest
wander about.
21 Young lions roar for prey;
they seek their food from God.[l]
22 When the sun rises, they steal away
and settle down in their dens.
23 People go out to their work,
to their labor till evening falls.

V

24 How varied are your works, LORD!
In wisdom you have made them all;
the earth is full of your creatures.[m]
25 There is the sea, great and wide!
It teems with countless beings,
living things both large and small.[n]
26 There ships ply their course
and Leviathan,* whom you formed to
play with.[o]

VI

27 All of these look to you
to give them food in due time.[p]
28 When you give it to them, they gather;
when you open your hand, they are
well filled.
29 *When you hide your face, they panic.
Take away their breath, they perish
and return to the dust.[q]
30 Send forth your spirit, they are created
and you renew the face of the earth.

VII

31 May the glory of the LORD endure
forever;
may the LORD be glad in his works!
32 Who looks at the earth and it trembles,
touches the mountains and they
smoke![r]
33 I will sing to the LORD all my life;
I will sing praise to my God while I
live.[s]
34 May my meditation be pleasing to him;
I will rejoice in the LORD.
35 May sinners vanish from the earth,
and the wicked be no more.
Bless the LORD, my soul! Hallelujah!*

## PSALM 105*

See RG 176

### *God's Fidelity to the Promise*

I

1 Give thanks to the LORD, invoke his name;[t]
make known among the peoples his
deeds![u]
2 Sing praise to him, play music;
proclaim all his wondrous deeds!
3 Glory in his holy name;
let hearts that seek the LORD rejoice!
4 Seek out the LORD and his might;
constantly seek his face.[v]
5 Recall the wondrous deeds he has done,
his wonders and words of judgment,
6 You descendants of Abraham his servant,
offspring of Jacob the chosen one!

II

7 He the LORD, is our God
whose judgments reach through all the
earth.
8 He remembers forever his covenant,
the word he commanded for a
thousand generations,
9 Which he made with Abraham,
and swore to Isaac,[w]
10 And ratified in a statute for Jacob,
an everlasting covenant for Israel:
11 "To you I give the land of Canaan,
your own allotted inheritance."[x]

III

12 When they were few in number,[y]
a handful, and strangers there,
13 Wandering from nation to nation,
from one kingdom to another people,

**104:26 Leviathan**: a sea monster symbolizing primeval chaos, cf. Ps 74:14; Is 27:1; Jb 40:25. God does not destroy chaos but makes it part of the created order.

**104:29–30** On one level, the spirit (or wind) of God is the fall and winter rains that provide food for all creatures. On another, it is the breath (or spirit) of God that makes beings live.

**104:35 Hallelujah**: a frequent word in the last third of the Psalter. The word combines the plural imperative of praise (*hallelu*) with an abbreviated form of the divine name Yah(weh).

**Psalm 105** A hymn to God who promised the land of Canaan to the holy people, cf. Ps 78; 106; 136. Israel is invited to praise and seek the presence of God (Ps 105:1–6), who is faithful to the promise of land to the ancestors (Ps 105:7–11). In every phase of the national story—the ancestors in the land of Canaan (Ps 105:12–15), Joseph in Egypt (Ps 105:16–22), Israel in Egypt (Ps 105:23–38), Israel in the desert on the way to Canaan (Ps 105:39–45)—God remained faithful, reiterating the promise of the land to successive servants.

*l:* Jb 38:39. *m:* Ps 92:6; Sir 39:16. *n:* Sir 43:26. *o:* Jb 3:8; 40:25, 29. *p:* Ps 136:25; 145:15–16. *q:* Ps 90:3; Jb 34:14–15; Eccl 3:20. *r:* Ps 144:5. *s:* Ps 146:2. *t:* 1 Chr 16:8–22. *u:* Ps 18:50; 96:3; 145:5; Is 12:4–5. *v:* Ps 24:6; 27:8. *w:* Gn 15:1ff; 26:3. *x:* Gn 12:7; 15:18. *y:* Dt 4:27; 26:5.

14 He let no one oppress them;
for their sake he rebuked kings:*
15 *"Do not touch my anointed ones,
to my prophets do no harm."

IV

16 Then he called down a famine on the land,
destroyed the grain that sustained them.*[z]
17 He had sent a man ahead of them,
Joseph, sold as a slave.[a]
18 They shackled his feet with chains;
collared his neck in iron,[b]
19 Till his prediction came to pass,
and the word of the LORD proved him
true.[c]
20 The king sent and released him;
the ruler of peoples set him free.[d]
21 He made him lord over his household,
ruler over all his possessions,[e]
22 To instruct his princes as he desired,
to teach his elders wisdom.

V

23 Then Israel entered Egypt;[f]
Jacob sojourned in the land of Ham.*
24 God greatly increased his people,
made them more numerous than their
foes.[g]
25 He turned their hearts to hate his people,
to treat his servants deceitfully.[h]
26 He sent his servant Moses,
and Aaron whom he had chosen.[i]
27 *They worked his signs in Egypt[j]
and wonders in the land of Ham.
28 He sent darkness and it grew dark,
but they rebelled against his word.
29 He turned their waters into blood
and killed their fish.
30 Their land swarmed with frogs,
even the chambers of their kings.
31 He spoke and there came swarms of flies,
gnats through all their country.
32 For rain he gave them hail,
flashes of lightning throughout their
land.
33 He struck down their vines and fig trees,
shattered the trees of their country.
34 He spoke and the locusts came,
grasshoppers without number.[k]
35 They devoured every plant in the land;
they devoured the crops of their fields.
36 He struck down every firstborn in the land,
the first fruits of all their vigor.
37 He brought his people out,
laden with silver and gold;[l]
no one among the tribes stumbled.
38 Egypt rejoiced when they left,
for fear had seized them.

VI

39 He spread a cloud out as a cover,
and made a fire to light up the night.[m]
40 They asked and he brought them quail;
with bread from heaven he filled them.[n]
41 He split the rock and water gushed forth;
it flowed through the desert like a river.[o]
42 For he remembered his sacred promise
to Abraham his servant.
43 He brought his people out with joy,
his chosen ones with shouts of triumph.
44 He gave them the lands of the nations,
they took possession of the wealth of
the peoples,[p]
45 That they might keep his statutes
and observe his teachings.[q]
Hallelujah!

## PSALM 106*

See RG 175

### *Israel's Confession of Sin*

1 Hallelujah!

A

Give thanks to the LORD, who is good,
whose mercy endures forever.[r]

**105:14 Kings**: Pharaoh and Abimelech of Gerar, cf. Gn 12:17; 20:6–7.

**105:15 My anointed ones . . . my prophets**: the patriarchs Abraham, Isaac, and Jacob, who were "anointed" in the sense of being consecrated and recipients of God's revelation.

**105:16 The grain that sustained them**: lit., every "staff of bread."

**105:23, 27 The land of Ham**: a synonym for Egypt, cf. Gn 10:6.

**105:27–38** This Psalm and Ps 78:43–51 have an account of the plagues differing in number or in order from Ex 7:14–12:30. Several versions of the exodus story were current.

**Psalm 106** Israel is invited to praise the God whose mercy has always tempered judgment of Israel (Ps 106:1–3). The speaker, on behalf of all, seeks solidarity with the people,

*z:* Gn 41:54, 57. *a:* Gn 37:28, 36; 45:5. *b:* Gn 39:20. *c:* Gn 40–41. *d:* Gn 41:14. *e:* Gn 41:41–44. *f:* Gn 46:1–47:12; Acts 7:15. *g:* Ex 1:7; Acts 7:17. *h:* Ex 1:8–14. *i:* Ex 3:10; 4:27. *j:* Ps 78:43–51; Ex 7–12. *k:* Jl 1:4. *l:* Ex 12:33–36. *m:* Ps 78:14; Ex 13:21–22; Wis 18:3. *n:* Ps 78:24–28; Ex 16:13–15; Nm 11:31ff; Wis 16:20. *o:* Ps 78:15–16; Ex 17:1–7; Nm 20:11. *p:* Dt 4:37–40. *q:* Dt 6:20–25; 7:8–11. *r:* Ps 100:5; 107:1; 1 Chr 16:34; Jer 33:11; Dn 3:89.

2 Who can recount the mighty deeds of the LORD,
proclaim in full God's praise?
3 Blessed those who do what is right,
whose deeds are always just.[s]
4 Remember me, LORD, as you favor your people;
come to me with your saving help,[t]
5 That I may see the prosperity of your chosen ones,
rejoice in the joy of your people,
and glory with your heritage.

B

6 We have sinned like our ancestors;[u]
we have done wrong and are guilty.

I

7 Our ancestors in Egypt
did not attend to your wonders.
They did not remember your manifold mercy;
they defied the Most High at the Red Sea.
8 Yet he saved them for his name's sake
to make his power known.[v]
9 He roared at the Red Sea and it dried up.
He led them through the deep as through a desert.[w]
10 He rescued them from hostile hands,
freed them from the power of the enemy.
11 The waters covered their oppressors;
not one of them survived.
12 Then they believed his words
and sang his praise.[x]

II

13 But they soon forgot all he had done;
they had no patience for his plan.
14 In the desert they gave in to their cravings,
tempted God in the wasteland.[y]
15 So he gave them what they asked
and sent a wasting disease against them.[z]

III

16 In the camp they challenged Moses[a]
and Aaron, the holy one of the LORD.
17 The earth opened and swallowed Dathan,
it closed on the followers of Abiram.
18 Against their company the fire blazed;
flames consumed the wicked.

IV

19 At Horeb they fashioned a calf,[b]
worshiped a metal statue.
20 They exchanged their glory*
for the image of a grass-eating bull.
21 They forgot the God who had saved them,
who had done great deeds in Egypt,[c]
22 Amazing deeds in the land of Ham,
fearsome deeds at the Red Sea.
23 He would have decreed their destruction,
had not Moses, his chosen one,
Withstood him in the breach*
to turn back his destroying anger.[d]

V

24 Next they despised the beautiful land;[e]
they did not believe the promise.
25 In their tents they complained;
they did not heed the voice of the LORD.
26 So with raised hand he swore
he would destroy them in the desert,
27 And scatter their descendants among the nations,
disperse them in foreign lands.

who can always count on God's fidelity despite their sin (Ps 106:4–5). Confident of God's mercy, the speaker invites national repentance (Ps 106:6) by reciting from Israel's history eight instances of sin, judgment, and forgiveness. The sins are the rebellion at the Red Sea (Ps 106:6–12; see Ex 14–15), the craving for meat in the desert (Ps 106:13–15; see Nm 11), the challenge to Moses' authority (Ps 106:16–18; see Nm 16), the golden calf episode (Ps 106:19–23; see Ex 32–34), the refusal to take Canaan by the southern route (Ps 106:24–27; see Nm 13–14 and Dt 1–2), the rebellion at Baal-Peor (Ps 106:28–31; see Nm 25:1–10), the anger of Moses (Ps 106:32–33; see Nm 20:1–13), and mingling with the nations (Ps 106:34–47). The last, as suggested by its length and generalized language, may be the sin that invites the repentance of the present generation. The text gives the site of each sin: Egypt (Ps 106:7), the desert (Ps 106:14), the camp (Ps 106:16), Horeb (Ps 106:19), in their tents (Ps 106:25), Baal-Peor (Ps 106:28), the waters of Meribah (Ps 106:32), Canaan (Ps 106:38).

**106:20 Their glory**: meant as a reference to God.

**106:23 Withstood him in the breach**: the image is that of Moses standing in a narrow break made in the wall to keep anyone from entering.

*s:* Is 56:1–2. *t:* Ps 25:7; Neh 5:19. *u:* Ps 78:11–17; Ex 14:11; Lv 26:40; 1 Kgs 8:47; Bar 2:12; Dn 9:5. *v:* Ez 36:20–22. *w:* Ex 14:21–31; Is 50:2; 63:11–14; Na 1:4. *x:* Ex 15:1–21. *y:* Ps 78:18; Ex 15:24; 16:3; Nm 11:1–6. *z:* Ps 78:26–31; Nm 11:33. *a:* Nm 16; Dt 11:6; Is 26:11. *b:* Ex 32; Dt 9:8–21; Jer 2:11; Acts 7:41; Rom 1:23. *c:* Ps 78:42–58; Dt 32:18; Jer 2:32. *d:* Ex 32:11; Dt 9:25; Ez 22:30. *e:* Lv 26:33; Nm 14; Dt 1:25–36; Ez 20:15, 23.

VI

28 They joined in the rites of Baal of Peor,[f]
ate food sacrificed to the dead.
29 They provoked him by their actions,
and a plague broke out among them.
30 Then Phinehas rose to intervene,
and the plague was brought to a halt.
31 This was counted for him as a righteous deed
for all generations to come.

VII

32 At the waters of Meribah they angered God,[g]
and Moses suffered because of them.*
33 They so embittered his spirit
that rash words crossed his lips.

VIII

34 They did not destroy the peoples
as the LORD had commanded them,[h]
35 But mingled with the nations
and imitated their ways.[i]
36 They served their idols
and were ensnared by them.[j]
37 They sacrificed to demons*
their own sons and daughters,
38 Shedding innocent blood,
the blood of their own sons and daughters,
Whom they sacrificed to the idols of Canaan,
desecrating the land with bloodshed.
39 They defiled themselves by their actions,
became adulterers by their conduct.
40 So the LORD grew angry with his people,
abhorred his own heritage.
41 He handed them over to the nations,
and their adversaries ruled over them.[k]
42 Their enemies oppressed them,
kept them under subjection.
43 Many times did he rescue them,
but they kept rebelling and scheming
and were brought low by their own guilt.[l]
44 Still God had regard for their affliction
when he heard their wailing.
45 For their sake he remembered his covenant
and relented in his abundant mercy,[m]
46 Winning for them compassion
from all who held them captive.

C

47 Save us, LORD, our God;
gather us from among the nations
That we may give thanks to your holy name
and glory in praising you.[n]
48 *Blessed be the LORD, the God of Israel,
from everlasting to everlasting!
Let all the people say, Amen![o]
Hallelujah!

## Fifth Book—Psalms 107–150

### PSALM 107*

See RG 175

### *God the Savior of Those in Distress*

1 "Give thanks to the LORD for he is good,
his mercy endures forever!"[p]
2 Let that be the prayer of the LORD's redeemed,
those redeemed from the hand of the foe,[q]
3 Those gathered from foreign lands,
from east and west, from north and south.[r]

I

4 Some had lost their way in a barren desert;
found no path toward a city to live in.

**106:32 Moses suffered because of them**: Moses was not allowed to enter the promised land because of his rash words (Nm 20:12). According to Dt 1:37, Moses was not allowed to cross because of the people's sin, not his own.

**106:37 Demons**: Hebrew *shedim* occurs in parallelism with "gods" in an important inscription from Transjordan and hence can also be translated "the gods."

**106:48** A doxology ending Book IV of the Psalter. It is not part of the Psalm.

**Psalm 107** A hymn inviting those who have been rescued by God to give praise (Ps 107:1–3). Four archetypal divine rescues are described, each ending in thanksgiving: from the sterile desert (Ps 107:4–9), from imprisonment in gloom (Ps 107:10–16), from mortal illness (Ps 107:17–22), and from the angry sea (Ps 107:23–32). The number four connotes totality, all the possible varieties of rescue. The same saving activity of God is shown in Israel's history (Ps 107:33–41); whenever the people were endangered God rescued them. The last verses invite people to ponder the persistent saving acts of God (Ps 107:42–43).

*f:* Nm 25; Dt 26:14; Sir 45:23–24. *g:* Ps 95:8–9; Ex 17:1–7; Nm 20:2–13; Dt 6:16; 33:8. *h:* Dt 7:1; Jgs 2:1–5. *i:* Lv 18:3; Jgs 1:27–35; 3:5. *j:* Lv 18:21; Nm 35:33; Dt 32:17; Jgs 2:11–13, 17, 19; 2 Kgs 16:3; Bar 4:7; 1 Cor 10:20. *k:* Jgs 2:14–23. *l:* Is 63:7–9. *m:* Lv 26:42. *n:* 1 Chr 16:35. *o:* Ps 41:14; 72:18; 89:53; 1 Chr 16:36; Neh 9:5. *p:* Ps 100:4–5; 106:1; Jer 33:11. *q:* Is 63:12. *r:* Is 43:5–6; 49:12; Zec 8:7.

5 They were hungry and thirsty;
their life was ebbing away.[s]
6 In their distress they cried to the LORD,
who rescued them in their peril,
7 [t]Guided them by a direct path
so they reached a city to live in.[u]
8 Let them thank the LORD for his mercy,
such wondrous deeds for the children
of Adam.
9 For he satisfied the thirsty,
filled the hungry with good things.[v]

II

10 Some lived in darkness and gloom,
imprisoned in misery and chains.
11 Because they rebelled against God's word,
and scorned the counsel of the Most
High,[w]
12 He humbled their hearts through
hardship;
they stumbled with no one to help.[x]
13 In their distress they cried to the LORD,
who saved them in their peril;
14 He brought them forth from darkness and
the shadow of death
and broke their chains asunder.[y]
15 Let them thank the LORD for his mercy,
such wondrous deeds for the children
of Adam.
16 For he broke down the gates of bronze
and snapped the bars of iron.

III

17 Some fell sick from their wicked ways,
afflicted because of their sins.
18 They loathed all manner of food;[z]
they were at the gates of death.
19 In their distress they cried to the LORD,
who saved them in their peril,
20 Sent forth his word to heal them,[a]
and snatched them from the grave.
21 Let them thank the LORD for his mercy,
such wondrous deeds for the children
of Adam.
22 Let them offer a sacrifice in thanks,
recount his works with shouts of joy.

IV

23 Some went off to sea in ships,
plied their trade on the deep waters.[b]
24 They saw the works of the LORD,
the wonders of God in the deep.
25 He commanded and roused a storm wind;
it tossed the waves on high.[c]
26 They rose up to the heavens, sank to the
depths;
their hearts trembled at the danger.
27 They reeled, staggered like drunkards;
their skill was of no avail.[d]
28 In their distress they cried to the LORD,
who brought them out of their peril;
29 He hushed the storm to silence,
the waves of the sea were stilled.[e]
30 They rejoiced that the sea grew calm,
that God brought them to the harbor
they longed for.
31 Let them thank the LORD for his mercy,
such wondrous deeds for the children
of Adam.
32 Let them extol him in the assembly of the
people,
and praise him in the council of the
elders.

V

33 *God changed rivers into desert,
springs of water into thirsty ground,[f]
34 Fruitful land into a salty waste,
because of the wickedness of its
people.[g]
35 He changed the desert into pools of
water,
arid land into springs of water,[h]
36 And settled the hungry there;
they built a city to live in.[i]
37 They sowed fields and planted vineyards,
brought in an abundant harvest.[j]
38 [k]God blessed them, and they increased
greatly,
and their livestock did not decrease.[l]
39 But he poured out contempt on princes,
made them wander trackless wastes,

**107:33–41** God destroyed Sodom and Gomorrah in Gn 18–19, which the Psalm sees as the destruction of the wicked inhabitants of Canaan to prepare the way for Israel (Ps 107:33–34). God then led Israel through the desert to give them a fertile land (Ps 107:35–38) and protected them from every danger (Ps 107:39–41).

*s:* Dt 8:15; 32:10; Is 49:10. *t:* Is 35:8; 40:3; 43:19. *u:* Dt 6:10. *v:* Lk 1:53. *w:* Is 42:7, 22; Jb 36:8–9; Prv 1:25. *x:* Ps 106:43. *y:* Is 42:7; 49:9; 51:14. *z:* Jb 6:6–7; 33:20. *a:* Ps 147:15; Wis 16:12; Is 55:11; Mt 8:8. *b:* Sir 43:25. *c:* Jon 1:4. *d:* Is 29:9. *e:* Ps 65:8; 89:10; Mt 8:26 par. *f:* Is 35:7; 42:15; 50:2. *g:* Gn 19:23–28; Dt 29:22; Sir 39:23. *h:* Ps 114:8; Is 41:8. *i:* Ez 36:35. *j:* Is 65:21; Jer 31:5. *k:* Jb 12:23–25. *l:* Dt 7:13–14.

[40] Where they were diminished and brought low
through misery and cruel oppression.
[41] While he released the poor man from affliction,
and increased their families like flocks.[m]
[42] The upright saw this and rejoiced;[n]
all wickedness shut its mouth.
[43] Whoever is wise will take note of these things,[o]
and ponder the merciful deeds of the LORD.

See RG 176

## PSALM 108*

### *Prayer for Victory*

[1] A song; a psalm of David.

I

[2] My heart is steadfast, God;[p]
my heart is steadfast.
Let me sing and chant praise.
[3] Awake, lyre and harp!
I will wake the dawn.[q]
[4] I will praise you among the peoples, LORD;
I will chant your praise among the nations.[r]
[5] For your mercy is greater than the heavens;
your faithfulness, to the skies.[s]

II

[6] Appear on high over the heavens, God;
your glory above all the earth.
[7] Help with your right hand and answer us
that your loved ones may escape.
[8] God speaks in his holiness:*[t]
"I will exult, I will apportion Shechem;
the valley of Succoth I will measure out.
[9] Gilead is mine, mine is Manasseh;
Ephraim is the helmet for my head,
Judah, my scepter.
[10] Moab is my washbowl;
upon Edom I cast my sandal;[u]
I will shout in triumph over Philistia."
[11] Who will bring me to the fortified city?
Who will lead me into Edom?
[12] Was it not you who rejected us, God?
Do you no longer march with our armies?[v]
[13] Give us aid against the foe;
worthless is human help.
[14] We will triumph with the help of God,
who will trample down our foes.

## PSALM 109*

See RG 175

### *Prayer of a Person Falsely Accused*

[1] For the leader. A psalm of David.

I

[2] O God, whom I praise, do not be silent,[w]
for wicked and treacherous mouths attack me.
They speak against me with lying tongues;
[3] with hateful words they surround me,
attacking me without cause.
[4] In return for my love they slander me,
even though I prayed for them.
[5] They repay me evil for good,
hatred for my love.[x]

II

[6] Appoint an evil one over him,
an accuser* to stand at his right hand,
[7] That he may be judged and found guilty,
that his plea may be in vain.
[8] May his days be few;
may another take his office.[y]

**Psalm 108** A prayer compiled from two other Psalms: Ps 108:2–6 are virtually the same as Ps 57:8–12; Ps 108:7–14 are the same as Ps 60:7–14. An old promise of salvation (Ps 108:8–10) is combined with a confident assurance (Ps 108:2–6, 13) and petition (Ps 108:7, 12–13).

**108:8 Holiness**: may also be translated as "sanctuary" or as referring to God's heavenly abode.

**Psalm 109** A lament notable for the length and vehemence of its prayer against evildoers (Ps 109:6–20); the cry to God (Ps 109:1) and the complaint (Ps 109:22–25) are brief in comparison. The psalmist is apparently the victim of a slander campaign, potentially devastating in a society where reputation and honor are paramount. In the emotional perspective of the Psalm, there are only two types of people: the wicked and their poor victims. The psalmist is a poor victim (Ps 109:22, 31) and by that fact a friend of God and enemy of the wicked. The psalmist seeks vindication not on the basis of personal virtue but because of God's promise to protect the poor.

**109:6 An accuser**: Hebrew *satan*, a word occurring in Job 1–2 and Zec 3:1–2. In the latter passage Satan stands at the right hand of the high priest to bring false accusations against him before God. Here the accuser is human.

*m:* Ps 113:7. *n:* Ps 58:11; 63:12. *o:* Hos 14:10. *p:* Ps 57:8–12. *q:* Jb 38:12. *r:* Ps 9:12; 18:50; 148:13. *s:* Ps 36:6; 71:19. *t:* Ps 60:8–14. *u:* Ru 4:7–8. *v:* Ps 44:10. *w:* Ps 35:22; 83:1. *x:* Ps 35:12; 38:21; Prv 17:13; Jer 18:20. *y:* Acts 1:20.

9 May his children be fatherless,
his wife, a widow.[z]
10 May his children wander and beg,
driven from their hovels.
11 May the usurer snare all he owns,
strangers plunder all he earns.
12 May no one treat him with mercy
or pity his fatherless children.
13 May his posterity be destroyed,[a]
their name rooted out in the next generation.
14 May his fathers' guilt be mentioned to the LORD;
his mother's sin not rooted out.[b]
15 May their guilt be always before the LORD,[c]
till their memory is banished from the earth,[d]
16 For he did not remember to show mercy,
but hounded the wretched poor
and brought death to the brokenhearted.
17 He loved cursing; may it come upon him;
he hated blessing; may none come to him.
18 May cursing clothe him like a robe;
may it enter his belly like water,
his bones like oil.
19 May it be near as the clothes he wears,
as the belt always around him.
20 *May this be the reward for my accusers from the LORD,
for those speaking evil against me.

III

21 But you, LORD, are my Lord,
deal kindly with me for your name's sake;
in your great mercy rescue me.
22 For I am poor and needy;
my heart is pierced within me.
23 Like a lengthening shadow I am gone,
I am shaken off like the locust.
24 My knees totter from fasting;[e]
my flesh has wasted away.
25 I have become a mockery to them;
when they see me, they shake their heads.
26 Help me, LORD, my God;
save me in your mercy.
27 Make them know this is your hand,
that you, LORD, have done this.
28 Though they curse, may you bless;
arise, shame them, that your servant may rejoice.
29 Clothe my accusers with disgrace;
make them wear their shame like a mantle.
30 I will give fervent thanks to the LORD;
before a crowd I will praise him.[f]
31 For he stands at the right hand of the poor
to save him from those who pass judgment on him.

## PSALM 110*

See RG 176, 178

### *God Appoints the King both King and Priest*

1 A psalm of David.

The LORD says to my lord:*
"Sit at my right hand,
while I make your enemies your footstool."*[g]
2 The scepter of your might:
the LORD extends your strong scepter from Zion.
Have dominion over your enemies!
3 Yours is princely power from the day of your birth.
In holy splendor before the daystar,
like dew I begot you.[h]
4 The LORD has sworn and will not waver:

**109:20 May this be the reward . . . from the LORD**: the psalmist prays that God ratify the curses of Ps 109:6–19 and bring them upon the wicked.

**Psalm 110** A royal Psalm in which a court singer recites three oracles in which God assures the king that his enemies are conquered (Ps 110:1–2), makes the king "son" in traditional adoption language (Ps 110:3), gives priestly status to the king and promises to be with him in future military ventures (Ps 110:4–7).

**110:1 The LORD says to my lord**: a polite form of address of an inferior to a superior, cf. 1 Sm 25:25; 2 Sm 1:10. The court singer refers to the king. Jesus in the synoptic gospels (Mt 22:41–46 and parallels) takes the psalmist to be David and hence "my lord" refers to the messiah, who must be someone greater than David. **Your footstool**: in ancient times victorious kings put their feet on the prostrate bodies of their enemies.

*z:* Ex 22:23; Jer 18:21. *a:* Ps 21:11; Prv 10:7. *b:* Ex 20:5. *c:* Ps 90:8. *d:* Ps 34:16. *e:* Ps 69:11–13. *f:* Ps 111:1. *g:* Mt 22:44; Acts 2:34–35; 1 Cor 15:25; Heb 1:13; 8:1; 10:12–13; 1 Pt 3:22. *h:* Ps 2:7; 89:27; Is 49:1.

PSALMS 111 AND 112, acrostic psalms introduced by "Hallelujah," are comprised of short lines that often quote traditional expressions containing wisdom ideas. They are somewhat disjointed and resemble answers to a student exercise: Compose a logical, complete acrostic of short lines using traditional statements. The simple style suggests that perhaps these were poems for teaching children. Stylistically, the two are so similar that they have been characterized as "twins."

"You are a priest forever in the manner
of Melchizedek."'*[i]
5 At your right hand is the Lord,
who crushes kings on the day of his
wrath,[j]
6 Who judges nations, heaps up corpses,
crushes heads across the wide earth,
7 *Who drinks from the brook by the
wayside
and thus holds high his head.[k]

## PSALM 111*

See RG 175–76

### *Praise of God for Goodness to Israel*

1 Hallelujah!

I will praise the LORD with all my heart[l]
in the assembled congregation of the
upright.*
2 Great are the works of the LORD,
studied by all who delight in them.
3 Majestic and glorious is his work,
his righteousness endures forever.
4 He won renown for his wondrous
deeds;
gracious and merciful is the LORD.[m]
5 He gives food to those who fear him,*
he remembers his covenant forever.
6 He showed his powerful deeds to his
people,
giving them the inheritance of the
nations.
7 The works of his hands are true and just,
reliable all his decrees,
8 Established forever and ever,
to be observed with truth and equity.
9 He sent release to his people,
decreed his covenant forever;
holy and fearsome is his name.
10 *The fear of the LORD is the beginning of
wisdom;[n]
prudent are all who practice it.
His praise endures forever.

## PSALM 112*

See RG 176

### *The Blessings of the Just*

1 Hallelujah!

Blessed the man who fears the LORD,
who greatly delights in his commands.[o]
2 His descendants shall be mighty in the
land,
a generation of the upright will be
blessed.
3 Wealth and riches shall be in his house;
his righteousness* shall endure forever.

**110:4 Melchizedek**: Melchizedek was the ancient king of Salem (Jerusalem) who blessed Abraham (Gn 14:18–20); like other kings of the time he performed priestly functions. Heb 7 sees in Melchizedek a type of Christ.

**110:7 Who drinks from the brook by the wayside**: the meaning is uncertain. Some see an allusion to a rite of royal consecration at the Gihon spring (cf. 1 Kgs 1:33, 38). Others find here an image of the divine warrior (or king) pursuing enemies so relentlessly that he does not stop long enough to eat and drink.

**Psalm 111** A Temple singer (Ps 111:1) tells how God is revealed in Israel's history (Ps 111:2–10). The deeds reveal God's very self, powerful, merciful, faithful. The poem is an acrostic, each verse beginning with a successive letter of the Hebrew alphabet.

**111:1 In the assembled congregation of the upright**: in the Temple, cf. Ps 149:1.

**111:5 Food to those who fear him**: probably a reference to the manna in the desert, which elsewhere is seen as a type of the Eucharist, cf. Jn 6:31–33, 49–51.

**111:10 The fear of the LORD**: reverence for God.

**Psalm 112** An acrostic poem detailing the blessings received by those who remain close to God by obedience to the commandments. Among their blessings are children (Ps 112:2), wealth that enables them to be magnanimous (Ps 112:3, 5, 9), and virtue by which they encourage others (Ps 112:4). The just person is an affront to the wicked, whose hopes remain unfulfilled (Ps 112:10). The logic resembles Ps 1; 111.

**112:3 Righteousness**: in the Second Temple period the word acquired the nuance of liberality and almsgiving, cf. Sir 3:30; 7:10; Mt 6:1–4.

*i:* Ps 89:35; 132:11; Gn 14:18; Heb 5:6; 7:21. *j:* Ps 2:9; Rev 2:27; 12:5; 19:15. *k:* Ps 3:4. *l:* Ps 138:1. *m:* Ps 103:8; 112:4. *n:* Prv 1:7; 9:10; Sir 1:16. *o:* Ps 1:1–2; 119:1–2; 128:1.

4 Light shines through the darkness for the
upright;[p]
gracious, compassionate, and righteous.
5 It is good for the man gracious in lending,
who conducts his affairs with justice.
6 For he shall never be shaken;
the righteous shall be remembered
forever.[q]
7 He shall not fear an ill report;
his heart is steadfast, trusting the LORD.
8 His heart is tranquil, without fear,
till at last he looks down on his foes.
9 Lavishly he gives to the poor;
his righteousness shall endure forever;[r]
his horn* shall be exalted in honor.
10 The wicked sees and is angry;
gnashes his teeth and wastes away;
the desire of the wicked come to
nothing.

## PSALM 113*

See RG 175

### *Praise of God's Care for the Poor*

1 Hallelujah!

I

Praise, you servants of the LORD,
praise the name of the LORD.[s]
2 Blessed be the name of the LORD
both now and forever.
3 From the rising of the sun to its setting[t]
let the name of the LORD be praised.

II

4 High above all nations is the LORD;
above the heavens his glory.[u]
5 Who is like the LORD our God,
enthroned on high,
6 [v]looking down on heaven and earth?
7 He raises the needy from the dust,
lifts the poor from the ash heap,[w]
8 Seats them with princes,
the princes of the people,
9 Gives the childless wife a home,
the joyful mother of children.[x]
Hallelujah!

## PSALM 114*

See RG 175

### *The Lord's Wonders at the Exodus*

1 When Israel came forth from Egypt,
the house of Jacob from an alien people,
2 Judah became God's sanctuary,
Israel, God's domain.[y]
3 *The sea saw and fled;
the Jordan turned back.[z]
4 The mountains skipped like rams;
the hills, like lambs.[a]
5 Why was it, sea, that you fled?
Jordan, that you turned back?
6 Mountains, that you skipped like rams?
You hills, like lambs?
7 Tremble, earth, before the Lord,[b]
before the God of Jacob,
8 *Who turned the rock into pools of water,
flint into a flowing spring.[c]

## PSALM 115*

See RG 175

### *The Greatness of the True God*

I

1 Not to us, LORD, not to us
but to your name give glory

**112:9 His horn**: the symbol for vitality and honor.

**Psalm 113** A hymn exhorting the congregation to praise God's name, i.e., the way in which God is present in the world; the name is mentioned three times in Ps 113:1–3. The divine name is especially honored in the Temple (Ps 113:1) but its recognition is not limited by time (Ps 113:2) and space (Ps 113:3), for God is everywhere active (Ps 113:4–5) especially in rescuing the lowly faithful (Ps 113:7–9).

**Psalm 114** A hymn celebrating Israel's escape from Egypt, journey through the wilderness, and entry into the promised land, and the miracles of nature that bore witness to God's presence in their midst. In the perspective of the Psalm, the people proceed directly from Egypt into the promised land (Ps 114:1–2). Sea and Jordan, which stood like soldiers barring the people from their land, flee before the mighty God as the earth recoils from the battle (Ps 114:3–4). The poet taunts the natural elements as one taunts defeated enemies (Ps 114:5–6).

**114:3–4** Pairs of cosmic elements such as sea and rivers, mountains and hills, are sometimes mentioned in creation accounts. Personified here as warriors, the pairs tremble in fear before the Divine Warrior. The quaking also recalls the divine appearance in the storm at Sinai (Ex 19:16–19) and elsewhere (Jgs 5:4–5; Ps 18:7–15).

**114:8** The miracles of giving drink to the people in the arid desert, cf. Ex 17:1–7; Is 41:17–18.

**Psalm 115** A response to the enemy taunt, "Where is your God?" This hymn to the glory of Israel's God (Ps 115:1–3) ridicules the lifeless idols of the nations (Ps 115:4–8), expresses in a litany the trust of the various classes of the people in God (Ps 115:9–11), invokes God's blessing on them as

*p:* Ps 37:6; 97:11; Prv 13:9; Is 58:10. *q:* Prv 10:7; Wis 8:13. *r:* Prv 22:9; 2 Cor 9:9. *s:* Ps 135:1. *t:* Mal 1:11. *u:* Ps 148:13. *v:* Ps 89:7–9. *w:* Ps 107:41; 1 Sm 2:7–8. *x:* 1 Sm 2:5; Is 54:1. *y:* Ex 19:6. *z:* Ps 66:6; 74:15; Ex 14:21ff; Jos 3:14ff. *a:* Ps 29:6; Wis 19:9. *b:* Ps 68:9. *c:* Ex 17:6; Nm 20:11.

because of your mercy and
faithfulness.[d]
2 Why should the nations say,
"Where is their God?"*[e]
3 Our God is in heaven
and does whatever he wills.[f]

II

4 Their idols are silver and gold,[g]
the work of human hands.[h]
5 They have mouths but do not speak,
eyes but do not see.
6 They have ears but do not hear,
noses but do not smell.
7 They have hands but do not feel,
feet but do not walk;
they produce no sound from their
throats.
8 Their makers will be like them,
and anyone who trusts in them.

III

9 *The house of Israel trusts in the LORD,[i]
who is their help and shield.[j]
10 The house of Aaron trusts in the LORD,
who is their help and shield.
11 Those who fear the LORD trust in the
LORD,
who is their help and shield.
12 The LORD remembers us and will
bless us,
will bless the house of Israel,
will bless the house of Aaron,
13 Will bless those who fear the LORD,
small and great alike.
14 May the LORD increase your number,
yours and your descendants.
15 May you be blessed by the LORD,
maker of heaven and earth.
16 *The heavens belong to the LORD,
but he has given the earth to the
children of Adam.[k]
17 *The dead do not praise the LORD,
not all those go down into silence.[l]
18 It is we who bless the LORD,
both now and forever.
Hallelujah!

## PSALM 116*

See RG 175

### *Thanksgiving to God Who Saves from Death*

I

1 I love the LORD, who listened
to my voice in supplication,
2 Who turned an ear to me
on the day I called.
3 I was caught by the cords of death;*[m]
the snares of Sheol had seized me;
I felt agony and dread.
4 Then I called on the name of the
LORD,
"O LORD, save my life!"

II

5 Gracious is the LORD and righteous;
yes, our God is merciful.[n]
6 The LORD protects the simple;
I was helpless, but he saved me.
7 Return, my soul, to your rest;
the LORD has been very good to you.[o]
8 For my soul has been freed from death,
my eyes from tears, my feet from
stumbling.[p]
9 I shall walk before the LORD
in the land of the living.*[q]

they invoke the divine name (Ps 115:12–15), and concludes as it began with praise of God. Ps 135:15–18 similarly mocks the Gentile gods and has a similar litany and hymn (Ps 135:19–21).

**115:2 Where is their God?**: implies that God cannot help them.

**115:9–11 The house of Israel . . . the house of Aaron . . . those who fear the LORD**: the laity of Israelite birth, the priests, and the converts to Judaism, cf. Ps 118:2–4; 135:19–21. In the New Testament likewise "those who fear the Lord" means converts to Judaism (cf. Acts 10:2, 22, 35; 13:16, 26).

**115:16 The heavens**: the Septuagint reads here "the heaven of heavens" or "the highest heavens," i.e., above the firmament. See note on Ps 148:4.

**115:17** See note on Ps 6:5.

**Psalm 116** A thanksgiving in which the psalmist responds to divine rescue from mortal danger (Ps 116:3–4) and from near despair (Ps 116:10–11) with vows and Temple sacrifices (Ps 116:13–14, 17–19). The Greek and Latin versions divide the Psalm into two parts: Ps 116:1–9 and Ps 116:10–19, corresponding to its two major divisions.

**116:3 The cords of death**: death is personified here; it attempts to capture the psalmist with snares and nets, cf. Ps 18:6.

**116:9 The land of the living**: the phrase elsewhere is an epithet of the Jerusalem Temple (cf. Ps 27:13; 52:5; Is 38:11). Hence the psalmist probably refers to being present to God in the Temple.

*d:* Ez 36:22–23. *e:* Ps 79:10. *f:* Ps 135:6. *g:* Ps 135:15–19; Wis 15:15–16; Is 44:9f; Jer 10:1–5. *h:* Is 40:19. *i:* Ps 118:2–4. *j:* Ps 33:20. *k:* Gn 1:28. *l:* Ps 6:6; 88:11ff; Sir 17:22f; Is 38:18. *m:* Ps 18:5; Jon 2:3. *n:* Ex 34:6. *o:* Ps 13:6. *p:* Ps 56:14; Is 25:8; Rev 21:4. *q:* Ps 27:13; 56:14; Is 38:11.

III

10 *I kept faith, even when I said,
"I am greatly afflicted!"[r]
11 I said in my alarm,
"All men are liars!"[s]
12 How can I repay the LORD
for all the great good done for me?
13 I will raise the cup of salvation*
and call on the name of the LORD.
14 I will pay my vows to the LORD
in the presence of all his people.
15 *Dear in the eyes of the LORD
is the death of his devoted.[t]
16 LORD, I am your servant,
your servant, the child of your
maidservant;[u]
you have loosed my bonds.
17 I will offer a sacrifice of praise
and call on the name of the LORD.[v]
18 I will pay my vows to the LORD[w]
in the presence of all his people,
19 In the courts of the house of the LORD,
in your midst, O Jerusalem.
Hallelujah!

See RG 175–76

## PSALM 117*

### *The Nations Called To Praise*

1 Praise the LORD, all you nations!
Extol him, all you peoples![x]
2 His mercy for us is strong;
the faithfulness of the LORD is forever.
Hallelujah!

See RG 179

## PSALM 118*

### *Hymn of Thanksgiving*

I

1 Give thanks to the LORD, for he is good,[y]
his mercy endures forever.
2 Let Israel say:
his mercy endures forever.
3 Let the house of Aaron say,
his mercy endures forever.
4 Let those who fear the LORD say,[z]
his mercy endures forever.

II

5 In danger I called on the LORD;
the LORD answered me and set me
free.
6 The LORD is with me; I am not afraid;
what can mortals do against me?[a]
7 The LORD is with me as my helper;
I shall look in triumph on my foes.
8 Better to take refuge in the LORD[b]
than to put one's trust in mortals.
9 Better to take refuge in the LORD
than to put one's trust in princes.

III

10 All the nations surrounded me;
in the LORD's name I cut them off.
11 They surrounded me on every side;
in the LORD's name I cut them off.
12 They surrounded me like bees;[c]
they burned up like fire among thorns;
in the LORD's name I cut them off.
13 I was hard pressed and falling,
but the LORD came to my help.[d]
14 The LORD, my strength and might,
has become my savior.[e]

IV

15 The joyful shout of deliverance
is heard in the tents of the righteous:
"The LORD's right hand works valiantly;
16 the LORD's right hand is raised;
the LORD's right hand works
valiantly."
17 I shall not die but live

**116:10 I kept faith, even when I said**: even in the days of despair, the psalmist did not lose all hope.

**116:13 The cup of salvation**: probably the libation of wine poured out in gratitude for rescue, cf. Ex 25:29; Nm 15:5, 7, 10.

**116:15 Dear in the eyes of the LORD**: the meaning is that the death of God's faithful is grievous to God, not that God is pleased with the death, cf. Ps 72:14. In Wis 3:5–6, God accepts the death of the righteous as a sacrificial burnt offering.

**Psalm 117** This shortest of hymns calls on the nations to acknowledge God's supremacy. The supremacy of Israel's God has been demonstrated to them by the people's secure existence, which is owed entirely to God's gracious fidelity.

**Psalm 118** A thanksgiving liturgy accompanying a procession of the king and the people into the Temple precincts. After an invocation in the form of a litany (Ps 118:1–4), the psalmist (very likely speaking in the name of the community) describes how the people confidently implored God's help (Ps 118:5–9) when hostile peoples threatened its life (Ps 118:10–14); vividly God's rescue is recounted (Ps 118:15–18). Then follows a possible dialogue at the Temple gates between the priests and the psalmist as the latter enters to offer the thanksgiving sacrifice (Ps 118:19–25). Finally, the priests impart their blessing (Ps 118:26–27), and the psalmist sings in gratitude (Ps 118:28–29).

*r:* 2 Cor 4:13. *s:* Ps 12:2. *t:* Ps 72:14; Is 43:4. *u:* Ps 86:16; 143:12; Wis 9:5. *v:* Lv 7:12ff. *w:* Jon 2:10. *x:* Rom 15:11. *y:* Ps 100:5; 136:1f. *z:* Ps 115:9–11. *a:* Ps 27:1; Heb 13:6. *b:* Ps 146:3. *c:* Dt 1:44. *d:* Ps 129:1–2. *e:* Ex 15:2; Is 12:2.

and declare the deeds of the LORD.
18 The LORD chastised me harshly,
but did not hand me over to death.

V

19 Open the gates of righteousness;
I will enter and thank the LORD.[f]
20 This is the LORD's own gate,
through it the righteous enter.
21 I thank you for you answered me;
you have been my savior.
22 *The stone the builders rejected
has become the cornerstone.[g]
23 By the LORD has this been done;
it is wonderful in our eyes.
24 This is the day the LORD has made;
let us rejoice in it and be glad.
25 LORD, grant salvation!*
LORD, grant good fortune!

VI

26 Blessed is he
who comes in the name of the LORD.[h]
We bless you from the house of the LORD.
27 The LORD is God and has
enlightened us.
Join in procession with leafy branches
up to the horns of the altar.

VII

28 You are my God, I give you thanks;
my God, I offer you praise.
29 Give thanks to the LORD, for he is good,
his mercy endures forever.

## PSALM 119*

See RG 176

### *A Prayer to God, the Lawgiver*

Aleph

1 Blessed those whose way is blameless,
who walk by the law of the LORD.[i]
2 Blessed those who keep his testimonies,
who seek him with all their heart.[j]
3 They do no wrong;
they walk in his ways.
4 You have given them the command
to observe your precepts with care.
5 May my ways be firm
in the observance of your statutes!
6 Then I will not be ashamed
to ponder all your commandments.
7 I will praise you with sincere heart
as I study your righteous judgments.
8 I will observe your statutes;
do not leave me all alone.

Beth

9 How can the young keep his way without
fault?
Only by observing your words.
10 With all my heart I seek you;
do not let me stray from your
commandments.
11 In my heart I treasure your promise,
that I may not sin against you.
12 Blessed are you, O LORD;
teach me your statutes.[k]
13 With my lips I recite
all the judgments you have spoken.
14 I find joy in the way of your testimonies
more than in all riches.
15 I will ponder your precepts
and consider your paths.
16 In your statutes I take delight;
I will never forget your word.

Gimel

17 Be kind to your servant that I may live,
that I may keep your word.
18 Open my eyes to see clearly

**118:22 The stone the builders rejected**: a proverb: what is insignificant to human beings has become great through divine election. The "stone" may originally have meant the foundation stone or capstone of the Temple. The New Testament interpreted the verse as referring to the death and resurrection of Christ (Mt 21:42; Acts 4:11; cf. Is 28:16 and Rom 9:33; 1 Pt 2:7).

**118:25 Grant salvation**: the Hebrew for this cry has come into English as "Hosanna." This cry and the words in Ps 118:26 were used in the gospels to welcome Jesus entering the Temple on Palm Sunday (Mk 11:9–10).

**Psalm 119** This Psalm, the longest by far in the Psalter, praises God for giving such splendid laws and instruction for people to live by. The author glorifies and thanks God for the Torah, prays for protection from sinners enraged by others' fidelity to the law, laments the cost of obedience, delights in the law's consolations, begs for wisdom to understand the precepts, and asks for the rewards of keeping them. Several expected elements do not appear in the Psalm: Mount Sinai with its story of God's revelation and gift to Israel of instruction and commandments, the Temple and other institutions related to revelation and laws (frequent in other Psalms). The Psalm is fascinated with God's word directing and guiding human life. The poem is an acrostic; its twenty-two stanzas (of eight verses each) are in the order of the Hebrew alphabet. Each of the eight verses within a stanza begins with the same letter. Each verse contains one word for "instruction." The translation here given attempts to translate each Hebrew

*f:* Is 26:2. *g:* Mt 21:42; Lk 20:17; Acts 4:11; Rom 9:33; 1 Pt 2:7. *h:* Mt 21:9; 23:39. *i:* Ps 1:1–2; 15:2; 112:1. *j:* Dt 4:29. *k:* Ps 25:4; 27:11; 86:11; 143:8, 10.

the wonders of your law.
19 I am a sojourner in the land;*[l]
do not hide your commandments from me.
20 At all times my soul is stirred
with longing for your judgments.
21 With a curse you rebuke the proud
who stray from your commandments.
22 Free me from disgrace and contempt,
for I keep your testimonies.
23 Though princes meet and talk against me,
your servant meditates on your statutes.
24 Your testimonies are my delight;
they are my counselors.

**Daleth**

25 My soul clings to the dust;[m]
give me life in accord with your word.
26 I disclosed my ways and you answered me;
teach me your statutes.
27 Make me understand the way of your precepts;
I will ponder your wondrous deeds.
28 My soul is depressed;
lift me up acccording to your word.
29 Lead me from the way of deceit;
favor me with your law.
30 The way of loyalty I have chosen;
I have kept your judgments.
31 I cling to your testimonies, LORD;
do not let me come to shame.
32 I will run the way of your commandments,
for you will broaden my heart.

**He**

33 LORD, teach me the way of your statutes;
I shall keep them with care.[n]
34 Give me understanding to keep your law,
to observe it with all my heart.
35 Lead me in the path of your commandments,[o]
for that is my delight.
36 Direct my heart toward your testimonies
and away from gain.
37 Avert my eyes from what is worthless;
by your way give me life.
38 For your servant, fulfill your promise
made to those who fear you.
39 Turn away from me the taunts I dread,
for your judgments are good.
40 See how I long for your precepts;
in your righteousness give me life.

**Waw**

41 Let your mercy come to me, LORD,
salvation in accord with your promise.
42 Let me answer my taunters with a word,
for I trust in your word.
43 Do not take the word of truth from my mouth,
for in your judgments is my hope.
44 I will keep your law always,
for all time and forever.
45 I will walk freely in an open space
because I cherish your precepts.
46 I will speak openly of your testimonies
without fear even before kings.
47 I delight in your commandments,
which I dearly love.
48 *I lift up my hands to your commandments;
I study your statutes, which I love.

**Zayin**

49 Remember your word to your servant
by which you give me hope.
50 This is my comfort in affliction,
your promise that gives me life.
51 Though the arrogant utterly scorn me,
I do not turn from your law.
52 When I recite your judgments of old
I am comforted, LORD.
53 Rage seizes me because of the wicked;
they forsake your law.
54 Your statutes become my songs
wherever I make my home.
55 Even at night I remember your name
in observance of your law, LORD.

word for "instruction" with the same English word. There are, however, nine words for "instruction," not eight, so the principle of a different word for "instruction" in each verse cannot be maintained with perfect consistency. The nine words for "instruction" in the translation are: law, statute, commandment, precept, testimony, word, judgment, way, and promise.

**119:19 A sojourner in the land**: like someone without the legal protection of a native inhabitant, the psalmist has a special need for the guidance of God's teaching.

**119:48 I lift up my hands to your commandments**: to lift up the hands was an ancient gesture of reverence to God. Here the picture is applied to God's law.

*l:* Ps 39:13. *m:* Ps 44:26. *n:* Ps 19:12. *o:* Ps 25:4; 27:11; 86:11; 143:8, 10.

for all your commandments are
righteous.
173 Keep your hand ready to help me,
for I have chosen your precepts.
174 I long for your salvation, LORD;
your law is my delight.
175 Let my soul live to praise you;
may your judgments give me help.
176 I have wandered like a lost sheep;
seek out your servant,
for I do not forget your
commandments.[h]

## PSALM 120*

See RG 175–76

### *Prayer of a Returned Exile*

1 A song of ascents.*

The LORD answered me
when I called in my distress:[i]
2 LORD, deliver my soul from lying lips,
from a treacherous tongue.[j]

3 What will he inflict on you,
O treacherous tongue,
and what more besides?*
4 A warrior's arrows
sharpened with coals of brush wood!*[k]

5 *Alas, I am a foreigner in Meshech,
I live among the tents of Kedar!
6 Too long do I live
among those who hate peace.
7 When I speak of peace,
they are for war.[l]

## PSALM 121*

See RG 175–76

### *The Lord My Guardian*

1 A song of ascents.

I raise my eyes toward the mountains.*
From whence shall come my help?[m]
2 My help comes from the LORD,
the maker of heaven and earth.[n]

3 He will not allow your foot to slip;[o]
or your guardian to sleep.
4 Behold, the guardian of Israel
never slumbers nor sleeps.
5 *The LORD is your guardian;
the LORD is your shade
at your right hand.[p]
6 By day the sun will not strike you,
nor the moon by night.[q]
7 The LORD will guard you from all
evil;
he will guard your soul.[r]
8 The LORD will guard your coming and
going
both now and forever.[s]

**Psalm 120** A thanksgiving, reporting divine rescue (Ps 120:1) yet with fervent prayer for further protection against lying attackers (Ps 120:2–4). The psalmist is acutely conscious of living away from God's own land where divine peace prevails (Ps 120:5–7).

**120:1 A song of ascents**: Ps 120–134 all begin with this superscription. Most probably these fifteen Psalms once formed a collection of Psalms sung when pilgrims went to Jerusalem, since one "ascended" to Jerusalem (1 Kgs 12:28; Ps 24:3; 122:4; Lk 2:42) or to the house of God or to an altar (1 Kgs 12:33; 2 Kgs 23:2; Ps 24:3). Less probable is the explanation that these Psalms were sung by the exiles when they "ascended" to Jerusalem from Babylonia (cf. Ezr 7:9). The idea, found in the Mishnah, that the fifteen steps on which the Levites sang corresponded to these fifteen Psalms (Middot 2:5) must underlie the Vulgate translation *canticum graduum*, "song of the steps" or "gradual song."

**120:3 More besides**: a common curse formula in Hebrew was "May the Lord do such and such evils to you [the evils being specified], and add still more to them," cf. 1 Sm 3:17; 14:44; 25:22. Here the psalmist is at a loss for a suitable malediction.

**120:4 Coals of brush wood**: coals made from the stalk of the broom plant burn with intense heat. The psalmist thinks of lighted coals cast at his enemies.

**120:5** Meshech was in the far north (Gn 10:2) and Kedar was a tribe of the north Arabian desert (Gn 25:13). The psalmist may be thinking generally of all aliens living among inhospitable peoples.

**Psalm 121** A blessing given to someone embarking on a dangerous journey whether a soldier going on a campaign or a pilgrim returning home from the Temple. People look anxiously at the wooded hills. Will God protect them on their journey (Ps 121:1)? The speaker declares that God is not confined to a place or a time (Ps 121:2), that every step is guarded (Ps 121:3–4); night and day (Ps 121:5–6) God watches over their every movement (Ps 121:7–8).

**121:1 The mountains**: possibly Mount Zion, the site of the Temple and hence of safety, but more probably mountains as a place of dangers, causing anxiety to the psalmist.

**121:5–6** The image of shade, a symbol of protection, is apt: God as shade protects from the harmful effects that ancients believed were caused by the sun and moon.

---

*h:* Is 53:6; Jer 50:6; Lk 15:1–7. *i:* Jon 2:3. *j:* Ps 12:3–5; Sir 51:3. *k:* Ps 11:6; 140:11; Prv 16:27. *l:* Ps 35:20; 140:3–4. *m:* Jer 3:23. *n:* Ps 124:8; 146:6. *o:* Ps 66:9; 91:12; 1 Sm 2:9; Prv 3:23. *p:* Ps 16:8; 73:23. *q:* Wis 18:3; Is 25:4; 49:10. *r:* Ps 97:10. *s:* Dt 28:6.

132 Turn to me and be gracious,[a]
according to your judgment for those
who love your name.
133 Steady my feet in accord with your
promise;
do not let iniquity lead me.
134 Free me from human oppression,
that I may observe your precepts.
135 Let your face shine upon your servant;
teach me your statutes.
136 My eyes shed streams of tears
because your law is not observed.

**Sadhe**

137 You are righteous, LORD,
and just are your judgments.[b]
138 You have given your testimonies in
righteousness
and in surpassing faithfulness.
139 I am consumed with rage,
because my foes forget your words.
140 Your servant loves your promise;
it has been proved by fire.
141 Though belittled and despised,
I do not forget your precepts.
142 Your justice is forever right,
your law true.
143 Though distress and anguish come
upon me,
your commandments are my delight.
144 Your testimonies are forever righteous;
give me understanding that I may live.
145 I call with all my heart, O LORD;
answer me that I may keep your
statutes.
146 I call to you to save me
that I may observe your testimonies.
147 I rise before dawn and cry out;
I put my hope in your words.
148 My eyes greet the night watches
as I meditate on your promise.[c]
149 Hear my voice in your mercy, O LORD;
by your judgment give me life.
150 Malicious persecutors draw near me;
they are far from your law.
151 You are near, O LORD;
reliable are all your commandments.
152 Long have I known from your
testimonies
that you have established them forever.

**Resh**

153 Look at my affliction and rescue me,
for I have not forgotten your law.
154 Take up my cause and redeem me;[d]
for the sake of your promise give me
life.
155 Salvation is far from sinners
because they do not cherish your
statutes.
156 Your compassion is great, O LORD;
in accord with your judgments, give
me life.
157 Though my persecutors and foes are
many,
I do not turn from your testimonies.
158 I view the faithless with loathing[e]
because they do not heed your
promise.
159 See how I love your precepts, LORD;
in your mercy give me life.
160 Your every word is enduring;
all your righteous judgments are
forever.

**Shin**

161 Princes persecute me without reason,
but my heart reveres only your word.
162 I rejoice at your promise,
as one who has found rich spoil.
163 Falsehood I hate and abhor;
your law I love.
164 Seven times a day I praise you
because your judgments are righteous.
165 Lovers of your law have much peace;[f]
for them there is no stumbling block.
166 I look for your salvation, LORD,
and I fulfill your commandments.
167 I observe your testimonies;
I love them very much.
168 I observe your precepts and testimonies;
all my ways are before you.

**Taw**

169 Let my cry come before you, LORD;[g]
in keeping with your word, give me
understanding.
170 Let my prayer come before you;
rescue me according to your promise.
171 May my lips pour forth your praise,
because you teach me your statutes.
172 May my tongue sing of your promise,

*a:* Ps 25:16; 86:16. *b:* Tb 3:2. *c:* Ps 63:7; 77:7. *d:* Ps 43:1. *e:* Ps 139:22. *f:* Ps 72:7. *g:* Ps 88:3.

92Had your law not been my delight,
I would have perished in my affliction.
93I will never forget your precepts;
through them you give me life.
94I am yours; save me,
for I cherish your precepts.
95The wicked hope to destroy me,
but I seek to understand your
testimonies.
96I have seen the limits of all perfection,
but your commandment is without
bounds.

**Mem**

97How I love your law, Lord!*
I study it all day long.
98Your commandment makes me wiser
than my foes,
as it is forever with me.
99I have more insight than all my teachers,
because I ponder your testimonies.
100I have more understanding than my elders,
because I keep your precepts.[v]
101I keep my steps from every evil path,
that I may observe your word.
102From your judgments I do not turn,
for you have instructed me.
103How sweet to my tongue is your
promise,
sweeter than honey to my mouth![w]
104Through your precepts I gain
understanding;
therefore I hate all false ways.

**Nun**

105Your word is a lamp for my feet,
a light for my path.[x]
106I make a solemn vow
to observe your righteous judgments.
107I am very much afflicted, LORD;
give me life in accord with your word.
108Accept my freely offered praise;[y]
LORD, teach me your judgments.
109My life is always at risk,
but I do not forget your law.
110The wicked have set snares for me,
but from your precepts I do not stray.
111Your testimonies are my heritage forever;
they are the joy of my heart.
112My heart is set on fulfilling your statutes;
they are my reward forever.

**Samekh**

113I hate every hypocrite;
your law I love.
114You are my refuge and shield;
in your word I hope.
115Depart from me, you wicked,[z]
that I may keep the commandments of
my God.
116Sustain me by your promise that I may
live;
do not disappoint me in my hope.
117Strengthen me that I may be safe,
ever to contemplate your statutes.
118You reject all who stray from your statutes,
for vain is their deceit.
119Like dross you regard all the wicked on
earth;
therefore I love your testimonies.
120My flesh shudders with dread of you;
I fear your judgments.

**Ayin**

121I have fulfilled your righteous judgment;
do not abandon me to my oppressors.
122Guarantee your servant's welfare;
do not let the arrogant oppress me.
123My eyes long to see your salvation
and the promise of your righteousness.
124Act with mercy toward your servant;
teach me your statutes.
125I am your servant; give me discernment
that I may know your testimonies.
126It is time for the LORD to act;
they have disobeyed your law.
127Truly I love your commandments
more than gold, more than the finest
gold.
128Thus, I follow all your precepts;
every wrong way I hate.

**Pe**

129Wonderful are your testimonies;
therefore I keep them.
130The revelation of your words sheds light,
gives understanding to the simple.
131I sigh with open mouth,
yearning for your commandments.

**119:97 Lord**: the inclusion of "Lord" follows the tradition of the Septuagint and the Vulgate.

*v:* Jb 32:6; Wis 4:8–9. *w:* Ps 19:11. *x:* Ps 18:29; Prv 6:23. *y:* Ps 50:14, 23; Heb 13:15. *z:* Ps 6:9; 139:19; Jb 21:14.

56 This is my good fortune,
for I have kept your precepts.

**Heth**

57 My portion is the LORD;
I promise to observe your words.
58 I entreat you with all my heart:
have mercy on me in accord with your promise.
59 I have examined my ways
and turned my steps to your testimonies.
60 I am prompt, I do not hesitate
in observing your commandments.
61 Though the snares of the wicked surround me,
your law I do not forget.
62 At midnight I rise to praise you
because of your righteous judgments.
63 I am the friend of all who fear you,
of all who observe your precepts.
64 The earth, LORD, is filled with your mercy;[p]
teach me your statutes.

**Teth**

65 You have treated your servant well,
according to your word, O LORD.
66 Teach me wisdom and knowledge,
for in your commandments I trust.
67 Before I was afflicted I went astray,
but now I hold to your promise.
68 You are good and do what is good;
teach me your statutes.
69 The arrogant smear me with lies,
but I keep your precepts with all my heart.
70 Their hearts are gross and fat;[q]
as for me, your law is my delight.
71 It was good for me to be afflicted,
in order to learn your statutes.
72 The law of your mouth is more precious to me
than heaps of silver and gold.

**Yodh**

73 Your hands made me and fashioned me;
give me understanding to learn your commandments.
74 Those who fear you rejoice to see me,
because I hope in your word.
75 I know, LORD, that your judgments are righteous;
though you afflict me, you are faithful.
76 May your mercy comfort me
in accord with your promise to your servant.
77 Show me compassion that I may live,
for your law is my delight.
78 Shame the proud for leading me astray with falsehood,
that I may study your testimonies.
79 Let those who fear you turn to me,
those who acknowledge your testimonies.
80 May I be wholehearted toward your statutes,
that I may not be put to shame.

**Kaph**

81 My soul longs for your salvation;
I put my hope in your word.[r]
82 My eyes long to see your promise.[s]
When will you comfort me?
83 I am like a wineskin shriveled by smoke,[t]
but I have not forgotten your statutes.
84 How long can your servant survive?
When will your judgment doom my foes?
85 The arrogant have dug pits for me;
defying your law.
86 All your commandments are steadfast.
Help me! I am pursued without cause.
87 They have almost put an end to me on earth,
but I do not forsake your precepts.
88 In your mercy give me life,
to observe the testimonies of your mouth.

**Lamedh**

89 *Your word, LORD, stands forever;[u]
it is firm as the heavens.
90 Through all generations your truth endures;
fixed to stand firm like the earth.
91 By your judgments they stand firm to this day,
for all things are your servants.

**119:89–91** God's word creates the world, which manifests that word by its permanence and reliability.

*p:* Ps 33:5. *q:* Ps 17:10; 73:7; Jb 15:27. *r:* Ps 130:6. *s:* Ps 25:15; 123:1–2; 141:8. *t:* Jb 30:30. *u:* Is 40:8.

See RG 175–76

## PSALM 122*

### *A Pilgrim's Prayer for Jerusalem*

[1] A song of ascents. Of David.

I

I rejoiced when they said to me,
"Let us go to the house of the LORD."[t]
[2] And now our feet are standing
within your gates, Jerusalem.
[3] Jerusalem, built as a city,
walled round about.*[u]
[4] There the tribes go up,
the tribes of the LORD,
As it was decreed for Israel,
to give thanks to the name of the
LORD.[v]
[5] There are the thrones of justice,
the thrones of the house of David.

II

[6] For the peace of Jerusalem pray:
"May those who love you prosper!
[7] May peace be within your ramparts,
prosperity within your towers."[w]
[8] For the sake of my brothers and friends
I say,
"Peace be with you."[x]
[9] For the sake of the house of the LORD,
our God,
I pray for your good.

See RG 175–76

## PSALM 123*

### *Reliance on the Lord*

[1] A song of ascents.

To you I raise my eyes,
to you enthroned in heaven.[y]
[2] Yes, like the eyes of servants
on the hand of their masters,
Like the eyes of a maid
on the hand of her mistress,
So our eyes are on the LORD our God,
till we are shown favor.
[3] Show us favor, LORD, show us favor,
for we have our fill of contempt.[z]
[4] Our souls are more than sated
with mockery from the insolent,
with contempt from the arrogant.

## PSALM 124*

See RG 176

### *God, the Rescuer of the People*

[1] A song of ascents. Of David.

Had not the LORD been with us,
let Israel say,[a]
[2] Had not the LORD been with us,
when people rose against us,
[3] Then they would have swallowed us
alive,[b]
for their fury blazed against us.
[4] Then the waters would have engulfed us,
the torrent overwhelmed us;[c]
[5] then seething water would have
drowned us.
[6] Blessed is the LORD, who did not leave
us
to be torn by their teeth.
[7] We escaped with our lives like a bird
from the fowler's snare;
the snare was broken,
and we escaped.
[8] *Our help is in the name of the LORD,
the maker of heaven and earth.[d]

**Psalm 122** A song of Zion, sung by pilgrims obeying the law to visit Jerusalem three times on a journey. The singer anticipates joining the procession into the city (Ps 122:1–3). Jerusalem is a place of encounter, where the people praise God (Ps 122:4) and hear the divine justice mediated by the king (Ps 122:5). The very buildings bespeak God's power (cf. Ps 48:13–15). May the grace of this place transform the people's lives (Ps 122:6–9)!

**122:3 Walled round about**: lit., "which is joined to it," probably referring both to the density of the buildings and to the dense population.

**Psalm 123** A lament that begins as a prayer of an individual (Ps 123:1), who expresses by a touching comparison exemplary confidence in God (Ps 123:2). The Psalm ends in prayer that God relieve the people's humiliation at the hands of the arrogant (Ps 123:3–4).

**Psalm 124** A thanksgiving which teaches that Israel's very existence is owed to God who rescues them. In the first part Israel's enemies are compared to the mythic sea dragon (Ps 124:2b–3a; cf. Jer 51:34) and Flood (Ps 124:3b–5; cf. Is 51:9–10). The Psalm heightens the malice of human enemies by linking them to the primordial enemies of God's creation. Israel is a bird freed from the trapper's snare (Ps 124:6–8)—freed originally from Pharaoh and now from the current danger.

**124:8 Our help is in the name**: for the idiom, see Ex 18:4.

*t:* Ps 43:3–4; 84:2–5. *u:* Ps 48:13–14. *v:* Dt 16:16. *w:* Ps 128:5. *x:* Jn 20:19ff. *y:* Ps 25:15; 119:82; 141:8. *z:* Ps 44:13–14; Jb 12:4. *a:* Ps 129:1. *b:* Prv 1:12. *c:* Ps 18:5; 69:2. *d:* Ps 121:2; 146:6.

## PSALM 125*

See RG 175–76

### *Israel's Protector*

[1] A song of ascents.

Those trusting in the LORD are like
Mount Zion,
unshakable, forever enduring.[e]
[2] As mountains surround Jerusalem,
the LORD surrounds his people
both now and forever.[f]

[3] The scepter of the wicked will not prevail
in the land allotted to the just,*
Lest the just themselves
turn their hands to evil.

[4] Do good, LORD, to the good,
to those who are upright of heart.[g]
[5] But those who turn aside to crooked ways
may the LORD send down with the
evildoers.[h]
Peace upon Israel![i]

## PSALM 126*

See RG 175–76

### *The Reversal of Zion's Fortunes*

[1] A song of ascents.

I

When the LORD restored the captives of
Zion,[j]
we thought we were dreaming.
[2] Then our mouths were filled with laughter;
our tongues sang for joy.[k]
Then it was said among the nations,
"The LORD had done great things for
them."
[3] The LORD has done great things for us;
Oh, how happy we were!
[4] Restore our captives, LORD,
like the dry stream beds of the Negeb.*

II

[5] Those who sow in tears
will reap with cries of joy.[l]
[6] Those who go forth weeping,
carrying sacks of seed,
Will return with cries of joy,
carrying their bundled sheaves.

## PSALM 127*

See RG 176

### *The Need of God's Blessing*

[1] A song of ascents. Of Solomon.

I

Unless the LORD build the house,
they labor in vain who build.
Unless the LORD guard the city,
in vain does the guard keep watch.
[2] It is vain for you to rise early
and put off your rest at night,
To eat bread earned by hard toil—
all this God gives to his beloved in
sleep.[m]

II

[3] Certainly sons are a gift from the LORD,
the fruit of the womb, a reward.[n]
[4] Like arrows in the hand of a warrior
are the sons born in one's youth.
[5] Blessed is the man who has filled his
quiver with them.
He will never be shamed
for he will destroy his foes at the
gate.*

**Psalm 125** In response to exilic anxieties about the ancient promises of restoration, the Psalm expresses confidence that God will surround the people as the mountains surround Zion (Ps 125:1–2). The just will not be contaminated by the wicked (Ps 125:3). May God judge between the two groups (Ps 125:4–5).

**125:3 The land allotted to the just**: lit., "the lot of the righteous." The promised land was divided among the tribes of Israel by lot (Nm 26:55; Jos 18). The righteous are the members of the people who are obedient to God. If the domination of the wicked were to continue in the land, even the just would be infected by their evil attitudes.

**Psalm 126** A lament probably sung shortly after Israel's return from exile. The people rejoice that they are in Zion (Ps 126:1–3) but mere presence in the holy city is not enough; they must pray for the prosperity and the fertility of the land (Ps 126:4). The last verses are probably an oracle of promise: the painful work of sowing will be crowned with life (Ps 126:5–6).

**126:4 Like the dry stream beds of the Negeb**: the psalmist prays for rain in such abundance that the dry riverbeds will run.

**Psalm 127** The Psalm puts together two proverbs (Ps 127:1–2, 3–5) on God establishing "houses" or families. The prosperity of human groups is not the work of human beings but the gift of God.

**127:5 At the gate**: the reference is not to enemies besieging the walls of a city but to adversaries in litigation. Law courts functioned in the open area near the main city gate. The more adult sons a man had, the more forceful he would appear in disputes, cf. Prv 31:23.

*e:* Prv 10:25. *f:* Dt 32:11. *g:* Ps 18:25ff. *h:* Prv 3:32. *i:* Ps 128:6. *j:* Ps 14:7. *k:* Jb 8:21. *l:* Bar 4:23; Is 65:19. *m:* Eccl 2:24. *n:* Ps 115:14; 128:3; Dt 28:11; Prv 17:6.

See RG 176

## PSALM 128*

### *The Blessed Home of the Just*

1 A song of ascents.

I

Blessed are all who fear the LORD,
and who walk in his ways.[o]
2 What your hands provide you will enjoy;
you will be blessed and prosper:[p]
3 Your wife will be like a fruitful vine
within your home,
Your children like young olive plants
around your table.[q]
4 Just so will the man be blessed
who fears the LORD.

II

5 May the LORD bless you from Zion;
may you see Jerusalem's prosperity
all the days of your life,[r]
6 and live to see your children's
children.[s]
Peace upon Israel![t]

See RG 175–76

## PSALM 129*

### *Against Israel's Enemies*

1 A song of ascents.

I

Viciously have they attacked me from
my youth,
let Israel say now.[u]
2 Viciously have they attacked me from
my youth,[v]
yet they have not prevailed against me.
3 Upon my back the plowers plowed,
as they traced their long furrows.[w]
4 But the just LORD cut me free
from the ropes of the wicked.*

II

5 May they recoil in disgrace,
all who hate Zion.
6 May they be like grass on the rooftops[x]
withered in early growth,*
7 Never to fill the reaper's hands,
nor the arms of the binders of sheaves,
8 And with none passing by to call out:
"The blessing of the LORD be upon you!*
We bless you in the name of the
LORD!"[y]

See RG 175–76

## PSALM 130*

### *Prayer for Pardon and Mercy*

1 A song of ascents.

I

Out of the depths* I call to you, LORD;
2 Lord, hear my cry!
May your ears be attentive
to my cry for mercy.[z]
3 If you, LORD, keep account of sins,
Lord, who can stand?[a]
4 But with you is forgiveness
and so you are revered.*

II

5 I wait for the LORD,
my soul waits
and I hope for his word.[b]
6 My soul looks for the Lord
more than sentinels for daybreak.[c]
More than sentinels for daybreak,
7 let Israel hope in the LORD,
For with the LORD is mercy,

**Psalm 128** A statement that the ever-reliable God will bless the reverent (Ps 128:1). God's blessing is concrete: satisfaction and prosperity, a fertile spouse and abundant children (Ps 128:2–4). The perspective is that of the adult male, ordinarily the ruler and representative of the household to the community. The last verses extend the blessing to all the people for generations to come (Ps 128:5–6).

**Psalm 129** A Psalm giving thanks for God's many rescues of Israel over the long course of their history (Ps 129:1–4); the people pray that their oppressors never know the joy of harvest (Ps 129:5–8).

**129:4 The ropes of the wicked**: usually understood as the rope for yoking animals to the plow. If it is severed, the plowing (cf. Ps 129:3) comes to a halt.

**129:6 Like grass on the rooftops**: after the spring rains, grass would sprout from the coat of mud with which the flat roofs of simple houses were covered, but when the dry summer began there was no moisture in the thin roof-covering to sustain the grass.

**129:8 The blessing of the LORD be upon you**: harvesters greeted one another with such blessings, cf. Ru 2:4.

**Psalm 130** This lament, a Penitential Psalm, is the *De profundis* used in liturgical prayers for the faithful departed. In deep sorrow the psalmist cries to God (Ps 130:1–2), asking for mercy (Ps 130:3–4). The psalmist's trust (Ps 130:5–6) becomes a model for the people (Ps 130:7–8).

**130:1 The depths**: Sheol here is a metaphor of total misery. Deep anguish makes the psalmist feel "like those descending to the pit" (Ps 143:7).

**130:4 And so you are revered**: the experience of God's mercy leads one to a greater sense of God.

*o:* Ps 112:1. *p:* Ps 112:3. *q:* Ps 144:12; Jb 29:5. *r:* Ps 20:3; 134:3. *s:* Jb 42:16; Prv 17:6. *t:* Ps 125:5. *u:* Ps 124:1. *v:* Ps 118:13. *w:* Is 51:23. *x:* Is 37:27. *y:* Ps 118:26. *z:* Ps 5:2–3; 55:2–3; 86:6; Lam 3:55–56; Jon 2:3. *a:* Na 1:6. *b:* Ps 119:81. *c:* Is 21:11; 26:9.

with him is plenteous redemption,[d]
8 And he will redeem Israel
from all its sins.[e]

## PSALM 131*

See RG 175–76

### *Humble Trust in God*

1 A song of ascents. Of David.

LORD, my heart is not proud;
nor are my eyes haughty.
I do not busy myself with great matters,
with things too sublime for me.[f]
2 Rather, I have stilled my soul,
Like a weaned child to its mother,
weaned is my soul.[g]
3 Israel, hope in the LORD,
now and forever.

## PSALM 132*

See RG 176

### *The Covenant Between David and God*

1 A song of ascents.

I

Remember, O LORD, for David
all his hardships;
2 How he swore an oath to the LORD,
vowed to the Mighty One of Jacob:*
3 "I will not enter the house where I live,[h]
nor lie on the couch where I sleep;
4 I will give my eyes no sleep,
my eyelids no rest,
5 Till I find a place for the LORD,
a dwelling for the Mighty One of Jacob."
6 "We have heard of it in Ephrathah;*
we have found it in the fields of Jaar.*
7 Let us enter his dwelling;
let us worship at his footstool."[i]
8 "Arise, LORD, come to your resting place,[j]
you and your mighty ark.
9 Your priests will be clothed with justice;
your devout will shout for joy."
10 For the sake of David your servant,
do not reject your anointed.

II

11 The LORD swore an oath to David in truth,
he will never turn back from it:[k]
"Your own offspring[l] I will set upon your throne.
12 If your sons observe my covenant,
and my decrees I shall teach them,
Their sons, in turn,
shall sit forever on your throne."
13 Yes, the LORD has chosen Zion,
desired it for a dwelling:
14 "This is my resting place forever;
here I will dwell, for I desire it.
15 I will bless Zion with provisions;
its poor I will fill with bread.
16 I will clothe its priests with salvation;
its devout shall shout for joy.[m]
17 There I will make a horn sprout for David;*[n]
I will set a lamp for my anointed.
18 His foes I will clothe with shame,
but on him his crown shall shine."

## PSALM 133*

See RG 176

### *A Vision of a Blessed Community*

1 A song of ascents. Of David.

How good and how pleasant it is,
when brothers* dwell together as one!

**Psalm 131** A song of trust, in which the psalmist gives up self-sufficiency (Ps 131:1), like a babe enjoying the comfort of its mother's lap (Ps 131:2), thus providing a model for Israel's faith (Ps 131:3).

**Psalm 132** A song for a liturgical ceremony in which the ark, the throne of Israel's God, was carried in procession to the Temple. The singer asks that David's care for the proper housing of the ark be regarded with favor (Ps 132:1–5), and tells how it was brought to Jerusalem (Ps 132:6–10). There follows God's promise of favor to the Davidic dynasty (Ps 132:11–12) and to Zion (Ps 132:13–17). The transfer of the ark to the tent in Jerusalem is described in 2 Sm 6.

**132:2, 132:5 Mighty One of Jacob**: one of the titles of Israel's God, cf. Gn 49:24; Is 49:26; 60:16.

**132:6 Ephrathah**: the homeland of David, cf. Ru 4:11. **The fields of Jaar**: poetic for Kiriath-jearim, a town west of Jerusalem, where the ark remained for several generations, cf. 1 Sm 7:1–2; 2 Sm 6:2; 1 Chr 13:5–6.

**132:17 A horn sprout for David**: the image of the horn, a symbol of strength, is combined with that of a "sprout," a term used for the Davidic descendant (cf. Jer 23:5; 33:15; Zec 3:8; 6:12). Early Christians referred the latter designation to Christ as son of David (Lk 1:69).

**Psalm 133** A benediction over a peaceful community, most probably the people Israel, but appropriate too for Israelite families (Ps 133:1). The history of Israel, whether of its an-

---

*d:* Ps 86:15; 100:5; 103:8. *e:* Ps 25:22; Mt 1:21. *f:* Ps 139:6. *g:* Is 66:12–13. *h:* 2 Sm 7; 1 Chr 28:2. *i:* Ps 99:5. *j:* Ps 2:2; 89:21; 95:11; Nm 10:35; 2 Chr 6:41–42; Sir 24:7. *k:* Ps 68:17; 1 Kgs 8:13; Sir 24:7. *l:* Ps 110:4; 2 Sm 7:12. *m:* 2 Chr 6:41; Is 61:10. *n:* Is 11:1; Jer 33:15; Ez 29:21; Zec 3:8; Lk 1:69.

2 Like fine oil on the head,*[o]
running down upon the beard,
Upon the beard of Aaron,
upon the collar of his robe.
3 Like dew* of Hermon* coming down
upon the mountains of Zion.[p]
There the LORD has decreed a blessing,
life for evermore![q]

### PSALM 134*

See RG 176

### *Exhortation to the Night Watch to Bless God*

1 A song of ascents.

O come, bless the LORD,
all you servants of the LORD*
You who stand in the house of the LORD
throughout the nights.[r]
2 Lift up your hands toward the sanctuary,[s]
and bless the LORD.
3 May the LORD bless you from Zion,
the Maker of heaven and earth.[t]

### PSALM 135*

See RG 175

### *Praise of God, the Ruler and Benefactor of Israel*

1 Hallelujah!

I

Praise the name of the LORD!
Praise, you servants of the LORD,[u]
2 Who stand in the house of the LORD,
in the courts of the house of our God![v]
3 Praise the LORD, for the LORD is good!
Sing to his name, for it brings joy!
4 *For the LORD has chosen Jacob for
himself,
Israel as his treasured possession.[w]

II

5 For I know that the LORD is great,
that our Lord is greater than all gods.[x]
6 Whatever the LORD desires
he does in heaven and on earth,
in the seas and all the depths.[y]
7 It is he who raises storm clouds from the
end of the earth,
makes lightning for the rain,
and brings forth wind from his
storehouse.[z]

III

8 He struck down Egypt's firstborn,[a]
of human being and beast alike,
9 And sent signs and wonders against you,
Egypt,
against Pharaoh and all his servants.
10 It is he who struck down many nations,[b]
and slew mighty kings—
11 Sihon, king of the Amorites,
and Og, king of Bashan,
all the kings of Canaan—
12 And made their land a heritage,
a heritage for Israel his people.
13 O LORD, your name is forever,
your renown, from generation to
generation![c]
14 For the LORD defends his people,
shows mercy to his servants.[d]

cestors in the Book of Genesis or of later periods, was a history of distinct groups struggling to live in unity. Here that unity is declared blessed, like the holy oils upon the priest Aaron or the dew of the rainless summer that waters the crops (Ps 133:2–3).

**133:1 Brothers**: in biblical Hebrew this word includes both the male and female members of a group united by blood relationships or by shared experiences and values. In this Psalm, the term could be applied most appropriately to the people of Israel, those privileged by God to be his chosen children.

**133:2 Oil on the head**: oil was used at the consecration of the high priest (Ex 30:22–33).

**133:3 Dew**: dew was an important source of moisture in the dry climate (Gn 27:28; Hos 14:6). **Hermon**: the majestic snow-capped mountain visible in the north of Palestine.

**Psalm 134** A brief liturgy exhorting all those who serve in the Jerusalem Temple during the night (cf. Is 30:29) to praise God with words and gestures. Although he is the Creator of the whole universe, God's blessings emanate in a unique way from Zion, the city of Jerusalem.

**134:1 Servants of the LORD**: priests and Levites, cf. Dt 10:8; Ps 113:1; 135:1; Dn 3:85.

**Psalm 135** The hymn begins and ends with an invitation to praise God (Ps 135:1–3, 19–20) for the great act of choosing Israel (Ps 135:4). The story of Israel's emergence as a people is told in Ps 135:5–14; God created and redeemed the people, easily conquering all opposition. God's defeat of hostile powers means that the powers themselves and their images are useless (Ps 135:15–18). The last three verses appear also in Ps 115:4–8.

**135:4** Though all nations are God's, Israel has a special status as God's "treasured" people: Ex 19:5; Dt 7:6; 14:2; 26:18; Mal 3:17.

*o:* Ex 30:25, 30. *p:* Hos 14:6. *q:* Dt 28:8; 30:20. *r:* Ps 135:1–2; 1 Chr 9:33. *s:* Ps 28:2; 141:2. *t:* Ps 20:3; 128:5; Nm 6:24. *u:* Ps 113:1. *v:* Ps 134:1. *w:* Ps 33:12; 144:15; Ex 19:6; Dt 7:6. *x:* Ps 95:3; Ex 18:11. *y:* Ps 115:3. *z:* Ps 148:8; Jer 10:13; 51:16; Jb 37:9. *a:* Ps 78:51; 105:27, 36; 136:10; Ex 12:29. *b:* Ps 136:17–22; Nm 21:21–35; Dt 2:24–3:17. *c:* Ps 102:13; Ex 3:15. *d:* Dt 32:36.

PSALM 136 IS known in Jewish liturgy as the Great Hallel and has been incorporated into the Passover Seder. Like 135, it is part of the introductory prayers to the morning service on Sabbath and festival days. The psalm is probably written to be chanted responsively, with the assembly chanting the refrain after each line. In Hebrew *hesed,* here translated "love," means a favor done out of loyalty. God's *hesed* to Israel is eternal. The psalm recounts in chronological order the many acts of *hesed* that God did for Israel in the past and the refrain confirms that these acts of *hesed* will continue.

IV

15 The idols of the nations are silver and gold,[e]
the work of human hands.
16 They have mouths but do not speak;
they have eyes but do not see;
17 They have ears but do not hear;
nor is there breath in their mouths.
18 Their makers will become like them,
and anyone who trusts in them.

V

19 House of Israel, bless the LORD![f]
House of Aaron, bless the LORD!
20 House of Levi, bless the LORD!
You who fear the LORD, bless the LORD!
21 Blessed be the LORD from Zion,
who dwells in Jerusalem!
Hallelujah!

## PSALM 136*

See RG 175

### *Hymn of Thanksgiving for God's Everlasting Mercy*

I

1 Praise the LORD, for he is good;[g]
for his mercy endures forever;
2 Praise the God of gods;
for his mercy endures forever;
3 Praise the Lord of lords;
for his mercy endures forever;

II

4 Who alone has done great wonders,[h]
for his mercy endures forever;
5 Who skillfully made the heavens,[i]
for his mercy endures forever;
6 Who spread the earth upon the waters,[j]
for his mercy endures forever;
7 Who made the great lights,
for his mercy endures forever;
8 The sun to rule the day,
for his mercy endures forever;
9 The moon and stars to rule the night,[k]
for his mercy endures forever;

III

10 Who struck down the firstborn of Egypt,[l]
for his mercy endures forever;
11 And led Israel from their midst,
for his mercy endures forever;
12 With mighty hand and outstretched arm,[m]
for his mercy endures forever;
13 Who split in two the Red Sea,
for his mercy endures forever;
14 And led Israel through its midst,
for his mercy endures forever;
15 But swept Pharaoh and his army into the Red Sea,[n]
for his mercy endures forever;
16 Who led the people through the desert,[o]
for his mercy endures forever;

IV

17 Who struck down great kings,[p]
for his mercy endures forever;
18 Slew powerful kings,
for his mercy endures forever;
19 Sihon, king of the Amorites,
for his mercy endures forever;
20 Og, king of Bashan,
for his mercy endures forever;
21 And made their lands a heritage,

**Psalm 136** The hymn praises Israel's God ("the God of gods," Ps 136:2), who has created the world in which Israel lives. The refrain occurring after every line suggests that a speaker and chorus sang the Psalm in antiphonal fashion. A single act of God is described in Ps 136:4–25. God arranges the heavens and the earth as the environment for human community, and then creates the community by freeing them and giving them land. In the final section (Ps 136:23–25) God, who created the people and gave them land, continues to protect and nurture them.

*e:* Ps 115:4–6, 8. *f:* Ps 118:2–4. *g:* Ps 100:5; 118:1. *h:* Ps 72:18. *i:* Gn 1:9–19. *j:* Ps 24:2. *k:* Jer 31:35. *l:* Ex 12:29, 51; 14:22, 27; 15:22; Ps 78:51–52; 135:8. *m:* Dt 4:34. *n:* Ex 14:21f. *o:* Dt 8:2, 15. *p:* Ps 135:10–12.

for his mercy endures forever;
22 *A heritage for Israel, his servant,
for his mercy endures forever.

V

23 The Lord remembered us in our low estate,
for his mercy endures forever;
24 Freed us from our foes,
for his mercy endures forever;
25 And gives bread to all flesh,
for his mercy endures forever.

VI

26 Praise the God of heaven,
for his mercy endures forever.

## PSALM 137*

See RG 175

### *Sorrow and Hope in Exile*

I

1 By the rivers of Babylon
there we sat weeping
when we remembered Zion.[q]
2 On the poplars in its midst
we hung up our harps.[r]
3 For there our captors asked us
for the words of a song;
Our tormentors, for joy:
"Sing for us a song of Zion!"
4 But how could we sing a song of the LORD
in a foreign land?

II

5 If I forget you, Jerusalem,
may my right hand forget.[s]
6 May my tongue stick to my palate
if I do not remember you,
If I do not exalt Jerusalem
beyond all my delights.

III

7 Remember, LORD, against Edom
that day at Jerusalem.
They said: "Level it, level it
down to its foundations!"[t]
8 Desolate Daughter Babylon, you shall be destroyed,
blessed the one who pays you back
what you have done us![u]
9 *Blessed the one who seizes your children
and smashes them against the rock.[v]

## PSALM 138*

See RG 175

### *Hymn of a Grateful Heart*

1 Of David.

I

I thank you, Lord, with all my heart;[w]
in the presence of the angels* to you I sing.
2 I bow low toward your holy temple;
I praise your name for your mercy and faithfulness.
For you have exalted over all
your name and your promise.
3 On the day I cried out, you answered;
you strengthened my spirit.

II

4 All the kings of earth will praise you, LORD,
when they hear the words of your mouth.
5 They will sing of the ways of the LORD:
"How great is the glory of the LORD!"
6 The LORD is on high, but cares for the lowly[x]
and knows the proud from afar.
7 Though I walk in the midst of dangers,
you guard my life when my enemies rage.
You stretch out your hand;
your right hand saves me.

**136:22 A heritage for Israel**: the land was given to Israel by God to be handed on to future generations.

**Psalm 137** A singer refuses to sing the people's sacred songs in an alien land despite demands from Babylonian captors (Ps 137:1–4). The singer swears an oath by what is most dear to a musician—hands and tongue—to exalt Jerusalem always (Ps 137:5–6). The Psalm ends with a prayer that the old enemies of Jerusalem, Edom and Babylon, be destroyed (Ps 137:7–9).

**137:9 Blessed the one who seizes your children and smashes them against the rock**: the children represent the future generations, and so must be destroyed if the enemy is truly to be eradicated.

**Psalm 138** A thanksgiving to God, who came to the rescue of the psalmist. Divine rescue was not the result of the psalmist's virtues but of God's loving fidelity (Ps 138:1–3). The act is not a private transaction but a public act that stirs the surrounding nations to praise God's greatness and care for the people (Ps 138:4–6). The psalmist, having experienced salvation, trusts that God will always be there in moments of danger (Ps 138:7–8).

**138:1 In the presence of the angels**: heavenly beings who were completely subordinate to Israel's God. The earthly Temple represents the heavenly palace of God.

*q:* Ez 3:15; Lam 3:48. *r:* Is 24:8; Lam 5:14. *s:* Jer 51:50. *t:* Jer 49:7; Lam 4:21–22; Ez 25:12–14. *u:* Is 47:1–3; Jer 50–51. *v:* Hos 14:1. *w:* Ps 9:1. *x:* Lk 1:51–52.

8 The LORD is with me to the end.
LORD, your mercy endures forever.
Never forsake the work of your hands!

See RG 176

## PSALM 139*

### *The All-knowing and Ever-present God*

1 For the leader. A psalm of David.

I

LORD, you have probed me, you know me:
2 you know when I sit and stand;*[y]
you understand my thoughts from afar.
3 You sift through my travels and my rest;
with all my ways you are familiar.
4 Even before a word is on my tongue,
LORD, you know it all.
5 Behind and before you encircle me
and rest your hand upon me.
6 Such knowledge is too wonderful for me,
far too lofty for me to reach.[z]

7 Where can I go from your spirit?
From your presence, where can I flee?
8 If I ascend to the heavens, you are there;
if I lie down in Sheol, there you are.[a]
9 If I take the wings of dawn*
and dwell beyond the sea,*
10 Even there your hand guides me,
your right hand holds me fast.
11 If I say, "Surely darkness shall hide me,
and night shall be my light"*—
12 Darkness is not dark for you,
and night shines as the day.
Darkness and light are but one.[b]

II

13 You formed my inmost being;
you knit me in my mother's womb.[c]
14 I praise you, because I am wonderfully
made;
wonderful are your works!
My very self you know.
15 My bones are not hidden from you,
When I was being made in secret,
fashioned in the depths of the earth.*
16 Your eyes saw me unformed;
in your book all are written down;[d]
my days were shaped, before one
came to be.

III

17 How precious to me are your designs,
O God;
how vast the sum of them!
18 Were I to count them, they would
outnumber the sands;
when I complete them, still you are
with me.[e]
19 When you would destroy the wicked,
O God,
the bloodthirsty depart from me![f]
20 Your foes who conspire a plot against you
are exalted in vain.

IV

21 Do I not hate, LORD, those who hate you?
Those who rise against you, do I not
loathe?[g]
22 With fierce hatred I hate them,
enemies I count as my own.

23 Probe me, God, know my heart;
try me, know my thoughts.[h]
24 See if there is a wicked path in me;
lead me along an ancient path.*

## PSALM 140*

See RG 175

### *Prayer for Deliverance from the Wicked*

1 For the leader. A psalm of David.

I

2 Deliver me, LORD, from the wicked;
preserve me from the violent,[i]

**Psalm 139** A hymnic meditation on God's omnipresence and omniscience. The psalmist is keenly aware of God's all-knowing gaze (Ps 139:1–6), of God's presence in every part of the universe (Ps 139:7–12), and of God's control over the psalmist's very self (Ps 139:13–16). Summing up Ps 139:1–16, 17–18 express wonder. There is only one place hostile to God's rule—wicked people. The psalmist prays to be removed from their company (Ps 139:19–24).

**139:2 When I sit and stand**: in all my physical movement.

**139:9 Take the wings of dawn**: go to the extremities of the east. **Beyond the sea**: uttermost bounds of the west; the sea is the Mediterranean.

**139:11 Night shall be my light**: night to me is what day is to others.

**139:15 The depths of the earth**: figurative language for the womb, stressing the hidden and mysterious operations that occur there.

**139:24 Lead me along an ancient path**: the manner of living of our ancestors, who were faithful to God's will, cf. Jer 6:16.

**Psalm 140** A lament seeking rescue from violent and

*y:* 2 Kgs 19:27; Jb 12:3. *z:* Ps 131:1. *a:* Jb 23:8–9; Jer 23:23–24. *b:* Jb 12:22. *c:* Wis 7:1; Eccl 11:5; Jb 1:21. *d:* Mal 3:16. *e:* Jb 11:7. *f:* Jb 21:14. *g:* Ps 119:158. *h:* Ps 17:3; 26:2. *i:* Ps 71:4.

3 From those who plan evil in their hearts,
who stir up conflicts every day,
4 *Who sharpen their tongue like a serpent,
venom of asps upon their lips.[j] *Selah*

II

5 Keep me, LORD, from the clutches of the wicked;
preserve me from the violent,
who plot to trip me up.[k]
6 *The arrogant have set a trap for me;
they have spread out ropes for a net,
laid snares for me by the wayside. *Selah*
7 I say to the LORD: You are my God;[l]
listen, LORD, to the words of my pleas.
8 LORD, my master, my strong deliverer,
you cover my head on the day of armed conflict.
9 LORD, do not grant the desires of the wicked one;
do not let his plot succeed. *Selah*

III

10 Those who surround me raise their heads;
may the mischief they threaten overwhelm them.
11 Drop burning coals upon them;[m]
cast them into the watery pit never more to rise.
12 Slanderers will not survive on earth;
evil will hunt down the man of violence to overthrow him.
13 For I know the LORD will take up the cause of the needy,
justice for the poor.
14 Then the righteous will give thanks to your name;
the upright will dwell in your presence.[n]

## PSALM 141*

See RG 175, 179

### *Prayer for Deliverance from the Wicked*

1 A psalm of David.

LORD, I call to you; hasten to me;
listen to my plea when I call.
2 Let my prayer be incense* before you;
my uplifted hands* an evening offering.[o]
3 Set a guard, LORD, before my mouth,
keep watch over the door of my lips.[p]
4 Do not let my heart incline to evil,
to perform deeds in wickedness.
On the delicacies of evildoers
let me not feast.
5 *Let a righteous person strike me; it is mercy if he reproves me.
Do not withhold oil from my head[q]
while my prayer opposes their evil deeds.
6 May their leaders be cast over the cliff,
so that they hear that my speeches are pleasing.
7 Like the plowing and breaking up of the earth,
our bones are strewn at the mouth of Sheol.
8 For my eyes are upon you, O LORD, my Lord;[r]
in you I take refuge; do not take away my soul.
9 Guard me from the trap they have set for me,
from the snares of evildoers.[s]
10 Let the wicked fall into their own nets,
while only I pass over them safely.

treacherous foes (Ps 140:2–6). The psalmist remains trusting (Ps 140:7–8), vigorously praying that the plans of the wicked recoil upon themselves (Ps 140:9–12). A serene statement of praise ends the Psalm (Ps 140:13). The psalmist is content to be known as one of "the needy," "the poor," "the just," "the upright" (Ps 140:13), a class of people expecting divine protection.

**140:4** Similar metaphors for a wicked tongue are used in Ps 52:2; 55:20; 58:3.

**140:6 Have set a trap . . . have spread out ropes for a net**: the same figure, of hunters setting traps, occurs in Ps 9:16; 31:5; 35:7; 64:6, cf. Mt 22:15; Lk 11:54.

**Psalm 141** A lament of an individual (Ps 141:1–2) who is keenly aware that only the righteous can worship God properly and who therefore prays to be protected from the doomed wicked (Ps 141:3–10).

**141:2 Incense**: lit., "smoke," i.e., the fragrant fumes arising from the altar at the burning of sacrificial animals or of aromatic spices; also used in Rev 5:8 as a symbol of prayer. **My uplifted hands**: the gesture of supplication, cf. Ps 28:2; 63:5; 88:10; 119:48; 134:2; 143:6.

**141:5–7** The Hebrew text is obscure.

*j:* Ps 64:4; Rom 3:13. *k:* Jer 18:22; Ps 56:7; 57:7. *l:* Ps 31:15. *m:* Ps 11:6; 120:4; Gn 19:24. *n:* Ps 11:7; 16:11; 17:15. *o:* Ps 134:2; Ex 30:8. *p:* Sir 22:27. *q:* Prv 9:8; 25:12. *r:* Ps 25:15; 123:1–2. *s:* Ps 142:4.

See RG 175

## PSALM 142*

### *A Prayer in Time of Trouble*

[1] A *maskil* of David, when he was in the cave.* A prayer.

[2] With my own voice I cry to the LORD;
with my own voice I beseech the LORD.
[3] Before him I pour out my complaint,
tell of my distress in front of him.
[4] When my spirit is faint within me,[t]
you know my path.[u]
As I go along this path,
they have hidden a trap for me.[v]
[5] I look to my right hand to see[w]
that there is no one willing to acknowledge me.
My escape has perished;
no one cares for me.
[6] I cry out to you, LORD,
I say, You are my refuge,[x]
my portion in the land of the living.[y]
[7] Listen to my cry for help,
for I am brought very low.[z]
Rescue me from my pursuers,
for they are too strong for me.
[8] Lead my soul from prison,
that I may give thanks to your name.
Then the righteous shall gather around me*
because you have been good to me.

See RG 175

## PSALM 143*

### *A Prayer in Distress*

[1] A psalm of David.

LORD, hear my prayer;
in your faithfulness listen to my pleading;
answer me in your righteousness.
[2] Do not enter into judgment with your servant;
before you no one can be just.[a]
[3] The enemy has pursued my soul;
he has crushed my life to the ground.[b]
He has made me dwell in darkness
like those long dead.[c]
[4] My spirit is faint within me;
my heart despairs.[d]
[5] I remember the days of old;
I ponder all your deeds;
the works of your hands I recall.[e]
[6] I stretch out my hands toward you,
my soul to you like a parched land.[f]
*Selah*
[7] Hasten to answer me, LORD;
for my spirit fails me.
Do not hide your face from me,
lest I become like those descending to the pit.[g]
[8] In the morning let me hear of your mercy,
for in you I trust.
Show me the path I should walk,
for I entrust my life to you.[h]
[9] Rescue me, LORD, from my foes,
for I seek refuge in you.
[10] Teach me to do your will,
for you are my God.
May your kind spirit guide me
on ground that is level.
[11] For your name's sake, LORD, give me life;
in your righteousness lead my soul out of distress.
[12] In your mercy put an end to my foes;
all those who are oppressing my soul,
for I am your servant.[i]

**Psalm 142** In this lament imploring God for help (Ps 142:2–4), the psalmist tells how enemies have set a trap (Ps 142:4–5), and prays for rescue (Ps 142:6–8). The speaker feels utterly alone (Ps 142:5), exhausted (Ps 142:7), and may even be imprisoned (Ps 142:7). Prison is possibly a metaphor for general distress. The last two verses are the vow of praise, made after receiving an assurance of divine help (Ps 142:7).

**142:1 In the cave**: cf. 1 Sm 22:1; 24:1–3; Ps 57:1.

**142:8 Then the righteous shall gather around me**: in the Temple, when the psalmist offers a thanksgiving sacrifice.

**Psalm 143** One of the Church's seven Penitential Psalms, this lament is a prayer to be freed from death-dealing enemies. The psalmist addresses God, aware that there is no equality between God and human beings; salvation is a gift (Ps 143:1–2). Victimized by evil people (Ps 143:3–4), the psalmist recites ("remembers") God's past actions on behalf of the innocent (Ps 143:5–6). The Psalm continues with fervent prayer (Ps 143:7–9) and a strong desire for guidance and protection (Ps 143:10–12).

*t:* Ps 143:4. *u:* Ps 139:24. *v:* Ps 141:9. *w:* Ps 16:8; 73:23; 121:5. *x:* Ps 91:2, 9. *y:* Ps 16:5; 27:13; 116:9; Is 38:11. *z:* Ps 79:8. *a:* Eccl 7:20; Jb 4:17; Rom 3:20. *b:* Ps 7:6. *c:* Lam 3:6. *d:* Ps 142:4; Jb 17:1. *e:* Ps 77:6, 12. *f:* Ps 42:2; 63:2. *g:* Ps 28:1; 30:4; 88:5; Prv 1:12. *h:* Ps 25:4; 27:11; 86:11; 119:12, 35. *i:* Ps 116:16.

See RG 176

## PSALM 144*

### *A Prayer for Victory and Prosperity*

1 Of David.

I

*Blessed be the LORD, my rock,
who trains my hands for battle,
my fingers for war;
2 My safeguard and my fortress,
my stronghold, my deliverer,
My shield, in whom I take refuge,
who subdues peoples under me.

II

3 *LORD, what is man that you take notice of him;
the son of man, that you think of him?[j]
4 *Man is but a breath,
his days are like a passing shadow.[k]
5 *LORD, incline your heavens and come down;
touch the mountains and make them smoke.[l]
6 Flash forth lightning and scatter my foes;
shoot your arrows and rout them.
7 Reach out your hand from on high;
deliver me from the many waters;
rescue me from the hands of foreign foes.
8 Their mouths speak untruth;
their right hands are raised in lying oaths.*
9 O God, a new song I will sing to you;
on a ten-stringed lyre I will play for you.[m]
10 You give victory to kings;
you delivered David your servant.[n]
From the menacing sword 11 deliver me;
rescue me from the hands of foreign foes.
Their mouths speak untruth;
their right hands are raised in lying oaths.

III

12 May our sons be like plants[o]
well nurtured from their youth,
Our daughters, like carved columns,
shapely as those of the temple.
13 May our barns be full
with every kind of store.
May our sheep increase by thousands,
by tens of thousands in our fields;
may our oxen be well fattened.
14 May there be no breach in the walls,
no exile, no outcry in our streets.[p]
15 Blessed the people so fortunate;
blessed the people whose God is the LORD.[q]

## PSALM 145*

See RG 175–76

### *The Greatness and Goodness of God*

1 Praise. Of David.

I will extol you, my God and king;
I will bless your name forever and ever.
2 Every day I will bless you;
I will praise your name forever and ever.[r]
3 Great is the LORD and worthy of much praise,[s]

**Psalm 144** The Psalm may reflect a ceremony in which the king, as leader of the army, asked God's help (Ps 144:1–8). In Ps 144:9 the poem shifts abruptly from pleading to thanksgiving, and (except for Ps 144:11) shifts again to prayer for the people. The first section (Ps 144:1–2) is a prayer of thanks for victory; the second (Ps 144:3–7a), a humble acknowledgment of human nothingness and a supplication that God show forth saving power; the third (Ps 144:9–11), a promise of future thanksgiving; the fourth (Ps 144:12–15), a wish for prosperity and peace. A prayer for deliverance from treacherous foes serves as a refrain after the second and third sections (Ps 144:7b–8, 11). Except for its final section, the Psalm is made up almost entirely of verses from other Psalms.

**144:1–2** Composed of phrases from Ps 18:3, 35, 47–48.

**144:3** Similar to Ps 8:4.

**144:4** Composed of phrases from Ps 39:6; 102:12.

**144:5–7** Adapted in large part from Ps 18:10, 15, 17; 104:32.

**144:8b, 11b Their right hands are raised in lying oaths**: the psalmist's enemies give false testimony.

**Psalm 145** A hymn in acrostic form; every verse begins with a successive letter of the Hebrew alphabet. Acrostic poems usually do not develop ideas but consist rather of loosely connected statements. The singer invites all to praise God (Ps 145:1–3, 21). The "works of God" make God present and invite human praise (Ps 145:4–7); they climax in a confession (Ps 145:8–9). God's mighty acts show forth divine kingship (Ps 145:10–20), a major theme in the literature of early Judaism and in Christianity.

*j:* Jb 7:17. *k:* Ps 62:10; 90:9–10; Jb 7:16; Eccl 6:12; Wis 2:5. *l:* Is 63:19. *m:* Ps 33:2–3. *n:* Ps 18:51. *o:* Ps 128:3. *p:* Is 65:19. *q:* Ps 33:12. *r:* Ps 34:2. *s:* Ps 48:2; 95:3; 96:4; Jb 36:26.

whose grandeur is beyond
understanding.
4 One generation praises your deeds to the
next
and proclaims your mighty works.[t]
5 They speak of the splendor of your
majestic glory,
tell of your wonderful deeds.[u]
6 They speak of the power of your
awesome acts
and recount your great deeds.[v]
7 They celebrate your abounding goodness
and joyfully sing of your justice.
8 The LORD is gracious and merciful,
slow to anger and abounding in
mercy.[w]
9 The LORD is good to all,
compassionate toward all your works.[x]
10 All your works give you thanks, LORD
and your faithful bless you.[y]
11 They speak of the glory of your reign
and tell of your mighty works,
12 Making known to the sons of men your
mighty acts,
the majestic glory of your rule.
13 Your reign is a reign for all ages,
your dominion for all generations.[z]
The LORD is trustworthy in all his words,
and loving in all his works.
14 The LORD supports all who are falling
and raises up all who are bowed
down.[a]
15 The eyes of all look hopefully to you;
you give them their food in due
season.[b]
16 You open wide your hand
and satisfy the desire of every living
thing.
17 The LORD is just in all his ways,
merciful in all his works.[c]
18 The LORD is near to all who call upon
him,
to all who call upon him in truth.[d]
19 He fulfills the desire of those who fear
him;
he hears their cry and saves them.[e]
20 The LORD watches over all who love
him,
but all the wicked he destroys.[f]
21 My mouth will speak the praises of the
LORD;
all flesh will bless his holy name
forever and ever.

## PSALM 146*

See RG 175

### *Trust in God the Creator and Redeemer*

1 Hallelujah!
2 Praise the LORD, my soul;
I will praise the LORD all my life,
sing praise to my God while I live.[g]

I

3 Put no trust in princes,
in children of Adam powerless to
save.[h]
4 Who breathing his last, returns to the
earth;
that day all his planning comes to
nothing.[i]

II

5 Blessed the one whose help is the God of
Jacob,
whose hope is in the LORD, his God,
6 The maker of heaven and earth,
the seas and all that is in them,[j]
Who keeps faith forever,
7 secures justice for the oppressed,[k]
who gives bread to the hungry.
The LORD sets prisoners free;[l]
8 the LORD gives sight to the blind.
The LORD raises up those who are bowed
down;[m]
the LORD loves the righteous.
9 The LORD protects the resident alien,
comes to the aid of the orphan and the
widow,[n]

**Psalm 146** A hymn of someone who has learned there is no other source of strength except the merciful God. Only God, not mortal human beings (Ps 146:3–4), can help vulnerable and oppressed people (Ps 146:5–9). The first of the five hymns that conclude the Psalter.

*t:* Ps 22:31–32; 48:14–15; 71:18; 78:4; Ex 10:2; Dt 4:9. *u:* Ps 96:3; 105:2. *v:* Ps 66:3. *w:* Ps 86:5, 15; 103:8; Ex 34:6; Sir 2:11. *x:* Ps 103:13; Wis 11:24. *y:* Dn 3:57. *z:* Ps 10:16; 102:13; 146:10; Lam 5:19; Dn 3:33; Rev 11:15. *a:* Ps 94:18; 146:8. *b:* Ps 136:25; 104:27–28; Mt 6:25–26. *c:* Dt 32:4. *d:* Dt 4:7; Is 55:6; 58:9. *e:* Ps 34:18. *f:* Jgs 5:31. *g:* Ps 103:1; 104:33. *h:* Ps 118:8–9. *i:* Ps 90:3; 104:29; 1 Mc 2:63; Jb 34:14–15; Eccl 3:20; 12:7; Sir 40:11; Is 2:22. *j:* Ps 121:2; 124:8; Ex 20:11; Acts 14:15; Rev 14:7. *k:* Ps 103:6. *l:* Ps 68:7; Is 49:9; 61:1. *m:* Ps 145:14. *n:* Ps 68:6; Dt 10:18.

but thwarts the way of the wicked.
10 The LORD shall reign forever,
your God, Zion, through all
generations![o]
Hallelujah!

## PSALM 147*

See RG 175-76

### *God's Word Restores Jerusalem*

1 Hallelujah!

I

How good to sing praise to our God;
how pleasant to give fitting praise.[p]
2 The LORD rebuilds Jerusalem,
and gathers the dispersed of Israel,[q]
3 Healing the brokenhearted,
and binding up their wounds.[r]
4 He numbers the stars,
and gives to all of them their names.[s]
5 Great is our Lord, vast in power,
with wisdom beyond measure.[t]
6 The LORD gives aid to the poor,
but casts the wicked to the ground.[u]

II

7 Sing to the LORD with thanksgiving;
with the lyre make music to our God,[v]
8 *Who covers the heavens with clouds,
provides rain for the earth,
makes grass sprout on the
mountains,[w]
9 Who gives animals their food
and young ravens what they cry for.[x]
10 *He takes no delight in the strength of
horses,
no pleasure in the runner's stride.[y]
11 Rather the LORD takes pleasure in those
who fear him,
those who put their hope in his mercy.

III

12 Glorify the LORD, Jerusalem;
Zion, offer praise to your God,
13 For he has strengthened the bars of your
gates,
blessed your children within you.[z]
14 He brings peace to your borders,
and satisfies you with finest wheat.[a]
15 *He sends his command to earth;
his word runs swiftly![b]
16 Thus he makes the snow like wool,
and spreads the frost like ash;[c]
17 He disperses hail like crumbs.
Who can withstand his cold?
18 Yet when again he issues his command,
it melts them;
he raises his winds and the waters
flow.
19 He proclaims his word to Jacob,
his statutes and laws to Israel.[d]
20 He has not done this for any other nation;
of such laws they know nothing.
Hallelujah!

## PSALM 148*

See RG 175, 178

### *All Creation Summoned To Praise*

1 Hallelujah!

I

Praise the LORD from the heavens;
praise him in the heights.
2 Praise him, all you his angels;
give praise, all you his hosts.[e]
3 Praise him, sun and moon;
praise him, all shining stars.
4 Praise him, highest heavens,*
you waters above the heavens.

**Psalm 147** The hymn is divided into three sections by the calls to praise in Ps 147:1, 7, 12. The first section praises the powerful creator who restores exiled Judah (Ps 147:1–6); the second section, the creator who provides food to animals and human beings; the third and climactic section exhorts the holy city to recognize it has been re-created and made the place of disclosure for God's word, a word as life-giving as water.

**147:8–9** God clothes the fields and feeds the birds, cf. Mt 6:26, 30.

**147:10–11** Acknowledging one's dependence upon God rather than claiming self-sufficiency pleases God, cf. Ps 20:8; 33:16–19.

**147:15–19** God speaks through the thunder of nature and the word of revealed law, cf. Is 55:10–11. The weather phenomena are well known in Jerusalem: a blizzard of snow and hail followed by a thunderstorm that melts the ice.

**Psalm 148** A hymn inviting the beings of heaven (Ps 148:1–6) and of earth (Ps 148:7–14) to praise God. The hymn does not distinguish between inanimate and animate (and rational) nature.

**148:4 Highest heavens**: lit., "the heavens of the heavens," i.e., the space above the firmament, where the "upper waters" are stored, cf. Gn 1:6–7; Dt 10:14; 1 Kgs 8:27; Ps 104:3, 13.

*o:* Ps 145:13; Lam 5:19. *p:* Ps 33:1; 92:2. *q:* Is 11:12; 56:8; Jer 31:10. *r:* Jb 5:18; Is 30:26; 61:1; Jer 33:6. *s:* Is 40:26. *t:* Jdt 16:13; Jer 51:15. *u:* Ps 146:9; 1 Sm 2:7–8. *v:* Ps 71:22. *w:* Ps 104:13f; Jb 5:10; Jer 14:22; Jl 2:23. *x:* Jb 38:41; Mt 6:26. *y:* Ps 20:8; 33:16–18. *z:* Ps 48:14. *a:* Ps 81:17. *b:* Ps 33:9. *c:* Jb 6:16; 37:10; 38:22. *d:* Ps 78:5; Bar 3:37; Dt 4:7–8. *e:* Ps 103:20f; Dn 3:58–63.

IN PSALM 150, the command to "give praise," *hallelu*, occurs in every verse. This psalm concludes the section and the book of Psalms as a whole, capturing the essence of the book. Instead of closing with a doxological verse, the book closes with an entire chapter that serves as a doxology.

5 Let them all praise the LORD's name;
for he commanded and they were
created,[f]
6 Assigned them their station forever,
set an order that will never change.

II

7 Praise the LORD from the earth,
you sea monsters and all the deeps of
the sea;[g]
8 Lightning and hail, snow and thick clouds,
storm wind that fulfills his command;
9 Mountains and all hills,
fruit trees and all cedars;[h]
10 Animals wild and tame,
creatures that crawl and birds that fly;[i]
11 Kings of the earth and all peoples,
princes and all who govern on earth;
12 Young men and women too,
old and young alike.
13 Let them all praise the LORD's name,
for his name alone is exalted,
His majesty above earth and heaven.[j]
14 *He has lifted high the horn of his people;
to the praise of all his faithful,
the Israelites, the people near to him.
Hallelujah!

## PSALM 149*

See RG 175

### *Praise God with Song and Sword*

[l]Hallelujah!

Sing to the LORD a new song,
his praise in the assembly of the
faithful.[k]
2 Let Israel be glad in its maker,
the people of Zion rejoice in their
king.
3 Let them praise his name in dance,
make music with tambourine and
lyre.*[l]
4 For the LORD takes delight in his people,
honors the poor with victory.
5 Let the faithful rejoice in their glory,
cry out for joy on their couches,*
6 With the praise of God in their mouths,
and a two-edged sword in their
hands,[m]
7 To bring retribution on the nations,
punishment on the peoples,[n]
8 To bind their kings in shackles,
their nobles in chains of iron,
9 To execute the judgments decreed for
them—
such is the glory* of all God's faithful.
Hallelujah!

## PSALM 150*

See RG 175

### *Final Doxology*

[l]Hallelujah!

Praise God in his holy sanctuary;*[o]
give praise in the mighty dome of
heaven.
2 Give praise for his mighty deeds,[p]
praise him for his great majesty.
3 Give praise with blasts upon the horn,[q]
praise him with harp and lyre.
4 Give praise with tambourines and dance,

**148:14 Has lifted high the horn of his people**: the horn symbolizes strength, the concrete noun for the abstract. Of all peoples, God has chosen Israel to return praise and thanks in a special way.

**Psalm 149** A hymn inviting the people of Israel to celebrate their God in song and festive dance (Ps 149:1–3, 5) because God has chosen them and given them victory (Ps 149:4). The exodus and conquest are the defining acts of Israel; the people must be ready to do again those acts in the future at the divine command (Ps 149:6–9).

**149:3 Make music with tambourine and lyre**: the verse recalls the great exodus hymn of Ex 15:20.

**149:5 On their couches**: the people reclined to banquet.

**149:9 The glory**: what brings honor to the people is their readiness to carry out the divine will, here conceived as punishing injustice done by the nations.

**Psalm 150** The Psalm is a closing doxology both for the

*f:* Ps 33:9; Gn 1:3f; Jdt 16:14. *g:* Ps 135:6; Gn 1:21. *h:* Is 44:23. *i:* Ps 30:5; Gn 1:21, 24f; Dt 4:7. *j:* Ps 30:5; Dt 4:7. *k:* Ps 22:23; 26:12; 35:18; 40:10; Jdt 16:1. *l:* Ps 68:26; 81:2–3; 87:7; 150:3–4. *m:* Neh 4:10–12; 2 Mc 15:27. *n:* Wis 3:8. *o:* Dn 3:53. *p:* Dt 3:24. *q:* Ps 81:3–4; 149:3; 2 Sm 6:5; 1 Chr 13:8; 16:5, 42; 2 Chr 5:12–13; 7:6.

praise him with strings and pipes.[r]
5 Give praise with crashing cymbals,
praise him with sounding cymbals.
6 Let everything that has breath
give praise to the LORD![s]
Hallelujah!

fifth book of the Psalms (Ps 107–149) and for the Psalter as a whole. Temple musicians and dancers are called to lead all beings on earth and in heaven in praise of God. The Psalm proclaims to whom praise shall be given, and where (Ps 150:1); what praise shall be given, and why (Ps 150:2); how praise shall be given (Ps 150:3–5), and by whom (Ps 150:6).

**150:1 His holy sanctuary**: God's Temple on earth. **The mighty dome of heaven**: lit., "[God's] strong vault"; heaven is here imagined as a giant plate separating the inhabited world from the waters of the heavens.

*r:* Ps 68:26; Ex 15:20. *s:* Rev 5:13.

See RG 180–82

# The Book of Proverbs

Proverbs is an anthology of collections of sayings and instructions. Many of the sayings and perhaps some instructions were composed in the monarchic period (late eleventh to the early sixth centuries). Editing of the whole book was done in the early postexilic period, in the view of most scholars; at that time chaps. 1–9 would have been added as the introduction. Whether the material originated among royal scribes (as 25:1 seems to suggest) imitating common literary genres, or whether it arose among tribal elders inculcating traditional ways, is disputed. The origin of the material, however, need not be imagined in an either/or scenario. Folk wisdom and observations could surely have been elaborated and re-expressed by learned scribes: "What oft was thought but ne'er so well expressed" (Alexander Pope). There can be no doubt, however, that Proverbs is sophisticated literature by talented writers, winning readers with its compelling portrait of wisdom and inviting them to see life afresh, "wisely," through its wit, originality, and shrewd observation.

The primary purpose of the book is to teach wisdom, not only to the young and inexperienced (1:2–4) but also to the advanced (1:5–6). Wisdom in the ancient Near East was not theoretical knowledge but practical expertise. Jewelers who cut precious stones were wise; kings who made their dominion peaceful and prosperous were wise. One could be wise in daily life, too, in knowing how to live successfully (having a prosperous household and living a long and healthy life) and without trouble in God's universe. Ultimately wisdom, or "sound guidance" (1:5), aims at the formation of character.

In the ancient Near East, people assumed that wisdom belonged to the gods, who were wise by reason of their divinity; human beings needed to have wisdom *granted* them by the gods. Creation accounts of neighboring cultures depict creation in two stages. In the first stage, human beings lived an animal-like existence, without clothes, writing, or kingship (proper governance). Over time, the gods came to realize that such a low grade of existence made the human race inadequate as their servants, so they endowed the race with "wisdom," which consisted of culture (e.g., kingship) and crafts (e.g., knowledge of farming, ability to weave). Such wisdom elevated the race to a "human" level and made them effective servants of the gods. Furthermore, divine wisdom was *mediated* to human beings through earthly institutions—the king, scribes (who produced wise writings), and heads of families (fathers, sometimes mothers). These traditional mediators appear in Proverbs: the book is credited to King Solomon, and kings are respectfully mentioned as pillars of society (e.g., 16:12–15); *writings* are a source of wisdom (1:1–7); the father instructing his son is the major paradigm of teaching. Proverbs differs, however, from other wisdom books in concentrating on wisdom itself, treating it as a virtually independent entity and personifying it as an attractive woman. Other books urge readers to perform wise acts, but Proverbs urges them to seek wisdom itself and portrays wisdom as a woman seeking human beings as disciples and companions.

Chapters 1–9 introduce the book, drawing attention to wisdom itself and its inherent value rather than exhorting to particular wise actions. The chapters personify wisdom as a woman and draw an extended analogy between finding a wife, or founding and maintaining a house(hold), and finding wisdom. The collections following chap. 9 consist largely of independent, two-line sayings, yielding their often indirect or paradoxical meaning only to readers willing to ponder them. To reflect on the sayings is perhaps what chaps. 1–9 mean by living with Wisdom and dwelling in her house.

The Book of Proverbs can make an important contribution to Christians and Jews today. First, it places the pursuit of wisdom over the performance of individual wise acts. To seek wisdom above all things is a fundamental option and a way of life. Second, it portrays the quest as filled with obstacles. There are men and women who offer a substitute for the real thing; discernment is required. Third, the book teaches that acquiring wisdom is both a human task and a divine gift. One can make oneself ready to receive by discipline, but one cannot take so divine a gift. Fourth, wisdom is in the world but it is not obvious to people entirely caught up with daily activities. The instructions and the aphorisms of the book can free the mind to see new things. Christians will see in personified Wisdom aspects of Jesus Christ, who they believe is divine wisdom sent to give human beings true and full life. Yet there is a universal dimension to Proverbs, for in its attention to human experience it creates a link to all people of good will.

The genres and themes of Proverbs continued on in Sirach, Wisdom of Solomon, and the later *Pirqe Abot* (The Sayings of the Fathers), a treatise in the Mishnah, which became the object of commentary in *Abot de Rabbi Nathan*. The New Testament saw Jesus as a wisdom teacher and employed the tradition of personified wisdom of chaps. 2 and 8 to express his incarnation. The Letter of James is an instruction resembling those in Proverbs. Wisdom traditions influenced the Gospels of Matthew and Luke through a common source (see, e.g., Mt 11:25–27 and Lk 10:21–22, which seem to derive their father-son language, at least in part, from the parental language of Proverbs). The Gospel of John regards Jesus as incarnate wisdom descended from on high to offer human beings life and truth and make disciples of them, a view largely reflected in Proverbs 1–9. In later Judaism, Hebrew ethical wills, in which parents hand on to their children their wisdom, borrowed from the genre of instruction.

The original audience of the instructions and sayings seems to have been male. The father addresses his son, marriage is finding a wife, success often is serving the king or farming effectively. The book itself, however, expands the traditional audience of youths (1:4) to include older, more experienced, people (1:5). It broadens the father-son language by mentioning the mother, and incorporates sayings on human experience generally. The father teaching his son becomes a model for anyone teaching a way of life to another person. The canonical process furthered such inclusiveness, for Proverbs was made part of the Bible that addresses *all* Israel.

The Book of Proverbs has nine sections:

- I. Title and Introduction (1:1–7)
- II. Instructions of Parents and of Woman Wisdom (1:8–9:18)
- III. First Solomonic Collection of Sayings (10:1–22:16)
- IV. Sayings of the Wise (22:17–24:22)
- V. Further Sayings of the Wise (24:23–34)
- VI. Second Solomonic Collection, Collected under King Hezekiah (25:1–29:27)
- VII. Sayings of Agur and Others (30:1–33)
- VIII. Sayings of King Lemuel (31:1–9)
- IX. Poem on the Woman of Worth (31:10–31)

Part II is judged by many scholars to contain ten instructions (1:8–19; chap. 2; 3:1–12, 21–35; 4:1–9, 10–19, 20–27; chap. 5; 6:20–35; chap. 7), three wisdom poems (1:20–33; chap. 8; 9:1–6 + 11, 13–18), and two interludes (3:13–20; 6:1–19).

# I. Title and Introduction

## CHAPTER 1

See RG 180–82

### *Purpose of the Proverbs of Solomon**

1 The proverbs* of Solomon,[a] the son of David,
king of Israel:

**1:1–7** The prologue explains the purpose of the book. The book has a sapiential, ethical, and religious dimension: to bring the inexperienced to knowledge and right conduct, to increase the facility of those already wise for interpreting proverbs, parables and riddles, and to encourage the fulfillment of one's duties to God.

**1:1 Proverbs**: the Hebrew word *mashal* is broader than English "proverb," embracing the instructions of chaps. 1–9

*a*: Prv 10:1; 25:1; 1 Kgs 4:32.

**Parental Advice on Leaving Home**

THE OPENING SCENE of a youth leaving his parents and home to establish his own household (1:8–19) sets the scene for the entire book of Proverbs. Every reader must establish a household in the sense of learning to live well as an adult, accepting traditional wisdom and discerning where true life is to be found.

2 That people may know wisdom and
discipline,*
may understand intelligent sayings;
3 May receive instruction in wise conduct,
in what is right, just and fair;
4 That resourcefulness may be imparted to
the naive,*
knowledge and discretion to the young.
5 The wise by hearing them will advance
in learning,
the intelligent will gain sound guidance,
6 To comprehend proverb and byword,
the words of the wise and their riddles.
7 Fear of the LORD* is the beginning of
knowledge;[b]
fools despise wisdom and discipline.

## II. Instructions of Parents and of Woman Wisdom

### *The Path of the Wicked: Greed and Violence**

8 Hear, my son, your father's instruction,
and reject not your mother's teaching;
9 A graceful diadem will they be for your
head;
a pendant for your neck.
10 My son, should sinners entice you,
11 do not go if they say, "Come along
with us!
Let us lie in wait for blood,
unprovoked, let us trap the innocent;
12 Let us swallow them alive, like Sheol,
whole, like those who go down to the
pit!
13 All kinds of precious wealth shall we
gain,
we shall fill our houses with booty;
14 Cast in your lot with us,
we shall all have one purse!"
15 My son, do not walk in the way with them,
hold back your foot from their path!
16 [For their feet run to evil,
they hasten to shed blood.[c]]
17 In vain a net is spread*
right under the eyes of any bird—
18 They lie in wait for their own blood,
they set a trap for their own lives.
19 This is the way of everyone greedy for
loot:
it takes away their lives.

### *Wisdom in Person Gives a Warning**

20 Wisdom cries aloud in the street,
in the open squares she raises her
voice;[d]

and the sayings, observations, and comparisons of chaps. 10–31.

**1:2 Discipline**: education or formation which dispels ignorance and corrects vice. Note the reprise of v. 2a in v. 7b.

**1:4 Naive**: immature, inexperienced, sometimes the young, hence easily influenced for good or evil.

**1:7 Fear of the LORD**: primarily a disposition rather than the emotion of fear; reverential awe and respect toward God combined with obedience to God's will.

**1:8–19** A parental warning to a young person leaving home, for them to avoid the company of the greedy and violent. Two ways lie before the hearer, a way that leads to death and a way that leads to life. The trap which the wicked set for the innocent (v. 11) in the end takes away the lives of the wicked themselves (v. 19). This theme will recur especially in chaps. 1–9. A second theme introduced here is that of founding (or managing) a household and choosing a spouse. A third theme is the human obstacles to attaining wisdom. Here (and in 2:12–15 and 4:10–19), the obstacle is men (always in the plural); in 2:16–19; 5:1–6; 6:20–35; chap. 7; 9:13–18, the obstacle to the quest is the "foreign" woman (always in the singular).

**1:17** A difficult verse. The most probable interpretation is that no fowler lifts up the net so the bird can see it. The verse might be paraphrased: God does not let those who walk on evil paths see the net that will entrap them. The passive construction ("a net is spread") is sometimes used to express divine activity. Verse 16 is a later attempt to add clarity. It is a quotation from Is 59:7 and is not in the best Greek manuscripts.

**1:20–33** Wisdom is personified as in chaps. 8 and 9:1–6. With divine authority she proclaims the moral order, threatening to leave to their own devices those who disregard her

*b:* Prv 9:10; Jb 28:28; Ps 111:10; Sir 1:16. *c:* Is 59:7. *d:* Prv 8:1–3; 9:3.

## The Blessings of Wisdom

CHAPTER 2 IS an acrostic poem of twenty-two lines (the number of consonants in the Hebrew alphabet). The first letter of the Hebrew alphabet ("aleph") dominates the first half (vv. 1–11; "aleph" is the initial letter in vv. 1, 3, 4, 5, and 9). The middle letter of the Hebrew alphabet ("lamed") dominates the second half (vv. 12–22; "lamed" is the initial letter of vv. 12, 16, 20). The main point of the poem is that if you seek wisdom with all your strength, the LORD will give it to you, and wisdom will safeguard you from wicked men and seductive women with the result that you can walk on the blessed path. Wisdom will be given to anyone who earnestly seeks it. However, one cannot directly take wisdom; it must be given as a gift.

21 Down the crowded ways she calls out,
at the city gates she utters her words:
22 * "How long, you naive ones, will you
love naivete,
23 How long will you turn away at my
reproof?
[The arrogant delight in their arrogance,
and fools hate knowledge.]
Lo! I will pour out to you my spirit,
I will acquaint you with my words:
24 'Because I called and you refused,
extended my hand and no one took
notice;[e]
25 Because you disdained all my counsel,
and my reproof you ignored—
26 I, in my turn, will laugh at your doom;
will mock when terror overtakes you;
27 When terror comes upon you like a storm,
and your doom approaches like a
whirlwind;
when distress and anguish befall you.'
28 Then they will call me, but I will not
answer;
they will seek me, but will not find me,
29 Because they hated knowledge,
and the fear of the LORD they did not
choose.
30 They ignored my counsel,
they spurned all my reproof;
31 Well, then, they shall eat the fruit* of
their own way,
and with their own devices be glutted.
32 For the straying of the naive kills them,
the smugness of fools destroys them.
33 But whoever obeys me dwells in security,
in peace, without fear of harm."[f]

### CHAPTER 2

See RG 180–82

### *The Blessings of Wisdom**

1 My son, if you receive my words
and treasure my commands,
2 Turning your ear to wisdom,*

invitation. All three speeches of Woman Wisdom have common features: a setting in city streets; an audience of simple or naive people; a competing appeal (chap. 7 is the competing appeal for chap. 8); an invitation to a relationship that brings long life, riches, repute.

The structure of the speeches is: A: setting (vv. 20–21); B: Wisdom's withdrawal, rebuke and announcement (vv. 22–23); reason and rejection I (vv. 24–27); reason and rejection II (vv. 28–31); summary (v. 32); C: the effects of Wisdom's presence (v. 33). Wisdom's opening speech is an extended threat ending with a brief invitation (v. 33). Her second speech is an extended invitation ending with a brief threat (8:36). The surprisingly abrupt and harsh tone of her speech is perhaps to be explained as a response to the arrogant words of the men in the previous scene (1:8–19).

**1:22–23** There is textual confusion. Verse 22bc (in the third person) is an addition, interrupting vv. 22a and 23a (in the second person). The addition has been put in brackets, to separate it from the original poem. The original verses do not ask for a change of heart but begin to detail the consequences of disobedience to Wisdom.

**1:31 Eat the fruit**: sinners are punished by the consequences of their sins. Wisdom's voice echoes that of the parents in vv. 8–19. The parents mediate wisdom in vv. 8–19, but here Wisdom herself speaks.

**2:1–22** Chapter 2 is a single poem, an acrostic of twenty-two lines, the number of consonants in the Hebrew alphabet. In vv. 1–11, the letter *aleph*, the first letter of the alphabet, predominates, and in vv. 12–22, the letter *lamed*, the first letter of the second half of the alphabet. A single structure runs through the whole: if (*aleph*) you search . . . then (*aleph*) the Lord/Wisdom will grant . . . saving (*lamed*) you from the wicked man/woman . . . thus (*lamed*) you can walk in the safe way. . . .

**2:2–3 Wisdom . . . understanding . . . intelligence**: various names or aspects of the same gift.

*e:* Is 65:2, 12; 66:4; Jer 7:13. *f:* Prv 8:33–34.

inclining your heart to understanding;
3 Yes, if you call for intelligence,
and to understanding raise your voice;
4 If you seek her like silver,
and like hidden treasures search her out,
5 Then will you understand the fear of the
LORD;
the knowledge of God you will find;
6 For the LORD gives wisdom,
from his mouth come knowledge and
understanding;[g]
7 He has success in store for the upright,
is the shield of those who walk honestly,
8 Guarding the paths of justice,
protecting the way of his faithful ones,
9 Then you will understand what is right
and just,
what is fair, every good path;
10 For wisdom will enter your heart,
knowledge will be at home in your soul,
11 Discretion will watch over you,
understanding will guard you;
12 * Saving you from the way of the wicked,
from those whose speech is perverse.
13 From those who have left the straight
paths
to walk in the ways of darkness,
14 Who delight in doing evil
and celebrate perversity;
15 Whose ways are crooked,
whose paths are devious;
16 * Saving you from a stranger,
from a foreign woman with her
smooth words,[h]
17 One who forsakes the companion of her
youth
and forgets the covenant of her God;
18 For her path sinks down to death,
and her footsteps lead to the shades.* [i]
19 None who enter there come back,
or gain the paths of life.
20 Thus you may walk in the way of the
good,
and keep to the paths of the just.
21 * For the upright will dwell in the land,[j]
people of integrity will remain in it;
22 But the wicked will be cut off from the
land,
the faithless will be rooted out of it.

## CHAPTER 3

See RG 180–82

### *Confidence in God Leads to Prosperity**

1 My son, do not forget* my teaching,
take to heart my commands;
2 For many days, and years of life,[k]
and peace, will they bring you.
3 Do not let love and fidelity forsake you;
bind them around your neck;
write them on the tablet of your heart.

**2:12–15** As in 1:8–19, there is an obstacle to the quest for wisdom—deceitful and violent men. Cf. also 4:10–19. They offer a way of life that is opposed to the way of wisdom.

**2:16–19** A second obstacle and counter-figure to Wisdom, personified as an attractive woman, is the "stranger," or "foreigner," from outside the territory or kinship group, hence inappropriate as a marriage partner. In Proverbs she comes to be identified with Woman Folly, whose deceitful words promise life but lead to death. Woman Folly appears also in chap. 5, 6:20–35, chap. 7 and 9:13–18. **Covenant**: refers to the vow uttered with divine sanction at the woman's previous marriage, as the parallel verse suggests. She is already married and relations with her would be adulterous.

**2:18 Shades**: the inhabitants of Sheol.

**2:21–22** Verses 21–22 echo the ending of Wisdom's speech in 1:32–33, in which refusing Wisdom's invitation meant death and obedience to her meant life. The same set of ideas is found in Ps 37 (especially vv. 3, 9, 11, 22, 29, 34, and 38): to live on (or inherit) the land and to be uprooted from the land are expressions of divine recompense.

**3:1–12** The instruction consists of a series of six four-line exhortations in which the second line of each exhortation mentions a reward or benefit. In the first five exhortations, the teacher promises a reward: long life, a good name, divine protection, health, abundant crops. The last exhortation, vv. 11–12, departs from the command-reward scheme, implying that being a disciple of the Lord does not guarantee unalloyed bliss: one must allow God freedom to "reprove" or educate. The process of education is like that described in chap. 2: the father first invites his son (or disciple) to memorize his teaching (v. 1), then to enter upon a relationship of trust with him (v. 3), and finally to place his trust in God, who takes up the parental task of education (v. 5). Education begun by the parent is brought to full completion by God.

**3:1 Do not forget**: this word and several others in the section such as "teaching," "commands," "years of life," and the custom of affixing written teaching to one's body, occur also in Deuteronomy. This vocabulary suggests that Proverbs and Deuteronomy had a common origin in the scribal class of Jerusalem. This section (and vv. 21–34) subtly elaborates Dt 6:5–9, "You shall love the LORD with all your heart (v. 5) . . . Take to heart these words (v. 1) . . . Recite them when you are at home and when you are away (v. 23) . . . when you lie down (v. 24) . . . Bind them (v. 3) on your arm as a sign and let them be a pendant on your forehead" (v. 21).

*g:* Jb 32:8; Wis 7:25; Sir 1:1; Jas 1:5. *h:* Prv 5:3, 20; 6:24; 7:5; 22:14. *i:* Prv 5:5; 7:27. *j:* Prv 10:7, 30; Jb 18:17; Ps 21:9–13; 37:22, 28. *k:* Prv 4:10; 9:11; 10:27.

4 Then will you win favor and esteem
before God and human beings.
5 Trust in the LORD with all your heart,
on your own intelligence do not rely;
6 In all your ways be mindful of him,
and he will make straight your paths.
7 Do not be wise in your own eyes,[l]
fear the LORD and turn away from evil;
8 This will mean health for your flesh
and vigor for your bones.
9 Honor the LORD with your wealth,
with first fruits of all your produce;[m]
10 Then will your barns be filled with
plenty,
with new wine your vats will overflow.
11 The discipline of the LORD, my son, do
not spurn;[n]
do not disdain his reproof;
12 * For whom the LORD loves he reproves,
as a father, the son he favors.[o]

### *The Benefits of Finding Wisdom**

13 Happy the one who finds wisdom,
the one who gains understanding![p]
14 Her profit is better than profit in silver,
and better than gold is her revenue;
15 She is more precious than corals,
and no treasure of yours can compare
with her.[q]
16 Long life is in her right hand,
in her left are riches and honor;
17 Her ways are pleasant ways,
and all her paths are peace;
18 She is a tree of life* to those who grasp
her,
and those who hold her fast are happy.[r]
19 The LORD by wisdom founded the earth,
established the heavens by
understanding;
20 By his knowledge the depths* are split,
and the clouds drop down dew.

### *Justice Toward One's Neighbor Brings Blessing**

21 My son, do not let these slip from your
sight:
hold to deliberation and planning;
22 So will they be life to your soul,*
and an adornment for your neck.
23 Then you may go your way securely;
your foot will never stumble;
24 When you lie down, you will not be afraid,

**3:12** One might be tempted to judge the quality of one's relationship to God by one's prosperity. It is an inadequate criterion, for God as a teacher might go counter to student expectations. The discipline of God can involve suffering.

**3:13–20** An encomium of Wisdom through the listing of her benefits to the human race and the depiction of her role in creation. Wisdom, or understanding, is more valuable than silver and gold. Its fruit is long life, riches, honor and happiness (vv. 13–18). Even the creation of the universe and its adornment (Gn 1) were not done without wisdom (vv. 19–20). The praise of Wisdom foreshadows the praise of a noble wife in the final poem (31:10–31), even to the singling out of the hands extended in a helpful way toward human beings.

**3:18 A tree of life**: in the Old Testament this phrase occurs only in Proverbs (11:30; 13:12; 15:4) and Genesis (2:9; 3:22, 24). The origins of the concept are obscure; there is no explicit mention of it in ancient Near Eastern literature, though on ancient seals trees are sometimes identified as trees of life. When the man and the woman were expelled from the garden, the tree of life was put off limits to them, lest they "eat of it and live forever" (Gn 3:22). The quest for wisdom gives access to the previously sequestered tree of life. The tree of life is mentioned also in the apocryphal work 1 Enoch 25:4–5. Rev 2 and 22 mention the tree of life as a source of eternal life.

**3:20 Depths**: for the Hebrews, the depths enclosed the great subterranean waters; the rain and dew descended from the waters above the firmament; cf. Gn 1:6–10; Jb 26:8, 12; Ps 18:15; 24:2. The cosmogony provides the reason why Wisdom offers such benefits to human beings: the world was created in wisdom so that all who live in accord with wisdom live in tune with the universe.

**3:21–35** As in other instructions, the father in vv. 21–26 urges the son to seek wisdom, which in this case means practicing the virtues of "deliberation and planning," a specification of wisdom. Practicing these virtues brings protection from violence (vv. 22–26) and friendship with God (vv. 32–35). The language is like Ps 91.

Verses 27–35 are arranged according to a clear order. Serving God requires serving one's neighbor through kindness (vv. 27–28), maintaining peace with the good (vv. 29–31), having no envy of the wicked (v. 31), because the Lord's friendship and kindness are with the just, not with the wicked. Matching the six exhortations of vv. 1–12, vv. 27–34 contain six prohibitions. The righteous/wicked contrast is progressively developed: in contrast to the wicked, the righteous are in God's inner circle, their houses are blessed, they deal with a merciful God, and obtain honor.

**3:22 Your soul**: Heb. *nephesh* means "throat, esophagus; life; soul." The meanings are connected. The throat area is the moist, breathing center of the body, which stands for life and for self. The figure of speech is called metonymy, in which one word is substituted for another on the basis of a causal relation, e.g., eye for sight, arm for power, or, as here, "throat area" for life. Proverbs sometimes plays on this concrete meaning of life (e.g., 21:23).

*l:* Rom 11:25; 12:16. *m:* Ex 34:26; Lv 27:30; Dt 26:2; Sir 7:31; 35:7. *n:* Heb 12:5–6. *o:* Jdt 8:27; Rev 3:19. *p:* Prv 8:34–35. *q:* Prv 8:11, 19; Wis 7:8–11. *r:* Prv 4:13; 8:35; 11:30; Gn 2:9; 3:22.

when you rest, your sleep will be sweet.
25 Do not be afraid of sudden terror,
of the ruin of the wicked when it comes;
26 For the LORD will be your confidence,
and will keep your foot from the snare.
27 Do not withhold any goods from the owner
when it is in your power to act.
28 Say not to your neighbor, "Go, come back tomorrow,
and I will give it to you," when all the while you have it.
29 Do not plot evil against your neighbors,
when they live at peace with you.
30 Do not contend with someone without cause,
with one who has done you no harm.
31 Do not envy the violent
and choose none of their ways:[s]
32 To the LORD the devious are an abomination,
but the upright are close to him.
33 The curse of the LORD is on the house of the wicked,
but the dwelling of the just he blesses;
34 Those who scoff, he scoffs at,[t]
but the lowly he favors.
35 The wise will possess glory,
but fools will bear shame.

## CHAPTER 4

See RG 180-82

### *The Teacher as Model Disciple**

1 Hear, O children, a father's instruction,
be attentive, that you may gain understanding!
2 Yes, excellent advice I give you;
my teaching do not forsake.
3 When I was my father's child,
tender, the darling of my mother,
4 He taught me and said to me:
"Let your heart hold fast my words:[u]
keep my commands, and live!
5 Get wisdom,* get understanding!
Do not forget or turn aside from the words of my mouth.
6 Do not forsake her, and she will preserve you;
love her, and she will safeguard you;
7 The beginning of wisdom is: get wisdom;
whatever else you get, get understanding.
8 Extol her, and she will exalt you;
she will bring you honors if you embrace her;
9 She will put on your head a graceful diadem;
a glorious crown will she bestow on you."

### *The Two Ways**

10 Hear, my son, and receive my words,
and the years of your life shall be many.[v]
11 On the way of wisdom I direct you,
I lead you on straight paths.
12 When you walk, your step will not be impeded,
and should you run, you will not stumble.
13 Hold fast to instruction, never let it go;
keep it, for it is your life.

**4:1–9** The teacher draws a parallel between his teaching the disciples now and his father's teaching him in his youth (vv. 3–4): what my father taught me about wisdom is what I am teaching you. The poem implies that the teacher has acquired wisdom and has in fact been protected and honored as his father promised long ago. Thus the teacher has the authority of someone who has been under wisdom's sway since earliest youth.

There are two sections, a call for attention and introduction of the speaker (vv. 1–3) and the father's quoting of his own father's teaching (vv. 4–9). Beginning with v. 5, the father's words are no longer quoted, wisdom herself becoming the active agent; she becomes the subject, not the object, of the verbs. Three Hebrew verbs are repeated in the two parts, "to forsake" in vv. 2 and 6, "to keep/guard" in vv. 4 and 6, and "to give/bestow" in vv. 2 and 9. Each verb in its first appearance has the father's words as its object; in its second appearance each verb has wisdom as its subject or object. The teaching process is like that in 2:1–22 and 3:1–12: heeding the words of one's parent puts one in touch with wisdom, who completes the process and bestows her gifts.

**4:5, 7 Get wisdom**: the same Hebrew word "to get" can mean to acquire merchandise and to acquire a wife (18:22; 31:10); both meanings are in keeping with Proverbs' metaphors of acquiring wisdom over gold and silver and of acquiring wisdom as a personified woman, a wife.

**4:10–19** A central metaphor of the poem is "the way." The way of wisdom leads directly to life (vv. 10–13); it is a light that grows brighter (v. 18). The wise are bound to shun (vv. 14–17) the dark and violent path of the wicked (v. 19). Singleness of purpose and right conduct proceed from the heart of the wise as from the source of life (vv. 23–26), saving them from destruction on evil paths (4:27; 5:21–23). As in 1:8–19 and 2:12–15, the obstacles to the quest are men and their way. Elsewhere in chaps. 1–9, the obstacle is the foreign woman (2:16–19; chap. 5; 6:20–35; chap. 7; 9:13–18).

*s:* Prv 23:17; 24:1, 19; Ps 37:1. *t:* Prv 1:26. *u:* Dt 6:1–6. *v:* Prv 3:2.

## The Two Ways

THE PROCESS OF gaining wisdom is essentially the same in all the instructions. One begins by memorizing the teaching and putting it into practice; then one receives wisdom as a gift. Proverbs 4:10–19 develops the doctrine of the two ways, in which a person's moral life is dramatized as two competing paths, the way of wisdom (vv. 10–13) and the path of the wicked (vv. 14–17). Each has its inherent destiny, represented here by the symbols of light and darkness (vv. 18–19). The two ways are not far removed from each other; one must struggle to stay on the right path. It is possible to leave one path and walk on the other.

14 * The path of the wicked do not enter,
nor walk in the way of the evil;
15 Shun it, do not cross it,
turn aside from it, pass on.
16 For they cannot rest unless they have done evil;
if they do not trip anyone they lose sleep.
17 For they eat the bread of wickedness
and drink the wine of violence.
18 But the path of the just is like shining light,
that grows in brilliance till perfect day.*
19 The way of the wicked is like darkness;
they do not know on what they stumble.

### *With Your Whole Being Heed My Words and Live**

20 My son, to my words be attentive,
to my sayings incline your ear;
21 Let them not slip from your sight,
keep them within your heart;
22 For they are life to those who find them,[w]
bringing health to one's whole being.
23 With all vigilance guard your heart,
for in it are the sources of life.
24 * Dishonest mouth put away from you,
deceitful lips put far from you.
25 Let your eyes look straight ahead
and your gaze be focused forward.
26 Survey the path for your feet,
and all your ways will be sure.
27 Turn neither to right nor to left,
keep your foot far from evil.

## CHAPTER 5

See RG 180–82

### *Warning Against Adultery**

1 My son, to my wisdom be attentive,
to understanding incline your ear,
2 That you may act discreetly,
and your lips guard what you know.
3 Indeed, the lips of the stranger drip honey,*

**4:14–15** One is always free to choose. The righteous may choose to leave their path to walk on the wicked path and the wicked may choose the righteous path.

**4:18 Till perfect day**: lit., "till the day is established"; this may refer to full daylight or to noonday.

**4:20–27** Acquiring wisdom brings life and health. The learning process involves two stages: (1) hearing the teacher's words and treasuring them in the heart; (2) speaking and acting in accord with the wisdom that one has stored in one's heart. Seven organs of the body are mentioned: ear, eyes, heart, mouth, lips, eyelids ("gaze," v. 25), feet. Each of the organs is to be strained to its limit as the disciple puts wisdom into practice. The physical organ stands for the faculty, e.g., the eye for sight, the foot for movement. The figure of speech is called metonymy; one word is substituted for another on the basis of a causal relation.

**4:24–27** In vv. 20–21 the faculties of hearing (ear) and seeing (eye) take in the teaching and the heart stores and ponders it, so in the second half of the poem, vv. 24–27, the faculties of speech, sight, and walking enable the disciple to put the teaching into practice.

**5:1–23** This is the first of three poems on the forbidden woman, the "stranger" outside the social boundaries (cf. 2:16–19); the other two are 6:20–35 and chap. 7. Understanding and discretion are necessary to avoid adultery, which leads astray and begets bitterness, bloodshed, and death (vv. 1–6). It destroys honor, wastes the years of life, despoils hard-earned wealth, and brings remorse in the end (vv. 7–14). Conjugal fidelity and love bring happiness and security (vv. 15–20). Cf. 6:20–7:27. The structure of the poem consists of a two-line introduction; part one consists of three stanzas of four lines each warning of the forbidden woman's effect on her lovers (vv. 3–14); part two consists of a stanza of twelve lines exhorting the disciple to marital fidelity (vv. 15–20); and a final stanza of six lines on the perils of the woman (vv. 21–23).

**5:3** A metaphorical level is established in the opening description of the forbidden woman: her lips drip honey and her

*w*: Prv 8:35.

and her mouth is smoother than oil;[x]
4 But in the end she is as bitter as
wormwood,
as sharp as a two-edged sword.
5 Her feet go down to death,
her steps reach Sheol;[y]
6 Her paths ramble, you know not where,
lest you see before you the road to life.
7 So now, children, listen to me,
do not stray from the words of my
mouth.
8 Keep your way far from her,[z]
do not go near the door of her house,
9 Lest you give your honor* to others,[a]
and your years to a merciless one;
10 Lest outsiders take their fill of your wealth,
and your hard-won earnings go to
another's house;
11 And you groan in the end,
when your flesh and your body are
consumed;
12 And you say, "Oh, why did I hate
instruction,
and my heart spurn reproof!
13 Why did I not listen to the voice of my
teachers,
incline my ear to my instructors!
14 I am all but ruined,
in the midst of the public assembly!"
15 Drink water* from your own cistern,
running water from your own well.
16 Should your water sources be dispersed
abroad,
streams of water in the streets?
17 Let them be yours alone,
not shared with outsiders;
18 Let your fountain be blessed and have
joy of the wife of your youth,
19 your lovely hind, your graceful doe.*
Of whose love you will ever have your
fill,
and by her ardor always be intoxicated.
20 Why then, my son, should you be
intoxicated with a stranger,
and embrace another woman?
21 Indeed, the ways of each person are plain
to the LORD's sight;
all their paths he surveys;[b]
22 By their own iniquities the wicked will
be caught,
in the meshes of their own sin they
will be held fast;
23 They will die from lack of discipline,
lost because of their great folly.

## CHAPTER 6

### *Miscellaneous Proverbs**

See RG 180–82

#### *Against Going Surety for One's Neighbor*

1 * My son, if you have become surety to
your neighbor,[c]
given your hand in pledge to another,

feet lead to death. By her lies, she leads people away from the wisdom that gives life.

**5:9 Honor**: the words "life" and "wealth" have also been read in this place. **A merciless one**: the offended husband; cf. 6:34–35.

**5:15–16 Water**: water may have an erotic meaning as in Sg 4:15, "[You are] a garden fountain, a well of living water." Eating and drinking can be metaphors expressing the mutuality of love. The wife is the opposite of the adulterous woman; she is not an outsider, not unfeeling, not a destroyer of her husband's self and goods. The best defense against adultery is appreciating and loving one's spouse. The best defense against folly is to appreciate and love wisdom.

**5:19 Lovely hind . . . graceful doe**: ancient Near Eastern symbols of feminine beauty and charm; cf. Sg 2:7, 9, 17.

**6:1–19** Four independent pieces akin to those in 30:1–5, 6–11, 12–15, and 16–19. Some judge the verses to be an ancient addition, but the fact that the pieces differ from the other material in chaps. 1–9 is not a strong argument against their originality. Ancient anthologies did not always have the symmetry of modern collections. An editor may have placed the four pieces in the midst of the three poems on the forbidden woman to shed light on some of their themes. Verses 1–5 warn against getting trapped by one's words to another person (the Hebrew word for "another" is the same used for the forbidden woman); vv. 6–11 proposes the ant as a model of forethought and diligence; vv. 12–15 describes the reprobate who bears some similarity to the seductive woman, especially as portrayed in chap. 7; vv. 16–19 depicts the typical enemy of God, underscoring the person's destructive words.

**6:1–5** Unlike other instructions that begin with "my son," this instruction does not urge the hearer to store up the father's words as a means to wisdom, but only to avoid one practice—going surety for one's neighbor. The warning is intensified by repetition of "neighbor" and "free yourself," the mention of bodily organs, and the imagery of hunting. **Given your hand in pledge**: lit., "struck your hands"; this was probably the legal method for closing a contract. To become surety meant intervening in favor of the insolvent debtor and assuming responsibility for the payment of the debt, either by obtaining it from the debtor or substituting oneself. Proverbs is strongly opposed to the practice (11:15; 17:18; 20:16; 22:26–27; 27:13) apparently because of the danger it poses to the freedom of the one providing surety.

*x:* Prv 7:5. *y:* Prv 2:18; 7:27. *z:* Prv 7:25. *a:* Sir 9:6. *b:* Jb 14:16; 31:4; 34:21. *c:* Prv 11:15; 22:26; Sir 8:13; 29:19.

## Four Short Pieces

PROVERBS 6:1–19 IS often judged to be an addition on the grounds that its topics and style are very different from the surrounding instructions. It is possible, however, that the editors wanted to insert related but miscellaneous material at this point. Thematically, the section is concerned not with external obstacles to acquiring wisdom, such as violent men and seductive women, but with internal obstacles, such as poor judgment (vv. 1–5) and laziness (vv. 6–11). It also sketches an evil character (vv. 12–15), who is wholly unacceptable to the LORD (vv. 16–19).

2 You have been snared by the utterance of
your lips,
caught by the words of your mouth;
3 So do this, my son, to free yourself,
since you have fallen into your
neighbor's power:
Go, hurry, rouse your neighbor!
4 Give no sleep to your eyes,
nor slumber to your eyelids;
5 Free yourself like a gazelle from the
hunter,
or like a bird from the hand of the
fowler.

### *The Ant and the Sluggard at Harvest*

6 * Go to the ant,[d] O sluggard,
study her ways and learn wisdom;
7 For though she has no chief,
no commander or ruler,
8 She procures her food in the summer,
stores up her provisions in the harvest.
9 How long, O sluggard, will you lie there?
when will you rise from your sleep?
10 A little sleep, a little slumber,
a little folding of the arms to rest—*
11 Then poverty will come upon you like a
robber,
and want like a brigand.

### *The Scoundrel*

12 * Scoundrels, villains, are they
who deal in crooked talk.
13 Shifty of eye,
feet ever moving,
pointing with fingers,
14 They have perversity in their hearts,
always plotting evil,
sowing discord.
15 Therefore their doom comes suddenly;
in an instant they are crushed beyond
cure.

### *What the Lord Rejects*

16 There are six things the LORD hates,
yes, seven* are an abomination to him;
17 * Haughty eyes, a lying tongue,
hands that shed innocent blood,
18 A heart that plots wicked schemes,
feet that are quick to run to evil,
19 The false witness who utters lies,
and the one who sows discord among
kindred.

### *Warning Against Adultery**

20 Observe, my son, your father's command,
and do not reject your mother's
teaching;

**6:6–11** The sluggard or lazybones is a type in Proverbs, like the righteous and the wicked. Sometimes the opposite type to the sluggard is the diligent person. Other extended passages on the sluggard are 24:30–34 and 26:13–16. The malice of the type is not low physical energy but the refusal to act. To describe human types, Proverbs often uses comparisons from the animal world, e.g., 27:8 (bird); 28:1, 15 (lion); 30:18–19 (eagle, snake); 30:24–28 (ant, badger, locust, lizard).

**6:10** This verse may be regarded as the sluggard's reply or as a continuation of the remonstrance.

**6:12–15** Proverbs uses types to make the point that certain ways of acting have inherent consequences. The typifying intensifies the picture. All the physical organs—mouth, eyes, feet, fingers—are at the service of evil. Cf. Rom 6:12–13: "Therefore, sin must not reign over your mortal bodies so that you obey their desires. And do not present the parts of your bodies to sin as weapons for wickedness, but present yourselves to God as raised from the dead to life and the parts of your bodies to God as weapons of righteousness."

**6:16 Six . . . seven**: this literary pattern (n, n + 1) occurs frequently; cf., e.g., Am 1–2; Prv 30:18–19.

**6:17–19** The seven vices, symbolized for the most part by bodily organs, are pride, lying, murder, intrigue, readiness to do evil, false witness, and the stirring up of discord.

**6:20–35** The second of three instructions on adultery (5:1–23; 6:20–35; and chap. 7). The instructions assume that wisdom will protect one from adultery and its consequences: loss of property and danger to one's person. In this poem, the

*d:* Prv 30:25.

21 Keep them fastened over your heart
always,
tie them around your neck.
22 When you lie down they* will watch over
you,
when you wake, they will share your
concerns;
wherever you turn, they will guide you.
23 For the command is a lamp, and the
teaching a light,
and a way to life are the reproofs that
discipline,
24 Keeping you from another's wife,
from the smooth tongue of the foreign
woman.[e]
25 Do not lust in your heart after her beauty,
do not let her captivate you with her
glance![f]
26 For the price of a harlot
may be scarcely a loaf of bread,
But a married woman
is a trap for your precious life.
27 * Can a man take embers into his bosom,
and his garments not be burned?
28 Or can a man walk on live coals,
and his feet not be scorched?
29 So with him who sleeps with another's
wife—
none who touches her shall go
unpunished.[g]
30 Thieves are not despised
if out of hunger they steal to satisfy
their appetite.
31 Yet if caught they must pay back
sevenfold,
yield up all the wealth of their house.
32 But those who commit adultery have no
sense;
those who do it destroy themselves.
33 * They will be beaten and disgraced,
and their shame will not be wiped
away;
34 For passion enrages the husband,
he will have no pity on the day of
vengeance;
35 He will not consider any restitution,
nor be satisfied by your many bribes.

## CHAPTER 7

See RG 180–82

### *The Seduction**

1 * My son, keep my words,
and treasure my commands.

father and the mother urge their son to keep their teaching constantly before his eyes. The teaching will light his way and make it a path to life (v. 23). The teaching will preserve him from the adulterous woman who is far more dangerous than a prostitute. Prostitutes may cost one money, but having an affair with someone else's wife puts one in grave danger. The poem bluntly urges self-interest as a motive to refrain from adultery.

The poem has three parts. I (vv. 20–24, ten lines), in which v. 23 repeats "command" and "teaching" of v. 20 and "keeping" in v. 24 completes the fixed pair initiated by "observe" in v. 20; II (vv. 25–29, ten lines) is a self-contained argument comparing the costs of a liaison with a prostitute and a married woman; III (vv. 30–35, twelve lines) draws conclusions from the comparison of adultery with theft: the latter involves property only but adultery destroys one's name and very self. The best protection against such a woman is heeding parental instruction, which is to be kept vividly before one's eyes like a written tablet.

**6:22 They**: Heb. has "she." If this verse is not out of place, then the antecedent of "she" is command (v. 20), or perhaps wisdom.

**6:27–29** There is a play on three words of similar sound, *'îsh*, "man," *'ishshâ*, "woman," and *'ēsh*, "fire, embers." The question, "Can a man (*'îsh*) take embers (*'ēsh*) into his bosom / and his garments not be burned?", has a double meaning. "Into his bosom" has an erotic meaning as in the phrase "wife of one's bosom" (Dt 13:6; 28:54; Sir 9:1). Hence one will destroy one's garments, which symbolize one's public position, by taking fire/another's wife into one's bosom.

**6:33–35** The nature of the husband's vengeance is disputed, some believing it is simply a physical beating whereas others hold it is public and involves the death penalty because Lv 20:20 and Dt 22:22 demand the death penalty.

**7:1–27** The third and climactic instruction on adultery and seduction is an example story, of the same type as the example story in 24:30–34. By its negative portrayal of the deceitful woman, who speaks in the night to a lone youth, it serves as a foil to trustworthy Wisdom in chap. 8, who speaks in broad daylight to all who pass in the street.

As in 6:20–24, the father warns his son to keep his teaching to protect him from the dangerous forbidden woman. The father's language in 7:4 ("Say to Wisdom, 'You are my sister,' and call Understanding 'Friend' ") sets this admonition apart, however; it is the language of courtship and love. If the son makes Woman Wisdom his companion and lover, she will protect him from the other woman. As in chap. 5, loving the right woman protects the man from the wrong woman.

As motivation, the father in vv. 6–23 tells his son of an incident he once observed while looking out his window—a young man went to the bed of an adulterous woman and wound up dead. As in chap. 5, the realistic details—the purposeful woman, the silent youth, the vow, the perfumed bed—have a metaphorical level. Ultimately the story is about two different kinds of love.

**7:1–3** Verses 1–3 are artistically constructed. "Keep" in v. 1a recurs in v. 2a; "commands" in v. 1b recurs in v. 2a; the im-

*e:* Prv 2:16; 7:5. *f:* Ex 20:17; Dt 5:21; Sir 9:8; 25:20; Mt 5:28. *g:* Sir 9:9.

2 Keep my commands and live,*
and my teaching as the apple of your eye;
3 Bind them on your fingers,
write them on the tablet of your heart.[h]
4 Say to Wisdom, "You are my sister!"*
Call Understanding, "Friend!"
5 That they may keep you from a stranger,
from the foreign woman with her smooth words.[i]
6 For at the window of my house,
through my lattice I looked out*
7 And I saw among the naive,
I observed among the young men,
a youth with no sense,
8 Crossing the street near the corner,
then walking toward her house,
9 In the twilight, at dusk of day,
in the very dark of night.
10 Then the woman comes to meet him,
dressed like a harlot, with secret designs.
11 She is raucous and unruly,
her feet cannot stay at home;
12 Now she is in the streets, now in the open squares,
lurking in ambush at every corner.
13 Then she grabs him, kisses him,
and with an impudent look says to him:
14 "I owed peace offerings,
and today I have fulfilled my vows;
15 So I came out to meet you,
to look for you, and I have found you!
16 With coverlets I have spread my couch,
with brocaded cloths of Egyptian linen;
17 I have sprinkled my bed* with myrrh,
with aloes, and with cinnamon.
18 Come, let us drink our fill of love,
until morning, let us feast on love!
19 For my husband is not at home,*
he has gone on a long journey;
20 A bag of money he took with him,
he will not return home till the full moon."
21 She wins him over by repeated urging,
with her smooth lips she leads him astray.* [j]
22 He follows her impulsively,
like an ox that goes to slaughter;
Like a stag that bounds toward the net,
23 till an arrow pierces its liver;
Like a bird that rushes into a snare,
unaware that his life is at stake.
24 So now, children, listen to me,*
be attentive to the words of my mouth!
25 Do not let your heart turn to her ways,
do not go astray in her paths;
26 For many are those she has struck down dead,
numerous, those she has slain.
27 Her house is a highway to Sheol,
leading down into the chambers of death.[k]

## CHAPTER 8

See RG 180-82

### *The Discourse of Wisdom**

1 Does not Wisdom call,
and Understanding raise her voice?[l]
2 On the top of the heights along the road,

perative verb "live" occurs in the very center of the three lines; v. 3, on preserving the teaching upon one's very person, matches vv. 1–2, on preserving the teaching internally by memorizing it.

**7:2 Live**: here as elsewhere (Gn 20:7; 42:18; 2 Kgs 18:32; Jer 27:12, 17; Ez 18:32), the imperative ("Live!") is uttered against the danger of death, e.g., "Do such and such and you will live (=survive the danger); why should you die?"

**7:4 You are my sister**: "sister" and "brother" are examples of love language in the ancient Near East, occurring in Egyptian love poetry and Mesopotamian marriage songs. In Sg 4:9, 10, 12; 5:1, the man calls the woman, "my sister, my bride." Intimate friendship with Woman Wisdom saves one from false and dangerous relationships.

**7:6–7 I looked out . . . I saw . . .** : the perspective is unusual. The narrator looks through a window upon the drama in the street.

**7:17 Bed**: a bed can designate a place of burial in Is 57:2; Ez 32:25; 2 Chr 16:14. **Myrrh . . . aloes**: the spices could be used for funerals as for weddings (Jn 19:39). It is possible that the language is ambivalent, speaking of death as it seems to speak of life. As the woman offers the youth a nuptial feast, she is in reality describing his funerary feast.

**7:19–20 For my husband is not at home**: the woman is calculating. She knows exactly how long her husband will be gone.

**7:21** The verbs "to win over" (lit., "to lead astray") and "to lead off" can be used of leading animals such as a donkey (Nm 22:23) or sheep (Jer 23:2 and 50:17). The animal imagery continues as the youth is compared to an ox, a fallow deer, and a bird in the moment they are slaughtered. None of the animals are aware of their impending death.

**7:24–27** The father addresses "children," a larger audience than his own son; the story is typical, intended for others as an example. The story is a foil to the speech of the other woman in chap. 8.

**8:1–36** Chapter 8 is Wisdom's longest speech in the book. Wisdom is here personified as in 1:20–33. She exalts her

*h:* Dt 6:8. *i:* Prv 2:16; 6:24. *j:* Prv 5:3; 6:24. *k:* Prv 2:18–19; 5:5. *l:* Prv 1:20–21; 9:3.

## The Personification of Wisdom

ONE OF THE most striking features of Proverbs is its vivid personification of wisdom as a woman. Personification is a way of presenting an idea, a natural force, or an abstract concept as if it were a person. "Woman Wisdom" gives two lengthy speeches in the town square (1:20–33 and 8:1–36), and she invites passers-by to the banquet dedicating her newly built palace (9:1–6).

The book of Proverbs presents a counter-figure to Woman Wisdom: the adulterous woman (2:16–19; 5:1–23; 6:20–35; 7:1–27) and the woman "Folly" (9:13–18). Ultimately, derived from warnings to young men against the wrong kind of women, the adulterous woman has a metaphorical dimension in the book: She seeks to seduce her hearers with words, promising them life but dealing them death. The book thus presents the moral life in dramatic terms; there are two voices (Wisdom and Folly), and there are two ways (the way of the righteous and the way of the wicked). Each person must choose one or the other.

Woman Wisdom's speeches in Proverbs contain no specific advice. Rather, she invites her hearers to become her disciples—to trust and obey her, and even to wait at her gates like a dear friend (8:32–36). She promises to bestow security (1:33), authority, wealth, and success (8:14–21). Her own authority rests on her intimacy and honored position with God; she was created before everything and has an intimate relationship with God. In fact, traditional love language is used to describe her relationship to God and to human beings (8:30–31, 34).

The personification of wisdom gives Proverbs a metaphorical dimension. The moral life is not simply a series of right actions but a fundamental option—seeking wisdom before all else.

at the crossroads she takes her stand;
3 By the gates at the approaches of the city,
in the entryways she cries aloud:
4 "To you, O people, I call;
my appeal is to you mortals.
5 You naive ones, gain prudence,
you fools,* gain sense.
6 Listen! for noble things I speak;
my lips proclaim honest words.
7 * Indeed, my mouth utters truth,
and my lips abhor wickedness.
8 All the words of my mouth are sincere,
none of them wily or crooked;
9 All of them are straightforward to the intelligent,
and right to those who attain knowledge.
10 Take my instruction instead of silver,
and knowledge rather than choice gold.
11 [For Wisdom is better than corals,
and no treasures can compare with her.[m]]

grandeur and origin, and invites all (vv. 1–11) to be attentive to her salutary influence in human society (vv. 12–21), for she was privileged to be present at the creation of the world (vv. 22–31). Finally, she promises life and the favor of God to those who are devoted to her, death to those who reject her.

The poem has four sections, each (except the fourth) with two parts of five lines each:

| | | | | |
|---|---|---|---|---|
| I. | A. | vv. 1–5 | B. | vv. 6–10 |
| II. | A. | vv. 12–16 | B. | vv. 17–21 |
| III. | A. | vv. 22–26 | B. | vv. 27–31 |
| IV. | | vv. 32–36 | | |

Within chaps. 1–9, chap. 8 is the companion piece to Wisdom's first speech in 1:20–33. There she spoke harshly, giving a promise only in the last line; here she speaks invitingly, giving a threat only in the last line.

Chapter 8 is the best-known chapter in Proverbs and has profoundly influenced Jewish and Christian thought. The most explicit and lengthy biblical comment is in Sir 24; it too has thirty-five lines in seven five-line stanzas and develops the theme of Wisdom's intimacy with God and desire to be with human beings. The Gospel of John portrays Jesus in the language of wisdom in Proverbs: Jesus, like Wisdom, calls out to people to listen to him, promises to tell them the truth, seeks disciples, invites them to a banquet, and gives them life. Writers in the patristic period used the language of pre-existent wisdom to express the idea of the pre-existent Word with God.

**8:5 Naive ones . . . fools**: see note on 1:4.

**8:7–8** The truth and sincerity of wisdom are absolute because they are of divine origin. They can neither deceive nor tolerate deception. The intelligent understand and accept this.

*m:* Prv 3:15; Wis 7:8.

12 I, Wisdom, dwell with prudence,
and useful knowledge I have.
13 [The fear of the LORD is hatred of evil;]
Pride, arrogance, the evil way,
and the perverse mouth I hate.[n]
14 Mine are counsel and advice;
Mine is strength; I am understanding.*
15 By me kings reign,
and rulers enact justice;
16 By me princes govern,
and nobles, all the judges of the earth.
17 Those who love me I also love,
and those who seek me find me.
18 With me are riches and honor,[o]
wealth that endures, and
righteousness.
19 My fruit is better than gold, even pure
gold,
and my yield than choice silver.[p]
20 On the way of righteousness I walk,
along the paths of justice,
21 Granting wealth to those who love me,
and filling their treasuries.

22 * "The LORD begot me, the beginning of
his works,
the forerunner of his deeds of long
ago;[q]
23 From of old I was formed,*
at the first, before the earth.[r]
24 * When there were no deeps I was
brought forth,
when there were no fountains or
springs of water;
25 Before the mountains were settled into
place,
before the hills, I was brought forth;
26 When the earth and the fields were not
yet made,
nor the first clods of the world.
27 When he established the heavens, there
was I,[s]
when he marked out the vault over the
face of the deep;
28 When he made firm the skies above,
when he fixed fast the springs of the
deep;
29 When he set for the sea its limit,
so that the waters should not transgress
his command;
When he fixed the foundations of earth,
30 then was I beside him as artisan;* [t]
I was his delight day by day,
playing before him all the while,
31 Playing over the whole of his earth,
having my delight with human beings.
32 * Now, children, listen to me;
happy are they who keep my ways.
33 Listen to instruction and grow wise,
do not reject it!
34 Happy the one who listens to me,
attending daily at my gates,
keeping watch at my doorposts;
35 For whoever finds me finds life,[u]
and wins favor from the LORD;
36 But those who pass me by do violence to
themselves;
all who hate me love death."

"Straight" and "crooked" in Hebrew and English are metaphors for true, trustworthy and false, deceitful.

**8:14** What is here predicated of Wisdom is elsewhere attributed to God (Jb 12:13–16).

**8:22–31** Wisdom is of divine origin. She is represented as existing before all things (vv. 22–26), when God planned and created the universe, adorning it with beauty and variety, and establishing its wonderful order (vv. 27–30). The purpose of the two cosmogonies (vv. 22–26 and 27–31) is to ground Wisdom's claims. The first cosmogony emphasizes that she was born before all else (and so deserving of honor) and the second underscores that she was with the Lord during the creation of the universe. The pre-existence of Woman Wisdom with God is developed in Sir 24 and in New Testament hymns to Christ, especially in Jn 1 and Col 1:15–20.

**8:23 Formed**: since the other verbs of the origin of Wisdom in these verses describe birth, it is likely that the somewhat uncertain verb is to be understood of birth as in Ps 139:13.

**8:24–26** Perhaps the formless mass from which God created the heavens and the earth; cf. Gn 1:1–2; 2:4–6.

**8:30 Artisan**: the translation of the Hebrew word *'āmôn* has been controverted since antiquity. There have been three main opinions: (1) artisan; (2) trustworthy (friend); (3) ward, nursling. The most likely explanation is that *'āmôn* is artisan, related to Akkadian *ummānu*, legendary sages and heroes who brought divine gifts and culture to the human race. **I was his delight**: the chiastic or ABBA structure of vv. 30–31 unifies the four lines and underscores the analogy between Woman Wisdom's intimate relation to the Lord and her intimate relation to human beings, i.e., "delight" + "playing" parallels "playing" + "delight." She is God's friend and intimate and invites human beings to a similar relationship to God through her.

**8:32–36** The final appeal of Woman Wisdom to her disciples is similar to the appeal of the father in 7:24–27.

*n:* Prv 6:16–17; 16:5. *o:* Prv 3:16. *p:* Prv 3:14. *q:* Wis 9:9; Sir 1:1; 24:9. *r:* Sir 1:4. *s:* Prv 3:19; Sir 24:4–5. *t:* Wis 9:9. *u:* Prv 3:13–18; 4:22.

## CHAPTER 9

See RG 180-82

### *The Two Women Invite Passersby to Their Banquets**

### *Woman Wisdom Issues Her Invitation*

1 Wisdom has built her house,*
she has set up her seven columns;
2 She has prepared her meat, mixed her wine,
yes, she has spread her table.
3 She has sent out her maidservants; she calls*
from the heights out over the city:[v]
4 "Let whoever is naive turn in here;
to any who lack sense I say,
5 Come, eat of my food,
and drink of the wine I have mixed!
6 Forsake foolishness that you may live;*
advance in the way of understanding."

### *Miscellaneous Aphorisms*

7 Whoever corrects the arrogant earns insults;
and whoever reproves the wicked incurs opprobrium.
8 Do not reprove the arrogant, lest they hate you;
reprove the wise, and they will love you.[w]
9 Instruct the wise, and they become still wiser;
teach the just, and they advance in learning.
10 The beginning of wisdom is fear of the LORD,
and knowledge of the Holy One is understanding.[x]
11 For by me your days will be multiplied
and the years of your life increased.[y]
12 If you are wise, wisdom is to your advantage;
if you are arrogant, you alone shall bear it.

### *Woman Folly Issues Her Invitation*

13 * Woman Folly is raucous,[z]
utterly foolish; she knows nothing.
14 She sits at the door of her house
upon a seat on the city heights,
15 Calling to passersby
as they go on their way straight ahead:

**9:1–6, 13–18** Wisdom and folly are represented as women, each inviting people to her banquet. Wisdom's banquet symbolizes joy and closeness to God. Unstable and senseless Folly furnishes stolen bread and water of deceit and vice that bring death to her guests. The opposition between wisdom and folly was stated at the beginning of chaps. 1–9 (folly in 1:8–19 and wisdom in 1:20–33) and is maintained throughout, down to this last chapter.

In comparable literature, gods might celebrate their sovereign by building a palace and inviting the other gods to come to a banquet and celebrate with them. Presumably, Woman Wisdom is celebrating her grandeur (just described in chap. 8); her grand house is a symbol of her status as the Lord's friend. In order to enter the sacred building and take part in the banquet ("eat of my food"), guests must leave aside their old ways ("forsake foolishness").

Verses 7–12 are unrelated to the two invitations to the banquet. They appear to be based on chap. 1, especially on 1:1–7, 22. The Greek version has added a number of verses after v. 12 and v. 18. In the confusion, 9:11 seems to have been displaced from its original position after 9:6. It has been restored to its original place in the text.

**9:1 House**: house has a symbolic meaning. Woman Wisdom encourages marital fidelity (2:16–19; 5; 6:20–35; 7), which builds up a household (cf. chap. 5). Some scholars propose that an actual seven-pillared house is referred to, but so far none have been unearthed by archaeologists. Seven may simply connote completeness—a great house.

Some scholars see a connection between the woman's house here and the woman's house in the final poem (31:10–31). In chap. 9, she invites the young man to enter her house and feast, i.e., to marry her. Chapter 31 shows what happens to the man who marries her; he has a house and enjoys "life" understood as consisting of a suitable wife, children, wealth, and honor.

**9:3 She calls**: i.e., invites; this is done indirectly through her maidservants, but the text could also mean that Wisdom herself publicly proclaims her invitation.

**9:6 That you may live**: life in Proverbs is this-worldly, consisting in fearing God or doing one's duty toward God, enjoying health and long life, possessing wealth, good reputation, and a family. Such a life cannot be attained without God's help. Hence Wisdom speaks not of life simply but of life with her; the guest is to live in Wisdom's house.

**9:13–18** Woman Folly is the mirror image of Woman Wisdom. Both make identical invitations but only one of the offers is trustworthy. Their hearers must discern which is the true offer. She is depicted with traits of the adulterous woman in 2:16–19; chap. 5; 6:20–35; chap. 7. Woman Folly is restless (cf. 7:11), her path leads to the underworld (2:18; 5:5; 7:27), and she is ignorant (5:6). In this final scene, she appears in single combat with her great nemesis, Woman Wisdom. Though the invitations of the two women appear at first hearing to be the same, they differ profoundly. Wisdom demands that her guests reject their ignorance, whereas Woman Folly trades on their ignorance.

*v:* Prv 8:1–2. *w:* Sir 10:27. *x:* Prv 1:7; Jb 28:28; Ps 111:10; Sir 1:16. *y:* Prv 3:2; 16:4, 10; 10:27. *z:* Prv 7:7–27.

**The Proverbs of Solomon**

NEARLY ALL OF chs 1–15 are antithetic proverbs, that is, the second line (B) restates the first line (A) in an opposite way. The section contrasts the wicked and the righteous person (treated as types) and emphasizes the consequences of human acts. Chapters 16–22, on the other hand, contain far fewer antitheses and many more exceptions to the rule. A key metaphor throughout all these chapters is founding or maintaining a house, which continues the same image as in chs 1–9. The chapters contain more than fifty references to father, mother, son, house, wife, or servant.

16 "Let those who are naive turn in here,
to those who lack sense I say,
17 Stolen water is sweet,
and bread taken secretly is pleasing!"*
18 Little do they know that the shades are there,
that her guests are in the depths of Sheol!*

## III. First Solomonic Collection of Sayings*

### CHAPTER 10

See RG 180–82

1The Proverbs of Solomon:
A wise son gives his father joy,
but a foolish son is a grief to his mother.* [a]
2 Ill-gotten treasures profit nothing,
but justice saves from death.* [b]
3 The LORD does not let the just go hungry,
but the craving of the wicked he thwarts.*
4 The slack hand impoverishes,
but the busy hand brings riches.[c]
5 A son who gathers in summer is a credit;
a son who slumbers during harvest, a disgrace.
6 Blessings are for the head of the just;
but the mouth of the wicked conceals violence.*
7 The memory of the just serves as blessing,
but the name of the wicked will rot.*

**9:17** "Stolen water" seems to refer to adultery, for "water" in 5:15–17 refers to the wife's sexuality; "stolen" refers to stealing the sexuality belonging to another's household. "Secret" evokes the furtive meeting of the wife and the youth in chap. 7.

**9:18** The banquet chamber of Folly is a tomb from which no one who enters it is released; cf. 7:27. **Shades**: the Rephaim, the inhabitants of the underworld.

**10:1–22:16** The Proverbs of Solomon are a collection of three hundred and seventy-five proverbs on a wide variety of subjects. No overall arrangement is discernible, but there are many clusters of sayings related by vocabulary and theme. One thread running through the whole is the relationship of the "son," the disciple, to the parents, and its effect upon the house(hold). In chaps. 10–14 almost all the proverbs are antithetical; "the righteous" and "the wicked" (ethical), "the wise" and "the foolish" (sapiential), and "the devout, the pious" and "the irreverent" (religious). Chapters 15–22 have fewer sharp antitheses. The sayings are generally witty, often indirect, and are rich in irony and paradox.

**10:1** The opening saying ties the whole collection to the first section, for "son," "father," and "mother" evoke the opening line of the first instruction, "Hear, my son, your father's instruction, and reject not your mother's teaching." The son is the subject of parental exhortation throughout chaps. 1–9. This is the first of many sayings on domestic happiness or unhappiness, between parents and children (e.g., 15:20; 17:21) and between husband and wife (e.g., 12:4; 14:1). Founding or maintaining a household is an important metaphor in the book.

Adult children represented the family (headed by the oldest married male) to the outside world. Foolishness, i.e., malicious ignorance, brought dishonor to the parents and the family.

**10:2 Death**: untimely, premature, or sorrowful. The word "death" can have other overtones (see Wis 1:15).

**10:3** The last of the three introductory sayings in the collection, which emphasize, respectively, the sapiential (v. 1), ethical (v. 2), and religious (v. 3) dimensions of wisdom. In this saying, God will not allow the appetite of the righteous to go unfulfilled. The appetite of hunger is singled out; it stands for all the appetites.

**10:6** This saying, like several others in the chapter, plays on the different senses of the verb "to cover." As in English, "to cover" can mean to fill (as in Is 60:2) and to conceal (as in Jb 16:18). Colon B can be read either "violence *fills* the mouth (= head) of the wicked" or "the mouth of the wicked *conceals* violence." The ambiguity is intentional; the proverb is meant to be read both ways.

**10:7** The name of the righteous continues to be used after their death in blessings such as "May you be as blessed as

*a:* Prv 1:1; 15:20; 17:25; 19:13; 25:1; 29:15. *b:* Prv 11:4, 6. *c:* Prv 6:11; 12:24; 13:4; 20:13; 28:19.

8 A wise heart accepts commands,
but a babbling fool will be overthrown.*
9 Whoever walks honestly walks securely,
but one whose ways are crooked will fare badly.
10 One who winks at a fault causes trouble,
but one who frankly reproves promotes peace.
11 The mouth of the just is a fountain of life,
but the mouth of the wicked conceals violence.
12 Hatred stirs up disputes,
[d] but love covers all offenses.*
13 On the lips of the intelligent is found wisdom,
but a rod for the back of one without sense.*
14 The wise store up knowledge,
but the mouth of a fool is imminent ruin.
15 The wealth of the rich is their strong city;
the ruin of the poor is their poverty.*
16 The labor of the just leads to life,
the gains of the wicked, to futility.* [e]
17 Whoever follows instruction is in the path to life,
but whoever disregards reproof goes astray.[f]
18 Whoever conceals hatred has lying lips,
and whoever spreads slander is a fool.
19 Where words are many, sin is not wanting;
but those who restrain their lips do well.[g]
20 Choice silver is the tongue of the just;
the heart of the wicked is of little worth.
21 The lips of the just nourish many,
but fools die for want of sense.*
22 It is the LORD's blessing that brings wealth,[h]
and no effort can substitute for it.*
23 Crime is the entertainment of the fool;
but wisdom is for the person of understanding.
24 What the wicked fear will befall them,
but the desire of the just will be granted.
25 When the tempest passes, the wicked are no more;
but the just are established forever.
26 As vinegar to the teeth, and smoke to the eyes,
are sluggards to those who send them.
27 Fear of the LORD prolongs life,
but the years of the wicked are cut short.[i]
28 The hope of the just brings joy,
but the expectation of the wicked perishes.*
29 The LORD is a stronghold to those who walk honestly,
downfall for evildoers.
30 The just will never be disturbed,
but the wicked will not abide in the land.
31 The mouth of the just yields wisdom,
but the perverse tongue will be cut off.
32 The lips of the just know favor,
but the mouth of the wicked, perversion.*

Abraham," but the wicked, being enemies of God, do not live on in anyone's memory. Their names rot with their bodies.

**10:8** The wise take in instruction from their teachers but those who expel or pour out folly through their words will themselves be expelled.

**10:12 Love covers all offenses**: a favorite maxim in the New Testament; cf. 1 Cor 13:7; Jas 5:20; 1 Pt 4:8. Cf. also Prv 17:9.

**10:13** An unusual juxtaposition of "lips" and "back." Those who have no wisdom on their lips (words) are fated to feel a punishing rod on their back.

**10:15** An observation rather than a moral evaluation of wealth and poverty; but cf. 18:10–11.

**10:16** Wages are a metaphor for reward and punishment. The Hebrew word does not mean "sin" here but falling short, a meaning that is frequent in Proverbs. Cf. Rom 6:1: "But what profit did you get then from the things of which you are now ashamed? For the end of those things is death."

**10:21** The wise by their words maintain others in life whereas the foolish cannot keep themselves from sin that leads to premature death.

**10:22** Human industry is futile without divine approval; cf. Ps 127:1–2; Mt 6:25–34.

**10:28** The thought is elliptical. Joy comes from fulfillment of one's plans, which the righteous can count on. The opposite of joy thus is not sadness but unfulfillment ("perishes").

**10:32** The word used for "favor" is favor shown by an authority (God or the king), not favor shown by a peer. A righteous person's words create a climate of favor and acceptance, whereas crooked words will not gain acceptance. In Hebrew as in English, straight and crooked are metaphors for good and wicked.

*d:* 1 Cor 13:4–7; 1 Pt 4:8. *e:* Prv 11:18–19. *f:* Prv 15:10. *g:* Prv 17:27; Sir 20:17; Jas 1:19. *h:* Sir 11:22. *i:* Prv 3:2; 4:10; 9:11; 14:27.

See RG 180–82

## CHAPTER 11

1 False scales are an abomination to
the LORD,
but an honest weight, his delight.*[j]
2 When pride comes, disgrace comes;
but with the humble is wisdom.*
3 The honesty of the upright guides them;
the faithless are ruined by their
duplicity.
4 Wealth is useless on a day of wrath,*[k]
but justice saves from death.
5 The justice of the honest makes their
way straight,
but by their wickedness the wicked
fall.*[l]
6 The justice of the upright saves them,
but the faithless are caught in their
own intrigue.
7 When a person dies, hope is destroyed;[m]
expectation pinned on wealth is
destroyed.*
8 The just are rescued from a tight spot,
but the wicked fall into it instead.
9 By a word the impious ruin their
neighbors,[n]
but through their knowledge the just
are rescued.*
10 When the just prosper, the city
rejoices;[o]
when the wicked perish, there is
jubilation.
11 Through the blessing of the upright the
city is exalted,
but through the mouth of the wicked it
is overthrown.
12 Whoever reviles a neighbor lacks sense,
but the intelligent keep silent.
13 One who slanders reveals secrets,[p]
but a trustworthy person keeps a
confidence.
14 For lack of guidance a people falls;
security lies in many counselors.[q]
15 Harm will come to anyone going surety
for another,[r]
but whoever hates giving pledges is
secure.*
16 A gracious woman gains esteem,
and ruthless men gain wealth.*
17 Kindly people benefit themselves,
but the merciless harm themselves.
18 The wicked make empty profits,
but those who sow justice have a sure
reward.[s]
19 Justice leads toward life,
but pursuit of evil, toward death.
20 The crooked in heart are an abomination
to the LORD,
but those who walk blamelessly are his
delight.*
21 Be assured, the wicked shall not go
unpunished,
but the offspring of the just shall
escape.

**11:1** The word pair "abomination" and "delight" (= acceptable) to God is common in Proverbs. Originally the language of ritual, the words came to be applied to whatever pleases or displeases God (cf. also 11:20). False weights were a constant problem even though weights were standardized. Cf. 20:23; Hos 12:8; Am 8:5.

**11:2** Disgrace is the very opposite of what the proud so ardently want. Those who do not demand their due receive wisdom.

**11:4** Cf. note on 10:2. A day of wrath is an unforeseen disaster (even death). Only one's relationship to God, which makes one righteous, is of any help on such a day.

**11:5** In Hebrew as in English, "way" means the course of one's life; similarly, "straight" and "crooked" are metaphors for morally straightforward and for bad, deviant, perverted.

**11:7** An ancient scribe added "wicked" to person in colon A, for the statement that hope ends at death seemed to deny life after death. The saying, however, is not concerned with life after death but with the fact that in the face of death all hopes based on one's own resources are vain. The aphorism is the climax of the preceding six verses; human resources cannot overcome mortality (cf. Ps 49:13).

**11:9** What the wicked express harms others; what the righteous leave unsaid protects. Verses 9–14 are related in theme: the effect of good and bad people, especially their words, on their community.

**11:15** Proverbs is opposed to providing surety for another's loan (see note on 6:1–5) and expresses this view throughout the book.

**11:16** Wealth and esteem are good things in Proverbs, but the means for acquiring them are flawed. As precious gifts, they must be granted, not taken. The esteem of others that depends on beauty is as fleeting as beauty itself (cf. 31:30) and the wealth acquired by aggressive behavior lasts only as long as one has physical strength.

**11:20** The terminology of ritual (acceptable and unacceptable sacrifice, "abomination" and "delight") is applied to human conduct as in v. 1. The whole of human life is under divine scrutiny, not just ritual.

*j:* Prv 16:11; 20:10; Lv 19:35–36. *k:* Prv 10:2. *l:* Prv 28:18. *m:* Prv 10:28; Wis 3:18. *n:* Prv 29:5. *o:* Prv 28:12; 29:2. *p:* Prv 20:19. *q:* Prv 15:22; 20:18; 24:6. *r:* Prv 6:1–2. *s:* Prv 10:16.

22 Like a golden ring in a swine's snout
is a beautiful woman without
judgment.*
23 The desire of the just ends only in good;
the expectation of the wicked is wrath.
24 One person is lavish yet grows still richer;
another is too sparing, yet is the
poorer.*
25 Whoever confers benefits will be amply
enriched,
and whoever refreshes others will be
refreshed.
26 Whoever hoards grain, the people curse,
but blessings are on the head of one
who distributes it!
27 Those who seek the good seek favor,
but those who pursue evil will have
evil come upon them.*
28 Those who trust in their riches will fall,
but like green leaves the just will
flourish.[t]
29 Those who trouble their household
inherit the wind,
and fools become slaves to the wise of
heart.
30 The fruit of justice is a tree of life,
and one who takes lives is a sage.*
31 If the just are recompensed on the earth,
how much more the wicked and the
sinner!* [u]

## CHAPTER 12

See RG 180–82

1 Whoever loves discipline loves
knowledge,
but whoever hates reproof is stupid.* [v]
2 A good person wins favor from the LORD,
but the schemer he condemns.*
3 No one is made secure by wickedness,
but the root of the just will never be
disturbed.*
4 A woman of worth is the crown of her
husband,[w]
but a disgraceful one is like rot in his
bones.*
5 The plans of the just are right;
the designs of the wicked are deceit.*
6 The words of the wicked are a deadly
ambush,
but the speech of the upright saves
them.*
7 Overthrow the wicked and they are no
more,
but the house of the just stands firm.
8 For their good sense people are praised,
but the perverse of heart are despised.*
9 Better to be slighted and have a servant
than put on airs and lack bread.[x]
10 The just take care of their livestock,
but the compassion of the wicked is
cruel.*

**11:22** Ear and nose rings were common jewelry for women. A humorous saying on the priority of wisdom over beauty in choosing a wife.

**11:24** A paradox: spending leads to more wealth.

**11:27** The saying is about seeking one thing and finding another. Striving for good leads to acceptance by God; seeking evil means only that trouble will come. The same Hebrew word means evil and trouble.

**11:30** Most translations emend Hebrew "wise person" in colon B on the basis of the Greek and Syriac translations to "violence" (similar in spelling), because the verb "to take a life" is a Hebrew idiom for "to kill" (as also in English). The emendation is unnecessary, however, for the saying deliberately plays on the odd meaning: the one who takes lives is not the violent but the wise person, for the wise have a profound influence upon life. There is a similar wordplay in 29:10.

**11:31** The saying is not about life after death; "on the earth" means life in the present world. The meaning is that divine judgment is exercised on all human action, even the best. The thought should strike terror into the hearts of habitual wrongdoers.

**12:1** Discipline in Proverbs is both doctrine and training. The path to wisdom includes obedience to teachers and parents, acceptance of the community's traditions.

**12:2** The antithesis is between the good person who, by reason of that goodness, already has divine acceptance, and the wicked person who, despite great effort, gains only condemnation.

**12:3** Human beings are described as "made secure" in Jb 21:8; Ps 101:7; 102:29. "Root" in the context means enduring to succeeding generations, as in Mal 3:19 and Jb 8:17.

**12:4** In Proverbs a crown is the result and sign of wise conduct. A good wife is a public sign of the husband's shrewd judgment and divine blessing (crown), whereas a bad wife brings him inner pain (rot in the bones).

**12:5** The opposite of "just" is not injustice but "deceit." The wicked will be deceived in their plans in the sense that their planning will not succeed.

**12:6** Words are a favorite theme of Proverbs. The words of the wicked effect harm to others whereas the words of the righteous protect themselves.

**12:8** The heart, the seat of intelligence, will eventually be revealed in the actions that people do, either for praise or for blame.

**12:10** The righteous are sympathetically aware of the

*t:* Ps 52:9–10. *u:* 1 Pt 4:18. *v:* Prv 15:5, 10; Sir 21:6. *w:* Prv 31:10; Sir 21:1, 16. *x:* Sir 10:26.

[11] Those who till their own land have food
in plenty,
but those who engage in idle pursuits
lack sense.* [y]
[12] A wicked person desires the catch of evil
people,
but the root of the righteous will bear
fruit.*
[13] By the sin of their lips the wicked are
ensnared,
but the just escape from a tight spot.
[14] From the fruit of their mouths people
have their fill of good,[z]
and the works of their hands come
back upon them.*
[15] The way of fools is right in their own eyes,
but those who listen to advice are the
wise.
[16] Fools immediately show their anger,
but the shrewd conceal contempt.
[17] Whoever speaks honestly testifies truly,
but the deceitful make lying
witnesses.* [a]
[18] The babble of some people is like sword
thrusts,
but the tongue of the wise is healing.
[19] Truthful lips endure forever,
the lying tongue, for only a moment.*
[20] Deceit is in the heart of those who plot
evil,
but those who counsel peace have joy.
[21] No harm befalls the just,
but the wicked are overwhelmed with
misfortune.
[22] Lying lips are an abomination to the
LORD,[b]
but those who are truthful, his delight.
[23] The shrewd conceal knowledge,
but the hearts of fools proclaim folly.*
[24] The diligent hand will govern,
but sloth makes for forced labor.[c]
[25] Worry weighs down the heart,
but a kind word gives it joy.[d]
[26] The just act as guides to their neighbors,
but the way of the wicked leads them
astray.
[27] Sloth does not catch its prey,
but the wealth of the diligent is
splendid.
[28] In the path of justice is life,
but the way of abomination leads to
death.

## CHAPTER 13

See RG 180–82

[1] A wise son loves correction,
but the scoffer heeds no rebuke.*
[2] From the fruit of the mouth one enjoys
good things,[e]
but from the throat of the treacherous
comes violence.*
[3] Those who guard their mouths preserve
themselves;*

needs of their livestock and prosper from their herd's good health. The wicked will pay the price for their self-centeredness and cruelty.

**12:11** The second line clarifies the first: idleness will give one plenty of nothing. "Lacking sense" is a common phrase for fools.

**12:12** A difficult, possibly corrupt saying, but there is no good alternative to the Hebrew text. The wicked desire what the malevolent have captured or killed, but their actions will go for naught because they invite punishment. The righteous, on the other hand, will bear fruit.

**12:14** The saying contrasts words and deeds. "Fruit" here is not what one normally eats, as in 1:31; 8:19; 31:16, 31, but the consequences of one's actions. In the second line the things that issue from one's hands (one's deeds) come back to one in recompense or punishment. Prv 13:2a and 18:20 are variants. Cf. Mt 7:17; Gal 6:8.

**12:17** What is the rule of thumb for judging legal testimony? Look to the ordinary conduct and daily speech of a witness.

**12:19** The saying has a double meaning: lies are quickly found out whereas truthful statements endure; truth-tellers, being favored by God, live long lives, whereas liars invite punishment.

**12:23** "Knowledge" here is "what one knows, has in one's heart," not knowledge in general. Fools reveal all they have stored in their heart and it naturally turns out to be folly. Revealing and concealing are constant themes in Proverbs.

**13:1** Another in the series on the household, this one on the relation of parents and children. See under 10:1. The scoffer in Proverbs condemns discipline and thus can never become wise. Wise adult children advertise to the community what they received from their parents, for children become wise through a dialectical process involving the parents. A foolish adult child witnesses to foolish parents.

**13:2** One's mouth normally eats food from outside, but in the moral life, things are reversed: one eats from the fruit of one's mouth, i.e., one experiences the consequences of one's own actions. Since the mouth of the treacherous is filled with violence, one must assume that they will some day endure violence.

**13:3** **Preserve themselves**: in Hebrew, literally to preserve the throat area, the moist breathing center of one's body, thus "life," "soul," or "self." There is wordplay: if you guard your

*y:* Prv 28:19; Sir 20:27. *z:* Prv 13:2; 18:20. *a:* Prv 14:5. *b:* Prv 6:17. *c:* Prv 10:4; 13:4. *d:* Prv 15:13; 17:22. *e:* Prv 12:14; 18:20.

those who open wide their lips bring
ruin.[f]
4 The appetite of the sluggard craves but
has nothing,
but the appetite of the diligent is
amply satisfied.
5 The just hate deceitful words,
but the wicked are odious and
disgraceful.
6 Justice guards one who walks honestly,
but sin leads the wicked astray.[g]
7 One acts rich but has nothing;
another acts poor but has great
wealth.*
8 People's riches serve as ransom for their
lives,
but the poor do not even hear a threat.*
9 The light of the just gives joy,
but the lamp* of the wicked goes out.[h]
10 The stupid sow discord by their
insolence,
but wisdom is with those who take
counsel.
11 Wealth won quickly dwindles away,
but gathered little by little, it grows.[i]
12 Hope deferred makes the heart sick,
but a wish fulfilled is a tree of life.*
13 Whoever despises the word must pay for
it,*
but whoever reveres the command will
be rewarded.
14 The teaching of the wise is a fountain of
life,
turning one from the snares of death.
15 Good sense brings favor,
but the way of the faithless is their
ruin.*
16 The shrewd always act prudently
but the foolish parade folly.*
17 A wicked messenger brings on disaster,
but a trustworthy envoy is a healing
remedy.
18 Poverty and shame befall those who let
go of discipline,
but those who hold on to reproof
receive honor.*
19 Desire fulfilled delights the soul,
but turning from evil is an
abomination to fools.
20 Walk with the wise and you become wise,
but the companion of fools fares
badly.[j]
21 Misfortune pursues sinners,
but the just shall be recompensed with
good.
22 The good leave an inheritance to their
children's children,
but the wealth of the sinner is stored
up for the just.
23 The tillage of the poor yields abundant
food,
but possessions are swept away for
lack of justice.*
24 Whoever spares the rod hates the child,
but whoever loves will apply
discipline.[k]
25 When the just eat, their hunger is
appeased;
but the belly of the wicked suffers
want.

mouth (= words) you guard your "soul." Fools, on the other hand, do not guard but open their lips and disaster strikes. A near duplicate is 21:23.

**13:7** Appearances can be deceiving; possessions do not always reveal the true state of a person.

**13:8** Related to v. 7. Possessions enable the wealthy to pay ransom but the poor are "protected" by lack of possessions: they never hear the threat of the pursuer. Cf. the use of the word "threat" in Is 30:17.

**13:9 Light. . . lamp**: symbols of life and prosperity; cf. 4:18–19.

**13:12** "Tree of life" occurs in Gn 2–3, Prv 3:18; 11:30; 13:12; 15:4, and Rev 2:7; 22:2, 14, 19. It provides food and healing.

**13:13 Must pay for it**: lit., "is pledge to it," i.e., just as one who has pledged or provided surety for another's loan is obligated to that pledge, so one is not free of a command until one performs it.

**13:15** As the behavior of the wise wins them favor that increases their prosperity, like Abigail with David in 1 Sm 25, so the way (= conduct) of the faithless ruins their lives.

**13:16** Like 12:23 and 15:2, 3, the saying is about revealing and concealing. The wise reveal their wisdom in their actions whereas fools "parade," spread out their folly for all to see. The verb is used of vendors spreading their wares and of birds spreading their wings.

**13:18** The saying plays on letting go and holding on. Wisdom consists in not rejecting discipline and being open to the comments of others, even if they are reproving comments.

**13:23** An observation on the poor. The lands of the poor are as fertile as anyone's, for nature does not discriminate against them. Their problem is lack of justice, which puts their harvest at risk from unscrupulous human beings.

*f:* Prv 18:7; 21:23. *g:* Prv 11:3, 5–6. *h:* Prv 24:20. *i:* Prv 28:20, 22. *j:* Sir 6:34; 8:8, 17. *k:* Prv 19:18; 22:15; 23:13–14; 29:15; Sir 30:1, 8–13.

See RG 180–82

## CHAPTER 14

1 Wisdom builds her house,
but Folly tears hers down with her own hands.*
2 Those who walk uprightly fear the LORD,
but those who are devious in their ways spurn him.
3 In the mouth of the fool is a rod for pride,
but the lips of the wise preserve them.
4 Where there are no oxen, the crib is clean;
but abundant crops come through the strength of the bull.*
5 A trustworthy witness does not lie,
but one who spouts lies makes a lying witness.* [l]
6 The scoffer seeks wisdom in vain,
but knowledge is easy for the intelligent.
7 Go from the face of the fool;
you get no knowledge from such lips.
8 The wisdom of the shrewd enlightens their way,
but the folly of fools is deceit.*
9 The wicked scorn a guilt offering,
but the upright find acceptance.
10 The heart knows its own bitterness,
and its joy no stranger shares.*
11 The house of the wicked will be destroyed,
but the tent of the upright will flourish.* [m]
12 Sometimes a way seems right,
but the end of it leads to death![n]
13 Even in laughter the heart may be sad,
and the end of joy may be sorrow.
14 From their own ways turncoats are sated,
from their own actions, the loyal.
15 The naive believe everything,
but the shrewd watch their steps.*
16 The wise person is cautious and turns from evil;
the fool is reckless and gets embroiled.
17 The quick-tempered make fools of themselves,
and schemers are hated.
18 The simple have folly as an adornment,
but the shrewd wear knowledge as a crown.*
19 The malicious bow down before the good,
and the wicked, at the gates of the just.
20 Even by their neighbors the poor are despised,
but a rich person's friends are many.[o]
21 Whoever despises the hungry comes up short,
but happy the one who is kind to the poor!*
22 Do not those who plan evil go astray?
But those who plan good win steadfast loyalty.
23 In all labor there is profit,
but mere talk tends only to loss.
24 The crown of the wise is wealth;
the diadem of fools is folly.
25 The truthful witness saves lives,
but whoever utters lies is a betrayer.
26 The fear of the LORD is a strong defense,
a refuge even for one's children.
27 The fear of the LORD is a fountain of life,
turning one from the snares of death.
28 A multitude of subjects is the glory of the king;
but if his people are few, a prince is ruined.

**14:1** The relationship between Wisdom, personified as a woman, and building a house is a constant theme. As elsewhere, the book here warns against the wrong woman and praises the right woman.

**14:4** If one has no animals, one does not have the burden of keeping the crib full, but without them one will have no crops to fill the barn. Colon B reverses the sense of colon A and also reverses the consonants of *bar* ("clean") to *rab* ("abundant").

**14:5** On discerning the truthfulness of witnesses; see 12:17.

**14:8** Wisdom enables the shrewd to know their path is right but folly leads fools on the wrong path ("deceit"), which calls down retribution.

**14:10** The heart in Proverbs is where a person's sense impressions are stored and reflected upon. It is thus one's most personal and individual part. One's sorrows and joys (= the full range of emotions) cannot be shared fully with another. Verse 13 expresses the same individuality of the human person.

**14:11** The traditional fixed pair "house" and "tent" is used to express the paradox that a house can be less secure than a tent if there is no justice.

**14:15** The naive gullibly rely on others' words whereas the shrewd watch their own steps.

**14:18** The inner quality of a person, simple or wise, will eventually be revealed.

**14:21** The paradox is that anyone who spurns the hungry will lack something, but anyone who shows mercy (presumably by giving to the poor) will gain prosperity.

*l:* Prv 12:17. *m:* Prv 3:33; 12:7; 15:25. *n:* Prv 16:25. *o:* Prv 19:4, 7; Sir 6:8, 12.

[29] Long-suffering results in great wisdom;
a short temper raises folly high.* [p]
[30] A tranquil mind gives life to the body,
but jealousy rots the bones.
[31] Those who oppress the poor revile their Maker,
but those who are kind to the needy honor him.[q]
[32] The wicked are overthrown by their wickedness,
but the just find a refuge in their integrity.
[33] Wisdom can remain silent in the discerning heart,
but among fools she must make herself known.* [r]
[34] Justice exalts a nation,
but sin is a people's disgrace.*
[35] The king favors the skillful servant,
but the shameless one incurs his wrath.

## CHAPTER 15

See RG 180–82

[1]* A mild answer turns back wrath,[s]
but a harsh word stirs up anger.*
[2] The tongue of the wise pours out knowledge,
but the mouth of fools spews folly.
[3] The eyes of the LORD are in every place,
keeping watch on the evil and the good.
[4] A soothing tongue is a tree of life,
but a perverse one breaks the spirit.
[5] The fool spurns a father's instruction,
but whoever heeds reproof is prudent.* [t]
[6] In the house of the just there are ample resources,
but the harvest of the wicked is in peril.
[7] The lips of the wise spread knowledge,
but the heart of fools is not steadfast.*
[8] The sacrifice of the wicked is an abomination to the LORD,[u]
but the prayer of the upright is his delight.
[9] The way of the wicked is an abomination to the LORD,
but he loves one who pursues justice.[v]
[10] Discipline seems bad to those going astray;
one who hates reproof will die.*
[11] Sheol and Abaddon* lie open before the LORD;
how much more the hearts of mortals!
[12] Scoffers do not love reproof;
to the wise they will not go.
[13] A glad heart lights up the face,
but an anguished heart breaks the spirit.[w]
[14] The discerning heart seeks knowledge,
but the mouth of fools feeds on folly.*
[15] All the days of the poor are evil,
but a good heart is a continual feast.*
[16] * Better a little with fear of the LORD
than a great fortune with anxiety.
[17] Better a dish of herbs where love is
than a fatted ox and hatred with it.
[18] The ill-tempered stir up strife,[x]
but the patient settle disputes.

**14:29** A series of puns on short and long; lit., "long of nostrils (idiom for "patient"), large in wisdom, / short in breath (idiom for "impatient"), makes folly tall."

**14:33** Wisdom can remain silent in a wise person as a welcome friend. But it must speak out among fools, for the dissonance is so strong.

**14:34** The rare noun "disgrace" occurs elsewhere only in Lv 20:17. In measuring the greatness of a nation, one is tempted to consider territory, wealth, history, but the most important criterion is its relationship to God ("justice").

**15:1–7** These verses form a section beginning and ending with the topic of words.

**15:1** Paradoxically, where words are concerned soft is powerful and hard is ineffective.

**15:5** One becomes wise by keeping and foolish by rejecting. One must accept the tradition of the community.

**15:7** "Lips" and "heart" are a fixed pair, in Proverbs signifying, respectively, expression and source. The wise disseminate what they have in their heart, but the wicked are unsound even in the source of their words, their hearts.

**15:10** Discipline, always a good thing in Proverbs, seems bad to those deliberately wandering from justice.

**15:11 Sheol and Abaddon**: terms for the abode of the dead, signifying the profound obscurity which is open nevertheless to the sight and power of God; cf. 27:20.

**15:14** The contrasts include heart (organ of reflection) and mouth (organ of expression), and the wise and fools. One type feeds its mind with wisdom and the other feeds its face with folly.

**15:15** Good heart does not refer to good intentions but to an instructed mind. Wisdom makes poverty not only bearable but even joyful like the joy of feast days.

**15:16–17** The sages favor wealth over poverty—but not at any price; cf. Ps 37:16.

*p:* Prv 16:32; 19:11; Jas 1:19. *q:* Prv 17:5. *r:* Prv 1:22; 8:1. *s:* Prv 25:15; Sir 6:5. *t:* Prv 12:1; 13:18. *u:* Prv 21:27; Eccl 4:17; Is 1:11–15. *v:* Prv 11:20; 21:21. *w:* Prv 12:25; 17:22; Sir 30:22. *x:* Prv 6:21; 29:22; Sir 28:11.

19 The way of the sluggard is like a thorn hedge,
but the path of the diligent is a highway.
20 A wise son gives his father joy,
but a fool despises his mother.[y]
21 Folly is joy* to the senseless,
but the person of understanding goes the straight way.
22 Plans fail when there is no counsel,
but they succeed when advisers are many.* [z]
23 One has joy from an apt response;
a word in season, how good it is!* [a]
24 The path of life leads upward for the prudent,
turning them from Sheol below.*
25 The LORD pulls down the house of the proud,
but preserves intact the widow's landmark.
26 The schemes of the wicked are an abomination to the LORD,[b]
but gracious words are pure.*
27 The greedy tear down their own house,
but those who hate bribes will live.*
28 The heart of the just ponders a response,
but the mouth of the wicked spews evil.
29 The LORD is far from the wicked,
but hears the prayer of the just.
30 A cheerful glance brings joy to the heart;
good news invigorates the bones.
31 The ear that listens to salutary reproof[c]
is at home among the wise.*
32 Those who disregard discipline hate themselves,
but those who heed reproof acquire understanding.
33 The fear of the LORD is training for wisdom,
and humility goes before honors.[d]

## CHAPTER 16

See RG 180–82

1 Plans are made in human hearts,
but from the LORD comes the tongue's response.*
2 All one's ways are pure* in one's own eyes,
but the measurer of motives is the LORD.[e]
3 Entrust your works to the LORD,
and your plans will succeed.
4 The LORD has made everything for a purpose,
even the wicked for the evil day.*
5 Every proud heart* is an abomination to the LORD;[f]
be assured that none will go unpunished.
6 By steadfast loyalty guilt is expiated,
and by the fear of the LORD evil is avoided.*
7 When the LORD is pleased with someone's ways,
he makes even enemies be at peace with them.
8 Better a little with justice,
than a large income with injustice.

**15:21** The word "joy" occurs in the first line of vv. 20, 21, and 23. The state of folly is joy to a fool but the wise person is totally absorbed in keeping on the right or straight road.

**15:22** Failure to consult makes it likely a plan will not succeed. The point is nicely made by contrasting the singular number in the first line ("no counsel") with the plural number in the second line ("many advisors").

**15:23** Conversation is the art of saying the right thing at the right time. It gives pleasure to speaker and hearer alike.

**15:24** Death is personified as Sheol, the underworld. "Up" and "down" in Hebrew as in English are metaphors for success and failure (see Dt 28:43). One who stays on the path of life need not fear the punishment that stalks sinners.

**15:26** "Pure" here means acceptable. The language of ritual (acceptable or pure) is applied to ordinary human actions. "Gracious words" are words that bring peace to the neighbor.

**15:27** The same lesson as the opening scene of Proverbs (1:8–19): one cannot build a house by unjust gain. Injustice will come back upon a house so built.

**15:31** To become wise, one must hear and integrate perspectives contrary to one's own, which means accepting "reproof." Wisdom does not isolate one but places one in the company of the wise.

**16:1** Words, like actions, often produce results different from those which were planned, and this comes under the agency of God.

**16:2** "Pure" in a moral sense for human action is found only in Job and Proverbs. As in v. 1, the contrast is between human intent and divine assessment.

**16:4** Even the wicked do not lie outside God's plan.

**16:5 Proud heart**: lit., "high of heart." To forget one is a fallible human being is so basic an error that one cannot escape exposure and punishment.

**16:6** As v. 5 used the language of worship to express what is acceptable or not to God, so this saying uses similar language to declare that lovingly loyal conduct undoes the effects of sin.

*y:* Prv 10:1; 29:3. *z:* Prv 11:14. *a:* Prv 25:11; Sir 20:6. *b:* Prv 6:18. *c:* Prv 25:12. *d:* Prv 1:7; 19:12; Sir 1:24. *e:* Prv 21:2. *f:* Prv 6:16–17; 8:13.

9 The human heart plans the way,
but the LORD directs the steps.* [g]
10 An oracle is upon the king's lips,
no judgment of his mouth is false.*
11 Balance and scales belong to the LORD;
every weight in the sack is his concern.[h]
12 Wrongdoing is an abomination to kings,
for by justice the throne endures.[i]
13 The king takes delight in honest lips,
and whoever speaks what is right he
loves.[j]
14 The king's wrath is a messenger of death,[k]
but a wise person can pacify it.
15 A king's smile means life,
and his favor is like a rain cloud in
spring.*
16 How much better to get wisdom than
gold!
To get understanding is preferable to
silver.* [l]
17 The path of the upright leads away from
misfortune;
those who attend to their way guard
their lives.*
18 Pride goes before disaster,
and a haughty spirit before a fall.
19 It is better to be humble with the poor
than to share plunder with the proud.[m]
20 Whoever ponders a matter will be
successful;
happy the one who trusts in the LORD!
21 The wise of heart is esteemed for
discernment,
and pleasing speech gains a reputation
for learning.
22 Good sense is a fountain of life to those
who have it,
but folly is the training of fools.
23 The heart of the wise makes for eloquent
speech,
and increases the learning on their lips.
24 Pleasing words are a honeycomb,
sweet to the taste and invigorating to
the bones.
25 Sometimes a way seems right,
but the end of it leads to death![n]
26 The appetite of workers works for them,
for their mouths urge them on.* [o]
27 Scoundrels are a furnace of evil,
and their lips are like a scorching fire.
28 Perverse speech sows discord,
and talebearing separates bosom
friends.[p]
29 The violent deceive their neighbors,
and lead them into a way that is not
good.
30 Whoever winks an eye plans perversity;
whoever purses the lips does evil.*
31 Gray hair is a crown of glory;[q]
it is gained by a life that is just.
32 The patient are better than warriors,
and those who rule their temper, better
than the conqueror of a city.[r]
33 Into the bag the lot is cast,
but from the LORD comes every
decision.*

## CHAPTER 17

See RG 180–82

1 Better a dry crust with quiet
than a house full of feasting with strife.*

**16:9** As in vv. 1–3, the antithesis is between human plans and divine disposal. The saying uses the familiar metaphor of path for the course of life.

**16:10** Six sayings on the king and his divine authority begin here, following the series of sayings about the Lord's governance in 15:33–16:9, in which "LORD" was mentioned nine times.

**16:15** The last of six sayings about the king. In the previous verse, royal wrath means death; in this verse royal favor means life. It is significant that royal favor is compared to something not under human control—the clouds preceding the spring rains.

**16:16** The point of comparison is the superiority of the pursuit of wisdom and gold, not the relative merits of wealth and wisdom.

**16:17** In the metaphor of the two ways, the way of the righteous is protected and the way of the wicked is unprotected. Since the path of the righteous leads therefore away from trouble, one's task is to stay on it, to "attend to" it.

**16:26** The adage puzzled ancient and modern commentators. The meaning seems to state the paradox that a person does not toil to feed the gullet but that the gullet itself "toils" in the sense that it forces the person to work. As often in Proverbs, the sense organ stands for the faculty by metonymy. Cf. Eccl 6:7.

**16:30** A restless or twitching eye or lip betrays the condition of the heart (cf. 6:13).

**16:33** Dice were given meanings of "yes" or "no" and then cast for their answer. What came out was the decision. Here the saying interprets the sequence of actions: a human being puts the dice in the bag but what emerges from the bag is the Lord's decision.

**17:1** A "better than" saying, stating the circumstances when a dry crust is better than a banquet. Peace and fellow-

---

*g:* Prv 19:21; 20:24; Jer 10:23. *h:* Prv 11:1. *i:* Prv 25:5. *j:* Prv 14:35; 22:11. *k:* Prv 19:12; 20:2. *l:* Prv 8:10–11. *m:* Prv 11:2. *n:* Prv 14:12. *o:* Prv 10:4. *p:* Prv 6:14, 19; 17:9; 26:22; Sir 28:15. *q:* Prv 20:29. *r:* Prv 14:29.

2 A wise servant will rule over an
unworthy son,
and will share the inheritance of the
children.*
3 The crucible for silver, and the furnace
for gold,
but the tester of hearts is the LORD.
4 The evildoer gives heed to wicked lips,
the liar, to a mischievous tongue.
5 Whoever mocks the poor reviles their
Maker;
whoever rejoices in their misfortune
will not go unpunished.[s]
6 Children's children are the crown of the
elderly,
and the glory of children is their
parentage.
7 Fine words ill fit a fool;
how much more lying lips, a noble!
8 A bribe seems a charm to its user;
at every turn it brings success.*
9 Whoever overlooks an offense fosters
friendship,
but whoever gossips about it separates
friends.*
10 A single reprimand does more for a
discerning person
than a hundred lashes for a fool.*
11 The wicked pursue only rebellion,
and a merciless messenger is sent
against them.*
12 Face a bear robbed of her cubs,
but never fools in their folly!*
13 If you return evil for good,
evil will not depart from your house.* [t]
14 The start of strife is like the opening of a
dam;
check a quarrel before it bursts forth!
15 Whoever acquits the wicked,[u] whoever
condemns the just—
both are an abomination to the LORD.
16 Of what use is money in the hands of
fools
when they have no heart to acquire
wisdom?*
17 A friend is a friend at all times,
and a brother is born for the time of
adversity.[v]
18 Those without sense give their hands in
pledge,
becoming surety for their neighbors.[w]
19 Those who love an offense love a fight;[x]
those who build their gate high* court
disaster.
20 The perverse in heart come to no good,
and the double-tongued fall into
trouble.*
21 Whoever conceives a fool has grief;
the father of a numskull has no joy.
22 A joyful heart is the health of the body,
but a depressed spirit dries up the
bones.[y]
23 A guilty person takes out a bribe from the
pocket,
thus perverting the course of justice.*
24 On the countenance of a discerning
person is wisdom,[z]
but the eyes of a fool are on the ends
of the earth.*
25 A foolish son is vexation to his father,

ship give joy to a meal, not the richness of the food. For a similar thought, see 15:16 and 16:8.

**17:2** Ability is esteemed more highly than ties of blood.

**17:8** An observation on the effect of the bribe upon the bribe-giver: it gives an intoxicating feeling of power ("seems"). In v. 23 the evil effects of a bribe are noted.

**17:9** A paradox. One finds (love, friend) by concealing (an offense), one loses (a friend) by revealing (a secret). In 10:12 love also covers over a multitude of offenses.

**17:10** A wonderful comment on the openness and sensitivity of the wise and the foolish. One type learns from a single word and for the other one hundred blows are not enough.

**17:11** The irony is that such people will meet up with what they so energetically pursue—in the form of an unrelenting emissary sent to them.

**17:12** Humorous hyperbole. An outraged dangerous beast poses less danger than a fool.

**17:13** The paradox is that to pay out evil for good means that the evil will never leave one's own house.

**17:16** The exhortation to acquire or purchase wisdom is common in Proverbs. Fools misunderstand the metaphor, assuming they can buy it with money. Their very misunderstanding shows they have no "heart" = mind, understanding. Money in the hand is no good without such a "heart" to store it in.

**17:19 Build their gate high**: a symbol of arrogance.

**17:20** The saying employs the familiar metaphors of walking = conducting oneself ("fall into trouble"), and of straight and crooked = right and wrong ("perverse," "double-tongued").

**17:23** A sharp look at the sly withdrawing of a bribe from the pocket and a blunt judgment on its significance.

**17:24** Wisdom is visible on the countenance (i.e., mouth, lips, tongue) of the wise person; its ultimate source is the heart. Fools have no such source of wisdom within them, a

*s:* Prv 14:31. *t:* Mt 5:39; Rom 12:17; 1 Thes 5:15; 1 Pt 3:9. *u:* Prv 24:24; Is 5:23. *v:* Prv 18:24. *w:* Prv 6:1–2; 11:15. *x:* Prv 15:18. *y:* Prv 12:25; 15:13. *z:* Eccl 8:1.

and bitter sorrow to her who bore him.[a]
26 It is wrong to fine an innocent person,
but beyond reason to scourge nobles.
27 Those who spare their words are truly knowledgeable,
and those who are discreet are intelligent.[b]
28 Even fools, keeping silent, are considered wise;
if they keep their lips closed, intelligent.*

## CHAPTER 18

See RG 180–82

1 One who is alienated seeks a pretext,
with all persistence picks a quarrel.
2 Fools take no delight in understanding,
but only in displaying what they think.*
3 With wickedness comes contempt,
and with disgrace, scorn.
4 The words of one's mouth are deep waters,
the spring of wisdom, a running brook.* [c]
5 It is not good to favor the guilty,
nor to reject the claim of the just.[d]
6 The lips of fools walk into a fight,
and their mouths are asking for a beating.*
7 The mouths of fools are their ruin;
their lips are a deadly snare.[e]
8 The words of a talebearer are like dainty morsels:
they sink into one's inmost being.[f]
9 Those slack in their work
are kin to the destroyer.
10 * The name of the LORD is a strong tower;
the just run to it and are safe.
11 The wealth of the rich is their strong city;[g]
they fancy it a high wall.
12 Before disaster the heart is haughty,[h]
but before honor is humility.
13 Whoever answers before listening,[i]
theirs is folly and shame.*
14 One's spirit supports one when ill,
but a broken spirit who can bear?*
15 The heart of the intelligent acquires knowledge,
and the ear of the wise seeks knowledge.*
16 Gifts clear the way for people,
winning access to the great.[j]
17 Those who plead the case first seem to be in the right;
then the opponent comes and cross-examines them.*
18 The lot puts an end to disputes,
and decides a controversy between the mighty.*
19 A brother offended is more unyielding than a stronghold;
such strife is more daunting than castle gates.*

point that is nicely made by referring to the eye of the fool, roving over the landscape.

**17:28** Related to v. 27. Words provide a glimpse into the heart. In the unlikely event that fools, who usually pour out words (15:2), were to say nothing, people would not be able to see their folly and would presume them intelligent. Alas, the saying is contrary to fact.

**18:2** One grows in wisdom by listening to others, but fools take delight in expounding the contents of their minds.

**18:4** Words express a person's thoughts ("deep waters"), which in turn become accessible to others. Cf. 20:5a.

**18:6** The bold personification of lips and mouth is similar to Ps 73:9, "They set their mouths against the heavens, their tongues roam the earth." Careless words can lead one into serious trouble.

**18:10–11** Contrast this judgment with the observation in 10:15.

**18:13** To speak without first listening is characteristic of a fool; cf. 10:14; Sir 11:8.

**18:14** The paradox is that something as slight as a column of air offers protection against the encroachment of death. If it is stilled, nothing, no matter how powerful, can substitute for it.

**18:15** "Knowledge" here refers to what one knows, not knowledge in itself. The mind acquires and stores it, the ear strains toward it.

**18:17** A persuasive speech in court can easily make one forget there is another side to the question. When the other party speaks, people realize they made a premature judgment. The experience at court is a lesson for daily life: there are two sides to every question.

**18:18** See note on 16:33.

**18:19** The Greek version, followed by several ancient versions, has the opposite meaning: "A brother helped by a brother is like a strong and lofty city; it is strong like a well-founded palace." The Greek is secondary as is shown by the need to supply the phrase "by a brother"; further, the parallelism is inadequate. The Hebrew is to be preferred.

*a:* Prv 10:1; 29:15. *b:* Prv 10:19; Sir 1:21; Jas 1:19. *c:* Prv 20:5; Jn 7:38. *d:* Prv 24:23; 28:21. *e:* Prv 10:14; 12:13; 13:3; Eccl 10:12. *f:* Prv 26:22. *g:* Prv 10:15. *h:* Prv 11:2; 16:18; Sir 10:15. *i:* Sir 11:8. *j:* Prv 21:14.

20 With the fruit of one's mouth one's belly is filled,
with the produce of one's lips one is sated.* [k]
21 Death and life are in the power of the tongue;[l]
those who choose one shall eat its fruit.*
22 To find a wife is to find happiness,
a favor granted by the LORD.[m]
23 The poor implore,
but the rich answer harshly.
24 There are friends who bring ruin,
but there are true friends more loyal than a brother.[n]

## CHAPTER 19

See RG 180–82

1 Better to be poor and walk in integrity
than rich and crooked in one's ways.[o]
2 Desire without knowledge is not good;
and whoever acts hastily, blunders.*
3 Their own folly leads people astray;
in their hearts they rage against the LORD.*
4 Wealth adds many friends,
but the poor are left friendless.[p]
5 The false witness will not go unpunished,
and whoever utters lies will not escape.* [q]
6 Many curry favor with a noble;
everybody is a friend of a gift giver.
7 All the kin of the poor despise them;
how much more do their friends shun them!*
8 Those who gain sense truly love themselves;
those who preserve understanding will find success.*
9 The false witness will not go unpunished,
and whoever utters lies will perish.
10 Luxury is not befitting a fool;
much less should a slave rule over princes.
11 It is good sense to be slow to anger,
and an honor to overlook an offense.*
12 The king's wrath is like the roar of a lion,
but his favor, like dew on the grass.* [r]
13 The foolish son is ruin to his father,[s]
and a quarrelsome wife is water constantly dripping.*
14 Home and possessions are an inheritance from parents,
but a prudent wife is from the LORD.[t]
15 Laziness brings on deep sleep,
and the sluggard goes hungry.[u]
16 Those who keep commands keep their lives,
but those who despise these ways will die.[v]
17 Whoever cares for the poor lends to the LORD,[w]
who will pay back the sum in full.
18 Discipline your son, for there is hope;
but do not be intent on his death.* [x]

**18:20** Fruit from the earth is our ordinary sustenance, but "the fruit of one's lips," i.e., our words, also affect our well-being. If our words and our deeds are right, then we are blessed, our "belly is filled."

**18:21** This enigmatic saying has provoked many interpretations, e.g., judicious speech brings a reward; those who love the tongue in the sense of rattling on must face the consequences of their loquacity. This translation interprets the verb "love" in colon B in its occasional sense of "choose" (e.g., 12:1; 20:13; Dt 4:37) and interprets its pronominal object as referring to both death and life in colon A. Death and life are set before every person (cf. Dt 30:15–20) and we have the power to choose either one by the quality of our deeds. Words (= "the tongue") are regarded here as the defining actions of human beings.

**19:2** When not guided by wisdom, appetite—or desire—is not good. "Running feet" (so the Hebrew) miss the mark, i.e., do not reach their destination.

**19:3** One's own folly destroys one's life. It is an indication of that folly that one blames God rather than oneself.

**19:5** The punishment fits the crime: those who abuse the legal system will be punished by the same system. They will not be acquitted.

**19:7** Closely related to vv. 4 and 6. An observation, not without sympathy, on the social isolation of poor people.

**19:8** Wisdom benefits the one who practices it.

**19:11** The paradox is that one obtains one thing by giving up another.

**19:12** An observation on the exercise of royal power. Both images suggest royal attitudes are beyond human control. Colon A is a variant of 20:2a and colon B of 16:15b.

**19:13** One of many sayings about domestic happiness. The perspective is male; the two greatest pains to a father is a malicious son and an unsuitable wife. The immediately following saying is on the noble wife, perhaps to make a positive statement about women.

**19:18** The pain of disciplining the young cannot be compared with the danger no discipline may bring. The chief reason for disciplining the young is their capacity to change;

---

*k:* Prv 12:14; 13:2. *l:* Sir 37:18. *m:* Prv 12:4; 19:14; Sir 7:26. *n:* Prv 17:17. *o:* Prv 28:6. *p:* Prv 14:20; Sir 13:20–23. *q:* Dt 19:16–20; Dn 13:61. *r:* Prv 20:2. *s:* Prv 10:1; 17:25. *t:* Prv 18:22. *u:* Prv 6:9–10. *v:* Prv 13:13; 16:17. *w:* Prv 14:21; 22:9; 28:27. *x:* Prv 13:24; 23:13–14.

19 A wrathful person bears the penalty;
after one rescue, you will have it to do again.
20 Listen to counsel and receive instruction,
that you may eventually become wise.
21 Many are the plans of the human heart,
but it is the decision of the LORD that endures.[y]
22 What is desired of a person is fidelity;
rather be poor than a liar.*
23 The fear of the LORD leads to life;
one eats and sleeps free from any harm.
24 The sluggard buries a hand in the dish;
not even lifting it to the mouth.[z]
25 Beat a scoffer and the naive learn a lesson;
rebuke the intelligent and they gain knowledge.[a]
26 Whoever mistreats a father or drives away a mother,
is a shameless and disgraceful child.* [b]
27 My son, stop attending to correction;
start straying from words of knowledge.*
28 An unprincipled witness scoffs at justice,
and the mouth of the wicked pours out iniquity.
29 Rods are prepared for scoffers,
and blows for the backs of fools.[c]

## CHAPTER 20

See RG 180–82

1 Wine is arrogant, strong drink is riotous;
none who are intoxicated by them are wise.* [d]
2 The terror of a king is like the roar of a lion;[e]
those who incur his anger forfeit their lives.
3 A person gains honor by avoiding strife,
while every fool starts a quarrel.*
4 In seedtime sluggards do not plow;
when they look for the harvest, it is not there.
5 The intention of the human heart is deep water,
but the intelligent draw it forth.* [f]
6 Many say, "My loyal friend,"
but who can find someone worthy of trust?
7 The just walk in integrity;
happy are their children after them!
8 A king seated on the throne of judgment
dispels all evil with his glance.*
9 Who can say, "I have made my heart clean,[g]
I am cleansed of my sin"?*
10 Varying weights, varying measures,
are both an abomination to the LORD.[h]
11 In their actions even children can playact
though their deeds be blameless and right.*
12 The ear that hears, the eye that sees—
the LORD has made them both.*
13 Do not love sleep lest you be reduced to poverty;

excluded thereby are revenge and punishment.

**19:22** The proverb has been read in two ways: (1) "Desire (greed) is a shame to a person," which assumes the rare Hebrew word for "shame" is being used; (2) "What is desired in a person is fidelity." The second interpretation is preferable. The context may be the court: better to forego money (a bribe) than perjure oneself.

**19:26** Children who disgrace the family equivalently plunder their father's wealth and expel their mother from the home.

**19:27** The meaning was disputed even in antiquity. The interpretation that most respects the syntax is to take it as ironic advice as in 22:6: to stop (listening) is to go (wandering).

**20:1** The cause stands for its effect (wine, drunken behavior). In Proverbs wine is a sign of prosperity and a symbol of feasting (3:10; 4:17; 9:2, 5) but also a potential threat to wisdom as in 20:1; 21:17; 23:29–35.

**20:3** The honor that one might seek to gain from fighting comes of itself to the person who refrains from fighting.

**20:5** The heart is where human plans are made and stored; they remain "deep water" until words reveal them to others. The wise know how to draw up those waters, i.e., express them. Cf. 18:4.

**20:8** The royal throne is established in justice and the king is the agent of that justice.

**20:9** A claim to sinlessness can be merely self-deception; see 16:2; cf. also 15:11.

**20:11** The verb in colon A can mean either "to make oneself known" or "to play another person" (as in Gn 42:7 and 1 Kgs 14:5, 6). The second meaning makes a better parallel to colon B. The meaning is that if a child can playact, an adult can do so even more. Actions do not always reveal character.

**20:12** Human judgments are not ultimate; the Lord expects proper use of these faculties.

*y:* Prv 16:9. *z:* Prv 26:15. *a:* Prv 17:10; 21:11. *b:* Sir 3:16. *c:* Prv 26:3. *d:* Prv 23:29–35. *e:* Prv 19:12. *f:* Prv 18:4. *g:* 1 Kgs 8:46; 2 Chr 6:36; Eccl 7:20; 1 Jn 1:8. *h:* Prv 11:1; 20:23.

keep your eyes open, have your fill of
food.
14 "Bad, bad!" says the buyer,
then goes away only to boast.*
15 One can put on gold and abundant
jewels,
but wise lips are the most precious
ornament.*
16 Take the garment of the one who became
surety for a stranger;[i]
if for foreigners, exact the pledge!*
17 Bread earned by deceit is sweet,
but afterward the mouth is filled with
gravel.
18 Plans made with advice succeed;
with wise direction wage your war.
19 A slanderer reveals secrets;
so have nothing to do with a babbler!
20 Those who curse father or mother—
their lamp will go out* in the dead of
night.[j]
21 Possessions greedily guarded at the
outset
will not be blessed in the end.*
22 Do not say, "I will repay evil!"
Wait for the LORD, who will help
you.* [k]
23 Varying weights are an abomination to
the LORD,
and false scales are not good.[l]
24 Our steps are from the LORD;[m]
how, then, can mortals understand
their way?*
25 It is a trap to pledge rashly a sacred gift,
and after a vow, then to reflect.*
26 A wise king winnows the wicked,
and threshes them under the
cartwheel.*
27 A lamp from the LORD is human life-
breath;
it searches through the inmost being.*
28 His steadfast loyalty safeguards the king,
and he upholds his throne by justice.[n]
29 The glory of the young is their strength,
and the dignity of the old is gray hair.[o]
30 Evil is cleansed away by bloody lashes,
and a scourging to the inmost being.

## CHAPTER 21

See RG 180–82

1 A king's heart is channeled water
in the hand of the LORD;
God directs it where he pleases.*
2 All your ways may be straight in your
own eyes,
but it is the LORD who weighs hearts.[p]
3 To do what is right and just[q]
is more acceptable to the LORD than
sacrifice.*
4 Haughty eyes and a proud heart—
the lamp of the wicked will fail.*

**20:14** Bartering invites playacting and masking one's true intent. The truth of words depends on their context.

**20:15** Wisdom is said to be preferable to gold in 3:14; 8:10, 19; 16:16. Colon B suggests that the gold and jewelry here are ornaments for the face (cf. Gn 24:53; Ex 3:22; Is 61:10). Wise lips are the most beautiful adornment, for they display the wisdom of the heart.

**20:16** The text is not clear. See 27:13. Caution in becoming surety is always advised (cf. 6:1–3), and it is especially advisable with strangers.

**20:20 Their lamp will go out**: misfortune, even death, awaits them; cf. 13:9; Ex 21:17.

**20:21** By definition, an inheritance is not gained by one's own efforts but is received as a gift. If, when one first receives the inheritance, one drives everyone away, one treats it as if one acquired it by one's own efforts. In an agricultural society, an inheritance would often be a field that would require God's blessing to be fertile.

**20:22** Appointing oneself an agent of divine retribution is dangerous. Better to wait for God to effect justice. Cf. 24:17–18.

**20:24** An indication of the Lord's inscrutable providence; cf. Jer 10:23; see Prv 21:2; cf. also 14:12.

**20:25** This verse cautions against making vows without proper reflection; cf. Dt 23:22–25; Eccl 5:4–5.

**20:26** The king is responsible for effecting justice. Judgment is portrayed in agricultural imagery—exposing grain to a current of air so that the chaff is blown away, and passing a wheel over the cereal to break the husk. Winnowing as image for judgment is found throughout the Bible.

**20:27** A parallel is drawn between the life-breath that is God's gift (Jb 32:8; 33:2) coursing through the human body (Is 2:22) and the lamp of God, which can be a symbol of divine scrutiny. In Zep 1:12, God declares, "And in that day I will search through Jerusalem with lamps."

**21:1** "Channeled water" in Is 32:2 and Prv 5:16 is water that fertilizes arid land. It takes great skill to direct water, whether it be water to fertilize fields or cosmic floods harnessed at creation, for water is powerful and seems to have a mind of its own. It also requires great skill to direct the heart of a king, for it is inscrutable and beyond ordinary human control.

**21:3** External rites or sacrifices do not please God unless accompanied by internal worship and right moral conduct; cf. 15:8; 21:27; Is 1:11–15; Am 5:22; Mal 1:12.

**21:4** Heart and eyes depict, respectively, the inner and the outer person. "Haughty eyes" peering out from a "proud

*i:* Prv 27:13. *j:* Prv 30:11, 17; Ex 21:17; Lv 20:9; Mt 15:4. *k:* Prv 24:29; Sir 28:1; Mt 5:39; Rom 12:17, 19; 1 Thes 5:15; 1 Pt 3:9. *l:* Prv 11:1; 20:10. *m:* Prv 16:9. *n:* Prv 16:12. *o:* Prv 16:31. *p:* Prv 16:2. *q:* 1 Sm 15:22; Hos 6:6.

5 The plans of the diligent end in profit,
but those of the hasty end in loss.*
6 Trying to get rich by lying
is chasing a bubble over deadly snares.
7 The violence of the wicked will sweep them away,
because they refuse to do what is right.
8 One's path may be winding and unfamiliar,
but one's conduct is blameless and right.*
9 It is better to dwell in a corner of the housetop
than in a mansion with a quarrelsome woman.* [r]
10 The soul of the wicked desires evil;
their neighbor finds no pity in their eyes.
11 When scoffers are punished the naive become wise;
when the wise succeed, they gain knowledge.[s]
12 The Righteous One appraises the house of the wicked,
bringing down the wicked to ruin.*
13 Those who shut their ears to the cry of the poor
will themselves call out and not be answered.
14 A secret gift allays anger,
and a present concealed, violent wrath.*
15 When justice is done it is a joy for the just,
downfall for evildoers.* [t]
16 Whoever strays from the way of good sense
will abide in the assembly of the shades.*
17 The lover of pleasure will suffer want;
the lover of wine and perfume will never be rich.
18 The wicked serve as ransom for the just,
and the faithless for the upright.* [u]
19 It is better to dwell in a wilderness
than with a quarrelsome wife and trouble.
20 Precious treasure and oil are in the house of the wise,
but the fool consumes them.
21 Whoever pursues justice and kindness
will find life and honor.*
22 The wise person storms the city of the mighty,
and overthrows the stronghold in which they trust.
23 Those who guard mouth and tongue
guard themselves* from trouble.[v]
24 Proud, boastful—scoffer is the name:
those who act with overbearing pride.
25 The desire of sluggards will slay them,
for their hands refuse to work.*

heart" show a thoroughly arrogant person. How can such a person flourish! Their lamp, which signifies life, will go out.

**21:5** The antitheses are diligent and impetuous. The metaphor characterizing each type is taken from the world of commerce. Planning is important; bustle leads to waste.

**21:8** One cannot always read others' hearts from their behavior. Unconventional conduct need not indicate evil motives.

**21:9** In Proverbs, two great obstacles to a happy household are foolish children and quarrelsome spouses. The nagging wife is also mentioned in 19:13 and 27:15; 25:24 is a duplicate.

**21:12** It is difficult to ascertain the subject of the saying. Some hold it is the Lord, the "Righteous One," who is normally the executor of justice in Proverbs. Others believe it is the just person who is the agent of divine justice. "Righteous One" is a title for God in Is 24:16. The best argument for making God the subject of the verb is that elsewhere in Proverbs righteous human beings never do anything to the wicked; only God does.

**21:14** Proverbs offers several remedies for anger—a soft word (15:1), patience, and a bribe. The last remedy implies a certain disdain for the disordered passion of anger, for it can be so easily assuaged by a discreetly offered "gift."

**21:15** The second line is a duplicate of 10:29b.

**21:16 Assembly of the shades**: those who dwell in Sheol.

**21:18** In this bold paradox, the ransom that protects the righteous is the wicked person who attracts, like a lightning rod, the divine wrath that might have been directed at the righteous.

**21:21** The paradox is that one comes upon something other than what one pursued. The way to (long and healthy) life and honor is the vigorous pursuit of virtue.

**21:23 Themselves**: see note on 13:3. To guard your "self" (lit., "throat," the moist and breathing center of the body, by metonymy, "life"), you must guard your tongue. Speech in Proverbs is the quintessential human activity and often has a meaning broader than speech alone; it can stand for all human activity. Acting rightly is the best way to protect yourself from evil.

**21:25** Desire, or appetite, is the impulse toward food and drink (see Ps 42:3) which spurs animals and human beings into action. But sluggards cannot lift hand to mouth; they bury their hand in the dish (19:24), and so their appetite is thwarted.

*r:* Prv 21:19; 25:24; 27:15; Sir 25:23. *s:* Prv 19:25. *t:* Prv 10:29. *u:* Prv 11:8. *v:* Prv 13:3.

26 Some are consumed with avarice all the day,
but the just give unsparingly.
27 The sacrifice of the wicked is an abomination,
the more so when they offer it with bad intent.[w]
28 The false witness will perish,[x]
but one who listens will give lasting testimony.
29 The face of the wicked hardens,
but the upright maintains a straight course.*
30 No wisdom, no understanding,
no counsel prevail against the LORD.
31 The horse is equipped for the day of battle,
but victory is the LORD's.

## CHAPTER 22

See RG 180–82

1 A good name is more desirable than great riches,
and high esteem, than gold and silver.* [y]
2 Rich and poor have a common bond:
the LORD is the maker of them all.[z]
3 The astute see an evil and hide,
while the naive continue on and pay the penalty.* [a]
4 The result of humility and fear of the LORD
is riches, honor and life.*
5 Thorns and snares are on the path of the crooked;
those who would safeguard their lives
will avoid them.
6 Train the young in the way they should go;
even when old, they will not swerve from it.*
7 The rich rule over the poor,
and the borrower is the slave of the lender.*
8 Those who sow iniquity reap calamity,[b]
and the rod used in anger will fail.*
9 The generous will be blessed,
for they share their food with the poor.
10 Expel the arrogant and discord goes too;
strife and insult cease.
11 The LORD loves the pure of heart;[c]
the person of winning speech has a king for a friend.
12 The eyes of the LORD watch over the knowledgeable,
but he defeats the projects of the faithless.
13 The sluggard says, "A lion is outside;[d]
I might be slain in the street."*
14 The mouth of the foreign woman is a deep pit;[e]
whoever incurs the LORD's anger will fall into it.
15 Folly is bound to the heart of a youth,
but the rod of discipline will drive it out.*
16 Oppressing the poor for enrichment,
giving to the rich: both are sheer loss.*

**21:29** The wicked cannot deter the righteous from walking the straight path, i.e., from practicing virtue.

**22:1** "Good name" (Heb. *shem*) and "high esteem" (Heb. *chen*) are declared to be of more value than great riches. Human beings belong to a community and without the acceptance of that community, which is built on esteem and trust, human life is grievously damaged. Riches are less essential to the human spirit.

**22:3** The wise see dangers before they are engulfed by them whereas fools, through dullness or boldness, march right on.

**22:4** Humiliation can be an occasion for knowing one's place in God's world. Such knowledge is part of fear (or revering) of the Lord. Revering the Lord brings the blessings of wealth, honor, and long life. The saying is perhaps meant to counter the view that humiliation is an unmixed evil; something good can come of it.

**22:6** One of the few exhortations in the collection (cf. 14:7; 16:3; 19:18, 20). "Way" in the first colon has been taken in two different senses: (1) the morally right way, "according to the way one ought to go"; (2) personal aptitude, i.e., the manner of life for which one is destined, as "the way of Egypt" (Is 10:24). Neither interpretation, however, accounts for the pronoun in the Hebrew phrase, lit., "his own way." The most natural solution is to take the whole as ironic advice (like 19:27): yes, go ahead and let the young do exactly what they want; they will become self-willed adults.

**22:7** An observation on money and power. One who borrows becomes poor in the sense of indebted, a slave to the lender.

**22:8** Agricultural metaphors express the failure of malicious actions. In the first line, bad actions are seeds yielding trouble. In the second line, "the rod" is a flail used to beat grains as in Is 28:27.

**22:13** To avoid the effort required for action, the sluggard exaggerates the difficulties that must be overcome.

**22:15** Folly is attached to children as the husk is attached to the grain. "Rod" here, as in v. 8, seems to be the flail. Discipline is the process of winnowing away the folly.

**22:16** A difficult saying. One possibility is to take it as a seemingly neutral observation on the plight of the poor: taking money from the poor is relatively easy for the powerful

*w:* Prv 15:8; Sir 34:21–23. *x:* Prv 19:5, 9. *y:* Eccl 7:1. *z:* Prv 29:13. *a:* Prv 27:12. *b:* Jb 4:8; Sir 7:3; Hos 8:7. *c:* Mt 5:8. *d:* Prv 26:13. *e:* Prv 23:27.

## IV. Sayings of the Wise*

17 The Words of the Wise:*
Incline your ear, and hear my words,[f]
and let your mind attend to my
teaching;
18 For it will be well if you hold them
within you,
if they all are ready on your lips.
19 That your trust may be in the LORD,
I make them known to you today—
yes, to you.
20 Have I not written for you thirty sayings,
containing counsels and knowledge,
21 To teach you truly
how to give a dependable report to one
who sends you?
22 Do not rob the poor because they are
poor,
nor crush the needy at the gate;*
23 For the LORD will defend their cause,[g]
and will plunder those who plunder
them.
24 Do not be friendly with hotheads,
nor associate with the wrathful,
25 Lest you learn their ways,
and become ensnared.
26 Do not be one of those who give their
hand in pledge,
those who become surety for debts;[h]
27 For if you are unable to pay,
your bed will be taken from under you.*
28 Do not remove the ancient landmark*
that your ancestors set up.[i]
29 Do you see those skilled at their work?
They will stand in the presence of kings,
but not in the presence of the obscure.

### CHAPTER 23

See RG 180–82

1 * When you sit down to dine with
a ruler,
mark well the one who is before you;

but it is dangerous as the poor have the Lord as their defender (24:22–23), who will punish their oppressors. Giving to the rich, perhaps to win their favor by presents and bribes, is equally a waste of money, for the rich will always do what they please in any case.

**22:17–24:22** This collection consists of an introduction (22:17–21) urging openness and stating the purpose of the Words and diverse admonitions, aphorisms, and counsels. It is written with faith in the Lord, shrewdness, and a satirical eye. The first part seems aimed at young people intent on a career (22:22–23:11); the second is taken up with the concerns of youth (23:12–35); the third part is interested in the ultimate fate of the good and the wicked (24:1–22). The whole can be described as a guidebook of professional ethics. The aim is to inculcate trust in the Lord and to help readers avoid trouble and advance their careers by living according to wisdom. Its outlook is very practical: avoid bad companions because in time you will take on some of their qualities; do not post bond for others because you yourself will be encumbered; do not promote yourself too aggressively because such promotion is self-defeating; do not abuse sex or alcohol because they will harm you; do not emulate your peers if they are wicked (23:14; 24:1, 19) because such people have no future. Rather, trust the vocation of a sage (22:29–23:9).

The Egyptian *Instructions of Amenemope* (written ca. 1100 B.C.) was discovered in 1923. Scholars immediately recognized it as a source of Prv 22:17–23:11. The Egyptian work has thirty chapters (cf. Prv 22:20); its preface resembled Prv 22:17–21; its first two admonitions matched the first two in Proverbs (Prv 22:22–25). There are many other resemblances as well, some of which are pointed out in the notes. The instruction of a father to his son (or an administrator to his successor) was a well-known genre in Egypt; seventeen works are extant, spanning the period from 2500 B.C. to the first century A.D. The instructions aimed to help a young person live a happy and prosperous life and avoid mistakes that cause difficulties. They make concrete and pragmatic suggestions rather than hold up abstract ideals. Pragmatic though they were, the instructions were religious; they assumed that the gods implanted an order in the world (Egyptian *maat*), which is found both in nature and in the human world. *Amenemope* represents a stage in the development of the Egyptian genre, displaying a new inwardness and quest for serenity while still assuming that the practice of virtue brings worldly success. Proverbs borrows from the Egyptian work with great freedom: it does not, for example, import as such the Egyptian concept of order; it engages the reader with its characteristic wit, irony, and paradox (e.g., 22:26–27; 23:1–3).

**22:17–23:35** The maxims warn against: robbing the poor and defenseless (22:22–23), anger (22:24–25), giving surety for debts (22:26–27), advancing oneself by socializing with rulers (23:1–2), anxiety for riches (23:4–5), forcing oneself on a grudging host (23:6–8), intemperance in food and drink (23:19–21, 29–35), and adultery (23:26–28). They exhort to: careful workmanship (22:29), respect for the rights of orphans (23:10–11), correction of the young (23:13–14), filial piety (23:15–16, 22–25), and fear of the Lord (23:17–18).

**22:22 At the gate**: of the city, where justice was administered and public affairs discussed; cf. Ru 4:1. Cf. also Ps 69:13; 127:5; Prv 24:7; 31:23, 31. The Lord will personally avenge those who have no one to defend them.

**22:27** Providing surety for a debtor puts one in danger of having the very basics of one's life suddenly seized.

**22:28 Landmark**: marks the boundary of property. To remove it is the equivalent of stealing land. A similar warning is contained in 23:10.

**23:1–9** Four admonitions for someone aspiring to be a sage: be careful about advancing your career by socializing with the great (vv. 1–3); avoid greed (vv. 4–5); do not force

*f*: Prv 5:1. *g*: Prv 23:11. *h*: Prv 6:1–2; 11:15; 17:18. *i*: Prv 23:10; Dt 19:14; 27:17.

2 Stick the knife in your gullet*
if you have a ravenous appetite.
3 Do not desire his delicacies;
it is food that deceives.
4 Do not wear yourself out to gain wealth,
cease to be worried about it;
5 When your glance flits to it, it is gone!
For assuredly it grows wings,
like the eagle that flies toward
heaven.*
6 * Do not take food with unwilling hosts,
and do not desire their delicacies;
7 For like something stuck in the throat is
that food.
"Eat and drink," they say to you,
but their hearts are not with you;
8 The little you have eaten you will
vomit up,
and you will have wasted your
agreeable words.
9 Do not speak in the hearing of fools;
they will despise the wisdom of your
words.[j]
10 Do not remove the ancient landmark,[k]
nor invade the fields of the fatherless;*
11 For their redeemer is strong;
he will defend their cause against you.[l]
12 Apply your heart to instruction,
and your ear to words of knowledge.
13 * Do not withhold discipline from youths;
if you beat them with the rod, they will
not die.[m]
14 Beat them with the rod,[n]
and you will save them from Sheol.
15 My son, if your heart is wise,
my heart also will rejoice;
16 And my inmost being will exult,
when your lips speak what is right.
17 Do not let your heart envy sinners,[o]
but only those who always fear the
LORD;*
18 For you will surely have a future,
and your hope will not be cut off.[p]
19 Hear, my son, and be wise,
and guide your heart in the right way.
20 Do not join with wine bibbers,
nor with those who glut themselves on
meat.
21 For drunkards and gluttons come to
poverty,
and lazing about clothes one in rags.
22 * Listen to your father who begot you,
do not despise your mother when she
is old.
23 Buy truth and do not sell:
wisdom, instruction, understanding!
24 The father of a just person will exult
greatly;
whoever begets a wise son will rejoice
in him.[q]

yourself on an unwilling host (vv. 6–8); do not waste your wisdom on those who cannot profit from it (v. 9).

**23:2 Stick the knife in your gullet**: a metaphor for self-restraint. The usual translation, "Put a knife to your throat," is misleading, for in English it is a death threat. The exhortation is humorously exaggerated: stick the table-knife in your own gullet rather than take too much food. It assumes that the young courtier is unused to opulent banquets and will be tempted to overindulgence.

**23:5** The frustration of covetous intent and elusiveness of wealth are portrayed by the sudden flight of an eagle. *Amenemope*, chap. 7, has a similar statement: "Do not set your heart on wealth. There is no ignoring Fate and Destiny; / Do not let your heart go straying." Proverbs imagines covetous intent as a flight of the eyes, whereas *Amenemope* imagines it as a straying of the heart.

**23:6–8** Some humorous advice on not trading on the courtesy of unwilling hosts who, for convention's sake, use the language of welcome. *Amenemope*, chap. 11, gives similar advice: "Do not intrude on a man in his house, / Enter when you have been called; / He may say 'Welcome' with his mouth, / Yet deride you in his thoughts." "Unwilling," lit., "evil of eye," is usually translated "stingy," but the context suggests unwilling. In v. 8, the unwanted guest vomits up the food, thus destroying the desired good impression. Proverbs regards the uninvited banqueters as thieves who will suffer the consequences of their theft. *Amenemope*, chap. 11, is relevant: "Do not covet a poor man's goods, . . . A poor man's goods are a block in the throat, / It makes the gullet vomit."

**23:10** In Israel ownership of property and other legal rights were vested mainly in the father as head of the family; thus the widow and fatherless child were vulnerable, left prey to those who would exploit them.

**23:13–14** The young will not die from instructional blows but from their absence, for (premature) death results from uncorrected folly. The sardonic humor means the exhortation is not to be taken literally, as an argument for corporal punishment. The next verses (vv. 15–16) are exceedingly tender toward the young.

**23:17** Those whom one admires or associates with exercise enormous influence. Do not join the wicked, who are a doomed group. The warning is repeated in 24:1–2, 19–20.

**23:22–23** Father and mother are associated with truth and wisdom. One should no more rid oneself of truth and wisdom than rid oneself of one's parents, who are their source.

*j:* Prv 9:7. *k:* Prv 22:28. *l:* Prv 22:23. *m:* Prv 13:24; 19:18; Sir 30:1. *n:* Prv 29:15, 17. *o:* Prv 3:31; 24:1, 19. *p:* Prv 24:14. *q:* Prv 10:1.

25 Let your father and mother rejoice;
let her who bore you exult.
26 * My son, give me your heart,
and let your eyes keep to my ways,
27 For the harlot is a deep pit,
and the foreign woman a narrow well;
28 Yes, she lies in wait like a robber,[r]
and increases the number of the faithless.
29 * Who scream? Who shout?
Who have strife? Who have anxiety?
Who have wounds for nothing?
Who have bleary eyes?
30 Whoever linger long over wine,
whoever go around quaffing wine.[s]
31 Do not look on the wine when it is red,
when it sparkles in the cup.
It goes down smoothly,
32 but in the end it bites like a serpent,
and stings like an adder.
33 Your eyes behold strange sights,
and your heart utters incoherent things;
34 You are like one sleeping on the high seas,
sprawled at the top of the mast.
35 "They struck me, but it did not pain me;
they beat me, but I did not feel it.
When can I get up,
when can I go out and get more?"*

## CHAPTER 24

See RG 180–82

1* Do not envy the wicked,
nor desire to be with them;[t]
2 For their hearts plot violence,
and their lips speak of foul play.
3 By wisdom a house is built,
by understanding it is established;
4 And by knowledge its rooms are filled
with every precious and pleasing possession.
5 The wise are more powerful than the strong,
and the learned, than the mighty,[u]
6 For by strategy war is waged,
and victory depends on many counselors.[v]
7 * Wise words are beyond fools' reach,[w]
in the assembly they do not open their mouth;
8 As they calculate how to do evil,
people brand them troublemakers.
9 The scheme of a fool gains no acceptance,
the scoffer is an abomination to the community.
10 * Did you fail in a day of adversity,
did your strength fall short?
11 Did you fail to rescue those who were being dragged off to death,*
those tottering, those near death,
12 because you said, "We didn't know about it"?
Surely, the Searcher of hearts knows
and will repay all according to their deeds.[x]
13 * If you eat honey, my son, because it is good,
if pure honey is sweet to your taste,
14 Such, you must know, is wisdom to your soul.

**23:26–28** The exhortation is a condensed version of chap. 7 with its emotional appeal to "my son" to avoid the forbidden woman (7:1–5), her traps (7:21–23), and her intent to add the youth to her list of victims (7:24–27). As in 23:15, 19, 22, a trustful and affectionate relationship between student and teacher is the basis of teaching. The danger of the woman is expressed in imagery that has sexual overtones (cf. 22:14).

**23:29–35** A vivid description of the evil effects, physical and psychological, of drunkenness. The emphasis is on the unwise behavior, the folly, caused by alcohol. Cf. 20:1.

**23:35** Drunkards become insensible to bodily and moral harm. Their one desire is to indulge again.

**24:1–22** A new section (24:1–14)—on the fates of the wicked and foolish—begins with a warning not to take the foolish as role models. The same admonition is repeated in 23:17–18 and 24:19–20. In 24:1, the verb means "to be jealous, zealous; to emulate." The motive stated in the other passages—the wicked have no future—is indirectly stated here.

**24:7–9** The verses are unclear; most scholars take them as two or even three single sayings, but, taken singly, the verses are banal. They are best taken as a single statement. Just as vv. 3–6 described the advantages of wisdom, so vv. 7–9 describe the disadvantages of its opposite, folly: it alienates one from the community (v. 7), for fools become notorious (v. 8), dooming their plans and ostracizing themselves.

**24:10–12** Excuses for not coming to the aid of one's neighbor in serious trouble do not suffice before God, who sees through self-serving excuses.

**24:11 Rescue . . . death**: perhaps refers to the legal rescue of those unjustly condemned to death.

**24:13–14** God's word is sometimes said to be sweeter than honey, e.g., Ps 119:101–103. Cf. also Ps 19:11; Prv 16:24; Ez 3:3; Sir 24:19–22.

*r:* Prv 7:10–27. *s:* Prv 20:1; Sir 19:2; Hos 4:11. *t:* Prv 3:31; 23:17; Ps 37:1. *u:* Prv 21:22. *v:* Prv 20:18. *w:* Sir 6:21. *x:* Ps 62:13; Sir 16:12; Mt 16:27; Rom 2:6.

If you find it, you will have a future,
and your hope will not be cut off.[y]
15 * Do not lie in wait at the abode of the just,
do not ravage their dwelling places;
16 Though the just fall seven times, they rise again,
but the wicked stumble from only one mishap.
17 * Do not rejoice when your enemies fall,
and when they stumble, do not let your heart exult,
18 Lest the LORD see it, be displeased with you,
and withdraw his wrath from your enemies.
19 Do not be provoked at evildoers,
do not envy the wicked;
20 For the evil have no future,
the lamp of the wicked will be put out.[z]
21 My son, fear the LORD and the king;
have nothing to do with those who hate them;
22 For disaster will issue suddenly,
and calamity from them both, who knows when?

## V. Further Sayings of the Wise *

23 These also are Words of the Wise:
To show partiality in judgment is not good.[a]
24 Whoever says to the guilty party, "You are innocent,"
will be cursed by nations, scorned by peoples;
25 But those who render just verdicts will fare well,
and on them will come the blessing of prosperity.
26 An honest reply—
a kiss on the lips.*
27 Complete your outdoor tasks,
and arrange your work in the field;
afterward you can build your house.*
28 Do not testify falsely against your neighbor[b]
and so deceive with your lips.
29 Do not say, "As they did to me, so will I do to them;[c]
I will repay them according to their deeds."*
30 * I passed by the field of a sluggard,
by the vineyard of one with no sense;
31 It was all overgrown with thistles;
its surface was covered with nettles,
and its stone wall broken down.
32 As I gazed at it, I reflected;
I saw and learned a lesson:
33 A little sleep, a little slumber,[d]
a little folding of the arms to rest—
34 Then poverty will come upon you like a robber,
and want like a brigand.

**24:15–16** The just will overcome every misfortune that oppresses them. *Seven times* is an indefinite number.

**24:17–18** The admonition is linked to the previous by the words "fall" and "stumble." Premature public celebration of the downfall of enemies equivalently preempts the retribution that belongs to God.

**24:23–34** A little collection between the thirty sayings of 22:17–24:22 and the Hezekiah collection in chaps. 25–29. Its title (v. 23) suggests that editors took it as an appendix. At this point, the Greek edition of Proverbs begins to arrange the later sections of the book in a different order than the Hebrew edition.

An editor has arranged originally separate sayings into two parallel groups.

| | I. | II. |
|---|---|---|
| Conduct in court: | Judges (vv. 24–25) | Witnesses (v. 28) |
| Speaking, thinking: | Good speech (v. 26) | Bad speech (v. 29) |
| Wisdom in work: | Positive (v. 27) | Negative (vv. 30–34) |

**24:26** The kiss is a gesture of respect and affection. The greatest sign of affection and respect for another is to tell that person the truth.

**24:27 House**: can refer to both the building and the family (cf. 2 Sm 7). In the context established by the placement noted above under 24:23, the saying means that neglect of one's field is a sign that one is not building the house properly. In an agricultural society especially, the concept of household includes fields for animals and crops. On the metaphorical level, one must lay a careful preparation before embarking on a great project. This verse is sometimes interpreted as advocating careful and practical preparation for marriage.

**24:29** Retribution is a long and complex process that belongs to the Lord, not to individuals. Cf. vv. 12d, 17–18.

**24:30–34** Neglect of one's fields through laziness ruins all plans to build a house (v. 27). This vignette is a teaching story, like those in 7:1–27; Ps 37:35–36.

*y:* Prv 23:18. *z:* Prv 13:9. *a:* Prv 18:5; 28:21; Lv 19:15; Dt 1:17; 16:19. *b:* Prv 19:5; 25:18. *c:* Prv 20:22. *d:* Prv 6:10–11.

## VI. Second Solomonic Collection, Collected under King Hezekiah*

### CHAPTER 25

See RG 180–82

1 These also are proverbs of Solomon.[e] The servants of Hezekiah,* king of Judah, transmitted them.

2 * It is the glory of God to conceal a matter,
and the glory of kings to fathom a matter.*
3 Like the heavens in height, and the earth in depth,
the heart of kings is unfathomable.
4 * Remove the dross from silver,
and it comes forth perfectly purified;
5 Remove the wicked from the presence of the king,
and his throne is made firm through justice.
6 * Claim no honor in the king's presence,
nor occupy the place of superiors;
7 For it is better to be told, "Come up closer!"
than to be humbled before the prince.[f]
8 What your eyes have seen
do not bring forth too quickly against an opponent;
For what will you do later on
when your neighbor puts you to shame?
9 * Argue your own case with your neighbor,
but the secrets of others do not disclose;
10 Lest, hearing it, they reproach you,
and your ill repute never ceases.
11 Golden apples in silver settings
are words spoken at the proper time.
12 A golden earring or a necklace of fine gold—
one who gives wise reproof to a listening ear.
13 Like the coolness of snow in the heat of the harvest
are faithful messengers for those who send them,
lifting the spirits of their masters.
14 Clouds and wind but no rain—
the one who boasts of a gift not given.
15 By patience is a ruler persuaded,[g]
and a soft tongue can break a bone.
16 * If you find honey, eat only what you need,
lest you have your fill and vomit it up.
17 Let your foot be seldom in your neighbors' house,
lest they have their fill of you—and hate you.
18 A club, sword, or sharp arrow—
the one who bears false witness against a neighbor.[h]
19 A bad tooth or an unsteady foot—
a trust betrayed in time of trouble.*
20 Like the removal of clothes on a cold day, or vinegar on soda,
is the one who sings to a troubled heart.

**25:1–29:27** Chaps. 25–29 make up the fifth collection in the book, and the third longest. King Hezekiah reigned in Judah in 715–687 B.C. According to 2 Kgs 18–20 and 2 Chr 29–32, he initiated political and religious reforms after the destruction of the Northern Kingdom in 722 B.C. Such reforms probably included copying and editing sacred literature such as Proverbs. Prv 25:1 is an important piece of evidence about the composition of the book, suggesting this collection was added to an already-existing collection also attributed to Solomon. The older collection is probably 10:1–22:16 (or part of it). By the end of the eighth century B.C., therefore, there existed in Israel two large collections of aphorisms.

Chap. 25 has two general themes: (1) social hierarchy, rank, or position; (2) social conflict and its resolution.

**25:1 The servants of Hezekiah**: presumably scribes at the court of Hezekiah. **Transmitted**: lit., "to move, transfer from," hence "to collect," and perhaps also to arrange and compose.

**25:2–7** The topic is the king—who he is (vv. 2–3) and how one is to behave in his presence (vv. 4–7).

**25:2** God and king were closely related in the ancient world and in the Bible. The king had a special responsibility for divine justice. Hence, God would give him special wisdom to search it out.

**25:4–5** Wisdom involves virtue as well as knowledge. As in Ps 101 the king cannot tolerate any wickedness in the royal service.

**25:6–7** An admonition with a practical motive for putting the teaching into practice. Pragmatic shrewdness suggests that we not promote ourselves but let others do it for us. See Lk 14:7–11.

**25:9–10** Another admonition on the use of law courts to settle personal disputes. Speak privately with your opponent lest others' personal business become public and they resent you.

**25:16–17** The two admonitions are complementary, expressing nicely the need to restrain the inclination for delightful things, whether for honey or friendship.

**25:19** "A time of trouble" defeats all plans (cf. 10:2; 11:4). At such times human resources alone are like a tooth that falls out as one bites or a foot that goes suddenly lame.

*e:* Prv 1:1. *f:* Lk 14:8–10. *g:* Prv 15:1, 4. *h:* Ex 20:16.

21 * If your enemies are hungry, give them
food to eat,
if thirsty, give something to drink;[i]
22 For live coals you will heap on their heads,
and the LORD will vindicate you.
23 The north wind brings rain,
and a backbiting tongue, angry looks.
24 It is better to dwell in a corner of the
housetop
than in a mansion with a quarrelsome
wife.* [j]
25 Cool water to one faint from thirst
is good news from a far country.
26 A trampled fountain or a polluted
spring—*
a just person fallen before the wicked.
27 To eat too much honey is not good;
nor to seek honor after honor.*
28 A city breached and left defenseless
are those who do not control their
temper.

## CHAPTER 26*

See RG 180–82

1 Like snow in summer, like rain in
harvest,
honor for a fool is out of place.*
2 Like the sparrow in its flitting, like the
swallow in its flight,
a curse uncalled-for never lands.*
3 The whip for the horse, the bridle for the
ass,
and the rod for the back of fools.[k]
4 * Do not answer fools according to their
folly,
lest you too become like them.
5 Answer fools according to their folly,
lest they become wise in their own
eyes.
6 Those who send messages by a fool
cut off their feet; they drink down
violence.
7 * A proverb in the mouth of a fool
hangs limp, like crippled legs.
8 Giving honor to a fool
is like entangling a stone in the sling.
9 A thorn stuck in the hand of a drunkard
is a proverb in the mouth of fools.
10 An archer wounding all who pass by
is anyone who hires a drunken fool.
11 As dogs return to their vomit,
so fools repeat their folly.[l]
12 You see those who are wise in their own
eyes?
There is more hope for fools than for
them.
13 * The sluggard says, "There is a lion in
the street,
a lion in the middle of the square!"[m]

**25:21–22** A memorable statement of humanity and moderation; such sentiments could be occasionally found even outside the Bible, e.g., "It is better to bless someone than to do harm to one who has insulted you" (Egyptian *Papyrus Insinger*). Cf. Ex 23:4 and Lv 19:17–18. Human beings should not take it upon themselves to exact vengeance, leaving it rather in God's hands. This saying has in view an enemy's vulnerability in time of need, in this case extreme hunger and thirst; such a need should not be an occasion for revenge. The motive for restraining oneself is to allow God's justice to take its own course, as in 20:22 and 24:17–19. **Live coals**: either remorse and embarrassment for the harm done, or increased punishment for refusing reconciliation. Cf. Mt 5:44. Rom 12:20 cites the Greek version and interprets it, "Do not be overcome by evil but overcome evil with good."

**25:24** A humorous saying about domestic unhappiness: better to live alone outdoors than indoors with an angry spouse. Prv 21:9 is identical and 21:19 is similar in thought.

**25:26** "Spring" is a common metaphor for source. The righteous should be a source of life for others. When they fail, it is as if a spring became foul and its water undrinkable. It is not clear whether the righteous person yielded to a scoundrel out of cowardice or was simply defeated by evil. The latter seems more likely, for other proverbs say the just person will never "fall" (lit., "be moved," 10:30; 12:3). The fall, even temporary, of a righteous person is a loss of life for others.

**25:27 Nor . . . honor**: the text is uncertain.

**26:1–28** Concrete images describe the vices of fools (vv. 1–12), of sluggards (vv. 13–16), of meddlers (vv. 17–19), of talebearers (vv. 20–22), and of flatterers (vv. 23–28).

**26:1** There is no fit ("out of place") between weather and agricultural season.

**26:2** The point is the similarity of actions: a hovering bird that never lands, a groundless curse that never "lands." It hangs in the air posing no threat to anyone.

**26:4–5** There is no contradiction between these two proverbs. In their answers, the wise must protect their own interests against fools. Or perhaps the juxtaposition of the two proverbs suggests that no single proverb can resolve every problem in life.

**26:7–9** Fools either abuse or are unable to use whatever knowledge they have. **A thorn**: a proverb is "words spoken at the proper time" (25:11). Fools have no sense of the right time; their statements are like thorns that fasten on clothing randomly.

**26:13–16** Each verse mentions the sluggard, whom Proverbs regards with derision. The criticism is not against low energy but failure to act and take responsibility. Proverbs' ideal is the active person who uses heart, lips, hands, feet to keep to the good path. The verses are examples of the sardonic humor of the book.

---

*i:* Rom 12:20. *j:* Prv 21:9. *k:* Prv 19:29; Sir 33:25. *l:* 2 Pt 2:22. *m:* Prv 22:13.

14 The door turns on its hinges
and sluggards, on their beds.
15 The sluggard buries a hand in the dish,
too weary to lift it to the mouth.[n]
16 In their own eyes sluggards are wiser
than seven who answer with good judgment.
17 Whoever meddles in the quarrel of another
is one who grabs a passing dog by the ears.
18 Like a crazed archer
scattering firebrands and deadly arrows,
19 Such are those who deceive their neighbor,
and then say, "I was only joking."
20 * Without wood the fire dies out;
without a talebearer strife subsides.
21 Charcoal for coals, wood for fire—
such are the quarrelsome, enkindling strife.[o]
22 The words of a talebearer are like dainty morsels:
they sink into one's inmost being.* [p]
23 Like a glazed finish on earthenware
are smooth lips and a wicked heart.*
24 With their lips enemies pretend,
but inwardly they maintain deceit;
25 When they speak graciously, do not trust them,[q]
for seven abominations* are in their hearts.
26 Hatred can be concealed by pretense,
but malice will be revealed in the assembly.*
27 Whoever digs a pit falls into it;
and a stone comes back upon the one who rolls it.[r]
28 The lying tongue is its owner's enemy,
and the flattering mouth works ruin.

## CHAPTER 27

See RG 180–82

1 Do not boast about tomorrow,
for you do not know what any day may bring forth.
2 Let another praise you, not your own mouth;
a stranger, not your own lips.
3 Stone is heavy, and sand a burden,
but a fool's provocation is heavier than both.[s]
4 Anger is cruel, and wrath overwhelming,
but before jealousy who can stand?*
5 * Better is an open rebuke
than a love that remains hidden.
6 Trustworthy are the blows of a friend,
dangerous, the kisses of an enemy.*
7 One who is full spurns honey;
but to the hungry, any bitter thing is sweet.
8 Like a bird far from the nest
so is anyone far from home.*
9 Perfume and incense bring joy to the heart,
but by grief the soul is torn asunder.
10 Do not give up your own friend and your father's friend;
do not resort to the house of your kindred when trouble strikes.
Better a neighbor near than kin far away.*

**26:20–22** The three proverbs have a common theme—the destructive power of slanderous words. Certain words are repeated: wood and fire, talebearer.

**26:22** Malicious gossip is compared to delicious food that is swallowed and lodges in the deepest recesses of one's body. Negative comments are seldom forgotten. Prv 18:8 is a duplicate.

**26:23** Heart = what is within, and lips (words) = what is expressed, are compared to an earthenware jar covered with glaze.

**26:25 Seven abominations**: many evil intentions.

**26:26** Hate may be concealed for a time, but it will eventually issue in a deed and become known in the public assembly. There is a play on words: the consonants of the word "hatred" (*śʾn*) are literally concealed in the word "pretense" (*mśʾn*).

**27:4** Anger generally subsides with time but jealousy coolly calculates and plots revenge.

**27:5–6** Verses 5 and 6 are concerned with true friendship. "Better than" sayings often declare one thing superior to another in view of some value, e.g., 15:17, vegetables are better than meat in view of a milieu of love. In v. 5, a rebuke is better than an act of affection in view of discipline that imparts wisdom.

**27:6** The present translation is conjectural. The meaning seems to be that a friend's rebuke can be life-giving and an enemy's kiss can be deadly (like the kiss of Judas in Mt 26:48).

**27:8** The bird symbolizes vulnerability as it flees before danger as in Is 10:14; 16:2; and Ps 11:1. For the importance of place in human life, see Jb 20:8–9. People are defined by their place, but, tragically, war, poverty, or illness can force them from it.

**27:10** The adage is about the difference between friends and kin in a crisis. Two admonitions are grounded in one maxim

*n:* Prv 19:24. *o:* Prv 15:18; 29:22. *p:* Prv 18:8. *q:* Sir 12:10; 27:33. *r:* Eccl 10:8; Sir 27:25–26. *s:* Sir 22:14–15.

11 Be wise, my son, and bring joy to my heart,
so that I can answer whoever taunts me.*
12 The astute see an evil and hide;
the naive continue on and pay the penalty.[t]
13 Take the garment of the one who became surety for a stranger;[u]
if for a foreign woman, exact the pledge!*
14 Those who greet their neighbor with a loud voice* in the early morning,
a curse can be laid to their charge.
15 For a persistent leak on a rainy day
the match is a quarrelsome wife;[v]
16 Whoever would hide her hides a stormwind
and cannot tell north from south.
17 Iron is sharpened by iron;
one person sharpens another.*
18 Those who tend a fig tree eat its fruit;
so those attentive to their master will be honored.
19 As face mirrors face in water,
so the heart reflects the person.
20 Sheol and Abaddon can never be satisfied;[w]
so the eyes of mortals can never be satisfied.*
21 The crucible for silver, the furnace for gold,
so you must assay the praise you receive.
22 Though you pound fools with a pestle,
their folly never leaves them.
23 * Take good care of your flocks,
give careful attention to your herds;
24 For wealth does not last forever,
nor even a crown from age to age.
25 When the grass comes up and the new growth appears,
and the mountain greens are gathered in,
26 The lambs will provide you with clothing,
and the goats, the price of a field,
27 And there will be ample goat's milk for your food,
food for your house, sustenance for your maidens.

## CHAPTER 28

See RG 180–82

1 The wicked flee though none pursue;
but the just, like a lion, are confident.
2 If a land is rebellious, its princes will be many;
but with an intelligent and wise ruler there is stability.*
3 One who is poor and extorts from the lowly
is a devastating rain that leaves no food.*
4 Those who abandon instruction* praise the wicked,
but those who keep instruction oppose them.
5 The evil understand nothing of justice,*

(colon C). The same Hebrew word means both "one who is near" and "friend." The whole proverb urges the reader to cultivate old family friends and neighbors and not to rely exclusively on kin in times of trouble, for kin may not be there for us.

**27:11** A father's command to a son to be wise, another way of saying that sons or daughters bring joy or shame to their parents.

**27:13** See note on 20:16.

**27:14** One interpretation takes the proverb as humorous and the other takes it as serious: (1) an overly loud and ill-timed greeting (lit., "blessing") invites the response of a curse rather than a "blessing" (greeting); (2) the loud voice suggests hypocrisy in the greeting.

**27:17** Iron sharpens the "face" (*panim* = surface, edge) of iron, and a human being sharpens the "face" (*panim* = face, words) of another. Human beings learn from each other and grow in wisdom by conversing.

**27:20** Sheol, the underworld abode of the dead, is personified as a force that is never satisfied and always desires more. Cf. Is 5:14 and Hos 13:14. The saying is applicable to modern consumerism.

**27:23–27** A little treatise on farming in the form of admonitions. It proposes the advantages of field and flock over other forms of wealth. Herds are the most productive wealth, for their value does not diminish; they are a source of money, clothing, and food. The thought is conservative and traditional but the development is vivid and concrete.

**28:2** The first line expresses the paradox that rebellion, far from doing away with rulers, actually multiplies them. The second line is corrupt.

**28:3** The reference may be to tax farmers who collected taxes and took a commission. The collectors' lack of wealth was the cause of their oppression of poor farmers. They are like a rain too violent to allow crops to grow.

**28:4 Instruction**: *torah*; the word is used both for the teaching of the wise and the law of Moses.

**28:5 Understanding nothing of justice** plays on the two-

*t:* Prv 22:3. *u:* Prv 20:16. *v:* Prv 21:9; 25:24. *w:* Prv 30:16; Eccl 4:8.

but those who seek the LORD
understand everything.
6 Better to be poor and walk in integrity
than rich and crooked in one's ways.[x]
7 Whoever heeds instruction is a wise son,
but whoever joins with wastrels
disgraces his father.
8 Whoever amasses wealth by interest and
overcharge*
gathers it for the one who is kind to the
poor.
9 Those who turn their ears from hearing
instruction,[y]
even their prayer is an abomination.
10 Those who mislead the upright into an
evil way
will themselves fall into their own pit,
but the blameless will attain
prosperity.
11 The rich are wise in their own eyes,
but the poor who are intelligent see
through them.
12 When the just triumph, there is great
glory;
but when the wicked prevail, people
hide.*
13 Those who conceal their sins do not
prosper,
but those who confess and forsake
them obtain mercy.*
14 Happy those who always fear;*
but those who harden their hearts fall
into evil.
15 A roaring lion or a ravenous bear
is a wicked ruler over a poor people.
16 The less prudent the rulers, the more
oppressive their deeds.
Those who hate ill-gotten gain prolong
their days.
17 Though a person burdened with blood
guilt is in flight even to the grave,
let no one offer support.
18 Whoever walks blamelessly is safe,
but one whose ways are crooked falls
into a pit.
19 Those who cultivate their land will have
plenty of food,
but those who engage in idle pursuits
will have plenty of want.[z]
20 The trustworthy will be richly blessed;
but whoever hastens to be rich will not
go unpunished.[a]
21 To show partiality is never good:[b]
for even a morsel of bread one may do
wrong.*
22 Misers hurry toward wealth,
not knowing that want is coming
toward them.*
23 Whoever rebukes another wins more
favor
than one who flatters with the tongue.
24 Whoever defrauds father or mother and
says, "It is no sin,"[c]
is a partner to a brigand.
25 The greedy person stirs up strife,
but the one who trusts in the LORD will
prosper.
26 Those who trust in themselves are fools,
but those who walk in wisdom are
safe.
27 Those who give to the poor have no
lack,[d]
but those who avert their eyes, many
curses.

fold sense of justice as righteousness and as punishment that comes on the wicked. On the other hand, **those who seek the LORD understand everything**, i.e., that the Lord punishes the wicked and rewards the righteous (themselves).

**28:8** Interest and overcharge were strictly forbidden in the old law among Israelites because it was presumed that the borrower was in distress; cf. Ex 22:25; Lv 25:35–37; Dt 23:20; Ps 15:5; Ez 18:8. Divine providence will take the offender's wealth; cf. Eccl 2:26.

**28:12** People react in opposite ways to the triumph of good and evil. To the triumph of good, they react by public display, public celebration, and to the triumph of evil, by hiding.

**28:13** Concealing the faults of another is a good thing in Proverbs (17:9), but concealing one's own sins is not. Ps 32:1–5 expresses the anguish caused by concealing one's sins rather than bringing them to light so they can be healed by God.

**28:14 Fear** is a different verb than in the phrase "to fear (or revere) the Lord." In its only other biblical occurrence (Is 51:13), the verb means to dread an oppressor. The saying states a paradox: those who fear in the sense of being cautious are declared happy, whereas those who are fearless will fall into traps they did not "fear." In short, there is good fear and bad fear.

**28:21** Cf. 24:23. Verse 21b warns that even in a light matter one must remain impartial.

**28:22** "Bad of eye" is the Hebrew idiom for miserly. Misers fail to see that poverty is hurrying toward them because of their wrong attitude toward wealth. Because misers are "bad of eye," they do not see the danger.

*x:* Prv 19:1. *y:* Prv 15:8; 21:27. *z:* Prv 12:11. *a:* Prv 13:11. *b:* Prv 24:23. *c:* Mk 7:11–13. *d:* Prv 19:17; Sir 4:3–8.

28 When the wicked prevail, people hide;
but at their fall the just abound.[e]

## CHAPTER 29

See RG 180–82

1 Those stiff-necked in the face of reproof
in an instant will be shattered beyond cure.*
2 When the just flourish, the people rejoice;
but when the wicked rule, the people groan.*[f]
3 Whoever loves wisdom gives joy to his father,
but whoever consorts with harlots squanders his wealth.
4 By justice a king builds up the land;
but one who raises taxes tears it down.*
5 Those who speak flattery to their neighbor
cast a net at their feet.*
6 The sin of the wicked is a trap,
but the just run along joyfully.[g]
7 The just care for the cause of the poor;
the wicked do not understand such care.*
8 Scoffers enflame the city,
but the wise calm the fury.[h]
9 If a wise person disputes with a fool,
there is railing and ridicule but no resolution.
10 The bloodthirsty hate the blameless,
but the upright seek his life.*
11 Fools give vent to all their anger;
but the wise, biding their time, control it.[i]
12 If rulers listen to lying words,
their servants all become wicked.
13 The poor and the oppressor meet:[j]
the LORD gives light to the eyes of both.
14 If a king is honestly for the rights of the poor,
his throne stands firm forever.[k]
15 The rod of correction gives wisdom,
but uncontrolled youths disgrace their mothers.[l]
16 When the wicked increase, crime increases;
but the just will behold their downfall.*
17 Discipline your children, and they will bring you comfort,
and give delight to your soul.
18 Without a vision the people lose restraint;
but happy is the one who follows instruction.*
19 Not by words alone can servants be trained;[m]
for they understand but do not respond.*
20 Do you see someone hasty in speech?[n]
There is more hope for a fool!
21 If servants are pampered from childhood
they will turn out to be stubborn.
22 The ill-tempered stir up strife,
and the hotheaded cause many sins.[o]

**29:1** The idiom "to stiffen one's neck" occurs in a context of not heeding a message in Dt 10:16 and 2 Kgs 17:14. To stiffen one's neck in this sense risks having it broken, as in 1 Sm 4:18.

**29:2** Popular response to a just or unjust ruler is expressed in sound—shouts of joy or groans of anguish. "Rejoice" can mean to express one's joy, i.e., joyous shouts.

**29:4** In Hebrew as in English high and low are metaphors for prosperity and depression. A king who is just "causes the land to stand up," i.e., to be prosperous, and one who makes taxes high brings a country low.

**29:5** When one addresses deceptive words to someone's face, one equivalently throws a net at their feet to snare them.

**29:7** As in 12:10 (on care for animals), the righteous care for those who are without a voice and often treated like animals. Colon B has a double meaning: the wicked have no such knowledge (care for the poor) and they have no knowledge (wisdom), for they are fools.

**29:10** An enigmatic saying in that "seek one's life" is a common idiom for killing. The saying probably plays on the idiom, interpreting "to seek the life of another" not as killing but as caring for another (as in 11:30).

**29:16** When the wicked grow numerous they sow the seeds of their own destruction, for there is a corresponding increase in offenses calling down divine retribution.

**29:18** This much-cited proverb has been interpreted in several different ways. "Vision" and "instruction" mean authoritative guidance for the community. People are demoralized without credible leadership, but any individual heeding traditional instruction can still find happiness. As in 15:15 wisdom enables an individual to surmount days of trouble.

**29:19** The give and take of reproving is not possible for servants or slaves. Ancient custom dictated silent acquiescence for them. There is no open and free dialogue, which is part of ancient discipline.

*e:* Prv 28:12. *f:* Prv 11:10; 28:12, 28. *g:* Prv 12:13. *h:* Prv 11:11. *i:* Prv 12:16; 25:28; Sir 21:26. *j:* Prv 22:2. *k:* Prv 16:12; 20:28; 25:5. *l:* Prv 13:24; 22:15; 23:13–14; Sir 22:6; 30:1. *m:* Sir 33:25–30. *n:* Sir 9:18; Prv 26:12. *o:* Prv 15:18; 22:24.

23 Haughtiness brings humiliation,
but the humble of spirit acquire honor.* [p]
24 Partners of a thief hate themselves;*
they hear the imprecation but do not testify.
25 Fear of others becomes a snare,
but the one who trusts in the LORD is safe.
26 Many curry favor with a ruler,
but it is from the LORD that one receives justice.
27 An abomination to the just, the evildoer;
an abomination to the wicked, one whose way is straight.

## VII. Sayings of Agur and Others

### CHAPTER 30

See RG 180–82

1* The words of Agur, son of Jakeh the Massaite:

The pronouncement of mortal man: "I am weary, O God;
I am weary, O God, and I am exhausted.
2 I am more brute than human being,
without even human intelligence;
3 * Neither have I learned wisdom,
nor have I the knowledge of the Holy One.
4 Who has gone up to heaven and come down again—
who has cupped the wind in the hollow of the hand?
Who has bound up the waters in a cloak—
who has established all the ends of the earth?
What is that person's name, or the name of his son?"*
5 * Every word of God is tested;[q]
he is a shield to those who take refuge in him.
6 Add nothing to his words,[r]
lest he reprimand you, and you be proved a liar.
7 * Two things I ask of you,
do not deny them to me before I die:
8 Put falsehood and lying far from me,
give me neither poverty nor riches;
provide me only with the food I need;
9 Lest, being full, I deny you,
saying, "Who is the LORD?"
Or, being in want, I steal,
and profane the name of my God.
10 Do not criticize servants to their master,
lest they curse you, and you have to pay the penalty.
11 * There are some who curse their fathers,
and do not bless their mothers.[s]
12 There are some pure in their own eyes,
yet not cleansed of their filth.
13 There are some—how haughty their eyes!
how overbearing their glance!
14 There are some—their teeth are swords,
their teeth are knives,

**29:23** One's prideful height brings one down and one's lowly state brings glory.

**29:24 Hate themselves**: because they not only incur guilt as accomplices but, by their silence, bring down on themselves the curse invoked on the unknown guilty partner. Such a case is envisioned in Lv 5:1. After a theft, a public proclamation was made, enforced by a curse. No one in a town or city could avoid hearing it. The curse hung over the accomplice. By doing nothing, neither directly stealing nor confessing, accomplices put themselves in serious danger.

**30:1–6** Scholars are divided on the original literary unit. Is it vv. 1–3, 1–4, 1–5, or 1–6? The unit is probably vv. 1–6, for a single contrast dominates: human fragility (and ignorance) and divine power (and knowledge). A similar contrast is found in Jb 28; Ps 73; Is 49:1–4. The language of self-abasement is hyperbolic; cf. 2 Sm 9:8; Ps 73:21–22; Jb 25:4–6. **Agur**: an unknown person. **Massaite**: from Massa in northern Arabia, elsewhere referred to as an encampment of the Ishmaelites (Gn 25:14). But Heb. *massa* may not be intended as a place name; it might signify "an oracle," "a prophecy," as in Is 15:1; 17:1; etc.

**30:3–4** Agur denies he has secret heavenly knowledge. The purpose of the denial is to underline that God directly gives wisdom to those whose conduct pleases him.

**30:4** The Hebrew text has the phrase "do you know?" at the end of v. 4, which is supported by the versions. The phrase, however, does not appear in the important Greek manuscripts Vaticanus and Sinaiticus and spoils the sense, for Agur, not God, is the questioner. The phrase seems to be an addition to the Hebrew text, borrowed from Job 38:5, where it also follows a cosmic question.

**30:5–6** Verse 5, like the confession of the king in Ps 18:31 (and its parallel, 2 Sm 22:31), expresses total confidence in the one who rescues from death. Agur has refused a word from any other except God and makes an act of trust in God.

**30:7–9** A prayer against lying words and for sufficiency of goods, lest reaction to riches or destitution lead to offenses against God.

**30:11–14** Perverted people are here classified as unfilial (v. 11), self-righteous (v. 12), proud (v. 13) and rapacious (v. 14).

---

*p:* Prv 11:2; 16:18; 18:12. *q:* Ps 12:7; 18:31. *r:* Dt 4:2; 13:1. *s:* Prv 20:20.

Devouring the needy from the earth,
and the poor from the human race.
15 * The leech has two daughters:
"Give," and "Give."
Three things never get their fill,
four never say, "Enough!"
16 Sheol, a barren womb,[t]
land that never gets its fill of water,
and fire, which never says, "Enough!"
17 The eye that mocks a father,
or scorns the homage due a mother,
Will be plucked out by brook ravens;
devoured by a brood of vultures.
18 * Three things are too wonderful for me,
yes, four I cannot understand:
19 The way of an eagle in the sky,
the way of a serpent upon a rock,
The way of a ship on the high seas,
and the way of a man with a woman.
20 This is the way of an adulterous woman:
she eats, wipes her mouth,
and says, "I have done no wrong."*
21 * Under three things the earth trembles,
yes, under four it cannot bear up:
22 Under a slave who becomes king,
and a fool who is glutted with food;[u]
23 Under an unloved woman who is wed,
and a maidservant who displaces her mistress.
24 * Four things are among the smallest on the earth,
and yet are exceedingly wise:
25 Ants—a species not strong,
yet they store up their food in the summer;
26 Badgers—a species not mighty,
yet they make their home in the crags;
27 Locusts—they have no king,
yet they march forth in formation;
28 Lizards—you can catch them with your hands,
yet they find their way into kings' palaces.
29 * Three things are stately in their stride,
yes, four are stately in their carriage:
30 The lion, mightiest of beasts,
retreats before nothing;
31 The strutting cock, and the he-goat,
and the king at the head of his people.
32 * If you have foolishly been proud
or presumptuous—put your hand on your mouth;
33 For as the churning of milk produces curds,
and the pressing of the nose produces blood,
the churning of anger produces strife.

## VIII. Sayings of King Lemuel*

### CHAPTER 31

See RG 180–82

1 The words of Lemuel, king of Massa,* the instruction his mother taught him:

**30:15–16** Here begins a series of numerical sayings; the pattern is n, n + 1. The slight variation in number (two and three, three and four) is an example of parallelism applied to numbers. The poetic technique is attested even outside the Bible. **Two daughters: "Give," and "Give"**: the text is obscure; as the leech (a bloodsucking worm) is insatiable in its desire for blood (v. 15), so are the nether world for victims, the barren womb for offspring, the earth for water, and fire for fuel (v. 16). **Sheol**: here not so much the place of the dead as a force (death) that eventually draws all the living into it; cf. 27:20; Is 5:14; Hb 2:5. **Land . . . fire**: land (especially the dry land of Palestine) always absorbs more water; fire always requires more fuel.

**30:18–19** The soaring flight of the eagle, the mysterious movement upon a rock of the serpent which has no feet, the path of the ship through the trackless deep, and the marvelous attraction between the sexes; there is a mysterious way common to them all.

**30:20** This verse portrays the indifference of an adulterous woman who casually dismisses her guilt because it cannot be traced.

**30:21–23** Shaking heavens are part of general cosmic upheaval in Is 14:16; Jl 2:10; Am 8:8; Jb 9:6. Disturbances in nature mirror the disturbance of unworthy people attaining what they do not deserve. **Glutted with food**: someone unworthy ends up with the fulfillment that befits a wise person. **Unloved woman**: an older woman who, contrary to expectation, finds a husband.

**30:24–28** The creatures may be small, but they are wise in knowing how to govern themselves—the definition of wisdom. **Badgers**: the rock badger is able to live on rocky heights that provide security from its enemies. **Locusts**: though vulnerable individually their huge swarms are impossible to deflect.

**30:29–31** Four beings with an imperiousness visible in their walk. Only the lion is described in detail; the reader is expected to transpose its qualities to the others.

**30:32–33** The same Hebrew verb, "to churn, shake," is applied to milk, the nose (sometimes a symbol of anger), and wrath. In each case something is eventually produced by the constant agitation. The wise make peace and avoid strife, for strife eventually harms those who provoke it.

**31:1–9** Though mothers are sources of wisdom in Proverbs

---

*t*: Prv 27:20. *u*: Prv 19:10; Eccl 10:6–7.

**Praise of the Capable Wife**

CHAPTER 31 (VV. 10–31) IS an acrostic poem of twenty-two lines, each line beginning with a successive letter of the alphabet. It is an encomium or hymn praising the capable wife. A hymn does not dwell on the inner feelings or the physical appearance of its hero but describes the hero's mighty feats of valor, in this case the wife's extraordinarily wise management of her great household.

2 What are you doing, my son!*
what are you doing, son of my womb;
what are you doing, son of my vows!
3 Do not give your vigor to women,
or your strength* to those who ruin kings.
4 It is not for kings, Lemuel,
not for kings to drink wine;
strong drink is not for princes,
5 Lest in drinking they forget what has been decreed,
and violate the rights of any who are in need.
6 Give strong drink to anyone who is perishing,
and wine to the embittered;
7 When they drink, they will forget their misery,
and think no more of their troubles.
8 Open your mouth in behalf of the mute,
and for the rights of the destitute;
9 Open your mouth, judge justly,
defend the needy and the poor!

## IX. Poem on the Woman of Worth*

10 Who can find* a woman of worth?[v]
Far beyond jewels is her value.
11 Her husband trusts her judgment;
he does not lack income.
12 She brings him profit, not loss,*
all the days of her life.
13 She seeks out wool and flax
and weaves with skillful hands.
14 Like a merchant fleet,*
she secures her provisions from afar.
15 She rises while it is still night,
and distributes food to her household,
a portion to her maidservants.
16 She picks out a field and acquires it;
from her earnings she plants a vineyard.
17 She girds herself with strength;
she exerts her arms with vigor.*
18 She enjoys the profit from her dealings;

(1:8; 6:20), the mother of Lemuel is special in being queen mother, which was an important position in the palace. Queen mothers played an important role in ancient palace life because of their longevity, knowledge of palace politics, and loyalty to their sons; they were in a good position to offer him sound counsel. The language of the poem contains Aramaisms, a sign of its non-Israelite origin.

The first section, vv. 3–5, warns against abuse of sex and alcohol (wine, strong drink) lest the king *forget* the *poor*. The second section, vv. 6–9, urges the use of alcohol (strong drink, wine) so that the downtrodden *poor* can *forget* their poverty. The real subject of the poem is justice for the poor.

**31:1 Massa**: see note on 30:1–6.

**31:2 My son**: in the Septuagint, "my son, my firstborn."

**31:3** The Hebrew word here translated "strength" normally means "ways," but the context and a cognate language support "authority" or "strength" here.

**31:10–31** An acrostic poem of twenty-two lines; each line begins with a successive letter of the Hebrew alphabet. As with many other acrostic poems in the Bible, the unity of the poem is largely extrinsic, coming not from the narrative logic but from the familiar sequence of letters. The topic is the ideal woman described through her activity as a wife. Some have suggested that the traditional hymn extolling the great deeds of a warrior has been transposed to extol a heroic wife; the focus is on her exploits. She runs a household distinguished by abundant food and clothing for all within, by its trade (import of raw materials and export of finished products), and by the renown of its head, her husband, in the community. At v. 28, the voice is no longer that of the narrator but of her children and husband as they praise her. The purpose of the poem has been interpreted variously: an encomium to offset the sometimes negative portrayal of women in the book, or, more symbolically (and more likely), a portrait of a household ruled by Woman Wisdom and a disciple of Woman Wisdom, i.e., he now has a worthy wife and children, a great household, renown in the community.

**31:10 Who can find . . . ?**: in 20:6 and Eccl 8:1 the question implies that finding such a person is well-nigh impossible.

**31:12 Profit, not loss**: a commercial metaphor.

**31:14 Like a merchant fleet**: she has her eye on the far horizon, like the ship of a merchant ready to bring supplies into her larder. It is the only simile ("like") in the poem.

**31:17** The metaphor of clothing oneself is used to show the

*v*: Prv 12:4; Sir 26:1–4, 13–18.

her lamp is never extinguished at night.*
19 She puts her hands to the distaff,
and her fingers ply the spindle.*
20 She reaches out her hands to the poor,
and extends her arms to the needy.
21 She is not concerned for her household
when it snows—
all her charges are doubly clothed.
22 She makes her own coverlets;
fine linen and purple are her clothing.
23 Her husband is prominent at the city
gates
as he sits with the elders of the land.*
24 She makes garments and sells them,
and stocks the merchants with belts.
25 She is clothed with strength and dignity,
and laughs at the days to come.*
26 She opens her mouth in wisdom;
kindly instruction is on her tongue.
27 She watches over* the affairs of her
household,
and does not eat the bread of idleness.
28 Her children rise up and call her blessed;
her husband, too, praises her:
29 "Many are the women of proven worth,
but you have excelled them all."
30 Charm is deceptive and beauty fleeting;
the woman who fears the LORD is to be
praised.*
31 Acclaim her for the work of her hands,
and let her deeds praise her at the city
gates.

woman's readiness. One can gird on weapons of war and might and splendor (Ps 69:7; Is 52:9).

**31:18 Her lamp is never extinguished at night**: indicates abundance of productive work and its accompanying prosperity; cf. 20:20; Jb 18:6.

**31:19** The wife weaves linen cloth from flax and wool from fleece, which she cultivated according to v. 13. **Distaff**: staff for holding the flax, tow, or wool, which in spinning was drawn out and twisted into yarn or thread by the spindle or round stick.

**31:23** The husband is mentioned for the first time since vv. 10–12 but as "her husband." He will not be mentioned again until v. 28, where he praises her.

**31:25 Laughs at the days to come**: anticipates the future with joy, free of anxiety.

**31:27 Watches over**: Hebrew *sopiyyâ*, perhaps a pun on the Greek *sophia* (= wisdom). **Bread of idleness**: she does not eat from the table of others but from her own labors.

**31:30** The true charm of this woman is her religious spirit, for she fears the Lord; cf. note on 1:7.

See RG 183–87

# The Book of Ecclesiastes

The Hebrew name of this book and of its author, Qoheleth, is actually a title, and it perhaps means "assembler" (of students, listeners) or "collector" (of wisdom sayings). The book's more common name, Ecclesiastes, is an approximate translation into Greek of this Hebrew word. The book comprises an extended reflective essay employing autobiographical narrative, proverbs, parables, and allegories. An almost unrelenting skepticism characterizes the tone or outlook. The issues with which the author deals and the questions he raises are aimed at those who would claim any absolute values in this life, including possessions, fame, success, or pleasure. Wisdom itself is challenged, but folly is condemned.

The refrain which begins and ends the book, "Vanity of vanities" (1:1; 12:8), recurs at key points throughout. The Hebrew word, *hebel* ("vanity"), has the sense of "emptiness, futility, absurdity": "I have seen all things that are done under the sun, and behold, all is vanity and a chase after wind" (1:14; 2:11, 17, 26; etc.). Everything in human life is subject to change, to qualification, to loss: "What profit have we from all the toil which we toil at under the sun?" (1:3). The answer is in the negative: No absolute profit or gain is possible. Even if some temporary profit or gain is achieved, it will ultimately be cancelled out by death, the great leveller (2:14–15; 3:19–20). Wisdom has some advantage over foolishness, but even wisdom's advantage is only a temporary and qualified one.

Many would locate Ecclesiastes in the third century B.C., when Judea was under the oppressive domination of Hellenistic kings from Egypt. These kings were highly efficient in their ruthless exploitation of the land and people (4:1; 5:7). The average Jew would have felt a sense of powerlessness and inability to change things for the better. For Qoheleth, God seems remote and uncommunicative, and we cannot hope to understand, much less influence, God's activity in the world (3:11; 8:16–17).

The book's honest and blunt appraisal of the

human condition provides a healthy corrective to the occasionally excessive self-assurance of other wisdom writers. Its radical skepticism is somewhat tempered by the resigned conclusions to rejoice in whatever gifts God may give (2:24; 3:12–13, 22; 5:17–18; 8:15; 9:7–9; 11:9).

The Book of Ecclesiastes is divided as follows:

I. Qoheleth's Investigation of Life (1:12–6:9)
II. Qoheleth's Conclusions (6:10–12:14)
  A. No One Can Find Out the Best Way of Acting (7:1–8:17)
  B. No One Knows the Future (9:1–12:14)

---

See RG 183–87

## CHAPTER 1

1 The words of David's son, Qoheleth,
king in Jerusalem:* [a]

2 Vanity of vanities,* says Qoheleth,
vanity of vanities! All things are
vanity![b]

### *Vanity of Human Toil*

3 What profit have we from all the toil
which we toil at under the sun?* [c]
4 One generation departs and another
generation comes,
but the world forever stays.
5 The sun rises and the sun sets;
then it presses on to the place where it
rises.
6 Shifting south, then north,
back and forth shifts the wind,
constantly shifting its course.
7 All rivers flow to the sea,
yet never does the sea become full.
To the place where they flow,
the rivers continue to flow.
8 All things are wearisome,*
too wearisome for words.
The eye is not satisfied by seeing
nor has the ear enough of hearing.[d]

9 What has been, that will be; what has
been done, that will be done. Nothing is new
under the sun![e] 10 Even the thing of which we
say, "See, this is new!" has already existed in
the ages that preceded us.[f] 11 There is no remembrance of past generations;[g] nor will future generations be remembered by those
who come after them.*

## I. Qoheleth's Investigation of Life

***Twofold Introduction.*** 12 I, Qoheleth, was
king over Israel in Jerusalem, 13 and I applied
my mind to search and investigate in wisdom all things that are done under the sun.[h]

A bad business God has given
to human beings to be busied with.

14 I have seen all things that are done under the sun, and behold, all is vanity and a
chase after wind.* [i]

15 What is crooked cannot be made straight,
and you cannot count what is not
there.*

16[j] Though I said to myself, "See, I have
greatly increased my wisdom beyond all
who were before me in Jerusalem, and my
mind has broad experience of wisdom and
knowledge," 17 yet when I applied my mind
to know wisdom and knowledge, madness
and folly, I learned that this also is a chase
after wind.[k]

**1:1 David's son . . . king in Jerusalem**: the intent of the author is to identify himself with Solomon. This is a literary device, by which the author hopes to commend his work to the public under the name of Israel's most famous sage (see 1 Kgs 5:9–14).

**1:2 Vanity of vanities**: a Hebrew superlative expressing the supreme degree of futility and emptiness.

**1:3 Under the sun**: used throughout this book to signify "on the earth."

**1:8 All things are wearisome**: or, "All speech is wearisome."

**1:11** Movement in nature and human activity appears to result in change and progress. The author argues that this change and progress are an illusion: "Nothing is new under the sun."

**1:14 A chase after wind**: an image of futile activity, like an attempt to corral the winds; cf. Hos 12:2. The ancient versions understood "affliction, dissipation of the spirit." This phrase concludes sections of the text as far as 6:9.

**1:15 You cannot count what is not there**: perhaps originally a commercial metaphor alluding to loss or deficit in the accounts ledger.

**1:18 Sorrow . . . grief**: these terms refer not just to a store of knowledge or to psychological or emotional pain. Corporal punishment, sometimes quite harsh, was also employed frequently by parents and teachers.

*a:* Eccl 1:12; 12:9–10. *b:* Eccl 12:8. *c:* Eccl 2:11, 22; 3:9; 5:15. *d:* Eccl 4:8; 5:9–11. *e:* Eccl 3:15; 6:10. *f:* Eccl 3:15. *g:* Eccl 2:16. *h:* Eccl 8:9. *i:* Eccl 2:11, 17. *j:* Eccl 2:9. *k:* Eccl 1:3; 8:16.

**Ecclesiastes and Wisdom Literature**

LIKE JOB, THE book of Ecclesiastes relates to the wisdom tradition in its own way. According to the tradition, as given for instance in the book of Proverbs, in the Wisdom of Solomon, and in Sirach (Ecclesiasticus), the regularity of life was what people relied on for guidance: "Charcoal for coals, wood for fire—such are the quarelsome, enkindling strife" (Prv 26:21). And just as human behavior follows in its regular course, good behavior regularly brings its reward: "Those who tend a fig tree eat its fruit, so those attentive to their master will be honored" (Prv 27:18). The book of Job denies that reward inevitably follows goodness. Ecclesiastes takes the idea of inevitability and repetition in life and turns it around: Instead of being an image of reliability, such regular recurrences as the returning seasons are the image of futility, "vanity." We may attempt to escape such futility by the pursuit of pleasure (Eccl 2:1–11); by attaining wisdom (vv. 12–17); or by working (vv. 18–26). But the realities of life will eventually bring us to recognize that all of these escapes are themselves futile. Implicitly, the argument of Ecclesiastes is that nothing in the natural life can be our ultimate goal: if we try to make it so, we will only learn that it is empty. Thus, without saying so, the book makes the point: Only God can truly satisfy every longing.

The issue of greed echoes through the centuries. One who seeks wealth for its own sake rather than for what it can provide when shared cannot be satisfied. Today we are still counseled to examine how we can share our time and our talent as well as our treasure. This can bring us closer to the wisdom taught here.

[18] For in much wisdom there is much sorrow;
whoever increases knowledge
increases grief.*

See RG 183–87

## CHAPTER 2

*Study of Pleasure-seeking.* [1]I said in
my heart,* "Come, now, let me try you with
pleasure and the enjoyment of good things."
See, this too was vanity. [2]Of laughter I said:
"Mad!" and of mirth: "What good does this
do?" [3]Guided by wisdom,* I probed with my
mind how to beguile my senses with wine
and take up folly, until I should understand
what is good for human beings to do under
the heavens during the limited days of their
lives.
[4]I undertook great works; I built myself
houses and planted vineyards; [5]I made gardens and parks, and in them set out fruit trees
of all sorts. [6]And I constructed for myself
reservoirs to water a flourishing woodland.
[7]I acquired male and female slaves, and had
slaves who were born in my house. I also
owned vast herds of cattle and flocks of
sheep, more than all who had been before
me in Jerusalem. [8]I amassed for myself silver and gold, and the treasures of kings and
provinces. I provided for myself male and
female singers and delights of men, many
women.* [9]I accumulated much more than all
others before me in Jerusalem; my wisdom,
too, stayed with me. [10]Nothing that my eyes
desired did I deny them, nor did I deprive
myself of any joy; rather, my heart rejoiced
in the fruit of all my toil. This was my share
for all my toil. [11]But when I turned to all the

**2:1–11** The author here assumes the role of Solomon who, as king, would have had the wealth and resources at his disposal to acquire wisdom and engage in pleasurable pursuits. Verses 4–8 in particular, with their description of abundant wealth and physical gratifications, parallel the descriptions in 1 Kgs 4–11 of the extravagances of Solomon's reign.

**2:3 Guided by wisdom**: using all the means money can buy, the author sets out on a deliberate search to discover if pleasure constitutes true happiness.

**2:8 Many women**: the final phrase of this verse is difficult to translate. One word, *shiddah*, which appears here in both singular and plural, is found nowhere else in the Hebrew Bible. A suggested meaning is "woman" or "concubine," as it is interpreted here: "many women." The rest of the section (2:1–12) seems to be a description of Solomon's kingdom, and the "many women" would represent his huge harem (1 Kgs 11:1–3). In rabbinic Hebrew the word comes to mean "chest" or "coffer."

*1:* Eccl 1:3, 17; Sir 44:9.

works that my hands had wrought, and to the
fruit of the toil for which I had toiled so
much, see! all was vanity and a chase after
wind. There is no profit under the sun.
12 What about one who succeeds a king? He
can do only what has already been done.*

***Study of Wisdom and Folly.*** I went on to
the consideration of wisdom, madness and
folly. 13 And I saw that wisdom has as much
profit over folly as light has over darkness.

14 Wise people have eyes in their heads,
 but fools walk in darkness.

Yet I knew that the same lot befalls
both.* [m] 15 So I said in my heart, if the fool's
lot is to befall me also, why should I be
wise? Where is the profit? And in my heart I
decided that this too is vanity. 16 [n] The wise
person will have no more abiding remembrance than the fool; for in days to come
both will have been forgotten. How is it that
the wise person dies* like the fool! 17 Therefore I detested life, since for me the work
that is done under the sun is bad; for all is
vanity and a chase after wind.

### *Study of the Fruits of Toil*

***To Others the Profits.*** 18 And I detested all the
fruits of my toil under the sun, because I
must leave them to the one who is to come
after me. 19 And who knows whether that one
will be wise or a fool? Yet that one will take
control of all the fruits of my toil and wisdom under the sun. This also is vanity. 20 So
my heart turned to despair over all the fruits
of my toil under the sun. 21 For here is one
who has toiled with wisdom and knowledge
and skill, and that one's legacy must be left
to another who has not toiled for it. This also
is vanity and a great evil. 22 [o] For what profit
comes to mortals from all the toil and anxiety of heart with which they toil under the
sun? 23 Every day sorrow and grief are their
occupation; even at night their hearts are not
at rest. This also is vanity.

24* [p] There is nothing better for mortals
than to eat and drink and provide themselves
with good things from their toil. Even this, I
saw, is from the hand of God. 25 For who can
eat or drink apart from God? 26* [q] For to the
one who pleases God, he gives wisdom and
knowledge and joy; but to the one who displeases, God gives the task of gathering possessions for the one who pleases God. This
also is vanity and a chase after wind.

## CHAPTER 3

See RG 183–87

### *No One Can Determine the Right Time To Act*

1 * There is an appointed time for
 everything,
 and a time for every affair under the
 heavens.
2 A time to give birth, and a time to die;
 a time to plant, and a time to uproot
 the plant.
3 A time to kill, and a time to heal;
 a time to tear down, and a time to build.
4 A time to weep, and a time to laugh;
 a time to mourn, and a time to dance.
5 A time to scatter stones, and a time to
 gather them;
 a time to embrace, and a time to be far
 from embraces.
6 A time to seek, and a time to lose;
 a time to keep, and a time to cast away.
7 A time to rend, and a time to sew;
 a time to be silent, and a time to speak.

**2:12 What . . . been done**: the verse is difficult and elliptical. The words "He can do only" have been added for clarity. The two halves of the verse have been reversed. The author argues that it is useless to repeat the royal experiment described in vv. 1–11. The results would only be the same.

**2:14 Yet I knew . . . befalls both**: the author quotes a traditional saying upholding the advantages of wisdom, but then qualifies it. Nothing, not even wisdom itself, can give someone absolute control over their destiny and therefore guarantee any advantage.

**2:16 The wise person dies**: death, until now only alluded to (vv. 14–15), takes center stage and will constantly appear in the author's reflections through the remainder of the book.

**2:24–26** The author is not advocating unrestrained indulgence. Rather he counsels acceptance of the good things God chooses to give. This is the first of seven similar conclusions that Qoheleth provides; see 3:12–13, 22; 5:17–18; 8:15; 9:7–9; 11:9.

**2:26** According to 7:15 and 9:1–3, God does not make an objective, evidential, moral distinction between saint and sinner. God "gives" as God pleases.

**3:1–8** The fourteen pairs of opposites describe various human activities. The poem affirms that God has determined the appropriate moment or "time" for each. Human beings cannot know that moment; further, the wider course of events and purposes fixed by God are beyond them as well.

*m:* Eccl 9:2–3. *n:* Eccl 1:11; Wis 2:4. *o:* Eccl 1:3. *p:* Eccl 3:12–13, 22; 5:17–19; 8:15. *q:* Eccl 7:26; Prv 13:22.

8 A time to love, and a time to hate;
a time of war, and a time of peace.

9[r] What profit have workers from their
toil? 10 I have seen the business that God has
given to mortals to be busied about. 11[s] God
has made everything appropriate to its time,
but has put the timeless* into their hearts so
they cannot find out, from beginning to end,
the work which God has done. 12[t] I recognized that there is nothing better than to rejoice and to do well during life. 13 Moreover,
that all can eat and drink and enjoy the good
of all their toil—this is a gift of God. 14 I recognized that whatever God does will endure
forever; there is no adding to it, or taking
from it. Thus has God done that he may be
revered. 15*[u] What now is has already been;
what is to be, already is: God retrieves what
has gone by.

***The Problem of Retribution.*** 16[v] And still
under the sun in the judgment place I saw
wickedness, and wickedness also in the seat
of justice. 17[w] I said in my heart, both the just
and the wicked God will judge, since a time
is set for every affair and for every work.* 18 I
said in my heart: As for human beings, it is
God's way of testing them and of showing
that they are in themselves like beasts. 19 For
the lot of mortals and the lot of beasts is the
same lot: The one dies as well as the other.
Both have the same life breath. Human beings have no advantage over beasts, but all is
vanity. 20[x] Both go to the same place; both
were made from the dust, and to the dust they
both return. 21 Who knows* if the life breath
of mortals goes upward and the life breath of
beasts goes earthward? 22[y] And I saw that
there is nothing better for mortals than to rejoice in their work; for this is their lot. Who
will let them see what is to come after them?[z]

## CHAPTER 4

See RG 183–87

***Vanity of Toil.*** 1 Again I saw all the oppressions that take place under the sun: the
tears of the victims with none to comfort*
them! From the hand of their oppressors
comes violence, and there is none to comfort
them![a] 2 And those now dead, I declared
more fortunate in death than are the living to
be still alive.[b] 3 And better off than both is the
yet unborn, who has not seen the wicked
work that is done under the sun. 4 Then I saw
that all toil and skillful work is the rivalry of
one person with another. This also is vanity
and a chase after wind.

5 "Fools fold their arms
and consume their own flesh"—*
6 Better is one handful with tranquility
than two with toil and a chase after
wind!

***Companions and Successors.*** 7 Again I
saw this vanity under the sun: 8 those all
alone with no companion, with neither child
nor sibling—with no end to all their toil, and
no satisfaction from riches. For whom do I
toil and deprive myself of good things? This
also is vanity and a bad business. 9 Two are
better than one: They get a good wage for
their toil. 10 If the one falls, the other will
help the fallen one. But woe to the solitary
person! If that one should fall, there is no
other to help. 11 So also, if two sleep together,
they keep each other warm. How can one

**3:11 The timeless**: others translate "eternity," "the world," or "darkness." The author credits God with keeping human beings ignorant about God's "work"—present and future.

**3:15** The verse is difficult. Literally it reads "and God seeks out what was pursued." It appears to be a variation of the theme in 1:9, "There is nothing new under the sun."

**3:17 A time is set . . . work**: another possible reading would see this verse referring to a judgment in or after death: "a time for every affair and for every work *there*" (that is, in death or in Sheol).

**3:21 Who knows**: the author presumes a negative answer: "No one knows." In place of speculation on impossible questions, the author counsels enjoyment of what is possible (cf. v. 22; but see also 2:10–11).

**4:1 Oppressions . . . victims . . . none to comfort**: the author obviously feels deeply about the plight of the oppressed, but he seems to feel powerless to do anything. The repetition of "none to comfort" is purposeful, and emphatic.

**4:5 Consume their own flesh**: an enigmatic statement. In the context of vv. 4 and 6 it seems to warn that those who refuse to work for the necessities of life will suffer hunger and impair their bodily health. But the verse could also be intended for the industrious: Even the lazy may manage to have "their own flesh," that is, have sufficient food to eat.

---

*r:* Eccl 1:3. *s:* Eccl 8:17; 11:5. *t:* Eccl 2:24. *u:* Eccl 1:9. *v:* Eccl 4:1. *w:* Eccl 8:6a; 11:9; 12:14. *x:* Eccl 12:7; Gn 3:19; Sir 17:2. *y:* Eccl 3:12–13; 5:17–18. *z:* Eccl 8:7; 10:14. *a:* Eccl 3:16; 5:7; 9:4–5. *b:* Eccl 6:3–5.

alone keep warm? 12 Where one alone may be overcome, two together can resist. A three-ply cord* is not easily broken.

13* Better is a poor but wise youth than an old but foolish king who no longer knows caution; 14 for from a prison house he came forth to reign; despite his kingship he was born poor. 15 I saw all the living, those who move about under the sun, with the second youth who will succeed him.* 16 There is no end to all this people, to all who were before them; yet the later generations will not have joy in him. This also is vanity and a chase after wind.

***Vanity of Many Words.*** 17[c] Guard your step when you go to the house of God.* Draw near for obedience, rather than for the fools' offering of sacrifice; for they know not how to keep from doing evil.

## CHAPTER 5

See RG 183–87

1* Be not hasty in your utterance and let not your heart be quick to utter a promise in God's presence. God is in heaven and you are on earth; therefore let your words be few.[d]

2 As dreams come along with many cares,
so a fool's voice along with a
multitude of words.

3[e] When you make a vow to God, delay not its fulfillment. For God has no pleasure in fools; fulfill what you have vowed. 4 It is better not to make a vow than make it and not fulfill it. 5 Let not your utterances make you guilty, and say not before his representative, "It was a mistake." Why should God be angered by your words and destroy the works of your hands? 6[f] Despite many dreams, futilities, and a multitude of words, fear God!

***Gain and Loss of Goods.*** 7[g] If you see oppression of the poor, and violation of rights and justice in the realm, do not be astonished by the fact, for the high official has another higher than he watching him and above these are others higher still—. 8 But profitable for a land in such circumstances is a king concerned about cultivation.*

9[h] The covetous are never satisfied with money, nor lovers of wealth with their gain; so this too is vanity. 10 Where there are great riches, there are also many to devour them. Of what use are they to the owner except as a feast for the eyes alone? 11 Sleep is sweet to the laborer, whether there is little or much to eat; but the abundance of the rich allows them no sleep.

12 This is a grievous evil which I have seen under the sun: riches hoarded by their owners to their own hurt. 13 Should the riches be lost through some misfortune, they may have offspring when they have no means. 14[i] As they came forth from their mother's womb, so again shall they return, naked as they came, having nothing from their toil to bring with them. 15 This too is a grievous evil, that they go just as they came. What then does it profit them to toil for the wind? 16 All their days they eat in gloom with great vexation, sickness and resentment.

17[j] Here is what I see as good: It is appropriate to eat and drink and prosper from all the toil one toils at under the sun during the limited days of life God gives us; for this is our lot. 18 Those to whom God gives riches and property, and grants power to partake of them, so that they receive their lot and find

**4:12 A three-ply cord**: an ancient proverb known centuries before biblical times. The progression ("two together . . . three-ply") seems to imply, "If two are good, three are even better."

**4:13–16** This passage deals with kingship and succession, but is obscure.

**4:15** The king is no sooner dead than the people transfer their allegiance to his successor.

**4:17 The house of God**: the Temple in Jerusalem. **Obedience . . . sacrifice**: the Temple was the place not only for sacrifice but also for instruction in the Law. Sacrifice without obedience was unacceptable; cf. 1 Sm 15:22; Hos 6:6.

**5:1–6** Further counsels on prudence and circumspection in fulfilling one's religious obligations. It is not the multitude of words but one's sincerity that counts in the acknowledgment of God's sovereignty (v. 1), especially through obedience (4:17) and reverence (v. 6).

**5:8 A king concerned about cultivation**: the Hebrew text is ambiguous and obscure. The author does not criticize the oppression he describes in v. 7. Now perhaps he expresses the hope that the king would use his power to upbuild agriculture in order to alleviate the hunger and suffering of the poor and oppressed.

*c:* 1 Sm 15:22; Ps 40:7–9; Prv 15:8; 21:3; Hos 6:6. *d:* Ps 115:3, 16; Mt 6:7; Jas 1:19. *e:* Nm 30:3; Dt 23:22–24; Prv 20:25; Sir 18:22–23. *f:* Eccl 3:14. *g:* Eccl 3:16; 4:1. *h:* Eccl 4:8; Prv 28:22. *i:* Jb 1:21; 1 Tm 6:7. *j:* Eccl 2:24.

joy in the fruits of their toil: This is a gift
from God. 19For they will hardly dwell on
the shortness of life, because God lets them
busy themselves with the joy of their heart.*

## CHAPTER 6

See RG 183–87

*Limited Worth of Enjoyment.* 1There
is another evil I have seen under the sun, and
it weighs heavily upon humankind: 2[k] There
is one to whom God gives riches and property and honor, and who lacks nothing the
heart could desire; yet God does not grant
the power to partake of them, but a stranger
devours them. This is vanity and a dire
plague. 3Should one have a hundred children
and live many years, no matter to what great
age, still if one has not the full benefit of
those goods, I proclaim that the child born
dead, even if left unburied, is more fortunate.* 4[l] Though it came in vain and goes
into darkness and its name is enveloped in
darkness, 5though it has not seen the sun or
known anything, yet the dead child has more
peace. 6Should such a one live twice a thousand years and not enjoy those goods, do not
both go to the same place?*

7All human toil is for the mouth,* yet the
appetite is never satisfied. 8What profit have
the wise compared to fools, or what profit
have the lowly in knowing how to conduct
themselves in life? 9"What the eyes see is
better than what the desires wander after."*
This also is vanity and a chase after wind.

# II. Qoheleth's Conclusions

10Whatever is, was long ago given its name,
and human nature is known; mortals cannot
contend in judgment with One who is
stronger.* 11For the more words, the more
vanity; what profit is there for anyone?
12[m] For who knows what is good for mortals
in life, the limited days of their vain life, spent
like a shadow? Because who can tell them
what will come afterward under the sun?[n]

### *A. No One Can Find Out the Best Way of Acting*

## CHAPTER 7

See RG 183–87

### *Critique of Sages on the Day of Adversity*

1 A good name is better than good
ointment,*
and the day of death than the day of
birth.[o]
2 It is better to go to the house of mourning
than to the house of feasting,
For that is the end of every mortal,
and the living should take it to heart.[p]
3 Sorrow is better than laughter;
when the face is sad, the heart grows
wise.
4 The heart of the wise is in the house of
mourning,
but the heart of fools is in the house of
merriment.
5 It is better to listen to the rebuke of the
wise
than to listen to the song of fools;
6 For as the crackling of thorns under a pot,
so is the fool's laughter.
This also is vanity.
7 Extortion can make a fool out of the
wise,
and a bribe corrupts the heart.
8 Better is the end of a thing than its
beginning;
better is a patient spirit than a lofty one.

**5:19** The joys of life, though temporary and never assured, keep one from dwelling on the ills which afflict humanity.

**6:3** Even a large family and exceptionally long life cannot compensate for the absence of good things and the joy which they bring.

**6:6 Same place**: the grave; cf. 3:20; 12:7.

**6:7 The mouth**: symbolic of human desires.

**6:9** Compare the English proverb, "A bird in the hand is worth two in the bush." However, it could also mean, "The seeing of the eyes is better than the wandering of the desire," with the emphasis on the actions of seeing and desiring. Seeing is a way of possessing whereas desire, by definition, can remain frustrated and unfulfilled.

**6:10–11 One who is stronger** is, of course, God. **The more vanity**: contending with God is futile.

**7:1 Ointment**: a good name can be affirmed only with death, when one is normally anointed. The author dialogues in this section (vv. 1–14) with traditional wisdom, alternately affirming or countering its assertions. The real value of traditional wisdom lies in its ability to provoke one to thought and reflection, and not to absolve one from such activity.

*k:* Eccl 2:18–19. *l:* Eccl 4:2–3; Jb 3:11, 16. *m:* Jb 8:9; 14:2; Ps 102:12. *n:* Eccl 3:22; 8:7. *o:* Eccl 4:2; Prv 22:1. *p:* Eccl 12:1.

9 Do not let anger upset your spirit,
for anger lodges in the bosom of a fool.

10 Do not say: How is it that former times
were better than these? For it is not out of
wisdom that you ask about this.

11 Wisdom is as good as an inheritance
and profitable to those who see the sun.

12* For the protection of wisdom is as the
protection of money; and knowledge is profitable because wisdom gives life to those
who possess it.
13 Consider the work of God. Who can
make straight what God has made crooked?[q]
14 On a good day enjoy good things, and on
an evil day consider: Both the one and the
other God has made, so that no one may find
the least fault with him.

***Critique of Sages on Justice and Wicked-ness.*** 15* I have seen all manner of things in
my vain days: the just perishing in their jus-
tice, and the wicked living long in their
wickedness. 16 "Be not just to excess, and be
not overwise. Why work your own ruin?
17 Be not wicked to excess, and be not foolish. Why should you die before your time?"
18 It is good to hold to this rule, and not to let
that one go; but the one who fears God will
succeed with both.
19 Wisdom is a better defense for the wise
than ten princes in the city, 20[r] yet there is no
one on earth so just as to do good and never
sin. 21 Do not give your heart to every word
that is spoken; you may hear your servant
cursing you, 22 for your heart knows that you
have many times cursed others.
23 All these things I probed in wisdom. I
said, "I will acquire wisdom"; but it was far
beyond me. 24 What exists is far-reaching; it
is deep, very deep:* Who can find it out?
25* [s] I turned my heart toward knowledge; I
sought and pursued wisdom and its design,
and I recognized that wickedness is foolishness and folly is madness.

***Critique of Advice on Women.*** 26[t] More
bitter than death I find the woman* who is a
hunter's trap, whose heart is a snare, whose
hands are prison bonds. The one who pleases
God will be delivered from her, but the one
who displeases will be entrapped by her.
27 See, this have I found, says Qoheleth,
adding one to one to find the sum. 28 What
my soul still seeks and has yet to find is this:
"One man out of a thousand have I found,
but a woman among them all I have not
found." 29 But this alone I have found: God
made humankind honest, but they have pursued many designs.

## CHAPTER 8

See RG 183–87

### Critique of Advice To Heed Authority

1 * Who is like the wise person,
and who knows the explanation of things?
Wisdom illumines the face
and transforms a grim countenance.

2 Observe the command of the king, in
view of your oath to God. 3 Be not hasty to
withdraw from the king; do not persist in an
unpleasant situation, for he does whatever
he pleases. 4 His word is sovereign, and who
can say to him, "What are you doing?"
5* [u] "Whoever observes a command

**7:12** St. Jerome's translation of v. 12b gives an edge to wisdom over money: "But learning and wisdom excel in this, that they bestow life on the one who possesses them."

**7:15–24** The author continues both to affirm and to counter traditional wisdom. He affirms a certain validity to wisdom, but challenges complacency and mindless optimism. His sense of life's uncertainty and insecurity finds expression, for example, in the irony evident when v. 16 is read in the light of vv. 20–24: How can one be "excessively" just or wise, when justice and wisdom may be out of reach to begin with? The only sure thing is to "fear God" (v. 18).

**7:24 Far-reaching . . . deep**: the spatial metaphor here emphasizes wisdom's inaccessibility, a frequent theme in wisdom literature; cf. Jb 28; Prv 30:1–4; Sir 24:28–29; Bar 3:14–23.

**7:25–29** The emphasis is on the devious designs of human beings in general, reflecting the viewpoint of Genesis.

**7:26 More bitter than death . . . the woman**: warnings against the scheming, adulterous woman are common in ancient wisdom (e.g., Prv 2:16–19, etc.).

**8:1–4** The author continues to quote traditional wisdom but then to counter and qualify it. He concedes wisdom's advantages (v. 1), but then describes the subservience and sometimes demeaning demands required of the sage in the court of the king (vv. 2–4).

**8:5–9** The wise exhibit keen insight about human nature and the course of events (vv. 5–6a). Yet their knowledge and wisdom confront certain limits, such as the mystery of evil and the time and inevitability of death (vv. 6b–9).

---

*q:* Eccl 1:15. *r:* Jb 9:2; 1 Kgs 8:46; Rom 3:23. *s:* Eccl 1:17. *t:* Prv 5:4. *u:* Prv 19:16.

knows no harm, and the wise heart knows times and judgments." [6v] Yes, there is a time and a judgment for everything. But it is a great evil for mortals [7w] that they are ignorant of what is to come; for who will make known to them how it will be? [8]No one is master of the breath of life so as to retain it, and none has mastery of the day of death. There is no exemption in wartime, nor does wickedness deliver those who practice it. [9]All these things I saw and I applied my heart to every work that is done under the sun, while one person tyrannizes over another for harm.

*The Problem of Retribution.* [10]Meanwhile I saw the wicked buried. They would come and go from the holy place. But those were forgotten in the city who had acted justly. This also is vanity.* [11]Because the sentence against an evil deed is not promptly executed, the human heart is filled with the desire to commit evil— [12*] because the sinner does evil a hundred times and survives. Though indeed I know that it shall be well with those who fear God, for their reverence toward him; [13]and that it shall not be well with the wicked, who shall not prolong their shadowy days, for their lack of reverence toward God.

[14]This is a vanity that occurs on earth: There are those who are just but are treated as though they had done evil, and those who are wicked but are treated as though they had done justly. This, too, I say is vanity. [15x] Therefore I praised joy, because there is nothing better for mortals under the sun than to eat and to drink and to be joyful; this will accompany them in their toil through the limited days of life God gives them under the sun.

[16]I applied my heart to know wisdom and to see the business that is done on earth, though neither by day nor by night do one's eyes see sleep, [17y] and I saw all the work of God: No mortal can find out the work that is done under the sun. However much mortals may toil in searching, no one finds it out; and even if the wise claim to know, they are unable to find it out.

See RG 183–87

### *B. No One Knows the Future*

## CHAPTER 9

[1]All this I have kept in my heart and all this I examined: The just, the wise, and their deeds are in the hand of God. Love from hatred* mortals cannot tell; both are before them. [2z] Everything is the same for everybody: the same lot for the just and the wicked, for the good, for the clean and the unclean, for the one who offers sacrifice and the one who does not. As it is for the good, so it is for the sinner; as it is for the one who takes an oath, so it is for the one who fears an oath. [3]Among all the things that are done under the sun, this is the worst, that there is one lot for all. Hence the hearts of human beings are filled with evil, and madness is in their hearts during life; and afterward—to the dead!

[4]For whoever is chosen among all the living has hope: "A live dog* is better off than a dead lion." [5a] For the living know that they are to die, but the dead no longer know anything. There is no further recompense for them, because all memory of them is lost. [6]For them, love and hatred and rivalry have long since perished. Never again will they have part in anything that is done under the sun.

**8:10** This difficult verse seems to contrast the wicked, who die enjoying a good reputation as pious individuals, and the just, who are quietly forgotten.

**8:12–17** The author admits that traditional wisdom affirms the long life and success of the just and the short unhappy life of the wicked (vv. 12b–13). But he points out clear exceptions: the wicked who live long, and the just who suffer for no apparent reason (v. 14). His puzzlement and frustration prompt a twofold response: acceptance of whatever joy God chooses to give each day, and honest acknowledgment that no one can discover "the work of God" (cf. 3:11; 7:13; 11:5).

**9:1–3 Love from hatred . . . everything is the same**: God seems to bestow divine favor or disfavor (love or hatred) indiscriminately on the just and wicked alike. More ominously, the arbitrariness and inevitability of death and adversity confront every human being, whether good or bad.

**9:4–6 A live dog . . . no further recompense**: human reason and experience persuaded Qoheleth that death with its finality and annihilating power cruelly negates the supreme value—life, and with it, all possibilities (cf. v. 10). Faith in eternal life has its foundation only in hope and trust in God's promise and in God's love.

*v:* Eccl 3:17; 9:12. *w:* Eccl 3:22; 6:12; 10:14. *x:* Eccl 2:24; 3:22; 5:17–18; 9:7. *y:* Eccl 3:11. *z:* Eccl 2:14; 3:15. *a:* Eccl 1:11; 2:16.

7[b] Go, eat your bread* with joy and drink
your wine with a merry heart, because it is
now that God favors your works. 8 At all times
let your garments be white, and spare not the
perfume for your head. 9 Enjoy life with the
wife you love, all the days of the vain life
granted you under the sun. This is your lot in
life, for the toil of your labors under the sun.
10 Anything you can turn your hand to, do
with what power you have; for there will be
no work, no planning, no knowledge, no wisdom in Sheol where you are going.

*The Time of Misfortune Is Not Known.*
11 Again I saw under the sun that the race is not
won by the swift, nor the battle by the valiant,
nor a livelihood by the wise, nor riches by the
shrewd, nor favor by the experts; for a time of
misfortune comes to all alike. 12 Human beings no more know their own time than fish
taken in the fatal net or birds trapped in the
snare; like these, mortals are caught when an
evil time suddenly falls upon them.

*The Uncertain Future and the Sages.* 13 On
the other hand I saw this wise deed under the
sun, which I thought magnificent. 14 Against
a small city with few inhabitants advanced a
mighty king, who surrounded it and threw
up great siegeworks about it. 15 But in the
city lived a man who, though poor, was wise,
and he delivered it through his wisdom. Yet
no one remembered this poor man.
16[c] Though I had said, "Wisdom is better
than force," yet the wisdom of the poor man
is despised and his words go unheeded.

17 The quiet words of the wise are better
heeded
than the shout of a ruler of fools.
18 Wisdom is better than weapons of war,
but one bungler destroys much good.

### CHAPTER 10

See RG 183–87

1 Dead flies corrupt and spoil the
perfumer's oil;
more weighty than wisdom or wealth
is a little folly!*
2 The wise heart turns to the right;
the foolish heart to the left.*

3 Even when walking in the street the fool,
lacking understanding, calls everyone a fool.*
4 Should the anger of a ruler burst upon
you, do not yield your place; for calmness*
abates great offenses.
5 I have seen under the sun another evil,
like a mistake that proceeds from a tyrant: 6 a
fool put in high position, while the great and
the rich sit in lowly places. 7 I have seen
slaves on horseback, while princes* went on
foot like slaves.

8 Whoever digs a pit may fall into it,[d]
and whoever breaks through a wall, a
snake may bite.
9 Whoever quarries stones may be hurt by
them,
and whoever chops wood* is in danger
from it.

10 If the ax becomes dull, and the blade is
not sharpened, then effort must be increased.
But the advantage of wisdom is success.

11 If the snake bites before it is charmed,
then there is no advantage in a charmer.*

**9:7–10 Go, eat your bread . . . enjoy life**: the author confesses his inability to imprison God in a fixed and predictable way of acting. Thus he ponders a practical and pragmatic solution: Seize whatever opportunity one has to find joy, if God grants it.

**10:1 Dead flies . . . a little folly**: wisdom is vulnerable to even the smallest amount of folly. The collection of proverbs and sayings in chaps. 10 and 11 demonstrates the author's sharp insight and strengthens his credentials as a sage. It thus adds weight to his critique of the wisdom tradition's tendencies to self-assurance and naive optimism.

**10:2 Right . . . left**: the right hand is identified with power, moral goodness, favor; the left hand with ineptness and bad luck.

**10:3 Calls everyone a fool**: or, "tells everyone that he (himself) is a fool."

**10:4 Calmness**: a frequent motif of wisdom; silence and reserve characterize the wise, while boisterousness and impetuosity identify the fool.

**10:6–7 A fool . . . the rich . . . slaves . . . princes**: another wisdom motif: astonishment at the reversal of the usual order in the world and in human affairs.

**10:8–9 A pit . . . a wall . . . stones . . . wood**: popular sayings reflecting the need for caution and alertness against the unexpected. Snakes could find a home in the stone walls of ancient Palestine; cf. Am 5:19.

**10:10–11 Ax . . . success . . . snake . . . charmer**: possession of the proper skill (a form of "wisdom") can ensure success, as in the case of a sharpened ax; but one must use it before it is too late (v. 11). Cf. Sir 12:13.

*b:* Eccl 2:24; 8:15; 11:9. *c:* Prv 24:5. *d:* Prv 26:27; Ps 7:16; Sir 27:29.

12 Words from the mouth of the wise win
favor,
but the lips of fools consume them.
13 [e] The beginning of their words is folly,
and the end of their talk is utter
madness;
14 yet fools multiply words.
No one knows what is to come,
for who can tell anyone what will be?[f]
15 The toil of fools wearies them,
so they do not know even the way to
town.

### *No One Knows What Evil Will Come*

16 Woe to you, O land, whose king is a
youth,*
and whose princes feast in the
morning!
17 Happy are you, O land, whose king is of
noble birth,
and whose princes dine at the right
time—
for vigor* and not in drinking bouts.
18 Because of laziness, the rafters sag;
when hands are slack, the house
leaks.
19 A feast is made for merriment
and wine gives joy to the living,
but money answers* for everything.
20 Even in your thoughts do not curse the
king,
nor in the privacy of your bedroom
curse the rich;
For the birds of the air may carry your
voice,
a winged creature* may tell what you
say.

## CHAPTER 11

See RG 183–87

1 * Send forth your bread upon the
face of the waters;
after a long time you may find it again.
2 Make seven, or even eight portions;
you know not what misfortune may
come upon the earth.

### *No One Knows What Good Will Come*

3 * When the clouds are full,
they pour out rain upon the earth.
Whether a tree falls to the south or to the
north,
wherever it falls, there shall it lie.
4 One who pays heed to the wind will
never sow,
and one who watches the clouds will
never reap.
5 Just as you do not know how the life breath
enters the human frame in the
mother's womb,
So you do not know the work of God,
who is working in everything.[g]
6 In the morning sow your seed,
and at evening do not let your hand be
idle:
For you do not know which of the two
will be successful,
or whether both alike will turn out well.

***Poem on Youth and Old Age.*** 7* Light is
sweet! and it is pleasant for the eyes to see
the sun. 8However many years mortals may
live, let them, as they enjoy them all, remember that the days of darkness will be
many. All that is to come is vanity.

**10:16 A youth**: thus too young and inexperienced to govern effectively. **Feast in the morning**: either concluding a whole night of revelry or beginning a new round of merry-making.

**10:17 For vigor**: or, "with self-control, restraint."

**10:19 Money answers**: a stark reminder that such a life requires money. It could also be an affirmation of the power of wealth: "Money conquers all."

**10:20 Birds of the air . . . winged creature**: a common motif in ancient literature, and a vivid reminder of the need for caution in dealing with the rich and powerful.

**11:1–2** These two sayings can be understood against a commercial background. They acknowledge the uncertainty and risk such activity involves. At the same time they encourage action and a spirit of adventure. The first (v. 1) speaks of trade and overseas investment: Export your grain ("bread") to foreign markets and you may be surprised at the substantial profits. The second (v. 2) encourages diversification of investment (seven, or even eight shipments of grain) to insure against heavy losses.

**11:3–6** Verses 3, 4, and 6 expand on the theme of uncertainty and human inability to assess accurately every situation. Verse 4, however, comments on the disadvantages of too much caution: Only those willing to risk will enjoy success. But only the Creator knows the mystery of the "work of God" (v. 5).

**11:7–10** The concluding part of the book opens with a final bittersweet homage to life and an enthusiastic encouragement to rejoice in its gifts while they are within grasp.

*e:* Eccl 5:2; 6:11. *f:* Eccl 3:22; 6:12; 10:14. *g:* Eccl 3:11; 7:13; 8:17.

9 Rejoice, O youth, while you are young
and let your heart be glad in the days
of your youth.
Follow the ways of your heart,
the vision of your eyes;
Yet understand regarding all this
that God will bring you to judgment.
10 Banish misery from your heart
and remove pain from your body,
for youth and black hair are fleeting.*

## CHAPTER 12

See RG 183–87

1* Remember your Creator in the
days of your youth,
before the evil days come
And the years approach of which you
will say,
"I have no pleasure in them";
2 Before the sun is darkened
and the light and the moon and the stars
and the clouds return after the rain;
3 * When the guardians of the house tremble,
and the strong men are bent;
When the women who grind are idle
because they are few,
and those who look through the
windows grow blind;
4 When the doors to the street are shut,
and the sound of the mill is low;
When one rises at the call of a bird,
and all the daughters of song are quiet;
5 When one is afraid of heights,
and perils in the street;
When the almond tree blooms,
and the locust grows sluggish
and the caper berry is without effect,
Because mortals go to their lasting home,
and mourners go about the streets;
6 * Before the silver cord is snapped
and the golden bowl is broken,
And the pitcher is shattered at the spring,
and the pulley is broken at the well,
7 And the dust returns to the earth as it
once was,
and the life breath returns to God who
gave it.* [h]
8 Vanity of vanities, says Qoheleth,
all things are vanity![i]

*Epilogue.* 9* Besides being wise, Qoheleth
taught the people knowledge, and weighed,
scrutinized and arranged many proverbs.
10 Qoheleth sought to find appropriate sayings, and to write down true sayings with
precision. 11 The sayings of the wise are like
goads; like fixed spikes are the collected sayings given by one shepherd.* 12 [j] As to more
than these,* my son, beware. Of the making
of many books there is no end, and in much
study there is weariness for the flesh.
13* [k] The last word, when all is heard: Fear
God and keep his commandments, for this
concerns all humankind; 14 [l] because God
will bring to judgment every work, with all
its hidden qualities, whether good or bad.

**11:10 Fleeting**: lit., "vanity."

**12:1–7** The homage to life of 11:7–10 is deliberately balanced by the sombre yet shimmering radiance of this poem on old age and death. The poem's enigmatic imagery has often been interpreted allegorically, especially in vv. 3–5. Above all it seeks to evoke an atmosphere as well as an attitude toward death and old age.

**12:3–5** An allegorical reading of these verses sees references to the human body—"guardians": the arms; "strong men": the legs; "women who grind": the teeth; "those who look": the eyes; "the doors": the lips; "daughters of song": the voice; "the almond tree blooms": resembling the white hair of old age; "the locust . . . sluggish": the stiffness in movement of the aged; "the caper berry": a stimulant for appetite.

**12:6** The golden bowl suspended by the silver cord is a symbol of life; the snapping of the cord and the breaking of the bowl, a symbol of death. **The pitcher . . . the pulley**: another pair of metaphors for life and its ending.

**12:7** Death is portrayed in terms of the description of creation in Gn 2:7; the body corrupts in the grave, and the life breath (lit., "spirit"), or gift of life, returns to God who had breathed upon what he had formed.

**12:9** A disciple briefly describes and praises the master's skill and reputation as a sage.

**12:11 One shepherd**: perhaps referring to the book's author, who gathers or "shepherds" together its contents. God could also be "the one shepherd," the ultimate depository and source of true wisdom.

**12:12 As to more than these**: the words seem to refer to the writings of Ecclesiastes and other sages. They are adequate and sufficient; any more involves exhaustive labor.

**12:13–14** These words reaffirm traditional wisdom doctrine such as fear of God and faithful obedience, perhaps lest some of the more extreme statements of the author be misunderstood. Although the epilogue has been interpreted as a criticism of the book's author, it is really a summary that betrays the unruffled spirit of later sages, who were not shocked by Qoheleth's statements. They honored him as a *hakam* or sage (v. 9), even as they preserved his statements about the futility of life (v. 8), and the mystery of divine judgment (8:17; 11:5).

*h:* Eccl 3:20–21; Jb 34:14–15. *i:* Eccl 1:2. *j:* Eccl 1:18. *k:* Eccl 5:6. *l:* Eccl 11:9.

See RG 187–92

# The Song of Songs

The Song of Songs (or Canticle of Canticles) is an exquisite collection of love lyrics, arranged to tell a dramatic tale of mutual desire and courtship. It presents an inspired portrayal of ideal human love, a resounding affirmation of the goodness of human sexuality that is applicable to the sacredness and the depth of married union.

Although the poem is attributed to Solomon in the traditional title (1:1), the language and style of the work, among other considerations, suggest a time after the end of the Babylonian exile (538 B.C.) when an unknown poet collected extant love poems, perhaps composing new material, and arranged the whole into the masterpiece we have before us. Some scholars argue the possibility of female authorship for at least portions of the Song.

The structure of the Song is difficult to analyze; this translation regards it as a lyric dialogue, with dramatic movement and interest. In both form and content, sections of the Song bear great similarity to the secular love songs of ancient Egypt and the "Sacred Marriage" cult songs of Mesopotamia which celebrate the union between divine partners.

While the lovers in the Song are clearly human figures, both Jewish and Christian traditions across the centuries have adopted "allegorical" interpretations. The Song is seen as a beautiful picture of the ideal Israel, the chosen people whom the Lord leads by degrees to a greater understanding and closer union in the bond of perfect love. Such readings of the Song build on Israel's covenant tradition. Isaiah (Is 5:1–7; 54:4–8; 62:5), Jeremiah (Jer 2:2, 3, 32), and Ezekiel (Ez 16; 23) all characterize the covenant between the Lord and Israel as a marriage. Hosea the prophet sees the idolatry of Israel in the adultery of Gomer (Hos 1–3). He also represents the Lord speaking to Israel's heart (Hos 2:16) and changing her into a new spiritual people, purified by the Babylonian captivity and betrothed anew to her divine Lover "in justice and uprightness, in love and mercy" (Hos 2:21). Similar imagery has also been used frequently in Jewish mystical texts. The Song offers a welcome corrective to negative applications of the theological metaphor of the marriage/covenant in some prophetic texts. It frequently proclaims a joyous reciprocity between the lovers and highlights the active role of the female partner, now a pure figure to be cherished rather than an adulterous woman to be punished and abused. See also Is 62:3–5.

Christian tradition has followed Israel's example in using marriage as an image for the relationship with God. This image is found extensively in the New Testament (Mt 9:15; 25:1–13; Jn 3:29; 2 Cor 11:2; Eph 5:23–32; Rev 19:7–9; 21:9–11). Thus the Song has been read as a sublime portrayal and praise of this mutual love of the Lord and his people. Christian writers have interpreted the Song in terms of the union between Christ and the Church and of the union between Christ and the individual soul, particularly in the writings of Origen and St. Bernard.

## CHAPTER 1

See RG 187–92

*1* The Song of Songs,* which is Solomon's.

### *The Woman Speaks of Her Lover*

W *2* *[a] Let him kiss me with kisses of his
mouth,
for your love is better than wine,*

**1:1 Song of Songs**: in Hebrew and Aramaic the idiom "the X of Xs" denotes the superlative (e.g., "king of kings" = "the highest king"; cf. Dt 10:17; Eccl 1:2; 12:8; Ezr 7:12; Dn 2:37). The ascription of authorship to Solomon is traditional. The heading may also mean "for Solomon" or "about Solomon."

**1:2–8:14** This translation augments the canonical text of the Song with the letters *W*, *M*, and *D*, placed in the margin, to indicate which of the characters in the Song is speaking: the woman, the man, or the "Daughters of Jerusalem." This interpretive gloss follows an early Christian scribal practice, attested in some Septuagint manuscripts from the first half of the first millennium A.D.

**1:2–7** The woman and her female chorus address the man, here viewed as king and shepherd (both are familiar metaphors for God; cf. Ps 23:1; Is 40:11; Jn 10:1–16). There is a wordplay between "kiss" (Hebrew *nashaq*) and "drink" (*shaqah*), anticipating 8:1–2. The change from third person ("let him kiss . . .") to second person (". . . for your love . . .") is not uncommon in the Song and elsewhere (1:4; 2:4; etc.;

*a:* Sg 4:10.

3 better than the fragrance of your
perfumes.*
Your name is a flowing perfume—
therefore young women love you.
4 b Draw me after you! Let us run!*
The king has brought me to his bed
chambers.
Let us exult and rejoice in you;
let us celebrate your love: it is
beyond wine!
Rightly do they love you!

### *Love's Boast*

**W** 5 I am black and beautiful,
Daughters of Jerusalem*—
Like the tents of Qedar,
like the curtains of Solomon.
6 Do not stare at me because I am so
black,*
because the sun has burned me.
The sons of my mother were angry
with me;
they charged me with the care of the
vineyards:
my own vineyard I did not take
care of.

### *Love's Inquiry*

**W** 7 Tell me, you whom my soul loves,
where you shepherd,* where you
give rest at midday.
Why should I be like one wandering
after the flocks of your companions?
**M** 8 If you do not know,
most beautiful among women,
Follow the tracks of the flock
and pasture your lambs*
near the shepherds' tents.

### *Love's Vision*

**M** 9 To a mare among Pharaoh's chariotry*
I compare you, my friend:
10 Your cheeks lovely in pendants,
your neck in jewels.
11 We will make pendants of gold for you,
and ornaments of silver.

### *How Near Is Love!*

**W** 12 While the king was upon his couch,
my spikenard* gave forth its
fragrance.
13 My lover* is to me a sachet of myrrh;
between my breasts he lies.
14 My lover is to me a cluster of henna*
from the vineyards of En-gedi.
**M** 15 c How beautiful you are, my friend,
how beautiful! your eyes are doves!*
**W** 16 How beautiful you are, my lover—
handsome indeed!
Verdant indeed is our couch;*
17 the beams of our house are cedars,
our rafters, cypresses.

Ps 23:1–3, 4–5, 6; etc.) and reflects the woman's move from interior monologue to direct address to her partner.

**1:3 Your perfumes**: *shemen* (perfume) is a play on *shem* (name).

**1:4** Another change, but from second to third person (cf. 1:2). The "king" metaphor recurs in 1:12; 3:5–11; 7:6. **Let us exult**: perhaps she is addressing young women, calling on them to join in the praise of her lover.

**1:5 Daughters of Jerusalem**: the woman contrasts herself with the elite city women, who act as her female "chorus" (5:9; 6:1). **Qedar**: a Syrian desert region whose name suggests darkness; tents were often made of black goat hair. **Curtains**: tent coverings, or tapestries. **Solomon**: it could also be read Salma, a region close to Qedar.

**1:6 So black**: tanned from working outdoors in her brothers' vineyards, unlike the city women she addresses. **My own vineyard**: perhaps the woman herself; see 8:8–10 for her relationship to her brothers.

**1:7 Shepherd**: a common metaphor for kings. Here and elsewhere in the Song (3:1; 5:8; 6:1), the woman expresses her desire to be in the company of her lover. The search for the lover and her failure to find him create a degree of tension. Only at the end (8:5–14) do the lovers finally possess each other.

**1:8 Pasture your lambs**: both the woman and the man act as shepherds in the Song.

**1:9–11** The man compares the woman's beauty to the rich adornment of the royal chariot of Pharaoh. **My friend**: a special feminine form of the word "friend," appearing only in the Song (1:15; 2:2, 10, 13; 4:1, 7; 5:2; 6:4) and used to express endearment and equality in love. Cf. Hos 3:1 for the use of the masculine form of the term in a context with sexual overtones.

**1:12 Spikenard**: a precious perfumed ointment from India; in 4:13–14, a metaphor for the woman herself.

**1:13 My lover**: the woman's favorite term for her partner (used 27 times). **Myrrh**: an aromatic resin of balsam or roses used in cosmetics, incense, and medicines.

**1:14 Henna**: a plant which bears white scented flowers, used in cosmetics and medicines. **En-gedi**: a Judean desert oasis overlooking the Dead Sea.

**1:15 Doves**: doves are pictured in the ancient world as messengers of love.

**1:16–17** Continuing the royal metaphor, the meeting place of the lovers, a shepherd's hut of green branches, becomes a

*b:* Sg 4:10. *c:* Sg 4:1, 7.

## Her Nighttime Search

IN CH 3 THE man does not return, and the woman takes the initiative to seek him. The book has a strong feminine orientation, speaking of the mother's house (v. 4; see also 1:6; 8:1–2; Ru 1:8) instead of the more normal house of the father. The woman seems to be at the center of every scene, either searching for her love, being praised by him, or in conversation with the daughters of Jerusalem.

See RG 187-92

### CHAPTER 2

*W* 1 I am a flower of Sharon,*
a lily of the valleys.
*M* 2 Like a lily among thorns,
so is my friend among women.
*W* 3 Like an apple tree among the trees of the woods,
so is my lover among men.
In his shadow* I delight to sit,
and his fruit is sweet to my taste.
4 [d] He brought me to the banquet hall*
and his glance at me signaled love.
5 [e] Strengthen me with raisin cakes,*
refresh me with apples,
for I am sick with love.
6 [f] His left hand is under my head
and his right arm embraces me.
7 [g] I adjure you, Daughters of Jerusalem,*
by the gazelles and the does of the field,
Do not awaken, or stir up love
until it is ready.

### *Her Lover's Visit Remembered*

*W* 8 The sound of my lover! here he comes*
springing across the mountains,
leaping across the hills.
9 My lover is like a gazelle*
or a young stag.
See! He is standing behind our wall,
gazing through the windows,
peering through the lattices.
10 My lover speaks and says to me,
*M* "Arise, my friend, my beautiful one,
and come!
11 For see, the winter is past,
the rains are over and gone.
12 The flowers appear on the earth,
the time of pruning the vines has come,
and the song of the turtledove is heard in our land.
13 The fig tree puts forth its figs,
and the vines, in bloom, give forth fragrance.
Arise, my friend, my beautiful one,
and come!
14 My dove in the clefts of the rock,*
in the secret recesses of the cliff,
Let me see your face,
let me hear your voice,
For your voice is sweet,
and your face is lovely."
*W* 15 Catch us the foxes,* the little foxes

palace with beams of cedar and rafters of cypress when adorned with their love.

**2:1 Flower of Sharon**: probably the narcissus, which grows in the fertile Plain of Sharon lying between Mount Carmel and Jaffa on the Mediterranean coast. **Lily**: the lotus plant.

**2:3 Shadow**: suggestive of protection (cf. Jgs 9:15; Ez 17:23; Ps 17:8; 121:5) and, here, of the woman's joy in the presence of her lover.

**2:4–6 The banquet hall**: the sweet things of the table, the embrace of the woman and man, express the richness of their affection and the intimacy of their love.

**2:5 Raisin cakes**: perhaps pastries used in the worship of the fertility goddess (cf. Hos 3:1; Jer 7:18; 44:19). **Apples**: this is the common translation of a fruit that cannot be identified (cf. 2:3; 8:5); it appears frequently in Sumerian love poetry associated with the worship of the goddess Inanna. **Sick**: love-sickness is a popular motif in ancient love poetry.

**2:7** Cf. 3:5; 5:8; 8:4. **By the gazelles and the does**: perhaps a mitigated invocation of the divinity based on the assonance in Hebrew of the names of these animals with terms for God.

**2:8–13** In this sudden change of scene, the woman describes a rendezvous and pictures her lover hastening toward her dwelling until his voice is heard calling her to him.

**2:9 Gazelle**: a frequent motif in ancient poems from Mesopotamia.

**2:14** The woman is addressed as though she were a dove in a mountain cleft out of sight and reach.

**2:15** A snatch of song in answer to the request of 2:14; cf. 8:13–14. **Foxes**: they threaten to disturb the security of vineyards. The vineyards are women sought after by young lovers, i.e., foxes.

*d:* Sg 1:4. *e:* Sg 5:8. *f:* Sg 8:3. *g:* Sg 3:5; 8:4.

**A Wedding Scene**

THE BOOK OF Songs' only description of a wedding, with Solomon present, occurs in 3:6–11. These verses have been variously assessed 1) as a later insertion, modeled on Ps 45 and intended to strengthen the book's connection with Solomon; or 2) as an extended royal image, in which the woman compares the sight of her lover to that of the extravagant entourage of a king known for his love of women (1 Kgs 11:1–3).

that damage the vineyards; for our
vineyards are in bloom!
16 h My lover belongs to me and I to him;
he feeds among the lilies.
17 i Until the day grows cool* and the
shadows flee,
roam, my lover,
Like a gazelle or a young stag
upon the rugged mountains.

## CHAPTER 3

See RG 187–92

### *Loss and Discovery*

W 1 j On my bed at night I sought him*
whom my soul loves—
I sought him but I did not find him.
2 "Let me rise then and go about the city,*
through the streets and squares;
Let me seek him whom my soul loves."
I sought him but I did not find him.
3 The watchmen found me,
as they made their rounds in the city:
"Him whom my soul loves—have
you seen him?"
4 k Hardly had I left them
when I found him whom my soul
loves.*
I held him and would not let him go
until I had brought him to my
mother's house,
to the chamber of her who
conceived me.
5 l I adjure you, Daughters of Jerusalem,
by the gazelles and the does of the
field,
Do not awaken or stir up love
until it is ready.

### *Solomon's Wedding Procession*

D 6 m Who is this coming up from the
desert,*
like columns of smoke
Perfumed with myrrh and
frankincense,
with all kinds of exotic powders?
7 See! it is the litter of Solomon;
sixty valiant men surround it,
of the valiant men of Israel:
8 All of them expert with the sword,
skilled in battle,
Each with his sword at his side
against the terrors* of the night.
9 King Solomon made himself an
enclosed litter
of wood from Lebanon.
10 He made its columns of silver,
its roof of gold,
Its seat of purple cloth,
its interior lovingly fitted.*
Daughters of Jerusalem, 11 go out
and look upon King Solomon
In the crown with which his mother
has crowned him

**2:17 Grows cool**: in the evening when the sun is going down. Cf. Gn 3:8. **Rugged**: Hebrew obscure; some interpret it as a geographical name; others, in the sense of spices (cf. 8:14); still others, of sacrifice (Gn 15:10); the image probably refers here to the woman herself.

**3:1–5** See the parallel in 5:2–8.

**3:2** The motif of seeking/finding here and elsewhere is used by later Christian and Jewish mystics to speak of the soul's search for the divine.

**3:4 Whom my soul loves**: the fourfold repetition of this phrase in vv. 1–4 highlights the depth of the woman's emotion and desire. **Mother's house**: cf. 8:2; a place of safety and intimacy, one which implicitly signifies approval of the lovers' relationship.

**3:6–11** This may be an independent poem. In context it portrays the lover as King Solomon, escorted by sixty armed men, coming in royal procession to meet a bride.

**3:8 Terrors**: cf. Ps 91:5; perhaps bandits lying in wait, unidentified dangers lurking in darkness.

**3:10 Lovingly fitted**: translation uncertain. The phrase "Daughters of Jerusalem" is read here with the following verse.

*h:* Sg 6:3; 7:10. *i:* Sg 4:6; 8:14. *j:* Sg 5:2–8. *k:* Sg 8:2. *l:* Sg 2:7; 8:4. *m:* Sg 6:10; 8:5.

on the day of his marriage,
on the day of the joy of his heart.

## CHAPTER 4

See RG 187–92

### *The Beauty of the Woman*

M 1 n,o How beautiful you are, my friend,
how beautiful you are!
Your eyes are doves
behind your veil.
Your hair is like a flock of goats
streaming down Mount Gilead.*
2 Your teeth* are like a flock of ewes to be shorn,
that come up from the washing,
All of them big with twins,
none of them barren.
3 Like a scarlet strand, your lips,
and your mouth—lovely!
Like pomegranate* halves, your cheeks
behind your veil.
4 p Like a tower of David, your neck,
built in courses,
A thousand shields hanging upon it,
all the armor of warriors.*
5 q Your breasts are like two fawns,
twins of a gazelle
feeding among the lilies.
6 r Until the day grows cool
and the shadows flee,
I shall go to the mountain of myrrh,
to the hill of frankincense.*
7 You are beautiful in every way, my friend,
there is no flaw in you!*
8 With me from Lebanon, my bride!
With me from Lebanon, come!
Descend from the peak of Amana,
from the peak of Senir and Hermon,*
From the lairs of lions,
from the leopards' heights.
9 s You have ravished my heart, my sister,* my bride;
you have ravished my heart with one glance of your eyes,
with one bead of your necklace.
10 t How beautiful is your love,
my sister, my bride,
How much better is your love than wine,
and the fragrance of your perfumes than any spice!
11 Your lips drip honey,* my bride,
honey and milk are under your tongue;
And the fragrance of your garments
is like the fragrance of Lebanon.

### *The Lover's Garden*

M 12 u A garden enclosed, my sister, my bride,
a garden enclosed, a fountain sealed!*
13 Your branches are a grove of pomegranates,
with fruits of choicest yield:
Henna with spikenard,
14 spikenard and saffron,
Sweet cane and cinnamon,
with all kinds of frankincense;
Myrrh and aloes,
with all the finest spices;*
15 A garden fountain, a well of living water,
streams flowing from Lebanon.
16 Awake,* north wind!
Come, south wind!

**4:1** This section (vv. 1–7) begins a *wasf*, a traditional poetic form describing the physical attributes of one's partner in terms of the natural world (cf. 5:10–16; 6:5b–7; 7:1–7). **Veil**: women of the region customarily veiled their faces for some occasions (cf. 4:3; 6:7; Gn 24:65–67; 38:14–19).

**4:2 Teeth**: praised for whiteness and evenness.

**4:3 Pomegranate**: a fruit with a firm skin and deep red color. The woman's cheek (or perhaps her brow) is compared, in roundness and tint, to a half-pomegranate.

**4:4** The ornaments about her neck are compared to the trophies and armaments on the city walls. Cf. 1 Kgs 10:10; 14:26–28; Ez 27:10.

**4:6 Mountain of myrrh . . . hill of frankincense**: spoken figuratively of the woman; cf. 8:14.

**4:7** Cf. the description of the church in Eph 5:27.

**4:8 Amana . . . Senir and Hermon**: these rugged heights symbolize obstacles that would separate the lovers; cf. 2:14.

**4:9 Sister**: a term of endearment; brother-sister language forms part of the conventional language of love used in this canticle, the Book of Tobit, and elsewhere in poetry from Egypt, Mesopotamia, and Syro-Palestine.

**4:11 Honey**: sweet words (cf. Prv 5:3) or perhaps kisses (1:2–3). **Honey and milk**: familiar descriptions for the fertile promised land (Ex 3:8, 17; Lv 20:24; Nm 13:27; Dt 6:3).

**4:12 Garden enclosed . . . fountain sealed**: reserved for the lover alone. Cf. Prv 5:15–19 for similar images used to describe fruitful, committed relationship.

**4:14** These plants are all known for their sweet fragrance.

**4:16 Awake**: the same verb is used of love in 3:5. The

*n:* Sg 6:5–7. *o:* Sg 1:15. *p:* Sg 7:5. *q:* Sg 7:4. *r:* Sg 2:17. *s:* Sg 6:5. *t:* Sg 1:2–3. *u:* Sg 6:2, 11.

Blow upon my garden
that its perfumes may spread abroad.
*W* Let my lover come to his garden
and eat its fruits of choicest yield.

CHAPTER 5

See RG 187–92

*M* 1 v I have come to my garden, my sister, my bride;
I gather my myrrh with my spices,
I eat my honeycomb with my honey,
I drink my wine with my milk.
*D?* Eat, friends; drink!
Drink deeply, lovers!*

### *A Fruitless Search*

*W* 2 w I was sleeping, but my heart was awake.*
The sound of my lover knocking!
"Open to me, my sister, my friend,
my dove, my perfect one!
For my head is wet with dew,
my hair, with the moisture of the night."
3 I have taken off my robe,*
am I then to put it on?
I have bathed my feet,
am I then to soil them?
4 My lover put his hand in through the opening:
my innermost being* trembled because of him.
5 I rose to open for my lover,
my hands dripping myrrh:
My fingers, flowing myrrh
upon the handles of the lock.
6 I opened for my lover—
but my lover had turned and gone!
At his leaving, my soul sank.
I sought him, but I did not find him;
I called out after him, but he did not answer me.*
7 The watchmen* found me,
as they made their rounds in the city;
They beat me, they wounded me,
they tore off my mantle,
the watchmen of the walls.
8 x I adjure you, Daughters of Jerusalem,
if you find my lover
What shall you tell him?
that I am sick with love.

### *The Lost Lover Described*

*D* 9 How does your lover differ from any other lover,
most beautiful among women?
How does your lover differ from any other,
that you adjure us so?
*W* 10 My lover is radiant and ruddy;*
outstanding among thousands.
11 His head is gold, pure gold,
his hair like palm fronds,
as black as a raven.
12 His eyes are like doves
beside streams of water,
Bathing in milk,
sitting* by brimming pools.
13 His cheeks are like beds of spices
yielding aromatic scents;
his lips are lilies
that drip flowing myrrh.
14 His arms are rods of gold
adorned with gems;
His loins, a work of ivory
covered with sapphires.
15 His legs, pillars of alabaster,
resting on golden pedestals.

woman may be the speaker of 16a, as it is she who issues the invitation of 16b. **His garden**: the woman herself.

**5:1 Eat . . . lovers**: the translation and meaning are uncertain.

**5:2–8** An experience of anticipation and loss similar to that in 3:1–5. The lover's abrupt appearance resembles that in 2:8–9.

**5:3 Robe**: knee-length undergarment worn by men and women. **Am I then . . . ?**: the woman's refusal is a form of gentle teasing; that she does not really reject her lover is shown by her actions in vv. 5–6. See 1:7–8; 2:14–15, for other teasing interchanges.

**5:4 My innermost being**: lit., "innards." In Gn 25:23, Is 49:1; Ps 71:6, the word appears to carry the meaning of "womb."

**5:6** The motif of the locked-out lover is common in classical Greek and Latin poetry.

**5:7 The watchmen**: they do not know the reason for the woman's appearance in the city streets; cf. 3:2–4.

**5:10–11** In answer to the question of 5:9 the woman sings her lover's praises (vv. 10–16). **Ruddy**: also used of David (1 Sm 16:12; 17:42). **Gold**: indicates how precious the lover is. **Palm fronds**: his thick, luxuriant growth of hair.

**5:12 Sitting . . .** : the translation of this line is uncertain; it may continue the metaphor of the lover's eyes, or refer to another part of his anatomy (e.g., teeth) which has been omitted from the text.

*v*: Sg 6:2. *w*: Sg 3:1–2. *x*: Sg 2:7; 8:4.

His appearance, like the Lebanon,
imposing as the cedars.
16 His mouth is sweetness itself;
he is delightful in every way.
Such is my lover, and such my friend,
Daughters of Jerusalem!

## CHAPTER 6

See RG 187–92

### *The Lost Lover Found*

*D* 1 Where has your lover gone,
most beautiful among women?
Where has your lover withdrawn
that we may seek him with you?*
*W* 2 *y* My lover has come down to his
garden,*
to the beds of spices,
To feed in the gardens
and to gather lilies.
3 *z* I belong to my lover, and my lover
belongs to me;
he feeds among the lilies.

### *The Beauty of the Woman*

*M* 4 Beautiful as Tirzah are you, my friend;*
fair as Jerusalem,
fearsome as celestial visions!
5 *a* Turn your eyes away from me,
for they stir me up.
Your hair is like a flock of goats
streaming down from Gilead.
6 *b* Your teeth are like a flock of ewes
that come up from the washing,
All of them big with twins,
none of them barren.
7 Like pomegranate halves,
your cheeks behind your veil.
8 Sixty are the queens, eighty the
concubines,
and young women without number—
9 One alone* is my dove, my perfect one,
her mother's special one,
favorite of the one who bore her.
Daughters see her and call her happy,
queens and concubines, and they
praise her:
10 *c* "Who* is this that comes forth like
the dawn,
beautiful as the white moon, pure as
the blazing sun,
fearsome as celestial visions?"

### *Love's Meeting*

*W* 11 *d* To the walnut grove* I went down,
to see the young growth of the
valley;
To see if the vines were in bloom,
if the pomegranates had blossomed.
12 Before I knew it, my desire had made
me
the blessed one of the prince's
people.*

## CHAPTER 7

See RG 187–92

### *The Beauty of the Beloved*

*D?* 1 Turn, turn, O Shulammite!*
turn, turn that we may gaze upon
you!
*W* How can you gaze upon the
Shulammite
as at the dance of the two camps?

**6:1** The Daughters of Jerusalem are won by this description of the lover and offer their aid in seeking him (cf. 5:6, 9).

**6:2–3** The woman implies here that she had never really lost her lover, for he has come down to his garden (cf. 2:16; 4:5). **Feed . . . lilies**: the imagery here evokes both a shepherd pasturing his flocks and erotic play between the lovers (2:16; 4:5, 12, 16).

**6:4–9** The man again celebrates the woman's beauty. **Tirzah**: probably meaning "pleasant"; it was the early capital of the Northern Kingdom of Israel (1 Kgs 16). **Celestial visions**: the meaning is uncertain. Military images may be implied here, i.e., the "heavenly hosts" who fight along with God on Israel's behalf (cf. Jgs 5:20), or perhaps a reference to the awesome goddesses of the region who combined aspects of both fertility and war.

**6:9 One alone**: the incomparability of the woman is a favorite motif in love poetry.

**6:10 "Who . . . "**: the speakers may be the women of vv. 8–9. **Moon . . . sun**: lit., "the white" and "the hot," respectively (cf. Is 24:23; 30:26). **Fearsome**: see note on 6:4–9.

**6:11 Walnut grove**: also a site of activity in a wedding hymn of the Syrian moon goddess Nikkal (cf. the woman compared to the moon in v. 10).

**6:12** The text is obscure in Hebrew and in the ancient versions. The Vulgate reads: "I did not know; my soul disturbed me because of the chariots of Aminadab." Based on a parallel in Jgs 5:24, "chariots" is here emended to "blessed one."

**7:1 Shulammite**: the woman is so designated because she is considered to be from Shulam (or Shunem) in the plain of Esdraelon (cf. 1 Kgs 1:3), or because the name may mean "the peaceful one," and thus recall the name of Solomon. **Turn**: she is asked to face the speaker(s). **How . . .** : she refuses to be regarded as a spectacle ("the dance of the two camps" is unknown). Some interpret the episode as an invitation to her to dance.

*y:* Sg 4:12; 5:1. *z:* Sg 2:16; 7:11. *a:* Sg 4:9. *b:* Sg 4:1–3. *c:* Sg 3:6; 8:5. *d:* Sg 4:12–5:1; 7:13.

M [2] How beautiful are your feet in sandals,*
O noble daughter!
Your curving thighs like jewels,
the product of skilled hands.
[3] Your valley,* a round bowl
that should never lack mixed wine.
Your belly, a mound of wheat,
encircled with lilies.
[4] [e] Your breasts are like two fawns,
twins of a gazelle.
[5] [f] Your neck like a tower of ivory;
your eyes, pools in Heshbon
by the gate of Bath-rabbim.
Your nose like the tower of Lebanon
that looks toward Damascus.*
[6] Your head rises upon you like Carmel;*
your hair is like purple;
a king is caught in its locks.

### *Love's Desires*

[7] How beautiful you are, how fair,
my love, daughter of delights!
[8] Your very form resembles a date-palm,*
and your breasts, clusters.
[9] I thought, "Let me climb the date-palm!
Let me take hold of its branches!
Let your breasts be like clusters of the
vine
and the fragrance of your breath like
apples,
[10] And your mouth like the best wine—
W that flows down smoothly for my
lover,
gliding* over my lips and teeth.
[11] [g] I belong to my lover,*
his yearning is for me.
[12] Come, my lover! Let us go out to the
fields,
let us pass the night among the henna.
[13] [h] Let us go early to the vineyards, and
see
if the vines are in bloom,
If the buds have opened,
if the pomegranates have blossomed;
There will I give you my love.
[14] The mandrakes* give forth fragrance,
and over our doors are all choice
fruits;
Fruits both fresh and dried, my lover,
have I kept in store for you.

## CHAPTER 8

See RG 187–92

[1] Would that you were a brother
to me,
nursed at my mother's breasts!
If I met you out of doors, I would kiss
you
and none would despise me.
[2] [i] I would lead you, bring you to my
mother's house,
where you would teach me,
Where I would give you to drink
spiced wine, my pomegranate* juice.
[3] [j] His left hand is under my head,
and his right arm embraces me.
[4] [k] I adjure you, Daughters of Jerusalem,
do not awaken or stir up love
until it is ready!

### *The Return from the Desert*

D? [5] [l] Who is this coming up from the
desert,

**7:2–6** Another description of the woman's charms. **Sandals**: the woman's sandaled foot was apparently considered quite seductive (Jdt 16:9). **Noble**: a possible connection to the enigmatic "prince" of 6:12. **Curving . . . jewels**: the meaning of these Hebrew words is not certain. Wine and wheat suggest fertility.

**7:3 Valley**: lit., navel; a discreet allusion to her sex.

**7:5** The comparison emphasizes the stateliness of her neck, and the clarity of her eyes. **Bath-rabbim**: a proper name which occurs only here; there was a city of Rabbah northeast of Heshbon in Transjordan. Cf. Jer 49:3.

**7:6 Carmel**: a prominent set of cliffs overlooking the Mediterranean.

**7:8–9 Date-palm**: a figure of stateliness. The lover is eager to enjoy the possession of his beloved.

**7:10 Gliding**: the beloved interrupts her partner's compliment by referring to the intoxication of their union. The translation rests on an emendation of the enigmatic "the lips of the sleepers."

**7:11–14** The woman's answer assures him of her love, and invites him to return with her to the rural delights associated with their love (cf. also 6:11–12). **Yearning**: used only here and in Gn 3:16; 4:7. The dependency and subordination of woman to man presented as a consequence of sin in the Genesis story is here transcended in the mutuality of true love.

**7:14 Mandrakes**: herbs believed to have power to arouse love and promote fertility; cf. Gn 30:14–16.

**8:2 Wine . . . pomegranate**: sexual connotations are implied, since the root "drink" (*shaqah*) is a wordplay on "kiss" (*nashaq*) in v. 1; cf. 1:2.

---

*e:* Sg 4:5. *f:* Sg 4:4. *g:* Sg 2:16; 6:3. *h:* Sg 6:11. *i:* Sg 3:4. *j:* Sg 2:6. *k:* Sg 2:7; 3:5. *l:* Sg 3:6; 6:10.

leaning upon her lover?

W Beneath the apple tree I awakened
you;*
there your mother conceived you;
there she who bore you conceived.

### *True Love*

6 Set me as a seal* upon your heart,
as a seal upon your arm;
For Love is strong as Death,
longing is fierce as Sheol.
Its arrows are arrows of fire,
flames of the divine.
7 m Deep waters* cannot quench love,
nor rivers sweep it away.
Were one to offer all the wealth of his
house for love,
he would be utterly despised.

### *An Answer to the Brothers*

W 8 "We have a little sister;*
she has no breasts as yet.
What shall we do for our sister
on the day she is spoken for?
9 If she is a wall,
we will build upon her a silver
turret;
But if she is a door,
we will board her up with cedar
planks."
10 I am a wall,*
and my breasts are like towers.
I became in his eyes
as one who brings peace.

### *A Boast*

M? 11 Solomon had a vineyard at
Baal-hamon;*
he gave over the vineyard to
caretakers.
For its fruit one would have to pay
a thousand silver pieces.
12 My vineyard is at my own disposal;
the thousand pieces are for you,
Solomon,
and two hundred for the caretakers
of its fruit.

### *The Lovers' Yearnings*

M 13 You who dwell in the gardens,*
my companions are listening for
your voice—
let me hear it!
W 14 n Swiftly, my lover,
be like a gazelle or a young stag
upon the mountains of spices.

**8:5 Awakened you**: the speakers in this verse are difficult to identify. Someone (the poet? Daughters?) hails the couple in v. 5a. According to the Masoretic vocalization, the woman is the speaker in v. 5b.

**8:6 Seal**: this could be worn bound to the arm, as here, or suspended at the neck, or as a ring (Jer 22:24). It was used for identification and signatures. **Strong . . . fierce**: in human experience, Death and Sheol are inevitable, unrelenting; in the end they always triumph. Love, which is just as certain of its victory, matches its strength against the natural enemies of life; waters cannot extinguish it nor floods carry it away. It is more priceless than all riches. **Flames of the divine**: the Hebrew is difficult: the short form (-Yah) of the divine name Yhwh found here may associate love with the Lord, or it may be acting as a superlative—i.e., god-sized flames.

**8:7 Deep waters**: often used to designate chaos (Ps 93:4; 144:7; Is 17:12–13; Hb 3:15). The fires of love cannot be extinguished, even by waters of chaos. **Wealth**: love cannot be bought.

**8:8–9** The woman quotes the course of action her elder brothers had decided on. While she is yet immature, they will shelter her in view of eventual marriage. **Wall . . . door**: if she is virtuous, she will be honored; if she is not, she will be kept under strict vigilance. **Silver turret**: a precious ornament.

**8:10** In reply to the officious and meddling attitude of the brothers, she answers with their terms: she is mature ("wall," "towers"). **Brings peace**: or, "finds peace."

**8:11–12** These enigmatic verses have been variously interpreted, depending on who is taken to be the speaker. In v. 11, if the woman, she boasts that she is a vineyard of great value. If the man, he boasts over his possession of her.

**8:13–14** As in 2:14, her lover asks for a word or a song and she replies in words similar to those found in 2:17.

---

*m:* Prv 6:31. *n:* Sg 2:9, 17; 4:6.

See RG 192–97

# The Book of Wisdom

The Book of Wisdom was written about fifty years before the coming of Christ. Its author, whose name is not known to us, was probably a member of the Jewish community at Alexandria, in Egypt. He wrote in Greek, in a style patterned on that of Hebrew verse. At times he speaks in the person of Solomon, placing his teachings on the lips of the wise king of Hebrew tradition in order to emphasize their value. His profound knowledge of the earlier Old Testament writings is reflected in almost every line of the book, and marks him, like Ben Sira, as an outstanding representative of religious devotion and learning among the sages of postexilic Judaism.

The primary purpose of the author was the edification of his co-religionists in a time when they had experienced suffering and oppression, in part at least at the hands of apostate fellow Jews. To convey his message he made use of the most popular religious themes of his time, namely the splendor and worth of divine wisdom (6:22–11:1), the glorious events of the exodus (11:2–16; 12:23–27; 15:18–19:22), God's mercy (11:17–12:22), the folly of idolatry (13:1–15:17), and the manner in which God's justice operates in rewarding or punishing the individual (1:1–6:21). The first ten chapters in particular provide background for the teaching of Jesus and for some New Testament theology about Jesus. Many passages from this section of the book, notably 3:1–8, are used by the church in the liturgy.

The principal divisions of the Book of Wisdom are:

I. The Reward of Righteousness (1:1–6:21).
II. Praise of Wisdom by Solomon (6:22–11:1).
III. Special Providence of God During the Exodus (11:2–16; 12:23–27; 15:18–19:22) with digressions on God's mercy (11:17–12:22) and on the folly and shame of idolatry (13:1–15:17).

---

## I. The Reward of Righteousness*

### CHAPTER 1

See RG 194–95

***Exhortation to Righteousness, the Key to Life***

1 Love righteousness,* you who judge the earth;[a]
think of the LORD in goodness,
and seek him in integrity of heart;[b]
2 Because he is found by those who do not test him,
and manifests himself to those who do not disbelieve him.[c]
3 For perverse counsels separate people from God,
and his power, put to the proof, rebukes the foolhardy;[d]
4 * Because into a soul that plots evil wisdom does not enter,
nor does she dwell in a body under debt of sin.[e]
5 For the holy spirit of discipline* flees deceit
and withdraws from senseless counsels
and is rebuked when unrighteousness occurs.[f]
6 For wisdom is a kindly spirit,
yet she does not acquit blasphemous lips;

**1:1–6:21** The reward is the gift of immortality, to the righteous (1:15; 3:1–3), but not to the wicked (5:1–13). Contrasts between these two groups dominate chaps. 1–5. The philosophy of the wicked and their persecution of the righteous are dramatically presented in 1:16–2:24. New light is shed on the suffering of the righteous (3:1–9), childlessness (3:13–15), and premature death (4:7–16)—in contrast to the fate of the wicked (3:10–12, 16–19; 4:3–6, 17–20).

**1:1 Righteousness**: not merely the cardinal virtue of justice (cf. 8:7), but the universal moral quality which is the application of wisdom to moral conduct. **You who judge**: "judges" and "kings" (cf. 6:1) are addressed in accordance with the literary customs of the times and with the putative Solomonic authorship, but the real audience is the Jewish community.

**1:4** In these verses personified Wisdom is identified with the spirit of the Lord; so also in 9:17.

**1:5 Discipline**: here and elsewhere, another name for Wisdom.

*a:* 1 Chr 29:17; Ps 2:10; Is 26:9. *b:* Sir 1:25. *c:* 1 Chr 28:9. *d:* Is 59:2. *e:* Sir 15:7–8; Rom 7:14. *f:* Is 63:10.

THE AUTHOR ASSUMES that human beings are composed of two parts, the *body* and the *soul* (1:4). Such an assumption is different from the traditional view of the Hebrew Bible about the nature of human beings, in which the human person is understood as an integrated whole; souls and bodies cannot exist apart from one another. The philosophical position that there are two separate, underlying aspects of reality, neither of which can be derived from the other, is called "dualism." Body/soul dualism developed from a more fundamental dualism common in Platonic thought: The substance of spiritual things is completely different from that of matter. A person's physical body consists of matter, while a soul exists as a nonmaterial substance that is potentially imperishable.

Because God is the witness of the inmost
self[g]
and the sure observer of the heart
and the listener to the tongue.[h]
7 For the spirit of the LORD fills the
world,[i]
is all-embracing, and knows whatever
is said.
8 Therefore those who utter wicked things
will not go unnoticed,
nor will chastising condemnation pass
them by.[j]
9 For the devices of the wicked shall be
scrutinized,
and the sound of their words shall
reach the LORD,
for the chastisement of their
transgressions;
10 Because a jealous ear hearkens to
everything,[k]
and discordant grumblings are not
secret.
11 Therefore guard against profitless
grumbling,
and from calumny* withhold your
tongues;
For a stealthy utterance will not go
unpunished,
and a lying mouth destroys the soul.
12 Do not court death* by your erring way
of life,
nor draw to yourselves destruction by
the works of your hands.
13 Because God did not make death,[l]
nor does he rejoice in the destruction
of the living.
14 For he fashioned all things that they
might have being,
and the creatures of the world are
wholesome;
There is not a destructive drug among
them
nor any domain of Hades* on earth,
15 For righteousness is undying.* [m]

### *The Wicked Reject Immortality and Righteousness Alike*

16 It was the wicked who with hands and
words invited death,
considered it a friend, and pined for it,
and made a covenant with it,
Because they deserve to be allied
with it.[n]

## CHAPTER 2

See RG 194–95

1 For, not thinking rightly, they
said among themselves:*
"Brief and troubled is our lifetime;[o]
there is no remedy for our dying,
nor is anyone known to have come
back from Hades.
2 For by mere chance were we born,

**1:11 Calumny**: speech against God and divine providence is meant.

**1:12 Death**: as will become clear, the author is not speaking of physical death but of spiritual death, the eternal separation from God.

**1:14 Hades**: the Greek term for the Hebrew Sheol, the dwelling place of the dead.

**1:15 Undying**: immortality is not seen as an innate quality of the soul but as a gift of God to the righteous.

**2:1–20** In this speech the wicked deny survival after death and indeed invite death by their evil deeds.

*g:* Jer 17:10. *h:* Jer 23:24–25. *i:* Wis 12:1. *j:* Prv 19:5. *k:* Nm 14:27–28. *l:* Ez 18:32; 33:11; 2 Pt 3:9. *m:* Is 51:6–8. *n:* Is 28:15. *o:* Jb 14:1; 7:9.

**Covenant with Death**

IN CH 1, V. 16, the author employs a rhetorical device from Hellenistic diatribe, a popular genre of the era intended for pedagogical purposes. The diatribe typically included dialogue with imaginary opponents. In this case the opponents represent those who deny that humans are immortal.

and hereafter we shall be as though we
had not been;
Because the breath in our nostrils is
smoke,
and reason a spark from the beating of
our hearts,
3 And when this is quenched, our body
will be ashes
and our spirit will be poured abroad
like empty air.[p]
4 Even our name will be forgotten in time,
and no one will recall our deeds.
So our life will pass away like the traces
of a cloud,
and will be dispersed like a mist
Pursued by the sun's rays
and overpowered by its heat.
5 For our lifetime is the passing of a shadow;
and our dying cannot be deferred
because it is fixed with a seal; and no
one returns.[q]
6 Come, therefore, let us enjoy the good
things that are here,
and make use of creation with youthful
zest.[r]
7 Let us have our fill of costly wine and
perfumes,
and let no springtime blossom pass
us by;
8 let us crown ourselves with rosebuds
before they wither.
9 Let no meadow be free from our
wantonness;
everywhere let us leave tokens of our
merriment,
for this is our portion, and this our lot.[s]
10 Let us oppress the righteous poor;
let us neither spare the widow
nor revere the aged for hair grown
white with time.[t]
11 But let our strength be our norm of
righteousness;
for weakness proves itself useless.
12 * Let us lie in wait for the righteous one,
because he is annoying to us;
he opposes our actions,
Reproaches us for transgressions of the
law*
and charges us with violations of our
training.[u]
13 He professes to have knowledge of God
and styles himself a child of the LORD.[v]
14 To us he is the censure of our thoughts;
merely to see him is a hardship for us,[w]
15 Because his life is not like that of others,
and different are his ways.
16 He judges us debased;
he holds aloof from our paths as from
things impure.
He calls blest the destiny of the righteous
and boasts that God is his Father.[x]
17 Let us see whether his words be true;
let us find out what will happen to him
in the end.[y]
18 For if the righteous one is the son of
God, God will help him
and deliver him from the hand of his
foes.[z]
19 With violence and torture let us put him
to the test
that we may have proof of his gentleness
and try his patience.
20 Let us condemn him to a shameful death;

**2:12–5:23** From 2:12 to 5:23 the author draws heavily on Is 52–62, setting forth his teaching in a series of characters or types taken from Isaiah and embellished with additional details from other texts. The description of the "righteous one" in 2:12–20 seems to undergird the New Testament passion narrative.

**2:12 Law**: the law of Moses; "training" has the same meaning.

*p:* Jb 7:9; Jas 4:14. *q:* Ps 144:4. *r:* Is 22:13; 1 Cor 15:32. *s:* Jer 13:25. *t:* Ex 22:21–23; Lv 19:32. *u:* Hos 8:1. *v:* Mt 27:43; Jn 8:55; 10:36–39. *w:* Mt 9:4. *x:* Jer 6:30. *y:* Gn 37:20. *z:* Ps 22:9; Is 42:1; Mt 27:43; Jn 5:18.

for according to his own words, God
will take care of him."[a]

[21] These were their thoughts, but they erred;
for their wickedness blinded them,[b]
[22] * And they did not know the hidden
counsels of God;
neither did they count on a
recompense for holiness
nor discern the innocent souls' reward.[c]
[23] For God formed us to be imperishable;
the image of his own nature he
made us.[d]
[24] But by the envy* of the devil, death
entered the world,
and they who are allied with him
experience it.[e]

## CHAPTER 3

See RG 194–95

### *The Hidden Counsels of God**

#### *A. On Suffering**

[1] The souls of the righteous are in the hand
of God,[f]
and no torment shall touch them.
[2] They seemed, in the view of the foolish,
to be dead;
and their passing away was thought an
affliction
[3] and their going forth from us, utter
destruction.
But they are in peace.[g]
[4] For if to others, indeed, they seem
punished,
yet is their hope full of immortality;
[5] Chastised a little, they shall be greatly
blessed,
because God tried them
and found them worthy of himself.[h]
[6] As gold in the furnace, he proved them,
and as sacrificial offerings* he took
them to himself.[i]
[7] In the time of their judgment* they shall
shine
and dart about as sparks through
stubble;[j]
[8] They shall judge nations and rule over
peoples,
and the LORD shall be their King
forever.[k]
[9] Those who trust in him shall understand
truth,
and the faithful shall abide with him in
love:
Because grace and mercy are with his
holy ones,[l]
and his care is with the elect.
[10] But the wicked shall receive a punishment
to match their thoughts,*
since they neglected righteousness and
forsook the LORD.
[11] For those who despise wisdom and
instruction are doomed.[m]
Vain is their hope, fruitless their labors,
and worthless their works.[n]
[12] Their wives are foolish and their children
wicked,
accursed their brood.[o]

#### *B. On Childlessness**

[13] Yes, blessed is she who, childless and
undefiled,
never knew transgression of the
marriage bed;

**2:22** This verse announces the subject of the next section.

**2:24 Envy**: perhaps because Adam was in the image of God or because Adam had control over all creation. **Devil**: the first biblical text to equate the serpent of Gn 3 with the devil.

**3:1–4:19** The central section of chaps. 1–6. The author begins by stating that immortality is the reward of the righteous, and then in the light of that belief comments on three points of the traditional discussion of the problem of retribution (suffering, childlessness, early death) each of which was often seen as a divine punishment.

**3:1–12** The author affirms that, for the righteous, sufferings are not punishments but purification and opportunities to show fidelity, whereas for the wicked suffering is truly a punishment.

**3:6 Offerings**: the image is that of the burnt offering, in which the victim is completely consumed by fire.

**3:7 Judgment**: the Greek *episkopē* is God's loving judgment of those who have been faithful to him; the same word is used in 14:11 for the punishment of the wicked at God's judgment. Cf. also v. 13.

**3:10 To match their thoughts**: a fate as empty as that which they describe in 2:1–5.

**3:13–4:6** The true fruit of life is not children but virtue which leads to immortality. The many children of the wicked will be a disappointing fruit.

*a:* Jas 5:6. *b:* Rom 1:21. *c:* Ps 18:24–25; Prv 11:18; Mt 11:25. *d:* Gn 1:26–27; Is 54:16 LXX. *e:* Gn 3:1–24; Rom 5:12. *f:* Jb 12:10. *g:* Is 57:2. *h:* Tb 12:13; 2 Cor 4:17; 1 Pt 1:6–7. *i:* Ps 51:19; Prv 17:3; Sir 2:5; Is 48:10. *j:* Dn 12:3; Ob 18; Mal 3:3; Mt 13:43. *k:* Wis 8:14; Prv 8:16; Dn 7:22; 1 Cor 6:2; Rev 20:4. *l:* Wis 4:15; Jb 10:12; Jn 15:10. *m:* Prv 1:7. *n:* Sir 41:8. *o:* Dt 28:18.

## Childlessness

IN WIS 3:13 to 4:6 the author offers an impassioned diatribe against the traditional devaluation of childlessness. The inability to bear children was typically regarded as a curse and was grounds for a husband to divorce his wife. In traditional Israelite religion, the continuation of one's family line through one's progeny constitutes a form of immortality. Because the author of the Wisdom of Solomon advocates a belief in immortality for righteous individuals, producing heirs becomes less important.

for she shall bear fruit at the judgment
of souls.*
14 So also the eunuch whose hand wrought
no misdeed,
who held no wicked thoughts against
the LORD—
For he shall be given fidelity's choice
reward*
and a more gratifying heritage in the
LORD's temple.[p]
15 For the fruit of noble struggles is a
glorious one;
and unfailing is the root of
understanding.* [q]
16 But the children of adulterers* will
remain without issue,
and the progeny of an unlawful bed
will disappear.[r]
17 For should they attain long life, they will
be held in no esteem,
and dishonored will their old age be in
the end;
18 Should they die abruptly, they will have
no hope
nor comfort in the day of scrutiny;
19 for dire is the end of the wicked
generation.[s]

### CHAPTER 4

See RG 194–95

1 Better is childlessness with virtue;
for immortal is the memory of virtue,
acknowledged both by God and
human beings.[t]
2 When it is present people imitate it,
and they long for it when it is gone;
Forever it marches crowned in triumph,
victorious in unsullied deeds of valor.
3 But the numerous progeny of the wicked
shall be of no avail;
their spurious offshoots shall not strike
deep root
nor take firm hold.[u]
4 For even though their branches flourish
for a time,
they are unsteady and shall be rocked
by the wind
and, by the violence of the winds,
uprooted;[v]
5 Their twigs shall be broken off untimely,
their fruit useless, unripe for eating,
fit for nothing.
6 For children born of lawless unions
give evidence of the wickedness of
their parents, when they are
examined.

### *C. On Early Death**

7 But the righteous one, though he die
early, shall be at rest.[w]
8 For the age that is honorable comes not
with the passing of time,[x]
nor can it be measured in terms of years.
9 Rather, understanding passes for gray hair,
and an unsullied life is the attainment
of old age.
10 * The one who pleased God was loved,[y]

**3:13** See vv. 7–9.

**3:14 Fidelity's choice reward**: cf. Is 56:1–8. **More gratifying**: better than sons and daughters; cf. Is 56:5.

**3:15 Root of understanding**: the root that is understanding (wisdom).

**3:16 Adulterers**: understood here as a type of sinners in general; cf. Is 57:3–5.

**4:7–19** Early death is not a punishment for the righteous because genuine old age is the attainment of perfection and early death is a preservation from corruption. The old age and death of the wicked, however, will not be honorable.

**4:10–11** There are allusions here to Enoch (Gn 5:21–24), who was young by patriarchal standards, and to Lot (Gn 19:10–11; 2 Pt 2:7–8). Cf. also Is 57:1–2.

*p:* Is 56:2–5. *q:* Sir 1:18. *r:* 2 Sm 12:14. *s:* Ps 34:22. *t:* Prv 3:3–4; Sir 16:1–3. *u:* Sir 23:25. *v:* Sir 40:15; Is 40:24. *w:* Wis 3:3. *x:* Jb 12:12; 32:9; Sir 25:4–6. *y:* Gn 5:24; Sir 44:16; Heb 11:5.

living among sinners, was
transported—
11 Snatched away, lest wickedness pervert
his mind
or deceit beguile his soul;[z]
12 For the witchery of paltry things
obscures what is right
and the whirl of desire transforms the
innocent mind.[a]
13 Having become perfect in a short while,
he reached the fullness of a long
career;
14 for his soul was pleasing to the LORD,
therefore he sped him out of the midst
of wickedness.[b]
But the people saw and did not
understand,
nor did they take that consideration
into account.*
16 Yes, the righteous one who has died will
condemn
the sinful who live;
And youth, swiftly completed, will
condemn
the many years of the unrighteous who
have grown old.[c]
17 For they will see the death of the wise
one
and will not understand what the LORD
intended,
or why he kept him safe.
18 They will see, and hold him in contempt;
but the LORD will laugh them to scorn.[d]
19 And they shall afterward become
dishonored corpses[e]
and an unceasing mockery among the
dead.
For he shall strike them down speechless
and prostrate[f]
and rock them to their foundations;
They shall be utterly laid waste
and shall be in grief
and their memory shall perish.

### *The Judgment of the Wicked*

20 Fearful shall they come, at the counting
up of their sins,
and their lawless deeds shall convict
them to their face.

## CHAPTER 5

See RG 194–95

1 * Then shall the righteous one with
great assurance confront[g]
his oppressors who set at nought his
labors.[h]
2 Seeing this, the wicked shall be shaken
with dreadful fear,
and be amazed at the unexpected
salvation.
3 They shall say among themselves, rueful
and groaning through anguish of spirit:
"This is the one whom once we held as a
laughingstock
and as a type for mockery,
4 fools that we were!
His life we accounted madness,
and death dishonored.
5 See how he is accounted among the
heavenly beings;*
how his lot is with the holy ones![i]
6 We, then, have strayed from the way of
truth,[j]
and the light of righteousness did not
shine for us,
and the sun did not rise for us.[k]
7 We were entangled in the thorns of
mischief and of ruin;
we journeyed through trackless
deserts,
but the way of the LORD we never
knew.
8 What did our pride avail us?
What have wealth and its boastfulness
afforded us?[l]
9 All of them passed like a shadow
and like a fleeting rumor;[m]
10 Like a ship traversing the heaving water:

**4:14** Verse 15 is omitted because it repeats the last two lines of 3:9.

**5:1–13** In contrast to their speech in chap. 2 the wicked now regret their assessment of life and righteousness.

**5:5 Heavenly beings**: lit., "sons of God." These are the holy ones, members of the heavenly court, among whom the righteous are to be found. A bodily resurrection does not seem to be envisioned.

*z:* Is 57:1–2. *a:* Wis 2:21; Dn 13:9. *b:* Gn 19:22, 29; 2 Pt 2:7. *c:* Mt 12:41–42. *d:* Ps 37:13. *e:* Neh 1:10 LXX; Ps 18:8; Is 14:19; Jer 23:39–40. *f:* 2 Mc 3:29. *g:* 2 Thes 1:6–7. *h:* Col 2:15. *i:* Acts 26:18; Col 1:12. *j:* Prv 4:18–19; Jn 12:35. *k:* Prv 22:5; Is 59:6–14. *l:* Ps 49:7; Prv 10:2. *m:* 1 Chr 20:15; Jb 9:25–26 LXX; Ps 144:4.

when it has passed, no trace can be
found,
no path of its keel in the waves.
11 Or like a bird flying through the air;
no evidence of its course is to be
found—
But the fluid air, lashed by the beating of
pinions,
and cleft by the rushing force
Of speeding wings, is traversed;
and afterward no mark of passage can
be found in it.
12 Or as, when an arrow has been shot at a
mark,
the parted air straightway flows
together again
so that none discerns the way it went—
13 Even so, once born, we abruptly came to
nought
and held no sign of virtue to display,
but were consumed in our wickedness."[n]

14 * Yes, the hope of the wicked is like chaff
borne by the wind,
and like fine, storm-driven snow;
Like smoke scattered by the wind,
and like the passing memory of the
nomad camping for a single day.[o]
15 But the righteous live forever,
and in the LORD is their recompense,
and the thought of them is with the
Most High.[p]
16 Therefore shall they receive the splendid
crown,
the beautiful diadem, from the hand of
the LORD,
For he will shelter them with his right
hand,
and protect them with his arm.[q]
17 He shall take his zeal for armor[r]
and arm creation to requite the enemy,
18 Shall put on righteousness for a
breastplate,
wear sure judgment for a helmet,
19 Shall take invincible holiness for a
shield,[s]
20 and sharpen his sudden anger for a
sword.
The universe will war with him against
the foolhardy;
21 Well-aimed bolts of lightning will go
forth
and from the clouds will leap to the
mark as from a well-drawn bow;[t]
22 and as from a sling, wrathful
hailstones shall be hurled.
The waters of the sea will be enraged
and flooding rivers will overwhelm
them;[u]
23 A mighty wind will confront them
and winnow them like a tempest;
Thus lawlessness will lay waste the
whole earth
and evildoing overturn the thrones of
the mighty.[v]

## CHAPTER 6

### *Exhortation to Seek Wisdom**

See RG 194–95

1 Hear, therefore, kings, and understand;[w]
learn, you magistrates* of the earth's
expanse!
2 Give ear, you who have power over
multitudes
and lord it over throngs of peoples!
3 Because authority was given you by the
Lord
and sovereignty by the Most High,
who shall probe your works and
scrutinize your counsels![x]
4 Because, though you were ministers of
his kingdom, you did not judge
rightly,
and did not keep the law,*
nor walk according to the will of God,
5 Terribly and swiftly he shall come
against you,

**5:14–23** A picture of the reward of the righteous which develops into an apocalyptic description of the divine warrior's destruction of evil. The author utilizes Is 59–62.

**6:1–21** The first part of the book closes with an exhortation comparable to 1:1–15, and it leads into "Solomon's" personal comments on wisdom in chaps. 7–9.

**6:1 Kings . . . magistrates**: note the inclusion with v. 21 ("kings"). The address to earthly powers is in accord with the opening (1:1), but the true audience remains the Jewish community.

**6:4 Law**: that of Moses; cf. 2:12; 6:10.

*n:* Ez 33:10. *o:* Jb 21:18; Ps 1:4; 37:20; Is 17:13. *p:* Is 62:11; Ez 18:9. *q:* Ex 33:22; Is 62:3; 2 Tm 4:8; 1 Pt 5:4. *r:* Is 59:17. *s:* Dt 32:40–43. *t:* Hb 3:9–11. *u:* Dt 11:4. *v:* Wis 11:20; Sir 10:13–14. *w:* Wis 1:1; Ps 2:10; Sir 33:19; Mi 3:1, 9. *x:* 2 Chr 36:23; Prv 8:15–16; Jn 19:11; Rom 13:1.

DESCRIPTIONS OF WISDOM personified as a female figure, "Sophia," such as in Wis 6:12–21, are common in wisdom literature (e.g., see Prv 8; Sir 1:1–10; 24:1–22). Both the Greek word *sophia* and the Hebrew word *hokhma,* meaning "wisdom," are feminine.

because severe judgment awaits the exalted—
6 For the lowly may be pardoned out of mercy[y]
but the mighty shall be mightily put to the test.
7 For the Ruler of all shows no partiality,
nor does he fear greatness,[z]
Because he himself made the great as well as the small,
and provides for all alike;
8 but for those in power a rigorous scrutiny impends.
9 To you, therefore, O princes, are my words addressed[a]
that you may learn wisdom and that you may not fall away.
10 For those who keep the holy precepts hallowed will be found holy,
and those learned in them will have ready a response.*
11 Desire therefore my words;
long for them and you will be instructed.

12 Resplendent and unfading is Wisdom,
and she is readily perceived by those who love her,
and found by those who seek her.[b]
13 She hastens to make herself known to those who desire her;[c]
14 one who watches for her at dawn will not be disappointed,
for she will be found sitting at the gate.
15 For setting your heart on her is the perfection of prudence,
and whoever keeps vigil for her is quickly free from care;
16 Because she makes her rounds, seeking those worthy of her,
and graciously appears to them on the way,
and goes to meet them with full attention.[d]
17 * For the first step toward Wisdom is an earnest desire for discipline;[e]
18 then, care for discipline is love of her;
love means the keeping of her laws;
To observe her laws is the basis for incorruptibility;
19 and incorruptibility makes one close to God;
20 thus the desire for Wisdom leads to a kingdom.
21 If, then, you find pleasure in throne and scepter, you princes of peoples,
honor Wisdom, that you may reign as kings forever.

## II. Praise of Wisdom by Solomon*

### *Introduction*

22 Now what wisdom is, and how she came to be I shall proclaim;
and I shall conceal no secrets from you,
But from the very beginning I shall search out
and bring to light knowledge of her;
I shall not diverge from the truth.[f]
23 Neither shall I admit consuming jealousy to my company,
because that can have no fellowship with Wisdom.[g]
24 A multitude of the wise is the safety of the world,

**6:10 Response**: a suitable plea before the great Judge. Cf. Prv 22:21; Jb 31:14; Hb 2:1; Sir 8:9.

**6:17–20** This type of reasoning approximates the rhetorical sorites, a series of statements in which the predicate of each becomes the subject of the next. Cf. Rom 5:3–5.

**6:22–9:18** In these verses the author identifies with Solomon (without mentioning that name anywhere), and praises the beauty of Wisdom, describing how he sought her out. Thus the readers of the book can find a model in their search for Wisdom.

*y:* Lk 12:48. *z:* Dt 1:17; Prv 22:2. *a:* Dt 4:10; Ps 2:12; Sir 32:14; 1 Jn 3:7. *b:* Wis 7:10; Prv 8:17; Jer 29:13. *c:* Prv 8:3, 17, 34. *d:* Prv 8:20–21; Sir 15:1–5. *e:* Ps 2:10–12; Prv 4:4–9; 7:1–4; 8:15–16; Dn 7:27; Jn 14:15, 21; 1 Jn 5:3. *f:* Tb 12:7, 11; Mt 13:11; Jn 15:15. *g:* Wis 7:13; Jas 3:14–15.

and a prudent king, the stability of the people;[h]
25 so take instruction from my words, to your profit.

See RG 195–96

## CHAPTER 7

### *Solomon Is Like All Others*

1 I too am a mortal, the same as all the rest,[i]
and a descendant of the first one formed of earth.*
And in my mother's womb I was molded into flesh
2 in a ten-month period*—body and blood,
from the seed of a man, and the pleasure that accompanies marriage.
3 And I too, when born, inhaled the common air,
and fell upon the kindred earth;
wailing, I uttered that first sound common to all.
4 In swaddling clothes and with constant care I was nurtured.
5 For no king has any different origin or birth;
6 one is the entry into life for all,
and in one same way they leave it.[j]

### *Solomon Prayed and Wisdom and Riches Came to Him*

7 Therefore I prayed, and prudence was given me;
I pleaded and the spirit of Wisdom came to me.[k]
8 I preferred her to scepter and throne,[l]
And deemed riches nothing in comparison with her,
9 nor did I liken any priceless gem to her;
Because all gold, in view of her, is a bit of sand,
and before her, silver is to be accounted mire.
10 Beyond health and beauty I loved her,
And I chose to have her rather than the light,
because her radiance never ceases.[m]
11 Yet all good things together came to me with her,[n]
and countless riches at her hands;
12 I rejoiced in them all, because Wisdom is their leader,
though I had not known that she is their mother.* [o]

### *Solomon Prays for Help to Speak Worthily of Wisdom*

13 Sincerely I learned about her, and ungrudgingly do I share—
her riches I do not hide away;[p]
14 For she is an unfailing treasure;
those who gain this treasure win the friendship of God,
being commended by the gifts that come from her discipline.*
15 Now God grant I speak suitably
and value these endowments at their worth:
For he is the guide of Wisdom
and the director of the wise.
16 For both we and our words are in his hand,
as well as all prudence and knowledge of crafts.[q]
17 * For he gave me sound knowledge of what exists,
that I might know the structure of the universe and the force of its elements,
18 The beginning and the end and the midpoint of times,
the changes in the sun's course and the variations of the seasons,
19 Cycles of years, positions of stars,
20 natures of living things, tempers of beasts,

**7:1 First one formed of earth**: Adam. The author omits throughout the book the proper names of the characters in sacred history of whom he speaks; see especially chap. 10.

**7:2 In a ten-month period**: ten lunar months.

**7:12 Mother**: lit., "she who begets." Although Wisdom herself is begotten of God (Prv 8:22–24), she is here the one who brings into being.

**7:14 Discipline**: cf. note on 1:5.

**7:17–22a** Wisdom teaches not only righteousness and friendship with God but also sound knowledge of the world, the universe, plants, animals and human beings. See also 1 Kgs 5:9–14; these specialties reflect Hellenistic culture.

*h:* Prv 11:14; 24:6; 29:4; Sir 10:1–5. *i:* Wis 10:1; Gn 2:7; Jb 10:9–12; 33:6; 1 Cor 15:47–49. *j:* Jb 1:21; Lk 2:12; 1 Tm 6:7–8. *k:* 1 Kgs 3:5–15; Prv 2:3–11. *l:* Wis 8:5; 1 Kgs 10:21; Jb 28:15–19; Prv 3:14–16; 8:10, 18–19. *m:* Prv 6:23. *n:* Prv 8:21. *o:* Prv 8:14–15. *p:* Wis 6:23. *q:* Wis 3:1.

Powers of the winds and thoughts of
human beings,
uses of plants and virtues of roots—
21 Whatever is hidden or plain I learned,
22 for Wisdom, the artisan of all,
taught me.[r]

### *Nature and Incomparable Dignity of Wisdom*

* For in her is a spirit
intelligent, holy, unique,
Manifold, subtle, agile,
clear, unstained, certain,
Never harmful, loving the good, keen,[s]
23 unhampered, beneficent, kindly,
Firm, secure, tranquil,
all-powerful, all-seeing,
And pervading all spirits,
though they be intelligent, pure and
very subtle.

24 For Wisdom is mobile beyond all motion,
and she penetrates and pervades all
things by reason of her purity.[t]
25 * For she is a breath of the might of God
and a pure emanation of the glory of
the Almighty;
therefore nothing defiled can enter into
her.
26 For she is the reflection of eternal light,
the spotless mirror of the power of
God,
the image of his goodness.[u]
27 Although she is one, she can do all things,
and she renews everything while
herself perduring;
Passing into holy souls from age to age,
she produces friends of God and
prophets.[v]
28 For God loves nothing so much as the
one who dwells with Wisdom.
29 For she is fairer than the sun[w]
and surpasses every constellation of
the stars.
Compared to light, she is found more
radiant;
30 though night supplants light,
wickedness does not prevail over
Wisdom.

## CHAPTER 8

See RG 195–96

1 Indeed, she spans the world from
end to end mightily
and governs all things well.[x]

### *Wisdom, the Source of Blessings*

2 Her I loved and sought after from my
youth;
I sought to take her for my bride*
and was enamored of her beauty.[y]
3 She adds to nobility the splendor of
companionship with God;
even the Ruler of all loved her.
4 For she leads into the understanding of
God,
and chooses his works.[z]
5 If riches are desirable in life,
what is richer than Wisdom, who
produces all things?[a]
6 And if prudence is at work,[b]
who in the world is a better artisan
than she?
7 Or if one loves righteousness,
whose works are virtues,
She teaches moderation and prudence,
righteousness and fortitude,*
and nothing in life is more useful than
these.
8 Or again, if one yearns for wide
experience,
she knows the things of old, and infers
the things to come.
She understands the turns of phrases and
the solutions of riddles;

**7:22b–23** The twenty-one (7 × 3) attributes of the spirit in Wisdom reflect the influence of contemporary philosophy, especially the Stoa, but the personification rests also on Prv 8:22–31 and Sir 24.

**7:25–26** Five strong metaphors underline the origins and closeness of Wisdom with God. See the use of this language in Heb 1:3; Col 1:15.

**8:2 I loved . . . my bride**: the erotic quality in the pursuit of and living with Woman Wisdom, who is the Lord's consort (9:4) and loved by him, continues throughout this chapter (vv. 16, 18). It is reflected already in Prv 4:5–9; 7:4–5. See also Sir 15:2–5; 51:13–21.

**8:7 Moderation . . . fortitude**: known also as the cardinal virtues, and recognized in Greek philosophy (Plato).

*r:* Wis 14:2; Prv 8:30. *s:* Heb 4:12–13; Jas 3:17. *t:* Wis 8:1. *u:* 2 Cor 4:4; Col 1:15; Heb 1:3. *v:* Ex 33:11; Jb 42:2; Ps 104:29; Jl 3:1. *w:* Sg 6:3, 9. *x:* Wis 7:24; 15:1. *y:* Prv 5:13–18; 8:17. *z:* Prv 8:27–31. *a:* Prv 8:18–19. *b:* Prv 8:14–15.

signs and wonders she knows in
advance
and the outcome of times and ages.[c]

### *Wisdom as Solomon's Counselor and Comfort*

9 So I determined to take her to live with me,
knowing that she would be my
counselor while all was well,
and my comfort in care and grief.
10 Because of her I have glory among the
multitudes,[d]
and esteem from the elders, though I
am but a youth.
11 I shall become keen in judgment,
and shall be a marvel before rulers.
12 They will wait while I am silent and
listen when I speak;
and when I shall speak the more,
they will put their hands upon their
mouths.*
13 Because of her I shall have immortality
and leave to those after me an
everlasting memory.[e]
14 I shall govern peoples, and nations will
be my subjects—[f]
15 tyrannical princes, hearing of me, will
be afraid;
in the assembly I shall appear noble,
and in war courageous.
16 Entering my house, I shall take my
repose beside her;
For association with her involves no
bitterness
and living with her no grief,
but rather joy and gladness.[g]

### *Wisdom Is a Gift of God*

17 Reflecting on these things,
and considering in my heart
That immortality lies in kinship with
Wisdom,[h]
18 great delight in love of her,
and unfailing riches in the works of
her hands;
And that in associating with her there is
prudence,
and fair renown in sharing her
discourses,
I went about seeking to take her for
my own.
19 * Now, I was a well-favored child,
and I came by a noble nature;
20 or rather, being noble, I attained an
unblemished body.
21 And knowing that I could not otherwise
possess her unless God gave it—
and this, too, was prudence, to know
whose gift she is—
I went to the LORD and besought him,[i]
and said with all my heart:

## CHAPTER 9

See RG 195–96

### *Solomon's Prayer**

1 * God of my ancestors, Lord of mercy,[j]
you who have made all things by your
word[k]
2 And in your wisdom have established
humankind
to rule the creatures produced by you,[l]
3 And to govern the world in holiness and
righteousness,
and to render judgment in integrity of
heart:[m]
4 Give me Wisdom, the consort at your
throne,
and do not reject me from among your
children;[n]
5 For I am your servant, the child of your
maidservant,

**8:12 Hands upon their mouths**: a sign of respect for unanswerable wisdom; cf. Jb 40:4.

**8:19–20** Here the author mentions first bodily, then spiritual, excellence. To make it plain that the latter is the governing factor in the harmonious development of the human person, he then reverses the order. The Platonic doctrine of the pre-existence of the soul is often read into these lines, but such an anthropology does not seem to be the intent of the author (cf. 7:1–6). Verse 20 appears to rule out any misunderstanding of v. 19. Verse 21 emphasizes that he did not bring talent to his "birth"; his wisdom is the gift of God.

**9:1–18** The author presents his version of Solomon's prayer (1 Kgs 3:6–9; 2 Chr 1:8–10).

**9:1–2** The author identifies Wisdom with the word of God just as he again identifies Wisdom with the spirit of God in v. 17. All three are alternate ways of expressing God's activity in relationship with the world and its inhabitants.

*c:* Prv 1:6; Sir 39:1–3; 42:19–20; Dn 2:21. *d:* 1 Kgs 3:28; Jb 29:8–10, 21–22. *e:* Sir 15:6; 41:12–13; Is 56:5. *f:* Wis 3:8; Ps 18:48; 47:4. *g:* Prv 29:6; Sir 15:6; Bar 3:38. *h:* Prv 3:18. *i:* 1 Kgs 3:9; 1 Kgs 5:9; Prv 2:6; Jas 1:5. *j:* Ps 86:15. *k:* Gn 1; Ps 33:6; Prv 3:19; Jer 10:12; Jn 1:3, 10. *l:* Ps 8:7–9; Sir 17:3–4. *m:* 1 Kgs 3:6; 9:4–5; Ps 9:8–9. *n:* 2 Chr 1:10.

a man weak and short-lived
and lacking in comprehension of
judgment and of laws.[o]
6 Indeed, though one be perfect among
mortals,
if Wisdom, who comes from you, be
lacking,
that one will count for nothing.[p]

7 You have chosen me king over your
people
and magistrate over your sons and
daughters.[q]
8 You have bid me build a temple on your
holy mountain
and an altar in the city that is your
dwelling place,
a copy of the holy tabernacle which
you had established from of old.[r]
9 Now with you is Wisdom, who knows
your works
and was present when you made the
world;
Who understands what is pleasing in
your eyes
and what is conformable with your
commands.[s]
10 Send her forth from your holy heavens
and from your glorious throne dispatch
her
That she may be with me and work with
me,
that I may know what is pleasing to
you.[t]
11 For she knows and understands all things,
and will guide me prudently in my
affairs
and safeguard me by her glory;[u]
12 Thus my deeds will be acceptable,
and I will judge your people justly
and be worthy of my father's throne.[v]
13 For who knows God's counsel,
or who can conceive what the Lord
intends?[w]
14 For the deliberations of mortals are timid,
and uncertain our plans.
15 * For the corruptible body burdens the
soul
and the earthly tent weighs down the
mind with its many concerns.[x]
16 Scarcely can we guess the things on earth,
and only with difficulty grasp what is
at hand;
but things in heaven, who can search
them out?[y]
17 Or who can know your counsel, unless
you give Wisdom
and send your holy spirit from on high?[z]
18 * Thus were the paths of those on earth
made straight,
and people learned what pleases you,
and were saved by Wisdom.[a]

## CHAPTER 10*

See RG 195–96

### *Wisdom Preserves Her Followers*

1 She preserved the first-formed father* of
the world[b]
when he alone had been created;[c]
And she raised him up from his fall,
2 and gave him power to rule all things.[d]
3 But when an unrighteous man* withdrew
from her in his anger,
he perished through his fratricidal
wrath.[e]
4 When on his account the earth was
flooded, Wisdom again saved it,
piloting the righteous man* on frailest
wood.[f]
5 She, when the nations were sunk in
universal wickedness,

**9:15–17** Although the expressions in v. 15 draw on the language of Plato concerning the human condition, the conclusion is very biblical: God remains a mystery (Jb 38–39; Eccl 8:17; Is 40:12–14; Rom 11:33–34). The plight of humankind is clearly one of ignorance, unless the "holy spirit" is sent from God.

**9:18** An announcement of the next section.

**10:1–21** This chapter prepares for the following section (Wis 11:2–19:22) on the history of Israel in the exodus, by reviewing the dealings of Wisdom with the patriarchs. It has a parallel in Sir 44–50; cf. also Wis 18:9.

**10:1–2** Adam.

**10:3** Cain.

**10:4** Noah.

*o:* 1 Kgs 3:7; Ps 116:16. *p:* Wis 3:17; 1 Kgs 11:4; 1 Cor 3:18–21. *q:* 1 Chr 28:5. *r:* Ex 25:8–9; 2 Sm 7:13; 1 Chr 28:5; 2 Chr 6:1–2; 7:7; Tb 1:4; Ps 15:1; 48:2–3. *s:* Dt 6:17–18; Prv 8:22–31; Jn 1:1–3, 10. *t:* Wis 18:15; Mt 5:34; Jn 3:17; 20:21. *u:* Wis 8:8. *v:* 1 Kgs 3:6–9. *w:* Is 40:13; Bar 3:31. *x:* Jb 4:19. *y:* Sir 1:3; Jn 3:12. *z:* Jn 14:26. *a:* Wis 10:9; Prv 28:26. *b:* Heb 11:17–27. *c:* Wis 7:1. *d:* Gn 1:28. *e:* Gn 4:1–16. *f:* Wis 14:5–6; Gn 6:5–9.

## The Wicked and the Just

IN CH 10 THERE is richness in the presentation of Wisdom and the followers who are just, by contrasting how the unjust are destroyed and the just enriched. Cain and Noah (vv. 3–4) are contrasts of the wicked and the just. So, too, the stories of Abraham and the Tower of Babel are opposites (vv. 5–8).

knew the righteous man,* kept him
blameless before God,
and preserved him resolute against
pity for his child.[g]
6 She rescued a righteous man* from
among the wicked who were
being destroyed,[h]
when he fled as fire descended upon
the Pentapolis—
7 Where as a testimony to its wickedness,
even yet there remain a smoking
desert,
Plants bearing fruit that never ripens,
and the tomb of a disbelieving soul,* a
standing pillar of salt.[i]
8 For those who forsook Wisdom
not only were deprived of knowledge
of the good,
But also left the world a memorial of
their folly,
so that they could not even be hidden
in their fall.
9 But Wisdom rescued from tribulations
those who served her.[j]
10 She, when a righteous man* fled from his
brother's anger,[k]
guided him in right ways,
Showed him the kingdom of God
and gave him knowledge of holy things;
She prospered him in his labors
and made abundant the fruit of his
works,
11 Stood by him against the greed of his
defrauders,
and enriched him;[l]
12 She preserved him from foes,
and secured him against ambush,
And she gave him the prize for his hard
struggle
that he might know that devotion to
God* is mightier than all else.[m]
13 She did not abandon a righteous man*
when he was sold,[n]
but rescued him from sin.[o]
14 She went down with him into the
dungeon,
and did not desert him in his bonds,
Until she brought him the scepter of
royalty
and authority over his oppressors,
Proved false those who had defamed him,
and gave him eternal glory.
15 The holy people and their blameless
descendants—it was she
who rescued them from the nation that
oppressed them.[p]
16 She entered the soul of the Lord's
servant,*
and withstood fearsome kings with
signs and wonders;[q]
17 she gave the holy ones the reward of
their labors,[r]
Conducted them by a wondrous road,
became a shelter for them by day
a starry flame by night.
18 She took them across the Red Sea
and brought them through the deep
waters.

**10:5** Abraham.

**10:6** Lot. **Pentapolis**: the five cities, including Sodom; cf. Gn 14:2.

**10:7 Disbelieving soul**: Lot's wife; cf. Gn 19:26.

**10:10–12** Jacob.

**10:12 Devotion to God**: in the Greek this signifies "piety" or "religion," and is the equivalent of the Hebrew "fear of the Lord"; cf. Prv 1:7.

**10:13–14** Joseph.

**10:16** Moses.

*g:* Gn 22:7–10. *h:* Gn 18:22–33; 19:15–25; 2 Pt 2:6–7. *i:* Gn 19:26; Lk 17:32. *j:* Wis 16:8. *k:* Gn 27:43–45; 28:12–15. *l:* Gn 30:29–30; 31:5–12. *m:* Gn 32:24–29; 1 Tm 4:8. *n:* Gn 37–45. *o:* Gn 39:7–10. *p:* Ex 3:9; 14:30; 19:6. *q:* Wis 1:4; 7:27; Ex 4:10; Ps 76:13. *r:* Wis 14:3; 19:7; Ex 13:21–22; Ex 14–15; Ps 77:20–21; 78:13, 53; Is 4:5–6.

19 Their enemies she overwhelmed,
and churned them up* from the bottom of the depths.
20 Therefore the righteous despoiled the wicked;
and they sang of your holy name, Lord,
and praised in unison your conquering hand,[s]
21 Because Wisdom opened the mouths of the mute,
and gave ready speech to infants.[t]

CHAPTER 11

See RG 195–96

1 She prospered their affairs through the holy prophet.[u]

## III. Special Providence of God During the Exodus*

### *Introduction*

2 They journeyed through the uninhabited desert,
and in lonely places they pitched their tents;[v]
3 they withstood enemies and warded off their foes.[w]
4 When they thirsted, they called upon you,
and water was given them from the sheer rock,
a quenching of their thirst from the hard stone.
5 For by the things through which their foes were punished
they in their need were benefited.[x]

### *First Example: Water Punishes the Egyptians and Benefits the Israelites*

6 Instead of a river's* perennial source,
troubled with impure blood[y]
7 as a rebuke to the decree for the slaying of infants,
You gave them abundant water beyond their hope,
8 after you had shown by the thirst they experienced
how you punished their adversaries.
9 For when they had been tried, though only mildly chastised,[z]
they recognized how the wicked, condemned in anger, were being tormented.
10 You tested your own people, admonishing them as a father;
but as a stern king you probed and condemned the wicked.
11 Those near and far were equally afflicted:[a]
12 for a twofold grief* took hold of them[b]
and a groaning at the remembrance of the ones who had departed.
13 For when they heard that the cause of their own torments
was a benefit to these others, they recognized the Lord.
14 For though they had mocked and rejected him who had been cast out and abandoned long ago,
in the final outcome, they marveled at him,
since their thirst proved unlike that of the righteous.[c]

### *Second Example: Animals Punish the Egyptians and Benefit the Israelites*

15 In return for their senseless, wicked thoughts,
which misled them into worshiping dumb* serpents and worthless insects,

**10:19 Churned them up**: casting their bodies on the shore.

**11:2–19:22** Few verses in chaps. 11–19 can be fully understood without consulting the passages in the Pentateuch which are indicated in the cross-references. The theme of this part of the book is expressed in v. 5 and is illustrated in the following chapters by five examples drawn from Exodus events.

**11:6–8 River**: the Nile; the contrast is between the first plague of Egypt (Ex 7:17–24) and the water drawn from the rock in Horeb (Ex 17:5–7; Nm 20:8–11).

**11:12 Twofold grief**: the double distress described in vv. 13–14.

**11:15 Dumb**: that is, irrational.

*s:* Ex 12:35–36; 15:1–21. *t:* Ex 4:10–15; Ps 8:3; Mt 11:25. *u:* Dt 2:7; Hos 12:14. *v:* Ex 17:2–6; Nm 20:1–13; Ps 63:2; 107:4–7; Jer 2:6. *w:* Ex 17:8–16; Nm 21:1–3, 21–35; 31:1–12; Ps 118:10–12. *x:* Wis 16:1–2. *y:* Wis 18:5; Ex 1:22; 7:17–24. *z:* Wis 3:5; 16:3–4; Dt 8:2–5; 2 Mc 6:12–16; Ps 6:2; Prv 3:12. *a:* Ps 6:2. *b:* Wis 16:8; Ex 14:4, 18. *c:* Ex 2:3.

You sent upon them swarms of dumb
creatures for vengeance;[d]
16 that they might recognize that one is
punished by the very things
through which one sins.[e]

### *Digression on God's Mercy*

17 For not without means was your
almighty hand,[f]
that had fashioned the universe from
formless matter,*
to send upon them many bears or
fierce lions,
18 Or newly created, wrathful, unknown
beasts
breathing forth fiery breath,
Or pouring out roaring smoke,
or flashing terrible sparks from their
eyes.
19 Not only could these attack and
completely destroy them;
even their frightful appearance itself
could slay.
20 Even without these, they could have been
killed at a single blast,
pursued by justice
and winnowed by your mighty spirit.
But you have disposed all things by
measure and number and weight.[g]
21 For great strength is always present with
you;
who can resist the might of your arm?[h]
22 Indeed, before you the whole universe is
like a grain from a balance,*
or a drop of morning dew come down
upon the earth.[i]
23 * But you have mercy on all, because you
can do all things;
and you overlook sins for the sake of
repentance.[j]
24 For you love all things that are
and loathe nothing that you have made;
for you would not fashion what you
hate.[k]
25 How could a thing remain, unless you
willed it;
or be preserved, had it not been called
forth by you?[l]
26 But you spare all things, because they are
yours,
O Ruler and Lover of souls,[m]
12:1 for your imperishable spirit is in all
things![n]

## CHAPTER 12

See RG 196

2 Therefore you rebuke offenders
little by little,
warn them, and remind them of the
sins they are committing,
that they may abandon their wickedness
and believe in you, Lord!
3 For truly, the ancient inhabitants of your
holy land,[o]
4 whom you hated for deeds most
odious—
works of sorcery and impious
sacrifices;
5 These merciless murderers of children,
devourers of human flesh,*
and initiates engaged in a blood ritual,
6 and parents who took with their own
hands defenseless lives,[p]
You willed to destroy by the hands of our
ancestors,
7 that the land that is dearest of all to
you
might receive a worthy colony of
God's servants.[q]
8 But even these you spared, since they
were but mortals
and sent wasps as forerunners of your
army

**11:17 Formless matter**: a Greek philosophical concept is used to interpret the chaos of Gn 1:2.

**11:22 Grain from a balance**: a tiny particle used for weighing on sensitive scales.

**11:23** The combination of divine mercy and power is an unusual paradox, but cf. 12:15–18; Ps 62:12–13; Sir 2:18. The main emphasis is on a creating that is motivated by love; the divine "imperishable spirit" (either Wisdom as in 1:4, 7, or perhaps the breath of life as in Gn 2:7) is in everything (12:1).

**12:5** The horrible crimes here attributed to the Canaanites (cf. also 14:23) were not unheard of in the ancient world.

*d:* Wis 12:23–24; 15:18–16:1; Ex 7:26–8:11. *e:* Wis 12:23, 27; Ex 10:16; Prv 1:31–32; 26:27. *f:* Wis 12:8–9; 16:1, 5; Gn 1:1–2; Dt 32:24; 2 Kgs 17:25–26; Hos 13:4–8. *g:* Jb 4:9. *h:* Wis 12:12; 2 Chr 20:6. *i:* Hos 13:3. *j:* Wis 12:10; Dt 9:27; Acts 17:30; Rom 2:4; 11:32; 2 Pt 3:9. *k:* Ps 145:9. *l:* Is 41:4. *m:* Wis 12:16; Is 63:9. *n:* Wis 1:7. *o:* Wis 14:23; Dt 18:9–12; Ps 5:6; 106:28, 34–39; Jer 19:4–5; Ez 16:3, 20–21, 36. *p:* Nm 33:52. *q:* Dt 11:12.

that they might exterminate them by
degrees.[r]
9 Not that you were without power to have
the wicked vanquished in battle
by the righteous,
or wiped out at once by terrible beasts
or by one decisive word;[s]
10 But condemning them by degrees, you
gave them space for repentance.
You were not unaware that their origins
were wicked
and their malice ingrained,[t]
And that their dispositions would never
change;
11 for they were a people accursed from
the beginning.
Neither out of fear for anyone
did you grant release from their
sins.[u]
12 For who can say to you, "What have you
done?"
or who can oppose your decree?
Or when peoples perish, who can
challenge you, their maker;
or who can come into your presence to
vindicate the unrighteous?[v]
13 For neither is there any god besides you
who have the care of all,
that you need show you have not
unjustly condemned;[w]
14 Nor can any king or prince confront you
on behalf of those you have
punished.[x]
15 But as you are righteous, you govern all
things righteously;
you regard it as unworthy of your
power
to punish one who has incurred no
blame.[y]
16 For your might is the source of
righteousness;
your mastery over all things makes
you lenient to all.[z]
17 For you show your might when the
perfection of your power is
disbelieved;
and in those who know you, you
rebuke insolence.* [a]
18 But though you are master of might, you
judge with clemency,
and with much lenience you govern us;
for power, whenever you will, attends
you.
19 You taught your people, by these deeds,[b]
that those who are righteous must be
kind;
And you gave your children reason to
hope
that you would allow them to repent
for their sins.
20 For these were enemies of your servants,
doomed to death;
yet, while you punished them with
such solicitude and indulgence,
granting time and opportunity to
abandon wickedness,
21 With what exactitude you judged your
children,
to whose ancestors you gave the sworn
covenants of goodly promises![c]
22 Therefore to give us a lesson you punish
our enemies with measured
deliberation
so that we may think earnestly of your
goodness when we judge,
and, when being judged, we may look
for mercy.

### *Second Example Resumed*

23 Hence those unrighteous who lived a life
of folly,
you tormented through their own
abominations.[d]
24 For they went far astray in the paths of
error,
taking for gods the worthless and
disgusting among beasts,

**12:17** The brunt of divine anger and justice is borne by those who know God but defy divine authority and might. Cf. 1:2; 15:2, but also 12:27; 18:13.

*r:* Ex 23:28–30; Dt 7:17–24. *s:* Wis 11:18; 18:15; Nm 16:21. *t:* Wis 11:23; Ps 55:20; Sir 16:9. *u:* Gn 9:25. *v:* 2 Sm 16:10; Eccl 8:4; Sir 46:19; Is 45:9; Dn 4:32; Rom 9:19–21. *w:* Wis 6:7; Dt 3:24; 32:39; Is 44:6, 8. *x:* Jer 49:19; 50:44. *y:* Gn 18:23–32; Dt 32:4. *z:* Wis 2:11; 11:26; Ps 103:19. *a:* Wis 15:2–3; Ex 9:16. *b:* Wis 11:23; Sir 17:24. *c:* Wis 18:22; Gn 50:24; Dt 7:6–14; Ps 105:8–11. *d:* Wis 11:16; 16:1.

**Worship of Creation, Rather Than Creator**

IN CH 13 THE beauty of the natural world reflects the nature of God, or less specifically, the plan of an intelligent mind. This is known as the "argument from design," a proof for the existence of God used in many different eras. The argument in antiquity represents a well-known strategy for undermining nature worship to demonstrate that the invisible God lies behind the visible world; it appears in Stoic writings, in Philo, and in truncated form in Paul (Rom 1:18–25).

being deceived like senseless infants.[e]
25 Therefore as though upon unreasoning children,
you sent your judgment on them as a mockery;[f]
26 But they who took no heed of a punishment which was but child's play
were to experience a condemnation worthy of God.
27 For by the things through which they suffered distress,
being tortured by the very things they deemed gods,
They saw and recognized the true God whom formerly they had refused to know;
with this, their final condemnation* came upon them.[g]

### CHAPTER 13

See RG 196

#### *Digression on False Worship*

##### *A. Nature Worship**

1 Foolish by nature were all who were in ignorance of God,
and who from the good things seen did not succeed in knowing the one who is,*
and from studying the works did not discern the artisan;[h]
2 Instead either fire, or wind, or the swift air,
or the circuit of the stars, or the mighty water,
or the luminaries of heaven, the governors* of the world, they considered gods.[i]
3 Now if out of joy in their beauty they thought them gods,
let them know how far more excellent is the Lord than these;
for the original source of beauty fashioned them.[j]
4 Or if they were struck by their might and energy,
let them realize from these things how much more powerful is the one who made them.[k]
5 For from the greatness and the beauty of created things
their original author, by analogy, is seen.
6 But yet, for these the blame is less;*
For they have gone astray perhaps,
though they seek God and wish to find him.
7 For they search busily among his works,
but are distracted by what they see,
because the things seen are fair.
8 But again, not even these are pardonable.
9 For if they so far succeeded in knowledge
that they could speculate about the world,
how did they not more quickly find its Lord?

**12:27 Condemnation**: the death of Egyptian firstborn and the destruction of their army in the sea.

**13:1–9** The author holds a relatively benign view of the efforts of the philosophers to come to know God from various natural phenomena. This is not a question of proving the existence of God in scholastic style. The author thinks that the beauty and might of the world should have pointed by analogy (v. 5) to the Maker. Instead, those "in ignorance of God" remained fixed on the elements (v. 2, three named, along with the stars). His Greek counterparts are not totally blameless; they should have gone further and acknowledged the creator of nature's wonders (vv. 4–5). Cf. Rom 1:18–23; Acts 17:27–28.

**13:1 One who is**: this follows the Greek translation of the sacred name for God in Hebrew; cf. Ex 3:14.

**13:2 Governors**: the sun and moon (cf. Gn 1:16).

**13:6 The blame is less**: the greater blame is incurred by those mentioned in v. 10; 15:14–16.

*e:* Dt 11:28; Jer 5:28; Rom 1:23. *f:* Jer 4:22. *g:* Wis 16:16; Ex 14:4, 28. *h:* Acts 14:17; Eph 4:17–19. *i:* Gn 1:14–19; Dt 4:19; Jb 31:26–28. *j:* Ps 8:4. *k:* Jer 10:2; Bar 6:39.

### *B. Idolatry**

10 But wretched are they, and in dead things
are their hopes,
who termed gods things made by
human hands:
Gold and silver, the product of art, and
images of beasts,
or useless stone, the work of an
ancient hand.[l]

### *The Carpenter and Wooden Idols*

11 A carpenter may cut down a suitable
tree[m]
and skillfully scrape off all its bark,
And deftly plying his art
produce something fit for daily use,[n]
12 And use the scraps from his handiwork
in preparing his food, and have his fill;
13 Then the good-for-nothing refuse from
these remnants,
crooked wood grown full of knots,
he takes and carves to occupy his spare
time.[o]
This wood he models with mindless skill,
and patterns it on the image of a
human being
14 or makes it resemble some worthless
beast.
When he has daubed it with red and
crimsoned its surface with red
stain,
and daubed over every blemish in it,[p]
15 He makes a fitting shrine for it
and puts it on the wall, fastening it
with a nail.[q]
16 Thus he provides for it lest it fall down,
knowing that it cannot help itself;
for, truly, it is an image and needs help.[r]
17 But when he prays about his goods or
marriage or children,[s]
he is not ashamed to address the thing
without a soul.
For vigor he invokes the powerless;
18 for life he entreats the dead;
For aid he beseeches the wholly
incompetent;
for travel, something that cannot even
walk;
19 For profit in business and success with
his hands
he asks power of a thing with hands
utterly powerless.

## CHAPTER 14

See RG 196

1 Again, one preparing for a voyage
and about to traverse the wild
waves
cries out to wood more unsound than
the boat that bears him.[t]
2 For the urge for profits devised this latter,
and Wisdom the artisan produced it.
3 * But your providence, O Father! guides
it,
for you have furnished even in the sea
a road,
and through the waves a steady path,[u]
4 Showing that you can save from any
danger,
so that even one without skill may
embark.[v]
5 But you will that the products of your
Wisdom be not idle;
therefore people trust their lives even
to most frail wood,
and were safe crossing the waves on a
raft.[w]
6 For of old, when the proud giants were
being destroyed,
the hope of the universe, who took
refuge on a raft,*
left to the world a future for the human
family, under the guidance of
your hand.
7 For blest is the wood through which
righteousness comes about;
8 but the handmade idol is accursed, and
its maker as well:

**13:10–19** The second digression is an example of the polemic against idolatry (cf. Is 44:9–20; Jer 10:3–9; Ps 135:15–18). Whether the idols be of wood or clay, they were made by human beings and have become the source of evil.

**14:3–6** The wooden ship mentioned in vv. 1–2 prompts a short meditation on the providence of God, who in fact has watched over boats in their dangerous courses. The wood as described in v. 7 became a favorite patristic type for the wood of the cross.

**14:6** Noah.

*l:* Wis 3:11; 15:5, 17; Dt 4:25–28; 7:25; 27:15; Ps 115:4; Hos 14:4; Acts 17:29. *m:* Is 44:9–20. *n:* Wis 15:7; Bar 6:58. *o:* Dt 4:16. *p:* Jer 10:9. *q:* Is 40:20; 41:7; 44:13. *r:* 1 Sm 5:3–5; Bar 6:57. *s:* Wis 15:15. *t:* Is 46:7. *u:* Ps 107:23–30; Is 43:16. *v:* Wis 16:8. *w:* Wis 10:4.

he for having produced it, and the
corruptible thing, because it was
termed a god.[x]
9 Equally odious to God are the evildoer
and the evil deed;
10 and the thing made will be punished
with its maker.
11 Therefore upon even the idols of the
nations shall a judgment come,
since they became abominable among
God's works,
Snares for human souls
and a trap for the feet of the senseless.[y]

### *The Origin and Evils of Idolatry*

12 For the source of wantonness is the
devising of idols;
and their invention, a corruption of
life.[z]
13 For in the beginning they were not,
nor can they ever continue;[a]
14 for from human emptiness they came
into the world,
and therefore a sudden end is devised
for them.
15 * For a father, afflicted with untimely
mourning,
made an image of the child so quickly
taken from him,
And now honored as a god what once
was dead
and handed down to his household
mysteries and sacrifices.
16 Then, in the course of time, the impious
practice gained strength and was
observed as law,
and graven things were worshiped by
royal decrees.[b]
17 People who lived so far away that they
could not honor him in his
presence
copied the appearance of the distant
king
And made a public image of him they
wished to honor,
out of zeal to flatter the absent one as
though present.
18 And to promote this observance among
those to whom it was strange,
the artisan's ambition provided a
stimulus.
19 For he, perhaps in his determination to
please the ruler,
labored over the likeness* to the best
of his skill;[c]
20 And the masses, drawn by the charm of
the workmanship,
soon took as an object of worship the
one who shortly before was
honored as a human being.[d]
21 And this became a snare for the world,
that people enslaved to either grief or
tyranny
conferred the incommunicable Name
on stones and wood.
22 Then it was not enough for them to err in
their knowledge of God;[e]
but even though they live in a great
war resulting from ignorance,
they call such evils peace.[f]
23 For while they practice either child
sacrifices or occult mysteries,
or frenzied carousing in exotic rites,[g]
24 They no longer respect either lives or
purity of marriage;
but they either waylay and kill each
other, or aggrieve each other by
adultery.
25 And all is confusion—blood and murder,
theft and guile,[h]
corruption, faithlessness, turmoil,
perjury,
26 Disturbance of good people, neglect of
gratitude,
besmirching of souls, unnatural lust,
disorder in marriage, adultery and
shamelessness.
27 For the worship of infamous idols
is the reason and source and extreme
of all evil.[i]

**14:15–21** The author develops two examples of idolatry: cult of the dead, and cult of the king.
**14:19 Likeness**: he made this more flattering than the reality.

*x:* Rom 1:23. *y:* Wis 3:7; Nm 33:4; Jos 23:13; Ps 115:4; Jer 6:15; 10:15; 46:25; Hos 9:15. *z:* Rom 1:23–32. *a:* Is 2:18. *b:* 1 Mc 1:47–50; Dn 3:4–7. *c:* Is 44:12–13 LXX. *d:* Wis 15:4. *e:* Jer 2:20; 3:1–25; Hos 4:1–2, 9–19; Rom 1:26–31; Gal 5:19–21; 1 Tm 1:9–10. *f:* Jer 6:14; Ez 13:10. *g:* Wis 12:4–5; 14:15; Is 57:5. *h:* Jer 7:8–9; 22:17. *i:* Ex 23:13.

## Idol Worship

BOTH IDOL WORSHIP and deviant sexual behavior (14:26–27) invert the proper social order. Jews often stereotyped Gentiles as sexually licentious and make a connection between idolatry and such behavior.

28 For they either go mad with enjoyment,
or prophesy lies,
or live lawlessly or lightly perjure
themselves.[j]
29 For as their trust is in lifeless idols,
they expect no harm when they have
sworn falsely.
30 But on both counts justice shall overtake
them:
because they thought perversely of
God by devoting themselves to
idols,[k]
and because they deliberately swore
false oaths, despising piety.*
31 For it is not the might of those by whom
they swear,
but the just retribution of sinners,
that ever follows upon the
transgression of the wicked.*

### CHAPTER 15

See RG 196

1* But you, our God, are good and
true,
slow to anger, and governing all with
mercy.[l]
2 For even if we sin, we are yours, and
know your might;
but we will not sin, knowing that we
belong to you.[m]
3 For to know you well is complete
righteousness,
and to know your might is the root of
immortality.[n]
4 For the evil creation of human fancy did
not deceive us,
nor the fruitless labor of painters,[o]
A form smeared with varied colors,
5 the sight of which arouses yearning in
a fool,
till he longs for the inanimate form of
a dead image.
6 Lovers of evil things, and worthy of such
hopes
are they who make them and long for
them and worship them.[p]

### *The Potter's Clay Idols*

7 For the potter, laboriously working the
soft earth,
molds for our service each single article:
He fashions out of the same clay
both the vessels that serve for clean
purposes
and their opposites, all alike;
As to what shall be the use of each vessel
of either class
the worker in clay is the judge.[q]
8 * With misspent toil he molds a
meaningless god from the
selfsame clay,
though he himself shortly before was
made from the earth,
And is soon to go whence he was taken,
when the life that was lent him is
demanded back.[r]
9 But his concern is not that he is to die
nor that his span of life is brief;
Rather, he vies with goldsmiths and
silversmiths
and emulates molders of bronze,
and takes pride in fashioning
counterfeits.[s]

**14:30 Piety**: the sanctity of oaths.

**14:31** Perjury is a form of deceit which calls for punishment even though it be practiced in the name of a lifeless idol.

**15:1–3** As often before (11:26; 12:2; 14:3–6), the author addresses God directly, so that chaps. 11–19 can be conceived as a more or less continuous prayer (cf. 11:7 and 19:22). This is the living God who is in stark contrast to the deadness of the idols that have been discussed. The merciful God (cf. Ex 34:6) is the source of immortality (1:15) for the community.

**15:8–9** The author matches the irony of his words about the carpenter in 13:15–19 with this description of the potter's vain work.

*j:* Jer 5:31; 29:26. *k:* Wis 1:1, 8; 11:20; Jer 5:2, 7. *l:* Ex 34:6–7; Ps 86:5, 15; 145:8, 9, 14. *m:* Jb 10:14–15 LXX. *n:* Wis 3:15; Jn 17:3. *o:* Wis 13:14. *p:* Ps 115:8. *q:* Wis 13:11; Jer 18:3–4; Rom 9:21; 2 Tm 2:20–21. *r:* Gn 3:19; Eccl 12:7. *s:* Bar 6:46.

[10] Ashes his heart is!* more worthless than
earth is his hope,[t]
more ignoble than clay his life;
[11] Because he knew not the one who
fashioned him,
and breathed into him a quickening
soul,
and infused a vital spirit.[u]
[12] Instead, he esteemed our life a mere
game,
and our span of life a holiday for gain;
"For one must," says he, "make a profit
in every way, be it even from
evil."[v]
[13] For more than anyone else he knows that
he is sinning,
when out of earthen stuff he creates
fragile vessels and idols alike.

[14] But most stupid of all and worse than
senseless in mind,
are the enemies of your people who
enslaved them.[w]
[15] For they esteemed all the idols of the
nations as gods,
which cannot use their eyes to see,
nor nostrils to breathe the air,
Nor ears to hear,
nor fingers on their hands for feeling;
even their feet are useless to walk
with.[x]
[16] For it was a mere human being who
made them;[y]
one living on borrowed breath who
fashioned them.
For no one is able to fashion a god like
himself;
[17] he is mortal, and what he makes with
lawless hands is dead.
For he is better than the things he
worships;
he at least lives, but never his idols.

*Second Example Resumed*

[18] * Besides, they worship the most
loathsome beasts—[z]
as regards stupidity, these are worse
than the rest,*
[19] For beasts are neither good-looking nor
desirable;
they have escaped both the approval of
God and his blessing.[a]

### CHAPTER 16

See RG 196

[1] Therefore they* were fittingly
punished by similar creatures,
and were tormented by a swarm of
insects.[b]
[2] Instead of this punishment, you benefited
your people
with a novel dish, the delight they
craved,
by providing quail for their food,[c]
[3] So that those others, when they desired
food,
should lose their appetite even for
necessities,
since the creatures sent to plague them
were so loathsome,
While these, after a brief period of
privation,
partook of a novel dish.[d]
[4] For inexorable want had to come upon
those oppressors;
but these needed only to be shown
how their enemies were being
tormented.[e]

[5] For when the dire venom of beasts came
upon them[f]
and they were dying from the bite of
crooked serpents,
your anger endured not to the end.
[6] But as a warning, for a short time they
were terrorized,

**15:10 Ashes his heart is!**: the words of this cry are taken from Is 44:20 (the Septuagint).

**15:18–19** The author here returns (11:15; 12:23–27) to the main theme of chaps. 11–19, which was interrupted by the digression of 13:1–15:17.

**15:18 Worse than the rest**: this may mean that the creatures worshiped by the Egyptians (e.g., crocodiles, serpents, scarabs, etc.) were less intelligent than the general run of beasts.

**16:1 They**: the Egyptian idolaters, who are punished according to the principle laid down in 11:5, 15–16.

*t:* Jb 13:12 LXX. *u:* Gn 2:7; Zec 12:1. *v:* Jas 4:13–14. *w:* Ex 1:13. *x:* Wis 14:11; Dt 4:28; Ps 115:4–7; 135:15–18. *y:* Wis 13:10. *z:* Wis 11:15; 12:24. *a:* Gn 1:25; 3:14. *b:* Wis 11:15–16; 12:23, 27; Ex 7:27; 8:12, 17. *c:* Wis 11:13; 19:11–12; Ex 16:13; Nm 11:31–32; Ps 105:40. *d:* Wis 11:15; Ex 8:10; 16:3. *e:* Wis 11:8–9. *f:* Nm 21:4–9; Dt 32:24; Jer 8:17 LXX.

though they had a sign* of salvation, to
remind them of the precept of
your law.
7 For the one who turned toward it was
saved,
not by what was seen,
but by you, the savior of all.
8 By this also you convinced our foes
that you are the one who delivers from
all evil.[g]
9 For the bites of locusts and of flies slew
them,
and no remedy was found to save their
lives
because they deserved to be punished
by such means;[h]
10 But not even the fangs of poisonous
reptiles overcame your children,
for your mercy came forth and healed
them.[i]
11 For as a reminder of your injunctions,
they were stung,
and swiftly they were saved,
Lest they should fall into deep forgetfulness
and become unresponsive to your
beneficence.[j]
12 For indeed, neither herb nor application
cured them,
but your all-healing word, O LORD![k]
13 * For you have dominion over life and
death;[l]
you lead down to the gates of Hades
and lead back.
14 Human beings, however, may kill
another with malice,
but they cannot bring back the
departed spirit,
or release the soul that death has
confined.
15 Your hand no one can escape.

### *Third Example: A Rain of Manna for Israel Instead of the Plague of Storms*

16 For the wicked who refused to know you
were punished by the might of your
arm,
Were pursued by unusual rains and
hailstorms and unremitting
downpours,
and were consumed by fire.[m]
17 For against all expectation, in water
which quenches everything,
the fire grew more active;
For the universe fights on behalf of the
righteous.[n]
18 Then the flame was tempered[o]
so that the beasts that were sent upon
the wicked might not be burnt up,
but that these might see and know that
they were struck by the judgment
of God;
19 And again, even in the water, fire blazed
beyond its strength
so as to consume the produce of the
wicked land.
20 Instead of this, you nourished your
people with food of angels*
and furnished them bread from heaven,
ready to hand, untoiled-for,
endowed with all delights and
conforming to every taste.[p]
21 For this substance of yours revealed your
sweetness toward your children,
and serving the desire of the one who
received it,
was changed to whatever flavor each
one wished.[q]
22 Yet snow and ice* withstood fire and
were not melted,
so that they might know that their
enemies' fruits

**16:6 Sign**: the brazen serpent, as related in Numbers 21, but the author deliberately avoids any misunderstanding by addressing the Lord as responsible for the healing, since he is "the savior of all" (v. 7; see also vv. 12 and 26 for the role of the "word" of God).

**16:13–14** The author recognizes the power of the Lord over life and death, as expressed in 1 Sm 2:6; Tb 13:2. The traditional imagery of Sheol (gates and confinement) colors the passage.

**16:20 Food of angels**: the famous phrase (cf. the hymn "Panis Angelicus") is taken from Ps 78:24 as rendered by the Septuagint. The "bread from heaven" (cf. Ex 16:4; Ps 105:40) with its marvelous "sweetness" becomes a type of the "bread come down from heaven" in Jn 6:32–51, and plays a large role in later Christian devotion.

**16:22 Snow and ice**: the manna; cf. v. 27; 19:21.

*g:* Gn 48:16; 2 Mc 1:24–25. *h:* Ex 8:16–28; 10:4–19; Ps 78:45–46; 105:31, 34; Rev 9:1–11. *i:* Dt 32:33. *j:* Ps 78:11. *k:* Ex 15:26. *l:* Dt 32:39; 1 Sm 2:6; Tb 13:2; 2 Mc 6:26; 7:23; Ps 78:34, 39; Eccl 8:8; Dn 5:19. *m:* Wis 11:21; 12:27; Ex 5:2; 9:29–34. *n:* Wis 10:20; 19:20; Ex 9:23–28; 2 Mc 8:36; 14:34. *o:* Wis 19:20–21. *p:* Ex 16:4; Nm 11:8; Ps 78:24–25; Jn 6:31. *q:* Ps 34:9.

Were consumed by a fire that blazed in
the hail
and flashed lightning in the rain.[r]

23 But this fire, again, in order that the
righteous might be nourished,
forgot even its proper strength;[s]
24 For your creation, serving you, its maker,
grows tense for punishment against the
wicked,
but is relaxed in benefit for those who
trust in you.[t]
25 Therefore at that very time, transformed
in all sorts of ways,
it was serving your all-nourishing
bounty
according to what they needed and
desired;
26 That your children whom you loved
might learn, O LORD,
that it is not the various kinds of fruits
that nourish,
but your word that preserves those
who believe you![u]
27 For what was not destroyed by fire,
melted when merely warmed by a
momentary sunbeam;[v]
28 To make known that one must give you
thanks before sunrise,
and turn to you at daybreak.[w]
29 For the hope of the ungrateful melts like
a wintry frost
and runs off like useless water.[x]

## CHAPTER 17

See RG 196

### *Fourth Example: Darkness Afflicts the Egyptians, While the Israelites Have Light**

1 For great are your judgments, and hard to
describe;
therefore the unruly souls went
astray.[y]
2 For when the lawless thought to enslave
the holy nation,
they themselves lay shackled with
darkness, fettered by the long
night,
confined beneath their own roofs as
exiles from the eternal
providence.[z]
3 For they, who supposed their secret sins
were hid[a]
under the dark veil of oblivion,
Were scattered in fearful trembling,
terrified by apparitions.
4 For not even their inner chambers kept
them unafraid,
for crashing sounds on all sides
terrified them,
and mute phantoms with somber looks
appeared.
5 No fire had force enough to give light,
nor did the flaming brilliance of the
stars
succeed in lighting up that gloomy
night.[b]
6 But only intermittent, fearful fires
flashed through upon them;
And in their terror they thought
beholding these was worse
than the times when that sight was no
longer to be seen.[c]
7 And mockeries of their magic art* failed,
and there was a humiliating refutation
of their vaunted shrewdness.[d]
8 For they who undertook to banish fears
and terrors from the sick soul
themselves sickened with ridiculous
fear.
9 For even though no monstrous thing
frightened them,
they shook at the passing of insects
and the hissing of reptiles,[e]
10 And perished trembling,

**17:1–18:4** The description of the darkness of the ninth plague is a very creative development of Ex 10:21–29. It betrays a wide knowledge of contemporary thought. For the first and only time in the Septuagint the Greek word for "conscience" occurs, in 17:11. There is no Hebrew word that is equivalent; the idea is expressed indirectly. The horrendous darkness is illumined by "fires" (v. 6), i.e., lightnings that only contributed to the terror.

**17:7 Magic art**: the Egyptian magicians who were successful at first (Ex 7:11, 22) and then failed (Ex 8:14; 9:11) are now powerless against the darkness and the phantoms and are totally discredited.

*r:* Ex 9:25–31; 10:12; Ps 148:8. *s:* Wis 19:21. *t:* Wis 5:17, 20; 19:6; Sir 39:25–27. *u:* Dt 8:3; Mt 4:4. *v:* Ex 16:21. *w:* Ps 57:9–10; 92:3. *x:* Wis 5:14; 2 Sm 14:14. *y:* Ex 6:6 LXX. *z:* Wis 18:4; Ex 1:13–14; 9:6; 10:21–23. *a:* Wis 1:7–8; 10:8; 18:17. *b:* Wis 10:17; Jer 23:24 LXX. *c:* Ex 9:23–24. *d:* Wis 12:25–26; Ex 7:11–12, 22; 8:3; 9:11; 10:2. *e:* Wis 16:1; Jer 26:22 LXX.

reluctant to face even the air that they
could nowhere escape.
11 For wickedness, of its nature cowardly,
testifies in its own condemnation,
and because of a distressed
conscience, always magnifies
misfortunes.[f]
12 For fear is nought but the surrender of
the helps that come from reason;
13 and the more one's expectation is of
itself uncertain,
the more one makes of not knowing
the cause that brings on torment.
14 So they, during that night, powerless
though it was,
since it had come upon them from the
recesses of a powerless* Hades,
while all sleeping the same sleep,
15 Were partly smitten by fearsome
apparitions
and partly stricken by their souls'
surrender;
for fear overwhelmed them, sudden
and unexpected.[g]
16 Thus, then, whoever was there fell
into that prison without bars and was
kept confined.[h]
17 For whether one was a farmer, or a
shepherd,
or a worker at tasks in the wasteland,
Taken unawares, each served out the
inescapable sentence;
18 for all were bound by the one bond of
darkness.[i]
And were it only the whistling wind,
or the melodious song of birds in the
spreading branches,
Or the steady sound of rushing water,
19 or the rude crash of overthrown rocks,
Or the unseen gallop of bounding
animals,
or the roaring cry of the fiercest beasts,
Or an echo resounding from the hollow
of the hills—
these sounds, inspiring terror,
paralyzed them.
20 For the whole world shone with brilliant
light[j]
and continued its works without
interruption;
21 But over them alone was spread
oppressive night,
an image of the darkness* that was
about to come upon them.
Yet they were more a burden to
themselves than was the
darkness.

## CHAPTER 18

See RG 196

1 But your holy ones had very great
light;
And those others, who heard their voices
but did not see their forms,
counted them blest for not having
suffered;
2 And because they who formerly had been
wronged did not harm them, they
thanked them,
and because of the difference between
them,* pleaded with them.
3 Instead of this, you furnished the flaming
pillar,
a guide on the unknown way,
and the mild sun for an honorable
migration.[k]
4 * For they deserved to be deprived of
light and imprisoned by darkness,
they had kept your children confined,
through whom the imperishable light
of the law was to be given to the
world.[l]

### *Fifth Example: Death of the Egyptian Firstborn; the Israelites Are Spared*

5 When they determined to put to death the
infants of the holy ones,
and when a single boy* had been cast
forth and then saved,

**17:14 Powerless**: Hades (or Sheol), i.e., the nether world, is often portrayed in the Old Testament as a hostile power, since all must die (Ps 49:8–13), but it has no power against God.

**17:21 Darkness**: of Hades or Sheol; see note on 16:13–14.

**18:2 The difference between them:** God's distinctive manner of treating the Israelites and the Egyptians according to their respective deeds. **Pleaded**: perhaps, for their departure.

**18:4** The discussion of physical light climaxes with a reference to the "imperishable light" of the torah.

**18:5 Single boy**: Moses.

*f:* Wis 4:6; 10:7; Rom 2:15. *g:* Ex 11:9–10. *h:* Wis 18:4; Ex 10:23. *i:* Lv 26:36. *j:* Ex 10:23; Is 9:1; 60:1–3; 2 Pt 2:17. *k:* Ex 13:21. *l:* Wis 17:2; Ps 119:105; Is 2:3, 5.

As a reproof you carried off a multitude of their children
and made them perish all at once in the mighty water.[m]
6 That night was known beforehand to our ancestors,
so that, with sure knowledge of the oaths in which they put their faith, they might have courage.[n]
7 The expectation of your people
was the salvation of the righteous and the destruction of their foes.[o]
8 For by the same means with which you punished our adversaries,
you glorified us whom you had summoned.[p]
9 For in secret the holy children of the good were offering sacrifice
and carried out with one mind the divine institution,*
So that your holy ones should share alike the same blessings and dangers,
once they had sung the ancestral hymns of praise.[q]
10 But the discordant cry of their enemies echoed back,
and the piteous wail of mourning for children was borne to them.[r]
11 And the slave was smitten with the same retribution as the master;
even the commoner suffered the same as the king.[s]
12 And all alike by one common form of death
had countless dead;
For the living were not even sufficient for the burial,
since at a single instant their most valued offspring had been destroyed.[t]
13 For though they disbelieved at every turn on account of sorceries,
at the destruction of the firstborn they acknowledged that this people*
was God's son.[u]
14 * For when peaceful stillness encompassed everything
and the night in its swift course was half spent,
15 Your all-powerful word from heaven's royal throne
leapt into the doomed land,[v]
16 a fierce warrior bearing the sharp sword of your inexorable decree,
And alighted, and filled every place with death,
and touched heaven, while standing upon the earth.[w]
17 Then, at once, visions in horrible dreams perturbed them[x]
and unexpected fears assailed them;
18 And cast half-dead, one here, another there,
they revealed why they were dying.
19 For the dreams that disturbed them had proclaimed this beforehand,
lest they perish unaware of why they endured such evil.
20 The trial of death touched even the righteous,
and in the desert a plague struck the multitude;
Yet not for long did the anger last.[y]
21 For the blameless man* hastened to be their champion,
bearing the weapon of his special office,
prayer and the propitiation of incense;
He withstood the wrath and put a stop to the calamity,
showing that he was your servant.
22 He overcame the bitterness
not by bodily strength, not by force of arms;
But by word he overcame the smiter,*

**18:9 Divine institution**: the Passover. **Ancestral hymns of praise**: possibly the Hallel psalms, the psalms sung at the end of the Passover meal; cf. Mt 26:30; Mk 14:26.

**18:13 People**: the Israelites (cf. Ex 4:22).

**18:14–16** These verses attribute to the personified "word" the actions of the Lord mentioned in Ex 12:13–17 (note the role of the "destroyer" in Ex 12:23 and compare Wis 18:22, 25).

**18:21 Blameless man**: Aaron, acting according to his office of high priest and intercessor (cf. Nm 17:9–15; Ex 28:15–21, 31–38).

**18:22 Smiter**: the destroying angel; cf. v. 25.

*m:* Wis 11:7, 14; Ex 1:16, 22; 2:3, 6–10; 15:10; Neh 9:11. *n:* Wis 12:21; Ex 6:8; 13:5. *o:* Ex 14:13. *p:* Wis 19:22; Ex 3:18; Is 43:3–4. *q:* Ex 12:21–28; Sir 44–50. *r:* Ex 12:30; Jer 9:17, 19. *s:* Ex 11:5; 12:29. *t:* Nm 33:4. *u:* Wis 17:7; Ex 4:22–23; 12:12, 29; 13:2, 13, 15. *v:* Wis 9:10; Ex 15:3. *w:* 1 Chr 21:16; Heb 4:12; Rev 1:16. *x:* Wis 17:3–4. *y:* Wis 16:5; Nm 17:9–15.

recalling the sworn covenants with
their ancestors.[z]
23 For when corpses had already fallen one
on another in heaps,
he stood in the midst and checked the
anger,
and cut off its way to the living.[a]
24 For on his full-length robe was the whole
world,
and ancestral glories were carved on
the four rows of stones,
and your grandeur* was on the crown
upon his head.[b]
25 To these the destroyer yielded, these he
feared;
for this sole trial of anger sufficed.[c]

## CHAPTER 19

See RG 196

1 But merciless wrath assailed the
wicked until the end,
for God knew beforehand what they
were yet to do:[d]
2 That though they themselves had agreed
to the departure
and had anxiously sent them on their
way,
they would regret it and pursue them.[e]
3 For while they were still engaged in
funeral rites
and mourning at the burials of the dead,
They adopted another senseless plan:
those whom they had driven out with
entreaties
they now pursued as fugitives.[f]
4 For a compulsion appropriate to this
ending drew them on,
and made them forget what had
befallen them,
That they might complete the torments of
their punishment,
5 and your people might experience a
glorious* journey
while those others met an
extraordinary death.
6 * For all creation, in its several kinds,
was being made over anew,
serving your commands, that your
children might be preserved
unharmed.[g]
7 The cloud overshadowed their camp;
and out of what had been water, dry
land was seen emerging:
Out of the Red Sea an unimpeded road,
and a grassy plain out of the mighty
flood.[h]
8 Over this crossed the whole nation
sheltered by your hand,
and they beheld stupendous wonders.
9 For they ranged about like horses,
and leapt like lambs,
praising you, LORD, their deliverer.[i]
10 For they were still mindful of what had
happened in their sojourn:
how instead of the young of animals
the land brought forth gnats,
and instead of fishes the river swarmed
with countless frogs.[j]
11 And later they saw also a new kind of
bird[k]
when, prompted by desire, they asked
for pleasant foods;
12 For to appease them quail came to them
from the sea.
13 And the punishments came upon the
sinners
not without forewarnings from the
violence of the thunderbolts.

For they justly suffered for their own
misdeeds,
since they treated their guests with the
more grievous* hatred.[l]
14 For those others* did not receive
unfamiliar visitors,[m]

**18:24 Glories . . . grandeur**: the name of God and the names of the tribes were inscribed on the high priest's apparel.

**19:5 Glorious**: more precisely, "wondrous," but the word reflects "glorified" in 18:8 and 19:22.

**19:6** The cooperation of creation in Israel's deliverance (vv. 7–12) under the direction of the Lord is a favorite theme; cf. 16:24–25.

**19:13 More grievous**: than that of the people of Sodom (Gn 19) with whom the Egyptians are compared.

**19:14 Others**: the people of Sodom refused to receive strangers. **Beneficent**: because of the services rendered by Joseph.

*z:* Wis 12:21; Ex 32:12–13; Ps 20:8. *a:* Nm 14:29–30. *b:* Ex 28:15–21, 31–38; Sir 45:8–12; 50:11. *c:* 1 Chr 21:15. *d:* Ex 14:4. *e:* Ex 12:33; 14:5, 8. *f:* Wis 18:10, 12; Ex 12:30–36. *g:* Wis 5:17; 16:24. *h:* Ex 14:21–29. *i:* Wis 10:20; 16:8; Ex 15:1–18; Ps 114:4–6. *j:* Ex 7:27–8:3; 8:12–15; Ps 105:30–31. *k:* Wis 16:2; Ps 78:18. *l:* 2 Mc 7:18, 32.

but these were enslaving beneficent
guests.
15 And not that only; but what punishment
was to be theirs*
since they received strangers
unwillingly!
16 Yet these,* after welcoming them with
festivities,
oppressed with awful toils
those who had shared with them the
same rights.[n]
17 And they were struck with blindness,*
as those others had been at the doors
of the righteous man—
When, surrounded by yawning
darkness,
each sought the entrance of his own
door.[o]
18 For the elements, in ever-changing
harmony,
like strings of the harp, produce new
melody,
while the flow of music steadily
persists.
And this can be perceived exactly from a
review of what took place.
19 For land creatures were changed into
water creatures,
and those that swam went over on land.
20 Fire in water maintained its own strength,[p]
and water forgot its quenching nature;
21 Flames, by contrast, neither consumed
the flesh
of the perishable animals that went
about in them,
nor melted the icelike, quick-melting
kind of ambrosial food.
22 For every way, LORD! you magnified and
glorified your people;
unfailing, you stood by them in every
time and circumstance.[q]

**19:15 Theirs**: the people of Sodom.
**19:16 These**: the Egyptians.
**19:17 Blindness**: the plague of darkness. **Righteous man**: Lot (Gn 19:11).

*m:* Gn 15:13; Ex 2:22. *n:* Gn 45:17–20; 47:4–6; Ex 1:11. *o:* Wis 17:2; Gn 19:11. *p:* Wis 16:17–19, 22–23, 27. *q:* Wis 18:8; Lv 26:44; Ps 126:3.

See RG 198–200

# The Wisdom of Ben Sira (Ecclesiasticus)

The Wisdom of Ben Sira derives its title from the author, "Yeshua [Jesus], son of Eleazar, son of Sira" (50:27). This seems to be the earliest title of the book. The designation "Liber Ecclesiasticus," meaning "Church Book," appended to some Greek and Latin manuscripts, is perhaps due to the extensive use the church made of this book in presenting moral teaching to catechumens and to the faithful. The title "Sirach" comes from the Greek form of the author's name.

The author, a sage who lived in Jerusalem, was thoroughly imbued with love for the wisdom tradition, and also for the law, priesthood, Temple, and divine worship. As a wise and experienced observer of life he addressed himself to his contemporaries with the motive of helping them to maintain religious faith and integrity through study of the books sacred to the Jewish tradition.

The book contains numerous well-crafted maxims, grouped by affinity, and dealing with a variety of subjects such as the individual, the family, and the community in their relations with one another and with God. It treats of friendship, education, poverty and wealth, laws, religious worship, and many other matters that reflect the religious and social customs of the time.

Written in Hebrew in the early years of the second century B.C., the book was finished by ca. 175. The text was translated into Greek by the author's grandson after 117 B.C. He also wrote a foreword which contains valuable information about the book, its author, and himself as translator. Until the close of the nineteenth century the Wisdom of Ben Sira was known to Christians in translations, of which the Greek rendering was the most important. From it the Latin version was made. Between 1896 and 1900, again in 1931, and several times since 1956, incomplete manuscripts were discovered, so that more than two thirds of the book in Hebrew is available; these

Hebrew texts agree substantially with the Greek. One such text, from Masada, is pre-Christian in date. The New American Bible provides a critical translation based on the evidence of all the ancient texts.

Though not included in the Jewish Bible after the first century A.D., nor, therefore, accepted by Protestants, the Wisdom of Ben Sira has been recognized by the Catholic Church as inspired and canonical. The Foreword, though not properly part of the book, is always included with it because of its antiquity and importance.

The contents of the Wisdom of Ben Sira are of a discursive nature, not easily divided into separate parts. Chapters 1–43 deal largely with moral instruction; 44:1–50:24 contain a eulogy of the heroes of Israel. There are two appendixes in which the author expresses his gratitude to God (51:1–12), and invites the unschooled to acquire true wisdom (51:13–30).

---

### FOREWORD*

*1*Inasmuch as many and great truths have been given to us through the Law, the prophets, and the authors who followed them,* for which the instruction and wisdom of Israel merit praise, it is the duty of those who read the scriptures not only to become knowledgeable themselves but also to use their love of learning in speech and in writing to help others less familiar. So my grandfather Jesus, who had long devoted himself to the study of the law, the prophets, and the rest of the books of our ancestors, and had acquired great familiarity with them, was moved to write something himself regarding instruction and wisdom. He did this so that those who love learning might, by accepting what he had written, make even greater progress in living according to the Law.

You are invited therefore to read it with good will and attention, with indulgence for any failure on our part, despite earnest efforts, in the interpretation of particular passages. For words spoken originally in Hebrew do not have the same effect when they are translated into another language. That is true not only of this book but of the Law itself, the prophecies, and the rest of the books, which differ no little when they are read in the original.

I arrived in Egypt in the thirty-eighth year of the reign of King Euergetes, and while there, I had access to no little learning. I therefore considered it my duty to devote some diligence and industry to the translation of this book. During this time I applied my skill for many sleepless hours to complete the book and publish it for those living abroad who wish to acquire learning and are disposed to live their lives according to the Law.

## The Wisdom of Ben Sira

### CHAPTER 1

See RG 198–200

### *God's Gift of Wisdom**

*1* All wisdom* is from the Lord
and remains with him forever.[a]
*2* The sands of the sea, the drops of rain,
the days of eternity—who can count them?
*3* Heaven's height, earth's extent,
the abyss and wisdom—who can explore them?
*4* Before all other things wisdom was created;
and prudent understanding, from eternity.†

*6* The root of wisdom—to whom has it been revealed?

**Foreword The Law, the prophets, and the authors who followed them**: an indication of the eventual tripartite division of the Hebrew Scriptures: Law (*torah*), Prophets (*nebi'im*), and Writings (*ketubim*), shortened in the acronym Tanak. **Thirty-eighth . . . Euergetes**: 132 B.C. The reference is to Ptolemy VII, Physkon Euergetes II (170–163; 145–117 B.C.).

**1:1–10** This brief poem serves as an introduction to the book. The Lord is the source and preserver of all wisdom, which he pours out upon all. See Jb 28:20–28; Prv 2:6; 8:22–31; Wis 7:25–27.

**1:1 Wisdom**: throughout the book Ben Sira describes in great detail just what wisdom is: sometimes divine (1:6, 8), sometimes a synonym for God's law (24:22–23). Ben Sira makes clear that all wisdom comes from God.

† **1:4** Other ancient texts read as v. 5:

The wellspring of wisdom is the word of God in the heights,
and its runlets are the ageless commandments.

*a:* 1 Kgs 3:9.

### The Fear of the LORD

TAKING HIS CUE from Psalm 111:10, "The fear of the LORD is the beginning of wisdom," which is similarly stated in Ben Sira 1:14, Ben Sira equates the possession of wisdom with the fear of the LORD. Since the pursuit of wisdom is a common goal found across cultures, the fear of the LORD may be a way of specifying what counts as Jewish wisdom. Because Ben Sira does not entertain the possibility of an afterlife, the rewards and blessings of wisdom are manifest in one's earthly life; they include happiness, long life, and lack of want (1:11–20). Such a perspective is comparable to that of Deuteronomy 6. The teachings of Ben Sira deal mostly with practical wisdom that could just as easily apply to Gentiles as well as Jews. The reference to the commandments (1:26), which fills out the meaning of the fear of the LORD, helps maintain a connection between Ben Sira's general instructions for living and the explicitly Jewish teachings of the Torah (see also 2:16; 38:34b–39:1). One who lacks wisdom inevitably disobeys God, which results in dishonor (1:28–30). Ben Sira's ethical teachings are based on a system of honor and shame (dishonor). Dishonor is not an internal feeling of guilt but, rather, a diminishment of one's esteem in the eyes of others. God's way of punishing anyone guilty of secret transgressions is to expose and thereby shame the culprit publicly.

Her subtleties—who knows them?† [b]
8 * There is but one, wise and truly awesome,
seated upon his throne—the Lord.
9 It is he who created her,
saw her and measured her,[c]
Poured her forth upon all his works,
10 upon every living thing according to his bounty,
lavished her upon those who love him.

### *Fear of the Lord Is Wisdom**

11 The fear of the Lord* is glory and exultation,
gladness and a festive crown.
12 The fear of the Lord rejoices the heart,
giving gladness, joy, and long life.†
13 Those who fear the Lord will be happy at the end,
even on the day of death they will be blessed.
14 The beginning of wisdom is to fear the Lord;
she is created with the faithful in the womb.[d]
15 With the godly she was created from of old,
and with their descendants she will keep faith.
16 The fullness of wisdom is to fear the Lord;
she inebriates them with her fruits.[e]
17 Their entire house she fills with choice foods,
their granaries with her produce.
18 The crown of wisdom is the fear of the Lord,

† **1:6** Other ancient texts read as v. 7:
An understanding of wisdom—to whom has this been disclosed;
her resourcefulness, who has known?

**1:8–10** In contrast to Jb 28, wisdom is not only with God, but given to all, especially Israel; see Bar 3:9; 4:4.

**1:11–30** This is one of several poems of 22 bicola, or poetic lines, corresponding to the number of letters in the Hebrew alphabet. Ben Sira uses the expression "fear of the Lord" twelve times and the noun "wisdom" seven times to emphasize the connection between the two ideas. He describes the blessings that come to those who fear the Lord, i.e., those who practice true religion by loving and serving God and keeping the Law (2:7–10, 15–17; 4:11–16; see Dt 6:1–5, 24). Such blessings recur throughout the book.

**1:11 Fear of the Lord**: Ben Sira identifies wisdom with the fear of the Lord (vv. 26–27).

† **1:12** Other ancient texts read as v. 12cd:
Fear of the Lord is the Lord's gift;
also for love he makes firm paths.

† **1:18** Other ancient texts read as v. 18cd:
Both are gifts of God toward peace;
splendor opens out for those who love him.

*b:* Bar 3:15; Jb 28:10, 20. *c:* Jb 28:27. *d:* Jb 28:28; Ps 111:10; Prv 1:7; 9:10. *e:* Eccl 12:13.

flowering with peace and perfect
health.†
19 Knowledge and full understanding she
rains down;
she heightens the glory of those who
possess her.
20 The root of wisdom is to fear the Lord;
her branches are long life.
21 The fear of the Lord drives away sins;
where it abides it turns back all anger.
22 Unjust anger can never be justified;
anger pulls a person to utter ruin.
23 * Until the right time, the patient remain
calm,
then cheerfulness comes back to them.
24 Until the right time they hold back their
words;
then the lips of many will tell of their
good sense.

25 Among wisdom's treasures is the model
for knowledge;
but godliness is an abomination to the
sinner.
26 If you desire wisdom, keep the
commandments,
and the Lord will bestow her upon
you;
27 For the fear of the Lord is wisdom and
discipline;
faithfulness and humility are his
delight.
28 Do not disobey the fear of the Lord,*
do not approach it with duplicity of
heart.[f]
29 Do not be a hypocrite before others;
over your lips keep watch.
30 Do not exalt yourself lest you fall
and bring dishonor upon yourself;

For then the Lord will reveal your secrets
and cast you down in the midst of the
assembly.
Because you did not approach the fear of
the Lord,
and your heart was full of deceit.

## CHAPTER 2

See RG 198–200

### *Trust in God*

1 My child, when you come to serve the
Lord,*
prepare yourself for trials.[g]
2 Be sincere of heart and steadfast,
and do not be impetuous in time of
adversity.
3 Cling to him, do not leave him,
that you may prosper in your last days.
4 Accept whatever happens to you;
in periods of humiliation be patient.
5 For in fire gold is tested,
and the chosen, in the crucible of
humiliation.[h]
6 Trust in God, and he will help you;
make your ways straight and hope in
him.
7 You that fear the Lord, wait for his
mercy,
do not stray lest you fall.
8 You that fear the Lord, trust in him,
and your reward will not be lost.
9 You that fear the LORD, hope for good
things,
for lasting joy and mercy.
10 Consider the generations long past and
see:
has anyone trusted in the Lord and
been disappointed?
Has anyone persevered in his fear and
been forsaken?
has anyone called upon him and been
ignored?[i]
11 For the Lord is compassionate and
merciful;
forgives sins and saves in time of
trouble.

**1:23–24** Ben Sira pays close attention to *kaîros*, the right time, occurring some sixty times in his book.

**1:28–30** Attempting to serve the Lord with duplicity of heart is hypocrisy and self-exaltation, deserving of public disgrace.

**2:1–11** Serving the Lord is not without its trials (v. 1); but no matter what happens, the genuine believer will remain sincere, steadfast, and faithful (vv. 2–3). Misfortune and humiliation are means of purification to prove one's worth (vv. 4–5). Ben Sira believed that patience and unwavering trust in God are ultimately rewarded with the benefits of God's mercy and of lasting joy (vv. 6–11).

**2:12–18** A stern warning to those who compromise their

*f:* Jas 1:8; 2:8. *g:* 2 Tm 3:10–12. *h:* Prv 17:3; Wis 3:6; Is 48:10; 1 Pt 1:7. *i:* Ps 31:2; 145:18–20.

12 Woe to timid hearts and drooping hands,*
to the sinner who walks a double path!
13 Woe to the faint of heart! For they do not trust,
and therefore have no shelter!
14 Woe to you that have lost hope!
what will you do at the Lord's visitation?

15 Those who fear the Lord do not disobey his words;
those who love him keep his ways.[j]
16 Those who fear the Lord seek to please him;
those who love him are filled with his law.
17 Those who fear the Lord prepare their hearts
and humble themselves before him.

18 Let us fall into the hands of the Lord
and not into the hands of mortals,
For equal to his majesty is his mercy;
and equal to his name are his works.[k]

## CHAPTER 3

See RG 198–200

### *Responsibilities to Parents**

1 Children, listen to me, your father;
act accordingly, that you may be safe.
2 For the Lord sets a father in honor over his children
and confirms a mother's authority over her sons.
3 Those who honor their father atone for sins;
4 they store up riches who respect their mother.
5 Those who honor their father will have joy in their own children,
and when they pray they are heard.
6 Those who respect their father will live a long life;
those who obey the Lord honor their mother.

7 Those who fear the Lord honor their father,
and serve their parents as masters.
8 In word and deed honor your father,
that all blessings may come to you.[l]
9 A father's blessing gives a person firm roots,
but a mother's curse uproots the growing plant.[m]
10 Do not glory in your father's disgrace,
for that is no glory to you!
11 A father's glory is glory also for oneself;
they multiply sin who demean their mother.[n]

12 My son, be steadfast in honoring your father;
do not grieve him as long as he lives.[o]
13 Even if his mind fails, be considerate of him;
do not revile him because you are in your prime.
14 Kindness to a father will not be forgotten;
it will serve as a sin offering—it will take lasting root.
15 In time of trouble it will be recalled to your advantage,
like warmth upon frost it will melt away your sins.
16 Those who neglect their father are like blasphemers;
those who provoke their mother are accursed by their Creator.[p]

### *Humility**

17 My son, conduct your affairs with humility,
and you will be loved more than a giver of gifts.

faith in time of affliction; they fail in courage and trust and therefore have no security (vv. 12–14). But those who fear the Lord through obedience, reverence, love, and humility find his "mercy equal to his majesty" (vv. 15–18).

**3:1–16** Besides the virtues that must characterize our conduct toward God, special duties are enjoined, such as honor and respect toward parents, with corresponding blessings (vv. 1–9). By showing such respect especially to old and infirm parents (vv. 10–13), the sins of children are pardoned (vv. 14–15). Failure to honor father and mother is blasphemy and merits a curse from God (v. 16). Cf. Ex 20:12; Eph 6:2–3.

**3:17–24** Humility gives you a true estimate of yourself (vv. 17–20; cf. 10:28), so that you will do what should be done, and avoid what is beyond your understanding and strength (vv. 21–23). Intellectual pride, however, leads you astray (v. 24). Ben Sira is perhaps warning his students against the perils of Greek philosophy.

*j:* Jn 14:23. *k:* Sir 17:29. *l:* Ex 20:12; Dt 5:16; Mt 15:4; 19:19; Mk 7:10; 10:19; Lk 18:20; Eph 6:2–3. *m:* Gn 27:27–29; 49:2–27. *n:* Prv 17:6. *o:* Prv 23:22. *p:* Prv 19:26; 30:11, 14, 17.

**Care for Those in Need**

CARE FOR THOSE who of necessity depend on the good will of others for their survival (4:1–10) reflects a standard of ethical piety that is well-represented in the various parts of the biblical tradition: in legal texts (Dt 24:17–22); in the prophets (Am 2:6–7); and elsewhere in wisdom literature (Jb 29:12–20; Prv 19:17, though compare Prv 19:6–7; Sir 10:27–31).

18 Humble yourself the more, the greater
you are,
and you will find mercy in the sight of
God.† [q]
20 For great is the power of the Lord;
by the humble he is glorified.
21 What is too sublime for you, do not seek;
do not reach into things that are hidden
from you.[r]
22 What is committed to you, pay heed to;
what is hidden is not your concern.
23 In matters that are beyond you do not
meddle,
when you have been shown more than
you can understand.
24 Indeed, many are the conceits of human
beings;
evil imaginations lead them astray.

### *Docility**

25 Without the pupil of the eye, light is
missing;
without knowledge, wisdom is missing.
26 A stubborn heart will fare badly in the
end;
those who love danger will perish in it.
27 A stubborn heart will have many a hurt;
adding sin to sin is madness.
28 When the proud are afflicted, there is no
cure;
for they are offshoots of an evil plant.[s]
29 The mind of the wise appreciates proverbs,
and the ear that listens to wisdom
rejoices.

### *Alms for the Poor*

30 As water quenches a flaming fire,
so almsgiving atones for sins.[t]
31 The kindness people have done crosses
their paths later on;
should they stumble, they will find
support.

## CHAPTER 4

See RG 198–200

1 My child, do not mock the life of
the poor;
do not keep needy eyes* waiting.[u]
2 Do not grieve the hungry,
nor anger the needy.
3 Do not aggravate a heart already angry,
nor delay giving to the needy.
4 A beggar's request do not reject;
do not turn your face away from the
poor.
5 From the needy do not turn your eyes;
do not give them reason to curse you.
6 If in their pain they cry out bitterly,
their Rock will hear the sound of their
cry.

### *Social Conduct*

7 Endear yourself to the assembly;
before the city's ruler bow your head.
8 Give a hearing to the poor,
and return their greeting with
deference;
9 Deliver the oppressed from their
oppressors;[v]
right judgment should not be
repugnant to you.
10 Be like a father to orphans,
and take the place of a husband to
widows.
Then God will call you his child,
and he will be merciful to you and
deliver you from the pit.

† **3:18** Other ancient texts read as v. 19:
Many are lofty and famous,
but to the humble he reveals his plan.

**3:25–29** The antidote for stubbornness is to be found in the search for knowledge and wisdom.

**4:1 Needy eyes**: when the poor look for help; cf. 18:18.

*q:* Mt 23:12; Lk 1:52; 14:11; 18:14. *r:* Ps 131:1. *s:* Dt 32:32; Wis 12:10. *t:* Sir 7:32–36; 29:8–13; Dt 15:7–11; Tb 12:9; Dn 4:24. *u:* Tb 4:7–11. *v:* Jb 29:12, 17.

### *The Rewards of Wisdom**

11 Wisdom teaches her children
and admonishes all who can understand her.
12 Those who love her love life;
those who seek her out win the LORD's favor.
13 Those who hold her fast will attain glory,
and they shall abide in the blessing of the LORD.
14 Those who serve her serve the Holy One;
those who love her the Lord loves.[w]

15 "Whoever obeys me will judge nations;
whoever listens to me will dwell in my inmost chambers.
16 If they remain faithful, they will possess me;
their descendants too will inherit me.

17 "I will walk with them in disguise,
and at first I will test them with trials.
Fear and dread I will bring upon them
and I will discipline them with my constraints.
When their hearts are fully with me,
18 then I will set them again on the straight path
and reveal my secrets to them.
19 But if they turn away from me, I will abandon them
and deliver them over to robbers."

### *Sincerity and Justice**

20 My son, watch for the right time; fear what is evil;
do not bring shame upon yourself.
21 There is a shame heavy with guilt,
and a shame that brings glory and respect.
22 Show no favoritism to your own discredit;
let no one intimidate you to your own downfall.
23 Do not refrain from speaking at the proper time,
and do not hide your wisdom;
24 For wisdom becomes known through speech,
and knowledge through the tongue's response.

25 Never speak against the truth,
but of your own ignorance be ashamed.
26 Do not be ashamed to acknowledge your sins,
and do not struggle against a rushing stream.
27 Do not abase yourself before a fool;
do not refuse to do so before rulers.
28 Even to the death, fight for what is right,
and the LORD will do battle for you.

29 Do not be haughty in your speech,
or lazy and slack in your deeds.
30 Do not be like a lion at home,
or sly and suspicious with your servants.
31 Do not let your hand be open to receive,
but clenched when it is time to give.

## CHAPTER 5

See RG 198–200

### *Against Presumption**

1 Do not rely on your wealth,
or say, "I have the power."[x]
2 Do not rely on your strength
in following the desires of your heart.
3 Do not say, "Who can prevail against me?"
for the LORD will exact punishment.
4 Do not say, "I have sinned, yet what has happened to me?"
for the LORD is slow to anger!
5 Do not be so confident of forgiveness
that you add sin upon sin.
6 Do not say, "His mercy is great;
my many sins he will forgive."

**4:11–19** The Hebrew text in vv. 15–19 presents wisdom speaking in the first person, as in chap. 24. The precious fruits of wisdom—life, favor, glory, blessings, God's love—arouse desire for her (vv. 11–14). Her disciples are like ministers (v. 14) and judges (v. 15), whose descendants have her for their heritage (v. 16). They enjoy happiness and learn her secrets after surviving her tests (vv. 17–18). Those who fail her are abandoned to destruction (v. 19).

**4:20–31** The student of wisdom is warned about interior trials of discipline and external dangers to sincerity and justice, namely evil, human respect (vv. 20–22), compromise of liberty in speech and action (vv. 23–25), false shame (v. 26). The student must fight for the truth (vv. 25, 28), avoiding cynicism and laziness (v. 29), and inconsistency (v. 30).

**5:1–8** The vices of the rich are pride and independence (vv. 1–2), presumption (v. 3), false security (vv. 4–6), and impenitence (v. 7), which cannot escape the divine wrath (vv. 7–8). Cf. Prv 18:23; 19:1; 28:6.

*w:* Wis 7:28. *x:* Sir 11:24; Prv 27:1; Lk 12:19; 1 Tm 6:17.

## The Dangers of Money, Talk, and Passion

A TWENTY-TWO-LINE POEM (5:1–6:4) provides an overview of three topics of central importance throughout the text of Ben Sira: wealth, speech, and desire. All three have the potential to bring ruin. Wealth should not be gained by thievery (5:8, 14b). Speech must not be double-tongued (5:14a), meaning it should never be deceitful or self-serving. Desire must be subordinate to wisdom.

For mercy and anger alike are with him;
his wrath comes to rest on the wicked.
7 Do not delay turning back to the LORD,
do not put it off day after day.
For suddenly his wrath will come forth;
at the time of vengeance, you will perish.
8 Do not rely on deceitful wealth,
for it will be no help on the day of wrath.[y]

### *Use and Abuse of the Tongue**

9 Do not winnow in every wind,
nor walk in every path.*
10 Be steadfast regarding your knowledge,
and let your speech be consistent.
11 Be swift to hear,
but slow to answer.[z]
12 If you can, answer your neighbor;
if not, place your hand over your mouth!
13 Honor and dishonor through speaking!
The tongue can be your downfall.
14 Do not be called double-tongued;
and with your tongue do not slander a neighbor.
For shame has been created for the thief,
and sore disgrace for the double-tongued.
15 In little or in much, do not act corruptly;

### CHAPTER 6

See RG 198–200

1 Do not be a foe instead of a friend.
A bad name, disgrace, and dishonor you will inherit.
Thus the wicked, the double-tongued!*

### *Unruly Passions*

2 Do not fall into the grip of your passion,[a]
lest like fire it consume your strength.
3 It will eat your leaves and destroy your fruits,
and you will be left like a dry tree.
4 For fierce passion destroys its owner
and makes him the sport of his enemies.

### *True Friendship**

5 Pleasant speech multiplies friends,
and gracious lips, friendly greetings.
6 Let those who are friendly to you be many,
but one in a thousand your confidant.
7 When you gain friends, gain them through testing,[b]
and do not be quick to trust them.
8 For there are friends when it suits them,
but they will not be around in time of trouble.
9 Another is a friend who turns into an enemy,
and tells of the quarrel to your disgrace.
10 Others are friends, table companions,
but they cannot be found in time of affliction.
11 When things go well, they are your other self,
and lord it over your servants.
12 If disaster comes upon you, they turn against you
and hide themselves.
13 Stay away from your enemies,
and be on guard with your friends.

**5:9–6:1** Proper use of the tongue requires constancy in speech (v. 10), prudence (vv. 11–12), good judgment (v. 13), charity (5:15; 6:1); detraction, calumny (v. 14), and double-talk bring shame and disgrace (5:14; 6:1).

**5:9** The metaphors indicate careless behavior.

**6:1 Thus . . . double-tongued!**: people will say this against those disgraced by lying and double-talk.

**6:5–17** One of several poems Ben Sira wrote on friendship; see also 9:10–16; 12:8–18; 13:1–23; 19:13–17; 22:19–26; 27:16–21. True friends are discerned not by prosperity (v. 11), but through the trials of adversity: distress, quarrels (v. 9), sorrow (v. 10) and misfortune (v. 12). Such friends are rare, a gift from God (vv. 14–17).

y: Prv 10:2; 11:4, 28; Ps 52:9. z: Prv 29:20; Eccl 5:1; Jas 1:19. a: Sir 9:8; 23:16; 25:21; 41:20, 22; Jb 31:12. b: Sir 12:8–9; 37:1–5; Prv 19:4.

14 Faithful friends are a sturdy shelter;
whoever finds one finds a treasure.
15 Faithful friends are beyond price,
no amount can balance their worth.
16 Faithful friends are life-saving medicine;
those who fear God will find them.
17 Those who fear the Lord enjoy stable friendship,
for as they are, so will their neighbors be.

### *Blessings of Wisdom**

18 My child, from your youth choose discipline;
and when you have gray hair you will find wisdom.
19 As though plowing and sowing, draw close to her;
then wait for her bountiful crops.
For in cultivating her you will work but little,
and soon you will eat her fruit.

20 She is rough ground to the fool!
The stupid cannot abide her.
21 She will be like a burdensome stone to them,
and they will not delay in casting her aside.
22 For discipline* is like her name,
she is not accessible to many.

23 Listen, my child, and take my advice;
do not refuse my counsel.
24 Put your feet into her fetters,
and your neck under her yoke.
25 Bend your shoulders and carry her
and do not be irked at her bonds.

26 With all your soul draw close to her;
and with all your strength keep her ways.
27 Inquire and search, seek and find;
when you get hold of her, do not let her go.
28 Thus at last you will find rest in her,
and she will become your joy.

29 Her fetters will be a place of strength;
her snare, a robe of spun gold.
30 Her yoke will be a gold ornament;[c]
her bonds, a purple cord.
31 You will wear her as a robe of glory,
and bear her as a splendid crown.

32 If you wish, my son, you can be wise;
if you apply yourself, you can be shrewd.
33 If you are willing to listen, you can learn;
if you pay attention, you can be instructed.

34 Stand in the company of the elders;
stay close to whoever is wise.
35 Be eager to hear every discourse;
let no insightful saying escape you.[d]
36 If you see the intelligent, seek them out;
let your feet wear away their doorsteps!

37 Reflect on the law of the Most High,
and let his commandments be your constant study.
Then he will enlighten your mind,
and make you wise as you desire.[e]

## CHAPTER 7

See RG 198–200

### *Conduct Toward God and Neighbor**

1 Do no evil, and evil will not overtake you;*
2 avoid wickedness, and it will turn away from you.
3 Do not sow in the furrows of injustice,
lest you harvest it sevenfold.[f]
4 Do not seek from God authority

**6:18–37** The various figures in each of the eight stanzas urge the search for wisdom through patience (vv. 18–19), persistence (vv. 20–22), docility and perseverance (vv. 23–28). Wisdom bestows rich rewards (vv. 29–31) on those who apply themselves and learn from the wise (vv. 32–36). Although one must strive for wisdom, it is God who grants it (v. 37). Cf. 4:11–19.

**6:22 Discipline**: *musar* (in the sense of wisdom) is a perfect homonym for *musar*, "removed, withdrawn"; thus the path of discipline is not accessible to many.

**7:1–17** In the conduct of social relations wisdom forbids evil and injustice (vv. 1–3), pride (vv. 5, 15–17), ambition and partiality (vv. 4, 6), public disorder (v. 7), presumption and impatience toward God (vv. 9–10), ridicule (v. 11), mischief and deceit toward one's neighbor (vv. 8, 12–13). See the several wisdom poems in Prv 1–9.

**7:1** There is a play on "evil" which means both moral wrong and material calamity.

*c:* Is 62:3. *d:* Sir 8:8–9. *e:* Ps 1:2. *f:* Jb 4:8; Prv 22:8; Hos 8:7.

or from the king a place of honor.
5 Do not parade your righteousness before the LORD,
and before the king do not flaunt your wisdom.[g]
6 Do not seek to become a judge
if you do not have the strength to root out crime,
Lest you show fear in the presence of the prominent
and mar your integrity.
7 Do not be guilty of any evil before the city court
or disgrace yourself before the assembly.
8 Do not plot to repeat a sin;
even for one, you will not go unpunished.
9 Do not say, "He will appreciate my many gifts;
the Most High God will accept my offerings."[h]
10 Do not be impatient in prayer
or neglect almsgiving.
11 Do not ridicule the embittered;
Remember: there is One who exalts and humbles.*
12 Do not plot mischief against your relative
or against your friend and companion.
13 Refuse to tell lie after lie,
for it never results in good.
14 Do not babble in the assembly of the elders
or repeat the words of your prayer.* [i]
15 Do not hate hard work;
work was assigned by God.[j]
16 Do not esteem yourself more than your compatriots;
remember, his wrath will not delay.
17 More and more, humble your pride;
what awaits mortals is worms.* [k]

***Duties of Family Life, Religion and Charity****

18 Do not barter a friend for money,
or a true brother for the gold of Ophir.*
19 Do not reject a sensible wife;
a gracious wife is more precious than pearls.
20 Do not mistreat a servant who works faithfully,
or laborers who devote themselves to their task.[l]
21 Love wise servants as yourself;
do not refuse them freedom.*
22 Do you have livestock? Look after them;
if they are dependable, keep them.
23 Do you have sons? Correct them
and cure their stubbornness* in their early youth.[m]
24 Do you have daughters? Keep them chaste,
and do not be indulgent to them.[n]
25 Give your daughter in marriage, and a worry comes to an end;
but give her to a sensible man.
26 Do you have a wife? Do not mistreat her,
but do not trust the wife you hate.
27 With your whole heart honor your father;
your mother's birth pangs do not forget.[o]
28 Remember, of these parents you were born;
what can you give them for all they gave you?
29 With all your soul fear God
and revere his priests.
30 With all your strength love your Maker

**7:11 One who exalts and humbles**: God; cf. 1 Sm 2:7; Ps 75:8; Lk 1:52.

**7:14 Repeat . . . prayer**: brevity of speech is a wisdom ideal; toward superiors and God it is a sign of respect; cf. Eccl 5:1; Mt 6:7.

**7:17 Worms**: i.e., corruption; the Septuagint adds "fire."

**7:18–36** Respect and appreciation, justice and kindness should characterize relations toward members of the household (vv. 18–28), God and the priests (vv. 29–31), the poor and afflicted, the living and the dead (vv. 32–35).

**7:18 Ophir**: the port, at present unidentified, to which the ships of Solomon sailed and from which they brought back gold and silver; cf. note on Ps 45:10.

**7:21** After six years of service a Hebrew slave was entitled to freedom; cf. Ex 21:2; Dt 15:12–15.

**7:23 Cure their stubbornness**: keep them from rebellious pride; so with the Greek. Cf. 30:1–13. The Hebrew text, probably not original here, reads: "Choose wives for them while they are young."

*g:* Jb 9:2; Ps 143:2; Prv 25:6; 1 Cor 4:4. *h:* Sir 34:21–24; 35:14–15. *i:* Sir 32:7–10; Mt 6:7. *j:* Gn 2:15; 3:17. *k:* Sir 10:11; Jb 17:14; Is 66:24. *l:* Lv 19:13; Dt 24:14–15; Jas 5:4. *m:* Sir 30:1–13; Prv 13:24; 19:18; 23:13–14; 29:15, 17. *n:* Sir 42:9–12. *o:* Sir 3:1–16; Ex 20:12; Dt 5:16; Tb 4:3–4; Prv 23:22.

and do not neglect his ministers.
31 Honor God and respect the priest;
give him his portion as you have been commanded:[p]
First fruits and contributions,
his portion of victims and holy offerings.*
32 To the poor also extend your hand,
that your blessing may be complete.
33 Give your gift to all the living,
and do not withhold your kindness from the dead.*
34 Do not avoid those who weep,
but mourn with those who mourn.[q]
35 Do not hesitate to visit the sick,
because for such things you will be loved.[r]
36 In whatever you do, remember your last days,
and you will never sin.*

See RG 198–200

## CHAPTER 8

### *Prudence in Dealing with Others**

1 Do not contend with the mighty,
lest you fall into their power.
2 Do not quarrel with the rich,
lest they pay out the price of your downfall.
For gold has unsettled many,
and wealth perverts the character of princes.[s]
3 Do not quarrel with loud-mouths,
or heap wood upon their fire.* [t]
4 Do not associate with the senseless,
lest your ancestors be insulted.
5 Do not reproach one who turns away from sin;[u]
remember, we all are guilty.*
6 Do not insult one who is old,
for some of us will also grow old.
7 Do not rejoice when someone dies;
remember, we are all to be gathered in.
8 Do not neglect the discourse of the wise,[v]
but busy yourself with their proverbs;
For in this way you will acquire the training
to stand in the presence of princes.
9 Do not reject the tradition of the elders
which they have heard from their ancestors;
For from it you will learn
how to answer when the need arises.
10 Do not kindle the coals of sinners,
lest you be burned in their flaming fire.
11 Do not give ground before scoundrels;
it will set them in ambush against you.*
12 Do not lend to one more powerful than yourself;
or if you lend, count it as lost.[w]
13 Do not give collateral beyond your means;
consider any collateral a debt you must pay.
14 Do not go to court against a judge,
for the case will be settled in his favor.
15 Do not travel with the ruthless
lest they weigh you down with calamity;
For they will only go their own way,
and through their folly you will also perish.
16 Do not defy the quick-tempered,
or ride with them through the desert.
For bloodshed is nothing to them;
when there is no one to help, they will destroy you.

**7:31 First fruits . . . holy offerings**: cf. Ex 29:27; Lv 7:31–34; Nm 18:8–20; Dt 18:1–5.

**7:33** This seems to refer to the observances ordained toward the dead, that is, proper mourning and burial. Cf. 2 Sm 21:12–14; Tb 1:17–18; 12:12.

**7:36 Never sin**: because the last days of the sinner, it was presumed, would be troubled.

**8:1–19** The prudent will be circumspect, avoiding conflict with the powerful, the rich and insolent, the impious, the irascible, and judges (vv. 1–3, 10–12, 14, 16). They will not associate with the undisciplined (v. 4) or the ruthless (v. 15), with fools or strangers (vv. 17–19), but with the wise and the elders of the people (vv. 8–9). Caution is a recurring theme in Ben Sira.

**8:3** One should avoid increasing the ire of those who are hotheaded; cf. vv. 10, 16.

**8:5 We all are guilty**: cf. 1 Kgs 8:46; 2 Chr 6:36; Jb 25:4; Eccl 7:20; Rom 3:9–10; 5:12; 1 Jn 1:8.

**8:11** Giving in to the wicked only encourages them to take advantage.

*p:* Lv 7:31; Nm 18:18. *q:* Rom 12:15. *r:* Mt 25:36. *s:* Sir 31:5–6; Dt 16:19. *t:* Prv 26:20–21. *u:* 1 Kgs 8:46; 1 Jn 1:8. *v:* Sir 6:34–36. *w:* Sir 29:4–7; Prv 17:18.

17 Do not take counsel with simpletons,
for they cannot keep a confidence.
18 Before a stranger do nothing that should be kept secret,
for you do not know what it will produce later on.* [x]
19 Open your heart to no one,
do not banish your happiness.

## CHAPTER 9

See RG 198–200

### *Advice Concerning Women**

1 Do not be jealous of the wife of your bosom,
lest you teach her to do evil against you.*
2 Do not give a woman power over you
to trample on your dignity.[y]
3 Do not go near a strange woman,
lest you fall into her snares.
4 Do not dally with a singer,
lest you be captivated by her charms.
5 Do not entertain any thoughts about a virgin,
lest you be enmeshed in damages for her.*
6 Do not give yourself to a prostitute
lest you lose your inheritance.[z]
7 Do not look around the streets of the city
or wander through its squares.
8 Avert your eyes from a shapely woman;
do not gaze upon beauty that is not yours;
Through woman's beauty many have been ruined,
for love of it burns like fire.[a]
9 Never recline at table with a married woman,
or drink intoxicants with her,
Lest your heart be drawn to her
and you go down in blood* to the grave.

### *Choice of Friends**

10 Do not abandon old friends;
new ones cannot equal them.
A new friend is like new wine—
when it has aged, you drink it with pleasure.
11 Do not envy the wicked
for you do not know when their day will come.
12 Do not delight in the pleasures of the ungodly;
remember, they will not die unpunished.
13 Keep away from those who have power to kill,
and you will not be filled with the dread of death.
But if you come near them, do not offend them,
lest they take away your life.
Know that you are stepping among snares
and walking over a net.
14 As best you can, answer your neighbor,
and associate with the wise.
15 With the learned exchange ideas;
and let all your conversation be about the law of the Most High.
16 Take the righteous for your table companions;
and let your glory be in the fear of God.

### *Concerning Rulers**

17 Work by skilled hands will earn praise;
but the people's leader is proved wise by his words.
18 Loud mouths are feared in their city,
and whoever is reckless in speech is hated.

**8:18** To keep a secret, or a confidence, is a major concern of Ben Sira; cf. 1:30; 22:22; 27:16–21; 37:10; 42:1.

**9:1–9** Ben Sira writes about women only from the androcentric viewpoint of his culture. Cf. 25:13–26:27.

**9:1** Jealousy may lead to suspicion and may prompt a wife to those actions her husband fears.

**9:5** Cf. Ex 22:15–16; Dt 22:28–29; Jb 31:1. Cf. note on Ex 22:16.

**9:9 In blood**: perhaps refers to blood revenge; cf. Lv 20:10.

**9:10–16** The second of Ben Sira's poems on friendship; cf. note on 6:5–17. In choosing friends, adherence to the law of the Lord should serve as a guide (v. 15). Associate with true friends (v. 10), with the righteous and the learned (vv. 14–16); avoid the company of the mighty and of sinners (vv. 11–13). Cf. 8:1–19.

**9:17–10:5** Public office as conducted justly or unjustly benefits or destroys the people, according to the axiom, "as the prince, so the people." God, however, has sovereignty over both.

*x:* Prv 25:9–10. *y:* Sir 25:21. *z:* Prv 5:1–14; 6:24; 29:3. *a:* Sir 25:20; 41:21; Prv 6:25–29.

## CHAPTER 10

See RG 198–200

1 A wise magistrate gives stability to his people,
and government by the intelligent is well ordered.[b]
2 As the people's judge, so the officials;[c]
as the head of a city, so the inhabitants.
3 A reckless king destroys his people,
but a city grows through the intelligence of its princes.[d]
4 Sovereignty over the earth is in the hand of God,
who appoints the right person for the right time.
5 Sovereignty over everyone is in the hand of God,
who imparts his majesty to the ruler.

### *The Sin of Pride*

6 No matter what the wrong, never harm your neighbor
or go the way of arrogance.[e]
7 Odious to the Lord and to mortals is pride,
and for both oppression is a crime.
8 Sovereignty is transferred from one people to another
because of the lawlessness of the proud.
9 Why are dust and ashes proud?*
Even during life the body decays.
10 A slight illness—the doctor jests;
a king today—tomorrow he is dead.
11 When a people die,
they inherit corruption and worms, gnats and maggots.[f]
12 The beginning of pride is stubbornness
in withdrawing the heart from one's Maker.
13 For sin is a reservoir of insolence,
a source which runs over with vice;
Because of it God sends unheard-of afflictions
and strikes people with utter ruin.[g]
14 God overturns the thrones of the proud
and enthrones the lowly in their place.
15 God plucks up the roots of the proud,
and plants the lowly in their place.
16 The Lord lays waste the lands of the nations,
and destroys them to the very foundations of the earth.
17 He removes them from the earth, destroying them,
erasing their memory from the world.
18 Insolence does not befit mortals,
nor impudent anger those born of women.

### *True Glory**

19 Whose offspring can be honorable?
Human offspring.
Those who fear the LORD are honorable offspring.
Whose offspring can be disgraceful?
Human offspring.
Those who transgress the commandment are disgraceful offspring.
20 Among relatives their leader is honored;
but whoever fears God is honored among God's people.†
22 Resident alien, stranger, foreigner, pauper—
their glory is the fear of the LORD.
23 It is not right to despise anyone wise but poor,
nor proper to honor the lawless.[h]
24 The prince, the ruler, the judge are in honor;
but none is greater than the one who fears God.
25 When the free serve a wise slave,
the wise will not complain.[i]
26 Do not flaunt your wisdom in managing your affairs,
or boast in your time of need.

**10:9–10** The general implication is that a slight illness today may be followed by death tomorrow. The uncertainty of life leaves no room for pride.

**10:19–11:6** Genuine honor comes not from one's place in society but from fear of the Lord and a true estimate of oneself. The Lord exalts the lowly and oppressed; transgressors of the commandment merit dishonor and disgrace.

† **10:20** Other ancient texts read as v. 21:
The beginning of acceptance is the fear of the Lord;
the beginning of rejection, effrontery and pride.

*b:* Prv 29:4; Wis 6:24. *c:* Ez 16:44; Prv 29:12. *d:* Prv 29:4–8. *e:* Lv 19:18. *f:* Sir 7:17; Jb 17:14; Is 66:24. *g:* Prv 11:2; 16:18; 18:12. *h:* Jas 2:1–4. *i:* Prv 17:2.

**Who Is Deserving of Honor?**

IN CONTRAST TO the previous section, which described the proud and powerful who seemingly possess honor but ultimately lack it, Ben Sira 10:19–11:6 addresses those who genuinely deserve honor. The opening questions emphasize that all people are worthy of honor if they fear the LORD. The prince, the ruler and the judge (10:24) should be honored not because of their professional station, but because they fear the LORD. Ben Sira points out that the same man will be more honored if he is rich than if he is poor. Such a sentiment seems to contrast with other of Ben Sira's teachings about the insignificance of wealth (11:14–28), but it may simply reflect reality and his pragmatic approach to life (13:22–25).

27 Better the worker who has goods in plenty
than the boaster who has no food.[j]

28 My son, with humility have self-esteem;
and give yourself the esteem you deserve.

29 Who will acquit those who condemn themselves?
Who will honor those who disgrace themselves?

30 The poor are honored for their wisdom;
the rich are honored for their wealth.

31 Honored in poverty, how much more so in wealth!
Disgraced in wealth, in poverty how much the more!

## CHAPTER 11

See RG 198–200

1 The wisdom of the poor lifts their head high
and sets them among princes.

2 Do not praise anyone for good looks;
or despise anyone because of appearance.

3 The bee is least among winged creatures,
but it reaps the choicest of harvests.

4 Do not mock the one who wears only a loin-cloth,
or scoff at a person's bitter day.
For strange are the deeds of the LORD,
hidden from mortals his work.*

5 Many are the oppressed who rise to the throne;
some that none would consider wear a crown.*

6 Many are the exalted who fall into utter disgrace,
many the honored who are given into the power of the few.

### *Moderation and Patience**

7 Before investigating, do not find fault;
examine first, then criticize.

8 Before listening, do not say a word,
interrupt no one in the midst of speaking.[k]

9 Do not dispute about what is not your concern;
in the quarrels of the arrogant do not take part.

10 My son, why increase your anxiety,
since whoever is greedy for wealth will not be blameless?
Even if you chase after it, you will never overtake it;
and by fleeing you will not escape.

11 One may work and struggle and drive,
and fall short all the same.[l]

12 Others go their way broken-down drifters,
with little strength and great misery—
Yet the eye of the LORD looks favorably upon them,
shaking them free of the stinking mire.

**11:4** The implication is similar to Eccl 7:13; 8:17: the mysterious work of God.

**11:5** Cf. 1 Sm 2:8; Ps 75:8; 105:17–22; Lk 1:52.

**11:7–28** Discretion should regulate conduct toward others (vv. 7–9); as regards personal interests, one should avoid solicitude for the passing external benefits of life and property (vv. 10–14, 18–19, 21, 23–25) and cultivate the lasting inward gifts of wisdom, virtue (vv. 20, 22), and patience (vv. 25–28).

**11:14** In mysterious ways God ultimately governs the lives

*j:* Prv 12:9. *k:* Prv 18:13. *l:* Ps 127:2; Eccl 4:8.

[13] He lifts up their heads and exalts them
to the amazement of the many.

[14] * Good and evil, life and death,[m]
poverty and riches—all are from the
LORD.†
[17] The Lord's gift remains with the devout;
his favor brings lasting success.
[18] Some become rich through a miser's life,
and this is their allotted reward:
[19] When they say: "I have found rest,[n]
now I will feast on my goods,"
They do not know how long it will be
till they die and leave them to others.*
[20] My child, stand by your agreement and
attend to it,
grow old while doing your work.
[21] Do not marvel at the works of a sinner,
but trust in the LORD and wait for his
light;
For it is easy in the eyes of the LORD
suddenly, in an instant, to make the
poor rich.

[22] God's blessing is the lot of the
righteous,
and in due time their hope bears fruit.
[23] Do not say: "What do I need?
What further benefits can be mine?"
[24] Do not say: "I am self-sufficient.
What harm can come to me now?"
[25] The day of prosperity makes one forget
adversity;
the day of adversity makes one forget
prosperity.[o]
[26] For it is easy for the Lord on the day of
death*
to repay mortals according to their
conduct.
[27] A time of affliction brings forgetfulness
of past delights;
at the end of life one's deeds are
revealed.
[28] Call none happy before death,
for how they end, they are known.

### *Care in Choosing Friends*

[29] Not everyone should be brought into
your house,
for many are the snares of the crafty.
[30] Like a decoy partridge in a cage, so is the
heart of the proud,
and like a spy they will pick out the
weak spots.
[31] For they lie in wait to turn good into evil,
and to praiseworthy deeds they attach
blame.
[32] One spark kindles many coals;
a sinner lies in wait for blood.
[33] Beware of scoundrels, for they breed
only evil,
and they may give you a lasting stain.
[34] Admit strangers into your home, and
they will stir up trouble
and make you a stranger to your own
family.

## CHAPTER 12

See RG 198–200

[1] If you do good, know for whom
you are doing it,*
and your kindness will have its effect.
[2] Do good to the righteous and reward will
be yours,
if not from them, from the LORD.[p]
[3] No good comes to those who give
comfort to the wicked,
nor is it an act of mercy that they do.
[4] Give to the good but refuse the sinner;
[5] refresh the downtrodden but give
nothing to the proud.
No arms for combat should you give them,
lest they use these against you;
Twofold evil you will obtain for every
good deed you do for them.
[6] For God also hates sinners,
and takes vengeance on evildoers.*

of men and women.

† **11:14** Other ancient texts read as vv. 15–16:
[15] Wisdom and understanding and knowledge of the Law,
love and virtuous paths, are from the Lord.
[16] Error and darkness were formed with sinners from their birth,
and evil grows old with those who exult in evil.

**11:19** Cf. the parable of the rich man, Lk 12:16–21.

**11:26–28** Ben Sira thought that divine retribution took place only in the present life, and even at the end of life; cf. 9:12; 14:16–17.

**12:1** The import of this verse is brought out in vv. 4–5.

**12:6** Verse 7 is a variant of verse 4 and is omitted.

*m:* Jb 1:21; 2:10. *n:* Eccl 4:8; 6:2; Lk 12:19. *o:* Sir 18:24–25. *p:* Dt 14:29.

8 In prosperity we cannot know our friends;*
in adversity an enemy will not remain concealed.[q]
9 When one is successful even an enemy is friendly;
but in adversity even a friend disappears.[r]
10 Never trust your enemies,
for their wickedness is like corrosion in bronze.
11 Even though they act deferentially and peaceably toward you,
take care to be on your guard against them.[s]
Treat them as those who reveal secrets,*
and be certain that in the end there will still be envy.
12 Do not let them stand near you,
lest they push you aside and take your place.
Do not let them sit at your right hand,
or they will demand your seat,
And in the end you will appreciate my advice,
when you groan with regret, as I warned.
13 Who pities a snake charmer when he is bitten,*
or anyone who goes near a wild beast?
14 So it is with the companion of the proud,
who is involved in their sins:
15 While you stand firm, they make no move;
but if you slip, they cannot hold back.
16 With their lips enemies speak sweetly,
but in their heart they scheme to plunge you into the abyss.
Though enemies have tears in their eyes,
given the chance, they will never have enough of your blood.[t]
17 If evil comes upon you, you will find them at hand;
pretending to help, they will trip you up,
18 Then they will shake their heads and clap their hands
and hiss repeatedly, and show their true faces.

## CHAPTER 13

See RG 198–200

### *Caution Regarding Associates**

1 Touch pitch and you blacken your hand;
associate with scoundrels and you learn their ways.
2 Do not lift a weight too heavy for you,
or associate with anyone wealthier than you.
How can the clay pot go with the metal cauldron?
When they knock together, the pot will be smashed:
3 The rich do wrong and boast of it,
while the poor are wronged and beg forgiveness.
4 As long as the rich can use you they will enslave you,
but when you are down and out they will abandon you.
5 As long as you have anything they will live with you,
but they will drain you dry without remorse.
6 When they need you they will deceive you
and smile at you and raise your hopes;
they will speak kindly to you and say, "What do you need?"
7 They will embarrass you at their dinner parties,
and finally laugh at you.
Afterwards, when they see you, they will pass you by,
and shake their heads at you.
8 Be on guard: do not act too boldly;
do not be like those who lack sense.
9 When the influential draw near, keep your distance;
then they will urge you all the more.

**12:8–18** Adversity distinguishes friends from enemies; to trust the latter or permit them intimacy is to invite disaster. Cf. note on 6:5–17.

**12:11** Ben Sira has harsh words for those who reveal secrets; see also 8:18; 27:16–21; 42:1; Prv 11:13; 20:19.

**12:13** For v. 13a, see especially Eccl 10:11.

**13:1–14:2** By means of various images, most of them unfavorable to the rich, Ben Sira indicates the practical impossibility of genuine and sincere companionship between the poor and the rich. He lays down a principle of associating with equals (13:6–19).

q: Prv 17:17. r: Prv 19:4–7. s: Prv 26:24–26. t: Jer 9:7.

10 Do not draw too close, lest you be rebuffed,
but do not keep too far away lest you be regarded as an enemy.
11 Do not venture to be free with them,
do not trust their many words;
For by prolonged talk they will test you,
and though smiling they will probe you.
12 Mercilessly they will make you a laughingstock,
and will not refrain from injury or chains.
13 Be on your guard and take care
never to accompany lawless people.†

15 Every living thing loves its own kind,
and we all love someone like ourselves.
16 Every living being keeps close to its own kind;
and people associate with their own kind.
17 Is a wolf ever allied with a lamb?
So the sinner with the righteous.[u]
18 Can there be peace between the hyena and the dog?
Or peace between the rich and the poor?*
19 Wild donkeys of the desert are lion's prey;
likewise the poor are feeding grounds for the rich.
20 Humility is an abomination to the proud;
and the poor are an abomination to the rich.
21 When the rich stumble they are supported by friends;
when the poor trip they are pushed down by friends.
22 When the rich speak they have many supporters;
though what they say is repugnant, it wins approval.
When the poor speak people say, "Come, come, speak up!"
though they are talking sense, they get no hearing.
23 When the rich speak all are silent,
their wisdom people extol to the clouds.
When the poor speak people say: "Who is that?"
If they stumble, people knock them down.[v]

24 Wealth is good where there is no sin;*
but poverty is evil by the standards of the proud.
25 The heart changes one's face,
either for good or for evil.[w]
26 The sign of a good heart is a radiant face;
withdrawn and perplexed is the toiling schemer.

## CHAPTER 14

See RG 198–200

1 * Happy those whose mouth causes them no grief,
those who are not stung by remorse for sin.[x]
2 Happy are those whose conscience does not reproach them,
those who have not lost hope.

### *The Use of Wealth*

3 Wealth is not appropriate for the mean-spirited;*
to misers, what use is gold?
4 What they deny themselves they collect for someone else,
and strangers will live sumptuously on their possessions.[y]
5 To whom will they be generous that are stingy with themselves
and do not enjoy what is their own?

† **13:13** Other ancient texts read as v. 14:
If you hear these things in your sleep, wake up!
With your whole life, love the Lord
and call on him for your salvation.

**13:18** The hostility between the dogs which guard the flocks (Jb 30:1) and the rapacious hyenas (Jer 12:9) is proverbial in Palestine.

**13:24** Ben Sira allows that the rich can be virtuous—but with difficulty; cf. 31:1–11.

**14:1–2** A clear conscience, the result of honoring personal commitments and responsibilities, brings contentment and peace.

**14:3–10** Ben Sira offers a case study about the miserable life of the "small-hearted" (Heb. *leb qaṭan*) to verify vv. 1–2. They are evil because they do not use their wealth properly to benefit themselves or others. While they are never satisfied that they have enough, they ignore their own needs and hospitality itself, feeding on the generosity of others, in order to protect their own resources. Ironically, after their death, strangers, with no obligation to keep their memory alive, enjoy their wealth.

*u:* 2 Cor 6:14–17. *v:* Prv 14:20; 19:4, 7. *w:* Prv 15:13. *x:* Sir 5:13–14; 19:16; 25:8; Jas 1:26; 3:2. *y:* Eccl 2:18–19; 6:2.

6 None are worse than those who are
stingy with themselves;
they punish their own avarice.
7 If ever they do good, it is by mistake;
in the end they reveal their meanness.
8 Misers are evil people,
they turn away and disregard others.
9 The greedy see their share as not enough;
greedy injustice dries up the soul.
10 The eye of the miserly is rapacious for
food,
but there is none of it on their own
table.

11 * My son, if you have the means, treat
yourself well,
and enjoy life as best you can.[z]
12 Remember that death does not delay,
and you have not been told the grave's
appointed time.
13 Before you die, be good to your friends;
give them a share in what you
possess.[a]
14 Do not deprive yourself of good things
now
or let a choice portion escape you.
15 Will you not leave your riches to others,
and your earnings to be divided by lot?
16 Give and take, treat yourself well,
for in Sheol there are no joys to seek.
17 All flesh grows old like a garment;
the age-old law is: everyone must die.[b]
18 As with the leaves growing on a
luxuriant tree—
one falls off and another sprouts—
So with the generations of flesh and
blood:
one dies and another flourishes.[c]
19 All human deeds surely perish;
the works they do follow after them.

*The Search for Wisdom and Her Blessings**

20 Happy those who meditate on Wisdom,
and fix their gaze on knowledge;[d]
21 Who ponder her ways in their heart,
and understand her paths;
22 Who pursue her like a scout,
and watch at her entry way;
23 Who peep through her windows,
and listen at her doors;
24 Who encamp near her house
and fasten their tent pegs next to her
walls;
25 Who pitch their tent beside her,
and dwell in a good place;*
26 * Who build their nest in her leaves,
and lodge in her branches;
27 Who take refuge from the heat in her
shade
and dwell in her home.

## CHAPTER 15

See RG 198–200

1 Whoever fears the LORD will do
this;
whoever is practiced in the Law will
come to Wisdom.
2 She will meet him like a mother;
like a young bride she will receive him,
3 * She will feed him with the bread of
learning,
and give him the water of
understanding to drink.[e]
4 He will lean upon her and not fall;
he will trust in her and not be put to
shame.
5 She will exalt him above his neighbors,
and in the assembly she will make him
eloquent.
6 Joy and gladness he will find,
and an everlasting name he will inherit.[f]
7 The worthless will not attain her,

**14:11–19** Three realities govern Ben Sira's attitude toward a proper use of wealth: the inevitability and uncertainty of death, the ephemeral nature of human accomplishments, the lack of reward or punishment after death. He advises generous enjoyment of God's gift of wealth before death.

**14:20–15:10** This poem charts the growing intimacy between those seeking Wisdom and Wisdom herself. They move from static reflection to playful pursuit, from camping outside the walls of her house to nesting inside her leafy shade. Ben Sira portrays Wisdom as both mother and bride, a feminine figure who is the fullness of womanhood according to his androcentric society.

**14:25 In a good place:** i.e., where Wisdom dwells.

**14:26–27** The shift in imagery creates a more intimate relationship. Those seeking Wisdom dwell within her as a bird nests within a leafy tree.

**15:3–6** In this role reversal Woman Wisdom teaches, nourishes, supports, and protects the vulnerable man. For similar imagery cf. Prv 8:4–21, 34–35; 9:1–5; 31:10–31.

*z:* Eccl 5:17–19. *a:* Prv 3:27–28; Tb 4:7. *b:* Ps 103:14–16; Jb 14:1–2; Is 40:6; Jas 1:10; 1 Pt 1:24. *c:* Eccl 1:4. *d:* Ps 1:2. *e:* Jn 4:10; 6:31–33. *f:* Sir 6:28–33.

and the haughty will not behold her.
8 She is far from the impious;
liars never think of her.
9 * Praise is unseemly on the lips of sinners,
for it has not been allotted to them by God.
10 But praise is uttered by the mouth of the wise,
and its rightful owner teaches it.

### *Free Will**

11 Do not say: "It was God's doing that I fell away,"
for what he hates he does not do.
12 Do not say: "He himself has led me astray,"
for he has no need of the wicked.[g]
13 Abominable wickedness the LORD hates
and he does not let it happen to those who fear him.
14 God in the beginning created human beings
and made them subject to their own free choice.[h]
15 If you choose, you can keep the commandments;
loyalty is doing the will of God.
16 Set before you are fire and water;
to whatever you choose, stretch out your hand.
17 Before everyone are life and death,
whichever they choose will be given them.[i]
18 Immense is the wisdom of the LORD;
mighty in power, he sees all things.
19 The eyes of God behold his works,
and he understands every human deed.[j]
20 He never commands anyone to sin,
nor shows leniency toward deceivers.*

## CHAPTER 16

See RG 198–200

### *God's Punishment of Sinners**

1 Do not yearn for worthless children,
or rejoice in wicked offspring.
2 Even if they be many, do not rejoice in them
if they do not have fear of the LORD.
3 Do not count on long life for them,[k]
or have any hope for their future.
For one can be better than a thousand;
rather die childless than have impious children!
4 Through one wise person a city can be peopled;
but through a clan of rebels it becomes desolate.

5 Many such things my eye has seen,
and even more than these my ear has heard.
6 Against a sinful band fire is kindled,[l]
upon a godless people wrath blazes.*
7 He did not forgive the princes of old*
who rebelled long ago in their might.[m]
8 He did not spare the neighbors of Lot,* [n]
abominable in their pride.
9 He did not spare the doomed people,*
dispossessed because of their sin;
10 Nor the six hundred thousand foot soldiers,* [o]

**15:9–10** There is an intimate association between wisdom and praise of the Lord.

**15:11–20** Here Ben Sira links freedom of the will with human responsibility. God, who sees everything, is neither the cause nor the occasion of sin. We have the power to choose our behavior and we are responsible for both the good and the evil we do (vv. 15–17).

**15:20 Deceivers**: those who hold the Lord responsible for their sins.

**16:1–23** One child who does God's will is a greater blessing than many sinful offspring (vv. 1–4), for history and experience show that God punishes sin (vv. 5–10). God judges everyone according to their deeds (vv. 11–14); no one can hide from God or escape retribution at his hand (vv. 17–23).

**16:6** For Korah and his band (v. 6a), see 45:18–19; Nm 16:1–35; Ps 106:18; for the disgruntled Israelites (v. 6b), Ps 78:21–22.

**16:7 The princes of old**: e.g., the mighty destroyed in the flood (Gn 6:1–4; Wis 14:6; Bar 3:26–28), as well as the king of Babylon (Is 14:4–21) and Nebuchadnezzar (Dn 4:7–30).

**16:8 Neighbors of Lot**: the people of Sodom and Gomorrah, condemned elsewhere for their sexual violence (Gn 19:24–25) and failure at hospitality (Ez 16:49–50).

**16:9 Doomed people**: the Canaanite tribes whose aberrant religious practices, at least in Israelite opinion, caused their downfall: Ex 23:23–24, 27–33; 33:2; 34:11–16; Dt 7:1–2; Wis 12:3–7.

**16:10 Six hundred thousand foot soldiers**: the number given for those rescued by Moses, who murmured against the Lord in the wilderness and died there: 46:1, 7–8; Nm 11:20; 14:1–12, 22–24, 29, 36–38; 26:65; Dt 1:35–38.

---

*g:* Jas 1:13. *h:* Gn 1:27. *i:* Dt 30:15–20. *j:* Ps 33:18; 34:16; Heb 4:13. *k:* Wis 4:1–2. *l:* Sir 21:9. *m:* Gn 6:4; Wis 14:6; Bar 3:26–28. *n:* Gn 19:24–25. *o:* Nm 14:29.

sent to their graves for the arrogance
of their hearts.
11 Had there been but one stiff-necked*
person,
it would be a wonder had he gone
unpunished.
For mercy and anger alike are with him;
he remits and forgives, but also pours
out wrath.
12 Great as his mercy is his punishment;
he judges people, each according to
their deeds.
13 Criminals do not escape with their
plunder;
the hope of the righteous, God never
leaves unfulfilled.
14 Whoever does good has a reward;
each receives according to their deeds.†
17 Do not say: "I am hidden from God;
and on high who remembers me?
Among so many people I am unknown;
what am I in the world of spirits?
18 Look, the heavens and the highest
heavens,
the abyss and the earth tremble at his
visitation.
19 The roots of the mountains and the
earth's foundations—
at his mere glance they quiver and
quake.
20 Of me, therefore, he will take no notice;
with my ways who will be concerned?
21 If I sin, no eye will see me;
if all in secret I act deceitfully, who is
to know?[p]
22 Who tells him about just deeds?
What can I expect for doing my duty?"
23 Such the thoughts of the senseless;
only the foolish entertain them.

### *Divine Wisdom Seen in Creation**

24 Listen to me, my son, and take my
advice,
and apply your mind to my words,
25 While I pour out my spirit by measure
and impart knowledge with care.
26 When at the first God created his works
and, as he made them, assigned their
tasks,[q]
27 He arranged for all time what they were
to do,
their domains from generation to
generation.
They were not to go hungry or grow
weary,
or ever cease from their tasks.
28 Never does a single one crowd its
neighbor,
or do any ever disobey his word.
29 Then the Lord looked upon the earth,
and filled it with his blessings.[r]
30 Its surface he covered with every kind of
living creature
which must return into it again.

## CHAPTER 17

See RG 198–200

### *Creation of Human Beings*

1 The Lord created human beings from the
earth,
and makes them return to earth again.[s]
2 A limited number of days he gave them,[t]
but granted them authority over
everything on earth.
3 He endowed them with strength like his
own,
and made them in his image.
4 He put fear of them in all flesh,
and gave them dominion over beasts
and birds.†

**16:11 Stiff-necked**: sinful Israelites; cf. Ex 32:9; 33:3, 5. Not even one Israelite would have gone unpunished for insolence or pride.

† **16:14** Other ancient texts read as vv. 15–16:

15 The LORD hardened the heart of Pharaoh so that he
did not recognize him
whose acts were manifest under the heavens;
16 His mercy was seen by all his creatures,
and his light and his darkness he apportioned to
humankind.

**16:24–17:23** In harmony with Gn 1–2, the author describes God's wisdom in creating the universe and everything in it (vv. 24–30), endowing human beings with a moral nature, with wisdom, knowledge, and freedom of will (cf. 15:14) according to his own image (17:1–3, 7). Now they can govern the earth (vv. 3–4), praise God's name (vv. 9–10), obey his law (vv. 11–14), and render to him an account of their deeds (v. 23). Cf. Ps 19; 104.

† **17:4** Other ancient texts read as v. 5:

They received the use of the Lord's five faculties;
of mind, the sixth, he granted them a share,
as also of speech, the seventh, the interpreter of his
actions.

*p:* Sir 23:18–20. *q:* Gn 1:3–30. *r:* Gn 1:11–31. *s:* Gn 2:7; 3:19. *t:* Gn 1:26–28; Ps 8:4–9.

[6] Discernment, tongues, and eyes,
ears, and a mind for thinking he gave them.
[7] With knowledge and understanding he filled them;
good and evil he showed them.
[8] He put fear of him into their hearts
to show them the grandeur of his works,
[9] That they might describe the wonders of his deeds
[10] and praise his holy name.
[11] He set before them knowledge,
and allotted to them the law of life.
[12] An everlasting covenant he made with them,
and his commandments* he revealed to them.
[13] His majestic glory their eyes beheld,
his glorious voice their ears heard.
[14] He said to them, "Avoid all evil";
to each of them he gave precepts about their neighbor.
[15] Their ways are ever known to him,
they cannot be hidden from his eyes.†
[17] Over every nation he appointed a ruler,*
but Israel is the Lord's own portion.† [u]
[19] All their works are clear as the sun to him,
and his eyes are ever upon their ways.
[20] Their iniquities cannot be hidden from him;
all their sins are before the Lord.†
[22] Human goodness is like a signet ring with God,
and virtue he keeps like the apple of his eye.
[23] Later he will rise up and repay them,
requiting each one as they deserve.[v]

*Appeal for a Return to God**

[24] But to the penitent he provides a way back
and encourages those who are losing hope!
[25] Turn back to the Lord and give up your sins,
pray before him and make your offenses few.
[26] Turn again to the Most High and away from iniquity,
and hate intensely what he loathes.
[27] * Who in Sheol can glorify the Most High[w]
in place of the living who offer their praise?
[28] The dead can no more give praise than those who have never lived;
they who are alive and well glorify the Lord.
[29] How great is the mercy of the Lord,
and his forgiveness for those who return to him!
[30] For not everything is within human reach,
since human beings are not immortal.
[31] Is anything brighter than the sun? Yet it can be eclipsed.
How worthless* then the thoughts of flesh and blood!

**17:12 An everlasting covenant . . . his commandments**: God made several covenants, e.g., Gn 9:8–17; 15:17–21; 17:1–22, entered into with humankind, especially on Mount Sinai, where the people saw God's glory and heard his voice (v. 13; cf. Ex 19:16–24:18).

† **17:15** Other ancient texts read as v. 16:
Their ways are directed toward evils from their youth,
and they are unable to make their hearts flesh rather than stone.

**17:17 Ruler**: this may refer to civil officials or to heavenly beings placed over nations as guardians; see note on Dt 32:8, and the cross-references.

† **17:17** Other ancient texts read as v. 18:
Israel, as his firstborn, he cares for with chastisement;
the light of his love he shares with him without neglect.

† **17:20** Other ancient texts read as v. 21:
But the Lord, being good and knowing how they are formed,
neither neglected them nor ceased to spare them.

**17:24–32** Ben Sira opens this poem with a prophetic summons to repent, urging sinners to give up their sins and to pray for forgiveness (vv. 24–26, 29). Ben Sira reflects the belief of his day that there was no life after death (vv. 27–28, 30; see note on 11:26–28). Cf. Ez 18:23, 30–32; 33:11–16. See note on Ps 6:6.

**17:27–28** True life consists in praise of God; this is not possible in Sheol.

**17:31 Worthless**: cf. Gn 6:5. Though moral fault is not excluded, the thought here is the inability to understand the designs of God. Cf. Wis 9:14–18.

*u:* Ex 19:5; Dt 4:19–20; 32:8–9; Dn 10:13–21; 12:1. *v:* Ps 7:17; Jl 4:4, 7; Jer 23:19; Ez 22:31. *w:* Ps 6:6; 88:4–7; 115:17; Is 38:18.

32 God holds accountable the hosts of
highest heaven,
while all mortals are dust and ashes.

## CHAPTER 18

See RG 198–200

### *The Divine Power and Mercy**

1 He who lives forever created the whole
universe;
2 the LORD alone is just.†
4 To whom has he given power to describe
his works,
and who can search out his mighty
deeds?
5 Who can measure his majestic power,
or fully recount his mercies?
6 No one can lessen, increase,
or fathom the wonders of the Lord.
7 When mortals finish, they are only
beginning,
and when they stop they are still
bewildered.
8 What are mortals? What are they worth?
What is good in them, and what is
evil?
9 The number of their days seems great
if it reaches a hundred years.[x]
10 Like a drop of water from the sea and a
grain of sand,
so are these few years among the days
of eternity.
11 That is why the Lord is patient with
them
and pours out his mercy on them.
12 He sees and understands that their death
is wretched,
and so he forgives them all the more.
13 Their compassion is for their neighbor,
but the Lord's compassion reaches all
flesh,
Reproving, admonishing, teaching,
and turning them back, as a shepherd
his flock.[y]
14 He has compassion on those who accept
his discipline,
who are eager for his precepts.

### *The Need for Prudence*

15 My child, add no reproach to your
charity,*
or spoil any gift by harsh words.
16 Does not the dew give relief from the
scorching heat?
So a word can be better than a gift.
17 Indeed does not a word count more than
a good gift?
But both are offered by a kind person.
18 The fool is ungracious and abusive,
and a grudging gift makes the eyes
smart.[z]
19 Before you speak, learn;
before you get sick, prepare the cure.
20 Before you are judged, examine
yourself,
and at the time of scrutiny you will
have forgiveness.
21 Before you fall ill, humble yourself;
and when you have sinned, show
repentance.*
Do not delay forsaking your sins;
do not neglect to do so until you are in
distress.
22 Let nothing prevent the prompt payment
of your vows;
do not wait until death to fulfill them.[a]
23 Before making a vow prepare yourself;
do not be like one who puts the Lord
to the test.
24 Think of wrath on the day of death,
the time of vengeance when he will
hide his face.[b]
25 Think of the time of hunger in the time of
plenty,
poverty and need in the day of wealth.[c]

**18:1–14** Not only are God's justice and power beyond human understanding (vv. 1–7), his mercy also is boundless and surpasses all human compassion (vv. 8–14); he pities human frailty and mortality.

† **18:2** Other ancient texts read as v. 3:

He controls the world within the span of his hand,
and everything obeys his will;
For he in his might is the King of all,
separating what is holy among them from what is profane.

**18:15–27** The practice of charity, especially almsgiving, is an art which avoids every offense to another (vv. 15–18). Prudence directs the changing circumstances of daily life in view of the time of scrutiny (i.e., the day of reckoning, or death, v. 24).

**18:21** Sickness was often viewed as a punishment for sin; hence, the need for repentance. Cf. 38:9–10; Jb 15:20–24.

*x:* Ps 90:10. *y:* Ps 23:1–4; Is 40:11; 49:9–10; Jn 10:11–16; Heb 13:20–21; Rev 7:17. *z:* Sir 20:14–15. *a:* Nm 30:3; Dt 23:22; Ps 50:14; Prv 20:25; Eccl 5:4. *b:* Sir 7:16. *c:* Sir 11:25–27.

26 Between morning and evening there is a change of time;
before the Lord all things are fleeting.

27 The wise are discreet in all things;
where sin is rife they keep themselves from wrongdoing.
28 Every wise person teaches wisdom,*
and those who know her declare her praise;
29 Those skilled in words become wise themselves,
and pour forth apt proverbs.

### Self-Control*

30 Do not let your passions be your guide,[d]
but keep your desires in check.
31 If you allow yourself to satisfy your passions,
they will make you the laughingstock of your enemies.
32 Take no pleasure in too much luxury
which brings on poverty redoubled.
33 Do not become a glutton and a drunkard
with nothing in your purse.

See RG 198–200

## CHAPTER 19

1 Whoever does this grows no richer;
those who waste the little they have will be stripped bare.
2 Wine and women make the heart lustful,
and the companion of prostitutes becomes reckless.[e]
3 Rottenness and worms will possess him,
and the reckless will be snatched away.[f]
4 Whoever trusts others too quickly has a shallow mind,
and those who sin wrong themselves.

### The Proper Use of Speech*

5 Whoever gloats over evil will be destroyed,
6 and whoever repeats gossip has no sense.
7 Never repeat gossip,
and no one will reproach you.[g]
8 Tell nothing to friend or foe;
and unless it be a sin for you, do not reveal a thing.[h]
9 For someone may have heard you and watched you,
and in time come to hate you.
10 Let anything you hear die with you;
never fear, it will not make you burst!
11 Having heard something, the fool goes into labor,
like a woman giving birth to a child.
12 Like an arrow stuck in a fool's thigh,
so is gossip in the belly of a fool.
13 Admonish your friend—he may not have done it;
and if he did, that he may not do it again.[i]
14 Admonish your neighbor—he may not have said it;
and if he did, that he may not say it again.
15 Admonish your friend—often it may be slander;
do not believe every story.
16 Then, too, a person can slip and not mean it;
who has not sinned with his tongue?[j]
17 Admonish your neighbor before you break with him;
and give due place to the Law of the Most High.† [k]

**18:28–29** A general statement on the teaching of wisdom, serving either as a conclusion to the preceding section or as an introduction to the following one.

**18:30–19:4** Inordinate gratification of the senses makes people unreasonable, slaves of passion, the laughingstock of their enemies, and it leads to an untimely death.

**19:5–17** An excellent commentary on bearing false witness (Ex 20:16; Dt 5:20). Ben Sira speaks harshly about calumny, rash judgment, and detraction (vv. 5–7), and urges discreet silence (vv. 8–12). Justice requires that an accused neighbor be given a hearing, and charity urges fraternal correction; both together fulfill the law of the Most High (vv. 13–17); cf. Mt 7:1–2; 18:15–16.

† **19:17** Other ancient texts read as vv. 18–19:
18 Fear of the Lord is the beginning of acceptance;
and wisdom from him obtains love.
19 Knowledge of the Lord's commandments is life-giving instruction;
those who do what pleases him will harvest the fruit of the tree of immortality.

*d:* Rom 6:12; 13:14; 2 Tm 2:22; Jas 1:14–15. *e:* Prv 20:1; 23:20–28. *f:* Gal 6:8. *g:* Prv 25:10. *h:* Sir 8:18–19. *i:* Lv 19:17; Mt 18:15; Lk 17:3. *j:* Sir 14:1; Jas 3:2. *k:* Lv 19:17.

### *How to Recognize True Wisdom**

20 All wisdom is fear of the LORD;
and in all wisdom, the observance of the Law.† [l]
22 The knowledge of wickedness is not wisdom,
nor is there prudence in the counsel of sinners.
23 There is a shrewdness that is detestable,
while the fool may be free from sin.
24 Better are the God-fearing who have little understanding
than those of great intelligence who violate the Law.
25 There is a shrewdness keen but dishonest,
and there are those who are duplicitous to win a judgment.
26 There is the villain bowed in grief,
but full of deceit within.
27 He hides his face and pretends not to hear,
but when not observed, he will take advantage of you:
28 Even if his lack of strength keeps him from sinning,
when he finds the right time he will do harm.
29 People are known by their appearance;
the sensible are recognized as such when first met.
30 One's attire, hearty laughter, and gait
proclaim him for what he is.

See RG 198–200

## CHAPTER 20

### *Conduct of the Wise and the Foolish*

1 There is an admonition that is untimely,*
but the silent person is the wise one.
2 It is much better to admonish than to lose one's temper;
3 one who admits a fault will be kept from disgrace.
4 Like a eunuch lusting to violate a young woman
is the one who does right under compulsion.*
5 One is silent and is thought wise;
another, for being talkative, is disliked.
6 One is silent, having nothing to say;
another is silent, biding his time.[m]
7 The wise remain silent till the right time comes,
but a boasting fool misses the proper time.
8 Whoever talks too much is detested;
whoever pretends to authority is hated.

9 There is the misfortune that brings success;*
and there is the gain that turns into loss.
10 There is the gift that profits you nothing,
and there is the gift that must be paid back double.
11 There is the loss for the sake of glory,
and there is the one who rises above humble circumstances.
12 There is one who buys much for little,
but pays for it seven times over.
13 The wise make themselves beloved by a few words,
but the courtesies of fools are wasted.
14 A gift from a fool will do you no good,
for in his eyes this one gift is equal to many.
15 He gives little, criticizes often,
and opens his mouth like a town crier.
He lends today and asks for it tomorrow;
such a person is hateful.
16 A fool says, "I have no friends
nor thanks for my generosity."
Those who eat his bread have a mocking tongue.
17 How many will ridicule him, and how often!

**19:20–30** True wisdom is contrasted with a dishonest shrewdness.

† **19:20** Other ancient texts read as v. 21:

The slave who says to his master, "What pleases you I will not do"—
even if he does it later, provokes the one who feeds him.

**20:1–8** The wise know the proper times for speech and silence, that is, the occasions when the most benefit can be gained from them. On the ambiguity of silences, see Prv 17:27–28.

**20:4** Force can prevent an external act of sin or compel a good deed, but it does not eliminate the internal sin or desire of wrongdoing.

**20:9–17** In a series of paradoxes the author indicates how much true and lasting values differ from apparent ones.

*l:* Sir 1:1, 12, 14; Jb 28:28; Ps 111:10; Prv 1:7; 9:10. *m:* Prv 17:27–28.

18 A slip on the floor is better than a slip of
the tongue;*
in like manner the downfall of the
wicked comes quickly.
19 A coarse person, an untimely story;
the ignorant are always ready to offer it.
20 A proverb spoken by a fool is
unwelcome,
for he does not tell it at the proper time.
21 There is a person whose poverty prevents
him from sinning,
but when he takes his rest he has no
regrets.
22 There is a person who is destroyed
through shame,
and ruined by foolish posturing.
23 There is one who promises a friend out
of shame,
and so makes an enemy needlessly.
24 A lie is a foul blot in a person,
yet it is always on the lips of the
ignorant.
25 A thief is better than an inveterate liar,
yet both will suffer ruin.
26 A liar's way leads to dishonor,
and his shame remains ever with him.

27 The wise gain promotion with few words,*
the prudent please the great.
28 Those who work the land have abundant
crops,
and those who please the great are
pardoned their faults.
29 Favors and gifts blind the eyes;
like a muzzle over the mouth they
silence reproofs.[n]
30 Hidden wisdom and unseen treasure—
what value has either?
31 Better are those who hide their folly
than those who hide their wisdom.†

## CHAPTER 21

See RG 198–200

### *Dangers from Sin**

1 My child, if you have sinned, do so no
more,
and for your past sins pray to be
forgiven.
2 Flee from sin as from a serpent
that will bite you if you go near it;
Its teeth, lion's teeth,
destroying human lives.
3 All lawlessness is like a two-edged sword;
when it cuts, there is no healing.[o]
4 Panic and pride wipe out wealth;
so too the house of the proud is
uprooted.
5 Prayer from the lips of the poor is heard
at once,
and justice is quickly granted them.
6 Whoever hates correction walks the
sinner's path,[p]
but whoever fears the Lord repents in
his heart.
7 Glib speakers are widely known,
but when they slip the sensible
perceive it.
8 Those who build their houses with
someone else's money
are like those who collect stones for
their funeral mounds.
9 A band of criminals is like a bundle of
tow;
they will end in a flaming fire.[q]
10 The path of sinners is smooth stones,
but its end is the pit of Sheol.*

### *The Wise and Foolish: A Contrast**

11 Those who keep the Law control their
thoughts;
perfect fear of the Lord is wisdom.

**20:18–26** The ill-timed speech brings disaster (vv. 18–20); human respect may lead to rash promises and enmity (vv. 22–23); lies bring dishonor and lasting disgrace (vv. 24–26).

**20:27–31** Through prudent speech the wise gain honor and esteem among the great (vv. 27–28). They must beware, however, of accepting bribes, lest they share in evil through silence when they should reprove (vv. 29–31).

† **20:31** Other ancient texts read as v. 32:

It is better to await the inevitable while serving the
Lord
than to be the ungoverned helmsman for the
careening of one's life.

**21:1–10** Under various figures, the consequences of sin are described as destructive of wealth, and even of life, deserving of death (vv. 2–4, 6a, 8–10). Fear of the Lord motivates repentance (vv. 5, 6b).

**21:10 The path of sinners . . . Sheol**: Ben Sira refers to the death that awaits unrepentant sinners; see notes on 11:26–28; 17:24–32.

**21:11–28** The mind of the wise is a fountain of knowledge (vv. 13, 15); their will is trained to keep the Law (v. 11); their

*n:* Ex 23:8; Dt 16:19. *o:* Prv 5:4. *p:* Prv 12:1. *q:* Sir 16:6; Ps 21:10.

12 One who is not clever can never be taught,
but there is a cleverness filled with bitterness.

13 The knowledge of the wise wells up like a flood,
and their counsel like a living spring.[r]
14 A fool's mind is like a broken jar:
it cannot hold any knowledge at all.

15 When the intelligent hear a wise saying,
they praise it and add to it.
The wanton hear it with distaste
and cast it behind their back.

16 A fool's chatter is like a load on a journey,
but delight is to be found on the lips of the intelligent.
17 The views of the prudent are sought in an assembly,
and their words are taken to heart.

18 Like a house in ruins is wisdom to a fool;
to the stupid, knowledge is incomprehensible chatter.
19 To the senseless, education is fetters on the feet,
like manacles on the right hand.
20 Fools raise their voice in laughter,
but the prudent at most smile quietly.[s]
21 Like a gold ornament is education to the wise,
like a bracelet on the right arm.

22 A fool steps boldly into a house,
while the well-bred are slow to make an entrance.[t]
23 A boor peeps through the doorway of a house,
but the educated stay outside.
24 It is rude for one to listen at a door;
the discreet person would be overwhelmed by the disgrace.

25 The lips of the arrogant talk of what is not their concern,
but the discreet carefully weigh their words.
26 The mind of fools is in their mouths,
but the mouth of the wise is in their mind.*
27 When the godless curse their adversary,*
they really curse themselves.
28 Slanderers sully themselves,
and are hated by their neighbors.

## CHAPTER 22

See RG 198–200

### *On Laziness and Foolishness*

1 * The sluggard is like a filthy stone;*
everyone hisses at his disgrace.
2 The sluggard is like a lump of dung;
whoever touches it shakes it off the hands.

3 An undisciplined child is a disgrace to its father;
if it be a daughter, she brings him to poverty.[u]
4 A thoughtful daughter obtains a husband of her own;
a shameless one is her father's grief.
5 A hussy shames her father and her husband;
she is despised by both.

6 Like music at the time of mourning is ill-timed talk,*
but lashes and discipline are at all times wisdom.†

words are gracious, valued, carefully weighed, sincere (vv. 16–17, 25–26); their conduct is respectful, cultured and restrained (vv. 20, 22–24). The mind of the foolish is devoid of knowledge and impenetrable to it (vv. 12, 14, 18–19); their will rejects it (v. 15); their talk is burdensome (v. 16), their laughter unrestrained (v. 20), their conversation shallow and meddlesome (vv. 25–26); their conduct is bold and rude (vv. 22–24); their abuse of others redounds on themselves (vv. 27–28).

**21:26** A clever play on words.

**21:27 Curse their adversary**: the curse of the godless often recoils on their own head; cf. Gn 27:29; Nm 24:9.

**22:1–15** To Ben Sira, a lazy person and an unruly child are a cause of shame and disgrace; everyone wishes to be rid of them (vv. 1–5). Speaking with a wicked fool is as senseless as talking with someone who is asleep or dead (v. 10). The fool is an intolerable burden that merits a lifetime of mourning (v. 12). Seven days was the usual mourning period. Cf. Gn 50:10; Jdt 16:24.

**22:1 Stone**: used then and even today for wiping oneself after a bowel movement.

**22:6** As a joyful song is out of place among mourners so a rebuke may be insufficient when corporal punishment is called for.

† **22:6** Other ancient texts read as vv. 7–8:

7 Children whose upbringing leads to a wholesome life
veil over the lowly origins of their parents.

*r:* Prv 13:14; 16:22; 18:4. *s:* Eccl 7:6. *t:* Prv 25:17. *u:* Prv 10:1; 17:21, 25; 19:13.

9 Teaching a fool is like gluing a broken pot,[v]
or rousing another from deep sleep.
10 Whoever talks with a fool talks to someone asleep;
when it is over, he says, "What was that?"
11 Weep over the dead, for their light has gone out;
weep over the fool, for sense has left him.
Weep but less bitterly over the dead, for they are at rest;
worse than death is the life of a fool.
12 Mourning for the dead, seven days—[w]
but for the wicked fool, a whole lifetime.
13 Do not talk much with the stupid,
or visit the unintelligent.
Beware of them lest you have trouble
and be spattered when they shake themselves off.
Avoid them and you will find rest
and not be wearied by their lack of sense.
14 What is heavier than lead?
What is its name but "Fool"?
15 Sand, salt, and an iron weight
are easier to bear than the stupid person.[x]
16 A wooden beam firmly bonded into a building*
is not loosened by an earthquake;
So the mind firmly resolved after careful deliberation
will not be afraid at any time.
17 The mind solidly backed by intelligent thought
is like a stucco decoration on a smooth wall.
18 Small stones lying on an open height
will not remain when the wind blows;
So a timid mind based on foolish plans
cannot stand up to fear of any kind.

### *The Preservation of Friendship**

19 Whoever jabs the eye brings tears;
whoever pierces the heart bares its feelings.
20 Whoever throws a stone at birds drives them away;
whoever insults a friend breaks up the friendship.
21 Should you draw a sword against a friend,
do not despair, for it can be undone.
22 Should you open your mouth against a friend,
do not worry, for you can be reconciled.
But a contemptuous insult, a confidence broken,
or a treacherous attack will drive any friend away.
23 Win your neighbor's trust while he is poor,
so that you may rejoice with him in his prosperity.
In time of trouble remain true to him,
so that you may share in his inheritance when it comes.
24 The billowing smoke of a furnace precedes the fire,
so insults precede bloodshed.
25 I am not ashamed to shelter a friend,
and I will not hide from him.
26 But if harm should come to me because of him,
all who hear of it will beware of him.

### *Prayer**

27 Who will set a guard over my mouth,
an effective seal on my lips,
That I may not fail through them,
and my tongue may not destroy me?[y]

[8] Children whose pride is in scornful misconduct
besmirch the nobility of their own family.

**22:16–18** A prudent mind firmly resolved is undisturbed by violent and conflicting thoughts, whereas a foolish person is tossed about by the winds of fear, like small stones whipped about by high winds.

**22:19–26** Disputes and violence weaken friendship, and disloyalty and abuse of confidence destroy it utterly (vv. 19–22, 24, 26); but kindness to a poor person in time of poverty and adversity builds up friendship and merits a share in his prosperity and inheritance (vv. 23, 25).

**22:27–23:6** Ben Sira implores the divine assistance to preserve him through stern discipline from sins of the tongue (22:27; 23:1), from ignorance of mind and weakness of will (vv. 2–3), and from inclinations of the senses and the flesh, lest he fall into the hands of his enemies or become a prey of shameful desires (vv. 4–6).

*v:* Prv 23:9. *w:* Gn 50:10; Jdt 16:24. *x:* Prv 27:3. *y:* Ps 141:3.

## CHAPTER 23

See RG 198–200

1 Lord, Father and Master of my life,*
do not abandon me to their designs,
do not let me fall because of them!

2 Who will apply the lash to my thoughts,
and to my mind the rod of discipline,
That my failings may not be spared
or the sins of my heart overlooked?
3 Otherwise my failings may increase,
and my sins be multiplied;
And I fall before my adversaries,
and my enemy rejoice over me?
4 Lord, Father and God of my life,
do not give me haughty eyes;
5 remove evil desire from my heart.
6 Let neither gluttony nor lust overcome me;
do not give me up to shameless desires.[z]

### *Proper Use of the Tongue**

7 Listen, my children, to instruction concerning the mouth,
for whoever keeps it will not be ensnared.
8 Through the lips the sinner is caught;
by them the reviler and the arrogant are tripped up.
9 Do not accustom your mouth to oaths,
or habitually utter the Holy Name.[a]
10 Just as a servant constantly under scrutiny
will not be without bruises,
So one who swears continually by the Holy Name
will never remain free from sin.
11 Those who swear many oaths heap up offenses;
and the scourge will never be far from their houses.
If they swear in error, guilt is incurred;
if they neglect their obligation, the sin is doubly great.[b]
If they swear without reason they cannot be declared innocent,
for their households will be filled with calamities.

12 There are words comparable to death;
may they never be heard in the inheritance of Jacob.
To the devout all such words are foreign;
they do not wallow in sin.
13 Do not accustom your mouth to coarse talk,
for it involves sinful speech.
14 Keep your father and mother in mind
when you sit among the mighty,[c]
Lest you forget yourself in their presence
and disgrace your upbringing.
Then you will wish you had never been born
and will curse the day of your birth.
15 Those accustomed to using abusive language
will never acquire discipline as long as they live.

### *Sins of the Flesh**

16 Two types of people multiply sins,
and a third* draws down wrath:
Burning passion is like a blazing fire,
not to be quenched till it burns itself out;
One unchaste with his kindred
never stops until fire breaks forth.
17 To the unchaste all bread is sweet;
he is never through till he dies.[d]
18 The man who dishonors his marriage bed
says to himself, "Who can see me?
Darkness surrounds me, walls hide me,
no one sees me. Who can stop me from sinning?"[e]

**23:1–6 Lord, Father and Master of my life**: these words express the tender personal relationship Ben Sira experiences with God, and introduce his prayer for divine assistance and providence in avoiding sins of pride and lust.

**23:7–15** A warning against sins of the tongue through misuse of the sacred Name, against thoughtless swearing (vv. 7–11), blasphemy (v. 12), coarse talk (vv. 13–14), and abusive language (v. 15).

**23:16–27** Ben Sira treats sexual sins and their consequences. Lust destroys its victims (vv. 16–17, 22–26). A false sense of security aggravates the adulterer's inevitable fate (vv. 18–21).

**23:16 Two types . . . a third**: a numerical proverb, as in 25:1–2, 7–11; 26:5–6, 28; 50:25–26; Prv 6:16–19; 30:15b–16, 18–19, 21–23, 29–31. Ben Sira condemns three kinds of sexual sin: incest (v. 16), fornication (v. 17), and adultery (vv. 18–26).

---

z: Rom 13:13. a: Ex 20:7; Lv 19:12; 24:16; Dt 5:11; Mt 5:33–37; Jas 5:12. b: Lv 5:4–10. c: Sir 7:27; Ex 20:12; Dt 5:16. d: Prv 9:17. e: Jb 24:15; Prv 15:3, 11; 17:3; 24:12; Is 29:15; Ez 8:12.

He is not mindful of the Most High,
19 fearing only human eyes.
He does not realize that the eyes of the Lord,
ten thousand times brighter than the sun,
Observe every step taken
and peer into hidden corners.
20 The one who knows all things before they exist
still knows them all after they are made.
21 Such a man will be denounced in the streets of the city;[f]
and where he least suspects it, he will be apprehended.

22 So it is with the woman unfaithful to her husband,
who offers him an heir by another man.
23 First of all, she has disobeyed the law of the Most High;
second, she has wronged her husband;
Third, through her wanton adultery
she has brought forth children by another man.
24 Such a woman will be dragged before the assembly,*
and her punishment will extend to her children.
25 Her children will not take root;
her branches will not bring forth fruit.
26 She will leave behind an accursed memory;
her disgrace will never be blotted out.
27 Thus all who dwell on the earth shall know,
all who remain in the world shall understand,
That nothing is better than the fear of the Lord,
nothing sweeter than obeying the commandments of the Lord.[g] †

## CHAPTER 24

See RG 198–200

### Praise of Wisdom

1 Wisdom sings her own praises,*
among her own people she proclaims her glory.
2 In the assembly of the Most High she opens her mouth,
in the presence of his host she tells of her glory:

3 "From the mouth of the Most High I came forth,[h]
and covered the earth like a mist.
4 In the heights of heaven I dwelt,
and my throne was in a pillar of cloud.
5 The vault of heaven I compassed alone,
and walked through the deep abyss.
6 Over waves of the sea, over all the land,
over every people and nation I held sway.
7 Among all these I sought a resting place.
In whose inheritance should I abide?
8 "Then the Creator of all gave me his command,
and my Creator chose the spot for my tent.
He said, 'In Jacob make your dwelling,
in Israel your inheritance.'
9 Before all ages, from the beginning, he created me,
and through all ages I shall not cease to be.
10 In the holy tent I ministered before him,
and so I was established in Zion.
11 In the city he loves as he loves me, he gave me rest;
in Jerusalem, my domain.
12 I struck root among the glorious people,
in the portion of the Lord, his heritage.

13 "Like a cedar in Lebanon I grew tall,
like a cypress on Mount Hermon;
14 I grew tall like a palm tree in Engedi,

**23:24–25** The judgment of the assembly determined the illegitimacy of children born of adultery or incest and excluded them from the "community of the Lord" (Dt 23:3). Cf. Wis 3:16–19; 4:3–6.

† **23:27** Other ancient texts read as v. 28:
It is a great glory to follow after God,
and for you to be received by him is length of days.

**24:1–29** Wisdom speaks in the first person, describing her origin, her dwelling place in Israel, and the reward she gives her followers. As in Proverbs 8, Wisdom is personified as coming from God, yet distinct from him. This description is reflected in the Johannine *logos*, or Word (Jn 1:1–14). It is used extensively in the Roman liturgy.

*f:* Lv 18:20; 20:10; Dt 22:21–22. *g:* Sir 1:11–30; Prv 3:1–2. *h:* Sir 1:1–4; Prv 2:6; 8:22–36; Wis 7:24–25.

like rosebushes in Jericho;
Like a fair olive tree in the field,
like a plane tree beside water I grew tall.
15 Like cinnamon and fragrant cane,
like precious myrrh I gave forth perfume;
Like galbanum and onycha and mastic,[i]
like the odor of incense in the holy tent.*

16 "I spread out my branches like a terebinth,
my branches so glorious and so graceful.
17 I bud forth delights like a vine;
my blossoms are glorious and rich fruit.†
19 Come to me, all who desire me,
and be filled with my fruits.*
20 You will remember me as sweeter than honey,
better to have than the honeycomb.
21 Those who eat of me will hunger still,*
those who drink of me will thirst for more.[j]
22 Whoever obeys me will not be put to shame,
and those who serve me will never go astray."
23 All this is the book of the covenant of the Most High God,[k]
the Law which Moses commanded us*
as a heritage for the community of Jacob.†
25 It overflows, like the Pishon, with wisdom,[l]
and like the Tigris at the time of first fruits.
26 It runs over, like the Euphrates, with understanding,
and like the Jordan at harvest time.
27 It floods like the Nile with instruction,
like the Gihon* at vintage time.
28 The first human being never finished comprehending wisdom,
nor will the last succeed in fathoming her.
29 For deeper than the sea are her thoughts,
and her counsels, than the great abyss.

30 Now I, like a stream from a river,*
and like water channeling into a garden—
31 I said, "I will water my plants,
I will drench my flower beds."
Then suddenly this stream of mine became a river,
and this river of mine became a sea.
32 Again I will make my teachings shine forth like the dawn;
I will spread their brightness afar off.
33 Again I will pour out instruction like prophecy
and bestow it on generations yet to come.

## CHAPTER 25

See RG 198–200

### *Those Who Are Worthy of Praise*

1 * With three things I am delighted,
for they are pleasing to the Lord and to human beings:

**24:15** These substances, associated with worship, are mentioned in Ex 30:23–28, 34–35 as the ingredients of the anointing oil and the sacred incense. Israel was a priestly nation (Ex 19:6; Is 61:6).

† **24:17** Other ancient texts read as v. 18:

I am the mother of fair love, of reverence,
of knowledge, and of holy hope;
To all my children I give
to be everlasting: to those named by Him.

**24:19** Mt 11:28–30 contains a similar invitation.

**24:21** The paradox of wisdom is that, far from being satiated, those who partake of her will always desire more.

**24:23** Ben Sira now identifies Wisdom and the law of Moses; see also Bar 4:1.

† **24:23** Other ancient texts read as v. 24:

Do not grow weary of striving with the Lord's help,
but cling to him that he may reinforce you.
The Lord Almighty alone is God,
and apart from him there is no savior.

**24:27 Gihon**: understood by some to have been a name for the Nile; cf. Gn 2:13.

**24:30–33** Ben Sira again speaks about himself. He had at first drawn a small portion of the water of wisdom for his own private benefit, but finding it so useful, he soon began to let others share in this boon by teaching them the lessons of wisdom. Like the words of the prophets, Ben Sira's instruction is valuable for all generations (v. 33). The comparison to prophecy is bold and unique.

**25:1–2** A numerical saying in threes.

*i:* Ex 30:23–28, 34–35. *j:* Is 55:1; Jn 4:10–14; 6:35. *k:* Ex 24:7. *l:* Gn 2:11–14.

Harmony among relatives, friendship
among neighbors,
and a wife and a husband living
happily together.
2 Three kinds of people I hate,
and I loathe their manner of life:
A proud pauper, a rich liar,
and a lecherous old fool.
3 In your youth you did not gather.
How will you find anything in your
old age?
4 How appropriate is sound judgment in
the gray-haired,
and good counsel in the elderly!
5 How appropriate is wisdom in the aged,
understanding and counsel in the
venerable!
6 The crown of the elderly, wide
experience;
their glory, the fear of the Lord.
7 There are nine who come to mind as
blessed,
a tenth whom my tongue proclaims:*
The man who finds joy in his children,
and the one who lives to see the
downfall of his enemies.
8 Happy the man who lives with a sensible
woman,
and the one who does not plow with an
ox and a donkey combined.*
Happy the one who does not sin with the
tongue,
who does not serve an inferior.
9 Happy the one who finds a friend,
who speaks to attentive ears.
10 How great is the one who finds
wisdom,
but none is greater than the one who
fears the Lord.
11 Fear of the Lord surpasses all else.
To whom can we compare the one who
has it?†

*Wicked and Virtuous Women**

13 Any wound, but not a wound of the heart!
Any wickedness, but not the
wickedness of a woman!
14 Any suffering, but not suffering from
one's foes!
Any vengeance, but not the vengeance
of one's enemies!
15 There is no poison worse than that of a
serpent,
no venom greater than that of a woman.
16 I would rather live with a dragon or a
lion
than live with a wicked woman.[m]
17 A woman's wicked disposition changes
her appearance,
and makes her face as dark as a bear.
18 When her husband sits among his
neighbors,
a bitter sigh escapes him unawares.
19 There is hardly an evil like that in a
woman;
may she fall to the lot of the sinner!
20 Like a sandy hill to aged feet
is a garrulous wife to a quiet husband.
21 Do not be enticed by a woman's beauty,
or be greedy for her wealth.
22 Harsh is the slavery and great the shame
when a wife supports her husband.
23 Depressed mind, gloomy face,
and a wounded heart—a wicked
woman.
Drooping hands and quaking knees,
any wife who does not make her
husband happy.
24 With a woman sin had a beginning,
and because of her we all die.*
25 Allow water no outlet,
and no boldness of speech to a wicked
woman.
26 If she does not go along as you direct,
cut her away from you.

**25:7–11** A numerical proverb (9 + 1), in which the tenth element, "the one who fears the Lord," is the most important.

**25:8 An ox and a donkey combined**: the reference is to a man married to two incompatible women (cf. 37:11a); the imagery derives from Dt 22:10.

† **25:11** Other ancient texts read as v. 12:

Fear of the Lord is the beginning of loving him,
and fidelity is the beginning of clinging to him.

**25:13–26** The harsh statements Ben Sira makes about women reflect the kind of instruction young Jewish males were exposed to in the early second century B.C. His patriarchal perspective is as unfair as it is one-sided.

**25:24** Ben Sira refers to the story of the first sin in Gn 3:1–6. Cf. 2 Cor 11:3 and 1 Tm 2:14. St. Paul, however, singles out Adam; cf. Rom 5:12–19; 1 Cor 15:22.

*m:* Prv 21:9, 19; 25:24; 27:15.

## CHAPTER 26

See RG 198–200

1 Happy the husband of a good wife;*
the number of his days will be doubled.[n]
2 A loyal wife brings joy to her husband,
and he will finish his years in peace.
3 A good wife is a generous gift
bestowed upon him who fears the Lord.[o]
4 Whether rich or poor, his heart is content,
a smile ever on his face.

5 There are three things I dread,
and a fourth which terrifies me:
Public slander, the gathering of a mob,
and false accusation—all harder to bear than death.
6 A wife jealous of another wife is heartache and mourning;*
everyone feels the lash of her tongue.
7 A wicked wife is a chafing yoke;
taking hold of her is like grasping a scorpion.
8 A drunken wife arouses great anger,
for she does not hide her shame.
9 By her haughty stare and her eyelids
an unchaste wife can be recognized.
10 Keep a strict watch over an unruly wife,
lest, finding an opportunity, she use it;[p]
11 Watch out for her impudent eye,
and do not be surprised if she betrays you:
12 As a thirsty traveler opens his mouth
and drinks from any water nearby,
So she sits down before every tent peg
and opens her quiver for every arrow.

13 A gracious wife delights her husband;
her thoughtfulness puts flesh on his bones.
14 A silent wife is a gift from the Lord;
nothing is worth more than her self-discipline.
15 A modest wife is a supreme blessing;
no scales can weigh the worth of her chastity.
16 The sun rising in the Lord's heavens—
the beauty of a good wife in her well-ordered home.
17 The light which shines above the holy lampstand—*
a beautiful face on a stately figure.
18 Golden columns on silver bases—
so her shapely legs and steady feet.†

### *Dangers to Integrity and Friendship*

28 * Two things bring grief to my heart,
and a third arouses my anger:
The wealthy reduced to want,
the intelligent held in contempt,
And those who pass from righteousness to sin—

**26:1–4, 13–18** A good wife is as a gift from God, bringing joy and peace, happiness and contentment to her husband (vv. 1–4) through her thoughtfulness, reserve, modesty and chastity, beauty, grace, and virtue (vv. 13–18).

**26:6–12** A repetition of the thought expressed in 25:13–26.

**26:17–18** The lampstand and the columns were located in the holy place of the ancient tabernacle (Ex 25:31–40; 26:32).

† **26:18** Other ancient texts read as vv. 19–27:

19 My child, keep intact the bloom of your youth,
and do not give your strength to strangers.
20 Seek out a fertile field from all the land,
and sow it with your own seed, confident in your fine stock.
21 So shall your offspring prosper,
and grow great, confident in their good descent.
22 A woman for hire is regarded as spittle,
but a married woman is a deadly snare for her lovers.
23 A godless wife will be given to the lawless man as his portion,
but a godly wife will be given to the man who fears the Lord.
24 A shameless woman wears out reproach,
but a virtuous daughter will be modest even before her husband.
25 A headstrong wife is regarded as a bitch,
but the one with a sense of shame fears the Lord.
26 The wife who honors her husband will seem wise to everyone,
but if she dishonors him in her pride, she will be known to everyone as ungodly.
Happy is the husband of a good wife,
for the number of his years will be doubled.
27 A loud-mouthed and garrulous wife will be regarded as a trumpet sounding the charge,
And every person who lives like this
will spend his life in the anarchy of war.

**26:28–27:15** From proper conduct in family life, Ben Sira proceeds to social morality, warning especially against injustice in business (26:29–27:3), and perversity of speech in daily life (27:4–7). The pursuit of justice in these matters is all the more meritorious as it is difficult (27:8–10). The discourses of the godly are marked with wisdom, but the conversations of the wicked with offense, swearing, cursing,

*n:* Sir 25:8; Prv 18:22. *o:* Sir 36:27–29. *p:* Sir 42:11.

the Lord prepares them for the
sword.[q]

29 A merchant can hardly keep from
wrongdoing,
nor can a shopkeeper stay free from sin;

CHAPTER 27

See RG 198–200

1 For the sake of profit many sin,
and the struggle for wealth blinds the
eyes.[r]
2 A stake will be driven between fitted
stones—
sin will be wedged in between buying
and selling.
3 Unless one holds fast to the fear of the
Lord,
with sudden swiftness will one's house
be thrown down.

4 When a sieve is shaken, the husks
appear;
so do people's faults when they speak.*
5 The furnace tests the potter's vessels;
the test of a person is in conversation.[s]
6 The fruit of a tree shows the care it has
had;
so speech discloses the bent of a
person's heart.[t]
7 Praise no one before he speaks,
for it is then that people are tested.

8 If you strive after justice, you will attain it,
and wear it like a splendid robe.
9 Birds nest with their own kind,
and honesty comes to those who work
at it.
10 A lion lies in wait for prey,
so does sin for evildoers.
11 The conversation of the godly is always
wisdom,
but the fool changes like the moon.
12 Limit the time you spend among the
stupid,
but frequent the company of the
thoughtful.
13 The conversation of fools is offensive,
and their laughter is wanton sin.
14 Their oath-filled talk makes the hair
stand on end,
and their brawls make one stop the
ears.
15 The wrangling of the proud ends in
bloodshed,
and their cursing is painful to hear.[u]

16 Whoever betrays a secret destroys
confidence,*
and will never find a congenial friend.[v]
17 Cherish your friend, keep faith with him;
but if you betray his secrets, do not go
after him;
18 For as one might kill another,
you have killed your neighbor's
friendship.
19 Like a bird released from your hand,
you have let your friend go and cannot
recapture him.
20 Do not go after him, for he is far away,
and has escaped like a gazelle from a
snare.
21 For a wound can be bandaged, and an
insult forgiven,
but whoever betrays secrets does
hopeless damage.[w]

### *Malice, Anger and Vengeance*

22 Whoever has shifty eyes plots mischief
and those who know him will keep
their distance;
23 In your presence he uses honeyed talk,
and admires your words,
But later he changes his tone
and twists the words to your ruin.[x]
24 I have hated many things but not as much
as him,
and the Lord hates him as well.[y]

quarrels, and even bloodshed (27:11–15).

**27:4–7, 11–15** The importance of effective speech is a favorite wisdom topic; e.g., cf. 20:1–8, 18–20; 22:27–23:15.

**27:16–28:11** Betrayal of confidence through indiscretion destroys friendship and does irreparable harm (27:16–21); cf. 22:22. False friendship based on hypocrisy and deceit is hateful to Ben Sira and, he adds, to God as well (27:22–24); it soon becomes a victim of its own treachery (27:25–27). The same fate awaits the malicious and vengeful (27:28–28:1). They can obtain mercy and forgiveness only by first forgiving their neighbor, being mindful of death and of the commandments of the Most High (28:2–7). And they must avoid quarrels and strife (28:8–11).

*q:* Ez 18:24–29. *r:* Sir 7:18; 31:5–6; Prv 30:7–9. *s:* 1 Pt 1:7. *t:* Mt 7:20. *u:* Sir 23:8–15. *v:* Prv 11:13; 20:19. *w:* Sir 22:20. *x:* Prv 26:24–28. *y:* Prv 6:16–19.

25 A stone falls back on the head of the one who throws it high,[z]
and a treacherous blow causes many wounds.
26 Whoever digs a pit falls into it,
and whoever lays a snare is caught in it.*
27 The evil anyone does will recoil on him
without knowing how it came upon him.
28 Mockery and abuse will befall the arrogant,
and vengeance lies in wait for them like a lion.
29 Those who rejoice in the downfall of the godly will be caught in a snare,
and pain will consume them before they die.
30 Wrath and anger, these also are abominations,
yet a sinner holds on to them.

## CHAPTER 28

See RG 198–200

1 The vengeful will face the Lord's vengeance;
indeed he remembers their sins in detail.[a]
2 Forgive your neighbor the wrong done to you;
then when you pray, your own sins will be forgiven.[b]
3 Does anyone nourish anger against another
and expect healing from the LORD?[c]
4 Can one refuse mercy to a sinner like oneself,
yet seek pardon for one's own sins?
5 If a mere mortal cherishes wrath,
who will forgive his sins?
6 Remember your last days and set enmity aside;
remember death and decay, and cease from sin![d]
7 Remember the commandments and do not be angry with your neighbor;
remember the covenant of the Most High, and overlook faults.
8 Avoid strife and your sins will be fewer,
for the hot-tempered kindle strife;
9 The sinner disrupts friendships
and sows discord among those who are at peace.[e]
10 The more the wood, the greater the fire,[f]
the more the cruelty, the fiercer the strife;
The greater the strength, the sterner the anger,
the greater the wealth, the greater the wrath.
11 Pitch and resin make fire flare up,
and a hasty quarrel provokes bloodshed.

### *The Evil Tongue**

12 If you blow on a spark, it turns into flame,
if you spit on it, it dies out;
yet both you do with your mouth!
13 Cursed be gossips and the double-tongued,
for they destroy the peace of many.[g]
14 A meddlesome tongue subverts many,
and makes them refugees among peoples.
It destroys strong cities,
and overthrows the houses of the great.
15 A meddlesome tongue drives virtuous women from their homes,
and robs them of the fruit of their toil.
16 Whoever heed it will find no rest,
nor will they dwell in peace.
17 A blow from a whip raises a welt,
but a blow from the tongue will break bones.
18 Many have fallen by the edge of the sword,
but not as many as by the tongue.[h]
19 Happy the one who is sheltered from it,
and has not endured its wrath;

**27:26** This expresses a popular idea of act and consequence; an evil (or good) deed is repaid by an evil (or good) result. The frequent metaphor is the digging of a hole for another to fall into; cf. Prv 26:27; Ps 7:14; 9:16; Eccl 10:8.

**28:12–26** Further treatment of sins of the tongue and the havoc that results; cf. 5:9–6:1; 19:5–17; 20:18–26; 23:7–15. Gossips and the double-tongued destroy domestic peace (vv. 12–16). The whip, the sword, chains, even Sheol, are not so cruel as the suffering inflicted by an evil tongue (vv. 17–21). Not the godly but those who forsake the Lord are victims of their evil tongues (vv. 22–23). Therefore, guard your mouth and tongue as you would guard treasure against an enemy (vv. 24–26).

*z:* Ps 7:16–17; Prv 26:27; Eccl 10:8. *a:* Dt 32:35; Rom 12:19. *b:* Mt 6:14. *c:* Mt 18:23–35. *d:* Sir 7:36; 38:20. *e:* Prv 15:18. *f:* Prv 26:20–21. *g:* Sir 5:13–6:1. *h:* Jas 3:5–12.

Who has not borne its yoke
nor been bound with its chains.
20 For its yoke is a yoke of iron,
and its chains are chains of bronze;
21 The death it inflicts is an evil death,
even Sheol is preferable to it.
22 It will have no power over the godly,
nor will they be burned in its flame.
23 But those who forsake the Lord will fall victim to it,
as it burns among them unquenchably;
It will hurl itself against them like a lion,
and like a leopard, it will tear them to pieces.
24 As you fence in your property with thorns,
so make a door and a bolt for your mouth.[i]
25 As you lock up your silver and gold,
so make balances and scales for your words.
26 Take care not to slip by your tongue
and fall victim to one lying in ambush.

See RG 198–200

## CHAPTER 29

### *Loans, Alms and Surety**

1 The merciful lend to their neighbor,
by holding out a helping hand, they keep the commandments.[j]
2 Lend to your neighbor in his time of need,
and pay back your neighbor in time.[k]
3 Keep your promise and be honest with him,
and at all times you will find what you need.
4 Many borrowers ask for a loan
and cause trouble for those who help them.
5 Till he gets a loan, he kisses the lender's hand
and speaks softly of his creditor's money,
But at time of payment, delays,
makes excuses, and finds fault with the timing.
6 If he can pay, the lender will recover barely half,
and will consider that a windfall.
If he cannot pay, the lender is cheated of his money
and acquires an enemy at no extra charge;
With curses and insults the borrower will repay,
and instead of honor will repay with abuse.
7 Many refuse to lend, not out of meanness,
but from fear of being cheated needlessly.
8 But with those in humble circumstances be patient;
do not keep them waiting for your alms.
9 Because of the commandment, help the poor,
and in their need, do not send them away empty-handed.[l]
10 Lose your money for relative or friend;
do not hide it under a stone to rot.
11 Dispose of your treasure according to the commandments of the Most High,
and that will profit you more than the gold.[m]
12 * Store up almsgiving in your treasury,
and it will save you from every evil.
13 Better than a mighty shield and a sturdy spear
it will fight for you against the enemy.
14 * A good person will be surety for a neighbor,
but whoever has lost a sense of shame will fail him.[n]
15 Do not forget the kindness of your backer,
for he has given his very life for you.
16 A sinner will turn the favor of a pledge into misfortune,

**29:1–20** Some practical maxims concerning the use of wealth. Give to the poor (vv. 8–9), lend to a needy neighbor, but repay when a loan falls due lest the lender's burden be increased (vv. 1–5) and his kindness abused (vv. 6–7); through charity build up defense against evil (vv. 10–13). Help your neighbor according to your means, but take care not to fall (v. 20), for the shameless play false and bring their protectors and themselves to misfortune and ruin (vv. 14–19).

**29:12–13** In Ben Sira's day, almsgiving and righteousness were practically identified.

**29:14–17** Ben Sira is more lenient on going surety than earlier sages; cf. Prv 6:1–5.

*i:* Sir 22:27; Ps 141:3. *j:* Dt 15:8; Ps 112:5; Prv 19:17. *k:* Ex 22:24–26; Lv 25:36; Mt 5:42. *l:* Sir 4:1–6; Lv 19:9–10; 23:22. *m:* Sir 17:22–23; Tb 4:7–11. *n:* Sir 8:13.

17 and the ungrateful will abandon his
rescuer.
18 Going surety has ruined many who were
prosperous
and tossed them about like waves of
the sea;[o]
It has exiled the prominent
and sent them wandering through
foreign lands.
19 The sinner will come to grief through
surety,
and whoever undertakes too much will
fall into lawsuits.
20 Help your neighbor according to your
means,
but take care lest you fall yourself.

### *Frugality and Its Rewards**

21 Life's prime needs are water, bread, and
clothing,
and also a house for decent privacy.[p]
22 Better is the life of the poor under the
shadow of their own roof
than sumptuous banquets among
strangers.[q]
23 Whether little or much, be content with
what you have:
then you will hear no reproach as a
parasite.
24 It is a miserable life to go from house to
house,
for where you are a guest you dare not
open your mouth.
25 You will entertain and provide drink
without being thanked;
besides, you will hear these bitter words:
26 "Come here, you parasite, set the table,
let me eat the food you have there!
27 Go away, you parasite, for one more
worthy;
for my relative's visit I need the room!"
28 Painful things to a sensitive person
are rebuke as a parasite and insults
from creditors.

## CHAPTER 30

See RG 198–200

### *The Training of Children**

1 Whoever loves a son will chastise him
often,
that he may be his joy when he
grows up.[r]
2 Whoever disciplines a son will benefit
from him,
and boast of him among acquaintances.
3 Whoever educates a son will make his
enemy jealous,
and rejoice in him among his friends.
4 At the father's death, he will seem not
dead,
for he leaves after him one like
himself,
5 Whom he looked upon through life with
joy,
and in death, without regret.
6 Against his enemies he has left an
avenger,
and one to repay his friends with
kindness.

7 Whoever spoils a son will have wounds
to bandage,
and will suffer heartache at every cry.
8 An untamed horse turns out stubborn;
and a son left to himself grows up
unruly.
9 Pamper a child and he will be a terror for
you,
indulge him, and he will bring you
grief.
10 Do not laugh with him lest you share
sorrow with him,
and in the end you will gnash your
teeth.
11 Do not give him his own way in his
youth,
and do not ignore his follies.
12 Bow down his head in his youth,
beat his sides while he is still young,

**29:21–28** Those who provide their own basic needs of food, clothing and dwelling, and are content with what they have, preserve their freedom and self-respect (vv. 21–23). But if they live as guests, even among the rich, they expose themselves to insult and rebuke (vv. 24–28).

**30:1–13** Sound discipline (which would include physical beating) and careful education of children correct self-indulgence and stubbornness, prevent remorse and humiliation, and bring to parents lasting joy and delight, prestige among friends, jealousy of enemies, perpetuation and vindication of themselves through their offspring (vv. 1–6). Lack of discipline and overindulgence of children bring sorrow and disappointment, terror and grief (vv. 7–13).

*o:* Prv 6:1–2; 11:15. *p:* Sir 39:26. *q:* Sir 40:29. *r:* Prv 13:24; 19:18; 22:15; 23:13; 29:15; Heb 12:7.

Lest he become stubborn and disobey you,
and leave you disconsolate.[s]
13 Discipline your son and make heavy his yoke,
lest you be offended by his shamelessness.

*Health and Cheerfulness**

14 Better the poor in vigorous health
than the rich with bodily ills.
15 I would rather have bodily health than any gold,
and contentment of spirit than pearls.
16 No riches are greater than a healthy body;
and no happiness than a joyful heart.
17 Better is death than a wretched life,[t]
everlasting sleep than constant illness.
18 Good things set before one who cannot eat
are like food offerings placed before a tomb.* [u]
19 What good is an offering to an idol
that can neither eat nor smell?
So it is with the one being punished by the Lord,
20 who groans at what his eyes behold.

21 Do not give in to sadness,
or torment yourself deliberately.[v]
22 Gladness of heart is the very life of a person,
and cheerfulness prolongs his days.
23 Distract yourself and renew your courage,
drive resentment far away from you;
For grief has killed many,[w]
and nothing is to be gained from resentment.
24 Envy and anger shorten one's days,
and anxiety brings on premature old age.
25 Those who are cheerful and merry at table
benefit from their food.* [x]

## CHAPTER 31

See RG 198–200

*The Proper Attitude Toward Riches**

1 Wakefulness over wealth wastes away the flesh,
and anxiety over it drives away sleep.
2 Wakeful anxiety banishes slumber;
more than a serious illness it disturbs repose.
3 The rich labor to pile up wealth,
and if they rest, it is to enjoy pleasure;
4 The poor labor for a meager living,
and if they ever rest, they become needy.
5 The lover of gold will not be free from sin;
whoever pursues money will be led astray by it.
6 Many have come to ruin for the sake of gold,
yet destruction lay before their very eyes;[y]
7 It is a stumbling block for fools;
any simpleton will be ensnared by it.
8 Happy the rich person found without fault,
who does not turn aside after wealth.[z]
9 Who is he, that we may praise him?
For he has done wonders among his people.
10 Who has been tested by gold and been found perfect?
Let it be for him his glory;
Who could have sinned but did not,
and could have done evil but did not?
11 So his good fortune is secure,
and the assembly will recount his praises.[a]

**30:14–25** Health of mind and body and joy of heart Ben Sira judges to be more precious than wealth (vv. 14–16), whereas bitterness, constant illness, and affliction are more difficult to bear than death (vv. 17–20). Sadness, resentment, anxiety, envy, and anger shorten days; they should be dispelled by cheerfulness and gladness of heart, which help to prolong one's days (vv. 21–25).

**30:18** The saying ridicules the practice of putting food and drink on the tombs of the dead.

**30:25(27)** Because of the dislocation of the Greek text, the numbering of this verse follows Ziegler's edition. There are no verses 25–26.

**31:1–11** Solicitude for acquiring wealth and anxiety over preserving it disturb repose and easily lead to sin and ruin (vv. 1–7). Cf. Mt 6:25–34. The rich who have not sinned or been seduced by wealth are worthy of highest praise (vv. 8–11).

*s:* Sir 7:23; Prv 23:14. *t:* Sir 41:2. *u:* Tb 4:17. *v:* Prv 12:25; 15:13; 17:22. *w:* Sir 38:18–19. *x:* Prv 15:15. *y:* Sir 8:2. *z:* Sir 5:1, 8. *a:* Prv 29:14.

### *Table Etiquette**

12 Are you seated at the table of the great?
Bring to it no greedy gullet,
Nor say, "How much food there is here!"
13 Remember that the greedy eye is evil.
What has been created more greedy than
the eye?
Therefore, it weeps for any cause.[b]
15 Recognize that your neighbor feels as
you do,
and keep in mind everything you
dislike.
14 Toward what he looks at, do not put out a
hand;
nor reach for the same dish when he
does.
16 Eat, like anyone else, what is set before
you,
but do not eat greedily, lest you be
despised.
17 Be the first to stop, as befits good
manners;
and do not gorge yourself, lest you
give offense.[c]
18 If there are many with you at table,
do not be the first to stretch out your
hand.
19 Does not a little suffice for a well-bred
person?
When he lies down, he does not
wheeze.[d]
20 Moderate eating ensures sound slumber
and a clear mind on rising the next
day.
The distress of sleeplessness and of nausea
and colic are with the glutton!
21 Should you have eaten too much,
get up to vomit* and you will have
relief.

22 Listen to me, my child, and do not
scorn me;
later you will find my advice good.
In whatever you do, be moderate,
and no sickness will befall you.
23 People bless one who is generous with
food,
and this testimony to his goodness is
lasting.[e]
24 The city complains about one who is
stingy with food,
and this testimony to his stinginess is
lasting.
25 Let not wine be the proof of your strength,
for wine has been the ruin of many.
26 As the furnace tests the work of the smith,
so does wine the hearts of the insolent.
27 Wine is very life to anyone,
if taken in moderation.
Does anyone really live who lacks the
wine
which from the beginning was created
for joy?[f]
28 Joy of heart, good cheer, and delight
is wine enough, drunk at the proper
time.
29 Headache, bitterness, and disgrace
is wine drunk amid anger and strife.
30 Wine in excess is a snare for the fool;
it lessens strength and multiplies
wounds.
31 Do not wrangle with your neighbor when
wine is served,
nor despise him while he is having a
good time;
Say no harsh words to him
nor distress him by making demands.

## CHAPTER 32

See RG 198–200

1 If you are chosen to preside at a
dinner, do not be puffed up,
but with the guests be as one of them;
Take care of them first and then sit down;
2 see to their needs, and then take your
place,
To share in their joy
and receive a wreath for a job well
done.

**31:12–32:13** Whoever observes etiquette at table avoids greed and selfishness (31:12–13), is considerate of a neighbor's likes and dislikes and is generous toward him (31:15, 14, 23, 24), observes proper manners (31:16–18), is moderate in eating and drinking (31:19–20, 25–30). A good host is solicitous for the guests (32:1–2), provides conversation and diversion (32:3–6), is modest in speech (32:7, 8, 10), is respectful of elders (32:9), polite in comportment and grateful to God for his favors (32:11–13).

**31:21 Get up to vomit**: the practice of induced vomiting, well-known among Romans, and less well-known among the Jews, seems to be referred to here.

*b:* Prv 23:1–2. *c:* Sir 37:27–31. *d:* Eccl 5:11. *e:* Prv 22:9. *f:* Ps 104:15; 1 Tm 5:23.

[3] You who are older, it is your right to speak,
but temper your knowledge and do not interrupt the singing.
[4] Where there is entertainment, do not pour out discourse,
and do not display your wisdom at the wrong time.
[5] Like a seal of carnelian in a setting of gold:
a concert of music at a banquet of wine.
[6] A seal of emerald in a work of gold:
the melody of music with delicious wine.
[7] Speak, young man, only when necessary,[g]
when they have asked you more than once.
[8] Be brief, say much in few words;
be knowledgeable and yet quiet.
[9] When among elders do not be forward,
and with officials do not be too insistent.
[10] The lightning that flashes before a hailstorm:
the esteem that shines on modesty.
[11] Leave in good time and do not be the last;
go home quickly without delay.
[12] There enjoy doing as you wish,
but do not sin through words of pride.
[13] Above all, bless your Maker,
who showers his favors upon you.

### *The Providence of God*

[14] Whoever seeks God must accept discipline;*
and whoever resorts to him obtains an answer.[h]
[15] Whoever seeks the law will master it,
but the hypocrite will be ensnared by it.[i]
[16] Whoever fears the LORD will understand what is right,
and out of obscurity he will draw forth a course of action.[j]
[17] The lawless turn aside warnings
and distort the law to suit their purpose.[k]
[18] The sensible will not neglect direction;
the proud and insolent are deterred by no fear.
[19] Do nothing without deliberation;
then once you have acted, have no regrets.[l]
[20] Do not go on a way set with snares,
and do not stumble on the same thing twice.
[21] Do not trust the road, because of bandits;
[22] be careful on your paths.
[23] Whatever you do, be on your guard,
for whoever does so keeps the commandments.
[24] Whoever keeps the law preserves himself;
and whoever trusts in the LORD shall not be put to shame.

## CHAPTER 33

See RG 198–200

[1] No evil can harm the one who fears the LORD;
through trials, again and again he is rescued.[m]
[2] Whoever hates the law is without wisdom,
and is tossed about like a boat in a storm.
[3] The prudent trust in the word of the LORD,
and the law is dependable for them as a divine oracle.*
[4] Prepare your words and then you will be listened to;
draw upon your training, and give your answer.
[5] Like the wheel of a cart is the mind of a fool,
and his thoughts like a turning axle.

**32:14–33:4** God is shown to reveal himself through the discipline of his law, a clear and safe plan of life for the pious. Direction and deliberation are aids in following it (32:14–16, 18–24; 33:1, 3–4). Sinners and hypocrites, hating the law or distorting it, fail in wisdom and are devoid of security (32:15b, 17, 18b; 33:2).

**33:3 Oracle**: as the answer given through the Urim and Thummim to the high priest is true, so the law proves itself true to those who obey it. Cf. Ex 28:30; Nm 27:21.

*g:* Sir 7:14. *h:* Sir 4:13. *i:* Sir 2:16. *j:* Ps 37:6. *k:* Sir 21:6; Prv 12:1. *l:* Sir 37:16; Tb 4:18. *m:* Ps 91:10–13; Mt 4:6; Lk 4:10–11.

6 A mocking friend is like a stallion
that neighs, no matter who the rider
may be.
7 * Why is one day more important than
another,
when the same sun lights up every day
of the year?
8 By the LORD's knowledge they are kept
distinct;
and he designates the seasons and
feasts.[n]
9 Some he exalts and sanctifies,
and others he lists as ordinary days.[o]
10 Likewise, all people are of clay,
and from earth humankind was formed;[p]
11 In the fullness of his knowledge the Lord
distinguished them,
and he designated their different ways.
12 Some he blessed and exalted,
and some he sanctified and drew to
himself.
Others he cursed and brought low,
and expelled them from their place.
13 Like clay in the hands of a potter,
to be molded according to his pleasure,
So are people in the hands of their Maker,
to be dealt with as he decides.[q]
14 As evil contrasts with good, and death
with life,
so are sinners in contrast with the
godly.[r]
15 See now all the works of the Most High:
they come in pairs, one the opposite of
the other.

16 Now I am the last to keep vigil,*
like a gleaner following the
grape-pickers;
17 Since by the Lord's blessing I have made
progress
till like a grape-picker I have filled my
wine press,
18 Consider that not for myself only have I
labored,
but for all who seek instruction.

### *Property and Servants**

19 Listen to me, leaders of the people;
rulers of the congregation, pay heed![s]
20a Let neither son nor wife, neither brother
nor friend,
have power over you as long as you
live.
21 While breath of life is still in you,
let no one take your place.
20b Do not give your wealth to another,
lest you must plead for support
yourself.
22 Far better that your children plead with
you
than that you should look for a
handout from them.
23 Keep control over all your affairs;
bring no stain on your honor.
24 When your few days reach their limit,
at the time of death distribute your
inheritance.

25 Fodder and whip and loads for a
donkey;
food, correction and work for a slave.
26 Make a slave work, and he will look for
rest;
let his hands be idle and he will seek to
be free.[t]
27 The yoke and harness will bow the neck;
and for a wicked slave, punishment in
the stocks.
28 Force him to work that he be not idle,
29 for idleness teaches much mischief.
30 Put him to work, as is fitting for him;

**33:7–15** An important doctrine of Ben Sira is his view of the polarities in creation and history; cf. v. 15; 42:24. Contrasts observable in the physical universe as well as in the moral order serve the purposes of divine wisdom (vv. 5–9). All creatures are like clay in the hands of their Maker—the fool and the wise, the sinner and the just (vv. 10–15). This does not imply that some are created to be sinners: God is not the author of wickedness. Divine determinism and human freedom are a mysterious mix.

**33:16–18** Ben Sira refers to himself as the most recent of the biblical writers who have endeavored to present true wisdom to their readers.

**33:19–33** Public officials should reject every influence that would restrict their freedom in the management of their affairs. They must make their own household subservient to them rather than be subservient to it (vv. 19–24). Slaves are to be given food and work and correction but never to be treated unjustly (vv. 25–30). Great care should be taken of good slaves (vv. 31–33).

*n:* Gn 1:14. *o:* Ex 20:11; Dt 5:13–14. *p:* Gn 2:7. *q:* Wis 15:7; Jer 18:1–6; Rom 9:20–21. *r:* Sir 42:25. *s:* Wis 6:1–2. *t:* Prv 29:19.

and if he does not obey, load him with chains.
But never lord it over any human being,
and do nothing unjust.
31 If you have but one slave, treat him like yourself,
for you have acquired him with your life's blood;
If you have but one slave, deal with him as a brother,
for you need him as you need your life.[u]
32 If you mistreat him and he runs away,
33 in what direction will you look for him?

## CHAPTER 34

See RG 198–200

### *Trust in the Lord and Not in Dreams**

1 Empty and false are the hopes of the senseless,
and dreams give wings to fools.
2 Like one grasping at shadows or chasing the wind,
so anyone who believes in dreams.
3 What is seen in dreams is a reflection,
the likeness of a face looking at itself.
4 How can the unclean produce what is clean?
How can the false produce what is true?[v]
5 Divination, omens, and dreams are unreal;
what you already expect, the mind fantasizes.
6 Unless they are specially sent by the Most High,
do not fix your heart on them.
7 For dreams have led many astray,
and those who put their hope in them have perished.
8 Without such deceptions the Law will be fulfilled,
and in the mouth of the faithful is complete wisdom.
9 A much-traveled person knows many things;
and one with much experience speaks sense.
10 An inexperienced person knows little,
11 whereas with travel one adds to resourcefulness.
12 I have seen much in my travels,
and learned more than I could ever say.
13 Often I was in danger of death,
but by these experiences I was saved.
14 Living is the spirit of those who fear the Lord,
15 for their hope is in their savior.
16 Whoever fear the Lord are afraid of nothing
and are never discouraged, for he is their hope.[w]
17 Happy the soul that fears the Lord!
18 In whom does he trust, and who is his support?
19 The eyes of the Lord are upon those who love him;
he is their mighty shield and strong support,
A shelter from the heat, a shade from the noonday sun,
a guard against stumbling, a help against falling.[x]
20 He lifts up spirits, brings a sparkle to the eyes,
gives health and life and blessing.

### *True Worship of God**

21 Ill-gotten goods offered in sacrifice are tainted.
22 Presents from the lawless do not win God's favor.[y]
23 The Most High is not pleased with the gifts of the godless,
nor for their many sacrifices does he forgive their sins.
24 One who slays a son in his father's presence—

**34:1–20** Confidence placed in dreams, divinations, and omens is false because these are devoid of reality (vv. 1–8). True confidence is founded on knowledge and experience (vv. 9–13), and above all on the fear of the Lord, with its accompanying blessings of divine assistance and protection (vv. 14–20).

**34:21–31** To be acts of true religion, sacrifice and penance must be accompanied by the proper moral dispositions. To offer to God goods taken from the poor (vv. 21–27), or to practice penance without interior reform, is a mockery, worthless in the sight of God (vv. 28–31). Cf. Mt 15:4–7; Mk 7:9–13.

*u:* Sir 7:20–21. *v:* Jb 14:4. *w:* Ps 23:4; 112:7–8; Prv 3:23–24; 28:1. *x:* Ps 33:18–19; 34:16. *y:* Sir 35:14–15; Prv 21:27.

whoever offers sacrifice from the
holdings of the poor.
25 The bread of charity is life itself for the
needy;[z]
whoever withholds it is a murderer.
26 To take away a neighbor's living is to
commit murder;
27 to deny a laborer wages is to shed
blood.

28 If one builds up and another tears down,
what do they gain but trouble?
29 If one prays and another curses,
whose voice will God hear?
30 If one again touches a corpse after
bathing,
what does he gain by the purification?[a]
31 So one who fasts for sins,
but goes and commits them again:
Who will hear his prayer,
what is gained by mortification?

## CHAPTER 35*

See RG 198–200

1 To keep the law is to make many
offerings;[b]
2 whoever observes the commandments
sacrifices a peace offering.
3 By works of charity one offers fine flour,*
4 and one who gives alms presents a
sacrifice of praise.
5 To refrain from evil pleases the Lord,
and to avoid injustice is atonement.

6 Do not appear before the Lord empty-
handed,
7 for all that you offer is in fulfillment of
the precepts.[c]
8 The offering of the just enriches the altar:
a sweet odor before the Most High.
9 The sacrifice of the just is accepted,
never to be forgotten.
10 With a generous spirit pay homage to the
Lord,
and do not spare your freewill gifts.[d]
11 With each contribution show a cheerful
countenance,
and pay your tithes in a spirit of joy.[e]
12 Give to the Most High as he has given to
you,
generously, according to your means.
13 For he is a God who always repays
and will give back to you sevenfold.[f]

14 But offer no bribes; these he does not
accept!
15 Do not trust in sacrifice of the fruits of
extortion,[g]
For he is a God of justice,
who shows no partiality.[h]
16 He shows no partiality to the weak
but hears the grievance of the
oppressed.*
17 He does not forsake the cry of the
orphan,[i]
nor the widow when she pours out her
complaint.
18 Do not the tears that stream down her
cheek
19 cry out against the one that causes
them to fall?
20 Those who serve God to please him are
accepted;
their petition reaches the clouds.
21 The prayer of the lowly pierces the
clouds;
it does not rest till it reaches its goal;
Nor will it withdraw till the Most High
responds,
22 judges justly and affirms the right.[j]

God indeed will not delay,
and like a warrior, will not be still[k]
Till he breaks the backs of the merciless
23 and wreaks vengeance upon the nations;
Till he destroys the scepter of the proud,
and cuts off the staff of the wicked;

**35:1–26** Keeping the commandments of the law and avoiding injustice constitute sacrifice pleasing and acceptable to God (vv. 1–5). Offerings also should be made to him, cheerfully and generously; these he repays sevenfold (vv. 6–13). Extortion from widows and orphans is injustice, and God will hear their cries (vv. 14–22a). Punishing the proud and the merciless and coming to the aid of the distressed, he requites everyone according to their deeds (vv. 22b–26).

**35:3 Fine flour**, together with oil and frankincense, was a prescribed offering to God; cf. Lv 2:1–3.

**35:16** Cf. Lv 19:15; Dt 1:17. The divine impartiality is paradoxical, for it is tilted toward the poor.

*z:* Lv 19:13; Dt 24:14–15; Tb 4:14. *a:* Nm 19:11–12; Prv 26:11; 2 Pt 2:22. *b:* 1 Sm 15:22; Ps 51:18–19; Is 1:11–18; Hos 6:6; Am 5:21–24. *c:* Ex 23:15; 34:20; Dt 16:16. *d:* Sir 7:31. *e:* Dt 14:22; 2 Cor 9:7. *f:* Prv 19:17; Mt 25:34–40. *g:* Sir 34:21–23; Prv 15:8; 21:27. *h:* Dt 10:17; 2 Chr 19:7; Jb 34:19; Wis 6:7; Acts 10:34; Rom 2:11; Gal 2:6; 1 Pt 1:17. *i:* Ex 22:22. *j:* Lk 18:7. *k:* Is 42:13–16; 2 Pt 3:9.

## A Prayer for Israel

THE PRAYER IN ch 36 reflects a political and theological perspective different from the rest of Ben Sira. Typical of wisdom literature, Ben Sira generally does not contain teachings about the end times, but focuses on providing guidance for living out one's life in the world as it currently exists. This section of the text is a petition for the overturning of the present world. As such, it presages a time in Jewish history, immediately following the time of Ben Sira, when Hellenistic rule reaches an intolerable level and results in the Maccabean revolt. It is difficult to know whether Ben Sira prays generically for a utopian time in the distant future when all God's promises to Israel would be fulfilled, or whether he prays more particularly for immediate deliverance from the foreign domination of the Seleucid dynasty. Comments like "crush the heads of the hostile rulers" (v. 12) and "gather all the tribes of Jacob, that they may inherit the land as of old" (vv. 13, 16) sound explicitly political. They call for the reestablishment of Israel as a nation distinct from other nations and for the return of the Diaspora Jews, so that Israel in general and Jerusalem in particular can be restored to glory. Part of the motivation for the reestablishment of Israel is to demonstrate Israel's preeminent creed (Dt 6:4)—that there is only one God, the God of Israel.

24 Till he requites everyone according to
their deeds,
and repays them according to their
thoughts;
25 Till he defends the cause of his people,
and makes them glad by his salvation.
26 Welcome is his mercy in time of distress
as rain clouds in time of drought.

### CHAPTER 36

See RG 198–200

*A Prayer for God's People**

1 Come to our aid, O God of the universe,
2 and put all the nations in dread of you!
3 Raise your hand against the foreign
people,
that they may see your mighty deeds.
4 As you have used us to show them your
holiness,*
so now use them to show us your glory.
5 Thus they will know, as we know,
that there is no God but you.

6 Give new signs and work new wonders;
7 show forth the splendor of your right
hand and arm.
8 Rouse your anger, pour out wrath;
9 humble the enemy, scatter the foe.[l]
10 Hasten the ending, appoint the time,
and let people proclaim your mighty
deeds.
11 Let raging fire consume the fugitive,
and your people's oppressors meet
destruction.
12 Crush the heads of the hostile rulers
who say, "There is no one besides me."

13 Gather all the tribes of Jacob,*
16 that they may inherit the land as in
days of old.
17 Show mercy to the people called by your
name:
Israel, whom you named your
firstborn.[m]
18 Take pity on your holy city:
Jerusalem, your dwelling place.[n]
19 Fill Zion with your majesty,
your temple with your glory.

20 Give evidence of your deeds of old;
fulfill the prophecies spoken in your
name.
21 Reward those who have hoped in you,
and let your prophets be proved true.

**36:1–22** A prayer that God hasten the day for the gathering of the tribes of Israel, and Zion once more be filled with the divine glory. All the earth will then know that the Lord is the eternal God.

**36:4 Show . . . holiness**: this cultic language is used to indicate God's liberation of his people; cf. Ez 20:41; 28:25.

**36:13** This verse marks the end of a major dislocation in the Greek text of Sirach (which is followed here) at the head of chap. 33. The verse numbers 1–13 come from the placement of these verses in Greek. Verse 13 here is the first half of a bicolon, the matching half of which is numbered in the Greek 36:16b. Thus although the numbering for vv. 14–15 is not used, none of the text is missing.

*l:* Ps 79:6; Jer 10:25. *m:* Ex 4:22. *n:* 2 Chr 6:41; Ps 132:8, 14; Is 2:1–3; Mi 4:1–3.

[22] Hear the prayer of your servants,
according to your good will toward your people.
Thus all the ends of the earth will know
that you are the eternal God.

*Choice of Associates**

[23] The throat can swallow any food,
yet some foods are more agreeable than others.
[24] The palate tests delicacies put forward as gifts,
so does a keen mind test deceitful tidbits.
[25] One with a tortuous heart brings about grief,
but an experienced person can turn the tables on him.
[26] A woman will accept any man as husband,
but one woman will be preferable to another.
[27] A woman's beauty makes her husband's face light up,
for it surpasses all else that delights the eye.[o]
[28] And if, besides, her speech is soothing,
her husband's lot is beyond that of mortal men.
[29] A wife is her husband's richest treasure,
a help like himself and a staunch support.[p]
[30] A vineyard with no hedge will be overrun;
and a man with no wife becomes a homeless wanderer.
[31] Who will trust an armed band
that shifts from city to city?
Or a man who has no nest,
who lodges wherever night overtakes him?[q]

## CHAPTER 37

See RG 198–200

[1] Every friend declares friendship,
but there are friends who are friends in name only.[r]
[2] Is it not a sorrow unto death
when your other self becomes your enemy?
[3] "Alas, my companion! Why were you created
to fill the earth with deceit?"
[4] A harmful friend will look to your table,
but in time of trouble he stands aloof.
[5] A good friend will fight with you against the foe,
and against your enemies he will hold up your shield.
[6] Do not forget your comrade during the battle,
and do not neglect him when you distribute your spoils.
[7] Every counselor points out a way,
but some counsel ways of their own.
[8] Watch out when one offers advice;
find out first of all what he wants.
For he also may be thinking of himself—
Why should the opportunity fall to him?
[9] He may tell you how good your way will be,
and then stand by to see you impoverished.
[10] Seek no advice from your father-in-law,
and from one who is envious of you, keep your intentions hidden.
[11] Seek no advice from a woman about her rival,
from a coward about war,
from a merchant about business,
from a buyer about value,
from a miser about generosity,
from a cruel person about well-being,
from a worthless worker about his work,
from a seasonal laborer about the harvest,
from an idle slave about a great task—
pay no attention to any advice they give.

**36:23–37:15** In the choice of wife, friend, or associate, experience is a discerner of character (36:23–26). Beauty and soothing speech make a woman desirable as wife (36:27–28). The good wife becomes her husband's richest treasure, his help in establishing his household (36:29–31). Good friends fight for comrades and share the spoils with them (37:5–6); false friends deceive and abandon in time of need (37:1–4). A true counselor and associate should be sought among those who keep the commandments, not among those who break them and seek their own advantage (37:7–12). In all things one should pray to God for light and follow conscience (37:13–15).

*o:* Sir 26:13–18; Prv 12:4; 18:22; 19:14. *p:* Gn 2:18. *q:* Prv 27:8. *r:* Sir 6:7–17.

12 Instead, associate with a religious person,
who you know keeps the
commandments;
Who is like-minded with yourself
and will grieve for you if you fall.
13 Then, too, heed your own heart's
counsel;
for there is nothing you can depend on
more.
14 The heart can reveal your situation
better than seven sentinels on a tower.
15 Then with all this, pray to God
to make your steps firm in the true path.

### *Wisdom and Temperance*

16 A word is the source of every deed;*
a thought, of every act.[s]
17 The root of all conduct is the heart;
18 four branches it shoots forth:
Good and evil, death and life,
and their absolute mistress is the
tongue.[t]
19 One may be wise and benefit many,
yet appear foolish to himself.
20 One may be wise, but if his words are
rejected,
he will be deprived of all enjoyment.*
22 When one is wise to his own advantage,
the fruits of knowledge are seen in his
own person.
23 When one is wise to the advantage of
people,
the fruits of knowledge are lasting.[u]
24 One wise for himself has full enjoyment,
and all who see him praise him.
25 The days of one's life are numbered,
but the life of Israel, days without
number.
26 One wise among the people wins a
heritage of glory,
and his name lives on and on.[v]
27 My son, while you are well, govern your
appetite,*
and see that you do not allow it what is
bad for you.
28 For not everything is good for everyone,
nor is everything suited to every
taste.[w]
29 Do not go to excess with any enjoyment,[x]
neither become a glutton for choice
foods;
30 For sickness comes with overeating,
and gluttony brings on nausea.
31 Through lack of self-control many have
died,
but the abstemious one prolongs life.

## CHAPTER 38

See RG 198–200

### *Sickness and Death*

1 Make friends with the doctor, for he is
essential to you;*
God has also established him in his
profession.
2 From God the doctor has wisdom,
and from the king he receives
sustenance.
3 Knowledge makes the doctor
distinguished,
and gives access to those in authority.
4 God makes the earth yield healing herbs
which the prudent should not neglect;
5 Was not the water sweetened by a twig,
so that all might learn his power?[y]
6 He endows people with knowledge,
to glory in his mighty works,
7 Through which the doctor eases pain,
8 and the druggist prepares his
medicines.
Thus God's work continues without
cease
in its efficacy on the surface of the
earth.

**37:16–26** Thoughts determine action. Wisdom is the source of good and life; folly, of evil and death (vv. 16–18). If the fruits of a person's wisdom benefit himself, he may be praised in his own lifetime; if they benefit others, the praise endures after him, in their lives (vv. 19–26).

**37:20** Verse 21 appears only in Greek, but not in the Hebrew, which is the basis for the translation here.

**37:27–31** Temperance and self-control should govern appetite for food, which is intended not to destroy but to preserve life.

**38:1–15** The profession of medicine comes from God, who makes the earth yield healing herbs and gives the physician knowledge of their power (vv. 1–8). In illness the sick should cleanse their soul from sin and petition God for help through an offering of sacrifice; the physician, too, does well to invoke God that he may understand the illness and apply the proper remedy (vv. 9–14). The sinner, in contrast, defies both his Maker and the doctor (v. 15).

*s:* Sir 32:19. *t:* Prv 18:21. *u:* Sir 39:10–11. *v:* Sir 39:9; 44:13–16. *w:* 1 Cor 6:12; 10:23. *x:* Sir 31:13, 16–21. *y:* Ex 15:25.

9 My son, when you are ill, do not delay,
but pray to God, for it is he who heals.[z]
10 Flee wickedness and purify your hands;
cleanse your heart of every sin.
11 Offer your sweet-smelling oblation and memorial,
a generous offering according to your means.[a]
12 Then give the doctor his place
lest he leave; you need him too,
13 For there are times when recovery is in his hands.
14 He too prays to God
That his diagnosis may be correct
and his treatment bring about a cure.
15 Whoever is a sinner before his Maker
will be defiant toward the doctor.

16 My son, shed tears for one who is dead*
with wailing and bitter lament;
As is only proper, prepare the body,
and do not absent yourself from the burial.
17 Weeping bitterly, mourning fully,
pay your tribute of sorrow, as deserved:
A day or two, to prevent gossip;
then compose yourself after your grief.
18 For grief can bring on death,
and heartache can sap one's strength.[b]
19 When a person is carried away, sorrow is over;
and the life of the poor one is grievous to the heart.
20 Do not turn your thoughts to him again;
cease to recall him; think rather of the end.[c]
21 Do not recall him, for there is no hope of his return;
you do him no good, and you harm yourself.[d]
22 Remember that his fate will also be yours;
for him it was yesterday, for you today.[e]
23 With the dead at rest, let memory cease;
be consoled, once the spirit has gone.

### *Vocations of the Skilled Worker and the Scribe**

24 The scribe's wisdom increases wisdom;
whoever is free from toil can become wise.
25 How can one become learned who guides the plow,
and thrills in wielding the goad like a lance,
Who guides the ox and urges on the bullock,
and whose every concern is for cattle?
26 His concern is to plow furrows,
and he is careful to fatten the livestock.

27 So with every engraver and designer
who, laboring night and day,
Fashions carved seals,
and whose concern is to vary the pattern.
His determination is to produce a lifelike impression,
and he is careful to finish the work.

28 So too the smith sitting by the anvil,
intent on the iron he forges.
The flame from the fire sears his flesh,
yet he toils away in the furnace heat.
The clang of the hammer deafens his ears;
his eyes are on the object he is shaping.
His determination is to finish the work,
and he is careful to perfect it in detail.

29 So also the potter sitting at his labor,
revolving the wheel with his feet.
He is always concerned for his products,
and turns them out in quantity.

**38:16–23** A period of mourning for the deceased and care for their burial are proper (vv. 16–17). But grief should not be excessive, for it cannot help the dead, who will not return, and may do harm to the living. The mourner should be realistic (vv. 18–23).

**38:24–39:11** Ben Sira has a balanced view of the various vocations of skilled laborers—the farmer, engraver, smith and potter—but the profession of scribe is more excellent (38:24–34). He studies and meditates on the law of the Most High, seeks him in prayer of thanksgiving, petition and repentance for sin (39:1, 5, 7), explores the wisdom of the past and present, travels abroad to observe the conduct of many peoples, and attends rulers and great men. Through the spirit of understanding granted by God, he will show forth his wisdom to the glory of God's law, gaining renown for generations to come (39:2–4, 6–11).

*z:* Is 38:1–3. *a:* Lv 2:1–3. *b:* Prv 12:25; 15:13; 17:22. *c:* Sir 7:36; 18:24; 30:21. *d:* 2 Sm 12:23; Wis 2:1. *e:* Jas 4:13–15.

30 With his hands he molds the clay,
and with his feet softens it.
His determination is to complete the glazing,
and he is careful to fire the kiln.

31 All these are skilled with their hands,
each one an expert at his own work;
32 Without them no city could be lived in,
and wherever they stay, they do not go hungry.
But they are not sought out for the council of the people,
33 nor are they prominent in the assembly.
They do not sit on the judge's bench,
nor can they understand law and justice.
They cannot expound discipline or judgment,
nor are they found among the rulers.
34 Yet they maintain the fabric of the world,
and their concern is for exercise of their skill.

### CHAPTER 39

See RG 198–200

How different the person who devotes himself
to the study of the law of the Most High!
1 He explores the wisdom of all the ancients
and is occupied with the prophecies;
2 He preserves the discourses of the famous,
and goes to the heart of involved sayings;
3 He seeks out the hidden meaning of proverbs,
and is busied with the enigmas found in parables.

4 He is in attendance on the great,
and appears before rulers.
He travels among the peoples of foreign lands
to test what is good and evil among people.
5 His care is to rise early
to seek the Lord his Maker,
to petition the Most High,
To open his mouth in prayer,
to ask pardon for his sins.

6 If it pleases the Lord Almighty,
he will be filled with the spirit of understanding;
He will pour forth his words of wisdom
and in prayer give praise to the Lord.
7 He will direct his knowledge and his counsel,
as he meditates upon God's mysteries.
8 He will show the wisdom of what he has learned
and glory in the Law of the Lord's covenant.

9 Many will praise his understanding;
his name can never be blotted out;
Unfading will be his memory,
through all generations his name will live;[f]
10 Peoples will speak of his wisdom,
and the assembly will declare his praise.
11 While he lives he is one out of a thousand,
and when he dies he leaves a good name.

### *Praise of God the Creator**

12 Once more I will set forth my theme
to shine like the moon in its fullness!
13 Listen to me, my faithful children: open up your petals,
like roses planted near running waters;
14 Send up the sweet odor of incense,
break forth in blossoms like the lily.
Raise your voices in a chorus of praise;
bless the Lord for all his works!
15 Proclaim the greatness of his name,
loudly sing his praises,

**39:12–35** Ben Sira invites his disciples to join him in joyfully proclaiming his favorite theme: The works of God are all good; God supplies for every need in its own time (vv. 12–16, 32–35). The sage describes God's omniscience, supreme power and wisdom, whereby all created things, good in themselves, are ever present to him, obey him, and fulfill their intended purpose (vv. 17–21), bringing blessing to the virtuous, but evil and punishment to the wicked who misuse them (vv. 22–31). Cf. similar hymns of praise, 36:1–22; 42:15–43:33.

*f:* Sir 37:26; 44:14.

With music on the harp and all stringed instruments;
sing out with joy as you proclaim:
16 The works of God are all of them good;
he supplies for every need in its own time.[g]
17 At his word the waters become still as in a flask;
he had but to speak and the reservoirs were made.[h]
18 He has but to command and his will is done;
nothing can limit his saving action.
19 The works of all humankind are present to him;
nothing is hidden from his eyes.[i]
20 His gaze spans all the ages:
is there any limit to his saving action?
To him, nothing is small or insignificant,
and nothing too wonderful or hard for him.
21 No cause then to say: "What is the purpose of this?"
Everything is chosen to satisfy a need.
22 His blessing overflows like the Nile;
like the Euphrates it enriches the surface of the earth.
23 Even so, his wrath dispossesses the nations
and turns fertile land into a salt marsh.[j]
24 For the virtuous his paths are level,
to the haughty they are clogged with stones.
25 Good things for the good he provided from the beginning,
but for the wicked good things and bad.
26 Chief of all needs for human life
are water and fire, iron and salt,
The heart of the wheat, milk and honey,
the blood of the grape, and oil, and clothing.[k]
27 For the good all these are good,
but for the wicked they turn out evil.
28 There are stormwinds created to punish;
in their fury they can dislodge mountains.
In a time of destruction they hurl their force
and calm the anger of their Maker.
29 Fire and hail, famine and disease:
these too were created for punishment.
30 Ravenous beasts, scorpions, vipers,
and the avenging sword to exterminate the wicked:
All these were created to meet a need,
and are kept in his storehouse for the proper time.
31 When he commands them, they rejoice,
in their assigned tasks they do not disobey his command.

32 That is why from the first I took my stand,
and wrote down as my theme:
33 The works of God are all of them good;
he supplies for every need in its own time.[l]
34 There is no cause then to say: "This is not as good as that";
for each shows its worth at the proper time.
35 So now with full heart and voice proclaim
and bless his name!

## CHAPTER 40

See RG 198–200

### *Joys and Miseries of Life*

1 A great anxiety has God allotted,*
and a heavy yoke, to the children of Adam,[m]
From the day they leave their mother's womb
until the day they return to the mother of all the living.*
2 Troubled thoughts and fear of heart are theirs
and anxious foreboding until death.
3 Whether one sits on a lofty throne
or grovels in dust and ashes,

**40:1–17** The former idyllic description of the universe is contrasted with the picture of the evils afflicting humanity. Every person, high or low, is burdened from birth to death with fears, anxieties, and troubles, by day and often by night, the time appointed for rest (vv. 1–7). For sinners, the suffering is much greater (vv. 8–10). What they gained by violence and injustice is quickly destroyed; but righteousness will prevail (vv. 14–17).

**40:1 Mother of all the living**: the earth from which human beings were taken. Cf. Gn 2:7; 3:19–20; Jb 1:21; Ps 139:15.

*g:* Sir 39:33; Gn 1:29–31; Eccl 3:11. *h:* Gn 1:6–10; Ex 14:21–22; Jos 3:15–16. *i:* Sir 15:18–19; 42:18–20. *j:* Gn 13:10; 19:24–28; Dt 29:22; Jos 1:2–6; Ps 107:34; Wis 10:7. *k:* Sir 29:21. *l:* Sir 39:16; Gn 1:29–31; Eccl 3:11. *m:* Gn 3:17–19; Jb 7:1; 14:1–2; Eccl 2:23.

4 Whether one wears a splendid crown
or is clothed in the coarsest of garments—
5 There is wrath and envy, trouble and dread,
terror of death, fury and strife.
Even when one lies on his bed to rest,
his cares disturb his sleep at night.
6 So short is his rest it seems like none,
till in his dreams he struggles as he did by day,
Troubled by the visions of his mind,
like a fugitive fleeing from the pursuer.
7 As he reaches safety, he wakes up,
astonished that there was nothing to fear.
8 To all flesh, human being and beast,
but for sinners seven times more,
9 Come plague and bloodshed, fiery heat and drought,
plunder and ruin, famine and death.[n]
10 For the wicked evil was created,
and because of them destruction hastens.

11 All that is of earth returns to earth,
and what is from above returns above.*
12 All that comes from bribes or injustice will be wiped out,
but loyalty remains forever.
13 Wealth from injustice is like a flooding wadi,
like a mighty stream with lightning and thunder,
14 Which, in its rising, rolls along the stones,
but suddenly, once and for all, comes to an end.[o]
15 The offshoot of violence will not flourish,
for the root of the godless is on sheer rock.
16 They are like reeds on riverbanks,
withered before all other plants;
17 But goodness, like eternity, will never be cut off,
and righteousness endures forever.

18 Wealth or wages can make life sweet,*
but better than either, finding a treasure.
19 A child or a city will preserve one's name,
but better than either, finding wisdom.
Cattle and orchards make a person flourish;
but better than either, a devoted wife.[p]
20 Wine and strong drink delight the soul,
but better than either, love of friends.[q]
21 Flute and harp offer sweet melody,
but better than either, a pure tongue.
22 Grace and beauty delight the eye,
but better than either, the produce of the field.
23 A friend and a neighbor are timely guides,
but better than either, a sensible wife.
24 Relatives and helpers for times of stress;
but better than either, charity that rescues.
25 Gold and silver make one's way secure,
but better than either, sound judgment.
26 Wealth and vigor make the heart exult,
but better than either, fear of God.
In the fear of the Lord there is no want;
whoever has it need seek no other support.
27 The fear of God is a paradise of blessings;
its canopy is over all that is glorious.[r]

28 My son, do not live the life of a beggar;*
better to die than to beg.
29 When one has to look to a stranger's table,
life is not worth living.
The delicacies offered bring revulsion of spirit,
and to the intelligent, inward torture.[s]

**40:11 All that is of earth . . . returns above**: a reference to bodily mortality and to the divine origin of life. Cf. 41:10; Gn 2:7; 3:19; Jb 34:14–15; Ps 104:29–30; 146:4; Eccl 12:7. The Greek and the Latin render the second half of the verse: "all waters shall return to the sea."

**40:18–27** Of the many treasures making life sweet, such as children, friends, music, vigor, the best are called true married love, wisdom, and above all, fear of God; cf. 25:6–11.

**40:28–30** Among the Jews, begging was considered degrading to human dignity; it was agreeable only to the shameless, who had lost their sense of honor. Cf. 29:22–23.

*n:* Sir 39:28–31. *o:* Sir 23:25–26; Wis 4:3–6. *p:* Prv 18:22; 19:14. *q:* Ps 104:15. *r:* Is 4:5–6. *s:* Sir 29:24.

30 In the mouth of the shameless begging is sweet,
but within him it burns like fire.

## CHAPTER 41

See RG 198–200

1 O death! How bitter is the thought of you*
for the one at peace in his home,
For the one who is serene and always successful,
who can still enjoy life's pleasures.
2 O death! How welcome is your sentence to the weak, failing in strength,
Stumbling and tripping on everything, with sight gone and hope lost.[t]
3 Do not fear death's decree for you;
remember, it embraces those before you and those to come.[u]
4 This decree for all flesh is from God;
why then should you reject a law of the Most High?
Whether one has lived a thousand years, a hundred, or ten,
in Sheol there are no arguments about life.

5 The children of sinners are a reprobate line,[v]
and witless offspring are in the homes of the wicked.
6 The inheritance of children of sinners will perish,
and on their offspring will be perpetual disgrace.
7 Children curse their wicked father,
for they suffer disgrace because of him.
8 Woe to you, O wicked people,
who forsake the Law of the Most High.
9 If you have children, calamity will be theirs;
and if you beget them, it will be only for groaning.
When you stumble, there is lasting joy;
and when you die, you become a curse.
10 All that is nought returns to nought,
so too the godless—from void to void.[w]

11 The human body is a fleeting thing,
but a virtuous name will never be annihilated.[x]
12 Have respect for your name, for it will stand by you
more than thousands of precious treasures.[y]
13 The good things of life last a number of days,
but a good name, for days without number.

### *True and False Shame**

14b Hidden wisdom and concealed treasure,
of what value is either?
15 Better is the person who hides his folly
than the one who hides his wisdom.
14a My children, listen to instruction about shame;
16a judge of disgrace according to my rules,
16b Not every kind of shame is shameful,
nor is every kind of disgrace to be recognized.
17 Before father and mother be ashamed of immorality,
before prince and ruler, of falsehood;
18 Before master and mistress, of deceit;
before the public assembly, of crime;
Before associate and friend, of disloyalty,
19 and in the place where you settle, of theft.
Be ashamed of breaking an oath or a covenant,
and of stretching your elbow at dinner;
Of refusing to give when asked,
21 of rebuffing your own relatives;
Of defrauding another of his appointed share,
20a of failing to return a greeting;

**41:1–13** Whether death seems bitter to one who enjoys peace, success, and pleasure, or welcome to one who is weak and in despair, it comes to all and must be accepted as the will of God (vv. 1–4). The human body passes away (v. 11). Sinners as well as their offspring pass away as if they had never been (vv. 5–10). Only the good name of the virtuous endures (vv. 11–13).

**41:14–42:8** Ben Sira illustrates the subject of true and false shame with numerous and detailed examples of wrongdoing (41:14–22) and virtue (42:1–8), following the norm of the commandments.

*t:* Sir 30:17. *u:* Sir 38:20–22. *v:* Sir 3:9–11; Wis 3:16–19. *w:* Sir 40:11; Wis 4:19. *x:* Prv 10:7. *y:* Prv 22:1; Eccl 7:1.

21c Of gazing at a man's wife,
20b of entertaining thoughts about another
woman;[z]
22 Of trifling with a servant girl you have,
of violating her bed;
Of using harsh words with friends,
of following up your gifts with insults;[a]

## CHAPTER 42

See RG 198–200

1 Of repeating what you hear,
of betraying any secret.[b]
Be ashamed of the right things,
and you will find favor in the sight of
all.

But of these things do not be ashamed,
lest you sin to save face:[c]
2 Of the Law of the Most High and his
precepts,
or of justice that acquits the ungodly;
3 Of sharing the expenses of a business or
a journey,
of dividing an inheritance or property;
4 Of accuracy of scales and balances,
of tested measures and weights;[d]
Of acquiring much or little,
5 of bargaining in dealing with a
merchant;
Of constant training of children,
of beating the sides of a wicked
servant;[e]
6 Of a seal to keep a foolish wife at home,
of a key where there are many hands;
7 Of numbering every deposit,
of recording all that is taken in and
given out;
8 Of chastisement for the silly and the
foolish,
for the aged and infirm answering for
wanton conduct.
Thus you will be truly refined
and recognized by all as discreet.

### *A Father's Care for His Daughter**

9 A daughter is a treasure that keeps her
father wakeful,
and worry over her drives away sleep:[f]
Lest in her youth she remain unmarried,
or when she is married, lest she be
childless;
10 While unmarried, lest she be defiled,
or in her husband's house, lest she
prove unfaithful;
Lest she become pregnant in her father's
house,
or be sterile in that of her husband.
11 My son, keep a close watch on your
daughter,
lest she make you a laughingstock for
your enemies,
A byword in the city and the assembly of
the people,
an object of derision in public
gatherings.[g]
See that there is no lattice in her room,
or spot that overlooks the approaches
to the house.
12 Do not let her reveal her beauty to any
male,[h]
or spend her time with married women;
13 For just as moths come from garments,
so a woman's wickedness comes from
a woman.
14 Better a man's harshness than a woman's
indulgence,
a frightened daughter than any disgrace.

### *The Works of God in Nature**

15 Now will I recall God's works;
what I have seen, I will describe.
By the LORD's word his works were
brought into being;
he accepts the one who does his will.[i]
16 As the shining sun is clear to all,

**42:9–14** Ben Sira considers a daughter to be a source of anxiety to her father, lest she fail to marry, or be defiled, or lest, marrying, she be childless, prove unfaithful, or find herself sterile (vv. 9–10). He is advised to keep a close watch on her and on her companions, lest he suffer on her account among the people (vv. 11–12). The exhortations, which take into account only a father's concern, are quite unflattering to young women. The concluding statements (vv. 13–14) show the limitations of Ben Sira's perspective in the male-oriented society of his day.

**42:15–43:33** These verses comprise another hymn; cf. 16:24–18:14. In them Ben Sira contemplates God's power, beauty, and goodness as manifested in the mighty work of creating and preserving the universe (42:15–17, 22–25; 43:1–26), his omniscience (42:18–20), perfect wisdom and eternity (42:21). The conclusion is a fervent hymn of praise (43:27–31).

*z:* Sir 9:8; Mt 5:28. *a:* Sir 18:15; 20:14. *b:* Sir 27:16. *c:* Prv 24:23; Jas 2:1. *d:* Lv 19:35; Prv 11:1; 16:11; 20:10. *e:* Sir 30:1–13; 33:25–33. *f:* Sir 7:24–25. *g:* Dt 22:20–21. *h:* Sir 9:1–9. *i:* Ps 77:12–13.

so the glory of the LORD fills all his
works;
17 Yet even God's holy ones must fail
in recounting the wonders of the
LORD,
Though God has given his hosts the
strength
to stand firm before his glory.
18 He searches out the abyss and penetrates
the heart;
their secrets he understands.
For the Most High possesses all
knowledge,
and sees from of old the things that are
to come.
19 He makes known the past and the future,
and reveals the deepest secrets.
20 He lacks no understanding;
no single thing escapes him.[j]
21 He regulates the mighty deeds of his
wisdom;
he is from all eternity one and the
same,
With nothing added, nothing taken away;
no need of a counselor for him![k]
22 How beautiful are all his works,
delightful to gaze upon and a joy to
behold!
23 Everything lives and abides forever;
and to meet each need all things are
preserved.
24 All of them differ, one from another,
yet none of them has he made in vain;
25 For each in turn, as it comes, is good;
can one ever see enough of their
splendor?[l]

## CHAPTER 43

See RG 198–200

1 The beauty of the celestial height
and the pure firmament,[m]
heaven itself manifests its glory.
2 The sun at its rising shines at its fullest,
a wonderful instrument, the work of
the Most High!
3 At noon it scorches the earth,
and who can bear its fiery heat?
4 Like a blazing furnace of solid metal,
the sun's rays set the mountains aflame;
Its fiery tongue consumes the world;
the eyes are burned by its fire.
5 Great indeed is the LORD who made it,
at whose orders it urges on its steeds.
6 It is the moon that marks the changing
seasons,
governing the times, their lasting
sign.[n]
7 By it we know the sacred seasons and
pilgrimage feasts,
a light which wanes in its course:
8 The new moon like its name* renews
itself;
how wondrous it is when it changes:
A military signal for the waterskins on
high,
it paves the firmament with its
brilliance,
9 The beauty of the heavens and the glory
of the stars,
a shining ornament in the heights of
God.[o]
10 By the LORD's command the moon keeps
its appointed place,
and does not fade as the stars keep
watch.
11 Behold the rainbow! Then bless its Maker,
for majestic indeed is its splendor;[p]
12 It spans the heavens with its glory,
the hand of God has stretched it out in
power.
13 His rebuke marks out the path for the
hail,
and makes the flashes of his judgment
shine forth.
14 For his own purposes he opens the
storehouse
and makes the rain clouds fly like
vultures.
15 His might gives the clouds their strength,
and breaks off the hailstones.
16 The thunder of his voice makes the earth
writhe;

**43:8 Like its name**: there is a play in the Hebrew text on the words for moon and renewal. **Waterskins**: clouds as source of rain.

*j:* Sir 39:19; Wis 1:6–9. *k:* Wis 9:13; Is 40:13; Rom 11:34; 1 Cor 2:11. *l:* Sir 33:15. *m:* Ps 19:2–5. *n:* Lv 23:5; Nm 28:11–14; Ps 81:4–6. *o:* Ps 8:4. *p:* Gn 9:13.

by his power he shakes the mountains.
17 A word from him drives on the south wind,
whirlwind, hurricane, and stormwind.
He makes the snow fly like birds;
it settles down like swarms of locusts.
18 Its shining whiteness blinds the eyes,
the mind marvels at its steady fall.
19 He scatters frost like salt;
it shines like blossoms on the thornbush.
20 He sends cold northern blasts
that harden the ponds like solid ground,
Spreads a crust over every body of water,
and clothes each pool with a coat of armor.
21 When mountain growth is scorched by heat,
and flowering plains as by fire,
22 The dripping clouds restore them all,
and the scattered dew enriches the parched land.
23 His is the plan that calms the deep,
and plants the islands in the sea.
24 Those who go down to the sea recount its extent,
and when we hear them we are thunderstruck;[q]
25 In it are his creatures, stupendous, amazing,
all kinds of life, and the monsters of the deep.
26 For him each messenger succeeds,
and at his bidding accomplishes his will.[r]

27 More than this we need not add;
let the last word be, he is the all!*
28 Let us praise him the more, since we cannot fathom him,
for greater is he than all his works;
29 Awesome indeed is the LORD,
and wonderful his power.
30 Lift up your voices to glorify the LORD
as much as you can, for there is still more.
Extol him with renewed strength,
do not grow weary, for you cannot fathom him.
31 For who has seen him and can describe him?
Who can praise him as he is?[s]
32 Beyond these, many things lie hidden;
only a few of his works have I seen.
33 It is the LORD who has made all things;
to those who fear him he gives wisdom.[t]

## CHAPTER 44

See RG 198–200

### *Praise of Israel's Great Ancestors**

1 I will now praise the godly,
our ancestors, in their own time,*
2 The abounding glory of the Most High's portion,
his own part, since the days of old.[u]
3 Subduers of the land in kingly fashion,
renowned for their might,
Counselors in their prudence,
seers of all things in prophecy,[v]
4 Resolute princes of the flock,
lawgivers and their rules,
Sages skilled in composition,
authors of sharp proverbs,
5 Composers of melodious psalms,
writers of lyric poems;
6 Stalwart, solidly established,
at peace in their own estates—
7 All these were glorious in their time,
illustrious in their day.
8 Some of them left behind a name
so that people recount their praises.
9 Of others no memory remains,
for when they perished, they perished,
As if they had never lived,

**43:27 The all**: the perfections reflected in creation are found in a transcendent way in God, who alone is their source.

**44:1–50:24** As in the previous section God's glory shone forth in the works of nature, so in these chapters it is revealed through the history of God's people as seen in the lives of their ancestors, prophets, priests, and rulers. The example of these great people, whose virtues are recalled here, constitutes a high point of Ben Sira's teaching.

**44:1–15** The reader is here introduced to those people of Israel, later mentioned by name, who through various achievements and beneficial social activities have acquired great renown (vv. 1–8, 14–15); and also to those who, though forgotten, endure through the fruit of their virtues and through their families because of God's covenant with them (vv. 9–15).

*q:* Ps 104:25–26. *r:* Ps 33:6. *s:* Ps 106:2. *t:* Sir 1:10. *u:* Dt 32:8–9. *v:* Sir 39:1.

**Praise of the Heroes**

THE FINAL CHAPTERS of Ben Sira form a distinct unit in which Ben Sira sings the praises of Israel's heroes. It is the best-known passage in Ben Sira and represents a kind of finale. With the exception of the last hero, Simon son of Onias, all the heroes are known from biblical literature. Thus, this long poem of praise partly functions as a retelling of biblical history. Its primary function is to recall the legacy of these renowned men (no women are included on the list), because they illustrate what it means to be truly honored. They are the paradigmatic examples of Ben Sira's claim that a good name lasts forever (41:13).

they and their children after them.
10 Yet these also were godly;
their virtues have not been forgotten.
11 Their wealth remains in their families,
their heritage with their descendants.
12 Through God's covenant their family endures,
and their offspring for their sake.
13 And for all time their progeny will endure,
their glory will never be blotted out;
14 Their bodies are buried in peace,
but their name lives on and on.[w]
15 At gatherings their wisdom is retold,
and the assembly proclaims their praises.

*The Early Ancestors*

16 [ENOCH* walked with the LORD and was taken,[x]
that succeeding generations might learn by his example.]
17 NOAH, found just and perfect,
renewed the race in the time of devastation.[y]
Because of his worth there were survivors,
and with a sign to him the deluge ended.
18 A lasting covenant was made with him,
that never again would all flesh be destroyed.
19 ABRAHAM, father of many peoples,
kept his glory without stain:[z]
20 He observed the Most High's command,
and entered into a covenant with him;
In his own flesh he incised the ordinance,*
and when tested was found loyal.[a]
21 For this reason, God promised him with an oath
to bless the nations through his descendants,
To make him numerous as grains of dust,
and to exalt his posterity like the stars,
Giving them an inheritance from sea to sea,
and from the River* to the ends of the earth.
22 For ISAAC, too, he renewed the same promise
because of Abraham, his father.
The covenant with all his forebears was confirmed,
23 and the blessing rested upon the head of ISRAEL.[b]
God acknowledged him as the firstborn,
and gave him his inheritance.
He fixed the boundaries for his tribes
and their division into twelve.

**44:16 Enoch**: because of his friendship with God and his unusual disappearance from the earth, this prophet's renown was great among the chosen people, particularly in the two centuries just before the coming of Christ; cf. Gn 5:21–24; Heb 11:5. The present verse is an expansion of the original text; cf. 49:14.

**44:20 In his own flesh . . . ordinance**: the covenant of circumcision; cf. Gn 17:10–14. **And when tested . . . loyal**: Abraham's willingness to sacrifice his son Isaac at the Lord's command; cf. Gn 22:1–12.

**44:21 The River**: the Euphrates; cf. Gn 2:14.

**44:23(end)–45:5** Moses manifested God's power through marvels (vv. 1–3), God's authority through the commandments and the Law (v. 5), and God's mercy through the intimacy granted him by the Lord for his own faithfulness and meekness (v. 4).

*w:* Wis 3:2–3. *x:* Sir 49:14; Gn 5:18–24; Heb 11:5. *y:* Gn 6:8–9:29; Heb 11:7. *z:* Gn 12:1–25:10; Rom 4:3; Gal 3:6; Heb 11:8–19; Jas 2:23. *a:* Gn 17:10–14; 22:1–12. *b:* Gn 26:3–5, 24; 27:28–29; 28:13–15.

## CHAPTER 45

See RG 198–200

### *Praise of Moses, Aaron, and Phinehas*

1 From him came the man*
who would win the favor of all the living:[c]
Dear to God and human beings,
MOSES, whose memory is a blessing.
2 God made him like the angels in honor,
and strengthened him with fearful powers.[d]
3 At his words God performed signs
and sustained him in the king's presence.
He gave him the commandments for his people,
and revealed to him his glory.[e]
4 Because of his trustworthiness and meekness
God selected him from all flesh;[f]
5 He let him hear his voice,
and led him into the cloud,
Where he handed over the commandments,
the law of life and understanding,*
That he might teach his precepts to Jacob,
his judgments and decrees to Israel.

6 He also raised up, like Moses in holiness,*
his brother AARON, of the tribe of Levi.[g]
7 He made his office perpetual
and bestowed on him priesthood for his people;
He established him in honor
and crowned him with lofty majesty.
8 He clothed him in splendid garments,
and adorned him with glorious vestments:
Breeches, tunic, and robe
9 with pomegranates at the hem
And a rustle of bells round about,
whose pleasing sound at each step
Would make him heard within the sanctuary,
a reminder for the people;
10 The sacred vestments of gold, violet,
and crimson, worked with embroidery;
The breastpiece for decision, the ephod and cincture
11 with scarlet yarn, the work of the weaver;
Precious stones with seal engravings
in golden settings, the work of the jeweler,
To commemorate in incised letters
each of the tribes of Israel;
12 On his turban a diadem of gold,
its plate engraved with the sacred inscription—
Majestic, glorious, renowned for splendor,
a delight to the eyes, supremely beautiful.
13 Before him, no one had been adorned with these,
nor may they ever be worn by any other
Except his sons and them alone,
generation after generation, for all time.
14 His grain offering is wholly burnt
as an established offering twice each day;
15 For Moses ordained him
and anointed him with the holy oil,
In a lasting covenant with him and his family,
as permanent as the heavens,
That he should serve God in the priesthood
and bless the people in his name.
16 He chose him from all the living
to sacrifice burnt offerings and choice portions,

**45:5** On God's intimacy with Moses, see Ex 33:11; Nm 12:8; Dt 34:10.

**45:6–25** Ben Sira here expresses his reverence and esteem for the priesthood of the old covenant. He recalls God's choice of Aaron and his sons for this sublime office (vv. 6–7), and describes in detail the beauty of the high priest's vestments (vv. 8–13). He relates the ordination of Aaron at the hands of Moses (v. 15), and describes the priestly functions, namely, offering sacrifice to God (v. 16), and blessing (v. 15), teaching, governing, and judging the people (v. 17); the inheritance of the high priest (vv. 20–22); the punishment of those who were jealous of Aaron (vv. 18–19); and the confirmation of the covenant of the priesthood with Aaron's descendants through Phinehas (vv. 23–25).

*c:* Ex 2:2; 11:3; 33:11; Nm 12:7. *d:* Ex 7–Dt 34. *e:* Ex 7:1–7; 20:2–17; Dt 5:6–21. *f:* Nm 12:3, 7. *g:* Ex 28–29; Wis 18:24.

To burn incense, sweet odor as a memorial,
and to atone for the people of Israel.
17 He gave to him the laws,
and authority to prescribe and to judge:
To teach precepts to the people,
and judgments to the Israelites.
18 Strangers rose in anger against him,
grew jealous of him in the desert—
The followers of Dathan and Abiram,
and the band of Korah in their defiance.[h]
19 When the LORD saw this he became angry,
and destroyed them in his burning wrath.
He brought against them a marvel,
and consumed them in flaming fire.
20 Then he increased the glory of Aaron[i]
and bestowed upon him his inheritance:
The sacred offerings he allotted to him,
with the showbread* as his portion;
21 The oblations of the LORD are his food,
a gift to him and his descendants.
22 But he holds no land among the people
nor shares with them their heritage;
For the LORD himself is his portion and inheritance
among the Israelites.

23 PHINEHAS too, the son of Eleazar,
was the courageous third of his line
When, zealous for the God of all,
he met the crisis of his people[j]
And, at the prompting of his noble heart,
atoned for the children of Israel.
24 Therefore, on him also God conferred the right,
in a covenant of friendship, to provide for the sanctuary,
So that he and his descendants
should possess the high priesthood forever.
25 For even his covenant with David,
the son of Jesse of the tribe of Judah,
Was an individual heritage through one son alone;[k]
but the heritage of Aaron is for all his descendants.

So now bless* the LORD
who has crowned you with glory!
26 May he grant you wisdom of heart
to govern his people in justice,
Lest the benefits you confer should be forgotten,
or your authority, throughout all time.

## CHAPTER 46

See RG 198–200

### *Joshua, Caleb, the Judges, and Samuel*

1 Valiant warrior was JOSHUA,* son of Nun,
aide to Moses in the prophetic office,
Formed to be, as his name implies,
the great savior of God's chosen ones,
To punish the enemy
and to give to Israel their heritage.[l]
2 What glory was his when he raised his hand,
to brandish his sword against the city![m]
3 Who could withstand him
when he fought the battles of the LORD?*
4 Was it not by that same hand the sun stopped,
so that one day became two?[n]
5 He called upon the Most High God
when his enemies beset him on all sides,
And God Most High answered him
with hailstones of tremendous power,
6 That rained down upon the hostile army
till on the slope he destroyed the foe;
That all the doomed nations might know
the LORD was watching over his people's battles.
He was indeed a devoted follower of God
7 and showed himself loyal in Moses' lifetime.
He and CALEB,* son of Jephunneh,

**45:20 Showbread**: cf. note on Ex 25:29–30.

**45:25–26 So now bless**: Ben Sira addresses the whole line of high priests, especially Simon II; cf. 50:1.

**46:1–6 Joshua**: whose name means "the Lord is savior" (v. 1), was the instrument through which God delivered his people in marvelous ways (vv. 2–6) by destroying their enemies, whose land he gave to the Israelites as a heritage (v. 1).

**46:3 The battles of the Lord**: cf. Jos 6–11.

**46:7–10 Caleb**: with Joshua he advised Moses to enter

*h:* Nm 16:1–35. *i:* Nm 18:11–24; Dt 10:9. *j:* Nm 25:7–13; 1 Mc 2:26, 54; Ps 106:30–31. *k:* 2 Sm 7:12–16. *l:* Ex 17:9; Nm 27:18–23; Dt 34:9; Jos 1:1–9. *m:* Jos 8:18–19. *n:* Jos 10:12–13.

when they opposed the rebel assembly,
Averted God's anger from the people
and suppressed the wicked complaint.[o]
8 Because of this, these two alone were spared
from the six hundred thousand infantry,
To lead the people into their heritage,
the land flowing with milk and honey.[p]
9 The strength God gave to Caleb
remained with him even in old age
Till he won his way onto the summits of the land;
his family too received a heritage,[q]
10 That all the offspring of Jacob might know
how good it is to be a devoted follower of the LORD.

11 The JUDGES,* each one of them,
whose hearts were not deceived,
Who did not abandon God—
may their memory be ever blessed![r]
12 May their bones flourish with new life where they lie,
and their names receive fresh luster in their children!
13 Beloved of his people, dear to his Maker,
pledged in a vow from his mother's womb,
As one consecrated to the LORD in the prophetic office,
was SAMUEL, the judge who offered sacrifice.
At God's word he established the kingdom
and anointed princes to rule the people.[s]
14 By the law of the LORD he judged the congregation,
and visited the encampments of Jacob.
15 As a trustworthy prophet he was sought out
and his words proved him to be a true seer.
16 He, too, called upon the mighty Lord
when his enemies pressed him on every side,
and offered up a suckling lamb.[t]
17 Then the LORD thundered from heaven,
and the tremendous roar of his voice was heard.[u]
18 He brought low the rulers of the enemy
and destroyed all the lords of the Philistines.
19 When Samuel neared the end of life,
he testified before the LORD and his anointed prince,
"No bribe or secret gift have I taken from anyone!"
and no one could accuse him.[v]
20 Even after death his guidance was sought;
he made known to the king his fate.
From the grave he spoke in prophecy
to put an end to wickedness.[w]

## CHAPTER 47

See RG 198–200

### *Nathan, David, and Solomon*

1 After him came NATHAN*
who served in David's presence.[x]
2 Like the choice fat of sacred offerings,
so was DAVID in Israel.[y]
3 He played with lions as though they were young goats,
and with bears, like lambs of the flock.[z]
4 As a youth he struck down the giant
and wiped out the people's disgrace;
His hand let fly the slingstone
that shattered the pride of Goliath.[a]
5 For he had called upon the Most High God,
who gave strength to his right arm
To defeat the skilled warrior
and establish the might of his people.
6 Therefore the women sang his praises
and honored him for "the tens of thousands."
When he received the royal crown, he battled[b]

Canaan, despite the counsel of their companion scouts and the rebellion of the people. He led the next generation of Israelites into the promised land. He received a portion of land which he himself had conquered; cf. Jos 15:13–14.

**46:11–20** Of the judges praised and blessed for their fidelity to God in opposing idolatry, Samuel was the greatest (vv. 11–13, 19). He was judge, prophet, and priest. Through his sacrificial offering he obtained victory over the Philistines. He established the kingdom, anointed kings (vv. 13–18), and even after his death foretold the king's fate (v. 20).

**47:1–11** An idealized portrait of David; cf. 1 Chronicles.

*o:* Nm 13:30; 14:1–3. *p:* Nm 14:22–38. *q:* Jos 14:6–13; 15:13. *r:* Jgs 1:1–16:31. *s:* 1 Sm 1:10–20; 8:4–10:1; 16:12–13. *t:* 1 Sm 7:9. *u:* 1 Sm 7:10–13. *v:* 1 Sm 12:3. *w:* 1 Sm 28:14–19. *x:* 2 Sm 7:2–17. *y:* 1 Sm 16:11–13. *z:* 1 Sm 17:34–36. *a:* 1 Sm 17:49. *b:* 1 Sm 18:7.

7 and subdued the enemy on every side.
He campaigned against the hostile Philistines
and shattered their power till our own day.[c]
8 With his every deed he offered thanks
to God Most High, in words of praise.
With his whole heart he loved his Maker
9 and daily had his praises sung;
10 He added beauty to the feasts
and solemnized the seasons of each year
9b With string music before the altar,
providing sweet melody for the psalms[d]
10b So that when the Holy Name was praised,
before daybreak the sanctuary would resound.
11 The LORD forgave him his sins
and exalted his strength forever;
He conferred on him the rights of royalty
and established his throne in Israel.[e]

12 Because of his merits he had as successor*
a wise son, who lived in security:[f]
13 SOLOMON reigned during an era of peace,
for God brought rest to all his borders.
He built a house to the name of God,
and established a lasting sanctuary.[g]
14 How wise you were when you were young,
overflowing with instruction, like the Nile in flood![h]
15 Your understanding covered the whole earth,
and, like a sea, filled it with knowledge.
16 Your fame reached distant coasts,
and you were beloved for your peaceful reign.
17 With song and proverb and riddle,
and with your answers, you astounded the nations.
18 You were called by that glorious name
which was conferred upon Israel.*
Gold you gathered like so much iron;
you heaped up silver as though it were lead.
19 But you abandoned yourself to women
and gave them dominion over your body.[i]
20 You brought a stain upon your glory,
shame upon your marriage bed,
Wrath upon your descendants,
and groaning upon your deathbed.
21 Thus two governments came into being,
when in Ephraim kingship was usurped.[j]
22 But God does not withdraw his mercy,
nor permit even one of his promises to fail.
He does not uproot the posterity of the chosen,
nor destroy the offspring of his friends.
So he gave to Jacob a remnant,
to David a root from his own family.[k]

### *Rehoboam and Jeroboam*

23 Solomon finally slept with his ancestors,
and left behind him one of his sons,
Broad* in folly, narrow in sense,
whose policy made the people rebel.
Then arose the one who should not be remembered,
the sinner who led Israel into sin,[l]
Who brought ruin to Ephraim
24 and caused them to be exiled from their land.

### *Elijah and Elisha*

25 Their sinfulness grew more and more,
and they gave themselves to every evil*

**47:12–24** The standard view of Solomon is echoed by Ben Sira, but he affirms the divine promise (v. 22) to David's line.

**47:18** Cf. 2 Sm 12:25, where Solomon is called Jedidiah, "beloved of the Lord." A similar term is used of Israel in Jer 11:15.

**47:23 Broad**: the name Rehoboam means "the people is broad, or expansive," that is, widespread. **The sinner**: Jeroboam; cf. 1 Kgs 12:1, 20, 26–32.

**47:25–48:11** The prophetic ministry of Elijah amid widespread idolatry is here described as a judgment by fire (48:1). Through his preaching, marvels, and acts of vengeance against God's enemies, he succeeded for a time in restoring faith in and worship of the Lord (vv. 2–8). His mysterious departure from this life gave rise to the belief that he did not die but would return before the day of the Lord. Cf. Mal 3:23–24; Mt 17:9–13.

*c:* 2 Sm 5:6–25. *d:* 1 Chr 16:4–37; 23:5; 25:1–7. *e:* 2 Sm 12:13; 7:12–16. *f:* 1 Kgs 2:12. *g:* 1 Kgs 5:1, 5; 6:2–38. *h:* 1 Kgs 5:9–14; 10:14–29. *i:* 1 Kgs 11:1–10. *j:* 1 Kgs 12:1–25. *k:* 2 Sm 7:15; Ps 89:34–38. *l:* 1 Kgs 11:43; 12:13, 21; 13:34; 2 Kgs 17:6–22.

## CHAPTER 48

See RG 198–200

1 Until like fire a prophet appeared,
his words a flaming furnace.[m]
2 The staff of life, their bread, he shattered,
and in his zeal he made them few in number.
3 By God's word he shut up the heavens
and three times brought down fire.[n]
4 How awesome are you, ELIJAH!
Whose glory is equal to yours?
5 You brought a dead body back to life
from Sheol, by the will of the LORD.[o]
6 You sent kings down to destruction,
and nobles, from their beds of sickness.[p]
7 You heard threats at Sinai,
at Horeb avenging judgments.[q]
8 You anointed the agent of these punishments,
the prophet to succeed in your place.[r]
9 You were taken aloft in a whirlwind,
in a chariot with fiery horses.[s]
10 You are destined, it is written, in time to come
to put an end to wrath before the day of the LORD,
To turn back the hearts of parents toward their children,
and to re-establish the tribes of Israel.[t]
11 Blessed is the one who shall have seen you before he dies!*
12 When Elijah was enveloped in the whirlwind,
ELISHA was filled with his spirit;*
He worked twice as many marvels,[u]
and every utterance of his mouth was wonderful.
During his lifetime he feared no one,
nor was anyone able to intimidate his will.
13 Nothing was beyond his power;[v]
and from where he lay buried, his body prophesied.*
14 In life he performed wonders,
and after death, marvelous deeds.
15 Despite all this the people did not repent,
nor did they give up their sins,
Until they were uprooted from their land
and scattered all over the earth.

### *Judah*

But Judah remained, a tiny people,
with its ruler from the house of David.[w]
16 Some of them did what was right,
but others were extremely sinful.

### *Hezekiah and Isaiah**

17 HEZEKIAH fortified his city
and had water brought into it;[x]
With bronze tools he cut through the rocks
and dammed up a mountain site for water.*
18 During his reign Sennacherib led an invasion
and sent his adjutant;
He shook his fist at Zion
and blasphemed God in his pride.[y]
19 The people's hearts melted within them,
and they were in anguish like that of childbirth.
20 But they called upon the Most High God
and lifted up their hands to him;
He heard the prayer they uttered,
and saved them through ISAIAH.[z]
21 God struck the camp of the Assyrians
and routed them with a plague.[a]
22 For Hezekiah did what was right

**48:11** Verse 11b is not extant in the Hebrew; it is represented in the Greek tradition by "for we too shall certainly live." But this can hardly be the original reading.

**48:12–16** Elisha continued Elijah's work (vv. 12–14), but the obstinacy of the people eventually brought on the destruction of the kingdom of Israel and the dispersion of its subjects. Judah, however, survived under the rule of Davidic kings, both good and bad (vv. 15–16).

**48:13** The reference in v. 13b seems to be to 2 Kgs 13:21 where it is related that a dead man, thrown into Elisha's grave, came back to life.

**48:17–25** The fidelity of King Hezekiah (vv. 17, 22), the zeal of the prophet Isaiah, and the prayer of the people (v. 20) were effective. The Assyrian oppressors under Sennacherib withdrew (vv. 18–19, 21). The king's life was prolonged. The people were consoled by Isaiah's words about the future (vv. 23–25); the "consolations" refer to Is 40–66.

**48:17** The reference is to the famous Siloam tunnel in present-day Jerusalem.

*m:* 1 Kgs 17:1. *n:* 2 Kgs 1:9–14. *o:* 1 Kgs 17:17–23. *p:* 1 Kgs 21:19; 2 Kgs 1:17. *q:* 1 Kgs 19:8–15. *r:* 1 Kgs 19:16–17. *s:* 2 Kgs 2:11. *t:* Mal 3:23–24; Mt 17:10. *u:* 2 Kgs 2:9–12. *v:* 2 Kgs 13:21. *w:* 2 Kgs 15:29; 18:11–12. *x:* 2 Kgs 20:20; 2 Chr 32:30. *y:* 2 Kgs 18:13–37; Is 36:1–22. *z:* 2 Kgs 19:20. *a:* 2 Kgs 19:35; Is 37:36.

and held fast to the paths of David,
As ordered by the illustrious prophet
Isaiah, who saw truth in visions.
23 In his lifetime he turned back the sun
and prolonged the life of the king.[b]
24 By his powerful spirit he looked into the
future[c]
and consoled the mourners of Zion;
25 He foretold what would happen till the
end of time,
hidden things yet to be fulfilled.

## CHAPTER 49

See RG 198–200

### *Josiah and the Prophets**

1 The name JOSIAH is like blended incense,
made lasting by a skilled perfumer.[d]
Precious is his memory, like honey to the
taste,
like music at a banquet.
2 For he grieved over our betrayals,
and destroyed the abominable idols.
3 He kept his heart fixed on God,
and in times of lawlessness practiced
virtue.
4 Except for David, Hezekiah, and Josiah,
they all were wicked;
They abandoned the Law of the Most
High,
these kings of Judah, right to the very
end.
5 So he gave over their power to others,
their glory to a foreign nation
6 Who burned the holy city
and left its streets desolate,
7 As foretold by JEREMIAH.[e] They
mistreated him
who even in the womb had been made
a prophet,
To root out, pull down, and destroy,
and then to build and to plant.[f]
8 EZEKIEL beheld a vision
and described the different creatures of
the chariot;[g]
9 He also referred to JOB,
who always persevered in the right
path.[h]
10 Then, too, the TWELVE PROPHETS—
may their bones flourish with new life
where they lie!—
They gave new strength to Jacob
and saved him with steadfast hope.

### *The Heroes After the Exile*

11 How to extol ZERUBBABEL?*
He was like a signet ring on the right
hand,[i]
12 And JESHUA, Jozadak's son?
In their time they rebuilt the altar
And erected the holy temple,
destined for everlasting glory.
13 Exalted be the memory of NEHEMIAH!
He rebuilt our ruined walls,
Restored our shattered defenses,
and set up gates and bars.[j]

### *The Earliest Patriarchs*

14 Few on earth have been created like
ENOCH;*
he also was taken up bodily.[k]
15 Was ever a man born like JOSEPH?
Even his dead body was provided for.[l]
16 Glorious, too, were SHEM and SETH and
ENOSH;
but beyond that of any living being
was the splendor of ADAM.[m]

## CHAPTER 50

See RG 198–200

### *Simeon, Son of Jochanan*

1 Greatest of his family, the glory of his
people,
was SIMEON the priest, son of
Jochanan,*

**49:1–10** Ben Sira's praise of King Josiah (vv. 1–3) and of the prophets Jeremiah and Ezekiel and the minor prophets (vv. 7–10) derives from their spirit of fidelity to the Lord and his Law (vv. 4–6, 10).

**49:11–13** The rebuilding of the Temple and the repair of the walls of the Holy City led to a restoration of religious worship and civil authority.

**49:14–16** The patriarchs here mentioned were glorious because of their spirit of religion, i.e., their profound reverence for God and obedience to him. **The splendor of Adam**: suggests his direct origin from God (Gn 1:26–27; 2:7).

**50:1–21 Son of Jochanan**: Simeon II, in whose time as high priest (219–196 B.C.) great works were accomplished for the benefit of public worship and welfare (vv. 1–4). Ben Sira, a contemporary, describes detailed liturgical action, perhaps

*b:* 2 Kgs 20:11; Is 38:8. *c:* 2 Kgs 20:17; Is 40:1–11; 42:9; 46:10; 48:6; 61:2–3. *d:* 2 Kgs 22:1–2, 10–13, 19; 23:4–15, 19–20, 24; 2 Chr 34:1–7. *e:* 2 Kgs 25:9; 2 Chr 36:19. *f:* Jer 1:5, 10. *g:* Ez 1:4–21. *h:* Ez 14:14, 20. *i:* Ezr 3:2; Hg 1:12; Zec 3:1. *j:* Neh 1:1–3:32. *k:* Sir 44:16; Gn 5:18–24. *l:* Gn 37; 39–50; Ex 13:19; Jos 24:32. *m:* Gn 1:26–30; 2:7; 4:25–26.

In whose time the house of God was
renovated,
in whose days the temple was
reinforced.
2 In his time also the retaining wall was
built
with powerful turrets for the temple
precincts.
3 In his time the reservoir was dug,
a pool as vast as the sea.
4 He protected the people against brigands
and strengthened the city against the
enemy.
5 How splendid he was as he looked out
from the tent,
as he came from behind the veil!
6 Like a star shining among the clouds,
like the full moon at the festal season;
7 Like sun shining upon the temple of the
King,
like a rainbow appearing in the cloudy
sky;
8 Like blossoms on the branches in
springtime,
like a lily by running waters;
Like a green shoot on Lebanon in
summer,
9 like the fire of incense at sacrifice;
Like a vessel of hammered gold,
studded with all kinds of precious
stones;
10 Like a luxuriant olive tree heavy with
fruit,
a plant with branches abounding in oil;
11 Wearing his glorious robes,
and vested in sublime magnificence,[n]
As he ascended the glorious altar
and lent majesty to the court of the
sanctuary.
12 When he received the portions from the
priests
while he stood before the sacrificial
wood,
His sons stood round him like a garland,
like young cedars on Lebanon;
And like poplars by the brook they
surrounded him,
13 all the sons of Aaron in their glory,
With the offerings to the LORD in their
hands,
in the presence of the whole assembly
of Israel.
14 Once he had completed the service at the
altar
and arranged the sacrificial hearth for
the Most High,
15 And had stretched forth his hand for the
cup,
to offer blood of the grape,
And poured it out at the foot of the altar,
a sweet-smelling odor to God the Most
High,[o]
16 Then the sons of Aaron would sound a
blast,
the priests, on their trumpets of beaten
metal;
A blast to resound mightily
as a reminder before the Most High.[p]
17 All the people with one accord
would fall with face to the ground
In adoration before the Most High,
before the Holy One of Israel.
18 Then hymns would re-echo,
and over the throng sweet strains of
praise resound.
19 All the people of the land would shout
for joy,
praying to the Merciful One,
As the high priest completed the service
at the altar
by presenting to God the fitting
sacrifice.
20 Then coming down he would raise his
hands
over all the congregation of Israel;
The blessing of the LORD would be upon
his lips,
the name of the LORD would be his
glory.[q]
21 The people would again fall down
to receive the blessing of the Most High.

22 And now, bless the God of all,*
who has done wonders on earth;

pertaining to the Day of Atonement (Yom Kippur, cf. Lv 16).
**50:22–24** Ben Sira urges the reader to praise and bless God for his wondrous works and then invokes a blessing on all that they may enjoy peace and gladness of heart and the abiding goodness of the Most High.

*n:* Sir 45:8–13; Ex 28:2–43; 39:1–31. *o:* Nm 15:5; 28:7. *p:* Nm 10:10. *q:* Nm 6:23–27.

Who fosters growth from the womb,
fashioning it according to his will!
23 May he grant you a wise heart
and abide with you in peace;
24 May his goodness toward Simeon last forever;
may he fulfill for him the covenant with Phinehas
So that it may not be abrogated for him
or his descendants while the heavens last.

### *Epilogue*

25 My whole being loathes two nations,
the third is not even a people:*
26 The inhabitants of Seir* and Philistia,
and the foolish people who dwell in Shechem.[r]
27 Wise instruction, appropriate proverbs,*
I have written in this book—
I, Yeshua Ben Eleazar Ben Sira—
as they poured forth from my heart's understanding.
28 Happy those who meditate upon these things;
wise those who take them to heart!
29 If they put them into practice, they can cope with anything,
for the fear of the LORD is their lamp.

## CHAPTER 51

See RG 198–200

### *A Prayer of Thanksgiving*

1 I give you thanks, LORD and King,*
I praise you, God my savior!
I declare your name, refuge of my life,[s]
2 because you have ransomed my life from death;
You held back my body from the pit,
and delivered my foot from the power of Sheol.[t]

You have preserved me from the scourge of the slanderous tongue,
and from the lips of those who went over to falsehood.
You were with me against those who rise up against me;
3 You have rescued me according to your abundant mercy[u]
From the snare of those who look for my downfall,
and from the power of those who seek my life.

From many dangers you have saved me,
4 from flames that beset me on every side,[v]
From the midst of fire till there was not a whiff of it,*
5 from the deep belly of Sheol,
From deceiving lips and painters of lies,
6 from the arrows of a treacherous tongue.
I was at the point of death,
my life was nearing the depths of Sheol;[w]
7 I turned every way, but there was no one to help;
I looked for support but there was none.[x]
8 Then I remembered the mercies of the LORD,
his acts of kindness through ages past;
For he saves those who take refuge in him,
and rescues them from every evil.
9 So I raised my voice from the grave;
from the gates of Sheol I cried for help.
10 I called out: LORD, you are my Father,
my champion, my savior!
Do not abandon me in time of trouble,
in the midst of storms and dangers.[y]
11 I will always praise your name
and remember you in prayer!
Then the LORD heard my voice,
and listened to my appeal.

**50:25 Not even a people**: the Samaritans.

**50:26 Seir:** Mount Seir in the territory of the Edomites. **Shechem**: a city in Samaria.

**50:27** This colophon may have been the original ending of the book. It is unusual for a biblical writer to append his name.

**51:1–30** This chapter contains two appendixes: a prayer (vv. 1–12) and an autobiographical poem praising wisdom (vv. 13–30).

**51:4** So complete is the deliverance from fire that even the smell of smoke cannot be detected. Cf. Dn 3:27.

*r:* 2 Kgs 17:24; Jn 4:9. *s:* Ps 138:1. *t:* Ps 91:3. *u:* Ps 56:10–12; 124:2. *v:* Ps 66:12. *w:* Ps 88:4; 94:17. *x:* Ps 22:12; 142:5. *y:* Ps 89:27; 95:1.

12 He saved me from every evil
and preserved me in time of trouble.
For this reason I thank and praise him;
I bless the name of the LORD.*

### *Ben Sira's Pursuit of Wisdom*

13 * When I was young and innocent,
I sought wisdom.[z]
14 She came to me in her beauty,
and until the end I will cultivate her.

15 As the blossoms yielded to ripening grapes,
the heart's joy,
My feet kept to the level path
because from earliest youth I was familiar with her.

16 In the short time I paid heed,
I met with great instruction.
17 Since in this way I have profited,
I will give my Teacher grateful praise.

18 I resolved to tread her paths;
I have been jealous for the good and will not turn back.
19 I burned with desire for her,
never relenting.
I became preoccupied with her,
never weary of extolling her.

I spread out my hands to the heavens
and I came to know her secrets.
20 For her I purified my hands;
in cleanness I attained to her.

At first acquaintance with her, I gained understanding
such that I will never forsake her.[a]
21 My whole being was stirred to seek her;
therefore I have made her my prize possession.
22 The LORD has rewarded me with lips,
with a tongue for praising him.

23 Come aside to me, you untutored,
and take up lodging in the house of instruction;* [b]
24 How long will you deprive yourself of wisdom's food,
how long endure such bitter thirst?
25 I open my mouth and speak of her:
gain wisdom for yourselves at no cost.[c]

**51:12** After this verse the Hebrew text gives the litany of praise contained below. It is similar to Ps 136. Though not found in any versions, and therefore of doubtful authenticity, the litany seems from internal evidence to go back to the time of Ben Sira.

Give praise to the LORD, for he is good, for God's love endures forever;
Give praise to the God of glory, for God's love endures forever;
Give praise to the Guardian of Israel, for God's love endures forever;
Give praise to the creator of all things, for God's love endures forever;
Give praise to the redeemer of Israel, for God's love endures forever;
Give praise to God who gathers the dispersed of Israel, for God's love endures forever;
Give praise to God who builds the city and sanctuary, for God's love endures forever;
Give praise to God who makes a horn sprout forth for the house of David, for God's love endures forever;
Give praise to God who has chosen the sons of Zadok as priests, for God's love endures forever;
Give praise to the Shield of Abraham, for God's love endures forever;
Give praise to the Rock of Isaac, for God's love endures forever;
Give praise to the Mighty One of Jacob, for God's love endures forever;
Give praise to God who has chosen Zion, for God's love endures forever;
Give praise to the King, the king of kings, for God's love endures forever.
He has lifted up the horn of his people! Let this be his praise from all the faithful,
From Israel, the people near to him. Hallelujah! (Cf. Ps 148:14.)

**51:13–30** A Hebrew manuscript from Qumran demonstrates the acrostic style of vv. 13–20. This is an elegant twenty-three-line alphabetic acrostic hymn that describes Ben Sira's relationship to wisdom: (a) his approach to wisdom through prayer, persistent study, and instruction (vv. 13–17); (b) his purification from sin, his enlightenment, and ardent desire to possess wisdom (vv. 18–22). Ben Sira concludes with an urgent invitation to his students to receive instruction in wisdom from him, and to live by it, because wisdom gives herself to those who seek her (vv. 23–26); and for their labor, God will reward them in his own time (vv. 27–30). Cf. Mt 11:28; Eccl 12:14.

**51:23 House of instruction**: this may be a metaphor for Ben Sira's teaching.

*z:* Sir 34:9–13; Prv 8:17. *a:* Prv 4:6. *b:* Prv 8:5. *c:* Sir 6:19; Is 55:1–3.

26 Take her yoke upon your neck;
that your mind may receive her teaching.
For she is close to those who seek her,
and the one who is in earnest finds her.[d]
27 See for yourselves! I have labored only a little,
but have found much.
28 Acquire but a little instruction,
and you will win silver and gold through her.
29 May your soul rejoice in God's mercy;
do not be ashamed to give him praise.
30 Work at your tasks in due season,
and in his own time God will give you your reward.[e]

*d:* Sir 6:26–28. *e:* Sir 2:8; Jb 34:11; Jn 9:4.

See RG 201–203

# THE PROPHETIC BOOKS

The prophetic books bear the names of the four major and twelve minor prophets, in addition to Lamentations and Baruch. The terms "major" and "minor" refer to the length of the respective compositions and not to their relative importance. Jonah is a story about a prophet rather than a collection of prophetic pronouncements. In the Hebrew Bible, Lamentations and Daniel are listed among the Writings (Hagiographa), not among the prophetic books. The former contains a series of laments over the destruction of Jerusalem by the Babylonians. The latter is considered to be a prophetic book, though it consists of a collection of six edifying diaspora tales (chaps. 1–6) and four apocalyptic visions about the end time (chaps. 7–12). Baruch is not included in the Hebrew canon, but is in the Septuagint or Old Greek version of the Bible, and the Church has from the beginning acknowledged its sacred and inspired character.

The prophetic books contain a deposit of prophetic preaching, and several of them in addition are filled out with narrative about prophets (e.g., Is 7; 36–39; Jer 26–29; 36–45; Am 7:10–17). In ancient Israel a prophet was understood to be an intermediary between God and the community, someone called to proclaim the word of God. Prophets received such communications through various means, including visions and dreams, often in a state of transformed consciousness, and transmitted them to the people as God's messengers through oracular utterances, sermons, writings, and symbolic actions.

It would be misleading to think of these works as books in our sense of the term. While some prophecies originated as written material, prophetic activity more commonly took the form of public speaking. Prophetic discourse addressed to different audiences in different situations would, typically, be committed first to memory, then to writing, often by the prophet's followers, sometimes by the prophet himself (e.g., Is 8:1–4, 16; Jer 36:1–2; Hb 2:2). Small compilations of such pronouncements and discourses would be put together, arranged according to subject matter (e.g., pronouncements against foreign nations), audience (e.g., Jeremiah to King Zedekiah, Jer 21:1–24:10), chronological sequence (e.g., in Ezekiel generally), or by verbal association (e.g., catchwords). These units would be circulated, edited, expanded and interpreted as the need arose to bring out the contemporary relevance of older prophecies, and eventually integrated into larger collections. The titles would have been added at a later date, in some instances centuries after the time of the prophet in question.

The office of the prophet came about as the result of a direct call from God. Unlike that of the priest, the prophetic function was not hereditary and did not correspond to a fixed office. In Israel as elsewhere in the ancient Near East and Levant, there were, however, prophets (*nəḇîʾîm* in Hebrew) who were employed in temples and at royal courts, and some of the canonical prophets may have started out as "professionals" of this kind. Prophecy also differed from priesthood in ancient Israel in that there were both male and female prophets. Though none of the prophetic books is named for a female prophet, Miriam (Ex 15:20) and Deborah (Jgs 4:4) played important roles at the beginning of Israel's history and Huldah (2 Kgs 22:14) toward the end. The Bible gives great importance to the call or commissioning of the prophet, which was often accompanied by visionary or other extraordinary experiences (e.g., Jer 23:21–22; Ez 1–2). In these accounts the prophetic intermediary can be represented as a messenger commissioned by the Lord as king (e.g., Micaiah in 1 Kgs 22:19–23, and Isaiah in Is 6:1–13), and therefore prophetic speech is often introduced with the form used in the delivery of a message: "thus says the Lord" or some similar formula. Sometimes the prophetic calling could be expected to involve struggle, persecution, and suffering.

While prophetic messages sometimes bore on the future, their primary concern was with contemporary events in the public sphere of social life and politics, national and international. They focus on public morality, the treatment of the poor and disadvantaged, and the abuse of power, especially of the judicial system. They pass judgment in the strongest terms on the moral conduct of rulers and the ruling class, in the belief that a society that does not practice justice and righteousness will not survive. With equal rigor, they also condemn a religious formalism that would legitimate such a society (e.g., Is 1:10–17; Jer 7:1–15; Am 5:21–24). They view international affairs, the rise and fall of the great empires, in the light of their own passionate belief in the God of Israel and the destiny of Israel. The prophets never take political and military power as absolutes. They do not preach a new morality. They are radicals only in the sense of a radical commitment to and interpretation of the religious, legal, and moral traditions inherited from Israel's past.

Prophetic speech is not, however, confined to judgment and condemnation. The prophets also exhort, cajole, encourage; they announce salvation and a good prognosis for the future. Sometimes present realities and situations shade off into, or are taken up into, a panorama of a more distant future. In many instances, too, prophetic pronouncements are developed by a cumulative and incremental editorial process into a more inclusive and total vision of a final salvation and a final judgment, with or without the presence of a messianic figure. This process is particularly evident throughout the Book of Isaiah, and played an important part in the self-understanding of early Christian churches and their interpretation of the person and mission of Jesus. For early Christianity, therefore, prophetic texts were used to describe the new reality of Christ and the church (e.g., Mt 1:23; Acts 2:14–21; Gal 4:27).

**See RG 204–212**

# The Book of Isaiah

Isaiah, one of the greatest of the prophets, appeared at a critical moment in Israel's history. The Northern Kingdom collapsed, under the hammer-like blows of Assyria, in 722/721 B.C., and in 701 Jerusalem itself saw the army of Sennacherib drawn up before its walls. In the year that Uzziah, king of Judah, died (742), Isaiah received his call to the prophetic office in the Temple of Jerusalem. Close attention should be given to chap. 6, where this divine summons to be the ambassador of the Most High is circumstantially described.

The vision of the Lord enthroned in glory stamps an indelible character on Isaiah's ministry and provides a key to the understanding of his message. The majesty, holiness and glory of the Lord took possession of his spirit and, at the same time, he gained a new awareness of human pettiness and sinfulness. The enormous abyss between God's sovereign holiness and human sinfulness overwhelmed the prophet. Only the purifying coal of the seraphim could cleanse his lips and prepare him for acceptance of the call: "Here I am, send me!"

The ministry of Isaiah extended from the death of Uzziah in 742 B.C. to Sennacherib's siege of Jerusalem in 701 B.C., and it may have continued even longer, until after the death of Hezekiah in 687 B.C. Later legend (the Martyrdom and Ascension of Isaiah) claims that Hezekiah's son, Manasseh, executed Isaiah by having him sawed in two; cf. Heb 11:37. During this long ministry, the prophet returned again and again to the same themes, and there are indications that he may have sometimes re-edited his older prophecies to fit new occasions. There is no evidence that the present arrangement of the oracles in the book reflects a chronological order. Indeed, it appears that there were originally separate smaller collections of oracles (note especially chaps. 6–12), each with its own logic for ordering, that were preserved fairly intact as blocks when the material was finally put together as a single literary work.

Isaiah's oracles cluster around several key historical events of the late eighth century: the Syro-Ephraimite War (735–732 B.C.), the accession of Hezekiah (715 B.C.), the revolt of Ashdod (714–711 B.C.), the death of Sargon (705 B.C.), and the revolt against Sennacherib (705–701 B.C.). In 738 B.C., with the Assyrian defeat of Calno/Calneh (Is 10:9; Am 6:2), the anti-Assyrian league, of which Judah may have been the ringleader, collapsed, and both Israel and the Arameans of Damascus paid tribute to Assyria. By 735 B.C., however, Rezin of Damascus had created a new anti-Assyrian league, and when Ahaz refused to join, the league attempted to remove Ahaz from the throne of Judah. The resulting Syro-Ephraimite War was the original occasion for many of Isaiah's oracles (cf. chaps. 7–8), in which he tried to reassure Ahaz of God's protection and dissuade him from seeking protection by an alliance with Assyria. Ahaz refused Isaiah's message, however.

When Hezekiah came to the throne in 715 B.C., Isaiah appears to have put great hopes in this new scion of David, and he undoubtedly supported the religious reform that Hezekiah undertook. But the old intrigues began again, and the king was sorely tempted to join with neighboring states in an alliance sponsored by Egypt against Assyria. Isaiah succeeded in keeping Hezekiah out of Ashdod's abortive revolt against Assyria, but when Sargon died in 705 B.C., with both Egypt and Babylon encouraging revolt, Hezekiah was won over to the pro-Egyptian party. Isaiah denounced this "covenant with death" (28:15, 18), and again summoned Judah to faith in the Lord as the only hope. But it was too late; the revolt had already begun. Assyria acted quickly and its army, after ravaging Judah, laid siege to Jerusalem (701). "I shut up Hezekiah like a bird in his cage," boasts the famous inscription of Sennacherib. The city was spared but at the cost of paying a huge indemnity to Assyria. Isaiah may have lived and prophesied for another dozen years after 701. There is material in the book that may plausibly be associated with Sennacherib's campaign against Babylon and its Arabian allies in 694–689 B.C.

For Isaiah, the vision of God's majesty was so overwhelming that military and political power faded into insignificance. He constantly called his people back to a reliance on God's promises and away from vain attempts to find security in human plans and intrigues. This vision also led him to insist on the ethical behavior that was required of human beings who wished to live in the presence of such a holy God. Isaiah couched this message in oracles of singular poetic beauty and power, oracles in which surprising shifts in syntax, audacious puns, and double- or triple-entendre are a constant feature.

The complete Book of Isaiah is an anthology of poems composed chiefly by the great prophet, but also by disciples, some of whom came many years after Isaiah. In 1–39 most of the oracles come from Isaiah and reflect the situation in eighth-century Judah. Sections such as the Apocalypse of Isaiah (24–27), the oracles against Babylon (13–14), and probably the poems of 34–35 were written by followers deeply influenced by the prophet, in some cases reusing earlier Isaianic material; cf., e.g., 27:2–8 with 5:1–7.

Chapters 40–55 (Second Isaiah, or Deutero-Isaiah) are generally attributed to an anonymous poet who prophesied toward the end of the Babylonian exile. From this section come the great oracles known as the Servant Songs, which are reflected in the New Testament understanding of the passion and glorification of Christ. Chapters 56–66 (Third Isaiah, or Trito-Isaiah) contain oracles from the postexilic period and were composed by writers imbued with the spirit of Isaiah who continued his work.

The principal divisions of the Book of Isaiah are the following:

I. Isaiah 1–39
   A. Indictment of Israel and Judah (1:1–5:30)
   B. The Book of Emmanuel (6:1–12:6)
   C. Oracles Against the Foreign Nations (13:1–23:18)
   D. Apocalypse of Isaiah (24:1–27:13)
   E. The Lord Alone, Israel's and Judah's Salvation (28:1–33:24)
   F. The Lord, Zion's Avenger (34:1–35:10)
   G. Historical Appendix (36:1–39:8)

**The Indictment and Complaint**

THE POEM IN ch 1 consists of a legal complaint concerning covenant violation by the Israelites, who are depicted as ungrateful and also less intelligent than farm animals (vv. 2–4). In ancient Israelite thinking, heaven and earth serve as witnesses to the covenant between God and Israel (see Dt 4:26; 32:1); hence, God calls on them to hear the charges against Israel.



# I. Isaiah 1—39

## A. Indictment of Israel and Judah

### CHAPTER 1

See RG 207–208

1* The vision which Isaiah, son of Amoz, saw concerning Judah and Jerusalem in the days of Uzziah, Jotham, Ahaz and Hezekiah, kings of Judah.

### *Accusation and Appeal*

2 * Hear, O heavens, and listen, O earth,
for the LORD speaks:
Sons have I raised and reared,
but they have rebelled against me![a]
3 An ox knows its owner,
and an ass,* its master's manger;
But Israel does not know,
my people has not understood.[b]
4 Ah!* Sinful nation, people laden with wickedness,
evil offspring, corrupt children!
They have forsaken the LORD,
spurned the Holy One of Israel,
apostatized,[c]
5 Why* would you yet be struck,
that you continue to rebel?
The whole head is sick,
the whole heart faint.
6 From the sole of the foot to the head
there is no sound spot in it;
Just bruise and welt and oozing wound,
not drained, or bandaged,
or eased with salve.
7 Your country is waste,
your cities burnt with fire;
Your land—before your eyes
strangers devour it,
a waste, like the devastation of Sodom.* [d]
8 And daughter Zion* is left
like a hut in a vineyard,
Like a shed in a melon patch,

**1:1** The title, or inscription, of the book is an editorial addition to identify the prophet and the circumstances of his ministry. **Isaiah**: meaning "the salvation of the Lord," or "the Lord is salvation." **Amoz**: not Amos the prophet. **Judah**: the Southern Kingdom of the tribes of Judah and Benjamin. **Uzziah**: also called Azariah; cf. 2 Kgs 15:1; 2 Chr 26:1.

**1:2–31** This chapter is widely considered to be a collection of oracles from various periods in Isaiah's ministry, chosen by the editor as a compendium of his most characteristic teachings.

**1:3 Ox . . . ass**: Isaiah uses animals proverbial for their stupidity and stubbornness to underline Israel's failure to respond to God. **Israel**: a term Isaiah (and other prophets) frequently applies to Judah, especially after the fall of the Northern Kingdom (which Isaiah normally calls Ephraim, as in 7:2, 9, 17; 9:8), but sometimes applies to the entire chosen people, as in 8:14.

**1:4 Ah**: see note on 5:8–24. **Holy One of Israel**: a title used frequently in the Book of Isaiah, rarely elsewhere in the Old Testament (see 5:19, 24; 10:20; 12:6; 17:7; 29:19; 30:11, 12, 15; 31:1; 37:23; 41:14, 16, 20; 43:3, 14; 45:11; 47:4; 48:17; 49:7; 54:5; 55:5; 60:9, 14).

**1:5–6** The Hebrew expression translated "Why?" may also be translated "Where?" The ambiguity is probably intentional: "Why, O Israel, would you still be beaten, and where on your bruised body do you want the next blow?" The bruised body is a metaphor for the historical disaster that has overtaken Israel (see v. 7) because of its sins.

**1:7 Sodom**: Sodom and Gomorrah (see vv. 9–10; cf. Gn 19) were proverbial as wicked cities completely overthrown and destroyed by God. Judah, more fortunate, survives at least as a remnant. The devastation of the land and the isolation of Jerusalem suggest the time of Sennacherib's invasion of 701.

**1:8 Daughter Zion**: Jerusalem, as isolated as a little hut erected in a field for the shelter of watchmen and laborers.

*a:* Dt 32:1, 5–6, 18. *b:* Jer 8:7; Lk 2:12. *c:* Is 5:24; Dt 32:15. *d:* Is 13:19; Dt 29:22; Jer 49:18; 50:40; Am 4:11.

## Rite and Right

THE SACRIFICES AND prayers offered by Isaiah's contemporaries are useless because they are not accompanied by ethical action (vv. 10–20). This is a frequent prophetic theme; see especially Amos 5:21–25; Isaiah 58:1–9.

like a city blockaded.
9 If the LORD of hosts* had not
left us a small remnant,
We would have become as Sodom,
would have resembled Gomorrah.[e]

10 * Hear the word of the LORD,
princes of Sodom!
Listen to the instruction of our God,
people of Gomorrah!
11 What do I care for the multitude of your
sacrifices?
says the LORD.
I have had enough of whole-burnt rams
and fat of fatlings;
In the blood of calves, lambs, and goats
I find no pleasure.[f]
12 When you come to appear before me,
who asks these things of you?
13 Trample my courts no more!
To bring offerings is useless;
incense is an abomination to me.
New moon and sabbath, calling
assemblies—
festive convocations with wickedness—
these I cannot bear.[g]
14 Your new moons and festivals I detest;[h]
they weigh me down, I tire of the load.
15 When you spread out your hands,
I will close my eyes to you;
Though you pray the more,
I will not listen.
Your hands are full of blood!* [i]
16 Wash yourselves clean!
Put away your misdeeds from before my
eyes;
cease doing evil;
17 learn to do good.
Make justice your aim: redress the
wronged,
hear the orphan's plea, defend the
widow.[j]

18 Come now, let us set things right,*
says the LORD:
Though your sins be like scarlet,
they may become white as snow;
Though they be red like crimson,
they may become white as wool.[k]
19 If you are willing, and obey,
you shall eat the good things of the
land;
20 But if you refuse and resist,
you shall be eaten by the sword:
for the mouth of the LORD has spoken!

### *The Purification of Jerusalem*

21 How she has become a prostitute,
the faithful city,* so upright!
Justice used to lodge within her,

**1:9 LORD of hosts**: God, who is the Creator and Ruler of the armies of Israel, the angels, stars, etc.

**1:10–17** A powerful indictment of the religious hypocrisy of rulers and others who neglect just judgment and oppress the weaker members, yet believe they can please God with sacrifices and other external forms of worship. The long list of observances suggests the Lord's tedium with such attempts. **Sodom . . . Gomorrah**: the names are picked up from v. 9, but now to emphasize their wickedness rather than the good fortune of escaping total destruction.

**1:15–16 Hands . . . blood**: oppression of the poor is likened to violence that bloodies the hands, which explains why the hands spread out in prayer (v. 15) are not regarded by the Lord. This climax of the accusations is followed by positive admonitions for reversing the evil situation.

**1:18–20 Let us set things right**: the Hebrew word refers to the arbitration of legal disputes (Jb 23:7). God offers to settle his case with Israel on the basis of the change of behavior demanded above. For Israel it is a life or death choice; life in conformity with God's will or death for continued disobedience.

**1:21–28 Faithful city**: the phrase, found in v. 21 and v. 28, forms an *inclusio* which marks off the passage and also suggests three chronological periods: the city's former ideal state, its present wicked condition (described in vv. 21b–23), and the future ideal conditions intended by God. This will be brought about by a purging judgment directed primarily against the leaders ("judges . . . counselors").

*e:* Rom 9:29. *f:* Ps 50:8–13; Sir 34:23; Mi 6:7. *g:* Prv 15:8; Jer 6:20. *h:* Am 5:21–24. *i:* Prv 1:28; Sir 34:25–31. *j:* Ex 23:6; Dt 24:17; Sir 4:9–10; Jer 22:3; Ez 22:7; Am 5:14–15; Zec 7:9–10. *k:* Ps 51:9.

but now, murderers.[l]
22 Your silver is turned to dross,
your wine is mixed with water.
23 Your princes are rebels
and comrades of thieves;
Each one of them loves a bribe
and looks for gifts.
The fatherless they do not defend,
the widow's plea does not reach them.[m]
24 Now, therefore, says the Lord,
the LORD of hosts, the Mighty One of Israel:
Ah! I will take vengeance on my foes
and fully repay my enemies![n]
25 I will turn my hand against you,
and refine your dross in the furnace,
removing all your alloy.
26 I will restore your judges* as at first,
and your counselors as in the beginning;
After that you shall be called
city of justice, faithful city.[o]
27 * Zion shall be redeemed by justice,
and her repentant ones by righteousness.
28 Rebels and sinners together shall be crushed,
those who desert the LORD shall be consumed.

### *Judgment on the Sacred Groves*

29 * You shall be ashamed of the terebinths
which you desired,
and blush on account of the gardens
which you chose.
30 You shall become like a terebinth whose leaves wither,
like a garden that has no water.
31 The strong tree shall turn to tinder,
and the one who tends it shall become a spark;
Both of them shall burn together,
and there shall be none to quench them.

## CHAPTER 2

See RG 207–208

1* This is what Isaiah, son of Amoz, saw concerning Judah and Jerusalem.

### *Zion, the Royal City of God*

2 * In days to come,
The mountain of the LORD's house
shall be established as the highest mountain
and raised above the hills.
All nations shall stream toward it.[p]
3 Many peoples shall come and say:
"Come, let us go up to the LORD's mountain,
to the house of the God of Jacob,

**1:26 Judges**: the reference must be to royal judges appointed by David and his successors, not to the tribal judges of the Book of Judges, since the "beginning" of Jerusalem as an Israelite city dates only to the time of David. The Davidic era is idealized here; obtaining justice in the historical Jerusalem of David's time was more problematic (see 2 Sm 15:1–6).

**1:27–28** These verses expand the oracle that originally ended at v. 26. The expansion correctly interprets the preceding text as proclaiming a purifying judgment on Zion in which the righteous are saved while the wicked perish. The meaning of "by justice" and "by righteousness" is ambiguous. Do these terms refer to God's judgment or to the justice and righteousness of Zion's surviving inhabitants? Is 33:14–16 suggests the latter interpretation.

**1:29–31** These verses were secondarily inserted here on the catchword principle; like v. 28 they pronounce judgment on certain parties "together" (v. 31). The terebinths and gardens refer to the sacred groves or asherahs that functioned as idolatrous cultic symbols at the popular shrines or high places (1 Kgs 14:23; 2 Kgs 17:10). Hezekiah cut down these groves during his reform (2 Kgs 18:4); they were a religious issue during Isaiah's ministry (cf. Is 17:7–11). Isaiah threatens those who cultivate these symbols with the same fate that befalls trees when deprived of water.

**2:1** This editorial heading probably introduced the collection of chaps. 2–12, to which chap. 1 with its introduction was added later (see note on 1:2–31).

**2:2–22** These verses contain two very important oracles, one on the pilgrimage of nations to Mount Zion (vv. 2–4—completed with an invitation to the "house of Jacob," v. 5), the other on the day of the Lord (see note on Am 5:18), which was probably composed from at least two earlier pieces. Whereas vv. 6–8 indict Judah for trust in superstitious practices and human resources rather than in the Lord, the following verses are directed against humankind in general and emphasize the effect of the "day of the Lord," the humbling of human pride. This may be taken as a precondition for the glorious vision of vv. 2–4. This vision of Zion's glorious future, which is also found in a slightly variant form in Mi 4:1–4, is rooted in the early Zion tradition, cultivated in the royal cult in Jerusalem. It celebrated God's choice of Jerusalem as the divine dwelling place, along with God's choice of the Davidic dynasty (Ps 68:16–17; 78:67–72; 132:13–18). **Highest mountain**: the Zion tradition followed earlier mythological conceptions that associate the abode of deities with very high mountains (Ps 48:2–3). The lifting of Mount Zion is a metaphor for universal recognition of the Lord's authority.

*l:* Jer 3:8; Hos 2:7. *m:* Ex 23:8; Dt 16:19. *n:* Dt 32:41. *o:* Jer 33:7–11; Zec 8:8. *p:* Mi 4:1–4.

**Jerusalem of the Future and of the Present**

THIS LONG SECTION (2:2–4:6) begins and ends with a description of Jerusalem as it should and will be: a city of peace, equity, and divine presence. The prophet Micah shared this vision. The long middle section (2:6–4:1) focuses on the sinfulness of the current inhabitants and their grim fate. The nation's sins—magic; amassing extraordinary amounts of wealth; pursuing military power; pride; and idolatry—are criticized here. All these vices embody inappropriate confidence in humanity's own powers. This confidence is not only mistaken, but is offensive to God.

That he may instruct us in his ways,
and we may walk in his paths."[q]
For from Zion shall go forth instruction,
and the word of the LORD from Jerusalem.
4 * He shall judge between the nations,
and set terms for many peoples.
They shall beat their swords into plowshares
and their spears into pruning hooks;[r]
One nation shall not raise the sword against another,
nor shall they train for war again.[s]
5 * House of Jacob, come,
let us walk in the light of the LORD!

*The Lord's Day of Judgment on Pride*

6 You have abandoned your people,
the house of Jacob!
Because they are filled with diviners,
and soothsayers, like the Philistines;
with foreigners they clasp hands.[t]
7 Their land is full of silver and gold,
there is no end to their treasures;
Their land is full of horses,
there is no end to their chariots.
8 Their land is full of idols;
they bow down to the works of their hands,
what their fingers have made.[u]
9 So all shall be abased,
each one brought low.*
Do not pardon them!
10 Get behind the rocks,
hide in the dust,
From the terror of the LORD
and the splendor of his majesty!
11 The eyes of human pride shall be lowered,
the arrogance of mortals shall be abased,
and the LORD alone will be exalted, on that day.*
12 For the LORD of hosts will have his day
against all that is proud and arrogant,
against all that is high, and it will be brought low;
13 Yes, against all the cedars of Lebanon*
and against all the oaks of Bashan,
14 Against all the lofty mountains
and all the high hills,
15 Against every lofty tower
and every fortified wall,
16 Against all the ships of Tarshish
and all stately vessels.
17 Then human pride shall be abased,
the arrogance of mortals brought low,
And the LORD alone will be exalted on that day.
18 The idols will vanish completely.
19 People will go into caves in the rocks
and into holes in the earth,
At the terror of the LORD
and the splendor of his majesty,
as he rises to overawe the earth.
20 On that day people shall throw to moles and bats
their idols of silver and their idols of gold

**2:4** Once the nations acknowledge God as sovereign, they go up to Jerusalem to settle their disputes, rather than having recourse to war.

**2:5** This verse is added as a conclusion to vv. 2–4; cf. Mi 4:4–5, where a quite different conclusion is provided for the parallel version of this oracle.

**2:9** Bowing down to idols will not bring deliverance to Israel, but rather total abasement. **Do not pardon them**: this line is so abrupt that it is almost certainly an intrusion in the text.

**2:11 That day**: i.e., the day of the Lord; cf. note on Am 5:18.

**2:13 Lebanon**: Mount Lebanon in Syria, famed for its cedars. **Bashan**: the fertile uplands east of the Sea of Galilee.

*q:* Is 56:7; 2 Kgs 17:26–28; Jer 31:6–14; Zec 8:20–23. *r:* Jl 4:10. *s:* Is 9:7; 11:4; Ps 46:10; Zec 9:10. *t:* Is 10:32. *u:* Is 17:7–8; 31:1–3.

which they made for themselves to
worship.
21 And they shall go into caverns in the
rocks
and into crevices in the cliffs,
At the terror of the LORD
and the splendor of his majesty,
as he rises to overawe the earth.
22 * As for you, stop worrying about mortals,
in whose nostrils is but a breath;
for of what worth are they?

See RG 207–208

## CHAPTER 3

### *Judgment on Jerusalem and Judah*

1 * The Lord, the LORD of hosts,
will take away from Jerusa'em and
from Judah
Support and staff—
all support of bread,
all support of water:[v]
2 Hero and warrior,
judge and prophet, diviner and elder,
3 The captain of fifty and the nobleman,
counselor, skilled magician, and expert
charmer.
4 I will place boys as their princes;
the fickle will govern them,[w]
5 And the people will oppress one another,
yes, each one the neighbor.
The child will be insolent toward the elder,
and the base toward the honorable.[x]
6 When anyone seizes a brother
in their father's house, saying,
"You have clothes! Be our ruler,
and take in hand this ruin!"—
7 He will cry out in that day:
"I cannot be a healer,[y]
when there is neither bread nor
clothing in my own house!
You will not make me a ruler of the
people!"
8 Jerusalem has stumbled, Judah has
fallen;
for their speech and deeds affront the
LORD,
a provocation in the sight of his
majesty.
9 Their very look bears witness against
them;[z]
they boast of their sin like Sodom,[a]
They do not hide it.
Woe to them!
They deal out evil to themselves.
10 Happy the just, for it will go well with
them,
the fruit of their works they will eat.
11 Woe to the wicked! It will go ill with
them,
with the work of their hands they will
be repaid.
12 My people—infants oppress them,
women rule over them!
My people, your leaders deceive you,[b]
they confuse the paths you should
follow.
13 * The LORD rises to accuse,
stands to try his people.
14 The Lord enters into judgment
with the people's elders and princes:
You, you who have devoured the
vineyard;
the loot wrested from the poor is in
your houses.
15 What do you mean by crushing my
people,
and grinding down the faces of the
poor?
says the Lord, the GOD of hosts.

**2:22** The meaning of this verse, certainly a later addition, is not clear. It is not addressed to God but to a plural subject.

**3:1–12** These verses suggest deportation, with resulting social upheaval, and thus may date to sometime after Ahaz submitted as vassal to Assyria. The deportation practiced by Assyria, as later by Babylon, exiled the leading elements of society, such as those named in vv. 2–3; cf. 2 Kgs 24:12, 14–16 for a similar list of those exiled by the Babylonians. Denuding society of its leaders opens the way to near anarchy and a situation in which leadership is seized by or thrust upon those unqualified for it (vv. 5–7). The situation has been provoked by sinfully inept leadership (vv. 4, 8–9, 12). Some suggest that vv. 4 and 12 refer to Ahaz, who may have come to the throne at an early age. Verses 10–11 form a wisdom couplet that was inserted later.

**3:13–15** The princes and the elders, here accused of despoiling the poor, are the very ones who should be their defenders. **Loot**: by the Hebrew term (*gazela*) Isaiah conveys the idea of violent seizure, though 10:1–4 suggests the poor could be plundered by legal means.

*v:* Lv 26:26; Ez 4:16. *w:* Eccl 10:16. *x:* Mi 7:5–6. *y:* Is 1:6. *z:* Jer 3:3. *a:* Is 1:10. *b:* Mi 3:5.

## Announcement of Judgment against the Women of Jerusalem

FIRST, REASONS FOR punishment are given in terms of the posture of the daughters of Zion (3:16); next, a judgment is announced that fits the crime (vv. 17–24). The humiliations which the women will suffer are common to military defeat and exile. The list of finery is a prose elaboration of vv. 17, 24.

### *The Haughty Women of Zion**

16 The LORD said:[c]
Because the daughters of Zion are haughty,
and walk with necks outstretched,
Ogling and mincing as they go,
their anklets tinkling with every step,
17 The Lord shall cover the scalps of Zion's daughters with scabs,
and the LORD shall lay bare their heads.* [d]

18* On that day the LORD will do away with
the finery of the anklets, sunbursts, and crescents; 19 the pendants, bracelets, and veils;
20 the headdresses, bangles, cinctures, perfume boxes, and amulets; 21 the signet rings,
and the nose rings; 22 the court dresses,
wraps, cloaks, and purses; 23 the lace gowns,
linen tunics, turbans, and shawls.

24 Instead of perfume there will be stench,
instead of a girdle, a rope,
And instead of elaborate coiffure, baldness;
instead of a rich gown, a sackcloth skirt.
Then, instead of beauty, shame.
25 Your men will fall by the sword,
and your champions,* in war;[e]
26 Her gates will lament and mourn,
as the city sits desolate on the ground.[f]

### CHAPTER 4

See RG 207–208

1 Seven women will take hold of one man*
on that day, saying:
"We will eat our own food
and wear our own clothing;
Only let your name be given us,
put an end to our disgrace!"

### *Jerusalem Purified*

2 * On that day,
The branch* of the LORD will be beauty and glory,
and the fruit of the land will be honor and splendor
for the survivors of Israel.
3 Everyone who remains in Zion,
everyone left in Jerusalem
Will be called holy:
everyone inscribed for life* in Jerusalem.[g]
4 When the Lord washes away
the filth of the daughters of Zion,
And purges Jerusalem's blood from her midst
with a blast of judgment, a searing blast,[h]
5 Then will the LORD create,
over the whole site of Mount Zion
and over her place of assembly,

**3:16–4:1** Here and again in 32:9–14 Isaiah condemns the women of the ruling class for their part in Jerusalem's plight.

**3:17** A shaven head is a mark of social disgrace; cf. Nm 5:18.

**3:18–23** The long list of women's apparel in these verses suggests luxury and vanity; it contains a number of rare words, and the precise meaning of many of the terms is uncertain.

**3:25 Your men . . . your champions**: the second person feminine singular pronoun here shows that the prophet has shifted his attention from the women of Zion to the personified city of Zion.

**4:1 Seven women . . . one man**: deportation (cf. note on 3:1–12) would result in a disproportion of the sexes and leave the female population without enough male partners. The women are willing to marry, not for support, but to avoid disgrace.

**4:2–6** Usually judged a later addition to the oracles of Isaiah. It relieves the threatening tone of the surrounding chaps. 3 and 5.

**4:2 Branch**: the term (Heb. *semah*) that is sometimes used of the ideal Davidic king of the future (cf. Jer 23:5; 33:15; Zec 3:8; 6:12). However, the parallel "fruit of the land" does not favor that usage here.

**4:3 Inscribed for life**: in God's list of the elect; cf. Ex 32:32.

*c:* Is 32:9–14; Ez 16:50; Am 4:1–3. *d:* Jer 13:26; Ez 16:37. *e:* Hos 14:1. *f:* Is 47:1; Lam 2:10. *g:* Is 6:13; Ob 17; Mal 3:16. *h:* Is 1:21–28.

**A Poem of Rebuke**

CHAPTER 5 IS a parable in which God is the farmer and Israel the vineyard. At first, the identity of the characters is not evident, and only gradually does the audience realize that it is they themselves who are being rebuked.

A smoking cloud by day
and a light of flaming fire by night.[i]
6 For over all, his glory will be shelter and protection:
shade from the parching heat of day,
refuge and cover from storm and rain.[j]

## CHAPTER 5

See RG 207–208

### *The Song of the Vineyard**

1 Now let me sing of my friend,
my beloved's song about his vineyard.
My friend had a vineyard
on a fertile hillside;
2 He spaded it, cleared it of stones,
and planted the choicest vines;
Within it he built a watchtower,
and hewed out a wine press.
Then he waited for the crop of grapes,
but it yielded rotten grapes.[k]
3 Now, inhabitants of Jerusalem, people of Judah,
judge between me and my vineyard:
4 What more could be done for my vineyard
that I did not do?[l]
Why, when I waited for the crop of grapes,
did it yield rotten grapes?
5 Now, I will let you know
what I am going to do to my vineyard:
Take away its hedge, give it to grazing,
break through its wall, let it be trampled!*
6 Yes, I will make it a ruin:
it shall not be pruned or hoed,
but will be overgrown with thorns and briers;
I will command the clouds
not to rain upon it.
7 The vineyard of the LORD of hosts is the house of Israel,
the people of Judah, his cherished plant;
He waited for judgment, but see, bloodshed!
for justice, but hark, the outcry!*

### *Oracles of Reproach**

8 * Ah! Those who join house to house,
who connect field with field,
Until no space remains, and you alone dwell
in the midst of the land![m]
9 In my hearing the LORD of hosts has sworn:[n]
Many houses shall be in ruins,
houses large and fine, with nobody living there.[o]
10 Ten acres of vineyard
shall yield but one bath,*
And a homer of seed
shall yield but an ephah.

**5:1–7 Vineyard**: although the term is sometimes used in an erotic context (Sg 1:6; 8:12), "vineyard" or "vine" is used more frequently as a metaphor for God's people (27:2; Ps 80:9, 14, 15; Jer 2:21; 12:10; Ez 17:7; Hos 10:1; Na 2:2). The terms translated "friend" (*yadid*) and "beloved" (*dod*) suggest the Lord's favor (Dt 33:12; 2 Sm 12:25; Ps 127:2) and familial background rather than introducing the piece as a "love song," as is sometimes suggested. The prophet disguises the real theme (the people's infidelity) so that the hearers will participate in the unfavorable judgment called for (vv. 3–4). Cf. the reversal of this parable in 27:2–6.

**5:5–6 Trampled ... thorns and briers**: this judgment is echoed in the description of the devastated land in 7:23–25.

**5:7 Judgment ... bloodshed ... justice ... outcry**: in Hebrew there is an impressive play on words: *mishpat* parallels *mispah*, *sedaqah* parallels *se'aqah*. See also the threefold "waited for" in vv. 2, 4, 7.

**5:8–24** These verses contain a series of short oracles introduced by the Hebrew particle *hoy* ("Ah!"), an emphatic exclamation, sometimes translated "Woe!"

**5:8–10** An oracle against land-grabbers (v. 8); they will be impoverished instead of enriched (vv. 9–10).

**5:10 Ten acres**: a field with ten times the surface area a yoke of oxen could plow in one day. **Bath**: a liquid measure equal to about twelve gallons. **Homer**: a dry measure equal to what a donkey can carry, calculated to be about ten bushels. **Ephah**: a dry measure of about one bushel. So small a harvest is the fruit of the land-grabbers' greed.

*i:* Ex 13:21. *j:* Is 32:1–2. *k:* Dt 32:32. *l:* Mi 6:3–5. *m:* Mi 2:1–3. *n:* Is 22:14. *o:* Is 6:12.

## A Series of Woe Indictments

EACH ACCUSATION IN ch 5 begins with the cry "Ah!" (vv. 8, 11, 18, 20, 21, 22). Isaiah 10:1–4 may also belong to this series. Each unit describes a group in terms of its immoral actions, and fitting punishments are handed out: against the rich who take the land of the poor; against those whose pursuit of pleasure obscures their perception of the LORD's activity and the needs of the people; against those who dare the LORD to act; against those who reverse morality; against those who are proud of their wisdom; and against drunkards who pervert justice.

11 * Ah! Those who rise early in the morning
in pursuit of strong drink,
lingering late
inflamed by wine,
12 Banqueting on wine with harp and lyre,
timbrel and flute,[p]
But the deed of the LORD they do not regard,
the work of his hands they do not see![q]
13 Therefore my people go into exile
for lack of understanding,[r]
Its nobles starving,
its masses parched with thirst.
14 Therefore Sheol enlarges its throat
and opens its mouth beyond measure;[s]
Down into it go nobility and masses,
tumult and revelry.
15 All shall be abased, each one brought low,
and the eyes of the haughty lowered,[t]
16 But the LORD of hosts shall be exalted by judgment,
by justice the Holy God shown holy.[u]
17 Lambs shall graze as at pasture,
young goats shall eat in the ruins of the rich.
18 Ah! Those who tug at guilt with cords of perversity,
and at sin as if with cart ropes!
19 * Who say, "Let him make haste,
let him speed his work, that we may see it;
On with the plan of the Holy One of Israel!
let it come to pass, that we may know it!"[v]
20 Ah! Those who call evil good, and good evil,
who change darkness to light, and light into darkness,
who change bitter to sweet, and sweet into bitter![w]
21 Ah! Those who are wise in their own eyes,
prudent in their own view![x]
22 Ah! Those who are champions at drinking wine,
masters at mixing drink!
23 Those who acquit the guilty for bribes,
and deprive the innocent of justice![y]
24 Therefore, as the tongue of fire licks up stubble,
as dry grass shrivels in the flame,
Their root shall rot
and their blossom scatter like dust;
For they have rejected the instruction of the LORD of hosts,
and scorned the word of the Holy One of Israel.

25 * Therefore the wrath of the LORD blazes against his people,
he stretches out his hand to strike them;

**5:11–13** An oracle against debauchery and indifference. **Strong drink**: the Hebrew word *shekar* means either beer or a type of wine, perhaps date wine, not distilled liquor.

**5:19** An indication that some, presumably of the ruling class, scoff at Isaiah's teaching on the Lord's "plan" and "work" (cf. v. 12; 14:26–27; 28:9–14; 30:10–11).

**5:25–30** These verses do not suit their present context. Apparently v. 25 was originally the conclusion of the poem of 9:7–20 directed against the Northern Kingdom; cf. the refrain that occurs here and in 9:11, 16, and 20. Verses 26–30 look to an invasion by Assyria and might originally have come immediately after the poem of 9:1–20 plus 5:25. The insertion of chaps. 6–8 may have occasioned the dislocation, as well as that of 10:1–4a, which may have originally belonged with the "reproach" oracles of 5:8–23.

*p:* Is 5:22; Am 6:1–7. *q:* Is 5:19; 10:12; 14:24–27; 19:12, 17; 23:9; 28:21; 30:1. *r:* Hos 4:6. *s:* Hb 2:5. *t:* Is 2:9, 11, 17. *u:* Is 1:27. *v:* Jer 17:15; 2 Pt 3:3–4. *w:* Is 32:4–5. *x:* Prv 3:7; 26:12; Rom 11:25; 12:16. *y:* Ex 23:8; Prv 17:15.

The mountains quake,[z]
their corpses shall be like refuse in the
streets.
For all this, his wrath is not turned back,
his hand is still outstretched.

### *Invasion**

26 He will raise a signal to a far-off nation,
and whistle for it from the ends of the
earth.[a]
Then speedily and promptly they will
come.
27 None among them is weary, none
stumbles,
none will slumber, none will sleep.
None with waist belt loose,
none with sandal thong broken.
28 Their arrows are sharp,
and all their bows are bent,
The hooves of their horses like flint,
and their chariot wheels like the
whirlwind.
29 They roar like the lion,
like young lions, they roar;
They growl and seize the prey,
they carry it off and none can rescue.
30 They will growl over it, on that day,
like the growling of the sea,
Look to the land—
darkness closing in,
the light dark with clouds![b]

## B. The Book of Emmanuel

### CHAPTER 6

See RG 207–208

***The Sending of Isaiah.*** 1 In the year
King Uzziah died,* I saw the Lord seated on
a high and lofty throne,[c] with the train of his
garment filling the temple. 2 Seraphim* were
stationed above; each of them had six wings:
with two they covered their faces, with two
they covered their feet, and with two they
hovered.[d] 3 One cried out to the other:

"Holy, holy, holy* is the LORD of hosts!
All the earth is filled with his glory!"

4 At the sound of that cry, the frame of the door
shook and the house was filled with smoke.*[e]
5 Then I said, "Woe is me, I am doomed!*
For I am a man of unclean lips, living among
a people of unclean lips,[f] and my eyes have
seen the King, the LORD of hosts!" 6 Then
one of the seraphim flew to me, holding an
ember which he had taken with tongs from
the altar.
7 He touched my mouth with it. "See," he
said, "now that this has touched your lips,* your
wickedness is removed, your sin purged."[g]
8 Then I heard the voice of the Lord saying, "Whom shall I send? Who will go for
us?" "Here I am," I said; "send me!" 9* And
he replied: Go and say to this people:

**5:26–30** This oracle threatens a future judgment, an invasion of the Assyrian army, God's instrument for punishing Judah (10:5, 15).

**6:1 In the year King Uzziah died**: probably 742 B.C., although the chronology of this period is disputed. **A high and lofty throne**: within the holy of holies of the Jerusalem Temple stood two cherubim, or winged sphinxes, whose outstretched wings served as the divine throne (1 Kgs 6:23–28; Ez 1:4–28; 10:1, 20). The ark of the covenant was God's footstool (Ps 132:7–8; 1 Chr 28:2), placed under the cherubim (1 Kgs 8:6–7). **Temple**: the holy place, just in front of the holy of holies.

**6:2 Seraphim**: the plural of *saraph* ("to burn"), a term used to designate the "fiery" serpents of the wilderness (Nm 21:8; Dt 8:15), and to refer to "winged" serpents (Is 14:29; 30:6). Here, however, it is used adjectivally of the cherubim, who are not serpent-like, as seen in the fact that they have faces and sexual parts ("feet"). See the adaptation of these figures by Ezekiel (Ez 1:10–12; 10:4–15).

**6:3 Holy, holy, holy**: these words have been used in Christian liturgy from the earliest times.

**6:4 Smoke**: reminiscent of the clouds which indicated God's presence at Mount Sinai (Ex 19:16–19; Dt 4:11) and which filled the tabernacle (Ex 40:34–38) and the Temple (1 Kgs 8:10–11) at their dedication.

**6:5 Doomed**: there are two roots from which the verb here could be derived; one means "to perish, be doomed," the other "to become silent," and given Isaiah's delight in puns and double entendre, he probably intended to sound both notes. "I am doomed!" is suggested by the popular belief that to see God would lead to one's death; cf. Gn 32:31; Ex 33:20; Jgs 13:22. "I am struck silent!" is suggested by the emphasis on the lips in vv. 5–6, and such silence is attested elsewhere as the appropriate response to the vision of the Lord in the Temple (Hb 2:20).

**6:7 Touched your lips**: Isaiah is thus symbolically purified of sin in preparation for his mission as God's prophet.

**6:9–10** Isaiah's words give evidence that he attempted in every way, through admonition, threat, and promise, to bring the people to conversion (cf. 1:18–20), so it is unlikely that this charge to "harden" is to be understood as Isaiah's task; more probably it reflects the refusal of the people, more particularly the leaders, who were supposed to "see," "hear," and

*z:* Am 1:1; Zec 14:5; cf. Is 9:18a. *a:* Is 7:18; 11:12; Jer 4:6; 50:2. *b:* Is 8:22. *c:* 1 Kgs 22:19–23; Jn 12:41. *d:* Rev 4:8. *e:* Rev 15:8. *f:* Is 29:13; Mt 15:1–11; Mk 7:1–13; Col 2:20–23. *g:* Jer 1:9; Dn 10:16.

Listen carefully, but do not understand!
Look intently, but do not perceive![h]
10 Make the heart of this people sluggish,
dull their ears and close their eyes;
Lest they see with their eyes, and hear
with their ears,
and their heart understand,
and they turn and be healed.[i]

11"How long, O Lord?" I asked. And he
replied:

* Until the cities are desolate,
without inhabitants,
Houses, without people,
and the land is a desolate waste.
12 Until the LORD sends the people far away,
and great is the desolation in the midst
of the land.
13 If there remain a tenth part in it,
then this in turn shall be laid waste;
As with a terebinth or an oak
whose trunk remains when its leaves
have fallen.* [j]
Holy offspring is the trunk.

See RG 208

## CHAPTER 7

### *The Syro-Ephraimite War**

***Crisis in Judah.*** 1In the days of Ahaz,* king of
Judah, son of Jotham, son of Uzziah, Rezin,
king of Aram, and Pekah, king of Israel, son
of Remaliah, went up to attack Jerusalem, but
they were not able to conquer it.[k] 2When word
came to the house of David that Aram had allied itself with Ephraim, the heart of the king
and heart of the people trembled, as the trees
of the forest tremble in the wind.

3Then the LORD said to Isaiah: Go out to
meet Ahaz, you and your son Shear-jashub,*
at the end of the conduit of the upper pool,
on the highway to the fuller's field, 4and say
to him: Take care you remain calm and do
not fear; do not let your courage fail before
these two stumps of smoldering brands,[l] the
blazing anger of Rezin and the Arameans
and of the son of Remaliah— 5because
Aram, with Ephraim and the son of Remaliah, has planned* evil against you. They say,
6"Let us go up against Judah, tear it apart,
make it our own by force, and appoint the
son of Tabeel* king there."

7 Thus says the Lord GOD:
It shall not stand, it shall not be![m]
8 * The head of Aram is Damascus,
and the head of Damascus is Rezin;
9 The head of Ephraim is Samaria,
and the head of Samaria is the son of
Remaliah.
Within sixty-five years,
Ephraim shall be crushed, no longer a
nation.

"understand," a refusal which would then lead to a disastrous outcome (vv. 11–12).

**6:11–12** The desolation described would be the result of the sort of deportation practiced by the Assyrians and later by the Babylonians. Isaiah seems to expect this as an eventual consequence of Judah's submission as vassal to the Assyrians; cf. 3:1–3; 5:13.

**6:13 When its leaves have fallen**: the meaning of the Hebrew is uncertain, and the text may be corrupt. **Holy offspring**: part of the phrase is missing from the Septuagint and may be a later addition; it provides a basis for hope for the future.

**7:1–8:18** These verses (often termed Isaiah's "Memoirs") contain a series of oracles and narratives (some in first person), all closely related to the Syro-Ephraimite war of 735–732 B.C. Several passages feature three children whose symbolic names refer to the Lord's purposes: Shear-jashub (7:3), Emmanuel (7:10–17; 8:8–10), and Maher-shalal-hash-baz (8:1–4). Judah and its Davidic dynasty should trust God's promises and not fear the combined armies of Israel and Syria; within a very short time these two enemy states will be destroyed, and David's dynasty will continue.

**7:1 Days of Ahaz**: who ruled from 735 to 715 B.C. This attack against Jerusalem by the kings of Aram (Syria) and Israel in 735 B.C. was occasioned by the refusal of Ahaz to enter with them into an anti-Assyrian alliance; cf. 2 Kgs 16.

**7:3 Shear-jashub**: this name means "a remnant will return" (cf. 10:20–22).

**7:5 Planned**: the plans of those who plot against Ahaz shall not be accomplished (v. 7). What the Lord plans will unfailingly come to pass, whereas human plans contrary to those of the Lord are doomed to frustration; cf. 8:10; 14:24–27; 19:11–14; 29:15; 30:1. See further the note on 14:24–27.

**7:6 Son of Tabeel**: a puppet of Jerusalem's enemies. His appointment would interrupt the lawful succession from David.

**7:8–9** God had chosen and made a commitment to David's dynasty and his capital city Jerusalem, not to Rezin and his capital Damascus, nor to the son of Remaliah and his capital Samaria (2 Sm 7:12–16; Ps 2:6; 78:68–72; 132:11–18). **Within sixty-five years . . . nation**: this text occurs at the end of v. 8 in the Hebrew. Ahaz would not have been reassured by so distant a promise; the phrase is probably a later addition.

---

*h:* Mt 13:10–17; Mk 4:10–12; Lk 8:9–10; Acts 28:25–28. *i:* Jer 5:21; Jn 12:40. *j:* Is 10:22. *k:* 2 Kgs 16:5; 2 Chr 28:5–15. *l:* Is 8:12; 30:15. *m:* Is 8:10; Ps 33:10.

Unless your faith is firm,
you shall not be firm![n]

*Emmanuel.* 10 Again the LORD spoke to
Ahaz: 11 Ask for a sign from the LORD, your
God; let it be deep as Sheol, or high as the
sky!* 12 But Ahaz answered, "I will not ask! I
will not tempt the LORD!"* 13 Then he said:
Listen, house of David! Is it not enough that
you weary human beings? Must you also
weary my God? 14 Therefore the Lord himself will give you a sign;* the young woman,
pregnant and about to bear a son, shall name
him Emmanuel. 15 Curds and honey* he will
eat so that he may learn to reject evil and
choose good; 16 for before the child learns to
reject evil and choose good, the land of those
two kings whom you dread shall be deserted.
17 The LORD shall bring upon you and your
people and your father's house such days as
have not come since Ephraim seceded* from
Judah (the king of Assyria). 18 On that day

The LORD shall whistle
for the fly in the farthest streams of
Egypt,
and for the bee in the land of Assyria.[o]
19 All of them shall come and settle
in the steep ravines and in the rocky
clefts,
on all thornbushes and in all pastures.

20* On that day the Lord shall shave with
the razor hired from across the River (the
king of Assyria) the head, and the hair of the
feet; it shall also shave off the beard.[p]
21 On that day a man shall keep alive a
young cow or a couple of sheep, 22 and from
their abundant yield of milk he shall eat
curds; curds and honey shall be the food of
all who are left in the land. 23* On that day
every place where there were a thousand
vines worth a thousand pieces of silver shall
become briers and thorns. 24 One shall have
to go there with bow and arrows, for all the
country shall be briers and thorns.[q] 25 But as
for all the hills which were hoed with a mat-
tock, for fear of briers and thorns you will
not go there; they shall become a place for
cattle to roam and sheep to trample.[r]

## CHAPTER 8

See RG 208

*A Son of Isaiah.* 1 The LORD said to
me: Take a large tablet, and inscribe on it
with an ordinary stylus,* "belonging to Maher-shalal-hash-baz,"[s] 2 and call reliable witnesses* for me, Uriah the priest, and
Zechariah, son of Jeberechiah.
3 Then I went to the prophetess and she
conceived and bore a son. The LORD said to
me: Name him Maher-shalal-hash-baz, 4 for
before the child learns to say, "My father,
my mother," the wealth of Damascus and the
spoils of Samaria shall be carried off by the
king of Assyria.

**7:11 Deep . . . sky**: an extraordinary or miraculous sign that would prove God's firm will to save the royal house of David from its oppressors.

**7:12 Tempt the LORD**: Ahaz prefers to depend upon the might of Assyria rather than the might of God.

**7:14** Isaiah's sign seeks to reassure Ahaz that he need not fear the invading armies of Syria and Israel in the light of God's promise to David (2 Sm 7:12–16). The oracle follows a traditional announcement formula by which the birth and sometimes naming of a child is promised to particular individuals (Gn 16:11; Jgs 13:3). **The young woman**: Hebrew *'almah* designates a young woman of marriageable age without specific reference to virginity. The Septuagint translated the Hebrew term as *parthenos*, which normally does mean virgin, and this translation underlies Mt 1:23. **Emmanuel**: the name means "with us is God." Since for the Christian the incarnation is the ultimate expression of God's willingness to "be with us," it is understandable that this text was interpreted to refer to the birth of Christ.

**7:15–16 Curds and honey**: the only diet available to those who are left after the devastation of the land; cf. vv. 21–25.

**7:17 Such days as have not come since Ephraim seceded**: the days of the kingdom prior to the secession of Ephraim and the other northern tribes (1 Kgs 12). **The king of Assyria**: the final comment appears to be a later editorial gloss indicating days worse than any since the secession.

**7:20** God will use the Assyrians from across the River (the Euphrates) as his instrument ("razor") to inflict disgrace and suffering upon his people. Ahaz paid tribute to the Assyrian king Tiglath-pileser III, who decimated Syria and Israel in his campaigns of 734–732 B.C. (cf. 2 Kgs 16:7–9). **The feet**: euphemism for sexual parts; cf. Is 6:2.

**7:23–25** Cf. note on 5:5–6.

**8:1 Ordinary stylus**: lit., "stylus of men." **Maher-shalal-hash-baz**: a symbolic name to be given to another son of Isaiah (v. 3); it means "quick spoils; speedy plunder," and describes what the Assyrians will do to Syria and Israel.

**8:2 Reliable witnesses**: who would testify that Isaiah had indeed prophesied the future destruction. **Uriah the priest**: cf. 2 Kgs 16:10.

---

*n:* 2 Chr 20:20. *o:* Is 5:26. *p:* Is 3:24; 2 Sm 10:4–6; Ez 5:1. *q:* Is 32:13. *r:* Is 5:5; 32:14. *s:* Is 10:6.

*The Choice: The Lord or Assyria.* 5 Again
the LORD spoke to me:

6 Because this people* has rejected
the waters of Shiloah that flow gently,
And melts with fear at the display of
Rezin and Remaliah's son,
7 Therefore the Lord is bringing up against
them
the waters of the River, great and
mighty,
the king of Assyria and all his glory.
It shall rise above all its channels,
and overflow all its banks.
8 It shall roll on into Judah,
it shall rage and pass on—
up to the neck it shall reach.[t]
But his outspread wings will fill
the width of your land, Emmanuel!
9 Band together, O peoples, but be
shattered!
Give ear, all you distant lands!
Arm yourselves, but be shattered! Arm
yourselves, but be shattered!
10 Form a plan, it shall be thwarted;
make a resolve, it shall not be carried
out,
for "With us is God!"* [u]

*Disciples of Isaiah.* 11 For thus said the
LORD—his hand strong upon me—warning
me not to walk in the way of this people:

12 * Do not call conspiracy what this people
calls conspiracy,
nor fear what they fear, nor feel dread.
13 But conspire with the LORD of hosts;
he shall be your fear, he shall be your
dread.[v]
14 He shall be a snare,
a stone for injury,
A rock for stumbling
to both the houses of Israel,
A trap and a snare
to those who dwell in Jerusalem;[w]
15 And many among them shall stumble;
fallen and broken;
snared and captured.[x]

16 Bind up my testimony, seal the instruction
with my disciples.* 17 I will trust in the LORD,
who is hiding his face from the house of Jacob; yes, I will wait for him. 18 Here am I and
the children whom the LORD has given me: we
are signs* and portents in Israel from the LORD
of hosts, who dwells on Mount Zion.[y]

19 And when they say to you, "Inquire of
ghosts and soothsayers who chirp and mutter;* [z] should not a people inquire of their
gods, consulting the dead on behalf of the
living, 20 for instruction and testimony?"
Surely, those who speak like this are the
ones for whom there is no dawn.*

21 He will pass through it hard-pressed and
hungry,
and when hungry, shall become
enraged,
and curse king and gods.
He will look upward,
22 and will gaze at the earth,
But will see only distress and darkness,
oppressive gloom,
murky, without light.*

**8:6–8 This people**: Judah. **Waters of Shiloah**: the stream that flows from the Gihon spring into the pool of Shiloah in Jerusalem and provides a sure supply in time of siege; here it symbolizes the divine protection which Judah has rejected by seeking Assyrian support, symbolized by "the River" (i.e., the Euphrates). Ultimately Assyrian power will devastate Judah. **His outspread wings**: the Lord's wings, a recurring symbol for divine protection (Ps 17:8; 36:8; 57:2; 61:5; 91:4; Ru 2:12). Some understand the image to refer to the sides of the flooding river, but this use of the Hebrew word for "wings" is unparalleled elsewhere in classical Hebrew.

**8:10** The plan of Israel's enemies will be thwarted because, as the name "Emmanuel" signifies, "with us is God."

**8:12–14** Because Isaiah and his followers resisted the official policy of seeking help from Assyria they were labeled "conspirators"; Isaiah uses the term to express what is really the case, cooperating with the Lord.

**8:16 Bind . . . seal . . . with my disciples**: because the prophet's message was not well received at the time, he wanted to preserve it until the future had vindicated him as God's true prophet (cf. 30:8–9).

**8:18 Signs**: in the meantime, while awaiting the vindication of his message, Isaiah and his children with their symbolic names stood as a reminder of God's message to Israel.

**8:19 Chirp and mutter**: a mocking reference to necromancers.

**8:20 Surely . . . no dawn**: reliance on necromancy brings futility.

**8:22 Oppressive gloom . . . . without light**: the meaning of the Hebrew here is quite uncertain.

*t:* Is 30:28. *u:* Is 7:7; 17:12–14. *v:* Is 29:23; 1 Pt 3:14–15. *w:* Lk 2:34; Rom 9:32–33; 1 Pt 2:7–8. *x:* Mt 21:44. *y:* Is 2:2–5; 4:5; 11:9; 14:32; 28:16; 31:9; 33:5. *z:* Is 29:4.

***The Promise of Salvation Under a New Davidic King.**** [23]There is no gloom where there had been distress. Where once he degraded the land of Zebulun and the land of Naphtali, now he has glorified the way of the Sea, the land across the Jordan, Galilee of the Nations.*

## CHAPTER 9

See RG 208

[1]The people who walked in darkness
have seen a great light;
Upon those who lived in a land of gloom
a light has shone.[a]
[2] You have brought them abundant joy
and great rejoicing;
They rejoice before you as people rejoice
at harvest,
as they exult when dividing the spoils.
[3] For the yoke that burdened them,
the pole on their shoulder,
The rod of their taskmaster,
you have smashed, as on the day of
Midian.* [b]
[4] For every boot that tramped in battle,
every cloak rolled in blood,
will be burned as fuel for fire.[c]
[5] For a child* is born to us, a son is given
to us;
upon his shoulder dominion rests.
They name him Wonder-Counselor,
God-Hero,[d]
Father-Forever, Prince of Peace.
[6] His dominion is vast
and forever peaceful,
Upon David's throne, and over his
kingdom,
which he confirms and sustains
By judgment and justice,
both now and forever.[e]
The zeal of the LORD of hosts will do
this!

***Judgment on the Northern Kingdom****

[7] The Lord has sent a word against Jacob,
and it falls upon Israel;
[8] And all the people know it—
Ephraim and those who dwell in
Samaria—
those who say in arrogance and pride
of heart,
[9] "Bricks have fallen,
but we will rebuild with cut stone;
Sycamores have been felled,
but we will replace them with cedars."[f]
[10] So the LORD raises up their foes against
them
and stirs up their enemies to action—
[11] Aram* from the east and the Philistines
from the west—
they devour Israel with open mouth.
For all this, his wrath is not turned back,

**8:23–9:6** The meaning of 8:23 is somewhat uncertain, for example, whether the expressions translated "once" and "now" refer to times or to individuals, and also whether the verbs speak of degrading and glorifying the territories. If this traditional translation is correct, the passage would seem to promise the former Northern Kingdom of Israel deliverance from the Assyrians and might relate to Hezekiah's program of trying to reincorporate the northern territories into the kingdom of Judah and thus restore the boundaries of the country as it was under David.

**8:23** The territories mentioned in this verse are those which the Assyrian king Tiglath-pileser III took from Israel and incorporated into the Assyrian provincial system as a result of the Syro-Ephraimite War of 735–732 B.C. (2 Kgs 15:29). **Zebulun ... Naphtali**: regions of the former Northern Kingdom of Israel. **The way of the Sea**: the area along the Mediterranean coast south of Mount Carmel which became the Assyrian province of Dor. **Land across the Jordan**: the province of Gilead east of the Jordan. **Galilee of the Nations**: the territory north of Mount Carmel which was incorporated in the Assyrian province of Megiddo. Galilee apparently had a large non-Israelite population. Mt 4:15–16 cites this verse in the context of the beginning of Jesus' public mission in Galilee.

**9:3 Day of Midian**: when God used the judge Gideon to deliver these northern territories from Midianite oppression (Jgs 6–7).

**9:5 A child**: perhaps to be identified with the Emmanuel of 7:14 and 8:8; cf. 11:1–2, 9. This verse may reflect a coronation rather than a birth. **Upon his shoulder**: the reference may be to a particular act in the ritual in which a symbol of the king's authority was placed on his shoulder (cf. 2 Kgs 11:12; Is 22:22).

**9:7–20 + 5:25–30** These verses describe a series of judgments God sent against the Northern Kingdom of Israel because of its sins. Despite the judgments, however, Israel continued to rebel, and God's anger remained unabated, as the recurring refrain emphasizes (9:11, 16, 20). The refrain ties Is 9:7–20 together as a unit, but 9:20 is far too abrupt to be the original conclusion to the oracle. With its series of past judgments and repeated refrain, the oracle resembles Am 4:6–12; by analogy with that model one expects a conclusion in which the prophet turns from the narration of past judgments to the announcement of a future judgment. Is 5:25–30 fits the pattern found in 9:7–20 and provides a suitable and possibly original conclusion for the whole oracle.

**9:11 Aram**: the Syrian kingdom, with its capital at Damascus.

*a:* Mt 4:15–16. *b:* Is 10:26; Jgs 7:22–25. *c:* Ps 46:10. *d:* Is 10:21. *e:* Jer 23:5; Lk 1:32–33. *f:* Mal 1:4.

and his hand is still outstretched!
12 The people do not turn back to the one
who struck them,
nor do they seek the LORD of hosts.
13 So the LORD cuts off from Israel head
and tail,
palm branch and reed in one day.[g]
14 (The elder and the noble are the head,
the prophet who teaches falsehood is
the tail.)[h]
15 Those who lead this people lead them
astray,
and those who are led are swallowed up.[i]
16 That is why the Lord does not spare their
young men,
and their orphans and widows he does
not pity;
For they are totally impious and wicked,
and every mouth speaks folly.
For all this, his wrath is not turned back,
his hand is still outstretched!
17 For wickedness burns like fire,
devouring brier and thorn;
It kindles the forest thickets,
which go up in columns of smoke.[j]
18 At the wrath of the LORD of hosts the
land quakes,
and the people are like fuel for fire;
no one spares his brother.[k]
19 They hack on the right, but remain hungry;
they devour on the left, but are not
filled.
Each devours the flesh of the neighbor;
20 Manasseh devours Ephraim,* and
Ephraim Manasseh,
together they turn on Judah.
For all this, his wrath is not turned back,
his hand is still outstretched!

## CHAPTER 10

See RG 208

### *Perversion of Justice*

1 * Ah! Those who enact unjust statutes,
who write oppressive decrees,[l]
2 Depriving the needy of judgment,
robbing my people's poor of justice,
Making widows their plunder,
and orphans their prey![m]
3 What will you do on the day of
punishment,
when the storm comes from afar?
To whom will you flee for help?
Where will you leave your wealth,
4 Lest it sink beneath the captive
or fall beneath the slain?
For all this, his wrath is not turned
back,
his hand is still outstretched!*

### *Judgment on Assyria*

5 * Ah! Assyria, the rod of my wrath,
the staff I wield in anger.[n]
6 Against an impious nation* I send him,
and against a people under my wrath I
order him
To seize plunder, carry off loot,
and to trample them like the mud of
the street.
7 But this is not what he intends,
nor does he have this in mind;
Rather, it is in his heart to destroy,
to make an end of not a few nations.
8 For he says, "Are not my commanders all
kings?"
9 * "Is not Calno like Carchemish,
Or Hamath like Arpad,
or Samaria like Damascus?

**9:20 Manasseh . . . Ephraim**: two of the leading tribes of the Northern Kingdom. The reference is to the civil wars that marked the final decades of the Northern Kingdom (2 Kgs 15:10, 14–16, 25; cf. Hos 7:3–7).

**10:1–4** This is another *hoy*-oracle; cf. note on 5:8–24. It may originally have been part of the collection at 5:8–24.

**10:4 For all this . . . outstretched!**: this refrain appears to be out of place here; cf. 9:11, 16, 20.

**10:5–34** These verses contain a series of oracles directed against Assyria. Verses 5–15 portray Assyria as simply the rod God uses to punish Israel, though Assyria does not realize this. The original conclusion to this unit may be the judgment found in vv. 24–27a, which continues the imagery and motifs found in vv. 5–15. Verses 16–23, because of the quite different imagery and motifs, may originally have been an insertion directed against Aram and Israel at the time of the Syro-Ephraimite War.

**10:6 Impious nation**: Judah. It was God's intention to use Assyria merely to punish, not to destroy, the nation.

**10:9–10** The cities mentioned were all cities captured, some more than once, by the Assyrians in the eighth century B.C. Verse 9 suggests a certain historical order in the fall of these cities, and v. 10 suggests that all of them had fallen before Samaria (cf. Am 6:2). That implies that one should think primarily of events during the reign of Tiglath-pileser III (745–727).

*g:* Is 19:15; Dt 28:13, 44. *h:* Is 28:7. *i:* Is 3:12. *j:* Is 5:24; 33:11–12. *k:* Is 3:5. *l:* Jer 8:8. *m:* Is 1:23; 3:14–15. *n:* Jer 51:20–23.

## Assyria, Rod of God's Anger

ASSYRIA IS THE LORD's means of punishing the people, but that nation also will be judged for its arrogance. God's purpose to punish Israel, carried out by Assyria, is just, but Assyria's own purpose is to plunder and conquer. While the king of Assyria boasts about his victories, God will destroy them when Assyria has served its purpose.

10 Just as my hand reached out to idolatrous kingdoms
that had more images than Jerusalem and Samaria—
11 Just as I treated Samaria and her idols,
shall I not do to Jerusalem and her graven images?"

12 But when the LORD has brought to an
end all his work on Mount Zion and in Jerusalem,

I will punish the utterance
of the king of Assyria's proud heart,
and the boastfulness of his haughty eyes.
13 For he says:
"By my own power I have done it,
and by my wisdom, for I am shrewd.
I have moved the boundaries of peoples,
their treasures I have pillaged,
and, like a mighty one, I have brought down the enthroned.
14 My hand has seized, like a nest,
the wealth of nations.
As one takes eggs left alone,
so I took in all the earth;
No one fluttered a wing,
or opened a mouth, or chirped!"
15 Will the ax boast against the one who hews with it?
Will the saw exalt itself above the one who wields it?
As if a rod could sway the one who lifts it,
or a staff could lift the one who is not wood!
16 Therefore the Lord, the LORD of hosts,
will send leanness among his fat ones,*
And under his glory there will be a kindling
like the kindling of fire.[o]
17 The Light of Israel will become a fire,
the Holy One, a flame,
That burns and consumes its briers
and its thorns in a single day.[p]
18 And the glory of its forests and orchards
will be consumed, soul and body,
and it will be like a sick man who wastes away.
19 And the remnant of the trees in his forest
will be so few,
that any child can record them.
20 On that day
The remnant of Israel,
the survivors of the house of Jacob,
will no more lean upon the one who struck them;
But they will lean upon the LORD,
the Holy One of Israel, in truth.
21 A remnant will return,* the remnant of Jacob,
to the mighty God.
22 Though your people, O Israel,
were like the sand of the sea,[q]
Only a remnant of them will return;
their destruction is decreed,
as overflowing justice demands.[r]

23 For the Lord, the GOD of hosts, is about to
carry out the destruction decreed in the
midst of the whole land.[s]
24* Therefore thus says the Lord, the GOD
of hosts: My people, who dwell in Zion, do
not fear the Assyrian, though he strikes you
with a rod, and raises his staff against you as
did the Egyptians. 25 For just a brief moment

**10:16 His fat ones**: the strong men of the enemy army.
**10:21 A remnant will return**: in Hebrew, *shear-jashub*, an allusion to the name of Isaiah's son, Shear-jashub; cf. 7:3.
**10:24** This verse with its reference to Assyria's rod may introduce the original conclusion to vv. 5–15.

*o:* Is 17:4. *p:* Is 9:17–18; 30:27–33; 31:9; 33:14. *q:* Hos 2:1; Rom 9:27–28. *r:* Is 28:16–18. *s:* Is 28:22.

more, and my wrath shall be over, and my
anger shall be set for their destruction.
26 Then the LORD of hosts will raise against
them a scourge such as struck Midian at the
rock of Oreb;[t] and he will raise his staff over
the sea as he did in Egypt.[u] 27 On that day,

His burden shall be taken from your
shoulder,
and his yoke shattered from your neck.[v]

*The March of an Enemy Army**

He has come up from Rimmon,
28 he has reached Aiath, passed through
Migron,
at Michmash he has stored his supplies.
29 He has crossed the ravine,
at Geba he has camped for the night.
Ramah trembles,
Gibeah of Saul has fled.
30 Cry and shriek, Bath-Gallim!
Hearken, Laishah! Answer her,
Anathoth!
31 Madmenah is in flight,
the inhabitants of Gebim seek refuge.
32 Even today he will halt at Nob,
he will shake his fist at the mount of
daughter Zion,
the hill of Jerusalem!
33 * Now the Lord, the LORD of hosts,
is about to lop off the boughs with
terrible violence;
The tall of stature shall be felled,
and the lofty ones shall be brought low;
34 He shall hack down the forest thickets
with an ax,
and Lebanon in its splendor shall fall.

## CHAPTER 11*

See RG 208

### *The Ideal Davidic King**

1 But a shoot shall sprout from the stump*
of Jesse,
and from his roots a bud shall
blossom.[w]
2 * The spirit of the LORD shall rest upon
him:[x]
a spirit of wisdom and of understanding,
A spirit of counsel and of strength,
a spirit of knowledge and of fear of the
LORD,
3 and his delight shall be the fear of the
LORD.
Not by appearance shall he judge,
nor by hearsay shall he decide,
4 But he shall judge the poor with justice,
and decide fairly for the land's
afflicted.[y]
He shall strike the ruthless with the rod
of his mouth,
and with the breath of his lips he shall
slay the wicked.[z]
5 Justice shall be the band around his
waist,
and faithfulness a belt upon his hips.[a]
6 * Then the wolf shall be a guest of the
lamb,
and the leopard shall lie down with the
young goat;

**10:27b–32** A poetic description of the march of an enemy army from the north, advancing south to the very gates of Jerusalem, where the enemy waves his hand in a gesture of derision against the city. Though Sennacherib's troops took a different route, advancing down the coast and then approaching Jerusalem from the southeast, the arrogant attitude toward God's chosen city was the same. **Aiath**: the Ai of Jos 7:22–8:29. **Migron**: modern Makrun north of Michmash. **The ravine**: the deep valley between Michmash and Geba (cf. 1 Sm 14:1–5). **Ramah . . . Gibeah . . . Bath-Gallim . . . Laishah . . . Anathoth . . . Madmenah . . . Gebim**: cities north of Jerusalem threatened by the sudden appearance of this enemy army. **Nob**: probably to be identified with the present Mount Scopus from where one has a clear view of Jerusalem.

**10:33–34** Just when the enemy is about to capture Jerusalem, God intervenes and destroys the hostile army. Cf. 29:1–8; 31:4–9.

**11:1–16** Isaiah 11 contains a prophecy of the rise of a new Davidic king who will embody the ancient ideal of Davidic kingship (vv. 1–9), an elaboration of that prophecy in a further description of that king's rule (v. 10), and a prophecy of God's deliverance of the chosen people from exile and cessation of enmities (vv. 11–16).

**11:1–9 (10)** Here Isaiah looks forward to a new Davidide who will realize the ancient ideals (see Ps 72). The oracle does not seem to have a particular historical person in mind.

**11:1 Shoot . . . stump**: the imagery suggests the bankruptcy of the monarchy as embodied in the historical kings, along with the need for a new beginning, to spring from the very origin from which David and his dynasty arose. **Jesse**: David's father (cf. 1 Sm 16:1–13).

**11:2–3** The source of the traditional names of the gifts of the Holy Spirit. The Septuagint and the Vulgate read "piety" for "fear of the Lord" in its first occurrence, thus listing seven gifts.

**11:6–9** This picture of the idyllic harmony of paradise is a

*t:* Is 9:3; Jgs 7:25. *u:* Ex 14:16. *v:* Is 9:3. *w:* Is 4:2; 53:2; Jer 23:5–6; 33:14–16; Zec 3:8; 6:12; Rev 22:16. *x:* Is 42:1; 1 Sm 16:13; Mt 3:16; Mk 1:10; Jn 1:32. *y:* Ps 72:2, 4; 98:9. *z:* 2 Thes 2:8; Rev 2:16. *a:* Eph 6:14.

## A Song of Thanksgiving

ISAIAH HAS BEEN constructed to form a series of "books within books." In ch 12 a song of thanksgiving for the salvation of God that will surely come to Jerusalem concludes the section that began in Isaiah 5:1. These shorter collections display a broad editorial structure where hope and promise follow threats and warnings. Even the punitive fires of judgment are placed within this larger context of the saving purpose of God.

The calf and the young lion shall browse
together,
with a little child to guide them.[b]
7 The cow and the bear shall graze,
together their young shall lie down;
the lion shall eat hay like the ox.[c]
8 The baby shall play by the viper's den,
and the child lay his hand on the
adder's lair.
9 They shall not harm or destroy on all my
holy mountain;
for the earth shall be filled with
knowledge of the LORD,
as water covers the sea.

### *Restoration**

10 On that day,
The root of Jesse,
set up as a signal for the peoples—
Him the nations will seek out;
his dwelling shall be glorious.[d]
11 On that day,
The Lord shall again take it in hand
to reclaim the remnant of his people
that is left from Assyria and Egypt,
Pathros, Ethiopia, and Elam,
Shinar, Hamath, and the isles of the sea.[e]
12 He shall raise a signal to the nations[f]
and gather the outcasts of Israel;
The dispersed of Judah he shall assemble
from the four corners of the earth.
13 The envy of Ephraim shall pass away,
and those hostile to Judah shall be cut
off;
Ephraim shall not envy Judah,
and Judah shall not be hostile to
Ephraim;
14 But they shall swoop down on the
foothills
of the Philistines to the west,
together they shall plunder the people
of the east;*
Edom and Moab shall be their
possessions,
and the Ammonites their subjects.
15 The LORD shall dry up the tongue* of the
Sea of Egypt,
and wave his hand over the Euphrates
with his fierce wind,
And divide it into seven streamlets,
so that it can be crossed in sandals.[g]
16 There shall be a highway for the remnant
of his people
that is left from Assyria,
As there was for Israel
when it came up from the land of
Egypt.[h]

## CHAPTER 12

See RG 208

### *Song of Thanksgiving**

1 On that day, you will say:
I give you thanks, O LORD;

dramatic symbol of universal peace and justice under the rule of the new Davidic king. The peace and harmony even among carnivores and their natural prey in this description suggest a paradisiac aspect of the reign of the new king.

**11:10–16** This passage, with its reference to God's people in widely scattered lands, is probably from a much later period. God will restore them to their own land. The reconciliation of Ephraim (i.e., the Northern Kingdom) and Judah reverses what Isaiah saw as a disastrous event of the past (cf. 7:17). God's action is likened to a new exodus, analogous to the time God first acquired Israel in bringing them out of the land of Egypt. **Pathros**: upper Egypt. **Elam**: east of Babylonia. **Shinar**: Babylonia. **Hamath**: on the Orontes River in Syria. **Isles**: or coastlands, in the Mediterranean.

**11:14 People of the east**: tribes in the Arabian Desert (cf. Jgs 6:3, 33; 7:12).

**11:15 Tongue**: perhaps to be identified with the Gulf of Suez.

**12:1–6** Israel's thanksgiving to the Lord, expressed in language like that of the Psalms.

*b:* Hos 2:20. *c:* Is 65:25. *d:* Is 2:2–4; Rom 15:12. *e:* Ex 3:20; Jer 23:7–8; 31:1–22; Zec 10:10. *f:* Is 18:3. *g:* Zec 10:11; Rev 16:12. *h:* Is 51:10; Ex 14:29.

though you have been angry with me,
your anger has abated, and you have consoled me.
2 God indeed is my salvation;
I am confident and unafraid.
For the LORD is my strength and my might,
and he has been my salvation.[i]
3 With joy you will draw water
from the fountains of salvation,[j]
4 And you will say on that day:
give thanks to the LORD, acclaim his name;
Among the nations make known his deeds,
proclaim how exalted is his name.[k]
5 Sing praise to the LORD for he has done glorious things;
let this be known throughout all the earth.[l]
6 Shout with exultation, City of Zion,
for great in your midst
is the Holy One of Israel![m]

## C. Oracles Against the Foreign Nations*

### CHAPTER 13

See RG 209

*Babylon.** 1 An oracle* concerning
Babylon; a vision of Isaiah, son of Amoz.

2 Upon the bare mountains set up a signal;
cry out to them,*
Beckon for them to enter
the gates of the nobles.[n]
3 I have commanded my consecrated ones,*
I have summoned my warriors,
eager and bold to carry out my anger.[o]
4 Listen! the rumble on the mountains:
that of an immense throng!
Listen! the noise of kingdoms, nations assembled!
The LORD of hosts is mustering
an army for battle.[p]
5 They come from a far-off country,
and from the end of the heavens,
The LORD and the instruments of his wrath,
to destroy all the land.
6 Howl, for the day of the LORD* is near;
as destruction from the Almighty it comes.[q]
7 Therefore all hands fall helpless,[r]
every human heart melts,
8 and they are terrified,
Pangs and sorrows take hold of them,
like a woman in labor they writhe;
They look aghast at each other,
their faces aflame.[s]
9 Indeed, the day of the LORD comes,
cruel, with wrath and burning anger;
To lay waste the land
and destroy the sinners within it![t]
10 The stars of the heavens and their constellations
will send forth no light;
The sun will be dark at its rising,
and the moon will not give its light.[u]
11 Thus I will punish the world for its evil
and the wicked for their guilt.
I will put an end to the pride of the arrogant,

**13:1–23:18** These chapters, which probably existed at one time as an independent collection, consist primarily of oracles from various sources against foreign nations. While some of the material is Isaianic, in many cases it has been reworked by later editors or writers.

**13:1–22** Although attributed to Isaiah (v. 1), this oracle does not reflect conditions of Isaiah's time. Babylon did not achieve imperial status until a century later, after its victory over Assyria in 609 B.C. The mention of the Medes (v. 17) rather than Persia suggests a date prior to 550 B.C., when the Median empire of Astyages fell to Cyrus the Persian. Tension is created in that the attackers are not named until v. 17 and the foe to be attacked until v. 19.

**13:1 Oracle**: Heb. *massa'*; used eight more times in this collection.

**13:2 To them**: the Medes (v. 17), who are being summoned to destroy Babylon. **Gates of the nobles**: the reference is apparently to the gates of Babylon and involves a wordplay on the city name (Babylon = *bab ilani*, "gate of the gods").

**13:3 Consecrated ones**: in the sense that they will wage a "holy war" and carry out God's plan.

**13:6–8 Day of the LORD**: described often in prophetic writings, it generally signified the coming of the Lord in power and majesty to destroy his enemies. The figures used convey the idea of horror and destruction (Am 5:18–20). **The Almighty**: Heb. *shaddai*; there is a play on words between destruction (*shod*) and Shaddai, a title for God traditionally rendered as "the Almighty" (cf. Gn 17:1; Ex 6:3).

*i:* Ex 15:2; Ps 118:14. *j:* Jgs 5:11; Jer 2:13; Jn 4:10, 14. *k:* Ps 105:1; 148:13. *l:* Is 11:9; Ex 15:1. *m:* Is 52:8–9; 54:1; Zep 3:14–15. *n:* Is 5:26; Jer 50:2. *o:* Jl 4:9. *p:* Jer 50:9. *q:* Is 2:12–21; Jer 46:10; Am 5:18–20; Jl 1:15; Zep 1:7; Rev 6:17. *r:* Jer 6:24; Ez 7:17. *s:* Is 21:3; Ps 48:7; Mi 4:9. *t:* Jer 4:7; 18:16; Mal 3:19. *u:* Is 24:23; Jer 4:23; Zep 1:15; Mt 24:29.

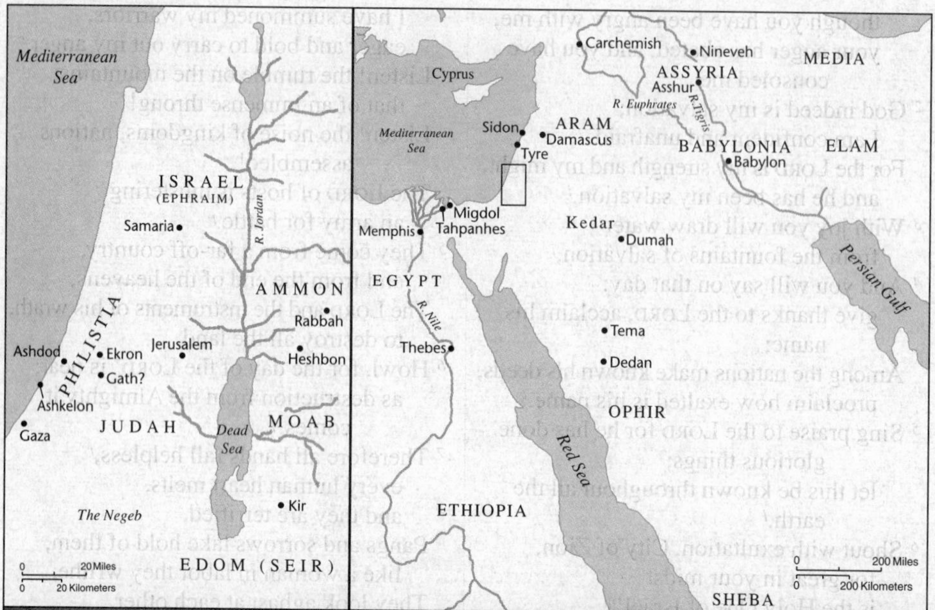

**Places Mentioned in the Oracles against the Nations**

the insolence of tyrants I will humble.[v]
12 I will make mortals more rare than pure gold,
human beings, than the gold of Ophir.* [w]
13 For this I will make the heavens tremble
and the earth shall be shaken from its place,
At the wrath of the Lord of hosts
on the day of his burning anger.[x]
14 Like a hunted gazelle,
or a flock that no one gathers,
They shall turn each to their own people
and flee each to their own land.[y]
15 Everyone who is taken shall be run through;
and everyone who is caught shall fall by the sword.
16 Their infants shall be dashed to pieces in their sight;
their houses shall be plundered
and their wives ravished.[z]
17 I am stirring up against them the Medes,
who think nothing of silver
and take no delight in gold.[a]
18 With their bows they shall shatter the young men,
And the fruit of the womb they shall not spare,
nor shall their eye take pity on children.
19 And Babylon, the jewel of kingdoms,
the glory and pride of the Chaldeans,
Shall become like Sodom and Gomorrah,
overthrown by God.[b]
20 It shall never be inhabited,
nor dwelt in, from age to age;

**13:12 Ophir**: cf. note on Ps 45:10.

*v:* Is 2:17; Jer 50:32. *w:* 1 Kgs 9:28; Jb 22:24. *x:* Hg 2:6; Lam 1:12. *y:* 1 Kgs 22:17; Jer 50:16; 51:9. *z:* 2 Kgs 8:12; Ps 137:9; Na 3:10. *a:* Is 21:2; Jer 51:11, 28. *b:* Dt 29:22; Is 1:7; Jer 49:18; 50:40; Am 4:11.

ISAIAH 13:15 IS one of the only verses in First Isaiah (RG 205) that anticipates the Israelites and Judeans taking vengeance on their enemies. It contradicts not only the prediction of a nonviolent messianic age earlier in this chapter, but also the consistent rejection of national revenge in Isaiah's prophecies.

## A Mocking Lament for the Death of the King of Babylon

THE BABYLONIAN THREAT occupies most of chs 40–55, so this great world power takes on a symbolic role as the supreme example of oppression. The editorial note in 14:1–2 provides a summary of the message of hope (chs 56–66; see also Is 11:12–16). In vv. 3–11, a brilliant, mocking lament for the death of the king of Babylon ironically contrasts the king's power in life and powerlessness in death and celebrates the passing of Babylon as a world power.

Arabians shall not pitch their tents there,
nor shepherds rest their flocks there.[c]
21 But desert demons shall rest there
and owls shall fill the houses;
There ostriches shall dwell,
and satyrs* shall dance.[d]
22 Wild dogs shall dwell in its castles,
and jackals in its luxurious palaces.
Its time is near at hand
and its days shall not be prolonged.[e]

### CHAPTER 14

See RG 209

*Restoration of Israel.* 1 But the LORD
will take pity on Jacob and again choose Israel, and will settle them on their own land;
foreigners will join them and attach themselves to the house of Jacob.[f] 2 The nations
will take them and bring them to their place,
and the house of Israel will possess them* as
male and female slaves on the Lord's land;
they will take captive their captors and rule
over their oppressors.[g]

*Downfall of the King of Babylon.* 3 On the
day when the LORD gives you rest from your
sorrow and turmoil, from the hard service
with which you served,[h] 4 you will take up
this taunt-song* against the king of Babylon:[i]

How the oppressor has come to an end!
how the turmoil has ended!
5 The LORD has broken the rod of the
wicked,
the staff of the tyrants[j]
6 That struck the peoples in wrath
with relentless blows;
That ruled the nations in anger,
with boundless persecution.[k]
7 The whole earth rests peacefully,
song breaks forth;
8 The very cypresses rejoice over you,
the cedars of Lebanon:
"Now that you are laid to rest,
no one comes to cut us down."[l]
9 Below, Sheol is all astir
preparing for your coming;
Awakening the shades to greet you,
all the leaders of the earth;
Making all the kings of the nations
rise from their thrones.
10 All of them speak out
and say to you,
"You too have become weak like us,
you are just like us!
11 Down to Sheol your pomp is brought,
the sound of your harps.
Maggots are the couch beneath you,
worms your blanket."[m]
12 How you have fallen from the heavens,
O Morning Star,* son of the dawn!
How you have been cut down to the
earth,

**13:21 Satyrs**: in the popular mind, demons of goatlike form dwelling in ruins, symbols of immorality; cf. Lv 17:7; Is 34:14.

**14:2 Possess them**: Israel will make slaves of the nations who escort it back to its land.

**14:4–21** This taunt-song, a satirical funeral lament, is a beautiful example of classical Hebrew poetry. According to the prose introduction and the prosaic conclusion (vv. 22–23), it is directed against the king of Babylon, though Babylon is mentioned nowhere in the song itself. If the reference to Babylon is accurate, the piece was composed long after the time of Isaiah, for Babylon was not a threat to Judah in the eighth century. Some have argued that Isaiah wrote it at the death of an Assyrian king and the references to Babylon were made by a later editor, but this is far from certain.

**14:12 Morning Star**: term addressed to the king of Babylon. The Vulgate translates as "Lucifer," a name applied by the church Fathers to Satan. **Son of the dawn**: Heb., *ben shahar*, may reflect the name of a pagan deity.

*c:* Jer 51:62. *d:* Is 34:13–14; 35:7. *e:* Ez 32:23. *f:* Is 56:3; 60:4; Ps 102:14; Jer 24:6; Zec 1:17. *g:* Is 49:22–23; 60:14; 66:20. *h:* Ex 33:14; Jos 1:13; Jer 30:10. *i:* Hb 2:6. *j:* Is 10:24–27. *k:* Is 10:5–7. *l:* Is 37:24; 44:23; 55:12; Ez 31:16. *m:* Sir 10:11.

you who conquered nations![n]
13 In your heart you said:
"I will scale the heavens;
Above the stars of God*
I will set up my throne;
I will take my seat on the Mount of Assembly,
on the heights of Zaphon.[o]
14 I will ascend above the tops of the clouds;
I will be like the Most High!"[p]
15 No! Down to Sheol you will be brought
to the depths of the pit![q]
16 When they see you they will stare,
pondering over you:
"Is this the man who made the earth tremble,
who shook kingdoms?
17 Who made the world a wilderness,
razed its cities,
and gave captives no release?"
18 All the kings of the nations lie in glory,
each in his own tomb;[r]
19 But you are cast forth without burial,
like loathsome carrion,
Covered with the slain, with those struck by the sword,
a trampled corpse,
Going down to the very stones of the pit.[s]
20 You will never be together with them
in the grave,
For you have ruined your land,
you have slain your people!
Let him never be named,
that offshoot of evil!
21 Make ready to slaughter his sons
for the guilt of their fathers;[t]
Lest they rise and possess the earth,
and fill the breadth of the world with cities.*

22 I will rise up against them, says the LORD of hosts, and cut off from Babylon name and remnant, progeny and offspring, says the LORD.[u] 23 I will make it a haunt of hoot owls and a marshland; I will sweep it with the broom of destruction, oracle of the LORD of hosts.

### *God's Plan for Assyria**

24 The LORD of hosts has sworn:
As I have resolved,
so shall it be;
As I have planned,
so shall it stand:
25 To break the Assyrian in my land
and trample him on my mountains;
Then his yoke shall be removed from them,
and his burden from their shoulder.[v]
26 This is the plan proposed for the whole earth,
and this the hand outstretched over all the nations.*
27 The LORD of hosts has planned;
who can thwart him?
His hand is stretched out;
who can turn it back?[w]

***Philistia.**** 28 In the year that King Ahaz died,* there came this oracle:

**14:13–15 God**: not Elohim, the common word for God, but El, the name of the head of the pantheon in Canaanite mythology, a god who was early identified with the Lord in Israelite thought. **Mount of Assembly**: mountain where the council of the gods met, according to Canaanite mythology. **Zaphon**: the sacred mountain of Baal, originally the Jebel el-Aqra north of Ugarit, but other mountains have been identified with it, including Mount Zion in Jerusalem (Ps 48:3). The attempt to usurp the place of God (v. 14), coupled with the dramatic reversal ("above the stars of God" to "the depths of the pit") occasioned the interpretation that saw here the rebellion and fall of Satan.

**14:21 Cities**: if the text is correct, it presumably refers to cities as expressions of human pride, authority, and oppression (cf. Gn 11:1–9; Na 3:1–4).

**14:24–27** The motif of God's plan or work is a recurring thread running through Isaiah's oracles. The plans of Judah's enemies will not come to pass (7:5–7; 8:9–10; 10:7), but God's plan for his work of disciplining his own people (5:12, 19; 28:21), and then for punishing the foreign agents God used to administer that discipline (10:12) will come to pass.

**14:26 Hand outstretched over all the nations**: as it was once outstretched over Israel (9:11, 16, 20; 5:25).

**14:28–31** This oracle seems to reflect the political situation soon after the death of Ahaz in 715 B.C., when Ashdod and the other Philistine cities were trying to create a united front to rebel against Assyria. Ahaz had refused to join the rebels in 735 B.C. and remained loyal to Assyria during the rest of his reign, but the Philistines may have had higher hopes for his son Hezekiah. Judah, however, did not join in Ashdod's disastrous revolt in 713–711 B.C. (cf. 20:1).

**14:28 The year that King Ahaz died**: 715 B.C.

*n:* Jb 14:10. *o:* Jer 51:53; Am 9:2. *p:* Ez 28:2; Zep 2:15; 2 Thes 2:4. *q:* Ez 28:8–9; 32:23; Mt 11:23; Acts 12:23. *r:* Jb 3:14–15. *s:* Is 66:24. *t:* Ex 20:5; Mt 23:35. *u:* Jer 51:62; Jb 18:19. *v:* Is 9:3; 10:27a. *w:* Is 23:8–9; Jb 40:8; Jer 4:28.

29 * Do not rejoice, Philistia, not one of you,
that the rod which struck you is broken;
For out of the serpent's root shall come
an adder,
its offspring shall be a flying saraph.
30 In my pastures the poor shall graze,
and the needy lie down in safety;
But I will kill your root with famine
that shall slay even your remnant.
31 Howl, O gate; cry out, O city!
Philistia, all of you melts away!
For there comes a smoke from the north,*
without a straggler in its ranks.
32 What will one answer the messengers of
the nations?*
"The LORD has established Zion,
and in her the afflicted of his people
find refuge."

## CHAPTER 15

See RG 209

### *Moab**

1 Oracle on Moab:
Laid waste in a night,
Ar of Moab is destroyed;
Laid waste in a night,
Kir of Moab is destroyed.
2 Daughter Dibon has gone up
to the high places to weep;
Over Nebo and over Medeba
Moab is wailing.
Every head is shaved,
every beard sheared off.* [x]
3 In the streets they wear sackcloth,
and on the rooftops;
In the squares
everyone wails, streaming with tears.[y]
4 Heshbon and Elealeh cry out,
they are heard as far as Jahaz.
At this the loins of Moab tremble,
his soul quivers within him;[z]
5 My heart cries out for Moab,
his fugitives reach Zoar,
Eglath-shelishiyah:
The ascent of Luhith
they ascend weeping;
On the way to Horonaim
they utter rending cries;[a]
6 The waters of Nimrim
have become a waste,
The grass is withered,
new growth is gone,
nothing is green.
7 So now whatever they have acquired or
stored away
they carry across the Wadi of the
Poplars.
8 The cry has gone round
the territory of Moab;
As far as Eglaim his wailing,
even at Beer-elim his wailing.
9 * The waters of Dimon are filled with
blood,
but I will bring still more upon Dimon:
Lions for those who are fleeing from
Moab
and for those who remain in the land!

## CHAPTER 16

See RG 209

1 Send them forth,* hugging the
earth like reptiles,
from Sela across the desert,
to the mount of daughter Zion.
2 Like flushed birds,
like scattered nestlings,
Are the daughters of Moab
at the fords of the Arnon.* [b]

**14:29** The occasion for this oracle is usually taken to be the death of an Assyrian king; the Philistines were vassals of Assyria, whereas no victories of Ahaz over the Philistines are recorded. The chronological notice (*in the year that King Ahaz died*) may be incorrect, for no Assyrian king died around 715, the date usually assigned for the death of Ahaz. **Flying saraph**: a winged cobra, often portrayed in Egyptian art and on Israelite seals. The Hebrew *saraph* means "to burn" and perhaps is applied to the cobra because of the burning sensation of its bite.

**14:31 Smoke from the north**: the dust raised from the approach of the Assyrian army.

**14:32 Messengers of the nations**: envoys from Philistia, and from Egypt and Ethiopia, the real powers behind the Philistine revolt (20:1–6; cf. 18:1–2).

**15:1–16:14** Both the historical situation reflected in this oracle against Moab and the date of composition are uncertain. Variants of the same poem are found in Jer 48, and there are connections with Nm 21:27–30 as well.

**15:2 Shaved . . . sheared off**: traditional signs of grief.

**15:9** There is a play on words between "Dimon" and *dam*, the Hebrew word for blood.

**16:1 Send them forth**: the Hebrew text is disturbed; it could also be understood to refer to tribute (a lamb) sent from Moab to Zion, presumably to encourage the king to receive the Moabite refugees.

**16:2 The Arnon**: principal river of Moab.

*x:* Jer 48:37; Ez 7:18; Am 8:10. *y:* Is 22:12; Jer 48:38. *z:* Jer 48:34. *a:* Jer 48:5, 34. *b:* Nm 21:13.

3 * Offer counsel, take their part;
at high noon make your shade like the night;
Hide the outcasts,
do not betray the fugitives.
4 Let the outcasts of Moab live with you,
be their shelter from the destroyer.
When there is an end to the oppressor,
when destruction has ceased,
and the marauders have vanished from the land,
5 A throne shall be set up in mercy,
and on it shall sit in fidelity,
in David's tent,
A judge upholding right,
prompt to do justice.[c]
6 We have heard of the pride of Moab,
how very proud he is,
Of his haughtiness, pride, and arrogance
that his empty words do not match.[d]
7 * Therefore let Moab wail,
let everyone wail for Moab;
For the raisin cakes* of Kir-hareseth
let them sigh, stricken with grief.
8 The terraced slopes of Heshbon languish,
the vines of Sibmah,
Whose clusters once overpowered
the lords of nations,
Reaching as far as Jazer
winding through the wilderness,*
Whose branches spread forth,
crossing over the sea.
9 Therefore I weep with Jazer
for the vines of Sibmah;
I drench you with my tears,
Heshbon and Elealeh;
For on your summer fruits and harvests
the battle cry* has fallen.[e]
10 From the orchards are taken away
joy and gladness,
In the vineyards there is no singing,
no shout of joy;
In the wine presses no one treads grapes,
the vintage shout is stilled.[f]
11 Therefore for Moab
my heart moans like a lyre,
my inmost being for Kir-hareseth.[g]
12 * When Moab wears himself out on the high places,
and enters his sanctuary to pray,
it shall avail him nothing.[h]

13* That is the word the LORD spoke
against Moab in times past. 14But now the
LORD speaks: In three years, like the years of
a hired laborer, the glory of Moab shall be
empty despite all its great multitude; and the
remnant shall be very small and weak.[i]

## CHAPTER 17

See RG 209

### *Damascus*

1 Oracle on Damascus:*
See, Damascus shall cease to be a city
and become a pile of ruins;[j]
2 Her cities shall be forever abandoned,
for flocks to lie in undisturbed.
3 The fortress shall vanish from Ephraim*
and dominion from Damascus;
The remnant of Aram shall become like the glory
of the Israelites—
oracle of the LORD of hosts.

**16:3–5** Directed to Jerusalem, which should receive the suffering Moabites with mercy, as befits the city of David's family, who were partly descended from Ruth the Moabite; and cf. 1 Sm 22:3–4. This would be a gracious act on Judah's part, since its relations with Moab were strained at best.

**16:7–14** Moab had been prosperous; now it has become a desert.

**16:7 Raisin cakes**: masses of dried compressed grapes used as food (cf. 2 Sm 6:19; 1 Chr 16:3; Sg 2:5), and also in the worship of other gods (Hos 3:1).

**16:8 Wilderness**: i.e., eastward. **Sea**: i.e., westward.

**16:9–10 Battle cry . . . shout of joy**: the same Hebrew word (*hedad*), which normally refers to the joyful shout of those treading the grapes (cf. Jer 25:30), here is used both for the triumphant shout of the enemy (v. 9) and for the vintagers' shout, which has ceased.

**16:12** In vain do the Moabites appeal to their god Chemosh.

**16:13–14** A prose application of the preceding poetic oracle against Moab (15:1–16:12); cf. Jer 4:8. **Like the years of a hired laborer**: the fixed period of time for which the hired laborer contracted his services; cf. Is 21:16.

**17:1 Damascus**: capital of Aram or Syria, conquered by Tiglath-pileser III at the end of the Syro-Ephraimite War in 732 B.C.

**17:3 Ephraim**: Israel, leagued with Aram against Judah in the Syro-Ephraimite War. Assyria ravaged and captured most of Israelite territory in 734–733 B.C. **Like the glory of the Israelites**: the remnant of Aram will be no more impressive than the pitiful remnant of the Northern Kingdom.

*c:* Is 9:6; 11:3–4; 32:1; Jer 23:5; Ps 89:14; Prv 20:28. *d:* Jer 48:29–30. *e:* Is 15:5; Jer 48:32. *f:* Is 24:8. *g:* Is 15:5; Jer 48:36. *h:* Jer 48:13. *i:* Dt 15:18. *j:* 2 Kgs 16:9; Jer 49:23; Am 1:3; Zec 9:1.

4 On that day
The glory of Jacob shall fade,
and his full body shall grow thin.[k]
5 Like the reaper's mere armful of stalks,
when he gathers the standing grain;
Or as when one gleans the ears
in the Valley of Rephaim.*
6 * Only gleanings shall be left in it,
as when an olive tree has been beaten—
Two or three olives at the very top,
four or five on its most fruitful branches—
oracle of the LORD, the God of Israel.[l]
7 On that day people shall turn to their maker,
their eyes shall look to the Holy One of Israel.[m]
8 They shall not turn to the altars, the work of their hands,
nor shall they look to what their fingers have made:
the asherahs* or the incense stands.
9 On that day his strong cities shall be
like those abandoned by the Hivites and Amorites
When faced with the Israelites;
and there shall be desolation.[n]
10 Truly, you have forgotten the God who saves you,
the Rock, your refuge, you have not remembered.[o]
Therefore, though you plant plants for the Pleasant One,*
and set out cuttings for a foreign one,[p]
11 Though you make them grow the day you plant them
and make them blossom the morning you set them out,
The harvest shall disappear on a day of sickness
and incurable pain.
12 Ah! the roaring of many peoples—*
a roar like the roar of the seas!
The thundering of nations—
thunder like the thundering of mighty waters![q]
13 * But God shall rebuke them,
and they shall flee far away,
Driven like chaff on the mountains before a wind,
like tumbleweed before a storm.[r]
14 At evening, there is terror,
but before morning, they are gone!
Such is the portion of those who despoil us,
the lot of those who plunder us.[s]

## CHAPTER 18

See RG 209

### *Ethiopia*

1 Ah! Land of buzzing insects,*
beyond the rivers of Ethiopia,[t]
2 Sending ambassadors by sea,
in papyrus boats on the waters!
Go, swift messengers,
to a nation tall and bronzed,
To a people dreaded near and far,
a nation strong and conquering,
whose land is washed by rivers.[u]
3 * All you who inhabit the world,
who dwell on earth,

**17:5 Valley of Rephaim**: a fertile plain just to the southwest of Jerusalem (cf. Jos 15:8; 2 Sm 5:18). Since it was near a large population center, the fields there would be thoroughly gleaned by the poor after the harvest, leaving very few ears of grain.

**17:6** Olives not easily picked by hand were knocked from the tree by means of a long stick; cf. 24:13.

**17:8 Asherahs**: see note on Ex 34:13. **Incense stands**: small altars on which incense was burned; cf. Is 27:9; Lv 26:30.

**17:10 The Pleasant One**: an epithet for a foreign god of fertility, probably Adonis, in whose honor saplings were planted.

**17:12 Many peoples**: the hordes that accompanied the invading Assyrians, whom God repels just as he vanquished the primeval waters of chaos; see notes on Jb 3:8; 7:12; Ps 89:11.

**17:13–14** The passage seems to evoke the motif of invincibility, part of the early Zion tradition that Jerusalem could not be conquered because God protected it (Ps 48:1–8).

**18:1–2 Land of buzzing insects**: the region of the Upper Nile where these multiplied with great rapidity. **Ethiopia**: in Hebrew, *Kush*. The center of this ancient kingdom corresponds geographically to the modern Sudan, Roman Nubia. **Papyrus boats**: light and serviceable vessels made of bundles of papyrus stalks and sealed with pitch. Egypt, ruled by a dynasty from Ethiopia, had invited Judah to join a coalition against Assyria, but Isaiah told the ambassadors to return to their own people.

**18:3–6** A more general address but probably relating to the same topic. The Lord will not act at once, but later there will be a "harvest" of terrible destruction, probably directed against Assyria (cf. 14:24–27).

*k:* Is 10:16. *l:* Is 24:13. *m:* Is 5:12. *n:* Is 27:10. *o:* Ps 106:13, 21; Jer 2:32; Hos 8:14. *p:* Is 1:29–31. *q:* Ps 46:3–7; 93:3–4. *r:* Ps 76:7; 83:14. *s:* Is 29:8. *t:* Zep 3:10. *u:* Is 18:7.

When the signal is raised on the mountain, look!
When the trumpet blows, listen!
4 For thus says the LORD to me:
I will be quiet, looking on from where I dwell,[v]
Like the shimmering heat in sunshine,
like a cloud of dew at harvest time.
5 Before the vintage, when the flowering has ended,
and the blooms are succeeded by ripening grapes,
Then comes the cutting of branches with pruning hooks,
and the discarding of the lopped-off shoots.
6 They shall all be left to the mountain vultures
and to the beasts of the earth;
The vultures shall summer on them,
all the beasts of the earth shall winter on them.

7Then will gifts be brought to the LORD of
hosts—to the place of the name of the LORD
of hosts, Mount Zion—from a people tall
and bronzed, from a people dreaded near
and far, a nation strong and conquering,
whose land is washed by rivers.[w]

## CHAPTER 19

See RG 209

### *Egypt*

1 Oracle on Egypt:
See, the LORD is riding on a swift cloud
on his way to Egypt;
The idols of Egypt tremble before him,
the hearts of the Egyptians melt within them.[x]
2 I will stir up Egypt against Egypt:
brother will war against brother,
Neighbor against neighbor,
city against city, kingdom against kingdom.
3 The courage of the Egyptians shall ebb away within them,
and I will bring their counsel to nought;
They shall consult idols and charmers,
ghosts and clairvoyants.[y]
4 I will deliver Egypt
into the power of a cruel master,
A harsh king* who shall rule over them—
oracle of the Lord, the LORD of hosts.[z]
5 The waters shall be drained from the sea,
the river shall parch and dry up;[a]
6 Its streams shall become foul,
and the canals of Egypt shall dwindle and parch.[b]
Reeds and rushes shall wither away,
7 and bulrushes on the bank of the Nile;[c]
All the sown land along the Nile
shall dry up and blow away, and be no more.
8 The fishermen shall mourn and lament,
all who cast hook in the Nile;
Those who spread their nets in the water
shall pine away.
9 The linen-workers shall be disappointed,
the combers and weavers shall turn pale;[d]
10 The spinners shall be crushed,
all the hired laborers shall be despondent.
11 Utter fools are the princes of Zoan!*
the wisest of Pharaoh's advisers give stupid counsel.
How can you say to Pharaoh,
"I am a descendant of wise men, of ancient kings"?
12 Where then are your wise men?
Let them tell you and make known
What the LORD of hosts has planned
against Egypt.[e]
13 The princes of Zoan have become fools,
the princes of Memphis have been deceived.
The chiefs of its tribes
have led Egypt astray.[f]
14 The LORD has prepared among them
a spirit of dizziness,

**19:4 Cruel master . . . harsh king**: possibly the Nubian (Ethiopian) Shabaka who gained control of all of Egypt around 712 B.C.

**19:11, 13 Zoan**, later known as Tanis, and **Memphis** (Hebrew *Noph*) were key cities in the Nile Delta.

*v:* Is 8:18; 18:7; 2 Chr 6:30; Ps 33:14. *w:* Is 45:14; Ps 68:30; Zep 3:10; Mal 1:11. *x:* Is 13:7. *y:* Is 8:19; 44:25; Lv 19:31. *z:* Ez 29:19; 30:10. *a:* Jer 51:36; Ez 30:12; 32:2. *b:* 2 Kgs 19:24. *c:* Jb 8:11. *d:* Ez 27:7. *e:* Is 14:26; 41:22–23. *f:* Jer 2:16; Hos 9:6.

## Threats concerning Egypt

THROUGHOUT THE PERIOD when Assyria and Babylonia were assaulting Israel and Judah, Egypt repeatedly promised protection, yet consistently failed to carry through. Egypt's help was "futile and vain" (30:7). The people famed throughout antiquity for learning and literary skill could offer no defense against a ruthless invader (19:11–15). In spite of these failures, Judah's relations with Egypt were prolonged and often close. The prophet looks beyond the turmoil of Mesopotamian rule to the time when a community would dwell there who spoke the language of Canaan (v. 18) and swore allegiance to the LORD of hosts. Even Assyria would one day become with Egypt and Israel a blessing in the midst of the land (v. 24). This series of remarkable short prophecies builds on the aftermath of the disasters that befell Jerusalem at the hands of the Assyrians and Babylonians. Many citizens fled to Egypt, and, from the sixth century B.C. onward, substantial settlements of exiled Judeans took refuge there. In this bold look across the spiritual boundaries of the ancient world, a genuine religious universalism begins to appear (vv. 23–24). The knowledge of God revealed to Israel would be shared among other peoples, replacing the failed learning of the Egyptian sages (v. 11).

And they have made Egypt stagger in
whatever she does,
as a drunkard staggers in his vomit.[g]
15 Egypt shall accomplish nothing—
neither head nor tail, palm branch nor
reed,* shall accomplish anything.

16 On that day the Egyptians shall be like
women, trembling with fear, because of the
LORD of hosts shaking his fist at them.[h]
17 And the land of Judah shall be a terror to
the Egyptians. Every time they think of Judah, they shall stand in dread because of the
plan the LORD of hosts has in mind for them.
18 On that day there shall be five cities* in
the land of Egypt that speak the language of
Canaan and swear by the LORD of hosts; one
shall be called "City of the Sun."
19 On that day there shall be an altar to the
LORD at the center of Egypt, and a sacred pillar to the LORD near its boundary. 20 This will
be a sign and witness to the LORD of hosts in
the land of Egypt, so that when they cry out
to the LORD because of their oppressors, he
will send them a savior to defend and deliver
them.[i] 21 The LORD shall make himself
known to Egypt, and the Egyptians shall
know the LORD in that day; they shall offer
sacrifices and oblations, make vows to the
LORD and fulfill them.[j] 22 Although the LORD
shall smite Egypt severely, he shall heal
them; they shall turn to the LORD and he shall
be moved by their entreaty and heal them.[k]
23 On that day there shall be a highway
from Egypt to Assyria; the Assyrians shall
enter Egypt, and the Egyptians enter Assyria, and the Egyptians shall worship with
the Assyrians.
24 On that day Israel shall be a third party
with Egypt and Assyria, a blessing in the
midst of the earth,[l] 25 when the LORD of hosts
gives this blessing: "Blessed be my people
Egypt, and the work of my hands Assyria,
and my heritage, Israel."

### CHAPTER 20

See RG 209

*Isaiah's Warning Against Trust in
Egypt and Ethiopia.* 1 In the year the general
sent by Sargon, king of Assyria, came to
Ashdod,* fought against it, and captured it—

**19:15 Head . . . reed**: the leaders and the people; cf. 9:13–14.

**19:18 Five cities**: colonies of Jews living together and speaking their native language; cf. Jer 43. **City of the Sun**: the meaning is uncertain, but the reference seems to be to the city known later as Heliopolis.

**20:1 Ashdod**: a city of Philistia. In 713 B.C., Azuri, the king of Ashdod was deposed by Sargon for plotting rebellion, but the citizens of Ashdod rejected the ruler installed by the Assyrian king and followed a certain Yamani, who in 712 B.C., with the protection of Egypt, attempted to draw Edom, Moab, and Judah into a coalition against Assyria. In 711 B.C., Sargon's general marched against Ashdod, and Yamani fled to

*g:* Is 28:7; Jer 48:26. *h:* Na 3:13. *i:* Ex 2:23; Jgs 2:18. *j:* Zec 14:16, 18. *k:* Hos 6:1. *l:* Gn 12:2; Zec 8:13.

2* at that time the LORD had spoken through
Isaiah, the son of Amoz: Go and take off the
sackcloth from your waist, and remove the
sandals from your feet. This he did, walking
naked and barefoot.[m] 3 Then the LORD said:
Just as my servant Isaiah has gone naked and
barefoot for three years as a sign and portent
against Egypt and Ethiopia,[n] 4 so shall the
king of Assyria lead away captives from
Egypt, and exiles from Ethiopia, young and
old, naked and barefoot, with buttocks uncovered, the shame of Egypt.[o] 5 They shall be
dismayed and ashamed because of Ethiopia,
their hope, and because of Egypt, their
boast.[p] 6 The inhabitants of this coastland
shall say on that day, "See what has happened to those we hoped in, to whom we fled
for help and deliverance from the king of
Assyria! What escape is there for us now?"[q]

## CHAPTER 21

See RG 209

### *Fall of Babylon**

1 Oracle on the wastelands by the sea:*
Like whirlwinds sweeping through the
Negeb,
it comes from the desert,
from the fearful land.[r]
2 A harsh vision has been announced to me:
"The traitor betrays,
the despoiler spoils.[s]
Go up, O Elam; besiege, O Media;*
put an end to all its groaning!"[t]
3 Therefore my loins are filled with anguish,
pangs have seized me like those of a
woman in labor;
I am too bewildered to hear,
too dismayed to look.[u]
4 My mind reels,
shuddering assails me;
The twilight I yearned for
he has turned into dread.[v]
5 They set the table,
spread out the rugs;
they eat, they drink.* [w]
Rise up, O princes,
oil the shield!
6 For thus my Lord said to me:
Go, station a watchman,
let him tell what he sees.
7 If he sees a chariot,
a pair of horses,
Someone riding a donkey,
someone riding a camel,
Then let him pay heed,
very close heed.
8 Then the watchman cried,
"On the watchtower, my Lord,
I stand constantly by day;
And I stay at my post
through all the watches of the night.[x]
9 Here he comes—
a single chariot,
a pair of horses—
He calls out and says,
'Fallen, fallen is Babylon!
All the images of her gods
are smashed to the ground!' "[y]
10 To you, who have been threshed,
beaten on my threshing floor,
What I have heard
from the LORD of hosts,
The God of Israel,
I have announced to you.[z]

### *Dumah*

11 Oracle on Dumah:*
They call to me from Seir,
"Watchman, how much longer the night?

Ethiopia. Ashdod was captured, and a short time later Ethiopia handed Yamani over to the Assyrians for punishment.

**20:2–6** Isaiah's nakedness is a symbolic act to convey the message that Assyria would lead the Egyptians and Ethiopians away as captives. The Judeans and their allies would then realize the folly of having trusted in them. The purpose of the oracle was to dissuade Hezekiah, the Judean king, from being drawn into Ashdod's anti-Assyrian coalition (14:28–32).

**21:1–10** This oracle against Babylon is probably to be dated to the period just before the fall of Babylon to the Persians in 539 B.C. (v. 9).

**21:1 Wastelands by the sea**: Babylonia. **Negeb**: the wilderness south of Judah.

**21:2 Elam . . . Media**: nations which, under the leadership of Cyrus, captured Babylon in 539 B.C. **End to all its groaning**: those who were captive of Babylon will be freed.

**21:5** Babylon is destroyed while its leaders are feasting; cf. Dn 5. **Oil the shield**: shields were oiled and greased so as to divert blows more easily; cf. 2 Sm 1:21.

**21:11–12 Dumah**: an oasis in north Arabia (cf. Gn 25:14

*m:* 1 Sm 19:24. *n:* Is 8:18. *o:* 2 Sm 10:4. *p:* Is 30:3, 5. *q:* Is 31:3; 36:6. *r:* Is 30:6; Dt 1:19; Jer 2:6. *s:* Is 24:16; 33:1. *t:* Is 13:17; Jer 49:34. *u:* Is 16:11; Ps 38:8. *v:* Dt 28:67. *w:* Dn 5:5. *x:* Hb 2:1. *y:* Is 46:1; Jer 50:2; 51:8; Rev 14:8; 18:2. *z:* Is 51:23; Jer 51:33; Mi 4:13; Hb 3:12.

Watchman, how much longer the night?"
12 The watchman replies,
"Morning has come, and again night.
If you will ask, ask; come back again."

### *In the Steppe*

13 Oracle: in the steppe:*
In the thicket in the steppe you will
spend the night,
caravans of Dedanites.
14 Meet the thirsty, bring them water,
inhabitants of the land of Tema,
greet the fugitives with bread.[a]
15 For they have fled from the sword,
from the drawn sword;
From the taut bow,
from the thick of battle.

16For thus the Lord has said to me: In another
year, like the years of a hired laborer,* all the
glory of Kedar shall come to an end. 17Few of
Kedar's stalwart archers shall remain, for the
LORD, the God of Israel, has spoken.

## CHAPTER 22

See RG 209

### *The Valley of Vision*

1 Oracle on the Valley of Vision:* [b]
What is the matter with you now, that
you have gone up,
all of you, to the housetops,
2 * You who were full of noise,
tumultuous city,
exultant town?[c]
Your slain are not slain with the sword,
nor killed in battle.
3 All your leaders fled away together,
they were captured without use of bow;
All who were found were captured
together,
though they had fled afar off.
4 That is why I say: Turn away from me,
let me weep bitterly;
Do not try to comfort me
for the ruin of the daughter of my
people.[d]
5 It is a day of panic, rout and confusion,
from the Lord, the GOD of hosts, in the
Valley of Vision*
Walls crash;
a cry for help to the mountains.
6 Elam takes up the quiver,
Aram mounts the horses
and Kir* uncovers the shields.
7 Your choice valleys are filled with
chariots,
horses are posted at the gates—
8 and shelter over Judah is removed.*

On that day you looked to the weapons in
the House of the Forest; 9* you saw that the

and 1 Chr 1:30), may be identified with the north Arabian Adummatu mentioned in Assyrian records of Sennacherib's campaign against north Arabia. **Seir**: a site in Edom. The Edomites ask the prophet how much longer they must suffer ("the night" of suffering); he answers ambiguously: "Liberation ("morning") and further suffering ("night")," but perhaps they will later receive a more encouraging answer ("ask; come back again").

**21:13–14 In the steppe**: the north Arabian steppe where the oases referred to were located. **Dedanites**: a north Arabian tribe associated with the oasis of Tema; cf. Gn 10:7; 25:3; Jer 25:23.

**21:16 Year . . . of a hired laborer**: see note on 16:13–14. **Kedar**: a nomadic tribe in Arabia; cf. 42:11; 60:7; Ps 120:5.

**22:1–14** The title "oracle on the valley of vision," like the other oracle headings in chaps. 13–23, was supplied by an editor and is taken from v. 5. In all probability it relates to the events of 701, the lifting of Sennacherib's siege of Jerusalem. The death of the Assyrian king Sargon II in 705 occasioned the revolt of many of the vassal nations subject to Assyria, a revolt in which Hezekiah joined, over Isaiah's bitter opposition. The biblical and other data concerning the outcome of this adventure are conflicting and confusing. While 2 Kgs 19 (Is 37) tells of a miraculous deliverance of the city after the siege had been renewed, Assyrian documents and 2 Kgs 18:13–16 report that Sennacherib, Sargon II's successor, devastated Judah (the destruction of 46 cities is mentioned in Assyrian records); Hezekiah had to surrender and paid Sennacherib a heavy indemnity, taken from the Temple treasury and adornments. The inhabitants of Jerusalem apparently took the lifting of the siege as occasion for great rejoicing, a response that Isaiah condemns. They should be mourning the dead and learning that their confidence in allies rather than in the Lord leads to disaster.

**22:2–3** The retreat of Judah's soldiers is a further reason that rejoicing is not in order.

**22:5 Valley of Vision**: frequently identified as the Hinnom Valley, west of Jerusalem.

**22:6 Elam . . . Kir**: the Assyrian forces presumably included auxiliary troops from various places.

**22:8 Shelter over Judah is removed**: the reference is obscure; it has been suggested that Judah's protection was Jerusalem itself, and with the fall of the city the country was exposed. **House of the Forest**: an armory built by Solomon; its columns of wood suggested the trees of a forest; cf. 1 Kgs 7:2; 10:17.

**22:9–11** Frenetic efforts made to fortify the city before the impending siege; cf. 2 Kgs 20:20; 2 Chr 32:3–4, 30. Some suggest that the description of these preparations comes from

*a:* Jb 6:19. *b:* Is 21:2. *c:* Is 32:13. *d:* Jer 6:26; 9:1; 14:17.

breaches in the City of David were many;
you collected the water of the lower pool.
10 You numbered the houses of Jerusalem,
tearing some down to strengthen the wall;
11 you made a reservoir between the two
walls for the water of the old pool. But you
did not look to the city's Maker, nor consider
the one who fashioned it long ago.

12 On that day the Lord,
the GOD of hosts, called
For weeping and mourning,
for shaving the head and wearing
sackcloth.
13 But look! instead, there was celebration
and joy,
slaughtering cattle and butchering
sheep,
Eating meat and drinking wine:
"Eat and drink, for tomorrow we die!"[e]
14 This message was revealed in my hearing
from the LORD of hosts:

This iniquity will not be forgiven you
until you die,
says the Lord, the GOD of hosts.

### *Shebna and Eliakim*

15 Thus says the Lord, the GOD of hosts:
Up, go to that official,
Shebna,* master of the palace,
16 * "What have you here? Whom have you
here,
that you have hewn for yourself a
tomb here,
Hewing a tomb on high,
carving a resting place in the rock?"
17 The LORD shall hurl you down headlong,
mortal man!
He shall grip you firmly,
18 And roll you up and toss you like a ball
into a broad land.
There you will die, there with the
chariots you glory in,
you disgrace to your master's house!
19 I will thrust you from your office
and pull you down from your station.
20 On that day I will summon my servant
Eliakim,* son of Hilkiah;[f]
21 I will clothe him with your robe,
gird him with your sash,
confer on him your authority.
He shall be a father to the inhabitants of
Jerusalem,
and to the house of Judah.[g]
22 I will place the key* of the House of
David on his shoulder;
what he opens, no one will shut,
what he shuts, no one will open.[h]
23 I will fix him as a peg in a firm place,
a seat of honor for his ancestral house;
24 On him shall hang all the glory of his
ancestral house:*
descendants and offspring,
all the little dishes, from bowls to jugs.

25 On that day, says the LORD of hosts, the
peg fixed in a firm place shall give way,
break off and fall, and the weight that hung
on it shall be done away with; for the LORD
has spoken.

## CHAPTER 23

See RG 209

### *Tyre and Sidon*

1 * Oracle on Tyre:
Wail, ships of Tarshish,
for your port is destroyed;
From the land of the Kittim*

the time of Nebuchadnezzar's assault on Jerusalem in 588. **You did not look to the city's Maker**: Isaiah here makes the crucial point. Jerusalem's safety lay not in military forces nor in alliances with other nations nor in playing power politics but in the Lord, here presented as the creator and founder of the city. Isaiah may be alluding to the belief that the city was inviolable.

**22:15 Shebna**: by the time of the siege of Jerusalem in 36:3, Shebna, the scribe, no longer held the office of master of the palace.

**22:16** What is probably Shebna's inscribed tomb has been discovered in the village of Silwan on the eastern slope of Jerusalem.

**22:20 Eliakim**: by the time of the events described in 36:3, Eliakim had replaced Shebna as master of the palace.

**22:22 Key**: symbol of authority; cf. Mt 16:19; Rev 3:7.

**22:24–25** Apparently Eliakim proved to be a disappointment, so an oracle of judgment was added to the originally positive oracle to Eliakim.

**23:1–17** This oracle, a satire directed against the Phoenician cities of Tyre and Sidon, is perhaps to be situated at the time of Sennacherib's campaign against the Phoenican cities in 701 B.C, following his subjugation of their Babylonian allies in 703 B.C.

**23:1 Kittim**: Cyprus. The Hebrew word is derived from

*e*: Is 56:12; Wis 2:6; 1 Cor 15:32. *f*: 2 Kgs 18:18, 37. *g*: Jb 29:16. *h*: Rev 3:7.

the news reaches them.[i]
2 Silence! you who dwell on the coast,
you merchants of Sidon,
Whose messengers crossed the sea
3 over the deep waters,
Whose revenue was the grain of
Shihor,* the harvest of the Nile,
you who were the merchant among the
nations.[j]
4 Be ashamed, Sidon, fortress on the sea,
for the sea* has spoken,
"I have not been in labor, nor given
birth,
nor raised young men,
nor reared young women."
5 When the report reaches Egypt
they shall be in anguish at the report
about Tyre.
6 Pass over to Tarshish,*
wail, you who dwell on the coast!
7 Is this your exultant city,
whose origin is from old,
Whose feet have taken her
to dwell in distant lands?
8 Who has planned such a thing
against Tyre, the bestower of
crowns,
Whose merchants are princes,
whose traders are the earth's honored
men?
9 The LORD of hosts has planned it,
to disgrace the height of all beauty,
to degrade all the honored of the
earth.[k]
10 Cross to your own land,
ship of Tarshish;
the harbor is no more.
11 His hand he stretches out over the sea,
he shakes kingdoms;
The LORD commanded the destruction
of Canaan's strongholds:* [l]
12 Crushed, you shall exult no more,
virgin daughter Sidon.
Arise, pass over to the Kittim,
even there you shall find no rest.[m]
13 * Look at the land of the Chaldeans,
the people that has ceased to be.
Assyria founded it for ships,
raised its towers,
Only to tear down its palaces,
and turn it into a ruin.[n]
14 Lament, ships of Tarshish,
for your stronghold is destroyed.

15 On that day, Tyre shall be forgotten for seventy years,* the lifetime of one king. At the end of seventy years, the song about the prostitute will be Tyre's song:

16 Take a harp, go about the city,
forgotten prostitute;
Pluck the strings skillfully, sing many
songs,
that you may be remembered.

17 At the end of the seventy years the LORD shall visit Tyre. She shall return to her hire and serve as prostitute* with all the world's kingdoms on the face of the earth.[o]
18 But her merchandise and her hire shall be sacred to the LORD. It shall not be stored up or laid away; instead, her merchandise shall belong to those who dwell before the LORD, to eat their fill and clothe themselves in choice attire.

the term for the well-known city of Cyprus, Kition. In later centuries the term Kittim is used for the Greeks, the Romans, and other distant peoples.

**23:3 Shihor**: a synonym for the Nile.

**23:4 The sea**: here personified, it brings to distant coasts the news that Sidon must disown her children; her people are dispersed.

**23:6–7 Tarshish**: perhaps Tartessus in Spain. **Distant lands**: the reference is to the far-flung colonies established by the Phoenicians throughout the Mediterranean, including North Africa, Spain, and Sardinia. Oceangoing vessels were therefore called Tarshish ships.

**23:11 Canaan's strongholds**: the fortresses of Phoenicia.

**23:13** The reference here seems to be to Assyria's subjugation of Babylon in 703 B.C., which left the coastal cities of Phoenicia as well as Judah open to Sennacherib's invasion in 701 B.C. **Founded it . . . its palaces . . . turn it**: the city of Babylon.

**23:15 Seventy years**: a conventional expression for a long period of time; cf. Jer 25:11 and 29:10.

**23:17–18 Her hire . . . prostitute**: the international trade engaged in by Tyre will become a source of wealth to God's people (cf. 45:14; 60:4–14; Zec 14:14).

*i:* Jer 25:22; Ez 26; Am 1:9; Zec 9:2, 4. *j:* Ez 27:3. *k:* Is 14:24–27; 22:11; Ez 28:7. *l:* Is 14:27; Ps 65:8. *m:* Ez 28:21–22. *n:* Is 13:21; 34:14; Jer 50:39. *o:* Rev 17:5; 18:3, 11, 13.

## D. Apocalypse of Isaiah*

### CHAPTER 24

See RG 209

### *Judgment upon the World and the Lord's Enthronement on Mount Zion**

1 See! The LORD is about to empty the
earth and lay it waste;
he will twist its surface,
and scatter its inhabitants:[p]
2 People and priest shall fare alike:
servant and master,
Maid and mistress,
buyer and seller,
Lender and borrower,
creditor and debtor.[q]
3 The earth shall be utterly laid waste,
utterly stripped,
for the LORD has decreed this word.
4 The earth mourns and fades,
the world languishes and fades;
both heaven and earth languish.[r]
5 The earth is polluted because of its
inhabitants,
for they have transgressed laws,
violated statutes,
broken the ancient covenant.*[s]
6 Therefore a curse devours the earth,
and its inhabitants pay for their guilt;
Therefore they who dwell on earth have
dwindled,
and only a few are left.[t]
7 The new wine mourns, the vine
languishes,
all the merry-hearted groan.[u]
8 Stilled are the cheerful timbrels,
ended the shouts of the jubilant,
stilled the cheerful harp.[v]
9 They no longer drink wine and sing;
strong brew is bitter to those who
drink it.[w]
10 Broken down is the city of chaos,*
every house is shut against entry.[x]
11 In the streets they cry out for lack of wine;
all joy has grown dim,
cheer is exiled from the land.[y]
12 In the city nothing remains but desolation,
gates battered into ruins.
13 For thus it shall be in the midst of the
earth,
among the peoples,
As when an olive tree has been beaten,
as with a gleaning when the vintage is
done.[z]
14 These* shall lift up their voice,
they shall sing for joy in the majesty of
the LORD,
they shall shout from the western sea:
15 "Therefore, in the east
give glory to the LORD!
In the coastlands of the sea,
to the name of the LORD, the God of
Israel!"[a]
16 From the end of the earth we hear songs:
"Splendor to the Just One!"
But I said, "I am wasted, wasted away.
Woe is me! The traitors betray;
with treachery have the traitors
betrayed![b]
17 Terror, pit, and trap
for you, inhabitant of the earth![c]
18 One who flees at the sound of terror
will fall into the pit;
One who climbs out of the pit
will be caught in the trap.

**24:1–27:13** Although it has become traditional to call these chapters "Apocalypse of Isaiah," and although they do contain some apocalyptic traits, many others are lacking, so that the title is imprecise as a designation. These chapters are not a unified composition and their growth into their present form was a long, complicated process. They echo many themes from chaps. 13–23, "Oracles Against the Foreign Nations," as well as from earlier parts of Isaiah (e.g., the reversal of the "vineyard song," 5:1–7, in 27:2–5). Of particular interest is an unnamed city (24:10–13; 25:2; 26:5–6; 27:10–11), a wicked city, doomed to destruction; to the extent that it is identifiable, it may be Babylon, but more generally it symbolizes all forces hostile to God. And it stands in contrast to another city, also unnamed but no doubt to be identified with Jerusalem (26:1–2).

**24:1–23** The world is about to be shaken by a devastating judgment that will overthrow both the human and divine enemies of the Lord, who will then reign in glory over his people on Mount Zion.

**24:5 Ancient covenant**: God's commandments to all humankind (cf. Gn 9:4–6).

**24:10 City of chaos**: a godless city which appears several times in chaps. 24–27; see note on 24:1–27:13.

**24:14 These**: the saved.

*p:* Is 13:9; Na 2:3, 11. *q:* Hos 4:9. *r:* Is 33:9. *s:* Nm 35:33; Hos 4:2–3. *t:* Lv 26:15–16. *u:* Jl 1:10–12. *v:* Jer 7:34; Hos 2:13. *w:* Am 6:5–7. *x:* Is 25:2. *y:* Jer 48:33; Lam 5:14–15. *z:* Is 17:6; Mi 7:1. *a:* Is 42:10, 12; Zep 2:11. *b:* Is 21:2; 33:1. *c:* Jer 48:43.

**The Banquet of the LORD of Hosts**

THE GREAT FESTIVAL to be celebrated in Jerusalem on the holy mountain (ch 25) gives pictorial expression to the praise of God (vv. 1–5). Even in the most violent trouble, God is a refuge to the needy in distress (v. 4). The prophetic vision, however, recognizes that there are wrongs and sufferings on earth that cannot be put right by stilling the blast of the ruthless. The ultimate resolution of injustice can come only when God overcomes the power of death itself (vv. 7–8a; cf Is 26:19).

For the windows on high are open
and the foundations of the earth shake.[d]
19 The earth will burst asunder,
the earth will be shaken apart,
the earth will be convulsed.
20 The earth will reel like a drunkard,
sway like a hut;
Its rebellion will weigh it down;
it will fall, never to rise again."[e]
21 On that day the LORD will punish
the host of the heavens* in the heavens,
and the kings of the earth on the earth.
22 They will be gathered together
like prisoners into a pit;
They will be shut up in a dungeon,
and after many days they will be
punished.[f]
23 Then the moon will blush
and the sun be ashamed,[g]
For the LORD of hosts will reign
on Mount Zion and in Jerusalem,
glorious in the sight of the elders.* [h]

## CHAPTER 25

See RG 209

### *Praise for God's Deliverance and the Celebration in Zion**

1 O LORD, you are my God,
I extol you, I praise your name;
For you have carried out your wonderful
plans of old,
faithful and true.[i]
2 For you have made the city a heap,
the fortified city a ruin,
The castle of the insolent, a city no more,
not ever to be rebuilt.[j]
3 Therefore a strong people will honor
you,
ruthless nations will fear you.
4 For you have been a refuge to the poor,
a refuge to the needy in their distress;
Shelter from the rain,
shade from the heat.[k]
When the blast of the ruthless was like a
winter rain,
5 the roar of strangers like heat in the
desert,
You subdued the heat with the shade of a
cloud,
the rain of the tyrants was vanquished.
6 On this mountain* the LORD of hosts
will provide for all peoples
A feast of rich food and choice wines,
juicy, rich food and pure, choice wines.
7 On this mountain he will destroy
the veil that veils all peoples,
The web that is woven over all nations.
8 He will destroy death forever.
The Lord GOD will wipe away
the tears from all faces;
The reproach of his people he will remove
from the whole earth; for the LORD has
spoken.[l]
9 On that day it will be said:
"Indeed, this is our God; we looked to
him, and he saved us!
This is the LORD to whom we looked;
let us rejoice and be glad that he has
saved us!"[m]

**24:21 Host of the heavens**: the stars, which were often regarded as gods; cf. Dt 4:19; Jer 8:2.

**24:23 The elders**: the tradition in Ex 24:9–11 suggests that this refers to the people of God who are to share in the banquet on Mount Zion (Is 25:6–8).

**25:1–9** These verses praise God for carrying out his plan to destroy the enemy and to save the poor of his people in Zion (14:32), and they announce the victory banquet to be celebrated in the Lord's city.

**25:6 This mountain**: i.e., Jerusalem's mountain, Zion.

*d:* Gn 7:11; Am 5:19. *e:* Am 5:2. *f:* 2 Pt 2:4; Jude 6. *g:* Is 13:10; Jl 3:3–4; 4:15. *h:* Is 4:5; 60:1–3; Ex 24:9–11; Mi 4:7; Rev 19:4–6. *i:* Is 12:1, 4; 22:11; 28:29; 37:26. *j:* Is 17:1; Jer 51:37. *k:* Is 14:32; 32:2; Na 1:7. *l:* Is 60:1, 3; 1 Cor 15:53–55; Rev 7:17; 21:4. *m:* Is 30:18–19.

*Judgment on Moab**

10 For the hand of the LORD will rest on this
mountain,
but Moab will be trodden down
as straw is trodden down in the mire.[n]
11 He will spread out his hands in its midst,
as a swimmer spreads out his hands to
swim;
His pride will be brought low
despite his strokes.[o]
12 The high-walled fortress he will raze,
bringing it low, leveling it to the
ground, to the very dust.[p]

See RG 209

CHAPTER 26

*Judah's Praise and Prayer for Deliverance.** 1 On that day this song shall be sung in the land of Judah:

"A strong city* have we;
he sets up victory as our walls and
ramparts.[q]
2 Open up the gates
that a righteous nation may enter,
one that keeps faith.[r]
3 With firm purpose you maintain peace;
in peace, because of our trust in you."[s]
4 Trust in the LORD forever!
For the LORD is an eternal Rock.[t]
5 He humbles those who dwell on high,
the lofty city he brings down,
Brings it down to the ground,
levels it to the dust.[u]
6 The feet of the needy trample on it—
the feet of the poor.
7 The way of the just is smooth;
the path of the just you make level.[v]
8 The course of your judgments, LORD, we
await;
your name and your memory are the
desire of our souls.
9 My soul yearns for you at night,
yes, my spirit within me seeks you at
dawn;
When your judgment comes upon the
earth,
the world's inhabitants learn justice.[w]
10 The wicked, when spared, do not learn
justice;
in an upright land they act
perversely,
and do not see the majesty of the
LORD.[x]
11 LORD, your hand is raised high,
but they do not perceive it;
Let them be put to shame when they see
your zeal for your people:
let the fire prepared for your enemies
consume them.[y]
12 LORD, you will decree peace for us,
for you have accomplished all we have
done.[z]
13 LORD, our God, lords other than you
have ruled us;
only because of you can we call upon
your name.
14 Dead they are, they cannot live,
shades that cannot rise;
Indeed, you have punished and destroyed
them,
and wiped out all memory of them.
15 You have increased the nation, LORD,
you have increased the nation, have
added to your glory,
you have extended far all the
boundaries of the land.[a]
16 LORD, oppressed by your punishment,
we cried out in anguish under your
discipline.[b]
17 As a woman about to give birth
writhes and cries out in pain,
so were we before you, LORD.[c]
18 We conceived and writhed in pain,
giving birth only to wind;
Salvation we have not achieved for the
earth,
no inhabitants for the world were
born.[d]

**25:10–12 Moab**: one of Israel's bitterest enemies.

**26:1–19** This text is a mixture of praise for the salvation that will take place, a confession of Judah's inability to achieve deliverance on its own, and earnest prayer that God may quickly bring about the longed-for salvation.

**26:1 Strong city**: Jerusalem, the antithesis of the "city of chaos" (24:10); see note on 24:1–27:13.

*n:* Zep 2:9–10. *o:* Is 16:6–7, 14. *p:* Is 26:5. *q:* Is 60:18. *r:* Ps 118:19–20. *s:* Is 32:17–18; Ps 112:7. *t:* Is 17:10; 30:29; Ps 62:8. *u:* Is 25:11–12; 32:19. *v:* Ps 23:3–4; Prv 11:3, 5. *w:* Ps 63:2. *x:* Is 5:12; Eccl 8:11. *y:* Is 9:6; 30:27; 37:32. *z:* Jer 29:11; Phil 2:13. *a:* Is 54:2–3. *b:* Hos 5:15. *c:* Mi 4:10. *d:* Is 37:3.

19 * But your dead shall live, their corpses
shall rise!
Awake and sing, you who lie in the
dust!
For your dew is a dew of light,
and you cause the land of shades to
give birth.[e]

*The Lord's Response**

20 Go, my people, enter your chambers,
and close the doors behind you;
Hide yourselves for a brief moment,
until the wrath is past.[f]
21 See, the LORD goes forth from his place,
to punish the wickedness of the earth's
inhabitants;
The earth will reveal the blood shed
upon it,
and no longer conceal the slain.[g]

## CHAPTER 27

See RG 209

### *The Judgment and Deliverance of Israel*

1 On that day,
The LORD will punish with his sword
that is cruel, great, and strong,
Leviathan the fleeing serpent,
Leviathan the coiled serpent;
he will slay the dragon* in the sea.[h]

2 * On that day—
The pleasant vineyard, sing about it![i]
3 I, the LORD, am its keeper,
I water it every moment;
Lest anyone harm it,
night and day I guard it.[j]
4 I am not angry.
But if I were to find briers and thorns,
In battle I would march against it;
I would burn it all.[k]
5 But if it holds fast to my refuge,
it shall have peace with me;[l]
it shall have peace with me.

6 In days to come Jacob shall take root,
Israel shall sprout and blossom,
covering all the world with fruit.[m]
7 * Was he smitten as his smiter was
smitten?
Was he slain as his slayer was slain?
8 Driving out and expelling, he struggled
against it,
carrying it off with his cruel wind on a
day of storm.[n]
9 This, then, shall be the expiation of
Jacob's guilt,
this the result of removing his sin:
He shall pulverize all the stones of the
altars
like pieces of chalk;
no asherahs or incense altars shall stand.
10 For the fortified city shall be desolate,
an abandoned pasture, a forsaken
wilderness;
There calves shall graze, there they shall
lie down,
and consume its branches.
11 When its boughs wither, they shall be
broken off;
and women shall come to kindle fires
with them.
For this is not an understanding people;
therefore their maker shall not spare
them;
their creator shall not be gracious to
them.[o]

**26:19** This verse refers not to resurrection of the dead, but to the restoration of the people; cf. Ez 37. The population of Judah was radically reduced by the slaughter and deportations that the historical disasters of the late eighth and seventh centuries B.C. brought upon the country. In this context, a major concern for the future was for an increase in the population, a rebirth of the nation's life.

**26:20–21** The time of wrath for Judah would soon be over, and the just punishment of its enemies would begin (cf. Hb 2:1–3).

**27:1 Leviathan . . . dragon**: the description of Leviathan is almost identical to a passage from a much earlier Ugaritic text. The sea dragon became a symbol of the forces of evil which God vanquishes even as he overcame primeval chaos; cf. notes on 30:7; 51:9–10; Jb 3:8; 7:12; no power can challenge God. Leviathan is even spoken of playfully in Ps 104:26.

**27:2–5** This passage mitigates the harsh words on Israel as the Lord's vineyard in 5:1–7; here is given the rain there withheld, though Israel's welfare is still made dependent on fidelity.

**27:7–9** Israel was not treated as sternly as were its enemies whom God used to punish it. God did, however, drive Israel from its land, and if it wants to make peace with God, it must change its former cultic practices, destroying its altars and sacred groves (cf. 17:7–11).

*e:* Ez 37:5–14; Dn 12:2; Hos 6:2. *f:* Is 10:25. *g:* Gn 4:10; Jb 16:18; Ps 106:38; Mi 1:3. *h:* Jb 40:25–32; Ps 74:12–14; Ez 32:2. *i:* Is 5:1; Am 5:11. *j:* Is 5:2–7. *k:* Is 10:17. *l:* Jb 22:21. *m:* Is 37:31–32; Hos 14:5–6. *n:* Jer 18:17. *o:* Is 1:3; 5:13; Jer 4:22.

12 On that day,
The LORD shall beat out grain
from the channel of the Euphrates to
the Wadi of Egypt,
and you shall be gleaned* one by one,
children of Israel.
13 On that day,*
A great trumpet shall blow,
and the lost in the land of Assyria
and the outcasts in the land of Egypt
Shall come and worship the LORD
on the holy mountain, in Jerusalem.[p]

## E. The Lord Alone, Israel's and Judah's Salvation

### CHAPTER 28

See RG 209

*The Fate of Samaria**

1 Ah! majestic garland
of the drunkards of Ephraim,*
Fading blooms of his glorious beauty,
at the head of the fertile valley,
upon those stupefied with wine.[q]
2 See, the LORD has a strong one, a mighty
one,*
who, like an onslaught of hail, a
destructive storm,
Like a flood of water, great and
overflowing,
levels to the ground with violence;[r]
3 With feet that will trample
the majestic garland of the drunkards
of Ephraim.
4 The fading blooms of his glorious beauty
at the head of the fertile valley
Will be like an early fig before summer:
whoever sees it,
swallows it as soon as it is in hand.[s]
5 On that day the LORD of hosts
will be a glorious crown
And a brilliant diadem
for the remnant of his people,
6 A spirit of judgment
for the one who sits in judgment,
And strength for those
who turn back the battle at the gate.

*Against Judah*

7 But these also stagger from wine
and stumble from strong drink:
Priest and prophet stagger from strong
drink,
overpowered by wine;
They are confused by strong drink,
they stagger in their visions,
they totter when giving judgment.[t]
8 Yes, all the tables
are covered with vomit,
with filth, and no place left clean.
9 * "To whom would he impart knowledge?
To whom would he convey the message?
To those just weaned from milk,
those weaned from the breast?
10 For he says,
'Command on command, command on
command,
rule on rule, rule on rule,
here a little, there a little!' "
11 * Yes, with stammering lips and in a
strange language
he will speak to this people,[u]
12 to whom he said:
"This is the resting place,

**27:12 Gleaned**: God will harvest his people who have been scattered from Assyria to Egypt. Note the same language of gleaning to describe the remnant of the Northern Kingdom in 17:5–6.

**27:13** The remnant of Israel will return to Jerusalem for worship; cf. 11:10–16.

**28:1–6** These verses once constituted an independent oracle against the Northern Kingdom, probably originally spoken during the time between its overthrow by Assyria in 732 and its destruction in 722/721. Isaiah has reused them as an introduction to his oracle against Judah (vv. 7–22), because the leaders of Judah were guilty of the same excesses that had once marked Ephraim's leadership.

**28:1 Ephraim**: the Northern Kingdom. Its capital, Samaria, was built upon a hill, suggestive of a majestic garland adorning a human head. The characterization of the leadership of Ephraim as drunken underscores its inattention to justice and good government (cf. 5:11–13; Am 6:1–6).

**28:2 A strong one, a mighty one**: Assyria (cf. 8:7–8).

**28:9–10** The words of those who ridicule Isaiah. The Hebrew of v. 10, by its very sound, conveys the idea of mocking imitation of what the prophet says, as though he spoke like a stammering child: "sau lasau, sau lasau, kau lakau, kau lakau, ze'er sham, ze'er sham." But in v. 13 God repeats these words in deadly earnest, putting them in the mouth of the victorious Assyrian army.

**28:11** God will answer the mockers and defend Isaiah. **Strange language**: spoken by the invading army.

*p:* Is 11:11–16. *q:* Hos 7:5; Am 6:1–6. *r:* Is 25:4–5; 28:17–18; 30:30. *s:* Is 17:6; Na 3:12. *t:* Is 5:11–12; Mi 2:11. *u:* Jer 5:15; 1 Cor 14:21; Dt 28:49; Bar 4:15.

give rest to the weary;
And this is the place of repose"—
but they refused to hear.[v]
13 So for them the word of the LORD shall be:
"Command on command, command
on command,
Rule on rule, rule on rule,
here a little, there a little!"
So that when they walk, they shall
stumble backward,
broken, ensnared, and captured.[w]
14 Therefore, hear the word of the LORD,
you scoffers,
who rule* this people in Jerusalem:[x]
15 You have declared, "We have made a
covenant with death,
with Sheol* we have made a pact;
When the raging flood passes through,
it will not reach us;
For we have made lies our refuge,
and in falsehood we have found a
hiding place,"—[y]
16 Therefore, thus says the Lord GOD:
See, I am laying a stone in Zion,*
a stone that has been tested,
A precious cornerstone as a sure
foundation;
whoever puts faith in it will not waver.[z]
17 I will make judgment a measuring line,
and justice a level.—*
Hail shall sweep away the refuge of lies,
and waters shall flood the hiding place.
18 Your covenant with death shall be
canceled
and your pact with Sheol shall not stand.
When the raging flood passes through,
you shall be beaten down by it.[a]
19 Whenever it passes, it shall seize you;
morning after morning it shall pass,
by day and by night.
Sheer terror
to impart the message!
20 For the bed shall be too short to stretch
out in,
and the cover too narrow to wrap in.
21 For the LORD shall rise up as on Mount
Perazim,
bestir himself as in the Valley of
Gibeon,*
To carry out his work—strange his work!
to perform his deed—alien his deed!
22 Now, cease scoffing,
lest your bonds be tightened,
For I have heard a decree of destruction
from the Lord, the GOD of hosts,
for the whole land.[b]

### *The Parable of the Farmer*

23 * Give ear and hear my voice,
pay attention and hear my word:
24 Is the plowman forever plowing in order
to sow,
always loosening and harrowing the
field?
25 When he has leveled the surface,
does he not scatter caraway and sow
cumin,*
Put in wheat and barley,

**28:14 Who rule**: there is a play on words; the same expression could also mean, "Proverb makers," that is, scoffers of this people.

**28:15, 18 A covenant with death, with Sheol**: an alliance with foreign powers, such as Egypt and Babylon. **Have made lies ... a hiding place**: this confidence in human aid will prove to be false and deceitful, incapable of averting the dreaded disaster. **Raging flood**: the Assyrian invasion; cf. 8:7–8.

**28:16 A stone in Zion**: the true and sure foundation of salvation, i.e., the presence of God, who had chosen and founded Zion as his city (Ps 78:68–69; Is 14:32) and had chosen the Davidic dynasty to rule over his people (Ps 78:70–72; Is 9:1–6; 11:1–10). **Cornerstone**: the assurance of salvation, rejected by the people of Judah in the prophet's time, is picked up in Ps 118:22 and later applied to Christ; cf. Mt 21:42; Lk 20:17; Acts 4:11; Rom 9:33; 1 Pt 2:7. Chapters 28–31 alternate between threats of the danger of rebelling against Assyria (with implied trust in Egypt) with assurances of the power and protection of the Lord.

**28:17 Line ... level**: instruments used in constructing a building, to keep it true. They are used metaphorically here to refer to the qualities that Zion, the city of God, must manifest, judgment and justice, not bloodshed (Mi 3:10), nor deceit and violence, which would result in a bulging unstable wall doomed to destruction (Is 30:12–14). Cf. 1 Cor 3:10–17.

**28:21 Mount Perazim ... Valley of Gibeon**: where David defeated the Philistines; cf. 2 Sm 5:20, 25; 1 Chr 14:11, 16. God's new work will be strange, because instead of fighting for Judah as the Lord did in David's time, God will now fight against Jerusalem (see 29:1–4).

**28:23–29** The practical variation of the farmer's work reflects the way God deals with his people, wisely adapted to circumstances; he does not altogether crush them in their weakness.

**28:25 Caraway ... cumin**: herbs used in seasoning food. **Spelt**: a variety of wheat.

*v:* Is 30:9. *w:* Is 8:15. *x:* Is 3:1–4; 5:18–21. *y:* Wis 1:16; Jer 5:12. *z:* Ps 118:22; Mt 21:42; Acts 4:11; Rom 9:33; 1 Pt 2:6. *a:* Is 28:2–3. *b:* Is 5:18–19; 10:23.

**The Lesson of the Farmer's Year**

ONE OF THE most instructive prophetic parables of the Hebrew Scriptures appears in 28:23–29. The variety of activities that make up the farmer's year illustrates the force of vv. 21–22. To the question, "Would not destroying the city where the temple stands be a strange work for God the protector?" the prophet's answer is that, like the farmer, God has many varied tasks to perform—and judging a rebellious people is one of them.

with spelt as its border?
26 His God has taught him this rule,
he has instructed him.
27 For caraway is not threshed with a sledge,
nor does a cartwheel roll over cumin.
But caraway is beaten out with a staff,
and cumin with a rod.
28 Grain is crushed for bread, but not forever;
though he thresh it thoroughly,
and drive his cartwheel and horses
over it,
he does not pulverize it.
29 This too comes from the LORD of hosts;
wonderful is his counsel and great his
wisdom.[c]

See RG 209

## CHAPTER 29

### *Judgment and Deliverance of Jerusalem*

1 Ah! Ariel, Ariel,*
city where David encamped!
Let year follow year,
and feast follow feast,[d]
2 But I will bring distress upon Ariel,
and there will be mourning and
moaning.
You shall be to me like Ariel:[e]
3 I will encamp like David against you;
I will circle you with outposts
and set up siege works against you.[f]
4 You shall speak from beneath the earth,
and from the dust below, your words
shall come.
Your voice shall be that of a ghost from
the earth,
and your words shall whisper from the
dust.[g]
5 The horde of your arrogant shall be like
fine dust,
a horde of tyrants like flying chaff.[h]
Then suddenly, in an instant,
6 you shall be visited by the LORD of
hosts,
With thunder, earthquake, and great
noise,
whirlwind, storm, and the flame of
consuming fire.[i]
7 * Then like a dream,
a vision of the night,
Shall be the horde of all the nations
who make war against Ariel:
All the outposts, the siege works against it,
all who distress it.
8 As when a hungry man dreams he is eating
and awakens with an empty stomach,
Or when a thirsty man dreams he is
drinking
and awakens faint, his throat parched,
So shall the horde of all the nations be,
who make war against Mount Zion.

### *Blindness and Perversity*

9 * Stupefy yourselves and stay stupid;
blind yourselves and stay blind!
You who are drunk, but not from wine,
who stagger, but not from strong drink![j]

**29:1–2 Ariel**: a poetic name for Jerusalem. It has been variously interpreted to mean "lion of God," "altar hearth of God" (Ez 43:15–16), "city of God," or "foundation of God." In v. 2 the term refers to "altar hearth," i.e., a place of burning for its people (cf. 30:33; 31:9). God will attack Jerusalem, as David did long ago.

**29:7–8** Just when the attackers think their capture of Jerusalem is certain, the Lord will snatch victory from their hands and save the city. The sudden shift from the Lord's attack on the city to its deliverance by him is surprising and unexplained; it may reflect the account related in 37:36.

**29:9–16** Despite their show of piety, Judah's leaders refused to accept the prophet's words of assurance. They rejected prophetic advice (cf. 30:10–11), did not consult the prophetic oracle in forming their political plans (30:1–2; 31:1), and tried to hide their plans even from God's prophet

*c:* Rom 11:33. *d:* 2 Sm 5:6–9. *e:* Is 33:7. *f:* 2 Kgs 25:1; Ez 4:2. *g:* Is 8:19; 1 Sm 28:14. *h:* Is 17:13; Ps 18:43; Jb 21:18. *i:* Is 30:27, 30. *j:* Is 19:14; 28:7–8.

10 For the LORD has poured out on you
a spirit of deep sleep.
He has shut your eyes (the prophets)
and covered your heads (the seers).* [k]

11 For you the vision of all this has become
like the words of a sealed scroll. When it is
handed to one who can read, with the request,
"Read this," the reply is, "I cannot, because it
is sealed." 12 When the scroll is handed to one
who cannot read, with the request, "Read
this," the reply is, "I cannot read."

13 The Lord said:
Since this people draws near with words
only
and honors me with their lips alone,
though their hearts are far from me,
And fear of me has become
mere precept of human teaching,[l]
14 Therefore I will again deal with this people
in surprising and wondrous fashion:
The wisdom of the wise shall perish,
the prudence of the prudent shall
vanish.[m]
15 Ah! You who would hide a plan
too deep for the LORD!
Who work in the dark, saying,
"Who sees us, who knows us?"[n]
16 Your perversity is as though the potter
were taken to be the clay:
As though what is made should say of its
maker,
"He did not make me!"
Or the vessel should say of the potter,
"He does not understand."[o]

### *Redemption**

17 Surely, in a very little while,
Lebanon shall be changed into an
orchard,
and the orchard be considered a forest![p]
18 On that day the deaf shall hear
the words of a scroll;
And out of gloom and darkness,
the eyes of the blind shall see.[q]
19 The lowly shall again find joy in the LORD,
the poorest rejoice in the Holy One of
Israel.[r]
20 For the tyrant shall be no more,
the scoffer shall cease to be;
All who are ready for evil shall be cut off,[s]
21 those who condemn with a mere word,
Who ensnare the defender at the gate,
and leave the just with an empty
claim.[t]
22 Therefore thus says the LORD,
the God of the house of Jacob,
who redeemed Abraham:*
No longer shall Jacob be ashamed,
no longer shall his face grow pale.[u]
23 For when his children see
the work of my hands in his midst,
They shall sanctify my name;
they shall sanctify the Holy One of
Jacob,
be in awe of the God of Israel.[v]
24 Those who err in spirit shall acquire
understanding,
those who find fault shall receive
instruction.

## CHAPTER 30

See RG 209

### *Oracle on the Futility of an Alliance with Egypt**

1 Ah! Rebellious children,
oracle of the LORD,
Who carry out a plan that is not mine,
who make an alliance* I did not inspire,
thus adding sin upon sin;[w]
2 They go down to Egypt,

(v. 15), who, they thought, simply did not understand military and political reality.

**29:10 Prophets . . . seers**: interpretive glosses.

**29:17–24** The prophet presents the positive aspects of God's plan in terms of a series of reversals: an end to pride, ignorance, and injustice. Cf. 32:3–5.

**29:22 Who redeemed Abraham**: perhaps by revealing himself and delivering Abraham from idolatrous worship; cf. Gn 12:1–3; 17:1; Jos 24:2–3.

**30:1–17** Several independent oracles against making an alliance with Egypt have been strung together in this chapter: vv. 1–5, vv. 6–7, and vv. 8–17. That these were originally separate oracles is indicated by the fact that the oracle in vv. 6–7 is still introduced by its own heading: Oracle on the Beasts of the Negeb.

**30:1 Make an alliance**: lit., "pour out a libation," namely, as part of the ritual of treaty making.

*k:* Is 6:10; Rom 11:8. *l:* Ez 33:31; Mt 15:8–9; Mk 7:6–7. *m:* Jer 49:7; 1 Cor 1:19. *n:* Is 30:1–2; 31:1; Ez 8:12; Jn 3:19–20. *o:* Is 45:9; Jer 18:6; Rom 9:20. *p:* Is 32:15. *q:* Is 35:5; 42:6–7. *r:* Is 61:1–2. *s:* Is 28:22. *t:* Is 5:23; 10:1–2; Am 5:10, 12. *u:* Is 45:17. *v:* Is 8:12–13. *w:* Is 1:4; 5:21; 28:15; 29:15.

without asking my counsel,*
To seek strength in Pharaoh's protection
and take refuge in Egypt's shadow.[x]
3 Pharaoh's protection shall become your
shame,
refuge in Egypt's shadow your
disgrace.[y]
4 When his princes are at Zoan
and his messengers reach Hanes,[z]
5 All shall be ashamed
of a people that gain them nothing,
Neither help nor benefit,
but only shame and reproach.[a]
6 Oracle on the Beasts of the Negeb.
Through the distressed and troubled
land*
of the lioness and roaring lion,
of the viper and flying saraph,
They carry their riches on the backs of
donkeys
and their treasures on the humps of
camels
To a people good for nothing,
7 to Egypt whose help is futile and vain.
Therefore I call her
"Rahab* Sit-still."
8 * Now come, write it on a tablet they can
keep,
inscribe it on a scroll;
That in time to come it may be
an eternal witness.[b]
9 For this is a rebellious people,
deceitful children,
Children who refuse
to listen to the instruction of the LORD;[c]
10 Who say to the seers, "Do not see";
to the prophets,* "Do not prophesy
truth for us;
speak smooth things to us, see visions
that deceive![d]
11 Turn aside from the way! Get out of the
path!
Let us hear no more
of the Holy One of Israel!"[e]
12 Therefore, thus says the Holy One of
Israel:
Because you reject this word,
And put your trust in oppression and
deceit,
and depend on them,[f]
13 This iniquity of yours shall be
like a descending rift
Bulging out in a high wall
whose crash comes suddenly, in an
instant,[g]
14 Crashing like a potter's jar
smashed beyond rescue,
And among its fragments cannot be found
a sherd to scoop fire from the hearth
or dip water from the cistern.[h]
15 For thus said the Lord GOD,
the Holy One of Israel:
By waiting and by calm you shall be
saved,
in quiet and in trust shall be your
strength.
But this you did not will.[i]
16 "No," you said,
"Upon horses we will flee."
Very well, you shall flee!
"Upon swift steeds we will ride."
Very well, swift shall be your
pursuers![j]
17 A thousand shall tremble at the threat of
one—
if five threaten, you shall flee.

**30:2 Without asking my counsel**: it was a practice to consult God through the prophets or through the priestly oracle before making a major political decision (1 Sm 23:1–12; 1 Kgs 22:5), but Judah's leadership, in its concern for security, was apparently trying to keep its plan for a treaty with Egypt secret even from the prophets, thus implicitly from God (29:15).

**30:6 Distressed . . . land**: the wilderness between Judah and Egypt, through which Judahite messengers had to pass, carrying their tribute to Egypt to buy assistance in the struggle against Assyria. **Flying saraph**: see notes on 6:2; 14:29.

**30:7** Here as elsewhere (cf. Ps 87:4) Egypt is compared to Rahab, the raging, destructive sea monster (cf. Is 51:9; Jb 26:12; Ps 89:11); yet Egypt, when asked for aid by Judah, becomes silent and "sits still."

**30:8** Isaiah will write down his condemnation of the foolish policy pursued so that the truth of his warning of its dire consequences (vv. 12–17) may afterward be recognized.

**30:10 Seers . . . prophets**: the two terms are synonyms for prophetic figures such as Isaiah (1:1; 2:1; 6:1, 5). There is wordplay between the nouns and their cognate verbs, both of which mean "to see." The authorities are depicted as forbidding prophets to contradict their secret political and military policies.

*x:* Is 31:1; 36:6. *y:* Is 20:5; Jer 2:36–37. *z:* Is 19:11. *a:* Is 36:6. *b:* Is 8:1, 16; Jer 36:2; Hb 2:2. *c:* Is 1:4; 28:12; Jer 7:28. *d:* Is 29:10; Jer 5:31; 11:21; Am 2:12. *e:* Jb 21:14–15. *f:* Is 28:15; Ps 62:11. *g:* Is 28:17; Ez 13:14. *h:* Jer 19:11. *i:* Is 7:4; 8:6; 28:12. *j:* Is 31:3.

EGYPT WAS FAMOUS for palaces and monuments, and as the gateway to Africa for the caravans that brought wealth and luxuries (see 1 Kgs 10). In Is 30:6–26, the prophet contrasts such exotic wealth with the worthlessness of the promises of Egyptian help. The description "crashing like a potter's jar" (v. 14) emphasizes the suddenness and completeness of the disaster that is to come. Hezekiah's attempt to build security through an alliance with Egypt will prove disastrously misjudged. The poetry of waiting, calm, quiet and trust (v. 15) attests that God alone is the defense of Jerusalem.

You will then be left like a flagstaff on a
mountaintop,
like a flag on a hill.[k]

### *Zion's Future Deliverance*

18 Truly, the LORD is waiting to be gracious
to you,
truly, he shall rise to show you mercy;
For the LORD is a God of justice:
happy are all who wait for him![l]
19 Yes, people of Zion, dwelling in
Jerusalem,
you shall no longer weep;
He will be most gracious to you when
you cry out;
as soon as he hears he will answer you.[m]
20 The Lord will give you bread in adversity
and water in affliction.
No longer will your Teacher* hide himself,
but with your own eyes you shall see
your Teacher,[n]
21 And your ears shall hear a word behind
you:
"This is the way; walk in it,"
when you would turn to the right or
the left.
22 You shall defile your silver-plated idols
and your gold-covered images;
You shall throw them away like filthy rags,
you shall say, "Get out!"[o]
23 He will give rain for the seed
you sow in the ground,
And the bread that the soil produces
will be rich and abundant.
On that day your cattle will graze
in broad meadows;[p]
24 The oxen and the donkeys that till the
ground
will eat silage tossed to them
with shovel and pitchfork.
25 Upon every high mountain and lofty hill
there will be streams of running water.
On the day of the great slaughter,
when the towers fall,
26 The light of the moon will be like the
light of the sun,
and the light of the sun will be seven
times greater,
like the light of seven days,
On the day the LORD binds up the
wounds of his people
and heals the bruises left by his blows.[q]

### *Divine Judgment on Assyria**

27 See, the name of the LORD is coming
from afar,
burning with anger, heavy with threat,
His lips filled with fury,
tongue like a consuming fire,[r]
28 Breath like an overflowing torrent
that reaches up to the neck!
He will winnow the nations with a
destructive winnowing
and bridle the jaws of the peoples to
send them astray.[s]
29 For you, there will be singing
as on a night when a feast is observed,
And joy of heart
as when one marches along with a flute
Going to the mountain of the LORD,

**30:20 Teacher**: God, who in the past made the people blind and deaf through the prophetic message (6:9–10) and who in his anger hid his face from the house of Jacob (8:17), shall in the future help them to understand his teaching clearly (cf. Jer 31:34).

**30:27–33** God's punishment of Assyria. **The name of the LORD**: here, God himself; cf. Ps 20:2.

*k:* Is 11:10; Dt 32:30. *l:* Ex 34:6; Ps 34:9; Jer 17:7. *m:* Is 25:8; 58:9; 65:24. *n:* Is 6:9–10; 8:17; 29:18. *o:* Is 2:20; 27:9; 31:7. *p:* Lv 26:3–5. *q:* Is 1:6; Jer 30:17; Hos 6:1. *r:* Is 10:17; 29:6. *s:* Is 8:7–8; 37:29.

to the Rock of Israel.
30 The LORD will make his glorious voice
heard,
and reveal his arm coming down
In raging fury and flame of consuming
fire,
in tempest, and rainstorm, and hail.[t]
31 For at the voice of the LORD, Assyria will
be shattered,
as he strikes with the rod;
32 And every sweep of the rod of his
punishment,
which the LORD will bring down on
him,
Will be accompanied by timbrels and
lyres,
while he wages war against him.[u]
33 For his tophet* has long been ready,
truly it is prepared for the king;
His firepit made both deep and wide,
with fire and firewood in abundance,
And the breath of the LORD, like a stream
of sulfur,
setting it afire.[v]

See RG 209

## CHAPTER 31

### *Against the Egyptian Alliance*

1 Ah! Those who go down to Egypt for
help,
who rely on horses;
Who put their trust in chariots because of
their number,
and in horsemen because of their
combined power,
But look not to the Holy One of Israel
nor seek the LORD!* [w]
2 Yet he too is wise and will bring disaster;
he will not turn from his threats.
He will rise up against the house of the
wicked
and against those who help
evildoers.[x]
3 The Egyptians are human beings, not
God,
their horses flesh, not spirit;
When the LORD stretches forth his hand,
the helper shall stumble, the one
helped shall fall,
and both of them shall perish together.[y]
4 For thus says the LORD to me:
As a lion or its young
growling over the prey,
With a band of shepherds
assembled against it,
Is neither dismayed by their shouts
nor cowed by their noise,
So shall the LORD of hosts come down
to wage war upon Mount Zion, upon
its height.[z]
5 Like hovering birds, so the LORD of
hosts
shall shield Jerusalem,
To shield and deliver,
to spare and rescue.[a]

6 Return, O Israelites, to him whom you
have utterly deserted.[b] 7 On that day each one
of you shall reject his idols of silver and
gold, which your hands have made.[c]

8 Assyria shall fall by a sword, not wielded
by human being,
no mortal sword shall devour him;
He shall flee before the sword,
and his young men shall be impressed
as laborers.[d]
9 He shall rush past his crag* in panic,
and his princes desert the standard in
terror,
Says the LORD who has a fire in Zion
and a furnace in Jerusalem.[e]

**30:33 Tophet**: a site, near Jerusalem, where children were sacrificed by fire to Molech (2 Kgs 23:10), and where, probably, Ahaz sacrificed his son (2 Kgs 16:3). Here, Isaiah speaks of "his tophet," the site prepared for burning up the king of Assyria. **King**: there seems to be a play on words between the Heb. word for king (*melek*) and the name Molech. This defeat of Assyria becomes the occasion for Israel's festal rejoicing (v. 32).

**31:1 Seek the LORD**: a technical expression for seeking a prophetic or priestly oracle, similar to the expression "asking my counsel" in 30:2. The prophet complains that Judah has decided on its policy of alliance with Egypt without first consulting the Lord.

**31:9 Crag**: the king as the rallying point of the princes. **Panic**: terror is an element of Israel's holy war tradition, in which defeat of the enemy is accomplished by the Lord rather than by human means (cf. v. 8).

*t:* Is 10:17; 28:2; 29:6. *u:* Is 10:24–26; 14:24–27. *v:* Gn 19:24; Ez 38:22. *w:* Is 5:12, 24; 18:2; 22:11; 29:15; 30:2; 36:6. *x:* Is 28:21. *y:* Ps 146:3–5. *z:* Hos 5:14; Am 1:2; 3:8, 12. *a:* Is 37:35; Dt 32:11; Ps 91:4. *b:* Is 1:2–4; Jer 3:12. *c:* Is 2:20; 30:22. *d:* Is 27:1; 34:5–6; 37:36. *e:* Is 30:17, 33.

See RG 209

## CHAPTER 32

### *The Kingdom of Justice*

1 See, a king will reign justly
and princes will rule rightly.[f]
2 Each of them will be like a shelter from the wind,
a refuge from the rain.
They will be like streams of water in a dry country,
like the shade of a great rock in a parched land.[g]
3 The eyes of those who see will not be closed;
the ears of those who hear will be attentive.[h]
4 The hasty of heart shall take thought to know,
and tongues of stutterers shall speak readily and clearly.
5 No more will the fool be called noble,
nor the deceiver be considered honorable.[i]
6 For the fool speaks folly,
his heart plans evil:
Godless actions,
perverse speech against the LORD,
Letting the hungry go empty
and the thirsty without drink.[j]
7 The deceits of the deceiver are evil,
he plans devious schemes:
To ruin the poor with lies,
and the needy when they plead their case.[k]
8 But the noble plan noble deeds,
and in noble deeds they persist.

### *The Women of Jerusalem*

9 You women so complacent, rise up and hear my voice,
daughters so confident, give heed to my words.[l]
10 In a little more than a year
your confidence will be shaken;
For the vintage will fail,
no fruit harvest will come in.[m]
11 Tremble, you who are so complacent!
Shudder, you who are so confident!
Strip yourselves bare,
with only a loincloth for cover.[n]
12 Beat your breasts
for the pleasant fields,
for the fruitful vine;[o]
13 For the soil of my people,
overgrown with thorns and briers;
For all the joyful houses,
the exultant city.[p]
14 The castle* will be forsaken,
the noisy city deserted;
Citadel and tower will become wasteland forever,
the joy of wild donkeys, the pasture of flocks;[q]
15 * Until the spirit from on high
is poured out on us.
And the wilderness becomes a garden land
and the garden land seems as common as forest.[r]
16 Then judgment will dwell in the wilderness
and justice abide in the garden land.
17 The work of justice will be peace;
the effect of justice, calm and security forever.[s]
18 My people will live in peaceful country,
in secure dwellings and quiet resting places.[t]
19 And the forest will come down completely,
the city will be utterly laid low.* [u]
20 Happy are you who sow beside every stream,
and let the ox and the donkey go freely![v]

**32:14 The castle**: the fortified royal palace in Jerusalem. **Citadel**: Ophel, the fortified hill, with its stronghold called "the great projecting tower" (Neh 3:27).

**32:15–18, 20** Extraordinary peace and prosperity will come to Israel under just rulers.

**32:19** Probably from a different context, perhaps after v. 14a.

*f:* Is 9:6; 11:4; 16:5; Ps 72:1–4; Jer 23:5–6. *g:* Is 4:6; 16:4; 25:4. *h:* Is 6:10; 29:18; 35:5. *i:* Is 5:20. *j:* Prv 15:2. *k:* Is 29:20–21; Mi 2:1. *l:* Is 3:16–24; Am 6:1. *m:* Zep 1:13. *n:* Is 20:2; Jer 4:8; Mi 1:8. *o:* Is 16:9. *p:* Is 5:6; 7:23–25; 22:2; 34:13. *q:* Is 7:25; 24:10–11. *r:* Is 44:3; Ps 104:30; Ez 37:9–10; Jl 3:1–2. *s:* Is 9:6; 30:15; 33:15–16; Ps 72:2–3, 7; Jas 3:18. *t:* Jer 23:6; Mi 4:4. *u:* Is 10:33–34; 26:5. *v:* Is 7:25; 30:18, 23.

See RG 209

## CHAPTER 33

### *Overthrow of Assyria**

1 Ah! You destroyer never destroyed,
betrayer never betrayed!
When you have finished destroying, you will be destroyed;
when you have stopped betraying, you will be betrayed.[w]
2 LORD, be gracious to us; for you we wait.
Be our strength every morning,
our salvation in time of trouble![x]
3 At the roaring sound, peoples flee;
when you rise in your majesty, nations are scattered.[y]
4 Spoil is gathered up as caterpillars gather,
an onrush like the rush of locusts.[z]
5 The LORD is exalted, enthroned on high;
he fills Zion with right and justice.[a]
6 That which makes her seasons certain,
her wealth, salvation, wisdom, and knowledge,
is the fear of the LORD, her treasure.[b]
7 See, the men of Ariel cry out in the streets,
the messengers of Shalem* weep bitterly.
8 The highways are desolate,
travelers have quit the paths,
Covenants are broken, witnesses spurned;
yet no one gives it a thought.[c]
9 The country languishes in mourning,
Lebanon withers with shame;
Sharon* is like the Arabah,
Bashan and Carmel are stripped bare.[d]
10 Now I will rise up, says the LORD,
now exalt myself,
now lift myself up.[e]
11 You conceive dry grass, bring forth stubble;
my spirit shall consume you like fire.
12 The peoples shall be burned to lime,
thorns cut down to burn in fire.[f]
13 Hear, you who are far off, what I have done;
you who are near, acknowledge my might.
14 In Zion sinners are in dread,
trembling grips the impious:
"Who of us can live with consuming fire?
who of us can live with everlasting flames?"[g]
15 Whoever walks righteously and speaks honestly,
who spurns what is gained by oppression,
Who waves off contact with a bribe,
who stops his ears so as not to hear of bloodshed,
who closes his eyes so as not to look on evil—[h]
16 That one shall dwell on the heights,
with fortresses of rock for stronghold,
food and drink in steady supply.
17 Your eyes will see a king* in his splendor,
they will look upon a vast land.[i]
18 Your mind will dwell on the terror:
"Where is the one who counted, where the one who weighed?
Where the one who counted the towers?"[j]
19 You shall no longer see a defiant people,
a people of speech too obscure to comprehend,
stammering in a tongue not understood.[k]
20 Look to Zion, the city of our festivals;
your eyes shall see Jerusalem
as a quiet abode, a tent not to be struck,
Whose pegs will never be pulled up,
nor any of its ropes severed.[l]
21 Indeed the LORD in majesty will be there for us

**33:1–24** After an introductory address to Assyria (v. 1), there follows a prayer on behalf of Jerusalem which recalls what God had done in the past (vv. 2–6) and a description of the present situation (vv. 7–9). In response, the Lord announces a judgment on Assyria (vv. 10–12) that will lead to the purification of Jerusalem's inhabitants (vv. 13–16). The text ends with an idealized portrait of the redeemed Jerusalem of the future (vv. 17–24).

**33:7 Ariel . . . Shalem**: Jerusalem; cf. 29:1; Gn 14:18; Ps 76:3. There is a play on words between "Shalem," the city name, and *shalom*, Heb. for "peace."

**33:9 Sharon**: the fertile plain near the Mediterranean.

**33:17 King**: either the ideal Davidic king or God; cf. v. 22.

*w:* Is 10:12; 16:4; 21:2; 24:16. *x:* Is 25:9; 30:18–19. *y:* Is 17:13; Nm 10:35; Ps 68:2. *z:* Is 9:2; 33:23. *a:* Is 1:26–27; 2:11, 17; 32:1; 33:16. *b:* Is 11:2; 13:22; 60:22. *c:* Is 24:5; Jgs 5:6. *d:* Na 1:4. *e:* Ps 12:6; Zep 3:8. *f:* Is 10:17. *g:* Is 30:27, 30, 32; 31:9. *h:* Ps 15:2–6; 24:4–5. *i:* Is 26:15. *j:* Ps 48:13–14. *k:* Is 28:11. *l:* Is 32:18; Ps 46:6; 122:1–4.

**Restoration of Zion**

THE CATASTROPHES THAT had befallen Jerusalem had cast doubt on the future of the Davidic kingship. The message of Is 11:1–5 reveals how eagerly the people awaited a descendant of Judah's royal dynasty, and this hope is repeated at the end of ch 33. Instead of the hated representatives of foreign domination—zealous only for plunder and gain (v. 18)—there would be a king upholding justice and building prosperity (v. 17).

a place of rivers and wide streams
on which no galley may go,
where no majestic ship* may pass.[m]
22 For the LORD is our judge,
the LORD is our lawgiver,
the LORD is our king;
he it is who will save us.
23 The rigging hangs slack;
it cannot hold the mast in place,
nor keep the sail spread out.
Then the blind will divide great spoils
and the lame will carry off the loot.[n]
24 No one who dwells there will say, "I am sick";
the people who live there will be forgiven their guilt.[o]

## F. The Lord, Zion's Avenger*

### CHAPTER 34

See RG 209

### *Judgment upon Edom*

1 Come near, nations, and listen;
be attentive, you peoples!
Let the earth and what fills it listen,
the world and all it produces.[p]
2 The LORD is angry with all the nations,
enraged against all their host;
He has placed them under the ban,
given them up to slaughter.[q]
3 Their slain shall be cast out,
their corpses shall send up a stench;
the mountains shall run with their blood,[r]
4 All the host of heaven shall rot;
the heavens shall be rolled up like a scroll.
All their host shall wither away,
as the leaf wilts on the vine,
or as the fig withers on the tree.[s]
5 When my sword has drunk its fill in the heavens,
it shall come down upon Edom for judgment,
upon a people under my ban.[t]
6 The LORD has a sword sated with blood,
greasy with fat,
With the blood of lambs and goats,
with the fat of rams' kidneys;
For the LORD has a sacrifice in Bozrah,
a great slaughter in the land of Edom.[u]
7 Wild oxen shall be struck down with fatlings,
and bullocks with bulls;
Their land shall be soaked with blood,
and their soil greasy with fat.
8 * For the LORD has a day of vengeance,
a year of requital for the cause of Zion.[v]
9 Edom's streams shall be changed into pitch,
its soil into sulfur,

**33:21–23 Galley . . . majestic ship**: of a foreign oppressor. Though the broad streams of the future Jerusalem will make it accessible by boat, no foreign invader will succeed in a naval attack on the city, for the Lord will protect it, the enemy fleet will be disabled, and even the weakest inhabitants will gather much plunder from the defeated enemy.

**34:1–35:10** These two chapters form a small collection which looks forward to the vindication of Zion, first by defeat of its enemies (chap. 34), then by its restoration (chap. 35). They are generally judged to be later than the time of Isaiah (eighth century), perhaps during the Babylonian exile or thereafter; they are strongly influenced by Deutero-Isaiah (sixth century). In places they reflect themes from other parts of the Isaian collection.

**34:8–17** The extreme hostility against Edom in this passage is reflected in a number of other prophetic texts from the seventh and sixth centuries B.C. (cf. e.g., 63:1–6; Jer 49:7–22; Ez 25:12–14). The animus was probably prompted by Edomite infiltration of the southern territories of Judah, especially after the Babylonian conquest of Judah.

*m:* Ez 47:1–12; Ps 46:5; 48:7. *n:* 2 Sm 8:6–7. *o:* Mi 7:18–19. *p:* Mi 1:2. *q:* Is 24:21. *r:* Ez 32:4, 6. *s:* Is 13:10; 24:23; Ez 32:7; Jl 3:3–4; Mt 24:29; 2 Pt 3:10; Rev 6:12–14. *t:* Jer 46:10. *u:* Is 63:1; Lv 3:4; 2 Sm 1:22; Jer 49:12–13; Zep 1:7. *v:* Is 13:9; 63:4.

and its land shall become burning
pitch;
[10] Night and day it shall not be quenched,
its smoke shall rise forever.
From generation to generation it shall lie
waste,
never again shall anyone pass
through it.[w]
[11] But the desert owl and hoot owl shall
possess it,
the screech owl and raven shall dwell
in it.
The LORD will stretch over it the
measuring line of chaos,
the plumb line of confusion.* [x]
[12] Its nobles shall be no more,
nor shall kings be proclaimed there;
all its princes are gone.[y]
[13] Its castles shall be overgrown with thorns,
its fortresses with thistles and briers.
It shall become an abode for jackals,
a haunt for ostriches.[z]
[14] Wildcats shall meet with desert beasts,
satyrs* shall call to one another;
There shall the lilith repose,
and find for herself a place to rest.
[15] There the hoot owl shall nest and lay eggs,
hatch them out and gather them in her
shadow;
There shall the kites assemble,
each with its mate.
[16] Search through the book of the LORD*
and read:
not one of these shall be lacking,
For the mouth of the LORD has ordered it,
and his spirit gathers them there.
[17] It is he who casts the lot for them;
his hand measures off* their portions;
They shall possess it forever,
and dwell in it from generation to
generation.[a]

## CHAPTER 35

See RG 209

### *Israel's Deliverance**

[1] The wilderness and the parched land will
exult;
the Arabah will rejoice and bloom;[b]
[2] Like the crocus it shall bloom
abundantly,
and rejoice with joyful song.
The glory of Lebanon will be given to it,
the splendor of Carmel and Sharon;
They will see the glory of the LORD,
the splendor of our God.[c]
[3] Strengthen hands that are feeble,
make firm knees that are weak,[d]
[4] Say to the fearful of heart:
Be strong, do not fear!
Here is your God,
he comes with vindication;
With divine recompense
he comes to save you.[e]
[5] Then the eyes of the blind shall see,
and the ears of the deaf be opened;[f]
[6] Then the lame shall leap like a stag,
and the mute tongue sing for joy.
For waters will burst forth in the
wilderness,
and streams in the Arabah.[g]
[7] The burning sands will become pools,
and the thirsty ground, springs of water;
The abode where jackals crouch
will be a marsh for the reed and
papyrus.
[8] A highway will be there,
called the holy way;
No one unclean may pass over it,
but it will be for his people;

**34:11 Chaos . . . confusion**: *tohu . . . bohu* in Hebrew, the terms used to describe the primeval chaos in Gn 1:2.

**34:14 Satyrs**: see note on 13:21. **The lilith**: a female demon thought to roam about the desert.

**34:16 Book of the LORD**: a list of God's creatures; cf. Ex 32:32–33; Ps 69:29, "the book of the living"; Ps 139:16, "your book."

**34:17 Casts the lot . . . measures off**: an ironic reference to how land might be distributed to new possessors (cf. Jos 14–21; Mi 2:5).

**35:1–10** This chapter contains a number of themes similar to those in Deutero-Isaiah (chaps. 40–55), for example, the blossoming of the wilderness (vv. 1–2; cf. 41:18–19), which is now well-irrigated (v. 7; cf. 43:19–20); sight to the blind (vv. 5–6; cf. 42:7, 16); a highway in the wilderness (v. 8; cf. 41:3); and the return of the redeemed/ransomed to Zion (vv. 9–10; cf. 51:11). Nevertheless, it forms a unit with chap. 34 (see note on 34:1–35:10) and reflects, along with that chapter, themes found in chaps. 1–33.

*w*: Mal 1:4; Rev 14:11; 18:18. *x*: Is 14:23; 28:17; 2 Kgs 21:13; Zep 2:14. *y*: Ob 18. *z*: Is 13:21; Hos 9:6. *a*: Jos 18:10; Ps 78:55. *b*: Is 41:18–19; 55:12–13. *c*: Is 40:5; 60:13. *d*: Is 40:29–30; Jb 4:3–4; Heb 12:12. *e*: Is 41:10; Zec 8:13. *f*: Is 29:18; 32:3. *g*: Is 32:3–4; 41:18; 43:19–20; 44:3; Mt 11:5.

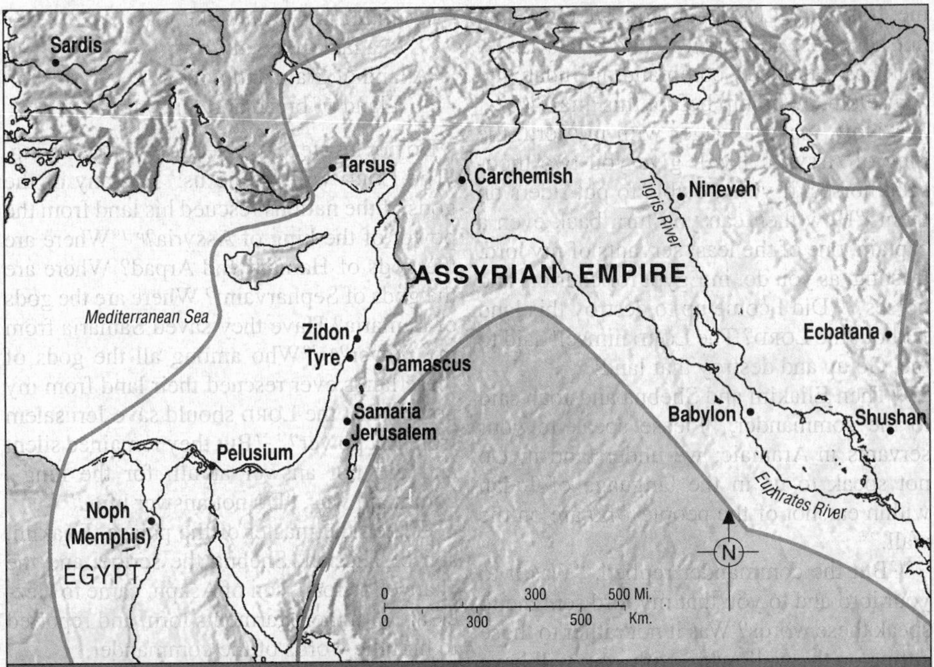


The Assyrian Empire

no traveler, not even fools, shall go
astray on it.[h]
9 No lion shall be there,
nor any beast of prey approach,
nor be found.
But there the redeemed shall walk,[i]
10 And the ransomed of the LORD shall
return,
and enter Zion singing,
crowned with everlasting joy;
They meet with joy and gladness,
sorrow and mourning flee away.[j]

## G. Historical Appendix*

### CHAPTER 36

See RG 209–210

*Invasion of Sennacherib.* [1]In the fourteenth year of King Hezekiah, Sennacherib,
king of Assyria, went up against all the fortified cities of Judah and captured them.*[k]
[2]From Lachish the king of Assyria sent his
commander with a great army to King Hezekiah in Jerusalem. When he stopped at the
conduit of the upper pool, on the highway of
the fuller's field, [3]there came out to him the
master of the palace, Eliakim, son of Hilkiah, and Shebna the scribe, and the chancellor, Joah, son of Asaph. [4]The commander
said to them, "Tell Hezekiah: Thus says the
great king, the king of Assyria: On what do
you base this trust of yours? [5]Do you think
mere words substitute for strategy and might
in war? In whom, then, do you place your
trust, that you rebel against me? [6]Do you
trust in Egypt, that broken reed of a staff
which pierces the hand of anyone who leans
on it? That is what Pharaoh, king of Egypt,
is to all who trust in him.[l] [7]Or do you say to

**36:1–39:8** Except for 38:9–20 (Hezekiah's prayer of thanksgiving), this historical appendix describing the siege, etc., is paralleled in 2 Kgs 18:13–20:19, which, however, has certain details proper to itself. The events are also reflected in the cuneiform inscriptions of Sennacherib.

**36:1** The occasion for this Assyrian attack was Hezekiah's attempt to reject Judah's status as vassal to Assyria, relying on help from Egypt, a course of action condemned by Isaiah (see notes on 28:15, 18; 28:16; 29:7–8; 30:1–17; etc.). 2 Kgs 19:14–16 reports that Hezekiah surrendered to the Assyrians and paid the tribute imposed on him—a report omitted in the Isaiah text.

*h:* Is 11:16; 43:19; 49:11. *i:* Is 62:10; Lv 26:6. *j:* Is 51:11. *k:* 2 Kgs 18:13; 2 Chr 32:1. *l:* Is 30:2–3, 7.

me: It is in the LORD, our God, we trust? Is it not he whose high places and altars Hezekiah has removed,* commanding Judah and Jerusalem, ‘Worship before this altar’?[m]

8 “Now, make a wager with my lord, the king of Assyria: I will give you two thousand horses, if you are able to put riders on them. 9 How then can you turn back even a captain, one of the least servants of my lord, trusting, as you do, in Egypt for chariots and horses? 10 Did I come up to destroy this land without the LORD? The LORD himself said to me, Go up and destroy that land!”[n]

11 Then Eliakim and Shebna and Joah said to the commander, “Please speak to your servants in Aramaic; we understand it. Do not speak to us in the language of Judah within earshot of the people who are on the wall.”*

12 But the commander replied, “Was it to your lord and to you that my lord sent me to speak these words? Was it not rather to those sitting on the wall, who, with you, will have to eat their own excrement and drink their own urine?” 13 Then the commander stepped forward and cried out in a loud voice in the language of Judah, “Listen to the words of the great king, the king of Assyria. 14 Thus says the king: Do not let Hezekiah deceive you, for he cannot rescue you. 15 And do not let Hezekiah induce you to trust in the LORD, saying, ‘The LORD will surely rescue us, and this city will not be handed over to the king of Assyria.’ 16 Do not listen to Hezekiah, for thus says the king of Assyria:

Make peace with me
 and surrender to me!
Eat, each of you, from your vine,
 each from your own fig tree.
Drink water, each from your own well,[o]
17 until I arrive and take you
 to a land like your own,
A land of grain and wine,
 a land of bread and vineyards.

18 Do not let Hezekiah seduce you by saying, ‘The LORD will rescue us.’ Has any of the gods of the nations rescued his land from the power of the king of Assyria?[p] 19 Where are the gods of Hamath and Arpad? Where are the gods of Sepharvaim? Where are the gods of Samaria? Have they saved Samaria from my power?[q] 20 Who among all the gods of these lands ever rescued their land from my power, that the LORD should save Jerusalem from my power?” 21 But they remained silent and did not answer at all, for the king's command was, “Do not answer him.”

22 Then the master of the palace, Eliakim, son of Hilkiah, Shebna the scribe, and the chancellor Joah, son of Asaph, came to Hezekiah with their garments torn, and reported to him the words of the commander.

## CHAPTER 37

See RG 209–210

1 * When King Hezekiah heard this, he tore his garments, covered himself with sackcloth, and went into the house of the LORD. 2 He sent Eliakim, the master of the palace, and Shebna the scribe, and the elders of the priests, covered with sackcloth, to tell the prophet Isaiah, son of Amoz,

3 “Thus says Hezekiah:
A day of distress and rebuke,
 a day of disgrace is this day!
Children are due to come forth,
 but the strength to give birth is
  lacking.* [r]

4 Perhaps the LORD, your God, will hear the words of the commander, whom his lord, the

**36:7** The Assyrians assert that Hezekiah's removal of the high places and altars (unofficial sanctuaries) was taken by the Lord as an insult. They declare to Jerusalem's emissaries that the city therefore no longer has a right to the Lord's protection and that they are the ones who truly carry out his will (cf. v. 10).

**36:11** The emissaries of King Hezekiah ask that the conversation be carried on in Aramaic, not in Hebrew, for they fear the effect of the Assyrian claims upon the morale of the people.

**37:1–35** There appear to be parallel accounts of Hezekiah's appeal and the response received (vv. 1–7 and vv. 14–35): in each, Hezekiah goes to the Temple, refers to the Assyrian boasts (found in 36:15–20; 37:10–14), and receives a favorable response from Isaiah.

**37:3** A proverbial expression. In the Bible the pangs of childbirth often typify extreme anguish; cf. 13:8; Jer 6:24; Mi 4:9–10. In this instance there is reference to the desperate situation of Hezekiah from which he would scarcely be able to free himself.

*m:* 2 Kgs 18:4. *n:* Is 10:5–6. *o:* 1 Kgs 5:5; Zec 3:10. *p:* Is 37:11. *q:* Is 10:9; 37:13. *r:* Is 26:18.

king of Assyria, sent to taunt the living God,
and will rebuke him for the words which the
LORD, your God, has heard. So lift up a
prayer for the remnant that is here."
5 When the servants of King Hezekiah had
come to Isaiah, 6 he said to them: "Tell this to
your lord: Thus says the LORD: Do not be
frightened by the words you have heard, by
which the deputies of the king of Assyria
have blasphemed me.[s]

7 I am putting in him such a spirit
that when he hears a report
he will return to his land.
I will make him fall by the sword in
his land."

8 When the commander, on his return,
heard that the king of Assyria had withdrawn
from Lachish, he found him besieging Libnah. 9 The king of Assyria heard a report:
"Tirhakah,* king of Ethiopia, has come out to
fight against you." Again he sent messengers
to Hezekiah to say: 10 "Thus shall you say to
Hezekiah, king of Judah: Do not let your God
in whom you trust deceive you by saying,
'Jerusalem will not be handed over to the
king of Assyria.'[t] 11 You, certainly, have heard
what the kings of Assyria have done to all the
lands: they put them under the ban! And are
you to be delivered? 12 Did the gods of the nations whom my fathers destroyed deliver
them—Gozan, Haran, Rezeph, and the Edenites in Telassar? 13 Where are the king of Hamath, the king of Arpad, or a king of the cities Sepharvaim, Hena or Ivvah?"
14 Hezekiah took the letter from the hand
of the messengers and read it; then he went
up to the house of the LORD, and spreading it
out before the LORD, 15 Hezekiah prayed to
the LORD:

16 "LORD of hosts, God of Israel,
enthroned on the cherubim!
You alone are God
over all the kingdoms of the earth.
It is you who made
the heavens and the earth.*
17 Incline your ear, LORD, and listen!
open your eyes, LORD, and see!
Hear all the words Sennacherib has sent
to taunt the living God.
18 Truly, O LORD,
the kings of Assyria have laid waste
the nations and their lands.
19 They gave their gods to the fire
—they were not gods at all,
but the work of human hands—
Wood and stone, they destroyed them.[u]
20 Therefore, LORD, our God,
save us from this man's power,
That all the kingdoms of the earth may
know
that you alone, LORD, are God."

21* Then Isaiah, son of Amoz, sent this
message to Hezekiah: "Thus says the LORD,
the God of Israel, to whom you have prayed
concerning Sennacherib, king of Assyria: I
have listened! 22 This is the word the LORD
has spoken concerning him:[v]

She despises you, laughs you to scorn,
the virgin daughter Zion;
Behind you she wags her head,
daughter Jerusalem.
23 Whom have you insulted and
blasphemed,
at whom have you raised your voice
And lifted up your eyes on high?
At the Holy One of Israel![w]
24 Through the mouths of your messengers
you have insulted the Lord when you
said:
'With my many chariots I went up
to the tops of the peaks,
to the recesses of Lebanon,
To cut down its lofty cedars,

**37:9 Tirhakah**: may have been general of the Egyptian army in 701 B.C.; later he became Pharaoh, one of the Ethiopian dynasty of Egyptian kings (ca. 690–664 B.C.). Many consider that this account in Isaiah combines features of two originally distinct sieges of Jerusalem by Sennacherib.

**37:16** In contrast to the empty boasting of the Assyrians, Hezekiah proclaims the Lord as "God over all the kingdoms of the earth."

**37:21–37** The reversal of Isaiah's attitude toward Hezekiah's revolt (see note on 36:1) and a wonderful deliverance after Hezekiah had already submitted and paid tribute raise questions difficult to answer. See note on 22:1–14. Some have postulated that chaps. 36–37 combine accounts of two different Assyrian invasions.

*s:* Is 7:4; 10:24. *t:* Is 36:14. *u:* Jer 16:20. *v:* 2 Kgs 19:21. *w:* Is 10:12.

its choice cypresses;
I reached the farthest shelter,
the forest ranges.
25 I myself dug wells
and drank foreign water;
Drying up all the rivers of Egypt
beneath the soles of my feet.'
26 Have you not heard?
A long time ago I prepared it,
from days of old I planned it,
Now I have brought it about:
You are here to reduce
fortified cities to heaps of ruins,[x]
27 Their people powerless,
dismayed and distraught,
They are plants of the field,
green growth,
thatch on the rooftops,
Grain scorched by the east wind.
28 I know when you stand or sit,
when you come or go,
and how you rage against me.
29 Because you rage against me
and your smugness has reached my
ears,
I will put my hook in your nose
and my bit in your mouth,
And make you leave by the way you
came.[y]
30 This shall be a sign* for you:
This year you shall eat the aftergrowth,
next year, what grows of itself;
But in the third year, sow and reap,
plant vineyards and eat their fruit!
31 The remaining survivors of the house of
Judah
shall again strike root below
and bear fruit above.[z]
32 For out of Jerusalem shall come a remnant,
and from Mount Zion, survivors.
The zeal of the LORD of hosts shall do this.[a]

33 Therefore, thus says the LORD about the
king of Assyria:

He shall not come as far as this city,
nor shoot there an arrow,
nor confront it with a shield,
Nor cast up a siege-work against it.
34 By the way he came he shall leave,
never coming as far as this city,
oracle of the LORD.
35 I will shield and save this city
for my own sake and the sake of David
my servant."[b]

36 Then the angel of the LORD went forth
and struck down one hundred and eighty-
five thousand in the Assyrian camp. Early
the next morning, there they were, all those
corpses, dead!* [c] 37 So Sennacherib, the king
of Assyria, broke camp, departed, returned
home, and stayed in Nineveh.
38 When he was worshiping in the temple
of his god Nisroch, his sons Adrammelech
and Sharezer struck him down with the
sword and fled into the land of Ararat.* His
son Esarhaddon reigned in his place.

## CHAPTER 38

See RG 209–210

### *Sickness and Recovery of Hezekiah.*

1* In those days,* when Hezekiah was mortally ill, the prophet Isaiah, son of Amoz,
came and said to him: "Thus says the LORD:
Put your house in order, for you are about to
die; you shall not recover."[d] 2 Hezekiah
turned his face to the wall and prayed to the
LORD:

3 "Ah, LORD, remember how faithfully
and wholeheartedly I conducted myself in
your presence, doing what was good in your
sight!" And Hezekiah wept bitterly.[e]
4 Then the word of the LORD came to Isaiah: 5 Go, tell Hezekiah:* Thus says the LORD,

**37:30 A sign**: sets a time limit. After two years the normal conditions of life will be resumed. See the similar use of time limits as signs in 7:15–16; 8:4; 16:14; and 21:16. **You**: Hezekiah.

**37:36** The destruction of Sennacherib's army is also recorded by Herodotus, a Greek historian of the fifth century B.C. It was possibly owing to a plague, which the author interprets as God's activity.

**37:38** The violent death of Sennacherib (681 B.C.) is also mentioned in non-biblical sources. It occurred twenty years after his invasion of Judah. **Ararat**: the land of Urartu in the mountains north of Assyria.

**38:1–39:8** The events of this section—sickness and recovery of Hezekiah, embassy of Merodach-baladan—anticipate the rise of Babylon (chaps. 40–66). They occurred prior to the events of 36:1–37:38, which point back to Assyria (1:1–35:10).

**38:1 In those days**: before the siege of Jerusalem in 701 B.C.

**38:5** Since Hezekiah died in 687 B.C., his sickness may have occurred in 702 B.C., that is, fifteen years before.

*x:* Is 10:6, 15. *y:* Is 30:28. *z:* Is 27:6. *a:* Is 9:6. *b:* Is 31:5; 1 Kgs 15:4. *c:* Is 10:12; 17:14. *d:* 2 Kgs 20:1. *e:* 2 Kgs 18:5–6.

## Hezekiah's Sickness and Recovery

HEZEKIAH'S PIETY (38:3) is illustrated in the story of his illness and recovery. His total submissiveness to the will of the LORD God and his subsequent recovery from the sickness are inseparably related to the wonderful deliverance of Jerusalem from the forces of Assyria (v. 6). Hezekiah's hymn of thanksgiving in vv. 10–20 is not included in 2 Kings 20:1–11, but is added here as further evidence of the king's piety. It is a personal psalm of thanksgiving for recovery from serious illness. It includes a lamentation during the time of distress (vv. 10–15) and thanksgiving for recovery (vv. 16–20).

the God of your father David: I have heard
your prayer; I have seen your tears. Now I
will add fifteen years to your life. 6 I will rescue you and this city from the hand of the
king of Assyria; I will be a shield to this city.[f]
7 This will be the sign for you from the
LORD that the LORD will carry out the word
he has spoken: 8 See, I will make the shadow
cast by the sun on the stairway to the terrace
of Ahaz* go back the ten steps it has advanced. So the sun came back the ten steps it
had advanced.[g]

***Hezekiah's Hymn of Thanksgiving.*** 9 The
song of Hezekiah, king of Judah, after he had
been sick and had recovered from his illness:

10 In the noontime of life* I said,
I must depart!
To the gates of Sheol I have been consigned
for the rest of my years.[h]
11 I said, I shall see the LORD* no more
in the land of the living.
Nor look on any mortals
among those who dwell in the world.
12 My dwelling, like a shepherd's tent,
is struck down and borne away from me;
You have folded up my life, like a weaver
who severs me from the last thread.* [i]
From morning to night you make an end of me;
13 I cry out even until the dawn.
Like a lion he breaks all my bones;
from morning to night you make an end of me.[j]
14 Like a swallow I chirp;
I moan like a dove.
My eyes grow weary looking heavenward:
Lord, I am overwhelmed; go security for me!
15 * What am I to say or tell him?
He is the one who has done it!
All my sleep has fled,
because of the bitterness of my soul.
16 Those live whom the LORD protects;
yours is the life of my spirit.
You have given me health and restored my life!
17 Peace in place of bitterness!
You have preserved my life
from the pit of destruction;
Behind your back
you cast all my sins.*
18 * For it is not Sheol that gives you thanks,
nor death that praises you;
Neither do those who go down into the pit
await your kindness.[k]

**38:8 Stairway to the terrace of Ahaz**: this interpretation is based on a reading of the Hebrew text revised according to the Dead Sea Scroll of Isaiah; cf. 2 Kgs 23:12. Many translate the phrase as "steps of Ahaz" and understand this as referring to a sundial.

**38:10 In the noontime of life**: long before the end of a full span of life; cf. Ps 55:24; 102:25.

**38:11 See the LORD**: go to the Temple and take part in its service.

**38:12** These two metaphors emphasize the suddenness and finality of death.

**38:15–16** The Hebrew text is very problematic and its meaning uncertain.

**38:17 Behind your back you cast all my sins**: figurative language to express the divine forgiveness of sins, as if God no longer saw or cared about them.

**38:18–19** See note on Ps 6:6.

*f:* Is 37:35. *g:* 2 Kgs 20:9–11. *h:* Jb 17:11–13; Ps 102:25. *i:* Jb 7:6. *j:* Jb 23:14. *k:* Ps 6:6; 88:11–13.

[19] The living, the living give you thanks,
as I do today.
Parents declare to their children,
O God, your faithfulness.
[20] The LORD is there to save us.
We shall play our music
In the house of the LORD
all the days of our life.

[21]* Then Isaiah said, "Bring a poultice of
figs and apply it to the boil for his recovery."
[22]Hezekiah asked, "What is the sign that I
shall go up to the house of the LORD?"

### CHAPTER 39

See RG 209–210

*Embassy from Merodach-baladan.*
[1]At that time Merodach-baladan,* son of
Baladan, king of Babylon, sent letters and
gifts to Hezekiah, when he heard that he had
been sick and had recovered.[l] [2]Hezekiah was
pleased at their coming, and then showed the
messengers his treasury, the silver and gold,
the spices and perfumed oil, his whole armory, and everything in his storerooms;
there was nothing in his house or in all his
realm that Hezekiah did not show them.[m]
[3]Then Isaiah the prophet came to King
Hezekiah and asked him, "What did these
men say to you? Where did they come
from?" Hezekiah replied, "They came to me
from a distant land, from Babylon." [4]He
asked, "What did they see in your house?"
Hezekiah answered, "They saw everything
in my house. There is nothing in my storerooms that I did not show them." [5]Then Isaiah said to Hezekiah, "Hear the word of the
LORD of hosts: [6]The time is coming when all
that is in your house, everything that your
ancestors have stored up until this day, shall
be carried off to Babylon;* nothing shall be
left, says the LORD.[n] [7]Some of your own descendants, your progeny, shall be taken and
made attendants in the palace of the king of
Babylon."[o] [8]Hezekiah replied to Isaiah,
"The word of the LORD which you have spoken is good."* For he thought, "There will be
peace and stability in my lifetime."

# II. Isaiah 40—55*

## A. The Lord's Glory in Israel's Liberation

### CHAPTER 40

See RG 210

*Promise of Salvation*
[1] * Comfort, give comfort to my people,
says your God.

**38:21–22** These verses are clearly out of place. Logically they should come after v. 6, as they do in the parallel account in 2 Kgs 20, but the two accounts are not identical, and it appears that the version in Isaiah is abbreviated from that in Kings. If that is so, Is 38:21–22 would be a secondary addition from Kings, inserted by a later reader who thought the account incomplete.

**39:1 Merodach-baladan**: twice king of Babylon, probably from 721 to 710 B.C., and again for nine months, in 704–703. This visit of his messengers, certainly before 701, was in reality a political one. Babylon hoped to lead an anti-Assyrian confederation composed of neighboring states and wanted Judah to join.

**39:6** Because Judah preferred to follow a pro-Babylonian policy, instead of trusting in the Lord, it would later be exiled to Babylon.

**39:8** Hezekiah was relieved that the disaster would not occur in his lifetime.

**40:1–55:13** Chapters 40–55 are usually designated Second Isaiah (or Deutero-Isaiah) and are believed to have been written by an anonymous prophet toward the end of the Babylonian exile. Isaiah, who is named frequently in chaps. 1–39, does not appear here; the Assyrians, the great threat during the eighth century, hardly appear; the Judeans are in Babylon, having been taken there by the victorious Babylonians; Cyrus, the Persian king, is named; he will defeat Babylon and release the captives. Second Isaiah, who sees this not as a happy circumstance but as part of God's age-old plan, exhorts the Judeans to resist the temptations of Babylonian religion and stirs up hopes of an imminent return to Judah, where the Lord will again be acknowledged as King (52:7). Because the prophet proclaimed the triumph of Persia over Babylon, his message would have been considered seditious, and it is very likely for this reason that the collection would have circulated anonymously. At some point it was appended to Is 1–39 and consequently was long considered the work of Isaiah of Jerusalem of the eighth century. But the fact that it is addressed to Judean exiles in Babylon indicates a sixth-century date. Nevertheless, this eloquent prophet in many ways works within the tradition of Isaiah and develops themes found in the earlier chapters, such as the holiness of the Lord (cf. note on 1:4) and his lordship of history. Second Isaiah also develops other Old Testament themes, such as the Lord as Israel's redeemer or deliverer (cf. Ex 3:8; 6:6; 15:13; 18:8).

**40:1** The "voices" of vv. 3, 6 are members of the heavenly court addressing the prophet; then v. 1 can be understood as the Lord addressing them. It is also possible to translate, with the Vulgate, "Comfort, give comfort, O my people" (i.e., the exiles are called to comfort Jerusalem). The juxtaposition of

*l:* 2 Kgs 20:12. *m:* 2 Chr 32:25–31. *n:* 2 Kgs 24:13; 25:13–17. *o:* Dn 1:3–19.

2 Speak to the heart of Jerusalem, and
proclaim to her
that her service* has ended,
that her guilt is expiated,
That she has received from the hand of
the LORD
double for all her sins.[p]

3 A voice proclaims:*
In the wilderness prepare the way of the
LORD!
Make straight in the wasteland a
highway for our God![q]
4 Every valley shall be lifted up,
every mountain and hill made low;
The rugged land shall be a plain,
the rough country, a broad valley.
5 Then the glory of the LORD shall be
revealed,
and all flesh shall see it together;
for the mouth of the LORD has spoken.

6 A voice says, "Proclaim!"
I answer, "What shall I proclaim?"
"All flesh is grass,
and all their loyalty like the flower of
the field.[r]
7 The grass withers, the flower wilts,
when the breath of the LORD blows
upon it."
"Yes, the people is grass!
8 The grass withers, the flower wilts,
but the word of our God stands
forever."

9 Go up onto a high mountain,
Zion, herald of good news!*
Cry out at the top of your voice,
Jerusalem, herald of good news!
Cry out, do not fear!
Say to the cities of Judah:
Here is your God!
10 Here comes with power
the Lord GOD,
who rules by his strong arm;
Here is his reward with him,
his recompense before him.
11 Like a shepherd he feeds his flock;
in his arms he gathers the lambs,
Carrying them in his bosom,
leading the ewes with care.[s]

### *Power of God and the Vanity of Idols*

12 Who has measured with his palm the
waters,
marked off the heavens with a span,
held in his fingers the dust of the earth,
weighed the mountains in scales
and the hills in a balance?*
13 Who has directed the spirit of the LORD,
or instructed him as his counselor?[t]
14 Whom did he consult to gain knowledge?
Who taught him the path of judgment,
or showed him the way of
understanding?
15 See, the nations count as a drop in the
bucket,
as a wisp of cloud on the scales;
the coastlands weigh no more than a
speck.*
16 Lebanon would not suffice for fuel,*
nor its animals be enough for burnt
offerings.
17 Before him all the nations are as nought,
as nothing and void he counts them.
18 To whom can you liken God?[u]
With what likeness can you confront
him?

"my people" and "your God" recalls the covenant formulary.

**40:2 Service**: servitude (cf. Jb 7:1) and exile.

**40:3–5** A description of the return of the exiles from Babylon to Jerusalem (Zion). The language used here figuratively describes the way the exiles will take. The Lord leads them, so their way lies straight across the wilderness rather than along the well-watered routes usually followed from Mesopotamia to Israel. Mt 3:3 and gospel parallels adapt these verses to the witness of John the Baptizer to Jesus.

**40:9 Herald of good news**: i.e., of the imminent restoration of the people to their land. This theme of the proclamation of the good news occurs elsewhere in Second Isaiah; cf. also 41:27; 52:7.

**40:12** The implicit answer is "the hand of the LORD" (v. 2). **Waters ... heavens ... earth**: together form the universe; cf. Gn 1:1–2. **Span**: the distance between the extended little finger and the thumb. **Fingers**: lit., "three fingers" (i.e., thumb, index, and middle).

**40:15 Drop ... wisp of cloud ... a speck**: the smallest constituent parts of the cosmic waters, heavens, and earth mentioned in v. 12.

**40:16 Lebanon ... fuel**: the famed cedars would not be enough to keep the fires of sacrifice burning.

---

*p:* Is 50:21. *q:* Mt 3:3; Mk 1:3; Lk 2:27; Jn 1:23. *r:* Jb 8:12; 14:2; Ps 37:2; Sir 14:18; Jas 1:10; 1 Pt 1:24. *s:* Is 49:9–10; 63:11; Ez 34:23; 37:24; Jn 10:11. *t:* Wis 9:13; Rom 11:34; 1 Cor 2:16; Jb 38:1–11. *u:* Acts 17:29.

19 An idol? An artisan casts it,
the smith plates it with gold,
fits it with silver chains.* v
20 Is mulberry wood the offering?
A skilled artisan picks out
a wood that will not rot,
Seeks to set up for himself
an idol that will not totter.w

21 Do you not know? Have you not heard?
Was it not told you from the beginning?
Have you not understood from the founding of the earth?
22 The one who is enthroned above the vault of the earth,
its inhabitants like grasshoppers,
Who stretches out the heavens like a veil
and spreads them out like a tent to dwell in.x
23 Who brings princes to nought
and makes the rulers of the earth as nothing.
24 Scarcely are they planted, scarcely sown,
scarcely their stem rooted in the earth,
When he breathes upon them and they wither,
and the stormwind carries them away like straw.

25 To whom can you liken me as an equal?
says the Holy One.
26 Lift up your eyes on high
and see who created* these:
He leads out their army and numbers them,
calling them all by name.
By his great might and the strength of his power
not one of them is missing!y
27 Why, O Jacob, do you say,*
and declare, O Israel,
"My way is hidden from the LORD,
and my right is disregarded by my God"?
28 Do you not know?
Have you not heard?
The LORD is God from of old,
creator of the ends of the earth.
He does not faint or grow weary,
and his knowledge is beyond scrutiny.
29 He gives power to the faint,
abundant strength to the weak.
30 Though young men faint and grow weary,
and youths stagger and fall,
31 They that hope in the LORD will renew their strength,
they will soar on eagles' wings;
They will run and not grow weary,
walk and not grow faint.

## CHAPTER 41

See RG 210

### *The Liberator of Israel*

1 Keep silence before me, O coastlands;*
let the nations renew their strength.
Let them draw near and speak;
let us come together for judgment.
2 Who has stirred up from the East the champion of justice,
and summoned him to be his attendant?
To him he delivers nations
and subdues kings;
With his sword he reduces them to dust,
with his bow, to driven straw.
3 He pursues them, passing on without loss,
by a path his feet scarcely touch.
4 Who has performed these deeds?
Who has called forth the generations from the beginning?z
I, the LORD, am the first,

**40:19 Chains**: needed to hold the idol steady when carried in processions; cf. v. 20; Jer 10:4.

**40:26 Created**: see note on Gn 1:1–2:3. **By name**: for he is their Creator.

**40:27–28** The exiles, here called Jacob-Israel (Gn 32:29), must not give way to discouragement: their Lord is the eternal God.

**41:1–4** Earlier prophets had spoken of the Assyrians and Babylonians as the Lord's instruments for the punishment of Israel's sins; here the Lord is described as raising up and giving victory to a foreign ruler in order to deliver Israel from the Babylonian exile. The ruler is Cyrus (44:28; 45:1), king of Anshan in Persia, a vassal of the Babylonians. He rebelled against the Babylonian overlords in 556 B.C., and after a series of victories, entered Babylon as victor in 539; the following year he issued a decree which allowed the Jewish captives to return to their homeland (2 Chr 36:22–23; Ezr 1:1–4). For Second Isaiah, the meteoric success of Cyrus was the work of the Lord to accomplish the deliverance promised by earlier prophets.

*v:* Ps 115:4–7; Jer 10:4. *w:* Is 44:13. *x:* Ps 104:2. *y:* Ps 147:4–5. *z:* Is 44:7; 46:10.

and at the last* I am he.
5 The coastlands see, and fear;
the ends of the earth tremble:
they approach, they come on.

6 Each one helps his neighbor,
one says to the other, "Courage!"
7 The woodworker encourages the goldsmith,
the one who beats with the hammer,
him who strikes on the anvil,
Saying of the soldering, "It is good!"
then fastening it with nails so it will not totter.

8 But you, Israel, my servant,[a]
Jacob, whom I have chosen,
offspring of Abraham my friend—
9 You whom I have taken from the ends of the earth
and summoned from its far-off places,
To whom I have said, You are my servant;
I chose you, I have not rejected you—
10 Do not fear: I am with you;
do not be anxious: I am your God.
I will strengthen you, I will help you,
I will uphold you with my victorious right hand.
11 Yes, all shall be put to shame and disgrace
who vent their anger against you;
Those shall be as nothing and perish
who offer resistance.
12 You shall seek but not find
those who strive against you;
They shall be as nothing at all
who do battle with you.

13 For I am the LORD, your God,
who grasp your right hand;
It is I who say to you, Do not fear,
I will help you.
14 Do not fear, you worm Jacob,
you maggot Israel;
I will help you—oracle of the LORD;
the Holy One of Israel is your redeemer.*
15 I will make of you a threshing sledge,
sharp, new, full of teeth,
To thresh the mountains and crush them,
to make the hills like chaff.
16 When you winnow them, the wind shall carry them off,
the storm shall scatter them.
But you shall rejoice in the LORD;
in the Holy One of Israel you shall glory.

17 The afflicted and the needy seek water in vain,
their tongues are parched with thirst.
I, the LORD, will answer them;
I, the God of Israel, will not forsake them.
18 I will open up rivers on the bare heights,
and fountains in the broad valleys;
I will turn the wilderness into a marshland,
and the dry ground into springs of water.
19 In the wilderness I will plant the cedar,
acacia, myrtle, and olive;
In the wasteland I will set the cypress,
together with the plane tree and the pine,
20 That all may see and know,
observe and understand,
That the hand of the LORD has done this,
the Holy One of Israel has created it.

21 Present your case, says the LORD;*
bring forward your arguments, says the King of Jacob.
22 Let them draw near and foretell to us
what it is that shall happen!
What are the things of long ago?
Tell us, that we may reflect on them
and know their outcome;

**41:4 The first . . . the last**: God as the beginning and end encompasses all reality. The same designation is used in 44:6 and 48:12.

**41:14 Redeemer**: in Hebrew, *go'el*, one who frees others from slavery and avenges their sufferings; cf. Lv 25:48; Dt 19:6, 12. Cf. note on Ru 2:20.

**41:21–29** This indictment of Babylonian gods is patterned on a legal trial, in which they are challenged to prove power over events of history and so justify their status as gods (vv. 21–24). Israel's God, on the other hand, has foretold and now brings to pass Israel's deliverance (vv. 25–27). The accused are unable to respond (vv. 28–29). By such polemics (see also 43:12) the prophet declares that all gods other than the Lord are nonexistent; this implicit claim of monotheism later becomes explicit (see 43:10–11; 45:5–7, 14, 18, 21–22; 46:9; and note on 44:6).

*a:* Is 44:1–2, 21; 45:4.

Or declare to us the things to come,*
23 tell what is to be in the future,
that we may know that you are gods!
Do something, good or evil,
that will put us in awe and in fear.
24 Why, you are nothing
and your work is nought;
to choose you is an abomination!

25 I have stirred up one from the north, and he comes;
from the east I summon him* by name;
He shall trample the rulers down like mud,
like a potter treading clay.
26 Who announced this from the beginning,
that we might know;
beforehand, that we might say,
"True"?
Not one of you foretold it, not one spoke;
not one heard you say,
27 "The first news for Zion: here they come,"
or, "I will give Jerusalem a herald of good news."
28 When I look, there is not one,
not one of them to give counsel,
to make an answer when I question them.
29 Ah, all of them are nothing,
their works are nought,
their idols, empty wind!

## CHAPTER 42

See RG 210

### *The Servant of the Lord*

1 Here is my servant* whom I uphold,
my chosen one with whom I am pleased.
Upon him I have put my spirit;
he shall bring forth justice to the nations.[b]
2 He will not cry out, nor shout,
nor make his voice heard in the street.
3 A bruised reed* he will not break,
and a dimly burning wick he will not quench.
He will faithfully bring forth justice.
4 He will not grow dim or be bruised
until he establishes justice on the earth;
the coastlands* will wait for his teaching.

5 Thus says God, the LORD,
who created the heavens and stretched them out,
who spread out the earth and its produce,
Who gives breath to its people
and spirit to those who walk on it:
6 I, the LORD, have called you for justice,
I have grasped you by the hand;
I formed you, and set you
as a covenant for the people,
a light for the nations,[c]
7 To open the eyes of the blind,
to bring out prisoners from confinement,
and from the dungeon, those who live in darkness.
8 I am the LORD, LORD is my name;
my glory I give to no other,
nor my praise to idols.
9 See, the earlier things have come to pass,
new ones I now declare;
Before they spring forth
I announce them to you.

### *The Lord's Purpose for Israel*

10 Sing to the LORD a new song,
his praise from the ends of the earth:
Let the sea and what fills it resound,
the coastlands, and those who dwell in them.

**41:22 Things of long ago . . . things to come**: there are no predictions attributed to idols that have since been fulfilled. Second Isaiah makes frequent reference to "things of long ago," sometimes in conjunction with "things to come" or "new things" in connection with the Lord's activity (cf. 42:9; 43:9, 18; 46:9–10; 48:3–8); both the old things (e.g., creation, exodus) and the new things (release from exile) God brings to pass (cf. 51:9–11), which is why he can declare them beforehand.

**41:25 I summon him**: Cyrus.

**42:1–4 Servant**: three other passages have been popularly called "servant of the Lord" poems: 49:1–7; 50:4–11; 52:13–53:12. Whether the servant is an individual or a collectivity is not clear (e.g., contrast 49:3 with 49:5). More important is the description of the mission of the servant. In the early Church and throughout Christian tradition, these poems have been applied to Christ; cf. Mt 12:18–21.

**42:3 Bruised reed . . .**: images to express the gentle manner of the servant's mission.

**42:4 Coastlands**: for Israel, the world to the west: the islands and coastal nations of the Mediterranean.

*b:* Is 45:6; 49:6. *c:* Is 45:13.

11 Let the wilderness and its cities cry out,
the villages where Kedar* dwells;
Let the inhabitants of Sela exult,
and shout from the top of the mountains.
12 Let them give glory to the LORD,
and utter his praise in the coastlands.
13 The LORD goes forth like a warrior,
like a man of war he stirs up his fury;
He shouts out his battle cry,
against his enemies he shows his might:[d]
14 For a long time I have kept silent,
I have said nothing, holding myself back;
Now I cry out like a woman in labor,
gasping and panting.
15 * I will lay waste mountains and hills,
all their undergrowth I will dry up;
I will turn the rivers into marshes,
and the marshes I will dry up.[e]
16 I will lead the blind on a way they do not know;
by paths they do not know I will guide them.
I will turn darkness into light before them,
and make crooked ways straight.
These are my promises:
I made them, I will not forsake them.[f]

17 They shall be turned back in utter shame
who trust in idols;
Who say to molten images,
"You are our gods."
18 You deaf ones, listen,*
you blind ones, look and see!
19 Who is blind but my servant,
or deaf like the messenger I send?
Who is blind like the one I restore,
blind like the servant of the LORD?
20 You see many things but do not observe;
ears open, but do not hear.
21 It was the LORD's will for the sake of his justice
to make his teaching great and glorious.

22 This is a people* plundered and despoiled,
all of them trapped in holes,
hidden away in prisons.
They are taken as plunder, with no one to rescue them,
as spoil, with no one to say, "Give back!"
23 Who among you will give ear to this,
listen and pay attention from now on?
24 Who was it that gave Jacob to be despoiled,
Israel to the plunderers?*
Was it not the LORD, against whom we have sinned?
In his ways they refused to walk,
his teaching they would not heed.
25 So he poured out wrath upon them,
his anger, and the fury of battle;
It blazed all around them, yet they did not realize,
it burned them, but they did not take it to heart.

## CHAPTER 43

See RG 210

### *Promises of Redemption and Restoration*

1 But now, thus says the LORD,
who created you, Jacob, and formed you, Israel:
Do not fear, for I have redeemed you;
I have called you by name: you are mine.
2 When you pass through waters, I will be with you;
through rivers, you shall not be swept away.
When you walk through fire, you shall not be burned,
nor will flames consume you.

**42:11 Kedar**: cf. note on 21:16. **Sela**: Petra, the capital of Edom.

**42:15–16** Active once more, God will remove the obstacles that hinder the exiles' return, and will lead them by new roads to Jerusalem; cf. 40:3–4.

**42:18–20** The Lord rebukes his people for their failures, but their role and their mission endure: they remain his servant, his messenger to the nations.

**42:22 A people**: Israel in exile.

**42:24 Plunderers**: the Assyrians and Babylonians. **We . . . they**: the switch from first- to third-person speech, though puzzling, does not obscure the fact that "the people" is meant.

*d:* Ex 14:3. *e:* Ex 9:25; 10:15; 14:21; Ps 105:33–35. *f:* Ex 13:21.

3 For I, the LORD, am your God,
the Holy One of Israel, your savior.
I give Egypt as ransom for you,
Ethiopia and Seba* in exchange for you.
4 Because you are precious in my eyes
and honored, and I love you,
I give people in return for you
and nations in exchange for your life.[g]
5 Fear not, for I am with you;
from the east I will bring back your offspring,
from the west I will gather you.
6 I will say to the north: Give them up!
and to the south: Do not hold them!
Bring back my sons from afar,
and my daughters from the ends of the earth:[h]
7 All who are called by my name
I created for my glory;
I formed them, made them.
8 Lead out the people, blind though they have eyes,
deaf though they have ears.

9 Let all the nations gather together,
let the peoples assemble!
Who among them could have declared this,
or announced to us the earlier things?*
Let them produce witnesses to prove themselves right,
that one may hear and say, "It is true!"
10 You are my witnesses*—oracle of the LORD—
my servant whom I have chosen
To know and believe in me
and understand that I am he.
Before me no god was formed,
and after me there shall be none.
11 I, I am the LORD;
there is no savior but me.
12 It is I who declared, who saved,
who announced, not some strange god among you;
You are my witnesses—oracle of the LORD.
I am God,
13 yes, from eternity I am he;
There is none who can deliver from my hand:
I act and who can cancel it?[i]

14 Thus says the LORD, your redeemer,*
the Holy One of Israel:
For your sake I send to Babylon;
I will bring down all her defenses,
and the Chaldeans shall cry out in lamentation.
15 I am the LORD, your Holy One,
the creator of Israel, your King.
16 Thus says the LORD,
who opens a way in the sea,
a path in the mighty waters,[j]
17 Who leads out chariots and horsemen,
a powerful army,
Till they lie prostrate together, never to rise,
snuffed out, quenched like a wick.[k]
18 Remember not* the events of the past,
the things of long ago consider not;
19 See, I am doing something new!
Now it springs forth, do you not perceive it?
In the wilderness I make a way,

**43:3–4 Egypt . . . Ethiopia and Seba**: countries which God permitted the Persians to conquer in return for having given Israel its freedom.

**43:9 Who among them . . . ?**: God, and only God, can foretell the future because it is he who brings it to pass. The argument from prediction is an important theme in Second Isaiah and occurs also in 41:22; 43:10; 44:7–8, 26.

**43:10 You are my witnesses**: Israel's role as chosen people now takes a new turn as they are given the active role of bearing witness before humankind to the Lord's role in history by proclaiming events beforehand and bringing them to pass; see also 44:8. The false gods, on the other hand, cannot produce such witnesses (v. 9; cf. 44:9). **I am he**: this formula of self-identification, repeated in vv. 13 and 25, is used here to support the assertion that the Lord alone is God; see also 41:4; 46:4; 48:12; 51:12; 52:6. This expression in part may be behind the self-identification formula used by Jesus in John's gospel (cf. Jn 8:58). **Before . . . after**: another example of the same assertion, that the Lord alone is God; see also note on 44:6.

**43:14–17** The destruction of Babylon is described in language that recalls the drowning of the Egyptian army in the Red Sea (Ex 14–15).

**43:18 Remember not**: God's new act of delivering Israel from the Babylonian captivity is presented as so great a marvel as to eclipse even the memory of the exodus from Egypt. This comparison of the return from Babylon to the exodus from Egypt recurs throughout Second Isaiah (cf. 41:17–20; 43:18–21; 48:20–21; 49:8–13; 51:9–11).

*g:* Dt 4:37; Hos 11:1. *h:* Is 49:22; Ez 16:20. *i:* Is 41:4. *j:* Is 51:10–11; Ex 14:21. *k:* Ex 15:4.

in the wasteland, rivers.
20 Wild beasts honor me,
jackals and ostriches,
For I put water in the wilderness
and rivers in the wasteland
for my chosen people to drink,
21 The people whom I formed for myself,
that they might recount my praise.
22 Yet you did not call upon me, Jacob,*
for you grew weary of me, Israel.
23 You did not bring me sheep for your
burnt offerings,
nor honor me with your sacrifices.
I did not exact from you the service of
offerings,
nor weary you for frankincense.[l]
24 You did not buy me sweet cane,*
nor did you fill me with the fat of your
sacrifices;
Instead, you burdened me with your sins,
wearied me with your crimes.
25 It is I, I, who wipe out,
for my own sake, your offenses;
your sins I remember no more.
26 Would you have me remember, have us
come to trial?
Speak up, prove your innocence!
27 Your first father* sinned;
your spokesmen rebelled against me
28 Till I repudiated the holy princes,
put Jacob under the ban,
exposed Israel to scorn.

## CHAPTER 44

See RG 210

1 Hear then, Jacob, my servant,
Israel, whom I have chosen.
2 Thus says the LORD who made you,
your help, who formed you from the
womb:
Do not fear, Jacob, my servant,
Jeshurun,* whom I have chosen.
3 I will pour out water upon the thirsty
ground,
streams upon the dry land;
I will pour out my spirit upon your
offspring,
my blessing upon your descendants.
4 They shall spring forth amid grass
like poplars beside flowing waters.[m]
5 One shall say, "I am the LORD's,"
another shall be named after Jacob,
And this one shall write on his hand,*
"The LORD's,"
and receive the name Israel.[n]

### *The True God and False Gods*

6 * Thus says the LORD, Israel's king,
its redeemer, the LORD of hosts:
I am the first, I am the last;
there is no God but me.* [o]
7 Who is like me? Let him stand up and
declare,
make it evident, and confront me with it.
Who of old announced future events?
Let them foretell to us the things to
come.
8 Do not fear or be troubled.
Did I not announce it to you long ago?
I declared it, and you are my witnesses.
Is there any God but me?
There is no other Rock,* I know of
none![p]
9 * Those who fashion idols are all
nothing;
their precious works are of no avail.
They are their witnesses:*
they see nothing, know nothing,
and so they are put to shame.[q]

**43:22–28** The reason for the liberation of the Israelites is not their constancy but rather God's faithfulness to his promise (cf. 40:6–8).

**43:24 Sweet cane**: a fragrant substance used in making incense and the sacred anointing oil; cf. Ex 30:23; Jer 6:20.

**43:27 First father**: Jacob. **Spokesmen**: leaders, priests, prophets.

**44:2 Jeshurun**: see note on Dt 32:15; cf. also Dt 33:5, 26.

**44:5 Write on his hand**: an allusion to the Babylonian custom of tattooing the owner's name on the hand of his slave.

**44:6–8** Prediction and fulfillment are here seen as the hallmarks of true divinity. See note on 43:9.

**44:6 No god but me**: with Second Isaiah, Israel's faith is declared to be explicitly monotheistic. However implicit it may have been, earlier formulas did not exclude the existence of other gods, not even that of the first commandment: "You shall not have other gods besides me" (Ex 20:3). Cf. also note on 41:21–29.

**44:8 Rock**: place of refuge, a title here used of God; cf., e.g., Dt 32:4, 18; 1 Sm 2:2; Ps 18:3.

**44:9–20** A satire on the makers and worshipers of idols.

**44:9 Their witnesses**: Israel has been called to bear witness to the awesome power of God (cf. 43:10, 12; 44:8), but

*l:* Jer 6:20. *m:* Is 54:1–3. *n:* Is 43:7; 45:14. *o:* Is 41:4; 43:15; 45:21; 48:3, 12; 51:15; 54:5. *p:* Is 43:10, 12; Dt 32:4. *q:* Is 48:5, 7.

10 Who would fashion a god or cast an idol,
that is of no use?
11 Look, all its company will be shamed;
they are artisans, mere human beings!
They all assemble and stand there,
only to cower in shame.
12 The ironsmith fashions a likeness,
he works it over the coals,
Shaping it with hammers,
working it with his strong arm.
With hunger his strength wanes,
without water, he grows faint.[r]
13 The woodworker stretches a line,
and marks out a shape with a stylus.
He shapes it with scraping tools,
with a compass measures it off,
Making it the copy of a man,*
human display, enthroned in a shrine.
14 He goes out to cut down cedars,
takes a holm tree or an oak.
He picks out for himself trees of the forest,
plants a fir, and the rain makes it grow.
15 It is used for fuel:
with some of the wood he warms himself,
makes a fire and bakes bread.
Yet he makes a god and worships it,
turns it into an idol and adores it!
16 Half of it he burns in the fire,
on its embers he roasts meat;
he eats the roast and is full.
He warms himself and says, "Ah!
I am warm! I see the flames!"
17 The rest of it he makes into a god,
an image to worship and adore.
He prays to it and says,
"Help me! You are my god!"
18 They do not know, do not understand;
their eyes are too clouded to see,
their minds, to perceive.
19 He does not think clearly;
he lacks the wit and knowledge to say,
"Half the wood I burned in the fire,
on its embers I baked bread,
I roasted meat and ate.
Shall I turn the rest into an abomination?
Shall I worship a block of wood?"
20 He is chasing ashes!*
A deluded mind has led him astray;
He cannot save himself,
does not say, "This thing in my right hand—is it not a fraud?"

21 Remember these things, Jacob,
Israel, for you are my servant!
I formed you, a servant to me;
Israel, you shall never be forgotten by me:
22 I have brushed away your offenses like a cloud,
your sins like a mist;
return to me, for I have redeemed you.

23 Raise a glad cry, you heavens—the LORD has acted!
Shout, you depths of the earth.
Break forth, mountains, into song,
forest, with all your trees.
For the LORD has redeemed Jacob,
shows his glory through Israel.

### *Cyrus, Anointed of the Lord, Agent of Israel's Liberation*

24 Thus says the LORD, your redeemer,
who formed you from the womb:
I am the LORD, who made all things,
who alone stretched out the heavens,
I spread out the earth by myself.[s]
25 I bring to nought the omens of babblers,
make fools of diviners,
Turn back the wise
and make their knowledge foolish.
26 I confirm the words of my servant,
carry out the plan my messengers announce.
I say to Jerusalem, Be inhabited!
To the cities of Judah, Be rebuilt!
I will raise up their ruins.
27 I say to the deep, Be dry!
I will dry up your rivers.[t]
28 I say of Cyrus,* My shepherd!
He carries out my every wish,

idol makers cannot testify in support of their creations, for idols cannot act (Dt 4:28; Ps 135:15–18).

**44:13 Copy of a man**: in the biblical view human beings are made in the image of God; here gods are made in the image of human beings.

**44:20 Chasing ashes**: an exercise in futility.

**44:28 Cyrus**: king of Persia (559–529 B.C.); cf. note on 41:1–4.

*r:* Wis 13:11–16. *s:* Is 40:22; Jb 9:8. *t:* Is 42:15; 51:10.

## The Election of Cyrus

THE LORD ANNOUNCES that Israel will be ransomed through a foreign king. Cyrus, king of Persia (559–529 B.C.) and victor over Babylon (539 B.C.), issued the edict that Jerusalem and the temple be rebuilt; see Ezra 1:1–4. Cyrus is the only non-Israelite called "anointed" (Is 45:1) because he carried out God's purpose of liberating Israel. God leads Cyrus by the hand so that he may accomplish his task without fail.

Saying of Jerusalem, "Let it be rebuilt,"
and of the temple, "Lay its
foundations."[u]

See RG 210

### CHAPTER 45

1 Thus says the LORD to his anointed,*
Cyrus,
whose right hand I grasp,
Subduing nations before him,
stripping kings of their strength,
Opening doors before him,
leaving the gates unbarred:
2 I will go before you
and level the mountains;
Bronze doors* I will shatter,
iron bars I will snap.[v]
3 I will give you treasures of darkness,
riches hidden away,
That you may know I am the LORD,
the God of Israel, who calls you by
name.
4 For the sake of Jacob, my servant,
of Israel my chosen one,
I have called you by name,
giving you a title, though you do not
know me.[w]
5 I am the LORD, there is no other,
there is no God besides me.
It is I who arm you, though you do not
know me,
6 so that all may know, from the rising
of the sun
to its setting, that there is none
besides me.*
I am the LORD, there is no other.
7 I form the light, and create the
darkness,
I make weal and create woe;*
I, the LORD, do all these things.
8 Let justice descend, you heavens, like
dew from above,
like gentle rain let the clouds drop it
down.
Let the earth open and salvation bud
forth;
let righteousness spring up with
them!*
I, the LORD, have created this.[x]
9 Woe to anyone who contends with their
Maker;[y]
a potsherd among potsherds of the
earth!*
Shall the clay say to the potter, "What are
you doing?"
or, "What you are making has no
handles"?
10 Woe to anyone who asks a father, "What
are you begetting?"
or a woman, "What are you giving
birth to?"
11 Thus says the LORD,
the Holy One of Israel, his maker:
Do you question me about my children,
tell me how to treat the work of my
hands?

**45:1 Anointed**: in Hebrew, *mashiah*, from which the word "Messiah" is derived; from its Greek translation, *Christos*, we have the title "Christ." Applied to kings, "anointed" originally referred only to those of Israel, but it is here given to Cyrus because he is the agent of the Lord.

**45:2 Bronze doors**: those defending the city gates of Babylon.

**45:6** The nations will come to know that Israel's God is the only God; cf. also vv. 20–25.

**45:7 Create woe**: God created and controls all aspects of creation (light and darkness, order and chaos).

**45:8** The Vulgate rendering gave a messianic sense to this verse, using "just one" and "savior" in place of "justice" and "salvation," phraseology taken over in the Advent liturgy, e.g., the "Rorate coeli."

**45:9** No one may challenge God's freedom of action, exemplified here by the selection of Cyrus as his anointed.

*u:* Jer 3:15; Ez 34:23. *v:* Ps 107:16. *w:* Is 40:26; 44:5. *x:* Ps 72:6; 85:11. *y:* Jer 18:6; Rom 9:20.

12 It was I who made the earth
and created the people upon it;
It was my hands that stretched out the heavens;
I gave the order to all their host.
13 It was I who stirred him* up for justice;
all his ways I make level.
He shall rebuild my city
and let my exiles go free
Without price or payment,
says the LORD of hosts.

14 Thus says the LORD:
The earnings of Egypt, the gain of Ethiopia,
and the Sabeans,* tall of stature,
Shall come over to you and belong to you;
they shall follow you, coming in chains.
Before you they shall bow down,
saying in prayer:
"With you alone is God; and there is none other,
no other god![z]
15 Truly with you God is hidden,*
the God of Israel, the savior![a]
16 They are put to shame and disgrace, all of them;
they go in disgrace who carve images.
17 Israel has been saved by the LORD,
saved forever!
You shall never be put to shame or disgrace
in any future age."

18 For thus says the LORD,
The creator of the heavens,
who is God,
The designer and maker of the earth
who established it,
Not as an empty waste* did he create it,
but designing it to be lived in:
I am the LORD, and there is no other.
19 I have not spoken in secret
from some place in the land of darkness,
I have not said to the descendants of Jacob,
"Look for me in an empty waste."
I, the LORD, promise justice,
I declare what is right.

20 Come and assemble, gather together,
you fugitives from among the nations!
They are without knowledge who bear wooden idols*
and pray to gods that cannot save.
21 Come close and declare;
let them take counsel together:
Who announced this from the beginning,
declared it from of old?
Was it not I, the LORD,
besides whom there is no other God?
There is no just and saving God
but me.

22 Turn to me and be safe,
all you ends of the earth,
for I am God; there is no other!
23 By myself I swear,
uttering my just decree,
a word that will not return:
To me every knee shall bend;
by me every tongue shall swear,[b]
24 Saying, "Only in the LORD
are just deeds and power.
Before him in shame shall come
all who vent their anger against him.
25 In the LORD all the descendants of Israel
shall have vindication and glory."

**45:13 Him**: Cyrus, called by God for the deliverance and restoration of Israel. **Justice**: the Hebrew word (*sedeq*) has multiple connotations; here it relates to the saving victory that the Lord will give to Cyrus for the deliverance of his people Israel. This word and others from the same root frequently have this connotation in Second Isaiah, occurring as a parallel term with "deliverance," "salvation," etc. Cf. its use in 41:10 (rendered "victorious") and 51:5 (rendered "victory").

**45:14 Egypt . . . Ethiopia . . . Sabeans**: the Egyptians and their allies who, when conquered by Cyrus, are seen as acknowledging the God of Israel; cf. 43:3.

**45:15 God is hidden**: i.e., the one known only to Israel, who cannot be represented by wooden or molten images. The concept of the "Deus absconditus," "the hidden God," becomes an important theme in later theology.

**45:18 Empty waste**: an allusion to Gn 1:2, where the earth is waste and void; the same Hebrew word, *tohu*, is used in both passages. Here it points to devastated Judah and Jerusalem, where God wishes to resettle the returning exiles.

**45:20 Who bear wooden idols**: in their religious processions. Such gods have feet but cannot walk; cf. Ps 115:7; Bar 6:25.

*z:* Is 43:3. *a:* Is 55:8; Prv 25:2. *b:* Rom 14:11; Phil 2:10.

See RG 210

## CHAPTER 46

### *The Gods of Babylon*

1 Bel bows down, Nebo* stoops,
their idols set upon beasts and cattle;
They must be borne upon shoulders,
a load for weary animals.
2 They stoop and bow down together;
unable to deliver those who bear them,
they too go into captivity.

3 Hear me, O house of Jacob,
all the remnant of the house of Israel,
My burden from the womb,
whom I have carried since birth.[c]
4 Even to your old age I am he,
even when your hair is gray I will carry you;
I have done this, and I will lift you up,
I will carry you to safety.

5 To whom would you liken me as an equal,
compare me, as though we were alike?
6 There are those who pour out gold from a purse
and weigh out silver on the scales;
They hire a goldsmith to make it into a god
before which they bow down in worship.
7 They lift it to their shoulders to carry;
when they set it down, it stays,
and does not move from the place.
They cry out to it, but it cannot answer;
it delivers no one from distress.

8 Remember this and be firm,
take it to heart, you rebels;
9 remember the former things, those long ago:
I am God, there is no other;
I am God, there is none like me.
10 At the beginning I declare the outcome;
from of old, things not yet done.
I say that my plan shall stand,
I accomplish my every desire.
11 I summon from the east a bird of prey,*
from a distant land, one to carry out my plan.
Yes, I have spoken, I will accomplish it;
I have planned it, and I will do it.
12 Listen to me, you fainthearted,
far from the victory of justice:
13 I am bringing on that victory, it is not far off,
my salvation shall not tarry;
I will put salvation within Zion,
give to Israel my glory.

## CHAPTER 47

See RG 210

### *The Fall of Babylon**

1 Come down, sit in the dust,
virgin daughter Babylon;
Sit on the ground, dethroned,
daughter of the Chaldeans.
No longer shall you be called
dainty and delicate.[d]
2 Take the millstone and grind flour,
remove your veil;
Strip off your skirt, bare your legs,
cross through the streams.
3 Your nakedness shall be uncovered,
and your shame be seen;
I will take vengeance,
I will yield to no entreaty,
says 4 our redeemer,
Whose name is the LORD of hosts,
the Holy One of Israel.

5 Go into darkness and sit in silence,
daughter of the Chaldeans,
No longer shall you be called
sovereign mistress of kingdoms.
6 Angry at my people,
I profaned my heritage
And gave them into your power;
but you showed them no mercy;
Upon the aged
you laid a very heavy yoke.
7 You said, "I shall remain always,
a sovereign mistress forever!"
You did not take these things to heart,

**46:1–4 Bel . . . Nebo**: gods of Babylon; their complete helplessness is here contrasted with God's omnipotence; whereas they must be carried about, the Lord carries Israel as a parent does a child.

**46:11 From the east a bird of prey**: Cyrus; cf. 41:2–4.

**47:1–15** A taunt-song, mocking Babylon, once queen of the nations, now a mere slave.

*c:* Is 44:2. *d:* Dt 28:56.

but disregarded their outcome.[e]
8 Now hear this, voluptuous one,
enthroned securely,
Saying in your heart,
"I, and no one else!"*
I shall never be a widow,
bereft of my children"—[f]
9 Both these things shall come to you
suddenly, in a single day:
Complete bereavement and widowhood
shall come upon you
Despite your many sorceries
and the full power of your spells;*
10 Secure in your wickedness,
you said, "No one sees me."
Your wisdom and your knowledge
led you astray,
And you said in your heart,
"I, and no one else!"
11 But upon you shall come an evil
you will not be able to charm away;
Upon you shall fall a disaster
you cannot ward off.
Upon you shall suddenly come
a ruin you cannot imagine.

12 Keep on with your spells
and your many sorceries,
at which you toiled from your youth.
Perhaps you can prevail,
perhaps you can strike terror!
13 You wore yourself out with so many
consultations!
Let the astrologers stand forth to save
you,
The stargazers who forecast at each new
moon
what would happen to you.
14 See, they are like stubble,
fire consumes them;
They cannot deliver themselves
from the spreading flames.
This is no warming ember,
no fire to sit before!
15 Thus do your wizards serve you
with whom you have toiled from your
youth;
They wander their separate ways,
with none to save you.

## CHAPTER 48

See RG 210

### *Exhortations to the Exiles*

1 Hear this, house of Jacob
called by the name Israel,
sprung from the stock of Judah,
You who swear by the name of the LORD
and invoke the God of Israel
without sincerity, without justice,
2 Though you are named after the holy city
and rely on the God of Israel,
whose name is the LORD of hosts.
3 Things of the past I declared long ago,
they went forth from my mouth, I
announced them;
then suddenly I took action and they
came to be.
4 Because I know that you are stubborn
and that your neck is an iron sinew
and your forehead bronze,
5 I declared them to you of old;
before they took place I informed you,
That you might not say, "My idol did
them,
my statue, my molten image
commanded them."
6 Now that you have heard, look at all this;
must you not admit it?[g]
From now on I announce new things to
you,
hidden events you never knew.
7 Now, not from of old, they are created,
before today you did not hear of them,
so that you cannot claim, "I have
known them."
8 You never heard, you never knew,
they never reached your ears
beforehand.
Yes, I know you are utterly treacherous,
a rebel you were named from the
womb.[h]
9 For the sake of my name I restrain my
anger,
for the sake of my renown I hold it
back from you,

**47:8, 10 I, and no one else**: Babylon is mockingly presented as making the same claim as the Lord (cf. 45:6, 14, 22; 46:9), a claim that events will soon prove to be false and foolish (v. 11).

**47:9–13, 15** Babylon was known for its sorcery and astrology.

*e:* Is 14:13–14. *f:* Zep 2:15; Rev 18:7. *g:* Is 42:9. *h:* Is 43:22–24.

lest I destroy you.
10 See, I refined you, but not like silver;
I tested you in the furnace of affliction.[i]
11 For my sake, for my own sake, I do this;
why should my name be profaned?
My glory I will not give to another.

12 Listen to me, Jacob,
Israel, whom I called!
I, it is I who am the first,
and am I the last.[j]
13 Yes, my hand laid the foundations of the earth;
my right hand spread out the heavens.
When I summon them,
they stand forth at once.[k]

14 All of you assemble and listen:
Who among you declared these things?
The one the LORD loves* shall do his will
against Babylon and the offspring of Chaldea.
15 I myself have spoken, I have summoned him,
I have brought him, and his way succeeds!
16 Come near to me and hear this!
From the beginning I did not speak in secret;
At the time it happens, I am there:
"Now the Lord GOD has sent me, and his spirit."*

17 Thus says the LORD, your redeemer,
the Holy One of Israel:
I am the LORD, your God,
teaching you how to prevail,
leading you on the way you should go.
18 If only you would attend to my commandments,
your peace would be like a river,
your vindication like the waves of the sea,
19 Your descendants like the sand,
the offspring of your loins like its grains,
Their name never cut off
or blotted out from my presence.
20 Go forth from Babylon, flee from Chaldea!
With shouts of joy declare this,
announce it;
Make it known to the ends of the earth,
Say: "The LORD has redeemed his servant Jacob.
21 They did not thirst
when he led them through dry lands;
Water from the rock he set flowing for them;
he cleft the rock, and waters welled forth."[l]

22 There is no peace* for the wicked,
says the LORD.

## B. Expiation of Sin, Spiritual Liberation of Israel

### CHAPTER 49

See RG 210

*The Servant of the Lord**

1 Hear me, coastlands,
listen, distant peoples.[m]
Before birth the LORD called me,
from my mother's womb he gave me my name.*
2 He made my mouth like a sharp-edged sword,
concealed me, shielded by his hand.
He made me a sharpened arrow,
in his quiver he hid me.
3 He said to me, You are my servant,
in you, Israel,* I show my glory.

**48:14 The one the LORD loves**: the reference is no doubt to Cyrus, who does the Lord's will by overcoming Babylon and releasing Israel from captivity.

**48:16 "Now the Lord . . . spirit"**: said by Cyrus; cf. v. 14.

**48:22 No peace**: while the good news proclaimed by the prophet is directed to the people as a whole, "peace," which can represent the fullness of God's blessings and which would here include deliverance from exile, is not extended to all regardless of disposition.

**49:1–7** The second of the four "servant of the Lord" oracles (cf. note on 42:1–4).

**49:1 Gave me my name**: designated me for a special task or mission (cf. Jer 1:5).

**49:3 Israel**: the servant is identified with the people of Israel as their ideal representative; however, vv. 5–6 seem to distinguish the servant from Israel.

*i:* Is 1:25; Jer 6:29–30; Zec 13:9; Mal 3:2. *j:* Is 41:4; 44:6; 48:12; Rev 1:8, 17. *k:* Is 40:22, 26; 45:12, 18. *l:* Ex 17:6; Nm 20:11. *m:* Is 41:9; 43:1; 44:2, 24; 46:3.

4 Though I thought I had toiled in vain,
for nothing and for naught spent my strength,
Yet my right is with the LORD,
my recompense is with my God.[n]
5 For now the LORD has spoken
who formed me as his servant from the womb,
That Jacob may be brought back to him
and Israel gathered to him;
I am honored in the sight of the LORD,
and my God is now my strength!
6 It is too little, he says, for you to be my servant,
to raise up the tribes of Jacob,
and restore the survivors of Israel;[o]
I will make you a light to the nations,
that my salvation may reach to the ends of the earth.*
7 Thus says the LORD,
the redeemer, the Holy One of Israel,
To the one despised, abhorred by the nations,
the slave of rulers:
When kings see you, they shall stand up,
and princes shall bow down
Because of the LORD who is faithful,
the Holy One of Israel who has chosen you.[p]

### *The Liberation and Restoration of Zion*

8 Thus says the LORD:
In a time of favor I answer you,*
on the day of salvation I help you;
I form you and set you
as a covenant for the people,
To restore the land
and allot the devastated heritages,[q]
9 To say to the prisoners: Come out!
To those in darkness: Show yourselves!
Along the roadways they shall find pasture,
on every barren height shall their pastures be.[r]
10 They shall not hunger or thirst;
nor shall scorching wind or sun strike them;
For he who pities them leads them
and guides them beside springs of water.[s]
11 I will turn all my mountains into roadway,
and make my highways level.[t]
12 See, these shall come from afar:
some from the north and the west,
others from the land of Syene.*
13 Sing out, heavens, and rejoice, earth,
break forth into song, you mountains,
For the LORD comforts his people
and shows mercy to his afflicted.

14 But Zion said, "The LORD has forsaken me;
my Lord has forgotten me."[u]
15 Can a mother forget her infant,
be without tenderness for the child of her womb?
Even should she forget,
I will never forget you.[v]
16 See, upon the palms of my hands I have engraved you;*
your walls are ever before me.
17 Your children hasten—
your levelers, your destroyers
go forth from you;
18 Look about and see,
they are all gathering and coming to you.
As I live—oracle of the LORD—
you shall don them as jewels,
bedeck yourself like a bride.

19 Though you were waste and desolate,
a land of ruins,
Now you shall be too narrow for your inhabitants,
while those who swallowed you up
will be far away.

**49:6** The servant's vocation extends beyond the restoration of Israel in order to bring the knowledge of Israel's God to the rest of the earth; cf. Lk 2:32.

**49:8 You**: the individual is not named; perhaps Cyrus or the prophet.

**49:12 Syene**: now called Aswan, at the first cataract of the Nile in southern Egypt.

**49:16 Upon the palms . . . you**: for continual remembrance; cf. Ex 13:9, 16; Dt 6:6–9.

**50:1** Responding to the people's complaint of utter aban-

*n:* Is 40:27. *o:* Is 42:1–6; 44:5; 45:14; Lk 2:32; Acts 13:46–47. *p:* Is 49:23; 55:5. *q:* 2 Cor 6:2. *r:* Is 42:7, 18–20. *s:* Is 51:14; Rev 7:16. *t:* Is 40:3–4. *u:* Is 40:27. *v:* Is 43:4; 44:21; 46:3–4.

20 The children of whom you were bereft
shall yet say in your hearing,
"This place is too narrow for me,
make room for me to live in."
21 You shall ask yourself:
"Who has borne me these,
when I was bereft and barren?
Exiled and repudiated,
who has reared them?
I was left all alone;
where then do these come from?"[w]
22 Thus says the Lord GOD:
See, I will lift up my hand to the nations,
and to the peoples raise my signal;
They shall bring your sons in their arms,
your daughters shall be carried on their shoulders.[x]
23 Kings shall be your guardians,
their princesses your nursemaids;
Face to the ground, they shall bow down before you
and lick the dust at your feet.
Then you shall know that I am the LORD,
none who hope in me shall be ashamed.
24 Can plunder be taken from a warrior,
or captives rescued from a tyrant?
25 Thus says the LORD:
Yes, captives can be taken from a warrior,
and plunder rescued from a tyrant;
Those who oppose you I will oppose,
and your sons I will save.
26 I will make your oppressors eat their own flesh,
and they shall be drunk with their own blood
as though with new wine.
All flesh shall know
that I, the LORD, am your savior,
your redeemer, the Mighty One of Jacob.[y]

## CHAPTER 50

See RG 210

### *Salvation Through the Lord's Servant*

1 Thus says the LORD:
Where is the bill of divorce
with which I dismissed your mother?*
Or to which of my creditors
have I sold you?
It was for your sins you were sold,
for your rebellions your mother was dismissed.[z]

2 Why was no one there when I came?
Why did no one answer when I called?*
Is my hand too short to ransom?
Have I not the strength to deliver?
See, with my rebuke I dry up the sea,
I turn rivers into wilderness;
Their fish rot for lack of water,
and die of thirst.[a]
3 I clothe the heavens in black,
and make sackcloth their covering.

4 * The Lord GOD has given me
a well-trained tongue,
That I might know how to answer the weary
a word that will waken them.
Morning after morning
he wakens my ear to hear as disciples do;
5 The Lord GOD opened my ear;
I did not refuse,
did not turn away.*
6 I gave my back to those who beat me,
my cheeks to those who tore out my beard;*
My face I did not hide
from insults and spitting.[b]

7 The Lord GOD is my help,
therefore I am not disgraced;

donment by God, the prophet asserts that their sins were responsible for their banishment. Since there was no bill of divorce, the bond between the Lord and his people still exists and he has the power to deliver them (v. 2).

**50:2** Israel's faith in God is weak; the people do not answer God's call, nor believe promises of deliverance.

**50:4–11** The third of the four "servant of the Lord" oracles (cf. note on 42:1–4); in vv. 4–9 the servant speaks; in vv. 10–11 God addresses the people directly.

**50:5** The servant, like a well-trained disciple, does not refuse the divine vocation.

**50:6** He willingly submits to insults and beatings. **Tore out my beard**: a grave and painful insult.

*w:* Is 54:1–3. *x:* Is 5:26; 13:2. *y:* Is 19:2; Ez 38:21; Zec 14:13. *z:* Is 54:6–8; Dt 24:1–4; Mt 19:3; Mk 10:2–4. *a:* Ex 7:18; Ps 105:29. *b:* 2 Sm 10:4–6; Mt 26:67; 27:30.

Therefore I have set my face like flint,
knowing that I shall not be put to shame.[c]
8 He who declares my innocence is near.
Who will oppose me?
Let us appear together.
Who will dispute my right?
Let them confront me.
9 See, the Lord GOD is my help;
who will declare me guilty?
See, they will all wear out like a garment,
consumed by moths.[d]
10 Who among you fears the LORD,*
heeds his servant's voice?
Whoever walk in darkness,
without any light,
Yet trust in the name of the LORD
and rely upon their God![e]
11 All you who kindle flames
and set flares alight,
Walk by the light of your own fire
and by the flares you have burnt!
This is your fate from my hand:
you shall lie down in a place of torment.

See RG 210

## CHAPTER 51

### *Exhortation To Trust in the Lord*

1 Listen to me, you who pursue justice,
who seek the LORD;
Look to the rock from which you were hewn,
to the quarry* from which you were taken;[f]
2 Look to Abraham, your father,
and to Sarah, who gave you birth;
Though he was but one when I called him,
I blessed him and made him many.[g]
3 Yes, the LORD shall comfort Zion,
shall comfort all her ruins;
Her wilderness he shall make like Eden,
her wasteland like the garden of the LORD;
Joy and gladness shall be found in her,
thanksgiving and the sound of song.
4 Be attentive to me, my people;*
my nation, give ear to me.
For teaching shall go forth from me,
and my judgment, as light to the peoples.[h]
5 I will make my victory come swiftly;
my salvation shall go forth
and my arm shall judge the nations;
In me the coastlands shall hope,
and my arm they shall await.
6 Raise your eyes to the heavens,
look at the earth below;
Though the heavens vanish like smoke,
the earth wear out like a garment
and its inhabitants die like flies,
My salvation shall remain forever
and my victory shall always be firm.*
7 Hear me, you who know justice,
you people who have my teaching at heart:
Do not fear the reproach of others;
remain firm at their revilings.
8 They shall be like a garment eaten by moths,
like wool consumed by grubs;
But my victory shall remain forever,
my salvation, for all generations.[i]
9 Awake, awake, put on strength,
arm of the LORD!
Awake as in the days of old,
in ages long ago!
Was it not you who crushed Rahab,*
you who pierced the dragon?[j]
10 Was it not you who dried up the sea,
the waters of the great deep,*
You who made the depths of the sea into a way

**50:10–11** The Lord offers a choice to those who walk in darkness: either trust in the true light (v. 10), or walk in their false light and suffer the consequences.

**51:1 Rock . . . quarry**: your glorious ancestry.

**51:4–5** The conversion of the nations.

**51:6** While the heavens and the earth appear eternal and changeless, they are not so firm and lasting as God's saving will for Israel.

**51:9 Rahab**: see note on 30:7. **The dragon**: see notes on 27:1; Ps 74:12–17.

**51:10 Great deep**: a reference to the primeval chaos (cf. Gn 1:2; 7:11; 49:25; Jb 28:14; Ps 36:7; Jon 2:4).

*c:* Ez 3:9. *d:* Is 51:6–8; Ps 102:27. *e:* Is 43:1–2; 44:1–2. *f:* Rom 9:30–31. *g:* Ez 33:24; Gn 12:2–4; 22:17. *h:* Is 2:3. *i:* Is 50:9. *j:* Ex 15:16; Jb 9:13; 26:12; Ps 74:13; 89:11.

for the redeemed to pass through?
11 Those whom the LORD has ransomed will return
and enter Zion singing,
crowned with everlasting joy;
They will meet with joy and gladness,
sorrow and mourning will flee.
12 I, it is I who comfort you.
Can you then fear mortals who die,
human beings who are just grass,
13 And forget the LORD, your maker,
who stretched out the heavens
and laid the foundations of earth?
All the day you are in constant dread
of the fury of the oppressor
When he prepares himself to destroy;
but where is the oppressor's fury?
14 The captives shall soon be released;
they shall not die and go down into the pit,
nor shall they want for bread.
15 For I am the LORD, your God,
who stirs up the sea so that its waves roar;
the LORD of hosts by name.[k]
16 I have put my words into your mouth,
I covered you, shielded by my hand,
Stretching out the heavens,
laying the foundations of the earth,
saying to Zion: You are my people.

### *The Cup of the Lord*

17 Wake up, wake up!
Arise, Jerusalem,
You who drank at the LORD's hand
the cup of his wrath;
Who drained to the dregs
the bowl of staggering![l]
18 She has no one to guide her
of all the children she bore;
She has no one to take her by the hand,
of all the children she reared!—
19 Your misfortunes are double;
who is there to grieve with you?
Desolation and destruction, famine and sword!
Who is there to comfort you?
20 Your children lie helpless
at every street corner
like antelopes in a net.
They are filled with the wrath of the LORD,
the rebuke of your God.
21 But now, hear this, afflicted one,
drunk, but not with wine,[m]
22 Thus says the LORD, your Master,
your God, who defends his people:
See, I am taking from your hand
the cup of staggering;
The bowl of my wrath
you shall no longer drink.
23 I will put it into the hands of your tormentors,
those who said to you,
"Bow down, that we may walk over you."
So you offered your back like the ground,
like the street for them to walk on.

## CHAPTER 52

See RG 210

### *Let Zion Rejoice*

1 Awake, awake!
Put on your strength, Zion;
Put on your glorious garments,
Jerusalem, holy city.
Never again shall the uncircumcised
or the unclean enter you.
2 Arise, shake off the dust,
sit enthroned, Jerusalem;
Loose the bonds from your neck,
captive daughter Zion!
3 For thus says the LORD:
For nothing you were sold,
without money you shall be redeemed.
4 For thus says the Lord GOD:
To Egypt long ago my people went down,
to sojourn there;
Assyria, too, oppressed them for nought.
5 But now, what am I to do here?
—oracle of the LORD.
My people have been taken away for nothing;
their rulers mock, oracle of the LORD;
constantly, every day, my name is reviled.

*k:* Jer 31:35. *l:* Jer 25:15–17; Ez 23:32–34. *m:* Is 29:9.

## The Suffering Servant

ISRAEL, THE SERVANT of God, has suffered as a humiliated individual. However, the servant endured without complaint because it was suffering for others. Nations and kings (52:15) will be surprised to see the unattractive, rejected servant exalted. In traditional Hebrew thought, the good person prospers like a tree by water, but the wicked is like a plant growing in parched ground; see Ps 1:3–6. The phrase in Is 53:3, "turn your face" was used in relation to lepers, whose sickness was considered a sign of sin. In the end, however, this reviled, condemned character is restored and exalted for accepting punishment for the transgressions of others.

6 Therefore my people shall know my name
on that day, that it is I who speaks:
Here I am!
7 How beautiful upon the mountains*
are the feet of the one bringing good
news,
Announcing peace, bearing good news,
announcing salvation, saying to Zion,
"Your God is King!"[n]

8 Listen! Your sentinels raise a cry,
together they shout for joy,
For they see directly, before their eyes,
the LORD's return to Zion.[o]
9 Break out together in song,
O ruins of Jerusalem!
For the LORD has comforted his people,
has redeemed Jerusalem.
10 The LORD has bared his holy arm
in the sight of all the nations;
All the ends of the earth can see
the salvation of our God.

11 Depart, depart, go out from there,
touch nothing unclean!
Out from there!* Purify yourselves,
you who carry the vessels of the LORD.
12 But not in hurried flight will you go out,
nor leave in headlong haste,
For the LORD goes before you,
and your rear guard is the God of
Israel.[p]

### *Suffering and Triumph of the Servant of the Lord**

13 See, my servant shall prosper,
he shall be raised high and greatly
exalted.
14 Even as many were amazed at him—
so marred were his features,
beyond that of mortals
his appearance, beyond that of human
beings—[q]
15 So shall he startle many nations,
kings shall stand speechless;
For those who have not been told shall
see,
those who have not heard shall
ponder it.[r]

### CHAPTER 53

See RG 210

1 Who would believe what we have
heard?*

**52:7–10** God leads the people back from Babylon to Zion, from whose ruined walls sentinels greet the returning exiles.

**52:11 From there**: from Babylon. **Vessels of the LORD**: taken to Babylon by Nebuchadnezzar, now carried back by the exiles returning in procession to Zion; cf. Ezr 1:7.

**52:13–53:12** The last of the "servant of the Lord" oracles (see note on 42:1–4). Taken together, these oracles depict a figure of one called by God for a vocation to Israel and the nations (42:4; 49:5–6); the servant's exaltation both opens and closes the passage (52:13; 53:12). The servant responded in fidelity but has suffered opposition (50:4–6). In this fourth oracle the servant is characterized as "a man of suffering" (53:3) and appears to be unjustly put to death (53:8–9). Those who have witnessed his career somehow recognize that he is innocent, has undergone suffering for their sins (53:4–6), and his death is referred to as a reparation offering (see note on 53:10–11). The servant is described in ways that identify him with Israel (which is frequently referred to as "servant" in the context of Second Isaiah—e.g., 41:8, 9; 44:2, 21; 43:4) and is designated as "Israel" in 49:3; yet Israel outside the "servant of the Lord" oracles is not presented as sinless, but rather in exile because of sin (40:2; 42:21–25) and even as servant as deaf and blind (42:18–19). The servant is thus both identified with Israel and distinguished from it. As with the previous servant poems, this chapter helped the followers of Jesus to interpret his suffering, death, and resurrection; see especially the passion narratives.

**53:1–10 What we have heard**: this fourth servant oracle is introduced by words of the Lord (52:13–15) but is now continued by speakers who are not identified, perhaps those re-

*n:* Is 40:9; Rom 10:15. *o:* Is 62:6. *p:* Ex 12:11. *q:* Ps 69:8.

To whom has the arm of the LORD
been revealed?[s]
2 He grew up like a sapling before him,[t]
like a shoot from the parched earth;
He had no majestic bearing to catch our eye,
no beauty to draw us to him.
3 He was spurned and avoided by men,
a man of suffering, knowing pain,
Like one from whom you turn your face,
spurned, and we held him in no esteem.[u]

4 Yet it was our pain that he bore,
our sufferings he endured.
We thought of him as stricken,
struck down by God* and afflicted,[v]
5 But he was pierced for our sins,
crushed for our iniquity.
He bore the punishment that makes us whole,
by his wounds we were healed.[w]
6 We had all gone astray like sheep,
all following our own way;
But the LORD laid upon him*
the guilt of us all.[x]

7 Though harshly treated, he submitted
and did not open his mouth;
Like a lamb led to slaughter
or a sheep silent before shearers,
he did not open his mouth.[y]
8 Seized and condemned, he was taken away.
Who would have thought any more of his destiny?
For he was cut off from the land of the living,
struck for the sins of his people.
9 He was given a grave among the wicked,
a burial place with evildoers,
Though he had done no wrong,
nor was deceit found in his mouth.[z]
10 But it was the LORD's will to crush him with pain.
By making his life as a reparation offering,*
he shall see his offspring, shall lengthen his days,
and the LORD's will shall be accomplished through him.
11 Because of his anguish he shall see the light;
because of his knowledge he shall be content;
My servant, the just one, shall justify the many,
their iniquity he shall bear.
12 Therefore I will give him his portion among the many,
and he shall divide the spoils with the mighty,
Because he surrendered himself to death,
was counted among the transgressors,
Bore the sins of many,
and interceded for the transgressors.[a]

## CHAPTER 54

See RG 210

### *The New Zion*

1 Raise a glad cry, you barren one* who never bore a child,
break forth in jubilant song, you who have never been in labor,
For more numerous are the children of the deserted wife
than the children of her who has a husband,
says the LORD.[b]

ferred to in 52:15, perhaps Israel (cf. "struck for the sins of his people"—v. 8). The Lord is again the speaker in vv. 11–13.

**53:4 Struck down by God**: the Bible often sees suffering as a punishment for sin (e.g., Ps 6:2; 32:1–5), yet sin sometimes appears to go unpunished and the innocent often suffer (cf. Ps 73; the Book of Job). In the case of the servant, the onlookers initially judge him guilty because of his suffering but, in some way not explained, they come to understand that his sufferings are for the sins of others. One notes the element of surprise, for such vicarious suffering, in the form described here, is without parallel in the Old Testament.

**53:6 The LORD laid upon him**: the servant's suffering is no accidental or casual matter, but part of God's plan; see also v. 10. The bystanders' speculation of v. 4 is verified, but not in the sense intended by them.

**53:10–11 Reparation offering**: the Hebrew term *'asham* is used of a particular kind of sacrifice, one that is intended as compensation for that which is due because of guilt. See Lv 5:14–26 and note. **Justify**: the verb means "to be acquitted," "declared innocent," but since the servant bears "their iniquity," an effective rather than simply legal action is suggested.

**54:1** Jerusalem, pictured as a wife who had been barren and deserted, now suddenly finds herself with innumerable children (the returning exiles); cf. Gal 4:27 for an application to a new context.

*r:* Mi 7:16. *s:* Is 52:10; Jn 12:38; Rom 10:16. *t:* Is 11:1. *u:* Jb 19:18; Ps 31:11–13; Mk 9:11. *v:* Jer 10:19; Mt 8:17. *w:* 1 Cor 15:3; 1 Pt 2:24. *x:* Lv 16:21–22. *y:* Mt 26:63; Acts 8:32. *z:* 1 Pt 2:22–23; 1 Jn 3:5. *a:* Mk 15:28; Lk 22:37. *b:* Gal 4:27.

[2] Enlarge the space for your tent,
spread out your tent cloths unsparingly;
lengthen your ropes and make firm
your pegs.[c]
[3] For you shall spread abroad to the right
and left;
your descendants shall dispossess the
nations
and shall people the deserted cities.*

[4] * Do not fear, you shall not be put to
shame;
do not be discouraged, you shall not be
disgraced.
For the shame of your youth you shall
forget,
the reproach of your widowhood no
longer remember.
[5] For your husband is your Maker;
the LORD of hosts is his name,
Your redeemer,* the Holy One of Israel,
called God of all the earth.

[6] The LORD calls you back,
like a wife forsaken and grieved in
spirit,
A wife married in youth and then cast off,
says your God.[d]
[7] For a brief moment I abandoned you,
but with great tenderness I will take
you back.
[8] In an outburst of wrath, for a moment
I hid my face from you;
But with enduring love I take pity on
you,
says the LORD, your redeemer.

[9] This is for me like the days of Noah:
As I swore then that the waters of Noah
should never again flood the earth,
So I have sworn now not to be angry
with you,
or to rebuke you.[e]
[10] Though the mountains fall away
and the hills be shaken,
My love shall never fall away from you
nor my covenant of peace* be shaken,
says the LORD, who has mercy on you.[f]

[11] O afflicted one,* storm-battered and
unconsoled,
I lay your pavements in carnelians,
your foundations in sapphires;[g]
[12] I will make your battlements of rubies,
your gates of jewels,
and all your walls of precious stones.
[13] All your children shall be taught by the
LORD;
great shall be the peace of your children.
[14] In justice shall you be established,
far from oppression, you shall not fear,
from destruction, it cannot come near.
[15] If there be an attack, it is not my doing;
whoever attacks shall fall before you.

[16] See, I have created the smith
who blows on the burning coals
and forges weapons as his work;
It is I also who have created
the destroyer to work havoc.
[17] Every weapon fashioned against you
shall fail;
every tongue that brings you to trial
you shall prove false.
This is the lot of the servants of the LORD,
their vindication from me—oracle of
the LORD.

## CHAPTER 55

See RG 210

### *An Invitation to Grace*

[1] All you who are thirsty,*
come to the water!
You who have no money,

**54:3** Those who had taken advantage of the exile to encroach on Jerusalem's territory will be driven out, and the returning exiles will repopulate the cities of Judah.

**54:4–8** As with some other Old Testament themes, Second Isaiah uses that of Israel as the Lord's bride in a new manner. Whereas Hosea and Jeremiah had depicted Israel as the Lord's spouse to emphasize both Israel's infidelity and the Lord's continued love (Hos 1–3; Jer 2:2; 3:1–15) and Ezekiel to accuse Israel unsparingly (Ez 16; 23), Second Isaiah speaks only of the love with which the Lord restores the people, speaking tender words with no hint of reproach.

**54:5 Redeemer**: cf. note on 41:14.

**54:10 Covenant of peace**: this whole section, vv. 9–17, is given to various assurances of God's love for Israel and of safety from various possible threats; the phrase sums up both the positive aspects of *shalom*, which implies a fullness of blessing, and protection from all that might harm. Cf. also 55:3; Nm 25:12; Ez 34:25; 37:26; Mal 2:5.

**54:11 Afflicted one**: Jerusalem.

**55:1–3** The prophet invites all to return, under the figure of a banquet; cf. the covenant banquet in Ex 24:9–11 and wis-

*c:* Is 49:20. *d:* Mal 2:14–15. *e:* Gn 9:15. *f:* Ps 46:3; 76:5. *g:* Rev 21:18–21.

come, buy grain and eat;
Come, buy grain without money,
wine and milk without cost![h]
2 Why spend your money for what is not bread;
your wages for what does not satisfy?
Only listen to me, and you shall eat well,
you shall delight in rich fare.
3 Pay attention and come to me;
listen, that you may have life.
I will make with you an everlasting covenant,
the steadfast loyalty promised to David.[i]
4 As I made him a witness to peoples,
a leader and commander of peoples,
5 So shall you summon a nation you knew not,
and a nation* that knew you not shall run to you,
Because of the LORD, your God,
the Holy One of Israel, who has glorified you.[j]

6 * Seek the LORD while he may be found,
call upon him while he is near.
7 Let the wicked forsake their way,
and sinners their thoughts;
Let them turn to the LORD to find mercy;
to our God, who is generous in forgiving.
8 For my thoughts are not your thoughts,
nor are your ways my ways—oracle of the LORD.
9 For as the heavens are higher than the earth,
so are my ways higher than your ways,
my thoughts higher than your thoughts.
10 * Yet just as from the heavens
the rain and snow come down
And do not return there
till they have watered the earth,
making it fertile and fruitful,
Giving seed to the one who sows
and bread to the one who eats,
11 So shall my word be
that goes forth from my mouth;
It shall not return to me empty,
but shall do what pleases me,
achieving the end for which I sent it.
12 Yes, in joy you shall go forth,
in peace you shall be brought home;
Mountains and hills shall break out in song before you,
all trees of the field shall clap their hands.
13 In place of the thornbush, the cypress shall grow,
instead of nettles,* the myrtle.
This shall be to the LORD's renown,
as an everlasting sign that shall not fail.

## III. Isaiah 56—66

### CHAPTER 56

See RG 211

### *Salvation for the Just**

1 * Thus says the LORD:
Observe what is right, do what is just,
for my salvation is about to come,
my justice, about to be revealed.[k]

dom's banquet in Prv 9:1–6. The Lord's covenant with David (2 Sm 7) is now to be extended beyond his dynasty.

**55:5** The "nation" is Persia under Cyrus, but the perspective is worldwide.

**55:6–9** The invitation to seek the Lord is motivated by the mercy of a God whose "ways" are completely mysterious.

**55:10–11** The efficacy of the word of God recalls 40:5, 8.

**55:13 Thornbush . . . nettles**: suggestive of the desert and therefore symbolic of suffering and hardship; **cypress . . . myrtle**: suggestive of fertile land and therefore symbolic of joy and strength. **To the LORD's renown**: lit., "to the name of the Lord."

**56:1–8** This poem inaugurates the final section of the Book of Isaiah, often referred to as Third or Trito-Isaiah. While Second or Deutero-Isaiah (Is 40–55) gave numerous references to the hopes of the community of Israel during the Babylonian exile (ca. 587–538 B.C.), Third Isaiah witnesses to the struggles and hoped-for blessings of the postexilic community now back in the homeland of Israel. In this opening poem, the references to "keeping the sabbath" (vv. 2, 4, 6), "holding fast to the covenant" (vv. 4, 6) and "God's holy mountain" as a house of prayer (v. 7), all tell of the postexilic community that was establishing itself again in the land according to the pattern of God's word given through the prophet. The poem can be classified as a "prophetic exhortation" in which the prophet gives instruction for those who wish to live according to God's word and covenant. What is important to note are the conditions placed upon the people of God; while Is 40–55 show an unconditional promise of redemption, these final chapters delineate clear expectations for receiving God's salvific promises. Both the expectations and the great promises of God will unfold in the succeeding chapters of Third Isaiah.

**56:1** This opening verse echoes themes that are well known throughout the Book of Isaiah: justice and right judg-

*h:* Jn 4:10–15; 6:35; 7:37–39; Rev 21:6; 22:17. *i:* 2 Sm 7:12–16. *j:* Acts 13:34. *k:* Is 59:9, 14, 19–20.

2 Happy is the one who does this,
whoever holds fast to it:
Keeping the sabbath without profaning it,
keeping one's hand from doing any evil.[l]

### *Obligations and Promises To Share in the Covenant*

3 * The foreigner joined to the LORD
should not say,
"The LORD will surely exclude me
from his people";
Nor should the eunuch say,
"See, I am a dry tree."[m]
4 For thus says the LORD:
To the eunuchs who keep my sabbaths,
who choose what pleases me,
and who hold fast to my covenant,[n]
5 I will give them, in my house
and within my walls, a monument and
a name*
Better than sons and daughters;
an eternal name, which shall not be cut
off, will I give them.
6 And foreigners who join themselves to
the LORD,
to minister to him,
To love the name of the LORD,
to become his servants—
All who keep the sabbath without
profaning it
and hold fast to my covenant,
7 * Them I will bring to my holy mountain
and make them joyful in my house of
prayer;
Their burnt offerings and their sacrifices
will be acceptable on my altar,
For my house shall be called
a house of prayer for all peoples.[o]
8 * Oracle of the Lord GOD,
who gathers the dispersed of Israel—
Others will I gather to them
besides those already gathered.[p]

### *Unworthy Shepherds**

9 All you beasts of the field,*
come to devour,
all you beasts in the forest![q]
10 * All the sentinels of Israel are blind,
they are without knowledge;
They are all mute dogs,
unable to bark;
Dreaming, reclining,
loving their sleep.
11 Yes, the dogs have a ravenous appetite;
they never know satiety,
Shepherds who have no understanding;
all have turned their own way,
each one covetous for gain:
12 "Come, let me bring wine;
let us fill ourselves with strong drink,
And tomorrow will be like today,
or even greater."[r]

## CHAPTER 57

See RG 211

1 The just have perished,
but no one takes it to heart;
The steadfast are swept away,
while no one understands.

ment (1:27; 5:7, 16; 9:6; 16:5; 26:9; 28:17; 32:1, 16; 33:5; 42:1, 4, 6; 45:8, 13, 19), salvation and deliverance (12:3; 26:18; 33:2; 45:8, 21; 46:13; 51:5, 6, 8). These themes will be developed also throughout Third Isaiah.

**56:3** Eunuchs had originally been excluded from the community of the Lord; cf. Dt 23:2; Neh 13:1–3; Wis 3:14.

**56:5 A monument and a name**: literally in Hebrew, "a hand and a name"; a memorial inscription to prevent oblivion for one who had no children; cf. 2 Sm 18:18; Neh 7:5; 13:14.

**56:7** This verse continues the theme of universalism found in Is 49:6. As Israel was to be "a light to the nations" so that God's "salvation may reach to the ends of the earth," so now does that come to pass as foreigners, faithful to the divine commands, are brought to the Temple by God and joined to the covenant community of Israel.

**56:8** For the gathering of the dispersed people of Israel, cf. Jer 23:3; 31:8–9; Ez 11:17. Here the Lord not only gathers the displaced of Israel, but also unites other peoples to them. Cf. Is 60:3–10; 66:18–21.

**56:9–57:21** This section is made up of two pronouncements of judgment (56:9–57:2; 57:3–13) and an oracle of salvation (57:14–21), each of which ends with a reversal of imagery and language. While there are harsh indictments against the corrupt leaders of Israel (56:9–12), a promise of peace is offered to those who are just (57:1–2). Then the judgment and its subsequent punishment for idolaters (57:3–13a) change to an announcement of reward for those who place their trust in God (57:13c). And the promises of salvation (57:14–19) then shift to a word of warning to the wicked (57:20–21).

**56:9 Beasts of the field**: foreign nations, which are invited to come and ravage Israel.

**56:10–11** These shepherds of Israel are without "knowledge," a theme developed earlier in the Isaian corpus; cf. 1:3; 6:9–10. Ezekiel 34 has similar condemnatory words against the unfaithful shepherds of Israel.

*l:* Is 1:13; 58:13–14; Ex 23:12. *m:* Dt 23:3–5; Neh 13:1–3. *n:* Wis 3:14. *o:* 1 Kgs 8:29–30, 41; Mt 21:13. *p:* Ps 147:2. *q:* Jer 12:9–10; Ez 34:5. *r:* Is 22:13; 28:7; Wis 2:7.

All these the wind shall carry off,
a mere breath shall bear them away;
But whoever takes refuge in me shall
inherit the land,
and possess my holy mountain.

### *The Way to Peace for God's People*

14 And I say:
Build up, build up, prepare the way,
remove every obstacle from my
people's way.* [v]
15 * For thus says the high and lofty One,
the One who dwells forever, whose
name is holy:
I dwell in a high and holy place,
but also with the contrite and lowly of
spirit,
To revive the spirit of the lowly,
to revive the heart of the crushed.
16 For I will not accuse forever,
nor always be angry;
For without me their spirit fails,
the life breath that I have given.[w]
17 Because of their wicked avarice I grew
angry;
I struck them, hiding myself from
them in wrath.
But they turned back, following the way
of their own heart.[x]
18 I saw their ways,
but I will heal them.
I will lead them and restore full comfort
to them
and to those who mourn for them,[y]
19 creating words of comfort.*
Peace! Peace to those who are far and near,
says the LORD; and I will heal them.
20 But the wicked are like the tossing sea
which cannot be still,
Its waters cast up mire and mud.[z]
21 There is no peace for the wicked!
says my God.[a]

## CHAPTER 58

See RG 211

### *Reasons for Judgment**

1 Cry out full-throated and unsparingly,
lift up your voice like a trumpet blast;
Proclaim to my people their
transgression,
to the house of Jacob their sins.[b]
2 They seek me day after day,
and desire to know my ways,
Like a nation that has done what is just
and not abandoned the judgment of
their God;
They ask of me just judgments,
they desire to draw near to God.
3 "Why do we fast, but you do not see it?
afflict ourselves, but you take no note?"
See, on your fast day you carry out your
own pursuits,
and drive all your laborers.[c]
4 See, you fast only to quarrel and fight
and to strike with a wicked fist!
Do not fast as you do today
to make your voice heard on high!
5 Is this the manner of fasting I would
choose,
a day to afflict oneself?
To bow one's head like a reed,
and lie upon sackcloth and ashes?
Is this what you call a fast,
a day acceptable to the LORD?[d]

### *Authentic Fasting That Leads to Blessing**

6 Is this not, rather, the fast that I choose:
releasing those bound unjustly,
untying the thongs of the yoke;
Setting free the oppressed,
breaking off every yoke?[e]
7 Is it not sharing your bread with the
hungry,
bringing the afflicted and the homeless
into your house;

**57:14 The way . . . my people's way**: the language and imagery are reminiscent of 40:1–2, but in this context, when the people have already returned, the physical road through the desert is replaced by the spiritual way that leads to redemption.

**57:15** The God of Israel is presented in both a transcendent and an immanent manner. God's holiness is the transcendent quality; the immanence is shown in the choice of dwelling among the downtrodden and humble.

**57:19 Creating words of comfort**: lit., "fruit of the lips," perhaps referring to praise and thanksgiving for the divine healing; cf. Hos 14:3.

**58:1–5** The prophet is commanded to condemn the formalism of the people, specifically their hypocritical fasting.

**58:6–12** Fasting is not genuine without reforming one's way of life. A true social morality will ensure prosperity.

*v:* Is 40:3–4. *w:* Gn 2:7. *x:* Is 56:11. *y:* Is 61:2. *z:* Jon 2:3–7. *a:* Is 48:22. *b:* Lv 25:9. *c:* 1 Sm 7:6; 1 Kgs 21:12; 1 Mc 3:47; Jl 1:1–2:17. *d:* Zec 7:5. *e:* Is 35:5–6.

Yet the just are taken away from the
presence of evil,
2 * and enter into peace;
They rest upon their couches,
the sincere, who walk in integrity.[s]

### *An Idolatrous People**

3 But you, draw near,
you children of a sorceress,
offspring of an adulterer and a
prostitute!*
4 Against whom do you make sport,
against whom do you open wide your
mouth,
and stick out your tongue?
Are you not rebellious children,
deceitful offspring—
5 You who burn with lust among the oaks,
under every green tree;
You who immolate children in the
wadies,
among the clefts of the rocks?* [t]
6 Among the smooth stones* of the wadi is
your portion,
they, they are your allotment;
Indeed, you poured out a drink offering
to them,
and brought up grain offerings.
With these things, should I be
appeased?
7 Upon a towering and lofty mountain
you set up your bed,
and there you went up to offer
sacrifice.[u]
8 Behind the door and the doorpost
you set up your symbol.
Yes, deserting me, you carried up your
bedding;
and spread it wide.
You entered an agreement with them,
you loved their couch, you gazed upon
nakedness.*
9 You approached the king* with oil,
and multiplied your perfumes;
You sent your ambassadors far away,
down even to deepest Sheol.
10 Though worn out with the length of your
journey,
you never said, "It is hopeless";
You found your strength revived,
and so you did not weaken.
11 Whom did you dread and fear,
that you told lies,
And me you did not remember
nor take to heart?
Am I to keep silent and conceal,
while you show no fear of me?
12 I will proclaim your justice*
and your works;
but they shall not help you.
13 * When you cry out,
let your collection of idols save you.

**57:2** Despite their sad fate, the just will ultimately attain peace (most likely in this world); cf. v. 13.

**57:3–13** In this courtroom imagery, the idolaters are summoned before the judge (v. 3), their crimes are graphically described (vv. 4–11), their guilt is established, and condemnation is carried out (vv. 12–13b). In contrast to this, v. 13c describes the inheritance of God's land and holy mountain given to those who place their confidence in God instead of in idols.

**57:3** Language of sexual infidelity is often used in a figurative way to describe idolatry. Cf. Ez 16:15–22; Hos 2:4–7; Col 3:5.

**57:5** Child sacrifice is also attested in 2 Kgs 23:10; Jer 7:31; Ez 16:20; 20:28, 31; 23:37–39.

**57:6 Smooth stones**: the Hebrew word for this expression has the same consonants as the word for "portion"; instead of making the Lord their portion (cf. Ps 16:5), the people adored slabs of stone which they took from the streambeds in valleys and set up as idols; cf. Jer 3:9. Therefore, it is implied, they will be swept away as by a sudden torrent of waters carrying them down the rocky-bottomed gorge to destruction and death without burial.

**57:8 Nakedness**: literally in Hebrew, "hand." In this context, it may euphemistically refer to a phallus.

**57:9 The king**: in Hebrew, the word for king is *melek*, similar in sound to the Canaanite god Molech, to whom children were offered as a sacrifice in pagan ritual. The expression "your ambassadors" could be a figurative expression for the children whose death served as an offering to this deity.

**57:12 Justice**: here used sarcastically. The activity described in these verses is far from the justice which God demands of those who are aligned with the covenant (cf. 56:1, 4, 6). In the larger context of Third Isaiah and the whole of the Isaian tradition, justice is a key theological motif. The justice to which God calls Israel will eventually come to its fulfillment in an act of divine intervention (cf. 60:21; 61:3c). Until then, the people of God must strive to live in the ways of justice and right judgment (56:1).

**57:13** In v. 6, the smooth stones of the valley are the portion which the unfaithful will receive as their due reward (cf. note on v. 6); while in v. 13c, an inheritance of the land and possession of God's holy mountain will be the portion of the upright.

*s:* Wis 3:1–3. *t:* Dt 12:2; 2 Kgs 17:10; Jer 7:31; 19:5; Ez 20:28, 31. *u:* Jer 2:20; Ez 6:13; Hos 4:13.

Clothing the naked when you see them,
and not turning your back on your own flesh?[f]
8 Then your light shall break forth like the dawn,
and your wound shall quickly be healed;
Your vindication shall go before you,
and the glory of the LORD shall be your rear guard.
9 Then you shall call, and the LORD will answer,
you shall cry for help, and he will say: "Here I am!"
If you remove the yoke from among you,
the accusing finger, and malicious speech;[g]
10 If you lavish your food on the hungry
and satisfy the afflicted;
Then your light shall rise in the darkness,
and your gloom shall become like midday;
11 Then the LORD will guide you always
and satisfy your thirst in parched places,
will give strength to your bones
And you shall be like a watered garden,
like a flowing spring whose waters never fail.[h]
12 Your people shall rebuild the ancient ruins;
the foundations from ages past you shall raise up;
"Repairer of the breach," they shall call you,
"Restorer of ruined dwellings."[i]

### *Authentic Sabbath Observance That Leads to Blessing**

13 If you refrain from trampling the sabbath,
from following your own pursuits on my holy day;
If you call the sabbath a delight,
the LORD's holy day glorious;
If you glorify it by not following your ways,
seeking your own interests, or pursuing your own affairs—
14 Then you shall delight in the LORD,
and I will make you ride upon the heights of the earth;
I will nourish you with the heritage of Jacob, your father,
for the mouth of the LORD has spoken.[j]

## CHAPTER 59

See RG 211

### *Salvation Delayed*

1 * No, the hand of the LORD is not too short to save,
nor his ear too dull to hear.[k]
2 Rather, it is your crimes
that separate you from your God,
It is your sins that make him hide his face
so that he does not hear you.
3 For your hands are defiled with blood,
and your fingers with crime;
Your lips speak falsehood,
and your tongue utters deceit.[l]
4 No one brings suit justly,
no one pleads truthfully;
They trust an empty plea and tell lies;
they conceive mischief and bring forth malice.
5 * They hatch adders' eggs,
and weave spiders' webs:
Whoever eats the eggs will die,
if one of them is crushed, it will hatch a viper;[m]
6 Their webs cannot serve as clothing,
nor can they cover themselves with their works.
Their works are evil works,
and deeds of violence are in their hands.
7 Their feet run to evil,
and they hasten to shed innocent blood;
Their thoughts are thoughts of wickedness,

**58:13–14** Sabbath observance becomes a cornerstone of postexilic piety; cf. 56:2, 4, 6.

**59:1–20** This poem brings together a lament of the postexilic community and a harsh word of judgment from the prophet. After the opening rhetorical question, each of the stanzas begins with a reference to the justice and right judgment which are lacking among the people (vv. 4, 9, 14). Toward the end of the poem, God is depicted as a Divine Warrior (vv. 16–20) who is the only one who can intervene in order to bring redemption. This same Divine Warrior imagery is repeated in a similar fashion in 63:1–6.

**59:5–6** The eggs signify evil works, doing positive harm; the webs are devices that serve no useful purpose.

*f:* Ez 18:7, 16; Mt 25:35. *g:* Am 5:7. *h:* Is 51:3; Ps 24. *i:* Is 61:4. *j:* Hb 3:19. *k:* Is 50:2; Nm 11:23. *l:* Is 1:15. *m:* Jb 20:12–16.

violence and destruction are on their
highways.[n]
8 The way of peace they know not,
and there is no justice on their paths;
Their roads they have made crooked,
no one who walks in them knows peace.

### *Acknowledgment of Transgressions*

9 * That is why judgment is far from us
and justice does not reach us.
We look for light, but there is darkness;
for brightness, and we walk in gloom![o]
10 Like those who are blind we grope along
the wall,
like people without eyes we feel our
way.
We stumble at midday as if at twilight,
among the vigorous, we are like the
dead.
11 Like bears we all growl,
like doves we moan without ceasing.
We cry out for justice, but it is not there;
for salvation, but it is far from us.[p]
12 For our transgressions before you are
many,
our sins bear witness against us.
Our transgressions are present to us,
and our crimes we acknowledge:
13 Transgressing, and denying the LORD,
turning back from following our God,
Planning fraud and treachery,
uttering lying words conceived in the
heart.
14 Judgment is turned away,
and justice stands far off;
For truth stumbles in the public square,
and uprightness cannot enter.[q]
15 Fidelity is lacking,
and whoever turns from evil is
despoiled.

### *Divine Intervention*

The LORD saw this, and was aggrieved
that there was no justice.
16 He saw that there was no one,
was appalled that there was none to
intervene;
Then his own arm brought about the
victory,
and his justice sustained him.
17 He put on justice as his breastplate,
victory as a helmet on his head;
He clothed himself with garments of
vengeance,
wrapped himself in a mantle of zeal.[r]
18 According to their deeds he repays his
enemies
and requites his foes with wrath;
to the coastlands he renders recompense.
19 Those in the west shall fear the name of
the LORD,
and those in the east, his glory,
Coming like a pent-up stream
driven on by the breath of the LORD.
20 Then for Zion shall come a redeemer,
to those in Jacob who turn from
transgression—oracle of the
LORD.[s]
21 * This is my covenant with them,
which I myself have made, says the
LORD:
My spirit which is upon you
and my words that I have put in your
mouth
Shall not depart from your mouth,
nor from the mouths of your children
Nor the mouths of your children's
children
from this time forth and forever, says
the LORD.[t]

## CHAPTER 60

See RG 211

### *The Dawning of Divine Glory for Zion*

1 * Arise! Shine, for your light has come,
the glory of the LORD has dawned
upon you.[u]
2 Though darkness covers the earth,

**59:9–15** The turning point in the poem comes when the people acknowledge their transgressions and describe the horror of their present state. Light is a metaphor for salvation (cf. 9:1; 42:16; 60:1–3, 19–20) and darkness represents sin and disaster.

**59:21** This verse makes the transition from chaps. 56–59 to chaps. 60–62. Oracles of judgment yield to oracles about God's redemptive action.

**60:1–9** The light the prophet proclaims to Zion symbolizes the blessing to come to her: the glory of the Lord, the return

*n:* Prv 1:15, 19; 2:8–9, 12–13, 15, 18–19; Rom 3:15. *o:* Am 5:18–19. *p:* Is 38:14. *q:* Jb 28:28. *r:* Wis 5:17–20; Eph 6:14–16; 1 Thes 5:8. *s:* Is 35:4; Rom 11:26–27. *t:* Is 1:27. *u:* Is 40:5; 49:14–26; 51:17–23.

and thick clouds, the peoples,
Upon you the LORD will dawn,
and over you his glory will be seen.
3 Nations shall walk by your light,
kings by the radiance of your dawning.[v]

### *The Nations Come to Zion*

4 Raise your eyes and look about;
they all gather and come to you—
Your sons from afar,
your daughters in the arms of their nurses.[w]
5 Then you shall see and be radiant,
your heart shall throb and overflow.
For the riches of the sea shall be poured out before you,
the wealth of nations shall come to you.
6 Caravans of camels shall cover you,
dromedaries of Midian and Ephah;
All from Sheba shall come
bearing gold and frankincense,
and heralding the praises of the LORD.
7 All the flocks of Kedar shall be gathered for you,
the rams of Nebaioth shall serve your needs;
They will be acceptable offerings on my altar,
and I will glorify my glorious house.
8 Who are these that fly along like a cloud,
like doves to their cotes?
9 The vessels of the coastlands are gathering,
with the ships of Tarshish in the lead,
To bring your children from afar,
their silver and gold with them—
For the name of the LORD, your God,
for the Holy One of Israel who has glorified you.

### *Honor and Service for Zion**

10 Foreigners shall rebuild your walls,
their kings shall minister to you;
Though in my wrath I struck you,
yet in my good will I have shown you mercy.[x]
11 Your gates shall stand open constantly;
day and night they shall not be closed
So that they may bring you the wealth of nations,
with their kings in the vanguard.[y]
12 For the nation or kingdom that will not serve you shall perish;
such nations shall be utterly destroyed![z]
13 The glory of Lebanon shall come to you—
the juniper, the fir, and the cypress all together—
To bring beauty to my sanctuary,
and glory to the place where I stand.[a]
14 The children of your oppressors shall come,
bowing before you;
All those who despised you,
shall bow low at your feet.
They shall call you "City of the LORD,"
"Zion of the Holy One of Israel."
15 No longer forsaken and hated,
with no one passing through,
Now I will make you the pride of the ages,
a joy from generation to generation.
16 You shall suck the milk of nations,
and be nursed at royal breasts;
And you shall know that I, the LORD, am your savior,
your redeemer, the Mighty One of Jacob.
17 Instead of bronze I will bring gold,
instead of iron I will bring silver;
Instead of wood, bronze;
instead of stones, iron.
I will appoint peace your governor,
and justice your ruler.[b]
18 No longer shall violence be heard of in your land,
or plunder and ruin within your borders.
You shall call your walls "Salvation"
and your gates "Praise."

### *Eternal Light for Zion*

19 * No longer shall the sun
be your light by day,

of her children, the wealth of nations who themselves will walk by her light. The passage is famous from its use in the Latin liturgy for the feast of Epiphany.

**60:10–18** The glorious promises for the future continue: the wealth of the nations (vv. 5, 10), tribute from kings, glorification of the Temple, peace and justice (cf. Ps 85:11).

**60:19–20** The theme of light is taken up again, but in an

*v:* Is 42:6; 45:14; 49:6. *w:* Is 49:18. *x:* Is 54:11–12. *y:* Rev 21:25. *z:* Is 61:2. *a:* Is 35:2; 66:1. *b:* Ps 85:11.

Nor shall the brightness of the moon
give you light by night;
Rather, the LORD will be your light forever,
your God will be your glory.[c]
20 No longer will your sun set,
or your moon wane;
For the LORD will be your light forever,
and the days of your grieving will be over.
21 Your people will all be just;
for all time they will possess the land;
They are the shoot that I planted,
the work of my hands, that I might be glorified.[d]
22 The least one shall become a clan,
the smallest, a mighty nation;
I, the LORD, will swiftly accomplish
these things when the time comes.[e]

See RG 211

## CHAPTER 61

### *The Anointed Bearer of Glad Tidings*

1 * The spirit of the Lord GOD is upon me,
because the LORD has anointed me;
He has sent me to bring good news to the afflicted,
to bind up the brokenhearted,
To proclaim liberty to the captives,
release to the prisoners,[f]
2 To announce a year of favor from the LORD
and a day of vindication by our God;
To comfort all who mourn;[g]
3 to place on those who mourn in Zion
a diadem instead of ashes,
To give them oil of gladness instead of mourning,
a glorious mantle instead of a faint spirit.

### *Restoration and Blessing*

They will be called oaks of justice,
the planting of the LORD to show his glory.
4 They shall rebuild the ancient ruins,
the former wastes they shall raise up
And restore the desolate cities,
devastations of generation upon generation.[h]
5 Strangers shall stand ready to pasture your flocks,
foreigners shall be your farmers and vinedressers.
6 * You yourselves shall be called "Priests of the LORD,"
"Ministers of our God" you shall be called.
You shall eat the wealth of the nations
and in their riches you will boast.[i]
7 Because their shame was twofold*
and disgrace was proclaimed their portion,
They will possess twofold in their own land;
everlasting joy shall be theirs.[j]

### *God's Word of Promise*

8 For I, the LORD, love justice,
I hate robbery and wrongdoing;
I will faithfully give them their recompense,
an everlasting covenant I will make with them.[k]
9 Their offspring shall be renowned among the nations,
and their descendants in the midst of the peoples;
All who see them shall acknowledge them:
"They are offspring the LORD has blessed."

### *Thanksgiving for God's Deliverance*

10 * I will rejoice heartily in the LORD,
my being exults in my God;
For he has clothed me with garments of salvation,

apocalyptic vein: the Lord's radiant presence replaces physical light.

**61:1–2** The prophet proclaims that he has been anointed by the Lord to bring good news (cf. 40:9) to the afflicted and to comfort Zion. The background to the "year of favor" is the jubilee year of release from debts (Lv 25:10–11; Is 49:8).

**61:6** The bestowal of a new name suggests a new identity and mission. The whole people will be priests (cf. Ex 19:6), even ministering to nations who will serve God's people.

**61:7 Twofold**: Israel was punished double for infidelity (40:2); the blessings of its restoration will also be double.

**61:10–11** The new life of the restored Zion is expressed in nuptial (cf. also 62:5) and agricultural (cf. v. 3; 60:21) imagery.

*c:* Is 2:5; Rev 21:23; 22:5. *d:* Is 57:13c. *e:* Gn 12:2; 17:6. *f:* Is 40:9; 42:1; 48:16; 52:7; 58:7; Lk 4:18–19. *g:* Mt 5:4. *h:* Is 58:12. *i:* Ex 19:6; 1 Pt 2:9. *j:* Is 40:2. *k:* Is 55:3; 54:9–10; 59:21.

and wrapped me in a robe of justice,
Like a bridegroom adorned with a diadem,
as a bride adorns herself with her jewels.[l]
11 As the earth brings forth its shoots,
and a garden makes its seeds spring up,
So will the Lord GOD make justice spring up,
and praise before all the nations.

## CHAPTER 62

See RG 211

### *A New Name for Zion*

1 * For Zion's sake I will not be silent,
for Jerusalem's sake I will not keep still,
Until her vindication shines forth like the dawn
and her salvation like a burning torch.[m]
2 Nations shall behold your vindication,
and all kings your glory;
You shall be called by a new name
bestowed by the mouth of the LORD.[n]
3 You shall be a glorious crown in the hand of the LORD,
a royal diadem in the hand of your God.
4 No more shall you be called "Forsaken,"
nor your land called "Desolate,"
But you shall be called "My Delight is in her,"
and your land "Espoused."
For the LORD delights in you,
and your land shall be espoused.[o]
5 For as a young man marries a virgin,
your Builder shall marry you;
And as a bridegroom rejoices in his bride
so shall your God rejoice in you.
6 Upon your walls, Jerusalem,
I have stationed sentinels;
By day and by night,
they shall never be silent.
You who are to remind the LORD,
take no rest,
7 And give him no rest,
until he re-establishes Jerusalem
And makes it the praise of the earth.

### *The Blessings of Salvation for God's People*

8 * The LORD has sworn by his right hand
and by his mighty arm:
No more will I give your grain
as food to your enemies;
Nor shall foreigners drink the wine,
for which you toiled.[p]
9 But those who harvest shall eat,
and praise the LORD;
Those who gather shall drink
in my holy courts.[q]
10 * Pass through, pass through the gates,
prepare a way for the people;[r]
Build up, build up the highway, clear it of stones,
raise up a standard over the nations.
11 The LORD has proclaimed
to the ends of the earth:
Say to daughter Zion,
"See, your savior comes!
See, his reward is with him,
his recompense before him."[s]
12 They shall be called "The Holy People,"
"The Redeemed of the LORD."
And you shall be called "Cared For,"
"A City Not Forsaken."[t]

## CHAPTER 63

See RG 211-12

### *The Divine Warrior**

1 Who is this that comes from Edom,
in crimsoned garments, from Bozrah?
Who is this, glorious in his apparel,
striding in the greatness of his strength?
"It is I, I who announce vindication,
mighty to save."[u]
2 Why is your apparel red,
and your garments like one who treads the wine press?[v]
3 "The wine press I have trodden alone,

**62:1–12** As in chap. 60, the prophet addresses Zion, announcing the reversal of her fortune. Several motifs reappear: light and glory (60:1–3, 19–20), tribute of nations (60:11), and especially the marriage (61:10; cf. also 54:5–8).

**62:8–9** Peace and prosperity are indicated by the absence of invaders who would live off the land.

**62:10–11** The gates of Babylon are to be opened for the exiles to return, led by the Lord, as in 40:3–5, 10.

**63:1–6** Two questions are raised at the approach of a majestic figure coming from Edom. It is the Lord, his garments red with the blood from the judgment battle. Edom (its capital Bozrah) plundered Judah after the fall of Jerusalem; cf. 34:5–17. **Wine press**: here a symbol of a bloody judgment; cf. Lam 1:15; Jl 4:13.

*l:* 1 Sm 2:1; Ps 138:1–2. *m:* Is 42:14; 64:22. *n:* Rev 2:17; 3:12. *o:* Is 49:15–16; 54:7–8. *p:* Is 52:10. *q:* Dt 12:17–18; 14:23. *r:* Is 58:14. *s:* Is 40:10. *t:* Is 62:4. *u:* Is 34:6; 49:19. *v:* Rev 19:13.

and from the peoples no one was
with me.
I trod them in my anger,
and trampled them down in my wrath;
Their blood spurted on my garments,
all my apparel I stained.
4 For a day of vindication was in my heart,
my year for redeeming had come.[w]
5 I looked about, but there was no one to
help,
I was appalled that there was no one to
lend support;
So my own arm brought me victory
and my own wrath lent me support.[x]
6 I trampled down the peoples in my
anger,
I made them drunk in my wrath,
and I poured out their blood upon the
ground."

***Prayer for the Return of God's Favor***

7 * The loving deeds of the LORD I will
recall,
the glorious acts of the LORD,
Because of all the LORD has done for us,
the immense goodness to the house of
Israel,
Which he has granted according to his
mercy
and his many loving deeds.[y]
8 He said: "They are indeed my people,
children who are not disloyal."
So he became their savior
9 in their every affliction.
It was not an envoy or a messenger,
but his presence that saved them.
Because of his love and pity
the LORD redeemed them,
Lifting them up and carrying them
all the days of old.[z]
10 But they rebelled
and grieved his holy spirit;
So he turned to become their enemy,
and warred against them.[a]
11 Then they remembered the days of old, of
Moses, his servant:
Where is the one who brought up out of
the sea
the shepherd of his flock?
Where is the one who placed in their midst
his holy spirit,[b]
12 Who guided Moses by the hand,
with his glorious arm?
Where is the one who divided the waters
before them—
winning for himself an everlasting
renown—
13 Who guided them through the depths,
like horses in open country?
14 As cattle going down into the valley,
they did not stumble.
The spirit of the LORD guided them.
Thus you led your people,
to make for yourself a glorious name.
15 Look down from heaven and regard us
from your holy and glorious palace!
Where is your zealous care and your might,
your surge of pity?[c]
Your mercy hold not back!
16 For you are our father.
Were Abraham not to know us,
nor Israel to acknowledge us,
You, LORD, are our father,
our redeemer you are named from of
old.
17 Why do you make us wander, LORD,
from your ways,
and harden our hearts so that we do
not fear you?*
Return for the sake of your servants,
the tribes of your heritage.
18 Why have the wicked invaded your holy
place,
why have our enemies trampled your
sanctuary?
19 * Too long have we been like those you
do not rule,

**63:7–64:11** This lament of the exilic community recalls God's protection, and especially the memories of the exodus (vv. 7–14), before begging the Lord to come once more to their aid (63:15–64:3), as they confess their sins (64:4–11). The prayer is marked by God's "holy spirit" (63:10–11, 14) and fatherhood (63:8, 9, 16; 64:7).

**63:17** The hardening of the heart (Ex 4:21; 7:3) serves to explain Israel's sins—a motif to induce the Lord to relent.

**63:19–64:3** A new theophany, like Sinai of old, is invoked so that Israel's enemies will be humbled by God's intervention.

*w:* Is 34:8; 61:2. *x:* Is 59:16. *y:* Is 26:15. *z:* Dt 4:37–40. *a:* Dt 32:15; Ps 51:12. *b:* Heb 13:20. *c:* Dt 26:15; Bar 2:16.

on whom your name is not invoked.
Oh, that you would rend the heavens and come down,
with the mountains quaking before you,[d]

## CHAPTER 64

See RG 211-12

1 As when brushwood is set ablaze,
or fire makes the water boil!
Then your name would be made known to your enemies
and the nations would tremble before you,
2 While you worked awesome deeds we could not hope for,*
3 such as had not been heard of from of old.
No ear has ever heard, no eye ever seen,
any God but you
working such deeds for those who wait for him.[e]
4 Would that you might meet us doing right,
that we might be mindful of you in our ways!
Indeed, you are angry; we have sinned,
we have acted wickedly.
5 We have all become like something unclean,
all our just deeds are like polluted rags;
We have all withered like leaves,
and our crimes carry us away like the wind.[f]
6 There are none who call upon your name,
none who rouse themselves to take hold of you;
For you have hidden your face from us
and have delivered us up to our crimes.

### *A Final Plea*

7 * Yet, LORD, you are our father;
we are the clay and you our potter:
we are all the work of your hand.
8 Do not be so very angry, LORD,
do not remember our crimes forever;
look upon us, who are all your people!
9 Your holy cities have become a wilderness;
Zion has become wilderness,
Jerusalem desolation![g]
10 Our holy and glorious house
in which our ancestors praised you
Has been burned with fire;
all that was dear to us is laid waste.
11 Can you hold back, LORD, after all this?
Can you remain silent, and afflict us so severely?

## CHAPTER 65

See RG 211-12

1 * I was ready to respond to those who did not ask,
to be found by those who did not seek me.
I said: Here I am! Here I am!
To a nation that did not invoke my name.[h]
2 I have stretched out my hands all day
to a rebellious people,
Who walk in a way that is not good,
following their own designs;[i]
3 A people who provoke me
continually to my face,
Offering sacrifices in gardens
and burning incense on bricks,
4 Sitting in tombs
and spending the night in caves,
Eating the flesh of pigs,
with broth of unclean meat in their dishes;
5 Crying out, "Hold back,
do not come near me, lest I render you holy!"*
These things are smoke in my nostrils,
a fire that burns all the day.
6 See, it stands written before me;

**64:2** The translation here omits some words repeated in the Hebrew from 63:19 ("would that you would come down, with the mountains trembling before you").

**64:7–11** The motifs of father (63:16) and creator (clay and potter, 29:16; 45:9) are adduced to move the Lord to action in view of the damage done to his "holy cities" and "glorious house."

**65:1–7** These verses serve as a response to the preceding questions about God's inaction (64:6, 11). It is not God who has been absent, but the people who have walked away from God by idolatrous acts and rituals (vv. 3–4). That is the reason for their punishment (vv. 6–7).

**65:5 Render you holy**: unclean food is what these people claim has made them sacred! The prophet ridicules them. Sacredness was understood as something communicable (cf. Ex 19:9–15).

*d:* Ps 144:5; Mk 1:10. *e:* 1 Cor 2:9. *f:* Is 1:30; 34:4. *g:* Ps 79:1; Lam 1. *h:* Rom 10:20. *i:* Rom 10:21.

I will not remain quiet until I have
repaid in full
7 Your crimes and the crimes of your
ancestors as well,
says the LORD.
Since they burned incense on the
mountains,
and insulted me on the hills,
I will at once pour out in full measure
their recompense into their laps.

### *Fate of the Just and Unjust in Israel*

8 * Thus says the LORD:
As when the juice is pressed from a
cluster,
and someone says, "Do not destroy it,
for there is still good in it,"
So will I do for the sake of my servants:
I will not destroy them all.
9 From Jacob I will bring forth offspring,
from Judah, those who are to possess
my mountains;
My chosen ones shall possess the land,
my servants shall dwell there.
10 Sharon shall become a pasture for the
flocks,
the Valley of Achor a resting place for
the cattle,
for my people who have sought me.[j]
11 But you who forsake the LORD,
who forget my holy mountain,
Who spread a table for Fortune
and fill cups of mixed wine for Destiny,*
12 You I will destine for the sword;
you shall all bow down for slaughter;
Because I called and you did not answer,
I spoke and you did not listen,
But did what is evil in my sight
and things I do not delight in, you
chose,[k]
13 therefore thus says the Lord GOD:
My servants shall eat,
but you shall go hungry;
My servants shall drink,
but you shall be thirsty;
My servants shall rejoice,
but you shall be put to shame;
14 My servants shall shout
for joy of heart,
But you shall cry out for grief of heart,
and howl for anguish of spirit.
15 You will leave your name for a curse to
my chosen ones
when the Lord GOD slays you,
and calls his servants by another name.
16 Whoever invokes a blessing in the land
shall bless by the God of truth;*
Whoever takes an oath in the land
shall swear by the God of truth;
For the hardships of the past shall be
forgotten
and hidden from my eyes.

### *A World Renewed*

17 * See, I am creating new heavens
and a new earth;
The former things shall not be
remembered
nor come to mind.[l]
18 Instead, shout for joy and be glad forever
in what I am creating.
Indeed, I am creating Jerusalem to be a
joy
and its people to be a delight;
19 I will rejoice in Jerusalem
and exult in my people.
No longer shall the sound of weeping be
heard there,
or the sound of crying;
20 No longer shall there be in it
an infant who lives but a few days,
nor anyone who does not live a full
lifetime;
One who dies at a hundred years shall be
considered a youth,
and one who falls short of a hundred
shall be thought accursed.[m]
21 They shall build houses and live in them,

**65:8** This verse reflects the remnant theology found elsewhere in the Book of Isaiah: 1:8–9; 4:3; 6:11–13; etc.

**65:11–12 Destiny**: the play on words is found in the Hebrew, in which "destiny" and "destine" are *menî* and *manîthî*.

**65:16 God of truth**: lit., "God of Amen," i.e., the one who keeps his word.

**65:17–18** The new creation (cf. 66:22) is described with apocalyptic exuberance: long life, material prosperity, and so forth. As the former events in 43:18 are to be forgotten, so also the new creation wipes out memory of the first creation.

*j:* Hos 2:17. *k:* Is 66:4; Prv 1:24; Jer 7:13. *l:* Is 66:22; Rev 21:1. *m:* Dt 4:40.

they shall plant vineyards and eat their
fruit;
22 They shall not build and others live
there;
they shall not plant and others eat.
As the years of a tree, so the years of my
people;
and my chosen ones shall long enjoy
the work of their hands.
23 They shall not toil in vain,
nor beget children for sudden
destruction;
For they shall be a people blessed by the
LORD
and their descendants with them.
24 Before they call, I will answer;
while they are yet speaking, I will hear.
25 * The wolf and the lamb shall pasture
together,
and the lion shall eat hay like the ox—
but the serpent's food shall be dust.[n]
None shall harm or destroy
on all my holy mountain, says the LORD.

See RG 211–12

## CHAPTER 66

### *True and False Worship*

1 * Thus says the LORD:
The heavens are my throne,
the earth, my footstool.
What house can you build for me?
Where is the place of my rest?[o]
2 My hand made all these things
when all of them came to be—oracle
of the LORD.
This is the one whom I approve:
the afflicted one, crushed in spirit,
who trembles at my word.[p]
3 * The one slaughtering an ox, striking a
man,
sacrificing a lamb, breaking a dog's
neck,
Making an offering of pig's blood,
burning incense, honoring an idol—
These have chosen their own ways,
and taken pleasure in their own
abominations.[q]
4 I in turn will choose affliction for them
and bring upon them what they fear.
Because when I called, no one answered,
when I spoke, no one listened.
Because they did what was evil in my
sight,
and things I do not delight in they
chose,[r]
5 Hear the word of the LORD,
you who tremble at his word!
Your kin who hate you
and cast you out because of my name
say,
"May the LORD show his glory,
that we may see your joy";
but they shall be put to shame.
6 A voice roaring from the city,
a voice from the temple;
The voice of the LORD
rendering recompense to his enemies![s]

### *Blessings of Prosperity and Consolation*

7 * Before she is in labor,
she gives birth;[t]
Before her pangs come upon her,
she delivers a male child.
8 Who ever heard of such a thing,
or who ever saw the like?
Can a land be brought forth in one day,
or a nation be born in a single
moment?
Yet Zion was scarcely in labor
when she bore her children.
9 Shall I bring a mother to the point of birth,
and yet not let her child be born? says
the LORD.
Or shall I who bring to birth
yet close her womb? says your God.
10 * Rejoice with Jerusalem and be glad
because of her,

**65:25** The imagery reflects the ideal era described in 11:6–9; see note there.

**66:1–2** The Lord rejects the abuses associated with Temple worship in order to emphasize his concern for the sincere worshiper.

**66:3–6** The sacrificial abuses listed will only merit punishment. The true worshipers, the downtrodden, are those who "tremble" (vv. 2, 5) at God's word. Although they are ridiculed by those who reject them (v. 5), the latter will be afflicted with divine punishment; their "choice" will be met by the Lord's choice (v. 4).

**66:7–9** The renewal of Zion is pictured in terms of a miraculous, instantaneous birth, facilitated by God's intervention.

**66:10–16** The poet addresses the children born of Jerusa-

*n:* Is 11:6–9. *o:* 2 Sm 7:4–7; 1 Kgs 8:27; Acts 7:49; 17:24. *p:* Ps 24:1–2. *q:* Lv 11:7. *r:* Is 65:12; Prv 1:24; Jer 7:13. *s:* Jl 4:16; Am 1:2. *t:* Is 49:18–21; 54:1.

all you who love her;
Rejoice with her in her joy,
all you who mourn over her—[u]
11 So that you may nurse and be satisfied
from her consoling breast;
That you may drink with delight
at her abundant breasts!
12 For thus says the LORD:
I will spread prosperity over her like a
river,
like an overflowing torrent,
the wealth of nations.
You shall nurse, carried in her arms,
cradled upon her knees;
13 As a mother comforts her child,
so I will comfort you;
in Jerusalem you shall find your
comfort.[v]
14 You will see and your heart shall exult,
and your bodies shall flourish like the
grass;
The LORD's power shall be revealed to
his servants,
but to his enemies, his wrath.
15 For see, the LORD will come in fire,
his chariots like the stormwind;
To wreak his anger in burning rage
and his rebuke in fiery flames.
16 For with fire the LORD shall enter into
judgment,
and, with his sword, against all flesh;
Those slain by the LORD shall be
many.[w]

17* Those who sanctify and purify themselves to go into the gardens, following one
who stands within, eating pig's flesh, abominable things, and mice, shall all together
come to an end, with their deeds and purposes—oracle of the LORD.

*God Gathers the Nations.* 18* I am coming
to gather all nations and tongues; they shall
come and see my glory.[x] 19 I will place a sign
among them; from them I will send survivors to the nations: to Tarshish, Put and
Lud, Mosoch, Tubal and Javan, to the distant
coastlands which have never heard of my
fame, or seen my glory; and they shall proclaim my glory among the nations. 20 They
shall bring all your kin from all the nations
as an offering to the LORD, on horses and in
chariots, in carts, upon mules and dromedaries, to Jerusalem, my holy mountain, says
the LORD, just as the Israelites bring their
grain offering in a clean vessel to the house
of the LORD. 21 Some of these I will take as
priests and Levites, says the LORD.

22 Just as the new heavens and the new earth
which I am making
Shall endure before me—oracle of the
LORD—
so shall your descendants and your
name endure.[y]
23 From new moon to new moon,
and from sabbath to sabbath,
All flesh shall come to worship
before me, says the LORD.[z]
24 * They shall go out and see the corpses[a]
of the people who rebelled against me;
For their worm shall not die,
their fire shall not be extinguished;
and they shall be an abhorrence to all
flesh.

lem, their mother. In v. 13 the metaphor switches to the Lord as mother (cf. 49:15), comforting her charges but destroying the enemies.

**66:17** This verse seems to have some connection with 65:2–3.

**66:18–21** God summons the neighboring nations to Zion and from among them will send some to far distant lands to proclaim the divine glory. **All your kin**: Jews in exile. The "gathering of the people and the nations" is an eschatological motif common in the prophetic tradition; cf. 56:8.

**66:24** God's enemies lie dead outside the walls of the New Jerusalem; just as in the past, corpses, filth and refuse lay in the Valley of Hinnom (Gehenna) outside the city; cf. 34:1–4; 2 Kgs 23:10.

*u:* Tb 13:14. *v:* Is 40:1; 49:13. *w:* Lv 11:29. *x:* Is 56:1, 8; 59:20. *y:* Is 65:17; Rev 21:1. *z:* Is 1:13. *a:* Is 1:27–28; Mk 9:45.

See RG 213–19

# The Book of Jeremiah

The Book of Jeremiah combines history, biography, and prophecy. It portrays a nation in crisis and introduces the reader to an extraordinary person whom the Lord called to prophesy under the trying circumstances of the final days of the kingdom of Judah. Jeremiah was born, perhaps about 650 B.C., of a priestly family from the village of Anathoth, two and a half miles northeast of Jerusalem. He was called to his task in the thirteenth year of King Josiah (Jer 1:2). Josiah's reform, begun with enthusiasm and hope, ended with his death on the battlefield of Megiddo (609 B.C.) as he attempted to stop the northward march of the Egyptian Pharaoh Neco, who was going to provide assistance to the Assyrians who were in retreat before the Babylonians.

Nineveh, the capital of Assyria, fell in 612 B.C., preparing the way for the new colossus, Babylon, which was soon to put an end to the independence of Judah.

The prophet supported the reform of King Josiah (2 Kgs 22–23), but after the death of Josiah the old idolatry returned. Jeremiah opposed this as well as royal policy toward Babylon. Arrest, imprisonment, and public disgrace were his lot. In the nation's apostasy Jeremiah saw the sealing of its doom. Nebuchadnezzar captured Jerusalem (598 B.C.) and carried King Jehoiachin into exile (Jer 22:24).

During the years 598–587, Jeremiah counseled Zedekiah in the face of bitter opposition. The false prophet Hananiah proclaimed that the yoke of Babylon was broken and a strong pro-Egyptian party in Jerusalem induced Zedekiah to revolt. Nebuchadnezzar took swift vengeance; Jerusalem was destroyed in 587 and its leading citizens sent into exile.

The prophet remained in Jerusalem, but was later forced into Egyptian exile. We do not know the details of his death. The influence of Jeremiah was greater after his death than before. The exiled community read and meditated on the lessons of the prophet; his influence is evident in Ezekiel, some of the psalms, Is 40–66, and Daniel. In the postexilic period, the Book of Jeremiah circulated in various editions.

The book may be divided as follows:

I. Oracles in the Days of Josiah (1:1–6:30)
II. Oracles Primarily from the Days of Jehoiakim (7:1–20:18)
III. Oracles in the Last Years of Jerusalem (21:1–25:38)
IV. The Temple Sermon (26:1–24; cf. 7:1–15)
V. Controversies with the False Prophets (27:1–29:32)
VI. Oracles of the Restoration of Israel and Judah (30:1–35:19)
VII. Jeremiah and the Fall of Jerusalem (36:1–45:5)
VIII. Oracles Against the Nations (46:1–51:64)
IX. Historical Appendix (52:1–34)

---

## I. Oracles in the Days of Josiah

### CHAPTER 1

See RG 216

1 The words of Jeremiah, son of Hilkiah, one of the priests from Anathoth,* in
the land of Benjamin. 2 The word of the
LORD came to him in the days of Josiah, son
of Amon, king of Judah, in the thirteenth
year of his reign,[a] 3 and again in the days of
Jehoiakim, son of Josiah, king of Judah, until the end of the eleventh year of Zedekiah,
son of Josiah, king of Judah—down to the
exile of Jerusalem, in the fifth month.[b]

*Call of Jeremiah*

4 The word of the LORD came to me:
5 Before I formed you in the womb I knew
you,
before you were born I dedicated you,
a prophet to the nations I appointed
you.*[c]
6 "Ah, Lord GOD!" I said,

**1:1 Anathoth**: a village about three miles northeast of Jerusalem, to which Solomon had exiled Abiathar the priest (1 Kgs 2:26–27); it is likely that Jeremiah belonged to that priestly family.

**1:5** Jeremiah was destined to become a prophet before his birth; cf. Is 49:1, 5; Lk 1:15; Gal 1:15–16. **I knew you**: I

*a*: Jer 25:3. *b*: Jer 25:1. *c*: Jer 49:1; Gal 1:15–16.

TO UNDERSTAND THE book of Jeremiah, it is probably best first to skim the whole book to get a sense of the book's many voices and different kinds of literature. Then it will be helpful to return to the first chapter, Jeremiah's call, and think of it is as an introduction to the book's major themes. It is important to recall that the book is not arranged in sequence. Time does not move in a straight line. Events in the past, promises about the future, and appeals to the reader in the present are braided together. Memories about the past shape the present and remain alive in it, just as future hope changes perceptions of the present. This overlapping of time is particularly true for survivors of trauma and loss. The present and the past weave together, and hopeful anticipation for the future can burst in without preparation upon the present.

"I do not know how to speak. I am too
young!"*
7 But the LORD answered me,
Do not say, "I am too young."
To whomever I send you, you shall go;
whatever I command you, you shall
speak.
8 Do not be afraid of them,
for I am with you to deliver you—
oracle of the LORD.

9 Then the LORD extended his hand and
touched my mouth, saying to me,

See, I place my words in your mouth![d]
10 Today I appoint you
over nations and over kingdoms,
To uproot and to tear down,
to destroy and to demolish,
to build and to plant.

11 The word of the LORD came to me: What
do you see, Jeremiah? "I see a branch of the
almond tree,"* I replied. 12 Then the LORD said
to me: You have seen well, for I am watching
over my word to carry it out. 13[e] A second
time the word of the LORD came to me: What
do you see? I replied, "I see a boiling kettle
whose mouth is tipped away from the north."*
14 The LORD said to me, And from the
north evil will pour out over all who dwell in
the land.[f]

15 Look, I am summoning
all the kingdoms of the north—oracle
of the LORD—
Each king shall come and set up his
throne
in the gateways of Jerusalem,
Against all its surrounding walls
and against all the cities of Judah.[g]
16 I will pronounce my sentence against
them
for all their wickedness in
forsaking me,
In burning incense to other gods,
in bowing down to the works of their
hands.[h]
17 But you, prepare yourself;
stand up and tell them
all that I command you.
Do not be terrified on account of
them,
or I will terrify you before them;
18 For I am the one who today
makes you a fortified city,
A pillar of iron, a wall of bronze,
against the whole land:
Against Judah's kings and princes,
its priests and the people of the land.[i]
19 They will fight against you, but not
prevail over you,
for I am with you to deliver you—
oracle of the LORD.

loved you and chose you. **I dedicated you**: I set you apart to be a prophet. **The nations**: the neighbors of Judah, along with Assyria, Babylonia, and Egypt.

**1:6 I am too young**: like Moses (Ex 3:11, 13; 4:10), Jeremiah at first resists God's call. This narrative is perhaps patterned after the story of Moses' call in order to identify Jeremiah as the prophet "like me" in Dt 18:15.

**1:11** There is wordplay between the Hebrew noun *shaqed*, "almond tree," and the Hebrew verb *shoqed*, "watcher/watching." Because the almond tree begins to bloom in late winter in Palestine, it is called "the watcher" for the coming of spring. God is also "watcher," observing the fulfillment of the prophetic word.

**1:13 Kettle . . . the north**: symbol of an invasion from the north; cf. vv. 14–15.

*d:* Dt 18:18; Is 6:7. *e:* Ez 11:3, 7; 24:3. *f:* Jer 4:6; 6:1. *g:* Jer 6:22. *h:* Is 2:8. *i:* Jer 6:27; 15:20; Ez 3:8.

## Jeremiah's Call

THE INTRODUCTORY VERSES of the book tell who Jeremiah was and when he prophesied. His call came during the time of King Josiah and extended until the fall of Jerusalem in 587 B.C., a 40-year period that symbolically links him with Moses' 40 years of leadership in the wilderness. Jeremiah is presented as a prophet like Moses, as promised in Deuteronomy 18:18.

In a poetic conversation between God and Jeremiah (Jer 1:4–10), Jeremiah receives his mission. His call before birth indicates that his prophecy was not his own invention but given to him by God. His resistance on the grounds that he is too young and so cannot speak properly also indicates that God has sent him; he has not chosen this task for himself. God tells him not to be afraid, promises to be with him, and touches his mouth. This gesture symbolizes the divine origin of the words Jeremiah speaks and the words recorded in this book. The short poem in verse 10 gives Jeremiah and his book authority in the face of opposition.

Jeremiah's mission gains substance from two visions written in prose. In verses 11–13, Jeremiah sees a branch of an almond tree, a *shaqed* in Hebrew. In a play on words, God says, "I am watching" (*shoqed*) "to carry it out." What God says through Jeremiah will happen. Next Jeremiah sees a "boiling kettle whose mouth is tipped away from the north." The boiling pot is a symbol of destruction, overflowing and burning. The north may refer to a historical enemy, but more likely the threat from the north refers to a mythic enemy, coming like a superhuman monster. The tilting pot will spill out an army of invaders who will stream upon the land. God is "summoning all the kingdoms of the north" to invade Jerusalem. Only in Jeremiah 20:4 will the foe from the north be identified as Babylon. Jeremiah himself should have courage to deliver God's judgment, for God will be with him.

See RG 216–17

### CHAPTER 2

*Infidelity of Israel.** 1 The word of the
LORD came to me: 2 Go, cry out this message
for Jerusalem to hear!

I remember the devotion* of your youth,
how you loved me as a bride,
Following me in the wilderness,
in a land unsown.[j]
3 Israel was dedicated to the LORD,
the first fruits* of his harvest;
All who ate of it were held guilty,
evil befell them—oracle of the LORD.[k]
4 Listen to the word of the LORD, house of
Jacob!
All you clans of the house of Israel,
5 thus says the LORD:
What fault did your ancestors find in me
that they withdrew from me,
Went after emptiness,
and became empty themselves?[l]
6 They did not ask, "Where is the LORD
who brought us up from the land of
Egypt,
Who led us through the wilderness,
through a land of wastes and ravines,
A land of drought and darkness,
a land which no one crosses,
where no one dwells?"[m]
7 I brought you into the garden land
to eat its fine fruits,
But you entered and defiled my land,
you turned my heritage into an
abomination.[n]
8 The priests did not ask,

**2:1–3:5** These chapters may contain some of Jeremiah's early preaching. He portrays Israel as the wife of the Lord, faithful only in the beginning, when she walked behind him (2:2–3, 5; 3:1). Consistent with the marriage metaphor, he describes her present unfaithfulness as adultery (2:20; 3:2–3); now she walks behind the Baals.

**2:2 Devotion**: Heb. *hesed*; Israel's gratitude, fidelity, and love for God.

**2:3 First fruits**: the first yield of a harvest offered as a sign of dependence on and gratitude toward the Lord of the land, thus divine property. Israel, then, is a gift made to God, set apart for his use; cf. Ex 23:19.

*j:* Dt 2:7; 32:9–12; Mi 6:4. *k:* Jer 12:14; Ex 4:22; Dt 7:6; 14:2. *l:* 2 Kgs 17:15; Is 5:4; Mi 6:3. *m:* Ex 20:2–3; Dt 8:14; Is 63:11–14. *n:* Lv 18:24–25; Dt 8:7–10; 32:13–14.

"Where is the LORD?"
The experts in the law* did not know me:
the shepherds rebelled against me.
The prophets prophesied by Baal,
and went after useless idols.[o]
9 Therefore I will again accuse you—
oracle of the LORD—
even your children's children I will
accuse.[p]
10 Cross to the coast of Cyprus and see,
send to Kedar* and carefully inquire:
Where has anything like this been
done?
11 Does any other nation change its gods?—
even though they are not gods at all!
But my people have changed their glory
for useless things.[q]
12 Be horrified at this, heavens;
shudder, be appalled—oracle of the
LORD.
13 Two evils my people have done:
they have forsaken me, the source of
living waters;
They have dug themselves cisterns,
broken cisterns that cannot hold
water.[r]
14 Is Israel a slave, a house-born servant?*
Why then has he become plunder?
15 Against him lions roar,
they raise their voices.
They have turned his land into a waste;
his cities are charred ruins, without an
inhabitant.[s]
16 Yes, the people of Memphis* and
Tahpanhes
shave the crown of your head.
17 Has not forsaking the LORD, your God,
done this to you?[t]
18 And now, why go to Egypt,*
to drink the waters of the Nile?
Why go to Assyria,
to drink the waters of the River?
19 Your own wickedness chastises you,
your own infidelities punish you.
Know then, and see, how evil and bitter
is your forsaking the LORD, your God,
And your showing no fear of me,
oracle of the Lord, the GOD of hosts.[u]
20 Long ago you broke your yoke,[v]
you tore off your bonds.
You said, "I will not serve."
On every high hill, under every green
tree,
you sprawled and served as a
prostitute.*
21 But I had planted you as a choice vine,
all pedigreed stock;
How could you turn out so obnoxious to
me,
a spurious vine?[w]
22 Even if you scour it with lye,
and use much soap,
The stain of your guilt is still before me,
oracle of the Lord GOD.[x]
23 How can you say, "I am not defiled,
I have not pursued the Baals"?
Consider your conduct in the Valley,*
recall what you have done:
A skittish young camel,
running back and forth,
24 a wild donkey bred in the wilderness,
Sniffing the wind in her desire—
who can restrain her lust?
None seeking her need tire themselves;
in her time they will find her.
25 Stop wearing out your feet
and parching your throat!
But you say, "No use! No!

**2:8 Experts in the law**: the priests. **The shepherds**: the kings and nobles.

**2:10 Kedar**: a nomadic tribe in north Arabia. Cyprus and Kedar represent west and east.

**2:14 House-born servant**: one born in the master's house, in contrast to a slave acquired by purchase or as a captive; cf. Lv 22:11.

**2:16 Memphis**: the capital of Lower Egypt. **Tahpanhes**: a frontier city of Egypt, east of the Delta. **Shave the crown of your head**: an image for Egypt plundering Judah; perhaps a reference to the capture of King Jehoahaz in 609 B.C. (2 Kgs 23:34).

**2:18** Egypt and Assyria were the competing foreign powers favored by rival parties within Judah. The desire for such foreign alliances is a further desertion of the Lord, the source of living waters (v. 13), in favor of the above-named powers, symbolized by the waters of the Nile and the Euphrates rivers.

**2:20 Served as a prostitute**: idolatry (because Israel is the "bride" of God); cf. vv. 2–3.

**2:23 The Valley**: probably Ben-hinnom, south of Jerusalem, site of the sanctuary of Topheth, where children were sacrificed to Molech; cf. 7:31.

*o:* Jer 8:8–9; 23:1, 13. *p:* Ex 20:5. *q:* Jer 16:20; Ps 106:20. *r:* Jer 17:13; Ps 36:9; Is 1:4. *s:* Jer 9:11. *t:* Jer 4:18; 30:15. *u:* Prv 5:22; Hos 5:5. *v:* Jer 3:6, 13; Jgs 10:6. *w:* Ex 15:17; Ps 80:9; Is 5:4. *x:* Jb 9:30.

How I love these strangers,
after them I must go."[y]
26 As the thief is shamed when caught,
so shall the house of Israel be shamed:
They, their kings, their princes,
their priests and their prophets;[z]
27 They say to a piece of wood, "You are my father,"
and to a stone, "You gave me birth."
They turn their backs to me, not their faces;
yet in their time of trouble they cry out,
"Rise up and save us!"
28 Where are the gods you made for yourselves?
Let them rise up!
Will they save you in your time of trouble?
For as numerous as your cities
are your gods, O Judah!
And as many as the streets of Jerusalem
are the altars you have set up for Baal.[a]
29 Why are you arguing with me?
You have all rebelled against me—
oracle of the LORD.
30 In vain I struck your children;
correction they did not take.
Your sword devoured your prophets
like a ravening lion.[b]
31 You people of this generation,
consider the word of the Lord:
Have I become a wilderness to Israel,
a land of gloom?
Why then do my people say, "We have moved on,
we will not come to you any more"?
32 Does a young woman forget her jewelry,
a bride her sash?
Yet my people have forgotten me
days without number.[c]
33 How well you pick your way
when seeking love!
In your wickedness,
you have gone by ways unclean!
34 On your clothing is
the life-blood of the innocent,
you did not find them committing burglary;
35 Nonetheless you say, "I am innocent;
at least, his anger is turned away from me."
Listen! I will judge you
on that word of yours, "I have not sinned."
36 How frivolous you have become
in changing your course!
By Egypt you will be shamed,
just as you were shamed by Assyria.[d]
37 From there too you will go out,
your hands upon your head;
For the LORD has rejected those in whom you trust,
with them you will have no success.[e]

## CHAPTER 3

See RG 216–17

1 If a man divorces his wife[f]
and she leaves him
and then becomes the wife of another,
Can she return to the first?*
Would not this land be wholly defiled?
But you have played the prostitute with many lovers,
and yet you would return to me!—
oracle of the LORD.
2 Raise your eyes to the heights, and look,
where have men not lain with you?
Along the roadways you waited for them
like an Arabian* in the wilderness.
You defiled the land
by your wicked prostitution.[g]
3 Therefore the showers were withheld,
the spring rain did not fall.
But because you have a prostitute's brow,
you refused to be ashamed.[h]
4 Even now do you not call me, "My father,
you are the bridegroom of my youth?

**3:1 Can she return to the first?**: i.e., her first husband. Here the Hebrew is emended in light of the Septuagint and Dt 24:1–4, which forbids a man to take back a woman once he has divorced her. The prophet uses this analogy to illustrate the presumption of Judah, the unfaithful wife, who assumes she can easily return to the Lord after worshiping other gods.

**3:2 An Arabian**: here depicted as a marauder lying in wait for caravans.

*y:* Jer 18:12. *z:* Jer 48:27; Rom 6:21. *a:* Jer 11:13; Dt 32:38; Jgs 10:14. *b:* Jer 5:3; Neh 9:26. *c:* Jer 13:25; Dt 32:18. *d:* 2 Chr 28:16–21. *e:* 2 Sm 13:19. *f:* Dt 24:1–4. *g:* Ex 16:24–25. *h:* Jer 6:15; 8:12.

CHAPTERS 2 AND 3 use marriage and family symbolism to describe historical situations. Both the northern and southern kingdoms have betrayed God and been cast off. The northern kingdom of Israel fell to Assyria in 721 B.C., and the text explains that historical tragedy in the symbolic terms of betrayal in a marriage. The divine husband sends Jeremiah to speak to the first wife and invite her to return. The text reports no response from her. Then the invitation to return is addressed to the children (3:14). Their father promises them restoration and reunification of the whole people in Jerusalem (vv. 15–18).

5 Will he keep his wrath forever,
will he hold his grudge to the end?"
This is what you say; yet you do
all the evil you can.

*Judah and Israel.* 6The LORD said to me in
the days of King Josiah: Do you see what rebellious Israel has done? She has gone up
every high mountain, and under every green
tree she has played the prostitute.[i] 7And I
thought: After she has done all this, she will
return to me. But she did not return. Then,
even though that traitor her sister Judah, saw
8that, in response to all the adulteries rebel
Israel had committed, I sent her away and
gave her a bill of divorce, nevertheless Judah, the traitor, her sister, was not frightened; she too went off and played the prostitute.[j] 9With her casual prostitution, she
polluted the land, committing adultery with
stone and wood.[k] 10In spite of all this, Judah,
the traitor, her sister, did not return to me
wholeheartedly, but insincerely—oracle of
the LORD.

*Restoration of Israel.* 11Then the LORD
said to me: Rebel Israel is more just than
traitor Judah.[l] 12Go, proclaim these words
toward the north, and say:

Return, rebel Israel—oracle of the LORD—
I will not remain angry with you;
For I am merciful, oracle of the LORD,
I will not keep my anger forever.[m]
13 Only admit your guilt:
how you have rebelled against the LORD, your God,
How you ran here and there to strangers
under every green tree
and would not listen to my voice—
oracle of the LORD.[n]
14 Return, rebellious children—oracle of the LORD—*
for I am your master;
I will take you, one from a city, two from a clan,
and bring you to Zion.[o]
15 I will appoint for you shepherds after my own heart,
who will shepherd you wisely and prudently.[p]
16 When you increase in number and are fruitful in the land—
oracle of the LORD—
They will in those days no longer say,
"The ark of the covenant of the LORD!"
They will no longer think of it, or remember it,
or miss it, or make another one.

17At that time they will call Jerusalem "the
LORD's throne." All nations will gather together there to honor the name of the LORD
at Jerusalem, and they will no longer stubbornly follow their wicked heart.[q] 18In those
days the house of Judah will walk alongside
the house of Israel; together they will come
from the land of the north to the land which
I gave your ancestors as a heritage.[r]

**3:14–18** A remnant of Israel (v. 14) will reunite with Judah (v. 18). The former Israelite community, represented by the ark of the covenant, will be replaced by a universal alliance, symbolized by Jerusalem, the Lord's throne, to which all nations will be gathered (v. 17).

*i:* Jer 2:20; Dt 12:2. *j:* 2 Kgs 17:6, 18–23; Ez 23:11. *k:* Jer 2:27. *l:* Ez 16:51; 23:11. *m:* Dt 4:29–31. *n:* Jer 2:20, 25; Lv 26:40. *o:* Jer 23:3; Is 10:21–22. *p:* Ez 34:23; Jn 21:15. *q:* Is 2:2. *r:* Jer 30:3; 31:8.

### *Conditions for Forgiveness*

19 I thought:
How I would like to make you my children!
So I gave you a pleasant land,
the most beautiful heritage among the nations!
You would call me, "My Father," I thought,
and you would never turn away from me.[s]
20 But like a woman faithless to her lover,
thus have you been faithless to me,
house of Israel—oracle of the LORD.[t]
21 A cry is heard on the heights!
the plaintive weeping of Israel's children,
Because they have perverted their way,
they have forgotten the LORD, their God.
22 Return, rebellious children!
I will heal your rebellions.
"Here we are! We belong to you,
for you are the LORD, our God.[u]
23 Deceptive indeed are the hills,
the mountains, clamorous;
Only in the LORD our God
is Israel's salvation.[v]
24 The shameful thing* has devoured
our ancestors' worth from our youth,
Their sheep and cattle,
their sons and daughters.
25 Let us lie down in our shame,
let our disgrace cover us,
for we have sinned against the LORD, our God,
We and our ancestors, from our youth to this day;
we did not listen to the voice of the LORD, our God."[w]

## CHAPTER 4

See RG 216–17

1 If you return, Israel—oracle of the LORD—
return to me.
If you put your detestable things out of my sight,
and do not stray,[x]
2 And swear, "As the LORD lives,"*
in truth, in judgment, and in justice,
Then the nations shall bless themselves in him
and in him glory.[y]

3 For to the people of Judah and Jerusalem, thus says the LORD:

Till your untilled ground,
and do not sow among thorns.[z]
4 Be circumcised for the LORD,*
remove the foreskins of your hearts,
people of Judah and inhabitants of Jerusalem;
Or else my anger will break out like fire,
and burn so that no one can quench it,
because of your evil deeds.[a]

### *The Invasion from the North*

5 Proclaim it in Judah,
in Jerusalem announce it;
Blow the trumpet throughout the land,
call out, "Fill the ranks!"
Say, "Assemble, let us march
to the fortified cities."
6 Raise the signal—to Zion!
Seek refuge! Don't stand there!
Disaster I bring from the north,
and great destruction.
7 Up comes the lion from its lair,
the destroyer of nations has set out,
has left its place,
To turn your land into a desolation,
your cities into an uninhabited waste.[b]
8 So put on sackcloth,
mourn and wail:
"The blazing anger of the LORD
has not turned away from us."[c]
9 In that day—oracle of the LORD—
The king will lose heart, and the princes;

**3:24 The shameful thing**: Heb. *bosheth* ("shame"), a term often substituted for the name of Baal, a Canaanite god worshiped at local shrines.

**4:2 As the LORD lives**: this oath, made sincerely, implies Israel's return and loyal adherence to God. Thus the ancient promises are fulfilled; cf. Gn 12:3; 18:18; 22:18; 26:4; Ps 72:17.

**4:4** The external rite of circumcision accomplishes nothing unless it is accompanied by the removal of blindness and obstinacy of heart. Jeremiah's view is reflected in Rom 2:25, 29; 1 Cor 7:19; Gal 5:6; 6:13, 15.

*s:* Jer 31:9, 20; Is 63:16. *t:* Jer 5:11. *u:* Hos 3:5. *v:* Jer 14:8. *w:* Jer 16:11–12; 22:21. *x:* Jer 25:5. *y:* Jer 12:16; Dt 10:20; Is 65:16. *z:* Hos 10:12; Mt 13:7, 22. *a:* Jer 9:24. *b:* Jer 2:15; 5:6. *c:* Jer 6:26; Is 5:25.

the priests will be horrified,
and the prophets stunned.
10 "Ah! Lord GOD," they will say,
"You really did deceive* us
When you said: You shall have peace,
while the sword was at our very throats."[d]
11 At that time it will be said
to this people and to Jerusalem,
A scorching wind from the bare heights comes
through the wilderness toward my daughter, the people.*
Not to winnow, not to cleanse,
12 a strong wind from there comes at my bidding.
Now I too pronounce
sentence upon them.[e]
13 See! like storm clouds he advances,
like a whirlwind, his chariots;
Swifter than eagles, his horses:
"Woe to us! we are ruined."
14 Cleanse your heart of evil, Jerusalem,
that you may be saved.
How long will you entertain
wicked schemes?
15 A voice proclaims it from Dan,
announces wickedness from Mount Ephraim:
16 "Make this known to the nations,
announce it against Jerusalem:
Besiegers are coming from the distant land,
shouting their war cry against the cities of Judah."[f]
17 Like watchers in the fields they surround her,
for she has rebelled against me—
oracle of the LORD.[g]
18 Your conduct, your deeds, have done this to you;
how bitter is this evil of yours,
how it reaches to your very heart![h]
19 My body! my body! how I writhe!*
The walls of my heart!
My heart beats wildly,
I cannot be still;
For I myself have heard the blast of the horn,
the battle cry.
20 Ruin upon ruin is reported;
the whole land is laid waste.
In an instant my tents are ravaged;
in a flash, my shelters.[i]
21 How long must I see the signal,
hear the blast of the horn!
22 My people are fools,
they do not know me;
They are senseless children,
without understanding;
They are wise at evil,
but they do not know how to do good.[j]
23 I looked at the earth—it was waste and void;
at the heavens—their light had gone out![k]
24 I looked at the mountains—they were quaking!
All the hills were crumbling!
25 I looked—there was no one;
even the birds of the air had flown away!
26 I looked—the garden land was a wilderness,
with all its cities destroyed
before the LORD, before his blazing anger.[l]
27 For thus says the LORD:
The whole earth shall be waste,
but I will not wholly destroy it.[m]
28 Because of this the earth shall mourn,
the heavens above shall darken;
I have spoken, I will not change my mind,
I have decided, I will not turn back.[n]
29 At the shout of rider and archer
each city takes to flight;
They shrink into the thickets,
they scale the rocks:

**4:10 You really did deceive**: Jeremiah complains that the Lord misled the people by fostering their complacency, leaving them unprepared and unrepentant as judgment approaches.

**4:11 My daughter, the people**: the covenant people personified as a young woman. Ezekiel 16 presents Israel and Judah as female infants whom the Lord adopts and then abandons and punishes because they desire other lords.

**4:19–21** Probably the prophet's own anguish at the coming destruction of Judah.

*d:* Jer 6:14. *e:* Jer 1:16. *f:* Jer 5:15. *g:* Jer 6:3. *h:* Jer 2:17, 19. *i:* Jer 10:20. *j:* Dt 32:5–6, 28. *k:* Is 24:1, 3. *l:* Lv 26:31. *m:* Jer 5:18. *n:* Is 24:4.

**God's Reluctance to Send the Attackers**

THE LOOSELY CONNECTED poems in ch 5 show that God does not wish to destroy the nation. Instead, the people are at fault because they will not act justly or repent. God is neither arbitrary nor whimsical in orchestrating the attack on the nation. In fact, God will not destroy the nation if Jeremiah can find one righteous person (v. 1). Though he runs up and down the streets of Jerusalem to the rich and the poor, Jeremiah's search is unsuccessful. God promises invasions by wild animals (v. 6), which symbolize the invading enemy.

All the cities are abandoned,
no one lives in them.
30 You now who are doomed, what are you doing
dressing in purple,
bedecking yourself with gold,
Enlarging your eyes with kohl?
You beautify yourself in vain!
Your lovers reject you,
they seek your life.
31 Yes, I hear the cry, like that of a woman in labor,
like the anguish of a mother bearing her first child—
The cry of daughter Zion gasping,
as she stretches out her hands:
"Ah, woe is me! I sink exhausted
before my killers!"[o]

## CHAPTER 5

See RG 216–17

### *Universal Corruption*

1 Roam the streets of Jerusalem,
look about and observe,
Search through her squares,
to find even one
Who acts justly
and seeks honesty,
and I will pardon her!
2 They say, "As the LORD lives,"
but in fact they swear falsely.
3 LORD, do your eyes not search for honesty?
You struck them, but they did not flinch;
you laid them low, but they refused correction;
They set their faces harder than stone,
and refused to return.[p]
4 I thought: These are only the lowly,
they behave foolishly;
For they do not know the way of the LORD,
the justice of their God.[q]
5 Let me go to the leaders
and speak with them;
For they must know the way of the LORD,
the justice of their God.
But, one and all, they have broken the yoke,
torn off the harness.[r]
6 Therefore, lions from the forest slay them,
wolves of the desert ravage them,
Leopards keep watch round their cities:
all who come out are torn to pieces,
For their crimes are many,
their rebellions numerous.
7 Why should I pardon you?
Your children have forsaken me,
they swear by gods that are no gods.
I fed them, but they commit adultery;
to the prostitute's house they throng.
8 They are lustful stallions,
each neighs after the other's wife.[s]
9 Should I not punish them for this?—
oracle of the LORD;
on a nation like this should I not take vengeance?
10 Climb her terraces, and ravage them,
destroy them completely.
Tear away her tendrils,
they do not belong to the LORD.[t]
11 For they have openly rebelled against me,
both the house of Israel and the house of Judah—
oracle of the LORD.[u]
12 They denied the LORD,*
saying, "He is nothing,

**5:12 They denied the LORD**: the people act as though God does not matter and will not interfere.

*o:* Jer 6:24. *p:* Jer 2:30. *q:* Jer 8:7. *r:* Jer 6:13. *s:* Jer 13:27. *t:* Jer 2:21. *u:* Jer 3:20.

No evil shall come to us,
neither sword nor famine shall we see.[v]
13 The prophets are wind,
and the word is not with them.
Let it be done to them!"
14 Therefore, thus says the LORD, the God of hosts,
because you have said this—
See! I make my words
a fire in your mouth,
And this people the wood
that it shall devour!—
15 Beware! I will bring against you
a nation from far away,
O House of Israel—oracle of the LORD;
A long-lived nation, an ancient nation,
a people whose language you do not know,
whose speech you cannot understand.[w]
16 Their quivers are like open graves;
all of them are warriors.
17 They will devour your harvest and your bread,
devour your sons and your daughters,
Devour your sheep and cattle,
devour your vines and fig trees;
With their swords they will beat down
the fortified cities in which you trust.[x]

18 Yet even in those days—oracle of the
LORD—I will not completely destroy you.[y]
19 And when they ask, "Why has the LORD
our God done all these things to us?" say to
them, "As you have abandoned me to serve
foreign gods in your own land, so shall you
serve foreigners in a land not your own."

20 Announce this to the house of Jacob,
proclaim it in Judah:
21 Pay attention to this,
you foolish and senseless people,
Who have eyes and do not see,
who have ears and do not hear.[z]
22 Should you not fear me—oracle of the LORD—
should you not tremble before me?
I made the sandy shore the sea's limit,
which by eternal decree it may not overstep.
Toss though it may, it is to no avail;
though its billows roar, they cannot overstep.[a]
23 But this people's heart is stubborn and rebellious;
they turn and go away,
24 And do not say in their hearts,
"Let us fear the LORD, our God,
Who gives us rain
early and late,* in its time;
Who watches for us
over the appointed weeks of harvest."[b]
25 Your crimes have prevented these things,
your sins have turned these blessings away from you.[c]
26 For criminals lurk among my people;
like fowlers they set traps,
but it is human beings they catch.[d]
27 Their houses are as full of treachery
as a bird-cage is of birds;
Therefore they grow powerful and rich,
28 fat and sleek.
They pass over wicked deeds;
justice they do not defend
By advancing the claim of the orphan
or judging the cause of the poor.[e]
29 Shall I not punish these things?—oracle of the LORD;
on a nation such as this shall I not take vengeance?
30 Something shocking and horrible
has happened in the land:
31 The prophets prophesy falsely,
and the priests teach on their own authority;
Yet my people like it this way;
what will you do when the end comes?[f]

## CHAPTER 6

See RG 216-17

### *The Enemy at the Gates*

1 Seek refuge, Benjaminites,
from the midst of Jerusalem!
Blow the trumpet in Tekoa,
raise a signal over Beth-haccherem;

**5:24 Rain early and late**: autumn and spring rains respectively. **Appointed weeks of harvest**: the seven weeks between the Passover (Dt 16:9–10) and the feast of Weeks (Pentecost), when it did not ordinarily rain.

*v:* Jer 14:13; Is 28:15. *w:* Dt 28:49. *x:* Dt 28:31. *y:* Jer 4:27. *z:* Is 6:9. *a:* Jb 38:10–11. *b:* Gn 8:22; Dt 11:14. *c:* Jer 2:17, 19. *d:* Prv 1:11. *e:* Jer 12:1; Is 1:23. *f:* Jer 14:14; Mi 2:11.

For disaster threatens from the north,
and mighty destruction.[g]
2 Lovely and delicate
daughter Zion, you are ruined!
3 Against her, shepherds come with their
flocks;*
all around, they pitch their tents
against her;
each one grazes his portion.[h]
4 "Prepare for war against her,
Up! let us rush upon her at midday!"
"Woe to us! the day is waning,
evening shadows lengthen!"
5 "Up! let us rush upon her by night,
destroy her palaces!"[i]
6 For thus says the LORD of hosts:
Hew down her trees,
throw up a siege mound against
Jerusalem.
Woe to the city marked for punishment;
there is nothing but oppression within
her![j]
7 As a well keeps its waters fresh,
so she keeps fresh her wickedness.
Violence and destruction resound in her;
ever before me are wounds and blows.[k]
8 Be warned, Jerusalem,
or I will be estranged from you,
And I will turn you into a wilderness,
a land where no one dwells.
9 Thus says the LORD of hosts:
Glean, glean like a vine
the remnant of Israel;
Pass your hand, like a vintager,
repeatedly over the tendrils.
10 To whom shall I speak?
whom shall I warn, and be heard?
See! their ears are uncircumcised,
they cannot pay attention;
See, the word of the LORD has become
for them
an object of scorn, for which they have
no taste.[l]
11 But the wrath of the LORD brims up
within me,
I am weary of holding it in.
I will pour it out upon the child in the
street,
upon the young men gathered together.
Yes, husband and wife will be taken,
elder with ancient.[m]
12 Their houses will fall to others,
their fields and their wives as well;
For I will stretch forth my hand
against those who dwell in the land—
oracle of the LORD.[n]
13 Small and great alike, all are greedy for
gain;
prophet and priest, all practice fraud.[o]
14 They have treated lightly
the injury to my people:
"Peace, peace!" they say,
though there is no peace.[p]
15 They have acted shamefully, committing
abominations,
yet they are not at all ashamed,
they do not know how to blush.
Therefore they will fall among the fallen;
in the time of their punishment they
shall stumble,
says the LORD.[q]
16 Thus says the LORD:
Stand by the earliest roads,
ask the pathways of old,*
"Which is the way to good?" and walk it;
thus you will find rest for yourselves.
But they said, "We will not walk it."[r]
17 I raised up watchmen* for them:
"Pay attention to the sound of the
trumpet!"
But they said, "We will not pay
attention!"
18 Therefore hear, O nations,
and know, O earth,
what I will do with them:
19 See, I bring evil upon this people,
the fruit of their own schemes,
Because they did not pay attention to my
words,
because they rejected my law.[s]

**6:3 Shepherds come with their flocks**: foreign invaders with their armies.
**6:16 Pathways of old**: history and the lessons to be learned from it.
**6:17 Watchmen**: the prophets who, like Jeremiah, had upheld God's moral law.

*g:* Jer 1:14–15. *h:* Jer 4:17. *i:* 2 Chr 36:19. *j:* Jer 32:24; Zep 3:1–4. *k:* Is 57:20. *l:* Jer 7:26; 20:8. *m:* Ez 9:6. *n:* Jer 8:10; Dt 28:30–32. *o:* Jer 8:10; 23:11. *p:* Jer 8:11. *q:* Jer 3:3; 8:12. *r:* Jer 7:23–24; 18:15. *s:* Prv 1:31.

20 Of what use to me is incense that comes
from Sheba,
or sweet cane from far-off lands?
Your burnt offerings find no favor
with me,
your sacrifices do not please me.[t]
21 Therefore, thus says the LORD:
See, I will place before this people
obstacles to trip them up;
Parents and children alike,
neighbors and friends shall perish.[u]
22 Thus says the LORD:
See, a people comes from the land of the
north,
a great nation, rising from the very
ends of the earth.[v]
23 Bow and javelin they wield;
cruel and pitiless are they.
They sound like the roaring sea
as they ride forth on horses,
Each in his place for battle
against you, daughter Zion.
24 We hear news of them;
our hands hang helpless,
Anguish takes hold of us,
pangs like a woman in childbirth.[w]
25 Do not go out into the field,
do not step into the street,
For the enemy has a sword;
terror on every side!
26 Daughter of my people, dress in sackcloth,
roll in the ashes.
Mourn as for an only child
with bitter wailing:
"How suddenly the destroyer
comes upon us!"[x]
27 * A tester for my people I have appointed
you,
to search and test their way.[y]
28 Arch-rebels are they all,
dealers in slander,
bronze and iron, all of them,
destroyers they are.
29 The bellows are scorched,
the lead is consumed by the fire;
In vain has the refiner refined,
the wicked are not drawn off.
30 "Silver rejected" they shall be called,
for the LORD has rejected them.

## II. Oracles Primarily from the Days of Jehoiakim

### CHAPTER 7

See 21

*The Temple Sermon.** 1 The word came to
Jeremiah from the LORD: 2 Stand at the gate
of the house of the LORD and proclaim this
message there: Hear the word of the LORD,
all you of Judah who enter these gates to
worship the LORD! 3 Thus says the LORD of
hosts, the God of Israel: Reform your ways
and your deeds so that I may dwell with you
in this place.[z] 4 Do not put your trust in these
deceptive words: "The temple of the LORD!
The temple of the LORD! The temple of the
LORD!"[a] 5 Only if you thoroughly reform
your ways and your deeds; if each of you
deals justly with your neighbor; 6 if you no
longer oppress the alien,* the orphan, and the
widow; if you no longer shed innocent blood
in this place or follow after other gods to
your own harm,[b] 7 only then will I let you
continue to dwell in this place, in the land I
gave your ancestors long ago and forever.[c]
8 But look at you! You put your trust in deceptive words to your own loss! 9 Do you
think you can steal and murder, commit
adultery and perjury, sacrifice to Baal, follow other gods that you do not know,[d] 10 and
then come and stand in my presence in this
house, which bears my name, and say: "We
are safe! We can commit all these abominations again!"?[e] 11 Has this house which bears
my name become in your eyes a den of
thieves? I have seen it for myself!—oracle
of the LORD.[f] 12 Go to my place at Shiloh,*
where I made my name dwell in the begin-

**6:27–30** God appoints Jeremiah to be a "tester" of his people. The passage uses the metaphor of the refining of silver: the silver was extracted from lead ore, but the process in ancient times was inexact, so that sometimes all that was left was a scummy mess, to be thrown out.

**7:1–15** The Temple of the Lord will not guarantee safety against enemy invasion or any other misfortune.

**7:6 The alien**: specially protected within Israelite society; cf. Ex 22:20; Nm 9:14; 15:14; Dt 5:14; 28:43.

**7:12 Shiloh**: an important sanctuary where the ark of the covenant was kept, according to the Books of Joshua, Judges,

*t:* Is 1:11; 43:24. *u:* Is 8:14–15. *v:* Jer 1:15; 5:15. *w:* Jer 4:31. *x:* Jer 25:34; Am 8:10. *y:* Jer 1:18. *z:* Jer 18:11; 26:13. *a:* Mi 3:11. *b:* Ex 22:21–24. *c:* Dt 4:40. *d:* Jer 44:17. *e:* Jer 32:34. *f:* Mt 21:13.

## The Temple Sermon

THE LONG PROSE sermon in chs 7–8, which is presented by Jeremiah at the temple in Jerusalem, appears to interrupt the poetry of chs 1–10. The poetry contains multiple images and voices that intrude upon each other, but the prose sermon contains only the voice of Jeremiah as the divine spokesperson. The sermon's subject is the hypocrisy and arrogance of the people's worship, and it focuses attention on the people's sinfulness. The people themselves, not God, should be blamed for the destruction of the nation. Judah and its capital city, Jerusalem, fell to Babylon because their worship was false.

The sermon must have been immensely shocking for its original audience. Since the time of David, the king and the temple had been closely bound together in the people's thinking. When David came to the throne, God promised that David's son would build the temple and that David and his throne would be established forever (1 Sm 7:1–7). A century earlier than Jeremiah, the prophet Isaiah had interpreted the promises to David as an unconditional assurance of Jerusalem's safety (Is 36–37). By the time of Jeremiah, the people of Judah seemed to think they were safe no matter what they did.

ning. See what I did to it because of the wickedness of my people Israel.[g] [13]And now, because you have committed all these deeds—oracle of the LORD—because you did not listen, though I spoke to you untiringly, and because you did not answer, though I called you, [14]I will do to this house, which bears my name, in which you trust, and to the place which I gave you and your ancestors, exactly what I did to Shiloh.[h] [15]I will cast you out of my sight, as I cast away all your kindred, all the offspring of Ephraim.[i]

***Abuses in Worship.*** [16]You, now, must not intercede for this people! Do not raise a cry or prayer in their behalf![j] Do not press me, for I will not listen to you! [17]Do you not see what they are doing in the cities of Judah, in the streets of Jerusalem? [18]The children gather wood, their fathers light the fire, and the women knead dough to make cakes for the Queen of Heaven,* while libations are poured out to other gods—all to offend me![k] [19]Are they really offending me—oracle of the LORD—or rather themselves, to their own disgrace?[l] [20]Therefore, thus says the Lord GOD: my anger and my wrath will pour out upon this place, upon human being and beast, upon the trees of the field and the fruits of the earth; it will burn and not be quenched.[m]

[21]Thus says the LORD of hosts, the God of Israel: Heap your burnt offerings upon your sacrifices; eat up the meat! [22]In speaking to your ancestors on the day I brought them out of the land of Egypt, I gave them no command* concerning burnt offering or sacrifice. [23]This rather is what I commanded them: Listen to my voice; then I will be your God and you shall be my people. Walk exactly in the way I command you, so that you may prosper.[n]

[24]But they did not listen to me, nor did they pay attention. They walked in the stubbornness of their evil hearts and turned their backs, not their faces, to me.[o] [25]From the day that your ancestors left the land of Egypt even to this day, I kept on sending all my servants the prophets to you.[p] [26]Yet they have not listened to me nor have they paid attention; they have stiffened their necks and done worse than their ancestors.[q] [27]When

and 1 Samuel. In response to the corrupt behavior of the priests serving there, God allows the Philistines to destroy Shiloh and take the ark of the covenant. Cf. 1 Sm 1:9; 4:3–4; Ps 78:60, 68–69.

**7:18 Queen of Heaven**: probably Astarte, goddess of fertility (cf. 1 Sm 31:10; 1 Kgs 11:5), worshiped particularly by women (cf. Jer 44:15–19). Such worship was evidently reinforced during the reign of King Manasseh (2 Kgs 21:3–7) and was revived after Josiah's death.

**7:22 I gave them no command**: right conduct rather than formal ritual was God's will concerning his people (v. 23).

*g:* Jos 18:1. *h:* Jer 26:9. *i:* 1 Kgs 9:7; 2 Kgs 17:23. *j:* Jer 11:14; 14:11. *k:* Jer 44:17, 19. *l:* Jb 35:6. *m:* Jer 36:29; 2 Kgs 22:17. *n:* Jer 11:4; Lv 26:3, 12. *o:* Jer 17:23. *p:* 2 Chr 36:15–16; Bar 1:19. *q:* Jer 19:15; 2 Chr 30:8.

you speak all these words to them, they will
not listen to you either. When you call to
them, they will not answer you. 28 Say to
them: This is the nation which does not listen to the voice of the LORD, its God, or take
correction. Faithfulness has disappeared; the
word itself is banished from their speech.

29 [r] Cut off your hair* and throw it away!
on the heights raise a lament;
The LORD has indeed rejected and cast off
the generation that draws down his wrath.

30 The people of Judah have done what is
evil in my eyes—oracle of the LORD. They
have set up their detestable things in the
house which bears my name, thereby defiling it.[s] 31 In the Valley of Ben-hinnom* they
go on building the high places of Topheth to
sacrifice their sons and daughters by fire,
something I never commanded or considered. 32 Be assured! Days are coming—oracle
of the LORD—when they will no longer say
"Topheth" or "Valley of Ben-hinnom" but
"Valley of Slaughter." For want of space, Topheth will become burial ground.[t] 33 The
corpses of this people will be food for the
birds of the sky and beasts of the earth, which
no one will drive away.[u] 34 I will silence the
cry of joy, the cry of gladness, the voice of
the bridegroom and the voice of the bride, in
the cities of Judah and in the streets of Jerusalem; for the land will be turned to rubble.[v]

See RG 217

## CHAPTER 8

1 At that time—oracle of the LORD—
the bones of the kings and princes of Judah,
the bones of the priests and the prophets, and
the bones of the inhabitants of Jerusalem
will be brought out of their graves[w] 2 and
spread out before the sun, the moon, and the
whole host of heaven,* which they loved and
served, which they followed, consulted, and
worshiped. They will not be gathered up for
burial, but will lie like dung upon the
ground.[x] 3 Death will be preferred to life by
all the survivors of this wicked people who
remain in any of the places to which I banish
them—oracle of the LORD of hosts.

### *Israel's Conduct Incomprehensible*

4 Tell them: Thus says the LORD:
When someone falls, do they not rise again?
if they turn away, do they not turn back?
5 Why then do these people resist
with persistent rebellion?
Why do they cling to deception,
refuse to turn back?[y]
6 I have listened closely:
they speak what is not true;
No one regrets wickedness,
saying, "What have I done?"
Everyone keeps on running their course,
like a horse dashing into battle.[z]
7 Even the stork in the sky
knows its seasons;
Turtledove, swift, and thrush
observe the time of their return,
But my people do not know
the order of the LORD.[a]
8 How can you say, "We are wise,[b]
we have the law of the LORD"?
See, that has been changed into falsehood
by the lying pen of the scribes!*
9 The wise are put to shame,
terrified, and trapped;
Since they have rejected the word of the LORD,
what sort of wisdom do they have?[c]

### *Shameless in Their Crimes*

10 Therefore, I will give their wives to other men,
their fields to new owners.

**7:29 Hair**: the unshorn hair of the nazirite, regarded as sacred because of a vow, temporary or permanent, to abstain from cutting or shaving the hair; nazirites also avoided contact with a corpse and with all products of the vine; cf. Nm 6:4–8. The cutting of this hair was a sign of extreme mourning.

**7:31 Valley of Ben-hinnom**: this valley was probably south of Jerusalem. **Topheth**: perhaps, "fire pit."

**8:2 Host of heaven**: the stars, worshiped by other nations and even by the inhabitants of Jerusalem, particularly during the reigns of Manasseh and Amon.

**8:8 Lying pen of the scribes**: because the teachings and interpretations of the scribes ran counter to the word of the Lord.

*r:* Jer 9:17–21. *s:* Jer 32:34. *t:* Jer 19:6; 32:35. *u:* Jer 16:4; 34:20. *v:* Jer 16:9. *w:* Bar 2:24. *x:* Dt 4:19. *y:* Jer 5:3; 7:24, 26. *z:* Jb 34:31–32. *a:* Is 1:3. *b:* Mal 2:8; Rom 2:17–23. *c:* 1 Cor 3:20.

GILEAD (8:22) IS THE part of Israel located to the east of the Jordan River, south of Bashan (Golan Heights) and north of Moab. It was apparently a site where balm and other healing substances could be extracted from local plants (see Gn 37:25).

Small and great alike, all are greedy for gain,
prophet and priest, all practice fraud.[d]
11 They have treated lightly
the injury to the daughter of my people:*
"Peace, peace!" they say,
though there is no peace.[e]
12 They have acted shamefully; they have done abominable things,
yet they are not at all ashamed,
they do not know how to blush.
Hence they shall be among those who fall;
in their time of punishment they shall stumble,
says the LORD.[f]

### *Threats of Punishment*

13 I will gather them all in—oracle of the LORD:
no grapes on the vine,
No figs on the fig trees,
foliage withered!
Whatever I have given them is gone.
14 Why do we remain here?
Let us assemble and flee to the fortified cities,
where we will meet our doom;
For the LORD our God has doomed us,
he has given us poisoned water to drink,
because we have sinned against the LORD.[g]
15 We wait for peace to no avail;
for a time of healing, but terror comes instead.[h]
16 From Dan is heard
the snorting of horses;
The neighing of stallions
shakes the whole land.
They come to devour the land and everything in it,
the city and its inhabitants.
17 Yes, I will send against you
poisonous snakes.
Against them no charm will work
when they bite you—oracle of the LORD.[i]

### *The Prophet's Grief over the People's Suffering*

18 My joy is gone,
grief is upon me,
my heart is sick.
19 Listen! the cry of the daughter of my people,
far and wide in the land!
"Is the LORD no longer in Zion,
is her King no longer in her midst?"
Why do they provoke me with their idols,
with their foreign nonentities?[j]
20 "The harvest is over, the summer ended,
but we have not yet been saved!"
21 I am broken by the injury of the daughter of my people.
I am in mourning; horror has seized me.[k]
22 Is there no balm in Gilead,*
no healer there?
Why does new flesh not grow
over the wound of the daughter of my people?[l]
23 Oh, that my head were a spring of water,
my eyes a fountain of tears,
That I might weep day and night
over the slain from the daughter of my people!

**8:11 Daughter of my people**: see note on 4:11.

**8:22 Gilead**: a region southeast of the Sea of Galilee noted for its healing balm.

*d:* Jer 6:13; Dt 28:30. *e:* Jer 6:14. *f:* Jer 6:15. *g:* Jer 9:14; 23:15. *h:* Jer 14:19. *i:* Dt 32:24. *j:* Dt 32:21; Mi 4:9. *k:* Jer 14:17. *l:* Jer 46:11.

See RG 217

## CHAPTER 9

### *The Corruption of the People*

1 Oh, that I had in the wilderness
a travelers' lodging!
That I might leave my people
and depart from them.
They are all adulterers,
a band of traitors.
2 They ready their tongues like a drawn bow;
with lying, and not with truth,
they are powerful in the land.
They go from evil to evil,
and me they do not know—oracle of the LORD.
3 Be on your guard, everyone against his neighbor;
put no trust in any brother.
Every brother imitates Jacob, the supplanter,*
every neighbor is guilty of slander.
4 Each one deceives the other,
no one speaks the truth.
They have accustomed their tongues to lying,
they are perverse and cannot repent.[m]
5 Violence upon violence,
deceit upon deceit:
They refuse to know me—
oracle of the LORD.
6 Therefore, thus says the LORD of hosts:
I will refine them and test them;
how else should I deal with the daughter of my people?
7 A murderous arrow is their tongue,
their mouths utter deceit;
They speak peaceably with their neighbors,
but in their hearts they lay an ambush![n]
8 Should I not punish them for these deeds—oracle of the LORD;
on a nation such as this should I not take vengeance?[o]

### *Dirge over the Ravaged Land*

9 Over the mountains I shall break out in cries of lamentation,
over the pastures in the wilderness, in a dirge:
They are scorched, and no one crosses them,
no sound of lowing cattle;
Birds of the air as well as beasts,
all have fled and are gone.[p]
10 I will turn Jerusalem into a heap of ruins,
a haunt of jackals;
The cities of Judah I will make a waste,
where no one dwells.[q]

11 Who is wise enough to understand this?
To whom has the mouth of the LORD spoken? Let him declare it!

Why is the land ravaged,
scorched like a wilderness no one crosses?[r]

12 The LORD said: Because they have
abandoned my law, which I set before them,
and did not listen to me or follow it, 13 but
followed instead their stubborn hearts and
the Baals, as their ancestors had taught
them,[s] 14 therefore, thus says the LORD of
hosts, the God of Israel: See now, I will give
this people wormwood to eat and poisoned
water to drink.[t] 15 I will scatter them among
nations whom neither they nor their ancestors have known; I will send the sword to
pursue them until I have completely destroyed them.[u]

16 Thus says the LORD of hosts:
Inquire, and call the wailing women to come;
summon the most skilled of them.
17 Let them come quickly
and raise for us a dirge,
That our eyes may run with tears,
our pupils flow with water.[v]
18 The sound of the dirge is heard from Zion:
We are ruined and greatly ashamed;

**9:3 Jacob, the supplanter**: in Hebrew, a play on words. In the popular etymology given in Gn 25:26, the name Jacob means "he supplants," for he deprived his brother Esau of his birthright (cf. Gn 25:33).

**9:25 Shave their temples**: some Arabian tribes practiced this custom. None of the nations who practice circumcision understand the meaning of their action, not even Israel; no one conforms to life under the covenant.

*m:* Jer 12:6. *n:* Ps 28:3; 62:4. *o:* Jer 5:9, 29. *p:* Jer 4:25; 12:4. *q:* Is 13:22. *r:* Ps 107:43; Hos 14:10. *s:* Jer 7:24; 19:4–5. *t:* Jer 23:15. *u:* Lv 26:33; Dt 28:36, 64. *v:* Jer 14:17.

## Hymn of Praise

THE FIRST 16 VERSES of ch 10 contain a hymn that expresses loyalty to the one true God and makes fun of other gods as worthless idols. The hymn serves as a model of repentance and reconciliation for the exiles surviving the nation's collapse. The poem is similar in subject and worship style to the repentance of the children from the broken family (3:22–25). The people should neither become like the nations around them nor adopt their idolatrous customs. Israel's God is the true king of the nations; by contrast, the gods of the nations are stupid, human creations. Only the God of Israel is the Creator whose wisdom made the world. Israel is God's special inheritance. In this hymn, creation's harmony is reestablished.

We have left the land,
given up our dwellings!
19 Hear, you women, the word of the LORD,
let your ears receive the word of his mouth.
Teach your daughters a dirge,
and each other a lament:
20 Death has come up through our windows,
has entered our citadels,
To cut down children in the street,
young people in the squares.[w]
21 Corpses shall fall
like dung in the open field,
Like sheaves behind the harvester,
with no one to gather them.

### True Glory

22 Thus says the LORD:
Let not the wise boast of his wisdom,
nor the strong boast of his strength,
nor the rich man boast of his riches;
23 But rather, let those who boast, boast of this,
that in their prudence they know me,[x]
Know that I, the LORD, act with fidelity,
justice, and integrity on earth.
How I take delight in these—oracle of the LORD.

***False Circumcision.*** 24 See, days are coming—oracle of the LORD—when I will demand an account of all those circumcised in
the foreskin:[y] 25 Egypt and Judah, Edom and
the Ammonites, Moab, and those who live in
the wilderness and shave their temples.* For
all the nations are uncircumcised, even the
whole house of Israel is uncircumcised at
heart.

### CHAPTER 10

See RG 217

***The Folly of Idolatry.*** 1 Hear the word
the LORD speaks to you, house of Israel.
2 Thus says the LORD:

Do not learn the ways of the nations,
and have no fear of the signs in the heavens,*
even though the nations fear them.[z]
3 For the carvings of the nations are nonentities,
wood cut from the forest,
Fashioned by artisans with the adze,[a]
4 adorned with silver and gold.
With nails and hammers they are fastened,
so they do not fall.[b]
5 Like a scarecrow in a cucumber field are they,
they cannot speak;
They must be carried about,
for they cannot walk.
Do not fear them, they can do no harm,
neither can they do good.[c]
6 No one is like you, LORD,
you are great,
great and mighty is your name.[d]
7 Who would not fear you,
King of the nations,
for it is your due!

**10:2 Signs in the heavens**: phenomena in the sky, such as eclipses or comets, used to predict disasters.

*w:* Jer 14:16. *x:* Prv 21:30. *y:* Jer 4:4. *z:* Bar 6:6. *a:* Wis 13:11; Is 44:9. *b:* Is 40:19; 41:7. *c:* Ps 115:4–8; Bar 6:15. *d:* Ps 86:8–10.

Among all the wisest of the nations,
and in all their domains,
there is none like you.[e]
8 One and all they are stupid and senseless,
the instruction from nonentities—only
wood!
9 Silver plates brought from Tarshish,
and gold from Ophir,
The work of the artisan
and the handiwork of the smelter,
Clothed with violet and purple—
all of them the work of skilled
workers.
10 The LORD is truly God,
he is the living God, the eternal King,
Before whose anger the earth quakes,
whose wrath the nations cannot
endure.[f]

11 Thus shall you say of them: The gods
that did not make heaven and earth—let
these perish from earth and from beneath
heaven!* [g]

12 The one who made the earth by his
power,
established the world by his wisdom,
and by his skill stretched out the
heavens.[h]
13 When he thunders, the waters in the
heavens roar,
and he brings up clouds from the end
of the earth,
Makes lightning flash in the rain,
and brings forth the wind from his
storehouses.
14 Everyone is too stupid to know;
every artisan is put to shame by his
idol:
He has molded a fraud,
without breath of life.[i]
15 They are nothing, objects of ridicule;
they will perish in their time of
punishment.
16 Jacob's portion is nothing like them:
for he is the maker of everything!
Israel is his very own tribe,
LORD of hosts is his name.[j]

### *Abandonment of Judah*

17 Gather up your bundle from the land,
City living under siege!
18 For thus says the LORD:
Now, at this time
I will sling away the inhabitants of the
land;
I will hem them in,
that they may be taken.
19 Woe is me! I am undone,
my wound is beyond healing.
Yet I had thought:
if I make light of my sickness, I can
bear it.
20 My tent is ruined,
all its cords are severed.
My children have left me, they are no
more:
no one to pitch my tent,
no one to raise its curtains.[k]
21 How stupid are the shepherds!
The LORD they have not sought;
For this reason they have failed,
and all their flocks scattered.[l]
22 Listen! a rumor! here it comes,
a great commotion from the land of
the north:
To make the cities of Judah a desolation,
the haunt of jackals.

### *Prayer of Jeremiah*

23 I know, LORD,
that no one chooses their way,
Nor determines their course
nor directs their own step.
24 Correct me, LORD, but with equity,
not in anger, lest you diminish me.
25 Pour out your wrath on the nations that
do not know you,
on the tribes that do not call your name;
For they have utterly devoured Jacob,
and laid waste his home.[m]

## CHAPTER 11

See RG 217

***Plea for Fidelity to the Covenant.*** 1 The word that came to Jeremiah from the
LORD: 2 Speak to the people of Judah and the

**10:11** This verse is in Aramaic.

*e:* Jer 5:22; Ps 47:2, 8. *f:* Ps 10:16. *g:* Ps 96:5. *h:* Ps 104:5. *i:* Rom 1:22–23. *j:* Ps 33:12; Jer 31:35. *k:* Jer 4:20. *l:* Jer 23:1; Ez 34:5–6. *m:* Ps 79:6–7.

inhabitants of Jerusalem, 3 and say to them:
Thus says the LORD, the God of Israel:
Cursed be anyone who does not observe the
words of this covenant,[n] 4 which I commanded your ancestors the day I brought
them up out of the land of Egypt, that iron
furnace, saying: Listen to my voice and do
all that I command you. Then you shall be
my people, and I will be your God.[o] 5 Thus I
will fulfill the oath I swore to your ancestors,
to give them a land flowing with milk and
honey, the one you have today. "Amen,
LORD," I answered.
6 Then the LORD said to me: Proclaim all
these words in the cities of Judah and in the
streets of Jerusalem: Hear the words of this
covenant and obey them. 7 I warned your ancestors unceasingly from the day I brought
them up out of the land of Egypt even to this
day: obey my voice. 8 But they did not listen or
obey. They each walked in the stubbornness of
their evil hearts, till I brought upon them all
the threats of this covenant which they had
failed to observe as I commanded them.[p]
9 A conspiracy has been found, the LORD
said to me, among the people of Judah and
the inhabitants of Jerusalem: 10 They have returned to the crimes of their ancestors who
refused to obey my words. They also have
followed and served other gods; the house of
Israel and the house of Judah have broken
the covenant I made with their ancestors.[q]
11 Therefore, thus says the LORD: See, I am
bringing upon them a disaster they cannot
escape. Though they cry out to me, I will not
listen to them.[r] 12 Then the cities of Judah
and the inhabitants of Jerusalem will go and
cry out to the gods to whom they have been
offering incense. But these gods will give
them no help whatever in the time of their
disaster.[s]

13 For as many as your cities
are your gods, O Judah!
As many as the streets of Jerusalem
are the altars for sacrifice to Baal.[t]

14 Now, you must not intercede for this people; do not raise on their behalf a cry or
prayer! I will not listen when they call to me
in the time of their disaster.[u]

### Sacrifices of No Avail

15 What right has my beloved in my house,
while she devises her plots?
Can vows and sacred meat turn away
your disaster from you?
Will you still be jubilant
16 when you hear the great tumult?
The LORD has named you
"a spreading olive tree, a pleasure to
behold";
Now he sets fire to it,
its branches burn.

17 The LORD of hosts who planted you has
decreed disaster for you because of the evil
done by the house of Israel and by the house
of Judah, who provoked me by sacrificing to
Baal.[v]

***The Plot Against Jeremiah.*** 18 I knew it because the LORD informed me: at that time
you showed me their doings.
19 Yet I was like a trusting lamb led to
slaughter, not knowing that they were hatch-
ing plots against me: "Let us destroy the tree
in its vigor; let us cut him off from the land
of the living, so that his name will no longer
be remembered."[w]

20 But, you, LORD of hosts, just Judge,
searcher of mind and heart,
Let me witness the vengeance you take
on them,
for to you I have entrusted my cause![x]

21 Therefore, thus says the LORD concerning the men of Anathoth who seek your life
and say, "Do not prophesy in the name of the
LORD; otherwise you shall die by our hand."[y]
22 Therefore, thus says the LORD of hosts: I
am going to punish them. The young men
shall die by the sword; their sons and daughters shall die by famine.[z] 23 None shall be
spared among them, for I will bring disaster
upon the men of Anathoth, the year of their
punishment.[a]

---

*n:* Dt 27:26. *o:* Dt 4:20; 1 Kgs 8:51. *p:* 2 Kgs 17:14. *q:* Dt 31:16; Ez 20:21–30. *r:* Jer 14:12; Mi 3:4. *s:* Dt 32:37–38. *t:* Jer 2:28; Hos 10:1. *u:* Jer 7:16; 14:11. *v:* Is 5:2. *w:* Jer 18:18; 20:10; Wis 2:20. *x:* Jer 15:15. *y:* Am 7:13, 16. *z:* Jer 18:21–22. *a:* Jer 23:12.

## Jeremiah's Lament

CHAPTER 12 OPENS with the first of several laments of Jeremiah (12:1–6, 19–23; 15:10–21; 17:14–18; 18:18–23; 20:7–13; 20:14–18), in which he complains to God concerning his own suffering for announcing divine judgment to the people. The language is typical of complaint language of the Psalms (e.g., Ps 7) and Lamentations, but it nevertheless provides an intimate glimpse of the prophet's own feelings. These laments, sometimes called "confessions," typify Jeremiah, in whose book there is more biographical information than in those of all of the other prophets combined.

### CHAPTER 12

See RG 217

1 You would be in the right, O LORD,
if I should dispute with you;
even so, I must lay out the case against you.
Why does the way of the wicked prosper,
why do all the treacherous live in contentment?[b]
2 You planted them; they have taken root,
they flourish and bear fruit as well.
You are upon their lips,
but far from their thoughts.[c]
3 LORD, you know me, you see me,
you have found that my heart is with you.[d]
Pick them out like sheep for the butcher,
set them apart for the day of slaughter.*
4 How long must the land mourn,
the grass of the whole countryside wither?
Because of the wickedness of those who dwell in it
beasts and birds disappear,
for they say, "God does not care about our future."

5 If running against men has wearied you,
how will you race against horses?
And if you are safe only on a level stretch,
what will you do in the jungle of the Jordan?
6 Your kindred and your father's house, even they betray you; they have recruited a force against you. Do not believe them, even when they speak fair words to you.[e]

*The Lord's Complaint*

7 I have abandoned my house,
cast off my heritage;
The beloved of my soul I have delivered
into the hand of her foes.[f]
8 My heritage has become for me
like a lion in the thicket;
She has raised her voice against me,
therefore she has incurred my hatred.[g]
9 My heritage is a prey for hyenas,
is surrounded by vultures;
Come, gather together, all you wild animals,
come and eat![h]
10 Many shepherds have ravaged my vineyard,
have trampled down my heritage;
My delightful portion they have turned
into a desert waste.[i]
11 They have made it a mournful waste,
desolate before me,
Desolate, the whole land,
because no one takes it to heart.
12 Upon every height in the wilderness
marauders have appeared.
The LORD has a sword that consumes
the land from end to end:
no peace for any living thing.[j]
13 They have sown wheat and reaped thorns,

**12:3** Jeremiah calls the Lord to account for allowing the wicked to flourish while he himself is persecuted for his fidelity to the Lord's mission; cf. 20:12. See Jesus' judgment, Mk 9:42. The metaphors indicate that Jeremiah has even greater trials ahead of him.

*b:* Jb 21:7; Mal 3:15. *c:* Is 29:13. *d:* Jer 17:18; Jb 23:10. *e:* Jer 9:4. *f:* Ps 78:62; Lam 2:1–2. *g:* Ps 106:40. *h:* 2 Kgs 24:2; Is 56:9. *i:* Jer 6:3; Is 63:18. *j:* Is 42:25; 57:21.

they have tired themselves out for no
purpose;
They are shamed by their harvest,
the burning anger of the LORD.

***Judah's Neighbors.*** 14 Thus says the LORD,
against all my evil neighbors* who plunder
the heritage I gave my people Israel as their
own: See, I will uproot them from their land;
the house of Judah I will uproot in their
midst.[k]
15 But after uprooting them, I will have
compassion on them again and bring them
back, each to their heritage, each to their
land.[l] 16 And if they truly learn my people's
custom of swearing by my name, "As the
LORD lives," just as they taught my people to
swear by Baal, then they shall be built up in
the midst of my people.[m] 17 But if they do not
obey, I will uproot and destroy that nation
entirely—oracle of the LORD.[n]

## CHAPTER 13

See RG 217

***Judah's Corruption.**** 1 The LORD said
to me: Go buy yourself a linen loincloth;
wear it on your loins, but do not put it in water. 2 I bought the loincloth, as the LORD commanded, and put it on. 3 A second time the
word of the LORD came to me thus: 4 Take the
loincloth which you bought and are wearing,
and go at once to the Perath; hide it there in
a cleft of the rock. 5 Obedient to the LORD's
command, I went to the Perath and buried
the loincloth. 6 After a long time, the LORD
said to me: Go now to the Perath and fetch
the loincloth which I told you to hide there.
7 So I went to the Perath, looked for the loincloth and took it from the place I had hidden
it. But it was rotted, good for nothing! 8 Then
the word came to me from the LORD: 9 Thus
says the LORD: So also I will allow the pride
of Judah to rot, the great pride of Jerusalem.[o]
10 This wicked people who refuse to obey my
words, who walk in the stubbornness of their
hearts and follow other gods, serving and
worshiping them, will be like this loincloth,
good for nothing.[p] 11 For, as the loincloth
clings to a man's loins, so I made the whole
house of Israel and the whole house of Judah
cling to me—oracle of the LORD—to be my
people, my fame, my praise, my glory. But
they did not listen.[q]

***The Broken Wineflask.*** 12 Now speak to
them this word: Thus says the LORD, the
God of Israel: Every wineflask should be
filled with wine. If they reply, "Do we not
know that every wineflask should be filled
with wine?" 13 say to them: Thus says the
LORD: Beware! I am making all the inhabitants of this land drunk, the kings who sit on
David's throne, the priests and prophets, and
all the inhabitants of Jerusalem.[r] 14 I will
smash them against each other, parents and
children together—oracle of the LORD—
showing no compassion, I will neither spare
nor pity, but I will destroy them.[s]

### *A Last Warning*

15 Listen and give ear, do not be arrogant,
for the LORD speaks.
16 Give glory to the LORD, your God,
before he brings darkness;
Before your feet stumble
on mountains at twilight;
Before the light you look for turns to
darkness,
changes into black clouds.[t]
17 If you do not listen to this in your pride,
I will weep many tears in secret;
My eyes will run with tears
for the LORD's flock, led away to
exile.[u]

### *Exile*

18 Say to the king and to the queen mother:
come down from your throne;
From your heads
your splendid crowns will fall.[v]

**12:14 My evil neighbors**: nations surrounding Israel, the land belonging to the Lord; cf. Is 8:8.

**13:1–11** In this symbolic action, Jeremiah probably went to the village and spring of Parah, two and a half miles northeast of Anathoth, whose name closely resembled the Hebrew name of the river Euphrates (*Perath*), in order to dramatize the religious corruption of Judah at the hands of the Babylonians.

*k:* 2 Kgs 24:2. *l:* Am 9:14. *m:* Dt 6:13. *n:* Is 60:12. *o:* Prv 16:18. *p:* Jer 2:20; 7:24; 16:11. *q:* Ex 19:5; Dt 26:18–19. *r:* Jer 25:15–18; Is 51:17. *s:* Jer 19:10–11. *t:* Prv 4:18–19; Is 5:30; Am 8:9. *u:* Jer 14:17; Ps 119:136. *v:* Jer 22:26; 2 Kgs 24:12, 15.

19 The cities of the Negeb are besieged,
with no one to relieve them;
Judah is taken into exile—all of it—
in total exile.

*Jerusalem's Disgrace*

20 Lift up your eyes and see
those coming in from the north.
Where is the flock entrusted to you,
your splendid sheep?[w]
21 What will you say when rulers are
appointed over you,
those you taught to be allies?
Will not pains seize you
like those of a woman giving birth?[x]
22 If you say to yourself:
"Why have these things happened
to me?"
For your great guilt your skirts are
stripped away
and you are violated.[y]
23 Can Ethiopians change their skin,
leopards their spots?
As easily would you be able to do good,
accustomed to evil as you are.[z]
24 I will scatter them like chaff that flies
on the desert wind.[a]
25 This is your lot, the portion I have
measured out to you—
oracle of the LORD.
Because you have forgotten me,
and trusted in deception,*[b]
26 I now will strip away your skirts,
so that your shame is visible.[c]
27 Your adulteries, your neighings,
your shameless prostitutions:
On the hills, in the fields
I see your detestable crimes.
Woe to you, Jerusalem! How long will
it be
before you are clean?[d]

See RG 217

## CHAPTER 14

***The Great Drought.*** 1 The word of the LORD that came to Jeremiah concerning the drought:[e]

2 Judah mourns,
her gates are lifeless;
They are bowed to the ground,
and the outcry of Jerusalem goes up.[f]
3 The nobles send their servants for water,
but when they come to the cisterns
They find no water
and return with empty jars.[g]
Confounded, despairing, they cover their
heads
4 because of the ruined soil;
Because there is no rain in the land
the farmers are confounded, they cover
their heads.[h]
5 Even the doe in the field deserts her
young
because there is no grass.
6 The wild donkeys stand on the bare
heights,
gasping for breath like jackals;
Their eyes grow dim;
there is no grass.
7 Even though our crimes bear witness
against us,
act, LORD, for your name's sake—
Even though our rebellions are many,
and we have sinned against you.[i]
8 Hope of Israel, LORD,
our savior in time of need!
Why should you be a stranger in the land,
like a traveler stopping only for a
night?
9 Why are you like someone bewildered,
a champion who cannot save?
You are in our midst, LORD,
your name we bear:
do not forsake us![j]
10 Thus says the LORD about this people:
They so love to wander
that they cannot restrain their feet.
The LORD takes no pleasure in them;
now he remembers their guilt,
and will punish their sins.[k]

11 Then the LORD said to me: Do not intercede for the well-being of this people.[l] 12 If they fast, I will not listen to their supplica-

**13:25** Heb. *sheqer*: lit., "deception," often used to designate an idol.

*w:* Jer 6:22–23. *x:* 2 Kgs 16:7. *y:* Is 47:2–3. *z:* Ps 55:20. *a:* Ps 1:4; 83:14. *b:* Jb 20:29. *c:* Ez 16:32. *d:* Jer 2:20. *e:* Lv 26:19–20. *f:* Is 3:26. *g:* Am 4:8. *h:* Dt 28:23. *i:* Dn 9:4–14. *j:* Is 59:1–2; 63:19. *k:* Jer 2:25. *l:* Jer 11:14; Ex 32:10.

**Jeremiah's Lament over Jerusalem's Inevitable Punishment**

THE THEME OF Jerusalem's punishment continues in ch 15, and Jeremiah laments his task and the city's fate. Jerusalem's punishment is inevitable; not even Moses and Samuel, the great earlier prophetic intercessors, could convince God to reverse the decision. The four punishments—death, sword, famine, and captivity—represent a comprehensive list of punishments not unlike those mentioned in Ezekiel ch 5. Even animals participate in the judgment.

tion. If they sacrifice burnt offerings or grain
offerings, I will take no pleasure in them.
Rather, I will destroy them with the sword,
famine, and plague.[m]
13 "Ah! Lord GOD," I replied, "it is the
prophets who say to them, 'You shall not see
the sword; famine shall not befall you. Indeed,
I will give you lasting peace in this place.' "[n]
14 These prophets utter lies in my name,
the LORD said to me: I did not send them; I
gave them no command, nor did I speak to
them. They prophesy to you lying visions,
foolish divination, deceptions from their
own imagination.[o]
15 Therefore, thus says the
LORD: Concerning the prophets who prophesy in my name, though I did not send them,
and who say, "Sword and famine shall not
befall this land": by sword and famine shall
these prophets meet their end.[p]
16 The people
to whom they prophesy shall be thrown out
into the streets of Jerusalem because of
famine and the sword. No one shall bury
them, their wives, their sons, or their daughters, for I will pour out upon them their own
wickedness.[q]
17 Speak to them this word:

Let my eyes stream with tears
night and day, without rest,
Over the great destruction which
overwhelms
the virgin daughter of my people,
over her incurable wound.[r]

18 If I walk out into the field,
look! those slain by the sword;
If I enter the city,
look! victims of famine.
Both prophet and priest ply their trade
in a land they do not know.

19 Have you really cast Judah off?
Is Zion loathsome to you?
Why have you struck us a blow
that cannot be healed?
We wait for peace, to no avail;
for a time of healing, but terror comes
instead.[s]

20 We recognize our wickedness, LORD,
the guilt of our ancestors:
we have sinned against you.[t]

21 Do not reject us, for your name's sake,
do not disgrace your glorious throne.
Remember! Do not break your
covenant with us.[u]

22 Among the idols of the nations are there
any that give rain?
Or can the mere heavens send showers?
Is it not you, LORD,
our God, to whom we look?
You alone do all these things.[v]

## CHAPTER 15

See RG 217

1 The LORD said to me: Even if Moses
and Samuel stood before me, my heart
would not turn toward this people. Send
them away from me and let them go.[w]
2 If
they ask you, "Where should we go?" tell
them, Thus says the LORD: Whoever is
marked for death, to death; whoever is
marked for the sword, to the sword; whoever
is marked for famine, to famine; whoever is
marked for captivity, to captivity.[x]
3 Four
kinds of scourge I have decreed against
them—oracle of the LORD—the sword to
kill them; dogs to drag them off; the birds of
the sky and the beasts of the earth to devour
and destroy them.[y]
4 And I will make them an
object of horror to all the kingdoms of the

*m:* Jer 6:20; Is 1:11, 13. *n:* Jer 4:10; 5:12. *o:* Jer 5:31; 23:16. *p:* Jer 5:12–13. *q:* Jer 7:33; 19:7. *r:* Jer 9:17. *s:* Jer 8:15; 2 Chr 36:16. *t:* Ps 106:6; Dn 9:5, 8. *u:* Jer 14:7; Lv 26:44; Ps 25:11. *v:* Jer 5:24; Zec 10:1. *w:* Ps 99:6; Ez 14:14, 16. *x:* Jer 14:12; Ez 5:12. *y:* Ez 14:21.

earth because of what Manasseh, son of Hezekiah, king of Judah, did in Jerusalem.[z]

### *Scene of Tragedy*

5 Who will pity you, Jerusalem,
who will grieve for you?
Who will stop to ask
about your welfare?[a]
6 It is you who have disowned me—oracle of the LORD—
turned your back upon me;
I stretched out my hand to destroy you,
because I was weary of relenting.[b]
7 I winnowed them with a winnowing fork
at the gates of the land;
I have bereaved, destroyed my people;
they have not turned from their evil ways.[c]
8 Their widows were more numerous before me
than the sands of the sea.
I brought against the mother of youths
the destroyer at midday;
Suddenly I struck her
with anguish and terror.
9 The mother of seven faints away,
breathing out her life;
Her sun sets in full day,
she is ashamed, abashed.
Their survivors I will give to the sword
in the presence of their enemies—
oracle of the LORD.[d]

### *Jeremiah's Complaint*

10 Woe to me, my mother, that you gave me birth!
a man of strife and contention to all the land!
I neither borrow nor lend,
yet everyone curses me.[e]
11 Tell me, LORD, have I not served you for their good?
Have I not interceded with you
in time of misfortune and anguish?[f]
12 Can one break iron,
iron from the north, and bronze?
13 * Your wealth and your treasures
I give as plunder, demanding no payment,
because of all your sins, throughout all your territory.
14 And I shall enslave you to your enemies
in a land you do not know,
For fire has broken out from my anger,
it is kindled against you.
15 You know, LORD:
Remember me and take care of me,
avenge me on my persecutors.
Because you are slow to anger, do not banish me;
know that for you I have borne insult.[g]
16 When I found your words, I devoured them;
your words were my joy, the happiness of my heart,
Because I bear your name,
LORD, God of hosts.
17 I did not sit celebrating
in the circle of merrymakers;
Under the weight of your hand I sat alone
because you filled me with rage.[h]
18 Why is my pain continuous,
my wound incurable, refusing to be healed?
To me you are like a deceptive brook,
waters that cannot be relied on![i]
19 Thus the LORD answered me:
If you come back and I take you back,
in my presence you shall stand;
If you utter what is precious and not what is worthless,
you shall be my mouth.
Then they will be the ones who turn to you,
not you who turn to them.
20 And I will make you toward this people
a fortified wall of bronze.
Though they fight against you,
they shall not prevail,
For I am with you,

**15:13–14** Though the wording of these verses is close to that in 17:3–4, the present passage is evidently God's word to Jeremiah, whereas 17:3–4 is evidently a word of judgment on Judah. It is noteworthy that the references to "you" in the present passage are singular, until a shift to plural in "against you" in the last line; this "you" is then doubtless a reference to both the prophet and his enemies.

*z:* Jer 24:9; 2 Kgs 21:11–16; 23:26; 24:3–4. *a:* Is 51:19. *b:* Am 7:8. *c:* Is 41:16. *d:* 1 Sm 2:5. *e:* Jer 20:14. *f:* Jer 39:11–14. *g:* Jer 11:20; 12:3; Ps 69:8. *h:* Ps 25:4. *i:* Jer 14:19; 30:15.

to save and rescue you—oracle of the
LORD.[j]
21 I will rescue you from the hand of the
wicked,
and ransom you from the power of the
violent.

## CHAPTER 16

See RG 217

***Jeremiah's Life a Warning.*** 1This word
came to me from the LORD: 2Do not take a
wife and do not have sons and daughters in
this place, 3for thus says the LORD concerning the sons and daughters born in this place,
the mothers who give them birth, the fathers
who beget them in this land: 4Of deadly disease they shall die. Unlamented and unburied
they will lie like dung on the ground. Sword
and famine will make an end of them, and
their corpses will become food for the birds
of the sky and the beasts of the earth.[k]
5Thus says the LORD: Do not go into a
house of mourning; do not go there to
lament or grieve for them. For I have withdrawn my peace from this people—oracle of
the LORD—my love and my compassion.[l]
6They shall die, the great and the lowly, in
this land, unburied and unlamented.* No one
will gash themselves or shave their heads for
them.[m] 7They will not break bread with the
bereaved to offer consolation for the dead;
they will not give them the cup of consolation to drink over the death of father or
mother.[n]
8Do not enter a house of feasting to sit eating and drinking with them. 9For thus says
the LORD of hosts, the God of Israel: Before
your eyes and in your lifetime, I will silence
in this place the song of joy and the song of
gladness, the song of the bridegroom and the
song of the bride.[o]
10When you proclaim all these words to
this people and they ask you: "Why has the
LORD pronounced all this great disaster
against us? What is our crime? What sin
have we committed against the LORD, our
God?"—[p] 11[q] you shall answer them: It is because your ancestors have forsaken me—oracle of the LORD—and followed other gods
that they served and worshiped; but me they
have forsaken, and my law they did not
keep. 12And you have done worse than your
ancestors. Here you are, every one of you,
walking in the stubbornness of your evil
heart instead of listening to me.[r] 13I will
throw you out of this land into a land that
neither you nor your ancestors have known;
there you can serve other gods day and night
because I will not show you mercy.
***Return from Exile.*** 14Therefore, days are
coming—oracle of the LORD—when it will
no longer be said, "As the LORD lives, who
brought the Israelites out of Egypt";[s] 15but
rather, "As the LORD lives, who brought the
Israelites out of the land of the north and out
of all the countries to which he had banished
them." I will bring them back to the land I
gave their ancestors.[t]
***Double Punishment.*** 16Look!—oracle of
the LORD—I will send many fishermen to
catch them. After that, I will send many
hunters to hunt them out from every mountain and hill and rocky crevice.[u] 17For my
eyes are upon all their ways; they are not
hidden from me, nor does their guilt escape
my sight.[v] 18I will at once repay them double
for their crime and their sin because they
profaned my land with the corpses of their
detestable idols, and filled my heritage with
their abominations.[w]

### *Conversion of the Nations*

19 LORD, my strength, my fortress,
my refuge in the day of distress!
To you nations will come
from the ends of the earth, and say,
"Our ancestors inherited mere frauds,
empty, worthless."[x]
20 Can human beings make for themselves
gods?
But these are not gods at all![y]
21 Therefore, I will indeed give them
knowledge;

**16:6–7** These verses refer to popular mourning practices in the land; cf. Dt 14:1–2.

*j:* Jer 1:18; 6:27. *k:* Jer 7:33; 22:18. *l:* Ez 24:16–17. *m:* Lv 19:28; Dt 14:1. *n:* Ez 24:17. *o:* Jer 7:34; 25:10. *p:* Jer 2:35; 5:19; 13:22. *q:* Jer 22:9; Dt 29:25. *r:* Jer 7:24–26. *s:* Jer 23:7–8. *t:* Jer 24:6. *u:* 2 Kgs 24:2; Lam 4:19. *v:* Jer 32:19; Jb 34:21. *w:* Is 40:2. *x:* Jer 2:11; Is 2:2–3. *y:* Jer 2:11; Gal 4:8.

this time I will make them
acknowledge
My strength and my power:
they shall know that my name is LORD.[z]

## CHAPTER 17

See RG 217

### *The Sin of Judah and Its Punishment*

1 The sin of Judah is written
with an iron stylus,
Engraved with a diamond point
upon the tablets of their hearts,[a]

And the horns of their altars, 2 when their
children remember their altars and their
asherahs, beside the green trees, on the high
hills, 3 the peaks in the country.

Your wealth and all your treasures
I give as plunder,
As payment for all your sins
throughout your territory,
4 You will relinquish your hold on your
heritage
which I have given you.
I will enslave you to your enemies
in a land you do not know:
For a fire has broken out from my anger,
burning forever.[b]

### *True Wisdom*

5 Thus says the LORD:
Cursed is the man who trusts in human
beings,
who makes flesh his strength,
whose heart turns away from the
LORD.[c]
6 He is like a barren bush in the wasteland
that enjoys no change of season,
But stands in lava beds in the wilderness,
a land, salty and uninhabited.
7 Blessed are those who trust in the LORD;
the LORD will be their trust.[d]
8 They are like a tree planted beside the
waters
that stretches out its roots to the
stream:
It does not fear heat when it comes,
its leaves stay green;
In the year of drought it shows no
distress,
but still produces fruit.[e]
9 More tortuous than anything is the
human heart,
beyond remedy; who can understand it?
10 I, the LORD, explore the mind
and test the heart,
Giving to all according to their ways,
according to the fruit of their deeds.[f]
11 A partridge that broods but does not
hatch
are those who acquire wealth unjustly:
In midlife it will desert them;
in the end they are only fools.[g]

### *The Source of Life*

12 A throne of glory, exalted from the
beginning,
such is our holy place.[h]
13 O Hope of Israel, LORD!
all who forsake you shall be put to
shame;
The rebels shall be enrolled in the
netherworld;
they have forsaken the LORD, source
of living waters.[i]

### *Prayer for Vengeance*

14 Heal me, LORD, that I may be healed;
save me, that I may be saved,
for you are my praise.
15 See how they say to me,
"Where is the word of the LORD?
Let it come to pass!"[j]
16 Yet I did not press you to send disaster;
the day without remedy I have not
desired.
You know what passed my lips;
it is present before you.
17 Do not become a terror to me,
you are my refuge in the day of
disaster.[k]
18 Let my persecutors be confounded—
not me!
let them be terrified—not me!
Bring upon them the day of disaster,
crush them with double destruction.[l]

*z:* Am 5:8. *a:* Jb 19:24. *b:* Jer 5:19; Dt 32:22. *c:* Ps 146:2–3. *d:* Ps 1:3. *e:* Is 58:11. *f:* Jer 32:19; 1 Sm 16:7; Eccl 12:14. *g:* Prv 13:11; Lk 12:20. *h:* Jer 14:21. *i:* Jer 2:13. *j:* Is 5:19; 2 Pt 3:4. *k:* Jer 16:19. *l:* Jer 15:15; 18:20–23; Ps 35:5–6.

*Observance of the Sabbath.* [19]Thus said
the LORD to me: Go, stand at the Gate of
Benjamin,* where the kings of Judah enter
and leave, and at the other gates of Jerusalem.[m] [20]There say to them: Hear the word of
the LORD, you kings of Judah, and all Judah,
and all you inhabitants of Jerusalem who enter these gates! [21]Thus says the LORD: As
you love your lives, take care not to carry
burdens on the sabbath, to bring them in
through the gates of Jerusalem.[n] [22]Bring no
burden from your homes on the sabbath. Do
no work whatever, but keep holy the sabbath
day, as I commanded your ancestors,[o]
[23]though they did not listen or give ear, but
stiffened their necks so they could not hear
or take correction.[p] [24]If you truly obey me—
oracle of the LORD—and carry no burden
through the gates of this city on the sabbath,
keeping the sabbath day holy and abstaining
from all work on it,[q] [25]then, through the
gates of this city, kings who sit upon the
throne of David will continue to enter, riding
in their chariots or upon their horses, along
with their princes, and the people of Judah,
and the inhabitants of Jerusalem. This city
will remain inhabited forever.[r] [26]To it people
will come from the cities of Judah and the
neighborhood of Jerusalem, from the land of
Benjamin and from the Shephelah, from the
hill country and the Negeb, to bring burnt offerings and sacrifices, grain offerings, incense, and thank offerings to the house of
the LORD.[s] [27]But if you do not obey me and
keep holy the sabbath day, if you carry burdens and come through the gates of Jerusalem on the sabbath, I will set fire to its
gates—a fire never to be extinguished—and
it will consume the palaces of Jerusalem.[t]

## CHAPTER 18

See RG 217

*The Potter's Vessel.** [1]This word came
to Jeremiah from the LORD: [2]Arise and go
down to the potter's house; there you will
hear my word. [3]I went down to the potter's
house and there he was, working at the
wheel. [4]Whenever the vessel of clay he was
making turned out badly in his hand, he tried
again, making another vessel of whatever
sort he pleased.[u] [5]Then the word of the LORD
came to me: [6]Can I not do to you, house of Israel, as this potter has done?—oracle of the
LORD. Indeed, like clay in the hand of the potter, so are you in my hand, house of Israel.[v]
[7][w] At one moment I may decree concerning a
nation or kingdom that I will uproot and tear
down and destroy it; [8]but if that nation
against whom I have decreed turns from its
evil, then I will have a change of heart regarding the evil which I have decreed.[x] [9]At
another moment, I may decree concerning a
nation or kingdom that I will build up and
plant it; [10]but if that nation does what is evil
in my eyes, refusing to obey my voice, then I
will have a change of heart regarding the
good with which I planned to bless it.[y]

[11]And now, tell this to the people of Judah
and the inhabitants of Jerusalem: Thus says
the LORD: Look, I am fashioning evil against
you and making a plan. Return, all of you,
from your evil way; reform your ways and
your deeds.[z] [12]But they will say, "No use!
We will follow our own devices; each one of
us will behave according to the stubbornness
of our evil hearts!"[a]

### *Unnatural Apostasy*

13 Therefore thus says the LORD:
Ask among the nations—
who has ever heard the like?
Truly horrible things
virgin Israel has done![b]
14 Does the snow of Lebanon*
desert the rocky heights?
Do the gushing waters dry up
that flow fresh down the mountains?

**17:19 The Gate of Benjamin**: this gate, probably part of the Temple area, is otherwise unknown.

**18:1–12** The lesson of the potter is that God has the power to destroy or restore, changing his plans accordingly as these nations disobey him or fulfill his will. Cf. Jon 3:10.

**18:14 Lebanon**: here apparently including Mount Hermon, whose snow-capped peak can be seen from parts of Palestine all year round. The prophet contrasts the certainties of nature with Israel's unnatural desertion of the Lord for idols (v. 15).

*m:* Jer 7:2. *n:* Neh 13:15–19. *o:* Ex 20:8; 23:12. *p:* Jer 5:3; 7:24. *q:* Is 58:14. *r:* Jer 22:4. *s:* Jer 32:44. *t:* Ez 22:8. *u:* Rom 9:20–21. *v:* Wis 15:7; Is 45:9. *w:* Jer 1:10. *x:* Jer 26:3; Is 55:7; Ez 18:21, 27; Jon 3:10. *y:* Nm 14:22–23. *z:* Jer 7:3; 25:5; 35:15. *a:* Jer 2:25; 7:24. *b:* Jer 2:10–11; 5:30.

15 Yet my people have forgotten me:
they offer incense in vain.
They stumble off their paths,
the ways of old,
Traveling on bypaths,
not the beaten track.[c]
16 Their land shall be made a waste,
an object of endless hissing:*
All passersby will be horrified,
shaking their heads.[d]
17 Like the east wind, I will scatter them
before their enemies;
I will show them my back, not my face,
in their day of disaster.[e]

*Another Prayer for Vengeance.* 18"Come,"
they said, "let us devise a plot against Jeremiah, for instruction will not perish from the
priests, nor counsel from the wise, nor the
word from the prophets. Come, let us destroy him by his own tongue. Let us pay
careful attention to his every word."[f]

19 Pay attention to me, O LORD,
and listen to what my adversaries say.
20 Must good be repaid with evil
that they should dig a pit to take my
life?
Remember that I stood before you
to speak on their behalf,
to turn your wrath away from them.[g]
21 So now, give their children* to famine,[h]
deliver them to the power of the sword.
Let their wives be childless and widows;
let their husbands die of pestilence,
their youths be struck down by the
sword in battle.
22 May cries be heard from their homes,
when suddenly you send plunderers
against them.
For they have dug a pit to capture me,
they have hidden snares for my feet;
23 But you, LORD, know
all their planning for my death.
Do not forgive their crime,
and their sin do not blot out from your
sight!
Let them stumble before you,
in the time of your anger act against
them.[i]

## CHAPTER 19

See RG 217

*Symbol of the Potter's Flask.* 1Thus
said the LORD: Go, buy a potter's earthenware flask. Take along some of the elders of
the people and some of the priests, 2and go
out toward the Valley of Ben-hinnom, at the
entrance of the Potsherd Gate;* there proclaim the words which I will speak to you:
3You shall say, Listen to the word of the
LORD, kings of Judah and inhabitants of Jerusalem: Thus says the LORD of hosts, the God
of Israel: I am going to bring such evil upon
this place that the ears of all who hear of it
will ring. 4All because they have forsaken me
and profaned this place by burning incense to
other gods which neither they nor their ancestors knew; and because the kings of Judah
have filled this place with innocent blood,[j]
5building high places for Baal to burn their
children in fire as offerings to Baal—something I never considered or said or commanded.[k] 6* Therefore, days are coming—
oracle of the LORD—when this place will no
longer be called Topheth, or the Valley of
Ben-hinnom, but rather, the Valley of
Slaughter.[l] 7In this place I will foil the plan of
Judah and Jerusalem; I will make them fall
by the sword before their enemies, at the
hand of those who seek their lives. Their
corpses I will give as food to the birds of the
sky and the beasts of the earth.[m] 8I will make
this city a waste and an object of hissing. Because of all its wounds, every passerby will
be horrified and hiss. 9I will have them eat
the flesh of their sons and daughters; they
shall eat one another's flesh during the harsh
siege under which their enemies and those
who seek their lives will confine them.[n]

**18:16 Hissing**: in some ancient Near Eastern cultures hissing was not only a sign of derision but a magical means of keeping demons away; people hissed in order to ward off danger, like whistling in a cemetery.

**18:21 Give their children**: often an extended family is meant, to be rewarded or punished as a unit.

**19:2 Potsherd Gate**: perhaps in the south wall of Jerusalem, through which potsherds and other refuse were thrown into the Valley of Ben-hinnom.

**19:6** Cf. note on 7:31.

*c:* Jer 2:13, 32. *d:* Jer 19:8; Lv 26:32; 1 Kgs 9:8. *e:* Prv 1:24–31. *f:* Jer 11:19; Ps 35:15–16. *g:* Ps 35:12. *h:* Ps 109:9–10. *i:* Neh 4:5; Ps 35:4; 37:32–33. *j:* Jer 1:16; 2 Kgs 21:16; 24:4. *k:* Jer 7:31–32; 32:35. *l:* Jer 7:32. *m:* Jer 7:33. *n:* Lv 26:29.

10 And you shall break the flask in the sight
of the men who went with you, 11 and say to
them: Thus says the LORD of hosts: Thus will
I smash this people and this city, as one
smashes a clay pot so that it cannot be repaired. And Topheth shall be its burial place,
for there will be no other place for burial.[o]
12 Thus I will do to this place and to its inhabitants—oracle of the LORD; I will make this
city like Topheth.[p] 13 And the houses of Jerusalem and the houses of the kings of Judah
shall be defiled like the place of Topheth, all
the houses upon whose roofs they burnt incense to the whole host of heaven and poured
out libations to other gods.[q]
14 When Jeremiah returned from Topheth,
where the LORD had sent him to prophesy, he
stood in the court of the house of the LORD
and said to all the people:[r] 15 Thus says the
LORD of hosts, the God of Israel: I will bring
upon this city all the evil I have spoken
against it, because they have become stubborn and have not obeyed my words.[s]

### CHAPTER 20

See RG 217

1 Now the priest Pashhur,[t] son of Immer, chief officer in the house of the LORD,*
heard Jeremiah prophesying these things.
2 So he struck the prophet and put him in the
stocks at the upper Gate of Benjamin in the
house of the LORD.[u] 3 The next morning, after Pashhur had released Jeremiah from the
stocks, the prophet said to him:[v] "Instead of
Pashhur, the LORD names you 'Terror on
every side.'* 4 For thus says the LORD: Indeed, I will hand you over to terror, you and
all your friends. Your own eyes shall see
them fall by the sword of their enemies. All
Judah I will hand over to the power of the
king of Babylon,* who shall take them captive to Babylon or strike them down with the
sword. 5 All the wealth of this city, all its resources and its valuables, all the treasures of
the kings of Judah, I will hand over to their
enemies, who will plunder it and carry it
away to Babylon.[w] 6 You, Pashhur, and all
the members of your household shall go into
exile. To Babylon you shall go; there you
shall die and be buried, you and all your
friends, because you have prophesied lies to
them."[x]

### *Jeremiah's Interior Crisis*

7 You seduced me,* LORD, and I let myself
be seduced;
you were too strong for me, and you
prevailed.
All day long I am an object of laughter;
everyone mocks me.
8 Whenever I speak, I must cry out,
violence and outrage I proclaim;
The word of the LORD has brought me
reproach and derision all day long.
9 I say I will not mention him,
I will no longer speak in his name.
But then it is as if fire is burning in my
heart,
imprisoned in my bones;
I grow weary holding back,
I cannot![y]
10 Yes, I hear the whisperings of many:
"Terror on every side!
Denounce! let us denounce him!"
All those who were my friends
are on the watch for any misstep of
mine.
"Perhaps he can be tricked; then we will
prevail,
and take our revenge on him."[z]
11 But the LORD is with me, like a mighty
champion:
my persecutors will stumble, they will
not prevail.
In their failure they will be put to utter
shame,
to lasting, unforgettable confusion.[a]
12 LORD of hosts, you test the just,
you see mind and heart,

**20:1 Chief officer in the house of the LORD**: head of the Temple police; cf. 29:26. By entering the Temple court (19:14), Jeremiah had put himself under Pashhur's jurisdiction.

**20:3 Terror on every side**: the name indicates the siege that will beset Jerusalem.

**20:4 Babylon**: mentioned here for the first time in Jeremiah as the land of exile. The prophecy dates from after 605 B.C., when Nebuchadnezzar defeated Egypt and made the Babylonian (Chaldean) empire dominant in Syria and Palestine.

**20:7 You seduced me**: Jeremiah accuses the Lord of having deceived him; cf. 15:18.

*o:* Jer 7:32. *p:* 2 Kgs 23:10. *q:* Jer 32:29. *r:* Jer 26:2. *s:* Jer 7:26; Prv 29:1. *t:* Jer 21:1. *u:* Jer 29:26. *v:* Jer 6:25. *w:* 2 Kgs 20:17; 24:12–16. *x:* Jer 14:13–14; 28:15. *y:* Jer 6:11; Jb 32:18. *z:* Jb 19:19; Ps 31:13; Lk 20:20. *a:* Jer 1:8; 15:20.

**A Curse**

JEREMIAH CURSES THE day of his birth (20:14), like Job (Jb 3). This curse closes the section on the covenant's destruction that was begun by the curse against the nation in ch 11. Jeremiah's curse speaks of the tragedy of his mission to announce disaster so that he wishes he had never been born. If his life represents that of the people, then his captivity, the fulfillment of his word, and his curse enact and bring about their captivity.

Let me see the vengeance you take on
them,
for to you I have entrusted my cause.[b]
13 Sing to the LORD,
praise the LORD,
For he has rescued the life of the poor
from the power of the evildoers![c]

14 Cursed be the day*
on which I was born!
May the day my mother gave me birth
never be blessed![d]
15 Cursed be the one who brought the news
to my father,
"A child, a son, has been born to you!"
filling him with great joy.
16 Let that man be like the cities
which the LORD relentlessly overthrew;
Let him hear war cries in the morning,
battle alarms at noonday,[e]
17 because he did not kill me in the womb!
Then my mother would have been my
grave,
her womb confining me forever.[f]
18 Why did I come forth from the womb,
to see sorrow and pain,
to end my days in shame?[g]

## III. Oracles in the Last Years of Jerusalem

### CHAPTER 21

See RG 217

*Fate of Zedekiah and Jerusalem.* 1 The
word which came to Jeremiah from the
LORD when King Zedekiah* sent Pashhur,
son of Malchiah, and the priest Zephaniah,
son of Maaseiah, to him with this request:
2 Inquire for us of the LORD, because Nebuchadnezzar, king of Babylon, is attacking us.
Perhaps the LORD will act for us in accord
with his wonderful works by making him
withdraw from us. 3 But Jeremiah answered
them: This is what you shall report to Zedekiah: 4 Thus says the LORD, the God of Israel:
I will turn against you the weapons with
which you are fighting the king of Babylon
and the Chaldeans who besiege you outside
the walls. These weapons I will pile up in the
midst of this city,[h] 5 and I myself will fight
against you with outstretched hand and
mighty arm, in anger, wrath, and great rage![i]
6 I will strike down the inhabitants of this
city, human being and beast; they shall die in
a great pestilence.[j] 7 After that—oracle of the
LORD—I will hand over Zedekiah, king of
Judah, and his ministers and the people in
this city who survive pestilence, sword, and
famine, to Nebuchadnezzar, king of Babylon, to their enemies and those who seek
their lives. He shall strike them down with
the edge of the sword, without quarter, without mercy or compassion.[k] 8 And to this people you shall say: Thus says the LORD: See,
I am giving you a choice between the way to
life and the way to death.[l] 9 Whoever remains
in this city shall die by the sword or famine
or pestilence. But whoever leaves and surrenders to the Chaldeans who are besieging
you shall live and escape with his life. 10 I
have set my face against this city, for evil

**20:14–18** Deception, sorrow and terror have brought the prophet to the point of despair; nevertheless he maintains confidence in God (vv. 11–13); cf. Jb 3:3–12.

**21:1 Zedekiah**: brother of Jehoiakim, appointed king by Nebuchadnezzar after he had carried Jehoiachin away to captivity (2 Kgs 24:17). **Pashhur**: different from the one in 20:1–3 but also one of Jeremiah's enemies; cf. 38:1, 4.

*b:* Jer 11:20. *c:* Ps 35:9–10; 109:30–31. *d:* Jer 15:10; Jb 3:1–10; 10:18. *e:* Gn 19:25; Is 13:19. *f:* Jb 3:10–11; 10:19. *g:* Jb 14:1. *h:* Jer 37:8–10. *i:* Is 63:10; Lam 2:4–5. *j:* Jer 16:4. *k:* Jer 24:8–10; Dt 28:49–50. *l:* Jer 21:9; Dt 30:15, 19.

and not for good—oracle of the LORD. It
shall be given into the power of the king of
Babylon who shall set it on fire.*

### *Oracles Regarding the Kings**

11 To the royal house of Judah:
Hear the word of the LORD,
12 house of David!
Thus says the LORD:
Each morning dispense justice,
rescue the oppressed from the hand of the oppressor,
Or my fury will break out like fire
and burn with no one to quench it
because of your evil deeds.[m]
13 Beware! I am against you, Ruler of the Valley,
Rock of the Plain*—oracle of the LORD.
You say, "Who will attack us,
who can storm our defenses?"
14 I will punish you—oracle of the LORD—
as your deeds deserve!
I will kindle a fire in its forest*
that shall devour all its surroundings.[n]

## CHAPTER 22

See RG 217

1 Thus says the LORD: Go down to the
palace of the king of Judah and there deliver
this word: 2 You shall say: Listen to the word
of the LORD, king of Judah, who sit on the
throne of David, you, your ministers, and
your people who enter by these gates![o]
3 Thus says the LORD: Do what is right and
just. Rescue the victims from the hand of
their oppressors. Do not wrong or oppress
the resident alien, the orphan, or the widow,
and do not shed innocent blood in this
place.[p] 4 If you carry out these commands,
kings who succeed to the throne of David
will continue to enter the gates of this house,
riding in chariots or mounted on horses, with
their ministers, and their people. 5 But if you
do not obey these commands, I swear by
myself—oracle of the LORD: this house shall
become rubble. 6 For thus says the LORD concerning the house of the king of Judah:

Though you be to me like Gilead,
like the peak of Lebanon,
I swear I shall turn you into a waste,
with cities uninhabited.
7 Against you I will send destroyers,
each with their tools:
They shall cut down your choice cedars,
and cast them into the fire.[q]

8 Many nations will pass by this city and
ask one another: "Why has the LORD done
this to so great a city?"[r] 9 And they will be
told: "Because they have deserted their covenant with the LORD, their God, by worshiping and serving other gods."[s]

### *Jehoahaz*

10 Do not weep for him who is dead,*
nor mourn for him!
Weep rather for him who is going away;
never again to see
the land of his birth.[t]

11 Thus says the LORD concerning Shallum,*
son of Josiah, king of Judah, his father's successor, who left this place: He shall never return, 12 but in the place where they exiled
him, there he shall die; he shall never see this
land again.

### *Jehoiakim*

13 Woe to him who builds his house on
wrongdoing,

**21:10** Jeremiah consistently pointed out the uselessness of resistance to Babylon, since the Lord had delivered Judah to Nebuchadnezzar (27:6). Because of this the prophet was denounced and imprisoned as a traitor (37:13–14).

**21:11–23:8** This section contains an editor's collection of Jeremiah's oracles against the kings of Judah. They are placed in the chronological order of the kings, and are prefaced by oracles against the kings of Judah in general (21:11–22:9).

**21:13 Ruler of the Valley, Rock of the Plain**: Mount Zion, surrounded by valleys, was regarded by the royal house as impregnable. Despite this natural fortification, God derides it as no more than a rock rising from the plain, useless against the attack of his fury.

**21:14 Its forest**: probably the royal palace, built of cedar wood; cf. 22:14; in 1 Kgs 7:2 the palace is called "the house of the forest of Lebanon."

**22:10 Him who is dead**: Josiah. His successor, Jehoahaz, was deported by Pharaoh Neco to Egypt, where he died (2 Kgs 23:33–34).

**22:11 Shallum**: i.e., Jehoahaz; cf. 1 Chr 3:15. This may have been his name at birth, in which case Jehoahaz would have been his throne name.

*m:* Jer 4:4; 22:3; Zec 7:9. *n:* 2 Kgs 25:9; 2 Chr 36:19. *o:* Jer 17:20. *p:* Jer 21:12; Ex 22:21–24; Dt 24:17. *q:* Jer 21:14. *r:* Dt 29:24–27. *s:* Jer 19:4; 40:2–3. *t:* 2 Chr 35:23–25.

his roof-chambers on injustice;
Who works his neighbors without pay,*
and gives them no wages.[u]
14 Who says, "I will build myself a spacious house,
with airy rooms,"
Who cuts out windows for it,
panels it with cedar,
and paints it with vermilion.
15 Must you prove your rank among kings*
by competing with them in cedar?
Did not your father eat and drink,
And act justly and righteously?
Then he prospered.[v]
16 Because he dispensed justice to the weak and the poor,
he prospered.
Is this not to know me?—
oracle of the LORD.[w]
17 But your eyes and heart are set on nothing
except your own gain,
On shedding innocent blood
and practicing oppression and extortion.[x]

18 Therefore, thus says the LORD concerning Jehoiakim, son of Josiah, king of Judah:

They shall not lament him,
"Alas! my brother"; "Alas! sister."*
They shall not lament him,
"Alas, Lord! alas, Majesty!"[y]
19 The burial of a donkey* he shall be given,
dragged forth and cast out
beyond the gates of Jerusalem.[z]

### *Jeconiah*

20 Climb Lebanon and cry out,*
in Bashan lift up your voice;
Cry out from Abarim,
for all your lovers are crushed.[a]
21 I spoke to you when you were secure,
but you answered, "I will not listen."
This has been your way from your youth,
not to listen to my voice.
22 The wind shall shepherd all your shepherds,
your lovers shall go into exile.
Surely then you shall be ashamed and confounded
because of all your wickedness.
23 You who dwell on Lebanon,
who nest in the cedars,
How you shall groan when pains come upon you,
like the pangs of a woman in childbirth!

24 As I live—oracle of the LORD—even if
you, Coniah,* son of Jehoiakim, king of Judah, were a signet ring[b] on my right hand, I
would snatch you off. 25 I will hand you over
to those who seek your life, to those you
dread: Nebuchadnezzar, king of Babylon,
and the Chaldeans.[c] 26 I will cast you out, you
and the mother who bore you,* into a land

**22:13 Without pay**: either by forced labor in public works, or by defrauding the workers. Despite the impoverishment caused in Judah by the payment of foreign tribute, Jehoiakim embarked on a building program in Jerusalem (v. 14); cedar was an expensive building material which had to be imported. Social injustice is the cause of much of the prophetic condemnation of the kings (v. 17).

**22:15–16** The rule of Josiah, Jehoiakim's father, shows that authentic kingship is rooted in knowledge of the Lord and creates a society in which the most disadvantaged can expect and receive justice.

**22:18 "Alas! my brother"; "Alas! sister"**: customary cries of mourning.

**22:19 The burial of a donkey**: no burial at all, except to be cast outside the city as refuse. This prophecy describes the popular feeling toward Jehoiakim rather than the actual circumstances of his burial. According to 2 Kgs 24:5 he was buried with his ancestors in Jerusalem.

**22:20–23** The prophet first bids Jerusalem to scale Lebanon, Bashan, and Abarim, i.e., the highest surrounding mountains to the north, northeast, and southeast, and gaze on the ruin of its lovers, i.e., the false leaders of Judah, called its shepherds (v. 22); cf. 2:8. Jerusalem still stands (v. 23), apparently as secure as the heights of Lebanon, but destruction is to follow (cf. v. 6).

**22:24 Coniah**: a shortened form of Jeconiah, the name Jeremiah gives King Jehoiachin (cf. 24:1). **A signet ring**: the seal used by kings and other powerful figures—a symbol of their power and status—mounted in a ring worn constantly on the hand. The Lord says that even were Jehoiachin such a precious possession, he would reject him. Hg 2:23 uses the same imagery to signal the restoration of Zerubbabel. The words in Jer 22:24–30 date from the short three-month reign of Jehoiachin, before he was deported by Nebuchadnezzar.

**22:26 You and the mother who bore you**: the queen mother held a special position in the monarchy of Judah, and in the Books of Kings she is invariably mentioned by name along with the king (1 Kgs 15:2; 2 Kgs 18:2). Jehoiachin did indeed die in Babylon.

*u:* Lv 19:13; Dt 24:14; Hb 2:9, 12. *v:* 2 Sm 5:11; 7:2; 2 Kgs 23:25. *w:* Prv 31:9. *x:* Ez 22:13, 27. *y:* Jer 16:4–7; 1 Kgs 13:30. *z:* Jer 36:30. *a:* Jer 30:14–15; Dt 32:49. *b:* Hg 2:23. *c:* Jer 21:7; 34:20.

different from the land of your birth; and
there you will die;[d] 27 Neither shall return to
the land for which they yearn.[e]

28 Is this man Coniah a thing despised, to be
broken,
a vessel that no one wants?
Why are he and his offspring cast out?
why thrown into a land they do not
know?
29 O land, land, land,
hear the word of the LORD—
30 Thus says the LORD:
[f] Write this man down as childless,*
a man who will never prosper in his life!
Nor shall any of his descendants prosper,
to sit upon the throne of David,
to rule again over Judah.

## CHAPTER 23

See RG 217

*A Just Shepherd.** 1 [g] Woe to the shepherds who destroy and scatter the flock of
my pasture—oracle of the LORD. 2 Therefore, thus says the LORD, the God of Israel,
against the shepherds who shepherd my
people: You have scattered my sheep and
driven them away. You have not cared for
them, but I will take care to punish your evil
deeds.[h] 3 I myself will gather the remnant of
my flock from all the lands to which I have
banished them and bring them back to their
folds; there they shall be fruitful and multiply.[i] 4 I will raise up shepherds for them who
will shepherd them so that they need no
longer fear or be terrified; none shall be
missing—oracle of the LORD.[j]

5 See, days are coming—oracle of the
LORD—
when I will raise up a righteous branch
for David;
As king he shall reign and govern wisely,
he shall do what is just and right in the
land.[k]
6 In his days Judah shall be saved,
Israel shall dwell in security.
This is the name to be given him:
"The LORD our justice."[l]

7 [m] Therefore, the days are coming—oracle of the LORD—when they shall no longer
say, "As the LORD lives, who brought the Israelites out of the land of Egypt"; 8 but rather,
"As the LORD lives, who brought the descendants of the house of Israel up from the
land of the north"—and from all the lands to
which I banished them; they shall again live
on their own soil.

### *The False Prophets**

9 Concerning the prophets:
My heart is broken within me,
all my bones tremble;
I am like a drunk,
like one overcome by wine,
Because of the LORD,
because of his holy words.
10 The land is filled with adulterers;
because of the curse the land mourns,
the pastures of the wilderness are
withered.[n]
Theirs is an evil course,
theirs is unjust power.
11 Both prophet and priest are godless!
In my very house I find their
wickedness—
oracle of the LORD.[o]
12 Hence their way shall become for them

**22:30 Childless**: Jehoiachin is considered childless because none of his seven sons became king. His grandson Zerubbabel presided for a time over the Judahite community after the return from exile, but not as king. According to Ezekiel, whose oracles are dated by Jehoiachin's fictitious regnal years, the people expected Jehoiachin to return. Jeremiah's prophecy dispels this hope, despite the words of Hananiah (28:4).

**23:1–8** With the false rulers (shepherds) who have governed his people the Lord contrasts himself, the true shepherd, who will in the times of restoration appoint worthy rulers (vv. 1–4). He will provide a new king from David's line who will rule justly, fulfilling royal ideals (vv. 5, 6). "The Lord our justice" is an ironic wordplay on the name of the weak King Zedekiah ("The Lord is justice"). Unlike Zedekiah, the future king will be true to the name he bears. Verses 7–8 may have been added during the exile.

**23:9–40** After the collection of oracles against the kings, the editor of the book placed this collection of oracles against the false prophets. With them are associated the priests, for both have betrayed their trust as instructors in the ways of the Lord; cf. 2:8; 4:9; 6:13–14.

*d:* 2 Kgs 24:15. *e:* Jer 44:14. *f:* Jer 36:30; 1 Chr 3:16–17; Mt 1:12. *g:* Jer 22:22. *h:* Ez 34:4–10; Zec 11:16–17. *i:* Jer 29:14; 32:37. *j:* Jer 3:15; Ez 34:11–12. *k:* Jer 33:14–16; Is 4:2; 9:5–6; 11:1–5. *l:* Dn 9:24. *m:* Jer 16:14–15. *n:* Jer 4:22; 5:7–8; 9:2, 10. *o:* Jer 6:13.

slippery ground.
Into the darkness they shall be driven,
and fall headlong;
For I will bring disaster upon them,
the year of their punishment—oracle
of the LORD.[p]
13 Among Samaria's prophets
I saw something unseemly:
They prophesied by Baal
and led my people Israel astray.[q]
14 But among Jerusalem's prophets
I saw something more shocking:
Adultery, walking in deception,*
strengthening the power of the wicked,
so that no one turns from evil;
To me they are all like Sodom,
its inhabitants like Gomorrah.[r]

15 Therefore, thus says the LORD of hosts
against the prophets:

Look, I will give them wormwood to eat,
and poisoned water to drink;
For from Jerusalem's prophets
ungodliness has gone forth into the
whole land.[s]
16 Thus says the LORD of hosts:
Do not listen to the words of your
prophets,
who fill you with emptiness;
They speak visions from their own fancy,
not from the mouth of the LORD.[t]
17 They say to those who despise the word
of the LORD,*
"Peace shall be yours";
And to everyone who walks in hardness
of heart,
"No evil shall overtake you."[u]
18 Now, who has stood in the council of the
LORD,
to see him and to hear his word?
Who has heeded his word so as to
announce it?[v]
19 See, the storm of the LORD!
His wrath breaks forth
In a whirling storm
that bursts upon the heads of the
wicked.[w]
20 The anger of the LORD shall not abate
until he has carried out completely
the decisions of his heart.
In days to come
you will understand fully.
21 I did not send these prophets,
yet they ran;
I did not speak to them,
yet they prophesied.[x]
22 Had they stood in my council,
they would have proclaimed my words
to my people,
They would have brought them back
from their evil ways
and from their wicked deeds.
23 Am I a God near at hand only—oracle of
the LORD—[y]
and not a God far off?*
24 Can anyone hide in secret
without my seeing them?—oracle of
the LORD.
Do I not fill
heaven and earth?—oracle of the
LORD.

25 I have heard the prophets who prophesy
lies in my name say, "I had a dream! I had a
dream!" 26 How long? Will the hearts of the
prophets who prophesy lies and their own
deceitful fancies ever turn back? 27 By the
dreams they tell each other, they plan to
make my people forget my name, just as
their ancestors forgot my name for Baal.[z]
28 Let the prophets who have dreams tell
their dreams; let those who have my word
speak my word truthfully!

What has straw to do with wheat?*
—oracle of the LORD.[a]

**23:14** Cf. note on 13:25.

**23:17–20** Not only are the false prophets personally immoral, but they encourage immorality by prophesying good for evildoers. The true prophet, on the other hand, sees the inevitable consequences of evil behavior.

**23:23–24 Near at hand only . . . far off**: a divine claim that no one can hide from God and that God is aware of all that happens.

**23:28–29 Straw . . . wheat**: a contrast between false and true prophecy. True prophecy is also like fire (cf. 5:14; 20:9), producing violent results (v. 29); Jeremiah's own life is a testimony of this.

*p:* Ps 35:6. *q:* 1 Kgs 18:19. *r:* Jer 29:21–23; Is 1:9–10. *s:* Jer 8:14; 9:14. *t:* Jer 14:14. *u:* Jer 5:12; Ez 13:10; Mi 3:11; Zec 10:2. *v:* Jb 15:8; Is 40:13; 1 Cor 2:16. *w:* Jer 30:23. *x:* Jer 29:9. *y:* Jer 16:17; Ps 139:8. *z:* Jgs 3:7; 8:33. *a:* Nm 12:6.

29 Is not my word like fire—oracle of the
LORD—
like a hammer shattering rock?

30 Therefore I am against the prophets—
oracle of the LORD—those who steal my
words from each other.[b] 31 Yes, I am against
the prophets—oracle of the LORD—those
who compose their own speeches and call
them oracles. 32 Yes, I am against the prophets who tell lying dreams—oracle of the
LORD—those who lead my people astray by
recounting their reckless lies. It was not I
who sent them or commanded them; they do
this people no good at all—oracle of the
LORD.[c]

33* And when this people or a prophet or
a priest asks you, "What is the burden of the
LORD?" you shall answer, "You are the burden, and I cast you off"—oracle of the
LORD. 34 If a prophet or a priest or anyone
else mentions "the burden of the LORD," I
will punish that man and his household.
35 Thus you shall ask, when speaking to one
another, "What answer did the LORD give?"
or "What did the LORD say?" 36 But "the burden of the LORD" you shall mention no
more. For each of you, your own word becomes the burden so that you pervert the
words of the living God, the LORD of hosts,
our God. 37 Thus shall you ask the prophet,
"What answer did the LORD give?" or
"What did the LORD say?" 38 But if you ask
about "the burden of the LORD," then thus
says the LORD: Because you use this phrase,
"the burden of the LORD," though I forbade
you to use it, 39 therefore I will lift you on
high and cast you from my presence, you
and the city which I gave to you and your
ancestors. 40 And I will bring upon you eternal reproach, eternal shame, never to be forgotten.[d]

## CHAPTER 24

See RG 217

*The Two Baskets of Figs.** 1 The LORD
showed me two baskets of figs placed before the temple of the LORD.[e] This was after
Nebuchadnezzar, king of Babylon, had exiled from Jerusalem Jeconiah,* son of Jehoiakim, king of Judah, and the princes of
Judah, the artisans and smiths, and brought
them to Babylon. 2 One basket contained
excellent figs, those that ripen early. But
the other basket contained very bad figs, so
bad they could not be eaten. 3 Then the
LORD said to me: What do you see, Jeremiah?[f] "Figs," I replied; "the good ones are
very good, but the bad ones very bad, so
bad they cannot be eaten." 4 Thereupon this
word of the LORD came to me: 5 Thus says
the LORD, the God of Israel: Like these
good figs, I will also regard with favor Judah's exiles whom I sent away from this
place into the land of the Chaldeans.[g] 6 I
will look after them for good and bring
them back to this land, to build them up, not
tear them down; to plant them, not uproot
them.[h] 7 I will give them a heart to know me,
that I am the LORD. They shall be my people and I will be their God, for they shall return to me with their whole heart.[i] 8 But like
the figs that are bad, so bad they cannot be
eaten—yes, thus says the LORD—even so
will I treat Zedekiah, king of Judah, and his
princes, the remnant of Jerusalem remaining in this land and those who have settled
in the land of Egypt.[j] 9 I will make them an
object of horror to all the kingdoms of the
earth, a reproach and a byword, a taunt and
a curse, in all the places to which I will
drive them.[k] 10 I will send upon them sword,
famine, and pestilence, until they have disappeared from the land which I gave them
and their ancestors.[l]

**23:33–40** A wordplay on *massa'*, which means both "oracle" (usually of woe) and "burden." In vv. 34–40 the word *massa'* itself is forbidden to the people under the meaning of a divine oracle.

**24:1–10** For Jeremiah, as for Ezekiel, no good could be expected from the people who had been left in Judah under Zedekiah or who had fled into Egypt; a future might be expected only for those who would pass through the purifying experience of the exile to form the new Israel.

**24:1 Jeconiah**: alternative form of Jehoiachin (cf. note on 22:24).

*b:* Dt 18:20. *c:* Jer 28:15–17. *d:* Jer 20:11. *e:* Am 8:1–2. *f:* Jer 1:11. *g:* Jer 29:11; Lv 26:44–45. *h:* Jer 12:15; Am 9:15. *i:* Jer 30:22; 31:1; 32:37; Bar 2:31. *j:* Jer 29:18. *k:* Jer 15:4; Dt 28:37. *l:* Jer 14:12.

## CHAPTER 25

See RG 217

***Seventy Years of Exile.*** 1 The word that came to Jeremiah concerning all the people of Judah, in the fourth year of Jehoiakim,* son of Josiah, king of Judah (the first year of Nebuchadnezzar, king of Babylon).[m] 2 This word the prophet Jeremiah spoke to all the people of Judah and all the inhabitants of Jerusalem: 3 Since the thirteenth year of Josiah, son of Amon, king of Judah, to this day—that is, twenty-three years—the word of the LORD has come to me and I spoke to you untiringly, but you would not listen.[n] 4 The LORD kept sending you all his servants the prophets,[o] but you refused to listen or pay attention 5 to this message: Turn back, each of you, from your evil way and from your evil deeds; then you shall remain in the land which the LORD gave you and your ancestors, from of old and forever. 6 Do not follow other gods to serve and bow down to them; do not provoke me with the works of your hands, or I will bring evil upon you.[p] 7 But you would not listen to me—oracle of the LORD—and so you provoked me with the works of your hands to your own harm.[q] 8 Hence, thus says the LORD of hosts: Since you would not listen to my words, 9 I am about to send for and fetch all the tribes from the north—oracle of the LORD—and I will send for Nebuchadnezzar, king of Babylon, my servant; I will bring them against this land, its inhabitants, and all these neighboring nations. I will doom them, making them an object of horror, of hissing, of everlasting reproach.[r] 10 Among them I will put to an end the song of joy and the song of gladness, the voice of the bridegroom and the voice of the bride, the sound of the millstone and the light of the lamp. 11 This whole land shall be a ruin and a waste. Seventy years these nations shall serve the king of Babylon;[s] 12 but when the seventy years have elapsed, I will punish the king of Babylon and that nation and the land of the Chaldeans for their guilt—oracle of the LORD. Their land I will turn into everlasting waste.[t] 13 Against that land I will fulfill all the words I have spoken against it, all that is written in this book, which Jeremiah prophesied against all the nations. 14 They also shall serve many nations and great kings, and thus I will repay them according to their own deeds and according to the works of their hands.[u]

***The Cup of Judgment on the Nations.*** 15* For thus said the LORD, the God of Israel, to me: Take this cup of the wine of wrath* from my hand and have all the nations to whom I will send you drink it.[v] 16 They shall drink, and retch, and go mad, because of the sword I will send among them.[w] 17 I took the cup from the hand of the LORD and gave it as drink to all the nations to whom the LORD sent me: 18 to Jerusalem, the cities of Judah, its kings and princes, to make them a ruin and a waste, an object of hissing and cursing, as they are today; 19 to Pharaoh, king of Egypt, and his servants, princes, all his people 20 and those of mixed ancestry; all the kings of the land of Uz;* all the kings of the land of the Philistines: Ashkelon, Gaza, Ekron, and the remnant of Ashdod; 21 Edom, Moab, and the Ammonites; 22 all the kings of Tyre, of Sidon, and of the shores beyond the sea;* 23 Dedan and Tema and Buz,* all the desert dwellers who shave their temples; 24 all the kings of Arabia; 25 all the kings of

**25:1–14 The fourth year of Jehoiakim**: 605 B.C. Officially, the first year of Nebuchadnezzar began the following year; but as early as his victory over Egypt at Carchemish in 605, Nebuchadnezzar wielded dominant power in the Near East. Jeremiah saw in him the fulfillment of his prophecy of the enemy to come from the north (cf. 1:13; 6:22–24). In vv. 11–12 the prophecy of the seventy years' exile occurs for the first time; cf. 29:10. This number signifies that the present generation must die out; cf. forty in the exodus tradition (Nm 14:20–23).

**25:15–17** Jeremiah is a prophet to the nations (cf. 1:5) as well as to his own people. All the nations mentioned here appear again in the more extensive collection of Jeremiah's oracles against the nations in chaps. 46–51.

**25:15 Cup . . . wrath**: a metaphor for destruction that occurs often in the Old Testament (cf. Ps 11:6; 75:9; Hb 2:15–16; Ez 23:31–33, etc.).

**25:20 Uz**: the homeland of legendary Job, in Edomite or Arabian territory.

**25:22 The shores beyond the sea**: Phoenician commercial colonies located throughout the Mediterranean world.

**25:23 Dedan and Tema and Buz**: North Arabian tribes.

*m:* Jer 36:1. *n:* Jer 1:2. *o:* 2 Chr 36:15. *p:* Jer 7:6–7. *q:* Jer 7:17–19. *r:* Jer 1:15; 43:10. *s:* Lv 26:32–35. *t:* Is 13:20–22. *u:* Jer 27:7; 50:9, 41–42; 51:6, 24. *v:* Rev 14:10. *w:* Jer 51:7.

**Jeremiah on Trial**

CHAPTER 26 SHOWS that Jeremiah faced great conflict but that he is the true prophet, and hence, is to be heeded. The chapter refers to Jeremiah's temple sermon (7:1–8:3) and summarizes it. What is of interest here, however, is the community's response to the sermon. Some accept it; priests, prophets, and King Jehoiakim reject it. Some of the leaders put Jeremiah on trial. Jeremiah responds to the charges by claiming that it was God who sent him (v. 12). The trial concludes with a declaration of Jeremiah's innocence.

Zimri, of Elam, of the Medes; 26 all the kings
of the north, near and far, one after the other;
all the kingdoms upon the face of the earth
and after them the king of Sheshach* shall
drink.
27 Tell them: Thus says the LORD of hosts,
the God of Israel: Drink! Get drunk and
vomit! Fall, never to rise, before the sword
that I will send among you![x] 28 If they refuse
to take the cup from your hand and drink,
say to them: Thus says the LORD of hosts:
You must drink![y] 29 Now that I am inflicting
evil on this city, called by my name, how can
you possibly escape? You shall not escape! I
am calling down the sword upon all the inhabitants of the earth—oracle of the LORD of
hosts. 30 As for you, prophesy against them
all these words and say to them:

The LORD roars from on high,
from his holy dwelling he raises his
voice;
Mightily he roars over his sheepfold,
a shout like that of vintagers echoes[z]
over all the inhabitants of the earth.
31 The uproar spreads
to the end of the earth;
For the LORD has an indictment against
the nations,
he enters into judgment against all
flesh:
The wicked shall be given to the
sword—
oracle of the LORD.
32 Thus says the LORD of hosts:
Look! disaster stalks
nation after nation;
A violent storm surges
from the recesses of the earth.

33 On that day, those whom the LORD has
slain will be strewn from one end of the
earth to the other. They will not be mourned,
they will not be gathered, they will not be
buried; they shall lie like dung upon the
ground.[a]

34 Howl, you shepherds, and wail!
roll on the ground, leaders of the
flock!
The time for your slaughter has come;
like choice rams you shall fall.
35 There is no flight for the shepherds,
no escape for the leaders of the
flock.[b]
36 Listen! Wailing from the shepherds,
howling from the leaders of the
flock!
For the LORD lays waste their grazing
place;
37 desolate are the peaceful pastures,
from the burning wrath of the LORD.
38 Like a lion he leaves his lair,
and their land is made desolate
By the sweeping sword,
and the burning wrath of the LORD.[c]

## IV. The Temple Sermon

### CHAPTER 26

See RG 217

***Jeremiah Threatened with Death.*** 1 In
the beginning of the reign* of Jehoiakim, son
of Josiah, king of Judah, this word came

**25:26 Sheshach**: a contrived word from the Hebrew letters of Babylon.

**26:1 The beginning of the reign**: a technical expression for the time between a king's accession to the throne and the beginning of his first official (calendar) year as king. Jehoiakim's first regnal year was 608 B.C.

*x:* Ob 16. *y:* Jer 49:12. *z:* Jer 51:14. *a:* Jer 8:2; 16:4, 6. *b:* Jer 32:4. *c:* Jer 4:7.

from the LORD: [2]Thus says the LORD: Stand in the court of the house of the LORD and speak to the inhabitants of all the cities of Judah who come to worship in the house of the LORD; whatever I command you, tell them, and hold nothing back.[d] [3]Perhaps they will listen and turn, all of them from their evil way, so that I may repent of the evil I plan to inflict upon them for their evil deeds.[e] [4]Say to them: Thus says the LORD: If you do not obey me, by walking according to the law I set before you [5]and listening to the words of my servants the prophets, whom I kept sending you, even though you do not listen to them,[f] [6]I will treat this house like Shiloh, and make this city a curse for all the nations of the earth.[g]

[7]Now the priests, the prophets, and all the people heard Jeremiah speaking these words in the house of the LORD. [8]When Jeremiah finished speaking all that the LORD commanded him to speak to all the people, then the priests, the prophets, and all the people laid hold of him, crying, "You must die! [9]Why do you prophesy in the name of the LORD: 'This house shall become like Shiloh,' and 'This city shall be desolate, without inhabitant'?" And all the people crowded around Jeremiah in the house of the LORD.

[10]When the princes of Judah heard about these things, they came up from the house of the king to the house of the LORD and convened at the New Gate of the house of the LORD. [11]The priests and prophets said to the princes and to all the people, "Sentence this man to death! He has prophesied against this city! You heard it with your own ears."[h] [12]Jeremiah said to the princes and all the people: "It was the LORD who sent me to prophesy against this house and city everything you have heard. [13]Now, therefore, reform your ways and your deeds; listen to the voice of the LORD your God, so that the LORD will have a change of heart regarding the evil he has spoken against you.[i] [14]As for me, I am in your hands; do with me what is good and right in your eyes. [15]But you should certainly know that by putting me to death, you bring innocent blood on yourselves, on this city and its inhabitants. For in truth it was the LORD who sent me to you, to speak all these words for you to hear."

[16]Then the princes and all the people said to the priests and the prophets, "This man does not deserve a death sentence; it is in the name of the LORD, our God, that he speaks to us." [17]At this, some of the elders of the land arose and said to the whole assembly of the people, [18]"Micah of Moresheth* used to prophesy in the days of Hezekiah, king of Judah, and he said to all the people of Judah: Thus says the LORD of hosts:

Zion shall be plowed as a field,
  Jerusalem, a heap of ruins,
 and the temple mount,
  a forest ridge.[j]

[19]Did Hezekiah, king of Judah, and all Judah condemn him to death? Did he not fear the LORD and entreat the favor of the LORD, so that the LORD had a change of heart regarding the evil he had spoken against them? We, however, are about to do great evil against ourselves."[k]

***The Fate of Uriah.*** [20]There was another man who used to prophesy in the name of the LORD, Uriah, son of Shemaiah, from Kiriath-jearim; he prophesied against this city and this land the same message as Jeremiah. [21]When King Jehoiakim and all his officers and princes heard his words, the king sought to have him killed. But Uriah heard of it and fled in fear to Egypt. [22]Then King Jehoiakim sent Elnathan, son of Achbor, and others with him into Egypt, [23]and they brought Uriah out of Egypt and took him to Jehoiakim the king, who struck him down with the sword and threw his corpse into the common burial ground. [24]But the hand of Ahikam, son of Shaphan,* protected Jeremiah, so they did not hand him over to the people to be put to death.

**26:18 Micah of Moresheth**: the prophet Micah, who appears among the canonical minor prophets (cf. Mi 1:1).

**26:24 Ahikam, son of Shaphan**: one of Josiah's officials (2 Kgs 22:12) and Jeremiah's friend. He was the father of Gedaliah, who was governor of Judah after Zedekiah's deportation (cf. Jer 39:14; 40:5–7).

*d:* Jer 7:2. *e:* Jer 18:3. *f:* Jer 25:4. *g:* Jer 7:12, 14. *h:* Jer 38:4. *i:* Jer 7:3. *j:* Mi 1:1; 3:12. *k:* 2 Chr 32:26.

### How the Nation Will Survive

THE FIRST "BOOK" (chs 1–25) accused Judah of infidelity, promised destruction and exile, and defended God from accusations of injustice. The second "book" (chs 26–52) presents stories and poems that reveal how to survive the period after the nation's fall to Babylon. The book's audience lives with the community's failure to repent. They themselves must repent and endure. Jeremiah appears here as a model of faithful endurance. Jeremiah's companion Baruch also appears in this part of the book. Baruch has traditionally been named as the writer of stories about Jeremiah, particularly in chs 37–45. The period of the exile was a time of great conflict about how to survive. This book insists that survival requires continued submission to Babylon, repentance, and obedience as set out in the book of Jeremiah.

## V. Controversies with the False Prophets*

### CHAPTER 27

See RG 217

***Serve Babylon or Perish.*** 1In the beginning of the reign of Zedekiah,* son of Josiah, king of Judah, this word came to Jeremiah from the LORD: 2The LORD said to me:
Make for yourself thongs and yoke bars and
put them on your shoulders. 3Send them to
the kings of Edom, Moab, the Ammonites,
Tyre, and Sidon, through the ambassadors
who have come to Jerusalem to Zedekiah,
king of Judah,* 4and command them to tell
their lords: Thus says the LORD of hosts, the
God of Israel, Thus shall you say to your
lords: 5It was I who made the earth, human
being and beast on the face of the earth, by
my great power, with my outstretched arm;
and I can give them to whomever I think fit.[l]
6Now I have given all these lands into the
hand of Nebuchadnezzar, king of Babylon,
my servant; even the wild animals I have
given him to serve him.[m] 7All nations shall
serve him and his son and his grandson, until the time comes for him and his land; then
many nations and great kings will enslave
him.[n] 8Meanwhile, the nation or the kingdom that will not serve him, Nebuchadnezzar, king of Babylon, or bend its neck under
the yoke of the king of Babylon, I will punish that nation with sword, famine, and
pestilence—oracle of the LORD—until I finish them by his hand.[o]
9You, however, must not listen to your
prophets,* to your diviners and dreamers, to
your soothsayers and sorcerers, who say to
you, "Do not serve the king of Babylon."[p]
10For they prophesy lies to you, so as to
drive you far from your land, making me
banish you so that you perish.[q] 11The people
that bends the neck to the yoke of the king of
Babylon to serve him, I will leave in peace
on its own land—oracle of the LORD—to
cultivate it and dwell on it.[r]
12To Zedekiah, king of Judah, I spoke the
same words: Bend your necks to the yoke of
the king of Babylon; serve him and his people, so that you may live.[s] 13Why should you
and your people die by sword, famine, and
pestilence, in accordance with the word the
LORD has spoken to the nation that will not
serve the king of Babylon?[t] 14Do not listen to
the words of the prophets who say to you,
"Do not serve the king of Babylon." They
prophesy lies to you![u] 15I did not send
them—oracle of the LORD—but they proph-

**27:1–29:32** A special collection of Jeremiah's prophecies dealing with false prophets. Stylistic peculiarities evident in the Hebrew suggest that these three chapters once existed as an independent work.

**27:1 Zedekiah**: The Hebrew text actually has "Jehoiakim," but the content of the chapter indicates that Zedekiah is intended.

**27:3** The time is the fourth year of Zedekiah, 594 B.C., the occasion of a delegation from the neighboring states, doubtless for the purpose of laying plans against Nebuchadnezzar.

**27:9 Your prophets**: seers and diviners served non-Israelite kings just as the professional prophets served the kings of Judah.

*l:* Jer 32:17. *m:* Jer 25:9; 43:10; Ez 30:21, 25. *n:* Jer 25:11; 2 Chr 36:20. *o:* Jer 25:9; Bar 2:22. *p:* Jer 29:8. *q:* Jer 14:13–16. *r:* Bar 2:21. *s:* Jer 38:17. *t:* Jer 24:8–10. *u:* Jer 14:14; 23:21.

esy falsely in my name. As a result I must banish you, and you will perish, you and the prophets who are prophesying to you.[v]

16[w] To the priests and to all the people I said: Thus says the LORD: Do not listen to the words of your prophets who prophesy to you: "The vessels of the house of the LORD will soon be brought back from Babylon," for they prophesy lies to you. 17 Do not listen to them! Serve the king of Babylon that you may live. Why should this city become rubble? 18 If they were prophets, if the word of the LORD were with them, then they would intercede with the LORD of hosts, that the vessels remaining in the house of the LORD and in the house of the king of Judah and in Jerusalem should not also go to Babylon. 19 For thus says the LORD of hosts concerning the pillars, the sea, the stands, and the rest of the vessels remaining in this city, 20 which Nebuchadnezzar, king of Babylon, did not take when he exiled Jeconiah, son of Jehoiakim, king of Judah, from Jerusalem to Babylon, along with all the nobles of Judah and Jerusalem— 21 thus says the LORD of hosts, the God of Israel, concerning the vessels remaining in the house of the LORD, in the house of the king of Judah, and in Jerusalem:[x] 22 To Babylon they shall go, and there they shall remain, until the day I look for them—oracle of the LORD; then I will bring them back and restore them to this place.

See RG 217

## CHAPTER 28

*The Two Yokes.* 1 That same year, in the beginning of the reign of Zedekiah, king of Judah, in the fifth month of the fourth year, Hananiah the prophet, son of Azzur, from Gibeon, said to me in the house of the LORD in the sight of the priests and all the people: 2 "Thus says the LORD of hosts, the God of Israel: I have broken the yoke of the king of Babylon. 3 Within two years I will restore to this place all the vessels of the house of the LORD which Nebuchadnezzar, king of Babylon, took from this place and carried away to Babylon. 4 And Jeconiah, son of Jehoiakim, king of Judah, and all the exiles of Judah who went to Babylon, I will bring back to this place—oracle of the LORD—for I will break the yoke of the king of Babylon."

5 Jeremiah the prophet answered the prophet Hananiah in the sight of the priests and all the people standing in the house of the LORD, 6 and said: Amen! thus may the LORD do! May the LORD fulfill your words that you have prophesied, by bringing back the vessels of the house of the LORD and all the exiles from Babylon to this place! 7 But now, listen to the word I am about to speak in your hearing and the hearing of all the people. 8 In the past, the prophets who came before you and me prophesied war, disaster, and pestilence against many lands and mighty kingdoms. 9 But the prophet who prophesies peace is recognized as the prophet whom the LORD has truly sent only when his word comes to pass.[y]

10 Thereupon Hananiah the prophet took the yoke bar from the neck of Jeremiah the prophet and broke it. 11 He said in the sight of all the people: "Thus says the LORD: Like this, within two years I will break the yoke of Nebuchadnezzar, king of Babylon, from the neck of all the nations." At that, the prophet Jeremiah went on his way.

12 After Hananiah the prophet had broken the yoke bar off the neck of the prophet Jeremiah, the word of the LORD came to Jeremiah: 13 Go tell Hananiah this: Thus says the LORD: By breaking a wooden yoke bar, you make an iron yoke! 14 For thus says the LORD of hosts, the God of Israel: A yoke of iron I have placed on the necks of all these nations serving Nebuchadnezzar, king of Babylon, and they shall serve him; even the wild animals I have given him.[z] 15 And Jeremiah the prophet said to Hananiah the prophet: Listen to this, Hananiah! The LORD has not sent you, and you have led this people to rely on deception. 16 For this, says the LORD, I am sending you from the face of the earth; this very year you shall die, because you have preached rebellion against the LORD.[a] 17 Hananiah the prophet died in that year, in the seventh month.

*v:* Jer 20:6. *w:* Jer 28:3; 2 Chr 36:7, 10, 18. *x:* 2 Kgs 25:13–17; 2 Chr 36:18, 22. *y:* Dt 18:22. *z:* Jer 27:6–7; Dt 28:48. *a:* Dt 13:6.

## CHAPTER 29

See RG 217

*Letter to the Exiles in Babylon.* [1]These are the words of the scroll which Jeremiah the prophet sent from Jerusalem to the remaining elders among the exiles, to the priests, the prophets, and all the people whom Nebuchadnezzar exiled from Jerusalem to Babylon. [2]This was after King Jeconiah and the queen mother, the court officials, the princes of Judah and Jerusalem, the artisans and smiths had left Jerusalem.[b] [3]Delivered in Babylon by Elasah,* son of Shaphan, and by Gemariah, son of Hilkiah, whom Zedekiah, king of Judah, sent to the king of Babylon, the letter read:

[4]Thus says the LORD of hosts, the God of Israel, to all the exiles whom I exiled from Jerusalem to Babylon: [5]Build houses and live in them; plant gardens and eat their fruits. [6]Take wives and have sons and daughters; find wives for your sons and give your daughters to husbands, so that they may bear sons and daughters. Increase there; do not decrease. [7]Seek the welfare of the city to which I have exiled you; pray for it to the LORD, for upon its welfare your own depends.[c] [8]For thus says the LORD of hosts, the God of Israel: Do not be deceived by the prophets and diviners who are among you; do not listen to those among you who dream dreams,[d] [9]for they prophesy lies to you in my name; I did not send them—oracle of the LORD.[e]

[10]For thus says the LORD: Only after seventy years have elapsed for Babylon will I deal with you and fulfill for you my promise to bring you back to this place.[f] [11]For I know well the plans I have in mind for you—oracle of the LORD—plans for your welfare and not for woe, so as to give you a future of hope. [12]When you call me, and come and pray to me, I will listen to you.[g] [13]When you look for me, you will find me. Yes, when you seek me with all your heart, [14]I will let you find me—oracle of the LORD—and I will change your lot; I will gather you together from all the nations and all the places to which I have banished you—oracle of the LORD—and bring you back to the place from which I have exiled you.[h] [15]As for your saying, "The LORD has raised up for us prophets here in Babylon"—

[16]Thus says the LORD concerning the king sitting on David's throne and all the people living in this city, your kinsmen who did not go with you into exile; [17]thus says the LORD of hosts: I am sending against them sword, famine, and pestilence. I will make them like rotten figs, so spoiled that they cannot be eaten. [18]I will pursue them with sword, famine, and pestilence, and make them an object of horror to all the kingdoms of the earth, a curse, a desolation, a hissing, and a reproach to all the nations among which I have banished them,[i] [19]because they did not listen to my words—oracle of the LORD—even though I kept sending them my servants the prophets, but they would not listen to them—oracle of the LORD.[j]

[20]As for you, listen to the word of the LORD, all you exiles whom I sent away from Jerusalem to Babylon. [21]This is what the LORD of hosts, the God of Israel, says about Ahab, son of Kolaiah, and Zedekiah, son of Maaseiah, who prophesy lies to you in my name: I am handing them over to Nebuchadnezzar, king of Babylon, who will kill them before your eyes.[k] [22]And because of them this curse will be used by all the exiles of Judah in Babylon: "May the LORD make you like Zedekiah and Ahab, whom the king of Babylon roasted in fire," [23]because they have committed an outrage in Israel, committing adultery with their neighbors' wives, and alleging in my name things I did not command. I know, I am witness—oracle of the LORD.[l]

*The False Prophet Shemaiah.* [24]To Shemaiah, the Nehelamite, say: [25]Thus says the

**29:3 Elasah**: probably the brother of Ahikam (cf. 26:24). **Gemariah**: probably the son of the high priest Hilkiah; cf. 2 Kgs 22:4. Zedekiah had dispatched these men to Nebuchadnezzar for some other purpose, possibly the payment of tribute, but Jeremiah took advantage of their mission to send his letter with them.

*b:* 2 Kgs 24:15. *c:* 1 Tm 2:1–2. *d:* Jer 27:9, 14. *e:* Jer 5:31. *f:* Jer 25:11; 2 Chr 36:21–22; Ezr 1:1; Dn 9:2; Zec 1:12; 7:5. *g:* Jer 33:3. *h:* Jer 23:3, 8. *i:* Jer 15:4; 24:9; 34:17–18. *j:* Jer 25:4. *k:* Jer 14:14. *l:* Jer 23:14.

LORD of hosts, the God of Israel: Because
you sent documents in your own name to all
the people in Jerusalem, to Zephaniah, the
priest, son of Maaseiah, and to all the priests
saying: 26* "It is the LORD who has appointed you priest in place of the priest Jehoiada, to provide officers for the house of
the LORD, that you may confine in stocks or
pillory any madman who poses as a prophet.
27 Why, then, have you not rebuked Jeremiah
of Anathoth who poses as a prophet among
you? 28 For he sent this message to us in Babylon: It will be a long time; build houses to
live in; plant gardens and eat their fruit. . . ."
29 When the priest Zephaniah read this letter to Jeremiah the prophet, 30 the word of the
LORD came to Jeremiah: 31 Send to all the exiles: Thus says the LORD concerning Shemaiah, the Nehelamite: Because Shemaiah
prophesies to you, although I did not send
him, and has led you to rely on a lie, 32 therefore thus says the LORD, I will punish Shemaiah, the Nehelamite, and his descendants.
None of them shall dwell among this people
to see the good I will do for this people—oracle of the LORD—because he preached rebellion against the LORD.

## VI. Oracles of the Restoration of Israel and Judah

### CHAPTER 30

See RG 217–18

*The Restoration.** 1 This word came to
Jeremiah from the LORD: 2 Thus says the
LORD, the God of Israel: Write down on a
scroll all the words I have spoken to you.[m]
3 For indeed, the days are coming—oracle of
the LORD—when I will restore the fortunes
of my people Israel and Judah—oracle of the
LORD. I will bring them back to the land
which I gave to their ancestors, and they
shall take possession of it.[n]
4 These are the words the LORD spoke to
Israel and to Judah: 5 Thus says the LORD:

We hear a cry of fear:
  terror, not peace.
6 Inquire and see:
  does a male give birth?
Why, then, do I see all these men,
  their hands on their loins
Like women in labor,
  all their faces drained of color?[o]
7 Ah! How mighty is that day—
  there is none like it!
A time of distress for Jacob,
  though he shall be saved from it.[p]

8 On that day—oracle of the LORD of
hosts—I will break his yoke off your neck
and snap your bonds. Strangers shall no
longer enslave them;[q] 9 instead, they shall
serve the LORD, their God, and David, their
king,* whom I will raise up for them.[r]

10 But you, my servant Jacob, do not
    fear!—oracle of the LORD—
  do not be dismayed, Israel!
For I will soon deliver you from places
    far away,
  your offspring from the land of their
    exile;
Jacob shall again find rest,
  secure, with none to frighten him,[s]
11 for I am with you—oracle of the
    LORD—to save you.
I will bring to an end all the nations
  among whom I have scattered you;

**29:26–29** Jeremiah's message to Shemaiah is not completely preserved in the current Hebrew text, hence the incomplete sentence in vv. 25–28.

**30:1–31:40** These two chapters contain salvation oracles that originally expressed the double expectation that the Lord would return the exiled survivors of the Northern Kingdom of Israel and reunite Israel and Judah as one kingdom under a just Davidic king. They were probably composed early in Josiah's reign (the reference of v. 9), when he took advantage of Assyria's internal disintegration and asserted control over northern Israel (cf. 2 Kgs 23:15–17). With the destruction of Jerusalem, the oracles were re-worked to include Judah and their fulfillment along with the renewal of the Davidic dynasty became associated with the eschatological "day of the Lord."

**30:9 David, their king**: a descendant of David ("his leader" in v. 21) who, like his ancestor, would rule a unified kingdom and "walk in the ways of the Lord," as the Deuteronomistic historians claimed David did. Other prophets also refer to this idealized ruler as "David"; cf. Ez 34:23–24; 37:24–25; Hos 3:5.

*m:* Jer 36:2; Hb 2:2; Rev 1:11. *n:* Jer 29:14; 31:8, 10, 23; 32:37, 44; Ez 39:25; Am 9:14. *o:* Jer 6:24; 50:43. *p:* Am 5:18; Zep 1:14–15. *q:* Is 14:5–6; Ez 34:27. *r:* Ez 34:23; 37:24; Hos 3:5; Lk 1:69. *s:* Jer 46:27; Is 43:5.

## Little Book of Consolation

THESE CHAPTERS COMBINE poetry (chs 30–31) and prose (chs 32–33) to depict a harmonious, idealized future for Israel and Judah. The placement of these chapters of hope and healing toward the center of the book is puzzling. Stories and poems of accusation and conflict surround them as if to temper the hope the chapters create. This structure may reflect the situation of the exilic audience, for whom escape from captivity remains a distant possibility. The chapters create a vision of what lies ahead, but they do not present a program for escape. Instead, they create unimagined possibilities that may help the community endure for a new day.

but you I will not bring to an end.
I will chastise you as you deserve,
I will not let you go unpunished.[t]
12 For thus says the LORD:
Incurable is your wound,
grievous your injury;[u]
13 There is none to plead your case,
no remedy for your running sore,
no healing for you.
14 All your lovers have forgotten you,
they do not seek you out.
I struck you as an enemy would strike,
punishing you cruelly.[v]
15 Why cry out over your wound?
There is no relief for your pain.
Because of your great guilt,
your numerous sins,
I have done this to you.[w]
16 Yet all who devour you shall be devoured,
all your enemies shall go into exile.
All who plunder you shall become plunder,
all who pillage you I will hand over to
be pillaged.[x]
17 For I will restore your health;
I will heal your injuries—oracle of the
LORD.
"The outcast" they have called you,
"whom no one looks for."[y]
18 Thus says the LORD:
See! I will restore the fortunes of Jacob's
tents,
on his dwellings I will have compassion;
A city shall be rebuilt upon its own ruins,
a citadel restored where it should be.[z]
19 From them will come praise,
the sound of people rejoicing.
I will increase them, they will not decrease,
I will glorify them, they will not be
insignificant.[a]
20 His children shall be as of old,
his assembly shall stand firm in my
presence,
I will punish all his oppressors.[b]
21 His leader* shall be one of his own,
and his ruler shall emerge from his
ranks.
He shall approach me when I summon
him;
Why else would he dare
approach me?—oracle of the LORD.
22 You shall be my people,
and I will be your God.[c]
23 Look! The storm of the LORD!
His wrath breaks out
In a whirling storm
that bursts upon the heads of the
wicked.[d]
24 The anger of the LORD will not abate
until he has carried out completely
the decisions of his heart.
In days to come
you will fully understand it.[e]

### CHAPTER 31

See RG 217–18

### *Good News of the Return*

1 At that time—oracle of the LORD—
I will be the God of all the families of
Israel,

**30:21 His leader**: cf. v. 9. **Approach me**: i.e., in the sanctuary of the Temple for worship. This new David is given a priestly function to perform on behalf of the assembly. To approach God on one's own brings death; cf. Lv 16:1–2.

*t:* Jer 46:28; Ez 11:16–17; Am 9:8–9. *u:* Jer 10:19; 14:17; 15:18. *v:* Jer 22:22; Lam 1:19. *w:* Jer 15:18. *x:* Jer 2:3. *y:* Jer 33:6. *z:* Jer 33:7, 11; Ezr 6:3–15; Ez 36:10. *a:* Is 35:10; 51:11. *b:* Is 49:26. *c:* Jer 24:7; 31:1, 33; 32:38; Lv 26:12; Ez 11:20; 36:28. *d:* Jer 23:19. *e:* Jer 23:20.

and they shall be my people.[f]

2 * Thus says the LORD:
The people who escaped the sword
find favor in the wilderness.
As Israel comes forward to receive rest,
3 from afar the LORD appears:
With age-old love I have loved you;
so I have kept my mercy toward you.[g]
4 Again I will build you, and you shall stay built,
virgin Israel;
Carrying your festive tambourines,
you shall go forth dancing with merrymakers.
5 You shall again plant vineyards
on the mountains of Samaria;
those who plant them shall enjoy their fruits.[h]
6 Yes, a day will come when the watchmen
call out on Mount Ephraim:
"Come, let us go up to Zion,
to the LORD, our God."[i]

### *The Road of Return*

7 For thus says the LORD:
Shout with joy for Jacob,
exult at the head of the nations;
proclaim your praise and say:
The LORD has saved his people,
the remnant of Israel.[j]
8 Look! I will bring them back
from the land of the north;
I will gather them from the ends of the earth,
the blind and the lame in their midst,
Pregnant women, together with those in labor—
an immense throng—they shall return.[k]
9 With weeping they shall come,
but with compassion I will guide them;
I will lead them to streams of water,
on a level road, without stumbling.
For I am a father to Israel,
Ephraim is my firstborn.[l]
10 Hear the word of the LORD, you nations,
proclaim it on distant coasts, and say:
The One who scattered Israel, now gathers them;
he guards them as a shepherd his flock.
11 The LORD shall ransom Jacob,
he shall redeem him from a hand too strong for him.[m]
12 Shouting, they shall mount the heights of Zion,
they shall come streaming to the LORD's blessings:
The grain, the wine, and the oil,
flocks of sheep and cattle;
They themselves shall be like watered gardens,
never again neglected.[n]
13 Then young women shall make merry and dance,
young men and old as well.
I will turn their mourning into joy,
I will show them compassion and have them rejoice after their sorrows.
14 I will lavish choice portions on the priests,
and my people shall be filled with my blessings—
oracle of the LORD.

### *End of Rachel's Mourning*

15 Thus says the LORD:
In Ramah* is heard the sound of sobbing,
bitter weeping!
Rachel mourns for her children,
she refuses to be consoled
for her children—they are no more![o]
16 Thus says the LORD:
Cease your cries of weeping,
hold back your tears!
There is compensation for your labor—
oracle of the LORD—

**31:2–3** Jeremiah describes the exiles of the Northern Kingdom on their way home from the nations where the Assyrians had resettled them (722/721 B.C.). The favor they discover in the wilderness is the appearance of the Lord (v. 3) coming to guide them to Jerusalem. Implicit in these verses is the presentation of the people's return from captivity as a second exodus, a unifying theme in Second Isaiah (chaps. 40–55).

**31:15 Ramah**: a village about five miles north of Jerusalem, where one tradition locates Rachel's tomb (1 Sm 10:2). The wife of Jacob/Israel, Rachel is the matriarchal ancestor of Ephraim, chief among the northern tribes. She personified Israel as a mother whose grief for her lost children is especially poignant because she had to wait a long time to

*f:* Jer 30:22. *g:* Dt 7:8; 10:15; Is 43:4; 63:9; Hos 11:1, 4. *h:* Dt 28:30; Is 65:21; Am 9:14. *i:* Is 2:3; 27:13; Mi 4:2. *j:* Is 12:6. *k:* Jer 3:18; 23:3, 8; Is 35:5–6. *l:* Ex 4:22. *m:* Is 44:23; 48:20. *n:* Is 58:11. *o:* Mt 2:18.

## Israel as Rachel

THE PORTRAYAL OF Israel as Rachel weeping for her lost children (31:15) draws upon the tragic tradition of Rachel, Jacob's beloved wife, who died while giving birth to Benjamin. Although Genesis 35:16–21 places her tomb on the road to Bethlehem, where the current structure stands, 1 Samuel 10:2 suggests that her tomb was on the road to Ramah, near modern Ramallah. The present text portrays Rachel weeping not for herself but for her lost children who have gone into exile.

they shall return from the enemy's land.
17 There is hope for your future—oracle of the LORD—
your children shall return to their own territory.[p]
18 Indeed, I heard Ephraim rocking in grief:
You chastised me, and I was chastised;
I was like an untamed calf.
Bring me back, let me come back,
for you are the LORD, my God.[q]
19 For after I turned away, I repented;
after I came to myself, I struck my thigh;*
I was ashamed, even humiliated,
because I bore the disgrace of my youth.[r]
20 Is Ephraim not my favored son,
the child in whom I delight?
Even though I threaten him,
I must still remember him!
My heart stirs for him,
I must show him compassion!—oracle of the LORD.[s]

### *Summons To Return Home*

21 Set up road markers,
put up signposts;
Turn your attention to the highway,
the road you walked.
Turn back, virgin Israel,
turn back to these your cities.
22 How long will you continue to hesitate,
rebellious daughter?
The LORD has created a new thing upon the earth:
woman encompasses man.*

23 Thus says the LORD of hosts, the God of
Israel: When I restore their fortunes in the
land of Judah and in its cities, they shall
again use this greeting: "May the LORD bless
you, Tent of Justice, Holy Mountain!"[t] 24 Judah and all its cities, the farmers and those
who lead the flock shall dwell there together.
25 For I will slake the thirst of the faint; the
appetite of all the weary I will satisfy. 26 At
this I awoke and opened my eyes; my sleep
was satisfying.*
27 See, days are coming—oracle of the
LORD—when I will sow the house of Israel
and the house of Judah with the seed of human beings and the seed of animals. 28 As I
once watched over them to uproot and tear
down, to demolish, to destroy, and to harm,
so I will watch over them to build and to
plant—oracle of the LORD.[u] 29 In those days
they shall no longer say,

"The parents ate unripe grapes,[v]
and the children's teeth are set on edge,"*

30 but all shall die because of their own iniquity: the teeth of anyone who eats unripe grapes shall be set on edge.

bear them. Mt 2:18 applies this verse to Herod's slaughter of the innocents.

**31:19 Struck my thigh**: a gesture signifying grief and dread (cf. Ez 21:17).

**31:22** No satisfactory explanation has been given for this text. Jerome, for example, saw the image as a reference to the infant Jesus enclosed in Mary's womb. Since Jeremiah often uses marital imagery in his description of a restored Israel, the phrase may refer to a wedding custom, perhaps women circling the groom in a dance. It may also be a metaphor describing the security of a new Israel, a security so complete that it defies the imagination and must be expressed as hyperbolic role reversal: any danger will be so insignificant that women can protect their men.

**31:26 I awoke . . . satisfying**: an intrusive comment.

**31:29 "The parents . . . on edge"**: Jeremiah's opponents use this proverb to complain that they are being punished for sins of their ancestors. Jeremiah, however, insists that the Lord knows the depth of their wickedness and holds them accountable for their actions.

*p*: Jer 29:10–14. *q*: Lv 26:40–42. *r*: Dt 30:1–3. *s*: Hos 11:8. *t*: Jer 30:3; Ps 122:8. *u*: Jer 1:10; 18:7. *v*: Dt 24:16; Ez 18:2.

*The New Covenant.** 31 See, days are coming—oracle of the LORD—when I will make
a new covenant with the house of Israel and
the house of Judah.[w] 32 It will not be like the
covenant I made with their ancestors the
day I took them by the hand to lead them out
of the land of Egypt. They broke my covenant, though I was their master—oracle of
the LORD.[x] 33 But this is the covenant I will
make with the house of Israel after those
days—oracle of the LORD. I will place my
law within them, and write it upon their
hearts; I will be their God, and they shall be
my people.[y] 34 They will no longer teach
their friends and relatives, "Know the
LORD!" Everyone, from least to greatest,
shall know me—oracle of the LORD—for I
will forgive their iniquity and no longer remember their sin.[z]

### *Certainty of God's Promise*

35 Thus says the LORD,
Who gives the sun to light the day,
moon and stars to light the night;
Who stirs up the sea so that its waves
roar,
whose name is LORD of hosts:[a]
36 If ever this fixed order gives way
before me—oracle of the LORD—
Then would the offspring of Israel cease
as a people before me forever.[b]
37 Thus says the LORD:
If the heavens on high could be measured,
or the foundations below the earth be
explored,
Then would I reject all the offspring of
Israel
because of all they have done—oracle
of the LORD.

***Jerusalem Rebuilt.**** 38 See, days are coming—oracle of the LORD—when the city
shall be rebuilt as the LORD's,[c] from the
Tower of Hananel to the Corner Gate. 39 A
measuring line shall be stretched from there
straight to the hill Gareb and then turn to
Goah. 40 The whole valley of corpses and
ashes, all the terraced slopes toward the
Wadi Kidron, as far as the corner of the
Horse Gate at the east, shall be holy to the
LORD. Never again shall the city be uprooted
or demolished.

## CHAPTER 32

See RG 217–18

***Pledge of Restoration.**** 1 The word
came to Jeremiah from the LORD in the tenth
year of Zedekiah,* king of Judah, the eighteenth year of Nebuchadnezzar. 2 At that time
the army of the king of Babylon was besieging Jerusalem, while Jeremiah the prophet
was confined to the court of the guard, in the
house of the king of Judah.[d] 3 Zedekiah, king
of Judah, had confined him there, saying:
"How dare you prophesy: Thus says the
LORD: I am handing this city over to the king
of Babylon that he may capture it.[e] 4 Zedekiah, king of Judah, shall not escape the
hands of the Chaldeans: he shall indeed be
handed over to the king of Babylon. He shall
speak with him face to face and see him eye

**31:31–34** The new covenant is an occasional prophetic theme, beginning with Hosea. According to Jeremiah, (a) it lasts forever; (b) its law (*torah*) is written in human hearts; (c) it gives everyone true knowledge of God, making additional instruction (*torah*) unnecessary. The Dead Sea Scroll community claimed they were partners in a "new covenant." The New Testament presents the death and resurrection of Jesus of Nazareth as inaugurating a new covenant open to anyone who professes faith in Jesus the Christ. Cf. Lk 22:20; 1 Cor 11:25; Heb 8:8–12. **Know the LORD**: cf. note on 22:15–16.

**31:38–40** The landmarks in these verses outline the borders of Jerusalem during the time of Nehemiah: the Tower of Hananel (Neh 3:1; 12:39) in the northeast and the Corner Gate (2 Kgs 14:13) in the northwest; Goah in the southeast and Gareb Hill in the southwest; the Valley of Ben-hinnom ("the Valley of corpses and ashes"), which met the Wadi Kidron in the southeast, and the Horse Gate in the eastern wall at the southeast corner of the Temple area.

**32:1–44** This chapter recounts a prophecy "in action." At the Lord's command, Jeremiah fulfills his family duty to purchase the land of his cousin, carrying out all the legal details, even putting the deed away for safekeeping against the day he will have to produce it to verify his ownership of the land. The Lord defines the meaning of this symbolic action: In the future, Judah will be restored and daily life will return to normal.

**32:1 The tenth year of Zedekiah**: 588 B.C. **The eighteenth year of Nebuchadnezzar**: dating his reign from his victory at Carchemish; see note on 25:1–14.

**32:6–9** Jeremiah's imprisonment by the weak-willed Zedekiah was a technical custody that did not deprive him of all freedom of action.

*w:* Jer 32:40; Heb 9:15. *x:* Ex 24:7–8; Dt 5:2. *y:* Jer 32:40; Ez 37:26; Heb 10:16. *z:* Is 54:13. *a:* Gn 1:14–18. *b:* Jer 33:20–21. *c:* Neh 12:38; Zec 14:10–11. *d:* Jer 33:1; 37:20; 38:6; 39:14. *e:* Jer 26:9; 34:2; 37:6–10.

to eye.[f] 5He shall take Zedekiah to Babylon.
There he shall remain, until I attend to him—
oracle of the LORD. If you fight against the
Chaldeans, you cannot win!"[g]
6* Jeremiah said, This word came to me
from the LORD: 7Hanamel, son of your uncle
Shallum, will come to you with the offer:[h]
"Purchase my field in Anathoth, since you,
as nearest relative, have the first right of purchase."* 8And, just as the LORD had said, my
cousin Hanamel came to me in the court of
the guard and said, "Please purchase my
field in Anathoth, in the territory of Benjamin; as nearest relative, you have the first
right of possession—purchase it for yourself." Then I knew this was the word of the
LORD. 9So I bought the field in Anathoth
from my cousin Hanamel, weighing out for
him the silver, seventeen shekels of silver.
10When I had written and sealed the deed,
called witnesses and weighed out the silver
on the scales, 11I accepted the deed of purchase, both the sealed copy, containing title
and conditions, and the open copy.* 12I gave
this deed of purchase to Baruch, son of Neriah, son of Mahseiah, in the presence of my
cousin Hanamel and the witnesses who had
signed the deed of purchase and before all
the Judahites sitting around in the court of
the guard.[i]
13In their presence I gave Baruch this
charge: 14Thus says the LORD of hosts, the
God of Israel: Take these deeds of purchase,
both the sealed and the open deeds, and put
them in an earthenware jar,* so they can last
a long time. 15For thus says the LORD of
hosts, the God of Israel: They shall again
purchase houses and fields and vineyards in
this land.
16After I had given the deed of purchase to
Baruch, son of Neriah, I prayed to the LORD:
17Ah, my Lord GOD! You made the heavens
and the earth with your great power and your
outstretched arm; nothing is too difficult for
you.[j] 18You continue your kindness through
a thousand generations; but you repay the
ancestors' guilt upon their children who follow them. Great and mighty God, whose
name is LORD of hosts,[k] 19great in counsel,
mighty in deed, whose eyes are fixed on all
the ways of mortals, giving to all according
to their ways, according to the fruit of their
deeds:[l] 20you performed signs and wonders
in the land of Egypt and to this day, in Israel
and among all peoples, you have made a
name for yourself as on this day.[m] 21You
brought your people Israel out of the land of
Egypt with signs and wonders, with a strong
hand and an outstretched arm, and great terror. 22And you gave them this land, as you
had sworn to their ancestors to give them, a
land flowing with milk and honey.[n] 23They
went in and took possession of it, but they
did not listen to your voice. They did not live
by your law; they did not do anything you
commanded them to do. Then you made all
this evil fall upon them.[o] 24See, the siegeworks have arrived at this city to capture it;
the city is handed over to the Chaldeans who
are attacking it, with sword, starvation, and
disease. What you threatened has happened—you can see it for yourself.[p] 25Yet
you told me, my Lord GOD: Purchase the
field with silver and summon witnesses,
when the city has already been handed over
to the Chaldeans!
26Then this word of the LORD came to Jeremiah: 27I am the LORD, the God of all the
living! Is anything too difficult for me?
28Therefore the LORD says: I am handing
over this city to the Chaldeans and to Nebuchadnezzar, king of Babylon, and he shall
capture it. 29The Chaldeans who are attacking this city shall go in and set the city on

**32:7 The first right of purchase**: the obligation of the closest relative to redeem the property of a family member in economic distress so that the ancestral land remains within the family (Lv 25:25–28); see note on Ru 2:20.

**32:11 The sealed copy . . . and the open copy**: the legal deed of sale was written on a scroll, which was then rolled up and sealed; a second scroll containing a copy of the legal deed was then rolled around it and left unsealed so the contents of the legal deed would be accessible without destroying the original seal.

**32:14 In an earthenware jar**: to protect the scroll from drying out and disintegrating. Some of the Dead Sea Scrolls were found in such jars.

*f:* Jer 34:3; 38:18, 23; 39:4–7. *g:* Jer 39:7; 52:11. *h:* Lv 25:24–34; Ru 4:4. *i:* Jer 36:4. *j:* 2 Kgs 19:15; Jb 42:2. *k:* Ex 20:5–6; 34:6; Dt 5:9. *l:* Jb 34:21; Ps 33:13–15. *m:* Ex 6:6; Dt 4:34; Ps 135:9. *n:* Jer 11:5; Gn 15:18; 17:8; 26:3. *o:* Jer 7:24–26; Dn 9:10–14. *p:* Jer 21:5; 33:4.

fire, burning it and the houses, on whose roofs incense was burned to Baal and libations were poured out to other gods in order to provoke me.[q] [30]From their youth the Israelites and the Judahites have been doing only what is evil in my eyes; the Israelites have been provoking me with the works of their hands—oracle of the LORD.[r] [31]This city has so stirred my anger and wrath, from the day it was built to this day, that I must put it out of my sight, [32]for all the evil the Israelites and Judahites have done to provoke me—they, their kings, their princes, their priests, and their prophets, the people of Judah and the inhabitants of Jerusalem.[s] [33]They turned their backs to me, not their faces; though I taught them persistently, they would not listen or accept correction.[t] [34]Instead they set up their abominations in the house which bears my name in order to defile it.[u] [35]They built high places to Baal in the Valley of Ben-hinnom to sacrifice their sons and daughters to Molech;* I never commanded them to do this, nor did it even enter my mind that they would practice this abomination, so as to bring sin upon Judah.[v]

[36]Now, therefore, thus says the LORD, the God of Israel, concerning this city, which you say is being handed over to the king of Babylon by means of the sword, starvation, and disease: [37]See, I am gathering them from all the lands to which I drove them in my rising fury and great anger; I will bring them back to this place and settle them here in safety.[w] [38]They shall be my people, and I will be their God.[x] [39]I will give them one heart and one way, that they may fear me always, for their own good and the good of their children after them. [40]With them I will make an everlasting covenant, never to cease doing good to them; I will put fear of me in their hearts so that they never turn away from me.[y] [41]I will take delight in doing good to them: I will plant them firmly in this land, with all my heart and soul.[z]

[42]For thus says the LORD: Just as I have brought upon this people all this great evil, so I will bring upon them all the good I have promised them.[a] [43]Fields shall be purchased in this land, about which you say, "It is a wasteland, without human beings or animals, handed over to the Chaldeans."[b] [44]They will purchase fields with silver, write up deeds, seal them, and have them witnessed in the land of Benjamin, in the neighborhood of Jerusalem, in the cities of Judah and of the hill country, in the cities of the Shephelah and the Negeb, when I restore their fortunes—oracle of the LORD.[c]

## CHAPTER 33

See RG 217-18

***Restoration of Jerusalem.*** [1]The word of the LORD came to Jeremiah a second time while he was still confined in the court of the guard: [2]Thus says the LORD who made the earth, giving it shape and stability, LORD is his name: [3]Call to me, and I will answer you; I will tell you great things beyond the reach of your knowledge.[d] [4]Thus says the LORD, the God of Israel, concerning the houses of this city and the houses of the kings of Judah, which are being torn down because of the siegeworks and the sword:[e] [5]men come to battle the Chaldeans, and to fill these houses with the corpses of those whom I have struck down in my raging anger, when I hid my face from this city because of all their wickedness.[f]

[6]Look! I am bringing the city recovery and healing; I will heal them and reveal to them an abundance of lasting peace.[g] [7]I will restore the fortunes of Judah and Israel, and rebuild them as they were in the beginning.[h] [8]I will purify them of all the guilt they incurred by sinning against me; I will forgive all their offenses by which they sinned and rebelled against me.[i] [9]Then this city shall become joy for me, a name of praise and pride, before all the nations of the earth, as they hear of all the good I am doing for them.

**32:35 Molech**: a god to whom human sacrifice was offered in the Valley of Ben-hinnom. Here, as in 19:5, he is called "Baal"; see note on Lv 18:21.

*q:* Jer 21:10; 37:8–10. *r:* Jer 3:25; 44:8. *s:* Jer 2:26; Is 3:8. *t:* Jer 7:24. *u:* Jer 7:30; 2 Kgs 21:4–5. *v:* Jer 7:31; 19:5; Ps 106:37–38. *w:* Jer 23:3; 29:14; Is 11:12; Ez 11:17. *x:* Jer 24:7; 31:33. *y:* Jer 31:31–33. *z:* Dt 30:9. *a:* Jer 33:10–14; Zec 8:13. *b:* Jer 33:10. *c:* Jer 17:26; 33:7. *d:* Is 48:6. *e:* Jer 32:24. *f:* Jer 21:4–6. *g:* Is 57:18. *h:* Jer 30:3; 32:44. *i:* Ez 36:25.

They shall fear and tremble because of all the prosperity I give it.

10 Thus says the LORD: In this place, about which you say: "It is a waste without people or animals!" and in the cities of Judah, in the streets of Jerusalem now deserted, without people, without inhabitant, without animal, there shall yet be heard[j] 11 the song of joy, the song of gladness, the song of the bridegroom, the song of the bride, the song of those bringing thank offerings to the house of the LORD: "Give thanks to the LORD of hosts, for the LORD is good; God's love endures forever." For I will restore the fortunes of this land as they were in the beginning, says the LORD.[k]

12 Thus says the LORD of hosts: In this place, now a waste, without people or animals, and in all its cities there shall again be sheepfolds for the shepherds to rest their flocks. 13 In the cities of the hill country, of the Shephelah and the Negeb, in the land of Benjamin and the neighborhood of Jerusalem, and in the cities of Judah, flocks will again pass under the hands of the one who counts them, says the LORD.

14* The days are coming—oracle of the LORD—when I will fulfill the promise I made to the house of Israel and the house of Judah. 15 In those days, at that time, I will make a just shoot spring up for David; he shall do what is right and just in the land.[l] 16 In those days Judah shall be saved and Jerusalem shall dwell safely; this is the name they shall call her: "The LORD our justice." 17 For thus says the LORD: David shall never lack a successor on the throne of the house of Israel,[m] 18 nor shall the priests of Levi ever be lacking before me, to sacrifice burnt offerings, to burn cereal offerings, and to make sacrifices.[n]

19 This word of the LORD also came to Jeremiah: 20 Thus says the LORD: If you can break my covenant with day[o] and my covenant with night so that day and night no longer appear in their proper time, 21 only then can my covenant with my servant David be broken, so that he will not have a descendant to act as king upon his throne, and my covenant with the priests of Levi who minister to me. 22 Just as the host of heaven cannot be numbered and the sands of the sea cannot be counted, so I will multiply the descendants of David my servant and the Levites who minister to me.

23 This word of the LORD came to Jeremiah: 24 Have you not noticed what these people are saying: "The LORD has rejected the two tribes he had chosen"? They hold my people in contempt as if it were no longer a nation in their eyes.[p] 25[q] Thus says the LORD: If I have no covenant with day and night, if I did not establish statutes for heaven and earth, 26 then I will also reject the descendants of Jacob and of David my servant, no longer selecting from his descendants rulers for the offspring of Abraham, Isaac, and Jacob. Yes, I will restore their fortunes and show them mercy.

## CHAPTER 34

See RG 217

*Fate of Zedekiah.* 1 The word which came to Jeremiah from the LORD while Nebuchadnezzar, king of Babylon, and all his army and all the earth's kingdoms under his rule, and all the peoples were attacking Jerusalem and all her cities:[r] 2 Thus says the LORD, the God of Israel: Go to Zedekiah, king of Judah, and tell him: Thus says the LORD: I am handing this city over to the king of Babylon; he will burn it with fire.[s] 3 You yourself shall not escape his hand; rather you will be captured and fall into his hand. You shall see the king of Babylon eye to eye and speak to him face to face. Then you shall go to Babylon.[t]

4 Just hear the word of the LORD, Zedekiah, king of Judah! Then, says the LORD concerning you, you shall not die by the sword. 5 You shall die in peace, and they will

**33:14–26** This is the longest continuous passage in the Hebrew text of Jeremiah that is missing from the Greek text of Jeremiah. It is probably the work of a postexilic writer who applied parts of Jeremiah's prophecies to new situations. The hope for an eternal Davidic dynasty (vv. 14–17; cf. 2 Sm 7:11–16) and for a perpetual priesthood and sacrificial system (v. 18) was not realized after the exile. On the canonical authority of the Septuagint, see note on Dn 13:1–14:42.

---

*j:* Jer 32:43. *k:* 1 Chr 16:34; Ezr 3:11; Ps 136:1. *l:* Jer 23:5; Ps 72:1–4, 12–14; Is 11:1. *m:* 2 Sm 7:16; 1 Kgs 2:4; Ps 89:4–5, 29, 36–37. *n:* Ez 44:15–16. *o:* Jer 31:36–37; Ps 89:37–38. *p:* Rom 11:1–2. *q:* Jer 31:36–37; 32:44. *r:* Jer 52:4; 2 Kgs 25:1. *s:* Jer 21:10; 32:3, 28. *t:* Jer 32:4; 52:11.

burn spices for you as they did for your ancestors, the earlier kings who preceded you,
and they shall make lament over you, "Alas,
Lord." I myself make this promise—oracle
of the LORD.
6Jeremiah the prophet told all these things
to Zedekiah, king of Judah, in Jerusalem,
7while the army of the king of Babylon was
attacking Jerusalem and the remaining cities
of Judah, Lachish, and Azekah.* Only these
fortified cities were left standing out of all
the cities of Judah!
*The Pact Broken.** 8This is the word that
came to Jeremiah from the LORD after King
Zedekiah had made a covenant with all the
people in Jerusalem to proclaim freedom:
9Everyone must free their Hebrew slaves,
male and female, so that no one should hold
another Judahite in servitude.[u] 10All the
princes and the people who entered this covenant agreed to set free their slaves, their
male and female servants, so that they
should no longer be in servitude. But even
though they agreed and freed them, 11after-
ward they took back their male and female
servants whom they had set free and again
forced them into servitude.
12Then this word of the LORD came to Jeremiah: 13Thus says the LORD, the God of Israel: I myself made a covenant with your ancestors the day I brought them out of the
land of Egypt, out of the house of slavery:
14Every seventh year each of you must set
free all Hebrews who have sold themselves
to you; six years they shall serve you, but
then you shall let them go free. Your ancestors, however, did not listen to me or obey
me. 15As for you, today you repented and did
what is right in my eyes by proclaiming freedom for your neighbor and making a covenant before me in the house which bears
my name. 16But then you again profaned my
name by taking back your male and female
slaves whom you had just set free for life;
you forced them to become your slaves
again.[v] 17Therefore, thus says the LORD: You
for your part did not obey me by proclaiming freedom for your families and neighbors.
So I now proclaim freedom for you—oracle
of the LORD—for the sword, starvation, and
disease. I will make you an object of horror
to all the kingdoms of the earth. 18* Those
who violated my covenant and did not observe the terms of the covenant they made in
my presence—I will make them like the calf
which they cut in two so they could pass between its parts— 19the princes of Judah and
of Jerusalem, the court officials, the priests,
and all the people of the land, who passed
between the parts of the calf. 20These I will
hand over to their enemies, to those who
seek their lives: their corpses shall become
food for the birds of the air and the beasts of
the field.[w]
21Zedekiah, king of Judah, and his
princes, I will hand also over to their enemies, to those who seek their lives, to the
army of the king of Babylon which is now
withdrawing from you.[x] 22I am giving the
command—oracle of the LORD—to bring
them back to this city. They shall attack and
capture it, and burn it with fire; the cities of
Judah I will turn into a waste, where no one
dwells.[y]

## CHAPTER 35

See RG 217

*The Faithful Rechabites.* 1The word
that came to Jeremiah from the LORD in the

**34:7 Lachish, and Azekah**: fortress towns southwest of Jerusalem which Nebuchadnezzar besieged to prevent any help coming to Jerusalem from Egypt. At Lachish, archaeologists found several letters written on ostraca (pottery fragments) dated to 598 or 588 B.C., which mention both Lachish and Azekah.

**34:8–22** During the siege of Jerusalem, its citizens made a covenant at Zedekiah's instigation to free Judahites they held in servitude, thus providing additional defenders for the city, leaving slave owners with fewer mouths to feed, and making reparation for past violations of the law, which dictated that Hebrew slaves should serve no longer than six years (Dt 15:12–15). But when the siege was temporarily lifted, when the assistance promised by Pharaoh Hophra arrived (cf. Jer 37:5), the inhabitants of Jerusalem broke the covenant and once more pressed their fellow citizens into slavery (v. 11).

**34:18–19** Both the Old Testament (Gn 15:10–17) and the eighth century B.C. Sefire inscription indicate that sometimes contracting parties ratified an agreement by walking between dismembered animals, invoking upon themselves the animals' fate if they failed to keep their word. **The covenant**: that mentioned in vv. 10, 15.

*u:* Ex 21:2–4; Lv 25:39, 46; Dt 15:12–15. *v:* Lv 19:12. *w:* Jer 7:33; 16:4; 19:7. *x:* Jer 37:5, 11. *y:* Jer 37:8; 52:7–13; 2 Chr 36:17, 19.

days of Jehoiakim,* son of Josiah, king of
Judah: 2Go to the house* of the Rechabites,
speak to them, and bring them to the house
of the LORD, to one of the rooms there, and
give them wine to drink. 3So I took Jaazaniah, son of Jeremiah, son of Habazziniah,
his brothers and all his sons—the whole
house of the Rechabites— 4and I brought
them to the house of the LORD, to the room
of the sons of Hanan,* son of Igdaliah, the
man of God, next to the room of the
princes above the room of Maaseiah, son
of Shallum, the guard at the entrance. 5I set
before the Rechabites bowls full of wine,
and cups, and said to them, "Drink some
wine."
6"We do not drink wine," they said to me;
"Jonadab,* Rechab's son, our father, commanded us, 'Neither you nor your children
shall ever drink wine.[z] 7Build no house and
sow no seed; do not plant vineyards or own
any. You must dwell in tents all your lives, so
that you may live long on the land where you
live as resident aliens.' 8We have obeyed
Jonadab, Rechab's son, our father, in everything that he commanded us: not drinking
wine as long as we live—neither we nor our
wives nor our sons nor our daughters; 9not
building houses to live in; not owning vineyards or fields or crops. 10We live in tents,
doing everything our father Jonadab commanded us. 11But when Nebuchadnezzar,
king of Babylon, invaded this land, we said,
'Come, let us go into Jerusalem to escape the
army of the Chaldeans and the army of the
Arameans.'* That is why we are now living
in Jerusalem."[a]

12Then the word of the LORD came to Jeremiah: 13Thus says the LORD of hosts, the
God of Israel: Go, say to the people of Judah
and to the inhabitants of Jerusalem: Will you
not take correction and obey my words?—
oracle of the LORD.[b] 14The words of Jonadab, Rechab's son, by which he commanded
his children not to drink wine, have been upheld: to this day they have not drunk wine;
they obeyed their ancestor's command. I,
however, have spoken to you time and
again. But you did not obey me![c] 15Time and
again I sent you all my servants the prophets,
saying: Turn away, each of you, from your
evil way and reform your actions! Do not
follow other gods to serve them that you
may remain in the land which I gave you and
your ancestors. But you did not pay attention. You did not obey me.[d] 16Yes, the children of Jonadab, Rechab's son, upheld the
command which their father laid on them.
But this people has not obeyed me! 17Now,
therefore, says the LORD God of hosts, the
God of Israel: I will soon bring upon Judah
and all the inhabitants of Jerusalem every
evil with which I threatened them because I
spoke but they did not obey, I called but they
did not answer.[e]
18But to the house of the Rechabites Jeremiah said: Thus says the LORD of hosts, the
God of Israel: Since you have obeyed the
command of Jonadab, your father, kept all
his commands and done everything he commanded you, 19therefore, thus says the LORD
of hosts, the God of Israel: Never shall there
fail to be a descendant of Jonadab, Rechab's
son, standing in my presence.

**35:1 In the days of Jehoiakim**: probably in 599 or 598 B.C. (cf. 2 Kgs 24:1–2).

**35:2 House**: both members of the family of Rechab (cf. v. 3) and the place where they live; cf. note on v. 11. **The Rechabites**: traditionalists who rejected the settled agricultural and urban cultures to which other Israelites had assimilated, maintaining their loyalty to the Lord by perpetuating the semi-nomadic life of their distant ancestors (cf. 2 Kgs 10:15–17). Jeremiah contrasts their adherence to their vows with the Judahites' disregard for divine commands.

**35:4 The sons of Hanan**: probably disciples of Hanan. **Man of God**: occurring only here in Jeremiah, the title frequently is applied to prophets: e.g., Samuel (1 Sm 9:6–10), Elijah (2 Kgs 1:9–13), Elisha (2 Kgs 4–13). Whatever the function of the sons of Hanan, they encourage Jeremiah by lending him their room. **Maaseiah**: perhaps the father of the priest Zephaniah (29:25; 37:3). **Guard at the entrance**: an important priestly responsibility (cf. 52:24).

**35:6 Jonadab**: another spelling of Jehonadab, a contemporary of King Jehu; cf. 2 Kgs 10:15–17.

**35:11 The army of the Arameans**: Nebuchadnezzar enlisted the help of Judah's neighbors in his assault on Jerusalem. **Living in Jerusalem**: the current military threat and the prospect of being killed or captured as plunder drove the Rechabites into the city and away from their tents.

*z:* Jgs 4:17, 24; 1 Sm 15:6; 2 Kgs 10:15–17. *a:* 2 Kgs 24:1–2. *b:* Jer 32:33. *c:* Jer 7:13; 25:3; 2 Chr 36:15–16. *d:* Jer 25:4–5, 7. *e:* Jer 11:8–9.

## VII. Jeremiah and the Fall of Jerusalem

### CHAPTER 36

See RG 217

*Baruch, the Scribe of Jeremiah.* 1In
the fourth year of Jehoiakim, son of Josiah,
king of Judah, this word came to Jeremiah
from the LORD: 2Take a scroll and write on it
all the words I have spoken to you about Israel, Judah, and all the nations, from the day
I first spoke to you, from the days of Josiah,
until today. 3Perhaps, if the house of Judah
hears all the evil I have in mind to do to
them, so that all of them turn from their evil
way, then I can forgive their wickedness and
their sin.[f] 4So Jeremiah called Baruch, son of
Neriah, and he wrote down on a scroll what
Jeremiah said, all the words which the LORD
had spoken to him. 5Then Jeremiah commanded Baruch: "I cannot enter the house of
the LORD; I am barred* from it. 6So you
yourself must go. On a fast day in the hearing of the people in the LORD's house, read
the words of the LORD from the scroll you
wrote at my dictation; read them also to all
the people of Judah who come up from their
cities. 7Perhaps they will present their supplication before the LORD and will all turn
back from their evil way; for great is the
anger and wrath with which the LORD has
threatened this people."[g]
8Baruch, son of Neriah, did everything
Jeremiah the prophet commanded; from the
scroll he read the LORD's words in the
LORD's house. 9In the ninth month, in the
fifth year of Jehoiakim, son of Josiah, king
of Judah, all the people of Jerusalem and all
those who came from Judah's cities to Jerusalem proclaimed a fast before the LORD.
10So Baruch read the words of Jeremiah
from the scroll in the room of Gemariah,*
son of the scribe Shaphan, in the upper court
of the LORD's house, at the entrance of the
New Temple Gate, in the hearing of all the
people.
11Now Micaiah, son of Gemariah, son of
Shaphan, heard all the words of the LORD
read from the scroll. 12So he went down to the
house of the king, into the scribe's chamber,*
where the princes were meeting in session:
Elishama, the scribe; Delaiah, son of Shemaiah; Elnathan, son of Achbor; Gemariah, son
of Shaphan; Zedekiah, son of Hananiah; and
the other princes. 13Micaiah reported to them
all that he had heard Baruch read from his
scroll in the hearing of the people. 14The
princes immediately sent Jehudi, son of
Nethaniah, son of Shelemiah, son of Cushi,
to Baruch with the order: "The scroll you
read in the hearing of the people—bring it
with you and come." Scroll in hand, Baruch,
son of Neriah, went to them. 15"Sit down,"
they said to him, "and read it in our hearing."
Baruch read it in their hearing, 16and when
they had heard all its words, they turned to
each other in alarm and said to Baruch, "We
have to tell the king all these things." 17Then
they asked Baruch: "Tell us, please, how did
you come to write down all these words? Was
it at his dictation?" 18"Yes, he would dictate
all these words to me," Baruch answered
them, "while I wrote them down with ink in
the scroll." 19The princes said to Baruch, "Go
into hiding, you and Jeremiah; do not let anyone know where you are."
20They went in to the king, into the courtyard; they had deposited the scroll in the
room of Elishama the scribe. When they told
the king everything that had happened, 21the
king sent Jehudi to get the scroll. Jehudi
brought it from the room of Elishama the
scribe, and read it to the king and to all the
princes who were attending the king. 22Now
the king was sitting in his winter house, since
it was the ninth month, and a fire was burning in the brazier before him. 23Each time Jehudi finished reading three or four columns,

**36:5 I am barred**: Jeremiah could have been forbidden to enter the Temple for any number of reasons: e.g., his inflammatory preaching (the Temple sermon, 7:1–15; the broken pot); the hostility of Temple guards; the restrictions of arrest.

**36:10 Gemariah**: member of a family friendly to Jeremiah with rights to a room in the gateway fortress overlooking the court of the Temple. His father Shaphan had been Josiah's secretary of state (2 Kgs 22:3). From a window in this room Baruch read Jeremiah's scroll to the people.

**36:12 The scribe's chamber**: the office of the royal secretary.

*f:* Jer 26:3; Is 55:6–7. *g:* 2 Kgs 22:13.

he would cut off the piece with a scribe's knife* and throw it into the fire in the brazier, until the entire scroll was consumed in the fire in the brazier. 24As they were listening to all these words the king and all his officials did not become alarmed, nor did they tear their garments. 25And though Elnathan, Delaiah, and Gemariah urged the king not to burn the scroll, he would not listen to them. 26He commanded Jerahmeel, a royal prince, and Seraiah, son of Azriel, and Shelemiah, son of Abdeel, to arrest Baruch, the scribe, and Jeremiah the prophet. But the LORD had hidden them away.

27The word of the LORD came to Jeremiah, after the king burned the scroll and the words Jeremiah had dictated to Baruch: 28Take another scroll, and write on it all the words in the first scroll, which Jehoiakim, king of Judah, burned. 29And against Jehoiakim, king of Judah, say this: Thus says the LORD: You are the one who burned that scroll, saying, "Why did you write on it: Babylon's king shall surely come and ravage this land, emptying it of every living thing"? 30The LORD now says of Jehoiakim, king of Judah:[h] No descendant of his shall sit on David's throne; his corpse shall be thrown out, exposed to heat by day, frost by night.* 31I will punish him and his descendants and his officials for their wickedness; upon them, the inhabitants of Jerusalem, and the people of Judah I will bring all the evil threats to which they did not listen.

32Then Jeremiah took another scroll and gave it to his scribe, Baruch, son of Neriah, who wrote on it at Jeremiah's dictation all the words contained in the scroll which Jehoiakim, king of Judah, had burned in the fire, adding many words like them.

## CHAPTER 37

See RG 217

***Jeremiah in the Dungeon.*** 1Zedekiah, son of Josiah, became king, succeeding Coniah, son of Jehoiakim; Nebuchadnezzar, king of Babylon, appointed him king over the land of Judah.[i] 2Neither he, nor his officials, nor the people of the land would listen to the words which the LORD spoke through Jeremiah the prophet. 3Yet King Zedekiah sent Jehucal, son of Shelemiah, and Zephaniah, son of Maaseiah the priest, to Jeremiah the prophet with this request: "Please appeal to the LORD, our God, for us."[j] 4At this time Jeremiah still came and went freely among the people; he had not yet been put into prison.* 5Meanwhile, Pharaoh's army* had set out from Egypt, and when the Chaldeans who were besieging Jerusalem heard this report, they withdrew from the city.[k]

6Then the word of the LORD came to Jeremiah the prophet: 7Thus says the LORD, the God of Israel: Thus you must say to the king of Judah who sent you to consult me: Listen! Pharaoh's army, which has set out to help you, will return to Egypt, its own land.[l] 8The Chaldeans shall return and attack this city; they shall capture it and destroy it by fire.[m]

9Thus says the LORD: Do not deceive yourselves, saying: "The Chaldeans are surely leaving us forever." They are not! 10Even if you could defeat the whole Chaldean army that is now attacking you, and only the wounded remained, each in his tent, these would rise up and destroy the city with fire.[n]

11Now when the Chaldean army withdrew from Jerusalem because of the army of Pharaoh,[o] 12Jeremiah set out from Jerusalem to go to the territory of Benjamin, to receive his share of property among the people. 13But at the Gate of Benjamin, the captain of the guard, by the name of Irijah, son of Shelemiah, son of Hananiah, arrested Jeremiah the prophet, saying, "You are deserting to the Chaldeans!" 14"That is a lie!" Jeremiah answered, "I am not deserting to the Chaldeans." Without listening to him, Irijah

**36:23 A scribe's knife**: used to sharpen reed pens.

**36:30** Jehoiakim's son Jehoiachin was named king, but reigned only three months; he was better known for his long exile in Babylon. **His corpse shall be thrown out**: just as Jehoiakim had thrown pieces of the scroll into the fire (cf. 22:19).

**37:4 Put into prison**: as described in 32:1–3. Chronologically, the present episode follows 34:1–7.

**37:5 Pharaoh's army**: the force sent by Pharaoh Hophra; when they arrived, the Chaldeans temporarily lifted the siege against Jerusalem (cf. 34:21).

*h:* Jer 22:19. *i:* Jer 52:1; 2 Kgs 24:17; 2 Chr 36:10. *j:* Jer 21:1. *k:* Ez 17:15; 29:6–7. *l:* Ez 17:17. *m:* Jer 34:22. *n:* Jer 21:4. *o:* Zec 14:10.

kept Jeremiah in custody and brought him to
the princes.
15The princes were enraged at Jeremiah
and had Jeremiah beaten and imprisoned in
the house of Jonathan the scribe, for they
were using it as a jail.[p] 16And so Jeremiah
went into a room in the dungeon, where he
remained many days.
17Then King Zedekiah had him brought to
his palace, and he asked him secretly, "Is
there any word from the LORD?" "There is!"
Jeremiah answered: "You shall be handed
over to the king of Babylon."[q] 18Jeremiah
then asked King Zedekiah: "How have I
wronged you or your officials or this people,
that you should put me in prison?[r] 19Where
are your own prophets who prophesied for
you, saying: 'The King of Babylon will not
attack you or this land'? 20Please hear me,
my lord king! Grant my petition: do not send
me back into the house of Jonathan the
scribe, or I shall die there."
21So King Zedekiah ordered that Jeremiah
be confined in the court of the guard and
given a ration of bread every day from the
bakers' street until all the bread in the city
was eaten up. Thus Jeremiah remained in the
court of the guard.[s]

See RG 217

## CHAPTER 38

***Jeremiah in the Muddy Cistern.***
1Shephatiah, son of Mattan, Gedaliah, son of
Pashhur, Jucal, son of Shelemiah, and Pashhur, son of Malchiah, heard the words Jeremiah was speaking to all the people:* 2Thus
says the LORD: Those who remain in this city
shall die by means of the sword, starvation,
and disease; but those who go out to the
Chaldeans shall live. Their lives shall be
spared them as spoils of war that they may
live.[t] 3Thus says the LORD: This city shall
certainly be handed over to the army of the
king of Babylon; he shall capture it.
4Then the princes said to the king, "This
man ought to be put to death. He is weakening the resolve* of the soldiers left in this
city and of all the people, by saying such
things to them; he is not seeking the welfare
of our people, but their ruin."[u] 5King Zedekiah answered: "He is in your hands," for the
king could do nothing with them. 6And so
they took Jeremiah and threw him into the
cistern of Prince Malchiah, in the court of
the guard, letting him down by rope. There
was no water in the cistern, only mud, and
Jeremiah sank down into the mud.[v]
7Now Ebed-melech, an Ethiopian, a court
official in the king's house, heard that they
had put Jeremiah in the cistern. The king happened to be sitting at the Gate of Benjamin,
8and Ebed-melech went there from the house
of the king and said to him, 9"My lord king,
these men have done wrong in all their treatment of Jeremiah the prophet, throwing him
into the cistern. He will starve to death on the
spot, for there is no more bread in the city."[w]
10Then the king ordered Ebed-melech the
Ethiopian: "Take three men with you, and get
Jeremiah the prophet out of the cistern before
he dies." 11Ebed-melech took the men with
him, and went first to the linen closet in the
house of the king. He took some old, tattered
rags and lowered them by rope to Jeremiah in
the cistern. 12Then he said to Jeremiah, "Put
these old, tattered rags between your armpits
and the ropes." Jeremiah did so, 13and they
pulled him up by rope out of the cistern. But
Jeremiah remained in the court of the guard.
14King Zedekiah summoned Jeremiah the
prophet to meet him at the third entrance of
the house of the LORD. "I have a question to
ask you," the king said to Jeremiah. "Do not
hide anything from me."[x] 15Jeremiah answered Zedekiah: "If I tell you anything,
will you not have me put to death? If I counsel you, you will not listen to me!"[y] 16But
King Zedekiah swore to Jeremiah secretly:
"As the LORD lives who gave us our lives, I
will not kill you, nor will I hand you over to
those men who seek your life."

**38:1** Jeremiah enjoyed sufficient liberty in the court of the guard (37:21) to speak to the people; cf. 32:6–9. **Gedaliah, son of Pashhur**: the latter is possibly the Pashhur of 20:1. **Pashhur, son of Malchiah**: mentioned in 21:1.

**38:4 He is weakening the resolve**: lit., "he weakens the hands." One of the Lachish ostraca (cf. note on 34:7) makes the same claim against the princes in Jerusalem.

*p*: Jer 38:6–13. *q*: Jer 21:7; 32:3; 34:21. *r*: Jer 26:19. *s*: Jer 32:2; 38:28. *t*: Jer 21:9–10; 39:18; 45:5. *u*: Jer 26:11. *v*: Jer 37:14–15. *w*: Jer 52:6. *x*: Jer 37:16. *y*: Lk 22:67–68.

17 Jeremiah then said to Zedekiah: "Thus says the LORD God of hosts, the God of Israel: If you will only surrender to the princes of Babylon's king, you shall save your life; this city shall not be destroyed by fire, and you and your household shall live.[z] 18 But if you do not surrender to the princes of Babylon's king, this city shall fall into the hand of the Chaldeans, who shall destroy it by fire, and you shall not escape their hand."[a]

19 King Zedekiah said to Jeremiah, "I am afraid of the Judahites who have deserted to the Chaldeans; I could be handed over to them, and they will mistreat me."[b] 20 "You will not be handed over to them," Jeremiah answered. "I beg you! Please listen to the voice of the LORD regarding what I tell you so that it may go well with you and your life be spared.[c] 21 But if you refuse to surrender, this is what the LORD has shown: 22 I see all the women who remain in the house of Judah's king being brought out to the princes of Babylon's king, and they are crying:

'They betrayed you, outdid you,
your good friends!
Now that your feet are sunk in mud,
they slink away.'[d]

23 All your wives and children shall be brought out to the Chaldeans, and you shall not escape their hands; you shall be handed over to the king of Babylon, and this city shall be destroyed by fire."[e]

24 Then Zedekiah said to Jeremiah, "Let no one know about this conversation, or you shall die. 25 If the princes should hear I spoke with you and if they should come and ask you, 'Tell us what you said to the king; do not hide it from us, or we will kill you,' or, 'What did the king say to you?' 26 then give them this answer: 'I petitioned the king not to send me back to Jonathan's house lest I die there.' " 27 When all the princes came to Jeremiah and questioned him, he answered them with the very words the king had commanded. They said no more to him, for nothing had been overheard of the conversation. 28 Thus Jeremiah stayed in the court of the guard until the day Jerusalem was taken.[f]

## CHAPTER 39

See RG 217

*The Capture of Jerusalem.* When Jerusalem was taken, 1 in the ninth year of Zedekiah,[g] king of Judah, in the tenth month,* Nebuchadnezzar, king of Babylon, and all his army marched against Jerusalem and placed it under siege. 2 In the eleventh year of Zedekiah, on the ninth day of the fourth month,* the city wall was breached. 3 All the princes of the king of Babylon came and took their seats at the middle gate: Nergal-sharezer of Simmagir, a chief officer; Nebushazban, a high dignitary; and all the rest of the princes of the king of Babylon.* 4 When Zedekiah, king of Judah, and all his warriors saw this, they fled, leaving the city at night by way of the king's garden,* through a gate between the two walls. He went in the direction of the Arabah,[h] 5 but the Chaldean army pursued them; they caught up with Zedekiah in the wilderness near Jericho and took him prisoner. They brought him to Nebuchadnezzar, king of Babylon, in Riblah,* in the land of Hamath, and he pronounced sentence upon him.[i] 6 The king of Babylon executed the sons of Zedekiah at Riblah before his very eyes; the king of Babylon also executed all the nobles of Judah.[j] 7 He then blinded Zedekiah and bound him in chains to bring him to Babylon.[k]

**39:1 In the ninth year . . . in the tenth month**: the month Tebet (mid-December to mid-January) of the year 589/588 B.C., according to the Babylonian calendar, whose New Year began in March/April.

**39:2 In the eleventh year . . . the ninth day of the fourth month**: in July, 587 B.C.

**39:3** The Babylonian officers act as a military tribunal or government, headed by Nergal-sharezer, Nebuchadnezzar's son and successor.

**39:4 By way of the king's garden**: along the southeast side of the city; the royal garden was in the Kidron Valley. **A gate between the two walls**: the southernmost city gate, at the end of the Tyropoeon Valley. **The Arabah**: the southern Jordan Valley. Zedekiah was perhaps trying to escape across the Jordan when he was captured near Jericho.

**39:5 Riblah**: Nebuchadnezzar's headquarters north of Damascus; Pharaoh Neco had once used the town as a military post (2 Kgs 23:33).

*z:* Jer 27:12–13; 2 Kgs 24:12. *a:* Jer 32:4. *b:* 1 Sm 31:4. *c:* 2 Chr 20:20. *d:* Jb 6:15; 19:13–14, 19. *e:* Jer 41:10. *f:* Jer 39:14. *g:* Jer 52:4–16; 2 Kgs 25:1–12; Ez 24:1. *h:* Jer 52:7. *i:* Jer 32:4–5; 38:18. *j:* Jer 34:21. *k:* Jer 32:4–5; Ez 12:13.

8 The Chaldeans set fire to the king's house and the houses of the people and tore down the walls of Jerusalem.[l] 9 Nebuzaradan, captain of the bodyguard, deported to Babylon the rest of the people left in the city, those who had deserted to him, and the rest of the workers.[m] 10 But Nebuzaradan, captain of the bodyguard, left in the land of Judah some of the poor who had nothing and at the same time gave them vineyards and farms.[n]

***Jeremiah Released to Gedaliah's Custody.*** 11 Concerning Jeremiah, Nebuchadnezzar, king of Babylon, gave these orders through Nebuzaradan, captain of the bodyguard: 12 "Take him and look after him; do not let anything happen to him. Whatever he may ask, you must do for him."[o] 13 Thereupon Nebuzaradan, captain of the bodyguard, and Nebushazban, a high dignitary, and Nergal-sharezer, a chief officer, and all the nobles of the king of Babylon, 14 had Jeremiah taken out of the courtyard of the guard and entrusted to Gedaliah, son of Ahikam, son of Shaphan, to bring him home. And so he remained among the people.[p]

***A Word of Comfort for Ebed-melech.*** 15 While Jeremiah was still imprisoned in the court of the guard, the word of the LORD came to him: 16 Go, tell this to Ebed-melech the Ethiopian: Thus says the LORD of hosts, the God of Israel: See, I am now carrying out my words against this city, for evil and not for good; this will happen in your presence on that day.[q] 17 But on that day I will deliver you—oracle of the LORD; you shall not be handed over to the men you dread. 18 I will make certain that you escape and do not fall by the sword. Your life will be your spoils of war because you trusted in me—oracle of the LORD.[r]

## CHAPTER 40

See RG 217

***Jeremiah Still in Judah.*** 1 The word* which came to Jeremiah from the LORD, after Nebuzaradan, captain of the bodyguard, had released him in Ramah, where he found him a prisoner in chains among the captives of Jerusalem and Judah being exiled to Babylon.[s] 2 The captain of the bodyguard took charge of Jeremiah and said to him, "The LORD, your God, decreed ruin for this place. 3 Now he has made it happen, accomplishing what he decreed; because you sinned against the LORD and did not listen to his voice, this decree has been realized against you. 4 Now, I release you today from the chains upon your hands; if you want to come with me to Babylon, then come: I will look out for you. But if you do not want to come to Babylon, very well. See, the whole land lies before you; go wherever you think good and proper.[t] 5 Or go to Gedaliah, son of Ahikam, son of Shaphan, whom the king of Babylon has set over the cities of Judah. Stay with him among the people. Or go wherever you want!" The captain of the bodyguard gave him food and gifts and let him go.[u] 6 So Jeremiah went to Gedaliah, son of Ahikam, in Mizpah,* and dwelt with him among the people left in the land.[v]

7 When the military leaders still in the field with their soldiers heard that the king of Babylon had set Gedaliah, son of Ahikam, over the land and had put him in charge of men, women, and children, from the poor of the land who had not been deported to Babylon, 8 they and their soldiers came to Gedaliah in Mizpah: Ishmael, son of Nethaniah; Johanan, son of Kareah; Seraiah, son of Tanhumeth; the sons of Ephai of Netophah; and Jezaniah of Beth-maacah. 9 Gedaliah, son of Ahikam, son of Shaphan, swore an oath to them and their men: "Do not be afraid to serve the Chaldeans. Stay in the land and serve the king of Babylon, so that everything may go well with you.[w] 10 As for me, I will remain in Mizpah, as your representative be-

**40:1 The word**: this "word" does not actually appear until 42:7.

**40:6** While Jerusalem had suffered a great deal of damage, the Babylonian leaders' selection of Mizpah as their local headquarters was probably as much a symbolic statement as it was a utilitarian move: Jerusalem and its political and religious worldview had given way to disorder and no longer existed as a symbol of order.

**40:14** In an attempt, perhaps, to weaken Babylon's hold on the area and to add Judah to the Ammonite kingdom, Baalis supported Ishmael's claim to the throne of David (cf. 41:1 for Ishmael's genealogy).

*l:* Jer 21:10; 34:2; 52:13. *m:* 2 Kgs 25:11. *n:* 2 Kgs 25:12, 22. *o:* Jer 40:4. *p:* Jer 26:24; 38:28. *q:* Jer 21:10; Dn 9:12. *r:* Jer 45:5; Ps 25:3; 37:40. *s:* Jer 39:14. *t:* Jer 39:12. *u:* Jer 39:14; 2 Kgs 25:22. *v:* Jer 39:14. *w:* Jer 27:12–13; 2 Kgs 25:24.

fore the Chaldeans when they come to us.
You, for your part, harvest the wine, the
fruit, and the oil, store them in jars, and remain in the cities you occupied." [11]Then all
the Judahites in Moab, in Ammon, in Edom,
and those in all other lands heard that the
king of Babylon had left a remnant in Judah
and had set over them Gedaliah, son of Ahikam, son of Shaphan. [12]They all returned to
the land of Judah from the places to which
they had scattered. They went to Gedaliah at
Mizpah and had a rich harvest of wine and
fruit.

***Assassination of Gedaliah.*** [13]Now Johanan, son of Kareah, and all the military leaders in the field came to Gedaliah in Mizpah
[14]and said to him, "Surely you are aware that
Baalis, the Ammonite king,* has sent Ishmael, son of Nethaniah, to assassinate
you?"[x] But Gedaliah, son of Ahikam, would
not believe them. [15]Then Johanan, son of
Kareah, said secretly to Gedaliah in Mizpah:
"Please let me go and kill Ishmael, son of
Nethaniah; no one will know it. What if he
assassinates you? All the Judahites who
have now rallied behind you would scatter
and the remnant of Judah would perish."
[16]Gedaliah, son of Ahikam, answered Johanan, son of Kareah, "You must not do that.
What you are saying about Ishmael is a lie!"

## CHAPTER 41

See RG 217

[1]In the seventh month, Ishmael, son
of Nethaniah, son of Elishama, of royal descent, one of the king's nobles, came with
ten men to Gedaliah, son of Ahikam, at Mizpah.[y] While they were together at table in
Mizpah, [2]Ishmael, son of Nethaniah, and the
ten with him, stood up and struck down Gedaliah, son of Ahikam, son of Shaphan, with
swords. They killed him, since the king of
Babylon had set him over the land; [3]Ishmael
also killed all the Judahites of military age
who were with Gedaliah and the Chaldean
soldiers stationed there.

[4]The day after the murder of Gedaliah, before anyone learned about it, [5]eighty men, in
ragged clothes, with beards shaved off and
gashes on their bodies, came from Shechem,
Shiloh, and Samaria, bringing grain offerings and incense for the house of the LORD.
[6]Weeping as he went, Ishmael son of Nethaniah, set out from Mizpah to meet them.
"Come to Gedaliah, son of Ahikam," he said
as he met them. [7]Once they were inside the
city, Ishmael, son of Nethaniah, and his men
slaughtered them and threw them into the
cistern. [8]Ten of them said to Ishmael: "Do
not kill us! We have stores of wheat and barley, oil and honey hidden in the field." So he
spared them and did not kill them as he had
killed their companions. [9]The cistern into
which Ishmael threw all the bodies of the
men he had killed was the large one King
Asa made to defend himself against Baasha,
king of Israel; Ishmael, son of Nethaniah,
filled this cistern with the slain.[z]

[10]Ishmael led away the rest of the people
left in Mizpah, including the princesses,*
whom Nebuzaradan, captain of the bodyguard, had consigned to Gedaliah, son of
Ahikam. With these captives, Ishmael, son
of Nethaniah, set out to cross over to the
Ammonites.

***Flight to Egypt.*** [11]But when Johanan, son
of Kareah, and the other army leaders with
him heard about the crimes Ishmael, son of
Nethaniah, had committed, [12]they took all
their men and set out to attack Ishmael, son
of Nethaniah. They overtook him at the great
pool in Gibeon.* [13]At the sight of Johanan,
son of Kareah, and the other army leaders,
the people with Ishmael rejoiced; [14]all of
those whom Ishmael had taken captive from
Mizpah went back to Johanan, son of Kareah. [15]But Ishmael, son of Nethaniah, escaped from Johanan with eight men and fled
to the Ammonites. [16]Then Johanan, son of
Kareah, and all the military leaders took
charge of all the rest of the people whom
Ishmael, son of Nethaniah, had taken away
from Mizpah after he killed Gedaliah, son of
Ahikam—the soldiers, the women with children, and court officials, whom he brought

**41:10 The princesses**: the women of Judah's royal house.

**41:12 Gibeon**: modern El-Jib; northwest of Jerusalem. A huge pit carved into limestone provided water in time of siege, here called the great pool, lit., "many waters"; cf. 2 Sm 2:12–14.

---

*x:* Jer 41:1–3, 10. *y:* Jer 40:14–16; 2 Kgs 25:25. *z:* 1 Kgs 15:16; 2 Chr 16:6.

back from Gibeon. 17They set out and stopped at Geruth Chimham near Bethlehem, intending to go into Egypt. 18They were afraid of the Chaldeans, because Ishmael, son of Nethaniah, had slain Gedaliah, son of Ahikam, whom the king of Babylon had set over the land.

## CHAPTER 42

See RG 217

1Then all the military leaders, including Johanan, son of Kareah, Azariah, son of Hoshaiah, and all the people, from the least to the greatest, 2approached Jeremiah the prophet and said, "Please grant our petition; pray for us to the LORD, your God, for all this remnant. As you see, only a few of us remain, but once we were many. 3May the LORD, your God, show us the way we should take and what we should do." 4"Very well!" Jeremiah the prophet answered them: "I will pray to the LORD, your God, as you desire; whatever the LORD answers, I will tell you; I will withhold nothing from you."[a] 5And they said to Jeremiah, "May the LORD be a true and faithful witness against us if we do not follow all the instructions the LORD, your God, sends us through you.[b] 6Whether we like it or not, we will obey the command of the LORD, our God, to whom we are sending you, so that it may go well with us for obeying the command of the LORD, our God."[c]

7Ten days passed before the word of the LORD came to Jeremiah. 8Then he called Johanan, son of Kareah, his army leaders, and all the people, from the least to the greatest, 9and said to them: Thus says the LORD, the God of Israel, to whom you sent me to offer your petition: 10If indeed you will remain in this land, I will build you up, and not tear you down; I will plant you, not uproot you; for I repent of the evil I have done you.[d] 11Do not fear the king of Babylon, as you do now. Do not fear him—oracle of the LORD—for I am with you to save you, to rescue you from his power.[e] 12I will take pity on you, so that he will have pity on you and let you return to your land.[f] 13But if you keep saying, "We will not stay in this land," thus disobeying the voice of the LORD, your God, 14and saying, "No, we will go to the land of Egypt, where we will not see war, nor hear the trumpet alarm, nor hunger for bread. There we will live!"[g] 15then listen to the word of the LORD, remnant of Judah: Thus says the LORD of hosts, the God of Israel: If you are set on going to Egypt and settling down there once you arrive, 16the sword you fear shall overtake you in the land of Egypt; the hunger you dread shall pursue you to Egypt and there you shall die.[h] 17All those determined to go to Egypt to live shall die by the sword, famine, and disease: not one shall survive or escape the evil that I am bringing upon them.[i]

18For thus says the LORD of hosts, the God of Israel: Just as my furious wrath was poured out upon the inhabitants of Jerusalem, so shall my anger be poured out on you when you reach Egypt. You shall become a malediction and a horror, a curse and a reproach, and you shall never see this place again.[j]

19The LORD has spoken to you, remnant of Judah. Do not go to Egypt! Mark well that I am warning you this day. 20At the cost of your lives you have been deceitful, for you yourselves sent me to the LORD, your God, saying, "Pray for us to the LORD, our God; whatever the LORD, our God, shall say, tell us and we will do it." 21Today I have told you, but you have not listened to the voice of the LORD your God, in anything that he has sent me to tell you.[k] 22Have no doubt about this: you shall die by the sword, famine, and disease in the place where you want to go and live.[l]

## CHAPTER 43

See RG 217

1When Jeremiah finished telling the people all the words the LORD, their God, sent to them, 2Azariah, son of Hoshaiah, Johanan, son of Kareah, and all the others had the insolence to say to Jeremiah: "You lie; the LORD, our God, did not send you to tell us, 'Do not to go to Egypt to live there.' 3Baruch, son of Neriah, is inciting you against us, to hand us over to the Chaldeans to be killed or exiled to Babylon."[m]

---

*a:* 1 Sm 3:18. *b:* Jgs 11:10. *c:* Jer 7:23; Dt 5:33; 6:3. *d:* Jer 31:28; 32:41. *e:* Jer 30:10–11. *f:* Ps 106:45–46; Prv 16:7. *g:* Dt 28:68. *h:* Jer 44:13–14, 27. *i:* Jer 29:17–18; 44:14, 28. *j:* Jer 44:12. *k:* Zec 7:11–12. *l:* Jer 44:12; Hos 9:6. *m:* Jer 38:4.

## Emigration to Egypt

JEREMIAH IS AN ally of Babylon and an opponent of Egypt in the international power struggles that afflict Judah at this time. Chapters 42–44 reflect anti-Egyptian viewpoints. They accuse survivors who go to Egypt of refusing to listen and engaging in idolatry. Paradoxically, Jeremiah and his scribe Baruch are also forced into exile.

4 So Johanan, son of Kareah, and the rest of the leaders and the people did not listen to the voice of the LORD to stay in the land of Judah.[n] 5 Instead, Johanan, son of Kareah, and the military leaders took along all the remnant of Judah who had been dispersed among the nations and then had returned to dwell in the land of Judah: 6 men, women, and children, the princesses and everyone whom Nebuzaradan, captain of the bodyguard, had consigned to Gedaliah, son of Ahikam, son of Shaphan; also Jeremiah, the prophet, and Baruch, son of Neriah.[o] 7 They went to Egypt—they did not listen to the voice of the LORD—and came to Tahpanhes.[p]

***Jeremiah in Egypt.*** 8 The word of the LORD came to Jeremiah in Tahpanhes: 9 Take some large stones in your hand and set them in mortar in the terrace at the entrance to the house of Pharaoh in Tahpanhes, while the Judahites watch. 10 Then say to them: Thus says the LORD of hosts, the God of Israel: I will send for my servant Nebuchadnezzar, king of Babylon. He will place his throne upon these stones which I, Jeremiah, have set up, and stretch his canopy above them.[q] 11 He shall come and strike the land of Egypt: with death, those marked for death; with exile, those marked for exile; with the sword, those marked for the sword.[r] 12 He shall set fire to the temples of Egypt's gods, burn the gods and carry them off. He shall pick the land of Egypt clean, as a shepherd picks lice off his cloak, and then depart victorious.[s] 13 He shall smash the obelisks at the Temple of the Sun in the land of Egypt and destroy with fire the temples of the Egyptian gods.

### CHAPTER 44

See RG 217

1 The word that came to Jeremiah for all the Judahites who were living in Egypt, those living in Migdol, Tahpanhes, and Memphis, and in Upper Egypt: 2* Thus says the LORD of hosts, the God of Israel: You yourselves have seen all the evil I brought upon Jerusalem and the other cities of Judah. Today they lie in ruins uninhabited,[t] 3 because of the evil they did to provoke me, going after other gods, offering incense and serving other gods they did not know, neither they, nor you, nor your ancestors.[u] 4 Though I repeatedly sent you all my servants the prophets, saying: "You must not commit this abominable deed I hate," 5 they did not listen or incline their ears in order to turn from their evil, no longer offering incense to other gods.[v] 6 Therefore the fury of my anger poured forth and kindled fire in the cities of Judah and the streets of Jerusalem, to turn them into the ruined wasteland they are today.

7 Now thus says the LORD God of hosts, the God of Israel: Why inflict so great an evil upon yourselves, cutting off from Judah man and woman, child and infant, not leaving yourselves even a remnant? 8 Why do you provoke me with the works of your hands, offering sacrifice to other gods here in the land of Egypt where you have come to live? Will you cut yourselves off and become a curse, a reproach among all the nations of the earth?[w] 9 Have you forgotten the evil of your ancestors, the evil of the kings of Judah, the evil of their wives, and your own evil and the evil of your wives—all that they did in the

**44:2–30** Chronologically, these are the last of Jeremiah's words to his people. As the narrative ends, Jeremiah meets with rejection. According to tradition, recorded in a much later work, he was murdered in Egypt by fellow Judahites.

*n:* Jer 41:16. *o:* Jer 41:10. *p:* Jer 42:13–14; 44:1. *q:* Jer 27:6; Ez 29:19. *r:* Jer 46:13; Ez 30:10. *s:* Jer 46:25; Ez 30:13–14. *t:* Jer 34:22; Lv 26:32–33. *u:* Jer 11:17; Dt 32:17. *v:* Jer 7:24, 26; 19:4. *w:* Jer 25:6–7.

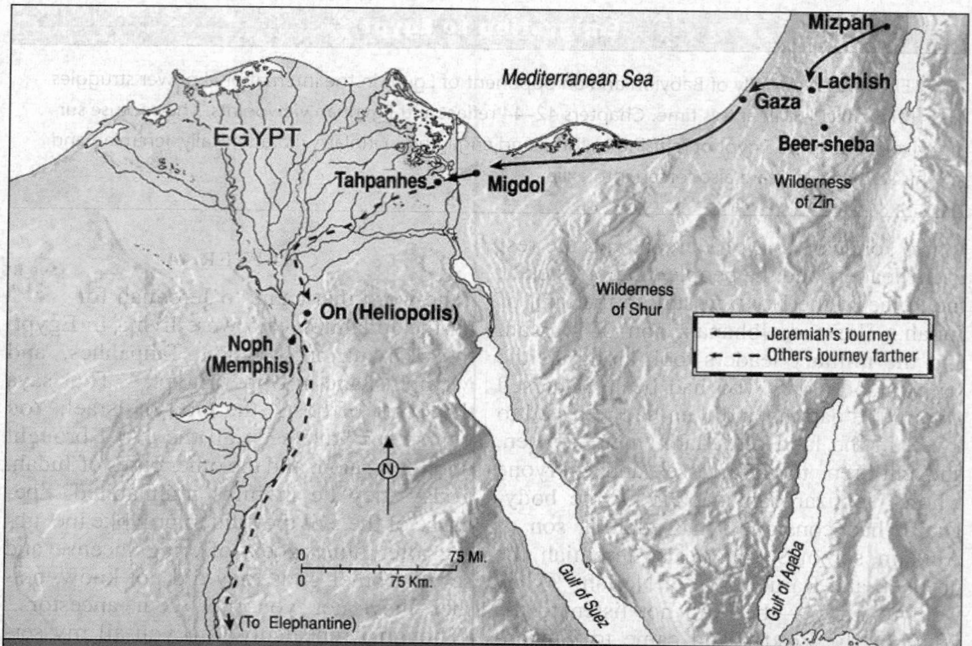


Jeremiah's Journey to Egypt

land of Judah and in the streets of Jerusalem?[x] [10]To this day they have not been
crushed down, nor have they shown fear.
They have not followed my law and my statutes that I set before you and your ancestors.[y]
[11]Therefore, thus says the LORD of hosts,
the God of Israel: I have set my face against
you for evil, to cut off all Judah. [12]I will take
away the remnant of Judah who insisted on
going to the land of Egypt to live there; in
the land of Egypt they shall meet their end.
They shall fall by the sword or be consumed
by hunger. From the least to the greatest,
they shall die by sword or hunger; they shall
become a malediction, a horror, a curse, a reproach.[z] [13]Thus I will punish those who live
in Egypt, just as I punished Jerusalem, with
sword, hunger, and disease, [14]so that none of
the remnant of Judah who came to live in the
land of Egypt shall escape or survive.[a] No
one shall return to the land of Judah. Even
though they long to return and live there,
they shall not return except as refugees.
[15]They answered Jeremiah—all the men
who knew that their wives were offering
sacrifices to other gods, all the women
standing there in the immense crowd, and all
the people who lived in Lower and Upper
Egypt: [16]"Regarding the word you have spoken to us in the name of the LORD, we are not
listening to you.[b] [17]Rather we will go on doing what we proposed; we will offer incense
to the Queen of Heaven and pour out libations to her, just as we have done, along with
our ancestors, our kings and princes, in the
cities of Judah and in the streets of Jerusalem. Then we had plenty to eat, we prospered, and we suffered no misfortune.[c] [18]But
ever since we stopped offering sacrifices to
the Queen of Heaven and pouring out libations to her, we lack everything and are being destroyed by sword and hunger." [19]And
the women said, "When we offered sacrifices to the Queen of Heaven and poured out
libations to her, did we bake cakes in her image and pour out libations to her without our
husbands' consent?"[d]
[20]To all the people, men and women, who

*x:* 1 Kgs 11:1, 8; Ezr 9:7, 14. *y:* Jer 7:24. *z:* Jer 42:15, 18, 22. *a:* Jer 43:11. *b:* Jer 6:16–17. *c:* Jer 5:3; 7:18. *d:* Jer 7:18.

gave him this answer, Jeremiah said: 21 As for the sacrifices you offered in the cities of Judah and in the streets of Jerusalem—you, your ancestors, your kings and princes, and the people of the land—did not the LORD remember them? Did it not enter his mind?[e] 22 The LORD could no longer bear the evil of your deeds, the abominations you were doing; then your land became a waste, a horror, a curse, without even one inhabitant, as it is today.[f] 23 Because you offered sacrifice and sinned against the LORD, not listening to the voice of the LORD, not following his law, his statutes, and his decrees, therefore this evil has overtaken you, as it is today.[g]

24 Jeremiah said to all the people and to all the women: Hear the word of the LORD, all you Judahites in the land of Egypt: 25 Thus says the LORD of hosts, the God of Israel: You and your wives have carried out with your hands what your mouths have spoken: "We will go on fulfilling the vows we have made to offer sacrifice to the Queen of Heaven and to pour out libations to her." Very well! keep your vows, fulfill your vows! 26 And then listen to the word of the LORD, all you Judahites living in Egypt; I swear by my own great name, says the LORD: in the whole land of Egypt, my name shall no longer be pronounced by the lips of any Judahite, saying, "As the Lord GOD lives." 27 I am watching over them for evil, not for good. All the Judahites in Egypt shall come to an end by sword or famine until they are completely destroyed.[h] 28 Those who escape the sword to return from the land of Egypt to the land of Judah shall be few in number. The whole remnant of Judah who came to Egypt to live shall know whose word stands, mine or theirs.[i]

29 And this shall be a sign to you—oracle of the LORD—I will punish you in this place so that you will know that my words stand solidly against you for evil. 30 Thus says the LORD: See! I will hand over Pharaoh Hophra,* king of Egypt, to his enemies, to those seeking his life, just as I handed over Zedekiah, king of Judah, to his enemy Nebuchadrezzar, king of Babylon, to the one seeking his life.[j]

## CHAPTER 45

See RG 217

*A Message to Baruch.** 1 The word that Jeremiah the prophet spoke to Baruch, son of Neriah, when he wrote on a scroll words from Jeremiah's own mouth in the fourth year of Jehoiakim, son of Josiah, king of Judah:[k] 2 Thus says the LORD, God of Israel, to you, Baruch. 3 You said, "Woe is me! the LORD has added grief to my pain.[l] I have worn myself out with groaning; rest eludes me." 4 You must say this to him. Thus says the LORD: What I have built, I am tearing down; what I have planted, I am uprooting: all this land.[m] 5 And you, do you seek great things for yourself? Do not seek them! I am bringing evil on all flesh—oracle of the LORD—but I will grant you your life as spoils of war, wherever you may go.[n]

# VIII. Oracles Against the Nations*

## CHAPTER 46

See RG 218

1 The word of the LORD that came to Jeremiah the prophet concerning the nations.

*Against Egypt.* 2 Concerning Egypt. Against the army of Pharaoh Neco, king of Egypt, defeated at Carchemish on the Euphrates* by Nebuchadrezzar, king of Babylon, in the fourth year of Jehoiakim, son of Josiah, king of Judah:

**44:30 Hophra**: killed by his own people. Hophra's successor, Amasis, ruled Egypt when Nebuchadnezzar took control of the country.

**45:1–5** At the conclusion of his narrative, Baruch appends a message Jeremiah had given him when he first wrote down Jeremiah's words (cf. 36:4). The future revealed by the prophet overwhelmed Baruch; now he learns his own safety is assured, even though the Lord will destroy Judah.

**46:1–51:64** A collection of oracles against foreign nations constitutes the final section of the Hebrew text of Jeremiah; in the Greek text they follow 25:13. The oracles here appear to be arranged in loose chronological order: 46:2 mentions the fourth year of Jehoiakim; the oracles in 50:1–51:64 are evidently from the end of Jeremiah's life.

**46:2 Carchemish on the Euphrates**: the western terminus of the Mesopotamian trade route, where Nebuchadnezzar defeated Pharaoh Neco in 605 B.C., thus gaining undisputed control of Syria and Palestine.

*e:* Jer 11:13. *f:* Jer 15:6. *g:* 2 Kgs 17:15; Dn 9:11–12. *h:* Ezr 7:3–7. *i:* Dt 28:62; Is 10:22. *j:* Jer 39:5–7; 46:25–26; Ez 29:3–4; 30:21. *k:* Jer 36:4, 18, 32. *l:* Lam 1:3; 5:5. *m:* Jer 18:7; Is 5:5–6. *n:* Jer 25:26–29.

3 Prepare buckler and shield!
move forward to battle!
4 Harness the horses,
charioteers, mount up!
Fall in, with helmets on;
polish your spears, put on your armor.
5 What do I see?
Are they panicking, falling apart?
Their warriors are hammered back,
They flee headlong
never making a stand.
Terror on every side—
oracle of the LORD![o]
6 The swift cannot flee,
nor the warrior escape:
There up north, on the banks of the
Euphrates
they stumble and fall.
7 Who is this? Like the Nile, it rears up;
like rivers, its waters surge.
8 Egypt rears up like the Nile,
like rivers, its waters surge.
"I will rear up," it says, "and cover the
earth,
destroying the city and its people.[p]
9 Forward, horses!
charge, chariots!
March forth, warriors,
Cush and Put, bearing shields,
Archers of Lud, stretching bows!"
10 Today belongs to the Lord GOD of hosts,
a day of vengeance, vengeance on his
foes!
The sword devours and is sated, drunk
with their blood:
for the Lord GOD of hosts holds a
sacrifice
in the land of the north, on the River
Euphrates.[q]
11 Go up to Gilead, procure balm,
Virgin daughter Egypt!
No use to multiply remedies;
for you there is no healing.[r]
12 The nations hear your cries,
your screaming fills the earth.
Warrior stumbles against warrior,
both collapse together.[s]

13[t] The word that the LORD spoke to Jeremiah the prophet when Nebuchadrezzar,
king of Babylon, came to attack the land of
Egypt:*

14 Proclaim in Egypt, announce in Migdol,
announce in Memphis and Tahpanhes!
Say: Fall in, get ready,
the sword has devoured your
neighbors.[u]
15 Why has Apis* fled?
Your champion did not stand,
Because the LORD thrust him down;
16 he stumbled repeatedly then collapsed.
They said to each other,
"Get up! We must return to our own
people,
To the land of our birth,
away from the destroying sword."[v]
17 Give Pharaoh, king of Egypt, the name
"Braggart-missed-his-chance."*
18 As I live, says the King
whose name is LORD of hosts,
Like Tabor above mountains,
like Carmel* above the sea, he comes.
19 Pack your bags for exile,
enthroned daughter Egypt;
Memphis shall become a wasteland,
an empty ruin.
20 Egypt is a beautiful heifer,
a horsefly from the north keeps
coming.
21 Even the mercenaries in her ranks
are like fattened calves;
They too turn and flee together—
they do not stand their ground,
For their day of ruin comes upon them,
their time of punishment.
22 Her voice is like a snake!

**46:13** In 601 B.C. Nebuchadnezzar advanced into Egypt itself, but finally had to withdraw to Syria.

**46:15 Apis**: the chief god of Memphis; the black bull honored as an incarnation of the god Ptah and, later, of the god Osiris.

**46:17 "Braggart-missed-his-chance"**: the Hebrew phrase may contain a pun on the Pharaoh's name or royal title.

**46:18 Tabor . . . Carmel:** mountains in Palestine that seem to tower over their surroundings as Nebuchadnezzar towers over the nations in his path as he makes his way toward Egypt.

*o:* Jer 6:25; 49:29. *p:* Ez 29:3; 32:2. *q:* Dt 32:42; Is 13:9; Ez 39:17–20. *r:* Jer 8:22; 51:8; Ez 30:21–22. *s:* Ez 32:9–12. *t:* Jer 43:10–11; 44:30; Is 19:1. *u:* Jer 44:1. *v:* Lv 26:37.

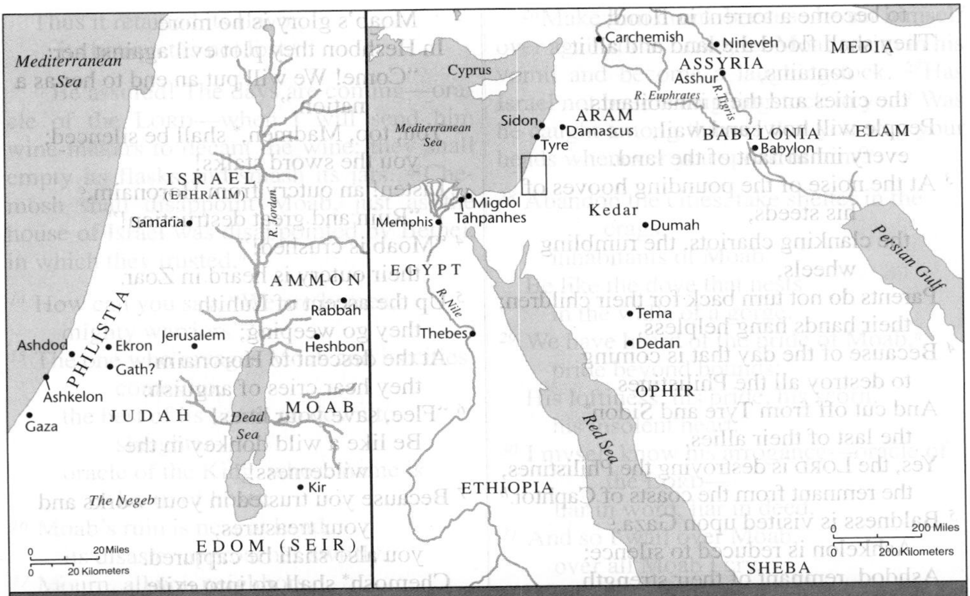

**Places Mentioned in the Oracles against the Nations**

Yes, they come in force;
They attack her with axes,
like those who fell trees.
23 They cut down her forest—oracle of the LORD—
impenetrable though it be;
More numerous than locusts,
they cannot be counted.
24 Shamed is daughter Egypt,
handed over to a people from the north.

25 The LORD of hosts, the God of Israel, has said: See! I will punish Amon* of Thebes and Egypt, gods, kings, Pharaoh, and those who trust in him.[w] 26 I will hand them over to those who seek their lives, to Nebuchadrezzar, king of Babylon, and to his officers. But later, Egypt shall be inhabited again, as in days of old—oracle of the LORD.[x]

27 But you, my servant Jacob, do not fear;
do not be dismayed, Israel!
Listen! I will deliver you from far-off lands;
your offspring, from the land of their exile.
Jacob shall again find rest,
secure, with none to frighten him.[y]
28 You, Jacob my servant, must not fear—
oracle of the LORD—
for I am with you;
I will make an end of all the nations
to which I have driven you,
But of you I will not make an end:
I will chastise you as you deserve,
I cannot let you go unpunished.[z]

## CHAPTER 47

See RG 218

*Against the Philistines.* 1 The word of the LORD that came to Jeremiah the prophet concerning the Philistines, before Pharaoh attacked Gaza:[a]

2 Thus says the LORD:
* See: waters are rising from the north,

**46:25 Amon**: the sun-god worshiped at Thebes in Upper Egypt.

**47:2–7** Nebuchadnezzar's military campaign against Ashkelon in 604 B.C. may provide some historical background for this poem.

*w:* Ez 30:15–16. *x:* Jer 44:30; Ez 30:4; 32:11–12. *y:* Jer 30:10; 43:5. *z:* Jer 30:11. *a:* Ez 25:15–16; Zep 2:4.

loins are draped in sackcloth.[s] 38 On all the
rooftops of Moab and in all its squares there is
mourning. I have shattered Moab like a pot
that no one wants—oracle of the LORD. 39 How
terrified they are, how they wail! How Moab
turns its back in shame! Moab has become a
laughingstock and a horror to all its neighbors!

40 For thus says the LORD:
Look there! Like an eagle he swoops,
spreading his wings over Moab.[t]
41 Cities are captured,
strongholds seized:
On that day the hearts of Moab's warriors
become like the heart of a woman in
labor.[u]
42 Moab shall be wiped out, a people no
more,
because it set itself over against the
LORD.[v]
43 Terror, pit, and trap be upon you,
enthroned Moab—oracle of the LORD.[w]
44 Those fleeing the terror
fall into the pit;
Those climbing out of the pit
are caught in the trap;
Ah, yes! I will bring these things upon
Moab
in the year of their punishment—
oracle of the LORD.
45 In Heshbon's shadow the fugitives
stop short, exhausted;
For fire blazes up from Heshbon,
and flames up from the house of Sihon:
It consumes the forehead of Moab,
the scalp of the noisemakers.[x]
46 Woe to you, Moab!
You are finished, people of Chemosh!
Your sons are taken into exile,
your daughters into captivity.
47 Yet I will restore the fortunes of Moab
in the days to come—oracle of the
LORD.[y]

Thus far the judgment on Moab.

## CHAPTER 49

See RG 218

*Against the Ammonites.* 1 Concerning
the Ammonites. Thus says the LORD:

Has Israel no sons?
none to inherit?
Why has Milcom* disinherited Gad,
why are his people living in its cities?
2 Therefore the days are coming—oracle
of the LORD—
when I will sound the battle alarm
against Rabbah of the Ammonites;
It shall become a mound of ruins,
and its villages destroyed by fire.
Israel shall then inherit those who
disinherited it—
oracle of the LORD.[z]
3 Wail, Heshbon, "The ruin is destroyed!"
shriek, villages of Rabbah!
Put on sackcloth and lament!
Run back and forth in the sheepfolds.
For Milcom is going into exile,
taking priest and prince with him.[a]
4 Why boast in your strength,
your ebbing strength, rebellious
daughter?
Why trust in your treasures, saying,
"Who would dare attack me?"
5 See, I am bringing terror upon you—
oracle of the Lord GOD of hosts—
from all around you;
You shall be scattered, each in headlong
flight,
with no one to gather the fugitives.[b]
6 But afterward I will restore the fortunes
of the Ammonites—oracle of the
LORD.

*Against Edom.** 7 Concerning Edom. Thus
says the LORD of hosts:

Is there no more wisdom in Teman,*
has counsel perished from the prudent,
is their wisdom gone?
8 Flee, retreat, hide deep for lodging,

**49:1 Milcom**: chief god of the Ammonites (cf. 1 Kgs 11:5). The Ammonites shared a border with Gad, an Israelite tribe in Transjordan (Jos 13:8–10); the Ammonites occupied its territory after the collapse of the Northern Kingdom.

**49:7–22 Edom**: southeast of the Dead Sea, a traditional enemy who profited from Judah's downfall; cf. Ps 137:7; Lam 4:21–22; Ob 11–12.

**49:7** Teman, a district of Edom (cf. Jb 2:11), represents the whole country, which was famous for the wisdom of its sages.

*s:* Jer 47:5; Is 15:2–3; Ez 7:18. *t:* Jer 49:22. *u:* Jer 6:24; 30:6. *v:* Zep 2:9–10. *w:* Is 24:17–18. *x:* Nm 21:28–29. *y:* Jer 49:39. *z:* Am 1:14. *a:* Is 15:2–5. *b:* Jer 48:47.

inhabitants of Dedan:
For I bring disaster upon Esau*
when I come to punish them.[c]
9 If vintagers came upon you,
they would leave no gleanings;
If thieves by night,
they would destroy as they pleased.[d]
10 So I myself will strip Esau;
I will uncover his lairs so he cannot hide.
Offspring and family are destroyed,
neighbors, too; he is no more.[e]
11 Leave your orphans behind, I will keep them alive;
your widows, let them trust in me.[f]

12 For thus says the LORD: Look, even those
not sentenced to drink the cup must drink it!
Shall you then go unpunished? You shall not!
You shall drink every bit of it![g] 13 By myself I
have sworn—oracle of the LORD—Bozrah*
shall become an object of horror, a disgrace, a
desolation, and a curse. Bozrah and all its cities shall become ruins forever.[h]

14 I have heard a report from the LORD,
a herald has been sent among the nations:
"Gather together, move against it,
get ready for battle!"
15 I will make you the least among the nations,
despised by all people![i]
16 The terror you spread,
the pride of your heart, beguiled you.
You denizens of rocks and crevices,
occupying towering peaks:
Though you build your nest high as the eagle,
from there I will bring you down—
oracle of the LORD.[j]

17 Edom shall become an object of horror.
Passersby recoil in terror, hissing at all its
wounds. 18 As when Sodom, Gomorrah, and
their neighbors were overthrown—oracle of
the LORD—no one shall live in it, nor anyone
settle there.[k]

19 As when a lion comes up from a thicket of the Jordan
to a permanent pasture,
So in an instant, I will chase them off;
I will establish there whomever I choose.
For who is like me? Who holds me accountable?
What shepherd can stand against me?[l]
20 Therefore, listen to the strategy
the LORD devised for Edom;
The plans he has drawn up
against the inhabitants of Teman:
They shall be dragged away, even the smallest of the flock;
their pasture shall be aghast because of them.
21 With the din of their collapse the earth quakes,
to the Red Sea the outcry is heard!
22 Look! like an eagle he soars aloft,
and spreads his wings over Bozrah;
On that day the hearts of Edom's warriors become
like the heart of a woman in labor.[m]

*Against Damascus.* 23 Concerning Damascus.

Hamath and Arpad* are shamed,
for they have heard bad news;
Anxious, they surge like the sea
which cannot calm down.[n]
24 Damascus loses heart, turns to flee;
panic has seized it.
Distress and pangs take hold,
like the pain of a woman in labor.
25 How can the glorious city be abandoned,
the town of joy!
26 But now its young men shall fall in its squares,
all the warriors destroyed on that day—
oracle of the LORD of hosts.

**49:8 Esau**: Jacob's brother, the traditional ancestor of the Edomites; cf. Gn 36:1.

**49:13 Bozrah**: capital of Edom.

**49:23 Hamath and Arpad**: independent Aramean states north of Damascus, the direction from which the invasion is coming. Cf. Is 10:9–10.

*c:* Ez 25:13. *d:* Ob 5. *e:* Mal 1:3. *f:* Dt 10:18; Ps 68:6. *g:* Jer 25:15, 28; Lam 4:21–22. *h:* Is 34:6; Ez 35:3–9; Ob 16. *i:* Ob 2. *j:* Jer 48:29–30. *k:* Jer 50:40; Dt 29:23. *l:* Jer 12:5; 25:9; 50:44–45. *m:* Jer 4:13. *n:* Is 36:19; 37:13.

27 I will set fire to the wall of Damascus;
it shall devour the palaces of Ben-hadad.*

*Against Arabia.* 28 About Kedar and the kingdoms of Hazor, which Nebuchadnezzar, king of Babylon, defeated.

Thus says the LORD:
Rise up, attack Kedar,
destroy the people from the east.[o]
29 Their tents and flocks shall be taken away,
their tent curtains and all their goods;
Their camels they carry off,
they shout over them, "Terror on every side!"[p]
30 Flee! wander about, hide deep for lodging,
inhabitants of Hazor—oracle of the LORD;
For Nebuchadnezzar, king of Babylon,
has devised a strategy against you,
drawn up a plan against you,
31 Get up! set out against a tranquil nation,
living in security—oracle of the LORD—
Without gates or bars,
dwelling alone.
32 Their camels shall become spoils,
their hordes of cattle, plunder;
I will scatter to the winds those who shave their temples;
from every side I will bring their ruin—
oracle of the LORD.[q]
33 Hazor shall become a haunt for jackals,
a wasteland forever,
Where no one lives,
no mortal stays.

*Against Elam.* 34 The word of the LORD that came to Jeremiah the prophet concerning Elam* at the beginning of the reign of Zedekiah, king of Judah:

35 Thus says the LORD of hosts:
Look! I will break the bow of Elam,
the mainstay of their might.
36 I will bring upon Elam the four winds
from the four ends of the heavens:
I will scatter them to all these winds,
until there is no nation
to which the outcasts of Elam have not gone.
37 I will terrify Elam before their foes,
those seeking their life;
I will bring evil upon them,
my burning wrath—oracle of the LORD.
I will send sword after them
until I have finished them off;
38 I will set up my throne in Elam
and destroy from there king and princes—
oracle of the LORD.
39 But at the end of days I will restore
the fortunes of Elam—oracle of the LORD.

## CHAPTER 50

See RG 218

*The First Oracle Against Babylon.*
1 The word the LORD spoke against Babylon,* against the land of the Chaldeans, through Jeremiah the prophet:[r]

2 Proclaim this among the nations,
announce it!
Announce it, do not hide it, but say:
Babylon is captured, Bel* put to shame,
Marduk terrified;
its images are put to shame, its idols shattered.
3 A nation from the north advances against it,
making the land desolate
So that no one can live there;
human beings and animals have fled.[s]
4 In those days and at that time—oracle of the LORD—
Israelite and Judahite shall come together,

**49:27 Ben-hadad**: a dynastic name for some of the kings who ruled in Damascus; cf. 1 Kgs 15:18, 20.

**49:34 Elam**: an ancient kingdom east of Babylonia.

**50:1–51:58** A collection of miscellaneous oracles against Babylon introducing the story in 51:59–64.

**50:2 Bel**: originally the title of the god of Nippur in Mesopotamia, later associated with *Merodach* (Marduk), chief god of Babylon (cf. Is 46:1).

*o:* Is 21:16. *p:* Jer 4:20. *q:* Jer 9:25. *r:* Jer 51:1; Is 13:1–14; 21:1–10. *s:* Jer 51:48; Is 13:17.

Weeping as they come, to seek the LORD,
their God;[t]
5 They shall ask for Zion,
seeking out the way.
"Come, let us join ourselves to the LORD
in an everlasting covenant, never to be
forgotten."[u]
6 Lost sheep were my people,
their shepherds misled them,
leading them astray on the mountains;
From mountain to hill they wandered,
forgetting their fold.[v]
7 Whoever happened upon them devoured
them;
their enemies said, "We are not guilty,
Because they sinned against the LORD,
the abode of justice, the hope of their
ancestors."[w]
8 Flee from the midst of Babylon,
leave the land of the Chaldeans,
be like rams at the head of the flock.[x]
9 See, I am stirring up against Babylon
a band of great nations from the land
of the north;
They are arrayed against her,
from there she shall be taken.
Their arrows are like the arrows of a
skilled warrior
who never returns empty-handed.[y]
10 Chaldea shall become plunder;
all its plunderers shall be enriched—
oracle of the LORD.
11 Yes, rejoice and exult,
you that plunder my heritage;
Frisk like calves on the grass,
neigh like stallions!
12 Your mother will indeed be put to shame,
she that bore you shall be abashed;
See, the last of the nations,
a wilderness, a dry wasteland.[z]
13 Because of the LORD's wrath it shall be
uninhabited,
become an utter wasteland;
Everyone who passes by Babylon will be
appalled
and hiss at all its wounds.[a]
14 Take your posts encircling Babylon,
you who bend the bow;
Shoot at it, do not spare your arrows,[b]
15 raise the war cry against it on every
side.
It surrenders, its bastions fall,
its walls are torn down:*
This is retribution from the LORD! Take
retribution on her,
as she has done, do to her;
for she sinned against the LORD.[c]
16 Cut off the sower from Babylon
and those who wield sickles at harvest
time!
Before the destroying sword,
all of them turn back to their own
people,
all flee to their own land.[d]
17 Israel was a stray sheep
that lions pursued;
The king of Assyria once devoured him;
now Nebuchadnezzar of Babylon
gnaws his bones.[e]
18 Therefore, thus says the LORD of hosts,
the God of Israel:
I will punish the king of Babylon and his
land,
as I once punished the king of
Assyria;[f]
19 But I will bring Israel back to its
pasture,
to feed on Carmel and Bashan,
And on Mount Ephraim and Gilead,
until they have their fill.[g]

20 In those days, at that time—oracle of the LORD:

The guilt of Israel may be sought, but it
no longer exists,
the sin of Judah, but it can no longer
be found;
for I will forgive the remnant I
preserve.[h]
21 Attack the land of Merathaim,

**50:15 Its walls are torn down**: the prophet describes the downfall of Babylon in conventional language. Babylon surrendered peacefully to the Persians in 539 B.C.

*t:* Jer 3:18; Ps 126:6. *u:* Jer 31:31; 32:40. *v:* Is 53:6; 1 Pt 2:25. *w:* Jer 31:23. *x:* Jer 51:6, 45; Is 48:20. *y:* Jer 51:27. *z:* Jer 51:43; Is 13:20–22. *a:* Jer 25:12. *b:* Jer 51:11; Is 21:2. *c:* Jer 51:11, 44, 58; Ps 137:8. *d:* Is 13:14. *e:* 2 Kgs 17:24; 18:14. *f:* Is 10:12; 14:24–25. *g:* Jer 23:3; Ez 34:13–14. *h:* Jer 31:34; Is 43:25; Mi 7:19.

and those who live in Pekod;*
Slaughter and put them under the ban—
oracle of the LORD—
do all I have commanded you.
22 Battle alarm in the land,
great destruction!
23 How the hammer of the whole earth
has been cut off and broken!
What an object of horror
Babylon has become among the
nations![i]
24 You ensnared yourself and were caught,
Babylon, before you knew it!
You were discovered and seized,
because you challenged the LORD.[j]
25 The LORD opens his armory,
brings out the weapons of his wrath;
The Lord GOD of hosts has work to do
in the land of the Chaldeans.[k]
26 Come upon them from every side,
open their granaries,
Pile them up in heaps and put them under
the ban;
do not leave a remnant.
27 Slay all the oxen,
take them down to slaughter;
Woe to them! their day has come,
the time of their punishment.
28 Listen! the fugitives, the refugees
from the land of Babylon:
They announce in Zion
the retribution of the LORD, our God.[l]
29 Call archers out against Babylon,
all who bend the bow;
Encamp around them;
let no one escape.
Repay them for their deeds;
what they have done, do to them,
For they insulted the LORD,
the Holy One of Israel.[m]
30 Therefore their young men shall fall in
the squares,
all their warriors shall be stilled on
that day—
oracle of the LORD.[n]
31 I am against you, O Insolence—
oracle of the Lord GOD of hosts;
For your day has come,
the time for me to punish you.
32 Insolence stumbles and falls;
there is no one to raise him up.
I will kindle a fire in his cities
to devour everything around him.
33 Thus says the LORD of hosts:
Oppressed are the people of Israel,
together with the people of Judah;
All their captors hold them fast
and refuse to let them go.
34 Strong is their Redeemer,
whose name is LORD of hosts,
The sure defender of their cause,
who gives rest to their land,
but unrest to those who live in
Babylon.[o]
35 A sword upon the Chaldeans—oracle of
the LORD—
upon the inhabitants of Babylon, her
princes and sages!
36 A sword upon the soothsayers,
and they become fools!
A sword upon the warriors,
and they tremble;
37 A sword upon their motley throng,
and they become women!
A sword upon their treasures,
and they are plundered;[p]
38 A drought upon the waters,
and they dry up!
For it is a land of idols,
soon made frantic by phantoms.[q]
39 Hence, wildcats shall dwell there with
hyenas,
and ostriches occupy it;
Never again shall it be inhabited or settled,
from age to age.[r]
40 As happened when God overturned
Sodom
and Gomorrah and their neighbors—
oracle of the LORD—
No one shall dwell there,
no mortal shall settle there.[s]
41 See, a people comes from the north,

**50:21 Merathaim . . . Pekod**: "twice bitter," "punishment," symbolic terms for Babylon that recall the names of regions in the country.

*i:* Jer 51:20; Is 14:6. *j:* Jer 51:57. *k:* Jer 51:11–12; Is 13:5. *l:* Jer 51:10–11. *m:* Jer 51:56. *n:* Jer 49:26; 51:4. *o:* Jer 51:36. *p:* Jer 51:30; Na 3:13. *q:* Jer 51:32, 36. *r:* Jer 51:37; Is 13:21–22. *s:* Jer 51:43.

a great nation, and mighty kings
rising from the ends of the earth.[t]
42 Bow and javelin they wield,
cruel and pitiless are they;
They sound like the roaring sea,
as they ride forth on horses,
Each in place for battle
against you, daughter Babylon.
43 The king of Babylon hears news of them,
and his hands hang helpless;
Anguish takes hold of him,
like the pangs of a woman giving birth.[u]
44 As happens when a lion comes up from a thicket of the Jordan
to permanent pasture,
So I, in an instant, will chase them off,
and establish there whomever I choose!
For who is like me? Who can call me to account?
What shepherd can stand against me?[v]
45 Therefore, hear the strategy of the LORD,
which he has devised against Babylon;
Hear the plans drawn up
against the land of the Chaldeans:
They shall be dragged away, even the smallest sheep;
their own pasture aghast because of them.[w]
46 At the cry "Babylon is captured!" the earth quakes;
the outcry is heard among the nations.[x]

## CHAPTER 51

See RG 218

### *The Second Oracle Against Babylon*

1 Thus says the LORD:
See! I rouse against Babylon,
and the inhabitants of Chaldea,
a destroyer wind.*
2 To Babylon I will send winnowers
to winnow and lay waste the land;
They shall besiege it on every side
on the day of affliction.[y]
3 How can the archers draw back their bows,
lift their armor?
Do not spare her young men,
put the entire army under the ban.[z]
4 The slain shall fall in the land of Chaldea,
the wounded, in its streets;[a]
5 For Israel and Judah are not left widowed
by their God, the LORD of hosts,
Even though the land is full of guilt
against the Holy One of Israel.
6 Flee from Babylon;
each of you save your own life,
do not perish because of her guilt;
This is a time of retribution from the LORD,
7 who pays out her due.[b]
Babylon was a golden cup in the hand of the LORD
making the whole earth drunk;
The nations drank its wine,
thus they have gone mad.[c]
8 Babylon suddenly falls and is broken:
wail over her!
Bring balm for her wounds,
in case she can be healed.[d]
9 "We have tried to heal Babylon,
but she cannot be healed.
Leave her, each of us must go to our own land."
The judgment against her reaches the heavens,
it touches the clouds.[e]
10 The LORD has brought forth our vindication;
come, let us tell in Zion
what the LORD, our God, has done.[f]
11 Sharpen the arrows,
fill the quivers;
The LORD has stirred up the spirit of the kings of the Medes,*
for his resolve is Babylon's destruction.
Yes, it is retribution from the LORD,
retribution for his temple.[g]
12 Over the walls of Babylon raise a signal,
reinforce the watch;

**51:1** The destroyer wind is the fierce dry wind from the east (cf. 4:11).
**51:11 Kings of the Medes**: the Medes and the Persians lived in the area known today as Iran.

*t:* Jer 51:27–28. *u:* Is 13:7. *v:* Jer 49:19. *w:* Jer 51:12, 29. *x:* Jer 51:29. *y:* Jer 15:7; Is 41:16. *z:* Jer 50:14, 29. *a:* Jer 50:30. *b:* Jer 50:8, 15, 29; Is 48:20. *c:* Rev 14:8; 17:4. *d:* Rev 18:9–18. *e:* Is 13:14; Rev 18:5. *f:* Jer 50:28. *g:* 2 Kgs 17:6; Is 13:17.

Post sentries,
arrange ambushes!
For the LORD has both planned and carried out
what he spoke against the inhabitants of Babylon.
13 You who dwell by mighty waters,
rich in treasure,
Your end has come,
the time at which you shall be cut off![h]
14 The LORD of hosts has sworn by himself:
I will fill you with people as numerous as locusts,
who shall raise over you a joyous shout!
15 He made the earth by his power,
established the world by wisdom,
and by his skill stretched out the heavens.[i]
16 When he thunders, the waters in the heavens roar,
he summons clouds from the ends of the earth,
Makes lightning flash in the rain,
and brings out winds from their storehouses.
17 Every man is stupid, ignorant;
every artisan is put to shame by his idol:
He molds a fraud,
without life-breath.
18 They are nothing, a ridiculous work,
that will perish at the time of punishment.
19 Jacob's portion is nothing like them:
he is the creator of all things.
Israel is his very own tribe;
LORD of hosts is his name.
20 You are my hammer,
a weapon for war;
With you I shatter nations,
with you I destroy kingdoms.
21 With you I shatter horse and rider,
with you I shatter chariot and driver.[j]
22 With you I shatter man and woman,
with you I shatter old and young,
with you I shatter the young man and young woman.[k]
23 With you I shatter shepherd and flock,
with you I shatter farmer and team,
with you I shatter governors and officers.
24 Thus I will repay Babylon,
all the inhabitants of Chaldea,
For all the evil they committed against Zion,
before your very eyes—oracle of the LORD.[l]
25 Beware! I am against you,
destroying mountain—oracle of the LORD—
destroyer of the entire earth,
I will stretch forth my hand against you,
roll you down over the cliffs,
and make you a burnt mountain:[m]
26 They will not take from you a cornerstone,
or a foundation stone;
You shall remain ruins forever—
oracle of the LORD.[n]
27 Raise a signal in the land,
sound the trumpet among the nations;
Dedicate nations for war against her,
summon against her the kingdoms:
Ararat, Minni, and Ashkenaz;*
Appoint a recruiting officer against her,
dispatch horses like bristling locusts.[o]
28 Dedicate nations for war against her:
the king of the Medes,
Its governors and all its officers,
every land in its domain.
29 The earth quakes and writhes,
the LORD's plan against Babylon is carried out,
Turning the land of Babylon
into a wasteland without inhabitants.
30 Babylon's warriors have ceased to fight,
they remain in their strongholds;
Dried up is their strength,
they have become women.
Burned down are their homes,
broken their gates.
31 One runner meets another,
herald meets herald,
Telling the king of Babylon

**51:27 Ararat, Minni, and Ashkenaz**: regions in eastern Asia Minor under the control of the Medes.

*h:* Na 2:1. *i:* Jer 10:12. *j:* Dn 7:7, 19, 23. *k:* Is 13:16, 18. *l:* Jer 25:14; 50:29; Ps 137:8. *m:* Rev 8:7; 18:8–9. *n:* Jer 25:12; Ps 118:22. *o:* Na 3:17.

that his entire city has been taken.[p]
32 The fords have been seized,
marshes set on fire,
warriors panic.

33 For thus says the LORD of hosts, the God of Israel:

Daughter Babylon is like a threshing
floor
at the time of treading;
Yet a little while,
and the harvest time will come for
her.[q]
34 "He consumed me, defeated me,
Nebuchadnezzar, king of Babylon;
he left me like an empty vessel,
Swallowed me like a sea monster,
filled his belly with my delicacies and
cast me out.
35 Let my torn flesh be visited upon
Babylon,"
says enthroned Zion;
"My blood upon the inhabitants of
Chaldea,"
says Jerusalem.
36 But now, thus says the LORD:
I will certainly defend your cause,
I will certainly avenge you;
I will dry up her sea,
and drain her fountain.
37 Babylon shall become a heap of ruins,
a haunt of jackals;
A place of horror and hissing,
without inhabitants.[r]
38 They roar like lions,
growl like lion cubs.[s]
39 When they are parched, I will set drink
before them
to make them drunk, that they may be
overcome
with everlasting sleep, never to
awaken—
oracle of the LORD.
40 I will bring them down like lambs to
slaughter,
like rams and goats.
41 How she has been seized, taken captive,
the glory of the whole world!
What a horror Babylon has become
among the nations:[t]
42 against Babylon the sea rises,
she is overwhelmed by roaring waves!
43 Her cities have become wasteland,
a parched and arid land
Where no one lives,
no one passes through.
44 I will punish Bel in Babylon,
and make him vomit up what he
swallowed;
nations shall no longer stream to him.
Even the wall of Babylon falls!
45 Leave her, my people; each of you
save your own life
from the burning wrath of the LORD.

46 Do not be discouraged when rumors
spread through the land; this year one rumor
comes, next year another: "Violence in the
land!" or "Ruler against ruler!"[u] 47 Realize
that the days are coming when I will punish
the idols of Babylon; the whole land shall be
put to shame, all her slain shall fall in her
midst. 48 Then heaven and earth and everything in them shall shout over Babylon with
joy, when the destroyers come against her
from the north—oracle of the LORD.[v] 49 Babylon, too, must fall, you slain of Israel, because by the hand of Babylon the slain of all
the earth have fallen.

50 You who have escaped the sword,
go, do not stand idle;
Remember the LORD from far away,
let Jerusalem come to mind.
51 We are ashamed because we have heard
taunts,
disgrace covers our faces;
strangers have entered sanctuaries in
the LORD's house.[w]
52 Therefore see, the days are coming—
oracle of the LORD—
when I will punish her idols,
and throughout the land the wounded
will groan.
53 Though Babylon scale the heavens,
and make her strong heights
inaccessible,

*p:* 2 Chr 30:6; Jb 1:14–18. *q:* Rev 14:15. *r:* Is 25:2. *s:* Na 2:11–12. *t:* Is 13:19. *u:* Mt 24:6–7. *v:* Rev 18:20. *w:* Ps 44:16–17; 78:1–4.

my destroyers shall reach her—oracle
of the LORD.[x]
54 A sound of crying from Babylon,
great destruction from the land of the
Chaldeans;
55 For the LORD lays Babylon waste,
silences her loud cry,
Waves roaring like mighty waters,
a clamor resounding.
56 For the destroyer comes upon her, upon
Babylon;
warriors are captured, their bows
broken;
The LORD is a God of recompense,
he will surely repay.[y]

57 I will make her princes and sages drunk,
with her governors, officers, and warriors,
so that they sleep an everlasting sleep, never
to awaken—oracle of the King, whose name
is LORD of hosts.

58 Thus says the LORD of hosts:
The walls of spacious Babylon shall be
leveled to the ground,
its lofty gates destroyed by fire.
The toil of the peoples is for nothing;
the nations weary themselves for what
the flames consume.[z]

***The Prophecy Sent to Babylon.*** 59 The mission Jeremiah the prophet gave to Seraiah,*
son of Neriah, son of Mahseiah, when he
went to Babylon with King Zedekiah, king
of Judah, in the fourth year of his reign; Seraiah was chief quartermaster. 60 Jeremiah
wrote down on one scroll the disaster that
would befall Babylon;* all these words were
written against Babylon. 61 And Jeremiah
said to Seraiah: "When you reach Babylon,
see that you read all these words aloud,[a]
62 and then say: LORD, you yourself spoke
against this place in order to cut it down so
that nothing, human being or beast, could
live in it, because it is to remain a wasteland
forever. 63 When you have finished reading
this scroll, tie a stone to it and throw it into
the Euphrates,[b] 64 and say: Thus Babylon
shall sink. It will never rise, because of the
disaster I am bringing upon it." Thus far the
words of Jeremiah.

## IX. Historical Appendix*

### CHAPTER 52

See RG 218

***Capture of Jerusalem.*** 1 Zedekiah was
twenty-one years old when he became king;
he reigned eleven years in Jerusalem.[c] His
mother's name was Hamutal, daughter of
Jeremiah from Libnah. 2 He did what was evil
in the sight of the LORD, just as Jehoiakim
had done. 3 Indeed, the things done in Jerusalem and in Judah so angered the LORD that he
cast them out from his presence. Thus Zedekiah rebelled against the king of Babylon.
4[d] In the tenth month of the ninth year of his
reign, on the tenth day of the month,* Nebuchadnezzar, king of Babylon, and his entire
army advanced against Jerusalem, encamped
around it, and built siege walls on every side.
5 The siege of the city continued until the
eleventh year of King Zedekiah.

6 On the ninth day of the fourth month,
when famine had gripped the city and the
people had no more bread, 7 the city walls
were breached. All the soldiers fled and left
the city by night through the gate between
the two walls which was near the king's garden. With the Chaldeans surrounding the
city, they went in the direction of the Arabah.
8 But the Chaldean army pursued the king
and overtook Zedekiah in the wilderness
near Jericho; his whole army fled from him.

9 The king, therefore, was arrested and
brought to Riblah, in the land of Hamath, to
the king of Babylon, who pronounced judgment on him. 10 As Zedekiah looked on, the

**51:59 Seraiah**: the brother of Baruch; cf. 32:12. He may have gone to Babylon to explain away the presence of foreign ambassadors in Jerusalem that same year; cf. 27:3.

**51:60** Jeremiah prophesied against Babylon, even as he foretold Judah's release from Babylon's power (3:14–18; 32:15; 33:6–9, 12–13); but his scroll against Babylon was thrown in the Euphrates (v. 63). Some of the preceding oracles may have been composed by later writers; see note on 50:1–51:58.

**52:1–34** One of the editors of the Book of Jeremiah took most of this supplement from 2 Kgs 24:18–25:30 and placed it here to show the fulfillment of Jeremiah's prophecies. The supplement repeats part of the history given in Jeremiah 39–41, but omits the history of Gedaliah in 2 Kgs 25:22–26.

**52:4 In the tenth month of the ninth year of his reign, on the tenth day of the month**: January 15, 588 B.C. Cf. 39:1.

*x:* Is 14:13. *y:* Na 1:2. *z:* Hb 2:13. *a:* Jer 50:1–51. *b:* Rev 18:21. *c:* 2 Kgs 24:18–25:21. *d:* Jer 39:1–10.

king of Babylon slaughtered his sons before his eyes! All the nobles of Judah were slaughtered at Riblah. [11]And the eyes of Zedekiah he then blinded, bound him with chains, and the King of Babylon brought him to Babylon and kept him in prison until the day he died.

***Destruction of Jerusalem.*** [12]On the tenth day of the fifth month, this was in the nineteenth year* of Nebuchadnezzar, king of Babylon, Nebuzaradan, captain of the bodyguard, came to Jerusalem as the representative of the king of Babylon. [13]He burned the house of the LORD, the palace of the king, and all the houses of Jerusalem; every large building he destroyed with fire. [14]Then the Chaldean troops with the captain of the guard tore down all the walls that surrounded Jerusalem.

[15]Nebuzaradan, captain of the guard, led into exile the remnant of people left in the city, those who had deserted to the king of Babylon, and the rest of the artisans. [16]But Nebuzaradan, captain of the guard, left behind some of the country's poor as vinedressers and farmers.

[17]The bronze pillars that belonged to the house of the LORD, and the wheeled carts and the bronze sea in the house of the LORD, the Chaldeans broke into pieces; they carried away all the bronze to Babylon. [18]They also took the pots, shovels, snuffers, bowls, pans, and all the bronze vessels used for service; [19]the basins, fire holders, bowls, pots, lampstands, pans, the sacrificial bowls made of gold or silver. Along with these furnishings the captain of the guard carried off [20]the two pillars, the one sea and its base of twelve oxen cast in bronze, and the wheeled carts King Solomon had commissioned for the house of the LORD. The bronze from all these furnishings was impossible to weigh.

[21]As for the pillars, each of them was eighteen cubits high and twelve cubits in diameter; each was four fingers thick and hollow inside. [22]A bronze capital five cubits high crowned the one pillar, and a network with pomegranates encircled the capital, all of bronze; and so for the other pillar, with pomegranates. [23]There were ninety-six pomegranates on the sides, a hundred pomegranates surrounding the network.

[24]The captain of the guard also took Seraiah the high priest, Zephaniah the second priest, and the three keepers of the entrance. [25]From the city he took one courtier, a commander of soldiers, and seven men in the personal service of the king still in the city, the scribe of the army commander who mustered the people of the land, and sixty of the common people remaining in the city. [26]The captain of the guard, Nebuzaradan, arrested them and brought them to the king of Babylon at Riblah, [27]who had them struck down and executed in Riblah, in the land of Hamath.

Thus Judah was exiled from the land. [28]* This is the number of people Nebuchadnezzar led away captive: in his seventh year, three thousand twenty-three people of Judah; [29]in the eighteenth year of Nebuchadnezzar, eight hundred thirty-two persons from Jerusalem; [30]in the twenty-third year of Nebuchadnezzar, Nebuzaradan, captain of the guard, deported seven hundred forty-five Judahites: four thousand six hundred persons in all.

***Favor Shown to Jehoiachin.**** [31][e] In the thirty-seventh year of the exile of Jehoiachin, king of Judah, on the twenty-fifth day of the twelfth month, Evil-merodach, king of Babylon, in the inaugural year of his reign, raised up Jehoiachin, king of Judah, and released him from prison. [32]He spoke kindly to him and gave him a throne higher than the thrones of the other kings* who were with him in Babylon. [33]Jehoiachin took off his prison garb and ate at the king's table as long as he lived. [34]The allowance given him by the king of Babylon was a perpetual allowance, in fixed daily amounts, all the days of his life until the day of his death.

**52:12 On the tenth day of the fifth month . . . nineteenth year**: the tenth of Ab—July/August in 587/586 B.C.

**52:28–30** These verses, missing in the Greek text, do not come from 2 Kgs 25 but from a source using a different chronology. Besides the deportations of 598 and 587 B.C., this passage mentions a final deportation in 582/581, possibly a response to the murder of Gedaliah; cf. Jer 41:2.

**52:31–34** In the year 561/560 B.C., Nebuchadnezzar's successor Awel-Marduk (Evil-merodach), who reigned only two years, released Jehoiachin. Babylonian records confirm that Jehoiachin and his family were supported at public expense.

**52:32 The other kings**: heads of state brought as captives to Babylon.

*e*: 2 Kgs 25:27–30.

See RG 219–23

# The Book of Lamentations

The Book of Lamentations is a collection of five poems that serve as an anguished response to the destruction of Jerusalem in 587 B.C., after a long siege by the invading Babylonian army. (See 2 Kgs 25 for a prose account of the fall of Jerusalem.) Although the poems are traditionally ascribed to the prophet Jeremiah, this is unlikely. The Hebrew text of the book does not mention Jeremiah at all, and it is difficult to square some of the content of the poetry with what one finds in the Book of Jeremiah itself (cf. Lam 1:10; 2:9; 4:17, 20). While there are connections in theme and vocabulary among all five chapters (and especially between chaps. 1 and 2), the poems may have been composed separately and grouped together later. In any case, they are anonymous compositions probably used by survivors of the catastrophe of 587 B.C. in a communal expression of grief and mourning.

Jewish liturgical tradition considers the book one of the "scrolls" (*megillot*); it is read once a year on the ninth of Av (August–September), a fast day commemorating the destruction of both the first Temple in 587 B.C. and the second Temple in A.D. 70. While passages from chap. 3 are often incorporated into Christian services for Holy Thursday or Good Friday, the Church has otherwise tended to neglect the book. It is not hard to see why; a more anguished piece of writing is scarcely imaginable: from its portrayal of Jerusalem in chaps. 1 and 2 as an abandoned widow exposed to endless dangers, to the broken man of chap. 3, to the bleak description in chap. 4 of the inhabitants of the devastated city, to the final unanswered communal lament of chap. 5, the reader is not so much engaged by the Book of Lamentations as assaulted by it. But with its unsparing focus on destruction, pain, and suffering the book serves an invaluable function as part of Scripture, witnessing to a biblical faith determined to express honestly the harsh realities of a violent world and providing contemporary readers the language to do the same.

As a literary work, the Book of Lamentations combines elements of communal and individual laments (in which the speakers attempt to persuade God to intervene in the face of an acute crisis), funeral dirges (in which a death is mourned), and ancient Near Eastern city-laments (in which the destruction of a city is mourned). The meter is called *Qinah* (lament), that is, each verse normally has three beats followed by two. The poems are acrostics: in chaps. 1–4, the separate stanzas begin with successive letters of the Hebrew alphabet from the first to the last. The last chapter, while not strictly an acrostic, nevertheless partially conforms to the pattern in its use of 22 lines, the number of letters in the Hebrew alphabet. Far from destroying the spontaneous pathos of the songs, this feature conveys the expression of a profound grief that might otherwise seem to be without limit (cf. 2:13).

The book may be divided as follows:

I. The Desolation of Jerusalem (1:1–22).
II. The Lord's Wrath and Zion's Ruin (2:1–22).
III. The Voice of a Suffering Individual (3:1–66).
IV. Miseries of the Besieged City (4:1–22).
V. The Community's Lament to the Lord (5:1–22).

## CHAPTER 1

See RG 219–23

### *The Desolation of Jerusalem**

1 How solitary sits the city,
once filled with people.
She who was great among the nations
is now like a widow.
Once a princess among the provinces,
now a toiling slave.

2 She weeps incessantly in the night,
her cheeks damp with tears.
She has no one to comfort her
from all her lovers;*

**1:1–22** In this poem the poet first takes on the persona of an observer describing Jerusalem's abject state after the destruction wrought by the Babylonian army (vv. 1–11a); but the detached tone gives way to a more impassioned appeal when the city itself—personified as the grieving widow and mother Zion—abruptly intrudes upon this description (vv. 9c, 11c–16, 18–22) to demand that God look squarely at her misery.

**1:2 Lovers**: language of love was typically used to de-

## A Poet Laments Jerusalem

AS IN MANY prophetic books (Hosea, Jeremiah, Ezekiel), Jerusalem is personified as a woman (Lam 1:1–11). In a striking series of contrasts, she who was great is now destitute like a widow; once a princess, she is now a slave. Political allies are called Jerusalem's dear ones or lovers (see also Hs 2:7). Public activities (feasts and gateways, where people gather) have ceased. Priests and virgins are among the many categories of people that the book shows as suffering. All of this, the book repeatedly claims, is because the Lord has punished Israel (v. 5).

Her friends have all betrayed her,
and become her enemies.[a]

3 Judah has gone into exile,
after oppression and harsh labor;
She dwells among the nations,
yet finds no rest:[b]
All her pursuers overtake her
in the narrow straits.

4 The roads to Zion mourn,
empty of pilgrims to her feasts.
All her gateways are desolate,
her priests groan,
Her young women grieve;
her lot is bitter.[c]

5 Her foes have come out on top,
her enemies are secure;
Because the LORD has afflicted her
for her many rebellions.
Her children have gone away,
captive before the foe.

6 From daughter Zion has gone
all her glory:
Her princes have become like rams
that find no pasture.
They have gone off exhausted
before their pursuers.

7 Jerusalem remembers
in days of wretched homelessness,
All the precious things she once had
in days gone by.
But when her people fell into the hands
of the foe,
and she had no help,
Her foes looked on and laughed
at her collapse.

8 Jerusalem has sinned grievously,
therefore she has become a mockery;
Those who honored her now demean her,
for they saw her nakedness;
She herself groans out loud,
and turns away.[d]

9 Her uncleanness is on her skirt;
she has no thought of her future.
Her downfall is astonishing,
with no one to comfort her.
"Look, O LORD, at my misery;
how the enemy triumphs!"*

10 The foe stretched out his hands
to all her precious things;
She has seen the nations
enter her sanctuary,
Those you forbade to come
into your assembly.[e]

11 All her people groan,
searching for bread;
They give their precious things for food,
to retain the breath of life.
"Look, O LORD, and pay attention
to how I have been demeaned!

12 Come, all who pass by the way,
pay attention and see:
Is there any pain like my pain,
which has been ruthlessly inflicted
upon me,

scribe the relationship between treaty partners, thus here it connotes Judah's allies (see v. 19).

**1:9** Zion breaks in on the poet's description in v. 9c, albeit briefly, to demand that the Lord face squarely her misery. She takes up the lament in a more sustained fashion in v. 11c.

*a:* Jer 30:14; Ez 16:37. *b:* Dt 28:65; Jer 45:3. *c:* Is 33:8–9; Jer 14:2. *d:* Is 47:2–3; Jer 13:22, 26; Na 3:5. *e:* Dt 23:3–6; Ps 74:4–8; Is 56:6; 66:20–21; Jer 51:51.

## Acrostic Poems in Hebrew

AN ACROSTIC POEM is one in which the initial letters of each line of poetry follow some sort of pattern. In the Hebrew Bible, all of the acrostic poems are alphabetical acrostics: that is, the first letters of each line (or each group of lines) form the Hebrew alphabet of twenty-two letters.

The following passages in the Bible are acrostics: Psalms 9–10, 25, 34, 37, 111, 112, 119, 145; Proverbs 31:10–31; each chapter in Lamentations except chapter 5, which nevertheless has twenty-two lines; Nahum 1:2–8 (or perhaps 2–10; the acrostic is incomplete). The Hebrew text of Sirach 51:13–30 is also an acrostic. Psalms 34, 37, 112, 119, Proverbs 31, and Sirach 51 are all examples of wisdom literature, and if these texts were used in schools, the acrostic feature may have been an aid to memorization.

We can compare the use of rhyme in English poetry. Rhyme is a pattern involving similar sounds at the ends of lines; it is therefore like an acrostic in combining a pattern of sound and meaning. We can admire the artistry involved in such a combination, and perhaps that will give us insight into the enjoyment that acrostic poems may have provided to their original audiences.

In the case of Lamentations, where chapters 1–4 are acrostics, and chapter 5 continues the pattern with its twenty-two lines, there may be a deeper meaning. By expressing grief in a pattern that completes the alphabet, the poet may be expressing two things: the completeness of grief—covering it "from A to Z," as we might say—and also its end. The poetical form helps the poet to channel and contain grief, as mourning rituals can do in other social settings.

With which the LORD has tormented me
on the day of his blazing wrath?

13 From on high he hurled fire down
into my very bones;
He spread out a net for my feet,
and turned me back.
He has left me desolate,
in misery all day long.[f]

14 The yoke of my rebellions is bound together,
fastened by his hand.
His yoke is upon my neck;
he has made my strength fail.
The Lord has delivered me into the grip
of those I cannot resist.

15 All my valiant warriors
my Lord has cast away;
He proclaimed a feast against me
to crush my young men;
My Lord has trodden in the wine press
virgin daughter Judah.

16 For these things I weep—My eyes! My eyes!
They stream with tears!
How far from me is anyone to comfort,
anyone to restore my life.
My children are desolate;
the enemy has prevailed."[g]

17 Zion stretches out her hands,
with no one to comfort her;
The LORD has ordered against Jacob
his foes all around;
Jerusalem has become in their midst
a thing unclean.

18 "The LORD is in the right;
I had defied his command.
Listen, all you peoples,
and see my pain:
My young women and young men
have gone into captivity.[h]

19 I cried out to my lovers,
but they failed me.[i]
My priests and my elders
perished in the city;

*f:* Ez 12:13. *g:* Ps 69:21; Eccl 4:1; Jer 13:17; 14:17; Na 3:7. *h:* Dt 28:41. *i:* Jer 30:14.

How desperately they searched for food,
to save their lives!

20 Look, O LORD, at the anguish I suffer!
My stomach churns,
And my heart recoils within me:
How bitter I am!
Outside the sword bereaves—
indoors, there is death.[j]

21 Hear how I am groaning;
there is no one to comfort me.
All my enemies hear of my misery and rejoice
over what you have done.
Bring on the day you proclaimed,
and let them become like me!

22 Let all their evil come before you
and deal with them
As you have so ruthlessly dealt with me
for all my rebellions.
My groans are many,
my heart is sick."[k]

## CHAPTER 2

See RG 219–23

### *The Lord's Wrath and Zion's Ruin**

1 How the Lord in his wrath
has abhorred daughter Zion,
Casting down from heaven to earth
the glory of Israel,*
Not remembering his footstool
on the day of his wrath!

2 The Lord has devoured without pity
all of Jacob's dwellings;
In his fury he has razed
daughter Judah's defenses,
Has brought to the ground in dishonor
a kingdom and its princes.

3 In blazing wrath, he cut down entirely
the horn* of Israel;
He withdrew the support of his right hand
when the enemy approached;
He burned against Jacob like a blazing fire
that consumes everything in its path.

4 He bent his bow like an enemy;
the arrow in his right hand
Like a foe, he killed
all those held precious;
On the tent of daughter Zion
he poured out his wrath like fire.

5 The Lord has become the enemy,
he has devoured Israel:
Devoured all its strongholds,
destroyed its defenses,
Multiplied moaning and groaning
throughout daughter Judah.

6 He laid waste his booth like a garden,
destroyed his shrine;*
The LORD has blotted out in Zion
feast day and sabbath,
Has scorned in fierce wrath
king and priest.[l]

7 The Lord has rejected his altar,
spurned his sanctuary;
He has handed over to the enemy
the walls of its strongholds.
They shout in the house of the LORD
as on a feast day.[m]

8 The LORD was bent on destroying
the wall of daughter Zion:
He stretched out the measuring line;*
did not hesitate to devour,
Brought grief on rampart and wall
till both succumbed.[n]

9 Her gates sank into the ground;
he smashed her bars to bits.

**2:1–22** This chapter continues to move between the voice of the poet (vv. 1–20) and that of personified Zion (vv. 20–22). The persona of the poet, first portrayed in chap. 1 as a detached observer recounting both the desolation as well as the sins of the city, becomes in this chapter an advocate for Zion in her appeal to the Lord and never once mentions her sins.

**2:1 The glory of Israel**: the Temple. **His footstool**: the ark of the covenant (1 Chr 28:2; Ps 99:5; 132:7); or again, the Temple (Ez 43:7).

**2:3 Horn**: a symbol of power and strength; cf. v. 17; 1 Sm 2:1, 10; Ps 89:18, 25; 92:11; 112:9.

**2:6 Booth . . . shrine**: synonyms for the Temple; cf. Ps 27:5; 74:4, 8. The term for "shrine" in Hebrew (*mo'ed*) figures prominently in the pentateuchal expression "tent of meeting" (*'ohel mo'ed*).

**2:8 The measuring line**: normally used for building, here employed ironically as an instrument of destruction; cf. Is 34:11; 2 Kgs 21:13.

*j*: Lam 2:11. *k*: Lam 3:64. *l*: Is 1:13; 5:5. *m*: Ez 24:21. *n*: Jer 52:12–14.

Her king and her princes are among the nations;
instruction is wanting,
Even her prophets do not obtain
any vision from the LORD.[o]

10 The elders of daughter Zion
sit silently on the ground;
They cast dust* on their heads
and dress in sackcloth;
The young women of Jerusalem
bow their heads to the ground.[p]

11 My eyes are spent with tears,
my stomach churns;*
My bile is poured out on the ground
at the brokenness of the daughter of my people,
As children and infants collapse
in the streets of the town.[q]

12 They cry out to their mothers,
"Where is bread and wine?"
As they faint away like the wounded
in the streets of the city,
As their life is poured out
in their mothers' arms.

13 To what can I compare you*—to what can I liken you—
O daughter Jerusalem?
What example can I give in order to comfort you,
virgin daughter Zion?
For your breach is vast as the sea;
who could heal you?[r]

14 Your prophets provided you visions
of whitewashed illusion;
They did not lay bare your guilt,
in order to restore your fortunes;
They saw for you only oracles
of empty deceit.[s]

15 All who pass by on the road,
clap their hands at you;
They hiss and wag their heads
over daughter Jerusalem:
"Is this the city they used to call
perfect in beauty and joy of all the earth?"[t]

16 They open their mouths against you,
all your enemies;
They hiss and gnash their teeth,
saying, "We have devoured her!
How we have waited for this day—
we have lived to see it!"[u]

17 The LORD has done what he planned.
He has fulfilled the threat
Decreed from days of old,
destroying without pity!
He let the enemy gloat over you
and exalted the horn of your foes.[v]

18 Cry out to the Lord from your heart,
wall of daughter Zion!
Let your tears flow like a torrent
day and night;
Give yourself no rest,
no relief for your eyes.

19 Rise up! Wail in the night,
at the start of every watch;
Pour out your heart like water
before the Lord;
Lift up your hands to him
for the lives of your children,
Who collapse from hunger
at the corner of every street.*

**2:10 They cast dust**: as a sign of mourning; cf. Jos 7:6; Jb 2:12; Ez 27:30.

**2:11 My eyes are spent with tears, my stomach churns**: the poet appropriates the emotional language used by Zion in 1:16 and 1:20 to express a progressively stronger commitment to her cause. After describing the systematic dismantling of the city in vv. 5–9, the poet turns to the plight of the inhabitants in vv. 10–12. It is the description of children dying in the streets that finally brings about the poet's emotional breakdown, even as it did for Zion in 1:16.

**2:13 To what can I compare you . . . ?**: the author calls attention to the poetic task: to find language that speaks adequately of the atrocities and incomparable suffering experienced by Zion, and thus to attempt to offer comfort.

**2:19** The poet urges Zion to appeal to the Lord once more on behalf of her dying children. The image of Zion's children effectively condenses the metaphorical sense of all residents of the city (young and old alike) into the more poignant picture of actual children at the point of death. It was precisely this image, no doubt well known to survivors of besieged cities, that led to the emotional breakdown of both Zion (1:16) and the poet (2:11). The hope is that the Lord will be similarly affected by such a poignant image and respond with mercy.

*o:* Dt 28:36. *p:* Is 3:26. *q:* Lam 1:16, 20; 3:48; Jer 8:18. *r:* Lam 1:12; Jer 8:21. *s:* Is 58:1; Jer 2:8; 23:16; Ez 13:9; 22:28. *t:* Ps 48:3; 50:12; Jer 18:16. *u:* Lam 3:46. *v:* Dt 28:15.

20 "Look, O LORD, and pay attention:
to whom have you been so ruthless?
Must women eat their own offspring,*
the very children they have borne?
Are priest and prophet to be slain
in the sanctuary of the Lord?[w]

21 They lie on the ground in the streets,
young and old alike;
Both my young women and young men
are cut down by the sword;
You killed them on the day of your wrath,
slaughtered without pity.[x]

22 You summoned as to a feast day
terrors on every side;
On the day of the LORD's wrath,
none survived or escaped.
Those I have borne and nurtured,
my enemy has utterly destroyed."[y]

## CHAPTER 3

See RG 219–23

### *The Voice of a Suffering Individual**

1 I am one who has known affliction
under the rod of God's anger,[z]
2 One whom he has driven and forced to walk
in darkness, not in light;
3 Against me alone he turns his hand—
again and again all day long.

4 He has worn away my flesh and my skin,
he has broken my bones;[a]
5 He has besieged me all around
with poverty and hardship;
6 He has left me to dwell in dark places
like those long dead.[b]

7 He has hemmed me in with no escape,
weighed me down with chains;
8 Even when I cry for help,
he stops my prayer;[c]
9 He has hemmed in my ways with fitted stones,
and made my paths crooked.

10 He has been a bear lying in wait for me,
a lion in hiding![d]
11 He turned me aside and tore me apart,
leaving me ravaged.[e]
12 He bent his bow, and set me up
as a target for his arrow.[f]

13 He pierced my kidneys
with shafts from his quiver.[g]
14 I have become a laughingstock to all my people,
their taunt all day long;[h]
15 He has sated me with bitterness,
filled me with wormwood.[i]

16 He has made me eat gravel,
trampled me into the dust;
17 My life is deprived of peace,
I have forgotten what happiness is;
18 My enduring hope, I said,
has perished before the LORD.

19 The thought of my wretched homelessness
is wormwood and poison;
20 Remembering it over and over,
my soul is downcast.
21 But this I will call to mind;*
therefore I will hope:

22 The LORD's acts of mercy are not exhausted,
his compassion is not spent;[j]
23 They are renewed each morning—
great is your faithfulness!
24 The LORD is my portion, I tell myself,
therefore I will hope in him.[k]

**2:20 Must women eat their own offspring**: extreme famine in a besieged city sometimes led to cannibalism; this becomes a stereotypical way of expressing the nearly unthinkable horrors of war; cf. Lam 4:10; Dt 28:53; 2 Kgs 6:28–29; Bar 2:3; Ez 5:10.

**3:1–66** This chapter is focused less on the destruction of Jerusalem than are chaps. 1 and 2 and more on the suffering of an individual. The identity of the individual is never given, and one probably should not search for a specific identification of the speaker. The figure of the representative sufferer makes concrete the pain of the people in a way similar to the personification of Zion as a woman in chaps. 1 and 2. Indeed, in vv. 40–48 the individual voice gives way to a communal voice, returning in vv. 49–66 to the individual sufferer.

**3:21–24** In the midst of a description of suffering, the speaker offers this brief but compelling statement of hope in God's ultimate mercy. It is a hard-won and precarious hope, nearly submerged by the volume and intensity of the surrounding lament, but it is hope nonetheless.

*w:* Lam 4:10. *x:* Lam 3:43; 2 Chr 36:17; Jer 6:11. *y:* Jer 42:17. *z:* Jer 20:18. *a:* Jb 30:30; Is 38:13. *b:* Ps 143:3. *c:* Ps 18:41; 22:2; 88:14–15. *d:* Jb 10:16; Hos 13:8. *e:* Lam 1:13. *f:* Lam 2:4; Jb 16:12. *g:* Jb 6:4; Ps 38:3. *h:* Jb 30:9; Ps 69:13. *i:* Jer 9:14; 23:15. *j:* 1 Sm 20:15; Neh 9:31. *k:* Ps 16:5; 73:26.

### A Teaching on God's Goodness

IN A JARRING shift at the center of the book, Lam 3:25–41 offers beautiful statements of God's mercy, faithfulness, and compassion and teaches silence in the face of suffering. Because some passages appear to contradict material that comes before and after (v. 39: Why should anyone complain?), these verses are often considered a later addition to the book. They function, however, to balance the community's expression of suffering with the book's insistent theme that God is justifiably punishing Judah for its sins. Because God has acted justly, Judah must examine its own wrongs.

25 The LORD is good to those who trust in him,
to the one that seeks him;[l]
26 It is good to hope in silence
for the LORD's deliverance.
27 It is good for a person, when young,
to bear the yoke,

28 To sit alone and in silence,
when its weight lies heavy,
29 To put one's mouth in the dust—*
there may yet be hope—
30 To offer one's cheek to be struck,
to be filled with disgrace.[m]

31 For the Lord does not
reject forever;[n]
32 Though he brings grief, he takes pity,
according to the abundance of his mercy;[o]
33 He does not willingly afflict
or bring grief to human beings.[p]

34 That someone tramples underfoot
all the prisoners in the land,
35 Or denies justice to anyone
in the very sight of the Most High,
36 Or subverts a person's lawsuit—
does the Lord not see?

37 Who speaks so that it comes to pass,
unless the Lord commands it?
38 Is it not at the word of the Most High
that both good and bad take place?[q]
39 What should the living complain about?
about their sins!

40 * Let us search and examine our ways,
and return to the LORD![r]
41 Let us lift up our hearts as well as our hands
toward God in heaven!
42 We have rebelled and been obstinate;
you have not forgiven us.

43 You wrapped yourself in wrath and pursued us,
killing without pity;[s]
44 You wrapped yourself in a cloud,
which no prayer could pierce.
45 You have made us filth and rubbish
among the peoples.[t]

46 They have opened their mouths against us,
all our enemies;
47 Panic and the pit have been our lot,
desolation and destruction;[u]
48 * My eyes stream with tears over the destruction
of the daughter of my people.[v]

49 My eyes will flow without ceasing,
without rest,
50 Until the LORD from heaven
looks down and sees.
51 I am tormented by the sight
of all the daughters of my city.

52 Without cause, my enemies snared me
as though I were a bird;
53 They tried to end my life in the pit,
pelting me with stones.

**3:29 To put one's mouth in the dust**: a sign of humiliation and submission; cf. v. 16; Ps 72:9.

**3:40–66** The plural voice in this lament suggests that a communal lament begins here; it then continues in the singular voice in vv. 55–66.

**3:48–51** These verses are more appropriate on the lips of the poet, who speaks of "my city" (v. 51). **Daughters of my city**: here as elsewhere "daughter" may refer to villages dependent on a larger city.

*l:* Ps 130:6; Is 30:18. *m:* Is 50:6; Mt 5:39. *n:* Ps 85:6; 103:9. *o:* 1 Sm 2:6–7; Tb 13:2; Is 54:8. *p:* Ex 34:6–7. *q:* Is 45:7. *r:* Jl 2:12–13. *s:* Lam 2:21. *t:* 1 Cor 4:13. *u:* Is 24:17–18; Jer 48:43–44. *v:* Lam 1:16; 2:11; Jer 8:23; 9:17.

**Jerusalem's Changed Fortunes**

IN LAM 4:1–10, the poet portrays a world upside down, where all that is normal has vanished. The once valuable is treated as worthless. Children, once treasured, are earthen jars, and scarce food is not given to them. Ostriches, to which the people are compared, have the reputation of neglecting their young (Jb 39:13–18). Purple, due to the costliness of its dye, was worn by royalty; thus in v. 5, the once privileged class now starves. In the most dramatic reversal, once compassionate mothers eat their children rather than feed them.

54 The waters flowed over my head:
and I said, "I am lost!"[w]

55 I have called upon your name,
O LORD,[x]
from the bottom of the pit;
56 You heard me call, "Do not let your ear
be deaf
to my cry for help."
57 You drew near on the day I called you;
you said, "Do not fear!"

58 You pleaded my case, Lord,
you redeemed my life.
59 You see, LORD, how I am wronged;
do me justice![y]
60 You see all their vindictiveness,
all their plots against me.

61 You hear their reproach, LORD,
all their plots against me,
62 The whispered murmurings of my
adversaries,
against me all day long;
63 Look! Whether they sit or stand,
I am the butt of their taunt.

64 Give them what they deserve, LORD,
according to their deeds;
65 Give them hardness of heart;
your curse be upon them;[z]
66 Pursue them in wrath and destroy them
from under the LORD's heaven!

## CHAPTER 4

See RG 219–23

### *Miseries of the Besieged City**

1 How the gold has lost its luster,
the noble metal changed;
Jewels* lie scattered
at the corner of every street.

2 And Zion's precious children,
worth their weight in gold—
How they are treated like clay jugs,
the work of any potter![a]

3 Even jackals offer their breasts
to nurse their young;
But the daughter of my people is as cruel
as the ostrich* in the wilderness.[b]

4 The tongue of the infant cleaves
to the roof of its mouth in thirst;
Children beg for bread,
but no one gives them a piece.

5 Those who feasted on delicacies
are abandoned in the streets;
Those who reclined on crimson*
now embrace dung heaps.[c]

6 The punishment of the daughter of my
people
surpassed the penalty of Sodom,
Which was overthrown in an instant
with no hand laid on it.[d]

**4:1–22** This chapter returns to the focus of chaps. 1 and 2, namely the horrors of a siege. Unlike chaps. 1 and 2, however, the character of personified Zion never interrupts the voice of the poet to protest her abject state. As a result, the emotion of the poem is less intense, while at the same time seeming more grim on account of its lack of petition to the Lord.

**4:1–2 Jewels**: lit., "holy stones." These precious things designate the children who are abandoned, starving, and killed in the siege of Jerusalem (cf. Zec 9:16). Another explanation is that these are the stones of the destroyed Temple.

**4:3 Cruel as the ostrich**: see note on Jb 39:14–16. Jerusalem, in her distress, has abandoned her children.

**4:5 Crimson**: a sign of luxury. Tyrian purple, a red-purple or blue-purple dye produced from shellfish, was very expensive and the only colorfast dye in the ancient Near East. Thus purple or crimson cloth was available only to the wealthy.

*w:* Ps 69:2–3; 88:8; Jon 2:4. *x:* Ps 130:1–2. *y:* Ps 35:23–24; 43:1; 119:154. *z:* Jer 11:20; 2 Tm 4:14. *a:* Jer 19:11. *b:* Jb 39:16. *c:* Dt 28:56. *d:* Gn 19:23–29; 2 Pt 2:6; Jude 7.

7 Her princes were brighter than snow,
whiter than milk,
Their bodies more ruddy than coral,
their beauty like the sapphire.

8 Now their appearance is blacker than soot,
they go unrecognized in the streets;
Their skin has shrunk on their bones,
and become dry as wood.[e]

9 Better for those pierced by the sword
than for those pierced by hunger,
Better for those who bleed from wounds
than for those who lack food.

10 The hands of compassionate women
have boiled their own children!
They became their food
when the daughter of my people was shattered.[f]

11 The LORD has exhausted his anger,
poured out his blazing wrath;
He has kindled a fire in Zion
that has consumed her foundations.[g]

12 The kings of the earth did not believe,
nor any of the world's inhabitants,
That foe or enemy could enter
the gates of Jerusalem.

13 Except for the sins of her prophets
and the crimes of her priests,
Who poured out in her midst
the blood of the just.[h]

14 They staggered blindly in the streets,
defiled with blood,
So that people could not touch
even their garments:[i]

15 "Go away! Unclean!" they cried to them,
"Away, away, do not touch!"
If they went away and wandered,
it would be said among the nations,
"They can no longer live here!

16 The presence of the LORD was their portion,
but he no longer looks upon them.
The priests are shown no regard,
the elders, no mercy.

17 Even now our eyes are worn out,
searching in vain for help;
From our watchtower we have watched
for a nation* unable to save.

18 They dogged our every step,
we could not walk in our squares;
Our end drew near, our time was up;
yes, our end had come.

19 Our pursuers were swifter
than eagles in the sky,
In the mountains they were hot on our trail,
they ambushed us in the wilderness.[j]

20 The LORD's anointed—our very lifebreath!—*
was caught in their snares,
He in whose shade we thought
to live among the nations.[k]

21 Rejoice and gloat, daughter Edom,
dwelling in the land of Uz,*
The cup will pass to you as well;
you shall become drunk and strip yourself naked![l]

22 Your punishment is completed, daughter Zion,
the Lord will not prolong your exile;
The Lord will punish your iniquity,
daughter Edom,
will lay bare your sins.[m]

## CHAPTER 5

See RG 219–23

### *The Community's Lament to the Lord*

1 Remember, LORD, what has happened to us,

**4:17 A nation**: probably Egypt, which failed to give effective aid against Babylon.

**4:20 Our very lifebreath**: lit., "the breath of our nostrils," that is, the king. This expression occurs in Egyptian texts of the late second millennium B.C., and may have survived as a royal epithet in the Jerusalem court. After the disaster of 598 B.C. (2 Kgs 24:1–17), Jerusalem could have hoped to live in peace amidst her neighbors; but they (vv. 21–22) as well as Babylon turned against her to ensure her total devastation in 587 B.C.

**4:21 Rejoice**: the address is sarcastic, since Edom (where Uz may have been located) ravaged the land after the fall of Jerusalem (cf. Ps 137).

*e:* Lam 3:4. *f:* Lam 2:20; Dt 28:56–57; 2 Kgs 6:29. *g:* Jer 7:20; Ez 5:13. *h:* Jer 6:13. *i:* Dt 28:29; Is 59:10. *j:* Jer 4:13; Hb 1:8. *k:* Lam 2:9; Ez 19:4, 8. *l:* Lam 1:21; Jer 25:15. *m:* Is 40:2.

THE POEM ENDS on a poignant note. God's power is undisputed, though God's care is questioned. The community asks that its broken relationship with God be healed but fears that God's anger may yet be too great.

pay attention, and see our disgrace:
2 Our heritage is turned over to strangers,
our homes, to foreigners.[n]
3 We have become orphans, without fathers;
our mothers are like widows.
4 We pay money to drink our own water,
our own wood comes at a price.
5 With a yoke on our necks, we are driven;
we are worn out, but allowed no rest.

6 We extended a hand to Egypt and Assyria,
to satisfy our need of bread.*
7 Our ancestors, who sinned, are no more;
but now we bear their guilt.
8 Servants* rule over us,
with no one to tear us from their hands.
9 We risk our lives just to get bread,
exposed to the desert heat;[o]
10 Our skin heats up like an oven,
from the searing blasts of famine.[p]

11 Women are raped in Zion,
young women in the cities of Judah;[q]
12 Princes have been hanged by them,
elders shown no respect.[r]
13 Young men carry millstones,
boys stagger under loads of wood;
14 The elders have abandoned the gate,*
the young men their music.

15 The joy of our hearts has ceased,
dancing has turned into mourning;[s]
16 The crown has fallen from our head:
woe to us that we sinned!
17 Because of this our hearts grow sick,
at this our eyes grow dim:
18 Because of Mount Zion, lying desolate,
and the jackals roaming there!

19 But you, LORD, are enthroned forever;
your throne stands from age to age.[t]
20 * Why have you utterly forgotten us,
forsaken us for so long?[u]
21 Bring us back to you, LORD, that we may return:
renew our days as of old.[v]
22 For now you have indeed rejected us
and utterly turned your wrath against us.[w]

**5:6 Extended a hand**: that is, made an alliance. In its state of abjection, Judah was forced to depend on the major powers to the west and the east for subsistence.

**5:8 Servants**: the Hebrew word for "servant" is also the word used for an official of relatively high status (servant of the ruler; cf. 2 Kgs 25:24, where the term is used to refer to Babylonian rulers over occupied Jerusalem); the author doubtless intends the double meaning here.

**5:14 The gate**: a place of assembly, where city decisions were made and judgment given by the elders and other community leaders; see note on Ru 4:1.

**5:20–22** Unlike most of the laments found in the Book of Psalms, the Book of Lamentations never moves from lament to thanksgiving. It ends with this question still unanswered by God: "Why have you utterly forgotten us?"

*n:* Ps 79:1. *o:* Lam 1:11. *p:* Lam 4:8. *q:* Zec 14:2. *r:* Lam 4:16. *s:* Jer 16:9; 25:10; Am 8:10. *t:* Ps 9:8; 45:7; 102:13, 27. *u:* Ps 13:2; 42:10; Is 49:14. *v:* Ps 80:19–20. *w:* Jer 14:19.

See RG 223–26

# The Book of Baruch

The opening verses ascribe the book to the well-known assistant to Jeremiah (Jer 32:12; 36:4, 32; 45:1). It is a collection of four very different compositions, ending with a work entitled "The Letter of Jeremiah," which circulated separately in major manuscripts of the Greek tradition. The original language may have been Hebrew, but only the Greek and other versions have been preserved. The fictional setting is Babylon, where Baruch reads his scroll to King Jechoniah (Jehoiachin) and the exiles; they react by sending gifts and the scroll to Jerusalem (1:1–14), presumably by the hand of Baruch (1:7). No certain date can be given for the book, but it may have

**The Community's Confession**

THE PIETY OF the exiled community is taken as a model for the Jews of the Diaspora during the time when Baruch was written. The people wept, fasted, and prayed, and then took up a collection so that those still in Jerusalem could offer sacrifices for them in absentia. God's punishment was seen as a result of Israel's sin (cf. Neh 9; Dn 9:4–19). The pattern of sin/punishment/repentance/salvation found in Deuteronomy 28–32 influences Baruch 1:5–3:8 and a number of other texts of the period (Jdt 5). The recitation of the mighty acts of God beginning in 2:11 was a standard part of the renewal of the covenant (Ex 19:3–6; Dt 6:12; Jos 24), but here it is incorporated into the confession of sins instigated by Baruch's reading of the scroll. The contrast of God's gracious act and Israel's ungrateful response is sharply drawn.

been edited in final form during the last two centuries B.C. The work attempts to explain the trauma of the exile in terms of a Deuteronomic cycle: sin (of Israel), punishment, repentance, and return (cf. Jgs 2; also Dt 28–33).

The prayer of the exiles (2:11–3:8) is a confession of sin and a request for mercy, and has remarkable similarities to Dn 9 and to parts of Jeremiah. The poem on personified Wisdom is concerned with three themes: the importance of Wisdom, the elusive character of Wisdom (cf. Jb 28), and the identification of Wisdom with Torah (cf. Sir 24:23). Baruch's Poem of Consolation resembles parts of Is 40–66, and it offers encouragement to the exiles in view of their eventual return; there are two addresses by personified Zion. The Letter of Jeremiah, unlike the letter in Jer 29, is a polemic against idolatry, a well-known theme (cf. Jer 10:2–11; Ps 115:4–8; 135:15–18; Is 44:9–20; Wis 13:10–15:17). It contains ten warnings that end in a kind of refrain that the idols are not gods and are not to be feared (vv. 14, 22, 28, 39, 44, 51, 56, 64, 68).

The book can be divided thus:

I. Letter to Jerusalem (1:1–3:8)
- A. Historical Setting (1:1–9)
- B. Confession of Guilt (1:10–2:10)
- C. Prayer for Deliverance (2:11–3:8)

II. Praise of Wisdom (3:9–4:4)
- A. Importance of Wisdom (3:9–23)
- B. Inaccessibility of Wisdom (3:24–36)
- C. Wisdom Contained in the Law (3:37–4:4)

III. Baruch's Poem of Consolation (4:5–5:9)
- A. Baruch Addresses Diaspora (4:5–9a)
- B. Jerusalem Addresses Neighbors (4:9b–16)
- C. Jerusalem Addresses Diaspora (4:17–29)
- D. Baruch Addresses Jerusalem (4:30–5:9)

IV. Letter of Jeremiah (6:1–72)

---

# I. Letter to Jerusalem

## CHAPTER 1

See RG 224–25

### *A. Historical Setting*

1 Now these are the words of the scroll which
Baruch, son of Neriah, son of Mahseiah, son
of Zedekiah, son of Hasadiah, son of Hilkiah, wrote in Babylon,[a] 2 in the fifth year, on
the seventh day of the month,* at the time the
Chaldeans took Jerusalem and destroyed it
with fire.[b] 3[c] Baruch read the words of this
scroll in the hearing of Jeconiah, son of Jehoiakim, king of Judah, and all the people
who came to the reading:[d] 4 the nobles,
kings' sons, elders, and all the people, small
and great—all who lived in Babylon by the
river Sud.*

5 They wept, fasted, and prayed before the
Lord, 6 and collected such funds as each

**1:2 In the fifth year, on the seventh day of the month**: Jerusalem fell on the seventh day of the fifth month in 587 B.C.; cf. 2 Kgs 25:8; Jer 52:12. Either the text read originally "the fifth month," or it refers to the observance of an anniversary of the fall of Jerusalem.

**1:4 The river Sud**: probably one of the Babylonian canals, not otherwise identified; or possibly a misreading of Ahava; cf. Ezr 8:21, 31.

*a:* Jer 32:12; 36:4; 45:1–5. *b:* 2 Kgs 25:8–10. *c:* 2 Kgs 23:1–2. *d:* 2 Kgs 24:8–17; Jer 22:24–30; 27:20; 51:59–64.

could afford.[e] 7These they sent to Jerusalem, to Jehoiakim the priest, son of Hilkiah, son of Shallum, and to the priests and the whole people who were with him in Jerusalem. 8(At the same time he* received the vessels of the house of the LORD that had been removed from the temple, to restore them to the land of Judah, on the tenth of Sivan. These silver vessels Zedekiah, son of Josiah, king of Judah, had had made 9[f] after Nebuchadnezzar, king of Babylon, carried off as captives Jeconiah and the princes, the skilled workers, the nobles, and the people of the land from Jerusalem, and brought them to Babylon.)

### *B. Confession of Guilt*

10The message was: "We send you funds, with which you are to procure burnt offerings, sin offerings, and frankincense, and to prepare grain offerings; offer these* on the altar of the LORD our God,[g] 11and pray for the life of Nebuchadnezzar, king of Babylon, and of Belshazzar, his son,* that their lifetimes may be as the days of the heavens above the earth.[h] 12Pray that the LORD may give us strength, and light to our eyes, that we may live under the protective shadow of Nebuchadnezzar, king of Babylon, and of Belshazzar, his son, to serve them many days, and find favor in their sight. 13Pray for us to the LORD, our God, for we have sinned against the LORD, our God. Even to this day the wrath of the LORD and his anger have not turned away from us. 14On the feast day and during the days of assembly, read aloud in the house of the LORD this scroll that we send you:[i]

15* "To the Lord our God belongs justice; to us, people of Judah and inhabitants of Jerusalem, to be shamefaced, as on this day—[j] 16to us, our kings, rulers, priests, and prophets, and our ancestors. 17We have sinned in the LORD's sight 18and disobeyed him. We have not listened to the voice of the LORD, our God, so as to follow the precepts the LORD set before us. 19From the day the LORD led our ancestors out of the land of Egypt until the present day, we have been disobedient to the LORD, our God, and neglected to listen to his voice. 20Even today evils cling to us, the curse the LORD pronounced to Moses, his servant, at the time he led our ancestors out of the land of Egypt to give us a land flowing with milk and honey.[k] 21For we did not listen to the voice of the LORD, our God, in all the words of the prophets he sent us, 22but each of us has followed the inclinations of our wicked hearts, served other gods, and done evil in the sight of the LORD, our God.

## CHAPTER 2

See RG 224–25

1"So the LORD carried out the warning he had uttered against us: against our judges, who governed Israel, against our kings and princes, and against the people of Israel and Judah. 2Nowhere under heaven has anything been done like what he did in Jerusalem, as was written in the law of Moses:*[l] 3that we would each eat* the flesh of our sons, each the flesh of our daughters. 4He has made us subject to all the kingdoms around us, an object of reproach and horror among all the peoples around us, where the LORD has scat-

**1:8–9 He**: apparently Baruch; less likely Jehoiakim the priest (v. 7). The silver vessels here described are distinct from the vessels referred to in 2 Kgs 25:14 and Ezr 1:7–9. The author of this note may have thought of the fifth year (v. 1) of Zedekiah, in view of Jer 28:1; 29:1–3. A "fifth year," again with no month mentioned, is given in Ez 1:2 for the inaugural vision of Ezekiel's prophetic career.

**1:10 Offer these**: since 2:26 suggests that the Temple is destroyed, the mention of sacrifices here may be an anachronism. Nevertheless, Jer 41:5 indicates that some people continued to worship at the Temple site after Nebuchadnezzar's destruction of the Temple.

**1:11 Nebuchadnezzar . . . Belshazzar, his son**: Belshazzar was the son of Nabonidus, the last king of Babylon, not of Nebuchadnezzar, the destroyer of Jerusalem. Belshazzar was co-regent for a few years while his father was away in Arabia. Later Jewish tradition seems to have simplified the end of the Babylonian empire (cf. Dn 5:1–2), for three kings came between Nebuchadnezzar and Nabonidus.

**1:15–2:10** This confession of sin is similar to Dn 9:7–14, and echoes ideas from Deuteronomy and Jeremiah; cf. also Neh 9.

**2:2 Law of Moses**: cf. Dt 28:53–57.

**2:3 We would each eat**: such dreadful events were the result of the prolonged siege of Jerusalem; cf. Lam 2:20.

*e:* Dt 16:17. *f:* Jer 24:1. *g:* Jer 17:26; 41:5. *h:* Dt 11:21; Ps 89:30; Jer 29:7; Dn 5:1–2; 1 Tm 2:1–2. *i:* Ex 23:14–17; Lv 23:35–36; Sir 50:6; Hos 9:5. *j:* Bar 2:6; 3:8; Ezr 9:6–15; Neh 9:6–37; Dn 9:4–19. *k:* Lv 26:14–39; Dt 28:15–68. *l:* Dt 28:52–57; 2 Kgs 6:28–29; Jer 19:9; Lam 2:20; 4:10; Ez 5:10; Dn 9:12.

tered us.[m] 5 We are brought low, not raised high,[n] because we sinned against the LORD, our God, not listening to his voice.

6 "To the LORD, our God, belongs justice; to us and to our ancestors, to be shamefaced, as on this day.[o] 7 All the evils of which the LORD had warned us have come upon us. 8 We did not entreat the favor of the LORD by turning, each one, from the designs of our evil hearts. 9 The LORD kept watch over the evils, and brought them home to us; for the LORD is just in all the works he commanded us to do,[p] 10 but we did not listen to his voice, or follow the precepts of the LORD which he had set before us.

### *C. Prayer for Deliverance*

11* "And now, LORD, God of Israel, who led your people out of the land of Egypt with a strong hand, with signs and wonders and great might, and with an upraised arm, so that you have made for yourself a name to the present day:[q] 12 we have sinned, we have committed sacrilege, we have violated all your statutes, LORD, our God.[r] 13 Withdraw your anger from us, for we are left few in number among the nations where you have scattered us. 14 Hear, LORD, our prayer of supplication, and deliver us for your own sake: grant us favor in the sight of those who brought us into exile, 15 that the whole earth may know that you are the LORD, our God, and that Israel* and his descendants bear your name.[s] 16 LORD, look down from your holy dwelling and take thought of us; LORD, incline your ear to hear us.[t] 17 Open your eyes and see: it is not the dead in Hades,* whose breath has been taken from within them, who will declare the glory and vindication to the LORD.[u] 18 The person who is deeply grieved, who walks bowed and feeble, with failing eyes and famished soul, will declare your glory and justice, LORD![v]

19 "Not on the just deeds of our ancestors and our kings do we base our plea for mercy in your sight, LORD, our God. 20 You have sent your wrath and anger upon us, as you had warned us through your servants the prophets: 21 Thus says the LORD: Bend your necks and serve the king of Babylon, that you may continue in the land I gave your ancestors;[w] 22* for if you do not listen to the LORD's voice so as to serve the king of Babylon, 23 I will silence from the cities of Judah and from the streets of Jerusalem the cry of joy and the cry of gladness, the voice of the bridegroom and the voice of the bride; and all the land shall be deserted, without inhabitants.[x] 24 But we did not listen to your voice, or serve the king of Babylon, and you carried out the threats you had made through your servants the prophets, that the bones of our kings and the bones of our ancestors would be brought out from their burial places.[y] 25 And indeed, they lie exposed* to the heat of day and the frost of night. They died in great suffering, by famine and sword and plague.[z] 26 And you reduced the house which bears your name* to what it is today, because of the wickedness of the house of Israel and the house of Judah.[a]

***God's Promises Recalled.*** 27 "But with us, Lord, our God, you have dealt in all your clemency and in all your great mercy. 28* Thus you spoke through your servant Moses, the day you ordered him to write down your law in the presence of the Israelites: 29 'If you do not listen to my voice, surely this great and numerous throng will dwindle away among the nations to which I will scat-

**2:11–35** An earnest appeal for divine mercy, along with confession of sin; cf. Dn 9:15–19.

**2:15 Israel**: the Israelites claimed descent from the patriarch Jacob, who had received the name Israel in a mysterious encounter with God (Gn 32:29). Thus the Deity was sometimes referred to as "the God of Israel" (Gn 33:20; Ex 5:1).

**2:17 Hades**: this is the Greek translation of Hebrew *sheol*, the nether world.

**2:22–24** These words are very similar to Jer 7:34; 27:9, 12.

**2:25 They lie exposed**: Jeremiah's words threatened Jehoiakim with being left unburied (Jer 22:19; 36:30).

**2:26 The house which bears your name**: the Temple of Jerusalem; cf. Dt 12:11; Jer 7:11. **What it is today**: during the exile it lay in ruins.

**2:28–35** These words do not actually quote anything Moses is recorded as having said, but they present the substance of a passage such as Dt 30:1–10, which envisions exile, repentance, and restoration.

*m:* Jer 29:18; Dn 9:16. *n:* Dt 28:13, 43–44. *o:* Bar 1:15; Dn 9:7. *p:* Jer 1:12; 31:28; 44:27; Dn 9:14. *q:* Dt 6:21–22. *r:* Ps 106:6. *s:* Gn 33:20; Sir 36:11; Jer 14:9; 35:17. *t:* Dt 26:15. *u:* Ps 6:6; Is 38:18. *v:* Zep 2:3. *w:* Jer 27:12. *x:* Jer 7:34. *y:* Jer 8:1–2. *z:* Jer 7:34; 14:12; 31:30. *a:* Jer 7:10–15; 11:17.

BARUCH 3:9–4:4 IS very similar to Proverbs 8–9, Job 28, Wisdom 7:15–22, and especially Sirach 24. However, unlike these, it lacks the role of wisdom in creation, and includes the theme of Israel's exile as punishment.

ter them.[b] 30 For I know they will not listen to
me, because they are a stiff-necked people.
But in the land of their exile they shall have
a change of heart;[c] 31 they shall know that I,
the LORD, am their God. I will give them a
heart and ears that listen;[d] 32 and they shall
praise me in the land of their exile, and shall
remember my name.[e] 33 Then they shall turn
back from their stiff-necked stubbornness,
and from their evil deeds, because they shall
remember the ways of their ancestors, who
sinned against the LORD.[f] 34 And I will bring
them back to the land I promised on oath to
their ancestors, to Abraham, Isaac, and Jacob; and they shall rule it. I will make them
increase; they shall not be few. 35 And I will
establish for them an eternal covenant: I will
be their God, and they shall be my people;
and I will never again remove my people Israel from the land I gave them.'[g]

## CHAPTER 3

See RG 224–25

1 "LORD Almighty, God of Israel, the
anguished soul, the dismayed spirit cries out
to you. 2 Hear, LORD, and have mercy, for
you are a merciful God; have mercy on us,
who have sinned against you: 3 for you are
enthroned forever, while we are perishing
forever.[h] 4 LORD Almighty, God of Israel,
hear the prayer of the dead of Israel, children
who sinned against you; they did not listen
to the voice of the LORD, their God, and their
evils cling to us.[i] 5 Do not remember the
wicked deeds of our ancestors, but remember at this time your power and your name,
6 for you are the LORD our God; and you,
LORD, we will praise! 7 This is why you put
into our hearts the fear of you: that we may
call upon your name, and praise you in our
exile, when we have removed from our
hearts all the wickedness of our ancestors
who sinned against you.[j] 8 See, today we are
in exile, where you have scattered us, an object of reproach and cursing and punishment
for all the wicked deeds of our ancestors,
who withdrew from the LORD, our God."

## II. Praise of Wisdom*

### *A. Importance of Wisdom*

9 Hear, Israel, the commandments of life:
listen, and know prudence![k]
10 How is it, Israel,
that you are in the land of your foes,
grown old in a foreign land,
11 Defiled with the dead,
counted among those destined for
Hades?[l]
12 You have forsaken the fountain of
wisdom![m]
13 Had you walked in the way of God,
you would have dwelt in enduring
peace.[n]

14 Learn where prudence is,
where strength, where understanding;
That you may know also
where are length of days, and life,
where light of the eyes, and peace.[o]
15 Who has found the place of wisdom?[p]
Who has entered into her treasuries?
16 Where are the rulers of the nations,
who lorded it over the wild beasts of
the earth,[q]
17 made sport of the birds in the heavens,
Who heaped up the silver,
the gold in which people trust,
whose possessions were unlimited,

**3:9–4:4** This poem in praise of personified Wisdom utilizes the theme of Jb 28 (where is wisdom to be found?) and it identifies wisdom and law, as in Sir 24:22–23.

*b:* Lv 26:39. *c:* Dt 30:1–2; 31:27. *d:* Ps 40:7; Jer 24:7; Ez 36:26. *e:* Tb 13:6. *f:* Lv 26:42–45; Dt 30:1–10. *g:* Jer 31:31; Lam 4:22. *h:* Ps 29:10; 102:12–13. *i:* Jer 31:29. *j:* Jer 31:33. *k:* Dt 6:4–5; Prv 4:20–22. *l:* Ps 88:5. *m:* Jer 2:13; Jn 4:10, 14. *n:* Is 48:18. *o:* Prv 3:2; 8:14. *p:* Jb 28:1–28. *q:* Jer 27:6; 1 Cor 1:20.

18 Who schemed anxiously for money,
their doings beyond discovery?
19 They have vanished, gone down to Hades,
and others have risen up in their stead.
20 Later generations have seen the light of day,
have dwelt on the earth,
But the way to understanding they have not known,
21 they have not perceived her paths or reached her;
their children remain far from the way to her.
22 She has not been heard of in Canaan,*
nor seen in Teman.[r]
23 The descendants of Hagar who seek knowledge on earth,
the merchants of Medan and Tema,[s]
the storytellers and those seeking knowledge—
These have not known the way to wisdom,
nor have they kept her paths in mind.

### *B. Inaccessibility of Wisdom*

24 O Israel, how vast is the dwelling of God,*
how broad the scope of his dominion:
25 Vast and endless,
high and immeasurable!
26 In it were born the giants,*
renowned at the first,
huge in stature, skilled in war.[t]
27 These God did not choose,
nor did he give them the way of understanding;[u]
28 They perished for lack of prudence,
perished through their own folly.[v]

29 Who has gone up to the heavens and taken her,
bringing her down from the clouds?[w]
30 Who has crossed the sea and found her,
bearing her away rather than choice gold?
31 None knows the way to her,
nor has at heart her path.
32 But the one who knows all things knows her;
he has probed her by his knowledge—
The one who established the earth for all time,
and filled it with four-footed animals,
33 Who sends out the lightning, and it goes,
calls it, and trembling it obeys him;
34 Before whom the stars at their posts
shine and rejoice.
35 When he calls them, they answer, "Here we are!"
shining with joy for their Maker.[x]
36 Such is our God;
no other is to be compared to him:

### *C. Wisdom Contained in the Law*

37 * He has uncovered the whole way of understanding,
and has given her to Jacob, his servant,
to Israel, his beloved.[y]

38 Thus she has appeared on earth,
is at home with mortals.[z]

## CHAPTER 4

See RG 225

1 * She is the book of the precepts of God,
the law that endures forever;
All who cling to her will live,
but those will die who forsake her.[a]
2 Turn, O Jacob, and receive her:
walk by her light toward splendor.[b]
3 Do not give your glory to another,
your privileges to an alien nation.
4 Blessed are we, O Israel;
for what pleases God is known to us![c]

**3:22–23** Despite the renown for wisdom of the peoples of Canaan and Phoenicia (Ez 28:3–4), of Teman (Jer 49:7), of the descendants of Hagar or the Arabians of Medan and Tema, they did not possess true wisdom, which is found only in the law of God (Bar 4:1).

**3:24 The dwelling of God**: here, the whole universe; cf. Is 66:1.

**3:26 The giants**: Gn 6:1–4 reflects a tradition about giants who existed before the flood; this was developed in the non-canonical Book of Enoch.

**3:37–38** As in Sir 24:8, Wisdom is given to Israel but also is said to live with all human beings (Prv 8:31).

**4:1–4** The poem ends with the identification of Wisdom and Torah, as in Sir 24:22–23; cf. also Dt 4:5–8.

*r:* Jb 2:11; Jer 49:7; Ez 28:4–5; Zec 9:2. *s:* Gn 25:2, 15; Jb 6:19; Jer 25:23. *t:* Gn 6:4; Wis 14:6; Sir 16:7. *u:* 1 Sm 16:7–10. *v:* Sir 10:8. *w:* Dt 30:12–13; Sir 24:4; Rom 10:6–7. *x:* Jb 38:7; Ps 147:4; Is 40:26. *y:* Ps 147:19; Sir 24:8–12. *z:* Wis 9:18; Jn 1:14. *a:* Dt 4:6–8; Prv 8:35–36; Sir 24:22. *b:* Prv 4:13, 19. *c:* Dt 4:32–37; 33:29.

ZION, REPRESENTING JERUSALEM, is personified as a grieving widow in 4:9–29. This section is heavily indebted to Isaiah 51:17–20 and Lamentations 1:1; 2:19–22, but it is longer and addresses the needs of a different audience and situation. Many of Baruch's earlier motifs are present here, especially the explanation of God's punishment as recompense for forsaking the law of God.

## III. Baruch's Poem of Consolation*

### *A. Baruch Addresses Diaspora*

5 Take courage, my people!
Remember, O Israel,
6 You were sold to the nations
not for destruction;
It was because you angered God
that you were handed over to your foes.[d]
7 For you provoked your Maker[e]
with sacrifices to demons and not to God;
8 You forgot the eternal God who nourished you,
and you grieved Jerusalem who nurtured you.
9 She indeed saw coming upon you
the wrath of God; and she said:

### *B. Jerusalem Addresses Neighbors*

"Hear, you neighbors of Zion!
God has brought great mourning upon me,
10 For I have seen the captivity
that the Eternal One has brought
upon my sons and daughters.
11 With joy I nurtured them;
but with mourning and lament I sent them away.
12 Let no one gloat over me,
a widow, bereft of many;
For the sins of my children I am left desolate,
because they turned from the law of God,[f]
13 and did not acknowledge his statutes;
In the ways of God's commandments
they did not walk,
nor did they tread the disciplined paths
of his justice.
14 "Let Zion's neighbors come—
Remember the captivity of my sons
and daughters,
brought upon them by the Eternal One.
15 He has brought against them a nation
from afar,
a nation ruthless and of alien speech,
That has neither reverence for old age
nor pity for the child;[g]
16 They have led away this widow's
beloved sons,
have left me solitary, without daughters.

### *C. Jerusalem Addresses Diaspora*

17 What can I do to help you?
18 The one who has brought this evil
upon you
must himself deliver you from your
enemies' hands.[h]
19 Farewell, my children, farewell;
I am left desolate.
20 I have taken off the garment of peace,
have put on sackcloth for my prayer of supplication;
while I live I will cry out to the Eternal One.[i]

21 "Take courage, my children; call upon God;
he will deliver you from oppression,
from enemy hands.[j]
22 I have put my hope for your deliverance
in the Eternal One,
and joy has come to me from the Holy One

**4:5–5:9** The poet addresses the exiles (vv. 5–9a), and then Zion personified is introduced, speaking to the nations and mourning the loss of her children (vv. 9b–16). She then addresses the exiles (vv. 17–29). Finally (4:30–5:9) the poet issues three calls to Jerusalem (4:30, 36; 5:5): she will see her children returning (4:22, 36–37; 5:5).

*d:* Jgs 2:14; Is 50:1; 52:3. *e:* Dt 32:13–18; 1 Cor 10:20. *f:* Lam 1:1, 2, 7. *g:* Dt 28:49–50; Jer 5:15; 6:22–23. *h:* Jer 32:42. *i:* Jdt 9:1; Est 4:16. *j:* Jer 51:5.

Because of the mercy that will swiftly
reach you
from your eternal Savior.
23 With mourning and lament I sent you
away,
but God will give you back to me
with gladness and joy forever.[k]
24 As Zion's neighbors lately saw you taken
captive,
so shall they soon see God's salvation
come to you,
with great glory and the splendor of
the Eternal One.[l]
25 "My children, bear patiently the wrath[m]
that has come upon you from God;
Your enemies have persecuted you,
but you will soon see their destruction
and trample upon their necks.*
26 My pampered children have trodden
rough roads,
carried off by their enemies like sheep
in a raid.[n]
27 Take courage, my children; call out to God!
The one who brought this upon you
will remember you.[o]
28 As your hearts have been disposed to
stray from God,
so turn now ten times the more to seek
him;
29 For the one who has brought disaster
upon you
will, in saving you, bring you eternal
joy."[p]

### *D. Baruch Addresses Jerusalem*

30 Take courage, Jerusalem!
The one who gave you your name will
console you.[q]
31 Wretched shall be those who harmed you,
who rejoiced at your downfall;
32 Wretched shall be the cities where your
children were enslaved,
wretched the city that received your
children.[r]
33 As that city rejoiced at your collapse,[s]
and made merry at your downfall,
so shall she grieve over her own
desolation.
34 I will take from her the rejoicing
crowds,
and her exultation shall be turned to
mourning:
35 For fire shall come upon her[t]
from the Eternal One, for many a day,
to be inhabited by demons for a long
time.*
36 Look to the east, Jerusalem;
see the joy that comes to you from
God![u]
37 Here come your children whom you sent
away,
gathered in from east to west
By the word of the Holy One,
rejoicing in the glory of God.

## CHAPTER 5

See RG 225

1 Jerusalem, take off your robe of
mourning and misery;
put on forever the splendor of glory
from God:[v]
2 Wrapped in the mantle of justice from
God,
place on your head the diadem
of the glory of the Eternal One.[w]
3 For God will show your splendor to all
under the heavens;
4 you will be named by God forever:
the peace of justice, the glory of God's
worship.[x]
5 Rise up, Jerusalem! stand upon the
heights;
look to the east and see your children
Gathered from east to west
at the word of the Holy One,
rejoicing that they are remembered by
God.
6 Led away on foot by their enemies they
left you:

**4:25 Trample upon their necks**: a sign of victory over the enemy (cf. Ps 44:6; Is 14:25). The Israelites considered their enemies to be God's enemies as well.

**4:35** Deserts and desolate places were looked upon as the habitation of demons; cf. Tb 8:3; Lk 11:24.

*k:* Jer 31:12–13. *l:* Is 60:1–7. *m:* Is 51:23. *n:* Lam 2:22. *o:* Is 40:1. *p:* Is 35:10. *q:* Ps 46:5; Is 60:14. *r:* Jer 51:43. *s:* Is 13:20–22; 47:1–11; Jer 50:13. *t:* Is 34:9–14. *u:* Is 60:4–5. *v:* Is 52:1. *w:* Ex 39:30; Wis 18:24; Is 61:10; 62:3. *x:* Is 1:26; 32:17; Jer 33:16.

but God will bring them back to you
carried high in glory as on royal
thrones.[y]
7 For God has commanded
that every lofty mountain
and the age-old hills be made low,
That the valleys be filled to make level
ground,
that Israel may advance securely in the
glory of God.[z]
8 The forests and every kind of fragrant
tree
have overshadowed Israel at God's
command;[a]
9 For God is leading Israel in joy
by the light of his glory,
with the mercy and justice that are his.

## IV. Letter of Jeremiah

### CHAPTER 6

See RG 225

1 A copy of the letter which Jeremiah
sent to those led captive to Babylon by the
king of the Babylonians, to tell them what
God had commanded him:[b]
For the sins you committed before God,
you are being led captive to Babylon by
Nebuchadnezzar, king of the Babylonians.
2 When you reach Babylon you will be there
many years, a long time—seven generations;* after that I will bring you back from
there in peace. 3 And now in Babylon you
will see gods of silver and gold and wood,
carried shoulder high, to cast fear upon the
nations.[c] 4* Take care that you yourselves do
not become like these foreigners and let not
such fear possess you. 5 When you see the
crowd before them and behind worshiping
them, say in your hearts, "You, Lord, are the
one to be worshiped!"[d] 6 For my angel* is
with you, and he will keep watch on you.[e]
7 Their tongues are smoothed by woodworkers; they are covered with gold and silver—but they are frauds, and cannot speak.[f]
8 People bring gold, as though for a girl fond
of dressing up, 9 and prepare crowns for the
heads of their gods. Then sometimes the
priests filch the gold and silver from their
gods and spend it on themselves, 10 or give
part of it to harlots* in the brothel. They
dress them up in clothes like human beings,
these gods of silver and gold and wood.
11 Though they are wrapped in purple clothing, they are not safe from rust and corrosion. 12 Their faces are wiped clean of the
cloud of dust which is thick upon them.
13 Each has a scepter, like the human ruler of
a district, but none can do away with those
that offend against it. 14 Each has in its right
hand an ax or dagger, but it cannot save itself
from war or pillage. Thus it is known they
are not gods; do not fear them.
15 As useless as a broken pot[g] 16 are their
gods, set up in their temples, their eyes full
of dust from the feet of those who enter.
17 Their courtyards are walled in like those of
someone brought to execution for a crime
against the king; the priests reinforce their
temples with gates and bars and bolts, so
they will not be carried off by robbers.
18 They light more lamps for them than for
themselves, yet not one of these can they
see. 19 They are like any timber in the temple;
their hearts, it is said, are eaten away.
Though crawling creatures from the ground
consume them and their garments, they do
not feel it. 20 Their faces become sooty from
the smoke in the temple. 21 Bats and swal-

**6:2 Seven generations**: this number may be symbolic. If it is not, it may indicate the date of this composition by an author writing for his contemporaries for whom the conditions of the exile were still realities. He has multiplied the seventy years of Jer 29:10 by three or four.

**6:4–72** This whole chapter is a sustained argument against the temptation to worship Babylonian gods. A pattern is repeated throughout the chapter: various reasons are set forth to prove that the idols in the Babylonian temples are not gods (e.g., they are weak, helpless, attended by unworthy ministers); each section is followed by an exhortation not to be deceived, not to worship them. Note the refrain at vv. 14, 22, 28, 39, 44, 51, 56, 64. Israelite religion was aniconic, i.e., it prohibited images; as elsewhere in the Old Testament (e.g., Is 42:17; 44:9–20), the polemic against idols here oversimplifies by identifying the god worshiped with the image that represents it.

**6:6 My angel**: the prophet assures the people that God's watchful care is with them, just as he was with their ancestors during their journey to the promised land (Ex 23:20).

**6:10 Harlots**: cult prostitutes, common in some religions of the ancient Near East.

*y:* Is 49:22. *z:* Is 40:3–4. *a:* Is 41:19. *b:* Jer 29:1. *c:* Is 46:7; Jer 10:1–16. *d:* Dt 6:13; 10:20; Mt 4:10; Lk 4:8. *e:* Ex 23:20. *f:* Ps 135:16. *g:* Jer 22:28.

lows alight on their bodies and heads—any bird, and cats as well. [22]Know, therefore, that they are not gods; do not fear them.

[23]Gold adorns them, but unless someone wipes away the corrosion, they do not shine; they felt nothing when they were molded. [24]They are bought at whatever price, but there is no spirit in them. [25]Since they have no feet, they are carried shoulder high, displaying to all how worthless they are; even those who worship them are put to shame[h] [26]because, if they fall to the ground, the worshipers must pick them up. They neither move of themselves if one sets them upright, nor come upright if they are tipped over; offerings are set out for them as for the dead.[i] [27]* Their priests sell their sacrifices for their own advantage. Likewise their wives cure some of the meat, but they do not share it with the poor and the weak;[j] [28]women ritually unclean or at childbirth handle their sacrifices. From such things, know that they are not gods; do not fear them.

[29]How can they be called gods? Women set out the offerings for these gods of silver and gold and wood, [30]and in their temples the priests squat with torn tunic and with shaven hair and beard, and with their heads uncovered.[k] [31]They shout and wail before their gods as others do at a funeral banquet. [32]The priests take some of the clothing from their gods and put it on their wives and children. [33]* Whether these gods are treated well or badly by anyone, they cannot repay it. They can neither set up nor remove a king.[l] [34]They cannot give anyone riches or pennies; if one fails to fulfill a vow to them, they will not exact it. [35]They neither save anyone from death, nor deliver the weak from the strong,[m] [36]nor do they restore sight to the blind, or rescue anyone in distress. [37]The widow they do not pity, the orphan they do not help. [38]These gilded and silvered wooden statues are no better than stones from the mountains; their worshipers will be put to shame. [39]How then can it be thought or claimed that they are gods?

[40]Even the Chaldeans themselves have no respect for them; for when they see a deaf mute, unable to speak, they bring forward Bel* and expect him to make a sound, as though he could hear. [41]They themselves are unable to reflect and abandon these gods, for they have no sense. [42]* And the women, with cords around them, sit by the roads, burning chaff for incense;[n] [43]and whenever one of them is taken aside by some passerby who lies with her, she mocks her neighbor who has not been thought thus worthy, and has not had her cord broken. [44]All that is done for these gods is a fraud; how then can it be thought or claimed that they are gods?

[45]They are produced by woodworkers and goldsmiths; they are nothing other than what these artisans wish them to be. [46]Even those who produce them are not long-lived; [47]how then can the things they have produced be gods? They have left frauds and disgrace to their successors. [48]For when war or disaster comes upon them, the priests deliberate among themselves where they can hide with them. [49]How then can one not understand that these are not gods, who save themselves neither from war nor from disaster? [50]Beings that are wooden, gilded and silvered, they will later be known for frauds. To all nations and kings it will be clear that they are not gods, but human handiwork; and that God's work is not in them. [51]Is it not obvious that they are not gods?

[52]* They set no king over the land, nor do they give rain. [53]They neither vindicate their own rights, nor do they rescue anyone wronged, for they are powerless. [54]They are

**6:27–31** From the viewpoint of Jewish ritual law, the practices named here were grotesque and depraved; cf. Lv 12:2–8; 15:19–23.

**6:33–39** All that the Babylonian gods cannot do, the true God does; they have neither power nor inclination to save those in need, unlike the God of Israel, who champions the cause of the weak over the strong, and who defends the widow and the orphan. Cf. 1 Sm 2:7; Ps 68:6; 146:7–9; Is 35:4–5.

**6:40 Bel**: cf. note on Jer 50:2.

**6:42–43** Perhaps a reference to the Babylonian practice of cultic prostitution mentioned by Herodotus, the fifth-century Greek historian. The unbroken cord was a sign that this service had not yet been rendered.

**6:52–53** Unlike the God of Israel, the Babylonian gods are unable to set up and depose kings, or to provide life-giving rain.

*h:* Wis 13:16. *i:* Sir 30:18–19. *j:* Lv 12:4; 15:19–20; Dt 14:28–29. *k:* Lv 10:6; 21:5, 10. *l:* Dn 2:21. *m:* Ps 68:6; 146:7–9. *n:* Jer 3:2.

like crows in midair. For when fire breaks
out in the temple of these wooden or gilded
or silvered gods, though the priests flee and
are safe, they themselves are burned up in
the fire like timbers. [55]They cannot resist a
king or enemy forces. [56]How then can it be
admitted or thought that they are gods?

They are safe from neither thieves nor
bandits, these wooden and silvered and
gilded gods. [57]Anyone who can will strip off
the gold and the silver, and go away with the
clothing that was on them; they cannot help
themselves. [58]How much better to be a king
displaying his valor, or a handy tool in a
house, the joy of its owner, than these false
gods; better the door of a house, protecting
whatever is within, than these false gods;
better a wooden post in a palace, than these
false gods![o] [59]* The sun and moon and stars
are bright, obedient in the task for which
they are sent. [60]Likewise the lightning, when
it flashes, is a great sight; and the one wind
blows over every land. [61]The clouds, too,
when commanded by God to proceed across
the whole world, fulfill the command; [62]and
fire, sent from on high to burn up the mountains and the forests, carries out its command. But these false gods are not their
equal, whether in appearance or in power.
[63]So it is unthinkable, and cannot be claimed
that they are gods. They can neither execute
judgment, nor benefit anyone. [64]Know,
therefore, that they are not gods; do not fear
them.

[65]Kings they can neither curse nor bless.
[66]They show the nations no signs in the
heavens, nor do they shine like the sun, nor
give light like the moon. [67]The beasts are
better than they—beasts can help themselves by fleeing to shelter. [68]Thus is it in no
way apparent to us that they are gods; so do
not fear them.

[69]For like a scarecrow in a cucumber
patch,[p] providing no protection, are their
wooden, gilded, silvered gods. [70]Just like a
thornbush in a garden on which perches
every kind of bird, or like a corpse hurled
into darkness, are their wooden, gilded, silvered gods. [71]From the rotting of the purple
and the linen upon them, you can know that
they are not gods; they themselves will in
the end be consumed, and be a disgrace in
the land. [72]Better the just who has no idols;
such shall be far from disgrace!

**6:59–62** The elements of nature, obedient to God's orders and accomplishing the divine purpose, are better than the Babylonian gods.

*o:* Wis 13:10–15; 15:7–17. *p:* Jer 10:5.

See RG 226–29

# The Book of Ezekiel

In response to the rebellion of Jehoiakim of Judah in 601 B.C., Nebuchadnezzar, the Babylonian ruler, besieged Jerusalem. When Jehoiakim's successor, Jehoiachin, surrendered in 597, Nebuchadnezzar appointed Zedekiah king and deported to Babylon Jehoiachin and the royal family, along with members of the upper class, including Ezekiel the priest. Five years later, as Zedekiah planned his own revolt against Babylon, Ezekiel became the first prophet to be commissioned outside Judah or Israel (chaps. 1–3). Before Jerusalem is destroyed (587 B.C.), Ezekiel is concerned to convince his audience that they are responsible for the punishment of exile and to justify the Lord's decision to destroy their city and Temple. Later, Ezekiel argues that the Judahites who embrace his preaching are the people whom the Lord has chosen as a new Israel, enlivened by a new heart, imbued with new breath (chaps. 36–37), and restored to a re-created land, Temple, and covenant relationship (chaps. 40–48). Ezekiel is clear on one point: the Lord punishes and restores for one reason—for the sake of his name, in order to demonstrate once and for all that he is Lord.

Ezekiel's symbolic actions or performances foreshadow the inevitable destruction of Jerusalem (4:1–5:4; 12:1–20; 24:15–24). The closely related judgment oracles are directed against increasingly larger groups: the inhabitants of Jerusalem

(5:5–17); refugees who have fled into the mountains (6:1–14); Judah's total population, "the four corners of the land" (7:1–27). Particularly chilling is Ez 8–11, the prophet's vision of the violent injustice and idolatrous worship that fills Jerusalem. When Ezekiel protests the Lord's order to slaughter Jerusalem's wicked inhabitants, the Lord refuses to relent; the Lord's glory leaves the Temple, affirming his judgment on Jerusalem (11:22–25), whom Ezekiel portrays as a promiscuous woman, rebel from the beginning, more violent and sinful than Sodom (chap. 16). Appeals for a speedy end to the exile on the basis of a past relationship with the Lord or of Jerusalem's privileged status are futile gestures.

Ezekiel uses stereotypic oracles against the nations (chaps. 25–32) to claim universal sovereignty for Israel's God, to exemplify the consequences of arrogant national pride, and to set the stage for Israel's restoration. In order to demonstrate to all the nations that "I am the Lord," God becomes Israel's just shepherd (34:15) under whose rule a restored people (37:1–14) enjoy prosperity in a restored land. God again acts "for the sake of my name" when the mysterious forces of Gog attack Israel (chaps. 38–39). Their defeat is prelude to Ezekiel's vision of a new Israel whose source of life and prosperity is a well-ordered cult in a new Temple, where the divine glory again dwells (chaps. 40–48).

The Book of Ezekiel has the following divisions:

I. Call of the Prophet (1:1–3:27)
II. Before the Siege of Jerusalem (4:1–24:27)
III. Prophecies Against Foreign Nations (25:1–32:32)
IV. Hope for the Future (33:1–39:29)
V. The New Israel (40:1–48:35)

# I. Call of the Prophet

## CHAPTER 1

See RG 230

### *The Vision: God on the Cherubim.*

1 In the thirtieth year,* on the fifth day of the
fourth month, while I was among the exiles
by the river Chebar, the heavens opened, and
I saw divine visions.[a]— 2 On the fifth day of
the month—this was the fifth year* of King
Jehoiachin's exile[b]— 3 the word of the LORD
came to the priest Ezekiel, the son of Buzi,
in the land of the Chaldeans by the river
Chebar. There the hand of the LORD came
upon him.[c]
4 As I watched, a great stormwind came
from the North,* a large cloud with flashing
fire, a bright glow all around it, and something like polished metal gleamed at the center of the fire.[d] 5 From within it figures in the
likeness of four living creatures* appeared.
This is what they looked like:[e] 6 They were in
human form, but each had four faces and
four wings,[f] 7 and their legs were straight, the
soles of their feet like the hooves of a bull,
gleaming like polished brass.[g] 8 Human
hands were under their wings, and the wings
of one touched those of another.[h] 9 Their
faces and their wings looked out on all their
four sides; they did not turn when they
moved, but each went straight ahead.[i]
10* Their faces were like this:[j] each of the
four had a human face, and on the right the
face of a lion, and on the left, the face of an
ox, and each had the face of an eagle. 11 Such
were their faces. Their wings were spread
out above. On each one, two wings touched
one another, and the other two wings covered the body.[k] 12 Each went straight ahead.

**1:1 The thirtieth year,** which corresponds to the fifth year of exile (v. 2), has never been satisfactorily explained; possibly it refers to the prophet's age, or the anniversary of the finding of the book of the law in the Temple during Josiah's reform of 622 (2 Kgs 22:1–13). **The river Chebar**: probably a canal near Nippur, southeast of Babylon, one of the sites on which the Jewish exiles were settled.

**1:2 The fifth day . . . the fifth year**: the end of July, 593 B.C.; cf. v. 1.

**1:4 The North**: Zaphon, the traditional abode of the gods; see notes on Jb 37:22; Ps 48:3; Is 14:13–15.

**1:5 Four living creatures**: identified as cherubim in 10:1–2, 20. Known from Assyrian religion as minor guardian deities of palaces and temples, the cherubim were usually portrayed in gigantic sculpture with the bodies of bulls or lions, wings like an eagle and a human head. In the Jerusalem Temple, the Lord was enthroned above in the holy of holies (Is 6:1–2).

**1:10** The four faces together represent animate creation: wild animals, domesticated livestock, birds, and human beings. Christian tradition associates them with the four evangelists: the lion with Mark, the ox with Luke, the eagle with John, and the man with Matthew.

*a:* Ez 10:20; 11:24–25; 43:3; Ps 137:1. *b:* 2 Kgs 24:15. *c:* Ez 3:14, 22; 8:1; 33:22; 37:1; 40:1; 2 Kgs 3:15; Is 8:11. *d:* Ez 8:2; Jb 38:1. *e:* Is 6:2. *f:* Ez 10:14. *g:* Rev 1:15. *h:* Ez 10:8. *i:* Ez 10:22. *j:* Ez 10:14; Rev 4:6–7. *k:* Is 6:2.

## Introduction

EZEKIEL PRESENTS SOME of the most theologically challenging and dynamic material among the prophetic books of the Hebrew Bible. It wrestles with the problem of the Babylonian exile in a manner not unlike the modern problem of the Shoah or Holocaust: Why did God allow Jerusalem and the temple to be destroyed, and why did God allow the people of Israel to be carried away into exile? In arguing that God made a deliberate decision to destroy the temple to purify Israel, Ezekiel draws upon his own priestly background in which sacrifice at the altar of the temple is an essential element in self-purification, which aids in restoring one's relationship with God. The book develops its ideas in two major sections: Chapters 1–32 focus on God's plans to punish both Israel (chs 1–24) and a select group of nations that would fall to Babylon (chs 25–32); chs 33–48 focus on God's plans to restore a purified Israel (chs 33–39) with the Jerusalem temple at the center of Israel and all creation (chs 40–48).

Ezekiel was a Zadokite priest, a descendant of Zadok, one of the priests of David. Ezekiel was exiled to Babylonia together with King Jehoiachin in 597 B.C. He began his prophetic career five years later with a vision in which "the glory of the LORD" appeared to him in the form of a divine throne chariot, from which God instructed him to speak. Ezekiel's prophetic career continued for more than 20 years and culminated in his vision of the restored Jerusalem temple. His last oracle with a specified date is from 571 B.C. (Ez 29:17–21). The book was originally written in an effort to explain the Babylonian exile and to prepare the exiled Judahite community for its return to Jerusalem.

Wherever the spirit would go, they went;
they did not change direction when they
moved.[l] 13* And the appearance of the living
creatures seemed like burning coals of fire.
Something indeed like torches moved back
and forth among the living creatures. The
fire gleamed intensely, and from it lightning
flashed. 14 The creatures darting back and
forth flashed like lightning.
15* As I looked at the living creatures, I
saw wheels on the ground, one alongside
each of the four living creatures.[m] 16 The
wheels and their construction sparkled like
yellow topaz, and all four of them looked the
same: their construction seemed as though
one wheel was inside the other. 17 When they
moved, they went in any of the four directions without veering as they moved. 18[n] The
four of them had rims, high and fearsome—
eyes filled the four rims all around. 19 When
the living creatures moved, the wheels
moved with them; and when the living creatures were raised from the ground, the
wheels also were raised. 20 Wherever the
spirit would go, they went. And they were
raised up together with the living creatures,
for the spirit of the living creatures was in
the wheels. 21 Wherever the living creatures
moved, the wheels moved; when they stood
still, the wheels stood still. When they were
lifted up from the earth, the wheels were
lifted up with them.[o] For the spirit of the living creatures was in the wheels.
22* Above the heads of the living creatures
was a likeness of the firmament; it was awesome, stretching upwards like shining crystal
over their heads.[p] 23 Beneath the firmament
their wings stretched out toward one another;
each had two wings covering the body.
24 Then I heard the sound of their wings, like
the roaring of mighty waters, like the voice
of the Almighty. When they moved, the

**1:13–14** The coals and flashing lightning moving among the four creatures and yet coming from them identify this vision as a theophany. See note on 10:2–13.

**1:15–21** The repetitions and inconsistencies in the description of the wheels and the direction of their movements evoke the vision's mysterious quality and emphasize the difficulty of describing the divine world in human language.

**1:22–23, 26** This symbolic description of God's throne is similar to that in Ex 24:9–10.

*l:* Ez 10:16–19. *m:* Ez 10:2. *n:* Ez 10:12; Rev 4:6, 8. *o:* Ez 10:9–12. *p:* Ez 10:1; Gn 1:6.

## Heavenly Beasts and Beings

IN CH 1 OF Ezekiel, the prophet sees a vision of the throne of the LORD that moves like a chariot on wheels that are connected to four living creatures—creatures that provide the motive power for the movement. The creatures are, like many of those described in ancient Near Eastern literature, composite beings: they are human in form, but with feet like calves, and they have wings. Each one has four faces: a human face, a lion's face, an ox's face, and an eagle's face.

These creatures are probably developments of the traditional idea of the cherub, a creature with a lion's or ox's body, wings, and the head of a human being. (The Sphinx in Egypt is a sort of cherub-figure.) Cherubim were guardians of holy places (Gn 3:24) and of palaces; in Exodus 25:18–22, they are the guardians of the ark of the covenant. In 2 Samuel 22:11 the LORD rides on a cherub. Ezekiel's beasts are more elaborate, because they symbolize more than speed or protection. The wings and the eagle's face symbolize the creature's ability to move swiftly through the air; the ox's face and the hoofed feet symbolize strength; the lion's face symbolizes royalty; and the human face symbolizes reason. The fact that there are four creatures symbolizes the four directions, thereby including all space, and the central throne that the creatures carry symbolizes God's presence at the center of creation.

Chapter 6 of Isaiah envisions a different sort of creature: the seraph, a fiery being that lives in the very presence of God (*saraph* is the Hebrew verb for "burn," and *seraphim* are therefore "burning ones"). As with the cherubim in Ezekiel, the seraph's physical description is symbolic, not literal: it "burns" with adoration for the LORD of hosts, and the fire also represents the purity of the heavenly beings, a purity that is transferred to the prophet when one of the seraphs touches his lips with a burning coal. The hymn that the seraphim sing in verse 3 is the basis of the Sanctus, said or sung before the Eucharistic Prayer. It is also the basis of one of the blessings in the synagogue service.

sound of the tumult was like the din of an
army. And when they stood still, they lowered their wings.[q] 25While they stood with
their wings lowered, a voice came from
above the firmament over their heads.
26Above the firmament over their heads
was the likeness of a throne that looked like
sapphire; and upon this likeness of a throne
was seated, up above, a figure that looked
like a human being.*[r] 27And I saw something like polished metal, like the appearance of fire enclosed on all sides, from what
looked like the waist up; and from what
looked like the waist down, I saw something
like the appearance of fire and brilliant light
surrounding him.[s] 28Just like the appearance
of the rainbow in the clouds on a rainy day
so was the appearance of brilliance that surrounded him. Such was the appearance of
the likeness of the glory of the LORD. And
when I saw it, I fell on my face and heard a
voice speak.[t]

### CHAPTER 2

See RG 230

***Eating of the Scroll.*** 1The voice said
to me: Son of man,* stand up! I wish to speak
to you. 2As he spoke to me, the spirit* entered into me and set me on my feet, and I
heard the one who was speaking[u] 3say to me:
Son of man, I am sending you to the Israelites, a nation of rebels who have rebelled
against me; they and their ancestors have

**1:26 Looked like a human being**: the God who transcends the powers of the human imagination is pictured here in the likeness of an enthroned human king.

**2:1 Son of man**: in Hebrew, "son/daughter of . . ." is a common idiom expressing affiliation in a group; in this case, "a human being." The title is God's habitual way of addressing the prophet throughout this book, probably used to emphasize the separation of the divine and the human.

**2:2 The spirit**: lit., wind, breath; a vital power, coming from God, which enables the prophet to hear the divine word; cf. 8:3; 11:1, 24.

*q:* Ez 3:13; 10:5; 43:2; Rev 1:15. *r:* Rev 1:13. *s:* Ez 8:2. *t:* Rev 4:2–3. *u:* Ez 3:24; Dn 8:18.

been in revolt against me to this very day.[v]
4 Their children are bold of face and stubborn
of heart—to them I am sending you. You
shall say to them: Thus says the Lord GOD.[w]
5 And whether they hear or resist—they are a
rebellious house—they shall know that a
prophet has been among them.[x] 6 But as for
you, son of man, do not fear them or their
words. Do not fear, even though there are
briers or thorns and you sit among scorpions.* Do not be afraid of their words or be
terrified by their looks for they are a rebellious house.[y] 7 You must speak my words to
them, whether they hear or resist, because
they are rebellious.[z] 8 But you, son of man,
hear me when I speak to you and do not rebel
like this rebellious house. Open your mouth
and eat what I am giving you.[a]

9[b] It was then I saw a hand stretched out to
me; in it was a written scroll. 10 He unrolled
it before me; it was covered with writing
front and back. Written on it was: Lamentation, wailing, woe![c]

## CHAPTER 3

See RG 230

1 He said to me: Son of man, eat what
you find here: eat this scroll, then go, speak
to the house of Israel. 2 So I opened my
mouth, and he gave me the scroll to eat.
3[d] Son of man, he said to me, feed your
stomach and fill your belly with this scroll I
am giving you. I ate it, and it was as sweet as
honey* in my mouth. 4 Then he said to me,
Son of man, go now to the house of Israel,
and speak my words to them.

5 Not to a people with obscure speech and
difficult language am I sending you, but to
the house of Israel.[e] 6 Nor to many nations of
obscure speech and difficult language whose
words you cannot understand. For if I were
to send you to these, they would listen to
you.[f] 7 But the house of Israel will refuse to
listen to you, since they refuse to listen to
me. For the whole house of Israel is stubborn
of brow and hard of heart.[g] 8* Look! I make
your face as hard as theirs, and your brow as
stubborn as theirs.[h] 9 Like diamond, harder
than flint, I make your brow. Do not be
afraid of them, or be terrified by their looks,
for they are a rebellious house.[i]

10 Then he said to me, Son of man, take
into your heart all my words that I speak to
you; hear them well. 11 Now go to the exiles,
to your own people, and speak to them. Say
to them, whether they hear or refuse to hear:
Thus says the LORD God!

12 Then the spirit lifted me up, and I heard
behind me a loud rumbling noise as the
glory of the LORD* rose from its place:[j] 13 the
noise of the wings of the living creatures
beating against one another, and the noise of
the wheels alongside them, a loud rumbling.[k] 14 And the spirit lifted me up and took
me away, and I went off, my spirit angry and
bitter, for the hand of the LORD pressed hard
on me. 15 Thus I came to the exiles who lived
at Tel-abib* by the river Chebar; and there
where they dwelt, I stayed among them distraught for seven days. 16[l] At the end of the
seven days, the word of the LORD came to
me:

***The Prophet as Sentinel.**** 17 Son of man, I
have appointed you a sentinel for the house
of Israel.[m] When you hear a word from my
mouth, you shall warn them for me.

18 If I say to the wicked, You shall surely
die—and you do not warn them or speak out
to dissuade the wicked from their evil conduct in order to save their lives—then they
shall die for their sin, but I will hold you responsible for their blood. 19 If, however, you
warn the wicked and they still do not turn

**2:6 And you sit among scorpions**: the prophet must be prepared for bitter opposition.

**3:3 As sweet as honey**: though the prophet must foretell terrible things, the word of God is sweet to the one who receives it.

**3:8** Cf. Jer 1:18. The prophet must face fierce opposition with the determination and resistance shown by his opponents.

**3:12 The glory of the LORD**: the divine presence, manifested here in audible form. Cf. Ex 40:34; Lk 2:9.

**3:15 Tel-abib**: one of the sites where the exiles were settled, probably near Nippur.

**3:17–21** This passage refers to the prophet's role as sentinel, placed here and in chap. 33 as introductions to sections containing judgment oracles and salvation oracles respectively; cf. Hb 2:1.

*v:* Ez 20:8, 13. *w:* Ex 32:9. *x:* Ez 3:11, 27; 33:33. *y:* Dt 31:6. *z:* Ez 3:10–11; Jer 7:27. *a:* Jer 15:16. *b:* Ez 8:3; Rev 10:2. *c:* Zec 5:3; Rev 5:1. *d:* Jer 15:16; Rev 10:9–10. *e:* Is 28:11. *f:* cf. Mt 11:21. *g:* Jer 7:27. *h:* Jer 1:18. *i:* Is 48:4. *j:* Ez 8:3; 43:5. *k:* Ez 10:16–17. *l:* Ez 33:7–9; cf. 18:5–18. *m:* Is 52:8; Jer 1:17; Hb 2:1.

PROPHETS PERFORM SYMBOLIC actions to dramatize their statements and enable them to take effect (Is 20; Jer 13; 19). Ezekiel builds a model of Jerusalem under siege. The action draws upon the imagery of Jeremiah 1:18. The background of "three hundred and ninety" and "forty" (4:5–6) is not exactly certain, and the Septuagint (the Greek version of the Hebrew Bible), contains entirely different figures. If one counts backward from the destruction of the Temple in 587 B.C., the total of 430 years points to the time of the establishment of the united monarchy of Israel under Saul in 1017 B.C. Counting forward 390 years from that date takes one to 627 B.C., the twelfth year of Josiah's reign and the year in which his reforms begin (2 Chr 34:3; cf 2 Kgs 22:3). Josiah failed in his attempt to reunite Israel and Judah. The remaining 40 years accounts for the time between the beginning of Josiah's reform and the destruction of Jerusalem. Also see note below on 4:5–6.

from their wickedness and evil conduct, they
shall die for their sin, but you shall save your
life.
20But if the just turn away from their right
conduct and do evil when I place a stumbling block before them, then they shall die.
Even if you warned them about their sin,
they shall still die, and the just deeds that
they performed will not be remembered on
their behalf. I will, however, hold you responsible for their blood.[n] 21If, on the other
hand, you warn the just to avoid sin, and
they do not sin, they will surely live because
of the warning, and you in turn shall save
your own life.

*Ezekiel Mute.* 22The hand of the LORD
came upon me there and he said to me: Get
up and go out into the plain, where I will
speak with you.[o] 23[p] So I got up and went out
into the plain. There it was! The glory of the
LORD was standing there like the glory I had
seen by the river Chebar. Then I fell on my
face, 24but the spirit entered into me, set me
on my feet; he spoke to me, and said: Go,
shut yourself in your house. 25As for you,
son of man, know that they will put ropes on
you and bind you with them, so that you cannot go out among them.[q] 26And I will make
your tongue stick to the roof of your mouth
so that you will be mute,* no longer one who
rebukes them for being a rebellious house.[r]
27Only when I speak to you and open your
mouth, shall you say to them: Thus says the
LORD God: Let those who hear, hear! Let
those who resist, resist! They are truly a rebellious house.

## II. Before the Siege of Jerusalem

### CHAPTER 4

See RG 230–31

*Acts Symbolic of Siege and Exile.*
1* You, son of man, take a clay tablet; place
it in front of you, and draw on it a city, Jerusalem. 2Lay siege to it: build up siege works,
raise a ramp against it, pitch camps and set
up battering rams all around it. 3Then take
an iron pan and set it up as an iron wall between you and the city. Set your face toward
it and put it under siege. So you must lay
siege to it as a sign for the house of Israel.[s]
4Then lie down on your left side, while I
place the guilt of the house of Israel upon
you. As many days as you lie like this, you
shall bear their guilt. 5I allot you three hundred and ninety days* during which you
must bear the guilt of the house of Israel, the
same number of years they sinned. 6When
you have completed this, you shall lie down
a second time, on your right side to bear the
guilt of the house of Judah forty days; I allot
you one day for each year.[t] 7Turning your
face toward the siege of Jerusalem, with

**3:26–27 Mute**: here the prophet's inability to speak to the people in exile while Jerusalem was being besieged is seen as a consequence of God's direct intervention (cf. 24:27).

**4:1–5:4** The symbolic actions in this section prepare for the series of oracles that follow in 5:5–7:27.

**4:5–6 Three hundred and ninety days . . . forty days**: a symbol to represent the respective lengths of exile for the Northern Kingdom of Israel and the Southern Kingdom of Judah. Israel had already fallen to Assyria in 722/721 B.C. The numerical value of the Hebrew consonants in the phrase translated "the days of your siege" (v. 8) is three hundred and ninety. Forty years conventionally represents one generation.

**4:7 Bared arm**: a symbol of unrestrained power.

*n:* Is 8:14. *o:* Ez 1:3; 8:4. *p:* Ez 10:15; 40:3. *q:* Ez 4:8. *r:* Ps 22:15. *s:* Is 8:18. *t:* Dn 9:24–25; 12:11–12.

bared arm* you shall prophesy against it. 8 See, I bind you with ropes so that you cannot turn from one side to the other until you have completed the days of your siege.[u]

9* Then take wheat and barley, beans and lentils, millet and spelt; put them into a single pot and make them into bread. Eat it for as many days as you lie upon your side, three hundred and ninety days. 10 The food you eat shall be twenty shekels a day by weight; each day you shall eat it. 11 And the water you drink shall be the sixth of a hin* by measure; each day you shall drink it. 12 And the barley cake you eat you must bake on human excrement in the sight of all. 13 The LORD said: Thus the Israelites shall eat their food, unclean, among the nations where I drive them.[v] 14 "Oh no, Lord GOD," I protested. "Never have I defiled myself nor have I eaten carrion flesh or flesh torn by wild beasts, nor from my youth till now has any unclean meat entered my mouth."[w] 15 Very well, he replied, I will let you use cow manure in place of human dung. You can bake your bread on that. 16 Then he said to me: Son of man, I am about to break the staff of bread* in Jerusalem so they shall eat bread which they have weighed out anxiously and drink water which they have measured out fearfully.[x] 17 Because they lack bread and water they shall be devastated; each and every one will waste away because of their guilt.[y]

## CHAPTER 5

See RG 230–31

1 Now you, son of man, take a sharp sword and use it like a barber's razor, to shave your head and your beard. Then take a balance scale for weighing and divide the hair.[z] 2 Set a third on fire within the city,* when the days of your siege are completed; place another third around the city and strike it with the sword; the final third scatter to the wind and then unsheathe the sword after it.[a] 3 But take a few of the hairs and tie them in the hem of your garment. 4 Take some of these and throw them into the fire and burn them in the fire. Because of this, fire will flash out against the whole house of Israel.

5 Thus says the Lord GOD: This is Jerusalem! I placed it in the midst of the nations, surrounded by foreign lands. 6 But it rebelled against my ordinances more wickedly than the nations, and against my statutes more than the foreign lands around it; they rejected my ordinances and did not walk in my statutes.[b] 7 Therefore, thus says the Lord GOD: Because you have caused more uproar than the nations surrounding you, not living by my statutes nor carrying out my judgments, nor even living by the ordinances of the surrounding nations; 8 therefore, thus says the Lord GOD: See, I am coming against you!* I will carry out judgments among you while the nations look on.[c] 9 Because of all your abominations I will do to you what I have never done before, the like of which I will never do again. 10 Therefore, parents will eat their children in your midst, and children will eat their parents.* I will inflict punishments upon you and scatter all who remain to the winds.[d]

11 Therefore, as I live, says the Lord GOD, because you have defiled my sanctuary with all your atrocities and all your abominations, I will surely withdraw and not look upon you with pity nor spare you.[e] 12 A third of your people shall die of disease or starve to death within you; another third shall fall by the sword all around you; a third I will scatter to the winds and pursue them with the sword.[f]

13 Thus my anger will spend itself; I will vent my wrath against them until I am satisfied. Then they will know that I the LORD

**4:9–13** This action represents the scarcity of food during the siege of Jerusalem, and the consequent need to eat whatever is at hand. **Twenty shekels**: about nine ounces. **The sixth of a hin**: about one quart.

**4:11 Hin**: see note on 45:24.

**4:16 Break the staff of bread**: reducing the supply of bread that supports life as the walking staff supports a traveler; cf. 5:16; 14:13; Lv 26:26; Ps 105:16; Is 3:1.

**5:2 The city**: the one drawn on the tablet (4:1).

**5:8 I am coming against you**: an expression borrowed from the language of warfare in which an enemy attacked another with the sword. "You" in vv. 8–17 is Jerusalem.

**5:10 Parents will eat their children . . . parents**: the prophet describes the consequences of the prolonged Babylonian siege of Jerusalem in 587/586 B.C. See note on Lam 2:20.

*u:* Ez 3:25. *v:* Hos 9:4. *w:* Dn 1:8. *x:* Ez 5:16; Lv 26:26. *y:* Lv 26:39. *z:* Is 7:20. *a:* Jer 13:24. *b:* Ez 16:47–51. *c:* Jer 21:5. *d:* Lv 26:29, 33; Dt 28:53; Jer 19:9. *e:* Ez 7:4, 9; 8:18. *f:* Ez 6:11–12; Rev 6:8.

spoke in my passion when I spend my wrath upon them.[g] [14]I will make you a desolation and a reproach among the nations around you, in the sight of every passerby.[h] [15]And you will be a reproach and a taunt, a warning and a horror to the nations around you when I execute judgments against you in angry wrath, with furious chastisements. I, the LORD, have spoken! [16]When I loose against you the deadly arrows of starvation that I am sending to destroy you, I will increase starvation and will break your staff of bread.[i] [17]I will send against you starvation and wild beasts who will leave you childless, while disease and bloodshed sweep through you. I will bring the sword against you. I, the LORD, have spoken.[j]

See RG 230–31

## CHAPTER 6

***Against the Mountains of Israel.*** [1]The word of the LORD came to me: [2]Son of man, set your face toward the mountains of Israel and prophesy against them:[k] [3]You shall say: Mountains of Israel, hear the word of the Lord GOD. Thus says the Lord GOD to the mountains and hills, to the ravines and valleys:[l] Pay attention! I am bringing a sword against you, and I will destroy your high places.* [4]Your altars shall be laid waste, your incense stands smashed, and I will throw your slain down in front of your idols. [5]Yes, I will lay the corpses of the Israelites in front of their idols, and scatter your bones around your altars.* [m] [6]Wherever you live, cities shall be ruined and high places laid waste, in order that your altars be laid waste and devastated, your idols broken and smashed, your incense altars hacked to pieces, and whatever you have made wiped out.[n] [7]The slain shall fall in your midst, and you shall know that I am the LORD.* [o] [8]But I will spare some of you from the sword to live as refugees among the nations when you are scattered to foreign lands. [9]Then your refugees will remember me among the nations to which they have been exiled, after I have broken their lusting hearts that turned away from me and their eyes that lusted after idols. They will loathe themselves for all the evil they have done, for all their abominations.[p] [10]Then they shall know that I the LORD did not threaten in vain to inflict this evil on them.

[11]Thus says the Lord GOD: Clap your hands, stamp your feet,* and cry "Alas!" for all the evil abominations of the house of Israel! They shall fall by the sword, starvation, and disease.[q] [12]Those far off shall die of disease, those nearby shall fall by the sword, and those who survive and are spared shall perish by starvation; thus will I spend my fury upon them. [13]They shall know that I am the LORD, when their slain lie among their idols, all around their altars, on every high hill and mountaintop, beneath every green tree and leafy oak*—any place they offer sweet-smelling oblations to all their idols.[r] [14]I will stretch out my hand against them; I will make the land a desolate waste, from the wilderness to Riblah,* wherever they live. Thus they shall know that I am the LORD.[s]

## CHAPTER 7

See RG 230–31

***The End Has Come.*** [1]The word of the LORD came to me: [2]Son of man, now say: Thus says the Lord GOD to the land of Israel: An end! The end comes upon the four corners of the land![t] [3]Now the end is upon you;

**6:3 High places**: raised platforms usually built on hills outside towns for making sacrifices to the Lord or to Canaanite deities. They became synonymous with places of idolatry after the centralization of worship in the Jerusalem Temple.

**6:5 Scatter your bones . . . altars**: the bones of the dead defiled a place; cf. 2 Kgs 23:14.

**6:7 You shall know that I am the LORD**: this formula is repeated after most of Ezekiel's oracles from this point on. Whatever happens to Israel happens at the Lord's command; because the Lord uses the nations to punish or reward Israel for its behavior, Israel will learn that its God has sole rule over the nations and the universe, and will acknowledge that rule in obedience.

**6:11 Clap your hands, stamp your feet**: these gestures may express grief, even horror, at Israel's infidelities; in 25:6, they are signs of gloating.

**6:13 Every green tree and leafy oak**: trees often identified with fertility deities and the "tree of life"; sacred groves had a long history in Palestine and throughout the Mediterranean basin as places of worship; cf. Dt 12:2.

**6:14 From the wilderness to Riblah**: the whole land, from the far south to the far north.

*g:* Ez 16:42. *h:* Lv 26:32. *i:* Ez 4:16; 14:13; Lv 26:26. *j:* Lv 26:25. *k:* Ez 36:1. *l:* Ez 36:4; Lv 26:30. *m:* Lv 26:30; Jer 8:12. *n:* Lv 26:30. *o:* Ez 11:10–12. *p:* Ez 20:7, 24; Ps 137:1. *q:* Ez 21:14–17. *r:* Ez 20:28; Lv 26:30. *s:* Jer 48:22. *t:* Rev 7:1; 20:8.

I will unleash my anger against you, judge you according to your ways, and hold against you all your abominations. 4 My eye will not spare you, nor will I have pity; but I will hold your conduct against you, since your abominations remain within you; then shall you know that I am the LORD.[u]

5 Thus says the Lord GOD: Evil upon evil! See it coming! 6 An end is coming, the end is coming; it is ripe for you! See it coming! 7 The crisis has come for you who dwell in the land! The time has come, near is the day: panic, no rejoicing on the mountains.[v] 8 Soon now I will pour out my fury upon you and spend my anger against you; I will judge you according to your ways and hold against you all your abominations.[w] 9 My eye will not spare, nor will I take pity; I will hold your conduct against you since your abominations remain within you, then you shall know that it is I, the LORD, who strikes.[x]

10 The day is here! Look! it is coming! The crisis has come! Lawlessness is blooming, insolence budding; 11 the violent have risen up to wield a scepter of wickedness. But none of them shall remain; none of their crowd, none of their wealth, for none of them are innocent. 12* The time has come, the day dawns. The buyer must not rejoice, nor the seller mourn, for wrath is coming upon all the throng.[y] 13 Assuredly, the seller shall not regain what was sold, as long as they all live; for the vision is for the whole crowd: it shall not be revoked! Yes, because of their guilt, they shall not hold on to life. 14 They will sound the trumpet and get everything ready, but no one will go out to battle, for my wrath weighs upon all the crowd.

15 The sword is outside; disease and hunger are within. Whoever is in the fields will die by the sword; whoever is in the city disease and hunger will devour.[z] 16 If their survivors flee, they will die on the mountains, moaning like doves of the valley on account of their guilt. 17 All their hands will hang limp, and all their knees* turn to water.[a] 18b They put on sackcloth, horror clothes them; shame is on all their faces, all their heads are shaved bald.* 19 They fling their silver into the streets, and their gold is considered unclean.[c] Their silver and gold cannot save them on the day of the LORD's wrath. They cannot satisfy their hunger or fill their bellies, for it has been the occasion of their sin. 20* In their beautiful ornaments they took pride; out of them they made their abominable images, their detestable things. For this reason I will make them unclean.[d] 21 I will hand them over as spoils to foreigners, as plunder to the wicked of the earth, so that they may defile them. 22 I will turn my face away from them. My treasure will be defiled; the violent will enter and defile it.[e] 23 They will wreak slaughter, for the land is filled with bloodshed and the city with violence.[f] 24 I will bring in the worst of the nations to take possession of their houses. I will put an end to their proud strength,* and their sanctuaries will be defiled.[g] 25 When anguish comes, they will seek peace, but there is none.[h] 26 Disaster after disaster, rumor upon rumor. They keep seeking a vision from the prophet; instruction from the priest is missing, and counsel from the elders.[i] 27 The king mourns, the prince is terror-stricken, the hands of the common people tremble. I will deal with them according to their ways, and according to their judgments I will judge them. They shall know that I am the LORD.

## CHAPTER 8

See RG 230–31

1 In the sixth year, on the fifth day of the sixth month,* as I was sitting in my

**7:12–13** Normal affairs will cease to have any meaning in view of the disaster that is to come.

**7:17 Hands . . . knees**: image of profound terror; loss of control of body movement and functions.

**7:18 Shaved bald**: shaving the head was a sign of mourning.

**7:20** Assyrian wall paintings show that statues of deities were often cast in precious metals and then decorated with jewelry. Cf. Is 40:19–20; 41:6–7; 44:9–20.

**7:24 Proud strength**: misplaced trust in the might and power of their kings and army. Cf. v. 22; 33:28 and related ideas in Is 2:12; 10:12; 13:11; Jer 48:29; Ez 24:21; 30:18.

**8:1 In the sixth year, on the fifth day of the sixth month**: September, 592 B.C.

*u:* Ez 5:11; Jer 13:14. *v:* Ez 12:23; 30:3; Am 5:18–19; Zep 1:14. *w:* Ez 20:8, 13, 21. *x:* Ez 22:31; Jer 21:7. *y:* Is 24:2; cf. Mt 24:17–18. *z:* Dt 32:25. *a:* Jer 47:3. *b:* Is 15:2–3; Jer 4:8; 48:3. *c:* Zep 1:7, 18; 2:2. *d:* Jer 10:3–4. *e:* Ps 74:7–8. *f:* Ez 22:9; 24:6. *g:* Lam 2:7. *h:* Jer 6:1. *i:* Jer 18:18; Mi 3:6–7.

house, with the elders of Judah sitting before me, the hand of the Lord GOD fell upon me there.[j] [2]I looked up and there was a figure that looked like a man.* Downward from what looked like his waist, there was fire; from his waist upward, like the brilliance of polished bronze.[k]

***Vision of Abominations in the Temple.*** [3]He stretched out the form of a hand and seized me by the hair of my head. The spirit lifted me up* between earth and heaven and brought me in divine vision to Jerusalem[l] to the entrance of the inner gate facing north where the statue of jealousy that provokes jealousy stood. [4]There I saw the glory of the God of Israel, like the vision I had seen in the plain.[m] [5]He said to me: Son of man, lift your eyes to the north! I looked to the north and there in the entry north of the altar gate was this statue of jealousy.[n] [6]He asked, Son of man, do you see what they are doing? Do you see the great abominations that the house of Israel is practicing here, so that I must depart from my sanctuary? You shall see even greater abominations![o]

[7]Then he brought me to the entrance of the courtyard, and there I saw a hole in the wall. [8]Son of man, he ordered, dig through the wall. I dug through the wall—there was a doorway. [9]Go in, he said to me, and see the evil abominations they are doing here. [10]I went in and looked—figures of all kinds of creeping things and loathsome beasts,* all the idols of the house of Israel,[p] pictured around the wall. [11]Before them stood seventy of the elders of the house of Israel. Among them stood Jaazaniah, son of Shaphan, each with censer in hand; a cloud of incense drifted upward.[q] [12]Then he said to me: Do you see, son of man, what the elders of the house of Israel are doing in the dark, each in his idol chamber? They think: "The LORD cannot see us; the LORD has forsaken the land."[r] [13]He said: You will see them practicing even greater abominations.

[14]Then he brought me to the entrance of the north gate of the house of the LORD. There women sat and wept for Tammuz.* [s] [15]He said to me: Do you see this, son of man? You will see other abominations, greater than these!

[16]Then he brought me into the inner court of the house of the LORD. There at the door of the LORD's temple, between the porch and the altar, were about twenty-five men with their backs to the LORD's temple and their faces toward the east; they were bowing eastward* to the sun.[t] [17]He said: Do you see, son of man? Are the abominable things the house of Judah has done here so slight that they should also fill the land with violence, provoking me again and again? Now they are putting the branch to my nose!* [18]Therefore I in turn will act furiously: my eye will not spare, nor will I take pity. Even if they cry out in a loud voice for me to hear, I shall not listen to them.

## CHAPTER 9

See RG 230–31

***Slaughter of the Idolaters.*** [1]Then he cried aloud for me to hear: Come, you scourges of the city! [2]And there were six

**8:2 Looked like a man**: the divine presence which accompanies Ezekiel in these visions. Cf. 40:3–4.

**8:3 The spirit lifted me up**: the prophet is transported in vision from Babylon to Jerusalem. Ezekiel may be drawing on his memory of the Temple from before his exile in 598 B.C. **The statue of jealousy**: the statue which provokes the Lord's outrage against the insults of his own people; perhaps the statue of the goddess Asherah set up by Manasseh, king of Judah (cf. 2 Kgs 21:7; 2 Chr 33:7, 15). Although his successor, Josiah, had removed it (2 Kgs 23:6), the statue may have been set up again after his death.

**8:10 Creeping things and loathsome beasts**: perhaps images of Egyptian deities, often represented in animal form. During the last days of Jerusalem Zedekiah, king of Judah, was allied with Egypt, hoping for protection against the Babylonians.

**8:14 Wept for Tammuz**: the withering of trees and plants that began in late spring was attributed to the descent of Tammuz, the Mesopotamian god of fertility, to the world of the dead beneath the earth. During the fourth month of the year, female worshipers of Tammuz would wail and mourn the god's disappearance.

**8:16 Bowing eastward**: sun worship was perhaps introduced as a condition of alliance with other nations. While Josiah removed some elements of this worship (2 Kgs 23:11), Manasseh, for example, built altars to all the "hosts of heaven" in two Temple courtyards (2 Kgs 21:5).

**8:17 Putting the branch to my nose**: the meaning is uncertain. It may be connected with the social injustice mentioned in v. 17b and in 9:9, e.g., "with their violence they tweak my nose," i.e., "goad my fury." The Masoretic text reads "their noses" as a euphemism for "my nose," thus avoiding the impropriety of these idolaters coming into contact with God even figuratively.

*j:* Ez 14:1; 33:31. *k:* Ez 1:4, 26–27. *l:* Ez 2:9; 3:12; Dn 14:6. *m:* Ez 3:22. *n:* Ps 78:58. *o:* Ps 78:60. *p:* Ez 23:14. *q:* Nm 11:16. *r:* Is 29:15. *s:* cf. Dn 11:37. *t:* Jb 31:26–28.

## The Slaughter of Jerusalem

SACRIFICIAL SLAUGHTER AT the altar of the temple portrays the killing of the people of Jerusalem. The six men (9:2) come from the upper gate to the north with weapons in their hands to begin the slaughter. The Babylonian army would have entered Judah from the north (see Jer 1:13–16). The man clothed in linen (9:3) wears the apparel of a priest who serves at the altar (Ex 28:39; Lv 6:10) and carries a writing case to record the sacrifices. The bronze altar had been moved to the north by Ahaz to accommodate the Assyrian altar (2 Kgs 16:14). The mark (the ancient letter "taw," translated "mark," looks like an X) placed on the foreheads of those who groan over all the abominations would have reminded the Israelites of the mark on the doorpost that protected the Israelites from God's plague against the Egyptians (Ex 12:23). Ezekiel attempts to intercede as Moses did (Ex 32:1–14; Nm 14), but God states that the people believe that God lacks power.

men coming from the direction of the upper
gate which faces north, each with a weapon
of destruction in his hand. In their midst was
a man dressed in linen, with a scribe's case
at his waist. They entered and stood beside
the bronze altar.[u] 3Then the glory of the God
of Israel moved off the cherub and went up
to the threshold of the temple. He called to
the man dressed in linen with the scribe's
case at his waist,[v] 4[w] and the LORD said to
him:* Pass through the city, through the
midst of Jerusalem, and mark an X on the
foreheads of those who grieve and lament
over all the abominations practiced within it.
5To the others he said in my hearing: Pass
through the city after him and strike! Do not
let your eyes spare; do not take pity. 6Old
and young, male and female, women and
children—wipe them out! But do not touch
anyone marked with the X. Begin at my
sanctuary. So they began with the elders
who were in front of the temple.[x] 7Defile the
temple, he said to them, fill its courts with
the slain. Then go out and strike in the city.
8As they were striking, I was left alone. I
fell on my face, crying out, "Alas, Lord
GOD! Will you destroy all that is left of Israel
when you pour out your fury on Jerusalem?"
9He answered me: The guilt of the house of
Israel and the house of Judah is too great to
measure; the land is filled with bloodshed,
the city with lawlessness. They think that the
LORD has abandoned the land, that he does
not see them. 10My eye, however, will not
spare, nor shall I take pity, but I will bring
their conduct down upon their heads.
11Just then the man dressed in linen with
the scribe's case at his waist made his report:
"I have done as you commanded!"

### CHAPTER 10

See RG 230–31

1Then I looked and there above the firmament over the heads of the cherubim was
something like a sapphire, something that
looked like a throne.[y] 2* And he said to the
man dressed in linen: Go within the wheelwork under the cherubim; fill both your
hands with burning coals from the place
among the cherubim, then scatter them over
the city. As I watched, he entered.[z] 3Now the
cherubim were standing to the south of the
temple when the man went in and a cloud
filled the inner court. 4The glory of the LORD
had moved off the cherubim to the threshold
of the temple; the temple was filled with the
cloud, the whole court brilliant with the glory
of the LORD. 5The sound of the wings of the
cherubim could be heard as far as the outer
court; it was like the voice of God Almighty
speaking.[a] 6He commanded the man dressed

**9:4** Ezekiel emphasizes personal accountability; the innocent inhabitants of Jerusalem are spared while the idolatrous are punished. **An X**: lit., the Hebrew letter *taw*.

**10:2–13** The burning coals, a sign of the divine presence (cf. 28:14; Ps 18:9), represent the judgment of destruction that God is visiting upon the city; they may also represent the judgment of purification that prepares the land to become the Lord's sanctuary (cf. Is 6:6–7).

*u:* Ez 10:2; Dn 10:5; 12:6; Rev 8:2; 15:6. *v:* Ez 11:22. *w:* Ex 12:7; Rev 7:2–4; 13:16. *x:* Gn 4:15; Ex 12:7. *y:* Ex 24:10; Rev 4:2. *z:* Rev 8:2. *a:* Jb 40:9.

in linen: Take fire from within the wheelwork among the cherubim. The man entered and stood by one of the wheels. 7 Thereupon a cherub stretched out a hand from among the cherubim toward the fire in the midst of the cherubim, took some, and put it in the hands of the one dressed in linen. He took it and came out. 8 Something like a human hand was visible under the wings of the cherubim. 9 I also saw four wheels beside the cherubim, one wheel beside each cherub, and the wheels appeared to have the sparkle of yellow topaz. 10 And the appearance of the four all seemed alike, as though one wheel were inside the other. 11 When they moved, they went in any of the four directions without veering as they moved; in whatever direction the first cherub faced, the others followed without veering as they went. 12 Their entire bodies—backs, hands, and wings—and wheels were covered with eyes all around like the four wheels.[b] 13 I heard the wheels called "wheelwork." 14 Each living creature had four faces: the first a cherub, the second a human being, the third a lion, the fourth an eagle.[c] 15* When the cherubim rose up, they were indeed the living creatures I had seen by the river Chebar.[d] 16 When the cherubim moved, the wheels went beside them; when the cherubim lifted up their wings to rise from the earth, even then the wheels did not leave their sides. 17 When they stood still, the wheels stood still; when they rose up, the wheels rose up with them, for the spirit of the living creatures was in them. 18 Then the glory of the LORD left the threshold of the temple and took its place upon the cherubim. 19 The cherubim lifted their wings and rose up from the earth before my eyes as they departed with the wheels beside them. They stopped at the entrance of the eastern gate of the LORD's house, and the glory of the God of Israel was up above them.[e] 20* These were the living creatures I had seen beneath the God of Israel by the river Chebar. Now I knew they were cherubim.[f] 21 Each of them had four faces and four wings, and something like human hands under their wings. 22 Their faces looked just like the faces I had seen by the river Chebar; and each one went straight ahead.

## CHAPTER 11

See RG 230-31

### *Death for the Remnant in Jerusalem.*

1 The spirit lifted me up and brought me to the east gate of the house of the LORD facing east. There at the entrance of the gate were twenty-five men; among them I saw the public officials Jaazaniah, son of Azzur, and Pelatiah, son of Benaiah. 2 The LORD said to me: Son of man, these are the men who are planning evil and giving wicked counsel in this city. 3 They are saying, "No need to build houses! The city is the pot, and we are the meat."* [g] 4 Therefore prophesy against them, son of man, prophesy! 5 Then the spirit of the LORD fell upon me and told me to say: Thus says the LORD: This is how you talk, house of Israel. I know the things that come into your mind! 6 You have slain many in this city, filled its streets with the slain. 7 Therefore thus says the Lord GOD: The slain whom you piled up in it, that is the meat, the pot is the city. But you I will bring out of it.[h] 8 You fear the sword—that sword I will bring upon you—oracle of the Lord GOD.[i] 9 I will bring you out of the city, hand you over to foreigners, and execute judgments against you. 10 By the sword you shall fall. At the borders of Israel I will judge you so that you will know that I am the LORD. 11 The city shall not be a pot for you, nor shall you be

**10:15–19** The throne represents God's presence as ruler and protector of the land. In chap. 1, God is revealed as the lord of the world who can appear even in a far-off land; here God is about to abandon the Temple, that is, hand the city over to its enemies. God and the throne return again in 43:1–3.

**10:20–22** The repetition of description from the preceding verses is a device intended to suggest the rapid, constantly changing motion of the vision and the difficulty of describing the divine in human language.

**11:3 No need to build houses . . . meat**: this advice is based on the conviction that invincible Jerusalem will protect its citizens from further danger just as a pot shields the meat inside from the fire. The poorer citizens of Jerusalem and the refugees from nearby villages can now appropriate the property abandoned by the city's wealthier upper class when they were deported (v. 15). The metaphor of the pot and its contents reappears in chap. 24.

*b*: Ez 1:15–20; Rev 4:6–8. *c*: cf. Gn 3:24. *d*: Ps 137:1. *e*: Ez 43:4. *f*: Ez 1:1. *g*: Ez 24:3; Jer 1:13. *h*: Mi 3:2–3. *i*: Lv 26:25.

meat within it. At the borders of Israel I will judge you,[j] 12 so you shall know that I am the LORD, whose statutes you did not follow, whose ordinances you did not keep. Instead, you acted according to the ordinances of the nations around you.

13 While I was prophesying, Pelatiah, the son of Benaiah, dropped dead. I fell down on my face and cried out in a loud voice: "Alas, Lord GOD! You are finishing off what remains of Israel!"*[k]

***Restoration for the Exiles.*** 14 The word of the LORD came to me: 15* Son of man, the inhabitants of Jerusalem are saying about all your relatives, the other exiles, and all the house of Israel, "They are far away from the LORD. The land is given to us as a possession."[l] 16 Therefore say: Thus says the Lord GOD: I have indeed sent them far away among the nations, scattered them over the lands, and have been but little sanctuary for them in the lands to which they have gone. 17 Therefore, thus says the Lord GOD, I will gather you from the nations and collect you from the lands through which you were scattered, so I can give you the land of Israel.[m] 18 They will enter it and remove all its atrocities and abominations. 19[n] And I will give them another heart and a new spirit I will put within them. From their bodies I will remove the hearts of stone, and give them hearts of flesh, 20 so that they walk according to my statutes, taking care to keep my ordinances. Thus they will be my people, and I will be their God.[o] 21 But as for those whose hearts are devoted to their atrocities and abominations, I will bring their conduct down upon their heads—oracle of the Lord GOD.

22 Then the cherubim lifted their wings and the wheels alongside them, with the glory of the God of Israel above them.[p] 23* The glory of the LORD rose up from the middle of the city and came to rest on the mountain east of the city.[q] 24 In a vision, the spirit lifted me up and brought me back to the exiles in Chaldea, by the spirit of God. The vision I had seen left me,[r] 25 and I told the exiles everything the LORD had shown me.[s]

## CHAPTER 12

See RG 230–31

***Acts Symbolic of the Exile.*** 1 The word of the LORD came to me: 2 Son of man, you live in the midst of a rebellious house; they have eyes to see, but do not see, and ears to hear but do not hear. They are such a rebellious house![t] 3 Now, son of man, during the day while they watch, pack a bag for exile,* and again while they watch, go into exile from your place to another place; perhaps they will see that they are a rebellious house. 4 During the day, while they watch, bring out your bag, an exile's bag. In the evening, again while they watch, go out as if into exile.[u] 5 While they watch, dig a hole through the wall* and go out through it. 6 While they watch, shoulder your load and go out in darkness. Cover your face so you cannot see the land, for I am making you a sign for the house of Israel![v]

7 I did just as I was commanded. During the day I brought out my bag, an exile's bag. In the evening while they watched, I dug a hole through the wall with my hands and set out in darkness, shouldering my load.

8 In the morning, the word of the LORD came to me: 9 Son of man, did not the house of Israel, that house of rebels, say, "What are you doing?"[w] 10 Tell them: Thus says the Lord

**11:13** In Ezekiel's vision Pelatiah represents the people left in Jerusalem, "the remnant of Israel." His sudden death in the vision, but not in reality, is a figure for the judgment described in vv. 8–10 and prompts Ezekiel's anguished question about the survival of the people left in the land after the deportations in 597.

**11:15–21** Ezekiel insists that those who remained in Judah are doomed; the exiles, under a new covenant, will constitute a new Israel. Cf. chap. 36; Jer 24:7; 29.

**11:23** The glory of the Lord departs toward the east, to the exiles in Babylon; it will return once the Temple is rebuilt (43:1–3).

**12:3–10** An exile's bag contains bare necessities, probably no more than a bowl, a mat, and a waterskin. The prophet's action foreshadows the fate of ruler and people (vv. 11–14).

**12:5 Through the wall**: mud-brick outer wall of a private home. In this symbolic action, Ezekiel represents the enemy forces, and the house wall, the city wall of Jerusalem breached by the Babylonian army.

*j:* 2 Kgs 25:20–21. *k:* Ez 9:8. *l:* Ez 33:24. *m:* Ez 34:13; 36:28. *n:* Ez 18:31; 36:26; 2 Cor 3:3. *o:* Ex 6:7; Jer 31:33; 32:38. *p:* Ex 24:16. *q:* Zec 14:4. *r:* Ez 37:1. *s:* Ez 3:4, 11. *t:* Is 6:9–10; Jer 5:21; cf. Mt 13:15; Mk 4:12; 8:18. *u:* 2 Kgs 25:4. *v:* Is 8:18. *w:* Ez 20:49; 24:19.

GOD: This load is the prince in Jerusalem and the whole house of Israel within it. 11 Say, I am a sign for you: just as I have done, so it shall be done to them; into exile, as captives they shall go.[x] 12 The prince among them shall shoulder his load in darkness and go out through the hole they dug in the wall to bring him out. His face shall be covered so that he cannot even see the ground.[y] 13[z] I will spread my net over him and he shall be caught in my snare. I will bring him into Babylon, to the land of the Chaldeans, though he shall not see it,* and there he shall die. 14 All his retinue, his aides and all his troops, I will scatter to the winds and pursue them with the sword.[a] 15 Then they shall know that I am the LORD, when I disperse them among the nations and scatter them throughout the lands.[b] 16 But I will let a few of them escape the sword, starvation, and plague, so that they may recount all their abominations among the nations to which they go. Thus they may know that I am the LORD.*

17 The word of the LORD came to me: 18 Son of man, eat your bread trembling and drink your water shaking with fear.[c] 19 And say to the people of the land:* Thus says the Lord GOD about the inhabitants of Jerusalem in the land of Israel: they shall eat their bread in fear and drink their water in horror, because the land will be emptied of what fills it—the lawlessness of all its inhabitants. 20 Inhabited cities shall be in ruins, the land a desolate place. Then you shall know that I am the LORD.

***Prophecy Ridiculed.*** 21 The word of the LORD came to me: 22 Son of man, what is this proverb you have in the land of Israel: "The days drag on, and every vision fails"?*[d] 23 Say to them therefore: Thus says the Lord GOD: I will put an end to that proverb; they shall never use it again in Israel. Say to them instead: "The days are at hand and every vision fulfilled."[e] 24 No longer shall there be any false visions or deceitful divinations within the house of Israel,[f] 25 for whatever word I speak shall happen without delay. In your days, rebellious house, whatever I speak I will bring about—oracle of the Lord GOD.[g]

26 The word of the LORD came to me: 27 Son of man, listen! The house of Israel is saying, "The vision he sees is a long time off; he prophesies for distant times!"[h] 28 Say to them therefore: Thus says the Lord GOD: None of my words shall be delayed any longer. Whatever I say is final; it shall be done—oracle of the Lord GOD.

## CHAPTER 13

See RG 231

***Against the Prophets of Peace.*** 1 The word of the LORD came to me: 2 Son of man, prophesy against the prophets of Israel, prophesy! Say to those who prophesy their own thoughts: Hear the word of the LORD![i] 3 Thus says the Lord GOD: Woe to those prophets, the fools who follow their own spirit and see nothing.[j] 4 Like foxes among ruins are your prophets, Israel! 5 You did not step into the breach, nor repair the wall around the house of Israel so it would stand firm against attack on the day of the LORD. 6 False visions! Lying divinations! They say, "The oracle of the LORD," even though the LORD did not send them. Then they expect their word to be confirmed![k] 7 Was not the vision you saw false? Did you not report a lying divination when you said, "Oracle of the LORD," even though I never spoke? 8 Therefore thus says the Lord GOD: Because you have spoken falsehood and seen lying visions, therefore, for certain I am coming at you—oracle of the Lord GOD. 9 My hand is against the prophets who see false visions and who make lying divinations. They shall

**12:13 Though he shall not see it**: according to a Targum, an allusion to Nebuchadnezzar having Zedekiah blinded before deporting him to Babylonia (cf. 2 Kgs 25:7); according to the Septuagint, the king is ashamed of his flight from the city and disguises himself so others will not recognize him.

**12:16** Both exiles and nations shall know that the exile is divine punishment for Israel's betrayal of the Lord and the covenant, not evidence that the Lord is too weak to fight off the Babylonian deity.

**12:19 The people of the land**: the exiles in Babylon who, ironically, are now outside the land.

**12:22–28** This proverb conveys the skepticism the people of Jerusalem have; cf. Jer 20:7–9.

*x:* 2 Kgs 25:7; Jer 52:15. *y:* Jer 23:33; 52:7. *z:* Ez 17:20; 19:8; 32:3. *a:* 2 Kgs 25:5; Jer 21:7. *b:* Lv 26:33. *c:* Lam 5:9. *d:* Ps 49:4. *e:* Ez 7:7. *f:* Ez 13:23; Jer 14:14; Zec 13:2–4. *g:* Hb 2:3. *h:* cf. Mt 24:48; 2 Pt 3:4. *i:* Jer 23:16, 21–22; 28:15. *j:* Ez 14:9; Nm 16:28; Is 32:6; Jer 23:1, 16, 25–40; Mi 2:11. *k:* cf. Is 30:10.

not belong to the community of my people. They shall not be written in the register of the house of Israel, nor shall they enter the land of Israel. Thus you shall know that I am the LORD.[l]

[10]Because they led my people astray, saying, "Peace!" when there is no peace, and when a wall is built, they cover it with whitewash,* [11]say then to the whitewashers: I will bring down a flooding rain; hailstones shall fall, and a stormwind shall break forth.[m] [12]When the wall has fallen, will you not be asked: "Where is the whitewash you spread on it?"

[13]Therefore thus says the Lord GOD: In my fury I will let loose stormwinds; because of my anger there will be flooding rain, and hailstones will fall with destructive wrath.[n] [14]I will tear down the wall you whitewashed and level it to the ground, laying bare its foundations. When it falls, you shall be crushed beneath it. Thus you shall know that I am the LORD. [15]When I have poured out my fury on the wall and its whitewashers, it will fall. Then I will say to you: No wall! No whitewashers— [16]the prophets of Israel who prophesy to Jerusalem and see visions of peace for it when there is no peace—oracle of the Lord GOD.[o]

*Against Witches.* [17]As for you, son of man, now set your face against the daughters of your people who play the prophet from their own thoughts, and prophesy against them.[p] [18]You shall say, Thus says the Lord GOD: Woe to those who sew amulets for the wrists of every arm and make veils* for every head size to snare lives! You ensnare the lives of my people, even as you preserve your own lives! [19]You have profaned me among my people for handfuls of barley and crumbs of bread,* slaying those who should not be slain, and keeping alive those who should not live, lying to my people, who listen to lies. [20]Therefore thus says the Lord GOD: See! I am coming after your amulets by which you ensnare lives like prey. I will tear them from your arms and set free the lives of those you have ensnared like prey.[q] [21]I will tear off your veils and deliver my people from your power, so that they shall never again be ensnared by your hands. Thus you shall know that I am the LORD. [22]Because you discourage the righteous with lies when I did not want them to be distressed, and encourage the wicked so they do not turn from their evil ways and save their lives,[r] [23]therefore you shall no longer see false visions or practice divination again. I will deliver my people from your hand. Thus you shall know that I am the LORD.

## CHAPTER 14

See RG 231

*Idolatry and Unfaithfulness.* [1]Some elders of Israel came and sat down before me.[s] [2]Then the word of the LORD came to me: [3]Son of man, these men keep the memory of their idols alive in their hearts, setting the stumbling block of their sin before them. Should I allow myself to be consulted by them? [4]Therefore say to them: Thus says the Lord GOD: If any of the house of Israel who keep the memory of their idols in their hearts, setting the stumbling block of their sin before them, come to a prophet, I the LORD will answer in person because of their many idols, [5]in order to catch the hearts of the house of Israel, estranged from me because of all their idols.

[6]Therefore say to the house of Israel: Thus says the Lord GOD: Return, turn away from your idols; from all your abominations, turn your faces.[t] [7]For if anyone of the house of Israel or any alien residing in Israel who are estranged from me and who keep their idols in their hearts, setting the stumbling block of their sin before them, come to ask a prophet to consult me on their behalf, I the LORD will answer them in person. [8]I will set

**13:10** The false prophets contributed to popular illusions of security by predictions of peace, like those who whitewash a wall to conceal its defects.

**13:18 Sew amulets . . . make veils**: used by sorcerers to mark individuals for life or for death. For a small price (v. 19), these women promised protection for the wicked, who, in the Lord's estimation, "should not live" (v. 19), and death for the righteous, "who should not be slain" (v. 19). Both decisions belong to the Lord.

**13:19 Handfuls of barley and crumbs of bread**: payment for the amulets and scarves.

*l:* Ex 32:32. *m:* cf. Ps 18:7–15; 77:17–18. *n:* Rev 11:19; 16:21. *o:* Jer 6:14. *p:* Rev 2:20. *q:* Ps 124:7. *r:* Ez 18:21; 33:14–16. *s:* Ez 8:1; 20:1. *t:* Is 2:20; cf. Ez 18:30; 33:11.

## Concerning Individual Righteousness

AFTER STATING THAT God deceives false prophets and leads them to destruction, Ezekiel claims in 14:12–23 that the people are responsible for their own moral action and safety from punishment. Noah, Daniel, and Job (v. 14) were exemplary righteous persons who had the capacity to save others. Noah saved his family during the flood (Gn 6–9), and Job saved his three friends who spoke wrongly about God (Jb 42:7–9). In the Canaanite legend of Aqhat, the righteous Dan-El saves his son Aqhat from death. Dan-El in Ezekiel is spelled according to the Canaanite pattern; see note below on 14:14. In this instance, however, Noah, Job, and Daniel would have no power to save: Each individual must face the consequences of his or her breaking faith with God.

my face against them and make them a sign
and a byword, and cut them off from the
midst of my people. Thus you shall know
that I am the LORD.
9[u] As for the prophet, if he speaks a deceiving word, I the LORD am the one who deceives that prophet.* I will stretch out my
hand against him and destroy him from the
midst of my people Israel. 10 They will be
punished for their own sins, the inquirer and
the prophet alike, 11 so that the house of Israel may no longer stray from me, no longer
defile themselves by all their sins. Then they
shall be my people, and I shall be their
God—oracle of the Lord GOD.
*Just Cause.** 12 The word of the LORD
came to me: 13[v] Son of man, if a land sins
against me by breaking faith, and I stretch
out my hand against it, breaking its staff of
bread and setting famine loose upon it, cutting off from it human being and beast
alike— 14 even if these three were in it,
Noah, Daniel, and Job,* they could only save
themselves by their righteousness—oracle
of the Lord GOD.[w] 15 If I summoned wild
beasts to prowl the land, depopulating it so
that it became a wasteland which no one
would cross because of the wild beasts,[x]
16 and these three were in it, as I live—oracle
of the Lord GOD—I swear they could save
neither sons nor daughters; they alone would
be saved, but the land would become a
wasteland.[y] 17 Or if I bring the sword upon
this land, commanding the sword to pass
through the land cutting off from it human
being and beast alike,[z] 18 and these three
were in it, as I live—oracle of the Lord
GOD—they could save neither sons nor
daughters; they alone would be saved. 19 Or
if I send plague into this land, pouring out
upon it my bloody wrath, cutting off from it
human being and beast alike, 20 even if Noah,
Daniel, and Job were in it, as I live—oracle
of the Lord GOD—they could save neither
son nor daughter; they would save only
themselves by their righteousness.
21 Thus says the Lord GOD: Even though I
send against Jerusalem my four evil punishments—sword, famine, wild beasts, and
plague—to cut off from it human being and
beast alike,[a] 22 there will still be some survivors in it who will bring out sons and
daughters. When they come out to you and
you see their ways and their deeds, you shall
be consoled regarding the evil I brought on
Jerusalem, everything I brought upon it.
23 They shall console you when you see their
ways and their deeds, and you shall know

**14:9** The ancient Israelites thought that God could use deception as a means of promoting divine justice; cf. 2 Sm 24:1–3; 1 Kgs 22:19–23.

**14:12–23** According to Ezekiel, the people in Jerusalem deserve destruction because they are corrupt. Yet he admits an exception to the principle of individual responsibility when he affirms that some of those deserving death will survive and be reunited with family in exile. The depravity of Jerusalem testifies that the punishment of Jerusalem was just and necessary.

**14:14 Noah, Daniel, and Job**: righteous folk heroes whom Israel shared with other ancient Near Eastern cultures. Daniel was the just judge celebrated in Ugaritic literature, perhaps the model for the hero of Dn 13.

*u*: cf. 1 Kgs 22:23; 2 Chr 18:22. *v*: Lv 26:26. *w*: Ez 28:3; Dn 1:6; cf. Gn 6:9; Jb 1:1. *x*: cf. Lv 26:22. *y*: cf. Ez 18:20. *z*: Lv 26:25. *a*: cf. Rev 6:8.

## The Allegory of the Useless Vine

IN CH 15, EZEKIEL uses rhetorical questions to compare the inhabitants of Jerusalem to the wood of a vine, which is entirely useless except for burning (see Jgs 9:7–21). It cannot be used to make anything, because vine branches are twisted and weak. Even when burned, the charred ends are useless. Similarly, Jerusalem will be burned.

that not without reason did I do to it everything I did—oracle of the Lord GOD.[b]

### CHAPTER 15

See RG 231

*Parable of the Vine.* 1* The word of the LORD came to me:

2 Son of man,
what makes the wood of the vine
Better than the wood of branches
found on the trees in the forest?[c]
3 Can wood be taken from it
to make something useful?
Can someone make even a peg out of it
on which to hang a vessel?
4 Of course not! If it is fed to the fire for
fuel,
and the fire devours both ends of it,
Leaving the middle charred,
is it useful for anything then?
5 Even when it is whole
it cannot be used for anything;
So when fire has devoured and charred it,
how useful can it be?
6 Therefore, thus says the Lord GOD:
Like vine wood among forest trees,
which I have given as fuel for fire,
So I will give the inhabitants of
Jerusalem.
7 I will set my face against them:
Although they have escaped the fire,
the fire will still devour them;
You shall know that I am the LORD,
when I set my face against them.[d]
8 Yes, I will make the land desolate,
because they are so unfaithful—
oracle of the Lord GOD.

### CHAPTER 16

See RG 231

*A Parable of Infidelity.* 1 The word of
the LORD came to me: 2 Son of man, make
known to Jerusalem her abominations.[e]
3 You shall say, Thus says the Lord GOD to
Jerusalem: By origin and birth you belong to
the land of the Canaanites; your father was
an Amorite, your mother a Hittite.*[f] 4* As
for your birth, on the day you were born your
navel cord was not cut; you were not washed
with water or anointed; you were not rubbed
with salt or wrapped in swaddling clothes.[g]
5 No eye looked on you with pity or compassion to do any of these things for you.
Rather, on the day you were born you were
left out in the field, rejected.

6 Then I passed by and saw you struggling
in your blood, and I said to you in your blood,
"Live!" 7 I helped you grow up like a field
plant, so that you grew, maturing into a
woman with breasts developed and hair
grown; but still you were stark naked. 8 I
passed by you again and saw that you were
now old enough for love. So I spread the corner of my cloak* over you to cover your

**15:1–8** Verses 2–5 point out that the wood of the vinestock may be burned for fuel, fit only for destruction. In vv. 6–8 Ezekiel asserts that Jerusalem has the same destiny.

**16:3–4 By origin and birth . . . Hittite**: Jerusalem's pre-Israelite origins are the breeding ground for its inability to respond faithfully to the Lord's generosity.

**16:4–5** In this chapter, Ezekiel represents Jerusalem and Samaria as unwanted, abandoned sisters whom the Lord rescues and cares for. Here the prophet depicts Jerusalem as a newborn female, abandoned and left to die, an accepted practice in antiquity for females, who were considered financial liabilities by their families. That the infant has no one, not even her mother, to tie off her umbilical cord, wash her clean, and wrap her in swaddling clothes emphasizes Jerusalem's death-like isolation and accentuates the Lord's gracious action in her behalf. The practice of rubbing the skin of newborns with salt is an attested Palestinian custom that survived into the twentieth century.

**16:8 I spread the corner of my cloak**: one way to acquire a woman for marriage; cf. Ru 3:9. In Dt 23:1 a son's illicit sexual relations with his father's wife is described as "uncovering the edge of the father's garment."

*b:* Jer 22:8–9. *c:* cf. Ps 80; Is 5:1–7. *d:* Is 24:18; Am 9:1–4. *e:* cf. Ez 8:17. *f:* cf. Dt 26:5; Gn 23:10; 48:22. *g:* cf. Lk 2:2.

## The Abandoned Infant

GOD COMMANDS THE abandoned infant in 16:6 to live but does nothing to care for her. She grows up like a plant but remains naked. Only after taking Jerusalem in marriage does God wash the blood from her and clothe her (vv. 8–9). The description of the clothing, jewelry, and food (see also Is 3:18–23) demonstrates God's generosity to the unwanted Jerusalem.

nakedness; I swore an oath to you and entered
into covenant with you—oracle of the Lord
GOD—and you became mine.[h] 9 Then I bathed
you with water, washed away your blood, and
anointed you with oil.[i] 10 I clothed you with an
embroidered gown, put leather sandals on
your feet; I gave you a fine linen sash and silk
robes to wear.[j] 11 I adorned you with jewelry,
putting bracelets on your arms, a necklace
about your neck,[k] 12 a ring in your nose, earrings in your ears, and a beautiful crown on
your head. 13 Thus you were adorned with
gold and silver; your garments made of fine
linen, silk, and embroidered cloth. Fine flour,
honey, and olive oil were your food. You were
very, very beautiful, fit for royalty.[l] 14 You
were renowned among the nations for your
beauty, perfected by the splendor I showered
on you—oracle of the Lord GOD.

15 But you trusted in your own beauty and
used your renown to serve as a prostitute. You
poured out your prostitution on every
passerby—let it be his.[m] 16* You took some of
your garments and made for yourself gaudy
high places, where you served as a prostitute.
It has never happened before, nor will it happen again![n] 17 You took the splendid gold and
silver ornaments that I had given you and
made for yourself male images and served as
a prostitute with them. 18 You took your embroidered garments to cover them; my oil and
my incense you set before them; 19 the food I
had given you, the fine flour, the oil, and the
honey with which I fed you, you set before
them as a pleasant odor, says the Lord GOD.[o]
20* [p] The sons and daughters you bore for me
you took and offered as sacrifices for them to
devour! Was it not enough that you had become a prostitute? 21 [q] You slaughtered and
immolated my children to them, making them
pass through fire. 22 In all your abominations
and prostitutions you did not remember the
days of your youth when you were stark
naked, struggling in your blood.[r]

23 Then after all your evildoing—woe,
woe to you! oracle of the Lord GOD— 24 you
built yourself a platform and raised up a
dais* in every public place.[s] 25 [t] At every intersection you built yourself a dais so that
you could degrade your beauty by spreading
your legs for every passerby, multiplying
your prostitutions. 26 You served as a prostitute with the Egyptians, your big-membered
neighbors, and multiplied your prostitutions
to provoke me. 27 Therefore I stretched out
my hand against you and reduced your allotment, and delivered you over to the whim of
your enemies, the Philistines,* who were revolted by your depraved conduct.[u] 28 You
also served as a prostitute for the Assyrians,
because you were not satisfied. Even after
serving as a prostitute for them, you were
still not satisfied.[v] 29 You increased your
prostitutions again, now going to Chaldea,
the land of traders; but despite this, you were
still not satisfied.[w]

**16:16** In the allegory of this chapter the viewpoint often shifts from the figure (prostitution) to the reality (idolatry). A symbol of the woman's depravity supersedes her parents' cruel abandonment when she was an infant. It overrides the loyalty she owes her covenant partner and the care she owes their children.

**16:20–21** Also a reference to the practice of child sacrifice introduced under Judah's impious kings; cf. 2 Kgs 16:3; 17:17; Jer 7:31; 19:5; 32:35.

**16:24 A platform . . . a dais**: associated with rituals borrowed from the Canaanites.

**16:27 Philistines**: lit., "daughters of the Philistines," a common expression when referring to the various towns that make up a territory.

*h:* cf. Ez 16:59; Ru 3:9. *i:* cf. Ru 3:3. *j:* cf. Ps 45:14. *k:* cf. Ez 23:40–42. *l:* Dt 32:13–14; Hos 2:8. *m:* Is 57:7–8. *n:* cf. 2 Kgs 23:7. *o:* Hos 2:13. *p:* Jer 7:31; cf. Lv 18:21; Dt 18:10; 2 Kgs 21:6; 23:10. *q:* cf. 2 Kgs 16:3; 17:17. *r:* Jer 2:2; Hos 2:15; 11:1. *s:* Is 57:7. *t:* Jer 2:20; 3:2; 5:7; Hos 2:4. *u:* cf. 2 Chr 28:18. *v:* 2 Kgs 16:7. *w:* cf. Ez 23:14–17.

30 How wild your lust!—oracle of the Lord
GOD—that you did all these works of a
shameless prostitute, 31 when you built your
platform at every intersection and set up
your high place in every public square. But
unlike a prostitute, you disdained payment.
32 Adulterous wife, taking strangers in place
of her husband! 33 Prostitutes usually receive
gifts. But you bestowed gifts on all your
lovers, bribing them to come to you for prostitution from every side.[x] 34 Thus in your
prostitution you were different from any
other woman. No one solicited you for prostitution. Instead, you yourself offered payment; what a reversal!

35 Therefore, prostitute, hear the word of
the LORD! 36 Thus says the Lord GOD: Because you poured out your lust and exposed
your nakedness in your prostitution with
your lovers and your abominable idols, because you gave the life-blood of your children to them, 37[y] therefore, I will now gather
together all your lovers with whom you
found pleasure, both those you loved and
those you hated; I will gather them against
you from all sides and expose you naked for
them to see. 38* I will inflict on you the sentence of adultery and murder; I will bring on
you bloody wrath and jealous anger.[z] 39 I will
hand you over to them to tear down your
platform and demolish your high place, to
strip you of your garments and take away
your splendid ornaments, leaving you stark
naked.[a] 40 They shall lead an assembly
against you to stone you and hack you to
pieces with their swords.[b] 41[c] They shall set
fire to your homes and inflict punishments
on you while many women watch. Thus I
will put an end to your prostitution, and you
shall never again offer payment. 42 When I
have spent my fury upon you I will stop being jealous about you, and calm down, no
longer angry. 43 Because you did not remember the days of your youth but enraged me
with all these things, see, I am bringing
down your ways upon your head—oracle of
the Lord GOD. Have you not added depravity to your other abominations?

44 See, everyone who makes proverbs will
make this proverb about you, "Like mother,
like daughter." 45 Yes, you are truly the
daughter of your mother* who rejected her
husband and children: you are truly a sister
to your sisters who rejected their husbands
and children—your mother was a Hittite and
your father an Amorite.[d] 46* Your elder sister
was Samaria with her daughters to the north
of you; and your younger sister was Sodom
and her daughters, south of you.[e] 47 Not only
did you walk in their ways and act as abom-
inably as they did, but in a very short time
you became more corrupt in all your ways
than they were.[f] 48 As I live—oracle of the
Lord GOD—I swear that your sister Sodom
with her daughters have not done the things
you and your daughters have done![g] 49[h] Now
look at the guilt of your sister Sodom: she
and her daughters were proud, sated with
food, complacent in prosperity. They did not
give any help to the poor and needy. 50 Instead, they became arrogant and committed
abominations before me; then, as you have
seen, I removed them.[i] 51 Samaria did not
commit half the sins you did. You have done
more abominable things than they did. You
even made your sisters look righteous, with
all the abominations you have done. 52 You,
then, must bear your disgrace, for you have
made a case for your sisters! Because your
sins are more abominable than theirs, they
seem righteous compared to you. Blush for
shame, and bear the disgrace of having made
your sisters appear righteous.

53 I will restore their fortunes, the fortunes

**16:38** As a jealous husband, Yhwh severely punishes Jerusalem for her adultery: i.e., her worship of idols. Adultery was considered a capital crime in ancient Israel; cf. Lv 20:10–14; Nm 5:11–28; Dt 22:22.

**16:45 Truly the daughter of your mother**: Jerusalem's depraved behavior follows from the bad behavior of its non-Israelite forebears; cf. v. 3.

**16:46–47** Jerusalem is so much more corrupt than Samaria, the elder sister in size, and the smaller Sodom that both now appear just and righteous. Ezekiel's reference to Sodom indicates that the city's identification with wickedness and evil was already an established tradition in fifth century B.C. Judah.

*x:* Hos 8:9–10. *y:* cf. Ez 23:10, 22; Is 47:3; Rev 17:16. *z:* Lv 20:10; Dt 22:22. *a:* cf. 2 Kgs 18:11. *b:* cf. Ez 23:47; Jn 8:5, 7. *c:* 2 Kgs 25:9; cf. Jgs 12:1; 15:6. *d:* cf. Ez 23:2. *e:* Jer 3:8–11; Rev 11:8. *f:* cf. Dt 29:23; 32:32; Is 1:9–10. *g:* cf. Gn 19:25; Mt 10:15; 11:23–24. *h:* cf. Is 1:10; cf. Gn 49:24. *i:* cf. Gn 18:20–21.

of Sodom and her daughters, the fortunes of
Samaria and her daughters—and your fortunes along with them. 54 Thus you must bear
your disgrace and be ashamed of all you
have done to bring them comfort. 55 Yes,
your sisters, Sodom and her daughters,
Samaria and her daughters, shall return to
the way they were,[j] and you and your daughters shall return to the way you were. 56 Did
you not hold your sister Sodom in bad repute
while you felt proud of yourself, 57 before
your evil was exposed? Now you are like
her, reproached by the Arameans and all
their neighbors, despised on all sides by the
Philistines.[k] 58 The penalty of your depravity
and your abominations—you must bear it
all—oracle of the LORD.
59 For thus says the Lord GOD: I will deal
with you for what you did; you despised an
oath by breaking a covenant.[l] 60 But I will remember the covenant I made with you when
you were young; I will set up an everlasting
covenant* with you.[m] 61 Then you shall remember your ways and be ashamed when
you receive your sisters, those older and
younger than you; I give them to you as
daughters, but not by reason of your covenant. 62 For I will re-establish my covenant
with you, that you may know that I am the
LORD,[n] 63 that you may remember and be
ashamed, and never again open your mouth
because of your disgrace, when I pardon you
for all you have done—oracle of the Lord
GOD.[o]

## CHAPTER 17

See RG 231

***The Eagles and the Vine.*** 1 The word
of the LORD came to me: 2 Son of man, propose a riddle, and tell this proverb to the
house of Israel: 3 Thus says the Lord GOD:

The great eagle, with wide wingspan
and long feathers, with thick plumage,
many-hued, came to Lebanon.
He plucked the crest of the cedar,[p]
4 broke off its topmost branch,
And brought it to a land of merchants,
set it in a city of traders.
5 Then he took some native seed
and planted it in fertile soil;
A shoot beside plentiful waters,
like a willow he planted it,[q]
6 That it might sprout and become a vine,
dense and low-lying,
With its branches turned toward him,
its roots beneath it.
Thus it became a vine, produced
branches,
and put forth shoots.
7 Then another great eagle appeared,
with wide wingspan, rich in plumage,
And see! This vine bent its roots to him,
sent out branches for him to water.
From the bed where it was planted,[r]
8 it was transplanted to a fertile field
By abundant waters, to produce branches,
to bear fruit, to become a majestic vine.
9 Say: Thus says the Lord GOD: Can it
thrive?
Will he not tear up its roots
and strip its fruit?
Then all its green leaves will wither—
neither strong arm nor mighty nation
is needed to uproot it.
10 True, it is planted; but will it thrive?
Will it not wither up
When the east wind strikes it,
wither in the very bed where it
sprouted?[s]

11* The word of the LORD came to me:
12 Now say to the rebellious house:
Do you not understand this? Tell them!
The king of Babylon came to Jerusalem
and took away its king and officials

**16:60 Everlasting covenant**: Ezekiel foresees God renewing the covenant of Sinai in a new and spirit-empowered way that will not be fatally broken as in the present exile or force God to abandon Israel again; cf. 11:19–21; 36:25–27; 37:26–28.

**17:11–21** These verses explain the allegory in vv. 3–10. In 597 B.C., Nebuchadnezzar removed Jehoiachin from the throne and took him into exile; in his place he set Zedekiah, Jehoiachin's uncle, on the throne and received from him the oath of loyalty. But Zedekiah was persuaded to rebel by Pharaoh Hophra of Egypt and thus deserved punishment; cf. 2 Kgs 24:10–25:7.

*j:* cf. Ez 36:11. *k:* cf. Ez 25:12–14; 35:1–15; 2 Kgs 16:6. *l:* cf. Ez 17:19. *m:* cf. Ez 37:26; Is 55:3; Jer 32:40. *n:* Dt 29:14. *o:* Dn 9:7–8. *p:* Dt 28:49; Jer 49:22; Dn 7:4. *q:* cf. 2 Kgs 24:17. *r:* cf. Ez 31:4–5; Jer 37:5; 44:30. *s:* cf. Ez 19:12.

and brought them to him in Babylon.[t]
13 After removing the nobles from the land,
he then took one of the royal line
And made a covenant with him,
binding him under oath,[u]
14 To be a humble kingdom,
without high aspirations,
to keep his covenant and so survive.
15 But this one rebelled against him
by sending envoys to Egypt
To obtain horses and a mighty army.
Can he thrive?
Can he escape if he does this?
Can he break a covenant and go free?[v]
16 As I live—oracle of the Lord GOD—
in the house of the king who set him
up to rule,
Whose oath he ignored and whose
covenant he broke,
there in Babylon I swear he shall die![w]
17 Pharaoh shall not help him on the day of
battle,
with a great force and mighty horde,
When ramps are thrown up and siege
works built
for the cutting down of many lives.
18 He ignored his oath, breaking his
covenant;
even though he gave his hand, he did
all these things—
he shall not escape![x]
19 Therefore, thus says the Lord GOD:
As I live, my oath which he spurned,
And my covenant which he broke,
I will bring down on his head.
20 I will spread my net over him,
and he will be caught in my snare.
I will bring him to Babylon
to judge him there
because he broke faith with me.[y]
21 Any among his forces who escape
will fall by the sword,
And whoever might survive
will be scattered to the winds.[z]
Thus you will know that I the LORD have
spoken.
22 Thus says the Lord GOD:
I, too, will pluck from the crest of the
cedar
the highest branch.
From the top a tender shoot
I will break off and transplant*
on a high, lofty mountain.
23 On the mountain height of Israel
I will plant it.
It shall put forth branches and bear fruit,
and become a majestic cedar.
Every small bird will nest under it,
all kinds of winged birds will dwell
in the shade of its branches.[a]
24 Every tree of the field will know
that I am the LORD.
I bring low the high tree,
lift high the lowly tree,
Wither up the green tree,
and make the dry tree bloom.[b]
As I, the LORD, have spoken, so will I do!

## CHAPTER 18

See RG 231

*Personal Responsibility.* 1 The word of
the LORD came to me: Son of man, 2 what is
the meaning of this proverb you recite in the
land of Israel:

"Parents eat sour grapes,[c]
but the children's teeth are set on
edge"?*

3 As I live—oracle of the Lord GOD: I swear
that none of you will ever repeat this proverb
in Israel. 4 For all life is mine: the life of the
parent is like the life of the child, both are
mine. Only the one who sins shall die!
5 If a man is just—if he does what is right,
6 if he does not eat on the mountains,* or raise
his eyes to the idols of the house of Israel; if
he does not defile a neighbor's wife, or have
relations with a woman during her period;[d]
7e if he oppresses no one, gives back the

**17:22–23** The Lord will undo the actions of the Babylonian king by rebuilding the Davidic dynasty so the nations realize that only Israel's God can restore a people's destiny.

**18:2 Parents . . . on edge**: a proverb the people quoted to complain that they were being punished for their ancestors' sins; cf. Jer 31:29.

**18:6 Eat on the mountains**: take part in meals after sacrifice at the high places.

*t:* 2 Kgs 24:15. *u:* 2 Chr 36:13. *v:* Jer 52:3. *w:* 2 Kgs 24:17; 25:7; Jer 52:11. *x:* cf. 2 Kgs 10:15. *y:* cf. Ez 12:13; 32:3. *z:* Lv 26:33; 2 Kgs 25:5. *a:* Dn 4:12; Hos 14:5–7. *b:* Dn 5:21. *c:* Jer 31:29; cf. Ez 21:19. *d:* Lv 15:19–24; cf. Hos 4:13. *e:* Ex 22:26; Is 58:7; Mt 25:35.

## Guilt and Reward

THE SON OF a righteous person who sins is responsible and will die. The son of a sinner who does right will be spared. Ezekiel's opponents contend that the son is guilty for the sins of the father, but Ezekiel states that only the person who commits sins will be punished for them (18:19–20). Then a new principle enters the debate. Ezekiel contends that a wicked person who repents will be saved, but a righteous person who sins will be condemned.

pledge received for a debt, commits no robbery; gives food to the hungry and clothes the naked; 8 if he does not lend at interest or exact usury; if he refrains from evildoing and makes a fair judgment between two opponents;[f] 9 if he walks by my statutes and is careful to observe my ordinances, that man is just—he shall surely live—oracle of the Lord GOD.[g]

10 But if he begets a son who is violent and commits murder, or does any of these things,[h] 11 even though the father does none of them—a son who eats on the mountains, defiles the wife of his neighbor, 12 oppresses the poor and needy, commits robbery, does not give back a pledge, raises his eyes to idols, does abominable things, 13 lends at interest and exacts usury—this son certainly shall not live. Because he practiced all these abominations, he shall surely be put to death; his own blood shall be on him.[i]

14 But, in turn, if he begets a son who sees all the sins his father commits, yet fears and does not imitate him— 15 a son who does not eat on the mountains, or raise his eyes to the idols of the house of Israel, or defile a neighbor's wife; 16 who does not oppress anyone, or exact a pledge, or commit robbery; who gives his food to the hungry and clothes the naked;[j] 17 who refrains from evildoing, accepts no interest or usury, but keeps my ordinances and walks in my statutes—this one shall not die for the sins of his father. He shall surely live! 18 Only the father, since he committed extortion and robbed his brother, and did what was not good among his people—he will die because of his sin! 19 You ask: "Why is not the son charged with the guilt of his father?" Because the son has done what is just and right and has been careful to observe all my statutes—he shall surely live! 20[k] Only the one who sins shall die. The son shall not be charged with the guilt of his father, nor shall the father be charged with the guilt of his son. Justice belongs to the just, and wickedness to the wicked.

21 But if the wicked man turns away from all the sins he has committed, if he keeps all my statutes and does what is just and right, he shall surely live. He shall not die! 22 None of the crimes he has committed shall be remembered against him; he shall live because of the justice he has shown. 23[l] Do I find pleasure in the death of the wicked—oracle of the Lord GOD? Do I not rejoice when they turn from their evil way and live?

24 And if the just turn from justice and do evil, like all the abominations the wicked do, can they do this evil and still live? None of the justice they did shall be remembered, because they acted treacherously and committed these sins; because of this, they shall die.[m] 25[n] You say, "The LORD's way is not fair!"* Hear now, house of Israel: Is it my way that is unfair? Are not your ways unfair? 26 When the just turn away from justice to do evil and die, on account of the evil they did they must die. 27 But if the wicked turn from the wickedness they did and do what is right and just, they save their lives; 28 since they turned away from all the sins they committed, they shall live; they shall not die. 29 But the house of Israel says, "The Lord's

**18:25 The LORD's way is not fair**: this chapter rejects the idea that punishment is transferred from one generation to the next and emphasizes individual responsibility and accountability.

*f:* Ex 22:25; Lv 25:35–37; Dt 23:19–20. *g:* Lv 18:5. *h:* cf. Ez 22:6–9. *i:* Ex 22:25; Lv 20:9–11. *j:* cf. Ez 16:49; Is 58:7–10. *k:* Dt 24:16; 2 Kgs 14:6; cf. Mt 16:27; Jn 9:2. *l:* cf. Ez 33:11; 2 Pt 3:9. *m:* cf. 2 Pt 2:20–22. *n:* cf. Ez 33:20.

way is not fair!" Is it my way that is not fair,
house of Israel? Is it not your ways that are
not fair?
30[o] Therefore I will judge you, house of
Israel, all of you according to your ways—
oracle of the Lord GOD. Turn, turn back
from all your crimes, that they may not be a
cause of sin for you ever again. 31 Cast away
from you all the crimes you have committed,
and make for yourselves a new heart and a
new spirit. Why should you die, house of Israel?[p] 32[q] For I find no pleasure in the death
of anyone who dies—oracle of the Lord
GOD. Turn back and live!

### CHAPTER 19

See RG 231

### *Allegory of the Lions**

1 As for you, raise a lamentation over the
princes of Israel, 2 and say:

What a lioness was your mother,
a lion among lions!
She made her lair among young lions,
to raise her cubs;
3 One cub she raised up,
a young lion he became;
He learned to tear apart prey,
he devoured people.[r]
4 Nations heard about him;
in their pit he was caught;
They took him away with hooks
to the land of Egypt.* [s]
5 When she realized she had waited in vain,
she lost hope.
She took another of her cubs,
and made him a young lion.
6 He prowled among the lions,
became a young lion;
He learned to tear apart prey,
he devoured people.[t]
7 He ravaged their strongholds,
laid waste their cities.
The earth and everything in it were
terrified
at the sound of his roar.
8 Nations laid out against him
snares all around;
They spread their net for him,
in their pit he was caught.[u]
9 They put him in fetters and took him away
to the king of Babylon,
So his roar would no longer be heard
on the mountains of Israel.

### *Allegory of the Vine Branch*

10 Your mother was like a leafy vine*
planted by water,
Fruitful and full of branches
because of abundant water.
11 One strong branch grew
into a royal scepter.
So tall it towered among the clouds,
conspicuous in height,
with dense foliage.[v]
12 But she was torn out in fury
and flung to the ground;
The east wind withered her up,
her fruit was plucked away;
Her strongest branch dried up,
fire devoured it.[w]
13 Now she is planted in a wilderness,
in a dry, parched land.[x]
14 Fire flashed from her branch,
and devoured her shoots;
Now she does not have a strong branch,
a royal scepter![y]

This is a lamentation and serves as a
lamentation.

### CHAPTER 20

See RG 231

***Israel's History of Infidelity.*** 1 In the
seventh year, on the tenth day of the fifth
month,* some of the elders of Israel came to

**19:1–9** Some commentators identify Jehoahaz and Zedekiah, sons of the same mother, as the "two young lions"; they were deported to Egypt and Babylon respectively. Cf. 2 Kgs 23:31–34; 24:18–20.

**19:4** A common fate for royal prisoners: e.g., Assurbanipal claims he put a ring in the jaw of a captive king and a dog collar around his neck (cf. v. 9). A wall relief shows Esarhaddon holding two royal captives with ropes tied to rings in their lips.

**19:10–14 Vine**: Judah. **One strong branch**: the Davidic king. This allegory describes the deportation of the Davidic dynasty to Babylon and laments the destruction of the house of David. From Ezekiel's perspective, the arrogance of Judah's kings leads to this tragedy (vv. 12–14).

**20:1 The seventh year . . . the fifth month**: August 14, 591 B.C.

*o:* Jer 35:15; cf. Mt 3:2; Lk 3:3. *p:* cf. Ez 11:19; 36:26. *q:* cf. Ez 18:23; 33:11. *r:* 2 Kgs 23:31–34. *s:* 2 Chr 36:4. *t:* 2 Kgs 24:9. *u:* 2 Kgs 24:2–15. *v:* Dn 4:11. *w:* Hos 13:15. *x:* cf. Ez 20:35. *y:* cf. Ez 20:47.

consult the LORD and sat down before me.[z]
2 Then the word of the LORD came to me:
3 Son of man, speak to the elders of Israel and
say to them: Thus says the Lord GOD: Have
you come to consult me? As I live, I will not
allow myself to be consulted by you!—oracle of the Lord GOD.
4 Will you judge them? Will you judge,
son of man? Tell them about the abominations of their ancestors,[a] 5 and say to them:
Thus says the Lord GOD: The day I chose Israel, I swore to the descendants of the house
of Jacob; I revealed myself to them in the
land of Egypt and swore to them, saying: I
am the LORD, your God. 6 That day I swore to
bring them out of the land of Egypt to the
land I had searched out for them, a land
flowing with milk and honey, a jewel among
all lands.[b] 7 Then I said to them: Throw away,
each of you, the detestable things* that held
your eyes; do not defile yourselves with the
idols of Egypt: I am the LORD, your God.[c]
8 But they rebelled and refused to listen to
me; none of them threw away the detestable
things that held their eyes, nor did they abandon the idols of Egypt. Then I considered
pouring out my fury and spending my anger
against them there in the land of Egypt.[d] 9 I
acted for the sake of my name, that it should
not be desecrated in the eyes of the nations
among whom they were: in the eyes of the
nations I had made myself known to them, to
bring them out of the land of Egypt.[e]
10 Therefore I led them out of the land of
Egypt and brought them into the wilderness.
11[f] Then I gave them my statutes and made
known to them my ordinances, so that
everyone who keeps them has life through
them. 12[g] I also gave them my sabbaths to be
a sign between me and them, to show that it
is I, the LORD, who makes them holy.
13 But the house of Israel rebelled against
me in the wilderness. They did not observe
my statutes, and they rejected my ordinances
that bring life to those who keep them. My
sabbaths, too, they desecrated grievously.
Then I considered pouring out my fury on
them in the wilderness to put an end to
them,[h] 14 but I acted for the sake of my name,
so it would not be desecrated in the eyes of
the nations in whose sight I had brought
them out.[i] 15 Nevertheless in the wilderness I
swore to them that I would not bring them
into the land I had given them—a land flowing with milk and honey, a jewel among all
the lands. 16 Their hearts followed after their
idols so closely that they did not live by my
statutes, but rejected my ordinances and desecrated my sabbaths. 17 But I looked on them
with pity, not wanting to destroy them, so I
did not put an end to them in the wilderness.
18 Then I said to their children in the wilderness: Do not follow the statutes of your
parents. Do not keep their ordinances. Do not
defile yourselves with their idols. 19 I am the
LORD, your God: follow my statutes and be
careful to observe my ordinances; 20 keep
holy my sabbaths as a sign between me and
you so that you may know that I am the
LORD, your God.[j] 21 But their children rebelled against me: they did not follow my
statutes or keep my ordinances that bring life
to those who observe them; my sabbaths they
desecrated. Then I considered pouring out
my fury on them, spending my anger against
them in the wilderness; 22 but I stayed my
hand, acting for the sake of my name, lest it
be desecrated in the eyes of the nations, in
whose sight I had brought them out. 23 Nevertheless I swore to them in the wilderness that
I would disperse them among the nations and
scatter them in other lands, 24 because they
did not carry out my ordinances, but rejected
my statutes and desecrated my sabbaths, having eyes only for the idols of their ancestors.
25 Therefore I gave them statutes that were
not good,* and ordinances through which
they could not have life.[k] 26 I let them become

**20:7 Detestable things**: in the Book of Ezekiel, Israel's continued worship of idols in Egypt and in the wilderness, despite the Lord's powerful deeds on their behalf, is the reason God punishes them so severely; they must learn and acknowledge that he is their only Lord. Cf., e.g., Exodus (5:1–6:9; 14:10–30; 16:1–36) and Numbers (11:1–15; 14:1–12; 20:1–9), where the people's failure to trust Moses and the Lord brings punishment.

**20:25–26 I gave them statutes that were not good**: because Israel rejected the Lord's life-giving laws, he "gave"

*z:* cf. Ez 8:1. *a:* cf. Ez 16:2; Mt 23:32. *b:* Ex 3:8; 6:8; Dt 8:7–10. *c:* Ex 20:2–4. *d:* cf. Ez 16:26; Ex 32:7. *e:* cf. Ez 36:22. *f:* Lv 18:5; Dt 4:7–8; Rom 10:5. *g:* Ex 20:8, 10; 31:13; Dt 5:12; Neh 13:17–18. *h:* Jer 11:7–8; 17:21–23. *i:* Is 48:11. *j:* Ex 31:13. *k:* cf. Rom 1:28.

defiled by their offerings, by having them make a fiery offering of every womb's firstborn, in order to ruin them so they might know that I am the LORD.[l]

27 Therefore speak to the house of Israel, son of man, and tell them: Thus says the Lord GOD: In this way also your ancestors blasphemed me, breaking faith with me. 28 When I brought them to the land I had sworn to give them, and they saw all its high hills and leafy trees, there they offered sacrifices, there they made offerings to provoke me, there they sent up sweet-smelling oblations, there they poured out their libations.[m] 29 So I said to them, "What is this high place* to which you go?" Thus its name became "high place" even to this day.[n] 30 Therefore say to the house of Israel: Thus says the Lord GOD: Will you defile yourselves in the way your ancestors did? Will you lust after their detestable idols? 31 By offering your gifts, by making your children pass through the fire, you defile yourselves with all your idols even to this day. Shall I let myself be consulted by you, house of Israel? As I live—oracle of the Lord GOD—I swear I will not let myself be consulted by you![o]

32 What has entered your mind shall never happen: You are thinking, "We shall be like the nations, like the peoples of foreign lands, serving wood and stone." 33 As I live—oracle of the Lord GOD—with mighty hand and outstretched arm, with wrath poured out, I swear I will be king over you![p] 34 With mighty hand and outstretched arm, with wrath poured out, I will bring you out from the nations and gather you from the countries over which you are scattered;[q] 35* I will lead you to the wilderness of the peoples and enter into judgment with you face to face. 36 Just as I entered into judgment with your ancestors in the wilderness of the land of Egypt, so will I enter into judgment with you—oracle of the Lord GOD. 37 Thus I will make you pass under the staff* and will impose on you the terms of the covenant.[r] 38 I will sort out from you those who defied me and rebelled against me; from the land where they resided as aliens I will bring them out, but they shall not return to the land of Israel. Thus you shall know that I am the LORD.

39 As for you, house of Israel, thus says the Lord GOD: Go! each of you, and worship your idols. Listen to me! You shall never again desecrate my holy name with your offerings and your idols![s] 40 For on my holy mountain,* on the highest mountain in Israel—oracle of the Lord GOD—there the whole house of Israel shall worship me; there in the land I will accept them all, there I will claim your tributes, the best of your offerings, from all your holy things.[t] 41 As a sweet-smelling oblation I will accept you, when I bring you from among the nations and gather you out of the lands over which you were scattered; and through you I will manifest my holiness in the sight of the nations.[u] 42 Thus you shall know that I am the LORD, when I bring you back to the soil of Israel, the land I swore to give your ances-

laws (e.g., the sacrifice of every firstborn) that would lead only to death and destruction. Dt 12:29–31; Jer 7:31; 19:4–5 may address a popular assumption that the Lord accepted and perhaps required child sacrifice, especially as evidence of great trust during national emergencies (2 Kgs 3:27; Mi 6:7). By combining language from Ex 22:28 with the vocabulary of child sacrifice, Ezekiel suggests that firstborn sons were regularly sacrificed in Israel.

**20:29 High place**: a cultic site, originally a hilltop, but often a raised platform in a sacred area. Until Deuteronomy's insistence that official and legitimate worship of the Lord take place only in Jerusalem, these local shrines were popular places for worship (e.g., 1 Sm 9–10) or for consulting the Lord (1 Kgs 3:4–5). In order to unite the Kingdom of Judah politically and religiously, Dt 12:2 demands destruction of the high places. Ezekiel, like other prophets, condemns Israelite worship at these places and identifies this illegitimate worship as one reason for the punishment of exile.

**20:35–38** Exile among other lands occasions a new exodus and a new wilderness journey back to Israel. The Lord will eliminate the rebellious, as he did on the first journey, and use the surviving remnant to reveal his power to the nations.

**20:37 Pass under the staff**: in Lv 27:32–33, a method of counting off animals to select those to be dedicated for the tithe. In Ezekiel, on the other hand, those who survive the selection process are marked for destruction for violating the covenant.

**20:40 Holy mountain**: the Temple mount and Jerusalem in contrast to "every high hill" in v. 28 (cf. the royal Zion theology in Ps 48:2). Acceptable worship takes place here among a restored people, a theme taken up in chaps. 40–48 (cf. 40:2).

*l:* Lv 18:21. *m:* Ps 78:57–58. *n:* cf. Ez 16:16. *o:* Ps 106:37–39. *p:* Dt 4:34; 5:1. *q:* Ps 106:47. *r:* Lv 27:3; Jer 33:13. *s:* Ex 20:7. *t:* cf. Ps 2:6; Is 11:9; 56:7. *u:* cf. 2 Cor 2:14.

tors. 43 There you shall remember your ways, all the deeds by which you defiled yourselves; and you shall loathe yourselves because of all the evil you did.[v] 44 And you shall know that I am the LORD when I deal with you thus, for the sake of my name, not according to your evil ways and wanton deeds, house of Israel—oracle of the Lord GOD.[w]

See RG 231

## CHAPTER 21

*The Sword of the Lord.* 1 The word of the LORD came to me: 2* Son of man, turn your face to the south: preach against the south, prophesy against the forest land in the south. 3 Say to the forest in the south: Hear the word of the LORD! Thus says the Lord GOD: See! I am kindling a fire in you that shall devour every green tree as well as every dry tree. The blazing flame shall not be quenched so that from south to north every face shall be scorched by it. 4 All flesh shall see that I, the LORD, have kindled it; it shall not be quenched.[x]

5 But I said, "Ah! Lord GOD, they are saying about me, 'Is not this the one who is forever spinning parables?' " 6 Then the word of the LORD came to me: 7 Son of man, turn your face toward Jerusalem: preach against its sanctuary, prophesy against the land of Israel.[y] 8 Say to the land of Israel: Thus says the LORD: See! I am coming against you; I will draw my sword from its scabbard and cut off from you the righteous and the wicked.* 9 Thus my sword shall come out from its scabbard against all flesh from south to north 10 and all flesh shall know that I, the LORD, have drawn my sword from its scabbard. It cannot return again.[z]

*Act Symbolic of the City's Fall.* 11 As for you, son of man, groan! with shattered loins and bitter grief, groan in their sight. 12 When they ask you, "Why are you groaning?" you shall say: Because of what I heard!* When it comes every heart shall melt, every hand fall helpless; every spirit will grow faint, and every knee run with water. See, it is coming, it is here!—oracle of the Lord GOD.

*Song of the Sword.* 13 The word of the LORD came to me:[a] 14 Son of man, prophesy! say: Thus says the LORD:

A sword, a sword has been sharpened,
a sword, a sword has been burnished:[b]
15 Sharpened to make a slaughter,
burnished to flash lightning!
Why should I stop now?
You have rejected the rod and every judgment!
16 I have given it over to the burnisher
that he might hold it in his hand,
A sword sharpened and burnished
to be put in the hands of an executioner.
17 Cry out and howl, son of man,
for it is destined for my people,
For all the princes of Israel,
victims of the sword with my people.
Therefore, slap your thigh,*
18 for it is tested, and why not?
Since you rejected my staff,
should it not happen?—
oracle of the Lord GOD.
19 As for you, son of man, prophesy,
and clap your hands!
Let the sword strike twice, a third time.
It is a sword of slaughter,
A sword for slaughtering,
whirling around them all,
20 That every heart may tremble;
for many will be made to stumble.
At all their gates
I have stationed the sword for slaughter,
Made it flash lightning,
drawn for slaughter.
21 Slash to the right!
turn to the left,
Wherever your edge is directed![c]
22 Then I, too, shall clap my hands,*

**21:2–4** In Babylon Ezekiel looks toward Judah, pictured as a forest about to be destroyed by fire.

**21:8 Cut off from you the righteous and the wicked**: a more complete devastation of Jerusalem than that described in 9:6.

**21:12 What I heard**: the news of the fall of Jerusalem; cf. 33:21–22.

**21:17 Slap your thigh**: a gesture signifying grief and dread; cf. Jer 31:19.

**21:22 Clap my hands**: the Lord declares himself no longer

*v:* Lv 26:41. *w:* cf. Ez 36:22. *x:* Lv 26:25. *y:* Lv 26:36. *z:* Is 34:5–6. *a:* Gn 49:10. *b:* cf. 2 Kgs 13:18–19. *c:* Prv 16:33; Zec 10:2.

and spend my fury.
I, the LORD, have spoken.

*Nebuchadnezzar at the Crossroads.* 23 The
word of the LORD came to me: 24 Son of man,
make for yourself two roads over which the
sword of the king of Babylon can come.
Both roads shall start out from the same
land. Then put a signpost at the head of each
road 25 so the sword can come to Rabbah of
the Ammonites or to Judah and its fortress,
Jerusalem. 26 For the king of Babylon is
standing at the fork of the two roads to read
the omens:* he shakes out the arrows, in-
quires of the teraphim, inspects the liver.[d]
27 Into his right hand has fallen the lot
marked "Jerusalem":* to order the slaughter,
to raise the battle cry, to set the battering
rams against the gates, to throw up a ramp,
to build siege works. 28 In the eyes of those
bound by oath this seems like a false omen;
yet the lot taken in hand exposes the wickedness for which they, still bound by oath, will
be taken in hand.

29 Therefore thus says the Lord GOD: Because your guilt has been exposed, your
crimes laid bare, your sinfulness revealed in
all your deeds—because you have been exposed, you shall be taken in hand.[e] 30 And as
for you, depraved and wicked prince of Israel,
a day is coming to end your life of crime.[f]
31 Thus says the Lord GOD: Off with the turban and away with the crown! Nothing shall
be as it was! Exalt the lowly and bring the exalted low! 32 A ruin, a ruin, a ruin, I shall make
it! Nothing will be the same until the one
comes to whom I have given it for judgment.[g]

*To the Ammonites.** 33 As for you, son of
man, prophesy: Thus says the Lord GOD to
the Ammonites and their insults:

O sword, sword drawn for slaughter,
burnished to consume, to flash lightning!
34 Your false visions and lying omens,
Set you over the necks of the slain,
the wicked whose day had come—
an end to their life of crime.
35 Return to your scabbard!
In the place you were created,
In the land of your origin,
I will judge you.
36 I will pour out my anger upon you,
breathing my fiery wrath against you;
I will hand you over to ravagers,
artisans of destruction!
37 You shall be fuel for the fire,
your blood shall flow throughout the
land;
You shall not be remembered,
for I, the LORD, have spoken.

## CHAPTER 22

See RG 231

*Crimes of Jerusalem.* 1 The word of
the LORD came to me: 2 You,* son of man,
will you judge? will you judge the city of
bloodshed? Then make known all its abominations, 3 and say: Thus says the Lord GOD:
O city that sheds blood within itself so that
its time has come, that has made idols for its
own defilement: 4 By the blood you shed you
have become guilty, and by the idols you
made you have become defiled. You have
brought on your day, you have come to the
end of your years. Therefore I make you an
object of scorn for the nations and a laughingstock for all lands.[h] 5 Those near and
those far off will mock you: "Defiled of
Name! Queen of Tumult!" 6 See! the princes
of Israel within you use their power to shed
blood.* 7 Within you, father and mother are

responsible for Judah; cf. 22:13; Nm 24:10; Jb 27:23; Lam 2:15.

**21:26** Three forms of divination are mentioned: arrow divination, consisting in the use of differently marked arrows extracted or shaken from a case at random; the consultation of the teraphim or household idols; and liver divination, scrutiny of the configurations of the livers of newly slaughtered animals, a common form of divination in Mesopotamia.

**21:27–28** A lot marked "Jerusalem" falls out, which marks the guilt of the city's inhabitants.

**21:33–37** In vv. 23–32 Ezekiel imagines Nebuchadnezzar deciding whether to attack Jerusalem or Rabbath-Ammon. As it happened, the Babylonians decided to attack Jerusalem first. Here (vv. 33–37) Ezekiel prophesies to the Ammonites that a nation which serves as an instrument of the Lord's judgment will itself be judged.

**22:2–16** This first oracle focuses on Jerusalem as a "city of bloodshed" (cf. Na 3:1). Here transgressions involving blood, the oppression of the poor, and improper cultic practices are seen as interrelated, for blood as the carrier of life is fundamental to both the cultic and social spheres of life.

**22:6 To shed blood**: a very serious charge in light of the solemn command of God to Noah in Gn 9:6 against human bloodshed.

*d:* Is 28:5; Ps 75:8. *e:* Jer 8:11–12; 27:9–10. *f:* cf. Ez 16:3. *g:* Mal 3:19. *h:* Ps 44:13–14.

### Purification

JUST AS METALS are smelted to remove dross, Israel will be purified in fire to remove its sins and impurities (22:17–31; Is 1:21–26). The prophet names all classes of people in Jerusalem, including its princes, its priests, its officials, its prophets and the people of the land.

dishonored; they extort the resident alien in your midst; within you, they oppress orphans and widows.[i] 8 What I consider holy you have rejected, and my sabbaths you have desecrated. 9* In you are those who slander to cause bloodshed; within you are those who feast on the mountains; in your midst are those whose actions are depraved.[j] 10 In you are those who uncover the nakedness of their fathers; in you those who coerce women to intercourse during their period.[k] 11l There are those in you who do abominable things with their neighbors' wives, men who defile their daughters-in-law by incest, men who coerce their sisters to intercourse, the daughters of their own fathers. 12 There are those in you who take bribes to shed blood. You exact interest and usury; you extort profit from your neighbor by violence. But me you have forgotten—oracle of the Lord GOD.[m]

13 See, I am clapping my hands because of the profits you extorted and the blood shed in your midst. 14 Will your heart remain firm, will your hands be strong, in the days when I deal with you? I am the LORD; I have spoken, and I will act! 15 I will disperse you among the nations and scatter you over other lands, so that I may purge your filth. 16 In you I will allow myself to be desecrated in the eyes of the nations; thus you shall know that I am the LORD.

17 The word of the LORD came to me: 18* Son of man, the house of Israel has become dross to me. All of them are copper, tin, iron, and lead within a furnace; they have become the dross from silver.[n] 19 Therefore thus says the Lord GOD: Because all of you have become dross, See! I am gathering you within Jerusalem. 20 Just as silver, copper, iron, lead, and tin are gathered within a furnace to be blasted with fire to smelt it, so I will gather you together in my furious wrath, put you in, and smelt you.[o] 21 When I have assembled you, I will blast you with the fire of my anger and smelt you with it. 22 Just as silver is smelted in a furnace, so you shall be smelted in it. Thus you shall know that I, the LORD, have poured out my fury on you.

23 The word of the LORD came to me: 24* Son of man, say to her: You are an unclean land receiving no rain at the time of my fury. 25 A conspiracy of its princes is like a roaring lion tearing prey; they devour people, seizing their wealth and precious things, making many widows within her.[p] 26 Her priests violate my law and desecrate what I consider holy; they do not distinguish between holy and common, nor teach the difference between unclean and clean; they pay no attention to my sabbaths, so that I have been desecrated in their midst.[q] 27r Within her, her officials are like wolves tearing prey, shedding blood and destroying lives to extort profit. 28s And her prophets cover them with whitewash, seeing false visions and performing lying divinations, saying, "Thus says the Lord GOD," although the LORD has not spoken. 29 The people of the land practice extortion and commit robbery; they wrong the poor and the needy, and oppress the resident alien without justice. 30 Thus I have searched among them for someone who would build a wall or stand in

**22:9–11** The charges against Jerusalem echo the commandments of Lv 20:10–18.

**22:18–22** The image of smelting metals for purifying the people by the attacks of their enemies is common among the prophets; cf. Is 1:22, 25; Jer 6:27–30.

**22:24–31** For a similar oracle, cf. Zep 3:1–8.

---

*i:* Ex 22:21–22; 23:9; Dt 5:16. *j:* cf. Ez 18:11. *k:* Lv 18:7–8, 19. *l:* Lv 18:7–20; 20:10–21; Dt 23:1–30; Jer 5:8. *m:* Ez 18:8; Dt 27:25; Am 5:12. *n:* Is 1:21–26; 48:10; Jer 6:27–30. *o:* Hos 8:10; Mal 3:2. *p:* Jer 15:8. *q:* Lv 20:25; Hg 2:11–14. *r:* Mi 3:11; Zep 3:3. *s:* cf. Ez 13:2–10.

the breach before me to keep me from destroying the land; but I found no one. 31 Therefore I have poured out my fury upon them; with my fiery wrath I have consumed them, bringing down their ways upon their heads—oracle of the Lord GOD.

See RG 231

## CHAPTER 23

***The Two Sisters.*** 1[t] The word of the LORD came to me: 2 Son of man, there were two women, daughters of the same mother.[u] 3 Even as young girls, they were prostitutes, serving as prostitutes in Egypt. There the Egyptians fondled their breasts and caressed their virgin nipples.[v] 4 Oholah was the name of the elder, and the name of her sister was Oholibah.* They became mine and gave birth to sons and daughters.[w] As for their names: Samaria was Oholah and Jerusalem, Oholibah. 5[x] Oholah became a prostitute while married to me and lusted after her lovers, the Assyrians: warriors 6 dressed in purple, governors and officers, all of them handsome young soldiers, mounted on horses. 7 She gave herself as a prostitute to them, to all the Assyrian elite; with all those for whom she lusted, she also defiled herself with their idols. 8 She did not abandon the prostitution she had begun with the Egyptians, who had lain with her when she was young, fondling her virgin breasts and pouring out their lust upon her.[y] 9 Therefore I handed her over to her lovers, to the Assyrians for whom she lusted. 10[z] They exposed her nakedness; her sons and daughters they took away, and her they killed with the sword. She became a byword for women because of the sentence carried out against her.

11 Although her sister Oholibah saw all this, her lust was more depraved than her sister's; she outdid her in prostitution.[a] 12 She too lusted after the Assyrians, governors and officers, warriors impeccably clothed, mounted on horses, all of them handsome young soldiers.[b] 13 I saw that she had defiled herself—now both had gone down the same path. 14 She went further in her prostitution: She saw male figures drawn on the wall, images of Chaldeans drawn with vermilion, 15 with sashes tied about their waists, flowing turbans on their heads, all looking like chariot warriors, images of Babylonians, natives of Chaldea. 16 As soon as she set eyes on them she lusted for them, and she sent messengers to them in Chaldea.[c] 17 The Babylonians came to her, to her love couch; they defiled her with their impurities. But as soon as they had defiled her, she recoiled from them. 18 When her prostitution was discovered and her shame revealed, I recoiled from her as I had recoiled from her sister. 19 But she increased her prostitution, recalling the days of her youth when she had served as a prostitute in the land of Egypt. 20 She lusted for the lechers of Egypt, whose members are like those of donkeys, whose thrusts are like those of stallions.

21 You reverted to the depravity of your youth, when Egyptians fondled your breasts, caressing your young nipples. 22 Therefore, Oholibah, thus says the Lord GOD: I will now stir up your lovers against you, those from whom you recoiled, and I will bring them against you from every side: 23 the men of Babylon and all of Chaldea, Pekod, Shoa and Koa,* along with all the Assyrians, handsome young soldiers, all of them governors and officers, charioteers and warriors, all of them horsemen. 24 They shall invade you with armor, chariots and wagons, a horde of peoples; they will array against you on every side bucklers and shields and helmets. I will give them the right of judgment, and they will judge you according to their standards.[d] 25 I will direct my jealousy against you, so that they deal with you in fury, cutting off your nose and ears; what is left of you shall fall by the sword. They shall take away your sons and daughters, and what is left of you shall be devoured by fire.

**23:4 Oholah . . . Oholibah**: symbolic names for Samaria, "her own tent," and Jerusalem, "my tent is in her." Cf. Ps 15:1 where "tent" is a synonym for "holy mountain." The names refer to the temple set up in the Northern Kingdom of Samaria (1 Kgs 12:28–29) and the Jerusalem Temple.

**23:23 Pekod, Shoa and Koa**: nations along the Tigris River, part of "greater Babylonia."

*t:* cf. Ez 16. *u:* Jer 3:7. *v:* Is 1:21. *w:* Jer 3:6–12. *x:* Hos 5:3; 8:9. *y:* cf. Ez 20:5–8. *z:* cf. Ez 16:37. *a:* Jer 3:8–11. *b:* 2 Kgs 16:7–15; 2 Chr 28:16. *c:* Is 57:8–9. *d:* Jer 30:5–6.

26 They shall strip off your clothes and seize your splendid jewelry. 27 I will put an end to your depravity and to your prostitution from the land of Egypt; you shall no longer look to them, nor even remember Egypt again.

28 For thus says the Lord GOD: I am now handing you over to those whom you hate, to those from whom you recoil. 29 They shall treat you with hatred, seizing all that you worked for and leaving you stark naked, so that your indecent nakedness is exposed.[e] Your depravity and prostitution 30 brought these things upon you because you served as a prostitute for the nations, defiling yourself with their idols.[f]

31 Because you followed your sister's path, I will put her cup into your hand.*[g]

32 Thus says the Lord GOD:[h]
The cup of your sister you shall drink,
deep and wide;
It brings ridicule and mockery,
it holds so much;
33 You will be filled with drunkenness and grief—
A cup of horror and devastation,
the cup of your sister Samaria;
34 You shall drink it dry,
its very sherds you will gnaw;
And you shall tear out your breasts;
for I have spoken—oracle of the Lord GOD.

35 Therefore thus says the Lord GOD: You have forgotten me and cast me behind your back; now suffer for your depravity and prostitution.

36* Then the LORD said to me: Son of man, would you judge Oholah and Oholibah? Then make known to them their abominations.[i] 37 For they committed adultery, and blood covers their hands. They committed adultery with their idols; even the children they bore for me they burnt as food for them. 38 And they also did this to me: on that day, they defiled my sanctuary and desecrated my sabbaths. 39 On the very day they slaughtered their children for their idols, they entered my sanctuary to desecrate it. Thus they acted within my house![j] 40 Moreover, they sent for men who had to come from afar; when a messenger was sent to them, they came. On their account you bathed, painted your eyes, and put on jewelry.[k] 41 You sat on a magnificent couch, set before it a table, on which to lay my incense and oil. 42 The cries of a mob! The shouts of men coming in from the wilderness! They put bracelets on the women's arms and splendid crowns on their heads. 43 I said: "That worn-out one still has adulteries in her! Now they engage her as a prostitute and she . . . 44 And indeed they did come in to her as men come in to a prostitute. Thus they came to Oholah and Oholibah, the depraved women. 45 The righteous shall certainly punish them with sentences given to adulterers and murderers, for they committed adultery, and blood is on their hands.[l]

46 Indeed, thus says the Lord GOD: Raise up an army against them and hand them over to terror and plunder. 47 The army will stone them and hack them to pieces with their swords. They will kill their sons and daughters and set fire to their houses. 48 Thus I will put an end to depravity in the land, and all women will be warned not to imitate your depravity. 49 They shall inflict on you the penalty of your depravity, and you shall pay for your sins of idolatry. Then you shall know that I am the Lord GOD.[m]

## CHAPTER 24

See RG 231

***Allegory of the Pot.**** 1 On the tenth day of the tenth month, in the ninth year,* the word of the LORD came to me:[n] 2 Son of man,

**23:31** The cup is a metaphor for divine punishment, the lot of all who rebel against the Lord (cf. Ps 75:9; Jer 25:15–16; 51:7; Is 51:21–23; Lam 4:21; Hb 2:15–16).

**23:36–49** Unlike vv. 1–35, this short poem juxtaposes the careers of the two sisters and looks to a future punishment. The male lovers of the first poem become the sisters' executioners, and the guests at the love feast a lynch mob. So corrupt and depraved are the two sisters that their executioners win the esteemed title "righteous," for they have acted appropriately as agents of the Lord's judgment.

**24:1–14** As the Babylonian siege of Jerusalem begins (588 B.C.), Ezekiel uses allegory to depict Jerusalem and its overconfident inhabitants as a pot of meat set on the fire for boiling (vv. 3–5; cf. 11:3) and left there until only burnt bones remain (v. 10). In vv. 6–8, the innocent blood shed by Jerusa-

*e:* Jer 13:27; Mi 1:11. *f:* Ps 106:37–38. *g:* Ps 75:8; Ob 16; Mt 20:22; Rev 14:10. *h:* Jer 25:15–16. *i:* Is 58:1; Mi 3:8. *j:* 2 Kgs 21:4. *k:* Jer 27:3. *l:* Lv 20:10. *m:* cf. Ez 24:13. *n:* cf. Ez 8:1.

write down today's date this very day, for on
this very day the king of Babylon lays siege
to Jerusalem. 3 [o] Propose this parable to the
rebellious house and say to them: Thus says
the Lord GOD:

Put the pot on, put it on!
  Pour in some water;
4 Add to it pieces of meat,
  all choice pieces;
With thigh and shoulder,
  with choice cuts fill it.
5 Choose the pick of the flock,
  then pile logs beneath it;
Bring it to a boil,
  cook all the pieces in it.[p]
6 Therefore thus says the Lord GOD:
  Woe to the city full of blood![q]
A pot containing filth,
  whose filth cannot be removed!
Take out its pieces one by one,
  for no lot has fallen on their behalf.
7 For her blood is still in her midst;
  on a bare rock she left it;
She did not pour it on the ground
  to be covered with dirt.*
8 To arouse wrath, to exact vengeance,
  I have left her blood on bare rock
  not to be covered.
9 Therefore, thus says the Lord GOD:
Woe to the city full of blood!
  I will make the pyre great!
10 Pile on the wood, kindle the fire.
Cook the meat, stir the spicy mixture,
  char the bones!
11 Then set it empty on the coals,
  to heat up until its copper glows,
So its impurities melt,
  its filth disappears.
12 * The toil is exhausting,
  but the great filth will not come out—
  Filth, even with fire.
13 Even in defiling yourself with depravity
  I would still have cleansed you,
  but you would not have your impurity
    cleansed.
You will not be cleansed now
  until I wreak my fury on you.[r]
14 I, the LORD, have spoken;
  it will happen!
I will do it and not hold back!
  I will not have pity or relent.
By your conduct and deeds you shall be
    judged—
  oracle of the Lord GOD.

*Ezekiel as a Sign for the Exiles.* 15 The
word of the LORD came to me: 16 Son of man,
with a sudden blow I am taking away from
you the delight of your eyes, but do not
mourn or weep or shed any tears.[s] 17 Groan,
moan for the dead, but make no public
lament; bind on your turban, put your sandals on your feet, but do not cover your
beard or eat the bread of mourners.* 18 I
spoke to the people in the morning. In the
evening my wife died. The next morning I
did as I had been commanded.[t] 19 Then the
people asked me, "Will you not tell us what
all these things you are doing mean for us?"
20 I said to them, The word of the LORD came
to me: 21 Say to the house of Israel: Thus says
the Lord GOD: I will now desecrate my sanctuary, the pride of your strength, the delight
of your eyes, the concern of your soul. The
sons and daughters you left behind shall fall
by the sword.[u] 22* Then you shall do as I
have done, not covering your beards nor eating the bread of mourning. 23 [v] Your turbans
shall remain on your heads, your sandals on
your feet. You shall not mourn or weep, but
you shall waste away because of your sins

lem's inhabitants is the rust that, despite efforts to remove it, coats the interior of the pot filled with meat. Once emptied (v. 8), the rust-encrusted pot is set on hot coals (v. 11), but the rust remains (v. 12). Only the brunt of the Lord's fury can cleanse Jerusalem of its guilt (vv. 13–14).

**24:1 The tenth day . . . the ninth year**: January 15, 588 B.C. The same wording appears in 2 Kgs 25:1 (Jer 52:4).

**24:7 Blood . . . to be covered with dirt**: since blood was sacred to God, it had to be covered with earth (Gn 37:26; Lv 17:13); the blood of innocent victims left uncovered cried out for vengeance; cf. Gn 4:10; Jb 16:18; Is 26:21.

**24:12** A cryptic line in Hebrew.

**24:17 The bread of mourners**: a post-burial meal that mourners shared to comfort one another; cf. 2 Sm 3:35; Jer 16:7. The other gestures mentioned here were also popular mourning customs. Because Ezekiel does not observe any of the mourning customs mentioned, the people are puzzled and ask him to explain.

**24:22–24** The fall of the city will be so sudden and final that the exiles will have no time to go into mourning.

*o:* cf. Ez 11:3–12. *p:* Jer 52:24–27. *q:* Na 3:1; Hb 2:12. *r:* Is 22:14; Jer 6:28–30. *s:* Jer 16:5–7. *t:* cf. Ez 12:9. *u:* Lv 26:31. *v:* Is 20:2–3.

and groan to one another. [24]Ezekiel shall be a sign for you: everything he did, you shall do. When it happens, you shall know that I am the Lord GOD.

***End of Ezekiel's Muteness.*** [25][w] As for you, son of man, truly, on the very day I take away from them their strength, their glorious joy, the delight of their eyes, the desire of their soul, the pride of their hearts, their sons and daughters, [26]on that day a survivor will come to you so that you may hear it with your own ears.[x] [27]On that day, with the survivor, your mouth shall be opened; you shall speak and be mute* no longer. You shall be a sign to them, and they shall know that I am the LORD.

## III. Prophecies Against Foreign Nations*

### CHAPTER 25*

See RG 231

***Against Ammon.*** [1]The word of the LORD came to me: [2]Son of man, turn toward the Ammonites and prophesy against them.[y] [3]Say to the Ammonites: Hear the word of the LORD! Thus says the Lord GOD: Because you jeered at my sanctuary when it was desecrated, at the land of Israel when it was destroyed, and at the house of Judah when they went into exile, [4]therefore I am giving you to people from the east* as a possession. They shall set up their encampments among you and pitch their tents in your midst; they shall eat your produce and drink your milk.[z] [5]And I will turn Rabbah into a pasture for camels and all of Ammon into a grazing place for flocks. Then you shall know that I am the LORD.

[6]For thus says the Lord GOD: Because you rejoiced over the land of Israel with scorn in your heart, clapping your hands and stamping your feet, [7]therefore, see, I am stretching out my hand against you and giving you up as plunder to the nations. I will cut you off from the peoples and wipe you out of the lands. I will destroy you, and you shall know that I am the LORD.[a]

***Against Moab.*** [8][b] Thus says the Lord GOD: Because Moab said, "See! the house of Judah is like all the other nations," [9]therefore, I am exposing the whole flank of Moab* with its cities, the jewels of its land: Beth-jesimoth, Baalmeon, and Kiriathaim. [10]I will hand it over, along with the Ammonites, to the people from the east that it may not be remembered among the nations. [11]I will execute judgment upon Moab that they may know that I am the LORD.[c]

***Against Edom.*** [12][d] Thus says the Lord GOD: Because Edom took vengeance on the house of Judah and incurred terrible guilt by taking vengeance on them, [13]therefore thus says the Lord GOD: I will stretch out my hand against Edom and cut off from it human being and beast alike. I will turn it into ruins from Teman to Dedan; they shall fall by the sword.[e] [14]I will put my vengeance against Edom into the hands of my people Israel; they will deal with Edom in accord with my furious anger. Thus they shall know my vengeance!—oracle of the Lord GOD.[f]

***Against the Philistines.*** [15]Thus says the Lord GOD: Because the Philistines acted vengefully and exacted vengeance with intentional malice, destroying with undying hostility,[g] [16]therefore thus says the Lord GOD: See! I am stretching out my hand against the Philistines, and I will cut off the Cherethites* and wipe out the remnant on the

**24:27 Mute**: unable to preach anything but the Lord's judgment against Judah and Jerusalem; cf. 3:27 and note on 33:21–22.

**25:1–32:32** These chapters form a body of oracles directed against foreign nations. They follow the prophet's condemnation of Judah and oracles announcing its destruction. The unit precedes the announcement of Judah's salvation in chaps. 33–48.

**25:1–17** Ezekiel condemns four nations for their reactions to Judah's destruction and exile: Ammon to the east (vv. 2–7); Moab to the southeast (vv. 8–11); Edom to the south (vv. 12–14); Philistia to the west (vv. 15–17). Their hostility was not unprovoked; at one time or another, each one either lost territory to Israel or had been under Israelite control.

**25:4 People from the east**: nomadic tribes from the desert east of Ammon and Moab (cf. Is 11:14; Jer 49:28), often a threat to outlying towns and villages.

**25:9 The whole flank of Moab**: the eastern edge of the Moabite plateau, perhaps lightly fortified because the vast desert to the east provided a natural barrier to invasion.

**25:16 Cherethites**: people from the island of Crete in the

*w:* cf. Ez 3:22–27. *x:* cf. Ez 33:22. *y:* Jer 49:1–6; Am 1:13–15; Zep 2:8–11. *z:* Dt 28:33, 51. *a:* Am 1:14–15. *b:* Sir 50:26; Is 15–16; Jer 48; Am 2:1–3. *c:* Am 2:1–3. *d:* 2 Sm 8:13–14; 2 Chr 28:17; Ob 11–14. *e:* cf. Ez 35; Is 34:5–17; 63:1–6; Jer 49:7–11. *f:* cf. Ez 35:11. *g:* Is 14:29–31; Jer 47:1–7; Am 1:6–8; Zep 2:4–7.

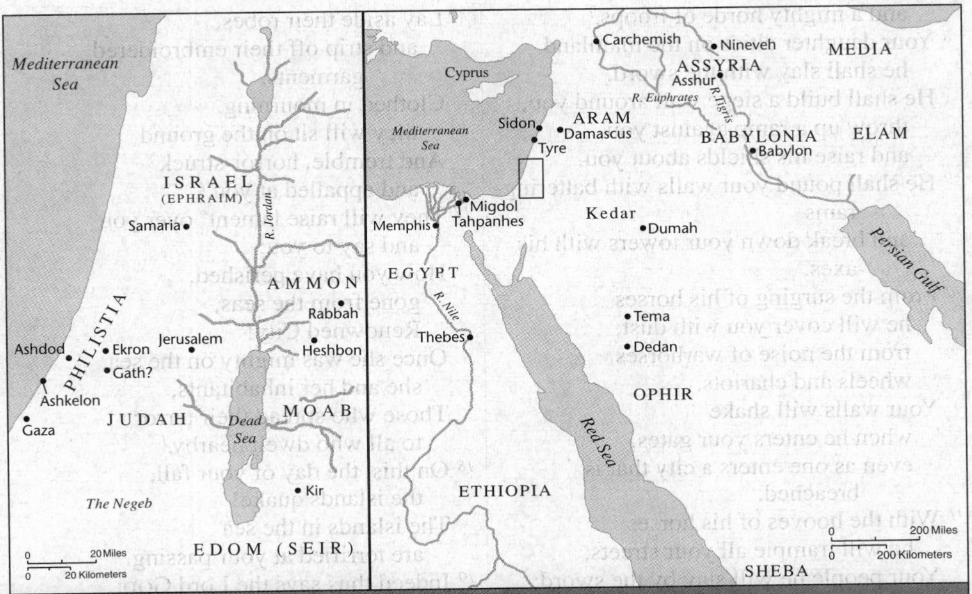

**Places Mentioned in the Oracles against the Nations**

seacoast. 17 Thus I will execute great acts of
vengeance on them, punishing them furiously. Then they shall know that I am the
LORD, when I wreak my vengeance on them.

## CHAPTER 26

See RG 231

*Against the City of Tyre.* 1* On the first
day of the eleventh month of the eleventh
year, the word of the LORD came to me:

2 * Son of man, because Tyre said of
Jerusalem:
“Aha! The gateway of the peoples is
smashed!
It has been turned over to me;
I will be enriched by its ruin!”[h]
3 therefore thus says the Lord GOD:
See! I am coming against you, Tyre;
I will churn up against you many
nations,
just as the sea churns up its waves.
4 They will destroy the walls of Tyre
and tear down its towers;
I will scrape off its debris
and leave it a bare rock.*
5 It will become a place for drying nets
in the midst of the sea.
For I have spoken—oracle of the Lord
GOD:
she will become plunder for the
nations.
6 Her daughter cities* on the mainland
will be slaughtered by the sword;
then they shall know that I am the
LORD.
7 Indeed thus says the Lord GOD:
I am bringing up against Tyre
from the north, Nebuchadnezzar,
King of Babylon, king of kings,
with horses and chariots, with cavalry,

Aegean, the Philistines’ point of origin. In Zep 2:5, the terms “Philistines,” “Cherethites,” and “seacoast people” describe the same group of people.

**26:1** The Hebrew text does not give a number with the month. This translation assumes a scribal error, the omission of the second occurrence of the number eleven.

**26:2** Tyre is pictured rejoicing over Jerusalem’s fall to Babylon because now the wealth from caravans and other trade will go to Tyrian merchants.

**26:4–5 A bare rock**: the Tyre of Ezekiel’s time was situated on a rocky island just off the Phoenician coast. During the time of Alexander the Great a causeway was built to connect it to the mainland.

**26:6 Daughter cities**: tributary towns and villages on the mainland.

*h*: Is 23:1–18; Jl 3:4–5; Am 1:9–10; Zec 9:2–4.

and a mighty horde of troops.[i]
8 Your daughter cities on the mainland
he shall slay with the sword.
He shall build a siege wall around you,
throw up a ramp against you,
and raise his shields about you.
9 He shall pound your walls with battering-rams
and break down your towers with his axes.
10 From the surging of his horses
he will cover you with dust;
from the noise of warhorses,
wheels and chariots.
Your walls will shake
when he enters your gates,
even as one enters a city that is breached.
11 With the hooves of his horses
he will trample all your streets;
Your people he will slay by the sword;
your mighty pillars will collapse.[j]
12 They shall plunder your wealth
and pillage your goods;
They will tear down your walls
and demolish your splendid houses.
Your stones, timbers, and debris
they will cast into the sea.
13 I will bring an end to the noise of your songs;
the music of your lyres will be heard no more.
14 I will turn you into bare rock,
you will become a place for drying nets.
You shall never be rebuilt,
for I the LORD have spoken—
oracle of the Lord GOD.
15 Thus says the Lord GOD to Tyre:
At the sound of your downfall,
at the groaning of the wounded,
When victims are slain within you,
will the islands not quake?
16 All the princes of the sea*
will step down from their thrones,
Lay aside their robes,
and strip off their embroidered garments.
Clothed in mourning,
they will sit on the ground
And tremble, horror-struck
and appalled at you.[k]
17 They will raise lament* over you
and say to you:
How you have perished,
gone from the seas,
Renowned City!
Once she was mighty on the sea,
she and her inhabitants,
Those who spread their terror
to all who dwelt nearby.[l]
18 On this, the day of your fall,
the islands quake!
The islands in the sea
are terrified at your passing.
19 Indeed thus says the Lord GOD:
When I make you a ruined city
like cities no longer inhabited,
When I churn up the deep
and its mighty waters cover you,
20 Then I will thrust you down
with those who go down to the pit,*
to those of the bygone age;
I will make you dwell in the netherworld,
in the everlasting ruins,
with those who have gone down to the pit,
So you will never return
or have a place in the land of the living.[m]
21 I will make you a horror,
and you shall be no more;
You shall be sought for,
but never found again—
oracle of the Lord GOD.

## CHAPTER 27

See RG 231

*The Ship Tyre.* 1 The word of the LORD
came to me: 2 You, son of man, raise a lament
over Tyre, 3 and say to Tyre, who sits at the

**26:16 The princes of the sea**: the rulers of the islands and coastal cities leagued commercially with Tyre.

**26:17 Lament**: the princes sing a funeral dirge at the burial of the personified Tyre; cf. the similar lamentation over Egypt in 32:3–8.

**26:20 Those who go down to the pit**: the dead, pictured as dwelling in Sheol, a place or cave of darkness. Cf. 32:17–32; Is 14:4–21 for other examples.

*i*: Jer 27:6; Na 2:3–4. *j*: Na 3:11. *k*: cf. Ez 32:10. *l*: cf. Ez 19:1. *m*: cf. Ez 31:14; 32:18, 24, 30.

entrance to the sea, trader to peoples on many coastlands, Thus says the Lord GOD:

Tyre, you said, "I am a ship,
perfect in beauty;[n]
4 In the heart of the sea was your territory;
your builders perfected your beauty.[o]
5 With juniper wood from Senir*
they built all your decks;
A cedar from Lebanon they took
to make you a mast.
6 With oaks of Bashan*
they fashioned your oars,
Your bridge, of ivory-inlaid cypress wood
from the coasts of Kittim.
7 Fine embroidered linen from Egypt
became your sail;
Your awnings were made of purple and
scarlet
from the coasts of Elishah.* [p]
8 Inhabitants of Sidon* and Arvad
were your oarsmen;
Your own sages, Tyre, were on board,
serving as your sailors.[q]
9 The elders and sages of Gebal
were with you to caulk your seams.
Every ship and sailor on the sea
came to you to carry on trade.[r]
10 Persia and Lud and Put
were warriors in your army;
Shield and helmet they hung on you
to enhance your splendor.
11 The men of Arvad and Helech*
were on your walls all around
And Gamadites on your towers;
they hung their shields around your
walls,
they made your beauty perfect.
12 Tarshish traded with you,
so great was your wealth,
Exchanging for your wares
silver, iron, tin, and lead.
13 Javan, Tubal, and Meshech
also traded with you,
Exchanging slaves and bronze vessels
for your merchandise.[s]
14 Horses, steeds, and mules from
Beth-togarmah
were exchanged for your wares.
15 Men of Rhodes trafficked with you;
many coastlands were your agents;
Ivory tusks and ebony wood
they brought back as your payment.
16 Edom traded with you for your many
wares:
garnets, purple dye, embroidered cloth,
Fine linen, coral, and rubies
they gave you as merchandise.
17 Judah and the land of Israel
trafficked with you:
Minnith wheat, grain,* honey, oil, and
balm[t]
they gave you as merchandise.
18 Damascus traded with you for your many
wares,
so great was your wealth,
exchanging Helbon wine and Zahar
wool.
19 Javan exchanged wrought iron, cassia,
and aromatic cane
from Uzal for your wares.
20 Dedan traded with you for riding gear.[u]
21 Arabia and the sheikhs of Kedar were
your agents,
dealing in lambs, rams, and goats.[v]
22 The merchants of Sheba and Raamah
also traded with you,
exchanging for your wares the very
best spices,
all kinds of precious stones, and gold.
23 Haran, Canneh, and Eden,
the merchants of Sheba, Asshur, and
Chilmad,
24 Traded with you, marketing rich garments,
purple cloth, embroidered fabric,
varicolored carpets, and braided cords.
25 The ships of Tarshish sailed for you with
your goods;

**27:5 Senir**: another name for Mount Hermon; cf. Dt 3:9.

**27:6 Bashan**: an area in northern Transjordan, noted for its lush growth and great forests (cf. Is 2:13). **Kittim**: here, probably Cyprus.

**27:7 Elishah**: perhaps another term for Cyprus.

**27:8–9 Sidon . . . Gebal**: Phoenician cities in Tyre's orbit of influence; Gebal is classical Byblos.

**27:11 Helech**: perhaps in Asia Minor; otherwise unknown.

**27:17 Grain**: most commentators have read "figs," but Hebrew *panag* more properly describes milled grains or prepared meal.

*n:* Is 23:9. *o:* cf. Ez 28:1. *p:* Is 19:9–10. *q:* cf. Ez 28:20–23. *r:* Ps 104:26. *s:* cf. Ez 38:2; 39:1. *t:* 1 Kgs 5:9. *u:* Is 21:13. *v:* Is 21:17; Jer 49:28.

## Ezekiel's Oracles Concerning the Nations

LIKE OTHER PROPHETIC books (Is 13–23; Jer 46–51), Ezekiel contains a section of oracles concerning foreign nations (Ez 25–32), which are intended to demonstrate God's power throughout the world. The nations included here, Ammon, Moab, Edom, Philistia, Tyre, and Egypt, would all be considered as targets of the Babylonian empire, although Egypt was never taken. Ezekiel identifies the projected expansion of Babylonia as an act of God.

You were full and heavily laden
in the heart of the sea.
26 Out into deep waters
your oarsmen brought you;
The east wind shattered you
in the heart of the sea.[w]
27 Your wealth, your goods, your wares,
your sailors, your crew,
The caulkers of your seams,
those who traded for your goods,
All the warriors with you,
the whole crowd with you
Sank into the heart of the sea
on the day of your downfall.[x]
28 At the sound of your sailors' shouts
the waves shudder,[y]
29 Down from their ships
come all who ply the oars;
Sailors, all the seafaring crew,
stand on the shore.
30 They raise their voices over you
and shout their bitter cries;
They pour dust on their heads
and cover themselves with ashes.
31 For you they shave their heads bald
and put on sackcloth;
For you they weep bitterly,
in anguished lament.[z]
32 They raise a lament for you;
they wail over you:
"Who was ever destroyed like Tyre
in the midst of the sea?"[a]
33 By exporting your goods by sea
you satisfied many peoples,
With your great wealth and merchandise
you enriched the kings of the earth.[b]
34 Now you are wrecked in the sea,
in the watery depths;
Your wares and all your crew
have fallen down with you.
35 All who dwell on the coastlands
are aghast over you;
Their kings are terrified,
their faces distorted.
36 The traders among the peoples
now hiss at you;
You have become a horror,
you shall be no more.

### CHAPTER 28

See RG 231

*The Prince of Tyre.* 1* The word of the
LORD came to me: 2Son of man, say to the
prince of Tyre: Thus says the Lord GOD:

Because you are haughty of heart,
you say, "I am a god!
I sit on a god's throne
in the heart of the sea!"
But you are a man, not a god;
yet you pretend
you are a god at heart!
3 Oh yes, you are wiser than Daniel,*
nothing secret is too obscure for you![c]
4 By your wisdom and intelligence
you made yourself rich,
filling your treasuries with gold and
silver.
5 Through your great wisdom in trading
you heaped up riches for yourself—
your heart is haughty because of your
riches.
6 Therefore thus says the Lord GOD:
Because you pretend you are a god at
heart,

**28:1–10** Ezekiel mocks the arrogance of Tyre's leader, who mistakes the city's commercial success for evidence of his divinity. At the hands of a foreign army, commissioned by the only God worthy of the name, this leader dies a humiliating, unceremonious death.

**28:3 Wiser than Daniel**: see note on 14:14.

*w:* Ps 48:7; Jer 18:17. *x:* cf. Ez 28:8. *y:* Jer 49:21. *z:* Is 15:2; Jer 48:37. *a:* Is 23:1–6. *b:* cf. Ez 28:4–5. *c:* cf. Ez 14:14; Dn 1:20; 2:20–23.

7 Therefore, I will bring against you
strangers, the most bloodthirsty of
nations.
They shall draw their swords
against your splendid wisdom,
and violate your radiance.[d]
8 They shall thrust you down into the pit:
you shall die a violent death
in the heart of the sea.
9 Then, face to face with your killers,
will you still say, "I am a god"?
No, you are a man, not a god,
handed over to those who slay you.
10 You shall die the death of the
uncircumcised
handed over to strangers,
for I have spoken—oracle of the Lord
GOD.[e]

11 The word of the LORD came to me: 12 Son
of man, raise a lament over the king of Tyre,
and say to him: Thus says the Lord GOD:

* You were a seal of perfection,
full of wisdom, perfect in beauty.[f]
13 In Eden, the garden of God, you lived;
precious stones of every kind were
your covering:
Carnelian, topaz, and beryl,
chrysolite, onyx, and jasper,
sapphire, garnet, and emerald.
Their mounts and settings
were wrought in gold,
fashioned for you the day you were
created.[g]
14 With a cherub I placed you;
I put you on the holy mountain of God,*
where you walked among fiery stones.
15 Blameless were you in your ways
from the day you were created,
Until evil was found in you.
16 Your commerce was full of
lawlessness, and you sinned.
Therefore I banished you from the
mountain of God;
the cherub drove you out
from among the fiery stones.[h]
17 Your heart had grown haughty
because of your beauty;
You corrupted your wisdom
because of your splendor.
I cast you to the ground,
I made you a spectacle
in the sight of kings.[i]
18 Because of the enormity of your guilt,
and the perversity of your trade,
you defiled your sanctuary.
I brought fire out of you;
it devoured you;
I made you ashes on the ground
in the eyes of all who see you.[j]
19 All the nations who knew you
are appalled on account of you;
You have become a horror,
never to be again.[k]

*Against Sidon.* 20 The word of the LORD
came to me: 21 Son of man, turn your face toward Sidon and prophesy against it. 22 Thus
says the Lord GOD:

Watch out! I am against you, Sidon;
I will win glory for myself in your midst.
They shall know that I am the LORD,
when I deliver judgment upon it
and manifest my holiness in it.
23 I will send disease into it;
blood will fill its streets,
Within it shall fall
those slain by the sword
raised against it on every side.
Then they shall know that I am the LORD.
24 No longer will there be a thorn that tears
or a brier that scratches for the house
of Israel
From the surrounding neighbors
who despise them;
thus they shall know that I am the
LORD.[l]

25 Thus says the Lord GOD: When I gather
the house of Israel from the peoples among

**28:12–19** Ezekiel describes the leader of Tyre in language that recalls the imagery of Gn 2–3.

**28:14 The holy mountain of God**: the residence of gods in Israelite and non-Israelite myth; cf. Is 14:13. **Fiery stones**: associated with the divine presence; cf. Ez 1:13; Ps 18:13.

*d:* cf. Ez 30:11; 31:12; 32:12. *e:* cf. Ez 32:19, 24. *f:* Is 14:12–15. *g:* cf. Ez 31:8–9; Gn 2:8, 15. *h:* Gn 3:24. *i:* Is 10:12. *j:* Ob 18. *k:* Lv 26:12. *l:* Nm 33:55.

whom they are scattered, and I manifest my holiness through them in the sight of the nations, then they shall live on the land I gave my servant Jacob.[m] 26 They shall dwell on it securely, building houses and planting vineyards. They shall dwell securely while I execute judgment on all their neighbors who treated them with contempt; then they shall know that I, the LORD, am their God.[n]

See RG 231

## CHAPTER 29

*Egypt the Crocodile.* 1 In the tenth year, on the twelfth day of the tenth month,* the word of the LORD came to me: 2 Son of man, turn your face toward Pharaoh, king of Egypt, and prophesy against him and against all Egypt.* [o] 3 Say to him: Thus says the Lord GOD:

Pay attention! I am against you,
Pharaoh, king of Egypt,
Great dragon* crouching
in the midst of the Nile,
Who says, "The Nile belongs to me;
I made it myself!"[p]
4 * I will put hooks in your jaws
and make all the fish of your Nile
Cling to your scales;
I will drag you up from your Nile,
With all the fish of your Nile
clinging to your scales.[q]
5 I will hurl you into the wilderness,
you and all the fish of your Nile.
You will fall into an open field,
you will not be picked up or gathered
together.
To the beasts of the earth
and the birds of the sky
I give you as food.[r]
6 [s] Then all the inhabitants of Egypt
will know that I am the LORD.
Because you were a staff of reeds*
for the house of Israel:
7 When they took hold of you, you would
splinter,
throwing shoulders out of joint.
When they leaned on you, you would
break,
pitching them down headlong.
8 Therefore thus says the Lord GOD:
Look! I am bringing the sword against
you
to cut off from you people and
animals.
9 The land of Egypt shall become a
desolate waste;
then they shall know that I am the
LORD.
Because you said, "The Nile belongs
to me;
I made it!"
10 Beware! I am against you
and against your Nile.
I will turn the land of Egypt into ruins,
into a dry, desolate waste,
From Migdol to Syene,*
up to the border of Ethiopia.[t]
11 No foot shall pass through it,
no human being or beast cross it;
it will remain uninhabited for forty
years.
12 I will make the land of Egypt the most
desolate
among desolate lands;
Its cities, the most deserted
among deserted cities for forty years;
I will scatter the Egyptians among the
nations

**29:1** The date is calculated to be January 7, 587 B.C. The siege of Jerusalem had begun a year earlier; cf. 24:1.

**29:2** Egypt was allied with Judah against the Babylonians.

**29:3 Dragon**: Hebrew reads *tannim*, usually translated "jackals," here a byform of *tannin*, the mythical dragon, or sea monster, representing chaos (cf. Is 27:1; 51:9; Jer 51:34; Ps 91:13; Jb 7:12), and the crocodile native to the Nile. **Nile**: the many rivulets of the Nile that branch out into the Delta.

**29:4–5** Ezekiel's repetition of detail creates a vivid picture of Egypt's destruction: God hauls the crocodile (Pharaoh) and the fish clinging to it for protection (the Egyptian populace) out of the Nile and lands them in an open field, where their corpses are torn apart by wildlife rather than being properly buried (cf. Dt 28:26; 2 Kgs 9:36–37; Jer 34:20; Ez 39:17–20).

**29:6 Staff of reeds**: Pharaoh is like a reed that looks sturdy but breaks under pressure. For a similar image, cf. 2 Kgs 18:21 (Is 36:6).

**29:10 From Migdol to Syene**: from the northeastern to the southern limits of Egypt. Syene is the modern Aswan, at the first cataract of the Nile; Ethiopia (Heb. *kush*) is the territory south of Aswan.

*m:* cf. Ez 20:41. *n:* Lv 25:18–19; Jer 23:6. *o:* Is 19:1–17; Jer 25:19. *p:* cf. Ez 32:2. *q:* Is 19:5. *r:* Jer 7:33. *s:* 2 Kgs 18:21; Is 36:6. *t:* cf. Ez 30:4, 6.

and disperse them throughout other
lands.[u]
13 But thus says the Lord GOD:
At the end of forty years
I will gather the Egyptians
from among the peoples
where they are scattered;
14 I will restore Egypt's fortunes,
bringing them back to the land of
Pathros,*
the land of their origin.
But there it will be a lowly kingdom,
15 lower than any other kingdom,
no longer able to set itself above the
nations.
I will make them few in number,
so they cannot rule other nations.
16 No longer shall they be security
for the house of Israel,
But a reminder of its iniquity
in turning away to follow them.
Then they shall know that I am the Lord
GOD.[v]

***Wages for Nebuchadnezzar.*** 17In the
twenty-seventh year on the first day of the
first month,* the word of the LORD came to
me: 18Son of man, Nebuchadnezzar, the king
of Babylon, has made his army wage a hard
campaign against Tyre;* their heads grew
bald, their shoulders rubbed raw, yet neither
he nor his army received compensation from
Tyre for all the effort they expended against
it.[w] 19Therefore thus says the Lord GOD:[x]
See! I am giving to Nebuchadnezzar, king of
Babylon, the land of Egypt! He will carry off
its wealth, plundering and pillaging whatever he can find to provide pay for his army.
20As payment for his toil I give him the land
of Egypt—oracle of the Lord GOD.
21On that day I will make a horn* sprout
for the house of Israel, and I will let you
again open your mouth in their midst; then
they shall know that I am the LORD.[y]

## CHAPTER 30

See RG 231

***The Day of the Lord Against Egypt.***
1The word of the LORD came to me: 2Son of
man, prophesy and say: Thus says the Lord
GOD:

Wail: "Alas the day!"
3 Yes, a day approaches,
a day of the Lord approaches:
A day of dark cloud,
a time appointed for the nations.[z]
4 A sword will come against Egypt,
there will be anguish in Ethiopia,
When the slain fall in Egypt
when its hordes are seized,
its foundations razed.[a]
5 Ethiopia, Put, and Lud,
all the mixed rabble* and Kub,
and the people of allied lands
shall fall by the sword with them.
6 Thus says the LORD:
The pillars of Egypt shall fall,
and its proud strength sink;
From Migdol to Syene,
its people will fall by the sword—
oracle of the Lord GOD.[b]
7 It shall be the most desolate
among desolate lands,
Its cities the most ruined
among ruined cities.
8 They shall know that I am the LORD,
when I set fire to Egypt,
and all its allies are shattered.[c]
9 On that day, messengers from me
will go forth in ships
to terrorize confident Ethiopia.
Anguish will be among them

**29:14 Pathros**: an Egyptian word for upper, i.e., southern, Egypt, above Memphis/Thebes. As silt filled the Delta region and richer land became available there, the population spread north, creating the tradition of a migration from the south (Is 11:11; Jer 44:1, 15).

**29:17 In the twenty-seventh year on the first day of the first month**: April 26, 571 B.C. This is the latest date attached to any of Ezekiel's prophecies.

**29:18–19** Nebuchadnezzar's thirteen-year siege (587–574 B.C.) ended with Tyre's surrender on the condition that the Babylonian army would not loot and pillage (*pace* 26:3–14). According to Ezekiel, Nebuchadnezzar and his army should collect their wages for serving as God's instrument in Tyre's punishment, by plundering and controlling Egypt.

**29:21 A horn**: God will give Israel renewed strength. For horn as a symbol of strength, cf. Dt 33:17; Ps 92:11; 132:17. Ezekiel suggests that the Babylonian conquest of Egypt precedes Israel's restoration, an event he expects to witness and acknowledge when God removes his muteness.

**30:5 Mixed rabble**: mercenaries.

*u:* Jer 46:19. *v:* Ps 40:5; Is 20:5. *w:* Is 26:7–14. *x:* Is 19:4. *y:* Ps 132:17; Lk 1:69. *z:* cf. Ez 7:7; Is 13:6. *a:* Jer 25:19–20. *b:* cf. Ez 29:10. *c:* Jer 49:27.

on Egypt's day—it is certainly
coming!*
10 Thus says the Lord GOD:
I will put an end to Egypt's hordes
by the hand of Nebuchadnezzar, king
of Babylon:
11 He and his army with him,
the most ruthless of nations,
will be brought in to devastate the land.
They will draw their swords against Egypt
and fill the land with the slain.
12 Then I will dry up the streams of the Nile,
and sell the land into evil hands;
By the hand of foreigners I will devastate
the land and everything in it.
I, the LORD, have spoken.[d]
13 * Thus says the Lord GOD:
I will destroy idols,
and put an end to images in Memphis.
There will never again be a prince
over the land of Egypt.
Instead, I will spread fear
throughout the land of Egypt.[e]
14 I will devastate Pathros,
set fire to Zoan,
and execute judgment against Thebes.[f]
15 I will pour out my wrath on Pelusium,
the fortress of Egypt,
and cut off the troops of Thebes.
16 I will set fire to Egypt;
Pelusium will writhe in anguish,
Thebes will be breached,
and Memphis besieged in daylight.
17 The warriors of On and Pi-beseth
will fall by the sword,
the cities taken captive.
18 In Tahpanhes, the day will turn dark
when I break the scepter of Egypt there
and put an end to its proud strength.
Dark clouds will cover it,
and its women will go into captivity.[g]
19 I will execute judgment against Egypt
that they may know that I am the LORD.

***Pharaoh's Broken Arm.*** 20 On the seventh
day of the first month in the eleventh year,*
the word of the LORD came to me: 21* Son of
man, I have broken the arm of Pharaoh, king
of Egypt. See! It has not been immobilized
for healing, nor set with a splint to make it
strong enough to grasp a sword.[h] 22 Therefore thus says the Lord GOD: See! I am coming against Pharaoh, king of Egypt. I will
break both his arms, the strong one and the
broken one, making the sword fall from his
hand. 23 I will scatter the Egyptians among
the nations and disperse them throughout
other lands. 24 I will, however, strengthen the
arms of the king of Babylon and put my
sword in his hand so he can bring it against
Egypt for plunder and pillage.[i] 25 When I
strengthen the arms of the king of Babylon,
and the arms of Pharaoh collapse, they shall
know that I am the LORD, because I put my
sword into the hand of the king of Babylon
to wield against the land of Egypt. 26 When I
scatter the Egyptians among the nations and
disperse them throughout other lands, they
shall know that I am the LORD.

## CHAPTER 31

See RG 231

***Allegory of the Cedar.*** 1 On the first
day of the third month in the eleventh year,*
the word of the LORD came to me: 2 Son of
man, say to Pharaoh, the king of Egypt, and
to his hordes: In your greatness, whom do
you resemble?

3 Assyria! It is Assyria!*
A cedar of Lebanon—
Beautiful branches,

**30:9** God spreads panic throughout Ethiopia, ancient Cush, by sending messengers with news of Egypt's fall. Rivers at its borders insulated Ethiopia and made it inaccessible except by boat.

**30:13–19** The prophet enumerates a list of major Egyptian cities that shall each bear the judgment proclaimed in the previous oracle, vv. 1–12.

**30:20 The seventh day of the first month in the eleventh year**: April 29, 587 B.C.

**30:21–26** This oracle was delivered more than a year into the siege of Jerusalem (24:1). When Pharaoh Hophra came to help Jerusalem, the Babylonians temporarily lifted the siege; cf. Jer 34:21; 37:6–7. In Ezekiel's eyes, Hophra was interfering with the punishment God intended the Babylonians to inflict on Judah. The Babylonians routed the Egyptians, who could not offer Jerusalem any more help; cf. chap. 31.

**31:1 The first day of the third month in the eleventh year**: June 21, 587 B.C.

**31:3 Assyria**: this translates *te'ashshur*, which some interpret as "cypress tree." The oracle, however, compares the fate

*d:* Is 19:6. *e:* Is 19:13. *f:* Is 19:11, 13; Jer 46:25. *g:* Jer 43:4–7. *h:* Jer 37:10; 44:30; 48:25. *i:* cf. Ez 21:14.

## Seven Oracles Concerning Egypt and Its Rulers

THE ORACLES AGAINST Egypt are found in chs 29–32. Egypt played a major role in instigating the revolt against its enemy Babylon. When Pharaoh Hophra attempted to relieve Jerusalem from the Babylonian siege in 588 B.C., he was repulsed (Jer 37; 44:30; see also Jer 32).

thick shade,
Towering heights,
its crown in the clouds![j]
4 The waters made it grow,
the deep made it tall,
Letting its currents flow
around the place it was planted,
Then sending its channels
to all the other trees of the field.[k]
5 Thereupon it towered in height
above all the trees in the field;
Its branches were numerous
and its boughs long,
Because of the many waters
sent to its shoots.
6 In its branches nested
all the birds of the sky;
Under its boughs all the wild animals
gave birth,
And in its shade* dwelt
all the mighty nations.[l]
7 It was magnificent in size
and in the length of its branches,
For its roots reached down
to the many waters.
8 In the garden of God,
no cedars could rival it,
No juniper could equal its branches,
no plane tree match its boughs.
No tree in the garden of God
could match its beauty.[m]
9 I made it beautiful
with abundant foliage,
So that all the trees in Eden
were envious of it.*
10 Therefore, thus says the Lord GOD:
Because it was arrogant about its height,
lifting its crown among the clouds
and exalting itself because of its size,[n]
11 I handed it over to a ruler of nations
to deal with it according to its evil.
I have cast it off,
12 and foreigners have cut it down,
The most ruthless nations,
have hurled it on the mountains.
Its boughs fell into every valley
and its branches lay broken
in every ravine in the land.
All the peoples of the earth
departed from its shade
when it was hurled down.[o]
13 On its fallen trunk
sit all the birds of the sky;
Beside its fallen branches,
are found all the beasts of the field.
14 This has happened so no well-watered
tree
will gain such lofty height,
or lift its crown to the clouds.
Not one of those fed by water
will tower in height over the rest.
For all of them are destined for death,
for the underworld, among mere
mortals,
with those who go down to the pit.
15 Thus says the Lord GOD:
On the day it went down to Sheol,
I made the deep close up
in mourning for it.
I restrained the currents of the deep,
and held back the many waters.
I darkened Lebanon because of it,
and all the trees of the field
languished because of it.
16 At the sound of its fall,
I made nations shudder,

of Pharaoh to the terrible demise of Assyria because of its arrogant pride (cf. Na 1–3). Ezekiel may have drawn on an ancient myth of a cosmic tree of life to emphasize the greatness of Egypt's fall.

**31:6 Shade**: a metaphor for protection (cf. Lam 4:20).

**31:9** Here Israel's God is responsible for Assyria's splendor, whereas in Is 10:13 Assyria claims to have created its own might.

*j:* Ps 92:12; Jer 50:18. *k:* Dn 4:10. *l:* Dn 4:12; cf. Mt 13:32. *m:* Ps 80:10. *n:* Is 2:11. *o:* Dn 4:14.

When I cast it down to Sheol
with those who go down to the pit.
In the underworld
all the trees of Eden took comfort:
Lebanon's choicest and best,
all that were fed by the waters.[p]
17 They too will go down to Sheol,
to those slain by the sword,
Its allies* who dwelt
in its shade among the nations.
18 To whom among the trees of Eden
do you compare in glory and greatness?
You will be brought down
with the trees of Eden to the underworld,
And lie among the uncircumcised,
with those slain by the sword.
Such is Pharaoh and all his hordes—
oracle of the Lord GOD.

## CHAPTER 32

See RG 231

*Lament over Pharaoh.* 1 On the first day of the twelfth month in the twelfth year,* the word of the LORD came to me: 2 Son of man, utter a lament over Pharaoh, the king of Egypt, and say to him:

You liken yourself to a lion among nations,
but you are like the monster in the sea!
Thrashing about in your streams,
churning the water with your feet,
polluting the streams.[q]
3 Thus says the Lord GOD:
I will cast my net over you
by assembling many armies,
and I will hoist you up in my mesh.
4 I will hurl you onto the land,
cast you into an open field.
I will make all the birds of the sky
roost upon you,
The beasts of the whole earth
gorge themselves on you.
5 I will strew your flesh on the mountains,
and fill the valleys with your corpse.[r]
6 I will drench the land,
pouring out your blood on the mountain;
filling up the ravines with you.
7 When I extinguish you,
I will cover the heavens
and darken all its stars.
The sun I will cover with clouds;
the moon will not give light.[s]
8 All the shining lights in the heavens
I will darken over you;
I will spread darkness over your land—
oracle of the Lord GOD.
9 I will trouble the hearts
of many peoples,
When I bring you captive
among the nations,
to lands you do not know.
10 I will fill many nations with horror;
their kings will shudder at you,
when I brandish my sword in their faces.
They will tremble violently
fearing for their lives on the day of your fall.[t]
11 For thus says the Lord GOD:
The sword of the king of Babylon
will come against you.
12 I will cut down your hordes
with the swords of warriors,
all of them, ruthless nations;
They will lay waste the glory of Egypt,
and all its hordes will be destroyed.
13 I will wipe out all the livestock
from the banks of its many waters;
No human foot will disturb them again,
no animal hoof stir them up.
14 Then I will make their waters clear
and their streams flow like oil—
oracle of the Lord GOD.
15 When I make Egypt a wasteland
and the land destitute of everything,
When I strike down all its inhabitants
they shall know that I am the LORD.
16 This is the lamentation
women of all nations will chant;
They will raise it over Egypt;
over all its hordes they will chant it—
oracle of the Lord GOD.

**31:17 Allies**: lit., "arm."

**32:1 The first day of the twelfth month in the twelfth year**: March 3, 585 B.C.

*p:* Is 14:8, 15. *q:* cf. Ez 19:1; 20:3. *r:* Is 34:3. *s:* Is 3:10. *t:* Rev 18:9–10; 32:12; cf. Ez 31:11–12.

***Another Lament over Egypt.*** 17* On the fifteenth day of that month in the twelfth year, the word of the LORD came to me:

18 Son of man, wail over the hordes of Egypt—
you and the women of mighty nations—
Send them down to the underworld,
with those who go down into the pit.
19 Whom do you excel in beauty? Go down!
Be laid to rest with the uncircumcised!
20 Among those slain by the sword they will fall,
for the sword has been appointed!
Seize Egypt and all its hordes.[u]
21 Out of Sheol the mighty warriors
will speak to him and his allies:
Let them descend and lie down among the uncircumcised,
those slain by the sword![v]
22 There is Assyria and all its company,
around it are its graves,
all of them slain, fallen by the sword.
23 The graves are set
in the recesses of the pit;
Its company is assembled
around its grave,
All of them slain, fallen by the sword,
those who spread terror in the land of the living.[w]
24 There is Elam and all its horde
around its grave,
All of them slain, fallen by the sword;
they descended uncircumcised
into the underworld,
Those who spread their terror
in the land of the living.
They bear their disgrace
with those who go down into the pit.
25 Among the slain is set its bed,
with all its horde around its grave;
All of them uncircumcised,
slain by the sword
Because of the terror they spread
in the land of the living.
They bear their disgrace
with those who go down into the pit.
Among the slain it is set!
26 There is Meshech and Tubal* and all the hordes
surrounding it with their graves.
All of them uncircumcised,
slain by the sword
Because they spread their terror
in the land of the living.[x]
27 They do not rest with the warriors
who fell in ancient times,
who went down to Sheol fully armed.
Their swords were placed under their heads
and their shields laid over their bones;
For there was terror of these warriors
in the land of the living.
28 But as for you, among the uncircumcised
you will be broken and laid to rest
with those slain by the sword.
29 There is Edom, all its kings and princes,
who, despite their might,
are put with those slain by the sword.
They lie among the uncircumcised,
with those who go down into the pit.[y]
30 There are the generals of the north
and all the Sidonians
Who have gone down with the slain,
because of the terror their might inspired.
They lie uncircumcised
with those slain by the sword,
And bear their shame with those
who have gone down into the pit.[z]
31 When Pharaoh sees them,
he will be consoled on behalf of all his hordes,
slain by the sword—
Pharaoh and all his army—
oracle of the Lord GOD.
32 I spread terror of him
in the land of the living;
Now he is laid among the uncircumcised,
with those slain by the sword—
Pharaoh and all his horde—
oracle of the Lord GOD.

**32:17–32** The description of Pharaoh in Sheol shifts rapidly between the single individual and the collective body, between corpses speaking and corpses lying inert, between singular (his, hers, its) and plural (them, theirs) pronouns to emphasize that all the enemies of Israel come to the same end.

**32:26 Meshech and Tubal**: see note on 38:2.

*u:* cf. Ez 31:17–18. *v:* Is 14:9. *w:* Is 14:15. *x:* cf. Ez 27:13. *y:* Is 34:5–15. *z:* Jer 25:26.

## IV. Hope for the Future

### CHAPTER 33

See RG 231–32

***The Prophet as Sentinel.*** 1 The word of the LORD came to me: 2 Son of man, speak to your people and tell them: When I bring the sword against a land, if the people of that land select one of their number as a sentinel* for them,[a] 3 and the sentinel sees the sword coming against the land, he should blow the trumpet to warn the people.[b] 4 If they hear the trumpet but do not take the warning and a sword attacks and kills them, their blood will be on their own heads.[c] 5 They heard the trumpet blast but ignored the warning; their blood is on them. If they had heeded the warning, they could have escaped with their lives. 6 If, however, the sentinel sees the sword coming and does not blow the trumpet, so that the sword attacks and takes someone's life, his life will be taken for his own sin, but I will hold the sentinel responsible for his blood.

7[d] You, son of man—I have appointed you as a sentinel for the house of Israel; when you hear a word from my mouth, you must warn them for me. 8 When I say to the wicked, "You wicked, you must die," and you do not speak up to warn the wicked about their ways, they shall die in their sins, but I will hold you responsible for their blood. 9 If, however, you warn the wicked to turn from their ways, but they do not, then they shall die in their sins, but you shall save your life.

***Individual Retribution.*** 10 As for you, son of man, speak to the house of Israel: You people say, "Our crimes and our sins weigh us down; we are rotting away because of them. How can we survive?"[e] 11[f] Answer them: As I live—oracle of the Lord GOD—I swear I take no pleasure in the death of the wicked, but rather that they turn from their ways and live. Turn, turn from your evil ways! Why should you die, house of Israel?

12 As for you, son of man, say to your people: The justice of the just will not save them on the day they sin; the wickedness of the wicked will not bring about their downfall on the day they turn from their wickedness. No, the just cannot save their lives on the day they sin.[g] 13 Even though I say to the just that they shall surely live, if they, relying on their justice, do wrong, none of their just deeds shall be remembered; because of the wrong they have done, they shall die.[h] 14 And though I say to the wicked that they shall die, if they turn away from sin and do what is just and right—15 returning pledges, restoring stolen goods, walking by statutes that bring life, doing nothing wrong—they shall surely live; they shall not die.[i] 16 None of the sins they committed shall be remembered against them. If they do what is right and just, they shall surely live.

17 Your people say, "The way of the LORD is not fair!" But it is their way that is not fair. 18 When the just turn away from justice and do wrong, they shall die for it.[j] 19 When the wicked turn away from wickedness and do what is right and just, because of this they shall live. 20 But still you say, "The way of the LORD is not fair!" I will judge each of you according to your ways, house of Israel.

***The Survivor from Jerusalem.*** 21 On the fifth day of the tenth month,* in the twelfth year of our exile, the survivor came to me from Jerusalem and said, "The city is taken!"[k] 22 The hand of the LORD had come upon me the evening before the survivor arrived and opened my mouth when he reached me in the morning. My mouth was opened, and I was mute no longer.[l]

***Those Left in Judah.**** 23 The word of the LORD came to me: 24 Son of man, these who

**33:2 Sentinel**: the theme of the sentinel's duty initiates a new commission to announce salvation (chaps. 33–48), just as the same command (3:17–21) opened Ezekiel's ministry to announce judgment (chaps. 3–24).

**33:21–22 The fifth day of the tenth month**: January 8, 585 B.C. According to Jeremiah (39:2), Jerusalem was taken in July, 587. Some manuscripts read "eleventh" for "twelfth" year (January, 586); even so, there was ample time between the fall of Jerusalem and the arrival of the survivor from that city to journey to Babylon. However, this is the survivor sent to fulfill the promise of Ez 24:25–27, the eyewitness whose arrival would release Ezekiel from his muteness; cf. 3:26–27.

**33:23–29** News brought by the survivor furnished the oc-

*a:* Lv 26:25. *b:* Hos 5:8; 8:1. *c:* Lv 20:9; Jer 6:17. *d:* Jer 1:17. *e:* Lv 26:16, 39. *f:* Jer 44:7–8; cf. Ez 18:23. *g:* cf. Ez 3:20. *h:* Heb 10:38. *i:* Ex 22:1–4, 26. *j:* Jer 18:7–10. *k:* 2 Kgs 25:4, 10; Is 39:1–2. *l:* cf. Ez 3:26–27.

live among the ruins in the land of Israel are
saying: “Abraham was only one person, yet
he was given possession of the land. Since
we are many, the land must be given to us as
our possession.”[m] 25 Therefore say to them:
Thus says the Lord GOD: You eat on the
mountains, you raise your eyes to your idols,
you shed blood—yet you would keep possession of the land?[n] 26 You rely on your
swords, you commit abominations, each defiles his neighbor’s wife—yet you would
keep possession of the land? 27 Say this to
them: Thus says the Lord GOD: As I live,
those among the ruins shall fall by the
sword; those in the open field I have made
food for the wild beasts; and those in rocky
hideouts and caves shall die by the plague.
28 I will make the land a desolate waste, so
that its proud strength will come to an end,
and the mountains of Israel shall be so desolate that no one will cross them. 29 Thus they
shall know that I am the LORD, when I make
the land a desolate waste because of all the
abominations they committed.

***Popular Misunderstanding.*** 30 As for you,
son of man, your people are talking about
you beside the walls and in the doorways of
houses. They say to one another, “Let’s go
hear the latest word that comes from the
LORD.” 31 My people come to you, gathering
as a crowd and sitting in front of you to hear
your words, but they will not act on them.
Love songs are on their lips, but in their
hearts they pursue dishonest gain.[o] 32 For
them you are only a singer* of love songs,
with a pleasant voice and a clever touch.
They listen to your words, but they do not
obey them. 33 But when it comes—and it is
surely coming!—they shall know that there
was a prophet among them.

## CHAPTER 34

See RG 231-32

***Parable of the Shepherds.*** 1 The word
of the LORD came to me: 2 Son of man,
prophesy against the shepherds* of Israel.
Prophesy and say to them: To the shepherds,
thus says the Lord GOD: Woe to the shepherds of Israel who have been pasturing
themselves![p] Should not shepherds pasture
the flock? 3 You consumed milk, wore wool,
and slaughtered fatlings, but the flock you
did not pasture.[q] 4 You did not strengthen the
weak nor heal the sick nor bind up the injured. You did not bring back the stray or
seek the lost but ruled them harshly and bru-
tally.[r] 5 So they were scattered for lack of a
shepherd, and became food for all the wild
beasts. They were scattered[s] 6 and wandered
over all the mountains and high hills; over
the entire surface of the earth my sheep were
scattered. No one looked after them or
searched for them.

7 Therefore, shepherds, hear the word of
the LORD: 8 As I live—oracle of the Lord
GOD—because my sheep became plunder,
because my sheep became food for wild
beasts, for lack of a shepherd, because my
shepherds did not look after my sheep, but
pastured themselves and did not pasture my
sheep,[t] 9 therefore, shepherds, hear the word
of the LORD: 10 Thus says the Lord GOD:
Look! I am coming against these shepherds.
I will take my sheep out of their hand and put
a stop to their shepherding my flock, so that
these shepherds will no longer pasture them.
I will deliver my flock from their mouths so
it will not become their food.[u]

11 For thus says the Lord GOD: Look! I myself will search for my sheep and examine
them. 12 As a shepherd examines his flock
while he himself is among his scattered
sheep, so will I examine my sheep. I will deliver them from every place where they were
scattered on the day of dark clouds.[v] 13 I will
lead them out from among the peoples and
gather them from the lands; I will bring them
back to their own country and pasture them
upon the mountains of Israel, in the ravines

casion for this prophecy. Like Jeremiah, Ezekiel rejects the idea that those left in Judah have any claim to the land. The new Israel is to be formed from the exiles.

**33:32 Singer**: perhaps the term indicates an entertainer whom one enjoys and then forgets.

**34:2 Shepherds**: the leaders of the people. A frequent title for kings and deities in the ancient Near East; the ideal ruler took care of his subjects and anticipated their needs. Ezekiel’s oracle broadens the reference to include the whole class of Jerusalem’s leaders (v. 17). The prophet assures his audience, the exiles in Babylon, that God holds these leaders responsi-

*m:* Is 51:2. *n:* Gn 9:4; Jer 7:9–10. *o:* cf. Ez 8:1; Mt 13:22. *p:* Ps 78:70–72; Jn 10:11. *q:* Is 56:11. *r:* Ex 1:13; Zec 11:15–17; Mt 18:12–14. *s:* cf. Mk 6:34. *t:* Jude 12. *u:* Ps 72:14. *v:* Is 40:11; Lk 19:10.

and every inhabited place in the land.[w] 14In good pastures I will pasture them; on the mountain heights of Israel will be their grazing land. There they will lie down on good grazing ground; in rich pastures they will be pastured on the mountains of Israel.[x] 15I myself will pasture my sheep; I myself will give them rest—oracle of the Lord GOD. 16The lost I will search out, the strays I will bring back, the injured I will bind up, and the sick I will heal; but the sleek and the strong I will destroy. I will shepherd them in judgment.

*Separation of the Sheep.* 17As for you, my flock, thus says the Lord GOD: I will judge between one sheep and another, between rams and goats.[y] 18Was it not enough for you to graze on the best pasture, that you had to trample the rest of your pastures with your hooves? Or to drink the clearest water, that you had to pollute the rest with your hooves? 19Thus my flock had to graze on what your hooves had trampled and drink what your hooves had polluted. 20Therefore thus says the Lord GOD: Now I will judge between the fat and the lean. 21Because you push with flank and shoulder, and butt all the weak sheep with your horns until you drive them off, 22I will save my flock so they can no longer be plundered; I will judge between one sheep and another. 23[z] I will appoint one shepherd* over them to pasture them, my servant David; he shall pasture them and be their shepherd. 24I, the LORD, will be their God, and my servant David will be prince in their midst. I, the LORD, have spoken.[a]

25I will make a covenant of peace with them and rid the country of wild beasts so they will dwell securely in the wilderness and sleep in the forests.[b] 26I will settle them around my hill and send rain in its season, the blessing of abundant rain. 27The trees of the field shall bear their fruits, and the land its crops, and they shall dwell securely on their own soil. They shall know that I am the LORD when I break the bars of their yoke and deliver them from the power of those who enslaved them.[c] 28They shall no longer be plundered by the nations nor will wild beasts devour them, but they shall dwell securely, with no one to frighten them.[d] 29I will prepare for them peaceful fields for planting so they are never again swept away by famine in the land or bear taunts from the nations. 30Thus they shall know that I, the LORD, their God, am with them, and that they are my people, the house of Israel—oracle of the Lord GOD.[e] 31Yes, you are my flock: you people are the flock of my pasture, and I am your God—oracle of the Lord GOD.[f]

## CHAPTER 35

See RG 231-32

*Against Edom.** 1The word of the LORD came to me: 2Son of man, set your face against Mount Seir and prophesy against it. 3Say to it: Thus says the Lord GOD: Watch out! I am against you, Mount Seir. I will stretch out my hand against you and turn you into a desolate waste.[g] 4Your cities I will turn into ruins, and you shall be a desolation; then you shall know that I am the LORD.[h]

5Because you nursed a long-standing hatred and handed the Israelites over to the sword at the time of their collapse, at the time of their final punishment,* [i] 6therefore, as I live—oracle of the Lord GOD—you are guilty of blood, and blood, I swear, shall pursue you. 7I will make Mount Seir a desolate waste and cut off from it anyone who travels across it and back.[j] 8I will fill its mountains with the slain; those slain by the sword shall fall on your hills, into your valleys and all your ravines.

ble for what has happened to Jerusalem and will give Israel a new shepherd worthy of the title.

**34:23 One shepherd**: a future king to rule over a unified, restored Israel, in the image of the idealized David present in the Book of Kings (cf., e.g., 1 Kgs 3:3; 11:38; 2 Kgs 14:3; 22:2). **My servant David**: a common characterization of David; e.g., 1 Kgs 11:34, 36, 38; 2 Kgs 8:19; Ps 36:1; 78:70. See Ez 37:25.

**35:1–15** After the fall of Jerusalem, Edom assisted the Babylonians in devastating the land and subduing the population in order to occupy part of Judah's former territory. For this reason these oracles against Edom are found in the context of the city's fall.

**35:5 Final punishment**: throughout this oracle the prophet echoes the threat against the mountains of Israel found in chaps. 6–7.

*w:* cf. Ez 36:24, 29–30. *x:* Ps 23:2; Is 40:11. *y:* Mt 25:32–33. *z:* Ps 89:4, 20; Jer 23:5–6. *a:* cf. Ez 36:28; Ps 89:49; Jn 10:16. *b:* Is 11:6–9. *c:* Lv 26:13; Ps 72:16; Jer 28:10–13. *d:* Jer 30:10. *e:* Ex 6:7. *f:* Ps 28:9. *g:* cf. Ez 25:12–14. *h:* Ob 13. *i:* Ob 11–15. *j:* Jer 46:19.

9 I will make you a desolation forever,
your cities will not be inhabited,
and you shall know that I am the LORD.[k]

10 Because you said: The two nations and
the two lands* belong to me; let us take possession of them—although the LORD was
there— 11 therefore, as I live—oracle of the
Lord GOD—I will deal with you according to
the anger and envy you dealt out to them in
your hatred, and I will make myself known to
them when I execute judgment on you,[l]
12 then you shall know that I am the LORD.
I have heard all the insults you spoke
against the mountains of Israel, saying: They
are desolate; they have been given to us to
devour. 13 You boasted against me with your
mouths and used insolent words against me.
I heard everything! 14 Thus says the Lord
GOD: Because you rejoiced that the whole
land was desolate, so I will do to you. 15 As
you rejoiced over the devastation of the heritage of the house of Israel, the same I will
do to you: you will become a ruin, Mount
Seir, and the whole of Edom, all of it! Then
they shall know that I am the LORD.[m]

## CHAPTER 36

See RG 231-32

*Regeneration of the Land.* 1 As for
you, son of man, prophesy to the mountains
of Israel and say: Mountains of Israel, hear
the word of the LORD! 2 Thus says the Lord
GOD: Because the enemy said about you,
"Ha! the ancient heights have become our
possession," 3 therefore prophesy and say:
Thus says the Lord GOD: because you have
been ridiculed and hounded on all sides for
becoming a possession for the remaining nations and have become a byword and a popular jeer,[n] 4 therefore, mountains of Israel,
hear the word of the Lord GOD: Thus says
the Lord GOD to the mountains and hills, to
the ravines and valleys, to the desolate ruins
and abandoned cities, plundered and
mocked by the nations remaining around
you:[o] 5 therefore thus says the Lord GOD:
Truly, with burning jealousy I speak against
the remaining nations and against Edom;
they all took possession of my land for plunder with wholehearted joy and utter contempt. 6 Therefore, prophesy concerning the
land of Israel and say to the mountains and
hills, to the ravines and valleys: Thus says
the Lord GOD: See! in my jealous fury I
speak, because you endured the reproach of
the nations. 7 Therefore, thus says the Lord
GOD: I raise my hand and swear: the nations
around you shall bear their own reproach.
8 But you, mountains of Israel, you will
sprout branches and bear fruit for my people
Israel, for they are coming soon.[p] 9 Look! I
am for you! I will turn my face toward you;
you will be plowed and planted.[q] 10 Upon you
I will multiply the whole house of Israel; cities shall be resettled and ruins rebuilt.[r]
11 Upon you I will multiply people and animals so they can multiply and be fruitful. I
will resettle you as in the past, and make you
more prosperous than at your beginning;
then you shall know that I am the LORD.[s]
12 Upon you I will have them walk, my
people Israel. They shall possess you, and
you shall be their heritage. Never again shall
you rob them of their children.
13 Thus says the Lord GOD: Because they
say of you, "You devour your own people,*
you rob your nation of its children,"[t] 14 therefore, you shall never again devour your people or rob your nation of its children—oracle
of the Lord GOD. 15 I will no longer make you
listen to the reproach of nations. You will
never again endure insults from the peoples.
Never again shall you rob your nation of its
children—oracle of the Lord GOD.
*Regeneration of the People.* 16 The word of
the LORD came to me: 17 Son of man, when

**35:10 The two nations and the two lands**: by presenting Edom's excursion into the southern territory of Judah as its claim to both kingdoms, Ezekiel exaggerates Edom's greed and arrogance. **LORD was there**: Edom's betrayal of Judah becomes an attack on Judah's God, the land's sovereign. In 11:15 and 33:24, Ezekiel condemns Judahites who annex land that does not belong to them. Now the exiles in Babylon learn that even though God had left Jerusalem (chap. 11), he witnesses Edom's insolence and pronounces judgment against it. Cf. 48:35, "The LORD is there!"

**36:13 You devour your own people**: i.e., the land destroys its own population; this phrase also occurs in Nm 13:32, where Israelite spies describe Canaan as "a land that devours its inhabitants."

*k:* Is 34:5–6; Ob 10. *l:* Ob 15. *m:* Is 34:11; Ob 12. *n:* Ob 13. *o:* cf. Ez 6:3. *p:* Lv 26:3–5. *q:* Lv 26:9. *r:* Is 49:8, 17–23. *s:* cf. Gn 1:22, 28. *t:* Nm 13:32.

the house of Israel lived in its land, they defiled it with their behavior and their deeds.
In my sight their behavior was like the impurity of a woman in menstruation.[u] 18 So I
poured out my fury upon them for the blood
they poured out on the ground and for the
idols with which they defiled it. 19 I scattered
them among the nations, and they were dispersed through other lands; according to
their behavior and their deeds I carried out
judgment against them.[v] 20* But when they
came to the nations, where they went, they
desecrated my holy name, for people said of
them: "These are the people of the LORD, yet
they had to leave their land." 21 So I relented
because of my holy name which the house of
Israel desecrated among the nations to
which they came. 22 Therefore say to the
house of Israel: Thus says the Lord GOD:
Not for your sake do I act, house of Israel,
but for the sake of my holy name, which you
desecrated among the nations to which you
came.[w] 23 But I will show the holiness of my
great name, desecrated among the nations,
in whose midst you desecrated it. Then the
nations shall know that I am the LORD—oracle of the Lord GOD—when through you I
show my holiness before their very eyes.[x] 24 I
will take you away from among the nations,
gather you from all the lands, and bring you
back to your own soil. 25* [y] I will sprinkle
clean water over you to make you clean;
from all your impurities and from all your
idols I will cleanse you. 26 [z] I will give you a
new heart, and a new spirit I will put within
you. I will remove the heart of stone from
your flesh and give you a heart of flesh.[a] 27 I
will put my spirit within you so that you
walk in my statutes, observe my ordinances,
and keep them.[b] 28 You will live in the land I
gave to your ancestors; you will be my people, and I will be your God.[c] 29 I will deliver
you from all your impurities. I will summon
the grain and make it plentiful; I will not
send famine against you. 30 I will increase the
fruit on your trees and the crops in your
fields so that you no longer endure reproach
from the nations because of famine.[d] 31 Then
you will remember your evil behavior and
your deeds that were not good; you will
loathe yourselves for your sins and your
abominations. 32 Not for your sake do I act—
oracle of the Lord GOD. Let this be known to
you! Be ashamed and humbled because of
your behavior, house of Israel.
33 Thus says the Lord GOD: When I cleanse
you of all your guilt, I will resettle the cities
and the ruins will be rebuilt.[e] 34 The desolate
land will be tilled—once a wasteland in the
eyes of every passerby. 35 They will say,
"This once-desolate land has become like the
garden of Eden. The cities once ruined, laid
waste and destroyed, are now resettled and
fortified."[f] 36 Then the surrounding nations
that remain shall know that I, the LORD, have
rebuilt what was destroyed and replanted
what was desolate. I, the LORD, have spoken:
I will do it. 37 Thus says the Lord GOD: This
also I will be persuaded to do for the house of
Israel: to multiply them like sheep. 38 Like
sheep for sacrifice, like the sheep of Jerusalem on its feast days, the ruined cities shall be
filled with flocks of people; then they shall
know that I am the LORD.[g]

## CHAPTER 37

See RG 231–32

*Vision of the Dry Bones.** 1 The hand
of the LORD came upon me, and he led me

**36:20–24** These verses make clear that Israel's restoration is God's initiative, independent of the people's shame and repentance (v. 31). By their wickedness, Israel provoked the exile; its presence among the nations gave the impression that God could not protect his people. God's gracious return of Israel to its land will restore his honor among these same nations.

**36:25–26** God's initiative to cleanse Israel (cf. 24:13–14) is the first act in the creation of a new people, no longer disposed to repeating Israel's wicked past (chap. 20). To make this restoration permanent, God replaces Israel's rebellious and obdurate interiority ("heart of stone") with an interiority ("heart of flesh") susceptible to and animated by God's intentions ("my spirit," v. 27).

**37:1–14** This account is a figurative description of God's creation of a new Israel. Even though that creation begins with the remains of the old Israel, the exiles under the image of dry bones, depicting a totally hopeless situation, the new Israel is radically different: it is an ideal people, shaped by God's spirit to live the covenant faithfully, something the old Israel, exiles included, were unable to do. While this passage

*u:* Ps 106:37–38. *v:* Lv 18:24–28. *w:* cf. Ez 20:44; Dt 9:4–6; Is 37:35. *x:* cf. Ez 20:41; Is 37:23. *y:* Ezr 6:21; Ps 51:2–7. *z:* Jer 31:33–34. *a:* cf. Rom 8:5–8. *b:* Ps 51:7–11. *c:* Jer 30:22; 31:33. *d:* Lv 26:4–5. *e:* Lv 26:31. *f:* cf. Ez 28:13; 31:9. *g:* 1 Kgs 8:63.

### The Valley of Dry Bones

EZEKIEL'S VISION OF dry bones symbolizes the restoration of the people of Israel. Many assume that it is based upon his observation of a battlefield filled with the bones of dead soldiers. The vision plays upon priestly concepts of purity, in that a priest must have no contact with the dead (Lv 21:1–12; those who do have contact with a corpse are defiled for a period of seven days, Nm 19:10b–22). Because such impurity is the epitome of defilement in priestly thought, this image of new life is a very powerful metaphor for the restoration and purification of Israel.

out in the spirit of the LORD and set me in the center of the broad valley. It was filled with bones. [2]He made me walk among them in every direction. So many lay on the surface of the valley! How dry they were! [3]He asked me: Son of man, can these bones come back to life? "Lord GOD," I answered, "you alone know that."[h] [4]Then he said to me: Prophesy over these bones, and say to them: Dry bones, hear the word of the LORD! [5]Thus says the Lord GOD to these bones: Listen! I will make breath enter you so you may come to life. [6]I will put sinews on you, make flesh grow over you, cover you with skin, and put breath into you so you may come to life. Then you shall know that I am the LORD. [7]I prophesied as I had been commanded. A sound started up, as I was prophesying, rattling like thunder. The bones came together, bone joining to bone. [8]As I watched, sinews appeared on them, flesh grew over them, skin covered them on top, but there was no breath in them. [9]Then he said to me: Prophesy to the breath, prophesy, son of man! Say to the breath: Thus says the Lord GOD: From the four winds come, O breath, and breathe into these slain that they may come to life.* [i] [10]I prophesied as he commanded me, and the breath entered them; they came to life and stood on their feet, a vast army.[j] [11]He said to me: Son of man, these bones are the whole house of Israel! They are saying, "Our bones are dried up, our hope is lost, and we are cut off." [12]Therefore, prophesy and say to them: Thus says the Lord GOD: Look! I am going to open your graves; I will make you come up out of your graves, my people, and bring you back to the land of Israel.[k] [13]You shall know that I am the LORD, when I open your graves and make you come up out of them, my people! [14]I will put my spirit in you that you may come to life, and I will settle you in your land. Then you shall know that I am the LORD. I have spoken; I will do it—oracle of the LORD.[l]

***The Two Sticks.*** [15]* Thus the word of the LORD came to me: [16]As for you, son of man, take one stick and write on it, "Judah and those Israelites associated with it." Then take another stick and write on it: "Joseph, Ephraim's stick, and the whole house of Israel associated with it." [17]Join the two sticks together so they become one stick in your hand. [18]When your people ask you, "Will you not tell us what you mean by all this?" [19]answer them: Thus says the Lord GOD: I will take the stick of Joseph, now in Ephraim's hand, and the tribes of Israel associated with it, and join to it the stick of Judah, making them one stick; they shall become one in my hand.[m] [20]The sticks on which you write, you must hold in your hand in their sight. [21]Say to them: Thus says the Lord GOD: I will soon take the Israelites from

in its present context is not about the doctrine of individual or communal resurrection, many Jewish and Christian commentators suggest that the doctrine is foreshadowed here.

**37:9** The Hebrew word *rûah* has multiple related meanings expressed by different English words: wind, spirit, breath. In this translation, *rûah* is rendered "spirit," a powerful force that creates vision and insight (v. 1); "breath," physical energy that quickens and enlivens (vv. 5–6); "wind," invisible physical energy, sometimes destructive, sometimes invigorating (e.g., the rain-bearing winter winds), also a metaphor for restoration and new life (vv. 9–10); "my spirit," a share in God's power so the people observe the law that assures them life in the land (v. 14).

**37:15–22** The symbolic action of joining two sticks into one continues Ezekiel's description of God's future saving action: the unification of Judah and Israel under an ideal ruler.

*h:* Is 26:19. *i:* Ps 104:30; Is 32:15; Dn 7:2. *j:* cf. Rev 11:11. *k:* Is 26:19; Jer 19:14. *l:* cf. Ez 36:27–28; Jer 43:2; Jl 3:1–2. *m:* Zec 10:6.

among the nations to which they have gone
and gather them from all around to bring
them back to their land. 22I will make them
one nation in the land, upon the mountains of
Israel, and there shall be one king for them
all. They shall never again be two nations,
never again be divided into two kingdoms.[n]
23No longer shall they defile themselves
with their idols, their abominations, and all
their transgressions. I will deliver them from
all their apostasy through which they sinned.
I will cleanse them so that they will be my
people, and I will be their God.[o] 24[p] David
my servant shall be king over them; they
shall all have one shepherd. They shall walk
in my ordinances, observe my statutes, and
keep them. 25They shall live on the land I
gave to Jacob my servant, the land where
their ancestors lived; they shall live on it always, they, their children, and their children's children, with David my servant as
their prince forever. 26[q] I will make a covenant of peace with them; it shall be an everlasting covenant with them. I will multiply
them and put my sanctuary among them forever. 27My dwelling shall be with them; I
will be their God, and they will be my people.[r] 28Then the nations shall know that I, the
LORD, make Israel holy, by putting my sanctuary among them forever.

See RG 232

## CHAPTER 38

***First Prophecy Against Gog.*** 1The
word of the LORD came to me:* 2Son of man,
turn your face against Gog* of the land of
Magog, the chief prince of Meshech and Tubal, and prophesy against him.[s] 3Say: Thus
says the Lord GOD: See! I am coming
against you, Gog, chief prince of Meshech
and Tubal. 4I will turn you around and put
hooks in your jaws to lead you out with all
your army, horses and riders, all well armed,
a great company, all of them with bucklers
and shields, carrying swords: 5[t] Persia,
Cush, and Put with them, all with shields
and helmets; 6Gomer and all its troops,
Beth-togarmah from the recesses of Zaphon
and all its troops—many nations will accompany you. 7Prepare and get ready, you
and the company mobilized for you, but in
my service. 8After many days you will be
called to battle; in the last years you will invade a land that has survived the sword—a
people gathered from many nations back to
the long-deserted mountains of Israel,
brought forth from the nations to dwell securely.[u] 9You shall come up like a sudden
storm, covering the land like a cloud, you
and all your troops and the many nations
with you.[v]
10Thus says the Lord GOD: On that day
thoughts shall cross your mind, and you
shall devise an evil plan. 11You will say, "I
will invade a land of open villages and attack a peaceful people who live in security—all of them living without city walls,
bars, or gates"—[w] 12in order to plunder and
pillage, turning your hand against resettled
ruins, against a people gathered from the nations, a people whose concern is cattle and
goods, dwelling at the center* of the earth.
13Sheba and Dedan, the merchants of Tarshish and all its "young lions" shall ask you:
"Have you come here to plunder? Have you
summoned your army for pillage, to carry
off silver and gold, to take away cattle and
goods, to seize much plunder?"[x]
***Second Prophecy Against Gog.*** 14There-
fore, prophesy, son of man, and say to Gog:
Thus says the Lord GOD: On that day, when
my people Israel dwell securely, will you not
take action, 15leaving your base in the recesses of Zaphon,* you and many nations
with you, all mounted on horses, a great

**38:1–39:20** These three oracles against Gog (38:2–13; 14–23; 39:1–20) describe a mythic attack of God against a final enemy of his people sometime in the future. Like the oracles against the nations, their purpose is to strengthen Israel's hope in God, since they end with God's triumph on behalf of the people.

**38:2 Gog**: the name is symbolic, probably derived from Gyges, king of Lydia. The gloss Magog may be an Akkadian expression, *mat-Gog*, "the land of Gog." Meshech and Tubal, as well as Gomer and Beth-togarmah (v. 6), were countries around the Black Sea, the northernmost countries known to the Israelites. The north was the traditional direction from which invasion was expected; cf. Jer 1:13–15.

**38:12 Center**: lit., "navel." Many ancient peoples spoke of their own homelands as "the navel," that is, the center of the earth.

**38:15 Zaphon**: cf. note on Jb 37:22.

*n:* cf. Ez 17:22; 34:13–14. *o:* cf. Ez 11:18; 36:28; Na 2:2. *p:* Ps 78:70–71; Is 55:4. *q:* Gn 9:16; Nm 25:12; Heb 13:20. *r:* Lv 26:11. *s:* cf. Gn 10:2; Ez 27:13. *t:* Gn 10:2–3, 6. *u:* Is 24:22. *v:* Is 25:4; Jer 4:13; Rev 20:8. *w:* Zec 2:4–5. *x:* Gn 10:4, 7.

company, a mighty army?[y] 16 You shall rise up over my people Israel like a cloud covering the land. In those last days, I will let you invade my land so that the nations acknowledge me, when in their sight I show my holiness through you, Gog.

17 Thus says the Lord GOD: About you I spoke in earlier times through my servants, the prophets of Israel, who prophesied at that time that I would let you invade them. 18 But on that day, the day Gog invades the land of Israel—oracle of the Lord GOD—my fury will flare up in my anger, 19 and in my jealousy, with fiery wrath, I swear on that day there will be a great earthquake in the land of Israel.[z] 20 Before me will tremble the fish of the sea and the birds of the air, the beasts of the field and everything that crawls on the ground, and everyone on the face of the earth. Mountains will be overturned, terraces will collapse, and every wall will fall to the ground.[a] 21 Against him I will summon every terror—oracle of the Lord GOD; every man's sword will be raised against his brother.[b] 22 I will execute judgment on him: disease and bloodshed; flooding rain and hailstones, fire and brimstone, I will rain down on him, on his troops and on the many nations with him.[c] 23 And so I will show my greatness and holiness and make myself known in the sight of many nations. Then they shall know that I am the LORD.[d]

## CHAPTER 39

See RG 232

*Third Prophecy Against Gog.* 1 You, son of man, prophesy against Gog, saying: Thus says the Lord GOD: Here I am, Gog, coming at you, chief prince of Meshech and Tubal. 2 I will turn you around, even though I urged you on and brought you up from the recesses of Zaphon and let you attack the mountains of Israel.[e] 3 Then I will strike the bow from your left hand and make the arrows drop from your right. 4 Upon the mountains of Israel you shall fall, you and all your troops and the peoples with you. I will give you as food to birds of prey of every kind and to wild beasts to be eaten. 5 In the open field you shall fall, for I have spoken—oracle of the Lord GOD.[f]

6 I will send fire against Magog and against those who live securely on the seacoast, and they will know that I am the LORD.[g] 7 I will reveal my holy name among my people Israel, and I will never again allow my holy name to be defiled. Then the nations shall know that I am the LORD, the Holy One of Israel.[h] 8 Yes, it is coming! It shall happen—oracle of the Lord GOD. This is the day I decreed.

9 Everyone living in the cities of Israel shall go out and set fire to the weapons, buckler and shield, bows and arrows, clubs and spears; for seven years they shall make fires with them.[i] 10 They will not need to bring in wood from the fields or cut down trees in the forests, for they will make fires with the weapons, plundering those who plundered them, pillaging those who pillaged them—oracle of the Lord GOD.

11 On that day I will give Gog a place for his tomb in Israel, the Valley of Abarim,* east of the sea. It will block the way of travelers. There Gog shall be buried with all his horde; it shall be called "Valley of Hamon-Gog."[j] 12 For seven months the house of Israel shall bury them in order to cleanse the land. 13 All the people of the land shall take part in the burials, making a name for themselves on the day I am glorified—oracle of the Lord GOD. 14 Men shall be permanently assigned to pass through the land, burying those who lie unburied in order to cleanse the land. For seven months they shall keep searching. 15 When these pass through the land and see a human bone, they must set up a marker beside it, until the gravediggers bury it in the Valley of Hamon-Gog. 16 Also the name of the city is Hamonah. Thus the land will be cleansed.

17 As for you, son of man, thus says the Lord GOD: Say to birds of every kind and to

**39:11 The Valley of Abarim**: in the Abarim mountains, east of the Jordan. "Abarim" plays on the word *'oberim*, "travelers." **Hamon-Gog**: "the horde of Gog."

*y:* cf. Ez 39:2. *z:* Is 24:18; Rev 6:12. *a:* Is 42:15. *b:* Is 34:5–6; 66:16. *c:* cf. Rev 9:17; 16:21. *d:* Rev 20:8. *e:* cf. Ez 32:30; 38:6, 15. *f:* cf. Ez 32:4. *g:* Rev 20:9. *h:* Is 12:6. *i:* Ps 46:9; 76:3. *j:* cf. Ez 38:2.

every wild beast: "Assemble! Come from all sides for the sacrifice I am making for you, a great slaughter on the mountains of Israel. You shall eat flesh and drink blood! 18You shall eat the flesh of warriors and drink the blood of the princes of the earth: rams, lambs, and goats, bulls and fatlings from Bashan, all of them.[k] 19From the sacrifice I slaughtered for you, you shall eat fat until you are sated and drink blood until you are drunk. 20At my table you shall be sated with horse and rider, with warrior and soldier of every kind—oracle of the Lord GOD.

***Israel's Return.*** 21Then I will display my glory among the nations, and all the nations will see the judgment I executed, the hand I laid upon them. 22From that day forward the house of Israel shall know that I am the LORD, their God. 23The nations shall know that the house of Israel went into exile because of its sins. Because they betrayed me, I hid my face from them, handing them over to their foes, so they all fell by the sword.[l] 24According to their defilement and their crimes I dealt with them, hiding my face from them.[m]

25Therefore, thus says the Lord GOD: Now I will restore the fortunes of Jacob and take pity on the whole house of Israel; I am zealous for my holy name.[n] 26They will forget their shame and all the infidelities they committed against me when they live securely on their own land with no one to frighten them. 27When I bring them back from the nations and gather them from the lands of their enemies, I will show my holiness through them in the sight of many nations.[o] 28Thus they shall know that I, the LORD, am their God, since I who exiled them among the nations will gather them back to their land, not leaving any of them behind. 29I will no longer hide my face from them once I pour out my spirit upon the house of Israel—oracle of the Lord GOD.[p]

## V. The New Israel*

### *The New Temple*

### CHAPTER 40

See RG 232

***The Man with a Measure.*** 1In the twenty-fifth year of our exile, at the beginning of the year, on the tenth day of the month, fourteen years after the city had been captured, on that very day the hand of the LORD came upon me and brought me back there.[q] 2In a divine vision he brought me to the land of Israel, where he set me down on a very high mountain. In front of me, there was something like a city built on it.[r] 3He brought me there, and there standing in the gateway was a man whose appearance was like bronze! He held in his hand a linen cord and a measuring rod.[s] 4The man said to me, "Son of man, look carefully and listen intently. Pay strict attention to everything I show you, for you have been brought here so that I might show it to you. Then you must tell the house of Israel everything you see." 5There an outer wall completely surrounded the temple. The measuring rod in the man's hand was six cubits long, each cubit being a cubit plus a handbreadth;* he measured the width of the structure, one rod, and its height, one rod.

***The East Gate.**** 6Going to the gate facing east, he climbed its steps and measured the threshold of the outer gateway as one rod wide.[t] 7Each cell was one rod long and one

**40:1–48:35** This lengthy vision of a new Temple and a restored Israel is dated in v. 1 to April 28, 573 B.C. The literary form of the vision is sometimes compared to a mandala, a sacred model through which one can move symbolically to reach the world of the divine. Ezekiel describes the Temple through its boundaries, entrances, and exits in chaps. 40–43; by its sacred and profane use and space in 44–46; and by its central place within the land itself in 47–48. The prophet could not have expected a literal fulfillment of much of what he described. The passage doubtless went through several editorial stages, both from the prophet and from later writers.

**40:5 A cubit plus a handbreadth**: a great cubit. The ordinary cubit consisted of six handbreadths; the great cubit, of seven. In measuring the Temple, a rod six great cubits long was used. The ordinary cubit was about one and a half feet, or, more exactly, 17.5 inches; the large cubit, 20.4 inches.

**40:6–16** The gate facing east, leading into the outer court of the Temple, is described more fully than the north and south gates, which, however, have the same dimensions. On the west side of the outer court there is a large building instead of a gate (cf. 41:12).

*k:* Jer 51:40; Rev 19:17–21. *l:* Ps 30:7; Is 54:8. *m:* 2 Kgs 17:23. *n:* Is 27:13. *o:* cf. Ez 20:41. *p:* cf. Ez 37:9; Is 11:2. *q:* 2 Kgs 25:7; Jer 39:1–10; 52:4–11. *r:* Is 2:2; Mi 4:1; Zec 14:10; cf. Rev 21:10. *s:* Zec 2:1–2; Rev 1:15; 11:1; 21:15. *t:* cf. Ez 8:16.

### The Temple

EZEKIEL'S TEMPLE (40:48–41:26) is constructed according to a three-room pattern, like that of Solomon's temple (1 Kgs 6) and other examples of temples and royal palaces from Canaan and Syria. The three rooms are the vestibule (35 feet by 21 feet), an entry or reception room; the nave (71 feet by 25 feet), the main hall where the temple furnishings are placed; and the inner room (35 feet by 35 feet), also known as the holy of holies, God's throne room which houses the ark of the covenant. Ezekiel does not enter the inner room because this is restricted to the high priest on Yom Kippur or the Day of Atonement (Lv 16).

rod wide, and there were five cubits between the cells; the threshold of the inner gateway adjoining the vestibule of the gate facing the temple was one rod wide. [8]He also measured the vestibule of the inner gate, [9]eight cubits, and its posts, two cubits each. The vestibule faced the inside. [10]On each side of the east gatehouse were three cells, all the same size; their posts were all the same size. [11]He measured the width of the gate's entryway, ten cubits, and the length of the gate itself, thirteen cubits. [12]The borders in front of the cells on both sides were one cubit, while the cells themselves measured six cubits by six cubits from one opening to the next. [13]Next he measured the gatehouse from the back wall of one cell to the back wall of the cell on the opposite side through the openings facing each other, a width of twenty-five cubits. [14]All around the courtyard of the gatehouse were posts six cubits high. [15]From the front of the gatehouse at its outer entry to the gateway of the porch facing inward, the length was fifty cubits. [16]There were recessed windows in the cells on all sides and in the posts on the inner side of the gate. Posts and windows were all around the inside, with palm trees decorating the posts.[u]

***The Outer Court.*** [17]Then he brought me to the outer court,* where there were chambers and pavement laid all around the courtyard: thirty chambers facing the pavement.[v] [18]The pavement lay alongside the gatehouses, the same length as the gates; this was the lower pavement. [19]He measured the length of the pavement from the front of the lower gate to the outside of the inner gate, one hundred cubits. He then moved from the east to the north side.

***The North Gate.*** [20]He measured the length and width of the north gate of the outer courtyard. [21]Its cells, three on each side, its posts, and its vestibule had the same measurements as those of the first gate, fifty cubits long and twenty-five cubits wide. [22]Its windows, its vestibule, and its palm decorations had the same proportions as those of the gate facing east. Seven steps led up to it, and its vestibule faced the inside. [23]The inner court had a gate opposite the north gate, just as at the east gate; he measured one hundred cubits from one gate to the other.

***The South Gate.*** [24]Then he led me to the south. There, too, facing south, was a gate! He measured its posts and vestibule; they were the same size as the others. [25]The gate and its vestibule had windows on both sides, like the other windows, fifty cubits long and twenty-five cubits wide. [26]Seven steps led up to it, its vestibule faced inside; and palms decorated each of the posts opposite one another. [27]The inner court also had a gate facing south. He measured it from gate to gate, facing south, one hundred cubits.

***Gates of the Inner Court.**** [28]Then he brought me to the inner courtyard by the south gate, where he measured the south gateway; its measurements were the same as the others. [29]Its cells, posts, and vestibule were the same size as the others, fifty cubits long and

**40:17 The outer court**: the court outside the Temple area proper, which had its own inner court (vv. 28–37).

**40:28–37** The gates leading into the inner court of the Temple area correspond to the gates leading into the outer court, with the exception that their vestibules are on the outer rather than the inner side.

*u:* 1 Kgs 6:29, 32, 35. *v:* cf. Ez 41:6; 42:1.

twenty-five cubits wide. [30]* The vestibules all around were twenty-five cubits long and five cubits wide. [31]Its vestibule faced the outer court; palms decorated its posts, and its stairway had eight steps. [32]Then he brought me to the inner courtyard on the east and measured the gate there; its dimensions were the same as the others. [33]Its cells, posts, and vestibule were the same size as the others. The gate and its vestibule had windows on both sides, fifty cubits long and twenty-five cubits wide. [34]Its vestibule faced the outer court, palms decorated the posts opposite each other, and it had a stairway of eight steps. [35]Then he brought me to the north gate,[w] where he measured the dimensions [36]of its cells, posts, and vestibule; they were the same. The gate and its vestibule had windows on both sides, fifty cubits long and twenty-five cubits wide. [37]Its vestibule faced the outer court; palm trees decorated its posts opposite each other, and it had a stairway of eight steps.

*Side Rooms.* [38]There was a chamber opening off the vestibule of the gate where burnt offerings were washed.[x] [39]In the vestibule of the gate there were two tables on either side for slaughtering the burnt offerings, purification offerings, and reparation offerings.[y] [40]Two more tables stood along the wall of the vestibule by the entrance of the north gate, and two tables on the other side of the vestibule of the gate. [41]There were thus four tables on one side of the gate and four tables on the other side, eight tables in all, for slaughtering. [42]The four tables for burnt offerings were made of cut stone, one and a half cubits long, one and a half cubits wide, and one cubit high; the instruments used for slaughtering burnt offerings and other sacrifices were kept [43]on shelves the width of one hand, fixed all around the room; but on the tables themselves was the meat for the sacrifices. [44]Outside the inner gatehouse there were two rooms on the inner courtyard, one beside the north gate, facing south, and the other beside the south gate, facing north. [45]He said to me, "This chamber facing south is reserved for the priests who have charge of the temple area, [46]while this chamber facing north is reserved for the priests who have charge of the altar; they are the sons of Zadok,* the only Levites who may come near to minister to the LORD." [47]He measured the courtyard, a square one hundred cubits long and a hundred cubits wide, with the altar standing in front of the temple.[z]

***The Temple Building.**** [48][a] Then he brought me into the vestibule of the temple and measured the posts, five cubits on each side. The gateway was fourteen cubits wide, its side walls three cubits. [49]The vestibule was twenty cubits long and twelve cubits wide; ten steps led up to it, and there were columns by the posts, one on each side.

## CHAPTER 41

See RG 232

[1]Then he brought me to the nave and measured the posts; each was six cubits wide.[b] [2]The width of the entrance was ten cubits, and the walls on either side measured five cubits. He measured the nave, forty cubits long and twenty cubits wide.

[3]Then he went inside and measured the posts at the other entrance, two cubits wide. The entrance was six cubits wide, with walls seven cubits long on each side. [4]Next he measured the length and width of the room beyond the nave, twenty cubits long and twenty cubits wide. He said to me, "This is the holy of holies."* [c]

[5]Then he measured the wall of the temple, six cubits wide, and the width of the side chambers stretching all around the temple, four cubits each. [6]* There were thirty side

**40:30** The reference to vestibules all around is uncertain, and the verse may have arisen as a partial repetition of v. 29.

**40:46 Sons of Zadok**: descendants of the priestly line of Zadok; cf. 2 Sm 15:24–29; 1 Kgs 1:32–34; 2:35.

**40:48–41:15** The description of Ezekiel's visionary Temple closely follows the description of the Temple of Solomon (1 Kgs 6), along with some crucial differences.

**40:49–41:4 Vestibule . . . nave . . . holy of holies**: the three divisions of the Temple building in progressing order of sanctity. The last is called "the inner sanctuary" in 1 Kgs 6.

**41:6** The description of the three stories of rooms surrounding the Temple building can be compared with Solomon's Temple in 1 Kgs 6:6; there a step-like or terraced retaining wall supported the Temple building so no beams or nails from these chambers would enter the Temple wall itself.

*w:* cf. Ez 44:4; 47:2. *x:* 2 Chr 4:6. *y:* cf. Ez 46:2. *z:* cf. Ez 41:13–14; 43:14–17. *a:* 1 Kgs 6:2. *b:* 1 Kgs 6:3–5. *c:* 1 Kgs 6:20; cf. Ex 26:33; Heb 9:3–8.

chambers, chamber upon chamber in three stories; terraces on the outside wall of the temple enclosing the side chambers provided support, but there were no supports for the temple wall itself. 7 A broad passageway led up the side chambers, for the house was enclosed all the way up and all the way around. Thus the temple was widened by the ascent that went from the lowest story through the middle one to the highest story.[d] 8 I saw a raised platform all around the temple, the foundation for the side chambers; the width of this terrace was a full rod, six cubits. 9 The width of the outside wall enclosing the side chambers was five cubits. There was an open space between the side chambers of the temple 10 and the other chambers that measured twenty cubits around the temple on all sides. 11 The side chambers had entrances to the open space, one entrance on the north and the other on the south. The width of the wall surrounding the open space was five cubits. 12 The building* opposite the restricted area on the west side was seventy cubits long and ninety cubits wide, with walls five cubits thick all around it. 13 Thus he measured the temple, one hundred cubits long. The restricted area, its building and walls, measured a hundred cubits in length. 14 The temple facade, along with the restricted area to the east, was also one hundred cubits wide. 15 He then measured the building opposite the restricted area which was behind it, together with its terraces on both sides, one hundred cubits.

***Interior of the Temple.*** The inner nave and the outer vestibule 16 were paneled; the windows had recesses and precious wood trim around all three sides except the sill. Paneling covered the walls from the floor up to the windows and even the window sections.[e] 17 Even above the doorway and in the inner part of the temple and outside as well, around all the walls inside and out, 18 were figures of cherubim and palm trees: a palm tree between each pair of cherubim. Each cherub had two faces:[f] 19 the face of a human being looked toward one palm tree and the face of a lion looked toward the other palm tree. Thus the figures covered all the walls around the temple. 20 From the floor to the lintel of the door, cherubim and palm trees decorated the walls. 21 The nave had a square door frame, and inside facing the holy place was something that looked like 22 a wooden altar,* three cubits high, two cubits long, and two cubits wide. It had corners and a wooden base and sides. He said to me, "This is the table that stands before the LORD."[g] 23 The nave had a double door,[h] and the holy place 24 also had a double door; each door had two sections that could move; two sections on one door, and two on the other.[i] 25 Cherubim and palm trees decorated the doors of the nave like the decoration on the walls. Outside a wooden lattice faced the vestibule. 26 There were recessed windows and palm trees on the side walls of the vestibule. The side chambers of the temple also had latticework.

## CHAPTER 42

See RG 232

***Other Structures.*** 1 Then he led me north to the outer court, bringing me to some chambers on the north side opposite the restricted area and the north building.[j] 2 They were a hundred cubits long on the north side and fifty cubits wide. 3 Built in rows at three different levels, they stood between the twenty cubits of the inner court and the pavement of the outer court. 4 In front of the chambers was a walkway ten cubits wide on the inside of a wall one cubit wide. The doorways faced north. 5* The upper chambers were shorter because they lost space to the lower and middle tiers of the building. 6 Because they were in three tiers, they did not have foundations like the court, but were set back from the lower and middle levels from the ground up. 7 The outside walls ran parallel to the chambers along the outer court, a length of fifty cubits. 8 The chambers

**41:12 The building**: the function of this structure behind the Temple is never specified.

**41:22 A wooden altar**: the altar of incense, standing in the nave at the entrance to the holy of holies.

**42:5–6** The three rows of identical chambers, on different ground levels, necessarily had roofs on correspondingly different levels.

*d:* 1 Kgs 6:8. *e:* 1 Kgs 6:4, 15. *f:* 1 Kgs 6:18, 29; 7:36. *g:* Ex 25:23; Lv 24:5–9. *h:* 1 Kgs 6:32. *i:* 1 Kgs 6:34. *j:* Ex 27:9.

facing the outer court were fifty cubits long; thus the wall along the nave was a hundred cubits. [9]At the base of these chambers, there was an entryway from the east so that one could enter from the outer court [10]where the wall of the court began.

To the south along the side of the restricted area and the building there were also chambers [11]with a walkway in front of them. They looked like the chambers on the north side in length and width, in their exits, their design, and their doorways. [12]At the base of the chambers on the south side there was an entry at the end of a walkway in front of the protective wall by which one could enter from the east. [13]He said to me, "The north and south chambers facing the restricted area are the chambers of the holy place where the priests who approach the LORD shall eat the most holy meals. Here they shall place the most holy offerings: the grain offerings, the purification offerings, and the reparation offerings; for the place is holy.* [k] [14]When the priests have entered, they must not go out again from the holy place into the outer court without leaving the garments in which they ministered because they are holy. They shall put on other garments before approaching the area for the people."[l]

*Measuring the Outer Court.* [15]When he finished measuring the interior of the temple area, he brought me out by way of the gate facing east and measured all around it. [16]He measured the east side, five hundred cubits by his measuring rod. Then he turned [17]and measured the north side: five hundred cubits by his measuring rod. He turned [18]and measured the south side, five hundred cubits by his measuring rod. [19]He turned and measured the west side, also five hundred cubits by his measuring rod. [20]Thus he measured it on the four sides. It was surrounded by a wall five hundred cubits long and five hundred cubits wide, to separate the sacred from the profane.

## *Restoration of the Temple*

### CHAPTER 43

See RG 232

*The Glory of the Lord Returns.* [1]Then he led me to the gate facing east,[m] [2]and there was the glory of the God of Israel coming from the east! His voice was like the roar of many waters, and the earth shone with his glory. [3]The vision I saw was like the vision I had seen when he came to destroy the city and like the vision I had seen by the river Chebar—I fell on my face. [4]The glory of the LORD entered the temple by way of the gate facing east.[n] [5]Then the spirit lifted me up and brought me to the inner court. And there the glory of the LORD filled the temple![o] [6]I heard someone speaking to me from the temple, but the man was standing beside me. [7]The voice said to me: Son of man, do you see the place for my throne, and the place for the soles of my feet? Here I will dwell among the Israelites forever. The house of Israel, neither they nor their kings, will never again defile my holy name, with their prostitutions and the corpses of their kings at their death.[p] [8]When they placed their threshold against my threshold* and their doorpost next to mine, with only a wall between me and them, they defiled my holy name by the abominations they committed, and I devoured them in my wrath.[q] [9]From now on, let them put their prostitution and the corpses of their kings far from me, and I will dwell in their midst forever.[r]

*The Law of the Temple.* [10]As for you, son of man, describe the temple to the house of Israel so they are ashamed for their sins. Let them measure its layout. [11]If they are ashamed for all they have done, tell them about the layout and design of the temple, its exits and entrances, with all its regulations and instructions; write it down for them to see, that they may carefully observe all its laws and statutes. [12]This is the law for the

**42:13** The function of these chambers is explained again in 46:19–20.

**43:8 They placed their threshold against my threshold**: in preexilic Jerusalem, the Temple and the palace belonged to the same complex of buildings; kings like Ahaz and Manasseh treated it as their private chapel for the religious practices Ezekiel condemns. In the new Israel the Temple is free, even spatially, from civil jurisdiction; cf. 45:7–8. This is an instance of Ezekiel's broader program to separate the sacred from the secular.

*k:* Lv 10:12–13, 17. *l:* Ex 29:9; Lv 8:7–9. *m:* 1 Chr 9:18. *n:* cf. Ez 10:19. *o:* cf. Ez 11:24. *p:* 1 Chr 28:2; Ps 132:7; Is 6:1; Jer 3:17. *q:* 1 Kgs 7:1–12. *r:* cf. Ez 37:26–28.

temple: the entire area on top of the mountain all around will be a most holy place.
This is the law for the temple.

***The Altar.*** 13These were the dimensions of
the altar* in cubits, a cubit being one cubit
plus a handbreadth. The channel was one cubit deep by one cubit wide, and its rim had a
lip one span wide all around it.[s] The height
of the altar itself was as follows: 14from the
channel at floor level up to the lower ledge
was two cubits, with the ledge one cubit
wide; from the lower ledge to the upper
ledge, four cubits, with the ledge one cubit
wide. 15The altar hearth was four cubits
high, and extending up from the top of the
hearth were four horns. 16The hearth was
twelve cubits long and twelve cubits wide, a
square with four equal sides. 17The upper
ledge was fourteen cubits long and fourteen
cubits wide on all four sides. The rim around
it was half a cubit, with a channel one cubit
all around. The steps faced east.[t]

18Then he said to me: Son of man, thus
says the Lord GOD: These are the statutes for
the altar when it is set up for sacrificing burnt
offerings and splashing blood on it.[u] 19A
young bull must be brought as a purification
offering to the priests, the Levites descended
from Zadok, who come near to serve me—
oracle of the Lord GOD.[v] 20You shall take
some of its blood and smear it on the four
horns of the altar, and on the four corners of
the ledge, and all around its rim. Thus you
shall purify and purge it.[w] 21Then take the
bull as purification offering and burn it in the
appointed place outside the sanctuary.[x] 22On
the second day present an unblemished male
goat as a purification offering, to purify the
altar as you did with the bull. 23When you
have completed the purification,[y] you must
bring an unblemished young bull and an unblemished ram from the flock 24and present
them before the LORD. The priests shall
throw salt on them and sacrifice them as
burnt offerings to the LORD. 25Daily for
seven days you shall give a male goat as a purification offering; and a young bull and a
ram from the flock, all unblemished,[z] shall be
offered 26for seven days. Thus they shall
purge the altar, in order to cleanse and dedicate it. 27And when these days are over, from
the eighth day on, the priests shall sacrifice
your burnt offerings and communion offerings on the altar. Then I will be pleased with
you—oracle of the Lord GOD.

## CHAPTER 44

See RG 232

***The Closed Gate.*** 1Then he brought
me back to the outer gate of the sanctuary
facing east, but it was closed. 2The LORD
said to me: This gate must remain closed; it
must not be opened, and no one should come
through it. Because the LORD, the God of Israel, came through it, it must remain closed.
3Only the prince may sit in it to eat a meal in
the presence of the LORD; he must enter
through the vestibule of the gate and leave
the same way.*[a]

### *The New Law*

***Admission to the Temple.*** 4Then he brought
me by way of the north gate to the facade of
the temple. I looked—and the glory of the
LORD filled the LORD's house! I fell on my
face.[b] 5The LORD said to me: Son of man, pay
close attention, look carefully, and listen intently to everything I tell you about all the
statutes and laws of the LORD's house. Pay
close attention to the entrance into the temple
and all the exits of the sanctuary. 6Say to that
rebellious house, the house of Israel: Thus
says the Lord GOD: Enough of all your abominations, house of Israel! 7You have admitted
foreigners, uncircumcised in heart and flesh,
into my sanctuary to profane it when you offered me food, the fat and blood.* Thus you

**43:13–17 The altar**: like altars from Assyria and other parts of the ancient Near East, this altar has three parts: a base, a pedestal, and an upper block with a channel cut into the surface on all sides. The rim around the upper block (v. 17) stopped blood and other sacrificial material from falling to the ground.

**44:3** Ezekiel imagines a scene like this: The prince stands at the eastern gate of the inner court while his sacrifice is being offered (46:2); he then goes to the vestibule of the outer court to eat the sacrificial meal. The closed outer gate on the eastern side signifies that the Lord has entered the Temple permanently, not to depart again.

**44:7–14** According to Ezekiel, the Levites' priestly role is

*s:* cf. Ex 20:24. *t:* Ex 20:26. *u:* Ex 29:16; Lv 4:6; 5:9. *v:* Lv 4:3. *w:* Lv 4:7. *x:* Ex 29:14; Lv 4:12; 8:17; cf. Heb 13:11–13. *y:* Ex 29:1. *z:* Ex 29:37; Lv 8:33. *a:* Ex 24:9–11; 2 Chr 26:16–20. *b:* Is 6:4; Rev 15:8.

have broken my covenant by all your abominations.[c] 8 Instead of caring for the service of my sanctuary, you appointed these foreigners to care for the service of my sanctuary. 9 Thus says the Lord GOD: No foreigners, uncircumcised in heart and flesh, shall ever enter my sanctuary: not even any of the foreigners who live among the Israelites.[d]

*Levites.* 10 As for the Levites who went far away from me when Israel strayed from me after their idols, they will bear the consequences of their sin. 11 They will serve in my sanctuary only as gatekeepers and temple servants; they will slaughter burnt offerings and sacrifices for the people. They will stand before the people to serve them.[e] 12 Because they used to serve them before their idols, thus becoming a stumbling block to the house of Israel, therefore I have sworn an oath against them, says the Lord GOD, and they will bear the consequences of their sin. 13 They shall no longer come near to serve as my priests, nor shall they touch any of my sacred things or my most sacred offerings, for they must bear their shame, the abominations they committed. 14 Instead I will make them responsible for the service of the temple and all its work, for everything that must be done in it.[f]

*Priests.* 15 As for the levitical priests, sons of Zadok, who took charge of my sanctuary when the Israelites strayed from me, they may approach me to serve me and stand before me to offer the fat and the blood—oracle of the Lord GOD.[g] 16 They may enter my sanctuary; they may approach my table to serve me and carry out my service.[h] 17 Whenever they enter the gates of the inner court, they shall wear linen garments; they shall not put on anything woolen when they serve at the gates of the inner court or within the temple. 18[i] They shall have linen turbans on their heads and linen undergarments on their loins; they shall not gird themselves with anything that causes sweat. 19[j] And when they go out to the people in the outer court, they shall take off the garments in which they served and leave them in the rooms of the sanctuary, and put on other garments so they do not transmit holiness to the people* by their garments.

20[k] They shall not shave their heads nor let their hair hang loose, but they shall keep their hair carefully trimmed. 21 No priest shall drink wine before he enters the inner court. 22[l] They shall not take as wives either widows or divorced women, but only unmarried women from the line of Israel; however, they may take as wives widows who are widows of priests. 23[m] They shall teach my people to distinguish between sacred and profane and make known to them the difference between clean and unclean. 24[n] In legal cases they shall stand as judges, judging according to my ordinances. They shall observe all my laws and statutes regarding all my appointed feasts, and they shall keep my sabbaths holy.

25[o] They shall not make themselves unclean by going near a dead body; only for their father, mother, son, daughter, brother, or unmarried sister may they make themselves unclean. 26 After he is again clean, he must wait an additional seven days; 27 on the day he enters the inner court to serve in the sanctuary, he shall present a purification offering for himself—oracle of the Lord GOD. 28[p] I will be their heritage: I am their heritage! You shall not give them any property in Israel, for I am their property! 29[q] They shall eat grain offerings, purification offerings, and reparation offerings; anything under the ban* in Israel belongs to them; 30[r] all the choicest first fruits of every kind and all the best of your offerings of every kind shall belong to the priests; the best of your dough

reduced to the performance of menial tasks as punishment for their misdeeds (cf. vv. 10–14). This demotion was enforced during the restoration of Temple worship under Ezra and Nehemiah; this may explain the small number of Levites willing to return to Jerusalem after the exile.

**44:19 Transmit holiness to the people**: holiness was considered to have a physical quality that could be communicated from person to person. It is a danger to those who have not prepared themselves to be in God's presence. The priests remove their ceremonial garments out of concern for the people.

**44:29 Under the ban**: dedicated to the Lord.

*c:* Lv 26:41. *d:* Jl 4:17; Neh 13:8. *e:* Nm 3:5–37; 1 Chr 26:12–19. *f:* 1 Chr 23:28–32. *g:* 1 Chr 6:50–53. *h:* Lv 3:16–17. *i:* Ex 28:39, 42. *j:* Ex 39:27–29; Lv 6:10–11. *k:* Lv 21:5. *l:* Lv 21:7. *m:* Hg 2:10–13. *n:* Dt 17:8–9. *o:* Lv 21:1–4. *p:* Nm 18:23–24; Dt 18:1–2. *q:* Lv 6:16; 27:28. *r:* Nm 15:18–21; 18:12–13.

you shall also give to the priests to bring a
blessing upon your house. 31[s] The priests
shall not eat anything, whether bird or animal, that died naturally or was killed by wild
beasts.

## CHAPTER 45

See RG 232

*The Holy Portion.* 1 When you apportion the land heritage by heritage, you shall
set apart a holy portion for the LORD, holier
than the rest of the land—twenty-five thousand cubits long and twenty thousand cubits
wide; the entire area shall be holy. 2 Of this
land a square plot, five hundred by five hundred cubits, shall be assigned to the sanctuary, with fifty cubits of free space around it.
3 From this tract also measure off a length of
twenty-five thousand cubits and a width of
ten thousand cubits; on it the sanctuary, the
holy of holies, shall stand. 4 This shall be the
sacred part of the land belonging to the
priests, the ministers of the sanctuary, who
draw near to minister to the LORD; it shall be
a place for their homes and an area set apart
for the sanctuary. 5 There shall also be a strip
twenty-five thousand cubits long and ten
thousand wide for the Levites, the ministers
of the temple, so they have cities to live in.
6 You shall assign a strip five thousand cubits
wide and twenty-five thousand long as the
property of the city parallel to the sacred
tract; this shall belong to the whole house of
Israel. 7 A section shall belong to the prince,
bordering both sides of the sacred tract and
city combined, extending westward on the
west side and eastward on the east side, corresponding in length to one of the tribal portions from the west boundary to the east
boundary 8 of the land. This shall be his
property in Israel so that my princes will no
longer oppress my people, but will leave the
land to the house of Israel according to its
tribes. 9 Thus says the Lord GOD: Enough,
you princes of Israel! Put away violence and
oppression, and do what is just and right!
Stop evicting my people!—oracle of the
Lord GOD.

*Weights and Measures.** 10[t] You shall have
honest scales, an honest ephah, and an honest bath. 11 The ephah and the bath shall be
the same size: the bath equal to one tenth of
a homer, and the ephah equal to one tenth of
a homer; their capacity is based on the homer. 12 The shekel shall be twenty gerahs.
Twenty shekels plus twenty-five shekels
plus fifteen shekels make up a mina* for you.

*Offerings.* 13 This is the offering you must
make: one sixth of an ephah from each homer of wheat and one sixth of an ephah from
each homer of barley. 14 This is the regulation for oil: for every bath of oil, one tenth of
a bath, computed by the kor,* made up of ten
baths, that is, a homer, for ten baths make a
homer. 15 Also, one sheep from the flock for
every two hundred from the pasture land of
Israel, for the grain offering, the burnt offering, and communion offerings, to make
atonement on their behalf—oracle of the
Lord GOD.[u] 16 All the people of the land shall
be responsible for these offerings to the
prince in Israel. 17 It shall be the duty of the
prince to provide burnt offerings, grain offerings, and libations on feast days, new
moons, and sabbaths, on all the festivals of
the house of Israel. He shall provide the purification offering, grain offering, burnt offering, and communion offerings, to make
atonement on behalf of the house of Israel.[v]

*The Passover.* 18 Thus says the Lord GOD:
On the first day of the first month you shall
take an unblemished young bull to purify the
sanctuary.[w] 19 The priest shall take some of
the blood from the purification offering and
smear it on the doorposts of the house, on the
four corners of the ledge of the altar, and on
the doorposts of the gates of the inner courtyard.[x] 20 You shall repeat this on the seventh
day of the month for those who have sinned

**45:10–12** Besides the land monopoly fostered by royal greed and collusion with the wealthy (Mi 2:2; Is 3:12–15; 5:8–10), one grave social evil of preexilic Israel was dishonesty in business; cf. Hos 12:8; Am 8:5. **Ephah, bath**: see note on Is 5:10.

**45:12 Mina**: before the exile, a mina was worth fifty shekels; later, in imitation of Babylonian practice, its value increased to sixty shekels. A shekel weighed slightly less than half an ounce. A shekel's monetary value depended on whether it was gold or silver.

**45:14 Kor**: a liquid and a dry measure, equal to a homer.

*s:* Lv 11:39. *t:* Lv 19:35–36; Dt 25:13–16; Mi 6:10–12. *u:* Lv 1:4; 6:23. *v:* cf. Ez 46:4–12. *w:* Lv 16:33. *x:* Lv 16:18–19.

inadvertently or out of ignorance; thus you shall purge the temple.[y] 21On the fourteenth day of the first month you shall observe the feast of Passover; for seven days unleavened bread must be eaten. 22On that day the prince shall sacrifice, on his own behalf and on behalf of all the people of the land, a bull as a purification offering. 23On each of the seven days of the feast he shall sacrifice, as a burnt offering to the LORD, seven bulls and seven rams without blemish, and as a purification offering he shall sacrifice one male goat each day.[z] 24As a grain offering he shall offer one ephah for each bull and one ephah for each ram and one hin* of oil for each ephah.[a]

***The Feast of Booths.*** 25In the seventh month, on the fifteenth day of the seventh month, on the feast day and for the next seven days, he shall make the same offerings: the same purification offerings, burnt offerings, grain offerings, and offerings of oil.[b]

## CHAPTER 46

See RG 232

***Sabbaths.*** 1Thus says the Lord GOD: The gate of the inner court facing east shall remain closed throughout the six working days, but on the sabbath and on the day of the new moon it shall be open. 2* Then the prince shall enter from outside by way of the vestibule of the gate and remain standing at the doorpost of the gateway while the priests sacrifice his burnt offerings and communion offerings; then he shall bow down in worship at the opening of the gate and leave. But the gate shall not be closed until evening. 3The people of the land also shall bow down in worship before the LORD at the opening of this gate on the sabbaths and new moons. 4The burnt offerings which the prince sacrifices to the LORD on the sabbath shall consist of six unblemished lambs and an unblemished ram, 5together with a grain offering of one ephah for the ram and whatever he pleases for the lambs, and a hin of oil for each ephah. 6[c] On the day of the new moon, he shall provide an unblemished young bull, six lambs, and a ram without blemish, 7with a grain offering of one ephah for the bull and an ephah for the ram, and for the lambs whatever he can, and for each ephah a hin of oil.[d]

***Ritual Laws.*** 8When the prince enters, he shall always enter and depart by the vestibule of the gate. 9When the people of the land come before the LORD to bow down on the festivals, if they enter by the north gate they shall leave by the south gate, and if they enter by the south gate they shall leave by the north gate. They shall not go back by the gate through which they entered; everyone shall leave by the opposite gate. 10When they come in, the prince shall be with them; he shall also leave with them. 11On feasts and festivals, the grain offering shall be an ephah for a bull, an ephah for a ram, but for the lambs whatever they please, and a hin of oil with each ephah. 12When the prince makes a freewill offering to the LORD, whether a burnt offering or communion offering, the gate facing east shall be opened for him, and he shall bring his burnt offering or peace offering as he does on the sabbath. Then he shall leave, and the gate shall be closed after his departure. 13[e] Every day you shall bring as a burnt offering to the LORD an unblemished year-old lamb; you shall offer it every morning, 14and with it every morning a grain offering of one sixth of an ephah, with a third of a hin of oil to moisten the fine flour. This grain offering for the LORD is a perpetual statute. 15[f] The lamb, the grain offering, and the oil you must bring every morning as a perpetual burnt offering.

***The Prince and the Land.*** 16Thus says the Lord GOD: If the prince makes a gift of part of his heritage to any of his sons, it belongs to his sons; that property is their heritage. 17But if he makes a gift of part of his heritage

**45:24 Hin**: one sixth of the liquid measure known as a bath.

**46:2–12** The prophet describes the inner eastern gateway opening on the inner court of the priests in front of the Temple itself where the altar of sacrifice stands. The people may watch the priests making offerings on sabbaths and feast days only by looking through the open gate; the prince, however, may stand inside the gate, in the vestibule on the edge of the inner court, to observe the offerings. Only priests could stand in the court itself.

*y:* Lv 4:27. *z:* Nm 22:40; 28:16–25. *a:* Nm 28:12–13. *b:* Ex 23:16; 34:22; Lv 23:34–43; Nm 29:12–38. *c:* Lv 22:20. *d:* cf. Nm 28:12. *e:* Ex 29:38; Nm 28:3–8. *f:* Ex 29:42; Nm 28:5–6.

### The Role of the Temple

ONCE THE TEMPLE is reestablished, water streams up from below the threshold of the temple (47:1) to water the land of Israel. This indicates the role of the temple as the center of creation (the Garden of Eden, Gn 2:10–14; Ps 46:4). The course of the water reflects that of the Gihon spring (cf the Edenic river, Gn 2:10, 13), and emerges east of the city of David where its waters flow south into the Siloam pool (see 1 Kgs 1:32–40; Is 7:3; 2 Chr 32:4). The water flows into the Jordan Valley and eventually into the Arabah (the Jordan rift where the Dead Sea is located) to transform the waters of the Dead Sea into fresh water that supports fish and fruit trees (see Gn 2:1–14). Everywhere it flows, the stream brings abundant life and food, a strong counterpoint to the desolation described earlier in Ezekiel and by other prophets.

to one of his servants, it belongs to him until the year of release;* then it reverts to the prince. Only the heritage given to his sons belongs to him.[g] 18The prince shall not seize any part of the heritage of the people by forcing them off their property. From his own property he shall provide heritage for his sons, so that none of my people will be driven off their property.

*The Temple Kitchens.* 19Then he brought me through the entrance at the side of the gateway to the chambers reserved for the priests, which faced north. There I saw a place at the far west end, 20about which he said to me, "This is the place where the priests cook the reparation offerings and the purification offerings and bake the grain offerings, so they do not have to bring them into the outer court and so transmit holiness to the people."* [h] 21Then he led me into the outer court and had me cross to the four corners of the court, and there, in each corner, was another court! 22In all four corners of the courtyard there were courts set off, each forty cubits long by thirty cubits wide, all four of them the same size. 23A stone wall surrounded them on four sides, and ovens were built along the bottom of the walls all the way around. 24He said to me, "These are the kitchens where the temple ministers cook the sacrifices of the people."

## CHAPTER 47

See RG 232

*The Wonderful Stream.** 1Then he brought me back to the entrance of the temple, and there! I saw water flowing out from under the threshold of the temple toward the east, for the front of the temple faced east. The water flowed out toward the right side of the temple to the south of the altar.[i] 2He brought me by way of the north gate and around the outside to the outer gate facing east; there I saw water trickling from the southern side. 3When he continued eastward with a measuring cord in his hand, he measured off a thousand cubits and had me wade through the water; it was ankle-deep. 4He measured off another thousand cubits and once more had me wade through the water; it was up to the knees. He measured another thousand cubits and had me wade through the water; it was up to my waist. 5Once more he measured off a thousand cubits. Now it was a river I could not wade across. The water had risen so high, I would have to swim—a river that was impassable. 6Then he asked me, "Do you see this, son of man?" He brought me to the bank of the river and had me sit down. 7As I was returning, I saw along the bank of the river a great many trees on each side.[j] 8He said to me, "This water flows out into the eastern district, runs down

**46:17 The year of release**: the jubilee year; cf. Lv 25:23–55.

**46:20** Cf. note on 44:19.

**47:1–12** The life and refreshment produced wherever the Temple stream flows evoke the order and abundance of paradise (cf. Gn 1:20–22; 2:10–14; Ps 46:5) and represent the coming transformation Ezekiel envisions for the exiles and their land. Water signifies great blessings and evidence of the Lord's presence (cf. Jl 2:14).

*g:* Lv 25:8–17. *h:* Lv 6:20. *i:* cf. Gn 2:10; Ps 46:4; Rev 22:1. *j:* Rev 22:2.

into the Arabah and empties into the polluted
waters of the sea* to freshen them.[k] 9Wher-
ever it flows, the river teems with every kind
of living creature; fish will abound. Where
these waters flow they refresh; everything
lives where the river goes. 10Fishermen will
stand along its shore from En-gedi to En-
eglaim;* it will become a place for drying
nets, and it will abound with as many kinds
of fish as the Great Sea.[l] 11Its marshes and
swamps shall not be made fresh, but will be
left for salt. 12Along each bank of the river
every kind of fruit tree will grow; their
leaves will not wither, nor will their fruit
fail. Every month they will bear fresh fruit
because the waters of the river flow out from
the sanctuary. Their fruit is used for food,
and their leaves for healing."[m]

### *The New Israel*

*Boundaries of the Land.** 13Thus says the
Lord GOD: These are the boundaries of the
land which you shall apportion among the
twelve tribes of Israel, with Joseph having
two portions.[n] 14You shall apportion it
equally because I swore to give it to your ancestors as a heritage; this land, then, is your
heritage.[o] 15[p] These are the borders of the
land: on the northern side, from the Great
Sea in the direction of Hethlon, Lebo-hamath to Zedad, 16Berothah, and Sibraim,
along the frontiers of Damascus and Hamath, to Hazar-enon, on the border of Hauran.[q] 17Thus the border extends from the sea
to Hazar-enon, north of the border of Damascus, the frontier of Hamath to the north.
This is the northern boundary. 18The eastern
border shall be between Damascus and Hauran, while the Jordan will form the border
between Gilead and the land of Israel down
to the eastern sea as far as Tamar. This is the
eastern boundary. 19The southern border
shall go southward from Tamar to the waters
of Meribath-kadesh, on to the Wadi of
Egypt, and into the Great Sea. This is the
southern boundary.[r] 20The western border
shall have the Great Sea as a boundary as far
as a point opposite Lebo-hamath. This is the
western boundary.

*The Northern Portions.* 21You shall divide
this land according to the tribes of Israel.
22[s] You shall allot it as heritage for yourselves
and for the resident aliens in your midst who
have fathered children among you. You shall
treat them like native Israelites; along with
you they shall receive a heritage among the
tribes of Israel. 23In whatever tribe the resident alien lives, there you shall assign his
heritage—oracle of the Lord GOD.

## CHAPTER 48

See RG 232

1These are the names* of the tribes:
At the northern end, along the side of the
way to Hethlon, Lebo-hamath, and Hazar-
enon, the border of Damascus, and northward up to the frontier with Hamath, from
the eastern border to the western: Dan, one
portion. 2Along the territory of Dan from the
eastern border to the western border: Asher,
one portion.[t] 3Along the territory of Asher
from the eastern border to the western border: Naphtali, one portion.[u] 4Along the territory of Naphtali from the eastern border to
the western border: Manasseh, one portion.[v]
5Along the territory of Manasseh from the
eastern border to the western border:
Ephraim, one portion.[w] 6Along the territory
of Ephraim from the eastern border to the
western border: Reuben, one portion.[x]
7Along the territory of Reuben from the
eastern border to the western border: Judah,
one portion.[y]

**47:8 The sea**: the Dead Sea, in which nothing can live. This vision of the Temple stream which transforms places of death into places of life is similar in purpose to the oracle of dry bones in 37:1–14: it offers the exiles hope for the future.

**47:10 From En-gedi to En-eglaim**: En-gedi is about halfway down the western shore of the Dead Sea; En-eglaim may have been at its northern end.

**47:13–20** These boundaries for a restored Israel correspond to the boundaries of the Davidic kingdom at its fullest extent; they are the "ideal boundaries" of the promised land; cf. Nm 34:3–12.

**48:1–29** This distribution of the land among the tribes does not correspond to the geographical realities of Palestine. It is another idealizing element in Ezekiel's representation of a restored and transformed Israel.

*k:* Zec 14:8. *l:* Ps 104:25. *m:* Ps 1:3; Jer 17:8. *n:* Gn 48:16; Nm 34:2–12. *o:* Gn 12:7; 15:9–21. *p:* Nm 34:1–12. *q:* 2 Sm 8:8. *r:* Nm 34:4; Dt 32:51. *s:* Lv 24:22; Nm 15:29; 26:55–56; Is 56:6–7. *t:* Jos 19:24–31. *u:* Jos 19:32–39. *v:* Jos 17:1–11. *w:* Jos 16:5–9. *x:* Jos 13:15–21. *y:* Jos 15:1–63.

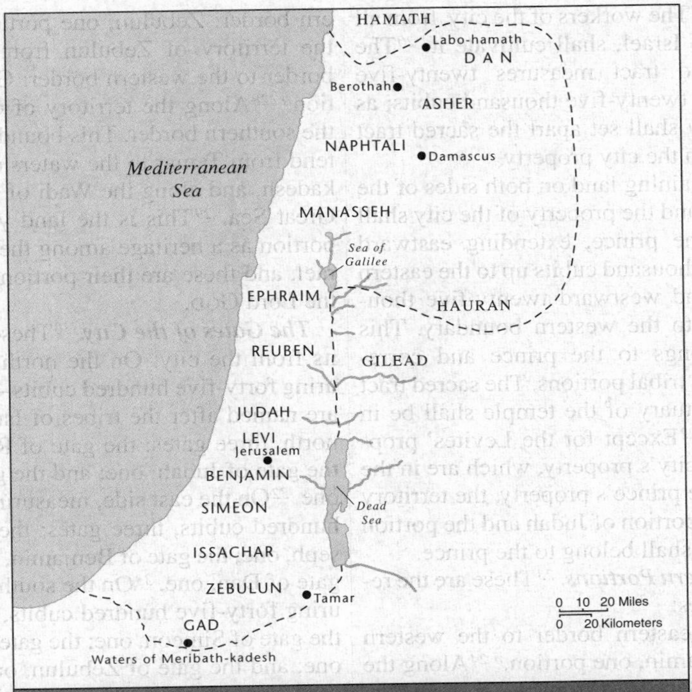


**Tribal Territories in the Restored Israel**

*The Sacred Tract.* 8Along the territory of
Judah from the eastern border to the western
border is the tract you shall set apart, twenty-
five thousand cubits wide and as long as one
of the portions from the eastern border to the
western border. The sanctuary shall stand in
the center of the tract. 9The tract you set
apart for the LORD shall be twenty-five thousand cubits long by twenty thousand wide.
10The sacred tract will be given to the following: the priests shall have twenty-five
thousand cubits on the north, ten thousand
on the west, ten thousand on the east, and
twenty-five thousand on the south. The sanctuary of the LORD shall be in its center. 11The
consecrated priests, the Zadokites, who fulfilled my service and did not stray with the
Israelites as the Levites did, 12shall have
their own tract set apart, next to the territory
of the Levites, separate from the most holy
tract. 13The Levites shall have territory corresponding to that of the priests, twenty-five
thousand cubits long and ten thousand cubits
wide. The whole tract shall be twenty-five
thousand cubits long and twenty thousand
wide. 14They may not sell or exchange or
transfer any of it, the best part of the land, for
it is sacred to the LORD. 15The remaining section, five thousand cubits long and twenty-
five thousand cubits wide, is profane land,
assigned to the city for dwellings and pasture. The city is at its center. 16These are the
dimensions of the city: the north side, forty-
five hundred cubits; the south side, forty-five
hundred cubits; the east side, forty-five hundred cubits; and the west side, forty-five
hundred cubits.[z] 17The pasture land for the
city extends north two hundred fifty cubits,
south two hundred fifty cubits, east two hundred fifty cubits, and west two hundred fifty
cubits. 18The remaining section runs eastward along the sacred tract for ten thousand
cubits and westward ten thousand cubits. Its
produce shall provide food for the workers

z: Rev 21:16.

of the city. [19]The workers of the city, from all the tribes of Israel, shall cultivate it. [20]The entire sacred tract measures twenty-five thousand by twenty-five thousand cubits; as a square you shall set apart the sacred tract together with the city property.

[21]The remaining land on both sides of the sacred tract and the property of the city shall belong to the prince, extending eastward twenty-five thousand cubits up to the eastern boundary, and westward twenty-five thousand cubits to the western boundary. This portion belongs to the prince and corresponds to the tribal portions. The sacred tract and the sanctuary of the temple shall be in the middle. [22]Except for the Levites' property and the city's property, which are in the middle of the prince's property, the territory between the portion of Judah and the portion of Benjamin shall belong to the prince.

***The Southern Portions.*** [23]These are the remaining tribes:

From the eastern border to the western border: Benjamin, one portion.[a] [24]Along the territory of Benjamin from the eastern border to the western border: Simeon, one portion.[b] [25]Along the territory of Simeon from the eastern border to the western border: Issachar, one portion.[c] [26]Along the territory of Issachar from the eastern border to the western border: Zebulun, one portion.[d] [27]Along the territory of Zebulun from the eastern border to the western border: Gad, one portion.[e] [28]Along the territory of Gad shall be the southern border. This boundary shall extend from Tamar to the waters of Meribath-kadesh, and along the Wadi of Egypt to the Great Sea. [29]This is the land you shall apportion as a heritage among the tribes of Israel, and these are their portions—oracle of the Lord GOD.

***The Gates of the City.*** [30]These are the exits from the city: On the north side, measuring forty-five hundred cubits— [31]the gates are named after the tribes of Israel—on the north, three gates: the gate of Reuben, one; the gate of Judah, one; and the gate of Levi, one. [32]On the east side, measuring forty-five hundred cubits, three gates: the gate of Joseph, one; the gate of Benjamin, one; and the gate of Dan, one. [33]On the south side, measuring forty-five hundred cubits, three gates: the gate of Simeon, one; the gate of Issachar, one; and the gate of Zebulun, one. [34]On the west side, measuring forty-five hundred cubits, three gates: the gate of Gad, one; the gate of Asher, one; and the gate of Naphtali, one.[f] [35]The circuit of the city shall be eighteen thousand cubits. From now on the name of the city is "The LORD is there."[g]

*a:* Jos 18:11–28. *b:* Jos 19:1–9. *c:* Jos 19:17–23. *d:* Jos 19:10–16. *e:* Jos 13:24–28. *f:* Rev 21:12–13. *g:* Is 2:6; Rev 3:12; 21:3.

See RG 233–38

# The Book of Daniel

This book takes its name not from the author, who is actually unknown, but from its hero, who was allegedly among the first Jews deported to Babylon, where he lived at least until 538 B.C. Strictly speaking, the book does not belong to the prophetic writings but rather to a distinctive type of literature known as "apocalyptic," of which it is an early specimen. Apocalyptic writing first appears about 200 B.C. and flourished among Jews and Christians down to the Middle Ages, especially in times of persecution. Apocalyptic literature has its roots in the older teaching of the prophets, who often pointed ahead to the day of the Lord, the consummation of history. For both prophet and apocalyptist there was one Lord of history, who would ultimately vindicate the chosen people. Apocalyptic also has roots in the wisdom tradition. Daniel has the gift of discernment from God. Greek wisdom (represented by the Babylonian "magicians and enchanters") is ridiculed (see especially chaps. 2 and 5), whereas God reveals hidden things to faithful servants.

This work was composed during the bitter persecution carried on by Antiochus IV Epiphanes (167–164 B.C.) and was written to strengthen and comfort the Jewish people in their ordeal. The persecution was occasioned by Antiochus's efforts to unify his kingdom, in face of the rising power of Rome, by continuing the hellenization begun by Alexander the Great; Antiochus tried to force Jews to adopt Greek ways, including religious practices. Severe penalties, including death, were exacted against those who refused (cf., e.g., 1 Mc 1:41–63).

The book contains traditional stories (chaps. 1–6), which tell of the trials and triumphs of the wise Daniel and his three companions. The moral is that people of faith can resist temptation and conquer adversity. The stories bristle with historical problems and have the character of historical novels rather than factual records. What is more important than the question of historicity, and closer to the intention of the author, is the fact that persecuted Jews of the second century B.C. would quickly see the application of these stories to their own plight.

There follows in chaps. 7–12 a series of visions promising deliverance and glory to the Jews in the days to come. The great nations of the ancient world have risen in vain against the Lord; his kingdom shall overthrow existing powers and last forever; in the end the dead will be raised for reward or punishment. Under this apocalyptic imagery some of the best elements of prophetic and sapiential teaching are synthesized: the insistence on right conduct, the divine control over events, the certainty that the kingdom of God will ultimately triumph and humanity attain the goal intended for it at the beginning of creation. The arrival of the kingdom is a central theme of the gospels, where Jesus is identified as the human figure (or "Son of Man") who appears in Daniel's vision in chap. 7. The message in both parts of the first twelve chapters (i.e., chaps. 1–6 and chaps. 7–12) is that history unrolls under the watchful eye of God, who does not abandon those who trust in him and will finally deliver and re-establish them. Moreover, it can be pointed out that chaps. 2 and 7 present the same teaching in different symbolism; 2:31 even describes the king's dream as a "vision."

The added episodes of Susanna, Bel, and the Dragon, found only in the Greek version, are edifying short stories with a didactic purpose (chaps. 13–14). The Greek version also adds a long prayer, numbered in the NAB and the Greek, 3:24–90, between 3:23–24 in the Hebrew text.

These three sections constitute the divisions of the Book of Daniel:

I. Daniel and the Kings of Babylon (1:1–6:29)

II. Daniel's Visions (7:1–12:13)

III. Appendix: Susanna, Bel, and the Dragon (13:1–14:42)

# I. Daniel and the Kings of Babylon

## CHAPTER 1

See RG 234–35

***The Food Test.*** [1]In the third year of the
reign of Jehoiakim,* king of Judah, King
Nebuchadnezzar of Babylon came and laid
siege to Jerusalem.[a] [2b] The Lord handed
over to him Jehoiakim, king of Judah, and
some of the vessels of the temple of God,
which he carried off to the land of Shinar*
and placed in the temple treasury of his god.
[3]The king told Ashpenaz,* his chief chamberlain, to bring in some of the Israelites,
some of the royal line and of the nobility.
[4]They should be young men without any defect, handsome, proficient in wisdom, well
informed, and insightful, such as could take
their place in the king's palace; he was to
teach them the language and literature of the
Chaldeans. [5]The king allotted them a daily
portion of food and wine from the royal
table. After three years' training they were to
enter the king's service. [6]Among these were
Judeans, Daniel, Hananiah, Mishael, and
Azariah. [7*] The chief chamberlain changed
their names: Daniel to Belteshazzar, Hananiah to Shadrach, Mishael to Meshach, and
Azariah to Abednego.

**1:1** According to 2 Kgs 24, the siege of Jerusalem took place after the death of Jehoiakim, but 2 Chr 36:5–8 says that Jehoiakim was taken to Babylon.

**1:2 Shinar**: ancient name for Babylonia, a deliberate archaism in this text; cf. Gn 10:10; 11:2.

**1:3** The proper name Ashpenaz is sometimes taken as a title, major-domo.

**1:7** Other prominent Jews with Babylonian names include Sheshbazzar and Zerubabbel, who were leaders of the post-exilic community.

*a:* 2 Kgs 24:1; 2 Chr 36:6; Jer 25:1. *b:* Dn 5:2; 2 Chr 36:7; Gn 10:10.

8 But Daniel was resolved not to defile himself with the king's food or wine; so he begged the chief chamberlain to spare him this defilement.* 9 Though God had given Daniel the favor and sympathy of the chief chamberlain, 10 he said to Daniel, "I am afraid of my lord the king, who allotted your food and drink. If he sees that you look thinner in comparison to the other young men of your age, you will endanger my life with the king." 11 Then Daniel said to the guardian whom the chief chamberlain had put in charge of Daniel, Hananiah, Mishael, and Azariah, 12 "Please test your servants for ten days. Let us be given vegetables to eat and water to drink. 13 Then see how we look in comparison with the other young men who eat from the royal table, and treat your servants according to what you see." 14 He agreed to this request, and tested them for ten days; 15 after ten days they looked healthier and better fed than any of the young men who ate from the royal table. 16 So the steward continued to take away the food and wine they were to receive, and gave them vegetables.

17 To these four young men God gave knowledge and proficiency in all literature and wisdom, and to Daniel the understanding of all visions and dreams. 18 At the end of the time the king had specified for their preparation, the chief chamberlain brought them before Nebuchadnezzar. 19 When the king had spoken with all of them, none was found equal to Daniel, Hananiah, Mishael, and Azariah; and so they entered the king's service. 20 In any question of wisdom or understanding which the king put to them, he found them ten times better than any of the magicians and enchanters in his kingdom. 21[c] Daniel remained there until the first year of King Cyrus.*

## CHAPTER 2

*Nebuchadnezzar's Dream.** 1 In the second year of his reign, King Nebuchadnezzar had a dream which left his spirit no rest and robbed him of his sleep. 2 So he ordered that the magicians, enchanters, sorcerers, and Chaldeans* be summoned to interpret the dream for him. When they came and presented themselves to the king, 3 he said to them, "I had a dream which will allow my spirit no rest until I know what it means." 4 The Chaldeans answered the king in Aramaic:* "O king, live forever! Tell your servants the dream and we will give its meaning." 5 The king answered the Chaldeans, "This is what I have decided: unless you tell me the dream and its meaning, you shall be cut to pieces and your houses made into a refuse heap. 6 But if you tell me the dream and its meaning, you shall receive from me gifts and presents and great honors. Therefore tell me the dream and its meaning."

7 Again they answered, "Let the king tell his servants the dream and we will give its meaning." 8 But the king replied: "I know for certain that you are bargaining for time, since you know what I have decided. 9 If you do not tell me the dream, there can be but one decree for you. You have conspired to present a false and deceitful interpretation to me until the crisis is past. Tell me the dream, therefore, that I may be sure that you can also give its correct interpretation."

10 The Chaldeans answered the king: "There is not a man on earth who can do what you ask, O king; never has any king, however great and mighty, asked such a

**1:8 This defilement**: the bread, meat, and wine of the Gentiles were unclean (Hos 9:3; Tb 1:12; Jdt 10:5; 12:1–2) because they might have been offered to idols; and the meat may not have been drained of blood, as Jewish dietary law requires. This test relates to the attempt of Antiochus to force Jews to eat forbidden foods in contempt of their religion (1 Mc 1:62–63; 2 Mc 6:18; 7:1).

**1:21 The first year of King Cyrus**: the year of this Persian king's conquest of Babylon, 539/538 B.C.

**2:1–49** The chronology of v. 1 is in conflict with that of 1:5, 18, and in 2:25 Daniel appears to be introduced to the king for the first time. It seems that the story of this chapter was originally entirely independent of chap. 1 and later retouched slightly to fit its present setting. The Septuagint (Papyrus 967) reads the twelfth year instead of the second.

**2:2 Chaldeans**: because the Babylonians gave serious study to the stars and planets, "Chaldeans" were identified with astrologers throughout the Hellenistic world.

**2:4 Aramaic**: a gloss to indicate that at this point the text switches from Hebrew to Aramaic, which continues through the end of chap. 7; at 8:1, the text switches back to Hebrew.

*c:* Dn 6:29.

thing of any magician, enchanter, or Chaldean. 11What you demand, O king, is too difficult; there is no one who can tell it to the
king except the gods, who do not dwell
among people of flesh." 12At this the king
became violently angry and ordered all the
wise men* of Babylon to be put to death.
13When the decree was issued that the wise
men should be slain, Daniel and his companions were also sought out.

14Then Daniel prudently took counsel
with Arioch, the chief of the king's guard,
who had set out to kill the wise men of Babylon. 15He asked Arioch, the officer of the
king, "What is the reason for this harsh order
from the king?" When Arioch told him,
16Daniel went and asked for time from the
king, that he might give him the interpretation.

17Daniel went home and informed his
companions Hananiah, Mishael, and Azariah, 18that they might implore the mercy of
the God of heaven in regard to this mystery,
so that Daniel and his companions might not
perish with the rest of the wise men of Babylon. 19During the night the mystery was revealed to Daniel in a vision, and he blessed
the God of heaven:

20 "Blessed be the name of God forever and ever,
for wisdom and power are his.
21 He causes the changes of the times and seasons,
establishes kings and deposes them.
He gives wisdom to the wise
and knowledge to those who understand.
22 He reveals deep and hidden things
and knows what is in the darkness,
for the light dwells with him.[d]
23 To you, God of my ancestors,
I give thanks and praise,
because you have given me wisdom and power.
Now you have shown me what we asked of you,
you have made known to us the king's dream."

24So Daniel went to Arioch, whom the
king had appointed to destroy the wise men
of Babylon, and said to him, "Do not put the
wise men of Babylon to death. Bring me before the king, and I will tell him the interpretation of the dream." Arioch quickly
brought Daniel to the king and said, 25"I
have found a man among the Judean exiles
who can give the interpretation to the king."
26The king asked Daniel, whose name was
Belteshazzar, "Can you tell me the dream
that I had and its meaning?" 27In the king's
presence Daniel made this reply:

"The mystery about which the king has
inquired, the wise men, enchanters, magicians, and diviners could not explain to the
king. 28But there is a God in heaven who reveals mysteries, and he has shown King
Nebuchadnezzar what is to happen in the
last days; this was your dream, the visions*
you saw as you lay in bed. 29To you in your
bed there came thoughts about what should
happen in the future, and he who reveals
mysteries showed you what is to be. 30To me
also this mystery has been revealed; not that
I am wiser than any other living person, but
in order that its meaning may be made
known to the king, that you may understand
the thoughts of your own mind.

31"In your vision, O king, you saw a
statue, very large and exceedingly bright,
terrifying in appearance as it stood before
you. 32Its head was pure gold, its chest and
arms were silver, its belly and thighs bronze,
33its legs iron, its feet partly iron and partly
clay.* 34While you watched, a stone was

**2:12 Wise men**: the satire, although directed against the Babylonian diviners in the text, refers to the Hellenistic Greeks, who made special claims to wisdom; the assertion here is that true wisdom comes from God and resides with the Jews. Cf. also chap. 5.

**2:28 The visions**: lit., "the visions of your head," a phrasing which distinguishes visionary experiences that are personal from those that are observable by others (see 4:2, 7, 10). That Daniel, unlike the Chaldeans, has access to these visions testifies to his God-given wisdom. Actually, this "dream" is more properly an apocalyptic vision; cf. the very similar message in Daniel's vision of chap. 7.

**2:33 Clay**: it has been suggested that the motif of iron mixed with clay implies a hollow metal statue packed with clay to stabilize it. In the interpretation of the dream, however, the mixture is taken as a sign of weakness.

*d:* Jn 1:9; 8:12; 1 Cor 4:5; 1 Jn 1:6.

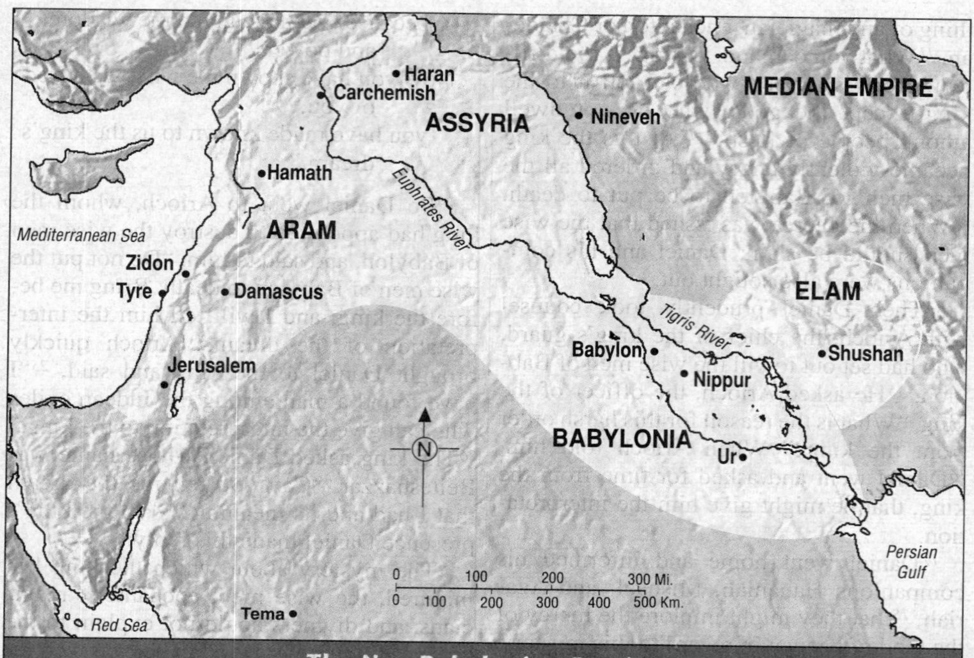


**The Neo-Babylonian Empire**

hewn from a mountain without a hand being
put to it, and it struck its iron and clay feet,
breaking them in pieces. 35The iron, clay,
bronze, silver, and gold all crumbled at once,
fine as the chaff on the threshing floor in
summer, and the wind blew them away without leaving a trace. But the stone that struck
the statue became a great mountain and
filled the whole earth.
36* "This was the dream; the interpretation
we shall also give in the king's presence.
37You, O king, are the king of kings; to you
the God of heaven has given dominion and
strength, power and glory; 38human beings,
wild beasts, and birds of the air, wherever
they may dwell, he has handed over to you,
making you ruler over them all; you are the
head of gold. 39Another kingdom shall take
your place, inferior to yours, then a third
kingdom, of bronze, which shall rule over the
whole earth. 40There shall be a fourth kingdom, strong as iron; it shall break in pieces
and subdue all these others, just as iron breaks
in pieces and crushes everything else. 41The
feet and toes you saw, partly of clay and
partly of iron, mean that it shall be a divided
kingdom, but yet have some of the hardness
of iron. As you saw the iron mixed with clay
tile, 42and the toes partly iron and partly clay,
the kingdom shall be partly strong and partly
fragile. 43The iron mixed with clay means that
they shall seal their alliances by intermarriage, but they shall not stay united, any more
than iron mixes with clay. 44In the lifetime of
those kings the God of heaven will set up a
kingdom that shall never be destroyed or delivered up to another people; rather, it shall
break in pieces all these kingdoms and put an

**2:36–45** The four successive kingdoms in this apocalyptic perspective are the Babylonian (gold), the Median (silver), the Persian (bronze), and the Hellenistic (iron). The last, after Alexander's death, was divided among his generals (vv. 41–42). Of the kingdoms which emerged from this partitioning, the two that most affected the Jews were the dynasties of the Ptolemies in Egypt and the Seleucids in Syria. They tried in vain, by war and through intermarriage, to restore the unity of Alexander's empire (v. 43). The stone hewn from the mountain is the kingdom of God awaited by the Jews (vv. 44–45). Compare the image of the stone applied to Jesus in Luke 20:17–18.

end to them, and it shall stand forever.
45e That is the meaning of the stone you saw
hewn from the mountain without a hand being put to it, which broke in pieces the iron,
bronze, clay, silver, and gold. The great God
has revealed to the king what shall be in the
future; this is exactly what you dreamed, and
its meaning is sure."
46 Then King Nebuchadnezzar fell down
and worshiped Daniel and ordered sacrifice
and incense offered to him. 47 To Daniel the
king said, "Truly your God is the God of
gods and Lord of kings and a revealer of
mysteries; that is why you were able to reveal this mystery." 48 He advanced Daniel to
a high post, gave him many generous presents, made him ruler of the whole province
of Babylon and chief prefect over all the
wise men of Babylon. 49 At Daniel's request
the king made Shadrach, Meshach, and
Abednego administrators of the province of
Babylon, while Daniel himself remained at
the king's court.

## CHAPTER 3

See RG 234–35

*The Fiery Furnace.* 1 King Nebuchadnezzar had a golden statue made, sixty cubits high and six cubits wide, which he set
up in the plain of Dura* in the province of
Babylon. 2 He then ordered the satraps,* prefects, and governors, the counselors, treasurers, judges, magistrates and all the officials of the provinces to be summoned to the
dedication of the statue which he had set up.
3 The satraps, prefects, and governors, the
counselors, treasurers, judges, magistrates
and all the officials of the provinces came together for the dedication and stood before
the statue which King Nebuchadnezzar had
set up. 4 A herald cried out: "Nations and
peoples of every language, 5* when you hear
the sound of the horn, pipe, zither, dulcimer,
harp, double-flute, and all the other musical
instruments, you must fall down and worship the golden statue which King Nebuchadnezzar has set up. 6 Whoever does not
fall down and worship shall be instantly cast
into a white-hot furnace." 7 Therefore, as
soon as they heard the sound of the horn,
pipe, zither, dulcimer, harp, double-flute,
and all the other musical instruments, the nations and peoples of every language all fell
down and worshiped the golden statue
which King Nebuchadnezzar had set up.
8 At that point, some of the Chaldeans
came and accused the Jews 9 to King Nebuchadnezzar: "O king, live forever! 10 O king,
you issued a decree that everyone who heard
the sound of the horn, pipe, zither, dulcimer,
harp, and double-flute, and all the other musical instruments should fall down and worship the golden statue; 11 whoever did not
was to be cast into a white-hot furnace.
12 There are certain Jews whom you have
made administrators of the province of Babylon: Shadrach, Meshach, and Abednego;
these men, O king, have paid no attention to
you; they will not serve your god or worship
the golden statue which you set up."
13 Nebuchadnezzar flew into a rage and
sent for Shadrach, Meshach, and Abednego,
who were promptly brought before the king.
14 King Nebuchadnezzar questioned them:
"Is it true, Shadrach, Meshach, and Abednego, that you will not serve my god, or worship the golden statue that I set up? 15 Now, if
you are ready to fall down and worship the
statue I made, whenever you hear the sound
of the horn, pipe, zither, dulcimer, harp, double-flute, and all the other musical instruments, then all will be well;* if not, you shall
be instantly cast into the white-hot furnace;
and who is the God who can deliver you out
of my hands?" 16 Shadrach, Meshach, and
Abednego answered King Nebuchadnezzar,
"There is no need for us to defend ourselves
before you in this matter. 17 If our God,
whom we serve, can save us* from the

**3:1 Dura**: several places in Babylonia bore this name. Probably the present reference is to one located close to Babylon. Giant statues of the type mentioned here were not uncommon in antiquity; a cubit was about a foot and a half. The unrealistic proportions of this statue suggest a comic effect.

**3:2 Satraps**: Persian provincial governors.

**3:5** The precise identification of the instruments is disputed. Several of the names are Greek.

**3:15 Then all will be well**: lacking in Aramaic; this phrase is supplied from the context.

**3:17 If our God . . . can save us**: the youths do not question the efficacy of the divine power, but whether it will be exercised (v. 18).

*e:* Mt 21:44; Lk 20:18.

white-hot furnace and from your hands, O
king, may he save us! [18]But even if he will
not, you should know, O king, that we will
not serve your god or worship the golden
statue which you set up."
[19]Nebuchadnezzar's face became livid
with utter rage against Shadrach, Meshach,
and Abednego. He ordered the furnace to be
heated seven times more than usual [20]and
had some of the strongest men in his army
bind Shadrach, Meshach, and Abednego and
cast them into the white-hot furnace. [21]They
were bound and cast into the white-hot furnace with their trousers, shirts, hats and
other garments, [22]for the king's order was
urgent. So huge a fire was kindled in the furnace that the flames devoured the men who
threw Shadrach, Meshach, and Abednego
into it. [23]But these three fell, bound, into the
midst of the white-hot furnace.
***Prayer of Azariah.****[24]They walked about
in the flames, singing to God and blessing
the Lord. [25]Azariah* stood up in the midst of
the fire and prayed aloud:

[26] "Blessed are you, and praiseworthy,
O Lord, the God of our ancestors,
and glorious forever is your name.
[27] For you are just in all you have done;
all your deeds are faultless, all your
ways right,
and all your judgments proper.
[28] You have executed proper judgments
in all that you have brought upon us
and upon Jerusalem, the holy city of
our ancestors.
By a proper judgment you have done all
this
because of our sins;
[29] For we have sinned and transgressed
by departing from you,
and we have done every kind of evil.
[30] Your commandments we have not
heeded or observed,
nor have we done as you ordered us
for our good.
[31] Therefore all you have brought upon us,
all you have done to us,
you have done by a proper judgment.
[32] You have handed us over to our enemies,
lawless and hateful rebels;
to an unjust king, the worst in all the
world.
[33] Now we cannot open our mouths;
shame and reproach have come upon us,
your servants, who revere you.
[34] For your name's sake, do not deliver us
up forever,
or make void your covenant.
[35] Do not take away your mercy from us,
for the sake of Abraham, your beloved,
Isaac your servant, and Israel your
holy one,
[36] To whom you promised to multiply their
offspring
like the stars of heaven,
or the sand on the shore of the sea.
[37] For we are reduced, O Lord, beyond any
other nation,
brought low everywhere in the world
this day
because of our sins.
[38] We have in our day no prince, prophet, or
leader,
no burnt offering, sacrifice, oblation,
or incense,
no place to offer first fruits, to find
favor with you.
[39] But with contrite heart and humble spirit
let us be received;
As though it were burnt offerings of rams
and bulls,
or tens of thousands of fat lambs,
[40] So let our sacrifice be in your presence
today
and find favor before you;
for those who trust in you cannot be
put to shame.
[41] And now we follow you with our whole
heart,
we fear you and we seek your face.
Do not put us to shame,
[42] but deal with us in your kindness and
great mercy.

**3:24–90** These verses are additions to the Aramaic text of Daniel, translated from the Greek form of the book. They were probably first composed in Hebrew or Aramaic, but are no longer extant in the original language. The Roman Catholic Church has always regarded them as part of the canonical Scriptures.

**3:25 Azariah**: i.e., Abednego; cf. Dn 1:7.

43 Deliver us in accord with your wonders,
and bring glory to your name, O Lord:
44 Let all those be put to shame
who inflict evils on your servants;
Let them be shamed and powerless,
and their strength broken;
45 Let them know that you alone are the
Lord God,
glorious over the whole world."

46Now the king's servants who had
thrown them in continued to stoke the furnace with naphtha, pitch, tow, and brush.
47The flames rose forty-nine cubits above
the furnace, 48and spread out, burning the
Chaldeans that it caught around the furnace.
49But the angel of the Lord went down into
the furnace with Azariah and his companions, drove the fiery flames out of the furnace, 50and made the inside of the furnace as
though a dew-laden breeze were blowing
through it. The fire in no way touched them
or caused them pain or harm. 51Then these
three in the furnace with one voice sang, glorifying and blessing God:

52 "Blessed are you, O Lord, the God of our
ancestors,
praiseworthy and exalted above all
forever;
And blessed is your holy and glorious
name,
praiseworthy and exalted above all for
all ages.
53 Blessed are you in the temple of your
holy glory,
praiseworthy and glorious above all
forever.
54 Blessed are you on the throne of your
kingdom,
praiseworthy and exalted above all
forever.
55 Blessed are you who look into the depths
from your throne upon the cherubim,
praiseworthy and exalted above all
forever.
56 Blessed are you in the firmament of
heaven,
praiseworthy and glorious forever.
57 Bless the Lord, all you works of the Lord,
praise and exalt him above all forever.
58 Angels of the Lord, bless the Lord,
praise and exalt him above all forever.
59 You heavens, bless the Lord,
praise and exalt him above all forever.[f]
60 All you waters above the heavens, bless
the Lord,
praise and exalt him above all forever.
61 All you powers, bless the Lord;
praise and exalt him above all forever.
62 Sun and moon, bless the Lord;
praise and exalt him above all forever.
63 Stars of heaven, bless the Lord;
praise and exalt him above all forever.
64 Every shower and dew, bless the Lord;
praise and exalt him above all forever.
65 All you winds, bless the Lord;
praise and exalt him above all forever.
66 Fire and heat, bless the Lord;
praise and exalt him above all forever.
67 Cold and chill, bless the Lord;
praise and exalt him above all forever.
68 Dew and rain, bless the Lord;
praise and exalt him above all forever.
69 Frost and chill, bless the Lord;
praise and exalt him above all forever.
70 Hoarfrost and snow, bless the Lord;
praise and exalt him above all forever.
71 Nights and days, bless the Lord;
praise and exalt him above all forever.
72 Light and darkness, bless the Lord;
praise and exalt him above all forever.
73 Lightnings and clouds, bless the Lord;
praise and exalt him above all forever.
74 Let the earth bless the Lord,
praise and exalt him above all forever.
75 Mountains and hills, bless the Lord;
praise and exalt him above all forever.
76 Everything growing on earth, bless the
Lord;
praise and exalt him above all forever.
77 You springs, bless the Lord;
praise and exalt him above all forever.
78 Seas and rivers, bless the Lord;
praise and exalt him above all forever.
79 You sea monsters and all water creatures,
bless the Lord;
praise and exalt him above all forever.
80 All you birds of the air, bless the Lord;

*f:* Ps 148:4.

praise and exalt him above all forever.
81 All you beasts, wild and tame, bless the
Lord;
praise and exalt him above all forever.
82 All you mortals, bless the Lord;
praise and exalt him above all forever.
83 O Israel, bless the Lord;
praise and exalt him above all forever.
84 Priests of the Lord, bless the Lord;
praise and exalt him above all forever.
85 Servants of the Lord, bless the Lord;
praise and exalt him above all forever.
86 Spirits and souls of the just, bless the
Lord;
praise and exalt him above all forever.
87 Holy and humble of heart, bless the Lord;
praise and exalt him above all forever.
88 Hananiah, Azariah, Mishael, bless the
Lord;
praise and exalt him above all forever.
For he has delivered us from Sheol,
and saved us from the power of death;
He has freed us from the raging flame
and delivered us from the fire.
89 Give thanks to the Lord, who is good,
whose mercy endures forever.
90 Bless the God of gods, all you who fear
the Lord;
praise and give thanks,
for his mercy endures forever."

***Deliverance from the Furnace.*** 91 Then
King Nebuchadnezzar was startled and rose
in haste, asking his counselors, "Did we not
cast three men bound into the fire?" "Certainly, O king," they answered. 92 "But," he
replied, "I see four men unbound and unhurt,
walking in the fire, and the fourth looks like
a son of God." 93 Then Nebuchadnezzar came
to the opening of the white-hot furnace and
called: "Shadrach, Meshach, and Abednego,
servants of the Most High God, come out."
Thereupon Shadrach, Meshach, and Abednego came out of the fire. 94 When the satraps, prefects, governors, and counselors of
the king came together, they saw that the fire
had had no power over the bodies of these
men; not a hair of their heads had been
singed, nor were their garments altered; there
was not even a smell of fire about them.
95 Nebuchadnezzar exclaimed, "Blessed be
the God of Shadrach, Meshach, and Abednego, who sent his angel to deliver the servants that trusted in him; they disobeyed the
royal command and yielded their bodies
rather than serve or worship any god except
their own God. 96 Therefore I decree for nations and peoples of every language that
whoever blasphemes the God of Shadrach,
Meshach, and Abednego shall be cut to
pieces and his house made into a refuse heap.
For there is no other God who can rescue like
this." 97 Then the king promoted Shadrach,
Meshach, and Abednego in the province of
Babylon.

98* King Nebuchadnezzar to the nations
and peoples of every language, wherever
they dwell on earth: May your peace
abound! 99 It has seemed good to me to publish the signs and wonders which the Most
High God has accomplished in my regard.

100 How great are his signs, how mighty his
wonders;
his kingship is an everlasting kingship,
and his dominion endures through all
generations.[g]

## CHAPTER 4

See RG 234–35

***Nebuchadnezzar's Madness.*** 1 I, Nebuchadnezzar, was at home in my palace,
content and prosperous. 2 I had a terrifying
dream as I lay in bed, and the images and my
visions frightened me. 3 So I issued a decree
that all the wise men of Babylon should be
brought before me to give the interpretation
of the dream. 4 When the magicians, enchanters, Chaldeans, and diviners had come
in, I related the dream before them; but none
of them could tell me its meaning. 5 Finally
there came before me Daniel, whose name is
Belteshazzar after the name of my god,* and

**3:98–4:34** This section has the form of a letter written by Nebuchadnezzar to his subjects.

**4:5 After the name of my god**: Belteshazzar, the Babylonian name given to Daniel at the king's orders (1:7), is *Balāṭ-šu-uṣur*, "protect his life." This passage implies a name connected with Bel, a Babylonian god. **A spirit of the holy gods**: or a holy divine spirit; or spirit of a holy God. See also vv. 6, 15; 5:11–12, 14; 6:4.

*g:* Dn 4:31; 7:14.

in whom is a spirit of the holy gods.[h] I repeated the dream to him: 6“Belteshazzar, chief of the magicians, I know that a spirit of the holy gods is in you and no mystery is too difficult for you; this is the dream that I saw, tell me its meaning.

7“These were the visions I saw while in bed: I saw a tree of great height at the center of the earth. 8It was large and strong, with its top touching the heavens, and it could be seen to the ends of the earth. 9Its leaves were beautiful, its fruit abundant, providing food for all. Under it the wild beasts found shade, in its branches the birds of the air nested; all flesh ate of it. 10In the vision I saw while in bed, a holy watcher* came down from heaven 11and cried aloud in these words:

‘Cut down the tree and lop off its
branches,
strip off its leaves and scatter its fruit;
Let the beasts flee from beneath it, and
the birds from its branches,
12 but leave its stump in the earth.
Bound with iron and bronze,
let him be fed with the grass of the
field
and bathed with the dew of heaven;
let his lot be with the beasts in the
grass of the earth.
13 Let his mind be changed from a human
one;
let the mind of a beast be given him,
till seven years pass over him.
14 By decree of the watchers is this
proclamation,
by order of the holy ones, this sentence;
That all who live may know
that the Most High is sovereign over
human kingship,
Giving it to whom he wills,
and setting it over the lowliest of
mortals.’[i]

15“This is the dream that I, King Nebuchadnezzar, had. Now, Belteshazzar, tell me its meaning. None of the wise men in my kingdom can tell me the meaning, but you can, because the spirit of the holy gods is in you.”

16Then Daniel, whose name was Belteshazzar, was appalled for a time, dismayed by his thoughts. “Belteshazzar,” the king said to him, “do not let the dream or its meaning dismay you.” “My lord,” Belteshazzar replied, “may this dream be for your enemies, and its meaning for your foes. 17The tree that you saw, large and strong, its top touching the heavens, that could be seen by the whole earth, 18its leaves beautiful, its fruit abundant, providing food for all, under which the wild beasts lived, and in whose branches the birds of the air dwelt— 19you are that tree, O king, large and strong! Your majesty has become so great as to touch the heavens, and your rule reaches to the ends of the earth. 20As for the king’s vision of a holy watcher, who came down from heaven and proclaimed: ‘Cut down the tree and destroy it, but leave its stump in the earth. Bound with iron and bronze, let him be fed with the grass of the field, and bathed with the dew of heaven; let his lot be with wild beasts till seven years pass over him’— 21here is its meaning, O king, here is the sentence that the Most High has passed upon my lord king: 22[j] You shall be cast out from human society and dwell with wild beasts; you shall be given grass to eat like an ox and be bathed with the dew of heaven; seven years shall pass over you, until you know that the Most High is sovereign over human kingship and gives it to whom he will. 23The command that the stump of the tree is to be left means that your kingdom shall be preserved for you, once you have learned that heaven is sovereign. 24Therefore, O king, may my advice be acceptable to you; atone for your sins by good deeds,* and for your misdeeds by kindness to the poor; then your contentment will be long lasting.”

25All this happened to King Nebuchadnezzar. 26Twelve months later, as he was

**4:10 A holy watcher**: lit., “a watcher and a holy one.” Two terms for angels. The term watcher is found in the Bible only in this chapter of Daniel, but it is common in extra-canonical Jewish literature. In 1 Enoch, the fallen angels are called watchers.

**4:24 Good deeds**: the Aramaic word *sidqâ* has the root meaning of “righteousness,” but in a late text such as this could mean “almsgiving.”

*h:* Gn 41:38. *i:* 1 Sm 2:8. *j:* Dn 5:21.

walking on the roof of the royal palace in Babylon, 27the king said, "Babylon the great! Was it not I, with my great strength, who built it as a royal residence for my splendor and majesty?" 28While these words were still on the king's lips, a voice spoke from heaven, "It has been decreed for you, King Nebuchadnezzar, that your kingship is taken from you! 29You shall be cast out from human society, and shall dwell with wild beasts; you shall be given grass to eat like an ox, and seven years shall pass over you, until you learn that the Most High is sovereign over human kingship and gives it to whom he will." 30* At once this was fulfilled. Nebuchadnezzar was cast out from human society, he ate grass like an ox, and his body was bathed with the dew of heaven, until his hair grew like the feathers of an eagle, and his nails like the claws of a bird.

31When this period was over, I, Nebuchadnezzar, raised my eyes to heaven; my reason was restored to me, and I blessed the Most High, I praised and glorified the One who lives forever,

Whose dominion is an everlasting dominion,
and whose kingdom endures through all generations.[k]
32 All who live on the earth are counted as nothing;
he does as he wills with the powers of heaven
and with those who live on the earth.
There is no one who can stay his hand
or say to him, "What have you done?"

33At the same time my reason returned to me, and for the glory of my kingdom, my majesty and my splendor returned to me. My counselors and nobles sought me out; I was restored to my kingdom and became much greater than before. 34Now, I, Nebuchadnezzar, praise and exalt and glorify the King of heaven, all of whose works are right and ways just; and who is able to humble those who walk in pride.

## CHAPTER 5

See RG 234–35

*The Writing on the Wall.* 1King Belshazzar gave a great banquet for a thousand of his nobles, with whom he drank. 2Under the influence of the wine, he ordered the gold and silver vessels which Nebuchadnezzar, his father,* had taken from the temple in Jerusalem, to be brought in so that the king, his nobles, his consorts, and his concubines might drink from them. 3When the gold vessels taken from the temple, the house of God in Jerusalem, had been brought in, and while the king, his nobles, his consorts, and his concubines were drinking 4wine from them, they praised their gods of gold and silver, bronze and iron, wood and stone.

5Suddenly, opposite the lampstand, the fingers of a human hand appeared, writing on the plaster of the wall in the king's palace. When the king saw the hand that wrote, 6his face became pale; his thoughts terrified him, his hip joints shook, and his knees knocked. 7The king shouted for the enchanters, Chaldeans, and diviners to be brought in. "Whoever reads this writing and tells me what it means," he said to the wise men of Babylon, "shall be clothed in purple, wear a chain of gold around his neck, and be third in governing the kingdom." 8But though all the king's wise men came in, none of them could either read the writing or tell the king what it meant. 9Then King Belshazzar was greatly terrified; his face became pale, and his nobles were thrown into confusion.

10When the queen heard of the discussion between the king and his nobles, she entered the banquet hall and said, "O king, live forever! Do not let your thoughts terrify you, or your face become so pale! 11There is a man in your kingdom in whom is a spirit of the

**4:30–32** There is no historical record that these events happened to Nebuchadnezzar. Scholars have long suspected that the story originally involved Nabonidus, the father of Belshazzar, who was absent from Babylon and lived at Teima in the Arabian desert for a number of years. This suggestion is now strengthened by the Prayer of Nabonidus, found at Qumran, which is closely related to chap. 4. The biblical author's chief interest was not in the historicity of this popular tale, but in the object lesson it contained for the proud "divine" kings of the Seleucid dynasty.

**5:2 Nebuchadnezzar, his father**: between Nebuchadnezzar and Belshazzar several kings ruled in Babylon. Belshazzar was the son of Nabonidus, and he acted as regent in Babylon during his father's absence.

*k:* Dn 3:33; 7:14.

holy gods; during the lifetime of your father he showed brilliant insight and god-like wisdom. King Nebuchadnezzar, your father, made him chief of the magicians, enchanters, Chaldeans, and diviners. [12]Because this Daniel, whom the king named Belteshazzar, has shown an extraordinary spirit, knowledge, and insight in interpreting dreams, explaining riddles and solving problems, let him now be summoned to tell you what this means."

[13]Then Daniel was brought into the presence of the king. The king asked him, "Are you the Daniel, one of the Jewish exiles, whom my father, the king, brought from Judah? [14]I have heard that the spirit of the gods is in you, that you have shown brilliant insight and extraordinary wisdom. [15]The wise men and enchanters were brought in to me to read this writing and tell me its meaning, but they could not say what the words meant. [16]But I have heard that you can give interpretations and solve problems; now, if you are able to read the writing and tell me what it means, you shall be clothed in purple, wear a chain of gold around your neck, and be third in governing the kingdom."

[17]Daniel answered the king: "You may keep your gifts, or give your presents to someone else; but the writing I will read for the king, and tell what it means. [18]The Most High God gave your father Nebuchadnezzar kingship, greatness, splendor, and majesty. [19]Because he made him so great, the nations and peoples of every language dreaded and feared him. Whomever he willed, he would kill or let live; whomever he willed, he would exalt or humble. [20]But when his heart became proud and his spirit hardened by insolence, he was put down from his royal throne and deprived of his glory; [21 l]he was cast out from human society and his heart was made like that of a beast; he lived with wild asses, and ate grass like an ox; his body was bathed with the dew of heaven, until he learned that the Most High God is sovereign over human kingship and sets over it whom he will. [22]You, his son, Belshazzar, have not humbled your heart, though you knew all this; [23]you have rebelled against the Lord of heaven. You had the vessels of his temple brought before you, so that you and your nobles, your consorts and your concubines, might drink wine from them; and you praised the gods of silver and gold, bronze and iron, wood and stone, that neither see nor hear nor have intelligence. But the God in whose hand is your very breath and the whole course of your life, you did not glorify. [24]By him was the hand sent, and the writing set down.

[25]"This is the writing that was inscribed: MENE, TEKEL, and PERES.* These words mean: [26]* MENE, God has numbered your kingdom and put an end to it; [27]TEKEL, you have been weighed on the scales and found wanting; [28]PERES, your kingdom has been divided and given to the Medes and Persians."

[29]Then by order of Belshazzar they clothed Daniel in purple, with a chain of gold around his neck, and proclaimed him third in governing the kingdom. [30]That very night Belshazzar, the Chaldean king, was slain:

## CHAPTER 6

See RG 234–35

[1]And Darius the Mede* succeeded to the kingdom at the age of sixty-two.

***The Lions' Den.*** [2]Darius decided to appoint over his entire kingdom one hundred and twenty satraps. [3]These were accountable to three ministers, one of whom was Daniel; the satraps reported to them, so that

**5:25 MENE, TEKEL, and PERES**: these seem to be the Aramaic names of weights and monetary values: the mina, the shekel (the sixtieth part of a mina), and the parsu (a half-mina).

**5:26–28** Daniel interprets these three terms by a play on the words: *MENE*, connected with the verb meaning to number; *TEKEL*, with the verb meaning to weigh; *PERES*, with the verb meaning to divide. There is also a play on the last term with the word for Persians.

**6:1 Darius the Mede**: unknown outside of the Book of Daniel. The Median kingdom did not exist at this time because it had already been conquered by Cyrus the Persian. Apparently the author of Daniel is following an apocalyptic view of history, linked to prophecy (cf. Is 13:17–19; Jer 51:11, 28–30), according to which the Medes formed the second of four world kingdoms preceding the messianic times; see note on Dn 2:36–45. The character of Darius the Mede has probably been modeled on that of the Persian king Darius the Great (522–486 B.C.), the second successor of Cyrus. The Persian Darius did appoint satraps over his empire.

*l:* Dn 4:22.

the king should suffer no loss. 4 Daniel outshone all the ministers and satraps because an extraordinary spirit was in him, and the king considered setting him over the entire kingdom. 5 Then the ministers and satraps tried to find grounds for accusation against Daniel regarding the kingdom. But they could not accuse him of any corruption. Because he was trustworthy, no fault or corruption was to be found in him. 6 Then these men said to themselves, "We shall find no grounds for accusation against this Daniel except in connection with the law of his God." 7 So these ministers and satraps stormed in to the king and said to him, "King Darius, live forever! 8* [m] All the ministers of the kingdom, the prefects, satraps, counselors, and governors agree that the following prohibition ought to be put in force by royal decree: for thirty days, whoever makes a petition to anyone, divine or human, except to you, O king, shall be thrown into a den of lions. 9 Now, O king, let the prohibition be issued over your signature, immutable and irrevocable* according to the law of the Medes and Persians." 10 So King Darius signed the prohibition into law.

11 Even after Daniel heard that this law had been signed, he continued his custom of going home to kneel in prayer and give thanks to his God in the upper chamber three times a day, with the windows open toward Jerusalem. 12 So these men stormed in and found Daniel praying and pleading before his God. 13 Then they went to remind the king about the prohibition: "Did you not sign a decree, O king, that for thirty days, whoever makes a petition to anyone, divine or human, except to you, O king, shall be cast into a den of lions?" The king answered them, "The decree is absolute, irrevocable under the law of the Medes and Persians." 14 To this they replied, "Daniel, one of the Jewish exiles, has paid no attention to you, O king, or to the prohibition you signed; three times a day he offers his prayer." 15 The king was deeply grieved at this news and he made up his mind to save Daniel; he worked till sunset to rescue him. 16 But these men pressed the king. "Keep in mind, O king," they said, "that under the law of the Medes and Persians every royal prohibition or decree is irrevocable." 17 So the king ordered Daniel to be brought and cast into the lions' den.* To Daniel he said, "Your God, whom you serve so constantly, must save you." 18 To forestall any tampering, the king sealed with his own ring and the rings of the lords the stone that had been brought to block the opening of the den.

19 Then the king returned to his palace for the night; he refused to eat and he dismissed the entertainers. Since sleep was impossible for him, 20 the king rose very early the next morning and hastened to the lions' den. 21 As he drew near, he cried out to Daniel sorrowfully, "Daniel, servant of the living God, has your God whom you serve so constantly been able to save you from the lions?" 22 Daniel answered the king: "O king, live forever! 23 My God sent his angel and closed the lions' mouths so that they have not hurt me.[n] For I have been found innocent before him; neither have I done you any harm, O king!" 24 This gave the king great joy. At his order Daniel was brought up from the den; he was found to be unharmed because he trusted in his God. 25 The king then ordered the men who had accused Daniel, along with their children and their wives, to be cast into the lions' den. Before they reached the bottom of the den, the lions overpowered them and crushed all their bones.

26 Then King Darius wrote to the nations and peoples of every language, wherever they dwell on the earth: "May your peace abound! 27 I decree that throughout my royal domain the God of Daniel is to be reverenced and feared:

**6:8–11** The Jews of the second century B.C. could relate the king's attempt to force upon them, under pain of death, the worship of a foreign deity to the decrees of Antiochus IV; cf. 1 Mc 1:41–50.

**6:9 Immutable and irrevocable**: Est 1:19 and 8:8 also refer to the immutability of Medo-Persian laws. The same idea is found in the historian Diodorus Siculus with reference to the time of Darius III (335–331 B.C.), the last of the Persian kings. Cf. Dn 6:13, 16.

**6:17 The lions' den**: a pit too deep to be easily scaled; its opening was blocked with a stone (v. 18).

*m:* Est 1:19. *n:* 1 Mc 2:60.

"For he is the living God, enduring
forever,
whose kingdom shall not be destroyed,
whose dominion shall be without end,
28 A savior and deliverer,
working signs and wonders in heaven
and on earth,
who saved Daniel from the lions'
power."

29 So Daniel fared well during the reign of
Darius and the reign of Cyrus the Persian.[o]

## II. Daniel's Visions

### CHAPTER 7

See RG 235–37

*The Beasts and the Judgment.** 1 In the
first year of King Belshazzar of Babylon, as
Daniel lay in bed he had a dream, visions in
his head. Then he wrote down the dream; the
account began: 2 In the vision I saw during
the night, suddenly the four winds of heaven
stirred up the great sea,* 3 from which
emerged four immense beasts,[p] each different from the others. 4 The first was like a
lion, but with eagle's wings.* While I
watched, the wings were plucked; it was
raised from the ground to stand on two feet
like a human being, and given a human
mind. 5 The second beast was like a bear;* it
was raised up on one side, and among the
teeth in its mouth were three tusks. It was
given the order, "Arise, devour much flesh."
6 After this I looked and saw another beast,
like a leopard;* on its back were four wings
like those of a bird, and it had four heads. To
this beast dominion was given. 7* After this,
in the visions of the night I saw a fourth
beast, terrifying, horrible, and of extraordinary strength; it had great iron teeth with
which it devoured and crushed, and it trampled with its feet what was left. It differed
from the beasts that preceded it. It had ten
horns. 8 I was considering the ten horns it
had, when suddenly another, a little horn,
sprang out of their midst, and three of the
previous horns were torn away to make
room for it. This horn had eyes like human
eyes, and a mouth that spoke arrogantly.
9* As I watched,

Thrones were set up
and the Ancient of Days took his
throne.
His clothing was white as snow,
the hair on his head like pure wool;
His throne was flames of fire,
with wheels of burning fire.
10 A river of fire surged forth,
flowing from where he sat;
Thousands upon thousands were
ministering to him,
and myriads upon myriads stood
before him.[q]

The court was convened, and the books
were opened. 11 I watched, then, from the
first of the arrogant words which the horn
spoke, until the beast was slain and its body

**7:1–27** This vision continues the motif of the four kingdoms from chap. 2; see note on 2:36–45. To the four succeeding world kingdoms, Babylonian, Median, Persian, and Greek, is opposed the heavenly kingdom of God and the kingdom of God's people on earth. The beast imagery of this chapter has been used extensively in the Book of Revelation, where it is applied to the Roman empire, the persecutor of the Church.

**7:2 The great sea**: the primordial ocean beneath the earth, according to ancient Near Eastern cosmology (Gn 7:11; 49:25). It was thought to contain various monsters (Is 27:1; Jb 7:12), and in particular mythological monsters symbolizing the chaos which God had vanquished in primordial times (Jb 9:13; 26:12; Is 51:9–10; etc.).

**7:4** In ancient times the Babylonian empire was commonly represented as a winged lion, in the rampant position (raised up on one side). The two wings that were plucked may represent Nebuchadnezzar and Belshazzar. **On two feet like a human being . . . a human mind**: contrasts with what is said in 4:13, 30.

**7:5 A bear**: represents the Median empire, its three tusks symbolizing its destructive nature; hence, the command: "Arise, devour much flesh."

**7:6 A leopard**: used to symbolize the swiftness with which Cyrus the Persian established his kingdom. **Four heads**: corresponding to the four Persian kings of 11:2.

**7:7–8** Alexander's empire was different from all the others in that it was Western rather than Eastern in inspiration, and far exceeded the others in power. The ten horns represent the kings of the Seleucid dynasty, the only part of the Hellenistic empire that concerned the author. The little horn is Antiochus IV Epiphanes (175–164 B.C.), who usurped the throne and persecuted the Jews.

**7:9–10** A vision of the heavenly throne of God (the Ancient of Days), who sits in judgment over the nations. Some of the details of the vision, depicting the divine majesty and omnipotence, are to be found in Ezekiel 1. Others are paralleled in 1 Enoch, a contemporary Jewish apocalypse.

*o:* Dn 1:21. *p:* Rev 13:1. *q:* Rev 5:11.

destroyed and thrown into the burning fire.
12 As for the other beasts, their dominion was
taken away, but they were granted a prolongation of life for a time and a season. 13 As
the visions during the night continued, I saw
coming with the clouds of heaven[r]

One like a son of man.*
When he reached the Ancient of Days
and was presented before him,
14 He received dominion, splendor, and kingship;
all nations, peoples and tongues will serve him.
His dominion is an everlasting dominion
that shall not pass away,
his kingship, one that shall not be destroyed.[s]

15 Because of this, my spirit was anguished and I, Daniel, was terrified by my
visions. 16 I approached one of those present
and asked him the truth of all this; in answer,
he made known to me its meaning: 17 "These
four great beasts stand for four kings which
shall arise on the earth. 18 But the holy ones*
of the Most High shall receive the kingship,
to possess it forever and ever."

19 Then I wished to make certain about the
fourth beast, so very terrible and different
from the others, devouring and crushing
with its iron teeth and bronze claws, and
trampling with its feet what was left; 20 and
about the ten horns on its head, and the other
one that sprang up, before which three horns
fell; and about the horn with the eyes and the
mouth that spoke arrogantly, which appeared greater than its fellows. 21 For, as I
watched, that horn made war against the
holy ones and was victorious 22 until the Ancient of Days came, and judgment was pronounced in favor of the holy ones of the
Most High, and the time arrived for the holy
ones to possess the kingship. 23 He answered
me thus:

"The fourth beast shall be a fourth kingdom on earth,
different from all the others;
The whole earth it shall devour,
trample down and crush.
24 The ten horns shall be ten kings
rising out of that kingdom;
another shall rise up after them,
Different from those before him,
who shall lay low three kings.
25 He shall speak against the Most High
and wear down the holy ones of the Most High,
intending to change the feast days and the law.*
They shall be handed over to him
for a time, two times, and half a time.
26 But when the court is convened,
and his dominion is taken away
to be abolished and completely destroyed,
27 Then the kingship and dominion and majesty
of all the kingdoms under the heavens
shall be given to the people of the holy ones of the Most High,
Whose kingship shall be an everlasting kingship,
whom all dominions shall serve and obey."

28 This is the end of the report. I, Daniel, was
greatly terrified by my thoughts, and my face
became pale, but I kept the matter to myself.*

**7:13–14 One like a son of man**: In contrast to the worldly kingdoms opposed to God, which are represented as grotesque beasts, the coming Kingdom of God is represented by a human figure. Scholars disagree as to whether this figure should be taken as a collective symbol for the people of God (cf. 7:27) or identified as a particular individual, e.g., the archangel Michael (cf. 12:1) or the messiah. The phrase "Son of Man" becomes a title for Jesus in the gospels, especially in passages dealing with the Second Coming (Mk 13 and parallels).

**7:18** "Holy ones" in Hebrew and Aramaic literature are nearly always members of the heavenly court or angels (cf. 4:10, 14, 20; 8:13), though here the term is commonly taken to refer to Israel.

**7:25** The reference is to the persecution of Antiochus IV and specifically to the disruption of the Temple cult (1 Mc 1:41–64). **A time, two times, and half a time**: an indefinite, evil period of time. Probably here, three and a half years, which becomes the standard period of tribulation in apocalyptic literature (Rev 11:2; 13:5 [in months]; 11:3 [in days]; and cf. 12:14). As seven is the Jewish "perfect" number, half of it signifies great imperfection. Actually, the Temple was desecrated for three years (1 Mc 4:52–54). The duration of the persecution was a little longer, since it was already under way before the Temple was desecrated.

**7:28** This verse ends the Aramaic part of the Book of Daniel.

*r:* Mk 13:26; 14:62. *s:* Dn 3:33; 4:31.

## CHAPTER 8

See RG 235–37
*The Ram and the He-goat.** 1 After this
first vision, I, Daniel, had another, in the
third year of the reign of King Belshazzar.
2 In my vision I saw myself in the fortress of
Susa* in the province of Elam; I was beside
the river Ulai. 3 I looked up and saw standing
by the river a ram with two great horns, the
one larger and newer than the other. 4 I saw
the ram butting toward the west, north, and
south. No beast could withstand it or be rescued from its power; it did what it pleased
and grew powerful.

5 As I was reflecting, a he-goat with a
prominent horn on its forehead suddenly
came from the west across the whole earth
without touching the ground. 6 It came to the
two-horned ram I had seen standing by the
river, and rushed toward it with savage
force. 7 I saw it reach the ram; enraged, the
he-goat attacked and shattered both its
horns. The ram did not have the strength to
withstand it; the he-goat threw the ram to the
ground and trampled upon it. No one could
rescue the ram from its power.

8 The he-goat grew very powerful, but at
the height of its strength the great horn was
shattered, and in its place came up four others, facing the four winds of heaven. 9 Out of
one of them came a little horn* which grew
and grew toward the south, the east, and the
glorious land. 10 It grew even to the host of
heaven,* so that it cast down to earth some of
the host and some of the stars and trampled
on them. 11 It grew even to the Prince of the
host, from whom the daily sacrifice was removed, and whose sanctuary was cast down.
12 The host was given over together with the
daily sacrifice in the course of transgression.
It cast truth to the ground, and was succeeding in its undertaking.

13 I heard a holy one speaking, and another
said to whichever one it was that spoke,
"How long shall the events of this vision last
concerning the daily sacrifice, the desolating
sin,* the giving over of the sanctuary and the
host for trampling?" 14 He answered him,
"For two thousand three hundred evenings
and mornings; then the sanctuary shall be set
right."

15 While I, Daniel, sought the meaning of
the vision I had seen, one who looked like a
man stood before me, 16 and on the Ulai I
heard a human voice that cried out, "Gabriel,*
explain the vision to this man." 17 When he
came near where I was standing, I fell prostrate in terror. But he said to me, "Understand,
O son of man, that the vision refers to the end
time."* 18 As he spoke to me, I fell forward unconscious; he touched me and made me stand
up. 19 "I will show you," he said, "what is to
happen in the last days of wrath; for it is for
the appointed time of the end.

20 "The two-horned ram you saw represents the kings of the Medes and Persians.*
21 The he-goat is the king of the Greeks, and
the great horn on its forehead is the first
king. 22 The four that rose in its place when
it was shattered are four kingdoms that will
issue from his nation, but without his
strength.

**8:1–27** This vision continues images of the preceding one, and develops it in more detail. As explained in vv. 20–22 the two-horned ram represents the combined kingdom of the Medes and Persians, destroyed by Alexander's Hellenistic empire originating in the west. Once again the author is interested only in the Seleucid dynasty, which emerged from the dissolution of Alexander's empire after his death in 323 B.C.

**8:2 The fortress of Susa**: the royal palace of the Persian kings in the ancient territory of Elam, east of Babylonia. **The river Ulai**: a canal along the northern side of Susa. Some scholars argue that the Hebrew word understood as "river" here should instead be translated "gate."

**8:9 A little horn**: as in chap. 7, Antiochus IV. **The glorious land**: Israel.

**8:10–12 The host of heaven**: the angelic host, symbolized by the stars. **The Prince of the host**: the Most High God, whose worship Antiochus suppressed (1 Mc 1:45).

**8:13 The desolating sin**: the Hebrew contains a wordplay (*shomem*) on the name Baal Shamem ("lord of the heavens," identified by some as the Greek Zeus Olympios). The reference is to some object with which Antiochus profaned the Temple of Jerusalem (2 Mc 6:2), most probably a pagan altar.

**8:16** The angel Gabriel is mentioned here for the first time in the Bible. There is wordplay in the preceding verse on *geber*, "manlike figure."

**8:17 The end time**: the time when God sits in judgment on the wicked (v. 19).

**8:20 The Medes and Persians**: the Medes had been allies of the Babylonians in destroying the Assyrian empire (late seventh century B.C.), and Cyrus the Persian defeated the Medes en route to conquering the Babylonians. The Book of Daniel, however, treats the Medes and Persians as a dual kingdom; cf. also 5:28; 6:9; and note on 6:1.

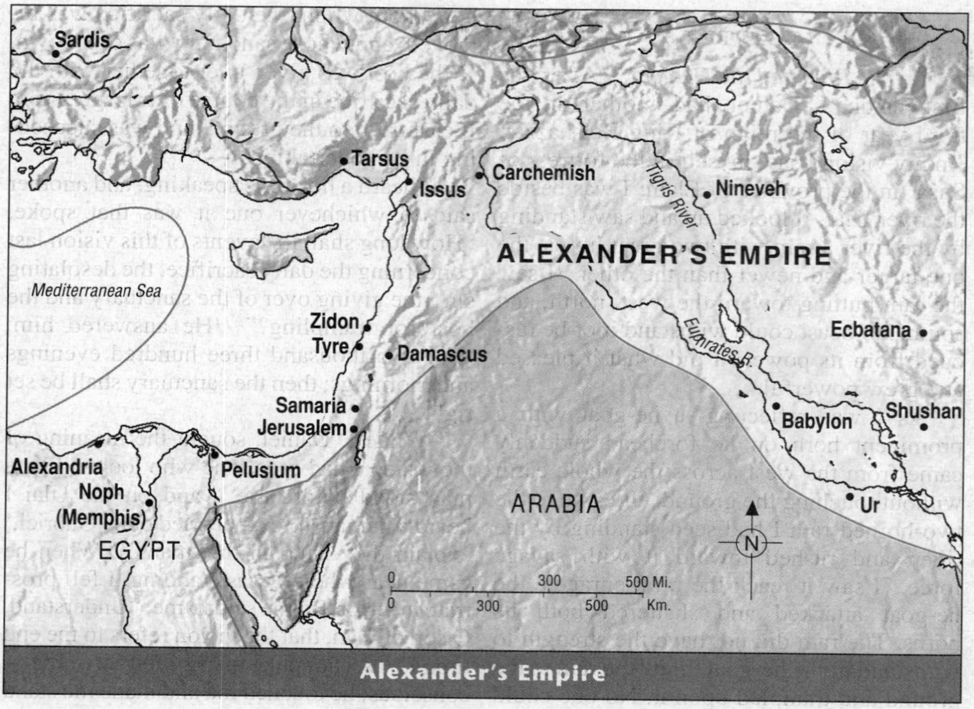

Alexander's Empire

23 "At the end of their reign,
when sinners have reached their measure,
There shall arise a king,
impudent, and skilled in intrigue.
24 He shall be strong and powerful,
bring about fearful ruin,
and succeed in his undertaking.
He shall destroy powerful peoples;
25 his cunning shall be against the holy ones,
his treacherous conduct shall succeed.
He shall be proud of heart
and destroy many by stealth.
But when he rises against the Prince of princes,
he shall be broken without a hand being raised.
26 As for the vision of the evenings and the mornings,
what was spoken is true.
But you, keep this vision secret:
it is for the distant future."

27 I, Daniel, was weak and ill for some
days; then I arose and took care of the king's
affairs. But the vision left me desolate, without understanding.

## CHAPTER 9

See RG 235–37

*The Seventy Weeks of Years.* 1 It was
the first year that Darius,* son of Ahasuerus,
of the race of the Medes, reigned over the
kingdom of the Chaldeans; 2 t in the first year
of his reign, I, Daniel, perceived in the books
the number of years the LORD had decreed to
the prophet Jeremiah: Jerusalem was to lie in
ruins for seventy years.*

3 I turned to the Lord God, to seek help, in
prayer and petition, with fasting, sackcloth,
and ashes. 4 u I prayed to the LORD, my God,
and confessed, "Ah, Lord, great and awe-

**9:1 Darius**: see note on 6:1.

**9:2 Seventy years**: Jeremiah was understood to prophesy a Babylonian captivity of seventy years, a round number signifying the complete passing away of the existing generation (Jer 25:11; 29:10). On this view Jeremiah's prophecy was seen to be fulfilled in the capture of Babylon by Cyrus and the

*t*: Jer 25:11; 29:10. *u*: Ezr 9:6–14; Neh 9:6–37.

some God, you who keep your covenant and
show mercy toward those who love you and
keep your commandments and your precepts! 5We have sinned, been wicked and
done evil; we have rebelled and turned from
your commandments and your laws. 6We
have not obeyed your servants the prophets,
who spoke in your name to our kings, our
princes, our ancestors, and all the people of
the land. 7Justice, O Lord, is on your side;
we are shamefaced even to this day: the men
of Judah, the residents of Jerusalem, and all
Israel, near and far, in all the lands to which
you have scattered them because of their
treachery toward you. 8O LORD, we are
ashamed, like our kings, our princes, and our
ancestors, for having sinned against you.
9But to the Lord, our God, belong compassion and forgiveness, though we rebelled
against him 10and did not hear the voice of
the LORD, our God, by walking in his laws
given through his servants the prophets.
11v The curse and the oath written in the law
of Moses, the servant of God, were poured
out over us for our sins, because all Israel
transgressed your law and turned aside, refusing to hear your voice. 12He fulfilled the
words he spoke against us and against those
who ruled us, by bringing upon us an evil—
no evil so great has happened under heaven
as happened in Jerusalem. 13As it is written*
in the law of Moses, this evil has come upon
us. We did not appease the LORD, our God,
by turning back from our wickedness and
acting according to your truth, 14so the LORD
kept watch over the evil and brought it upon
us. The LORD, our God, is just in all that he
has done: we did not listen to his voice.

15"Now, Lord, our God, who led your
people out of the land of Egypt with a strong
hand, and made a name for yourself even to
this day, we have sinned, we are guilty.
16Lord, in keeping with all your just deeds,
let your anger and your wrath be turned
away from your city Jerusalem, your holy
mountain. On account of our sins and the
crimes of our ancestors, Jerusalem and your
people have become the reproach of all our
neighbors. 17Now, our God, hear the prayer
and petition of your servant; and for your
own sake, Lord, let your face shine upon
your desolate sanctuary. 18Give ear, my God,
and listen; open your eyes and look upon our
desolate city upon which your name is invoked. When we present our petition before
you, we rely not on our just deeds, but on
your great mercy. 19Lord, hear! Lord, pardon! Lord, be attentive and act without delay, for your own sake, my God, because
your name is invoked upon your city and
your people!"

20I was still praying to the LORD, my God,
confessing my sin and the sin of my people
Israel, presenting my petition concerning the
holy mountain of my God—21I was still
praying, when the man, Gabriel, whom I had
seen in vision before, came to me in flight at
the time of the evening offering.* 22He instructed me in these words: "Daniel, I have
now come to give you understanding.
23When you began your petition, an answer
was given which I have come to announce,
because you are beloved. Therefore, mark
the answer and understand the vision.

24 "Seventy weeks* are decreed
for your people and for your holy city:
Then transgression will stop and sin will
end,
guilt will be expiated,
Everlasting justice will be introduced,
vision and prophecy ratified,
and a holy of holies will be anointed.
25 Know and understand:

subsequent return of the Jews to Palestine. However, the author of Daniel, living during the persecution of Antiochus, extends Jeremiah's number to seventy weeks of years (Dn 9:24), i.e., seven times seventy years, to encompass the period of Seleucid persecution.

**9:13 As it is written**: the first time that this formula of Scriptural citation is used in the Bible. The reference (v. 11) is to the sanctions of Lv 26:14–16; Dt 28:15–17.

**9:21 At the time of the evening offering**: between three and four in the afternoon.

**9:24 Seventy weeks**: i.e., of years. Just as Jeremiah's seventy years was an approximation (see note on v. 2), the four hundred and ninety years here is not to be taken literally. Similarly, the distribution of the "weeks" in the following verses indicates only relative proportions of the total figure. **A holy of holies**: or "most holy"; could be understood as a place (e.g., the Jerusalem Temple) or a person (cf. 1 Chr 23:13).

*v*: Dt 27:15.

From the utterance of the word
that Jerusalem was to be rebuilt*
Until there is an anointed ruler,
there shall be seven weeks.
In the course of sixty-two weeks
it shall be rebuilt,
With squares and trenches,
in time of affliction.
26 After the sixty-two weeks
an anointed one* shall be cut down
with no one to help him.
And the people of a leader who will
come
shall destroy the city and the sanctuary.
His end shall come in a flood;
until the end of the war, which is
decreed,
there will be desolation.
27 For one week* he shall make
a firm covenant with the many;
Half the week
he shall abolish sacrifice and offering;
In their place shall be the desolating
abomination
until the ruin that is decreed
is poured out upon the desolator."[w]

## CHAPTER 10

See RG 237

*An Angelic Vision.** 1 In the third year
of Cyrus, king of Persia, a revelation was
given to Daniel, who had been named Belteshazzar. The revelation was certain: a great
war;* he understood this from the vision. 2 In
those days, I, Daniel, mourned three full
weeks. 3 I ate no savory food, took no meat
or wine, and did not anoint myself at all until the end of the three weeks.
4 On the twenty-fourth day of the first
month* I was on the bank of the great river,
the Tigris. 5 As I looked up, I saw a man*
dressed in linen with a belt of fine gold
around his waist.[x] 6 His body was like chrysolite, his face shone like lightning, his eyes
were like fiery torches, his arms and feet
looked like burnished bronze, and the sound
of his voice was like the roar of a multitude.
7 I alone, Daniel, saw the vision; but great
fear seized those who were with me; they
fled and hid themselves, although they did
not see the vision. 8 So I was left alone to see
this great vision. No strength remained in
me; I turned the color of death and was powerless. 9 When I heard the sound of his voice,
I fell face forward unconscious.
10 But then a hand touched me, raising me
to my hands and knees. 11 "Daniel, beloved,"
he said to me, "understand the words which
I am speaking to you; stand up, for my mission now is to you." When he said this to me,
I stood up trembling. 12 "Do not fear, Daniel," he continued; "from the first day you
made up your mind to acquire understanding
and humble yourself before God, your
prayer was heard. Because of it I started out,
13 but the prince of the kingdom of Persia*
stood in my way for twenty-one days, until
finally Michael, one of the chief princes,
came to help me. I left him there with the
prince of the kingdom of Persia, 14 and came
to make you understand what shall happen

**9:25 From the utterance . . . to be rebuilt**: from the time of Jeremiah's prophecy. **Anointed ruler**: either Cyrus, who was called the anointed of the Lord to end the exile (Is 45:1), or the high priest Jeshua who presided over the rebuilding of the altar of sacrifice after the exile (Ezr 3:2). **Seven weeks**: forty-nine years, an approximation of the time of the exile. **In the course of sixty-two weeks . . . rebuilt**: a period of four hundred thirty-four years, roughly approximating the interval between the rebuilding of Jerusalem after the exile and the beginning of the Seleucid persecution.

**9:26 An anointed one**: the high priest Onias III, murdered in 171 B.C., from which the author dates the beginning of the persecution. Onias was in exile when he was killed. **A leader**: Antiochus IV.

**9:27 One week**: the final phase of the period in view, the time of Antiochus' persecution. **He**: Antiochus himself. **The many**: the faithless Jews who allied themselves with the Seleucids; cf. 1 Mc 1:11–13. **Half the week**: three and a half years; the Temple was desecrated by Antiochus from 167 to 164 B.C. **The desolating abomination**: see note on 8:13; probably a pagan altar. Jesus refers to this passage in his prediction of the destruction of Jerusalem in Mt 24:15.

**10:1–12:13** This final vision is concerned with history from the time of Cyrus to the death of Antiochus Epiphanes.

**10:1 A great war**: or "the service was great," or "a mighty host." The Hebrew is ambiguous.

**10:4 The first month**: the month Nisan (mid-March to mid-April).

**10:5–6** The heavenly person of the vision is probably the angel Gabriel, as in 9:21. **Chrysolite**: or topaz, a yellowish precious stone. Cf. the visions in Ez 1 and 8.

**10:13 The prince of the kingdom of Persia**: the angelic guardian of Persia. Where older texts speak of the gods of various countries (Dt 32:8), Daniel speaks of "princes." **Michael**: the patron angel of Israel (v. 21).

*w:* Mt 24:15; 1 Mc 1:54. *x:* Ez 10:2.

to your people in the last days; for there is
yet a vision concerning those days."
15While he was speaking thus to me, I fell
forward and kept silent. 16Then something
like a hand touched my lips; I opened my
mouth and said to the one standing before
me, "My lord, I was seized with pangs at the
vision and I was powerless. 17How can my
lord's servant speak with you, my lord? For
now no strength or even breath is left in me."
18The one who looked like a man touched
me again and strengthened me, saying,
19"Do not fear, beloved. Peace! Take
courage and be strong." When he spoke to
me, I grew strong and said, "Speak, my lord,
for you have strengthened me." 20"Do you
know," he asked, "why I have come to you?
Soon I must fight the prince of Persia again.
When I leave, the prince of Greece will
come; 21but I shall tell you what is written in
the book of truth.* No one supports me
against these except Michael,[y] your prince,
11:1and in the first year of Darius the Mede I
stood to strengthen him and be his refuge.

## CHAPTER 11

See RG 237

*The Hellenistic Age.* 2"Now I shall tell
you the truth.
"Three kings of Persia* are yet to appear;
and a fourth shall acquire the greatest riches
of all. Strengthened by his riches, he shall
stir up all kingdoms, even that of Greece.
3But a powerful king* shall appear and rule
with great might, doing as he wills. 4No
sooner shall he appear than his kingdom
shall be broken and divided in four directions under heaven; but not among his descendants or in keeping with his mighty rule,
for his kingdom shall be torn to pieces and
belong to others.
5* "The king of the south shall grow
strong, but one of his princes shall grow
stronger still and govern a domain greater
than his. 6* After some years they shall become allies: the daughter of the king of the
south shall come to the king of the north to
carry out the alliance. But she shall not retain power: and his offspring shall not survive, and she shall be given up, together
with those who brought her, her son, and her
supporter in due time. 7A descendant of her
line shall succeed to his place, and shall
come against the army, enter the stronghold
of the king of the north, attack and conquer
them. 8Even their gods, with their molten
images and their precious vessels of silver
and gold, he shall carry away as spoils of
war into Egypt. For years he shall have nothing to do with the king of the north. 9Then
the latter shall invade the land of the king of
the south, and return to his own country.
10"But his sons shall be aroused and assemble a great armed host, which shall pass
through like a flood and again surge around
the stronghold. 11* The king of the south, enraged, shall go out to fight against the king
of the north, who shall field a great host, but
the host shall be given into his hand. 12When
the host is carried off, in the pride of his
heart he shall bring down tens of thousands,
but he shall not triumph. 13* For the king of
the north shall raise another army, greater
than before; after some years he shall attack
with this large army and great resources. 14In
those times many shall resist the king of the
south, and violent ones among your people
shall rise up in fulfillment of vision, but they
shall stumble. 15* When the king of the north
comes, he shall set up siegeworks and take
the fortified city by storm. The forces of the

**10:21 The book of truth**: a heavenly book in which future events are already recorded; cf. 7:10; 12:1.

**11:2 Three kings of Persia**: it is unclear which kings are intended because there were more than three Persian kings between Cyrus and the dissolution of the kingdom. The fourth is Xerxes I (486–465 B.C.), the great campaigner against Greece.

**11:3 A powerful king**: Alexander the Great, who broke Persian dominance by his victory at Issus in 333 B.C.

**11:5–45** These verses describe the dynastic histories of the Ptolemies in Egypt (the king of the south) and the Seleucids in Syria (the king of the north), the two divisions of the Hellenistic empire that were of interest to the author (v. 6). Verses 10–20 describe the struggle between the two kingdoms for the control of Palestine; the Seleucids were eventually victorious.

**11:6** The marriage of Antiochus II Theos and Berenice of Egypt about 250 B.C., which ended in tragedy.

**11:11** The battle of Raphia (217 B.C.), in which Egypt defeated Syria.

**11:13** Syria defeated Egypt at the battle of Paneas in 200 B.C. Judea then passed under Syrian rule.

**11:15** The siege of Sidon after the battle of Paneas.

*y:* Rev 12:7.

south shall not withstand him, and not even
his picked troops shall have the strength to
withstand. 16 The invader shall do as he wills,
with no one to withstand him. He shall stop
in the glorious land, and it shall all be in his
power. 17* He shall resolve to come with the
entire strength of his kingdom. He shall
make an alliance with him and give him a
daughter in marriage in order to destroy him,
but this shall not stand. 18* He shall turn to
the coastland and take many prisoners, but a
commander shall put an end to his shameful
conduct, so that he cannot retaliate. 19 He
shall turn to the strongholds of his own land,
but shall stumble and fall, to be found no
more. 20* In his stead one shall arise who
will send a collector of tribute through the
glorious kingdom, but he shall soon be destroyed, though not in conflict or in battle.

21* "There shall arise in his place a despi-
cable person, to whom the royal insignia
shall not be given. He shall enter by stealth
and seize the kingdom by fraud. 22 Armed
forces shall be completely overwhelmed by
him and crushed, even the prince of the covenant.* 23 After making alliances, he shall
treacherously rise to power with only a few
supporters. 24 By stealth he shall enter prosperous provinces and do that which his fathers or grandfathers never did; he shall distribute spoil, plunder, and riches among
them and devise plots against their strongholds. 25 He shall rouse his strength and
courage to meet the king of the south with a
great army; the king of the south shall go
into battle with a very large and strong army,
but he shall not stand because of the plots
devised against him. 26 Even his table companions shall seek to destroy him, his army
shall be overwhelmed, and many shall be
struck down. 27 The two kings, resolved on
evil, shall sit at table together and exchange
lies, but they shall have no success, because
the appointed end is not yet.

28 "He* shall turn back toward his land
with great riches, his mind set against the
holy covenant; he shall take action and return to his land. 29 At the time appointed he
shall come again to the south, but this time it
shall not be as before. 30 When ships of the
Kittim* confront him, he shall lose heart and
retreat. Then he shall rage against the holy
covenant and take action; he shall again favor those who forsake the holy covenant.
31 Armed forces shall rise at his command
and defile the sanctuary stronghold, abolishing the daily sacrifice and setting up the desolating abomination. 32 By his deceit he shall
make some who were disloyal forsake the
covenant; but those who remain loyal to
their God shall take strong action. 33 Those
with insight among the people shall instruct
the many; though for a time the sword,
flames, exile, and plunder will cause them to
stumble. 34 When they stumble, they will be
helped,* but only a little; many shall join
them, but out of treachery. 35 Some of those
with insight shall stumble so that they may
be tested, refined, and purified, until the end
time which is still appointed to come.

36 "The king shall do as he wills, exalting
himself and making himself greater than any
god; he shall utter dreadful blasphemies
against the God of gods. He shall prosper
only till the wrath is finished, for what is determined must take place. 37 He shall have no
regard for the gods of his ancestors or for the
one in whom women delight;* for no god
shall he have regard, because he shall make
himself greater than all. 38 Instead, he shall

**11:17** Antiochus III, the Great, betrothed his daughter to Ptolemy Epiphanes in 197 B.C.

**11:18** The Roman general Scipio defeated Antiochus at Magnesia in 190 B.C.

**11:20** Seleucus IV, who sent Heliodorus to Jerusalem (cf. 2 Mc 3).

**11:21** Here begins the career of Antiochus IV Epiphanes.

**11:22 The prince of the covenant**: the high priest Onias III, who was murdered.

**11:28 He**: the king of the north, probably Antiochus IV.

**11:30 Kittim**: originally this word meant Cypriots or other westerners. It is sometimes used for the Greeks (1 Mc 1:1). Here it refers to the Romans, who forced Antiochus to withdraw from Egypt during his second campaign there.

**11:34 Helped**: this may be a reference to the Maccabean revolt. The apocalyptic author expects deliverance from God and has little regard for human efforts. In fact, the Maccabees routed the Syrian troops, recaptured Jerusalem, purified and rededicated the Temple, and brought to an end the Syrian persecution.

**11:37 The one in whom women delight**: Tammuz. Antiochus favored the cult of Zeus. Daniel takes this to imply the neglect of all other gods, although this does not appear to have been the case.

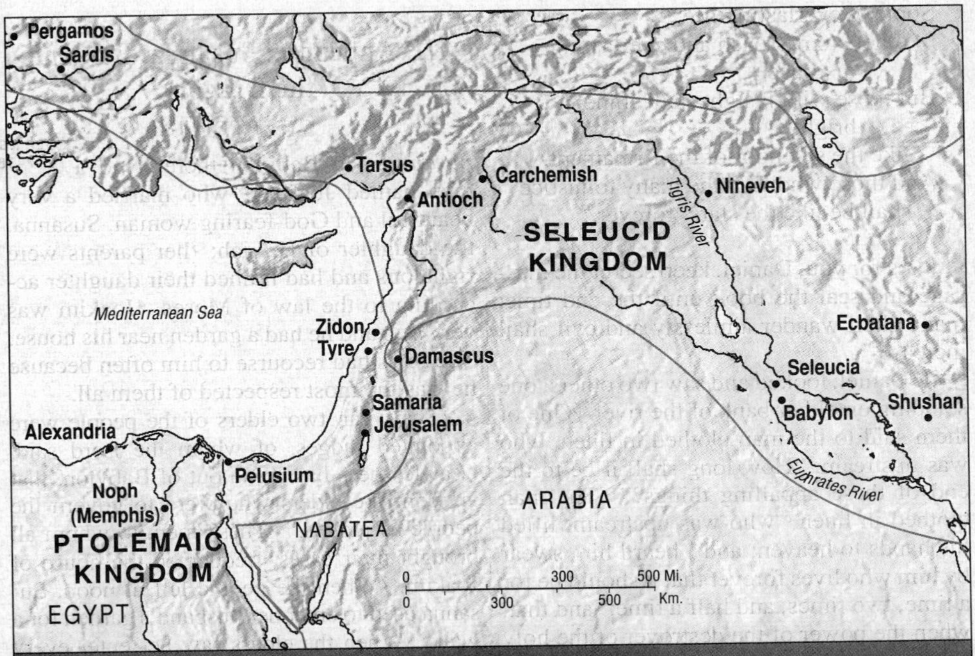


**The Ptolemaic and Seleucid Kingdoms**

give glory to the god of strongholds;* a god
unknown to his ancestors he shall glorify
with gold, silver, precious stones, and other
treasures. 39 He shall act for those who fortify
strongholds, a people of a foreign god,
whom he has recognized. He shall greatly
honor them; he shall make them rule over
the many and distribute the land as a reward.

40* "At the end time the king of the south
shall engage him in battle but the king of the
north shall overwhelm him with chariots and
horsemen and a great fleet, passing through
the lands like a flood. 41 He shall enter the
glorious land and many shall fall, except
Edom, Moab, and the chief part of Ammon,
which shall escape his power. 42 He shall extend his power over the land, and not even
Egypt shall escape. 43 He shall control the
riches of gold and silver and all the treasures
of Egypt; Libya and Ethiopia shall be in his
entourage. 44 When reports from the east and
the north disturb him, he shall set out with
great fury to destroy many, putting them under the ban. 45 He shall pitch the tents of his
royal pavilion between the sea and the glorious holy mountain, but he shall come to his
end with none to help him.

## CHAPTER 12

See RG 237

### *The Resurrection*

1 "At that time there shall arise Michael,[z]
the great prince,
guardian of your people;
It shall be a time unsurpassed in distress
since the nation began until that time.
At that time your people shall escape,
everyone who is found written in the
book.*
2 Many of those who sleep*
in the dust of the earth shall awake;

**11:38 The god of strongholds**: the god worshiped in the fortress Akra, which Antiochus established in Jerusalem.

**11:40–45** In these concluding verses, the events described no longer correspond to the history of the Maccabean period. Daniel imagines the death of Antiochus on the model of Gog in Ez 38–39. Antiochus actually died in Persia.

**12:1 Written in the book**: cf. 10:21.

**12:2 Many of those who sleep**: Daniel does not envisage the universal resurrection as later developed. Two groups are distinguished, one that rises to eternal life, the other to re-

*z:* Rev 12:7.

Some to everlasting life,
others to reproach and everlasting
disgrace.[a]
3 But those with insight shall shine
brightly
like the splendor of the firmament,
And those who lead the many to justice
shall be like the stars* forever.[b]

4“As for you, Daniel, keep secret the message and seal the book until the end time;
many shall wander aimlessly and evil shall
increase.”
5I, Daniel, looked and saw two others, one
standing on either bank of the river. 6One of
them said to the man clothed in linen, who
was upstream, “How long shall it be to the
end of these appalling things?” 7The man
clothed in linen,[c] who was upstream, lifted
his hands to heaven; and I heard him swear
by him who lives forever that it should be for
a time, two times, and half a time;* and that,
when the power of the destroyer of the holy
people was brought to an end, all these
things should end. 8I heard, but I did not understand; so I asked, “My lord, what follows
this?” 9“Go, Daniel,” he said, “because the
words are to be kept secret and sealed until
the end time. 10Many shall be refined, purified, and tested, but the wicked shall prove
wicked; the wicked shall have no understanding, but those with insight shall.
11* From the time that the daily sacrifice is
abolished and the desolating abomination is
set up, there shall be one thousand two hundred and ninety days. 12Blessed are they who
have patience and persevere for the one
thousand three hundred and thirty-five days.
13Go, take your rest, you shall rise for your
reward at the end of days.”

# III. Appendix: Susanna, Bel, and the Dragon*

## CHAPTER 13

See RG 237-38

*Susanna.* 1In Babylon there lived a
man named Joakim, 2who married a very
beautiful and God-fearing woman, Susanna,
the daughter of Hilkiah; 3her parents were
righteous and had trained their daughter according to the law of Moses. 4Joakim was
very rich and he had a garden near his house.
The Jews had recourse to him often because
he was the most respected of them all.
5That year, two elders of the people were
appointed judges, of whom the Lord said,
“Lawlessness has come out of Babylon, that
is, from the elders who were to govern the
people as judges.” 6These men, to whom all
brought their cases, frequented the house of
Joakim. 7When the people left at noon, Susanna used to enter her husband’s garden for a
walk. 8When the elders saw her enter every
day for her walk, they began to lust for her.
9They perverted their thinking; they would not
allow their eyes to look to heaven, and did not
keep in mind just judgments. 10Though both
were enamored of her, they did not tell each
other their trouble, 11for they were ashamed to
reveal their lustful desire to have her. 12Day by
day they watched eagerly for her. 13One day
they said to each other, “Let us be off for
home, it is time for the noon meal.” So they
went their separate ways. 14But both turned
back and arrived at the same spot. When they
asked each other the reason, they admitted
their lust, and then they agreed to look for an
occasion when they could find her alone.
15One day, while they were waiting for the
right moment, she entered as usual, with two

proach and disgrace. Then “those with insight” (11:33–35) are singled out for special honor.

**12:3 Like the stars**: like the heavenly host, or angels. Cf. Mt 22:30.

**12:7 A time, two times, and half a time**: see note on 7:25.

**12:11** The specific numbers of days given in vv. 11–12 represent attempts to calculate the precise duration of the three and a half years. Most probably, when the first date (1,290 days) passed, the author attempted another calculation. Another, earlier calculation is preserved in 8:14. It is noteworthy, however, that the contradictory numbers were allowed to stand in the text; this is a reminder that it is not possible to calculate a precise date for God’s judgment; cf. Mk 13:32.

**13:1–14:42** The short stories in these two chapters exist now only in Greek and other translations, but probably were first composed in Hebrew or Aramaic. They were never part of the Hebrew-Aramaic Book of Daniel, or of the Hebrew Bible. They are excluded from the Protestant canon of Scripture, but the Catholic Church has always included them among the inspired writings; they existed in the Septuagint, which was used as its Bible by the early church.

*a:* Is 66:24; Mt 25:46; Jn 5:29. *b:* Wis 3:7. *c:* Rev 10:5–6.

maids only, wanting to bathe in the garden,
for the weather was warm. 16Nobody else
was there except the two elders, who had
hidden themselves and were watching her.
17“Bring me oil and soap,” she said to the
maids, “and shut the garden gates while I
bathe.” 18They did as she said; they shut the
garden gates and left by the side gate to fetch
what she had ordered, unaware that the elders were hidden inside.

19As soon as the maids had left, the two
old men got up and ran to her. 20“Look,”
they said, “the garden doors are shut, no one
can see us, and we want you. So give in to
our desire, and lie with us. 21If you refuse,
we will testify against you that a young man
was here with you and that is why you sent
your maids away.”

22“I am completely trapped,” Susanna
groaned. “If I yield, it will be my death; if I refuse, I cannot escape your power. 23Yet it is
better for me not to do it and to fall into your
power than to sin before the Lord.” 24Then Susanna screamed, and the two old men also
shouted at her, 25as one of them ran to open the
garden gates. 26When the people in the house
heard the cries from the garden, they rushed in
by the side gate to see what had happened to
her. 27At the accusations of the old men, the
servants felt very much ashamed, for never
had any such thing been said about Susanna.

28When the people came to her husband
Joakim the next day, the two wicked old men
also came, full of lawless intent to put Susanna
to death. 29Before the people they ordered:
“Send for Susanna, the daughter of Hilkiah,
the wife of Joakim.” When she was sent for,
30she came with her parents, children and all
her relatives. 31Susanna, very delicate and
beautiful, 32was veiled; but those transgressors of the law ordered that she be exposed so
as to sate themselves with her beauty. 33All her
companions and the onlookers were weeping.

34In the midst of the people the two old
men rose up and laid their hands on her head.
35As she wept she looked up to heaven, for
she trusted in the Lord wholeheartedly. 36The
old men said, “As we were walking in the
garden alone, this woman entered with two
servant girls, shut the garden gates and sent
the servant girls away. 37A young man, who
was hidden there, came and lay with her.
38When we, in a corner of the garden, saw
this lawlessness, we ran toward them. 39We
saw them lying together, but the man we
could not hold, because he was stronger than
we; he opened the gates and ran off. 40Then
we seized this one and asked who the young
man was, 41but she refused to tell us. We testify to this.” The assembly believed them,
since they were elders and judges of the people, and they condemned her to death.

42But Susanna cried aloud: “Eternal God,
you know what is hidden and are aware of
all things before they come to be: 43you
know that they have testified falsely against
me. Here I am about to die, though I have
done none of the things for which these men
have condemned me.”

44The Lord heard her prayer. 45As she was
being led to execution, God stirred up the
holy spirit of a young boy named Daniel,
46and he cried aloud: “I am innocent of this
woman’s blood.” 47All the people turned and
asked him, “What are you saying?” 48He
stood in their midst and said, “Are you such
fools, you Israelites, to condemn a daughter
of Israel without investigation and without
clear evidence? 49Return to court, for they
have testified falsely against her.”

50Then all the people returned in haste. To
Daniel the elders said, “Come, sit with us
and inform us, since God has given you the
prestige of old age.” 51But he replied, “Separate these two far from one another, and I
will examine them.”

52After they were separated from each
other, he called one of them and said: “How
you have grown evil with age! Now have
your past sins come to term: 53passing unjust
sentences, condemning the innocent, and
freeing the guilty,[d] although the Lord says,
‘The innocent and the just you shall not put to
death.’ 54Now, then, if you were a witness, tell
me under what tree you saw them together.”
55“Under a mastic tree,”* he answered. “Your

**13:55–59** The contrast between the mastic tree, which is small, and the majestic oak emphasizes the contradiction between the statements of the two elders. In the Greek text there is a play on words between the names of these two trees and

*d:* Ex 23:7.

fine lie has cost you your head,” said Daniel;
“for the angel of God has already received the
sentence from God and shall split you in
two.” 56Putting him to one side, he ordered
the other one to be brought. “Offspring of Canaan, not of Judah,” Daniel said to him,
“beauty has seduced you, lust has perverted
your heart. 57This is how you acted with the
daughters of Israel, and in their fear they
yielded to you; but a daughter of Judah did
not tolerate your lawlessness. 58Now, then,
tell me under what tree you surprised them together.” 59“Under an oak,” he said. “Your fine
lie has cost you also your head,” said Daniel;
“for the angel of God waits with a sword to
cut you in two so as to destroy you both.”

60The whole assembly cried aloud, blessing God who saves those who hope in him.
61They rose up against the two old men, for
by their own words Daniel had convicted
them of bearing false witness.[e] They condemned them to the fate they had planned
for their neighbor: 62in accordance with the
law of Moses they put them to death. Thus
was innocent blood spared that day.

63Hilkiah and his wife praised God for
their daughter Susanna, with Joakim her
husband and all her relatives, because she
was found innocent of any shameful deed.
64And from that day onward Daniel was
greatly esteemed by the people.

## CHAPTER 14

See RG 237–38

*Bel and the Dragon.** 1After King
Astyages* was gathered to his ancestors, Cyrus the Persian succeeded to his kingdom.
2Daniel was a companion of the king and was
held in higher honor than any of the Friends of
the King. 3The Babylonians had an idol called
Bel,* and every day they provided for it six
bushels of fine flour, forty sheep, and six
measures of wine. 4The king revered it and
went every day to worship it; but Daniel worshiped only his God. 5When the king asked
him, “Why do you not worship Bel?” Daniel
replied, “Because I do not revere idols made
with hands, but only the living God who made
heaven and earth and has dominion over all
flesh.” 6Then the king continued, “You do not
think Bel is a living god? Do you not see how
much he eats and drinks every day?” 7Daniel
began to laugh. “Do not be deceived, O king,”
he said; “it is only clay inside and bronze outside; it has never eaten or drunk anything.”
8Enraged, the king called his priests and said
to them, “Unless you tell me who it is that consumes these provisions, you shall die. But if
you can show that Bel consumes them, Daniel
shall die for blaspheming Bel.” 9Daniel said to
the king, “Let it be as you say!”

There were seventy priests of Bel, besides
their wives and children. 10* When the king
went with Daniel into the temple of Bel, 11the
priests of Bel said, “See, we are going to leave.
You, O king, set out the food and prepare the
wine; then shut the door and seal it with your
ring. 12* If you do not find that Bel has eaten it
all when you return in the morning, we are to
die; otherwise Daniel shall die for his lies
against us.” 13They were not perturbed, because under the table they had made a secret
entrance through which they always came in

the mortal punishment decreed by Daniel for the elders. The mastic tree (*schinon*) sounds like the verb “to split” (*schisai*). The oak tree (*prinon*) suggests a play on *poisai* (to saw).

**14:1–22** In chap. 14, readings in the Septuagint differ markedly from those in Theodotion, which is followed here. See individual notes on 1–3a, 10–11, 12–14, 15–17 and 21–22; the translation is that of Collins, *Daniel*, pp. 405ff, with brackets indicating additions to the Septuagint according to Collins.

**14:1–3a** These verses in the Septuagint Greek text read: “From the prophecy of Habakkuk, son of Joshua, of the tribe of Levi. 2 There was a certain man, a priest, whose name was Daniel, son of Abal, a companion of the king of Babylon. 3 There was an idol, Bel, which the Babylonians revered, . . .” This may represent an earlier form of the story, before it was attached to the Book of Daniel. **King Astyages**: the last of the Median kings, defeated by Cyrus in 550 B.C. This story preserves the fiction of a successive Median and Persian rule of Babylon.

**14:3 Bel**: see note on 4:5.

**14:10–11** These verses in the Septuagint Greek text read: “(Now, there were seventy priests of Bel, apart from women and children.) They led the king to the idol shrine. 11 The food was set out in the presence of the king and of Daniel, and mixed wine was brought in and set before Bel. Daniel said, ‘You yourself see that these things are laid out, O king. You, therefore, seal the door of temple when it is closed.’ [The word pleased the king.]”

**14:12–14** Theodotion’s vv. 12–13 and 14’s “After they departed the king set the food before Bel” are lacking in the Septuagint Greek text, which continues vv. 15–17 from v. 11 as follows: “Then Daniel commanded his attendants to make everyone go out from the temple and sprinkle the whole tem-

*e:* Dt 19:18–19.

to consume the food. 14 After they departed the king set the food before Bel, while Daniel ordered his servants to bring some ashes, which they scattered through the whole temple; the king alone was present. Then they went outside, sealed the closed door with the king's ring, and departed. 15* The priests entered that night as usual, with their wives and children, and they ate and drank everything.

16 Early the next morning, the king came with Daniel. 17 "Are the seals unbroken, Daniel?" he asked. And Daniel answered, "They are unbroken, O king." 18 As soon as he had opened the door, the king looked at the table and cried aloud, "You are great, O Bel; there is no deceit in you." 19* But Daniel laughed and kept the king from entering. He said, "Look at the floor and consider whose footprints these are." 20 "I see the footprints of men, women, and children!" said the king. 21* In his wrath the king arrested the priests, their wives, and their children. They showed him the secret door by which they used to enter to consume what was on the table. 22 The king put them to death, and handed Bel over to Daniel, who destroyed it and its temple.

23 There was a great dragon* which the Babylonians revered. 24 The king said to Daniel, "You cannot deny that this is a living god, so worship it." 25 But Daniel answered, "I worship the Lord, my God, for he is the living God. 26 Give me permission, O king, and I will kill this dragon without sword or club." "I give you permission," the king said. 27 Then Daniel took some pitch, fat, and hair; these he boiled together and made into cakes. He put them into the mouth of the dragon, and when the dragon ate them, he burst. "This," he said, "is what you revered."

28 When the Babylonians heard this, they were angry and turned against the king. "The king has become a Jew," they said; "he has destroyed Bel, killed the dragon, and put the priests to death." 29 They went to the king and demanded: "Hand Daniel over to us, or we will kill you and your family." 30 When he saw himself threatened with violence, the king was forced to hand Daniel over to them. 31 They threw Daniel into a lions' den,* where he remained six days. 32 In the den were seven lions. Two carcasses and two sheep had been given to them daily, but now they were given nothing, so that they would devour Daniel.

33 The prophet Habakkuk was in Judea. He mixed some bread in a bowl with the stew he had boiled, and was going to bring it to the reapers in the field, 34 when an angel of the Lord told him, "Take the meal you have to Daniel in the lions' den at Babylon." 35 But Habakkuk answered, "Sir, I have never seen Babylon, and I do not know the den!" 36 The angel of the Lord seized him by the crown of his head and carried him by the hair;[f] with the speed of the wind, he set him down in Babylon above the den. 37 "Daniel, Daniel," cried Habakkuk, "take the meal God has sent you." 38 "You have remembered me, O God," said Daniel; "you have not forsaken those who love you." 39 So Daniel ate, but the angel of God at once brought Habakkuk back to his own place.

40 On the seventh day the king came to mourn for Daniel. As he came to the den and looked in, there was Daniel, sitting there. 41 The king cried aloud, "You are great, O Lord, the God of Daniel, and there is no other besides you!" 42 He brought Daniel out, but those who had tried to destroy him he threw into the den, and they were devoured in a moment before his eyes.

ple with ashes, unknown to anyone outside. Then he ordered them to apply the seal with the king's ring [and the seals of certain illustrious priests, and so it was done]."

**14:15–17** These verses in the Septuagint Greek text read: "15 On the next day they came to the place. But the priests of Bel had entered through false doors and had eaten all that was set forth for Bel and drunk the wine. Daniel said, 'See whether your seals remain, O priests, and you, O king, see that nothing has happened that seems improper to you.' They found the seal as it had been, and they removed the seal."

**14:19** Note that here the king seems unaware of Daniel's ruse.

**14:21–22** These verses in the Septuagint Greek text read: "21 And he went to the house where the priests had come, and he found Bel's food and the wine, and Daniel showed the king the false doors through which the priests entered and consumed what had been set before Bel. 22 The king led them out of the temple of Bel and gave them over to Daniel. He gave Daniel what was expended on him and destroyed Bel."

**14:23 Dragon**: or "serpent," and see v. 27. Sacred snakes are well attested in the ancient world (e.g., in the temple of the god of healing Asclepius at Epidaurus), though evidence for their veneration in Babylon is doubtful.

**14:31 A lions' den**: this story provides a different account from chap. 6 as to why Daniel was associated with the lions' den.

*f*: Ez 8:3.

See RG 240–44

# The Book of Hosea

Hosea, a prophet from the Northern Kingdom, preached in his homeland, which he addresses as Israel, Jacob or, frequently, Ephraim. Hosea began his mission in a period of prosperity, the last years of Jeroboam II (783–743 B.C.). This was followed by a period of internal instability, with intrigues at the royal court leading to the assassination of several kings. Hosea witnessed the revival of Assyria, the Syro-Ephraimite war, and the numerous treaties the Israelite kings made with Egypt and Assyria to survive. Hosea's long ministry (ca. 750–725) seems to have ended before the capture of Samaria in 722/721.

The only information the text provides us about the life of Hosea concerns his marriage. Even if we cannot reconstruct what happened exactly, the text as it now stands speaks of three moments in the relationship: first love, separation, reunion. This marriage is a symbol of the covenant between the Lord and Israel. Hosea speaks about the first love, the short period of Israel's loyalty in the desert, which was then followed by a long history of unfaithfulness lasting until his day. Hosea accuses Israel of three crimes in particular. Instead of putting their trust in the Lord alone, the people break the covenant: (1) by counting on their own military strength, (2) by making treaties with foreign powers (Assyria and Egypt), and (3) by running after the Baals, the gods of fertility. Israel thus forgets that the Lord is its strength, its covenant partner, and giver of fertility. This unfaithful behavior will lead to Israel's destruction by Assyria, but God's love will have the last word. The back and forth movement from doom to salvation is typical of the Book of Hosea.

Hosea began the Old Testament tradition of describing the relation between the Lord and Israel in terms of marriage (e.g., Jer 3:1; Ez 16:23; Is 50:1). The New Testament uses the marriage imagery to describe the union between Christ and the Church (e.g., Mk 2:19–20; Eph 5:25).

The Hebrew of the Book of Hosea is challenging to translate, possibly because the text is corrupt or because it is written in a nonstandard dialect of Hebrew. As a result, the English translations of the book sometimes offer very different readings of the same passage.

The book, which opens with a superscription (1:1) and ends with a final challenge (14:10), is divided into two major parts:

I. The Prophet's Marriage and Its Symbolism (1:2–3:5)

II. Israel's Guilt, Punishment, and Restoration (4:1–14:9)

## CHAPTER 1

See RG 241–44

1* The word of the LORD that came to
Hosea son of Beeri, in the days of Uzziah,
Jotham, Ahaz, Hezekiah, kings of Judah,
and in the days of Jeroboam, son of Joash,
king of Israel.*

## I. The Prophet's Marriage and Its Symbolism

*Marriage of Hosea and Gomer.* 2When the
LORD began to speak with Hosea, the LORD
said to Hosea: Go, get for yourself a woman
of prostitution* and children of prostitution,
for the land prostitutes itself,[a] turning away
from the LORD.
3So he went and took Gomer, daughter of
Diblaim; and she conceived and bore him a
son. 4Then the LORD said to him: Give him
the name "Jezreel,"* for in a little while I will
punish the house of Jehu for the bloodshed at

**1:1–3** This section begins with Hosea's marriage to Gomer, which symbolizes Israel's relationship to God. Hence the symbolic names of Hosea's children and their later renaming (1:2–9; 2:1–3). The prophet foresees God's punishment for the unfaithful covenant partner, but knows that God's last word is always hope (2:4–25).

**1:1** This superscription is from a Judean editor, who lists the kings of Judah in the south first, even though Hosea preached in the Northern Kingdom of Israel.

**1:2 A woman of prostitution**: this does not necessarily mean that Gomer was a prostitute when Hosea married her; the verse describes the event in its final consequences. Prostitution here may refer to Gomer's participation in the worship of other gods.

**1:4 Give him the name "Jezreel"**: the names of the three children are symbolic, and predict God's punishment in a

*a:* Jer 2:20, 23; Ez 23:3.

Jezreel and bring to an end the kingdom of
the house of Israel; 5on that day I will break
the bow of Israel in the valley of Jezreel.

6She conceived again and bore a daughter.
The LORD said to him: Give her the name
"Not-Pitied,"* for I will no longer feel pity
for the house of Israel: rather, I will utterly
abhor them. 7* Yet for the house of Judah I
will feel pity; I will save them by the LORD,
their God; but I will not save them by bow or
sword, by warfare, by horses or horsemen.[b]

8After she weaned Not-Pitied, she conceived and bore a son. 9Then the LORD said:
Give him the name "Not-My-People,"* for
you are not my people, and I am not "I am"
for you.

## CHAPTER 2

See RG 241–44

1* The number of the Israelites
will be like the sand of the sea,
which can be neither measured nor counted.[c]
Instead of being told,
"You are Not-My-People,"
They will be called,
"Children of the living God."[d]
2 Then the people of Judah and of Israel
will gather together;
They will appoint for themselves one head
and rise up from the land;
great indeed shall be the day of Jezreel!
3 Say to your brothers, "My People,"
and to your sisters, "Pitied."

### *The Lord and Israel His Spouse**

4 Accuse your mother, accuse!
for she is not my wife,
and I am not her husband.*
Let her remove her prostitution from her face,
her adultery from between her breasts,
5 Or I will strip her naked,*
leaving her as on the day of her birth;
I will make her like the wilderness,
make her like an arid land,
and let her die of thirst.
6 I will have no pity on her children,
for they are children of prostitution.
7 Yes, their mother has prostituted herself;
she who conceived them has acted shamefully.
For she said, "I will go after my lovers,*
who give me my bread and my water,
my wool and my flax, my oil and my drink."[e]
8 * Therefore, I will hedge in her way with thorns
and erect a wall against her,
so that she cannot find her paths.
9 If she runs after her lovers, she will not overtake them;

crescendo. These names are frequently repeated in chaps. 1–2. **Jezreel**: (lit., "God will sow") the strategic valley in northern Israel where Jehu brought the dynasty of Omri to an end through bloodshed (2 Kgs 9–10). Jeroboam II was the next to the last king of the house of Jehu. The prophecy in this verse of the end of the house of Jehu was fulfilled by the murder of Zechariah, son of Jeroboam II (2 Kgs 15:8–10).

**1:6 "Not-Pitied"**: in Hebrew *lo-ruhama*.

**1:7** Probably written by a later editor when the prophecies of Hosea circulated in the south, after the dissolution of the Northern Kingdom had occurred. The second part of the verse emphasizes the power of the Lord, who needs no human agents to fulfill the divine will. It may refer to the deliverance of Jerusalem from the siege of Sennacherib in 701 (2 Kgs 19:35–37).

**1:9 "Not-My-People"**: in Hebrew *lo-ammi*. **I am not "I am" for you**: a reference to the divine name revealed to Moses, "I am" (Ex 3:14). This reversal of the relationship marks the end of the covenant (Ex 6:7).

**2:1–3** These verses abruptly reverse the tone of the judgments of 1:2–9 with words of hope for the covenant people: the name Jezreel is given a positive interpretation in contrast to its negative meaning in 1:4; the child named "Not-Pitied" in 1:6 is renamed "Pitied" in 2:3; the child named "Not-My-People" is renamed "My People." The reversal of these names occurs again in 2:25.

**2:4–25** The section contains three oracles of doom (vv. 4–6, 7–9, 10–15), a transition (vv. 16–17), and three oracles of salvation (vv. 18–19, 20–22, 23–25).

**2:4** The Lord speaks of Israel, still using the example of Hosea's wife.

**2:5 I will strip her naked**: it was the husband's responsibility to provide food and clothing for his wife (Ex 21:10) and now, because of her adultery, he takes back his support.

**2:7 My lovers**: even though Israel had experienced the Lord as the God of the desert, covenant and conquest, the people were inclined to turn to the local fertility deities, the Baals, who were believed to be responsible for agricultural success. They easily forgot that the Lord provides them with everything (v. 10; cf. Dt 7:13), and thus prostituted themselves by worshiping other gods.

**2:8** The crop failures sent by the Lord are meant to make Israel see the folly of its ways.

*b:* Zec 4:6. *c:* Gn 15:5; 22:17; 32:13. *d:* Rom 9:26–27. *e:* Jer 2:25.

if she seeks them she will not find them.
Then she will say,
"I will go back to my first husband,
for I was better off then than now."[f]

10 She did not know
that it was I who gave her
the grain, the wine, and the oil,
I who lavished upon her silver,
and gold, which they used for Baal,*
11 Therefore I will take back my grain in its time,
and my wine in its season;
I will snatch away my wool and my flax,
which were to cover her nakedness.
12 Now I will lay bare her shame
in full view of her lovers,[g]
and no one can deliver her out of my hand.[h]
13 I will put an end to all her joy,
her festivals, her new moons, her sabbaths—
all her seasonal feasts.
14 I will lay waste her vines and fig trees,
of which she said, "These are the fees
my lovers have given me";
I will turn them into rank growth
and wild animals shall devour them.
15 I will punish her for the days of the Baals,*
for whom she burnt incense,
When she decked herself out with her rings and her jewelry,
and went after her lovers—
but me she forgot—oracle of the LORD.[i]
16 Therefore,* I will allure her now;
I will lead her into the wilderness[j]
and speak persuasively to her.
17 Then I will give her the vineyards she had,
and the valley of Achor* as a door of hope.[k]
There she will respond as in the days of her youth,
as on the day when she came up from the land of Egypt.

18 On that day—oracle of the LORD—
You shall call me "My husband,"
and you shall never again call me "My baal."*
19 I will remove from her mouth the names of the Baals;
they shall no longer be mentioned by their name.

20 I will make a covenant for them on that day,[l]
with the wild animals,
With the birds of the air,
and with the things that crawl on the ground.
Bow and sword and warfare
I will destroy from the land,
and I will give them rest in safety.
21 I will betroth you to me forever:
I will betroth you to me with* justice
and with judgment,
with loyalty and with compassion;
22 I will betroth you to me with fidelity,
and you shall know the LORD.
23 On that day I will respond—oracle of the LORD—
I will respond to the heavens,
and they will respond to the earth;

**2:10 For Baal**: as an offering to Baal or to make statues of Baal.

**2:15 The days of the Baals**: feast days of the Baal cult (v. 13), or the whole period of Israel's apostasy.

**2:16 Therefore**: this word in Hebrew normally introduces an oracle of doom; here, surprisingly, it leads to hope. **Allure**: as though seducing a virgin (Ex 22:15–16). Ordinarily this word connotes deception (Jgs 14:15; 16:5; 1 Kgs 22:20–22).

**2:17 Valley of Achor**: lit., valley of trouble (Jos 7:26). Here this valley becomes a valley of hope, a new entry into the promised land.

**2:18–19 Baal**: the word means "lord, master." It was commonly used by women of their husbands, but it is to be shunned as a title for the Lord because of its association with the fertility gods, the Baals. Many Israelites saw little if any difference between the worship of the Lord and the worship of the Baals, thereby dishonoring the true source of the land's fertility.

**2:21–22 Betroth ... with**: the betrothal was the legal moment before cohabitation when the dowry was paid to the father of the bride. In this remarriage the Lord gives the bride price to Israel herself "forever." **Justice ... judgment**: refer to equity and fairness of conduct. The next two terms, "loyalty" (*hesed*), the steadfast love between the covenant partners, and "compassion," maternal love (cf. 1:6; 2:3, 25) are characteristic of Hosea. **You shall know**: not an abstract but a practical knowledge which means acknowledgment of God's will and obedience to his law (4:1; 5:4; 6:3, 6).

*f*: Lk 15:17–18. *g*: Ez 16:37. *h*: Jn 10:29. *i*: Jer 2:32. *j*: Jer 2:2–7. *k*: Jos 7:24–26. *l*: Gn 9:8–11; Ez 34:25; Jb 5:23.

### Hosea Marries an Adulteress

THE DETAILS OF the account in ch 3 are so sketchy that it is difficult to decide whether it describes 1) Hosea's first marriage to Gomer in ch 1, but from the first-person rather than third-person perspective; 2) Hosea's marriage to a second woman; or 3) Hosea's remarriage to Gomer. In any case, the point of his symbolic act is clear: Israel has been an unfaithful wife, but God desires her return.

In v. 4 Hosea predicts a coming judgment in which Israel will lose both political and religious leadership. But Israel will return to God, in the same way an unfaithful wife returns to her husband: with humility and seeking forgiveness.

24 The earth will respond to the grain, and
wine, and oil,
and these will respond to Jezreel.
25 I will sow her for myself in the land,
and I will have pity on Not-Pitied.
I will say to Not-My-People, "You are
my people,"[m]
and he will say, "My God!"

### CHAPTER 3

See RG 241–44

*Hosea and His Wife Reunited** 1 Again
the LORD said to me:

Go, love a woman
who is loved by her spouse but
commits adultery;
Just as the LORD loves the Israelites,
though they turn to other gods
and love raisin cakes.*

2* So I acquired her for myself for fifteen
pieces of silver and a homer and a lethech of
barley. 3 Then I said to her:

"You will wait for me for many days;
you will not prostitute yourself
Or belong to any man;
I in turn will wait for you."
4 * For the Israelites will remain many
days
without king or prince,
Without sacrifice or sacred pillar,
without ephod or household gods.
5 Afterward the Israelites will turn back
and seek the LORD, their God,
and David, their king;* [n]
They will come trembling to the LORD
and to his bounty, in the last days.

## II. Israel's Guilt, Punishment, and Restoration

### CHAPTER 4

See RG 241–44

*Indictment of Israel**
1 Hear the word of the LORD, Israelites,
for the LORD has a dispute
with the inhabitants of the land:[o]
There is no fidelity, no loyalty,
no knowledge of God in the land.
2 Swearing, lying, murder,

**3:1–5** Just as the Lord is ready to take Israel back, Hosea takes his wife back. She must undergo a period of purification, just as Israel must experience purification before the restoration of the covenant relationship.

**3:1 Raisin cakes**: offerings to the fertility goddess Asherah, the female counterpart of Baal, cf. Jer 7:18; 44:19; Dn 14:5–8.

**3:2** Just as the Lord offered a new bride price to Israel (2:21–22), so Hosea offers a new bride price to his wife. He returns to her what he has taken away from her (2:5): "fifteen (shekels) of silver"; "a homer of barley," a unit of dry measurement, which according to the etymology means "a mule load"; and "a lethech of barley," which is a half-homer.

**3:4** Israel will lose its political and cultic institutions. **Sacred pillar**: originally perhaps a phallic symbol, representing Baal. These were also used in Israelite worship (cf. notes on Gn 28:18; Ex 34:13). **Ephod**: an instrument used in consulting the deity (1 Sm 23:6–12; 30:7; cf. notes on Ex 28:6, 15–30). **Household gods**: in Hebrew, *teraphim*; images regarded as the tutelary deities of the household (Gn 31:19; Jgs 17:5; 18:14, 17–18).

**3:5 David, their king**: the king belonging to the line of David who will restore the Israelite nation (Jer 23:5; Ez 34:23, 24). **The last days**: a future time of transformation.

**4:1–3** The introduction to the oracles (chaps. 4–11) which begin with "Hear the word of the Lord" (4:1) and end with "oracle of the Lord" (11:11).

*m:* Rom 9:25–26; 1 Pt 2:10. *n:* Jer 30:9; Ez 34:23. *o:* Is 3:10–15; Mi 6:1–5.

stealing and adultery break out;*
bloodshed follows bloodshed.[p]
3 Therefore the land dries up,
and everything that dwells in it
languishes:
The beasts of the field,
the birds of the air,
and even the fish of the sea perish.[q]

### *Guilt of Priest and of People*

4 But let no one accuse, let no one rebuke;
with you is my dispute, priest!*
5 You will stumble in the day,
and the prophet will stumble with you
at night;
I will make an end of your mother.*
6 My people are ruined for lack of
knowledge!
Since you have rejected knowledge,
I will reject you from serving as my
priest;
Since you have forgotten the law of your
God,
I will also forget your children.
7 The more they multiplied, the more they
sinned against me,
I will change their glory* into shame.[r]
8 They feed on the sin of my people,
and are greedy for their iniquity.*
9 Like people, like priest:[s]
I will punish them for their ways,
and repay them for their deeds.
10 They will eat but not be satisfied,[t]
they will promote prostitution* but not
increase,
Because they have abandoned the LORD,
devoting themselves
11 to prostitution.
Aged wine and new wine
take away understanding.[u]
12 My people consult their piece of wood,*
and their wand makes pronouncements
for them,
For the spirit of prostitution has led them
astray;
they prostitute themselves, forsaking
their God.
13 On the mountaintops they offer sacrifice
and on the hills they burn incense,
Beneath oak and poplar and terebinth,
because of their pleasant shade.*
Therefore your daughters prostitute
themselves,
and your daughters-in-law commit
adultery.
14 I will not punish your daughters for their
prostitution,
nor your daughters-in-law for their
adultery,
Because the men themselves consort
with prostitutes,
and with temple women* they offer
sacrifice!
Thus a people without understanding
comes to ruin.
15 Though you prostitute yourself, Israel,
do not let Judah become guilty!
Do not come to Gilgal,*
do not go up to Beth-aven,[v]
do not swear, "As the Lord lives!"[w]

**4:2** Similar to the decalogue (Ex 20:1–17; cf. Jer 7:9).

**4:4–6** Hosea is particularly severe with the priests in the Northern Kingdom who had led the way in the general apostasy from God's law. The prophets here associated with the priests (v. 5) were doubtless cult prophets; cf. Jer 2:8; 4:9–10; 6:13–14; 23:9–40.

**4:5 Your mother**: the one who gave life to the priest, understood here as an extension of the punishment to his whole family (Am 7:17), or "mother" taken as a metaphor for the community of Israel, of which the priest is a member (Hos 2:4).

**4:7 Their glory**: possibly connoting "their children." See 9:11: Is 22:24. Or "Glory" may refer to the Lord in contrast to Ba'al. The Hebrew word for shame, *bosheth*, is often substituted for Ba'al in biblical names. See Ishbaal (Heb. *Ishbosheth*, 2 Sm 2:8, 10, 12, 15) and Meribaal (Heb. *Mephibosheth*, 2 Sm 9:6, 10–13).

**4:8** The priest receives part of the sacrifice (Lv 6:19; 7:7).

**4:10–11 Prostitution**: often a synonym for idolatry. The covenant bond was symbolized as the relationship between husband and wife (see chaps. 1–2). Thus, abandoning the Lord for a foreign god was called prostitution or adultery.

**4:12 Piece of wood**: a derogatory term for an idol. **Wand**: a sacred wooden object, perhaps some kind of staff, used for divination.

**4:13** The shrines on the "high places" typically had an altar, a grove of trees, and a stone pillar representing a god (Dt 12:2; Jer 2:20).

**4:14 Temple women**: plural of Heb. *qedesha*; the exact import of the term is disputed. See notes on Gn 38:21 and Dt 23:18–19.

**4:15 Gilgal**: close to Jericho (Jos 4:19–20; 5:2–9). **Beth-**

*p:* Ex 20:13–17. *q:* Is 24:4–7; Zep 1:2–3. *r:* Jer 2:11; Ps 106:20. *s:* Is 24:2. *t:* Mi 6:14. *u:* Is 28:7. *v:* Am 4:4. *w:* Am 8:14.

16 For like a stubborn cow,
Israel is stubborn;
Will the LORD now pasture them,
like lambs in a broad meadow?
17 Ephraim* is bound to idols,
let him alone!
18 * When their drinking is over,
they give themselves to prostitution;[x]
they love shame more than their honor.
19 A wind* has bound them up in its wings;[y]
they shall be ashamed because of their altars.[z]

## CHAPTER 5

See RG 241–44

### *Guilt of the Religious and Political Leaders*

1 Hear this, priests,
Pay attention, house of Israel,
Household of the king, give ear![a]
For you are responsible for judgment.*
But you have been a snare at Mizpah,*
a net spread upon Tabor,
2 a pit dug deep in Shittim.
Now I will discipline them all.

3 I know Ephraim,
and Israel is not hidden from me:
Now, Ephraim, you have practiced prostitution,
Israel is defiled.
4 Their deeds do not allow them
to return to their God;[b]
For the spirit of prostitution is in them,
and they do not know the LORD.
5 The arrogance of Israel bears witness
against him;
Israel and Ephraim stumble because of their iniquity,
and Judah stumbles with them.
6 With their flocks and herds they will go
to seek the LORD, but will not find him;[c]
he has withdrawn from them.
7 They have betrayed the LORD,
for they have borne illegitimate children;
Now the new moon* will devour them
together with their fields.

### *Political Upheavals**

8 Blow the ram's horn in Gibeah,
the trumpet in Ramah!
Sound the alarm in Beth-aven:[d]
"Look behind you, Benjamin!"*
9 Ephraim shall become a wasteland
on the day of punishment:
Among the tribes of Israel
I announce what is sure to be.
10 The princes of Judah have become
like those who move a boundary line;* [e]
Upon them I will pour out
my wrath like water.
11 Ephraim is oppressed, crushed by judgment,

**aven**: (lit., "house of iniquity") Hosea's derogatory term for the sanctuary of Bethel (lit., "house of God"), the major shrine of the Northern Kingdom (10:5, 8; cf. Am 5:5). **As the Lord lives**: a legitimate oath formula (1 Sm 26:10, 16), but unacceptable here because Israel is guilty of religious syncretism and the idolatrous worship of other gods.

**4:17 Ephraim**: the name of one of the sons of Joseph, son of Jacob (Gn 41:52), also used to designate one of the tribes living in the heartland of the Northern Kingdom. Hosea often uses the name Ephraim to refer to the whole Northern Kingdom of Israel. During the latter part of his ministry, after the Assyrians occupied Galilee, Ephraim was all that remained of Israel.

**4:18** Cf. v. 11.

**4:19 A wind**: (Heb. *ruah*), a metaphor for Israel's addiction to the Baal cult, which is nothing but wind, a "spirit (*ruah*) of prostitution" (v. 12).

**5:1 For you . . . judgment**: possibly "for you are called to judgment."

**5:1–2 Mizpah**: several places bear this name; the best known is in Benjamin (1 Sm 7:6, 16; 10:17). Perhaps this is a wordplay on *mishpat*, "justice," "judgment." **Tabor**: the mountain that dominates the valley of Jezreel. **Shittim**: in Transjordan, where Israel committed its first act of idolatry with the Baal of Peor (9:10; cf. Nm 25). At these three places the leaders had misled the people by an idolatrous cult or by an abuse of justice.

**5:7 New moon**: normally a feast day of joy (2:13), but, because of infidelity, it will be a day of destruction.

**5:8–14** This passage describes political and military conflict between Judah and Israel. Perhaps some allusion is made to the Syro-Ephraimite war of 735–734 B.C., when a coalition of Arameans and Israelites attempted to dethrone the king of Judah (2 Kgs 16:5; Is 7:1–9). Judah repulsed the attempt with the aid of Assyria, and the latter devastated both Aram and Israel.

**5:8** A vision of invasion, from Gibeah and Ramah in northern Judah, into Israel.

**5:10 Move a boundary line**: invasion by Judah (v. 8) is compared to a case of social injustice (Dt 19:14; 27:17; Prv 23:10–11).

*x:* Am 2:8. *y:* Jer 4:11–12. *z:* Is 1:29. *a:* Mi 3:1. *b:* Jer 13:23. *c:* Is 55:6; Jer 29:13; Am 5:4–6; 8:12; Jn 7:34. *d:* Jer 4:5; Jl 2:1. *e:* Dt 19:14; 27:17.

for he has willingly gone after filth!*
12 I am like a moth for Ephraim,[f]
like rot for the house of Judah.
13 When Ephraim saw his infirmity,
and Judah his sore,
Ephraim went to Assyria,
and sent to the great king.* [g]
But he cannot heal you,
nor take away your sore.
14 For I am like a lion to Ephraim,
like a young lion to the house of Judah;[h]
It is I who tear the prey and depart,
I carry it away and no one can save it.[i]

### Insincere Conversion

15 I will go back to my place
until they make reparation
and seek my presence.
In their affliction, they shall look for me.[j]

## CHAPTER 6

See RG 241–44

1 "Come, let us return to the LORD,[k]
For it is he who has torn, but he will
heal us;
he has struck down, but he will bind
our wounds.
2 He will revive us after two days;
on the third day* he will raise us up,[l]
to live in his presence.
3 Let us know, let us strive to know the
LORD;
as certain as the dawn is his coming.
He will come to us like the rain,
like spring rain that waters the earth."[m]
4 What can I do with you, Ephraim?
What can I do with you, Judah?
Your loyalty is like morning mist,
like the dew that disappears early.
5 For this reason I struck them down
through the prophets,
I killed them by the words of my
mouth;* [n]
my judgment shines forth like the light.
6 For it is loyalty that I desire, not sacrifice,
and knowledge of God rather than
burnt offerings.[o]

### Further Crimes of Israel

7 But they, at Adam,* violated the covenant;
there they betrayed me.
8 Gilead* is a city of evildoers,
tracked with blood.
9 Like brigands lying in wait
is the band of priests.
They murder on the road to Shechem,*
indeed they commit a monstrous crime.
10 In the house of Israel I have seen a
horrible thing:
there is found Ephraim's prostitution,
Israel is defiled.
11 For you also, Judah,
a harvest* has been appointed!

## CHAPTER 7

See RG 241–44

When I would have restored the
fortunes of my people,
1 when I would have healed Israel,
The guilt of Ephraim was revealed,
the wickedness of Samaria:
They practiced falsehood.
Thieves break in,
bandits roam outside.
2 Yet they do not call to mind
that I remember all their wickedness.[p]
Now their crimes surround them,
present to my sight.[q]

**5:11 Filth**: Ephraim's reliance on foreign nations and their gods.

**5:13 Ephraim went . . . king**: in 738 the Israelite king Menahem had to pay tribute to the Assyrian king Tiglath-pileser III, whose vassal he became (2 Kgs 15:19–20). Under the threat of the Syro-Ephraimite invasion King Ahaz of Judah also submitted to Tiglath-pileser (2 Kgs 16:7–9). **Great king**: Heb. *melek-yarev*; may be a proper name: King Yarev, but unknown; or "the defender king": irony about the great king of Assyria (see note on 10:6).

**6:2 After two days; on the third day**: presumptuous Israel expects that soon God will renew them (cf. Ez 37).

**6:5** The word of God proclaimed by the prophets is effective, it accomplished what it promised: punishment.

**6:7 At Adam**: the violation of the covenant at Adam is mentioned nowhere else in the Bible. The place Adam, the location of which is unknown, may be referred to in Jos 3:16.

**6:8 Gilead**: city in Transjordan (Gn 31:46–48; 2 Kgs 15:25).

**6:9 Shechem**: an important ancient religious and political center (Jos 24).

**6:11 Harvest**: God's judgment, when Judah will reap what it has sown.

*f:* Is 50:9. *g:* 2 Kgs 15:19–20; 16:7–9. *h:* Is 5:29; Am 1:2; 3:12. *i:* Dt 32:39. *j:* Jer 29:13; Ps 78:34. *k:* Lam 3:40. *l:* Lk 24:7, 46; 1 Cor 15:4. *m:* Dt 11:14; Ps 72:6. *n:* Is 11:4; 49:2; Jer 5:14; Heb 4:12–13. *o:* 1 Sm 15:22; Am 5:22–24; Mi 6:6–8; Eccl 4:17; Mt 9:13; 12:7. *p:* Ps 10:11. *q:* Prv 5:21–22.

### *Israel's Domestic Politics**

3 With their wickedness they make the
king rejoice,
the princes too, with their treacherous
deeds.
4 They are all adulterers,*
like a blazing oven,
Which the baker quits stoking,
after the dough's kneading until its
rising.
5 On the day of our king,
they made the princes sick with
poisoned wine;
he extended his hand to the
scoffers.
6 For they draw near in ambush
with their hearts like an oven.
All the night their anger sleeps;
in the morning it flares like a blazing
fire.
7 They are all heated like ovens,
and consume their rulers.
All their kings have fallen;
none of them calls upon me.

### *Israel's Foreign Politics*

8 Ephraim is mixed with the nations,*
Ephraim is an unturned cake.
9 Strangers have consumed his strength,
but he does not know it;[r]
Gray hairs are strewn on his head,
but he takes no notice of it.
10 The arrogance of Israel bears witness
against him;
yet they do not return to the LORD,
their God,
nor seek him, despite all this.[s]
11 Ephraim is like a dove,
silly and senseless;
They call upon Egypt,
they go to Assyria.
12 When they go I will spread my net
around them,
like birds in the air I will bring them
down.[t]
I will chastise them when I hear of
their assembly.
13 Woe to them, for they have strayed
from me!
Ruin to them, for they have rebelled
against me!
Though I wished to redeem them,
they spoke lies against me.
14 They have not cried to me from their
hearts
when they wailed upon their beds;
For wheat and wine they lacerated
themselves;*
they rebelled against me.
15 Though I trained and strengthened their
arms,
yet they devised evil against me.
16 They have again become useless,
they have been like a treacherous bow.[u]
Their princes shall fall by the sword
because of the insolence of their
tongues;
thus they shall be mocked in the land
of Egypt.

## CHAPTER 8

See RG 241–44

### *Corruption of Cult, Domestic and Foreign Politics*

1 Put the trumpet to your lips![v]
One like an eagle* is over the house of
the LORD!
Because they have violated my covenant,
and rebelled against my law,
2 They cry out to me,
"My God! We know you!"
3 But Israel has rejected what is good;
the enemy* shall pursue him.

**7:3–7** This passage perhaps refers to a conspiracy at the royal court. Between the death of Jeroboam II (743 B.C.) and the fall of Samaria (722/721), nearly all the kings were murdered (2 Kgs 15:10, 14, 25, 30).

**7:4 Adulterers**: the unfaithful nobles who kill the king. Their passion is compared to the fire of the oven. The point of the metaphor is that, like this oven whose fire is always ready to blaze up again, the conspirators are always ready for rebellion.

**7:8 Is mixed with the nations**: the people reject exclusive allegiance to the Lord, and they now try to find their salvation in alliances with foreign nations. **An unturned cake**: burnt on one side, but not baked at all on the other, and thus worthless.

**7:14 Lacerated themselves**: a ritual to obtain a good harvest from Baal (2:7–10; 1 Kgs 18:28; Jer 16:6; 41:5). This practice was forbidden (Lv 19:28; Dt 14:1).

**8:1 Eagle**: perhaps an image for Tiglath-pileser III of Assyria, who overran the land of Israel in 733 B.C. (Jer 48:40; 49:22; Ez 17:3).

**8:3 Enemy**: Assyria.

*r:* Jer 5:3; Rev 3:17. *s:* Is 9:12; Am 4:6. *t:* Ez 12:13; 32:3. *u:* Ps 78:57. *v:* Jl 2:1.

### Prophets and Gender

HOSEA'S PRIMARY IMAGE for Israel's disloyalty to God is the wife who is unfaithful to her husband and has become a prostitute. One reason Hosea chose this image is the fact that his audience was primarily male—the men held the power and wealth in ancient patriarchal societies such as biblical Israel. For these men, faithless wives were a stinging shame. Hosea wanted to shock them, so they would see the seriousness of their crimes. The image of the faithless wife gave Hosea a forceful means of criticizing the abuses of Israel's male elite. The problem of the image is that it leads some readers to connect disloyalty and sin with women in particular, a connection that must be clearly rejected to keep such an image from being used to disparage and mistreat women. In fact, Hosea only refers to one specific woman who is described as unfaithful. Nowhere does Hosea imply that all women are the same; rather, it is the priests and leaders who are condemned as a group (Hos 4:4–7).

4 * They made kings, but not by my
authority;
they established princes, but without
my knowledge.
With their silver and gold
they made idols for themselves,
to their own destruction.
5 He has rejected your calf,* Samaria![w]
My wrath is kindled against them;
How long will they be incapable of
innocence
in Israel?
6 An artisan made it,
it is no god at all.[x]
The calf of Samaria
will be dashed to pieces.
7 When they sow the wind,
they will reap the whirlwind;[y]
The stalk of grain that forms no head
can yield no flour;
Even if it could,
strangers would swallow it.
8 Israel is swallowed up;
now they are among the nations,
like a useless vessel.
9 For they went up to Assyria—*
a wild ass off on its own—
Ephraim bargained for lovers.[z]
10 Even though they bargain with the nations,
I will now gather them* together;
They will soon succumb
under the burden of king and princes.
11 * When Ephraim made many altars to
expiate sin,
they became altars for sinning.
12 Though I write for him my many
instructions,
they are considered like a stranger's.
13 They love sacrifice,
they sacrifice meat and eat it,
but the LORD is not pleased with
them.[a]
Now he will remember their guilt
and punish their sins;[b]
they shall return to Egypt.* [c]
14 Israel has forgotten his maker[d]
and has built palaces.
Judah, too, has fortified many cities,
but I will send fire upon his cities,
to devour their strongholds.[e]

**8:4** Hosea is not against the monarchy, but against the conspiracies at the royal court (see note on 7:3–7). The king should be chosen by God (1 Kgs 19:15–16).

**8:5 Calf**: a cultic object introduced by Jeroboam I after the separation of the Northern Kingdom from the Southern Kingdom (1 Kgs 12:26–30; cf. Ex 32).

**8:9 They went up to Assyria**: a reference to the politics of appealing to Assyria (cf. 5:13; 7:11). There is a play on the Hebrew word for "wild ass" (*pere*) and "Ephraim."

**8:10 I will now gather them**: for judgment and for deportation.

**8:11** The altars had become places of self-serving worship (cf. v. 13).

**8:13 Return to Egypt**: to punish their violation of the covenant they will experience a reversal of the exodus.

*w:* 1 Kgs 12:28. *x:* Ex 20:4; 34:17; Is 40:19–20; 44:9–20; Jer 10:1–16. *y:* Jb 4:8; Prv 22:8; 2 Cor 9:6; Gal 6:7–8. *z:* Ez 16:32–34. *a:* Am 5:22. *b:* Jer 14:10. *c:* Dt 28:68. *d:* Dt 32:15, 18; Is 51:13. *e:* Am 1:7, 10, 12, 14; 2:2, 5.

See RG 241–44

## CHAPTER 9

### *From Days of Celebration to Days of Punishment*

1 Do not rejoice, Israel,
do not exult like the nations!
For you have prostituted yourself,
abandoning your God,
loving a prostitute's fee
upon every threshing floor.*
2 Threshing floor and wine press will not nourish them,
the new wine will fail them.

3 They will not dwell in the LORD's land;
Ephraim will return to Egypt,
and in Assyria they will eat unclean food.
4 They will not pour libations of wine to the LORD,
and their sacrifices will not please him.
Their bread will be like mourners' bread,*[f]
that makes unclean all who eat of it;
Their food will be for their own appetites;
it cannot enter the house of the LORD.

5 What will you do on the festival day,
the day of the LORD's feast?*
6 * When they flee from the devastation,
Egypt will gather them, Memphis will bury them.
Weeds will overgrow their silver treasures,
and thorns, their tents.

7 They have come, the days of punishment!
they have come, the days of recompense!
Let Israel know it!
"The prophet is a fool,[g]
the man of the spirit is mad!"
Because your iniquity is great,
great, too, is your hostility.
8 * The watchman of Ephraim, the people of my God, is the prophet;[h]
yet a fowler's snare is on all his ways,
hostility in the house of his God.
9 They have sunk to the depths of corruption,
as in the days of Gibeah;*[i]
God will remember their iniquity
and punish their sins.

### *From Former Glory to a History of Corruption*

10 Like grapes in the desert,
I found Israel;
Like the first fruits of the fig tree, its first to ripen,[j]
I looked on your ancestors.
But when they came to Baal-peor*[k]
and consecrated themselves to the Shameful One,
they became as abhorrent as the thing they loved.
11 Ephraim is like a bird:
their glory flies away—
no birth, no pregnancy, no conception.[l]
12 Even though they bring up their children,
I will make them childless, until no one is left.
Indeed, woe to them
when I turn away from them!
13 Ephraim, as I saw, was a tree
planted in a meadow;
But now Ephraim will bring out
his children to the slaughterer!
14 Give them, LORD!

**9:1 Threshing floor**: an allusion to harvest festivals in honor of Baal, to whom the Israelites had attributed the fertility of the land; cf. 2:7.

**9:4 Mourners' bread**: bread eaten at funeral rites (Dt 26:14). The presence of a corpse also made all food prepared in that house unclean (Jer 16:5–7).

**9:5 The LORD's feast**: probably the important autumn feast of Booths, the most important of the Israelite public celebrations (Lv 23:34).

**9:6** Instead of gathering for celebration (v. 5), they will be gathered for death. **Memphis**: known for the monumental pyramid tombs. **Silver treasures**: the silver statues of Baal (8:4).

**9:8** Prophets, like Hosea himself, are called to be sentinels for Israel, warning Israel of God's coming wrath (see Ez 3:17; 33:7), but often meet rejection.

**9:9 The days of Gibeah**: the precise allusion is not clear. Perhaps it is a reference to the outrage committed at Gibeah in the days of the judges (Jgs 19–21), or to questions surrounding Saul's kingship at Gibeah (1 Sm 10:26; 14:2; 22:6).

**9:10 Baal-peor**: where the Israelites consecrated themselves for the first time to Baal (Nm 25; see note on Hos 5:1–2). Baal is here called the Shameful One.

---

*f:* Dt 26:14. *g:* 2 Kgs 9:11; Jn 10:20. *h:* Jer 6:17; Ez 3:17; 33:2, 6, 7. *i:* Jgs 19–21. *j:* Is 28:4; Jer 2:2. *k:* Nm 25. *l:* Dt 28:18.

give them what?
Give them a miscarrying womb,
and dry breasts![m]
15 All their misfortune began in Gilgal;*
yes, there I rejected them.
Because of their wicked deeds
I will drive them out of my house.
I will love them no longer;
all their princes are rebels.
16 * Ephraim is stricken,
their root is dried up;[n]
they will bear no fruit.[o]
Were they to bear children,
I would slay the beloved of their womb.
17 My God will disown them
because they have not listened to him;
they will be wanderers among the
nations.[p]

## CHAPTER 10

See RG 241–44

### *Destruction of Idolatrous Cultic Objects*

1 [q] Israel is a luxuriant vine
whose fruit matches its growth.
The more abundant his fruit,
the more altars he built;
The more productive his land,
the more sacred pillars* he set up.
2 Their heart is false!
Now they will pay for their guilt:
God will break down their altars
and destroy their sacred pillars.
3 For now they will say,
"We have no king!*
Since we do not fear the LORD,
the king—what could he do for us?"
4 They make promises,
swear false oaths, and make covenants,
While lawsuits sprout
like poisonous weeds* in the furrows
of a field!
5 The inhabitants of Samaria are afraid
for the calf of Beth-aven;*
Its people mourn for it
and its idolatrous priests wail over it,
—over its glory which has departed
from it.[r]
6 It too will be carried to Assyria,
as an offering to the great king.* [s]
Ephraim will be put to shame,
Israel will be shamed by his schemes.
7 Samaria and her king will disappear,
like a twig upon the waters.
8 The high places of Aven* will be
destroyed,
the sin of Israel;
thorns and thistles will overgrow their
altars.
Then they will cry out to the mountains,
"Cover us!"
and to the hills, "Fall upon us!"[t]

### *War Because of Israel's Wickedness*

9 Since the days of Gibeah[u]
you have sinned, Israel.
There they took their stand;
will war not reach them in Gibeah?
Against a perverse people
10 I came and I chastised them;
Peoples will be gathered against them
when I bind them to their two crimes.*
11 Ephraim was a trained heifer,
that loved to thresh;
I myself laid a yoke
upon her beautiful neck;
I will make Ephraim break ground, Judah
must plow,

**9:15 Gilgal**: possibly a reference to Saul's disobedience to Samuel (1 Sm 13:7–14; 15), or to the idolatry practiced in that place (see note on Hos 4:15).

**9:16** Wordplay on the Hebrew word for "fruit" (*peri*) and Ephraim (see note on 8:9). The whole passage (vv. 10–17) presents a reversal of Ephraim's name (Gn 41:52). He will have no fruit, a condition which will result in extinction.

**10:1 Sacred pillars**: see note on 3:4.

**10:3 No king**: the instability of the monarchy (7:3–7) and its vassalage to foreign kings (7:8–16) render the monarchy ineffective. The kings do the opposite of what they are supposed to do (10:4).

**10:4 Lawsuits . . . like poisonous weeds**: the administration of justice, which should have been the mainstay of the people, has in corrupt hands become another instrument of oppression; cf. Am 6:12.

**10:5 The calf of Beth-aven**: see note on 4:15.

**10:6 The great king**: a title used by the Assyrian kings. See also note on 5:13.

**10:8 Aven**: wickedness, first of all at Bethel (v. 5), but also at all the high places.

**10:10 Two crimes**: the allusion is not clear; a possible reference is the outrage described in Jgs 19.

*m:* Jb 3:11–12; Lk 23:29. *n:* Am 2:9. *o:* Mt 21:19. *p:* Gn 4:12, 14; Dt 28:64–65. *q:* Is 5:1–7. *r:* 1 Sm 4:21–22. *s:* Am 5:27. *t:* Is 2:10, 19; Lk 23:30; Rev 6:16. *u:* Jgs 19–21.

Jacob must harrow for himself:
12 "Sow for yourselves justice,
reap the reward of loyalty;
Break up for yourselves a new field,[v]
for it is time to seek the LORD,
till he comes and rains justice upon
you."[w]
13 But you have plowed wickedness,
reaped perversity,
and eaten the fruit of falsehood.
Because you have trusted in your own
power,
and in your many warriors,[x]
14 The clamor of war shall break out among
your people
and all your fortresses shall be ravaged
As Salman ravaged Beth-arbel* on the
day of war,
smashing mothers along with their
children.[y]
15 So it will be done to you, Bethel,
because of your utter wickedness:
At dawn* the king of Israel
will utterly disappear.

## CHAPTER 11

See RG 241–44

### *The Disappointment of a Parent*

1 * When Israel was a child I loved him,[z]
out of Egypt* I called my son.[a]
2 The more I called them,
the farther they went from me,
Sacrificing to the Baals
and burning incense to idols.
3 Yet it was I who taught Ephraim to walk,
who took them in my arms;[b]
but they did not know that I cared for
them.
4 I drew them with human cords,
with bands of love;*
I fostered them like those
who raise an infant to their cheeks;
I bent down to feed them.[c]

5 He shall return to the land of Egypt,[d]
Assyria shall be his king,
because they have refused to repent.
6 The sword shall rage in his cities:
it shall destroy his diviners,
and devour them because of their
schemings.
7 My people have their mind set on
apostasy;
though they call on God in unison,
he shall not raise them up.

### *But Love Is Stronger and Restores*

8 How could I give you up, Ephraim,
or deliver you up, Israel?
How could I treat you as Admah,
or make you like Zeboiim?* [e]
My heart is overwhelmed,
my pity is stirred.
9 I will not give vent to my blazing anger,
I will not destroy Ephraim again;
For I am God and not a man,[f]
the Holy One present among you;
I will not come in wrath.
10 They shall follow the LORD,
who roars like a lion;[g]
When he roars,
his children shall come frightened
from the west,
11 Out of Egypt they shall come trembling,
like birds,
like doves, from the land of Assyria;
And I will resettle them in their homes,
oracle of the LORD.

**10:14 As Salman ravaged Beth-arbel**: perhaps Salamanu, king of Moab, mentioned in an inscription of Tiglath-pileser III, after an invasion in Gilead (Transjordan), where there was a Beth-arbel, close to present Irbid.

**10:15 At dawn**: normally the moment of God's victory over Israel's enemies, and thus his salvation (Is 17:14; Ps 46:6). Here it is a reversal of this expectation.

**11:1–3** After the image of husband-wife (chaps. 1–3), Hosea uses the image of parent-child (Ex 4:22; Is 1:2; Jer 3:19).

**11:1 Out of Egypt**: Hosea dates the real beginning of Israel from the time of the exodus. Mt 2:15 applies this text to the return of Jesus from Egypt.

**11:4 I drew them . . . with bands of love**: perhaps a reversal of the yoke imagery of the previous chapter, i.e., not forcing them like draft animals, but drawing them with kindness and affection.

**11:8 Admah . . . Zeboiim**: cities in the vicinity of Sodom and Gomorrah (Gn 14:2, 8) and destroyed with them (Gn 19:24–25; Dt 29:22).

*v:* Jer 4:3. *w:* Is 45:8; Jl 2:23. *x:* Is 31:1. *y:* Ps 137:9; Am 1:13. *z:* Dt 7:8; 10:15; Jer 2:1–9. *a:* Ex 4:22; Mt 2:15. *b:* Dt 1:31; 8:5. *c:* Dt 8:16. *d:* Dt 17:16. *e:* Dt 29:22. *f:* Nm 23:19; Is 31:3; Ez 28:2. *g:* Jl 4:16; Am 1:2; Jer 25:30.

## CHAPTER 12

See RG 241–44

### *Infidelity of Israel**

1 Ephraim has surrounded me with lies,
the house of Israel, with deceit;
Judah still wanders about with gods,
and is faithful to holy ones.*
2 * Ephraim shepherds the wind,
and pursues the east wind all day long.
He multiplies lies and violence:
They make a covenant with Assyria,
and oil is carried to Egypt.

3 The LORD has a dispute with Judah,
and will punish Jacob* for his conduct,
and repay him for his deeds.
4 In the womb he supplanted his brother,[h]
and in his vigor he contended with a divine being;
5 He contended with an angel and prevailed,[i]
he wept and entreated him.
At Bethel he met with him,
and there he spoke with him.[j]
6 The LORD is the God of hosts,
the LORD is his name![k]
7 You must return to your God.
Maintain loyalty and justice
and always hope in your God.

8 A merchant who holds a false balance,
he loves to extort!
9 Ephraim has said,
"How rich I have become;
I have made a fortune!"[l]
All his gain will not suffice
for the guilt of his sin.
10 I the LORD have been your God,
since the land of Egypt;[m]
I will again have you live in tents,
as on feast days.
11 I spoke to the prophets,
I granted many visions,[n]
and through the prophets I told parables.
12 In Gilead is falsehood, they have come to nothing;
in Gilgal they sacrifice bulls,
But their altars are like heaps of stones[o]
in the furrows of the field.

13 Jacob fled to the land of Aram,
and Israel served for a wife;
for a wife he tended sheep.[p]
14 But by a prophet* the LORD brought Israel out of Egypt,
and by a prophet Israel was tended.[q]
15 Ephraim has aroused bitter anger,
so his Lord shall cast his bloodguilt upon him
and repay him for his scorn.

## CHAPTER 13

See RG 241–44

### *The Death of Ephraim*

1 When Ephraim spoke there was terror;
he was exalted in Israel;*
but he became guilty through Baal and died.

2 Now they continue to sin,
making for themselves molten images,
Silver idols according to their skill,[r]
all of them the work of artisans.
"To these, offer sacrifice," they say.
People kiss calves!* [s]
3 Therefore, they will be like a morning cloud
or like the dew that vanishes with the dawn,
Like chaff storm-driven from the threshing floor[t]
or like smoke out of the window.

4 I, the LORD, am your God,
since the land of Egypt;* [u]

**12:1–15** This chapter draws a parallel between the history of Israel and events in the life of Jacob-Israel, the ancestor.

**12:1** An attack on the idolatry of both kingdoms, Israel and Judah. **Holy ones**: subordinate gods, members of the divine council.

**12:2** Hosea frequently condemns the alliances with Assyria and Egypt, the two world powers (7:8–16).

**12:3 Jacob**: whose name was changed to Israel (Gn 35:10).

**12:14 A prophet**: Moses.

**13:1 Exalted in Israel**: Ephraim enjoyed a privileged position in Israel (Gn 48:14–19).

**13:2 Kiss calves**: apparently a reference to a ritual gesture associated with the worship of Baal represented as a calf (1 Kgs 19:18).

**13:4 I, the LORD . . . land of Egypt**: according to 1 Kgs 12:28, Jeroboam introduced the calves used in the worship at

*h:* Gn 25:26; 27:35–36. *i:* Gn 32:25–30. *j:* Gn 28:12–19; 35:15. *k:* Ex 3:15; Am 4:13. *l:* Rev 3:17. *m:* Ex 20:2. *n:* Ps 74:9. *o:* Gn 31:45–54; Jos 4–5. *p:* Gn 28:5; 29:15–30; 30:31. *q:* Ex 3:7–10; Dt 18:18. *r:* Is 40:19–20; 44:9–20. *s:* 1 Kgs 19:18. *t:* Is 17:13; Zep 2:2; Ps 1:4. *u:* Ex 20:2.

Gods apart from me you do not know;
there is no savior but me.[v]
5 I fed you in the wilderness,
in the parched land.
6 When I fed them, they were satisfied;
when satisfied, they became proud,
therefore they forgot me.
7 So, I will be like a lion to them,
like a leopard by the road I will keep
watch.
8 w I will attack them like a bear robbed of
its young,
and tear their hearts from their
breasts;
I will devour them on the spot like a lion,
as a wild animal would rip them open.
9 * I destroy you, Israel!
who is there to help you?
10 Where now is your king,
that he may rescue you?
And all your princes,
that they may defend you?
Of whom you said,
"Give me a king and princes"?[x]
11 I give you a king in my anger,
and I take him away in my wrath.*
12 The guilt of Ephraim is wrapped up,
his sin is stored away.
13 * The birth pangs will come for him,[y]
but this is an unwise child,
Who, when it is time, does not present
himself
at the mouth of the womb.[z]
14 * Shall I deliver them from the power of
Sheol?
shall I redeem them from death?
Where are your plagues, O death!
where is your sting, Sheol![a]
Compassion is hidden from my eyes.
15 Though Ephraim* may flourish among
his brothers,
an east wind[b] will come, a wind from
the LORD,
rising from the wilderness,
That will dry up his spring,
and leave his fountain dry.
It will loot his treasury
of every precious thing.

## CHAPTER 14

See RG 241–44

1 Samaria* has become guilty,
for she has rebelled against her God.
They shall fall by the sword,
their infants shall be dashed to pieces,[c]
their pregnant women shall be ripped
open.[d]

### *Sincere Conversion and New Life*

2 Return, Israel, to the LORD, your God;
you have stumbled because of your
iniquity.
3 Take with you words,
and return to the LORD;
Say to him, "Forgive all iniquity,
and take what is good.
Let us offer the fruit of our lips.[e]
4 * Assyria will not save us,
nor will we mount horses;[f]
We will never again say, 'Our god,'
to the work of our hands;
for in you the orphan finds
compassion."[g]
5 I will heal their apostasy,
I will love them freely;

the sanctuaries in Bethel and Dan with the words: "Here are your gods, O Israel, who brought you up from the land of Egypt."

**13:9–10** Only God can save Israel, not the king, whom Israel had requested from the Lord (1 Sm 8:1–9).

**13:11 I give you a king . . . in my wrath**: the Lord punished the people of the Northern Kingdom by giving them kings who were soon deposed (see notes on 7:3–7 and 8:4).

**13:13** Ephraim will die along with its stored-up sin, just as a mother dies along with a child that she cannot deliver.

**13:14** God calls upon "death" and "Sheol" to send their auxiliaries, "plagues" and "sting," to punish Israel (Hb 3:5; Ps 91:6). Paul uses this text in a different way to speak about the victory over death (1 Cor 15:54–55).

**13:15** Although "Ephraim" is not explicitly mentioned in the text (the Hebrew text has the word "he"), the wordplay with the Hebrew word for "flourish" (*yaphri*) suggests the use of "Ephraim" in the translation. **Wind**: possibly Assyria.

**14:1 Samaria**: the capital of the Northern Kingdom will fall; this is the punishment predicted for Ephraim, the Northern Kingdom.

**14:4** These good intentions promise a reversal of Israel's sins: no more reliance on "Assyria," i.e., on foreign alliances (see notes on 8:9 and 12:2), on "horses," i.e., on human power (10:13), and on idolatry (8:4–6; 13:2). Israel will trust in the Lord alone.

*v:* Is 43:11. *w:* 2 Sm 17:8. *x:* 1 Sm 8:5. *y:* Is 26:17–18; Jer 6:24; 22:23. *z:* Is 37:3. *a:* 1 Cor 15:55. *b:* Ez 19:12. *c:* Ps 137:9. *d:* Am 1:13. *e:* Heb 13:15. *f:* Is 31:1. *g:* Lam 5:3.

for my anger is turned away from
them.
6 I will be like the dew for Israel:[h]
he will blossom like the lily;
He will strike root like the Lebanon
cedar,
7 and his shoots will go forth.[i]
His splendor will be like the olive tree
and his fragrance like Lebanon
cedar.[j]
8 Again they will live in his shade;
they will raise grain,
They will blossom like the vine,
and his renown will be like the wine of
Lebanon.
9 Ephraim! What more have I to do with
idols?[k]
I have humbled him, but I will take
note of him.
I am like a verdant cypress tree.*
From me fruit will be found for you!

### *Epilogue*

10 * Who is wise enough to understand
these things?[l]
Who is intelligent enough to know
them?
Straight are the paths of the LORD,[m]
the just walk in them,[n]
but sinners stumble in them.

**14:9 Verdant cypress tree**: the symbol of lasting life, the opposite of the sacred trees of the Baal cult (4:13). The Lord provides the "fruit" (*peri*) to Israel (2:7, 10), another instance of the wordplay on Ephraim (see notes on 9:16 and 13:15).

**14:10** A challenge to the reader in the style of the wisdom literature.

*h:* Is 26:19. *i:* Is 27:6. *j:* Sg 4:11. *k:* 2 Cor 6:16. *l:* Ps 107:43; Jer 9:11; Eccl 8:1. *m:* Dt 32:4. *n:* Dt 8:6; 11:22; Mi 6:8.

See RG 244–46

# The Book of Joel

In the two speeches that make up this book, Joel uses an agricultural crisis to measure his audience's knowledge of its God, warn them of a worse disaster if they ignore his preaching, and express his conviction that all faithful Judahites would someday enjoy a secure future. Although the superscription, or title (1:1), does not place Joel's preaching or the book's composition in a specific historical context, internal evidence favors a postexilic date for its composition, probably 450–400 B.C. This evidence includes: Joel's reliance on an established, possibly written, prophetic tradition; the existence of an organized temple liturgy; the dominance of priests and the absence of a king; and vocabulary characteristic of later material like Chronicles and Zechariah.

Inadequate winter rains and a spring locust infestation have devastated Judah's grain fields, vineyards, and orchards. Because the people carry on with business as usual, unaware that this crisis is the work of the Lord in their midst, Joel fears that the Lord may soon deliver a death blow by withholding the rains that normally fall in the late autumn. However, Joel's efforts to avert this crisis are successful. The first speech ends with Joel's assurance that at the end of the next agricultural year the people will enjoy a superabundant harvest.

The second speech begins with a summary description (chap. 3) of the prophet's hope that Judah's God will one day destroy its enemies and make Jerusalem secure once and for all. This divine intervention will create a more inclusive community, cutting across boundaries of gender, class, and age. In Peter's first public speech at Pentecost (Acts 2:16–21), the author uses Jl 3:1–5 to announce the formation of such a community among Christians in Jerusalem and the proximity of the day of the Lord. The rest of Joel's second speech (chap. 4) uses the imagery of drought and locusts from the first speech and introduces the metaphor of a grape harvest and wine making to describe the attack of the Lord's heavenly army on Judah's enemies. In the renewal of Judah's hillsides by the winter rains, the prophet sees the revitalization of the people because the Lord dwells with them.

The Book of Joel may be divided as follows:

I. Announcement of Unprecedented Disaster (1:2–20)
II. The Day of the Lord (2:1–27)
III. The Lord's Final Judgment (3:1–4:21)

**The Desert Locust**

THE DESERT LOCUST is a distant cousin of the American grasshopper. It lives and breeds in the great desert stretching from the Sahara in Africa to the Arabian Peninsula, including the Sinai and Judean deserts. In the right conditions, it multiplies rapidly, crowds into dense swarms, and sweeps into neighboring fertile areas, where it eats its own weight in green food each day. A swarm of desert locusts in Somaliland in 1957 was estimated to include 16 billion locusts and to weigh 50,000 tons. The desert locust's threat to Middle Eastern societies is recorded in the earliest human records and continues into the present, where it is monitored and combated by the United Nations Food and Agriculture Organization's (UNFAO) Emergency Center for Locust Operations.

## CHAPTER 1

See RG 245

1 The word of the LORD which came to Joel, the son of Pethuel.

## I. Announcement of Unprecedented Disaster

2 Listen to this, you elders!
Pay attention, all who dwell in the land!
Has anything like this ever happened in your lifetime,
or in the lifetime of your ancestors?
3 Report it to your children.
Have your children report it to their children,
and their children to the next generation.
4 What the cutter left,
the swarming locust has devoured;
What the swarming locust left,
the hopper has devoured;
What the hopper left,
the consuming locust* has devoured.
5 Wake up, you drunkards,* and weep;
wail, all you wine drinkers,
Over the new wine,
taken away from your mouths.
6 For a nation* invaded my land,
powerful and past counting,
With teeth like a lion's,
fangs like those of a lioness.
7 It has stripped bare my vines,
splintered my fig tree,
Shearing off its bark and throwing it away,
until its branches turn white.
8 Wail like a young woman* dressed in sackcloth
for the husband of her youth.
9 Grain offering and libation are cut off
from the house of the LORD;
In mourning are the priests,
the ministers of the LORD.
10 The field is devastated;
the farmland mourns,*
Because the grain is devastated,
the wine has dried up,
the oil has failed.
11 Be appalled, you farmers!
wail, you vinedressers,
Over the wheat and the barley,
because the harvest in the field is ruined.
12 The vine has dried up,
the fig tree has withered;
The pomegranate, even the date palm
and the apple—

**1:4 Cutter . . . swarming locust . . . hopper . . . consuming locust**: these names may refer to various species of locusts, or to some phases in the insect's life cycle, or to successive waves of locusts ravaging the countryside.

**1:5 Drunkards**: this metaphor expresses both the urgency behind Joel's preaching and his ironic assessment of his audience. There are no grapes to process into new wine, yet people view their situation as just another agricultural crisis. Joel argues that the problems they now face are lessons the Lord is using to provide the knowledge they lack.

**1:6 A nation**: the locusts are compared to an invading army, whose numbers are overwhelming. The ravaged landscape resembles the wasteland left behind by marauding troops; the order and peace associated with agricultural productivity (1 Kgs 5:5; Mi 4:4) has been destroyed.

**1:8 Like a young woman**: this simile personifies Jerusalem as a youthful widow, left unprotected and without resources by her husband's sudden death.

**1:10 The farmland mourns**: or "the farmland is dried up."

every tree in the field has dried up.
Joy itself has dried up
among the people.

### *Cry Out to the Lord*

13 * Gird yourselves and lament, you priests!
wail, ministers of the altar!
Come, spend the night in sackcloth,
ministers of my God!
For the grain offering and the libation
are withheld from the house of your God.[a]
14 Proclaim a holy fast!
Call an assembly!
Gather the elders,
all who dwell in the land,
To the house of the LORD, your God,
and cry out to the LORD![b]
15 O! The day!*
For near is the day of the LORD,
like destruction from the Almighty it is coming![c]
16 Before our very eyes*
has not food been cut off?
And from the house of our God,
joy and gladness?
17 The seed lies shriveled beneath clods of dirt;*
the storehouses are emptied.
The granaries are broken down,
for the grain is dried up.
18 * How the animals groan!
The herds of cattle are bewildered!
Because they have no pasture,
even the flocks of sheep are starving.
19 To you, LORD, I cry!
for fire has devoured the wilderness pastures,
flame has scorched all the trees in the field.
20 Even the animals in the wild
cry out to you;
For the streams of water have run dry,
and fire has devoured the wilderness pastures.[d]

## II. The Day of the Lord

### CHAPTER 2

See RG 245

### *The Day Approaches*

1 * Blow the horn in Zion,
sound the alarm on my holy mountain!
Let all the inhabitants of the land tremble,
for the day of the LORD is coming![e]
Yes, it approaches,
2 a day of darkness and gloom,
a day of thick clouds!
Like dawn* spreading over the mountains,
a vast and mighty army!
Nothing like it has ever happened in ages past,
nor will the future hold anything like it,
even to the most distant generations.[f]
3 Before it,* fire devours,
behind it flame scorches.
The land before it is like the garden of Eden,

**1:13** Judah's situation is so grave and the day of the Lord so imminent that priests must lament day and night if they hope to reverse the divine punishment.

**1:15** As in Am 5:18–20, the day of the Lord in Joel's first speech brings punishment, not victory, for Judah. In his second speech, this event means victory for those faithful to the Lord and death for the nations who are the Lord's enemies. **Almighty**: Hebrew *shaddai*. There is wordplay between *shod* ("destruction") and *shaddai*.

**1:16 Before our very eyes**: Joel's audience should have discerned the significance of the winter drought and the locust invasion they witnessed. **Joy and gladness**: the loss of field crops has reduced Joel's audience to subsistence living, with no means for liturgical or personal celebration, as in v. 12.

**1:17 The seed . . . clods of dirt**: the meaning of the Hebrew is uncertain. Most commentators use the translation given here, since it fits the prophet's description of an agricultural year plagued by winter drought and a spring locust infestation.

**1:18–19** In figurative language, Joel describes how the insufficient winter rain, the locust invasions, and summer's heat on pasture lands and water sources drive domestic and wild animals to cry out for rain.

**2:1–11** Joel warns the people about the destruction he sees galloping toward Jerusalem. He combines the imagery of the locust invasion (chap. 1) with language from the holy war tradition in order to describe the Lord leading a heavenly army against the enemy, in this case, Jerusalem.

**2:2 Like dawn**: from the east comes dark destruction rather than a new day's light.

**2:3 Before it**: fire precedes and follows the army's advance. Even the ravaged landscape of chap. 1 looks like a lush garden compared to the devastation this army leaves behind.

*a:* Jer 4:8. *b:* Jl 2:15. *c:* Is 13:6; Ez 30:2–3; Ob 15; Zep 1:7. *d:* Ps 42:2. *e:* Is 13:9; Jer 4:5; 6:1; 51:27; Hos 5:8; Zep 1:16. *f:* Is 13:14; Zep 1:4–15.

and behind it, a desolate wilderness;
from it nothing escapes.[g]
4 Their appearance is that of horses;
like war horses they run.
5 Like the rumble of chariots
they hurtle across mountaintops;
Like the crackling of fiery flames
devouring stubble;
Like a massive army
in battle formation.[h]
6 Before them peoples tremble,
every face turns pale.[i]
7 Like warriors they run,
like soldiers they scale walls,
Each advancing in line,
without swerving from the course.
8 No one crowds the other;
each advances in its own track;
They plunge through the weapons;
they are not checked.
9 They charge the city,
they run upon the wall,
they climb into the houses;
Through the windows
they enter like thieves.

10 Before them the earth trembles;
the heavens shake;
Sun and moon are darkened,
and the stars withhold their
brightness.[j]
11 The LORD raises his voice
at the head of his army;
How immense is his host!
How numerous those who carry out
his command!
How great is the day of the LORD!
Utterly terrifying! Who can survive it?[k]

### *Return to the Lord*

12 Yet even now—oracle of the LORD—
return to me with your whole heart,
with fasting, weeping, and mourning.
13 Rend your hearts, not your garments,
and return to the LORD, your God,
For he is gracious and merciful,
slow to anger, abounding in steadfast
love,
and relenting in punishment.[l]
14 Perhaps he will again relent
and leave behind a blessing,*
Grain offering and libation
for the LORD, your God.[m]
15 Blow the horn in Zion!
Proclaim a fast,
call an assembly![n]
16 Gather the people,
sanctify the congregation;
Assemble the elderly;
gather the children,
even infants nursing at the breast;
Let the bridegroom leave his room,
and the bride* her bridal tent.
17 Between the porch and the altar*
let the priests weep,
let the ministers of the LORD weep and
say:
"Spare your people, LORD!
do not let your heritage become a
disgrace,
a byword among the nations!
Why should they say among the peoples,
'Where is their God?' "[o]

***The Lord Relents.*** 18Then the LORD grew
jealous* for his land and took pity on his
people. 19In response the LORD said to his
people:
I am sending you
grain, new wine, and oil,
and you will be satisfied by them;
Never again will I make you
a disgrace among the nations.

**2:14 Blessing**: the rain that makes possible the grapes and grain (v. 19) that workers will process into Temple offerings.

**2:16 Elderly . . . infants . . . bridegroom . . . bride**: Jerusalem is in such great danger that even those normally excused from fasting or working are called upon to participate in activities to ward off the imminent catastrophe.

**2:17 Between the porch and the altar**: the priests stood in the open space between the outdoor altar for burnt offerings and the Temple building.

**2:18 Jealous**: the Hebrew word describes the passionate empathetic bond the Lord has with Israel. The people's wholehearted participation in Joel's call for fasting and prayer sparks the Lord's longing to protect and love his people Israel. This desire moves him to withhold punishment and to send the blessing of v. 14 instead.

*g:* Is 13:9; 51:3; Ez 36:35. *h:* Jer 6:23. *i:* Na 2:11. *j:* Jl 4:15; Is 13:10, 13; Ez 32:7–8; Mt 24:29; Mk 13:24; Lk 21:25–26. *k:* Jer 30:7; Am 5:18; Zep 1:15. *l:* Ex 34:6; Ps 86:5; Jon 4:2. *m:* Jon 3:9. *n:* Jl 1:14. *o:* Ps 42:4, 11; 79:10; 115:2.

**The Day of the LORD**

APPEARING FIVE TIMES in Joel (1:15; 2:1; 2:11; 3:4; 4:14), this expression is used in the Bible for a decisive divine act in human affairs. In its earliest occurrence, Amos uses it to describe an act of God's judgment on Israel (Am 5, 18–20). But because Amos implies that his audience believes this expression referred to an act of God's salvation, scholars think the day of the LORD originally may have had a positive meaning, describing God's victory on Israel's behalf. In some cases, in fact, this phrase is used for God's judgment on the nations and restoration of Judah (Ob 15–21; Zec 14:1–9). Scholars disagree whether the day of the LORD is used both ways in Joel—for judgment in Joel 1:15; 2:1; 2:11 and for salvation in Joel 3:4; 4:14—or whether all uses point toward the final salvation described in ch 3.

20 The northerner* I will remove far from you,
driving them out into a dry and
desolate land,
Their vanguard to the eastern sea,
their rearguard to the western sea,
And their stench will rise,
their stink will ascend,
What great deeds the Lord has done!
21 Do not fear, O land!
delight and rejoice,
for the LORD has done great things![p]
22 Do not fear, you animals in the wild,
for the wilderness pastures sprout
green grass.
The trees bear fruit,
the fig tree and the vine produce their
harvest.
23 Children of Zion, delight
and rejoice in the LORD, your God!
For he has faithfully given you the early
rain,*
sending rain down on you,
the early and the late rains as before.[q]
24 The threshing floors will be full of grain,
the vats spilling over with new wine
and oil.
25 I will repay you double
what the swarming locust has eaten,
The hopper, the consuming locust, and
the cutter,
my great army I sent against you.[r]
26 You will eat until you are fully satisfied,
then you will praise the name of the
LORD, your God,
Who acts so wondrously on your behalf!
My people will never again be put to
shame.
27 Then you will know that I am in the
midst of Israel:
I, the LORD, am your God, and there is
no other;
my people will never again be put to
shame.[s]

## III. The Lord's Final Judgment

### CHAPTER 3

See RG 245

*The Day of the Lord*[t]

1 * It shall come to pass
I will pour out my spirit upon all flesh.
Your sons and daughters will prophesy,
your old men will dream dreams,

**2:20 The northerner**: the locusts, pictured as an invading army, which traditionally came from the north (Jer 1:14–15; Ez 26:7; 38:6, 15). Locusts are not usually an annual threat in Palestine, nor are they often associated with the north. However, to demonstrate the extent of the Lord's care for Judah and control over what happens within its borders, Joel assures his audience that the Lord will quickly drive the locusts out of Judah the coming spring, should they reappear. Dead locusts will litter the shores of the "eastern" (the Dead Sea) and the "western" (the Mediterranean) seas.

**2:23** This autumn rain teaches the people to recognize God's compassionate presence in nature and history. There is a play on the double meaning of the Hebrew word *moreh*: "early rain" and "teacher." In the Dead Sea Scrolls, the word is used in the phrase "teacher (= *moreh*) of righteousness."

**3:1–5** In many places in the Old Testament, Hebrew *ruah* is God's power, or spirit, bestowed on chosen individuals. The word can also mean "breath" or "wind." In this summary introduction to his second speech, Joel anticipates that the Lord will someday renew faithful Judahites with the divine spirit. In Acts 2:17–21 the author has Peter cite Joel's words to suggest that the newly constituted Christian community,

*p:* Ps 126:3. *q:* Hos 10:12. *r:* Jer 5:17. *s:* Is 45:5–6, 18; 46:9.

your young men will see visions.
2 Even upon your male and female
servants,
in those days, I will pour out my spirit.
3 I will set signs in the heavens and on the
earth,
blood, fire, and columns of smoke;
4 The sun will darken,
the moon turn blood-red,
Before the day of the LORD arrives,
that great and terrible day.[u]
5 Then everyone who calls upon the name
of the LORD
will escape harm.
For on Mount Zion there will be a
remnant,
as the LORD has said,
And in Jerusalem survivors
whom the LORD will summon.[v]

See RG 246

## CHAPTER 4

### *The Lord's Case Against the Nations*

1 For see, in those days and at that time,[w]
when I restore the fortunes
of Judah and Jerusalem,
2 I will gather all the nations
and bring them down to the Valley of
Jehoshaphat.*
There I will enter into judgment with
them
on behalf of my people, my heritage,
Israel;
Because they scattered them among the
nations,
they divided up my land.[x]
3 For my people they cast lots,
trading a young boy for the price of a
prostitute,
exchanging a young girl for the wine
they drank.[y]

4* Moreover, what are you doing to me,
Tyre and Sidon, and all the regions of Philistia? Are you paying me back for something?
If you are, I will very quickly turn your
deeds back upon your own head.[z] 5 You took
my silver and my gold and brought my
priceless treasures into your temples! 6 You
sold the people of Judah and Jerusalem to
the Greeks, taking them far from their own
country! 7 Look! I am rousing them from the
place to which you sold them, and I will turn
your deeds back upon your own head. 8 I will
sell your sons and daughters to the Judahites
who will sell them to the Sabeans,* a distant
nation. The LORD has spoken!

### *The Nations Destroyed*

9 Announce this to the nations:
Proclaim a holy war!
Alert the warriors!
Let all the soldiers
report and march![a]
10 * Beat your plowshares into swords,
and your pruning knives into spears;
let the weakling boast, "I am a
warrior!"[b]
11 Hurry and come, all you neighboring
peoples,
assemble there!
Bring down, LORD, your warriors!
12 Let the nations rouse themselves and
come up
to the Valley of Jehoshaphat;
For there I will sit in judgment
upon all the neighboring nations.

filled with divine life and power, inaugurates the Lord's Day, understood as salvation for all who believe that Jesus of Nazareth is the Christ.

**4:2 Valley of Jehoshaphat**: one of the symbolic names of the place of punishment for Judah's enemies; the other is "Valley of Decision" (v. 14). The name Jehoshaphat means "the Lord judges." If the popular identification of this place as the Kidron Valley is accurate, Joel may imagine the Lord seated above the valley on Mount Zion directing his troops in the destruction of nations in the valley below.

**4:4–8** This prose material may be a later addition to the book. It illustrates a common biblical theme (cf. Ps 7:16; 9:16; 35:8; 37:14–15; 57:7), having one's evil deed (selling Judahites into slavery) turned into one's own punishment (being sold into slavery by the Judahites).

**4:8 Sabeans**: traders from the southwestern tip of the Arabian peninsula, present-day Yemen (cf. 1 Kgs 10:1–2; Ps 72:10; Jer 6:20).

**4:10** The Lord directs the troops to forge military weapons out of the agricultural tools necessary for life during peacetime. In Is 2:4 and Mi 4:3, both in contexts presuming the defeat of Israel's enemies, this imagery is reversed.

*t:* Is 44:3; Ez 39:28–29; Acts 2:17–21. *u:* Jl 2:10; Mal 3:23. *v:* Ob 17–18; Rom 10:13. *w:* Jer 33:15; 50:4, 20. *x:* Is 66:18; Zec 14:2. *y:* Ob 11, 16. *z:* Ob 15. *a:* Jer 6:4. *b:* Is 2:4; Mi 4:3.

13 Wield the sickle,[c]
for the harvest is ripe;
Come and tread,
for the wine press is full;
The vats overflow,
for their crimes are numerous.*
14 Crowds upon crowds
in the Valley of Decision;
For near is the day of the LORD
in the Valley of Decision.[d]
15 Sun and moon are darkened,
and the stars withhold their
brightness,[e]
16 The LORD roars from Zion,
and from Jerusalem raises his voice,[f]
The heavens and the earth quake,
but the LORD will be a shelter for his
people,
a fortress for the people of Israel.

### *A Secure Future for Judah*

17 Then you will know* that I the LORD am
your God,[g]
dwelling on Zion, my holy mountain;
Jerusalem will be holy,
and strangers will never again travel
through her.
18 * On that day
the mountains will drip new wine,
and the hills flow with milk,
All the streams of Judah
will flow with water.
A spring will rise from the house of the
LORD,
watering the Valley of Shittim.[h]
19 Egypt will be a waste,
Edom a desolate wilderness,
Because of violence done to the
Judahites,
because they shed innocent blood in
their land.[i]
20 But Judah will be inhabited forever,
and Jerusalem for all generations.
21 I will avenge their blood,
and I will not acquit the guilt.
The LORD dwells in Zion.

**4:13 Their crimes are numerous**: the nations are ripe for punishment. Joel uses the vocabulary of the autumn grape harvest to describe the assault of the Lord's army against these nations. In Is 63:1–6, grape harvest imagery also controls the description of the Lord's return from Edom with blood-spattered clothing after having trod his enemies into the ground as if they were grapes (cf. Jer 25:30).

**4:17 Then you will know**: this verse further develops the motif of knowledge introduced in 2:27. The Judahites will learn that the Lord is present in their economic prosperity and political autonomy, even though they did not associate God's presence with their crop failure.

**4:18** Images of agricultural abundance illustrate the harmony and order Joel expects the Lord to establish in Judah; like 2:18–27, this section reverses the deprivation and drought of chap. 1. **A spring ... house of the LORD**: streams of water flowing from the Temple of an ideal Jerusalem also appear in Ez 47:1. **The Valley of Shittim**: or "the ravine of the acacia trees"; while there is a Shittim east of the Jordan, the reference here is probably to that rocky part of the Kidron Valley southeast of Jerusalem, an arid region where acacia trees flourished.

*c:* Is 63:1–6; Rev 14:15. *d:* Ob 15. *e:* Jl 2:10; 3:4. *f:* Jer 25:30; Am 1:2. *g:* Ob 17; Na 2:1. *h:* Ez 47:1–12; Am 9:13; Zec 14:8. *i:* Ob 10.

See RG 246–50

# The Book of Amos

Amos was a sheepbreeder of Tekoa in Judah, who delivered his oracles in the Northern Kingdom during the prosperous reign of Jeroboam II (786–746 B.C.). He prophesied in Israel at the great cult center of Bethel, from which he was finally expelled by the priest in charge of this royal sanctuary (7:10–17). The poetry of Amos, who denounces the hollow prosperity of the Northern Kingdom, is filled with imagery and language taken from his own pastoral background. The book is an anthology of his oracles and was compiled either by the prophet or by some of his disciples.

The prophecy begins with a sweeping indictment of Damascus, Philistia, Tyre, and Edom; but the forthright herdsman saves his climactic denunciation for Israel, whose injustice and idolatry are sins against the light granted to her. Israel could indeed expect the day of the Lord, but it would be a day of darkness and not light (5:18). When Amos prophesied the overthrow of the sanctuary, the fall of the royal house, and the captivity of the people, it was more than Israelite officialdom could bear. The priest of Bethel drove Amos from the shrine—but not before hearing a terrible sentence pronounced upon himself.

Amos is a prophet of divine judgment, and the sovereignty of the Lord in nature and history dominates his thought. But he was no innovator; his conservatism was in keeping with the whole prophetic tradition calling the people back to the high moral and religious demands of the Lord's revelation.

Amos's message stands as one of the most powerful voices ever to challenge hypocrisy and injustice. He boldly indicts kings, priests, and leaders (6:1; 7:9, 16–17). He stresses the importance and the divine origin of the prophetic word (3:3–8); one must either heed that word in its entirety or suffer its disappearance (8:11–12). Religion without justice is an affront to the God of Israel and, far from appeasing God, can only provoke divine wrath (5:21–27; 8:4–10). The Lord is not some petty national god but the sovereign creator of the cosmos (4:13; 5:8; 9:5–6). Amos alludes to historical forces at work through which God would exercise judgment on Israel (6:14). Several times he mentions deportation as the fate that awaits the people and their corrupt leaders (4:3; 5:5, 27; 7:17), a standard tactic of Assyrian foreign policy during this period. Through the prophetic word and various natural disasters (4:6–12) the Lord has tried to bring Israel to repentance, but to no avail. Israel's rebelliousness has exhausted the divine patience and the destruction of Israel as a nation and as God's people is inevitable (2:4, 13–16; 7:8–9). As it is presented in this book, Amos's message is one of almost unrelieved gloom (but see 5:14–15). A later appendix (9:11–15), however, ends the book on a hopeful note, looking beyond the judgment that had already taken place in fulfillment of Amos's word.

The Book of Amos may be divided as follows:

I. Editorial Introduction (1:1–2)
II. Oracles Against the Nations (1:3–2:16)
III. Threefold Summons to Hear the Word of the Lord (3:1–5:9)
IV. Three Woes (5:7–6:14)
V. Symbolic Visions (7:1–9:10)
VI. Epilogue: Restoration Under a Davidic King (9:11–15)

## I. Editorial Introduction

### CHAPTER 1

See RG 248–49

1 The words of Amos, who was one of
the sheepbreeders from Tekoa,[a] which he received in a vision concerning Israel in the
days of Uzziah, king of Judah, and in the
days of Jeroboam, son of Joash, king of Israel, two years before the earthquake.* 2 He
said:

The LORD roars from Zion,*
and raises his voice from Jerusalem;
The pastures of the shepherds languish,
and the summit of Carmel withers.[b]

## II. Oracles Against the Nations*

### *Aram*

3 Thus says the LORD:

For three crimes of Damascus, and now four—*
I will not take it back—
Because they threshed Gilead
with sledges of iron,
4 I will send fire upon the house of Hazael,
and it will devour the strongholds of Ben-hadad.*[c]
5 I will break the barred gate of Damascus;

**1:1 The earthquake**: a major earthquake during the reign of Uzziah (ca. 783–742 B.C.), so devastating that it was remembered long afterwards (cf. Zec 14:5). See the description of an earthquake in Amos's final vision (9:1).

**1:2** Significantly, the roar comes to the Northern Kingdom from Jerusalem. This verse, perhaps an editorial remark, sets the tone of Amos's message.

**1:3–2:16** All the nations mentioned here may have been part of the ideal empire of David-Solomon (cf. 1 Kgs 5:1; 2 Kgs 14:25). Certain standards of conduct were expected not only in their relations with Israel but also with one another.

**1:3 For three crimes . . . and now four**: this formula (N, N+1) is frequent in poetry (e.g., Prv 6:16–19; 30:18–19). The progression "three" followed by "four" here suggests a climax. The fourth crime is one too many and exhausts the Lord's forbearance.

**1:4 Hazael . . . Ben-hadad**: kings of the Arameans whose capital was Damascus (v. 5); they fought against Israel (2 Kgs 13:3) and had long occupied the region of Gilead (v. 3) in Transjordan.

*a*: Zec 14:5. *b*: Jer 25:30; Jl 4:16. *c*: 2 Kgs 13:3–7; Hos 8:14.

## Judgments on Israel's Neighbors

IN TYPICAL TWO-PART judgment speeches, containing indictments and sentences, Amos announces divine judgment on seven of Israel's closest neighbors. The indictments in each case involve acts of brutality against neighboring peoples. The phrase "says the LORD," which begins and ends these speeches, identifies them as divine oracles and the prophet as a divine spokesperson.

From the Valley of Aven* I will cut off
the one enthroned,
And the sceptered ruler from Beth-eden;
the people of Aram shall be exiled to
Kir,[d] says the LORD.

*Philistia*

6 Thus says the LORD:

For three crimes of Gaza, and now
four—
I will not take it back—
Because they exiled an entire population,
handing them over to Edom,
7 I will send fire upon the wall of Gaza,
and it will devour its strongholds;
8 From Ashdod I will cut off the one
enthroned
and the sceptered ruler from Ashkelon;
I will turn my hand against Ekron,
and the last of the Philistines shall
perish,
says the Lord GOD.

*Tyre*

9 Thus says the LORD:

For three crimes of Tyre, and now
four—
I will not take it back—
Because they handed over an entire
population to Edom,
and did not remember their covenant
of brotherhood,*
10 I will send fire upon the wall of Tyre,
and it will devour its strongholds.

*Edom*

11 Thus says the LORD:

For three crimes of Edom, and now four—
I will not take it back—
Because he pursued his brother* with the
sword,
suppressing all pity,
Persisting in his anger,
his wrath raging without end,
12 I will send fire upon Teman,
and it will devour the strongholds of
Bozrah.*

*Ammon*

13 Thus says the LORD:

For three crimes of the Ammonites, and
now four—
I will not take it back—
Because they ripped open pregnant
women in Gilead,[e]
in order to extend their territory,
14 I will kindle a fire upon the wall of
Rabbah,*
and it will devour its strongholds
Amid war cries on the day of battle,
amid stormwind on the day of tempest.
15 Their king shall go into exile,
he and his princes with him, says the
LORD.

**1:5 Valley of Aven**: lit., "valley of wickedness," perhaps a distortion of a place name in Aramean territory, identity unknown. **Beth-eden**: an Aramean city-state on the Euphrates, about two hundred miles northeast of Damascus, called *Bit-adini* in Assyro-Babylonian texts. **Kir**: cf. 9:7; probably to be identified with the city of Emar on the Euphrates, a major Aramean center in the Late Bronze Age. One text from this site calls the king of Emar "the king of the people of the land of Kir."

**1:9 Did not remember their covenant of brotherhood**: standard diplomatic language of this period, meaning "violated the treaty." The violation may not have been against Israel itself but against a fellow "subject" nation of the ideal Davidic-Solomonic empire (cf. 2:1).

**1:11 Pursued his brother**: "brother" here may denote a fellow vassal or subject of Israel.

**1:12 Teman . . . Bozrah**: two of the chief cities of Edom; cf. Jer 49:20.

**1:14 Rabbah**: now called Amman, the modern capital of Jordan.

*d:* 2 Kgs 16:9. *e:* 2 Kgs 8:12; 15:16.

## Israel's Stubbornness

A BRIEF HISTORICAL summary in 2:9–12 stresses Israel's stubbornness by contrasting it with God's acts of salvation on Israel's behalf. The judgment imposed for Israel's crimes (vv. 13–16) will bring an end to Israel's strongest defenses: its fast runners, its strongest warriors, its most skilled archers, and its best horsemen.

See RG 248–49

### CHAPTER 2

#### *Moab*

1 Thus says the LORD:

For three crimes of Moab, and now four—
I will not take it back—
Because he burned to ashes*
the bones of Edom's king,
2 I will send fire upon Moab,
and it will devour the strongholds of Kerioth;
Moab shall meet death amid uproar,
battle cries and blasts of the ram's horn.
3 I will cut off the ruler from its midst,
and all the princes I will slay with him,
says the LORD.

#### *Judah*

4* Thus says the LORD:

For three crimes of Judah, and now four—
I will not take it back—
Because they spurned the instruction of the LORD,[f]
and did not keep his statutes;
Because the lies* which their ancestors followed
have led them astray,
5 I will send fire upon Judah,
and it will devour the strongholds of Jerusalem.

#### *Israel*

6 Thus says the LORD:

For three crimes of Israel,* and now four—
I will not take it back—
Because they hand over the just for silver,
and the poor for a pair of sandals;[g]
7 They trample the heads of the destitute
into the dust of the earth,
and force the lowly out of the way.
Son and father sleep with the same girl,*
profaning my holy name.
8 Upon garments taken in pledge
they recline beside any altar.* [h]
Wine at treasury expense
they drink in their temples.
9 Yet it was I who destroyed the Amorites before them,
who were as tall as cedars,
and as strong as oak trees.
I destroyed their fruit above
and their roots beneath.[i]
10 It was I who brought you up from the land of Egypt,

**2:1 He burned to ashes**: to the peoples of the Near East, burning the bones of the dead was a particularly heinous crime, as it was believed to cause the spirits of these dead to wander without any hope of interment in their graves, where they could rest in peace.

**2:4–8, 12** Unlike the crimes of the nations detailed in this section, which are wrongs against other nations, those of Judah and Israel named here are violations of the Lord's demands.

**2:4 The lies**: false gods worshiped by the Judahites.

**2:6 Israel**: Amos's audience would applaud his condemnation of foreign kingdoms in the foregoing seven oracles, especially of Judah. But now he adds an eighth, unexpected oracle—against Israel itself. This is the real "punch line" of this whole section, to which the preceding oracles serve mainly as introduction.

**2:7 Son and father sleep with the same girl**: the crime condemned here may be the misuse of power by the rich who take unfair advantage of young women from the ranks of the poor and force themselves on them, thus adding oppression to the sin of impurity.

**2:8 Upon garments . . . any altar**: creditors kept the garments taken as pledges from the poor instead of returning them to their owners before nightfall as the law commanded (Ex 22:25; cf. Dt 24:12). **Wine . . . in their temples**: lavish feasts for the rich, serving the finest wines in great abundance (see 6:4–7) and funded by the treasuries of local temples (e.g., at Dan and Bethel). The Hebrew in this verse is difficult. Another possible translation would be: "And the wine of those who have been fined / they drink in the house of their god."

---

*f*: Is 5:24. *g*: Am 8:6; Sir 46:19. *h*: Dt 24:12–13. *i*: Nm 21:21–32; Dt 2:24–37; Jb 18:16; Hos 9:16.

**Judgment on Bethel**

LOCATED IN THE southern part of Israel, Bethel, together with Dan in the north, was one of Israel's major religious centers. The judgment against Israel's houses (3:15) that follows the judgment on Bethel contains an implicit criticism of the rich. Israel's wealthiest citizens built winter houses in the Jordan valley to escape the cold winter climate in the mountains of Samaria, and they made furniture inlaid with ivory for their homes (6:4).

and who led you through the desert for
forty years,
to occupy the land of the Amorites;
11 I who raised up prophets among your
children,
and nazirites* among your young men.
Is this not so, Israelites?—
oracle of the LORD.
12 But you made the nazirites drink wine,
and commanded the prophets, "Do not
prophesy!"[j]
13 Look, I am groaning beneath you,
as a wagon groans when laden with
sheaves.
14 Flight shall elude the swift,
and the strong shall not retain
strength;[k]
The warrior shall not save his life,
15 nor shall the archer stand his ground;
The swift of foot shall not escape,
nor shall the horseman save his life.
16 And the most stouthearted of warriors
shall flee naked on that day—
oracle of the LORD.

## III. Threefold Summons to Hear the Word of the Lord

### CHAPTER 3

See RG 249

*First Summons*

1 Hear this word, Israelites, that the LORD
speaks concerning you,
concerning the whole family I brought
up from the land of Egypt:
2 You alone I have known,*
among all the families of the earth;[l]
Therefore I will punish you
for all your iniquities.

3 * Do two journey together
unless they have agreed?
4 Does a lion roar in the forest
when it has no prey?
Does a young lion cry out from its den
unless it has seized something?
5 Does a bird swoop down on a trap on the
ground
when there is no lure for it?
Does a snare spring up from the ground
without catching anything?
6 Does the ram's horn sound in a city
without the people becoming
frightened?
Does disaster befall a city
unless the LORD has caused it?[m]

7 (Indeed, the Lord GOD does nothing without revealing his plan to his servants the prophets.)

8 The lion has roared,
who would not fear?[n]
The Lord GOD has spoken,
who would not prophesy?
9 Proclaim this in the strongholds of
Assyria,*

**2:11 Nazirites**: see note on Nm 6:2–21. **Oracle of the LORD**: a phrase used extensively in prophetic books to indicate divine speech.

**3:2 You alone I have known**: precisely because Israel enjoyed a special status among the nations of the world in the eyes of the Lord (but see 9:7) it was called to a high degree of fidelity to God. Because Israel has failed in this expectation, it must experience God's punishment.

**3:3–8** The metaphors in these sayings illustrate the principle of cause and effect, and lead up to the conclusion in v. 8.

**3:9 Assyria**: following the Greek version, the Hebrew text has "Ashod." It is supposed that this was a copyist's error: "Assyria" seems intended, in order to parallel "Egypt" in the next line.

**3:9** With a keen sense of irony, Amos invites the most powerful oppressors in Israel's memory, past and present—Egypt and Assyria—to see and marvel at the great oppression and

*j:* Am 7:13; Nm 6:1–4; Is 30:10; Jer 11:21. *k:* Ps 33:16. *l:* Gn 18:19; Dt 7:6. *m:* Jl 2:1. *n:* Am 1:2.

## Judgment on Samaria's Elite Women

IN THIS INDICTMENT of their oppression of the poor (4:1), Amos compares Israel's leading women to cattle grazing in Israel's prime pasture land, Bashan.

in the strongholds of the land of Egypt:
"Gather on the mount of Samaria,
and see the great disorders within it,
the oppressions within its midst."*
10 They do not know how to do what is right—
oracle of the LORD—
Storing up in their strongholds
violence and destruction.
11 Therefore thus says the Lord GOD:
An enemy shall surround the land,
tear down your fortresses,
and pillage your strongholds.
12 Thus says the LORD:
As the shepherd rescues from the mouth of the lion
a pair of sheep's legs or the tip of an ear,
So shall the Israelites escape,
those who dwell in Samaria,
With the corner of a couch
or a piece of a cot.*

13 Hear and bear witness against the house of Jacob—
an oracle of the Lord GOD, the God of hosts:
14 On the day when I punish Israel for its crimes,
I will also punish the altars of Bethel;
The horns of the altar shall be broken off
and fall to the ground.* [o]
15 I will strike the winter house
and the summer house;
The houses of ivory shall lie in ruin,
and their many rooms shall be no more—
oracle of the LORD.

### CHAPTER 4

See RG 249

*Second Summons*

1 Hear this word, you cows of Bashan,*
who live on the mount of Samaria:
Who oppress the destitute
and abuse the needy;
Who say to your husbands,
"Bring us a drink!"
2 The Lord GOD has sworn by his holiness:
Truly days are coming upon you
when they shall drag you away with ropes,
your children with fishhooks;
3 You shall go out through the breached walls
one in front of the other,
And you shall be exiled to Harmon—*
oracle of the LORD.

4 Come to Bethel* and sin,
to Gilgal and sin all the more!
Each morning bring your sacrifices,
every third day your tithes;
5 Burn leavened bread as a thanksgiving sacrifice,
proclaim publicly your voluntary offerings,
For so you love to do, Israelites—
oracle of the Lord GOD.
6 Though I made your teeth
clean of food in all your cities,
and made bread scarce in all your dwellings,
Yet you did not return to me—
oracle of the LORD.[p]
7 [q] And I withheld the rain from you

injustice being wrought within Samaria by the people of Israel.

**3:12** The "escape" is clearly a disaster, not a deliverance.

**3:14** On Bethel, see also 4:4; 5:5–6; and 7:13. The prophet is condemning the religiosity and formalism of the worship by Israel's leaders.

**4:1 Cows of Bashan**: the pampered women of Samaria; Bashan was a region east of the Sea of Galilee, famous for its rich pasture and fattened herds.

**4:3 Harmon**: or perhaps "Mount Mon"; an unidentified site, probably far to the north of Israel, under the control of Assyria.

**4:4 Come to Bethel**: Amos's invitation to the people to come and "sin" at two of the major religious centers in Samaria is sarcastic. His point is that sacrifice and worship without justice is an abomination to the God of Israel; cf. 5:21–24.

*o:* Am 9:1; 1 Kgs 13:1–5. *p:* Wis 12:2, 10. *q:* Jer 14:1–6.

when the harvest was still three
months away;
I sent rain upon one city
but not upon another;
One field was watered by rain,
but the one I did not water dried up;
8 Two or three cities staggered to another
to drink water
but were not satisfied;
Yet you did not return to me—
oracle of the LORD.
9 I struck you with blight and mildew;
locusts devoured your gardens and
vineyards,
the caterpillar consumed your fig trees
and olive trees;
Yet you did not return to me—
oracle of the LORD.[r]
10 I sent upon you pestilence like that of
Egypt;[s]
with the sword I killed your young
men and your captured horses,
and to your nostrils I brought the
stench of your camps;
Yet you did not return to me—
oracle of the LORD.
11 I overthrew you
as when God overthrew Sodom and
Gomorrah;
you were like a brand plucked from
the fire,[t]
Yet you did not return to me—
oracle of the LORD.
12 Therefore thus I will do to you,* Israel:
and since I will deal thus with you,
prepare to meet your God, O Israel!
13 The one who forms mountains and
creates winds,
and declares to mortals their thoughts;
Who makes dawn into darkness
and strides upon the heights of the
earth,
the LORD, the God of hosts, is his
name!

## CHAPTER 5

See RG 249

### *Third Summons**

1 Hear this word which I utter concerning
you,
this dirge, house of Israel:
2 She is fallen, to rise no more,
virgin Israel;
She lies abandoned on her land,
with no one to raise her up.[u]
3 For thus says the Lord GOD
to the house of Israel:
The city that marched out with a
thousand
shall be left with a hundred,
Another that marched out with a hundred
shall be left with ten.
4 For thus says the LORD*
to the house of Israel:
Seek me, that you may live,[v]
5 but do not seek Bethel;
Do not come to Gilgal,
and do not cross over to Beer-sheba;
For Gilgal shall be led into exile
and Bethel shall be no more.
6 * Seek the LORD, that you may live,
lest he flare up against the house of
Joseph* like a fire
that shall consume the house of Israel,
with no one to quench it.
8 The one who made the Pleiades and
Orion,
who turns darkness into dawn,
and darkens day into night;
Who summons the waters of the sea,

**4:12 Therefore thus I will do to you**: this climax of vv. 6–12, announcing the sentence the Lord intends to pass on Israel, is open-ended.

**5:1–17** These verses form a chiastic section beginning and ending with a lament over Israel (vv. 2, 16–17) and containing a double appeal to "seek" the Lord (vv. 4, 14). This editorial arrangement gives the whole section a negative cast, in effect nullifying the only hopeful verse in Amos (v. 15). Israel is as good as dead.

**5:4–5 For thus says the LORD . . . Bethel shall be no more**: these two verses continue the sarcasm of 4:4–5, verses in which Amos invites the people to come and "sin" at Bethel and Gilgal. The cult cities of Samaria should have been places where God could be "sought" but, because of the sins of the Northern Kingdom, these cities would cease to exist.

**5:6** These verses have been rearranged to achieve the proper sequence according to the best possible manuscript tradition. Cf. the Textual Notes accompanying the translation.

**5:6 House of Joseph**: the kingdom of Israel or Northern Kingdom, the chief tribes of which were descended from Ephraim and Manasseh, the sons of Joseph; cf. 5:15; 6:6.

*r:* Dt 28:22; Jl 1:4; 2:25; Hg 2:17. *s:* Dt 7:15; 28:27. *t:* Gn 19:24–25; Zec 3:2. *u:* Am 8:13. *v:* Hos 5:6; 10:12.

and pours them out on the surface of
the earth;[w]
9 Who makes destruction fall suddenly
upon the stronghold
and brings ruin upon the fortress,
the LORD is his name.

## IV. Three Woes

### *First Woe*

7 Woe to those who turn justice into
wormwood
and cast righteousness to the ground,
10 They hate those who reprove at the gate
and abhor those who speak with
integrity;
11 Therefore, because you tax the destitute
and exact from them levies of grain,
Though you have built houses of hewn
stone,
you shall not live in them;
Though you have planted choice
vineyards,
you shall not drink their wine.[x]
12 Yes, I know how many are your crimes,
how grievous your sins:
Oppressing the just, accepting bribes,
turning away the needy at the gate.
13 (Therefore at this time the wise are struck
dumb
for it is an evil time.)
14 Seek good and not evil,
that you may live;
Then truly the LORD, the God of hosts,
will be with you as you claim.
15 Hate evil and love good,
and let justice prevail at the gate;
Then it may be that the LORD, the God of
hosts,
will have pity on the remnant of
Joseph.[y]
16 Therefore, thus says the LORD,
the God of hosts, the Lord:
In every square there shall be lamentation,
and in every street they shall cry, "Oh,
no!"
They shall summon the farmers to wail
and the professional mourners to
lament.
17 And in every vineyard there shall be
lamentation
when I pass through your midst, says
the LORD.

### *Second Woe*

18 Woe to those who yearn
for the day of the LORD!*
What will the day of the LORD mean for
you?
It will be darkness, not light![z]
19 As if someone fled from a lion
and a bear met him;
Or as if on entering the house
he rested his hand against the wall,
and a snake bit it.
20 Truly, the day of the LORD will be
darkness, not light,
gloom without any brightness!
21 * [a] I hate, I despise your feasts,
I take no pleasure in your solemnities.
22 Even though you bring me your burnt
offerings and grain offerings
I will not accept them;
Your stall-fed communion offerings,
I will not look upon them.
23 Take away from me
your noisy songs;
The melodies of your harps,
I will not listen to them.
24 Rather let justice surge like waters,
and righteousness like an unfailing
stream.

**5:18 The day of the LORD**: first mentioned in Amos, this refers to a specific time in the future, known to the Lord alone, when God's enemies would be decisively defeated. The common assumption among Israelites was that the Lord's foes and Israel's foes were one and the same. But Amos makes it clear that because the people have become God's enemies by refusing to heed the prophetic word, they too would experience the divine wrath on that fateful day. However, during the exile this expression comes to mean a time when God would avenge Israel against its oppressors and bring about its restoration (Jer 50:27; Ez 30:3–5).

**5:21–27** The prophet does not condemn cultic activity as such but rather the people's attempt to offer worship with hands unclean from oppression of their fellow Israelites (cf. Ps 15:2–5; 24:3–4). But worship from those who disregard justice and righteousness (v. 24) is never acceptable to the God of Israel. Through the Sinai covenant the love of God and the love of neighbor are inextricably bound together.

*w:* Am 9:6; Jb 9:9; 38:31. *x:* Am 9:14; Dt 28:30; Zep 1:13. *y:* Jl 2:14; Rom 12:9. *z:* Jer 14:16; Jl 2:1–2, 11; Zep 1:14–18. *a:* Is 1:10–17; Jer 6:20.

25 [b] Did you bring me sacrifices and grain offerings
for forty years in the desert, O house of Israel?[c]
26 Yet you will carry away Sukuth,* your king,
and Kaiwan, your star-image,
your gods that you have made for yourselves,[d]
27 As I exile you beyond Damascus,
says the LORD,
whose name is the God of hosts.

## CHAPTER 6

See RG 249

### *Third Woe*

1 Woe to those who are complacent in Zion,
secure on the mount of Samaria,
Leaders of the first among nations,
to whom the people of Israel turn.
2 Pass over to Calneh and see,
go from there to Hamath the great,
and down to Gath* of the Philistines.
Are you better than these kingdoms,
or is your territory greater than theirs?
3 You who would put off the day of disaster,
yet hasten the time of violence!
4 Those who lie on beds of ivory,
and lounge upon their couches;
Eating lambs taken from the flock,
and calves from the stall;
5 Who improvise to the music of the harp,
composing on musical instruments like David,
6 Who drink wine from bowls,
and anoint themselves with the best oils,
but are not made ill by the collapse of Joseph;
7 Therefore, now they shall be the first to go into exile,
and the carousing of those who lounged shall cease.
8 The Lord GOD has sworn by his very self—
an oracle of the LORD, the God of hosts:
I abhor the pride of Jacob,
I hate his strongholds,
and I will hand over the city with everything in it;[e]
9 Should there remain ten people
in a single house, these shall die.
10 When a relative or one who prepares the body picks up the remains
to carry them out of the house,
If he says to someone in the recesses of the house,
"Is anyone with you?" and the answer is, "No one,"
Then he shall say, "Silence!"
for no one must mention the name of the LORD.* [f]
11 Indeed, the LORD has given the command
to shatter the great house to bits,
and reduce the small house to rubble.
12 Can horses run over rock,
or can one plow the sea with oxen?
Yet you have turned justice into gall,
and the fruit of righteousness into wormwood,[g]
13 You who rejoice in Lodebar,
and say, "Have we not, by our own strength,
seized Karnaim* for ourselves?"
14 Look, I am raising up against you, house of Israel—
oracle of the LORD, the God of hosts—
A nation* that shall oppress you

**5:26 Sukuth**: probably a hebraized form of Assyro-Babylonian *Shukudu* ("the Arrow"), a name of Sirius, the brightest star in the night sky. It was associated with the god Ninurta, who was widely worshiped in Mesopotamia. According to 2 Kgs 17:30 the cult of Sirius was introduced into Samaria by deportees from Babylonia. **Kaiwan:** a hebraized form of an Akkadian name for the planet Saturn, also worshiped as a deity in Mesopotamia.

**6:2 Calneh . . . Hamath . . . Gath**: city-states overcome by the Assyrians in the eighth century B.C., whose fate should be a lesson to the Israelites. The prophet castigates the leaders for being more intent on pursuing a luxurious lifestyle (vv. 1, 4–6) than reading the signs of the times.

**6:10** In this desperate situation there seems to be a profound fear of the Lord, who is the cause of the deaths (cf. 3:6).

**6:13 Lodebar . . . Karnaim**: two towns recaptured from Judah by Israelite forces during the reign of Jeroboam II (see 2 Kgs 14:25). Some mockery of at least the first of these victories is probably intended by the prophet here, as Lodebar can be translated "nothing."

**6:14 A nation**: Assyria. **Lebo-hamath . . . Wadi Arabah**:

*b:* Acts 7:42–43. *c:* Jer 7:21–26. *d:* 2 Kgs 17:30; Jer 2:28. *e:* Is 28:1–4; Jer 51:14. *f:* Zep 1:7. *g:* Am 5:7.

from Lebo-hamath even to the Wadi
Arabah.

## V. Symbolic Visions

### CHAPTER 7

See RG 249–50

*First Vision: The Locust Swarm*

[1]This is what the Lord GOD showed me: He
was forming a locust swarm when the late
growth began to come up (the late growth
after the king's mowing*). [2]When they had
finished eating the grass in the land, I said:

Forgive, O Lord GOD!
Who will raise up Jacob?
He is so small!

[3]The LORD relented concerning this.
"This shall not be," said the Lord GOD.

*Second Vision: The Rain of Fire*

[4]This is what the Lord GOD showed me: He
was summoning a rain of fire. It had devoured the great abyss and was consuming
the fields. [5]Then I said:

Cease, O Lord GOD!
Who will raise up Jacob?
He is so small!

[6]The LORD relented concerning this.
"This also shall not be," said the Lord GOD.

*Third Vision: The Plummet*

[7][h] This is what the Lord GOD showed me: He
was standing, plummet in hand, by a wall
built with a plummet.* [8]The Lord GOD asked
me, "What do you see, Amos?" And I answered, "A plummet." Then the LORD said:

See, I am laying the plummet
in the midst of my people Israel;
I will forgive them no longer.

[9] The high places of Isaac shall be laid
waste,
and the sanctuaries of Israel made
desolate;
and I will attack the house of
Jeroboam with the sword.

*Biographical Interlude: Amos and Amaziah*

[10]Amaziah, the priest of Bethel, sent word to
Jeroboam, king of Israel: "Amos has conspired against you within the house of Israel;
the country cannot endure all his words.
[11]For this is what Amos says:

'Jeroboam shall die by the sword,
and Israel shall surely be exiled from
its land.'"

[12]To Amos, Amaziah said: "Off with you,
seer, flee to the land of Judah and there earn
your bread by prophesying! [13]But never again
prophesy in Bethel;[i] for it is the king's sanctuary and a royal temple." [14]Amos answered
Amaziah, "I am not a prophet,* nor do I belong
to a company of prophets. I am a herdsman and
a dresser of sycamores,[j] [15]but the LORD took
me from following the flock, and the LORD
said to me, 'Go, prophesy to my people Israel.'[k] [16]Now hear the word of the LORD:

You say: 'Do not prophesy against Israel,
do not preach against the house of
Isaac.'

[17] Therefore thus says the LORD:
Your wife shall become a prostitute in
the city,
and your sons and daughters shall fall
by the sword.
Your land shall be parcelled out by
measuring line,
and you yourself shall die in an
unclean land;

the territorial limits of Solomon's kingdom, north and south respectively, as re-established by Jeroboam II (see 2 Kgs 14:25).

**7:1 The king's mowing**: the first harvesting of the crops apparently belonged to the king as a kind of tax.

**7:7 A plummet**: with this vision, the pleas of the prophet (vv. 1–6) disappear, and disaster is announced. One use of the plummet in ancient times was to see how far out of line a wall or building had become, to determine whether it could be repaired or would have to be torn down. Like a structure that had become architecturally unsound, Israel was unsalvageable and would have to be demolished (cf. 2 Kgs 21:13; Is 34:11; Lam 2:8).

**7:14 I am not a prophet**: Amos reacts strongly to Amaziah's attempt to classify him as a "prophet-for-hire" who "earns [his] bread" by giving oracles in exchange for payment (cf. 1 Sm 9:3–10; Mi 3:5). To disassociate himself from this kind of "professional" prophet, Amos rejects outright the title of *nabi'* ("prophet"). By profession he is a herdsman/sheepbreeder and a dresser of sycamore trees, but God's call has commissioned him to prophesy to Israel.

*h:* Jer 1:11–14. *i:* Am 2:12. *j:* Am 1:1; 2 Sm 7:8. *k:* Am 3:8.

**Judgment on Israel's Businessmen**

IN THE JUDGMENT speech beginning in 8:4, Amos indicts Israel's merchants for economic abuses (vv. 4–6) and announces a sentence of widespread devastation (vv. 7–14). The new moon and the sabbath are religious holidays (Is 1:13; Hos 2:11) considered an annoyance by merchants who cannot make a profit during their observance. God's judgment will turn their current condition on its head: the wealthy will starve, and joy will become mourning. Those who currently ignore their God will seek God out but be unable to find the word of the LORD.

and Israel shall be exiled from its
land."

See RG 249–50

## CHAPTER 8

### *Fourth Vision: The Summer Fruit*

1 This is what the Lord GOD showed me: a
basket of end-of-summer fruit.* 2 He asked,
"What do you see, Amos?" And I answered,
"A basket of end-of-summer fruit." And the
LORD said to me:

The end has come for my people Israel;
I will forgive them no longer.
3 The temple singers will wail on that day—
oracle of the Lord GOD.
Many shall be the corpses,
strewn everywhere—Silence![l]
4 Hear this, you who trample upon the needy
and destroy the poor of the land:
5 "When will the new moon be over," you ask,
"that we may sell our grain,
And the sabbath,
that we may open the grain-bins?
We will diminish the ephah,*
add to the shekel,
and fix our scales for cheating![m]
6 We will buy the destitute for silver,
and the poor for a pair of sandals;[n]
even the worthless grain we will sell!"
7 The LORD has sworn by the pride of Jacob:
Never will I forget a thing they have done!
8 Shall not the land tremble because of this,
and all who dwell in it mourn?
It will all rise up and toss like the Nile,
and subside like the river of Egypt.[o]
9 On that day—oracle of the Lord GOD—
I will make the sun set at midday
and in broad daylight cover the land with darkness.
10 I will turn your feasts into mourning
and all your songs into dirges.
I will cover the loins of all with sackcloth
and make every head bald.
I will make it like the time of mourning for an only child,
and its outcome like a day of bitter weeping.[p]
11 See, days are coming—oracle of the Lord GOD—
when I will send a famine upon the land:
Not a hunger for bread, or a thirst for water,
but for hearing the word of the LORD.
12 They shall stagger from sea to sea
and wander from north to east
In search of the word of the LORD,
but they shall not find it.[q]
13 On that day, beautiful young women and young men
shall faint from thirst,
14 Those who swear by Ashima of Samaria,*[r]
and who say, "By the life of your god, O Dan,"

**8:1–2 End-of-summer fruit . . . the end has come**: the English translation attempts to capture the wordplay of the Hebrew. The Hebrew word for "fruit picked late in the season" is *qayis*, while the word for "end" is *qes*.

**8:5 Ephah**: see note on Is 5:10.

**8:14 Ashima of Samaria**: a high-ranking goddess worshiped in Hamath, whose cult was transplanted by the people

*l:* Am 6:10. *m:* Dt 25:13; Hos 12:8. *n:* Am 2:6. *o:* Am 1:1; 9:1, 5. *p:* Tb 2:6; Zec 12:10. *q:* Hos 5:6. *r:* 2 Kgs 17:30.

**Amos's Visions Concluded**

LIKE AMOS'S OTHER visions (Am 7:1–9; 8:1–3), the vision in 9:1–4 shows God's coming judgment to Amos, but the judgment predicted here is the harshest and most complete of them all.

"By the life of the Power of Beer-sheba!"
They shall fall, never to rise again.

## CHAPTER 9

See RG 249–50

### *Fifth Vision: The Destruction of the Sanctuary*

1 I saw the Lord standing beside the altar. And he said:

Strike the capitals
so that the threshold shakes!
Break them off on the heads of them all!
Those who are left I will slay with the sword.
Not one shall get away,
no survivor shall escape.* [s]
2 Though they dig down to Sheol,
even from there my hand shall take them;
Though they climb to the heavens,
even from there I shall bring them down.[t]
3 Though they hide on the summit of Carmel,
there too I will hunt them down and take them;
Though they hide from my gaze at the bottom of the sea,
there I will command the serpent* to bite them.[u]
4 Though they go into captivity before their enemies,
there I will command the sword to slay them.
I will fix my gaze upon them
for evil and not for good.
5 The Lord GOD of hosts,
Who melts the earth with his touch,
so that all who dwell on it mourn,
So that it will all rise up like the Nile,
and subside like the river of Egypt;[v]
6 Who has built his upper chamber in heaven,
and established his vault over the earth;
Who summons the waters of the sea
and pours them upon the surface of the earth—
the LORD is his name.[w]
7 Are you not like the Ethiopians to me,
O Israelites?—oracle of the LORD—
Did I not bring the Israelites from the land of Egypt
as I brought the Philistines from Caphtor
and the Arameans* from Kir?
8 See, the eyes of the Lord GOD are on this sinful kingdom,
and I will destroy it from the face of the earth—
But I will not destroy the house of Jacob completely—
oracle of the LORD.

of that city when they were deported to Samaria by the Assyrians (2 Kgs 17:30). **The Power of Beer-sheba**: possibly an epithet of a deity worshiped in Beer-sheba, either a syncretistic form of the worship of Israel's God or of another god. **Dan ... Beer-sheba**: the traditional designation for the northern and southern limits of Israel to which the Israelites made pilgrimages.

**9:1** This vision may describe the destruction of the temple at Bethel and the fulfillment of the oracle in 3:14, linking God's judgment upon Israel with the "punishment" of the altars of Bethel. This dramatic event (perhaps to be identified with the earthquake mentioned in 1:1) symbolizes the end of the Northern Kingdom as the Lord's people, the consequence of their steadfast refusal to heed the prophetic word and return to the God of Israel.

**9:3 The serpent**: a name for the primeval chaos monster, vanquished by God at the time of creation but not annihilated. He was a personification of the sea, another primary archetype of chaos in the ancient Near East.

**9:7 The Ethiopians ... the Philistines ... the Arameans**: although Israel's relationship to the Lord was special, even unique in some respects (3:2), Israel was not the only people on earth that God cared for. Striking here is the reference to divine intervention in the history of the Philistines and Arameans, not unlike the Lord's saving intervention to bring Israel out of Egypt. **Caphtor**: the island of Crete.

*s*: Am 2:13–16. *t*: Ps 139:7–12; Jb 20:6. *u*: Jb 7:12; Is 27:1. *v*: Am 8:8. *w*: Am 5:8.

**Vision of Renewal**

THE RUINED STATE of the hut of David (Am 9:11), a reference to the Davidic monarchy that ruled Judah, appears to place this concluding speech after the fall of Jerusalem in 587 B.C. This image also suggests that this text was written from the perspective of Judah, the southern kingdom, rather than from the perspective of the northern kingdom, which Amos addressed. It anticipates the return of the Babylonian exiles to rebuild their ruined country.

9 For see, I have given the command
to sift the house of Israel among all the nations,
As one sifts with a sieve,
letting no pebble fall to the ground.
10 All sinners among my people shall die by the sword,
those who say, "Disaster will not reach or overtake us."[x]

## VI. Epilogue: Restoration Under a Davidic King

11 * On that day I will raise up
the fallen hut of David;
I will wall up its breaches,
raise up its ruins,
and rebuild it as in the days of old,[y]
12 That they may possess the remnant of Edom,
and all nations claimed in my name—
oracle of the LORD, the one who does this.
13 Yes, days are coming—
oracle of the LORD—
When the one who plows shall overtake the one who reaps
and the vintager, the sower of the seed;
The mountains shall drip with the juice of grapes,
and all the hills shall run with it.[z]
14 I will restore my people Israel,
they shall rebuild and inhabit their ruined cities,
Plant vineyards and drink* the wine,
set out gardens and eat the fruits.[a]
15 I will plant them upon their own ground;
never again shall they be plucked
From the land I have given them—
the LORD, your God, has spoken.

**9:11–15** These verses are most likely an editorial supplement to Amos, added to bring the book into harmony with the positive thrust of the prophetic books in general, especially those written after the exile, when the final edition of Amos was probably completed. The editors would have seen the destruction of Samaria in 722/721 B.C. as the fulfillment of Amos's prophecies, but in this epilogue they express the view that destruction was not the Lord's final word for Israel. In Acts 15:15–17, James interprets this passage in a messianic sense. **The fallen hut of David**: the Davidic kingdom, which included what later became the divided Northern and Southern Kingdoms. **All nations claimed in my name**: lit., "all nations over whom my name has been pronounced." This idiom denotes ownership.

**9:14 Rebuild ... inhabit ... plant ... drink**: in this era of restoration, the Lord nullifies the curse of 5:11, which uses these same four verbs, and turns it into a blessing for Israel.

*x:* Jer 5:12; 23:17. *y:* Acts 15:16–17. *z:* Jl 4:18. *a:* Is 65:21–22.

See RG 250–51

# The Book of Obadiah

This book, the shortest among the twelve minor prophets, is a single twenty-one-verse oracle against Edom. Nothing is known of the author, although his prophecy against Edom, a neighbor and rival of Israel, indicates a date of composition sometime after the Babylonian destruction of Jerusalem in 587 B.C., when the Edomites apparently took advantage of the helpless people of Judah and Jerusalem (v. 11; Ps 137:7). The relations and rivalries between Israel and Edom are reflected in oracles against Edom (Is 34; Ez 35) and in the stories of their ancestors, the brothers Jacob and Esau (Gn 25–33).

The prophecy is a bitter cry for vengeance against Edom for its pride and its crimes. Mount Esau in Edom will be occupied and ravaged by the enemy, while Mount Zion will be restored to its former sanctity and security. The triumphant refrain of Israelite eschatology will be heard once more: "The kingdom is the Lord's!" The opening verses of this prophecy (vv. 1–5) are very similar to part of an oracle against Edom in Jer 49 (vv. 9, 14–16), suggesting that Israel's prophets drew upon traditional language and idioms in the composition of prophetic speech.

The book may be divided as follows:

I. Edom's Fall Decreed (1–7)
II. Edom's Betrayal of Judah (8–14)
III. Edom's Fall and Judah's Restoration (15–21)

---

### *Edom's Fall Decreed*

*1* The vision of Obadiah.
Thus says the Lord GOD concerning Edom:
We have heard a message from the LORD,
and a herald has been sent among the nations:
"Rise up, so we may go to war against it!"[a]
*2* Now I make you least among the nations;
you are utterly contemptible.
*3* The pride of your heart has deceived you—
you who dwell in mountain crevices,
in your lofty home,*
Who say in your heart,
"Who will bring me down to earth?"
*4* Though you soar like the eagle,
and your nest is set among the stars,
From there I will bring you down—
oracle of the LORD.
*5* If thieves came to you, robbers by night
—how you have been destroyed!—
would they not steal merely till they had enough?
If grape pickers came to you,
would they not leave some gleanings?*[b]
*6* * How Esau has been searched out,
his treasures hunted down!
*7* To the border they have driven you—
all your allies;
Your partners have deceived you,
they have overpowered you;
Those who eat your bread*
will replace you with foreigners,
who have no understanding.

### *Edom's Betrayal of Judah*

*8* On that day—oracle of the LORD—will I not
make the wise disappear from Edom,
and understanding from Mount Esau?[c]
*9* Teman,* your warriors will be terror-stricken,
so that everyone on Mount Esau will be cut down.
*10* Because of violence to your brother* Jacob,
disgrace will cover you,
you will be done away with forever![d]
*11* On the day you stood by,
the day strangers carried off his possessions,
And foreigners entered his gates
and cast lots for Jerusalem,
you too were like one of them.*[e]

*12* * Do not gloat over the day of your brother,
the day of his disaster;

**3** Edom occupied the mountains southeast of Israel and the Dead Sea.

**5** Something of value may escape the thief, and the grape picker always leaves something for the gleaners, but God's devastation of Edom will be complete.

**6** With the past tense in vv. 5–7, the prophet presents a future event as if it had already happened.

**7 Those who eat your bread**: alliances were often established by covenant meals (cf. Gn 31:44–46). When Edom is destroyed, foreigners will replace the Edomites, who were known for wisdom (cf. v. 8; Jer 49:7; Jb 2:11).

**9 Teman**: a synonym for Edom; perhaps the name of a region or a city, the part representing the whole. **Mount Esau**: whatever its geographic reference, the phrase is an effective representation of Edom's arrogance.

**10 Your brother**: used with a double meaning referring to the common lineage of Israel and Edom, in which their ancestors were brothers, Jacob and Esau (Gn 25:19–26), and referring also to their political alliance, in which allies were called brothers (cf. Am 1:9, 11).

**11** In 587 B.C., Edomites joined the invading Babylonian forces (v. 13) and captured escaping Judahites. The destruction of Jerusalem strengthened and expanded Edom's hold on Judah's southern territory.

**12–14** The commands in vv. 12–14 are not to be understood as future prohibitions but as descriptions of crimes Edom in fact already committed on the day of Jerusalem's fall described in v. 11.

---

*a:* Jer 49:14–16. *b:* Jer 49:9. *c:* Is 29:14; 1 Cor 1:19. *d:* Gn 27:41–45; Ez 25:12–14. *e:* Ps 137:7.

Do not exult over the people of Judah
on the day of their ruin;
Do not speak haughtily
on the day of distress!
13 Do not enter the gate of my people
on the day of their calamity;
Do not gloat—especially you—over his misfortune
on the day of his calamity;
Do not lay hands upon his possessions
on the day of his calamity!
14 Do not stand at the crossroads
to cut down his survivors;
Do not hand over his fugitives
on the day of distress!

### *Edom's Fall and Judah's Restoration*

15 Near is the day of the LORD[f]
against all the nations!
As you have done, so will it be done to you,
your conduct will come back upon your own head;
16 As you drank* upon my holy mountain,
so will all the nations drink continually.
Yes, they will drink and swallow,
and will become as though they had not been.
17 But on Mount Zion there will be some who escape;*
the mountain will be holy,
And the house of Jacob will take possession
of those who dispossessed them.[g]
18 The house of Jacob will be a fire,
the house of Joseph a flame,
and the house of Esau stubble.
They will set it ablaze and devour it;
none will survive of the house of Esau,
for the LORD has spoken.

19 They will take possession of the Negeb,*
Mount Esau, the Shephelah, and Philistia,
possess the countryside of Ephraim, the
countryside of Samaria, Benjamin, and Gilead.[h] 20 The exiles of this Israelite army will
possess the Canaanite land as far as
Zarephath,* and the exiles of Jerusalem who
are in Sepharad will possess the cities of the
Negeb. 21 And deliverers* will ascend Mount
Zion to rule Mount Esau, and the kingship
shall be the LORD's.

**16 As you drank**: i.e., Judah has suffered the punishment of divine wrath in 587 B.C. The oracle promises a similar fate for the nations, especially Edom (v. 18). The metaphor "drinking the cup of God's wrath" occurs often in the Bible; cf. Jb 21:20; Is 51:17–23; Jer 25:15–16; Rev 14:10.

**17–19** The Israelites will be restored and will occupy the lands of those who oppressed them. The survivors of Judah will be rejoined by the returned exiles from northern Israel.

**19 Negeb**: the area south of Judah and west of Edom. **Gilead**: east of the Jordan River.

**20 Zarephath**: a town in Phoenicia, north of Tyre; cf. 1 Kgs 17:10. **Sepharad**: perhaps Sardis in western Asia Minor. The later rabbis thought it was Spain.

**21 Deliverers**: the victorious Israelites who will rule over their enemies, as the ancient judges did; cf. Jgs 3:9, 15, 31; 10:1.

*f:* Jl 4:11–12, 14. *g:* Jer 49:2. *h:* Jer 50:19.

See RG 251–53

# The Book of Jonah

The story of Jonah has great theological import. It concerns a disobedient prophet who rejected his divine commission, was cast overboard in a storm and swallowed by a great fish, rescued in a marvelous manner, and returned to his starting point. Now he obeys and goes to Nineveh, the capital of Israel's ancient enemy. The Ninevites listen to his message of doom and repent immediately. All, from king to lowliest subject, humble themselves in sackcloth and ashes. Seeing their repentance, God does not carry out the punishment planned for them. At this, Jonah complains, angry because the Lord spares them. This fascinating story caricatures a narrow mentality which would see God's interest extending only to Israel, whereas God is presented as concerned with and merciful to even the inhabitants of Nineveh (4:11), the capital of the Assyrian empire which brought the Northern Kingdom of Israel to an end and devastated Jerusalem in 701. The Lord is free to "repent" and change his mind. Jonah seems to realize this possibility and wants no part in it (4:2; cf. Ex 34:6). But the story also conveys something of the ineluctable character of the prophetic calling.

## Jonah's Prayer

JONAH'S PRAYER IN ch 2, an appeal to God in poetic form, may be a traditional text taken over by the narrator to represent Jonah's petition. It is composed in the form of a lament, a common psalm type in which the worshiper pleads for God's help in a time of great distress (Pss 3; 5; 7). The lament opens with an address, in which the worshiper calls out to God. The description of distress follows the opening address. The image of deep waters swallowing the worshiper is common in such descriptions of distress (Ps 69:1–2, 14–15). A petition to God follows the description of distress. Laments customarily end, as does this one, with the worshiper anticipating God's aid and promising to thank God by presenting a sacrifice at the temple. God answers Jonah's prayer, but when God does the same for Nineveh, Jonah responds much differently.

The book is replete with irony, wherein much of its humor lies. The name "Jonah" means "dove" in Hebrew, but Jonah's character is anything but dove-like. Jonah is commanded to go east to Nineveh but flees toward the westernmost possible point (1:2–3), only to be swallowed by a great fish and dumped back at this starting point (2:1, 11). The sailors pray to their gods, but Jonah is asleep in the hold (1:5–6). The prophet's preaching is a minimum message of destruction, while it is the king of Nineveh who calls for repentance and conversion (3:4–10); the instant conversion of the Ninevites is greeted by Jonah with anger and sulking (4:1). He reproaches the Lord in words that echo Israel's traditional praise of his mercy (4:2; cf. Ex 34:6–7). Jonah is concerned about the loss of the gourd but not about the possible destruction of 120,000 Ninevites (4:10–11).

Unlike other prophetic books, this is not a collection of oracles but the story of a disobedient, narrow-minded prophet who is angry at the outcome of the sole message he delivers (3:4). It is difficult to date but almost certainly is postexilic and may reflect the somewhat narrow, nationalistic reforms of Ezra and Nehemiah. As to genre, it has been classified in various ways, such as parable or satire. The "sign" of Jonah is interpreted in two ways in the New Testament: His experience of three days and nights in the fish is a "type" of the experience of the Son of Man (Mt 12:39–40), and the Ninevites' reaction to the preaching of Jonah is contrasted with the failure of Jesus' generation to obey the preaching of one who is "greater than Jonah" (Mt 12:41–42; Lk 11:29–32).

The Book of Jonah may be divided as follows:

I. Jonah's Disobedience and Flight (1:1–16)
II. Jonah's Prayer (2:1–11)
III. Jonah's Obedience and the Ninevites' Repentance (3:1–10)
IV. Jonah's Anger and God's Reproof (4:1–11)

### CHAPTER 1

See RG 251–53

*Jonah's Disobedience and Flight.*
1 The word of the LORD came to Jonah,[a] son
of Amittai:* 2 Set out for the great city* of
Nineveh, and preach against it; for their
wickedness has come before me.[b] 3 But Jonah made ready to flee to Tarshish,* away
from the LORD. He went down to Joppa,
found a ship going to Tarshish, paid the fare,
and went down in it to go with them to Tarshish, away from the LORD.

4[c] The LORD, however, hurled a great
wind upon the sea, and the storm was so
great that the ship was about to break up.
5 Then the sailors were afraid and each one
cried to his god. To lighten the ship for themselves, they threw its cargo into the sea.
Meanwhile, Jonah had gone down into the

**1:1 Jonah, son of Amittai**: a prophet of this name lived at the time of Jeroboam II (786–746 B.C.).

**1:2 Great city**: exaggeration is characteristic of this book; the word "great" (Heb. *gadol*) occurs fourteen times.

**1:3 Tarshish**: identified by many with Tartessus, an ancient Phoenician colony in southwest Spain; precise identification with any particular Phoenician center in the western Mediterranean is uncertain. To the Israelites it stood for the far west.

*a:* 2 Kgs 14:25. *b:* Jon 3:3; 4:11. *c:* Mk 4:37–38.

hold of the ship, and lay there fast asleep.
6 The captain approached him and said,
"What are you doing asleep? Get up, call on
your god! Perhaps this god will be mindful
of us so that we will not perish."
7 Then they said to one another, "Come, let
us cast lots to discover on whose account
this evil has come to us." So they cast lots,
and the lot fell on Jonah.[d] 8 They said to him,
"Tell us why this evil has come to us! What
is your business? Where do you come from?
What is your country, and to what people do
you belong?" 9 "I am a Hebrew," he replied;
"I fear the LORD, the God of heaven, who
made the sea and the dry land."
10 Now the men were seized with great fear
and said to him, "How could you do such a
thing!"—They knew that he was fleeing
from the LORD, because he had told them.
11 They asked, "What shall we do with you,
that the sea may calm down for us?" For the
sea was growing more and more stormy.
12 Jonah responded, "Pick me up and hurl me
into the sea and then the sea will calm down
for you. For I know that this great storm has
come upon you because of me."
13 Still the men rowed hard to return to dry
land, but they could not, for the sea grew
more and more stormy. 14 Then they cried to
the LORD: "Please, O LORD, do not let us perish for taking this man's life; do not charge us
with shedding innocent blood, for you, LORD,
have accomplished what you desired."*
15 Then they picked up Jonah and hurled him
into the sea, and the sea stopped raging.
16 Seized with great fear of the LORD, the men
offered sacrifice to the LORD and made vows.

## CHAPTER 2

See RG 251–53

*Jonah's Prayer.* 1 But the LORD sent a
great fish to swallow Jonah, and he remained in the belly of the fish three days and
three nights.[e] 2 Jonah prayed to the LORD, his
God, from the belly of the fish:

3 * Out of my distress I called to the LORD,
and he answered me;
From the womb of Sheol* I cried for
help,
and you heard my voice.[f]
4 You cast me into the deep, into the heart
of the sea,
and the flood enveloped me;
All your breakers and your billows
passed over me.[g]
5 Then I said, "I am banished from your
sight!
How will I again look upon your holy
temple?"[h]

6 The waters surged around me up to my
neck;
the deep enveloped me;
seaweed wrapped around my head.[i]
7 I went down to the roots of the
mountains;
to the land whose bars closed behind
me forever,
But you brought my life up from the pit,
O LORD, my God.[j]

8 When I became faint,
I remembered the LORD;
My prayer came to you
in your holy temple.[k]
9 Those who worship worthless idols
abandon their hope for mercy.[l]
10 But I, with thankful voice,
will sacrifice to you;
What I have vowed I will pay:
deliverance is from the LORD.[m]

11 Then the LORD commanded the fish to
vomit Jonah upon dry land.

## CHAPTER 3

See RG 251–53

*Jonah's Obedience and the Ninevites' Repentance.* 1 The word of the LORD came to
Jonah a second time: 2 Set out for the great
city of Nineveh, and announce to it the message that I will tell you. 3 So Jonah set out for

**1:14** Aware that this disaster is a divine punishment on Jonah, the sailors ask that in ridding themselves of him they not be charged with the crime of murder.

**2:3–10** These verses, which may have originally been an independent composition, are a typical example of a song of thanksgiving, a common psalm genre (e.g., Ps 116; Is 38:9–20). Such a song is relevant here, since Jonah has not drowned, and the imagery of vv. 4, 6 is appropriate.

**2:3 Sheol**: Cf. note on Ps 6:6.

*d:* Jos 7:16–18; 1 Sm 14:40–42. *e:* Mt 12:40; 16:4; Lk 11:30; 1 Cor 15:4. *f:* Ps 18:7; 120:1. *g:* Ps 42:8. *h:* Ps 31:23; Is 38:11. *i:* Ps 18:5; 69:2. *j:* Ps 16:10; 30:4. *k:* Ps 5:8; 18:7; 88:3. *l:* Ps 31:7. *m:* Ps 50:14.

Nineveh, in accord with the word of the LORD. Now Nineveh was an awesomely great city; it took three days to walk through it. [4]Jonah began his journey through the city, and when he had gone only a single day's walk announcing, "Forty days more and Nineveh shall be overthrown," [5]the people of Nineveh believed God; they proclaimed a fast and all of them, great and small,* put on sackcloth.[n]

[6]When the news reached the king of Nineveh, he rose from his throne, laid aside his robe, covered himself with sackcloth, and sat in ashes. [7]Then he had this proclaimed throughout Nineveh:* "By decree of the king and his nobles, no man or beast, no cattle or sheep, shall taste anything; they shall not eat, nor shall they drink water. [8]Man and beast alike must be covered with sackcloth and call loudly to God; they all must turn from their evil way and from the violence of their hands. [9]* Who knows? God may again repent and turn from his blazing wrath, so that we will not perish."[o] [10]When God saw by their actions how they turned from their evil way, he repented of the evil he had threatened to do to them; he did not carry it out.

## CHAPTER 4

See RG 251–53

### *Jonah's Anger and God's Reproof.*

[1]But this greatly displeased Jonah, and he became angry.* [2]He prayed to the LORD, "O LORD, is this not what I said while I was still in my own country? This is why I fled at first toward Tarshish. I knew that you are a gracious and merciful God, slow to anger, abounding in kindness, repenting of punishment.*[p] [3]So now, LORD, please take my life from me; for it is better for me to die than to live."[q] [4]But the LORD asked, "Are you right to be angry?"*

[5]Jonah then left the city for a place to the east of it, where he built himself a hut and waited* under it in the shade, to see what would happen to the city. [6]Then the LORD God provided a gourd plant.* And when it grew up over Jonah's head, giving shade that relieved him of any discomfort, Jonah was greatly delighted with the plant. [7]But the next morning at dawn God provided a worm that attacked the plant, so that it withered. [8]And when the sun arose, God provided a scorching east wind; and the sun beat upon Jonah's head till he became faint. Then he wished for death, saying, "It is better for me to die than to live."

[9]But God said to Jonah, "Do you have a right to be angry over the gourd plant?" Jonah answered, "I have a right to be angry—angry enough to die." [10]Then the LORD said, "You are concerned* over the gourd plant which cost you no effort and which you did not grow; it came up in one night and in one night it perished. [11]And should I not be concerned over the great city of Nineveh, in which there are more than a hundred and twenty thousand persons who cannot know their right hand from their left, not to mention all the animals?"*

**3:5 Great and small**: the contrast can refer to distinctions of social class (prominent citizens and the poor).

**3:7–8** Fasting and wearing sackcloth are signs of human repentance; here they are legislated even for the animals—a humorous touch, perhaps anticipating 4:11.

**3:9–10** Scripture frequently presents the Lord as repenting (or, changing his mind) of the evil that he threatens; e.g., Gn 6:6–7; Jer 18:8.

**4:1 He became angry**: because of his narrow vindictiveness, Jonah did not wish the Lord to forgive the Ninevites.

**4:2 Punishment**: lit., "evil"; see 1:2, 7, 8; 3:8, 10; 4:1.

**4:4** The Lord's question is as unexpected as it is pithy. It is also a mysterious reply to Jonah's wish to die; perhaps it serves to invite Jonah to think over his situation. However, it goes unanswered, and the request and reply will be repeated in vv. 8–9.

**4:5 Waited**: Jonah still hopes his threat of doom will be fulfilled.

**4:6 Gourd plant**: the Hebrew word, *qiqayon*, means here a wide-leafed plant of the cucumber or castor-bean variety.

**4:10 Concerned**: the meaning of the Hebrew verb suggests "pity, care for," and this appears in the Lord's attitude to Nineveh in v. 11. Jonah has shown only a selfish concern over the plant in contrast to the Lord's true "concern" for his creatures.

**4:11** A selfish Jonah bemoans his personal loss of a gourd plant for shade without any concern over the threat of loss of life to the Ninevites through the destruction of their city. If a solicitous God provided the plant for a prophet without the latter's effort or merit, how much more is God disposed to show love and mercy toward all people, Jew and Gentile, when they repent of their sins and implore divine pardon. God's care goes beyond human beings to all creation, as in Job 38.

*n:* Mt 12:41; Lk 11:32. *o:* Jl 2:14. *p:* Ex 34:6–7; Ps 86:5; Jl 2:13. *q:* 1 Kgs 19:4.

See RG 253–55

# The Book of Micah

This book consists of a collection of speeches, proclamations of punishment and of salvation, attributed to the prophet Micah. Following its superscription (1:1), the book has two major sections, each with two parts. The organization of the material is thematic, moving from judgment to salvation in both major sections. In the first section (Mi 1–5), chaps. 1–3 consist almost entirely of prophecies of punishment, and chaps. 4–5 of prophecies of salvation. The second section (chaps. 6–7) also moves from prophecies of punishment (6:1–7:6) to confidence in God's salvation (7:7–20).

Micah was a contemporary of the prophet Isaiah. The book's superscription (1:1) places his prophetic activity during the reigns of three kings of Judah: Jotham, Ahaz, and Hezekiah. It identifies him as a resident of Moresheth, a village in the Judean foothills. The solitary reference to Micah outside the book (Jer 26:17–18) places him in the reign of Hezekiah and reports that he went from his small town to proclaim the word of the Lord in the capital, and asserts that his announcements of judgment against Jerusalem moved the king and the people to repentance. Unlike Isaiah, who was a native of the holy city, Micah was an outsider from the countryside and must have been a controversial figure. He would have been unpopular with the leaders whom he condemned (3:1–4) and the wealthy whom he criticized (2:1–5). He was quick to separate himself from priests and other prophets, whom he considered to be corrupt (3:5–8).

Just how much of the Book of Micah can be traced to the eighth-century prophet is uncertain. Tradition considers all of the words to be the recorded speeches of Micah, and some contemporary commentators agree. On the other hand, some modern scholars have thought of Micah as exclusively a prophet of doom, and therefore attributed as few as three of the seven chapters to him. The style, content, theological viewpoint, and historical perspective of some of the material reflect not the period of the Assyrian threat to Judah in the eighth century but the Babylonian exile in the sixth century B.C. and later. This is particularly evident in chap. 7, but also at other points in the book. The composition of this book, like most other prophetic texts, involved a complex editorial process. This is apparent from the fact that the stirring prophecy of peace and justice in 4:1–5 is virtually identical to Is 2:2–5.

Like Is 1–39, the Book of Micah is focused on Jerusalem, Zion, and the Judean leadership. The Micah who speaks in this prophetic book knows the tradition that Zion is the Lord's chosen place, but he is critical of the popular view that this election ensures the city's security (2:6–13; 3:9–12). Through the prophetic voice, the Lord announces the impending punishment of God's people by means of military defeat and exile because of their failure to establish justice. After that punishment God will bring the people back to their land and establish perpetual peace. The will of God for human beings is that they do justice, love goodness, and walk humbly with God (6:6–8).

The Book of Micah is divided as follows:

I. Oracles of Punishment (1:2–3:12)
II. Oracles of Salvation (4:1–5:14)
III. Announcement of Judgment (6:1–7:6)
IV. Confidence in God's Future (7:7–20)

## CHAPTER 1

See RG 254

1 The word of the LORD which came to Micah of Moresheth in the days of Jotham, Ahaz, and Hezekiah, kings of Judah, which he saw concerning Samaria and Jerusalem.

## I. Oracles of Punishment

2 Hear, O peoples, all of you,
give heed, O earth, and all that is in it![a]
Let the Lord GOD be witness against you,

**1:2** The prophet summons all the peoples to hear the divine accusations against them. What follows in 1:2–3:12 is a series of prophecies of punishment addressed to the capital cities of both the Northern and Southern Kingdoms, Samaria and Jerusalem. The prophecies indict the leaders and main officials, including prophets. Because of the corruption and selfishness of their leaders, Samaria and Jerusalem will fall to their enemies.

*a:* Dt 32:1; Is 1:2.

## Judgment on Samaria and Jerusalem

MICAH'S OPENING SPEECH focuses on his primary audience: the ruling elite in the capitals of Israel and Judah. Samaria and Jerusalem (v. 5) are viewed as the centers of corruption in their respective kingdoms.

the Lord from his holy temple!*
3 For see, the LORD goes out from his place[b]
and descending, treads upon the
heights of the earth.*
4 The mountains melt under him
and the valleys split open,
Like wax before the fire,
like water poured down a slope.
5 All this is for the crime of Jacob,
for the sins of the house of Israel.*
What is the crime of Jacob? Is it not
Samaria?
And what is the sin of the house of Judah?
Is it not Jerusalem?
6 So I will make Samaria a ruin in the field,
a place to plant vineyards;
I will throw its stones into the valley,
and lay bare its foundations.*
7 All its carved figures shall be broken to
pieces,[c]
all its wages shall be burned in the fire,
and all its idols I will destroy.
As the wages of a prostitute* it gathered
them,
and to the wages of a prostitute they
shall return.
8 * For this I will lament and wail,
go barefoot and naked;
I will utter lamentation like the jackals,
mourning like the ostriches,[d]
9 For her wound is incurable;
it has come even to Judah.
It has reached to the gate of my people,
even to Jerusalem.
10 * Do not announce it in Gath,
do not weep at all;
In Beth-leaphrah
roll in the dust.[e]
11 Pass by,
you who dwell in Shaphir!
The inhabitants of Zaanan
do not come forth from their city.
There is lamentation in Beth-ezel.
It will withdraw its support from you.
12 The inhabitants of Maroth
hope for good,
But evil has come down from the LORD
to the gate of Jerusalem.
13 Harness steeds to the chariots,
inhabitants of Lachish;
You are the beginning of sin
for daughter Zion,
For in you were found
the crimes of Israel.
14 Therefore you must give back the dowry
to Moresheth-gath;
The houses of Achzib* are a dry stream
bed

**1:3** The Lord comes in a theophany which has devastating effects on the natural world (1:4).

**1:5** Although the summons (1:2) had been addressed to all people, the Lord speaks against Israel and Judah, identifying their crimes with the respective capital cities of Samaria and Jerusalem. Only Samaria, however, is scheduled for destruction in the announcement of punishment (vv. 6–7).

**1:6** The punishment of Samaria will be a military disaster such as the one that actually came at the hands of the Assyrian army in 722/721 B.C.

**1:7 The wages of a prostitute**: as often in the prophets, prostitution is a metaphor for idolatry (Hos 1–3; 4:14). **They shall return**: i.e., Samaria's idols shall come to nothing just as the wages of a prostitute are counted as nothing.

**1:8–16** The prophet laments and wails, singing a funeral song or dirge over the city of Jerusalem. Finally (1:16) he calls upon the people of Jerusalem to join in the mourning.

**1:10–15** Not all of the cities and villages in this long list can be located with certainty. However, those which can be identified, including the prophet's hometown, lie southwest of Jerusalem. In the Hebrew, wordplays on the names of these cities abound. The territory involved corresponds to that decimated by the Assyrian king Sennacherib in 701 B.C., during the reign of Hezekiah. **Do not weep at all**: some commentators and translators understand the Hebrew differently. They argue that the translation "in (unknown place name) weep!" fits the context better.

**1:14 The houses of Achzib**: there is a wordplay here. In the Hebrew, the word translated here as "dry stream bed" is

*b:* Is 26:21; Na 1:5; Hb 3:10. *c:* Hos 9:1. *d:* Jb 30:29. *e:* 2 Sm 1:20.

to the kings of Israel.
15 Again I will bring the conqueror to you,
inhabitants of Mareshah;
The glory of Israel shall come
even to Adullam.
16 Make yourself bald, cut off your hair,
for the children whom you cherish;
Make yourself bald as a vulture,
for they are taken from you into exile.*

## CHAPTER 2

See RG 254

1* Ah! you plotters of iniquity,
who work out evil on your beds!
In the morning light you carry it out
for it lies within your power.
2 * You covet fields, and seize them;
houses, and take them;
You cheat owners of their houses,
people of their inheritance.
3 Therefore thus says the LORD:
Look, I am planning against this family
an evil
from which you cannot free your necks;
Nor shall you walk with head held high,
for it will be an evil time.
4 On that day you shall be mocked,
and there will be bitter lament:
"Our ruin is complete,
our fields are divided among our
captors,
The fields of my people are measured
out,
and no one can get them back!'"*
5 Thus you shall have no one
in the assembly of the LORD
to allot to you a share of land.
6 * "Do not preach," they preach,
"no one should preach of these things!
Shame will not overtake us."
7 How can it be said, house of Jacob,
"Is the LORD short of patience;
are these the Lord's deeds?"
Do not my words promise good
to the one who walks in justice?
8 But you rise up against my people as an
enemy:
you have stripped off the garment
from the peaceful,
From those who go their way in
confidence,
as though it were spoils of war.
9 The women of my people you drive out
from their pleasant houses;
From their children you take away
forever the honor I gave them.
10 * "Get up! Leave,
this is no place to rest";
Because of uncleanness that destroys
with terrible destruction.
11 If one possessed of a lying spirit[f]
speaks deceitfully, saying,
"I will preach to you wine and strong
drink,"
that one would be the preacher for this
people.
12 * I will gather you, Jacob, each and every
one,

*'achzab*; this word is sometimes translated as "deception" or "disappointment."

**1:16** Shaving the head was a sign of mourning; cf. Is 3:24; Am 8:10.

**2:1–5** The cry "Ah" (*hoy*) begins a typical prophetic speech that is usually continued, as here (vv. 1–2), by a description of the addressees in terms of their unrighteous activities. This description is an indictment which gives the reasons for punishment announced to a particular group of people (vv. 3–5). The prophet spells out the crimes; the Lord announces the punishment, which corresponds to the crime: those who take the land of others will have their own land taken.

Those who plot iniquity and have the power to do it are wealthy landowners. The evil which they do consists in coveting the fields and houses of others and taking them.

**2:2** To covet the "house" and other property of the neighbor was a violation of the Decalogue (Ex 20:17; 34:24; Dt 5:21).

The Lord, as owner of the earth, allotted the land by tribes and families to the people of Israel (Jos 13–19). Losing one's inheritance diminished one's place in the community and threatened the family's economic viability and existence. According to Micah, those who used their power to expand their estates at the expense of weaker Israelites took more than land from them: they were tampering with the divine order.

**2:4** Those who take land from the less powerful will in turn have their land taken away by invaders.

**2:6–11** This unit is a disputation, an argument in which the prophet is debating with his opponents. The words of the opponents are given to us only as the prophet quotes them. The opponents accuse Micah of being a false prophet, and he reacts by accusing them of injustice and of preferring prophets and preachers who speak lies (v. 11).

**2:10** The meaning of the Hebrew is uncertain.

**2:12–13** This announcement of salvation to the "remnant of Israel" stands out dramatically in the context, and is probably a later addition to the words of Micah, coming from the

*f.* 1 Kgs 22:22–23.

## God Rules from Jerusalem

CHAPTER 4 BEGINS a new collection of speeches that announce salvation rather than judgment. They stress the return of the Israelite exiles and the restoration of Jerusalem to its former power and prestige. Sections of these speeches (Mi 4:3; 5:1) are often read during Advent as passages that point to the coming of the Messiah.

with justice and with might;
To declare to Jacob his crimes
and to Israel his sins.

9 * Hear this, you leaders of the house of Jacob,
you rulers of the house of Israel!
You who abhor justice,
and pervert all that is right;
10 Who build up Zion with bloodshed,
and Jerusalem with wickedness!
11 Its leaders render judgment for a bribe,
the priests teach for pay,
the prophets divine for money,
While they rely on the LORD, saying,
"Is not the LORD in the midst of us?
No evil can come upon us!"[j]
12 Therefore, because of you,
Zion shall be plowed like a field,
and Jerusalem reduced to rubble,
And the mount of the temple
to a forest ridge.[k]

## II. Oracles of Salvation

### CHAPTER 4

See RG 254

1* In days to come
the mount of the LORD's house
Shall be established as the highest mountain;
it shall be raised above the hills,
And peoples shall stream to it:[l]
2 Many nations shall come, and say,
"Come, let us climb the LORD's mountain,
to the house of the God of Jacob,
That he may instruct us in his ways,
that we may walk in his paths."
For from Zion shall go forth instruction,
and the word of the LORD from Jerusalem.
3 He shall judge between many peoples
and set terms for strong and distant nations;
They shall beat their swords into plowshares,
and their spears into pruning hooks;
One nation shall not raise the sword against another,
nor shall they train for war again.
4 They shall all sit under their own vines,
under their own fig trees, undisturbed;
for the LORD of hosts has spoken.[m]
5 Though all the peoples walk,
each in the name of its god,
We will walk in the name of the LORD,
our God, forever and ever.
6 * On that day—oracle of the LORD—
I will gather the lame,
And I will assemble the outcasts,
and those whom I have afflicted.

**3:9–12** This is the most comprehensive of Micah's prophecies of punishment concerning the leaders in Jerusalem. The indictment (vv. 9–11) includes all political and religious leaders. They combine corruption and greed with a false confidence that the Lord is on their side. But the announcement of judgment (v. 12) is not limited to the punishment of the leaders but includes Mount Zion where the Temple stands and the entire city, thus encompassing the entire population.

**4:1–4** This magnificent prophecy of salvation is almost identical to Is 2:2–5, with the exception of its last verse. See also Jl 4:9–10, which transforms the promise into a call to war. It is not known if Micah or an editor of the book picked up the announcement from his contemporary Isaiah or if Isaiah borrowed it from Micah. Perhaps both Isaiah and Micah depended upon another, more ancient tradition. The ground of the prophetic hope voiced here is the justice and grace of the God who has chosen Israel. The basis for peace shall be a just order where all are obedient to the divine will. While the vision is a universal one, including all peoples and nations (vv. 3–4), its center and wellspring is the Temple of the Lord of Israel on Mount Zion in Jerusalem.

**4:6–8** An announcement of salvation proclaiming that the Lord will restore the lame and afflicted people of God as a nation on Mount Zion. **Oracle of the LORD**: a phrase used extensively in prophetic books to indicate divine speech.

*j:* Ez 22:27; Zep 3:3. *k:* Jer 26:18. *l:* Is 2:2–4. *m:* Hos 14:8; Am 9:14.

## Judgment on the Ruling Elite

CHAPTER 3 IS composed of three typical judgment speeches. The first judgment speech, directed to political officials, includes an indictment (vv. 1–3), accusing them of devouring their people by their injustices, and a sentence (v. 4), according to which they are abandoned by God. The second judgment speech, directed to the false prophets, indicts them for accepting bribes to give favorable prophecies (v. 5). The sentence by which they are blocked from receiving further revelations (vv. 6–7) is contrasted with Micah's own power to preach (v. 8). The third judgment speech indicts Jerusalem's political and religious leaders alike: its political leaders, its priests, and its prophets (vv. 9–11), who are driven by greed rather than faithfulness to the LORD. Micah announces the sentence: the destruction of Jerusalem (v. 12).

I will assemble all the remnant of
Israel;
I will group them like a flock in the fold,
like a herd in its pasture;
the noise of the people will resound.
13 The one who makes a breach goes up
before them;
they make a breach and pass through
the gate;
Their king shall go through before them,
the LORD at their head.

### CHAPTER 3

See RG 254

1 * And I said:
Hear, you leaders of Jacob,
rulers of the house of Israel!
Is it not your duty to know what is right,
2 you who hate what is good, and love
evil?
You who tear their skin from them,
and their flesh from their bones;[g]
3 Who eat the flesh of my people,
flay their skin from them,
and break their bones;
Who chop them in pieces like flesh in a
kettle,
like meat in a pot.
4 When they cry to the LORD,
he will not answer them;
He will hide his face from them at that
time,
because of the evil they have done.
5 * Thus says the LORD regarding the
prophets:
O you who lead my people astray,
When your teeth have something to bite
you announce peace,
But proclaim war against the one
who fails to put something in your
mouth.[h]
6 Therefore you shall have night, not
vision,
darkness, not divination;
The sun shall go down upon the
prophets,
and the day shall be dark for them.[i]
7 Then the seers shall be put to shame,
and the diviners confounded;
They shall all cover their lips,
because there is no answer from God.
8 But as for me, I am filled with power,
with the spirit of the LORD,

time of the Babylonian exile. The content of the promise and the images are similar to those found in Second Isaiah, the great poet of Israel's salvation and restoration (see Is 40:11; 43:5).

**3:1–4** This prophecy of punishment has an introductory call to hear (v. 1a–b) and two major parts, the indictment or reasons for punishment (vv. 1c–3) and the announcement of judgment (v. 4). The prophet accuses the leaders and rulers of Israel of treating the people so badly that their actions are comparable to cannibalism. Those who, above all, should know and maintain justice are the most corrupt of all. In the time of trouble the Lord will withdraw (v. 4); that is, God will abandon the leaders to their fate and refuse to answer their prayers.

**3:5–8** This prophecy of punishment concerns and is addressed to false prophets. The prophets in Jerusalem who mislead the people are corrupt because their word can be bought (v. 5). Therefore such prophets, seers, and diviners shall be disgraced, put to shame, left in the dark without vision or answer (vv. 6–7). But Micah is convinced that he is filled with power and the spirit of the Lord, which corresponds to justice and might (v. 8).

*g*: Am 2:7. *h*: Ez 13:10. *i*: Jer 15:9; Am 8:9; Zec 13:3.

### A New Ruler

BY ASSOCIATING THE new ruler over a restored Israel with Bethlehem, David's home town, and with Ephrathah, David's clan (1 Sm 17:12), the author announces in Mi 5:1 that the coming ruler will revive the dynasty of David, which ruled in Jerusalem before it fell to the Babylonians in 587 B.C.

7 I will make of the lame a remnant,
and of the weak a strong nation;
The LORD shall be king over them on
Mount Zion,
from now on and forever.[n]

8 And you, O tower of the flock,*
hill of daughter Zion!
To you it shall come:
the former dominion shall be restored,
the reign of daughter Jerusalem.

9 Now why do you cry out so?
Are you without a king?
Or has your adviser perished,
That you are seized with pains
like a woman in labor?
10 * Writhe, go into labor,
O daughter Zion,
like a woman giving birth;
For now you shall leave the city
and camp in the fields;
To Babylon you shall go,
there you shall be rescued.
There the LORD shall redeem you
from the hand of your enemies.

11 * And now many nations are gathered
against you!
They say, "Let her be profaned,
let our eyes see Zion's downfall!"
12 But they do not know the thoughts of the
LORD,
nor understand his plan:
He has gathered them
like sheaves to the threshing floor.
13 Arise and thresh, O daughter Zion;
your horn I will make iron
And your hoofs I will make bronze,
that you may crush many peoples;
You shall devote their spoils to the LORD,*
their riches to the Lord of the whole
earth.[o]

14 Now grieve, O grieving daughter!*
"They have laid siege against us!"
With the rod they strike on the cheek
the ruler of Israel.

## CHAPTER 5

See RG 254

1 * But you, Bethlehem-Ephrathah[p]
least among the clans of Judah,
From you shall come forth for me
one who is to be ruler in Israel;
Whose origin is from of old,
from ancient times.
2 Therefore the Lord will give them up,
until the time
when she who is to give birth has borne,*
Then the rest of his kindred shall return
to the children of Israel.[q]
3 He shall take his place as shepherd
by the strength of the LORD,
by the majestic name of the LORD, his
God;
And they shall dwell securely, for now
his greatness

**4:8 Tower of the flock**: in Hebrew *migdal-eder,* a place name in Gn 35:21.

**4:10** Frequently the prophets personify the city of Jerusalem as a woman, and here as a woman in labor.

**4:11–13** The nations who have ridiculed Zion (v. 11) will be threshed like grain (v. 13).

**4:13 Devote their spoils to the LORD**: the fulfillment of the ancient ordinance of the holy war in which all plunder taken in the war was "put under the ban," i.e., belonged to the Lord.

**4:14 Grieve, O grieving daughter!**: the Hebrew actually reflects the ancient Near Eastern mourning practice of afflicting oneself with cuts and gashes, as evidence of grief. A literal rendering would be "gash yourself, O woman who gashes."

**5:1–6** Salvation will come through a "messiah," an anointed ruler. The Book of Micah shares with Isaiah the expectation that God will deliver Israel through a king in the line of David. Bethlehem-Ephrathah is the home of the Davidic line.

**5:2** These words are sometimes understood as a reference to Isaiah's Emmanuel oracle, given some thirty years earlier (Is 7:14). The Gospel of Matthew reports that the chief priests and scribes cite this passage as the ancient promise of a messiah in the line of David to be born in Bethlehem (Mt 2:5–6).

*n:* Is 6:13; Dn 7:14; Zep 3:19; Lk 1:32. *o:* Is 41:15; Hos 10:11. *p:* Ru 1:2; 1 Sm 17:12; Mt 2:6; Jn 7:42. *q:* Is 7:14; 11:1–2.

**God Demands Justice Above All**

THE FIRST HALF of ch 6, beginning the second collection from the eighth-century prophet Micah (Mi 6:1–7:7), describes God's message to Israel as a lawsuit brought against the people. A dialogue between God and the people ends, in v. 8, with God's instruction for how they can answer the LORD's complaint.

shall reach to the ends of the earth:
4 he shall be peace.*
If Assyria invades our country
and treads upon our land,
We shall raise against it seven shepherds,
eight of royal standing;
5 They shall tend the land of Assyria with the sword,
and the land of Nimrod* with the drawn sword;
They will deliver us from Assyria,
when it invades our land,
when it treads upon our borders.

6 The remnant of Jacob shall be
in the midst of many peoples,
Like dew coming from the LORD,
like showers on the grass,
Which wait for no one,
delay for no human being.
7 And the remnant of Jacob shall be among the nations,
in the midst of many peoples,
Like a lion among beasts of the forest,
like a young lion among flocks of sheep;
When it passes through it tramples;
it tears and no one can rescue.
8 Your hand shall be lifted above your foes,
and all your enemies shall be cut down.

9 * On that day—oracle of the LORD—
I will destroy the horses from your midst
and ruin your chariots;
10 I will destroy the cities of your land
and tear down all your fortresses.
11 I will destroy the sorcery you practice,
and there shall no longer be
soothsayers among you.
12 I will destroy your carved figures
and the sacred stones* from your midst;
And you shall no longer worship
the works of your hands.[r]
13 I will tear out the asherahs from your midst,
and destroy your cities.
14 I will wreak vengeance in anger and wrath
upon the nations that have not listened.

## III. Announcement of Judgment

### CHAPTER 6

See RG 254

1 * Hear, then, what the LORD says:
Arise, plead your case before the mountains,
and let the hills hear your voice![s]
2 Hear, O mountains, the LORD's case,
pay attention, O foundations of the earth!
For the LORD has a case against his people;
he enters into trial with Israel.
3 My people, what have I done to you?
how have I wearied you? Answer me![t]
4 I brought you up from the land of Egypt,

**5:4 Peace**: he will not only symbolize but also bring about harmony and wholeness.

**5:5 Nimrod**: the legendary ancestor of the Mesopotamians; cf. Gn 10:10–12.

**5:9–13** The Lord will destroy all those features of the nation's life that have stood between the people and their God. These false supports include horses, chariots, fortifications, and forbidden practices such as sorcery and idolatry.

**5:12–13 Sacred stones . . . asherahs**: the Hebrew *asherah* is a sacred pole. All forms of idolatry (standing stones and sacred poles were part of forbidden cult practices) were violations of Israel's covenant with the Lord.

**6:1–5** The Lord, through the prophet, initiates a legal case against the people. The initial calls (vv. 1–2) signal the beginning of a trial, and the proclamation that the Lord intends to enter into a legal dispute with Israel. One would expect accusations to follow such an introduction, but instead the Lord speaks in self-defense, reciting mighty acts done in behalf of Israel (vv. 3–5).

*r:* Hos 3:4; 10:1–2. *s:* Is 6:2; Ob 1. *t:* Jer 2:5.

## Judgment on Israel's Businessmen

MICAH RESUMES HIS attack on Israel's leadership, indicting its wealthy citizens for cheating the poor (6:9–12) and imposing a sentence by which they will be unable to enjoy the profits they have earned unfairly (vv. 13–16).

from the place of slavery I ransomed you;
And I sent before you Moses,
Aaron, and Miriam.[u]
5 * My people, remember what Moab's King Balak planned,
and how Balaam, the son of Beor, answered him.
Recall the passage from Shittim to Gilgal,
that you may know the just deeds of the LORD.[v]
6 * With what shall I come before the LORD,
and bow before God most high?
Shall I come before him with burnt offerings,
with calves a year old?[w]
7 Will the LORD be pleased with thousands of rams,
with myriad streams of oil?
* Shall I give my firstborn for my crime,
the fruit of my body for the sin of my soul?
8 * You have been told, O mortal, what is good,
and what the LORD requires of you:
Only to do justice and to love goodness,
and to walk humbly with your God.[x]
9 * The LORD cries aloud to the city
(It is prudent to fear your name!):
Hear, O tribe and city assembly,
10 Am I to bear criminal hoarding
and the accursed short ephah?*
11 Shall I acquit crooked scales,
bags of false weights?
12 You whose wealthy are full of violence,
whose inhabitants speak falsehood
with deceitful tongues in their mouths!
13 I have begun to strike you
with devastation because of your sins.
14 You shall eat, without being satisfied,
food that will leave you empty;
What you acquire, you cannot save;
what you do save, I will deliver up to the sword.[y]
15 You shall sow, yet not reap,
tread out the olive, yet pour no oil,
crush the grapes, yet drink no wine.[z]
16 You have kept the decrees of Omri,
and all the works of the house of Ahab,
and you have walked in their counsels;
Therefore I will deliver you up to ruin,
and your citizens to derision;
and you shall bear the reproach of the nations.

**6:5** The Lord calls for the people to remember the saving events of the past, from the encounters with Balak and Balaam (Nm 22:23) during the wandering in the wilderness to the entrance into the promised land ("from Shittim to Gilgal," Jos 3–5).

**6:6–8** These verses continue the previous unit (6:1–5), the dialogue between the Lord and the people in the pattern of a trial. The Lord has initiated proceedings against them, and they ask how to re-establish the broken relationship with God (vv. 6–7), and are given an answer (v. 8). The form of the passage borrows from a priestly liturgical pattern. When worshipers came to the temple, they inquired of the priest concerning the appropriate offering or sacrifice, and the priest answered them (see Ps 15; 24; Is 1:10–17; Am 5:21–24).

**6:7** The questions reach their climax with the possibility of child sacrifice, a practice known in antiquity (cf. 2 Kgs 16:3; 21:6).

**6:8 To do justice** refers to human behavior in relationship to others. **To love goodness** refers to the kind of love and concern which is at the heart of the covenant between the Lord and Israel; it is persistently faithful. **To walk humbly with your God** means to listen carefully to the revealed will of God.

**6:9–16** The language of the trial resumes as the Lord accuses the people of their sins (vv. 9–12, 16a) and announces their punishment (vv. 13–15, 16b). The city is Jerusalem, and those addressed are its inhabitants. Their wickedness includes cheating in business with false weights and measures, violence, lies, and following the practices of the Israelite kings Omri and Ahab (v. 16a), whose reigns came to symbolize a time of syncretistic worship. The punishment, which has already begun, will include a series of disasters. Finally, the Lord will destroy the city and see that its inhabitants are ridiculed (v. 16b).

**6:10 Ephah**: see note on Is 5:10.

*u:* Ex 15:20. *v:* Nm 22:23; Jos 3–5. *w:* Hos 6:6; 8:13; Am 5:21. *x:* Dt 26:16; Zec 7:9; Mt 23:23. *y:* Dt 28:38; Am 5:11; Hg 1:6. *z:* Hos 4:10.

**Judgment on the Powerful**

FROM THE OPENING speech (ch 1), in which Micah singles out for criticism the capitals of Israel and Judah, to the concluding speech in 7:1–7 (Mi 7:8–20 is an exilic supplement), the abuse of power is a central concern in Micah's message. In this speech, Micah laments the spread of corruption from the powerful (vv. 1–4) to friends and family (vv. 5–6).

See RG 254–55

## CHAPTER 7

1 Woe is me! I am like the one who
gathers summer fruit,
when the vines have been gleaned;
There is no cluster to eat,
no early fig that I crave.
2 The faithful have vanished from the earth,
no mortal is just!
They all lie in wait to shed blood,
each one ensnares the other.[a]
3 Their hands succeed at evil;
the prince makes demands,
The judge is bought for a price,
the powerful speak as they please.[b]
4 The best of them is like a brier,
the most honest like a thorn hedge.
The day announced by your sentinels!
Your punishment has come;
now is the time of your confusion.
5 Put no faith in a friend,
do not trust a companion;
With her who lies in your embrace
watch what you say.[c]
6 For the son belittles his father,
the daughter rises up against her mother,
The daughter-in-law against her mother-in-law,
and your enemies are members of your household.[d]

## IV. Confidence in God's Future

7 But as for me, I will look to the LORD,
I will wait for God my savior;
my God will hear me![e]
8 * Do not rejoice over me, my enemy!*
though I have fallen, I will arise;
though I sit in darkness, the LORD is
my light.
9 I will endure the wrath of the LORD
because I have sinned against him,
Until he pleads my case,
and establishes my right.
He will bring me forth to the light;
I will see his righteousness.
10 When my enemy sees this,
shame shall cover her:
She who said to me,
"Where is the LORD, your God?"
My eyes shall see her downfall;
now she will be trampled* underfoot,
like mud in the streets.
11 * It is the day for building your walls;
on that day your boundaries shall be
enlarged.
12 It is the day when those from Assyria to
Egypt
shall come to you,
And from Tyre even to the River,
from sea to sea, and from mountain to
mountain;[f]
13 And the earth shall be a waste
because of its inhabitants,
as a result of their deeds.

14 * Shepherd your people with your staff,
the flock of your heritage,
That lives apart[g] in a woodland,

**7:8–20** The book concludes with a collection of confident prayers for deliverance, affirmations of faith, and announcements of salvation. Most of these verses bear the marks of use in worship, and probably arose in the exilic or postexilic periods.

**7:8–10** An individual, possibly personified Jerusalem, expresses confidence that the Lord will deliver her from her enemy (cf. Ps 23).

**7:10 She who said . . . she will be trampled**: in the Old Testament, cities are often personified as women. Here, the prophet is speaking of the enemies' cities.

**7:11–13** An announcement of salvation to Zion. The walls of Jerusalem will be rebuilt, its inhabitants who are now scattered from Assyria to Egypt shall return, but the other peoples will suffer for their evil deeds.

**7:14–17** A prayer that God will care for the people as in ancient days (v. 14) is answered (vv. 15–17) when the Lord

*a:* Is 1:21; Hos 4:2. *b:* Is 1:23. *c:* Jer 9:3. *d:* Mt 10:35–36. *e:* Is 8:17. *f:* Zec 14:16. *g:* Nm 23:9.

in the midst of an orchard.
Let them feed in Bashan and Gilead,
as in the days of old;
15 As in the days when you came from the land of Egypt,
show us wonderful signs.
16 The nations will see and will be put to shame,
in spite of all their strength;
They will put their hands over their mouths;
their ears will become deaf.
17 They will lick the dust like a snake,
like crawling things on the ground;
They will come quaking from their strongholds;
they will tremble in fear of you, the LORD, our God.
18 * Who is a God like you, who removes guilt
and pardons sin for the remnant of his inheritance;
Who does not persist in anger forever,
but instead delights in mercy,[h]
19 And will again have compassion on us,
treading underfoot our iniquities?
You will cast into the depths of the sea all our sins;
20 You will show faithfulness to Jacob,
and loyalty to Abraham,
As you have sworn to our ancestors
from days of old.[i]

promises to do marvelous things. The nations shall be afraid and turn to the Lord.

**7:18–20** The final lines of the book contain a hymn of praise for the incomparable God, who pardons sin and delights in mercy. Thus the remnant, those left after the exile, is confident in God's compassion and in the ancient promises sworn to the ancestors.

*h*: Jer 10:6; Acts 10:43. *i*: Ps 105:6; Is 41:8; 63:16.

See RG 255–56

# The Book of Nahum

Shortly before the fall of Nineveh, the capital of Assyria, in 612 B.C., Nahum uttered his prophecy against the hated city. To understand the prophet's exultant outburst of joy over the impending destruction it is necessary to recall the savage cruelty of Assyria, which had made it the scourge of the ancient Near East for almost three centuries. The royal inscriptions of Assyria afford the best commentary on Nahum's burning denunciation of "the bloody city." In the wake of their conquests, mounds of heads, impaled bodies, enslaved citizens, and avaricious looters testified to the ruthlessness of the Assyrians. Just such a conquest was suffered by Israel, when its capital Samaria fell to the Assyrians in 722/721 B.C., and by Judah, when its capital Jerusalem nearly fell to invading Assyrian armies twenty years later. Little wonder that in 3:19 Judah is shown as joining in the general outburst of joy over the destruction of Nineveh!

But Nahum is not a prophet of unrestrained revenge. He asserts God's moral government of the world. Nineveh's doom is evidence that God stands against oppression and the abuse of power. As an ancient Near Eastern superpower, Assyria had terrorized its smaller and weaker neighbors, exploiting their economies and subjugating their people for its own ends. Thus Nineveh's demise is viewed as an act of divine justice, and it is greeted by the small, oppressed countries as a time of deliverance, as a moment of renewal, and as a message of peace (2:1; 3:19).

The book is divided as follows:

I. God's Terrifying Appearance (1:2–8)
II. Nineveh's Judgment and Judah's Restoration (1:9–2:1)
III. The Attack on Nineveh (2:2–3:7)
IV. Nineveh's Inescapable Fate (3:8–19)

## CHAPTER 1

See RG 255–56

1 Oracle* concerning Nineveh. The book of the vision of Nahum of Elkosh.

**1:1 Oracle**: (Heb. *Massa'*) a word used frequently to describe a prophetic statement against a foreign nation or occasionally Israel; it is used favorably for Israel in Zec 12:1 and Mal 1:1. **Nahum of Elkosh**: Nahum means "comfort." Elkosh is a clan or village of unknown location, perhaps in southern Judah.

### *God's Terrifying Appearance*

2 * A jealous and avenging God* is the LORD,
an avenger is the LORD, full of wrath;
The LORD takes vengeance on his adversaries,
and rages against his enemies;
3 The LORD is slow to anger, yet great in power;
the LORD will not leave the guilty unpunished.[a]
In stormwind* and tempest he comes,
and clouds are the dust at his feet;
4 He roars at the sea and leaves it dry,
and all the rivers he dries up.
Laid low are Bashan and Carmel,
and the bloom of Lebanon withers;*
5 The mountains quake before him,
and the hills dissolve;
The earth is laid waste before him,
the world and all who dwell in it.
6 * Before his wrath, who can stand firm,
and who can face his blazing anger?[b]
His fury is poured out like fire,
and boulders break apart before him.
7 The LORD is good to those who wait for him,
a refuge on the day of distress,
Taking care of those who look to him for protection,
8 when the flood rages;
He makes an end of his opponents,
and pursues his enemies into darkness.

### *Nineveh's Judgment and Judah's Restoration*

9 What do you plot against the LORD,
the one about to bring total destruction?
No opponent rises a second time!
10 * Like a thorny thicket, they are tangled,
and like drunkards, they are drunk;
like dry stubble, they are utterly consumed.
11 From you has come
one plotting evil against the LORD,
one giving sinister counsel.*
12 Thus says the LORD:
though fully intact and so numerous,
they* shall be mown down and disappear.
Though I have humbled you,
I will humble you no more.
13 Now I will break his yoke off of you,
and tear off your bonds.[c]

14 The LORD has commanded regarding you:*
no descendant will again bear your name;
From the house of your gods I will abolish
the carved and the molten image;
I will make your grave a dung heap.

## CHAPTER 2

See RG 255–56

1 At this moment on the mountains
the footsteps of one bearing good news,
of one announcing peace![d]
Celebrate your feasts, Judah,
fulfill your vows!
For never again will destroyers invade you;*
they are completely cut off.

**1:2–8** A poem written in the style of the alphabetic psalms (cf. Ps 9; 25; 111; 119) in which each verse unit begins with a successive letter of the Hebrew alphabet. The second half of the alphabet is not represented here.

**1:2 A jealous . . . God**: see note on Ex 20:5.

**1:3–6 In stormwind**: the power of God is often pictured by natural forces and cosmic disruption (Ex 19:9–25; Ps 18:8–16; 104:1–9).

**1:4** Bashan, Carmel, and Lebanon were famous for their mountainous terrain and lush forests.

**1:6–7** When God comes in judgment those who oppose God will be destroyed, and those who trust in God will be saved.

**1:10** Thorns (Is 34:13), drunkenness (Lam 4:21; Na 3:11), and burning stubble (Ob 18) are all images of the judgment of God's enemies.

**1:11 From you . . . giving sinister counsel**: addressed to Nineveh, the capital city of Sennacherib, king of Assyria, who besieged Jerusalem ca. 700 B.C.

**1:12–13 They**: the enemies of Judah. **You**: Judah. **His yoke**: the dominion of the Assyrian king over Judah.

**1:14 You**: the king of Assyria.

**2:1 For never again will destroyers invade you**: prophets are not always absolutely accurate in the things they foresee. Nineveh was destroyed, as Nahum expected, but Judah was later invaded by the Babylonians and (much later) by the Romans. The prophets were convinced that Israel held a key place in God's plan and looked for the people to survive all catastrophes, always blessed by the Lord, though the manner was not always as they expected; the "fallen hut of David"

*a:* Ex 34:6–7; Jl 2:13. *b:* Is 30:27–28; Zep 1:15. *c:* Is 9:4; 10:27. *d:* Is 52:7; Rom 10:15.

*The Attack on Nineveh*

2 One who scatters has come up against
you;*
guard the rampart,
Watch the road, brace yourselves,
marshal all your strength!
3 * The LORD will restore the vine of Jacob,
the honor of Israel,
Because ravagers have ravaged them
and ruined their branches.
4 The shields of his warriors are
crimsoned,
the soldiers clad in scarlet;
Like fire are the trappings of the chariots
on the day he prepares for war;
the cavalry is agitated!
5 The chariots dash madly through the
streets
and wheel in the squares,
Looking like torches,
bolting like lightning.
6 His picked troops are called,
ranks break at their charge;
To the wall they rush,
their screen* is set up.
7 The river gates* are opened,
the palace is washed away.
8 The mistress is led forth captive,
and her maidservants* led away,
Moaning like doves,
beating their breasts.
9 Nineveh is like a pool
whose waters escape;
"Stop! Stop!"
but none turns back.[e]
10 "Plunder the silver, plunder the gold!"
There is no end to the treasure,
to wealth in every precious thing!
11 Emptiness, desolation, waste;
melting hearts and trembling knees,
Churning in every stomach,
every face turning pale![f]
12 Where is the lionesses' den,
the young lions' cave,
Where the lion* went in and out,
and the cub, with no one to disturb
them?[g]
13 The lion tore apart enough for his cubs,
and strangled for his lionesses;
He filled his lairs with prey,
and his dens with torn flesh.
14 I now come against you—
oracle of the LORD of hosts—
I will consume your chariots in smoke,
and the sword will devour your young
lions;
Your preying on the land I will bring to
an end,
the cry of your lionesses will be heard
no more.

## CHAPTER 3

See RG 255–56

1 Ah! The bloody city,
all lies,
Full of plunder,
whose looting never stops![h]
2 The crack of the whip,
the rumbling of wheels;
Horses galloping,
chariots bounding,
3 Cavalry charging,
the flash of the sword,
the gleam of the spear;
A multitude of slain,
a mass of corpses,
Endless bodies
to stumble upon!
4 For the many debaucheries of the
prostitute,
a charming mistress of witchcraft,
Who enslaved nations with her
prostitution,

was not rebuilt as Am 9:11 suggests, except in the coming of Jesus, and in a way far different than the prophet expected. Often the prophet speaks in hyperbole, as when Second Isaiah speaks of the restored Jerusalem being built with precious stones (Is 54:12) as a way of indicating a glorious future.

**2:2 One who scatters has come up against you**: the enemy is about to crush Nineveh, dispersing and deporting its people (v. 8; 3:18).

**2:3** This verse does not fit its context well; it may have been the conclusion for the preceding section and have once followed v. 1, or it may be a later scribal addition.

**2:6 Their screen**: that is, a mantelet, a movable military shelter protecting the besiegers.

**2:7 River gates**: a network of canals brought water into Nineveh from the Tigris and Khosr Rivers on which the city was located.

**2:8 Mistress . . . and her maidservants**: either the queen of Nineveh with the ladies of her court, or the city of Nineveh itself, pictured as a noblewoman (3:4).

**2:12 The lion**: the king of Assyria.

*e*: Is 8:7–8. *f*: Jl 2:6. *g*: Ez 19:2–7. *h*: Is 10:13–14; Hb 2:12.

NAHUM'S FINAL VERSE summarizes the image of Nineveh held by all who had suffered as a result of its imperial ambitions. Jonah shared this opinion, hence his resistance to God's instruction to prophesy to Nineveh and his anger when God spared the city.

and peoples by her witchcraft:[i]
5 * I now come against you—
oracle of the LORD of hosts—
and I will lift your skirt above your face;
I will show your nakedness to the nations,
to the kingdoms your shame![j]
6 I will cast filth upon you,
disgrace you and make you a spectacle;
7 Until everyone who sees you
runs from you saying,
"Nineveh is destroyed;
who can pity her?
Where can I find
any to console you?"

### *Nineveh's Inescapable Fate*

8 Are you better than No-amon* [k]
that was set among the Nile's canals,
Surrounded by waters,
with the river for her rampart
and water for her wall?
9 Ethiopia was her strength,
and Egypt without end;
Put* and the Libyans
were her allies.
10 Yet even she became an exile,
and went into captivity;
Even her little ones were dashed to pieces
at the corner of every street;
For her nobles they cast lots,
and all her great ones were put into chains.
11 You, too, will drink of this;
you will be overcome;[l]
You, too, will seek
a refuge from the foe.
12 But all your fortresses are fig trees,
bearing early figs;*
When shaken, they fall
into the devourer's mouth.
13 Indeed your troops
are women in your midst;
To your foes are open wide
the gates of your land,
fire has consumed their bars.
14 Draw water for the siege,*
strengthen your fortresses;
Go down into the mud
and tread the clay,
take hold of the brick mold!
15 There the fire will consume you,
the sword will cut you down;
it will consume you like the grasshoppers.

Multiply like the grasshoppers,
multiply like the locusts![m]
16 You have made your traders* more numerous
than the stars of the heavens;
like grasshoppers that shed their skins
and fly away.
17 Your sentries are like locusts,
and your scribes like locust swarms
Gathered on the rubble fences
on a cold day!
Yet when the sun rises, they vanish,
and no one knows where they have gone.

18 Your shepherds slumber,
O king of Assyria,

**3:5–6** The punishment for adulterous women.

**3:8 No-amon**: "No" was the Egyptian name of the capital of Upper Egypt, called Thebes by the Greeks; its patron deity was Amon. This great city was destroyed by the Assyrians in 663 B.C.

**3:9 Put**: a North African people often associated with Egypt and Ethiopia (Jer 46:8–9).

**3:12 Early figs**: the refugees from Nineveh who escape to presumably secure fortresses.

**3:14** An ironic exhortation to prepare the city for a futile defense. **Go down . . . brick mold**: make bricks for the city walls.

**3:16 Traders**: agents of the economic exploitation that sustained and enriched the Assyrian empire.

*i:* Mi 1:7; Rev 17:1. *j:* Is 47:3; Jer 13:26. *k:* Jer 46:25. *l:* Jer 25:15–16; Ob 16. *m:* Jer 46:23.

your nobles have gone to rest;
Your people are scattered upon the
mountains,
with none to gather them.
19 There is no healing for your hurt,
your wound is fatal.
All who hear this news of you
clap their hands over you;
For who has not suffered
under your endless malice?

See RG 256–58

# The Book of Habakkuk

Habakkuk is the only prophet to devote his entire work to the question of the justice of God's government of the world. In the Bible as a whole, only Job delivers a more pointed challenge to divine rule. Habakkuk's challenge is set up as a dialogue between the prophet and God, in which Habakkuk's opening complaint about injustices in Judean society (1:2–4) is followed in 1:5–11 by God's promise that the perpetrators will be punished by invading Chaldeans, i.e., Babylonians. Habakkuk's second complaint about the violence of the Chaldeans themselves (1:12–2:1) is followed by a second divine response assuring the prophet of the reliability of God's rule and calling for human faithfulness (2:2–4).

This dialogue is followed by a series of observations on the disastrous nature of tyranny (2:5–20), and by a vivid description in chap. 3 of God's appearance to save the people. Chapter 3 may be the prophet's prayer that God fulfill the promises made earlier to Habakkuk, or a hymn praising God's power added to Habakkuk's speeches by editors. In either case, the description of the theophany draws heavily upon ancient traditions in which God establishes order by defeating chaos, symbolized by rebellious waters (see Jb 7:12; Ps 74:13–14; 77:17–21; 89:10–11; Is 51:9).

Two important events frame Habakkuk's prophecy: the great Babylonian (Chaldean) victory over the Egyptians at Carchemish (605 B.C.) and the second Babylonian invasion of Judah (587 B.C.), which ended with the destruction of Jerusalem. The desperate conditions in Judah during these years, arising from internal and external threats, provoked Habakkuk's struggle with difficult and important theological questions about divine justice.

The book may be divided as follows:

I. Habakkuk's First Complaint (1:2–4)
II. God's Response (1:5–11)
III. Habakkuk's Second Complaint (1:12–2:1)
IV. God's Response (2:2–4)
V. Sayings Against Tyrants (2:5–20)
VI. Hymn About God's Reign (3:1–19)

---

## CHAPTER 1

See RG 257

1 The oracle which Habakkuk the prophet received in a vision.

### *Habakkuk's First Complaint*

2 How long, O LORD, must I cry for help*
and you do not listen?[a]
Or cry out to you, "Violence!"
and you do not intervene?
3 Why do you let me see iniquity?
why do you simply gaze at evil?
Destruction and violence are before me;[b]
there is strife and discord.
4 This is why the law is numb*
and justice never comes,
For the wicked surround the just;[c]
this is why justice comes forth
perverted.

### *God's Response*

5 * Look over the nations and see!
Be utterly amazed!
For a work is being done in your days

**1:2–4** The prophet complains about God's apparent disregard for Judah's internal evils in language that echoes the preaching of prophets like Amos, Isaiah, and Jeremiah.

**1:4 The law is numb**: because the Lord has been silent, the Law, whether in the form of the scroll found in the Temple in the time of Josiah (2 Kgs 22) or in the form of divine instruction given by priests and prophets, has proved ineffective and so appeared to be cold, unreceptive, and powerless. For the Law to be credible, the Lord must see to it that the wicked are punished and the just rewarded.

**1:5–7** Habakkuk interprets the Babylonian defeat of Egypt at Carchemish (605 B.C.) as the answer to his complaint: the

*a:* Ps 13:2. *b:* Ez 45:9. *c:* Is 29:20–21.

that you would not believe, were it
told.[d]
6 For now I am raising up the Chaldeans,[e]
that bitter and impulsive people,
Who march the breadth of the land
to take dwellings not their own.
7 They are terrifying and dreadful;
their right and their exalted position
are of their own making.
8 Swifter than leopards are their horses,
and faster than desert wolves.
Their horses spring forward;
they come from far away;
they fly like an eagle hastening to
devour.
9 All of them come for violence,
their combined onslaught, a stormwind
to gather up captives like sand.
10 They scoff at kings,
ridicule princes;
They laugh at any fortress,
heap up an earthen ramp, and
conquer it.
11 Then they sweep through like the wind
and vanish—
they make their own strength their god!*

### *Habakkuk's Second Complaint*

12 Are you not from of old, O LORD,
my holy God, immortal?[f]
LORD, you have appointed them for
judgment,*
O Rock,* you have set them in place to
punish!
13 Your eyes are too pure to look upon
wickedness,
and the sight of evil you cannot endure.
Why, then, do you gaze on the faithless
in silence
while the wicked devour those more
just than themselves?
14 You have made mortals like the fish in
the sea,
like creeping things without a leader.
15 He* brings them all up with a hook,
and hauls them away with his net;
He gathers them in his fishing net,
and then rejoices and exults.
16 Therefore he makes sacrifices to his net,*
and burns incense to his fishing net;
For thanks to them his portion is rich,
and his meal lavish.
17 Shall they, then, keep on drawing his
sword
to slaughter nations without mercy?

## CHAPTER 2

See RG 257

1 I will stand at my guard post,
and station myself upon the rampart;[g]
I will keep watch to see what he will say
to me,
and what answer he will give to my
complaint.

### *God's Response*

2 Then the LORD answered me and said:
Write down the vision;* [h]
Make it plain upon tablets,
so that the one who reads it may run.
3 For the vision is a witness for the
appointed time,
a testimony to the end; it will not
disappoint.
If it delays, wait for it,
it will surely come, it will not be late.
4 See, the rash have no integrity;
but the just one who is righteous
because of faith shall live.* [i]

Lord will send the Chaldean empire against Judah as punishment for their sins.

**1:11** The primary aim of military campaigns by ancient Near Eastern rulers was usually the gathering of spoils and the collection of tribute rather than the annexation of territory. However, in the eighth century B.C., the Assyrians began to administer many conquered territories as provinces.

**1:12–2:1 Appointed them for judgment**: this complaint is directed against the violent Babylonians, the very nation God chose to punish Judah.

**1:12 Rock**: an ancient title celebrating the Lord's power and fidelity; cf. Dt 32:4; Is 26:4; 30:29; Ps 18:3, 32, 47; 95:1.

**1:15 He**: the Babylonian king (cf. vv. 6, 13), who easily conquers other nations and treats them as objects for his entertainment and enrichment.

**1:16 He makes sacrifices to his net**: the leader attributes victory to the military weapons he wields; he and his weapons have won victory, not any god.

**2:2 Write down the vision**: the vision is written down for two reasons: so that a herald may carry and proclaim its contents to the people, and so that the reception of the vision and its truth can be verified by its fulfillment (v. 3).

**2:4 The just one who is righteous because of faith shall**

*d:* Acts 13:41. *e:* Jer 32:28. *f:* Ps 90:2. *g:* Is 21:8. *h:* Is 30:8. *i:* Rom 1:17; Gal 3:11; Heb 10:38.

### *Sayings Against Tyrants*

5 * Indeed wealth is treacherous;
a proud man does not succeed.
He who opens wide his throat like Sheol,
and is insatiable as death,
Who gathers to himself all the nations,
and collects for himself all the
peoples—
6 Shall not all these take up a taunt against
him,[j]
and make a riddle about him, saying:

Ah! you who store up what is not yours
—how long can it last!—
you who load yourself down with
collateral.
7 Will your debtors* not rise suddenly?
Will they not awake, those who make
you tremble?
You will become their spoil!
8 Because you plundered many nations,
the remaining peoples shall plunder
you;
Because of the shedding of human blood,
and violence done to the land,
to the city and to all who live in it.

9 Ah! you who pursue evil gain for your
household,
setting your nest on high
to escape the reach of misfortune!
10 You have devised shame for your
household,
cutting off many peoples, forfeiting
your own life;
11 For the stone in the wall shall cry out,*
and the beam in the frame shall
answer it!

12 Ah! you who build a city by bloodshed,
and who establish a town with
injustice![k]
13 Is this not from the LORD of hosts:
peoples toil* for what the flames
consume,
and nations grow weary for nothing!
14 But the earth shall be filled
with the knowledge of the LORD's
glory,
just as the water covers the sea.[l]

15 Ah! you who give your neighbors
the cup of your wrath to drink, and
make them drunk,
until their nakedness is seen![m]
16 You are filled with shame instead of
glory;
drink, you too, and stagger!
The cup from the LORD's right hand shall
come around to you,
and utter shame shall cover your glory.
17 For the violence done to Lebanon* shall
cover you,[n]
and the destruction of the animals shall
terrify you;
Because of the shedding of human blood,
and violence done to the land,
to the city and to all who live in it.

18 Of what use is the carved image,*
that its maker should carve it?
Or the molten image, the lying oracle,
that its very maker should trust in it,
and make mute idols?
19 Ah! you who say to wood, "Awake!"
to silent stone, "Arise!"
Can any such thing give oracles?[o]

**live**: the faithful survive the impending doom because they trust in God's justice and wait patiently for God to carry it out. Several New Testament passages cite these words (Rom 1:17; Gal 3:11; cf. Heb 10:38) to confirm the teaching that people receive justification and supernatural life through faith in Christ.

**2:5** This verse describes any tyrant who, like the Babylonians, possesses insatiable greed.

**2:7 Debtors**: the Hebrew term can mean either debtors or creditors, and this double meaning is likely intended: the debtor nations rise up against their creditor nation and become its creditors in the reversal of affairs described here.

**2:11–12** The palaces, built at the expense of gross injustice (vv. 6–10), call down vengeance on their builders. This is typical prophetic language for the condemnation of social crimes within Israel and Judah.

**2:13 Peoples toil**: those oppressed by the Babylonians do not benefit from their work. Verses 13–14 break the pattern of reversal in the oracles that precede and may have been added by an editor.

**2:17 The violence done to Lebanon**: the destruction of the cedar forests of Lebanon, used in lavish building projects by the great conquerors; cf. Is 14:8; 37:24. **The destruction of the animals**: the killing off of the wild animals through excessive hunting by the same conquerors; cf. Bar 3:16.

**2:18–20** Idolatrous worship is here shown to be folly by contrasting idols with the majesty of the one true God. Verse 18 may originally have followed v. 19, since the term "Ah!" begins each new saying in this section.

*j*: Is 14:4. *k*: Ez 24:6; Mi 3:10; Na 3:1. *l*: Is 11:9. *m*: Jer 51:7; Lam 4:21. *n*: Is 14:8. *o*: Is 44:18–19.

## A Hymn Praising God's Rule

THE HYMN IN ch 3 describes a theophany, a direct appearance of God (vv. 3–15), placed in a framework describing the poet's response to it (vv. 2, 16–19).

In the earlier chapters, the prophet lamented how God could allow the injustices he described. Now Habakkuk concludes with a petition to God to manifest his power, and he describes what will happen when the LORD comes into the world. Finally, he expresses a prayer of confidence in the LORD.

It is only overlaid with gold and silver,
there is no breath in it at all.
20 But the LORD is in his holy temple;
silence before him, all the earth![p]

See RG 257

### CHAPTER 3

### *Hymn About God's Reign*

1 Prayer of Habakkuk, the prophet. According to Shigyonot.*

2 O LORD, I have heard your renown,
and am in awe, O LORD, of your work.
In the course of years revive it,*
in the course of years make yourself known;
in your wrath remember compassion!

3 * God came from Teman,*
the Holy One from Mount Paran.[q]
*Selah*

His glory covered the heavens,
and his praise filled the earth;
4 his splendor spread like the light.
He raised his horns high,[r]
he rejoiced on the day of his strength.

5 Before him went pestilence,
and plague* followed in his steps.
6 He stood and shook the earth;
he looked and made the nations tremble.
Ancient mountains were shattered,
the age-old hills bowed low,
age-old orbits* collapsed.
7 The tents of Cushan trembled,
the pavilions of the land of Midian.*
8 Was your anger against the rivers, O LORD?
your wrath against the rivers,
your rage against the sea,*[s]
That you mounted your steeds,
your victorious chariot?
9 You readied your bow,
you filled your bowstring with arrows.
*Selah*

You split the earth with rivers;
10 at the sight of you the mountains writhed.
The clouds poured down water;
the deep roared loudly.

**3:1 Shigyonot**: a Hebrew technical term no longer understood, but probably a musical notation regarding the following hymn. This term, the references to the leader and stringed instruments at the end of the hymn (v. 19), and the use of the term *selah* in vv. 3, 9, and 13 are found elsewhere in the Bible only in the Psalter, and they indicate that, like the psalms, this poem was once used in worship.

**3:2 In the course of years revive it**: a plea for God to renew the works of the past.

**3:3–15** Cf. the theophanies in Dt 33:2–3; Jgs 5:4–5; Ps 18:8–16; 68:8–9; 77:17–21; 97:1–5; Na 1:3–6, etc. Conventional language is employed to describe the appearance of the Lord, as in Ex 19:16–19.

**3:3 Teman**: a region in Edom. **Mount Paran**: in the territory of Edom, or the northern part of the Sinai peninsula.

**3:5 Pestilence . . . plague**: these may be figures who are part of the heavenly armies God leads into battle.

**3:6 Age-old orbits**: the regular paths through the skies of heavenly bodies are disrupted at the appearance of the divine warrior, as are the ancient mountains on earth. Such cosmic disruption is typical of divine appearances (Ps 18:8; Na 1:5).

**3:7 Cushan . . . Midian**: the inhabitants of the area southeast of Judah where the divine march originates (Teman, Mount Paran), who are shaken, together with the cosmos, at God's appearance.

**3:8 Rivers . . . sea**: the forces of chaos personified as *yam* (Sea) and *nahar* (River) try to destroy the order God imposed at creation by sweeping past their boundaries and covering the earth. Their mention here and in v. 15 emphasizes that God is both creator and deliverer, subduing historical enemies and cosmic forces.

*p:* Ps 11:4. *q:* Dt 33:2. *r:* Ps 18:3. *s:* Ps 74:13; 89:11; Is 51:9; Na 1:4.

The sun* forgot to rise,
11 the moon left its lofty station,[t]
At the light of your flying arrows,
at the gleam of your flashing spear.

12 In wrath you marched on the earth,
in fury you trampled the nations.
13 You came forth to save your people,
to save your anointed one.*
You crushed the back of the wicked,
you laid him bare, bottom to neck.
*Selah*

14 * You pierced his head with your shafts;
his princes you scattered with your stormwind,
as food for the poor in unknown places.
15 You trampled the sea with your horses
amid the churning of the deep waters.

16 I hear, and my body trembles;
at the sound, my lips quiver.
Decay invades my bones,
my legs tremble beneath me.
I await the day of distress
that will come upon the people who attack us.

17 For though the fig tree does not blossom,
and no fruit appears on the vine,
Though the yield of the olive fails
and the terraces produce no nourishment,
Though the flocks disappear from the fold
and there is no herd in the stalls,
18 Yet I will rejoice in the LORD
and exult in my saving God.
19 GOD, my Lord, is my strength;
he makes my feet swift as those of deer
and enables me to tread upon the heights.* [u]

For the leader; with stringed instruments.

**3:10–11 Sun . . . moon**: heavenly figures who, like pestilence and plague (v. 5), serve in God's army, or are startled at God's appearance, as are the ancient constellations (v. 6).

**3:13 Your anointed one**: the theocratic king, the head of God's people. **The back of the wicked**: this may refer both to God's cosmic enemy, River/Sea, and to the leader of Israel's historical enemy.

**3:14** The last two lines of this verse are obscure in Hebrew and difficult to translate.

**3:19 The heights**: this term can also mean "backs" and may be an image of conquest over the poet's foes.

---

*t:* Jos 10:12–13. *u:* Ps 18:32–34.

See RG 258–59

# The Book of Zephaniah

Zephaniah's prophecy of judgment on Judah and Jerusalem emphasizes, perhaps more than any other prophecy, the devastation and death that divine judgment will bring. Described as the day of the Lord, the day of judgment is pictured as a time of darkness, of anguish and distress, of destruction and plunder of cities, and of threat to all life, human and animal alike. The major sins motivating this judgment, in Zephaniah's view, are Judah's worship of other deities (1:4–9) and its unjust and abusive leadership (3:1–4).

The title of the prophecy informs us that the ministry of Zephaniah took place during the reign of Josiah (640–609 B.C.), not long before the fall of Jerusalem in 587 B.C. The protest against the worship of false gods and the condemnation of foreign practices (1:8–9) may indicate that Zephaniah spoke during the height of Assyrian influence in the early years of Josiah's reign, before Josiah launched the religious reforms praised by Israel's historians (2 Kgs 22:1–23:30). If so, the prophecy of Zephaniah would be contemporary with the early prophecy of Jeremiah, with which it shares both language and ideas.

Following are the book's four sections:

I. The Day of the Lord: Judgment on Judah (1:2–2:3)
II. Judgment on the Nations (2:4–15)
III. Jerusalem Reproached (3:1–7)
IV. The Nations Punished and Jerusalem Restored (3:8–20)

## CHAPTER 1

See RG 258

1 The word of the LORD which came to Zephaniah, the son of Cushi, the son of Gedaliah, the son of Amariah, the son of Hezekiah,* in the days of Josiah, the son of Amon, king of Judah.

### *The Day of the Lord: Judgment on Judah*

2 I will completely sweep away all things
from the face of the land—oracle of
the LORD.
3 I will sweep away human being and
beast alike,
I will sweep away the birds of the sky,
and the fish of the sea.
I will make the wicked stumble;
I will eliminate the people
from the face of the land—oracle of
the LORD.[a]
4 I will stretch out my hand against
Judah,
and against all the inhabitants of
Jerusalem;
I will eliminate from this place
the last vestige of Baal,
the name of the idolatrous priests.
5 And those who bow down on the roofs
to the host of heaven,*
And those who bow down to the LORD
but swear by Milcom;[b]
6 And those who have turned away from
the LORD,
and those who have not sought the
LORD,
who have not inquired of him.
7 Silence in the presence of the Lord GOD!
for near is the day of the LORD,
Yes, the LORD has prepared a sacrifice,
he has consecrated his guests.* [c]
8 On the day of the LORD's sacrifice
I will punish the officials and the king's
sons,
and all who dress in foreign apparel.
9 I will punish, on that day,
all who leap over the threshold,*
Who fill the house of their master
with violence and deceit.
10 On that day—oracle of the LORD—
A cry will be heard from the Fish Gate,
a wail from the Second Quarter,*
loud crashing from the hills.
11 Wail, O inhabitants of Maktesh!
for all the merchants are destroyed,
all who weigh out silver, done away
with.
12 At that time,
I will search Jerusalem with lamps,
I will punish the people
who settle like dregs in wine,*
Who say in their hearts,
"The Lord will not do good,
nor will he do harm."
13 Their wealth shall be given to plunder
and their houses to devastation;
They will build houses,
but not dwell in them;
They will plant vineyards,
but not drink their wine.[d]
14 Near is the great day of the LORD,
near and very swiftly coming.
The sound of the day of the LORD!
Piercing—
there a warrior shrieks!
15 A day of wrath is that day,
a day of distress and anguish,
a day of ruin and desolation,
A day of darkness and gloom,
a day of thick black clouds,[e]
16 A day of trumpet blasts and battle cries
against fortified cities,
against lofty battlements.[f]

**1:1 Hezekiah**: it is possible, but not certain, that Zephaniah's ancestor was King Hezekiah who reigned in Judah from 715 to 687 B.C. (2 Kgs 18–20).

**1:5 The host of heaven**: the sun, moon, planets, and stars, the worship of which became widespread in Judah under Assyrian influence. **Milcom**: the god of the Ammonites; cf. 1 Kgs 11:5, 7, 33; 2 Kgs 23:13.

**1:7 He has consecrated his guests**: God has consecrated the troops, presumably foreign, who have been invited to share in the spoil on the day of slaughter.

**1:9 Leap over the threshold**: the reference may be to a religious ritual like that practiced by the priests of the Philistine deity Dagon (1 Sm 5:5).

**1:10–11 The Second Quarter . . . Maktesh**: sections of Jerusalem (cf. 2 Kgs 22:14).

**1:12 Settle like dregs in wine**: those who are overconfident because, like the sediment that settles to the bottom of a bottle of wine, they have remained at peace and undisturbed for a long time.

*a:* Hos 4:3. *b:* Jer 8:2; 2 Kgs 23:13. *c:* Is 34:6; Am 5:18. *d:* Am 5:11. *e:* Is 13:9; Jl 2:1–2. *f:* Am 2:2.

## The Day of the LORD: Judah Is Judged

ZEPHANIAH'S SPEECH (1:2–2:3) includes an indictment of Judah's sins (vv. 4–9), but, as is customary in prophetic judgment speeches, the prophet emphasizes the sentence, God's punishment on Judah and its people. Verses 2–3 give one of the most desolate images of judgment in prophetic literature (cf Jer 4:23–26). In effect, this is a vision of "uncreation" that parallels the creation story in Genesis ch 1, insofar as it involved living things. Zephaniah describes the process of undoing God's creative act, the judgment of God on humankind's evil.

17 I will hem the people in
till they walk like the blind,
because they have sinned against the LORD;
And their blood shall be poured out like dust,
and their bowels like dung.
18 Neither their silver nor their gold
will be able to save them.
On the day of the LORD's wrath,
in the fire of his passion,
all the earth will be consumed.
For he will make an end, yes, a sudden end,
of all who live on the earth.[g]

### CHAPTER 2

See RG 258–59

1* Gather, gather yourselves together,
O nation without shame!
2 Before you are driven away,
like chaff that disappears;
Before there comes upon you
the blazing anger of the LORD;
Before there comes upon you
the day of the LORD's anger.
3 Seek the LORD,
all you humble of the land,
who have observed his law;
Seek justice,
seek humility;
Perhaps you will be sheltered
on the day of the LORD's anger.[h]

### *Judgment on the Nations*

4 For Gaza shall be forsaken,
and Ashkelon shall be a waste,
Ashdod they shall drive out at midday,
and Ekron* shall be uprooted.[i]
5 Ah! You who dwell by the seacoast,
the nation of Cherethites,*
the word of the LORD is against you!
O Canaan, land of the Philistines,
I will leave you to perish without an inhabitant!
6 You shall become fields for shepherds,
and folds for flocks.
7 The seacoast shall belong
to the remnant of the house of Judah;
by the sea they shall pasture.
In the houses of Ashkelon
they shall lie down in the evening.
For the LORD their God will take care of them,
and bring about their restoration.

8 I have heard the taunts uttered by Moab,
and the insults of the Ammonites,*
When they taunted my people
and made boasts against their territory.[j]
9 Therefore, as I live—
oracle of the LORD of hosts—
the God of Israel,
Moab shall become like Sodom,
the Ammonites like Gomorrah:

**2:1–3** This oracle is a classic description of the day of the Lord as an overwhelming disaster, concluding with a call for repentance and reform. **Nation without shame**: Judah.

**2:4 Gaza . . . Ashkelon . . . Ashdod . . . Ekron**: cities of the Philistine confederation.

**2:5 Cherethites**: a synonym for, or subgroup of, the Philistines, which may be associated with Crete, a part of the larger Aegean area from which the Philistines came.

**2:8 Moab . . . Ammonites**: Judah's neighbors to the East across the Jordan.

*g*: Zep 3:8; Jer 4:26–27. *h*: Am 5:14–15. *i*: Jer 47:5; Am 1:6–8. *j*: Jer 48:1; 49:1.

A field of weeds,
a salt pit,
a waste forever.
The remnant of my people shall plunder them,
the survivors of my nation dispossess them.
10 This will be the recompense for their pride,
because they taunted and boasted against
the people of the LORD of hosts.
11 The LORD shall inspire them with terror
when he makes all the gods of earth waste away;
Then the distant shores of the nations,
each from its own place,
shall bow down to him.

12 You too, O Cushites,*
shall be slain by the sword of the LORD.[k]
13 He will stretch out his hand against the north,
to destroy Assyria;
He will make Nineveh a waste,
dry as the desert.[l]
14 In her midst flocks shall lie down,
all the wild life of the hollows;
The screech owl and the desert owl
shall roost in her columns;
The owl shall hoot from the window,
the raven croak from the doorway.[m]
15 Is this the exultant city*
that dwelt secure,
That told itself,
"I and there is no one else"?
How it has become a waste,
a lair for wild animals!
Those who pass by it
hiss, and shake their fists!

See RG 259

## CHAPTER 3

### *Jerusalem Reproached*

1 Ah! Rebellious and polluted,
the tyrannical city!*
2 It listens to no voice,
accepts no correction;
In the LORD it has not trusted,
nor drawn near to its God.[n]
3 Its officials within it
are roaring lions;
Its judges are desert wolves
that have no bones to gnaw by morning.[o]
4 Its prophets are reckless,
treacherous people;
Its priests profane what is holy,
and do violence to the law.[p]
5 But the LORD in its midst is just,
doing no wrong;
Morning after morning rendering judgment
unfailingly, at dawn;
the wicked, however, know no shame.

6 I have cut down nations,
their battlements are laid waste;
I have made their streets deserted,
with no one passing through;
Their cities are devastated,
with no one dwelling in them.[q]
7 I said, "Surely now you will fear me,
you will accept correction;
They cannot fail to see
all I have brought upon them."
Yet the more eagerly they have done
all their corrupt deeds.

### *The Nations Punished and Jerusalem Restored*

8 Therefore, wait for me—oracle of the LORD—
until the day when I arise as accuser;
For it is my decision to gather nations,
to assemble kingdoms,
In order to pour out upon them my wrath,
all my blazing anger;
For in the fire of my passion
all the earth will be consumed.[r]

9 For then I will make pure
the speech of the peoples,

**2:12 Cushites**: the Ethiopians, who had ruled Egypt a generation before Zephaniah's career.
**2:15 The exultant city**: Nineveh. **Hiss, and shake their fists**: gestures of derision.
**3:1 The tyrannical city**: Jerusalem.

*k:* 2 Chr 14:7–14. *l:* Na 3:7. *m:* Is 34:11. *n:* Jer 2:30; 7:28. *o:* Ez 22:27; Mi 3:11. *p:* Ez 22:26; Hb 1:4. *q:* Jer 2:15. *r:* Zep 1:18; Jl 4:2.

That they all may call upon the name of
the LORD,
to serve him with one accord;
10 From beyond the rivers of Ethiopia
and as far as the recesses of the North,
they shall bring me offerings.

11 On that day
You will not be ashamed
of all your deeds,
when you rebelled against me;
For then I will remove from your midst
the proud braggarts,
And you shall no longer exalt yourself
on my holy mountain.
12 But I will leave as a remnant in your
midst
a people humble and lowly,
Who shall take refuge in the name of the
LORD—[s]
13 the remnant of Israel.
They shall do no wrong
and speak no lies;
Nor shall there be found in their mouths
a deceitful tongue;
They shall pasture and lie down
with none to disturb them.[t]
14 Shout for joy, daughter Zion!
sing joyfully, Israel!
Be glad and exult with all your heart,
daughter Jerusalem![u]
15 The LORD has removed the judgment
against you,
he has turned away your enemies;
The King of Israel, the LORD, is in your
midst,
you have no further misfortune to
fear.
16 On that day, it shall be said to
Jerusalem:
Do not fear, Zion,
do not be discouraged!
17 The LORD, your God, is in your midst,
a mighty savior,
Who will rejoice over you with gladness,
and renew you in his love,
Who will sing joyfully because of you,[v]
18 as on festival days.
I will remove disaster from among you,
so that no one may recount your
disgrace.
19 At that time I will deal
with all who oppress you;
I will save the lame,
and assemble the outcasts;
I will give them praise and renown
in every land where they were
shamed.[w]
20 At that time I will bring you home,
and at that time I will gather you;
For I will give you renown and praise,
among all the peoples of the earth,
When I bring about your restoration
before your very eyes, says the
LORD.[x]

*s:* Is 57:13; Ob 17. *t:* Mi 4:4. *u:* Zec 9:9. *v:* Jl 2:27. *w:* Mi 4:6. *x:* Jl 4:1.

See RG 259–60

# The Book of Haggai

Haggai's words concern conditions in the Persian province of Judah at the beginning of the postexilic period during the reign of the Persian king Darius I (522–486 B.C.). The community in Judah is struggling with its identity in light of the loss of its statehood through the demise of the monarchy and the destruction of the Temple. Haggai's oracles address both these problems. First, the provincial government, despite its subordination to Persian hegemony, is seen as the legitimate heir to the Davidic monarchy; the governor Zerubbabel, himself a descendant of the Davidic line, and the high priest Joshua together provide political, economic, and religious leadership for the survivors of the Babylonian destruction and the returnees from the Babylonian exile who live together in Judah. Still, the possibility for restoration of Davidic rule is not relinquished but rather is shifted to the eschatological future. Second, the Temple's ruined state is addressed by a rebuilding program. The prophet links the well-being of the community to the work of Temple restoration, and his exhortations to the leaders and the people to begin work on this project are apparently

## The Charge to Rebuild the Temple

HAGGAI'S FIRST SPEECH (Hg 1:1–15a) directs those who have returned to Jerusalem from exile to begin reconstruction of the temple.

heeded. The brief period of Haggai's ministry (August to December 520 B.C.) marks the resumption of work on the Temple, the symbol of divine presence among the people.

Six date formulas (1:1, 15; 2:1, 10, 18, 20) are an important feature of the Book of Haggai. In their specificity and in their link to the reign of a foreign king (Darius), the dates underscore God's control over history, as do similar chronological references in Zechariah, a prophetic book connected in literary and thematic ways to Haggai.

The prophecies of Haggai can be divided into two major parts:

I. The Restoration of the Temple (1:1–15)
II. Oracles of Encouragement (2:1–23)

---

See RG 260

### CHAPTER 1

***Prophetic Call To Work on the Temple.*** 1 On the first day of the sixth month in
the second year* of Darius the king, the
word of the LORD came through Haggai the
prophet to the governor of Judah, Zerubbabel,[a] son of Shealtiel, and to the high priest
Joshua, son of Jehozadak:[b] 2 Thus says the
LORD of hosts: This people has said: "Now
is not the time to rebuild the house of the
LORD."

3 Then the word of the LORD came through
Haggai the prophet: 4 Is it time for you to
dwell in your paneled houses while this
house lies in ruins?*[c]

5 Now thus says the LORD of hosts:
Reflect on your experience!*
6 You have sown much, but have brought in little;
you have eaten, but have not been satisfied;[d]
You have drunk, but have not become intoxicated;
you have clothed yourselves, but have not been warmed;
And the hired worker labors for a bag full of holes.
7 Thus says the LORD of hosts:

Reflect on your experience!
8 Go up into the hill country;
bring timber, and build the house
That I may be pleased with it,
and that I may be glorified,* says the LORD.
9 You expected much, but it came to little;
and what you brought home, I blew away.
Why is this?—oracle of the LORD* of hosts—
Because my house is the one which lies in ruins,
while each of you runs to your own house.
10 Therefore, the heavens withheld the dew,
and the earth its yield.
11 And I have proclaimed a devastating heat*
upon the land and upon the mountains,

**1:1 First day of the sixth month in the second year**: August 29, 520 B.C. This is the first of six chronological indicators in Haggai. **Darius**: Darius I, emperor of Persia from 522 to 486 B.C. **Governor**: term used for local rulers of provinces in the Persian imperial structure. **Zerubbabel**: grandson of King Jehoiachin (cf. 2 Kgs 24:8–17).

**1:4 Your paneled houses . . . house lies in ruins**: the contrast here is between the unfinished Temple and the completed houses of the Judeans.

**1:5 Reflect on your experience**: the prophet exhorts the people to consider the futility of their efforts as a result of their neglecting work on the Temple. The following verses call attention to harsh conditions in Judah after the return from exile and the preoccupation of the people with their personal concerns.

**1:8 That I may be glorified**: for the prophet, the rebuilding of the Temple restores the glory God had lost in the eyes of the nations by the Temple's destruction.

**1:9 Oracle of the LORD**: a phrase used extensively in prophetic books to indicate divine speech.

**1:11 Devastating heat**: this pronouncement of natural disaster, which functions as a warning to the people for their failure to rebuild the Temple, concludes the opening oracular section of Haggai.

---

*a:* Zec 4:6–10. *b:* Zec 3:1–10. *c:* 2 Sm 7:2. *d:* Lv 26:26; Hos 4:10.

**The Glory of the Temple**

TO THOSE WHO are disappointed with the rebuilt temple, which pales in comparison to the temple of Solomon, God has a powerful reminder in ch 2. The glory of the temple comes not from earthly riches or fine building materials, but from the LORD's residing there. For the returning exiles, there is no greater treasure than the ability to worship the LORD in the temple.

Upon the grain, the new wine, and the
olive oil,
upon all that the ground brings forth;
Upon human being and beast alike,
and upon all they produce.

*Response of Leaders and People.* 12 Then
Zerubbabel, son of Shealtiel, and the high
priest Joshua, son of Jehozadak, and all the
remnant of the people* obeyed the LORD
their God, and the words of Haggai the
prophet, since the LORD their God had sent
him; thus the people feared the LORD.
13 Then Haggai, the messenger of the LORD,
proclaimed to the people as the message of
the LORD: I am with you!—oracle of the
LORD.
14 And so the LORD stirred up the spirit of
the governor of Judah, Zerubbabel, son of
Shealtiel, and the spirit of the high priest
Joshua, son of Jehozadak, and the spirit of
all the remnant of the people,[e] so that they
came to do the work in the house of the
LORD of hosts, their God, 15 on the twenty-
fourth day of the sixth month in the second
year* of Darius the king.

## CHAPTER 2

See RG 260

*Assurance of God's Presence.* 1 On the
twenty-first day of the seventh month,* the
word of the LORD came through Haggai the
prophet: 2 Speak to the governor of Judah,
Zerubbabel, son of Shealtiel, and to the high
priest Joshua, son of Jehozadak, and to the
remnant of the people:

3 Who is left among you*
who saw this house in its former
glory?
And how do you see it now?
Does it not seem like nothing in your
eyes?[f]
4 Now be strong, Zerubbabel—oracle of
the LORD—
be strong, Joshua, son of Jehozadak,
high priest,
Be strong, all you people of the land—
oracle of the LORD—
and work! For I am with you—oracle
of the LORD of hosts.
5 This is the commitment I made to you
when you came out of Egypt.
My spirit remains in your midst;
do not fear!

6 For thus says the LORD of hosts:*

In just a little while,
I will shake the heavens and the earth,[g]
the sea and the dry land.
7 I will shake all the nations,

**1:12 The remnant of the people**: here the phrase appears to refer to the prophet's audience, but the "remnant" theme, though often in different Hebrew terminology, suggesting especially those whom the Lord will call back from exile and re-establish as his people, is important in the prophets (cf. Is 4:3; 37:31–32; Jl 3:5; Mi 4:7; Ob 17) and in the New Testament (cf. Rom 11:1–10).

**1:15 Twenty-fourth day of the sixth month in the second year**: September 21, 520 B.C. The resumption of work on the Temple occurred twenty-three days from the beginning of Haggai's prophecy. This date formula repeats in reverse order the formula of v. 1, thereby bringing to conclusion chap. 1; it also initiates the next unit in 2:1.

**2:1 Twenty-first day of the seventh month**: October 17, 520 B.C.

**2:3 Who is left among you**: i.e., who is old enough to have seen the first Temple prior to its destruction in 587 B.C.? Compare the reaction of priests who were alive then (Ezr 3:12–13).

**2:6–9** These verses emphasize that the total fulfillment of God's promises to Israel is on the horizon. Such an eschatological event, which will shake the nations (v. 6; cf. v. 21), finds an echo not only in the political revolts in the Persian empire in 521 but also in the formative events of Israel's history (Ex 19:18; Jgs 5:4; Ps 68:8–9) when God intervened on behalf of the Israelites. The bringing of treasures of all the nations (v. 7) to Jerusalem recalls the visionary passages of Isaiah of the pilgrimage of all nations to Jerusalem (Is 2:2–4; 60:6–9).

*e:* Ezr 1:5; 5:1–2. *f:* Ezr 3:10–13. *g:* Heb 12:26.

so that the treasures of all the nations
will come in.
And I will fill this house with glory—
says the LORD of hosts.[h]

8 Mine is the silver and mine the gold—oracle of the LORD of hosts.

9 Greater will be the glory of this house[i]
the latter more than the former—says
the LORD of hosts;
And in this place I will give you peace—*
oracle of the LORD of hosts.

***Priestly Ruling with Prophetic Interpretation.**** 10 On the twenty-fourth day of the
ninth month in the second year* of Darius,
the word of the LORD came to Haggai the
prophet: 11 Thus says the LORD of hosts: Ask
the priests for a ruling:* 12 If someone carries
sanctified meat in the fold of a garment and
the fold touches bread, soup, wine, oil, or
any other food, do they become sanctified?
"No," the priests answered. 13 Then Haggai
asked: "If a person defiled from contact with
a corpse touches any of these, do they become defiled?" The priests answered, "They
become defiled."[j] 14 Then Haggai replied:

So is this people,* and so is this nation
in my sight—oracle of the LORD—
And so is all the work of their hands;
what they offer there is defiled.

15 Now reflect,* from this day forward—
before you set stone to stone in the temple of
the LORD, 16 what was your experience?

When one went to a heap of grain for
twenty ephahs,
there were only ten;
When one went to a vat to draw fifty
ephahs,*
there were only twenty.[k]
17 I struck you, and all the work of your
hands,
with searing wind, blight, and hail,
yet you did not return to me—oracle
of the LORD.[l]

18 Reflect from this day forward, from the
twenty-fourth day of the ninth month.* From
the day on which the temple of the LORD was
founded, reflect!
19 Is there still seed in the storehouse?
Have the vine, the fig, the
pomegranate,
and the olive tree still not borne fruit?
From this day, I will bless you.*

***Future Hope.**** 20 The word of the LORD
came a second time to Haggai on the twenty-fourth day of the month:* 21 Speak to Zerubbabel, the governor of Judah:
I will shake the heavens and the earth;
22 I will overthrow the thrones of
kingdoms,

**2:9 Peace**: after God's presence or glory has returned to the Temple, Jerusalem will receive the treasures from the nations, making the Temple more glorious than ever; and from that place God will extend *shalom*, a peace which embraces prosperity, well-being, harmony.

**2:10–14** A request for a priestly ruling (Heb. *torah*) is made in the form of a dialogue between Haggai and the priests. Explicit examples where such priestly rulings are quoted are rare in prophetic books. The interchange illustrates an essential role of the priesthood: the interpretation of God's law (cf. Lv 10:9–11).

**2:10 Twenty-fourth day of the ninth month in the second year**: December 18, 520 B.C.

**2:11 Ask the priests for a ruling**: i.e., a determination on whether defilement and sanctity can be physically transmitted. The priests are expected to make a legal decision. The answer is that sanctity cannot be transmitted (v. 12) but defilement can (v. 13). Priestly duties are enumerated in Lv 10:10–20.

**2:14 So is this people**: the prophet's interpretation is that the restored sacrifices were not acceptable because the people's behavior was tainted.

**2:15–19** This prophecy is retrospective and should be read with 1:5–11, a description of the conditions of economic deprivation before the rebuilding of the Temple.

**2:16 Ephahs**: see note on Is 5:10.

**2:18 Twenty-fourth day of the ninth month**: December 18, 520 B.C., the date of the refounding of the Temple (vv. 10, 20), the central date in Haggai.

**2:19 I will bless you**: from the day of the refounding of the Temple, agricultural plenty and fertility are assured. This link between temple and prosperity is part of the ancient Near Eastern temple ideology that underlies Haggai and Zec 1–8.

**2:20–23** This final oracle of hope is uttered on the day of the refounding of the Temple. Unlike the other oracles it is addressed to Zerubbabel alone, who, as a Davidic descendant, will have a servant role in God's future Israelite kingdom to be established when God intervenes to overthrow the nations.

**2:20 Twenty-fourth day of the month**: December 18, 520 B.C. (as in v. 18).

*h:* Is 60:7–11. *i:* 1 Kgs 8:11. *j:* Lv 22:4–7. *k:* Hos 4:3a. *l:* Am 4:9.

and destroy the power of the kingdoms
of the nations.
I will overthrow the chariots and their
riders,
and the riders with their horses
will fall by each other's swords.[m]

23 On that day—oracle of the LORD of
hosts—I will take you, my servant, Zerubbabel, son of Shealtiel—oracle of the
LORD—and I will make you like a signet
ring,* for I have chosen you—oracle of the
LORD of hosts.[n]

**2:23 Like a signet ring**: this promise to Zerubbabel reverses the punishment of his grandfather (Jer 22:23–25). A signet is a ring or other instrument used to mark documents or materials with the equivalent of an official signature. A lower official could thus be authorized to act on behalf of a higher official. Like a signet ring, Zerubbabel represents the Lord.

*m:* Sir 49:11. *n:* Zec 6:12–13.

See RG 261–63

# The Book of Zechariah

The Book of Zechariah, because of its great variation in style, content, and language, is widely believed to be a composite work. Made up of First Zechariah (chaps. 1–8) and Second Zechariah (chaps. 9–14), the book has been attributed to at least two different prophets. The prophecies of First Zechariah can be dated to the late sixth century B.C., contemporary with those of Haggai; the oracles of Second Zechariah are somewhat later.

The most striking feature of First Zechariah is a series of visions in which the prophet describes the centrality of Jerusalem, its Temple, and its leaders, who function both in the politics of the region and of the Persian empire and in God's universal rule. These visions clearly relate to the Temple restoration begun in 520 B.C.

The prophecies of First Zechariah can be divided into three literary units. A brief introductory unit (1:1–6) links the prophecies of chaps. 1–8 with those of Haggai. The visionary unit (1:7–6:15) consists of seven visionary images plus an associated vision dealing with the high priest Joshua. The third unit (7:1–8:23) consists of two parts: (1) an address (7:1–14) to a delegation sent from Bethel in anticipation of the end of the seventy years of exile; (2) a series of oracles (8:1–23): seven oracles dealing with the restoration of Judah and Zion (vv. 1–17), followed by three oracles of hope concerning Judah and the nations (vv. 18–23).

Coming nearly a century later, the prophecies of Second Zechariah are extraordinarily diverse. A complex assortment of literary genres appears in these six chapters, which consist of two distinct parts (chaps. 9–11 and chaps. 12–14), each introduced by an unusual Hebrew word for "oracle." Despite the diversity of materials, the structural links among the chapters along with verbal and thematic connections point to an overall integrity for Zec 9–14.

Second Zechariah draws heavily on the words and ideas of earlier biblical prophets. The prophet is acutely aware of the devastation that comes from disobedience to God's word, as had been spoken by God's prophetic emissaries. Yet, it was now clear in this century after the rebuilding of the Temple and the repatriation of many of the exiles, that Judah would not soon regain political autonomy and a Davidic king. So the various poems, narratives, oracles, and parables of Second Zechariah maintain the hope of previous prophets by depicting a glorious eschatological restoration. At that time all nations will recognize Jerusalem's centrality and acknowledge God's universal sovereignty.

## CHAPTER 1

See RG 261–62

*Call for Obedience.* 1 In the second
year of Darius,* in the eighth month, the
word of the LORD came to the prophet
Zechariah, son of Berechiah, son of Iddo:

**1:1 Darius**: Darius I, emperor of Persia from 522 to 486 B.C. **The second year . . . eighth month**: October/November 520 B.C., i.e., prior to the latest date in Haggai (Dec. 18, 520 B.C., Hg 2:10). Unlike other prophets, Haggai and Zechariah 1–8 contain specific chronological information, probably because they were sensitive to the imminent end of the expected seventy years of exile. See note on Zec 1:12.

## Zechariah's Opening Speech

Zechariah's visions (Zec 1:7–6:8) are introduced and concluded (chs 7–8) by speeches in which Zechariah urges his listeners to embrace the social responsibilities and just behavior preached by the prophets before him.

[2]The LORD was very angry with your ancestors.* [a] [3]Say to them: Thus says the LORD of hosts, Return to me—oracle of the LORD* of hosts—and I will return to you, says the LORD of hosts. [4]Do not be like your ancestors to whom the earlier prophets* proclaimed: Thus says the LORD of hosts: Turn from your evil ways and from your wicked deeds.[b] But they did not listen or pay attention to me[c]—oracle of the LORD.— [5]Your ancestors, where are they? And the prophets, can they live forever? [6]But my words and my statutes, with which I charged my servants the prophets, did these not overtake your ancestors?[d] Then they repented* and admitted: "Just as the LORD of hosts intended to treat us according to our ways and deeds, so the LORD has done."

***First Vision: Horses Patrolling the Earth.***[e] [7]In the second year of Darius, on the twenty-fourth day of Shebat, the eleventh month,* the word of the LORD came to the prophet Zechariah, son of Berechiah, son of Iddo: [8]* I looked out in the night,* and there was a man mounted on a red horse standing in the shadows among myrtle trees; and behind him were red, sorrel, and white horses. [9]I asked, "What are these, my lord?"* Then the angel who spoke with me answered, "I will show you what these are." [10]Then the man who was standing among the myrtle trees spoke up and said, "These are the ones whom the LORD has sent to patrol the earth."[f] [11]And they answered the angel of the LORD,* who was standing among the myrtle trees: "We have been patrolling the earth, and now the whole earth rests quietly." [12]Then the angel of the LORD replied, "LORD of hosts, how long will you be without mercy for Jerusalem and the cities of Judah that have felt your anger these seventy years?"* [g] [13]To the angel who spoke with me, the LORD replied favorably, with comforting words.

***Oracular Response.*** [14]The angel who spoke with me then said to me, Proclaim: Thus says the LORD of hosts:

I am jealous for Jerusalem
    and for Zion* intensely jealous.[h]
[15] I am consumed with anger
    toward the complacent nations;*
When I was only a little angry,

**1:2 Your ancestors**: refers to the preexilic people of Judah, who were subjected to Babylonian destruction and exile.

**1:3 Oracle of the LORD**: a phrase used extensively in prophetic books to indicate divine speech.

**1:4 Earlier prophets**: preexilic prophets of the Lord. There are many allusions to them in Zechariah, indicating their influence on the postexilic community (see 7:7, 12).

**1:6 Repented**: the Hebrew word *shub* literally means "turn back." This term is often used to speak of repentance as a return to the covenantal relationship between Israel and the Lord.

**1:7 The second year . . . eleventh month**: February 15, 519 B.C. The largest set of visions (1:7–6:15) is dated to a time just prior to the beginning of the new year in the spring.

**1:8–11** Four riders on horses of three different colors are sent by God to patrol the four corners of the earth. Compare the four chariots of the seventh vision, 6:1–8.

**1:8 In the night**: nighttime, or this night. This setting of darkness is meant only for the first vision.

**1:9 My lord**: this expression in Hebrew (*'adoni*) is used as a polite form of address. **Angel who spoke with me**: angelic being (not identical to the angel of the Lord who is one of the four horsemen) who serves as an interpreter, bringing a message from God to the prophet, who himself is a messenger of God.

**1:11 Angel of the LORD**: chief angelic figure in God's heavenly court, and perhaps the "man" of 1:8.

**1:12 These seventy years**: allusion to the period of divine anger mentioned in Jer 25:11–12 and 29:10. Here the symbolic number seventy is understood to mark the period without a Temple in Jerusalem. Since these seventy years would have been almost over at this point, this symbolic number would have provided motivation for rebuilding the Temple as a sign of the end of the exile.

**1:14 For Jerusalem and for Zion**: rather than the usual order, Zion and Jerusalem, elsewhere in the Bible. The reversal highlights the centrality of Jerusalem, which is mentioned in all three of the brief oracles of 1:14–17.

*a:* Mi 3:7. *b:* Is 55:7. *c:* Lk 20:15. *d:* Zec 7:7–14. *e:* Zec 6:1–7; Rev 5:6; 6:1–9. *f:* Zec 7:5; Jer 25:11–12; 29:10. *g:* Rev 6:10. *h:* Zec 8:2.

they compounded the disaster.[i]
16 Therefore, thus says the LORD:
I return to Jerusalem in mercy;[j]
my house* will be rebuilt there[k]—
oracle of the LORD of hosts—
and a measuring line will be stretched
over Jerusalem.
17 Proclaim further: Thus says the LORD of
hosts:
My cities will again overflow with
prosperity;
the LORD will again comfort Zion,
and will again choose Jerusalem.[l]

## CHAPTER 2

See RG 261–62

***Second Vision: The Four Horns and***
***the Four Smiths.*** 1 I raised my eyes and
looked and there were four horns.* 2 Then I
asked the angel who spoke with me, "What
are those?" He answered, "Those are the
horns that scattered* Judah, Israel, and Jerusalem."[m]
3 Then the LORD showed me four workmen.* 4 And I said, "What are these coming
to do?" And the LORD said, "Those are the
horns that scattered Judah, so that none
could raise their heads any more;[n] and these
have come to terrify them—to cut down the
horns of the nations that raised their horns to
scatter the land of Judah."
***Third Vision: The Man with the Measur-***
***ing Cord.*** 5 I raised my eyes and looked, and
there was a man with a measuring cord* in
his hand.[o] 6 I asked, "Where are you going?"
And he said, "To measure Jerusalem—to see
how great its width is and how great its
length."
7 Then the angel who spoke with me advanced as another angel came out to meet
him 8 and he said to the latter, "Run, speak to
that official:* Jerusalem will be unwalled,
because of the abundance of people and
beasts in its midst.[p] 9 I will be an encircling
wall of fire* for it—oracle of the LORD—and
I will be the glory in its midst."[q]
***Expansion on the Themes of the First***
***Three Visions.*** 10 Up! Up! Flee from the land
of the north*—oracle of the LORD;—For like
the four winds of heaven I have dispersed
you—oracle of the LORD.[r] 11 Up, Zion! Escape, you who dwell in daughter Babylon!
12 For thus says the LORD of hosts after the
LORD's glory had sent me, concerning the
nations that have plundered you: Whoever
strikes you strikes me directly in the eye.[s]
13 Now I wave my hand over them, and they
become plunder for their own servants.[t]
Thus you shall know that the LORD of hosts
has sent me. 14 Sing and rejoice, daughter
Zion! Now, I am coming to dwell in your
midst—oracle of the LORD. 15 Many nations
will bind themselves to the LORD on that
day.[u] They will be my people,* and I will
dwell in your midst. Then you shall know
that the LORD of hosts has sent me to you.
16 The LORD will inherit Judah[v] as his portion

**1:15 Complacent nations**: probably a reference to the Persian empire, which in its imperial extent included many national groups that maintained separate identities. **Compounded the disaster**: the surrounding nations took advantage of the Lord's anger against Judah to further their own interests.

**1:16 My house**: the Temple. See note on Hg 1:4. **Measuring line**: a builder's string, not for devastation, as in Is 34:11, but for reconstruction.

**2:1 Four horns**: symbols of the total political and military might of Judah's imperial adversaries, probably representing Assyria, Babylonia, and Persia. The number four represents universality rather than any specific number of foes.

**2:2 Scattered**: sent part of the population into exile. This was standard imperial policy initiated in the ancient Near East by the Assyrians for dealing with a conquered state.

**2:3 Four workmen**: four agents of God's power. The imagery follows that of four horns: the workers cut down, or make ineffectual, the horns, i.e., enemy.

**2:5 Measuring cord**: a string for measuring, as opposed to a builder's string, 1:16.

**2:8 That official**: probably the man with the measuring cord of v. 5.

**2:9 Encircling wall of fire**: divine protection for an unwalled Jerusalem. Urban centers were generally walled, and Jerusalem's walls were eventually rebuilt in the late fifth century B.C. (Neh 2:17–20).

**2:10 Land of the north**: refers to Babylon (v. 11), in a geographic rather than a political sense, as the place from which exiles will return. The designation is "north" because imperial invaders historically entered Palestine from that direction (see Jer 3:18; 23:8).

**2:15 Many nations . . . my people**: a way of expressing God's relationship to people in covenant language. The covenant between God and Israel (see Jer 31:33; 32:38) is here universalized to include all nations.

*i:* Is 47:6. *j:* Is 54:6–10. *k:* Zec 2:5–9. *l:* Zec 2:15; 13:9. *m:* Dt 33:17; Dn 7:8. *n:* Jer 48:25. *o:* Jer 31:38–39; Ez 41:13; Rev 11:1; 21:15. *p:* Is 49:19–20; 54:2–3; Jer 31:27; Ez 38:11. *q:* Rev 21:23; 22:3–5. *r:* Zec 6:5; Is 48:20; Jer 50:8; 51:6. *s:* Dt 32:10; Ps 17:8. *t:* Is 14:2; Zep 3:15. *u:* Is 56:6; 66:18. *v:* Zec 1:17.

of the holy land,* and the LORD will again choose Jerusalem. 17Silence, all people, in the presence of the LORD, who stirs forth from his holy dwelling.[w]

See RG 261-62

## CHAPTER 3

***Prophetic Vision: Joshua the High Priest.*** 1Then he showed me Joshua the high priest standing before the angel of the LORD, while the adversary* stood at his right side to accuse him.[x] 2And the angel of the LORD said to the adversary, "May the LORD rebuke you, O adversary; may the LORD who has chosen Jerusalem rebuke you![y] Is this not a brand plucked from the fire?"[z]

3* Now Joshua was standing before the angel, clad in filthy garments. 4Then the angel said to those standing before him, "Remove his filthy garments."[a] And to him he said, "Look, I have taken your guilt from you,[b] and I am clothing you in stately robes." 5Then he said, "Let them put a clean turban on his head." And they put a clean turban on his head and clothed him with the garments while the angel of the LORD was standing by. 6Then the angel of the LORD charged Joshua: 7"Thus says the LORD of hosts: If you walk in my ways and carry out my charge, you will administer my house and watch over my courts;* and I will give you access to those standing here."

***Supplementary Oracle.*** 8"Hear, O Joshua, high priest! You and your associates who sit before you! For they are signs of things to come!*[c] I will surely bring my servant the Branch. 9Look at the stone[d] that I have placed before Joshua. On this one stone with seven facets*[e] I will engrave its inscription—oracle of the LORD of hosts—and I will take away the guilt of that land in one day. 10On that day—oracle of the LORD of hosts—you will invite one another under your vines and fig trees."[f]

## CHAPTER 4

See RG 261-62

***Fourth Vision: The Lampstand and the Two Olive Trees.*** 1Then the angel who spoke with me returned and aroused me, like one awakened from sleep. 2He said to me, "What do you see?" I replied, "I see a lampstand* all of gold,[g] with a bowl on top of it. There are seven lamps on it, with seven spouts on each of the lamps that are on top of it. 3And beside it are two olive trees,* one on the right of the bowl and one to its left." 4Then I said to the angel who spoke with me, "What are these things, my lord?" 5And the angel who spoke with me replied, "Do you not know what these things are?" I said, "No, my lord."

***An Oracle.*** 6Then he said to me: "This is the word of the LORD to Zerubbabel: Not by

**2:16 The holy land**: the Lord's earthly territory, a designation found only rarely in the Old Testament.

**3:1 Adversary**: Hebrew *satan*, here, the prosecuting attorney, a figure in the Lord's heavenly courtroom. Cf. Jb 1:6–2:7. Later tradition understands this figure to be Satan.

**3:3–4** The filthy garments of Joshua symbolized the guilt of the Israelite people who have become unclean by going into exile. The angel of the Lord purifies the high priest by the removal of his garments.

**3:7 If you walk . . . watch over my courts**: four components of priestly activity: (1) following God's commandments and teaching them to the people, (2) carrying out cultic functions, (3) participating in the judicial system in certain difficult cases, and (4) administering the laborers and lands in the Temple's domain.

**3:8 Signs of things to come**: the restoration of the priesthood is a sign of the expected restoration of the Davidic line. **The Branch**: a tree metaphor for the expected future ruler as a descendant of the Davidic dynasty. This imagery also appears in Is 11:1, 10; Jer 23:5; 33:15; and Zec 6:12.

**3:9 Stone with seven facets**: represents both the precious stones that were part of the high priest's apparel and the building stone (see 4:7, 10) that initiated a major construction project. The seven facets (or "eyes") indicate the totality of its role as an instrument of God's vigilance and action. **Inscription**: can refer both to words engraved on the high priest's apparel (Ex 28:9, 11) and to words chiseled on a cornerstone.

**4:2 Lampstand**: receptacle for lamps and one of the furnishings of the main room of the Temple. This visionary object does not correspond to the biblical descriptions of the menorah in either the tabernacle (Ex 25:31–40) or the Solomonic Temple (1 Kgs 7:49) but rather has properties of both. **Seven lamps . . . seven spouts**: seven lamps, each with seven pinched wick holes. Such objects were part of the repertoire of cultic vessels throughout the Old Testament period. Here they symbolize God's eyes, i.e., divine omniscience; see v. 10.

**4:3 Olive trees**: visionary image that picks up the botanical language describing the Israelite cultic lampstands, with the olive trees specifically connoting fertility, permanence, and righteousness.

*w:* Hb 2:20; Zep 1:7; Rev 8:1a. *x:* Jb 1:6–2:7; 1 Chr 21:1. *y:* Jude 9. *z:* Am 4:11. *a:* Lk 15:22; Rev 19:8. *b:* Is 6:7; Jer 31:34; Ez 36:33. *c:* Is 8:18. *d:* Zec 4:7, 10; Is 28:16. *e:* Rev 5:6. *f:* 1 Kgs 5:5; Mi 4:4. *g:* Ex 25:31–40; 1 Kgs 7:49; Rev 11:4.

might, and not by power, but by my spirit,*[h]
says the LORD of hosts. 7Who are you, O great
mountain?* Before Zerubbabel you become a
plain. He will bring forth the first stone amid
shouts of 'Favor, favor be upon it!' "
8Then the word of the LORD came to me:
9The hands of Zerubbabel have laid the
foundations of this house, and his hands will
finish it. Thus you shall know that the LORD
of hosts has sent me to you. 10For whoever
has scorned such a day of small things will
rejoice to see the capstone* in the hand of
Zerubbabel.

***Resumption of the Vision: Explanation of Lamps and Trees.*** "These seven are the eyes
of the LORD that range over the whole earth."[i]
11I then asked him, "What are these two olive
trees, on the right of the lampstand and on its
left?" 12A second time I asked, "What are the
two streams from the olive trees that pour out
golden oil through two taps of gold?" 13He
said to me, "Do you not know what these
are?" I answered, "No, my lord." 14Then he
said, "These are the two anointed ones* who
stand by the Lord of the whole earth."[j]

## CHAPTER 5

See RG 261–62

***Fifth Vision: The Flying Scroll.*** 1Then
I raised my eyes again and saw a flying
scroll. 2He asked me, "What do you see?" I
answered, "I see a flying scroll, twenty cubits long and ten cubits wide."*[k] 3Then he
said to me: "This is the curse which is to go
forth over the whole land. According to it,
every thief and every perjurer* will be expelled. 4I will send it forth—oracle of the
LORD of hosts—so that it will come to the
house of the thief, and into the house of the
one who swears falsely by my name.[l] It shall
lodge within each house, consuming it, timber and stones."

***Sixth Vision: The Basket of Wickedness.***
5Then the angel who spoke with me came
forward and said to me, "Raise your eyes
and look. What is this that comes forth?" 6I
said, "What is it?" And he answered, "This
is the basket* that is coming." And he said,
"This is their guilt in all the land." 7Then a
leaden cover was lifted, and there was a
woman sitting inside the basket.* 8He said,
"This is Wickedness," and he thrust her inside the basket, pushing the leaden weight
into the opening.
9Then I raised my eyes and saw two
women coming forth with wind under their
wings*—they had wings like the wings of a
stork—and they lifted the basket into the air.
10I said to the angel who spoke with me,
"Where are they taking the basket?" 11He
replied, "To build a temple for it in the land

**4:6 Not by might . . . my spirit**: one of the most quoted verses from the Old Testament, particularly in Jewish tradition, which connects it with the theme of Hanukkah, sometimes called the Festival of Lights.

**4:7 Great mountain**: part of symbolic imagery for the Temple on Mount Zion, as embodiment of the cosmic mountain where heaven and earth connect. **Plain**: leveled ground serving as the foundation area for the construction of the Temple, and symbolizing the foundation of the cosmos. **First stone**: foundation stone of a major public building. Such stones were laid with great ceremony in foundation rituals when monumental buildings were newly built or rebuilt in the biblical world.

**4:10 Capstone**: topmost stone of a structure, which finishes the construction. This translation is based on the context. Other translations read: "stone of distinction," "plummet," "tin-stone."

**4:14 Two anointed ones**: two leadership positions in the ideal restored nation. The concept of a state headed by both priestly and political leaders harks back to premonarchic traditions (Aaron and Moses) and finds an echo in the two messianic figures—a Davidic and a levitical messiah—in the Dead Sea Scrolls and in apocryphal literature. See also the two crowns of 6:11–14.

**5:2 Twenty cubits long and ten cubits wide**: ca. thirty feet by fifteen feet. These dimensions may represent the ratio of height to width in the exposed portion of a scroll being opened for liturgical reading; at the same time it may symbolize the approach to God's presence since the entryway to the Temple has the same measurements (1 Kgs 6:3). The scroll itself may represent God's covenant with the people, insofar as it contains curses against those who break the law.

**5:3 Thief . . . perjurer**: a pair of miscreants representing all those who disobey God's covenant (see note on v. 2) and who must therefore be punished according to covenant curses.

**5:6 Basket**: literally, ephah, a dry measure; see note on Is 5:10.

**5:7 Woman sitting inside the basket**: figure representing wickedness or foreign idolatry being transported back to Babylonia (vv. 1–11). Returning exiles were apparently worshiping deities they had learned to accept in Babylonia, and that "wickedness" (v. 8) must be removed.

**5:9 Two women . . . wings**: composite beings, part human and part animal, similar to the cherubim flanking the holy ark (Ex 25:18–22; 1 Kgs 6:23–28; Ez 10:18–22). Such creatures accompany foreign deities as here, or the biblical God.

*h:* Hos 1:7. *i:* Zec 1:11; 6:7; Rev 5:6. *j:* Jos 3:11; Mi 4:13; Rev 11:4. *k:* Ez 2:9–10; Rev 10:9–11. *l:* Ex 20:7, 16.

**Rituals of Practice**

BY RESPONDING TO a question about mourning rituals (7:3) with a charge to create a just society, Zechariah appears to side with his predecessors, the former prophets, who claimed that religious rituals were meaningless apart from the practice of justice in all areas of life (Am 5:21–24).

of Shinar.* When the temple is constructed, they will set it there on its base."

## CHAPTER 6

See RG 261–62

***Seventh Vision: Four Chariots.***[m] 1Again I raised my eyes and saw four chariots* coming out from between two mountains; and the mountains were of bronze. 2The first chariot had red horses, the second chariot black horses, 3the third chariot white horses, and the fourth chariot dappled horses—all of them strong horses. 4I asked the angel who spoke with me, "What are these, my lord?" 5The angel answered me, "These are the four winds of the heavens,* which are coming forth after presenting themselves before the LORD of all the earth.[n] 6The one with the black horses is going toward the land of the north, and the white horses go toward the west, and the dappled ones go toward the land of the south." 7These strong horses went out, eager to set about patrolling the earth, for he said, "Go, patrol the earth!" So they patrolled the earth. 8Then he cried out to me and said, "See, those who go forth to the land of the north provide rest for my spirit in the land of the north."*

***The Crowning.*** 9Then the word of the LORD came to me: 10Take from the exiles—Heldai, Tobijah, Jedaiah—and go the same day to the house of Josiah, son of Zephaniah. (These had come from Babylon.) 11You will take silver and gold, and make crowns;* place one on the head of Joshua, son of Jehozadak, the high priest. 12And say to him: Thus says the LORD of hosts: There is a man whose name is Branch*[o]—and from his place he will branch out and he will build the temple of the LORD. 13He will build the temple of the LORD, and taking up the royal insignia, he will sit as ruler upon his throne. The priest will be at his right hand, and between the two of them there will be peaceful understanding.*[p] 14The other crown will be in the temple of the LORD as a gracious reminder to Heldai, Tobijah, Jedaiah, and the son of Zephaniah. 15And they who are from afar will come and build the temple of the LORD, and you will know that the LORD of hosts has sent me to you. This will happen if you truly obey the LORD your God.[q]

## CHAPTER 7

See RG 261–62

***A Question About Fasting.*** 1In the fourth year of Darius the king, the word of the LORD came to Zechariah, on the fourth day of the ninth month, Kislev.* 2Bethelsarezer sent Regem-melech and his men to implore the favor of the LORD 3and to ask the priests of the house of the LORD of hosts, and the prophets, "Must I weep and abstain in the fifth month* as I have been doing these

**5:11 Shinar**: land of Babylonia; this name for Babylonia is found also in Gn 1:10; 11:2; 14:1; Is 11:11; and Dn 1:2.

**6:1 Four chariots**: vehicles with horses of four different colors (vv. 2–3) represent God's presence throughout the world and correspond to the four horses of 1:7–11.

**6:5 Four winds of the heavens**: four compass directions and therefore the whole world.

**6:8 Land of the north**: the enemy (cf. 2:10). This emphasis on the land of the north refers to the fact that God will deal with Israel's foes and order will be re-established.

**6:11 Crowns**: two crowns made of precious metals and representing two high offices (compare the symbolism of the two olive trees in 4:14). One crown is for the high priest Joshua, who, with the governor Zerubbabel, was one of the recognized rulers of the Persian province of Judah. The other crown would have been for a royal ruler, a Davidic descendant. Zerubbabel was a Davidide but could not be king because the Persians would not allow such autonomy. The second crown was thus put in storage in the Temple (v. 14) for the crowning of a future king, or "branch" (see 3:8), from the house of David.

**6:12 Branch**: future Davidic ruler. See note on 3:8.

**6:13 Peaceful understanding**: harmonious rule of both the high priest and the king.

**7:1 The fourth year of Darius . . . the ninth month, Kislev**: December 7, 518 B.C., the last chronological heading in Zechariah.

**7:3 Weep . . . fifth month**: a mourning ritual commemo-

*m:* Rev 6:2–8. *n:* Rev 7:1. *o:* Zec 3:8; Jer 23:5. *p:* Zec 4:14. *q:* Dt 28:1.

many years?" 4Then the word of the LORD of
hosts came to me: 5Say to all the people of
the land and to the priests: When you fasted
and lamented in the fifth and in the seventh
month* these seventy years, was it really for
me that you fasted?[r] 6When you were eating
and drinking, was it not for yourselves that
you ate and for yourselves that you drank?
7Are these not the words which the LORD
proclaimed through the earlier prophets,*
when Jerusalem and its surrounding cities
were inhabited and secure, when the Negeb
and the Shephelah were inhabited? 8The
word of the LORD came to Zechariah: 9Thus
says the LORD of hosts: Judge with true justice, and show kindness and compassion toward each other.[s] 10Do not oppress the
widow or the orphan, the resident alien or
the poor;* do not plot evil against one another in your hearts.[t] 11But they refused to
listen; they stubbornly turned their backs
and stopped their ears so as not to hear.[u]
12And they made their hearts as hard as diamond[v] so as not to hear the instruction and
the words that the LORD of hosts had sent by
his spirit through the earlier prophets. So
great anger came from the LORD of hosts:
13Just as when I called out and they did not
listen, so they will call out and I will not listen, says the LORD of hosts. 14And I will
scatter them among all the nations that they
do not know.[w] So the land was left desolate
behind them with no one moving about, and
they made a pleasant land into a wasteland.

## CHAPTER 8

See RG 261–62

***Seven Oracles: Judah and Zion Re-
stored.*** 1Then the word of the LORD of hosts
came: 2Thus says the LORD of hosts:

I am intensely jealous for Zion,[x]
stirred to jealous wrath for her.

3Thus says the LORD:

I have returned to Zion,
and I will dwell within Jerusalem;
Jerusalem will be called the faithful
city,* [y]
and the mountain of the LORD of hosts,
the holy mountain.

4Thus says the LORD of hosts:
Old men and old women will again sit in
the streets of Jerusalem, each with staff in
hand because of old age.[z] 5The city will be
filled with boys and girls playing in its
streets.
6Thus says the LORD of hosts:
Even if this should seem impossible in the
eyes of the remnant of this people in those
days, should it seem impossible in my eyes
also?[a]—oracle of the LORD of hosts.
7Thus says the LORD of hosts:
I am going to rescue my people from the
land of the rising sun, and from the land of
the setting sun. 8I will bring them back to
dwell within Jerusalem. They will be my
people, and I will be their God,[b] in faithfulness and justice.
9Thus says the LORD of hosts:
Let your hands be strong, you who now
hear these words which were spoken by the
prophets when the foundation of the house
of the LORD of hosts was laid* for the building of the temple.[c] 10For before those days,
there were no wages for people, nor hire for
animals. Those who came and went were not
safe from the enemy, for I set neighbor
against neighbor. 11But now I will not deal

rating the destruction of Jerusalem and the Temple on the seventh day of the fifth month in the nineteenth year of Nebuchadnezzar's reign (ca. 587/586 B.C.; see 2 Kgs 25:8).

**7:5 Seventh month**: the time of a fast in memory of the murder of Gedaliah, the governor installed by the Babylonians after they conquered Jerusalem (see 2 Kgs 25:25; Jer 41:1–3). **Seventy years**: see note on 1:12.

**7:7, 12 Earlier prophets**: see note on 1:4.

**7:10 Widow . . . orphan . . . resident alien . . . poor**: four categories of socially and economically marginalized persons. Concern for their well-being is commanded in both pentateuchal and prophetic literature.

**8:3 Faithful city**: a unique biblical epithet for Jerusalem, signaling the importance of the holy city and its leaders for establishing justice in society (see also vv. 8, 16, 19). **Holy mountain**: Jerusalem and its Temple, the sacred center of the holy land (2:16) and of the whole world.

**8:9 When the foundation . . . was laid**: December 18, 520 B.C., the date of the Temple refoundation ceremony, marking the beginning of the project to restore the Temple (see Hg 2:10, 18, 20).

*r:* Am 5:21. *s:* Is 1:17; 58:6. *t:* Ex 22:20–24; Dt 24:17; Jer 5:28; Mi 2:1. *u:* Ex 32:9; Is 48:4. *v:* Ez 11:19. *w:* Dt 4:27. *x:* Zec 1:14. *y:* Is 1:26. *z:* Dt 4:40. *a:* Jer 32:27. *b:* Zec 13:9; Jer 31:33. *c:* Hg 1:14.

with the remnant of this people as in former
days—oracle of the LORD of hosts.

12 For there will be a sowing of peace:
the vine will yield its fruit,
the land will yield its crops,
and the heavens* will yield their dew.

I will give all these things to the remnant of
this people to possess. 13 Just as you became
a curse among the nations, O house of Judah
and house of Israel, so will I save you that
you may be a blessing.[d] Do not fear; let your
hands be strong.
14 Thus says the LORD of hosts:
Just as I intended to harm you when your
ancestors angered me—says the LORD of
hosts—and I did not relent, 15 so again in
these days I intend to favor Jerusalem and
the house of Judah; do not fear! 16 These then
are the things you must do: Speak the truth
to one another;[e] judge with honesty and
complete justice in your gates.*[f] 17 Let none
of you plot evil against another in your heart,
nor love a false oath. For all these things I
hate—oracle of the LORD.

*Three Oracles: Judah and the Nations.*
18 The word of the LORD of hosts came to me:
19 Thus says the LORD of hosts:
The fast days of the fourth, the fifth, the
seventh, and the tenth months*[g] will become occasions of joy and gladness, and
happy festivals for the house of Judah.[h] So
love faithfulness and peace!
20 Thus says the LORD of hosts:
There will yet come peoples and inhabitants of many cities;[i] 21 and the inhabitants of
one city will approach those of another, and
say, "Come! let us go to implore the favor of
the LORD and to seek the LORD of hosts. I too
am going." 22 Many peoples and strong nations
will come to seek the LORD of hosts in Jerusalem and to implore the favor of the LORD.
23 Thus says the LORD of hosts:
In those days ten people from nations of
every language will take hold,[j] yes, will take
hold of the cloak of every Judahite and say,
"Let us go with you, for we have heard that
God is with you."

## CHAPTER 9

See RG 262–63

### *Restoration of the Land of Israel**

1 An oracle:* the word of the LORD is
against the land of Hadrach,
and Damascus is its destination,
For the cities of Aram are the LORD's,
as are all the tribes of Israel.
2 Hamath also on its border,
Tyre too, and Sidon, no matter how
clever they be.
3 Tyre built itself a stronghold,
and heaped up silver like dust,
and gold like the mud of the streets.
4 But now the Lord will dispossess it,
and cast its wealth into the sea,
and it will be devoured by fire.
5 Ashkelon will see it and be afraid;
Gaza too will be in great anguish;
Ekron also, for its hope will wither.
The king will disappear from Gaza,
Ashkelon will not be inhabited,
6 and the illegitimate will rule in
Ashdod.
I will destroy the pride of the Philistines
7 and take from their mouths their
bloody prey,

**8:12 Vine . . . land . . . heavens**: future prosperity, reversing the hardships of Hg 1:10.

**8:16 Gates**: important gathering places in ancient Near Eastern cities, where legal proceedings were often carried out.

**8:19 Fast days of the fourth, the fifth, the seventh, and the tenth months**: all these fast days were probably held in connection with Jerusalem's demise. The fasts of the fourth month (commemorating the departure of Judahite leadership from Jerusalem, 2 Kgs 25:3–7) and of the tenth month (marking the beginning of the siege of Jerusalem, 2 Kgs 25:1) were added to the fasts of the fifth and seventh months mentioned in Zec 7:3 and 5 (see notes).

**9:1–8** The opening verses of Second Zechariah delineate the ideal boundaries of a restored Israel. Echoing the ideas of Haggai and First Zechariah (chaps. 1–8), the prophet reiterates the notion that the rebuilt Temple will bring about peace. The areas to be returned to Israel include Syria (Aram), with the cities of Hadrach and Damascus; Phoenicia, with the cities of Tyre and Sidon; and Philistia, with the cities of Ashkelon, Gaza, Ekron, and Ashdod.

**9:1 An oracle**: this designation also introduces Zec 12:1 and Mal 1:1, suggesting a connection among the three units. The term functions as both a title to the larger literary unit (Zec 9–11) and a part of the message of the opening oracular statement.

*d:* Gn 12:3; Ps 72:17. *e:* Eph 4:25. *f:* Zec 7:9; Dt 21:19; 22:24; Ru 4:1, 11. *g:* Zec 7:1–3; Mt 9:14–15. *h:* Is 35:10; Jer 31:13. *i:* 1 Kgs 8:43. *j:* 1 Sm 15:27; Tb 13:11.

their disgusting meat from between
their teeth.
They will become merely a remnant for
our God,[k]
and will be like a clan in Judah;
Ekron will be like the Jebusites.*
8 I will encamp at my house,
a garrison against invaders;
No oppressor will overrun them again,
for now I have seen their affliction.

### *The King's Entry into Jerusalem**

9 Exult greatly, O daughter Zion!
Shout for joy, O daughter Jerusalem!
Behold: your king* is coming to you,
a just savior is he,
Humble, and riding on a donkey,
on a colt, the foal of a donkey.[l]
10 He shall banish the chariot from Ephraim,[m]
and the horse from Jerusalem;
The warrior's bow will be banished,
and he will proclaim peace to the
nations.[n]
His dominion will be from sea to sea,
and from the River* to the ends of the
earth.[o]

### *Restoration of the People*

11 As for you, by the blood of your
covenant,* [p]
I have freed your prisoners from a
waterless pit.
12 Return to a fortress,*
O prisoners of hope;
This very day, I announce
I am restoring double to you.
13 For I have bent Judah as my bow,
I have set Ephraim as its arrow;
I will arouse your sons, O Zion,
against your sons, O Yavan,*
and I will use you as a warrior's
sword.
14 The LORD will appear over them,
God's arrow will shoot forth as
lightning;
The Lord GOD will sound the ram's horn,
and come in a storm from the south.[q]
15 The LORD of hosts will protect them;
they will devour and conquer with
sling stones,
they will drink and become heated as
with wine;
they will be full like bowls—like the
corners of the altar.[r]
16 And the LORD their God will save them:
the people, like a flock on that day;[s]
For like gemstones of a crown*
they will shine on the land.
17 Then how good and how lovely!
Grain will make the young men
flourish,
and new wine the young women.[t]

## CHAPTER 10

See RG 262–63

### *The Lord Strengthens Judah and Rescues Ephraim*

1 Ask the LORD for rain in the spring
season,[u]
the LORD who brings storm clouds,
and heavy rains,[v]

**9:7 The Jebusites**: the pre-Israelite inhabitants of Jerusalem, conquered by David and incorporated into Israel.

**9:9–10** These two verses form the centerpiece of chap. 9. The restoration of a royal figure connects the first part of the chapter (vv. 1–8), which depicts the restored land of Israel, with the second part (vv. 11–17), which concerns the restoration of the people Israel.

**9:9 Your king**: a just savior, a figure of humble demeanor, but riding on a donkey like royalty in the ancient Near East (Gn 49:11; Jgs 5:10; 10:4). The announcement of the coming of such a king marks a departure from the view of the royal figure as a conquering warrior. This depiction is in keeping with the tone of First Zechariah (3:8; 4:6–10; 6:12) but contrasts with Haggai (2:20–23). New Testament authors apply this prophecy to Jesus' triumphant entry into Jerusalem (Mt 21:4–5; Jn 12:14–15).

**9:10 The River**: probably the Euphrates; see note on Ps 72:8.

**9:11 The blood of your covenant**: the covenant between the Lord and Israel sealed with sacrificial blood (Ex 24:8).

**9:12 Fortress**: the Hebrew word for "fortress" (*bissaron*) plays upon the Hebrew word for Zion (*siyyon*). Those who return to Zion will be protected by the Lord. **O prisoners of hope**: imagery of exile, conveying a sense that the future in Israel will be better.

**9:13 Your sons, O Yavan**: the reference is to the Greeks and their struggle with the Persians for control of Syria-Palestine and the eastern Mediterranean in the mid-fifth century B.C.

**9:16 Like gemstones of a crown**: imagery reminiscent of First Zechariah (3:9; 4:7, 10; 6:11, 14) and evocative of the Temple and the priestly headgear (cf. Ex 29:6 and Lv 8:9).

*k:* Is 4:3. *l:* Is 9:6; 62:11; Jer 23:5; Mt 21:5; Jn 12:15. *m:* Mi 5:9. *n:* Is 2:4; 11:6; Hos 2:20; Eph 2:17. *o:* Ps 72:8. *p:* Ex 24:4–8; Mt 26:28; Heb 13:20. *q:* Dt 33:2; Ps 18:14; Hb 3:4. *r:* Ex 27:3; 38:3; Nm 4:14. *s:* Ez 34:11. *t:* Jer 31:12–13. *u:* Dt 11:14. *v:* Ps 135:7.

**Land of Israel**

IN THE VISION in 10:6–12, God will gather all the people of Israel together, recalling them from exile and rebuilding Israel to be greater than ever, taking over neighboring territories, and bringing low Israel's traditional enemies. The house of Joseph and Ephraim are references to the northern kingdom of Israel. Egypt and Assyria are two of the countries to which Israelites were exiled (2 Kgs 17:5–6; 25:26). Gilead and Lebanon are territories to the north of Israel.

who gives to everyone grain in the fields.
2 For the teraphim* have spoken nonsense,[w]
the diviners have seen false visions;
Deceitful dreams they have told,
empty comfort they have offered.
This is why they wandered like sheep,
wretched, for they have no shepherd.[x]
3 My wrath is kindled against the shepherds,*
and I will punish the leaders.
For the LORD of hosts attends to the flock, the house of Judah,
and will make them like a splendid horse in battle.
4 From them will come the tower,
from them the tent peg,
from them the bow of war,
from them every officer.
5 Together they will be like warriors,
trampling the mud of the streets in battle.
They will wage war because the LORD is with them,
and will put the horsemen to shame.
6 I will strengthen the house of Judah,[y]
the house of Joseph* I will save;
I will bring them back, because I have mercy on them;
they will be as if I had never cast them off,
for I am the LORD their God, and I will answer them.[z]
7 Then Ephraim will be like a hero,
and their hearts will be cheered as by wine.[a]
Their children will see and rejoice—
their hearts will exult in the LORD.
8 I will whistle for them and gather them in;
for I will redeem them
and they will be as numerous as before.*
9 I sowed them among the nations,
yet in distant lands they will remember me;
they will bear their children and return.[b]
10 I will bring them back from the land of Egypt,
and gather them from Assyria.
To the land of Gilead and to Lebanon I will bring them,
until no room is found for them.
11 I will cross over to Egypt
and smite the waves of the sea,
and all the depths of the Nile will dry up.
The pride of Assyria will be cast down,
and the scepter of Egypt disappear.
12 I will strengthen them in the LORD,[c]
in whose name they will walk—oracle of the LORD.

## CHAPTER 11

See RG 262–63

### *The Cry of Trees, Shepherds, and Lions*

1 Open your doors, Lebanon,
that fire may devour your cedars!
2 Wail, cypress trees,

**10:2 Teraphim**: household idols or cult objects (see Gn 31:19, 30–35; Jgs 17:5; 1 Sm 19:11–17), or ancestor statuettes (see 2 Kgs 23:24; Hos 3:4).

**10:3 Against the shepherds**: bad leaders or false prophets.

**10:6 The house of Joseph**: represents the Northern Kingdom (Israel), as does Ephraim in v. 7 below.

**10:8 Gather them in . . . be as numerous as before**: God's intention is to bring back the exiles and redeem them as at the time of the exodus. This image, resumed in vv. 10–11, anticipates an expanded population, echoes the ancestral promise (Gn 1:22, 28; 9:1, 7; 35:11), and also suggests an awareness of the acute demographic decline of Jews in Palestine in the Persian period.

*w:* 1 Sm 15:23. *x:* Ez 34:5; Mt 9:36. *y:* Zec 12:5. *z:* Is 41:17. *a:* Ps 104:15. *b:* Dt 30:1–3; Bar 2:30–32. *c:* Zec 12:5.

for the cedars are fallen,
the mighty are destroyed!
Wail, oaks of Bashan,
for the dense forest is cut down!
3 Listen! the wailing of shepherds,
their glory has been destroyed.
Listen! the roaring of young lions,
the thickets of the Jordan are
destroyed.

***The Shepherd Narrative.**** [d] 4 Thus says the
LORD, my God: Shepherd the flock to be
slaughtered.[e] 5 For they who buy them slay
them and are not held accountable; while
those who sell them say, "Blessed be the
LORD, I have become rich!" Even their own
shepherds will not pity them. 6 For I will no
longer pity the inhabitants of the earth—oracle of the LORD.—Yes, I will deliver them
into each other's power, or into the power of
their kings; they will crush the earth, and I
will not deliver it out of their power.

7 So I shepherded the flock to be slaughtered for the merchants of the flock. I took
two staffs: one I called Delight, and the other
Union. Thus I shepherded the flock. 8 In a
single month, I did away with the three shepherds, for I wearied of them, and they disdained me. 9 "I will not shepherd you," I
said. "Whoever is to die shall die; whoever
is to be done away with shall be done away
with; and those who are left shall devour one
another's flesh."

10 Then I took my staff Delight and
snapped it in two, breaking my covenant
which I had made with all peoples. 11 So it
was broken on that day. The merchants of
the flock, who were watching me, understood that this was the word of the LORD.
12 Then I said to them, "If it seems good to
you, give me my wages; but if not, withhold
them."[f] And they counted out my wages,[g]
thirty pieces of silver. 13 Then the LORD said
to me, Throw it in the treasury—the handsome price at which they valued me. So I
took the thirty pieces of silver and threw
them into the treasury in the house of the
LORD. 14 Then I snapped in two my second
staff, Union, breaking the kinship between
Judah and Israel.

15 The LORD said to me: This time take the
gear of a foolish shepherd.[h] 16 For I am raising up a shepherd in the land who will take
no note of those that disappear, nor seek the
strays, nor heal the injured,[i] nor feed the exhausted; but he will eat the flesh of the fat
ones and tear off their hoofs!

### *Oracle to the Worthless Shepherd*

17 Ah! my worthless shepherd
who forsakes the flock![j]
May the sword fall upon his arm
and upon his right eye;
His arm will surely wither,
and his right eye surely go blind!

## CHAPTER 12

See RG 263

***Oracles Concerning the Nations and
Judah.**** 1 An oracle:* The word of the LORD
concerning Israel—oracle of the LORD, who
spreads out the heavens, lays the founda-

**11:4–17** This narrative has features of an allegory, a parable, and a commissioning narrative. The use of a symbolic action (vv. 7, 10, 14), however, places this text squarely in the tradition of classical prophecy. For example, the staff "Delight" signifies the Mosaic covenant, and the staff "Union" signifies the union of Israel and Judah. Breaking the staffs signifies the breaking of the Mosaic covenant (resulting in the destruction of Jerusalem and the exile) and the historical schism between north and south. In this narrative the prophet is the "shepherd" of God's flock, which is to be slaughtered. The "three shepherds" of v. 8 represent either leaders responsible for the decay in Israelite society or false prophets (cf. vv. 15, 17 and 13:2–6). The service of the good shepherd is contemptuously valued at thirty pieces of silver, the legal indemnity for a gored slave (Ex 21:32). The prophet throws the money into the Temple treasury, showing how poorly God's love is requited (cf. Mt 26:14–16; 27:5). With great rhetorical irony, payment is rejected. The entire wage-payment scenario may be regarded as another symbolic action, embedded within the primary action.

**12:1–10** The oracles deal with (1) the status of Judah in relation to other political powers in the world that threaten its existence and (2) the reordering of Judah's internal structures so that its future can be realized. That future is linked to the fortunes of the house of David, which is mentioned five times between 12:7 and 13:1 (12:7, 8, 10, 12; 13:1).

**12:1 An oracle**: part two of Second Zechariah begins with the same heading as that of part one (9:1; also Mal 1:1), suggesting two distinct blocks of material. The unusual cluster of introductory terms that follow the heading greatly intensifies the claim of prophetic authority, apparently an issue in postexilic prophecy.

*d:* Ez 34:1. *e:* Jer 12:3. *f:* Mt 27:3–10. *g:* 2 Kgs 12:11; 22:4. *h:* Ez 34:1–10. *i:* Is 42:3; Mt 12:20. *j:* Jer 23:1; Jn 10:12–13.

tions of the earth, and fashions the human spirit within:[k] 2 See, I will make Jerusalem a cup of reeling* for all peoples round about.[l] Judah will be besieged, even Jerusalem. 3 On that day I will make Jerusalem a heavy stone for all peoples. All who attempt to lift it will injure themselves badly, though all the nations of the earth will gather against it. 4 On that day—oracle of the LORD—I will strike every horse with fright, and its rider with madness. But over the house of Judah I will keep watch, while I strike blind all the horses of the peoples. 5 Then the clans of Judah will say to themselves, "The inhabitants of Jerusalem have their strength in the LORD of hosts, their God."[m] 6 On that day I will make the clans of Judah like a brazier of fire in the woodland and like a burning torch among sheaves, and they will devour right and left all the surrounding peoples; but Jerusalem will again inhabit its own place.[n]

7 The LORD will save the tents of Judah first, that the glory of the house of David and the glory of the inhabitants of Jerusalem may not be exalted over Judah. 8 On that day the LORD will shield the inhabitants of Jerusalem, so that the weakest among them will be like David on that day; and the house of David will be like God, like the angel of the LORD before them.

9 On that day I will seek the destruction of all nations that come against Jerusalem.[o] 10 I will pour out on the house of David and on the inhabitants of Jerusalem a spirit of mercy and supplication, so that when they look on him whom they have thrust through,*[p] they will mourn for him as one mourns for an only child, and they will grieve for him as one grieves over a firstborn.[q]

***Catalogue of Mourners.*** 11 On that day the mourning in Jerusalem will be as great as the mourning for Hadadrimmon in the plain of Megiddo.* 12 And the land shall mourn, each family apart: the family of the house of David, and their women; the family of the house of Nathan, and their women; 13 the family of the house of Levi, and their women; the family of Shimei, and their women; 14 and all the rest of the families, each family apart, and the women apart.

## CHAPTER 13

See RG 263

***Oracles Concerning the End of False Prophecy.**** 1 On that day a fountain will be opened for the house of David* and the inhabitants of Jerusalem, to purify from sin and uncleanness.[r]

2 On that day—oracle of the LORD of hosts—I will destroy the names of the idols from the land, so that they will be mentioned no more; I will also remove the prophets and the spirit of uncleanness from the land. 3 If any still prophesy, their father and mother who bore them will say, "You will not live, because you have spoken a lie in the name of the LORD." Their father and mother who bore them will thrust them through when they prophesy.[s]

4 On that day, all prophets will be ashamed of the visions they prophesy; and they will

**12:2 Cup of reeling**: like a cup filled with intoxicating drink, Jerusalem will cause the nations to stumble and fall (cf. Is 51:17, 22; Jer 25:15; 49:12; Lam 4:21).

**12:10 They look on him . . . thrust through**: another possible rendering is "they shall look to me concerning him . . . thrust through." In either case, the victim is an enigmatic figure, perhaps referring to a Davidic descendant, a priestly leader, or even a true prophet. Some historical event, unknown to us from any surviving source, may underlie this reference. The Gospel of John applies this text to the piercing of Christ's side after his death (19:37).

**12:11** The mourning for the pierced victim in Jerusalem is compared to the annual ritual mourning in the plain of Megiddo over the death of the Phoenician fertility god, Hadadrimmon. According to others, Hadadrimmon is the name of a place near Megiddo, and the reference would then be to the mourning over the death of King Josiah at the hands of Pharaoh Neco in 609 B.C.; cf. 2 Kgs 23:29–30; 2 Chr 35:22–25.

**13:1–6** False prophecy is a major theme of Second Zechariah (chaps. 9–14) and figures in many other passages (10:1–2; 11; 12:10). Problems of idolatry and false prophecy occurred in postexilic Judah as they had in preexilic times. The understanding of the role of the prophet as an intermediary was challenged because (1) there was no king in Jerusalem, and (2) the texts of earlier prophets were beginning to be accorded the authority of prophetic tradition.

**13:1 For the house of David**: anticipation that a cleansed leadership will enable the re-established monarchy to be rid of the misdeeds of its past.

**13:4 Hairy mantle**: worn by prophets as a sign of their calling, for example, Elijah (1 Kgs 19:13; 2 Kgs 1:8) and John the Baptist (Mt 3:4).

*k:* Gn 2:7; Is 42:5. *l:* Is 51:17. *m:* Zec 10:6, 12. *n:* Zec 14:10. *o:* Zec 14:3. *p:* Jn 19:37; Rev 1:7. *q:* Am 8:10. *r:* Ez 36:25; 47:1; Jn 7:38. *s:* Jn 19:34.

not put on the hairy mantle* to mislead,[t] 5 but
each will say, "I am not a prophet. I am a
tiller of the soil, for I have owned land since
my youth."[u] 6 And if anyone asks, "What are
these wounds on your chest?"* each will answer, "I received these wounds in the house
of my friends."[v]

### *The Song of the Sword*

7 Awake, O sword, against my shepherd,
against the one who is my associate
—oracle of the LORD of hosts.
Strike the shepherd
that the sheep may be scattered;*[w]
I will turn my hand against the little
ones.
8 In all the land—oracle of the LORD—
two thirds of them will be cut off and
perish,
and one third will be left.
9 I will bring the one third through the fire;
I will refine them as one refines silver,[x]
and I will test them as one tests gold.
They will call upon my name, and I will
answer them;[y]
I will say, "They are my people,"[z]
and they will say, "The LORD is my
God."

## CHAPTER 14

See RG 263

***Devastation and Rescue of Jerusalem.***
1* A day is coming for the LORD when the
spoils taken from you will be divided in your
midst. 2 And I will gather all the nations
against Jerusalem for battle: The city will be
taken, houses will be plundered, women
raped; half the city will go into exile, but the
rest of the people will not be removed from
the city. 3 Then the LORD will go forth and
fight against those nations, fighting as on a
day of battle.[a] 4 On that day God's feet will
stand* on the Mount of Olives, which is opposite Jerusalem to the east. The Mount of
Olives will be split in two from east to west
by a very deep valley,[b] and half of the mountain will move to the north and half of it to
the south. 5 You will flee by the valley between the mountains, for the valley between
the mountains will reach to Azal. Thus you
will flee as you fled because of the earthquake* in the days of Uzziah king of Judah.[c]
Then the LORD, my God, will come, and all
his holy ones with him.[d]
***Jerusalem Restored.*** 6 On that day there
will no longer be cold or frost. 7 There will be
one continuous day—it is known to the
LORD—not day and night, for in the evening
there will be light. 8 On that day, fresh water
will flow from Jerusalem,[e] half to the eastern
sea, and half to the western sea. This will be
so in summer and in winter. 9 The LORD will
be king over the whole earth;[f] on that day the
LORD will be the only one, and the LORD's
name the only one. 10 All the land will turn
into a plain, from Geba to Rimmon, south of
Jerusalem, which will stand exalted in its
place—from the Gate of Benjamin to the
place of the first gate, to the Corner Gate and

**13:6 Wounds on your chest**: lit., "wounds between your hands." The false prophets, like the prophets of Baal (1 Kgs 18:28), apparently inflicted wounds on themselves. Here it seems that persons accused of false prophecy deny having inflicted wounds on themselves and instead claim that they have received them at the houses of their friends.

**13:7 Strike the shepherd . . . may be scattered**: in Matthew's Gospel (26:31) Jesus makes use of this text before his arrest in the Garden of Gethsemane and the flight of the disciples.

**14:1–21** The marked eschatological thrust of Zec 9–14 culminates in this apocalyptic description, with its astonishing images of the day of the Lord. This last and longest chapter focuses on the restoration of Jerusalem and the return of the people of Zion so that the rest of the world will acknowledge God's sovereignty. Four units constitute this chapter: vv. 1–5 concentrate on the destruction and rescue of Jerusalem and the escape of a remnant; vv. 6–11 describe the transformation of the climate and the topography of Jerusalem; vv. 12–15 depict the defeat of Jerusalem's enemies; and vv. 16–21 outline a vision for the end time, in which even foreign nations will make the pilgrimage to Jerusalem to acknowledge God's universal reign.

**14:4 God's feet will stand**: a remarkable anthropomorphic image adds emphasis to the traditional Old Testament scene of God appearing on a mountain and causing extreme reactions such as quaking, melting, shattering (see Ex 19:18; Ps 97:5; Hb 3:6). The Mount of Olives is split, which opens a way for those fleeing from the Lord's appearance to escape from Jerusalem.

**14:5 Earthquake**: Amos 1:1 mentions an earthquake in the time of King Uzziah (cf. Is 6:4).

*t:* 2 Kgs 1:8; Mt 3:4. *u:* Am 7:14. *v:* 1 Kgs 18:28. *w:* Ez 34:1–8; Mt 26:31. *x:* Is 1:25; 48:10. *y:* Ps 91:15; Is 65:24. *z:* Zec 8:8; Jer 31:31. *a:* Is 31:4. *b:* Mi 1:4. *c:* Am 1:1. *d:* Dt 33:2–3; Mt 16:27; 1 Thes 3:13. *e:* Zec 13:1; Ez 47:1–8; Jl 4:18. *f:* Ps 96:7–10; 97:1; 98:4–6; Rev 11:15.

from the Tower of Hananel to the king's wine presses. 11 The city will be inhabited; never again will it be doomed. Jerusalem will dwell securely.[g]

***The Fate of Jerusalem's Foes.*** 12 And this will be the plague with which the LORD will strike all the peoples that have fought against Jerusalem: their flesh will rot while they stand on their feet, and their eyes will rot in their sockets, and their tongues will rot in their mouths.[h] 13 On that day a great panic from the LORD will be upon them.[i] They will seize each other's hands, and their hands will be raised against each other. 14 Even Judah will fight against Jerusalem. The riches of all the surrounding nations will be gathered together—gold, silver, and garments—in great abundance. 15 Like the plague on human beings will be the plague upon the horses, mules, camels, donkeys, and upon all the beasts that are in those camps.

***The Future: Jerusalem, Judah, and the Nations.*** 16 Everyone who is left of all the nations that came against Jerusalem will go up year after year to bow down to the King, the LORD of hosts, and to celebrate the feast of Booths.*[j] 17 Should any of the families of the earth[k] not go up to Jerusalem to bow down to the King, the LORD of hosts, then there will be no rain for them. 18 And if the family of Egypt does not go up or enter, upon them will fall the plague,[l] with which the LORD strikes the nations that do not go up to celebrate the feast of Booths. 19 This will be the punishment of Egypt and the punishment of all the nations that do not go up to celebrate the feast of Booths.

20 On that day, "Holy to the LORD"[m] will be written on the horses' bells.* The pots in the house of the LORD will be as the basins before the altar. 21 Every pot* in Jerusalem and in Judah will be holy to the LORD of hosts. All who come to sacrifice will take them and cook in them. No longer will there be merchants in the house of the LORD of hosts on that day.

**14:16 Feast of Booths**: fall harvest festival, also known as the "festival of Ingathering" (Ex 23:16; 34:22) or "Booths" (Lv 23:33–36; Dt 16:13–15; 31:9–13). The singling out of this festival indicates its special status in the sacred calendar; it is frequently referred to as "the feast" (1 Kgs 8:1–2; 2 Chr 5:3; Ez 45:25).

**14:20 Horses' bells**: even these bells, part of the trappings of animals used for war, will become holy in the end time, like the bells of the high priest's garb (cf. Ex 28:34).

**14:21 Every pot**: vessels used for mundane food preparation will, in the end time, be as holy as Temple vessels.

*g:* Dt 33:28; Jer 31:40; Rev 22:3. *h:* Is 66:24. *i:* 1 Sm 5:9, 11; 14:18–20; Is 22:5. *j:* Lv 23:33–36; Dt 16:13–15. *k:* Zec 8:20–23; Is 2:1–4; Mi 4:1–3. *l:* Ex 5:3; 9:15. *m:* Lv 23:20; 27:30, 32.

See RG 263–65

# The Book of Malachi

This short book may have been written before Nehemiah's first return to Jerusalem in 445 B.C.; it is also possible that it was written while Nehemiah was there, or even later. What seems to be the author's name, *mal'ākî*, is found in 1:1 ("the word of the Lord to Israel through Malachi"), but many believe that this is a pseudonym based on *mal'ākî*, "my messenger," in 3:1 and that the author's real name is unknown. In any case, he shows us attitudes and behaviors characteristic of the Jewish community a few generations after the end of the Babylonian exile, and describes God's response.

God loves Israel (1:2–5), but the people return that love poorly. Taking advantage of the negligent attitude of the priests, they withhold tithes and sacrificial contributions (3:6–11) and cheat God by providing defective goods for sacrifice (1:6–14). People divorce their spouses and marry worshipers of other gods (2:10–16). Sorcerers, adulterers, perjurers, and people who take advantage of workers and the needy abound (3:5). Priests, who could strengthen discipline by their instruction, connive with the people, telling them what they want to hear (2:1–9). Underlying all this is a weary attitude, a cynical notion that nothing is to be gained by doing what God wants and that wrongdoers prosper (2:17; 3:14–15). God condemns the wrongdoing and the underlying attitude, issuing a challenge to immediate reform (3:10–12), but also announcing a general reckoning at a future moment (3:16–21).

### The Priests' Sins

MAKING UP ONE-THIRD of the entire book of Malachi, the accusation in 1:6 to 2:9 singles out two priestly sins: making improper offerings (1:6–2:3) and giving improper instruction (2:4–9). The importance of proper sacrifice and truthful, relevant teaching of the Torah were central to Jewish priesthood. Just as Judah's priests are not following their obligations for proper worship at the temple, so Judah's people are not fulfilling theirs. They are not bringing to the temple the full tithes of their produce required by Israelite law (Lv 27:30–33; Dt 14:22–29).

The Book of Malachi may be divided as follows:

I. Israel Preferred to Edom (1:2–5)
II. Offense in Sacrifice and Priestly Duty (1:6–2:9)
III. Marriage and Divorce (2:10–16)
IV. Purification and Just Judgment (2:17)
V. The Messenger of the Covenant (3:1–5)
VI. Gifts for God, Blessings for the People (3:6–12)
VII. The Need To Serve God (3:13–21)
VIII. Moses and Elijah (3:22–24)

## CHAPTER 1

See RG 264

1* An oracle. The word of the LORD to Israel through Malachi.

### *Israel Preferred to Edom*

2 a I love you, says the LORD;
but you say, "How do you love us?"
3 * b Was not Esau Jacob's brother?—
oracle of the LORD.
I loved Jacob, but rejected Esau;
I made his mountains a waste,
his heritage a desert for jackals.
4 c If Edom says, "We have been crushed,
but we will rebuild the ruins,"
Thus says the LORD of hosts:
They indeed may build, but I will tear down,
And they shall be called "territory of wickedness,"
the people with whom the LORD is angry forever.
5 d Your own eyes will see it, and you will say,
"Great is the LORD, even beyond the territory of Israel."

### *Offense in Sacrifice and Priestly Duty*

6 e A son honors his father,
and a servant fears his master;
If, then, I am a father,
where is the honor due to me?
And if I am a master,
where is the fear due to me?
So says the LORD of hosts to you, O priests,
who disdain my name.
But you ask, "How have we disdained your name?"
7 By offering defiled food on my altar!
You ask, "How have we defiled it?"
By saying that the table of the LORD may be disdained!
8 * f When you offer a blind animal for sacrifice,
is there no wrong in that?
When you offer a lame or sick animal,
is there no wrong in that?
Present it to your governor!
Will he be pleased with you—or show you favor?
says the LORD of hosts.
9 So now implore God's favor, that he may have mercy on us!
You are the ones who have done this;
Will he show favor to any of you?
says the LORD of hosts.

**1:1** See note on Zec 9:1.

**1:3–5** The thought passes from the person Esau to his descendants, Edom, and from the person Jacob to his descendants, Israel; cf. Gn 25:21–23. In the New Testament, Paul uses this passage as an example of God's freedom of choice in calling the Gentiles to faith (Rom 9:13).

**1:8** The sacrificial offering of a lame, sick, or blind animal was forbidden in the law (Lv 22:17–25; Dt 17:1).

*a:* Dt 7:8; Ez 16; Hos 11:1; Am 1:11. *b:* Gn 25:23; Rom 9:13. *c:* Is 34:2–15; 63:1–6; Jer 49:7–22; Ob 21. *d:* Is 60. *e:* Prv 1:7; Is 29:13. *f:* Lv 22:17–25; Dt 15:21; 17:1.

10 * Oh, that one of you would just shut the temple gates
to keep you from kindling fire on my altar in vain!
I take no pleasure in you, says the LORD of hosts;
and I will not accept any offering from your hands!
11 g From the rising of the sun to its setting,
my name is great among the nations;
Incense offerings are made to my name everywhere,
and a pure offering;
For my name is great among the nations,
says the LORD of hosts.
12 But you profane it by saying
that the LORD's table is defiled,
and its food may be disdained.
13 You say, "See what a burden this is!"
and you exasperate me, says the LORD of hosts;
You bring in what is mutilated, or lame, or sick;
you bring it as an offering!
Will I accept it from your hands?
says the LORD.
14 Cursed is the cheat who has in his flock an intact male,
and vows it, but sacrifices to the LORD a defective one instead;
For a great king am I, says the LORD of hosts,
and my name is feared among the nations.

## CHAPTER 2

See RG 264

1 And now, priests, this commandment is for you:
If you do not listen,
2 h And if you do not take to heart
giving honor to my name, says the LORD of hosts,
I will send a curse upon you
and your blessing I will curse.
In fact, I have already cursed it,
because you do not take it to heart.
3 I will rebuke your offspring;
I will spread dung on your faces,
Dung from your feasts,
and will carry you to it.
4 You should know that I sent you this commandment
so that my covenant with Levi might endure,
says the LORD of hosts.
5 i My covenant with him was the life and peace which I gave him,
and the fear he had for me,
standing in awe of my name.
6 j Reliable instruction was in his mouth,
no perversity was found upon his lips;
He walked with me in integrity and uprightness,
and turned many away from evil.
7 k For a priest's lips preserve knowledge,
and instruction is to be sought from his mouth,
because he is the messenger of the LORD of hosts.
8 But you have turned aside from the way,
and have caused many to stumble by your instruction;
You have corrupted the covenant of Levi,*
says the LORD of hosts.
9 I, therefore, have made you contemptible
and base before all the people,
For you do not keep my ways,
but show partiality in your instruction.

**1:10–11** The imperfect sacrifices offered by the people of Judah are displeasing to the Lord. **Kindling fire on my altar**: kindle the altar fire for sacrifice. In contrast, the Lord is pleased with the sacrifices offered by other peoples in other places (**the rising of the sun**: the far east; **its setting**: the far west). Since the people of other nations could not be expected to know the Lord's name as did the people of Judah, the rhetorical purpose of this statement is to shame the latter. **Incense offerings**: in the ancient world, the hallmark of an offering made to a god was the smoke it produced on an altar. In the Old Testament, this was true not only of animals (Lv 8:20–21) but also of incense (Ex 30:7), suet (Lv 3:11), and grain offerings (Lv 6:8). In a Christian interpretation of Mal 1:10–11, the "pure offering" of Mal 1:11 is seen as a reference to sacrifice in the Messianic Age. The Council of Trent endorsed this interpretation (DS 1724).

**2:8 The covenant of Levi**: not mentioned elsewhere in the Bible. The covenant with Phinehas the grandson of Aaron (Nm 25:11–13) and the Blessing of Levi (Dt 33:8–11) may lie in the background.

*g*: Ps 113:3; Is 59:19. *h*: Lv 26:14–45; Dt 28:15. *i*: Ez 37:26. *j*: Dt 33:8–11. *k*: Lv 10:10–11; Dt 17:9–10; Hg 2:11–13.

### *Marriage and Divorce*

10 * *l* Have we not all one father?
Has not one God created us?
Why, then, do we break faith with each other,
profaning the covenant of our ancestors?
11 *m* Judah has broken faith; an abominable thing
has been done in Israel and in Jerusalem.
Judah has profaned the LORD's holy place, which he loves,
and has married a daughter of a foreign god.*
12 May the LORD cut off from the man who does this
both witness and advocate from the tents of Jacob,
and anyone to bring an offering to the LORD of hosts!
13 This also you do: the altar of the LORD you cover
with tears, weeping, and groaning,
Because the Lord no longer takes note of your offering
or accepts it favorably from your hand.
14 *n* And you say, "Why?"—
Because the LORD is witness
between you and the wife of your youth
With whom you have broken faith,
though she is your companion, your covenanted wife.*
15 *o* Did he not make them one, with flesh and spirit?
And what does the One require? Godly offspring!
You should be on guard, then, for your life,
and do not break faith with the wife of your youth.
16 For I hate divorce,
says the LORD, the God of Israel,
And the one who covers his garment with violence,
says the LORD of hosts.
You should be on guard, then, for your life,
and you must not break faith.

### *Purification and Just Judgment*

17 You have wearied the LORD with your words,
yet you say, "How have we wearied him?"
By saying, "All evildoers
are good in the sight of the LORD,
And he is pleased with them,"
or "Where is the just God?"

## CHAPTER 3

See RG 264–65

### *The Messenger of the Covenant*

1 *p* Now I am sending my messenger—
he will prepare the way before me;*
And the lord whom you seek will come suddenly to his temple;
The messenger of the covenant whom you desire—
see, he is coming! says the LORD of hosts.
2 But who can endure the day of his coming?
Who can stand firm when he appears?

**2:10–16** Intermarriage of Israelites with foreigners was forbidden according to Dt 7:1–4. After the exile, attempts were made to enforce this law (Ezr 9–10). Foreign marriages are here portrayed as a covenantal violation (v. 10). They were all the more reprehensible when they were accompanied by the divorce of Israelite wives (vv. 14–16), and God finds their sacrifices unacceptable (vv. 13–14). In Mk 10:2–12, Jesus forbids divorce; in Mt 19:3–12, this ideal is maintained with the provision that unlawful marriage may be grounds for divorce (see 1 Cor 7:10–16). **You should be on guard, then, for your life**: a warning of punishment for failure to obey God (cf. Dt 4:9; Jos 23:11; Jer 17:21).

**2:11 Daughter of a foreign god**: this unusual phrase connotes a woman who does not share the same father/creator (v. 10), since she does not share the same covenant.

**2:14 Companion . . . covenanted wife**: the Hebrew word *haberet* signifies an equal, a partner. This woman, in contrast to the daughter of a foreign god, shares with her husband the same covenant with the Lord.

**3:1 My messenger . . . before me**: Mt 11:10 applies these words to John the Baptist; Mt 11:14 further identifies John as Elijah (see Mal 3:23). Some take God's messenger in v. 1a to be a person distinct from "the lord" and "the messenger of the covenant" in v. 1b; others hold that they are one and the same person. Some consider "the lord" and "the messenger of the covenant" to be divine, while others hold that in the text's literal sense he is a messianic earthly ruler.

*l:* Dt 32:6; Jb 31:15; Mt 23:9; Eph 4:6. *m:* Ezr 9:2; Neh 13:25. *n:* Gn 31:49–50; Prv 5:18–19. *o:* Gn 2:7, 22–24. *p:* Ex 23:20–22; Is 40:3; Mt 11:10; Mk 1:2; Lk 1:17; 7:27.

For he will be like a refiner's fire,
like fullers' lye.
3 [q] He will sit refining and purifying silver,
and he will purify the Levites,
Refining them like gold or silver,
that they may bring offerings to the
LORD in righteousness.
4 Then the offering of Judah and Jerusalem
will please the LORD,
as in ancient days, as in years gone by.
5 I will draw near to you for judgment,
and I will be swift to bear witness
Against sorcerers, adulterers, and
perjurers,
those who deprive a laborer of wages,
Oppress a widow or an orphan,
or turn aside a resident alien,
without fearing me, says the LORD of
hosts.

### *Gifts for God, Blessings for the People*

6 For I, the LORD, do not change,*
and you, sons of Jacob, do not cease to
be.
7 [r] Since the days of your ancestors you
have turned aside
from my statutes and have not kept
them.
Return to me, that I may return to you,
says the LORD of hosts.
But you say, "Why should we return?"
8 [s] Can anyone rob God? But you are
robbing me!
And you say, "How have we robbed
you?"
Of tithes and contributions!
9 You are indeed accursed,
for you, the whole nation, rob me.
10 [t] Bring the whole tithe
into the storehouse,*
That there may be food in my house.
Put me to the test, says the LORD of
hosts,
And see if I do not open the floodgates of
heaven for you,
and pour down upon you blessing
without measure!
11 I will rebuke the locust for you
so that it will not destroy your crops,
And the vine in the field will not be
barren,
says the LORD of hosts.
12 [u] All the nations will call you blessed,
for you will be a delightful land,
says the LORD of hosts.

### *The Need To Serve God*

13 Your words are too much for me, says the
LORD.
You ask, "What have we spoken
against you?"
14 [v] You have said, "It is useless to serve
God;
what do we gain by observing God's
requirements,
And by going about as mourners*
before the LORD of hosts?
15 But we call the arrogant blessed;
for evildoers not only prosper
but even test God and escape."
16 [w] Then those who fear the LORD spoke
with one another,
and the LORD listened attentively;
A record book* was written before him
of those who fear the LORD and esteem
his name.
17 [x] They shall be mine, says the LORD of
hosts,
my own special possession, on the day
when I take action.
And I will have compassion on them,
as a man has compassion on his son
who serves him.
18 Then you will again distinguish
between the just and the wicked,
Between the person who serves God,

**3:6–7 Not change**: God remains faithful to the covenant even when the human partners break it.
**3:10 Storehouse**: the temple treasury.
**3:14 As mourners**: the adverb translated "as mourners" means something like "with a long face."
**3:16 Record book**: see note on Ex 32:32.

*q:* Is 1:25; Zec 13:9. *r:* Zec 1:3–4; Acts 7:51. *s:* Neh 13:10–14. *t:* Dt 28:2, 12; 2 Chr 31:10–11; Neh 10:38; 13:12; Prv 3:9–10. *u:* Dt 28:10; Is 61:9. *v:* Jb 21:14–15; 22:17; Ps 73:11–12; Is 58:3; Zec 7:2–7. *w:* Rev 20:12. *x:* Ex 19:5; Dt 7:6; Ps 103:13; 135:4.

and the one who does not.
19 y For the day is coming, blazing like an oven,
when all the arrogant and all evildoers will be stubble,
And the day that is coming will set them on fire,
leaving them neither root nor branch,
says the LORD of hosts.
20 z But for you who fear my name, the sun of justice
will arise with healing in its wings;*
And you will go out leaping like calves from the stall
21 and tread down the wicked;
They will become dust under the soles of your feet,
on the day when I take action, says the LORD of hosts.

### *Moses and Elijah*

22 a Remember the law of Moses my servant,
whom I charged at Horeb
With statutes and ordinances
for all Israel.
23 b Now I am sending to you
Elijah* the prophet,
Before the day of the LORD comes,
the great and terrible day;
24 He will turn the heart of fathers to their sons,
and the heart of sons to their fathers,
Lest I come and strike
the land with utter destruction.

**3:20 Wings**: a common symbol of the manifestation of a god in the ancient Near East is the winged sun disk found, for example, on premonarchic jar handles. Cf. Nm 6:25; Ps 4:7; 31:17; 34:6; 84:12.

**3:23 Elijah**: taken up in a whirlwind, according to 2 Kgs 2:11. Here his return seems to be foretold. A Jewish tradition interpreted this literally; the gospels saw Elijah in the person of John the Baptist (Mt 11:13–14; 17:10–13; Mk 9:9–13).

*y:* Is 13:9; 34:8; Jl 3:3; Zep 1:18; 2 Pt 3:7. *z:* Lk 1:78–79. *a:* Ex 20; Lv 26; Dt 4:1, 5–6. *b:* 2 Kgs 2:10–12; Sir 48:10; Mt 11:13–14; 17:10–13; Mk 9:9–13; Lk 1:17.

# THE NEW TESTAMENT

## NEW AMERICAN BIBLE

# PREFACE TO THE *NEW AMERICAN BIBLE*

## First Edition of the New Testament

The New Testament translation has been approached with essentially the same fidelity to the thought and individual style of the biblical writers as was applied in the Old Testament. In some cases, however, the problem of marked literary peculiarities had to be met. What by any Western standard are the limited vocabularies and stylistic infelicities of the evangelists cannot be retained in the exact form in which they appear in the originals without displeasing the modern ear. A compromise is here attempted whereby some measure of the poverty of the evangelists' expression is kept and placed at the service of their message in its richness. Similarly, the syntactical shortcomings of Paul, his frequent lapses into anacoluthon, and the like, are rendered as they occur in his epistles rather than "smoothed out." Only thus, the translators suppose, will contemporary readers have some adequate idea of the kind of writing they have before them. When the prose of the original flows more smoothly, as in Luke, Acts, and Hebrews, it is reflected in the translation.

The Gospel according to John comprises a special case. Absolute fidelity to his technique of reiterated phrasing would result in an assault on the English ear, yet the softening of the vocal effect by substitution of other words and phrases would destroy the effectiveness of his poetry. Again, resort is had to compromise. This is not an easy matter when the very repetitiousness which the author deliberately employed is at the same time regarded by those who read and speak English to be a serious stylistic defect. Only those familiar with the Greek originals can know what a relentless tattoo Johannine poetry can produce. A similar observation could be made regarding other New Testament books as well. Matthew and Mark are given to identical phrasing twice and three times in the same sentence. As for the rhetorical overgrowth and mixed figures of speech in the letters of Peter, James, and Jude, the translator must resist a powerful compulsion to tidy them up if only to render these letters intelligibly.

Without seeking refuge in complaints against the inspired authors, however, the translators of *The New American Bible* here state that what they have attempted is a translation rather than a paraphrase. To be sure, all translation can be called paraphrase by definition. Any striving for complete fidelity will shortly end in infidelity. Nonetheless, it must be pointed out that the temptation to improve overladen sentences by the consolidation or elimination of multiplied adjectives, or the simplification of clumsy hendiadys, has been resisted here. For the most part, rhetorically ineffective words and phrases are retained in this translation in some form, even when it is clear that a Western contemporary writer would never have employed them.

The spelling of proper names in *The New American Bible* follows the customary forms found in most English Bibles since the Authorized Version.

Despite the arbitrary character of the divisions into numbered verses (a scheme which in its present form is only four centuries old), the translators have made a constant effort to keep within an English verse the whole verbal content of the Greek verse. At times the effort has not seemed worth the result since it often does violence to the original author's flow of expression, which preceded it by so many centuries. If this translation had been prepared for purposes of public reading only, the editors would have foregone the effort at an early stage. But since they never departed from the threefold objective of preparing a translation suitable for liturgical use, private reading, and the purposes of students, the last-named consideration prevailed. Those familiar with Greek should be able to discover how the translators of the New Testament have rendered any given original verse of scripture, if their exegetical or theological tasks require them to know this. At the same time, the fact should be set down here that the editors did not commit themselves in the synoptic gospels to rendering repeated words or phrases identically.

This leads to a final consideration: the Greek text used for the New Testament. Here, punctuation and verse division are at least as important as variant readings. In general, Nestle-Aland's *Novum Testamentum Graece* (25th edition, 1963) was followed. Additional help was derived from *The Greek New Testament* (Aland, Black, Metzger, Wikgren), produced for the use of translators by the United Bible Societies in 1966. However, the editors did not confine themselves strictly to these texts; at times, they inclined toward readings otherwise attested. The omission of alternative translations does not mean that the translators think them without merit, but only that in every case they had to make a choice.

Poorly attested readings do not occur in this translation. Doubtful readings of some merit appear within brackets; public readers may include such words or phrases, or omit them entirely without any damage to sense. Parentheses are used, as ordinarily in English, as a punctuation device. Material they enclose is in no sense textually doubtful. It is simply thought to be parenthetical in the intention of the biblical author, even though there is no such punctuation mark in Greek. The difficulty in dealing with quotation marks is well known. Since they do not appear in any form in the original text, wherever they occur here they constitute an editorial decision.

# PREFACE TO THE REVISED EDITION

The New Testament of *The New American Bible,* a fresh translation from the Greek text, was first published in complete form in 1970, together with the Old Testament translation that had been completed the previous year. Portions of the New Testament had appeared earlier, in somewhat different form, in the provisional Mass lectionary of 1964 and in the *Lectionary for Mass* of 1970.

Since 1970 many different printings of the New Testament have been issued by a number of publishers, both separately and in complete Bibles, and the text has become widely known both in the United States and in other English-speaking countries. Most American Catholics have been influenced by it because of its widespread use in the liturgy, and it has received a generally favorable reception from many other Christians as well. It has taken its place among the standard contemporary translations of the New Testament, respected for its fidelity to the original and its attempt to render this into current American English.

Although the scriptures themselves are timeless, translations and explanations of them quickly become dated in an era marked by rapid cultural change to a degree never previously experienced. The explosion of biblical studies that has taken place in our century and the changing nature of our language itself require periodic adjustment both in translations and in the accompanying explanatory materials. The experience of actual use of the New Testament of *The New American Bible*, especially in oral proclamation, has provided a basis for further improvement. Accordingly, it was decided in 1978 to proceed with a thorough revision of the New Testament to reflect advances in scholarship and to satisfy needs identified through pastoral experience.

For this purpose a steering committee was formed to plan, organize, and direct the work of revision, to engage collaborators, and to serve as an editorial board to coordinate the work of the various revisers and to determine the final form of the text and the explanatory materials. Guidelines were drawn up and collaborators selected in 1978 and early 1979, and November of 1980 was established as the deadline for manuscripts. From December 1980 through September 1986 the editorial board met a total of fifty times and carefully reviewed and revised all the material in order to ensure accuracy and consistency of approach. The editors also worked together with the bishops' ad hoc committee that was appointed by the National Conference of Catholic Bishops in 1982 to oversee the revision.

The threefold purpose of the translation that was expressed in the preface to the first edition has been maintained in the revision: to provide a version suitable for liturgical proclamation, for private reading, and for purposes of study. Special attention has been given to the first of these purposes, since oral proclamation demands special qualities in a translation, and experience had provided insights and suggestions that could lead to improvement in this area. Efforts have also been made, however, to facilitate devotional reading by providing suitable notes and introductory materials, and to assist the student by achieving greater accuracy and consistency in the translation and supplying more abundant information in the introductions and notes.

The primary aim of the revision is to produce a version as accurate and faithful to the meaning of the Greek original as is possible for a translation. The editors have consequently moved in the direction of a formal-equivalence approach to translation, matching the vocabulary, structure, and even word order of the original as closely as possible in the receptor language. Some other contemporary biblical versions have adopted, in varying degrees, a dynamic-equivalence approach, which attempts to respect the individuality of each language by expressing the meaning of the original in a linguistic structure suited to English, even though this may be very different from the corresponding Greek structure. While this approach often results in fresh and brilliant renderings, it has the disadvantages of more or less radically abandoning traditional biblical and liturgical terminology and phraseology, of expanding the text to include what more properly belongs in notes, commentaries, or preaching, and of tending toward paraphrase. A more formal approach seems better suited to the specific purposes intended for this translation.

At the same time, the editors have wished to produce a version in English that reflects contemporary American usage and is readily understandable to ordinary educated people, but one that will be recognized as dignified speech, on the level of formal rather than colloquial usage. These aims are not in fact contradictory, for there are different levels of language in current use: the language of formal situations is not that of colloquial conversation, though people understand both and may pass from one to the other without adverting to the transition. The liturgy is a formal situation that requires a level of discourse more dignified, formal, and hieratic than the world of business, sport, or informal communication. People readily understand this more formal level even though they may not often use it; our passive vocabulary is much larger than our active vocabulary. Hence this revision, while avoiding archaisms, does not shrink from traditional biblical terms that are easily understood even though not in common use in everyday speech. The level of language consciously aimed at is one appropriate for liturgical proclamation; this may also permit the translation to serve the purposes of devotional reading and serious study.

A particular effort has been made to insure consistency of vocabulary. Always to translate a given Greek word by the same English equivalent would lead to ludicrous results and to infidelity to the meaning of the text. But in passages where a particular Greek term retains the same meaning, it has been rendered in the same way insofar as this has been feasible; this is particularly significant in the case of terms that have a specific theological meaning. The synoptic gospels have been carefully translated so as to reveal both the similarities and the differences of the Greek.

An especially sensitive problem today is the question of discrimination in language. In recent years there has been much discussion about allegations of anti-Jewish expressions in the New Testament and of language that discriminates against various minorities. Above all, however, the question of discrimination against women affects the largest number of people and arouses the greatest degree of interest and concern. At present there is little agreement about these problems or about the best way to deal with them. In all these areas the present translation attempts to display a sensitivity appropriate to the present state of the questions under discussion, which are not yet resolved and in regard to which it is impossible to please everyone, since intelligent and sincere participants in the debate hold mutually contradictory views.

The primary concern in this revision is fidelity to what the text says. When the meaning of the Greek is inclusive of both sexes, the translation seeks to reproduce such inclusivity insofar as this is possible in normal English usage, without resort to inelegant circumlocutions or neologisms that would offend against the dignity of the language. Although the generic sense of *man* is traditional in English, many today reject it; its use has therefore generally been avoided, though it is retained in cases where no fully satisfactory equivalent could be found. English does not possess a gender-inclusive third personal pronoun in the singular, and this translation continues to use the masculine resumptive pronoun after *everyone* or *anyone*, in the traditional way, where this cannot be avoided without infidelity to the meaning.

The translation of the Greek word *adelphos,* particularly in the plural form *adelphoi,* poses an especially delicate problem. While the term literally means *brothers* or other male blood relatives, even in profane Greek the plural can designate two persons, one of either sex, who were born of the same parents. It was adopted by the early Christians to designate, in a figurative sense, the members of the Christian community, who were conscious of a new familial relationship to one another by reason of their adoption as children of God. They are consequently addressed as *adelphoi.* This has traditionally been rendered into English by *brothers* or, more archaically, *brethren.* There has never been any doubt that this designation includes *all* the members of the Christian community, both male and female. Given the absence in English of a corresponding term that explicitly includes both sexes, this translation retains the usage of *brothers,* with the inclusive meaning that has been traditionally attached to it in this biblical context.

Since the New Testament is the product of a particular time and culture, the views expressed in it and the language in which they are expressed reflect a particular cultural conditioning, which sometimes makes them quite different from contemporary ideas and concerns. Discriminatory language should be eliminated insofar as possible whenever it is unfaithful to the meaning of the New Testament, but the text should not be altered in order to adjust it to contemporary concerns. This translation does not introduce any changes, expansions, additions to, or subtractions from the text of scripture. It further retains the traditional biblical ways of speaking about God and about Christ, including the use of masculine nouns and pronouns.

The Greek text followed in this translation is that of the third edition of *The Greek New Testament*, edited by Kurt Aland, Matthew Black, Carlo Martini, Bruce Metzger, and Allen Wikgren, and published by the United Bible Societies in 1975. The same text, with a different critical apparatus and variations in punctuation and typography, was published as the twenty-sixth edition of the Nestle-Aland *Novum Testamentum Graece* in 1979 by the Deutsche Bibelstiftung, Stuttgart. This edition has also been consulted. When variant readings occur, the translation, with few exceptions, follows the reading that was placed in the text of these Greek editions, though the occurrence of the principal variants is pointed out in the notes.

The editors of the Greek text placed square brackets around words or portions of words of which the authenticity is questionable because the evidence of textual witnesses is inconclusive. The same has been done in the translation insofar as it is possible to reproduce this convention in English. It should be possible to read the text either with or without the disputed words, but in English it is not always feasible to provide this alternative, and in some passages the bracketed words must be included to make sense. As in the first edition, parentheses do not indicate textual uncertainty, but are simply a punctuation device to indicate a passage that in the editors' judgment appears parenthetical to the thought of the author.

Citations from the Old Testament are placed within quotation marks; longer citations are set off as block quotations in a separate indented paragraph. The sources of such citations, as well as those of many more or less subtle allusions to the Old Testament, are identified in the biblical cross-reference section at the bottom of each page. Insofar as possible, the translation of such Old Testament citations agrees with that of *The New American Bible* Old Testament whenever the underlying Greek agrees with the Hebrew (or, in some cases, the Aramaic or Greek) text from which the Old Testament translation was made. But citations in the New Testament frequently follow the Septuagint or some other version, or were made from memory; hence, in many cases the translation in the New Testament passage will not agree with what appears in the Old Testament. Some of these cases are explained in the notes.

It is a further aim of the revised edition to supply explanatory materials more abundantly than in the first edition. In most cases the introductions and notes have been entirely rewritten and expanded, and the cross-references checked and revised. It is intended that these materials should reflect the present state of sound biblical scholarship and should be presented in such a form that they can be assimilated by the ordinary intelligent reader without specialized biblical training. While they have been written with the ordinary educated Christian in mind, not all technical vocabulary can be entirely dispensed with in approaching the Bible, any more than in any other field. It is the hope of the editors that these materials, even if they sometimes demand an effort, will help the reader to a fuller and more intelligent understanding of the New Testament and a fruitful appropriation of its meaning for personal spiritual growth.

*The New American Bible* is a Roman Catholic translation. This revision, however, like the first edition, has been accomplished with the collaboration of scholars from other Christian churches, both among the revisers and on the editorial board, in response to the encouragement of Vatican Council II (*Dei Verbum,* 22). The editorial board expresses gratitude to all who have collaborated in the revision: to all the revisers, consultants, and bishops who contributed to it, to reviewers of the first edition, and to those who voluntarily submitted suggestions. May this translation fulfill its threefold purpose, "so that the word of the Lord may speed forward and be glorified" (2 Thes 3:1).

*The Feast of St. Jerome*
*September 30, 1986*

# THE GOSPELS

See RG 266–75

The collection of writings that constitutes the New Testament begins with four gospels. Next comes the Acts of the Apostles, followed by twenty-one letters that are attributed to Paul, James, Peter, John, and Jude. Finally, at the end of the early church's scriptures stands the Revelation to John. Virtually all Christians agree that these twenty-seven books constitute the "canon," a term that means "rule" and designates the list of writings that are regarded as authoritative for Christian faith and life.

It is the purpose of this Introduction to describe those features that are common to the four gospels. A similar treatment of the letters of the New Testament is provided in the two Introductions that appear before the Letter to the Romans and before the Letter of James, respectively. The Acts of the Apostles, a work that is both historical and theological, and Revelation, an apocalyptic work, have no counterparts in the New Testament; the special Introductions prefixed to these books treat of the literary characteristics proper to each of them.

While the New Testament contains four writings called "gospels," there is in reality only one gospel running through all of the Christian scriptures, the gospel of and about Jesus Christ. Our English word "gospel" translates the Greek term *euangelion*, meaning "good news." This noun was used in the plural by the Greek translators of the Old Testament to render the Hebrew term for "good news" (2 Sm 4:10; possibly also 2 Sm 18:20, 25). But it is the corresponding verb *euangelizomai*, "to proclaim good news," that was especially significant in preparing for the New Testament idea of "gospel," since this term is used by Deutero-Isaiah of announcing the great victory of God that was to establish his universal kingship and inaugurate the new age (Is 40:9; 52:7; 61:1).

Paul used the word *euangelion* to designate the message that he and the other apostles proclaimed, the "gospel of God" (Rom 1:1; 15:16; 2 Cor 11:7; 1 Thes 2:2, 8–9). He often referred to it simply as "the gospel" (Rom 1:16; 10:16; 11:28; etc) or, because of its content and origin, as "the gospel of Christ" (Rom 15:19; 1 Cor 9:12; 1 Thes 3:2; etc). Because of its personal meaning for him and his own particular manner of telling the story about Jesus Christ and of explaining the significance of his cross and resurrection, Paul also referred to this message as "my gospel" (Rom 2:16; cf. Gal 1:11; 2:2) or "our gospel" (2 Cor 4:3; 1 Thes 1:5; 2 Thes 2:14).

It was Mark, as far as we know, who first applied the term "gospel" to a book telling the story of Jesus; see Mk 1:1 and the note there. This form of presenting Jesus' life, works, teachings, passion, and resurrection was developed further by the other evangelists; see the Introduction to each gospel. The first three of the canonical gospels, Matthew, Mark, and Luke, are so similar at many points when viewed together, particularly when arranged in parallel columns or lines, that they are called "synoptic" gospels, from the Greek word for such a general view. The fourth gospel, John, often differs significantly from the synoptics in outline and approach. This work never uses the word "gospel" or its corresponding verb; nevertheless, its message concerns the same Jesus, and the reader is urged to believe in him as the Messiah, "that through this belief you may have life in his name" (Jn 20:31).

From the second century onward, the practice arose of designating each of these four books as a "gospel," understood as a title, and of adding a phrase with a name that identified the traditional author, e.g., "The Gospel according to Matthew." The arrangement of the canon that was adopted, with the four gospels grouped together at the beginning followed by Acts, provides a massive focus upon Jesus and allows Acts to serve as a framework for the letters of the New Testament. This order, however, conceals the fact that Luke's two volumes, a gospel and Acts, were intended by their author to go together. It further obscures the point that Paul's letters were written before any of our gospels, though the sayings and deeds of Jesus stand behind all the New Testament writings.

See RG 275–91

# The Gospel According to Matthew

The position of the Gospel according to Matthew as the first of the four gospels in the New Testament reflects both the view that it was the first to be written, a view that goes back to the late second century A.D., and the esteem in which it was held by the church; no other was so frequently quoted in the noncanonical literature of earliest Christianity. Although the majority of scholars now reject the opinion about the time of its composition, the high estimation of this work remains. The reason for that becomes clear upon study of the way in which Matthew presents his story of Jesus, the demands of Christian discipleship, and the breaking-in of the new and final age through the ministry but particularly through the death and resurrection of Jesus.

The gospel begins with a narrative prologue (Mt 1:1–2:23), the first part of which is a genealogy of Jesus starting with Abraham, the father of Israel (Mt 1:1–17). Yet at the beginning of that genealogy Jesus is designated as "the son of David, the son of Abraham" (Mt 1:1). The kingly ancestor who lived about a thousand years after Abraham is named first, for this is the genealogy of Jesus Christ, the Messiah, the royal anointed one (Mt 1:16). In the first of the episodes of the infancy narrative that follow the genealogy, the mystery of Jesus' person is declared. He is conceived of a virgin by the power of the Spirit of God (Mt 1:18–25). The first of the gospel's fulfillment citations, whose purpose it is to show that he was the one to whom the prophecies of Israel were pointing, occurs here (Mt 1:23): he shall be named Emmanuel, for in him God is with us.

The announcement of the birth of this newborn king of the Jews greatly troubles not only King Herod but all Jerusalem (Mt 2:1–3), yet the Gentile magi are overjoyed to find him and offer him their homage and their gifts (Mt 2:10–11). Thus his ultimate rejection by the mass of his own people and his acceptance by the Gentile nations is foreshadowed. He must be taken to Egypt to escape the murderous plan of Herod. By his sojourn there and his subsequent return after the king's death he relives the Exodus experience of Israel. The words of the Lord spoken through the prophet Hosea, "Out of Egypt I called my son," are fulfilled in him (Mt 2:15); if Israel was God's son, Jesus is so in a way far surpassing the dignity of that nation, as his marvelous birth and the unfolding of his story show (see Mt 3:17; 4:1–11; 11:27; 14:33; 16:16; 27:54). Back in the land of Israel, he must be taken to Nazareth in Galilee because of the danger to his life in Judea, where Herod's son Archelaus is now ruling (Mt 2:22–23). The sufferings of Jesus in the infancy narrative anticipate those of his passion, and if his life is spared in spite of the dangers, it is because his destiny is finally to give it on the cross as "a ransom for many" (Mt 20:28). Thus the word of the angel will be fulfilled, ". . . he will save his people from their sins" (Mt 1:21; cf. Mt 26:28).

In Mt 4:12 Matthew begins his account of the ministry of Jesus, introducing it by the preparatory preaching of John the Baptist (Mt 3:1–12), the baptism of Jesus that culminates in God's proclaiming him his "beloved Son" (Mt 3:13–17), and the temptation in which he proves his true sonship by his victory over the devil's attempt to deflect him from the way of obedience to the Father (Mt 4:1–11). The central message of Jesus' preaching is the coming of the kingdom of heaven and the need for repentance, a complete change of heart and conduct, on the part of those who are to receive this great gift of God (Mt 4:17). Galilee is the setting for most of his ministry; he leaves there for Judea only in Mt 19:1, and his ministry in Jerusalem, the goal of his journey, is limited to a few days (Mt 21:1–25:46).

In this extensive material there are five great discourses of Jesus, each concluding with the formula "When Jesus finished these words" or one closely similar (Mt 7:28; 11:1; 13:53; 19:1; 26:1). These are an important structure of the gospel. In every case the discourse is preceded by a narrative section, each narrative and discourse together constituting a "book" of the gospel. The discourses are, respectively, the "Sermon on the Mount" (Mt 5:3–7:27), the missionary discourse (Mt 10:5–42), the parable discourse (Mt 13:3–52), the "church order" discourse (Mt 18:3–35), and the eschatological discourse (Mt 24:4–25:46). In large measure the material of these discourses came to Matthew from his tradition, but his work in modifying and adding to what he had received is abundantly evident. No other evangelist gives the teaching of Jesus with such elegance and order as he.

In the "Sermon on the Mount" the theme of righteousness is prominent, and even at this early stage of the ministry the note of opposition is struck between Jesus and the Pharisees, who are designated as "the hypocrites" (Mt 6:2, 5, 16). The righteousness of his disciples must surpass that of the scribes and Pharisees; otherwise, in spite of their alleged following of Jesus, they will not enter into the kingdom of heaven (Mt 5:20). Righteousness means doing the will of the heavenly Father (Mt 7:21), and his will is proclaimed in a manner that is startling to all who have identified it with the law of Moses. The antitheses of the Sermon (Mt 5:21–48) both accept (Mt 5:21–30, 43–48) and reject (Mt 5:31–42) elements of that law, and in the former case the understanding of the law's demands is deepened and extended. The antitheses are the best commentary on the meaning of Jesus' claim that he has come not to abolish but to fulfill the law (Mt 5:17). What is meant by fulfillment of the law is not the demand to keep it exactly as it stood before the coming of Jesus, but rather his bringing the law to be a lasting expression of the will of God, and in that fulfillment there is much that will pass away. Should this appear contradictory to his saying that "until heaven and earth pass away" not even the smallest part of the law will pass (Mt 5:18), that time of fulfillment is not the dissolution of the universe but the coming of the new age, which will occur with Jesus' death and resurrection. While righteousness in the new age will continue to mean conduct that is in accordance with the law, it will be conduct in accordance with the law as expounded and interpreted by Jesus (cf. Mt 28:20, ". . . all that I have commanded you").

Though Jesus speaks harshly about the Pharisees in the Sermon, his judgment is not solely a condemnation of them. The Pharisees are portrayed as a negative example for his disciples, and his condemnation of those who claim to belong to him while disobeying his word is no less severe (Mt 7:21–23, 26–27).

In Mt 4:23 a summary statement of Jesus' activity speaks not only of his teaching and proclaiming the gospel but of his "curing every disease and illness among the people"; this is repeated almost verbatim in Mt 9:35. The narrative section that follows the Sermon on the Mount (Mt 8:1–9:38) is composed principally of accounts of those merciful deeds of Jesus, but it is far from being simply a collection of stories about miraculous cures. The nature of the community that Jesus will establish is shown; it will always be under the protection of him whose power can deal with all dangers (Mt 8:23–27), but it is only for those who are prepared to follow him at whatever cost (Mt 8:16–22), not only believing Israelites but Gentiles who have come to faith in him (Mt 8:10–12). The disciples begin to have some insight, however imperfect, into the mystery of Jesus' person. They wonder about him whom "the winds and the sea obey" (Mt 8:27), and they witness his bold declaration of the forgiveness of the paralytic's sins (Mt 9:2). That episode of the narrative moves on two levels. When the crowd sees the cure that testifies to the authority of Jesus, the Son of Man, to forgive sins (Mt 9:6), they glorify God "who had given such authority to human beings" (Mt 9:8). The forgiveness of sins is now not the prerogative of Jesus alone but of "human beings," that is, of the disciples who constitute the community of Jesus, the church. The ecclesial character of this narrative section could hardly be more plainly indicated.

The end of the section prepares for the discourse on the church's mission (Mt 10:5–42). Jesus is moved to pity at the sight of the crowds who are like sheep without a shepherd (Mt 9:36), and he sends out the twelve disciples to make the proclamation with which his own ministry began, "The kingdom of heaven is at hand" (Mt 10:7; cf. Mt 4:17), and to drive out demons and cure the sick as he has done (Mt 10:1). Their mission is limited to Israel (Mt 10:5–6) as Jesus' own was (Mt 15:24), yet in Mt 15:16 that perspective broadens and the discourse begins to speak of the mission that the disciples will have after the resurrection and of the severe persecution that will attend it (Mt 10:18). Again, the discourse moves on two levels: that of the time of Jesus and that of the time of the church.

The narrative section of the third book (Mt 11:2–12:50) deals with the growing opposition to Jesus. Hostility toward him has already been manifested (Mt 8:10; 9:3, 10–13, 34), but here it becomes more intense. The rejection of Jesus comes, as before, from Pharisees, who take "counsel against him to put him to death" (Mt 12:14) and repeat their earlier accusation that he drives out demons because he is in league with demonic power (Mt 12:22–24). But they are not alone in their rejection. Jesus complains of the lack of faith of "this generation" of Israelites (Mt 11:16–19) and reproaches the towns "where most of his mighty deeds had been done" for not heeding his call to repentance (Mt 11:20–24). This dark picture is relieved by Jesus' praise of the Father who has enabled "the childlike" to accept him (Mt 11:25–27), but on the whole the story is one of opposition to his word and blindness to the meaning of his deeds. The whole section ends with his declaring that not even the most intimate blood relationship with him counts for anything; his only true relatives are those who do the will of his heavenly Father (Mt 12:48–50).

The narrative of rejection leads up to the parable discourse (Mt 13:3–52). The reason given for Jesus' speaking to the crowds in parables is that they have hardened themselves against his clear teaching, unlike the disciples to whom knowledge of "the mysteries of the kingdom has been granted" (Mt 13:10–16). In Mt 13:36 he dismisses the crowds and continues the discourse to his disciples alone, who claim, at the end, to have understood all that he has said (Mt 13:51). But, lest the impression be given that the church of Jesus is made up only of true disciples, the explanation of the parable of the weeds among the wheat (Mt 13:37–43), as well as the parable of the net thrown into the sea "which collects fish of every kind" (Mt 13:47–49), shows that it is composed of both the righteous and the wicked, and that separation between the two will be made only at the time of the final judgment.

In the narrative that constitutes the first part of the fourth book of the gospel (Mt 13:54–17:27), Jesus is shown preparing for the establishment of his church with its teaching authority that will supplant the blind guidance of the Pharisees (Mt 15:13–14), whose teaching, curiously said to be that of the Sadducees also, is repudiated by Jesus as the norm for his disciples (Mt 16:6, 11–12). The church of Jesus will be built on Peter (Mt 16:18), who will be given authority to bind and loose on earth, an authority whose exercise will be confirmed in heaven (Mt 16:19). The metaphor of binding and loosing has a variety of meanings, among them that of giving authoritative teaching. This promise is made to Peter directly after he has confessed Jesus to be the Messiah, the Son of the living God (Mt 16:16), a confession that he has made as the result of revelation given to him by the heavenly Father (Mt 16:17); Matthew's ecclesiology is based on his high christology.

Directly after that confession Jesus begins to instruct his disciples about how he must go the way of suffering and death (Mt 16:21). Peter, who has been praised for his confession, protests against this and receives from Jesus the sharpest of rebukes for attempting to deflect Jesus from his God-appointed destiny. The future rock upon whom the church will be built is still a man of "little faith" (see Mt 14:31). Both he and the other disciples must know not only that Jesus will have to suffer and die but that they too will have to follow him on the way of the cross if they are truly to be his disciples (Mt 16:24–25).

The discourse following this narrative (Mt 18:1–35) is often called the "church order" discourse, although that title is perhaps misleading since the emphasis is not on the structure of the church but on the care that the disciples must have for one another in respect to guarding each other's faith in Jesus (Mt 18:6–7), to seeking out those who have wandered from the fold (Mt 18:10–14), and to repeated forgiving of their fellow disciples who have offended them (Mt 18:21–35). But there is also the obligation to correct the sinful fellow Christian and, should one refuse to be corrected, separation from the community is demanded (Mt 18:15–18).

The narrative of the fifth book (Mt 19:1–23:39) begins with the departure of Jesus and his disciples from Galilee for Jerusalem. In the course of their journey Jesus for the third time predicts the passion that awaits him at Jerusalem and also his resurrection (Mt 20:17–19). At his entrance into the city he is hailed as the Son of David by the crowds accompanying him (Mt 21:9). He cleanses the temple (Mt 21:12–17), and in the few days of his Jerusalem ministry he engages in a series of controversies with the Jewish religious leaders (Mt 21:23–27; 22:15–22, 23–33, 34–40, 41–46), meanwhile speaking parables against them (Mt 21:28–32, 33–46), against all those Israelites who have rejected God's invitation to the messianic banquet (Mt 22:1–10), and against all, Jew and Gentile, who have accepted but have shown themselves unworthy of it (Mt 22:11–14). Once again, the perspective of the evangelist includes not only the time of Jesus' ministry but that of the preaching of the gospel after his resurrection. The narrative culminates in Jesus' denunciation of the scribes and Pharisees, reflecting not only his own opposition to them but that of Matthew's church (Mt 23:1–36), and in Jesus' lament over Jerusalem (Mt 23:37–39).

In the discourse of the fifth book (Mt 24:1–25:46), the last of the great structural discourses of the gospel, Jesus predicts the destruction of the temple and his own final coming. The time of the latter is unknown (Mt 24:36, 44), and the disciples are exhorted in various parables to live in readiness for it, a readiness that entails faithful attention to the duties of the interim period (Mt 24:45–25:30). The coming of Jesus will bring with it the great judgment by which the everlasting destiny of all will be determined (Mt 25:31–46).

The story of Jesus' passion and resurrection (Mt 26:1–28:20), the climax of the gospel, throws light on all that has preceded. In Matthew "righteousness" means both the faithful response to the will of God demanded of all to whom that will is announced and also the saving activity of God for his people (see Mt 3:15; 5:6; 6:33). The passion supremely exemplifies both meanings of that central Matthean word. In Jesus' absolute faithfulness to the Father's will that he drink the cup of suffering (Mt 26:39), the incomparable model for Christian obedience is given; in his death "for the forgiveness of sins" (Mt 26:28), the saving power of God is manifested as never before.

Matthew's portrayal of Jesus in his passion combines both the majestic serenity of the obedient Son who goes his destined way in fulfillment of the scriptures (Mt 26:52–54), confident of his ultimate vindication by God, and the depths of fear and abandonment that he feels in face of death (Mt 26:38–39; 27:46). These two aspects are expressed by an Old Testament theme that occurs often in the narrative, i.e., the portrait of the suffering Righteous One who complains to God in his misery, but is certain of eventual deliverance from his terrible ordeal.

The passion-resurrection of God's Son means nothing less than the turn of the ages, a new stage of history, the coming of the Son of Man in his kingdom (Mt 28:18; cf. Mt 16:28). That is the sense of the apocalyptic signs that accompany Jesus' death (Mt 27:51–53) and resurrection (Mt 28:2). Although the old age continues, as it will until the manifestation of Jesus' triumph at his parousia, the final age has now begun. This is known only to those who have seen the Risen One and to those, both Jews and Gentiles, who have believed in their announcement of Jesus' triumph and have themselves become his disciples (cf. Mt 28:19). To them he is constantly, though invisibly, present (Mt 28:20), verifying the name Emmanuel, "God is with us" (cf. Mt 1:23).

The questions of authorship, sources, and the time of composition of this gospel have received many answers, none of which can claim more than a greater or lesser degree of probability. The one now favored by the majority of scholars is the following.

The ancient tradition that the author was the disciple and apostle of Jesus named Matthew (see Mt 10:3) is untenable because the gospel is based, in large part, on the Gospel according to Mark (almost all the verses of that gospel have been utilized in this), and it is hardly likely that a companion of Jesus would have followed so extensively an account that came from one who admittedly never had such an association rather than rely on his own memories. The attribution of the gospel to the disciple Matthew may have been due to his having been responsible for some of the traditions found in it, but that is far from certain.

The unknown author, whom we shall continue to call Matthew for the sake of convenience, drew not only upon the Gospel according to Mark but upon a large body of material (principally, sayings of Jesus) not found in Mark that corresponds, sometimes exactly, to material found also in the Gospel according to Luke. This material, called "Q" (probably from the first letter of the German word Quelle, meaning "source"), represents traditions, written and oral, used by both Matthew and Luke. Mark and Q are sources common to the two other synoptic gospels; hence the name the "Two-Source Theory" given to this explanation of the relation among the synoptics.

In addition to what Matthew drew from Mark and Q, his gospel contains material that is found only there. This is often designated "M," written or oral tradition that was available to the author. Since Mark was written shortly before or shortly after A.D. 70 (see Introduction to Mark), Matthew was composed certainly after that date, which marks the fall of Jerusalem to the Romans at the time of the First Jewish Revolt (A.D. 66–70), and probably at least a decade later since Matthew's use of Mark presupposes a wide diffusion of that gospel. The post-A.D. 70 date is confirmed within the text by Mt 22:7, which refers to the destruction of Jerusalem.

As for the place where the gospel was composed, a plausible suggestion is that it was Antioch, the capital of the Roman province of Syria. That large and important city had a mixed population of Greek-speaking Gentiles and Jews. The tensions between Jewish and Gentile Christians there in the time of Paul (see Gal 2:1–14) in respect to Christian obligation to observe Mosaic law are partially similar to tensions that can be seen between the two groups in Matthew's gospel. The church of Matthew, originally strongly Jewish Christian, had become one in which Gentile Christians were predominant. His gospel answers the question how obedience to the will of God is to be expressed by those who live after the "turn of the ages," the death and resurrection of Jesus.

The principal divisions of the Gospel according to Matthew are the following:

- I. The Infancy Narrative (1:1–2:23)
- II. The Proclamation of the Kingdom (3:1–7:29)
- III. Ministry and Mission in Galilee (8:1–11:1)
- IV. Opposition from Israel (11:2–13:53)
- V. Jesus, the Kingdom, and the Church (13:54–18:35)
- VI. Ministry in Judea and Jerusalem (19:1–25:46)
- VII. The Passion and Resurrection (26:1–28:20)

# I. The Infancy Narrative

## CHAPTER 1

See RG 279–80

*The Genealogy of Jesus.** 1[a] The book
of the genealogy of Jesus Christ, the son of
David, the son of Abraham.*
2[b] Abraham became the father of Isaac,
Isaac the father of Jacob, Jacob the father of
Judah and his brothers.[c] 3 Judah became the
father of Perez and Zerah, whose mother
was Tamar.[d] Perez became the father of Hezron, Hezron the father of Ram, 4[e] Ram the
father of Amminadab. Amminadab became
the father of Nahshon, Nahshon the father of
Salmon, 5[f] Salmon the father of Boaz, whose
mother was Rahab. Boaz became the father

**1:1–2:23** The infancy narrative forms the prologue of the gospel. Consisting of a genealogy and five stories, it presents the coming of Jesus as the climax of Israel's history, and the events of his conception, birth, and early childhood as the fulfillment of Old Testament prophecy. The genealogy is probably traditional material that Matthew edited. In its first two sections (Mt 1:2–11) it was drawn from Ru 4:18–22; 1 Chr 1–3. Except for Jechoniah, Shealtiel, and Zerubbabel, none of the names in the third section (Mt 1:12–16) is found in any Old Testament genealogy. While the genealogy shows the continuity of God's providential plan from Abraham on, discontinuity is also present. The women Tamar (Mt 1:3), Rahab and Ruth (Mt 1:5), and the wife of Uriah, Bathsheba (Mt 1:6), bore their sons through unions that were in varying degrees strange and unexpected. These "irregularities" culminate in the supreme "irregularity" of the Messiah's birth of a virgin mother; the age of fulfillment is inaugurated by a creative act of God.

Drawing upon both biblical tradition and Jewish stories, Matthew portrays Jesus as reliving the Exodus experience of Israel and the persecutions of Moses. His rejection by his own people and his passion are foreshadowed by the troubled reaction of "all Jerusalem" to the question of the magi who are seeking the "newborn king of the Jews" (Mt 2:2–3), and by Herod's attempt to have him killed. The magi who do him homage prefigure the Gentiles who will accept the preaching of the gospel. The infancy narrative proclaims who Jesus is, the savior of his people from their sins (Mt 1:21), Emmanuel in whom "God is with us" (Mt 1:23), and the Son of God (Mt 2:15).

**1:1 The Son of David, the son of Abraham**: two links of the genealogical chain are singled out. Although the later, David is placed first in order to emphasize that Jesus is the royal Messiah. The mention of Abraham may be due not only to his being the father of the nation Israel but to Matthew's interest in the universal scope of Jesus' mission; cf. Gn 22:18 ". . . in your descendants all the nations of the earth shall find blessing."

*a:* Gn 5:1; 1 Chr 17:11; Gn 22:18. *b:* Lk 3:23–38. *c:* Gn 21:3; 25:26; 29:35; 1 Chr 2:1. *d:* Gn 38:29–30; Ru 4:18; 1 Chr 2:4–9. *e:* Ru 4:19–20; 1 Chr 2:10–11. *f:* Ru 4:21–22; 1 Chr 2:11–12.

of Obed, whose mother was Ruth. Obed became the father of Jesse, 6[g] Jesse the father
of David the king.

David became the father of Solomon,
whose mother had been the wife of Uriah.
7*[h] Solomon became the father of Rehoboam, Rehoboam the father of Abijah, Abijah the father of Asaph. 8 Asaph became the
father of Jehoshaphat, Jehoshaphat the father of Joram, Joram the father of Uzziah.
9 Uzziah became the father of Jotham, Jotham the father of Ahaz, Ahaz the father of
Hezekiah. 10 Hezekiah became the father of
Manasseh, Manasseh the father of Amos,*
Amos the father of Josiah. 11 Josiah became
the father of Jechoniah and his brothers at
the time of the Babylonian exile.

12[i] After the Babylonian exile, Jechoniah
became the father of Shealtiel, Shealtiel the
father of Zerubbabel, 13 Zerubbabel the father
of Abiud. Abiud became the father of Eliakim,
Eliakim the father of Azor, 14 Azor the father of
Zadok. Zadok became the father of Achim,
Achim the father of Eliud, 15 Eliud the father of
Eleazar. Eleazar became the father of Matthan, Matthan the father of Jacob, 16 Jacob the
father of Joseph, the husband of Mary. Of her
was born Jesus who is called the Messiah.

17 Thus the total number of generations
from Abraham to David is fourteen generations; from David to the Babylonian exile,
fourteen generations; from the Babylonian
exile to the Messiah, fourteen generations.*

*The Birth of Jesus.** 18 Now this is how the
birth of Jesus Christ came about. When his
mother Mary was betrothed to Joseph,* but
before they lived together, she was found with
child through the holy Spirit. 19 Joseph her
husband, since he was a righteous man,* yet
unwilling to expose her to shame, decided to
divorce her quietly. 20[j] Such was his intention
when, behold, the angel of the Lord* appeared
to him in a dream and said, "Joseph, son of
David, do not be afraid to take Mary your wife
into your home. For it is through the holy
Spirit that this child has been conceived in her.
21 She will bear a son and you are to name him
Jesus,* because he will save his people from
their sins." 22 All this took place to fulfill what
the Lord had said through the prophet:

**1:7** The successor of Abijah was not Asaph but Asa (see 1 Chr 3:10). Some textual witnesses read the latter name; however, **Asaph** is better attested. Matthew may have deliberately introduced the psalmist Asaph into the genealogy (and in Mt 1:10 the prophet Amos) in order to show that Jesus is the fulfillment not only of the promises made to David (see 2 Sm 7) but of all the Old Testament.

**1:10 Amos**: some textual witnesses read **Amon**, who was the actual successor of Manasseh (see 1 Chr 3:14).

**1:17** Matthew is concerned with fourteen generations, probably because fourteen is the numerical value of the Hebrew letters forming the name of David. In the second section of the genealogy (Mt 1:6b–11), three kings of Judah, Ahaziah, Joash, and Amaziah, have been omitted (see 1 Chr 3:11–12), so that there are fourteen generations in that section. Yet the third (Mt 1:12–16) apparently has only thirteen. Since Matthew here emphasizes that each section has fourteen, it is unlikely that the thirteen of the last was due to his oversight. Some scholars suggest that **Jesus who is called the Messiah** (Mt 1:16b) doubles the final member of the chain: **Jesus**, born within the family of David, opens up the new age as **Messiah**, so that in fact there are fourteen generations in the third section. This is perhaps too subtle, and the hypothesis of a slip not on the part of Matthew but of a later scribe seems likely. On **Messiah**, see note on Lk 2:11.

**1:18–25** This first story of the infancy narrative spells out what is summarily indicated in Mt 1:16. The virginal conception of Jesus is the work of the Spirit of God. Joseph's decision to divorce Mary is overcome by the heavenly command that he take her into his home and accept the child as his own. The natural genealogical line is broken but the promises to David are fulfilled; through Joseph's adoption the child belongs to the family of David. Matthew sees the virginal conception as the fulfillment of Is 7:14.

**1:18 Betrothed to Joseph**: betrothal was the first part of the marriage, constituting a man and woman as husband and wife. Subsequent infidelity was considered adultery. The betrothal was followed some months later by the husband's taking his wife into his home, at which time normal married life began.

**1:19 A righteous man**: as a devout observer of the Mosaic law, Joseph wished to break his union with someone whom he suspected of gross violation of the law. It is commonly said that the law required him to do so, but the texts usually given in support of that view, e.g., Dt 22:20–21 do not clearly pertain to Joseph's situation. **Unwilling to expose her to shame**: the penalty for proved adultery was death by stoning; cf. Dt 22:21–23.

**1:20 The angel of the Lord**: in the Old Testament a common designation of God in communication with a human being. **In a dream**: see Mt 2:13, 19, 22. These dreams may be meant to recall the dreams of Joseph, son of Jacob the patriarch (Gn 37:5–11:19). A closer parallel is the dream of Amram, father of Moses, related by Josephus (*Antiquities* 2:112, 215–16).

**1:21 Jesus**: in first-century Judaism the Hebrew name Joshua (Greek *Iēsous*) meaning "Yahweh helps" was interpreted as "Yahweh saves."

*g:* 2 Sm 12:24; 1 Chr 2:15; 3:5. *h:* 2 Kgs 25:1–21; 1 Chr 3:10–15. *i:* 1 Chr 3:16–19. *j:* 2:13, 19; Lk 1:35.

23 * [k] "Behold, the virgin shall be with child
and bear a son,
and they shall name him Emmanuel,"

which means "God is with us." 24 When Joseph awoke, he did as the angel of the Lord
had commanded him and took his wife into
his home. 25 He had no relations with her until she bore a son,* and he named him Jesus.[l]

## CHAPTER 2

See RG 279–80

***The Visit of the Magi.**** 1 When Jesus
was born in Bethlehem of Judea, in the days
of King Herod,* behold, magi from the east
arrived in Jerusalem, 2 saying, "Where is the
newborn king of the Jews? We saw his star*
at its rising and have come to do him homage."[m] 3 When King Herod heard this, he was
greatly troubled, and all Jerusalem with him.
4 Assembling all the chief priests and the
scribes of the people, he inquired of them
where the Messiah was to be born.* 5 [n] They
said to him, "In Bethlehem of Judea, for thus
it has been written through the prophet:

6 'And you, Bethlehem, land of Judah,
are by no means least among the rulers
of Judah;
since from you shall come a ruler,
who is to shepherd my people
Israel.' "

7 Then Herod called the magi secretly and ascertained from them the time of the star's appearance. 8 He sent them to Bethlehem and
said, "Go and search diligently for the child.
When you have found him, bring me word,
that I too may go and do him homage." 9 After their audience with the king they set out.
And behold, the star that they had seen at its
rising preceded them, until it came and
stopped over the place where the child was.
10 They were overjoyed at seeing the star,
11* [o] and on entering the house they saw the
child with Mary his mother. They prostrated
themselves and did him homage. Then they
opened their treasures and offered him gifts
of gold, frankincense, and myrrh. 12 And
having been warned in a dream not to return
to Herod, they departed for their country by
another way.

***The Flight to Egypt.*** 13* When they had departed, behold, the angel of the Lord appeared
to Joseph in a dream and said, "Rise, take the
child and his mother, flee to Egypt,* and stay
there until I tell you. Herod is going to search
for the child to destroy him." 14 Joseph rose
and took the child and his mother by night
and departed for Egypt. 15* He stayed there
until the death of Herod, that what the Lord
had said through the prophet[p] might be fulfilled, "Out of Egypt I called my son."

**1:23 God is with us**: God's promise of deliverance to Judah in Isaiah's time is seen by Matthew as fulfilled in the birth of Jesus, in whom God is with his people. The name Emmanuel is alluded to at the end of the gospel where the risen Jesus assures his disciples of his continued presence, ". . . I am with you always, until the end of the age" (Mt 28:20).

**1:25 Until she bore a son**: the evangelist is concerned to emphasize that Joseph was not responsible for the conception of Jesus. The Greek word translated "until" does not imply normal marital conduct after Jesus' birth, nor does it exclude it.

**2:1–12** The future rejection of Jesus by Israel and his acceptance by the Gentiles are retrojected into this scene of the narrative.

**2:1 In the days of King Herod**: Herod reigned from 37 to 4 B.C. **Magi**: originally a designation of the Persian priestly caste, the word became used of those who were regarded as having more than human knowledge. Matthew's magi are astrologers.

**2:2 We saw his star**: it was a common ancient belief that a new star appeared at the time of a ruler's birth. Matthew also draws upon the Old Testament story of Balaam, who had prophesied that "A star shall advance from Jacob" (Nm 24:17), though there the star means not an astral phenomenon but the king himself.

**2:4** Herod's consultation with the chief priests and scribes has some similarity to a Jewish legend about the child Moses in which the "sacred scribes" warn Pharaoh about the imminent birth of one who will deliver Israel from Egypt and the king makes plans to destroy him.

**2:11** Cf. Ps 72:10, 15; Is 60:6. These Old Testament texts led to the interpretation of the magi as kings.

**2:13–23** Biblical and nonbiblical traditions about Moses are here applied to the child Jesus, though the dominant Old Testament type is not Moses but Israel (Mt 2:15).

**2:13 Flee to Egypt**: Egypt was a traditional place of refuge for those fleeing from danger in Palestine (see 1 Kgs 11:40; Jer 26:21), but the main reason why the child is to be taken to Egypt is that he may relive the Exodus experience of Israel.

**2:15** The fulfillment citation is taken from Hos 11:1. Israel, God's son, was called out of Egypt at the time of the Exodus; Jesus, the Son of God, will similarly be called out of that land in a new exodus. The father-son relationship between God and the nation is set in a higher key. Here the son is not a group adopted as "son of God," but the child who, as conceived by the holy Spirit, stands in unique relation to God. He is son of David and of Abraham, of Mary and of Joseph, but, above all, of God.

*k:* Is 7:14 LXX. *l:* Lk 2:7. *m:* Nm 24:17. *n:* Mi 5:1; 2 Sm 5:2. *o:* Ps 72:10–11, 15; Is 60:6. *p:* Hos 11:1.

*The Massacre of the Infants.* [16]When
Herod realized that he had been deceived by
the magi, he became furious. He ordered the
massacre of all the boys in Bethlehem and
its vicinity two years old and under, in accordance with the time he had ascertained
from the magi. [17]Then was fulfilled what
had been said through Jeremiah the prophet:

[18]* [q] "A voice was heard in Ramah,
sobbing and loud lamentation;
Rachel weeping for her children,
and she would not be consoled,
since they were no more."

*The Return from Egypt.* [19]When Herod
had died, behold, the angel of the Lord appeared in a dream to Joseph in Egypt [20]and
said,[r] "Rise, take the child and his mother
and go to the land of Israel, for those who
sought the child's life are dead."* [21]He rose,
took the child and his mother, and went to
the land of Israel. [22]But when he heard that
Archelaus was ruling over Judea in place of
his father Herod,* he was afraid to go back
there. And because he had been warned in a
dream, he departed for the region of Galilee.
[23]* [s] He went and dwelt in a town called Nazareth, so that what had been spoken through
the prophets might be fulfilled, "He shall be
called a Nazorean."

## II. The Proclamation of the Kingdom

### CHAPTER 3

See RG 280–81

*The Preaching of John the Baptist.** [t]
[1]In those days John the Baptist appeared,
preaching in the desert of Judea* [2][and] saying, "Repent,* for the kingdom of heaven is
at hand!"[u] [3]* It was of him that the prophet
Isaiah[v] had spoken when he said:

"A voice of one crying out in the desert,
'Prepare the way of the Lord,
make straight his paths.'"

[4]* [w] John wore clothing made of camel's hair
and had a leather belt around his waist. His

**2:18** Jer 31:15 portrays Rachel, wife of the patriarch Jacob, weeping for her children taken into exile at the time of the Assyrian invasion of the northern kingdom (722–21 B.C.). Bethlehem was traditionally identified with Ephrath, the place near which Rachel was buried (see Gn 35:19; 48:7), and the mourning of Rachel is here applied to her lost children of a later age. **Ramah**: about six miles north of Jerusalem. The lamentation of Rachel is so great as to be heard at a far distance.

**2:20 For those who sought the child's life are dead**: Moses, who had fled from Egypt because the Pharaoh sought to kill him (see Ex 2:15), was told to return there, "for all the men who sought your life are dead" (Ex 4:19).

**2:22** With the agreement of the emperor Augustus, Archelaus received half of his father's kingdom, including Judea, after Herod's death. He had the title "ethnarch" (i.e., "ruler of a nation") and reigned from 4 B.C. to A.D. 6.

**2:23 Nazareth . . . he shall be called a Nazorean**: the tradition of Jesus' residence in Nazareth was firmly established, and Matthew sees it as being in accordance with the foreannounced plan of God. The town of Nazareth is not mentioned in the Old Testament, and no such prophecy can be found there. The vague expression "through the prophets" may be due to Matthew's seeing a connection between Nazareth and certain texts in which there are words with a remote similarity to the name of that town. Some such Old Testament texts are Is 11:1 where the Davidic king of the future is called "a bud" (*nēṣer*) that shall blossom from the roots of Jesse, and Jgs 13:5, 7 where Samson, the future deliverer of Israel from the Philistines, is called one who shall be consecrated (a *nāzîr*) to God.

**3:1–12** Here Matthew takes up the order of Jesus' ministry found in the gospel of Mark, beginning with the preparatory preaching of John the Baptist.

**3:1** Unlike Luke, Matthew says nothing of the Baptist's origins and does not make him a relative of Jesus. **The desert of Judea**: the barren region west of the Dead Sea extending up the Jordan valley.

**3:2 Repent**: the Baptist calls for a change of heart and conduct, a turning of one's life from rebellion to obedience towards God. **The kingdom of heaven is at hand**: "heaven" (lit., "the heavens") is a substitute for the name "God" that was avoided by devout Jews of the time out of reverence. The expression "the kingdom of heaven" occurs only in the gospel of Matthew. It means the effective rule of God over his people. In its fullness it includes not only human obedience to God's word, but the triumph of God over physical evils, supremely over death. In the expectation found in Jewish apocalyptic, the kingdom was to be ushered in by a judgment in which sinners would be condemned and perish, an expectation shared by the Baptist. This was modified in Christian understanding where the kingdom was seen as being established in stages, culminating with the parousia of Jesus.

**3:3** See note on Jn 1:23.

**3:4** The clothing of John recalls the austere dress of the prophet Elijah (2 Kgs 1:8). The expectation of the return of Elijah from heaven to prepare Israel for the final manifestation of God's kingdom was widespread, and according to Matthew this expectation was fulfilled in the Baptist's ministry (Mt 11:14; 17:11–13).

---

*q:* Jer 31:15. *r:* Ex 4:19. *s:* 13:54; Mk 1:9; Lk 2:39; 4:34; Jn 19:19. *t:* Mk 1:2–8; Lk 3:2–17. *u:* 4:17; 10:7. *v:* Is 40:3. *w:* 11:7–8; 2 Kgs 1:8; Zec 13:4.

food was locusts and wild honey. [5]At that
time Jerusalem, all Judea, and the whole region around the Jordan were going out to him
[6]and were being baptized by him in the Jordan River as they acknowledged their sins.*
[7]When he saw many of the Pharisees and
Sadducees* coming to his baptism, he said to
them, "You brood of vipers! Who warned you
to flee from the coming wrath?[x] [8]Produce
good fruit as evidence of your repentance.
[9]And do not presume to say to yourselves,
'We have Abraham as our father.' For I tell
you, God can raise up children to Abraham
from these stones.[y] [10]Even now the ax lies at
the root of the trees. Therefore every tree that
does not bear good fruit will be cut down and
thrown into the fire. [11][z] I am baptizing you
with water, for repentance, but the one who is
coming after me is mightier than I. I am not
worthy to carry his sandals. He will baptize
you with the holy Spirit and fire.* [12]* [a] His
winnowing fan is in his hand. He will clear
his threshing floor and gather his wheat into
his barn, but the chaff he will burn with unquenchable fire."

***The Baptism of Jesus.**** [13][b] Then Jesus
came from Galilee to John at the Jordan to
be baptized by him. [14]* John tried to prevent
him, saying, "I need to be baptized by you,
and yet you are coming to me?" [15]Jesus said
to him in reply, "Allow it now, for thus it is
fitting for us to fulfill all righteousness."
Then he allowed him. [16]* [c] After Jesus was
baptized, he came up from the water and behold, the heavens were opened [for him],
and he saw the Spirit of God descending like
a dove [and] coming upon him. [17]And a
voice came from the heavens, saying, "This
is my beloved Son,* with whom I am well
pleased."[d]

## CHAPTER 4

See RG 280-81

***The Temptation of Jesus.*** [1]* [e] Then
Jesus was led by the Spirit into the desert to

**3:6** Ritual washing was practiced by various groups in Palestine between 150 B.C. and A.D. 250. John's baptism may have been related to the purificatory washings of the Essenes at Qumran.

**3:7 Pharisees and Sadducees**: the former were marked by devotion to the law, written and oral, and the scribes, experts in the law, belonged predominantly to this group. The Sadducees were the priestly aristocratic party, centered in Jerusalem. They accepted as scripture only the first five books of the Old Testament, followed only the letter of the law, rejected the oral legal traditions, and were opposed to teachings not found in the Pentateuch, such as the resurrection of the dead. Matthew links both of these groups together as enemies of Jesus (Mt 16:1, 6, 11, 12; cf. Mk 8:11–13, 15). The threatening words that follow are addressed to them rather than to "the crowds" as in Lk 3:7. **The coming wrath**: the judgment that will bring about the destruction of unrepentant sinners.

**3:11 Baptize you with the holy Spirit and fire**: the water baptism of John will be followed by an "immersion" of the repentant in the cleansing power of the Spirit of God, and of the unrepentant in the destroying power of God's judgment. However, some see **the holy Spirit** and **fire** as synonymous, and the effect of this "baptism" as either purification or destruction. See note on Lk 3:16.

**3:12** The discrimination between the good and the bad is compared to the procedure by which a farmer separates wheat and chaff. The **winnowing fan** was a forklike shovel with which the threshed wheat was thrown into the air. The kernels fell to the ground; the light chaff, blown off by the wind, was gathered and burned up.

**3:13–17** The baptism of Jesus is the occasion on which he is equipped for his ministry by the holy Spirit and proclaimed to be the Son of God.

**3:14–15** This dialogue, peculiar to Matthew, reveals John's awareness of Jesus' superiority to him as the mightier one who is coming and who will baptize with the holy Spirit (Mt 3:11). His reluctance to admit Jesus among the sinners whom he is baptizing with water is overcome by Jesus' response. **To fulfill all righteousness**: in this gospel to **fulfill** usually refers to fulfillment of prophecy, and **righteousness** to moral conduct in conformity with God's will. Here, however, as in Mt 5:6; 6:33, **righteousness** seems to mean the saving activity of God. **To fulfill all righteousness** is to submit to the plan of God for the salvation of the human race. This involves Jesus' identification with sinners; hence the propriety of his accepting John's baptism.

**3:16 The Spirit . . . coming upon him**: cf. Is 42:1.

**3:17 This is my beloved Son**: the Marcan address to Jesus (Mk 1:11) is changed into a proclamation. The Father's voice speaks in terms that reflect Is 42:1; Ps 2:7; Gn 22:2.

**4:1–11** Jesus, proclaimed Son of God at his baptism, is subjected to a triple temptation. Obedience to the Father is a characteristic of true sonship, and Jesus is tempted by the devil to rebel against God, overtly in the third case, more subtly in the first two. Each refusal of Jesus is expressed in language taken from the Book of Deuteronomy (Dt 8:3; 6:13, 16). The testings of Jesus resemble those of Israel during the wandering in the desert and later in Canaan, and the victory of Jesus, the true Israel and the true Son, contrasts with the failure of the ancient and disobedient "son," the old Israel. In the temptation account Matthew is almost identical with Luke; both seem to have drawn upon the same source.

---

*x:* 12:34; 23:33; Is 59:5. *y:* Jn 8:33, 39; Rom 9:7–8; Gal 4:21–31. *z:* Jn 1:26–27, 33; Acts 1:5. *a:* 13:30; Is 41:16; Jer 15:7. *b:* Mk 1:9–11; Lk 3:21–22; Jn 1:31–34. *c:* Is 42:1. *d:* 12:18; 17:5; Gn 22:2; Ps 2:7; Is 42:1. *e:* Mk 1:12–13; Lk 4:1–13.

be tempted by the devil. 2[f] He fasted for
forty days and forty nights,* and afterwards
he was hungry. 3 The tempter approached
and said to him, "If you are the Son of God,
command that these stones become loaves
of bread." 4* He said in reply, "It is written:[g]

'One does not live by bread alone,
but by every word that comes forth
from the mouth of God.' "

5* Then the devil took him to the holy city,
and made him stand on the parapet of the
temple, 6 and said to him, "If you are the Son
of God, throw yourself down. For it is written:

'He will command his angels concerning
you'
and 'with their hands they will support
you,
lest you dash your foot against a
stone.' "[h]

7 Jesus answered him, "Again it is written,
'You shall not put the Lord, your God, to the
test.' "[i] 8 Then the devil took him up to a very
high mountain, and showed him all the kingdoms of the world in their magnificence,
9 and he said to him, "All these I shall give to
you, if you will prostrate yourself and worship me."* 10 At this, Jesus said to him, "Get
away, Satan! It is written:

'The Lord, your God, shall you worship
and him alone shall you serve.' "[j]

11 Then the devil left him and, behold, angels
came and ministered to him.

*The Beginning of the Galilean Ministry.**
12[k] When he heard that John had been arrested, he withdrew to Galilee. 13 He left
Nazareth and went to live in Capernaum by
the sea, in the region of Zebulun and Naphtali,[l] 14 that what had been said through Isaiah the prophet might be fulfilled:

15 "Land of Zebulun and land of Naphtali,[m]
the way to the sea, beyond the Jordan,
Galilee of the Gentiles,
16 the people who sit in darkness
have seen a great light,
on those dwelling in a land
overshadowed by death
light has arisen."[n]

17* From that time on, Jesus began to preach
and say,[o] "Repent, for the kingdom of
heaven is at hand."

*The Call of the First Disciples.** 18[p] As he
was walking by the Sea of Galilee, he saw
two brothers, Simon who is called Peter, and
his brother Andrew, casting a net into the
sea; they were fishermen. 19 He said to them,
"Come after me, and I will make you fishers
of men." 20* At once they left their nets and
followed him. 21 He walked along from there
and saw two other brothers, James, the son
of Zebedee, and his brother John. They were
in a boat, with their father Zebedee, mending
their nets. He called them, 22 and immedi-

**4:2 Forty days and forty nights**: the same time as that during which Moses remained on Sinai (Ex 24:18). The time reference, however, seems primarily intended to recall the forty years during which Israel was tempted in the desert (Dt 8:2).

**4:4** Cf. Dt 8:3. Jesus refuses to use his power for his own benefit and accepts whatever God wills.

**4:5–7** The devil supports his proposal by an appeal to the scriptures, Ps 91:11a, 12. Unlike Israel (Dt 6:16), Jesus refuses to "test" God by demanding from him an extraordinary show of power.

**4:9** The worship of Satan to which Jesus is tempted is probably intended to recall Israel's worship of false gods. His refusal is expressed in the words of Dt 6:13.

**4:12–17** Isaiah's prophecy of the light rising upon Zebulun and Naphtali (Is 8:22–9:1) is fulfilled in Jesus' residence at Capernaum. The territory of these two tribes was the first to be devastated (733–32 B.C.) at the time of the Assyrian invasion. In order to accommodate Jesus' move to Capernaum to the prophecy, Matthew speaks of that town as being "in the region of Zebulun and Naphtali" (Mt 4:13), whereas it was only in the territory of the latter, and he understands the sea of the prophecy, the Mediterranean, as the sea of Galilee.

**4:17** At the beginning of his preaching Jesus takes up the words of John the Baptist (Mt 3:2) although with a different meaning; in his ministry the kingdom of heaven has already begun to be present (Mt 12:28).

**4:18–22** The call of the first disciples promises them a share in Jesus' work and entails abandonment of family and former way of life. Three of the four, Simon, James, and John, are distinguished among the disciples by a closer relation with Jesus (Mt 17:1; 26:37).

**4:20** Here and in Mt 4:22, as in Mark (Mk 1:16–20) and unlike the Lucan account (Lk 5:1–11), the disciples' response is motivated only by Jesus' invitation, an element that emphasizes his mysterious power.

*f:* Ex 24:18; Dt 8:2. *g:* Dt 8:3. *h:* Ps 91:11–12. *i:* Dt 6:16. *j:* 16:23; Dt 6:13. *k:* Mk 1:14–15; Lk 4:14, 31. *l:* Jn 2:12. *m:* Is 8:23 LXX; 9:1. *n:* Lk 1:79. *o:* 3:2. *p:* Mk 1:16–20; Lk 5:1–11.

ately they left their boat and their father and
followed him.
*Ministering to a Great Multitude.** 23 He
went around all of Galilee, teaching in their
synagogues,* proclaiming the gospel of the
kingdom, and curing every disease and illness among the people.[q] 24* His fame spread
to all of Syria, and they brought to him all
who were sick with various diseases and
racked with pain, those who were possessed,
lunatics, and paralytics, and he cured them.
25[r] And great crowds from Galilee, the Decapolis,* Jerusalem, and Judea, and from beyond the Jordan followed him.

See RG 281–82

## CHAPTER 5

*The Sermon on the Mount.* 1* When
he saw the crowds,* he went up the mountain, and after he had sat down, his disciples
came to him. 2 He began to teach them, saying:

### The Beatitudes*

3 "Blessed are the poor in spirit,*
for theirs is the kingdom of heaven.[s]
4 * Blessed are they who mourn,[t]
for they will be comforted.
5 * Blessed are the meek,[u]
for they will inherit the land.
6 Blessed are they who hunger and thirst
for righteousness,*
for they will be satisfied.
7 Blessed are the merciful,
for they will be shown mercy.[v]
8 * Blessed are the clean of heart,[w]
for they will see God.
9 Blessed are the peacemakers,
for they will be called children of God.
10 Blessed are they who are persecuted for
the sake of righteousness,*
for theirs is the kingdom of heaven.[x]
11 Blessed are you when they insult you and

**4:23–25** This summary of Jesus' ministry concludes the narrative part of the first book of Matthew's gospel (Mt 3–4). The activities of his ministry are teaching, proclaiming the gospel, and healing; cf. Mt 9:35.

**4:23 Their synagogues**: Matthew usually designates the Jewish synagogues as **their synagogue(s)** (Mt 9:35; 10:17; 12:9; 13:54) or, in address to Jews, **your synagogues** (Mt 23:34), an indication that he wrote after the break between church and synagogue.

**4:24 Syria**: the Roman province to which Palestine belonged.

**4:25 The Decapolis**: a federation of Greek cities in Palestine, originally ten in number, all but one east of the Jordan.

**5:1–7:29** The first of the five discourses that are a central part of the structure of this gospel. It is the discourse section of the first book and contains sayings of Jesus derived from Q and from M. The Lucan parallel is in that gospel's "Sermon on the Plain" (Lk 6:20–49), although some of the sayings in Matthew's "Sermon on the Mount" have their parallels in other parts of Luke. The careful topical arrangement of the sermon is probably not due only to Matthew's editing; he seems to have had a structured discourse of Jesus as one of his sources. The form of that source may have been as follows: four beatitudes (Mt 5:3–4, 6, 11–12), a section on the new righteousness with illustrations (Mt 5:17, 20–24, 27–28, 33–48), a section on good works (Mt 6:1–6, 16–18), and three warnings (Mt 7:1–2, 15–21, 24–27).

**5:1–2** Unlike Luke's sermon, this is addressed not only to the disciples but to the crowds (see Mt 7:28).

**5:3–12** The form **Blessed are (is)** occurs frequently in the Old Testament in the Wisdom literature and in the psalms. Although modified by Matthew, the first, second, fourth, and ninth beatitudes have Lucan parallels (Mt 5:3 // Lk 6:20; Mt 5:4 // Lk 6:21b; Mt 5:6 // Lk 6:21a; Mt 5:11–12 // Lk 5:22–23). The others were added by the evangelist and are probably his own composition. A few manuscripts, Western and Alexandrian, and many versions and patristic quotations give the second and third beatitudes in inverted order.

**5:3 The poor in spirit**: in the Old Testament, the poor (*'ănāwîm*) are those who are without material possessions and whose confidence is in God (see Is 61:1; Zep 2:3; in the NAB the word is translated **lowly** and **humble**, respectively, in those texts). Matthew added **in spirit** in order either to indicate that only the devout poor were meant or to extend the beatitude to all, of whatever social rank, who recognized their complete dependence on God. The same phrase **poor in spirit** is found in the Qumran literature (1QM 14:7).

**5:4** Cf. Is 61:2, "(The Lord has sent me) . . . to comfort all who mourn." **They will be comforted**: here the passive is a "theological passive" equivalent to the active "God will comfort them"; so also in Mt 5:6, 7.

**5:5** Cf. Ps 37:11, ". . . the meek shall possess the land." In the psalm "the land" means the land of Palestine; here it means the kingdom.

**5:6 For righteousness**: a Matthean addition. For the meaning of **righteousness** here, see note on Mt 3:14–15.

**5:8** Cf. Ps 24:4. Only one "pure of heart" can take part in the temple worship. To be with God in the temple is described in Ps 42:3 as "see[ing] the face of God," but here the promise to **the clean of heart** is that they will **see God** not in the temple but in the coming kingdom.

**5:10 Righteousness** here, as usually in Matthew, means conduct in conformity with God's will.

*q:* 9:35; Mk 1:39; Lk 4:15, 44. *r:* Mk 3:7–8; Lk 6:17–19. *s:* Lk 6:20–23. *t:* Is 61:2–3; Rev 21:4. *u:* Gn 13:15; Ps 37:11. *v:* 18:33; Jas 2:13. *w:* Ps 24:4–5; 73:1. *x:* 1 Pt 2:20; 3:14; 4:14. *y:* 10:22; Acts 5:41.

persecute you and utter every kind of evil against you [falsely] because of me.[y] 12* Rejoice and be glad, for your reward will be great in heaven.[z] Thus they persecuted the prophets who were before you.

***The Similes of Salt and Light.**** 13a "You are the salt of the earth. But if salt loses its taste, with what can it be seasoned? It is no longer good for anything but to be thrown out and trampled underfoot.* 14 You are the light of the world. A city set on a mountain cannot be hidden.[b] 15 Nor do they light a lamp and then put it under a bushel basket; it is set on a lampstand, where it gives light to all in the house.[c] 16 Just so, your light must shine before others, that they may see your good deeds and glorify your heavenly Father.[d]

***Teaching About the Law.*** 17* "Do not think that I have come to abolish the law or the prophets. I have come not to abolish but to fulfill. 18 Amen, I say to you, until heaven and earth pass away, not the smallest letter or the smallest part of a letter will pass from the law, until all things have taken place.[e] 19 Therefore, whoever breaks one of the least of these commandments and teaches others to do so will be called least in the kingdom of heaven. But whoever obeys and teaches these commandments will be called greatest in the kingdom of heaven.* 20 I tell you, unless your righteousness surpasses that of the scribes and Pharisees, you will not enter into the kingdom of heaven.

***Teaching About Anger.**** 21 "You have heard that it was said to your ancestors,[f] 'You shall not kill; and whoever kills will be liable to judgment.'* 22* But I say to you, whoever is angry* with his brother will be liable to judgment,[g] and whoever says to his brother, 'Raqa,' will be answerable to the Sanhedrin, and whoever says, 'You fool,' will be liable to

**5:12 The prophets who were before you**: the disciples of Jesus stand in the line of the persecuted prophets of Israel. Some would see the expression as indicating also that Matthew considered all Christian disciples as prophets.

**5:13–16** By their deeds the disciples are to influence the world for good. They can no more escape notice than **a city set on a mountain**. If they fail in good works, they are as useless as flavorless salt or as a lamp whose light is concealed.

**5:13** The unusual supposition of salt losing its flavor has led some to suppose that the saying refers to the salt of the Dead Sea that, because chemically impure, could lose its taste.

**5:17–20** This statement of Jesus' position concerning the Mosaic law is composed of traditional material from Matthew's sermon documentation (see note on Mt 5:1–7:29), other Q material (cf. Mt 18; Lk 16:17), and the evangelist's own editorial touches. **To fulfill** the law appears at first to mean a literal enforcement of the law in the least detail: **until heaven and earth pass away** nothing of the law **will pass** (Mt 5:18). Yet the "passing away" of heaven and earth is not necessarily the end of the world understood, as in much apocalyptic literature, as the dissolution of the existing universe. The "turning of the ages" comes with the apocalyptic event of Jesus' death and resurrection, and those to whom this gospel is addressed are living in the new and final age, prophesied by Isaiah as the time of "new heavens and a new earth" (Is 65:17; 66:22). Meanwhile, during Jesus' ministry when the kingdom is already breaking in, his mission remains within the framework of the law, though with significant anticipation of the age to come, as the following antitheses (Mt 5:21–48) show.

**5:19** Probably **these commandments** means those of the Mosaic law. But this is an interim ethic "until heaven and earth pass away."

**5:21–48** Six examples of the conduct demanded of the Christian disciple. Each deals with a commandment of the law, introduced by **You have heard that it was said to your ancestors** or an equivalent formula, followed by Jesus' teaching in respect to that commandment, **But I say to you**; thus their designation as "antitheses." Three of them accept the Mosaic law but extend or deepen it (Mt 5:21–22; 27–28; 43–44); three reject it as a standard of conduct for the disciples (Mt 5:31–32; 33–37; 38–39).

**5:21** Cf. Ex 20:13; Dt 5:17. The second part of the verse is not an exact quotation from the Old Testament, but cf. Ex 21:12.

**5:22–26** Reconciliation with an offended brother is urged in the admonition of Mt 5:23–24 and the parable of Mt 5:25–26 (// Lk 12:58–59). The severity of the judge in the parable is a warning of the fate of unrepentant sinners in the coming judgment by God.

**5:22** Anger is the motive behind murder, as the insulting epithets are steps that may lead to it. They, as well as the deed, are all forbidden. **Raqa**: an Aramaic word *rēqāʾ* or *rēqâ* probably meaning "imbecile," "blockhead," a term of abuse. The ascending order of punishment, **judgment** (by a local council?), trial before **the Sanhedrin**, condemnation to **Gehenna**, points to a higher degree of seriousness in each of the offenses. **Sanhedrin**: the highest judicial body of Judaism. **Gehenna**: in Hebrew *gê-hinnōm*, "Valley of Hinnom," or *gê ben-hinnōm*, "Valley of the son of Hinnom," southwest of Jerusalem, the center of an idolatrous cult during the monarchy in which children were offered in sacrifice (see 2 Kgs 23:10; Jer 7:31). In Jos 18:16 (Septuagint, Codex Vaticanus) the Hebrew is transliterated into Greek as *gaienna*, which appears in the New Testament as *geenna*. The concept of punishment of sinners by fire either after death or after the final judgment is found in Jewish apocalyptic literature (e.g., Enoch 90:26) but the name *geenna* is first given to the place of punishment in the New Testament.

*z:* 2 Chr 36:16; Heb 11:32–38; Jas 5:10. *a:* Mk 9:50; Lk 14:34–35. *b:* Jn 8:12. *c:* Mk 4:21; Lk 8:16; 11:33. *d:* Jn 3:21. *e:* Lk 16:17. *f:* Ex 20:13; Dt 5:17. *g:* Jas 1:19–20.

fiery Gehenna. [23]Therefore, if you bring your gift to the altar, and there recall that your brother has anything against you,[h] [24]leave your gift there at the altar, go first and be reconciled with your brother, and then come and offer your gift. [25]Settle with your opponent quickly while on the way to court with him.[i] Otherwise your opponent will hand you over to the judge, and the judge will hand you over to the guard, and you will be thrown into prison. [26]Amen, I say to you, you will not be released until you have paid the last penny.

*Teaching About Adultery.* [27*] "You have heard that it was said,[j] 'You shall not commit adultery.' [28]But I say to you, everyone who looks at a woman with lust has already committed adultery with her in his heart. [29*] If your right eye causes you to sin, tear it out and throw it away.[k] It is better for you to lose one of your members than to have your whole body thrown into Gehenna. [30]And if your right hand causes you to sin, cut it off and throw it away. It is better for you to lose one of your members than to have your whole body go into Gehenna.

*Teaching About Divorce.* [31*] "It was also said, 'Whoever divorces his wife must give her a bill of divorce.'[l] [32]But I say to you, whoever divorces his wife (unless the marriage is unlawful) causes her to commit adultery, and whoever marries a divorced woman commits adultery.[m]

*Teaching About Oaths.* [33*] [n] "Again you have heard that it was said to your ancestors, 'Do not take a false oath, but make good to the Lord all that you vow.' [34][o] But I say to you, do not swear at all;* not by heaven, for it is God's throne; [35]nor by the earth, for it is his footstool; nor by Jerusalem, for it is the city of the great King. [36]Do not swear by your head, for you cannot make a single hair white or black. [37*] Let your 'Yes' mean 'Yes,' and your 'No' mean 'No.' Anything more is from the evil one.

*Teaching About Retaliation.* [38*] "You have heard that it was said,[p] 'An eye for an eye and a tooth for a tooth.' [39][q] But I say to you, offer no resistance to one who is evil. When someone strikes you on [your] right cheek, turn the other one to him as well. [40]If anyone wants to go to law with you over your tunic, hand him your cloak as well. [41]Should anyone press you into service for one mile,* go with him for two miles.[r] [42]Give to the one who asks of you, and do not turn your back on one who wants to borrow.[s]

**5:27** See Ex 20:14; Dt 5:18.

**5:29–30** No sacrifice is too great to avoid total destruction in **Gehenna**.

**5:31–32** See Dt 24:1–5. The Old Testament commandment that a bill of divorce be given to the woman assumes the legitimacy of divorce itself. It is this that Jesus denies. **(Unless the marriage is unlawful)**: this "exceptive clause," as it is often called, occurs also in Mt 19:9, where the Greek is slightly different. There are other sayings of Jesus about divorce that prohibit it absolutely (see Mk 10:11–12; Lk 16:18; cf. 1 Cor 7:10, 11b), and most scholars agree that they represent the stand of Jesus. Matthew's "exceptive clauses" are understood by some as a modification of the absolute prohibition. It seems, however, that the unlawfulness that Matthew gives as a reason why a marriage must be broken refers to a situation peculiar to his community: the violation of Mosaic law forbidding marriage between persons of certain blood and/or legal relationship (Lv 18:6–18). Marriages of that sort were regarded as incest (*porneia*), but some rabbis allowed Gentile converts to Judaism who had contracted such marriages to remain in them. Matthew's "exceptive clause" is against such permissiveness for Gentile converts to Christianity; cf. the similar prohibition of *porneia* in Acts 15:20, 29. In this interpretation, the clause constitutes no exception to the absolute prohibition of divorce when the marriage is lawful.

**5:33** This is not an exact quotation of any Old Testament text, but see Ex 20:7; Dt 5:11; Lv 19:12. The purpose of an oath was to guarantee truthfulness by one's calling on God as witness.

**5:34–36** The use of these oath formularies that avoid the divine name is in fact equivalent to swearing by it, for all the things sworn by are related to God.

**5:37 Let your 'Yes' mean 'Yes,' and your 'No' mean 'No'**: literally, "let your speech be 'Yes, yes,' 'No, no.'" Some have understood this as a milder form of oath, permitted by Jesus. In view of Mt 5:34, "Do not swear at all," that is unlikely. **From the evil one**: i.e., from the devil. Oath-taking presupposes a sinful weakness of the human race, namely, the tendency to lie. Jesus demands of his disciples a truthfulness that makes oaths unnecessary.

**5:38–42** See Lv 24:20. The Old Testament commandment was meant to moderate vengeance; the punishment should not exceed the injury done. Jesus forbids even this proportionate retaliation. Of the five examples that follow, only the first deals directly with retaliation for evil; the others speak of liberality.

**5:41** Roman garrisons in Palestine had the right to requisition the property and services of the native population.

*h:* Mk 11:25. *i:* 18:34–35; Lk 12:58–59. *j:* Ex 20:14; Dt 5:18. *k:* 18:8–9; Mk 9:43–47. *l:* 19:3–9; Dt 24:1. *m:* Lk 16:18; 1 Cor 7:10–11. *n:* Lv 19:12; Nm 30:3. *o:* Ps 48:3; Sir 23:9; Is 66:1; Jas 5:12. *p:* Ex 21:24; Lv 24:19–20. *q:* Lk 6:29–30. *r:* Lam 3:30. *s:* Dt 15:7–8.

*Love of Enemies.** [t] 43 “You have heard that it was said, ‘You shall love your neighbor and hate your enemy.’[u] 44 But I say to you, love your enemies, and pray for those who persecute you, 45 that you may be children of your heavenly Father, for he makes his sun rise on the bad and the good, and causes rain to fall on the just and the unjust. 46 For if you love those who love you, what recompense will you have? Do not the tax collectors* do the same? 47 And if you greet your brothers only, what is unusual about that? Do not the pagans do the same?* 48 So be perfect,* just as your heavenly Father is perfect.[v]

## CHAPTER 6

See RG 281–82

*Teaching About Almsgiving.** 1 “[But] take care not to perform righteous deeds in order that people may see them;[w] otherwise, you will have no recompense from your heavenly Father. 2 When you give alms, do not blow a trumpet before you, as the hypocrites* do in the synagogues and in the streets to win the praise of others. Amen, I say to you, they have received their reward.[x] 3 But when you give alms, do not let your left hand know what your right is doing, 4 so that your almsgiving may be secret. And your Father who sees in secret will repay you.

*Teaching about Prayer.* 5 “When you pray, do not be like the hypocrites, who love to stand and pray in the synagogues and on street corners so that others may see them. Amen, I say to you, they have received their reward. 6 But when you pray, go to your inner room, close the door, and pray to your Father in secret. And your Father who sees in secret will repay you. 7* In praying, do not babble like the pagans, who think that they will be heard because of their many words.* 8 Do not be like them. Your Father knows what you need before you ask him.

*The Lord's Prayer.* 9* “This is how you are to pray:[y]

Our Father in heaven,*
hallowed be your name,

**5:43–48** See Lv 19:18. There is no Old Testament commandment demanding hatred of one's enemy, but the “neighbor” of the love commandment was understood as one's fellow countryman. Both in the Old Testament (Ps 139:19–22) and at Qumran (1QS 9:21) hatred of evil persons is assumed to be right. Jesus extends the love commandment to the enemy and the persecutor. His disciples, as children of God, must imitate the example of their Father, who grants his gifts of sun and rain to both the good and the bad.

**5:46 Tax collectors**: Jews who were engaged in the collection of indirect taxes such as tolls and customs. See note on Mk 2:14.

**5:47** Jesus' disciples must not be content with merely usual standards of conduct; see Mt 5:20 where the verb “surpass” (Greek *perisseuō*) is cognate with the **unusual** (*perisson*) of this verse.

**5:48 Perfect**: in the gospels this word occurs only in Matthew, here and in Mt 19:21. The Lucan parallel (Lk 6:36) demands that the disciples be **merciful**.

**6:1–18** The sermon continues with a warning against doing good in order to be seen and gives three examples, almsgiving (Mt 6:2–4), prayer (Mt 6:5–15), and fasting (Mt 6:16–18). In each, the conduct of the hypocrites (Mt 6:2) is contrasted with that demanded of the disciples. The sayings about reward found here and elsewhere (Mt 5:12, 46; 10:41–42) show that this is a genuine element of Christian moral exhortation. Possibly to underline the difference between the Christian idea of reward and that of the hypocrites, the evangelist uses two different Greek verbs to express the rewarding of the disciples and that of the hypocrites; in the latter case it is the verb *apechō*, a commercial term for giving a receipt for what has been paid in full (Mt 6:2, 5, 16).

**6:2 The hypocrites**: the scribes and Pharisees, see Mt 23:13, 15, 23, 25, 27, 29. The designation reflects an attitude resulting not only from the controversies at the time of Jesus' ministry but from the opposition between Pharisaic Judaism and the church of Matthew. **They have received their reward**: they desire praise and have received what they were looking for.

**6:7–15** Matthew inserts into his basic traditional material an expansion of the material on prayer that includes the model prayer, the “Our Father.” That prayer is found in Lk 11:2–4 in a different context and in a different form.

**6:7** The example of what Christian prayer should be like contrasts it now not with the prayer of the hypocrites but with that of **the pagans**. Their babbling probably means their reciting a long list of divine names, hoping that one of them will force a response from the deity.

**6:9–13** Matthew's form of the “Our Father” follows the liturgical tradition of his church. Luke's less developed form also represents the liturgical tradition known to him, but it is probably closer than Matthew's to the original words of Jesus.

**6:9 Our Father in heaven**: this invocation is found in many rabbinic prayers of the post-New Testament period. **Hallowed be your name**: though the “hallowing” of the divine name could be understood as reverence done to God by human praise and by obedience to his will, this is more probably a petition that God hallow his own name, i.e., that he manifest his glory by an act of power (cf. Ez 36:23), in this case, by the establishment of his kingdom in its fullness.

*t:* Lk 6:27, 32–36. *u:* Lv 19:18. *v:* Lv 11:44; 19:2; Dt 18:13; Jas 1:4; 1 Pt 1:16; 1 Jn 3:3. *w:* 23:5. *x:* Jn 12:43. *y:* Lk 11:2–4.

10 your kingdom come,*
your will be done,
on earth as in heaven.[z]
11 * [a] Give us today our daily bread;
12 and forgive us our debts,*
as we forgive our debtors;[b]
13 and do not subject us to the final test,*
but deliver us from the evil one.[c]

14* If you forgive others their transgressions,
your heavenly Father will forgive you.[d]
15 But if you do not forgive others, neither
will your Father forgive your transgressions.[e]

*Teaching about Fasting.* 16 "When you
fast,* do not look gloomy like the hypocrites.
They neglect their appearance, so that they
may appear to others to be fasting. Amen, I
say to you, they have received their reward.
17 But when you fast, anoint your head and
wash your face, 18 so that you may not appear
to others to be fasting, except to your Father
who is hidden. And your Father who sees
what is hidden will repay you.

*Treasure in Heaven.* 19* "Do not store up
for yourselves treasures on earth, where
moth and decay destroy, and thieves break in
and steal.[f] 20 But store up treasures in heaven,
where neither moth nor decay destroys, nor
thieves break in and steal. 21 For where your
treasure is, there also will your heart be.[g]

*The Light of the Body.** 22 "The lamp of the
body is the eye. If your eye is sound, your
whole body will be filled with light; 23 but if
your eye is bad, your whole body will be in
darkness. And if the light in you is darkness,
how great will the darkness be.[h]

*God and Money.* 24* "No one can serve
two masters.[i] He will either hate one and
love the other, or be devoted to one and despise the other. You cannot serve God and
mammon.

*Dependence on God.** 25 [j] "Therefore I tell
you, do not worry about your life, what you
will eat [or drink], or about your body, what
you will wear. Is not life more than food and
the body more than clothing? 26 Look at the
birds in the sky; they do not sow or reap,
they gather nothing into barns, yet your
heavenly Father feeds them. Are not you
more important than they?[k] 27 Can any of you
by worrying add a single moment to your
life-span?* 28 Why are you anxious about
clothes? Learn from the way the wild flowers grow. They do not work or spin. 29 But I
tell you that not even Solomon in all his

**6:10 Your kingdom come**: this petition sets the tone of the prayer, and inclines the balance toward divine rather than human action in the petitions that immediately precede and follow it. **Your will be done, on earth as in heaven**: a petition that the divine purpose to establish the kingdom, a purpose present now **in heaven**, be executed **on earth**.

**6:11 Give us today our daily bread**: the rare Greek word *epiousios*, here **daily**, occurs in the New Testament only here and in Lk 11:3. A single occurrence of the word outside of these texts and of literature dependent on them has been claimed, but the claim is highly doubtful. The word may mean **daily** or "future" (other meanings have also been proposed). The latter would conform better to the eschatological tone of the whole prayer. So understood, the petition would be for a speedy coming of the kingdom (**today**), which is often portrayed in both the Old Testament and the New under the image of a feast (Is 25:6; Mt 8:11; 22:1–10; Lk 13:29; 14:15–24).

**6:12 Forgive us our debts**: the word **debts** is used metaphorically of sins, "debts" owed to God (see Lk 11:4). The request is probably for forgiveness at the final judgment.

**6:13** Jewish apocalyptic writings speak of a period of severe trial before the end of the age, sometimes called the "messianic woes." This petition asks that the disciples be spared that **final test**.

**6:14–15** These verses reflect a set pattern called "Principles of Holy Law." Human action now will be met by a corresponding action of God at the final judgment.

**6:16** The only fast prescribed in the Mosaic law was that of the Day of Atonement (Lv 16:31), but the practice of regular fasting was common in later Judaism; cf. *Didache* 9:1.

**6:19–34** The remaining material of this chapter is taken almost entirely from Q. It deals principally with worldly possessions, and the controlling thought is summed up in Mt 6:24: the disciple can serve only one master and must choose between God and wealth (**mammon**). See further the note on Lk 16:9.

**6:22–23** In this context the parable probably points to the need for the disciple to be enlightened by Jesus' teaching on the transitory nature of earthly riches.

**6:24 Mammon**: an Aramaic word meaning wealth or property.

**6:25–34** Jesus does not deny the reality of human needs (Mt 6:32), but forbids making them the object of anxious care and, in effect, becoming their slave.

**6:27 Life-span**: the Greek word can also mean "stature." If it is taken in that sense, the word here translated **moment** (literally, "cubit") must be translated literally as a unit not of time but of spatial measure. The cubit is about eighteen inches.

*z:* 26:42. *a:* Prv 30:8–9. *b:* 18:21–22; Sir 28:2. *c:* Jn 17:15; 2 Thes 3:3. *d:* 18:35; Sir 28:1–5; Mk 11:25. *e:* Jas 2:13. *f:* Jas 5:2–3. *g:* Lk 12:33–34. *h:* Lk 11:34–36. *i:* Lk 16:13. *j:* Lk 12:22–31. *k:* Ps 145:15–16; 147:9.

splendor was clothed like one of them. [30*] If God so clothes the grass of the field, which grows today and is thrown into the oven tomorrow, will he not much more provide for you, O you of little faith? [31] So do not worry and say, 'What are we to eat?' or 'What are we to drink?' or 'What are we to wear?' [32] All these things the pagans seek. Your heavenly Father knows that you need them all. [33] But seek first the kingdom [of God] and his righteousness,* and all these things will be given you besides. [34] Do not worry about tomorrow; tomorrow will take care of itself. Sufficient for a day is its own evil.

See RG 281–82

## CHAPTER 7

***Judging Others.*** [1*] [l] "Stop judging,* that you may not be judged.[m] [2] For as you judge, so will you be judged, and the measure with which you measure will be measured out to you.[n] [3] Why do you notice the splinter in your brother's eye, but do not perceive the wooden beam in your own eye? [4] How can you say to your brother, 'Let me remove that splinter from your eye,' while the wooden beam is in your eye? [5] You hypocrite,* remove the wooden beam from your eye first; then you will see clearly to remove the splinter from your brother's eye.

***Pearls Before Swine.*** [6] "Do not give what is holy to dogs,* or throw your pearls before swine, lest they trample them underfoot, and turn and tear you to pieces.[o]

***The Answer to Prayers.*** [7] [p] "Ask and it will be given to you; seek and you will find; knock and the door will be opened to you.[q] [8] For everyone who asks, receives; and the one who seeks, finds; and to the one who knocks, the door will be opened.[r] [9] Which one of you would hand his son a stone when he asks for a loaf of bread,* [10] or a snake when he asks for a fish? [11] If you then, who are wicked, know how to give good gifts to your children, how much more will your heavenly Father give good things to those who ask him.[s]

***The Golden Rule.*** [12*] "Do to others whatever you would have them do to you.[t] This is the law and the prophets.

***The Narrow Gate.*** [13*] "Enter through the narrow gate;* for the gate is wide and the road broad that leads to destruction, and those who enter through it are many.[u] [14] How narrow the gate and constricted the road that leads to life. And those who find it are few.

***False Prophets.**** [15] "Beware of false prophets, who come to you in sheep's clothing, but underneath are ravenous wolves.[v] [16] [w] By their fruits you will know them. Do

**6:30 Of little faith**: except for the parallel in Lk 12:28, the word translated **of little faith** is found in the New Testament only in Matthew. It is used by him of those who are disciples of Jesus but whose faith in him is not as deep as it should be (see Mt 8:26; 14:31; 16:8 and the cognate noun in Mt 17:20).

**6:33 Righteousness**: see note on Mt 3:14–15.

**7:1–12** In Mt 7:1 Matthew returns to the basic traditional material of the sermon (Lk 6:37–38, 41–42). The governing thought is the correspondence between conduct toward one's fellows and God's conduct toward the one so acting.

**7:1** This is not a prohibition against recognizing the faults of others, which would be hardly compatible with Mt 7:5, 6 but against passing judgment in a spirit of arrogance, forgetful of one's own faults.

**7:5 Hypocrite**: the designation previously given to the scribes and Pharisees is here given to the Christian disciple who is concerned with the faults of another and ignores his own more serious offenses.

**7:6 Dogs** and **swine** were Jewish terms of contempt for Gentiles. This saying may originally have derived from a Jewish Christian community opposed to preaching the gospel (**what is holy, pearls**) to Gentiles. In the light of Mt 28:19 that can hardly be Matthew's meaning. He may have taken the saying as applying to a Christian dealing with an obstinately impenitent fellow Christian (Mt 18:17).

**7:9–10** There is a resemblance between a stone and a round loaf of bread and between a serpent and the scaleless fish called *barbut*.

**7:12** See Lk 6:31. This saying, known since the eighteenth century as the "Golden Rule," is found in both positive and negative form in pagan and Jewish sources, both earlier and later than the gospel. **This is the law and the prophets** is an addition probably due to the evangelist.

**7:13–28** The final section of the discourse is composed of a series of antitheses, contrasting two kinds of life within the Christian community, that of those who obey the words of Jesus and that of those who do not. Most of the sayings are from Q and are found also in Luke.

**7:13–14** The metaphor of the "two ways" was common in pagan philosophy and in the Old Testament. In Christian literature it is found also in the *Didache* (1–6) and the *Epistle of Barnabas* (18–20).

**7:15–20** Christian disciples who claimed to speak in the name of God are called **prophets** (Mt 7:15) in Mt 10:41; Mt 23:34. They were presumably an important group within the church of Matthew. As in the case of the Old Testament prophets, there were both true and false ones, and for Matthew the

*l:* Lk 6:37–38, 41–42. *m:* Rom 2:1–2; 1 Cor 4:5. *n:* Wis 12:22; Mk 4:24. *o:* Prv 23:9. *p:* Mk 11:24; Lk 11:9–13. *q:* 18:19. *r:* Lk 18:1–8; Jn 14:13. *s:* 1 Jn 5:14–15. *t:* Lk 6:31. *u:* Lk 13:24. *v:* 2 Pt 2:1. *w:* 12:33; Lk 6:43–44.

people pick grapes from thornbushes, or figs from thistles? 17 Just so, every good tree bears good fruit, and a rotten tree bears bad fruit. 18 A good tree cannot bear bad fruit, nor can a rotten tree bear good fruit. 19 Every tree that does not bear good fruit will be cut down and thrown into the fire. 20 So by their fruits you will know them.[x]

*The True Disciple.* 21 "Not everyone who says to me, 'Lord, Lord,' will enter the kingdom of heaven,* but only the one who does the will of my Father in heaven.[y] 22 Many will say to me on that day,[z] 'Lord, Lord, did we not prophesy in your name? Did we not drive out demons in your name? Did we not do mighty deeds in your name?'[a] 23 Then I will declare to them solemnly, 'I never knew you.* Depart from me, you evildoers.'[b]

*The Two Foundations.* 24* "Everyone who listens to these words of mine and acts on them will be like a wise man who built his house on rock.[c] 25 The rain fell, the floods came, and the winds blew and buffeted the house.[d] But it did not collapse; it had been set solidly on rock. 26 And everyone who listens to these words of mine but does not act on them will be like a fool who built his house on sand. 27 The rain fell, the floods came, and the winds blew and buffeted the house. And it collapsed and was completely ruined."

28* When Jesus finished these words, the crowds were astonished at his teaching, 29*[e] for he taught them as one having authority, and not as their scribes.

## III. Ministry and Mission in Galilee*

### CHAPTER 8

See RG 282-83

*The Cleansing of a Leper.* 1[f] When Jesus came down from the mountain, great crowds followed him. 2 And then a leper* approached, did him homage, and said, "Lord, if you wish, you can make me clean." 3 He stretched out his hand, touched him, and said, "I will do it. Be made clean." His leprosy was cleansed immediately. 4* Then Jesus said to him, "See that you tell no one, but go show yourself to the priest, and offer the gift that Moses prescribed;[g] that will be proof for them."

*The Healing of a Centurion's Servant.** 5[h] When he entered Capernaum,* a centurion

difference could be recognized by the quality of their deeds, the **fruits** (Mt 7:16). The mention of **fruits** leads to the comparison with trees, some producing good fruit, others bad.

**7:21–23** The attack on the false prophets is continued, but is broadened to include those disciples who perform works of healing and exorcism in the name of Jesus (**Lord**) but live evil lives. Entrance into the kingdom is only for those who do the will of the Father. On the day of judgment (**on that day**) the morally corrupt prophets and miracle workers will be rejected by Jesus.

**7:23 I never knew you**: cf. Mt 10:33. **Depart from me, you evildoers**: cf. Ps 6:9.

**7:24–27** The conclusion of the discourse (cf. Lk 6:47–49). Here the relation is not between saying and doing as in Mt 7:15–23 but between hearing and doing, and the words of Jesus are applied to every Christian (**everyone who listens**).

**7:28–29 When Jesus finished these words**: this or a similar formula is used by Matthew to conclude each of the five great discourses of Jesus (cf. Mt 11:1; 13:53; 19:1; 26:1).

**7:29 Not as their scribes**: scribal instruction was a faithful handing down of the traditions of earlier teachers; Jesus' teaching is based on his own authority. **Their scribes**: for the implications of **their**, see note on Mt 4:23.

**8:1–9:38** This narrative section of the second book of the gospel is composed of nine miracle stories, most of which are found in Mark, although Matthew does not follow the Marcan order and abbreviates the stories radically. The stories are arranged in three groups of three, each group followed by a section composed principally of sayings of Jesus about discipleship. Mt 9:35 is an almost verbatim repetition of Mt 4:23. Each speaks of Jesus' teaching, preaching, and healing. The teaching and preaching form the content of Mt 5–7; the healing, that of Mt 8–9. Some scholars speak of a portrayal of Jesus as "Messiah of the Word" in Mt 5–7 and "Messiah of the Deed" in Mt 8–9. That is accurate so far as it goes, but there is also a strong emphasis on discipleship in Mt 8–9; these chapters have not only christological but ecclesiological import.

**8:2 A leper**: see note on Mk 1:40.

**8:4** Cf. Lv 14:2–9. **That will be proof for them**: the Greek can also mean "that will be proof against them." It is not clear whether **them** refers to the priests or the people.

**8:5–13** This story comes from Q (see Lk 7:1–10) and is also reflected in Jn 4:46–54. The similarity between the Q story and the Johannine is due to a common oral tradition, not to a common literary source. As in the later story of the daughter of the Canaanite woman (Mt 15:21–28) Jesus here breaks with his usual procedure of ministering only to Israelites and anticipates the mission to the Gentiles.

**8:5 A centurion**: a military officer commanding a hundred men. He was probably in the service of Herod Antipas, tetrarch of Galilee; see note on Mt 14:1.

*x:* 3:10. *y:* Is 29:13; Lk 6:46. *z:* Lk 13:26–27. *a:* 25:11–12. *b:* Ps 5:5; 6:9. *c:* Lk 6:47–49. *d:* Prv 10:25. *e:* Mk 1:22; Lk 4:32. *f:* Mk 1:40–44; Lk 5:12–14. *g:* Lv 14:2–32; Lk 17:14. *h:* Lk 7:1–10; Jn 4:46–53.

approached him and appealed to him, 6 saying, "Lord, my servant is lying at home paralyzed, suffering dreadfully." 7 He said to
him, "I will come and cure him." 8 The centurion said in reply,* "Lord, I am not worthy
to have you enter under my roof; only say the
word and my servant will be healed. 9 For I
too am a person subject to authority, with soldiers subject to me. And I say to one, 'Go,'
and he goes; and to another, 'Come here,'
and he comes; and to my slave, 'Do this,' and
he does it." 10 When Jesus heard this, he was
amazed and said to those following him,
"Amen, I say to you, in no one in Israel* have
I found such faith. 11[i] I say to you,* many will
come from the east and the west, and will recline with Abraham, Isaac, and Jacob at the
banquet in the kingdom of heaven, 12 but the
children of the kingdom will be driven out
into the outer darkness, where there will be
wailing and grinding of teeth." 13 And Jesus
said to the centurion, "You may go; as you
have believed, let it be done for you." And at
that very hour [his] servant was healed.

***The Cure of Peter's Mother-in-Law.****
14[j] Jesus entered the house of Peter, and saw
his mother-in-law lying in bed with a fever.
15 He touched her hand, the fever left her, and
she rose and waited on him.[k]

***Other Healings.*** 16 When it was evening,
they brought him many who were possessed
by demons, and he drove out the spirits by a
word* and cured all the sick, 17 to fulfill what
had been said by Isaiah the prophet:*[l]

"He took away our infirmities
and bore our diseases."

***The Would-be Followers of Jesus.****
18[m] When Jesus saw a crowd around him, he
gave orders to cross to the other side.* 19[n] A
scribe approached and said to him,
"Teacher,* I will follow you wherever you
go." 20 Jesus answered him, "Foxes have
dens and birds of the sky have nests, but the
Son of Man* has nowhere to rest his head."
21 Another of [his] disciples said to him,
"Lord, let me go first and bury my father."
22* But Jesus answered him, "Follow me,
and let the dead bury their dead."

***The Calming of the Storm at Sea.*** 23*[o] He
got into a boat and his disciples followed
him. 24 Suddenly a violent storm* came up on

**8:8–9** Acquainted by his position with the force of a command, the centurion expresses faith in the power of Jesus' mere word.

**8:10 In no one in Israel**: there is good textual attestation (e.g., Codex Sinaiticus) for a reading identical with that of Lk 7:9, "not even in Israel." But that seems to be due to a harmonization of Matthew with Luke.

**8:11–12** Matthew inserts into the story a Q saying (see Lk 13:28–29) about the entrance of Gentiles into the kingdom and the exclusion of those Israelites who, though descended from the patriarchs and members of the chosen nation (**the children of the kingdom**), refused to believe in Jesus. **There will be wailing and grinding of teeth**: the first occurrence of a phrase used frequently in this gospel to describe final condemnation (Mt 13:42, 50; 22:13; 24:51; 25:30). It is found elsewhere in the New Testament only in Lk 13:28.

**8:14–15** Cf. Mk 1:29–31. Unlike Mark, Matthew has no implied request by others for the woman's cure. Jesus acts on his own initiative, and the cured woman rises and waits not on "them" (Mk 1:31) but on **him**.

**8:16 By a word**: a Matthean addition to Mk 1:34; cf. 8:8.

**8:17** This fulfillment citation from Is 53:4 follows the MT, not the LXX. The prophet speaks of the Servant of the Lord who suffers vicariously for the sins ("infirmities") of others; Matthew takes the **infirmities** as physical afflictions.

**8:18–22** This passage between the first and second series of miracles about following Jesus is taken from Q (see Lk 9:57–62). The third of the three sayings found in the source is absent from Matthew.

**8:18 The other side**: i.e., of the Sea of Galilee.

**8:19 Teacher**: for Matthew, this designation of Jesus is true, for he has Jesus using it of himself (Mt 10:24, 25; 23:8; 26:18), yet when it is used of him by others they are either his opponents (Mt 9:11; 12:38; 17:24; 22:16, 24, 36) or, as here and in Mt 19:16, well-disposed persons who cannot see more deeply. Thus it reveals an inadequate recognition of who Jesus is.

**8:20 Son of Man**: see note on Mk 8:31. This is the first occurrence in Matthew of a term that appears in the New Testament only in sayings of Jesus, except for Acts 7:56 and possibly Mt 9:6 (// Mk 2:10; Lk 5:24). In Matthew it refers to Jesus in his ministry (seven times, as here), in his passion and resurrection (nine times, e.g., Mt 17:22), and in his glorious coming at the end of the age (thirteen times, e.g., Mt 24:30).

**8:22 Let the dead bury their dead**: the demand of Jesus overrides what both the Jewish and the Hellenistic world regarded as a filial obligation of the highest importance. See note on Lk 9:60.

**8:23 His disciples followed him**: the first miracle in the second group (Mt 8:23–9:8) is introduced by a verse that links it with the preceding sayings by the catchword "follow." In Mark the initiative in entering the boat is taken by the disciples (Mk 4:35–41); here, Jesus enters first and the disciples follow.

**8:24 Storm**: literally, "earthquake," a word commonly used in apocalyptic literature for the shaking of the old world

*i:* 13:42, 50; 22:13; 24:51; 25:30; Lk 13:28–29. *j:* Mk 1:29–34; Lk 4:38–41. *k:* 9:25. *l:* Is 53:4. *m:* Mk 4:35. *n:* Lk 9:57–60. *o:* Mk 4:35–40; Lk 8:22–25.

the sea, so that the boat was being swamped by waves; but he was asleep. 25[p] They came and woke him, saying, "Lord, save us!* We are perishing!" 26 He said to them, "Why are you terrified, O you of little faith?"* Then he got up, rebuked the winds and the sea, and there was great calm. 27 The men were amazed and said, "What sort of man is this, whom even the winds and the sea obey?"

***The Healing of the Gadarene Demoniacs.*** 28[q] When he came to the other side, to the territory of the Gadarenes,* two demoniacs who were coming from the tombs met him. They were so savage that no one could travel by that road. 29 They cried out, "What have you to do with us,* Son of God? Have you come here to torment us before the appointed time?" 30 Some distance away a herd of many swine was feeding.* 31 The demons pleaded with him, "If you drive us out, send us into the herd of swine."[r] 32 And he said to them, "Go then!" They came out and entered the swine, and the whole herd rushed down the steep bank into the sea where they drowned. 33 The swineherds ran away, and when they came to the town they reported everything, including what had happened to the demoniacs. 34 Thereupon the whole town came out to meet Jesus, and when they saw him they begged him to leave their district.

## CHAPTER 9

See RG 283

***The Healing of a Paralytic.*** 1* [s] He entered a boat, made the crossing, and came into his own town. 2 And there people brought to him a paralytic lying on a stretcher. When Jesus saw their faith, he said to the paralytic, "Courage, child, your sins are forgiven."[t] 3 At that, some of the scribes* said to themselves, "This man is blaspheming." 4 Jesus knew what they were thinking, and said, "Why do you harbor evil thoughts? 5 Which is easier, to say, 'Your sins are forgiven,' or to say, 'Rise and walk'? 6* But that you may know that the Son of Man has authority on earth to forgive sins"—he then said to the paralytic, "Rise, pick up your stretcher, and go home."[u] 7 He rose and went home. 8* When the crowds saw this they were struck with awe and glorified God who had given such authority to human beings.

***The Call of Matthew.**** 9 As Jesus passed on

when God brings in his kingdom. All the synoptics use it in depicting the events preceding the parousia of the Son of Man (Mt 24:7; Mk 13:8; Lk 21:11). Matthew has introduced it here and in his account of the death and resurrection of Jesus (Mt 27:51–54; 28:2).

**8:25** The reverent plea of the disciples contrasts sharply with their reproach of Jesus in Mk 4:38.

**8:26 You of little faith**: see note on Mt 6:30. **Great calm**: Jesus' calming the sea may be meant to recall the Old Testament theme of God's control over the chaotic waters (Ps 65:8; 89:10; 93:3–4; 107:29).

**8:28 Gadarenes**: this is the reading of Codex Vaticanus, supported by other important textual witnesses. The original reading of Codex Sinaiticus was Gazarenes, later changed to Gergesenes, and a few versions have Gerasenes. Each of these readings points to a different territory connected, respectively, with the cities Gadara, Gergesa, and Gerasa (modern Jerash). There is the same confusion of readings in the parallel texts, Mk 5:1 and Lk 8:26; there the best reading seems to be "Gerasenes," whereas "Gadarenes" is probably the original reading in Matthew. The town of Gadara was about five miles southeast of the Sea of Galilee, and Josephus (*Life* 9:42) refers to it as possessing territory that lay on that sea. **Two demoniacs**: Mark (5:1–20) has one.

**8:29 What have you to do with us?**: see note on Jn 2:4. **Before the appointed time**: the notion that evil spirits were allowed by God to afflict human beings until the time of the final judgment is found in Enoch 16:1 and Jubilees 10:7–10.

**8:30** The tending of pigs, animals considered unclean by Mosaic law (Lv 11:6–7), indicates that the population was Gentile.

**9:1 His own town**: Capernaum; see Mt 4:13.

**9:3 Scribes**: see note on Mk 2:6. Matthew omits the reason given in the Marcan story for the charge of blasphemy: "Who but God alone can forgive sins?" (Mk 2:7).

**9:6** It is not clear whether **"But that you may know . . . to forgive sins"** is intended to be a continuation of the words of Jesus or a parenthetical comment of the evangelist to those who would hear or read this gospel. In any case, Matthew here follows the Marcan text.

**9:8 Who had given such authority to human beings**: a significant difference from Mk 2:12 ("They . . . glorified God, saying, 'We have never seen anything like this' "). Matthew's extension to **human beings** of the authority to forgive sins points to the belief that such authority was being claimed by Matthew's church.

**9:9–17** In this section the order is the same as that of Mk 2:13–22.

**9:9 A man named Matthew**: Mark names this tax collector Levi (Mk 2:14). No such name appears in the four lists of the twelve who were the closest companions of Jesus (Mt 10:2–4; Mk 3:16–19; Lk 6:14–16; Acts 1:13 [eleven, because of the defection of Judas Iscariot]), whereas all four list a Matthew, designated in Mt 10:3 as "the tax collector." The evangelist may have changed the "Levi" of his source

*p:* Ps 107:28–29. *q:* Mk 5:1–17; Lk 8:26–37. *r:* Lk 4:34, 41. *s:* Mk 2:3–12; Lk 5:18–26. *t:* Lk 7:48. *u:* Jn 5:27.

from there,[v] he saw a man named Matthew* sitting at the customs post. He said to him, "Follow me." And he got up and followed him. [10]While he was at table in his house,* many tax collectors and sinners came and sat with Jesus and his disciples.[w] [11]The Pharisees saw this and said to his disciples, "Why does your teacher* eat with tax collectors and sinners?" [12]He heard this and said, "Those who are well do not need a physician, but the sick do.* [13]Go and learn the meaning of the words,[x] 'I desire mercy, not sacrifice.'* I did not come to call the righteous but sinners."

***The Question About Fasting.*** [14y] Then the disciples of John approached him and said, "Why do we and the Pharisees fast (much), but your disciples do not fast?" [15]Jesus answered them, "Can the wedding guests mourn as long as the bridegroom is with them? The days will come when the bridegroom is taken away from them, and then they will fast.* [16]No one patches an old cloak with a piece of unshrunken cloth,* for its fullness pulls away from the cloak and the tear gets worse. [17]People do not put new wine into old wineskins. Otherwise the skins burst, the wine spills out, and the skins are ruined. Rather, they pour new wine into fresh wineskins, and both are preserved."

***The Official's Daughter and the Woman with a Hemorrhage.*** [18*] While he was saying these things to them,[z] an official* came forward, knelt down before him, and said, "My daughter has just died. But come, lay your hand on her, and she will live." [19]Jesus rose and followed him, and so did his disciples. [20]A woman suffering hemorrhages for twelve years came up behind him and touched the tassel* on his cloak. [21]She said to herself, "If only I can touch his cloak, I shall be cured."[a] [22]Jesus turned around and saw her, and said, "Courage, daughter! Your faith has saved you." And from that hour the woman was cured.

[23]When Jesus arrived at the official's house and saw the flute players and the crowd who were making a commotion, [24]he said, "Go away! The girl is not dead but sleeping."* And they ridiculed him. [25]When the crowd was put out, he came and took her by the hand, and the little girl arose. [26]And news of this spread throughout all that land.

***The Healing of Two Blind Men.**** [27b] And

to **Matthew** so that this man, whose call is given special notice, like that of the first four disciples (Mt 4:18–22), might be included among the twelve. Another reason for the change may be that the disciple Matthew was the source of traditions peculiar to the church for which the evangelist was writing.

**9:10 His house**: it is not clear whether **his** refers to Jesus or Matthew. **Tax collectors**: see note on Mt 5:46. Table association with such persons would cause ritual impurity.

**9:11 Teacher**: see note on Mt 8:19.

**9:12** See note on Mk 2:17.

**9:13 Go and learn . . . not sacrifice**: Matthew adds the prophetic statement of Hos 6:6 to the Marcan account (see also Mt 12:7). If mercy is superior to the temple sacrifices, how much more to the laws of ritual impurity.

**9:15** Fasting is a sign of mourning and would be as inappropriate at this time of joy, when Jesus is proclaiming the kingdom, as it would be at a marriage feast. Yet the saying looks forward to the time when Jesus will no longer be with the disciples visibly, the time of Matthew's church. **Then they will fast**: see *Didache* 8:1.

**9:16–17** Each of these parables speaks of the unsuitability of attempting to combine the old and the new. Jesus' teaching is not a patching up of Judaism, nor can the gospel be contained within the limits of Mosaic law.

**9:18–34** In this third group of miracles, the first (Mt 9:18–26) is clearly dependent on Mark (Mk 5:21–43). Though it tells of two miracles, the cure of the woman had already been included within the story of the raising of the official's daughter, so that the two were probably regarded as a single unit. The other miracles seem to have been derived from Mark and Q respectively, though there Matthew's own editing is much more evident.

**9:18 Official**: literally, "ruler." Mark calls him "one of the synagogue officials" (Mk 5:22). **My daughter has just died**: Matthew heightens the Marcan "my daughter is at the point of death" (Mk 5:23).

**9:20 Tassel**: possibly "fringe." The Mosaic law prescribed that tassels be worn on the corners of one's garment as a reminder to keep the commandments (see Nm 15:37–39; Dt 22:12).

**9:24 Sleeping**: sleep is a biblical metaphor for death (see Ps 87:6 LXX; Dn 12:2; 1 Thes 5:10). Jesus' statement is not a denial of the child's real death, but an assurance that she will be roused from her sleep of death.

**9:27–31** This story was probably composed by Matthew out of Mark's story of the healing of a blind man named Bartimaeus (Mk 10:46–52). Mark places the event late in Jesus' ministry, just before his entrance into Jerusalem, and Matthew has followed his Marcan source at that point in his gospel also (see Mt 20:29–34). In each of the Matthean stories the single blind man of Mark becomes two. The reason

*v:* Mk 2:14–17; Lk 5:27–32. *w:* 11:19; Lk 15:1–2. *x:* 12:7; Hos 6:6. *y:* Mk 2:18–22; Lk 5:33–39. *z:* Mk 5:22–43; Lk 8:41–56. *a:* 14:36; Nm 15:37. *b:* 20:29–34.

as Jesus passed on from there, two blind men
followed [him], crying out, "Son of David,*
have pity on us!"[c] 28 When he entered the
house, the blind men approached him and
Jesus said to them, "Do you believe that I
can do this?" "Yes, Lord," they said to him.
29 Then he touched their eyes and said, "Let
it be done for you according to your faith."
30 And their eyes were opened. Jesus warned
them sternly, "See that no one knows about
this." 31 But they went out and spread word
of him through all that land.

*The Healing of a Mute Person.* 32 [d] As they
were going out,* a demoniac who could not
speak was brought to him, 33 and when the
demon was driven out the mute person
spoke. The crowds were amazed and said,
"Nothing like this has ever been seen in Israel."[e] 34* But the Pharisees said,[f] "He drives
out demons by the prince of demons."

*The Compassion of Jesus.* 35* [g] Jesus went
around to all the towns and villages, teaching in their synagogues, proclaiming the
gospel of the kingdom, and curing every disease and illness. 36 [h] At the sight of the
crowds, his heart was moved with pity for
them because they were troubled and abandoned,* like sheep without a shepherd.
37* [i] Then he said to his disciples, "The harvest is abundant but the laborers are few;
38 so ask the master of the harvest to send out
laborers for his harvest."

## CHAPTER 10

See RG 283

*The Mission of the Twelve.* 1* Then he
summoned his twelve disciples* and gave
them authority over unclean spirits to drive
them out and to cure every disease and every
illness.[j] 2 The names of the twelve apostles*
are these: first, Simon called Peter, and his
brother Andrew; James, the son of Zebedee,
and his brother John; 3 Philip and
Bartholomew, Thomas and Matthew the tax
collector; James, the son of Alphaeus, and
Thaddeus; 4 Simon the Cananean, and Judas
Iscariot who betrayed him.

*The Commissioning of the Twelve.* 5 [k] Jesus
sent out these twelve* after instructing them

why Matthew would have given a double version of the Marcan story and placed the earlier one here may be that he wished to add a story of Jesus' curing the blind at this point in order to prepare for Jesus' answer to the emissaries of the Baptist (Mt 11:4–6) in which Jesus, recounting his works, begins with his giving sight to the blind.

**9:27 Son of David**: this messianic title is connected once with the healing power of Jesus in Mark (Mk 10:47–48) and Luke (Lk 18:38–39) but more frequently in Matthew (see also Mt 12:23; 15:22; 20:30–31).

**9:32–34** The source of this story seems to be Q (see Lk 11:14–15). As in the preceding healing of the blind, Matthew has two versions of this healing, the later in Mt 12:22–24 and the earlier here.

**9:34** This spiteful accusation foreshadows the growing opposition to Jesus in Mt 11; 12.

**9:35** See notes on Mt 4:23–25; Mt 8:1–9:38.

**9:36** See Mk 6:34; Nm 27:17; 1 Kgs 22:17.

**9:37–38** This Q saying (see Lk 10:2) is only imperfectly related to this context. It presupposes that only God (**the master of the harvest**) can take the initiative in sending out preachers of the gospel, whereas in Matthew's setting it leads into Mt 10 where Jesus does so.

**10:1–11:1** After an introductory narrative (Mt 10:1–4), the second of the discourses of the gospel. It deals with the mission now to be undertaken by the disciples (Mt 10:5–15), but the perspective broadens and includes the missionary activity of the church between the time of the resurrection and the parousia.

**10:1 His twelve disciples**: although, unlike Mark (Mk 3:13–14) and Luke (Lk 6:12–16), Matthew has no story of Jesus' choosing the Twelve, he assumes that the group is known to the reader. The earliest New Testament text to speak of it is 1 Cor 15:5. The number probably is meant to recall the twelve tribes of Israel and implies Jesus' authority to call all Israel into the kingdom. While Luke (Lk 6:13) and probably Mark (Mk 4:10, 34) distinguish between the Twelve and a larger group also termed disciples, Matthew tends to identify the disciples and the Twelve. **Authority . . . every illness**: activities the same as those of Jesus; see Mt 4:23; Mt 9:35; 10:8. The Twelve also share in his proclamation of the kingdom (Mt 10:7). But although he teaches (Mt 4:23; 7:28; 9:35), they do not. Their commission to teach comes only after Jesus' resurrection, after they have been fully instructed by him (Mt 28:20).

**10:2–4** Here, for the only time in Matthew, the Twelve are designated **apostles**. The word "apostle" means "one who is sent," and therefore fits the situation here described. In the Pauline letters, the place where the term occurs most frequently in the New Testament, it means primarily one who has seen the risen Lord and has been commissioned to proclaim the resurrection. With slight variants in Luke and Acts, the names of those who belong to this group are the same in the four lists given in the New Testament (see note on Mt 9:9). **Cananean**: this represents an Aramaic word meaning "zealot." The meaning of that designation is unclear (see note on Lk 6:15).

**10:5–6** Like Jesus (Mt 15:24), the Twelve are sent only to Israel. This saying may reflect an original Jewish Christian refusal of the mission to the Gentiles, but for Matthew it expresses rather the limitation that Jesus himself observed during his ministry.

*c:* 15:22. *d:* 12:22–24; Lk 11:14–15. *e:* Mk 2:12; 7:37. *f:* 10:25; Mk 3:22. *g:* 4:23; Lk 8:1. *h:* Nm 27:17; 1 Kgs 22:17; Jer 50:6; Ez 34:5; Mk 6:34. *i:* Lk 10:2; Jn 4:35. *j:* Mk 3:14–19; Lk 6:13–16; Acts 1:13. *k:* Mk 6:7–13; Lk 9:1–6.

thus, "Do not go into pagan territory or enter
a Samaritan town. [6][l] Go rather to the lost
sheep of the house of Israel. [7]As you go,
make this proclamation: 'The kingdom of
heaven is at hand.'[m] [8]* Cure the sick, raise the
dead, cleanse lepers, drive out demons. Without cost you have received; without cost you
are to give. [9][n] Do not take gold or silver or
copper for your belts; [10][o] no sack for the
journey, or a second tunic, or sandals, or
walking stick. The laborer deserves his keep.
[11][p] Whatever town or village you enter, look
for a worthy person in it, and stay there until
you leave. [12]As you enter a house, wish it
peace. [13]If the house is worthy, let your peace
come upon it; if not, let your peace return to
you.* [14]* [q] Whoever will not receive you or
listen to your words—go outside that house
or town and shake the dust from your feet.
[15]Amen, I say to you, it will be more tolerable for the land of Sodom and Gomorrah on
the day of judgment than for that town.[r]

***Coming Persecutions.*** [16][s] "Behold, I am
sending you like sheep in the midst of
wolves; so be shrewd as serpents and simple
as doves. [17]* But beware of people,[t] for they
will hand you over to courts and scourge you
in their synagogues,[u] [18]and you will be led
before governors and kings for my sake as a
witness before them and the pagans. [19]When
they hand you over, do not worry about how
you are to speak or what you are to say. You
will be given at that moment what you are to
say.[v] [20]For it will not be you who speak but
the Spirit of your Father speaking through
you. [21]* [w] Brother will hand over brother to
death, and the father his child; children will
rise up against parents and have them put to
death. [22]You will be hated by all because of
my name, but whoever endures to the end*
will be saved. [23]When they persecute you in
one town, flee to another. Amen, I say to
you, you will not finish the towns of Israel
before the Son of Man comes.* [24][x] No disciple is above his teacher, no slave above his
master. [25]It is enough for the disciple that he
become like his teacher, for the slave that he
become like his master. If they have called
the master of the house Beelzebul,* how
much more those of his household!

***Courage Under Persecution.*** [26][y] "Therefore do not be afraid of them. Nothing is
concealed that will not be revealed, nor secret that will not be known.* [z] [27]What I say to
you in the darkness, speak in the light; what
you hear whispered, proclaim on the housetops. [28]And do not be afraid of those who kill
the body but cannot kill the soul; rather, be
afraid of the one who can destroy both soul
and body in Gehenna.[a] [29]Are not two sparrows sold for a small coin? Yet not one of
them falls to the ground without your Father's knowledge. [30]Even all the hairs of
your head are counted. [31]So do not be afraid;

**10:8–11** The Twelve have received their own call and mission through God's gift, and the benefits they confer are likewise to be given freely. They are not to take with them money, provisions, or unnecessary clothing; their lodging and food will be provided by those who receive them.

**10:13** The greeting of peace is conceived of not merely as a salutation but as an effective word. If it finds no worthy recipient, it will return to the speaker.

**10:14 Shake the dust from your feet**: this gesture indicates a complete disassociation from such unbelievers.

**10:17** The persecutions attendant upon the post-resurrection mission now begin to be spoken of. Here Matthew brings into the discourse sayings found in Mk 13 which deals with events preceding the parousia.

**10:21** See Mi 7:6 which is cited in Mt 10:35, 36.

**10:22 To the end**: the original meaning was probably "until the parousia." But it is not likely that Matthew expected no missionary disciples to suffer death before then, since he envisages the martyrdom of other Christians (Mt 10:21). For him, **the end** is probably that of the individual's life (see Mt 10:28).

**10:23 Before the Son of Man comes**: since the coming of the Son of Man at the end of the age had not taken place when this gospel was written, much less during the mission of the Twelve during Jesus' ministry, Matthew cannot have meant the coming to refer to the parousia. It is difficult to know what he understood it to be: perhaps the "proleptic parousia" of Mt 28:16–20, or the destruction of the temple in A.D. 70, viewed as a coming of Jesus in judgment on unbelieving Israel.

**10:25 Beelzebul**: see Mt 9:34 for the charge linking Jesus with "the prince of demons," who is named **Beelzebul** in Mt 12:24. The meaning of the name is uncertain; possibly, "lord of the house."

**10:26** The **concealed** and **secret** coming of the kingdom is to be proclaimed by them, and no fear must be allowed to deter them from that proclamation.

*l:* 15:24. *m:* 3:2; 4:17. *n:* Mk 6:8–9; Lk 9:3; 10:4. *o:* Lk 10:7; 1 Cor 9:14; 1 Tm 5:18. *p:* Mk 6:10–11; Lk 9:4–5; 10:5–12. *q:* Acts 13:51; 18:6. *r:* 11:24; Gn 19:1–29; Jude 7. *s:* Lk 10:3. *t:* Mk 13:9–13; Lk 21:12–19. *u:* Acts 5:40. *v:* Ex 4:11–12; Jer 1:6–10; Lk 12:11–12. *w:* 24:9, 13. *x:* Lk 6:40; Jn 13:16; 15:20. *y:* Lk 12:2–9. *z:* Mk 4:22; Lk 8:17; 1 Tm 5:25. *a:* Jas 4:12.

you are worth more than many sparrows. 32* Everyone who acknowledges me before others I will acknowledge before my heavenly Father. 33 But whoever denies me before others, I will deny before my heavenly Father.[b]

***Jesus: A Cause of Division.*** 34[c] "Do not think that I have come to bring peace upon the earth. I have come to bring not peace but the sword. 35 For I have come to set

a man 'against his father,
  a daughter against her mother,
and a daughter-in-law against her
    mother-in-law;
36 and one's enemies will be those of his
    household.'

***The Conditions of Discipleship.*** 37[d] "Whoever loves father or mother more than me is not worthy of me, and whoever loves son or daughter more than me is not worthy of me; 38 and whoever does not take up his cross* and follow after me is not worthy of me. 39*[e] Whoever finds his life will lose it, and whoever loses his life for my sake will find it.

***Rewards.*** 40 "Whoever receives you receives me,* and whoever receives me receives the one who sent me.[f] 41* Whoever receives a prophet because he is a prophet will receive a prophet's reward, and whoever receives a righteous man because he is righteous will receive a righteous man's reward. 42 And whoever gives only a cup of cold water to one of these little ones to drink because he is a disciple—amen, I say to you, he will surely not lose his reward."[g]

### CHAPTER 11

See RG 283–84

1 When Jesus finished giving these commands to his twelve disciples,* he went away from that place to teach and to preach in their towns.

## IV. Opposition from Israel

***The Messengers from John the Baptist.*** 2*[h] When John heard in prison* of the works of the Messiah, he sent his disciples to him 3* with this question, "Are you the one who is to come, or should we look for another?" 4 Jesus said to them in reply, "Go and tell John what you hear and see: 5* the blind regain their sight, the lame walk, lepers are cleansed, the deaf hear, the dead are raised, and the poor have the good news proclaimed to them.[i] 6 And blessed is the one who takes no offense at me."

***Jesus' Testimony to John.**** 7 As they were going off, Jesus began to speak to the crowds

**10:32–33** In the Q parallel (Lk 12:8–9), the Son of Man will acknowledge those who have acknowledged Jesus, and those who deny him will be denied (by the Son of Man) before the angels of God at the judgment. Here Jesus and the Son of Man are identified, and the acknowledgment or denial will be before his heavenly Father.

**10:38** The first mention of the cross in Matthew, explicitly that of the disciple, but implicitly that of Jesus (**and follow after me**). Crucifixion was a form of capital punishment used by the Romans for offenders who were not Roman citizens.

**10:39** One who denies Jesus in order to save one's earthly life will be condemned to everlasting destruction; loss of earthly life for Jesus' sake will be rewarded by everlasting life in the kingdom.

**10:40–42** All who receive the disciples of Jesus receive him, and God who sent him, and will be rewarded accordingly.

**10:41** **A prophet**: one who speaks in the name of God; here, the Christian prophets who proclaim the gospel. **Righteous man**: since righteousness is demanded of all the disciples, it is difficult to take the **righteous man** of this verse and **one of these little ones** (Mt 10:42) as indicating different groups within the followers of Jesus. Probably all three designations are used here of Christian missionaries as such.

**11:1** The closing formula of the discourse refers back to the original addressees, the Twelve.

**11:2–12:50** The narrative section of the third book deals with the growing opposition to Jesus. It is largely devoted to disputes and attacks relating to faith and discipleship and thus contains much sayings-material, drawn in large part from Q.

**11:2** **In prison**: see Mt 4:12; 14:1–12. **The works of the Messiah**: the deeds of Mt 8–9.

**11:3** The question probably expresses a doubt of the Baptist that Jesus is **the one who is to come** (cf. Mal 3:1) because his mission has not been one of fiery judgment as John had expected (Mt 3:2).

**11:5–6** Jesus' response is taken from passages of Isaiah (Is 26:19; 29:18–19; 35:5–6; 61:1) that picture the time of salvation as marked by deeds such as those that Jesus is doing. The beatitude is a warning to the Baptist not to disbelieve because his expectations have not been met.

**11:7–19** Jesus' rebuke of John is counterbalanced by a reminder of the greatness of the Baptist's function (Mt 11:7–15) that is followed by a complaint about those who have heeded neither John nor Jesus (Mt 11:16–19).

*b:* Mk 8:38; Lk 9:26; 2 Tm 2:12; Rev 3:5. *c:* Lk 12:51–53. *d:* 16:24–25; Lk 14:26–27. *e:* Mk 8:35; Lk 9:24; Jn 12:25. *f:* Lk 10:16; Jn 12:44; 13:20. *g:* 25:40; Mk 9:41. *h:* Lk 7:18–28. *i:* Is 26:19; 29:18–19; 35:5–6; 61:1.

about John, "What did you go out to the
desert to see? A reed swayed by the wind?[j]
8 Then what did you go out to see? Someone
dressed in fine clothing? Those who wear
fine clothing are in royal palaces. 9 Then why
did you go out? To see a prophet?* Yes, I tell
you, and more than a prophet. 10 This is the
one about whom it is written:

'Behold, I am sending my messenger
ahead of you;
he will prepare your way before you.'[k]

11 Amen, I say to you, among those born of
women there has been none greater than
John the Baptist; yet the least in the kingdom
of heaven is greater than he.* 12 From the
days of John the Baptist until now, the kingdom of heaven suffers violence,* and the violent are taking it by force.[l] 13 All the prophets and the law* prophesied up to the time of
John. 14 And if you are willing to accept it, he
is Elijah, the one who is to come.[m] 15 Whoever has ears ought to hear.
16[n] "To what shall I compare this generation?* It is like children who sit in marketplaces and call to one another, 17 'We played
the flute for you, but you did not dance, we
sang a dirge but you did not mourn.' 18 For
John came neither eating nor drinking, and
they said, 'He is possessed by a demon.'[o]
19 The Son of Man came eating and drinking
and they said, 'Look, he is a glutton and a
drunkard, a friend of tax collectors and sinners.' But wisdom is vindicated by her
works."[p]

***Reproaches to Unrepentant Towns.***
20[q] Then he began to reproach the towns
where most of his mighty deeds had been
done, since they had not repented. 21 "Woe to
you, Chorazin! Woe to you, Bethsaida! For if
the mighty deeds done in your midst had been
done in Tyre and Sidon,* they would long ago
have repented in sackcloth and ashes.[r] 22 But I
tell you, it will be more tolerable for Tyre and
Sidon on the day of judgment than for you.
23* And as for you, Capernaum:

'Will you be exalted to heaven?[s]
You will go down to the netherworld.'

For if the mighty deeds done in your midst
had been done in Sodom, it would have remained until this day. 24 But I tell you, it will
be more tolerable for the land of Sodom on
the day of judgment than for you."[t]

***The Praise of the Father.*** 25[u] At that time
Jesus said in reply,* "I give praise to you, Father, Lord of heaven and earth, for although
you have hidden these things from the wise
and the learned you have revealed them to
the childlike. 26 Yes, Father, such has been

**11:9–10** In common Jewish belief there had been no prophecy in Israel since the last of the Old Testament prophets, Malachi. The coming of a new prophet was eagerly awaited, and Jesus agrees that John was such. Yet he was **more than a prophet**, for he was the precursor of the one who would bring in the new and final age. The Old Testament quotation is a combination of Mal 3:1; Ex 23:20 with the significant change that the **before me** of Malachi becomes **before you**. The messenger now precedes not God, as in the original, but Jesus.

**11:11** John's preeminent greatness lies in his function of announcing the imminence of the kingdom (Mt 3:1). But to be in the kingdom is so great a privilege that the least who has it is greater than the Baptist.

**11:12** The meaning of this difficult saying is probably that the opponents of Jesus are trying to prevent people from accepting the kingdom and to snatch it away from those who have received it.

**11:13 All the prophets and the law**: Matthew inverts the usual order, "law and prophets," and says that both have **prophesied**. This emphasis on the prophetic character of the law points to its fulfillment in the teaching of Jesus and to the transitory nature of some of its commandments (see note on Mt 5:17–20).

**11:16–19** See Lk 7:31–35. The meaning of the parable (Mt 11:16–17) and its explanation (Mt 11:18–19b) is much disputed. A plausible view is that the **children** of the parable are two groups, one of which proposes different entertainments to the other that will not agree with either proposal. The first represents John, Jesus, and their disciples; the second those who reject John for his asceticism and Jesus for his table association with those despised by the religiously observant. Mt 11:19c (**her works**) forms an inclusion with Mt 11:2 ("the works of the Messiah"). The original form of the saying is better preserved in Lk 7:35 ". . . wisdom is vindicated by all her children." There John and Jesus are the children of Wisdom; here the works of Jesus the Messiah are those of divine Wisdom, of which he is the embodiment. Some important textual witnesses, however, have essentially the same reading as in Luke.

**11:21** Tyre and Sidon were pagan cities denounced for their wickedness in the Old Testament; cf. Jl 4:4–7.

**11:23** Capernaum's pride and punishment are described in language taken from the taunt song against the king of Babylon (Is 14:13–15).

**11:25–27** This Q saying, identical with Lk 10:21–22 except

*j:* 3:3, 5. *k:* Ex 23:20; Mal 3:1; Mk 1:2; Lk 1:76. *l:* Lk 16:16. *m:* 17:10–13; Mal 3:23; Lk 1:17. *n:* Lk 7:31–35. *o:* Lk 1:15. *p:* 9:10–11. *q:* Lk 10:12–15. *r:* Jl 4:4–7. *s:* Is 14:13–15. *t:* 10:15. *u:* Lk 10:21–22.

your gracious will. 27 All things have been handed over to me by my Father. No one knows the Son except the Father, and no one knows the Father except the Son and anyone to whom the Son wishes to reveal him.[v]

*The Gentle Mastery of Christ.* 28* "Come to me, all you who labor and are burdened,* and I will give you rest. 29* [w] Take my yoke upon you and learn from me, for I am meek and humble of heart; and you will find rest for yourselves. 30 For my yoke is easy, and my burden light."

## CHAPTER 12

See RG 283–84

*Picking Grain on the Sabbath.* 1* At that time Jesus was going through a field of grain on the sabbath.[x] His disciples were hungry and began to pick the heads* of grain and eat them.[y] 2 When the Pharisees saw this, they said to him, "See, your disciples are doing what is unlawful to do on the sabbath." 3 He said to them,* "Have you not read what David[z] did when he and his companions were hungry, 4 how he went into the house of God and ate the bread of offering,[a] which neither he nor his companions but only the priests could lawfully eat? 5* Or have you not read in the law that on the sabbath the priests serving in the temple violate the sabbath and are innocent?[b] 6 I say to you, something greater than the temple is here. 7* If you knew what this meant, 'I desire mercy, not sacrifice,'[c] you would not have condemned these innocent men. 8* [d] For the Son of Man is Lord of the sabbath."

*The Man with a Withered Hand.* 9[e] Moving on from there, he went into their synagogue. 10 And behold, there was a man there who had a withered hand. They questioned him, "Is it lawful to cure on the sabbath?"* so that they might accuse him. 11* He said to them, "Which one of you who has a sheep that falls into a pit on the sabbath will not take hold of it and lift it out? 12 How much more valuable a person is than a sheep. So it is lawful to do good on the sabbath." 13 Then he said to the man, "Stretch out your hand." He stretched it out, and it was restored as sound as the other. 14 But the Pharisees* went out and took counsel against him to put him to death.[f]

for minor variations, introduces a joyous note into this section, so dominated by the theme of unbelief. **While the wise and the learned**, the scribes and Pharisees, have rejected Jesus' preaching and the significance of his mighty deeds, **the childlike** have accepted them. Acceptance depends upon the Father's revelation, but this is granted to those who are open to receive it and refused to the arrogant. Jesus can speak of all mysteries because he is **the Son** and there is perfect reciprocity of knowledge between him and the Father; what has been **handed over** to him is revealed only to those whom he wishes.

**11:28–29** These verses are peculiar to Matthew and are similar to Ben Sirach's invitation to learn wisdom and submit to her yoke (Sir 51:23, 26).

**11:28 Who labor and are burdened**: burdened by the law as expounded by the scribes and Pharisees (Mt 23:4).

**11:29** In place of the yoke of the law, complicated by scribal interpretation, Jesus invites the burdened to take the yoke of obedience to his word, under which they **will find rest**; cf. Jer 6:16.

**12:1–14** Matthew here returns to the Marcan order that he left in Mt 9:18. The two stories depend on Mk 2:23–28; 3:1–6 respectively, and are the only places in either gospel that deal explicitly with Jesus' attitude toward sabbath observance.

**12:1–2** The picking of the heads of grain is here equated with reaping, which was forbidden on the sabbath (Ex 34:21).

**12:3–4** See 1 Sm 21:2–7. In the Marcan parallel (Mk 2:25–26) the high priest is called Abiathar, although in 1 Samuel this action is attributed to Ahimelech. The Old Testament story is not about a violation of the sabbath rest; its pertinence to this dispute is that a violation of the law was permissible because of David's men being without food.

**12:5–6** This and the following argument (Mt 12:7) are peculiar to Matthew. The temple service seems to be the changing of the showbread on the sabbath (Lv 24:8) and the doubling on the sabbath of the usual daily holocausts (Nm 28:9–10). The argument is that the law itself requires work that breaks the sabbath rest, because of the higher duty of temple service. If temple duties outweigh the sabbath law, how much more does the presence of Jesus, with his proclamation of the kingdom (**something greater than the temple**), justify the conduct of his disciples.

**12:7** See note on Mt 9:13.

**12:8** The ultimate justification for the disciples' violation of the sabbath rest is that Jesus, the Son of Man, has supreme authority over the law.

**12:10** Rabbinic tradition later than the gospels allowed relief to be given to a sufferer on the sabbath if life was in danger. This may also have been the view of Jesus' Pharisaic contemporaries. But the case here is not about one in danger of death.

**12:11** Matthew omits the question posed by Jesus in Mk 3:4 and substitutes one about rescuing a sheep on the sabbath, similar to that in Lk 14:5.

**12:14** See Mk 3:6. Here the plan to bring about Jesus' death is attributed to the Pharisees only. This is probably due to the situation of Matthew's church, when the sole opponents were the Pharisees.

*v:* Jn 3:35; 6:46; 7:28; 10:15. *w:* Sir 51:26; Jer 6:16. *x:* Mk 2:23–28; Lk 6:1–5. *y:* Dt 23:26. *z:* 1 Sm 21:2–7. *a:* Lv 24:5–9. *b:* Lv 24:8; Nm 28:9–10. *c:* Hos 6:6. *d:* Jn 5:16–17. *e:* Mk 3:1–6; Lk 6:6–11. *f:* Jn 5:18.

***The Chosen Servant.**** 15 When Jesus realized this, he withdrew from that place. Many
[people] followed him, and he cured them
all,* 16 but he warned them not to make him
known. 17 This was to fulfill what had been
spoken through Isaiah the prophet:

18 "Behold, my servant whom I have
chosen,[g]
my beloved in whom I delight;
I shall place my spirit upon him,
and he will proclaim justice to the
Gentiles.
19 He will not contend* or cry out,
nor will anyone hear his voice in the
streets.
20 A bruised reed he will not break,
a smoldering wick he will not quench,
until he brings justice to victory.
21 And in his name the Gentiles will
hope."*

***Jesus and Beelzebul.**** 22 [h] Then they
brought to him a demoniac who was blind
and mute. He cured the mute person so that
he could speak and see. 23* [i] All the crowd
was astounded, and said, "Could this perhaps be the Son of David?" 24* [j] But when
the Pharisees heard this, they said, "This
man drives out demons only by the power of
Beelzebul, the prince of demons." 25 [k] But he
knew what they were thinking and said to
them,* "Every kingdom divided against itself will be laid waste, and no town or house
divided against itself will stand. 26 And if Satan drives out Satan, he is divided against
himself; how, then, will his kingdom stand?
27 And if I drive out demons by Beelzebul, by
whom do your own people* drive them out?
Therefore they will be your judges. 28* [l] But
if it is by the Spirit of God that I drive out
demons, then the kingdom of God has come
upon you. 29* How can anyone enter a strong
man's house and steal his property, unless he
first ties up the strong man? Then he can
plunder his house. 30* [m] Whoever is not with
me is against me, and whoever does not
gather with me scatters. 31 [n] Therefore, I say
to you, every sin and blasphemy will be forgiven people, but blasphemy against the
Spirit* will not be forgiven. 32 And whoever
speaks a word against the Son of Man will
be forgiven; but whoever speaks against the
holy Spirit will not be forgiven, either in this
age or in the age to come.

**12:15–21** Matthew follows Mk 3:7–12 but summarizes his source in two verses (Mt 12:15, 16) that pick up the withdrawal, the healings, and the command for silence. To this he adds a fulfillment citation from the first Servant Song (Is 42:1–4) that does not correspond exactly to either the Hebrew or the LXX of that passage. It is the longest Old Testament citation in this gospel, emphasizing the meekness of Jesus, the Servant of the Lord, and foretelling the extension of his mission to the Gentiles.

**12:15** Jesus' knowledge of the Pharisees' plot and his healing all are peculiar to Matthew.

**12:19** The servant's not contending is seen as fulfilled in Jesus' withdrawal from the disputes narrated in Mt 12:1–14.

**12:21** Except for a minor detail, Matthew here follows the LXX, although the meaning of the Hebrew ("the coastlands will wait for his teaching") is similar.

**12:22–32** For the exorcism, see note on Mt 9:32–34. The long discussion combines Marcan and Q material (Mk 3:22–30; Lk 11:19–20, 23; 12:10). Mk 3:20–21 is omitted, with a consequent lessening of the sharpness of Mt 12:48.

**12:23** See note on Mt 9:27.

**12:24** See note on Mt 10:25.

**12:25–26** Jesus' first response to the Pharisees' charge is that if it were true, Satan would be destroying his own kingdom.

**12:27** Besides pointing out the absurdity of the charge, Jesus asks how the work of Jewish exorcists (**your own people**) is to be interpreted. Are they, too, to be charged with collusion with Beelzebul? For an example of Jewish exorcism see Josephus, *Antiquities* 8:42–49.

**12:28** The Q parallel (Lk 11:20) speaks of the "finger" rather than of the "spirit" of God. While the difference is probably due to Matthew's editing, he retains **the kingdom of God** rather than changing it to his usual "kingdom of heaven." **Has come upon you**: see Mt 4:17.

**12:29** A short parable illustrates what Jesus is doing. The **strong man** is Satan, whom Jesus has tied up and whose **house** he is plundering. Jewish expectation was that Satan would be chained up in the last days (Rev 20:2); Jesus' exorcisms indicate that those days have begun.

**12:30** This saying, already attached to the preceding verses in Q (see Lk 11:23), warns that there can be no neutrality where Jesus is concerned. Its pertinence in a context where Jesus is addressing not the neutral but the bitterly opposed is not clear. The accusation of scattering, however, does fit the situation. Jesus is the shepherd of God's people (Mt 2:6), his mission is to the lost sheep of Israel (Mt 15:24); the Pharisees, who oppose him, are guilty of scattering the sheep.

**12:31** **Blasphemy against the Spirit**: the sin of attributing to Satan (Mt 12:24) what is the work of the Spirit of God (Mt 12:28).

*g:* Is 42:1–4. *h:* 9:32–34; Lk 11:14–15. *i:* 9:27. *j:* 10:25; Mk 3:22. *k:* Mk 3:23–27; Lk 11:17–22. *l:* Lk 11:20. *m:* Lk 11:23. *n:* Mk 3:28–30; Lk 12:10.

*A Tree and Its Fruits.* [33][o] "Either declare*
the tree good and its fruit is good, or declare
the tree rotten and its fruit is rotten, for a tree
is known by its fruit. [34]* [p] You brood of
vipers, how can you say good things when
you are evil? For from the fullness of the
heart the mouth speaks. [35]A good person
brings forth good out of a store of goodness,
but an evil person brings forth evil out of a
store of evil. [36]* [q] I tell you, on the day of
judgment people will render an account for
every careless word they speak. [37]By your
words you will be acquitted, and by your
words you will be condemned."

*The Demand for a Sign.** [38]Then some of
the scribes and Pharisees said to him,
"Teacher,* we wish to see a sign from you."[r]
[39]He said to them in reply, "An evil and unfaithful* generation seeks a sign, but no sign
will be given it except the sign of Jonah the
prophet. [40]Just as Jonah was in the belly of
the whale three days and three nights,* so
will the Son of Man be in the heart of the
earth three days and three nights. [41]* At the
judgment, the men of Nineveh will arise with
this generation and condemn it, because they
repented at the preaching of Jonah; and there
is something greater than Jonah here. [42]At
the judgment the queen of the south will arise
with this generation and condemn it, because
she came from the ends of the earth to hear
the wisdom of Solomon; and there is something greater than Solomon here.[s]

*The Return of the Unclean Spirit.**
[43][t] "When an unclean spirit goes out of a person it roams through arid regions searching
for rest but finds none. [44]Then it says, 'I will
return to my home from which I came.' But
upon returning, it finds it empty, swept
clean, and put in order. [45]Then it goes and
brings back with itself seven other spirits
more evil than itself, and they move in and
dwell there; and the last condition of that
person is worse than the first. Thus it will be
with this evil generation."

*The True Family of Jesus.** [46][u] While he
was still speaking to the crowds, his mother
and his brothers appeared outside, wishing
to speak with him. [47][Someone told him,
"Your mother and your brothers are standing
outside, asking to speak with you."]* [48]But
he said in reply to the one who told him,
"Who is my mother? Who are my brothers?"
[49]And stretching out his hand toward his disciples, he said, "Here are my mother and my
brothers. [50]For whoever does the will of my
heavenly Father is my brother, and sister,
and mother."

**12:33 Declare**: literally, "make." The meaning of this verse is obscure. Possibly it is a challenge to the Pharisees either to declare Jesus and his exorcisms good or both of them bad. A tree is known by its fruit; if the fruit is good, so must the tree be. If the driving out of demons is good, so must its source be.

**12:34** The admission of Jesus' goodness cannot be made by the Pharisees, for they are evil, and the words that proceed from their evil hearts cannot be good.

**12:36–37** If on the day of judgment people will be held accountable for even their **careless** words, the vicious accusations of the Pharisees will surely lead to their condemnation.

**12:38–42** This section is mainly from Q (see Lk 11:29–32). Mk 8:11–12, which Matthew has followed in Mt 16:1–4, has a similar demand for a sign. The scribes and Pharisees refuse to accept the exorcisms of Jesus as authentication of his claims and demand a sign that will end all possibility of doubt. Jesus' response is that no such sign will be given. Because his opponents are evil and see him as an agent of Satan, nothing will convince them.

**12:38 Teacher**: see note on Mt 8:19. In Mt 16:1 the request is for a sign "from heaven" (Mk 8:11).

**12:39 Unfaithful**: literally, "adulterous." The covenant between God and Israel was portrayed as a marriage bond, and unfaithfulness to the covenant as adultery; cf. Hos 2:4–14; Jer 3:6–10.

**12:40** See Jon 2:1. While in Q the sign was simply Jonah's preaching to the Ninevites (Lk 11:30, 32), Matthew here adds Jonah's sojourn **in the belly of the whale** for **three days and three nights**, a prefigurement of Jesus' sojourn in the abode of the dead and, implicitly, of his resurrection.

**12:41–42** The Ninevites who **repented** (see Jon 3:1–10) and **the queen of the south** (i.e., of Sheba; see 1 Kgs 10:1–13) were pagans who responded to lesser opportunities than have been offered to Israel in the ministry of Jesus, **something greater than Jonah** or **Solomon**. At the final judgment they will condemn the faithless **generation** that has rejected him.

**12:43–45** Another Q passage; cf. Mt 11:24–26. Jesus' ministry has broken Satan's hold over Israel, but the refusal of **this evil generation** to accept him will lead to a worse situation than what preceded his coming.

**12:46–50** See Mk 3:31–35. Matthew has omitted Mk 3:20–21 which is taken up in Mk 3:31 (see note on Mt 12:22–32), yet the point of the story is the same in both gospels: natural kinship with Jesus counts for nothing; only one who **does the will of** his **heavenly Father** belongs to his true family.

**12:47** This verse is omitted in some important textual witnesses, including Codex Sinaiticus (original reading) and Codex Vaticanus.

---

*o:* Lk 6:43–45. *p:* 3:7; 23:33; 15:11–12; Lk 3:7. *q:* Jas 3:1–2. *r:* 16:1–4; Jon 2:1; 3:1–10; Mk 8:11–12; Lk 11:29–32. *s:* 1 Kgs 10:1–10. *t:* Lk 11:24–26. *u:* Mk 3:31–35; Lk 8:19–21.

## CHAPTER 13

See RG 284–85

***The Parable of the Sower.*** 1* On that day, Jesus went out of the house and sat down by the sea.[v] 2 Such large crowds gathered around him that he got into a boat and sat down, and the whole crowd stood along the shore. 3* And he spoke to them at length in parables,* saying: "A sower went out to sow. 4 And as he sowed, some seed fell on the path, and birds came and ate it up. 5 Some fell on rocky ground, where it had little soil. It sprang up at once because the soil was not deep, 6 and when the sun rose it was scorched, and it withered for lack of roots. 7 Some seed fell among thorns, and the thorns grew up and choked it. 8 But some seed fell on rich soil, and produced fruit, a hundred or sixty or thirtyfold. 9 Whoever has ears ought to hear."

***The Purpose of Parables.*** 10 The disciples approached him and said, "Why do you speak to them in parables?" 11* He said to them in reply, "Because knowledge of the mysteries of the kingdom of heaven has been granted to you, but to them it has not been granted. 12[w] To anyone who has, more will be given* and he will grow rich; from anyone who has not, even what he has will be taken away. 13*[x] This is why I speak to them in parables, because 'they look but do not see and hear but do not listen or understand.' 14[y] Isaiah's prophecy is fulfilled in them, which says:

'You shall indeed hear but not understand
you shall indeed look but never see.
15 Gross is the heart of this people,
they will hardly hear with their ears,
they have closed their eyes,
lest they see with their eyes
and hear with their ears
and understand with their heart and be
converted,
and I heal them.'

**13:1–53** The discourse in parables is the third great discourse of Jesus in Matthew and constitutes the second part of the third book of the gospel. Matthew follows the Marcan outline (Mk 4:1–35) but has only two of Mark's parables, the five others being from Q and M. In addition to the seven parables, the discourse gives the reason why Jesus uses this type of speech (Mt 13:10–15), declares the blessedness of those who understand his teaching (Mt 13:16–17), explains the parable of the sower (Mt 13:18–23) and of the weeds (Mt 13:36–43), and ends with a concluding statement to the disciples (Mt 13:51–52).

**13:3–8** Since in Palestine sowing often preceded plowing, much of the seed is scattered on ground that is unsuitable. Yet while much is wasted, the seed that falls on good ground bears fruit in extraordinarily large measure. The point of the parable is that, in spite of some failure because of opposition and indifference, the message of Jesus about the coming of the kingdom will have enormous success.

**13:3 In parables**: the word "parable" (Greek *parabolē*) is used in the LXX to translate the Hebrew *māshāl*, a designation covering a wide variety of literary forms such as axioms, proverbs, similitudes, and allegories. In the New Testament the same breadth of meaning of the word is found, but there it primarily designates stories that are illustrative comparisons between Christian truths and events of everyday life. Sometimes the event has a strange element that is quite different from usual experience (e.g., in Mt 13:33 the enormous amount of dough in the parable of the yeast); this is meant to sharpen the curiosity of the hearer. If each detail of such a story is given a figurative meaning, the story is an allegory. Those who maintain a sharp distinction between parable and allegory insist that a parable has only one point of comparison, and that while parables were characteristic of Jesus' teaching, to see allegorical details in them is to introduce meanings that go beyond their original intention and even falsify it. However, to exclude any allegorical elements from a parable is an excessively rigid mode of interpretation, now abandoned by many scholars.

**13:11** Since a parable is figurative speech that demands reflection for understanding, only those who are prepared to explore its meaning can come to know it. To understand is a gift of God, granted to the disciples but not to the crowds. In Semitic fashion, both the disciples' understanding and the crowd's obtuseness are attributed to God. The question of human responsibility for the obtuseness is not dealt with, although it is asserted in Mt 13:13. **The mysteries**: as in Lk 8:10; Mk 4:11 has "the mystery." The word is used in Dn 2:18, 19, 27 and in the Qumran literature (1QpHab 7:8; 1QS 3:23; 1QM 3:9) to designate a divine plan or decree affecting the course of history that can be known only when revealed. **Knowledge of the mysteries of the kingdom of heaven** means recognition that the kingdom has become present in the ministry of Jesus.

**13:12** In the New Testament use of this axiom of practical "wisdom" (see Mt 25:29; Mk 4:25; Lk 8:18; 19:26), the reference transcends the original level. God gives further understanding to one who accepts the revealed mystery; from the one who does not, he will take it away (note the "theological passive," **more will be given, what he has will be taken away**).

**13:13 Because 'they look . . . or understand'**: Matthew softens his Marcan source, which states that Jesus speaks in parables so that the crowds may not understand (Mk 4:12), and makes such speaking a punishment given **because** they have not accepted his previous clear teaching. However, his citation of Is 6:9–10 in Mt 13:14 supports the harsher Marcan view.

*v:* Mk 4:1–12; Lk 8:4–10. *w:* 25:29; Mk 4:25; Lk 8:18; 19:26. *x:* Jn 9:39. *y:* Is 6:9–10; Jn 12:40; Acts 28:26–27; Rom 11:8.

***The Privilege of Discipleship.**** [16z] "But
blessed are your eyes, because they see, and
your ears, because they hear. [17] Amen, I say
to you, many prophets and righteous people
longed to see what you see but did not see it,
and to hear what you hear but did not hear it.
***The Explanation of the Parable of the
Sower.**** [18a] "Hear then the parable of the
sower. [19] The seed sown on the path is the
one who hears the word of the kingdom
without understanding it, and the evil one
comes and steals away what was sown in his
heart. [20] The seed sown on rocky ground is
the one who hears the word and receives it at
once with joy. [21] But he has no root and lasts
only for a time. When some tribulation or
persecution comes because of the word, he
immediately falls away. [22] The seed sown
among thorns is the one who hears the word,
but then worldly anxiety and the lure of
riches choke the word and it bears no fruit.
[23] But the seed sown on rich soil is the one
who hears the word and understands it, who
indeed bears fruit and yields a hundred or
sixty or thirtyfold."
***The Parable of the Weeds Among the
Wheat.*** [24] He proposed another parable to
them.* "The kingdom of heaven may be
likened to a man who sowed good seed in his
field. [25] While everyone was asleep his enemy came and sowed weeds* all through the
wheat, and then went off. [26] When the crop
grew and bore fruit, the weeds appeared as
well. [27] The slaves of the householder came
to him and said, 'Master, did you not sow
good seed in your field? Where have the
weeds come from?' [28] He answered, 'An enemy has done this.' His slaves said to him,
'Do you want us to go and pull them up?'
[29] He replied, 'No, if you pull up the weeds
you might uproot the wheat along with
them. [30] Let them grow together until harvest;* then at harvest time I will say to the
harvesters, "First collect the weeds and tie
them in bundles for burning; but gather the
wheat into my barn." '"[b]
***The Parable of the Mustard Seed.**** [31c] He
proposed another parable to them. "The
kingdom of heaven is like a mustard seed
that a person took and sowed in a field.
[32* d] It is the smallest of all the seeds, yet
when full-grown it is the largest of plants. It
becomes a large bush, and the 'birds of the
sky come and dwell in its branches.' "
***The Parable of the Yeast.*** [33] He spoke to
them another parable. "The kingdom of

**13:16–17** Unlike the unbelieving crowds, the disciples have seen that which the **prophets** and the **righteous** of the Old Testament **longed to see** without having their longing fulfilled.

**13:18–23** See Mk 4:14–20; Lk 8:11–15. In this explanation of the parable the emphasis is on the various types of soil on which the seed falls, i.e., on the dispositions with which the preaching of Jesus is received. The second and third types particularly are explained in such a way as to support the view held by many scholars that the explanation derives not from Jesus but from early Christian reflection upon apostasy from the faith that was the consequence of persecution and worldliness respectively. Others, however, hold that the explanation may come basically from Jesus even though it was developed in the light of later Christian experience. The four types of persons envisaged are (1) those who never accept **the word of the kingdom** (Mt 13:19); (2) those who believe for a while but fall away because of **persecution** (Mt 13:20–21); (3) those who believe, but in whom **the word** is choked by **worldly anxiety** and the seduction of **riches** (Mt 13:22); (4) those who respond to **the word** and produce **fruit** abundantly (Mt 13:23).

**13:24–30** This parable is peculiar to Matthew. The comparison in Mt 13:24 does not mean that **the kingdom of heaven may be likened** simply to the person in question but to the situation narrated in the whole story. The refusal of the **householder** to allow his **slaves** to separate **the wheat** from **the weeds** while they are still growing is a warning to the disciples not to attempt to anticipate the final judgment of God by a definitive exclusion of sinners from the kingdom. In its present stage it is composed of the good and the bad. The judgment of God alone will eliminate the sinful. Until then there must be patience and the preaching of repentance.

**13:25 Weeds**: darnel, a poisonous weed that in its first stage of growth resembles wheat.

**13:30 Harvest**: a common biblical metaphor for the time of God's judgment; cf. Jer 51:33; Jl 4:13; Hos 6:11.

**13:31–33** See Mk 4:30–32; Lk 13:18–21. The parables of the mustard seed and the yeast illustrate the same point: the amazing contrast between the small beginnings of the kingdom and its marvelous expansion.

**13:32** See Dn 4:7–9, 17–19 where the birds nesting in the tree represent the people of Nebuchadnezzar's kingdom. See also Ez 17:23; 31:6.

**13:33** Except in this Q parable and in Mt 16:12, **yeast** (or "leaven") is, in New Testament usage, a symbol of corruption (see Mt 16:6, 11–12; Mk 8:15; Lk 12:1; 1 Cor 5:6–8; Gal 5:9). **Three measures**: an enormous amount, enough to feed a hundred people. The exaggeration of this element of the parable points to the greatness of the kingdom's effect.

*z:* Lk 10:23–24; 1 Pt 1:10–12. *a:* Mk 4:13–20; Lk 8:11–15. *b:* 3:12. *c:* Mk 4:30–32; Lk 13:18–19. *d:* Ez 17:23; 31:6; Dn 4:7–9, 17–19.

heaven is like yeast* that a woman took and
mixed with three measures of wheat flour
until the whole batch was leavened."[e]

*The Use of Parables.* [34]*[f] All these things
Jesus spoke to the crowds in parables. He
spoke to them only in parables, [35]to fulfill
what had been said through the prophet:*

> "I will open my mouth in parables,
> I will announce what has lain hidden
> from the foundation [of the
> world]."[g]

***The Explanation of the Parable of the***
***Weeds.*** [36]Then, dismissing the crowds,* he
went into the house. His disciples approached him and said, "Explain to us the
parable of the weeds in the field." [37]* He said
in reply, "He who sows good seed is the Son
of Man, [38]the field is the world,* the good
seed the children of the kingdom. The weeds
are the children of the evil one, [39]and the enemy who sows them is the devil. The harvest
is the end of the age,* and the harvesters are
angels. [40]Just as weeds are collected and
burned [up] with fire, so will it be at the end
of the age. [41]The Son of Man will send his
angels, and they will collect out of his kingdom* all who cause others to sin and all evildoers. [42][h] They will throw them into the fiery
furnace, where there will be wailing and
grinding of teeth. [43]*[i] Then the righteous will
shine like the sun in the kingdom of their Father. Whoever has ears ought to hear.

*More Parables.** [44][j] "The kingdom of
heaven is like a treasure buried in a field,*
which a person finds and hides again, and
out of joy goes and sells all that he has and
buys that field. [45]Again, the kingdom of
heaven is like a merchant searching for fine
pearls. [46]When he finds a pearl of great
price, he goes and sells all that he has and
buys it. [47]Again, the kingdom of heaven is
like a net thrown into the sea, which collects
fish of every kind. [48]When it is full they haul
it ashore and sit down to put what is good
into buckets. What is bad they throw away.
[49]Thus it will be at the end of the age. The
angels will go out and separate the wicked
from the righteous [50]and throw them into the
fiery furnace, where there will be wailing
and grinding of teeth.

***Treasures New and Old.*** [51]"Do you understand* all these things?" They answered,
"Yes." [52]* And he replied, "Then every scribe

**13:34 Only in parables**: see Mt 13:10–15.

**13:35 The prophet**: some textual witnesses read "Isaiah the prophet." The quotation is actually from Ps 78:2; the first line corresponds to the LXX text of the psalm. The psalm's title ascribes it to Asaph, the founder of one of the guilds of temple musicians. He is called "the prophet" (NAB "the seer") in 2 Chr 29:30, but it is doubtful that Matthew averted to that; for him, any Old Testament text that could be seen as fulfilled in Jesus was prophetic.

**13:36 Dismissing the crowds**: the return of Jesus to the house marks a break with the crowds, who represent unbelieving Israel. From now on his attention is directed more and more to his disciples and to their instruction. The rest of the discourse is addressed to them alone.

**13:37–43** In the explanation of the parable of the weeds emphasis lies on the fearful end of the wicked, whereas the parable itself concentrates on patience with them until judgment time.

**13:38 The field is the world**: this presupposes the resurrection of Jesus and the granting to him of "all power in heaven and on earth" (Mt 28:18).

**13:39 The end of the age**: this phrase is found only in Matthew (13:40, 49; 24:3; 28:20).

**13:41 His kingdom**: the **kingdom** of **the Son of Man** is distinguished from that of the Father (Mt 13:43); see 1 Cor 15:24–25. The church is the place where Jesus' kingdom is manifested, but his royal authority embraces the entire world; see note on Mt 13:38.

**13:43** See Dn 12:3.

**13:44–50** The first two of the last three parables of the discourse have the same point. The **person** who **finds** a buried **treasure** and the **merchant** who finds a **pearl of great price** sell **all** that they have to acquire these finds; similarly, the one who understands the supreme value of the kingdom gives up whatever he must to obtain it. The **joy** with which this is done is made explicit in the first parable, but it may be presumed in the second also. The concluding parable of the fishnet resembles the explanation of the parable of the weeds with its stress upon the final exclusion of evil persons from the kingdom.

**13:44** In the unsettled conditions of Palestine in Jesus' time, it was not unusual to guard valuables by burying them in the ground.

**13:51** Matthew typically speaks of the understanding of the disciples.

**13:52** Since Matthew tends to identify the disciples and the Twelve (see note on Mt 10:1), this saying about the Christian **scribe** cannot be taken as applicable to all who accept the message of Jesus. While the Twelve are in many ways representative of all who believe in him, they are also distinguished from them in certain respects. The church of Matthew has leaders among whom are a group designated as "scribes" (Mt 23:34). Like the scribes of Israel, they are teachers. It is the Twelve and these their later counterparts to

*e:* Lk 13:20–21. *f:* Mk 4:33–34. *g:* Ps 78:2. *h:* 8:12; Rev 21:8. *i:* Dn 12:3. *j:* Prv 2:4; 4:7.

who has been instructed in the kingdom of
heaven is like the head of a household who
brings from his storeroom both the new and
the old." 53 When Jesus finished these parables, he went away from there.

## V. Jesus, the Kingdom, and the Church

***The Rejection at Nazareth.*** 54* He came to
his native place and taught the people in
their synagogue.[k] They were astonished* and
said, "Where did this man get such wisdom
and mighty deeds?[l] 55 Is he not the carpenter's son? Is not his mother named Mary and
his brothers James, Joseph, Simon, and Judas?[m] 56 Are not his sisters all with us?
Where did this man get all this?" 57 And they
took offense at him. But Jesus said to them,
"A prophet is not without honor except in his
native place and in his own house."[n] 58 And
he did not work many mighty deeds there
because of their lack of faith.

### CHAPTER 14

See RG 284–85

***Herod's Opinion of Jesus.*** 1* [o] At that
time Herod the tetrarch*[p] heard of the reputation of Jesus[q] 2 and said to his servants,
"This man is John the Baptist. He has been
raised from the dead; that is why mighty
powers are at work in him."

***The Death of John the Baptist.*** 3[r] Now
Herod had arrested John, bound [him], and put
him in prison on account of Herodias,* the
wife of his brother Philip, 4[s] for John had said
to him, "It is not lawful for you to have her."
5[t] Although he wanted to kill him, he feared
the people, for they regarded him as a prophet.
6 But at a birthday celebration for Herod, the
daughter of Herodias performed a dance before the guests and delighted Herod 7 so much
that he swore to give her whatever she might
ask for. 8 Prompted by her mother, she said,
"Give me here on a platter the head of John the
Baptist." 9 The king was distressed, but because of his oaths and the guests who were
present, he ordered that it be given, 10 and he
had John beheaded in the prison. 11 His head
was brought in on a platter and given to the
girl, who took it to her mother. 12 His disciples
came and took away the corpse and buried
him; and they went and told Jesus.

***The Return of the Twelve and the Feeding of the Five Thousand.*** * 13[u] When Jesus heard

whom this verse applies. **The scribe . . . instructed in the kingdom of heaven** knows both the teaching of Jesus (**the new**) and the law and prophets (**the old**) and provides in his own teaching **both the new and the old** as interpreted and fulfilled by **the new**. On the translation **head of a household** (for the same Greek word translated **householder** in Mt 13:27), see note on Mt 24:45–51.

**13:54–17:27** This section is the narrative part of the fourth book of the gospel.

**13:54–58** After the Sermon on the Mount the crowds are in admiring astonishment at Jesus' teaching (Mt 7:28); here the astonishment is of those who take **offense at him**. Familiarity with his background and family leads them to regard him as pretentious. Matthew modifies his Marcan source (Mt 6:1–6). Jesus is not the carpenter but **the carpenter's son** (Mt 13:55), "and among his own kin" is omitted (Mt 13:57), **he did not work many mighty deeds** in face of such unbelief (Mt 13:58) rather than the Marcan ". . . he was not able to perform any mighty deed there" (Mt 6:5), and there is no mention of his amazement at his townspeople's lack of faith.

**14:1–12** The murder of the Baptist by Herod Antipas prefigures the death of Jesus (see Mt 17:12). The Marcan source (Mk 6:14–29) is much reduced and in some points changed. In Mark Herod reveres John as a holy man and the desire to kill him is attributed to Herodias (Mk 6:19, 20), whereas here that desire is Herod's from the beginning (Mt 14:5).

**14:1 Herod the tetrarch**: Herod Antipas, son of Herod the Great. When the latter died, his territory was divided among three of his surviving sons, Archelaus who received half of it (Mt 2:23), Herod Antipas who became ruler of Galilee and Perea, and Philip who became ruler of northern Transjordan. Since he received a quarter of his father's domain, Antipas is accurately designated **tetrarch** ("ruler of a fourth [part]"), although in Mt 14:9 Matthew repeats the "king" of his Marcan source (Mk 6:26).

**14:3** Herodias was not the wife of Herod's half-brother Philip but of another half-brother, Herod Boethus. The union was prohibited by Lv 18:16; 20:21. According to Josephus (*Antiquities* 18:116–19), Herod imprisoned and then executed John because he feared that the Baptist's influence over the people might enable him to lead a rebellion.

**14:13–21** The feeding of the five thousand is the only miracle of Jesus that is recounted in all four gospels. The principal reason for that may be that it was seen as anticipating the Eucharist and the final banquet in the kingdom (Mt 8:11; 26:29), but it looks not only forward but backward, to the feeding of Israel with manna in the desert at the time of the Exodus (Ex 16), a miracle that in some contemporary Jewish expectation would be repeated in the messianic age (2 Bar 29:8). It may also be meant to recall Elisha's feeding a hundred men with small provisions (2 Kgs 4:42–44).

*k:* Mk 6:1–6; Lk 4:16–30. *l:* 2:23; Jn 1:46; 7:15. *m:* 12:46; 27:56; Jn 6:42. *n:* Jn 4:44. *o:* Mk 6:14–29. *p:* Lk 9:7–9. *q:* Lk 3:1. *r:* Lk 3:19–20. *s:* Lv 18:16; 20:21. *t:* 21:26. *u:* 15:32–38; Mk 6:32–44; Lk 9:10–17; Jn 6:1–13.

of it, he withdrew in a boat to a deserted
place by himself. The crowds heard of this
and followed him on foot from their towns.
14 When he disembarked and saw the vast
crowd, his heart was moved with pity for
them, and he cured their sick. 15 When it was
evening, the disciples approached him and
said, "This is a deserted place and it is already late; dismiss the crowds so that they
can go to the villages and buy food for themselves." 16 [Jesus] said to them, "There is no
need for them to go away; give them some
food yourselves." 17 But they said to him,
"Five loaves and two fish are all we have
here." 18 Then he said, "Bring them here to
me," 19 and he ordered the crowds to sit
down on the grass. Taking* the five loaves
and the two fish, and looking up to heaven,
he said the blessing, broke the loaves, and
gave them to the disciples, who in turn gave
them to the crowds. 20 They all ate and were
satisfied, and they picked up the fragments
left over*—twelve wicker baskets full.
21 Those who ate were about five thousand
men, not counting women and children.

***The Walking on the Water.**** 22v Then he
made the disciples get into the boat and precede him to the other side, while he dismissed the crowds. 23w After doing so, he
went up on the mountain by himself to pray.
When it was evening he was there alone.
24 Meanwhile the boat, already a few miles
offshore, was being tossed about by the
waves, for the wind was against it. 25 During
the fourth watch of the night,* he came toward them, walking on the sea. 26 When the
disciples saw him walking on the sea they
were terrified. "It is a ghost," they said, and
they cried out in fear. 27 At once [Jesus]
spoke to them, "Take courage, it is I;* do not
be afraid." 28 Peter said to him in reply,
"Lord, if it is you, command me to come to
you on the water." 29 He said, "Come." Peter
got out of the boat and began to walk on the
water toward Jesus. 30x But when he saw
how [strong] the wind was he became frightened; and, beginning to sink, he cried out,
"Lord, save me!" 31 Immediately Jesus
stretched out his hand and caught him, and
said to him, "O you of little faith,* why did
you doubt?" 32 After they got into the boat,
the wind died down. 33* y Those who were in
the boat did him homage, saying, "Truly,
you are the Son of God."

***The Healings at Gennesaret.*** 34z After
making the crossing, they came to land at
Gennesaret. 35 When the men of that place
recognized him, they sent word to all the surrounding country. People brought to him all
those who were sick 36a and begged him that
they might touch only the tassel on his cloak,
and as many as touched it were healed.

## CHAPTER 15

See RG 284–85

***The Tradition of the Elders.**** 1b Then
Pharisees and scribes came to Jesus from

**14:19** The **taking**, saying the blessing, breaking, and giving to the disciples correspond to the actions of Jesus over the bread at the Last Supper (Mt 26:26). Since they were usual at any Jewish meal, that correspondence does not necessarily indicate a eucharistic reference here. Matthew's silence about Jesus' dividing the fish among the people (Mk 6:41) is perhaps more significant in that regard.

**14:20 The fragments left over**: as in Elisha's miracle, food was **left over** after all had been fed. The word **fragments** (Greek *klasmata*) is used, in the singular, of the broken bread of the Eucharist in *Didache* 9:3–4.

**14:22–33** The disciples, laboring against the turbulent sea, are saved by Jesus. For his power over the waters, see note on Mt 8:26. Here that power is expressed also by his **walking on the sea** (Mt 14:25; cf. Ps 77:20; Jb 9:8). Matthew has inserted into the Marcan story (Mk 6:45–52) material that belongs to his special traditions on Peter (Mt 14:28–31).

**14:25 The fourth watch of the night**: between 3 a.m. and 6 a.m. The Romans divided the twelve hours between 6 p.m. and 6 a.m. into four equal parts called "watches."

**14:27 It is I**: see note on Mk 6:50.

**14:31 You of little faith**: see note on Mt 6:30. **Why did you doubt?**: the verb is peculiar to Matthew and occurs elsewhere only in Mt 28:17.

**14:33** This confession is in striking contrast to the Marcan parallel (Mk 6:51) where the disciples are "completely astounded."

**15:1–20** This dispute begins with the question of the Pharisees and scribes why Jesus' disciples are breaking **the tradition of the elders** about washing one's hands before eating (Mt 15:2). Jesus' counterquestion accuses his opponents of breaking **the commandment of God for the sake of** their **tradition** (Mt 15:3) and illustrates this by their interpretation of the commandment of the Decalogue concerning parents (Mt 15:4–6). Denouncing them as hypocrites, he applies to them a derogatory prophecy of Isaiah (Mt 15:7–8). Then with a wider audience (**the crowd**, Mt 15:10) he goes beyond the violation of tradition with which the dispute has started. The parable (Mt 15:11) is an attack on the Mosaic law concerning clean and un-

---

*v:* Mk 6:45–52; Jn 6:16–21. *w:* Mk 1:35; Lk 5:16; 6:12. *x:* 8:25–26. *y:* 16:16. *z:* Mk 6:53–56. *a:* 9:20–22. *b:* Mk 7:1–23.

Jerusalem and said, [2c]“Why do your disciples
break the tradition of the elders?* They do not
wash [their] hands when they eat a meal.” [3]He
said to them in reply, “And why do you break
the commandment of God* for the sake of
your tradition? [4d] For God said, ‘Honor your
father and your mother,’ and ‘Whoever curses
father or mother shall die.’ [5*] But you say,
‘Whoever says to father or mother, “Any support you might have had from me is dedicated
to God,” [6]need not honor his father.’ You have
nullified the word of God for the sake of your
tradition. [7]Hypocrites, well did Isaiah prophesy about you when he said:

[8 e] ‘This people honors me with their lips,*
but their hearts are far from me;
[9 f] in vain do they worship me,
teaching as doctrines human
precepts.’ ”

[10g] He summoned the crowd and said to
them, “Hear and understand. [11]It is not what
enters one’s mouth that defiles that person;
but what comes out of the mouth is what defiles one.” [12]Then his disciples approached
and said to him, “Do you know that the Pharisees took offense when they heard what you
said?” [13]He said in reply,* “Every plant that
my heavenly Father has not planted will be
uprooted. [14h] Let them alone; they are blind
guides (of the blind). If a blind person leads
a blind person, both will fall into a pit.”
[15]Then Peter* said to him in reply, “Explain
[this] parable to us.” [16]He said to them, “Are
even you still without understanding? [17]Do
you not realize that everything that enters
the mouth passes into the stomach and is expelled into the latrine? [18i] But the things that
come out of the mouth come from the heart,
and they defile. [19*] For from the heart come
evil thoughts, murder, adultery, unchastity,
theft, false witness, blasphemy. [20]These are
what defile a person, but to eat with unwashed hands does not defile.”

***The Canaanite Woman’s Faith.**** [21j] Then
Jesus went from that place and withdrew to
the region of Tyre and Sidon. [22]And behold,
a Canaanite woman of that district came and
called out, “Have pity on me, Lord, Son of
David! My daughter is tormented by a demon.” [23]But he did not say a word in answer
to her. His disciples came and asked him,
“Send her away, for she keeps calling out after us.” [24*] He said in reply, “I was sent only
to the lost sheep of the house of Israel.”
[25k] But the woman came and did him homage, saying, “Lord, help me.” [26]He said in
reply, “It is not right to take the food of the
children* and throw it to the dogs.” [27]She
said, “Please, Lord, for even the dogs eat the
scraps that fall from the table of their masters.” [28l] Then Jesus said to her in reply, “O

clean foods, similar to those antitheses that abrogate the law (Mt 5:31–32, 33–34, 38–39). After a warning to his disciples not to follow the moral guidance of the Pharisees (Mt 15:13–14), he explains the **parable** (Mt 15:15) to them, saying that defilement comes not from what **enters the mouth** (Mt 15:17) but from the evil thoughts and deeds that rise from within, **from the heart** (Mt 15:18–20). The last verse returns to the starting point of the dispute (eating **with unwashed hands**). Because of Matthew’s omission of Mk 7:19b, some scholars think that Matthew has weakened the Marcan repudiation of the Mosaic food laws. But that half verse is ambiguous in the Greek, which may be the reason for its omission here.

**15:2 The tradition of the elders**: see note on Mk 7:5. The purpose of the handwashing was to remove defilement caused by contact with what was ritually unclean.

**15:3–4** For the commandment see Ex 20:12 (// Dt 5:16); 21:17. The honoring of one’s parents had to do with supporting them in their needs.

**15:5** See note on Mk 7:11.

**15:8** The text of Is 29:13 is quoted approximately according to the Septuagint.

**15:13–14** Jesus leads his disciples away from the teaching authority of the Pharisees.

**15:15** Matthew specifies **Peter** as the questioner, unlike Mk 7:17. Given his tendency to present the disciples as more understanding than in his Marcan source, it is noteworthy that here he retains the Marcan rebuke, although in a slightly milder form. This may be due to his wish to correct the Jewish Christians within his church who still held to the food laws and thus separated themselves from Gentile Christians who did not observe them.

**15:19** The Marcan list of thirteen things that defile (Mk 7:21–22) is here reduced to seven that partially cover the content of the Decalogue.

**15:21–28** See note on Mt 8:5–13.

**15:24** See note on Mt 10:5–6.

**15:26 The children**: the people of Israel. **Dogs**: see note on Mt 7:6.

**15:28** As in the case of the cure of the centurion’s servant (Mt 8:10), Matthew ascribes Jesus’ granting the request to the woman’s **great faith**, a point not made equally explicit in the Marcan parallel (Mk 7:24–30).

*c:* Lk 11:38. *d:* Ex 20:12; 21:17; Lv 20:9; Dt 5:16; Prv 20:20. *e:* Is 29:13 LXX. *f:* Col 2:23. *g:* Mk 7:14. *h:* 23:16, 19, 24; Lk 6:39; Jn 9:40. *i:* 12:34. *j:* Mk 7:24–30. *k:* 10:6. *l:* 8:10.

woman, great is your faith!* Let it be done
for you as you wish." And her daughter was
healed from that hour.

*The Healing of Many People.* 29 Moving on
from there Jesus walked by the Sea of Galilee, went up on the mountain, and sat down
there. 30m Great crowds came to him, having
with them the lame, the blind, the deformed,
the mute, and many others. They placed
them at his feet, and he cured them. 31 The
crowds were amazed when they saw the
mute speaking, the deformed made whole,
the lame walking, and the blind able to see,
and they glorified the God of Israel.

*The Feeding of the Four Thousand.**
32n Jesus summoned his disciples and said,
"My heart is moved with pity for the crowd,
for they have been with me now for three
days and have nothing to eat. I do not want
to send them away hungry, for fear they may
collapse on the way." 33 The disciples said to
him, "Where could we ever get enough
bread in this deserted place to satisfy such a
crowd?" 34 Jesus said to them, "How many
loaves do you have?" "Seven," they replied,
"and a few fish." 35 He ordered the crowd to
sit down on the ground. 36 Then he took the
seven loaves and the fish, gave thanks,*
broke the loaves, and gave them to the disciples, who in turn gave them to the crowds.
37o They all ate and were satisfied. They
picked up the fragments left over—seven
baskets full. 38 Those who ate were four
thousand men, not counting women and
children. 39 And when he had dismissed the
crowds, he got into the boat and came to the
district of Magadan.

## CHAPTER 16

See RG 284–87

*The Demand for a Sign.* 1* p The Pharisees and Sadducees came and, to test him,
asked him to show them a sign from heaven.
2* He said to them in reply, "[In the evening
you say, 'Tomorrow will be fair, for the sky
is red'; 3q and, in the morning, 'Today will
be stormy, for the sky is red and threatening.' You know how to judge the appearance
of the sky, but you cannot judge the signs of
the times.] 4r An evil and unfaithful generation seeks a sign, but no sign will be given it
except the sign of Jonah."* Then he left them
and went away.

*The Leaven of the Pharisees and Sad-
ducees.* 5s In coming to the other side of the
sea,* the disciples had forgotten to bring
bread. 6t Jesus said to them, "Look out, and
beware of the leaven* of the Pharisees and
Sadducees." 7* They concluded among
themselves, saying, "It is because we have
brought no bread." 8 When Jesus became
aware of this he said, "You of little faith,
why do you conclude among yourselves that
it is because you have no bread? 9u Do you
not yet understand, and do you not remember the five loaves for the five thousand, and
how many wicker baskets you took up?
10v Or the seven loaves for the four thousand,
and how many baskets you took up? 11 How
do you not comprehend that I was not speaking to you about bread? Beware of the

**15:32–39** Most probably this story is a doublet of that of the feeding of the five thousand (Mt 14:13–21). It differs from it notably only in that Jesus takes the initiative, not the disciples (Mt 15:32), and in the numbers: the crowd has been with Jesus **three days** (Mt 15:32), **seven loaves** are multiplied (Mt 15:36), **seven baskets** of **fragments** remain after the feeding (Mt 15:37), and **four thousand** men are fed (Mt 15:38).

**15:36 Gave thanks**: see Mt 14:19, "said the blessing." There is no difference in meaning. The thanksgiving was a blessing of God for his benefits.

**16:1 A sign from heaven**: see note on Mt 12:38–42.

**16:2–3** The answer of Jesus in these verses is omitted in many important textual witnesses, and it is very uncertain that it is an original part of this gospel. It resembles Lk 12:54–56 and may have been inserted from there. It rebukes the Pharisees and Sadducees who are able to read indications of coming weather but not the indications of the coming kingdom in the signs that Jesus does offer, his mighty deeds and teaching.

**16:4** See notes on Mt 12:39, 40.

**16:5–12** Jesus' warning his disciples against **the teaching of the Pharisees and Sadducees** comes immediately before his promise to confer on Peter the authority to bind and to loose on earth (Mt 16:19), an authority that will be confirmed in heaven. Such authority most probably has to do, at least in part, with teaching. The rejection of the teaching authority of the Pharisees (see also Mt 12:12–14) prepares for a new one derived from Jesus.

**16:6 Leaven**: see note on Mt 13:33. **Sadducees**: Matthew's Marcan source speaks rather of "the leaven of Herod" (Mk 8:15).

**16:7–11** The disciples, men **of little faith**, misunderstand Jesus' metaphorical use of **leaven**, forgetting that, as the feeding of the crowds shows, he is not at a loss to provide them with bread.

*m:* Is 35:5–6. *n:* Mk 8:1–10. *o:* 16:10. *p:* Mk 8:11–21. *q:* Lk 12:54–56. *r:* 12:39; Jon 2:1. *s:* Mk 8:14–21. *t:* Lk 12:1. *u:* 14:17–21; Jn 6:9. *v:* 15:34–38.

leaven of the Pharisees and Sadducees."
12 Then they understood* that he was not
telling them to beware of the leaven of
bread, but of the teaching of the Pharisees
and Sadducees.

***Peter's Confession About Jesus.**** 13[w] When
Jesus went into the region of Caesarea Philippi* he asked his disciples, "Who do people
say that the Son of Man is?" 14[x] They replied,
"Some say John the Baptist,* others Elijah,
still others Jeremiah or one of the prophets."
15 He said to them, "But who do you say that
I am?" 16* [y] Simon Peter said in reply, "You
are the Messiah, the Son of the living God."
17 Jesus said to him in reply, "Blessed are you,
Simon son of Jonah. For flesh and blood* has
not revealed this to you, but my heavenly Father. 18[z] And so I say to you, you are Peter,
and upon this rock I will build my church,*
and the gates of the netherworld shall not prevail against it. 19[a] I will give you the keys to
the kingdom of heaven.* Whatever you bind

**16:12** After his rebuke, the disciples understand that by **leaven** he meant the corrupting influence of **the teaching of the Pharisees and Sadducees.** The evangelist probably understands this **teaching** as common to both groups. Since at the time of Jesus' ministry the two differed widely on points of teaching, e.g., the resurrection of the dead, and at the time of the evangelist the Sadducee party was no longer a force in Judaism, the supposed common teaching fits neither period. The disciples' eventual understanding of Jesus' warning contrasts with their continuing obtuseness in the Marcan parallel (Mk 8:14–21).

**16:13–20** The Marcan confession of Jesus as Messiah, made by Peter as spokesman for the other disciples (Mk 8:27–29; cf. also Lk 9:18–20), is modified significantly here. The confession is of Jesus both as **Messiah** and as **Son of the living God** (Mt 16:16). Jesus' response, drawn principally from material peculiar to Matthew, attributes the confession to a divine revelation granted to Peter alone (Mt 16:17) and makes him the **rock** on which Jesus **will build** his **church** (Mt 16:18) and the disciple whose authority in the church **on earth** will be confirmed in **heaven**, i.e., by God (Mt 16:19).

**16:13 Caesarea Philippi**: situated about twenty miles north of the Sea of Galilee in the territory ruled by Philip, a son of Herod the Great, tetrarch from 4 B.C. until his death in A.D. 34 (see note on Mt 14:1). He rebuilt the town of Paneas, naming it **Caesarea** in honor of the emperor, and **Philippi** ("of Philip") to distinguish it from the seaport in Samaria that was also called Caesarea. **Who do people say that the Son of Man is?**: although the question differs from the Marcan parallel (Mk 8:27: "Who . . . that I am?"), the meaning is the same, for Jesus here refers to himself as the **Son of Man** (cf. Mt 16:15).

**16:14 John the Baptist**: see Mt 14:2. **Elijah**: cf. Mal 3:23–24; Sir 48:10; and see note on Mt 3:4. **Jeremiah**: an addition of Matthew to the Marcan source.

**16:16 The Son of the living God**: see Mt 2:15; 3:17. The addition of this exalted title to the Marcan confession eliminates whatever ambiguity was attached to the title Messiah. This, among other things, supports the view proposed by many scholars that Matthew has here combined his source's confession with a post-resurrectional confession of faith in Jesus as **Son of the living God** that belonged to the appearance of the risen Jesus to Peter; cf. 1 Cor 15:5; Lk 24:34.

**16:17 Flesh and blood**: a Semitic expression for human beings, especially in their weakness. **Has not revealed this . . . but my heavenly Father**: that Peter's faith is spoken of as coming not through human means but through a revelation from God is similar to Paul's description of his recognition of who Jesus was; see Gal 1:15–16, ". . . when he [God] . . . was pleased to reveal his Son to me. . . ."

**16:18 You are Peter, and upon this rock I will build my church**: the Aramaic word *kēpā'* meaning **rock** and transliterated into Greek as *Kēphas* is the name by which Peter is called in the Pauline letters (1 Cor 1:12; 3:22; 9:5; 15:4; Gal 1:18; 2:9, 11, 14) except in Gal 2:7–8 ("Peter"). It is translated as *Petros* ("Peter") in Jn 1:42. The presumed original Aramaic of Jesus' statement would have been, in English, "You are the Rock (*Kēpā'*) and upon this rock (*kēpā'*) I will build my church." The Greek text probably means the same, for the difference in gender between the masculine noun *petros*, the disciple's new name, and the feminine noun *petra* (rock) may be due simply to the unsuitability of using a feminine noun as the proper name of a male. Although the two words were generally used with slightly different nuances, they were also used interchangeably with the same meaning, "rock." **Church**: this word (Greek *ekklēsia*) occurs in the gospels only here and in Mt 18:17 (twice). There are several possibilities for an Aramaic original. Jesus' **church** means the community that he **will** gather and that, like a building, will have Peter as its solid foundation. That function of Peter consists in his being witness to Jesus as **the Messiah, the Son of the living God. The gates of the netherworld shall not prevail against it**: the netherworld (Greek *Hadēs*, the abode of the dead) is conceived of as a walled city whose **gates** will not close in upon the church of Jesus, i.e., it will not be overcome by the power of death.

**16:19 The keys to the kingdom of heaven**: the image of the keys is probably drawn from Is 22:15–25 where Eliakim, who succeeds Shebna as master of the palace, is given "the key of the House of David," which he authoritatively "opens" and "shuts" (Is 22:22). **Whatever you bind . . . loosed in heaven**: there are many instances in rabbinic literature of the binding-loosing imagery. Of the several meanings given there to the metaphor, two are of special importance here: the giving of authoritative teaching, and the lifting or imposing of the ban of excommunication. It is disputed whether the image of the keys and that of binding and loosing are different metaphors meaning the same thing. In any case, the promise of **the keys** is given to Peter alone. In Mt 18:18 all the disciples are given the power of binding and loosing, but the context of that verse suggests that there the power of excommunication alone is intended. That **the keys** are those **to the kingdom of heaven** and that Peter's exercise of authority in the church **on earth** will be confirmed **in heaven** show an intimate connection between, but not an identification of, the church and **the kingdom of heaven.**

*w:* Mk 8:27–29; Lk 9:18–20. *x:* 14:2. *y:* Jn 6:69. *z:* Jn 1:42. *a:* Is 22:22; Rev 3:7.

on earth shall be bound in heaven; and whatever you loose on earth shall be loosed in
heaven." 20* [b] Then he strictly ordered his
disciples to tell no one that he was the Messiah.

***The First Prediction of the Passion.****
21 [c] From that time on, Jesus began to show
his disciples that he* must go to Jerusalem
and suffer greatly from the elders, the chief
priests, and the scribes, and be killed and on
the third day be raised.[d] 22* Then Peter took
him aside and began to rebuke him, "God
forbid, Lord! No such thing shall ever happen to you." 23 [e] He turned and said to Peter,
"Get behind me, Satan! You are an obstacle
to me. You are thinking not as God does, but
as human beings do."

***The Conditions of Discipleship.**** 24 [f] Then
Jesus said to his disciples, "Whoever wishes
to come after me must deny himself,* take
up his cross, and follow me. 25 [g] For whoever
wishes to save his life will lose it, but whoever loses his life for my sake will find it.*
26 What profit would there be for one to gain
the whole world and forfeit his life? Or what
can one give in exchange for his life?
27* [h] For the Son of Man will come with his
angels in his Father's glory, and then he will
repay everyone according to his conduct.
28* Amen, I say to you, there are some standing here who will not taste death until they
see the Son of Man coming in his kingdom."

## CHAPTER 17

See RG 285-87

***The Transfiguration of Jesus.**** 1 [i] After
six days Jesus took Peter, James, and John
his brother, and led them up a high mountain
by themselves.* 2* [j] And he was transfigured

**16:20** Cf. Mk 8:30. Matthew makes explicit that the prohibition has to do with speaking of Jesus as **the Messiah**; see note on Mk 8:27–30.

**16:21–23** This first prediction of the passion follows Mk 8:31–33 in the main and serves as a corrective to an understanding of Jesus' messiahship as solely one of glory and triumph. By his addition of **from that time on** (Mt 16:21) Matthew has emphasized that Jesus' revelation of his coming suffering and death marks a new phase of the gospel. Neither this nor the two later passion predictions (Mt 17:22–23; 20:17–19) can be taken as sayings that, as they stand, go back to Jesus himself. However, it is probable that he foresaw that his mission would entail suffering and perhaps death, but was confident that he would ultimately be vindicated by God (see Mt 26:29).

**16:21 He**: the Marcan parallel (Mk 8:31) has "the Son of Man." Since Matthew has already designated Jesus by that title (Mt 15:13), its omission here is not significant. The Matthean prediction is equally about the sufferings of the Son of Man. **Must**: this necessity is part of the tradition of all the synoptics; cf. Mk 8:31; Lk 9:21. **The elders, the chief priests, and the scribes**: see note on Mk 8:31. **On the third day**: so also Lk 9:22, against the Marcan "after three days" (Mk 8:31). Matthew's formulation is, in the Greek, almost identical with the pre-Pauline fragment of the kerygma in 1 Cor 15:4 and also with Hos 6:2, which many take to be the Old Testament background to the confession that Jesus was raised **on the third day**. Josephus uses "after three days" and "on the third day" interchangeably (*Antiquities* 7:280–81; 8:214, 218) and there is probably no difference in meaning between the two phrases.

**16:22–23** Peter's refusal to accept Jesus' predicted suffering and death is seen as a satanic attempt to deflect Jesus from his God-appointed course, and the disciple is addressed in terms that recall Jesus' dismissal of the devil in the temptation account (Mt 4:10: "Get away, Satan!"). Peter's satanic purpose is emphasized by Matthew's addition to the Marcan source of the words **You are an obstacle to me**.

**16:24–28** A readiness to follow Jesus even to giving up one's life for him is the condition for true discipleship; this will be repaid by him at the final judgment.

**16:24 Deny himself**: to deny someone is to disown him (see Mt 10:33; 26:34–35) and to deny oneself is to disown oneself as the center of one's existence.

**16:25** See notes on Mt 10:38, 39.

**16:27** The parousia and final judgment are described in Mt 25:31 in terms almost identical with these.

**16:28 Coming in his kingdom**: since the **kingdom** of the **Son of Man** has been described as "the world" and Jesus' sovereignty precedes his final coming in glory (Mt 13:38, 41), the coming in this verse is not the parousia as in the preceding but the manifestation of Jesus' rule after his resurrection; see notes on Mt 13:38, 41.

**17:1–8** The account of the transfiguration confirms that Jesus is the **Son** of God (Mt 17:5) and points to fulfillment of the prediction that he will come **in his Father's glory** at the end of the age (Mt 16:27). It has been explained by some as a resurrection appearance retrojected into the time of Jesus' ministry, but that is not probable since the account lacks many of the usual elements of the resurrection-appearance narratives. It draws upon motifs from the Old Testament and noncanonical Jewish apocalyptic literature that express the presence of the heavenly and the divine, e.g., brilliant light, white garments, and the overshadowing cloud.

**17:1** These three disciples are also taken apart from the others by Jesus in Gethsemane (Mt 26:37). **A high mountain**: this has been identified with Tabor or Hermon, but probably no specific mountain was intended by the evangelist or by his Marcan source (Mk 9:2). Its meaning is theological rather than geographical, possibly recalling the revelation to Moses on Mount Sinai (Ex 24:12–18) and to Elijah at the same place (1 Kgs 19:8–18; Horeb = Sinai).

*b:* Mk 8:30; Lk 9:21. *c:* Mk 8:31–9:1; Lk 9:22–27. *d:* 17:22–23; 20:17–19. *e:* 4:10. *f:* Lk 14:27. *g:* Lk 17:33; Jn 12:25. *h:* 25:31–33; Jb 34:11; Ps 62:13; Jer 17:10; 2 Thes 1:7–8. *i:* Mk 9:2–8; Lk 9:28–36.

before them; his face shone like the sun and
his clothes became white as light. 3* And behold, Moses and Elijah appeared to them,
conversing with him. 4Then Peter said to
Jesus in reply, "Lord, it is good that we are
here. If you wish, I will make three tents*
here, one for you, one for Moses, and one for
Elijah." 5[k] While he was still speaking, behold, a bright cloud cast a shadow over
them,* then from the cloud came a voice that
said, "This is my beloved Son, with whom I
am well pleased; listen to him." 6* When the
disciples heard this, they fell prostrate and
were very much afraid. 7But Jesus came and
touched them, saying, "Rise, and do not be
afraid." 8And when the disciples raised their
eyes, they saw no one else but Jesus alone.

***The Coming of Elijah.**** 9[l] As they were
coming down from the mountain, Jesus
charged them, "Do not tell the vision* to
anyone until the Son of Man has been raised
from the dead." 10*[m] Then the disciples
asked him, "Why do the scribes say that Elijah must come first?" 11[n] He said in reply,*
"Elijah will indeed come and restore all
things; 12[o] but I tell you that Elijah has already come, and they did not recognize him
but did to him whatever they pleased. So
also will the Son of Man suffer at their
hands." 13* Then the disciples understood
that he was speaking to them of John the
Baptist.

***The Healing of a Boy with a Demon.****
14[p] When they came to the crowd a man approached, knelt down before him, 15and
said, "Lord, have pity on my son, for he is a
lunatic* and suffers severely; often he falls
into fire, and often into water. 16I brought
him to your disciples, but they could not
cure him." 17[q] Jesus said in reply, "O faithless and perverse* generation, how long will
I be with you? How long will I endure you?

**17:2 His face shone like the sun**: this is a Matthean addition; cf. Dn 10:6. **His clothes became white as light**: cf. Dn 7:9, where the clothing of God appears "snow bright." For the white garments of other heavenly beings, see Rev 4:4; 7:9; 19:14.

**17:3** See note on Mk 9:5.

**17:4 Three tents**: the booths in which the Israelites lived during the feast of Tabernacles (cf. Jn 7:2) were meant to recall their ancestors' dwelling in booths during the journey from Egypt to the promised land (Lv 23:39–42). The same Greek word, *skēnē*, here translated **tents**, is used in the LXX for the booths of that feast, and some scholars have suggested that there is an allusion here to that liturgical custom.

**17:5 Cloud cast a shadow over them**: see note on Mk 9:7. **This is my beloved Son . . . listen to him**: cf. Mt 3:17. The voice repeats the baptismal proclamation about Jesus, with the addition of the command **listen to him**. The latter is a reference to Dt 18:15 in which the Israelites are commanded to **listen to** the prophet like Moses whom God will raise up for them. The command to listen to Jesus is general, but in this context it probably applies particularly to the preceding predictions of his passion and resurrection (Mt 16:21) and of his coming (Mt 16:27, 28).

**17:6–7** A Matthean addition; cf. Dn 10:9–10, 18–19.

**17:9–13** In response to the disciples' question about the expected return of Elijah, Jesus interprets the mission of the Baptist as the fulfillment of that expectation. But that was not suspected by those who opposed and finally killed him, and Jesus predicts a similar fate for himself.

**17:9 The vision**: Matthew alone uses this word to describe the transfiguration. **Until the Son of Man has been raised from the dead**: only in the light of Jesus' resurrection can the meaning of his life and mission be truly understood; until then no testimony to **the vision** will lead people to faith.

**17:10** See notes on Mt 3:4; 16:14.

**17:11–12** The preceding question and this answer may reflect later controversy with Jews who objected to the Christian claims for Jesus that Elijah had not yet come.

**17:13** See Mt 11:14.

**17:14–20** Matthew has greatly shortened the Marcan story (Mk 9:14–29). Leaving aside several details of the boy's illness, he concentrates on the need for faith, not so much on the part of the boy's father (as does Mark, for Matthew omits Mk 9:22b–24) but on that of his own disciples whose inability to drive out the demon is ascribed to their **little faith** (Mt 17:20).

**17:15 A lunatic**: this description of the boy is peculiar to Matthew. The word occurs in the New Testament only here and in Mt 4:24 and means one affected or struck by the moon. The symptoms of the boy's illness point to epilepsy, and attacks of this were thought to be caused by phases of the moon.

**17:17 Faithless and perverse**: so Matthew and Luke (Lk 9:41) against Mark's **faithless** (Mk 9:19). The Greek word here translated **perverse** is the same as that in Dt 32:5 LXX, where Moses speaks to his people. There is a problem in knowing to whom the reproach is addressed. Since the Matthean Jesus normally chides his disciples for their **little faith** (as in Mt 17:20), it would appear that the charge of lack of faith could not be made against them and that the reproach is addressed to unbelievers among the Jews. However in Mt 17:20b (**if you have faith the size of a mustard seed**), which is certainly addressed to the disciples, they appear to have not even the smallest faith; if they had, they would have been able to cure the boy. In the light of Mt 17:20b the reproach of Mt 17:17 could have applied to the disciples. There seems to be an inconsistency between the charge of **little faith** in Mt 17:20a and that of not even a little in Mt 17:20b.

*j:* 28:3; Dn 7:9; 10:6; Rev 4:4; 7:9; 19:14. *k:* 3:17; Dt 18:15; 2 Pt 1:17. *l:* Mk 9:9–13. *m:* Mal 3:23–24. *n:* Lk 1:17. *o:* 11:14. *p:* Mk 9:14–29; Lk 9:37–43. *q:* Dt 32:5 LXX.

Bring him here to me." 18 Jesus rebuked him
and the demon came out of him,* and from
that hour the boy was cured. 19 Then the disciples approached Jesus in private and said,
"Why could we not drive it out?" 20*[r] He
said to them, "Because of your little faith.
Amen, I say to you, if you have faith the size
of a mustard seed, you will say to this mountain, 'Move from here to there,' and it will
move. Nothing will be impossible for
you." [21]*

***The Second Prediction of the Passion.****
22[s] As they were gathering in Galilee, Jesus
said to them, "The Son of Man is to be
handed over to men, 23 and they will kill him,
and he will be raised on the third day." And
they were overwhelmed with grief.

***Payment of the Temple Tax.**** 24[t] When they
came to Capernaum, the collectors of the temple tax* approached Peter and said, "Doesn't
your teacher pay the temple tax?" 25 "Yes," he
said.* When he came into the house, before he
had time to speak, Jesus asked him, "What is
your opinion, Simon? From whom do the
kings of the earth take tolls or census tax?
From their subjects or from foreigners?"
26* When he said, "From foreigners," Jesus
said to him, "Then the subjects are exempt.
27 But that we may not offend them,* go to the
sea, drop in a hook, and take the first fish that
comes up. Open its mouth and you will find a
coin worth twice the temple tax. Give that to
them for me and for you."

## CHAPTER 18*

See RG 285–87

***The Greatest in the Kingdom.*** 1[u] At
that time the disciples* approached Jesus
and said, "Who is the greatest in the king-

**17:18 The demon came out of him**: not until this verse does Matthew indicate that the boy's illness is a case of demoniacal possession.

**17:20** The entire verse is an addition of Matthew who (according to the better attested text) omits the reason given for the disciples' inability in Mk 9:29. **Little faith**: see note on Mt 6:30. **Faith the size of a mustard seed . . . and it will move**: a combination of a Q saying (cf. Lk 17:6) with a Marcan saying (cf. Mk 11:23).

**17:21** Some manuscripts add, "But this kind does not come out except by prayer and fasting"; this is a variant of the better reading of Mk 9:29.

**17:22–23** The second passion prediction (cf. Mt 16:21–23) is the least detailed of the three and may be the earliest. In the Marcan parallel the disciples do not understand (Mk 9:32); here they understand and are **overwhelmed with grief** at the prospect of Jesus' death (Mt 17:23).

**17:24–27** Like Mt 14:28–31 and Mt 16:16b–19, this episode comes from Matthew's special material on Peter. Although the question of **the collectors** concerns Jesus' payment of **the temple tax**, it is put to **Peter**. It is he who receives instruction from Jesus about freedom from the obligation of payment and yet why it should be made. The means of doing so is provided miraculously. The pericope deals with a problem of Matthew's church, whether its members should pay the temple tax, and the answer is given through a word of Jesus conveyed to Peter. Some scholars see here an example of the teaching authority of Peter exercised in the name of Jesus (see Mt 16:19). The specific problem was a Jewish Christian one and may have arisen when the Matthean church was composed largely of that group.

**17:24 The temple tax**: before the destruction of the Jerusalem temple in A.D. 70 every male Jew above nineteen years of age was obliged to make an annual contribution to its upkeep (cf. Ex 30:11–16; Neh 10:33). After the destruction the Romans imposed upon Jews the obligation of paying that tax for the temple of Jupiter Capitolinus. There is disagreement about which period the story deals with.

**17:25 From their subjects or from foreigners?**: the Greek word here translated **subjects** literally means "sons."

**17:26 Then the subjects are exempt**: just as **subjects** are not bound by laws applying to **foreigners**, neither are Jesus and his disciples, who belong to the kingdom of heaven, bound by the duty of paying the temple tax imposed on those who are not of the kingdom. If the Greek is translated "sons," the freedom of Jesus, the Son of God, and of his disciples, children ("sons") of the kingdom (cf. Mt 13:38), is even more clear.

**17:27 That we may not offend them**: though they are exempt (Mt 17:26), Jesus and his disciples are to avoid giving offense; therefore the tax is to be paid. **A coin worth twice the temple tax**: literally, "a stater," a Greek coin worth two double drachmas. Two double drachmas were equal to the Jewish shekel and the tax was a half-shekel. **For me and for you**: not only Jesus but Peter pays the tax, and this example serves as a standard for the conduct of all the disciples.

**18:1–35** This discourse of the fourth book of the gospel is often called the "church order" discourse, but it lacks most of the considerations usually connected with church order, such as various offices in the church and the duties of each, and deals principally with the relations that must obtain among the members of the church. Beginning with the warning that greatness in **the kingdom of heaven** is measured not by rank or power but by childlikeness (Mt 18:1–5), it deals with the care that the disciples must take not to cause the **little ones to sin** or to neglect them if they stray from the community (Mt 18:6–14), the correction of members who sin (Mt 18:15–18), the efficacy of the prayer of the disciples because of the presence of Jesus (Mt 18:19–20), and the forgiveness that must be repeatedly extended to sinful members who repent (Mt 18:21–35).

**18:1** The initiative is taken not by Jesus as in the Marcan parallel (Mk 9:33–34) but by the disciples. **Kingdom of heaven**: this may mean **the kingdom** in its fullness, i.e., after the parousia and the final judgment. But what follows about causes of sin, church discipline, and forgiveness, all dealing

*r:* 21:21; Lk 17:6; 1 Cor 13:2. *s:* 16:21; 20:18–19. *t:* Ex 30:11–16; Neh 10:33. *u:* Mk 9:36–37; Lk 9:46–48.

dom of heaven?" [2]He called a child over,
placed it in their midst, [3y] and said, "Amen,
I say to you, unless you turn and become like
children,* you will not enter the kingdom of
heaven. [4w] Whoever humbles himself like
this child is the greatest in the kingdom of
heaven. [5*] And whoever receives one child
such as this in my name receives me.

***Temptations to Sin.*** [6x] "Whoever causes
one of these little ones* who believe in me to
sin, it would be better for him to have a great
millstone hung around his neck and to be
drowned in the depths of the sea. [7*] Woe to
the world because of things that cause sin!
Such things must come, but woe to the one
through whom they come! [8y] If your hand or
foot causes you to sin,* cut it off and throw it
away. It is better for you to enter into life
maimed or crippled than with two hands or
two feet to be thrown into eternal fire. [9]And
if your eye causes you to sin, tear it out and
throw it away. It is better for you to enter
into life with one eye than with two eyes to
be thrown into fiery Gehenna.

***The Parable of the Lost Sheep.**** [10z] "See
that you do not despise one of these little
ones,* for I say to you that their angels in
heaven always look upon the face of my
heavenly Father. *[11]**[a] [12]What is your opinion? If a man has a hundred sheep and one of
them goes astray, will he not leave the
ninety-nine in the hills and go in search of
the stray? [13]And if he finds it, amen, I say to
you, he rejoices more over it than over the
ninety-nine that did not stray. [14]In just the
same way, it is not the will of your heavenly
Father that one of these little ones be lost.

***A Brother Who Sins.**** [15b] "If your brother*

with the present age, suggests that the question has to do with rank also in the church, where the kingdom is manifested here and now, although only partially and by anticipation; see notes on Mt 3:2; 4:17.

**18:3 Become like children**: the child is held up as a model for the disciples not because of any supposed innocence of children but because of their complete dependence on, and trust in, their parents. So must the disciples be, in respect to God.

**18:5** Cf. Mt 10:40.

**18:6 One of these little ones**: the thought passes from the child of Mt 18:2–4 to the disciples, **little ones** because of their becoming **like children.** It is difficult to know whether this is a designation of all who are disciples or of those who are insignificant in contrast to others, e.g., the leaders of the community. Since apart from this chapter the designation **little ones** occurs in Matthew only in Mt 10:42 where it means disciples as such, that is its more likely meaning here. **Who believe in me**: since discipleship is impossible without at least some degree of faith, this further specification seems superfluous. However, it serves to indicate that the warning against causing a **little one** to sin is principally directed against whatever would lead such a one to a weakening or loss of faith. The Greek verb *skandalizein*, here translated **causes . . . to sin**, means literally "causes to stumble"; what the stumbling is depends on the context. It is used of falling away from faith in Mt 13:21. According to the better reading of Mk 9:42, **in me** is a Matthean addition to the Marcan source. **It would be better . . . depths of the sea**: cf. Mk 9:42.

**18:7** This is a Q saying; cf. Lk 17:1. The inevitability of **things that cause sin** (literally, "scandals") does not take away the responsibility of **the one through whom they come.**

**18:8–9** These verses are a doublet of Mt 5:29–30. In that context they have to do with causes of sexual sin. As in the Marcan source from which they have been drawn (Mk 9:42–48), they differ from the first warning about scandal, which deals with causing another person to sin, for they concern what **causes** oneself **to sin** and they do not seem to be related to another's loss of faith, as the first warning is. It is difficult to know how Matthew understood the logical connection between these verses and Mt 18:6–7.

**18:10–14** The first and last verses are peculiar to Matthew. The parable itself comes from Q; see Lk 15:3–7. In Luke it serves as justification for Jesus' table-companionship with sinners; here, it is an exhortation for the disciples to seek out fellow disciples who have gone **astray**. Not only must no one cause a fellow disciple to sin, but those who have strayed must be sought out and, if possible, brought back to the community. The joy of the shepherd on finding the sheep, though not absent in Mt 18:13 is more emphasized in Luke. By his addition of Mt 18:10, 14 Matthew has drawn out explicitly the application of the parable to the care of the **little ones.**

**18:10 Their angels in heaven . . . my heavenly Father**: for the Jewish belief in angels as guardians of nations and individuals, see Dn 10:13, 20–21; Tb 5:4–7; 1QH 5:20–22; as intercessors who present the prayers of human beings to God, see Tb 13:12, 15. The high worth of the **little ones** is indicated by their being represented before God by these heavenly beings.

**18:11** Some manuscripts add, "For the Son of Man has come to save what was lost"; cf. Mt 9:13. This is practically identical with Lk 19:10 and is probably a copyist's addition from that source.

**18:15–20** Passing from the duty of Christian disciples toward those who have strayed from their number, the discourse now turns to how they are to deal with one who sins and yet remains within the community. First there is to be private correction (Mt 18:15); if this is unsuccessful, further correction before **two or three witnesses** (Mt 18:16); if this fails, the matter is to be brought before the assembled community (the church), and if the sinner refuses to attend to the correction of **the church**, he is to be expelled (Mt 18:17). The church's judgment will be ratified **in heaven**, i.e., by God (Mt

*v:* 19:14; Mk 10:15; Lk 18:17. *w:* 23:12. *x:* Mk 9:42; Lk 17:1–2. *y:* 5:29–30; Mk 9:43–47. *z:* Ez 34:1–3, 16; Lk 15:3–7. *a:* Lk 19:10. *b:* Lv 19:17; Sir 19:13; Gal 6:1.

sins [against you], go and tell him his fault
between you and him alone. If he listens to
you, you have won over your brother. [16]* [c] If
he does not listen, take one or two others
along with you, so that 'every fact may be
established on the testimony of two or three
witnesses.' [17][d] If he refuses to listen to them,
tell the church.* If he refuses to listen even to
the church, then treat him as you would a
Gentile or a tax collector. [18]* [e] Amen, I say to
you, whatever you bind on earth shall be
bound in heaven, and whatever you loose on
earth shall be loosed in heaven. [19]* [f] Again,
[amen,] I say to you, if two of you agree on
earth about anything for which they are to
pray, it shall be granted to them by my heavenly Father. [20]* [g] For where two or three are
gathered together in my name, there am I in
the midst of them."

*The Parable of the Unforgiving Servant.**
[21][h] Then Peter approaching asked him,
"Lord, if my brother sins against me, how
often must I forgive him? As many as seven
times?" [22]* Jesus answered, "I say to you,
not seven times but seventy-seven times.
[23][i] That is why the kingdom of heaven may
be likened to a king who decided to settle accounts with his servants. [24]* When he began
the accounting, a debtor was brought before
him who owed him a huge amount. [25] Since
he had no way of paying it back, his master
ordered him to be sold, along with his wife,
his children, and all his property, in payment
of the debt. [26]* At that, the servant fell down,
did him homage, and said, 'Be patient with
me, and I will pay you back in full.' [27] Moved
with compassion the master of that servant
let him go and forgave him the loan. [28] When

18:18). This three-step process of correction corresponds, though not exactly, to the procedure of the Qumran community; see 1QS 5:25–6:1; 6:24–7:25; CD 9:2–8. The section ends with a saying about the favorable response of God to prayer, even to that of a very small number, for Jesus is in the midst of any gathering of his disciples, however small (Mt 18:19–20). Whether this prayer has anything to do with the preceding judgment is uncertain.

**18:15 Your brother**: a fellow disciple; see Mt 23:8. The bracketed words, **against you**, are widely attested but they are not in the important codices Sinaiticus and Vaticanus or in some other textual witnesses. Their omission broadens the type of sin in question. **Won over**: literally, "gained."

**18:16** Cf. Dt 19:15.

**18:17 The church**: the second of the only two instances of this word in the gospels; see note on Mt 16:18. Here it refers not to the entire **church** of Jesus, as in Mt 16:18, but to the local congregation. **Treat him . . . a Gentile or a tax collector**: just as the observant Jew avoided the company of Gentiles and tax collectors, so must the congregation of Christian disciples separate itself from the arrogantly sinful member who refuses to repent even when convicted of his sin by the whole **church**. Such a one is to be set outside the fellowship of the community. The harsh language about **Gentile** and **tax collector** probably reflects a stage of the Matthean **church** when it was principally composed of Jewish Christians. That time had long since passed, but the principle of exclusion for such a sinner remained. Paul makes a similar demand for excommunication in 1 Cor 5:1–13.

**18:18** Except for the plural of the verbs **bind** and **loose**, this verse is practically identical with Mt 16:19b and many scholars understand it as granting to all the disciples what was previously given to Peter alone. For a different view, based on the different contexts of the two verses, see note on Mt 16:19.

**18:19–20** Some take these verses as applying to prayer on the occasion of the church's gathering to deal with the sinner of Mt 18:17. Unless an *a fortiori* argument is supposed, this seems unlikely. God's answer to the prayer of **two or three** envisages a different situation from one that involves the entire congregation. In addition, the object of this prayer is expressed in most general terms as **anything for which they are to pray**.

**18:20 For where two or three . . . midst of them**: the presence of Jesus guarantees the efficacy of the prayer. This saying is similar to one attributed to a rabbi executed in A.D. 135 at the time of the second Jewish revolt: ". . . When two sit and there are between them the words of the Torah, the divine presence (*Shekinah*) rests upon them" (*Pirqê 'Abôt* 3, 3).

**18:21–35** The final section of the discourse deals with the forgiveness that the disciples are to give to their fellow disciples who sin against them. To the question of Peter how often forgiveness is to be granted (Mt 18:21), Jesus answers that it is to be given without limit (Mt 18:22) and illustrates this with the parable of the unmerciful servant (Mt 18:23–34), warning that his **heavenly Father** will give those who do not forgive the same treatment as that given to the unmerciful servant (Mt 18:35). Mt 18:21–22 correspond to Lk 17:4; the parable and the final warning are peculiar to Matthew. That the parable did not originally belong to this context is suggested by the fact that it really does not deal with repeated forgiveness, which is the point of Peter's question and Jesus' reply.

**18:22 Seventy-seven times**: the Greek corresponds exactly to the LXX of Gn 4:24. There is probably an allusion, by contrast, to the limitless vengeance of Lamech in the Genesis text. In any case, what is demanded of the disciples is limitless forgiveness.

**18:24 A huge amount**: literally, "ten thousand talents." The talent was a unit of coinage of high but varying value depending on its metal (gold, silver, copper) and its place of origin. It is mentioned in the New Testament only here and in Mt 25:14–30.

**18:26 Pay you back in full**: an empty promise, given the size of the debt.

*c:* Dt 19:15; Jn 8:17; 1 Tm 5:19. *d:* 1 Cor 5:1–13. *e:* 16:19; Jn 20:23. *f:* 7:7–8; Jn 15:7. *g:* 1 Cor 5:4. *h:* 6:12; Lk 17:4. *i:* 25:19.

that servant had left, he found one of his fellow servants who owed him a much smaller
amount.* He seized him and started to choke
him, demanding, 'Pay back what you owe.'
[29]Falling to his knees, his fellow servant
begged him, 'Be patient with me, and I will
pay you back.' [30]But he refused. Instead, he
had him put in prison until he paid back the
debt. [31]Now when his fellow servants saw
what had happened, they were deeply disturbed, and went to their master and reported
the whole affair. [32]His master summoned
him and said to him, 'You wicked servant! I
forgave you your entire debt because you
begged me to. [33 j] Should you not have had
pity on your fellow servant, as I had pity on
you?' [34]Then in anger his master handed him
over to the torturers until he should pay back
the whole debt.* [35* k] So will my heavenly
Father do to you, unless each of you forgives
his brother from his heart."

## VI. Ministry in Judea and Jerusalem

### CHAPTER 19

See RG 285–87

*Marriage and Divorce.* [1*] When Jesus*
finished these words,* he left Galilee and
went to the district of Judea across the Jordan. [2]Great crowds followed him, and he
cured them there. [3 l] Some Pharisees approached him, and tested him,* saying, "Is it
lawful for a man to divorce his wife for any
cause whatever?" [4* m] He said in reply,
"Have you not read that from the beginning
the Creator 'made them male and female'
[5 n] and said, 'For this reason a man shall
leave his father and mother and be joined to
his wife, and the two shall become one
flesh'? [6]So they are no longer two, but one
flesh. Therefore, what God has joined together, no human being must separate."

**18:28 A much smaller amount**: literally, "a hundred denarii." A denarius was the normal daily wage of a laborer. The difference between the two debts is enormous and brings out the absurdity of the conduct of the Christian who has received the great forgiveness of God and yet refuses to forgive the relatively minor offenses done to him.

**18:34** Since the debt is so great as to be unpayable, the punishment will be endless.

**18:35** The Father's forgiveness, already given, will be withdrawn at the final judgment for those who have not imitated his forgiveness by their own.

**19:1–23:39** The narrative section of the fifth book of the gospel. The first part (Mt 19:1–20:34) has for its setting the journey of Jesus from Galilee to Jerusalem; the second (Mt 21:1–23:39) deals with Jesus' ministry in Jerusalem up to the final great discourse of the gospel (Mt 24–25). Matthew follows the Marcan sequence of events, though adding material both special to this gospel and drawn from Q. The second part ends with the denunciation of the scribes and Pharisees (Mt 23:1–36) followed by Jesus' lament over Jerusalem (Mt 23:37–39). This long and important speech raises a problem for the view that Matthew is structured around five other discourses of Jesus (see Introduction) and that this one has no such function in the gospel. However, it is to be noted that this speech lacks the customary concluding formula that follows the five discourses (see note on Mt 7:28), and that those discourses are all addressed either exclusively (Mt 10; 18; 24; 25) or primarily (Mt 5–7; 13) to the disciples, whereas this is addressed primarily to the scribes and Pharisees (Mt 23:13–36). Consequently, it seems plausible to maintain that the evangelist did not intend to give it the structural importance of the five other discourses, and that, in spite of its being composed of sayings-material, it belongs to the narrative section of this book. In that regard, it is similar to the sayings-material of Mt 11:7–30. Some have proposed that Matthew wished to regard it as part of the final discourse of Mt 24–25, but the intervening material (Mt 24:1–4) and the change in matter and style of those chapters do not support that view.

**19:1** In giving Jesus' teaching on divorce (Mt 19:3–9), Matthew here follows his Marcan source (Mk 10:2–12) as he does Q in Mt 5:31–32 (cf. Lk 16:18). Mt 19:10–12 are peculiar to Matthew.

**19:1 When Jesus finished these words**: see note on Mt 7:28–29. **The district of Judea across the Jordan**: an inexact designation of the territory. Judea did not extend **across the Jordan**; the territory east of the river was Perea. The route to Jerusalem by way of Perea avoided passage through Samaria.

**19:3 Tested him**: the verb is used of attempts of Jesus' opponents to embarrass him by challenging him to do something they think impossible (Mt 16:1; Mk 8:11; Lk 11:16) or by having him say something that they can use against him (Mt 22:18, 35; Mk 10:2; 12:15). **For any cause whatever**: this is peculiar to Matthew and has been interpreted by some as meaning that Jesus was being asked to take sides in the dispute between the schools of Hillel and Shammai on the reasons for divorce, the latter holding a stricter position than the former. It is unlikely, however, that to ask Jesus' opinion about the differing views of two Jewish schools, both highly respected, could be described as "testing" him, for the reason indicated above.

**19:4–6** Matthew recasts his Marcan source, omitting Jesus' question about Moses' command (Mk 10:3) and having him recall at once two Genesis texts that show the will and purpose of **the Creator** in making human beings **male and female** (Gn 1:27), namely, that a **man** may **be joined to his wife** in marriage in the intimacy of **one flesh** (Gn 2:24). **What God has** thus **joined** must not be separated by any human being. (The NAB translation of the Hebrew *bāśār* of Gn 2:24 as "body" rather than "flesh" obscures the reference of Matthew to that text.)

**19:7** See Dt 24:1–4

*j:* Sir 28:4. *k:* 6:15; Jas 2:13. *l:* Mk 10:2–12. *m:* Gn 1:27. *n:* Gn 2:24; 1 Cor 6:16; Eph 5:31. *o:* Dt 24:1–4.

7* o They said to him, "Then why did Moses
command that the man give the woman a bill
of divorce and dismiss [her]?" 8He said to
them, "Because of the hardness of your
hearts Moses allowed you to divorce your
wives, but from the beginning it was not so.
9p I say to you,* whoever divorces his wife
(unless the marriage is unlawful) and marries another commits adultery." 10[His] disciples said to him, "If that is the case of a
man with his wife, it is better not to marry."
11He answered, "Not all can accept [this]
word,* but only those to whom that is
granted. 12Some are incapable of marriage
because they were born so; some, because
they were made so by others; some, because
they have renounced marriage* for the sake
of the kingdom of heaven. Whoever can accept this ought to accept it."

*Blessing of the Children.** 13q Then children were brought to him that he might lay
his hands on them and pray. The disciples rebuked them, 14r but Jesus said, "Let the children come to me, and do not prevent them;
for the kingdom of heaven belongs to such
as these." 15After he placed his hands on
them, he went away.

*The Rich Young Man.** 16s Now someone
approached him and said, "Teacher, what
good must I do to gain eternal life?"* 17He
answered him, "Why do you ask me about
the good? There is only One who is good.* If
you wish to enter into life, keep the commandments." 18* t He asked him, "Which
ones?" And Jesus replied, " 'You shall not
kill; you shall not commit adultery; you shall
not steal; you shall not bear false witness;
19honor your father and your mother'; and
'you shall love your neighbor as yourself.' "
20* The young man said to him, "All of these

**19:9** Moses' concession to human sinfulness (**the hardness of your hearts**, Mt 19:8) is repudiated by Jesus, and the original will of the Creator is reaffirmed against that concession. (**Unless the marriage is unlawful**): see note on Mt 5:31–32. There is some evidence suggesting that Jesus' absolute prohibition of divorce was paralleled in the Qumran community (see 11QTemple 57:17–19; CD 4:12b–5:14). Matthew removes Mark's setting of this verse as spoken to the disciples alone "in the house" (Mk 10:10) and also his extension of the divorce prohibition to the case of a woman's divorcing her husband (Mk 10:12), probably because in Palestine, unlike the places where Roman and Greek law prevailed, the woman was not allowed to initiate the divorce.

**19:11 [This] word**: probably the disciples' **"it is better not to marry"** (Mt 19:10). Jesus agrees but says that celibacy is not for all but only for those **to whom that is granted** by God.

**19:12 Incapable of marriage**: literally, "eunuchs." Three classes are mentioned, eunuchs from birth, eunuchs by castration, and those who have voluntarily **renounced marriage** (literally, "have made themselves eunuchs") **for the sake of the kingdom**, i.e., to devote themselves entirely to its service. Some scholars take the last class to be those who have been divorced by their spouses and have refused to enter another marriage. But it is more likely that it is rather those who have chosen never to marry, since that suits better the optional nature of the decision: **whoever can . . . ought to accept it**.

**19:13–15** This account is understood by some as intended to justify the practice of infant baptism. That interpretation is based principally on the command not to **prevent** the children from coming, since that word sometimes has a baptismal connotation in the New Testament; see Acts 8:36.

**19:16–30** Cf. Mk 10:17–31. This story does not set up a "two-tier" morality, that of those who seek (only) **eternal life** (Mt 19:16) and that of those who **wish to be perfect** (Mt 19:21). It speaks rather of the obstacle that riches constitute for the following of Jesus and of the impossibility, humanly speaking, for one who has **many possessions** (Mt 19:22) **to enter the kingdom** (Mt 19:24). Actual renunciation of riches is not demanded of all; Matthew counts the rich Joseph of Arimathea as a disciple of Jesus (Mt 27:57). But only the poor in spirit (Mt 5:3) can **enter the kingdom** and, as here, such poverty may entail the sacrifice of one's **possessions**. The Twelve, who **have given up everything** (Mt 19:27) to follow Jesus, will have as their reward a share in Jesus' (the Son of Man's) **judging the twelve tribes of Israel** (Mt 19:28), and all who have similarly sacrificed family or property for his sake **will inherit eternal life** (Mt 19:29).

**19:16 Gain eternal life**: this is equivalent to "entering into life" (Mt 19:17) and "being saved" (Mt 19:25); the **life** is that of the new age after the final judgment (see Mt 25:46). It probably is also equivalent here to "entering the kingdom of heaven" (Mt 19:23) or "the kingdom of God" (Mt 19:24), but see notes on Mt 3:2; 4:17; 18:1 for the wider reference of **the kingdom** in Matthew.

**19:17** By Matthew's reformulation of the Marcan question and reply (Mk 10:17–18) Jesus' repudiation of the term "good" for himself has been softened. Yet the Marcan assertion that "no one is good but God alone" stands, with only unimportant verbal modification.

**19:18–19** The first five commandments cited are from the Decalogue (see Ex 20:12–16; Dt 5:16–20). Matthew omits Mark's "you shall not defraud" (Mk 10:19; see Dt 24:14) and adds Lv 19:18. This combination of commandments of the Decalogue with Lv 19:18 is partially the same as Paul's enumeration of the demands of Christian morality in Rom 13:9.

**19:20 Young man**: in Matthew alone of the synoptics the questioner is said to be a **young man**; thus the Marcan "from my youth" (Mk 10:20) is omitted.

---

*p:* 5:32; Lk 16:18; 1 Cor 7:10–11. *q:* Mk 10:13–16; Lk 18:15–17. *r:* 18:3; Acts 8:36. *s:* Mk 10:17–31; Lk 18:18–30. *t:* Ex 20:12–16; Dt 5:16–20 / Lv 19:18; Rom 13:9.

I have observed. What do I still lack?"
[21u] Jesus said to him, "If you wish to be perfect,* go, sell what you have and give to [the]
poor, and you will have treasure in heaven.
Then come, follow me." [22]When the young
man heard this statement, he went away sad,
for he had many possessions. [23*] Then Jesus
said to his disciples, "Amen, I say to you, it
will be hard for one who is rich to enter the
kingdom of heaven. [24v] Again I say to you, it
is easier for a camel to pass through the eye
of a needle than for one who is rich to enter
the kingdom of God." [25*] When the disciples
heard this, they were greatly astonished and
said, "Who then can be saved?" [26w] Jesus
looked at them and said, "For human beings
this is impossible, but for God all things are
possible." [27x] Then Peter said to him in reply,
"We have given up everything and followed
you. What will there be for us?" [28* y] Jesus
said to them, "Amen, I say to you that you
who have followed me, in the new age,
when the Son of Man is seated on his throne
of glory, will yourselves sit on twelve
thrones, judging the twelve tribes of Israel.
[29]And everyone who has given up houses or
brothers or sisters or father or mother or
children or lands for the sake of my name
will receive a hundred times more, and will
inherit eternal life. [30* z] But many who are
first will be last, and the last will be first.

## CHAPTER 20

See RG 285-87

*The Workers in the Vineyard.** [1]"The
kingdom of heaven is like a landowner who
went out at dawn to hire laborers for his
vineyard. [2]After agreeing with them for the
usual daily wage, he sent them into his vineyard. [3]Going out about nine o'clock, he saw
others standing idle in the marketplace,
[4*] and he said to them, 'You too go into my
vineyard, and I will give you what is just.'
[5]So they went off. [And] he went out again
around noon, and around three o'clock, and
did likewise. [6]Going out about five o'clock,
he found others standing around, and said to
them, 'Why do you stand here idle all day?'
[7]They answered, 'Because no one has hired
us.' He said to them, 'You too go into my
vineyard.' [8* a] When it was evening the
owner of the vineyard said to his foreman,
'Summon the laborers and give them their
pay, beginning with the last and ending with
the first.' [9]When those who had started about
five o'clock came, each received the usual
daily wage. [10]So when the first came, they
thought that they would receive more, but
each of them also got the usual wage. [11]And

**19:21 If you wish to be perfect**: **to be perfect** is demanded of all Christians; see Mt 5:48. In the case of this man, it involves selling his possessions and giving to the poor; only so can he **follow** Jesus.

**19:23–24** Riches are an obstacle to entering **the kingdom** that cannot be overcome by human power. The comparison with the impossibility of a camel's passing **through the eye of a needle** should not be mitigated by such suppositions as that **the eye of a needle** means a low or narrow gate. **The kingdom of God**: as in Mt 12:28; 21:31, 43 instead of Matthew's usual **kingdom of heaven.**

**19:25–26** See note on Mk 10:23–27.

**19:28** This saying, directed to the Twelve, is from Q; see Lk 22:29–30. **The new age**: the Greek word here translated "new age" occurs in the New Testament only here and in Ti 3:5. Literally, it means "rebirth" or "regeneration," and is used in Titus of spiritual rebirth through baptism. Here it means the "rebirth" effected by the coming of the kingdom. Since that coming has various stages (see notes on Mt 3:2; 4:17), **the new age** could be taken as referring to the time after the resurrection when the Twelve will govern the true Israel, i.e., the church of Jesus. (For "judge" in the sense of "govern," cf. Jgs 12:8, 9, 11; 15:20; 16:31; Ps 2:10). But since it is connected here with the time when **the Son of Man** will be **seated on his throne of glory**, language that Matthew uses in Mt 25:31 for the time of final judgment, it is more likely that what the Twelve are promised is that they will be joined with Jesus then in judging the people of Israel.

**19:30** Different interpretations have been given to this saying, which comes from Mk 10:31. In view of Matthew's associating it with the following parable (Mt 20:1–15) and substantially repeating it (in reverse order) at the end of that parable (Mt 20:16), it may be that his meaning is that all who respond to the call of Jesus, at whatever time (**first** or **last**), will be the same in respect to inheriting the benefits of the kingdom, which is the gift of God.

**20:1–16** This parable is peculiar to Matthew. It is difficult to know whether the evangelist composed it or received it as part of his traditional material and, if the latter is the case, what its original reference was. In its present context its close association with Mt 19:30 suggests that its teaching is the equality of all the disciples in the reward of inheriting eternal life.

**20:4 What is just**: although the wage is not stipulated as in the case of those first hired, it will be fair.

**20:8 Beginning with the last . . . the first**: this element of the parable has no other purpose than to show how **the first** knew what **the last** were given (Mt 20:12).

*u:* 5:48; 6:20. *v:* 7:14. *w:* Gn 18:14; Jb 42:2; Lk 1:37. *x:* 4:20, 22. *y:* 25:31; Dn 7:9, 22; Lk 22:30; Rev 3:21; 20:4. *z:* 20:16. *a:* Lv 19:13; Dt 24:15.

on receiving it they grumbled against the
landowner, [12]saying, 'These last ones
worked only one hour, and you have made
them equal to us, who bore the day's burden
and the heat.' [13]He said to one of them in reply, 'My friend, I am not cheating you.* Did
you not agree with me for the usual daily
wage? [14*] Take what is yours and go. What if
I wish to give this last one the same as you?
[15][Or] am I not free to do as I wish with my
own money? Are you envious because I am
generous?' [16*] Thus, the last will be first, and
the first will be last."

***The Third Prediction of the Passion.****
[17b] As Jesus was going up to Jerusalem, he
took the twelve [disciples] aside by themselves, and said to them on the way, [18]"Behold, we are going up to Jerusalem, and the
Son of Man will be handed over to the chief
priests and the scribes, and they will condemn
him to death, [19]and hand him over to the Gentiles to be mocked and scourged and crucified, and he will be raised on the third day."

***The Request of James and John.**** [20c] Then
the mother* of the sons of Zebedee approached him with her sons and did him homage, wishing to ask him for something. [21]He
said to her, "What do you wish?" She answered him, "Command that these two sons
of mine sit, one at your right and the other at
your left, in your kingdom." [22]Jesus said in
reply, "You do not know what you are asking.* Can you drink the cup that I am going to
drink?" They said to him, "We can." [23]He
replied, "My cup you will indeed drink, but to
sit at my right and at my left [, this] is not
mine to give but is for those for whom it has
been prepared by my Father." [24d] When the
ten heard this, they became indignant at the
two brothers. [25]But Jesus summoned them
and said, "You know that the rulers of the
Gentiles lord it over them, and the great ones
make their authority over them felt. [26]But it
shall not be so among you. Rather, whoever
wishes to be great among you shall be your
servant; [27e] whoever wishes to be first among
you shall be your slave. [28f] Just so, the Son of
Man did not come to be served but to serve
and to give his life as a ransom* for many."

***The Healing of Two Blind Men.**** [29g] As

**20:13 I am not cheating you**: literally, "I am not treating you unjustly."

**20:14–15** The owner's conduct involves no violation of justice (Mt 20:4, 13), and that all the workers receive the same wage is due only to his generosity to the latest arrivals; the resentment of the first comes from envy.

**20:16** See note on Mt 19:30.

**20:17–19** Cf. Mk 10:32–34. This is the third and the most detailed of the passion predictions (Mt 16:21–23; 17:22–23). It speaks of Jesus' being **handed over to the Gentiles** (Mt 27:2), his being **mocked** (Mt 27:27–30), **scourged** (Mt 27:26), and **crucified** (Mt 27:31, 35). In all but the last of these points Matthew agrees with his Marcan source, but whereas Mark speaks of Jesus' being killed (Mk 10:34), Matthew has the specific **to be . . . crucified.**

**20:20–28** Cf. Mk 10:35–45. The request of the sons of Zebedee, made through their mother, for the highest places of honor in the **kingdom**, and the indignation of **the** other **ten** disciples at this request, show that neither **the two brothers** nor the others have understood that what makes for greatness in the kingdom is not lordly power but humble service. Jesus gives the example, and his ministry of service will reach its highest point when he gives his life for the deliverance of the human race from sin.

**20:20–21** The reason for Matthew's making **the mother** the petitioner (cf. Mk 10:35) is not clear. Possibly he intends an allusion to Bathsheba's seeking the kingdom for Solomon; see 1 Kgs 1:11–21. **Your kingdom**: see note on Mt 16:28.

**20:22 You do not know what you are asking**: the Greek verbs are plural and, with the rest of the verse, indicate that the answer is addressed not to the woman but to her sons. **Drink the cup**: see note on Mk 10:38–40. Matthew omits the Marcan "or be baptized with the baptism with which I am baptized" (Mk 10:38).

**20:28 Ransom**: this noun, which occurs in the New Testament only here and in the Marcan parallel (Mk 10:45), does not necessarily express the idea of liberation by payment of some price. The cognate verb is used frequently in the LXX of God's liberating Israel from Egypt or from Babylonia after the Exile; see Ex 6:6; 15:13; Ps 77:16 (76 LXX); Is 43:1; 44:22. The liberation brought by Jesus' death will be **for many**; cf. Is 53:12. **Many** does not mean that some are excluded, but is a Semitism designating the collectivity who benefit from the service of the one, and is equivalent to "all." While there are few verbal contacts between this saying and the fourth Servant Song (Is 52:13–53:12), the ideas of that passage are reflected here.

**20:29–34** The cure of the blind men is probably symbolic of what will happen to the disciples, now blind to the meaning of Jesus' passion and to the necessity of their sharing his suffering. As the men are given sight, so, after the resurrection, will the disciples come to see that to which they are now blind. Matthew has abbreviated his Marcan source (Mk 10:46–52) and has made Mark's one man two. Such doubling is characteristic of this gospel; see Mt 8:28–34 (// Mk 5:1–20) and the note on Mt 9:27–31.

*b:* 16:21; 17:22–23; Mk 10:32–34; Lk 18:31–33. *c:* Mk 10:35–45. *d:* Lk 22:25–27. *e:* Mk 9:35. *f:* 26:28; Is 53:12; Rom 5:6; 1 Tm 2:6. *g:* Mk 10:46–52; Lk 18:35–43.

they left Jericho, a great crowd followed
him. [30h]Two blind men were sitting by the
roadside, and when they heard that Jesus
was passing by, they cried out, "[Lord,]* Son
of David, have pity on us!" [31]The crowd
warned them to be silent, but they called out
all the more, "Lord, Son of David, have pity
on us!" [32]Jesus stopped and called them and
said, "What do you want me to do for you?"
[33]They answered him, "Lord, let our eyes be
opened." [34]Moved with pity, Jesus touched
their eyes. Immediately they received their
sight, and followed him.

## CHAPTER 21

See RG 287–88

*The Entry into Jerusalem.** [1i]When
they drew near Jerusalem and came to Bethphage* on the Mount of Olives, Jesus sent
two disciples, [2]saying to them, "Go into the
village opposite you, and immediately you
will find an ass tethered, and a colt with her.*
Untie them and bring them here to me. [3]And
if anyone should say anything to you, reply,
'The master has need of them.' Then he will
send them at once." [4*]This happened so that
what had been spoken through the prophet
might be fulfilled:

[5j]"Say to daughter Zion,
'Behold, your king comes to you,
meek and riding on an ass,
and on a colt, the foal of a beast of burden.' "

[6]The disciples went and did as Jesus had ordered them. [7*]They brought the ass and the
colt and laid their cloaks over them, and he
sat upon them. [8*k]The very large crowd
spread their cloaks on the road, while others
cut branches from the trees and strewed
them on the road. [9l]The crowds preceding
him and those following kept crying out and
saying:

"Hosanna* to the Son of David;
blessed is he who comes in the name of the Lord;
hosanna in the highest."

[10]And when he entered Jerusalem the
whole city was shaken* and asked, "Who is
this?" [11]And the crowds replied, "This is

**20:30 [Lord,]**: some important textual witnesses omit this, but that may be because copyists assimilated this verse to Mt 9:27. **Son of David**: see note on Mt 9:27.

**21:1–11** Jesus' coming to Jerusalem is in accordance with the divine will that he must go there (cf. Mt 16:21) to suffer, die, and be raised. He prepares for his entry into the city in such a way as to make it a fulfillment of the prophecy of Zec 9:9 (Mt 21:2) that emphasizes the humility of the **king who comes** (Mt 21:5). That prophecy, absent from the Marcan parallel account (Mk 11:1–11) although found also in the Johannine account of the entry (Jn 12:15), is the center of the Matthean story. During the procession from Bethphage to Jerusalem, Jesus is acclaimed as the Davidic messianic king by the crowds who accompany him (Mt 21:9). On his arrival **the whole city was shaken**, and to the inquiry of the amazed populace about Jesus' identity the crowds with him reply that he is **the prophet, from Nazareth in Galilee** (Mt 21:10, 11).

**21:1 Bethphage**: a village that can no longer be certainly identified. Mark mentions it before Bethany (Mk 11:1), which suggests that it lay to the east of the latter. **The Mount of Olives**: the hill east of Jerusalem that is spoken of in Zec 14:4 as the place where the Lord will come to rescue Jerusalem from the enemy nations.

**21:2 An ass tethered, and a colt with her**: instead of the one animal of Mk 11:2, Matthew has two, as demanded by his understanding of Zec 9:9.

**21:4–5 The prophet**: this fulfillment citation is actually composed of two distinct Old Testament texts, Is 62:11 (**Say to daughter Zion**) and Zec 9:9. The **ass** and the **colt** are the same animal in the prophecy, mentioned twice in different ways, the common Hebrew literary device of poetic parallelism. That Matthew takes them as two is one of the reasons why some scholars think that he was a Gentile rather than a Jewish Christian who would presumably not make that mistake (see Introduction).

**21:7 Upon them**: upon the two animals; an awkward picture resulting from Matthew's misunderstanding of the prophecy.

**21:8 Spread . . . on the road**: cf. 2 Kgs 9:13. There is a similarity between the cutting and strewing of the branches and the festivities of Tabernacles (Lv 23:39–40); see also 2 Mc 10:5–8 where the celebration of the rededication of the temple is compared to that of Tabernacles.

**21:9 Hosanna**: the Hebrew means "(O LORD) grant salvation"; see Ps 118:25, but that invocation had become an acclamation of jubilation and welcome. **Blessed is he . . . in the name of the Lord**: see Ps 118:26 and the note on Jn 12:13. **In the highest**: probably only an intensification of the acclamation, although **Hosanna in the highest** could be taken as a prayer, "May God save (him)."

**21:10 Was shaken**: in the gospels this verb is peculiar to Matthew where it is used also of the earthquake at the time of the crucifixion (Mt 27:51) and of the terror of the guards of Jesus' tomb at the appearance of the angel (Mt 28:4). For Matthew's use of the cognate noun, see note on Mt 8:24.

**21:11 The prophet**: see Mt 16:14 ("one of the prophets") and 21:46.

*h:* 9:27. *i:* Mk 11:1–11; Lk 19:28–38; Jn 12:12–15. *j:* Is 62:11; Zec 9:9. *k:* 2 Kgs 9:13. *l:* Ps 118:25–26.

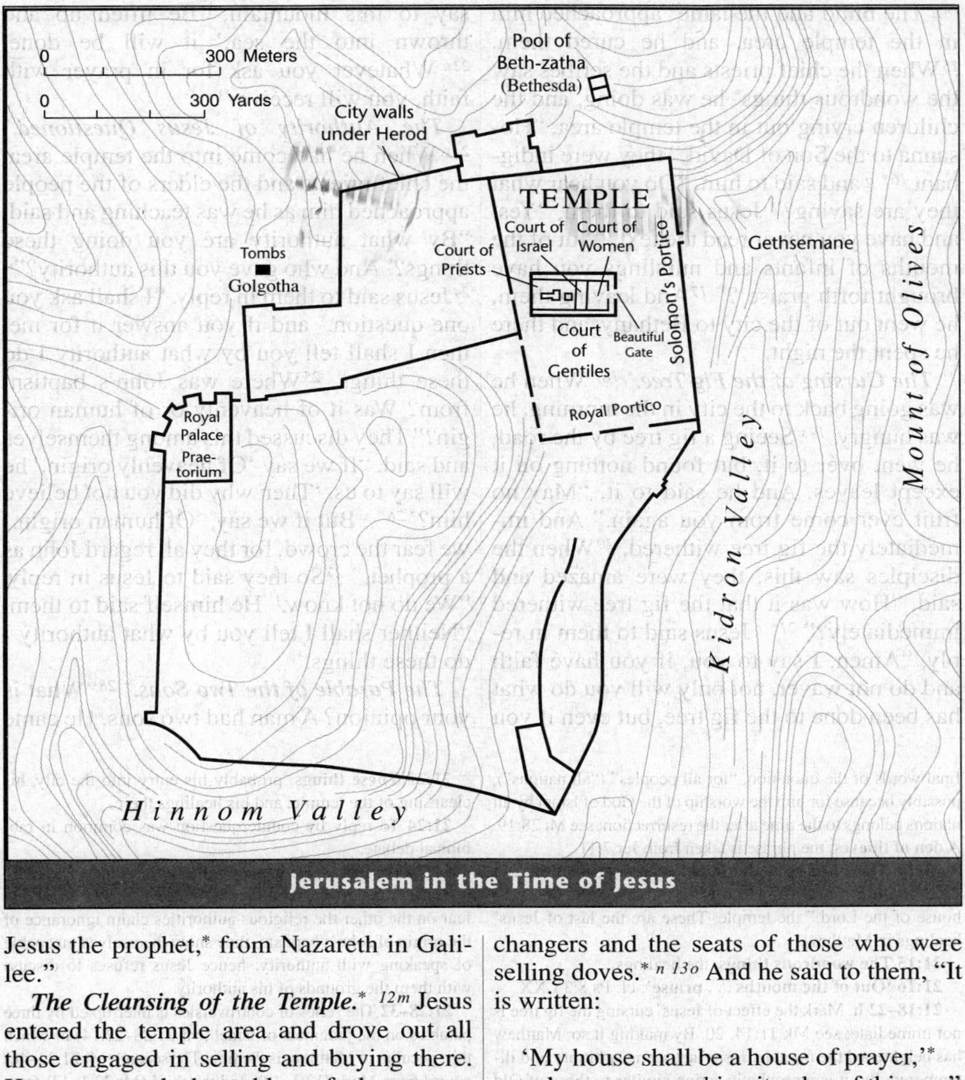


Jerusalem in the Time of Jesus

Jesus the prophet,* from Nazareth in Galilee."

*The Cleansing of the Temple.** 12m Jesus entered the temple area and drove out all those engaged in selling and buying there. He overturned the tables of the money changers and the seats of those who were selling doves.* n 13o And he said to them, "It is written:

'My house shall be a house of prayer,'*
but you are making it a den of thieves."

**21:12–17** Matthew changes the order of (Mk 11:11, 12, 15) and places the cleansing of the temple on the same day as the entry into Jerusalem, immediately after it. The activities going on in **the temple area** were not secular but connected with the temple worship. Thus Jesus' attack on those so engaged and his charge that they were **making** God's **house of prayer a den of thieves** (Mt 21:12–13) constituted a claim to authority over the religious practices of Israel and were a challenge to the priestly authorities. Mt 21:14–17 are peculiar to Matthew. Jesus' healings and his countenancing the children's cries of praise rouse the indignation of **the chief priests and the scribes** (Mt 21:15). These two groups appear in the infancy narrative (Mt 2:4) and have been mentioned in the first and third passion predictions (Mt 16:21; 20:18). Now, as the passion approaches, they come on the scene again, exhibiting their hostility to Jesus.

**21:12** These activities were carried on in the court of the Gentiles, the outermost court of **the temple area**. Animals for sacrifice were sold; the **doves** were for those who could not afford a more expensive offering; see Lv 5:7. **Tables of the money changers**: only the coinage of Tyre could be used for the purchases; other money had to be exchanged for that.

**21:13 'My house . . . prayer'**: cf. Is 56:7. Matthew omits the

*m:* Mk 11:15–19; Lk 19:45–48; Jn 2:14–22. *n:* Lv 5:7. *o:* Is 56:7; Jer 7:11.

[14p] The blind and the lame* approached him
in the temple area, and he cured them.
[15]When the chief priests and the scribes saw
the wondrous things* he was doing, and the
children crying out in the temple area, "Hosanna to the Son of David," they were indignant [16* q] and said to him, "Do you hear what
they are saying?" Jesus said to them, "Yes;
and have you never read the text, 'Out of the
mouths of infants and nurslings you have
brought forth praise'?" [17]And leaving them,
he went out of the city to Bethany, and there
he spent the night.

***The Cursing of the Fig Tree.**** [18r] When he
was going back to the city in the morning, he
was hungry. [19s] Seeing a fig tree by the road,
he went over to it, but found nothing on it
except leaves. And he said to it, "May no
fruit ever come from you again." And immediately the fig tree withered. [20]When the
disciples saw this, they were amazed and
said, "How was it that the fig tree withered
immediately?" [21* t] Jesus said to them in reply, "Amen, I say to you, if you have faith
and do not waver, not only will you do what
has been done to the fig tree, but even if you
say to this mountain, 'Be lifted up and
thrown into the sea,' it will be done.
[22u] Whatever you ask for in prayer with
faith, you will receive."

***The Authority of Jesus Questioned.****
[23v] When he had come into the temple area,
the chief priests and the elders of the people
approached him as he was teaching and said,
"By what authority are you doing these
things?* And who gave you this authority?"[w]
[24]Jesus said to them in reply, "I shall ask you
one question,* and if you answer it for me,
then I shall tell you by what authority I do
these things. [25]Where was John's baptism
from? Was it of heavenly or of human origin?" They discussed this among themselves
and said, "If we say 'Of heavenly origin,' he
will say to us, 'Then why did you not believe
him?' [26* x] But if we say, 'Of human origin,'
we fear the crowd, for they all regard John as
a prophet." [27]So they said to Jesus in reply,
"We do not know." He himself said to them,
"Neither shall I tell you by what authority I
do these things.*

***The Parable of the Two Sons.**** [28]"What is
your opinion? A man had two sons. He came

final words of the quotation, "for all peoples" ("all nations"), possibly because for him the worship of the God of Israel by all nations belongs to the time after the resurrection; see Mt 28:19. **A den of thieves**: the phrase is taken from Jer 7:11.

**21:14 The blind and the lame**: according to 2 Sm 5:8 LXX **the blind and the lame** were forbidden to enter "the house of the Lord," the temple. These are the last of Jesus' healings in Matthew.

**21:15 The wondrous things**: the healings.

**21:16 'Out of the mouths . . . praise'**: cf. Ps 8:3 LXX.

**21:18–22** In Mark the effect of Jesus' cursing the fig tree is not immediate; see Mk 11:14, 20. By making it so, Matthew has heightened the miracle. Jesus' act seems arbitrary and ill-tempered, but it is a prophetic action similar to those of Old Testament prophets that vividly symbolize some part of their preaching; see, e.g., Ez 12:1–20. It is a sign of the judgment that is to come upon the Israel that with all its apparent piety lacks the fruit of good deeds (Mt 3:10) and will soon bear the punishment of its fruitlessness (Mt 21:43). Some scholars propose that this story is the development in tradition of a parable of Jesus about the destiny of a fruitless tree, such as Lk 13:6–9. Jesus' answer to the question of the amazed disciples (Mt 21:20) makes the miracle an example of the power of prayer made with unwavering **faith** (Mt 21:21–22).

**21:21** See Mt 17:20.

**21:23–27** Cf. Mk 11:27–33. This is the first of five controversies between Jesus and the religious authorities of Judaism in Mt 21:23–22:46, presented in the form of questions and answers.

**21:23 These things**: probably his entry into the city, his cleansing of the temple, and his healings there.

**21:24** To reply by counterquestion was common in rabbinical debate.

**21:26 We fear . . . as a prophet**: cf. Mt 14:5.

**21:27** Since through embarrassment on the one hand and fear on the other the religious authorities claim ignorance of the origin of John's baptism, they show themselves incapable of speaking with authority; hence Jesus refuses to discuss with them the grounds of his authority.

**21:28–32** The series of controversies is interrupted by three parables on the judgment of Israel (Mt 21:28–22:14) of which this, peculiar to Matthew, is the first. The second (Mt 21:33–46) comes from Mark (12:1–12), and the third (Mt 22:1–14) from Q; see Lk 14:15–24. This interruption of the controversies is similar to that in Mark, although Mark has only one parable between the first and second controversy. As regards Matthew's first parable, Mt 21:28–30 if taken by themselves could point simply to the difference between saying and doing, a theme of much importance in this gospel (cf. Mt 7:21; 12:50); that may have been the parable's original reference. However, it is given a more specific application by the addition of Mt 21:31–32. The two sons represent, respectively, the religious leaders and the religious outcasts who followed John's call to repentance. By the answer they give to Jesus' question (Mt 21:31) the leaders con-

*p:* 2 Sm 5:8 LXX. *q:* Ps 8:2 LXX; Wis 10:21. *r:* Mk 11:12–14, 20–24. *s:* Jer 8:13; Lk 13:6–9. *t:* 17:20; Lk 17:6. *u:* 7:7; 1 Jn 3:22. *v:* Mk 11:27–33; Lk 20:1–8. *w:* Jn 2:18. *x:* 14:5.

to the first and said, 'Son, go out and work in
the vineyard today.' [29]He said in reply, 'I
will not,' but afterwards he changed his
mind and went. [30]The man came to the other
son and gave the same order. He said in reply, 'Yes, sir,' but did not go. [31]* Which of
the two did his father's will?" They answered, "The first." Jesus said to them,
"Amen, I say to you, tax collectors and prostitutes are entering the kingdom of God before you. [32]* [y] When John came to you in the
way of righteousness, you did not believe
him; but tax collectors and prostitutes did.
Yet even when you saw that, you did not
later change your minds and believe him.

*The Parable of the Tenants.** [33][z] "Hear another parable. There was a landowner who
planted a vineyard,* put a hedge around it,
dug a wine press in it, and built a tower.
Then he leased it to tenants and went on a
journey.[a] [34]When vintage time drew near, he
sent his servants* to the tenants to obtain his
produce. [35]But the tenants seized the servants and one they beat, another they killed,
and a third they stoned. [36]Again he sent
other servants, more numerous than the first
ones, but they treated them in the same way.
[37]Finally, he sent his son to them, thinking,
'They will respect my son.' [38]* But when the
tenants saw the son, they said to one another,
'This is the heir. Come, let us kill him and
acquire his inheritance.' [39]* [b] They seized
him, threw him out of the vineyard, and
killed him. [40]What will the owner of the
vineyard do to those tenants when he
comes?" [41]They answered* him, "He will
put those wretched men to a wretched death
and lease his vineyard to other tenants who
will give him the produce at the proper
times." [42]* [c] Jesus said to them, "Did you
never read in the scriptures:

'The stone that the builders rejected
  has become the cornerstone;
by the Lord has this been done,
  and it is wonderful in our eyes'?

[43]* Therefore, I say to you, the kingdom of

demn themselves. There is much confusion in the textual tradition of the parable. Of the three different forms of the text given by important textual witnesses, one has the leaders answer that the son who agreed to go but did not was the one who did the father's will. Although some scholars accept that as the original reading, their arguments in favor of it seem unconvincing. The choice probably lies only between a reading that puts the son who agrees and then disobeys before the son who at first refuses and then obeys, and the reading followed in the present translation. The witnesses to the latter reading are slightly better than those that support the other.

**21:31 Entering . . . before you**: this probably means "they enter; you do not."

**21:32** Cf. Lk 7:29–30. Although the thought is similar to that of the Lucan text, the formulation is so different that it is improbable that the saying comes from Q. **Came to you . . . way of righteousness**: several meanings are possible: that John himself was righteous, that he taught righteousness to others, or that he had an important place in God's plan of salvation. For the last, see note on Mt 3:14–15.

**21:33–46** Cf. Mk 12:1–12. In this parable there is a close correspondence between most of the details of the story and the situation that it illustrates, the dealings of God with his people. Because of that heavy allegorizing, some scholars think that it does not in any way go back to Jesus, but represents the theology of the later church. That judgment applies to the Marcan parallel as well, although the allegorizing has gone farther in Matthew. There are others who believe that while many of the allegorical elements are due to church sources, they have been added to a basic parable spoken by Jesus. This view is now supported by the Gospel of Thomas, 65, where a less allegorized and probably more primitive form of the parable is found.

**21:33 Planted a vineyard . . . a tower**: cf. Is 5:1–2. The **vineyard** is defined in Is 5:7 as "the house of Israel."

**21:34–35 His servants**: Matthew has two sendings of **servants** as against Mark's three sendings of a single servant (Mk 11:2–5a) followed by a statement about the sending of "many others" (Mk 11:2, 5b). That these servants stand for the prophets sent by God to Israel is clearly implied but not made explicit here, but see Mt 23:37. **His produce**: cf. Mk 12:2 "some of the produce." The **produce** is the good works demanded by God, and his claim to them is total.

**21:38 Acquire his inheritance**: if a Jewish proselyte died without heir, the tenants of his land would have final claim on it.

**21:39 Threw him out . . . and killed him**: the change in the Marcan order where the son is killed and his corpse then thrown out (Mk 12:8) was probably made because of the tradition that Jesus died outside the city of Jerusalem; see Jn 19:17; Heb 13:12.

**21:41 They answered**: in Mk 12:9 the question is answered by Jesus himself; here the leaders answer and so condemn themselves; cf. Mt 21:31. Matthew adds that the new **tenants** to whom the vineyard will be transferred **will give** the owner **the produce at the proper times**.

**21:42** Cf. Ps 118:22–23. The psalm was used in the early church as a prophecy of Jesus' resurrection; see Acts 4:11; 1 Pt 2:7. If, as some think, the original parable ended at Mt 21:39 it was thought necessary to complete it by a reference to Jesus' vindication by God.

**21:43** Peculiar to Matthew. **Kingdom of God**: see note on Mt

*y:* Lk 7:29–30. *z:* Mk 12:1–12; Lk 20:9–19. *a:* Is 5:1–2, 7. *b:* Heb 13:12. *c:* Ps 118:22–23; Is 28:16; Acts 4:11; 1 Pt 2:7.

God will be taken away from you and given
to a people that will produce its fruit.
44 [* The one who falls on this stone will be
dashed to pieces; and it will crush anyone on
whom it falls.]" 45 When the chief priests and
the Pharisees* heard his parables, they knew
that he was speaking about them. 46 And although they were attempting to arrest him,
they feared the crowds, for they regarded
him as a prophet.

See RG 287–88

## CHAPTER 22

*The Parable of the Wedding Feast.**
1d Jesus again in reply spoke to them in parables, saying, 2 "The kingdom of heaven may
be likened to a king who gave a wedding
feast* for his son. 3* He dispatched his servants to summon the invited guests to the
feast, but they refused to come. 4 A second
time he sent other servants, saying, 'Tell
those invited: "Behold, I have prepared my
banquet, my calves and fattened cattle are
killed, and everything is ready; come to the
feast."' 5 Some ignored the invitation and
went away, one to his farm, another to his
business. 6e The rest laid hold of his servants,
mistreated them, and killed them. 7* The king
was enraged and sent his troops, destroyed
those murderers, and burned their city. 8 Then
he said to his servants, 'The feast is ready, but
those who were invited were not worthy to
come. 9 Go out, therefore, into the main roads
and invite to the feast whomever you find.'
10 The servants went out into the streets and
gathered all they found, bad and good alike,*
and the hall was filled with guests. 11* But
when the king came in to meet the guests he
saw a man there not dressed in a wedding
garment. 12 He said to him, 'My friend, how
is it that you came in here without a wedding
garment?' But he was reduced to silence.
13* f Then the king said to his attendants,
'Bind his hands and feet, and cast him into
the darkness outside, where there will be
wailing and grinding of teeth.' 14 Many are invited, but few are chosen."

***Paying Taxes to the Emperor.**** 15g Then the
Pharisees* went off and plotted how they
might entrap him in speech. 16 They sent their
disciples to him, with the Herodians,* saying,

19:23–24. Its presence here instead of Matthew's usual "kingdom of heaven" may indicate that the saying came from Matthew's own traditional material. **A people that will produce its fruit**: believing Israelites and Gentiles, the church of Jesus.

**21:44** The majority of textual witnesses omit this verse. It is probably an early addition to Matthew from Lk 20:18 with which it is practically identical.

**21:45 The Pharisees**: Matthew inserts into the group of Jewish leaders (Mt 21:23) those who represented the Judaism of his own time.

**22:1–14** This parable is from Q; see Lk 14:15–24. It has been given many allegorical traits by Matthew, e.g., the burning of the **city** of the guests who refused the invitation (Mt 22:7), which corresponds to the destruction of Jerusalem by the Romans in A.D. 70. It has similarities with the preceding parable of the tenants: the sending of two groups of **servants** (Mt 22:3, 4), the murder of the **servants** (Mt 22:6), the punishment of the **murderers** (Mt 22:7), and the entrance of a new group into a privileged situation of which the others had proved themselves unworthy (Mt 22:8–10). The parable ends with a section that is peculiar to Matthew (Mt 22:11–14), which some take as a distinct parable. Matthew presents the **kingdom** in its double aspect, already present and something that can be entered here and now (Mt 22:1–10), and something that will be possessed only by those present members who can stand the scrutiny of the final judgment (Mt 22:11–14). The parable is not only a statement of God's judgment on Israel but a warning to Matthew's church.

**22:2 Wedding feast**: the Old Testament's portrayal of final salvation under the image of a banquet (Is 25:6) is taken up also in Mt 8:11; cf. Lk 13:15.

**22:3–4 Servants . . . other servants**: probably Christian missionaries in both instances; cf. Mt 23:34.

**22:7** See note on Mt 22:1–14.

**22:10 Bad and good alike**: cf. Mt 13:47.

**22:11 A wedding garment**: the repentance, change of heart and mind, that is the condition for entrance into the kingdom (Mt 3:2; 4:17) must be continued in a life of good deeds (Mt 7:21–23).

**22:13 Wailing and grinding of teeth**: the Christian who lacks the wedding garment of good deeds will suffer the same fate as those Jews who have rejected Jesus; see note on Mt 8:11–12.

**22:15–22** The series of controversies between Jesus and the representatives of Judaism (see note on Mt 21:23–27) is resumed. As in the first (Mt 21:23–27), here and in the following disputes Matthew follows his Marcan source with few modifications.

**22:15 The Pharisees**: while Matthew retains the Marcan union of Pharisees and Herodians in this account, he clearly emphasizes the Pharisees' part. They alone are mentioned here, and the Herodians are joined with them only in a prepositional phrase of Mt 22:16. **Entrap him in speech**: the question that they will pose is intended to force Jesus to take either a position contrary to that held by the majority of the people or one that will bring him into conflict with the Roman authorities.

**22:16 Herodians:** see note on Mk 3:6. They would favor payment of the tax; the Pharisees did not.

*d:* Lk 14:15–24. *e:* 21:35. *f:* 8:12; 25:30. *g:* Mk 12:13–17; Lk 20:20–26.

"Teacher, we know that you are a truthful
man and that you teach the way of God in accordance with the truth. And you are not concerned with anyone's opinion, for you do not
regard a person's status. 17* Tell us, then,
what is your opinion: Is it lawful to pay the
census tax to Caesar or not?" 18 Knowing
their malice, Jesus said, "Why are you testing
me, you hypocrites? 19* Show me the coin
that pays the census tax." Then they handed
him the Roman coin. 20 He said to them,
"Whose image is this and whose inscription?" 21h They replied, "Caesar's."* At that
he said to them, "Then repay to Caesar what
belongs to Caesar and to God what belongs
to God." 22 When they heard this they were
amazed, and leaving him they went away.

*The Question About the Resurrection.**
23i On that day Sadducees approached him,
saying that there is no resurrection.* They
put this question to him, 24j saying, "Teacher, Moses said, 'If a man dies* without children, his brother shall marry his wife and
raise up descendants for his brother.' 25 Now
there were seven brothers among us. The
first married and died and, having no descendants, left his wife to his brother. 26 The
same happened with the second and the
third, through all seven. 27 Finally the woman
died. 28 Now at the resurrection, of the seven,
whose wife will she be? For they all had
been married to her." 29* Jesus said to them
in reply, "You are misled because you do not
know the scriptures or the power of God.
30 At the resurrection they neither marry nor
are given in marriage but are like the angels
in heaven. 31 And concerning the resurrection of the dead, have you not read what was
said to you* by God, 32k 'I am the God of
Abraham, the God of Isaac, and the God of
Jacob'? He is not the God of the dead but of
the living." 33 When the crowds heard this,
they were astonished at his teaching.

*The Greatest Commandment.** 34l When

**22:17 Is it lawful**: the law to which they refer is the law of God.

**22:19 They handed him the Roman coin**: their readiness in producing the money implies their use of it and their acceptance of the financial advantages of the Roman administration in Palestine.

**22:21 Caesar's**: the emperor Tiberius (A.D. 14–37). **Repay to Caesar what belongs to Caesar**: those who willingly use the coin that is Caesar's should **repay** him in kind. The answer avoids taking sides in the question of the lawfulness of the tax. **To God what belongs to God**: Jesus raises the debate to a new level. Those who have hypocritically asked about tax in respect to its relation to the law of **God** should be concerned rather with repaying God with the good deeds that are his due; cf. Mt 21:41, 43.

**22:23–33** Here Jesus' opponents are the **Sadducees**, members of the powerful priestly party of his time; see note on Mt 3:7. Denying the resurrection of the dead, a teaching of relatively late origin in Judaism (cf. Dn 12:2), they appeal to a law of the Pentateuch (Dt 25:5–10) and present a case based on it that would make resurrection from the dead ridiculous (Mt 22:24–28). Jesus chides them for knowing neither **the scriptures** nor **the power of God** (Mt 22:29). His argument in respect to God's power contradicts the notion, held even by many proponents as well as by opponents of the teaching, that the life of those raised from the dead would be essentially a continuation of the type of life they had had before death (Mt 22:30). His argument based on the scriptures (Mt 22:31–32) is of a sort that was accepted as valid among Jews of the time.

**22:23 Saying that there is no resurrection**: in the Marcan parallel (Mk 22:12, 18) the Sadducees are correctly defined as those "who say there is no resurrection"; see also Lk 20:27. Matthew's rewording of Mark can mean that these particular Sadducees deny the resurrection, which would imply that he was not aware that the denial was characteristic of the party. For some scholars this is an indication of his being a Gentile Christian; see note on Mt 21:4–5.

**22:24 'If a man dies . . . his brother'**: this is known as the "law of the levirate," from the Latin *levir*, "brother-in-law." Its purpose was to continue the family line of the deceased brother (Dt 25:6).

**22:29** The sexual relationships of this world will be transcended; the risen body will be the work of the creative **power of God**.

**22:31–32** Cf. Ex 3:6. In the Pentateuch, which the Sadducees accepted as normative for Jewish belief and practice, God speaks even now (**to you**) of himself as the God of the patriarchs who died centuries ago. He identifies himself in relation to them, and because of their relation to him, the living God, they too are alive. This might appear no argument for the resurrection, but simply for life after death as conceived in Wis 3:1–3. But the general thought of early first-century Judaism was not influenced by that conception; for it human immortality was connected with the existence of the body.

**22:34–40** The Marcan parallel (Mk 12:28–34) is an exchange between Jesus and a scribe who is impressed by the way in which Jesus has conducted himself in the previous controversy (Mk 12:28), who compliments him for the answer he gives him (Mk 12:32), and who is said by Jesus to be "not far from the kingdom of God" (Mk 12:34). Matthew has sharpened that scene. The questioner, as the representative of other Pharisees, tests Jesus by his question (Mt 22:34–35), and both his reaction to Jesus' reply and Jesus' commendation of him are lacking.

*h:* Rom 13:7. *i:* Mk 12:18–27; Lk 20:27–40. *j:* Gn 38:8; Dt 25:5–6. *k:* Ex 3:6. *l:* Mk 12:28–34; Lk 10:25–28.

the Pharisees heard that he had silenced the
Sadducees, they gathered together, [35]and
one of them [a scholar of the law]* tested
him by asking, [36]"Teacher,* which commandment in the law is the greatest?" [37m] He
said to him,* "You shall love the Lord, your
God, with all your heart, with all your soul,
and with all your mind. [38]This is the greatest
and the first commandment. [39n] The second
is like it:* You shall love your neighbor as
yourself. [40*] [o] The whole law and the prophets depend on these two commandments."

***The Question About David's Son.**** 
[41p] While the Pharisees were gathered together, Jesus questioned them,* [42*] saying,
"What is your opinion about the Messiah?
Whose son is he?" They replied, "David's."
[43]He said to them, "How, then, does David,
inspired by the Spirit, call him 'lord,' saying:

[44] [q] 'The Lord said to my lord,
"Sit at my right hand
until I place your enemies under your
feet" '?

[45*] If David calls him 'lord,' how can he be
his son?" [46r] No one was able to answer him
a word, nor from that day on did anyone dare
to ask him any more questions.

## CHAPTER 23*

See RG 287-88

***Denunciation of the Scribes and Pharisees.*** [1s] Then Jesus spoke to the crowds
and to his disciples, [2*] saying, "The scribes
and the Pharisees have taken their seat on

**22:35 [A scholar of the law]**: meaning "scribe." Although this reading is supported by the vast majority of textual witnesses, it is the only time that the Greek word so translated occurs in Matthew. It is relatively frequent in Luke, and there is reason to think that it may have been added here by a copyist since it occurs in the Lucan parallel (Lk 10:25–28). **Tested**: see note on Mt 19:3.

**22:36** For the devout Jew all the commandments were to be kept with equal care, but there is evidence of preoccupation in Jewish sources with the question put to Jesus.

**22:37–38** Cf. Dt 6:5. Matthew omits the first part of Mark's fuller quotation (Mk 12:29; Dt 6:4–5), probably because he considered its monotheistic emphasis needless for his church. The love of God must engage the total person (**heart, soul, mind**).

**22:39** Jesus goes beyond the extent of the question put to him and joins **to the greatest and the first commandment** a **second**, that of **love** of **neighbor**, Lv 19:18; see note on Mt 19:18–19. This combination of the two commandments may already have been made in Judaism.

**22:40** The double commandment is the source from which **the whole law and the prophets** are derived.

**22:41–46** Having answered the questions of his opponents in the preceding three controversies, Jesus now puts a question to them about the sonship of the Messiah. Their easy response (Mt 22:43a) is countered by his quoting a verse of Ps 110 that raises a problem for their response (43b–45). They are unable to solve it and **from that day on** their questioning of him is ended.

**22:41 The Pharisees . . . questioned them**: Mark is not specific about who are questioned (Mk 12:35).

**22:42–44 David's**: this view of the Pharisees was based on such Old Testament texts as Is 11:1–9; Jer 23:5; and Ez 34:23; see also the extrabiblical Psalms of Solomon 17:21. **How, then . . . saying**: Jesus cites Ps 110:1, accepting the Davidic authorship of the psalm, a common view of his time. The psalm was probably composed for the enthronement of a Davidic king of Judah. Matthew assumes that the Pharisees interpret it as referring to the Messiah, although there is no clear evidence that it was so interpreted in the Judaism of Jesus' time. It was widely used in the early church as referring to the exaltation of the risen Jesus. **My lord**: understood as the Messiah.

**22:45** Since Matthew presents Jesus both as Messiah (Mt 16:16) and as Son of David (Mt 1:1; see also note on Mt 9:27), the question is not meant to imply Jesus' denial of Davidic sonship. It probably means that although he is the Son of David, he is someone greater, Son of Man and Son of God, and recognized as greater by David who calls him my **'lord.'**

**23:1–39** The final section of the narrative part of the fifth book of the gospel is a denunciation by Jesus of the scribes and the Pharisees (see note on Mt 3:7). It depends in part on Mark and Q (cf. Mk 12:38–39; Lk 11:37–52; 13:34–35), but in the main it is peculiar to Matthew. (For the reasons against considering this extensive body of sayings-material either as one of the structural discourses of this gospel or as part of the one that follows in Mt 24–25, see note on Mt 19:1–23:39.) While the tradition of a deep opposition between Jesus and the Pharisees is well founded, this speech reflects an opposition that goes beyond that of Jesus' ministry and must be seen as expressing the bitter conflict between Pharisaic Judaism and the church of Matthew at the time when the gospel was composed. The complaint often made that the speech ignores the positive qualities of Pharisaism and of its better representatives is true, but the complaint overlooks the circumstances that gave rise to the invective. Nor is the speech purely anti-Pharisaic. The evangelist discerns in his church many of the same faults that he finds in its opponents and warns his fellow Christians to look to their own conduct and attitudes.

**23:2–3 Have taken their seat . . . Moses**: it is uncertain whether this is simply a metaphor for Mosaic teaching authority or refers to an actual **chair** on which the teacher sat. It has been proved that there was a seat so designated in synagogues of a later period than that of this gospel. **Do and observe . . . they tell you**: since the Matthean Jesus abrogates Mosaic law (Mt 5:31–42), warns his disciples against the teaching of the Pharisees (Mt 14:1–12), and, in this speech, denounces the Pharisees as blind guides in respect to their teaching on oaths (Mt 23:16–22), this commandment **to ob-**

*m:* Dt 6:5. *n:* Lv 19:18; Jas 2:8. *o:* Rom 13:8–10; Gal 5:14. *p:* Mk 12:35–37; Lk 20:41–44. *q:* Ps 110:1; Acts 2:35; Heb 1:13. *r:* Lk 20:40. *s:* Mk 12:38–39; Lk 11:37–52; 13:34–35.

the chair of Moses. 3 Therefore, do and observe all things whatsoever they tell you, but
do not follow their example. For they preach
but they do not practice. 4 [t] They tie up heavy
burdens* [hard to carry] and lay them on
people's shoulders, but they will not lift a
finger to move them. 5* [u] All their works are
performed to be seen. They widen their phylacteries and lengthen their tassels. 6* [v] They
love places of honor at banquets, seats of
honor in synagogues, 7 greetings in marketplaces, and the salutation 'Rabbi.' 8* As for
you, do not be called 'Rabbi.' You have but
one teacher, and you are all brothers. 9 Call
no one on earth your father; you have but
one Father in heaven. 10 Do not be called
'Master'; you have but one master, the Messiah. 11 [w] The greatest among you must be
your servant. 12 [x] Whoever exalts himself
will be humbled; but whoever humbles himself will be exalted.
13* [y] "Woe to you, scribes and Pharisees,
you hypocrites. You lock the kingdom of
heaven* before human beings. You do not
enter yourselves, nor do you allow entrance
to those trying to enter. [14]*
15* "Woe to you, scribes and Pharisees,
you hypocrites. You traverse sea and land to
make one convert, and when that happens
you make him a child of Gehenna twice as
much as yourselves.
16* [z] "Woe to you, blind guides, who say, 'If

**serve all things whatsoever they** (the scribes and Pharisees) **tell you** cannot be taken as the evangelist's understanding of the proper standard of conduct for his church. The saying may reflect a period when the Matthean community was largely Jewish Christian and was still seeking to avoid a complete break with the synagogue. Matthew has incorporated this traditional material into the speech in accordance with his view of the course of salvation history, in which he portrays the time of Jesus' ministry as marked by the fidelity to the law, although with significant pointers to the new situation that would exist after his death and resurrection (see note on Mt 5:17–20). The crowds and the disciples (Mt 23:1) are exhorted not to **follow** the **example** of the Jewish leaders, whose deeds do not conform to their teaching (Mt 23:3).

**23:4 Tie up heavy burdens**: see note on Mt 11:28.

**23:5** To the charge of preaching but not practicing (Mt 23:3), Jesus adds that of acting in order to earn praise. The disciples have already been warned against this same fault (see note on Mt 6:1–18). **Phylacteries**: the Mosaic law required that during prayer small boxes containing parchments on which verses of scripture were written be worn on the left forearm and the forehead (see Ex 13:9, 16; Dt 6:8; 11:18). **Tassels**: see note on Mt 9:20. The widening of **phylacteries** and the lengthening of **tassels** were for the purpose of making these evidences of piety more noticeable.

**23:6–7** Cf. Mk 12:38–39. **'Rabbi'**: literally, "my great one," a title of respect for teachers and leaders.

**23:8–12** These verses, warning against the use of various titles, are addressed to the disciples alone. While only the title **'Rabbi'** has been said to be used in addressing the scribes and Pharisees (Mt 23:7), the implication is that **Father** and **'Master'** also were. The prohibition of these titles to the disciples suggests that their use was present in Matthew's church. The Matthean Jesus forbids not only the titles but the spirit of superiority and pride that is shown by their acceptance. **Whoever exalts . . . will be exalted**: cf. Lk 14:11.

**23:13–36** This series of seven "woes," directed against the **scribes and Pharisees** and addressed to them, is the heart of the speech. The phrase **woe to** occurs often in the prophetic and apocalyptic literature, expressing horror of a sin and punishment for those who commit it. **Hypocrites**: see note on Mt 6:2. The hypocrisy of the **scribes and Pharisees** consists in the difference between their speech and action (Mt 23:3) and in demonstrations of piety that have no other purpose than to enhance their reputation as religious persons (Mt 23:5).

**23:13 You lock the kingdom of heaven**: cf. Mt 16:19 where Jesus tells Peter that he will give him the keys to **the kingdom of heaven**. The purpose of the authority expressed by that metaphor is to give entrance into the kingdom (the kingdom is closed only to those who reject the authority); here the charge is made that the authority of the **scribes and Pharisees** is exercised in such a way as to be an obstacle to entrance. Cf. Lk 11:52 where the accusation against the "scholars of the law" (Matthew's **scribes**) is that they "have taken away the key of knowledge."

**23:14** Some manuscripts add a verse here or after Mt 23:12, "Woe to you, scribes and Pharisees, you hypocrites. You devour the houses of widows and, as a pretext, recite lengthy prayers. Because of this, you will receive a very severe condemnation." Cf. Mk 12:40; Lk 20:47. This "woe" is almost identical with Mk 12:40 and seems to be an interpolation derived from that text.

**23:15** In the first century A.D. until the First Jewish Revolt against Rome (A.D. 66–70), many Pharisees conducted a vigorous missionary campaign among Gentiles. **Convert**: literally, "proselyte," a Gentile who accepted Judaism fully by submitting to circumcision and all other requirements of Mosaic law. **Child of Gehenna**: worthy of everlasting punishment; for **Gehenna**, see note on Mt 5:22. **Twice as much as yourselves**: possibly this refers simply to the zeal of the **convert**, surpassing that of the one who converted him.

**23:16–22** An attack on the casuistry that declared some oaths binding (**one is obligated**) and others not (**it means nothing**) and held the binding oath to be the one made by something of lesser value (**the gold; the gift on the altar**). Such teaching, which inverts the order of values, reveals the teachers to be **blind guides**; cf. Mt 15:14. Since the Matthean Jesus forbids all oaths to his disciples (Mt 5:33–37), this woe does not set up a standard for Christian moral conduct, but ridicules the Pharisees on their own terms.

---

*t:* Lk 11:46. *u:* 6:1–6; Ex 13:9, 16; Nm 15:38–39; Dt 6:8; 11:18. *v:* Mk 12:38–39; Lk 11:43; 20:46. *w:* 20:26. *x:* Lk 14:11; 18:14. *y:* Lk 11:52. *z:* 15:14.

one swears by the temple, it means nothing,
but if one swears by the gold of the temple,
one is obligated.' [17]Blind fools, which is
greater, the gold, or the temple that made the
gold sacred? [18]And you say, 'If one swears by
the altar, it means nothing, but if one swears
by the gift on the altar, one is obligated.'
[19]You blind ones, which is greater, the gift, or
the altar that makes the gift sacred? [20a] One
who swears by the altar swears by it and all
that is upon it; [21]one who swears by the temple swears by it and by him who dwells in it;
[22]one who swears by heaven swears by the
throne of God and by him who is seated on it.
[23b] "Woe to you, scribes and Pharisees,
you hypocrites. You pay tithes* of mint and
dill and cummin, and have neglected the
weightier things of the law: judgment and
mercy and fidelity. [But] these you should
have done, without neglecting the others.
[24* c] Blind guides, who strain out the gnat
and swallow the camel!
[25* d] "Woe to you, scribes and Pharisees,
you hypocrites. You cleanse the outside of
cup and dish, but inside they are full of plunder and self-indulgence. [26]Blind Pharisee,
cleanse first the inside of the cup, so that the
outside also may be clean.
[27*] "Woe to you, scribes and Pharisees,
you hypocrites. You are like whitewashed
tombs, which appear beautiful on the outside, but inside are full of dead men's bones
and every kind of filth. [28e] Even so, on the
outside you appear righteous, but inside you
are filled with hypocrisy and evildoing.
[29*] "Woe to you, scribes and Pharisees,*
you hypocrites. You build the tombs of the
prophets and adorn the memorials of the
righteous, [30f] and you say, 'If we had lived in
the days of our ancestors, we would not have
joined them in shedding the prophets'
blood.' [31g] Thus you bear witness against
yourselves that you are the children of those
who murdered the prophets; [32]now fill up
what your ancestors measured out! [33h] You
serpents, you brood of vipers, how can you
flee from the judgment of Gehenna?
[34* i] Therefore, behold, I send to you proph-

**23:23** The Mosaic law ordered tithing of the produce of the land (Lv 27:30; Dt 14:22–23), and the scribal tradition is said here to have extended this law to even the smallest herbs. The practice is criticized not in itself but because it shows the Pharisees' preoccupation with matters of less importance while they neglect **the weightier things of the law**.

**23:24** Cf. Lv 11:41–45 that forbids the eating of any "swarming creature." The Pharisees' scrupulosity about minor matters and neglect of greater ones (Mt 23:23) is further brought out by this contrast between straining liquids that might contain a tiny "swarming creature" and yet swallowing **the camel**. The latter was one of the unclean animals forbidden by the law (Lv 11:4), but it is hardly possible that the scribes and Pharisees are being denounced as guilty of so gross a violation of the food laws. To **swallow the camel** is only a hyperbolic way of speaking of their neglect of what is important.

**23:25–26** The ritual washing of utensils for dining (cf. Mk 7:4) is turned into a metaphor illustrating a concern for appearances while inner purity is ignored. The **scribes and Pharisees** are compared to cups carefully washed on the outside but filthy within. **Self-indulgence**: the Greek word here translated means lack of self-control, whether in drinking or in sexual conduct.

**23:27–28** The sixth **woe**, like the preceding one, deals with concern for externals and neglect of what is **inside**. Since contact with dead bodies, even when one was unaware of it, caused ritual impurity (Nm 19:11–22), tombs were whitewashed so that no one would contract such impurity inadvertently.

**23:29–36** The final **woe** is the most serious indictment of all. It portrays the **scribes and Pharisees** as standing in the same line as their **ancestors** who murdered **the prophets** and **the righteous**.

**23:29–32** In spite of honoring the slain dead by building their **tombs** and adorning their **memorials**, and claiming that they would not have joined in their ancestors' crimes if they **had lived in** their **days**, the **scribes and Pharisees** are true children of their ancestors and are defiantly ordered by Jesus to **fill up** what those **ancestors measured out**. This order reflects the Jewish notion that there was an allotted measure of suffering that had to be completed before God's final judgment would take place.

**23:34–36** There are important differences between the Matthean and the Lucan form of this Q material; cf. Lk 11:49–51. In Luke the one who sends the emissaries is the "wisdom of God." If, as many scholars think, that is the original wording of Q, Matthew, by making Jesus the sender, has presented him as the personified divine wisdom. In Luke, wisdom's emissaries are the Old Testament "prophets" and the Christian "apostles." Matthew's **prophets and wise men and scribes** are probably Christian disciples alone; cf. Mt 10:41 and see note on Mt 13:52. **You will kill**: see Mt 24:9. **Scourge in your synagogues . . . town to town**: see Mt 10:17, 23 and the note on Mt 10:17. **All the righteous blood shed upon the earth**: the slaying of the disciples is in continuity with all the shedding of **righteous blood** beginning with that **of Abel.** The persecution of Jesus' disciples by **this generation** involves the persecutors in the guilt of their murderous ancestors. **The blood of Zechariah**: see note on Lk 11:51. By identifying him as **the son of Barachiah** Matthew understands him to be Zechariah the Old Testament minor prophet; see Zec 1:1.

*a:* 5:34–35. *b:* Lv 27:30; Dt 14:22; Lk 11:42. *c:* Lv 11:41–45. *d:* Mk 7:4; Lk 11:39. *e:* Lk 16:15; 18:9. *f:* Lk 11:47. *g:* Acts 7:52. *h:* 3:7; 12:34. *i:* 5:12; Gn 4:8; 2 Chr 24:20–22; Zec 1:1; Lk 11:49–51; Rev 18:24.

ets and wise men and scribes; some of them
you will kill and crucify, some of them you
will scourge in your synagogues and pursue
from town to town, 35 so that there may come
upon you all the righteous blood shed upon
earth, from the righteous blood of Abel to the
blood of Zechariah, the son of Barachiah,
whom you murdered between the sanctuary
and the altar. 36 Amen, I say to you, all these
things will come upon this generation.

*The Lament over Jerusalem.** 37[j] "Jerusalem, Jerusalem, you who kill the prophets
and stone those sent to you, how many times
I yearned to gather your children together, as
a hen gathers her young under her wings, but
you were unwilling![k] 38[l] Behold, your house
will be abandoned, desolate. 39[m] I tell you,
you will not see me again until you say,
'Blessed is he who comes in the name of the
Lord.' "

## CHAPTER 24

See RG 287–88

*The Destruction of the Temple Fore-
told.* 1* [n] Jesus left the temple area and was
going away, when his disciples approached
him to point out the temple buildings. 2* He
said to them in reply, "You see all these
things, do you not? Amen, I say to you, there
will not be left here a stone upon another
stone that will not be thrown down."

*The Beginning of Calamities.* 3 As he was
sitting on the Mount of Olives,* the disciples
approached him privately and said, "Tell us,
when will this happen, and what sign will
there be of your coming, and of the end of
the age?" 4* Jesus said to them in reply, "See
that no one deceives you. 5 For many will
come in my name, saying, 'I am the Messiah,' and they will deceive many. 6[o] You
will hear of wars* and reports of wars; see

**23:37–39** Cf. Lk 13:34–35. The denunciation of Pharisaic Judaism ends with this lament over **Jerusalem**, which has repeatedly rejected and murdered those whom God has **sent** to her. **How many times**: this may refer to various visits of Jesus to the city, an aspect of his ministry found in John but otherwise not in the synoptics. **As a hen . . . under her wings**: for imagery similar to this, see Ps 17:8; 91:4. **Your house . . . desolate**: probably an allusion to the destruction of the temple in A.D. 70. **You will not see me . . . in the name of the Lord**: Israel will not see Jesus again until he comes in glory for the final judgment. The acclamation has been interpreted in contrasting ways, as an indication that Israel will at last accept Jesus at that time, and as its troubled recognition of him as its dreaded judge who will pronounce its condemnation; in support of the latter view see Mt 24:30.

**24:1–25:46** The discourse of the fifth book, the last of the five around which the gospel is structured. It is called the "eschatological" discourse since it deals with the coming of the new age (the *eschaton*) in its fullness, with events that will precede it, and with how the disciples are to conduct themselves while awaiting an event that is as certain as its exact time is unknown to all but the Father (Mt 24:36). The discourse may be divided into two parts, Mt 24:1–44 and Mt 24:45–25:46. In the first, Matthew follows his Marcan source (Mk 13:1–37) closely. The second is drawn from Q and from the evangelist's own traditional material. Both parts show Matthew's editing of his sources by deletions, additions, and modifications. The vigilant waiting that is emphasized in the second part does not mean a cessation of ordinary activity and concentration only on what is to come, but a faithful accomplishment of duties at hand, with awareness that the end, for which the disciples must always be ready, will entail the great judgment by which the everlasting destiny of all will be determined.

**24:2** As in Mark, Jesus predicts the destruction of the temple. By omitting the Marcan story of the widow's contribution (Mk 12:41–44) that immediately precedes the prediction in that gospel, Matthew has established a close connection between it and Mt 23:38, ". . . your house will be abandoned desolate."

**24:3 The Mount of Olives**: see note on Mt 21:1. **The disciples**: cf. Mk 13:3–4 where only Peter, James, John, and Andrew put the question that is answered by the discourse. In both gospels, however, the question is put **privately**: the ensuing discourse is only for those who are **disciples** of Jesus. **When will this happen . . . end of the age?**: Matthew distinguishes carefully between the destruction of the temple (**this**) and the **coming** of Jesus that will bring **the end of the age**. In Mark the two events are more closely connected, a fact that may be explained by Mark's believing that the one would immediately succeed the other. **Coming**: this translates the Greek word *parousia*, which is used in the gospels only here and in Mt 24:27, 37, 39. It designated the official visit of a ruler to a city or the manifestation of a saving deity, and it was used by Christians to refer to the final coming of Jesus in glory, a term first found in the New Testament with that meaning in 1 Thes 2:19. **The end of the age**: see note on Mt 13:39.

**24:4–14** This section of the discourse deals with calamities in the world (Mt 24:6–7) and in the church (Mt 24:9–12). The former **must happen** before **the end** comes (Mt 24:6), but they are only **the beginning of the labor pains** (Mt 24:8). (It may be noted that the Greek word translated **the end** in Mt 24:6 and in Mt 24:13–14 is not the same as the phrase "the end of the age" in Mt 24:3, although the meaning is the same.) The latter are sufferings of the church, both from within and without, that will last until **the gospel** is **preached . . . to all nations**. **Then the end will come** and those who have endured the sufferings with fidelity **will be saved** (Mt 24:13–14).

**24:6–7** The disturbances mentioned here are a commonplace of apocalyptic language, as is the assurance that they **must happen** (see Dn 2:28 LXX), for that is the plan of God. **Kingdom against kingdom**: see Is 19:2.

*j:* Lk 13:34–35; 19:41–44. *k:* 21:35. *l:* Jer 12:7. *m:* Ps 118:26. *n:* Mk 13:1–37; Lk 21:5–36. *o:* Dn 2:28 LXX.

that you are not alarmed, for these things
must happen, but it will not yet be the end.
7p Nation will rise against nation, and kingdom against kingdom; there will be famines
and earthquakes from place to place. 8* All
these are the beginning of the labor pains.
9* q Then they will hand you over to persecution, and they will kill you. You will be
hated by all nations because of my name.
10 And then many will be led into sin; they
will betray and hate one another. 11 Many
false prophets will arise and deceive many;
12 and because of the increase of evildoing,
the love of many will grow cold. 13r But the
one who perseveres to the end will be saved.
14s And this gospel of the kingdom will be
preached throughout the world as a witness
to all nations,* and then the end will come.

***The Great Tribulation.**** 15t "When you see
the desolating abomination* spoken of through
Daniel the prophet standing in the holy place
(let the reader understand), 16 then those in Judea must flee* to the mountains, 17* u a person
on the housetop must not go down to get things
out of his house, 18 a person in the field must
not return to get his cloak. 19 Woe to pregnant
women and nursing mothers in those days.
20* Pray that your flight not be in winter or on
the sabbath, 21* v for at that time there will be
great tribulation, such as has not been since the
beginning of the world until now, nor ever will
be. 22 And if those days had not been shortened,

**24:8 The labor pains**: the tribulations leading up to the end of the age are compared to the pains of a woman about to give birth. There is much attestation for rabbinic use of the phrase "the woes (or birth pains) of the Messiah" after the New Testament period, but in at least one instance it is attributed to a rabbi who lived in the late first century A.D. In this Jewish usage it meant the distress of the time preceding the coming of the Messiah; here, the **labor pains** precede the coming of the Son of Man in glory.

**24:9–12** Matthew has used Mk 13:9–12 in his missionary discourse (Mt 10:17–21) and omits it here. Besides the sufferings, including death, and the hatred of **all nations** that the disciples will have to endure, there will be worse affliction within the church itself. This is described in Mt 24:10–12, which are peculiar to Matthew. **Will be led into sin**: literally, "will be scandalized," probably meaning that they will become apostates; see Mt 13:21 where "fall away" translates the same Greek word as here. **Betray**: in the Greek this is the same word as the **hand over** of Mt 24:9. The handing over to persecution and hatred from outside will have their counterpart within the church. **False prophets**: these are Christians; see note on Mt 7:15–20. **Evildoing**: see Mt 7:23. Because of the apocalyptic nature of much of this discourse, the literal meaning of this description of the church should not be pressed too hard. However, there is reason to think that Matthew's addition of these verses reflects in some measure the condition of his community.

**24:14** Except for the last part (**and then the end will come**), this verse substantially repeats Mk 13:10. The Matthean addition raises a problem since what follows in Mt 24:15–23 refers to the horrors of the First Jewish Revolt including the destruction of the temple, and Matthew, writing after that time, knew that the parousia of Jesus was still in the future. A solution may be that the evangelist saw the events of those verses as foreshadowing the cosmic disturbances that he associates with the parousia (Mt 24:29) so that the period in which the former took place could be understood as belonging to **the end**.

**24:15–28** Cf. Mk 13:14–23; Lk 17:23–24, 37. A further stage in the tribulations that will precede the coming of the Son of Man, and an answer to the question of Mt 24:3a, "when will this (the destruction of the temple) happen?"

**24:15 The desolating abomination**: in 167 B.C. the Syrian king Antiochus IV Epiphanes desecrated the temple by setting up in it a statue of Zeus Olympios (see 1 Mc 1:54). That event is referred to in Dn 12:11 LXX as the "desolating abomination" (NAB "horrible abomination") and the same Greek term is used here; cf. also Dn 9:27; 11:31. Although the desecration had taken place before Daniel was written, it is presented there as a future event, and Matthew sees that "prophecy" fulfilled in the desecration of the temple by the Romans. **In the holy place**: the temple; more precise than Mark's **where he should not** (Mk 13:14). **Let the reader understand**: this parenthetical remark, taken from Mk 13:14 invites **the reader** to realize the meaning of Daniel's "prophecy."

**24:16** The tradition that the Christians of Jerusalem fled from that city to Pella, a city of Transjordan, at the time of the First Jewish Revolt is found in Eusebius (*Ecclesiastical History* 3.5.3), who attributes the flight to "a certain oracle given by revelation before the war." The tradition is not improbable but the Matthean command, derived from its Marcan source, is vague in respect to the place of flight (**to the mountains**), although some scholars see it as applicable to the flight to Pella.

**24:17–19** Haste is essential, and the journey will be particularly difficult for women who are burdened with unborn or infant children.

**24:20 On the sabbath**: this addition to **in winter** (cf. Mk 13:18) has been understood as an indication that Matthew was addressed to a church still observing the Mosaic law of sabbath rest and the scribal limitations upon the length of journeys that might lawfully be made on that day. That interpretation conflicts with Matthew's view on sabbath observance (cf. Mt 12:1–14). The meaning of the addition may be that those undertaking on the sabbath a journey such as the one here ordered would be offending the sensibilities of law-observant Jews and would incur their hostility.

**24:21** For the unparalleled distress of that time, see Dn 12:1.

*p:* Is 19:2. *q:* 10:17. *r:* 10:22. *s:* 28:19; Rom 10:18. *t:* Dn 9:27; 11:31; 12:11; Mk 13:14. *u:* Lk 17:31. *v:* Dn 12:1.

no one would be saved; but for the sake of the
elect they will be shortened. 23w If anyone says
to you then, 'Look, here is the Messiah!' or,
'There he is!' do not believe it. 24 False messiahs and false prophets will arise, and they will
perform signs and wonders so great as to deceive, if that were possible, even the elect.
25 Behold, I have told it to you beforehand.
26 So if they say to you, 'He is in the desert,' do
not go out there; if they say, 'He is in the inner
rooms,' do not believe it.* 27x For just as lightning comes from the east and is seen as far as
the west, so will the coming of the Son of Man
be. 28 Wherever the corpse is, there the vultures
will gather.

***The Coming of the Son of Man.*** 29* y "Immediately after the tribulation of those days,

the sun will be darkened,
  and the moon will not give its light,
and the stars will fall from the sky,
  and the powers of the heavens will be
    shaken.

30z And then the sign of the Son of Man* will
appear in heaven, and all the tribes of the
earth will mourn, and they will see the Son of
Man coming upon the clouds of heaven with
power and great glory. 31a And he will send
out his angels* with a trumpet blast, and they
will gather his elect from the four winds,
from one end of the heavens to the other.

***The Lesson of the Fig Tree.**** 32 "Learn a lesson from the fig tree. When its branch becomes tender and sprouts leaves, you know
that summer is near. 33 In the same way, when
you see all these things, know that he is near,
at the gates. 34 Amen, I say to you, this generation* will not pass away until all these things
have taken place. 35b Heaven and earth will
pass away, but my words will not pass away.

***The Unknown Day and Hour.**** 36c "But of
that day and hour no one knows, neither the
angels of heaven, nor the Son,* but the Father alone. 37* d For as it was in the days of
Noah, so it will be at the coming of the Son
of Man. 38 In [those] days before the flood,
they were eating and drinking, marrying and
giving in marriage, up to the day that Noah
entered the ark. 39 They did not know until
the flood came and carried them all away. So
will it be [also] at the coming of the Son of
Man. 40* e Two men will be out in the field;

**24:26–28** Claims that the Messiah is to be found in some distant or secret place must be ignored. **The coming of the Son of Man** will be as clear as **lightning** is to all and as **the corpse** of an animal is to **vultures**; cf. Lk 17:24, 37. Here there is clear identification of **the Son of Man** and the Messiah; cf. Mt 24:23.

**24:29** The answer to the question of Mt 24:3b "What sign will there be of your coming?" **Immediately after . . . those days**: the shortening of time between the preceding **tribulation** and the parousia has been explained as Matthew's use of a supposed device of Old Testament prophecy whereby certainty that a predicted event will occur is expressed by depicting it as imminent. While it is questionable that that is an acceptable understanding of the Old Testament predictions, it may be applicable here, for Matthew knew that the parousia had not come **immediately after** the fall of Jerusalem, and it is unlikely that he is attributing a mistaken calculation of time to Jesus. **The sun . . . be shaken**: cf. Is 13:10, 13.

**24:30 The sign of the Son of Man**: perhaps this means **the sign** that is the glorious appearance **of the Son of Man**; cf. Mt 12:39–40 where "the sign of Jonah" is Jonah's being in the "belly of the whale." **Tribes of the earth will mourn**: peculiar to Matthew; cf. Zec 12:12–14. **Coming upon the clouds . . . glory**: cf. Dn 7:13, although there the "one like a son of man" comes to God to receive kingship; here **the Son of Man** comes from heaven for judgment.

**24:31 Send out his angels**: cf. Mt 13:41 where they are sent out to collect the wicked for punishment. **Trumpet blast**: cf. Is 27:13; 1 Thes 4:16.

**24:32–35** Cf. Mk 13:28–31.

**24:34** The difficulty raised by this verse cannot be satisfactorily removed by the supposition that **this generation** means the Jewish people throughout the course of their history, much less the entire human race. Perhaps for Matthew it means the **generation** to which he and his community belonged.

**24:36–44** The statement of Mt 24:34 is now counterbalanced by one that declares that the exact time of the parousia is known only to **the Father** (Mt 24:36), and the disciples are warned to be always ready for it. This section is drawn from Mark and Q (cf. Lk 17:26–27, 34–35; 12:39–40).

**24:36** Many textual witnesses omit **nor the Son**, which follows Mk 13:32. Since its omission can be explained by reluctance to attribute this ignorance to **the Son**, the reading that includes it is probably original.

**24:37–39** Cf. Lk 17:26–27. **In the days of Noah**: the Old Testament account of the flood lays no emphasis upon what is central for Matthew, i.e., the unexpected coming of the flood upon those who were unprepared for it.

**24:40–41** Cf. Lk 17:34–35. **Taken . . . left**: the former probably means **taken** into the kingdom; the latter, **left** for destruction. People in the same situation will be dealt with in opposite ways. In this context, the discrimination between them will be based on their readiness for the coming of the Son of Man.

*w:* Lk 17:23. *x:* Lk 17:24, 37. *y:* Is 13:10, 13; Ez 32:7; Am 8:9. *z:* Dn 7:13; Zec 12:12–14; Rev 1:7. *a:* Is 27:13; 1 Cor 15:52; 1 Thes 4:16. *b:* Is 40:8. *c:* Acts 1:7. *d:* Gn 6:5–7:23; Lk 17:26–27; 2 Pt 3:6. *e:* Lk 17:34–35.

one will be taken, and one will be left. 41 Two
women will be grinding at the mill; one will
be taken, and one will be left. 42* f Therefore,
stay awake! For you do not know on which
day your Lord will come. 43 g Be sure of this:
if the master of the house had known the
hour of night when the thief was coming, he
would have stayed awake and not let his
house be broken into. 44 So too, you also
must be prepared, for at an hour you do not
expect, the Son of Man will come.

*The Faithful or the Unfaithful Servant.**
45 h "Who, then, is the faithful and prudent
servant, whom the master has put in charge
of his household to distribute to them their
food at the proper time?* 46 Blessed is that
servant whom his master on his arrival finds
doing so. 47 Amen, I say to you, he will put
him in charge of all his property. 48* But if
that wicked servant says to himself, 'My
master is long delayed,' 49 and begins to beat
his fellow servants, and eat and drink with
drunkards, 50 the servant's master will come
on an unexpected day and at an unknown
hour 51 i and will punish him severely* and
assign him a place with the hypocrites, where
there will be wailing and grinding of teeth.

See RG 287–88

## CHAPTER 25

*The Parable of the Ten Virgins.**
1 "Then* the kingdom of heaven will be like
ten virgins who took their lamps and went
out to meet the bridegroom. 2* Five of them
were foolish and five were wise. 3 The foolish ones, when taking their lamps, brought
no oil with them, 4 but the wise brought
flasks of oil with their lamps. 5 Since the
bridegroom was long delayed, they all became drowsy and fell asleep. 6 At midnight,
there was a cry, 'Behold, the bridegroom!
Come out to meet him!' 7 Then all those virgins got up and trimmed their lamps. 8 The
foolish ones said to the wise, 'Give us some
of your oil, for our lamps are going out.'
9 But the wise ones replied, 'No, for there
may not be enough for us and you. Go instead to the merchants and buy some for
yourselves.' 10 While they went off to buy it,
the bridegroom came and those who were
ready went into the wedding feast with him.
Then the door was locked. 11* j Afterwards
the other virgins came and said, 'Lord, Lord,
open the door for us!' 12 But he said in reply,
'Amen, I say to you, I do not know you.'
13 k Therefore, stay awake,* for you know
neither the day nor the hour.

*The Parable of the Talents.** 14 l "It will be as
when a man who was going on a journey*
called in his servants and entrusted his possessions to them. 15 To one he gave five talents;* to another, two; to a third, one—to each
according to his ability. Then he went away.

**24:42–44** Cf. Lk 12:39–40. The theme of vigilance and readiness is continued with the bold comparison of the Son of Man to a thief who comes to break into a house.

**24:45–51** The second part of the discourse (see note on Mt 24:1–25:46) begins with this parable of **the faithful** or unfaithful **servant**; cf. Lk 12:41–46. It is addressed to the leaders of Matthew's church; **the servant has** been **put in charge** of his master's **household** (Mt 24:45) even though that household is composed of those who are his **fellow servants** (Mt 24:49).

**24:45 To distribute . . . proper time**: readiness for the master's return means a vigilance that is accompanied by faithful performance of the duty assigned.

**24:48 My master . . . delayed**: the note of delay is found also in the other parables of this section; cf. Mt 25:5, 19.

**24:51 Punish him severely**: the Greek verb, found in the New Testament only here and in the Lucan parallel (Lk 12:46), means, literally, "cut in two." **With the hypocrites**: see note on Mt 6:2. Matthew classes the unfaithful Christian leader with the unbelieving leaders of Judaism. **Wailing and grinding of teeth**: see note on Mt 8:11–12.

**25:1–13** Peculiar to Matthew.

**25:1 Then**: at the time of the parousia. **Kingdom . . . will be like**: see note on Mt 13:24–30.

**25:2–4 Foolish . . . wise**: cf. the contrasted "wise man" and "fool" of Mt 7:24, 26, where the two are distinguished by good deeds and lack of them, and such deeds may be signified by the **oil** of this parable.

**25:11–12 Lord, Lord**: cf. Mt 7:21. **I do not know you**: cf. Mt 7:23 where the Greek verb is different but synonymous.

**25:13 Stay awake**: some scholars see this command as an addition to the original parable of Matthew's traditional material, since in Mt 25:5 all the virgins, wise and foolish, fall asleep. But the wise virgins are adequately equipped for their task, and stay awake may mean no more than to be prepared; cf. Mt 24:42, 44.

**25:14–30** Cf. Lk 19:12–27.

**25:14 It will be as when . . . journey**: literally, "For just as a man who was going on a journey." Although the comparison is not completed, the sense is clear; the kingdom of heaven is like the situation here described. Faithful use of one's gifts will lead to participation in the fullness of the kingdom, lazy inactivity to exclusion from it.

**25:15 Talents**: see note on Mt 18:24.

*f:* 25:13; Lk 12:39–40. *g:* 1 Thes 5:2. *h:* Lk 12:41–46. *i:* 13:42; 25:30. *j:* 7:21, 23; Lk 13:25–27. *k:* 24:42; Mk 13:33. *l:* Lk 19:12–27.

Immediately [16]the one who received five talents went and traded with them, and made another five. [17]Likewise, the one who received
two made another two. [18]* But the man who
received one went off and dug a hole in the
ground and buried his master's money. [19]Af-
ter a long time the master of those servants
came back and settled accounts with them.
[20]The one who had received five talents came
forward bringing the additional five.* He said,
'Master, you gave me five talents. See, I have
made five more.' [21m] His master said to him,
'Well done, my good and faithful servant.
Since you were faithful in small matters, I will
give you great responsibilities. Come, share
your master's joy.' [22][Then] the one who had
received two talents also came forward and
said, 'Master, you gave me two talents. See, I
have made two more.' [23]His master said to
him, 'Well done, my good and faithful servant. Since you were faithful in small matters,
I will give you great responsibilities. Come,
share your master's joy.' [24]Then the one who
had received the one talent came forward and
said, 'Master, I knew you were a demanding
person, harvesting where you did not plant
and gathering where you did not scatter; [25]so
out of fear I went off and buried your talent in
the ground. Here it is back.' [26]His master said
to him in reply, 'You wicked, lazy servant!*
So you knew that I harvest where I did not
plant and gather where I did not scatter?
[27]Should you not then have put my money in
the bank so that I could have got it back with
interest on my return? [28]Now then! Take the
talent from him and give it to the one with ten.
[29]* [n] For to everyone who has, more will be
given and he will grow rich; but from the one
who has not, even what he has will be taken
away. [30]* And throw this useless servant into
the darkness outside, where there will be
wailing and grinding of teeth.'

***The Judgment of the Nations.**** [31o] "When
the Son of Man comes in his glory, and all the
angels with him, he will sit upon his glorious
throne, [32p] and all the nations* will be assembled before him. And he will separate them
one from another, as a shepherd separates the
sheep from the goats. [33]He will place the
sheep on his right and the goats on his left.
[34]Then the king will say to those on his right,
'Come, you who are blessed by my Father.
Inherit the kingdom prepared for you from
the foundation of the world. [35q] For I was
hungry and you gave me food, I was thirsty
and you gave me drink, a stranger and you
welcomed me, [36]naked and you clothed me,
ill and you cared for me, in prison and you
visited me.' [37]Then the righteous* will answer
him and say, 'Lord, when did we see you hun-

**25:18 Buried his master's money**: see note on Mt 13:44.

**25:20–23** Although the first two servants have received and doubled large sums, their faithful trading is regarded by the master as fidelity **in small matters** only, compared with the **great responsibilities** now to be given to them. The latter are unspecified. **Share your master's joy**: probably the joy of the banquet of the kingdom; cf. Mt 8:11.

**25:26–28 Wicked, lazy servant**: this man's inactivity is not negligible but seriously culpable. As punishment, he loses the gift he had received, that is now given to the first servant, whose possessions are already great.

**25:29** See note on Mt 13:12 where there is a similar application of this maxim.

**25:30** See note on Mt 8:11–12.

**25:31–46** The conclusion of the discourse, which is peculiar to Matthew, portrays the final judgment that will accompany the parousia. Although often called a "parable," it is not really such, for the only parabolic elements are the depiction of **the Son of Man** as a **shepherd** and of **the righteous** and the wicked as **sheep** and **goats** respectively (Mt 25:32–33). The criterion of judgment will be the deeds of mercy that have been done for the **least** of Jesus' **brothers** (Mt 25:40). A difficult and important question is the identification of these **least brothers**. Are they all people who have suffered hunger, thirst, etc. (Mt 25:35, 36) or a particular group of such sufferers? Scholars are divided in their response and arguments can be made for either side. But leaving aside the problem of what the traditional material that Matthew edited may have meant, it seems that a stronger case can be made for the view that in the evangelist's sense the sufferers are Christians, probably Christian missionaries whose sufferings were brought upon them by their preaching of the gospel. The criterion of judgment for **all the nations** is their treatment of those who have borne to the world the message of Jesus, and this means ultimately their acceptance or rejection of Jesus himself; cf. Mt 10:40, "Whoever receives you, receives me." See note on Mt 16:27.

**25:32 All the nations**: before the end the gospel will have been preached throughout the world (Mt 24:14); thus the Gentiles will be judged on their response to it. But the phrase **all the nations** includes the Jews also, for at the judgment "the Son of Man . . . will repay everyone according to his conduct" (Mt 16:27).

**25:37–40 The righteous** will be astonished that in caring for the needs of the sufferers they were ministering to the **Lord** himself. **One of these least brothers of mine**: cf. Mt 10:42.

*m:* Lk 16:10. *n:* 13:12; Mk 4:25; Lk 8:18; 19:26. *o:* 16:27; Dt 33:2 LXX. *p:* Ez 34:17. *q:* Is 58:7; Ez 18:7.

gry and feed you, or thirsty and give you
drink? [38]When did we see you a stranger and
welcome you, or naked and clothe you?
[39]When did we see you ill or in prison, and
visit you?' [40r] And the king will say to them in
reply, 'Amen, I say to you, whatever you did
for one of these least brothers of mine, you
did for me.' [41* s] Then he will say to those on
his left, 'Depart from me, you accursed, into
the eternal fire prepared for the devil and his
angels. [42t] For I was hungry and you gave me
no food, I was thirsty and you gave me no
drink, [43]a stranger and you gave me no welcome, naked and you gave me no clothing, ill
and in prison, and you did not care for me.'
[44*] Then they will answer and say, 'Lord,
when did we see you hungry or thirsty or a
stranger or naked or ill or in prison, and not
minister to your needs?' [45]He will answer
them, 'Amen, I say to you, what you did not
do for one of these least ones, you did not do
for me.' [46u] And these will go off to eternal
punishment, but the righteous to eternal life."

## VII. The Passion and Resurrection

### CHAPTER 26

See RG 288–89

*The Conspiracy Against Jesus.*
[1*] When Jesus finished all these words,* he
said to his disciples, [2v] "You know that in
two days' time it will be Passover, and the
Son of Man will be handed over to be crucified." [3*] Then the chief priests and the elders
of the people assembled in the palace of the
high priest, who was called Caiaphas, [4w] and
they consulted together to arrest Jesus by
treachery and put him to death. [5]But they
said, "Not during the festival,* that there
may not be a riot among the people."

*The Anointing at Bethany.** [6x] Now when
Jesus was in Bethany in the house of Simon
the leper, [7]a woman came up to him with an
alabaster jar of costly perfumed oil, and
poured it on his head while he was reclining
at table. [8]When the disciples saw this, they
were indignant and said, "Why this waste? [9]It
could have been sold for much, and the
money given to the poor." [10]Since Jesus knew
this, he said to them, "Why do you make trouble for the woman? She has done a good thing
for me. [11y] The poor you will always have
with you; but you will not always have me.
[12*] In pouring this perfumed oil upon my
body, she did it to prepare me for burial.
[13]Amen, I say to you, wherever this gospel is
proclaimed in the whole world, what she has
done will be spoken of, in memory of her."

*The Betrayal by Judas.* [14z] Then one of the
Twelve, who was called Judas Iscariot,*
went to the chief priests [15* a] and said, "What

**25:41 Fire prepared . . . his angels**: cf. 1 Enoch 10:13 where it is said of the evil angels and Semyaza, their leader, "In those days they will lead them into the bottom of the fire—and in torment—in the prison (where) they will be locked up forever."

**25:44–45** The **accursed** (Mt 25:41) will be likewise astonished that their neglect of the sufferers was neglect of the **Lord** and will receive from him a similar answer.

**26:1–28:20** The five books with alternating narrative and discourse (Mt 3:1–25:46) that give this gospel its distinctive structure lead up to the climactic events that are the center of Christian belief and the origin of the Christian church, the passion and resurrection of Jesus. In his passion narrative (Mt 26 and 27) Matthew follows his Marcan source closely but with omissions (e.g., Mk 14:51–52) and additions (e.g., Mt 27:3–10, 19). Some of the additions indicate that he utilized traditions that he had received from elsewhere; others are due to his own theological insight (e.g., Mt 26:28, ". . . for the forgiveness of sins"; Mt 27:52). In his editing Matthew also altered Mark in some minor details. But there is no need to suppose that he knew any passion narrative other than Mark's.

**26:1–2 When Jesus finished all these words**: see note on Mt 7:28–29. **"You know . . . crucified"**: Matthew turns Mark's statement of the time (Mk 14:1) into Jesus' final prediction of his passion. **Passover**: see note on Mk 14:1.

**26:3 Caiaphas** was high priest from A.D. 18 to 36.

**26:5 Not during the festival**: the plan to delay Jesus' arrest and execution until after **the festival** was not carried out, for according to the synoptics he was arrested on the night of Nisan 14 and put to death the following day. No reason is given why the plan was changed.

**26:6–13** See notes on Mk 14:3–9 and Jn 12:1–8.

**26:12 To prepare me for burial**: cf. Mk 14:8. In accordance with the interpretation of this act as Jesus' **burial** anointing, Matthew, more consistent than Mark, changes the purpose of the visit of the women to Jesus' tomb; they do not go to anoint him (Mk 16:1) but "to see the tomb" (Mt 28:1).

**26:14 Iscariot**: see note on Lk 6:16.

**26:15** The motive of avarice is introduced by Judas's question about the price for betrayal, which is absent in the Marcan source (Mk 14:10–11). **Hand him over**: the same Greek

*r:* 10:40, 42. *s:* 7:23; Lk 13:27. *t:* Jb 22:7; Jas 2:15–16. *u:* Dn 12:2. *v:* Mk 14:1–2; Lk 22:1–2. *w:* Jn 11:47–53. *x:* Mk 14:3–9; Jn 12:1–8. *y:* Dt 15:11. *z:* Mk 14:10–11; Lk 22:3–6. *a:* Zec 11:12.

are you willing to give me if I hand him over
to you?" They paid him thirty pieces of silver, 16 and from that time on he looked for an
opportunity to hand him over.

***Preparations for the Passover.*** 17[b] On the
first day of the Feast of Unleavened Bread,*
the disciples approached Jesus and said,
"Where do you want us to prepare for you to
eat the Passover?"[c] 18* He said, "Go into the
city to a certain man and tell him, 'The teacher
says, "My appointed time draws near; in your
house I shall celebrate the Passover with my
disciples." ' " 19 The disciples then did as Jesus
had ordered, and prepared the Passover.

***The Betrayer.*** 20 When it was evening, he
reclined at table with the Twelve. 21 And
while they were eating, he said, "Amen, I
say to you, one of you will betray me."*
22 Deeply distressed at this, they began to say
to him one after another, "Surely it is not I,
Lord?" 23 He said in reply, "He who has
dipped his hand into the dish with me is the
one who will betray me. 24* [d] The Son of
Man indeed goes, as it is written of him, but
woe to that man by whom the Son of Man is
betrayed. It would be better for that man if
he had never been born." 25* Then Judas, his
betrayer, said in reply, "Surely it is not I,
Rabbi?" He answered, "You have said so."

***The Lord's Supper.*** 26* [e] While they were
eating, Jesus took bread, said the blessing,
broke it, and giving it to his disciples said,
"Take and eat; this is my body."* [f] 27 Then he
took a cup, gave thanks,* and gave it to them,
saying, "Drink from it, all of you, 28[g] for this
is my blood of the covenant, which will be
shed on behalf of many for the forgiveness
of sins. 29* I tell you, from now on I shall not
drink this fruit of the vine until the day when
I drink it with you new in the kingdom of my
Father." 30* Then, after singing a hymn, they
went out to the Mount of Olives.

verb is used to express the saving purpose of God by which Jesus is handed over to death (cf. Mt 17:22; 20:18; 26:2) and the human malice that hands him over. **Thirty pieces of silver**: the price of the betrayal is found only in Matthew. It is derived from Zec 11:12 where it is the wages paid to the rejected shepherd, a cheap price (Zec 11:13). That amount is also the compensation paid to one whose slave has been gored by an ox (Ex 21:32).

**26:17 The first day of the Feast of Unleavened Bread**: see note on Mk 14:1. Matthew omits Mark's "when they sacrificed the Passover lamb."

**26:18** By omitting much of Mk 14:13–15, adding **My appointed time draws near,** and turning the question into a statement, **in your house I shall celebrate the Passover**, Matthew has given this passage a solemnity and majesty greater than that of his source.

**26:21** Given Matthew's interest in the fulfillment of the Old Testament, it is curious that he omits the Marcan designation of Jesus' betrayer as "one who is eating with me" (Mk 14:18), since that is probably an allusion to Ps 41:10. However, the shocking fact that the betrayer is one who shares table fellowship with Jesus is emphasized in Mt 26:23.

**26:24 It would be better . . . born**: the enormity of the deed is such that it would be better not to exist than to do it.

**26:25** Peculiar to Matthew. **You have said so**: cf. Mt 26:64; 27:11. This is a half-affirmative. Emphasis is laid on the pronoun and the answer implies that the statement would not have been made if the question had not been asked.

**26:26–29** See note on Mk 14:22–24. The Marcan-Matthean is one of the two major New Testament traditions of the words of Jesus when instituting the Eucharist. The other (and earlier) is the Pauline-Lucan (1 Cor 11:23–25; Lk 22:19–20). Each shows the influence of Christian liturgical usage, but the Marcan-Matthean is more developed in that regard than the Pauline-Lucan. The words over the bread and cup succeed each other without the intervening meal mentioned in 1 Cor 11:25; Lk 22:20; and there is parallelism between the consecratory words (**this is my body . . . this is my blood**). Matthew follows Mark closely but with some changes.

**26:26** See note on Mt 14:19. **Said the blessing**: a prayer blessing God. **Take and eat**: literally, **Take, eat**. **Eat** is an addition to Mark's "take it" (literally, "take"; Mk 14:22). **This is my body**: the bread is identified with Jesus himself.

**26:27–28 Gave thanks**: see note on Mt 15:36. **Gave it to them . . . all of you**: cf. Mk 14:23–24. In the Marcan sequence the disciples drink and then Jesus says the interpretative words. Matthew has changed this into a command to **drink** followed by those words. **My blood**: see Lv 17:11 for the concept that the **blood** is "the seat of life" and that when placed on the altar it "makes atonement." **Which will be shed**: the present participle, "being shed" or "going to be shed," is future in relation to the Last Supper. **On behalf of**: Greek *peri*; see note on Mk 14:24. **Many**: see note on Mt 20:28. **For the forgiveness of sins**: a Matthean addition. The same phrase occurs in Mk 1:4 in connection with John's baptism but Matthew avoids it there (Mt 3:11). He places it here probably because he wishes to emphasize that it is the sacrificial death of Jesus that brings **forgiveness of sins**.

**26:29** Although his death will interrupt the table fellowship he has had with the disciples, Jesus confidently predicts his vindication by God and a new table fellowship with them at the banquet of the kingdom.

**26:30** See note on Mk 14:26.

---

*b:* Mk 14:12–21; Lk 22:7–23. *c:* Ex 12:14–20. *d:* Is 53:8–10.
*e:* Mk 14:22–26; Lk 22:14–23; 1 Cor 11:23–25. *f:* 1 Cor 10:16.
*g:* Ex 24:8; Is 53:12.

***Peter's Denial Foretold.*** [31h] Then Jesus said to them, "This night all of you will have your faith in me shaken,* for it is written:[i]

'I will strike the shepherd,
and the sheep of the flock will be
dispersed';

[32]but after I have been raised up, I shall go before you to Galilee." [33]Peter said to him in reply, "Though all may have their faith in you shaken, mine will never be." [34*j] Jesus said to him, "Amen, I say to you, this very night before the cock crows, you will deny me three times."[k] [35]Peter said to him, "Even though I should have to die with you, I will not deny you." And all the disciples spoke likewise.

***The Agony in the Garden.*** [36*l] Then Jesus came with them to a place called Gethsemane,* and he said to his disciples, "Sit here while I go over there and pray."[m] [37n] He took along Peter and the two sons of Zebedee,* and began to feel sorrow and distress. [38o] Then he said to them, "My soul is sorrowful even to death.* Remain here and keep watch with me." [39p] He advanced a little and fell prostrate in prayer, saying, "My Father,* if it is possible, let this cup pass from me; yet, not as I will, but as you will." [40]When he returned to his disciples he found them asleep. He said to Peter, "So you could not keep watch with me for one hour? [41]Watch and pray that you may not undergo the test.* The spirit is willing, but the flesh is weak." [42*q] Withdrawing a second time, he prayed again, "My Father, if it is not possible that this cup pass without my drinking it, your will be done!" [43]Then he returned once more and found them asleep, for they could not keep their eyes open. [44]He left them and withdrew again and prayed a third time, saying the same thing again. [45r] Then he returned to his disciples and said to them, "Are you still sleeping and taking your rest? Behold, the hour is at hand when the Son of Man is to be handed over to sinners. [46]Get up, let us go. Look, my betrayer is at hand."

***The Betrayal and Arrest of Jesus.*** [47s] While he was still speaking, Judas, one of the Twelve, arrived, accompanied by a large crowd, with swords and clubs, who had come from the chief priests and the eld-

**26:31 Will have . . . shaken**: literally, "will be scandalized in me"; see note on Mt 24:9–12. **I will strike . . . dispersed**: cf. Zec 13:7.

**26:34 Before the cock crows**: see note on Mt 14:25. The third watch of the night was called "cockcrow." **Deny me**: see note on Mt 16:24.

**26:36–56** Cf. Mk 14:32–52. The account of Jesus in Gethsemane is divided between that of his agony (Mt 26:36–46) and that of his betrayal and arrest (Mt 26:47–56). Jesus' **sorrow and distress** (Mt 26:37) in face of death is unrelieved by the presence of his three disciples who, though urged to **watch with** him (Mt 26:38, 41), fall asleep (Mt 26:40, 43). He prays that **if . . . possible** his death may be avoided (Mt 26:39) but that his Father's will be done (Mt 26:39, 42, 44). Knowing then that his death must take place, he announces to his companions that **the hour** for his being **handed over** has come (Mt 26:45). Judas arrives with an armed band provided by the Sanhedrin and greets Jesus with a kiss, the prearranged sign for his identification (Mt 26:47–49). After his arrest, he rebukes a disciple who has attacked the **high priest's servant** with a **sword** (Mt 26:51–54), and chides those who have come out to seize him with **swords and clubs** as if he were a **robber** (Mt 26:55–56). In both rebukes Jesus declares that the treatment he is how receiving is the fulfillment of the scriptures (Mt 26:55, 56). The subsequent flight of **all the disciples** is itself the fulfillment of his own prediction (cf. 31). In this episode, Matthew follows Mark with a few alterations.

**26:36 Gethsemane**: the Hebrew name means "oil press" and designates an olive orchard on the western slope of the Mount of Olives; see note on Mt 21:1. The name appears only in Matthew and Mark. The place is called a "garden" in Jn 18:1.

**26:37 Peter and the two sons of Zebedee**: cf. Mt 17:1.

**26:38** Cf. Ps 42:6, 12. In the Septuagint (Ps 41:5, 12) the same Greek word for **sorrowful** is used as here. **To death**: i.e., "enough to die"; cf. Jon 4:9.

**26:39 My Father**: see note on Mk 14:36. Matthew omits the Aramaic *'abbā* and adds the qualifier **my. This cup**: see note on Mk 10:38–40.

**26:41 Undergo the test**: see note on Mt 6:13. In that verse "the final test" translates the same Greek word as is here translated **the test**, and these are the only instances of the use of that word in Matthew. It is possible that the passion of Jesus is seen here as an anticipation of the great tribulation that will precede the parousia (see notes on Mt 24:8; 24:21) to which Mt 6:13 refers, and that just as Jesus prays to be delivered from death (Mt 26:39), so he exhorts the disciples to pray that they will not have to **undergo the** great **test** that his passion would be for them. Some scholars, however, understand **not undergo** (literally, "not enter") **the test** as meaning not that the disciples may be spared **the test** but that they may not yield to the temptation of falling away from Jesus because of his passion even though they will have to endure it.

**26:42 Your will be done**: cf. Mt 6:10.

*h:* Mk 14:7–31. *i:* Zec 13:7; Jn 16:32. *j:* Lk 22:33–34; Jn 13:37–38. *k:* 26:69–75. *l:* Mk 14:32–42; Lk 22:39–46. *m:* Jn 18:1. *n:* Heb 5:7. *o:* Ps 42:6, 12; Jon 4:9. *p:* Jn 4:34; 6:38; Phil 2:8. *q:* 6:10; Heb 10:9. *r:* Jn 12:23; 13:1; 17:1. *s:* Mk 14:43–50; Lk 22:47–53; Jn 18:3–11.

ers of the people. 48 His betrayer had
arranged a sign with them, saying, "The
man I shall kiss is the one; arrest him."
49 Immediately he went over to Jesus and
said, "Hail, Rabbi!"* and he kissed him.
50 Jesus answered him, "Friend, do what you
have come for." Then stepping forward they
laid hands on Jesus and arrested him. 51 And
behold, one of those who accompanied
Jesus put his hand to his sword, drew it, and
struck the high priest's servant, cutting off
his ear. 52 Then Jesus said to him, "Put your
sword back into its sheath, for all who take
the sword will perish by the sword. 53 Do
you think that I cannot call upon my Father
and he will not provide me at this moment
with more than twelve legions of angels?
54 But then how would the scriptures be fulfilled which say that it must come to pass in
this way?" 55* At that hour Jesus said to the
crowds, "Have you come out as against a
robber, with swords and clubs to seize me?
Day after day I sat teaching in the temple
area, yet you did not arrest me. 56[t] But all
this has come to pass that the writings of the
prophets may be fulfilled." Then all the disciples left him and fled.

***Jesus Before the Sanhedrin.**** 57[u] Those
who had arrested Jesus led him away to Caiaphas* the high priest, where the scribes and
the elders were assembled. 58 Peter was following him at a distance as far as the high
priest's courtyard, and going inside he sat
down with the servants to see the outcome.
59 The chief priests and the entire Sanhedrin*
kept trying to obtain false testimony against
Jesus in order to put him to death, 60[v] but
they found none, though many false witnesses came forward. Finally two* came forward 61 who stated, "This man said, 'I can
destroy the temple of God and within three
days rebuild it.'" 62 The high priest rose and
addressed him, "Have you no answer? What
are these men testifying against you?"
63[w] But Jesus was silent.* Then the high
priest said to him, "I order you to tell us under oath before the living God whether you
are the Messiah, the Son of God." 64[x] Jesus
said to him in reply, "You have said so.* But
I tell you:

**26:49 Rabbi**: see note on Mt 23:6–7. Jesus is so addressed twice in Matthew (Mt 26:25), both times by Judas. For the significance of the closely related address "teacher" in Matthew, see note on Mt 8:19.

**26:55 Day after day . . . arrest me**: cf. Mk 14:49. This suggests that Jesus had taught for a relatively long period in Jerusalem, whereas Mt 21:1–11 puts his coming to the city for the first time only a few days before.

**26:57–68** Following Mk 14:53–65 Matthew presents the nighttime appearance of Jesus before the **Sanhedrin** as a real trial. After **many false witnesses** bring charges against him that do not suffice for the death sentence (Mt 26:60), **two came forward** who charge him with claiming to be able to **destroy the temple . . . and within three days to rebuild it** (Mt 26:60–61). Jesus makes no answer even when challenged to do so by **the high priest**, who then orders him to declare **under oath . . . whether** he is the **Messiah, the Son of God** (Mt 26:62–63). Matthew changes Mark's clear affirmative response (Mk 14:62) to the same one as that given to Judas (Mt 26:25), but follows Mark almost verbatim in Jesus' predicting that his judges will see him **(the Son of Man) seated at the right hand of** God **and coming on the clouds of heaven** (Mt 26:64). **The high priest** then charges him with blasphemy (Mt 26:65), a charge with which the other members of **the Sanhedrin** agree by declaring that **he deserves to die** (Mt 26:66). They then attack him (Mt 26:67) and mockingly demand that he **prophesy** (Mt 26:68). This account contains elements that are contrary to the judicial procedures prescribed in the Mishnah, the Jewish code of law that dates in written form from ca. A.D. 200, e.g., trial on a feast day, a night session of the court, pronouncement of a verdict of condemnation at the same session at which testimony was received. Consequently, some scholars regard the account entirely as a creation of the early Christians without historical value. However, it is disputable whether the norms found in the Mishnah were in force at the time of Jesus. More to the point is the question whether the Matthean-Marcan night trial derives from a combination of two separate incidents, a nighttime preliminary investigation (cf. Jn 18:13, 19–24) and a formal trial on the following morning (cf. Lk 22:66–71).

**26:57 Caiaphas**: see note on Mt 26:3.

**26:59 Sanhedrin**: see note on Lk 22:66.

**26:60–61 Two**: cf. Dt 19:15. **I can destroy . . . rebuild it**: there are significant differences from the Marcan parallel (Mk 14:58). Matthew omits "made with hands" and "not made with hands" and changes Mark's "will destroy" and "will build another" to **can destroy** and (can) **rebuild**. The charge is probably based on Jesus' prediction of the temple's destruction; see notes on Mt 23:37–39; 24:2; and Jn 2:19. A similar prediction by Jeremiah was considered as deserving death; cf. Jer 7:1–15; 26:1–8.

**26:63 Silent**: possibly an allusion to Is 53:7. **I order you . . . living God**: peculiar to Matthew; cf. Mk 14:61.

**26:64 You have said so**: see note on Mt 26:25. **From now on . . . heaven**: the Son of Man who is to be crucified (cf. Mt 20:19) will be seen in glorious majesty (cf. Ps 110:1) and **coming on the clouds of heaven** (cf. Dn 7:13). **The Power**: see note on Mk 14:61–62.

*t*: 26:31. *u*: Mk 14:53–65; Lk 22:54–55, 63–71; Jn 18:12–14, 19–24. *v*: Dt 19:15; Jn 2:19; Acts 6:14. *w*: Is 53:7. *x*: Ps 110:1; Dn 7:13.

From now on you will see 'the Son of
Man
seated at the right hand of the Power'
and 'coming on the clouds of
heaven.' "
65Then the high priest tore his robes and said, "He has blasphemed!* What further need have we of witnesses? You have now heard the blasphemy; 66what is your opinion?" They said in reply, "He deserves to die!" 67* y Then they spat in his face and struck him, while some slapped him, 68saying, "Prophesy for us, Messiah: who is it that struck you?"

***Peter's Denial of Jesus.*** 69z Now Peter was sitting outside in the courtyard. One of the maids came over to him and said, "You too were with Jesus the Galilean." 70* But he denied it in front of everyone, saying, "I do not know what you are talking about!" 71As he went out to the gate, another girl saw him and said to those who were there, "This man was with Jesus the Nazorean." 72Again he denied it with an oath, "I do not know the man!" 73* A little later the bystanders came over and said to Peter, "Surely you too are one of them; even your speech gives you away." 74At that he began to curse and to swear, "I do not know the man." And immediately a cock crowed. 75a Then Peter remembered the word that Jesus had spoken: "Before the cock crows you will deny me three times." He went out and began to weep bitterly.

## CHAPTER 27

See RG 288–89

***Jesus before Pilate.*** 1* When it was morning,[b] all the chief priests and the elders of the people took counsel* against Jesus to put him to death. 2They bound him, led him away, and handed him over to Pilate, the governor.

***The Death of Judas.*** 3c Then Judas, his betrayer, seeing that Jesus had been condemned, deeply regretted what he had done. He returned the thirty pieces of silver* to the chief priests and elders,[d] 4saying, "I have sinned in betraying innocent blood." They said, "What is that to us? Look to it yourself." 5* Flinging the money into the temple, he departed and went off and hanged himself. 6The chief priests gathered up the money, but said, "It is not lawful to deposit this in the temple treasury, for it is the price of blood." 7After consultation, they used it to buy the potter's field as a burial place for foreigners. 8That is why that field even today is called

**26:65 Blasphemed**: the punishment for **blasphemy** was death by stoning (see Lv 24:10–16). According to the Mishnah, to be guilty of blasphemy one had to pronounce "the Name itself," i.e. Yahweh; cf. *Sanhedrin* 7:4, 5. Those who judge the gospel accounts of Jesus' trial by the later Mishnah standards point out that Jesus uses the surrogate "the Power," and hence no Jewish court would have regarded him as guilty of blasphemy; others hold that the Mishnah's narrow understanding of blasphemy was a later development.

**26:67–68** The physical abuse, apparently done to Jesus by the members of the Sanhedrin themselves, recalls the sufferings of the Isaian Servant of the Lord; cf. Is 50:6. The mocking challenge to **prophesy** is probably motivated by Jesus' prediction of his future glory (Mt 26:64).

**26:70 Denied it in front of everyone**: see Mt 10:33. Peter's repentance (Mt 26:75) saves him from the fearful destiny of which Jesus speaks there.

**26:73 Your speech . . . away**: Matthew explicates Mark's "you too are a Galilean" (Mk 14:70).

**27:1–31** Cf. Mk 15:1–20. Matthew's account of the Roman trial before **Pilate** is introduced by a consultation of the Sanhedrin after which Jesus is **handed over to . . . the governor** (Mt 27:1–2). Matthew follows his Marcan source closely but adds some material that is peculiar to him, the death of **Judas** (Mt 27:3–10), possibly the name **Jesus** as the name of **Barabbas** also (Mt 27:16–17), the intervention of Pilate's **wife** (Mt 27:19), Pilate's washing **his hands** in token of his disclaiming responsibility for Jesus' death (Mt 27:24), and the assuming of that responsibility by **the whole people** (Mt 27:25).

**27:1** There is scholarly disagreement about the meaning of the Sanhedrin's taking **counsel** (*symboulion elabon*; cf. Mt 12:14; 22:15; 27:7; 28:12); see note on Mk 15:1. Some understand it as a discussion about the strategy for putting their death sentence against **Jesus** into effect since they lacked the right to do so themselves. Others see it as the occasion for their passing that sentence, holding that Matthew, unlike Mark (Mk 14:64), does not consider that it had been passed in the night session (Mt 26:66). Even in the latter interpretation, their handing **him over to Pilate** is best explained on the hypothesis that they did not have competence to put their sentence into effect, as is stated in Jn 18:31.

**27:3 The thirty pieces of silver**: see Mt 26:15.

**27:5–8** For another tradition about the death of Judas, cf. Acts 1:18–19. The two traditions agree only in the purchase of a field with **the money** paid to Judas for his betrayal of Jesus and the name given to the field, **the Field of Blood**. In Acts Judas himself buys the field and its name comes from his own blood shed in his fatal accident on it. **The potter's field**: this designation of the field is based on the fulfillment citation in Mt 27:10.

*y:* Wis 2:19; Is 50:6. *z:* Mk 14:66–72; Lk 22:56–62; Jn 18:17–18, 25–27. *a:* 26:34. *b:* Mk 15:1; Lk 23:1; Jn 18:28. *c:* Acts 1:18–19. *d:* 26:15.

the Field of Blood. [9]Then was fulfilled what
had been said through Jeremiah the prophet,*
"And they took the thirty pieces of silver, the
value of a man with a price on his head, a
price set by some of the Israelites, [10e] and
they paid it out for the potter's field just as
the Lord had commanded me."

***Jesus Questioned by Pilate.*** [11f] Now Jesus
stood before the governor, and he questioned him, "Are you the king of the Jews?"*
Jesus said, "You say so." [12g] And when he
was accused by the chief priests and elders,*
he made no answer. [13]Then Pilate said to
him, "Do you not hear how many things they
are testifying against you?" [14]But he did not
answer him one word, so that the governor
was greatly amazed.

***The Sentence of Death.*** [15* h] Now on the
occasion of the feast the governor was accustomed to release to the crowd one prisoner whom they wished. [16*] And at that time
they had a notorious prisoner called [Jesus]
Barabbas. [17]So when they had assembled,
Pilate said to them, "Which one do you want
me to release to you, [Jesus] Barabbas, or
Jesus called Messiah?" [18*] For he knew that
it was out of envy that they had handed him
over. [19*] While he was still seated on the
bench, his wife sent him a message, "Have
nothing to do with that righteous man. I suffered much in a dream today because of
him." [20i] The chief priests and the elders persuaded the crowds to ask for Barabbas but to
destroy Jesus. [21]The governor said to them
in reply, "Which of the two do you want me
to release to you?" They answered, "Barabbas!" [22*] Pilate said to them, "Then what
shall I do with Jesus called Messiah?" They
all said, "Let him be crucified!" [23]But he
said, "Why? What evil has he done?" They
only shouted the louder, "Let him be crucified!" [24* j] When Pilate saw that he was not

**27:9–10** Cf. Mt 26:15. Matthew's attributing this text to Jeremiah is puzzling, for there is no such text in that book, and **the thirty pieces of silver** thrown by Judas "into the temple" (Mt 27:5) recall rather Zec 11:12–13. It is usually said that the attribution of the text to Jeremiah is due to Matthew's combining the Zechariah text with texts from Jeremiah that speak of a **potter** (Jer 18:2–3), the buying of a **field** (Jer 32:6–9), or the breaking of a potter's flask at Topheth in the valley of Ben-Hinnom with the prediction that it will become a burial place (Jer 19:1–13).

**27:11 King of the Jews**: this title is used of Jesus only by pagans. The Matthean instances are, besides this verse, Mt 2:2; 27:29, 37. Matthew equates it with "Messiah"; cf. Mt 2:2, 4 and Mt 27:17, 22 where he has changed "the king of the Jews" of his Marcan source (Mk 15:9, 12) to "(Jesus) called Messiah." The normal political connotation of both titles would be of concern to the Roman **governor**. **You say so**: see note on Mt 26:25. An unqualified affirmative response is not made because Jesus' kingship is not what Pilate would understand it to be.

**27:12–14** Cf. Mt 26:62–63. As in the trial before the Sanhedrin, Jesus' silence may be meant to recall Is 53:7. **Greatly amazed**: possibly an allusion to Is 52:14–15.

**27:15–26** The choice that Pilate offers **the crowd** between **Barabbas** and **Jesus** is said to be in accordance with a custom of releasing at the Passover feast **one prisoner** chosen by **the crowd** (Mt 27:15). This custom is mentioned also in Mk 15:6 and Jn 18:39 but not in Luke; see note on Lk 23:17. Outside of the gospels there is no direct attestation of it, and scholars are divided in their judgment of the historical reliability of the claim that there was such a practice.

**27:16–17 [Jesus] Barabbas**: it is possible that the double name is the original reading; **Jesus** was a common Jewish name; see note on Mt 1:21. This reading is found in only a few textual witnesses, although its absence in the majority can be explained as an omission of **Jesus** made for reverential reasons. That name is bracketed because of its uncertain textual attestation. The Aramaic name **Barabbas** means "son of the father"; the irony of the choice offered between him and Jesus, the true son of the Father, would be evident to those addressees of Matthew who knew that.

**27:18** Cf. Mk 14:10. This is an example of the tendency, found in varying degree in all the gospels, to present Pilate in a relatively favorable light and emphasize the hostility of the Jewish authorities and eventually of the people.

**27:19** Jesus' innocence is declared by a Gentile woman. **In a dream**: in Matthew's infancy narrative, dreams are the means of divine communication; cf. Mt 1:20; 2:12, 13, 19, 22.

**27:22 Let him be crucified**: incited by the chief priests and elders (Mt 27:20), the crowds demand that Jesus be executed by crucifixion, a peculiarly horrible form of Roman capital punishment. The Marcan parallel, "Crucify him" (Mk 15:3), addressed to Pilate, is changed by Matthew to the passive, probably to emphasize the responsibility of the crowds.

**27:24–25** Peculiar to Matthew. **Took water . . . blood**: cf. Dt 21:1–8, the handwashing prescribed in the case of a murder when the killer is unknown. The elders of the city nearest to where the corpse is found must wash their hands, declaring, "Our hands did not shed this blood." **Look to it yourselves**: cf. Mt 27:4. **The whole people**: Matthew sees in those who speak these words **the** entire **people** (Greek *laos*) of Israel. **His blood . . . and upon our children**: cf. Jer 26:15. The responsibility for Jesus' death is accepted by the nation that was God's special possession (Ex 19:5), his own **people** (Hos 2:25), and they thereby lose that high privilege; see Mt 21:43 and the note on that verse. The controversy between Matthew's church and Pharisaic Judaism about which was the true people of God is reflected here. As the Second Vatican Council has pointed out, guilt for Jesus' death is not attributable to all the Jews of his time or to any Jews of later times.

*e:* Zec 11:12–13. *f:* Mk 15:2–5; Lk 23:2–3; Jn 18:29–38. *g:* Is 53:7. *h:* Mk 15:6–15; Lk 23:17–25; Jn 18:39–19:16. *i:* Acts 3:14. *j:* Dt 21:1–8.

succeeding at all, but that a riot was breaking out instead, he took water and washed his hands in the sight of the crowd, saying, "I am innocent of this man's blood. Look to it yourselves." 25 And the whole people said in reply, "His blood be upon us and upon our children." 26 Then he released Barabbas to them, but after he had Jesus scourged,* he handed him over to be crucified.

***Mockery by the Soldiers.*** 27k Then the soldiers of the governor took Jesus inside the praetorium* and gathered the whole cohort around him. 28 They stripped off his clothes and threw a scarlet military cloak* about him. 29l Weaving a crown out of thorns,* they placed it on his head, and a reed in his right hand. And kneeling before him, they mocked him, saying, "Hail, King of the Jews!" 30m They spat upon him* and took the reed and kept striking him on the head. 31 And when they had mocked him, they stripped him of the cloak, dressed him in his own clothes, and led him off to crucify him.

***The Way of the Cross.**** 32n As they were going out, they met a Cyrenian named Simon; this man they pressed into service to carry his cross.

***The Crucifixion.*** 33o And when they came to a place called Golgotha (which means Place of the Skull), 34p they gave Jesus wine to drink mixed with gall.* But when he had tasted it, he refused to drink. 35q After they had crucified him, they divided his garments* by casting lots; 36 then they sat down and kept watch over him there. 37 And they placed over his head the written charge* against him: This is Jesus, the King of the Jews. 38 Two revolutionaries* were crucified with him, one on his right and the other on his left. 39* r Those passing by reviled him, shaking their heads 40s and saying, "You who would destroy the temple and rebuild it in three days, save yourself, if you are the Son of God, [and] come down from the cross!" 41 Likewise the chief priests with the scribes and elders mocked him and said, 42 "He saved others; he cannot save himself. So he is the king of Israel!* Let him come down from the cross now, and we will believe in him. 43* t He trusted in God; let him deliver him now if he wants him. For he

**27:26 He had Jesus scourged**: the usual preliminary to crucifixion.

**27:27 The praetorium**: the residence of the Roman governor. His usual place of residence was at Caesarea Maritima on the Mediterranean coast, but he went to Jerusalem during the great feasts, when the influx of pilgrims posed the danger of a nationalistic riot. It is disputed whether **the praetorium** in Jerusalem was the old palace of Herod in the west of the city or the fortress of Antonia northwest of the temple area. **The whole cohort**: normally six hundred soldiers.

**27:28 Scarlet military cloak**: so Matthew as against the royal purple of Mk 15:17 and Jn 19:2.

**27:29 Crown out of thorns**: probably of long **thorns** that stood upright so that it resembled the "radiant" **crown**, a diadem with spikes worn by Hellenistic kings. The soldiers' purpose was mockery, not torture. **A reed**: peculiar to Matthew; a mock scepter.

**27:30 Spat upon him**: cf. Mt 26:67 where there also is a possible allusion to Is 50:6.

**27:32** See note on Mk 15:21. **Cyrenian named Simon**: Cyrenaica was a Roman province on the north coast of Africa and Cyrene was its capital city. The city had a large population of Greek-speaking Jews. **Simon** may have been living in Palestine or have come there for the Passover as a pilgrim. **Pressed into service**: see note on Mt 5:41.

**27:34 Wine . . . mixed with gall**: cf. Mk 15:23 where the drink is "wine drugged with myrrh," a narcotic. Matthew's text is probably an inexact allusion to Ps 69:22. That psalm belongs to the class called the individual lament, in which a persecuted just man prays for deliverance in the midst of great suffering and also expresses confidence that his prayer will be heard. That theme of the suffering Just One is frequently applied to the sufferings of Jesus in the passion narratives.

**27:35** The clothing of an executed criminal went to his executioner(s), but the description of that procedure in the case of Jesus, found in all the gospels, is plainly inspired by Ps 22:19. However, that psalm verse is quoted only in Jn 19:24.

**27:37** The offense of a person condemned to death by crucifixion was written on a tablet that was displayed on his cross. The **charge** against **Jesus** was that he had claimed to be the **King of the Jews** (cf. Mt 27:11), i.e., the Messiah (cf. Mt 27:17, 22).

**27:38 Revolutionaries**: see note on Jn 18:40 where the same Greek word as that found here is used for Barabbas.

**27:39–40 Reviled him . . . heads**: cf. Ps 22:8. **You who would destroy . . . three days**; cf. Mt 26:61. **If you are the Son of God**: the same words as those of the devil in the temptation of Jesus; cf. Mt 4:3, 6.

**27:42 King of Israel**: in their mocking of Jesus the members of the Sanhedrin call themselves and their people not "the Jews" but **Israel**.

**27:43** Peculiar to Matthew. **He trusted in God . . . wants him**: cf. Ps 22:9. **He said . . . of God**: probably an allusion to Wis 2:12–20 where the theme of the suffering Just One appears.

*k:* Mk 15:16–20; Jn 19:2–3. *l:* 27:11. *m:* Is 50:6. *n:* Mk 15:21; Lk 23:26. *o:* Mk 15:22–32; Lk 23:32–38; Jn 19:17–19, 23–24. *p:* Ps 69:21. *q:* Ps 22:19. *r:* Ps 22:8. *s:* 4:3, 6; 26:61. *t:* Ps 22:9; Wis 2:12–20.

said, 'I am the Son of God.' " 44 The revolutionaries who were crucified with him also
kept abusing him in the same way.
*The Death of Jesus.* 45* [u] From noon onward,[v] darkness came over the whole land
until three in the afternoon. 46[w] And about
three o'clock Jesus cried out in a loud voice,
"*Eli, Eli, lema sabachthani?*"* which means,
"My God, my God, why have you forsaken
me?" 47* Some of the bystanders who heard
it said, "This one is calling for Elijah."
48[x] Immediately one of them ran to get a
sponge; he soaked it in wine, and putting it
on a reed, gave it to him to drink. 49 But the
rest said, "Wait, let us see if Elijah comes to
save him." 50* But Jesus cried out again in a
loud voice, and gave up his spirit. 51[y] And
behold, the veil of the sanctuary was torn in
two from top to bottom.* The earth quaked,
rocks were split, 52[z] tombs were opened, and
the bodies of many saints who had fallen
asleep were raised. 53 And coming forth from
their tombs after his resurrection, they entered the holy city and appeared to many.
54* The centurion and the men with him who
were keeping watch over Jesus feared
greatly when they saw the earthquake and all
that was happening, and they said, "Truly,
this was the Son of God!" 55 There were
many women there, looking on from a distance,* who had followed Jesus from Galilee, ministering to him. 56[a] Among them
were Mary Magdalene and Mary the mother
of James and Joseph, and the mother of the
sons of Zebedee.
*The Burial of Jesus.** 57[b] When it was
evening, there came a rich man from Arimathea named Joseph, who was himself a disciple of Jesus.[c] 58 He went to Pilate and asked
for the body of Jesus; then Pilate ordered it
to be handed over. 59 Taking the body, Joseph
wrapped it [in] clean linen 60 and laid it in his

**27:45** Cf. Am 8:9 where on the day of the Lord "the sun will set at midday."

**27:46** *Eli, Eli, lema sabachthani?*: Jesus cries out in the words of Ps 22:2a, a psalm of lament that is the Old Testament passage most frequently drawn upon in this narrative. In Mark the verse is cited entirely in Aramaic, which Matthew partially retains but changes the invocation of God to the Hebrew *Eli*, possibly because that is more easily related to the statement of the following verse about Jesus' calling for Elijah.

**27:47 Elijah**: see note on Mt 3:4. This prophet, taken up into heaven (2 Kgs 2:11), was believed to come to the help of those in distress, but the evidences of that belief are all later than the gospels.

**27:50 Gave up his spirit**: cf. the Marcan parallel (Mk 15:37), "breathed his last." Matthew's alteration expresses both Jesus' control over his destiny and his obedient giving up of his life to God.

**27:51–53 Veil of the sanctuary . . . bottom**: cf. Mk 15:38; Lk 23:45. Luke puts this event immediately before the death of Jesus. There were two veils in the Mosaic tabernacle on the model of which the temple was constructed, the outer one before the entrance of the Holy Place and the inner one before the Holy of Holies (see Ex 26:31–36). Only the high priest could pass through the latter and that only on the Day of Atonement (see Lv 16:1–18). Probably the torn veil of the gospels is the inner one. The meaning of the scene may be that now, because of Jesus' death, all people have access to the presence of God, or that the temple, its holiest part standing exposed, is now profaned and will soon be destroyed. **The earth quaked . . . appeared to many**: peculiar to Matthew. The earthquake, the splitting of the **rocks**, and especially the resurrection of the dead **saints** indicate the coming of the final age. In the Old Testament the coming of God is frequently portrayed with the imagery of an earthquake (see Ps 68:9; 77:19), and Jesus speaks of the earthquakes that will accompany the "labor pains" that signify the beginning of the dissolution of the old world (Mt 24:7–8). For the expectation of the resurrection of the dead at the coming of the new and final age, see Dn 12:1–3. Matthew knows that the end of the old age has not yet come (Mt 28:20), but the new age has broken in with the death (and resurrection; cf. the earthquake in Mt 28:2) of Jesus; see note on Mt 16:28. **After his resurrection**: this qualification seems to be due to Matthew's wish to assert the primacy of Jesus' **resurrection** even though he has placed the resurrection of the dead **saints** immediately after Jesus' death.

**27:54** Cf. Mk 15:39. The Christian confession of faith is made by Gentiles, not only **the centurion**, as in Mark, but the other soldiers **who were keeping watch over Jesus** (cf. Mt 27:36).

**27:55–56 Looking on from a distance**: cf. Ps 38:12. **Mary Magdalene . . . Joseph**: these two women are mentioned again in Mt 27:61 and Mt 28:1 and are important as witnesses of the reality of the empty tomb. A **James** and **Joseph** are referred to in Mt 13:55 as brothers of Jesus.

**27:57–61** Cf. Mk 15:42–47. Matthew drops Mark's designation of **Joseph** of **Arimathea** as "a distinguished member of the council" (the Sanhedrin), and makes him **a rich man** and a **disciple of Jesus**. The former may be an allusion to Is 53:9 (the Hebrew reading of that text is disputed and the one followed in the NAB OT has nothing about the rich, but they are mentioned in the LXX version). That the tomb was the **new tomb** of **a rich man** and that it was seen by the women are indications of an apologetic intent of Matthew; there could be no question about the identity of Jesus' burial place. **The other Mary**: the mother of James and Joseph (Mt 27:56).

*u:* Mk 15:33–41; Lk 23:44–49; Jn 19:28–30. *v:* Am 8:9. *w:* Ps 22:2. *x:* Ps 69:21. *y:* Ex 26:31–36; Ps 68:9; 77:19. *z:* Dn 12:1–3. *a:* 13:55. *b:* Mk 15:42–47; Lk 23:50–56; Jn 19:38–42. *c:* Is 53:9.

new tomb that he had hewn in the rock. Then
he rolled a huge stone across the entrance to
the tomb and departed. 61 But Mary Magdalene and the other Mary remained sitting
there, facing the tomb.

*The Guard at the Tomb.** 62 The next day,
the one following the day of preparation,*
the chief priests and the Pharisees gathered
before Pilate 63[d] and said, "Sir, we remember
that this impostor while still alive said, 'After three days I will be raised up.' 64 Give orders, then, that the grave be secured until the
third day, lest his disciples come and steal
him and say to the people, 'He has been
raised from the dead.' This last imposture
would be worse than the first."* 65 Pilate said
to them, "The guard is yours;* go secure it as
best you can." 66 So they went and secured
the tomb by fixing a seal to the stone and setting the guard.

## CHAPTER 28*

See RG 289–90

*The Resurrection of Jesus.* 1[e] After
the sabbath, as the first day of the week was
dawning,* Mary Magdalene and the other
Mary came to see the tomb. 2*[f] And behold,
there was a great earthquake; for an angel of
the Lord descended from heaven, approached, rolled back the stone, and sat upon
it. 3[g] His appearance was like lightning and
his clothing was white as snow. 4 The guards
were shaken with fear of him and became
like dead men. 5 Then the angel said to the
women in reply, "Do not be afraid! I know
that you are seeking Jesus the crucified.
6* He is not here, for he has been raised just

**27:62–66** Peculiar to Matthew. The story prepares for Mt 28:11–15 and the Jewish charge that the tomb was empty because the disciples had stolen the body of Jesus (Mt 28:13, 15).

**27:62 The next day . . . preparation**: the sabbath. According to the synoptic chronology, in that year **the day of preparation** (for the sabbath) was the Passover; cf. Mk 15:42. **The Pharisees**: the principal opponents of Jesus during his ministry and, in Matthew's time, of the Christian church, join with **the chief priests** to guarantee against a possible attempt of Jesus' **disciples** to steal his body.

**27:64 This last imposture . . . the first**: the claim that Jesus **has been raised from the dead** is clearly the **last imposture; the first** may be either his claim that he would **be raised up** (Mt 27:63) or his claim that he was the one with whose ministry the kingdom of God had come (see Mt 12:28).

**27:65 The guard is yours**: literally, "have a guard" or "you have a guard." Either the imperative or the indicative could mean that Pilate granted the petitioners some Roman soldiers as guards, which is the sense of the present translation. However, if the verb is taken as an indicative it could also mean that Pilate told them to use their own Jewish guards.

**28:1–20** Except for Mt 28:1–8 based on Mk 16:1–8, the material of this final chapter is peculiar to Matthew. Even where he follows Mark, Matthew has altered his source so greatly that a very different impression is given from that of the Marcan account. The two points that are common to the resurrection testimony of all the gospels are that the tomb of Jesus had been found empty and that the risen Jesus had appeared to certain persons, or, in the original form of Mark, that such an appearance was promised as soon to take place (see Mk 16:7). On this central and all-important basis, Matthew has constructed an account that interprets the resurrection as the turning of the ages (Mt 28:2–4), shows the Jewish opposition to Jesus as continuing **to the present** in the claim that the resurrection is a deception perpetrated by the **disciples** who stole his body from the tomb (Mt 28:11–15), and marks a new stage in the mission of **the disciples** once limited to Israel (Mt 10:5–6); now they are to **make disciples of all nations.** In this work they will be strengthened by the presence of the exalted Son of Man, who will be with them **until** the kingdom comes in fullness at **the end of the age** (Mt 28:16–20).

**28:1 After the sabbath . . . dawning**: since the sabbath ended at sunset, this could mean in the early evening, for **dawning** can refer to the appearance of the evening star; cf. Lk 23:54. However, it is probable that Matthew means the morning dawn of the day after the sabbath, as in the similar though slightly different text of Mark, "when the sun had risen" (Mk 16:2). **Mary Magdalene and the other Mary**: see notes on Mt 27:55–56; 57–61. **To see the tomb**: cf. Mk 16:1–2 where the purpose of the women's visit is to anoint Jesus' body.

**28:2–4** Peculiar to Matthew. **A great earthquake**: see note on Mt 27:51–53. **Descended from heaven**: this trait is peculiar to Matthew, although his interpretation of the "young man" of his Marcan source (Mk 16:5) as an **angel** is probably true to Mark's intention; cf. Lk 24:23 where the "two men" of Mt 24:4 are said to be "angels." **Rolled back the stone . . . upon it**: not to allow the risen Jesus to leave the tomb but to make evident that the tomb is empty (see Mt 24:6). Unlike the apocryphal Gospel of Peter (9:35—11:44), the New Testament does not describe the resurrection of Jesus, nor is there anyone who sees it. **His appearance was like lightning . . . snow**: see note on Mt 17:2.

**28:6–7** Cf. Mk 16:6–7. **Just as he said**: a Matthean addition referring to Jesus' predictions of his resurrection, e.g., Mt 16:21; 17:23; 20:19. **Tell his disciples**: like the angel of the Lord of the infancy narrative, the angel interprets a fact and gives a commandment about what is to be done; cf. Mt 1:20–21. Matthew omits Mark's "and Peter" (Mk 16:7); considering his interest in Peter, this omission is curious. Perhaps the reason is that the Marcan text may allude to a first appearance of Jesus to Peter alone (cf. 1 Cor 15:5; Lk 24:34) which Matthew has already incorporated into his account of Peter's confession at Caesarea Philippi; see note on Mt 16:16. **He is going . . . Galilee**: like Mk 16:7, a reference to Jesus' prediction at the Last Supper (Mt 26:32; Mk 14:28). Matthew changes Mark's "as he told you" to a declaration of the angel.

*d*: 12:40; 16:21; 17:23; 20:19. *e*: Mk 16:1–8; Lk 24:1–12; Jn 20:1–10. *f*: 25:51. *g*: 17:2.

as he said. Come and see the place where he
lay. [7h] Then go quickly and tell his disciples,
'He has been raised from the dead, and he is
going before you to Galilee; there you will
see him.' Behold, I have told you." [8]Then
they went away quickly from the tomb, fearful yet overjoyed, and ran to announce* this
to his disciples. [9* i] And behold, Jesus met
them on their way and greeted them. They
approached, embraced his feet, and did him
homage. [10]Then Jesus said to them, "Do not
be afraid. Go tell my brothers to go to Galilee, and there they will see me."

***The Report of the Guard.**** [11]While they
were going, some of the guard went into the
city and told the chief priests all that had
happened. [12]They assembled with the elders
and took counsel; then they gave a large sum
of money to the soldiers, [13]telling them,
"You are to say, 'His disciples came by night
and stole him while we were asleep.' [14]And
if this gets to the ears of the governor, we
will satisfy [him] and keep you out of trouble." [15]The soldiers took the money and did
as they were instructed. And this story has
circulated among the Jews to the present
[day].

***The Commissioning of the Disciples.****
[16j] The eleven* disciples went to Galilee, to
the mountain to which Jesus had ordered
them. [17*] When they saw him, they worshiped, but they doubted. [18* k] Then Jesus
approached and said to them, "All power in
heaven and on earth has been given to me.
[19l] Go, therefore,* and make disciples of all
nations, baptizing them in the name of the
Father, and of the Son, and of the holy Spirit,
[20m] teaching them to observe all that I have
commanded you.* And behold, I am with
you always, until the end of the age."

**28:8** Contrast Mk 16:8 where the women in their fear "said nothing to anyone."

**28:9–10** Although these verses are peculiar to Matthew, there are similarities between them and John's account of the appearance of Jesus to Mary Magdalene (Jn 20:17). In both there is a touching of Jesus' body, and a command of Jesus to bear a message to his disciples, designated as his **brothers**. Matthew may have drawn upon a tradition that appears in a different form in John. Jesus' words to the women are mainly a repetition of those of the angel (Mt 28:5a, 7b).

**28:11–15** This account indicates that the dispute between Christians and Jews about the empty tomb was not whether the tomb was empty but why.

**28:16–20** This climactic scene has been called a "proleptic parousia," for it gives a foretaste of the final glorious coming of the Son of Man (Mt 26:64). Then his triumph will be manifest to all; now it is revealed only to **the disciples**, who are commissioned to announce it to **all nations** and bring them to belief in Jesus and obedience to his commandments.

**28:16 The eleven**: the number recalls the tragic defection of Judas Iscariot. **To the mountain . . . ordered them**: since the message to the **disciples** was simply that they were to go to Galilee (Mt 28:10), some think that **the mountain** comes from a tradition of the message known to Matthew and alluded to here. For the significance of **the mountain**, see note on Mt 17:1.

**28:17 But they doubted**: the Greek can also be translated, "but some doubted." The verb occurs elsewhere in the New Testament only in Mt 14:31 where it is associated with Peter's being of "little faith." For the meaning of that designation, see note on Mt 6:30.

**28:18 All power . . . me**: the Greek word here translated **power** is the same as that found in the LXX translation of Dn 7:13–14 where one "like a son of man" is given **power** and an everlasting kingdom by God. The risen Jesus here claims universal power, i.e., **in heaven and on earth**.

**28:19 Therefore**: since universal power belongs to the risen Jesus (Mt 28:18), he gives the eleven a mission that is universal. They are to **make disciples of all nations**. While **all nations** is understood by some scholars as referring only to all Gentiles, it is probable that it included the Jews as well. **Baptizing them**: baptism is the means of entrance into the community of the risen one, the Church. **In the name of the Father . . . holy Spirit**: this is perhaps the clearest expression in the New Testament of trinitarian belief. It may have been the baptismal formula of Matthew's church, but primarily it designates the effect of baptism, the union of the one baptized with the Father, Son, and holy Spirit.

**28:20 All that I have commanded you**: the moral teaching found in this gospel, preeminently that of the Sermon on the Mount (Mt 5–7). The commandments of Jesus are the standard of Christian conduct, not the Mosaic law as such, even though some of the Mosaic commandments have now been invested with the authority of Jesus. **Behold, I am with you always**: the promise of Jesus' real though invisible presence echoes the name Emmanuel given to him in the infancy narrative; see note on Mt 1:23. **End of the age**: see notes on Mt 13:39 and Mt 24:3.

---

*h:* 26:32. *i:* Jn 20:17. *j:* Mk 16:14–16; Lk 24:36–49; Jn 20:19–23. *k:* Dn 7:14 LXX. *l:* Acts 1:8. *m:* 1:23; 13:39; 24:3.

See RG 291–300

# The Gospel According to Mark

This shortest of all New Testament gospels is likely the first to have been written, yet it often tells of Jesus' ministry in more detail than either Matthew or Luke (for example, the miracle stories at Mk 5:1–20 or Mk 9:14–29). It recounts what Jesus did in a vivid style, where one incident follows directly upon another. In this almost breathless narrative, Mark stresses Jesus' message about the kingdom of God now breaking into human life as good news (Mk 1:14–15) and Jesus himself as the gospel of God (Mk 1:1; 8:35; 10:29). Jesus is the Son whom God has sent to rescue humanity by serving and by sacrificing his life (Mk 10:45).

The opening verse about good news in Mark (Mk 1:1) serves as a title for the entire book. The action begins with the appearance of John the Baptist, a messenger of God attested by scripture. But John points to a mightier one, Jesus, at whose baptism God speaks from heaven, declaring Jesus his Son. The Spirit descends upon Jesus, who eventually, it is promised, will baptize "with the holy Spirit." This presentation of who Jesus really is (Mk 1:1–13) is rounded out with a brief reference to the temptation of Jesus and how Satan's attack fails. Jesus as Son of God will be victorious, a point to be remembered as one reads of Jesus' death and the enigmatic ending to Mark's Gospel.

The key verses at Mk 1:14–15, which are programmatic, summarize what Jesus proclaims as gospel: fulfillment, the nearness of the kingdom, and therefore the need for repentance and for faith. After the call of the first four disciples, all fishermen (Mk 1:16–20), we see Jesus engaged in teaching (Mk 1:21, 22, 27), preaching (Mk 1:38, 39), and healing (Mk 1:29–31, 34, 40–45), and exorcising demons (Mk 1:22–27, 34–39). The content of Jesus' teaching is only rarely stated, and then chiefly in parables (Mk 4) about the kingdom. His cures, especially on the sabbath (Mk 3:1–5); his claim, like God, to forgive sins (Mk 2:3–12); his table fellowship with tax collectors and sinners (Mk 2:14–17); and the statement that his followers need not now fast but should rejoice while Jesus is present (Mk 2:18–22), all stir up opposition that will lead to Jesus' death (Mk 3:6).

In Mark, Jesus is portrayed as immensely popular with the people in Galilee during his ministry (Mk 2:2; 3:7; 4:1). He appoints twelve disciples to help preach and drive out demons, just as he does (Mk 3:13–19). He continues to work many miracles; the blocks Mk 4:35–6:44 and Mk 6:45–7:10 are cycles of stories about healings, miracles at the Sea of Galilee, and marvelous feedings of the crowds. Jesus' teaching in Mk 7 exalts the word of God over "the tradition of the elders" and sees defilement as a matter of the heart, not of unclean foods. Yet opposition mounts. Scribes charge that Jesus is possessed by Beelzebul (Mk 3:22). His relatives think him "out of his mind" (Mk 3:21). Jesus' kinship is with those who do the will of God, in a new eschatological family, not even with mother, brothers, or sisters by blood ties (Mk 3:31–35; cf. Mk 6:1–6). But all too often his own disciples do not understand Jesus (Mk 4:13, 40; 6:52; 8:17–21). The fate of John the Baptist (Mk 6:17–29) hints ominously at Jesus' own passion (Mk 9:13; cf. Mk 8:31).

A breakthrough seemingly comes with Peter's confession that Jesus is the Christ (Messiah; Mk 8:27–30). But Jesus himself emphasizes his passion (Mk 8:31; 9:31; 10:33–34), not glory in the kingdom (Mk 10:35–45). Momentarily he is glimpsed in his true identity when he is transfigured before three of the disciples (Mk 9:2–8), but by and large Jesus is depicted in Mark as moving obediently along the way to his cross in Jerusalem. Occasionally there are miracles (Mk 9:17–27; 10:46–52; 11:12–14, 20–21, the only such account in Jerusalem), sometimes teachings (Mk 10:2–11, 23–31), but the greatest concern is with discipleship (Mk 8:34–9:1; 9:33–50). For the disciples do not grasp the mystery being revealed (Mk 9:32; 10:32, 38). One of them will betray him, Judas (Mk 14:10–11, 43–45); one will deny him, Peter (Mk 14:27, 31, 54, 66–72); all eleven men will desert Jesus (Mk 14:27, 50).

The passion account, with its condemnation of Jesus by the Sanhedrin (Mk 14:53, 55–65; 15:1a) and sentencing by Pilate (Mk 15:1b–15), is prefaced with the entry into Jerusalem (Mk 11:1–11), ministry and controversies there (Mk 11:15–12:44), Jesus' Last Supper with the disciples (Mk 14:1–26), and his arrest at Gethsemane (Mk 14:32–52). A chapter of apocalyptic tone about the destruction of the temple (Mk 13:1–2, 14–23) and the coming of the Son of Man (Mk 13:24–27), a discourse filled with promises (Mk 13:11, 31) and admonitions to be watchful (Mk 13:2, 23, 37), is significant for Mark's Gospel, for it helps one see that God, in Jesus, will be victorious after the cross and at the end of history.

The Gospel of Mark ends in the most ancient manuscripts with an abrupt scene at Jesus' tomb, which the women find empty (Mk 16:1–8). His own prophecy of Mk 14:28 is reiterated, that Jesus goes before the disciples into Galilee; "there you will see him." These words may imply resurrection appearances there, or Jesus' parousia there, or the start of Christian mission, or a return to the roots depicted in Mk 1:9, 14–15 in Galilee. Other hands have attached additional endings after Mk 16:8; see note on Mk 16:9–20.

The framework of Mark's Gospel is partly geographical: Galilee (Mk 1:14–9:49), through the area "across the Jordan" (Mk 10:1) and through Jericho (Mk 10:46–52), to Jerusalem (Mk 11:1–16:8). Only rarely does Jesus go into Gentile territory (Mk 5:1–20; 7:24–37), but those who acknowledge him there and the centurion who confesses Jesus at the cross (Mk 15:39) presage the gospel's expansion into the world beyond Palestine.

Mark's Gospel is even more oriented to christology. Jesus is the Son of God (Mk 1:11; 9:7; 15:39; cf. Mk 1:1; 14:61). He is the Messiah, the anointed king of Davidic descent (Mk 12:35; 15:32), the Greek for which, *Christos*, has, by the time Mark wrote, become in effect a proper name (Mk 1:1; 9:41). Jesus is also seen as Son of Man, a term used in Mark not simply as a substitute for "I" or for humanity in general (cf. Mk 2:10, 27–28; 14:21) or with reference to a mighty figure who is to come (Mk 13:26; 14:62), but also in connection with Jesus' predestined, necessary path of suffering and vindication (Mk 8:31; 10:45).

The unfolding of Mark's story about Jesus is sometimes viewed by interpreters as centered around the term "mystery." The word is employed just once, at Mk 4:11, in the singular, and its content there is the kingdom, the open secret that God's reign is now breaking into human life with its reversal of human values. There is a related sense in which Jesus' real identity remained a secret during his lifetime, according to Mark, although demons and demoniacs knew it (Mk 1:24; 3:11; 5:7); Jesus warned against telling of his mighty deeds and revealing his identity (Mk 1:44; 3:12; 5:43; 7:36; 8:26, 30), an injunction sometimes broken (Mk 1:45; cf. Mk 5:19–20). Further, Jesus teaches by parables, according to Mark, in such a way that those "outside" the kingdom do not understand, but only those to whom the mystery has been granted by God.

Mark thus shares with Paul, as well as with other parts of the New Testament, an emphasis on election (Mk 13:20, 22) and upon the gospel as Christ and his cross (cf. 1 Cor 1:23). Yet in Mark the person of Jesus is also depicted with an unaffected naturalness. He reacts to events with authentic human emotion: pity (Mk 1:44), anger (Mk 3:5), triumph (Mk 4:40), sympathy (Mk 5:36; 6:34), surprise (Mk 6:9), admiration (Mk 7:29; 10:21), sadness (Mk 14:33–34), and indignation (Mk 14:48–49).

Although the book is anonymous, apart from the ancient heading "According to Mark" in manuscripts, it has traditionally been assigned to John Mark, in whose mother's house (at Jerusalem) Christians assembled (Acts 12:12). This Mark was a cousin of Barnabas (Col 4:10) and accompanied Barnabas and Paul on a missionary journey (Acts 12:25; 13:3; 15:36–39). He appears in Pauline letters (2 Tm 4:11; Phlm 24) and with Peter (1 Pt 5:13). Papias (ca. A.D. 135) described Mark as Peter's "interpreter," a view found in other patristic writers. Petrine influence should not, however, be exaggerated. The evangelist has put together various oral and possibly written sources—miracle stories, parables, sayings, stories of controversies, and the passion—so as to speak of the crucified Messiah for Mark's own day.

Traditionally, the gospel is said to have been written shortly before A.D. 70 in Rome, at a time of impending persecution and when destruction loomed over Jerusalem. Its audience seems to have been Gentile, unfamiliar with Jewish customs (hence Mk 7:3–4, 11). The book aimed to equip such Christians to stand faithful in the face of persecution (Mk 13:9–13), while going on with the proclamation of the gospel begun in Galilee (Mk 13:10; 14:9). Modern research often proposes as the author an unknown Hellenistic Jewish Christian, possibly in Syria, and perhaps shortly after the year 70.

The principal divisions of the Gospel according to Mark are the following:

I. The Preparation for the Public Ministry of Jesus (1:1–13)

II. The Mystery of Jesus (1:14–8:26)
III. The Mystery Begins to Be Revealed (8:27–9:32)
IV. The Full Revelation of the Mystery (9:33–16:8)
The Longer Ending (16:9–20)
The Shorter Ending
The Freer Logion (in the note on 16:9–20)

## I. The Preparation for the Public Ministry of Jesus*

### CHAPTER 1

See RG 294–95

[1]The beginning of the gospel of Jesus Christ [the Son of God].*

***The Preaching of John the Baptist.*** [2][a]As it is written in Isaiah the prophet:*[b]

"Behold, I am sending my messenger
ahead of you;
he will prepare your way.
[3][c]A voice of one crying out in the desert:
'Prepare the way of the Lord,
make straight his paths.' "

[4]John [the] Baptist appeared in the desert proclaiming a baptism of repentance for the forgiveness of sins. [5]People of the whole Judean countryside and all the inhabitants of Jerusalem were going out to him and were being baptized by him in the Jordan River as they acknowledged their sins. [6]John was clothed in camel's hair, with a leather belt around his waist.* He fed on locusts and wild honey. [7]And this is what he proclaimed: "One mightier than I is coming after me. I am not worthy to stoop and loosen the thongs of his sandals. [8]*[d]I have baptized you with water; he will baptize you with the holy Spirit."

***The Baptism of Jesus.*** [9][e]It happened in those days that Jesus came from Nazareth of Galilee and was baptized in the Jordan by John. [10]On coming up out of the water he saw the heavens being torn open and the Spirit, like a dove, descending upon him.* [11][f]And a voice came from the heavens, "You are my beloved Son; with you I am well pleased."

***The Temptation of Jesus.**** [12]At once the Spirit drove him out into the desert,[g] [13]and he remained in the desert for forty days, tempted by Satan. He was among wild beasts, and the angels ministered to him.

**1:1–13** The prologue of the Gospel according to Mark begins with the title (Mk 1:1) followed by three events preparatory to Jesus' preaching: (1) the appearance in the Judean wilderness of John, baptizer, preacher of repentance, and precursor of Jesus (Mk 1:2–8); (2) the baptism of Jesus, at which a voice from heaven acknowledges Jesus to be God's Son, and the holy Spirit descends on him (Mk 1:9–11); (3) the temptation of Jesus by Satan (Mk 1:12–13).

**1:1 The gospel of Jesus Christ [the Son of God]**: the "good news" of salvation in and through Jesus, crucified and risen, acknowledged by the Christian community as Messiah (Mk 8:29; 14:61–62) and Son of God (Mk 1:11; 9:7; 15:39), although some important manuscripts here omit **the Son of God**.

**1:2–3** Although Mark attributes the prophecy to Isaiah, the text is a combination of Mal 3:1; Is 40:3; Ex 23:20; cf. Mt 11:10; Lk 7:27. John's ministry is seen as God's prelude to the saving mission of his Son. **The way of the Lord**: this prophecy of Deutero-Isaiah concerning the end of the Babylonian exile is here applied to the coming of Jesus; John the Baptist is to prepare the way for him.

**1:6 Clothed in camel's hair . . . waist**: the Baptist's garb recalls that of Elijah in 2 Kgs 1:8. Jesus speaks of the Baptist as Elijah who has already come (Mk 9:11–13; Mt 17:10–12; cf. Mal 3:23–24; Lk 1:17).

**1:8–9** Through the life-giving baptism with the holy Spirit (Mk 1:8), Jesus will create a new people of God. But first he identifies himself with the people of Israel in submitting to John's baptism of repentance and in bearing on their behalf the burden of God's decisive judgment (Mk 1:9; cf. Mk 1:4). As in the desert of Sinai, so here in the wilderness of Judea, Israel's sonship with God is to be renewed.

**1:10–11 He saw the heavens . . . and the Spirit . . . upon him**: indicating divine intervention in fulfillment of promise. Here the descent of the Spirit on Jesus is meant, anointing him for his ministry; cf. Is 11:2; 42:1; 61:1; 63:9. **A voice . . . with you I am well pleased**: God's acknowledgment of Jesus as his unique Son, the object of his love. His approval of Jesus is the assurance that Jesus will fulfill his messianic mission of salvation.

**1:12–13** The same Spirit who descended on Jesus in his baptism now drives him into the desert for forty days. The result is radical confrontation and temptation by Satan who attempts to frustrate the work of God. The presence of wild beasts may indicate the horror and danger of the desert regarded as the abode of demons or may reflect the paradise motif of harmony among all creatures; cf. Is 11:6–9. The presence of ministering angels to sustain Jesus recalls the angel who guided the Israelites in the desert in the first Exodus (Ex 14:19; 23:20) and the angel who supplied nourishment to Elijah in the wilderness (1 Kgs 19:5–7). The combined forces

*a:* Mt 3:1–11; Lk 3:2–16. *b:* Mal 3:1. *c:* Is 40:3; Jn 1:23. *d:* Jn 1:27; Acts 1:5; 11:16. *e:* Mt 3:13–17; Lk 3:21–23; Jn 1:32–33. *f:* Ps 2:7. *g:* Mt 4:1–11; Lk 4:1–13.

## II. The Mystery of Jesus

***The Beginning of the Galilean Ministry.*** [14h] After John had been arrested,* Jesus came to Galilee proclaiming the gospel of God: [15i] "This is the time of fulfillment. The kingdom of God is at hand. Repent, and believe in the gospel."

***The Call of the First Disciples.**** [16j] As he passed by the Sea of Galilee, he saw Simon and his brother Andrew casting their nets into the sea; they were fishermen. [17]Jesus said to them, "Come after me, and I will make you fishers of men." [18]Then they abandoned their nets and followed him. [19]He walked along a little farther and saw James, the son of Zebedee, and his brother John. They too were in a boat mending their nets. [20]Then he called them. So they left their father Zebedee in the boat along with the hired men and followed him.

***The Cure of a Demoniac.*** [21* k] Then they came to Capernaum, and on the sabbath he entered the synagogue and taught. [22l] The people were astonished at his teaching, for he taught them as one having authority and not as the scribes. [23*] In their synagogue was a man with an unclean spirit; [24*] he cried out, "What have you to do with us,* Jesus of Nazareth? Have you come to destroy us? I know who you are—the Holy One of God!" [25]Jesus rebuked him and said, "Quiet! Come out of him!" [26]The unclean spirit convulsed him and with a loud cry came out of him. [27]All were amazed and asked one another, "What is this? A new teaching with authority. He commands even the unclean spirits and they obey him." [28]His fame spread everywhere throughout the whole region of Galilee.

***The Cure of Simon's Mother-in-Law.*** [29m] On leaving the synagogue he entered the house of Simon and Andrew with James and John. [30]Simon's mother-in-law lay sick with a fever. They immediately told him about her. [31]He approached, grasped her hand, and helped her up. Then the fever left her and she waited on them.

***Other Healings.*** [32]When it was evening, after sunset, they brought to him all who were ill or possessed by demons. [33]The whole town was gathered at the door. [34]He cured many who were sick with various diseases, and he drove out many demons, not permitting them to speak because they knew him.

***Jesus Leaves Capernaum.*** [35n] Rising very early before dawn, he left and went off to a deserted place, where he prayed. [36]Simon and those who were with him pursued him [37]and on finding him said, "Everyone is looking for you." [38]He told them, "Let us go on to the nearby villages that I may preach there also. For this purpose have I come." [39]So he went into their synagogues, preaching and driving out demons throughout the whole of Galilee.

***The Cleansing of a Leper.*** [40o] A leper* came to him [and kneeling down] begged

of good and evil were present to Jesus in the desert. His sustained obedience brings forth the new Israel of God there where Israel's rebellion had brought death and alienation.

**1:14–15 After John had been arrested**: in the plan of God, Jesus was not to proclaim the good news of salvation prior to the termination of the Baptist's active mission. **Galilee**: in the Marcan account, scene of the major part of Jesus' public ministry before his arrest and condemnation. **The gospel of God**: not only the good news from God but about God at work in Jesus Christ. **This is the time of fulfillment**: i.e., of God's promises. **The kingdom of God . . . Repent**: see note on Mt 3:2.

**1:16–20** These verses narrate the call of the first Disciples. See notes on Mt 4:18–22 and Mt 4:20.

**1:21–45** The account of a single day's ministry of Jesus on a sabbath in and outside the synagogue of Capernaum (Mk 1:21–31) combines teaching and miracles of exorcism and healing. Mention is not made of the content of the teaching but of the effect of astonishment and alarm on the people. Jesus' teaching with authority, making an absolute claim on the hearer, was in the best tradition of the ancient prophets, not of the scribes. The narrative continues with events that evening (Mk 1:32–34; see notes on Mt 8:14–17) and the next day (Mk 1:35–39). The cleansing in Mk 1:40–45 stands as an isolated story.

**1:23 An unclean spirit**: so called because of the spirit's resistance to the holiness of God. The spirit knows and fears the power of Jesus to destroy his influence; cf. Mk 1:32, 34; 3:11; 6:13.

**1:24–25 The Holy One of God**: not a confession but an attempt to ward off Jesus' power, reflecting the notion that use of the precise name of an opposing spirit would guarantee mastery over him. Jesus silenced the cry of the unclean spirit and drove him out of the man.

**1:24 What have you to do with us?**: see note on Jn 2:4.

**1:40 A leper**: for the various forms of skin disease, see Lv 13:1–50 and the note on Lv 13:2–4. There are only two instances in the Old Testament in which God is shown to have cured a leper (Nm 12:10–15; 2 Kgs 5:1–14). The law of Mo-

*h:* Mt 4:12–17; Lk 4:14–15. *i:* Mt 3:2. *j:* Mt 4:18–22; Lk 5:2–11. *k:* Lk 4:31–37. *l:* Mt 7:28–29. *m:* Mt 8:14–16; Lk 4:38–41. *n:* Lk 4:42–44. *o:* Mt 8:2–4; Lk 5:12–14.

## Tax Collectors and Sinners

LEVI (CALLED MATTHEW in Mt 9:9) was a customs officer at the border village of Capernaum. Such tax collectors were despised as Roman collaborators and extortionists. "Sinners" are those who deliberately place themselves apart from the observance of Torah. The Pharisees, a branch of Judaism that was dedicated to interpreting biblical law, likely including the extension of the sanctity of the temple to the home (including the table), regarded eating with them (Mk 2:16) as contact with impure people and social outcasts.

him and said, "If you wish, you can make me clean." [41]Moved with pity, he stretched out his hand, touched him, and said to him, "I do will it. Be made clean."[p] [42]The leprosy left him immediately, and he was made clean.[q] [43]Then, warning him sternly, he dismissed him at once. [44]Then he said to him, "See that you tell no one anything, but go, show yourself to the priest and offer for your cleansing what Moses prescribed; that will be proof for them."[r] [45]The man went away and began to publicize the whole matter. He spread the report abroad so that it was impossible for Jesus to enter a town openly. He remained outside in deserted places, and people kept coming to him from everywhere.

## CHAPTER 2

See RG 295–96

*The Healing of a Paralytic.* [1*] When Jesus returned to Capernaum[s] after some days, it became known that he was at home.* [2]Many gathered together so that there was no longer room for them, not even around the door, and he preached the word to them. [3]They came bringing to him a paralytic carried by four men. [4]Unable to get near Jesus because of the crowd, they opened up the roof above him. After they had broken through, they let down the mat on which the paralytic was lying. [5*] When Jesus saw their faith, he said to the paralytic, "Child, your sins are forgiven." [6*] Now some of the scribes were sitting there asking themselves, [7]"Why does this man speak that way?* He is blaspheming. Who but God alone can forgive sins?"[t] [8]Jesus immediately knew in his mind what they were thinking to themselves, so he said, "Why are you thinking such things in your hearts? [9]Which is easier, to say to the paralytic, 'Your sins are forgiven,' or to say, 'Rise, pick up your mat and walk'? [10*] But that you may know that the Son of Man has authority to forgive sins on earth"— [11]he said to the paralytic, "I say to you, rise, pick up your mat, and go home." [12]He rose, picked up his mat at once, and went away in the sight of everyone. They were all astounded and glorified God, saying, "We have never seen anything like this."

*The Call of Levi.* [13*] [u] Once again he went out along the sea. All the crowd came to him

ses provided for the ritual purification of a leper. In curing the leper, Jesus assumes that the priests will reinstate the cured man into the religious community. See also note on Lk 5:14.

**2:1–3:6** This section relates a series of conflicts between Jesus and the scribes and Pharisees in which the growing opposition of the latter leads to their plot to put Jesus to death (Mk 3:6).

**2:1–2 He was at home**: to the crowds that gathered in and outside the house Jesus **preached the word**, i.e., the gospel concerning the nearness of the kingdom and the necessity of repentance and faith (Mk 1:14).

**2:5** It was the faith of the paralytic and those who carried him that moved Jesus to heal the sick man. Accounts of other miracles of Jesus reveal more and more his emphasis on faith as the requisite for exercising his healing powers (Mk 5:34; 9:23–24; 10:52).

**2:6 Scribes**: trained in oral interpretation of the written law; in Mark's gospel, adversaries of Jesus, with one exception (Mk 12:28, 34).

**2:7 He is blaspheming**: an accusation made here and repeated during the trial of Jesus (Mk 14:60–64).

**2:10 But that you may know that the Son of Man . . . on earth**: although Mk 2:8–9 are addressed to the scribes, the sudden interruption of thought and structure in Mk 2:10 seems not addressed to them nor to the paralytic. Moreover, the early public use of the designation "Son of Man" to unbelieving scribes is most unlikely. The most probable explanation is that Mark's insertion of Mk 2:10 is a commentary addressed to Christians for whom he recalls this miracle and who already accept in faith that Jesus is Messiah and Son of God.

**2:13 He taught them**: see note on Mk 1:21–45.

*p:* 5:30. *q:* Lk 17:14. *r:* Lv 14:2–32. *s:* Mt 9:2–8; Lk 5:18–26. *t:* Is 43:25. *u:* 4:1.

and he taught them. 14[v] As he passed by,* he saw Levi, son of Alphaeus, sitting at the customs post. He said to him, "Follow me." And he got up and followed him. 15 While he was at table in his house,* many tax collectors and sinners sat with Jesus and his disciples; for there were many who followed him. 16* Some scribes who were Pharisees saw that he was eating with sinners and tax collectors and said to his disciples, "Why does he eat with tax collectors and sinners?" 17 Jesus heard this and said to them [that], "Those who are well do not need a physician,* but the sick do. I did not come to call the righteous but sinners."

***The Question About Fasting.**** 18 The disciples of John and of the Pharisees were accustomed to fast.[w] People came to him and objected, "Why do the disciples of John and the disciples of the Pharisees fast, but your disciples do not fast?" 19 Jesus answered them, "Can the wedding guests fast* while the bridegroom is with them? As long as they have the bridegroom with them they cannot fast. 20 But the days will come when the bridegroom is taken away from them, and then they will fast on that day. 21 No one sews a piece of unshrunken cloth on an old cloak. If he does, its fullness pulls away, the new from the old, and the tear gets worse. 22 Likewise, no one pours new wine into old wineskins. Otherwise, the wine will burst the skins, and both the wine and the skins are ruined. Rather, new wine is poured into fresh wineskins."

***The Disciples and the Sabbath.**** 23 As he was passing through a field of grain on the sabbath, his disciples began to make a path while picking the heads of grain.[x] 24 At this the Pharisees said to him, "Look, why are they doing what is unlawful on the sabbath?"[y] 25 He said to them, "Have you never read what David did* when he was in need and he and his companions were hungry? 26 How he went into the house of God when Abiathar was high priest and ate the bread of offering that only the priests could lawfully eat, and shared it with his companions?"[z] 27 Then he said to them, "The sabbath was made for man,* not man for the sabbath.[a] 28* That is why the Son of Man is lord even of the sabbath."

## CHAPTER 3

See RG 295–96

***A Man with a Withered Hand.***
1* Again he entered the synagogue.[b] There

**2:14 As he passed by**: see note on Mk 1:16–20. **Levi, son of Alphaeus**: see note on Mt 9:9. **Customs post**: such tax collectors paid a fixed sum for the right to collect customs duties within their districts. Since whatever they could collect above this amount constituted their profit, the abuse of extortion was widespread among them. Hence, Jewish customs officials were regarded as sinners (Mk 2:16), outcasts of society, and disgraced along with their families. **He got up and followed him**: i.e., became a disciple of Jesus.

**2:15 In his house**: cf. Mk 2:1; Mt 9:10. Lk 5:29 clearly calls it Levi's house.

**2:16–17** This and the following conflict stories reflect a similar pattern: a statement of fact, a question of protest, and a reply by Jesus.

**2:17 Do not need a physician**: this maxim of Jesus with its implied irony was uttered to silence his adversaries who objected that he ate with **tax collectors and sinners** (Mk 2:16). Because the scribes and Pharisees were self-righteous, they were not capable of responding to Jesus' call to repentance and faith in the gospel.

**2:18–22** This conflict over the question of fasting has the same pattern as Mk 2:16–17; see notes on Mt 9:15; 9:16–17.

**2:19 Can the wedding guests fast?**: the bridal metaphor expresses a new relationship of love between God and his people in the person and mission of Jesus to his disciples. It is the inauguration of the new and joyful messianic time of fulfillment and the passing of the old. Any attempt at assimilating the Pharisaic practice of fasting, or of extending the preparatory discipline of John's disciples beyond the arrival of the bridegroom, would be as futile as sewing **a piece of unshrunken cloth on an old cloak** or pouring **new wine into old wineskins** with the resulting destruction of both cloth and wine (Mk 2:21–22). Fasting is rendered superfluous during the earthly ministry of Jesus; cf. Mk 2:20.

**2:23–28** This conflict regarding the sabbath follows the same pattern as in Mk 2:18–22.

**2:25–26 Have you never read what David did?**: Jesus defends the action of his disciples on the basis of 1 Sm 21:2–7 in which an exception is made to the regulation of Lv 24:9 because of the extreme hunger of David and his men. According to 1 Samuel, the priest who gave the bread to David was Ahimelech, father of Abiathar.

**2:27 The sabbath was made for man**: a reaffirmation of the divine intent of the sabbath to benefit Israel as contrasted with the restrictive Pharisaic tradition added to the law.

**2:28 The Son of Man is lord even of the sabbath**: Mark's comment on the theological meaning of the incident is to benefit his Christian readers; see note on Mk 2:10.

**3:1–5** Here Jesus is again depicted in conflict with his adversaries over the question of sabbath-day observance. His opponents were already ill disposed toward him because they

*v:* Mt 9:9–13; Lk 5:27–32. *w:* Mt 9:14–17; Lk 5:33–39. *x:* Mt 12:1–8; Lk 6:1–5. *y:* Dt 23:25. *z:* 1 Sm 21:2–7; Lv 24:5–9. *a:* 2 Mc 5:19. *b:* Mt 12:9–14; Lk 6:6–11.

was a man there who had a withered hand.
2They watched him closely to see if he
would cure him on the sabbath so that they
might accuse him. 3He said to the man with
the withered hand, "Come up here before
us." 4Then he said to them, "Is it lawful to do
good on the sabbath rather than to do evil, to
save life rather than to destroy it?" But they
remained silent. 5Looking around at them
with anger and grieved at their hardness of
heart, he said to the man, "Stretch out your
hand." He stretched it out and his hand was
restored.[c] 6* The Pharisees went out and immediately took counsel with the Herodians
against him to put him to death.

***The Mercy of Jesus.*** 7* Jesus withdrew toward the sea with his disciples.[d] A large
number of people [followed] from Galilee
and from Judea. 8Hearing what he was doing,
a large number of people came to him also
from Jerusalem, from Idumea, from beyond
the Jordan, and from the neighborhood of
Tyre and Sidon. 9He told his disciples to have
a boat ready for him because of the crowd, so
that they would not crush him. 10He had
cured many and, as a result, those who had
diseases were pressing upon him to touch
him.[e] 11* And whenever unclean spirits saw
him they would fall down before him and
shout, "You are the Son of God."[f] 12He
warned them sternly not to make him known.

***The Mission of the Twelve.*** 13[g] He went up
the mountain* and summoned those whom
he wanted and they came to him. 14[h] He appointed twelve [whom he also named apos-
tles] that they might be with him* and he
might send them forth to preach 15and to
have authority to drive out demons: 16* [he
appointed the twelve:] Simon, whom he
named Peter; 17James, son of Zebedee, and
John the brother of James, whom he named
Boanerges, that is, sons of thunder;[i] 18An-
drew, Philip, Bartholomew, Matthew,
Thomas, James the son of Alphaeus; Thaddeus, Simon the Cananean, 19and Judas Iscariot who betrayed him.

***Blasphemy of the Scribes.*** 20* He came
home.* Again [the] crowd gathered, making
it impossible for them even to eat.[j] 21When
his relatives heard of this they set out to
seize him, for they said, "He is out of his
mind."[k] 22The scribes who had come from
Jerusalem said, "He is possessed by Beelzebul,"* and "By the prince of demons he
drives out demons."[l]

***Jesus and Beelzebul.*** 23Summoning them,

regarded Jesus as a violator of the sabbath. Jesus' question **Is it lawful to do good on the sabbath rather than to do evil?** places the matter in the broader theological context outside the casuistry of the scribes. The answer is obvious. Jesus heals the man with the withered hand in the sight of all and reduces his opponents to silence; cf. Jn 5:17–18.

**3:6** In reporting the plot of the Pharisees and Herodians to put Jesus to death after this series of conflicts in Galilee, Mark uses a pattern that recurs in his account of later controversies in Jerusalem (Mk 11:17–18; 12:13–17). The help of the Herodians, supporters of Herod Antipas, tetrarch of Galilee and Perea, is needed to take action against Jesus. Both series of conflicts point to their gravity and to the impending passion of Jesus.

**3:7–19** This overview of the Galilean ministry manifests the power of Jesus to draw people to himself through his teaching and deeds of power. The crowds of Jews from many regions surround Jesus (Mk 3:7–12). This phenomenon prepares the way for creating a new people of Israel. The choice and mission of the Twelve is the prelude (Mk 3:13–19).

**3:11–12** See note on Mk 1:24–25.

**3:13 He went up the mountain**: here and elsewhere the mountain is associated with solemn moments and acts in the mission and self-revelation of Jesus (Mk 6:46; 9:2–8; 13:3). Jesus acts with authority as he **summoned those whom he wanted and they came to him**.

**3:14–15 He appointed twelve [whom he also named apostles] that they might be with him**: literally "he made," i.e., instituted them as apostles to extend his messianic mission through them (Mk 6:7–13). See notes on Mt 10:1 and 10:2–4.

**3:16 Simon, whom he named Peter**: Mark indicates that Simon's name was changed on this occasion. Peter is first in all lists of the apostles (Mt 10:2; Lk 6:14; Acts 1:13; cf. 1 Cor 15:5–8).

**3:20–35** Within the narrative of the coming of Jesus' relatives (Mk 3:20–21) is inserted the account of the unbelieving scribes from Jerusalem who attributed Jesus' power over demons to Beelzebul (Mk 3:22–30); see note on Mk 5:21–43. There were those even among the relatives of Jesus who disbelieved and regarded Jesus as **out of his mind** (Mk 3:21). Against this background, Jesus is informed of the arrival of his mother and brothers [and sisters] (Mk 3:32). He responds by showing that not family ties but doing God's will (Mk 3:35) is decisive in the kingdom; cf. note on Mt 12:46–50.

**3:20 He came home**: cf. Mk 2:1–2 and see note on Mk 2:15.

**3:22 By Beelzebul**: see note on Mt 10:25. Two accusations are leveled against Jesus: (1) that **he is possessed** by an unclean spirit, and (2) **by the prince of demons he drives out demons**. Jesus answers the second charge by a parable (Mk 3:24–27) and responds to the first charge in Mk 3:28–29.

*c:* Lk 14:4. *d:* Mt 4:23–25; 12:15; Lk 6:17–19. *e:* 5:30. *f:* 1:34; Lk 4:41. *g:* Mt 10:1–4; Lk 6:12–16. *h:* 6:7. *i:* Mt 16:18; Jn 1:42. *j:* 2:2. *k:* Jn 10:20. *l:* Mt 12:24–32; Lk 11:15–22; 12:10.

**Rejections**

JESUS' FAMILY DOUBTS his sanity (3:21), and he replaces the biological family with the family of faith. The scribes accept Jesus' power but question the source of his authority; they ironically charge Jesus the exorcist with being possessed by Beelzebul, a false god (2 Kgs 1:2) or demon.

he began to speak to them in parables, "How can Satan drive out Satan? 24 If a kingdom is divided against itself, that kingdom cannot stand. 25 And if a house is divided against itself, that house will not be able to stand. 26 And if Satan has risen up against himself and is divided, he cannot stand; that is the end of him. 27 But no one can enter a strong man's house to plunder his property unless he first ties up the strong man. Then he can plunder his house. 28 Amen, I say to you, all sins and all blasphemies that people utter will be forgiven them.[m] 29 But whoever blasphemes against the holy Spirit* will never have forgiveness, but is guilty of an everlasting sin." 30 For they had said, "He has an unclean spirit."

***Jesus and His Family.*** 31[n] His mother and his brothers arrived. Standing outside they sent word to him and called him. 32 A crowd seated around him told him, "Your mother and your brothers* [and your sisters] are outside asking for you." 33 But he said to them in reply, "Who are my mother and [my] brothers?" 34 And looking around at those seated in the circle he said, "Here are my mother and my brothers. 35 [For] whoever does the will of God is my brother and sister and mother."

## CHAPTER 4

See RG 296–97

***The Parable of the Sower.*** 1* On another occasion[o] he began to teach by the sea.* A very large crowd gathered around him so that he got into a boat on the sea and sat down. And the whole crowd was beside the sea on land.[p] 2 And he taught them at length in parables, and in the course of his instruction he said to them, 3* "Hear this! A sower went out to sow. 4 And as he sowed, some seed fell on the path, and the birds came and ate it up. 5 Other seed fell on rocky ground where it had little soil. It sprang up at once because the soil was not deep. 6 And when the sun rose, it was scorched and it withered for lack of roots. 7 Some seed fell among thorns, and the thorns grew up and choked it and it produced no grain. 8 And some seed fell on rich soil and produced fruit. It came up and grew and yielded thirty, sixty, and a hundredfold." 9 He added, "Whoever has ears to hear ought to hear."

***The Purpose of the Parables.*** 10 And when he was alone, those present along with the Twelve questioned him about the parables. 11* He answered them, "The mystery of the kingdom of God has been granted to you. But to those outside everything comes in parables, 12 so that

**3:29 Whoever blasphemes against the holy Spirit**: this sin is called **an everlasting sin** because it attributes to Satan, who is the power of evil, what is actually the work of the holy Spirit, namely, victory over the demons.

**3:32 Your brothers**: see note on Mk 6:3.

**4:1–34 In parables** (Mk 4:2): see note on Mt 13:3. The use of parables is typical of Jesus' enigmatic method of teaching the crowds (Mk 4:2–9, 12) as compared with the interpretation of the parables he gives to his disciples (Mk 4:10–25, 33–34) to each group according to its capacity to understand (Mk 4:9–11). The key feature of the parable at hand is the sowing of the seed (Mk 4:3), representing the breakthrough of the kingdom of God into the world. The various types of soil refer to the diversity of response accorded the word of God (Mk 4:4–7). The climax of the parable is the harvest of thirty, sixty, and a hundredfold, indicating the consummation of the kingdom (Mk 4:8). Thus both the present and the future action of God, from the initiation to the fulfillment of the kingdom, is presented through this and other parables (Mk 4:26–29, 30–32).

**4:1 By the sea**: the shore of the Sea of Galilee or a boat near the shore (Mk 2:13; 3:7–8) is the place where Mark depicts Jesus teaching the crowds. By contrast the mountain is the scene of Jesus at prayer (Mk 6:46) or in the process of forming his disciples (Mk 3:13; 9:2).

**4:3–8** See note on Mt 13:3–8.

**4:11–12** These verses are to be viewed against their background in Mk 3:6, 22 concerning the unbelief and opposition Jesus encountered in his ministry. It is against this background that the distinction in Jesus' method becomes clear of presenting the kingdom to the disbelieving crowd in one manner and to the disciples in another. To the former it is pre-

*m:* Lk 12:10. *n:* Mt 12:46–50; Lk 8:19–21. *o:* Mt 13:1–13; Lk 8:4–10. *p:* 2:13; Lk 5:1.

'they may look and see but not perceive,
and hear and listen but not understand,
in order that they may not be converted
and be forgiven.' "[q]

13* Jesus said to them, "Do you not understand this parable?[r] Then how will you understand any of the parables? 14 The sower sows the word. 15 These are the ones on the path where the word is sown. As soon as they hear, Satan comes at once and takes away the word sown in them. 16 And these are the ones sown on rocky ground who, when they hear the word, receive it at once with joy. 17 But they have no root; they last only for a time. Then when tribulation or persecution comes because of the word, they quickly fall away. 18 Those sown among thorns are another sort. They are the people who hear the word, 19 but worldly anxiety, the lure of riches, and the craving for other things intrude and choke the word, and it bears no fruit. 20 But those sown on rich soil are the ones who hear the word and accept it and bear fruit thirty and sixty and a hundredfold."

***Parable of the Lamp.*** 21[s] He said to them, "Is a lamp brought in to be placed under a bushel basket or under a bed, and not to be placed on a lampstand?[t] 22 For there is nothing hidden except to be made visible; nothing is secret except to come to light.[u] 23 Anyone who has ears to hear ought to hear." 24 He also told them, "Take care what you hear. The measure with which you measure will be measured out to you, and still more will be given to you.[v] 25 To the one who has, more will be given; from the one who has not, even what he has will be taken away."[w]

***Seed Grows of Itself.*** 26 He said, "This is how it is with the kingdom of God;* it is as if a man were to scatter seed[x] on the land 27 and would sleep and rise night and day and the seed would sprout and grow, he knows not how. 28 Of its own accord the land yields fruit, first the blade, then the ear, then the full grain in the ear. 29 And when the grain is ripe, he wields the sickle at once, for the harvest has come."

***The Mustard Seed.*** 30[y] He said, "To what shall we compare the kingdom of God, or what parable can we use for it? 31 It is like a mustard seed that, when it is sown in the ground, is the smallest of all the seeds on the earth. 32* But once it is sown, it springs up and becomes the largest of plants and puts forth large branches, so that the birds of the sky can dwell in its shade." 33 With many such parables[z] he spoke the word to them as they were able to understand it. 34 Without parables he did not speak to them, but to his own disciples he explained everything in private.

***The Calming of a Storm at Sea.*** 35* On that day, as evening drew on, he said to them, "Let us cross to the other side."[a] 36 Leaving the crowd, they took him with them in the boat just as he was. And other boats were with him. 37 A violent squall came up and waves were breaking over the boat, so that it was already filling up. 38 Jesus was in the stern, asleep on a cushion. They woke him and said to him, "Teacher, do you not care that we are perishing?" 39 He woke up, rebuked the wind, and said to the sea, "Quiet! Be still!"* The wind ceased and there was great calm. 40 Then he asked them, "Why are you terrified? Do you not yet have faith?"

sented in parables and the truth remains hidden; for the latter the parable is interpreted and the mystery is partially revealed because of their faith; see notes on Mt 13:11 and Mt 13:13.

**4:13–20** See note on Mt 13:18–23.

**4:26–29** Only Mark records the parable of the seed's growth. Sower and harvester are the same. The emphasis is on the power of the seed to grow of itself without human intervention (Mk 4:27). Mysteriously it produces **blade** and **ear** and **full grain** (Mk 4:28). Thus the kingdom of God initiated by Jesus in proclaiming the word develops quietly yet powerfully until it is fully established by him at the final judgment (Mk 4:29); cf. Rev 14:15.

**4:32** The universality of the kingdom of God is indicated here; cf. Ez 17:23; 31:6; Dn 4:17–19.

**4:35–5:43** After the chapter on parables, Mark narrates four miracle stories: Mk 4:35–41; 5:1–20; and two joined together in Mk 5:21–43. See also notes on Mt 8:23–34 and 9:8–26.

**4:39 Quiet! Be still!:** as in the case of silencing a demon (Mk 1:25), Jesus rebukes the wind and subdues the turbulence of the sea by a mere word; see note on Mt 8:26.

**4:41** Jesus is here depicted as exercising power over wind and sea. In the Christian community this event was seen as a sign of Jesus' saving presence amid persecutions that threatened its existence.

*q:* Is 6:9; Jn 12:40; Acts 28:26; Rom 11:8. *r:* Mt 13:18–23; Lk 8:11–15. *s:* Lk 8:16–18. *t:* Mt 5:15; Lk 11:33. *u:* Mt 10:26; Lk 12:2. *v:* Mt 7:2; Lk 6:38. *w:* Mt 13:12; Lk 19:26. *x:* Jas 5:7. *y:* Mt 13:31–32; Lk 13:18–19. *z:* Mt 13:34. *a:* Mt 8:18, 23–37; Lk 8:22–25.

41*[b] They were filled with great awe and said to one another, "Who then is this whom even wind and sea obey?"

## CHAPTER 5

See RG 296–97

***The Healing of the Gerasene Demoniac.*** 1*[c] They came to the other side of the sea, to the territory of the Gerasenes. 2 When he got out of the boat, at once a man* from the tombs who had an unclean spirit met him. 3 The man had been dwelling among the tombs, and no one could restrain him any longer, even with a chain. 4 In fact, he had frequently been bound with shackles and chains, but the chains had been pulled apart by him and the shackles smashed, and no one was strong enough to subdue him. 5 Night and day among the tombs and on the hillsides he was always crying out and bruising himself with stones. 6 Catching sight of Jesus from a distance, he ran up and prostrated himself before him, 7 crying out in a loud voice, "What have you to do with me,* Jesus, Son of the Most High God? I adjure you by God, do not torment me!" 8 (He had been saying to him, "Unclean spirit, come out of the man!") 9* He asked him, "What is your name?" He replied, "Legion is my name. There are many of us."[d] 10 And he pleaded earnestly with him not to drive them away from that territory.

11 Now a large herd of swine* was feeding there on the hillside. 12 And they pleaded with him, "Send us into the swine. Let us enter them." 13 And he let them, and the unclean spirits came out and entered the swine. The herd of about two thousand rushed down a steep bank into the sea, where they were drowned. 14 The swineherds ran away and reported the incident in the town and throughout the countryside. And people came out to see what had happened. 15 As they approached Jesus, they caught sight of the man who had been possessed by Legion, sitting there clothed and in his right mind. And they were seized with fear. 16 Those who witnessed the incident explained to them what had happened to the possessed man and to the swine. 17 Then they began to beg him to leave their district. 18 As he was getting into the boat, the man who had been possessed pleaded to remain with him. 19 But he would not permit him but told him instead, "Go home* to your family and announce to them all that the Lord in his pity has done for you." 20 Then the man went off and began to proclaim in the Decapolis what Jesus had done for him; and all were amazed.

***Jairus's Daughter and the Woman with a Hemorrhage.**** 21 When Jesus had crossed again [in the boat] to the other side, a large crowd gathered around him, and he stayed close to the sea.[e] 22 One of the synagogue officials, named Jairus, came forward.[f] Seeing him he fell at his feet 23 and pleaded earnestly with him, saying, "My daughter is at the point of death. Please, come lay your hands on her* that she may get well and live." 24 He went off with him, and a large crowd followed him and pressed upon him.

25 There was a woman afflicted with hemorrhages for twelve years. 26 She had suffered greatly at the hands of many doctors and had spent all that she had. Yet she was not helped

**5:1 The territory of the Gerasenes**: the reference is to pagan territory; cf. Is 65:1. Another reading is "Gadarenes"; see note on Mt 8:28.

**5:2–6** The man was an outcast from society, dominated by unclean spirits (Mk 5:8, 13), living among the tombs. The prostration before Jesus (Mk 5:6) indicates Jesus' power over evil spirits.

**5:7 What have you to do with me?**: cf. Mk 1:24 and see note on Jn 2:4.

**5:9 Legion is my name**: the demons were numerous and the condition of the possessed man was extremely serious; cf. Mt 12:45.

**5:11 Herd of swine**: see note on Mt 8:30.

**5:19 Go home**: Jesus did not accept the man's request **to remain with him** as a disciple (Mk 5:18), yet invited him to announce to his own people what the Lord had done for him, i.e., proclaim the gospel message to his pagan family; cf. Mk 1:14, 39; 3:14; 13:10.

**5:21–43** The story of the raising to life of Jairus's daughter is divided into two parts: Mk 5:21–24; 5:35–43. Between these two separated parts the account of the cure of the hemorrhage victim (Mk 5:25–34) is interposed. This technique of intercalating or sandwiching one story within another occurs several times in Mk 3:19b–21; 3:22–30; 3:31–35; 6:6b–13; 6:14–29; 6:30; 11:12–14; 11:15–19; 11:20–25; 14:53; 14:54; 14:55–65; 14:66–73.

**5:23 Lay your hands on her**: this act for the purpose of healing is frequent in Mk 6:5; 7:32–35; 8:23–25; 16:18 and is also found in Mt 9:18; Lk 4:40; 13:13; Acts 9:17; 28:8.

*b:* 1:27. *c:* Mt 8:28–34; Lk 8:26–39. *d:* Mt 12:45; Lk 8:2; 11:26. *e:* 2:13. *f:* Mt 9:18–26; Lk 8:41–56.

but only grew worse. [27]She had heard about Jesus and came up behind him in the crowd and touched his cloak. [28]* She said, "If I but touch his clothes, I shall be cured." [29]Immediately her flow of blood dried up. She felt in her body that she was healed of her affliction. [30]Jesus, aware at once that power had gone out from him, turned around in the crowd and asked, "Who has touched my clothes?" [31]But his disciples said to him, "You see how the crowd is pressing upon you, and yet you ask, 'Who touched me?' " [32]And he looked around to see who had done it. [33]The woman, realizing what had happened to her, approached in fear and trembling. She fell down before Jesus and told him the whole truth. [34]He said to her, "Daughter, your faith has saved you. Go in peace and be cured of your affliction."[g]

[35]* While he was still speaking, people from the synagogue official's house arrived and said, "Your daughter has died; why trouble the teacher any longer?" [36]Disregarding the message that was reported, Jesus said to the synagogue official, "Do not be afraid; just have faith." [37]He did not allow anyone to accompany him inside except Peter, James, and John, the brother of James. [38]When they arrived at the house of the synagogue official, he caught sight of a commotion, people weeping and wailing loudly. [39]* [h] So he went in and said to them, "Why this commotion and weeping? The child is not dead but asleep." [40]And they ridiculed him. Then he put them all out. He took along the child's father and mother and those who were with him and entered the room where the child was. [41]* He took the child by the hand and said to her, *"Talitha koum,"* which means, "Little girl, I say to you, arise!" [42]The girl, a child of twelve, arose immediately and walked around. [At that] they were utterly astounded. [43]He gave strict orders that no one should know this and said that she should be given something to eat.

## CHAPTER 6

See RG 296-97

***The Rejection at Nazareth.*** [1] [i] He departed from there and came to his native place,* accompanied by his disciples. [2]* When the sabbath came he began to teach in the synagogue, and many who heard him were astonished. They said, "Where did this man get all this? What kind of wisdom has been given him? What mighty deeds are wrought by his hands! [3] [j] Is he not the carpenter,* the son of Mary, and the brother of James and Joses and Judas and Simon? And are not his sisters here with us?" And they took offense at him. [4]* [k] Jesus said to them, "A prophet is not without honor except in his native place and among his own kin and in

**5:28** Both in the case of Jairus and his daughter (Mk 5:23) and in the case of the hemorrhage victim, the inner conviction that physical contact (Mk 5:30) accompanied by faith in Jesus' saving power could effect a cure was rewarded.

**5:35** The faith of Jairus was put to a twofold test: (1) that his daughter might be cured and, now that she had died, (2) that she might be restored to life. His faith contrasts with the lack of faith of the crowd.

**5:39 Not dead but asleep**: the New Testament often refers to death as sleep (Mt 27:52; Jn 11:11; 1 Cor 15:6; 1 Thes 4:13–15); see note on Mt 9:24.

**5:41 Arise**: the Greek verb *egeirein* is the verb generally used to express resurrection from death (Mk 6:14, 16; Mt 11:5; Lk 7:14) and Jesus' own resurrection (Mk 16:6; Mt 28:6; Lk 24:6).

**6:1 His native place**: the Greek word *patris* here refers to Nazareth (cf. Mk 1:9; Lk 4:16, 23–24) though it can also mean native land.

**6:2–6** See note on Mt 13:54–58.

**6:3 Is he not the carpenter?**: no other gospel calls Jesus a carpenter. Some witnesses have "the carpenter's son," as in Mt 13:55. **Son of Mary**: contrary to Jewish custom, which calls a man the son of his father, this expression may reflect Mark's own faith that God is the Father of Jesus (Mk 1:1, 11; 8:38; 13:32; 14:36). **The brother of James . . . Simon**: in Semitic usage, the terms "brother," "sister" are applied not only to children of the same parents, but to nephews, nieces, cousins, half-brothers, and half-sisters; cf. Gn 14:16; 29:15; Lv 10:4. While one cannot suppose that the meaning of a Greek word should be sought in the first place from Semitic usage, the Septuagint often translates the Hebrew *'āh* by the Greek word *adelphos*, "brother," as in the cited passages, a fact that may argue for a similar breadth of meaning in some New Testament passages. For instance, there is no doubt that in v 17, "brother" is used of Philip, who was actually the half-brother of Herod Antipas. On the other hand, Mark may have understood the terms literally; see also Mk 3:31–32; Mt 12:46; 13:55–56; Lk 8:19; Jn 7:3, 5. The question of meaning here would not have arisen but for the faith of the church in Mary's perpetual virginity.

**6:4 A prophet is not without honor except . . . in his own house**: a saying that finds parallels in other literatures, especially Jewish and Greek, but without reference to a prophet. Comparing himself to previous Hebrew prophets whom the people rejected, Jesus intimates his own eventual rejection by the nation especially in view of the dishonor his own relatives had shown him (Mk 3:21) and now his townspeople as well.

*g:* Lk 7:30. *h:* Acts 9:40. *i:* Mt 13:54–58; Lk 4:16–30. *j:* 15:40; Mt 12:46; Jn 6:42. *k:* Jn 4:44.

his own house.” 5 So he was not able to perform any mighty deed there,* apart from curing a few sick people by laying his hands on
them. 6 He was amazed at their lack of faith.

*The Mission of the Twelve.* He went around
to the villages in the vicinity teaching. 7[l] He
summoned the Twelve* and began to send
them out two by two and gave them authority over unclean spirits. 8* He instructed them
to take nothing for the journey but a walking
stick—no food, no sack, no money in their
belts. 9 They were, however, to wear sandals
but not a second tunic. 10* He said to them,
“Wherever you enter a house, stay there until you leave from there. 11 Whatever place
does not welcome you or listen to you, leave
there and shake the dust off your feet in testimony against them.” 12 So they went off and
preached repentance. 13* They drove out
many demons, and they anointed with oil
many who were sick[m] and cured them.

*Herod’s Opinion of Jesus.** 14 King Herod*
heard about it, for his fame had become
widespread, and people were saying,[n] “John
the Baptist has been raised from the dead;
that is why mighty powers are at work in
him.”[o] 15 Others were saying, “He is Elijah”;
still others, “He is a prophet like any of the
prophets.”[p] 16 But when Herod learned of it,
he said, “It is John whom I beheaded. He
has been raised up.”

*The Death of John the Baptist.** 17 Herod
was the one who had John arrested and
bound in prison on account of Herodias, the
wife of his brother Philip, whom he had married.[q] 18 John had said to Herod, “It is not
lawful for you to have your brother’s wife.”[r]
19 Herodias* harbored a grudge against him
and wanted to kill him but was unable to do
so. 20 Herod feared John, knowing him to be
a righteous and holy man, and kept him in
custody. When he heard him speak he was
very much perplexed, yet he liked to listen to
him. 21 She had an opportunity one day when
Herod, on his birthday, gave a banquet for
his courtiers, his military officers, and the
leading men of Galilee. 22 Herodias’s own
daughter came in and performed a dance that
delighted Herod and his guests. The king
said to the girl, “Ask of me whatever you
wish and I will grant it to you.” 23 He even
swore [many things] to her, “I will grant you
whatever you ask of me, even to half of my
kingdom.”[s] 24 She went out and said to her
mother, “What shall I ask for?” She replied,
“The head of John the Baptist.” 25 The girl
hurried back to the king’s presence and
made her request, “I want you to give me at
once on a platter the head of John the Baptist.” 26 The king was deeply distressed, but
because of his oaths and the guests he did
not wish to break his word to her. 27[t] So he

**6:5 He was not able to perform any mighty deed there**: according to Mark, Jesus’ power could not take effect because of a person’s lack of faith.

**6:7–13** The preparation for the mission of the Twelve is seen in the call (1) of the first disciples to be fishers of men (Mk 1:16–20), (2) then of the Twelve set apart to be with Jesus and to receive authority to preach and expel demons (Mk 3:13–19). Now they are given the specific mission to exercise that authority in word and power as representatives of Jesus during the time of their formation.

**6:8–9** In Mark the use of a **walking stick** (Mk 6:8) and **sandals** (Mk 6:9) is permitted, but not in Mt 10:10 nor in Lk 10:4. Mark does not mention any prohibition to visit pagan territory and to enter Samaritan towns. These differences indicate a certain adaptation to conditions in and outside of Palestine and suggest in Mark’s account a later activity in the church. For the rest, Jesus required of his apostles a total dependence on God for food and shelter; cf. Mk 6:35–44; 8:1–9.

**6:10–11** Remaining in the same house as a guest (Mk 6:10) rather than moving to another offering greater comfort avoided any impression of seeking advantage for oneself and prevented dishonor to one’s host. Shaking the dust off one’s feet served as testimony against those who rejected the call to repentance.

**6:13 Anointed with oil . . . cured them**: a common medicinal remedy, but seen here as a vehicle of divine power for healing.

**6:14–16** The various opinions about Jesus anticipate the theme of his identity that reaches its climax in Mk 8:27–30.

**6:14 King Herod**: see note on Mt 14:1.

**6:17–29** Similarities are to be noted between Mark’s account of the imprisonment and death of John the Baptist in this pericope, and that of the passion of Jesus (Mk 15:1–47). Herod and Pilate, each in turn, acknowledges the holiness of life of one over whom he unjustly exercises the power of condemnation and death (Mk 6:26–27; 15:9–10, 14–15). The hatred of Herodias toward John parallels that of the Jewish leaders toward Jesus. After the deaths of John and of Jesus, well-disposed persons request the bodies of the victims of Herod and of Pilate in turn to give them respectful burial (Mk 6:29; 15:45–46).

**6:19 Herodias**: see note on Mt 14:3.

*l:* Mt 10:1, 9–14; Lk 9:15; 10:4–11. *m:* Jas 5:14. *n:* Mt 14:1–12. *o:* Lk 9:7–8. *p:* Mt 16:14. *q:* Lk 3:19–20. *r:* Lv 18:16. *s:* Est 5:3. *t:* Lk 9:9.

## The Problem of the Disciples

MARK'S PORTRAIT OF the twelve is highly problematic. On the one hand, they come when Jesus calls them; they do not hesitate to leave their boats, their property, and their families (1:16–20; 2:14; 10:28). They successfully complete their first mission, during which they perform exorcisms, anoint the sick with oil, and heal (6:12–30).

On the other hand, they consistently fail to understand Jesus' teachings, exhortations, and desires. As early as Mark 1:37, they interrupt Jesus, who has withdrawn from the crowds for prayer and solitude. Mark 4:13 recounts Jesus' impatience with their lack of understanding of the parables. In Mark 4:40, following the calming of the storm, Jesus asks, "Why are you terrified? Do you not yet have faith?" Upon the healing of the woman with the hemorrhages, they chide Jesus: "You see how the crowd is pressing upon you, and yet you ask, 'Who touched me?'" (5:31). The disciples are unable to recognize Jesus' power; as Mark states, "They were completely astounded. They had not understood the incident of the loaves. On the contrary, their hearts were hardened" (6:51–52). In Mark 7:17–18, confused by Jesus' discussion of dietary regulations, the twelve ask Jesus about his parable. Jesus responds, "Are you even likewise without understanding?" Following the miraculous feedings of first 5,000 and then 4,000, the disciples worry in Mark 8:16 that they have no bread.

In the latter half of the Gospel, the failure of the twelve intensifies. They are unable to accept the passion predictions; they have insufficient faith to heal the child with a mute spirit (9:18–19, 28–29); without warrant they reprove the exorcist who heals in Jesus' name (9:38–41); they attempt to prevent children from approaching Jesus (10:13–16); they yearn for positions of honor rather than service (10:35–40); and they display anger with each other (10:41–44). Judas betrays Jesus, Peter denies him, and the last collective action of the disciples in the Gospel is to forsake Jesus by fleeing from Gethsemane (14:50). Even the women who follow him from Galilee come to anoint the body: Had they known of, or believed in, the resurrection, this would not have been necessary. The last sentence of the original Gospel ends with the women fleeing from the tomb: "They said nothing to anyone, for they were afraid" (16:8).

Scholars debate the meaning of Mark's depiction of Jesus' followers. Perhaps Mark wanted the twelve to represent the range of believers; members of Mark's community may have doubted, denied Jesus under pressure of persecution, or failed to grasp the need for service. Perhaps Mark wanted readers to first to identify with the disciples and then, finally, to reject their misconceptions of Jesus' nature and mission.

promptly dispatched an executioner with orders to bring back his head. He went off and beheaded him in the prison. 28 He brought in the head on a platter and gave it to the girl. The girl in turn gave it to her mother. 29 When his disciples heard about it, they came and took his body and laid it in a tomb.

***The Return of the Twelve.*** 30 The apostles* gathered together with Jesus and reported all they had done and taught.[u] 31* He said to

**6:30 Apostles**: here, and in some manuscripts at Mk 3:14, Mark calls apostles (i.e., those sent forth) the Twelve whom Jesus sends as his emissaries, empowering them to preach, to expel demons, and to cure the sick (Mk 6:13). Only after Pentecost is the title used in the technical sense.

**6:31–34** The withdrawal of Jesus with his disciples to a desert place to rest attracts a great number of people to follow them. Toward this people of the new exodus Jesus is moved with pity; he satisfies their spiritual hunger by teaching them many things, thus gradually showing himself the faithful shepherd of a new Israel; cf. Nm 27:17; Ez 34:15.

*u*: Lk 9:10.

them, "Come away by yourselves to a deserted place and rest a while." People were
coming and going in great numbers, and
they had no opportunity even to eat.[v] 32 So
they went off in the boat by themselves to a
deserted place.[w] 33 People saw them leaving
and many came to know about it. They hastened there on foot from all the towns and arrived at the place before them.

***The Feeding of the Five Thousand.***
34 When he disembarked and saw the vast
crowd, his heart was moved with pity for
them, for they were like sheep without a
shepherd; and he began to teach them many
things. 35* By now it was already late and his
disciples approached him and said, "This is
a deserted place and it is already very late.
36 Dismiss them so that they can go to the
surrounding farms and villages and buy
themselves something to eat." 37 He said to
them in reply, "Give them some food yourselves." But they said to him, "Are we to buy
two hundred days' wages worth of food and
give it to them to eat?" 38 He asked them,
"How many loaves do you have? Go and
see." And when they had found out they
said, "Five loaves and two fish." 39 So he
gave orders to have them sit down in groups
on the green grass. 40* The people took their
places in rows by hundreds and by fifties.
41 Then, taking the five loaves and the two
fish and looking up to heaven, he said the
blessing, broke the loaves, and gave them to
[his] disciples to set before the people; he
also divided the two fish among them all.*
42 They all ate and were satisfied. 43 And they
picked up twelve wicker baskets full of fragments and what was left of the fish. 44 Those
who ate [of the loaves] were five thousand
men.

***The Walking on the Water.**** 45 Then he
made his disciples get into the boat[x] and precede him to the other side toward Bethsaida,* while he dismissed the crowd. 46* And
when he had taken leave of them, he went
off to the mountain to pray. 47 When it was
evening, the boat was far out on the sea and
he was alone on shore. 48 Then he saw that
they were tossed about while rowing, for the
wind was against them. About the fourth
watch of the night, he came toward them
walking on the sea.* He meant to pass by
them. 49 But when they saw him walking on
the sea, they thought it was a ghost and cried
out. 50* They had all seen him and were terrified. But at once he spoke with them,
"Take courage, it is I, do not be afraid!" 51 He
got into the boat with them and the wind
died down. They were [completely] astounded. 52 They had not understood the incident of the loaves.* On the contrary, their
hearts were hardened.[y]

***The Healings at Gennesaret.*** 53[z] After
making the crossing, they came to land at
Gennesaret and tied up there. 54 As they were
leaving the boat, people immediately recognized him. 55 They scurried about the surrounding country and began to bring in the

**6:35–44** See note on Mt 14:13–21. Compare this section with Mk 8:1–9. The various accounts of the multiplication of loaves and fishes, two each in Mark and in Matthew and one each in Luke and in John, indicate the wide interest of the early church in their eucharistic gatherings; see, e.g., Mk 6:41; 8:6; 14:22; and recall also the sign of bread in Ex 16; Dt 8:3–16; Ps 78:24–25; 105:40; Wis 16:20–21.

**6:40 The people . . . in rows by hundreds and by fifties**: reminiscent of the groupings of Israelites encamped in the desert (Ex 18:21–25) and of the wilderness tradition of the prophets depicting the transformation of the wasteland into pastures where the true shepherd feeds his flock (Ez 34:25–26) and makes his people beneficiaries of messianic grace.

**6:41** On the language of this verse as eucharistic (cf. Mk 14:22), see notes on Mt 14:19, 20. Jesus observed the Jewish table ritual of blessing God before partaking of food.

**6:45–52** See note on Mt 14:22–33.

**6:45 To the other side toward Bethsaida**: a village at the northeastern shore of the Sea of Galilee.

**6:46 He went off to the mountain to pray**: see Mk 1:35–38. In Jn 6:15 Jesus withdrew to evade any involvement in the false messianic hopes of the multitude.

**6:48 Walking on the sea**: see notes on Mt 14:22–33 and on Jn 6:19.

**6:50 It is I, do not be afraid!**: literally, "I am." This may reflect the divine revelatory formula of Ex 3:14; Is 41:4, 10, 14; 43:1–3, 10, 13. Mark implies the hidden identity of Jesus as Son of God.

**6:52 They had not understood . . . the loaves**: the revelatory character of this sign and that of the walking on the sea completely escaped the disciples. **Their hearts were hardened**: in Mk 3:5–6 hardness of heart was attributed to those who did not accept Jesus and plotted his death. Here the same disposition prevents the disciples from comprehending Jesus' self-revelation through signs; cf. Mk 8:17.

*v:* 3:20; Mt 14:13; Lk 9:10. *w:* Mt 14:13–21; Lk 9:10–17; Jn 6:1–13. *x:* Mt 14:22–32; Jn 6:15–21. *y:* 4:13. *z:* Mt 14:34–36.

sick on mats to wherever they heard he was.
56 Whatever villages or towns or countryside
he entered, they laid the sick in the marketplaces and begged him that they might touch
only the tassel on his cloak; and as many as
touched it were healed.[a]

## CHAPTER 7

See RG 296–97

*The Tradition of the Elders.** 1 Now
when the Pharisees with some scribes who
had come from Jerusalem gathered around
him,[b] 2 they observed that some of his disciples ate their meals with unclean, that is, unwashed, hands. 3 (For the Pharisees and, in
fact, all Jews, do not eat without carefully
washing their hands,* keeping the tradition
of the elders. 4 And on coming from the marketplace they do not eat without purifying
themselves. And there are many other things
that they have traditionally observed, the purification of cups and jugs and kettles [and
beds].) 5 So the Pharisees and scribes questioned him, "Why do your disciples not follow the tradition of the elders* but instead
eat a meal with unclean hands?" 6 He responded, "Well did Isaiah prophesy about
you hypocrites, as it is written:[c]

'This people honors me with their lips,
  but their hearts are far from me;
7 In vain do they worship me,
  teaching as doctrines human precepts.'

8 You disregard God's commandment but
cling to human tradition." 9 He went on to
say, "How well you have set aside the commandment of God in order to uphold your
tradition! 10 For Moses said, 'Honor your father and your mother,' and 'Whoever curses
father or mother shall die.'[d] 11 Yet you say, 'If
a person says to father or mother, "Any support you might have had from me is *qorban*"' * (meaning, dedicated to God), 12 you
allow him to do nothing more for his father
or mother. 13 You nullify the word of God in
favor of your tradition that you have handed
on. And you do many such things." 14[e] He
summoned the crowd again and said to
them, "Hear me, all of you, and understand.
15 Nothing that enters one from outside can
defile that person; but the things that come
out from within are what defile." *[16]**
17*[f] When he got home away from the
crowd his disciples questioned him about
the parable. 18 He said to them, "Are even
you likewise without understanding? Do
you not realize that everything that goes
into a person from outside cannot defile,
19*[g] since it enters not the heart but the
stomach and passes out into the latrine?"
(Thus he declared all foods clean.) 20 "But
what comes out of a person, that is what defiles. 21[h] From within people, from their
hearts, come evil thoughts, unchastity, theft,
murder, 22 adultery, greed, malice, deceit, licentiousness, envy, blasphemy, arrogance,
folly. 23 All these evils come from within
and they defile."

**7:1–23** See note on Mt 15:1–20. Against the Pharisees' narrow, legalistic, and external practices of piety in matters of purification (Mk 7:2–5), external worship (Mk 7:6–7), and observance of commandments, Jesus sets in opposition the true moral intent of the divine law (Mk 7:8–13). But he goes beyond contrasting the law and Pharisaic interpretation of it. The parable of Mk 7:14–15 in effect sets aside the law itself in respect to clean and unclean food. He thereby opens the way for unity between Jew and Gentile in the kingdom of God, intimated by Jesus' departure for pagan territory beyond Galilee. For similar contrast see Mk 2:1–3:6; 3:20–35; 6:1–6.

**7:3 Carefully washing their hands**: refers to ritual purification.

**7:5 Tradition of the elders**: the body of detailed, unwritten, human laws regarded by the scribes and Pharisees to have the same binding force as that of the Mosaic law; cf. Gal 1:14.

**7:11 Qorban**: a formula for a gift to God, dedicating the offering to the temple, so that the giver might continue to use it for himself but not give it to others, even needy parents.

**7:16** Mk 7:16, "Anyone who has ears to hear ought to hear," is omitted because it is lacking in some of the best Greek manuscripts and was probably transferred here by scribes from Mk 4:9, 23.

**7:17 Away from the crowd . . . the parable**: in this context of privacy the term *parable* refers to something hidden, about to be revealed to the disciples; cf. Mk 4:10–11, 34. Jesus sets the Mosaic food laws in the context of the kingdom of God where they are abrogated, and he declares moral defilement the only cause of uncleanness.

**7:19 (Thus he declared all foods clean)**: if this bold declaration goes back to Jesus, its force was not realized among Jewish Christians in the early church; cf. Acts 10:1–11:18.

---

*a:* 5:27–28; Acts 5:15. *b:* Mt 15:1–20. *c:* Is 29:13. *d:* Ex 21:17; Lv 20:9; Dt 5:16; Eph 6:2. *e:* Mt 15:10–20. *f:* 4:10, 13. *g:* Acts 10:15. *h:* Jer 17:9.

***The Syrophoenician Woman's Faith.***
24[i] From that place he went off to the district
of Tyre.* He entered a house and wanted no
one to know about it, but he could not escape
notice. 25 Soon a woman whose daughter had
an unclean spirit heard about him. She came
and fell at his feet. 26 The woman was a
Greek, a Syrophoenician by birth, and she
begged him to drive the demon out of her
daughter.[j] 27 He said to her, "Let the children
be fed first.* For it is not right to take the
food of the children and throw it to the
dogs." 28 She replied and said to him, "Lord,
even the dogs under the table eat the children's scraps." 29 Then he said to her, "For
saying this, you may go. The demon has
gone out of your daughter." 30 When the
woman went home, she found the child lying in bed and the demon gone.

***The Healing of a Deaf Man.*** 31[k] Again he
left the district of Tyre and went by way of
Sidon to the Sea of Galilee, into the district
of the Decapolis. 32 And people brought to
him a deaf man who had a speech impediment and begged him to lay his hand on him.
33 He took him off by himself away from the
crowd. He put his finger into the man's ears
and, spitting, touched his tongue; 34 then he
looked up to heaven and groaned, and said to
him, "*Ephphatha*!" (that is, "Be opened!")
35 And [immediately] the man's ears were
opened, his speech impediment was removed, and he spoke plainly. 36* He ordered
them not to tell anyone. But the more he ordered them not to, the more they proclaimed
it. 37 They were exceedingly astonished and
they said, "He has done all things well. He
makes the deaf hear and [the] mute speak."[l]

## CHAPTER 8

See RG 297–98

***The Feeding of the Four Thousand.**** 1 In
those days when there again was a great
crowd without anything to eat,[m] he summoned
the disciples and said, 2 "My heart is moved
with pity for the crowd, because they have
been with me now for three days and have
nothing to eat. 3 If I send them away hungry to
their homes, they will collapse on the way, and
some of them have come a great distance."
4 His disciples answered him, "Where can anyone get enough bread to satisfy them here in
this deserted place?" 5 Still he asked them,
"How many loaves do you have?" "Seven,"
they replied. 6* He ordered the crowd to sit
down on the ground. Then, taking the seven
loaves he gave thanks, broke them, and gave
them to his disciples to distribute, and they
distributed them to the crowd. 7 They also had
a few fish. He said the blessing over them and
ordered them distributed also. 8 They ate and
were satisfied. They picked up the fragments
left over—seven baskets. 9 There were about
four thousand people.

He dismissed them 10 and got into the boat
with his disciples and came to the region of
Dalmanutha.

***The Demand for a Sign.*** 11* The Pharisees
came forward and began to argue with him,[n]
seeking from him a sign from heaven to test
him.[o] 12 He sighed from the depth of his spirit

**7:24–37** The withdrawal of Jesus to the district of Tyre may have been for a respite (Mk 7:24), but he soon moved onward to Sidon and, by way of the Sea of Galilee, to the Decapolis. These districts provided a Gentile setting for the extension of his ministry of healing because the people there acknowledged his power (Mk 7:29, 37). The actions attributed to Jesus (Mk 7:33–35) were also used by healers of the time.

**7:27–28** The figure of a household in which children at table are fed first and then their leftover food is given to the dogs under the table is used effectively to acknowledge the prior claim of the Jews to the ministry of Jesus; however, Jesus accedes to the Gentile woman's plea for the cure of her afflicted daughter because of her faith.

**7:36 The more they proclaimed it**: the same verb *proclaim* attributed here to the crowd in relation to the miracles of Jesus is elsewhere used in Mark for the preaching of the gospel on the part of Jesus, of his disciples, and of the Christian community (Mk 1:14; 13:10; 14:9). Implied in the action of the crowd is a recognition of the salvific mission of Jesus; see note on Mt 11:5–6.

**8:1–10** The two accounts of the multiplication of loaves and fishes (Mk 8:1–10; 6:31–44) have eucharistic significance. Their similarity of structure and themes but dissimilarity of detail are considered by many to refer to a single event that, however, developed in two distinct traditions, one Jewish Christian and the other Gentile Christian, since Jesus in Mark's presentation (Mk 7:24–37) has extended his saving mission to the Gentiles.

**8:6** See note on Mk 6:41.

**8:11–12** The objection of the Pharisees that Jesus' miracles are unsatisfactory for proving the arrival of God's kingdom is comparable to the request of the crowd for a sign in Jn 6:30–31. Jesus' response shows that a sign originating in human demand will not be provided; cf. Nm 14:11, 22.

---

*i:* Mt 15:21–28. *j:* Mt 8:29. *k:* Mt 15:29–31. *l:* Mt 15:31. *m:* 6:34–44; Mt 15:32–39. *n:* Mt 12:38–39; 16:1–4. *o:* Lk 11:16.

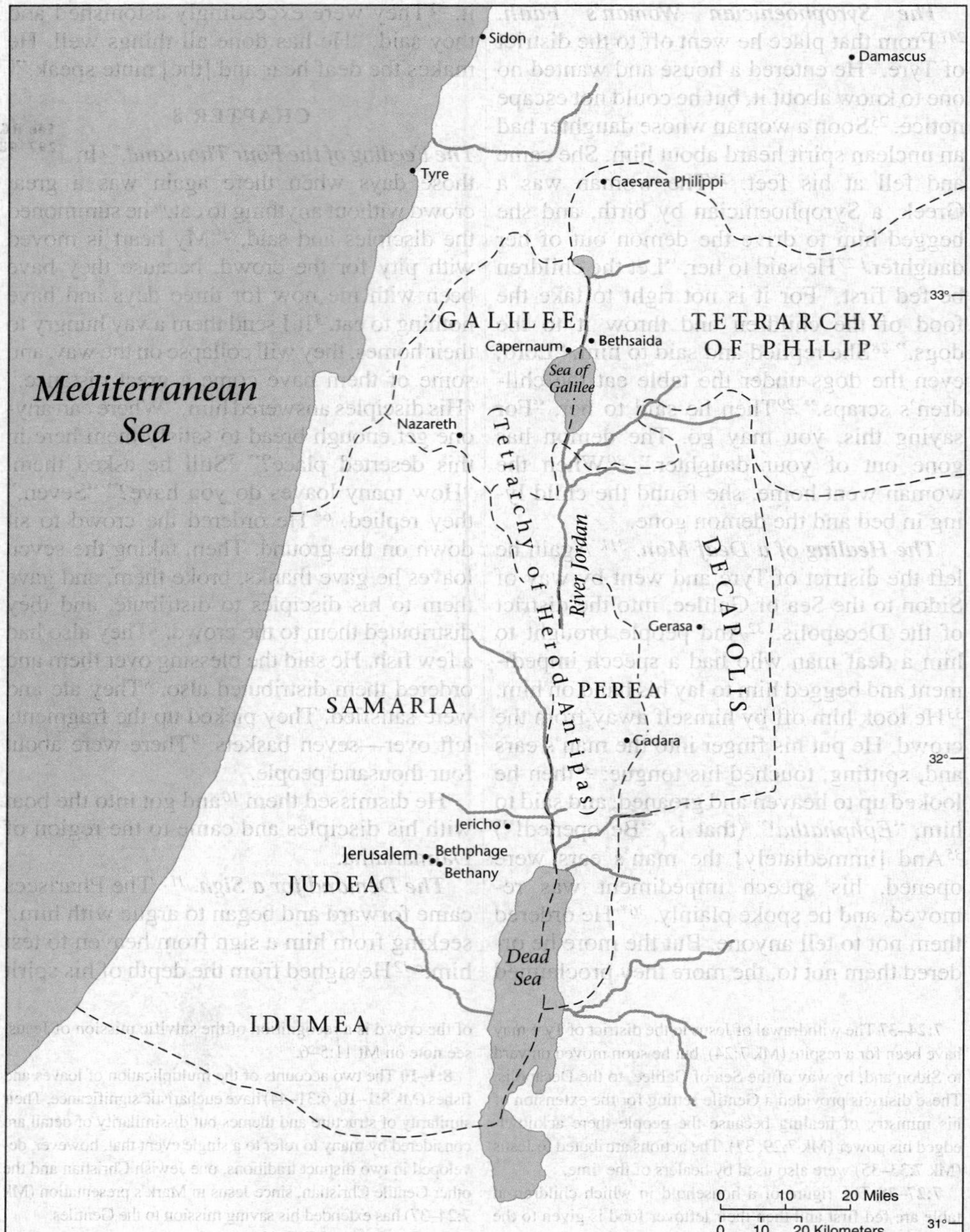


**Sites of Jesus' Travels in Galilee and Vicinity**

and said, "Why does this generation seek a sign? Amen, I say to you, no sign will be given to this generation." [13]Then he left them, got into the boat again, and went off to the other shore.

***The Leaven of the Pharisees.*** [14][p] They had forgotten to bring bread, and they had only one loaf with them in the boat. [15]* He enjoined them, "Watch out, guard against the leaven of the Pharisees and the leaven of Herod." [16]They concluded among themselves that it was because they had no bread. [17]When he became aware of this he said to them, "Why do you conclude that it is because you have no bread? Do you not yet understand or comprehend? Are your hearts hardened?[q] [18]Do you have eyes and not see, ears and not hear? And do you not remember,[r] [19]when I broke the five loaves for the five thousand, how many wicker baskets full of fragments you picked up?" They answered him, "Twelve." [20]"When I broke the seven loaves for the four thousand, how many full baskets of fragments did you pick up?" They answered [him], "Seven." [21]He said to them, "Do you still not understand?"

***The Blind Man of Bethsaida.**** [22]When they arrived at Bethsaida, they brought to him a blind man and begged him to touch him. [23]He took the blind man by the hand and led him outside the village. Putting spittle on his eyes he laid his hands on him and asked, "Do you see anything?"[s] [24]Looking up he replied, "I see people looking like trees and walking." [25]Then he laid hands on his eyes a second time and he saw clearly; his sight was restored and he could see everything distinctly. [26]Then he sent him home and said, "Do not even go into the village."

## III. The Mystery Begins to Be Revealed

***Peter's Confession About Jesus.**** [27]Now Jesus and his disciples set out for the villages of Caesarea Philippi.[t] Along the way he asked his disciples, "Who do people say that I am?" [28]They said in reply, "John the Baptist, others Elijah, still others one of the prophets." [29]And he asked them, "But who do you say that I am?" Peter said to him in reply, "You are the Messiah." [30]Then he warned them not to tell anyone about him.

***The First Prediction of the Passion.*** [31][u] He began to teach them that the Son of Man* must suffer greatly and be rejected by the elders, the chief priests, and the scribes, and be killed, and rise after three days. [32]He spoke this openly. Then Peter took him aside and began to rebuke him. [33]At this he turned

**8:15 The leaven of the Pharisees . . . of Herod**: the corruptive action of leaven (1 Cor 5:6–8; Gal 5:9) was an apt symbol of the evil dispositions both of the Pharisees (Mk 8:11–13; 7:5–13) and of Herod (Mk 6:14–29) toward Jesus. The disciples of Jesus are warned against sharing such rebellious attitudes toward Jesus; cf. Mk 8:17, 21.

**8:22–26** Jesus' actions and the gradual cure of the blind man probably have the same purpose as in the case of the deaf man (Mk 7:31–37). Some commentators regard the cure as an intended symbol of the gradual enlightenment of the disciples concerning Jesus' messiahship.

**8:27–30** This episode is the turning point in Mark's account of Jesus in his public ministry. Popular opinions concur in regarding him as a prophet. The disciples by contrast believe him to be the Messiah. Jesus acknowledges this identification but prohibits them from making his messianic office known to avoid confusing it with ambiguous contemporary ideas on the nature of that office. See further the notes on Mt 16:13–20.

**8:31 Son of Man**: an enigmatic title. It is used in Dn 7:13–14 has a symbol of "the saints of the Most High," the faithful Israelites who receive the everlasting kingdom from the Ancient One (God). They are represented by a human figure that contrasts with the various beasts who represent the previous kingdoms of the earth. In the Jewish apocryphal books of 1 Enoch and 4 Ezra the "Son of Man" is not, as in Daniel, a group, but a unique figure of extraordinary spiritual endowments, who will be revealed as the one through whom the everlasting kingdom decreed by God will be established. It is possible though doubtful that this individualization of the Son of Man figure had been made in Jesus' time, and therefore his use of the title in that sense is questionable. Of itself, this expression means simply a human being, or, indefinitely, someone, and there are evidences of this use in pre-Christian times. Its use in the New Testament is probably due to Jesus' speaking of himself in that way, "a human being," and the later church's taking this in the sense of the Jewish apocrypha and applying it to him with that meaning. **Rejected by the elders, the chief priests, and the scribes**: the supreme council called the Sanhedrin was made up of seventy-one members of these three groups and presided over by the high priest. It exercised authority over the Jews in religious matters. See note on Mt 8:20.

*p:* Mt 16:5–12; Lk 12:1. *q:* 4:13. *r:* Jer 5:21; Ez 12:2. *s:* 7:33; Jn 9:6. *t:* Mt 16:13–20; Lk 9:18–21. *u:* Mt 16:21–27; Lk 9:22–26.

around and, looking at his disciples, rebuked Peter and said, "Get behind me, Satan. You are thinking not as God does, but as human beings do."

***The Conditions of Discipleship.*** [34]He summoned the crowd with his disciples and said* to them, "Whoever wishes to come after me must deny himself, take up his cross, and follow me.[v] [35]For whoever wishes to save his life will lose it, but whoever loses his life for my sake and that of the gospel* will save it.[w] [36]What profit is there for one to gain the whole world and forfeit his life? [37]What could one give in exchange for his life? [38]Whoever is ashamed of me and of my words in this faithless and sinful generation, the Son of Man will be ashamed of when he comes in his Father's glory with the holy angels."[x]

## CHAPTER 9

See RG 297–98

[1]*[y] He also said to them, "Amen, I say to you, there are some standing here who will not taste death until they see that the kingdom of God has come in power."

***The Transfiguration of Jesus.**** [2]After six days Jesus took Peter, James, and John and led them up a high mountain apart by themselves.[z] And he was transfigured before them, [3]and his clothes became dazzling white, such as no fuller on earth could bleach them. [4]Then Elijah appeared to them along with Moses, and they were conversing with Jesus. [5]* Then Peter said to Jesus in reply, "Rabbi, it is good that we are here! Let us make three tents: one for you, one for Moses, and one for Elijah." [6]He hardly knew what to say, they were so terrified. [7]Then a cloud came, casting a shadow over them;* then from the cloud came a voice, "This is my beloved Son. Listen to him." [8]Suddenly, looking around, they no longer saw anyone but Jesus alone with them.

***The Coming of Elijah.**** [9]As they were coming down from the mountain, he charged them not to relate what they had seen to anyone, except when the Son of Man had risen from the dead.[a] [10]So they kept the matter to themselves, questioning what rising from the dead meant. [11][b] Then they asked him, "Why do the scribes say that Elijah must come first?" [12]He told them, "Elijah will indeed come first and restore all things, yet how is it written regarding the Son of Man that he must suffer greatly and be treated with contempt? [13]But I tell you that Elijah has come and they did to him whatever they pleased, as it is written of him."[c]

***The Healing of a Boy with a Demon.****

**8:34–35** This utterance of Jesus challenges all believers to authentic discipleship and total commitment to himself through self-renunciation and acceptance of the cross of suffering, even to the sacrifice of life itself. **Whoever wishes to save his life will lose it . . . will save it**: an expression of the ambivalence of life and its contrasting destiny. Life seen as mere self-centered earthly existence and lived in denial of Christ ends in destruction, but when lived in loyalty to Christ, despite earthly death, it arrives at fullness of life.

**8:35 For my sake and that of the gospel**: Mark here, as at Mk 10:29 equates Jesus with the gospel.

**9:1 There are some standing . . . come in power**: understood by some to refer to the establishment by God's power of his kingdom on earth in and through the church; more likely, as understood by others, a reference to the imminent parousia.

**9:2–8** Mark and Mt 17:1 place the transfiguration of Jesus six days after the first prediction of his passion and death and his instruction to the disciples on the doctrine of the cross; Lk 9:28 has "about eight days." Thus the transfiguration counterbalances the prediction of the passion by affording certain of the disciples insight into the divine glory that Jesus possessed. His glory will overcome his death and that of his disciples; cf. 2 Cor 3:18; 2 Pt 1:16–19. The heavenly voice (Mk 9:7) prepares the disciples to understand that in the divine plan Jesus must die ignominiously before his messianic glory is made manifest; cf. Lk 24:25–27. See further the note on Mt 17:1–8.

**9:5** Moses and Elijah represent respectively law and prophecy in the Old Testament and are linked to Mount Sinai; cf. Ex 19:16–20:17; 1 Kgs 19:2, 8–14. They now appear with Jesus as witnesses to the fulfillment of the law and the prophets taking place in the person of Jesus as he appears in glory.

**9:7 A cloud came, casting a shadow over them**: even the disciples enter into the mystery of his glorification. In the Old Testament the cloud covered the meeting tent, indicating the Lord's presence in the midst of his people (Ex 40:34–35) and came to rest upon the temple in Jerusalem at the time of its dedication (1 Kgs 8:10).

**9:9–13** At the transfiguration of Jesus his disciples had seen Elijah. They were perplexed because, according to the rabbinical interpretation of Mal 3:23–24, Elijah was to come first. Jesus' response shows that Elijah has come, in the person of John the Baptist, to prepare for the day of the Lord. Jesus **must suffer greatly and be treated with contempt** (Mk 9:12) like the Baptist (Mk 9:13); cf. Mk 6:17–29.

*v:* Mt 10:38–39; 16:24–27; Lk 14:26–27. *w:* Jn 12:25. *x:* Mt 10:33; Lk 12:8. *y:* Mt 16:28; Lk 9:27. *z:* Mt 17:1–13; Lk 9:28–36. *a:* 8:31. *b:* Is 53:3; Mal 3:23. *c:* 1 Kgs 19:2–10.

14 When they came to the disciples,[d] they saw a large crowd around them and scribes arguing with them. 15 Immediately on seeing him, the whole crowd was utterly amazed. They ran up to him and greeted him. 16 He asked them, "What are you arguing about with them?" 17 Someone from the crowd answered him, "Teacher, I have brought to you my son possessed by a mute spirit. 18 Wherever it seizes him, it throws him down; he foams at the mouth, grinds his teeth, and becomes rigid. I asked your disciples to drive it out, but they were unable to do so." 19 He said to them in reply, "O faithless generation, how long will I be with you? How long will I endure you? Bring him to me." 20 They brought the boy to him. And when he saw him, the spirit immediately threw the boy into convulsions. As he fell to the ground, he began to roll around and foam at the mouth. 21 Then he questioned his father, "How long has this been happening to him?" He replied, "Since childhood. 22 It has often thrown him into fire and into water to kill him. But if you can do anything, have compassion on us and help us." 23 Jesus said to him, " 'If you can!' Everything is possible to one who has faith." 24 Then the boy's father cried out, "I do believe, help my unbelief!" 25 Jesus, on seeing a crowd rapidly gathering, rebuked the unclean spirit and said to it, "Mute and deaf spirit, I command you: come out of him and never enter him again!" 26 Shouting and throwing the boy into convulsions, it came out. He became like a corpse, which caused many to say, "He is dead!" 27 But Jesus took him by the hand, raised him, and he stood up. 28 When he entered the house, his disciples asked him in private, "Why could we not drive it out?" 29* He said to them, "This kind can only come out through prayer."

***The Second Prediction of the Passion.*** 30[e] They left from there and began a journey through Galilee, but he did not wish anyone to know about it.[f] 31 He was teaching his disciples and telling them, "The Son of Man is to be handed over to men and they will kill him, and three days after his death he will rise." 32 But they did not understand the saying, and they were afraid to question him.

## IV. The Full Revelation of the Mystery

***The Greatest in the Kingdom.**** 33 They came to Capernaum and, once inside the house, he began to ask them, "What were you arguing about on the way?"[g] 34 But they remained silent. They had been discussing among themselves on the way who was the greatest. 35 Then he sat down, called the Twelve, and said to them, "If anyone wishes to be first, he shall be the last of all and the servant of all."[h] 36 Taking a child he placed it in their midst, and putting his arms around it he said to them, 37 "Whoever receives one child such as this in my name, receives me; and whoever receives me, receives not me but the One who sent me."[i]

***Another Exorcist.**** 38 John said to him,[j] "Teacher, we saw someone driving out demons in your name, and we tried to prevent him because he does not follow us." 39 Jesus replied, "Do not prevent him. There is no one who performs a mighty deed in my name who can at the same time speak ill of me. 40 For whoever is not against us is for us.[k] 41 Anyone who gives you a cup of water to drink because you belong to Christ, amen, I say to you, will surely not lose his reward.[l]

***Temptations to Sin.*** 42[m] "Whoever causes

**9:14–29** The disciples' failure to effect a cure seems to reflect unfavorably on Jesus (Mk 9:14–18, 22). In response Jesus exposes their lack of trust in God (Mk 9:19) and scores their lack of prayer (Mk 9:29), i.e., of conscious reliance on God's power when acting in Jesus' name. For Matthew, see note on Mt 17:14–20. Lk 9:37–43 centers attention on Jesus' sovereign power.

**9:29 This kind can only come out through prayer**: a variant reading adds "and through fasting."

**9:33–37** Mark probably intends this incident and the sayings that follow as commentary on the disciples' lack of understanding (Mk 9:32). Their role in Jesus' work is one of service, especially to the poor and lowly. Children were the symbol Jesus used for the *anawim*, the poor in spirit, the lowly in the Christian community.

**9:38–41** Jesus warns against jealousy and intolerance toward others, such as exorcists who do **not follow us**. The saying in Mk 9:40 is a broad principle of the divine tolerance. Even the smallest courtesies shown to those who teach in Jesus' name do not go unrewarded.

*d:* Mt 17:14–21; Lk 9:37–43. *e:* 8:31; Mt 17:22–23; Lk 9:43–45. *f:* Jn 7:1. *g:* Mt 18:1–5; Lk 9:46–48. *h:* Mt 20:27. *i:* Mt 10:40; 18:5; Jn 13:20. *j:* Nm 11:28; Lk 9:49–50; 1 Cor 12:3. *k:* Mt 12:30. *l:* Mt 10:42; 1 Cor 3:23. *m:* Mt 5:29–30; 18:6–9; Lk 17:1–2.

one of these little ones who believe [in me] to sin, it would be better for him if a great millstone were put around his neck and he were thrown into the sea. 43 If your hand causes you to sin, cut it off. It is better for you to enter into life maimed than with two hands to go into Gehenna,* into the unquenchable fire. [44]* 45 And if your foot causes you to sin, cut it off. It is better for you to enter into life crippled than with two feet to be thrown into Gehenna. [46] 47 And if your eye causes you to sin, pluck it out. Better for you to enter into the kingdom of God with one eye than with two eyes to be thrown into Gehenna, 48 where 'their worm does not die, and the fire is not quenched.'[n]

*The Simile of Salt.* 49* "Everyone will be salted with fire. 50 Salt is good, but if salt becomes insipid, with what will you restore its flavor? Keep salt in yourselves and you will have peace with one another."[o]

## CHAPTER 10

See RG 297–98

*Marriage and Divorce.* 1 He set out from there and went into the district of Judea [and] across the Jordan. Again crowds gathered around him and, as was his custom, he again taught them. 2* The Pharisees approached and asked, "Is it lawful for a husband to divorce his wife?" They were testing him.[p] 3 He said to them in reply, "What did Moses command you?" 4 They replied, "Moses permitted him to write a bill of divorce and dismiss her."[q] 5 But Jesus told them, "Because of the hardness of your hearts he wrote you this commandment. 6 But from the beginning of creation, 'God made them male and female.[r] 7 For this reason a man shall leave his father and mother [and be joined to his wife],[s] 8 and the two shall become one flesh.' So they are no longer two but one flesh. 9 Therefore what God has joined together, no human being must separate." 10 In the house the disciples again questioned him about this. 11[t] He said to them, "Whoever divorces his wife and marries another commits adultery against her; 12 and if she divorces her husband and marries another, she commits adultery."

*Blessing of the Children.* 13[u] And people were bringing children to him that he might touch them, but the disciples rebuked them.[v] 14 When Jesus saw this he became indignant and said to them, "Let the children come to me; do not prevent them, for the kingdom of God belongs to such as these. 15 Amen, I say to you, whoever does not accept the kingdom of God like a child* will not enter it."[w] 16 Then he embraced them and blessed them, placing his hands on them.

*The Rich Man.* 17[x] As he was setting out on a journey, a man ran up, knelt down before him, and asked him, "Good teacher, what must I do to inherit eternal life?" 18 Jesus answered him, "Why do you call me good?* No one is good but God alone. 19 You know the commandments: 'You shall not kill; you shall not commit adultery; you shall not steal; you shall not bear false witness; you shall not defraud; honor your father and your mother.' "[y] 20 He replied and said to him, "Teacher, all of these I have observed from my youth." 21 Jesus, looking at him, loved him and said to him, "You are lacking in one thing. Go, sell what you have, and

**9:43, 45, 47 Gehenna**: see note on Mt 5:22.

**9:44, 46** These verses, lacking in some important early manuscripts, are here omitted as scribal additions. They simply repeat Mk 9:48 itself a modified citation of Is 66:24.

**9:49 Everyone will be salted with fire**: so the better manuscripts. Some add "every sacrifice will be salted with salt." The purifying and preservative use of salt in food (Lv 2:13) and the refinement effected through fire refer here to comparable effects in the spiritual life of the disciples of Jesus.

**10:2–9** In the dialogue between Jesus and the Pharisees on the subject of divorce, Jesus declares that the law of Moses permitted divorce (Dt 24:1) only **because of the hardness of your hearts** (Mk 10:4–5). In citing Gn 1:27 and 2:24 Jesus proclaims permanence to be the divine intent from the beginning concerning human marriage (Mk 10:6–8). He reaffirms this with the declaration that **what God has joined together, no human being must separate** (Mk 10:9). See further the notes on Mt 5:31–32; 19:3–9.

**10:15 Whoever does not accept the kingdom of God like a child**: i.e., in total dependence upon and obedience to the gospel; cf. Mt 18:3–4.

**10:18 Why do you call me good?**: Jesus repudiates the term "good" for himself and directs it to God, the source of all goodness who alone can grant the gift of eternal life; cf. Mt 19:16–17.

*n:* Is 66:24. *o:* Lv 2:13; Mt 5:13; Lk 14:34–35; Col 4:6. *p:* Mt 19:3–9. *q:* Dt 24:1–4. *r:* Gn 1:27. *s:* Gn 2:24; 1 Cor 6:16; Eph 5:31. *t:* Mt 5:32; Lk 16:18; 1 Cor 7:10–11. *u:* Mt 19:13–15; Lk 18:15–17. *v:* Lk 9:47. *w:* Mt 18:3. *x:* Mt 19:16–30; Lk 18:18–30. *y:* Ex 20:12–16; Dt 5:16–21.

give to [the] poor and you will have treasure in heaven; then come, follow me." [22]At that statement his face fell, and he went away sad, for he had many possessions.

[23*] Jesus looked around and said to his disciples, "How hard it is for those who have wealth to enter the kingdom of God!"[z] [24]The disciples were amazed at his words. So Jesus again said to them in reply, "Children, how hard it is to enter the kingdom of God! [25]It is easier for a camel to pass through [the] eye of [a] needle than for one who is rich to enter the kingdom of God." [26]They were exceedingly astonished and said among themselves, "Then who can be saved?" [27]Jesus looked at them and said, "For human beings it is impossible, but not for God. All things are possible for God." [28]Peter began to say to him, "We have given up everything and followed you." [29]Jesus said, "Amen, I say to you, there is no one who has given up house or brothers or sisters or mother or father or children or lands for my sake and for the sake of the gospel [30]who will not receive a hundred times more now in this present age: houses and brothers and sisters and mothers and children and lands, with persecutions, and eternal life in the age to come. [31]But many that are first will be last, and [the] last will be first."[a]

***The Third Prediction of the Passion.*** [32b] They were on the way, going up to Jerusalem, and Jesus went ahead of them. They were amazed, and those who followed were afraid. Taking the Twelve aside again, he began to tell them what was going to happen to him. [33]"Behold, we are going up to Jerusalem, and the Son of Man will be handed over to the chief priests and the scribes, and they will condemn him to death and hand him over to the Gentiles [34]who will mock him, spit upon him, scourge him, and put him to death, but after three days he will rise."

***Ambition of James and John.*** [35c] Then James and John, the sons of Zebedee, came to him and said to him, "Teacher, we want you to do for us whatever we ask of you." [36]He replied, "What do you wish [me] to do for you?" [37]They answered him, "Grant that in your glory we may sit one at your right and the other at your left." [38* d] Jesus said to them, "You do not know what you are asking. Can you drink the cup that I drink or be baptized with the baptism with which I am baptized?" [39]They said to him, "We can." Jesus said to them, "The cup that I drink, you will drink, and with the baptism with which I am baptized, you will be baptized; [40]but to sit at my right or at my left is not mine to give but is for those for whom it has been prepared." [41]When the ten heard this, they became indignant at James and John. [42*] Jesus summoned them and said to them,[e] "You know that those who are recognized as rulers over the Gentiles lord it over them, and their great ones make their authority over them felt. [43]But it shall not be so among you. Rather, whoever wishes to be great among you will be your servant; [44]whoever wishes to be first among you will be the slave of all. [45]For the Son of Man did not come to be served but to serve and to give his life as a ransom for many."

***The Blind Bartimaeus.**** [46]They came to Jericho.[f] And as he was leaving Jericho with

**10:23–27** In the Old Testament wealth and material goods are considered a sign of God's favor (Jb 1:10; Ps 128:1–2; Is 3:10). The words of Jesus in Mk 10:23–25 provoke astonishment among the disciples because of their apparent contradiction of the Old Testament concept (Mk 10:24, 26). Since wealth, power, and merit generate false security, Jesus rejects them utterly as a claim to enter the kingdom. Achievement of salvation is beyond human capability and depends solely on the goodness of God who offers it as a gift (Mk 10:27).

**10:38–40 Can you drink the cup . . . I am baptized?**: the metaphor of drinking the cup is used in the Old Testament to refer to acceptance of the destiny assigned by God; see note on Psalm 11:6. In Jesus' case, this involves divine judgment on sin that Jesus the innocent one is to expiate on behalf of the guilty (Mk 14:24; Is 53:5). His baptism is to be his crucifixion and death for the salvation of the human race; cf. Lk 12:50. The request of James and John for a share in the glory (Mk 10:35–37) must of necessity involve a share in Jesus' sufferings, the endurance of tribulation and suffering for the gospel (Mk 10:39). The authority of assigning places of honor in the kingdom is reserved to God (Mk 10:40).

**10:42–45** Whatever authority is to be exercised by the disciples must, like that of Jesus, be rendered as service to others (Mk 10:45) rather than for personal aggrandizement (Mk 10:42–44). The service of Jesus is his passion and death for the sins of the human race (Mk 10:45); cf. Mk 14:24; Is 53:11–12; Mt 26:28; Lk 22:19–20.

**10:46–52** See notes on Mt 9:27–31 and 20:29–34.

*z:* Prv 11:28. *a:* Mt 19:30; Lk 13:30. *b:* 8:31; Mt 20:17–19; Lk 18:31–33. *c:* Mt 20:20–28. *d:* Lk 12:50. *e:* Lk 22:25–27. *f:* Mt 20:29–34; Lk 18:35–43.

his disciples and a sizable crowd, Bartimaeus, a blind man, the son of Timaeus, sat by the roadside begging. 47On hearing that it was Jesus of Nazareth, he began to cry out and say, "Jesus, son of David, have pity on me." 48And many rebuked him, telling him to be silent. But he kept calling out all the more, "Son of David, have pity on me." 49Jesus stopped and said, "Call him." So they called the blind man, saying to him, "Take courage; get up, he is calling you." 50He threw aside his cloak, sprang up, and came to Jesus. 51Jesus said to him in reply, "What do you want me to do for you?" The blind man replied to him, "Master, I want to see." 52Jesus told him, "Go your way; your faith has saved you." Immediately he received his sight and followed him on the way.

## CHAPTER 11

See RG 298

***The Entry into Jerusalem.**** 1When they drew near to Jerusalem,[g] to Bethphage and Bethany at the Mount of Olives, he sent two of his disciples 2and said to them, "Go into the village opposite you, and immediately on entering it, you will find a colt tethered on which no one has ever sat. Untie it and bring it here. 3If anyone should say to you, 'Why are you doing this?' reply, 'The Master has need of it and will send it back here at once.' " 4So they went off and found a colt tethered at a gate outside on the street, and they untied it. 5Some of the bystanders said to them, "What are you doing, untying the colt?" 6They answered them just as Jesus had told them to, and they permitted them to do it. 7So they brought the colt to Jesus and put their cloaks over it. And he sat on it. 8Many people spread their cloaks on the road, and others spread leafy branches that they had cut from the fields. 9Those preceding him as well as those following kept crying out:[h]

"Hosanna!
Blessed is he who comes in the name of the Lord!
10 Blessed is the kingdom of our father David that is to come!
Hosanna in the highest!"

11He entered Jerusalem and went into the temple area. He looked around at everything and, since it was already late, went out to Bethany with the Twelve.[i]

***Jesus Curses a Fig Tree.**** 12The next day as they were leaving Bethany he was hungry.[j] 13Seeing from a distance a fig tree in leaf, he went over to see if he could find anything on it. When he reached it he found nothing but leaves; it was not the time for figs. 14And he said to it in reply, "May no one ever eat of your fruit again!" And his disciples heard it.

***Cleansing of the Temple.**** 15They came to Jerusalem,[k] and on entering the temple area he began to drive out those selling and buying there. He overturned the tables of the money changers and the seats of those who were selling doves. 16He did not permit anyone to carry anything through the temple area. 17Then he taught them saying, "Is it not written:

'My house shall be called a house of prayer for all peoples'?
But you have made it a den of thieves."[l]

18The chief priests and the scribes came to hear of it and were seeking a way to put him to death, yet they feared him because the whole crowd was astonished at his teaching. 19When evening came, they went out of the city.[m]

***The Withered Fig Tree.*** 20[n] Early in the morning, as they were walking along, they saw the fig tree withered to its roots. 21Peter

**11:1–11** In Mark's account Jesus takes the initiative in ordering the preparation for his entry into Jerusalem (Mk 11:1–6) even as he later orders the preparation of his last Passover supper (Mk 14:12–16). In Mk 10:9–10 the greeting Jesus receives stops short of proclaiming him Messiah. He is greeted rather as the prophet of the coming messianic kingdom. Contrast Mt 21:9.

**11:12–14** Jesus' search for fruit on the fig tree recalls the prophets' earlier use of this image to designate Israel; cf. Jer 8:13; 29:17; Jl 1:7; Hos 9:10, 16. Cursing the fig tree is a parable in action representing Jesus' judgment (Mk 11:20) on barren Israel and the fate of Jerusalem for failing to receive his teaching; cf. Is 34:4; Hos 2:14; Lk 13:6–9.

**11:15–19** See note on Mt 21:12–17.

*g:* Mt 21:1–9; Lk 19:29–38; Jn 12:12–15. *h:* 2 Sm 7:16; Ps 118:26. *i:* Mt 21:10, 17. *j:* Mt 21:18–20; Lk 13:6–9. *k:* Mt 21:12–13; Lk 19:45–46; Jn 2:14–16. *l:* Is 56:7; Jer 7:11. *m:* Lk 21:37. *n:* Mt 21:20–22.

remembered and said to him, "Rabbi, look!
The fig tree that you cursed has withered."
22 Jesus said to them in reply, "Have faith in
God. 23 Amen, I say to you, whoever says to
this mountain, 'Be lifted up and thrown into
the sea,' and does not doubt in his heart but
believes that what he says will happen, it
shall be done for him.[o] 24 Therefore I tell you,
all that you ask for in prayer, believe that
you will receive it and it shall be yours.[p]
25 When you stand to pray, forgive anyone
against whom you have a grievance, so that
your heavenly Father may in turn forgive
you your transgressions."[q] [26]*

***The Authority of Jesus Questioned.****
27 They returned once more to Jerusalem.[r] As
he was walking in the temple area, the chief
priests, the scribes, and the elders approached him 28 and said to him, "By what
authority are you doing these things? Or
who gave you this authority to do them?"
29 Jesus said to them, "I shall ask you one
question. Answer me, and I will tell you by
what authority I do these things. 30 Was
John's baptism of heavenly or of human origin? Answer me." 31 They discussed this
among themselves and said, "If we say, 'Of
heavenly origin,' he will say, '[Then] why
did you not believe him?' 32 But shall we say,
'Of human origin'?"—they feared the
crowd, for they all thought John really was a
prophet. 33 So they said to Jesus in reply, "We
do not know." Then Jesus said to them,
"Neither shall I tell you by what authority I
do these things."

## CHAPTER 12

See RG 298

***Parable of the Tenants.**** 1 He began to
speak to them in parables.[s] "A man planted a
vineyard, put a hedge around it, dug a wine
press, and built a tower. Then he leased it to
tenant farmers and left on a journey.[t] 2 At the
proper time he sent a servant to the tenants to
obtain from them some of the produce of the
vineyard. 3 But they seized him, beat him,
and sent him away empty-handed. 4 Again he
sent them another servant. And that one they
beat over the head and treated shamefully.
5 He sent yet another whom they killed. So,
too, many others; some they beat, others
they killed. 6 He had one other to send, a
beloved son. He sent him to them last of all,
thinking, 'They will respect my son.' 7 But
those tenants said to one another, 'This is the
heir. Come, let us kill him, and the inheritance will be ours.' 8 So they seized him and
killed him, and threw him out of the vineyard. 9 What [then] will the owner of the
vineyard do? He will come, put the tenants
to death, and give the vineyard to others.
10 Have you not read this scripture passage:[u]

'The stone that the builders rejected
has become the cornerstone;
11 by the Lord has this been done,
and it is wonderful in our eyes'?"

12 They were seeking to arrest him, but they
feared the crowd, for they realized that he
had addressed the parable to them. So they
left him and went away.

***Paying Taxes to the Emperor.*** 13* They
sent some Pharisees[v] and Herodians to him
to ensnare him[w] in his speech.* 14 They came
and said to him, "Teacher, we know that you
are a truthful man and that you are not concerned with anyone's opinion. You do not regard a person's status but teach the way of
God in accordance with the truth. Is it lawful

**11:26** This verse, which reads, "But if you do not forgive, neither will your heavenly Father forgive your transgressions," is omitted in the best manuscripts. It was probably added by copyists under the influence of Mt 6:15.

**11:27–33** The mounting hostility toward Jesus came from the chief priests, the scribes, and the elders (Mk 11:27); the Herodians and the Pharisees (Mk 12:13); and the Sadducees (Mk 12:18). By their rejection of God's messengers, John the Baptist and Jesus, they incurred the divine judgment implied in Mk 11:27–33 and confirmed in the parable of the vineyard tenants (Mk 12:1–12).

**12:1–12** The vineyard denotes Israel (Is 5:1–7). The tenant farmers are the religious leaders of Israel. God is the owner of the vineyard. His servants are his messengers, the prophets. The beloved son is Jesus (Mk 1:11; 9:7; Mt 3:17; 17:5; Lk 3:22; 9:35). The punishment of the tenants refers to the religious leaders, and the transfer of the vineyard to others refers to the people of the new Israel.

**12:13–34** In the ensuing conflicts (cf. also Mk 2:1–3:6) Jesus vanquishes his adversaries by his responses to their questions and reduces them to silence (Mk 12:34).

**12:13–17** See note on Mt 22:15–22.

*o:* Mt 17:20–21; Lk 17:6. *p:* Mt 7:7; Jn 11:22; 14:13. *q:* Mt 6:14; 18:35. *r:* Mt 21:23–27; Lk 20:1–8. *s:* Mt 21:33–46; Lk 20:9–19. *t:* Is 5:1–7; Jer 2:21. *u:* Ps 118:22–23; Is 28:16. *v:* Mt 22:15–33; Lk 20:20–39. *w:* 3:6.

to pay the census tax to Caesar or not?
Should we pay or should we not pay?"
15 Knowing their hypocrisy he said to them,
"Why are you testing me? Bring me a denarius to look at." 16 They brought one to him
and he said to them, "Whose image and inscription is this?" They replied to him, "Caesar's." 17 So Jesus said to them, "Repay to
Caesar what belongs to Caesar and to God
what belongs to God." They were utterly
amazed at him.[x]

***The Question About the Resurrection.****
18 Some Sadducees, who say there is no resurrection, came to him and put this question
to him, 19 saying, "Teacher, Moses wrote for
us, 'If someone's brother dies, leaving a wife
but no child, his brother must take the wife
and raise up descendants for his brother.'[y]
20 Now there were seven brothers. The first
married a woman and died, leaving no descendants. 21 So the second married her and
died, leaving no descendants, and the third
likewise. 22 And the seven left no descendants. Last of all the woman also died. 23 At
the resurrection [when they arise] whose
wife will she be? For all seven had been
married to her." 24 Jesus said to them, "Are
you not misled because you do not know the
scriptures or the power of God? 25 When they
rise from the dead, they neither marry nor
are given in marriage, but they are like the
angels in heaven. 26 As for the dead being
raised, have you not read in the Book of Moses, in the passage about the bush, how God
told him, 'I am the God of Abraham, [the]
God of Isaac, and [the] God of Jacob'?[z] 27 He
is not God of the dead but of the living. You
are greatly misled."

***The Greatest Commandment.**** 28 One of
the scribes,[a] when he came forward and
heard them disputing and saw how well he
had answered them, asked him, "Which is
the first of all the commandments?" 29 Jesus
replied, "The first is this: 'Hear, O Israel!
The Lord our God is Lord alone! 30 You shall
love the Lord your God with all your heart,
with all your soul, with all your mind, and
with all your strength.'[b] 31 The second is this:
'You shall love your neighbor as yourself.'
There is no other commandment greater
than these."[c] 32 The scribe said to him, "Well
said, teacher. You are right in saying, 'He is
One and there is no other than he.' 33 And 'to
love him with all your heart, with all your
understanding, with all your strength, and to
love your neighbor as yourself' is worth
more than all burnt offerings and sacrifices."[d] 34 And when Jesus saw that [he] answered with understanding, he said to him,
"You are not far from the kingdom of God."
And no one dared to ask him any more questions.[e]

***The Question About David's Son.**** 35 As
Jesus was teaching in the temple area he
said,[f] "How do the scribes claim that the
Messiah is the son of David? 36 David himself, inspired by the holy Spirit, said:

'The Lord said to my lord,
"Sit at my right hand
until I place your enemies under your
feet." '[g]

37 David himself calls him 'lord'; so how is
he his son?" [The] great crowd heard this
with delight.

***Denunciation of the Scribes.**** 38 In the
course of his teaching he said,[h] "Beware of
the scribes, who like to go around in long
robes and accept greetings in the marketplaces, 39 seats of honor in synagogues, and
places of honor at banquets. 40 They devour
the houses of widows and, as a pretext, recite lengthy prayers. They will receive a
very severe condemnation."

***The Poor Widow's Contribution.**** 41 He sat
down opposite the treasury and observed

**12:18–27** See note on Mt 22:23–33.

**12:28–34** See note on Mt 22:34–40.

**12:35–37** Jesus questions the claim of the scribes about the Davidic descent of the Messiah, not to deny it (Mt 1:1; Acts 2:20, 34; Rom 1:3; 2 Tm 2:8) but to imply that he is more than this. His superiority derives from his transcendent origin, to which David himself attested when he spoke of the Messiah with the name "Lord" (Ps 110:1). See also note on Mt 22:41–46.

**12:38–40** See notes on Mk 7:1–23 and Mt 23:1–39.

**12:41–44** See note on Lk 21:1–4.

*x:* Rom 13:7. *y:* Dt 25:5. *z:* Ex 3:6. *a:* Mt 22:34–40; Lk 10:25–28. *b:* Dt 6:4–5. *c:* Lv 19:18; Rom 13:9; Gal 5:14; Jas 2:8. *d:* Dt 6:4; Ps 40:7–9. *e:* Mt 22:46; Lk 20:40. *f:* Mt 22:41–45; Lk 20:41–44. *g:* Ps 110:1. *h:* Mt 23:1–7; Lk 11:43; 20:45–47.

## Parables in the Synoptic Gospels

| Parable | Matthew | Mark | Luke |
|---|---|---|---|
| The Weeds among the Wheat | 13:24–30 | | |
| The Hidden Treasure | 13:44 | | |
| The Fine Pearl | 13:45–46 | | |
| The Net | 13:47–48 | | |
| The Unforgiving Servant | 18:23–35 | | |
| The Workers in the Vineyard | 20:1–16 | | |
| The Two Sons | 21:28–30 | | |
| The Wedding Feast | 22:2–14 | | |
| The Talents | 25:14–30 | | |
| The Judgment of the Nations | 25:31–46 | | |
| Seed Grows of Itself | | 4:26–29 | |
| Need for Watchfulness | | 13:32–37 | |
| The Two Debtors | | | 7:41–42 |
| The Good Samaritan | | | 10:30–35 |
| The Persistent Friend | | | 11:5–8 |
| The Rich Fool | | | 12:16–20 |
| The Vigilant and Faithful Servants | | | 12:35–40 |
| The Faithful and Wise Steward | | | 12:42–48 |
| The Barren Fig Tree | | | 13:6–9 |
| The Great Feast | | | 14:15–24 |
| The Tower | | | 14:28–30 |
| The King Marching into Battle | | | 14:31–33 |
| The Lost Coin | | | 15:8–10 |
| The Lost Son | | | 15:11–32 |
| The Dishonest Steward | | | 16:1–8 |
| The Rich Man and Lazarus | | | 16:19–31 |
| Attitude of a Servant | | | 17:7–10 |
| The Persistent Widow | | | 18:2–5 |
| The Pharisee and the Tax Collector | | | 18:9–14 |
| The Ten Gold Coins | | | 19:11–27 |
| The Two Foundations | 7:24–29 | | 6:46–49 |
| The Yeast | 13:33 | | 13:20–21 |
| The Lost Sheep | 18:10–14 | | 15:1–7 |
| The Lamp | 5:15 | 4:21 | 8:16; 11:33 |
| The New Cloth | 9:16 | 2:21 | 5:36 |
| The New Wine in Old Wineskins | 9:17 | 2:22 | 5:37–38 |
| The Sower | 13:1–9 | 4:1–9 | 8:4–8 |
| The Mustard Seed | 13:31–32 | 4:30–34 | 13:18–19 |
| The Tenants | 21:33–46 | 12:1–12 | 20:9–19 |
| The Lesson of the Fig Tree | 24:32–35 | 13:28–31 | 21:29 |

how the crowd put money into the treasury.[i] Many rich people put in large sums. 42 A poor widow also came and put in two small coins worth a few cents. 43 Calling his disciples to himself, he said to them, "Amen, I say to you, this poor widow put in more than all the other contributors to the treasury. 44 For they have all contributed from their surplus wealth, but she, from her poverty, has contributed all she had, her whole livelihood."

## CHAPTER 13

See RG 298

***The Destruction of the Temple Foretold.**** 1 As he was making his way out of the temple area one of his disciples said to him, "Look, teacher, what stones and what buildings!"[j] 2 Jesus said to him, "Do you see these great buildings? There will not be one stone left upon another that will not be thrown down."

***The Signs of the End.*** 3* As he was sitting on the Mount of Olives opposite the temple area, Peter, James, John, and Andrew asked him privately,[k] 4 "Tell us, when will this happen, and what sign will there be when all these things are about to come to an end?" 5 Jesus began to say to them, "See that no one deceives you.[l] 6 Many will come in my name saying, 'I am he,' and they will deceive many. 7 When you hear of wars and reports of wars do not be alarmed; such things must happen, but it will not yet be the end. 8 Nation will rise against nation and kingdom against kingdom. There will be earthquakes from place to place and there will be famines. These are the beginnings of the labor pains.

***The Coming Persecution.*** 9[m] "Watch out for yourselves. They will hand you over to the courts. You will be beaten in synagogues. You will be arraigned before governors and kings because of me, as a witness before them. 10 But the gospel must first be preached to all nations.* 11 When they lead you away and hand you over, do not worry beforehand about what you are to say.[n] But say whatever will be given to you at that hour. For it will not be you who are speaking but the holy Spirit. 12 Brother will hand over brother to death, and the father his child; children will rise up against parents and have them put to death. 13 You will be hated by all because of my name. But the one who perseveres to the end will be saved.

***The Great Tribulation.*** 14[o] "When you see the desolating abomination standing* where he should not (let the reader understand), then those in Judea must flee to the mountains,[p] 15 [and] a person on a housetop must not go down or enter to get anything out of his house,[q] 16 and a person in a field must not return to get his cloak. 17 Woe to pregnant women and nursing mothers in those days. 18 Pray that this does not happen in winter. 19 For those times will have tribulation such as has not been since the beginning of God's creation until now, nor ever will be.[r] 20 If the Lord had not shortened those days, no one would be saved; but for the sake of the elect whom he chose, he did shorten the days. 21 If anyone says to you then, 'Look, here is the Messiah!

**13:1–2** The reconstructed temple with its precincts, begun under Herod the Great ca. 20 B.C., was completed only some seven years before it was destroyed by fire in A.D. 70 at the hands of the Romans; cf. Jer 26:18; Mt 24:1–2. For the dating of the reconstruction of the temple, see further the note on Jn 2:20.

**13:3–37** Jesus' prediction of the destruction of the temple (Mk 13:2) provoked questions that the four named disciples put to him in private regarding the time and the sign when all **these things are about to come to an end** (Mk 13:3–4). The response to their questions was Jesus' eschatological discourse prior to his imminent death. It contained instruction and consolation exhorting the disciples and the church to faith and obedience through the trials that would confront them (Mk 13:5–13). The sign is the presence of **the desolating abomination** (Mk 13:14; see Dn 9:27), i.e., of the Roman power profaning the temple. Flight from Jerusalem is urged rather than defense of the city through misguided messianic hope (Mk 13:14–23). Intervention will occur only after destruction (Mk 13:24–27), which will happen before the end of the first Christian generation (Mk 13:28–31). No one but the Father knows the precise time, or that of the parousia (Mk 13:32); hence the necessity of constant vigilance (Mk 13:33–37). Luke sets the parousia at a later date, after "the time of the Gentiles" (Lk 21:24). See also notes on Mt 24:1–25:46.

**13:10 The gospel . . . to all nations**: the period of the Christian mission.

**13:14** The participle **standing** is masculine, in contrast to the neuter at Mt 24:15.

*i:* Lk 21:1–4. *j:* Mt 24:1–2; Lk 21:5–6. *k:* Mt 24:3–8; Lk 21:7–11. *l:* Eph 5:6; 2 Thes 2:3. *m:* Mt 24:9–14; Lk 21:12–19. *n:* Mt 10:19–22; Lk 12:11–12. *o:* Mt 24:15–22; Lk 21:20–24. *p:* Dn 9:27; Mt 24:15. *q:* Lk 17:31. *r:* Dn 12:1.

## Apocalyptic

THE TERM "APOCALYPTIC" derives from a Greek word meaning "to uncover, to reveal." It gives its name to the last book of the Christian canon, the Book of Revelation, which is also known as the Apocalypse of John (see Rv 1:1). The name also extends to the type of literature associated with the Book of Revelation: Apocalyptic materials contain elements such as a pessimistic view of the present world, a dualistic outlook that divides people into the few to be saved and the many damned, tours of heaven and hell, descriptions of future cataclysms, cryptic signs in need of interpretation, and angels to provide such interpretation.

Within the Gospel tradition, Mark 13—often called the Little Apocalypse to distinguish it from the Book of Revelation—contains several hallmarks of the genre: predictions of destruction, heavenly portents, the gathering of the elect, and so forth. Matthew uses much of this material but takes it out of its end-of-the-world context. What for Mark are signs of the end (persecution, family disintegration) are for Matthew indications that one is living according to Jesus' teaching.

Although the literature can be frightening, apocalyptic writing serves to encourage the group to which it is addressed. It urges steadfastness in the face of persecution, assures the reader of heavenly control of what appears to be a chaotic world, and offers the promise that, with the momentous entry of the divine into human history, the righteous will be rewarded and the wicked punished. Likely, not all early readers took the signs literally; rather, they recognized the conventional aspects of the genre.

Apocalyptic literature is found, cross-culturally, among both groups that are persecuted and groups that perceive themselves to be fully disenfranchised, with no hope of affecting their future. Scholars debate whether Jesus was an apocalyptic prophet or whether his early followers added apocalyptic statements to the collection of his sayings. On the one hand, the parables are not typically apocalyptic; they use quite mundane images to convey their points. On the other, Mark 13 and its parallels in Matthew and Luke, the writings of Paul (especially 1 Thessalonians), and quite likely the preaching of John the Baptist all suggest that apocalyptic thinking was part of Jesus' legacy.

Look, there he is!' do not believe it. 22 False
messiahs and false prophets will arise and
will perform signs and wonders in order to
mislead, if that were possible, the elect. 23 Be
watchful! I have told it all to you beforehand.

***The Coming of the Son of Man.*** 24 s "But in
those days after that tribulation

the sun will be darkened,
and the moon will not give its light,'
25 and the stars will be falling from the sky,
and the powers in the heavens will be
shaken.

26* u And then they will see 'the Son of Man
coming in the clouds' with great power and
glory, 27 and then he will send out the angels
and gather [his] elect from the four winds,
from the end of the earth to the end of the sky.

***The Lesson of the Fig Tree.*** 28 v "Learn a
lesson from the fig tree. When its branch becomes tender and sprouts leaves, you know
that summer is near. 29 In the same way,
when you see these things happening, know
that he is near, at the gates. 30 Amen, I say to
you, this generation will not pass away until
all these things have taken place. 31 Heaven

**13:26 Son of Man . . . with great power and glory**: Jesus cites this text from Dn 7:13 in his response to the high priest, **Are you the Messiah?** (Mk 14:61). In Ex 34:5; Lv 16:2; and Nm 11:25 the clouds indicate the presence of the divinity. Thus in his role of Son of Man, Jesus is a heavenly being who will come in power and glory.

*s:* Mt 24:29–31; Lk 21:25–27. *t:* Is 13:10; Ez 32:7; Jl 2:10. *u:* 14:62; Dn 7:13–14. *v:* Mt 24:32–36; Lk 21:29–33.

and earth will pass away, but my words will not pass away.

***Need for Watchfulness.*** 32 "But of that day or hour, no one knows, neither the angels in heaven, nor the Son, but only the Father. 33[w] Be watchful! Be alert! You do not know when the time will come. 34 It is like a man traveling abroad. He leaves home and places his servants in charge, each with his work, and orders the gatekeeper to be on the watch.[x] 35 Watch, therefore; you do not know when the lord of the house is coming, whether in the evening, or at midnight, or at cockcrow, or in the morning. 36 May he not come suddenly and find you sleeping. 37 What I say to you, I say to all: 'Watch!' "

See RG 298–99

## CHAPTER 14

***The Conspiracy Against Jesus.*** 1* The Passover and the Feast of Unleavened Bread* were to take place in two days' time.[y] So the chief priests and the scribes were seeking a way to arrest him by treachery and put him to death. 2 They said, "Not during the festival, for fear that there may be a riot among the people."

***The Anointing at Bethany.**** 3 When he was in Bethany reclining at table in the house of Simon the leper,[z] a woman came with an alabaster jar of perfumed oil, costly genuine spikenard. She broke the alabaster jar and poured it on his head. 4 There were some who were indignant. "Why has there been this waste of perfumed oil? 5 It could have been sold for more than three hundred days' wages and the money given to the poor." They were infuriated with her. 6 Jesus said, "Let her alone. Why do you make trouble for her? She has done a good thing for me. 7 The poor you will always have with you, and whenever you wish you can do good to them, but you will not always have me. 8 She has done what she could. She has anticipated anointing my body for burial. 9 Amen, I say to you, wherever the gospel is proclaimed to the whole world, what she has done will be told in memory of her."

***The Betrayal by Judas.*** 10[a] Then Judas Iscariot, one of the Twelve, went off to the chief priests to hand him over to them. 11 When they heard him they were pleased and promised to pay him money. Then he looked for an opportunity to hand him over.

***Preparations for the Passover.*** 12[b] On the first day of the Feast of Unleavened Bread, when they sacrificed the Passover lamb,* his disciples said to him, "Where do you want us to go and prepare for you to eat the Passover?" 13 He sent two of his disciples and said to them, "Go into the city and a man will meet you, carrying a jar of water.* Follow him. 14 Wherever he enters, say to the master of the house, 'The Teacher says, "Where is my guest room where I may eat the Passover with my disciples?" ' 15 Then he will show you a large upper room furnished and ready. Make the preparations for us there." 16 The disciples then went off, entered

**14:1–16:8** In the movement of Mark's gospel the cross is depicted as Jesus' way to glory in accordance with the divine will. Thus the passion narrative is seen as the climax of Jesus' ministry.

**14:1 The Passover and the Feast of Unleavened Bread**: the connection between the two festivals is reflected in Ex 12:3–20; 34:18; Lv 23:4–8; Nm 9:2–14; 28:16–17; Dt 16:1–8. The Passover commemorated the redemption from slavery and the departure of the Israelites from Egypt by night. It began at sundown after the Passover lamb was sacrificed in the temple in the afternoon of the fourteenth day of the month of Nisan. With the Passover supper on the same evening was associated the eating of unleavened bread. The latter was continued through Nisan 21, a reminder of the affliction of the Israelites and of the haste surrounding their departure. Praise and thanks to God for his goodness in the past were combined at this dual festival with the hope of future salvation. **The chief priests . . . to death**: the intent to put Jesus to death was plotted for a long time but delayed for fear of the crowd (Mk 3:6; 11:18; 12:12).

**14:3** At Bethany on the Mount of Olives, a few miles from Jerusalem, in **the house of Simon the leper**, Jesus defends a woman's loving action of anointing his head with perfumed oil in view of his impending death and burial as a criminal, in which case his body would not be anointed. See further the note on Jn 12:7. He assures the woman of the remembrance of her deed in the worldwide preaching of the good news.

**14:12 The first day of the Feast of Unleavened Bread . . . the Passover lamb**: a less precise designation of the day for sacrificing the Passover lamb as evidenced by some rabbinical literature. For a more exact designation, see note on Mk 14:1. It was actually Nisan 14.

**14:13 A man . . . carrying a jar of water**: perhaps a prearranged signal, for only women ordinarily carried water in jars. The Greek word used here, however, implies simply a person and not necessarily a male.

*w:* Mt 24:42; 25:13–15. *x:* Mt 25:14–30; Lk 19:12–27. *y:* Mt 26:2–5; Lk 22:1–2; Jn 11:45–53. *z:* Mt 26:6–13; Jn 12:1–8. *a:* Mt 26:14–16; Lk 22:3–6. *b:* Mt 26:17–19; Lk 22:7–13.

the city, and found it just as he had told them; and they prepared the Passover.

***The Betrayer.*** [17c] When it was evening, he came with the Twelve. [18*] And as they reclined at table and were eating, Jesus said, "Amen, I say to you, one of you will betray me, one who is eating with me." [19] They began to be distressed and to say to him, one by one, "Surely it is not I?" [20] He said to them, "One of the Twelve, the one who dips with me into the dish. [21] For the Son of Man indeed goes, as it is written of him,* but woe to that man by whom the Son of Man is betrayed. It would be better for that man if he had never been born."

***The Lord's Supper.*** [22*] While they were eating,[d] he took bread, said the blessing, broke it, and gave it to them, and said, "Take it; this is my body." [23] Then he took a cup, gave thanks, and gave it to them, and they all drank from it. [24] He said to them, "This is my blood of the covenant, which will be shed* for many. [25] Amen, I say to you, I shall not drink again the fruit of the vine until the day when I drink it new in the kingdom of God." [26] Then, after singing a hymn,* they went out to the Mount of Olives.[e]

***Peter's Denial Foretold.**** [27] Then Jesus said to them, "All of you will have your faith shaken, for it is written:

'I will strike the shepherd,
and the sheep will be dispersed.'[f]

[28] But after I have been raised up, I shall go before you to Galilee." [29] Peter said to him, "Even though all should have their faith shaken, mine will not be." [30] Then Jesus said to him, "Amen, I say to you, this very night before the cock crows twice you will deny me three times." [31] But he vehemently replied, "Even though I should have to die with you, I will not deny you." And they all spoke similarly.

***The Agony in the Garden.*** [32*] Then they came to a place named Gethsemane,[g] and he said to his disciples, "Sit here while I pray."[h] [33] He took with him Peter, James, and John, and began to be troubled and distressed. [34] Then he said to them, "My soul is sorrowful even to death. Remain here and keep watch." [35] He advanced a little and fell to the ground and prayed that if it were possible the hour might pass by him; [36] he said, "Abba, Father,* all things are possible to you. Take this cup away from me, but not what I will but what you will." [37] When he returned he found them asleep. He said to Peter, "Simon, are you asleep? Could you not keep watch for one hour? [38*] Watch and

**14:18 One of you will betray me, one who is eating with me**: contrasts the intimacy of table fellowship at the Passover meal with the treachery of the traitor; cf. Ps 41:10.

**14:21 The Son of Man indeed goes, as it is written of him**: a reference to Ps 41:10 cited by Jesus concerning Judas at the Last Supper; cf. Jn 13:18–19.

**14:22–24** The actions and words of Jesus express within the framework of the Passover meal and the transition to a new covenant the sacrifice of himself through the offering of his body and blood in anticipation of his passion and death. His **blood of the covenant** both alludes to the ancient rite of Ex 24:4–8 and indicates the new community that the sacrifice of Jesus will bring into being (Mt 26:26–28; Lk 22:19–20; 1 Cor 11:23–25).

**14:24 Which will be shed**: see note on Mt 26:27–28. **For many**: the Greek preposition *hyper* is a different one from that at Mt 26:28 but the same as that found at Lk 22:19, 20 and 1 Cor 11:24. The sense of both words is vicarious, and it is difficult in Hellenistic Greek to distinguish between them. For **many** in the sense of "all," see note on Mt 20:28.

**14:26 After singing a hymn**: Ps 114–118, thanksgiving songs concluding the Passover meal.

**14:27–31** Jesus predicted that the Twelve would waver in their faith, even abandon him, despite their protestations to the contrary. Yet he reassured them that after his resurrection he would regather them in Galilee (Mk 16:7; cf. Mt 26:32; 28:7, 10, 16; Jn 21), where he first summoned them to be his followers as he began to preach the good news (Mk 1:14–20).

**14:32–34** The disciples who had witnessed the raising to life of the daughter of Jairus (Mk 5:37) and the transfiguration of their Master (Mk 9:2) were now invited to witness his degradation and agony and to watch and pray with him.

**14:36 Abba, Father**: an Aramaic term, here also translated by Mark, Jesus' special way of addressing God with filial intimacy. The word *'abbā'* seems not to have been used in earlier or contemporaneous Jewish sources to address God without some qualifier. Cf. Rom 8:15; Gal 4:6 for other occurrences of the Aramaic word in the Greek New Testament. **Not what I will but what you will**: note the complete obedient surrender of the human will of Jesus to the divine will of the Father; cf. Jn 4:34; 8:29; Rom 5:19; Phil 2:8; Heb 5:8.

**14:38 The spirit is willing but the flesh is weak**: the spirit is drawn to what is good yet found in conflict with the flesh, inclined to sin; cf. Ps 51:7, 12. Everyone is faced with this struggle, the full force of which Jesus accepted on our behalf and, through his bitter passion and death, achieved the victory.

*c:* Mt 26:20–24; Lk 22:21–23; Jn 13:21–26. *d:* Mt 26:26–30; Lk 22:19–20; 1 Cor 11:23–25. *e:* Mt 26:30–35; Lk 22:34, 39; Jn 13:36–38. *f:* Zec 13:7; Jn 16:32. *g:* Mt 26:36–46; Lk 22:40–46. *h:* Jn 18:1.

pray that you may not undergo the test.[i] The spirit is willing but the flesh is weak." 39 Withdrawing again, he prayed, saying the same thing. 40 Then he returned once more and found them asleep, for they could not keep their eyes open and did not know what to answer him. 41 He returned a third time and said to them, "Are you still sleeping and taking your rest? It is enough. The hour has come. Behold, the Son of Man is to be handed over to sinners. 42 Get up, let us go. See, my betrayer is at hand."

***The Betrayal and Arrest of Jesus.*** 43[j] Then, while he was still speaking, Judas, one of the Twelve, arrived, accompanied by a crowd with swords and clubs who had come from the chief priests, the scribes, and the elders. 44 His betrayer had arranged a signal with them, saying, "The man I shall kiss is the one; arrest him and lead him away securely." 45 He came and immediately went over to him and said, "Rabbi." And he kissed him. 46 At this they laid hands on him and arrested him. 47 One of the bystanders drew his sword, struck the high priest's servant, and cut off his ear. 48 Jesus said to them in reply, "Have you come out as against a robber, with swords and clubs, to seize me? 49 Day after day I was with you teaching in the temple area, yet you did not arrest me; but that the scriptures may be fulfilled." 50 And they all left him and fled. 51 Now a young man followed him wearing nothing but a linen cloth about his body. They seized him, 52 but he left the cloth behind and ran off naked.

***Jesus before the Sanhedrin.*** 53*[k] They led Jesus away to the high priest, and all the chief priests and the elders and the scribes came together. 54 Peter followed him at a distance into the high priest's courtyard and was seated with the guards, warming himself at the fire. 55 The chief priests and the entire Sanhedrin kept trying to obtain testimony against Jesus in order to put him to death, but they found none. 56 Many gave false witness against him, but their testimony did not agree. 57* Some took the stand and testified falsely against him, alleging, 58 "We heard him say, 'I will destroy this temple made with hands and within three days I will build another not made with hands.' "[l] 59 Even so their testimony did not agree. 60 The high priest rose before the assembly and questioned Jesus, saying, "Have you no answer? What are these men testifying against you?" 61* But he was silent and answered nothing. Again the high priest asked him and said to him, "Are you the Messiah, the son of the Blessed One?" 62 Then Jesus answered, "I am;

and 'you will see the Son of Man
seated at the right hand of the Power
and coming with the clouds of
heaven.' "[m]

63 At that the high priest tore his garments and said, "What further need have we of witnesses? 64 You have heard the blasphemy. What do you think?" They all condemned him as deserving to die. 65 Some began to spit on him. They blindfolded him and struck him and said to him, "Prophesy!" And the guards greeted him with blows.[n]

***Peter's Denial of Jesus.*** 66[o] While Peter was below in the courtyard, one of the high priest's maids came along. 67 Seeing Peter warming himself, she looked intently at him and said, "You too were with the Nazarene, Jesus." 68* But he denied it saying, "I neither know nor understand what you are talking

**14:53 They led Jesus away . . . came together**: Mark presents a formal assembly of the whole Sanhedrin (chief priests, elders, and scribes) at night, leading to the condemnation of Jesus (Mk 14:64), in contrast to Lk 22:66, 71 where Jesus is condemned in a daytime meeting of the council; see also Jn 18:13, 19–24.

**14:57–58** See notes on Mt 26:60–61 and Jn 2:19.

**14:61–62 The Blessed One**: a surrogate for the divine name, which Jews did not pronounce. **I am**: indicates Jesus' acknowledgment that he is the Messiah and Son of God; cf. Mk 1:1. Contrast Mt 26:64 and Lk 22:67–70, in which Jesus leaves his interrogators to answer their own question. **You will see the Son of Man . . . with the clouds of heaven**: an allusion to Dn 7:13 and Ps 110:1 portending the enthronement of Jesus as judge in the transcendent glory of God's kingdom. **The Power**: another surrogate for the name of God.

**14:68 [Then the cock crowed]**: found in most manuscripts, perhaps in view of Mk 14:30, 72 but omitted in others.

*i:* Rom 7:5. *j:* Mt 26:47–56; Lk 22:47–53; Jn 18:3–11. *k:* Mt 26:57–68; Lk 22:54–55, 63–65, 67–71; Jn 18:12–13. *l:* 15:29; 2 Cor 5:1. *m:* 13:26; Ps 110:1; Dn 7:13; Mt 24:30. *n:* Lk 22:63–65. *o:* Mt 26:69–75; Lk 22:56–62; Jn 18:16–18, 25–27.

about." So he went out into the outer court. [Then the cock crowed.] 69 The maid saw him and began again to say to the bystanders, "This man is one of them." 70 Once again he denied it. A little later the bystanders said to Peter once more, "Surely you are one of them; for you too are a Galilean." 71 He began to curse and to swear, "I do not know this man about whom you are talking." 72 And immediately a cock crowed a second time. Then Peter remembered the word that Jesus had said to him, "Before the cock crows twice you will deny me three times." He broke down and wept.[p]

## CHAPTER 15

See RG 298–99

***Jesus Before Pilate.*** 1 [q] As soon as morning came,[r] the chief priests with the elders and the scribes, that is, the whole Sanhedrin, held a council.* They bound Jesus, led him away, and handed him over to Pilate. 2 Pilate questioned him, "Are you the king of the Jews?"* He said to him in reply, "You say so." 3 The chief priests accused him of many things. 4 Again Pilate questioned him, "Have you no answer? See how many things they accuse you of." 5 Jesus gave him no further answer, so that Pilate was amazed.

***The Sentence of Death.**** 6 Now on the occasion of the feast he used to release to them one prisoner whom they requested.[s] 7 A man called Barabbas* was then in prison along with the rebels who had committed murder in a rebellion. 8 The crowd came forward and began to ask him to do for them as he was accustomed. 9 Pilate answered, "Do you want me to release to you the king of the Jews?" 10 For he knew that it was out of envy that the chief priests had handed him over. 11 But the chief priests stirred up the crowd to have him release Barabbas for them instead. 12 Pilate again said to them in reply, "Then what [do you want] me to do with [the man you call] the king of the Jews?" 13* They shouted again, "Crucify him." 14 Pilate said to them, "Why? What evil has he done?" They only shouted the louder, "Crucify him." 15* So Pilate, wishing to satisfy the crowd, released Barabbas to them and, after he had Jesus scourged, handed him over to be crucified.

***Mockery by the Soldiers.*** 16* [t] The soldiers led him away inside the palace, that is, the praetorium, and assembled the whole cohort. 17 They clothed him in purple and, weaving a crown of thorns, placed it on him. 18 They began to salute him with, "Hail, King of the Jews!" 19 and kept striking his head with a reed and spitting upon him. They knelt before him in homage. 20 And when they had mocked him, they stripped him of the purple cloak, dressed him in his own clothes, and led him out to crucify him.

***The Way of the Cross.*** 21 They pressed into service a passer-by, Simon, a Cyrenian,* who was coming in from the country, the father of Alexander and Rufus, to carry his cross.[u]

***The Crucifixion.*** 22 [v] They brought him to the place of Golgotha (which is translated Place of the Skull). 23 They gave him wine drugged with myrrh, but he did not take it. 24* [w] Then they crucified him and divided his

**15:1 Held a council**: the verb here, *poieō*, can mean either "convene a council" or "take counsel." This reading is preferred to a variant "reached a decision" (cf. Mk 3:6), which Mk 14:64 describes as having happened at the night trial; see note on Mt 27:1–2. **Handed him over to Pilate**: lacking authority to execute their sentence of condemnation (Mk 14:64), the Sanhedrin had recourse to Pilate to have Jesus tried and put to death (Mk 15:15); cf. Jn 18:31.

**15:2 The king of the Jews**: in the accounts of the evangelists a certain irony surrounds the use of this title as an accusation against Jesus (see note on Mk 15:26). While Pilate uses this term (Mk 15:2, 9, 12), he is aware of the evil motivation of the chief priests who handed Jesus over for trial and condemnation (Mk 15:10; Lk 23:14–16, 20; Mt 27:18, 24; Jn 18:38; 19:4, 6, 12).

**15:6–15** See note on Mt 27:15–26.

**15:7 Barabbas**: see note on Mt 27:16–17.

**15:13 Crucify him**: see note on Mt 27:22.

**15:15** See note on Mt 27:26.

**15:16 Praetorium**: see note on Mt 27:27.

**15:21 They pressed into service . . . Simon, a Cyrenian**: a condemned person was constrained to bear his own instrument of torture, at least the crossbeam. The precise naming of Simon and his sons is probably due to their being known among early Christian believers to whom Mark addressed his gospel. See also notes on Mt 27:32; Lk 23:26–32.

**15:24** See notes on Mt 27:35 and Jn 19:23–25a.

*p:* Jn 13:38. *q:* Mt 27:1–2, 11–14; Lk 23:1–3. *r:* Jn 18:28. *s:* Mt 27:15–26; Lk 23:17–25; Jn 18:39–40. *t:* Mt 27:27–31; Jn 19:2–3. *u:* Mt 27:32; Lk 23:26. *v:* Mt 27:33–51; Lk 23:32–46; Jn 19:17–30. *w:* Ps 22:18.

garments by casting lots for them to see
what each should take. [25]It was nine o'clock
in the morning* when they crucified him.
[26*] The inscription of the charge against him
read, "The King of the Jews." [27]With him
they crucified two revolutionaries, one on
his right and one on his left.[x] [28*] [29*] Those
passing by reviled him, shaking their heads
and saying,[y] "Aha! You who would destroy
the temple and rebuild it in three days,
[30]save yourself by coming down from the
cross." [31]Likewise the chief priests, with the
scribes, mocked him among themselves and
said, "He saved others; he cannot save himself. [32]Let the Messiah, the King of Israel,
come down now from the cross that we may
see and believe." Those who were crucified
with him also kept abusing him.[z]

***The Death of Jesus.*** [33]At noon darkness
came over the whole land until three in the
afternoon. [34]And at three o'clock Jesus cried
out in a loud voice, "*Eloi, Eloi, lema
sabachthani?*"* which is translated, "My
God, my God, why have you forsaken me?"[a]
[35*] Some of the bystanders who heard it said,
"Look, he is calling Elijah." [36]One of them
ran, soaked a sponge with wine, put it on a
reed, and gave it to him to drink, saying,
"Wait, let us see if Elijah comes to take him
down." [37]Jesus gave a loud cry and breathed
his last. [38*] The veil of the sanctuary was
torn in two from top to bottom. [39*] [b] When
the centurion who stood facing him saw how
he breathed his last he said, "Truly this man
was the Son of God!" [40*] There were also
women looking on from a distance.[c] Among
them were Mary Magdalene, Mary the
mother of the younger James and of Joses,
and Salome. [41]These women had followed
him when he was in Galilee and ministered
to him. There were also many other women
who had come up with him to Jerusalem.

***The Burial of Jesus.*** [42][d] When it was already evening, since it was the day of preparation, the day before the sabbath, [43]Joseph
of Arimathea,* a distinguished member of
the council, who was himself awaiting the
kingdom of God, came and courageously
went to Pilate and asked for the body of
Jesus. [44]Pilate was amazed that he was already dead. He summoned the centurion and
asked him if Jesus had already died. [45]And
when he learned of it from the centurion, he
gave the body to Joseph. [46]Having bought a
linen cloth, he took him down, wrapped him
in the linen cloth and laid him in a tomb that
had been hewn out of the rock. Then he
rolled a stone against the entrance to the
tomb. [47]Mary Magdalene and Mary the
mother of Joses watched where he was laid.

## CHAPTER 16

See RG 299–300

***The Resurrection of Jesus.**** [1]When
the sabbath was over,[e] Mary Magdalene,

**15:25 It was nine o'clock in the morning**: literally, "the third hour," thus between 9 a.m. and 12 noon. Cf. Mk 15:33, 34, 42 for Mark's chronological sequence, which may reflect liturgical or catechetical considerations rather than the precise historical sequence of events; contrast the different chronologies in the other gospels, especially Jn 19:14.

**15:26 The inscription . . . the King of the Jews**: the political reason for the death penalty falsely charged by the enemies of Jesus. See further the notes on Mt 27:37 and Jn 19:19.

**15:28** This verse, "And the scripture was fulfilled that says, 'And he was counted among the wicked,' " is omitted in the earliest and best manuscripts. It contains a citation from Is 53:12 and was probably introduced from Lk 22:37.

**15:29** See note on Mt 27:39–40.

**15:34** An Aramaic rendering of Ps 22:2. See also note on Mt 27:46.

**15:35 Elijah**: a verbal link with Eloi (Mk 15:34). See note on Mk 9:9–13; cf. Mal 3:23–24. See also note on Mt 27:47.

**15:38** See note on Mt 27:51–53.

**15:39** The closing portion of Mark's gospel returns to the theme of its beginning in the Gentile centurion's climactic declaration of belief that Jesus **was the Son of God**. It indicates the fulfillment of the good news announced in the prologue (Mk 1:1) and may be regarded as the firstfruit of the passion and death of Jesus.

**15:40–41** See note on Mt 27:55–56.

**15:43 Joseph of Arimathea**: see note on Mt 27:57–61.

**16:1–8** The purpose of this narrative is to show that the tomb is empty and that Jesus **has been raised** (Mk 16:6) and is **going before you to Galilee** (Mk 16:7) in fulfillment of Mk 14:28. The women find the tomb empty, and an angel stationed there announces to them what has happened. They are told to proclaim the news to Peter and the disciples in order to prepare them for a reunion with him. Mark's composition of the gospel ends at Mk 16:8 with the women telling no one, because they were afraid. This abrupt termination causes some to believe that the original ending of this gospel may have been lost. See the following note.

*x:* Lk 23:33. *y:* Jn 2:19. *z:* Lk 23:39. *a:* Ps 22:2. *b:* Mt 27:54–56; Lk 23:47–49. *c:* 6:3; Lk 8:2–3. *d:* Mt 27:57–61; Lk 23:50–56; Jn 19:38–42. *e:* Mt 28:1–8; Lk 24:1–10; Jn 20:1–10. *f:* Mt 28:1; Lk 23:56.

Mary, the mother of James, and Salome
bought spices so that they might go and
anoint him.[f] 2 Very early when the sun had
risen, on the first day of the week, they came
to the tomb. 3 They were saying to one another, "Who will roll back the stone for us
from the entrance to the tomb?" 4 When they
looked up, they saw that the stone had been
rolled back; it was very large. 5 On entering
the tomb they saw a young man sitting on
the right side, clothed in a white robe, and
they were utterly amazed.[g] 6 He said to them,
"Do not be amazed! You seek Jesus of Nazareth, the crucified. He has been raised; he is
not here. Behold the place where they laid
him. 7 But go and tell his disciples and Peter,
'He is going before you to Galilee; there you
will see him, as he told you.' "[h] 8 Then they
went out and fled from the tomb, seized with
trembling and bewilderment. They said
nothing to anyone, for they were afraid.

## The Longer Ending *

***The Appearance to Mary Magdalene.***
[9[i] When he had risen, early on the first day
of the week, he appeared first to Mary Magdalene, out of whom he had driven seven
demons. 10[j] She went and told his companions who were mourning and weeping.
11 When they heard that he was alive and had
been seen by her, they did not believe.
***The Appearance to Two Disciples.*** 12[k] After this he appeared in another form to two of
them walking along on their way to the
country. 13 They returned and told the others;
but they did not believe them either.
***The Commissioning of the Eleven.***
14[l] [But] later, as the eleven were at table, he
appeared to them and rebuked them for their
unbelief and hardness of heart because they
had not believed those who saw him after he
had been raised. 15[m] He said to them, "Go
into the whole world and proclaim the
gospel to every creature. 16 Whoever believes and is baptized will be saved; whoever does not believe will be condemned.
17 These signs will accompany those who believe: in my name they will drive out
demons, they will speak new languages.
18 They will pick up serpents [with their
hands], and if they drink any deadly thing, it
will not harm them. They will lay hands on
the sick, and they will recover."[n]
***The Ascension of Jesus.*** 19 So then the
Lord Jesus, after he spoke to them, was
taken up into heaven and took his seat at the
right hand of God.[o] 20 But they went forth
and preached everywhere, while the Lord
worked with them and confirmed the word
through accompanying signs.][p]

## The Shorter Ending

[And they reported all the instructions briefly to Peter's companions. Afterwards Jesus himself, through them, sent forth from east to west the sacred and imperishable proclamation of eternal salvation. Amen.]

**16:9–20** This passage, termed the Longer Ending to the Marcan gospel by comparison with a much briefer conclusion found in some less important manuscripts, has traditionally been accepted as a canonical part of the gospel and was defined as such by the Council of Trent. Early citations of it by the Fathers indicate that it was composed by the second century, although vocabulary and style indicate that it was written by someone other than Mark. It is a general resume of the material concerning the appearances of the risen Jesus, reflecting, in particular, traditions found in Lk 24 and Jn 20.

The Shorter Ending: Found after Mk 16:8 before the Longer Ending in four seventh-to-ninth-century Greek manuscripts as well as in one Old Latin version, where it appears alone without the Longer Ending.

The Freer Logion: Found after v 14 in a fourth-fifth century manuscript preserved in the Freer Gallery of Art, Washington, DC, this ending was known to Jerome in the fourth century. It reads: "And they excused themselves, saying, 'This age of lawlessness and unbelief is under Satan, who does not allow the truth and power of God to prevail over the unclean things dominated by the spirits [or, does not allow the unclean things dominated by the spirits to grasp the truth and power of God]. Therefore reveal your righteousness now.' They spoke to Christ. And Christ responded to them, 'The limit of the years of Satan's power is completed, but other terrible things draw near. And for those who sinned I was handed over to death, that they might return to the truth and no longer sin, in order that they might inherit the spiritual and incorruptible heavenly glory of righteousness. But . . .' "

*g:* Jn 20:12. *h:* 14:28. *i:* Mt 28:1–10; Jn 20:11–18. *j:* Lk 24:10–11; Jn 20:18. *k:* Lk 24:13–35. *l:* Lk 24:36–49; 1 Cor 15:5. *m:* 13:10; Mt 28:18–20; Lk 24:47; Jn 20:21. *n:* Mt 10:1; Lk 10:19; Acts 28:3–6. *o:* Lk 24:50–53. *p:* 1 Tm 3:16.

See RG 300–19

# The Gospel According to Luke

The Gospel according to Luke is the first part of a two-volume work that continues the biblical history of God's dealings with humanity found in the Old Testament, showing how God's promises to Israel have been fulfilled in Jesus and how the salvation promised to Israel and accomplished by Jesus has been extended to the Gentiles. The stated purpose of the two volumes is to provide Theophilus and others like him with certainty—assurance—about earlier instruction they have received (Lk 1:4). To accomplish his purpose, Luke shows that the preaching and teaching of the representatives of the early church are grounded in the preaching and teaching of Jesus, who during his historical ministry (Acts 1:21–22) prepared his specially chosen followers and commissioned them to be witnesses to his resurrection and to all else that he did (Acts 10:37–42). This continuity between the historical ministry of Jesus and the ministry of the apostles is Luke's way of guaranteeing the fidelity of the Church's teaching to the teaching of Jesus.

Luke's story of Jesus and the church is dominated by a historical perspective. This history is first of all salvation history. God's divine plan for human salvation was accomplished during the period of Jesus, who through the events of his life (Lk 22:22) fulfilled the Old Testament prophecies (Lk 4:21; 18:31; 22:37; 24:26–27, 44), and this salvation is now extended to all humanity in the period of the church (Acts 4:12). This salvation history, moreover, is a part of human history. Luke relates the story of Jesus and the church to events in contemporary Palestinian (Lk 1:5; 3:1–2; Acts 4:6) and Roman (Lk 2:1–2; 3:1; Acts 11:28; 18:2, 12) history for, as Paul says in Acts 26:26, "this was not done in a corner." Finally, Luke relates the story of Jesus and the church to contemporaneous church history. Luke is concerned with presenting Christianity as a legitimate form of worship in the Roman world, a religion that is capable of meeting the spiritual needs of a world empire like that of Rome. To this end, Luke depicts the Roman governor Pilate declaring Jesus innocent of any wrongdoing three times (Lk 23:4, 14, 22). At the same time Luke argues in Acts that Christianity is the logical development and proper fulfillment of Judaism and is therefore deserving of the same toleration and freedom traditionally accorded Judaism by Rome (Acts 13:16–41; 23:6–9; 24:10–21; 26:2–23).

The prominence given to the period of the church in the story has important consequences for Luke's interpretation of the teachings of Jesus. By presenting the time of the church as a distinct phase of salvation history, Luke accordingly shifts the early Christian emphasis away from the expectation of an imminent parousia to the day-to-day concerns of the Christian community in the world. He does this in the gospel by regularly emphasizing the words "each day" (Lk 9:23; cf. Mk 8:34; Lk 11:3; 16:19; 19:47) in the sayings of Jesus. Although Luke still believes the parousia to be a reality that will come unexpectedly (Lk 12:38, 45–46), he is more concerned with presenting the words and deeds of Jesus as guides for the conduct of Christian disciples in the interim period between the ascension and the parousia and with presenting Jesus himself as the model of Christian life and piety.

Throughout the gospel, Luke calls upon the Christian disciple to identify with the master Jesus, who is caring and tender toward the poor and lowly, the outcast, the sinner, and the afflicted, toward all those who recognize their dependence on God (Lk 4:18; 6:20–23; 7:36–50; 14:12–14; 15:1–32; 16:19–31; 18:9–14; 19:1–10; 21:1–4), but who is severe toward the proud and self-righteous, and particularly toward those who place their material wealth before the service of God and his people (Lk 6:24–26; 12:13–21; 16:13–15, 19–31; 18:9–14, 15–25; cf. Lk 1:50–53). No gospel writer is more concerned than Luke with the mercy and compassion of Jesus (Lk 7:41–43; 10:29–37; 13:6–9; 15:11–32). No gospel writer is more concerned with the role of the Spirit in the life of Jesus and the Christian disciple (Lk 1:35, 41; 2:25–27; 4:1, 14, 18; 10:21; 11:13; 24:49), with the importance of prayer (Lk 3:21; 5:16; 6:12; 9:28; 11:1–13; 18:1–8), or with Jesus' concern for women (Lk 7:11–17, 36–50; 8:2–3; 10:38–42). While Jesus calls all humanity to repent (Lk 5:32; 10:13; 11:32; 13:1–5; 15:7–10; 16:30; 17:3–4; 24:47), he is particularly demanding of those who would be his disciples. Of them he demands absolute and total detachment from family and material possessions (Lk 9:57–62; 12:32–34; 14:25–35). To all who respond in faith and repentance to the word Jesus preaches, he brings salvation (Lk 2:30–32; 3:6; 7:50; 8:48, 50; 17:19; 19:9) and peace (Lk 2:14; 7:50; 8:48; 19:38, 42) and life (Lk 10:25–28; 18:26–30).

Early Christian tradition, from the late second century on, identifies the author of this gospel and of the Acts of the Apostles as Luke, a Syrian from Antioch, who is mentioned in the New Testament in Col 4:14, Phlm 24 and 2 Tm 4:11. The prologue of the gospel makes it clear that Luke is not part of the first generation of Christian disciples but is himself dependent upon the traditions he received from those who were eyewitnesses and ministers of the word (Lk 1:2). His two-volume work marks him as someone who was highly literate both in the Old Testament traditions according to the Greek versions and in Hellenistic Greek writings.

Among the likely sources for the composition of this gospel (Lk 1:3) were the Gospel of Mark, a written collection of sayings of Jesus known also to the author of the Gospel of Matthew (Q; see Introduction to Matthew), and other special traditions that were used by Luke alone among the gospel writers. Some hold that Luke used Mark only as a complementary source for rounding out the material he took from other traditions. Because of its dependence on the Gospel of Mark and because details in Luke's Gospel (Lk 13:35a; 19:43–44; 21:20; 23:28–31) imply that the author was acquainted with the destruction of the city of Jerusalem by the Romans in A.D. 70, the Gospel of Luke is dated by most scholars after that date; many propose A.D. 80–90 as the time of composition.

Luke's consistent substitution of Greek names for the Aramaic or Hebrew names occurring in his sources (e.g., Lk 23:33; Mk 15:22; Lk 18:41; Mk 10:51), his omission from the gospel of specifically Jewish Christian concerns found in his sources (e.g., Mk 7:1–23), his interest in Gentile Christians (Lk 2:30–32; 3:6, 38; 4:16–30; 13:28–30; 14:15–24; 17:11–19; 24:47–48), and his incomplete knowledge of Palestinian geography, customs, and practices are among the characteristics of this gospel that suggest that Luke was a non-Palestinian writing to a non-Palestinian audience that was largely made up of Gentile Christians.

The principal divisions of the Gospel according to Luke are the following:

I. The Prologue (1:1–4)
II. The Infancy Narrative (1:5–2:52)
III. The Preparation for the Public Ministry (3:1–4:13)
IV. The Ministry in Galilee (4:14–9:50)
V. The Journey to Jerusalem: Luke's Travel Narrative (9:51–19:27)
VI. The Teaching Ministry in Jerusalem (19:28–21:38)
VII. The Passion Narrative (22:1–23:56)
VIII. The Resurrection Narrative (24:1–53)

## I. The Prologue*

### CHAPTER 1

See RG 307-309

*1* Since many have undertaken to
compile a narrative of the events that have
been fulfilled among us,[a] *2* just as those who
were eyewitnesses from the beginning and
ministers of the word have handed them
down to us,[b] *3* I too have decided, after investigating everything accurately anew, to
write it down in an orderly sequence for
you, most excellent Theophilus, *4* so that
you may realize the certainty of the teachings you have received.

**1:1–4** The Gospel according to Luke is the only one of the synoptic gospels to begin with a literary prologue. Making use of a formal, literary construction and vocabulary, the author writes the prologue in imitation of Hellenistic Greek writers and, in so doing, relates his story about Jesus to contemporaneous Greek and Roman literature. Luke is not only interested in the words and deeds of Jesus, but also in the larger context of the birth, ministry, death, and resurrection of Jesus as the fulfillment of the promises of God in the Old Testament. As a second- or third-generation Christian, Luke acknowledges his debt to earlier **eyewitnesses** and **ministers of the word**, but claims that his contribution to this developing tradition is a complete and accurate account, told in an orderly manner, and intended to provide **Theophilus** ("friend of God," literally) and other readers with certainty about earlier teachings they have received.

*a:* Acts 1:1; 1 Cor 15:3. *b:* 24:48; Jn 15:27; Acts 1:21–22.

## II. The Infancy Narrative*

***Announcement of the Birth of John.*** [5]In the days of Herod, King of Judea,* there was a priest named Zechariah of the priestly division of Abijah; his wife was from the daughters of Aaron, and her name was Elizabeth.[c] [6]Both were righteous in the eyes of God, observing all the commandments and ordinances of the Lord blamelessly. [7]But they had no child,* because Elizabeth was barren and both were advanced in years.[d] [8]Once when he was serving as priest in his division's turn before God, [9]according to the practice of the priestly service, he was chosen by lot to enter the sanctuary of the Lord to burn incense.[e] [10]Then, when the whole assembly of the people was praying outside at the hour of the incense offering, [11]the angel of the Lord appeared to him, standing at the right of the altar of incense. [12]Zechariah was troubled by what he saw, and fear came upon him. [13]But the angel said to him, "Do not be afraid,* Zechariah, because your prayer has been heard. Your wife Elizabeth will bear you a son, and you shall name him John.[f] [14]And you will have joy and gladness, and many will rejoice at his birth, [15]for he will be great in the sight of [the] Lord. He will drink neither wine nor strong drink.* He will be filled with the holy Spirit even from his mother's womb,[g] [16]and he will turn many of the children of Israel to the Lord their God. [17]He will go before him in the spirit and power of Elijah* to turn the hearts of fathers toward children and the disobedient to the understanding of the righteous, to prepare a people fit for the Lord."[h] [18]Then Zechariah said to the angel, "How shall I know this? For I am an old man, and my wife is advanced in years." [19]And the angel said to him in reply, "I am Gabriel,* who stand before

**1:5–2:52** Like the Gospel according to Matthew, this gospel opens with an infancy narrative, a collection of stories about the birth and childhood of Jesus. The narrative uses early Christian traditions about the birth of Jesus, traditions about the birth and circumcision of John the Baptist, and canticles such as the Magnificat (Lk 1:46–55) and Benedictus (Lk 1:67–79), composed of phrases drawn from the Greek Old Testament. It is largely, however, the composition of Luke who writes in imitation of Old Testament birth stories, combining historical and legendary details, literary ornamentation and interpretation of scripture, to answer in advance the question, "Who is Jesus Christ?" The focus of the narrative, therefore, is primarily christological. In this section Luke announces many of the themes that will become prominent in the rest of the gospel: the centrality of Jerusalem and the temple, the journey motif, the universality of salvation, joy and peace, concern for the lowly, the importance of women, the presentation of Jesus as savior, Spirit-guided revelation and prophecy, and the fulfillment of Old Testament promises. The account presents parallel scenes (diptychs) of angelic announcements of the birth of John the Baptist and of Jesus, and of the birth, circumcision, and presentation of John and Jesus. In this parallelism, the ascendency of Jesus over John is stressed: John is prophet of the Most High (Lk 1:76); Jesus is Son of the Most High (Lk 1:32). John is great in the sight of the Lord (Lk 1:15); Jesus will be Great (a LXX attribute, used absolutely, of God) (Lk 1:32). John will go before the Lord (Lk 1:16–17); Jesus will be Lord (Lk 1:43; 2:11).

**1:5 In the days of Herod, King of Judea**: Luke relates the story of salvation history to events in contemporary world history. Here and in Lk 3:1–2 he connects his narrative with events in Palestinian history; in Lk 2:1–2 and Lk 3:1 he casts the Jesus story in the light of events of Roman history. Herod the Great, the son of the Idumean Antipater, was declared "King of Judea" by the Roman Senate in 40 B.C., but became the undisputed ruler of Palestine only in 37 B.C. He continued as king until his death in 4 B.C. **Priestly division of Abijah**: a reference to the eighth of the twenty-four divisions of priests who, for a week at a time, twice a year, served in the Jerusalem temple.

**1:7 They had no child**: though childlessness was looked upon in contemporaneous Judaism as a curse or punishment for sin, it is intended here to present Elizabeth in a situation similar to that of some of the great mothers of important Old Testament figures: Sarah (Gn 15:3; 16:1); Rebekah (Gn 25:21); Rachel (Gn 29:31; 30:1); the mother of Samson and wife of Manoah (Jgs 13:2–3); Hannah (1 Sm 1:2).

**1:13 Do not be afraid**: a stereotyped Old Testament phrase spoken to reassure the recipient of a heavenly vision (Gn 15:1; Jos 1:9; Dn 10:12, 19 and elsewhere in Lk 1:30; 2:10). **You shall name him John**: the name means "Yahweh has shown favor," an indication of John's role in salvation history.

**1:15 He will drink neither wine nor strong drink**: like Samson (Jgs 13:4–5) and Samuel (1 Sm 1:11 LXX and 4QSam[a]), John is to be consecrated by Nazirite vow and set apart for the Lord's service.

**1:17 He will go before him in the spirit and power of Elijah**: John is to be the messenger sent before Yahweh, as described in Mal 3:1–2. He is cast, moreover, in the role of the Old Testament fiery reformer, the prophet Elijah, who according to Mal 3:23 (4:5) is sent before "the great and terrible day of the Lord comes."

**1:19 I am Gabriel**: "the angel of the Lord" is identified as Gabriel, the angel who in Dn 9:20–25 announces the seventy weeks of years and the coming of an anointed one, a prince. By alluding to Old Testament themes in Lk 1:17, 19 such as the coming of the day of the Lord and the dawning of the messianic era, Luke is presenting his interpretation of the significance of the births of John and Jesus.

*c:* 1 Chr 24:10. *d:* Gn 18:11; Jgs 13:2–5; 1 Sm 1:5–6. *e:* Ex 30:7. *f:* 1:57, 60, 63; Mt 1:20–21. *g:* 7:33; Nm 6:1–21; Jgs 13:4; 1 Sm 1:11 LXX. *h:* Sir 48:10; Mal 3:1; 3:23–24; Mt 11:14; 17:11–13. *i:* Dn 8:16; 9:21.

God. I was sent to speak to you and to announce to you this good news.[i] 20 But now you will be speechless and unable to talk* until the day these things take place, because you did not believe my words, which will be fulfilled at their proper time."[j]

21 Meanwhile the people were waiting for Zechariah and were amazed that he stayed so long in the sanctuary. 22 But when he came out, he was unable to speak to them, and they realized that he had seen a vision in the sanctuary. He was gesturing to them but remained mute. 23 Then, when his days of ministry were completed, he went home. 24 After this time his wife Elizabeth conceived, and she went into seclusion for five months, saying, 25 "So has the Lord done for me at a time when he has seen fit to take away my disgrace before others."[k]

***Announcement of the Birth of Jesus.**** 26 In the sixth month, the angel Gabriel was sent from God to a town of Galilee called Nazareth, 27 to a virgin betrothed to a man named Joseph, of the house of David, and the virgin's name was Mary.[l] 28 And coming to her, he said, "Hail, favored one! The Lord is with you."[m] 29 But she was greatly troubled at what was said and pondered what sort of greeting this might be. 30 Then the angel said to her, "Do not be afraid, Mary, for you have found favor with God. 31[n] Behold, you will conceive in your womb and bear a son, and you shall name him Jesus. 32[o] He will be great and will be called Son of the Most High,* and the Lord God will give him the throne of David his father, 33 and he will rule over the house of Jacob forever, and of his kingdom there will be no end."[p] 34 But Mary said to the angel, "How can this be, since I have no relations with a man?"* 35 And the angel said to her in reply, "The holy Spirit will come upon you, and the power of the Most High will overshadow you. Therefore the child to be born will be called holy, the Son of God.[q] 36 And behold, Elizabeth, your relative, has also conceived* a son in her old age, and this is the sixth month for her who was called barren; 37 for nothing will be impossible for God."[r] 38 Mary said, "Behold, I am the handmaid of the Lord. May it be done to me according to your word." Then the angel departed from her.

***Mary Visits Elizabeth.*** 39 During those days Mary set out and traveled to the hill country in haste to a town of Judah, 40 where she entered the house of Zechariah and greeted Elizabeth. 41 When Elizabeth heard Mary's greeting, the infant leaped in her womb, and Elizabeth, filled with the holy Spirit,[s] 42 cried out in a loud voice and said, "Most blessed are you among women, and blessed is the fruit of your womb.[t] 43 And how does this happen to me, that the mother of my Lord* should come to me? 44 For at the moment the sound of your greeting reached my ears, the infant in my womb leaped for joy. 45 Blessed are you who believed* that

**1:20 You will be speechless and unable to talk**: Zechariah's becoming mute is the sign given in response to his question in v 18. When Mary asks a similar question in Lk 1:34, unlike Zechariah who was punished for his doubt, she, in spite of her doubt, is praised and reassured (Lk 1:35–37).

**1:26–38** The announcement to Mary of the birth of Jesus is parallel to the announcement to Zechariah of the birth of John. In both the angel Gabriel appears to the parent who is troubled by the vision (Lk 1:11–12, 26–29) and then told by the angel not to fear (Lk 1:13, 30). After the announcement is made (Lk 1:14–17, 31–33) the parent objects (Lk 1:18, 34) and a sign is given to confirm the announcement (Lk 1:20, 36). The particular focus of the announcement of the birth of Jesus is on his identity as Son of David (Lk 1:32–33) and Son of God (Lk 1:32, 35).

**1:32 Son of the Most High**: cf. Lk 1:76 where John is described as "prophet of the Most High." "Most High" is a title for God commonly used by Luke (Lk 1:35, 76; 6:35; 8:28; Acts 7:48; 16:17).

**1:34** Mary's questioning response is a denial of sexual relations and is used by Luke to lead to the angel's declaration about the Spirit's role in the conception of this child (Lk 1:35). According to Luke, the virginal conception of Jesus takes place through the holy Spirit, the power of God, and therefore Jesus has a unique relationship to Yahweh: he is Son of God.

**1:36–37** The sign given to Mary in confirmation of the angel's announcement to her is the pregnancy of her aged relative Elizabeth. If a woman past the childbearing age could become pregnant, why, the angel implies, should there be doubt about Mary's pregnancy, for **nothing will be impossible for God**.

**1:43** Even before his birth, Jesus is identified in Luke as the Lord.

**1:45 Blessed are you who believed**: Luke portrays Mary as a believer whose faith stands in contrast to the disbelief of Zechariah (Lk 1:20). Mary's role as believer in the infancy narrative should be seen in connection with the explicit mention of her presence among "those who believed" after the resurrection at the beginning of the Acts of the Apostles (Acts 1:14).

*j:* 1:45. *k:* Gn 30:23. *l:* 2:5; Mt 1:16, 18. *m:* Jgs 6:12; Ru 2:4; Jdt 13:18. *n:* Gn 16:11; Jgs 13:3; Is 7:14; Mt 1:21–23. *o:* 2 Sm 7:12, 13, 16; Is 9:7. *p:* Dn 2:44; 7:14; Mi 4:7; Mt 28:18. *q:* Mt 1:20. *r:* Gn 18:14; Jer 32:27; Mt 19:26. *s:* 1:15; Gn 25:22 LXX. *t:* 11:27–28; Jgs 5:24; Jdt 13:18; Dt 28:4.

what was spoken to you by the Lord would
be fulfilled."[u]

*The Canticle of Mary.* 46[v] And Mary
said:*

"My soul proclaims the greatness of the
Lord;[w]
47 my spirit rejoices in God my savior.[x]
48 For he has looked upon his handmaid's
lowliness;
behold, from now on will all ages call
me blessed.[y]
49 The Mighty One has done great things
for me,
and holy is his name.[z]
50 His mercy is from age to age
to those who fear him.[a]
51 He has shown might with his arm,
dispersed the arrogant of mind and
heart.[b]
52 He has thrown down the rulers from their
thrones
but lifted up the lowly.[c]
53 The hungry he has filled with good
things;
the rich he has sent away empty.[d]
54 He has helped Israel his servant,
remembering his mercy,[e]
55 according to his promise to our fathers,
to Abraham and to his descendants
forever."[f]

56 Mary remained with her about three
months and then returned to her home.

*The Birth of John.** 57 When the time arrived
for Elizabeth to have her child she gave birth
to a son. 58 Her neighbors and relatives heard
that the Lord had shown his great mercy toward her, and they rejoiced with her.[g]
59* When they came on the eighth day to circumcise[h] the child, they were going to call
him Zechariah after his father, 60 but his
mother said in reply, "No. He will be called
John."[i] 61 But they answered her, "There is no
one among your relatives who has this name."
62 So they made signs, asking his father what
he wished him to be called. 63 He asked for a
tablet and wrote, "John is his name," and all
were amazed. 64 Immediately his mouth was
opened, his tongue freed, and he spoke blessing God.[j] 65 Then fear came upon all their
neighbors, and all these matters were discussed throughout the hill country of Judea.
66 All who heard these things took them to
heart, saying, "What, then, will this child be?"
For surely the hand of the Lord was with him.

*The Canticle of Zechariah.* 67 Then
Zechariah his father, filled with the holy
Spirit, prophesied, saying:

68 * "Blessed be the Lord, the God of Israel,
for he has visited and brought
redemption to his people.[k]

**1:46–55** Although Mary is praised for being the mother of the Lord and because of her belief, she reacts as the servant in a psalm of praise, the Magnificat. Because there is no specific connection of the canticle to the context of Mary's pregnancy and her visit to Elizabeth, the Magnificat (with the possible exception of v 48) may have been a Jewish Christian hymn that Luke found appropriate at this point in his story. Even if not composed by Luke, it fits in well with themes found elsewhere in Luke: joy and exultation in the Lord; the lowly being singled out for God's favor; the reversal of human fortunes; the fulfillment of Old Testament promises. The loose connection between the hymn and the context is further seen in the fact that a few Old Latin manuscripts identify the speaker of the hymn as Elizabeth, even though the overwhelming textual evidence makes Mary the speaker.

**1:57–66** The birth and circumcision of John above all emphasize John's incorporation into the people of Israel by the sign of the covenant (Gn 17:1–12). The narrative of John's circumcision also prepares the way for the subsequent description of the circumcision of Jesus in Lk 2:21. At the beginning of his two-volume work Luke shows those who play crucial roles in the inauguration of Christianity to be wholly a part of the people of Israel. At the end of the Acts of the Apostles (Acts 21:20; 22:3; 23:6–9; 24:14–16; 26:2–8, 22–23) he will argue that Christianity is the direct descendant of Pharisaic Judaism.

**1:59** The practice of Palestinian Judaism at this time was to name the child at birth; moreover, though naming a male child after the father is not completely unknown, the usual practice was to name the child after the grandfather (see Lk 1:61). The naming of the child John and Zechariah's recovery from his loss of speech should be understood as fulfilling the angel's announcement to Zechariah in Lk 1:13, 20.

**1:68–79** Like the canticle of Mary (Lk 1:46–55) the canticle of Zechariah is only loosely connected with its context. Apart from Lk 1:76–77, the hymn in speaking of **a horn for our salvation** (Lk 1:69) and **the daybreak from on high** (Lk 1:78) applies more closely to Jesus and his work than to John.

*u:* 1:20. *v:* 1 Sm 2:1–10. *w:* Ps 35:9; Is 61:10; Heb 3:18. *x:* Ti 3:4; Jude 25. *y:* 11:27; 1 Sm 1:11; 2 Sm 16:12; 2 Kgs 14:26; Ps 113:7. *z:* Dt 10:21; Ps 71:19; 111:9; 126:2–3. *a:* Ps 89:2; 103:13, 17. *b:* Ps 89:10; 118:15; Jer 32:17 (39:17 LXX). *c:* 1 Sm 2:7; 2 Sm 22:28; Jb 5:11; 12:19; Ps 147:6; Sir 10:14; Jas 4:6; 1 Pt 5:5. *d:* 1 Sm 2:5; Ps 107:9. *e:* Ps 98:3; Is 41:8–9. *f:* Gn 13:15; 17:7; 18:18; 22:17–18; Mi 7:20. *g:* 1:14. *h:* 2:21; Gn 17:10, 12; Lv 12:3. *i:* 1:13. *j:* 1:20. *k:* 7:16; Ps 41:13; 72:18; 106:48; 111:9.

69 * He has raised up a horn for our salvation
within the house of David his servant,[l]
70 even as he promised through the mouth of his holy prophets from of old:
71 salvation from our enemies and from the hand of all who hate us,[m]
72 to show mercy to our fathers[n] and to be mindful of his holy covenant[o]
73 and of the oath he swore to Abraham our father,[p]
and to grant us that, 74 rescued from the hand of enemies,
without fear we might worship him 75 in holiness and righteousness
before him all our days.[q]
76 And you, child, will be called prophet of the Most High,
for you will go before the Lord* to prepare his ways,[r]
77 to give his people knowledge of salvation
through the forgiveness of their sins,
78 because of the tender mercy of our God[s]
by which the daybreak from on high* will visit us[t]
79 to shine on those who sit in darkness and death's shadow,
to guide our feet into the path of peace."

80 The child grew and became strong in
spirit, and he was in the desert until the day
of his manifestation to Israel.[u]

## CHAPTER 2

See RG 307–309

*The Birth of Jesus.* 1* In those days a
decree went out from Caesar Augustus* that
the whole world should be enrolled. 2 This
was the first enrollment, when Quirinius was
governor of Syria. 3 So all went to be enrolled,
each to his own town. 4 And Joseph too went
up from Galilee from the town of Nazareth to
Judea, to the city of David that is called Bethlehem, because he was of the house and family of David,[v] 5 to be enrolled with Mary, his
betrothed, who was with child.[w] 6 While they

Again like Mary's canticle, it is largely composed of phrases taken from the Greek Old Testament and may have been a Jewish Christian hymn of praise that Luke adapted to fit the present context by inserting Lk 1:76–77 to give Zechariah's reply to the question asked in Lk 1:66.

**1:69 A horn for our salvation**: the horn is a common Old Testament figure for strength (Ps 18:3; 75:5–6; 89:18; 112:9; 148:14). This description is applied to God in Ps 18:2 and is here transferred to Jesus. The connection of the phrase with **the house of David** gives the title messianic overtones and may indicate an allusion to a phrase in Hannah's song of praise (1 Sm 2:10), "the horn of his anointed."

**1:76 You will go before the Lord**: here **the Lord** is most likely a reference to Jesus (contrast Lk 1:15–17 where Yahweh is meant) and John is presented as the precursor of Jesus.

**1:78 The daybreak from on high**: three times in the LXX (Jer 23:5; Zec 3:8; 6:12), the Greek word used here for **daybreak** translates the Hebrew word for "scion, branch," an Old Testament messianic title.

**2:1–2** Although universal registrations of Roman citizens are attested in 28 B.C., 8 B.C., and A.D. 14 and enrollments in individual provinces of those who are not Roman citizens are also attested, such a universal census of the Roman world under Caesar Augustus is unknown outside the New Testament. Moreover, there are notorious historical problems connected with Luke's dating the census **when Quirinius was governor of Syria**, and the various attempts to resolve the difficulties have proved unsuccessful. P. Sulpicius Quirinius became legate of the province of Syria in A.D. 6–7 when Judea was annexed to the province of Syria. At that time, a provincial census of Judea was taken up. If Quirinius had been legate of Syria previously, it would have to have been before 10 B.C. because the various legates of Syria from 10 B.C. to 4 B.C. (the death of Herod) are known, and such a dating for an earlier census under Quirinius would create additional problems for dating the beginning of Jesus' ministry (Lk 3:1, 23). A previous legateship after 4 B.C. (and before A.D. 6) would not fit with the dating of Jesus' birth in the days of Herod (Lk 1:5; Mt 2:1). Luke may simply be combining Jesus' birth in Bethlehem with his vague recollection of a census under Quirinius (see also Acts 5:37) to underline the significance of this birth for the whole Roman world: through this child born in Bethlehem peace and salvation come to the empire.

**2:1 Caesar Augustus**: the reign of the Roman emperor Caesar Augustus is usually dated from 27 B.C. to his death in A.D. 14. According to Greek inscriptions, Augustus was regarded in the Roman Empire as "savior" and "god," and he was credited with establishing a time of peace, the *pax Augusta*, throughout the Roman world during his long reign. It is not by chance that Luke relates the birth of Jesus to the time of Caesar Augustus: the real savior (Lk 2:11) and peace-bearer (Lk 2:14; see also Lk 19:38) is the child born in Bethlehem. The great emperor is simply God's agent (like the Persian king Cyrus in Is 44:28–45:1) who provides the occasion for God's purposes to be accomplished. **The whole world**: that is, the whole Roman world: Rome, Italy, and the Roman provinces.

*l:* Ps 18:3. *m:* Ps 106:10. *n:* Gn 17:7; Lv 26:42; Ps 105:8–9; Mi 7:20. *o:* Ps 106:45–46. *p:* Gn 22:16–17. *q:* Ti 2:12. *r:* Is 40:3; Mal 3:1; Mt 3:3; 11:10. *s:* Is 60:1–2. *t:* Mal 3:20. *u:* 2:40; Mt 3:1. *v:* Mi 5:2; Mt 2:6. *w:* 1:27; Mt 1:18.

were there, the time came for her to have her
child, 7 and she gave birth to her firstborn
son.* She wrapped him in swaddling clothes
and laid him in a manger, because there was
no room for them in the inn.[x]
8* Now there were shepherds in that region living in the fields and keeping the
night watch over their flock. 9 The angel of
the Lord appeared to them and the glory of
the Lord shone around them, and they were
struck with great fear.[y] 10 The angel said to
them, "Do not be afraid; for behold, I proclaim to you good news of great joy that will
be for all the people. 11* [z] For today in the
city of David a savior has been born for you
who is Messiah and Lord. 12 And this will be
a sign for you: you will find an infant
wrapped in swaddling clothes and lying in a
manger." 13 And suddenly there was a multitude of the heavenly host with the angel,
praising God and saying:

14 * "Glory to God in the highest[a]
and on earth peace to those on whom
his favor rests."

*The Visit of the Shepherds.* 15 When the
angels went away from them to heaven, the
shepherds said to one another, "Let us go,
then, to Bethlehem to see this thing that has
taken place, which the Lord has made
known to us." 16 So they went in haste and
found Mary and Joseph, and the infant lying
in the manger. 17 When they saw this, they
made known the message that had been told
them about this child. 18 All who heard it
were amazed by what had been told them by
the shepherds. 19 And Mary kept all these
things, reflecting on them in her heart.
20 Then the shepherds returned, glorifying
and praising God for all they had heard and
seen, just as it had been told to them.

*The Circumcision and Naming of Jesus.*
21 When eight days were completed for his
circumcision,* he was named Jesus, the
name given him by the angel before he was
conceived in the womb.[b]

*The Presentation in the Temple.* 22* When
the days were completed for their purification* according to the law of Moses, they
took him up to Jerusalem to present him to

**2:7 Firstborn son**: the description of Jesus as **firstborn** son does not necessarily mean that Mary had other sons. It is a legal description indicating that Jesus possessed the rights and privileges of the firstborn son (Gn 27; Ex 13:2; Nm 3:12–13; 18:15–16; Dt 21:15–17). See notes on Mt 1:25; Mk 6:3. **Wrapped him in swaddling clothes**: there may be an allusion here to the birth of another descendant of David, his son Solomon, who though a great king was wrapped in swaddling clothes like any other infant (Wis 7:4–6). **Laid him in a manger**: a feeding trough for animals. A possible allusion to Is 1:3 LXX.

**2:8–20** The announcement of Jesus' birth to the shepherds is in keeping with Luke's theme that the lowly are singled out as the recipients of God's favors and blessings (see also Lk 1:48, 52).

**2:11** The basic message of the infancy narrative is contained in the angel's announcement: this child is **savior, Messiah**, and **Lord**. Luke is the only synoptic gospel writer to use the title **savior** for Jesus (Lk 2:11; Acts 5:31; 13:23; see also Lk 1:69; 19:9; Acts 4:12). As savior, Jesus is looked upon by Luke as the one who rescues humanity from sin and delivers humanity from the condition of alienation from God. The title *christos*, "Christ," is the Greek equivalent of the Hebrew *māšîaḥ*, "Messiah," "anointed one." Among certain groups in first-century Palestinian Judaism, the title was applied to an expected royal leader from the line of David who would restore the kingdom to Israel (see Acts 1:6). The political overtones of the title are played down in Luke and instead the Messiah of the Lord (Lk 2:26) or the Lord's anointed is the one who now brings salvation to all humanity, Jew and Gentile (Lk 2:29–32). Lord is the most frequently used title for Jesus in Luke and Acts. In the New Testament it is also applied to Yahweh, as it is in the Old Testament. When used of Jesus it points to his transcendence and dominion over humanity.

**2:14 On earth peace to those on whom his favor rests**: the peace that results from the Christ event is for those whom God has favored with his grace. This reading is found in the oldest representatives of the Western and Alexandrian text traditions and is the preferred one; the Byzantine text tradition, on the other hand, reads: "on earth peace, good will toward men." The peace of which Luke's gospel speaks (Lk 2:14; 7:50; 8:48; 10:5–6; 19:38, 42; 24:36) is more than the absence of war of the *pax Augusta*; it also includes the security and well-being characteristic of peace in the Old Testament.

**2:21** Just as John before him had been incorporated into the people of Israel through his circumcision, so too this child (see note on Lk 1:57–66).

**2:22–40** The presentation of Jesus in the temple depicts the parents of Jesus as devout Jews, faithful observers of the law of the Lord (Lk 2:23–24, 39), i.e., the law of Moses. In this respect, they are described in a fashion similar to the parents of John (Lk 1:6) and Simeon (Lk 2:25) and Anna (Lk 2:36–37).

**2:22 Their purification**: syntactically, **their** must refer to Mary and Joseph, even though the Mosaic law never mentions the purification of the husband. Recognizing the problem, some Western scribes have altered the text to read "his purification," understanding the presentation of Jesus in the temple as a form of purification; the Vulgate version has a Latin form that could be either "his" or "her." According to the Mosaic law (Lv 12:2–8), the woman who gives birth to a

*x:* Mt 1:25. *y:* 1:11, 26. *z:* Mt 1:21; 16:16; Jn 4:42; Acts 2:36; 5:31; Phil 2:11. *a:* 19:38. *b:* 1:31; Gn 17:12; Mt 1:21.

the Lord,[c] 23 just as it is written in the law of
the Lord, "Every male that opens the womb
shall be consecrated to the Lord,"[d] 24 and to
offer the sacrifice of "a pair of turtledoves or
two young pigeons," in accordance with the
dictate in the law of the Lord.

25 Now there was a man in Jerusalem
whose name was Simeon. This man was
righteous and devout, awaiting the consolation of Israel,* and the holy Spirit was upon
him. 26 It had been revealed to him by the
holy Spirit that he should not see death before he had seen the Messiah of the Lord.
27 He came in the Spirit into the temple; and
when the parents brought in the child Jesus
to perform the custom of the law in regard to
him, 28 he took him into his arms and blessed
God, saying:

29 "Now, Master, you may let your servant go
in peace, according to your word,
30 for my eyes have seen your salvation,[e]
31 which you prepared in sight of all the
peoples,
32 a light for revelation to the Gentiles,
and glory for your people Israel."[f]

33 The child's father and mother were
amazed at what was said about him; 34 and
Simeon blessed them and said to Mary his
mother, "Behold, this child is destined for
the fall and rise of many in Israel, and to be
a sign that will be contradicted[g] 35 (and you
yourself a sword will pierce)* so that the
thoughts of many hearts may be revealed."

36 There was also a prophetess, Anna, the
daughter of Phanuel, of the tribe of Asher.
She was advanced in years, having lived
seven years with her husband after her marriage, 37 and then as a widow until she was
eighty-four. She never left the temple, but
worshiped night and day with fasting and
prayer. 38 And coming forward at that very
time, she gave thanks to God and spoke
about the child to all who were awaiting the
redemption of Jerusalem.[h]

***The Return to Nazareth.*** 39 When they had
fulfilled all the prescriptions of the law of
the Lord, they returned to Galilee, to their
own town of Nazareth.[i] 40 The child grew
and became strong, filled with wisdom; and
the favor of God was upon him.[j]

***The Boy Jesus in the Temple.**** 41 Each year
his parents went to Jerusalem for the feast of
Passover,[k] 42 and when he was twelve years
old, they went up according to festival custom. 43 After they had completed its days, as
they were returning, the boy Jesus remained
behind in Jerusalem, but his parents did not
know it. 44 Thinking that he was in the caravan, they journeyed for a day and looked for
him among their relatives and acquaintances,
45 but not finding him, they returned to Jerusalem to look for him. 46 After three days they
found him in the temple, sitting in the midst
of the teachers, listening to them and asking
them questions, 47 and all who heard him
were astounded at his understanding and his
answers. 48 When his parents saw him, they

boy is unable for forty days to touch anything sacred or to enter the temple area by reason of her legal impurity. At the end of this period she is required to offer a year-old lamb as a burnt offering and a turtledove or young pigeon as an expiation of sin. The woman who could not afford a lamb offered instead two turtledoves or two young pigeons, as Mary does here. **They took him up to Jerusalem to present him to the Lord**: as the firstborn son (Lk 2:7) Jesus was consecrated to the Lord as the law required (Ex 13:2, 12), but there was no requirement that this be done at the temple. The concept of a presentation at the temple is probably derived from 1 Sm 1:24–28, where Hannah offers the child Samuel for sanctuary services. The law further stipulated (Nm 3:47–48) that the firstborn son should be redeemed by the parents through their payment of five shekels to a member of a priestly family. About this legal requirement Luke is silent.

**2:25 Awaiting the consolation of Israel**: Simeon here and later Anna who speak about the child to all who were awaiting the redemption of Jerusalem represent the hopes and expectations of faithful and devout Jews who at this time were looking forward to the restoration of God's rule in Israel. The birth of Jesus brings these hopes to fulfillment.

**2:35 (And you yourself a sword will pierce)**: Mary herself will not be untouched by the various reactions to the role of Jesus (Lk 2:34). Her blessedness as mother of the Lord will be challenged by her son who describes true blessedness as "hearing the word of God and observing it" (Lk 11:27–28 and Lk 8:20–21).

**2:41–52** This story's concern with an incident from Jesus' youth is unique in the canonical gospel tradition. It presents Jesus in the role of the faithful Jewish boy, raised in the traditions of Israel, and fulfilling all that the law requires. With this episode, the infancy narrative ends just as it began, in the setting of the Jerusalem temple.

*c:* Lv 12:2–8. *d:* Ex 13:2, 12. *e:* 3:6; Is 40:5 LXX; 52:10. *f:* Is 42:6; 46:13; 49:6; Acts 13:47; 26:23. *g:* 12:51; Is 8:14; Jn 9:39; Rom 9:33; 1 Cor 1:23; 1 Pt 2:7–8. *h:* Is 52:9. *i:* Mt 2:23. *j:* 1:80; 2:52. *k:* Ex 12:24–27; 23:15; Dt 16:1–8.

were astonished, and his mother said to him,
"Son, why have you done this to us? Your father and I have been looking for you with
great anxiety." 49 And he said to them, "Why
were you looking for me? Did you not know
that I must be in my Father's house?"* 50 But
they did not understand what he said to them.
51 He went down with them and came to Nazareth, and was obedient to them; and his
mother kept all these things in her heart.[l]
52 And Jesus advanced [in] wisdom and age
and favor before God and man.[m]

## III. The Preparation for the Public Ministry

### CHAPTER 3

See RG 309

***The Preaching of John the Baptist.****

1 In the fifteenth year of the reign of Tiberius
Caesar,* when Pontius Pilate was governor
of Judea,[n] and Herod was tetrarch of Galilee,
and his brother Philip tetrarch of the region
of Ituraea and Trachonitis, and Lysanias was
tetrarch of Abilene, 2 during the high priesthood of Annas and Caiaphas,* the word of
God came to John[o] the son of Zechariah in
the desert. 3* He went throughout [the]
whole region of the Jordan, proclaiming a
baptism of repentance for the forgiveness of
sins,[p] 4* as it is written in the book of the
words of the prophet Isaiah:[q]

"A voice of one crying out in the desert:
'Prepare the way of the Lord,[r]
make straight his paths.
5 Every valley shall be filled
and every mountain and hill shall be
made low.
The winding roads shall be made straight,
and the rough ways made smooth,
6 and all flesh shall see the salvation of
God.' "[s]

**2:49 I must be in my Father's house**: this phrase can also be translated, "I must be about my Father's work." In either translation, Jesus refers to God as his Father. His divine sonship, and his obedience to his heavenly Father's will, take precedence over his ties to his family.

**3:1–20** Although Luke is indebted in this section to his sources, the Gospel of Mark and a collection of sayings of John the Baptist, he has clearly marked this introduction to the ministry of Jesus with his own individual style. Just as the gospel began with a long periodic sentence (Lk 1:1–4), so too this section (Lk 3:1–2). He casts the call of John the Baptist in the form of an Old Testament prophetic call (Lk 3:2) and extends the quotation from Isaiah found in Mk 1:3 (Is 40:3) by the addition of Is 40:4–5 in Lk 3:5–6. In doing so, he presents his theme of the universality of salvation, which he has announced earlier in the words of Simeon (Lk 2:30–32). Moreover, in describing the expectation of the people (Lk 3:15), Luke is characterizing the time of John's preaching in the same way as he had earlier described the situation of other devout Israelites in the infancy narrative (Lk 2:25–26, 37–38). In Lk 3:7–18 Luke presents the preaching of John the Baptist who urges the crowds to reform in view of **the coming wrath** (Lk 3:7, 9: eschatological preaching), and who offers the crowds certain standards for reforming social conduct (Lk 3:10–14: ethical preaching), and who announces to the crowds the coming of **one mightier than** he (Lk 3:15–18: messianic preaching).

**3:1 Tiberius Caesar**: Tiberius succeeded Augustus as emperor in A.D. 14 and reigned until A.D. 37. The fifteenth year of his reign, depending on the method of calculating his first regnal year, would have fallen between A.D. 27 and 29. **Pontius Pilate**: prefect of Judea from A.D. 26 to 36. The Jewish historian Josephus describes him as a greedy and ruthless prefect who had little regard for the local Jewish population and their religious practices (see Lk 13:1). **Herod**: i.e., Herod Antipas, the son of Herod the Great. He ruled over Galilee and Perea from 4 B.C. to A.D. 39. His official title **tetrarch** means literally, "ruler of a quarter," but came to designate any subordinate prince. **Philip**: also a son of Herod the Great, tetrarch of the territory to the north and east of the Sea of Galilee from 4 B.C. to A.D. 34. Only two small areas of this territory are mentioned by Luke. **Lysanias**: nothing is known about this Lysanias who is said here to have been tetrarch of Abilene, a territory northwest of Damascus.

**3:2 During the high priesthood of Annas and Caiaphas**: after situating the call of John the Baptist in terms of the civil rulers of the period, Luke now mentions the religious leadership of Palestine (see note on Lk 1:5). Annas had been high priest A.D. 6–15. After being deposed by the Romans in A.D. 15 he was succeeded by various members of his family and eventually by his son-in-law, Caiaphas, who was high priest A.D. 18–36. Luke refers to Annas as high priest at this time (but see Jn 18:13, 19), possibly because of the continuing influence of Annas or because the title continued to be used for the ex-high priest. **The word of God came to John**: Luke is alone among the New Testament writers in associating the preaching of John with a call from God. Luke is thereby identifying John with the prophets whose ministries began with similar calls. In Lk 7:26 John will be described as "more than a prophet"; he is also the precursor of Jesus (Lk 7:27), a transitional figure inaugurating the period of the fulfillment of prophecy and promise.

**3:3** See note on Mt 3:2.

**3:4** The Essenes from Qumran used the same passage to explain why their community was in the desert studying and observing the law and the prophets (1QS 8:12–15).

*l:* 2:19. *m:* 1:80; 2:40; 1 Sm 2:26. *n:* Mt 3:1–12; Mk 1:1–8; Jn 1:19–28. *o:* 1:80. *p:* Acts 13:24; 19:4. *q:* Is 40:3–5. *r:* Jn 1:23. *s:* 2:30–31.

7He said to the crowds who came out to be
baptized by him, "You brood of vipers! Who
warned you to flee from the coming wrath?[t]
8Produce good fruits as evidence of your repentance; and do not begin to say to yourselves, 'We have Abraham as our father,' for
I tell you, God can raise up children to Abraham from these stones.[u] 9Even now the ax
lies at the root of the trees. Therefore every
tree that does not produce good fruit will be
cut down and thrown into the fire."[v]
10And the crowds asked him, "What then
should we do?" 11He said to them in reply,
"Whoever has two tunics should share with
the person who has none. And whoever has
food should do likewise." 12Even tax collectors came to be baptized and they said to
him, "Teacher, what should we do?"[w] 13He
answered them, "Stop collecting more than
what is prescribed." 14Soldiers also asked
him, "And what is it that we should do?" He
told them, "Do not practice extortion, do not
falsely accuse anyone, and be satisfied with
your wages."
15[x] Now the people were filled with expectation, and all were asking in their hearts
whether John might be the Messiah. 16* John
answered them all, saying,[y] "I am baptizing
you with water, but one mightier than I is
coming. I am not worthy to loosen the
thongs of his sandals. He will baptize you
with the holy Spirit and fire. 17His winnowing fan* is in his hand to clear his threshing
floor and to gather the wheat into his barn,
but the chaff he will burn with unquenchable
fire."[z] 18Exhorting them in many other ways,
he preached good news to the people.
19* Now Herod the tetrarch,[a] who had been
censured by him because of Herodias, his
brother's wife, and because of all the evil
deeds Herod had committed, 20added still
another to these by [also] putting John in
prison.

***The Baptism of Jesus.*** * 21[b] After all the
people had been baptized and Jesus also had
been baptized and was praying,* heaven was
opened 22* [c] and the holy Spirit descended
upon him in bodily form like a dove. And a
voice came from heaven, "You are my
beloved Son; with you I am well pleased."

***The Genealogy of Jesus.*** * 23[d] When Jesus
began his ministry he was about thirty years
of age. He was the son, as was thought, of
Joseph, the son of Heli,[e] 24the son of Matthat, the son of Levi, the son of Melchi, the
son of Jannai, the son of Joseph, 25the son of
Mattathias, the son of Amos, the son of Nahum, the son of Esli, the son of Naggai, 26the
son of Maath, the son of Mattathias, the son
of Semein, the son of Josech, the son of

**3:16 He will baptize you with the holy Spirit and fire**: in contrast to John's baptism with water, Jesus is said to baptize with the holy Spirit and with fire. From the point of view of the early Christian community, the Spirit and fire must have been understood in the light of the fire symbolism of the pouring out of the Spirit at Pentecost (Acts 2:1–4); but as part of John's preaching, the Spirit and fire should be related to their purifying and refining characteristics (Ez 36:25–27; Mal 3:2–3). See note on Mt 3:11.

**3:17 Winnowing fan**: see note on Mt 3:12.

**3:19–20** Luke separates the ministry of John the Baptist from that of Jesus by reporting the imprisonment of John before the baptism of Jesus (Lk 3:21–22). Luke uses this literary device to serve his understanding of the periods of salvation history. With John the Baptist, the time of promise, the period of Israel, comes to an end; with the baptism of Jesus and the descent of the Spirit upon him, the time of fulfillment, the period of Jesus, begins. In his second volume, the Acts of the Apostles, Luke will introduce the third epoch in salvation history, the period of the church.

**3:21–22** This episode in Luke focuses on the heavenly message identifying Jesus as Son and, through the allusion to Is 42:1, as Servant of Yahweh. The relationship of Jesus to the Father has already been announced in the infancy narrative (Lk 1:32, 35; 2:49); it occurs here at the beginning of Jesus' Galilean ministry and will reappear in Lk 9:35 before another major section of Luke's gospel, the travel narrative (Lk 9:51–19:27). Elsewhere in Luke's writings (Lk 4:18; Acts 10:38), this incident will be interpreted as a type of anointing of Jesus.

**3:21 Was praying**: Luke regularly presents Jesus at prayer at important points in his ministry: here at his baptism; at the choice of the Twelve (Lk 6:12); before Peter's confession (Lk 9:18); at the transfiguration (Lk 9:28); when he teaches his disciples to pray (Lk 11:1); at the Last Supper (Lk 22:32); on the Mount of Olives (Lk 22:41); on the cross (Lk 23:46).

**3:22 You are my beloved Son; with you I am well pleased**: this is the best attested reading in the Greek manuscripts. The Western reading, "You are my Son, this day I have begotten you," is derived from Ps 2:7.

**3:23–38** Whereas Mt 1:2 begins the genealogy of Jesus with Abraham to emphasize Jesus' bonds with the people of Israel, Luke's universalism leads him to trace the descent of Jesus beyond Israel to Adam and beyond that to God (Lk 3:38) to stress again Jesus' divine sonship.

*t:* Mt 12:34. *u:* Jn 8:39. *v:* Mt 7:19; Jn 15:6. *w:* 7:29. *x:* Acts 13:25. *y:* 7:19–20; Jn 1:27; Acts 1:5; 11:16. *z:* Mt 3:12. *a:* Mt 14:3–4; Mk 6:17–18. *b:* Mt 3:13–17; Mk 1:9–11. *c:* 9:35; Ps 2:7; Is 42:1; Mt 12:18; 17:5; Mk 9:7; Jn 1:32; 2 Pt 1:17. *d:* Mt 1:1–17. *e:* 4:22; Jn 6:42.

Joda, 27the son of Joanan, the son of Rhesa,
the son of Zerubbabel, the son of Shealtiel,
the son of Neri,[f] 28the son of Melchi, the son
of Addi, the son of Cosam, the son of Elma-
dam, the son of Er, 29the son of Joshua, the
son of Eliezer, the son of Jorim, the son of
Matthat, the son of Levi, 30the son of Simeon, the son of Judah, the son of Joseph, the
son of Jonam, the son of Eliakim, 31[g] the son
of Melea, the son of Menna, the son of Mat-
tatha, the son of Nathan, the son of David,*
32the son of Jesse,[h] the son of Obed, the son
of Boaz, the son of Sala, the son of Nahshon,
33the son of Amminadab, the son of Admin,
the son of Arni, the son of Hezron, the son of
Perez,[i] the son of Judah,[j] 34the son of Jacob,
the son of Isaac, the son of Abraham,[k] the
son of Terah, the son of Nahor, 35the son of
Serug, the son of Reu, the son of Peleg, the
son of Eber, the son of Shelah, 36the son of
Cainan, the son of Arphaxad, the son of
Shem,[l] the son of Noah, the son of Lamech,
37the son of Methuselah, the son of Enoch,
the son of Jared, the son of Mahalaleel, the
son of Cainan, 38the son of Enos, the son of
Seth, the son of Adam,[m] the son of God.

See RG 309–10

## CHAPTER 4

***The Temptation of Jesus.**** 1[n] Filled
with the holy Spirit,* Jesus returned from the
Jordan and was led by the Spirit into the
desert 2for forty days,* to be tempted by the
devil. He ate nothing during those days, and
when they were over he was hungry.[o] 3The
devil said to him, "If you are the Son of God,
command this stone to become bread."
4Jesus answered him, "It is written, 'One
does not live by bread alone.' "[p] 5Then he
took him up and showed him all the kingdoms of the world in a single instant. 6The
devil said to him, "I shall give to you all this
power and their glory; for it has been handed
over to me, and I may give it to whomever I
wish.[q] 7All this will be yours, if you worship
me." 8Jesus said to him in reply, "It is written:

'You shall worship the Lord, your God,
and him alone shall you serve.' "[r]

9* Then he led him to Jerusalem, made him
stand on the parapet of the temple, and said
to him, "If you are the Son of God, throw
yourself down from here, 10for it is written:

'He will command his angels concerning
you,
to guard you,'[s]

11and:

'With their hands they will support you,
lest you dash your foot against a
stone.' "[t]

12Jesus said to him in reply, "It also says,
'You shall not put the Lord, your God, to the
test.' "[u] 13* When the devil had finished
every temptation,[v] he departed from him for
a time.

# IV. The Ministry in Galilee

***The Beginning of the Galilean Ministry.***
14[w] Jesus returned to Galilee in the power of
the Spirit, and news of him spread* throughout the whole region.[x] 15He taught in their
synagogues and was praised by all.

**3:31 The son of Nathan, the son of David**: in keeping with Jesus' prophetic role in Luke and Acts (e.g., Lk 7:16, 39; 9:8; 13:33; 24:19; Acts 3:22–23; 7:37) Luke traces Jesus' Davidic ancestry through the prophet Nathan (see 2 Sm 7:2) rather than through King Solomon, as Mt 1:6–7.

**4:1–13** See note on Mt 4:1–11.

**4:1 Filled with the holy Spirit**: as a result of the descent of the Spirit upon him at his baptism (Lk 3:21–22), Jesus is now equipped to overcome the devil. Just as the Spirit is prominent at this early stage of Jesus' ministry (Lk 4:1, 14, 18), so too it will be at the beginning of the period of the church in Acts (Acts 1:4; 2:4, 17).

**4:2 For forty days**: the mention of forty days recalls the forty years of the wilderness wanderings of the Israelites during the Exodus (Dt 8:2).

**4:9 To Jerusalem**: the Lucan order of the temptations concludes on the parapet of the temple in Jerusalem, the city of destiny in Luke-Acts. It is in Jerusalem that Jesus will ultimately face his destiny (Lk 9:51; 13:33).

**4:13 For a time**: the devil's opportune time will occur before the passion and death of Jesus (Lk 22:3, 31–32, 53).

**4:14 News of him spread**: a Lucan theme; see Lk 4:37; 5:15; 7:17.

*f:* 1 Chr 3:17; Ez 3:2. *g:* 2 Sm 5:14. *h:* 1 Sm 16:1, 18. *i:* Ru 4:17–22; 1 Chr 2:1–15. *j:* Gn 29:35; 38:29. *k:* Gn 21:3; 25:26; 1 Chr 1:34; 28:34. *l:* Gn 11:10–26; 1 Chr 1:24–27. *m:* Gn 4:25–5:32; 1 Chr 1:1–4. *n:* Mt 4:1–11; Mk 1:12–13. *o:* Heb 4:15. *p:* Dt 8:3. *q:* Jer 27:5; Mt 28:18. *r:* Dt 6:13. *s:* Ps 91:11. *t:* Ps 91:12. *u:* Dt 6:16; 1 Cor 10:9. *v:* 22:3; Jn 13:2, 27; Heb 4:15. *w:* Mt 4:12–17; Mk 1:14–15. *x:* 5:15; Mt 3:16.

***The Rejection at Nazareth.***[*] [y] 16 He came
to Nazareth, where he had grown up, and
went according to his custom[*] into the synagogue on the sabbath day. He stood up to
read 17 and was handed a scroll of the prophet
Isaiah. He unrolled the scroll and found the
passage where it was written:

18 "The Spirit of the Lord is upon me,[*]
because he has anointed me
to bring glad tidings to the poor.[z]
He has sent me to proclaim liberty to
captives
and recovery of sight to the blind,
to let the oppressed go free,
19 and to proclaim a year acceptable to the
Lord."

20 Rolling up the scroll, he handed it back to
the attendant and sat down, and the eyes of
all in the synagogue looked intently at him.
21 He said to them, "Today this scripture passage is fulfilled in your hearing."[*] 22 And all
spoke highly of him and were amazed at the
gracious words that came from his mouth.
They also asked, "Isn't this the son of Joseph?"[a] 23 He said to them, "Surely you will
quote me this proverb, 'Physician, cure
yourself,' and say, 'Do here in your native
place the things that we heard were done in
Capernaum.' "[*] 24 And he said, "Amen, I say
to you, no prophet is accepted in his own native place. 25[*] Indeed, I tell you, there were
many widows in Israel in the days of Elijah
when the sky was closed for three and a half
years and a severe famine spread over the
entire land.[b] 26[*] It was to none of these that
Elijah was sent, but only to a widow in
Zarephath[c] in the land of Sidon. 27 Again,
there were many lepers in Israel during the
time of Elisha the prophet; yet not one of
them was cleansed, but only Naaman the
Syrian."[d] 28 When the people in the synagogue heard this, they were all filled with
fury. 29 They rose up, drove him out of the
town, and led him to the brow of the hill on
which their town had been built, to hurl him
down headlong. 30 But he passed through the
midst of them and went away.

***The Cure of a Demoniac.*** 31[*] Jesus then
went down to Capernaum,[e] a town of Galilee.[f] He taught them on the sabbath, 32 and
they were astonished at his teaching because

**4:16–30** Luke has transposed to the beginning of Jesus' ministry an incident from his Marcan source, which situated it near the end of the Galilean ministry (Mk 6:1–6a). In doing so, Luke turns the initial admiration (Lk 4:22) and subsequent rejection of Jesus (Lk 4:28–29) into a foreshadowing of the whole future ministry of Jesus. Moreover, the rejection of Jesus in his own hometown hints at the greater rejection of him by Israel (Acts 13:46).

**4:16 According to his custom**: Jesus' practice of regularly attending synagogue is carried on by the early Christians' practice of meeting in the temple (Acts 2:46; 3:1; 5:12).

**4:18 The Spirit of the Lord is upon me, because he has anointed me**: see note on Lk 3:21–22. As this incident develops, Jesus is portrayed as a prophet whose ministry is compared to that of the prophets Elijah and Elisha. Prophetic anointings are known in first-century Palestinian Judaism from the Qumran literature that speaks of prophets as God's anointed ones. **To bring glad tidings to the poor**: more than any other gospel writer Luke is concerned with Jesus' attitude toward the economically and socially poor (see Lk 6:20, 24; 12:16–21; 14:12–14; 16:19–26; 19:8). At times, the poor in Luke's gospel are associated with the downtrodden, the oppressed and afflicted, the forgotten and the neglected (Lk 4:18; 6:20–22; 7:22; 14:12–14), and it is they who accept Jesus' message of salvation.

**4:21 Today this scripture passage is fulfilled in your hearing**: this sermon inaugurates the time of fulfillment of Old Testament prophecy. Luke presents the ministry of Jesus as fulfilling Old Testament hopes and expectations (Lk 7:22); for Luke, even Jesus' suffering, death, and resurrection are done in fulfillment of the scriptures (Lk 24:25–27, 44–46; Acts 3:18).

**4:23 The things that we heard were done in Capernaum**: Luke's source for this incident reveals an awareness of an earlier ministry of Jesus in Capernaum that Luke has not yet made use of because of his transposition of this Nazareth episode to the beginning of Jesus' Galilean ministry. It is possible that by use of the future tense **you will quote me . . .**, Jesus is being portrayed as a prophet.

**4:25–26** The references to Elijah and Elisha serve several purposes in this episode: they emphasize Luke's portrait of Jesus as a prophet like Elijah and Elisha; they help to explain why the initial admiration of the people turns to rejection; and they provide the scriptural justification for the future Christian mission to the Gentiles.

**4:26 A widow in Zarephath in the land of Sidon**: like Naaman the Syrian in Lk 4:27, a non-Israelite becomes the object of the prophet's ministry.

**4:31–44** The next several incidents in Jesus' ministry take place in Capernaum and are based on Luke's source, Mk 1:21–39. To the previous portrait of Jesus as prophet (Lk 4:16–30) they now add a presentation of him as teacher (Lk 4:31–32), exorcist (Lk 4:32–37, 41), healer (Lk 4:38–40), and proclaimer of God's kingdom (Lk 4:43).

*y:* Mt 13:53–58; Mk 6:1–6. *z:* Is 61:1–2; 58:6. *a:* 3:23; Jn 6:42. *b:* 1 Kgs 17:1–7; 18:1; Jas 5:17. *c:* 1 Kgs 17:9. *d:* 2 Kgs 5:1–14. *e:* Mk 1:21–28. *f:* Mt 4:13; Jn 2:12.

he spoke with authority.[g] 33 In the synagogue
there was a man with the spirit of an unclean
demon,[h] and he cried out in a loud voice,
34 "Ha! What have you to do with us, Jesus of
Nazareth? Have you come to destroy us?* I
know who you are—the Holy One of God!"[i]
35 Jesus rebuked him and said, "Be quiet!
Come out of him!" Then the demon threw
the man down in front of them and came out
of him without doing him any harm. 36 They
were all amazed and said to one another,
"What is there about his word? For with authority and power he commands the unclean
spirits, and they come out." 37 And news of
him spread everywhere in the surrounding
region.

***The Cure of Simon's Mother-in-Law.***
38[j] After he left the synagogue, he entered
the house of Simon.* Simon's mother-in-law
was afflicted with a severe fever, and they
interceded with him about her. 39 He stood
over her, rebuked the fever, and it left her.
She got up immediately and waited on them.

***Other Healings.***[k] 40 At sunset, all who had
people sick with various diseases brought
them to him. He laid his hands on each of
them and cured them. 41* And demons also
came out from many, shouting, "You are the
Son of God."[l] But he rebuked them and did
not allow them to speak because they knew
that he was the Messiah.

***Jesus Leaves Capernaum.***[m] 42* At daybreak, Jesus left and went to a deserted place.
The crowds went looking for him, and when
they came to him, they tried to prevent him
from leaving them. 43 But he said to them,
"To the other towns also I must proclaim the
good news of the kingdom of God, because
for this purpose I have been sent."[n] 44 And he
was preaching in the synagogues of Judea.*

## CHAPTER 5

See RG 310–11

***The Call of Simon the Fisherman.**** [o]
1[p] While the crowd was pressing in on Jesus
and listening to the word of God, he was
standing by the Lake of Gennesaret. 2 He saw
two boats there alongside the lake; the fishermen had disembarked and were washing
their nets. 3 Getting into one of the boats, the
one belonging to Simon, he asked him to put
out a short distance from the shore. Then he
sat down and taught the crowds from the
boat. 4[q] After he had finished speaking, he
said to Simon, "Put out into deep water and
lower your nets for a catch." 5 Simon said in
reply, "Master, we have worked hard all
night and have caught nothing, but at your
command I will lower the nets." 6 When they

**4:34 What have you to do with us?**: see note on Jn 2:4. **Have you come to destroy us?**: the question reflects the current belief that before the day of the Lord control over humanity would be wrested from the evil spirits, evil destroyed, and God's authority over humanity reestablished. The synoptic gospel tradition presents Jesus carrying out this task.

**4:38 The house of Simon**: because of Luke's arrangement of material, the reader has not yet been introduced to Simon (cf. Mk 1:16–18, 29–31). Situated as it is before the call of Simon (Lk 5:1–11), it helps the reader to understand Simon's eagerness to do what Jesus says (Lk 5:5) and to follow him (Lk 5:11).

**4:41 They knew that he was the Messiah**: that is, the Christ (see note on Lk 2:11).

**4:42 They tried to prevent him from leaving them**: the reaction of these strangers in Capernaum is presented in contrast to the reactions of those in his hometown who rejected him (Lk 4:28–30).

**4:44 In the synagogues of Judea**: instead of **Judea**, which is the best reading of the manuscript tradition, the Byzantine text tradition and other manuscripts read "Galilee," a reading that harmonizes Luke with Mt 4:23 and Mk 1:39. Up to this point Luke has spoken only of a ministry of Jesus in Galilee. Luke may be using **Judea** to refer to the land of Israel, the territory of the Jews, and not to a specific portion of it.

**5:1–11** This incident has been transposed from his source, Mk 1:16–20, which places it immediately after Jesus makes his appearance in Galilee. By this transposition Luke uses this example of Simon's acceptance of Jesus to counter the earlier rejection of him by his hometown people, and since several incidents dealing with Jesus' power and authority have already been narrated, Luke creates a plausible context for the acceptance of Jesus by Simon and his partners. Many commentators have noted the similarity between the wondrous catch of fish reported here (Lk 4:4–9) and the post-resurrectional appearance of Jesus in Jn 21:1–11. There are traces in Luke's story that the post-resurrectional context is the original one: in Lk 4:8 Simon addresses Jesus as **Lord** (a post-resurrectional title for Jesus—see Lk 24:34; Acts 2:36—that has been read back into the historical ministry of Jesus) and recognizes himself as a sinner (an appropriate recognition for one who has denied knowing Jesus—Lk 22:54–62). As used by Luke, the incident looks forward to Peter's leadership in Luke-Acts (Lk 6:14; 9:20; 22:31–32; 24:34; Acts 1:15; 2:14–40; 10:11–18; 15:7–12) and symbolizes the future success of Peter as fisherman (Acts 2:41).

*g:* Mt 7:28–29. *h:* 8:28; Mt 8:29; Mk 1:23–24; 5:7. *i:* 4:41; Jn 6:69. *j:* Mt 8:14–15; Mk 1:29–31. *k:* Mt 8:16; Mk 1:32–34. *l:* 4:34; Mt 8:29; Mk 3:11–12. *m:* Mk 1:35–39. *n:* 8:1; Mk 1:14–15. *o:* Mt 4:18–22; Mk 1:16–20. *p:* Mt 13:1–2; Mk 2:13; 3:9–10; 4:1–2. *q:* Jn 21:1–11.

had done this, they caught a great number of fish and their nets were tearing. [7]They signaled to their partners in the other boat to come to help them. They came and filled both boats so that they were in danger of sinking. [8]When Simon Peter saw this, he fell at the knees of Jesus and said, "Depart from me, Lord, for I am a sinful man." [9]For astonishment at the catch of fish they had made seized him and all those with him, [10]and likewise James and John, the sons of Zebedee, who were partners of Simon. Jesus said to Simon, "Do not be afraid; from now on you will be catching men."[r] [11]When they brought their boats to the shore, they left everything* and followed him.[s]

***The Cleansing of a Leper.***[t] [12]Now there was a man full of leprosy* in one of the towns where he was; and when he saw Jesus, he fell prostrate, pleaded with him, and said, "Lord, if you wish, you can make me clean." [13]Jesus stretched out his hand, touched him, and said, "I do will it. Be made clean." And the leprosy left him immediately. [14]Then he ordered him not to tell anyone, but "Go, show yourself to the priest and offer for your cleansing what Moses prescribed;* that will be proof for them."[u] [15]The report about him spread all the more, and great crowds assembled to listen to him and to be cured of their ailments, [16]but he would withdraw to deserted places to pray.[v]

***The Healing of a Paralytic.***[w] [17]* One day as Jesus was teaching, Pharisees* and teachers of the law were sitting there who had come from every village of Galilee and Judea and Jerusalem, and the power of the Lord was with him for healing. [18]And some men brought on a stretcher a man who was paralyzed; they were trying to bring him in and set [him] in his presence. [19]But not finding a way to bring him in because of the crowd, they went up on the roof and lowered him on the stretcher through the tiles* into the middle in front of Jesus. [20]When he saw their faith, he said, "As for you, your sins are forgiven."* [21]Then the scribes* and Pharisees began to ask themselves, "Who is this who speaks blasphemies? Who but God alone can forgive sins?"[x] [22]Jesus knew their thoughts and said to them in reply, "What are you thinking in your hearts?[y] [23]Which is easier, to say, 'Your sins are forgiven,' or to say, 'Rise and walk'? [24]* [z] But that you may know that the Son of Man has authority on earth to forgive sins"—he said to the man who was paralyzed, "I say to you, rise, pick up your stretcher, and go home." [25]He stood up immediately before them, picked up what he had been lying on, and went home, glorifying God. [26]Then astonishment seized them all and they glorified God, and, struck with awe, they said, "We have seen incredible things today."

***The Call of Levi.***[a] [27]After this he went out and saw a tax collector named Levi sitting at the customs post. He said to him, "Follow me." [28]And leaving everything behind,* he

**5:11 They left everything**: in Mk 1:16–20 and Mt 4:18–22 the fishermen who follow Jesus leave their nets and their father; in Luke, they leave **everything** (see also Lk 5:28; 12:33; 14:33; 18:22), an indication of Luke's theme of complete detachment from material possessions.

**5:12 Full of leprosy**: see note on Mk 1:40.

**5:14 Show yourself to the priest . . . what Moses prescribed**: this is a reference to Lv 14:2–9 that gives detailed instructions for the purification of one who had been a victim of leprosy and thereby excluded from contact with others (see Lv 13:45–46, 49; Nm 5:2–3). **That will be proof for them**: see note on Mt 8:4.

**5:17–6:11** From his Marcan source, Luke now introduces a series of controversies with Pharisees: controversy over Jesus' power to forgive sins (Lk 5:17–26); controversy over his eating and drinking with tax collectors and sinners (Lk 5:27–32); controversy over not fasting (Lk 5:33–36); and finally two episodes narrating controversies over observance of the sabbath (Lk 5:1–11).

**5:17 Pharisees**: see note on Mt 3:7.

**5:19 Through the tiles**: Luke has adapted the story found in Mark to his non-Palestinian audience by changing "opened up the roof" (Mk 2:4 a reference to Palestinian straw and clay roofs) to **through the tiles**, a detail that reflects the Hellenistic Greco-Roman house with tiled roof.

**5:20 As for you, your sins are forgiven**: literally, "O man, your sins are forgiven you." The connection between the forgiveness of sins and the cure of the paralytic reflects the belief of first-century Palestine (based on the Old Testament: Ex 20:5; Dt 5:9) that sickness and infirmity are the result of sin, one's own or that of one's ancestors (see also Lk 13:2; Jn 5:14; 9:2).

**5:21 The scribes**: see note on Mk 2:6.

**5:24** See notes on Mt 9:6 and Mk 2:10.

**5:28 Leaving everything behind**: see note on Lk 5:11.

*r:* Jer 16:16. *s:* Mt 19:27. *t:* Mt 8:2–4; Mk 1:40–45. *u:* 8:56; Lv 14:2–32; Mk 7:36. *v:* Mk 1:35. *w:* Mt 9:1–8; Mk 2:1–12. *x:* 7:49; Is 43:25. *y:* 6:8; 9:47. *z:* Jn 5:8–9, 27. *a:* Mt 9:9–13; Mk 2:13–17.

got up and followed him. 29b Then Levi gave
a great banquet for him in his house, and a
large crowd of tax collectors and others were
at table with them. 30 The Pharisees and their
scribes complained to his disciples, saying,
"Why do you eat and drink with tax collectors
and sinners?" 31 Jesus said to them in reply,
"Those who are healthy do not need a physician, but the sick do. 32 I have not come to call
the righteous to repentance but sinners."
*The Question About Fasting.*[c] 33 And they
said to him, "The disciples of John fast often
and offer prayers, and the disciples of the
Pharisees do the same; but yours eat and
drink." 34* Jesus answered them, "Can you
make the wedding guests* fast while the
bridegroom is with them? 35 But the days will
come, and when the bridegroom is taken
away from them, then they will fast in those
days." 36* And he also told them a parable.
"No one tears a piece from a new cloak to
patch an old one. Otherwise, he will tear the
new and the piece from it will not match the
old cloak. 37 Likewise, no one pours new wine
into old wineskins. Otherwise, the new wine
will burst the skins, and it will be spilled, and
the skins will be ruined. 38 Rather, new wine
must be poured into fresh wineskins. 39 [And]
no one who has been drinking old wine desires new, for he says, 'The old is good.'"*

## CHAPTER 6

See RG 311

*Debates About the Sabbath.** 1d While
he was going through a field of grain on a sabbath, his disciples were picking the heads of
grain, rubbing them in their hands, and eating
them.[e] 2 Some Pharisees said, "Why are you
doing what is unlawful on the sabbath?"
3f Jesus said to them in reply, "Have you not
read what David did when he and those [who
were] with him were hungry? 4 [How] he
went into the house of God, took the bread of
offering,* which only the priests could lawfully eat, ate of it, and shared it with his companions."[g] 5 Then he said to them, "The Son of
Man is lord of the sabbath."
6h On another sabbath he went into the
synagogue and taught, and there was a man
there whose right hand was withered. 7 The
scribes and the Pharisees watched him
closely to see if he would cure on the sabbath so that they might discover a reason to
accuse him.[i] 8 But he realized their intentions
and said to the man with the withered hand,
"Come up and stand before us." And he rose
and stood there.[j] 9 Then Jesus said to them, "I
ask you, is it lawful to do good on the sabbath rather than to do evil, to save life rather
than to destroy it?" 10 Looking around at
them all, he then said to him, "Stretch out
your hand." He did so and his hand was restored. 11 But they became enraged and discussed together what they might do to Jesus.
*The Mission of the Twelve.** 12k In those
days he departed to the mountain to pray,
and he spent the night in prayer* to God.
13 When day came, he called his disciples to
himself, and from them he chose Twelve,*

**5:34–35** See notes on Mt 9:15 and Mk 2:19.

**5:34 Wedding guests**: literally, "sons of the bridal chamber."

**5:36–39** See notes on Mt 9:16–17 and Mk 2:19.

**5:39 The old is good**: this saying is meant to be ironic and offers an explanation for the rejection by some of the new wine that Jesus offers: satisfaction with old forms will prevent one from sampling the new.

**6:1–11** The two episodes recounted here deal with gathering grain and healing, both of which were forbidden on the sabbath. In his defense of his disciples' conduct and his own charitable deed, Jesus argues that satisfying human needs such as hunger and performing works of mercy take precedence even over the sacred sabbath rest. See also notes on Mt 12:1–14 and Mk 2:25–26.

**6:4 The bread of offering**: see note on Mt 12:5–6.

**6:12–16** See notes on Mt 10:1–11:1 and Mk 3:14–15.

**6:12 Spent the night in prayer**: see note on Lk 3:21.

**6:13 He chose Twelve**: the identification of this group as the **Twelve** is a part of early Christian tradition (see 1 Cor 15:5), and in Matthew and Luke, the **Twelve** are associated with the twelve tribes of Israel (Lk 22:29–30; Mt 19:28). After the fall of Judas from his position among the Twelve, the need is felt on the part of the early community to reconstitute this group before the Christian mission begins at Pentecost (Acts 1:15–26). From Luke's perspective, they are an important group who because of their association with Jesus from the time of his baptism to his ascension (Acts 1:21–22) provide the continuity between the historical Jesus and the church of Luke's day and who as the original eyewitnesses guarantee the fidelity of the church's beliefs and practices to the teachings of Jesus (Lk 1:1–4). **Whom he also named apostles**: only Luke among the gospel writers attributes to Jesus the bestowal of the name **apostles** upon the Twelve. See note on Mt 10:2–4. "Apostle" becomes a technical term in

*b:* 15:1–2. *c:* Mt 9:14–17; Mk 2:18–22. *d:* Mt 12:1–8; Mk 2:23–28. *e:* Dt 23:26. *f:* 1 Sm 21:1–6. *g:* Lv 24:5–9. *h:* Mt 12:9–14; Mk 3:1–6. *i:* 14:1. *j:* 5:22; 9:47. *k:* Mt 10:1–4; Mk 3:13–19.

whom he also named apostles: [14l] Simon, whom he named Peter,* and his brother Andrew, James, John, Philip, Bartholomew, [15] Matthew, Thomas, James the son of Alphaeus, Simon who was called a Zealot,* [16] and Judas the son of James, and Judas Iscariot,* who became a traitor.

***Ministering to a Great Multitude.***[m]
[17*] And he came down with them and stood on a stretch of level ground. A great crowd of his disciples and a large number of the people from all Judea and Jerusalem and the coastal region of Tyre and Sidon [18] came to hear him and to be healed of their diseases; and even those who were tormented by unclean spirits were cured. [19] Everyone in the crowd sought to touch him because power came forth from him and healed them all.

***Sermon on the Plain.***[n] [20*] And raising his eyes toward his disciples he said:

"Blessed are you who are poor,*
for the kingdom of God is yours.
[21] Blessed are you who are now hungry,
for you will be satisfied.
Blessed are you who are now weeping,
for you will laugh.[o]
[22] Blessed are you when people hate you,
and when they exclude and insult you,
and denounce your name as evil
on account of the Son of Man.[p]

[23] Rejoice and leap for joy on that day! Behold, your reward will be great in heaven. For their ancestors treated the prophets in the same way.[q]

[24] But woe to you who are rich,
for you have received your consolation.[r]
[25] But woe to you who are filled now,
for you will be hungry.
Woe to you who laugh now,
for you will grieve and weep.[s]
[26] Woe to you when all speak well of you,
for their ancestors treated the false
prophets in this way.[t]

***Love of Enemies.**** [27u] "But to you who hear I say, love your enemies, do good to those who hate you,[v] [28] bless those who curse you, pray for those who mistreat you.[w]

early Christianity for a missionary sent out to preach the word of God. Although Luke seems to want to restrict the title to the Twelve (only in Acts 4:4, 14 are Paul and Barnabas termed apostles), other places in the New Testament show an awareness that the term was more widely applied (1 Cor 15:5–7; Gal 1:19; 1 Cor 1:1; 9:1; Rom 16:7).

**6:14 Simon, whom he named Peter**: see note on Mk 3:16.

**6:15 Simon who was called a Zealot**: the Zealots were the instigators of the First Revolt of Palestinian Jews against Rome in A.D. 66–70. Because the existence of the Zealots as a distinct group during the lifetime of Jesus is the subject of debate, the meaning of the identification of Simon as a Zealot is unclear.

**6:16 Judas Iscariot**: the name **Iscariot** may mean "man from Kerioth."

**6:17 The coastal region of Tyre and Sidon**: not only Jews from Judea and Jerusalem, but even Gentiles from outside Palestine come to hear Jesus (see Lk 2:31–32; 3:6; 4:24–27).

**6:20–49** Luke's "Sermon on the Plain" is the counterpart to Matthew's "Sermon on the Mount" (Mt 5:1–7:27). It is addressed to the disciples of Jesus, and, like the sermon in Matthew, it begins with beatitudes (Lk 6:20–22) and ends with the parable of the two houses (Lk 6:46–49). Almost all the words of Jesus reported by Luke are found in Matthew's version, but because Matthew includes sayings that were related to specifically Jewish Christian problems (e.g., Mt 5:17–20; 6:1–8, 16–18) that Luke did not find appropriate for his predominantly Gentile Christian audience, the "Sermon on the Mount" is considerably longer. Luke's sermon may be outlined as follows: an introduction consisting of blessings and woes (Lk 6:20–26); the love of one's enemies (Lk 6:27–36); the demands of loving one's neighbor (Lk 6:37–42); good deeds as proof of one's goodness (Lk 6:43–45); a parable illustrating the result of listening to and acting on the words of Jesus (Lk 6:46–49). At the core of the sermon is Jesus' teaching on the love of one's enemies (Lk 6:27–36) that has as its source of motivation God's graciousness and compassion for all humanity (Lk 6:35–36) and Jesus' teaching on the love of one's neighbor (Lk 6:37–42) that is characterized by forgiveness and generosity.

**6:20–26** The introductory portion of the sermon consists of blessings and woes that address the real economic and social conditions of humanity (the poor—the rich; the hungry—the satisfied; those grieving—those laughing; the outcast—the socially acceptable). By contrast, Matthew emphasizes the religious and spiritual values of disciples in the kingdom inaugurated by Jesus ("poor in spirit," Mt 5:3; "hunger and thirst for righteousness," Mt 5:6). In the sermon, **blessed** extols the fortunate condition of persons who are favored with the blessings of God; the woes, addressed as they are to the disciples of Jesus, threaten God's profound displeasure on those so blinded by their present fortunate situation that they do not recognize and appreciate the real values of God's kingdom. In all the blessings and woes, the present condition of the persons addressed will be reversed in the future.

**6:27–36** See notes on Mt 5:43–48 and Mt 5:48.

*l:* Acts 1:13. *m:* Mt 4:23–25; Mk 3:7–10. *n:* Mt 5:1–12. *o:* Ps 126:5–6; Is 61:3; Jer 31:25; Rev 7:16–17. *p:* Jn 15:19; 16:2; 1 Pt 4:14. *q:* 11:47–48; 2 Chr 36:16; Mt 23:30–31. *r:* Jas 5:1. *s:* Is 65:13–14. *t:* Jas 4:4. *u:* Mt 5:38–48. *v:* Prv 25:21; Rom 12:20–21. *w:* Rom 12:14; 1 Pt 3:9.

[29]To the person who strikes you on one
cheek, offer the other one as well, and from
the person who takes your cloak, do not
withhold even your tunic. [30]Give to everyone who asks of you, and from the one who
takes what is yours do not demand it back.
[31]Do to others as you would have them do to
you.[x] [32]For if you love those who love you,
what credit is that to you? Even sinners love
those who love them. [33]And if you do good
to those who do good to you, what credit is
that to you? Even sinners do the same. [34]If
you lend money to those from whom you expect repayment, what credit [is] that to you?
Even sinners lend to sinners, and get back
the same amount.[y] [35]But rather, love your
enemies and do good to them, and lend expecting nothing back; then your reward will
be great and you will be children of the Most
High, for he himself is kind to the ungrateful
and the wicked.[z] [36]Be merciful, just as [also]
your Father is merciful.

***Judging Others.**** [37][a] "Stop judging and you
will not be judged. Stop condemning and you
will not be condemned. Forgive and you will
be forgiven.[b] [38]Give and gifts will be given to
you; a good measure, packed together, shaken
down, and overflowing, will be poured into
your lap. For the measure with which you
measure will in return be measured out to
you."[c] [39]And he told them a parable, "Can a
blind person guide a blind person? Will not
both fall into a pit?[d] [40]No disciple is superior
to the teacher; but when fully trained, every
disciple will be like his teacher.[e] [41]Why do
you notice the splinter in your brother's eye,
but do not perceive the wooden beam in your
own? [42]How can you say to your brother,
'Brother, let me remove that splinter in your
eye,' when you do not even notice the
wooden beam in your own eye? You hypocrite! Remove the wooden beam from your
eye first; then you will see clearly to remove
the splinter in your brother's eye.

***A Tree Known by Its Fruit.***[f] [43]* "A good
tree does not bear rotten fruit, nor does a rotten tree bear good fruit. [44]For every tree is
known by its own fruit. For people do not
pick figs from thornbushes, nor do they
gather grapes from brambles. [45]A good person out of the store of goodness in his heart
produces good, but an evil person out of a
store of evil produces evil; for from the fullness of the heart the mouth speaks.

***The Two Foundations.*** [46][g] "Why do you
call me, 'Lord, Lord,' but not do what I command? [47]* I will show you what someone is
like who comes to me, listens to my words,
and acts on them.[h] [48]That one is like a person
building a house, who dug deeply and laid
the foundation on rock; when the flood
came, the river burst against that house but
could not shake it because it had been well
built. [49]But the one who listens and does not
act is like a person who built a house on the
ground without a foundation. When the river
burst against it, it collapsed at once and was
completely destroyed."

## CHAPTER 7

See RG 311-12

***The Healing of a Centurion's Slave.***[i]
[1]* When he had finished all his words to the
people, he entered Capernaum.* [2]A centurion* there had a slave who was ill and about
to die, and he was valuable to him. [3]When he
heard about Jesus, he sent elders of the Jews
to him, asking him to come and save the life
of his slave. [4]They approached Jesus and

**6:37–42** See notes on Mt 7:1–12; 7:1; 7:5.

**6:43–46** See notes on Mt 7:15–20 and 12:33.

**6:47–49** See note on Mt 7:24–27.

**7:1–8:3** The episodes in this section present a series of reactions to the Galilean ministry of Jesus and reflect some of Luke's particular interests: the faith of a Gentile (Lk 7:1–10); the prophet Jesus' concern for a widowed mother (Lk 7:11–17); the ministry of Jesus directed to the afflicted and unfortunate of Is 61:1 (Lk 7:18–23); the relation between John and Jesus and their role in God's plan for salvation (Lk 7:24–35); a forgiven sinner's manifestation of love (Lk 7:36–50); the association of women with the ministry of Jesus (Lk 8:1–3).

**7:1–10** This story about the faith of the centurion, a Gentile who cherishes the Jewish nation (Lk 7:5), prepares for the story in Acts of the conversion by Peter of the Roman centurion Cornelius who is similarly described as one who is generous to the Jewish nation (Acts 10:2). See also Acts 10:34–35 in the speech of Peter: "God shows no partiality . . . whoever fears him and acts righteously is acceptable to him." See also notes on Mt 8:5–13 and Jn 4:43–54.

**7:2 A centurion**: see note on Mt 8:5.

*x:* Mt 7:12. *y:* Dt 15:7–8. *z:* Lv 25:35–36. *a:* Mt 7:1–5. *b:* Mt 6:14; Jas 2:13. *c:* Mk 4:24. *d:* Mt 15:14; 23:16–17, 24. *e:* Mt 10:24–25; Jn 13:16; 15:20. *f:* Mt 7:16–20; 12:33, 35. *g:* Mt 7:21; Rom 2:13; Jas 1:22. *h:* Mt 7:24–27. *i:* Mt 8:5–13; Jn 4:43–54.

strongly urged him to come, saying, "He deserves to have you do this for him, 5 for he loves our nation and he built the synagogue for us." 6 And Jesus went with them, but when he was only a short distance from the house, the centurion sent friends to tell him, "Lord, do not trouble yourself, for I am not worthy to have you enter under my roof.* 7 Therefore, I did not consider myself worthy to come to you; but say the word and let my servant be healed. 8 For I too am a person subject to authority, with soldiers subject to me. And I say to one, 'Go,' and he goes; and to another, 'Come here,' and he comes; and to my slave, 'Do this,' and he does it." 9 When Jesus heard this he was amazed at him and, turning, said to the crowd following him, "I tell you, not even in Israel have I found such faith." 10 When the messengers returned to the house, they found the slave in good health.

***Raising of the Widow's Son.**** 11[j] Soon afterward he journeyed to a city called Nain, and his disciples and a large crowd accompanied him. 12 As he drew near to the gate of the city, a man who had died was being carried out, the only son of his mother, and she was a widow. A large crowd from the city was with her.[k] 13 When the Lord saw her, he was moved with pity for her and said to her, "Do not weep." 14 He stepped forward and touched the coffin; at this the bearers halted, and he said, "Young man, I tell you, arise!" 15 The dead man sat up and began to speak, and Jesus gave him to his mother.[l] 16 Fear seized them all, and they glorified God, exclaiming, "A great prophet has arisen in our midst," and "God has visited his people."[m] 17 This report about him spread through the whole of Judea and in all the surrounding region.

***The Messengers from John the Baptist.**** 18[n] The disciples of John told him about all these things. John summoned two of his disciples 19 and sent them to the Lord to ask, "Are you the one who is to come, or should we look for another?"[o] 20 When the men came to him, they said, "John the Baptist has sent us to you to ask, 'Are you the one who is to come, or should we look for another?' " 21 At that time he cured many of their diseases, sufferings, and evil spirits; he also granted sight to many who were blind. 22 And he said to them in reply, "Go and tell John what you have seen and heard: the blind regain their sight, the lame walk, lepers are cleansed, the deaf hear, the dead are raised, the poor have the good news proclaimed to them.[p] 23 And blessed is the one who takes no offense at me."*

***Jesus' Testimony to John.*** 24* When the messengers of John had left, Jesus began to speak to the crowds about John.[q] "What did you go out to the desert to see—a reed swayed by the wind? 25 Then what did you go out to see? Someone dressed in fine garments? Those who dress luxuriously and live sumptuously are found in royal palaces. 26 Then what did you go out to see? A prophet? Yes, I tell you, and more than a prophet.[r] 27 This is the one about whom scripture says:

**7:6 I am not worthy to have you enter under my roof**: to enter the house of a Gentile was considered unclean for a Jew; cf. Acts 10:28.

**7:11–17** In the previous incident Jesus' power was displayed for a Gentile whose servant was dying; in this episode it is displayed toward a widowed mother whose only son has already died. Jesus' power over death prepares for his reply to John's disciples in Lk 7:22: "the dead are raised." This resuscitation in alluding to the prophet Elijah's resurrection of the only son of a widow of Zarephath (1 Kgs 7:8–24) leads to the reaction of the crowd: "A great prophet has arisen in our midst" (Lk 7:16).

**7:18–23** In answer to John's question, **Are you the one who is to come?**—a probable reference to the return of the fiery prophet of reform, Elijah, "before the day of the Lord comes, the great and terrible day" (Mal 3:23)—Jesus responds that his role is rather to bring the blessings spoken of in Is 61:1 to the oppressed and neglected of society (Lk 7:22; cf. Lk 4:18).

**7:23 Blessed is the one who takes no offense at me**: this beatitude is pronounced on the person who recognizes Jesus' true identity in spite of previous expectations of what "the one who is to come" would be like.

**7:24–30** In his testimony to John, Jesus reveals his understanding of the relationship between them: John is the precursor of Jesus (Lk 7:27); John is the messenger spoken of in Mal 3:1 who in Mal 3:19 is identified as Elijah. Taken with the previous episode, it can be seen that Jesus identifies John as precisely the person John envisioned Jesus to be: the Elijah who prepares the way for the coming of the day of the Lord.

*j:* 4:25–26; 1 Kgs 17:8–24. *k:* 8:42; 1 Kgs 17:17. *l:* 1 Kgs 17:23; 2 Kgs 4:36. *m:* 1:68; 19:44. *n:* Mt 11:2–6. *o:* Mal 3:1; Rev 1:4, 8; 4:8. *p:* 4:18; Is 35:5–6; 61:1. *q:* Mt 11:7–15. *r:* 1:76.

'Behold, I am sending my messenger
ahead of you,
he will prepare your way before you.'[s]

28 I tell you, among those born of women, no
one is greater than John; yet the least in the
kingdom of God is greater than he." 29[t] (All
the people who listened, including the tax
collectors, and who were baptized with the
baptism of John, acknowledged the righteousness of God; 30 but the Pharisees and
scholars of the law, who were not baptized
by him, rejected the plan of God for themselves.)

31* "Then to what shall I compare the people of this generation? What are they like?[u]
32 They are like children who sit in the marketplace and call to one another,

'We played the flute for you, but you did
not dance.
We sang a dirge, but you did not
weep.'

33 For John the Baptist came neither eating
food nor drinking wine, and you said, 'He is
possessed by a demon.' 34 The Son of Man
came eating and drinking and you said,
'Look, he is a glutton and a drunkard, a
friend of tax collectors and sinners.'[v] 35 But
wisdom is vindicated by all her children."

***The Pardon of the Sinful Woman.**** 36[w] A
Pharisee invited him to dine with him, and
he entered the Pharisee's house and reclined
at table.* 37 Now there was a sinful woman in
the city who learned that he was at table in
the house of the Pharisee.[x] Bringing an alabaster flask of ointment,[y] 38 she stood behind him at his feet weeping and began to
bathe his feet with her tears. Then she wiped
them with her hair, kissed them, and
anointed them with the ointment. 39 When
the Pharisee who had invited him saw this
he said to himself, "If this man were a
prophet, he would know who and what sort
of woman this is who is touching him, that
she is a sinner." 40 Jesus said to him in reply,
"Simon, I have something to say to you."
"Tell me, teacher," he said. 41 "Two people
were in debt to a certain creditor; one owed
five hundred days' wages* and the other
owed fifty. 42 Since they were unable to repay the debt, he forgave it for both. Which
of them will love him more?" 43 Simon said
in reply, "The one, I suppose, whose larger
debt was forgiven." He said to him, "You
have judged rightly." 44 Then he turned to
the woman and said to Simon, "Do you see
this woman? When I entered your house,
you did not give me water for my feet, but
she has bathed them with her tears and
wiped them with her hair. 45 You did not give
me a kiss, but she has not ceased kissing my
feet since the time I entered. 46 You did not
anoint my head with oil, but she anointed
my feet with ointment. 47 So I tell you, her
many sins have been forgiven; hence, she
has shown great love.* But the one to whom
little is forgiven, loves little." 48 He said to
her, "Your sins are forgiven."[z] 49 The others
at table said to themselves, "Who is this
who even forgives sins?"[a] 50 But he said to
the woman, "Your faith has saved you; go in
peace."

**7:31–35** See note on Mt 11:16–19.

**7:36–50** In this story of the pardoning of the sinful woman Luke presents two different reactions to the ministry of Jesus. A Pharisee, suspecting Jesus to be a prophet, invites Jesus to a festive banquet in his house, but the Pharisee's self-righteousness leads to little forgiveness by God and consequently little love shown toward Jesus. The sinful woman, on the other hand, manifests a faith in God (Lk 7:50) that has led her to seek forgiveness for her sins, and because so much was forgiven, she now overwhelms Jesus with her display of love; cf. the similar contrast in attitudes in Lk 18:9–14. The whole episode is a powerful lesson on the relation between forgiveness and love.

**7:36 Reclined at table**: the normal posture of guests at a banquet. Other oriental banquet customs alluded to in this story include the reception by the host with a kiss (Lk 7:45), washing the feet of the guests (Lk 7:44), and the anointing of the guests' heads (Lk 7:46).

**7:41 Days' wages**: one denarius is the normal daily wage of a laborer.

**7:47 Her many sins have been forgiven; hence, she has shown great love**: literally, "her many sins have been forgiven, seeing that she has loved much." That the woman's sins have been forgiven is attested by the great love she shows toward Jesus. Her love is the consequence of her forgiveness. This is also the meaning demanded by the parable in Lk 7:41–43.

*s:* Mal 3:1 / Is 40:3. *t:* 3:7, 12; Mt 21:32. *u:* Mt 11:16–19. *v:* 15:2. *w:* 11:37; 14:1. *x:* Mt 26:7; Mk 14:3. *y:* Jn 12:3. *z:* 5:20; Mt 9:20; Mk 2:5. *a:* 5:21.

## CHAPTER 8

See RG 311-12

***Galilean Women Follow Jesus.**** 1 Afterward he journeyed from one town and village to another, preaching and proclaiming the good news of the kingdom of God.[b] Accompanying him were the Twelve 2[c] and some women who had been cured of evil spirits and infirmities, Mary, called Magdalene, from whom seven demons had gone out, 3 Joanna, the wife of Herod's steward Chuza, Susanna, and many others who provided for them out of their resources.

***The Parable of the Sower.***[d] 4* When a large crowd gathered, with people from one town after another journeying to him, he spoke in a parable.* 5 "A sower went out to sow his seed. And as he sowed, some seed fell on the path and was trampled, and the birds of the sky ate it up. 6 Some seed fell on rocky ground, and when it grew, it withered for lack of moisture. 7 Some seed fell among thorns, and the thorns grew with it and choked it. 8 And some seed fell on good soil, and when it grew, it produced fruit a hundredfold." After saying this, he called out, "Whoever has ears to hear ought to hear."[e]

***The Purpose of the Parables.***[f] 9 Then his disciples asked him what the meaning of this parable might be. 10 He answered, "Knowledge of the mysteries of the kingdom of God has been granted to you; but to the rest, they are made known through parables so that 'they may look but not see, and hear but not understand.'[g]

***The Parable of the Sower Explained.**** 11[h] "This is the meaning of the parable. The seed is the word of God.[i] 12 Those on the path are the ones who have heard, but the devil comes and takes away the word from their hearts that they may not believe and be saved. 13 Those on rocky ground are the ones who, when they hear, receive the word with joy, but they have no root; they believe only for a time and fall away in time of trial. 14 As for the seed that fell among thorns, they are the ones who have heard, but as they go along, they are choked by the anxieties and riches and pleasures of life, and they fail to produce mature fruit. 15 But as for the seed that fell on rich soil, they are the ones who, when they have heard the word, embrace it with a generous and good heart, and bear fruit through perseverance.

***The Parable of the Lamp.**** 16[j] "No one who lights a lamp conceals it with a vessel or sets it under a bed; rather, he places it on a lampstand so that those who enter may see the light.[k] 17 For there is nothing hidden that will not become visible, and nothing secret that will not be known and come to light.[l] 18 Take care, then, how you hear. To anyone who has, more will be given, and from the one who has not, even what he seems to have will be taken away."[m]

***Jesus and His Family.***[n] 19 Then his mother and his brothers* came to him but were unable to join him because of the crowd. 20[o] He was told, "Your mother and your brothers are standing outside and they wish to see

**8:1–3** Luke presents Jesus as an itinerant preacher traveling in the company of the Twelve and of the Galilean women who are sustaining them out of their means. These Galilean women will later accompany Jesus on his journey to Jerusalem and become witnesses to his death (Lk 23:49) and resurrection (Lk 24:9–11, where Mary Magdalene and Joanna are specifically mentioned; cf. also Acts 1:14). The association of women with the ministry of Jesus is most unusual in the light of the attitude of first-century Palestinian Judaism toward women. The more common attitude is expressed in Jn 4:27, and early rabbinic documents caution against speaking with women in public.

**8:4–21** The focus in this section is on how one should hear the word of God and act on it. It includes the parable of the sower and its explanation (Lk 8:4–15), a collection of sayings on how one should act on the word that is heard (Lk 8:16–18), and the identification of the mother and brothers of Jesus as the ones who hear the word and act on it (Lk 8:19–21). See also notes on Mt 13:1–53 and Mk 4:1–34.

**8:4–8** See note on Mt 13:3–8.

**8:11–15** On the interpretation of the parable of the sower, see note on Mt 13:18–23.

**8:16–18** These sayings continue the theme of responding to the word of God. Those who hear the word must become a light to others (Lk 8:16); even the mysteries of the kingdom that have been made known to the disciples (Lk 8:9–10) must come to light (Lk 8:17); a generous and persevering response to the word of God leads to a still more perfect response to the word.

**8:19 His brothers**: see note on Mk 6:3.

*b:* 4:43. *c:* 23:49; 24:10; Mt 27:55–56; Mk 15:40–41; Jn 19:5. *d:* Mt 13:1–9; Mk 4:1–9. *e:* 14:35; Mt 11:15; 13:43; Mk 4:23. *f:* Mt 13:10–13; Mk 4:10–12. *g:* Is 6:9. *h:* Mt 13:18–23; Mk 4:13–20. *i:* 1 Pt 1:23. *j:* Mk 4:21–25. *k:* 11:33; Mt 5:15. *l:* 12:2; Mt 10:26. *m:* 19:26; Mt 13:12; 25:29. *n:* Mt 12:46–50; Mk 3:31–35. *o:* 11:27–28.

you." [21]He said to them in reply, "My mother and my brothers are those who hear the word of God and act on it."[*]

***The Calming of a Storm at Sea.***[p] [22*] One day he got into a boat with his disciples and said to them, "Let us cross to the other side of the lake." So they set sail, [23]and while they were sailing he fell asleep. A squall blew over the lake, and they were taking in water and were in danger. [24]They came and woke him saying, "Master, master, we are perishing!" He awakened, rebuked the wind and the waves, and they subsided and there was a calm. [25]Then he asked them, "Where is your faith?" But they were filled with awe and amazed and said to one another, "Who then is this, who commands even the winds and the sea, and they obey him?"

***The Healing of the Gerasene Demoniac.***[q] [26]Then they sailed to the territory of the Gerasenes,[*] which is opposite Galilee. [27]When he came ashore a man from the town who was possessed by demons met him. For a long time he had not worn clothes; he did not live in a house, but lived among the tombs. [28][r] When he saw Jesus, he cried out and fell down before him; in a loud voice he shouted, "What have you to do with me, Jesus, son of the Most High God? I beg you, do not torment me!" [29]For he had ordered the unclean spirit to come out of the man. (It had taken hold of him many times, and he used to be bound with chains and shackles as a restraint, but he would break his bonds and be driven by the demon into deserted places.) [30]Then Jesus asked him, "What is your name?"[*] He replied, "Legion," because many demons had entered him. [31]And they pleaded with him not to order them to depart to the abyss.[*]

[32]A herd of many swine was feeding there on the hillside, and they pleaded with him to allow them to enter those swine; and he let them. [33]The demons came out of the man and entered the swine, and the herd rushed down the steep bank into the lake and was drowned. [34]When the swineherds saw what had happened, they ran away and reported the incident in the town and throughout the countryside. [35]People came out to see what had happened and, when they approached Jesus, they discovered the man from whom the demons had come out sitting at his feet.[*] He was clothed and in his right mind, and they were seized with fear. [36]Those who witnessed it told them how the possessed man had been saved. [37]The entire population of the region of the Gerasenes asked Jesus to leave them because they were seized with great fear. So he got into a boat and returned. [38]The man from whom the demons had come out begged to remain with him, but he sent him away, saying, [39]"Return home and recount what God has done for you." The man went off and proclaimed throughout the whole town what Jesus had done for him.

***Jairus's Daughter and the Woman with a Hemorrhage.***[*] [40][s] When Jesus returned, the

**8:21** The family of Jesus is not constituted by physical relationship with him but by obedience to the word of God. In this, Luke agrees with the Marcan parallel (Mk 3:31–35), although by omitting Mk 3:33 and especially Mk 3:20–21 Luke has softened the Marcan picture of Jesus' natural family. Probably he did this because Mary has already been presented in Lk 1:38 as the obedient handmaid of the Lord who fulfills the requirement for belonging to the eschatological family of Jesus; cf. also Lk 11:27–28.

**8:22–56** This section records four miracles of Jesus that manifest his power and authority: (1) the calming of a storm on the lake (Lk 8:22–25); (2) the exorcism of a demoniac (Lk 8:26–39); (3) the cure of a hemorrhaging woman (Lk 8:40–48); (4) the raising of Jairus's daughter to life (Lk 8:49–56). They parallel the same sequence of stories at Mk 4:35–5:43.

**8:26 Gerasenes**: other manuscripts read Gadarenes or Gergesenes. See also note on Mt 8:28. **Opposite Galilee**: probably Gentile territory (note the presence in the area of pigs—unclean animals to Jews) and an indication that the person who receives salvation (Lk 8:36) is a Gentile.

**8:30 What is your name?**: the question reflects the popular belief that knowledge of the spirit's name brought control over the spirit. **Legion**: to Jesus' question the demon replies with a Latin word transliterated into Greek. The Roman legion at this period consisted of 5,000 to 6,000 foot soldiers; hence the name implies a very large number of demons.

**8:31 Abyss**: the place of the dead (Rom 10:7) or the prison of Satan (Rev 20:3) or the subterranean "watery deep" that symbolizes the chaos before the order imposed by creation (Gn 1:2).

**8:35 Sitting at his feet**: the former demoniac takes the position of a disciple before the master (Lk 10:39; Acts 22:3).

**8:40–56** Two interwoven miracle stories, one a healing and the other a resuscitation, present Jesus as master over sickness and death. In the Lucan account, faith in Jesus is responsible for the cure (Lk 8:48) and for the raising to life (Lk 8:50).

*p:* Mt 8:18, 23–27; Mk 4:35–41. *q:* Mt 8:28–34; Mk 5:1–20. *r:* 4:33–35; Mt 8:29; Mk 1:23–24. *s:* Mt 9:18–26; Mk 5:21–43.

crowd welcomed him, for they were all waiting for him. [41] And a man named Jairus, an official of the synagogue, came forward. He fell at the feet of Jesus and begged him to come to his house, [42] because he had an only daughter,* about twelve years old, and she was dying. As he went, the crowds almost crushed him. [43] And a woman afflicted with hemorrhages for twelve years,* who [had spent her whole livelihood on doctors and] was unable to be cured by anyone, [44] came up behind him and touched the tassel on his cloak. Immediately her bleeding stopped. [45] Jesus then asked, "Who touched me?" While all were denying it, Peter said, "Master, the crowds are pushing and pressing in upon you." [46] But Jesus said, "Someone has touched me; for I know that power has gone out from me."[t] [47] When the woman realized that she had not escaped notice, she came forward trembling. Falling down before him, she explained in the presence of all the people why she had touched him and how she had been healed immediately. [48] He said to her, "Daughter, your faith has saved you; go in peace."[u]

[49] While he was still speaking, someone from the synagogue official's house arrived and said, "Your daughter is dead; do not trouble the teacher any longer." [50] On hearing this, Jesus answered him, "Do not be afraid; just have faith and she will be saved." [51] When he arrived at the house he allowed no one to enter with him except Peter and John and James, and the child's father and mother. [52]* [v] All were weeping and mourning for her, when he said, "Do not weep any longer, for she is not dead, but sleeping." [53] And they ridiculed him, because they knew that she was dead. [54] But he took her by the hand and called to her, "Child, arise!" [55] Her breath returned and she immediately arose. He then directed that she should be given something to eat. [56] Her parents were astounded, and he instructed them to tell no one what had happened.

## CHAPTER 9

See RG 311–13

***The Mission of the Twelve.**** [1] [w] He summoned the Twelve and gave them power and authority over all demons and to cure diseases, [2] and he sent them to proclaim the kingdom of God and to heal [the sick]. [3] He said to them, "Take nothing for the journey,* neither walking stick, nor sack, nor food, nor money, and let no one take a second tunic. [4] Whatever house you enter, stay there and leave from there.[x] [5] And as for those who do not welcome you, when you leave that town, shake the dust from your feet* in testimony against them."[y] [6] Then they set out and went from village to village proclaiming the good news and curing diseases everywhere.

***Herod's Opinion of Jesus.***[z] [7]* Herod the tetrarch* heard about all that was happening, and he was greatly perplexed because some were saying, "John has been raised from the dead";[a] [8] others were saying, "Elijah has appeared"; still others, "One of the ancient prophets has arisen." [9]* [b] But Herod said,

**8:42 An only daughter**: cf. the son of the widow of Nain whom Luke describes as an "only" son (Lk 7:12; see also Lk 9:38).

**8:43 Afflicted with hemorrhages for twelve years**: according to the Mosaic law (Lv 15:25–30) this condition would render the woman unclean and unfit for contact with other people.

**8:52 Sleeping**: her death is a temporary condition; cf. Jn 11:11–14.

**9:1–6** Armed with the power and authority that Jesus himself has been displaying in the previous episodes, the Twelve are now sent out to continue the work that Jesus has been performing throughout his Galilean ministry: (1) proclaiming the kingdom (Lk 4:43; 8:1); (2) exorcising demons (Lk 4:33–37, 41; 8:26–39) and (3) healing the sick (Lk 4:38–40; 5:12–16, 17–26; 6:6–10; 7:1–10, 17, 22; 8:40–56).

**9:3 Take nothing for the journey**: the absolute detachment required of the disciple (Lk 14:33) leads to complete reliance on God (Lk 12:22–31).

**9:5 Shake the dust from your feet**: see note on Mt 10:14.

**9:7–56** This section in which Luke gathers together incidents that focus on the identity of Jesus is introduced by a question that Herod is made to ask in this gospel: "Who then is this about whom I hear such things?"(Lk 9:9) In subsequent episodes, Luke reveals to the reader various answers to Herod's question: Jesus is one in whom God's power is present and who provides for the needs of God's people (Lk 9:10–17); Peter declares Jesus to be "the Messiah of God" (Lk 9:18–21); Jesus says he is the suffering Son of Man (Lk 9:22, 43–45); Jesus is the Master to be followed, even to death (Lk 9:23–27); Jesus is God's son, his Chosen One (Lk 9:28–36).

**9:7 Herod the tetrarch**: see note on Lk 3:1.

**9:9 And he kept trying to see him**: this indication of Herod's interest in Jesus prepares for Lk 13:31–33 and for Lk 23:8–12 where Herod's curiosity about Jesus' power to perform miracles remains unsatisfied.

---

*t:* 6:19. *u:* 7:50; 17:19; 18:42. *v:* 7:13. *w:* Mt 10:1, 5–15; Mk 6:7–13. *x:* 10:5–7. *y:* 10:10–11; Acts 13:51. *z:* Mt 14:1–12; Mk 6:14–29. *a:* 9:19; Mt 16:14; Mk 8:28. *b:* 23:8.

"John I beheaded. Who then is this about whom I hear such things?" And he kept trying to see him.

***The Return of the Twelve and the Feeding of the Five Thousand.***[c] [10]When the apostles returned, they explained to him what they had done. He took them and withdrew in private to a town called Bethsaida. [11]The crowds, meanwhile, learned of this and followed him. He received them and spoke to them about the kingdom of God, and he healed those who needed to be cured. [12]As the day was drawing to a close, the Twelve approached him and said, "Dismiss the crowd so that they can go to the surrounding villages and farms and find lodging and provisions; for we are in a deserted place here." [13][d] He said to them, "Give them some food yourselves." They replied, "Five loaves and two fish are all we have, unless we ourselves go and buy food for all these people." [14]Now the men there numbered about five thousand. Then he said to his disciples, "Have them sit down in groups of [about] fifty." [15]They did so and made them all sit down. [16]Then taking[*] the five loaves and the two fish, and looking up to heaven, he said the blessing over them, broke them, and gave them to the disciples to set before the crowd.[e] [17]They all ate and were satisfied. And when the leftover fragments were picked up, they filled twelve wicker baskets.

***Peter's Confession About Jesus.***[*] [18][f] Once when Jesus was praying in solitude,[*] and the disciples were with him, he asked them, "Who do the crowds say that I am?" [19]They said in reply, "John the Baptist; others, Elijah; still others, 'One of the ancient prophets has arisen.' "[g] [20]Then he said to them, "But who do you say that I am?" Peter said in reply, "The Messiah of God."[*] [21]He rebuked them and directed them not to tell this to anyone.

***The First Prediction of the Passion.*** [22]He said, "The Son of Man must suffer greatly and be rejected by the elders, the chief priests, and the scribes, and be killed and on the third day be raised."[h]

***The Conditions of Discipleship.***[i] [23]Then he said to all, "If anyone wishes to come after me, he must deny himself and take up his cross daily[*] and follow me.[j] [24]For whoever wishes to save his life will lose it, but whoever loses his life for my sake will save it.[k] [25]What profit is there for one to gain the whole world yet lose or forfeit himself? [26]Whoever is ashamed of me and of my words, the Son of Man will be ashamed of when he comes in his glory and in the glory of the Father and of the holy angels.[l] [27]Truly I say to you, there are some standing here who will not taste death until they see the kingdom of God."

***The Transfiguration of Jesus.***[*] [28][m] About eight days after he said this, he took Peter, John, and James and went up the mountain to pray.[*] [29]While he was praying his face changed in appearance and his clothing became dazzling white. [30]And behold, two men were conversing with him, Moses and

**9:16 Then taking . . .**: the actions of Jesus recall the institution of the Eucharist in Lk 22:19; see also note on Mt 14:19.

**9:18–22** This incident is based on Mk 8:27–33, but Luke has eliminated Peter's refusal to accept Jesus as suffering Son of Man (Mk 8:32) and the rebuke of Peter by Jesus (Mk 8:33). Elsewhere in the gospel, Luke softens the harsh portrait of Peter and the other apostles found in his Marcan source (cf. Lk 22:39–46, which similarly lacks a rebuke of Peter that occurs in the source, Mk 14:37–38).

**9:18 When Jesus was praying in solitude**: see note on Lk 3:21.

**9:20 The Messiah of God**: on the meaning of this title in first-century Palestinian Judaism, see notes on Lk 2:11 and on Mt 16:13–20 and Mk 8:27–30.

**9:23 Daily**: this is a Lucan addition to a saying of Jesus, removing the saying from a context that envisioned the imminent suffering and death of the disciple of Jesus (as does the saying in Mk 8:34–35) to one that focuses on the demands of daily Christian existence.

**9:28–36** Situated shortly after the first announcement of the passion, death, and resurrection, this scene of Jesus' transfiguration provides the heavenly confirmation to Jesus' declaration that his suffering will end in glory (Lk 9:32); see also notes on Mt 17:1–8 and Mk 9:2–8.

**9:28 Up the mountain to pray**: the "mountain" is the regular place of prayer in Luke (see Lk 6:12; 22:39–41).

**9:30 Moses and Elijah**: the two figures represent the Old Testament law and the prophets. At the end of this episode, the heavenly voice will identify Jesus as the one to be listened to now (Lk 9:35). See also note on Mk 9:5.

*c:* Mt 14:13–21; Mk 6:30–44; Jn 6:1–14. *d:* 2 Kgs 4:42–44. *e:* 22:19; 24:30–31; Acts 2:42; 20:11; 27:35. *f:* Mt 16:13–20; Mk 8:27–30. *g:* 9:7–8. *h:* 24:7, 26; Mt 16:21; 20:18–19; Mk 8:31; 10:33–34. *i:* Mt 16:24–28; Mk 8:34–9:1. *j:* 14:27; Mt 10:38. *k:* 17:33; Mt 10:39; Jn 12:25. *l:* 12:9; Mt 10:33; 2 Tm 2:12. *m:* Mt 17:1–8; Mk 9:2–8.

Elijah,* 31* [n] who appeared in glory and spoke of his exodus that he was going to accomplish in Jerusalem. 32 Peter and his companions had been overcome by sleep, but becoming fully awake, they saw his glory* and the two men standing with him.[o] 33 As they were about to part from him, Peter said to Jesus, "Master, it is good that we are here; let us make three tents,* one for you, one for Moses, and one for Elijah." But he did not know what he was saying. 34* While he was still speaking, a cloud came and cast a shadow over them, and they became frightened when they entered the cloud. 35* [p] Then from the cloud came a voice that said, "This is my chosen Son; listen to him." 36 After the voice had spoken, Jesus was found alone. They fell silent and did not at that time* tell anyone what they had seen.

***The Healing of a Boy with a Demon.**** 37 [q] On the next day, when they came down from the mountain, a large crowd met him. 38 There was a man in the crowd who cried out, "Teacher, I beg you, look at my son; he is my only child. 39 For a spirit seizes him and he suddenly screams and it convulses him until he foams at the mouth; it releases him only with difficulty, wearing him out. 40 I begged your disciples to cast it out but they could not." 41 Jesus said in reply, "O faithless and perverse generation, how long will I be with you and endure you? Bring your son here." 42 As he was coming forward, the demon threw him to the ground in a convulsion; but Jesus rebuked the unclean spirit, healed the boy, and returned him to his father. 43 And all were astonished by the majesty of God.

***The Second Prediction of the Passion.***[r] While they were all amazed at his every deed, he said to his disciples, 44 "Pay attention to what I am telling you. The Son of Man is to be handed over to men." 45 But they did not understand this saying; its meaning was hidden from them so that they should not understand it, and they were afraid to ask him about this saying.

***The Greatest in the Kingdom.***[s] 46* An argument arose among the disciples about which of them was the greatest.[t] 47 Jesus realized the intention of their hearts and took a child and placed it by his side 48 and said to them, "Whoever receives this child in my name receives me, and whoever receives me receives the one who sent me. For the one who is least among all of you is the one who is the greatest."[u]

***Another Exorcist.***[v] 49 Then John said in reply, "Master, we saw someone casting out demons in your name and we tried to prevent him because he does not follow in our company." 50 Jesus said to him, "Do not prevent him, for whoever is not against you is for you."

## V. The Journey to Jerusalem: Luke's Travel Narrative*

***Departure for Jerusalem; Samaritan Inhospitality.*** 51* When the days for his being taken

**9:31 His exodus that he was going to accomplish in Jerusalem**: Luke identifies the subject of the conversation as the **exodus** of Jesus, a reference to the death, resurrection, and ascension of Jesus that will take place in Jerusalem, the city of destiny (see Lk 9:51). The mention of exodus, however, also calls to mind the Israelite Exodus from Egypt to the promised land.

**9:32 They saw his glory**: the **glory** that is proper to God is here attributed to Jesus (see Lk 24:26).

**9:33 Let us make three tents**: in a possible allusion to the feast of Tabernacles, Peter may be likening his joy on the occasion of the transfiguration to the joyful celebration of this harvest festival.

**9:34 Over them**: it is not clear whether **them** refers to Jesus, Moses, and Elijah, or to the disciples. For the cloud casting its shadow, see note on Mk 9:7.

**9:35** Like the heavenly voice that identified Jesus at his baptism prior to his undertaking the Galilean ministry (Lk 3:22), so too here before the journey to the city of destiny is begun (Lk 9:51) the heavenly voice again identifies Jesus as Son. **Listen to him**: the two representatives of Israel of old depart (Lk 9:33) and Jesus is left alone (Lk 9:36) as the teacher whose words must be heeded (see also Acts 3:22).

**9:36 At that time**: i.e., before the resurrection.

**9:37–43a** See note on Mk 9:14–29.

**9:46–50** These two incidents focus on attitudes that are opposed to Christian discipleship: rivalry and intolerance of outsiders.

**9:51–18:14** The Galilean ministry of Jesus finishes with the previous episode and a new section of Luke's gospel begins, the journey to Jerusalem. This journey is based on Mk

*n:* 9:22; 13:33. *o:* Jn 1:14; 2 Pt 1:16. *p:* 3:22; Dt 18:15; Ps 2:7; Is 42:1; Mt 3:17; 12:18; Mk 1:11; 2 Pt 1:17–18. *q:* Mt 17:14–18; Mk 9:14–27. *r:* 18:32–34; Mt 17:22–23; Mk 9:30–32. *s:* Mt 18:1–5; Mk 9:33–37. *t:* 22:24. *u:* 10:16; Mt 10:40; Jn 13:20. *v:* Mk 9:38–40.

up* were fulfilled, he resolutely determined to journey to Jerusalem,[w] 52* and he sent messengers ahead of him.[x] On the way they entered a Samaritan village to prepare for his reception there, 53 but they would not welcome him because the destination of his journey was Jerusalem. 54 When the disciples James and John saw this they asked, "Lord, do you want us to call down fire from heaven to consume them?"[y] 55 Jesus turned and rebuked them, 56 and they journeyed to another village.

*The Would-be Followers of Jesus.** 57[z] As they were proceeding on their journey someone said to him, "I will follow you wherever you go." 58 Jesus answered him, "Foxes have dens and birds of the sky have nests, but the Son of Man has nowhere to rest his head." 59 And to another he said, "Follow me." But he replied, "[Lord,] let me go first and bury my father." 60 But he answered him, "Let the dead bury their dead.* But you, go and proclaim the kingdom of God." 61[a] And another said, "I will follow you, Lord, but first let me say farewell to my family at home." 62 [To him] Jesus said, "No one who sets a hand to the plow and looks to what was left behind is fit for the kingdom of God."

## CHAPTER 10

See RG 312–13

*The Mission of the Seventy-two.** 1 After this the Lord appointed seventy [-two]* others whom he sent ahead of him in pairs to every town and place he intended to visit.[b] 2 He said to them, "The harvest is abundant but the laborers are few; so ask the master of the harvest to send out laborers for his harvest.[c] 3 Go on your way; behold, I am sending you like lambs among wolves.[d] 4* Carry no money bag,[e] no sack, no sandals;[f] and greet no one along the way. 5 Into whatever house you enter, first say, 'Peace to this household.'* 6 If a peaceful person* lives there, your peace

10:1–52 but Luke uses his Marcan source only in Lk 18:15–19:27. Before that point he has inserted into his gospel a distinctive collection of sayings of Jesus and stories about him that he has drawn from Q, a collection of sayings of Jesus used also by Matthew, and from his own special traditions. All of the material collected in this section is loosely organized within the framework of a journey of Jesus to Jerusalem, the city of destiny, where his exodus (suffering, death, resurrection, ascension) is to take place (Lk 9:31), where salvation is accomplished, and from where the proclamation of God's saving word is to go forth (Lk 24:47; Acts 1:8). Much of the material in the Lucan travel narrative is teaching for the disciples. During the course of this journey Jesus is preparing his chosen Galilean witnesses for the role they will play after his exodus (Lk 9:31): they are to be his witnesses to the people (Acts 10:39; 13:31) and thereby provide certainty to the readers of Luke's gospel that the teachings they have received are rooted in the teachings of Jesus (Lk 1:1–4).

**9:51–55** Just as the Galilean ministry began with a rejection of Jesus in his hometown, so too the travel narrative begins with the rejection of him by Samaritans. In this episode Jesus disassociates himself from the attitude expressed by his disciples that those who reject him are to be punished severely. The story alludes to 2 Kgs 1:10, 12 where the prophet Elijah takes the course of action Jesus rejects, and Jesus thereby rejects the identification of himself with Elijah.

**9:51 Days for his being taken up**: like the reference to his exodus in Lk 9:31 this is probably a reference to all the events (suffering, death, resurrection, ascension) of his last days in Jerusalem. **He resolutely determined**: literally, "he set his face."

**9:52 Samaritan**: Samaria was the territory between Judea and Galilee west of the Jordan river. For ethnic and religious reasons, the Samaritans and the Jews were bitterly opposed to one another (see Jn 4:9).

**9:57–62** In these sayings Jesus speaks of the severity and the unconditional nature of Christian discipleship. Even family ties and filial obligations, such as burying one's parents, cannot distract one no matter how briefly from proclaiming the kingdom of God. The first two sayings are paralleled in Mt 8:19–22; see also notes there.

**9:60 Let the dead bury their dead**: i.e., let the spiritually dead (those who do not follow) bury their physically dead. See also note on Mt 8:22.

**10:1–12** Only the Gospel of Luke contains two episodes in which Jesus sends out his followers on a mission: the first (Lk 10:1–6) is based on the mission in Mk 6:6b–13 and recounts the sending out of the Twelve; here in Lk 10:1–12 a similar report based on Q becomes the sending out of seventy-two in this gospel. The episode continues the theme of Jesus preparing witnesses to himself and his ministry. These witnesses include not only the Twelve but also the seventy-two who may represent the Christian mission in Luke's own day. Note that the instructions given to the Twelve and to the seventy-two are similar and that what is said to the seventy-two in Lk 10:4 is directed to the Twelve in Lk 22:35.

**10:1 Seventy[-two]**: important representatives of the Alexandrian and Caesarean text types read "seventy," while other important Alexandrian texts and Western readings have "seventy-two."

**10:4 Carry no money bag . . . greet no one along the way**: because of the urgency of the mission and the single-mindedness required of missionaries, attachment to material possessions should be avoided and even customary greetings should not distract from the fulfillment of the task.

**10:5 First say, 'Peace to this household'**: see notes on Lk 2:14 and Mt 10:13.

**10:6 A peaceful person**: literally, "a son of peace."

*w:* 9:53; 13:22, 33; 17:11; 18:31; 19:28; 24:51; Acts 1:2, 9–11, 22. *x:* Mal 3:1. *y:* 2 Kgs 1:10, 12. *z:* Mt 8:19–22. *a:* 1 Kgs 19:20. *b:* Mk 6:7. *c:* Mt 9:37–38; Jn 4:35. *d:* Mt 10:16. *e:* Mt 10:7–14. *f:* 9:3; 2 Kgs 4:29.

will rest on him; but if not, it will return to you. 7 Stay in the same house and eat and drink what is offered to you, for the laborer deserves his payment. Do not move about from one house to another.[g] 8 Whatever town you enter and they welcome you, eat what is set before you,[h] 9 cure the sick in it and say to them, 'The kingdom of God is at hand for you.'[i] 10 Whatever town you enter and they do not receive you, go out into the streets and say,[j] 11 'The dust of your town that clings to our feet, even that we shake off against you.' Yet know this: the kingdom of God is at hand.[k] 12 I tell you, it will be more tolerable for Sodom on that day than for that town.[l]

***Reproaches to Unrepentant Towns.****[*] 13[m] "Woe to you, Chorazin! Woe to you, Bethsaida![n] For if the mighty deeds done in your midst had been done in Tyre and Sidon, they would long ago have repented, sitting in sackcloth and ashes. 14 But it will be more tolerable for Tyre and Sidon at the judgment than for you. 15[*][o] And as for you, Capernaum, 'Will you be exalted to heaven? You will go down to the netherworld.' " 16 Whoever listens to you listens to me. Whoever rejects you rejects me. And whoever rejects me rejects the one who sent me."[p]

***Return of the Seventy-two.*** 17 The seventy [-two] returned rejoicing, and said, "Lord, even the demons are subject to us because of your name." 18 Jesus said, "I have observed Satan fall like lightning[*] from the sky.[q] 19 Behold, I have given you the power 'to tread upon serpents' and scorpions and upon the full force of the enemy and nothing will harm you.[r] 20 Nevertheless, do not rejoice because the spirits are subject to you, but rejoice because your names are written in heaven."[s]

***Praise of the Father.***[t] 21 At that very moment he rejoiced [in] the holy Spirit and said, "I give you praise, Father, Lord of heaven and earth, for although you have hidden these things from the wise and the learned you have revealed them to the childlike.[*] Yes, Father, such has been your gracious will.[u] 22 All things have been handed over to me by my Father. No one knows who the Son is except the Father, and who the Father is except the Son and anyone to whom the Son wishes to reveal him."[v]

***The Privileges of Discipleship.***[w] 23 Turning to the disciples in private he said, "Blessed are the eyes that see what you see. 24 For I say to you, many prophets and kings desired to see what you see, but did not see it, and to hear what you hear, but did not hear it."

***The Greatest Commandment.***[x] 25[*] There was a scholar of the law[*] who stood up to test him and said, "Teacher, what must I do to inherit eternal life?"[y] 26 Jesus said to him, "What is written in the law? How do you read it?" 27 He said in reply, "You shall love the Lord, your God, with all your heart, with all your being, with all your strength, and with all your mind, and your neighbor as yourself."[z] 28 He replied to him, "You have answered correctly; do this and you will live."[a]

**10:13–16** The call to repentance that is a part of the proclamation of the kingdom brings with it a severe judgment for those who hear it and reject it.

**10:15 The netherworld**: the underworld, the place of the dead (Acts 2:27, 31) here contrasted with heaven; see also note on Mt 11:23.

**10:18 I have observed Satan fall like lightning**: the effect of the mission of the seventy-two is characterized by the Lucan Jesus as a symbolic fall of Satan. As the kingdom of God is gradually being established, evil in all its forms is being defeated; the dominion of Satan over humanity is at an end.

**10:21 Revealed them to the childlike**: a restatement of the theme announced in Lk 8:10: the mysteries of the kingdom are revealed to the disciples. See also note on Mt 11:25–27.

**10:25–37** In response to a question from a Jewish legal expert about inheriting eternal life, Jesus illustrates the superiority of love over legalism through the story of the good Samaritan. The law of love proclaimed in the "Sermon on the Plain" (Lk 6:27–36) is exemplified by one whom the legal expert would have considered ritually impure (see Jn 4:9). Moreover, the identity of the "neighbor" requested by the legal expert (Lk 10:29) turns out to be a Samaritan, the enemy of the Jew (see note on Lk 9:52).

**10:25 Scholar of the law**: an expert in the Mosaic law, and probably a member of the group elsewhere identified as the scribes (Lk 5:21).

*g:* 9:4; Mt 10:10; 1 Cor 9:6–14; 1 Tm 5:18. *h:* 1 Cor 10:27. *i:* Mt 3:2; 4:17; Mk 1:15. *j:* 9:5. *k:* Acts 13:51; 18:6. *l:* Mt 10:15; 11:24. *m:* Mt 11:20–24. *n:* Is 23; Ez 26–28; Jl 3:4–8; Am 1:1–10; Zec 9:2–4. *o:* Is 14:13–15. *p:* Mt 10:40; Jn 5:23; 13:20; 15:23. *q:* Is 14:12; Jn 12:31; Rev 12:7–12. *r:* Ps 91:13; Mk 16:18. *s:* Ex 32:32; Dn 12:1; Mt 7:22; Phil 4:3; Heb 12:23; Rev 3:5; 21:27. *t:* Mt 11:25–27. *u:* 1 Cor 1:26–28. *v:* Jn 3:35; 10:15. *w:* Mt 13:16–17. *x:* Mt 22:34–40; Mk 12:28–34. *y:* 18:18; Mt 19:16; Mk 10:17. *z:* Lv 19:18; Dt 6:5; 10:12; Jos 22:5; Mt 19:19; 22:37–39; Rom 13:9; Gal 5:14; Jas 2:8. *a:* Lv 18:5; Prv 19:16; Rom 10:5; Gal 3:12.

*The Parable of the Good Samaritan.* 29 But because he wished to justify himself, he said to Jesus, "And who is my neighbor?" 30 Jesus replied, "A man fell victim to robbers as he went down from Jerusalem to Jericho. They stripped and beat him and went off leaving him half-dead. 31* A priest happened to be going down that road, but when he saw him, he passed by on the opposite side. 32 Likewise a Levite came to the place, and when he saw him, he passed by on the opposite side. 33 But a Samaritan traveler who came upon him was moved with compassion at the sight. 34 He approached the victim, poured oil and wine over his wounds and bandaged them. Then he lifted him up on his own animal, took him to an inn and cared for him. 35 The next day he took out two silver coins and gave them to the innkeeper with the instruction, 'Take care of him. If you spend more than what I have given you, I shall repay you on my way back.' 36 Which of these three, in your opinion, was neighbor to the robbers' victim?" 37 He answered, "The one who treated him with mercy." Jesus said to him, "Go and do likewise."

*Martha and Mary.** 38b As they continued their journey he entered a village where a woman whose name was Martha welcomed him. 39* She had a sister named Mary [who] sat beside the Lord at his feet listening to him speak. 40 Martha, burdened with much serving, came to him and said, "Lord, do you not care that my sister has left me by myself to do the serving? Tell her to help me." 41 The Lord said to her in reply, "Martha, Martha, you are anxious and worried about many things. 42* There is need of only one thing. Mary has chosen the better part and it will not be taken from her."

## CHAPTER 11

See RG 312–13

*The Lord's Prayer.*[c] 1* He was praying in a certain place, and when he had finished, one of his disciples said to him, "Lord, teach us to pray just as John taught his disciples."* 2* He said to them, "When you pray, say:

Father, hallowed be your name,
your kingdom come.
3 Give us each day our daily bread*
4 and forgive us our sins
for we ourselves forgive everyone in debt to us,
and do not subject us to the final test."

*Further Teachings on Prayer.*[d] 5 And he said to them, "Suppose one of you has a friend to whom he goes at midnight and says, 'Friend, lend me three loaves of bread, 6 for a friend of mine has arrived at my house from a journey and I have nothing to offer him,' 7 and he says in reply from within, 'Do not bother me; the door has already been locked and my children and I are already in bed. I cannot get up to give you anything.' 8 I tell you, if he does not get up to give him the loaves because of their friendship, he will get up to give him whatever he needs because of his persistence.

**10:31–32 Priest . . . Levite**: those religious representatives of Judaism who would have been expected to be models of "neighbor" to the victim pass him by.

**10:38–42** The story of Martha and Mary further illustrates the importance of hearing the words of the teacher and the concern with women in Luke.

**10:39 Sat beside the Lord at his feet**: it is remarkable for first-century Palestinian Judaism that a woman would assume the posture of a disciple at the master's feet (see also Lk 8:35; Acts 22:3), and it reveals a characteristic attitude of Jesus toward women in this gospel (see Lk 8:2–3).

**10:42 There is need of only one thing**: some ancient versions read, "there is need of few things"; another important, although probably inferior, reading found in some manuscripts is, "there is need of few things, or of one."

**11:1–13** Luke presents three episodes concerned with prayer. The first (Lk 11:1–4) recounts Jesus teaching his disciples the Christian communal prayer, the "Our Father"; the second (Lk 11:5–8), the importance of persistence in prayer; the third (Lk 11:9–13), the effectiveness of prayer.

**11:1–4** The Matthean form of the "Our Father" occurs in the "Sermon on the Mount" (Mt 6:9–15); the shorter Lucan version is presented while Jesus is at prayer (see note on Lk 3:21) and his disciples ask him to teach them to pray just as John taught his disciples to pray. In answer to their question, Jesus presents them with an example of a Christian communal prayer that stresses the fatherhood of God and acknowledges him as the one to whom the Christian disciple owes daily sustenance (Lk 11:3), forgiveness (Lk 11:4), and deliverance from the final trial (Lk 11:4). See also notes on Mt 6:9–13.

**11:2 Your kingdom come**: in place of this petition, some early church Fathers record: "May your holy Spirit come upon us and cleanse us," a petition that may reflect the use of the "Our Father" in a baptismal liturgy.

**11:3–4 Daily bread**: see note on Mt 6:11. **The final test**: see note on Mt 6:13.

*b:* Jn 11:1; 12:2–3. *c:* Mt 6:9–15. *d:* 18:1–5.

*The Answer to Prayer.*[e] 9"And I tell you,
ask and you will receive; seek and you will
find; knock and the door will be opened to
you.[f] 10For everyone who asks, receives; and
the one who seeks, finds; and to the one who
knocks, the door will be opened. 11What father among you would hand his son a snake
when he asks for a fish? 12Or hand him a
scorpion when he asks for an egg? 13If you
then, who are wicked, know how to give
good gifts to your children, how much more
will the Father in heaven give the holy
Spirit* to those who ask him?"

*Jesus and Beelzebul.*[g] 14He was driving
out a demon [that was] mute, and when the
demon had gone out, the mute person spoke
and the crowds were amazed. 15Some of
them said, "By the power of Beelzebul, the
prince of demons, he drives out demons."[h]
16Others, to test him, asked him for a sign
from heaven.[i] 17But he knew their thoughts
and said to them, "Every kingdom divided
against itself will be laid waste and house
will fall against house. 18And if Satan is divided against himself, how will his kingdom
stand? For you say that it is by Beelzebul
that I drive out demons. 19If I, then, drive out
demons by Beelzebul, by whom do your
own people* drive them out? Therefore they
will be your judges. 20But if it is by the finger of God that [I] drive out demons, then
the kingdom of God has come upon you.[j]
21When a strong man fully armed guards his
palace, his possessions are safe. 22But when
one stronger* than he attacks and overcomes
him, he takes away the armor on which he
relied and distributes the spoils. 23Whoever
is not with me is against me, and whoever
does not gather with me scatters.[k]

*The Return of the Unclean Spirit.*[l]
24"When an unclean spirit goes out of someone, it roams through arid regions searching
for rest but, finding none, it says, 'I shall return to my home from which I came.' 25But
upon returning, it finds it swept clean and put
in order. 26Then it goes and brings back seven
other spirits more wicked than itself who
move in and dwell there, and the last condition of that person is worse than the first."[m]

*True Blessedness.** 27While he was speaking, a woman from the crowd called out and
said to him, "Blessed is the womb that carried
you and the breasts at which you nursed."[n]
28He replied, "Rather, blessed are those who
hear the word of God and observe it."

*The Demand for a Sign.** 29While still
more people gathered in the crowd, he said
to them,[o] "This generation is an evil generation; it seeks a sign, but no sign will be given
it, except the sign of Jonah.[p] 30Just as Jonah
became a sign to the Ninevites, so will the
Son of Man be to this generation. 31At the
judgment the queen of the south will rise
with the men of this generation and she will
condemn them, because she came from the
ends of the earth to hear the wisdom of
Solomon, and there is something greater
than Solomon here.[q] 32At the judgment the
men of Nineveh will arise with this generation and condemn it, because at the preaching of Jonah they repented, and there is
something greater than Jonah here.[r]

*The Simile of Light.* 33"No one who lights
a lamp hides it away or places it [under a
bushel basket], but on a lampstand so that
those who enter might see the light.[s] 34The
lamp of the body is your eye.[t] When your eye
is sound, then your whole body is filled with

**11:13 The holy Spirit**: this is a Lucan editorial alteration of a traditional saying of Jesus (see Mt 7:11). Luke presents the gift of the holy Spirit as the response of the Father to the prayer of the Christian disciple.

**11:19 Your own people**: the Greek reads "your sons." Other Jewish exorcists (see Acts 19:13–20), who recognize that the power of God is active in the exorcism, would themselves convict the accusers of Jesus. See also note on Mt 12:27.

**11:22 One stronger**: i.e., Jesus. Cf. Lk 3:16 where John the Baptist identifies Jesus as "mightier than I."

**11:27–28** The beatitude in Lk 11:28 should not be interpreted as a rebuke of the mother of Jesus; see note on Lk 8:21. Rather, it emphasizes (like Lk 2:35) that attentiveness to God's word is more important than biological relationship to Jesus.

**11:29–32** The "sign of Jonah" in Luke is the preaching of the need for repentance by a prophet who comes from afar. Cf. Mt 12:38–42 (and see notes there) where the "sign of Jonah" is interpreted by Jesus as his death and resurrection.

*e:* Mt 7:7–11. *f:* Mt 21:22; Mk 11:24; Jn 14:13; 15:7; 1 Jn 5:14–15. *g:* Mt 12:22–30; Mk 3:20–27. *h:* Mt 9:34. *i:* Mt 12:38; 16:1; Mk 8:11; 1 Cor 1:22. *j:* Ex 8:19. *k:* 9:50; Mk 9:40. *l:* Mt 12:43–45. *m:* Jn 5:14. *n:* 1:28, 42, 48. *o:* Mt 12:38–42; Mk 8:12. *p:* Mt 16:1, 4; Jn 6:30; 1 Cor 1:22. *q:* 1 Kgs 10:1–10; 2 Chr 9:1–12. *r:* Jon 3:8, 10. *s:* 8:16; Mt 5:15; Mk 4:21. *t:* Mt 6:22–23.

light, but when it is bad, then your body is in darkness. [35]Take care, then, that the light in you not become darkness. [36]If your whole body is full of light, and no part of it is in darkness, then it will be as full of light as a lamp illuminating you with its brightness."

***Denunciation of the Pharisees and Scholars of the Law.*** * [37u] After he had spoken, a Pharisee invited him to dine at his home. He entered and reclined at table to eat.[v] [38]The Pharisee was amazed to see that he did not observe the prescribed washing before the meal.[w] [39]The Lord said to him, "Oh you Pharisees![x] Although you cleanse the outside of the cup and the dish, inside you are filled with plunder and evil. [40]You fools! Did not the maker of the outside also make the inside? [41]But as to what is within, give alms, and behold, everything will be clean for you. [42]Woe to you Pharisees! You pay tithes of mint and of rue and of every garden herb, but you pay no attention to judgment and to love for God. These you should have done, without overlooking the others.[y] [43]Woe to you Pharisees! You love the seat of honor in synagogues and greetings in marketplaces.[z] [44]Woe to you! You are like unseen graves* over which people unknowingly walk."[a]

[45]Then one of the scholars of the law* said to him in reply, "Teacher, by saying this you are insulting us too."[b] [46]And he said, "Woe also to you scholars of the law! You impose on people burdens hard to carry, but you yourselves do not lift one finger to touch them. [47c] Woe to you! You build the memorials of the prophets whom your ancestors killed. [48]Consequently, you bear witness and give consent to the deeds of your ancestors, for they killed them and you do the building. [49d]Therefore, the wisdom of God said, 'I will send to them prophets and apostles;* some of them they will kill and persecute' [50]in order that this generation might be charged with the blood of all the prophets shed since the foundation of the world, [51]from the blood of Abel to the blood of Zechariah* who died between the altar and the temple building. Yes, I tell you, this generation will be charged with their blood![e] [52]Woe to you, scholars of the law! You have taken away the key of knowledge. You yourselves did not enter and you stopped those trying to enter."[f] [53]When he left, the scribes and Pharisees began to act with hostility toward him and to interrogate him about many things,[g] [54]for they were plotting to catch him at something he might say.[h]

## CHAPTER 12

See RG 312-13

***The Leaven of the Pharisees.*** * [1]Meanwhile, so many people were crowding together that they were trampling one another underfoot.[i] He began to speak, first to his disciples, "Beware of the leaven—that is, the hypocrisy—of the Pharisees.

***Courage Under Persecution.*** * [2j]"There is nothing concealed that will not be revealed, nor secret that will not be known.[k] [3]Therefore whatever you have said in the darkness will be heard in the light, and what you have whispered behind closed doors will be proclaimed on the housetops. [4]I tell you, my

**11:37–54** This denunciation of the Pharisees (Lk 11:39–44) and the scholars of the law (Lk 11:45–52) is set by Luke in the context of Jesus' dining at the home of a Pharisee. Controversies with or reprimands of Pharisees are regularly set by Luke within the context of Jesus' eating with Pharisees (see Lk 5:29–39; 7:36–50; 14:1–24). A different compilation of similar sayings is found in Mt 23 (see also notes there).

**11:44 Unseen graves**: contact with the dead or with human bones or graves (see Nm 19:16) brought ritual impurity. Jesus presents the Pharisees as those who insidiously lead others astray through their seeming attention to the law.

**11:45 Scholars of the law**: see note on Lk 10:25.

**11:49 I will send to them prophets and apostles**: Jesus connects the mission of the church (apostles) with the mission of the Old Testament prophets who often suffered the rebuke of their contemporaries.

**11:51 From the blood of Abel to the blood of Zechariah**: the murder of Abel is the first murder recounted in the Old Testament (Gn 4:8). The Zechariah mentioned here may be the Zechariah whose murder is recounted in 2 Chr 24:20–22, the last murder presented in the Hebrew canon of the Old Testament.

**12:1** See notes on Mk 8:15 and Mt 16:5–12.

**12:2–9** Luke presents a collection of sayings of Jesus exhorting his followers to acknowledge him and his mission fearlessly and assuring them of God's protection even in times of persecution. They are paralleled in Mt 10:26–33.

*u:* 20:45–47; Mt 23:1–36; Mk 12:38–40. *v:* 7:36; 14:1. *w:* Mt 15:2; Mk 7:2–5. *x:* Mt 23:25–26. *y:* Lv 27:30; Mt 23:23. *z:* 20:46; Mt 23:6; Mk 12:38–39. *a:* Mt 23:27. *b:* Mt 23:4. *c:* Mt 23:29–32. *d:* Mt 23:34–36. *e:* Gn 4:8; 2 Chr 24:20–22. *f:* Mt 23:13. *g:* 6:11; Mt 22:15–22. *h:* 20:20. *i:* Mt 16:6; Mk 8:15. *j:* Mt 10:26–33. *k:* 8:17; Mk 4:22.

friends, do not be afraid of those who kill the body but after that can do no more. 5 I shall show you whom to fear. Be afraid of the one who after killing has the power to cast into Gehenna;* yes, I tell you, be afraid of that one. 6 Are not five sparrows sold for two small coins?* Yet not one of them has escaped the notice of God. 7 Even the hairs of your head have all been counted. Do not be afraid. You are worth more than many sparrows.[l] 8 I tell you, everyone who acknowledges me before others the Son of Man will acknowledge before the angels of God. 9 But whoever denies me before others will be denied before the angels of God.[m]

***Sayings About the Holy Spirit.**** 10 "Everyone who speaks a word against the Son of Man will be forgiven, but the one who blasphemes against the holy Spirit will not be forgiven.[n] 11 When they take you before synagogues and before rulers and authorities,[o] do not worry about how or what your defense will be or about what you are to say. 12 For the holy Spirit will teach you at that moment what you should say."

***Saying Against Greed.*** 13* Someone in the crowd said to him, "Teacher, tell my brother to share the inheritance with me." 14 He replied to him, "Friend, who appointed me as your judge and arbitrator?"[p] 15 Then he said to the crowd, "Take care to guard against all greed, for though one may be rich, one's life does not consist of possessions."[q]

***Parable of the Rich Fool.*** 16 Then he told them a parable. "There was a rich man whose land produced a bountiful harvest. 17 He asked himself, 'What shall I do, for I do not have space to store my harvest?' 18 And he said, 'This is what I shall do: I shall tear down my barns and build larger ones. There I shall store all my grain and other goods 19[r] and I shall say to myself, "Now as for you, you have so many good things stored up for many years, rest, eat, drink, be merry!" '[s] 20 But God said to him, 'You fool, this night your life will be demanded of you; and the things you have prepared, to whom will they belong?' 21 Thus will it be for the one who stores up treasure for himself but is not rich in what matters to God."*

***Dependence on God.*** 22[t] He said to [his] disciples, "Therefore I tell you, do not worry about your life and what you will eat, or about your body and what you will wear. 23 For life is more than food and the body more than clothing. 24 Notice the ravens: they do not sow or reap; they have neither storehouse nor barn, yet God feeds them. How much more important are you than birds![u] 25 Can any of you by worrying add a moment to your lifespan? 26 If even the smallest things are beyond your control, why are you anxious about the rest? 27 Notice how the flowers grow. They do not toil or spin. But I tell you, not even Solomon in all his splendor was dressed like one of them.[v] 28 If God so clothes the grass in the field that grows today and is thrown into the oven tomorrow, will he not much more provide for you, O you of little faith? 29 As for you, do not seek what you are to eat and what you are to drink, and do not worry anymore. 30 All the nations of the world seek for these things, and your Father knows that you need them. 31 Instead, seek his kingdom, and these other things will be given you besides. 32 Do not be afraid any longer, little flock, for your Father is pleased to give you the kingdom.[w] 33 Sell your belongings and

**12:5 Gehenna**: see note on Mt 5:22.

**12:6 Two small coins**: the Roman copper coin, the assarion (Latin *as*), was worth about one-sixteenth of a denarius (see note on Lk 7:41).

**12:10–12** The sayings about the holy Spirit are set in the context of fearlessness in the face of persecution (Lk 12:2–9; cf. Mt 12:31–32). The holy Spirit will be presented in Luke's second volume, the Acts of the Apostles, as the power responsible for the guidance of the Christian mission and the source of courage in the face of persecution.

**12:13–34** Luke has joined together sayings contrasting those whose focus and trust in life is on material possessions, symbolized here by the rich fool of the parable (Lk 12:16–21), with those who recognize their complete dependence on God (Lk 12:21), those whose radical detachment from material possessions symbolizes their heavenly treasure (Lk 12:33–34).

**12:21 Rich in what matters to God**: literally, "rich for God."

*l:* 12:24; 21:18; Acts 27:34. *m:* 9:26; Mk 8:38; 2 Tm 2:12. *n:* Mt 12:31–32; Mk 3:28–29. *o:* 21:12–15; Mt 10:17–20; Mk 13:11. *p:* Ex 2:14; Acts 7:27. *q:* 1 Tm 6:9–10. *r:* Mt 6:19–21; 1 Tm 6:17. *s:* Sir 11:19. *t:* Mt 6:25–34. *u:* 12:7. *v:* 1 Kgs 10:4–7; 2 Chr 9:3–6. *w:* 22:29; Rev 1:6.

give alms. Provide money bags for yourselves that do not wear out, an inexhaustible treasure in heaven that no thief can reach nor moth destroy.[x] [34]For where your treasure is, there also will your heart be.

***Vigilant and Faithful Servants.**** [35][y] "Gird your loins and light your lamps [36]and be like servants who await their master's return from a wedding, ready to open immediately when he comes and knocks.[z] [37]Blessed are those servants whom the master finds vigilant on his arrival. Amen, I say to you, he will gird himself, have them recline at table, and proceed to wait on them. [38]And should he come in the second or third watch and find them prepared in this way, blessed are those servants. [39][a] Be sure of this: if the master of the house had known the hour when the thief was coming, he would not have let his house be broken into. [40]You also must be prepared, for at an hour you do not expect, the Son of Man will come."

[41]Then Peter said, "Lord, is this parable meant for us or for everyone?" [42]And the Lord replied, "Who, then, is the faithful and prudent steward whom the master will put in charge of his servants to distribute [the] food allowance at the proper time? [43]Blessed is that servant whom his master on arrival finds doing so. [44]Truly, I say to you, he will put him in charge of all his property. [45]But if that servant says to himself, 'My master is delayed in coming,'* and begins to beat the menservants and the maidservants, to eat and drink and get drunk, [46]then that servant's master will come on an unexpected day and at an unknown hour and will punish him severely and assign him a place with the unfaithful. [47]That servant who knew his master's will but did not make preparations nor act in accord with his will shall be beaten severely;[b] [48]and the servant who was ignorant of his master's will but acted in a way deserving of a severe beating shall be beaten only lightly. Much will be required of the person entrusted with much, and still more will be demanded of the person entrusted with more.

***Jesus: A Cause of Division.**** [49]"I have come to set the earth on fire, and how I wish it were already blazing! [50]* There is a baptism with which I must be baptized, and how great is my anguish until it is accomplished![c] [51]Do you think that I have come to establish peace on the earth?[d] No, I tell you, but rather division.[e] [52]From now on a household of five will be divided, three against two and two against three; [53]a father will be divided against his son and a son against his father, a mother against her daughter and a daughter against her mother, a mother-in-law against her daughter-in-law and a daughter-in-law against her mother-in-law."[f]

***Signs of the Times.***[g] [54]He also said to the crowds, "When you see [a] cloud rising in the west you say immediately that it is going to rain—and so it does; [55]and when you notice that the wind is blowing from the south you say that it is going to be hot—and so it is. [56]You hypocrites! You know how to interpret the appearance of the earth and the sky; why do you not know how to interpret the present time?

***Settlement with an Opponent.***[h] [57]"Why do you not judge for yourselves what is right? [58]If you are to go with your opponent before a magistrate, make an effort to settle the matter on the way; otherwise your opponent will turn you over to the judge, and the judge hand you over to the constable, and the constable throw you into prison. [59]I say to you, you will not be released until you have paid the last penny."*

**12:35–48** This collection of sayings relates to Luke's understanding of the end time and the return of Jesus. Luke emphasizes for his readers the importance of being faithful to the instructions of Jesus in the period before the parousia.

**12:45 My master is delayed in coming**: this statement indicates that early Christian expectations for the imminent return of Jesus had undergone some modification. Luke cautions his readers against counting on such a delay and acting irresponsibly. Cf. the similar warning in Mt 24:48.

**12:49–53** Jesus' proclamation of the kingdom is a refining and purifying fire. His message that meets with acceptance or rejection will be a source of conflict and dissension even within families.

**12:50 Baptism**: i.e., his death.

**12:59 The last penny**: Greek, **lepton**, a very small amount. Mt 5:26 has for "the last penny" the Greek word *kodrantēs* (Latin *quadrans*, "farthing").

*x:* 18:22; Mt 6:20–21; Mk 10:21. *y:* Mt 24:45–51. *z:* Mt 25:1–13; Mk 13:35–37. *a:* Mt 24:43–44; 1 Thes 5:2. *b:* Jas 4:17. *c:* Mk 10:38–39. *d:* Mt 10:34–35. *e:* 2:14. *f:* Mi 7:6. *g:* Mt 16:2–3. *h:* Mt 5:25–26.

## CHAPTER 13

See RG 312-13

***A Call to Repentance.*** * 1 At that time some people who were present there told him about the Galileans whose blood Pilate* had mingled with the blood of their sacrifices. 2 He said to them in reply, "Do you think that because these Galileans suffered in this way they were greater sinners than all other Galileans?[i] 3 By no means! But I tell you, if you do not repent,[j] you will all perish as they did! 4 Or those eighteen people who were killed when the tower at Siloam fell on them*—do you think they were more guilty than everyone else who lived in Jerusalem? 5 By no means! But I tell you, if you do not repent, you will all perish as they did!"

***The Parable of the Barren Fig Tree.*** * 6[k] And he told them this parable: "There once was a person who had a fig tree planted in his orchard, and when he came in search of fruit on it but found none, 7 he said to the gardener, 'For three years now I have come in search of fruit on this fig tree but have found none. [So] cut it down. Why should it exhaust the soil?' 8 He said to him in reply, 'Sir, leave it for this year also, and I shall cultivate the ground around it and fertilize it; 9 it may bear fruit in the future. If not you can cut it down.'"

***Cure of a Crippled Woman on the Sabbath.*** * 10 He was teaching in a synagogue on the sabbath. 11 And a woman was there who for eighteen years had been crippled by a spirit; she was bent over, completely incapable of standing erect. 12 When Jesus saw her, he called to her and said, "Woman, you are set free of your infirmity." 13 He laid his hands on her, and she at once stood up straight and glorified God. 14[l] But the leader of the synagogue, indignant that Jesus had cured on the sabbath, said to the crowd in reply, "There are six days when work should be done. Come on those days to be cured, not on the sabbath day." 15* The Lord said to him in reply, "Hypocrites! Does not each one of you on the sabbath untie his ox or his ass from the manger and lead it out for watering?[m] 16* This daughter of Abraham, whom Satan has bound for eighteen years now, ought she not to have been set free on the sabbath day from this bondage?"[n] 17 When he said this, all his adversaries were humiliated; and the whole crowd rejoiced at all the splendid deeds done by him.

***The Parable of the Mustard Seed.***[o] 18* Then he said, "What is the kingdom of God like? To what can I compare it? 19 It is like a mustard seed that a person took and

**13:1–5** The death of the Galileans at the hands of Pilate (Lk 13:1) and the accidental death of those on whom the tower fell (Lk 13:4) are presented by the Lucan Jesus as timely reminders of the need for all to repent, for the victims of these tragedies should not be considered outstanding sinners who were singled out for punishment.

**13:1** The slaughter of the Galileans by Pilate is unknown outside Luke; but from what is known about Pilate from the Jewish historian Josephus, such a slaughter would be in keeping with the character of Pilate. Josephus reports that Pilate had disrupted a religious gathering of the Samaritans on Mount Gerizim with a slaughter of the participants (*Antiquities* 18:86–87), and that on another occasion Pilate had killed many Jews who had opposed him when he appropriated money from the temple treasury to build an aqueduct in Jerusalem (*Jewish Wars* 2:175–77; *Antiquities* 18:60–62).

**13:4** Like the incident mentioned in Lk 13:1 nothing of this accident in Jerusalem is known outside Luke and the New Testament.

**13:6–9** Following on the call to repentance in Lk 13:1–5, the parable of the barren fig tree presents a story about the continuing patience of God with those who have not yet given evidence of their repentance (see Lk 3:8). The parable may also be alluding to the delay of the end time, when punishment will be meted out, and the importance of preparing for the end of the age because the delay will not be permanent (Lk 13:8–9).

**13:10–17** The cure of the crippled woman on the sabbath and the controversy that results furnishes a parallel to an incident that will be reported by Luke in 14:1–6, the cure of the man with dropsy on the sabbath. A characteristic of Luke's style is the juxtaposition of an incident that reveals Jesus' concern for a man with an incident that reveals his concern for a woman; cf., e.g., Lk 7:11–17 and Lk 8:49–56.

**13:15–16** If the law as interpreted by Jewish tradition allowed for the untying of bound animals on the sabbath, how much more should this woman who has been bound by Satan's power be freed on the sabbath from her affliction.

**13:16 Whom Satan has bound**: affliction and infirmity are taken as evidence of Satan's hold on humanity. The healing ministry of Jesus reveals the gradual wresting from Satan of control over humanity and the establishment of God's kingdom.

**13:18–21** Two parables are used to illustrate the future proportions of the kingdom of God that will result from its deceptively small beginning in the preaching and healing ministry of Jesus. They are paralleled in Mt 13:31–33 and Mk 4:30–32.

*i:* Jn 9:2. *j:* Jn 8:24. *k:* Jer 8:13; Heb 3:17; Mt 21:19; Mk 11:13. *l:* 6:7; 14:3; Ex 20:8–11; Dt 5:12–15; Mt 12:10; Mk 3:2–4; Jn 5:16; 7:23; 9:14, 16. *m:* 14:5; Dt 22:4; Mt 12:11. *n:* 19:9. *o:* Mt 13:31–32; Mk 4:30–32.

planted in the garden. When it was fully grown, it became a large bush and 'the birds of the sky dwelt in its branches.' "[p]

*The Parable of the Yeast.*[q] 20 Again he said, "To what shall I compare the kingdom of God? 21 It is like yeast that a woman took and mixed [in] with three measures of wheat flour until the whole batch of dough was leavened."

*The Narrow Door; Salvation and Rejection.** 22 He passed through towns and villages, teaching as he went and making his way to Jerusalem. 23 Someone asked him, "Lord, will only a few people be saved?" He answered them, 24[r] "Strive to enter through the narrow door, for many, I tell you, will attempt to enter but will not be strong enough.[s] 25 After the master of the house has arisen and locked the door, then will you stand outside knocking and saying, 'Lord, open the door for us.' He will say to you in reply, 'I do not know where you are from.'[t] 26 And you will say, 'We ate and drank in your company and you taught in our streets.' 27[u] Then he will say to you, 'I do not know where [you] are from. Depart from me, all you evildoers!' 28[v] And there will be wailing and grinding of teeth when you see Abraham, Isaac, and Jacob and all the prophets in the kingdom of God and you yourselves cast out. 29 And people will come from the east and the west and from the north and the south and will recline at table in the kingdom of God.[w] 30 For behold, some are last who will be first, and some are first who will be last."[x]

*Herod's Desire to Kill Jesus.* 31 At that time some Pharisees came to him and said, "Go away, leave this area because Herod wants to kill you." 32 He replied, "Go and tell that fox, 'Behold, I cast out demons and I perform healings today and tomorrow, and on the third day I accomplish my purpose.* 33* Yet I must continue on my way today,[y] tomorrow, and the following day, for it is impossible that a prophet should die outside of Jerusalem.'

*The Lament over Jerusalem.*[z] 34 "Jerusalem, Jerusalem, you who kill the prophets and stone those sent to you, how many times I yearned to gather your children together as a hen gathers her brood under her wings, but you were unwilling! 35 Behold, your house will be abandoned. [But] I tell you, you will not see me until [the time comes when] you say, 'Blessed is he who comes in the name of the Lord.' "[a]

## CHAPTER 14

See RG 312-13

*Healing of the Man with Dropsy on the Sabbath.** 1[b] On a sabbath he went to dine at the home of one of the leading Pharisees, and the people there were observing him carefully.[c] 2 In front of him there was a man suffering from dropsy.* 3 Jesus spoke to the scholars of the law and Pharisees in reply, asking, "Is it lawful to cure on the sabbath or not?"[d] 4 But they kept silent; so he took the man and, after he had healed him, dismissed him. 5 Then he said to them, "Who among you, if your son or ox* falls into a cistern, would not immediately pull him out on the sabbath day?"[e] 6 But they were unable to answer his question.[f]

**13:22–30** These sayings of Jesus follow in Luke upon the parables of the kingdom (Lk 13:18–21) and stress that great effort is required for entrance into the kingdom (Lk 13:24) and that there is an urgency to accept the present opportunity to enter because the narrow door will not remain open indefinitely (Lk 13:25). Lying behind the sayings is the rejection of Jesus and his message by his Jewish contemporaries (Lk 13:26) whose places at table in the kingdom will be taken by Gentiles from the four corners of the world (Lk 13:29). Those called last (the Gentiles) will precede those to whom the invitation to enter was first extended (the Jews). See also Lk 14:15–24.

**13:32** Nothing, not even Herod's desire to kill Jesus, stands in the way of Jesus' role in fulfilling God's will and in establishing the kingdom through his exorcisms and healings.

**13:33 It is impossible that a prophet should die outside of Jerusalem**: Jerusalem is the city of destiny and the goal of the journey of the prophet Jesus. Only when he reaches the holy city will his work be accomplished.

**14:1–6** See note on Lk 13:10–17.

**14:2 Dropsy**: an abnormal swelling of the body because of the retention and accumulation of fluid.

**14:5 Your son or ox**: this is the reading of many of the oldest and most important New Testament manuscripts. Because of the strange collocation of **son** and **ox**, some copyists have altered it

*p:* Ez 17:23–24; 31:6. *q:* Mt 13:33. *r:* Mt 7:13–14, 21–23. *s:* Mk 10:25. *t:* Mt 25:10–12. *u:* Ps 6:9; Mt 7:23; 25:41. *v:* Mt 8:11–12. *w:* Ps 107:2–3. *x:* Mt 19:20; 20:16; Mk 10:31. *y:* 2:38; Jn 6:30; 8:20. *z:* 19:41–44; Mt 23:37–39. *a:* 19:38; 1 Kgs 9:7–8; Ps 118:26; Jer 7:4–7, 13–15; 12:7; 22:5. *b:* 6:6–11; 13:10–17. *c:* 11:37. *d:* 6:9; Mk 3:4. *e:* 13:15; Dt 22:4; Mt 12:11. *f:* Mt 22:46.

***Conduct of Invited Guests and Hosts.**** [7g] He told a parable to those who had been invited, noticing how they were choosing the places of honor at the table. [8h] "When you are invited by someone to a wedding banquet, do not recline at table in the place of honor. A more distinguished guest than you may have been invited by him, [9] and the host who invited both of you may approach you and say, 'Give your place to this man,' and then you would proceed with embarrassment to take the lowest place. [10] Rather, when you are invited, go and take the lowest place so that when the host comes to you he may say, 'My friend, move up to a higher position.' Then you will enjoy the esteem of your companions at the table. [11] For everyone who exalts himself will be humbled, but the one who humbles himself will be exalted."[i] [12] Then he said to the host who invited him, "When you hold a lunch or a dinner, do not invite your friends or your brothers or your relatives or your wealthy neighbors, in case they may invite you back and you have repayment.[j] [13] Rather, when you hold a banquet, invite the poor, the crippled, the lame, the blind; [14] blessed indeed will you be because of their inability to repay you. For you will be repaid at the resurrection of the righteous."[k]

***The Parable of the Great Feast.**** [15] One of his fellow guests on hearing this said to him, "Blessed is the one who will dine in the kingdom of God." [16l] He replied to him, "A man gave a great dinner to which he invited many. [17] When the time for the dinner came, he dispatched his servant to say to those invited, 'Come, everything is now ready.' [18] But one by one, they all began to excuse themselves. The first said to him, 'I have purchased a field and must go to examine it; I ask you, consider me excused.' [19] And another said, 'I have purchased five yoke of oxen and am on my way to evaluate them; I ask you, consider me excused.' [20] And another said, 'I have just married a woman, and therefore I cannot come.' [21] The servant went and reported this to his master. Then the master of the house in a rage commanded his servant, 'Go out quickly into the streets and alleys of the town and bring in here the poor and the crippled, the blind and the lame.' [22] The servant reported, 'Sir, your orders have been carried out and still there is room.' [23] The master then ordered the servant, 'Go out to the highways and hedgerows and make people come in that my home may be filled. [24] For, I tell you, none of those men who were invited will taste my dinner.' "

***Sayings on Discipleship.**** [25] Great crowds were traveling with him, and he turned and addressed them, [26m] "If any one comes to me without hating his father* and mother, wife and children, brothers and sisters, and even his own life, he cannot be my disciple.[n] [27] Whoever does not carry his own cross and come after me cannot be my disciple.[o] [28] Which of you wishing to construct a tower does not first sit down and calculate the cost to see if there is enough for its completion? [29] Otherwise, after laying the foundation and finding himself unable to finish the work the onlookers should laugh at him [30] and say, 'This one began to build but did not have the resources to finish.' [31] Or what king marching into battle would not first sit down and decide whether with ten thousand troops he can successfully oppose another king ad-

to "your ass or ox," on the model of the saying in Lk 13:15.

**14:7–14** The banquet scene found only in Luke provides the opportunity for these teachings of Jesus on humility and presents a setting to display Luke's interest in Jesus' attitude toward the rich and the poor (see notes on Lk 4:18; 6:20–26; 12:13–34).

**14:15–24** The parable of the great dinner is a further illustration of the rejection by Israel, God's chosen people, of Jesus' invitation to share in the banquet in the kingdom and the extension of the invitation to other Jews whose identification as the poor, crippled, blind, and lame (Lk 14:21) classifies them among those who recognize their need for salvation, and to Gentiles (Lk 14:23). A similar parable is found in Mt 22:1–10.

**14:25–33** This collection of sayings, most of which are peculiar to Luke, focuses on the total dedication necessary for the disciple of Jesus. No attachment to family (Lk 14:26) or possessions (Lk 14:33) can stand in the way of the total commitment demanded of the disciple. Also, acceptance of the call to be a disciple demands readiness to accept persecution and suffering (Lk 14:27) and a realistic assessment of the hardships and costs (Lk 14:28–32).

**14:26 Hating his father . . .**: cf. the similar saying in Mt 10:37. The disciple's family must take second place to the absolute dedication involved in following Jesus (see also Lk 9:59–62).

*g:* 11:43; Mt 23:6; Mk 12:38–39. *h:* Prv 25:6–7. *i:* 18:14. *j:* 6:32–35. *k:* Jn 5:29. *l:* Mt 22:2–10. *m:* Mt 10:37–38. *n:* 9:57–62; 18:29; Jn 12:25. *o:* 9:23; Mt 16:24; Mk 8:34.

vancing upon him with twenty thousand troops? 32 But if not, while he is still far away, he will send a delegation to ask for peace terms. 33 In the same way, everyone of you who does not renounce all his possessions cannot be my disciple.[p]

*The Simile of Salt.** 34 "Salt is good, but if salt itself loses its taste, with what can its flavor be restored?[q] 35 It is fit neither for the soil nor for the manure pile; it is thrown out. Whoever has ears to hear ought to hear."[r]

See RG 312–13

## CHAPTER 15

*The Parable of the Lost Sheep.*[s] 1* The tax collectors and sinners were all drawing near to listen to him, 2 but the Pharisees and scribes began to complain, saying, "This man welcomes sinners and eats with them."[t] 3 So to them he addressed this parable. 4[u] "What man among you having a hundred sheep and losing one of them would not leave the ninety-nine in the desert and go after the lost one[v] until he finds it?[w] 5 And when he does find it, he sets it on his shoulders with great joy 6 and, upon his arrival home, he calls together his friends and neighbors and says to them, 'Rejoice with me because I have found my lost sheep.' 7 I tell you, in just the same way there will be more joy in heaven over one sinner who repents than over ninety-nine righteous people who have no need of repentance.[x]

*The Parable of the Lost Coin.* 8 "Or what woman having ten coins* and losing one would not light a lamp and sweep the house, searching carefully until she finds it? 9 And when she does find it, she calls together her friends and neighbors and says to them, 'Rejoice with me because I have found the coin that I lost.' 10 In just the same way, I tell you, there will be rejoicing among the angels of God over one sinner who repents."

*The Parable of the Lost Son.* 11 Then he said, "A man had two sons, 12 and the younger son said to his father, 'Father, give me the share of your estate that should come to me.' So the father divided the property between them. 13 After a few days, the younger son collected all his belongings and set off to a distant country where he squandered his inheritance on a life of dissipation.[y] 14 When he had freely spent everything, a severe famine struck that country, and he found himself in dire need. 15 So he hired himself out to one of the local citizens who sent him to his farm to tend the swine. 16 And he longed to eat his fill of the pods on which the swine fed, but nobody gave him any. 17 Coming to his senses he thought, 'How many of my father's hired workers have more than enough food to eat, but here am I, dying from hunger. 18 I shall get up and go to my father and I shall say to him, "Father, I have sinned against heaven and against you. 19 I no longer deserve to be called your son; treat me as you would treat one of your hired workers." ' 20 So he got up and went back to his father. While he was still a long way off, his father caught sight of him, and was filled with compassion. He ran to his son, embraced him and kissed him. 21 His son said to him, 'Father, I have sinned against heaven and against you; I no longer deserve to be called your son.' 22 But his father ordered his servants, 'Quickly bring the finest robe and put it on him; put a ring on his finger and sandals on his feet. 23 Take the fattened calf and slaughter it. Then let us celebrate with a feast, 24 because this son of mine was dead, and has come to life again; he was lost, and has been found.' Then the celebration began. 25 Now the older son had been out in the field and, on his way back, as he neared the house, he heard the sound of music and dancing. 26 He called one of the servants and asked what this might mean. 27 The servant said to him, 'Your brother has returned and

**14:34–35** The simile of salt follows the sayings of Jesus that demanded of the disciple total dedication and detachment from family and possessions and illustrates the condition of one who does not display this total commitment. The half-hearted disciple is like salt that cannot serve its intended purpose. See the simile of salt in Mt 5:13 and the note there.

**15:1–32** To the parable of the lost sheep (Lk 15:1–7) that Luke shares with Matthew (Mt 18:12–14), Luke adds two parables (the lost coin, Lk 15:8–10; the prodigal son, Lk 15:11–32) from his own special tradition to illustrate Jesus' particular concern for the lost and God's love for the repentant sinner.

**15:8 Ten coins**: literally, "ten drachmas." A drachma was a Greek silver coin.

*p:* 5:11. *q:* Mt 5:13; Mk 9:50. *r:* 8:8; Mt 11:15; 13:9; Mk 4:9, 23. *s:* Mt 9:10–13. *t:* 5:30; 19:7. *u:* Mt 18:12–14. *v:* 19:10. *w:* Ez 34:11–12, 16. *x:* Ez 18:23. *y:* Prv 29:3.

your father has slaughtered the fattened calf
because he has him back safe and sound.’
28He became angry, and when he refused to
enter the house, his father came out and
pleaded with him. 29He said to his father in
reply, ‘Look, all these years I served you and
not once did I disobey your orders; yet you
never gave me even a young goat to feast on
with my friends. 30But when your son returns
who swallowed up your property with prostitutes, for him you slaughter the fattened
calf.’ 31He said to him, ‘My son, you are here
with me always; everything I have is yours.
32But now we must celebrate and rejoice, because your brother was dead and has come to
life again; he was lost and has been found.’ ”

## CHAPTER 16

See RG 312-13

### *The Parable of the Dishonest Steward.**

1Then he also said to his disciples, “A rich
man had a steward who was reported to him
for squandering his property. 2He summoned
him and said, ‘What is this I hear about you?
Prepare a full account of your stewardship,
because you can no longer be my steward.’
3The steward said to himself, ‘What shall I
do, now that my master is taking the position
of steward away from me? I am not strong
enough to dig and I am ashamed to beg. 4I
know what I shall do so that, when I am removed from the stewardship, they may welcome me into their homes.’ 5He called in his
master’s debtors one by one. To the first he
said, ‘How much do you owe my master?’
6* He replied, ‘One hundred measures of olive oil.’ He said to him, ‘Here is your promissory note. Sit down and quickly write one for
fifty.’ 7Then to another he said, ‘And you,
how much do you owe?’ He replied, ‘One
hundred kors* of wheat.’ He said to him,
‘Here is your promissory note; write one for
eighty.’ 8And the master commended that dishonest steward for acting prudently.

*Application of the Parable.** “For the children of this world are more prudent in dealing with their own generation than are the
children of light.*[z] 9I tell you, make friends
for yourselves with dishonest wealth,* so
that when it fails, you will be welcomed into
eternal dwellings.[a] 10* The person who is
trustworthy in very small matters is also
trustworthy in great ones; and the person
who is dishonest in very small matters is
also dishonest in great ones.[b] 11If, therefore,
you are not trustworthy with dishonest
wealth, who will trust you with true wealth?
12If you are not trustworthy with what belongs to another, who will give you what is
yours? 13No servant can serve two masters.*
He will either hate one and love the other, or
be devoted to one and despise the other. You
cannot serve God and mammon.”[c]

**16:1–8a** The parable of the dishonest steward has to be understood in the light of the Palestinian custom of agents acting on behalf of their masters and the usurious practices common to such agents. The dishonesty of the steward consisted in the squandering of his master’s property (Lk 16:1) and not in any subsequent graft. The master commends the dishonest steward who has forgone his own usurious commission on the business transaction by having the debtors write new notes that reflected only the real amount owed the master (i.e., minus the steward’s profit). The dishonest steward acts in this way in order to ingratiate himself with the debtors because he knows he is being dismissed from his position (Lk 16:3). The parable, then, teaches the prudent use of one’s material goods in light of an imminent crisis.

**16:6 One hundred measures:** literally, “one hundred baths.” A bath is a Hebrew unit of liquid measurement equivalent to eight or nine gallons.

**16:7 One hundred kors:** a **kor** is a Hebrew unit of dry measure for grain or wheat equivalent to ten or twelve bushels.

**16:8b–13** Several originally independent sayings of Jesus are gathered here by Luke to form the concluding application of the parable of the dishonest steward.

**16:8b–9** The first conclusion recommends the prudent use of one’s wealth (in the light of the coming of the end of the age) after the manner of the children of this world, represented in the parable by the dishonest steward.

**16:9 Dishonest wealth**: literally, “mammon of iniquity.” Mammon is the Greek transliteration of a Hebrew or Aramaic word that is usually explained as meaning “that in which one trusts.” The characterization of this wealth as **dishonest** expresses a tendency of wealth to lead one to dishonesty. **Eternal dwellings**: or, “eternal tents,” i.e., heaven.

**16:10–12** The second conclusion recommends constant fidelity to those in positions of responsibility.

**16:13** The third conclusion is a general statement about the incompatibility of serving God and being a slave to riches. To be dependent upon wealth is opposed to the teachings of Jesus who counseled complete dependence on the Father as one of the characteristics of the Christian disciple (Lk 12:22–39). **God and mammon**: see note on Lk 16:9. Mammon is used here as if it were itself a god.

*z:* Eph 5:8; 1 Thes 5:5. *a:* 12:33. *b:* 19:17; Mt 25:20–23. *c:* Mt 6:24.

***A Saying Against the Pharisees.*** 14* The Pharisees, who loved money,* heard all these things and sneered at him. 15 And he said to them, "You justify yourselves in the sight of others, but God knows your hearts; for what is of human esteem is an abomination in the sight of God.[d]

***Sayings About the Law.*** 16 "The law and the prophets lasted until John;* but from then on the kingdom of God is proclaimed, and everyone who enters does so with violence.[e] 17 It is easier for heaven and earth to pass away than for the smallest part of a letter of the law to become invalid.[f]

***Sayings About Divorce.*** 18 "Everyone who divorces his wife and marries another commits adultery, and the one who marries a woman divorced from her husband commits adultery.[g]

***The Parable of the Rich Man and Lazarus.**** 19 "There was a rich man* who dressed in purple garments and fine linen and dined sumptuously each day. 20 And lying at his door was a poor man named Lazarus, covered with sores,[h] 21 who would gladly have eaten his fill of the scraps that fell from the rich man's table. Dogs even used to come and lick his sores. 22 When the poor man died, he was carried away by angels to the bosom of Abraham. The rich man also died and was buried, 23 and from the netherworld,* where he was in torment, he raised his eyes and saw Abraham far off and Lazarus at his side. 24 And he cried out, 'Father Abraham, have pity on me. Send Lazarus to dip the tip of his finger in water and cool my tongue, for I am suffering torment in these flames.' 25 Abraham replied, 'My child, remember that you received what was good during your lifetime while Lazarus likewise received what was bad; but now he is comforted here, whereas you are tormented.[i] 26 Moreover, between us and you a great chasm is established to prevent anyone from crossing who might wish to go from our side to yours or from your side to ours.' 27 He said, 'Then I beg you, father, send him to my father's house, 28 for I have five brothers, so that he may warn them, lest they too come to this place of torment.' 29 But Abraham replied, 'They have Moses and the prophets. Let them listen to them.' 30* He said, 'Oh no, father Abraham, but if someone from the dead goes to them, they will repent.' 31 Then Abraham said, 'If they will not listen to Moses and the prophets, neither will they be persuaded if someone should rise from the dead.' "[j]

## CHAPTER 17

See RG 312–13

***Temptations to Sin.*** 1[k] He said to his disciples, "Things that cause sin will inevitably occur, but woe to the person through whom they occur. 2 It would be better for him if a millstone were put around his neck and he be thrown into the sea than for him to cause one of these little ones to sin. 3 Be on your guard!* If your brother sins, rebuke him; and if he repents, forgive him.[l] 4 And if he wrongs you seven times in one day and returns to you seven times saying, 'I am sorry,' you should forgive him."[m]

***Saying of Faith.*** 5 And the apostles said to

**16:14–18** The two parables about the use of riches in chap. 16 are separated by several isolated sayings of Jesus on the hypocrisy of the Pharisees (Lk 16:14–15), on the law (Lk 16:16–17), and on divorce (Lk 16:18).

**16:14–15** The Pharisees are here presented as examples of those who are slaves to wealth (see Lk 16:13) and, consequently, they are unable to serve God.

**16:16** John the Baptist is presented in Luke's gospel as a transitional figure between the period of Israel, the time of promise, and the period of Jesus, the time of fulfillment. With John, the fulfillment of the Old Testament promises has begun.

**16:19–31** The parable of the rich man and Lazarus again illustrates Luke's concern with Jesus' attitude toward the rich and the poor. The reversal of the fates of the rich man and Lazarus (Lk 16:22–23) illustrates the teachings of Jesus in Luke's "Sermon on the Plain" (Lk 6:20–21, 24–25).

**16:19** The oldest Greek manuscript of Luke dating from ca. A.D. 175–225 records the name of the rich man as an abbreviated form of "Nineveh," but there is very little textual support in other manuscripts for this reading. "Dives" of popular tradition is the Latin Vulgate's translation for "rich man" (Lk 16:19–31).

**16:23 The netherworld**: see note on Lk 10:15.

**16:30–31** A foreshadowing in Luke's gospel of the rejection of the call to repentance even after Jesus' resurrection.

**17:3 Be on your guard**: the translation takes Lk 17:3a as the conclusion to the saying on scandal in Lk 17:1–2. It is not impossible that it should be taken as the beginning of the saying on forgiveness in Lk 17:3b–4.

*d:* 18:9–14. *e:* Mt 11:12–13. *f:* Mt 5:18. *g:* Mt 5:32; 19:9; Mk 10:11–12; 1 Cor 7:10–11. *h:* Mt 15:27; Mk 7:28. *i:* 6:24–25. *j:* Jn 5:46–47; 11:44–48. *k:* Mt 18:6–7. *l:* Mt 18:15. *m:* Mt 6:14; 18:21–22, 35; Mk 11:25.

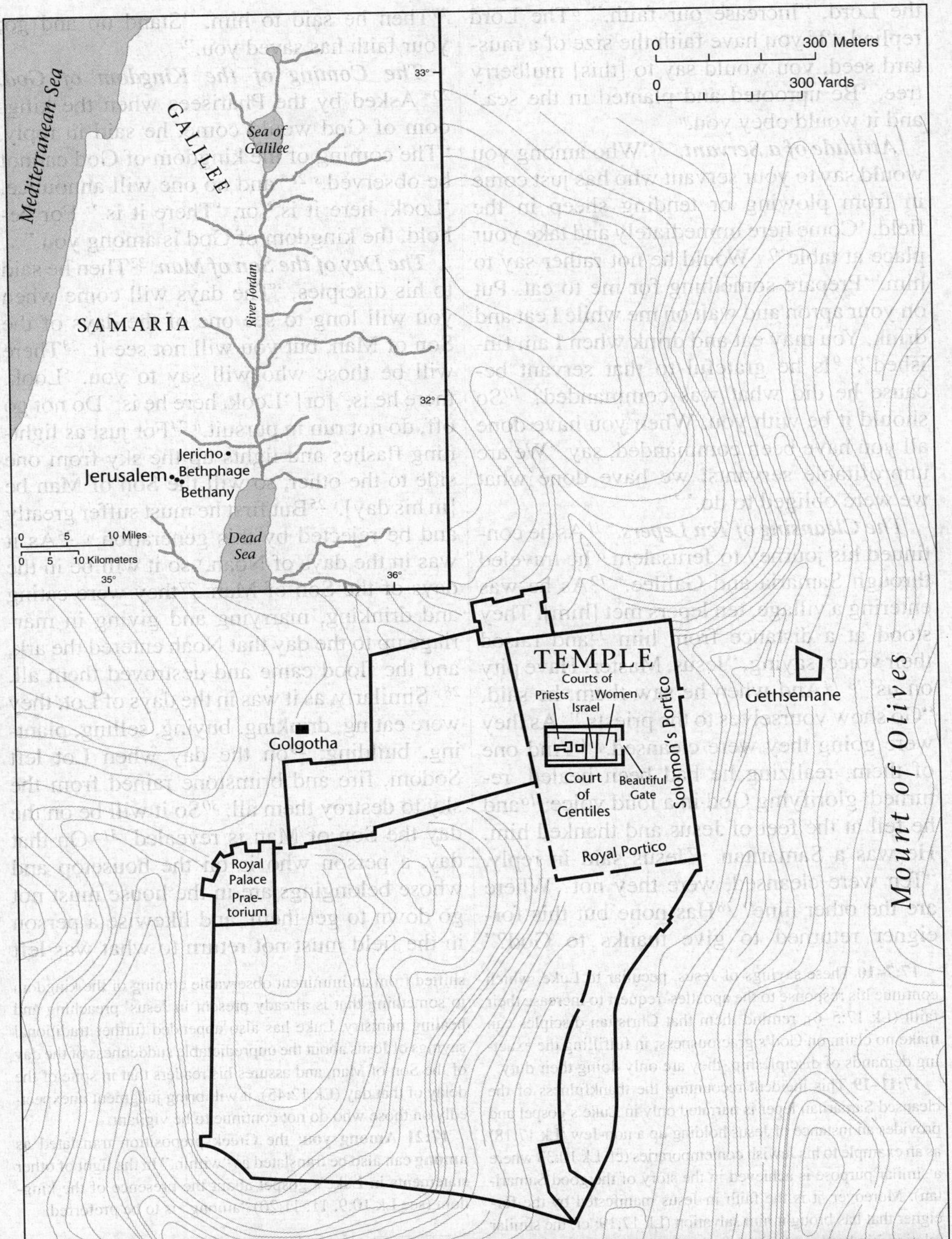


**Sites of Jesus' Journey to Jerusalem and within It**

the Lord, "Increase our faith." 6 The Lord
replied, "If you have faith the size of a mustard seed, you would say to [this] mulberry
tree, 'Be uprooted and planted in the sea,'
and it would obey you.[n]

***Attitude of a Servant.**** 7 "Who among you
would say to your servant who has just come
in from plowing or tending sheep in the
field, 'Come here immediately and take your
place at table'? 8 Would he not rather say to
him, 'Prepare something for me to eat. Put
on your apron and wait on me while I eat and
drink. You may eat and drink when I am finished'? 9 Is he grateful to that servant because he did what was commanded? 10 So
should it be with you. When you have done
all you have been commanded, say, 'We are
unprofitable servants; we have done what
we were obliged to do.' "

***The Cleansing of Ten Lepers.**** 11 As he continued his journey to Jerusalem,[o] he traveled
through Samaria and Galilee.* 12 As he was
entering a village, ten lepers met [him]. They
stood at a distance from him 13 and raised
their voice, saying, "Jesus, Master! Have pity
on us!"[p] 14 And when he saw them, he said,
"Go show yourselves to the priests."* As they
were going they were cleansed.[q] 15 And one
of them, realizing he had been healed, returned, glorifying God in a loud voice; 16 and
he fell at the feet of Jesus and thanked him.
He was a Samaritan. 17 Jesus said in reply,
"Ten were cleansed, were they not? Where
are the other nine? 18 Has none but this foreigner returned to give thanks to God?"
19 Then he said to him, "Stand up and go;
your faith has saved you."[r]

***The Coming of the Kingdom of God.***
20* Asked by the Pharisees when the kingdom of God would come, he said in reply,
"The coming of the kingdom of God cannot
be observed,[s] 21* and no one will announce,
'Look, here it is,' or, 'There it is.'[t] For behold, the kingdom of God is among you."

***The Day of the Son of Man.*** 22 Then he said
to his disciples, "The days will come when
you will long to see one of the days of the
Son of Man, but you will not see it. 23 There
will be those who will say to you, 'Look,
there he is,' [or] 'Look, here he is.' Do not go
off, do not run in pursuit.[u] 24 For just as lightning flashes and lights up the sky from one
side to the other, so will the Son of Man be
[in his day].[v] 25 But first he must suffer greatly
and be rejected by this generation.[w] 26 As it
was in the days of Noah,[x] so it will be in the
days of the Son of Man; 27 they were eating
and drinking, marrying and giving in marriage up to the day that Noah entered the ark,
and the flood came and destroyed them all.
28[y] Similarly, as it was in the days of Lot: they
were eating, drinking, buying, selling, planting, building; 29 on the day when Lot left
Sodom, fire and brimstone rained from the
sky to destroy them all. 30 So it will be on the
day the Son of Man is revealed. 31[z] On that
day, a person who is on the housetop and
whose belongings are in the house must not
go down to get them, and likewise a person
in the field must not return to what was left

**17:7–10** These sayings of Jesus, peculiar to Luke, which continue his response to the apostles' request to increase their faith (Lk 17:5–6), remind them that Christian disciples can make no claim on God's graciousness; in fulfilling the exacting demands of discipleship, they are only doing their duty.

**17:11–19** This incident recounting the thankfulness of the cleansed Samaritan leper is narrated only in Luke's gospel and provides an instance of Jesus holding up a non-Jew (Lk 17:18) as an example to his Jewish contemporaries (cf. Lk 10:33 where a similar purpose is achieved in the story of the good Samaritan). Moreover, it is the faith in Jesus manifested by the foreigner that has brought him salvation (Lk 17:19; cf. the similar relationship between faith and salvation in Lk 7:50; 8:48, 50).

**17:11 Through Samaria and Galilee**: or, "between Samaria and Galilee."

**17:14** See note on Lk 5:14.

**17:20–37** To the question of the Pharisees about the time of the coming of God's kingdom, Jesus replies that the kingdom is **among you** (Lk 17:20–21). The emphasis has thus been shifted from an imminent observable coming of the kingdom to something that is already present in Jesus' preaching and healing ministry. Luke has also appended further traditional sayings of Jesus about the unpredictable suddenness of the day of the Son of Man, and assures his readers that in spite of the delay of that day (Lk 12:45), it will bring judgment unexpectedly on those who do not continue to be vigilant.

**17:21 Among you**: the Greek preposition translated as **among** can also be translated as "within." In the light of other statements in Luke's gospel about the presence of the kingdom (see Lk 10:9, 11; 11:20) "among" is to be preferred.

---

*n:* Mt 17:20; 21:21; Mk 11:23. *o:* 9:51–53; 13:22, 33; 18:31; 19:28; Jn 4:4. *p:* 18:38; Mt 9:27; 15:22. *q:* 5:14; Lv 14:2–32; Mt 8:4; Mk 1:44. *r:* 7:50; 18:42. *s:* Jn 3:3. *t:* 17:23; Mt 24:23; Mk 13:21. *u:* 17:21; Mt 24:23, 26; Mk 13:21. *v:* Mt 24:27. *w:* 9:22; 18:32–33; Mt 16:21; 17:22–23; 20:18–19; Mk 8:31; 9:31; 10:33–34. *x:* Gn 6–8; Mt 24:37–39. *y:* Gn 18:20–21; 19:1–29. *z:* Gn 19:17, 26.

behind.[a] 32Remember the wife of Lot.
33Whoever seeks to preserve his life will lose
it, but whoever loses it will save it.[b] 34I tell
you, on that night there will be two people in
one bed; one will be taken, the other left.
35[c] And there will be two women grinding
meal together; one will be taken, the other
left." 36* 37They said to him in reply, "Where,
Lord?" He said to them, "Where the body is,
there also the vultures will gather."[d]

## CHAPTER 18

See RG 312–13

*The Parable of the Persistent Widow.*
1* Then he told them a parable about the necessity for them to pray always without becoming weary.[e] He said, 2"There was a judge
in a certain town who neither feared God nor
respected any human being. 3And a widow in
that town used to come to him and say, 'Render a just decision for me against my adversary.' 4For a long time the judge was unwilling, but eventually he thought, 'While it is true
that I neither fear God nor respect any human
being, 5* [f] because this widow keeps bothering
me I shall deliver a just decision for her lest
she finally come and strike me.' " 6The Lord
said, "Pay attention to what the dishonest
judge says. 7Will not God then secure the
rights of his chosen ones who call out to him
day and night? Will he be slow to answer
them? 8I tell you, he will see to it that justice is
done for them speedily. But when the Son of
Man comes, will he find faith on earth?"

*The Parable of the Pharisee and the Tax Collector.* 9He then addressed this parable to
those who were convinced of their own righ-
teousness and despised everyone else.[g]
10"Two people went up to the temple area to
pray; one was a Pharisee and the other was a
tax collector. 11The Pharisee took up his position and spoke this prayer to himself, 'O
God, I thank you that I am not like the rest of
humanity—greedy, dishonest, adulterous—
or even like this tax collector. 12I fast twice a
week, and I pay tithes on my whole income.'[h] 13But the tax collector stood off at a
distance and would not even raise his eyes to
heaven but beat his breast and prayed, 'O
God, be merciful to me a sinner.'[i] 14I tell
you, the latter went home justified, not the
former; for everyone who exalts himself will
be humbled, and the one who humbles himself will be exalted."[j]

*Saying on Children and the Kingdom.*
15* People were bringing even infants to him
that he might touch them,* and when the disciples saw this, they rebuked them.[k] 16Jesus,
however, called the children to himself and
said, "Let the children come to me and do
not prevent them; for the kingdom of God
belongs to such as these. 17Amen, I say to
you, whoever does not accept the kingdom
of God like a child will not enter it."[l]

*The Rich Official.* 18[m] An official asked
him this question, "Good teacher, what must
I do to inherit eternal life?"[n] 19Jesus answered him, "Why do you call me good? No
one is good but God alone. 20You know the

**17:36** The inclusion of Lk 17:36 "There will be two men in the field; one will be taken, the other left behind," in some Western manuscripts appears to be a scribal assimilation to Mt 24:40.

**18:1–14** The particularly Lucan material in the travel narrative concludes with two parables on prayer. The first (Lk 18:1–8) teaches the disciples the need of persistent prayer so that they not fall victims to apostasy (Lk 18:8). The second (Lk 18:9–14) condemns the self-righteous, critical attitude of the Pharisee and teaches that the fundamental attitude of the Christian disciple must be the recognition of sinfulness and complete dependence on God's graciousness. The second parable recalls the story of the pardoning of the sinful woman (Lk 7:36–50) where a similar contrast is presented between the critical attitude of the Pharisee Simon and the love shown by the pardoned sinner.

**18:5 Strike me**: the Greek verb translated as strike means "to strike under the eye" and suggests the extreme situation to which the persistence of the widow might lead. It may, however, be used here in the much weaker sense of "to wear one out."

**18:15–19:27** Luke here includes much of the material about the journey to Jerusalem found in his Marcan source (Lk 10:1–52) and adds to it the story of Zacchaeus (Lk 19:1–10) from his own particular tradition and the parable of the gold coins (minas) (Lk 19:11–27) from Q, the source common to Luke and Matthew.

**18:15–17** The sayings on children furnish a contrast to the attitude of the Pharisee in the preceding episode (Lk 18:9–14) and that of the wealthy official in the following one (Lk 18:18–23) who think that they can lay claim to God's favor by their own merit. The attitude of the disciple should be marked by the receptivity and trustful dependence characteristic of the child.

*a:* Mt 24:17–18; Mk 13:15–16. *b:* 9:24; Mt 10:39; 16:25; Mk 8:35; Jn 12:25. *c:* Mt 24:40–41. *d:* Jb 39:30; Mt 24:28. *e:* Rom 12:12; Col 4:2; 1 Thes 5:17. *f:* 11:8. *g:* 16:5; Mt 23:25–28. *h:* Mt 23:23. *i:* Ps 51:3. *j:* 14:11; Mt 23:12. *k:* Mt 19:13–15; Mk 10:13–16. *l:* Mt 18:3. *m:* Mt 19:16–30; Mk 10:17–31. *n:* 10:25.

commandments, 'You shall not commit adultery; you shall not kill; you shall not steal; you shall not bear false witness; honor your father and your mother.' "[o] [21] And he replied, "All of these I have observed from my youth." [22]* [p] When Jesus heard this he said to him, "There is still one thing left for you: sell all that you have and distribute it to the poor, and you will have a treasure in heaven. Then come, follow me." [23] But when he heard this he became quite sad, for he was very rich.

***On Riches and Renunciation.*** [24] Jesus looked at him [now sad] and said, "How hard it is for those who have wealth to enter the kingdom of God! [25] For it is easier for a camel to pass through the eye of a needle than for a rich person to enter the kingdom of God." [26] Those who heard this said, "Then who can be saved?" [27] And he said, "What is impossible for human beings is possible for God."[q] [28] Then Peter said, "We have given up our possessions and followed you." [29] [r] He said to them, "Amen, I say to you, there is no one who has given up house or wife or brothers or parents or children for the sake of the kingdom of God [30] who will not receive [back] an overabundant return in this present age and eternal life in the age to come."

***The Third Prediction of the Passion.***[s] [31]* Then he took the Twelve aside and said to them, "Behold, we are going up to Jerusalem and everything written by the prophets about the Son of Man will be fulfilled.* [32] [t] He will be handed over to the Gentiles and he will be mocked and insulted and spat upon; [33] and after they have scourged him they will kill him, but on the third day he will rise." [34] But they understood nothing of this; the word remained hidden from them and they failed to comprehend what he said.[u]

***The Healing of the Blind Beggar.***[v] [35] Now as he approached Jericho a blind man was sitting by the roadside begging, [36] and hearing a crowd going by, he inquired what was happening. [37] They told him, "Jesus of Nazareth is passing by." [38] [w] He shouted, "Jesus, Son of David,* have pity on me!" [39] The people walking in front rebuked him, telling him to be silent, but he kept calling out all the more, "Son of David, have pity on me!" [40] Then Jesus stopped and ordered that he be brought to him; and when he came near, Jesus asked him, [41] "What do you want me to do for you?" He replied, "Lord, please let me see."[x] [42] Jesus told him, "Have sight; your faith has saved you."[y] [43] He immediately received his sight and followed him, giving glory to God. When they saw this, all the people gave praise to God.

## CHAPTER 19

See RG 312–14

***Zacchaeus the Tax Collector.*** * [1] He came to Jericho and intended to pass through the town. [2] Now a man there named Zacchaeus, who was a chief tax collector and also a wealthy man, [3] was seeking to see who Jesus was; but he could not see him because of the crowd, for he was short in stature. [4] So he ran ahead and climbed a sycamore tree in order to see Jesus, who was about to pass that way.

**18:22** Detachment from material possessions results in the total dependence on God demanded of one who would inherit eternal life. **Sell all that you have**: the original saying (cf. Mk 10:21) has characteristically been made more demanding by Luke's addition of "all."

**18:31–33** The details included in this third announcement of Jesus' suffering and death suggest that the literary formulation of the announcement has been directed by the knowledge of the historical passion and death of Jesus.

**18:31 Everything written by the prophets . . . will be fulfilled**: this is a Lucan addition to the words of Jesus found in the Marcan source (Mk 10:32–34). Luke understands the events of Jesus' last days in Jerusalem to be the fulfillment of Old Testament prophecy, but, as is usually the case in Luke-Acts, the author does not specify which Old Testament prophets he has in mind; cf. Lk 24:25, 27, 44; Acts 3:8; 13:27; 26:22–23.

**18:38 Son of David**: the blind beggar identifies Jesus with a title that is related to Jesus' role as Messiah (see note on Lk 2:11). Through this Son of David, salvation comes to the blind man. Note the connection between salvation and house of David mentioned earlier in Zechariah's canticle (Lk 1:69). See also note on Mt 9:27.

**19:1–10** The story of the tax collector Zacchaeus is unique to this gospel. While a rich man (Lk 19:2), Zacchaeus provides a contrast to the rich man of Lk 18:18–23 who cannot detach himself from his material possessions to become a follower of Jesus. Zacchaeus, according to Luke, exemplifies the proper attitude toward wealth: he promises to give half of his possessions to the poor (Lk 19:8) and consequently is the recipient of salvation (Lk 19:9–10).

*o:* Ex 20:12–16; Dt 5:16–20. *p:* 12:33; Sir 29:11; Mt 6:20. *q:* Mk 14:36. *r:* 14:26. *s:* 24:25–27, 44; Mt 20:17–19; Mk 10:32–34; Acts 3:18. *t:* 9:22, 44. *u:* Mk 9:32. *v:* Mt 20:29–34; Mk 10:46–52. *w:* 17:13; Mt 9:27; 15:22. *x:* Mk 10:36. *y:* 7:50; 17:19.

5 When he reached the place, Jesus looked up
and said to him, "Zacchaeus, come down
quickly, for today I must stay at your house."
6 And he came down quickly and received
him with joy. 7 When they all saw this, they
began to grumble, saying, "He has gone to
stay at the house of a sinner."[z] 8 But Zacchaeus stood there and said to the Lord, "Behold,
half of my possessions, Lord, I shall give to
the poor, and if I have extorted anything
from anyone I shall repay it four times
over."[a] 9* And Jesus said to him, "Today salvation[b] has come to this house because this
man too is a descendant of Abraham.
10* [c] For the Son of Man has come to seek
and to save what was lost."

*The Parable of the Ten Gold Coins.**
11 [d] While they were listening to him speak, he
proceeded to tell a parable because he was
near Jerusalem and they thought that the
kingdom of God would appear there immediately. 12 So he said, "A nobleman went off to a
distant country to obtain the kingship for himself and then to return.[e] 13 He called ten of his
servants and gave them ten gold coins* and
told them, 'Engage in trade with these until I
return.' 14 His fellow citizens, however, despised him and sent a delegation after him to
announce, 'We do not want this man to be our
king.' 15 But when he returned after obtaining
the kingship, he had the servants called, to
whom he had given the money, to learn what
they had gained by trading. 16 The first came
forward and said, 'Sir, your gold coin has
earned ten additional ones.' 17 He replied,
'Well done, good servant! You have been
faithful in this very small matter; take charge
of ten cities.'[f] 18 Then the second came and reported, 'Your gold coin, sir, has earned five
more.' 19 And to this servant too he said, 'You,
take charge of five cities.' 20 Then the other
servant came and said, 'Sir, here is your gold
coin; I kept it stored away in a handkerchief,
21 for I was afraid of you, because you are a
demanding person; you take up what you did
not lay down and you harvest what you did
not plant.' 22 He said to him, 'With your own
words I shall condemn you, you wicked servant. You knew I was a demanding person,
taking up what I did not lay down and harvesting what I did not plant; 23 why did you
not put my money in a bank? Then on my return I would have collected it with interest.'
24 And to those standing by he said, 'Take the
gold coin from him and give it to the servant
who has ten.' 25 But they said to him, 'Sir, he
has ten gold coins.' 26 'I tell you, to everyone
who has, more will be given, but from the one
who has not, even what he has will be taken
away.[g] 27 Now as for those enemies of mine
who did not want me as their king, bring them
here and slay them before me.' "

## VI. The Teaching Ministry in Jerusalem*

*The Entry into Jerusalem.*[h] 28 After he had
said this, he proceeded on his journey up to

**19:9 A descendant of Abraham**: literally, "a son of Abraham." The tax collector Zacchaeus, whose repentance is attested by his determination to amend his former ways, shows himself to be a true descendant of Abraham, the true heir to the promises of God in the Old Testament. Underlying Luke's depiction of Zacchaeus as a descendant of Abraham, the father of the Jews (Lk 1:73; 16:22–31), is his recognition of the central place occupied by Israel in the plan of salvation.

**19:10** This verse sums up for Luke his depiction of the role of Jesus as savior in this gospel.

**19:11–27** In this parable Luke has combined two originally distinct parables: (1) a parable about the conduct of faithful and productive servants (Lk 19:13, 15b–26) and (2) a parable about a rejected king (Lk 19:12, 14–15a, 27). The story about the conduct of servants occurs in another form in Mt 25:14–20. The story about the rejected king may have originated with a contemporary historical event. After the death of Herod the Great, his son Archelaus traveled to Rome to receive the title of king. A delegation of Jews appeared in Rome before Caesar Augustus to oppose the request of Archelaus. Although not given the title of king, Archelaus was made ruler over Judea and Samaria. As the story is used by Luke, however, it furnishes a correction to the expectation of the imminent end of the age and of the establishment of the kingdom in Jerusalem (Lk 19:11). Jesus is not on his way to Jerusalem to receive the kingly power; for that, he must go away and only after returning from the distant country (a reference to the parousia) will reward and judgment take place.

**19:13 Ten gold coins**: literally, "ten minas." A mina was a monetary unit that in ancient Greece was the equivalent of one hundred drachmas.

**19:28–21:38** With the royal entry of Jesus into Jerusalem, a new section of Luke's gospel begins, the ministry of Jesus in Jerusalem before his death and resurrection. Luke suggests that this was a lengthy ministry in Jerusalem (Lk 19:47; 20:1;

*z:* 5:30; 15:2. *a:* Ex 21:37; Nm 5:6–7; 2 Sm 12:6. *b:* 13:16; Mt 21:31. *c:* 15:4–10; Ez 34:16. *d:* Mt 25:14–30. *e:* Mk 13:34. *f:* 16:10. *g:* 8:18; Mt 13:12; Mk 4:25. *h:* Mt 21:1–11; Mk 11:1–11; Jn 12:12–19.

Jerusalem. 29 As he drew near to Bethphage
and Bethany at the place called the Mount of
Olives, he sent two of his disciples.[i] 30 He said,
"Go into the village opposite you, and as you
enter it you will find a colt tethered on which
no one has ever sat. Untie it and bring it here.[j]
31 And if anyone should ask you, 'Why are
you untying it?' you will answer, 'The Master
has need of it.' " 32 So those who had been
sent went off and found everything just as he
had told them.[k] 33 And as they were untying
the colt, its owners said to them, "Why are
you untying this colt?" 34 They answered,
"The Master has need of it." 35[l] So they
brought it to Jesus, threw their cloaks over the
colt, and helped Jesus to mount. 36 As he rode
along, the people were spreading their cloaks
on the road; 37 and now as he was approaching
the slope of the Mount of Olives, the whole
multitude of his disciples began to praise God
aloud with joy for all the mighty deeds they
had seen. 38 They proclaimed:

"Blessed is the king who comes
in the name of the Lord.*
Peace in heaven
and glory in the highest."[m]

39 Some of the Pharisees in the crowd said to
him, "Teacher, rebuke your disciples."* 40 He
said in reply, "I tell you, if they keep silent,
the stones will cry out!"

***The Lament for Jerusalem.**** 41[n] As he
drew near, he saw the city and wept over it,[o]
42 saying, "If this day you only knew what
makes for peace—but now it is hidden from
your eyes.[p] 43* For the days are coming upon
you when your enemies will raise a palisade
against you; they will encircle you and hem
you in on all sides.[q] 44 They will smash you
to the ground and your children within you,
and they will not leave one stone upon another within you because you did not recognize the time of your visitation."[r]

***The Cleansing of the Temple.*** 45[s] Then
Jesus entered the temple area* and proceeded
to drive out those who were selling things,[t]
46 saying to them, "It is written, 'My house
shall be a house of prayer, but you have made
it a den of thieves.' "[u] 47 And every day he
was teaching in the temple area.[v] The chief
priests, the scribes, and the leaders of the
people, meanwhile, were seeking to put him
to death,[w] 48 but they could find no way to accomplish their purpose because all the people were hanging on his words.

## CHAPTER 20*

See RG 314–15

***The Authority of Jesus Questioned.***[x]
1 One day as he was teaching the people in
the temple area and proclaiming the good
news, the chief priests and scribes, together
with the elders, approached him 2 and said to

21:37–38; 22:53) and it is characterized by Jesus' daily teaching in the temple (Lk 21:37–38). For the story of the entry of Jesus into Jerusalem, see also Mt 21:1–11; Mk 11:1–10; Jn 12:12–19 and the notes there.

**19:38 Blessed is the king who comes in the name of the Lord**: only in Luke is Jesus explicitly given the title **king** when he enters Jerusalem in triumph. Luke has inserted this title into the words of Ps 118:26 that heralded the arrival of the pilgrims coming to the holy city and to the temple. Jesus is thereby acclaimed as **king** (see Lk 1:32) and as the one **who comes** (see Mal 3:1; Lk 7:19). **Peace in heaven . . .**: the acclamation of the disciples of Jesus in Luke echoes the announcement of the angels at the birth of Jesus (Lk 2:14). The peace Jesus brings is associated with the salvation to be accomplished here in Jerusalem.

**19:39 Rebuke your disciples**: this command, found only in Luke, was given so that the Roman authorities would not interpret the acclamation of Jesus as king as an uprising against them; cf. Lk 23:2–3.

**19:41–44** The lament for Jerusalem is found only in Luke. By not accepting Jesus (the one who mediates peace), Jerusalem will not find peace but will become the victim of devastation.

**19:43–44** Luke may be describing the actual disaster that befell Jerusalem in A.D. 70 when it was destroyed by the Romans during the First Revolt.

**19:45–46** Immediately upon entering the holy city, Jesus in a display of his authority enters the temple (see Mal 3:1–3) and lays claim to it after cleansing it that it might become a proper place for his teaching ministry in Jerusalem (Lk 19:47; 20:1; 21:37; 22:53). See Mt 21:12–17; Mk 11:15–19; Jn 2:13–17 and the notes there.

**20:1–47** The Jerusalem religious leaders or their representatives, in an attempt to incriminate Jesus with the Romans and to discredit him with the people, pose a number of questions to him (about his authority, Lk 20:2; about payment of taxes, Lk 20:22; about the resurrection, Lk 20:28–33).

*i:* Zec 14:4. *j:* Nm 19:2; Dt 21:3; 1 Sm 6:7; Zec 9:9. *k:* 22:13. *l:* 2 Kgs 9:13. *m:* 2:14; Ps 118:26. *n:* 13:34–35. *o:* 2 Kgs 8:11–12; Jer 14:17; 15:5. *p:* 8:10; Is 6:9–10; Mt 13:14; Mk 4:12; Acts 28:26–27; Rom 11:8, 10. *q:* Is 29:3. *r:* 1:68; 21:6; Ps 137:9; Mt 24:2; Mk 13:2. *s:* Mt 21:12–13; Mk 11:15–17; Jn 2:13–17. *t:* 3:1 / Hos 9:15. *u:* Is 56:7; Jer 7:11. *v:* 20:19; 22:2; Mt 21:46; Mk 11:18; 12:12; 14:1–2; Jn 5:18; 7:30. *w:* 21:37; 22:53; Jn 18:20. *x:* Mt 21:23–27; Mk 11:27–33. *y:* Acts 4:7.

him, "Tell us, by what authority are you doing these things? Or who is the one who
gave you this authority?"[y] 3He said to them
in reply, "I shall ask you a question. Tell me,
4was John's baptism of heavenly or of human origin?"[z] 5They discussed this among
themselves, and said, "If we say, 'Of heavenly origin,' he will say, 'Why did you not
believe him?'[a] 6But if we say, 'Of human
origin,' then all the people will stone us, for
they are convinced that John was a prophet."
7So they answered that they did not know
from where it came. 8Then Jesus said to
them, "Neither shall I tell you by what authority I do these things."

*The Parable of the Tenant Farmers.**
9b Then he proceeded to tell the people this
parable. "[A] man planted a vineyard, leased
it to tenant farmers, and then went on a journey for a long time.[c] 10At harvest time he
sent a servant[d] to the tenant farmers to receive some of the produce of the vineyard.
But they beat the servant and sent him away
empty-handed. 11So he proceeded to send
another servant, but him also they beat and
insulted and sent away empty-handed.
12Then he proceeded to send a third, but this
one too they wounded and threw out. 13The
owner of the vineyard said, 'What shall I do?
I shall send my beloved son; maybe they
will respect him.'[e] 14But when the tenant
farmers saw him they said to one another,
'This is the heir. Let us kill him that the inheritance may become ours.' 15So they
threw him out of the vineyard and killed
him.* What will the owner of the vineyard
do to them? 16He will come and put those
tenant farmers to death and turn over the
vineyard to others." When the people heard
this, they exclaimed, "Let it not be so!"
17But he looked at them and asked, "What
then does this scripture passage mean:

'The stone which the builders rejected
has become the cornerstone'?[f]

18Everyone who falls on that stone will be
dashed to pieces; and it will crush anyone on
whom it falls." 19The scribes and chief
priests sought to lay their hands on him at
that very hour, but they feared the people,
for they knew that he had addressed this parable to them.[g]

*Paying Taxes to the Emperor.*[h] 20* They
watched him closely and sent agents pretending to be righteous who were to trap him
in speech,[i] in order to hand him over to the
authority and power of the governor. 21They
posed this question to him, "Teacher, we
know that what you say and teach is correct,
and you show no partiality, but teach the
way of God in accordance with the truth.[j]
22Is it lawful for us to pay tribute to Caesar
or not?"* 23Recognizing their craftiness he
said to them, 24"Show me a denarius;* whose
image and name does it bear?" They replied,
"Caesar's." 25So he said to them, "Then repay to Caesar what belongs to Caesar and to
God what belongs to God."[k] 26They were
unable to trap him by something he might
say before the people, and so amazed were
they at his reply that they fell silent.

*The Question About the Resurrection.*[l]
27Some Sadducees,* those who deny that
there is a resurrection, came forward and put

**20:9–19** This parable about an absentee landlord and a tenant farmers' revolt reflects the social and economic conditions of rural Palestine in the first century. The synoptic gospel writers use the parable to describe how the rejection of the landlord's son becomes the occasion for the vineyard to be taken away from those to whom it was entrusted (the religious leadership of Judaism that rejects the teaching and preaching of Jesus; Lk 20:19).

**20:15 They threw him out of the vineyard and killed him**: cf. Mk 12:8. Luke has altered his Marcan source and reports that the murder of the son takes place outside the vineyard to reflect the tradition of Jesus' death outside the walls of the city of Jerusalem (see Heb 13:12).

**20:20 The governor**: i.e., Pontius Pilate, the Roman administrator responsible for the collection of taxes and maintenance of order in Palestine.

**20:22** Through their question the agents of the Jerusalem religious leadership hope to force Jesus to take sides on one of the sensitive political issues of first-century Palestine. The issue of nonpayment of taxes to Rome becomes one of the focal points of the First Jewish Revolt (A.D. 66–70) that resulted in the Roman destruction of Jerusalem and the temple. See also note on Mt 22:15–22.

**20:24 Denarius**: a Roman silver coin (see note on Lk 7:41).

**20:27 Sadducees**: see note on Mt 3:7.

*z:* 3:3, 16. *a:* Mt 21:32. *b:* Mt 21:33–46; Mk 12:1–12. *c:* Is 5:1–7. *d:* 2 Chr 36:15–16. *e:* 3:22. *f:* Ps 118:22; Is 28:16. *g:* 19:47–48; 22:2; Mt 21:46; Mk 11:18; 12:12; 14:1–2; Jn 5:18; 7:30. *h:* Mt 22:15–22; Mk 12:13–17. *i:* 11:54. *j:* Jn 3:2. *k:* Rom 13:6–7. *l:* Mt 22:23–33; Mk 12:18–27.

this question to him,[m] 28* saying, "Teacher,
Moses wrote for us, 'If someone's brother
dies leaving a wife but no child, his brother
must take the wife and raise up descendants
for his brother.'[n] 29Now there were seven
brothers; the first married a woman but died
childless. 30Then the second 31and the third
married her, and likewise all the seven died
childless. 32Finally the woman also died.
33Now at the resurrection whose wife will that
woman be? For all seven had been married to
her." 34Jesus said to them, "The children of
this age marry and are given in marriage; 35but
those who are deemed worthy to attain to the
coming age and to the resurrection of the dead
neither marry nor are given in marriage.
36They can no longer die, for they are like angels; and they are the children of God because
they are the ones who will rise.* 37That the
dead will rise even Moses made known in the
passage about the bush, when he called 'Lord'
the God of Abraham, the God of Isaac, and the
God of Jacob;[o] 38and he is not God of the
dead, but of the living, for to him all are
alive."[p] 39Some of the scribes said in reply,
"Teacher, you have answered well." 40And
they no longer dared to ask him anything.[q]

***The Question About David's Son.****

41[r] Then he said to them, "How do they claim
that the Messiah is the Son of David? 42For
David himself in the Book of Psalms says:[s]

'The Lord said to my lord,
"Sit at my right hand
43 till I make your enemies your
footstool."'

44Now if David calls him 'lord,' how can he
be his son?"

***Denunciation of the Scribes.***[t] 45Then, within
the hearing of all the people, he said to [his]
disciples, 46"Be on guard against the scribes,
who like to go around in long robes and love
greetings in marketplaces, seats of honor in
synagogues, and places of honor at banquets.[u]
47They devour the houses of widows and, as a
pretext, recite lengthy prayers. They will receive a very severe condemnation."

## CHAPTER 21

See RG 314-15

***The Poor Widow's Contribution.****

1[v] When he looked up he saw some wealthy
people putting their offerings into the treasury 2and he noticed a poor widow putting in
two small coins. 3He said, "I tell you truly,
this poor widow put in more than all the rest;
4for those others have all made offerings
from their surplus wealth, but she, from her
poverty, has offered her whole livelihood."

***The Destruction of the Temple Foretold.***[w]

5* While some people were speaking about
how the temple was adorned with costly
stones and votive offerings, he said, 6"All

**20:28–33** The Sadducees' question, based on the law of levirate marriage recorded in Dt 25:5–10, ridicules the idea of the resurrection. Jesus rejects their naive understanding of the resurrection (Lk 20:35–36) and then argues on behalf of the resurrection of the dead on the basis of the written law (Lk 20:37–38) that the Sadducees accept. See also notes on Mt 22:23–33.

**20:36 Because they are the ones who will rise**: literally, "being sons of the resurrection."

**20:41–44** After successfully answering the three questions of his opponents, Jesus now asks them a question. Their inability to respond implies that they have forfeited their position and authority as the religious leaders of the people because they do not understand the scriptures. This series of controversies between the religious leadership of Jerusalem and Jesus reveals Jesus as the authoritative teacher whose words are to be listened to (see Lk 9:35). See also notes on Mt 22:41–46.

**21:1–4** The widow is another example of the poor ones in this gospel whose detachment from material possessions and dependence on God leads to their blessedness (Lk 6:20). Her simple offering provides a striking contrast to the pride and pretentiousness of the scribes denounced in the preceding section (Lk 20:45–47). The story is taken from Mk 12:41–44.

**21:5–36** Jesus' eschatological discourse in Luke is inspired by Mk 13 but Luke has made some significant alterations to the words of Jesus found there. Luke maintains, though in a modified form, the belief in the early expectation of the end of the age (see Lk 21:27, 28, 31, 32, 36), but, by focusing attention throughout the gospel on the importance of the day-to-day following of Jesus and by reinterpreting the meaning of some of the signs of the end from Mk 13 he has come to terms with what seemed to the early Christian community to be a delay of the parousia. Mark, for example, described the desecration of the Jerusalem temple by the Romans (Mk 13:14) as the apocalyptic symbol (see Dn 9:27; 12:11) accompanying the end of the age and the coming of the Son of Man. Luke (Lk 21:20–24), however, removes the apocalyptic setting and separates the historical destruction of Jerusalem from the signs of the coming of the Son of Man by a period that he refers to as "the times of the Gentiles" (Lk 21:24). See also notes on Mt 24:1–36 and Mk 13:1–37.

*m:* Acts 23:8. *n:* Gn 38:8; Dt 25:5. *o:* Ex 3:2, 6, 15–16. *p:* Rom 14:8–9. *q:* Mt 22:46; Mk 12:34. *r:* Mt 22:41–45; Mk 12:35–37. *s:* Ps 110:1. *t:* 11:37–54; Mt 23:1–36; Mk 12:38–40. *u:* 14:7–11. *v:* Mk 12:41–44. *w:* Mt 24:1–2; Mk 13:1–2. *x:* 19:44.

that you see here—the days will come when there will not be left a stone upon another stone that will not be thrown down."[x]

*The Sign of the End.* 7[y] Then they asked him, "Teacher, when will this happen? And what sign will there be when all these things are about to happen?" 8 He answered, "See that you not be deceived, for many will come in my name, saying, 'I am he,' and 'The time has come.'* Do not follow them![z] 9 When you hear of wars and insurrections, do not be terrified; for such things must happen first, but it will not immediately be the end." 10 Then he said to them, "Nation will rise against nation, and kingdom against kingdom.[a] 11 There will be powerful earthquakes, famines, and plagues from place to place; and awesome sights and mighty signs will come from the sky.

*The Coming Persecution.* 12[b] "Before all this happens,* however, they will seize and persecute you, they will hand you over to the synagogues and to prisons, and they will have you led before kings and governors because of my name.[c] 13 It will lead to your giving testimony. 14 Remember, you are not to prepare your defense beforehand, 15[d] for I myself shall give you a wisdom in speaking* that all your adversaries will be powerless to resist or refute. 16[e] You will even be handed over by parents, brothers, relatives, and friends, and they will put some of you to death.[f] 17 You will be hated by all because of my name, 18 but not a hair on your head will be destroyed.[g] 19 By your perseverance you will secure your lives.[h]

*The Great Tribulation.** 20[i] "When you see Jerusalem surrounded by armies, know that its desolation is at hand.[j] 21 Then those in Judea must flee to the mountains. Let those within the city escape from it, and let those in the countryside not enter the city,[k] 22 for these days are the time of punishment when all the scriptures are fulfilled. 23 Woe to pregnant women and nursing mothers in those days, for a terrible calamity will come upon the earth and a wrathful judgment upon this people.[l] 24 They will fall by the edge of the sword and be taken as captives to all the Gentiles; and Jerusalem will be trampled underfoot by the Gentiles until the times of the Gentiles* are fulfilled.[m]

*The Coming of the Son of Man.*[n] 25 "There will be signs in the sun, the moon, and the stars, and on earth nations will be in dismay, perplexed by the roaring of the sea and the waves.[o] 26 People will die of fright in anticipation of what is coming upon the world, for the powers of the heavens* will be shaken.[p] 27 And then they will see the Son of Man coming in a cloud with power and great glory.[q] 28 But when these signs begin to happen, stand erect and raise your heads because your redemption is at hand."[r]

*The Lesson of the Fig Tree.*[s] 29 He taught them a lesson. "Consider the fig tree and all the other trees. 30 When their buds burst open, you see for yourselves and know that summer is now near; 31 in the same way, when you see these things happening, know that the kingdom of God is near. 32 Amen, I say to you, this generation will not pass away until all these things have taken place.[t] 33 Heaven and earth will pass away, but my words will not pass away.[u]

**21:8 The time has come**: in Luke, the proclamation of the imminent end of the age has itself become a false teaching.

**21:12 Before all this happens . . .**: to Luke and his community, some of the signs of the end just described (Lk 21:10–11) still lie in the future. Now in dealing with the persecution of the disciples (Lk 21:12–19) and the destruction of Jerusalem (Lk 21:20–24) Luke is pointing to eschatological signs that have already been fulfilled.

**21:15 A wisdom in speaking**: literally, "a mouth and wisdom."

**21:20–24** The actual destruction of Jerusalem by Rome in A.D. 70 upon which Luke and his community look back provides the assurance that, just as Jesus' prediction of Jerusalem's destruction was fulfilled, so too will be his announcement of their final redemption (Lk 21:27–28).

**21:24 The times of the Gentiles**: a period of indeterminate length separating the destruction of Jerusalem from the cosmic signs accompanying the coming of the Son of Man.

**21:26 The powers of the heavens**: the heavenly bodies mentioned in Lk 21:25 and thought of as cosmic armies.

*y:* Mt 24:3–14; Mk 13:3–13. *z:* 17:23; Mk 13:5, 6, 21; 1 Jn 2:18. *a:* 2 Chr 15:6; Is 19:2. *b:* 12:11–12; Mt 10:17–20; Mk 13:9–11. *c:* Jn 16:2; Acts 25:24. *d:* Acts 6:10. *e:* Mt 10:21–22. *f:* 12:52–53. *g:* 12:7; 1 Sm 14:45; Mt 10:30; Acts 27:34. *h:* 8:15. *i:* Mt 24:15–21; Mk 13:14–19. *j:* 19:41–44. *k:* 17:31. *l:* 1 Cor 7:26. *m:* Tb 14:5; Ps 79:1; Is 63:18; Jer 21:7; Rom 11:25; Rev 11:2. *n:* Mt 24:29–31; Mk 13:24–27. *o:* Wis 5:22; Is 13:10; Ez 32:7; Jl 2:10; 3:3–4; 4:15; Rev 6:12–14. *p:* Hg 2:6, 21. *q:* Dn 7:13–14; Mt 26:64; Rev 1:7. *r:* 2:38. *s:* Mt 24:32–35; Mk 13:28–31. *t:* 9:27; Mt 16:28. *u:* 16:17.

***Exhortation to Be Vigilant.*** 34 “Beware that your hearts do not become drowsy from carousing and drunkenness and the anxieties of daily life, and that day catch you by surprise[v] 35 like a trap. For that day will assault everyone who lives on the face of the earth. 36 Be vigilant at all times and pray that you have the strength to escape the tribulations that are imminent and to stand before the Son of Man.”[w]

***Ministry in Jerusalem.*** 37 During the day, Jesus was teaching in the temple area, but at night he would leave and stay at the place called the Mount of Olives.[x] 38 And all the people would get up early each morning to listen to him in the temple area.

## VII. The Passion Narrative*

### CHAPTER 22

See RG 315–16

***The Conspiracy Against Jesus.*** 1[y] Now the feast of Unleavened Bread, called the Passover,* was drawing near, 2[z] and the chief priests and the scribes were seeking a way to put him to death, for they were afraid of the people. 3[a] Then Satan entered into Judas,* the one surnamed Iscariot, who was counted among the Twelve,[b] 4 and he went to the chief priests and temple guards to discuss a plan for handing him over to them. 5 They were pleased and agreed to pay him money. 6 He accepted their offer and sought a favorable opportunity to hand him over to them in the absence of a crowd.

***Preparations for the Passover.***[c] 7 When the day of the feast of Unleavened Bread arrived, the day for sacrificing the Passover lamb,[d] 8 he sent out Peter and John, instructing them, “Go and make preparations for us to eat the Passover.” 9 They asked him, “Where do you want us to make the preparations?” 10 And he answered them, “When you go into the city, a man will meet you carrying a jar of water.* Follow him into the house that he enters 11 and say to the master of the house, ‘The teacher says to you, “Where is the guest room where I may eat the Passover with my disciples?” ’ 12 He will show you a large upper room that is furnished. Make the preparations there.” 13 Then they went off and found everything exactly as he had told them, and there they prepared the Passover.[e]

***The Last Supper.***[f] 14 When the hour came, he took his place at table with the apostles. 15 He said to them, “I have eagerly desired to eat this Passover* with you before I suffer, 16 for, I tell you, I shall not eat it [again] until there is fulfillment in the kingdom of God.”[g] 17 Then he took a cup,* gave thanks, and said, “Take this and share it among yourselves; 18 for I tell you [that] from this time on I shall not drink of the fruit of the vine until the kingdom of God comes.” 19* [h] Then he took the

**22:1–23:56a** The passion narrative. Luke is still dependent upon Mark for the composition of the passion narrative but has incorporated much of his own special tradition into the narrative. Among the distinctive sections in Luke are: (1) the tradition of the institution of the Eucharist (Lk 22:15–20); (2) Jesus' farewell discourse (Lk 22:21–38); (3) the mistreatment and interrogation of Jesus (Lk 22:63–71); (4) Jesus before Herod and his second appearance before Pilate (Lk 23:6–16); (5) words addressed to the women followers on the way to the crucifixion (Lk 23:27–32); (6) words to the penitent thief (Lk 23:39–41); (7) the death of Jesus (Lk 23:46, 47b–49). Luke stresses the innocence of Jesus (Lk 23:4, 14–15, 22) who is the victim of the powers of evil (Lk 22:3, 31, 53) and who goes to his death in fulfillment of his Father's will (Lk 22:42, 46). Throughout the narrative Luke emphasizes the mercy, compassion, and healing power of Jesus (Lk 22:51; 23:43) who does not go to death lonely and deserted, but is accompanied by others who follow him on the way of the cross (Lk 23:26–31, 49).

**22:1 Feast of Unleavened Bread, called the Passover**: see note on Mk 14:1.

**22:3 Satan entered into Judas**: see note on Lk 4:13.

**22:10 A man will meet you carrying a jar of water**: see note on Mk 14:13.

**22:15 This Passover**: Luke clearly identifies this last supper of Jesus with the apostles as a Passover meal that commemorated the deliverance of the Israelites from slavery in Egypt. Jesus reinterprets the significance of the Passover by setting it in the context of the kingdom of God (Lk 22:16). The “deliverance” associated with the Passover finds its new meaning in the blood that will be shed (Lk 22:20).

**22:17** Because of a textual problem in Lk 22:19–20 some commentators interpret this cup as the eucharistic cup.

**22:19c–20 Which will be given . . . do this in memory of me**: these words are omitted in some important Western text

*v:* 12:45–46; Mt 24:48–50; 1 Thes 5:3, 6–7. *w:* Mk 13:33. *x:* 19:47; 22:39. *y:* Mt 26:1–5; Mk 14:1–2; Jn 11:47–53. *z:* 19:47–48; 20:19; Mt 21:46; Mk 12:12; Jn 5:18; 7:30. *a:* Mt 26:14–16; Mk 14:10–11; Jn 13:2, 27. *b:* Acts 1:17. *c:* Mt 26:17–19; Mk 14:12–16. *d:* Ex 12:6, 14–20. *e:* 19:32. *f:* Mt 26:20, 26–30; Mk 14:17, 22–26; 1 Cor 11:23–25. *g:* 13:29. *h:* 24:30; Acts 27:35.

bread, said the blessing, broke it, and gave it
to them, saying, "This is my body, which will
be given for you; do this in memory of me."
20 And likewise the cup after they had eaten,
saying, "This cup is the new covenant in my
blood, which will be shed for you.[i]
*The Betrayal Foretold.*[j] 21 "And yet behold,
the hand of the one who is to betray me is
with me on the table; 22 for the Son of Man indeed goes as it has been determined; but woe
to that man by whom he is betrayed." 23 And
they began to debate among themselves who
among them would do such a deed.
*The Role of the Disciples.* 24* Then an argument broke out among them[k] about which
of them should be regarded as the greatest.
25* [l] He said to them, "The kings of the Gentiles lord it over them and those in authority
over them are addressed as 'Benefactors';
26 but among you it shall not be so. Rather, let
the greatest among you be as the youngest,
and the leader as the servant.[m] 27 For who is
greater: the one seated at table or the one
who serves? Is it not the one seated at table?
I am among you as the one who serves. 28 It
is you who have stood by me in my trials;
29 and I confer a kingdom on you, just as my
Father has conferred one on me,[n] 30 that you
may eat and drink at my table in my kingdom; and you will sit on thrones judging the
twelve tribes of Israel.[o]
*Peter's Denial Foretold.*[p] 31* "Simon, Simon, behold Satan has demanded to sift all
of you* like wheat,[q] 32 but I have prayed that
your own faith may not fail; and once you
have turned back, you must strengthen your
brothers." 33 He said to him, "Lord, I am prepared to go to prison and to die with you."[r]
34 But he replied, "I tell you, Peter, before the
cock crows this day, you will deny three
times that you know me."[s]
*Instructions for the Time of Crisis.* 35[t] He
said to them, "When I sent you forth without
a money bag or a sack or sandals, were you
in need of anything?" "No, nothing," they
replied. 36[u] He said to them,* "But now one
who has a money bag should take it, and
likewise a sack, and one who does not have
a sword should sell his cloak and buy one.
37 For I tell you that this scripture must be
fulfilled in me, namely, 'He was counted
among the wicked'; and indeed what is written about me is coming to fulfillment."[v]
38 Then they said, "Lord, look, there are two
swords here." But he replied, "It is
enough!"*
*The Agony in the Garden.*[w] 39 Then going
out he went, as was his custom, to the Mount
of Olives, and the disciples followed him.
40 When he arrived at the place he said to
them, "Pray that you may not undergo the
test."[x] 41 After withdrawing about a stone's
throw from them and kneeling, he prayed,[y]
42 saying, "Father, if you are willing, take
this cup away from me; still, not my will but
yours be done."[z] *[43 And to strengthen him

manuscripts and a few Syriac manuscripts. Other ancient text types, including the oldest papyrus manuscript of Luke dating from the late second or early third century, contain the longer reading presented here. The Lucan account of the words of institution of the Eucharist bears a close resemblance to the words of institution in the Pauline tradition (see 1 Cor 11:23–26). See also notes on Mt 26:26–29; 26:27–28; and Mk 14:22–24.

**22:24–38** The Gospel of Luke presents a brief farewell discourse of Jesus; compare the lengthy farewell discourses and prayer in Jn 13–17.

**22:25 'Benefactors'**: this word occurs as a title of rulers in the Hellenistic world.

**22:31–32** Jesus' prayer for Simon's faith and the commission to strengthen his brothers anticipates the post-resurrectional prominence of Peter in the first half of Acts, where he appears as the spokesman for the Christian community and the one who begins the mission to the Gentiles (Acts 10–11).

**22:31 All of you:** literally, "you." The translation reflects the meaning of the Greek text that uses a second person plural pronoun here.

**22:36** In contrast to the ministry of the Twelve and of the seventy-two during the period of Jesus (Lk 9:3; 10:4), in the future period of the church the missionaries must be prepared for the opposition they will face in a world hostile to their preaching.

**22:38 It is enough!**: the farewell discourse ends abruptly with these words of Jesus spoken to the disciples when they take literally what was intended as figurative language about being prepared to face the world's hostility.

**22:43–44** These verses, though very ancient, were probably not part of the original text of Luke. They are absent from the oldest papyrus manuscripts of Luke and from manuscripts of wide geographical distribution.

*i:* Ex 24:8; Jer 31:31; 32:40; Zec 9:11. *j:* Ps 41:10; Mt 26:21–25; Mk 14:18–21; Jn 13:21–30. *k:* 9:46; Mt 18:1; Mk 9:34. *l:* Mt 20:25–27; Mk 10:42–44; Jn 13:3–16. *m:* Mt 23:11; Mk 9:35. *n:* 12:32. *o:* Mt 19:28. *p:* Mt 26:33–35; Mk 14:29–31; Jn 13:37–38. *q:* Jb 1:6–12; Am 9:9. *r:* 22:54. *s:* 22:54–62. *t:* 9:3; 10:4; Mt 10:9–10; Mk 6:7–9. *u:* 22:49. *v:* Is 53:12. *w:* Mt 26:30, 36–46; Mk 14:26, 32–42; Jn 18:1–2. *x:* 22:46. *y:* Heb 5:7–8. *z:* Mt 6:10.

an angel from heaven appeared to him. 44 He was in such agony and he prayed so fervently that his sweat became like drops of blood falling on the ground.] 45 When he rose from prayer and returned to his disciples, he found them sleeping from grief. 46 He said to them, "Why are you sleeping? Get up and pray that you may not undergo the test."[a]

***The Betrayal and Arrest of Jesus.***[b] 47 While he was still speaking, a crowd approached and in front was one of the Twelve, a man named Judas. He went up to Jesus to kiss him. 48 Jesus said to him, "Judas, are you betraying the Son of Man with a kiss?" 49 His disciples realized what was about to happen, and they asked, "Lord, shall we strike with a sword?"[c] 50 And one of them struck the high priest's servant and cut off his right ear.[d] 51* But Jesus said in reply, "Stop, no more of this!" Then he touched the servant's ear and healed him. 52 And Jesus said to the chief priests and temple guards and elders who had come for him, "Have you come out as against a robber, with swords and clubs?[e] 53 Day after day I was with you in the temple area, and you did not seize me; but this is your hour, the time for the power of darkness."[f]

***Peter's Denial of Jesus.*** 54[g] After arresting him they led him away and took him into the house of the high priest; Peter was following at a distance.[h] 55 They lit a fire in the middle of the courtyard and sat around it, and Peter sat down with them. 56 When a maid saw him seated in the light, she looked intently at him and said, "This man too was with him." 57 But he denied it saying, "Woman, I do not know him." 58 A short while later someone else saw him and said, "You too are one of them"; but Peter answered, "My friend, I am not." 59 About an hour later, still another insisted, "Assuredly, this man too was with him, for he also is a Galilean." 60 But Peter said, "My friend, I do not know what you are talking about." Just as he was saying this, the cock crowed, 61 and the Lord turned and looked at Peter;* and Peter remembered the word of the Lord, how he had said to him, "Before the cock crows today, you will deny me three times."[i] 62 He went out and began to weep bitterly. 63[j] The men who held Jesus in custody were ridiculing and beating him. 64 They blindfolded him and questioned him, saying, "Prophesy! Who is it that struck you?" 65 And they reviled him in saying many other things against him.

***Jesus Before the Sanhedrin.**** 66[k] When day came the council of elders of the people met, both chief priests and scribes,[l] and they brought him before their Sanhedrin.* 67 They said, "If you are the Messiah, tell us," but he replied to them, "If I tell you, you will not believe,[m] 68 and if I question, you will not respond. 69 But from this time on the Son of Man will be seated at the right hand of the power of God."[n] 70 They all asked, "Are you then the Son of God?" He replied to them, "You say that I am." 71 Then they said, "What further need have we for testimony? We have heard it from his own mouth."

## CHAPTER 23

See RG 316

***Jesus Before Pilate.***[o] 1* Then the whole assembly of them arose and brought

**22:51 And healed him**: only Luke recounts this healing of the injured servant.

**22:61** Only Luke recounts that **the Lord turned and looked at Peter**. This look of Jesus leads to Peter's weeping bitterly over his denial (Lk 22:62).

**22:66–71** Luke recounts one daytime trial of Jesus (Lk 22:66–71) and hints at some type of preliminary nighttime investigation (Lk 22:54–65). Mark (and Matthew who follows Mark) has transferred incidents of this day into the nighttime interrogation with the result that there appear to be two Sanhedrin trials of Jesus in Mark (and Matthew); see note on Mk 14:53.

**22:66 Sanhedrin**: the word is a Hebraized form of a Greek word meaning a "council," and refers to the elders, chief priests, and scribes who met under the high priest's leadership to decide religious and legal questions that did not pertain to Rome's interests. Jewish sources are not clear on the competence of the Sanhedrin to sentence and to execute during this period.

**23:1–5, 13–25** Twice Jesus is brought before Pilate in Luke's account, and each time Pilate explicitly declares Jesus innocent of any wrongdoing (Lk 23:4, 14, 22). This stress on the innocence of Jesus before the Roman authorities is also characteristic of John's gospel (Jn 18:38; 19:4, 6). Luke pre-

*a:* 22:40. *b:* Mt 26:47–56; Mk 14:43–50; Jn 18:3–4. *c:* 22:36. *d:* Jn 18:26. *e:* 22:37. *f:* 19:47; 21:37; Jn 7:30; 8:20; Col 1:13. *g:* Mt 26:57–58, 69–75; Mk 14:53–54, 66–72; Jn 18:12–18, 25–27. *h:* 22:33. *i:* 22:34. *j:* Mt 26:67–68; Mk 14:65. *k:* Mt 26:59–66; Mk 14:55–64. *l:* Mt 27:1; Mk 15:1. *m:* Jn 3:12; 8:45; 10:24. *n:* Ps 110:1; Dn 7:13–14; Acts 7:56. *o:* Mt 27:1–2, 11–14; Mk 15:1–5; Jn 18:28–38.

him before Pilate. [2]They brought charges against him, saying, "We found this man misleading our people; he opposes the payment of taxes to Caesar and maintains that he is the Messiah, a king."[p] [3]Pilate asked him, "Are you the king of the Jews?" He said to him in reply, "You say so."[q] [4]Pilate then addressed the chief priests and the crowds, "I find this man not guilty." [5]But they were adamant and said, "He is inciting the people with his teaching throughout all Judea, from Galilee where he began even to here."[r]

***Jesus Before Herod.*** [6]* On hearing this Pilate asked if the man was a Galilean; [7]and upon learning that he was under Herod's jurisdiction, he sent him to Herod who was in Jerusalem at that time.[s] [8]Herod was very glad to see Jesus; he had been wanting to see him for a long time, for he had heard about him and had been hoping to see him perform some sign.[t] [9]He questioned him at length, but he gave him no answer.[u] [10]The chief priests and scribes, meanwhile, stood by accusing him harshly.[v] [11][Even] Herod and his soldiers treated him contemptuously and mocked him, and after clothing him in resplendent garb, he sent him back to Pilate.[w] [12]Herod and Pilate became friends that very day, even though they had been enemies formerly. [13]Pilate then summoned the chief priests, the rulers, and the people [14]and said to them, "You brought this man to me and accused him of inciting the people to revolt. I have conducted my investigation in your presence and have not found this man guilty of the charges you have brought against him,[x] [15]nor did Herod, for he sent him back to us. So no capital crime has been committed by him. [16y] Therefore I shall have him flogged and then release him." [17]*

***The Sentence of Death.***[z] [18]But all together they shouted out, "Away with this man! Release Barabbas to us." [19](Now Barabbas had been imprisoned for a rebellion that had taken place in the city and for murder.) [20]Again Pilate addressed them, still wishing to release Jesus, [21]but they continued their shouting, "Crucify him! Crucify him!" [22]Pilate addressed them a third time, "What evil has this man done? I found him guilty of no capital crime. Therefore I shall have him flogged and then release him." [23]With loud shouts, however, they persisted in calling for his crucifixion, and their voices prevailed. [24]The verdict of Pilate was that their demand should be granted. [25]So he released the man who had been imprisoned for rebellion and murder, for whom they asked, and he handed Jesus over to them to deal with as they wished.

***The Way of the Cross.**** [26a] As they led him away they took hold of a certain Simon, a Cyrenian, who was coming in from the country; and after laying the cross on him, they made him carry it behind Jesus. [27]A large crowd of people followed Jesus, including many women who mourned and lamented him. [28b] Jesus turned to them and said, "Daughters of Jerusalem, do not weep for me; weep instead for yourselves and for your children, [29]for indeed, the days are coming when people will say, 'Blessed are the barren, the wombs that never bore and the breasts that never nursed.' [30]At that time people will say to the mountains, 'Fall upon us!' and to the hills, 'Cover us!'[c] [31]for if these things are done when the wood is green what

sents the Jerusalem Jewish leaders as the ones who force the hand of the Roman authorities (Lk 23:1–2, 5, 10, 13, 18, 21, 23–25).

**23:6–12** The appearance of Jesus before Herod is found only in this gospel. Herod has been an important figure in Luke (Lk 9:7–9; 13:31–33) and has been presented as someone who has been curious about Jesus for a long time. His curiosity goes unrewarded. It is faith in Jesus, not curiosity, that is rewarded (Lk 7:50; 8:48, 50; 17:19).

**23:17** This verse, "He was obliged to release one prisoner for them at the festival," is not part of the original text of Luke. It is an explanatory gloss from Mk 15:6 (also Mt 27:15) and is not found in many early and important Greek manuscripts. On its historical background, see notes on Mt 27:15–26.

**23:26–32** An important Lucan theme throughout the gospel has been the need for the Christian disciple to follow in the footsteps of Jesus. Here this theme comes to the fore with the story of Simon of Cyrene who takes up the cross and follows Jesus (see Lk 9:23; 14:27) and with the large crowd who likewise follow Jesus on the way of the cross. See also note on Mk 15:21.

*p:* 20:22–25; Acts 17:7; 24:5. *q:* 22:70; 1 Tm 6:13. *r:* 23:14, 22, 41; Mt 27:24; Jn 19:4, 6; Acts 13:28. *s:* 3:1; 9:7. *t:* 9:9; Acts 4:27–28. *u:* Mk 15:5. *v:* Mt 27:12; Mk 15:3. *w:* Mt 27:28–30; Mk 15:17–19; Jn 19:2–3. *x:* 23:4, 22, 41. *y:* 23:22; Jn 19:12–14. *z:* Mt 27:20–26; Mk 15:6–7, 11–15; Jn 18:38b–40; 19:14–16; Acts 3:13–14. *a:* Mt 27:32, 38; Mk 15:21, 27; Jn 19:17. *b:* 19:41–44; 21:23–24. *c:* Hos 10:8; Rev 6:16.

will happen when it is dry?" 32 Now two others, both criminals, were led away with him to be executed.

*The Crucifixion.*[d] 33 When they came to the place called the Skull, they crucified him and the criminals there, one on his right, the other on his left.[e] 34 [Then Jesus said, "Father, forgive them, they know not what they do."]* They divided his garments by casting lots.[f] 35 The people stood by and watched; the rulers, meanwhile, sneered at him and said,[g] "He saved others, let him save himself if he is the chosen one, the Messiah of God."[h] 36 Even the soldiers jeered at him. As they approached to offer him wine[i] 37 they called out, "If you are King of the Jews, save yourself." 38 Above him there was an inscription that read, "This is the King of the Jews."

39* Now one of the criminals hanging there reviled Jesus, saying, "Are you not the Messiah? Save yourself and us." 40 The other, however, rebuking him, said in reply, "Have you no fear of God, for you are subject to the same condemnation? 41 And indeed, we have been condemned justly, for the sentence we received corresponds to our crimes, but this man has done nothing criminal."[j] 42 Then he said, "Jesus, remember me when you come into your kingdom."[k] 43 He replied to him, "Amen, I say to you, today you will be with me in Paradise."[l]

*The Death of Jesus.*[m] 44* It was now about noon[n] and darkness came over the whole land until three in the afternoon 45 because of an eclipse of the sun. Then the veil of the temple was torn down the middle.[o] 46 Jesus cried out in a loud voice, "Father, into your hands I commend my spirit"; and when he had said this he breathed his last.[p] 47 The centurion who witnessed what had happened glorified God and said, "This man was innocent* beyond doubt." 48 When all the people who had gathered for this spectacle saw what had happened, they returned home beating their breasts;[q] 49 but all his acquaintances stood at a distance, including the women who had followed him from Galilee and saw these events.[r]

*The Burial of Jesus.*[s] 50 Now there was a virtuous and righteous man named Joseph who, though he was a member of the council, 51 had not consented to their plan of action. He came from the Jewish town of Arimathea and was awaiting the kingdom of God.[t] 52 He went to Pilate and asked for the body of Jesus. 53 After he had taken the body down, he wrapped it in a linen cloth and laid him in a rock-hewn tomb in which no one had yet been buried.[u] 54 It was the day of preparation, and the sabbath was about to begin. 55 The women who had come from Galilee with him followed behind, and when they had seen the tomb and the way in which his body was laid in it,[v] 56 they returned and prepared spices and perfumed oils. Then they rested on the sabbath according to the commandment.[w]

## VIII. The Resurrection Narrative*

### CHAPTER 24

See RG 316–18

*The Resurrection of Jesus.* 1x But at daybreak on the first day of the week they

**23:34 [Then Jesus said, "Father, forgive them, they know not what they do."]**: this portion of Lk 23:34 does not occur in the oldest papyrus manuscript of Luke and in other early Greek manuscripts and ancient versions of wide geographical distribution.

**23:39–43** This episode is recounted only in this gospel. The penitent sinner receives salvation through the crucified Jesus. Jesus' words to the penitent thief reveal Luke's understanding that the destiny of the Christian is "to be with Jesus."

**23:44 Noon . . . three in the afternoon**: literally, the sixth and ninth hours. See note on Mk 15:25.

**23:47 This man was innocent**: or, "This man was righteous."

**24:1–53** The resurrection narrative in Luke consists of five sections: (1) the women at the empty tomb (Lk 23:56b–24:12); (2) the appearance to the two disciples on the way to Emmaus (Lk 24:13–35); (3) the appearance to the disciples in Jerusalem (Lk 24:36–43); (4) Jesus' final instructions (Lk 24:44–49); (5) the ascension (Lk 24:50–53). In Luke, all the resurrection appearances take place in and around Jerusalem; moreover, they are all recounted as having taken place on Easter Sunday. A con-

*d:* Mt 27:33–44; Mk 15:22–32; Jn 19:17–24. *e:* 22:37; Is 53:12. *f:* Nm 15:27–31; Ps 22:19; Mt 5:44; Acts 7:60. *g:* Ps 22:8–9. *h:* 4:23. *i:* Ps 69:22; Mt 27:48; Mk 15:36. *j:* 23:4, 14, 22. *k:* 9:27; 23:2, 3, 38. *l:* 2 Cor 12:3; Rev 2:7. *m:* Mt 27:45–56; Mk 15:33–41; Jn 19:25–30. *n:* Am 8:9. *o:* Ex 26:31–33; 36:35. *p:* Ps 31:6; Acts 7:59. *q:* 18:13; Zec 12:10. *r:* 8:1–3; 23:55–56; 24:10; Ps 38:12. *s:* Mt 27:57–61; Mk 15:42–47; Jn 19:38–42; Acts 13:29. *t:* 2:25, 38. *u:* 19:30; Acts 13:29. *v:* 8:2; 23:49; 24:10. *w:* Ex 12:16; 20:10; Dt 5:14. *x:* Mt 28:1–8; Mk 16:1–8; Jn 20:1–17.

took the spices they had prepared and went to the tomb. 2 They found the stone rolled away from the tomb; 3 but when they entered, they did not find the body of the Lord Jesus. 4 While they were puzzling over this, behold, two men in dazzling garments appeared to them.[y] 5 They were terrified and bowed their faces to the ground. They said to them, "Why do you seek the living one among the dead?[z] 6 He is not here, but he has been raised.* Remember what he said to you while he was still in Galilee, 7 that the Son of Man must be handed over to sinners and be crucified, and rise on the third day."[a] 8 And they remembered his words.[b] 9* [c] Then they returned from the tomb and announced all these things to the eleven and to all the others. 10 The women were Mary Magdalene, Joanna, and Mary the mother of James; the others who accompanied them also told this to the apostles,[d] 11 but their story seemed like nonsense and they did not believe them. 12* [e] But Peter got up and ran to the tomb, bent down, and saw the burial cloths alone; then he went home amazed at what had happened.

***The Appearance on the Road to Emmaus.****

13 Now that very day two of them were going to a village seven miles* from Jerusalem called Emmaus,[f] 14 and they were conversing about all the things that had occurred. 15 And it happened that while they were conversing and debating, Jesus himself drew near and walked with them, 16* [g] but their eyes were prevented from recognizing him. 17 He asked them, "What are you discussing as you walk along?" They stopped, looking downcast. 18 One of them, named Cleopas, said to him in reply, "Are you the only visitor to Jerusalem who does not know of the things that have taken place there in these days?" 19 And he replied to them, "What sort of things?" They said to him, "The things that happened to Jesus the Nazarene, who was a prophet mighty in deed and word before God and all the people,[h] 20 how our chief priests and rulers both handed him over to a sentence of death and crucified him. 21 [i] But we were hoping that he would be the one to redeem Israel; and besides all this, it is now the third day since this took place. 22 [j] Some women from our group, however, have astounded us: they were at the tomb early in the morning 23 and did not find his body; they came back and reported that they had indeed seen a vision of angels who announced that he was alive. 24 [k] Then some of those with us went to the tomb and found things just as the women had described, but him they did not see." 25 [l] And he said to them, "Oh, how foolish you are! How slow of heart to believe all that the prophets spoke! 26 Was it not necessary that the Messiah should suffer* these

sistent theme throughout the narrative is that the suffering, death, and resurrection of Jesus were accomplished in fulfillment of Old Testament promises and of Jewish hopes (Lk 24:19a, 21, 26–27, 44, 46). In his second volume, Acts, Luke will argue that Christianity is the fulfillment of the hopes of Pharisaic Judaism and its logical development (see Acts 24:10–21).

**24:6 He is not here, but he has been raised**: this part of the verse is omitted in important representatives of the Western text tradition, but its presence in other text types and the slight difference in wording from Mt 28:6 and Mk 16:6 argue for its retention.

**24:9** The women in this gospel do not flee from the tomb and tell no one, as in Mk 16:8 but return and tell the disciples about their experience. The initial reaction to the testimony of the women is disbelief (Lk 24:11).

**24:12** This verse is missing from the Western textual tradition but is found in the best and oldest manuscripts of other text types.

**24:13–35** This episode focuses on the interpretation of scripture by the risen Jesus and the recognition of him in the breaking of the bread. The references to the quotations of scripture and explanation of it (Lk 24:25–27), the kerygmatic proclamation (Lk 24:34), and the liturgical gesture (Lk 24:30) suggest that the episode is primarily catechetical and liturgical rather than apologetic.

**24:13 Seven miles**: literally, "sixty stades." A stade was 607 feet. Some manuscripts read "160 stades" or more than eighteen miles. The exact location of Emmaus is disputed.

**24:16** A consistent feature of the resurrection stories is that the risen Jesus was different and initially unrecognizable (Lk 24:37; Mk 16:12; Jn 20:14; 21:4).

**24:26 That the Messiah should suffer . . .**: Luke is the only New Testament writer to speak explicitly of a suffering Messiah (Lk 24:26, 46; Acts 3:18; 17:3; 26:23). The idea of a suffering Messiah is not found in the Old Testament or in other Jewish literature prior to the New Testament period, although the idea is hinted at in Mk 8:31–33. See notes on Mt 26:63 and 26:67–68.

*y:* 2 Mc 3:26; Acts 1:10. *z:* Acts 2:9. *a:* 9:22, 44; 17:25; 18:32–33; Mt 16:21; 17:22–23; Mk 9:31; Acts 17:3. *b:* Jn 2:22. *c:* Mk 16:10–11; Jn 20:18. *d:* 8:2–3; Mk 16:9. *e:* Jn 20:3–7. *f:* Mk 16:12–13. *g:* Jn 20:14; 21:4. *h:* Mt 2:23; 21:11; Acts 2:22. *i:* 1:54, 68; 2:38. *j:* 24:1–11; Mt 28:1–8; Mk 16:1–8. *k:* Jn 20:3–10. *l:* 9:22; 18:31; 24:44; Acts 3:24; 17:3.

things and enter into his glory?" 27 Then beginning with Moses and all the prophets, he interpreted to them what referred to him in all the scriptures.[m] 28 As they approached the village to which they were going, he gave the impression that he was going on farther. 29 But they urged him, "Stay with us, for it is nearly evening and the day is almost over." So he went in to stay with them. 30 And it happened that, while he was with them at table, he took bread, said the blessing, broke it, and gave it to them. 31 With that their eyes were opened and they recognized him, but he vanished from their sight. 32 Then they said to each other, "Were not our hearts burning [within us] while he spoke to us on the way and opened the scriptures to us?" 33 So they set out at once and returned to Jerusalem where they found gathered together the eleven and those with them 34 who were saying, "The Lord has truly been raised and has appeared to Simon!"[n] 35 Then the two recounted what had taken place on the way and how he was made known to them in the breaking of the bread.

***The Appearance to the Disciples in Jerusalem.*** 36* While they were still speaking about this,[o] he stood in their midst and said to them, "Peace be with you."[p] 37 But they were startled and terrified and thought that they were seeing a ghost.[q] 38 Then he said to them, "Why are you troubled? And why do questions arise in your hearts? 39* Look at my hands and my feet, that it is I myself. Touch me and see, because a ghost does not have flesh and bones as you can see I have." 40[r] And as he said this, he showed them his hands and his feet. 41 While they were still incredulous for joy and were amazed, he asked them, "Have you anything here to eat?" 42 They gave him a piece of baked fish;[s] 43 he took it and ate it in front of them.

44 He said to them, "These are my words that I spoke to you while I was still with you, that everything written about me in the law of Moses and in the prophets and psalms must be fulfilled."[t] 45 Then he opened their minds to understand the scriptures.[u] 46* And he said to them,[v] "Thus it is written that the Messiah would suffer and rise from the dead on the third day 47 and that repentance, for the forgiveness of sins, would be preached in his name to all the nations, beginning from Jerusalem.[w] 48 You are witnesses of these things.[x] 49 And [behold] I am sending the promise of my Father* upon you; but stay in the city until you are clothed with power from on high."[y]

***The Ascension.**** 50[z] Then he led them [out] as far as Bethany, raised his hands, and blessed them. 51 As he blessed them he parted from them and was taken up to heaven. 52 They did him homage and then returned to Jerusalem with great joy,[a] 53 and they were continually in the temple praising God.*

**24:36–43, 44–49** The Gospel of Luke, like each of the other gospels (Mt 28:16–20; Mk 16:14–15; Jn 20:19–23), focuses on an important appearance of Jesus to the Twelve in which they are commissioned for their future ministry. As in Lk 24:6, 12, so in Lk 24:36, 40 there are omissions in the Western text.

**24:39–42** The apologetic purpose of this story is evident in the concern with the physical details and the report that Jesus ate food.

**24:46** See note on Lk 24:26.

**24:49 The promise of my Father**: i.e., the gift of the holy Spirit.

**24:50–53** Luke brings his story about the time of Jesus to a close with the report of the ascension. He will also begin the story of the time of the church with a recounting of the ascension. In the gospel, Luke recounts the ascension of Jesus on Easter Sunday night, thereby closely associating it with the resurrection. In Acts 1:3, 9–11; 13:31 he historicizes the ascension by speaking of a forty-day period between the resurrection and the ascension. The Western text omits some phrases in Lk 24:51, 52 perhaps to avoid any chronological conflict with Acts 1 about the time of the ascension.

**24:53** The Gospel of Luke ends as it began (Lk 1:9), in the Jerusalem temple.

*m:* 24:44; Dt 18:15; Ps 22:1–18; Is 53; 1 Pt 1:10–11. *n:* 1 Cor 15:4–5. *o:* Mk 16:14–19; Jn 20:19–20. *p:* 1 Cor 15:5. *q:* Mt 14:26. *r:* Jn 21:5, 9–10, 13. *s:* Acts 10:41. *t:* 18:31; 24:27; Mt 16:21; Jn 5:39, 46. *u:* Jn 20:9. *v:* 9:22; Is 53; Hos 6:2. *w:* Mt 3:2; 28:19–20; Mk 16:15–16; Acts 10:41. *x:* Acts 1:8. *y:* Jn 14:26; Acts 1:4; 2:3–4. *z:* Mk 16:19; Acts 1:9–11. *a:* Acts 1:12.

See RG 319–34

# The Gospel According to John

The Gospel according to John is quite different in character from the three synoptic gospels. It is highly literary and symbolic. It does not follow the same order or reproduce the same stories as the synoptic gospels. To a much greater degree, it is the product of a developed theological reflection and grows out of a different circle and tradition. It was probably written in the 90s of the first century.

The Gospel of John begins with a magnificent prologue, which states many of the major themes and motifs of the gospel, much as an overture does for a musical work. The prologue proclaims Jesus as the preexistent and incarnate Word of God who has revealed the Father to us. The rest of the first chapter forms the introduction to the gospel proper and consists of the Baptist's testimony about Jesus (there is no baptism of Jesus in this gospel—John simply points him out as the Lamb of God), followed by stories of the call of the first disciples, in which various titles predicated of Jesus in the early church are presented.

The gospel narrative contains a series of "signs"—the gospel's word for the wondrous deeds of Jesus. The author is primarily interested in the significance of these deeds, and so interprets them for the reader by various reflections, narratives, and discourses. The first sign is the transformation of water into wine at Cana (Jn 2:1–11); this represents the replacement of the Jewish ceremonial washings and symbolizes the entire creative and transforming work of Jesus. The second sign, the cure of the royal official's son (Jn 4:46–54) simply by the word of Jesus at a distance, signifies the power of Jesus' life-giving word. The same theme is further developed by other signs, probably for a total of seven. The third sign, the cure of the paralytic at the pool with five porticoes in chap. 5, continues the theme of water offering newness of life. In the preceding chapter, to the woman at the well in Samaria Jesus had offered living water springing up to eternal life, a symbol of the revelation that Jesus brings; here Jesus' life-giving word replaces the water of the pool that failed to bring life. Jn 6 contains two signs, the multiplication of loaves and the walking on the waters of the Sea of Galilee. These signs are connected much as the manna and the crossing of the Red Sea are in the Passover narrative and symbolize a new exodus. The multiplication of the loaves is interpreted for the reader by the discourse that follows, where the bread of life is used first as a figure for the revelation of God in Jesus and then for the Eucharist. After a series of dialogues reflecting Jesus' debates with the Jewish authorities at the Feast of Tabernacles in Jn 7; 8, the sixth sign is presented in Jn 9, the sign of the young man born blind. This is a narrative illustration of the theme of conflict in the preceding two chapters; it proclaims the triumph of light over darkness, as Jesus is presented as the Light of the world. This is interpreted by a narrative of controversy between the Pharisees and the young man who had been given his sight by Jesus, ending with a discussion of spiritual blindness and spelling out the symbolic meaning of the cure. And finally, the seventh sign, the raising of Lazarus in chap. 11, is the climax of signs. Lazarus is presented as a token of the real life that Jesus, the Resurrection and the Life, who will now ironically be put to death because of his gift of life to Lazarus, will give to all who believe in him once he has been raised from the dead.

After the account of the seven signs, the "hour" of Jesus arrives, and the author passes from sign to reality, as he moves into the discourses in the upper room that interpret the meaning of the passion, death, and resurrection narratives that follow. The whole gospel of John is a progressive revelation of the glory of God's only Son, who comes to reveal the Father and then returns in glory to the Father. The author's purpose is clearly expressed in what must have been the original ending of the gospel at the end of Jn 20: "Now Jesus did many other signs in the presence of [his] disciples that are not written in this book. But these are written that you may [come to] believe that Jesus is the Messiah, the Son of God, and that through this belief you may have life in his name."

Critical analysis makes it difficult to accept the idea that the gospel as it now stands was written by one person. Jn 21 seems to have been added after the gospel was completed; it exhibits a Greek style somewhat different from that of the rest of the work. The prologue (Jn 1:1–18) apparently contains an independent hymn, subsequently adapted to serve as a preface to the gospel. Within the gospel itself there are also some inconsistencies, e.g., there are two endings of Jesus' discourse in the upper room (Jn 14:31; 18:1). To solve these problems, scholars have proposed various rearrangements that would produce a smoother order. However, most have come to the conclusion that the inconsistencies were probably produced by subsequent editing in which homogeneous materials were added to a shorter original.

Other difficulties for any theory of eyewitness authorship of the gospel in its present form are presented by its highly developed theology and by certain elements of its literary style. For instance, some of the wondrous deeds of Jesus have been worked into highly effective dramatic scenes (Jn 9); there has been a careful attempt to have these followed by discourses that explain them (Jn 5; 6); and the sayings of Jesus have been oven into long discourses of a quasi-poetic form resembling the speeches of personified Wisdom in the Old Testament.

The polemic between synagogue and church produced bitter and harsh invective, especially regarding the hostility toward Jesus of the authorities—Pharisees and Sadducees—who are combined and referred to frequently as "the Jews" (see note on Jn 1:19). These opponents are even described in Jn 8:44 as springing from their father the devil, whose conduct they imitate in opposing God by rejecting Jesus, whom God has sent. On the other hand, the author of this gospel seems to take pains to show that women are not inferior to men in the Christian community: the woman at the well in Samaria (Jn 4) is presented as a prototype of a missionary (Jn 4:4–42), and the first witness of the resurrection is a woman (Jn 20:11–18).

The final editing of the gospel and arrangement in its present form probably dates from between A.D. 90 and 100. Traditionally, Ephesus has been favored as the place of composition, though many support a location in Syria, perhaps the city of Antioch, while some have suggested other places, including Alexandria.

The principal divisions of the Gospel according to John are the following:

I. Prologue (1:1–18)
II. The Book of Signs (1:19–12:50)
III. The Book of Glory (13:1–20:31)
IV. Epilogue: The Resurrection Appearance in Galilee (21:1–25)

## I. Prologue*

### CHAPTER 1

See RG 324–25

1 In the beginning* was the Word,
and the Word was with God,
and the Word was God.[a]
2 He was in the beginning with God.
3 * All things came to be through him,
and without him nothing came to be.[b]
What came to be 4 through him was life,
and this life was the light of the human race;[c]
5 * the light shines in the darkness,[d]
and the darkness has not overcome it.

**1:1–18** The prologue states the main themes of the gospel: life, light, truth, the world, testimony, and the preexistence of Jesus Christ, the incarnate *Logos*, who reveals God the Father. In origin, it was probably an early Christian hymn. Its closest parallel is in other christological hymns, Col 1:15–20 and Phil 2:6–11. Its core (Jn 1:1–5, 10–11, 14) is poetic in structure, with short phrases linked by "staircase parallelism," in which the last word of one phrase becomes the first word of the next. Prose inserts (at least Jn 1:6–8, 15) deal with John the Baptist.

**1:1 In the beginning**: also the first words of the Old Testament (Gn 1:1). **Was**: this verb is used three times with different meanings in this verse: existence, relationship, and predication. **The Word** (Greek *logos*): this term combines God's dynamic, creative word (Genesis), personified preexistent Wisdom as the instrument of God's creative activity (Proverbs), and the ultimate intelligibility of reality (Hellenistic philosophy). **With God**: the Greek preposition here connotes communication with another. **Was God**: lack of a definite article with "God" in Greek signifies predication rather than identification.

**1:3 What came to be**: while the oldest manuscripts have no punctuation here, the corrector of Bodmer Papyrus $P^{75}$, some manuscripts, and the Ante-Nicene Fathers take this phrase with what follows, as staircase parallelism. Connection with Jn 1:3 reflects fourth-century anti-Arianism.

**1:5** The ethical dualism of light and darkness is paralleled in intertestamental literature and in the Dead Sea Scrolls. **Overcome**: "comprehend" is another possible translation, but cf. Jn 12:35; Wis 7:29–30.

*a:* 10:30; Gn 1:1–5; Jb 28:12–27; Prv 8:22–25; Wis 9:1–2; 1 Jn 1:1–2; Col 1:1, 15; Rev 3:14; 19:13. *b:* Ps 33:9; Wis 9:1; Sir 42:15; 1 Cor 8:6; Col 1:16; Heb 1:2; Rev 3:14. *c:* 5:26; 8:12; 1 Jn 1:2. *d:* 3:19; 8:12; 9:5; 12:35, 46; Wis 7:29–30; 1 Thes 5:4; 1 Jn 2:8.

6* A man named John was sent from God.[e]
7 He came for testimony,* to testify to the
light, so that all might believe through him.[f]
8 He was not the light, but came to testify to
the light.[g] 9 The true light, which enlightens
everyone, was coming into the world.[h]

10 He was in the world,
and the world came to be through him,
but the world did not know him.
11 He came to what was his own,
but his own people* did not accept him.

12 [i] But to those who did accept him he gave
power to become children of God, to those
who believe in his name, 13* [j] who were born
not by natural generation nor by human
choice nor by a man's decision but of God.

14 And the Word became flesh*
and made his dwelling among us,
and we saw his glory,
the glory as of the Father's only Son,
full of grace and truth.[k]

15* John testified to him and cried out, saying, "This was he of whom I said,[l] 'The one
who is coming after me ranks ahead of me
because he existed before me.' " 16 From his
fullness we have all received, grace in place
of grace,* 17 because while the law was given
through Moses, grace and truth came
through Jesus Christ.[m] 18 No one has ever
seen God. The only Son, God,* who is at the
Father's side, has revealed him.[n]

## II. The Book of Signs

### *John the Baptist's Testimony to Himself.*

19* And this is the testimony of John. When
the Jews* from Jerusalem sent priests and
Levites [to him] to ask him, "Who are you?"

**1:6** John was **sent** just as Jesus was "sent" (Jn 4:34) in divine mission. Other references to John the Baptist in this gospel emphasize the differences between them and John's subordinate role.

**1:7 Testimony**: the testimony theme of John is introduced, which portrays Jesus as if on trial throughout his ministry. All testify to Jesus: John the Baptist, the Samaritan woman, scripture, his works, the crowds, the Spirit, and his disciples.

**1:11 What was his own . . . his own people**: first a neuter, literally, "his own property/possession" (probably = Israel), then a masculine, "his own people" (the Israelites).

**1:13** Believers in Jesus become children of God not through any of the three natural causes mentioned but through God who is the immediate cause of the new spiritual life. **Were born**: the Greek verb can mean "begotten" (by a male) or "born" (from a female or of parents). The variant "he who was begotten," asserting Jesus' virginal conception, is weakly attested in Old Latin and Syriac versions.

**1:14 Flesh**: the whole person, used probably against docetic tendencies (cf. 1 Jn 4:2; 2 Jn 7). **Made his dwelling**: literally, "pitched his tent/tabernacle." Cf. the tabernacle or tent of meeting that was the place of God's presence among his people (Ex 25:8–9). The incarnate Word is the new mode of God's presence among his people. The Greek verb has the same consonants as the Aramaic word for God's presence (Shekinah). **Glory**: God's visible manifestation of majesty in power, which once filled the tabernacle (Ex 40:34) and the temple (1 Kgs 8:10–11, 27), is now centered in Jesus. **Only Son**: Greek, *monogenēs*, but see note on Jn 1:18. **Grace and truth**: these words may represent two Old Testament terms describing Yahweh in covenant relationship with Israel (cf. Ex 34:6), thus God's "love" and "fidelity." The Word shares Yahweh's covenant qualities.

**1:15** This verse, interrupting Jn 1:14, 16 seems drawn from Jn 1:30.

**1:16 Grace in place of grace**: replacement of the Old Covenant with the New (cf. Jn 1:17). Other possible translations are "grace upon grace" (accumulation) and "grace for grace" (correspondence).

**1:18 The only Son, God**: while the vast majority of later textual witnesses have another reading, "the Son, the only one" or "the only Son," the translation above follows the best and earliest manuscripts, *monogenēs theos*, but takes the first term to mean not just "Only One" but to include a filial relationship with the Father, as at Lk 9:38 ("only child") or Heb 11:17 ("only son") and as translated at Jn 1:14. The Logos is thus "only Son" and God but not Father/God.

**1:19–51** The testimony of John the Baptist about the Messiah and Jesus' self-revelation to the first disciples. This section constitutes the introduction to the gospel proper and is connected with the prose inserts in the prologue. It develops the major theme of testimony in four scenes: John's negative testimony about himself; his positive testimony about Jesus; the revelation of Jesus to Andrew and Peter; the revelation of Jesus to Philip and Nathanael.

**1:19 The Jews**: throughout most of the gospel, the "Jews" does not refer to the Jewish people as such but to the hostile authorities, both Pharisees and Sadducees, particularly in Jerusalem, who refuse to believe in Jesus. The usage reflects the atmosphere, at the end of the first century, of polemics between church and synagogue, or possibly it refers to Jews as representative of a hostile world (Jn 1:10–11).

*e:* Mt 3:1; Mk 1:4; Lk 3:2–3. *f:* 1:19–34; 5:33. *g:* 5:35. *h:* 3:19; 8:12; 9:39; 12:46. *i:* 3:11–12; 5:43–44; 12:46–50; Gal 3:26; 4:6–7; Eph 1:5; 1 Jn 3:2. *j:* 3:5–6. *k:* Ex 16:10; 24:17; 25:8–9; 33:22; 34:6; Sir 24:4, 8; Is 60:1; Ez 43:7; Jl 4:17; Heb 2:14; 1 Jn 1:2; 4:2; 2 Jn 7. *l:* 1:30; 3:27–30. *m:* 7:19; Ex 31:18; 34:28. *n:* 5:37; 6:46; Ex 33:20; Jgs 13:21–22; 1 Tm 6:16; 1 Jn 4:12.

20* he admitted and did not deny it, but admitted,[o] "I am not the Messiah." 21 So they
asked him, "What are you then? Are you Elijah?"* And he said, "I am not." "Are you the
Prophet?" He answered, "No."[p] 22 So they
said to him, "Who are you, so we can give an
answer to those who sent us? What do you
have to say for yourself?" 23 He said:

"I am 'the voice of one crying out in the
desert,[q]
"Make straight the way of the Lord," '*

as Isaiah the prophet said." 24 Some Pharisees* were also sent. 25 They asked him,
"Why then do you baptize if you are not the
Messiah or Elijah or the Prophet?"[r] 26 John
answered them, "I baptize with water;* but
there is one among you whom you do not
recognize,[s] 27 the one who is coming after
me, whose sandal strap I am not worthy to
untie." 28 This happened in Bethany across
the Jordan,* where John was baptizing.

***John the Baptist's Testimony to Jesus.***
29 The next day he saw Jesus coming toward
him and said, "Behold, the Lamb of God,*
who takes away the sin of the world.[t] 30* He
is the one of whom I said,[u] 'A man is coming
after me who ranks ahead of me because he
existed before me.' 31 I did not know him,*
but the reason why I came baptizing with
water was that he might be made known to
Israel." 32 John testified further, saying, "I
saw the Spirit come down like a dove* from
the sky and remain upon him. 33 I did not
know him,[v] but the one who sent me to baptize with water told me, 'On whomever you
see the Spirit come down and remain, he is
the one who will baptize with the holy
Spirit.'[w] 34* [x] Now I have seen and testified
that he is the Son of God."

***The First Disciples.***[y] 35 The next day John
was there again with two of his disciples,
36 and as he watched Jesus walk by, he said,
"Behold, the Lamb of God."* 37 The two disciples* heard what he said and followed
Jesus. 38 Jesus turned and saw them following
him and said to them, "What are you looking
for?" They said to him, "Rabbi" (which translated means Teacher), "where are you stay-

**1:20 Messiah**: the anointed agent of Yahweh, usually considered to be of Davidic descent. See further the note on Jn 1:41.

**1:21 Elijah**: the Baptist did not claim to be Elijah returned to earth (cf. Mal 3:19; Mt 11:14). **The Prophet**: probably the prophet like Moses (Dt 18:15; cf. Acts 3:22).

**1:23** This is a repunctuation and reinterpretation (as in the synoptic gospels and Septuagint) of the Hebrew text of Is 40:3 which reads, "A voice cries out: In the desert prepare the way of the LORD."

**1:24 Some Pharisees**: other translations, such as "Now they had been sent from the Pharisees," misunderstand the grammatical construction. This is a different group from that in Jn 1:19; the priests and Levites would have been Sadducees, not Pharisees.

**1:26 I baptize with water**: the synoptics add "but he will baptize you with the holy Spirit" (Mk 1:8) or ". . . holy Spirit and fire" (Mt 3:11; Lk 3:16). John's emphasis is on purification and preparation for a better baptism.

**1:28 Bethany across the Jordan**: site unknown. Another reading is "Bethabara."

**1:29 The Lamb of God**: the background for this title may be the victorious apocalyptic lamb who would destroy evil in the world (Rev 5–7; 17:14); the paschal lamb, whose blood saved Israel (Ex 12); and/or the suffering servant led like a lamb to the slaughter as a sin-offering (Is 53:7, 10).

**1:30 He existed before me**: possibly as Elijah (to come, Jn 1:27); for the evangelist and his audience, Jesus' preexistence would be implied (see note on Jn 1:1).

**1:31 I did not know him**: this gospel shows no knowledge of the tradition (Lk 1) about the kinship of Jesus and John the Baptist. **The reason why I came baptizing with water**: in this gospel, John's baptism is not connected with forgiveness of sins; its purpose is revelatory, that Jesus may be made known to Israel.

**1:32 Like a dove**: a symbol of the new creation (Gn 8:8) or the community of Israel (Hos 11:11). **Remain**: the first use of a favorite verb in John, emphasizing the permanency of the relationship between Father and Son (as here) and between the Son and the Christian. Jesus is the permanent bearer of the Spirit.

**1:34 The Son of God**: this reading is supported by good Greek manuscripts, including the Chester Beatty and Bodmer Papyri and the Vatican Codex, but is suspect because it harmonizes this passage with the synoptic version: "This is my beloved Son" (Mt 3:17; Mk 1:11; Lk 3:22). The poorly attested alternate reading, "God's chosen One," is probably a reference to the Servant of Yahweh (Is 42:1).

**1:36** John the Baptist's testimony makes his disciples' following of Jesus plausible.

**1:37 The two disciples**: Andrew (Jn 1:40) and, traditionally, John, son of Zebedee (see note on Jn 13:23).

*o:* 3:28; Lk 3:15; Acts 13:25. *p:* Dt 18:15, 18; 2 Kgs 2:11; Sir 48:10; Mal 3:1, 23; Mt 11:14; 17:11–13; Mk 9:13; Acts 3:22. *q:* Is 40:3; Mt 3:3; Mk 1:2; Lk 3:4. *r:* Ez 36:25; Zec 13:1; Mt 16:14. *s:* Mt 3:11; Mk 1:7–8; Lk 3:16; Acts 13:25. *t:* 1:36; Ex 12; Is 53:7; Rev 5–7; 17:14. *u:* 1:15; Mt 3:11; Mk 1:7; Lk 3:16. *v:* Sg 5:2; Is 11:2; Hos 11:11; Mt 3:16; Mk 1:10; Lk 3:21–22. *w:* Is 42:1; Mt 3:11; Mk 1:8; Lk 3:16. *x:* Is 42:1; Mt 3:17; Mk 1:11; Lk 9:35. *y:* Mt 4:18–22; Mk 1:16–20; Lk 5:1–11.

## The Lamb of God

"BEHOLD, THE LAMB of God, who takes away the sin of the world."

This phrase appears only in the Gospel of John (Jn 1:29, 36), where John the Baptist applies it to Jesus. The Gospel writer provides no guidance, however, to help us understand what it means. For that, we need to look within the biblical text itself.

Although various animals and birds, as well as flour and oil, could be sacrificed (see "Holiness and Sacrifice," p. 145), the lamb gradually came to stand for sacrifice in general. This may have been because, as a relatively small animal, it was more commonly sacrificed than the larger ones like oxen. It may also have come more readily to mind because it was the main part of the Passover meal (Ex 12:3–10). The blood of the Passover lamb marked the doorposts of the Jewish people, signaling that the LORD should not kill any of those within (Ex 12:21–23). In subsequent celebrations of the Passover, the people were told to recall this (Ex 12:24–27). Later (Lv 14:12), the lamb was used for the guilt offering (or "offering of reparation").

The prophets Isaiah and Jeremiah developed another part of the imagery of the sacrificial lamb. The fourth "Servant Song" (Is 52:13–53:12) compares the servant to "a lamb led to slaughter . . . [who] did not open his mouth" (53:7), and Jeremiah compares himself to "a trusting lamb led to slaughter" (11:19). On the natural level this is no doubt based on the fact that a lamb is a very docile animal, and it will often allow itself to be brought somewhere with little or no resistance. In the imagery of the prophets, however, it is transformed into the one who was betrayed (Jeremiah) and the one who went willingly to death (the servant of the Isaiah passage).

When the Gospel of John has John the Baptist call Jesus "the Lamb of God," therefore, it may be referring to this background of meaning. The Lamb is the willing sacrificial victim who makes reparation for sin. At the end of the Gospel of John, there is a subtle echo of this passage. According to John's chronology, the Last Supper takes place before Passover (Jn 13:1); the day of the crucifixion of Jesus was "preparation day" (Jn 19:31), the day during which the Passover meal was prepared before the supper that evening (Ex 12:16). Thus, as Jesus is dying on the cross, the lambs for the Passover meal are being slaughtered.

The image of the sacrificial lamb makes one other significant appearance in the Bible, in Revelation 5:6–12. There the scroll that contains the divine plan of salvation must be opened, and the only one able to open it is "the lion of the tribe of Judah" (Rv 5:5) who in fact is the "Lamb that seemed to have been slain" (Rv 5:6). That Lamb (Christ) is "worthy" of honor and worship (Rv 5:12–14) because of his willing self-sacrifice.

This acclamation in the Gospel formed the basis of a portion of the *Gloria in excelsis*—"Lord God, Lamb of God, you take away the sin of the world"—and of the *Agnus Dei,* now recited at the Fraction—"Lamb of God, you take away the sins of the world: have mercy on us/grant us peace."

ing?" 39 He said to them, "Come, and you will
see." So they went and saw where he was
staying, and they stayed with him that day. It
was about four in the afternoon.* 40 Andrew,
the brother of Simon Peter, was one of the
two who heard John and followed Jesus. 41 He
first found his own brother Simon and told
him, "We have found the Messiah"* (which is
translated Anointed).[z] 42 Then he brought him
to Jesus. Jesus looked at him and said, "You
are Simon the son of John;* you will be called
Cephas" (which is translated Peter).[a]

43 The next day he* decided to go to Galilee,
and he found Philip. And Jesus said to him,
"Follow me." 44 Now Philip was from Bethsaida, the town of Andrew and Peter. 45 Philip
found Nathanael and told him, "We have
found the one about whom Moses wrote in
the law, and also the prophets, Jesus, son of
Joseph, from Nazareth."[b] 46 But Nathanael
said to him, "Can anything good come from
Nazareth?" Philip said to him, "Come and
see." 47 Jesus saw Nathanael coming toward
him and said of him, "Here is a true Israelite.*
There is no duplicity in him." 48* [c] Nathanael
said to him, "How do you know me?" Jesus
answered and said to him, "Before Philip
called you, I saw you under the fig tree."
49 Nathanael answered him, "Rabbi, you are
the Son of God;* you are the King of Israel."[d]
50 Jesus answered and said to him, "Do you
believe because I told you that I saw you under the fig tree?* You will see greater things
than this." 51 And he said to him, "Amen,
amen,* I say to you, you will see the sky
opened and the angels of God ascending and
descending on the Son of Man."[e]

## CHAPTER 2

See RG 325–26

***The Wedding at Cana.*** 1* On the third
day there was a wedding* in Cana* in Galilee, and the mother of Jesus was there.[f]
2 Jesus and his disciples were also invited to
the wedding. 3 When the wine ran short, the
mother of Jesus said to him, "They have no
wine." 4* [And] Jesus said to her, "Woman,
how does your concern affect me? My hour
has not yet come."[g] 5 His mother said to the

**1:39 Four in the afternoon**: literally, the tenth hour, from sunrise, in the Roman calculation of time. Some suggest that the next day, beginning at sunset, was the sabbath; they would have stayed with Jesus to avoid travel on it.

**1:41 Messiah**: the Hebrew word *māšîaḥ*, "anointed one" (see note on Lk 2:11), appears in Greek as the transliterated *messias* only here and in Jn 4:25. Elsewhere the Greek translation *christos* is used.

**1:42 Simon, the son of John**: in Mt 16:17, Simon is called *Bariōna*, "son of Jonah," a different tradition for the name of Simon's father. **Cephas**: in Aramaic = the Rock; cf. Mt 16:18. Neither the Greek equivalent **Petros** nor, with one isolated exception, **Cephas** is attested as a personal name before Christian times.

**1:43 He**: grammatically, could be Peter, but logically is probably Jesus.

**1:47 A true Israelite. There is no duplicity in him**: Jacob was the first to bear the name "Israel" (Gn 32:29), but Jacob was a man of duplicity (Gn 27:35–36).

**1:48 Under the fig tree**: a symbol of messianic peace (cf. Mi 4:4; Zec 3:10).

**1:49 Son of God**: this title is used in the Old Testament, among other ways, as a title of adoption for the Davidic king (2 Sm 7:14; Ps 2:7; 89:27), and thus here, with **King of Israel**, in a messianic sense. For the evangelist, **Son of God** also points to Jesus' divinity (cf. Jn 20:28).

**1:50** Possibly a statement: "You [singular] believe because I saw you under the fig tree."

**1:51** The double "Amen" is characteristic of John. **You** is plural in Greek. The allusion is to Jacob's ladder (Gn 28:12).

**2:1–6:71** Signs revealing Jesus as the Messiah to all Israel. "Sign" (*sēmeion*) is John's symbolic term for Jesus' wondrous deeds (see Introduction). The Old Testament background lies in the Exodus story (cf. Dt 11:3; 29:2). John is interested primarily in what the *sēmeia* signify: God's intervention in human history in a new way through Jesus.

**2:1–11** The first sign. This story of replacement of Jewish ceremonial washings (Jn 2:6) presents the initial revelation about Jesus at the outset of his ministry. He manifests his glory; the disciples believe. There is no synoptic parallel.

**2:1 Cana**: unknown from the Old Testament. **The mother of Jesus**: she is never named in John.

**2:4** This verse may seek to show that Jesus did not work miracles to help his family and friends, as in the apocryphal gospels. **Woman**: a normal, polite form of address, but unattested in reference to one's mother. Cf. also Jn 19:26. **How does your concern affect me?**: literally, "What is this to me and to you?"—a Hebrew expression of either hostility (Jgs 11:12; 2 Chr 35:21; 1 Kgs 17:18) or denial of common interest (Hos 14:9; 2 Kgs 3:13). Cf. Mk 1:24; 5:7 used by demons to Jesus. **My hour has not yet come**: the translation as a question ("Has not my hour now come?"), while preferable grammatically and supported by Greek Fathers, seems unlikely from a comparison with Jn 7:6, 30. The "hour" is that of Jesus' passion, death, resurrection, and ascension (Jn 13:1).

---

*z:* 4:25. *a:* Mt 16:18; Mk 3:16. *b:* 21:2. *c:* Mi 4:4; Zec 3:10. *d:* 12:13; Ex 4:22; Dt 14:1; 2 Sm 7:14; Jb 1:6; 2:1; 38:7; Ps 2:7; 29:1; 89:27; Wis 2:18; Sir 4:10; Dn 3:92; Hos 11:1; Mt 14:33; 16:16; Mk 13:32. *e:* Gn 28:10–17; Dn 7:13. *f:* 4:46; Jgs 14:12; Tb 11:8. *g:* 7:30; 8:20; 12:23; 13:1; Jgs 11:12; 1 Kgs 17:18; 2 Kgs 3:13; 2 Chr 35:21; Hos 14:9; Mk 1:24; 5:7; 7:30; 8:20; 12:23; 13:1.

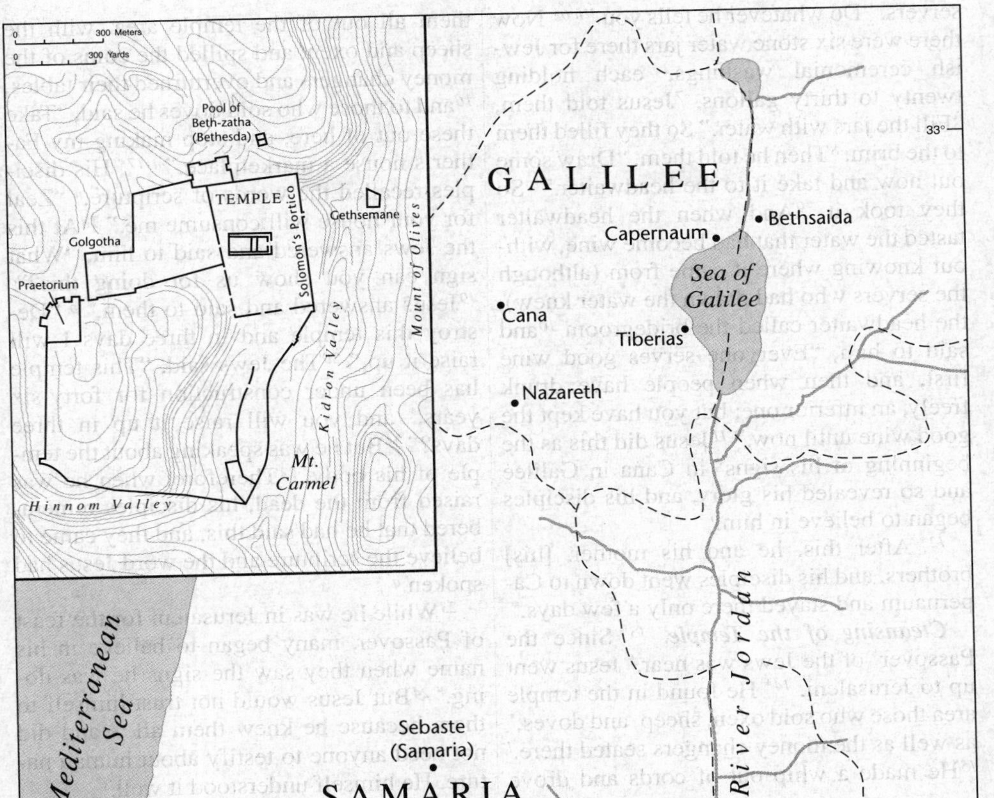


Geography of the Gospel of John

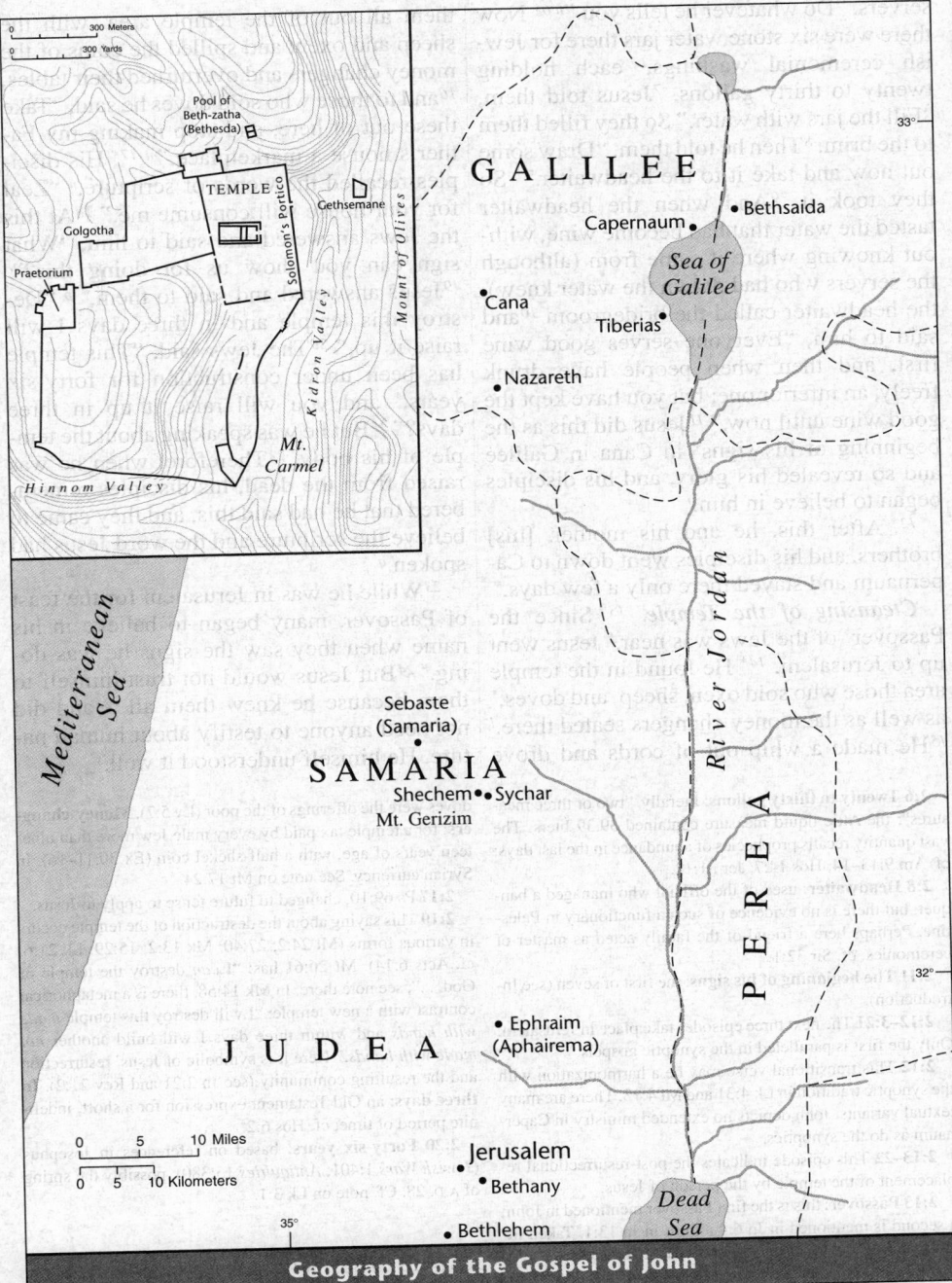

servers, "Do whatever he tells you."[h] 6* Now
there were six stone water jars there for Jewish ceremonial washings,[i] each holding
twenty to thirty gallons. 7 Jesus told them,
"Fill the jars with water." So they filled them
to the brim. 8 Then he told them, "Draw some
out now and take it to the headwaiter."* So
they took it. 9 And when the headwaiter
tasted the water that had become wine, without knowing where it came from (although
the servers who had drawn the water knew),
the headwaiter called the bridegroom 10 and
said to him, "Everyone serves good wine
first, and then when people have drunk
freely, an inferior one; but you have kept the
good wine until now." 11 Jesus did this as the
beginning of his signs* in Cana in Galilee
and so revealed his glory, and his disciples
began to believe in him.[j]

12* After this, he and his mother, [his]
brothers, and his disciples went down to Capernaum and stayed there only a few days.*

***Cleansing of the Temple.*** 13* Since the
Passover* of the Jews was near,[k] Jesus went
up to Jerusalem. 14* He found in the temple
area those who sold oxen, sheep, and doves,*
as well as the money changers seated there.[l]
15 He made a whip out of cords and drove
them all out of the temple area, with the
sheep and oxen, and spilled the coins of the
money changers and overturned their tables,
16 and to those who sold doves he said, "Take
these out of here, and stop making my Father's house a marketplace."[m] 17* His disciples recalled the words of scripture,[n] "Zeal
for your house will consume me." 18 At this
the Jews answered and said to him, "What
sign can you show us for doing this?"[o]
19 Jesus answered and said to them,* [p] "Destroy this temple and in three days I will
raise it up." 20 The Jews said, "This temple
has been under construction for forty-six
years,* and you will raise it up in three
days?" 21 But he was speaking about the temple of his body. 22 Therefore, when he was
raised from the dead, his disciples remembered that he had said this, and they came to
believe the scripture and the word Jesus had
spoken.[q]

23 While he was in Jerusalem for the feast
of Passover, many began to believe in his
name when they saw the signs he was doing.[r] 24 But Jesus would not trust himself to
them because he knew them all, 25 and did
not need anyone to testify about human nature. He himself understood it well.[s]

**2:6 Twenty to thirty gallons**: literally, "two or three measures"; the Attic liquid measure contained 39.39 liters. The vast quantity recalls prophecies of abundance in the last days; cf. Am 9:13–14; Hos 14:7; Jer 31:12.

**2:8 Headwaiter**: used of the official who managed a banquet, but there is no evidence of such a functionary in Palestine. Perhaps here a friend of the family acted as master of ceremonies; cf. Sir 32:1.

**2:11 The beginning of his signs**: the first of seven (see Introduction).

**2:12–3:21** The next three episodes take place in Jerusalem. Only the first is paralleled in the synoptic gospels.

**2:12** This transitional verse may be a harmonization with the synoptic tradition in Lk 4:31 and Mt 4:13. There are many textual variants. John depicts no extended ministry in Capernaum as do the synoptics.

**2:13–22** This episode indicates the post-resurrectional replacement of the temple by the person of Jesus.

**2:13 Passover**: this is the first Passover mentioned in John; a second is mentioned in Jn 6:4 a third in Jn 13:1. Taken literally, they point to a ministry of at least two years.

**2:14–22** The other gospels place the cleansing of the temple in the last days of Jesus' life (Matthew, on the day Jesus entered Jerusalem; Mark, on the next day). The order of events in the gospel narratives is often determined by theological motives rather than by chronological data.

**2:14 Oxen, sheep, and doves**: intended for sacrifice. The doves were the offerings of the poor (Lv 5:7). **Money-changers**: for a temple tax paid by every male Jew more than nineteen years of age, with a half-shekel coin (Ex 30:11–16), in Syrian currency. See note on Mt 17:24.

**2:17** Ps 69:10, changed to future tense to apply to Jesus.

**2:19** This saying about the destruction of the temple occurs in various forms (Mt 24:2; 27:40; Mk 13:2; 15:29; Lk 21:6; cf. Acts 6:14). Mt 26:61 has: "I *can* destroy the temple of God. . ."; see note there. In Mk 14:58, there is a metaphorical contrast with a new temple: "I will destroy this temple *made with hands* and within three days I will build another *not made with hands*." Here it is symbolic of Jesus' resurrection and the resulting community (see Jn 2:21 and Rev 21:2). **In three days**: an Old Testament expression for a short, indefinite period of time; cf. Hos 6:2.

**2:20 Forty-six years**: based on references in Josephus (*Jewish Wars* 1:401; *Antiquities* 15:380), possibly the spring of A.D. 28. Cf. note on Lk 3:1.

*h:* Gn 41:55. *i:* 3:25; Lv 11:33; Am 9:13–14; Mt 15:2; 23:25–26; Mk 7:2–4; Lk 11:38. *j:* 4:54. *k:* Mt 21:12–13; Mk 11:15–17; Lk 19:45–46. *l:* Ex 30:11–16; Lv 5:7. *m:* Zec 14:21. *n:* Ps 69:9. *o:* 6:30. *p:* Mt 24:2; 26:61; 27:40; Mk 13:2; 14:58; 15:29; Lk 21:6; Acts 6:14. *q:* 5:39; 12:16; 14:26; 20:9; Mt 12:6; Lk 24:6–8; Rev 21:22. *r:* 4:45. *s:* 1 Kgs 8:39; Ps 33:15; 94:11; Sir 42:18; Jer 17:10; 20:12.

## CHAPTER 3

See RG 326–27

***Nicodemus.*** * 1[t] Now there was a Pharisee named Nicodemus, a ruler of the Jews.*
2He came to Jesus at night and said to him,
"Rabbi, we know that you are a teacher who
has come from God, for no one can do these
signs that you are doing unless God is with
him."[u] 3Jesus answered and said to him,
"Amen, amen, I say to you, no one can see the
kingdom of God without being born* from
above." 4Nicodemus said to him, "How can a
person once grown old be born again? Surely
he cannot reenter his mother's womb and be
born again, can he?"[v] 5Jesus answered,
"Amen, amen, I say to you, no one can enter
the kingdom of God without being born of
water and Spirit.[w] 6What is born of flesh is
flesh and what is born of spirit is spirit.[x] 7Do
not be amazed that I told you, 'You must be
born from above.' 8The wind* blows where it
wills, and you can hear the sound it makes,
but you do not know where it comes from or
where it goes; so it is with everyone who is
born of the Spirit."[y] 9Nicodemus answered
and said to him, "How can this happen?"
10Jesus answered and said to him, "You are
the teacher of Israel and you do not understand this? 11Amen, amen, I say to you, we
speak of what we know and we testify to what
we have seen, but you people do not accept
our testimony.[z] 12If I tell you about earthly
things and you do not believe, how will you
believe if I tell you about heavenly things?[a]
13No one has gone up to heaven except the
one who has come down from heaven, the
Son of Man.[b] 14And just as Moses lifted up*
the serpent in the desert, so must the Son of
Man be lifted up,[c] 15* so that everyone who
believes in him may have eternal life."

16For God so loved the world that he gave*
his only Son, so that everyone who believes
in him might not perish but might have eternal life.[d] 17For God did not send his Son into
the world to condemn* the world, but that the
world might be saved through him.[e] 18Who-
ever believes in him will not be condemned,
but whoever does not believe has already
been condemned, because he has not believed
in the name of the only Son of God.[f] 19* And
this is the verdict,[g] that the light came into the
world, but people preferred darkness to light,
because their works were evil. 20For everyone
who does wicked things hates the light and
does not come toward the light, so that his
works might not be exposed.[h] 21But whoever
lives the truth comes to the light, so that his
works may be clearly seen as done in God.[i]

***Final Witness of the Baptist.*** 22* After this,
Jesus and his disciples went into the region of

**3:1–21** Jesus instructs Nicodemus on the necessity of a new birth from above. This scene in Jerusalem at Passover exemplifies the faith engendered by signs (Jn 2:23). It continues the self-manifestation of Jesus in Jerusalem begun in Jn 2. This is the first of the Johannine discourses, shifting from dialogue to monologue (Jn 3:11–15) to reflection of the evangelist (Jn 3:16–21). The shift from singular through Jn 3:10 to plural in Jn 3:11 may reflect the early church's controversy with the Jews.

**3:1 A ruler of the Jews**: most likely a member of the Jewish council, the Sanhedrin; see note on Mk 8:31.

**3:3 Born**: see note on Jn 1:13. **From above**: the Greek adverb *anōthen* means both "from above" and "again." Jesus means "from above" (see Jn 3:31) but Nicodemus misunderstands it as "again." This misunderstanding serves as a springboard for further instruction.

**3:8 Wind**: the Greek word *pneuma* (as well as the Hebrew *rûah*) means both "wind" and "spirit." In the play on the double meaning, "wind" is primary.

**3:14 Lifted up**: in Nm 21:9, Moses simply "mounted" a serpent upon a pole. John here substitutes a verb implying glorification. Jesus, exalted to glory at his cross and resurrection, represents healing for all.

**3:15 Eternal life**: used here for the first time in John, this term stresses quality of life rather than duration.

**3:16 Gave**: as a gift in the incarnation, and also "over to death" in the crucifixion; cf. Rom 8:32.

**3:17–19 Condemn**: the Greek root means both judgment and condemnation. Jesus' purpose is to save, but his coming provokes judgment; some condemn themselves by turning from the light.

**3:19** Judgment is not only future but is partially realized here and now.

**3:22–26** Jesus' ministry in Judea is only loosely connected with Jn 2:13–3:21; cf. Jn 1:19–36. Perhaps John the Baptist's further testimony was transposed here to give meaning to "water" in Jn 3:5. Jesus is depicted as baptizing (Jn 3:22); contrast Jn 4:2.

*t:* 7:50–51; 19:39. *u:* 9:4, 16, 33; 10:21; 11:10; 13:30; Mt 22:16; Mk 12:14; Lk 20:21. *v:* 1:13. *w:* 1:32; 7:39; 19:30, 34–35; Is 32:15; 44:3; Ez 36:25–27; Jl 3:1–2. *x:* 6:63; 1 Cor 15:44–50. *y:* Eccl 11:4–5; Acts 2:2–4. *z:* 3:32, 34; 8:14; Mt 11:27. *a:* 6:62–65; Wis 9:16–17; 1 Cor 15:40; 2 Cor 5:1; Phil 2:10; 3:19–20. *b:* 1:18; 6:62; Dn 7:13; Rom 10:6; Eph 4:9. *c:* 8:28; 12:32, 34; Nm 21:4–9; Wis 16:5–7. *d:* 1 Jn 4:9. *e:* 5:22, 30; 8:15–18; 12:47. *f:* 5:24; Mk 16:16. *g:* 1:5, 9–11; 8:12; 9:5. *h:* Jb 24:13–17. *i:* Gn 47:29 LXX; Jos 2:14 LXX; 2 Sm 2:6 LXX; 15:20 LXX; Tb 4:6 LXX; 13:6; Is 26:10 LXX; Mt 5:14–16.

Judea, where he spent some time with them baptizing.[j] 23 John was also baptizing in Aenon near Salim,* because there was an abundance of water there, and people came to be baptized, 24* [k] for John had not yet been imprisoned. 25 Now a dispute arose between the disciples of John and a Jew* about ceremonial washings. 26 So they came to John and said to him, "Rabbi, the one who was with you across the Jordan, to whom you testified, here he is baptizing and everyone is coming to him."[l] 27 John answered and said, "No one can receive anything except what has been given him from heaven.[m] 28 You yourselves can testify that I said [that] I am not the Messiah, but that I was sent before him.[n] 29 The one who has the bride is the bridegroom; the best man,* who stands and listens to him, rejoices greatly at the bridegroom's voice. So this joy of mine has been made complete.[o] 30 He must increase; I must decrease."[p]

***The One from Heaven.**** 31 The one who comes from above is above all. The one who is of the earth is earthly and speaks of earthly things. But the one who comes from heaven [is above all].[q] 32 He testifies to what he has seen and heard, but no one accepts his testimony.[r] 33 Whoever does accept his testimony certifies that God is trustworthy.[s] 34 For the one whom God sent speaks the words of God. He does not ration his gift* of the Spirit. 35 The Father loves the Son and has given everything over to him.[t] 36 Whoever believes in the Son has eternal life, but whoever disobeys the Son will not see life, but the wrath of God remains upon him.[u]

## CHAPTER 4

See RG 326–27

1* Now when Jesus learned that the Pharisees had heard that Jesus was making and baptizing more disciples than John 2 (although Jesus himself was not baptizing, just his disciples),* 3 he left Judea and returned to Galilee.

***The Samaritan Woman.*** 4 He had to* pass through Samaria. 5 So he came to a town of Samaria called Sychar,* near the plot of land that Jacob had given to his son Joseph.[v] 6 Jacob's well was there. Jesus, tired from his journey, sat down there at the well. It was about noon.

7 A woman of Samaria came to draw water. Jesus said to her, "Give me a drink." 8 His disciples had gone into the town to buy food. 9* The Samaritan woman said to him, "How can you, a Jew, ask me, a Samaritan woman, for a drink?"[w] (For Jews use nothing in common with Samaritans.) 10* Jesus answered and said to her,[x] "If you knew the gift of God and who is saying to you, 'Give me a drink,' you would have asked him and he would have given you living water." 11 [The woman]

**3:23 Aenon near Salim**: site uncertain, either in the upper Jordan valley or in Samaria.

**3:24** A remark probably intended to avoid objections based on a chronology like that of the synoptics (Mt 4:12; Mk 1:14).

**3:25 A Jew**: some think Jesus is meant. Many manuscripts read "Jews."

**3:29 The best man**: literally, "the friend of the groom," the *shoshben* of Jewish tradition, who arranged the wedding. Competition between him and the groom would be unthinkable.

**3:31–36** It is uncertain whether these are words by the Baptist, Jesus, or the evangelist. They are reflections on the two preceding scenes.

**3:34 His gift**: of God or to Jesus, perhaps both. This verse echoes Jn 3:5–8.

**4:1–42** Jesus in Samaria. The self-revelation of Jesus continues with his second discourse, on his mission to "half-Jews." It continues the theme of replacement, here with regard to cult (Jn 4:21). Water (Jn 4:7–15) serves as a symbol (as at Cana and in the Nicodemus episode).

**4:2** An editorial refinement of Jn 3:22, perhaps directed against followers of John the Baptist who claimed that Jesus imitated him.

**4:4 He had to**: a theological necessity; geographically, Jews often bypassed Samaria by taking a route across the Jordan.

**4:5 Sychar**: Jerome identifies this with Shechem, a reading found in Syriac manuscripts.

**4:9** Samaritan women were regarded by Jews as ritually impure, and therefore Jews were forbidden to drink from any vessel they had handled.

**4:10 Living water**: the water of life, i.e., the revelation that Jesus brings; the woman thinks of "flowing water," so much more desirable than stagnant well water. On John's device of such misunderstanding, cf. note on Jn 3:3.

**4:11 Sir**: the Greek *kyrios* means "master" or "lord," as a respectful mode of address for a human being or a deity; cf. Jn 4:19. It is also the word used in the Septuagint for the Hebrew *'adônai*, substituted for the tetragrammaton YHWH.

*j:* 4:1–2. *k:* Mt 4:12; 14:3; Mk 1:14; 6:17; Lk 3:20. *l:* 1:26, 32–34, 36. *m:* 19:11; 1 Cor 4:7; 2 Cor 3:5; Heb 5:4. *n:* 1:20–23; Lk 3:15. *o:* 15:11; 17:13; Mt 9:15. *p:* 2 Sm 3:1. *q:* 8:23. *r:* 3:11. *s:* 8:26; 12:44–50; 1 Jn 5:10. *t:* 13:3; Mt 11:27; 28:18; Lk 10:22. *u:* 3:16; 1 Jn 5:13. *v:* Gn 33:18–19; 48:22; Jos 24:32. *w:* Sir 50:25–26; Mt 10:5. *x:* Sir 24:20–21; Is 55:1; Jer 2:13.

said to him, “Sir,* you do not even have a
bucket and the well is deep; where then can
you get this living water? 12 Are you greater
than our father Jacob, who gave us this well
and drank from it himself with his children
and his flocks?”[y] 13 Jesus answered and said
to her, “Everyone who drinks this water will
be thirsty again; 14 but whoever drinks the
water I shall give will never thirst; the water
I shall give will become in him a spring of
water welling up to eternal life.”[z] 15 The
woman said to him, “Sir, give me this water,
so that I may not be thirsty or have to keep
coming here to draw water.”

16 Jesus said to her, “Go call your husband
and come back.” 17 The woman answered
and said to him, “I do not have a husband.”
Jesus answered her, “You are right in saying,
‘I do not have a husband.’ 18 For you have
had five husbands, and the one you have
now is not your husband. What you have
said is true.”[a] 19 The woman said to him, “Sir,
I can see that you are a prophet.[b] 20 Our ancestors worshiped on this mountain;* but
you people say that the place to worship is in
Jerusalem.”[c] 21 Jesus said to her, “Believe
me, woman, the hour is coming when you
will worship the Father neither on this
mountain nor in Jerusalem. 22 You people
worship what you do not understand; we
worship what we understand, because salvation is from the Jews.[d] 23 But the hour is coming, and is now here, when true worshipers
will worship the Father in Spirit and truth;*
and indeed the Father seeks such people to
worship him. 24 God is Spirit, and those who
worship him must worship in Spirit and
truth.”[e] 25* The woman said to him, “I know
that the Messiah is coming,[f] the one called
the Anointed; when he comes, he will tell us
everything.” 26 Jesus said to her, “I am he,*
the one who is speaking with you.”[g]

27 At that moment his disciples returned,
and were amazed that he was talking with a
woman,* but still no one said, “What are you
looking for?” or “Why are you talking with
her?” 28 The woman left her water jar and
went into the town and said to the people,
29 “Come see a man who told me everything
I have done. Could he possibly be the Messiah?” 30 They went out of the town and came
to him. 31 Meanwhile, the disciples urged
him, “Rabbi, eat.” 32 But he said to them, “I
have food to eat of which you do not know.”
33 So the disciples said to one another,
“Could someone have brought him something to eat?” 34 Jesus said to them, “My food
is to do the will of the one who sent me and
to finish his work.[h] 35 Do you not say, ‘In four
months* the harvest will be here’? I tell you,
look up and see the fields ripe for the harvest.[i] 36 The reaper is already* receiving his
payment and gathering crops for eternal life,
so that the sower and reaper can rejoice together.[j] 37 For here the saying is verified that
‘One sows and another reaps.’[k] 38 I sent you
to reap what you have not worked for; others
have done the work, and you are sharing the
fruits of their work.”

39 Many of the Samaritans of that town began to believe in him because of the word of
the woman* who testified, “He told me everything I have done.” 40 When the Samaritans
came to him, they invited him to stay with
them; and he stayed there two days. 41 Many
more began to believe in him because of his

**4:20 This mountain**: Gerizim, on which a temple was erected in the fourth century B.C. by Samaritans to rival Mount Zion in Jerusalem; cf. Dt 27:4 (Mount Ebal = the Jews' term for Gerizim).

**4:23 In Spirit and truth**: not a reference to an interior worship within one's own spirit. The Spirit is the spirit given by God that reveals truth and enables one to worship God appropriately (Jn 14:16–17). Cf. “born of water and Spirit” (Jn 3:5).

**4:25** The expectations of the Samaritans are expressed here in Jewish terminology. They did not expect a messianic king of the house of David but a prophet like Moses (Dt 18:15).

**4:26 I am he**: it could also be translated “I am,” an Old Testament self-designation of Yahweh (Is 43:3, etc.); cf. Jn 6:20; 8:24, 28, 58; 13:19; 18:5–6, 8. See note on Mk 6:50.

**4:27 Talking with a woman**: a religious and social restriction that Jesus is pictured treating as unimportant.

**4:35 ‘In four months . . . ’**: probably a proverb; cf. Mt 9:37–38.

**4:36 Already**: this word may go with the preceding verse rather than with Jn 4:36.

**4:39** The woman is presented as a missionary, described in virtually the same words as the disciples are in Jesus' prayer (Jn 17:20).

*y:* 8:53; Mt 12:41. *z:* 6:35, 58; 7:37–39; Is 44:3; 49:10; Jl 4:18; Rev 7:16; 21:6. *a:* 2 Kgs 17:24–34. *b:* 9:17; Hos 1:3. *c:* Dt 11:29; 27:4; Jos 8:33; Ps 122:1–5. *d:* 2 Kgs 17:27; Ps 76:2–3. *e:* 2 Cor 3:17. *f:* 1:41. *g:* 9:37. *h:* 5:30, 36; 6:38; 9:4; 17:4. *i:* Mt 9:37–38; Lk 10:2; Rev 14:15. *j:* Ps 126:5–6; Am 9:13–14. *k:* Dt 20:6; 28:30; Jb 31:8; Mi 6:15.

word, 42 and they said to the woman, "We no longer believe because of your word; for we have heard for ourselves, and we know that this is truly the savior of the world."[l]

***Return to Galilee.*** 43* After the two days, he left there for Galilee. 44* [m] For Jesus himself testified that a prophet has no honor in his native place. 45 When he came into Galilee, the Galileans welcomed him, since they had seen all he had done in Jerusalem at the feast; for they themselves had gone to the feast.

***Second Sign at Cana.**** 46[n] Then he returned to Cana in Galilee, where he had made the water wine. Now there was a royal official whose son was ill in Capernaum. 47 When he heard that Jesus had arrived in Galilee from Judea, he went to him and asked him to come down and heal his son, who was near death. 48 Jesus said to him, "Unless you people see signs and wonders, you will not believe."[o] 49 The royal official said to him, "Sir, come down before my child dies." 50 Jesus said to him, "You may go; your son will live." The man believed what Jesus said to him and left.[p] 51 While he was on his way back, his slaves met him and told him that his boy would live. 52 He asked them when he began to recover. They told him, "The fever left him yesterday, about one in the afternoon." 53 The father realized that just at that time Jesus had said to him, "Your son will live," and he and his whole household came to believe. 54 [Now] this was the second sign Jesus did when he came to Galilee from Judea.[q]

## CHAPTER 5*

See RG 327

***Cure on a Sabbath.*** 1 After this, there was a feast* of the Jews, and Jesus went up to Jerusalem.[r] 2 Now there is in Jerusalem at the Sheep [Gate]* a pool called in Hebrew Bethesda, with five porticoes.[s] 3 In these lay a large number of ill, blind, lame, and crippled.* [4]* 5 One man was there who had been ill for thirty-eight years. 6 When Jesus saw him lying there and knew that he had been ill for a long time, he said to him, "Do you want to be well?" 7 The sick man answered him, "Sir, I have no one to put me into the pool when the water is stirred up; while I am on my way, someone else gets down there before me." 8 Jesus said to him, "Rise, take up your mat, and walk."[t] 9 Immediately the man became well, took up his mat, and walked.[u]

Now that day was a sabbath. 10 So the Jews said to the man who was cured, "It is the sabbath, and it is not lawful for you to carry your mat."[v] 11 He answered them, "The

**4:43–54** Jesus' arrival in Cana in Galilee; the second sign. This section introduces another theme, that of the life-giving word of Jesus. It is explicitly linked to the first sign (Jn 2:11). The royal official believes (Jn 4:50). The natural life given his son is a sign of eternal life.

**4:44** Probably a reminiscence of a tradition as in Mk 6:4. Cf. Gospel of Thomas 31: "No prophet is acceptable in his village, no physician heals those who know him."

**4:46–54** The story of the cure of the royal official's son may be a third version of the cure of the centurion's son (Mt 8:5–13) or servant (Lk 7:1–10). Cf. also Mt 15:21–28; Mk 7:24–30.

**5:1–47** The self-revelation of Jesus continues in Jerusalem at a feast. The third sign (cf. Jn 2:11; 4:54) is performed, the cure of a paralytic by Jesus' life-giving word. The water of the pool fails to bring life; Jesus' word does.

**5:1** The reference in Jn 5:45–46 to Moses suggests that the feast was Pentecost. The connection of that feast with the giving of the law to Moses on Sinai, attested in later Judaism, may already have been made in the first century. The feast could also be Passover (cf. Jn 6:4). John stresses that the day was a sabbath (Jn 5:9).

**5:2** There is no noun with **Sheep**. "Gate" is supplied on the grounds that there must have been a gate in the NE wall of the temple area where animals for sacrifice were brought in; cf. Neh 3:1, 32; 12:39. **Hebrew**: more precisely, Aramaic. **Bethesda**: preferred to variants "Be(th)zatha" and "Bethsaida"; *bêt-eˆsdatayin* is given as the name of a double pool northeast of the temple area in the Qumran Copper Roll. **Five porticoes**: a pool excavated in Jerusalem actually has five porticoes.

**5:3** The Caesarean and Western recensions, followed by the Vulgate, add "waiting for the movement of the water." Apparently an intermittent spring in the pool bubbled up occasionally (see Jn 5:7). This turbulence was believed to cure.

**5:4** Toward the end of the second century in the West and among the fourth-century Greek Fathers, an additional verse was known: "For [from time to time] an angel of the Lord used to come down into the pool; and the water was stirred up, so the first one to get in [after the stirring of the water] was healed of whatever disease afflicted him." The angel was a popular explanation of the turbulence and the healing powers attributed to it. This verse is missing from all early Greek

*l:* 1 Jn 4:14. *m:* Mt 13:57; Mk 6:4; Lk 4:24. *n:* 2:1–11; Mt 8:5–13; 15:21–28; Mk 7:24–30; Lk 7:1–10. *o:* 2:18, 23; Wis 8:8; Mt 12:38; 1 Cor 1:22. *p:* 1 Kgs 17:23. *q:* 2:11. *r:* 6:4. *s:* Neh 3:1, 32; 12:39. *t:* Mt 9:6; Mk 2:11; Lk 5:24; Acts 3:6. *u:* Mk 2:12; Lk 5:25; 9:14. *v:* Ex 20:8; Jer 17:21–27; Mk 3:2; Lk 13:10 / 14:1.

man who made me well told me, 'Take up your mat and walk.' " 12They asked him, "Who is the man who told you, 'Take it up and walk'?" 13The man who was healed did not know who it was, for Jesus had slipped away, since there was a crowd there.[w] 14* After this Jesus found him in the temple area and said to him,[x] "Look, you are well; do not sin any more, so that nothing worse may happen to you." 15The man went and told the Jews that Jesus was the one who had made him well. 16Therefore, the Jews began to persecute Jesus because he did this on a sabbath.[y] 17* But Jesus answered them,[z] "My Father is at work until now, so I am at work." 18For this reason the Jews tried all the more to kill him, because he not only broke the sabbath but he also called God his own father, making himself equal to God.[a]

***The Work of the Son.*** 19* Jesus answered and said to them, "Amen, amen, I say to you, a son cannot do anything on his own, but only what he sees his father doing;[b] for what he does, his son will do also. 20For the Father loves his Son and shows him everything that he himself does, and he will show him greater works than these, so that you may be amazed.[c] 21For just as the Father raises the dead and gives life,* so also does the Son give life to whomever he wishes.[d] 22Nor does the Father judge anyone, but he has given all judgment* to his Son,[e] 23so that all may honor the Son just as they honor the Father. Whoever does not honor the Son does not honor the Father who sent him. 24Amen, amen, I say to you, whoever hears my word and believes in the one who sent me has eternal life and will not come to condemnation, but has passed from death to life.[f] 25Amen, amen, I say to you, the hour is coming and is now here when the dead will hear the voice of the Son of God, and those who hear will live.[g] 26For just as the Father has life in himself, so also he gave to his Son the possession of life in himself.[h] 27And he gave him power to exercise judgment, because he is the Son of Man.[i] 28* Do not be amazed at this, because the hour is coming in which all who are in the tombs will hear his voice[j] 29and will come out, those who have done good deeds to the resurrection of life, but those who have done wicked deeds to the resurrection of condemnation.[k]

30"I cannot do anything on my own; I judge as I hear, and my judgment is just, because I do not seek my own will but the will of the one who sent me.[l]

***Witnesses to Jesus.*** 31[m] "If I testify on my own behalf, my testimony cannot be verified. 32But there is another* who testifies on my behalf, and I know that the testimony he gives on my behalf is true. 33You sent emissaries to John, and he testified to the truth.[n] 34I do not accept testimony from a human being, but I say this so that you may be saved.[o] 35He was a burning and

manuscripts and the earliest versions, including the original Vulgate. Its vocabulary is markedly non-Johannine.

**5:14** While the cure of the paralytic in Mk 2:1–12 is associated with the forgiveness of sins, Jesus never drew a one-to-one connection between sin and suffering (cf. Jn 9:3; Lk 12:1–5), as did Ez 18:20.

**5:17** Sabbath observance (5:10) was based on God's resting on the seventh day (cf. Gn 2:2–3; Ex 20:11). Philo and some rabbis insisted that God's providence remains active on the sabbath, keeping all things in existence, giving life in birth and taking it away in death. Other rabbis taught that God rested from creating, but not from judging (=ruling, governing). Jesus here claims the same authority to work as the Father, and, in the discourse that follows, the same divine prerogatives: power over life and death (Jn 5:21, 24–26) and judgment (Jn 5:22, 27).

**5:19** This proverb or parable is taken from apprenticeship in a trade: the activity of a son is modeled on that of his father. Jesus' dependence on the Father is justification for doing what the Father does.

**5:21 Gives life**: in the Old Testament, a divine prerogative (Dt 32:39; 1 Sm 2:6; 2 Kgs 5:7; Tb 13:2; Is 26:19; Dn 12:2).

**5:22 Judgment**: another divine prerogative, often expressed as acquittal or condemnation (Dt 32:36; Ps 43:1).

**5:28–29** While Jn 5:19–27 present realized eschatology, Jn 5:28–29 are future eschatology; cf. Dn 12:2.

**5:32 Another**: likely the Father, who in four different ways gives testimony to Jesus, as indicated in the verse groupings Jn 5:33–34, 36, 37–38, 39–40.

*w:* Mt 8:18; 13:36; Mk 4:36; 7:17. *x:* 8:11; 9:2; Ez 18:20. *y:* 7:23; Mt 12:8. *z:* Ex 20:11. *a:* 7:1, 25; 8:37, 40; 10:33, 36; 14:28; Gn 3:5–6; Wis 2:16; Mt 26:4; 2 Thes 2:4. *b:* 3:34; 8:26; 12:49; 9:4; 10:30. *c:* 3:35. *d:* 11:25; Dt 32:39; 1 Sm 2:6; 2 Kgs 5:7; Tb 13:2; Wis 16:13; Is 26:19; Dn 7:10, 13; 12:2; Rom 4:17; 2 Cor 1:9. *e:* Acts 10:42; 17:31. *f:* 3:18; 8:51; 1 Jn 3:14. *g:* 5:28; 8:51; 11:25–26; Eph 2:1; 5:14; Rev 3:1. *h:* 1:4; 1 Jn 5:11. *i:* 5:22; Dn 7:13, 22; Mt 25:31; Lk 21:36. *j:* 11:43. *k:* Dn 12:2; Mt 16:27; 25:46; Acts 24:15; 2 Cor 5:10. *l:* 6:38. *m:* 8:13–14, 18. *n:* 1:19–27; Mt 11:10–11. *o:* 1 Jn 5:9.

shining lamp,* and for a while you were content to rejoice in his light.[p] 36But I have testimony greater than John's. The works that the Father gave me to accomplish, these works that I perform testify on my behalf that the Father has sent me.[q] 37Moreover, the Father who sent me has testified on my behalf. But you have never heard his voice nor seen his form,[r] 38and you do not have his word remaining in you, because you do not believe in the one whom he has sent.[s] 39You search* the scriptures, because you think you have eternal life through them; even they testify on my behalf.[t] 40But you do not want to come to me to have life.

***Unbelief of Jesus' Hearers.*** 41"I do not accept human praise;* 42moreover, I know that you do not have the love of God in you.[u] 43I came in the name of my Father, but you do not accept me; yet if another comes in his own name, you will accept him.[v] 44How can you believe, when you accept praise from one another and do not seek the praise that comes from the only God?[w] 45Do not think that I will accuse you before the Father: the one who will accuse you is Moses, in whom you have placed your hope.[x] 46For if you had believed Moses, you would have believed me, because he wrote about me.[y] 47But if you do not believe his writings, how will you believe my words?"

## CHAPTER 6

See RG 327-28

***Multiplication of the Loaves.**** 1[z] After this, Jesus went across the Sea of Galilee [of Tiberias].* 2A large crowd followed him, because they saw the signs he was performing on the sick. 3Jesus went up on the mountain, and there he sat down with his disciples. 4The Jewish feast of Passover was near.[a] 5* When Jesus raised his eyes and saw that a large crowd was coming to him, he said to Philip,[b] "Where can we buy enough food for them to eat?" 6* He said this to test him, because he himself knew what he was going to do. 7Philip answered him, "Two hundred days' wages* worth of food would not be enough for each of them to have a little [bit]."[c] 8One of his disciples, Andrew, the brother of Simon Peter, said to him, 9"There is a boy here who has five barley loaves* and two fish; but what good are these for so many?"[d] 10Jesus said, "Have the people recline." Now there was a great deal of grass* in that place. So the men reclined, about five thousand in number.[e] 11Then Jesus took the loaves, gave thanks, and distributed them to those who were reclining, and also as much of the fish as they wanted.[f] 12When they had had their fill, he said to his disciples, "Gather the fragments left over, so that nothing will be wasted." 13So they collected them, and filled twelve wicker baskets* with fragments from the five barley loaves that

**5:35 Lamp**: cf. Ps 132:17—"I will place a lamp for my anointed (= David)," and possibly the description of Elijah in Sir 48:1. But only **for a while**, indicating the temporary and subordinate nature of John's mission.

**5:39 You search**: this may be an imperative: "Search the scriptures, because you think that you have eternal life through them."

**5:41 Praise**: the same Greek word means "praise" or "honor" (from others) and "glory" (from God). There is a play on this in Jn 5:44.

**6:1–15** This story of the multiplication of the loaves is the fourth sign (cf. note on Jn 5:1–47). It is the only miracle story found in all four gospels (occurring twice in Mark and Matthew). See notes on Mt 14:13–21; 15:32–39. John differs on the roles of Philip and Andrew, the proximity of Passover (Jn 6:4), and the allusion to Elisha (see Jn 6:9). The story here symbolizes the food that is really available through Jesus. It connotes a new exodus and has eucharistic overtones.

**6:1 [Of Tiberias]**: the awkward apposition represents a later name of the Sea of Galilee. It was probably originally a marginal gloss.

**6:5** Jesus takes the initiative (in the synoptics, the disciples do), possibly pictured as (cf. Jn 6:14) the new Moses (cf. Nm 11:13).

**6:6** Probably the evangelist's comment; in this gospel Jesus is never portrayed as ignorant of anything.

**6:7 Days' wages**: literally, "denarii"; a Roman denarius is a day's wage in Mt 20:2.

**6:9 Barley loaves**: the food of the poor. There seems an allusion to the story of Elisha multiplying the barley bread in 2 Kgs 4:42–44.

**6:10 Grass**: implies springtime, and therefore Passover. **Five thousand**: so Mk 6:39, 44 and parallels.

**6:13 Baskets**: the word describes the typically Palestinian wicker basket, as in Mk 6:43 and parallels.

*p:* 1:8; Ps 132:17; Sir 48:1. *q:* 10:25. *r:* 8:18; Dt 4:12, 15; 1 Jn 5:9. *s:* 1 Jn 2:14. *t:* 12:16; 19:28; 20:9; Lk 24:27, 44; 1 Pt 1:10. *u:* 1 Jn 2:15. *v:* Mt 24:5, 24. *w:* 12:43. *x:* Dt 31:26. *y:* 5:39; Dt 18:15; Lk 16:31; 24:44. *z:* Mt 14:13–21; Mk 6:32–44; Lk 9:10–17. *a:* 2:13; 11:55. *b:* Nm 11:13. *c:* Mt 20:2. *d:* 2 Kgs 4:42–44. *e:* Mt 14:21; Mk 6:44. *f:* 21:13.

had been more than they could eat. 14When
the people saw the sign he had done, they
said, "This is truly the Prophet,* the one who
is to come into the world."[g] 15Since Jesus
knew that they were going to come and carry
him off to make him king, he withdrew
again to the mountain alone.[h]

*Walking on the Water.* * 16[i] When it was
evening, his disciples went down to the sea,
17embarked in a boat, and went across the
sea to Capernaum. It had already grown
dark, and Jesus had not yet come to them.
18The sea was stirred up because a strong
wind was blowing. 19When they had rowed
about three or four miles, they saw Jesus
walking on the sea* and coming near the
boat, and they began to be afraid.[j] 20But he
said to them, "It is I.* Do not be afraid."
21They wanted to take him into the boat, but
the boat immediately arrived at the shore to
which they were heading.

*The Bread of Life Discourse.* 22* The next
day, the crowd that remained across the sea
saw that there had been only one boat there,
and that Jesus had not gone along with his
disciples in the boat, but only his disciples
had left. 23* Other boats came from Tiberias
near the place where they had eaten the bread
when the Lord gave thanks. 24When the
crowd saw that neither Jesus nor his disciples
were there, they themselves got into boats
and came to Capernaum looking for Jesus.
25And when they found him across the sea
they said to him, "Rabbi, when did you get
here?" 26Jesus answered them and said,
"Amen, amen, I say to you, you are looking
for me not because you saw signs but because
you ate the loaves and were filled. 27Do not
work for food that perishes but for the food
that endures for eternal life,* which the Son of
Man will give you. For on him the Father,
God, has set his seal."[k] 28So they said to him,
"What can we do to accomplish the works of
God?" 29Jesus answered and said to them,
"This is the work of God, that you believe in
the one he sent." 30So they said to him, "What
sign can you do, that we may see and believe
in you? What can you do?[l] 31* Our ancestors
ate manna in the desert, as it is written:[m]

'He gave them bread from heaven to eat.' "

32So Jesus said to them, "Amen, amen, I say
to you, it was not Moses who gave the bread
from heaven; my Father gives you the true
bread from heaven.[n] 33For the bread of God
is that which comes down from heaven and
gives life to the world."

34[o] So they said to him, "Sir, give us this
bread always." 35* Jesus said to them, "I am
the bread of life; whoever comes to me will
never hunger, and whoever believes in me
will never thirst.[p] 36But I told you that although you have seen [me], you do not believe.[q] 37Everything that the Father gives me
will come to me, and I will not reject anyone
who comes to me, 38because I came down
from heaven not to do my own will but the
will of the one who sent me.[r] 39And this is the
will of the one who sent me, that I should not
lose anything of what he gave me, but that I

**6:14 The Prophet**: probably the prophet like Moses (see note on Jn 1:21). **The one who is to come into the world**: probably Elijah; cf. Mal 3:1; 4:5.

**6:16–21** The fifth sign is a nature miracle, portraying Jesus sharing Yahweh's power. Cf. the parallel stories following the multiplication of the loaves in Mk 6:45–52 and Mt 14:22–33.

**6:19 Walking on the sea**: although the Greek (cf. Jn 6:16) could mean "on the seashore" or "by the sea" (cf. Jn 21:1), the parallels, especially Mt 14:25, make clear that Jesus walked upon the water. John may allude to Jb 9:8: God "treads upon the crests of the sea."

**6:20 It is I**: literally, "I am." See also notes on Jn 4:26 and Mk 6:50.

**6:22–71** Discourse on the bread of life; replacement of the manna. Jn 6:22–34 serve as an introduction, Jn 6:35–59 constitute the discourse proper, Jn 6:60–71 portray the reaction of the disciples and Peter's confession.

**6:23** Possibly a later interpolation, to explain how the crowd got to Capernaum.

**6:27 The food that endures for eternal life**: cf. Jn 4:14, on water "springing up to eternal life."

**6:31 Bread from heaven**: cf. Ex 16:4, 15, 32–34 and the notes there; Ps 78:24. The manna, thought to have been hidden by Jeremiah (2 Mc 2:5–8), was expected to reappear miraculously at Passover, in the last days.

**6:35–59** Up to Jn 6:50 "bread of life" is a figure for God's revelation in Jesus; in Jn 6:51–58, the eucharistic theme comes to the fore. There may thus be a break between Jn 6:50–51.

*g:* Dt 18:15, 18; Mal 3:1, 23; Acts 3:22. *h:* 18:36. *i:* Mt 14:22–27; Mk 6:45–52. *j:* Jb 9:8; Ps 29:3–4; 77:20; Is 43:16. *k:* 6:50, 51, 54, 58. *l:* Mt 16:1–4; Lk 11:29–30. *m:* Ex 16:4–5; Nm 11:7–9; Ps 78:24. *n:* Mt 6:11. *o:* 4:15. *p:* Is 55:1–3; Am 8:11–13. *q:* 20:29. *r:* 4:34; Mt 26:39; Heb 10:9.

should raise it [on] the last day.[s] 40 For this is
the will of my Father, that everyone who sees
the Son and believes in him may have eternal
life, and I shall raise him [on] the last day."[t]
41 The Jews murmured about him because
he said, "I am the bread that came down
from heaven," 42 and they said, "Is this not
Jesus, the son of Joseph? Do we not know
his father and mother? Then how can he say,
'I have come down from heaven'?"[u] 43 Jesus
answered and said to them, "Stop murmuring* among yourselves.[v] 44 No one can come
to me unless the Father who sent me draw
him, and I will raise him on the last day. 45 It
is written in the prophets:

'They shall all be taught by God.'

Everyone who listens to my Father and
learns from him comes to me.[w] 46 Not that
anyone has seen the Father except the one
who is from God; he has seen the Father.[x]
47 Amen, amen, I say to you, whoever believes has eternal life. 48 I am the bread of life.
49 Your ancestors ate the manna in the desert,
but they died;[y] 50 this is the bread that comes
down from heaven so that one may eat it and
not die. 51 I am the living bread that came
down from heaven; whoever eats this bread
will live forever; and the bread that I will
give is my flesh for the life of the world."[z]
52 The Jews quarreled among themselves,
saying, "How can this man give us [his]
flesh to eat?" 53 Jesus said to them, "Amen,
amen, I say to you, unless you eat the flesh
of the Son of Man and drink his blood, you
do not have life within you. 54 Whoever eats*
my flesh and drinks my blood has eternal
life, and I will raise him on the last day. 55 For
my flesh is true food, and my blood is true
drink. 56 Whoever eats my flesh and drinks
my blood remains in me and I in him. 57 Just
as the living Father sent me and I have life
because of the Father, so also the one who
feeds on me will have life because of me.[a]
58 This is the bread that came down from
heaven. Unlike your ancestors who ate and
still died, whoever eats this bread will live
forever." 59 These things he said while teaching in the synagogue in Capernaum.

***The Words of Eternal Life.**** 60 Then many
of his disciples who were listening said,
"This saying is hard; who can accept it?"
61 Since Jesus knew that his disciples were
murmuring about this, he said to them,
"Does this shock you? 62 What if you were to
see the Son of Man ascending to where he
was before?* 63 It is the spirit that gives life,
while the flesh* is of no avail. The words I
have spoken to you are spirit and life. 64 But
there are some of you who do not believe."
Jesus knew from the beginning the ones who
would not believe and the one who would
betray him.[b] 65 And he said, "For this reason
I have told you that no one can come to me
unless it is granted him by my Father."
66 As a result of this, many [of] his disciples returned to their former way of life and
no longer accompanied him. 67 Jesus then
said to the Twelve, "Do you also want to
leave?" 68 Simon Peter answered him, "Master, to whom shall we go? You have the
words of eternal life. 69 We have come to believe and are convinced that you are the
Holy One of God."[c] 70 Jesus answered them,
"Did I not choose you twelve? Yet is not one
of you a devil?" 71 He was referring to Judas,
son of Simon the Iscariot; it was he who
would betray him, one of the Twelve.[d]

**6:43 Murmuring**: the word may reflect the Greek of Ex 16:2, 7–8.

**6:54–58 Eats**: the verb used in these verses is not the classical Greek verb used of human eating, but that of animal eating: "munch," "gnaw." This may be part of John's emphasis on the reality of the flesh and blood of Jesus (cf. Jn 6:55), but the same verb eventually became the ordinary verb in Greek meaning "eat."

**6:60–71** These verses refer more to themes of Jn 6:35–50 than to those of Jn 6:51–58 and seem to be addressed to members of the Johannine community who found it difficult to accept the high christology reflected in the bread of life discourse.

**6:62** This unfinished conditional sentence is obscure. Probably there is a reference to Jn 6:49–51. Jesus claims to be **the bread that comes down from heaven** (Jn 6:50); this claim provokes incredulity (Jn 6:60); and so Jesus is pictured as asking what his disciples will say when he goes up to heaven.

**6:63 Spirit . . . flesh**: probably not a reference to the eucharistic body of Jesus but to the supernatural and the natural, as in Jn 3:6. **Spirit and life**: all Jesus said about the bread of life is the revelation of the Spirit.

*s:* 10:28–29; 17:12; 18:9. *t:* 1 Jn 2:25. *u:* Mt 13:54–57; Mk 6:1–4; Lk 4:22. *v:* Ex 16:2, 7, 8; Lk 4:22. *w:* Is 54:13; Jer 31:33–34. *x:* 1:18; 7:29; Ex 33:20. *y:* 1 Cor 10:3, 5. *z:* Mt 26:26–27; Lk 22:19. *a:* 5:26. *b:* 13:11. *c:* 11:27; Mt 16:16; Mk 1:24; Lk 4:34. *d:* 12:4; 13:2, 27.

## CHAPTER 7

See RG 328–29

*The Feast of Tabernacles.* 1* After
this, Jesus moved about within Galilee; but
he did not wish to travel in Judea, because
the Jews were trying to kill him.[e] 2 But the
Jewish feast of Tabernacles was near.[f] 3 So
his brothers* said to him, "Leave here and go
to Judea, so that your disciples also may see
the works you are doing. 4 No one works in
secret if he wants to be known publicly. If
you do these things, manifest yourself to the
world."[g] 5 For his brothers did not believe in
him. 6* So Jesus said to them, "My time is
not yet here, but the time is always right for
you. 7 The world cannot hate you, but it hates
me, because I testify to it that its works are
evil.[h] 8 You go up to the feast. I am not going
up* to this feast, because my time has not yet
been fulfilled." 9 After he had said this, he
stayed on in Galilee.

10 But when his brothers had gone up to the
feast, he himself also went up, not openly but
[as it were] in secret. 11 The Jews were looking for him at the feast and saying, "Where is
he?" 12 And there was considerable murmuring about him in the crowds. Some said, "He
is a good man," [while] others said, "No; on
the contrary, he misleads the crowd." 13 Still,
no one spoke openly about him because they
were afraid of the Jews.[i]

*The First Dialogue.** 14 When the feast
was already half over, Jesus went up into
the temple area and began to teach. 15*[j] The
Jews were amazed and said, "How does he
know scripture without having studied?"
16 Jesus answered them and said, "My
teaching is not my own but is from the one
who sent me. 17 Whoever chooses to do his
will* shall know whether my teaching is
from God or whether I speak on my own.[k]
18 Whoever speaks on his own seeks his
own glory, but whoever seeks the glory of
the one who sent him is truthful, and there
is no wrong in him. 19 Did not Moses give
you the law? Yet none of you keeps the law.
Why are you trying to kill me?"[l] 20 The
crowd answered, "You are possessed!*
Who is trying to kill you?"[m] 21 Jesus answered and said to them, "I performed one
work* and all of you are amazed[n] 22 because
of it. Moses gave you circumcision—not
that it came from Moses but rather from the
patriarchs—and you circumcise a man on
the sabbath.[o] 23 If a man can receive circumcision on a sabbath so that the law of Moses may not be broken, are you angry with
me because I made a whole person well on
a sabbath?[p] 24 Stop judging by appearances,
but judge justly."[q]

25 So some of the inhabitants of Jerusalem
said, "Is he not the one they are trying to

**[7–8]** These chapters contain events about the feast of Tabernacles (Sukkoth, Ingathering: Ex 23:16; Tents, Booths: Dt 16:13–16), with its symbols of booths (originally built to shelter harvesters), rain (water from Siloam poured on the temple altar), and lights (illumination of the four torches in the Court of the Women). They continue the theme of the replacement of feasts (Passover, Jn 2:13; 6:4; Hanukkah, Jn 10:22; Pentecost, Jn 5:1), here accomplished by Jesus as the Living Water. These chapters comprise seven miscellaneous controversies and dialogues. There is a literary inclusion with Jesus in hiding in Jn 7:4, 10; 8:59. There are frequent references to attempts on his life: Jn 7:1, 13, 19, 25, 30, 32, 44; 8:37, 40, 59.

**7:3 Brothers**: these relatives (cf. Jn 2:12 and see note on Mk 6:3) are never portrayed as disciples until after the resurrection (Acts 1:14). Mt 13:55 and Mk 6:3 give the names of four of them. Jesus has already performed works/signs in Judea; cf. Jn 2:23; 3:2; 4:45; 5:8.

**7:6 Time**: the Greek word means "opportune time," here a synonym for Jesus' "hour" (see note on Jn 2:4), his death and resurrection. In the wordplay, any time is suitable for Jesus' brothers, because they are not dependent on God's will.

**7:8 I am not going up**: an early attested reading "not yet" seems a correction, since Jesus in the story does go up to the feast. "Go up," in a play on words, refers not only to going up to Jerusalem but also to exaltation at the cross, resurrection, and ascension; cf. Jn 3:14; 6:62; 20:17.

**7:14–31** Jesus teaches in the temple; debate with the Jews.

**7:15 Without having studied**: literally, "How does he know letters without having learned?" Children were taught to read and write by means of the scriptures. But here more than Jesus' literacy is being discussed; the people are wondering how he can teach like a rabbi. Rabbis were trained by other rabbis and traditionally quoted their teachers.

**7:17 To do his will**: presumably a reference back to the "work" of Jn 6:29: belief in the one whom God has sent.

**7:20 You are possessed**: literally, "You have a demon." The insane were thought to be possessed by a demoniacal spirit.

**7:21 One work**: the cure of the paralytic (Jn 5:1–9) because of the reference to the sabbath (Jn 7:22; 5:9–10).

*e:* 5:18; 8:37, 40. *f:* Ex 23:16; Lv 23:34; Nm 29:12; Dt 16:13–16; Zec 14:16–19. *g:* 14:22. *h:* 15:18. *i:* 9:22; 19:38; 20:19. *j:* Lk 2:47. *k:* 6:29. *l:* Acts 7:53. *m:* 8:48–49; 10:20. *n:* 5:1–9. *o:* Gn 17:10; Lv 12:3. *p:* 5:2–9, 16; Mt 12:11–12; Lk 14:5. *q:* 8:15; Lv 19:15; Is 11:3–4.

kill? [26]And look, he is speaking openly and
they say nothing to him. Could the authorities* have realized that he is the Messiah?
[27]But we know where he is from. When the
Messiah comes, no one will know where he
is from."[r] [28]So Jesus cried out in the temple
area as he was teaching and said, "You
know me and also know where I am from.
Yet I did not come on my own, but the one
who sent me, whom you do not know, is
true.[s] [29]I know him, because I am from him,
and he sent me."[t] [30]So they tried to arrest
him, but no one laid a hand upon him, because his hour had not yet come.[u] [31]But
many of the crowd began to believe in him,
and said, "When the Messiah comes, will he
perform more signs than this man has
done?"[v]

*Officers Sent to Arrest Jesus.** [32]The Pharisees heard the crowd murmuring about him
to this effect, and the chief priests and the
Pharisees sent guards to arrest him. [33]So
Jesus said, "I will be with you only a little
while longer, and then I will go to the one
who sent me.[w] [34]You will look for me but not
find [me], and where I am you cannot
come."[x] [35]So the Jews said to one another,
"Where is he going that we will not find
him? Surely he is not going to the dispersion* among the Greeks to teach the Greeks,
is he? [36]What is the meaning of his saying,
'You will look for me and not find [me], and
where I am you cannot come'?"

*Rivers of Living Water.** [37]On the last and
greatest day of the feast, Jesus stood up and
exclaimed, "Let anyone who thirsts come to
me and drink.[y] [38]Whoever believes in me, as
scripture says:

'Rivers of living water* will flow from
within him.' "[z]

[39]He said this in reference to the Spirit that
those who came to believe in him were to receive. There was, of course, no Spirit yet,*
because Jesus had not yet been glorified.[a]

***Discussion about the Origins of the Mes-
siah.**** [40]Some in the crowd who heard these
words said, "This is truly the Prophet."[b] [41]Oth-
ers said, "This is the Messiah." But others
said, "The Messiah will not come from Galilee, will he? [42]Does not scripture say that the
Messiah will be of David's family and come
from Bethlehem, the village where David
lived?"[c] [43]So a division occurred in the crowd
because of him. [44]Some of them even wanted
to arrest him, but no one laid hands on him.

[45]So the guards went to the chief priests
and Pharisees, who asked them, "Why did
you not bring him?" [46]The guards answered,
"Never before has anyone spoken like this
one." [47]So the Pharisees answered them,
"Have you also been deceived? [48]Have any
of the authorities or the Pharisees believed in
him?[d] [49]But this crowd, which does not
know the law, is accursed." [50]Nicodemus,
one of their members who had come to him
earlier, said to them,[e] [51]"Does our law condemn a person before it first hears him and
finds out what he is doing?"[f] [52]They answered and said to him, "You are not from
Galilee also, are you? Look and see that no
prophet arises from Galilee."

## CHAPTER 8

See RG 328–29

***A Woman Caught in Adultery.**** 
[[7:53]Then each went to his own house,

**7:26 The authorities**: the members of the Sanhedrin (same term as Jn 3:1).

**7:32–36** Jesus announces his approaching departure (cf. also Jn 8:21; 12:36; 13:33) and complete control over his destiny.

**7:35 Dispersion**: or "diaspora": Jews living outside Palestine. **Greeks**: probably refers to the Gentiles in the Mediterranean area; cf. Jn 12:20.

**7:37, 39** Promise of living water through the Spirit.

**7:38 Living water**: not an exact quotation from any Old Testament passage; in the gospel context the gift of the Spirit is meant; cf. Jn 3:5. **From within him**: either Jesus or the believer; if Jesus, it continues the Jesus-Moses motif (water from the rock, Ex 17:6; Nm 20:11) as well as Jesus as the new temple (cf. Ez 47:1). Grammatically, it goes better with the believer.

**7:39 No Spirit yet**: Codex Vaticanus and early Latin, Syriac, and Coptic versions add "given." In this gospel, the sending of the Spirit cannot take place until Jesus' glorification through his death, resurrection, and ascension; cf. Jn 20:22.

**7:40–53** Discussion of the Davidic lineage of the Messiah.

**7:53–8:11** The story of the woman caught in adultery is a later insertion here, missing from all early Greek manuscripts. A Western text-type insertion, attested mainly in Old Latin translations, it is found in different places in different manu-

*r:* Heb 7:3. *s:* 8:19. *t:* 6:46; 8:55. *u:* 7:44; 8:20; Lk 4:29–30. *v:* 2:11; 10:42; 11:45. *w:* 13:33; 16:16. *x:* 8:21; 12:36; 13:33, 36; 16:5; Dt 4:29; Prv 1:28; Is 55:6; Hos 5:6. *y:* Rev 21:6. *z:* 4:10, 14; 19:34; Is 12:3; Ez 47:1. *a:* 16:7. *b:* Dt 18:15, 18. *c:* 2 Sm 7:12–14; Ps 89:3–4; 132:11; Mi 5:1; Mt 2:5–6. *d:* 12:42. *e:* 3:1; 19:39. *f:* Dt 1:16–17.

1 while Jesus went to the Mount of Olives.* [g] 2 But early in the morning he arrived again in the temple area, and all the people started coming to him, and he sat down and taught them. 3 Then the scribes and the Pharisees brought a woman who had been caught in adultery and made her stand in the middle. 4 They said to him, "Teacher, this woman was caught in the very act of committing adultery. 5 Now in the law, Moses commanded us to stone such women.* So what do you say?"[h] 6 They said this to test him, so that they could have some charge to bring against him. Jesus bent down and began to write on the ground with his finger.* 7* But when they continued asking him, he straightened up and said to them,[i] "Let the one among you who is without sin be the first to throw a stone at her." 8 Again he bent down and wrote on the ground. 9 And in response, they went away one by one, beginning with the elders. So he was left alone with the woman before him. 10 Then Jesus straightened up and said to her, "Woman, where are they? Has no one condemned you?"[j] 11 She replied, "No one, sir." Then Jesus said, "Neither do I condemn you. Go, [and] from now on do not sin any more."][k]

***The Light of the World.**** 12 Jesus spoke to them again, saying, "I am the light of the world. Whoever follows me will not walk in darkness, but will have the light of life."[l] 13 So the Pharisees said to him, "You testify on your own behalf, so your testimony cannot be verified." 14 Jesus answered and said to them, "Even if I do testify on my own behalf, my testimony can be verified,* because I know where I came from and where I am going. But you do not know where I come from or where I am going.[m] 15 You judge by appearances,* but I do not judge anyone.[n] 16 And even if I should judge, my judgment is valid, because I am not alone, but it is I and the Father who sent me.[o] 17 Even in your law* it is written that the testimony of two men can be verified.[p] 18 I testify on my behalf and so does the Father who sent me."[q] 19 So they said to him, "Where is your father?" Jesus answered, "You know neither me nor my Father. If you knew me, you would know my Father also."[r] 20 He spoke these words while teaching in the treasury in the temple area. But no one arrested him, because his hour had not yet come.[s]

***Jesus, the Father's Ambassador.**** 21 He said to them again, "I am going away and you will look for me, but you will die in your sin.* Where I am going you cannot come."[t] 22* So the Jews said, "He is not going to kill himself, is he, because he said, 'Where I am going you cannot come'?" 23 He said to them, "You belong to what is below, I belong to what is above. You belong to this world, but I do not belong to this world.[u]

scripts: here, or after Jn 7:36 or at the end of this gospel, or after Lk 21:38, or at the end of that gospel. There are many non-Johannine features in the language, and there are also many doubtful readings within the passage. The style and motifs are similar to those of Luke, and it fits better with the general situation at the end of Lk 21, but it was probably inserted here because of the allusion to Jer 17:13 (cf. note on Jn 8:6) and the statement, "I do not judge anyone," in Jn 8:15. The Catholic Church accepts this passage as canonical scripture.

**8:1 Mount of Olives**: not mentioned elsewhere in the gospel tradition outside of passion week.

**8:5** Lv 20:10 and Dt 22:22 mention only death, but Dt 22:23–24 prescribes stoning for a betrothed virgin.

**8:6** Cf. Jer 17:13 (RSV): "Those who turn away from thee shall be written in the earth, for they have forsaken the LORD, the fountain of living water"; cf. Jn 7:38.

**8:7** The first stones were to be thrown by the witnesses (Dt 17:7).

**8:12–20** Jesus the light of the world. Jesus replaces the four torches of the illumination of the temple as the light of joy.

**8:14 My testimony can be verified**: this seems to contradict Jn 5:31, but the emphasis here is on Jesus' origin from the Father and his divine destiny. **Where I am going**: indicates Jesus' passion and glorification.

**8:15 By appearances**: literally, "according to the flesh." **I do not judge anyone**: superficial contradiction of Jn 5:22, 27, 30; here the emphasis is that the judgment is not by material standards.

**8:17 Your law**: a reflection of later controversy between church and synagogue.

**8:21–30** He whose ambassador I am is with me. Jesus' origin is from God; he can reveal God.

**8:21 You will die in your sin**: i.e., of disbelief; cf. Jn 8:24. **Where I am going you cannot come**: except through faith in Jesus' passion-resurrection.

**8:22** The Jews suspect that he is referring to his death. Johannine irony is apparent here; Jesus' death will not be self-inflicted but destined by God.

---

*g:* Lk 21:37–38. *h:* Lv 20:10; Dt 22:22–29. *i:* Dt 17:7. *j:* Ez 33:11. *k:* 5:14. *l:* 1:4–5, 9; 12:46; Ex 13:22; Is 42:6; Zec 14:8. *m:* 5:31. *n:* 12:47; 1 Sm 16:7. *o:* 5:30. *p:* Dt 17:6; 19:15; Nm 35:30. *q:* 5:23, 37. *r:* 7:28; 14:7; 15:21. *s:* 7:30. *t:* 7:34; 13:33. *u:* 3:31; 17:14; 18:36.

24 That is why I told you that you will die in
your sins. For if you do not believe that I
AM,* you will die in your sins."[v] 25* So they
said to him, "Who are you?"[w] Jesus said to
them, "What I told you from the beginning.
26 I have much to say about you in condemnation. But the one who sent me is true, and
what I heard from him I tell the world."[x]
27 They did not realize that he was speaking
to them of the Father. 28 So Jesus said [to
them], "When you lift up the Son of Man,
then you will realize that I AM, and that I do
nothing on my own, but I say only what the
Father taught me.[y] 29 The one who sent me is
with me. He has not left me alone, because I
always do what is pleasing to him." 30 Because he spoke this way, many came to believe in him.

***Jesus and Abraham.**** 31 Jesus then said to
those Jews who believed in him,* "If you remain in my word, you will truly be my disciples, 32 and you will know the truth, and the
truth will set you free."[z] 33 They answered
him, "We are descendants of Abraham and
have never been enslaved to anyone.* How
can you say, 'You will become free'?"[a]
34 Jesus answered them, "Amen, amen, I say
to you, everyone who commits sin is a slave
of sin.[b] 35 A slave does not remain in a household forever, but a son* always remains.[c]
36 So if a son frees you, then you will truly be
free. 37 I know that you are descendants of
Abraham. But you are trying to kill me, because my word has no room among you. 38* I
tell you what I have seen in the Father's
presence; then do what you have heard from
the Father."

39* They answered and said to him, "Our
father is Abraham." Jesus said to them,[d] "If
you were Abraham's children, you would be
doing the works of Abraham. 40 But now you
are trying to kill me, a man who has told you
the truth that I heard from God; Abraham did
not do this. 41 You are doing the works of
your father!" [So] they said to him, "We are
not illegitimate. We have one Father, God."[e]
42 Jesus said to them, "If God were your Father, you would love me, for I came from
God and am here; I did not come on my own,
but he sent me.[f] 43 Why do you not understand what I am saying? Because you cannot
bear to hear my word. 44 You belong to your
father the devil and you willingly carry out
your father's desires. He was a murderer
from the beginning and does not stand in
truth, because there is no truth in him. When
he tells a lie, he speaks in character, because
he is a liar and the father of lies.[g] 45 But because I speak the truth, you do not believe
me. 46 Can any of you charge me with sin? If
I am telling the truth, why do you not believe
me?[h] 47 Whoever belongs to God hears the
words of God; for this reason you do not listen, because you do not belong to God."[i]

48 The Jews answered and said to him,
"Are we not right in saying that you are a
Samaritan* and are possessed?" 49 Jesus answered, "I am not possessed; I honor my Father, but you dishonor me. 50 I do not seek my
own glory; there is one who seeks it and he

**8:24, 28 I AM**: an expression that late Jewish tradition understood as Yahweh's own self-designation (Is 43:10); see note on Jn 4:26. Jesus is here placed on a par with Yahweh.

**8:25 What I told you from the beginning**: this verse seems textually corrupt, with several other possible translations: "(I am) what I say to you"; "Why do I speak to you at all?" The earliest attested reading (Bodmer Papyrus P66) has (in a second hand), "I told you at the beginning what I am also telling you (now)." The answer here (cf. Prv 8:22) seems to hinge on a misunderstanding of Jn 8:24 "*that* I AM" as "*what* I am."

**8:31–59** Jesus' origin ("before Abraham") and destiny are developed; the truth will free them from sin (Jn 8:34) and death (Jn 8:51).

**8:31 Those Jews who believed in him**: a rough editorial suture, since in Jn 8:37 they are described as trying to kill Jesus.

**8:33 Have never been enslaved to anyone**: since, historically, the Jews were enslaved almost continuously, this verse is probably Johannine irony, about slavery to sin.

**8:35 A slave . . . a son**: an allusion to Ishmael and Isaac (Gn 16; 21), or to the release of a slave after six years (Ex 21:2; Dt 15:12).

**8:38 The Father**: i.e., God. It is also possible, however, to understand the second part of the verse as a sarcastic reference to descent of the Jews from the devil (Jn 8:44), "You do what you have heard from [your] father."

**8:39 The works of Abraham**: Abraham believed; cf. Rom 4:11–17; Jas 2:21–23.

**8:48 Samaritan**: therefore interested in magical powers; cf. Acts 7:14–24.

*v:* Ex 3:14; Dt 32:39; Is 43:10. *w:* 10:24. *x:* 12:44–50. *y:* 3:14; 12:32, 34. *z:* Is 42:7; Gal 4:31. *a:* Mt 3:9. *b:* Rom 6:16–17. *c:* Gn 21:10; Gal 4:30; Heb 3:5–6. *d:* Gn 26:5; Rom 4:11–17; Jas 2:21–23. *e:* Mal 2:10. *f:* 1 Jn 5:1. *g:* Gn 3:4; Wis 1:13; 2:24; Acts 13:10; 1 Jn 3:8–15. *h:* Heb 4:15; 1 Pt 2:22; 1 Jn 3:5. *i:* 10:26; 1 Jn 4:6.

is the one who judges.[j] 51 Amen, amen, I say to you, whoever keeps my word will never see death."[k] 52 [So] the Jews said to him, "Now we are sure that you are possessed. Abraham died, as did the prophets, yet you say, 'Whoever keeps my word will never taste death.' 53 Are you greater than our father Abraham,* who died? Or the prophets, who died? Who do you make yourself out to be?"[l] 54 Jesus answered, "If I glorify myself, my glory is worth nothing; but it is my Father who glorifies me, of whom you say, 'He is our God.' 55 You do not know him, but I know him. And if I should say that I do not know him, I would be like you a liar. But I do know him and I keep his word.[m] 56 Abraham your father rejoiced to see my day; he saw it* and was glad.[n] 57 So the Jews said to him, "You are not yet fifty years old and you have seen Abraham?"* 58* Jesus said to them,[o] "Amen, amen, I say to you, before Abraham came to be, I AM." 59 So they picked up stones to throw at him; but Jesus hid and went out of the temple area.[p]

See RG 329

## CHAPTER 9

***The Man Born Blind.*** 1* As he passed by he saw a man blind from birth.[q] 2* His disciples asked him,[r] "Rabbi, who sinned, this man or his parents, that he was born blind?" 3 Jesus answered, "Neither he nor his parents sinned; it is so that the works of God might be made visible through him.[s] 4 We have to do the works of the one who sent me while it is day. Night is coming when no one can work.[t] 5 While I am in the world, I am the light of the world."[u] 6 When he had said this, he spat on the ground and made clay with the saliva, and smeared the clay on his eyes,[v] 7 and said to him, "Go wash* in the Pool of Siloam" (which means Sent). So he went and washed, and came back able to see.[w]

8 His neighbors and those who had seen him earlier as a beggar said, "Isn't this the one who used to sit and beg?" 9 Some said, "It is," but others said, "No, he just looks like him." He said, "I am." 10 So they said to him, "[So] how were your eyes opened?" 11 He replied, "The man called Jesus made clay and anointed my eyes and told me, 'Go to Siloam and wash.' So I went there and washed and was able to see." 12 And they said to him, "Where is he?" He said, "I don't know."

13 They brought the one who was once blind to the Pharisees. 14 Now Jesus had made clay* and opened his eyes on a sabbath.[x] 15 So then the Pharisees also asked him how he was able to see. He said to them, "He put clay on my eyes, and I washed, and now I can see." 16 So some of the Pharisees said, "This man is not from God, because he does not keep the sabbath." [But] others said, "How can a sinful man do such signs?" And there was a division among them.[y] 17 So they said to the blind man again, "What do you have to say about him, since he opened your eyes?" He said, "He is a prophet."[z]

18 Now the Jews did not believe that he had been blind and gained his sight until they summoned the parents of the one who had gained his sight. 19 They asked them, "Is this your son, who you say was born blind? How does he

**8:53 Are you greater than our father Abraham?**: cf. Jn 4:12.

**8:56 He saw it**: this seems a reference to the birth of Isaac (Gn 17:7; 21:6), the beginning of the fulfillment of promises about Abraham's seed.

**8:57** The evidence of the third-century Bodmer Papyrus P75 and the first hand of Codex Sinaiticus indicates that the text originally read: "How can Abraham have seen you?"

**8:58 Came to be, I AM**: the Greek word used for "came to be" is the one used of all creation in the prologue, while the word used for "am" is the one reserved for the Logos.

**9:1–10:21** Sabbath healing of the man born blind. This sixth sign is introduced to illustrate the saying, "I am the light of the world" (Jn 8:12; 9:5). The narrative of conflict about Jesus contrasts Jesus (light) with the Jews (blindness, Jn 9:39–41). The theme of water is reintroduced in the reference to the pool of Siloam. Ironically, Jesus is being judged by the Jews, yet the Jews are judged by the Light of the world; cf. Jn 3:19–21.

**9:2** See note on Jn 5:14, and Ex 20:5, that parents' sins were visited upon their children. Jesus denies such a cause and emphasizes the purpose: the infirmity was providential.

**9:7 Go wash**: perhaps a test of faith; cf. 2 Kgs 5:10–14. The water tunnel Siloam (= Sent) is used as a symbol of Jesus, sent by his Father.

**9:14** In using spittle, kneading clay, and healing, Jesus had broken the sabbath rules laid down by Jewish tradition.

*j:* 7:18. *k:* 5:24–29; 6:40, 47; 11:25–26. *l:* 4:12. *m:* 7:28–29. *n:* Gn 17:17; Mt 13:17; Lk 17:22. *o:* 1:30; 17:5. *p:* 10:31, 39; 11:8; Lk 4:29–30. *q:* Is 42:7. *r:* Ex 20:5; Ez 18:20; Lk 13:2. *s:* 5:14; 11:4. *t:* 11:9–10; 12:35–36. *u:* 8:12. *v:* 5:11; Mk 7:33; 8:23. *w:* 2 Kgs 5:10–14. *x:* 5:9. *y:* 3:2; Mt 12:10–11; Lk 13:10–11; 14:1–4. *z:* 4:19.

now see?" [20]His parents answered and said, "We know that this is our son and that he was born blind. [21]We do not know how he sees now, nor do we know who opened his eyes. Ask him, he is of age; he can speak for himself." [22]* [a] His parents said this because they were afraid of the Jews, for the Jews had already agreed that if anyone acknowledged him as the Messiah, he would be expelled from the synagogue. [23]For this reason his parents said, "He is of age; question him."[b]

[24]So a second time they called the man who had been blind and said to him, "Give God the praise!* We know that this man is a sinner."[c] [25]He replied, "If he is a sinner, I do not know. One thing I do know is that I was blind and now I see." [26]So they said to him, "What did he do to you? How did he open your eyes?" [27]He answered them, "I told you already and you did not listen. Why do you want to hear it again? Do you want to become his disciples, too?" [28]They ridiculed him and said, "You are that man's disciple; we are disciples of Moses! [29]We know that God spoke to Moses, but we do not know where this one is from."[d] [30]The man answered and said to them, "This is what is so amazing, that you do not know where he is from, yet he opened my eyes. [31]We know that God does not listen to sinners, but if one is devout and does his will, he listens to him.[e] [32]* It is unheard of that anyone ever opened the eyes of a person born blind. [33]If this man were not from God, he would not be able to do anything."[f] [34]They answered and said to him, "You were born totally in sin, and are you trying to teach us?" Then they threw him out.

[35]When Jesus heard that they had thrown him out, he found him and said, "Do you believe in the Son of Man?" [36]He answered and said, "Who is he, sir, that I may believe in him?" [37]Jesus said to him, "You have seen him and the one speaking with you is he."[g] [38]He said, "I do believe, Lord," and he worshiped him. [39]* Then Jesus said, "I came into this world for judgment, so that those who do not see might see, and those who do see might become blind."[h]

[40]Some of the Pharisees who were with him heard this and said to him, "Surely we are not also blind, are we?"[i] [41]Jesus said to them, "If you were blind, you would have no sin; but now you are saying, 'We see,' so your sin remains.[j]

## CHAPTER 10

See RG 329

***The Good Shepherd.*** [1]* "Amen, amen, I say to you,[k] whoever does not enter a sheepfold* through the gate but climbs over elsewhere is a thief and a robber. [2]But whoever enters through the gate is the shepherd of the sheep. [3]The gatekeeper opens it for him, and the sheep hear his voice, as he calls his own sheep by name and leads them out. [4]* When he has driven out all his own, he walks ahead of them, and the sheep follow him,[l] because they recognize his voice. [5]But they will not follow a stranger; they will run away from him, because they do not recognize the voice of strangers." [6]Although Jesus used this figure of speech,* they did not realize what he was trying to tell them.

**9:22** This comment of the evangelist (in terms used again in Jn 12:42; 16:2) envisages a situation after Jesus' ministry. Rejection/excommunication from the synagogue of Jews who confessed Jesus as Messiah seems to have begun ca. A.D. 85, when the curse against the *mînîm* or heretics was introduced into the "Eighteen Benedictions."

**9:24 Give God the praise!**: an Old Testament formula of adjuration to tell the truth; cf. Jos 7:19; 1 Sm 6:5 LXX. Cf. Jn 5:41.

**9:32 A person born blind**: the only Old Testament cure from blindness is found in Tobit (cf. Tb 7:7; 11:7–13; 14:1–2), but Tobit was not born blind.

**9:39–41** These verses spell out the symbolic meaning of the cure; the Pharisees are not the innocent blind, willing to accept the testimony of others.

**10:1–21** The good shepherd discourse continues the theme of attack on the Pharisees that ends Jn 9. The figure is allegorical: the hired hands are the Pharisees who excommunicated the cured blind man. It serves as a commentary on Jn 9. For the shepherd motif, used of Yahweh in the Old Testament, cf. Ex 34; Gn 48:15; 49:24; Mi 7:14; Ps 23:1–4; 80:1.

**10:1 Sheepfold**: a low stone wall open to the sky.

**10:4 Recognize his voice**: the Pharisees do not recognize Jesus, but the people of God, symbolized by the blind man, do.

**10:6 Figure of speech**: John uses a different word for illustrative speech than the "parable" of the synoptics, but the idea is similar.

*a:* 7:13; 12:42; 16:2; 19:38. *b:* 12:42. *c:* Jos 7:19; 1 Sm 6:5 LXX. *d:* Ex 33:11. *e:* 10:21; Ps 34:16; 66:18; Prv 15:29; Is 1:15. *f:* 3:2. *g:* 4:26; Dn 7:13. *h:* Mt 13:33–35. *i:* Mt 15:14; 23:26; Rom 2:19. *j:* 15:22. *k:* Gn 48:15; 49:24; Ps 23:1–4; 80:2; Jer 23:1–4; Ez 34:1–31; Mi 7:14. *l:* Mi 2:12–13.

7* So Jesus said again, "Amen, amen, I say to you, I am the gate for the sheep. 8* All who came [before me] are thieves and robbers, but the sheep did not listen to them. 9 I am the gate. Whoever enters through me will be saved, and will come in and go out and find pasture. 10 A thief comes only to steal and slaughter and destroy; I came so that they might have life and have it more abundantly. 11 I am the good shepherd. A good shepherd lays down his life for the sheep.[m] 12 A hired man, who is not a shepherd and whose sheep are not his own, sees a wolf coming and leaves the sheep and runs away, and the wolf catches and scatters them.[n] 13 This is because he works for pay and has no concern for the sheep. 14 I am the good shepherd, and I know mine and mine know me, 15 just as the Father knows me and I know the Father; and I will lay down my life for the sheep.[o] 16 I have other sheep* that do not belong to this fold. These also I must lead, and they will hear my voice, and there will be one flock, one shepherd.[p] 17 This is why the Father loves me, because I lay down my life in order to take it up again.[q] 18 No one takes it from me, but I lay it down on my own. I have power to lay it down, and power to take it up again.* This command I have received from my Father."[r]

19 Again there was a division among the Jews because of these words.[s] 20 Many of them said, "He is possessed and out of his mind; why listen to him?"[t] 21 Others said, "These are not the words of one possessed; surely a demon cannot open the eyes of the blind, can he?"[u]

*Feast of the Dedication.* 22 The feast of the Dedication* was then taking place in Jerusalem. It was winter.[v] 23* And Jesus walked about in the temple area on the Portico of Solomon. 24 So the Jews gathered around him and said to him, "How long are you going to keep us in suspense?* If you are the Messiah, tell us plainly."[w] 25 Jesus answered them, "I told you* and you do not believe. The works I do in my Father's name testify to me.[x] 26 But you do not believe, because you are not among my sheep.[y] 27 My sheep hear my voice; I know them, and they follow me. 28 I give them eternal life, and they shall never perish. No one can take them out of my hand.[z] 29 My Father, who has given them to me, is greater than all,* and no one can take them out of the Father's hand.[a] 30* The Father and I are one."[b]

31 The Jews again picked up rocks to stone him.[c] 32 Jesus answered them, "I have shown you many good works from my Father. For which of these are you trying to stone me?" 33 The Jews answered him, "We are not stoning you for a good work but for blasphemy. You, a man, are making yourself God."[d] 34* Jesus answered them,[e] "Is it not written

**10:7–10** In Jn 10:7–8, the figure is of a gate for the shepherd to come to the sheep; in Jn 10:9–10, the figure is of a gate for the sheep to **come in and go out**.

**10:8 [Before me]**: these words are omitted in many good early manuscripts and versions.

**10:16 Other sheep**: the Gentiles, possibly a reference to "God's dispersed children" of Jn 11:52 destined to be gathered into one, or "apostolic Christians" at odds with the community of the beloved disciple.

**10:18 Power to take it up again**: contrast the role of the Father as the efficient cause of the resurrection in Acts 2:24; 4:10; etc.; Rom 1:4; 4:24. Yet even here is added: **This command I have received from my Father**.

**10:22 Feast of the Dedication**: an eight-day festival of lights (Hebrew, Hanukkah) held in December, three months after the feast of Tabernacles (Jn 7:2), to celebrate the Maccabees' rededication of the altar and reconsecration of the temple in 164 B.C., after their desecration by Antiochus IV Epiphanes (Dn 8:13; 9:27; cf. 1 Mc 4:36–59; 2 Mc 1:18–2:19; 10:1–8).

**10:23 Portico of Solomon**: on the east side of the temple area, offering protection against the cold winds from the desert.

**10:24 Keep us in suspense**: literally, "How long will you take away our life?" Cf. Jn 11:48–50. **If you are the Messiah, tell us plainly**: cf. Lk 22:67. This is the climax of Jesus' encounters with the Jewish authorities. There has never yet been an open confession before them.

**10:25 I told you**: probably at Jn 8:25 which was an evasive answer.

**10:29** The textual evidence for the first clause is very divided; it may also be translated: "As for the Father, what he has given me is greater than all," or "My Father is greater than all, in what he has given me."

**10:30** This is justification for Jn 10:29; it asserts unity of power and reveals that the words and deeds of Jesus are the words and deeds of God.

**10:34** This is a reference to the judges of Israel who, since they exercised the divine prerogative to judge (Dt 1:17), were

*m:* Ps 23:1–4; Is 40:11; 49:9–10; Heb 13:20; Rev 7:17. *n:* Zec 11:17. *o:* 15:13; 1 Jn 3:16. *p:* 11:52; Is 56:8; Jer 23:3; Ez 34:23; 37:24; Mi 2:12. *q:* Heb 10:10. *r:* 19:11. *s:* 7:43; 9:16. *t:* 7:20; 8:48. *u:* 3:2. *v:* 1 Mc 4:54, 59. *w:* Lk 22:67. *x:* 8:25 / 5:36; 10:38. *y:* 8:45, 47. *z:* Dt 32:39. *a:* Wis 3:1; Is 43:13. *b:* 1:1; 12:45; 14:9; 17:21. *c:* 8:59. *d:* 5:18; 19:7; Lv 24:16. *e:* Ps 82:6.

in your law, 'I said, "You are gods" '? 35 If it calls them gods to whom the word of God came, and scripture cannot be set aside, 36 can you say that the one whom the Father has consecrated* and sent into the world blasphemes because I said, 'I am the Son of God'?[f] 37 If I do not perform my Father's works, do not believe me; 38 but if I perform them, even if you do not believe me, believe the works, so that you may realize [and understand] that the Father is in me and I am in the Father."[g] 39 [Then] they tried again to arrest him; but he escaped from their power.

40 He went back across the Jordan to the place where John first baptized, and there he remained.[h] 41 Many came to him and said, "John performed no sign,* but everything John said about this man was true." 42 And many there began to believe in him.[i]

See RG 329

## CHAPTER 11

***The Raising of Lazarus.**** 1 Now a man was ill, Lazarus from Bethany,[j] the village of Mary and her sister Martha. 2 Mary was the one who had anointed the Lord with perfumed oil and dried his feet with her hair; it was her brother Lazarus who was ill. 3 So the sisters sent word to him, saying, "Master, the one you love is ill." 4 When Jesus heard this he said, "This illness is not to end in death,* but is for the glory of God, that the Son of God may be glorified through it."[k] 5 Now Jesus loved Martha and her sister and Lazarus. 6 So when he heard that he was ill, he remained for two days in the place where he was. 7 Then after this he said to his disciples, "Let us go back to Judea." 8 The disciples said to him, "Rabbi, the Jews were just trying to stone you, and you want to go back there?"[l] 9 Jesus answered, "Are there not twelve hours in a day? If one walks during the day,[m] he does not stumble, because he sees the light of this world.[n] 10 But if one walks at night, he stumbles, because the light is not in him."* 11 He said this, and then told them, "Our friend Lazarus is asleep, but I am going to awaken him." 12 So the disciples said to him, "Master, if he is asleep, he will be saved." 13 But Jesus was talking about his death, while they thought that he meant ordinary sleep.[o] 14 So then Jesus said to them clearly, "Lazarus has died. 15 And I am glad for you that I was not there, that you may believe. Let us go to him." 16 So Thomas, called Didymus,* said to his fellow disciples, "Let us also go to die with him."[p]

17 When Jesus arrived, he found that Lazarus had already been in the tomb for four days. 18 Now Bethany was near Jerusalem, only about two miles* away. 19 And many of the Jews had come to Martha and Mary to comfort them about their brother.[q] 20 When Martha heard that Jesus was coming, she went to meet him; but Mary sat at home. 21 Martha said to Jesus, "Lord, if you had been here, my brother would not have died.[r] 22 [But] even now I know that whatever you ask of God, God will give you." 23 Jesus said

called "gods"; cf. Ex 21:6, besides Ps 82:6, from which the quotation comes.

**10:36 Consecrated**: this may be a reference to the rededicated altar at the Hanukkah feast; see note on Jn 10:22.

**10:41 Performed no sign**: this is to stress the inferior role of John the Baptist. The Transjordan topography recalls the great witness of John the Baptist to Jesus, as opposed to the hostility of the authorities in Jerusalem.

**11:1–44** The raising of Lazarus, the longest continuous narrative in John outside of the passion account, is the climax of the signs. It leads directly to the decision of the Sanhedrin to kill Jesus. The theme of life predominates. Lazarus is a token of the real life that Jesus dead and raised will give to all who believe in him. Johannine irony is found in the fact that Jesus' gift of life leads to his own death. The story is not found in the synoptics, but cf. Mk 5:21 and parallels; Lk 7:11–17. There are also parallels between this story and Luke's parable of the rich man and poor Lazarus (Lk 16:19–31). In both a man named Lazarus dies; in Luke, there is a request that he return to convince his contemporaries of the need for faith and repentance, while in John, Lazarus does return and some believe but others do not.

**11:4 Not to end in death**: this is misunderstood by the disciples as referring to physical death, but it is meant as spiritual death.

**11:10 The light is not in him**: the ancients apparently did not grasp clearly the entry of light through the eye; they seem to have thought of it as being **in** the eye; cf. Lk 11:34; Mt 6:23.

**11:16 Called Didymus**: **Didymus** is the Greek word for twin. Thomas is derived from the Aramaic word for twin; in an ancient Syriac version and in the Gospel of Thomas (80:11–12) his given name, Judas, is supplied.

**11:18 About two miles**: literally, "about fifteen stades"; a stade was 607 feet.

*f:* 5:18. *g:* 14:10–11, 20. *h:* 1:28. *i:* 2:23; 7:31; 8:30. *j:* 12:1–8; Lk 10:38–42; 16:19–31. *k:* 9:3, 24. *l:* 8:59; 10:31. *m:* 12:35; 1 Jn 2:10. *n:* 8:12; 9:4. *o:* Mt 9:24. *p:* 14:5, 22. *q:* 12:9, 17–18. *r:* 11:32.

to her, "Your brother will rise." 24 Martha
said to him, "I know he will rise, in the resurrection on the last day."[s] 25 Jesus told her,
"I am the resurrection and the life; whoever
believes in me, even if he dies, will live,[t]
26 and everyone who lives and believes in me
will never die. Do you believe this?" 27*[u] She
said to him, "Yes, Lord. I have come to believe that you are the Messiah, the Son of
God, the one who is coming into the world."
28 When she had said this, she went and
called her sister Mary secretly, saying, "The
teacher is here and is asking for you." 29 As
soon as she heard this, she rose quickly and
went to him. 30 For Jesus had not yet come into
the village, but was still where Martha had
met him. 31 So when the Jews who were with
her in the house comforting her saw Mary get
up quickly and go out, they followed her, presuming that she was going to the tomb to weep
there. 32 When Mary came to where Jesus was
and saw him, she fell at his feet and said to
him, "Lord, if you had been here, my brother
would not have died." 33 When Jesus saw her
weeping and the Jews who had come with her
weeping, he became perturbed* and deeply
troubled, 34 and said, "Where have you laid
him?" They said to him, "Sir, come and see."
35 And Jesus wept.[v] 36 So the Jews said, "See
how he loved him." 37 But some of them said,
"Could not the one who opened the eyes of the
blind man have done something so that this
man would not have died?"
38 So Jesus, perturbed again, came to the
tomb. It was a cave, and a stone lay across it.
39 Jesus said, "Take away the stone." Martha,
the dead man's sister, said to him, "Lord, by
now there will be a stench; he has been dead
for four days." 40 Jesus said to her, "Did I not
tell you that if you believe you will see the
glory of God?" 41 So they took away the
stone. And Jesus raised his eyes and said,
"Father,* I thank you for hearing me. 42 I
know that you always hear me; but because
of the crowd here I have said this, that they
may believe that you sent me."[w] 43 And when
he had said this, he cried out in a loud voice,*
"Lazarus, come out!" 44 The dead man came
out, tied hand and foot with burial bands,
and his face was wrapped in a cloth. So Jesus
said to them, "Untie him and let him go."

*Session of the Sanhedrin.* 45 Now many of
the Jews who had come to Mary and seen
what he had done began to believe in him.[x]
46 But some of them went to the Pharisees
and told them what Jesus had done. 47 So the
chief priests and the Pharisees convened the
Sanhedrin and said, "What are we going to
do? This man is performing many signs.[y] 48 If
we leave him alone, all will believe in him,
and the Romans will come* and take away
both our land and our nation." 49[z] But one of
them, Caiaphas, who was high priest that
year,* said to them, "You know nothing,
50 nor do you consider that it is better for you
that one man should die instead of the people, so that the whole nation may not perish." 51 He did not say this on his own, but
since he was high priest for that year, he
prophesied that Jesus was going to die for
the nation, 52 and not only for the nation, but
also to gather into one the dispersed children
of God.* 53 So from that day on they planned
to kill him.[a]
54 So Jesus no longer walked about in public among the Jews, but he left for the region
near the desert, to a town called Ephraim,*
and there he remained with his disciples.

**11:27** The titles here are a summary of titles given to Jesus earlier in the gospel.

**11:33 Became perturbed**: a startling phrase in Greek, literally, "He snorted in spirit," perhaps in anger at the presence of evil (death).

**11:41 Father**: in Aramaic, *'abbā'*. See note on Mk 14:36.

**11:43 Cried out in a loud voice**: a dramatization of Jn 5:28; "the hour is coming when all who are in the tombs will hear his voice."

**11:48 The Romans will come**: Johannine irony; this is precisely what happened after Jesus' death.

**11:49 That year**: emphasizes the conjunction of the office and the year. Actually, Caiaphas was high priest A.D. 18–36. The Jews attributed a gift of prophecy, sometimes unconscious, to the high priest.

**11:52 Dispersed children of God**: perhaps the "other sheep" of Jn 10:16.

**11:54** Ephraim is usually located about twelve miles northeast of Jerusalem, where the mountains descend into the Jordan valley.

*s:* 5:29; 6:39–40, 44, 54; 12:48; Is 2:2; Mi 4:1; Acts 23:8; 24:15. *t:* 5:24; 8:51; 14:6; Dn 12:2. *u:* 1:9; 6:69. *v:* Lk 19:41. *w:* 12:30. *x:* Lk 16:31. *y:* 12:19; Mt 26:3–5; Lk 22:2; Acts 4:16. *z:* 18:13–14. *a:* 5:18; 7:1; Mt 12:14.

***The Last Passover.*** 55 Now the Passover of the Jews was near, and many went up from the country to Jerusalem before Passover to purify* themselves.[b] 56 They looked for Jesus and said to one another as they were in the temple area, "What do you think? That he will not come to the feast?" 57 For the chief priests and the Pharisees had given orders that if anyone knew where he was, he should inform them, so that they might arrest him.

See RG 329

## CHAPTER 12

***The Anointing at Bethany.***[c] 1* Six days before Passover Jesus came to Bethany, where Lazarus was, whom Jesus had raised from the dead.[d] 2 They gave a dinner for him there, and Martha served, while Lazarus was one of those reclining at table with him.[e] 3 Mary took a liter of costly perfumed oil made from genuine aromatic nard and anointed the feet of Jesus* and dried them with her hair; the house was filled with the fragrance of the oil.[f] 4 Then Judas the Iscariot, one [of] his disciples, and the one who would betray him, said, 5 "Why was this oil not sold for three hundred days' wages* and given to the poor?" 6 He said this not because he cared about the poor but because he was a thief and held the money bag and used to steal the contributions.[g] 7 So Jesus said, "Leave her alone. Let her keep this for the day of my burial.* 8 You always have the poor with you, but you do not always have me."[h]

9 [The] large crowd of the Jews found out that he was there and came, not only because of Jesus, but also to see Lazarus, whom he had raised from the dead.[i] 10 And the chief priests plotted to kill Lazarus too, 11 because many of the Jews were turning away and believing in Jesus because of him.[j]

***The Entry into Jerusalem.**** 12[k] On the next day, when the great crowd that had come to the feast heard that Jesus was coming to Jerusalem, 13 they took palm branches* and went out to meet him, and cried out:

"Hosanna!  
Blessed is he who comes in the name of the Lord,  
[even] the king of Israel."[l]

14 Jesus found an ass and sat upon it, as is written:

15 "Fear no more, O daughter Zion;*  
see, your king comes, seated upon an ass's colt."[m]

16 His disciples did not understand this at first, but when Jesus had been glorified they remembered that these things were written about him and that they had done this* for him.[n] 17* So the crowd that was with him when he called Lazarus from the tomb and raised him from death continued to testify. 18 This

**11:55 Purify**: prescriptions for purity were based on Ex 19:10–11, 15; Nm 9:6–14; 2 Chr 30:1–3, 15–18.

**12:1–8** This is probably the same scene of anointing found in Mk 14:3–9 (see note there) and Mt 26:6–13. The anointing by a penitent woman in Lk 7:36–38 is different. Details from these various episodes have become interchanged.

**12:3 The feet of Jesus**: so Mk 14:3; but in Mt 26:6, Mary anoints Jesus' head as a sign of regal, messianic anointing.

**12:5 Days' wages**: literally, "denarii." A denarius is a day's wage in Mt 20:2; see note on Jn 6:7.

**12:7** Jesus' response reflects the rabbinical discussion of what was the greatest act of mercy, almsgiving or burying the dead. Those who favored proper burial of the dead thought it an essential condition for sharing in the resurrection.

**12:12–19** In John, the entry into Jerusalem follows the anointing whereas in the synoptics it precedes. In John, the crowd, not the disciples, are responsible for the triumphal procession.

**12:13 Palm branches**: used to welcome great conquerors; cf. 1 Mc 13:51; 2 Mc 10:7. They may be related to the *lûlāb*, the twig bundles used at the feast of Tabernacles. **Hosanna**: see Ps 118:25–26. The Hebrew word means: "(O Lord), grant salvation." **He who comes in the name of the Lord**: referred in Ps 118:26 to a pilgrim entering the temple gates, but here a title for Jesus (see notes on Mt 11:3 and Jn 6:14; 11:27). **The king of Israel**: perhaps from Zep 3:14–15, in connection with the next quotation from Zec 9:9.

**12:15 Daughter Zion**: Jerusalem. **Ass's colt**: symbol of peace, as opposed to the war horse.

**12:16 They had done this**: the antecedent of **they** is ambiguous.

**12:17–18** There seem to be two different crowds in these verses. There are some good witnesses to the text that have another reading for Jn 12:17: "Then the crowd that was with him began to testify that he had called Lazarus out of the tomb and raised him from the dead."

*b:* 2:13; 5:1; 6:4; 18:28; Ex 19:10–11, 15; Nm 9:6–14; 19:12; Dt 16:6; 2 Chr 30:1–3, 15–18. *c:* Mt 26:6–13; Mk 14:3–9. *d:* 11:1. *e:* Lk 10:38–42. *f:* 11:2. *g:* 13:29. *h:* Dt 15:11. *i:* 11:19. *j:* 11:45. *k:* Mt 21:1–16; Mk 11:1–10; Lk 19:28–40. *l:* 1:49; Lv 23:40; 1 Mc 13:51; 2 Mc 10:7; Rev 7:9. *m:* Is 40:9; Zec 9:9. *n:* 2:22.

was [also] why the crowd went to meet him,
because they heard that he had done this sign.
19 So the Pharisees said to one another, "You
see that you are gaining nothing. Look, the
whole world* has gone after him."[o]

*The Coming of Jesus' Hour.** 20 Now there
were some Greeks* among those who had
come up to worship at the feast.[p] 21* They
came to Philip, who was from Bethsaida in
Galilee, and asked him, "Sir, we would like
to see Jesus."[q] 22 Philip went and told Andrew; then Andrew and Philip went and
told Jesus.[r] 23* Jesus answered them,[s] "The
hour has come for the Son of Man to be glorified. 24* Amen, amen, I say to you, unless
a grain of wheat falls to the ground and
dies, it remains just a grain of wheat;[t] but if
it dies, it produces much fruit. 25 Whoever
loves his life* loses it, and whoever hates
his life in this world will preserve it for
eternal life.[u] 26 Whoever serves me must
follow me, and where I am, there also will
my servant be. The Father will honor whoever serves me.[v]

27 "I am troubled* now. Yet what should I
say? 'Father, save me from this hour'? But it
was for this purpose that I came to this
hour.[w] 28 Father, glorify your name." Then a
voice came from heaven, "I have glorified it
and will glorify it again."[x] 29 The crowd there
heard it and said it was thunder; but others
said, "An angel has spoken to him."[y] 30 Jesus
answered and said, "This voice did not come
for my sake but for yours.[z] 31 Now is the time
of judgment on this world; now the ruler of
this world* will be driven out.[a] 32 And when
I am lifted up from the earth, I will draw
everyone to myself."[b] 33 He said this indicating the kind of death he would die. 34 So the
crowd answered him, "We have heard from
the law that the Messiah remains forever.*
Then how can you say that the Son of Man
must be lifted up? Who is this Son of Man?"[c]
35 Jesus said to them, "The light will be
among you only a little while. Walk while
you have the light, so that darkness may not
overcome you. Whoever walks in the dark
does not know where he is going.[d] 36 While
you have the light, believe in the light, so
that you may become children of the light."[e]

***Unbelief and Belief Among the Jews.*** After he had said this, Jesus left and hid from
them. 37*[f] Although he had performed so
many signs in their presence they did not believe in him, 38* in order that the word which
Isaiah the prophet spoke might be fulfilled:

"Lord, who has believed our preaching,
to whom has the might of the Lord
been revealed?"[g]

**12:19 The whole world**: the sense is that everyone is following Jesus, but John has an ironic play on **world**; he alludes to the universality of salvation (Jn 3:17; 4:42).

**12:20–36** This announcement of glorification by death is an illustration of "the whole world" (Jn 12:19) going after him.

**12:20 Greeks**: not used here in a nationalistic sense. These are probably Gentile proselytes to Judaism; cf. Jn 7:35.

**12:21–22 Philip . . . Andrew**: the approach is made through disciples who have distinctly Greek names, suggesting that access to Jesus was mediated to the Greek world through his disciples. Philip and Andrew were from Bethsaida (Jn 1:44); Galileans were mostly bilingual. **See**: here seems to mean "have an interview with."

**12:23** Jesus' response suggests that only after the crucifixion could the gospel encompass both Jew and Gentile.

**12:24** This verse implies that through his death Jesus will be accessible to all. **It remains just a grain of wheat**: this saying is found in the synoptic triple and double traditions (Mk 8:35; Mt 16:25; Lk 9:24; Mt 10:39; Lk 17:33). John adds the phrases (Jn 12:25) **in this world** and **for eternal life**.

**12:25 His life**: the Greek word *psychē* refers to a person's natural life. It does not mean "soul," for Hebrew anthropology did not postulate body/soul dualism in the way that is familiar to us.

**12:27 I am troubled**: perhaps an allusion to the Gethsemane agony scene of the synoptics.

**12:31 Ruler of this world**: Satan.

**12:34** There is no passage in the Old Testament that states precisely that the **Messiah remains forever**. Perhaps the closest is Ps 89:37.

**12:37–50** These verses, on unbelief of the Jews, provide an epilogue to the Book of Signs.

**12:38–41** John gives a historical explanation of the disbelief of the Jewish people, not a psychological one. The Old Testament had to be fulfilled; the disbelief that met Isaiah's message was a foreshadowing of the disbelief that Jesus encountered. In Jn 12:42 and also in Jn 3:20 we see that there is no negation of freedom.

*o:* 11:47–48. *p:* Acts 10:2. *q:* 1:44. *r:* 1:40. *s:* 2:4. *t:* Is 53:10–12; 1 Cor 15:36. *u:* Mt 10:39; 16:25; Mk 8:35; Lk 9:24; 17:33. *v:* 14:3; 17:24; Mt 16:24; Mk 8:34; Lk 9:23. *w:* 6:38; 18:11; Mt 26:38–39; Mk 14:34–36; Lk 22:42; Heb 5:7–8. *x:* 2:11; 17:5; Dn 4:31, 34. *y:* Ex 9:28; 2 Sm 22:14; Jb 37:4; Ps 29:3; Lk 22:43; Acts 23:9. *z:* 11:42. *a:* 16:11; Lk 10:18; Rev 12:9. *b:* 3:14; 8:28; Is 52:13. *c:* Ps 89:5; 110:4; Is 9:7; Dn 7:13–14; Rev 20:1–6. *d:* 9:4; 11:10; Jb 5:14. *e:* Eph 5:8. *f:* Dt 29:2–4; Mk 4:11–12; Rom 9–11. *g:* Is 53:1; Rom 10:16.

39 For this reason they could not believe,
because again Isaiah said:

40 "He blinded their eyes
and hardened their heart,
so that they might not see with their
eyes
and understand with their heart and be
converted,
and I would heal them."[h]

41 Isaiah said this because he saw his glory*
and spoke about him.[i] 42 Nevertheless, many,
even among the authorities, believed in him,
but because of the Pharisees they did not acknowledge it openly in order not to be expelled from the synagogue.[j] 43 For they preferred human praise to the glory of God.[k]

***Recapitulation.*** 44 Jesus cried out and said,
"Whoever believes in me believes not only
in me but also in the one who sent me,[l] 45 and
whoever sees me sees the one who sent me.[m]
46 I came into the world as light, so that
everyone who believes in me might not remain in darkness.[n] 47 And if anyone hears my
words and does not observe them, I do not
condemn him, for I did not come to condemn the world but to save the world.[o]
48 Whoever rejects me and does not accept
my words has something to judge him: the
word that I spoke, it will condemn him on
the last day,[p] 49 because I did not speak on my
own, but the Father who sent me commanded me what to say and speak.[q] 50 And I
know that his commandment is eternal life.
So what I say, I say as the Father told me."

# III. The Book of Glory*

## CHAPTER 13

See RG 329–31

***The Washing of the Disciples' Feet.****
1 Before the feast of Passover,* Jesus knew
that his hour had come to pass from this
world to the Father. He loved his own in the
world and he loved them to the end.[r] 2 The
devil had already induced* Judas, son of Simon the Iscariot, to hand him over. So, during supper,[s] 3 fully aware that the Father had
put everything into his power and that he
had come from God and was returning to
God,[t] 4 he rose from supper and took off his
outer garments. He took a towel and tied it
around his waist. 5* Then he poured water
into a basin and began to wash the disciples'
feet[u] and dry them with the towel around his
waist. 6 He came to Simon Peter, who said to
him, "Master, are you going to wash my
feet?" 7 Jesus answered and said to him,
"What I am doing, you do not understand
now, but you will understand later." 8 Peter
said to him, "You will never wash my feet."
Jesus answered him, "Unless I wash you,
you will have no inheritance with me."[v] 9 Simon Peter said to him, "Master, then not
only my feet, but my hands and head as
well." 10 Jesus said to him, "Whoever has
bathed* has no need except to have his feet
washed, for he is clean all over; so you are
clean, but not all."[w] 11 For he knew who
would betray him; for this reason, he said,
"Not all of you are clean."[x]

**12:41 His glory**: Isaiah saw the glory of Yahweh enthroned in the heavenly temple, but in John the antecedent of **his** is Jesus.

**13:1–19:42** The Book of Glory. There is a major break here; the word "sign" is used again only in Jn 20:30. In this phase of Jesus' return to the Father, the discourses (Jn 13–17) precede the traditional narrative of the passion (Jn 18–20) to interpret them for the Christian reader. This is the only extended example of esoteric teaching of disciples in John.

**13:1–20** Washing of the disciples' feet. This episode occurs in John at the place of the narration of the institution of the Eucharist in the synoptics. It may be a dramatization of Lk 22:27—"I am your servant." It is presented as a "model" ("pattern") of the crucifixion. It symbolizes cleansing from sin by sacrificial death.

**13:1 Before the feast of Passover**: this would be Thursday evening, before the day of preparation; in the synoptics, the Last Supper is a Passover meal taking place, in John's chronology, on Friday evening. **To the end**: or, "completely."

**13:2 Induced**: literally, "The devil put into the heart that Judas should hand him over."

**13:5** The act of washing another's feet was one that could not be required of the lowliest Jewish slave. It is an allusion to the humiliating death of the crucifixion.

**13:10 Bathed**: many have suggested that this passage is a symbolic reference to baptism. The Greek root involved is used in baptismal contexts in 1 Cor 6:11; Eph 5:26; Ti 3:5; Heb 10:22.

*h:* Is 6:9–10; Mt 13:13–15; Mk 4:12. *i:* 5:39; Is 6:1, 4. *j:* 9:22. *k:* 5:44. *l:* 13:20; 14:1. *m:* 14:7–9. *n:* 1:9; 8:12. *o:* 3:17. *p:* Lk 10:16; Heb 4:12. *q:* 14:10, 31; Dt 18:18–19. *r:* 2:4; 7:30; 8:20; Mt 26:17, 45; Mk 14:12, 41; Lk 22:7. *s:* 6:71; 17:12; Mt 26:20–21; Mk 14:17–18; Lk 22:3. *t:* 3:35. *u:* 1 Sm 25:41. *v:* 2 Sm 20:1. *w:* 15:3. *x:* 6:70.

[12]So when he had washed their feet [and] put his garments back on and reclined at table again, he said to them, "Do you realize what I have done for you? [13]You call me 'teacher' and 'master,' and rightly so, for indeed I am.[y] [14]If I, therefore, the master and teacher, have washed your feet, you ought to wash one another's feet. [15]I have given you a model to follow, so that as I have done for you, you should also do.[z] [16]Amen, amen, I say to you, no slave is greater than his master nor any messenger* greater than the one who sent him.[a] [17]If you understand this, blessed are you if you do it. [18]I am not speaking of all of you. I know those whom I have chosen. But so that the scripture might be fulfilled, 'The one who ate my food has raised his heel against me.'[b] [19]From now on I am telling you before it happens, so that when it happens you may believe that I AM. [20]Amen, amen, I say to you, whoever receives the one I send receives me, and whoever receives me receives the one who sent me."[c]

*Announcement of Judas's Betrayal.*[d] [21]When he had said this, Jesus was deeply troubled and testified, "Amen, amen, I say to you, one of you will betray me." [22]The disciples looked at one another, at a loss as to whom he meant. [23]One of his disciples, the one whom Jesus loved,* was reclining at Jesus' side.[e] [24]So Simon Peter nodded to him to find out whom he meant. [25]He leaned back against Jesus' chest and said to him, "Master, who is it?"[f] [26]Jesus answered, "It is the one to whom I hand the morsel* after I have dipped it." So he dipped the morsel and [took it and] handed it to Judas, son of Simon the Iscariot. [27]After he took the morsel, Satan entered him. So Jesus said to him, "What you are going to do, do quickly."[g] [28][Now] none of those reclining at table realized why he said this to him. [29]Some thought that since Judas kept the money bag, Jesus had told him, "Buy what we need for the feast," or to give something to the poor.[h] [30]So he took the morsel and left at once. And it was night.

*The New Commandment.* [31]* When he had left, Jesus said,* "Now is the Son of Man glorified, and God is glorified in him. [32][If God is glorified in him,] God will also glorify him in himself, and he will glorify him at once.[i] [33]My children, I will be with you only a little while longer. You will look for me, and as I told the Jews, 'Where I go you cannot come,' so now I say it to you.[j] [34]I give you a new commandment:* love one another. As I have loved you, so you also should love one another.[k] [35]This is how all will know that you are my disciples, if you have love for one another."

*Peter's Denial Predicted.* [36]Simon Peter said to him, "Master, where are you going?" Jesus answered [him], "Where I am going, you cannot follow me now, though you will follow later."[l] [37]Peter said to him, "Master, why can't I follow you now? I will lay down my life for you." [38]Jesus answered, "Will you lay down your life for me? Amen, amen, I say to you, the cock will not crow before you deny me three times."[m]

**13:16 Messenger**: the Greek has *apostolos*, the only occurrence of the term in John. It is not used in the technical sense here.

**13:23 The one whom Jesus loved**: also mentioned in Jn 19:26; 20:2; 21:7. A disciple, called "another disciple" or "the other disciple," is mentioned in Jn 18:15 and Jn 20:2; in the latter reference he is identified with the disciple whom Jesus loved. There is also an unnamed disciple in Jn 1:35–40; see note on Jn 1:37.

**13:26 Morsel**: probably the bitter herb dipped in salt water.

**13:31–17:26** Two farewell discourses and a prayer. These seem to be Johannine compositions, including sayings of Jesus at the Last Supper and on other occasions, modeled on similar farewell discourses in Greek literature and the Old Testament (of Moses, Joshua, David).

**13:31–38** Introduction: departure and return. Terms of coming and going predominate. These verses form an introduction to the last discourse of Jesus, which extends through Jn 14–17. In it John has collected Jesus' words to his own (Jn 13:1). There are indications that several speeches have been fused together, e.g., in Jn 14:31 and Jn 17:1.

**13:34 I give you a new commandment**: this puts Jesus on a par with Yahweh. The commandment itself is not new; cf. Lv 19:18 and the note there.

*y:* Mt 23:8, 10. *z:* Lk 22:27; 1 Pt 2:21. *a:* 15:20; Mt 10:24; Lk 6:40. *b:* Ps 41:10. *c:* Mt 10:40; Mk 9:37; Lk 9:48. *d:* Mt 26:21–25; Mk 14:18–21; Lk 22:21–23. *e:* 19:26; 20:2; 21:7, 20; Mt 10:37. *f:* 21:20. *g:* 13:2; Lk 22:3. *h:* 12:5–6. *i:* 17:1–5. *j:* 7:33; 8:21. *k:* 15:12–13, 17; Lv 19:18; 1 Thes 4:9; 1 Jn 2:7–10; 3:23; 2 Jn 5. *l:* Mk 14:27; Lk 22:23. *m:* 18:27; Mt 26:33–35; Mk 14:29–31; Lk 22:33–34.

## CHAPTER 14

See RG 330–31

*Last Supper Discourses.* 1* "Do not let your hearts be troubled. You have faith* in God; have faith also in me. 2 In my Father's house there are many dwelling places. If there were not, would I have told you that I am going to prepare a place for you? 3* And if I go and prepare a place for you, I will come back again and take you to myself, so that where I am you also may be.[n] 4 Where [I] am going you know the way."* 5 Thomas said to him, "Master, we do not know where you are going; how can we know the way?" 6 Jesus said to him, "I am the way and the truth* and the life. No one comes to the Father except through me.[o] 7 If you know me, then you will also know my Father.* From now on you do know him and have seen him."[p] 8 Philip said to him, "Master, show us the Father,* and that will be enough for us."[q] 9 Jesus said to him, "Have I been with you for so long a time and you still do not know me, Philip? Whoever has seen me has seen the Father. How can you say, 'Show us the Father'?[r] 10 Do you not believe that I am in the Father and the Father is in me? The words that I speak to you I do not speak on my own. The Father who dwells in me is doing his works.[s] 11 Believe me that I am in the Father and the Father is in me, or else, believe because of the works themselves.[t] 12 Amen, amen, I say to you, whoever believes in me will do the works that I do, and will do greater ones than these, because I am going to the Father.[u] 13 And whatever you ask in my name, I will do, so that the Father may be glorified in the Son.[v] 14 If you ask anything of me in my name, I will do it.

*The Advocate.* 15 "If you love me, you will keep my commandments.[w] 16 And I will ask the Father, and he will give you another Advocate* to be with you always,[x] 17 the Spirit of truth,* which the world cannot accept, because it neither sees nor knows it. But you know it, because it remains with you, and will be in you.[y] 18 I will not leave you orphans; I will come to you.* 19 In a little while the world will no longer see me, but you will see me, because I live and you will live.[z] 20 On that day you will realize that I am in my Father and you are in me and I in you.[a] 21 Whoever has my commandments and observes them is the one who loves me. And whoever loves me will be loved by my Father, and I will love him and reveal myself to him."[b] 22 Judas, not the Iscariot,* said to him, "Master, [then] what happened that you will reveal yourself to us and not to the world?"[c] 23 Jesus answered and said to him, "Whoever loves me will keep my

**14:1–31** Jesus' departure and return. This section is a dialogue marked off by a literary inclusion in Jn 14:1, 27: "Do not let your hearts be troubled."

**14:1 You have faith**: could also be imperative: "Have faith."

**14:3 Come back again**: a rare Johannine reference to the parousia; cf. 1 Jn 2:28.

**14:4 The way**: here, of Jesus himself; also a designation of Christianity in Acts 9:2; 19:9, 23; 22:4; 24:14, 22.

**14:6 The truth**: in John, the divinely revealed reality of the Father manifested in the person and works of Jesus. The possession of truth confers knowledge and liberation from sin (Jn 8:32).

**14:7** An alternative reading, "If you knew me, then you would have known my Father also," would be a rebuke, as in Jn 8:19.

**14:8 Show us the Father**: Philip is pictured asking for a theophany like Ex 24:9–10; 33:18.

**14:16 Another Advocate**: Jesus is the first advocate (*paraclete*); see 1 Jn 2:1, where Jesus is an advocate in the sense of intercessor in heaven. The Greek term derives from legal terminology for an advocate or defense attorney, and can mean spokesman, mediator, intercessor, comforter, consoler, although no one of these terms encompasses the meaning in John. The Paraclete in John is a teacher, a witness to Jesus, and a prosecutor of the world, who represents the continued presence on earth of the Jesus who has returned to the Father.

**14:17 The Spirit of truth**: this term is also used at Qumran, where it is a moral force put into a person by God, as opposed to the spirit of perversity. It is more personal in John; it will teach the realities of the new order (Jn 14:26), and testify to the truth (Jn 14:6). While it has been customary to use masculine personal pronouns in English for the Advocate, the Greek word for "spirit" is neuter, and the Greek text and manuscript variants fluctuate between masculine and neuter pronouns.

**14:18 I will come to you**: indwelling, not parousia.

**14:22 Judas, not the Iscariot**: probably not the brother of Jesus in Mk 6:3 // Mt 13:55 or the apostle named Jude in Lk 6:16, but Thomas (see note on Jn 11:16), although other readings have "Judas the Cananean."

*n:* 12:26; 17:24; 1 Jn 2:28. *o:* 8:31–47. *p:* 8:19; 12:45. *q:* Ex 24:9–10; 33:18. *r:* 1:18; 10:30; 12:45; 2 Cor 4:4; Col 1:15; Heb 1:3. *s:* 1:1; 10:37–38; 12:49. *t:* 10:38. *u:* 1:50; 5:20. *v:* 15:7, 16; 16:23–24; Mt 7:7–11. *w:* 15:10; Dt 6:4–9; Ps 119; Wis 6:18; 1 Jn 5:3; 2 Jn 6. *x:* 15:26; Lk 24:49; 1 Jn 2:1. *y:* 16:13; Mt 28:20; 2 Jn 1–2. *z:* 16:16. *a:* 10:38; 17:21; Is 2:17; 4:2–3. *b:* 16:27; 1 Jn 2:5; 3:24. *c:* 7:4; Acts 10:40–41.

word, and my Father will love him, and we will come to him and make our dwelling with him.[d] 24 Whoever does not love me does not keep my words; yet the word you hear is not mine but that of the Father who sent me.

25 "I have told you this while I am with you. 26 The Advocate, the holy Spirit that the Father will send in my name—he will teach you everything and remind you of all that [I] told you.[e] 27 Peace* I leave with you; my peace I give to you. Not as the world gives do I give it to you. Do not let your hearts be troubled or afraid.[f] 28* You heard me tell you, 'I am going away and I will come back to you.'[g] If you loved me, you would rejoice that I am going to the Father; for the Father is greater than I. 29 And now I have told you this before it happens, so that when it happens you may believe.[h] 30 I will no longer speak much with you, for the ruler of the world* is coming. He has no power over me, 31 but the world must know that I love the Father and that I do just as the Father has commanded me. Get up, let us go.[i]

## CHAPTER 15

See RG 330-31

*The Vine and the Branches.* 1* "I am the true vine,* and my Father is the vine grower.[j] 2 He takes away every branch in me that does not bear fruit, and every one that does he prunes* so that it bears more fruit. 3 You are already pruned because of the word that I spoke to you.[k] 4 Remain in me, as I remain in you. Just as a branch cannot bear fruit on its own unless it remains on the vine, so neither can you unless you remain in me. 5 I am the vine, you are the branches. Whoever remains in me and I in him will bear much fruit, because without me you can do nothing. 6* [l] Anyone who does not remain in me will be thrown out like a branch and wither; people will gather them and throw them into a fire and they will be burned. 7 If you remain in me and my words remain in you, ask for whatever you want and it will be done for you.[m] 8 By this is my Father glorified, that you bear much fruit and become my disciples.[n] 9 As the Father loves me, so I also love you. Remain in my love.[o] 10 If you keep my commandments, you will remain in my love, just as I have kept my Father's commandments and remain in his love.[p]

11 "I have told you this so that my joy may be in you and your joy may be complete.[q] 12 This is my commandment: love one another as I love you.[r] 13* No one has greater love than this,[s] to lay down one's life for one's friends. 14 You are my friends if you do what I command you. 15 I no longer call you slaves, because a slave does not know what his master is doing. I have called you friends,* because I have told you everything I have heard from my Father.[t] 16 It was not you who chose me, but I who chose you and appointed you to go and bear fruit that will remain, so that whatever you ask the Father in my name he may give you.[u] 17 This I command you: love one another.[v]

**14:27 Peace**: the traditional Hebrew salutation *šālôm*; but Jesus' "Shalom" is a gift of salvation, connoting the bounty of messianic blessing.

**14:28 The Father is greater than I**: because he **sent**, **gave**, etc., and Jesus is "a man who has told you the truth that I heard from God" (Jn 8:40).

**14:30 The ruler of the world**: Satan; cf. Jn 12:31; 16:11.

**15:1–16:4** Discourse on the union of Jesus with his disciples. His words become a monologue and go beyond the immediate crisis of the departure of Jesus.

**15:1–17** Like Jn 10:1–5, this passage resembles a parable. Israel is spoken of as a vineyard at Is 5:1–7; Mt 21:33–46 and as a vine at Ps 80:9–17; Jer 2:21; Ez 15:2; 17:5–10; 19:10; Hos 10:1. The identification of the vine as the Son of Man in Ps 80:15 and Wisdom's description of herself as a vine in Sir 24:17 are further background for portrayal of Jesus by this figure. There may be secondary eucharistic symbolism here; cf. Mk 14:25, "the fruit of the vine."

**15:2 Takes away . . . prunes**: in Greek there is a play on two related verbs.

**15:6** Branches were cut off and dried on the wall of the vineyard for later use as fuel.

**15:13 For one's friends**: or: "those whom one loves." In Jn 15:9–13a, the words for love are related to the Greek *agapaō*. In Jn 15:13b–15, the words for love are related to the Greek *phileō*. For John, the two roots seem synonymous and mean "to love"; cf. also Jn 21:15–17. The word *philos* is used here.

**15:15 Slaves . . . friends**: in the Old Testament, Moses (Dt 34:5), Joshua (Jos 24:29), and David (Ps 89:21) were called "servants" or "slaves of Yahweh"; only Abraham (Is 41:8; 2 Chr 20:7; cf. Jas 2:23) was called a "friend of God."

*d:* Rev 3:20. *e:* 15:26; 16:7, 13–14; Ps 51:13; Is 63:10. *f:* 16:33; Eph 2:14–18. *g:* 8:40. *h:* 13:19; 16:4. *i:* 6:38. *j:* Ps 80:9–17; Is 5:1–7; Jer 2:21; Ez 15:2; 17:5–10; 19:10. *k:* 13:10. *l:* Ez 15:6–7; 19:10–14. *m:* 14:13; Mt 7:7; Mk 11:24; 1 Jn 5:14. *n:* Mt 5:16. *o:* 17:23. *p:* 8:29; 14:15. *q:* 16:22; 17:13. *r:* 13:34. *s:* Rom 5:6–8; 1 Jn 3:16. *t:* Dt 34:5; Jos 24:29; 2 Chr 20:7; Ps 89:21; Is 41:8; Rom 8:15; Gal 4:7; Jas 2:23. *u:* 14:13; Dt 7:6. *v:* 13:34; 1 Jn 3:23; 4:21.

***The World's Hatred.**** 18"If the world hates you, realize that it hated me first.[w] 19If you belonged to the world, the world would love its own; but because you do not belong to the world, and I have chosen you out of the world, the world hates you.[x] 20Remember the word I spoke to you,* 'No slave is greater than his master.' If they persecuted me, they will also persecute you. If they kept my word, they will also keep yours.[y] 21And they will do all these things to you on account of my name,* because they do not know the one who sent me.[z] 22If I had not come and spoken* to them, they would have no sin; but as it is they have no excuse for their sin.[a] 23Whoever hates me also hates my Father.[b] 24If I had not done works among them that no one else ever did, they would not have sin; but as it is, they have seen and hated both me and my Father.[c] 25But in order that the word written in their law* might be fulfilled, 'They hated me without cause.'[d]

26"When the Advocate comes whom I will send* you from the Father, the Spirit of truth that proceeds from the Father, he will testify to me.[e] 27And you also testify, because you have been with me from the beginning.[f]

## CHAPTER 16

See RG 330–31

1"I have told you this so that you may not fall away. 2They will expel you from the synagogues; in fact, the hour* is coming when everyone who kills you will think he is offering worship to God.[g] 3They will do this because they have not known either the Father or me.[h] 4I have told you this so that when their hour comes you may remember that I told you.[i]

***Jesus' Departure; Coming of the Advocate.**** "I did not tell you this from the beginning, because I was with you. 5But now I am going to the one who sent me, and not one of you asks me,* 'Where are you going?'[j] 6But because I told you this, grief has filled your hearts. 7But I tell you the truth, it is better for you that I go. For if I do not go, the Advocate will not come to you.[k] But if I go, I will send him to you. 8* And when he comes he will convict the world in regard to sin and righteousness and condemnation: 9sin, because they do not believe in me;[l] 10righteousness, because I am going to the Father and you will no longer see me; 11condemnation, because the ruler of this world has been condemned.[m]

12"I have much more to tell you, but you cannot bear it now. 13* But when he comes, the Spirit of truth, he will guide you to all truth.[n] He will not speak on his own, but he will speak what he hears, and will declare to you the things that are coming. 14He will glorify me, because he will take from what is

**15:18–16:4** The hostile reaction of the world. There are synoptic parallels, predicting persecution, especially at Mt 10:17–25; 24:9–10.

**15:20 The word I spoke to you**: a reference to Jn 13:16.

**15:21 On account of my name**: the idea of persecution for Jesus' name is frequent in the New Testament (Mt 10:22; 24:9; Acts 9:14). For John, association with Jesus' name implies union with Jesus.

**15:22, 24** Jesus' words (**spoken**) and deeds (**works**) are the great motives of credibility. **They have seen and hated**: probably means that they have seen his works and still have hated; but the Greek can be read: "have seen both me and my Father and still have hated both me and my Father." **Works . . . that no one else ever did**: so Yahweh in Dt 4:32–33.

**15:25 In their law**: law is here used as a larger concept than the Pentateuch, for the reference is to Ps 35:19 or Ps 69:5. See notes on Jn 10:34; 12:34. **Their** law reflects the argument of the church with the synagogue.

**15:26 Whom I will send**: in Jn 14:16, 26, the Paraclete is to be sent by the Father, at the request of Jesus. Here the Spirit comes from both Jesus and the Father in mission; there is no reference here to the eternal procession of the Spirit.

**16:2 Hour**: of persecution, not Jesus' "hour" (see note on Jn 2:4).

**16:4b–33** A duplicate of Jn 14:1–31 on departure and return.

**16:5 Not one of you asks me**: the difficulty of reconciling this with Simon Peter's question in Jn 13:36 and Thomas' words in Jn 14:5 strengthens the supposition that the last discourse has been made up of several collections of Johannine material.

**16:8–11** These verses illustrate the forensic character of the Paraclete's role: in the forum of the disciples' conscience he prosecutes the world. He leads believers to see (a) that the basic sin was and is refusal to believe in Jesus; (b) that, although Jesus was found guilty and apparently died in disgrace, in reality righteousness has triumphed, for Jesus has returned to his Father; (c) finally, that it is the ruler of this world, Satan, who has been condemned through Jesus' death (Jn 12:32).

**16:13 Declare to you the things that are coming**: not a reference to new predictions about the future, but interpretation of what has already occurred or been said.

*w:* 7:7; 14:17; Mt 10:22; 24:9; Mk 13:13; Lk 6:22; 1 Jn 3:13. *x:* 17:14–16; 1 Jn 4:5. *y:* 13:16; Mt 10:24. *z:* 8:19; 16:3. *a:* 8:21, 24; 9:41. *b:* 5:23; Lk 10:16; 1 Jn 2:23. *c:* 3:2; 9:32; Dt 4:32–33. *d:* Ps 35:19; 69:4. *e:* 14:16, 26; Mt 10:19–20. *f:* Lk 1:2; Acts 1:8. *g:* 9:22; 12:42; Mt 10:17; Lk 21:12; Acts 26:11. *h:* 15:21. *i:* 13:19; 14:29. *j:* 7:33; 13:36; 14:5. *k:* 7:39; 14:16–17, 26; 15:26. *l:* 8:21–24; 15:22. *m:* 12:31. *n:* 14:17, 26; 15:26; Ps 25:5; 143:10; 1 Jn 2:27; Rev 7:17.

mine and declare it to you. 15 Everything that the Father has is mine; for this reason I told you that he will take from what is mine and declare it to you.

16 "A little while and you will no longer see me, and again a little while later and you will see me."[o] 17 So some of his disciples said to one another, "What does this mean that he is saying to us, 'A little while and you will not see me, and again a little while and you will see me,' and 'Because I am going to the Father'?" 18 So they said, "What is this 'little while' [of which he speaks]? We do not know what he means." 19 Jesus knew that they wanted to ask him, so he said to them, "Are you discussing with one another what I said, 'A little while and you will not see me, and again a little while and you will see me'? 20 Amen, amen, I say to you, you will weep and mourn, while the world rejoices; you will grieve, but your grief will become joy.[p] 21 When a woman is in labor, she is in anguish because her hour has arrived; but when she has given birth to a child, she no longer remembers the pain because of her joy that a child has been born into the world.[q] 22 So you also are now in anguish. But I will see you again, and your hearts will rejoice, and no one will take your joy away from you.[r] 23 On that day you will not question me about anything. Amen, amen, I say to you, whatever you ask the Father in my name he will give you.[s] 24 Until now you have not asked anything in my name; ask and you will receive, so that your joy may be complete.

25* [t] "I have told you this in figures of speech. The hour is coming when I will no longer speak to you in figures but I will tell you clearly about the Father. 26 On that day you will ask in my name, and I do not tell you that I will ask the Father for you.[u] 27 For the Father himself loves you, because you have loved me and have come to believe that I came from God. 28 I came from the Father and have come into the world. Now I am leaving the world and going back to the Father."[v] 29 His disciples said, "Now you are talking plainly, and not in any figure of speech. 30 Now we realize that you know everything and that you do not need to have anyone question you. Because of this we believe that you came from God."* 31 Jesus answered them, "Do you believe now? 32 Behold, the hour is coming and has arrived when each of you will be scattered* to his own home and you will leave me alone. But I am not alone, because the Father is with me.[w] 33 I have told you this so that you might have peace in me. In the world you will have trouble, but take courage, I have conquered the world."[x]

## CHAPTER 17

See RG 330–31

***The Prayer of Jesus.**** 1 When Jesus had said this, he raised his eyes to heaven* and said, "Father, the hour has come. Give glory to your son, so that your son may glorify you,[y] 2* just as you gave him authority over all people,[z] so that he may give eternal life to all you gave him. 3* Now this is eternal life,[a] that they should know you, the only true God, and the

**16:25** See note on Jn 10:6. Here, possibly a reference to Jn 15:1–16 or Jn 16:21.

**16:30** The reference is seemingly to the fact that Jesus could anticipate their question in Jn 16:19. The disciples naively think they have the full understanding that is the climax of "the hour" of Jesus' death, resurrection, and ascension (Jn 16:25), but the only part of the hour that is at hand for them is their share in the passion (Jn 16:32).

**16:32 You will be scattered**: cf. Mk 14:27 and Mt 26:31, where both cite Zec 13:7 about the sheep being dispersed.

**17:1–26** Climax of the last discourse(s). Since the sixteenth century, this chapter has been called the "high priestly prayer" of Jesus. He speaks as intercessor, with words addressed directly to the Father and not to the disciples, who supposedly only overhear. Yet the prayer is one of petition, for immediate (Jn 17:6–19) and future (Jn 17:20–21) disciples. Many phrases reminiscent of the Lord's Prayer occur. Although still in the world (Jn 17:13), Jesus looks on his earthly ministry as a thing of the past (Jn 17:4, 12). Whereas Jesus has up to this time stated that the disciples could follow him (Jn 13:33, 36), now he wishes them to be with him in union with the Father (Jn 17:12–14).

**17:1** The action of looking up to heaven and the address Father are typical of Jesus at prayer; cf. Jn 11:41 and Lk 11:2.

**17:2** Another possible interpretation is to treat the first line of the verse as parenthetical and the second as an appositive to the clause that ends v 1: **so that your son may glorify you (just as . . . all people), so that he may give eternal life. . . .**

**17:3** This verse was clearly added in the editing of the gospel as a reflection on the preceding verse; Jesus nowhere else refers to himself as Jesus Christ.

*o:* 7:33; 14:19. *p:* Ps 126:6. *q:* Is 26:17–18; Jer 31:13; Mi 4:9. *r:* 14:19; 15:11; 20:20. *s:* 14:13. *t:* Mt 13:34–35. *u:* 14:13. *v:* 1:1. *w:* 8:29; Zec 13:7; Mt 26:31; Mk 14:27. *x:* 14:27. *y:* 13:31. *z:* 3:35; Mt 28:18. *a:* 1:17; Wis 14:7; 15:3; 1 Jn 5:20.

one whom you sent, Jesus Christ. [4]I glorified you on earth by accomplishing the work that you gave me to do. [5]Now glorify me, Father, with you, with the glory that I had with you before the world began.[b]

[6]"I revealed your name* to those whom you gave me out of the world. They belonged to you, and you gave them to me, and they have kept your word. [7]Now they know that everything you gave me is from you, [8]because the words you gave to me I have given to them, and they accepted them and truly understood that I came from you, and they have believed that you sent me. [9]I pray for them. I do not pray for the world but for the ones you have given me, because they are yours,[c] [10]and everything of mine is yours and everything of yours is mine, and I have been glorified in them.[d] [11]And now I will no longer be in the world, but they are in the world, while I am coming to you. Holy Father, keep them in your name that you have given me, so that they may be one just as we are. [12]When I was with them I protected them in your name that you gave me, and I guarded them, and none of them was lost except the son of destruction, in order that the scripture might be fulfilled.[e] [13]But now I am coming to you. I speak this in the world so that they may share my joy completely.[f] [14]I gave them your word, and the world hated them, because they do not belong to the world any more than I belong to the world.[g] [15]* I do not ask that you take them out of the world[h] but that you keep them from the evil one. [16]They do not belong to the world any more than I belong to the world. [17]Consecrate them in the truth. Your word is truth.[i] [18]As you sent me into the world, so I sent them into the world.[j] [19]And I consecrate myself for them, so that they also may be consecrated in truth.

[20]"I pray not only for them, but also for those who will believe in me through their word, [21]so that they may all be one, as you, Father, are in me and I in you, that they also may be in us, that the world may believe that you sent me.[k] [22]And I have given them the glory you gave me, so that they may be one, as we are one, [23]I in them and you in me, that they may be brought to perfection as one, that the world may know that you sent me, and that you loved them even as you loved me. [24]Father, they are your gift to me. I wish that where I am* they also may be with me, that they may see my glory that you gave me, because you loved me before the foundation of the world.[l] [25]Righteous Father, the world also does not know you, but I know you, and they know that you sent me.[m] [26]I made known to them your name and I will make it known,* that the love with which you loved me may be in them and I in them."

## CHAPTER 18

See RG 331-32

***Jesus Arrested.**** [1]When he had said this, Jesus went out* with his disciples across the Kidron valley to where there was a garden, into which he and his disciples entered.[n] [2]Judas his betrayer also knew the place, because Jesus had often met there with his disciples. [3]So Judas got a band of soldiers* and guards from the chief priests and the Pharisees and went there with lanterns, torches, and weapons.[o] [4]Jesus, knowing everything that was going to happen to him, went out and said to them, "Whom are you looking for?"

**17:6 I revealed your name**: perhaps the name **I AM**; cf. Jn 8:24, 28, 58; 13:19.

**17:15** Note the resemblance to the petition of the Lord's Prayer, "deliver us from the evil one." Both probably refer to the devil rather than to abstract evil.

**17:24 Where I am**: Jesus prays for the believers ultimately to join him in heaven. Then they will not see his glory as in a mirror but clearly (2 Cor 3:18; 1 Jn 3:2).

**17:26 I will make it known**: through the Advocate.

**18:1–14** John does not mention the agony in the garden and the kiss of Judas, nor does he identify the place as Gethsemane or the Mount of Olives.

**18:1 Jesus went out**: see Jn 14:31, where it seems he is leaving the supper room. **Kidron valley**: literally, "the winter-flowing Kidron"; this wadi has water only during the winter rains.

**18:3 Band of soldiers**: seems to refer to Roman troops, either the full cohort of 600 men (1/10 of a legion), or more likely the maniple of 200 under their tribune (Jn 18:12). In this case, John is hinting at Roman collusion in the action against Jesus before he was brought to Pilate. The lanterns and torches may be symbolic of the hour of darkness.

*b:* 1:1, 2; 12:28; Phil 2:6, 9–11. *c:* 17:20. *d:* 16:15; 2 Thes 1:10, 12. *e:* 13:18; 18:9; Ps 41:10; Mt 26:24; Acts 1:16. *f:* 15:11. *g:* 15:19. *h:* Mt 6:13; 2 Thes 3:3; 1 Jn 5:18. *i:* 1 Pt 1:22 *j:* 20:21–22. *k:* 10:30; 14:10–11, 20. *l:* 14:3; 1 Thes 4:17. *m:* 1:10. *n:* 2 Sm 15:23; Mt 26:30, 36; Mk 14:26, 32; Lk 22:39. *o:* Mt 26:47–51; Mk 14:43–44; Lk 22:47.

5They answered him, "Jesus the Nazorean."* He said to them, "I AM." Judas his betrayer was also with them. 6When he said to them, "I AM," they turned away and fell to the ground. 7So he again asked them, "Whom are you looking for?" They said, "Jesus the Nazorean." 8Jesus answered, "I told you that I AM. So if you are looking for me, let these men go." 9* [p] This was to fulfill what he had said, "I have not lost any of those you gave me." 10Then Simon Peter, who had a sword, drew it, struck the high priest's slave, and cut off his right ear. The slave's name was Malchus.* 11Jesus said to Peter, "Put your sword into its scabbard. Shall I not drink the cup* that the Father gave me?"[q]

12[r] So the band of soldiers, the tribune, and the Jewish guards seized Jesus, bound him, 13and brought him to Annas* first. He was the father-in-law of Caiaphas, who was high priest that year.[s] 14It was Caiaphas who had counseled the Jews that it was better that one man should die rather than the people.[t]

***Peter's First Denial.***[u] 15Simon Peter and another disciple* followed Jesus. Now the other disciple was known to the high priest, and he entered the courtyard of the high priest with Jesus. 16But Peter stood at the gate outside. So the other disciple, the acquaintance of the high priest, went out and spoke to the gatekeeper and brought Peter in. 17Then the maid who was the gatekeeper said to Peter, "You are not one of this man's disciples, are you?" He said, "I am not." 18Now the slaves and the guards were standing around a charcoal fire that they had made, because it was cold, and were warming themselves. Peter was also standing there keeping warm.

***The Inquiry Before Annas.***[v] 19The high priest questioned Jesus about his disciples and about his doctrine. 20Jesus answered him, "I have spoken publicly to the world. I have always taught in a synagogue or in the temple area* where all the Jews gather, and in secret I have said nothing.[w] 21Why ask me? Ask those who heard me what I said to them. They know what I said." 22When he had said this, one of the temple guards standing there struck Jesus and said, "Is this the way you answer the high priest?"[x] 23Jesus answered him, "If I have spoken wrongly, testify to the wrong; but if I have spoken rightly, why do you strike me?" 24Then Annas sent him bound to Caiaphas* the high priest.[y]

***Peter Denies Jesus Again.***[z] 25Now Simon Peter was standing there keeping warm. And they said to him, "You are not one of his disciples, are you?" He denied it and said, "I am not." 26One of the slaves of the high priest, a relative of the one whose ear Peter had cut off, said, "Didn't I see you in the garden with him?" 27Again Peter denied it. And immediately the cock crowed.*

***The Trial Before Pilate.*** 28[a] Then they brought Jesus from Caiaphas to the praetorium.* It was morning. And they themselves did not enter the praetorium, in order not to

**18:5 Nazorean**: the form found in Mt 26:71 (see note on Mt 2:23) is here used, not **Nazarene** of Mark. **I AM**: or "I am he," but probably intended by the evangelist as an expression of divinity (cf. their appropriate response in Jn 18:6); see note on Jn 8:24. John sets the confusion of the arresting party against the background of Jesus' divine majesty.

**18:9** The citation may refer to Jn 6:39; 10:28; or 17:12.

**18:10** Only John gives the names of the two antagonists; both John and Luke mention the right ear.

**18:11** The theme of the cup is found in the synoptic account of the agony (Mk 14:36 and parallels).

**18:13 Annas**: only John mentions an inquiry before Annas; cf. Jn 18:16, 19–24; see note on Lk 3:2. It is unlikely that this nighttime interrogation before Annas is the same as the trial before Caiaphas placed by Matthew and Mark at night and by Luke in the morning.

**18:15–16 Another disciple . . . the other disciple**: see note on Jn 13:23.

**18:20 I have always taught . . . in the temple area**: cf. Mk 14:49 for a similar statement.

**18:24 Caiaphas**: see Mt 26:3, 57; Lk 3:2; and the notes there. John may leave room here for the trial before Caiaphas described in the synoptic gospels.

**18:27** Cockcrow was the third Roman division of the night, lasting from midnight to 3 a.m.

**18:28 Praetorium**: see note on Mt 27:27. **Morning**: literally, "the early hour," or fourth Roman division of the night, 3 to 6 a.m. **The Passover**: the synoptic gospels give the impression that the Thursday night supper was the Passover meal (Mk 14:12); for John that meal is still to be eaten Friday night.

*p:* 6:39; 10:28; 17:12. *q:* Mt 20:22; 26:39; Mk 10:38; Lk 22:42. *r:* Mt 26:57–58; Mk 14:53–54; Lk 22:54–55. *s:* Lk 3:2. *t:* 11:49–50. *u:* Mt 26:58, 69–70; Mk 14:54, 66–68; Lk 22:54–57. *v:* Mt 26:59–66; Mk 14:55–64; Lk 22:66–71. *w:* 6:59; 7:14, 26; Is 48:16; Mt 26:55; Mk 4:23; Lk 19:47; 22:53. *x:* Acts 23:2. *y:* Mt 26:57. *z:* Mt 26:71–75; Mk 14:69–72; Lk 22:58–62. *a:* Mt 27:1–2, 11–25; Mk 15:1–5; Lk 23:1–5.

be defiled so that they could eat the Passover. [29]So Pilate came out to them and said, "What charge do you bring [against] this man?" [30]They answered and said to him, "If he were not a criminal, we would not have handed him over to you." [31]At this, Pilate said to them, "Take him yourselves, and judge him according to your law." The Jews answered him, "We do not have the right to execute anyone,"* [32]* in order that the word of Jesus might be fulfilled that he said indicating the kind of death[b] he would die. [33]So Pilate went back into the praetorium and summoned Jesus and said to him, "Are you the King of the Jews?" [34]Jesus answered, "Do you say this on your own or have others told you about me?" [35]Pilate answered, "I am not a Jew, am I? Your own nation and the chief priests handed you over to me. What have you done?"[c] [36]Jesus answered, "My kingdom does not belong to this world. If my kingdom did belong to this world, my attendants [would] be fighting to keep me from being handed over to the Jews. But as it is, my kingdom is not here."[d] [37]So Pilate said to him, "Then you are a king?" Jesus answered, "You say I am a king.* For this I was born and for this I came into the world, to testify to the truth. Everyone who belongs to the truth listens to my voice."[e] [38]Pilate said to him, "What is truth?"[f]

When he had said this, he again went out to the Jews and said to them, "I find no guilt in him. [39]But you have a custom that I release one prisoner to you at Passover.* Do you want me to release to you the King of the Jews?" [40]They cried out again, "Not this one but Barabbas!"* Now Barabbas was a revolutionary.

## CHAPTER 19

See RG 331–32

[1]* [g] Then Pilate took Jesus and had him scourged. [2]And the soldiers wove a crown out of thorns and placed it on his head, and clothed him in a purple cloak, [3]and they came to him and said, "Hail, King of the Jews!" And they struck him repeatedly. [4]Once more Pilate went out and said to them, "Look, I am bringing him out to you, so that you may know that I find no guilt in him."[h] [5]So Jesus came out, wearing the crown of thorns and the purple cloak. And he said to them, "Behold, the man!"[i] [6]When the chief priests and the guards saw him they cried out, "Crucify him, crucify him!" Pilate said to them, "Take him yourselves and crucify him. I find no guilt in him."[j] [7]* The Jews answered,[k] "We have a law, and according to that law he ought to die, because he made himself the Son of God." [8]Now when Pilate heard this statement, he became even more afraid, [9]and went back into the praetorium and said to Jesus, "Where are you from?" Jesus did not answer him.[l] [10]So Pilate said to him, "Do you not speak to me? Do you not know that I have power to release you and I have power to crucify you?" [11]Jesus answered [him], "You would have no power over me if it had not been given to you from above. For this reason the one who handed me over to you has the greater sin."[m] [12]Consequently, Pilate tried to release him; but the

**18:31 We do not have the right to execute anyone**: only John gives this reason for their bringing Jesus to Pilate. Jewish sources are not clear on the competence of the Sanhedrin at this period to sentence and to execute for political crimes.

**18:32** The Jewish punishment for blasphemy was stoning (Lv 24:16). In coming to the Romans to ensure that Jesus would be crucified, the Jewish authorities fulfilled his prophecy that he would be exalted (Jn 3:14; 12:32–33). There is some historical evidence, however, for Jews crucifying Jews.

**18:37 You say I am a king**: see Mt 26:64 for a similar response to the high priest. It is at best a reluctant affirmative.

**18:39** See note on Mt 27:15.

**18:40 Barabbas**: see note on Mt 27:16–17. **Revolutionary**: a guerrilla warrior fighting for nationalistic aims, though the term can also denote a robber. See note on Mt 27:38.

**19:1** Luke places the mockery of Jesus at the midpoint in the trial when Jesus was sent to Herod. Mark and Matthew place the scourging and mockery at the end of the trial after the sentence of death. Scourging was an integral part of the crucifixion penalty.

**19:7 Made himself the Son of God**: this question was not raised in John's account of the Jewish interrogations of Jesus as it was in the synoptic account. Nevertheless, see Jn 5:18; 8:53; 10:36.

**19:12 Friend of Caesar**: a Roman honorific title bestowed upon high-ranking officials for merit.

*b:* 3:14; 8:28; 12:32–33. *c:* 1:11. *d:* 1:10; 8:23. *e:* 8:47; 1 Tm 6:13. *f:* Mt 27:15–26; Mk 15:6–15; Lk 23:18–25; Acts 3:14. *g:* Mt 27:27–31; Mk 15:16–20; Lk 23:13–25. *h:* 18:38. *i:* Is 52:14. *j:* 18:31; 19:15. *k:* 10:33–36; Lv 24:16. *l:* 7:28. *m:* 3:27; 10:18; Rom 13:1.

Jews cried out, "If you release him, you are
not a Friend of Caesar.* Everyone who
makes himself a king opposes Caesar."[n]
13 When Pilate heard these words he
brought Jesus out and seated him* on the
judge's bench in the place called Stone
Pavement, in Hebrew, Gabbatha. 14 It was
preparation day for Passover, and it was
about noon.* And he said to the Jews, "Behold, your king!" 15 They cried out, "Take
him away, take him away! Crucify him!" Pilate said to them, "Shall I crucify your
king?" The chief priests answered, "We
have no king but Caesar." 16 Then he handed
him over to them to be crucified.*

***The Crucifixion of Jesus.*** So they took
Jesus, 17[o] and carrying the cross himself* he
went out to what is called the Place of the
Skull, in Hebrew, Golgotha. 18 There they
crucified him, and with him two others, one
on either side, with Jesus in the middle.
19* Pilate also had an inscription written and
put on the cross. It read, "Jesus the Nazorean, the King of the Jews." 20 Now many of
the Jews read this inscription, because the
place where Jesus was crucified was near the
city; and it was written in Hebrew, Latin, and
Greek. 21 So the chief priests of the Jews said
to Pilate, "Do not write 'The King of the
Jews,' but that he said, 'I am the King of the
Jews.' "[p] 22 Pilate answered, "What I have
written, I have written."
23* When the soldiers had crucified
Jesus,[q] they took his clothes and divided
them into four shares, a share for each soldier.[r] They also took his tunic, but the tunic
was seamless, woven in one piece from the
top down. 24 So they said to one another,
"Let's not tear it, but cast lots for it to see
whose it will be," in order that the passage of
scripture might be fulfilled [that says]:

"They divided my garments among them,
and for my vesture they cast lots."

This is what the soldiers did. 25* [s] Standing
by the cross of Jesus were his mother and his
mother's sister, Mary the wife of Clopas,
and Mary of Magdala. 26 When Jesus saw his
mother* and the disciple there whom he
loved, he said to his mother, "Woman, be-

**19:13 Seated him**: others translate "(Pilate) sat down." In John's thought, Jesus is the real judge of the world, and John may here be portraying him seated on the judgment bench. **Stone Pavement**: in Greek *lithostrotos*; under the fortress Antonia, one of the conjectured locations of the praetorium, a massive stone pavement has been excavated. **Gabbatha** (Aramaic rather than Hebrew) probably means "ridge, elevation."

**19:14 Noon**: Mk 15:25 has Jesus crucified "at the third hour," which means either 9 a.m. or the period from 9 to 12. Noon, the time when, according to John, Jesus was sentenced to death, was the hour at which the priests began to slaughter Passover lambs in the temple; see Jn 1:29.

**19:16 He handed him over to them to be crucified**: in context this would seem to mean "handed him over to the chief priests." Lk 23:25 has a similar ambiguity. There is a polemic tendency in the gospels to place the guilt of the crucifixion on the Jewish authorities and to exonerate the Romans from blame. But John later mentions the Roman soldiers (Jn 19:23), and it was to these soldiers that Pilate handed Jesus over.

**19:17 Carrying the cross himself**: a different picture from that of the synoptics, especially Lk 23:26, where Simon of Cyrene is made to carry the cross, walking behind Jesus. In John's theology, Jesus remained in complete control and master of his destiny (cf. Jn 10:18). **Place of the Skull**: the Latin word for skull is *Calvaria*; hence "Calvary." **Golgotha** is actually an Aramaic rather than a Hebrew word.

**19:19** The inscription differs with slightly different words in each of the four gospels. John's form is fullest and gives the equivalent of the Latin *INRI = Iesus Nazarenus Rex Iudaeorum*. Only John mentions its polyglot character (Jn 19:20) and Pilate's role in keeping the title unchanged (Jn 19:21–22).

**19:23–25a** While all four gospels describe the soldiers casting lots to divide Jesus' garments (see note on Mt 27:35), only John quotes the underlying passage from Ps 22:19, and only John sees each line of the poetic parallelism literally carried out in two separate actions (Jn 19:23–24).

**19:25** It is not clear whether four women are meant, or three (i.e., **Mary the wife of Cl[e]opas** [cf. Lk 24:18] is in apposition with **his mother's sister**) or two (his mother and his mother's sister, i.e., Mary of Cl[e]opas and Mary of Magdala). Only John mentions the mother of Jesus here. The synoptics have a group of women looking on from a distance at the cross (Mk 15:40).

**19:26–27** This scene has been interpreted literally, of Jesus' concern for his mother; and symbolically, e.g., in the light of the Cana story in Jn 2 (the presence of the mother of Jesus, the address **woman**, and the mention of the **hour**) and of the upper room in Jn 13 (the presence of the beloved disciple; the **hour**). Now that the hour has come (Jn 19:28), Mary (a symbol of the church?) is given a role as the mother of Christians (personified by the beloved disciple); or, as a representative of those seeking salvation, she is supported by the disciple who interprets Jesus' revelation; or Jewish and Gentile Christianity (or Israel and the Christian community) are reconciled.

*n:* Acts 17:7. *o:* Mt 27:32–37; Mk 15:21–26; Lk 23:26–35. *p:* 18:33; Lk 19:14. *q:* Mt 27:38–44; Mk 15:27–32; Lk 23:36–43. *r:* Ps 22:19; Mt 27:35; Mk 15:24; Lk 23:34. *s:* Mt 27:55; Mk 15:40–41; Lk 8:2; 23:49.

hold, your son."[t] 27 Then he said to the disciple, "Behold, your mother." And from that hour the disciple took her into his home.

28[u] After this, aware that everything was now finished, in order that the scripture might be fulfilled,* Jesus said, "I thirst."[v] 29 There was a vessel filled with common wine.* So they put a sponge soaked in wine on a sprig of hyssop and put it up to his mouth. 30* When Jesus had taken the wine, he said, "It is finished."[w] And bowing his head, he handed over the spirit.

*The Blood and Water.* 31 Now since it was preparation day, in order that the bodies might not remain on the cross on the sabbath, for the sabbath day of that week was a solemn one, the Jews asked Pilate that their legs be broken and they be taken down.[x] 32 So the soldiers came and broke the legs of the first and then of the other one who was crucified with Jesus. 33 But when they came to Jesus and saw that he was already dead, they did not break his legs, 34* [y] but one soldier thrust his lance into his side, and immediately blood and water flowed out. 35 An eyewitness has testified, and his testimony is true; he knows* that he is speaking the truth, so that you also may [come to] believe.[z] 36 For this happened so that the scripture passage might be fulfilled:

"Not a bone of it will be broken."[a]

37 And again another passage says:

"They will look upon him whom they
have pierced."[b]

*The Burial of Jesus.** 38[c] After this, Joseph of Arimathea, secretly a disciple of Jesus for fear of the Jews, asked Pilate if he could remove the body of Jesus. And Pilate permitted it. So he came and took his body. 39 Nicodemus, the one who had first come to him at night, also came bringing a mixture of myrrh and aloes weighing about one hundred pounds.[d] 40 They took the body of Jesus and bound it with burial cloths along with the spices, according to the Jewish burial custom. 41 Now in the place where he had been crucified there was a garden, and in the garden a new tomb, in which no one had yet been buried. 42 So they laid Jesus there because of the Jewish preparation day; for the tomb was close by.

## CHAPTER 20*

See RG 331-32

*The Empty Tomb.** 1 On the first day of the week,[e] Mary of Magdala came to the tomb early in the morning, while it was still dark,* and saw the stone removed from the tomb.[f] 2 So she ran* and went to Simon Peter and to the other disciple whom Jesus loved, and told them, "They have taken the Lord from the tomb, and we don't know where

**19:28 The scripture . . . fulfilled**: either in the scene of Jn 19:25–27, or in the **I thirst** of Jn 19:28. If the latter, Ps 22:16; 69:22 deserve consideration.

**19:29 Wine**: John does not mention the drugged wine, a narcotic that Jesus refused as the crucifixion began (Mk 15:23), but only this final gesture of kindness at the end (Mk 15:36). **Hyssop**, a small plant, is scarcely suitable for carrying a sponge (Mark mentions a reed) and may be a symbolic reference to the hyssop used to daub the blood of the paschal lamb on the doorpost of the Hebrews (Ex 12:22).

**19:30 Handed over the spirit**: there is a double nuance of dying (giving up the last breath or spirit) and that of passing on the holy Spirit; see Jn 7:39, which connects the giving of the Spirit with Jesus' glorious return to the Father, and Jn 20:22, where the author portrays the conferral of the Spirit.

**19:34–35** John probably emphasizes these verses to show the reality of Jesus' death, against the docetic heretics. In the blood and water there may also be a symbolic reference to the Eucharist and baptism.

**19:35 He knows**: it is not certain from the Greek that this **he** is the **eyewitness** of the first part of the sentence. **May [come to] believe**: see note on Jn 20:31.

**19:38–42** In the first three gospels there is no anointing on Friday. In Matthew and Luke the women come to the tomb on Sunday morning precisely to anoint Jesus.

**20:1–31** The risen Jesus reveals his glory and confers the Spirit. This story fulfills the basic need for testimony to the resurrection. What we have here is not a record but a series of single stories.

**20:1–10** The story of the empty tomb is found in both the Matthean and the Lucan traditions; John's version seems to be a fusion of the two.

**20:1 Still dark**: according to Mark the sun had risen, Matthew describes it as "dawning," and Luke refers to early dawn. Mary sees the stone removed, not the empty tomb.

**20:2** Mary runs away, not directed by an angel/young man as in the synoptic accounts. The plural "we" in the second part of her statement might reflect a tradition of more women going to the tomb.

*t:* 13:23. *u:* Mt 27:45–56; Mk 15:33–41; Lk 23:44–49. *v:* Ps 22:16; 69:22. *w:* 4:34; 10:18; 17:4; Lk 23:46. *x:* Ex 12:16; Dt 21:23. *y:* Nm 20:11; 1 Jn 5:6. *z:* 7:37–39; 21:24. *a:* Ex 12:46; Nm 9:12; Ps 34:21. *b:* Nm 21:9; Zec 12:10; Rev 1:7. *c:* Mt 27:57–60; Mk 15:42–46; Lk 23:46–49. *d:* 3:1–2; 7:50; Ps 45:9. *e:* Mt 28:1–10; Mk 16:1–11; Lk 24:1–12. *f:* 19:25.

they put him." 3* So Peter and the other disciple went out and came to the tomb. 4They both ran, but the other disciple ran faster than Peter and arrived at the tomb first; 5he bent down and saw the burial cloths there, but did not go in. 6[g] When Simon Peter arrived after him, he went into the tomb and saw the burial cloths* there, 7and the cloth that had covered his head, not with the burial cloths but rolled up in a separate place.[h] 8Then the other disciple also went in, the one who had arrived at the tomb first, and he saw and believed. 9* [i] For they did not yet understand the scripture that he had to rise from the dead. 10Then the disciples returned home.

***The Appearance to Mary of Magdala.**** 11But Mary stayed outside the tomb weeping.[j] And as she wept, she bent over into the tomb 12and saw two angels in white sitting there, one at the head and one at the feet where the body of Jesus had been. 13And they said to her, "Woman, why are you weeping?" She said to them, "They have taken my Lord, and I don't know where they laid him." 14When she had said this, she turned around and saw Jesus there, but did not know it was Jesus.[k] 15Jesus said to her, "Woman, why are you weeping? Whom are you looking for?"[l] She thought it was the gardener and said to him, "Sir, if you carried him away, tell me where you laid him, and I will take him." 16Jesus said to her, "Mary!" She turned and said to him in Hebrew, "Rabbouni,"* which means Teacher. 17Jesus said to her, "Stop holding on to me,* for I have not yet ascended to the Father. But go to my brothers and tell them, 'I am going to my Father and your Father, to my God and your God.' "[m] 18Mary of Magdala went and announced to the disciples, "I have seen the Lord," and what he told her.

***Appearance to the Disciples.**** 19On the evening of that first day of the week,[n] when the doors were locked, where the disciples* were, for fear of the Jews, Jesus came and stood in their midst and said to them, "Peace be with you." 20When he had said this, he showed them his hands and his side.* The disciples rejoiced when they saw the Lord.[o] 21* [Jesus] said to them again,[p] "Peace be with you. As the Father has sent me, so I

**20:3–10** The basic narrative is told of Peter alone in Lk 24:12, a verse missing in important manuscripts and which may be borrowed from tradition similar to John. Cf. also Lk 24:24.

**20:6–8** Some special feature about the state of the burial cloths caused the beloved disciple to believe. Perhaps the details emphasized that the grave had not been robbed.

**20:9** Probably a general reference to the scriptures is intended, as in Lk 24:26 and 1 Cor 15:4. Some individual Old Testament passages suggested are Ps 16:10; Hos 6:2; Jon 2:1, 2, 10.

**20:11–18** This appearance to Mary is found only in John, but cf. Mt 28:8–10 and Mk 16:9–11.

**20:16 Rabbouni**: Hebrew or Aramaic for "my master."

**20:17 Stop holding on to me**: see Mt 28:9, where the women take hold of his feet. **I have not yet ascended**: for John and many of the New Testament writers, the ascension in the theological sense of going to the Father to be glorified took place with the resurrection as one action. This scene in John dramatizes such an understanding, for by Easter night Jesus is glorified and can give the Spirit. Therefore his ascension takes place immediately after he has talked to Mary. In such a view, the ascension after forty days described in Acts 1:1–11 would be simply a termination of earthly appearances or, perhaps better, an introduction to the conferral of the Spirit upon the early church, modeled on Elisha's being able to have a (double) share in the spirit of Elijah if he saw him being taken up (same verb as ascending) into heaven (2 Kgs 2:9–12). **To my Father and your Father, to my God and your God**: this echoes Ru 1:16: "Your people shall be my people, and your God my God." The Father of Jesus will now become the Father of the disciples because, once ascended, Jesus can give them the Spirit that comes from the Father and they can be reborn as God's children (Jn 3:5). That is why he calls them **my brothers**.

**20:19–29** The appearances to the disciples, without or with Thomas (cf. Jn 11:16; 14:5), have rough parallels in the other gospels only for Jn 20:19–23; cf. Lk 24:36–39; Mk 16:14–18.

**20:19 The disciples**: by implication from Jn 20:24 this means ten of the Twelve, presumably in Jerusalem. **Peace be with you**: although this could be an ordinary greeting, John intends here to echo Jn 14:27. The theme of rejoicing in Jn 20:20 echoes Jn 16:22.

**20:20 Hands and . . . side**: Lk 24:39–40 mentions "hands and feet," based on Ps 22:17.

**20:21** By means of this sending, the Eleven were made apostles, that is, "those sent" (cf. Jn 17:18), though John does not use the noun in reference to them (see note on Jn 13:16). A solemn mission or "sending" is also the subject of the post-resurrection appearances to the Eleven in Mt 28:19; Lk 24:47; Mk 16:15.

*g:* Lk 24:12. *h:* 11:44; 19:40. *i:* Acts 2:26–27; 1 Cor 15:4. *j:* Mk 16:9–11. *k:* 21:4; Mk 16:12; Lk 24:16; 1 Cor 15:43–44. *l:* Mt 28:9–10. *m:* Acts 1:9. *n:* Mt 28:16–20; Mk 16:14–18; Lk 24:36–44. *o:* 14:27. *p:* 17:18; Mt 28:19; Mk 16:15; Lk 24:47–48.

send you." 22* And when he had said this, he breathed on them and said to them,[q] "Receive the holy Spirit. 23* [r] Whose sins you forgive are forgiven them, and whose sins you retain are retained."

***Thomas.*** 24 Thomas, called Didymus, one of the Twelve, was not with them when Jesus came. 25 So the other disciples said to him, "We have seen the Lord." But he said to them, "Unless I see the mark of the nails in his hands and put my finger into the nailmarks and put my hand into his side, I will not believe."[s] 26 Now a week later his disciples were again inside and Thomas was with them. Jesus came, although the doors were locked, and stood in their midst and said, "Peace be with you."[t] 27 Then he said to Thomas, "Put your finger here and see my hands, and bring your hand and put it into my side, and do not be unbelieving, but believe." 28* [u] Thomas answered and said to him, "My Lord and my God!" 29* Jesus said to him, "Have you come to believe because you have seen me?[v] Blessed are those who have not seen and have believed."

***Conclusion.**** 30 Now Jesus did many other signs in the presence of [his] disciples that are not written in this book.[w] 31 But these are written that you may [come to] believe that Jesus is the Messiah, the Son of God, and that through this belief you may have life in his name.[x]

## IV. Epilogue: The Resurrection Appearance in Galilee

### CHAPTER 21

See RG 332

***The Appearance to the Seven Disciples.*** 1* After this, Jesus revealed himself again to his disciples at the Sea of Tiberias. He revealed himself in this way.[y] 2 Together were Simon Peter, Thomas called Didymus, Nathanael from Cana in Galilee, Zebedee's sons,* and two others of his disciples. 3* Simon Peter said to them, "I am going fishing." They said to him, "We also will come with you." So they went out and got into the boat, but that night they caught nothing.[z] 4 When it was already dawn, Jesus was standing on the shore; but the disciples did not realize that it was Jesus.[a] 5 Jesus said to them, "Children, have you caught anything to eat?" They answered him, "No."[b] 6 So he said to them, "Cast the net over the right side of the boat and you will find something." So they cast it, and were not able to pull it in because of the number of fish. 7 So the disciple whom Jesus loved said to Peter, "It is the Lord." When Simon Peter heard that it was the Lord, he tucked in his garment, for he was lightly clad, and jumped into the sea. 8 The other disciples came in the boat, for they were not far from shore, only about a hundred yards, dragging the net with the

**20:22** This action recalls Gn 2:7, where God breathed on the first man and gave him life; just as Adam's life came from God, so now the disciples' new spiritual life comes from Jesus. Cf. also the revivification of the dry bones in Ez 37. This is the author's version of Pentecost. Cf. also the note on Jn 19:30.

**20:23** The Council of Trent defined that this power to forgive sins is exercised in the sacrament of penance. See Mt 16:19; 18:18.

**20:28 My Lord and my God**: this forms a literary inclusion with the first verse of the gospel: "and the Word was God."

**20:29** This verse is a beatitude on future generations; faith, not sight, matters.

**20:30–31** These verses are clearly a conclusion to the gospel and express its purpose. While many manuscripts read **come to believe**, possibly implying a missionary purpose for John's gospel, a small number of quite early ones read "continue to believe," suggesting that the audience consists of Christians whose faith is to be deepened by the book; cf. Jn 19:35.

**21:1–23** There are many non-Johannine peculiarities in this chapter, some suggesting Lucan Greek style; yet this passage is closer to John than Jn 7:53–8:11. There are many Johannine features as well. Its closest parallels in the synoptic gospels are found in Lk 5:1–11 and Mt 14:28–31. Perhaps the tradition was ultimately derived from John but preserved by some disciple other than the writer of the rest of the gospel. The appearances narrated seem to be independent of those in Jn 20. Even if a later addition, the chapter was added before publication of the gospel, for it appears in all manuscripts.

**21:2 Zebedee's sons**: the only reference to James and John in this gospel (but see note on Jn 1:37). Perhaps the phrase was originally a gloss to identify, among the five, the **two others of his disciples**. The anonymity of the latter phrase is more Johannine (Jn 1:35). The total of seven may suggest the community of the disciples in its fullness.

**21:3–6** This may be a variant of Luke's account of the catch of fish; see note on Lk 5:1–11.

*q:* Gn 2:7; Ez 37:9; 1 Cor 15:45. *r:* Mt 16:19; 18:18. *s:* 1 Jn 1:1. *t:* 21:14. *u:* 1:1. *v:* 4:48; Lk 1:45; 1 Pt 1:8. *w:* 21:25. *x:* 3:14, 15; 1 Jn 5:13. *y:* Mt 26:32; 28:7. *z:* Mt 4:18; Lk 5:4–10. *a:* 20:14; Mt 28:17; Lk 24:16. *b:* Lk 24:41.

fish. 9* [c] When they climbed out on shore, they saw a charcoal fire with fish on it and bread. 10 Jesus said to them, "Bring some of the fish you just caught." 11 So Simon Peter went over and dragged the net ashore full of one hundred fifty-three* large fish. Even though there were so many, the net was not torn.[d] 12 Jesus said to them, "Come, have breakfast." And none of the disciples dared to ask him,* "Who are you?" because they realized it was the Lord. 13 Jesus came over and took the bread and gave it to them, and in like manner the fish.[e] 14* This was now the third time[f] Jesus was revealed to his disciples after being raised from the dead.

*Jesus and Peter.** 15 When they had finished breakfast, Jesus said to Simon Peter,* "Simon, son of John, do you love me more than these?"* He said to him, "Yes, Lord, you know that I love you." He said to him, "Feed my lambs." 16 He then said to him a second time, "Simon, son of John, do you love me?" He said to him, "Yes, Lord, you know that I love you." He said to him, "Tend my sheep." 17 He said to him the third time, "Simon, son of John, do you love me?" Peter was distressed that he had said to him a third time, "Do you love me?" and he said to him, "Lord, you know everything; you know that I love you." [Jesus] said to him, "Feed my sheep.[g] 18* Amen, amen, I say to you,[h] when you were younger, you used to dress yourself and go where you wanted; but when you grow old, you will stretch out your hands, and someone else will dress you and lead you where you do not want to go." 19 He said this signifying by what kind of death he would glorify God. And when he had said this, he said to him, "Follow me."[i]

***The Beloved Disciple.*** 20 Peter turned and saw the disciple following whom Jesus loved, the one who had also reclined upon his chest during the supper and had said, "Master, who is the one who will betray you?"[j] 21 When Peter saw him, he said to Jesus, "Lord, what about him?" 22 Jesus said to him, "What if I want him to remain until I come?* What concern is it of yours? You follow me."[k] 23* So the word spread among the brothers that that disciple would not die. But Jesus had not told him that he would not die, just "What if I want him to remain until I come? [What concern is it of yours?]"

***Conclusion.*** 24 It is this disciple who testifies to these things and has written them,* and we know that his testimony is true.[l] 25 There are also many other things that Jesus did, but if these were to be described individually, I do not think the whole world would contain the books that would be written.[m]

**21:9, 12–13** It is strange that Jesus already has fish since none have yet been brought ashore. This meal may have had eucharistic significance for early Christians since Jn 21:13 recalls Jn 6:11 which uses the vocabulary of Jesus' action at the Last Supper; but see also note on Mt 14:19.

**21:11** The exact number 153 is probably meant to have a symbolic meaning in relation to the apostles' universal mission; Jerome claims that Greek zoologists catalogued 153 species of fish. Or 153 is the sum of the numbers from 1 to 17. Others invoke Ez 47:10.

**21:12 None . . . dared to ask him**: is Jesus' appearance strange to them? Cf. Lk 24:16; Mk 16:12; Jn 20:14. The disciples do, however, recognize Jesus **before** the breaking of the bread (opposed to Lk 24:35).

**21:14** This verse connects Jn 20 and 21; cf. Jn 20:19, 26.

**21:15–23** This section constitutes Peter's rehabilitation and emphasizes his role in the church.

**21:15–17** In these three verses there is a remarkable variety of synonyms: two different Greek verbs for **love** (see note on Jn 15:13); two verbs for **feed/tend**; two nouns for **sheep**; two verbs for **know**. But apparently there is no difference of meaning. The threefold confession of Peter is meant to counteract his earlier threefold denial (Jn 18:17, 25, 27). The First Vatican Council cited these verses in defining that Jesus after his resurrection gave Peter the jurisdiction of supreme shepherd and ruler over the whole flock.

**21:15 More than these**: probably "more than these disciples do" rather than "more than you love them" or "more than you love these things [fishing, etc.]."

**21:18** Originally probably a proverb about old age, now used as a figurative reference to the crucifixion of Peter.

**21:22 Until I come**: a reference to the parousia.

**21:23** This whole scene takes on more significance if the disciple is already dead. The death of the apostolic generation caused problems in the church because of a belief that Jesus was to have returned first. Loss of faith sometimes resulted; cf. 2 Pt 3:4.

**21:24 Who . . . has written them**: this does not necessarily mean he wrote them with his own hand. The same expression is used in Jn 19:22 of Pilate, who certainly would not have written the inscription himself. **We know**: i.e., the Christian community; cf. Jn 1:14, 16.

*c:* Lk 24:41–43. *d:* 2 Chr 2:16. *e:* Lk 24:42. *f:* 20:19, 26. *g:* 13:37–38; 18:15–18, 25–27; Mt 26:69–75; Mk 14:66–72; Lk 22:55–62. *h:* Acts 21:11, 14; 2 Pt 1:14. *i:* 13:36. *j:* 13:25. *k:* Mt 16:28. *l:* 19:35. *m:* 20:30.

See RG 334–50

# The Acts of the Apostles

The Acts of the Apostles, the second volume of Luke's two-volume work, continues Luke's presentation of biblical history, describing how the salvation promised to Israel in the Old Testament and accomplished by Jesus has now under the guidance of the holy Spirit been extended to the Gentiles. This was accomplished through the divinely chosen representatives (Acts 10:41) whom Jesus prepared during his historical ministry (Acts 1:21–22) and commissioned after his resurrection as witnesses to all that he taught (Acts 1:8; 10:37–43; Lk 24:48). Luke's preoccupation with the Christian community as the Spirit-guided bearer of the word of salvation rules out of his book detailed histories of the activity of most of the preachers. Only the main lines of the roles of Peter and Paul serve Luke's interest.

Peter was the leading member of the Twelve (Acts 1:13, 15), a miracle worker like Jesus in the gospel (Acts 3:1–10; 5:1–11, 15; 9:32–35, 36–42), the object of divine care (Acts 5:17–21; 12:6–11), and the spokesman for the Christian community (Acts 2:14–36; 3:12–26; 4:8–12; 5:29–32; 10:34–43; 15:7–11), who, according to Luke, was largely responsible for the growth of the community in the early days (Acts 2:4; 4:4). Paul eventually joined the community at Antioch (Acts 11:25–26), which subsequently commissioned him and Barnabas to undertake the spread of the gospel to Asia Minor. This missionary venture generally failed to win the Jews of the diaspora to the gospel but enjoyed success among the Gentiles (Acts 13:14–14:27).

Paul's refusal to impose the Mosaic law upon his Gentile converts provoked very strong objection among the Jewish Christians of Jerusalem (Acts 15:1), but both Peter and James supported his position (Acts 15:6–21). Paul's second and third missionary journeys (Acts 16:36–21:16) resulted in the same pattern of failure among the Jews generally but of some success among the Gentiles. Paul, like Peter, is presented as a miracle worker (Acts 14:8–18; 19:12; 20:7–12; 28:7–10) and the object of divine care (Acts 16:25–31).

In Acts, Luke has provided a broad survey of the church's development from the resurrection of Jesus to Paul's first Roman imprisonment, the point at which the book ends. In telling this story, Luke describes the emergence of Christianity from its origins in Judaism to its position as a religion of worldwide status and appeal. Originally a Jewish Christian community in Jerusalem, the church was placed in circumstances impelling it to include within its membership people of other cultures: the Samaritans (Acts 8:4–25), at first an occasional Gentile (Acts 8:26–30; 10:1–48), and finally the Gentiles on principle (Acts 11:20–21). Fear on the part of the Jewish people that Christianity, particularly as preached to the Gentiles, threatened their own cultural heritage caused them to be suspicious of Paul's gospel (Acts 13:42–45; 15:1–5; 28:17–24). The inability of Christian missionaries to allay this apprehension inevitably created a situation in which the gospel was preached more and more to the Gentiles. Toward the end of Paul's career, the Christian communities, with the exception of those in Palestine itself (Acts 9:31), were mainly of Gentile membership. In tracing the emergence of Christianity from Judaism, Luke is insistent upon the prominence of Israel in the divine plan of salvation (see note on Acts 1:26; see also Acts 2:5–6; 3:13–15; 10:36; 13:16–41; 24:14–15) and that the extension of salvation to the Gentiles has been a part of the divine plan from the beginning (see Acts 15:13–18; 26:22–23).

In the development of the church from a Jewish Christian origin in Jerusalem, with its roots in Jewish religious tradition, to a series of Christian communities among the Gentiles of the Roman empire, Luke perceives the action of God in history laying open the heart of all humanity to the divine message of salvation. His approach to the history of the church is motivated by his theological interests. His history of the apostolic church is the story of a Spirit-guided community and a Spirit-guided spread of the Word of God (Acts 1:8). The travels of Peter and Paul are in reality the travels of the Word of God as it spreads from Jerusalem, the city of destiny for Jesus, to Rome, the capital of the civilized world of Luke's day. Nonetheless, the historical data he utilizes are of value for the understanding of the church's early life and development and as general background to the Pauline epistles. In the interpretation of Acts, care must be exercised to determine Luke's theological aims and interests and to evaluate his historical data without either exaggerating their literal accuracy or underestimating their factual worth.

Finally, an apologetic concern is evident throughout Acts. By stressing the continuity between Judaism and Christianity (Acts 13:16–41; 23:6–9; 24:10–21; 26:2–23), Luke argues that Christianity is deserving of the same toleration accorded Judaism by Rome. Part of Paul's defense before Roman authorities is to show that Christianity is not a disturber of the peace of the Roman Empire (Acts 24:5, 12–13; 25:7–8). Moreover, when he stands before Roman authorities, he is declared innocent of any crime against the empire (Acts 18:13–15; 23:29; 25:25–27; 26:31–32). Luke tells his story with the hope that Christianity will be treated as fairly.

Concerning the date of Acts, see the Introduction to the Gospel according to Luke.

The principal divisions of the Acts of the Apostles are the following:

I. The Preparation for the Christian Mission (1:1–2:13)
II. The Mission in Jerusalem (2:14–8:3)
III. The Mission in Judea and Samaria (8:4–9:43)
IV. The Inauguration of the Gentile Mission (10:1–15:35)
V. The Mission of Paul to the Ends of the Earth (15:36–28:31)

# I. The Preparation for the Christian Mission

## CHAPTER 1*

See RG 337–38

***The Promise of the Spirit.*** 1 In the first
book,[a] Theophilus, I dealt with all that Jesus
did and taught 2 until the day he was taken
up, after giving instructions through the holy
Spirit to the apostles whom he had chosen.[b]
3 He presented himself alive to them by
many proofs after he had suffered, appearing
to them during forty days* and speaking
about the kingdom of God.[c] 4 While meeting
with them, he enjoined them not to depart
from Jerusalem, but to wait for "the promise
of the Father* about which you have heard
me speak;[d] 5 for John baptized with water,
but in a few days you will be baptized with
the holy Spirit."[e]

***The Ascension of Jesus.*** 6 When they had
gathered together they asked him, "Lord, are
you at this time going* to restore the kingdom
to Israel?" 7* He answered them,[f] "It is not
for you to know the times or seasons that the
Father has established by his own authority.
8* But you will receive power when the holy
Spirit comes upon you,[g] and you will be my
witnesses in Jerusalem, throughout Judea
and Samaria, and to the ends of the earth."

**1:1–26** This introductory material (Acts 1:1–2) connects Acts with the Gospel of Luke, shows that the apostles were instructed by the risen Jesus (Acts 1:3–5), points out that the parousia or second coming in glory of Jesus will occur as certainly as his ascension occurred (Acts 1:6–11), and lists the members of the Twelve, stressing their role as a body of divinely mandated witnesses to his life, teaching, and resurrection (Acts 1:12–26).

**1:3 Appearing to them during forty days**: Luke considered especially sacred the interval in which the appearances and instructions of the risen Jesus occurred and expressed it therefore in terms of the sacred number forty (cf. Dt 8:2). In his gospel, however, Luke connects the ascension of Jesus with the resurrection by describing the ascension on Easter Sunday evening (Lk 24:50–53). What should probably be understood as one event (resurrection, glorification, ascension, sending of the Spirit—the paschal mystery) has been historicized by Luke when he writes of a visible ascension of Jesus after forty days and the descent of the Spirit at Pentecost. For Luke, the ascension marks the end of the appearances of Jesus except for the extraordinary appearance to Paul. With regard to Luke's understanding of salvation history, the ascension also marks the end of the time of Jesus (Lk 24:50–53) and signals the beginning of the time of the church.

**1:4 The promise of the Father**: the holy Spirit, as is clear from the next verse. This gift of the Spirit was first promised in Jesus' final instructions to his chosen witnesses in Luke's gospel (Lk 24:49) and formed part of the continuing instructions of the risen Jesus on the kingdom of God, of which Luke speaks in Acts 1:3.

**1:6** The question of the disciples implies that in believing Jesus to be the Christ (see note on Lk 2:11) they had expected him to be a political leader who would restore self-rule to Israel during his historical ministry. When this had not taken place, they ask if it is to take place at this time, the period of the church.

**1:7** This verse echoes the tradition that the precise time of the parousia is not revealed to human beings; cf. Mk 13:32; 1 Thes 5:1–3.

**1:8** Just as Jerusalem was the city of destiny in the Gospel of Luke (the place where salvation was accomplished), so here at the beginning of Acts, Jerusalem occupies a central position. It is the starting point for the mission of the Christian disciples to "the ends of the earth," the place where the apostles were situated and the doctrinal focal point in the early days of the community (Acts 15:2, 6). **The ends of the earth**: for Luke, this means Rome.

*a:* Lk 1:1–4. *b:* Mt 28:19–20; Lk 24:44–49; Jn 20:22; 1 Tm 3:16. *c:* 10:41; 13:31. *d:* Jn 14:16, 17, 26. *e:* 11:16; Mt 3:11; Mk 1:8; Lk 3:16; Jn 1:26; Eph 1:13. *f:* Mt 24:36; 1 Thes 5:1–2. *g:* 2:1–13; 10:39; Is 43:10; Mt 28:19; Lk 24:47–48.

[9]When he had said this, as they were looking on, he was lifted up, and a cloud took him from their sight.[h] [10]While they were looking intently at the sky as he was going, suddenly two men dressed in white garments stood beside them.[i] [11]They said, "Men of Galilee, why are you standing there looking at the sky? This Jesus who has been taken up from you into heaven will return in the same way as you have seen him going into heaven."[j] [12k] Then they returned to Jerusalem from the mount called Olivet, which is near Jerusalem, a sabbath day's journey away.

***The First Community in Jerusalem.*** [13]When they entered the city they went to the upper room where they were staying, Peter and John and James and Andrew, Philip and Thomas, Bartholomew and Matthew, James son of Alphaeus, Simon the Zealot, and Judas son of James. [14]All these devoted themselves with one accord to prayer, together with some women, and Mary the mother of Jesus, and his brothers.[l]

***The Choice of Judas's Successor.*** [15]During those days Peter stood up in the midst of the brothers (there was a group of about one hundred and twenty persons in the one place). He said, [16]"My brothers, the scripture had to be fulfilled which the holy Spirit spoke beforehand through the mouth of David, concerning Judas, who was the guide for those who arrested Jesus.[m] [17]He was numbered among us and was allotted a share in this ministry. [18n] He bought a parcel of land with the wages of his iniquity, and falling headlong, he burst open in the middle, and all his insides spilled out.* [19]This became known to everyone who lived in Jerusalem, so that the parcel of land was called in their language 'Akeldama,' that is, Field of Blood. [20]For it is written in the Book of Psalms:

> 'Let his encampment become desolate,
> and may no one dwell in it.'

And:

> 'May another take his office.'[o]

[21]Therefore, it is necessary that one of the men who accompanied us the whole time the Lord Jesus came and went among us, [22]beginning from the baptism of John until the day on which he was taken up from us, become with us a witness to his resurrection."[p] [23]So they proposed two, Joseph called Barsabbas, who was also known as Justus, and Matthias. [24]Then they prayed, "You, Lord, who know the hearts of all, show which one of these two you have chosen [25]to take the place in this apostolic ministry from which Judas turned away to go to his own place." [26* q] Then they gave lots to them, and the lot fell upon Matthias, and he was counted with the eleven apostles.

## CHAPTER 2

See RG 338–39

***The Coming of the Spirit.*** [1*] When the time for Pentecost was fulfilled, they were all in one place together.[r] [2]And suddenly there came from the sky a noise like a strong driving wind,* and it filled the entire house in which they were.[s] [3]Then there appeared to them tongues as of fire,* which parted and

**1:18** Luke records a popular tradition about the death of Judas that differs from the one in Mt 27:5, according to which Judas hanged himself. Here, although the text is not certain, Judas is depicted as purchasing a piece of property with the betrayal money and being killed on it in a fall.

**1:26** The need to replace Judas was probably dictated by the symbolism of the number twelve, recalling the twelve tribes of Israel. This symbolism also indicates that for Luke (see Lk 22:30) the Christian church is a reconstituted Israel.

**2:1–41** Luke's pentecostal narrative consists of an introduction (Acts 2:1–13), a speech ascribed to Peter declaring the resurrection of Jesus and its messianic significance (Acts 2:14–36), and a favorable response from the audience (Acts 2:37–41). It is likely that the narrative telescopes events that took place over a period of time and on a less dramatic scale. The Twelve were not originally in a position to proclaim publicly the messianic office of Jesus without incurring immediate reprisal from those religious authorities in Jerusalem who had brought about Jesus' death precisely to stem the rising tide in his favor.

**2:2 There came from the sky a noise like a strong driving wind**: wind and spirit are associated in Jn 3:8. The sound of a great rush of wind would herald a new action of God in the history of salvation.

**2:3 Tongues as of fire**: see Ex 19:18 where fire symbolizes the presence of God to initiate the covenant on Sinai. Here the holy Spirit acts upon the apostles, preparing them to proclaim the new covenant with its unique gift of the Spirit (Acts 2:38).

*h:* 2 Kgs 2:11; Mk 16:19; Lk 24:51. *i:* Jn 20:17. *j:* Lk 24:51; Eph 4:8–10; 1 Pt 3:22; Rev 1:7. *k:* Lk 6:14–16. *l:* Lk 23:49. *m:* Ps 41:10; Lk 22:47. *n:* Mt 27:3–10. *o:* Ps 69:26; 109:8; Jn 17:12. *p:* 1:8–9; 10:39. *q:* Prv 16:33. *r:* Lv 23:15–21; Dt 16:9–11. *s:* Jn 3:8.

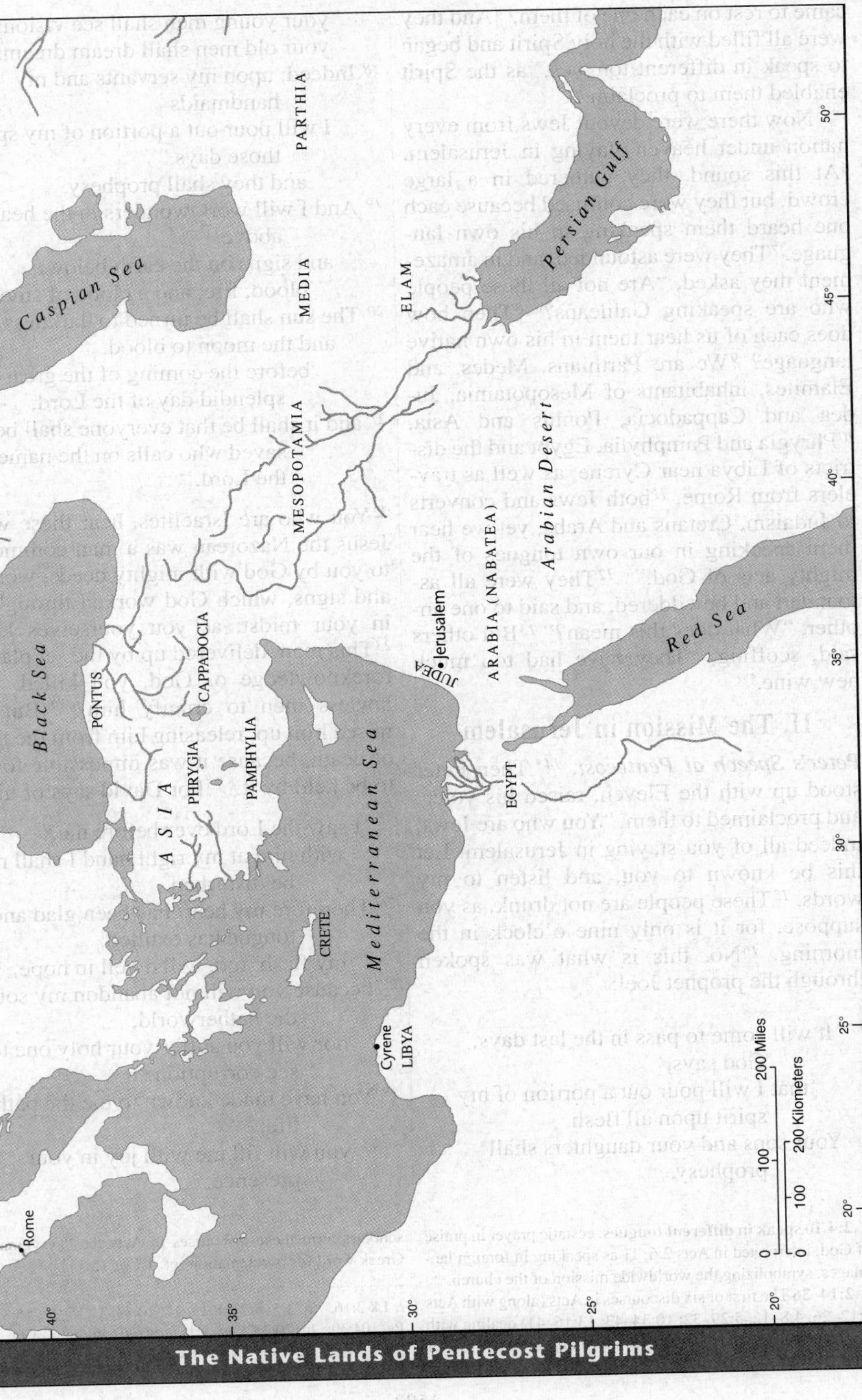

The Native Lands of Pentecost Pilgrims

came to rest on each one of them.[t] 4And they
were all filled with the holy Spirit and began
to speak in different tongues,* as the Spirit
enabled them to proclaim.[u]
5Now there were devout Jews from every
nation under heaven staying in Jerusalem.
6At this sound, they gathered in a large
crowd, but they were confused because each
one heard them speaking in his own language. 7They were astounded, and in amazement they asked, "Are not all these people
who are speaking Galileans?[v] 8Then how
does each of us hear them in his own native
language? 9We are Parthians, Medes, and
Elamites, inhabitants of Mesopotamia, Judea and Cappadocia, Pontus and Asia,
10Phrygia and Pamphylia, Egypt and the districts of Libya near Cyrene, as well as travelers from Rome, 11both Jews and converts
to Judaism, Cretans and Arabs, yet we hear
them speaking in our own tongues of the
mighty acts of God."[w] 12They were all astounded and bewildered, and said to one another, "What does this mean?" 13But others
said, scoffing, "They have had too much
new wine."[x]

## II. The Mission in Jerusalem

***Peter's Speech at Pentecost.*** 14* Then Peter
stood up with the Eleven, raised his voice,
and proclaimed to them, "You who are Jews,
indeed all of you staying in Jerusalem. Let
this be known to you, and listen to my
words. 15These people are not drunk, as you
suppose, for it is only nine o'clock in the
morning. 16No, this is what was spoken
through the prophet Joel:

17 'It will come to pass in the last days,'
God says,
'that I will pour out a portion of my
spirit upon all flesh.
Your sons and your daughters shall
prophesy,
your young men shall see visions,
your old men shall dream dreams.[y]
18 Indeed, upon my servants and my
handmaids
I will pour out a portion of my spirit in
those days,
and they shall prophesy.
19 And I will work wonders in the heavens
above
and signs on the earth below:
blood, fire, and a cloud of smoke.
20 The sun shall be turned to darkness,
and the moon to blood,
before the coming of the great and
splendid day of the Lord,
21 and it shall be that everyone shall be
saved who calls on the name of
the Lord.'[z]

22You who are Israelites, hear these words.
Jesus the Nazorean was a man commended
to you by God with mighty deeds, wonders,
and signs, which God worked through him
in your midst, as you yourselves know.[a]
23This man, delivered up by the set plan and
foreknowledge of God, you killed, using
lawless men to crucify him.[b] 24But God
raised him up, releasing him from the throes
of death, because it was impossible for him
to be held by it.[c] 25For David says of him:

'I saw the Lord ever before me,[d]
with him at my right hand I shall not
be disturbed.
26 Therefore my heart has been glad and my
tongue has exulted;
my flesh, too, will dwell in hope,
27 because you will not abandon my soul to
the netherworld,
nor will you suffer your holy one to
see corruption.[e]
28 You have made known to me the paths of
life;
you will fill me with joy in your
presence.'

**2:4 To speak in different tongues**: ecstatic prayer in praise of God, interpreted in Acts 2:6, 11 as speaking in foreign languages, symbolizing the worldwide mission of the church.

**2:14–36** The first of six discourses in Acts (along with Acts 3:12–26; 4:8–12; 5:29–32; 10:34–43; 13:16–41) dealing with the resurrection of Jesus and its messianic import. Five of these are attributed to Peter, the final one to Paul. Modern scholars term these discourses in Acts the "kerygma," the Greek word for proclamation (cf. 1 Cor 15:11).

*t:* Lk 3:16. *u:* 1:5; 4:31; 8:15, 17; 10:44; 11:15–16; 15:8; 19:6; Ps 104:30; Jn 20:33. *v:* 1:11. *w:* 10:46. *x:* 1 Cor 14:23. *y:* Is 2:2; 44:3; Jl 3:1–5. *z:* Rom 10:13. *a:* 10:38; Lk 24:19. *b:* 1 Thes 2:15. *c:* 13:34. *d:* Ps 16:8–11. *e:* 13:35.

29My brothers, one can confidently say to you
about the patriarch David that he died and was
buried, and his tomb is in our midst to this day.
30But since he was a prophet and knew that
God had sworn an oath to him that he would
set one of his descendants upon his throne,[f]
31he foresaw and spoke of the resurrection of
the Messiah, that neither was he abandoned to
the netherworld nor did his flesh see corruption.[g] 32God raised this Jesus; of this we are all
witnesses. 33Exalted at the right hand of God,*
he received the promise of the holy Spirit
from the Father and poured it forth, as you
(both) see and hear.[h] 34For David did not go
up into heaven, but he himself said:

'The Lord said to my Lord,
"Sit at my right hand[i]
35 until I make your enemies your
footstool." '

36Therefore let the whole house of Israel
know for certain that God has made him
both Lord and Messiah, this Jesus whom
you crucified."[j]

37Now when they heard this, they were cut
to the heart, and they asked Peter and the
other apostles, "What are we to do, my brothers?"[k] 38Peter [said] to them, "Repent and be
baptized,* every one of you, in the name of
Jesus Christ for the forgiveness of your sins;
and you will receive the gift of the holy
Spirit.[l] 39For the promise is made to you and
to your children and to all those far off,
whomever the Lord our God will call."[m] 40He
testified with many other arguments, and was
exhorting them, "Save yourselves from this
corrupt generation."[n] 41Those who accepted
his message were baptized, and about three
thousand persons were added that day.[o]

***Communal Life.**** 42[p] They devoted themselves to the teaching of the apostles and to
the communal life, to the breaking of the
bread and to the prayers.[q] 43Awe came upon
everyone, and many wonders and signs were
done through the apostles.[r] 44All who believed were together and had all things in
common;[s] 45they would sell their property
and possessions and divide them among all
according to each one's need. 46Every day
they devoted themselves to meeting together
in the temple area and to breaking bread in
their homes. They ate their meals with exultation and sincerity of heart, 47praising God
and enjoying favor with all the people. And
every day the Lord added to their number
those who were being saved.

## CHAPTER 3

See RG 338–39

***Cure of a Crippled Beggar.*** 1* Now Peter and John were going up to the temple

**2:33 At the right hand of God**: or "by the right hand of God."

**2:38 Repent and be baptized**: repentance is a positive concept, a change of mind and heart toward God reflected in the actual goodness of one's life. It is in accord with the apostolic teaching derived from Jesus (Acts 2:42) and ultimately recorded in the four gospels. Luke presents baptism in Acts as the expected response to the apostolic preaching about Jesus and associates it with the conferring of the Spirit (Acts 1:5; 10:44–48; 11:16).

**2:42–47** The first of three summary passages (along with Acts 4:32–37; 5:12–16) that outline, somewhat idyllically, the chief characteristics of the Jerusalem community: adherence to the teachings of the Twelve and the centering of its religious life in the eucharistic liturgy (Acts 2:42); a system of distribution of goods that led wealthier Christians to sell their possessions when the needs of the community's poor required it (Acts 2:44 and the note on Acts 4:32–37); and continued attendance at the temple, since in this initial stage there was little or no thought of any dividing line between Christianity and Judaism (Acts 2:46).

**3:1–4:31** This section presents a series of related events: the dramatic cure of a lame beggar (Acts 3:1–10) produces a large audience for the kerygmatic discourse of Peter (Acts 3:11–26). The Sadducees, taking exception to the doctrine of resurrection, have Peter, John, and apparently the beggar as well, arrested (Acts 4:1–4) and brought to trial before the Sanhedrin. The issue concerns the authority by which Peter and John publicly teach religious doctrine in the temple (Acts 4:5–7). Peter replies with a brief summary of the kerygma, implying that his authority is prophetic (Acts 4:8–12). The court warns the apostles to abandon their practice of invoking prophetic authority in the name of Jesus (Acts 4:13–18). When Peter and John reply that the prophetic role cannot be abandoned to satisfy human objections, the court nevertheless releases them, afraid to do otherwise since the beggar, lame from birth and over forty years old, is a well-known figure in Jerusalem and the facts of his cure are common property (Acts 4:19–22). The narrative concludes with a prayer of the Christian community imploring divine aid against threats of persecution (Acts 4:23–31).

**3:1 For the three o'clock hour of prayer**: literally, "at the ninth hour of prayer." With the day beginning at 6 a.m., the ninth hour would be 3 p.m.

*f:* 2 Sm 7:12; Ps 132:11. *g:* 13:35; Ps 16:10. *h:* 1:4–5. *i:* Ps 110:1. *j:* 9:22; Rom 10:9; Phil 2:11. *k:* Lk 3:10. *l:* 3:19; 16:31; Lk 3:3. *m:* Is 57:19; Jl 3:5; Eph 2:17. *n:* Dt 32:5; Ps 78:8; Lk 9:41; Phil 2:15. *o:* 2:47; 4:4; 5:14; 6:7; 11:21, 24; 21:20. *p:* 4:32–35. *q:* 1:14; 6:4. *r:* 5:12–16. *s:* 4:32, 34–35.

area for the three o'clock hour of prayer.*
2[t] And a man crippled from birth was carried
and placed at the gate of the temple called
"the Beautiful Gate" every day to beg for
alms from the people who entered the temple. 3 When he saw Peter and John about to
go into the temple, he asked for alms. 4 But
Peter looked intently at him, as did John, and
said, "Look at us." 5 He paid attention to
them, expecting to receive something from
them. 6* Peter said, "I have neither silver nor
gold, but what I do have I give you: in the
name of Jesus Christ the Nazorean, [rise
and] walk."[u] 7 Then Peter took him by the
right hand and raised him up, and immediately his feet and ankles grew strong. 8 He
leaped up, stood, and walked around, and
went into the temple with them, walking and
jumping and praising God.[v] 9 When all the
people saw him walking and praising God,
10 they recognized him as the one who used
to sit begging at the Beautiful Gate of the
temple, and they were filled with amazement and astonishment at what had happened to him.

***Peter's Speech.*** 11 As he clung to Peter and
John, all the people hurried in amazement toward them in the portico called "Solomon's
Portico."[w] 12 When Peter saw this, he addressed the people, "You Israelites, why are
you amazed at this, and why do you look so
intently at us as if we had made him walk by
our own power or piety?[x] 13 The God of Abraham, [the God] of Isaac, and [the God] of Jacob, the God of our ancestors, has glorified*
his servant Jesus whom you handed over and
denied in Pilate's presence, when he had decided to release him.[y] 14 You denied the Holy
and Righteous One* and asked that a murderer be released to you.[z] 15* The author of
life you put to death, but God raised him
from the dead; of this we are witnesses.[a]
16 And by faith in his name, this man, whom
you see and know, his name has made strong,
and the faith that comes through it has given
him this perfect health, in the presence of all
of you. 17 Now I know, brothers, that you
acted out of ignorance,* just as your leaders
did;[b] 18 but God has thus brought to fulfillment what he had announced beforehand
through the mouth of all the prophets,* that
his Messiah would suffer.[c] 19 Repent, therefore, and be converted, that your sins may be
wiped away,[d] 20 and that the Lord may grant
you times of refreshment and send you the
Messiah already appointed for you, Jesus,*
21 whom heaven must receive until the times
of universal restoration* of which God spoke

**3:6–10** The miracle has a dramatic cast; it symbolizes the saving power of Christ and leads the beggar to enter the temple, where he hears Peter's proclamation of salvation through Jesus.

**3:13 Has glorified**: through the resurrection and ascension of Jesus, God reversed the judgment against him on the occasion of his trial. **Servant**: the Greek word can also be rendered as "son" or even "child" here and also in Acts 3:26; 4:25 (applied to David); Acts 4:27; and Acts 4:30. Scholars are of the opinion, however, that the original concept reflected in the words identified Jesus with the suffering Servant of the Lord of Is 52:13–53:12.

**3:14 The Holy and Righteous One**: so designating Jesus emphasizes his special relationship to the Father (see Lk 1:35; 4:34) and emphasizes his sinlessness and religious dignity that are placed in sharp contrast with the guilt of those who rejected him in favor of Barabbas.

**3:15 The author of life**: other possible translations of the Greek title are "leader of life" or "pioneer of life." The title clearly points to Jesus as the source and originator of salvation.

**3:17 Ignorance**: a Lucan motif, explaining away the actions not only of the people but also of their leaders in crucifying Jesus. On this basis the presbyters in Acts could continue to appeal to the Jews in Jerusalem to believe in Jesus, even while affirming their involvement in his death because they were unaware of his messianic dignity. See also Acts 13:27 and Lk 23:34.

**3:18 Through the mouth of all the prophets**: Christian prophetic insight into the Old Testament saw the crucifixion and death of Jesus as the main import of messianic prophecy. The Jews themselves did not anticipate a suffering Messiah; they usually understood the Servant Song in Is 52:13–53:12 to signify their own suffering as a people. In his typical fashion (cf. Lk 18:31; 24:25, 27, 44), Luke does not specify the particular Old Testament prophecies that were fulfilled by Jesus. See also note on Lk 24:26.

**3:20 The Lord . . . and send you the Messiah already appointed for you, Jesus**: an allusion to the parousia or second coming of Christ, judged to be imminent in the apostolic age. This reference to its nearness is the only explicit one in Acts. Some scholars believe that this verse preserves a very early christology, in which the title "Messiah" (Greek "Christ") is applied to him as of his parousia, his second coming (contrast Acts 2:36). This view of a future messiahship of Jesus is not found elsewhere in the New Testament.

**3:21 The times of universal restoration**: like "the times of refreshment" (Acts 3:20), an apocalyptic designation of the messianic age, fitting in with the christology of Acts 3:20 that associates the messiahship of Jesus with his future coming.

---

*t:* 14:8–10. *u:* 4:10. *v:* Is 35:6; Lk 7:22. *w:* 5:12; Jn 10:23. *x:* 14:15. *y:* Ex 3:6, 15; Is 52:13; Lk 23:14–25. *z:* Mt 27:20–21; Mk 15:11; Lk 23:18; Jn 18:40. *a:* 4:10; 5:31 / 1:8; 2:32. *b:* 13:27; Lk 23:34; 1 Cor 2:8; 1 Tm 1:13. *c:* Lk 18:31. *d:* 2:38.

through the mouth of his holy prophets from
of old. [22]For Moses said:*

'A prophet like me will the Lord, your
God, raise up for you
from among your own kinsmen;
to him you shall listen in all that he may
say to you.[e]
[23] Everyone who does not listen to that
prophet
will be cut off from the people.'[f]

[24]Moreover, all the prophets who spoke,
from Samuel and those afterwards, also announced these days. [25]You are the children
of the prophets and of the covenant that God
made with your ancestors when he said to
Abraham, 'In your offspring all the families
of the earth shall be blessed.'[g] [26]For you
first, God raised up his servant and sent him
to bless you by turning each of you from
your evil ways."[h]

## CHAPTER 4

See RG 339

[1]While they were still speaking to the
people, the priests, the captain of the temple
guard, and the Sadducees* confronted them,
[2]disturbed that they were teaching the people and proclaiming in Jesus the resurrection
of the dead.[i] [3]They laid hands on them and
put them in custody until the next day, since
it was already evening. [4]But many of those
who heard the word came to believe and
[the] number of men grew to [about] five
thousand.

*Before the Sanhedrin.* [5]On the next day,
their leaders, elders, and scribes were assembled in Jerusalem, [6]with Annas the high
priest, Caiaphas, John, Alexander, and all
who were of the high-priestly class. [7]They
brought them into their presence and questioned them, "By what power or by what
name have you done this?" [8]Then Peter,
filled with the holy Spirit, answered them,
"Leaders of the people and elders:[j] [9]If we are
being examined today about a good deed
done to a cripple, namely, by what means he
was saved, [10]then all of you and all the people of Israel should know that it was in the
name of Jesus Christ the Nazorean whom
you crucified, whom God raised from the
dead; in his name this man stands before you
healed. [11][k] He is 'the stone rejected by you,*
the builders, which has become the cornerstone.' [12]*[l] There is no salvation through
anyone else, nor is there any other name under heaven given to the human race by
which we are to be saved."

[13]Observing the boldness of Peter and
John and perceiving them to be uneducated,
ordinary men, they were amazed, and they
recognized them as the companions of Jesus.
[14]Then when they saw the man who had
been cured standing there with them, they
could say nothing in reply. [15]So they ordered
them to leave the Sanhedrin, and conferred
with one another, saying, [16]"What are we to
do with these men? Everyone living in Jerusalem knows that a remarkable sign was
done through them, and we cannot deny it.
[17]But so that it may not be spread any further
among the people, let us give them a stern
warning never again to speak to anyone in
this name."[m]

[18]So they called them back and ordered
them not to speak or teach at all in the name
of Jesus. [19]Peter and John, however, said to
them in reply, "Whether it is right in the
sight of God for us to obey you rather than

**3:22** A loose citation of Dt 18:15, which teaches that the Israelites are to learn the will of Yahweh from no one but their prophets. At the time of Jesus, some Jews expected a unique prophet to come in fulfillment of this text. Early Christianity applied this tradition and text to Jesus and used them especially in defense of the divergence of Christian teaching from traditional Judaism.

**4:1 The priests, the captain of the temple guard, and the Sadducees**: the priests performed the temple liturgy; the temple guard was composed of Levites, whose captain ranked next after the high priest. The Sadducees, a party within Judaism at this time, rejected those doctrines, including bodily resurrection, which they believed alien to the ancient Mosaic religion. The Sadducees were drawn from priestly families and from the lay aristocracy.

**4:11** Early Christianity applied this citation from Ps 118:22 to Jesus; cf. Mk 12:10; 1 Pt 2:7.

**4:12** In the Roman world of Luke's day, salvation was often attributed to the emperor who was hailed as "savior" and "god." Luke, in the words of Peter, denies that deliverance comes through anyone other than Jesus.

*e:* 7:37; Dt 18:15, 18. *f:* Lv 23:29; Dt 18:19. *g:* Gn 12:3; 18:18; 22:18; Sir 44:19–21; Gal 3:8–9. *h:* 13:46; Rom 1:16. *i:* 23:6–8; 24:21. *j:* Mt 10:20. *k:* Ps 118:22; Is 28:16; Mt 21:42; Mk 12:10; Lk 20:17; Rom 9:33; 1 Pt 2:7. *l:* Mt 1:21; 1 Cor 3:11. *m:* 5:28.

God, you be the judges.[n] 20It is impossible
for us not to speak about what we have seen
and heard." 21After threatening them further,
they released them, finding no way to punish
them, on account of the people who were all
praising God for what had happened. 22For
the man on whom this sign of healing had
been done was over forty years old.

*Prayer of the Community.* 23After their release they went back to their own people and
reported what the chief priests and elders
had told them. 24And when they heard it,
they raised their voices to God with one accord and said, "Sovereign Lord, maker of
heaven and earth and the sea and all that is in
them, 25you said by the holy Spirit through
the mouth of our father David, your servant:

'Why did the Gentiles rage[o]
and the peoples entertain folly?
26 The kings of the earth took their stand
and the princes gathered together
against the Lord and against his
anointed.'

27Indeed they gathered in this city against
your holy servant Jesus whom you anointed,
Herod* and Pontius Pilate, together with the
Gentiles and the peoples of Israel,[p] 28to do
what your hand and [your] will had long ago
planned to take place. 29And now, Lord, take
note of their threats, and enable your servants to speak your word with all boldness,
30as you stretch forth [your] hand to heal,
and signs and wonders are done through the
name of your holy servant Jesus." 31* As
they prayed, the place where they were gathered shook, and they were all filled with the
holy Spirit and continued to speak the word
of God with boldness.[q]

*Life in the Christian Community.** 32The
community of believers was of one heart and
mind, and no one claimed that any of his
possessions was his own, but they had
everything in common. 33With great power
the apostles bore witness to the resurrection
of the Lord Jesus, and great favor was accorded them all. 34[r] There was no needy person among them, for those who owned property or houses would sell them, bring the
proceeds of the sale, 35and put them at the
feet of the apostles, and they were distributed to each according to need.

36[s] Thus Joseph, also named by the apostles Barnabas (which is translated "son of
encouragement"), a Levite, a Cypriot by
birth, 37sold a piece of property that he
owned, then brought the money and put it at
the feet of the apostles.

## CHAPTER 5

See RG 339

*Ananias and Sapphira.** 1A man
named Ananias, however, with his wife Sapphira, sold a piece of property. 2He retained
for himself, with his wife's knowledge,
some of the purchase price, took the remainder, and put it at the feet of the apostles. 3But
Peter said, "Ananias, why has Satan filled
your heart so that you lied to the holy Spirit
and retained part of the price of the land?[t]
4While it remained unsold, did it not remain
yours? And when it was sold, was it not still
under your control? Why did you contrive
this deed? You have lied not to human beings, but to God." 5When Ananias heard
these words, he fell down and breathed his

**4:27 Herod**: Herod Antipas, ruler of Galilee and Perea from 4 B.C. to A.D. 39, who executed John the Baptist and before whom Jesus was arraigned; cf. Lk 23:6–12.

**4:31 The place . . . shook**: the earthquake is used as a sign of the divine presence in Ex 19:18; Is 6:4. Here the shaking of the building symbolizes God's favorable response to the prayer. Luke may have had as an additional reason for using the symbol in this sense the fact that it was familiar in the Hellenistic world. Ovid and Virgil also employ it.

**4:32–37** This is the second summary characterizing the Jerusalem community (see note on Acts 2:42–47). It emphasizes the system of the distribution of goods and introduces Barnabas, who appears later in Acts as the friend and companion of Paul, and who, as noted here (Acts 4:37), endeared himself to the community by a donation of money through the sale of property. This sharing of material possessions continues a practice that Luke describes during the historical ministry of Jesus (Lk 8:3) and is in accord with the sayings of Jesus in Luke's gospel (Lk 12:33; 16:9, 11, 13).

**5:1–11** The sin of Ananias and Sapphira did not consist in the withholding of part of the money but in their deception of the community. Their deaths are ascribed to a lie to the holy Spirit (Acts 5:3, 9), i.e., they accepted the honor accorded them by the community for their generosity, but in reality they were not deserving of it.

*n:* 5:29–32. *o:* Ps 2:1–2. *p:* Lk 23:12–13. *q:* 2:4. *r:* 2:44–45. *s:* 9:27; 11:22, 30; 12:25; 13:15; 1 Cor 9:6; Gal 2:1, 9, 13; Col 4:10. *t:* Lk 22:3; Jn 13:2.

last, and great fear came upon all who heard of it. [6]The young men came and wrapped him up, then carried him out and buried him.

[7]After an interval of about three hours, his wife came in, unaware of what had happened. [8]Peter said to her, "Tell me, did you sell the land for this amount?" She answered, "Yes, for that amount." [9]Then Peter said to her, "Why did you agree to test the Spirit of the Lord? Listen, the footsteps of those who have buried your husband are at the door, and they will carry you out." [10]At once, she fell down at his feet and breathed her last. When the young men entered they found her dead, so they carried her out and buried her beside her husband. [11]And great fear came upon the whole church and upon all who heard of these things.[u]

***Signs and Wonders of the Apostles.**** [12]Many signs and wonders were done among the people at the hands of the apostles. They were all together in Solomon's portico.[v] [13]None of the others dared to join them, but the people esteemed them. [14]Yet more than ever, believers in the Lord, great numbers of men and women, were added to them. [15]Thus they even carried the sick out into the streets and laid them on cots and mats so that when Peter came by, at least his shadow might fall on one or another of them.[w] [16]A large number of people from the towns in the vicinity of Jerusalem also gathered, bringing the sick and those disturbed by unclean spirits, and they were all cured.

***Trial Before the Sanhedrin.**** [17]Then the high priest rose up and all his companions, that is, the party of the Sadducees, and, filled with jealousy,[x] [18]laid hands upon the apostles and put them in the public jail. [19]But during the night, the angel of the Lord opened the doors of the prison, led them out, and said,[y] [20]"Go and take your place in the temple area, and tell the people everything about this life." [21]When they heard this, they went to the temple early in the morning and taught. When the high priest and his companions arrived, they convened the Sanhedrin, the full senate of the Israelites, and sent to the jail to have them brought in. [22]But the court officers who went did not find them in the prison, so they came back and reported, [23]"We found the jail securely locked and the guards stationed outside the doors, but when we opened them, we found no one inside." [24]When they heard this report, the captain of the temple guard and the chief priests were at a loss about them, as to what this would come to. [25]Then someone came in and reported to them, "The men whom you put in prison are in the temple area and are teaching the people." [26]Then the captain and the court officers went and brought them in, but without force, because they were afraid of being stoned by the people.[z]

[27]When they had brought them in and made them stand before the Sanhedrin, the high priest questioned them, [28]"We gave you strict orders [did we not?] to stop teaching in that name. Yet you have filled Jerusalem with your teaching and want to bring this man's blood upon us."[a] [29]But Peter and the apostles said in reply, "We must obey God rather than men.[b] [30]* The God of our ancestors raised Jesus,[c] though you had him killed by hanging him on a tree. [31]God exalted him at his right hand* as leader and savior to grant Israel repentance and forgiveness of

**5:12–16** This, the third summary portraying the Jerusalem community, underscores the Twelve as its bulwark, especially because of their charismatic power to heal the sick; cf. Acts 2:42–47; 4:32–37.

**5:17–42** A second action against the community is taken by the Sanhedrin in the arrest and trial of the Twelve; cf. Acts 4:1–3. The motive is the jealousy of the religious authorities over the popularity of the apostles (Acts 5:17) who are now charged with the defiance of the Sanhedrin's previous order to them to abandon their prophetic role (Acts 5:28; cf. Acts 4:18). In this crisis the apostles are favored by a miraculous release from prison (Acts 5:18–24). (For similar incidents involving Peter and Paul, see Acts 12:6–11; 16:25–29.) The real significance of such an event, however, would be manifest only to people of faith, not to unbelievers; since the Sanhedrin already judged the Twelve to be inauthentic prophets, it could disregard reports of their miracles. When the Twelve immediately resumed public teaching, the Sanhedrin determined to invoke upon them the penalty of death (Acts 5:33) prescribed in Dt 13:6–10. Gamaliel's advice against this course finally prevailed, but it did not save the Twelve from the punishment of scourging (Acts 5:40) in a last endeavor to shake their conviction of their prophetic mission.

**5:30 Hanging him on a tree**: that is, crucifying him (cf. also Gal 3:13).

**5:31 At his right hand**: see note on Acts 2:33.

*u:* 2:43; 5:5; 19:17. *v:* 2:43; 6:8; 14:3; 15:12. *w:* 19:11–12; Mk 6:56. *x:* 4:1–3, 6. *y:* 12:7–10; 16:25–26. *z:* Lk 20:19. *a:* Mt 27:25. *b:* 4:19. *c:* 2:23–24.

sins.[d] 32 We are witnesses of these things, as is the holy Spirit that God has given to those who obey him."[e]

33 When they heard this, they became infuriated and wanted to put them to death. 34* But a Pharisee in the Sanhedrin named Gamaliel, a teacher of the law, respected by all the people, stood up, ordered the men to be put outside for a short time,[f] 35 and said to them, "Fellow Israelites, be careful what you are about to do to these men. 36* Some time ago, Theudas appeared, claiming to be someone important, and about four hundred men joined him, but he was killed, and all those who were loyal to him were disbanded and came to nothing. 37 After him came Judas the Galilean at the time of the census. He also drew people after him, but he too perished and all who were loyal to him were scattered. 38 So now I tell you, have nothing to do with these men, and let them go. For if this endeavor or this activity is of human origin, it will destroy itself. 39 But if it comes from God, you will not be able to destroy them; you may even find yourselves fighting against God." They were persuaded by him. 40 After recalling the apostles, they had them flogged, ordered them to stop speaking in the name of Jesus, and dismissed them.[g] 41 So they left the presence of the Sanhedrin, rejoicing that they had been found worthy to suffer dishonor for the sake of the name.[h] 42 And all day long, both at the temple and in their homes, they did not stop teaching and proclaiming the Messiah, Jesus.[i]

## CHAPTER 6

See RG 339–41

*The Need for Assistants.* 1* At that time, as the number of disciples continued to grow, the Hellenists complained against the Hebrews because their widows were being neglected in the daily distribution.[j] 2* So the Twelve called together the community of the disciples and said, "It is not right for us to neglect the word of God to serve at table.* 3 Brothers, select from among you seven reputable men, filled with the Spirit and wisdom, whom we shall appoint to this task, 4 whereas we shall devote ourselves to prayer and to the ministry of the word." 5 The proposal was acceptable to the whole community, so they chose Stephen, a man filled with faith and the holy Spirit, also Philip, Prochorus, Nicanor, Timon, Parmenas, and Nicholas of Antioch, a convert to Judaism. 6[k] They presented these men to the apostles who prayed and laid hands on them.* 7 The word of God continued to spread, and the number of the disciples in Jerusalem increased greatly; even a large group of priests were becoming obedient to the faith.[l]

*Accusation Against Stephen.* 8* Now Ste-

**5:34 Gamaliel**: in Acts 22:3, Paul identifies himself as a disciple of this Rabbi Gamaliel I who flourished in Jerusalem between A.D. 25 and 50.

**5:36–37** Gamaliel offers examples of unsuccessful contemporary movements to argue that if God is not the origin of this movement preached by the apostles it will perish by itself. The movement initiated by Theudas actually occurred when C. Cuspius Fadus was governor, A.D. 44–46. Luke's placing of Judas the Galilean after Theudas and at the time of the census (see note on Lk 2:1–2) is an indication of the vagueness of his knowledge of these events.

**6:1–7 The Hellenists . . . the Hebrews**: the Hellenists were not necessarily Jews from the diaspora, but were more probably Palestinian Jews who spoke only Greek. The Hebrews were Palestinian Jews who spoke Hebrew or Aramaic and who may also have spoken Greek. Both groups belong to the Jerusalem Jewish Christian community. The conflict between them leads to a restructuring of the community that will better serve the community's needs. The real purpose of the whole episode, however, is to introduce Stephen as a prominent figure in the community whose long speech and martyrdom will be recounted in Acts 7.

**6:2–4** The essential function of the Twelve is the "service of the word," including development of the kerygma by formulation of the teachings of Jesus.

**6:2 To serve at table**: some commentators think that it is not the serving of food that is described here but rather the keeping of the accounts that recorded the distribution of food to the needy members of the community. In any case, after Stephen and the others are chosen, they are never presented carrying out the task for which they were appointed (Acts 6:2–3). Rather, two of their number, Stephen and Philip, are presented as preachers of the Christian message. They, the Hellenist counterpart of the Twelve, are active in the ministry of the word.

**6:6 They . . . laid hands on them**: the customary Jewish way of designating persons for a task and invoking upon them the divine blessing and power to perform it.

**6:8–8:1** The summary (Acts 6:7) on the progress of the Jerusalem community, illustrated by the conversion of the priests, is followed by a lengthy narrative regarding Stephen. Stephen's defense is not a response to the charges made

*d:* 2:38. *e:* Lk 24:48; Jn 15:26. *f:* 22:3. *g:* Mt 10:17; Acts 4:17–18. *h:* Mt 5:10–11; 1 Pt 4:13. *i:* 2:46; 5:20–21, 25; 8:35; 17:3; 18:5, 28; 19:4–5. *j:* 2:45; 4:34–35. *k:* 1:24; 13:3; 14:23. *l:* 9:31; 12:24; 16:5; 19:20; 28:30–31.

phen, filled with grace and power, was working great wonders and signs among the people. 9 Certain members of the so-called Synagogue of Freedmen, Cyrenians, and Alexandrians, and people from Cilicia and Asia, came forward and debated with Stephen, 10 but they could not withstand the wisdom and the spirit with which he spoke.[m] 11 Then they instigated some men to say, "We have heard him speaking blasphemous words against Moses and God."[n] 12 They stirred up the people, the elders, and the scribes, accosted him, seized him, and brought him before the Sanhedrin. 13 They presented false witnesses* who testified, "This man never stops saying things against [this] holy place and the law. 14 For we have heard him claim that this Jesus the Nazorean will destroy this place and change the customs that Moses handed down to us."[o] 15 All those who sat in the Sanhedrin looked intently at him and saw that his face was like the face of an angel.

## CHAPTER 7

See RG 340–41

***Stephen's Discourses.*** 1 Then the high priest asked, "Is this so?" 2[p] And he replied,* "My brothers and fathers, listen. The God of glory appeared to our father Abraham while he was in Mesopotamia,* before he had settled in Haran, 3 and said to him, 'Go forth from your land and [from] your kinsfolk to the land that I will show you.'[q] 4 So he went forth from the land of the Chaldeans and settled in Haran. And from there, after his father died, he made him migrate to this land where you now dwell.[r] 5 Yet he gave him no inheritance in it, not even a foot's length, but he did promise to give it to him and his descendants as a possession, even though he was childless.[s] 6 And God spoke thus,[t] 'His descendants shall be aliens in a land not their own, where they shall be enslaved and oppressed for four hundred years; 7 but I will bring judgment on the nation they serve,' God said, 'and after that they will come out and worship me in this place.'[u] 8 Then he gave him the covenant of circumcision, and so he became the father of Isaac, and circumcised him on the eighth day, as Isaac did Jacob, and Jacob the twelve patriarchs.[v]

9 "And the patriarchs, jealous of Joseph, sold him into slavery in Egypt; but God was with him[w] 10 and rescued him from all his afflictions. He granted him favor and wisdom before Pharaoh, the king of Egypt, who put him in charge of Egypt and [of] his entire household.[x] 11 Then a famine and great affliction struck all Egypt and Canaan, and our ancestors could find no food;[y] 12 but when Jacob heard that there was grain in Egypt, he sent our ancestors there a first time.[z] 13 The second time, Joseph made himself known to his brothers, and Joseph's family became known to Pharaoh.[a] 14 Then Joseph sent for his father Jacob, inviting him and his whole clan, seventy-five persons;[b] 15 and Jacob

against him but takes the form of a discourse that reviews the fortunes of God's word to Israel and leads to a prophetic declaration: a plea for the hearing of that word as announced by Christ and now possessed by the Christian community.

The charges that Stephen depreciated the importance of the temple and the Mosaic law and elevated Jesus to a stature above Moses (Acts 6:13–14) were in fact true. Before the Sanhedrin, no defense against them was possible. With Stephen, who thus perceived the fuller implications of the teachings of Jesus, the differences between Judaism and Christianity began to appear. Luke's account of Stephen's martyrdom and its aftermath shows how the major impetus behind the Christian movement passed from Jerusalem, where the temple and law prevailed, to Antioch in Syria, where these influences were less pressing.

**6:13 False witnesses**: here, and in his account of Stephen's execution (Acts 7:54–60), Luke parallels the martyrdom of Stephen with the death of Jesus.

**7:2–53** Stephen's speech represents Luke's description of Christianity's break from its Jewish matrix. Two motifs become prominent in the speech: (1) Israel's reaction to God's chosen leaders in the past reveals that the people have consistently rejected them; and (2) Israel has misunderstood God's choice of the Jerusalem temple as the place where he is to be worshiped.

**7:2 God . . . appeared to our father Abraham . . . in Mesopotamia**: the first of a number of minor discrepancies between the data of the Old Testament and the data of Stephen's discourse. According to Gn 12:1, God first spoke to Abraham in Haran. The main discrepancies are these: in Acts 7:16 it is said that Jacob was buried in Shechem, whereas Gn 50:13 says he was buried at Hebron; in the same verse it is said that the tomb was purchased by Abraham, but in Gn 33:19 and Jos 24:32 the purchase is attributed to Jacob himself.

*m:* Lk 21:15. *n:* Mt 26:59–61; Mk 14:55–58; Acts 21:21. *o:* Mt 26:59–61; 27:40; Jn 2:19. *p:* Gn 11:31; 12:1; Ps 29:3. *q:* Gn 12:1. *r:* Gn 12:5; 15:7. *s:* Gn 12:7; 13:15; 15:2; 16:1; Dt 2:5. *t:* Gn 15:13–14. *u:* Ex 3:12. *v:* Gn 17:10–14; 21:2–4. *w:* Gn 37:11, 28; 39:2, 3, 21, 23. *x:* Gn 41:37–43; Ps 105:21; Wis 10:13–14. *y:* Gn 41:54–57; 42:5. *z:* Gn 42:1–2. *a:* Gn 45:3–4, 16. *b:* Gn 45:9–11, 18–19; 46:27; Ex 1:5 LXX; Dt 10:22.

went down to Egypt. And he and our ancestors died[c] [16]and were brought back to Shechem and placed in the tomb that Abraham had purchased for a sum of money from the sons of Hamor at Shechem.[d]

[17]"When the time drew near for the fulfillment of the promise that God pledged to Abraham, the people had increased and become very numerous in Egypt,[e] [18]until another king who knew nothing of Joseph came to power [in Egypt].[f] [19]He dealt shrewdly with our people and oppressed [our] ancestors by forcing them to expose their infants, that they might not survive. [20]At this time Moses was born, and he was extremely beautiful. For three months he was nursed in his father's house;[g] [21]but when he was exposed, Pharaoh's daughter adopted him and brought him up as her own son.[h] [22]Moses was educated [in] all the wisdom of the Egyptians and was powerful in his words and deeds.

[23][i]"When he was forty years old, he decided to visit his kinsfolk, the Israelites. [24]When he saw one of them treated unjustly, he defended and avenged the oppressed man by striking down the Egyptian. [25]He assumed [his] kinsfolk would understand that God was offering them deliverance through him, but they did not understand. [26][j]The next day he appeared to them as they were fighting and tried to reconcile them peacefully, saying, 'Men, you are brothers. Why are you harming one another?' [27]Then the one who was harming his neighbor pushed him aside, saying, 'Who appointed you ruler and judge over us? [28]Are you thinking of killing me as you killed the Egyptian yesterday?' [29]Moses fled when he heard this and settled as an alien in the land of Midian, where he became the father of two sons.[k]

[30][l]"Forty years later, an angel appeared to him in the desert near Mount Sinai in the flame of a burning bush. [31]When Moses saw it, he was amazed at the sight, and as he drew near to look at it, the voice of the Lord came, [32]'I am the God of your fathers, the God of Abraham, of Isaac, and of Jacob.' Then Moses, trembling, did not dare to look at it. [33]But the Lord said to him, 'Remove the sandals from your feet, for the place where you stand is holy ground. [34]I have witnessed the affliction of my people in Egypt and have heard their groaning, and I have come down to rescue them. Come now, I will send you to Egypt.' [35]This Moses, whom they had rejected with the words, 'Who appointed you ruler and judge?' God sent as [both] ruler and deliverer, through the angel who appeared to him in the bush.[m] [36]This man led them out, performing wonders and signs in the land of Egypt, at the Red Sea, and in the desert for forty years.[n] [37]It was this Moses who said to the Israelites, 'God will raise up for you, from among your own kinsfolk, a prophet like me.'[o] [38]It was he who, in the assembly in the desert, was with the angel who spoke to him on Mount Sinai and with our ancestors, and he received living utterances to hand on to us.[p]

[39]"Our ancestors were unwilling to obey him; instead, they pushed him aside and in their hearts turned back to Egypt,[q] [40]saying to Aaron, 'Make us gods who will be our leaders. As for that Moses who led us out of the land of Egypt, we do not know what has happened to him.'[r] [41][s]So they made a calf in those days, offered sacrifice to the idol, and reveled in the works of their hands. [42]Then God turned and handed them over to worship the host of heaven, as it is written in the book of the prophets:[t]

'Did you bring me sacrifices and
offerings
for forty years in the desert, O house
of Israel?[u]
[43]No, you took up the tent of Moloch
and the star of [your] god Rephan,
the images that you made to worship.
So I shall take you into exile beyond
Babylon.'

[44]"Our ancestors had the tent of testimony in the desert just as the One who spoke to Moses directed him to make it according to the

*c:* Gn 46:5–6; 49:33. *d:* Gn 23:3–20; 33:19; 49:29–30; 50:13; Jos 24:32. *e:* Ex 1:7. *f:* Ex 1:8. *g:* Ex 2:2; Heb 11:23. *h:* Ex 2:3–10. *i:* Ex 2:11–12. *j:* Ex 2:13–14. *k:* Ex 2:15, 21–22; 18:3–4. *l:* Ex 3:2–3. *m:* Ex 2:14. *n:* Ex 7:3, 10; 14:21; Nm 14:33. *o:* Dt 18:15; Acts 3:22. *p:* Ex 19:3; 20:1–17; Dt 5:4–22; 6:4–25. *q:* Nm 14:3. *r:* Ex 32:1, 23. *s:* Ex 32:4–6. *t:* Am 5:25–27. *u:* Jer 7:18; 8:2; 19:13.

pattern he had seen.[v] 45Our ancestors who inherited it brought it with Joshua when they dispossessed the nations that God drove out from before our ancestors, up to the time of David,[w] 46who found favor in the sight of God and asked that he might find a dwelling place for the house of Jacob.[x] 47But Solomon built a house for him.[y] 48Yet the Most High does not dwell in houses made by human hands. As the prophet says:[z]

49 'The heavens are my throne,
the earth is my footstool.
What kind of house can you build for me?
says the Lord,
or what is to be my resting place?[a]
50 Did not my hand make all these things?'

***Conclusion.*** 51"You stiff-necked people, uncircumcised in heart and ears, you always oppose the holy Spirit; you are just like your ancestors. 52Which of the prophets did your ancestors not persecute? They put to death those who foretold the coming of the righteous one, whose betrayers and murderers you have now become.[b] 53You received the law as transmitted by angels, but you did not observe it."[c]

***Stephen's Martyrdom.*** 54When they heard this, they were infuriated, and they ground their teeth at him. 55[d] But he, filled with the holy Spirit, looked up intently to heaven and saw the glory of God and Jesus standing at the right hand of God,* 56and he said, "Behold, I see the heavens opened and the Son of Man standing at the right hand of God." 57But they cried out in a loud voice, covered their ears,* and rushed upon him together. 58They threw him out of the city, and began to stone him. The witnesses laid down their cloaks at the feet of a young man named Saul.[e] 59As they were stoning Stephen,[f] he called out, "Lord Jesus, receive my spirit."* 60Then he fell to his knees and cried out in a loud voice, "Lord, do not hold this sin against them"; and when he said this, he fell asleep.[g]

## CHAPTER 8

See RG 340–41

1Now Saul was consenting to his execution.[h]

***Persecution of the Church.*** On that day, there broke out a severe persecution* of the church in Jerusalem, and all were scattered throughout the countryside of Judea and Samaria, except the apostles.* 2Devout men buried Stephen and made a loud lament over him. 3Saul, meanwhile, was trying to destroy the church;* entering house after house and dragging out men and women, he handed them over for imprisonment.[i]

# III. The Mission in Judea and Samaria

***Philip in Samaria.*** 4Now those who had been scattered went about preaching the word.[j] 5Thus Philip went down to [the] city of

**7:55 He . . . saw . . . Jesus standing at the right hand of God**: Stephen affirms to the Sanhedrin that the prophecy Jesus made before them has been fulfilled (Mk 14:62).

**7:57 Covered their ears**: Stephen's declaration, like that of Jesus, is a scandal to the court, which regards it as blasphemy.

**7:59** Compare Lk 23:34, 46.

**8:1–40** Some idea of the severity of the persecution that now breaks out against the Jerusalem community can be gathered from Acts 22:4 and Acts 26:9–11. Luke, however, concentrates on the fortunes of the word of God among people, indicating how the dispersal of the Jewish community resulted in the conversion of the Samaritans (Acts 8:4–17, 25). His narrative is further expanded to include the account of Philip's acceptance of an Ethiopian (Acts 8:26–39).

**8:1 All were scattered . . . except the apostles**: this observation leads some modern scholars to conclude that the persecution was limited to the Hellenist Christians and that the Hebrew Christians were not molested, perhaps because their attitude toward the law and temple was still more in line with that of their fellow Jews (see the charge leveled against the Hellenist Stephen in Acts 6:13–14). Whatever the facts, it appears that the Twelve took no public stand regarding Stephen's position, choosing, instead, to await the development of events.

**8:3 Saul . . . was trying to destroy the church**: like Stephen, Saul was able to perceive that the Christian movement contained the seeds of doctrinal divergence from Judaism. A pupil of Gamaliel, according to Acts 22:3, and totally dedicated to the law as the way of salvation (Gal 1:13–14), Saul accepted the task of crushing the Christian movement, at least insofar as it detracted from the importance of the temple and the law. His vehement opposition to Christianity reveals how difficult it was for a Jew of his time to accept a messianism that differed so greatly from the general expectation.

*v:* Ex 25:9, 40. *w:* Jos 3:14–17; 18:1; 2 Sm 7:5–7. *x:* 2 Sm 7:1–2; 1 Kgs 8:17; Ps 132:1–5. *y:* 1 Kgs 6:1; 1 Chr 17:12. *z:* 17:24. *a:* Is 66:1–2. *b:* 2 Chr 36:16; Mt 23:31, 34. *c:* Gal 3:19; Heb 2:2. *d:* Mt 26:64; Mk 14:62; Lk 22:69; Acts 2:34. *e:* 22:20. *f:* Ps 31:6; Lk 23:46. *g:* Mt 27:46, 50; Mk 15:34; Lk 23:46. *h:* 22:20. *i:* 9:1, 13; 22:4; 26:9–11; 1 Cor 5:9; Gal 1:13. *j:* 11:19.

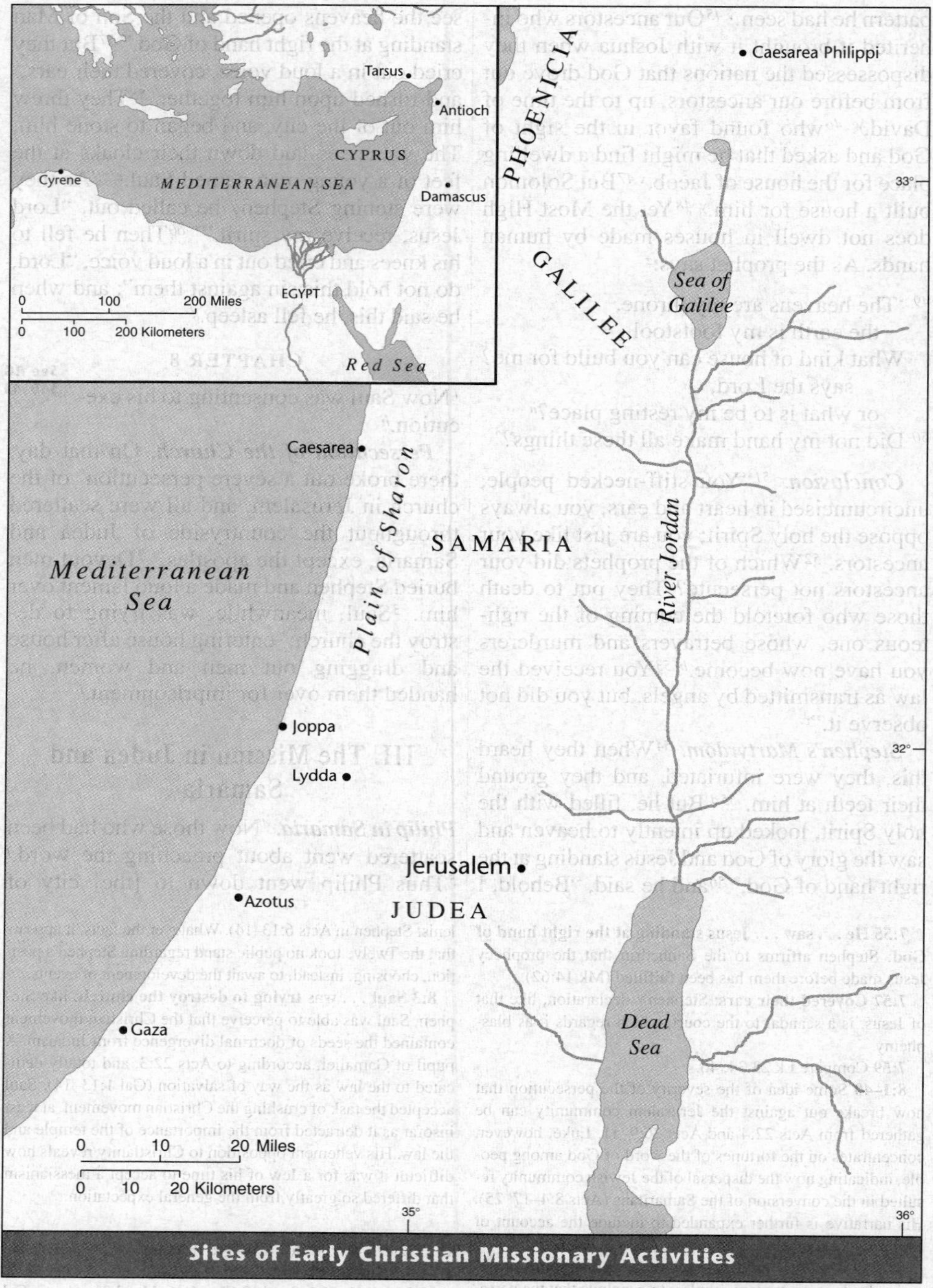


Sites of Early Christian Missionary Activities

Samaria and proclaimed the Messiah to them.[k] 6 With one accord, the crowds paid attention to what was said by Philip when they heard it and saw the signs he was doing. 7 For unclean spirits, crying out in a loud voice, came out of many possessed people, and many paralyzed and crippled people were cured.[l] 8 There was great joy in that city.

***Simon the Magician.*** 9 A man named Simon used to practice magic* in the city and astounded the people of Samaria, claiming to be someone great. 10 All of them, from the least to the greatest, paid attention to him, saying, "This man is the 'Power of God' that is called 'Great.' " 11 They paid attention to him because he had astounded them by his magic for a long time, 12 but once they began to believe Philip as he preached the good news about the kingdom of God and the name of Jesus Christ, men and women alike were baptized.[m] 13 Even Simon himself believed and, after being baptized, became devoted to Philip; and when he saw the signs and mighty deeds that were occurring, he was astounded.

14 Now when the apostles in Jerusalem heard that Samaria had accepted the word of God, they sent them Peter and John, 15 who went down and prayed for them, that they might receive the holy Spirit, 16 for it had not yet fallen upon any of them; they had only been baptized in the name of the Lord Jesus.* 17 Then they laid hands on them and they received the holy Spirit.[n]

18* When Simon saw that the Spirit was conferred by the laying on of the apostles' hands, he offered them money 19 and said, "Give me this power too, so that anyone upon whom I lay my hands may receive the holy Spirit." 20 But Peter said to him, "May your money perish with you, because you thought that you could buy the gift of God with money. 21 You have no share or lot in this matter, for your heart is not upright before God. 22 Repent of this wickedness of yours and pray to the Lord that, if possible, your intention may be forgiven. 23 For I see that you are filled with bitter gall and are in the bonds of iniquity." 24 Simon said in reply, "Pray for me to the Lord, that nothing of what you have said may come upon me." 25 So when they had testified and proclaimed the word of the Lord, they returned to Jerusalem and preached the good news to many Samaritan villages.

***Philip and the Ethiopian.**** 26 Then the angel of the Lord spoke to Philip, "Get up and head south on the road that goes down from Jerusalem to Gaza, the desert route." 27 So he got up and set out. Now there was an Ethiopian eunuch, a court official of the Candace,* that is, the queen of the Ethiopians, in charge of her entire treasury, who had come to Jerusalem to worship,[o] 28 and was returning home. Seated in his chariot, he was reading the prophet Isaiah. 29 The Spirit said to Philip, "Go and join up with that chariot." 30* Philip ran up and heard him reading Isaiah the prophet and said, "Do you understand what you are reading?" 31 He replied, "How can I, unless someone instructs me?" So he invited Philip to get in and sit with

**8:9–13, 18–24** Sorcerers were well known in the ancient world. Probably the incident involving Simon and his altercation with Peter is introduced to show that the miraculous charisms possessed by members of the Christian community (Acts 8:6–7) were not to be confused with the magic of sorcerers.

**8:16** Here and in Acts 10:44–48 and Acts 19:1–6, Luke distinguishes between baptism in the name of the Lord Jesus and the reception of the Spirit. In each case, the Spirit is conferred through members of the Twelve (Peter and John) or their representative (Paul). This may be Luke's way of describing the role of the church in the bestowal of the Spirit. Elsewhere in Acts, baptism and the Spirit are more closely related (Acts 1:5; 11:16).

**8:18–20** Simon attempts to buy the gift of God (Acts 8:20) with money. Peter's cursing of Simon's attempt so to use his money expresses a typically Lucan attitude toward material wealth (cf. Lk 6:24; 12:16–21; 16:13).

**8:26–40** In the account of the conversion of the Ethiopian eunuch, Luke adduces additional evidence to show that the spread of Christianity outside the confines of Judaism itself was in accord with the plan of God. He does not make clear whether the Ethiopian was originally a convert to Judaism or, as is more probable, a "God-fearer" (Acts 10:1), i.e., one who accepted Jewish monotheism and ethic and attended the synagogue but did not consider himself bound by other regulations such as circumcision and observance of the dietary laws. The story of his conversion to Christianity is given a strong supernatural cast by the introduction of an angel (Acts 8:26), instruction from the holy Spirit (Acts 8:29), and the strange removal of Philip from the scene (8:39).

**8:27 The Candace**: Candace is not a proper name here but the title of a Nubian queen.

**8:30–34** Philip is brought alongside the carriage at the very moment when the Ethiopian is pondering the meaning of Is 53:7–8, a passage that Christianity, from its earliest origins, has applied to Jesus; cf. note on Acts 3:13.

*k:* 6:5; 21:8–9. *l:* Mk 16:17. *m:* 1:3; 19:8; 28:23, 31. *n:* 2:4; 4:31; 10:44–47; 15:8–9; 19:2, 6. *o:* Is 56:3–5.

him.[p] 32 This was the scripture passage he
was reading:[q]

> "Like a sheep he was led to the slaughter,
> and as a lamb before its shearer is silent,
> so he opened not his mouth.
> 33 In [his] humiliation justice was denied him.
> Who will tell of his posterity?
> For his life is taken from the earth."

34 Then the eunuch said to Philip in reply, "I
beg you, about whom is the prophet saying
this? About himself, or about someone
else?" 35 Then Philip opened his mouth and,
beginning with this scripture passage, he
proclaimed Jesus to him. 36[r] As they traveled
along the road they came to some water, and
the eunuch said, "Look, there is water. What
is to prevent my being baptized?"
[37]* 38 Then he ordered the chariot to stop,
and Philip and the eunuch both went down
into the water, and he baptized him. 39 When
they came out of the water, the Spirit of the
Lord snatched Philip away, and the eunuch
saw him no more, but continued on his way
rejoicing.[s] 40 Philip came to Azotus, and went
about proclaiming the good news to all the
towns until he reached Caesarea.[t]

## CHAPTER 9

See RG 341–42

*Saul's Conversion.* 1* Now Saul, still
breathing murderous threats against the disciples of the Lord,[u] went to the high priest[v]
2 and asked him for letters to the synagogues
in Damascus, that, if he should find any men
or women who belonged to the Way,* he
might bring them back to Jerusalem in
chains. 3 On his journey, as he was nearing
Damascus, a light from the sky suddenly
flashed around him.[w] 4 He fell to the ground
and heard a voice saying to him, "Saul, Saul,
why are you persecuting me?"[x] 5 He said,
"Who are you, sir?" The reply came, "I am
Jesus, whom you are persecuting.[y] 6 Now get
up and go into the city and you will be told
what you must do."[z] 7 The men who were
traveling with him stood speechless, for they
heard the voice but could see no one.[a] 8 Saul
got up from the ground, but when he opened
his eyes he could see nothing;* so they led
him by the hand and brought him to Damascus.[b] 9 For three days he was unable to see,
and he neither ate nor drank.

*Saul's Baptism.* 10[c] There was a disciple in
Damascus named Ananias, and the Lord said
to him in a vision, "Ananias." He answered,
"Here I am, Lord." 11 The Lord said to him,
"Get up and go to the street called Straight
and ask at the house of Judas for a man from
Tarsus named Saul. He is there praying,[d]
12 and [in a vision] he has seen a man named
Ananias come in and lay [his] hands on him,
that he may regain his sight." 13 But Ananias
replied, "Lord, I have heard from many
sources about this man, what evil things he
has done to your holy ones* in Jerusalem.[e]
14 And here he has authority from the chief
priests to imprison all who call upon your
name."[f] 15 But the Lord said to him, "Go, for

**8:37** The oldest and best manuscripts of Acts omit this verse, which is a Western text reading: "And Philip said, 'If you believe with all your heart, you may.' And he said in reply, 'I believe that Jesus Christ is the Son of God.'"

**9:1–19** This is the first of three accounts of Paul's conversion (with Acts 22:3–16 and Acts 26:2–18) with some differences of detail owing to Luke's use of different sources. Paul's experience was not visionary but was precipitated by the appearance of Jesus, as he insists in 1 Cor 15:8. The words of Jesus, "Saul, Saul, why are you persecuting me?" related by Luke with no variation in all three accounts, exerted a profound and lasting influence on the thought of Paul. Under the influence of this experience he gradually developed his understanding of justification by faith (see the letters to the Galatians and Romans) and of the identification of the Christian community with Jesus Christ (see 1 Cor 12:27). That Luke would narrate this conversion three times is testimony to the importance he attaches to it. This first account occurs when the word is first spread to the Gentiles. At this point, the conversion of the hero of the Gentile mission is recounted. The emphasis in the account is on Paul as a divinely chosen instrument (Acts 9:15).

**9:2 The Way**: a name used by the early Christian community for itself (Acts 18:26; 19:9, 23; 22:4; 24:14, 22). The Essene community at Qumran used the same designation to describe its mode of life.

**9:8 He could see nothing**: a temporary blindness (Acts 9:18) symbolizing the religious blindness of Saul as persecutor (cf. Acts 26:18).

**9:13 Your holy ones**: literally, "your saints."

*p:* Jn 16:13. *q:* Is 53:7–8 LXX. *r:* 10:47. *s:* 1 Kgs 18:12. *t:* 21:8. *u:* 8:3; 9:13; 22:4; 1 Cor 15:9; Gal 1:13–14. *v:* 9:14; 26:10. *w:* 1 Cor 9:1; 15:8; Gal 1:16. *x:* 22:6; 26:14. *y:* 22:8; 26:15; Mt 25:40. *z:* 22:10; 26:16. *a:* 22:9; 26:13–14. *b:* 22:11. *c:* 22:12–16. *d:* 21:39. *e:* 8:3; 9:1. *f:* 9:1–2; 26:10; 1 Cor 1:2; 2 Tm 2:22.

this man is a chosen instrument of mine to
carry my name before Gentiles, kings, and
Israelites,[g] 16 and I will show him what he
will have to suffer for my name." 17 So Ananias went and entered the house; laying his
hands on him, he said, "Saul, my brother, the
Lord has sent me, Jesus who appeared to you
on the way by which you came, that you may
regain your sight and be filled with the holy
Spirit." 18 Immediately things like scales fell
from his eyes and he regained his sight. He
got up and was baptized, 19 and when he had
eaten, he recovered his strength.*

*Saul Preaches in Damascus.* He stayed
some days with the disciples in Damascus,
20 and he began at once to proclaim Jesus in
the synagogues, that he is the Son of God.*
21 All who heard him were astounded and
said, "Is not this the man who in Jerusalem
ravaged those who call upon this name, and
came here expressly to take them back in
chains to the chief priests?" 22 But Saul grew
all the stronger and confounded [the] Jews
who lived in Damascus, proving that this is
the Messiah.

*Saul Visits Jerusalem.* 23 After a long time
had passed, the Jews conspired to kill him,
24[h] but their plot became known to Saul.
Now they were keeping watch on the gates
day and night so as to kill him, 25 but his disciples took him one night and let him down
through an opening in the wall, lowering
him in a basket.

26[i] When he arrived in Jerusalem* he tried
to join the disciples, but they were all afraid
of him, not believing that he was a disciple.
27 Then Barnabas took charge of him and
brought him to the apostles, and he reported
to them how on the way he had seen the Lord
and that he had spoken to him, and how in
Damascus he had spoken out boldly in the
name of Jesus. 28 He moved about freely with
them in Jerusalem, and spoke out boldly in
the name of the Lord. 29 He also spoke and
debated with the Hellenists,* but they tried
to kill him. 30 And when the brothers learned
of this, they took him down to Caesarea and
sent him on his way to Tarsus.[j]

*The Church at Peace.* 31* The church
throughout all Judea, Galilee, and Samaria
was at peace. It was being built up and walked
in the fear of the Lord, and with the consolation of the holy Spirit it grew in numbers.

*Peter Heals Aeneas at Lydda.* 32 As Peter
was passing through every region, he went
down to the holy ones living in Lydda.
33 There he found a man named Aeneas, who
had been confined to bed for eight years, for
he was paralyzed. 34 Peter said to him, "Aeneas, Jesus Christ heals you. Get up and
make your bed." He got up at once. 35 And all
the inhabitants of Lydda and Sharon saw
him, and they turned to the Lord.

*Peter Restores Tabitha to Life.* 36 Now in
Joppa there was a disciple named Tabitha
(which translated means Dorcas).* She was
completely occupied with good deeds and
almsgiving. 37 Now during those days she
fell sick and died, so after washing her, they
laid [her] out in a room upstairs. 38 Since
Lydda was near Joppa, the disciples, hearing
that Peter was there, sent two men to him
with the request, "Please come to us without
delay." 39 So Peter got up and went with
them. When he arrived, they took him to the
room upstairs where all the widows came to
him weeping and showing him the tunics
and cloaks that Dorcas had made while she

**9:19–30** This is a brief resume of Paul's initial experience as an apostolic preacher. At first he found himself in the position of being regarded as an apostate by the Jews and suspect by the Christian community of Jerusalem. His acceptance by the latter was finally brought about through his friendship with Barnabas (Acts 9:27).

**9:20 Son of God**: the title "Son of God" occurs in Acts only here, but cf. the citation of Ps 2:7 in Paul's speech at Antioch in Pisidia (Acts 13:33).

**9:26** This visit of Paul to Jerusalem is mentioned by Paul in Gal 1:18.

**9:29 Hellenists**: see note on Acts 6:1–7.

**9:31–43** In the context of the period of peace enjoyed by the community through the cessation of Paul's activities against it, Luke introduces two traditions concerning the miraculous power exercised by Peter as he was making a tour of places where the Christian message had already been preached. The towns of Lydda, Sharon, and Joppa were populated by both Jews and Gentiles and their Christian communities may well have been mixed.

**9:36 Tabitha (Dorcas)**, respectively the Aramaic and Greek words for "gazelle," exemplifies the right attitude toward material possessions expressed by Jesus in the Lucan Gospel (Lk 6:30; 11:41; 12:33; 18:22; 19:8).

*g*: 22:15; 26:1; 27:24. *h*: 2 Cor 11:32–33. *i*: Gal 1:18. *j*: 11:25.

was with them. 40 Peter sent them all out and
knelt down and prayed. Then he turned to
her body and said, "Tabitha, rise up." She
opened her eyes, saw Peter, and sat up.[k] 41 He
gave her his hand and raised her up, and
when he had called the holy ones and the
widows, he presented her alive. 42 This became known all over Joppa, and many came
to believe in the Lord. 43* [l] And he stayed a
long time in Joppa with Simon, a tanner.

## IV. The Inauguration of the Gentile Mission

### CHAPTER 10

See RG 342–43

*The Vision of Cornelius.*[m] 1* Now in
Caesarea there was a man named Cornelius,
a centurion of the Cohort called the Italica,*
2 devout and God-fearing along with his
whole household, who used to give alms
generously* to the Jewish people and pray to
God constantly. 3 One afternoon about three
o'clock,* he saw plainly in a vision an angel
of God come in to him and say to him, "Cornelius." 4 He looked intently at him and,
seized with fear, said, "What is it, sir?" He
said to him, "Your prayers and almsgiving
have ascended as a memorial offering before
God. 5 Now send some men to Joppa and
summon one Simon who is called Peter. 6 He
is staying with another Simon, a tanner, who
has a house by the sea."[n] 7 When the angel
who spoke to him had left, he called two of
his servants and a devout soldier* from his
staff, 8 explained everything to them, and
sent them to Joppa.

*The Vision of Peter.* 9* The next day, while
they were on their way and nearing the city,
Peter went up to the roof terrace to pray at
about noontime.* 10 He was hungry and
wished to eat, and while they were making
preparations he fell into a trance. 11 [o] He saw
heaven opened and something resembling a
large sheet coming down, lowered to the
ground by its four corners. 12 In it were all the
earth's four-legged animals and reptiles and
the birds of the sky. 13 A voice said to him,
"Get up, Peter. Slaughter and eat." 14 But Peter said, "Certainly not, sir. For never have I
eaten anything profane and unclean."[p] 15 The
voice spoke to him again, a second time,
"What God has made clean, you are not to
call profane."[q] 16 This happened three times,
and then the object was taken up into the sky.

17* While Peter was in doubt about the
meaning of the vision he had seen, the men
sent by Cornelius asked for Simon's house
and arrived at the entrance. 18 They called out
inquiring whether Simon, who is called Peter, was staying there. 19 As Peter was pondering the vision, the Spirit said [to him],
"There are three men here looking for you.[r]
20 So get up, go downstairs, and accompany
them without hesitation, because I have sent
them." 21 Then Peter went down to the men

**9:43** The fact that Peter lodged with a tanner would have been significant to both the Gentile and Jewish Christians, for Judaism considered the tanning occupation unclean.

**10:1–48** The narrative centers on the conversion of Cornelius, a Gentile and a "God-fearer" (see note on Acts 8:26–40). Luke considers the event of great importance, as is evident from his long treatment of it. The incident is again related in Acts 11:1–18 where Peter is forced to justify his actions before the Jerusalem community and alluded to in Acts 15:7–11 where at the Jerusalem "Council" Peter supports Paul's missionary activity among the Gentiles. The narrative divides itself into a series of distinct episodes, concluding with Peter's presentation of the Christian kerygma (Acts 10:4–43) and a pentecostal experience undergone by Cornelius' household preceding their reception of baptism (Acts 10:44–48).

**10:1 The Cohort called the Italica**: this battalion was an auxiliary unit of archers formed originally in Italy but transferred to Syria shortly before A.D. 69.

**10:2 Used to give alms generously**: like Tabitha (Acts 9:36), Cornelius exemplifies the proper attitude toward wealth (see note on Acts 9:36).

**10:3 About three o'clock**: literally, "about the ninth hour." See note on Acts 3:1.

**10:7 A devout soldier**: by using this adjective, Luke probably intends to classify him as a "God-fearer" (see note on Acts 8:26–40).

**10:9–16** The vision is intended to prepare Peter to share the food of Cornelius' household without qualms of conscience (Acts 10:48). The necessity of such instructions to Peter reveals that at first not even the apostles fully grasped the implications of Jesus' teaching on the law. In Acts, the initial insight belongs to Stephen.

**10:9 At about noontime**: literally, "about the sixth hour."

**10:17–23** The arrival of the Gentile emissaries with their account of the angelic apparition illuminates Peter's vision: he is to be prepared to admit Gentiles, who were considered unclean like the animals of his vision, into the Christian community.

*k:* Mk 5:40–41. *l:* 10:6. *m:* 10:30–33. *n:* 9:43. *o:* 11:5–12. *p:* Lv 11:1–47; Ez 4:14. *q:* Mk 7:15–19; Gal 2:12. *r:* 13:2.

and said, "I am the one you are looking for. What is the reason for your being here?" 22 They answered, "Cornelius, a centurion, an upright and God-fearing man, respected by the whole Jewish nation, was directed by a holy angel to summon you to his house and to hear what you have to say."[s] 23 So he invited them in and showed them hospitality.

The next day he got up and went with them, and some of the brothers from Joppa went with him. 24* On the following day he entered Caesarea. Cornelius was expecting them and had called together his relatives and close friends. 25[t] When Peter entered, Cornelius met him and, falling at his feet, paid him homage. 26 Peter, however, raised him up, saying, "Get up. I myself am also a human being." 27 While he conversed with him, he went in and found many people gathered together 28[u] and said to them, "You know that it is unlawful for a Jewish man to associate with, or visit, a Gentile, but God has shown me that I should not call any person profane or unclean.* 29 And that is why I came without objection when sent for. May I ask, then, why you summoned me?"

30 Cornelius replied, "Four days ago* at this hour, three o'clock in the afternoon, I was at prayer in my house when suddenly a man in dazzling robes stood before me and said, 31 'Cornelius, your prayer has been heard and your almsgiving remembered before God. 32 Send therefore to Joppa and summon Simon, who is called Peter. He is a guest in the house of Simon, a tanner, by the sea.' 33 So I sent for you immediately, and you were kind enough to come. Now therefore we are all here in the presence of God to listen to all that you have been commanded by the Lord."

***Peter's Speech.**** 34 Then Peter proceeded to speak and said,* "In truth, I see that God shows no partiality.[v] 35 Rather, in every nation whoever fears him and acts uprightly is acceptable to him. 36* You know the word [that] he sent to the Israelites* as he proclaimed peace through Jesus Christ, who is Lord of all,[w] 37 what has happened all over Judea, beginning in Galilee after the baptism that John preached,[x] 38 how God anointed Jesus of Nazareth* with the holy Spirit and power. He went about doing good and healing all those oppressed by the devil, for God was with him.[y] 39 We are witnesses* of all that he did both in the country of the Jews and [in] Jerusalem. They put him to death by hanging him on a tree. 40 This man God raised [on] the third day and granted that he be visible, 41 not to all the people, but to us, the witnesses chosen by God in advance, who ate and drank with him after he rose from the dead.[z] 42 He

**10:24–27** So impressed is Cornelius with the apparition that he invites close personal friends to join him in his meeting with Peter. But his understanding of the person he is about to meet is not devoid of superstition, suggested by his falling down before him. For a similar experience of Paul and Barnabas, see Acts 14:11–18.

**10:28** Peter now fully understands the meaning of his vision; see note on Acts 10:17–23.

**10:30 Four days ago**: literally, "from the fourth day up to this hour."

**10:34–43** Peter's speech to the household of Cornelius typifies early Christian preaching to Gentiles.

**10:34–35** The revelation of God's choice of Israel to be the people of God did not mean he withheld the divine favor from other people.

**10:36–43** These words are more directed to Luke's Christian readers than to the household of Cornelius, as indicated by the opening words, "You know." They trace the continuity between the preaching and teaching of Jesus of Nazareth and the proclamation of Jesus by the early community. The emphasis on this divinely ordained continuity (Acts 10:41) is meant to assure Luke's readers of the fidelity of Christian tradition to the words and deeds of Jesus.

**10:36 To the Israelites**: Luke, in the words of Peter, speaks of the prominent position occupied by Israel in the history of salvation.

**10:38 Jesus of Nazareth**: God's revelation of his plan for the destiny of humanity through Israel culminated in Jesus of Nazareth. Consequently, the ministry of Jesus is an integral part of God's revelation. This viewpoint explains why the early Christian communities were interested in conserving the historical substance of the ministry of Jesus, a tradition leading to the production of the four gospels.

**10:39 We are witnesses**: the apostolic testimony was not restricted to the resurrection of Jesus but also included his historical ministry. This witness, however, was theological in character; the Twelve, divinely mandated as prophets, were empowered to interpret his sayings and deeds in the light of his redemptive death and resurrection. The meaning of these words and deeds was to be made clear to the developing Christian community as the bearer of the word of salvation (cf. Acts 1:21–26). **Hanging him on a tree**: see note on Acts 5:30.

*s:* Lk 7:4–5. *t:* 14:13–15; Rev 19:10. *u:* Gal 2:11–16. *v:* Dt 10:17; 2 Chr 19:7; Jb 34:19; Wis 6:7; Rom 2:11; Gal 2:6; Eph 6:9; 1 Pt 1:17. *w:* Is 52:7; Na 2:1. *x:* Mt 4:12; Mk 1:14; Lk 4:14. *y:* Is 61:1; Lk 4:18. *z:* Lk 24:41–43.

commissioned us[a] to preach to the people and testify that he is the one appointed by God as judge of the living and the dead.* 43To him all the prophets bear witness, that everyone who believes in him will receive forgiveness of sins through his name."

*The Baptism of Cornelius.* 44[b] While Peter was still speaking these things, the holy Spirit fell upon all who were listening to the word.* 45The circumcised believers who had accompanied Peter were astounded that the gift of the holy Spirit should have been poured out on the Gentiles also, 46for they could hear them speaking in tongues and glorifying God. Then Peter responded, 47"Can anyone withhold the water for baptizing these people, who have received the holy Spirit even as we have?"[c] 48He ordered them to be baptized in the name of Jesus Christ. 49Then they invited him to stay for a few days.

## CHAPTER 11

See RG 342–43

*The Baptism of the Gentiles Explained.** 1Now the apostles and the brothers who were in Judea heard that the Gentiles too had accepted the word of God. 2So when Peter went up to Jerusalem the circumcised believers confronted him, 3saying, "You entered* the house of uncircumcised people and ate with them." 4Peter began and explained it to them step by step, saying, 5[d] "I was at prayer in the city of Joppa when in a trance I had a vision, something resembling a large sheet coming down, lowered from the sky by its four corners, and it came to me. 6Looking intently into it, I observed and saw the four-legged animals of the earth, the wild beasts, the reptiles, and the birds of the sky. 7I also heard a voice say to me, 'Get up, Peter. Slaughter and eat.' 8But I said, 'Certainly not, sir, because nothing profane or unclean has ever entered my mouth.' 9But a second time a voice from heaven answered, 'What God has made clean, you are not to call profane.' 10This happened three times, and then everything was drawn up again into the sky. 11Just then three men appeared at the house where we were, who had been sent to me from Caesarea. 12The Spirit told me to accompany them without discriminating. These six brothers* also went with me, and we entered the man's house. 13He related to us how he had seen [the] angel standing in his house, saying, 'Send someone to Joppa and summon Simon, who is called Peter,[e] 14who will speak words to you by which you and all your household will be saved.' 15As I began to speak, the holy Spirit fell upon them as it had upon us at the beginning,[f] 16and I remembered the word of the Lord, how he had said, 'John baptized with water but you will be baptized with the holy Spirit.'[g] 17If then God gave them the same gift he gave to us when we came to believe in the Lord Jesus Christ, who was I to be able to hinder God?"[h] 18When they heard this, they stopped objecting and glorified God, saying, "God has then granted life-giving repentance to the Gentiles too."

*The Church at Antioch.** 19Now those who had been scattered by the persecution that arose because of Stephen went as far as Phoenicia, Cyprus, and Antioch, preaching the word to no one but Jews.[i] 20There were

**10:42 As judge of the living and the dead**: the apostolic preaching to the Jews appealed to their messianic hope, while the preaching to Gentiles stressed the coming divine judgment; cf. 1 Thes 1:10.

**10:44** Just as the Jewish Christians received the gift of the Spirit, so too do the Gentiles.

**11:1–18** The Jewish Christians of Jerusalem were scandalized to learn of Peter's sojourn in the house of the Gentile Cornelius. Nonetheless, they had to accept the divine directions given to both Peter and Cornelius. They concluded that the setting aside of the legal barriers between Jew and Gentile was an exceptional ordinance of God to indicate that the apostolic kerygma was also to be directed to the Gentiles. Only in Acts 15 at the "Council" in Jerusalem does the evangelization of the Gentiles become the official position of the church leadership in Jerusalem.

**11:3 You entered . . .**: alternatively, this could be punctuated as a question.

**11:12 These six brothers**: companions from the Christian community of Joppa (see Acts 10:23).

**11:19–26** The Jewish Christian antipathy to the mixed community was reflected by the early missionaries generally. The few among them who entertained a different view succeeded in introducing Gentiles into the community at Antioch (in Syria). When the disconcerted Jerusalem community sent Barnabas to investigate, he was so favorably impressed by what he observed that he persuaded his friend Saul to participate in the Antioch mission.

---

*a:* 1:8; 3:15; 17:31; Lk 24:48; Rom 14:9; 2 Tm 4:1. *b:* 11:15; 15:8. *c:* 8:36. *d:* 10:11–20. *e:* 10:3–5, 22, 30–32. *f:* 10:44. *g:* 1:5; 19:4; Lk 3:16. *h:* 15:8–9. *i:* 8:1–4.

some Cypriots and Cyrenians among them, however, who came to Antioch and began to speak to the Greeks as well, proclaiming the Lord Jesus. 21 The hand of the Lord was with them and a great number who believed turned to the Lord. 22 The news about them reached the ears of the church in Jerusalem, and they sent Barnabas [to go] to Antioch. 23 When he arrived and saw the grace of God, he rejoiced and encouraged them all to remain faithful to the Lord in firmness of heart, 24 for he was a good man, filled with the holy Spirit and faith. And a large number of people was added to the Lord. 25 Then he went to Tarsus to look for Saul, 26 and when he had found him he brought him to Antioch. For a whole year they met with the church and taught a large number of people, and it was in Antioch that the disciples were first called Christians.*

***The Prediction of Agabus.**** 27 At that time some prophets came down from Jerusalem to Antioch, 28 and one of them named Agabus stood up and predicted by the Spirit that there would be a severe famine all over the world, and it happened under Claudius.[j] 29 So the disciples determined that, according to ability,[k] each should send relief to the brothers who lived in Judea. 30* This they did, sending it to the presbyters in care of Barnabas and Saul.

## CHAPTER 12

See RG 343

***Herod's Persecution of the Christians.**** 1 About that time King Herod laid hands upon some members of the church to harm them. 2 He had James, the brother of John,* killed by the sword, 3* and when he saw that this was pleasing to the Jews he proceeded to arrest Peter also. (It was [the] feast of Unleavened Bread.) 4 He had him taken into custody and put in prison under the guard of four squads of four soldiers each. He intended to bring him before the people after Passover. 5 Peter thus was being kept in prison, but prayer by the church was fervently being made to God on his behalf.[l]

6 On the very night before Herod was to bring him to trial, Peter, secured by double chains, was sleeping between two soldiers, while outside the door guards kept watch on the prison. 7 Suddenly the angel of the Lord stood by him and a light shone in the cell. He tapped Peter on the side and awakened him, saying, "Get up quickly." The chains fell from his wrists. 8 The angel said to him, "Put on your belt and your sandals." He did so. Then he said to him, "Put on your cloak and follow me." 9 So he followed him out, not realizing that what was happening through the angel was real; he thought he was seeing a vision. 10 They passed the first guard, then the second, and came to the iron gate leading out to the city, which opened for them by itself. They emerged and made their way down an alley, and suddenly the angel left him. 11 Then Peter recovered his senses and said, "Now I know for certain that [the] Lord sent his angel and rescued me from the hand of Herod and from all that the Jewish people had been expecting." 12 When he realized this, he went to the house of Mary, the mother of John who is called Mark, where there were many people gathered in prayer.[m] 13 When he knocked on the gateway door, a maid named Rhoda came to answer it. 14 She was so overjoyed

**11:26 Christians**: "Christians" is first applied to the members of the community at Antioch because the Gentile members of the community enable it to stand out clearly from Judaism.

**11:27–30** It is not clear whether the prophets from Jerusalem came to Antioch to request help in view of the coming famine or whether they received this insight during their visit there. The former supposition seems more likely. Suetonius and Tacitus speak of famines during the reign of Claudius (A.D. 41–54), while the Jewish historian Josephus mentions a famine in Judea in A.D. 46–48. Luke is interested, rather, in showing the charity of the Antiochene community toward the Jewish Christians of Jerusalem despite their differences on mixed communities.

**11:30 Presbyters**: this is the same Greek word that elsewhere is translated "elders," primarily in reference to the Jewish community.

**12:1–19** Herod Agrippa ruled Judea A.D. 41–44. While Luke does not assign a motive for his execution of James and his intended execution of Peter, the broad background lies in Herod's support of Pharisaic Judaism. The Jewish Christians had lost the popularity they had had in Jerusalem (Acts 2:47), perhaps because of suspicions against them traceable to the teaching of Stephen.

**12:2 James, the brother of John**: this James, the son of Zebedee, was beheaded by Herod Agrippa ca. A.D. 44.

**12:3–4 Feast of Unleavened Bread . . . Passover**: see note on Lk 22:1.

*j:* 21:10. *k:* 12:25. *l:* Jas 5:16. *m:* 12:25; 15:37.

when she recognized Peter's voice that, instead of opening the gate, she ran in and announced that Peter was standing at the gate.
15They told her, "You are out of your mind,"
but she insisted that it was so. But they kept
saying, "It is his angel." 16But Peter continued to knock, and when they opened it, they
saw him and were astounded. 17He motioned to them with his hand to be quiet and
explained [to them] how the Lord had led
him out of the prison, and said, "Report this
to James* and the brothers." Then he left
and went to another place. 18At daybreak
there was no small commotion among the
soldiers over what had become of Peter.[n]
19Herod, after instituting a search but not
finding him, ordered the guards tried and
executed. Then he left Judea to spend some
time in Caesarea.

***Herod's Death.*** 20* He had long been very
angry with the people of Tyre and Sidon,
who now came to him in a body. After winning over Blastus, the king's chamberlain,
they sued for peace because their country
was supplied with food from the king's territory. 21On an appointed day, Herod, attired
in royal robes, [and] seated on the rostrum,
addressed them publicly. 22The assembled
crowd cried out, "This is the voice of a god,
not of a man." 23At once the angel of the
Lord struck him down because he did not ascribe the honor to God, and he was eaten by
worms and breathed his last. 24But the word
of God continued to spread and grow.[o]

***Mission of Barnabas and Saul.*** 25After
Barnabas and Saul completed their relief
mission, they returned to Jerusalem,* taking
with them John, who is called Mark.[p]

## CHAPTER 13

See RG 343

1* Now there were in the church at Antioch prophets and teachers: Barnabas,
Symeon who was called Niger, Lucius of Cyrene, Manaen who was a close friend of Herod
the tetrarch, and Saul. 2While they were worshiping the Lord and fasting, the holy Spirit
said, "Set apart for me Barnabas and Saul for
the work to which I have called them." 3Then,
completing their fasting and prayer, they laid
hands on them and sent them off.

***First Mission Begins in Cyprus.*** 4* So they,
sent forth by the holy Spirit, went down to
Seleucia and from there sailed to Cyprus.
5When they arrived in Salamis, they proclaimed the word of God in the Jewish synagogues. They had John* also as their assistant. 6When they had traveled through the
whole island as far as Paphos, they met a
magician named Bar-Jesus who was a Jewish false prophet.* 7He was with the proconsul Sergius Paulus, a man of intelligence,
who had summoned Barnabas and Saul and
wanted to hear the word of God. 8But Elymas the magician (for that is what his name

**12:17 To James**: this James is not the son of Zebedee mentioned in Acts 12:2, but is James, the "brother of the Lord" (Gal 1:19), who in Acts 15; 21 is presented as leader of the Jerusalem Christian community. **He left and went to another place**: the conjecture that Peter left for Rome at this time has nothing to recommend it. His chief responsibility was still the leadership of the Jewish Christian community in Palestine (see Gal 2:7). The concept of the great missionary effort of the church was yet to come (see Acts 13:1–3).

**12:20–23** Josephus gives a similar account of Herod's death that occurred in A.D. 44. Early Christian tradition considered the manner of it to be a divine punishment upon his evil life. See 2 Kgs 19:35 for the figure of the angel of the Lord in such a context.

**12:25 They returned to Jerusalem**: many manuscripts read "from Jerusalem," since Acts 11:30 implies that Paul and Barnabas are already in Jerusalem. This present verse could refer to a return visit or subsequent relief mission.

**13:1–3** The impulse for the first missionary effort in Asia Minor is ascribed to the prophets of the Antiochene community, under the inspiration of the holy Spirit. Just as the Jerusalem community had earlier been the center of missionary activity, so too Antioch becomes the center from which the missionaries Barnabas and Saul are sent out.

**13:4–14:27** The key event in Luke's account of the first missionary journey is the experience of Paul and Barnabas at Pisidian Antioch (Acts 13:14–52). The Christian kerygma proclaimed by Paul in the synagogue was favorably received. Some Jews and "God-fearers" (see note on Acts 8:26–40) became interested and invited the missionaries to speak again on the following sabbath (Acts 13:42). By that time, however, the appearance of a large number of Gentiles from the city had so disconcerted the Jews that they became hostile toward the apostles (Acts 13:44–50). This hostility of theirs appears in all three accounts of Paul's missionary journeys in Acts, the Jews of Iconium (Acts 14:1–2) and Beroea (Acts 17:11) being notable exceptions.

**13:5 John**: that is, John Mark (see Acts 12:12, 25).

**13:6 A magician named Bar-Jesus who was a Jewish false prophet**: that is, he posed as a prophet. Again Luke takes the opportunity to dissociate Christianity from the magical acts of the time (Acts 13:7–11); see also Acts 8:18–24.

*n:* 5:22–24. *o:* 6:7. *p:* 11:29–30.

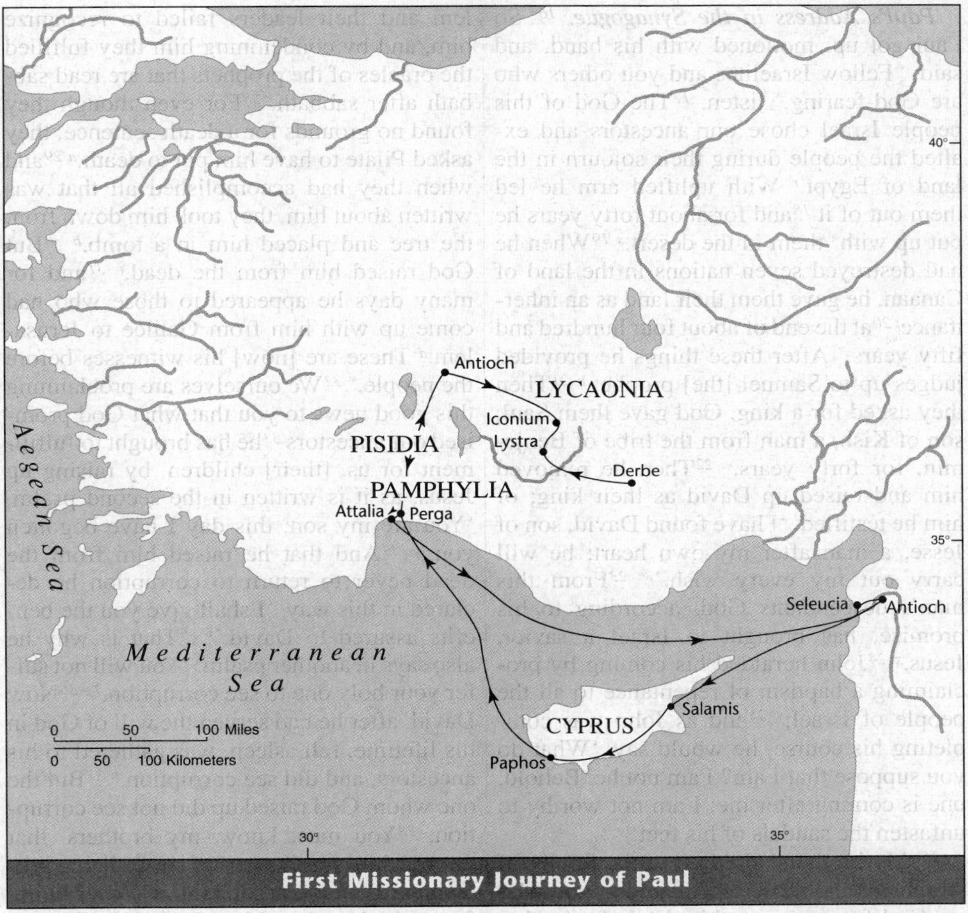

First Missionary Journey of Paul

means) opposed them in an attempt to turn the proconsul away from the faith. 9 But Saul, also known as Paul,* filled with the holy Spirit, looked intently at him 10 and said, "You son of the devil, you enemy of all that is right, full of every sort of deceit and fraud. Will you not stop twisting the straight paths of [the] Lord? 11 Even now the hand of the Lord is upon you. You will be blind, and unable to see the sun for a time." Immediately a dark mist fell upon him, and he went about seeking people to lead him by the hand. 12 When the proconsul saw what had happened, he came to believe, for he was astonished by the teaching about the Lord.

***Paul's Arrival at Antioch in Pisidia.*** 13 From Paphos, Paul and his companions set sail and arrived at Perga in Pamphylia. But John left them and returned to Jerusalem.[q] 14 They continued on from Perga and reached Antioch in Pisidia. On the sabbath they entered [into] the synagogue and took their seats. 15 After the reading of the law and the prophets, the synagogue officials sent word to them, "My brothers, if one of you has a word of exhortation for the people, please speak."

**13:9 Saul, also known as Paul**: there is no reason to believe that his name was changed from Saul to Paul upon his conversion. The use of a double name, one Semitic (Saul), the other Greco-Roman (Paul), is well attested (cf. Acts 1:23, Joseph Justus; Acts 12:12, 25, John Mark).

*q*: 15:38.

*Paul's Address in the Synagogue.* [16]* So Paul got up, motioned with his hand, and said, "Fellow Israelites and you others who are God-fearing,* listen. [17]The God of this people Israel chose our ancestors and exalted the people during their sojourn in the land of Egypt.[r] With uplifted arm he led them out of it [18]and for about forty years he put up with* them in the desert.[s] [19]When he had destroyed seven nations in the land of Canaan, he gave them their land as an inheritance[t] [20]at the end of about four hundred and fifty years.* After these things he provided judges up to Samuel [the] prophet.[u] [21]Then they asked for a king. God gave them Saul, son of Kish, a man from the tribe of Benjamin, for forty years.[v] [22]Then he removed him and raised up David as their king; of him he testified, 'I have found David, son of Jesse, a man after my own heart; he will carry out my every wish.'[w] [23]From this man's descendants God, according to his promise, has brought to Israel a savior, Jesus.[x] [24]John heralded his coming by proclaiming a baptism of repentance to all the people of Israel;[y] [25]and as John was completing his course, he would say, 'What do you suppose that I am? I am not he. Behold, one is coming after me; I am not worthy to unfasten the sandals of his feet.'[z]

[26]"My brothers, children of the family of Abraham, and those others among you who are God-fearing, to us this word of salvation has been sent. [27]The inhabitants of Jerusalem and their leaders failed to recognize him, and by condemning him they fulfilled the oracles of the prophets that are read sabbath after sabbath. [28]For even though they found no grounds for a death sentence, they asked Pilate to have him put to death,[a] [29]and when they had accomplished all that was written about him, they took him down from the tree and placed him in a tomb.[b] [30]But God raised him from the dead,[c] [31]and for many days he appeared to those who had come up with him from Galilee to Jerusalem.[d] These are [now] his witnesses before the people.* [32]We ourselves are proclaiming this good news to you that what God promised our ancestors [33]he has brought to fulfillment for us, [their] children, by raising up Jesus, as it is written in the second psalm, 'You are my son; this day I have begotten you.'[e] [34]And that he raised him from the dead never to return to corruption he declared in this way, 'I shall give you the benefits assured to David.'[f] [35]That is why he also says in another psalm, 'You will not suffer your holy one to see corruption.'[g] [36]Now David, after he had served the will of God in his lifetime, fell asleep, was gathered to his ancestors, and did see corruption.[h] [37]But the one whom God raised up did not see corruption. [38]You must know, my brothers, that through him forgiveness of sins is being proclaimed to you, [and] in regard to everything from which you could not be justified* under the law of Moses, [39]in him every believer is

**13:16–41** This is the first of several speeches of Paul to Jews proclaiming that the Christian church is the logical development of Pharisaic Judaism (see also Acts 24:10–21; 26:2–23).

**13:16 Who are God-fearing**: see note on Acts 8:26–40.

**13:18 Put up with**: some manuscripts read "sustained."

**13:20 At the end of about four hundred and fifty years**: the manuscript tradition makes it uncertain whether the mention of four hundred and fifty years refers to the sojourn in Egypt before the Exodus, the wilderness period and the time of the conquest (see Ex 12:40–41), as the translation here suggests, or to the time between the conquest and the time of Samuel, the period of the judges, if the text is read, "After these things, for about four hundred and fifty years, he provided judges."

**13:31** The theme of the Galilean witnesses is a major one in the Gospel of Luke and in Acts and is used to signify the continuity between the teachings of Jesus and the teachings of the church and to guarantee the fidelity of the church's teachings to the words of Jesus.

**13:38–39 Justified**: the verb is the same as that used in Paul's letters to speak of the experience of justification and, as in Paul, is here connected with the term "to have faith" ("every believer"). But this seems the only passage about Paul in Acts where justification is mentioned. In Lucan fashion it is paralleled with "forgiveness of sins" (a theme at Acts 2:38; 3:19; 5:31; 10:43) based on Jesus' resurrection (Acts 13:37) rather than his cross, and is put negatively (Acts 13:38). Therefore, some would translate, "in regard to everything from which you could not be acquitted . . . every believer is acquitted."

*r:* Ex 6:1, 6; 12:51. *s:* Ex 16:1, 35; Nm 14:34. *t:* Dt 7:1; Jos 14:1–2. *u:* Jgs 2:16; 1 Sm 3:20. *v:* 1 Sm 8:5, 19; 9:16; 10:1, 20–21, 24; 11:15. *w:* 1 Sm 13:14; 16:12–13; Ps 89:20–21. *x:* Is 11:1. *y:* Mt 3:1–2; Mk 1:4–5; Lk 3:2–3. *z:* Mt 3:11; Mk 1:7; Lk 3:16; Jn 1:20, 27. *a:* Mt 27:20, 22–23; Mk 15:13–14; Lk 23:4, 14–15, 21–23; Jn 19:4–6, 15. *b:* Mt 27:59–60; Mk 15:46; Lk 23:53; Jn 19:38, 41–42. *c:* 2:24, 32; 3:15; 4:10; 17:31. *d:* 1:3, 8; 10:39, 41; Mt 28:8–10, 16–20; Mk 16:9, 12–20; Lk 24:13–53; Jn 20:11–29; 21:1–23. *e:* Ps 2:7. *f:* Is 55:3. *g:* Ps 16:10. *h:* 2:29; 1 Kgs 2:10.

justified.[i] 40 Be careful, then, that what was
said in the prophets not come about:

41 'Look on, you scoffers,
be amazed and disappear.
For I am doing a work in your days,
a work that you will never believe
even if someone tells you.' "[j]

42 As they were leaving, they invited them to
speak on these subjects the following sabbath. 43 After the congregation had dispersed, many Jews and worshipers who
were converts to Judaism followed Paul and
Barnabas, who spoke to them and urged
them to remain faithful to the grace of God.

***Address to the Gentiles.*** 44 On the following sabbath almost the whole city gathered
to hear the word of the Lord. 45 When the
Jews saw the crowds, they were filled with
jealousy and with violent abuse contradicted
what Paul said. 46[k] Both Paul and Barnabas
spoke out boldly and said, "It was necessary
that the word of God be spoken to you first,
but since you reject it and condemn yourselves as unworthy of eternal life, we now
turn to the Gentiles.* 47 For so the Lord has
commanded us, 'I have made you a light to
the Gentiles, that you may be an instrument
of salvation to the ends of the earth.' "[l]

48 The Gentiles were delighted when they
heard this and glorified the word of the Lord.
All who were destined for eternal life came
to believe, 49 and the word of the Lord continued to spread through the whole region.
50 The Jews, however, incited the women of
prominence who were worshipers and the
leading men of the city, stirred up a persecution against Paul and Barnabas, and expelled
them from their territory. 51[m] So they shook
the dust from their feet in protest against
them and went to Iconium.* 52 The disciples
were filled with joy and the holy Spirit.

## CHAPTER 14

See RG 343

***Paul and Barnabas at Iconium.*** 1 In
Iconium they entered the Jewish synagogue
together and spoke in such a way that a great
number of both Jews and Greeks came to believe, 2 although the disbelieving Jews stirred
up and poisoned the minds of the Gentiles
against the brothers. 3 So they stayed for a
considerable period, speaking out boldly for
the Lord, who confirmed the word about his
grace by granting signs and wonders to occur
through their hands.[n] 4 The people of the city
were divided: some were with the Jews; others, with the apostles. 5 When there was an attempt by both the Gentiles and the Jews, together with their leaders, to attack and stone
them,[o] 6 they realized it and fled to the Lycaonian cities of Lystra and Derbe and to the
surrounding countryside, 7 where they continued to proclaim the good news.

***Paul and Barnabas at Lystra.*** 8* At Lystra
there was a crippled man, lame from birth,
who had never walked. 9 He listened to Paul
speaking, who looked intently at him, saw
that he had the faith to be healed, 10 and called
out in a loud voice, "Stand up straight on
your feet." He jumped up and began to walk
about. 11 When the crowds saw what Paul had
done, they cried out in Lycaonian, "The gods
have come down to us in human form."[p]
12 They called Barnabas "Zeus"* and Paul
"Hermes," because he was the chief speaker.
13 And the priest of Zeus, whose temple was
at the entrance to the city, brought oxen and
garlands to the gates, for he together with the
people intended to offer sacrifice.

14 The apostles Barnabas and Paul tore
their garments* when they heard this and

**13:46** The refusal to believe frustrates God's plan for his chosen people; however, no adverse judgment is made here concerning their ultimate destiny. Again, Luke, in the words of Paul, speaks of the priority of Israel in the plan for salvation (see Acts 10:36).

**13:51** See note on Lk 9:5.

**14:8–18** In an effort to convince his hearers that the divine power works through his word, Paul cures the cripple. However, the pagan tradition of the occasional appearance of gods among human beings leads the people astray in interpreting the miracle. The incident reveals the cultural difficulties with which the church had to cope. Note the similarity of the miracle worked here by Paul to the one performed by Peter in Acts 3:2–10.

**14:12 Zeus . . . Hermes**: in Greek religion, Zeus was the chief of the Olympian gods, the "father of gods and men"; Hermes was a son of Zeus and was usually identified as the herald and messenger of the gods.

**14:14 Tore their garments**: a gesture of protest.

*i:* Rom 3:20. *j:* Heb 1:5. *k:* 3:26; Rom 1:16. *l:* Is 49:6. *m:* Mt 10:14; Mk 6:11; Lk 9:5; 10:11. *n:* Mk 16:17–20. *o:* 2 Tm 3:11. *p:* 28:6.

rushed out into the crowd, shouting,
15* “Men, why are you doing this? We are of
the same nature as you, human beings. We
proclaim to you good news that you should
turn from these idols to the living God, ‘who
made heaven and earth and sea and all that is
in them.’[q] 16In past generations he allowed
all Gentiles to go their own ways;[r] 17yet, in
bestowing his goodness, he did not leave
himself without witness, for he gave you
rains from heaven and fruitful seasons, and
filled you with nourishment and gladness for
your hearts.”[s] 18Even with these words, they
scarcely restrained the crowds from offering
sacrifice to them.
19t However, some Jews from Antioch and
Iconium arrived and won over the crowds.
They stoned Paul and dragged him out of the
city, supposing that he was dead. 20But when
the disciples gathered around him, he got up
and entered the city. On the following day he
left with Barnabas for Derbe.
*End of the First Mission.* 21After they had
proclaimed the good news to that city and
made a considerable number of disciples,
they returned to Lystra and to Iconium and to
Antioch. 22They strengthened the spirits of
the disciples and exhorted them to persevere
in the faith, saying, “It is necessary for us to
undergo many hardships to enter the kingdom of God.”[u] 23They appointed presbyters*
for them in each church and, with prayer and
fasting, commended them to the Lord in
whom they had put their faith. 24Then they
traveled through Pisidia and reached Pamphylia. 25After proclaiming the word at Perga
they went down to Attalia. 26From there they
sailed to Antioch, where they had been commended to the grace of God for the work they
had now accomplished.[v] 27And when they arrived, they called the church together and reported what God had done with them and
how he had opened the door of faith to the
Gentiles. 28Then they spent no little time
with the disciples.

## CHAPTER 15

See RG 343-46

*Council of Jerusalem.* 1* Some who
had come down from Judea were instructing
the brothers,[w] “Unless you are circumcised
according to the Mosaic practice,[x] you cannot
be saved.”* 2Because there arose no little dissension and debate by Paul and Barnabas
with them, it was decided that Paul, Barnabas, and some of the others should go up to
Jerusalem to the apostles and presbyters
about this question. 3They were sent on their
journey by the church, and passed through
Phoenicia and Samaria telling of the conversion of the Gentiles, and brought great joy to
all the brothers. 4When they arrived in Jerusalem, they were welcomed by the church, as
well as by the apostles and the presbyters, and
they reported what God had done with them.
5But some from the party of the Pharisees
who had become believers stood up and said,
“It is necessary to circumcise them and direct
them to observe the Mosaic law.”
6* The apostles and the presbyters met
together to see about this matter. 7* After

**14:15–17** This is the first speech of Paul to Gentiles recorded by Luke in Acts (cf. Acts 17:22–31). Rather than showing how Christianity is the logical outgrowth of Judaism, as he does in speeches before Jews, Luke says that God excuses past Gentile ignorance and then presents a natural theology arguing for the recognition of God’s existence and presence through his activity in natural phenomena.

**14:23 They appointed presbyters**: the communities are given their own religious leaders by the traveling missionaries. The structure in these churches is patterned on the model of the Jerusalem community (Acts 11:30; 15:2, 5, 22; 21:18).

**15:1–35** The Jerusalem “Council” marks the official rejection of the rigid view that Gentile converts were obliged to observe the Mosaic law completely. From here to the end of Acts, Paul and the Gentile mission become the focus of Luke’s writing.

**15:1–5** When some of the converted Pharisees of Jerusalem discover the results of the first missionary journey of Paul, they urge that the Gentiles be taught to follow the Mosaic law. Recognizing the authority of the Jerusalem church, Paul and Barnabas go there to settle the question of whether Gentiles can embrace a form of Christianity that does not include this obligation.

**15:6–12** The gathering is possibly the same as that recalled by Paul in Gal 2:1–10. Note that in Acts 15:2 it is only the apostles and presbyters, a small group, with whom Paul and Barnabas are to meet. Here Luke gives the meeting a public character because he wishes to emphasize its doctrinal significance (see Acts 15:22).

**15:7–11** Paul’s refusal to impose the Mosaic law on the Gentile Christians is supported by Peter on the ground that within his own experience God bestowed the holy Spirit upon

*q:* 3:12; 10:26; Ex 20:11; Ps 146:6. *r:* 17:30. *s:* Wis 13:1. *t:* 2 Cor 11:25; 2 Tm 3:11. *u:* 1 Thes 3:3. *v:* 13:1–3. *w:* Gal 2:1–9. *x:* Lv 12:3; Gal 5:2.

much debate had taken place, Peter got up
and said to them, "My brothers, you are
well aware that from early days God made
his choice among you that through my
mouth the Gentiles would hear the word of
the gospel and believe.[y] 8And God, who
knows the heart, bore witness by granting
them the holy Spirit just as he did us.[z] 9He
made no distinction between us and them,
for by faith he purified their hearts.[a]
10Why, then, are you now putting God to
the test by placing on the shoulders of the
disciples a yoke that neither our ancestors
nor we have been able to bear?[b] 11On the
contrary, we believe that we are saved
through the grace of the Lord Jesus,[c] in the
same way as they."* 12The whole assembly
fell silent, and they listened while Paul and
Barnabas described the signs and wonders
God had worked among the Gentiles
through them.

*James on Dietary Law.* 13* After they had
fallen silent, James responded, "My brothers, listen to me. 14Symeon* has described
how God first concerned himself with acquiring from among the Gentiles a people
for his name. 15The words of the prophets
agree with this, as is written:

16 'After this I shall return[d]
and rebuild the fallen hut of David;
from its ruins I shall rebuild it
and raise it up again,
17 so that the rest of humanity may seek out
the Lord,
even all the Gentiles on whom my
name is invoked.
Thus says the Lord who accomplishes
these things,
18 known from of old.'

19e It is my judgment, therefore, that we
ought to stop troubling the Gentiles who turn
to God, 20but tell them by letter to avoid pollution from idols, unlawful marriage, the
meat of strangled animals, and blood.[f] 21For
Moses, for generations now, has had those
who proclaim him in every town, as he has
been read in the synagogues every sabbath."

*Letter of the Apostles.* 22Then the apostles
and presbyters, in agreement with the whole
church, decided to choose representatives
and to send them to Antioch with Paul and
Barnabas. The ones chosen were Judas, who
was called Barsabbas, and Silas, leaders
among the brothers. 23This is the letter delivered by them: "The apostles and the presbyters, your brothers, to the brothers in Antioch, Syria, and Cilicia of Gentile origin:
greetings. 24Since we have heard that some
of our number [who went out] without any
mandate from us have upset you with their
teachings and disturbed your peace of mind,
25we have with one accord decided to
choose representatives and to send them to
you along with our beloved Barnabas and
Paul, 26who have dedicated their lives to the
name of our Lord Jesus Christ. 27So we are
sending Judas and Silas who will also convey this same message by word of mouth:
28g 'It is the decision of the holy Spirit and of
us not to place on you any burden beyond
these necessities, 29namely, to abstain from
meat sacrificed to idols, from blood, from

Cornelius and his household without preconditions concerning the adoption of the Mosaic law (see Acts 10:44–47).

**15:11** In support of Paul, Peter formulates the fundamental meaning of the gospel: that all are invited to be saved through faith in the power of Christ.

**15:13–35** Some scholars think that this apostolic decree suggested by James, the immediate leader of the Jerusalem community, derives from another historical occasion than the meeting in question. This seems to be the case if the meeting is the same as the one related in Gal 2:1–10. According to that account, nothing was imposed upon Gentile Christians in respect to Mosaic law; whereas the decree instructs Gentile Christians of mixed communities to abstain from meats sacrificed to idols and from blood-meats, and to avoid marriage within forbidden degrees of consanguinity and affinity (Lv 18), all of which practices were especially abhorrent to Jews. Luke seems to have telescoped two originally independent incidents here: the first a Jerusalem "Council" that dealt with the question of circumcision, and the second a Jerusalem decree dealing mainly with Gentile observance of dietary laws (see Acts 21:25 where Paul seems to be learning of the decree for the first time).

**15:14 Symeon**: elsewhere in Acts he is called either Peter or Simon. The presence of the name Symeon here suggests that, in the source Luke is using for this part of the Jerusalem "Council" incident, the name may have originally referred to someone other than Peter (see Acts 13:1 where the Antiochene Symeon Niger is mentioned). As the text now stands, however, it is undoubtedly a reference to Simon Peter (Acts 15:7).

*y:* 10:27–43. *z:* 10:44–48. *a:* 10:34–35. *b:* Mt 23:4; Gal 5:1. *c:* Gal 2:16; 3:11; Eph 2:5–8. *d:* Am 9:11–12. *e:* 15:28–29; 21:25. *f:* Gn 9:4; Lv 3:17; 17:10–14. *g:* 15:19–20.

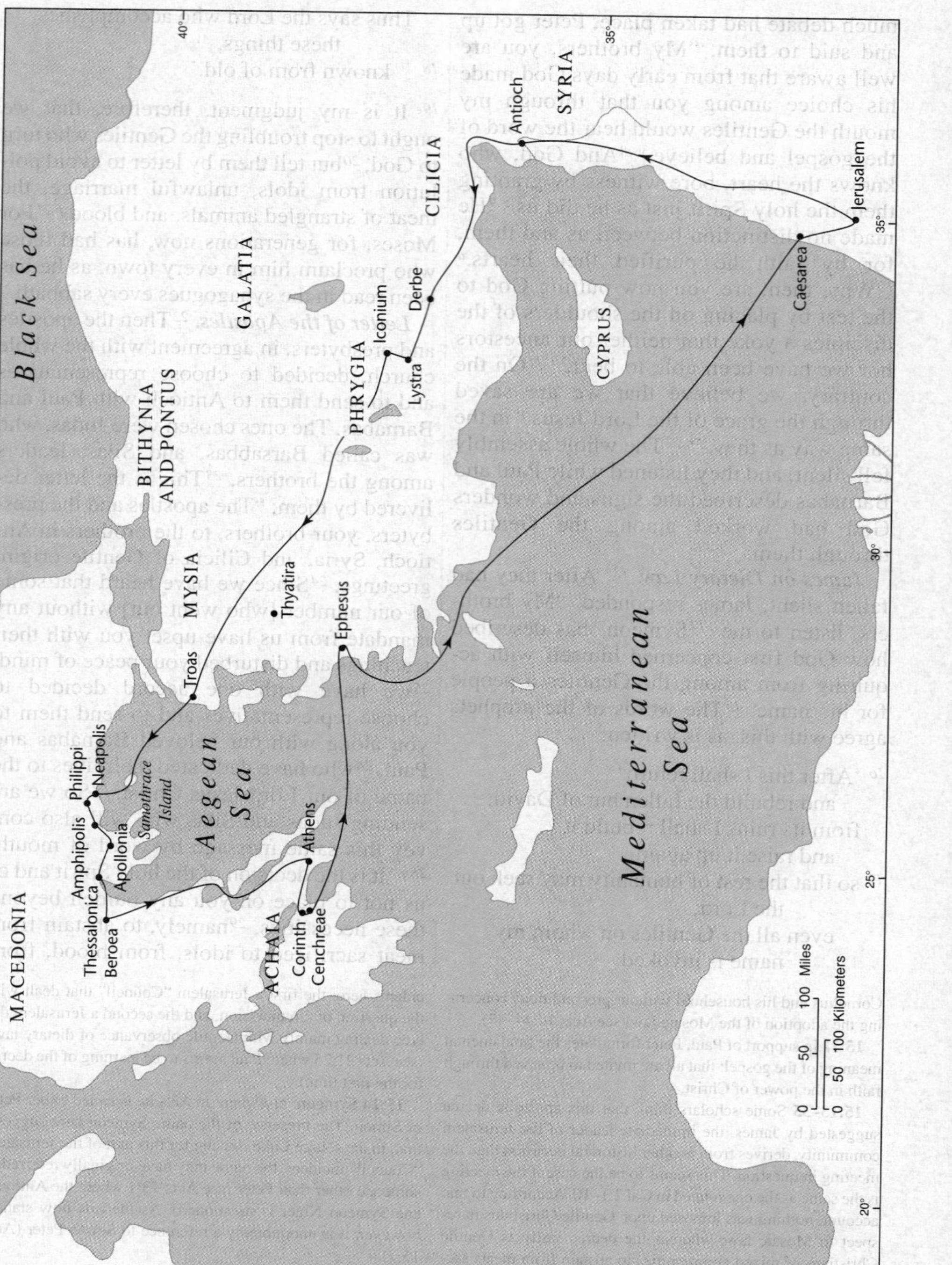


Second Missionary Journey of Paul

meats of strangled animals, and from unlawful marriage. If you keep free of these, you will be doing what is right. Farewell.' "[h]

***Delegates at Antioch.*** 30 And so they were sent on their journey. Upon their arrival in Antioch they called the assembly together and delivered the letter. 31 When the people read it, they were delighted with the exhortation. 32 Judas and Silas, who were themselves prophets, exhorted and strengthened the brothers with many words. 33 After they had spent some time there, they were sent off with greetings of peace from the brothers to those who had commissioned them. [34]* 35 But Paul and Barnabas remained in Antioch, teaching and proclaiming with many others the word of the Lord.

## V. The Mission of Paul to the Ends of the Earth

***Paul and Barnabas Separate.*** 36* After some time, Paul said to Barnabas, "Come, let us make a return visit to see how the brothers are getting on in all the cities where we proclaimed the word of the Lord." 37 Barnabas wanted to take with them also John, who was called Mark, 38 but Paul insisted that they should not take with them someone who had deserted them at Pamphylia and who had not continued with them in their work.[i] 39 So sharp was their disagreement that they separated. Barnabas took Mark and sailed to Cyprus. 40 But Paul chose Silas and departed after being commended by the brothers to the grace of the Lord. 41 He traveled through Syria and Cilicia bringing strength to the churches.

### CHAPTER 16

See RG 344–46

***Paul in Lycaonia: Timothy.*** 1 He reached [also] Derbe and Lystra where there was a disciple named Timothy, the son of a Jewish woman who was a believer, but his father was a Greek.[j] 2 The brothers in Lystra and Iconium spoke highly of him,[k] 3 and Paul wanted him to come along with him. On account of the Jews of that region, Paul had him circumcised,* for they all knew that his father was a Greek. 4 As they traveled from city to city, they handed on to the people for observance the decisions reached by the apostles and presbyters in Jerusalem. 5 Day after day the churches grew stronger in faith and increased in number.

***Through Asia Minor.*** 6 They traveled through the Phrygian and Galatian territory because they had been prevented by the holy Spirit from preaching the message in the province of Asia. 7 When they came to Mysia, they tried to go on into Bithynia, but the Spirit of Jesus* did not allow them, 8 so they crossed through Mysia and came down to Troas. 9 During [the] night Paul had a vision. A Macedonian stood before him and implored him with these words, "Come over to Macedonia and help us." 10 When he had seen the vision, we* sought passage to Macedonia at once, concluding that God had called us to proclaim the good news to them.

**15:34** Some manuscripts add, in various wordings, "But Silas decided to remain there."

**15:36–18:22** This continuous narrative recounts Paul's second missionary journey. On the internal evidence of the Lucan account, it lasted about three years. Paul first visited the communities he had established on his first journey (Acts 16:1–5), then pushed on into Macedonia, where he established communities at Philippi, Thessalonica, and Beroea (Acts 16:7–17:5). To escape the hostility of the Jews of Thessalonica, he left for Greece and while resident in Athens attempted, without success, to establish an effective Christian community there. From Athens he proceeded to Corinth and, after a stay of a year and a half, returned to Antioch by way of Ephesus and Jerusalem (Acts 17:16–18:22). Luke does not concern himself with the structure or statistics of the communities but aims to show the general progress of the gospel in the Gentile world as well as its continued failure to take root in the Jewish community.

**16:3 Paul had him circumcised**: he did this in order that Timothy might be able to associate with the Jews and so perform a ministry among them. Paul did not object to the Jewish Christians' adherence to the law. But he insisted that the law could not be imposed on the Gentiles. Paul himself lived in accordance with the law, or as exempt from the law, according to particular circumstances (see 1 Cor 9:19–23).

**16:7 The Spirit of Jesus**: this is an unusual formulation in Luke's writings. The parallelism with Acts 16:6 indicates its meaning, the holy Spirit.

**16:10–17** This is the first of the so-called "we-sections" in Acts, where Luke writes as one of Paul's companions. The other passages are Acts 20:5–15; 21:1–18; 27:1–28:16. Scholars debate whether Luke may not have used the first person plural simply as a literary device to lend color to the narrative. The realism of the narrative, however, lends weight to the argument that the "we" includes Luke or another companion of Paul whose data Luke used as a source.

*h:* Gn 9:4; Lv 3:17; 17:10–14. *i:* 13:13. *j:* 1 Tm 1:2; 2 Tm 1:5. *k:* Phil 2:20.

*Into Europe.* 11* We set sail from Troas, making a straight run for Samothrace, and on the next day to Neapolis, 12 and from there to Philippi, a leading city in that district of Macedonia and a Roman colony. We spent some time in that city. 13 On the sabbath we went outside the city gate along the river where we thought there would be a place of prayer. We sat and spoke with the women who had gathered there. 14 One of them, a woman named Lydia, a dealer in purple cloth, from the city of Thyatira, a worshiper of God,* listened, and the Lord opened her heart to pay attention to what Paul was saying. 15 After she and her household had been baptized, she offered us an invitation, "If you consider me a believer in the Lord, come and stay at my home," and she prevailed on us.

*Imprisonment at Philippi.* 16 As we were going to the place of prayer, we met a slave girl with an oracular spirit,* who used to bring a large profit to her owners through her fortune-telling. 17 She began to follow Paul and us, shouting, "These people are slaves of the Most High God, who proclaim to you a way of salvation." 18 She did this for many days. Paul became annoyed, turned, and said to the spirit, "I command you in the name of Jesus Christ to come out of her." Then it came out at that moment.

19 When her owners saw that their hope of profit was gone, they seized Paul and Silas and dragged them to the public square before the local authorities. 20 They brought them before the magistrates* and said, "These people are Jews and are disturbing our city 21 and are advocating customs that are not lawful for us Romans to adopt or practice." 22[l] The crowd joined in the attack on them, and the magistrates had them stripped and ordered them to be beaten with rods. 23 After inflicting many blows on them, they threw them into prison and instructed the jailer to guard them securely. 24 When he received these instructions, he put them in the innermost cell and secured their feet to a stake.

*Deliverance from Prison.* 25 About midnight, while Paul and Silas were praying and singing hymns to God as the prisoners listened, 26 there was suddenly such a severe earthquake that the foundations of the jail shook; all the doors flew open, and the chains of all were pulled loose. 27 When the jailer woke up and saw the prison doors wide open, he drew [his] sword and was about to kill himself, thinking that the prisoners had escaped. 28 But Paul shouted out in a loud voice, "Do no harm to yourself; we are all here." 29 He asked for a light and rushed in and, trembling with fear, he fell down before Paul and Silas. 30 Then he brought them out and said, "Sirs, what must I do to be saved?" 31 And they said, "Believe in the Lord Jesus and you and your household will be saved." 32 So they spoke the word of the Lord to him and to everyone in his house. 33 He took them in at that hour of the night and bathed their wounds; then he and all his family were baptized at once. 34 He brought them up into his house and provided a meal and with his household rejoiced at having come to faith in God.

35 But when it was day, the magistrates sent the lictors* with the order, "Release those men." 36 The jailer reported the[se] words to Paul, "The magistrates have sent orders that you be released. Now, then, come out and go in peace." 37 But Paul said to them, "They have beaten us publicly, even though we are Roman citizens and have not been tried, and have thrown us into prison.[m] And now, are they going to release us se-

**16:11–40** The church at Philippi became a flourishing community to which Paul addressed one of his letters (see Introduction to the Letter to the Philippians).

**16:14 A worshiper of God**: a "God-fearer." See note on Acts 8:26–40.

**16:16 With an oracular spirit**: literally, "with a Python spirit." The Python was the serpent or dragon that guarded the Delphic oracle. It later came to designate a "spirit that pronounced oracles" and also a ventriloquist who, it was thought, had such a spirit in the belly.

**16:20 Magistrates**: in Greek, *stratēgoi*, the popular designation of the *duoviri*, the highest officials of the Roman colony of Philippi.

**16:35 The lictors**: the equivalent of police officers, among whose duties were the apprehension and punishment of criminals.

**16:37** Paul's Roman citizenship granted him special privileges in regard to criminal process. Roman law forbade under severe penalty the beating of Roman citizens (see also Acts 22:25).

*l:* 2 Cor 11:25; Phil 1:30; 1 Thes 2:2. *m:* 22:25.

cretly? By no means. Let them come themselves and lead us out."'* 38The lictors reported these words to the magistrates, and they became alarmed when they heard that they were Roman citizens.[n] 39So they came and placated them, and led them out and asked that they leave the city. 40When they had come out of the prison, they went to Lydia's house where they saw and encouraged the brothers, and then they left.

## CHAPTER 17

See RG 344–46

***Paul in Thessalonica.*** 1When they took the road through Amphipolis and Apollonia, they reached Thessalonica, where there was a synagogue of the Jews.[o] 2Following his usual custom, Paul joined them, and for three sabbaths he entered into discussions with them from the scriptures, 3expounding and demonstrating that the Messiah had to suffer and rise from the dead, and that "This is the Messiah, Jesus, whom I proclaim to you."[p] 4Some of them were convinced and joined Paul and Silas; so, too, a great number of Greeks who were worshipers, and not a few of the prominent women. 5But the Jews became jealous and recruited some worthless men loitering in the public square, formed a mob, and set the city in turmoil. They marched on the house of Jason,[q] intending to bring them before the people's assembly. 6* When they could not find them, they dragged Jason and some of the brothers before the city magistrates, shouting, "These people who have been creating a disturbance all over the world have now come here, 7and Jason has welcomed them.[r] They all act in opposition to the decrees of Caesar and claim instead that there is another king, Jesus."'* 8They stirred up the crowd and the city magistrates who, upon hearing these charges, 9took a surety payment from Jason and the others before releasing them.

***Paul in Beroea.*** 10The brothers immediately sent Paul and Silas to Beroea during the night. Upon arrival they went to the synagogue of the Jews. 11These Jews were more fair-minded than those in Thessalonica, for they received the word with all willingness and examined the scriptures daily to determine whether these things were so.[s] 12Many of them became believers, as did not a few of the influential Greek women and men. 13But when the Jews of Thessalonica learned that the word of God had now been proclaimed by Paul in Beroea also, they came there too to cause a commotion and stir up the crowds. 14So the brothers at once sent Paul on his way to the seacoast, while Silas and Timothy remained behind.[t] 15After Paul's escorts had taken him to Athens, they came away with instructions for Silas and Timothy to join him as soon as possible.

***Paul in Athens.**** 16While Paul was waiting for them in Athens, he grew exasperated at the sight of the city full of idols. 17So he debated in the synagogue with the Jews and with the worshipers, and daily in the public square with whoever happened to be there. 18Even some of the Epicurean and Stoic philosophers* engaged him in discussion. Some asked, "What is this scavenger trying to say?"

**17:6–7** The accusations against Paul and his companions echo the charges brought against Jesus in Lk 23:2.

**17:7 There is another king, Jesus**: a distortion into a political sense of the apostolic proclamation of Jesus and the kingdom of God (see Acts 8:12).

**17:16–21** Paul's presence in Athens sets the stage for the great discourse before a Gentile audience in Acts 17:22–31. Although Athens was a politically insignificant city at this period, it still lived on the glories of its past and represented the center of Greek culture. The setting describes the conflict between Christian preaching and Hellenistic philosophy.

**17:18 Epicurean and Stoic philosophers**: for the followers of Epicurus (342–271 B.C.), the goal of life was happiness attained through sober reasoning and the searching out of motives for all choice and avoidance. The Stoics were followers of Zeno, a younger contemporary of Alexander the Great. Zeno and his followers believed in a type of pantheism that held that the spark of divinity was present in all reality and that, in order to be free, each person must live "according to nature." **This scavenger**: literally, "seed-picker," as of a bird that picks up grain. The word is later used of scrap collectors and of people who take other people's ideas and propagate them as if they were their own. **Promoter of foreign deities**: according to Xenophon, Socrates was accused of promoting new deities. The accusation against Paul echoes the charge against Socrates. **'Jesus' and 'Resurrection'**: the Athenians are presented as misunderstanding Paul from the outset; they think he is preaching about Jesus and a goddess named *Anastasis*, i.e., Resurrection.

*n:* 22:29. *o:* 1 Thes 2:1–2. *p:* 3:18; Lk 24:25–26, 46. *q:* Rom 16:21. *r:* Lk 23:2; Jn 19:12–15. *s:* Jn 5:39. *t:* 1 Thes 3:1–2.

Others said, "He sounds like a promoter of foreign deities," because he was preaching about 'Jesus' and 'Resurrection.' 19 They took him and led him to the Areopagus* and said, "May we learn what this new teaching is that you speak of?[u] 20 For you bring some strange notions to our ears; we should like to know what these things mean." 21 Now all the Athenians as well as the foreigners residing there used their time for nothing else but telling or hearing something new.

***Paul's Speech at the Areopagus.*** 22 Then Paul stood up at the Areopagus and said:*

"You Athenians, I see that in every respect you are very religious. 23 For as I walked around looking carefully at your shrines, I even discovered an altar inscribed, 'To an Unknown God.'* What therefore you unknowingly worship, I proclaim to you. 24 The God who made the world and all that is in it, the Lord of heaven and earth, does not dwell in sanctuaries made by human hands,[v] 25 nor is he served by human hands because he needs anything. Rather it is he who gives to everyone life and breath and everything. 26 He made from one* the whole human race to dwell on the entire surface of the earth, and he fixed the ordered seasons and the boundaries of their regions, 27 so that people might seek God, even perhaps grope for him and find him, though indeed he is not far from any one of us.[w] 28 For 'In him we live and move and have our being,'* as even some of your poets have said, 'For we too are his offspring.' 29 Since therefore we are the offspring of God, we ought not to think that the divinity is like an image fashioned from gold, silver, or stone by human art and imagination.[x] 30 God has overlooked the times of ignorance, but now he demands that all people everywhere repent 31 because he has established a day on which he will 'judge the world with justice' through a man he has appointed, and he has provided confirmation for all by raising him from the dead."[y]

32 When they heard about resurrection of the dead, some began to scoff, but others said, "We should like to hear you on this some other time." 33 And so Paul left them. 34 But some did join him, and became believers. Among them were Dionysius, a member of the Court of the Areopagus, a woman named Damaris, and others with them.

## CHAPTER 18

See RG 344–48

***Paul in Corinth.*** 1 After this he left Athens and went to Corinth. 2 There he met a Jew named Aquila,[z] a native of Pontus, who had recently come from Italy with his wife Priscilla* because Claudius had ordered all the Jews to leave Rome. He went to visit them 3 and, because he practiced the same trade, stayed with them and worked, for they were tentmakers by trade. 4 Every sabbath, he

**17:19 To the Areopagus:** the "Areopagus" refers either to the Hill of Ares west of the Acropolis or to the Council of Athens, which at one time met on the hill but which at this time assembled in the Royal Colonnade (**Stoa Basileios**).

**17:22–31** In Paul's appearance at the Areopagus he preaches his climactic speech to Gentiles in the cultural center of the ancient world. The speech is more theological than christological. Paul's discourse appeals to the Greek world's belief in divinity as responsible for the origin and existence of the universe. It contests the common belief in a multiplicity of gods supposedly exerting their powers through their images. It acknowledges that the attempt to find God is a constant human endeavor. It declares, further, that God is the judge of the human race, that the time of the judgment has been determined, and that it will be executed through a man whom God raised from the dead. The speech reflects sympathy with pagan religiosity, handles the subject of idol worship gently, and appeals for a new examination of divinity, not from the standpoint of creation but from the standpoint of judgment.

**17:23 'To an Unknown God'**: ancient authors such as Pausanias, Philostratus, and Tertullian speak of Athenian altars with no specific dedication as altars of "unknown gods" or "nameless altars."

**17:26 From one**: many manuscripts read "from one blood." **Fixed . . . seasons**: or "fixed limits to the epochs."

**17:28 'In him we live and move and have our being'**: some scholars understand this saying to be based on an earlier saying of Epimenides of Knossos (6th century B.C.). **'For we too are his offspring'**: here Paul is quoting Aratus of Soli, a third-century B.C. poet from Cilicia.

**18:2 Aquila . . . Priscilla**: both may already have been Christians at the time of their arrival in Corinth (see Acts 18:26). According to 1 Cor 16:19, their home became a meeting place for Christians. **Claudius**: the Emperor Claudius expelled the Jews from Rome ca. A.D. 49. The Roman historian Suetonius gives as reason for the expulsion disturbances among the Jews "at the instigation of Chrestos," probably meaning disputes about the messiahship of Jesus.

*u:* 1 Cor 1:22. *v:* 7:48–50; Gn 1:1; 1 Kgs 8:27; Is 42:5. *w:* Jer 23:23; Wis 13:6; Rom 1:19. *x:* 19:26; Is 40:18–20; 44:10–17; Rom 1:22–23. *y:* 10:42. *z:* Rom 16:3.

entered into discussions in the synagogue, attempting to convince both Jews and Greeks.
5 When Silas and Timothy came down from
Macedonia, Paul began to occupy himself totally with preaching the word, testifying to
the Jews that the Messiah was Jesus. 6 When
they opposed him and reviled him, he shook
out his garments* and said to them, "Your
blood be on your heads! I am clear of responsibility. From now on I will go to the Gentiles."[a] 7 So he left there and went to a house
belonging to a man named Titus Justus, a
worshiper of God;* his house was next to a
synagogue.[b] 8 Crispus,* the synagogue official,[c] came to believe in the Lord along with
his entire household, and many of the Corinthians who heard believed and were baptized.
9[d] One night in a vision the Lord said to Paul,
"Do not be afraid. Go on speaking, and do not
be silent, 10 for I am with you. No one will attack and harm you, for I have many people in
this city." 11 He settled there for a year and a
half and taught the word of God among them.
*Accusations Before Gallio.* 12 But when
Gallio was proconsul of Achaia,* the Jews
rose up together against Paul and brought
him to the tribunal, 13 saying, "This man is
inducing people to worship God contrary to
the law."* 14 When Paul was about to reply,
Gallio spoke to the Jews, "If it were a matter
of some crime or malicious fraud, I should
with reason hear the complaint of you Jews;
15 but since it is a question of arguments over
doctrine and titles and your own law, see to
it yourselves. I do not wish to be a judge of
such matters." 16 And he drove them away
from the tribunal. 17 They all seized Sosthenes, the synagogue official, and beat him
in full view of the tribunal. But none of this
was of concern to Gallio.
*Return to Syrian Antioch.* 18 Paul remained
for quite some time, and after saying farewell
to the brothers he sailed for Syria, together
with Priscilla and Aquila. At Cenchreae he
had his hair cut[e] because he had taken a vow.*
19 When they reached Ephesus, he left them
there, while he entered the synagogue and
held discussions with the Jews. 20 Although
they asked him to stay for a longer time, he
did not consent, 21 but as he said farewell he
promised, "I shall come back to you again,
God willing." Then he set sail from Ephesus.
22 Upon landing at Caesarea, he went up and
greeted the church* and then went down to
Antioch. 23* After staying there some time,
he left and traveled in orderly sequence
through the Galatian country and Phrygia,
bringing strength to all the disciples.
*Apollos.* 24 A Jew named Apollos,[f] a native
of Alexandria, an eloquent speaker, arrived
in Ephesus. He was an authority on the scriptures.* 25 He had been instructed in the Way of
the Lord and, with ardent spirit, spoke and
taught accurately about Jesus, although he
knew only the baptism of John. 26 He began
to speak boldly in the synagogue; but when
Priscilla and Aquila heard him, they took him
aside and explained to him the Way [of God]*
more accurately. 27 And when he wanted to
cross to Achaia, the brothers encouraged him
and wrote to the disciples there to welcome
him. After his arrival he gave great assistance

**18:6 Shook out his garments**: a gesture indicating Paul's repudiation of his mission to the Jews there; cf. Acts 28:17–31.

**18:7 A worshiper of God**: see note on Acts 8:26–40.

**18:8 Crispus**: in 1 Cor 1:14 Paul mentions that Crispus was one of the few he himself baptized at Corinth.

**18:12 When Gallio was proconsul of Achaia**: Gallio's proconsulship in Achaia is dated to A.D. 51–52 from an inscription discovered at Delphi. This has become an important date in establishing a chronology of the life and missionary work of Paul.

**18:13 Contrary to the law**: Gallio (Acts 18:15) understands this to be a problem of Jewish, not Roman, law.

**18:18 He had his hair cut because he had taken a vow**: a reference to a Nazirite vow (see Nm 6:1–21, especially Nm 6:18) taken by Paul (see also Acts 21:23–27).

**18:22 He went up and greeted the church**: "going up" suggests a visit to the church in Jerusalem.

**18:23–21:16** Luke's account of Paul's third missionary journey devotes itself mainly to his work at Ephesus (Acts 19:1–20:1). There is a certain restiveness on Paul's part and a growing conviction that the Spirit bids him return to Jerusalem and prepare to go to Rome (Acts 19:21).

**18:24–25** Apollos appears as a preacher who knows the teaching of Jesus in the context of John's baptism of repentance. Aquila and Priscilla instruct him more fully. He is referred to in 1 Cor 1:12; 3:5–6, 22.

**18:26 The Way [of God]**: for the Way, see note on Acts 9:2. Other manuscripts here read "the Way of the Lord," "the word of the Lord," or simply "the Way."

---

*a:* 13:51; Mt 10:14; 27:24–25; Mk 6:11; Lk 9:5; 10:10–11. *b:* 13:46–47; 28:28. *c:* 1 Cor 1:14. *d:* Jer 1:8. *e:* 21:24; Nm 6:18. *f:* 1 Cor 1:12.

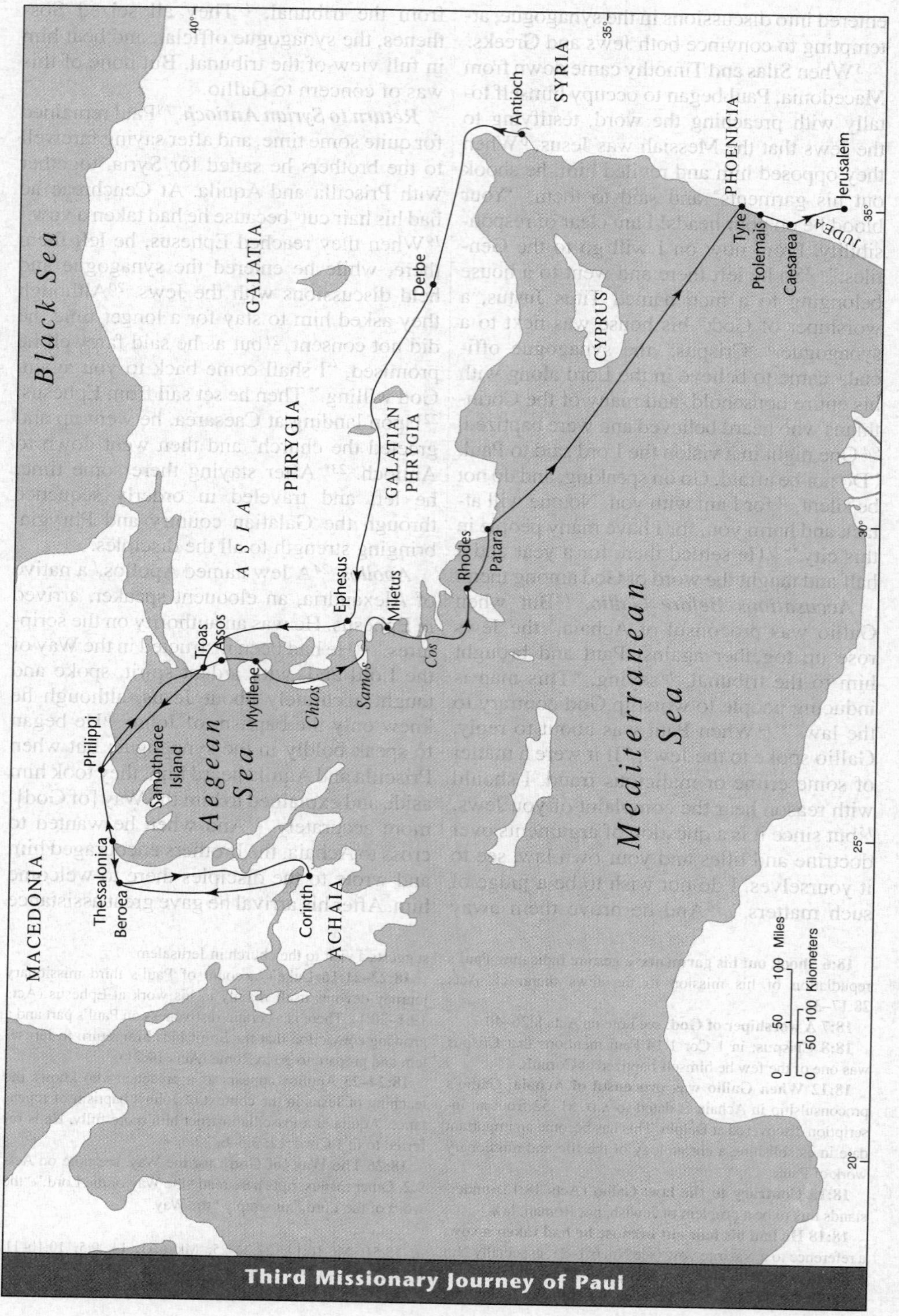


Third Missionary Journey of Paul

to those who had come to believe through grace. [28]He vigorously refuted the Jews in public, establishing from the scriptures that the Messiah is Jesus.

## CHAPTER 19

See RG 346–48

***Paul in Ephesus.*** [1]* While Apollos was in Corinth, Paul traveled through the interior of the country and came [down] to Ephesus where he found some disciples. [2]He said to them, "Did you receive the holy Spirit when you became believers?" They answered him, "We have never even heard that there is a holy Spirit." [3]He said, "How were you baptized?" They replied, "With the baptism of John." [4]Paul then said, "John baptized with a baptism of repentance, telling the people to believe in the one who was to come after him, that is, in Jesus."[g] [5]When they heard this, they were baptized in the name of the Lord Jesus. [6]And when Paul laid [his] hands on them, the holy Spirit came upon them, and they spoke in tongues and prophesied.[h] [7]Altogether there were about twelve men.

[8]He entered the synagogue, and for three months debated boldly with persuasive arguments about the kingdom of God. [9]But when some in their obstinacy and disbelief disparaged the Way before the assembly, he withdrew and took his disciples with him and began to hold daily discussions in the lecture hall of Tyrannus. [10]This continued for two years with the result that all the inhabitants of the province of Asia heard the word of the Lord, Jews and Greeks alike. [11]So extraordinary were the mighty deeds God accomplished at the hands of Paul [12]that when face cloths or aprons that touched his skin were applied to the sick, their diseases left them and the evil spirits came out of them.[i]

***The Jewish Exorcists.*** [13]Then some itinerant Jewish exorcists tried to invoke the name of the Lord Jesus over those with evil spirits, saying, "I adjure you by the Jesus whom Paul preaches." [14]When the seven sons of Sceva, a Jewish high priest, tried to do this, [15]the evil spirit said to them in reply, "Jesus I recognize, Paul I know, but who are you?" [16]The person with the evil spirit then sprang at them and subdued them all. He so overpowered them that they fled naked and wounded from that house. [17]When this became known to all the Jews and Greeks who lived in Ephesus, fear fell upon them all, and the name of the Lord Jesus was held in great esteem. [18]Many of those who had become believers came forward and openly acknowledged their former practices. [19]Moreover, a large number of those who had practiced magic collected their books and burned them in public. They calculated their value and found it to be fifty thousand silver pieces. [20]Thus did the word of the Lord continue to spread with influence and power.

***Paul's Plans.*** [21]When this was concluded, Paul made up his mind to travel through Macedonia and Achaia, and then to go on to Jerusalem, saying, "After I have been there, I must visit Rome also."[j] [22]Then he sent to Macedonia two of his assistants, Timothy and Erastus, while he himself stayed for a while in the province of Asia.

***The Riot of the Silversmiths.*** [23]About that time a serious disturbance broke out concerning the Way. [24]There was a silversmith named Demetrius who made miniature silver shrines of Artemis* and provided no little work for the craftsmen. [25]He called a meeting of these and other workers in related crafts and said, "Men, you know well that our prosperity derives from this work. [26]As you can now see and hear, not only in Ephesus but throughout most of the province of Asia this Paul has persuaded and misled a great number of people by saying that gods made by hands are not gods at all.[k] [27]The

**19:1–6** Upon his arrival in Ephesus, Paul discovers other people at the same religious stage as Apollos, though they seem to have considered themselves followers of Christ, not of the Baptist. On the relation between baptism and the reception of the Spirit, see note on Acts 8:16.

**19:24 Miniature silver shrines of Artemis**: the temple of Artemis at Ephesus was one of the seven wonders of the ancient world. Artemis, originally the Olympian virgin hunter, moon goddess, and goddess of wild nature, was worshiped at Ephesus as an Asian mother goddess and goddess of fertility. She was one of the most widely worshiped female deities in the Hellenistic world (see Acts 18:27).

*g*: 1:5; 11:16; 13:24–25; Mt 3:11; Mk 1:8; Lk 3:16. *h*: 8:15–17; 10:44, 46. *i*: 5:15–16; Lk 8:44–47. *j*: 23:11; Rom 1:13; 15:22–32. *k*: 17:29.

danger grows, not only that our business will be discredited, but also that the temple of the great goddess Artemis will be of no account, and that she whom the whole province of Asia and all the world worship will be stripped of her magnificence."

28When they heard this, they were filled with fury and began to shout, "Great is Artemis of the Ephesians!" 29The city was filled with confusion, and the people rushed with one accord into the theater, seizing Gaius and Aristarchus, the Macedonians, Paul's traveling companions.[l] 30Paul wanted to go before the crowd, but the disciples would not let him, 31and even some of the Asiarchs* who were friends of his sent word to him advising him not to venture into the theater. 32Meanwhile, some were shouting one thing, others something else; the assembly was in chaos, and most of the people had no idea why they had come together. 33Some of the crowd prompted Alexander, as the Jews pushed him forward, and Alexander signaled with his hand that he wished to explain something to the gathering. 34But when they recognized that he was a Jew, they all shouted in unison, for about two hours, "Great is Artemis of the Ephesians!" 35Finally the town clerk restrained the crowd and said, "You Ephesians, what person is there who does not know that the city of the Ephesians is the guardian of the temple* of the great Artemis and of her image that fell from the sky? 36Since these things are undeniable, you must calm yourselves and not do anything rash. 37The men you brought here are not temple robbers, nor have they insulted our goddess. 38If Demetrius and his fellow craftsmen have a complaint against anyone, courts are in session, and there are proconsuls. Let them bring charges against one another. 39If you have anything further to investigate, let the matter be settled in the lawful assembly, 40for, as it is, we are in danger of being charged with rioting because of today's conduct. There is no cause for it. We shall [not]* be able to give a reason for this demonstration." With these words he dismissed the assembly.

## CHAPTER 20

See RG 346–48

***Journey to Macedonia and Greece.*** 1When the disturbance was over, Paul had the disciples summoned and, after encouraging them, he bade them farewell and set out on his journey to Macedonia.[m] 2As he traveled throughout those regions, he provided many words of encouragement for them. Then he arrived in Greece, 3where he stayed for three months. But when a plot was made against him by the Jews as he was about to set sail for Syria, he decided to return by way of Macedonia.

***Return to Troas.*** 4[n] Sopater, the son of Pyrrhus, from Beroea, accompanied him, as did Aristarchus and Secundus from Thessalonica, Gaius from Derbe, Timothy, and Tychicus and Trophimus from Asia 5who went on ahead and waited for us* at Troas.[o] 6We sailed from Philippi after the feast of Unleavened Bread,* and rejoined them five days later in Troas, where we spent a week.

***Eutychus Restored to Life.*** 7On the first day of the week* when we gathered to break bread, Paul spoke to them because he was going to leave on the next day, and he kept on speaking until midnight. 8There were many lamps in the upstairs room where we

**19:31 Asiarchs**: the precise status and role of the Asiarchs is disputed. They appear to have been people of wealth and influence who promoted the Roman imperial cult and who may also have been political representatives in a league of cities in the Roman province of Asia.

**19:35 Guardian of the temple**: this title was accorded by Rome to cities that provided a temple for the imperial cult. Inscriptional evidence indicates that Ephesus was acknowledged as the temple keeper of Artemis and of the imperial cult. **That fell from the sky**: many scholars think that this refers to a meteorite that was worshiped as an image of the goddess.

**19:40** Some manuscripts omit the negative in **[not] be able**, making the meaning, "There is no cause for which we shall be able to give a reason for this demonstration."

**20:5** The second "we-section" of Acts begins here. See note on Acts 16:10–17.

**20:6 Feast of Unleavened Bread**: see note on Lk 22:1.

**20:7 The first day of the week**: the day after the sabbath and the first day of the Jewish week, apparently chosen originally by the Jerusalem community for the celebration of the liturgy of the Eucharist in order to relate it to the resurrection of Christ.

*l:* Col 4:10. *m:* 1 Cor 16:1. *n:* Rom 16:21. *o:* 21:29; 2 Tm 4:20.

were gathered, [9]and a young man named Eutychus who was sitting on the window sill was sinking into a deep sleep as Paul talked on and on. Once overcome by sleep, he fell down from the third story and when he was picked up, he was dead. [10][p] Paul went down,* threw himself upon him, and said as he embraced him, "Don't be alarmed; there is life in him." [11]Then he returned upstairs, broke the bread, and ate; after a long conversation that lasted until daybreak, he departed. [12]And they took the boy away alive and were immeasurably comforted.

***Journey to Miletus.*** [13]We went ahead to the ship and set sail for Assos where we were to take Paul on board, as he had arranged, since he was going overland. [14]When he met us in Assos, we took him aboard and went on to Mitylene. [15]We sailed away from there on the next day and reached a point off Chios, and a day later we reached Samos, and on the following day we arrived at Miletus. [16]* Paul had decided to sail past Ephesus in order not to lose time in the province of Asia, for he was hurrying to be in Jerusalem, if at all possible, for the day of Pentecost.

***Paul's Farewell Speech at Miletus.*** [17]From Miletus he had the presbyters of the church at Ephesus summoned. [18]When they came to him, he addressed them, "You know how I lived among you the whole time from the day I first came to the province of Asia. [19]I served the Lord with all humility and with the tears and trials that came to me because of the plots of the Jews, [20]and I did not at all shrink from telling you what was for your benefit, or from teaching you in public or in your homes. [21]I earnestly bore witness for both Jews and Greeks to repentance before God and to faith in our Lord Jesus. [22]But now, compelled by the Spirit, I am going to Jerusalem. What will happen to me there I do not know, [23]except that in one city after another the holy Spirit has been warning me that imprisonment and hardships await me.[q] [24]Yet I consider life of no importance to me, if only I may finish my course and the ministry that I received from the Lord Jesus, to bear witness to the gospel of God's grace.[r]

[25]"But now I know that none of you to whom I preached the kingdom during my travels will ever see my face again. [26]And so I solemnly declare to you this day that I am not responsible for the blood of any of you, [27]for I did not shrink from proclaiming to you the entire plan of God. [28][s] Keep watch over yourselves and over the whole flock of which the holy Spirit has appointed you overseers,* in which you tend the church of God that he acquired with his own blood. [29]I know that after my departure savage wolves will come among you, and they will not spare the flock.[t] [30]And from your own group, men will come forward perverting the truth to draw the disciples away after them.[u] [31]So be vigilant and remember that for three years, night and day, I unceasingly admonished each of you with tears.[v] [32]And now I commend you to God and to that gracious word of his that can build you up and give you the inheritance among all who are consecrated. [33]I have never wanted anyone's silver or gold or clothing. [34]You know well that these very hands have served my needs and my companions.[w] [35]In every way I have shown you that by hard work of that sort we must help the weak, and keep in mind the words of the Lord Jesus who himself said, 'It is more blessed to give than to receive.' "[x]

**20:10** The action of Paul in throwing himself upon the dead boy recalls that of Elijah in 1 Kgs 17:21 where the son of the widow of Zarephath is revived and that of Elisha in 2 Kgs 4:34 where the Shunamite woman's son is restored to life.

**20:16–35** Apparently aware of difficulties at Ephesus and neighboring areas, Paul calls the presbyters together at Miletus, about thirty miles from Ephesus. He reminds them of his dedication to the gospel (Acts 20:18–21), speaks of what he is about to suffer for the gospel (Acts 20:22–27), and admonishes them to guard the community against false prophets, sure to arise upon his departure (Acts 20:28–31). He concludes by citing a saying of Jesus (Acts 20:35) not recorded in the gospel tradition. Luke presents this farewell to the Ephesian presbyters as Paul's last will and testament.

**20:28 Overseers**: see note on Phil 1:1. **The church of God**: because the clause "that he acquired with his own blood" following "the church of God" suggests that "his own blood" refers to God's blood, some early copyists changed "the church of God" to "the church of the Lord." Some prefer the translation "acquired with the blood of his own," i.e., Christ.

*p:* 1 Kgs 17:17–24; 2 Kgs 4:30–37; Mt 9:24; Mk 5:39; Lk 8:52. *q:* 9:16. *r:* 2 Tm 4:7. *s:* Jn 21:15–17; 1 Pt 5:2. *t:* Jn 10:12. *u:* Mt 7:15; 2 Pt 2:1–3; 1 Jn 2:18–19. *v:* 1 Thes 2:11. *w:* 1 Cor 4:12; 1 Thes 2:9; 2 Thes 3:8. *x:* Sir 4:31.

36 When he had finished speaking he knelt down and prayed with them all. 37 They were all weeping loudly as they threw their arms around Paul and kissed him, 38 for they were deeply distressed that he had said that they would never see his face again. Then they escorted him to the ship.

## CHAPTER 21

See RG 346–48

*Arrival at Tyre.* 1* When we had taken leave of them we set sail, made a straight run for Cos, and on the next day for Rhodes, and from there to Patara. 2 Finding a ship crossing to Phoenicia, we went on board and put out to sea. 3 We caught sight of Cyprus but passed by it on our left and sailed on toward Syria and put in at Tyre where the ship was to unload cargo. 4 There we sought out the disciples and stayed for a week. They kept telling Paul through the Spirit not to embark for Jerusalem. 5 At the end of our stay we left and resumed our journey. All of them, women and children included, escorted us out of the city, and after kneeling on the beach to pray, 6 we bade farewell to one another. Then we boarded the ship, and they returned home.

*Arrival at Ptolemais and Caesarea.* 7 We continued the voyage and came from Tyre to Ptolemais, where we greeted the brothers and stayed a day with them. 8 On the next day we resumed the trip and came to Caesarea, where we went to the house of Philip the evangelist, who was one of the Seven,* and stayed with him.[y] 9 He had four virgin daughters gifted with prophecy. 10 We had been there several days when a prophet named Agabus* came down from Judea. 11[z] He came up to us, took Paul's belt, bound his own feet and hands with it, and said, "Thus says the holy Spirit: This is the way the Jews will bind the owner of this belt in Jerusalem, and they will hand him over to the Gentiles."* 12 When we heard this, we and the local residents begged him not to go up to Jerusalem. 13 Then Paul replied, "What are you doing, weeping and breaking my heart? I am prepared not only to be bound but even to die in Jerusalem for the name of the Lord Jesus." 14[a] Since he would not be dissuaded we let the matter rest, saying,[b] "The Lord's will be done."*

*Paul and James in Jerusalem.* 15 After these days we made preparations for our journey, then went up to Jerusalem. 16 Some of the disciples from Caesarea came along to lead us to the house of Mnason, a Cypriot, a disciple of long standing, with whom we were to stay. 17* When we reached Jerusalem the brothers welcomed us warmly. 18 The next day, Paul accompanied us on a visit to James, and all the presbyters were present. 19 He greeted them, then proceeded to tell them in detail what God had accomplished among the Gentiles through his ministry. 20 They praised God when they heard it but said to him, "Brother, you see how many thousands of believers there are from among the Jews, and they are all zealous observers of the law. 21 They have been informed that you are teaching all the Jews who live among the Gentiles to abandon Moses and that you are telling them not to circumcise their children or to observe their customary practices. 22 What is to be done? They will surely hear that you have arrived. 23* So do what we tell you. We have four men who have taken a vow.[c] 24 Take these men and purify yourself

**21:1–18** The third "we-section" of Acts (see note on Acts 16:10–17).

**21:8 One of the Seven**: see note on Acts 6:2–4.

**21:10 Agabus**: mentioned in Acts 11:28 as the prophet who predicted the famine that occurred when Claudius was emperor.

**21:11** The symbolic act of Agabus recalls those of Old Testament prophets. Compare Is 20:2; Ez 4:1; Jer 13:1.

**21:14** The Christian disciples' attitude reflects that of Jesus (see Lk 22:42).

**21:17–26** The leaders of the Jewish Christians of Jerusalem inform Paul that the Jews there believe he has encouraged the Jews of the diaspora to abandon the Mosaic law. According to Acts, Paul had no objection to the retention of the law by the Jewish Christians of Jerusalem and left the Jews of the diaspora who accepted Christianity free to follow the same practice.

**21:23–26** The leaders of the community suggest that Paul, on behalf of four members of the Jerusalem community, make the customary payment for the sacrifices offered at the termination of the Nazirite vow (see Nm 6:1–24) in order to impress favorably the Jewish Christians in Jerusalem with his high regard for the Mosaic law. Since Paul himself had once made this vow (Acts 18:18), his respect for the law would be on public record.

**21:24 Pay their expenses**: according to Nm 6:14–15 the Nazirite had to present a yearling lamb for a holocaust, a yearling ewe lamb for a sin offering, and a ram for a peace offering, along with food and drink offerings, upon completion of the period of the vow.

*y:* 6:5; 8:5–6. *z:* 11:28; 20:23. *a:* 19:15–16. *b:* Mt 6:10; 26:39; Mk 14:36; Lk 22:42. *c:* 18:18; Nm 6:1–21.

with them, and pay their expenses* that they may have their heads shaved. In this way everyone will know that there is nothing to the reports they have been given about you but that you yourself live in observance of the law. [25][d] As for the Gentiles who have come to believe, we sent them our decision that they abstain from meat sacrificed to idols, from blood, from the meat of strangled animals, and from unlawful marriage."* [26]So Paul took the men, and on the next day after purifying himself together with them entered the temple to give notice of the day when the purification would be completed and the offering made for each of them.[e]

***Paul's Arrest.*** [27]When the seven days were nearly completed, the Jews from the province of Asia noticed him in the temple, stirred up the whole crowd, and laid hands on him, [28][f] shouting, "Fellow Israelites, help us. This is the man who is teaching everyone everywhere against the people and the law and this place, and what is more, he has even brought Greeks into the temple and defiled this sacred place."* [29]For they had previously seen Trophimus the Ephesian in the city with him and supposed that Paul had brought him into the temple. [30]The whole city was in turmoil with people rushing together. They seized Paul and dragged him out of the temple, and immediately the gates were closed. [31]While they were trying to kill him, a report reached the cohort commander* that all Jerusalem was rioting. [32]He immediately took soldiers and centurions and charged down on them. When they saw the commander and the soldiers they stopped beating Paul. [33]The cohort commander came forward, arrested him, and ordered him to be secured with two chains; he tried to find out who he might be and what he had done. [34]Some in the mob shouted one thing, others something else; so, since he was unable to ascertain the truth because of the uproar, he ordered Paul to be brought into the compound. [35]When he reached the steps, he was carried by the soldiers because of the violence of the mob, [36]* [g] for a crowd of people followed and shouted, "Away with him!"

[37]Just as Paul was about to be taken into the compound, he said to the cohort commander, "May I say something to you?" He replied, "Do you speak Greek? [38]So then you are not the Egyptian* who started a revolt some time ago and led the four thousand assassins into the desert?"[h] [39]Paul answered, "I am a Jew, of Tarsus in Cilicia, a citizen of no mean city; I request you to permit me to speak to the people." [40]When he had given his permission, Paul stood on the steps and motioned with his hand to the people; and when all was quiet he addressed them in Hebrew.*

## CHAPTER 22

See RG 348

***Paul's Defense Before the Jerusalem Jews.**** [1]"My brothers and fathers, listen to what I am about to say to you in my defense." [2]When they heard him addressing them in Hebrew they became all the more quiet. And he continued, [3]"I am a Jew, born in Tarsus in Cilicia, but brought up in this

**21:25** Paul is informed about the apostolic decree, seemingly for the first time (see note on Acts 15:13–35). The allusion to the decree was probably introduced here by Luke to remind his readers that the Gentile Christians themselves were asked to respect certain Jewish practices deriving from the law.

**21:28** The charges against Paul by the diaspora Jews are identical to the charges brought against Stephen by diaspora Jews in Acts 6:13. **Brought Greeks into the temple**: non-Jews were forbidden, under penalty of death, to go beyond the Court of the Gentiles. Inscriptions in Greek and Latin on a stone balustrade marked off the prohibited area.

**21:31 Cohort commander**: literally, "the leader of a thousand in a cohort." At this period the Roman cohort commander usually led six hundred soldiers, a tenth of a legion; but the number in a cohort varied.

**21:36 "Away with him!"**: at the trial of Jesus before Pilate in Lk 23:18, the people similarly shout, "Away with this man."

**21:38 The Egyptian**: according to the Jewish historian Josephus, an Egyptian gathered a large crowd on the Mount of Olives to witness the destruction of the walls of Jerusalem that would fall at the Egyptian "prophet's" word. The commotion was put down by the Roman authorities and the Egyptian escaped, but only after thousands had been killed. **Four thousand assassins**: literally, *sicarii*. According to Josephus, these were political nationalists who removed their opponents by assassination with a short dagger, called in Latin a *sica*.

**21:40 In Hebrew**: meaning, perhaps, in Aramaic, which at this time was the Semitic tongue in common use.

**22:1–21** Paul's first defense speech is presented to the Jerusalem crowds. Luke here presents Paul as a devout Jew (Acts 22:3) and zealous persecutor of the Christian community (Acts 22:4–5), and then recounts the conversion of Paul for the second time in Acts (see note on Acts 9:1–19).

---

*d:* 15:19–20, 28–29. *e:* 1 Cor 9:20. *f:* Rom 15:31. *g:* 22:22; Lk 23:18; Jn 19:15. *h:* 5:36–37.

city. At the feet of Gamaliel I was educated strictly in our ancestral law and was zealous for God, just as all of you are today.[i] 4 I persecuted this Way to death, binding both men and women and delivering them to prison.[j] 5 Even the high priest and the whole council of elders can testify on my behalf. For from them I even received letters to the brothers and set out for Damascus to bring back to Jerusalem in chains for punishment those there as well.

6 "On that journey as I drew near to Damascus, about noon a great light from the sky suddenly shone around me.[k] 7 I fell to the ground and heard a voice saying to me, 'Saul, Saul, why are you persecuting me?'[l] 8 I replied, 'Who are you, sir?' And he said to me, 'I am Jesus the Nazorean whom you are persecuting.'[m] 9 My companions saw the light but did not hear the voice of the one who spoke to me.[n] 10 I asked, 'What shall I do, sir?' The Lord answered me, 'Get up and go into Damascus, and there you will be told about everything appointed for you to do.'[o] 11 Since I could see nothing because of the brightness of that light, I was led by hand by my companions and entered Damascus.[p]

12 [q] "A certain Ananias, a devout observer of the law, and highly spoken of by all the Jews who lived there, 13 came to me and stood there and said, 'Saul, my brother, regain your sight.' And at that very moment I regained my sight and saw him. 14 Then he said, 'The God of our ancestors designated you to know his will, to see the Righteous One, and to hear the sound of his voice; 15 for you will be his witness* before all to what you have seen and heard. 16 Now, why delay? Get up and have yourself baptized and your sins washed away, calling upon his name.'

17 "After I had returned to Jerusalem and while I was praying in the temple, I fell into a trance 18 and saw the Lord saying to me, 'Hurry, leave Jerusalem at once, because they will not accept your testimony about me.' 19 But I replied, 'Lord, they themselves know that from synagogue to synagogue I used to imprison and beat those who believed in you.[r] 20 And when the blood of your witness Stephen was being shed, I myself stood by giving my approval and keeping guard over the cloaks of his murderers.'[s] 21 Then he said to me,[t] 'Go, I shall send you far away to the Gentiles.' "*

***Paul Imprisoned.*** 22 [u] They listened to him until he said this, but then they raised their voices and shouted, "Take such a one as this away from the earth. It is not right that he should live."* 23 And as they were yelling and throwing off their cloaks and flinging dust into the air, 24 the cohort commander ordered him to be brought into the compound and gave instruction that he be interrogated under the lash to determine the reason why they were making such an outcry against him. 25 [v] But when they had stretched him out for the whips, Paul said to the centurion on duty, "Is it lawful for you to scourge a man who is a Roman citizen and has not been tried?"* 26 When the centurion heard this, he went to the cohort commander and reported it, saying, "What are you going to do? This man is a Roman citizen." 27 Then the commander came and said to him, "Tell me, are you a Roman citizen?" "Yes," he answered. 28 The commander replied, "I acquired this citizenship for a large sum of money." Paul said, "But I was born one." 29 At once those who were going to interrogate him backed away from him, and the commander became alarmed when he realized that he was a Roman citizen and that he had had him bound.

**22:15 His witness**: like the Galilean followers during the historical ministry of Jesus, Paul too, through his experience of the risen Christ, is to be a witness to the resurrection (compare Acts 1:8; 10:39–41; Lk 24:48).

**22:21** Paul endeavors to explain that his position on the law has not been identical with that of his audience because it has been his prophetic mission to preach to the Gentiles to whom the law was not addressed and who had no faith in it as a way of salvation.

**22:22** Paul's suggestion that his prophetic mission to the Gentiles did not involve his imposing the law on them provokes the same opposition as occurred in Pisidian Antioch (Acts 13:45).

**22:25 Is it lawful for you to scourge a man who is a Roman citizen and has not been tried?**: see note on Acts 16:37.

*i:* 5:34; 26:4–5; 2 Cor 11:22; Gal 1:13–14; Phil 3:5–6. *j:* 8:3; 9:1–2; 22:19; 26:9–11; Phil 3:6. *k:* 9:3; 26:13; 1 Cor 15:8. *l:* 9:4; 26:14. *m:* 9:5; 26:15; Mt 25:40. *n:* 9:7; 26:13–14. *o:* 9:6; 26:16. *p:* 9:8. *q:* 9:10–19. *r:* 8:3; 9:1–2; 22:4–5; 26:9–11. *s:* 7:58; 8:1. *t:* 9:15; Gal 2:7–9. *u:* 21:36; Lk 23:18; Jn 19:15. *v:* 16:37.

*Paul Before the Sanhedrin.* 30 The next day, wishing to determine the truth about why he was being accused by the Jews, he freed him and ordered the chief priests and the whole Sanhedrin to convene. Then he brought Paul down and made him stand before them.

## CHAPTER 23

See RG 348

1 Paul looked intently at the Sanhedrin and said, "My brothers, I have conducted myself with a perfectly clear conscience before God to this day."[w] 2 The high priest Ananias* ordered his attendants to strike his mouth. 3 Then Paul said to him, "God will strike you,* you whitewashed wall. Do you indeed sit in judgment upon me according to the law and yet in violation of the law order me to be struck?"[x] 4 The attendants said, "Would you revile God's high priest?" 5 Paul answered, "Brothers, I did not realize he was the high priest. For it is written,[y] 'You shall not curse a ruler of your people.' "*

6 Paul was aware that some were Sadducees and some Pharisees, so he called out before the Sanhedrin, "My brothers, I am a Pharisee, the son of Pharisees; [I] am on trial for hope in the resurrection of the dead."[z] 7 When he said this, a dispute broke out between the Pharisees and Sadducees, and the group became divided. 8 For the Sadducees say that there is no resurrection or angels or spirits, while the Pharisees acknowledge all three.[a] 9 A great uproar occurred, and some scribes belonging to the Pharisee party stood up and sharply argued, "We find nothing wrong with this man. Suppose a spirit or an angel has spoken to him?" 10 The dispute was so serious that the commander, afraid that Paul would be torn to pieces by them, ordered his troops to go down and rescue him from their midst and take him into the compound. 11* [b] The following night the Lord stood by him and said, "Take courage. For just as you have borne witness to my cause in Jerusalem, so you must also bear witness in Rome."

*Transfer to Caesarea.* 12 When day came, the Jews made a plot and bound themselves by oath not to eat or drink until they had killed Paul. 13 There were more than forty who formed this conspiracy. 14 They went to the chief priests and elders and said, "We have bound ourselves by a solemn oath to taste nothing until we have killed Paul. 15 You, together with the Sanhedrin, must now make an official request to the commander to have him bring him down to you, as though you meant to investigate his case more thoroughly. We on our part are prepared to kill him before he arrives." 16 The son of Paul's sister, however, heard about the ambush; so he went and entered the compound and reported it to Paul. 17 Paul then called one of the centurions* and requested, "Take this young man to the commander; he has something to report to him." 18 So he took him and brought him to the commander and explained, "The prisoner Paul called me and asked that I bring this young man to you; he has something to say to you." 19 The commander took him by the hand, drew him aside, and asked him privately, "What is it you have to report to me?" 20 He replied, "The Jews have conspired to ask you to bring Paul down to the Sanhedrin tomorrow, as though they meant to inquire about him more thoroughly, 21 but do not believe them. More than forty of them are lying in wait for him; they have bound themselves by oath not to eat or drink until they have killed him. They are now ready and only wait for your consent." 22 As the commander dismissed the young man he directed him, "Tell no one that you gave me this information."

**23:2 The high priest Ananias**: Ananias, son of Nedebaeus, was high priest from A.D. 47 to 59.

**23:3 God will strike you**: Josephus reports that Ananias was later assassinated in A.D. 66 at the beginning of the First Revolt.

**23:5** Luke portrays Paul as a model of one who is obedient to the Mosaic law. Paul, because of his reverence for the law (Ex 22:27), withdraws his accusation of hypocrisy, "whitewashed wall" (cf. Mt 23:27), when he is told Ananias is the high priest.

**23:11** The occurrence of the vision of Christ consoling Paul and assuring him that he will be his witness in Rome prepares the reader for the final section of Acts: the journey of Paul and the word he preaches to Rome under the protection of the Romans.

**23:17 Centurions**: a centurion was a military officer in charge of one hundred soldiers.

*w:* 24:16. *x:* Ez 13:10–15; Mt 23:27. *y:* Ex 22:27. *z:* 24:15, 21; 26:5; Phil 3:5. *a:* Mt 22:23; Lk 20:27. *b:* 19:21.

[23]Then he summoned two of the centurions and said, “Get two hundred soldiers ready to go to Caesarea by nine o’clock tonight,* along with seventy horsemen and two hundred auxiliaries. [24]Provide mounts for Paul to ride and give him safe conduct to Felix the governor.” [25]Then he wrote a letter with this content: [26]* “Claudius Lysias to his excellency the governor Felix, greetings.* [27]This man, seized by the Jews and about to be murdered by them, I rescued after intervening with my troops when I learned that he was a Roman citizen.[c] [28]I wanted to learn the reason for their accusations against him so I brought him down to their Sanhedrin. [29]I discovered that he was accused in matters of controversial questions of their law and not of any charge deserving death or imprisonment.[d] [30]Since it was brought to my attention that there will be a plot against the man, I am sending him to you at once, and have also notified his accusers to state [their case] against him before you.”

[31]So the soldiers, according to their orders, took Paul and escorted him by night to Antipatris. [32]The next day they re turned to the compound, leaving the horsemen to complete the journey with him. [33]When they arrived in Caesarea they delivered the letter to the governor and presented Paul to him. [34]When he had read it and asked to what province he belonged, and learned that he was from Cilicia, [35]he said, “I shall hear your case when your accusers arrive.” Then he ordered that he be held in custody in Herod’s praetorium.

See RG 348

## CHAPTER 24

***Trial Before Felix.*** [1]Five days later the high priest Ananias came down with some elders and an advocate, a certain Tertullus, and they presented formal charges against Paul to the governor. [2]When he was called, Tertullus began to accuse him, saying, “Since we have attained much peace through you, and reforms have been accomplished in this nation through your provident care, [3]we acknowledge this in every way and everywhere, most excellent Felix, with all gratitude. [4]But in order not to detain you further, I ask you to give us a brief hearing with your customary graciousness. [5][e] We found this man to be a pest; he creates dissension among Jews all over the world and is a ringleader of the sect of the Nazoreans.* [6]He even tried to desecrate our temple, but we arrested him.[f] [7]* [8]If you examine him you will be able to learn from him for yourself about everything of which we are accusing him.” [9]The Jews also joined in the attack and asserted that these things were so.

[10]* Then the governor motioned to him to speak and Paul replied, “I know that you have been a judge over this nation for many years and so I am pleased to make my defense before you. [11]As you can verify, not more than twelve days have passed since I went up to Jerusalem to worship. [12]Neither in the temple, nor in the synagogues, nor anywhere in the city did they find me arguing with anyone or instigating a riot among the people. [13]Nor can they prove to you the accusations they are now making against me. [14]But this I do admit to you, that according to the Way, which they call a sect, I worship the God of our ancestors and I believe everything that is in accordance with the law and written in the prophets.[g] [15]I have

**23:23 By nine o’clock tonight**: literally, “by the third hour of the night.” The night hours began at 6 p.m. **Two hundred auxiliaries**: the meaning of the Greek is not certain. It seems to refer to spearmen from the local police force and not from the cohort of soldiers, which would have numbered only 500–1000 men.

**23:26–30** The letter emphasizes the fact that Paul is a Roman citizen and asserts the lack of evidence that he is guilty of a crime against the empire. The tone of the letter implies that the commander became initially involved in Paul’s case because of his Roman citizenship, but this is not an exact description of what really happened (see Acts 21:31–33; 22:25–29).

**23:26** M. Antonius Felix was procurator of Judea from A.D. 52 to 60. His procuratorship was marked by cruelty toward and oppression of his Jewish subjects.

**24:5 Nazoreans**: that is, followers of Jesus of Nazareth.

**24:7** The Western text has added here a verse (really Acts 24:6b–8a) that is not found in the best Greek manuscripts. It reads, “and would have judged him according to our own law, but the cohort commander Lysias came and violently took him out of our hands and ordered his accusers to come before you.”

**24:10–21** Whereas the advocate Tertullus referred to Paul’s activities on his missionary journeys, the apostle narrowed the charges down to the riot connected with the incident in the temple (see Acts 21:27–30; 24:17–20). In his defense, Paul stresses the continuity between Christianity and Judaism.

*c:* 21:30–34; 22:27. *d:* 18:14–15; 25:18–19. *e:* 24:14; Lk 23:2. *f:* 21:28. *g:* 24:5.

the same hope in God as they themselves have that there will be a resurrection of the righteous and the unrighteous.[h] 16Because of this, I always strive to keep my conscience clear before God and man.[i] 17After many years, I came to bring alms for my nation and offerings,[j] 18While I was so engaged, they found me, after my purification, in the temple without a crowd or disturbance.[k] 19But some Jews from the province of Asia, who should be here before you to make whatever accusation they might have against me— 20or let these men themselves state what crime they discovered when I stood before the Sanhedrin, 21unless it was my one outcry as I stood among them, that 'I am on trial before you today for the resurrection of the dead.' "[l]

22Then Felix, who was accurately informed about the Way, postponed the trial, saying, "When Lysias the commander comes down, I shall decide your case." 23He gave orders to the centurion that he should be kept in custody but have some liberty, and that he should not prevent any of his friends from caring for his needs.

***Captivity in Caesarea.*** 24* Several days later Felix came with his wife Drusilla, who was Jewish. He had Paul summoned and listened to him speak about faith in Christ Jesus. 25But as he spoke about righteousness and self-restraint and the coming judgment, Felix became frightened and said, "You may go for now; when I find an opportunity I shall summon you again." 26At the same time he hoped that a bribe would be offered him by Paul, and so he sent for him very often and conversed with him.

27Two years passed and Felix was succeeded by Porcius Festus. Wishing to ingratiate himself with the Jews, Felix left Paul in prison.*

## CHAPTER 25

See RG 348

***Appeal to Caesar.*** 1Three days after his arrival in the province, Festus went up from Caesarea to Jerusalem 2where the chief priests and Jewish leaders presented him their formal charges against Paul.* They asked him 3as a favor to have him sent to Jerusalem, for they were plotting to kill him along the way. 4Festus replied that Paul was being held in custody in Caesarea and that he himself would be returning there shortly. 5He said, "Let your authorities come down with me, and if this man has done something improper, let them accuse him."

6After spending no more than eight or ten days with them, he went down to Caesarea, and on the following day took his seat on the tribunal and ordered that Paul be brought in. 7When he appeared, the Jews who had come down from Jerusalem surrounded him and brought many serious charges against him, which they were unable to prove. 8In defending himself Paul said, "I have committed no crime either against the Jewish law or against the temple or against Caesar." 9* Then Festus, wishing to ingratiate himself with the Jews, said to Paul in reply, "Are you willing to go up to Jerusalem and there stand trial before me on these charges?" 10Paul answered, "I am standing before the tribunal of Caesar; this is where I should be tried. I have committed no crime against the Jews, as you very well know. 11If I have committed a crime or done anything deserving death, I do not seek to escape the death penalty; but if there is no substance to the charges they are bringing against me, then no one has the right to hand me over to them. I appeal to Caesar." 12Then Festus, after conferring with his council, replied, "You have appealed to Caesar. To Caesar you will go."

**24:24–25** The way of Christian discipleship greatly disquiets Felix, who has entered into an adulterous marriage with Drusilla, daughter of Herod Agrippa I. This marriage provides the background for the topics Paul speaks about and about which Felix does not want to hear.

**24:27** Very little is known of Porcius Festus who was a procurator of Judea from A.D. 60 to 62.

**25:2** Even after two years the animosity toward Paul in Jerusalem had not subsided (see Acts 24:27).

**25:9–12** Paul refuses to acknowledge that the Sanhedrin in Jerusalem has any jurisdiction over him now (Acts 25:11). Paul uses his right as a Roman citizen to appeal his case to the jurisdiction of the Emperor (Nero, ca. A.D. 60) (Acts 25:12). This move broke the deadlock between Roman protective custody of Paul and the plan of his enemies to kill him (25:3).

*h:* Dn 12:2; Jn 5:28–29. *i:* 23:1. *j:* Rom 15:25–26; Gal 2:10. *k:* 21:26–30. *l:* 23:6; 24:15.

***Paul Before King Agrippa.*** [13]When a few days had passed, King Agrippa and Bernice* arrived in Caesarea on a visit to Festus. [14]Since they spent several days there, Festus referred Paul's case to the king, saying, "There is a man here left in custody by Felix.[m] [15]When I was in Jerusalem the chief priests and the elders of the Jews brought charges against him and demanded his condemnation. [16]I answered them that it was not Roman practice to hand over an accused person before he has faced his accusers and had the opportunity to defend himself against their charge. [17]So when [they] came together here, I made no delay; the next day I took my seat on the tribunal and ordered the man to be brought in. [18n] His accusers stood around him, but did not charge him with any of the crimes I suspected. [19]Instead they had some issues with him about their own religion and about a certain Jesus who had died but who Paul claimed was alive. [20]Since I was at a loss how to investigate this controversy, I asked if he were willing to go to Jerusalem and there stand trial on these charges. [21] And when Paul appealed that he be held in custody for the Emperor's decision, I ordered him held until I could send him to Caesar." [22]Agrippa said to Festus, "I too should like to hear this man." He replied, "Tomorrow you will hear him."

[23]The next day Agrippa and Bernice came with great ceremony and entered the audience hall in the company of cohort commanders and the prominent men of the city and, by command of Festus, Paul was brought in. [24]And Festus said, "King Agrippa and all you here present with us, look at this man about whom the whole Jewish populace petitioned me here and in Jerusalem, clamoring that he should live no longer. [25]I found, however, that he had done nothing deserving death, and so when he appealed to the Emperor, I decided to send him. [26]But I have nothing definite to write about him to our sovereign; therefore I have brought him before all of you, and particularly before you, King Agrippa, so that I may have something to write as a result of this investigation. [27]For it seems senseless to me to send up a prisoner without indicating the charges against him."

## CHAPTER 26

See RG 348

***King Agrippa Hears Paul.*** [1]Then Agrippa said to Paul, "You may now speak on your own behalf." So Paul stretched out his hand and began his defense. [2*] "I count myself fortunate, King Agrippa, that I am to defend myself before you today against all the charges made against me by the Jews, [3]especially since you are an expert in all the Jewish customs and controversies. And therefore I beg you to listen patiently. [4]My manner of living from my youth, a life spent from the beginning among my people* and in Jerusalem, all [the] Jews know. [5o] They have known about me from the start, if they are willing to testify, that I have lived my life as a Pharisee, the strictest party of our religion. [6p] But now I am standing trial because of my hope in the promise made by God to our ancestors. [7]Our twelve tribes hope to attain to that promise as they fervently worship God day and night; and on account of this hope I am accused by Jews, O king. [8]Why is it thought unbelievable among you that God raises the dead? [9q] I myself once thought that I had to do many things against the name of Jesus the Nazorean, [10]and I did so in Jerusalem. I imprisoned many of the holy ones with the authorization I received from the chief priests, and when they were to be put to death I cast my vote against them.[r] [11]Many times, in synagogue after synagogue, I punished them in an attempt to force them to blaspheme; I was so enraged against them that I pursued them even to foreign cities.

[12]"On one such occasion I was traveling to Damascus with the authorization and com-

**25:13 King Agrippa and Bernice**: brother and sister, children of Herod Agrippa I whose activities against the Jerusalem community are mentioned in Acts 12:1–19. Agrippa II was a petty ruler over small areas in northern Palestine and some villages in Perea. His influence on the Jewish population of Palestine was insignificant.

**26:2–23** Paul's final defense speech in Acts is now made before a king (see Acts 9:15). In the speech Paul presents himself as a zealous Pharisee and Christianity as the logical development of Pharisaic Judaism. The story of his conversion is recounted for the third time in Acts in this speech (see note on Acts 9:1–19).

**26:4 Among my people**: that is, among the Jews.

*m:* 24:27. *n:* 18:14–15; 23:29. *o:* Phil 3:5–6; Gal 1:13–14; 2 Cor 11:22. *p:* 23:6; 24:15, 21; 28:20. *q:* 8:3; 9:1–2; 22:19; Phil 3:6. *r:* 9:14.

mission of the chief priests. 13[s] At midday, along the way, O king, I saw a light from the sky, brighter than the sun, shining around me and my traveling companions.[t] 14 We all fell to the ground and I heard a voice saying to me in Hebrew, 'Saul, Saul, why are you persecuting me?[u] It is hard for you to kick against the goad.'* 15 And I said, 'Who are you, sir?' And the Lord replied, 'I am Jesus whom you are persecuting.[v] 16 Get up now, and stand on your feet.[w] I have appeared to you for this purpose, to appoint you as a servant and witness of what you have seen [of me] and what you will be shown.* 17 I shall deliver you from this people and from the Gentiles to whom I send you,[x] 18 to open their eyes* that they may turn from darkness to light and from the power of Satan to God, so that they may obtain forgiveness of sins and an inheritance among those who have been consecrated by faith in me.'[y]

19 "And so, King Agrippa, I was not disobedient to the heavenly vision. 20 On the contrary, first to those in Damascus and in Jerusalem and throughout the whole country of Judea, and then to the Gentiles, I preached the need to repent and turn to God, and to do works giving evidence of repentance. 21[z] That is why the Jews seized me [when I was] in the temple and tried to kill me. 22[a] But I have enjoyed God's help to this very day, and so I stand here testifying to small and great alike, saying nothing different from what the prophets and Moses foretold,* 23 that the Messiah must suffer* and that, as the first to rise from the dead, he would proclaim light both to our people and to the Gentiles."[b]

***Reactions to Paul's Speech.*** 24 While Paul was so speaking in his defense, Festus said in a loud voice, "You are mad, Paul; much learning is driving you mad." 25 But Paul replied, "I am not mad, most excellent Festus; I am speaking words of truth and reason. 26 The king knows about these matters and to him I speak boldly, for I cannot believe that [any] of this has escaped his notice; this was not done in a corner.* 27 King Agrippa, do you believe the prophets?* I know you believe." 28 Then Agrippa said to Paul, "You will soon persuade me to play the Christian." 29 Paul replied, "I would pray to God that sooner or later not only you but all who listen to me today might become as I am except for these chains."

30 Then the king rose, and with him the governor and Bernice and the others who sat with them. 31* And after they had withdrawn they said to one another, "This man is doing nothing [at all] that deserves death or imprisonment." 32 And Agrippa said to Festus, "This man could have been set free if he had not appealed to Caesar."[c]

## CHAPTER 27

See RG 348–49

***Departure for Rome.*** 1* When it was decided that we should sail to Italy, they handed Paul and some other prisoners over to

**26:14 In Hebrew**: see note on Acts 21:40. **It is hard for you to kick against the goad**: this proverb is commonly found in Greek literature and in this context signifies the senselessness and ineffectiveness of any opposition to the divine influence in his life.

**26:16** The words of Jesus directed to Paul here reflect the dialogues between Christ and Ananias (Acts 9:15) and between Ananias and Paul (Acts 22:14–15) in the two previous accounts of Paul's conversion.

**26:18 To open their eyes**: though no mention is made of Paul's blindness in this account (cf. Acts 9:8–9, 12, 18; 22:11–13), the task he is commissioned to perform is the removal of other people's spiritual blindness.

**26:22 Saying nothing different from what the prophets and Moses foretold**: see note on Lk 18:31.

**26:23 That the Messiah must suffer**: see note on Lk 24:26.

**26:26 Not done in a corner**: for Luke, this Greek proverb expresses his belief that he is presenting a story about Jesus and the church that is already well known. As such, the entire history of Christianity is public knowledge and incontestable. Luke presents his story in this way to provide "certainty" to his readers about the instructions they have received (Lk 1:4).

**26:27, 28** If the Christian missionaries proclaim nothing different from what the Old Testament prophets had proclaimed (Acts 26:22–23), then the logical outcome for the believing Jew, according to Luke, is to become a Christian.

**26:31–32** In recording the episode of Paul's appearance before Agrippa, Luke wishes to show that, when Paul's case was judged impartially, no grounds for legal action against him were found (see Acts 23:29; 25:25).

**27:1–28:16** Here Luke has written a stirring account of adventure on the high seas, incidental to his main purpose of showing how well Paul got along with his captors and how

*s:* 9:7. *t:* 9:3; 22:6. *u:* 9:4; 22:7. *v:* 9:5; 22:8; Mt 25:40. *w:* 9:6; 22:10; Ez 2:1. *x:* Jer 1:7. *y:* Is 42:7, 16; 61:1 LXX; Col 1:13. *z:* 21:31. *a:* 3:18; Lk 24:26–27, 44–47. *b:* Is 42:6; 49:6; Lk 2:32; 1 Cor 15:20–23. *c:* 25:11–12.

a centurion named Julius of the Cohort Augusta.* [2]We went on board a ship from Adramyttium bound for ports in the province of Asia and set sail. Aristarchus, a Macedonian from Thessalonica, was with us.[d] [3]On the following day we put in at Sidon where Julius was kind enough to allow Paul to visit his friends who took care of him. [4]From there we put out to sea and sailed around the sheltered side of Cyprus because of the headwinds, [5]and crossing the open sea off the coast of Cilicia and Pamphylia we came to Myra in Lycia.

***Storm and Shipwreck.*** [6]There the centurion found an Alexandrian ship that was sailing to Italy and put us on board. [7]For many days we made little headway, arriving at Cnidus only with difficulty, and because the wind would not permit us to continue our course we sailed for the sheltered side of Crete off Salmone. [8]We sailed past it with difficulty and reached a place called Fair Havens, near which was the city of Lasea.

[9]Much time had now passed and sailing had become hazardous because the time of the fast* had already gone by, so Paul warned them,[e] [10]"Men, I can see that this voyage will result in severe damage and heavy loss not only to the cargo and the ship, but also to our lives." [11]The centurion, however, paid more attention to the pilot and to the owner of the ship than to what Paul said. [12]Since the harbor was unfavorably situated for spending the winter, the majority planned to put out to sea from there in the hope of reaching Phoenix, a port in Crete facing west-northwest, there to spend the winter.

[13]A south wind blew gently, and thinking they had attained their objective, they weighed anchor and sailed along close to the coast of Crete. [14]Before long an offshore wind of hurricane force called a "Northeaster" struck. [15]Since the ship was caught up in it and could not head into the wind we gave way and let ourselves be driven. [16]We passed along the sheltered side of an island named Cauda and managed only with difficulty to get the dinghy under control. [17]They hoisted it aboard, then used cables to undergird the ship. Because of their fear that they would run aground on the shoal of Syrtis, they lowered the drift anchor and were carried along in this way. [18]We were being pounded by the storm so violently that the next day they jettisoned some cargo, [19]and on the third day with their own hands they threw even the ship's tackle overboard. [20]Neither the sun nor the stars were visible for many days, and no small storm raged. Finally, all hope of our surviving was taken away.

[21]When many would no longer eat, Paul stood among them and said, "Men, you should have taken my advice and not have set sail from Crete and you would have avoided this disastrous loss. [22]I urge you now to keep up your courage; not one of you will be lost, only the ship. [23]For last night an angel of the God to whom (I) belong and whom I serve stood by me [24]and said, 'Do not be afraid, Paul. You are destined to stand before Caesar; and behold, for your sake, God has granted safety to all who are sailing with you.'[f] [25]Therefore, keep up your courage, men; I trust in God that it will turn out as I have been told. [26]We are destined to run aground on some island."

[27]On the fourteenth night, as we were still being driven about on the Adriatic Sea, toward midnight the sailors began to suspect that they were nearing land. [28]They took soundings and found twenty fathoms; a little farther on, they again took soundings and found fifteen fathoms. [29]Fearing that we would run aground on a rocky coast, they dropped four anchors from the stern and prayed for day to come. [30]The sailors then tried to abandon ship; they lowered the dinghy to the sea on the pretext of going to lay out anchors from the bow. [31]But Paul

his prophetic influence saved the lives of all on board. The recital also establishes the existence of Christian communities in Puteoli and Rome. This account of the voyage and shipwreck also constitutes the final "we-section" in Acts (see note on Acts 16:10–17).

**27:1 Cohort Augusta**: the presence of a Cohort Augusta in Syria during the first century A.D. is attested in inscriptions. Whatever the historical background to this information given by Luke may be, the name Augusta serves to increase the prominence and prestige of the prisoner Paul whose custodians bear so important a Roman name.

**27:9 The time of the fast**: the fast kept on the occasion of the Day of Atonement (Lv 16:29–31), which occurred in late September or early October.

*d:* 19:29; 20:4. *e:* Lv 16:29–31. *f:* 23:11.

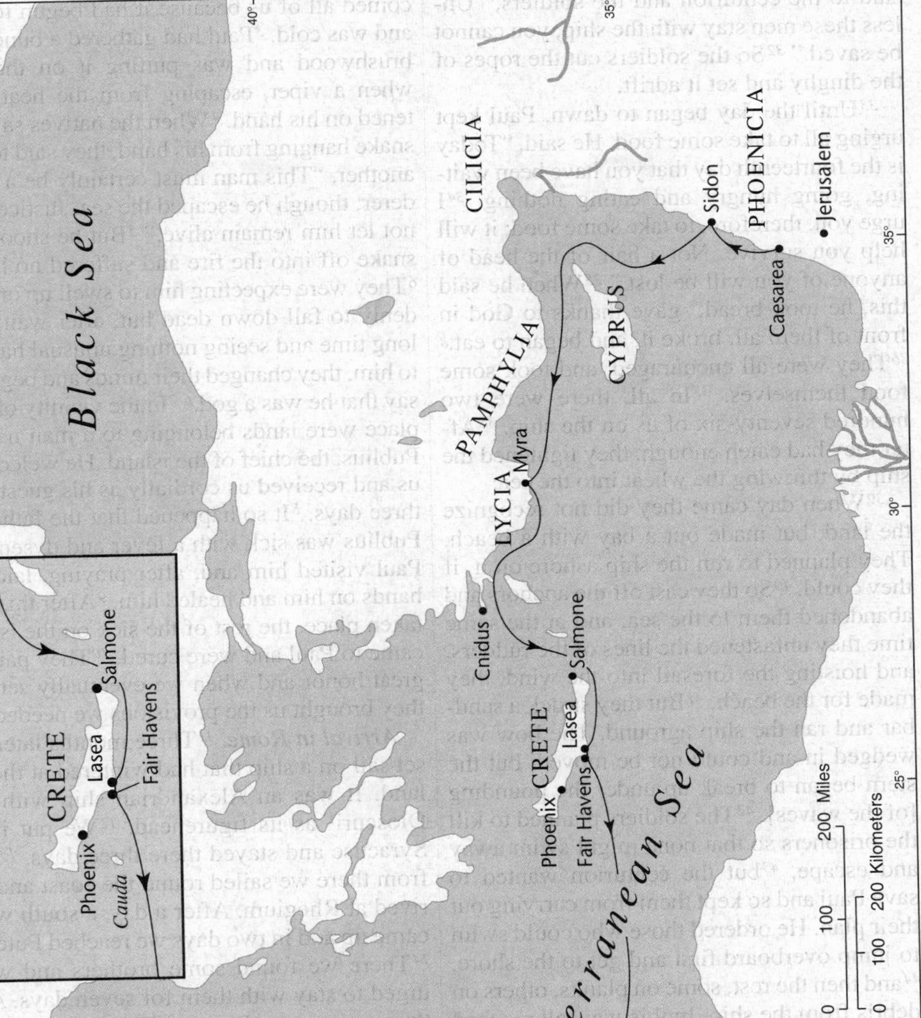

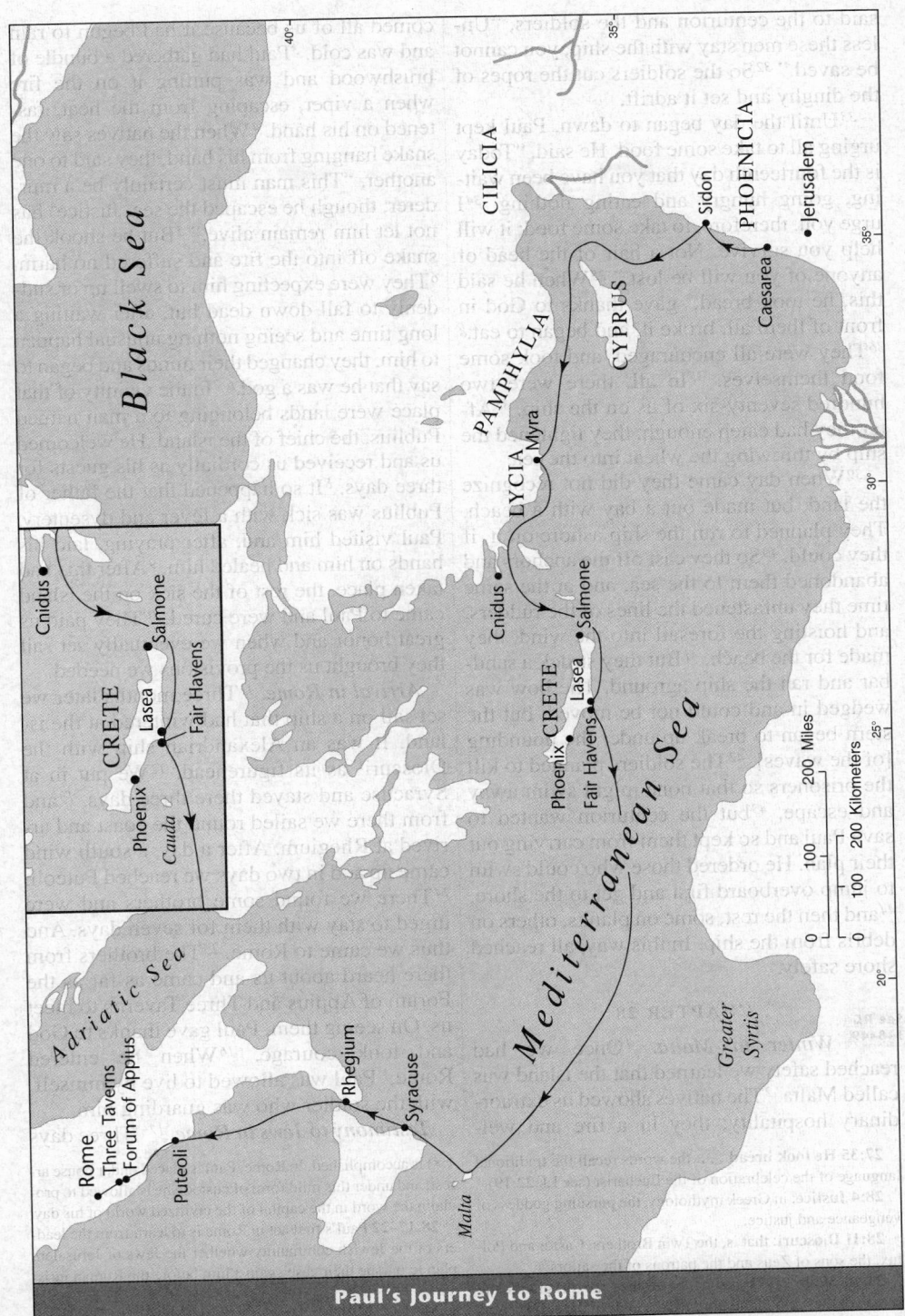


Paul's Journey to Rome

said to the centurion and the soldiers, "Unless these men stay with the ship, you cannot be saved." [32]So the soldiers cut the ropes of the dinghy and set it adrift.

[33]Until the day began to dawn, Paul kept urging all to take some food. He said, "Today is the fourteenth day that you have been waiting, going hungry and eating nothing. [34]I urge you, therefore, to take some food; it will help you survive. Not a hair of the head of anyone of you will be lost." [35]When he said this, he took bread,* gave thanks to God in front of them all, broke it, and began to eat.[g] [36]They were all encouraged, and took some food themselves. [37]In all, there were two hundred seventy-six of us on the ship. [38]After they had eaten enough, they lightened the ship by throwing the wheat into the sea.

[39]When day came they did not recognize the land, but made out a bay with a beach. They planned to run the ship ashore on it, if they could. [40]So they cast off the anchors and abandoned them to the sea, and at the same time they unfastened the lines of the rudders, and hoisting the foresail into the wind, they made for the beach. [41]But they struck a sandbar and ran the ship aground. The bow was wedged in and could not be moved, but the stern began to break up under the pounding [of the waves]. [42]The soldiers planned to kill the prisoners so that none might swim away and escape, [43]but the centurion wanted to save Paul and so kept them from carrying out their plan. He ordered those who could swim to jump overboard first and get to the shore, [44]and then the rest, some on planks, others on debris from the ship. In this way, all reached shore safely.

## CHAPTER 28

See RG 348–49

***Winter in Malta.*** [1]Once we had reached safety we learned that the island was called Malta. [2]The natives showed us extraordinary hospitality; they lit a fire and welcomed all of us because it had begun to rain and was cold. [3]Paul had gathered a bundle of brushwood and was putting it on the fire when a viper, escaping from the heat, fastened on his hand. [4]When the natives saw the snake hanging from his hand, they said to one another, "This man must certainly be a murderer; though he escaped the sea, Justice* has not let him remain alive." [5]But he shook the snake off into the fire and suffered no harm. [6]They were expecting him to swell up or suddenly to fall down dead but, after waiting a long time and seeing nothing unusual happen to him, they changed their minds and began to say that he was a god.[h] [7]In the vicinity of that place were lands belonging to a man named Publius, the chief of the island. He welcomed us and received us cordially as his guests for three days. [8]It so happened that the father of Publius was sick with a fever and dysentery. Paul visited him and, after praying, laid his hands on him and healed him. [9]After this had taken place, the rest of the sick on the island came to Paul and were cured. [10]They paid us great honor and when we eventually set sail they brought us the provisions we needed.

***Arrival in Rome.*** [11]Three months later we set sail on a ship that had wintered at the island. It was an Alexandrian ship with the Dioscuri* as its figurehead. [12]We put in at Syracuse and stayed there three days, [13]and from there we sailed round the coast and arrived at Rhegium. After a day, a south wind came up and in two days we reached Puteoli. [14]There we found some brothers and were urged to stay with them for seven days. And thus we came to Rome. [15]The brothers from there heard about us and came as far as the Forum of Appius and Three Taverns to meet us. On seeing them, Paul gave thanks to God and took courage. [16]When he entered Rome,* Paul was allowed to live by himself, with the soldier who was guarding him.

***Testimony to Jews in Rome.*** [17]* Three days

**27:35 He took bread . . .**: the words recall the traditional language of the celebration of the Eucharist (see Lk 22:19).

**28:4 Justice**: in Greek mythology, the pursuing goddess of vengeance and justice.

**28:11 Dioscuri**: that is, the Twin Brothers, Castor and Pollux, the sons of Zeus and the patrons of the sailors.

**28:16** With Paul's arrival in Rome, the programmatic spread of the word of the Lord to "the ends of the earth" (Acts 1:8) is accomplished. In Rome, Paul is placed under house arrest, and under this mild form of custody he is allowed to proclaim the word in the capital of the civilized world of his day.

**28:17–22** Paul's first act in Rome is to learn from the leaders of the Jewish community whether the Jews of Jerusalem plan to pursue their case against him before the Roman juris-

*g:* Mt 15:36; Mk 6:41; 8:6; Lk 22:19; 1 Cor 11:23–24. *h:* 14:11.

later he called together the leaders of the
Jews. When they had gathered he said to
them, "My brothers, although I had done
nothing against our people or our ancestral
customs, I was handed over to the Romans
as a prisoner from Jerusalem.[i] 18 After trying
my case the Romans wanted to release me,
because they found nothing against me deserving the death penalty.[j] 19 But when the
Jews objected, I was obliged to appeal to
Caesar, even though I had no accusation to
make against my own nation.[k] 20 This is the
reason, then, I have requested to see you and
to speak with you, for it is on account of the
hope of Israel* that I wear these chains."[l]
21 They answered him, "We have received no
letters from Judea about you, nor has any of
the brothers arrived with a damaging report
or rumor about you. 22 But we should like to
hear you present your views, for we know
that this sect is denounced everywhere."[m]
23 So they arranged a day with him and
came to his lodgings in great numbers. From
early morning until evening, he expounded
his position to them, bearing witness to the
kingdom of God and trying to convince
them about Jesus from the law of Moses and
the prophets. 24 Some were convinced by
what he had said, while others did not believe. 25* Without reaching any agreement
among themselves they began to leave; then
Paul made one final statement. "Well did the
holy Spirit speak to your ancestors through
the prophet Isaiah, saying:

26 'Go to this people and say:[n]
You shall indeed hear but not understand.
You shall indeed look but never see.
27 Gross is the heart of this people;
they will not hear with their ears;
they have closed their eyes,
so they may not see with their eyes
and hear with their ears
and understand with their heart and be
converted,
and I heal them.'

28[o] Let it be known to you that this salvation
of God has been sent to the Gentiles; they
will listen." [29]*
30* He remained for two full years in his
lodgings. He received all who came to him,
31 and with complete assurance and without
hindrance he proclaimed the kingdom of
God and taught about the Lord Jesus Christ.

diction. He is informed that no such plan is afoot, but that the Jews of Rome have heard the Christian teaching denounced. Paul's offer to explain it to them is readily accepted.

**28:20 The hope of Israel**: in the words of Paul (Acts 23:6), Luke has identified this hope as hope in the resurrection of the dead.

**28:25–28** Paul's final words in Acts reflect a major concern of Luke's writings: how the salvation promised in the Old Testament, accomplished by Jesus, and offered first to Israel (Acts 13:26), has now been offered to and accepted by the Gentiles. Quoting Is 6:9–10, Paul presents the scriptural support for his indictment of his fellow Jews who refuse to accept the message he proclaims. Their rejection leads to its proclamation among the Gentiles.

**28:29** The Western text has added here a verse that is not found in the best Greek manuscripts: "And when he had said this, the Jews left, seriously arguing among themselves."

**28:30–31** Although the ending of Acts may seem to be abrupt, Luke has now completed his story with the establishment of Paul and the proclamation of Christianity in Rome. Paul's confident and unhindered proclamation of the gospel in Rome forms the climax to the story whose outline was provided in Acts 1:8—"You will be my witnesses in Jerusalem . . . and to the ends of the earth."

*i:* 24:12–13; 25:8. *j:* 23:29; 25:25; 26:31–32. *k:* 25:11. *l:* 23:6; 24:15, 21; 26:6–8. *m:* 24:5, 14. *n:* Is 6:9–10; Mt 13:14–15; Mk 4:12; Lk 8:10; Jn 12:40; Rom 11:8. *o:* 13:46; 18:6; Ps 67:2; Is 40:5 LXX; Lk 3:6.

See RG 351–53

# NEW TESTAMENT LETTERS

In the New Testament canon, between the Acts of the Apostles and Revelation, there are twenty-one documents that take the form of letters or epistles. Most of these are actual letters, but some are more like treatises in the guise of letters. In a few cases even some of the more obvious elements of the letter form are absent; see the Introductions to Hebrews and to 1 John.

The virtually standard form found in these documents, though with some variation, is dependent upon the conventions of letter writing common in the ancient world, but these were modified to suit the purposes of Christian writers. The New Testament letters usually begin with a greeting including an identification of the sender or senders and of the recipients. Next comes a prayer, usually in the form of a thanksgiving. The body of the letter provides an exposition of Christian teaching, usually provoked by concrete circumstances, and generally also draws conclusions regarding ethical behavior. There often follows a discussion of practical matters, such as the writer's travel plans, and the letter concludes with further advice and a formula of farewell.

Fourteen of the twenty-one letters have been traditionally attributed to Paul. One of these, the Letter to the Hebrews, does not itself claim to be the work of Paul; when it was accepted into the canon after much discussion, it was attached at the very end of the Pauline corpus. The other thirteen identify Paul as their author, but most scholars believe that some of them were actually written by his disciples; see the Introductions to Ephesians, Colossians, 2 Thessalonians, and 1 Timothy.

Four of the letters in the Pauline corpus (Ephesians, Philippians, Colossians, and Philemon) are called the "Captivity Epistles" because in each of them the author speaks of being in prison at the time of writing. Three others (1–2 Timothy and Titus) are known as the "Pastoral Epistles" because, addressed to individuals rather than communities, they give advice to disciples about caring for the flock. The letters of the Pauline corpus are arranged in roughly descending order of length from Romans to Philemon, with Hebrews added at the end.

The other seven letters of the New Testament that follow the Pauline corpus are collectively referred to as the "Catholic Epistles." This term, which means "universal," refers to the fact that most of them are directed not to a single Christian community, as are most of the Pauline letters, but to a wider audience; see the Introduction to the catholic letters. Three of them (1–2–3 John) are closely related to the fourth gospel and thus belong to the Johannine corpus. The catholic letters, like those of the Pauline corpus, are also arranged in roughly descending order of length, but the three Johannine letters are kept together and Jude is placed at the end.

The genuine letters of Paul are earlier in date than any of our written gospels. The dates of the other New Testament letters are more difficult to determine, but for the most part they belong to the second and third Christian generations rather than to the first.

See RG 353–63

# The Letter to the Romans

Of all the letters of Paul, that to the Christians at Rome has long held pride of place. It is the longest and most systematic unfolding of the apostle's thought, expounding the gospel of God's righteousness that saves all who believe (Rom 1:16–17); it reflects a universal outlook, with special implications for Israel's relation to the church (Rom 9–11). Yet, like all Paul's letters, Romans too arose out of a specific situation, when the apostle wrote from Greece, likely Corinth, between A.D. 56 and 58 (cf. Acts 20:2–3).

Paul at that time was about to leave for Jerusalem with a collection of funds for the impoverished Jewish Christian believers there, taken up from his predominantly Gentile congregations (Rom 15:25–27). He planned then to travel on to Rome and to enlist support there for a mission to Spain (Rom 15:24, 28). Such a journey had long been on his mind (Rom 1:9–13; 15:23). Now, with much missionary preaching successfully accomplished in the East (Rom 15:19), he sought new opportunities in the West (Rom 15:20–21), in order to complete the divine plan of evangelization in the Roman world. Yet he recognized that the visit to Jerusalem would be hazardous (Rom 15:30–32), and we know from Acts that Paul was arrested there and came to Rome only in chains, as a prisoner (Acts 21–28, especially Acts 21:30–33 and Acts 28:14, 30–31).

The existence of a Christian community in Rome antedates Paul's letter there. When it arose, likely within the sizable Jewish population at Rome, and how, we do not know. The Roman historian Suetonius mentions an edict of the Emperor Claudius about A.D. 49 ordering the expulsion of Jews from Rome in connection with a certain "Chrestus," probably involving a dispute in the Jewish community over Jesus as the Messiah ("Christus"). According to Acts 18:2, Aquila and Priscilla (or Prisca, as in Rom 16:3) were among those driven out; from them, in Corinth, Paul may have learned about conditions in the church at Rome.

Opinions vary as to whether Jewish or Gentile Christians predominated in the house churches (cf. Rom 16:5) in the capital city of the empire at the time Paul wrote. Perhaps already by then Gentile Christians were in the majority. Paul speaks in Romans of both Jews and Gentiles (Rom 3:9, 29; see note on Rom 1:14). The letter also refers to those "weak in faith" (Rom 14:1) and those "who are strong" (Rom 15:1); this terminology may reflect not so much differences between believers of Jewish and of Gentile background, respectively, as an ascetic tendency in some converts (Rom 14:2) combined with Jewish laws about clean and unclean foods (Rom 14:14, 20). The issues were similar to problems that Paul had faced in Corinth (1 Cor 8). If Rom 16 is part of the letter to Rome (see note on Rom 16:1–23), then Paul had considerable information about conditions in Rome through all these people there whom he knew, and our letter does not just reflect a generalized picture of an earlier situation in Corinth.

In any case, Paul writes to introduce himself and his message to the Christians at Rome, seeking to enlist their support for the proposed mission to Spain. He therefore employs formulations likely familiar to the Christians at Rome; see note on the confessional material at Rom 1:3–4 and compare Rom 3:25–26; 4:25. He cites the Old Testament frequently (Rom 1:17; 3:10–18; 4; 9:7, 12–13, 15, 17, 25–29, 33; 10:5–13, 15–21; 15:9–12). The gospel Paul presents is meant to be a familiar one to those in Rome, even though they heard it first from other preachers.

As the outline below shows, this gospel of Paul (see Rom 16:25) finds its center in salvation and justification through faith in Christ (Rom 1:16–17). While God's wrath is revealed against all sin and wickedness of Gentile and Jew alike (Rom 1:18–3:20), God's power to save by divine righteous or justifying action in Christ is also revealed (Rom 1:16–17; 3:21–5:21). The consequences and implications for those who believe are set forth (Rom 6:1–8:39), as are results for those in Israel (Rom 9–11) who, to Paul's great sorrow (Rom 9:1–5), disbelieve. The apostle's hope is that, just as rejection of the gospel by some in Israel has led to a ministry of salvation for non-Jews, so one day, in God's mercy, "all Israel" will be saved (Rom 11:11–15, 25–29, 30–32). The fuller ethical response of believers is also drawn out, both with reference to life in

Christ's body (Rom 12) and with regard to the world (Rom 13:1–7), on the basis of the eschatological situation (Rom 13:11–14) and conditions in the community (Rom 14:1–15:13).

Others have viewed Romans more in the light of Paul's earlier, quite polemical Letter to the Galatians and so see the theme as the relationship between Judaism and Christianity, a topic judged to be much in the minds of the Roman Christians. Each of these religious faiths claimed to be the way of salvation based upon a covenant between God and a people chosen and made the beneficiary of divine gifts. But Christianity regarded itself as the prophetic development and fulfillment of the faith of the Old Testament, declaring that the preparatory Mosaic covenant must now give way to the new and more perfect covenant in Jesus Christ. Paul himself had been the implacable advocate of freedom of Gentiles from the laws of the Mosaic covenant and, especially in Galatia, had refused to allow attempts to impose them on Gentile converts to the gospel. He had witnessed the personal hostilities that developed between the adherents of the two faiths and had written his strongly worded Letter to the Galatians against those Jewish Christians who were seeking to persuade Gentile Christians to adopt the religious practices of Judaism. For him, the purity of the religious understanding of Jesus as the source of salvation would be seriously impaired if Gentile Christians were obligated to amalgamate the two religious faiths.

Still others find the theme of Israel and the church as expressed in Rom 9–11 to be the heart of Romans. Then the implication of Paul's exposition of justification by faith rather than by means of law is that the divine plan of salvation works itself out on a broad theological plane to include the whole of humanity, despite the differences in the content of the given religious system to which a human culture is heir. Romans presents a plan of salvation stretching from Adam through Abraham and Moses to Christ (Rom 4; 5) and on to the future revelation at Christ's parousia (Rom 8:18–25). Its outlook is universal.

Paul's Letter to the Romans is a powerful exposition of the doctrine of the supremacy of Christ and of faith in Christ as the source of salvation. It is an implicit plea to the Christians at Rome, and to all Christians, to hold fast to that faith. They are to resist any pressure put on them to accept a doctrine of salvation through works of the law (see note on Rom 10:4). At the same time they are not to exaggerate Christian freedom as an abdication of responsibility for others (Rom 12:1–2) or as a repudiation of God's law and will (see notes on Rom 3:9–26; 3:31; 7:7–12,13–25).

The principal divisions of the Letter to the Romans are the following:

- I. Address (1:1–15)
- II. Humanity Lost Without the Gospel (1:16–3:20)
- III. Justification Through Faith in Christ (3:21–5:21)
- IV. Justification and the Christian Life (6:1–8:39)
- V. Jews and Gentiles in God's Plan (9:1–11:36)
- VI. The Duties of Christians (12:1–15:13)
- VII. Conclusion (15:14–16:27)

# I. Address

## CHAPTER 1

See RG 355-58

*Greeting.** *1*Paul, a slave of Christ
Jesus,* called to be an apostle and set apart for
the gospel of God,[a] *2*which he promised previously through his prophets in the holy scrip-

**1:1–7** In Paul's letters the greeting or *praescriptio* follows a standard form, though with variations. It is based upon the common Greco-Roman epistolary practice, but with the addition of Semitic and specifically Christian elements. The three basic components are: name of sender; name of addressee; greeting. In identifying himself, Paul often adds phrases to describe his apostolic mission; this element is more developed in Romans than in any other letter. Elsewhere he associates co-workers with himself in the greeting: Sosthenes (1 Corinthians), Timothy (2 Corinthians; Philippians; Philemon) Silvanus (1 Thessalonians–2 Thessalonians). The standard secular greeting was the infinitive *chairein*, "greetings." Paul uses instead the similar-sounding *charis*, "grace," together with the Semitic greeting *šālôm* (Greek *eirēnē*), "peace." These gifts, foreshadowed in God's dealings with Israel (see Nm 6:24–26), have been poured out abundantly in Christ, and Paul wishes them to his readers. In Romans the Pauline *praescriptio* is expanded and expressed in a formal tone; it emphasizes Paul's office as apostle to the Gentiles. Rom 1:3–4 stress the gospel or *kerygma*, Rom 1:2 the fulfillment of God's promise, and Rom 1:1, 5 Paul's office. On his call, see Gal 1:15–16; 1 Cor 9:1; 15:8–10; Acts 9:1–22; 22:3–16; 26:4–18.

**1:1 Slave of Christ Jesus**: Paul applies the term slave to himself in order to express his undivided allegiance to the Lord of the church, the Master of all, including slaves and

*a:* Gal 1:10; Phil 1:1; Jas 1:1 / Acts 9:15; 13:2; 1 Cor 1:1; Gal 1:15; Ti 1:1. *b:* 16:25–26; Ti 1:2.

tures,[b] 3* the gospel about his Son, descended
from David according to the flesh,[c] 4 but established as Son of God in power according
to the spirit of holiness through resurrection
from the dead, Jesus Christ our Lord.[d]
5* Through him we have received the grace of
apostleship, to bring about the obedience of
faith, for the sake of his name, among all the
Gentiles,[e] 6 among whom are you also, who
are called to belong to Jesus Christ;[f] 7 to all the
beloved of God in Rome, called to be holy.*
Grace to you and peace from God our Father
and the Lord Jesus Christ.[g]

***Thanksgiving.*** 8 First, I give thanks* to my
God through Jesus Christ for all of you, because your faith is heralded throughout the
world.[h] 9 God is my witness, whom I serve
with my spirit in proclaiming the gospel of
his Son, that I remember you constantly,[i]
10* always asking in my prayers that somehow by God's will I may at last find my way
clear to come to you.[j] 11 For I long to see you,
that I may share with you some spiritual gift
so that you may be strengthened,[k] 12 that is,
that you and I may be mutually encouraged
by one another's faith, yours and mine. 13 I
do not want you to be unaware, brothers,*
that I often planned to come to you, though I
was prevented until now, that I might harvest some fruit among you, too, as among
the rest of the Gentiles.[l] 14 To Greeks* and
non-Greeks alike, to the wise and the ignorant, I am under obligation; 15 that is why I
am eager to preach the gospel also to you in
Rome.[m]

## II. Humanity Lost Without the Gospel

***God's Power for Salvation.**** 16 For I am not
ashamed of the gospel. It is the power of
God for the salvation of everyone who be-

masters. "No one can serve (i.e., be a slave to) two masters," said Jesus (Mt 6:24). It is this aspect of the slave-master relationship rather than its degrading implications that Paul emphasizes when he discusses Christian commitment.

**1:3–4** Paul here cites an early confession that proclaims Jesus' sonship as messianic descendant of David (cf. Mt 22:42; 2 Tm 2:8; Rev 22:16) and as Son of God by the resurrection. As "life-giving spirit" (1 Cor 15:45), Jesus Christ is able to communicate the Spirit to those who believe in him.

**1:5** Paul recalls his apostolic office, implying that the Romans know something of his history. **The obedience of faith**: as Paul will show at length in chaps. 6–8 and 12–15, faith in God's justifying action in Jesus Christ relates one to God's gift of the new life that is made possible through the death and resurrection of Jesus Christ and the activity of the holy Spirit (see especially Rom 8:1–11).

**1:7 Called to be holy**: Paul often refers to Christians as "the holy ones" or "the saints." The Israelite community was called a "holy assembly" because they had been separated for the worship and service of the Lord (see Lv 11:44; 23:1–44). The Christian community regarded its members as sanctified by baptism (Rom 6:22; 15:16; 1 Cor 6:11; Eph 5:26–27). Christians are called to holiness (1 Cor 1:2; 1 Thes 4:7), that is, they are called to make their lives conform to the gift they have already received.

**1:8** In Greco-Roman letters, the greeting was customarily followed by a prayer. The Pauline letters usually include this element (except Galatians and Titus) expressed in Christian thanksgiving formulas and usually stating the principal theme of the letter. In 2 Corinthians the thanksgiving becomes a blessing, and in Ephesians it is preceded by a lengthy blessing. Sometimes the thanksgiving is blended into the body of the letter, especially in 1 Thessalonians. In Romans it is stated briefly.

**1:10–12** Paul lays the groundwork for his more detailed statement in Rom 15:22–24 about his projected visit to Rome.

**1:13 Brothers** is idiomatic for all Paul's "kin in Christ," all those who believe in the gospel; it includes women as well as men (cf. Rom 4:3).

**1:14 Greeks and non-Greeks**: literally, "Greeks and barbarians." As a result of Alexander's conquests, Greek became the standard international language of the Mediterranean world. **Greeks** in Paul's statement therefore means people who know Greek or who have been influenced by Greek culture. **Non-Greeks** were people whose cultures remained substantially unaffected by Greek influences. Greeks called such people "barbarians" (cf. Acts 28:2), meaning people whose speech was foreign. Roman citizens would scarcely classify themselves as such, and Nero, who was reigning when Paul wrote this letter, prided himself on his admiration for Greek culture. **Under obligation**: Paul will expand on the theme of obligation in Rom 13:8; 15:1,27.

**1:16–17** The principal theme of the letter is salvation through faith. **I am not ashamed of the gospel**: Paul is not ashamed to proclaim the gospel, despite the criticism that Jews and Gentiles leveled against the proclamation of the crucified savior; cf. 1 Cor 1:23–24. Paul affirms, however, that it is precisely through the crucifixion and resurrection of Jesus that God's saving will and power become manifest. **Jew first** (cf. Rom 2:9–10) means that Jews especially, in view of the example of Abraham (Rom 4), ought to be the leaders in the response of faith.

---

*c:* 9:5; 2 Sm 7:12; Mt 1:1; Mk 12:35; Jn 7:42; Acts 13:22–23; 2 Tm 2:8; Rev 22:16. *d:* 10:9; Acts 13:33; Phil 3:10. *e:* 15:15; Gal 2:7, 9 / 15:18; Acts 9:15; 26:16–18; Gal 1:16; 2:7, 9. *f:* 1 Cor 1:9. *g:* Nm 6:25–26; 1 Cor 1:2–3; 2 Cor 1:1–2. *h:* 16:19; 1 Thes 1:8. *i:* 2 Cor 1:23; Eph 1:16; Phil 1:8; 1 Thes 1:2; 2:5, 10; 2 Tm 1:3. *j:* 15:23, 32; Acts 18:21; 1 Cor 4:19; 1 Thes 2:17. *k:* 1 Thes 2:17; 3:10. *l:* 15:22; Jn 15:16; Acts 19:21. *m:* Acts 28:30–31.

lieves: for Jew first, and then Greek.[n] [17]For
in it is revealed the righteousness of God
from faith to faith;* as it is written, "The one
who is righteous by faith will live."[o]

***Punishment of Idolaters.*** [18]* The wrath* of
God* is indeed being revealed from heaven
against every impiety and wickedness[p] of
those who suppress the truth by their wickedness. [19]For what can be known about God is
evident to them, because God made it evident
to them.[q] [20]Ever since the creation of the
world, his invisible attributes of eternal
power and divinity have been able to be understood and perceived in what he has made.[r]
As a result, they have no excuse; [21]for although they knew God they did not accord
him glory as God or give him thanks. Instead,
they became vain in their reasoning, and their
senseless minds were darkened.[s] [22]While
claiming to be wise,[t] they became fools [23]and
exchanged the glory of the immortal God for
the likeness of an image of mortal man or of
birds or of four-legged animals or of snakes.[u]
[24]Therefore, God handed them over to impurity through the lusts of their hearts* for
the mutual degradation of their bodies.[v]
[25]They exchanged the truth of God for a lie
and revered and worshiped the creature
rather than the creator, who is blessed forever. Amen.[w] [26]Therefore, God handed them
over to degrading passions. Their females
exchanged natural relations for unnatural,
[27]and the males likewise gave up natural relations with females and burned with lust for
one another. Males did shameful things with
males and thus received in their own persons
the due penalty for their perversity.[x] [28]And
since they did not see fit to acknowledge
God, God handed them over to their undiscerning mind to do what is improper.
[29][y]They are filled with every form of
wickedness, evil, greed, and malice; full of
envy, murder, rivalry, treachery, and spite.
They are gossips [30]and scandalmongers and
they hate God. They are insolent, haughty,
boastful, ingenious in their wickedness, and
rebellious toward their parents. [31]They are
senseless, faithless, heartless, ruthless. [32]Al-
though they know the just decree of God that
all who practice such things deserve death,
they not only do them but give approval to
those who practice them.[z]

**1:17 In it is revealed the righteousness of God from faith to faith**: the gospel centers in Jesus Christ, in whom God's saving presence and righteousness in history have been made known. Faith is affirmation of the basic purpose and meaning of the Old Testament as proclamation of divine promise (Rom 1:2; 4:13) and exposure of the inability of humanity to effect its salvation even through covenant law. Faith is the gift of the holy Spirit and denotes acceptance of salvation as God's righteousness, that is, God's gift of a renewed relationship in forgiveness and power for a new life. Faith is response to God's total claim on people and their destiny. **The one who is righteous by faith will live**: see note on Heb 2:4.

**1:18–3:20** Paul aims to show that all humanity is in a desperate plight and requires God's special intervention if it is to be saved.

**1:18–32** In this passage Paul uses themes and rhetoric common in Jewish-Hellenistic mission proclamation (cf. Wis 13:1–14:31) to indict especially the non-Jewish world. The close association of idolatry and immorality is basic, but the generalization needs in all fairness to be balanced against the fact that non-Jewish Christian society on many levels displayed moral attitudes and performance whose quality would challenge much of contemporary Christian culture. Romans themselves expressed abhorrence over devotion accorded to animals in Egypt. Paul's main point is that the wrath of God does not await the end of the world but goes into action at each present moment in humanity's history when misdirected piety serves as a facade for self-interest.

**1:18 The wrath of God**: God's reaction to human sinfulness, an Old Testament phrase that expresses the irreconcilable opposition between God and evil (see Is 9:11, 16, 18, 20; 10:4; 30:27). It is not contrary to God's universal love for his creatures, but condemns Israel's turning aside from the covenant obligations. Hosea depicts Yahweh as suffering intensely at the thought of having to punish Israel (Hos 11:8–9). God's wrath was to be poured forth especially on the "Day of Yahweh" and thus took on an eschatological connotation (see Zep 1:15).

**1:24** In order to expose the depth of humanity's rebellion against the Creator, **God handed them over to impurity through the lusts of their hearts.** Instead of curbing people's evil interests, God abandoned them to self-indulgence, thereby removing the facade of apparent conformity to the divine will. Subsequently Paul will show that the Mosaic law produces the same effect; cf. Rom 5:20; 7:13–24. The divine judgment expressed here is related to the theme of hardness of heart described in Rom 9:17–18.

---

*n:* Ps 119:46; 1 Cor 1:18, 24 / Rom 2:9; Acts 3:26; 13:46. *o:* 3:21–22; Heb 2:4; Gal 3:11; Heb 10:38. *p:* 2:5, 8–9; Is 66:15; Eph 5:6; Col 3:6. *q:* Wis 13–19; Acts 14:15–17; 17:23–29. *r:* Jb 12:7–9; Ps 8:4; 19:2; Sir 17:7–9; Is 40:26; Acts 14:17; 17:25–28. *s:* Eph 4:17–18. *t:* Wis 13:1–9; Is 5:21; Jer 10:14; Acts 17:29–30; 1 Cor 1:19–21. *u:* Dt 4:15–19; Ps 106:20; Wis 11:15; 12:24; 13:10–19; Jer 2:11. *v:* Wis 12:25; 14:22–31; Acts 7:41–42; Eph 4:19. *w:* 9:5; Jer 13:25–27. *x:* Lv 18:22; 20:13; Wis 14:26; 1 Cor 6:9; 1 Tm 1:10. *y:* 13:13; Mt 15:19; Mk 7:21–22; Gal 5:19–21; 2 Tm 3:2–4. *z:* Acts 8:1; 2 Thes 2:12.

## CHAPTER 2

See RG 357–58

***God's Just Judgment.*** 1* Therefore, you are without excuse,[a] every one of you who passes judgment.* For by the standard by which you judge another you condemn yourself, since you, the judge, do the very same things. 2 We know that the judgment of God on those who do such things is true. 3 Do you suppose, then, you who judge those who engage in such things and yet do them yourself, that you will escape the judgment of God?[b] 4 Or do you hold his priceless kindness, forbearance, and patience in low esteem, unaware that the kindness of God would lead you to repentance?[c] 5 By your stubbornness and impenitent heart,[d] you are storing up wrath for yourself for the day of wrath and revelation of the just judgment of God, 6[e] who will repay everyone according to his works:* 7 eternal life to those who seek glory, honor, and immortality through perseverance in good works, 8 but wrath and fury to those who selfishly disobey the truth and obey wickedness.[f] 9 Yes, affliction and distress will come upon every human being who does evil, Jew first and then Greek. 10[g] But there will be glory, honor, and peace for everyone who does good, Jew first and then Greek. 11*[h] There is no partiality with God.

***Judgment by the Interior Law.**** 12 All who sin outside the law will also perish without reference to it, and all who sin under the law will be judged in accordance with it.[i] 13 For it is not those who hear the law who are just in the sight of God; rather, those who observe the law will be justified.[j] 14 For when the Gentiles who do not have the law by nature observe the prescriptions of the law, they are a law for themselves even though they do not have the law.[k] 15 They show that the demands of the law are written in their hearts,* while their conscience also bears witness and their conflicting thoughts accuse or even defend them 16 on the day when, according to my gospel, God will judge people's hidden works through Christ Jesus.[l]

***Judgment by the Mosaic Law.**** 17 Now if you call yourself a Jew and rely on the law and boast of God[m] 18 and know his will and are able to discern what is important since you are instructed from the law,[n] 19 and if you are confident that you are a guide for the blind and a light for those in darkness,[o] 20 that you are a trainer of the foolish and teacher of the simple,[p] because in the law you have the formulation of knowledge and truth— 21 then you who teach another, are you failing to teach yourself? You who preach against stealing, do you steal?[q] 22 You who forbid adultery, do you commit adultery? You who detest idols, do you rob temples? 23 You who boast of the law, do you dis-

**2:1–3:20** After his general indictment of the Gentile, Paul shows that in spite of special revelation Jews enjoy no advantage in moral status before God (Rom 3:1–8). With the entire human race now declared guilty before God (Rom 3:9–20), Paul will then be able to display the solution for the total problem: salvation through God's redemptive work that is revealed in Christ Jesus for all who believe (Rom 3:21–31).

**2:1–11** As a first step in his demonstration that Jews enjoy no real moral supremacy over Gentiles, Paul explains that the final judgment will be a review of performance, not of privilege. From this perspective Gentiles stand on an equal footing with Jews, and Jews cannot condemn the sins of Gentiles without condemning themselves.

**2:6 Will repay everyone according to his works**: Paul reproduces the Septuagint text of Ps 62:12 and Prv 24:12.

**2:11 No partiality with God**: this sentence is not at variance with the statements in Rom 2:9–10. Since Jews are the first to go under indictment, it is only fair that they be given first consideration in the distribution of blessings. Basic, of course, is the understanding that God accepts no bribes (Dt 10:17).

**2:12–16** Jews cannot reasonably demand from Gentiles the standard of conduct inculcated in the Old Testament since God did not address its revelation to them. Rather, God made it possible for Gentiles to know instinctively the difference between right and wrong. But, as Paul explained in Rom 1:18–32, humanity misread the evidence of God's existence, power, and divinity, and "while claiming to be wise, they became fools" (Rom 1:22).

**2:15** Paul expands on the thought of Jer 31:33; Wis 17:11.

**2:17–29** Mere possession of laws is no evidence of virtue. By eliminating circumcision as an elitist moral sign, Paul clears away the last obstacle to his presentation of justification through faith without claims based on the receipt of circumcision and its attendant legal obligations.

---

*a:* Mt 7:1–2. *b:* Wis 16:15–16. *c:* 3:25–26; 9:22; Wis 11:23; 15:1; 2 Pt 3:9, 15. *d:* Ex 33:3; Acts 7:51; Rev 6:17; 11:18. *e:* Ps 62:12; Prv 24:12; Sir 16:14; Mt 16:27; Jn 5:29; 2 Cor 5:10. *f:* 2 Thes 1:8. *g:* 1:16; 3:9. *h:* Dt 10:17; 2 Chr 19:7; Sir 35:12–13; Acts 10:34; Gal 2:6; Eph 6:9; Col 3:25; 1 Pt 1:17. *i:* 3:19. *j:* Mt 7:21; Lk 6:46–49; 8:21; Jas 1:22–25; 1 Jn 3:7. *k:* Acts 10:35. *l:* Acts 10:42; 17:31. *m:* Is 48:1–2; Mi 3:11; Phil 3:4–6. *n:* Phil 1:10. *o:* Mt 15:14; Lk 6:39. *p:* 2 Tm 3:15. *q:* Ps 50:16–21; Mt 23:3–4.

honor God by breaking the law? 24[r] For, as it
is written, "Because of you the name of God
is reviled among the Gentiles."*
25[s] Circumcision, to be sure, has value if
you observe the law; but if you break the
law, your circumcision has become uncircumcision.[t] 26 Again, if an uncircumcised
man keeps the precepts of the law, will he
not be considered circumcised?[u] 27 Indeed,
those who are physically uncircumcised but
carry out the law will pass judgment on you,
with your written law and circumcision, who
break the law. 28 One is not a Jew outwardly.
True circumcision is not outward, in the
flesh.[v] 29 Rather, one is a Jew inwardly, and
circumcision is of the heart, in the spirit, not
the letter; his praise is not from human beings but from God.[w]

### CHAPTER 3

See RG 357–58

***Answers to Objections.*** 1* What advantage is there then in being a Jew? Or
what is the value of circumcision? 2 Much, in
every respect. [For] in the first place, they
were entrusted with the utterances of God.[x]
3 What if some were unfaithful? Will their infidelity nullify the fidelity of God?[y] 4 Of
course not! God must be true, though every
human being is a liar,* as it is written:

"That you may be justified in your
words,
and conquer when you are judged."[z]

5 But if our wickedness provides proof of
God's righteousness, what can we say? Is
God unjust, humanly speaking, to inflict his
wrath?[a] 6 Of course not! For how else is God
to judge the world? 7 But if God's truth redounds to his glory through my falsehood,
why am I still being condemned as a sinner?
8 And why not say—as we are accused and as
some claim we say—that we should do evil
that good may come of it? Their penalty is
what they deserve.[b]

***Universal Bondage to Sin.**** 9 Well, then,
are we better off? Not entirely, for we have
already brought the charge against Jews and
Greeks alike that they are all under the domination of sin,[c] 10 as it is written:[d]

"There is no one just, not one,
11 there is no one who understands,
there is no one who seeks God.
12 All have gone astray; all alike are
worthless;
there is not one who does good,
[there is not] even one.
13 Their throats are open graves;
they deceive with their tongues;
the venom of asps is on their lips;[e]
14 their mouths are full of bitter cursing.[f]
15 Their feet are quick to shed blood;[g]
16 ruin and misery are in their ways,
17 and the way of peace they know not.
18 There is no fear of God before their
eyes."[h]

19 Now we know that what the law* says is
addressed to those under the law, so that
every mouth may be silenced and the whole
world stand accountable to God,[i] 20 since no

**2:24** According to Is 52:5 the suffering of Israel prompts her enemies to revile God. Paul uses the passage in support of his point that the present immorality of Israelites is the cause of such defamation.

**3:1–4** In keeping with the popular style of diatribe, Paul responds to the objection that his teaching on the sinfulness of all humanity detracts from the religious prerogatives of Israel. He stresses that Jews have remained the vehicle of God's revelation despite their sins, though this depends on the fidelity of God.

**3:4 Though every human being is a liar**: these words reproduce the Greek text of Ps 116:11. The rest of the verse is from Ps 51:6.

**3:9–20 Well, then, are we better off?**: this phrase can also be translated "Are we at a disadvantage?" but the latter version does not substantially change the overall meaning of the passage. Having explained that Israel's privileged status is guaranteed by God's fidelity, Paul now demonstrates the infidelity of the Jews by a catena of citations from scripture, possibly derived from an existing collection of *testimonia.* These texts show that all human beings share the common burden of sin. They are linked together by mention of organs of the body: throat, tongue, lips, mouth, feet, eyes.

**3:19 The law**: Paul here uses the term in its broadest sense to mean all of the scriptures; none of the preceding texts is from the Torah or Pentateuch.

**3:20 No human being will be justified in his sight**: these words are freely cited from Ps 143:2. In place of the psalmist's "no living person," Paul substitutes "no human being" (literally "no flesh," a Hebraism), and he adds "by observing the law."

*r:* Is 52:5; Ez 36:20; 2 Pt 2:2. *s:* Jer 4:4; 9:24–25. *t:* 1 Cor 7:19; Gal 5:3. *u:* Gal 5:6. *v:* Jn 7:24; 8:15, 39. *w:* Dt 30:6; Jer 4:4; 9:25; Col 2:11 / 1 Cor 4:5; 2 Cor 10:18. *x:* 9:4; Dt 4:7–8; Ps 103:7; 147:19–20. *y:* 9:6; 11:1, 29; Ps 89:30–37; 2 Tm 2:13. *z:* Ps 116:11 / Ps 51:6. *a:* 9:14; Jb 34:12–17. *b:* 6:1. *c:* 1:18–2:25; 3:23; Sir 8:5. *d:* Ps 14:1–3; 53:2–4; Eccl 7:20. *e:* Ps 5:10; 140:4. *f:* Ps 10:7. *g:* Prv 1:16; Is 59:7–8. *h:* Ps 36:2. *i:* 7:7. *j:* Ps 143:2; Gal 2:16 / 7:7.

human being will be justified in his sight* by
observing the law; for through the law
comes consciousness of sin.[j]

## III. Justification Through Faith in Christ

*Justification apart from the Law.** 21 But
now* the righteousness of God has been
manifested apart from the law, though testified to by the law and the prophets,[k] 22 the
righteousness of God through faith in Jesus
Christ for all who believe. For there is no
distinction;[l] 23 all have sinned and are deprived of the glory of God.[m] 24 They are justified freely by his grace through the redemption in Christ Jesus,[n] 25 whom God set
forth as an expiation,* through faith, by his
blood, to prove his righteousness because of
the forgiveness of sins previously committed,[o] 26 through the forbearance of God—to
prove his righteousness in the present time,
that he might be righteous and justify the
one who has faith in Jesus.
27[p] What occasion is there then for boasting?* It is ruled out. On what principle, that of
works? No, rather on the principle of faith.*
28 For we consider that a person is justified by
faith apart from works of the law.[q] 29 Does
God belong to Jews alone? Does he not belong to Gentiles, too? Yes, also to Gentiles,[r]
30 for God is one and will justify the circumcised on the basis of faith and the uncircumcised through faith.[s] 31 Are we then annulling
the law by this faith? Of course not![t] On the
contrary, we are supporting the law.*

### CHAPTER 4*

See RG 358

*Abraham Justified by Faith.* 1 What
then can we say that Abraham found, our ancestor according to the flesh?[u] 2* Indeed, if
Abraham was justified on the basis of his
works, he has reason to boast; but this was
not so in the sight of God. 3[v] For what does

**3:21–31** These verses provide a clear statement of Paul's "gospel," i.e., the principle of justification by faith in Christ. God has found a means of rescuing humanity from its desperate plight: Paul's general term for this divine initiative is the righteousness of God (Rom 3:21). Divine mercy declares the guilty innocent and makes them so. God does this not as a result of the law but apart from it (Rom 3:21), and not because of any merit in human beings but through forgiveness of their sins (Rom 3:24), in virtue of the redemption wrought in Christ Jesus for all who believe (Rom 3:22, 24–25). God has manifested his righteousness in the coming of Jesus Christ, whose saving activity inaugurates a new era in human history.

**3:21 But now**: Paul adopts a common phrase used by Greek authors to describe movement from disaster to prosperity. The expressions indicate that Rom 3:21–26 are the consolatory answer to Rom 3:9–20.

**3:25 Expiation**: this rendering is preferable to "propitiation," which suggests hostility on the part of God toward sinners. As Paul will be at pains to point out (Rom 5:8–10), it is humanity that is hostile to God.

**3:27–31** People cannot boast of their own holiness, since it is God's free gift (Rom 3:27), both to the Jew who practices circumcision out of faith and to the Gentile who accepts faith without the Old Testament religious culture symbolized by circumcision (Rom 3:29–30).

**3:27 Principle of faith**: literally, "law of faith." Paul is fond of wordplay involving the term "law"; cf. Rom 7:21, 23; 8:2. Since "law" in Greek may also connote "custom" or "principle," his readers and hearers would have sensed no contradiction in the use of the term after the negative statement concerning law in Rom 3:20.

**3:31 We are supporting the law**: giving priority to God's intentions. God is the ultimate source of law, and the essence of law is fairness. On the basis of the Mosaic covenant, God's justice is in question if those who sinned against the law are permitted to go free (see Rom 3:23–26). In order to rescue all humanity rather than condemn it, God thinks of an alternative: the law or "principle" of faith (Rom 3:27). What can be more fair than to admit everyone into the divine presence on the basis of forgiveness grasped by faith? Indeed, this principle of faith antedates the Mosaic law, as Paul will demonstrate in Rom 4, and does not therefore mark a change in divine policy.

**4:1–25** This is an expanded treatment of the significance of Abraham's faith, which Paul discusses in Gal 3:6–18; see notes there.

**4:2–5** Rom 4:2 corresponds to Rom 4:4, and Rom 4:3–5. The Greek term here rendered **credited** means "made an entry." The context determines whether it is credit or debit. Rom 4:8 speaks of "recording sin" as a debit. Paul's repeated use of accountants' terminology in this and other passages can be traced both to the Old Testament texts he quotes and to his business activity as a tentmaker. The commercial term in Gn 15:6, "attributed it to him," reminds Paul in Rom 4:7–8 of Ps 32:2, in which the same term is used and applied to forgiveness of sins. Thus Paul is able to argue that Abraham's faith involved receipt of forgiveness of sins and that all believers benefit as he did through faith.

**4:3** Jas 2:24 appears to conflict with Paul's statement. However, James combats the error of extremists who used the doctrine of justification through faith as a screen for moral self-determination. Paul discusses the subject of holiness in greater detail than does James and beginning with Rom 6

---

*k:* Is 51:6–8; Acts 10:43. *l:* 1:17; Gal 2:16; Phil 3:9. *m:* 3:9; 5:12. *n:* Eph 2:8; Ti 3:7 / Rom 5:1–2; Eph 1:7. *o:* Lv 16:12–15; Acts 17:31; 1 Jn 4:10. *p:* 8:2; 1 Cor 1:29–31. *q:* 5:1; Gal 2:16. *r:* 10:12. *s:* Dt 6:4; Gal 3:20; Jas 2:19 / Rom 4:11–12. *t:* 8:4; Mt 5:17. *u:* Gal 3:6–9. *v:* Gn 15:6; Gal 3:6; Jas 2:14, 20–24.

the scripture say? "Abraham believed God,
and it was credited to him as righteousness."* 4 A worker's wage is credited not as a
gift, but as something due.[w] 5 But when one
does not work, yet believes in the one who
justifies the ungodly, his faith is credited as
righteousness. 6 So also David declares the
blessedness of the person to whom God
credits righteousness apart from works:

7 "Blessed are they whose iniquities are
forgiven[x]
and whose sins are covered.
8 Blessed is the man whose sin the Lord
does not record."

9 Does this blessedness* apply only to the circumcised, or to the uncircumcised as well?
Now we assert that "faith was credited to
Abraham as righteousness."[y] 10 Under what
circumstances was it credited? Was he circumcised or not? He was not circumcised,
but uncircumcised. 11 And he received the
sign of circumcision as a seal on the righteousness received through faith while he
was uncircumcised. Thus he was to be the
father of all the uncircumcised who believe,
so that to them [also] righteousness might be
credited,[z] 12 as well as the father of the circumcised who not only are circumcised, but
also follow the path of faith that our father
Abraham walked while still uncircumcised.
***Inheritance Through Faith.*** 13 It was not
through the law that the promise was made to
Abraham and his descendants that he would
inherit the world, but through the righteousness that comes from faith.[a] 14 For if those
who adhere to the law are the heirs, faith is
null and the promise is void.[b] 15 For the law
produces wrath;[c] but where there is no law,
neither is there violation.* 16 For this reason, it
depends on faith, so that it may be a gift, and
the promise may be guaranteed to all his descendants, not to those who only adhere to the
law but to those who follow the faith of Abraham, who is the father of all of us,[d] 17 as it is
written, "I have made you father of many nations." He is our father in the sight of God, in
whom he believed, who gives life to the dead
and calls into being what does not exist.[e] 18 He
believed, hoping against hope,[f] that he would
become "the father of many nations," according to what was said, "Thus shall your descendants be." 19[g] He did not weaken in faith
when he considered his own body as [al-
ready] dead (for he was almost a hundred
years old) and the dead womb of Sarah. 20 He
did not doubt God's promise in unbelief;*
rather, he was empowered by faith and gave
glory to God 21 and was fully convinced that
what he had promised he was also able to do.[h]
22 That is why "it was credited to him as righteousness."[i] 23 But it was not for him alone
that it was written that "it was credited to
him"; 24 it was also for us, to whom it will be
credited, who believe in the one who raised
Jesus our Lord from the dead,[j] 25 who was
handed over for our transgressions and was
raised for our justification.[k]

shows how justification through faith introduces one to the gift of a new life in Christ through the power of the holy Spirit.

**4:9 Blessedness**: evidence of divine favor.

**4:15** Law has the negative function of bringing the deep-seated rebellion against God to the surface in specific sins; see note on Rom 1:18–32.

**4:20 He did not doubt God's promise in unbelief**: any doubts Abraham might have had were resolved in commitment to God's promise. Heb 11:8–12 emphasizes the faith of Abraham and Sarah.

**5:1–11** Popular piety frequently construed reverses and troubles as punishment for sin; cf. Jn 9:2. Paul therefore assures believers that God's justifying action in Jesus Christ is a declaration of peace. The crucifixion of Jesus Christ displays God's initiative in certifying humanity for unimpeded access into the divine presence. Reconciliation is God's gift of pardon to the entire human race. Through faith one benefits personally from this pardon or, in Paul's term, is justified. The ultimate aim of God is to liberate believers from the pre-Christian self as described in Rom 1–3. Since this liberation will first find completion in the believer's resurrection, salvation is described as future in Rom 5:10. Because this fullness of salvation belongs to the future it is called the Christian hope. Paul's Greek term for hope does not, however, suggest a note of uncertainty, to the effect: "I wonder whether God really means it." Rather, God's promise in the gospel fills believers with expectation and anticipation for the climactic gift of unalloyed commitment in the holy Spirit to the performance of the will of God. The persecutions that attend Christian commitment are to teach believers patience and to strengthen this hope, which will not disappoint them because the holy Spirit dwells in their hearts and imbues them with God's love (Rom 5:5).

*w:* 11:6. *x:* Ps 32:1–2. *y:* 4:3. *z:* Gn 17:10–11; Gal 3:6–8. *a:* Gn 12:7; 18:18; 22:17–18; Sir 44:21; Gal 3:16–18, 29. *b:* Gal 3:18. *c:* 3:20; 5:13; 7:8; Gal 3:19. *d:* Sir 44:19; Gal 3:7–9. *e:* Gn 17:5; Heb 11:19 / Is 48:13. *f:* Gn 15:5. *g:* Gn 17:17; Heb 11:11. *h:* Gn 18:14; Lk 1:37. *i:* Gn 15:6. *j:* 10:9; 1 Pt 1:21. *k:* Is 53:4–5, 12; 1 Cor 15:17; 1 Pt 1:3 / Rom 8:11.

## CHAPTER 5

See RG 358–59

***Faith, Hope, and Love.**** 1 Therefore, since we have been justified by faith, we have peace* with God through our Lord Jesus Christ,[l] 2 through whom we have gained access [by faith] to this grace in which we stand, and we boast in hope of the glory of God.[m] 3 Not only that, but we even boast of our afflictions, knowing that affliction produces endurance, 4 and endurance, proven character, and proven character, hope,[n] 5 and hope does not disappoint, because the love of God has been poured out into our hearts through the holy Spirit that has been given to us.[o] 6 For Christ, while we were still helpless, yet died at the appointed time for the ungodly. 7 Indeed, only with difficulty does one die for a just person, though perhaps for a good person one might even find courage to die.* 8 But God proves his love for us in that while we were still sinners Christ died for us.[p] 9 How much more then, since we are now justified by his blood, will we be saved through him from the wrath.[q] 10 Indeed, if, while we were enemies, we were reconciled to God through the death of his Son, how much more, once reconciled, will we be saved by his life.[r] 11 Not only that, but we also boast of God through our Lord Jesus Christ, through whom we have now received reconciliation.

***Humanity's Sin Through Adam.*** 12* Therefore, just as through one person sin entered the world,[s] and through sin, death, and thus death came to all, inasmuch as all sinned*— 13 for up to the time of the law, sin was in the world, though sin is not accounted when there is no law.[t] 14 But death reigned from Adam to Moses, even over those who did not sin after the pattern of the trespass of Adam, who is the type of the one who was to come.[u]

***Grace and Life Through Christ.*** 15 But the gift is not like the transgression. For if by that one person's transgression the many died, how much more did the grace of God and the gracious gift of the one person Jesus Christ overflow for the many. 16 And the gift is not like the result of the one person's sinning. For after one sin there was the judgment that brought condemnation; but the gift, after many transgressions, brought acquittal. 17 For if, by the transgression of one person, death came to reign through that one, how much more will those who receive the abundance of grace and of the gift of justification come to reign in life through the one person Jesus Christ. 18 In conclusion, just as through one transgression condemnation came upon all, so through one righteous act acquittal and life came to all.[v] 19 For just as through the disobedience of one person the many were made sinners, so through the obedience of one the many will be made righteous.[w] 20 The law entered in* so that transgression might increase but, where sin increased, grace overflowed all the more,[x] 21 so that, as sin reigned in death, grace also might reign through justification for eternal life through Jesus Christ our Lord.[y]

**5:1 We have peace**: a number of manuscripts, versions, and church Fathers read "Let us have peace"; cf. Rom 14:19.

**5:7** In the world of Paul's time the **good person** is especially one who is magnanimous to others.

**5:12–21** Paul reflects on the sin of Adam (Gn 3:1–13) in the light of the redemptive mystery of Christ. Sin, as used in the singular by Paul, refers to the dreadful power that has gripped humanity, which is now in revolt against the Creator and engaged in the exaltation of its own desires and interests. But no one has a right to say, "Adam made me do it," for all are culpable (Rom 5:12): Gentiles under the demands of the law written in their hearts (Rom 2:14–15), and Jews under the Mosaic covenant. Through the Old Testament law, the sinfulness of humanity that was operative from the beginning (Rom 5:13) found further stimulation, with the result that sins were generated in even greater abundance. According to Rom 5:15–21, God's act in Christ is in total contrast to the disastrous effects of the virus of sin that invaded humanity through Adam's crime.

**5:12 Inasmuch as all sinned**: others translate "because all sinned," and understand v 13 as a parenthetical remark. Unlike Wis 2:24, Paul does not ascribe the entry of death to the devil.

**5:20 The law entered in**: sin had made its entrance (Rom 5:12); now the law comes in alongside sin. See notes on Rom 1:18–32; 5:12–21. **Where sin increased, grace overflowed all the more**: Paul declares that grace outmatches the productivity of sin.

*l:* 3:24–28; Gal 2:16. *m:* Eph 2:18; 3:12. *n:* 2 Cor 12:9–10; Jas 1:2–4; 1 Pt 1:5–7; 4:12–14. *o:* 8:14–16; Ps 22:5–6; 25:20. *p:* Jn 3:16; 1 Jn 4:10, 19. *q:* 1:18; 1 Thes 1:10. *r:* 8:7–8; 2 Cor 5:18; Col 1:21–22. *s:* Gn 2:17; 3:1–19; Wis 2:24 / Rom 3:19, 23. *t:* 4:15. *u:* 1 Cor 15:21. *v:* 1 Cor 15:21–22. *w:* Is 53:11; Phil 2:8–9. *x:* 4:15; 7:7–8; Gal 3:19. *y:* 6:23.

## IV. Justification and the Christian Life

### CHAPTER 6

See RG 358–59

***Freedom from Sin; Life in God.***

1* What then shall we say? Shall we persist in sin that grace may abound? Of course not![z] 2 How can we who died to sin yet live in it?[a] 3 Or are you unaware that we who were baptized into Christ Jesus were baptized into his death?[b] 4 We were indeed buried with him through baptism into death, so that, just as Christ was raised from the dead by the glory of the Father, we too might live in newness of life.[c]

5 For if we have grown into union with him through a death like his, we shall also be united with him in the resurrection.[d] 6 We know that our old self was crucified with him, so that our sinful body might be done away with, that we might no longer be in slavery to sin.[e] 7 For a dead person has been absolved from sin. 8 If, then, we have died with Christ, we believe that we shall also live with him.[f] 9 We know that Christ, raised from the dead, dies no more; death no longer has power over him.[g] 10 As to his death, he died to sin once and for all; as to his life, he lives for God.[h] 11 Consequently, you too must think of yourselves as [being] dead to sin and living for God in Christ Jesus.[i]

12* Therefore, sin must not reign over your mortal bodies so that you obey their desires.[j] 13 And do not present the parts of your bodies to sin as weapons for wickedness, but present yourselves to God as raised from the dead to life and the parts of your bodies to God as weapons for righteousness.[k] 14 For sin is not to have any power over you, since you are not under the law but under grace.[l]

15 What then? Shall we sin because we are not under the law but under grace? Of course not![m] 16 Do you not know that if you present yourselves to someone as obedient slaves,[n] you are slaves of the one you obey, either of sin, which leads to death, or of obedience, which leads to righteousness?[o] 17 But thanks be to God that, although you were once slaves of sin, you have become obedient from the heart to the pattern of teaching to which you were entrusted.* 18 Freed from sin, you have become slaves of righteousness. 19 I am speaking in human terms because of the weakness of your nature. For just as you presented the parts of your bodies as slaves to impurity and to lawlessness for lawlessness, so now present them as slaves to righteousness for sanctification. 20[p] For when you were slaves of sin, you were free from righteousness.* 21 But what profit did you get then from the things of which you are now ashamed? For the end of those things is death.[q] 22 But now that you have been freed from sin and have become slaves of God, the benefit that you have leads to sanctification,*

**6:1–11** To defend the gospel against the charge that it promotes moral laxity (cf. Rom 3:5–8), Paul expresses himself in the typical style of spirited diatribe. God's display of generosity or grace is not evoked by sin but, as stated in Rom 5:8 is the expression of God's love, and this love pledges eternal life to all believers (Rom 5:21). Paul views the present conduct of the believers from the perspective of God's completed salvation when the body is resurrected and directed totally by the holy Spirit. Through baptism believers share the death of Christ and thereby escape from the grip of sin. Through the resurrection of Christ the power to live anew becomes reality for them, but the fullness of participation in Christ's resurrection still lies in the future. But life that is lived in dedication to God now is part and parcel of that future. Hence anyone who sincerely claims to be interested in that future will scarcely be able to say, "Let us sin so that grace may prosper" (cf. Rom 6:1).

**6:12–19** Christians have been released from the grip of sin, but sin endeavors to reclaim its victims. The antidote is constant remembrance that divine grace has claimed them and identifies them as people who are alive only for God's interests.

**6:17** In contrast to humanity, which was handed over to self-indulgence (Rom 1:24–32), believers are **entrusted** ("handed over") to God's **pattern of teaching**, that is, the new life God aims to develop in Christians through the productivity of the holy Spirit. Throughout this passage Paul uses the slave-master model in order to emphasize the fact that one cannot give allegiance to both God and sin.

**6:20 You were free from righteousness**: expressed ironically, for such freedom is really tyranny. The commercial metaphors in Rom 6:21–23 add up only one way: sin is a bad bargain.

**6:22 Sanctification**: or holiness.

*z:* 3:5–8. *a:* 1 Pt 4:1. *b:* Gal 3:27. *c:* Col 2:12; 1 Pt 3:21–22. *d:* Phil 3:10–11; 2 Tm 2:11. *e:* Gal 5:24; 6:14; Eph 4:22–23. *f:* 1 Thes 4:17. *g:* Acts 13:34; 1 Cor 15:26; 2 Tm 1:10; Rev 1:18. *h:* Heb 9:26–28; 1 Pt 3:18. *i:* 2 Cor 5:15; 1 Pt 2:24. *j:* Gn 4:7. *k:* 12:1; Eph 2:5; 5:14 / Col 3:5. *l:* Gal 5:18; 1 Jn 3:6. *m:* 5:17, 21. *n:* Jn 8:32–36. *o:* Jn 8:31–34; 2 Pt 2:19. *p:* Jn 8:34. *q:* 8:6, 13; Prv 12:28; Ez 16:61, 63.

and its end is eternal life.[r] 23 For the wages of sin is death, but the gift of God is eternal life in Christ Jesus our Lord.[s]

## CHAPTER 7

See RG 359

***Freedom from the Law.*** * 1 Are you unaware, brothers (for I am speaking to people who know the law), that the law has jurisdiction over one as long as one lives? 2 Thus a married woman is bound by law to her living husband; but if her husband dies, she is released from the law in respect to her husband.[t] 3 Consequently, while her husband is alive she will be called an adulteress if she consorts with another man. But if her husband dies she is free from that law, and she is not an adulteress if she consorts with another man.

4 In the same way, my brothers, you also were put to death to the law through the body of Christ, so that you might belong to another, to the one who was raised from the dead in order that we might bear fruit for God. 5 For when we were in the flesh, our sinful passions, awakened by the law, worked in our members to bear fruit for death.[u] 6 But now we are released from the law, dead to what held us captive, so that we may serve in the newness of the spirit and not under the obsolete letter.[v]

***Acquaintance with Sin Through the Law.*** 7* What then can we say? That the law is sin? Of course not!* Yet I did not know sin except through the law, and I did not know what it is to covet except that the law said, "You shall not covet."[w] 8 But sin, finding an opportunity in the commandment, produced in me every kind of covetousness. Apart from the law sin is dead.[x] 9 I once lived outside the law, but when the commandment came, sin became alive; 10 then I died, and the commandment that was for life turned out to be death for me.[y] 11 For sin, seizing an opportunity in the commandment, deceived me and through it put me to death.[z] 12 So then the law is holy, and the commandment is holy and righteous and good.[a]

***Sin and Death.*** * 13 Did the good, then, become death for me? Of course not! Sin, in order that it might be shown to be sin, worked death in me through the good, so that sin might become sinful beyond measure through the commandment.[b] 14 We know that the law is spiritual; but I am carnal, sold into slavery to sin.[c] 15 What I do, I do not understand. For I do not do what I want, but I do what I hate. 16 Now if I do what I do not want, I concur that the law is good. 17 So now it is no longer I who do it, but sin that dwells in me. 18 For I know that good does not dwell in me, that is, in my flesh. The willing is ready at hand, but doing the good is not.[d] 19 For I do not do the good I want, but I do the evil I do not want. 20 Now if [I] do what I do not want, it is no longer I who do it, but sin that dwells in me. 21 So, then, I discover the principle that when I want to do right, evil is at hand. 22 For I take delight in the law of God, in my inner self, 23[e] but I see in my members another principle at war with the law of my mind, taking me captive to the law

**7:1–6** Paul reflects on the fact that Christians have a different understanding of the law because of their faith in Christ. Law binds the living, not the dead, as exemplified in marriage, which binds in life but is dissolved through death. Similarly, Christians who through baptism have died with Christ to sin (cf. Rom 6:2–4) are freed from the law that occasioned transgressions, which in turn were productive of death. Now that Christians are joined to Christ, the power of Christ's resurrection makes it possible for them to bear the fruit of newness of life for God.

**7:7–25** In this passage Paul uses the first person singular in the style of diatribe for the sake of argument. He aims to depict the disastrous consequences when a Christian reintroduces the law as a means to attain the objective of holiness pronounced in Rom 6:22.

**7:7–12** The apostle defends himself against the charge of identifying the law with sin. Sin does not exist in law but in human beings, whose sinful inclinations are not overcome by the proclamation of law.

**7:13–25** Far from improving the sinner, law encourages sin to expose itself in transgressions or violations of specific commandments (see Rom 1:24; 5:20). Thus persons who do not experience the justifying grace of God, and Christians who revert to dependence on law as the criterion for their relationship with God, will recognize a rift between their reasoned desire for the goodness of the law and their actual performance that is contrary to the law. Unable to free themselves from the slavery of sin and the power of death, they can only be rescued from defeat in the conflict by the power of God's grace working through Jesus Christ.

**7:23** As in Rom 3:27, Paul plays on the term **law**, which in Greek can connote custom, system, or **principle**.

*r:* 1 Pt 1:9. *s:* Gn 2:17; Gal 6:7–9; Jas 1:15. *t:* 1 Cor 7:39. *u:* 6:21; 8:6, 13. *v:* 8:2; 2 Cor 3:6. *w:* 3:20; Ex 20:17; Dt 5:21. *x:* 5:13, 20; 1 Cor 15:56 / Rom 4:15. *y:* Lv 18:5. *z:* Gn 3:13; Heb 3:13. *a:* 1 Tm 1:8. *b:* 4:15; 5:20. *c:* 8:7–8; Ps 51:7. *d:* Gn 6:5; 8:21; Phil 2:13. *e:* Gal 5:17; 1 Pt 2:11.

of sin that dwells in my members.* 24 Miserable one that I am! Who will deliver me from this mortal body? 25 Thanks be to God through Jesus Christ our Lord. Therefore, I myself, with my mind, serve the law of God but, with my flesh, the law of sin.[f]

## CHAPTER 8

See RG 359–60

***The Flesh and the Spirit.**** 1 Hence, now there is no condemnation for those who are in Christ Jesus. 2 For the law of the spirit of life in Christ Jesus has freed you from the law of sin and death.[g] 3 For what the law, weakened by the flesh, was powerless to do, this God has done: by sending his own Son in the likeness of sinful flesh and for the sake of sin, he condemned sin in the flesh,[h] 4 so that the righteous decree of the law might be fulfilled in us, who live not according to the flesh but according to the spirit.[i] 5 For those who live according to the flesh are concerned with the things of the flesh, but those who live according to the spirit with the things of the spirit. 6 The concern of the flesh is death, but the concern of the spirit is life and peace.[j] 7 For the concern of the flesh is hostility toward God; it does not submit to the law of God, nor can it;[k] 8 and those who are in the flesh cannot please God.[l] 9 But you are not in the flesh; on the contrary, you are in the spirit, if only the Spirit of God dwells in you. Whoever does not have the Spirit of Christ does not belong to him.[m] 10 But if Christ is in you, although the body is dead because of sin, the spirit is alive because of righteousness.[n] 11 If the Spirit of the one who raised Jesus from the dead dwells in you, the one who raised Christ from the dead will give life to your mortal bodies also, through his Spirit that dwells in you. 12 Consequently, brothers, we are not debtors to the flesh, to live according to the flesh. 13 For if you live according to the flesh, you will die, but if by the spirit you put to death the deeds of the body, you will live.[o]

***Children of God Through Adoption.**** 14 For those who are led by the Spirit of God are children of God.[p] 15 For you did not receive a spirit of slavery to fall back into fear, but you received a spirit of adoption, through which we cry, "Abba,* Father!"[q] 16 The Spirit itself bears witness with our spirit that we are children of God,[r] 17 and if children, then heirs, heirs of God and joint heirs with Christ, if only we suffer with him so that we may also be glorified with him.[s]

***Destiny of Glory.**** 18 I consider that the sufferings of this present time are as nothing compared with the glory to be revealed for us.[t] 19 For creation awaits with eager expectation the revelation of the children of God; 20 for creation was made subject to futility, not of its own accord but because of the one who subjected it,[u] in hope 21 that creation it-

**8:1–13** After his warning in Rom 7 against the wrong route to fulfillment of the objective of holiness expressed in Rom 6:22, Paul points his addressees to the correct way. Through the redemptive work of Christ, Christians have been liberated from the terrible forces of sin and death. Holiness was impossible so long as the **flesh** (or our "old self"), that is, self-interested hostility toward God (Rom 8:7), frustrated the divine objectives expressed in the law. What is worse, sin used the law to break forth into all manner of lawlessness (Rom 8:8). All this is now changed. At the cross God broke the power of sin and pronounced sentence on it (Rom 8:3). Christians still retain the flesh, but it is alien to their new being, which is life in the spirit, namely the new self, governed by the holy Spirit. Under the direction of the holy Spirit Christians are able to fulfill the divine will that formerly found expression in the law (Rom 8:4). The same Spirit who enlivens Christians for holiness will also resurrect their bodies at the last day (Rom 8:11). Christian life is therefore the experience of a constant challenge to put to death the evil deeds of the body through life of the spirit (Rom 8:13).

**8:14–17** Christians, by reason of the Spirit's presence within them, enjoy not only new life but also a new relationship to God, that of adopted children and heirs through Christ, whose sufferings and glory they share.

**8:15 Abba**: see note on Mk 14:36.

**8:18–27** The glory that believers are destined to share with Christ far exceeds the sufferings of the present life. Paul considers the destiny of the created world to be linked with the future that belongs to the believers. As it shares in the penalty of corruption brought about by sin, so also will it share in the benefits of redemption and future glory that comprise the ultimate liberation of God's people (Rom 8:19–22). After patient endurance in steadfast expectation, the full harvest of the Spirit's presence will be realized. On earth believers enjoy the first-fruits, i.e., the Spirit, as a guarantee of the total liberation of their bodies from the influence of the rebellious old self (Rom 8:23).

*f:* 1 Cor 15:57. *g:* 7:23–24; 2 Cor 3:17. *h:* Acts 13:38; 15:10 / Jn 3:16–17; 2 Cor 5:21; Gal 3:13; 4:4; Phil 2:7; Col 1:22; Heb 2:17; 4:15; 1 Jn 4:9. *i:* Gal 5:16–25. *j:* 6:21; 7:5; 8:13; Gal 6:8. *k:* 5:10; Jas 4:4. *l:* 1 Jn 2:16. *m:* 1 Cor 3:16. *n:* Gal 2:20; 1 Pt 4:6. *o:* Gal 5:24; 6:8; Eph 4:22–24. *p:* Gal 5:18. *q:* Mk 14:36; Gal 4:5–6; 2 Tm 1:7. *r:* Jn 1:12; Gal 3:26–29. *s:* Gal 4:7; 1 Pt 4:13; 5:1. *t:* 2 Cor 4:17. *u:* Gn 3:17–19. *v:* 2 Pt 3:12–13; Rev 21:1.

self would be set free from slavery to corruption and share in the glorious freedom of the children of God.[v] 22 We know that all creation is groaning in labor pains even until now;[w] 23 and not only that, but we ourselves, who have the firstfruits of the Spirit, we also groan within ourselves as we wait for adoption, the redemption of our bodies.[x] 24 For in hope we were saved. Now hope that sees for itself is not hope. For who hopes for what one sees?[y] 25 But if we hope for what we do not see, we wait with endurance.

26 In the same way, the Spirit too comes to the aid of our weakness; for we do not know how to pray as we ought, but the Spirit itself intercedes with inexpressible groanings. 27 And the one who searches hearts knows what is the intention of the Spirit, because it intercedes for the holy ones according to God's will.[z]

***God's Indomitable Love in Christ.*** 28* We know that all things work for good for those who love God,* who are called according to his purpose.[a] 29* For those he foreknew he also predestined to be conformed to the image of his Son, so that he might be the firstborn among many brothers.[b] 30 And those he predestined he also called; and those he called he also justified; and those he justified he also glorified.[c]

31* What then shall we say to this? If God is for us, who can be against us?[d] 32 He who did not spare his own Son but handed him over for us all, how will he not also give us everything else along with him?[e] 33 Who will bring a charge against God's chosen ones? It is God who acquits us.[f] 34 Who will condemn? It is Christ [Jesus] who died, rather, was raised, who also is at the right hand of God, who indeed intercedes for us.[g] 35 What will separate us from the love of Christ? Will anguish, or distress, or persecution, or famine, or nakedness, or peril, or the sword? 36 As it is written:[h]

"For your sake we are being slain all the day;
we are looked upon as sheep to be slaughtered."

37 No, in all these things we conquer overwhelmingly through him who loved us.[i] 38 For I am convinced that neither death, nor life, nor angels, nor principalities, nor present things,* nor future things, nor powers,[j] 39 nor height, nor depth,* nor any other creature will be able to separate us from the love of God in Christ Jesus our Lord.

# V. Jews and Gentiles in God's Plan*

## CHAPTER 9

See RG 360–61

***Paul's Love for Israel.**** 1 I speak the truth in Christ, I do not lie; my conscience joins with the holy Spirit in bearing me witness[k] 2 that I

**8:28–30** These verses outline the Christian vocation as it was designed by God: **to be conformed to the image of his Son**, who is to **be the firstborn among many brothers** (Rom 8:29). God's redemptive action on behalf of the believers has been in process before the beginning of the world. Those whom God chooses are **those he foreknew** (Rom 8:29) or elected. Those who are **called** (Rom 8:30) are **predestined** or predetermined. These expressions do not mean that God is arbitrary. Rather, Paul uses them to emphasize the thought and care that God has taken for the Christian's salvation.

**8:28 We know that all things work for good for those who love God**: a few ancient authorities have God as the subject of the verb, and some translators render: "We know that God makes everything work for good for those who love God . . . ."

**8:29 Image**: while man and woman were originally created in God's image (Gn 1:26–27), it is through baptism into Christ, the image of God (2 Cor 4:4; Col 1:15), that we are renewed according to the image of the Creator (Col 3:10).

**8:31–39** The all-conquering power of God's love has overcome every obstacle to Christians' salvation and every threat to separate them from God. That power manifested itself fully when God's own Son was delivered up to death for their salvation. Through him Christians can overcome all their afflictions and trials.

**8:38 Present things** and **future things** may refer to astrological data. Paul appears to be saying that the gospel liberates believers from dependence on astrologers.

**8:39 Height, depth** may refer to positions in the zodiac, positions of heavenly bodies relative to the horizon. In astrological documents the term for "height" means "exaltation" or the position of greatest influence exerted by a planet. Since hostile spirits were associated with the planets and stars, Paul includes **powers** (Rom 8:38) in his list of malevolent forces.

**9:1–11:36** Israel's unbelief and its rejection of Jesus as sav-

*w:* 2 Cor 5:2–5. *x:* 2 Cor 1:22; Gal 5:5. *y:* 2 Cor 5:7; Heb 11:1. *z:* Ps 139:1; 1 Cor 4:5. *a:* Eph 1:4–14; 3:11. *b:* Eph 1:5; 1 Pt 1:2. *c:* Is 45:25; 2 Thes 2:13–14. *d:* Ps 118:6; Heb 13:6. *e:* Jn 3:16. *f:* Is 50:8. *g:* Ps 110:1; Heb 7:25; 1 Jn 2:1. *h:* Ps 44:23; 1 Cor 4:9; 15:30; 2 Cor 4:11; 2 Tm 3:12. *i:* 1 Jn 5:4. *j:* 1 Cor 3:22; Eph 1:21; 1 Pt 3:22. *k:* 2 Cor 11:31; 1 Tm 2:7.

have great sorrow and constant anguish in my heart. 3For I could wish that I myself were accursed and separated from Christ for the sake of my brothers, my kin according to the flesh.[l] 4They are Israelites; theirs the adoption, the glory, the covenants, the giving of the law, the worship, and the promises;[m] 5theirs the patriarchs, and from them, according to the flesh, is the Messiah. God who is over all* be blessed forever. Amen.[n]

*God's Free Choice.* 6But it is not that the word of God has failed. For not all who are of Israel are Israel,[o] 7nor are they all children of Abraham because they are his descendants; but "It is through Isaac that descendants shall bear your name."[p] 8This means that it is not the children of the flesh who are the children of God, but the children of the promise are counted as descendants.[q] 9For this is the wording of the promise, "About this time I shall return and Sarah will have a son."[r] 10And not only that,[s] but also when Rebecca had conceived children by one husband, our father Isaac*— 11before they had yet been born or had done anything, good or bad, in order that God's elective plan might continue, 12not by works but by his call— she was told, "The older shall serve the younger."[t] 13As it is written:[u]

"I loved Jacob
but hated Esau."*

14* What then are we to say? Is there injustice on the part of God? Of course not![v] 15For he says to Moses:

"I will show mercy to whom I will,
I will take pity on whom I will."[w]

16So it depends not upon a person's will or exertion, but upon God, who shows mercy.[x] 17For the scripture says to Pharaoh, "This is why I have raised you up, to show my power through you that my name may be proclaimed throughout the earth."[y] 18Consequently, he has mercy upon whom he wills,[z] and he hardens whom he wills.*

19* You will say to me then, "Why [then] does he still find fault? For who can oppose his will?"[a] 20But who indeed are you, a human being, to talk back to God?[b] Will what

ior astonished and puzzled Christians. It constituted a serious problem for them in view of God's specific preparation of Israel for the advent of the Messiah. Paul addresses himself here to the essential question of how the divine plan could be frustrated by Israel's unbelief. At the same time, he discourages both complacency and anxiety on the part of Gentiles. To those who might boast of their superior advantage over Jews, he warns that their enjoyment of the blessings assigned to Israel can be terminated. To those who might anxiously ask, "How can we be sure that Israel's fate will not be ours?" he replies that only unbelief can deprive one of salvation.

**9:1–5** The apostle speaks in strong terms of the depth of his grief over the unbelief of his own people. He would willingly undergo a curse himself for the sake of their coming to the knowledge of Christ (Rom 9:3; cf. Lv 27:28–29). His love for them derives from God's continuing choice of them and from the spiritual benefits that God bestows on them and through them on all of humanity (Rom 9:4–5).

**9:5** Some editors punctuate this verse differently and prefer the translation, "Of whom is Christ according to the flesh, who is God over all." However, Paul's point is that God **who is over all** aimed to use Israel, which had been entrusted with every privilege, in outreach to the entire world through the Messiah.

**9:10 Children by one husband, our father Isaac**: Abraham had two children, Ishmael and Isaac, by two wives, Hagar and Sarah, respectively. In that instance Isaac, although born later than Ishmael, became the bearer of the messianic promise. In the case of twins born to Rebecca, God's elective procedure is seen even more dramatically, and again the younger, contrary to Semitic custom, is given the preference.

**9:13** The literal rendering, **"Jacob I loved, but Esau I hated,"** suggests an attitude of divine hostility that is not implied in Paul's statement. In Semitic usage "hate" means to love less; cf. Lk 14:26 with Mt 10:37. Israel's unbelief reflects the mystery of the divine election that is always operative within it. Mere natural descent from Abraham does not ensure the full possession of the divine gifts; it is God's sovereign prerogative to bestow this fullness upon, or to withhold it from, whomsoever he wishes; cf. Mt 3:9; Jn 8:39. The choice of Jacob over Esau is a case in point.

**9:14–18** The principle of divine election does not invite Christians to theoretical inquiry concerning the nonelected, nor does this principle mean that God is unfair in his dealings with humanity. The instruction concerning divine election is a part of the gospel and reveals that the gift of faith is the enactment of God's mercy (Rom 9:16). God raised up Moses to display that mercy, and Pharaoh to display divine severity in punishing those who obstinately oppose their Creator.

**9:18** The basic biblical principle is: those who will not see or hear *shall* not see or hear. On the other hand, the same God who thus makes stubborn or hardens the heart can reconstruct it through the work of the holy Spirit.

**9:19–29** The apostle responds to the objection that if God rules over faith through the principle of divine election, God

*l:* Ex 32:32. *m:* 3:2; Ex 4:22; Dt 7:6; 14:1–2. *n:* Mt 1:1–16; Lk 3:23–38 / Rom 1:25; Ps 41:14. *o:* Nm 23:19 / Mt 3:9. *p:* Gn 21:12; Gal 3:29. *q:* Gal 4:23, 28. *r:* Gn 18:10, 14. *s:* Gn 25:21. *t:* 11:5–6 / Gn 25:23–24. *u:* Mal 1:3. *v:* Dt 32:4. *w:* Ex 33:19. *x:* Eph 2:8; Ti 3:5. *y:* Ex 9:16. *z:* 11:30–32; Ex 4:21; 7:3. *a:* 3:7; Wis 12:12. *b:* Wis 15:7; Is 29:16; 45:9; Jer 18:6.

is made say to its maker, "Why have you
created me so?" 21Or does not the potter
have a right over the clay, to make out of the
same lump one vessel for a noble purpose
and another for an ignoble one? 22What if
God, wishing to show his wrath and make
known his power, has endured with much
patience the vessels of wrath made for destruction?[c] 23This was to make known the
riches of his glory to the vessels of mercy,
which he has prepared previously for glory,
24namely, us whom he has called, not only
from the Jews but also from the Gentiles.

***Witness of the Prophets.*** 25As indeed he
says in Hosea:

"Those who were not my people I will
call 'my people,'
and her who was not beloved* I will
call 'beloved.'"[d]
26 And in the very place where it was said
to them, 'You are not my people,'
there they shall be called children of
the living God."[e]

27[f] And Isaiah cries out concerning Israel,
"Though the number of the Israelites were
like the sand of the sea, only a remnant will
be saved; 28for decisively and quickly will
the Lord execute sentence upon the earth."
29And as Isaiah predicted:

"Unless the Lord of hosts had left us
descendants,
we would have become like Sodom
and have been made like Gomorrah."[g]

***Righteousness Based on Faith.**** 30What then
shall we say? That Gentiles, who did not pursue righteousness, have achieved it, that is,
righteousness that comes from faith;[h] 31but that
Israel, who pursued the law of righteousness,
did not attain to that law?[i] 32Why not? Because
they did it not by faith, but as if it could be done
by works.[j] They stumbled over the stone that
causes stumbling,* 33as it is written:

"Behold, I am laying a stone in Zion
that will make people stumble
and a rock that will make them fall,
and whoever believes in him shall not be
put to shame."[k]

## CHAPTER 10

See RG 360–61

1* Brothers, my heart's desire and
prayer to God on their behalf is for salvation.[l] 2I testify with regard to them that they
have zeal for God, but it is not discerning.[m]
3For, in their unawareness of the righteousness that comes from God and their attempt
to establish their own [righteousness], they
did not submit to the righteousness of God.[n]
4For Christ is the end* of the law for the justification of everyone who has faith.[o]

cannot then accuse unbelievers of sin (Rom 9:19). For Paul, this objection is in the last analysis a manifestation of human insolence, and his "answer" is less an explanation of God's ways than the rejection of an argument that places humanity on a level with God. At the same time, Paul shows that God is far less arbitrary than appearances suggest, for God endures **with much patience** (Rom 9:22) a person like the Pharaoh of the Exodus.

**9:25 Beloved**: in Semitic discourse means "preferred" or "favorite" (cf. Rom 9:13). See Hos 2:1.

**9:30–33** In the conversion of the Gentiles and, by contrast, of relatively few Jews, the Old Testament prophecies are seen to be fulfilled; cf. Rom 9:25–29. Israel feared that the doctrine of justification through faith would jeopardize the validity of the Mosaic law, and so they never reached their goal of righteousness that they had sought to attain through meticulous observance of the law (Rom 9:31). Since Gentiles, including especially Greeks and Romans, had a great regard for righteousness, Paul's statement concerning Gentiles in Rom 9:30 is to be understood from a Jewish perspective: quite evidently they had not been interested in "God's" righteousness, for it had not been revealed to them; but now in response to the proclamation of the gospel they respond in faith.

**9:32** Paul discusses Israel as a whole from the perspective of contemporary Jewish rejection of Jesus as Messiah. The Old Testament and much of Jewish noncanonical literature in fact reflect a fervent faith in divine mercy.

**10:1–13** Despite Israel's lack of faith in God's act in Christ, Paul does not abandon hope for her salvation (Rom 10:1). However, Israel must recognize that the Messiah's arrival in the person of Jesus Christ means the termination of the Mosaic law as the criterion for understanding oneself in a valid relationship to God. Faith in God's saving action in Jesus Christ takes precedence over any such legal claim (Rom 10:6).

**10:4** The Mosaic legislation has been superseded by God's action in Jesus Christ. Others understand end here in the sense that Christ is the goal of the law, i.e., the true meaning of the Mosaic law, which cannot be correctly understood apart from him. Still others believe that both meanings are intended.

*c:* 2:4; Wis 12:20–21; Jer 50:25. *d:* Hos 2:25. *e:* Hos 2:1. *f:* Is 10:22–23; Hos 2:1 / Rom 11:5 / Is 28:22. *g:* Is 1:9; Mt 10:15. *h:* 10:4, 20. *i:* 10:3. *j:* Is 8:14. *k:* Is 28:16; 1 Pt 2:6–8. *l:* 9:1, 3. *m:* Acts 22:3. *n:* 9:31–32; Phil 3:9. *o:* Acts 13:38–39; 2 Cor 3:14; Heb 8:13.

5* Moses writes about the righteousness that comes from [the] law, "The one who does these things will live by them."[p] 6 But the righteousness that comes from faith says,[q] "Do not say in your heart, 'Who will go up into heaven?' (that is, to bring Christ down) 7* or 'Who will go down into the abyss?' (that is, to bring Christ up from the dead)."[r] 8 But what does it say?

"The word is near you,
in your mouth and in your heart"[s]

(that is, the word of faith that we preach), 9 for, if you confess* with your mouth that Jesus is Lord and believe in your heart that God raised him from the dead, you will be saved.[t] 10 For one believes with the heart and so is justified, and one confesses with the mouth and so is saved. 11 For the scripture says, "No one who believes in him will be put to shame."[u] 12 For there is no distinction between Jew and Greek; the same Lord is Lord of all, enriching all who call upon him.[v] 13 For "everyone who calls on the name of the Lord will be saved."[w]

14* But how can they call on him in whom they have not believed? And how can they believe in him of whom they have not heard? And how can they hear without someone to preach?[x] 15 And how can people preach unless they are sent? As it is written,[y] "How beautiful are the feet of those who bring [the] good news!"* 16 But not everyone has heeded the good news; for Isaiah says, "Lord, who has believed what was heard from us?"[z] 17 Thus faith comes from what is heard, and what is heard comes through the word of Christ.[a] 18 But I ask, did they not hear? Certainly they did; for

"Their voice has gone forth to all the earth,
and their words to the ends of the world."[b]

19 But I ask, did not Israel understand?[c] First Moses says:

"I will make you jealous of those who are not a nation;
with a senseless nation I will make you angry."

20d Then Isaiah speaks boldly and says:

"I was found [by] those who were not seeking me;
I revealed myself to those who were not asking for me."

21 But regarding Israel he says, "All day long I stretched out my hands to a disobedient and contentious people."

## CHAPTER 11

See RG 360–61

*The Remnant of Israel.** 1 I ask, then, has God rejected his people? Of course not![e] For I too am an Israelite, a descendant of Abraham, of the tribe of Benjamin.[f] 2 God has not rejected his people whom he foreknew. Do you not know what the scripture says about Elijah, how he pleads with God against Israel? 3 "Lord, they have killed

**10:5–6** The subject of the verb **says** (Rom 10:6) is **righteousness** personified. Both of the statements in Rom 10:5, 6 derive from Moses, but Paul wishes to contrast the language of law and the language of faith.

**10:7** Here Paul blends Dt 30:13 and Ps 107:26.

**10:9–11** To confess Jesus as Lord was frequently quite hazardous in the first century (cf. Mt 10:18; 1 Thes 2:2; 1 Pt 2:18–21; 3:14). For a Jew it could mean disruption of normal familial and other social relationships, including great economic sacrifice. In the face of penalties imposed by the secular world, Christians are assured that **no one who believes in** Jesus **will be put to shame** (Rom 10:11).

**10:14–21** The gospel has been sufficiently proclaimed to Israel, and Israel has adequately understood God's plan for the messianic age, which would see the gospel brought to the uttermost parts of the earth. As often in the past, Israel has not accepted the prophetic message; cf. Acts 7:51–53.

**10:15 How beautiful are the feet of those who bring [the] good news**: in Semitic fashion, the parts of the body that bring the messenger with welcome news are praised; cf. Lk 11:27.

**11:1–10** Although Israel has been unfaithful to the prophetic message of the gospel (Rom 10:14–21), God remains faithful to Israel. Proof of the divine fidelity lies in the existence of Jewish Christians like Paul himself. The unbelieving Jews, says Paul, have been blinded by the Christian teaching concerning the Messiah.

*p:* Lv 18:5; Gal 3:12. *q:* Dt 9:4; 30:12. *r:* Dt 30:13; 1 Pt 3:19. *s:* Dt 30:14. *t:* 1 Cor 12:3. *u:* 9:33; Is 28:16. *v:* 1:16; 3:22, 29; Acts 10:34; 15:9, 11; Gal 3:28; Eph 2:14. *w:* Jl 3:5; Acts 2:21. *x:* Acts 8:31. *y:* Is 52:7; Na 2:1; Eph 6:15. *z:* Is 53:1; Jn 12:38. *a:* Jn 17:20. *b:* Ps 19:5; Mt 24:14. *c:* 11:11, 14; Dt 32:21. *d:* 9:30; Is 65:1–2. *e:* 1 Sm 12:22; Ps 94:14. *f:* 2 Cor 11:22; Phil 3:5. *g:* 1 Kgs 19:10, 14.

your prophets, they have torn down your altars, and I alone am left, and they are seeking my life.”[g] 4 But what is God’s response to him? “I have left for myself seven thousand men who have not knelt to Baal.”[h] 5 So also at the present time there is a remnant, chosen by grace.[i] 6 But if by grace, it is no longer because of works; otherwise grace would no longer be grace.[j] 7 What then? What Israel was seeking it did not attain, but the elect attained it; the rest were hardened,[k] 8 as it is written:

“God gave them a spirit of deep sleep,
eyes that should not see
and ears that should not hear,
down to this very day.”[l]

9 And David says:[m]

“Let their table become a snare and a trap,
a stumbling block and a retribution for them;
10 let their eyes grow dim so that they may not see,
and keep their backs bent forever.”

***The Gentiles’ Salvation.*** 11* Hence I ask, did they stumble so as to fall? Of course not! But through their transgression salvation has come to the Gentiles, so as to make them jealous.[n] 12 Now if their transgression is enrichment for the world, and if their diminished number is enrichment for the Gentiles, how much more their full number.

13 Now I am speaking to you Gentiles. Inasmuch then as I am the apostle to the Gentiles, I glory in my ministry[o] 14 in order to make my race jealous and thus save some of them. 15 For if their rejection is the reconciliation of the world, what will their acceptance be but life from the dead? 16* If the firstfruits are holy, so is the whole batch of dough; and if the root is holy, so are the branches.[p]

17 But if some of the branches were broken off, and you, a wild olive shoot, were grafted in their place and have come to share in the rich root of the olive tree,[q] 18 do not boast against the branches. If you do boast, consider that you do not support the root; the root supports you.[r] 19 Indeed you will say, “Branches were broken off so that I might be grafted in.” 20 That is so. They were broken off because of unbelief, but you are there because of faith. So do not become haughty, but stand in awe.[s] 21 For if God did not spare the natural branches, [perhaps] he will not spare you either.[t] 22 See, then, the kindness and severity of God: severity toward those who fell, but God’s kindness to you, provided you remain in his kindness; otherwise you too will be cut off.[u] 23 And they also, if they do not remain in unbelief, will be grafted in, for God is able to graft them in again.[v] 24 For if you were cut from what is by nature a wild olive tree, and grafted, contrary to nature, into a cultivated one, how much more will they who belong to it by nature be grafted back into their own olive tree.

***God’s Irrevocable Call.**** 25 I do not want you to be unaware of this mystery, brothers, so that you will not become wise [in] your own estimation: a hardening has come upon Israel in part, until the full number of the Gentiles comes in,[w] 26 and thus all Israel will be saved,[x] as it is written:[y]

**11:11–15** The unbelief of the Jews has paved the way for the preaching of the gospel to the Gentiles and for their easier acceptance of it outside the context of Jewish culture. Through his mission to the Gentiles Paul also hopes to fill his fellow Jews with jealousy. Hence he hastens to fill the entire Mediterranean world with the gospel. Once all the Gentile nations have heard the gospel, Israel as a whole is expected to embrace it. This will be tantamount to resurrection of the dead, that is, the reappearance of Jesus Christ with all the believers at the end of time.

**11:16–24** Israel remains holy in the eyes of God and stands as a witness to the faith described in the Old Testament because of **the firstfruits** (or the first piece baked) (Rom 11:16), that is, the converted remnant, and **the root** that **is holy**, that is, the patriarchs (Rom 11:16). The Jews’ failure to believe in Christ is a warning to Gentile Christians to be on guard against any semblance of anti-Jewish arrogance, that is, failure to recognize their total dependence on divine grace.

**11:25–29** In God’s design, Israel’s unbelief is being used to grant the light of faith to the Gentiles. Meanwhile, Israel remains dear to God (cf. Rom 9:13), still the object of special providence, the mystery of which will one day be revealed.

*h:* 1 Kgs 19:18. *i:* 9:27. *j:* 4:4; Gal 3:18. *k:* 9:31. *l:* Dt 29:3; Is 29:10; Mt 13:13–15; Acts 28:26–27. *m:* Ps 69:23–24; 35:8. *n:* Acts 13:46; 18:6; 28:28 / Rom 10:19; Dt 32:21. *o:* 1:5. *p:* Nm 15:17–21; Ez 44:30; Neh 10:36–38. *q:* Eph 2:11–19. *r:* 1 Cor 1:31. *s:* 12:16. *t:* 1 Cor 10:12. *u:* Jn 15:2, 4; Heb 3:14. *v:* 2 Cor 3:16. *w:* Prv 3:7 / Rom 12:16; Mk 13:10; Lk 21:24; Jn 10:16. *x:* Ps 14:7; Is 59:20–21. *y:* Mt 23:39.

"The deliverer will come out of Zion,
he will turn away godlessness from
Jacob;
27 and this is my covenant with them
when I take away their sins."[z]

28 In respect to the gospel, they are enemies
on your account; but in respect to election,
they are beloved because of the patriarchs.[a]
29 For the gifts and the call of God are irrevocable.[b]
***Triumph of God's Mercy.*** 30* Just as you
once disobeyed God but have now received
mercy because of their disobedience, 31 so
they have now disobeyed in order that, by
virtue of the mercy shown to you, they too
may [now] receive mercy. 32 For God delivered all to disobedience, that he might have
mercy upon all.[c]
33* Oh, the depth of the riches and wisdom
and knowledge of God! How inscrutable are
his judgments and how unsearchable his
ways![d]

34 "For who has known the mind of the
Lord*
or who has been his counselor?"[e]
35* "Or who has given him anything[f]
that he may be repaid?"

36 For from him and through him and for him
are all things. To him be glory forever.
Amen.[g]

## VI. The Duties of Christians*

### CHAPTER 12

See RG 361

***Sacrifice of Body and Mind.*** 1* I urge
you therefore, brothers, by the mercies of
God, to offer your bodies as a living sacrifice, holy and pleasing to God, your spiritual
worship.[h] 2 Do not conform yourselves to
this age but be transformed by the renewal
of your mind, that you may discern what is
the will of God, what is good and pleasing
and perfect.[i]
***Many Parts in One Body.*** 3[j] For by the
grace given to me I tell everyone among
you not to think of himself more highly
than one ought to think, but to think
soberly, each according to the measure of
faith that God has apportioned. 4[k] For as in
one body we have many parts, and all the
parts do not have the same function, 5 so we,
though many, are one body in Christ* and
individually parts of one another. 6[l] Since
we have gifts that differ according to the
grace given to us, let us exercise them:* if

**11:30–32** Israel, together with the Gentiles who have been handed over to all manner of vices (Rom 1), **has been delivered . . . to disobedience**. The conclusion of Rom 11:32 repeats the thought of Rom 5:20, "Where sin increased, grace overflowed all the more."

**11:33–36** This final reflection celebrates the wisdom of God's plan of salvation. As Paul has indicated throughout these chapters, both Jew and Gentile, despite the religious recalcitrance of each, have received the gift of faith. The methods used by God in making this outreach to the world stagger human comprehension but are at the same time a dazzling invitation to abiding faith.

**11:34** The citation is from the Greek text of Is 40:13. Paul does not explicitly mention Isaiah in this verse, nor Job in Rom 11:35.

**11:35** Paul quotes from an old Greek version of Jb 41:3a, which differs from the Hebrew text (Jb 41:11a).

**12:1–13:14** Since Christ marks the termination of the Mosaic law as the primary source of guidance for God's people (Rom 10:4), the apostle explains how Christians can function, in the light of the gift of justification through faith, in their relation to one another and the state.

**12:1–8** The Mosaic code included elaborate directions on sacrifices and other cultic observances. The gospel, however, invites believers to present their **bodies as a living sacrifice** (Rom 12:1). Instead of being limited by specific legal maxims, Christians are liberated for the exercise of good judgment as they are confronted with the many and varied decisions required in the course of daily life. To assist them, God distributes a variety of gifts to the fellowship of believers, including those of prophecy, teaching, and exhortation (Rom 12:6–8). Prophets assist the community to understand the will of God as it applies to the present situation (Rom 12:6). Teachers help people to understand themselves and their responsibilities in relation to others (Rom 12:7). One who **exhorts** offers encouragement to the community to exercise their faith in the performance of all that is pleasing to God (Rom 12:8). Indeed, this very section, beginning with Rom 12:1, is a specimen of Paul's own style of exhortation.

**12:5 One body in Christ**: on the church as the body of Christ, see 1 Cor 12:12–27.

**12:6** Everyone has some gift that can be used for the benefit of the community. When the instruction on justification through faith is correctly grasped, the possessor of a gift will understand that it is not an instrument of self-aggrandizement. Possession of a gift is not an index to quality of faith. Rather, the gift is a challenge to faithful use.

*z:* Is 27:9; Jer 31:33–34. *a:* 15:8; 1 Thes 2:15–16. *b:* 9:6; Nm 23:19; Is 54:10. *c:* Gal 3:22; 1 Tm 2:4. *d:* Jb 11:7–8; Ps 139:6, 17–18; Wis 17:1; Is 55:8–9. *e:* Jb 15:8; Wis 9:13; Is 40:13; Jer 23:18; 1 Cor 2:11–16. *f:* Jb 41:3; Is 40:14. *g:* 1 Cor 8:6; Col 1:16–17. *h:* 2 Cor 1:3 / Rom 6:13; 1 Pt 2:5. *i:* Eph 4:17, 22–23; 1 Pt 1:14 / Eph 5:10, 17; Phil 1:10. *j:* 15:15 / Phil 2:3 / 1 Cor 12:11; Eph 4:7. *k:* 1 Cor 12:12, 27; Eph 4:25. *l:* 1 Cor 12:4–11, 28–31; Eph 4:7–12; 1 Pt 4:10–11 / 2 Cor 9:7.

prophecy, in proportion to the faith; [7]if ministry, in ministering; if one is a teacher, in teaching; [8]if one exhorts, in exhortation; if one contributes, in generosity; if one is over others,* with diligence; if one does acts of mercy, with cheerfulness.

*Mutual Love.* [9]Let love be sincere; hate what is evil, hold on to what is good;[m] [10]love one another with mutual affection; anticipate one another in showing honor.[n] [11]Do not grow slack in zeal, be fervent in spirit, serve the Lord.[o] [12]Rejoice in hope, endure in affliction, persevere in prayer.[p] [13]Contribute to the needs of the holy ones,[q] exercise hospitality. [14]* Bless those who persecute [you],[r] bless and do not curse them.[s] [15]Rejoice with those who rejoice, weep with those who weep.[t] [16]Have the same regard for one another; do not be haughty but associate with the lowly; do not be wise in your own estimation.[u] [17]Do not repay anyone evil for evil; be concerned for what is noble in the sight of all.[v] [18]If possible, on your part, live at peace with all.[w] [19]Beloved, do not look for revenge but leave room for the wrath; for it is written, "Vengeance is mine, I will repay, says the Lord."[x] [20]Rather, "if your enemy is hungry, feed him; if he is thirsty, give him something to drink; for by so doing you will heap burning coals upon his head."[y] [21]Do not be conquered by evil but conquer evil with good.

## CHAPTER 13

See RG 361

*Obedience in Authority.** [1]Let every person be subordinate to the higher authorities, for there is no authority except from God, and those that exist have been established by God.[z] [2]Therefore, whoever resists authority opposes what God has appointed, and those who oppose it will bring judgment upon themselves. [3]For rulers are not a cause of fear to good conduct, but to evil.[a] Do you wish to have no fear of authority? Then do what is good and you will receive approval from it, [4]for it is a servant of God for your good. But if you do evil, be afraid, for it does not bear the sword without purpose; it is the servant of God to inflict wrath on the evildoer.[b] [5]Therefore, it is necessary to be subject not only because of the wrath but also because of conscience.[c] [6]This is why you also pay taxes, for the authorities are ministers of God, devoting themselves to this very thing. [7]Pay to all their dues, taxes to whom taxes are due, toll to whom toll is due, respect to whom respect is due, honor to whom honor is due.[d]

*Love Fulfills the Law.** [8]Owe nothing to anyone, except to love one another; for the

**12:8 Over others:** usually taken to mean "rule over" but possibly "serve as a patron." Wealthier members in Greco-Roman communities were frequently asked to assist in public service projects. In view of the references to contributing **in generosity** and to **acts of mercy**, Paul may have in mind people like Phoebe (Rom 16:1–2), who is called a **benefactor** (or "patron") because of the services she rendered to many Christians, including Paul.

**12:14–21** Since God has justified the believers, it is not necessary for them to take justice into their own hands by taking vengeance. God will ultimately deal justly with all, including those who inflict injury on the believers. This question of personal rights as a matter of justice prepares the way for more detailed consideration of the state as adjudicator.

**13:1–7** Paul must come to grips with the problem raised by a message that declares people free from the law. How are they to relate to Roman authority? The problem was exacerbated by the fact that imperial protocol was interwoven with devotion to various deities. Paul builds on the traditional instruction exhibited in Wis 6:1–3, according to which kings and magistrates rule by consent of God. From this perspective, then, believers who render obedience to the governing authorities are obeying the one who is highest in command. At the same time, it is recognized that Caesar has the responsibility to make just ordinances and to commend uprightness; cf. Wis 6:4–21. That Caesar is not entitled to obedience when such obedience would nullify God's prior claim to the believers' moral decision becomes clear in the light of the following verses.

**13:8–10** When love directs the Christian's moral decisions, the interest of law in basic concerns, such as familial relationships, sanctity of life, and security of property, is safeguarded (Rom 13:9). Indeed, says Paul, the same applies to any **other commandment** (Rom 13:9), whether one in the Mosaic code or one drawn up by local magistrates under imperial authority. Love anticipates the purpose of public legislation, namely, to secure the best interests of the citizenry. Since Caesar's obligation is to punish the wrongdoer (Rom 13:4), the Christian who acts in love is free from all legitimate indictment.

*m:* 2 Cor 6:6; 1 Tm 1:5; 1 Pt 1:22 / Am 5:15. *n:* Jn 13:34; 1 Thes 4:9; 1 Pt 2:17; 2 Pt 1:7 / Phil 2:3. *o:* Acts 18:25. *p:* 5:2–3; Col 4:2; 1 Thes 5:17. *q:* Heb 13:2; 1 Pt 4:9. *r:* Mt 5:38–48; 1 Cor 4:12; 1 Pt 3:9. *s:* Lk 6:27–28. *t:* Ps 35:13; Sir 7:34; 1 Cor 12:26. *u:* 15:5; Phil 2:2–3 / Rom 11:20; Prv 3:7; Is 5:21. *v:* Prv 3:4; 1 Thes 5:15; 1 Pt 3:9. *w:* Heb 12:14. *x:* Lv 19:18; Dt 32:35, 41; Mt 5:39; 1 Cor 6:6–7; Heb 10:30. *y:* Prv 25:21–22; Mt 5:44. *z:* Prv 8:15–16; Wis 6:3; Jn 19:11; 1 Pt 2:13–17; Ti 3:1. *a:* 1 Pt 2:13–14; 3:13. *b:* 12:19. *c:* 1 Pt 2:19. *d:* Mt 22:21; Mk 12:17; Lk 20:25.

one who loves another has fulfilled the law.[e]
9 The commandments, “You shall not commit adultery; you shall not kill; you shall not
steal; you shall not covet,” and whatever
other commandment there may be, are
summed up in this saying, [namely] “You
shall love your neighbor as yourself.”[f]
10 Love does no evil to the neighbor; hence,
love is the fulfillment of the law.[g]

***Awareness of the End of Time.**** 11 And do
this because you know the time; it is the hour
now for you to awake from sleep. For our
salvation is nearer now than when we first
believed;[h] 12 the night is advanced, the day is
at hand. Let us then throw off the works of
darkness [and] put on the armor of light;[i]
13 let us conduct ourselves properly as in the
day,* not in orgies and drunkenness, not in
promiscuity and licentiousness, not in rivalry and jealousy.[j] 14 But put on the Lord
Jesus Christ, and make no provision for the
desires of the flesh.[k]

See RG 361-62

## CHAPTER 14

***To Live and Die for Christ.*** 1* Welcome anyone who is weak in faith,[l] but not
for disputes over opinions.[m] 2 One person believes that one may eat anything, while the
weak person eats only vegetables.[n] 3 The one
who eats must not despise the one who abstains, and the one who abstains must not
pass judgment on the one who eats; for God
has welcomed him.[o] 4 Who are you to pass
judgment on someone else’s servant? Before
his own master he stands or falls. And he
will be upheld, for the Lord is able to make
him stand.[p] 5 [For] one person considers one
day more important than another, while another person considers all days alike.[q] Let
everyone be fully persuaded in his own
mind.* 6 Whoever observes the day, observes
it for the Lord. Also whoever eats, eats for
the Lord, since he gives thanks to God;
while whoever abstains, abstains for the
Lord and gives thanks to God. 7 None of us
lives for oneself, and no one dies for oneself.
8 For if we live, we live for the Lord,* and if
we die, we die for the Lord; so then, whether
we live or die, we are the Lord’s.[r] 9 For this is
why Christ died and came to life, that he
might be Lord of both the dead and the living.[s] 10 Why then do you judge your brother?
Or you, why do you look down on your
brother? For we shall all stand before the
judgment seat of God;[t] 11 for it is written:

“As I live, says the Lord, every knee
shall bend before me,
and every tongue shall give praise to
God.”[u]

12 So [then] each of us shall give an account
of himself [to God].[v]

***Consideration for the Weak Conscience.***
13 Then let us no longer judge one another, but
rather resolve never to put a stumbling block
or hindrance in the way of a brother.[w] 14 I

**13:11–14** These verses provide the motivation for the love that is encouraged in Rom 13:8–10.

**13:13 Let us conduct ourselves properly as in the day**: the behavior described in Rom 1:29–30 is now to be reversed. Secular moralists were fond of making references to people who could not wait for nightfall to do their carousing. Paul says that Christians claim to be people of the new day that will dawn with the return of Christ. Instead of planning for nighttime behavior they should be concentrating on conduct that is consonant with avowed interest in the Lord’s return.

**14:1–15:6** Since Christ spells termination of the law, which included observance of specific days and festivals as well as dietary instruction, the jettisoning of long-practiced customs was traumatic for many Christians brought up under the Mosaic code. Although Paul acknowledges that in principle no food is a source of moral contamination (Rom 14:14), he recommends that the consciences of Christians who are scrupulous in this regard be respected by other Christians (Rom 14:21). On the other hand, those who have scruples are not to sit in judgment on those who know that the gospel has liberated them from such ordinances (Rom 14:10). See 1 Cor 8; 10.

**14:5** Since the problem to be overcome was humanity’s perverted mind or judgment (Rom 1:28), Paul indicates that the **mind** of the Christian is now able to function with appropriate discrimination (cf. Rom 12:2).

**14:8 The Lord**: Jesus, our Master. The same Greek word, *kyrios*, was applied to both rulers and holders of slaves. Throughout the Letter to the Romans Paul emphasizes God’s total claim on the believer; see note on Rom 1:1.

*e:* Jn 13:34; Gal 5:14. *f:* Ex 20:13–17 / Lv 19:18; Dt 5:17–21; Mt 5:43–44; 19:18–19; 22:39; Mk 12:31; Lk 10:27; Gal 5:14; Jas 2:8. *g:* Mt 22:40; 1 Cor 13:4–7. *h:* Eph 5:8–16; 1 Thes 5:5–7. *i:* Jn 8:12; 1 Thes 5:4–8; 1 Jn 2:8 / 2 Cor 6:7; 10:4; Eph 5:11; 6:13–17. *j:* Lk 21:34; Eph 5:18. *k:* Gal 3:27; 5:16; Eph 4:24; 6:11. *l:* 1 Cor 8:1–13. *m:* 15:1, 7; 1 Cor 9:22. *n:* Gn 1:29; 9:3; 1 Cor 8:1–13; 10:14–33. *o:* Col 2:16. *p:* 2:1; Mt 7:11; Jas 4:11–12. *q:* Gal 4:10. *r:* Lk 20:38; 2 Cor 5:15; Gal 2:20; 1 Thes 5:10. *s:* Acts 10:42. *t:* Acts 17:31; 2 Cor 5:10. *u:* Is 49:18 / Is 45:23; Phil 2:10–11. *v:* Gal 6:5. *w:* 1 Cor 8:9, 13. *x:* Mk 7:5, 20; Acts 10:15; 1 Cor 10:25–27; 1 Tm 4:4.

know and am convinced in the Lord Jesus that nothing is unclean in itself; still, it is unclean for someone who thinks it unclean.[x] 15If your brother is being hurt by what you eat, your conduct is no longer in accord with love. Do not because of your food destroy him for whom Christ died.[y] 16So do not let your good be reviled.[z] 17For the kingdom of God is not a matter of food and drink, but of righteousness, peace, and joy in the holy Spirit;[a] 18whoever serves Christ in this way is pleasing to God and approved by others. 19Let us* then pursue what leads to peace and to building up one another.[b] 20For the sake of food, do not destroy the work of God.[c] Everything is indeed clean, but it is wrong for anyone to become a stumbling block by eating; 21it is good not to eat meat or drink wine or do anything that causes your brother to stumble. 22Keep the faith [that] you have to yourself in the presence of God; blessed is the one who does not condemn himself for what he approves. 23[d] But whoever has doubts is condemned if he eats, because this is not from faith; for whatever is not from faith is sin.*

## CHAPTER 15

See RG 361–62

***Patience and Self-Denial.*** 1We who are strong ought to put up with the failings of the weak and not to please ourselves;[e] 2let each of us please our neighbor for the good, for building up.[f] 3For Christ did not please himself; but, as it is written,[g] "The insults of those who insult you fall upon me."* 4For whatever was written previously was written for our instruction, that by endurance and by the encouragement of the scriptures we might have hope.[h] 5May the God of endurance and encouragement grant you to think in harmony* with one another, in keeping with Christ Jesus,[i] 6that with one accord you may with one voice glorify the God and Father of our Lord Jesus Christ.

***God's Fidelity and Mercy.**** 7Welcome one another, then, as Christ welcomed you, for the glory of God.[j] 8For I say that Christ became a minister of the circumcised to show God's truthfulness, to confirm the promises to the patriarchs,[k] 9but so that the Gentiles might glorify God for his mercy. As it is written:

"Therefore, I will praise you among the Gentiles
and sing praises to your name."[l]

10And again it says:[m]

"Rejoice, O Gentiles, with his people."*

11And again:

"Praise the Lord, all you Gentiles,
and let all the peoples praise him."[n]

12And again Isaiah says:

"The root of Jesse shall come,
raised up to rule the Gentiles;
in him shall the Gentiles hope."[o]

13May the God of hope fill you with all joy and peace in believing, so that you may abound in hope by the power of the holy Spirit.[p]

# VII. Conclusion

***Apostle to the Gentiles.*** 14* I myself am convinced about you, my brothers, that you yourselves are full of goodness,* filled with all

**14:19** some manuscripts, versions, and church Fathers read, "We then pursue . . ."; cf. Rom 5:1.

**14:23 Whatever is not from faith is sin**: Paul does not mean that all the actions of unbelievers are sinful. He addresses himself to the question of intracommunity living. **Sin** in the singular is the dreadful power described in Rom 5:12–14.

**15:3** Liberation from the law of Moses does not make the scriptures of the old covenant irrelevant. Much consolation and motivation for Christian living can be derived from the Old Testament, as in the citation from Ps 69:10. Because this psalm is quoted several times in the New Testament, it has been called indirectly messianic.

**15:5 Think in harmony**: a Greco-Roman ideal. Not rigid uniformity of thought and expression but thoughtful consideration of other people's views finds expression here.

**15:7–13** True oneness of mind is found in pondering the ultimate mission of the church: to bring it about that God's name be glorified throughout the world and that Jesus Christ be universally recognized as God's gift to all humanity. Paul here prepares his addressees for the climactic appeal he is about to make.

**15:10** Paul's citation of Dt 32:43 follows the Greek version.

**15:14–33** Paul sees himself as apostle and benefactor in

*y:* 1 Cor 8:11–13. *z:* 2:24; Ti 2:5. *a:* 1 Cor 8:8. *b:* 12:18 / 15:2. *c:* 1 Cor 8:11–13; 10:28–29; Ti 1:15. *d:* Ti 1:15; Jas 4:17. *e:* 14:1–2. *f:* 14:1, 19; 1 Cor 9:19; 10:24, 33. *g:* Ps 69:10. *h:* 4:23–24; 1 Mc 12:9; 1 Cor 10:11; 2 Tm 3:16. *i:* 12:16; Phil 2:2; 4:2. *j:* 14:1. *k:* Mt 15:24 / Mi 7:20; Acts 3:25. *l:* 11:30 / 2 Sm 22:50; Ps 18:50. *m:* Dt 32:43. *n:* Ps 117:1. *o:* Is 11:10; Rev 5:5; 22:16. *p:* 5:1–2.

knowledge, and able to admonish one another. [15]But I have written to you rather boldly in some respects to remind you, because of the grace given me by God[q] [16]to be a minister of Christ Jesus to the Gentiles in performing the priestly service of the gospel of God, so that the offering up of the Gentiles may be acceptable, sanctified by the holy Spirit.[r] [17]In Christ Jesus, then, I have reason to boast in what pertains to God. [18]For I will not dare to speak of anything except what Christ has accomplished through me to lead the Gentiles to obedience by word and deed,[s] [19]by the power of signs and wonders, by the power of the Spirit [of God], so that from Jerusalem all the way around to Illyricum* I have finished preaching the gospel of Christ. [20]Thus I aspire* to proclaim the gospel not where Christ has already been named, so that I do not build on another's foundation,[t] [21]but as it is written:[u]

"Those who have never been told of him
shall see,
and those who have never heard of
him shall understand."*

***Paul's Plans; Need for Prayers.*** [22]That is why I have so often been prevented from coming to you. [23]But now, since I no longer have any opportunity in these regions and since I have desired to come to you for many years,[v] [24]I hope to see you in passing as I go to Spain and to be sent on my way there by you, after I have enjoyed being with you for a time.[w] [25]* Now, however, I am going to Jerusalem to minister to the holy ones.[x] [26]For Macedonia and Achaia* have decided to make some contribution for the poor among the holy ones in Jerusalem;[y] [27]they decided to do it, and in fact they are indebted to them, for if the Gentiles have come to share in their spiritual blessings, they ought also to serve them in material blessings.[z] [28]So when I have completed this and safely handed over this contribution to them, I shall set out by way of you to Spain; [29]and I know that in coming to you I shall come in the fullness of Christ's blessing.

[30]I urge you, [brothers,] by our Lord Jesus Christ and by the love of the Spirit, to join me in the struggle by your prayers to God on my behalf,[a] [31]that I may be delivered from the disobedient in Judea, and that my ministry for Jerusalem may be acceptable to the holy ones, [32]so that I may come to you with joy by the will of God and be refreshed together with you. [33]The God of peace be with all of you. Amen.[b]

## CHAPTER 16

See RG 362

***Phoebe Commended.*** [1]* I commend to you Phoebe our sister, who is [also] a minister* of the church at Cenchreae,[c] [2]that you may receive her in the Lord in a manner wor-

the priestly service of the gospel and so sketches plans for a mission in Spain, supported by those in Rome.

**15:14 Full of goodness**: the opposite of what humanity was filled with according to Rom 1:29–30.

**15:19 Illyricum**: Roman province northwest of Greece on the eastern shore of the Adriatic.

**15:20 I aspire**: Paul uses terminology customarily applied to philanthropists. Unlike some philanthropists of his time, Paul does not engage in cheap competition for public acclaim. This explanation of his missionary policy is to assure the Christians in Rome that he is also not planning to remain in that city and build on other people's foundations (cf. 2 Cor 10:12–18). However, he does solicit their help in sending him on his way to Spain, which was considered the limit of the western world. Thus Paul's addressees realize that evangelization may be understood in the broader sense of mission or, as in Rom 1:15, of instruction within the Christian community that derives from the gospel.

**15:21** The citation from Is 52:15 concerns the Servant of the Lord. According to Isaiah, the Servant is first of all Israel, which was to bring the knowledge of Yahweh to the nations. In Rom 9–11 Paul showed how Israel failed in this mission. Therefore, he himself undertakes almost singlehandedly Israel's responsibility as the Servant and moves as quickly as possible with the gospel through the Roman empire.

**15:25–27** Paul may have viewed the contribution he was gathering from Gentile Christians for the poor in Jerusalem (cf. 2 Cor 8–9) as a fulfillment of the vision of Is 60:5–6. In confidence that the messianic fulfillment was taking place, Paul stresses in Rom 14–16 the importance of harmonious relationships between Jews and Gentiles.

**15:26 Achaia**: the Roman province of southern Greece.

**16:1–23** Some authorities regard these verses as a later addition to the letter, but in general the evidence favors the view that they were included in the original. Paul endeavors through the long list of greetings (Rom 16:3–16, 21–23) to establish strong personal contact with congregations that he has not personally encountered before. The combination of Jewish and Gentile names dramatically attests the unity in the

*q:* 1:5; 12:3. *r:* 11:13; Phil 2:17. *s:* Acts 15:12; 2 Cor 12:12. *t:* 2 Cor 10:13–18. *u:* Is 52:15. *v:* 1:10–13; Acts 19:21–22. *w:* 1 Cor 16:6. *x:* Acts 19:21; 20:22. *y:* 1 Cor 16:1; 2 Cor 8:1–4; 9:2, 12. *z:* 9:4 / 1 Cor 9:11. *a:* 2 Cor 1:11; Phil 1:27; Col 4:3; 2 Thes 3:1. *b:* 16:20; 2 Cor 13:11; Phil 4:9; 1 Thes 5:23; 2 Thes 3:16; Heb 13:20. *c:* Acts 18:18.

thy of the holy ones, and help her in whatever she may need from you, for she has been a benefactor to many and to me as well.

***Paul's Greetings.*** 3 Greet Prisca and Aquila,* my co-workers in Christ Jesus,[d] 4 who risked their necks for my life, to whom not only I am grateful but also all the churches of the Gentiles; 5 greet also the church at their house.* Greet my beloved Epaenetus, who was the firstfruits in Asia for Christ.[e] 6 Greet Mary, who has worked hard for you. 7 Greet Andronicus and Junia,* my relatives and my fellow prisoners; they are prominent among the apostles and they were in Christ before me. 8 Greet Ampliatus, my beloved in the Lord. 9 Greet Urbanus, our co-worker in Christ, and my beloved Stachys. 10 Greet Apelles, who is approved in Christ. Greet those who belong to the family of Aristobulus. 11 Greet my relative Herodion. Greet those in the Lord who belong to the family of Narcissus. 12 Greet those workers in the Lord, Tryphaena and Tryphosa. Greet the beloved Persis, who has worked hard in the Lord. 13 Greet Rufus,* chosen in the Lord, and his mother and mine.[f] 14 Greet Asyncritus, Phlegon, Hermes, Patrobas, Hermas, and the brothers who are with them. 15 Greet Philologus, Julia, Nereus and his sister, and Olympas, and all the holy ones who are with them. 16 Greet one another with a holy kiss. All the churches of Christ greet you.[g]

***Against Factions.*** 17* I urge you, brothers, to watch out for those who create dissensions and obstacles, in opposition to the teaching that you learned; avoid them.[h] 18 For such people do not serve our Lord Christ but their own appetites, and by fair and flattering speech they deceive the hearts of the innocent.[i] 19 For while your obedience is known to all, so that I rejoice over you, I want you to be wise as to what is good, and simple as to what is evil;[j] 20 then the God of peace will quickly crush Satan* under your feet. The grace of our Lord Jesus be with you.[k]

***Greetings from Corinth.*** 21 Timothy, my co-worker, greets you; so do Lucius and Jason and Sosipater, my relatives.[l] 22 I, Tertius, the writer of this letter, greet you in the Lord. 23[m] Gaius, who is host to me and to the whole church, greets you. Erastus,* the city treasurer, and our brother Quartus greet you. [24]*

***Doxology.**** [25 Now to him who can strengthen you, according to my gospel and the proclamation of Jesus Christ,[n] according to the revelation of the mystery kept secret for long ages* 26 but now manifested through the prophetic writings and, according to the command of the eternal God, made known to all nations to bring about the obedience of faith,[o] 27 to the only wise God, through Jesus Christ be glory forever and ever. Amen.][p]

gospel that transcends previous barriers of nationality, religious ceremony, or racial status.

**16:1 Minister**: in Greek, *diakonos*; see note on Phil 1:1.

**16:3 Prisca and Aquila**: presumably the couple mentioned at Acts 18:2; 1 Cor 16:19; 2 Tm 4:19.

**16:5 The church at their house**: i.e., that meets there. Such local assemblies (cf. 1 Cor 16:19; Col 4:15; Phlm 2) might consist of only one or two dozen Christians each. It is understandable, therefore, that such smaller groups might experience difficulty in relating to one another on certain issues. **Firstfruits**: cf. Rom 8:23; 11:16; 1 Cor 16:15.

**16:7** The name Junia is a woman's name. One ancient Greek manuscript and a number of ancient versions read the name "Julia." Most editors have interpreted it as a man's name, Junias.

**16:13** This Rufus cannot be identified to any degree of certainty with the Rufus of Mk 15:21.

**16:17–18** Paul displays genuine concern for the congregations in Rome by warning them against self-seeking teachers. It would be a great loss, he intimates, if their obedience, which is known to all (cf. Rom 1:8), would be diluted.

**16:20** This verse contains the only mention of Satan in Romans.

**16:23** This Erastus is not necessarily to be identified with the Erastus of Acts 19:22 or of 2 Tm 4:20.

**16:24** Some manuscripts add, similarly to Rom 16:20, "The grace of our Lord Jesus Christ be with you all. Amen."

**16:25–27** This doxology is assigned variously to the end of Rom 14; 15; 16 in the manuscript tradition. Some manuscripts omit it entirely. Whether written by Paul or not, it forms an admirable conclusion to the letter at this point.

**16:25** Paul's gospel reveals **the mystery kept secret for long ages**: justification and salvation through faith, with all the implications for Jews and Gentiles that Paul has developed in the letter.

*d:* Acts 18:2, 18–26; 1 Cor 16:19; 2 Tm 4:19. *e:* 1 Cor 16:19; Col 4:15; Phlm 2 / 1 Cor 16:15. *f:* Mk 15:21. *g:* 1 Cor 16:20; 2 Cor 13:12; 1 Thes 5:26; 1 Pt 5:14. *h:* Mt 7:15; Ti 3:10. *i:* Phil 3:18–19; Col 2:4; 2 Pt 2:3. *j:* 1:8; Mt 10:16; 1 Cor 14:20. *k:* 15:33; Gn 3:15; Lk 10:19 / 1 Cor 16:23; 1 Thes 5:28; 2 Thes 3:18. *l:* Acts 16:1–2; 19:22; 20:4; 1 Cor 4:17; 16:10; Phil 2:19–22; Heb 13:23. *m:* Acts 19:29; 1 Cor 1:14 / 2 Tm 4:20. *n:* 1 Cor 2:7; Eph 1:9; 3:3–9; Col 1:26. *o:* 2 Tm 1:10 / Rom 1:5; Eph 3:4–5, 9; 1 Pt 1:20. *p:* 11:36; Gal 1:5; Eph 3:20–21; Phil 4:20; 1 Tm 1:17; 2 Tm 4:18; Heb 13:21; 1 Pt 4:11; 2 Pt 3:18; Jude 25; Rev 1:6.

See RG 364–74

# The First Letter to the Corinthians

Paul's first letter to the church of Corinth provides us with a fuller insight into the life of an early Christian community of the first generation than any other book of the New Testament. Through it we can glimpse both the strengths and the weaknesses of this small group in a great city of the ancient world, men and women who had accepted the good news of Christ and were now trying to realize in their lives the implications of their baptism. Paul, who had founded the community and continued to look after it as a father, responds both to questions addressed to him and to situations of which he had been informed. In doing so, he reveals much about himself, his teaching, and the way in which he conducted his work of apostleship. Some things are puzzling because we have the correspondence only in one direction. For the person studying this letter, it seems to raise as many questions as it answers, but without it our knowledge of church life in the middle of the first century would be much poorer.

Paul established a Christian community in Corinth about the year 51, on his second missionary journey. The city, a commercial crossroads, was a melting pot full of devotees of various pagan cults and marked by a measure of moral depravity not unusual in a great seaport. The Acts of the Apostles suggests that moderate success attended Paul's efforts among the Jews in Corinth at first, but that they soon turned against him (Acts 18:1–8). More fruitful was his year and a half spent among the Gentiles (Acts 18:11), which won to the faith many of the city's poor and underprivileged (1 Cor 1:26). After his departure the eloquent Apollos, an Alexandrian Jewish Christian, rendered great service to the community, expounding "from the scriptures that the Messiah is Jesus" (Acts 18:24–28).

While Paul was in Ephesus on his third journey (1 Cor 16:8; Acts 19:1–20), he received disquieting news about Corinth. The community there was displaying open factionalism, as certain members were identifying themselves exclusively with individual Christian leaders and interpreting Christian teaching as a superior wisdom for the initiated few (1 Cor 1:10–4:21). The community lacked the decisiveness to take appropriate action against one of its members who was living publicly in an incestuous union (1 Cor 5:1–13). Other members engaged in legal conflicts in pagan courts of law (1 Cor 6:1–11); still others may have participated in religious prostitution (1 Cor 6:12–20) or temple sacrifices (1 Cor 10:14–22).

The community's ills were reflected in its liturgy. In the celebration of the Eucharist certain members discriminated against others, drank too freely at the agape, or fellowship meal, and denied Christian social courtesies to the poor among the membership (1 Cor 11:17–22). Charisms such as ecstatic prayer, attributed freely to the impulse of the holy Spirit, were more highly prized than works of charity (1 Cor 13:1–2, 8), and were used at times in a disorderly way (1 Cor 14:1–40). Women appeared at the assembly without the customary head-covering (1 Cor 11:3–16), and perhaps were quarreling over their right to address the assembly (1 Cor 14:34–35).

Still other problems with which Paul had to deal concerned matters of conscience discussed among the faithful members of the community: the eating of meat that had been sacrificed to idols (1 Cor 8:1–13), the use of sex in marriage (1 Cor 7:1–7), and the attitude to be taken by the unmarried toward marriage in view of the possible proximity of Christ's second coming (1 Cor 7:25–40). There was also a doctrinal matter that called for Paul's attention, for some members of the community, despite their belief in the resurrection of Christ, were denying the possibility of general bodily resurrection.

To treat this wide spectrum of questions, Paul wrote this letter from Ephesus about the year A.D. 56. The majority of the Corinthian Christians may well have been quite faithful. Paul writes on their behalf to guard against the threats posed to the community by the views and conduct of various minorities. He writes with confidence in the authority of his apostolic mission, and he presumes that the Corinthians, despite their deficiencies, will recognize and accept it. On the other hand, he does not hesitate to exercise his authority as his judgment dictates in each situation, even going so far as to promise a direct confrontation with recalcitrants, should the abuses he scores remain uncorrected (1 Cor 4:18–21).

The letter illustrates well the mind and character of Paul. Although he is impelled to insist on his office as founder of the community, he recognizes that he is only one servant of God among many and generously acknowledges the labors of Apollos (1 Cor 3:5–8). He provides us in this letter with many valuable examples of his method of theological reflection and exposition. He always treats the questions at issue on the level of the purity of Christian teaching and conduct. Certain passages of the letter are of the greatest importance for the understanding of early Christian teaching on the Eucharist (1 Cor 10:14–22; 11:17–34) and on the resurrection of the body (1 Cor 15:1–58).

Paul's authorship of 1 Corinthians, apart from a few verses that some regard as later interpolations, has never been seriously questioned. Some scholars have proposed, however, that the letter as we have it contains portions of more than one original Pauline letter. We know that Paul wrote at least two other letters to Corinth (see 1 Cor 5:9; 2 Cor 2:3–4) in addition to the two that we now have; this theory holds that the additional letters are actually contained within the two canonical ones. Most commentators, however, find 1 Corinthians quite understandable as a single coherent work.

The principal divisions of the First Letter to the Corinthians are the following:

- I. Address (1:1–9)
- II. Disorders in the Corinthian Community (1:10–6:20)
  - A. Divisions in the Church (1:10–4:21)
  - B. Moral Disorders (5:1–6:20)
- III. Answers to the Corinthians' Questions (7:1–11:1)
  - A. Marriage and Virginity (7:1–40)
  - B. Offerings to Idols (8:1–11:1)
- IV. Problems in Liturgical Assemblies (11:2–14:40)
  - A. Women's Headdresses (11:3–16)
  - B. The Lord's Supper (11:17–34)
  - C. Spiritual Gifts (12:1–14:40)
- V. The Resurrection (15:1–58)
  - A. The Resurrection of Christ (15:1–11)
  - B. The Resurrection of the Dead (15:12–34)
  - C. The Manner of the Resurrection (15:35–58)
- VI. Conclusion (16:1–24)

# I. Address*

## CHAPTER 1

See RG 366–67

***Greeting.*** 1Paul, called to be an apostle of Christ Jesus by the will of God,* and Sosthenes our brother,[a] 2to the church of God that is in Corinth, to you who have been sanctified in Christ Jesus, called to be holy, with all those everywhere who call upon the name of our Lord Jesus Christ, their Lord and ours.[b] 3Grace to you and peace from God our Father and the Lord Jesus Christ.

***Thanksgiving.*** 4I give thanks to my God always on your account for the grace of God bestowed on you in Christ Jesus, 5that in him you were enriched in every way, with all discourse and all knowledge, 6as the testimony* to Christ was confirmed among you, 7so that you are not lacking in any spiritual gift as you wait for the revelation of our Lord Jesus Christ.[c] 8He will keep you firm to the end, irreproachable on the day of our Lord Jesus [Christ].[d] 9God is faithful, and by him you were called to fellowship with his Son, Jesus Christ our Lord.[e]

# II. Disorders in the Corinthian Community

## A. Divisions in the Church*

***Groups and Slogans.*** 10I urge you, brothers, in the name of our Lord Jesus Christ, that

**1:1–9** Paul follows the conventional form for the opening of a Hellenistic letter (cf. Rom 1:1–7), but expands the opening with details carefully chosen to remind the readers of their situation and to suggest some of the issues the letter will discuss.

**1:1 Called . . . by the will of God**: Paul's mission and the church's existence are grounded in God's initiative. God's call, grace, and fidelity are central ideas in this introduction, emphasized by repetition and wordplays in the Greek.

**1:6 The testimony**: this defines the purpose of Paul's mission (see also 1 Cor 15:15 and the note on 1 Cor 2:1). The forms of his testimony include oral preaching and instruction, his letters, and the life he leads as an apostle.

**1:10–4:21** The first problem Paul addresses is that of divisions within the community. Although we are unable to re-

*a:* Rom 1:1. *b:* Acts 18:1–11. *c:* Ti 2:13. *d:* Phil 1:6. *e:* 1 Jn 1:3.

all of you agree in what you say, and that
there be no divisions among you, but that
you be united in the same mind and in the
same purpose.[f] 11For it has been reported to
me about you, my brothers, by Chloe's people, that there are rivalries among you. 12I
mean that each of you is saying, "I belong
to* Paul," or "I belong to Apollos," or "I belong to Cephas," or "I belong to Christ."[g]
13* Is Christ divided? Was Paul crucified
for you? Or were you baptized in the name
of Paul? 14I give thanks [to God] that I baptized none of you except Crispus and Gaius,[h] 15so that no one can say you were baptized in my name. 16(I baptized the
household of Stephanas also; beyond that I
do not know whether I baptized anyone
else.)[i] 17* For Christ did not send me to baptize but to preach the gospel, and not with
the wisdom of human eloquence,* so that
the cross of Christ might not be emptied of
its meaning.[j]

***Paradox of the Cross.*** 18The message of
the cross is foolishness to those who are perishing, but to us who are being saved it is the
power of God.[k] 19For it is written:

"I will destroy the wisdom of the wise,
and the learning of the learned I will
set aside."[l]

20Where is the wise one? Where is the
scribe? Where is the debater of this age? Has
not God made the wisdom of the world foolish?[m] 21* For since in the wisdom of God the
world did not come to know God through
wisdom, it was the will of God through the
foolishness of the proclamation to save
those who have faith. 22For Jews demand
signs and Greeks look for wisdom,[n] 23but we
proclaim Christ crucified, a stumbling block
to Jews and foolishness to Gentiles,[o] 24but to
those who are called, Jews and Greeks alike,
Christ the power of God and the wisdom of
God. 25For the foolishness of God is wiser
than human wisdom, and the weakness of
God is stronger than human strength.

***The Corinthians and Paul.**** 26Consider
your own calling, brothers. Not many of you
were wise by human standards, not many
were powerful, not many were of noble birth.
27Rather, God chose the foolish of the world
to shame the wise, and God chose the weak

construct the situation in Corinth completely, Paul clearly traces the divisions back to a false self-image on the part of the Corinthians, coupled with a false understanding of the apostles who preached to them (cf. 1 Cor 4:6, 9; 9:1–5) and of the Christian message itself. In these chapters he attempts to deal with those underlying factors and to bring the Corinthians back to a more correct perspective.

**1:12 I belong to**: the activities of Paul and Apollos in Corinth are described in Acts 18. **Cephas** (i.e., "the Rock," a name by which Paul designates Peter also in 1 Cor 3:22; 9:5; 15:5 and in Gal 1:18; 2:9, 11, 14) may well have passed through Corinth; he could have baptized some members of the community either there or elsewhere. The reference to **Christ** may be intended ironically here.

**1:13–17** The reference to baptism and the contrast with preaching the gospel in v 17a suggest that some Corinthians were paying special allegiance to the individuals who initiated them into the community.

**1:17b–18** The basic theme of 1 Cor 1–4 is announced. Adherence to individual leaders has something to do with differences in rhetorical ability and also with certain presuppositions regarding wisdom, eloquence, and effectiveness (power), which Paul judges to be in conflict with the gospel and the cross.

**1:17b Not with the wisdom of human eloquence**: both of the nouns employed here involve several levels of meaning, on which Paul deliberately plays as his thought unfolds. **Wisdom** (*sophia*) may be philosophical and speculative, but in biblical usage the term primarily denotes practical knowledge such as is demonstrated in the choice and effective application of means to achieve an end. The same term can designate the arts of building (cf. 1 Cor 3:10) or of persuasive speaking (cf. 1 Cor 2:4) or effectiveness in achieving salvation. **Eloquence** (*logos*): this translation emphasizes one possible meaning of the term *logos* (cf. the references to rhetorical style and persuasiveness in 1 Cor 2:1, 4). But the term itself may denote an internal reasoning process, plan, or intention, as well as an external word, speech, or message. So by his expression *ouk en sophia logou* in the context of gospel preaching, Paul may intend to exclude both human ways of reasoning or thinking about things and human rhetorical technique. **Human**: this adjective does not stand in the Greek text but is supplied from the context. Paul will begin immediately to distinguish between *sophia* and *logos* from their divine counterparts and play them off against each other.

**1:21–25** True wisdom and power are to be found paradoxically where one would least expect them, in the place of their apparent negation. To human eyes the crucified Christ symbolizes impotence and absurdity.

**1:26–2:5** The pattern of God's wisdom and power is exemplified in their own experience, if they interpret it rightly (1 Cor 1:26–31), and can also be read in their experience of Paul as he first appeared among them preaching the gospel (1 Cor 2:1–5).

---

*f:* Phil 2:2. *g:* 3:4, 22; 16:12; Acts 18:24–28. *h:* Acts 18:8 / Rom 16:23. *i:* 16:15–17. *j:* 2:1, 4. *k:* 2:14 / Rom 1:16. *l:* Is 29:14. *m:* Is 19:12. *n:* Mt 12:38; 16:1 / Acts 17:18–21. *o:* 2:2; Gal 3:1 / Gal 5:11. *p:* Jas 2:5.

of the world to shame the strong,[p] 28 and God
chose the lowly and despised of the world,
those who count for nothing, to reduce to
nothing those who are something, 29 so that
no human being might boast* before God.[q]
30 It is due to him that you are in Christ Jesus,
who became for us wisdom from God, as
well as righteousness, sanctification, and redemption,[r] 31 so that, as it is written, "Whoever boasts, should boast in the Lord."[s]

## CHAPTER 2

See RG 366-67

1 When I came to you, brothers, proclaiming the mystery of God,* I did not come
with sublimity of words or of wisdom.[t] 2 For I
resolved to know nothing while I was with
you except Jesus Christ, and him crucified.[u] 3 I
came to you in weakness* and fear and much
trembling, 4 and my message and my proclamation were not with persuasive [words of]
wisdom,* but with a demonstration of spirit
and power,[v] 5 so that your faith might rest not
on human wisdom but on the power of God.[w]

***The True Wisdom.**** 6 Yet we do speak a
wisdom to those who are mature, but not a
wisdom of this age, nor of the rulers of this
age who are passing away. 7 Rather, we
speak God's wisdom,* mysterious, hidden,
which God predetermined before the ages
for our glory, 8 and which none of the rulers
of this age* knew; for if they had known it,
they would not have crucified the Lord of
glory. 9 But as it is written:

"What eye has not seen, and ear has not
heard,
and what has not entered the human
heart,
what God has prepared for those who
love him,"[x]

10[y] this God has revealed to us through the
Spirit.

For the Spirit scrutinizes everything, even
the depths of God. 11 Among human beings,
who knows what pertains to a person except
the spirit of the person that is within? Similarly, no one knows what pertains to God except the Spirit of God. 12 We have not received the spirit of the world but the Spirit
that is from God, so that we may understand
the things freely given us by God. 13 And we
speak about them not with words taught by

**1:29–31** "Boasting (about oneself)" is a Pauline expression for the radical sin, the claim to autonomy on the part of a creature, the illusion that we live and are saved by our own resources. "Boasting in the Lord" (1 Cor 1:31), on the other hand, is the acknowledgment that we live only from God and for God.

**2:1 The mystery of God**: God's secret, known only to himself, is his plan for the salvation of his people; it is clear from 1 Cor 1:18–25; 2:2, 8–10 that this secret involves Jesus and the cross. In place of **mystery**, other good manuscripts read "testimony" (cf. 1 Cor 1:6).

**2:3** The **weakness** of the crucified Jesus is reflected in Paul's own bearing (cf. 2 Cor 10–13). **Fear and much trembling**: reverential fear based on a sense of God's transcendence permeates Paul's existence and preaching. Compare his advice to the Philippians to work out their salvation with "fear and trembling" (Phil 2:12), because God is at work in them just as his exalting power was paradoxically at work in the emptying, humiliation, and obedience of Jesus to death on the cross (Phil 2:6–11).

**2:4** Among many manuscript readings here the best is either "not with the persuasion of wisdom" or "not with persuasive words of wisdom," which differ only by a nuance. Whichever reading is accepted, the inefficacy of human wisdom for salvation is contrasted with the power of the cross.

**2:6–3:4** Paul now asserts paradoxically what he has previously been denying. To the Greeks who "are looking for wisdom" (1 Cor 1:22), he does indeed bring a wisdom, but of a higher order and an entirely different quality, the only wisdom really worthy of the name. The Corinthians would be able to grasp Paul's preaching as wisdom and enter into a wisdom-conversation with him if they were more open to the Spirit and receptive to the new insight and language that the Spirit teaches.

**2:7–10a God's wisdom**: his plan for our salvation. This was his own eternal secret that no one else could fathom, but in this new age of salvation he has graciously revealed it to us. For the pattern of God's secret, hidden to others and now revealed to the Church, cf. also Rom 11:25–36; 16:25–27; Eph 1:3–10; 3:3–11; Col 1:25–28.

**2:8 The rulers of this age**: this suggests not only the political leaders of the Jews and Romans under whom Jesus was crucified (cf. Acts 4:25–28) but also the cosmic powers behind them (cf. Eph 1:20–23; 3:10). **They would not have crucified the Lord of glory**: they became the unwitting executors of God's plan, which will paradoxically bring about their own conquest and submission (1 Cor 15:24–28).

**2:13 In spiritual terms**: the Spirit teaches spiritual people a new mode of perception (1 Cor 2:12) and an appropriate language by which they can share their self-understanding, their knowledge about what God has done in them. The final phrase in 1 Cor 2:13 can also be translated "describing spiritual realities to spiritual people," in which case it prepares for 1 Cor 2:14–16.

*q:* Eph 2:9. *r:* Rom 4:17 / 6:11; Rom 3:24–26; 2 Cor 5:21 / Eph 1:7; Col 1:14; 1 Thes 5:23. *s:* Jer 9:23; 2 Cor 10:17. *t:* 1:17. *u:* 1:23; Gal 6:14. *v:* 4:20; Rom 15:19; 1 Thes 1:5. *w:* 2 Cor 4:7. *x:* Is 64:3. *y:* Mt 11:25; 13:11; 16:17.

human wisdom, but with words taught by
the Spirit, describing spiritual realities in
spiritual terms.*
[14]Now the natural person* does not accept
what pertains to the Spirit of God, for to him
it is foolishness, and he cannot understand it,
because it is judged spiritually. [15]The spiritual person, however, can judge everything
but is not subject to judgment* by anyone.
[16]For "who has known the mind of the
Lord, so as to counsel him?" But we have the
mind of Christ.[z]

## CHAPTER 3

See RG 366–67

[1]* Brothers, I could not talk to you as
spiritual people, but as fleshly people,* as infants in Christ. [2]I fed you milk, not solid
food, because you were unable to take it. Indeed, you are still not able, even now,[a] [3]for
you are still of the flesh. While there is jealousy and rivalry among you,* are you not of
the flesh, and behaving in an ordinary human way?[b] [4]Whenever someone says, "I belong to Paul," and another, "I belong to
Apollos," are you not merely human?[c]
***The Role of God's Ministers.**** [5]What is
Apollos, after all, and what is Paul? Ministers* through whom you became believers,
just as the Lord assigned each one. [6]I planted,
Apollos watered, but God caused the
growth.[d] [7]Therefore, neither the one who
plants nor the one who waters is anything, but
only God, who causes the growth. [8]The one
who plants and the one who waters are equal,
and each will receive wages in proportion to
his labor. [9]For we are God's co-workers; you
are God's field, God's building.[e]
[10]* According to the grace of God given to
me, like a wise master builder I laid a foundation, and another is building upon it. But
each one must be careful how he builds upon
it, [11]for no one can lay a foundation other
than the one that is there, namely, Jesus
Christ. [12]If anyone builds on this foundation
with gold, silver, precious stones, wood, hay,
or straw, [13]the work of each will come to
light, for the Day* will disclose it. It will be
revealed with fire, and the fire [itself] will
test the quality of each one's work.[f] [14]If the
work stands that someone built upon the
foundation, that person will receive a wage.
[15]But if someone's work is burned up, that

**2:14 The natural person**: see note on 1 Cor 3:1.

**2:15 The spiritual person . . . is not subject to judgment**: since spiritual persons have been given knowledge of what pertains to God (1 Cor 2:11–12), they share in God's own capacity to judge. One to whom the mind of the Lord (and of Christ) is revealed (1 Cor 2:16) can be said to share in some sense in God's exemption from counseling and criticism.

**3:1–4** The Corinthians desire a sort of wisdom dialogue or colloquy with Paul; they are looking for solid, adult food, and he appears to disappoint their expectations. Paul counters: if such a dialogue has not yet taken place, the reason is that they are still at an immature stage of development (cf. 1 Cor 2:6).

**3:1 Spiritual people . . . fleshly people**: Paul employs two clusters of concepts and terms to distinguish what later theology will call the "natural" and the "supernatural." (1) The natural person (1 Cor 2:14) is one whose existence, perceptions, and behavior are determined by purely natural principles, the *psychē* (1 Cor 2:14) and the *sarx* (flesh, a biblical term that connotes creatureliness, 1 Cor 3:1, 3). Such persons are only infants (1 Cor 3:1); they remain on a purely human level (*anthrōpoi*, 1 Cor 3:4). (2) On the other hand, they are called to be animated by a higher principle, the *pneuma*, God's spirit. They are to become spiritual (*pneumatikoi*, 1 Cor 3:1) and mature (1 Cor 2:6) in their perceptions and behavior (cf. Gal 5:16–26). The culmination of existence in the Spirit is described in 1 Cor 15:44–49.

**3:3–4** Jealousy, rivalry, and divisions in the community are symptoms of their arrested development; they reveal the immaturity both of their self-understanding (1 Cor 3:4) and of the judgments about their apostles (1 Cor 3:21).

**3:5–4:5** The Corinthians tend to evaluate their leaders by the criteria of human wisdom and to exaggerate their importance. Paul views the role of the apostles in the light of his theology of spiritual gifts (cf. 1 Cor 12–14, where the charism of the apostle heads the lists). The essential aspects of all spiritual gifts (1 Cor 12:4–6 presents them as gifts of grace, as services, and as modes of activity) are exemplified by the apostolate, which is a gift of grace (1 Cor 3:10) through which God works (1 Cor 3:9) and a form of service (1 Cor 3:5) for the common good (elsewhere expressed by the verb "build up," suggested here by the image of the building, 1 Cor 3:9). The apostles serve the church, but their accountability is to God and to Christ (1 Cor 4:1–5).

**3:5 Ministers**: for other expressions of Paul's understanding of himself as minister or steward to the church, cf. 1 Cor 4:1; 9:17, 19–27; 2 Cor 3:6–9; 4:1; 5:18; 6:3–4; and 2 Cor 11:23 (the climax of Paul's defense).

**3:10–11** There are diverse functions in the service of the community, but each individual's task is serious, and each will stand accountable for the quality of his contribution.

**3:13 The Day**: the great day of Yahweh, the day of judgment, which can be a time of either gloom or joy. **Fire** both destroys and purifies.

**3:15 Will be saved**: although Paul can envision very harsh divine punishment (cf. 1 Cor 3:17), he appears optimistic about the success of divine corrective means both here and elsewhere (cf. 1 Cor 5:5; 11:32 [discipline]). The text of 1 Cor 3:15 has sometimes been used to support the notion of purgatory, though it does not envisage this.

*z:* Wis 9:13; Is 40:13; Rom 11:34. *a:* Heb 5:12–14. *b:* Jas 3:13–16. *c:* 1:12. *d:* Acts 18:1–11, 24–28. *e:* Eph 2:20–22; 1 Pt 2:5. *f:* Mt 3:11–12; 2 Thes 1:7–10.

one will suffer loss; the person will be
saved,* but only as through fire. 16 Do you
not know that you are the temple of God, and
that the Spirit of God dwells in you?[g] 17 If
anyone destroys God's temple, God will destroy that person; for the temple of God,
which you are, is holy.*

18 Let no one deceive himself. If any one
among you considers himself wise in this
age, let him become a fool so as to become
wise.[h] 19 For the wisdom of this world is foolishness in the eyes of God, for it is written:[i]

"He catches the wise in their own ruses,"

20 and again:

"The Lord knows the thoughts of the
wise, that they are vain."[j]

21* So let no one boast about human beings,
for everything belongs to you,[k] 22 Paul or
Apollos or Cephas, or the world or life or
death, or the present or the future: all belong
to you, 23 and you to Christ, and Christ to God.

## CHAPTER 4

See RG 366–67

1 Thus should one regard us: as servants of Christ and stewards of the mysteries
of God.[l] 2 Now it is of course required of
stewards that they be found trustworthy. 3 It
does not concern me in the least that I be
judged by you or any human tribunal; I do
not even pass judgment on myself; 4 I am not
conscious of anything against me, but I do
not thereby stand acquitted; the one who
judges me is the Lord.[m] 5 Therefore, do not
make any judgment before the appointed
time, until the Lord comes, for he will bring
to light what is hidden in darkness and will
manifest the motives of our hearts, and then
everyone will receive praise from God.

***Paul's Life as Pattern.**** 6 I have applied
these things to myself and Apollos for your
benefit, brothers, so that you may learn from
us not to go beyond what is written,* so that
none of you will be inflated with pride in favor of one person over against another. 7 Who
confers distinction upon you? What do you
possess that you have not received? But if
you have received it, why are you boasting as
if you did not receive it? 8 You are already
satisfied; you have already grown rich; you
have become kings* without us! Indeed, I
wish that you had become kings, so that we
also might become kings with you.

9* For as I see it, God has exhibited us
apostles as the last of all, like people sen-

**3:17 Holy**: i.e., "belonging to God." The cultic sanctity of the community is a fundamental theological reality to which Paul frequently alludes (cf. 1 Cor 1:2, 30; 6:11; 7:14).

**3:21–23** These verses pick up the line of thought of 1 Cor 1:10–13. If the Corinthians were genuinely wise (1 Cor 3:18–20), their perceptions would be reversed, and they would see everything in the world and all those with whom they exist in the church in their true relations with one another. Paul assigns all the persons involved in the theological universe a position on a scale: God, Christ, church members, church leaders. Read from top to bottom, the scale expresses ownership; read from bottom to top, the obligation to serve. This picture should be complemented by similar statements such as those in 1 Cor 8:6 and 1 Cor 15:20–28.

**4:6–21** This is an emotionally charged peroration to the discussion about divisions. It contains several exhortations and statements of Paul's purpose in writing (cf. 1 Cor 4:6, 14–17, 21) that counterbalance the initial exhortation at 1 Cor 1:10.

**4:6 That you may learn from us not to go beyond what is written**: the words "to go" are not in the Greek, but have here been added as the minimum necessary to elicit sense from this difficult passage. It probably means that the Corinthians should avoid the false wisdom of vain speculation, contenting themselves with Paul's proclamation of the cross, which is the fulfillment of God's promises in the Old Testament (what is written). **Inflated with pride**: literally, "puffed up," i.e., arrogant, filled with a sense of self-importance. The term is particularly Pauline, found in the New Testament only in 1 Cor 4:6, 18–19; 5:2; 8:1; 13:4; Col 2:18 (cf. the related noun at 2 Cor 12:20). It sometimes occurs in conjunction with the theme of "boasting," as in 1 Cor 4:6–7 here.

**4:8 Satisfied . . . rich . . . kings**: these three statements could also be punctuated as questions continuing the series begun in v 7. In any case these expressions reflect a tendency at Corinth toward an overrealized eschatology, a form of self-deception that draws Paul's irony. The underlying attitude has implications for the Corinthians' thinking about other issues, notably morality and the resurrection, that Paul will address later in the letter.

**4:9–13** A rhetorically effective catalogue of the circumstances of apostolic existence, in the course of which Paul ironically contrasts his own sufferings with the Corinthians' illusion that they have passed beyond the folly of the passion and have already reached the condition of glory. His language echoes that of the beatitudes and woes, which assert a future reversal of present conditions. Their present sufferings ("to this very hour," 11) place the apostles in the class of those to whom the beatitudes promise future relief (Mt 5:3–11; Lk 6:20–23); whereas the Corinthians' image of themselves as "already" filled, rich, ruling (1 Cor 4:8), as wise, strong, and honored (1 Cor 4:10)

*g:* 6:19; 2 Cor 6:16; Eph 2:20–22. *h:* 8:2; Is 5:21; Gal 6:3. *i:* 1:20 / Jb 5:13. *j:* Ps 94:11. *k:* 4:6 / Rom 8:32. *l:* Ti 1:7; 1 Pt 4:10. *m:* 2 Cor 1:12 / Rom 2:16; 2 Cor 5:10.

tenced to death, since we have become a spectacle to the world, to angels and human beings alike.[n] 10We are fools on Christ's account, but you are wise in Christ; we are weak, but you are strong; you are held in honor, but we in disrepute.[o] 11To this very hour we go hungry and thirsty, we are poorly clad and roughly treated, we wander about homeless[p] 12and we toil, working with our own hands. When ridiculed, we bless; when persecuted, we endure;[q] 13when slandered, we respond gently. We have become like the world's rubbish, the scum of all, to this very moment.

14I am writing you this not to shame you, but to admonish you as my beloved children.* 15Even if you should have countless guides to Christ, yet you do not have many fathers, for I became your father in Christ Jesus through the gospel.[r] 16Therefore, I urge you, be imitators of me.[s] 17For this reason I am sending you Timothy, who is my beloved and faithful son in the Lord; he will remind you of my ways in Christ [Jesus], just as I teach them everywhere in every church.[t]

18* Some have become inflated with pride, as if I were not coming to you. 19But I will come to you soon, if the Lord is willing, and I shall ascertain not the talk of these inflated people but their power. 20For the kingdom of God is not a matter of talk but of power.[u] 21Which do you prefer? Shall I come to you with a rod, or with love and a gentle spirit?[v]

## B. Moral Disorders

### CHAPTER 5

See RG 366–68

*A Case of Incest.** 1It is widely reported that there is immorality among you, and immorality of a kind not found even among pagans—a man living with his father's wife.[w] 2And you are inflated with pride.* Should you not rather have been sorrowful? The one who did this deed should be expelled from your midst. 3I, for my part, although absent in body but present in spirit, have already, as if present, pronounced judgment on the one who has committed this deed,[x] 4in the name of [our] Lord Jesus: when you have gathered together and I am with you in spirit with the power of the Lord Jesus, 5you are to deliver this man to Satan* for the destruction of his flesh, so that his spirit may be saved on the day of the Lord.[y]

6[z] Your boasting is not appropriate. Do you not know that a little yeast* leavens all

places them paradoxically in the position of those whom the woes threaten with future undoing (Lk 6:24–26). They have lost sight of the fact that the reversal is predicted for the future.

**4:14–17 My beloved children**: the close of the argument is dominated by the tender metaphor of the father who not only gives his children life but also educates them. Once he has begotten them through his preaching, Paul continues to present the gospel to them existentially, by his life as well as by his word, and they are to learn, as children do, by imitating their parents (1 Cor 4:16). The reference to the **rod** in 1 Cor 4:21 belongs to the same image-complex. So does the image of the **ways** in 1 Cor 4:17: the ways that Paul teaches everywhere, "his ways in Christ Jesus," mean a behavior pattern quite different from the human ways along which the Corinthians are walking (1 Cor 3:3).

**4:18–21** 1 Cor 4:20 picks up the contrast between a certain kind of talk (*logos*) and true power (*dynamis*) from 1 Cor 1:17–18 and 1 Cor 2:4–5. The kingdom, which many of them imagine to be fully present in their lives (1 Cor 4:8), will be rather unexpectedly disclosed in the strength of Paul's encounter with them, if they make a powerful intervention on his part necessary. Compare the similar ending to an argument in 2 Cor 13:1–4, 10.

**5:1–6:20** Paul now takes up a number of other matters that require regulation. These have come to his attention by hearsay (1 Cor 5:1), probably in reports brought by "Chloe's people" (1 Cor 1:11).

**5:1–13** Paul first deals with the incestuous union of a man with his stepmother (1 Cor 5:1–8) and then attempts to clarify general admonitions he has given about associating with fellow Christians guilty of immorality (1 Cor 5:9–13). Each of these three brief paragraphs expresses the same idea: the need of separation between the holy and the unholy.

**5:2 Inflated with pride**: this remark and the reference to **boasting** in 1 Cor 5:6 suggest that they are proud of themselves despite the infection in their midst, tolerating and possibly even approving the situation. The attitude expressed in 1 Cor 6:2, 13 may be influencing their thinking in this case.

**5:5 Deliver this man to Satan**: once the sinner is expelled from the church, the sphere of Jesus' lordship and victory over sin, he will be in the region outside over which Satan is still master. **For the destruction of his flesh**: the purpose of the penalty is medicinal: through affliction, sin's grip over him may be destroyed and the path to repentance and reunion laid open. With Paul's instructions for an excommunication ceremony here, contrast his recommendations for the reconciliation of a sinner in 2 Cor 2:5–11.

**5:6 A little yeast**: yeast, which induces fermentation, is a

*n:* 15:31; Rom 8:36; 2 Cor 4:8–12; 11:23 / Heb 10:33. *o:* 1:18; 3:18; 2 Cor 11:19 / 1 Cor 2:3; 2 Cor 13:9. *p:* Rom 8:35; 2 Cor 11:23–27. *q:* Acts 9:6–14; 18:3; 20:34; 1 Thes 2:9 / 1 Pt 3:9. *r:* Gal 4:19; Phlm 10. *s:* 11:1; Phil 3:17; 4:9; 1 Thes 1:6; 2 Thes 3:7, 9. *t:* 16:10; Acts 19:22. *u:* 2:4; 1 Thes 1:5. *v:* 2 Cor 1:23; 10:2. *w:* Lv 18:7–8; 20:11; Dt 27:20. *x:* Col 2:5. *y:* 1 Tm 1:20. *z:* Gal 5:9.

the dough? 7* Clear out the old yeast, so that you may become a fresh batch of dough, inasmuch as you are unleavened. For our paschal lamb, Christ, has been sacrificed.[a] 8 Therefore let us celebrate the feast, not with the old yeast, the yeast of malice and wickedness, but with the unleavened bread of sincerity and truth.[b]

9* I wrote you in my letter not to associate with immoral people, 10 not at all referring to the immoral of this world or the greedy and robbers or idolaters; for you would then have to leave the world.[c] 11 But I now write to you not to associate with anyone named a brother, if he is immoral, greedy, an idolater, a slanderer, a drunkard, or a robber, not even to eat with such a person.[d] 12 For why should I be judging outsiders? Is it not your business to judge those within? 13 God will judge those outside. "Purge the evil person from your midst."[e]

## CHAPTER 6

See RG 367-68

*Lawsuits Before Unbelievers.** 1 How can any one of you with a case against another dare to bring it to the unjust for judgment instead of to the holy ones? 2* Do you not know that the holy ones will judge the world? If the world is to be judged by you, are you unqualified for the lowest law courts?[f] 3 Do you not know that we will judge angels? Then why not everyday matters? 4 If, therefore, you have courts for everyday matters, do you seat as judges people of no standing in the church? 5 I say this to shame you. Can it be that there is not one among you wise enough to be able to settle a case between brothers? 6 But rather brother goes to court against brother, and that before unbelievers?

7 Now indeed [then] it is, in any case, a failure on your part that you have lawsuits against one another. Why not rather put up with injustice? Why not rather let yourselves be cheated?[g] 8 Instead, you inflict injustice and cheat, and this to brothers. 9* Do you not know that the unjust will not inherit the kingdom of God? Do not be deceived; neither fornicators nor idolaters nor adulterers nor boy prostitutes* nor sodomites[h] 10 nor thieves nor the greedy nor drunkards nor slanderers nor robbers will inherit the kingdom of God. 11 That is what some of you used to be; but now you have had yourselves washed, you were sanctified, you were justified in the name of the Lord Jesus Christ and in the Spirit of our God.[i]

*Sexual Immorality.** 12 "Everything is law-

natural symbol for a source of corruption that becomes all-pervasive. The expression is proverbial.

**5:7–8** In the Jewish calendar, Passover was followed immediately by the festival of Unleavened Bread. In preparation for this feast all traces of old bread were removed from the house, and during the festival only unleavened bread was eaten. The sequence of these two feasts provides Paul with an image of Christian existence: Christ's death (the true Passover celebration) is followed by the life of the Christian community, marked by newness, purity, and integrity (a perpetual feast of unleavened bread). Paul may have been writing around Passover time (cf. 1 Cor 16:5); this is a little Easter homily, the earliest in Christian literature.

**5:9–13** Paul here corrects a misunderstanding of his earlier directives against associating with immoral fellow Christians. He concedes the impossibility of avoiding contact with sinners in society at large but urges the Corinthians to maintain the inner purity of their own community.

**6:1–11** Christians at Corinth are suing one another before pagan judges in Roman courts. A barrage of rhetorical questions (1 Cor 6:1–9) betrays Paul's indignation over this practice, which he sees as an infringement upon the holiness of the Christian community.

**6:2–3** The principle to which Paul appeals is an eschatological prerogative promised to Christians: they are to share with Christ the judgment of the world (cf. Dn 7:22, 27). Hence they ought to be able to settle minor disputes within the community.

**6:9–10** A catalogue of typical vices that exclude from the kingdom of God and that should be excluded from God's church. Such lists (cf. 1 Cor 5:10) reflect the common moral sensibility of the New Testament period.

**6:9** The Greek word translated as **boy prostitutes** may refer to catamites, i.e., boys or young men who were kept for purposes of prostitution, a practice not uncommon in the Greco-Roman world. In Greek mythology this was the function of Ganymede, the "cupbearer of the gods," whose Latin name was Catamitus. The term translated **sodomites** refers to adult males who indulged in homosexual practices with such boys. See similar condemnations of such practices in Rom 1:26–27; 1 Tm 1:10.

**6:12–20** Paul now turns to the opinion of some Corinthians that sexuality is a morally indifferent area (1 Cor 6:12–13). This leads him to explain the mutual relation between the Lord Jesus and our bodies (1 Cor 6:13b) in a densely packed paragraph that contains elements of a profound theology of sexuality (1 Cor 6:15–20).

**6:12–13 Everything is lawful for me**: the Corinthians may have derived this slogan from Paul's preaching about Christian freedom, but they mean something different by it:

*a:* Ex 12:1–13; Dt 16:1–2; 1 Pt 1:19. *b:* Ex 12:15–20; 13:7; Dt 16:3. *c:* 10:27; Jn 17:15. *d:* Mt 18:17; 2 Thes 3:6, 14; 2 Jn 10. *e:* Dt 13:6; 17:7; 22:24. *f:* Wis 3:8; Mt 19:28; Rev 20:4. *g:* Mt 5:38–42; Rom 12:17–21; 1 Thes 5:15. *h:* 15:50; Gal 5:19–21; Eph 5:5. *i:* Ti 3:3–7.

ful for me,"* but not everything is beneficial.
"Everything is lawful for me," but I will not
let myself be dominated by anything.[j]
13"Food for the stomach and the stomach for
food," but God will do away with both the
one and the other. The body, however, is not
for immorality, but for the Lord, and the
Lord is for the body; 14God raised the Lord
and will also raise us by his power.[k]
15Do you not know that your bodies are
members of Christ? Shall I then take Christ's
members and make them the members of a
prostitute?* Of course not![l] 16[Or] do you not
know that anyone who joins himself to a prostitute becomes one body with her? For "the
two," it says, "will become one flesh."[m] 17But
whoever is joined to the Lord becomes one
spirit with him.[n] 18Avoid immorality. Every
other sin a person commits is outside the body,
but the immoral person sins against his own
body.* 19Do you not know that your body is a
temple* of the holy Spirit within you, whom
you have from God, and that you are not your
own?[o] 20For you have been purchased at a
price. Therefore, glorify God in your body.[p]

# III. Answers to the Corinthians' Questions

## A. Marriage and Virginity*

### CHAPTER 7

See RG 368

***Advice to the Married.**** 1Now in regard to the matters about which you wrote:
"It is a good thing for a man not to touch a
woman,"* 2but because of cases of immorality every man should have his own wife, and
every woman her own husband. 3The husband should fulfill his duty toward his wife,
and likewise the wife toward her husband.
4A wife does not have authority over her
own body, but rather her husband, and similarly a husband does not have authority over
his own body, but rather his wife. 5Do not
deprive each other, except perhaps by mutual consent for a time, to be free for prayer,
but then return to one another, so that Satan
may not tempt you through your lack of self-
control. 6This I say by way of concession,*
however, not as a command. 7Indeed, I wish
everyone to be as I am, but each has a par-

they consider sexual satisfaction a matter as indifferent as food, and they attribute no lasting significance to bodily functions (1 Cor 6:13a). Paul begins to deal with the slogan by two qualifications, which suggest principles for judging sexual activity. **Not everything is beneficial**: cf. 1 Cor 10:23, and the whole argument of 1 Cor 8–10 on the finality of freedom and moral activity. **Not let myself be dominated**: certain apparently free actions may involve in fact a secret servitude in conflict with the lordship of Jesus.

**6:15b–16 A prostitute**: the reference may be specifically to religious prostitution, an accepted part of pagan culture at Corinth and elsewhere; but the prostitute also serves as a symbol for any sexual relationship that conflicts with Christ's claim over us individually. **The two . . . will become one flesh**: the text of Gn 2:24 is applied positively to human marriage in Matthew and Mark, and in Eph 5:29–32: love of husband and wife reflect the love of Christ for his church. The application of the text to union with a prostitute is jarring, for such a union is a parody, an antitype of marriage, which does conflict with Christ's claim over us. This explains the horror expressed in 1 Cor 6:15b.

**6:18 Against his own body**: expresses the intimacy and depth of sexual disorder, which violates the very orientation of our bodies.

**6:19–20** Paul's vision becomes trinitarian. **A temple**: sacred by reason of God's gift, his indwelling Spirit. **Not your own**: but "for the Lord," who acquires ownership by the act of redemption. **Glorify God in your body**: the argument concludes with a positive imperative to supplement the negative "avoid immorality" of 1 Cor 6:18. Far from being a terrain that is morally indifferent, the area of sexuality is one in which our relationship with God (and his Christ and his Spirit) is very intimately expressed: he is either highly glorified or deeply offended.

**7:1–40** Paul now begins to answer questions addressed to him by the Corinthians (1 Cor 7:1–11:1). The first of these concerns marriage. This chapter contains advice both to the married (1–16) and to the unmarried (1 Cor 7:25–38) or widowed (1 Cor 7:39–40); these two parts are separated by 1 Cor 7:17–24, which enunciate a principle applicable to both.

**7:1–16** It seems that some Christians in Corinth were advocating asceticism in sexual matters. The pattern **it is a good thing . . ., but** occurs twice (1 Cor 7:1–2, 8–9; cf. 1 Cor 7:26), suggesting that in this matter as in others the Corinthians have seized upon a genuine value but are exaggerating or distorting it in some way. Once again Paul calls them to a more correct perspective and a better sense of their own limitations. The phrase it is a **good thing** (1 Cor 7:1) may have been the slogan of the ascetic party at Corinth.

**7:1–7** References to Paul's own behavior (1 Cor 7:7–8) suggest that his celibate way of life and his preaching to the unmarried (cf. 1 Cor 7:25–35) have given some the impression that asceticism within marriage, i.e., suspension of normal sexual relations, would be a laudable ideal. Paul points to their experience of widespread immorality to caution them against overestimating their own strength (1 Cor 7:2); as individuals they may not have the particular gift that makes such asceticism feasible (1 Cor 7:7) and hence are to abide by the principle to be explained in 1 Cor 7:17–24.

**7:6 By way of concession**: this refers most likely to the

*j:* 10:23. *k:* Rom 8:11; 2 Cor 4:14. *l:* 12:27; Rom 6:12–13; 12:5; Eph 5:30. *m:* Gn 2:24; Mt 19:5; Mk 10:8; Eph 5:31. *n:* Rom 8:9–10; 2 Cor 3:17. *o:* 3:16–17; Rom 5:5. *p:* 3:23; 7:23; Acts 20:28 / Rom 12:1; Phil 1:20. *q:* Mt 19:11–12.

ticular gift from God,* one of one kind and one of another.[q]

8* [r] Now to the unmarried and to widows, I say: it is a good thing for them to remain as they are, as I do, 9but if they cannot exercise self-control they should marry, for it is better to marry than to be on fire. 10[s] To the married, however, I give this instruction (not I, but the Lord):* A wife should not separate from her husband 11—and if she does separate she must either remain single or become reconciled to her husband—and a husband should not divorce his wife.

12To the rest* I say (not the Lord): if any brother has a wife who is an unbeliever, and she is willing to go on living with him, he should not divorce her; 13and if any woman has a husband who is an unbeliever, and he is willing to go on living with her, she should not divorce her husband. 14For the unbelieving husband is made holy through his wife, and the unbelieving wife is made holy through the brother. Otherwise your children would be unclean, whereas in fact they are holy.[t]

15If the unbeliever separates,* however, let him separate. The brother or sister is not bound in such cases; God has called you to peace. 16For how do you know, wife, whether you will save your husband; or how do you know, husband, whether you will save your wife?

***The Life That the Lord Has Assigned.**** 17Only, everyone should live as the Lord has assigned, just as God called each one. I give this order in all the churches. 18Was someone called after he had been circumcised? He should not try to undo his circumcision. Was an uncircumcised person called? He should not be circumcised.[u] 19Circumcision means nothing, and uncircumcision means nothing; what matters is keeping God's commandments.[v] 20Everyone should remain in the state in which he was called.

21Were you a slave when you were called? Do not be concerned but, even if you can gain your freedom, make the most of it. 22For the slave called in the Lord is a freed person in the Lord, just as the free person who has been called is a slave of Christ.[w] 23You have been purchased at a price. Do not become slaves to human beings.[x] 24Brothers, everyone should continue before God in the state in which he was called.

***Advice to Virgins and Widows.*** 25Now in regard to virgins, I have no commandment from the Lord,* but I give my opinion as one who by the Lord's mercy is trustworthy. 26So this is what I think best because of the present distress: that it is a good thing for a person to remain as he is.[y] 27Are you bound to a wife? Do not seek a separation. Are you free of a wife? Then do not look for a wife. 28If you marry, however, you do not sin, nor does an unmarried woman sin if she marries; but such people will experience affliction in their earthly life, and I would like to spare you that.

29* I tell you, brothers, the time is running out. From now on, let those having wives act

concession mentioned in 1 Cor 7:5a: temporary interruption of relations for a legitimate purpose.

**7:7 A particular gift from God**: use of the term *charisma* suggests that marriage and celibacy may be viewed in the light of Paul's theology of spiritual gifts (1 Cor 7:12–14).

**7:8** Paul was obviously unmarried when he wrote this verse. Some interpreters believe that he had previously been married and widowed; there is no clear evidence either for or against this view, which was expressed already at the end of the second century by Clement of Alexandria.

**7:10–11 (Not I, but the Lord)**: Paul reminds the married of Jesus' principle of nonseparation (Mk 10:9). This is one of his rare specific references to the teaching of Jesus.

**7:12–14 To the rest**: marriages in which only one partner is a baptized Christian. Jesus' prohibition against divorce is not addressed to them, but Paul extends the principle of nonseparation to such unions, provided they are marked by peacefulness and shared sanctification.

**7:15–16 If the unbeliever separates**: the basis of the "Pauline privilege" in Catholic marriage legislation.

**7:17–24** On the ground that distinct human conditions are less significant than the whole new existence opened up by God's call, Paul urges them to be less concerned with changing their states of life than with answering God's call where it finds them. The principle applies both to the married state (1 Cor 7:1–16) and to the unmarried (1 Cor 7:25–38).

**7:25–28** Paul is careful to explain that the principle of 1 Cor 7:17 does not bind under sin but that present earthly conditions make it advantageous for the unmarried to remain as they are (1 Cor 7:28). These remarks must be complemented by the statement about "particular gifts" from 1 Cor 7:7.

**7:29–31 The world . . . is passing away**: Paul advises Christians to go about the ordinary activities of life in a manner different from those who are totally immersed in them and unaware of their transitoriness.

*r:* 1 Tm 5:11–16 / 1 Cor 9:5. *s:* Mt 5:32; 19:9. *t:* Rom 11:16. *u:* 1 Mc 1:15 / Acts 15:1–2. *v:* Rom 2:25, 29; Gal 5:6; 6:15. *w:* Eph 6:5–9; Col 3:11; Phlm 16. *x:* 6:20. *y:* 7:8.

as not having them,[z] 30those weeping as not
weeping, those rejoicing as not rejoicing,
those buying as not owning, 31those using
the world as not using it fully. For the world
in its present form is passing away.

32I should like you to be free of anxieties.
An unmarried man is anxious about the
things of the Lord, how he may please the
Lord. 33But a married man is anxious about
the things of the world, how he may please
his wife,[a] 34and he is divided. An unmarried
woman or a virgin is anxious about the
things of the Lord, so that she may be holy in
both body and spirit. A married woman, on
the other hand, is anxious about the things of
the world, how she may please her husband.[b]
35I am telling you this for your own benefit,
not to impose a restraint upon you, but for
the sake of propriety and adherence to the
Lord without distraction.[c]

36* If anyone thinks he is behaving improperly toward his virgin, and if a critical
moment has come* and so it has to be, let
him do as he wishes. He is committing no
sin; let them get married. 37The one who
stands firm in his resolve, however, who is
not under compulsion but has power over his
own will, and has made up his mind to keep
his virgin, will be doing well. 38So then, the
one who marries his virgin does well; the
one who does not marry her will do better.

39* A wife is bound to her husband as long
as he lives. But if her husband dies, she is
free to be married to whomever she wishes,
provided that it be in the Lord.[d] 40She is
more blessed, though, in my opinion, if she
remains as she is, and I think that I too have
the Spirit of God.[e]

## B. Offerings to Idols*

### CHAPTER 8

See RG 368–69

*Knowledge Insufficient.* 1Now in regard to meat sacrificed to idols:* we realize
that "all of us have knowledge"; knowledge
inflates with pride, but love builds up.[f] 2If
anyone supposes he knows something, he
does not yet know as he ought to know. 3But
if one loves God, one is known by him.[g]

4So about the eating of meat sacrificed to
idols: we know that "there is no idol in the
world," and that "there is no God but one."[h]
5Indeed, even though there are so-called
gods in heaven and on earth (there are, to be
sure, many "gods" and many "lords"), 6* yet
for us there is

**7:36–38** The passage is difficult to interpret, because it is unclear whether Paul is thinking of a father and his unmarried daughter (or slave), or of a couple engaged in a betrothal or spiritual marriage. The general principles already enunciated apply: there is no question of sin, even if they should marry, but staying as they are is "better" (for the reasons mentioned in 1 Cor 7:28–35). Once again the **charisma** of 1 Cor 7:7 which applies also to the unmarried (1 Cor 7:8–9), is to be presupposed.

**7:36 A critical moment has come**: either because the woman will soon be beyond marriageable age, or because their passions are becoming uncontrollable (cf. 1 Cor 7:9).

**7:39–40** Application of the principles to the case of widows. If they do choose to remarry, they ought to prefer Christian husbands.

**8:1–11:1** The Corinthians' second question concerns meat that has been sacrificed to idols; in this area they were exhibiting a disordered sense of liberation that Paul here tries to rectify. These chapters contain a sustained and unified argument that illustrates Paul's method of theological reflection on a moral dilemma. Although the problem with which he is dealing is dated, the guidelines for moral decisions that he offers are of lasting validity. Essentially Paul urges them to take a communitarian rather than an individualistic view of their Christian freedom. Many decisions that they consider pertinent only to their private relationship with God have, in fact, social consequences. Nor can moral decisions be determined by merely theoretical considerations; they must be based on concrete circumstances, specifically on the value and needs of other individuals and on mutual responsibility within the community. Paul here introduces the theme of "building up" (*oikodomē*), i.e., of contributing by individual action to the welfare and growth of the community. This theme will be further developed in 1 Cor 14; see note on 1 Cor 14:3b–5. Several years later Paul would again deal with the problem of meat sacrificed to idols in Rom 14:1–15:6.

**8:1a Meat sacrificed to idols**: much of the food consumed in the city could have passed through pagan religious ceremonies before finding its way into markets and homes. **"All of us have knowledge"**: a slogan, similar to 1 Cor 6:12, which reveals the self-image of the Corinthians. 1 Cor 8:4 will specify the content of this knowledge.

**8:6** This verse rephrases the monotheistic confession of 1 Cor 8:4 in such a way as to contrast it with polytheism (1 Cor 8:5) and to express our relationship with the one God in concrete, i.e., in personal and Christian terms. **And for whom we exist**: since the Greek contains no verb here and the action intended must be inferred from the preposition *eis*, another translation is equally possible: "toward whom we return." **Through whom all things**: the earliest reference in the New Testament to Jesus' role in creation.

*z:* Rom 13:11. *a:* Lk 14:20. *b:* 1 Tm 5:5. *c:* Lk 10:39–42. *d:* Rom 7:2. *e:* 7:25. *f:* Rom 15:14 / 1 Cor 13:1–13; Rom 14:15, 19. *g:* Rom 8:29; Gal 4:9; *h:* 10:19; Dt 6:4. *i:* Mal 2:10 / Rom 11:36; Eph 4:5–6 / 1 Cor 1:2–3 / Jn 1:3; Col 1:16.

one God, the Father,
from whom all things are and for whom we exist,
and one Lord, Jesus Christ,
through whom all things are and through whom we exist.[i]

*Practical Rules.* [7]But not all have this knowledge. There are some who have been so used to idolatry up until now that, when they eat meat sacrificed to idols, their conscience, which is weak, is defiled.[j]

[8]* Now food will not bring us closer to God. We are no worse off if we do not eat, nor are we better off if we do.[k] [9]But make sure that this liberty of yours in no way becomes a stumbling block to the weak.[l] [10]If someone sees you, with your knowledge, reclining at table in the temple of an idol, may not his conscience too, weak as it is, be "built up" to eat the meat sacrificed to idols? [11]Thus through your knowledge, the weak person is brought to destruction, the brother for whom Christ died.[m] [12]When you sin in this way against your brothers and wound their consciences, weak as they are, you are sinning against Christ. [13]* [n] Therefore, if food causes my brother to sin, I will never eat meat again, so that I may not cause my brother to sin.

## CHAPTER 9*

See RG 369–70

***Paul's Rights as an Apostle.*** [1]Am I not free? Am I not an apostle? Have I not seen Jesus our Lord? Are you not my work in the Lord?[o] [2]Although I may not be an apostle for others, certainly I am for you, for you are the seal of my apostleship in the Lord.

[3]My defense against those who would pass judgment on me* is this. [4]* Do we not have the right to eat and drink? [5]Do we not have the right to take along a Christian wife, as do the rest of the apostles, and the brothers of the Lord, and Cephas? [6]Or is it only myself and Barnabas who do not have the right not to work?[p] [7]Who ever serves as a soldier at his own expense? Who plants a vineyard without eating its produce? Or who shepherds a flock without using some of the milk from the flock?[q] [8]Am I saying this on human authority, or does not the law also speak of these things? [9]It is written in the law of Moses, "You shall not muzzle an ox while it is treading out the grain."[r] Is God concerned about oxen, [10]or is he not really speaking for our sake? It was written for our sake, because the plowman should plow in hope, and the thresher in hope of receiving a share.[s] [11]If we have sown spiritual seed for you, is it a great thing that we reap a material harvest from you?[t] [12]If others

**8:8–9** Although the food in itself is morally neutral, extrinsic circumstances may make the eating of it harmful. **A stumbling block**: the image is that of tripping or causing someone to fall (cf. 1 Cor 8:13; 9:12; 10:12, 32; 2 Cor 6:3; Rom 14:13, 20–1). This is a basic moral imperative for Paul, a counterpart to the positive imperative to "build one another up"; compare the expression "giving offense" as opposed to "pleasing" in 1 Cor 10:32–33.

**8:13** His own course is clear: he will avoid any action that might harm another Christian. This statement prepares for the paradigmatic development in 1 Cor 9.

**9:1–27** This chapter is an emotionally charged expansion of Paul's appeal to his own example in 1 Cor 8:13; its purpose is to reinforce the exhortation of 1 Cor 8:9. The two opening questions introduce the themes of Paul's freedom and his apostleship (1 Cor 9:1), themes that the chapter will develop in reverse order, 1 Cor 9:1–18 treating the question of his apostleship and the rights that flow from it, and 1 Cor 9:19–27 exploring dialectically the nature of Paul's freedom. The language is highly rhetorical, abounding in questions, wordplays, paradoxes, images, and appeals to authority and experience. The argument is unified by repetitions; its articulations are highlighted by inclusions and transitional verses.

**9:3 My defense against those who would pass judgment on me**: the reference to a defense (*apologia*) is surprising, and suggests that Paul is incorporating some material here that he has previously used in another context. The defense will touch on two points: the fact of Paul's rights as an apostle (1 Cor 9:4–12a and 1 Cor 9:13–14) and his nonuse of those rights (1 Cor 9:12b and 1 Cor 9:15–18).

**9:4–12a** Apparently some believe that Paul is not equal to the other apostles and therefore does not enjoy equal privileges. His defense on this point (here and in 1 Cor 9:13–14) reinforces the assertion of his apostolic character in 1 Cor 9:2. It consists of a series of analogies from natural equity (1 Cor 9:7) and religious custom (1 Cor 9:13) designed to establish his equal right to support from the churches (1 Cor 9:4–6, 11–12a); these analogies are confirmed by the authority of the law (1 Cor 9:8–10) and of Jesus himself (1 Cor 9:14).

**9:12b** It appears, too, that suspicion or misunderstanding has been created by Paul's practice of not living from his preaching. The first reason he asserts in defense of this prac-

*j:* 10:28; Rom 14:23 / Rom 14:1; 15:1. *k:* Rom 14:17. *l:* Rom 14:13, 20–21. *m:* Rom 14:15, 20. *n:* Mt 18:6; Rom 14:20–21. *o:* 1 Cor 9:19 / 2 Cor 12:12 / 1 Cor 15:8–9 / Acts 9:17; 26:16. *p:* Acts 4:36–37; 13:1–2; Gal 2:1, 9, 13; Col 4:10. *q:* 2 Tm 2:3–4. *r:* Dt 25:4; 1 Tm 5:18. *s:* 2 Tm 2:6.

share this rightful claim on you, do not we still more?[u]

*Reason for Not Using His Rights.* Yet we have not used this right.* On the contrary, we endure everything so as not to place an obstacle to the gospel of Christ. [13]* Do you not know that those who perform the temple services eat [what] belongs to the temple, and those who minister at the altar share in the sacrificial offerings?[v] [14]In the same way, the Lord ordered that those who preach the gospel should live by the gospel.[w]

[15]* I have not used any of these rights, however, nor do I write this that it be done so in my case. I would rather die. Certainly no one is going to nullify my boast.[x] [16]If I preach the gospel, this is no reason for me to boast, for an obligation has been imposed on me, and woe to me if I do not preach it![y] [17]If I do so willingly, I have a recompense, but if unwillingly, then I have been entrusted with a stewardship.[z] [18]What then is my recompense? That, when I preach, I offer the gospel free of charge so as not to make full use of my right in the gospel.[a]

*All Things to All.* [19]* Although I am free in regard to all, I have made myself a slave to all so as to win over as many as possible.[b] [20]To the Jews I became like a Jew to win over Jews; to those under the law I became like one under the law—though I myself am not under the law—to win over those under the law. [21]To those outside the law I became like one outside the law—though I am not outside God's law but within the law of Christ—to win over those outside the law. [22]To the weak I became weak, to win over the weak. I have become all things to all, to save at least some.[c] [23]All this I do for the sake of the gospel, so that I too may have a share in it.

[24]* Do you not know that the runners in the stadium all run in the race, but only one wins the prize? Run so as to win.[d] [25]Every athlete exercises discipline in every way. They do it to win a perishable crown, but we an imperishable one.[e] [26]Thus I do not run aimlessly; I do not fight as if I were shadowboxing. [27]No, I drive my body and train it, for fear that, after having preached to others, I myself should be disqualified.*

## CHAPTER 10

See RG 369

*Warning Against Overconfidence.* [1]* I do not want you to be unaware, brothers, that our ancestors were all under the cloud and all passed through the sea,[f] [2]and all of them were baptized into Moses in the cloud and in the sea.[g] [3]All ate the same spiritual

tice is an entirely apostolic one; it anticipates the developments to follow in 1 Cor 9:19–22. He will give a second reason in 1 Cor 9:15–18.

**9:13–14** The position of these verses produces an interlocking of the two points of Paul's defense. These arguments by analogy (1 Cor 9:13) and from authority (1 Cor 9:14) belong with those of 1 Cor 9:7–10 and ground the first point. But Paul defers them until he has had a chance to mention "the gospel of Christ" (1 Cor 9:12b), after which it is more appropriate to mention Jesus' injunction to his preachers and to argue by analogy from the sacred temple service to his own liturgical service, the preaching of the gospel (cf. Rom 1:9; 15:16).

**9:15–18** Paul now assigns a more personal motive to his nonuse of his right to support. His preaching is not a service spontaneously undertaken on his part but a stewardship imposed by a sort of divine compulsion. Yet to merit any reward he must bring some spontaneous quality to his service, and this he does by freely renouncing his right to support. The material here is quite similar to that contained in Paul's "defense" at 2 Cor 11:5–12; 12:11–18.

**9:19–23** In a rhetorically balanced series of statements Paul expands and generalizes the picture of his behavior and explores the paradox of apostolic freedom. It is not essentially freedom from restraint but freedom for service—a possibility of constructive activity.

**9:24–27** A series of miniparables from sports, appealing to readers familiar with Greek gymnasia and the nearby Isthmian games.

**9:27 For fear that . . . I myself should be disqualified**: a final paradoxical turn to the argument: what appears at first a free, spontaneous renunciation of rights (1 Cor 9:12–18) seems subsequently to be required for fulfillment of Paul's stewardship (to preach effectively he must reach his hearers wherever they are, 1 Cor 9:19–22), and finally is seen to be necessary for his own salvation (1 Cor 9:23–27). Mention of the possibility of disqualification provides a transition to 1 Cor 10.

**10:1–5** Paul embarks unexpectedly upon a panoramic survey of the events of the Exodus period. The privileges of Israel in the wilderness are described in terms that apply strictly only to the realities of the new covenant ("baptism," "spiritual food and drink"); interpreted in this way they point forward to the Christian experience (1 Cor 10:1–4). But those privileges did not guarantee God's permanent pleasure (1 Cor 10:5).

*t:* Rom 15:27. *u:* 2 Cor 11:7–12; 12:13–18; 2 Thes 3:6–12. *v:* Nm 18:8, 31; Dt 18:1–5. *w:* Mt 10:10; Lk 10:7–8. *x:* 2 Cor 11:9–10. *y:* Acts 26:14–18. *z:* 4:1; Gal 2:7. *a:* 2 Cor 11:7–12. *b:* Mt 20:26–27. *c:* 10:33; Rom 15:1; 2 Cor 11:29. *d:* Heb 12:1. *e:* 2 Tm 2:5 / 2 Tm 4:7–8; Jas 1:12; 1 Pt 5:4. *f:* Ex 13:21–22; 14:19–20 / Ex 14:21–22, 26–30. *g:* Rom 6:3; Gal 3:27 / Ex 16:4–35.

food, 4and all drank the same spiritual drink, for they drank from a spiritual rock that followed them,* and the rock was the Christ.[h] 5Yet God was not pleased with most of them, for they were struck down in the desert.[i]

6* These things happened as examples for us, so that we might not desire evil things, as they did.[j] 7And do not become idolaters, as some of them did, as it is written, "The people sat down to eat and drink, and rose up to revel."[k] 8Let us not indulge in immorality as some of them did, and twenty-three thousand fell within a single day.[l] 9Let us not test Christ* as some of them did, and suffered death by serpents.[m] 10Do not grumble as some of them did, and suffered death by the destroyer.[n] 11These things happened to them as an example, and they have been written down as a warning to us, upon whom the end of the ages has come.* 12Therefore, whoever thinks he is standing secure should take care not to fall.* 13No trial has come to you but what is human. God is faithful and will not let you be tried beyond your strength; but with the trial he will also provide a way out, so that you may be able to bear it.[o]

***Warning Against Idolatry.**** 14Therefore, my beloved, avoid idolatry.[p] 15I am speaking as to sensible people; judge for yourselves what I am saying. 16The cup of blessing that we bless, is it not a participation in the blood of Christ? The bread that we break, is it not a participation in the body of Christ?[q] 17Because the loaf of bread is one, we, though many, are one body, for we all partake of the one loaf.[r]

18Look at Israel according to the flesh; are not those who eat the sacrifices participants in the altar?[s] 19So what am I saying? That meat sacrificed to idols is anything? Or that an idol is anything? 20No, I mean that what they sacrifice, [they sacrifice] to demons,* not to God, and I do not want you to become participants with demons.[t] 21You cannot drink the cup of the Lord and also the cup of demons. You cannot partake of the table of the Lord and of the table of demons.[u] 22Or are we provoking the Lord to jealous anger? Are we stronger than he?[v]

***Seek the Good of Others.**** 23"Everything is lawful," but not everything is beneficial.* "Everything is lawful," but not everything builds up.[w] 24No one should seek his own advantage, but that of his neighbor.[x] 25* Eat any-

**10:4 A spiritual rock that followed them**: the Torah speaks only about a rock from which water issued, but rabbinic legend amplified this into a spring that followed the Israelites throughout their migration. Paul uses this legend as a literary type: he makes the rock itself accompany the Israelites, and he gives it a spiritual sense. **The rock was the Christ**: in the Old Testament, Yahweh is the Rock of his people (cf. Dt 32, Moses' song to Yahweh the Rock). Paul now applies this image to the Christ, the source of the living water, the true Rock that accompanied Israel, guiding their experiences in the desert.

**10:6–13** This section explicitates the typological value of these Old Testament events: the desert experiences of the Israelites are examples, meant as warnings, to deter us from similar sins (idolatry, immorality, etc.) and from a similar fate.

**10:9 Christ**: to avoid Paul's concept of Christ present in the wilderness events, some manuscripts read "the Lord."

**10:11 Upon whom the end of the ages has come**: it is our period in time toward which past ages have been moving and in which they arrive at their goal.

**10:12–13 Take care not to fall**: the point of the whole comparison with Israel is to caution against overconfidence, a sense of complete security (1 Cor 10:12). This warning is immediately balanced by a reassurance, based, however, on God (1 Cor 10:13).

**10:14–22** The warning against idolatry from 1 Cor 10:7 is now repeated (1 Cor 10:14) and explained in terms of the effect of sacrifices: all sacrifices, Christian (1 Cor 10:16–17), Jewish (1 Cor 10:18), or pagan (1 Cor 10:20), establish communion. But communion with Christ is exclusive, incompatible with any other such communion (1 Cor 10:21). Compare the line of reasoning at 1 Cor 6:15.

**10:20 To demons**: although Jews denied divinity to pagan gods, they often believed that there was some nondivine reality behind the idols, such as the dead, or angels, or demons. The explanation Paul offers in 1 Cor 10:20 is drawn from Dt 32:17: the power behind the idols, with which the pagans commune, consists of demonic powers hostile to God.

**10:23–11:1** By way of peroration Paul returns to the opening situation (1 Cor 8) and draws conclusions based on the intervening considerations (1 Cor 9–10).

**10:23–24** He repeats in the context of this new problem the slogans of liberty from 1 Cor 6:12, with similar qualifications. Liberty is not merely an individual perfection, nor an end in itself, but is to be used for the common good. The language of 1 Cor 10:24 recalls the descriptions of Jesus' self-emptying in Phil 2.

**10:25–30** A summary of specific situations in which the eating of meat sacrificed to idols could present problems of conscience. Three cases are considered. In the first (the marketplace, 1 Cor 10:25–26) and the second (at table, 1 Cor 10:27), there is no need to be concerned with whether food has passed through a pagan

*h:* Ex 17:1–7; Nm 20:7–11; Dt 8:15. *i:* Nm 14:28–38; Jude 5. *j:* Nm 11:4, 34. *k:* Ex 32:6. *l:* Nm 25:1–9. *m:* Nm 21:5–9. *n:* Nm 14:2–37; 16:1–35. *o:* Mt 6:13; Jas 1:13–14 / 1 Cor 1:9. *p:* 1 Jn 5:21. *q:* Mt 26:26–29; Acts 2:42. *r:* Rom 12:5; Eph 4:4. *s:* Lv 7:6. *t:* Dt 32:17. *u:* 2 Cor 6:14–18. *v:* Dt 32:21 / Eccl 6:10. *w:* 6:12. *x:* Rom 15:2; Phil 2:4, 21.

thing sold in the market, without raising questions on grounds of conscience, [26]for "the earth and its fullness are the Lord's."[y] [27]If an unbeliever invites you and you want to go, eat whatever is placed before you, without raising questions on grounds of conscience. [28]But if someone says to you, "This was offered in sacrifice," do not eat it on account of the one who called attention to it and on account of conscience; [29]I mean not your own conscience, but the other's. For why should my freedom be determined by someone else's conscience? [30]If I partake thankfully, why am I reviled for that over which I give thanks?[z]

[31]So whether you eat or drink, or whatever you do, do everything for the glory of God. [32]* Avoid giving offense, whether to Jews or Greeks or the church of God, [33]just as I try to please everyone in every way, not seeking my own benefit but that of the many, that they may be saved.[a]

See RG 370–71

## CHAPTER 11

[1]Be imitators of me, as I am of Christ.[b]

## IV. Problems In Liturgical Assemblies*

[2]I praise you because you remember me in everything and hold fast to the traditions, just as I handed them on to you.[c]

### A. Women's Headdresses*

***Man and Woman.*** [3]But I want you to know that Christ is the head of every man, and a husband the head of his wife,* and God the head of Christ.[d] [4]* Any man who prays or prophesies with his head covered brings shame upon his head. [5]But any woman who prays or prophesies with her head unveiled brings shame upon her head, for it is one and the same thing as if she had had her head shaved. [6]For if a woman does not have her head veiled, she may as well have her hair cut off. But if it is shameful for a woman to have her hair cut off or her head shaved, then she should wear a veil.

[7]* A man, on the other hand, should not cover his head, because he is the image and glory of God, but woman is the glory of

sacrifice or not, for the principle of 1 Cor 8:4–6 still stands, and the whole creation belongs to the one God. But in the third case (1 Cor 10:28), the situation changes if someone present explicitly raises the question of the sacrificial origin of the food; eating in such circumstances may be subject to various interpretations, some of which could be harmful to individuals. Paul is at pains to insist that the enlightened Christian conscience need not change its judgment about the neutrality, even the goodness, of the food in itself (1 Cor 10:29–30); yet the total situation is altered to the extent that others are potentially endangered, and this calls for a different response, for the sake of others.

**10:32–11:1** In summary, the general rule of mutually responsible use of their Christian freedom is enjoined first negatively (1 Cor 10:32), then positively, as exemplified in Paul (1 Cor 10:33), and finally grounded in Christ, the pattern for Paul's behavior and theirs (1 Cor 11:1; cf. Rom 15:1–3).

**11:2–14:40** This section of the letter is devoted to regulation of conduct at the liturgy. The problems Paul handles have to do with the dress of women in the assembly (1 Cor 11:3–16), improprieties in the celebration of community meals (1 Cor 11:17–34), and the use of charisms or spiritual gifts (1 Cor 12:1–14:40). The statement in 1 Cor 11:2 introduces all of these discussions, but applies more appropriately to the second (cf. the mention of praise in 1 Cor 11:17 and of tradition in 1 Cor 11:23).

**11:3–16** Women have been participating in worship at Corinth without the head-covering normal in Greek society of the period. Paul's stated goal is to bring them back into conformity with contemporary practice and propriety. In his desire to convince, he reaches for arguments from a variety of sources, though he has space to develop them only sketchily and is perhaps aware that they differ greatly in persuasiveness.

**11:3 A husband the head of his wife**: the specific problem suggests to Paul the model of the head as a device for clarifying relations within a hierarchical structure. The model is similar to that developed later in greater detail and nuance in Eph 5:21–33. It is a hybrid model, for it grafts onto a strictly theological scale of existence (cf. 1 Cor 3:21–23) the hierarchy of sociosexual relations prevalent in the ancient world: men, dominant, reflect the active function of Christ in relation to his church; women, submissive, reflect the passive role of the church with respect to its savior. This gives us the functional scale: God, Christ, man, woman.

**11:4–6** From man's direct relation to Christ, Paul infers that his head should not be covered. But woman, related not directly to Christ on the scale but to her husband, requires a covering as a sign of that relationship. **Shameful . . . to have her hair cut off**: certain less honored classes in society, such as lesbians and prostitutes, are thought to have worn their hair close-cropped.

**11:7–9** The hierarchy of v 3 is now expressed in other metaphors: the image (*eikōn*) and the reflected glory (*doxa*). Paul is alluding basically to the text of Gn 1:27, in which mankind as a whole, the male-female couple, is created in God's image and given the command to multiply and together dominate the lower creation. But Gn 1:24 is interpreted here in the light of the second creation narrative in Gn 2, in which each of the sexes is created separately (first the man and then the woman from man and for him, to be his helpmate,

*y:* Ps 24:1; 50:12. *z:* Rom 14:6; 1 Tm 4:3–4. *a:* 9:22; Rom 15:2. *b:* 4:16; Phil 3:17. *c:* 15:3; 2 Thes 2:15. *d:* Eph 5:23. *e:* Gn 1:26–27; 5:1.

man.[e] 8For man did not come from woman, but woman from man;[f] 9nor was man created for woman, but woman for man;[g] 10for this reason a woman should have a sign of authority* on her head, because of the angels. 11* Woman is not independent of man or man of woman in the Lord.[h] 12For just as woman came from man, so man is born of woman; but all things are from God.[i]

13* Judge for yourselves: is it proper for a woman to pray to God with her head unveiled? 14Does not nature itself teach you that if a man wears his hair long it is a disgrace to him, 15whereas if a woman has long hair it is her glory, because long hair has been given [her] for a covering? 16But if anyone is inclined to be argumentative, we do not have such a custom, nor do the churches of God.

## B. The Lord's Supper*

***An Abuse at Corinth.*** 17In giving this instruction, I do not praise the fact that your meetings are doing more harm than good. 18First of all, I hear that when you meet as a church there are divisions among you, and to a degree I believe it;[j] 19there have to be factions among you in order that [also] those who are approved among you may become known.* 20When you meet in one place, then, it is not to eat the Lord's supper, 21for in eating, each one goes ahead with his own supper, and one goes hungry while another gets drunk. 22Do you not have houses in which you can eat and drink? Or do you show contempt for the church of God and make those who have nothing feel ashamed? What can I say to you? Shall I praise you? In this matter I do not praise you.[k]

***Tradition of the Institution.*** 23* For I received from the Lord what I also handed on to you,[l] that the Lord Jesus, on the night he was handed over, took bread, 24and, after he had given thanks, broke it and said, "This is my body that is for you. Do this in remembrance of me." 25In the same way also the cup, after supper, saying, "This cup is the new covenant in my blood. Do this, as often as you drink it, in remembrance of me."[m] 26For as often as you eat this bread and drink the cup, you proclaim the death of the Lord until he comes.

27Therefore whoever eats the bread or drinks the cup of the Lord unworthily will have to answer for the body and blood of the Lord.* 28A person should examine him-

Gn 2:20–23), and under the influence of the story of the fall, as a result of which the husband rules over the woman (Gn 3:16). This interpretation splits the single image of God into two, at different degrees of closeness.

**11:10 A sign of authority**: "authority" (*exousia*) may possibly be due to mistranslation of an Aramaic word for "veil"; in any case, the connection with 1 Cor 11:9 indicates that the covering is a sign of woman's subordination. **Because of the angels**: a surprising additional reason, which the context does not clarify. Presumably the reference is to cosmic powers who might inflict harm on women or whose function is to watch over women or the cult.

**11:11–12** These parenthetical remarks relativize the argument from Gn 2–3. **In the Lord**: in the Christian economy the relation between the sexes is characterized by a mutual dependence, which is not further specified. And even in the natural order conditions have changed: the mode of origin described in Gn 2 has been reversed (1 Cor 11:12a). But the ultimately significant fact is the origin that all things have in common (1 Cor 11:12b).

**11:13–16** The argument for conformity to common church practice is summed up and pressed home. 1 Cor 11:14–15 contain a final appeal to the sense of propriety that contemporary Greek society would consider "natural" (cf. 1 Cor 11:5–6).

**11:17–34** Paul turns to another abuse connected with the liturgy, and a more serious one, for it involves neglect of basic Christian tradition concerning the meaning of the Lord's Supper. Paul recalls that tradition for them and reminds them of its implications.

**11:19 That . . . those who are approved among you may become known**: Paul situates their divisions within the context of the eschatological separation of the authentic from the inauthentic and the final revelation of the difference. The notion of authenticity-testing recurs in the injunction to self-examination in view of present and future judgment (1 Cor 11:28–32).

**11:23–25** This is the earliest written account of the institution of the Lord's Supper in the New Testament. The narrative emphasizes Jesus' action of self-giving (expressed in the words over the bread and the cup) and his double command to repeat his own action.

**11:27** It follows that the only proper way to celebrate the Eucharist is one that corresponds to Jesus' intention, which fits with the meaning of his command to reproduce his action in the proper spirit. If the Corinthians eat and drink unworthily, i.e., without having grasped and internalized the meaning of his death for them, **they will have to answer for the body and blood**, i.e., will be guilty of a sin against the Lord himself (cf. 1 Cor 8:12).

*f:* Gn 2:21–23. *g:* Gn 2:18. *h:* Gal 3:27–28. *i:* 8:6; Rom 11:36. *j:* 1:10–12; Gal 5:20. *k:* Jas 2:1–7. *l:* 11:2; 15:3 / 10:16–17; Mt 26:26–29; Mk 14:22–25; Lk 22:14–20. *m:* Ex 24:8; 2 Cor 3:6; Heb 8:6–13.

self,* and so eat the bread and drink the cup. 29For anyone who eats and drinks without discerning the body, eats and drinks judgment* on himself. 30That is why many among you are ill and infirm, and a considerable number are dying. 31If we discerned ourselves, we would not be under judgment; 32but since we are judged by [the] Lord, we are being disciplined so that we may not be condemned along with the world.[n]

33Therefore, my brothers, when you come together to eat, wait for one another. 34If anyone is hungry, he should eat at home, so that your meetings may not result in judgment. The other matters I shall set in order when I come.

## C. Spiritual Gifts*

### CHAPTER 12

See RG 371

*Unity and Variety.* 1Now in regard to spiritual gifts, brothers, I do not want you to be unaware. 2* You know how, when you were pagans, you were constantly attracted and led away to mute idols.[o] 3Therefore, I tell you that nobody speaking by the spirit of God says, "Jesus be accursed." And no one can say, "Jesus is Lord," except by the holy Spirit.[p]

4* There are different kinds of spiritual gifts but the same Spirit;[q] 5there are different forms of service but the same Lord; 6there are different workings but the same God who produces all of them in everyone. 7To each individual the manifestation of the Spirit is given for some benefit. 8To one is given through the Spirit the expression of wisdom; to another the expression of knowledge according to the same Spirit;[r] 9to another faith by the same Spirit; to another gifts of healing by the one Spirit; 10to another mighty deeds; to another prophecy; to another discernment of spirits; to another varieties of tongues; to another interpretation of tongues.[s] 11But one and the same Spirit produces all of these, distributing them individually to each person as he wishes.[t]

*One Body, Many Parts.** 12As a body is one though it has many parts, and all the parts of the body, though many, are one body, so also Christ.[u] 13For in one Spirit we were all baptized into one body, whether Jews or Greeks, slaves or free persons, and we were all given to drink of one Spirit.[v]

14Now the body is not a single part, but many. 15If a foot should say, "Because I am not a hand I do not belong to the body," it does not for this reason belong any less to

**11:28 Examine himself**: the Greek word is similar to that for "approved" in 1 Cor 11:19, which means "having been tested and found true." The self-testing required for proper eating involves **discerning the body** (1 Cor 11:29), which, from the context, must mean understanding the sense of Jesus' death (1 Cor 11:26), perceiving the imperative to unity that follows from the fact that Jesus gives himself to all and requires us to repeat his sacrifice in the same spirit (1 Cor 11:18–25).

**11:29–32 Judgment**: there is a series of wordplays in these verses that would be awkward to translate literally into English; it includes all the references to judgment (*krima*, 1 Cor 11:29, 34; *krinō*, 1 Cor 11:31, 32) discernment (*diakrinō*, 1 Cor 11:29, 31), and condemnation (*katakrinō*, 1 Cor 11:32). The judgment is concretely described as the illness, infirmity, and death that have visited the community. These are signs that the power of Jesus' death is not yet completely recognized and experienced. Yet even the judgment incurred is an expression of God's concern; it is a medicinal measure meant to rescue us from condemnation with God's enemies.

**12:1–14:40** Ecstatic and charismatic activity were common in early Christian experience, as they were in other ancient religions. But the Corinthians seem to have developed a disproportionate esteem for certain phenomena, especially tongues, to the detriment of order in the liturgy. Paul's response to this development provides us with the fullest exposition we have of his theology of the charisms.

**12:2–3** There is an experience of the Spirit and an understanding of ecstatic phenomena that are specifically Christian and that differ, despite apparent similarities, from those of the pagans. It is necessary to discern which spirit is leading one; ecstatic phenomena must be judged by their effect (1 Cor 12:2). 1 Cor 12:3 illustrates this by an example: power to confess Jesus as Lord can come only from the Spirit, and it is inconceivable that the Spirit would move anyone to curse the Lord.

**12:4–6** There are some features common to all charisms, despite their diversity: all are **gifts** (*charismata*), grace from outside ourselves; all are **forms of service** (*diakoniai*), an expression of their purpose and effect; and all are workings (*energēmata*), in which God is at work. Paul associates each of these aspects with what later theology will call one of the persons of the Trinity, an early example of "appropriation."

**12:12–26** The image of **a body** is introduced to explain Christ's relationship with believers (1 Cor 12:12). 1 Cor 12:13 applies this model to the church: by baptism all, despite diversity of ethnic or social origins, are integrated into one organism. 1 Cor 12:14–26 then develop the need for diversity of function among the parts of a body without threat to its unity.

*n:* Dt 8:5; Heb 12:5–11. *o:* Eph 2:11–18. *p:* Rom 10:9; 1 Jn 4:2–3. *q:* Rom 12:6; Eph 4:7, 11. *r:* 2:6–13. *s:* 14:5, 26, 39; Acts 2:4. *t:* 7:7; Eph 4:7. *u:* 10:17; Rom 12:4–5; Eph 2:16; Col 3:15. *v:* Gal 3:28; Eph 2:13–18; Col 3:11 / Jn 7:37–39.

the body. 16 Or if an ear should say, "Because I am not an eye I do not belong to the body," it does not for this reason belong any less to the body. 17 If the whole body were an eye, where would the hearing be? If the whole body were hearing, where would the sense of smell be? 18 But as it is, God placed the parts, each one of them, in the body as he intended. 19 If they were all one part, where would the body be? 20 But as it is, there are many parts, yet one body. 21 The eye cannot say to the hand, "I do not need you," nor again the head to the feet, "I do not need you." 22 Indeed, the parts of the body that seem to be weaker are all the more necessary, 23 and those parts of the body that we consider less honorable we surround with greater honor, and our less presentable parts are treated with greater propriety, 24 whereas our more presentable parts do not need this. But God has so constructed the body as to give greater honor to a part that is without it, 25 so that there may be no division in the body, but that the parts may have the same concern for one another. 26 If [one] part suffers, all the parts suffer with it; if one part is honored, all the parts share its joy.

*Application to Christ.** 27 Now you are Christ's body, and individually parts of it.[w] 28 Some people God has designated in the church to be, first, apostles;* second, prophets; third, teachers; then, mighty deeds; then, gifts of healing, assistance, administration, and varieties of tongues.[x] 29 Are all apostles? Are all prophets? Are all teachers? Do all work mighty deeds? 30 Do all have gifts of healing? Do all speak in tongues? Do all interpret? 31 Strive eagerly for the greatest spiritual gifts.

*The Way of Love.* But I shall show you a still more excellent way.

## CHAPTER 13*

See RG 371

1 If I speak in human and angelic tongues* but do not have love, I am a resounding gong or a clashing cymbal.[y] 2 And if I have the gift of prophecy and comprehend all mysteries and all knowledge; if I have all faith so as to move mountains but do not have love, I am nothing.[z] 3 If I give away everything I own, and if I hand my body over so that I may boast but do not have love, I gain nothing.[a]

4* Love is patient, love is kind. It is not jealous, [love] is not pompous, it is not inflated,[b] 5 it is not rude, it does not seek its own interests, it is not quick-tempered, it does not brood over injury,[c] 6 it does not rejoice over wrongdoing but rejoices with the truth. 7 It bears all things, believes all things, hopes all things, endures all things.[d]

8* Love never fails. If there are prophecies, they will be brought to nothing; if tongues, they will cease; if knowledge, it will be brought to nothing. 9 For we know partially and we prophesy partially, 10 but when the

**12:27–30** Paul now applies the image again to the church as a whole and its members (1 Cor 12:27). The lists in 1 Cor 12:28–30 spell out the parallelism by specifying the diversity of functions found in the church (cf. Rom 12:6–8; Eph 4:11).

**12:28 First, apostles**: apostleship was not mentioned in 1 Cor 12:8–10, nor is it at issue in these chapters, but Paul gives it pride of place in his listing. It is not just one gift among others but a prior and fuller gift that includes the others. They are all demonstrated in Paul's apostolate, but he may have developed his theology of charisms by reflecting first of all on his own grace of apostleship (cf. 1 Cor 3:5–4:14; 9:1–27; 2 Cor 2:14–6:13; 10:1–13:30, esp. 1 Cor 11:23 and 12:12).

**13:1–13** This chapter involves a shift of perspective and a new point. All or part of the material may once have been an independent piece in the style of Hellenistic eulogies of virtues, but it is now integrated, by editing, into the context of 1 Cor 12–14 (cf. the reference to tongues and prophecy) and into the letter as a whole (cf. the references to knowledge and to behavior). The function of 1 Cor 13 within the discussion of spiritual gifts is to relativize all the charisms by contrasting them with the more basic, pervasive, and enduring value that gives them their purpose and their effectiveness. The rhetoric of this chapter is striking.

**13:1–3** An inventory of gifts, arranged in careful gradation: neither tongues (on the lowest rung), nor prophecy, knowledge, or faith, nor even self-sacrifice has value unless informed by love.

**13:4–7** This paragraph is developed by personification and enumeration, defining love by what it does or does not do. The Greek contains fifteen verbs; it is natural to translate many of them by adjectives in English.

**13:8–13** The final paragraph announces its topic, **Love never fails** (1 Cor 13:8), then develops the permanence of love in contrast to the charisms (1 Cor 13:9–12), and finally asserts love's superiority even over the other "theological virtues" (1 Cor 13:13).

*w:* Rom 12:5–8; Eph 1:23; 4:12; 5:30; Col 1:18, 24. *x:* Eph 2:20; 3:5; 4:11. *y:* 8:1; 16:14; Rom 12:9–10; 13:8–10. *z:* 4:1; 14:2 / 1:5; 8:1–3; 12:8 / Mt 17:20; 21:21; Col 2:3. *a:* Mt 6:2. *b:* Eph 4:2 / 1 Cor 4:6, 18; 5:2; 8:1. *c:* 10:24, 33; Phil 2:4, 21; 1 Thes 5:15. *d:* Prv 10:12; 1 Pt 4:8.

perfect comes, the partial will pass away.
*11* When I was a child, I used to talk as a child,
think as a child, reason as a child; when I became a man, I put aside childish things. *12* At
present we see indistinctly, as in a mirror, but
then face to face. At present I know partially;
then I shall know fully, as I am fully known.[e]
*13** So faith, hope, love remain, these three;[f]
but the greatest of these is love.

See RG 371

## CHAPTER 14

***Prophecy Greater than Tongues.***
*1** Pursue love, but strive eagerly for the
spiritual gifts, above all that you may prophesy.[g] *2** For one who speaks in a tongue does
not speak to human beings but to God, for no
one listens; he utters mysteries in spirit. *3* On
the other hand, one who prophesies does
speak to human beings, for their building
up,* encouragement, and solace.[h] *4* Whoever
speaks in a tongue builds himself up, but
whoever prophesies builds up the church.
*5* Now I should like all of you to speak in
tongues, but even more to prophesy. One
who prophesies is greater than one who
speaks in tongues, unless he interprets, so
that the church may be built up.
*6** Now, brothers, if I should come to you
speaking in tongues, what good will I do you
if I do not speak to you by way of revelation,
or knowledge, or prophecy, or instruction?
*7* Likewise, if inanimate things that produce
sound, such as flute or harp, do not give out
the tones distinctly, how will what is being
played on flute or harp be recognized? *8* And
if the bugle gives an indistinct sound, who
will get ready for battle? *9* Similarly, if you,
because of speaking in tongues, do not utter
intelligible speech, how will anyone know
what is being said? For you will be talking to
the air. *10* It happens that there are many different languages in the world, and none is
meaningless; *11* but if I do not know the
meaning of a language, I shall be a foreigner
to one who speaks it, and one who speaks it
a foreigner to me. *12* So with yourselves:
since you strive eagerly for spirits, seek to
have an abundance of them for building up
the church.

***Need for Interpretation.**** *13* Therefore, one
who speaks in a tongue should pray to be
able to interpret. *14* [For] if I pray in a tongue,
my spirit* is at prayer but my mind is unproductive. *15* So what is to be done? I will pray
with the spirit, but I will also pray with the
mind. I will sing praise with the spirit, but I

**13:13** In speaking of love, Paul is led by spontaneous association to mention faith and hope as well. They are already a well-known triad (cf. 1 Thes 1:3), three interrelated (cf. 1 Cor 13:7) features of Christian life, more fundamental than any particular charism. **The greatest . . . is love**: love is operative even within the other members of the triad (1 Cor 13:7), so that it has a certain primacy among them. Or, if the perspective is temporal, love will remain (cf. "never fails," 1 Cor 13:8) even when faith has yielded to sight and hope to possession.

**14:1–5** 1 Cor 14:1b returns to the thought of 1 Cor 12:31a and reveals Paul's primary concern. The series of contrasts in 1 Cor 14:2–5 discloses the problem at Corinth: a disproportionate interest in tongues, with a corresponding failure to appreciate the worth of prophecy. Paul attempts to clarify the relative values of those gifts by indicating the kind of communication achieved in each and the kind of effect each produces.

**14:2–3a** They involve two kinds of communication: tongues, private speech toward God in inarticulate terms that need interpretation to be intelligible to others (see 1 Cor 14:27–28); prophecy, communication with others in the community.

**14:3b–5** They produce two kinds of effect. One who speaks in tongues **builds himself up**; it is a matter of individual experience and personal perfection, which inevitably recalls Paul's previous remarks about being inflated, seeking one's own good, pleasing oneself. But a prophet **builds up the church**: the theme of "building up" or "edifying" others, the main theme of the letter, comes to clearest expression in this chapter (1 Cor 14:3, 4, 5, 12, 17). It has been anticipated at 1 Cor 8:1 and 1 Cor 10:23, and by the related concept of "the beneficial" in 1 Cor 6:12; 10:23; 12:7; etc.

**14:6–12** Sound, in order to be useful, must be intelligible. This principle is illustrated by a series of analogies from music (1 Cor 14:7–8) and from ordinary human speech (1 Cor 14:10–11); it is applied to the case at hand in 1 Cor 14:9, 12.

**14:13–19** The charism of interpretation lifts tongues to the level of intelligibility, enabling them to produce the same effect as prophecy (cf. 1 Cor 14:5, 26–28).

**14:14–15 My spirit**: Paul emphasizes the exclusively ecstatic, nonrational quality of tongues. The tongues at Pentecost are also described as an ecstatic experience (Acts 2:4, 12–13), though Luke superimposes further interpretations of his own. **My mind**: the ecstatic element, dominant in earliest Old Testament prophecy as depicted in 1 Sm 10:5–13; 19:20–24, seems entirely absent from Paul's notion of prophecy and completely relegated to tongues. He emphasizes the role of reason when he specifies instruction as a function of prophecy (1 Cor 14:6, 19, 31). But he does not exclude intuition and emotion; cf. references to encouragement and consolation (1 Cor 14:3, 31) and the scene describing the ideal exercise of prophecy (1 Cor 14:24–25).

*e*: 2 Cor 5:7; Heb 11:1 / 2 Tm 2:19; 1 Jn 3:2. *f*: Col 1:4; 1 Thes 1:3; 5:8. *g*: 5, 12, 39. *h*: 14:4–5, 12, 17, 26; 3:9; 8:1, 10; 10:23. *i*: Eph 5:19; Col 3:16.

will also sing praise with the mind.[i] [16]Other-
wise, if you pronounce a blessing [with] the
spirit, how shall one who holds the place of
the uninstructed say the "Amen" to your
thanksgiving, since he does not know what
you are saying? [17]For you may be giving
thanks very well, but the other is not built
up. [18]I give thanks to God that I speak in
tongues more than any of you, [19]but in the
church I would rather speak five words with
my mind, so as to instruct others also, than
ten thousand words in a tongue.

***Functions of These Gifts.*** [20*] Brothers,
stop being childish in your thinking. In respect to evil be like infants, but in your
thinking be mature.[j] [21]It is written in the law:

"By people speaking strange tongues
and by the lips of foreigners
I will speak to this people,
and even so they will not listen to me,[k]

says the Lord." [22]Thus, tongues are a sign
not for those who believe but for unbelievers, whereas prophecy is not for unbelievers
but for those who believe.

[23*] So if the whole church meets in one
place and everyone speaks in tongues, and
then uninstructed people or unbelievers
should come in, will they not say that you
are out of your minds?[l] [24]But if everyone is
prophesying, and an unbeliever or uninstructed person should come in, he will be
convinced by everyone and judged by
everyone, [25]and the secrets of his heart will
be disclosed, and so he will fall down and
worship God, declaring, "God is really in
your midst."[m]

***Rules of Order.*** [26*] So what is to be done,
brothers? When you assemble, one has a
psalm, another an instruction, a revelation, a
tongue, or an interpretation. Everything
should be done for building up.[n] [27]If anyone
speaks in a tongue, let it be two or at most
three, and each in turn, and one should interpret. [28]But if there is no interpreter, the person should keep silent in the church and
speak to himself and to God.

[29]Two or three prophets should speak, and
the others discern. [30]But if a revelation is
given to another person sitting there, the first
one should be silent. [31]For you can all prophesy one by one, so that all may learn and all
be encouraged. [32]Indeed, the spirits of prophets are under the prophets' control, [33]since he
is not the God of disorder but of peace.

As in all the churches of the holy ones,*
[34]women should keep silent in the churches,
for they are not allowed to speak, but should
be subordinate, as even the law says.[o] [35]But
if they want to learn anything, they should

**14:20–22** The Corinthians pride themselves on tongues as a sign of God's favor, a means of direct communication with him (2:28). To challenge them to a more mature appraisal, Paul draws from scripture a less flattering explanation of what speaking in tongues may signify. Isaiah threatened the people that if they failed to listen to their prophets, the Lord would speak to them (in punishment) through the lips of Assyrian conquerors (Is 28:11–12). Paul compresses Isaiah's text and makes God address his people directly. Equating tongues with foreign languages (cf. 1 Cor 14:10–11), Paul concludes from Isaiah that **tongues are a sign not for those who believe**, i.e., not a mark of God's pleasure for those who listen to him but a mark of his displeasure with those in the community who are faithless, who have not heeded the message that he has sent through the prophets.

**14:23–25** Paul projects the possible missionary effect of two hypothetical liturgical experiences, one consisting wholly of tongues, the other entirely of prophecy. **Uninstructed** (*idiōtai*): the term may simply mean people who do not speak or understand tongues, as in 1 Cor 14:16, where it seems to designate Christians. But coupled with the term "unbelievers" it may be another way of designating those who have not been initiated into the community of faith; some believe it denotes a special class of non-Christians who are close to the community, such as catechumens. **Unbelievers** (*apistoi*): he has shifted from the inner-community perspective of 1 Cor 14:22; the term here designates non-Christians (cf. 1 Cor 6:6; 7:15; 10:27).

**14:26–33a** Paul concludes with specific directives regarding exercise of the gifts in their assemblies. Verse 26 enunciates the basic criterion in the use of any gift: it must contribute to "building up."

**14:33b–36** Verse 33b may belong with what precedes, so that the new paragraph would begin only with 1 Cor 14:34. 1 Cor 14:34–35 change the subject. These two verses have the theme of submission in common with 1 Cor 14:11 despite differences in vocabulary, and a concern with what is or is not becoming; but it is difficult to harmonize the injunction to silence here with 1 Cor 11 which appears to take it for granted that women do pray and prophesy aloud in the assembly (cf. 1 Cor 11:5, 13). Hence the verses are often considered an interpolation, reflecting the discipline of later churches; such an interpolation would have to have antedated our manuscripts, all of which contain them, though some transpose them to the very end of the chapter.

*j:* Mt 10:16; Rom 16:19; Eph 4:14. *k:* Is 28:11–12; Dt 28:49. *l:* Acts 2:6, 13. *m:* 4:5 / Is 45:14; Zec 8:23. *n:* Eph 4:12. *o:* 1 Tm 2:11–15; 1 Pt 3:1.

ask their husbands at home. For it is improper for a woman to speak in the church. 36Did the word of God go forth from you? Or has it come to you alone?

37If anyone thinks that he is a prophet or a spiritual person, he should recognize that what I am writing to you is a commandment of the Lord. 38If anyone does not acknowledge this, he is not acknowledged. 39So, [my] brothers, strive eagerly to prophesy, and do not forbid speaking in tongues, 40but everything must be done properly and in order.

## V. The Resurrection

### A. The Resurrection of Christ

#### CHAPTER 15*

See RG 371–72

*The Gospel Teaching.** 1Now I am reminding you, brothers, of the gospel I preached to you, which you indeed received and in which you also stand. 2Through it you are also being saved, if you hold fast to the word I preached to you, unless you believed in vain. 3* For I handed on to you as of first importance what I also received: that Christ died for our sins in accordance with the scriptures;[p] 4that he was buried; that he was raised on the third day in accordance with the scriptures;[q] 5that he appeared to Cephas, then to the Twelve.[r] 6After that, he appeared to more than five hundred brothers at once, most of whom are still living, though some have fallen asleep. 7After that he appeared to James, then to all the apostles. 8Last of all, as to one born abnormally, he appeared to me.[s] 9For I am the least* of the apostles, not fit to be called an apostle, because I persecuted the church of God.[t] 10But by the grace of God I am what I am, and his grace to me has not been ineffective. Indeed, I have toiled harder than all of them; not I, however, but the grace of God [that is] with me. 11Therefore, whether it be I or they, so we preach and so you believed.

### B. The Resurrection of the Dead

***Results of Denial.*** * 12But if Christ is preached as raised from the dead, how can some among you say there is no resurrection of the dead? 13If there is no resurrection of the dead, then neither has Christ been raised.[u] 14And if Christ has not been raised, then empty [too] is our preaching; empty, too, your faith. 15Then we are also false witnesses to God, because we testified against God that he raised Christ, whom he did not raise if in fact the dead are not raised.[v] 16For if the dead are not raised, neither has Christ been raised, 17and if Christ

**15:1–58** Some consider this chapter an earlier Pauline composition inserted into the present letter. The problem that Paul treats is clear to a degree: some of the Corinthians are denying the resurrection of the dead (1 Cor 15:12), apparently because of their inability to imagine how any kind of bodily existence could be possible after death (1 Cor 15:35). It is plausibly supposed that their attitude stems from Greek anthropology, which looks with contempt upon matter and would be content with the survival of the soul, and perhaps also from an overrealized eschatology of gnostic coloration, such as that reflected in 2 Tm 2:18, which considers the resurrection a purely spiritual experience already achieved in baptism and in the forgiveness of sins. Paul, on the other hand, will affirm both the essential corporeity of the resurrection and its futurity. His response moves through three steps: a recall of the basic kerygma about Jesus' resurrection (1 Cor 15:1–11), an assertion of the logical inconsistencies involved in denial of the resurrection (1 Cor 15:12–34), and an attempt to perceive theologically what the properties of the resurrected body must be (1 Cor 15:35–58).

**15:1–11** Paul recalls the tradition (1 Cor 15:3–7), which he can presuppose as common ground and which provides a starting point for his argument. This is the fundamental content of all Christian preaching and belief (1 Cor 15:1–2, 11).

**15:3–7** The language by which Paul expresses the essence of the "gospel" (1 Cor 15:1) is not his own but is drawn from older credal formulas. This credo highlights Jesus' death for our sins (confirmed by his burial) and Jesus' resurrection (confirmed by his appearances) and presents both of them as fulfillment of prophecy. **In accordance with the scriptures**: conformity of Jesus' passion with the scriptures is asserted in Mt 16:1; Lk 24:25–27, 32, 44–46. Application of some Old Testament texts (Ps 2:7; 16:8–11) to his resurrection is illustrated by Acts 2:27–31; 13:29–39; and Is 52:13–53:12 and Hos 6:2 may also have been envisaged.

**15:9–11** A persecutor may have appeared disqualified (*ouk . . . hikanos*) from apostleship, but in fact God's grace has qualified him. Cf. the remarks in 2 Corinthians about his qualifications (2 Cor 2:16; 3:5) and his greater labors (2 Cor 11:23). These verses are parenthetical, but a nerve has been touched (the references to his abnormal birth and his activity as a persecutor may echo taunts from Paul's opponents), and he is instinctively moved to self-defense.

**15:12–19** Denial of the resurrection (1 Cor 15:12) involves logical inconsistencies. The basic one, stated twice (1 Cor 15:13, 16), is that if there is no such thing as (bodily) resurrection, then it has not taken place even in Christ's case.

*p:* 11:23 / 1 Pt 2:24; 3:18 / Is 53:4–12. *q:* Acts 2:23–24 / Ps 16:8–11; Hos 6:1–2; Jon 2:1. *r:* Mk 16:14; Mt 28:16–17; Lk 24:36; Jn 20:19. *s:* 9:1; Acts 9:3–6; Gal 1:16. *t:* Acts 8:3; 9:1–2; Gal 1:23; Eph 3:8; 1 Tm 1:15. *u:* 1 Thes 4:14. *v:* Acts 5:32.

has not been raised,* your faith is vain; you
are still in your sins. 18Then those who have
fallen asleep in Christ have perished. 19If for
this life only we have hoped in Christ, we are
the most pitiable people of all.

***Christ the Firstfruits.**** 20[w] But now Christ
has been raised from the dead, the firstfruits*
of those who have fallen asleep. 21* For
since death came through a human being,
the resurrection of the dead came also
through a human being. 22For just as in
Adam all die, so too in Christ shall all be
brought to life,[x] 23but each one in proper order: Christ the firstfruits; then, at his coming, those who belong to Christ;[y] 24then
comes the end,* when he hands over the
kingdom to his God and Father, when he has
destroyed every sovereignty and every authority and power.[z] 25For he must reign until
he has put all his enemies under his feet.[a]
26* The last enemy[b] to be destroyed is death,
27* for "he subjected everything under his
feet."[c] But when it says that everything has
been subjected, it is clear that it excludes the
one who subjected everything to him.
28When everything is subjected to him, then
the Son himself will [also] be subjected to
the one who subjected everything to him, so
that God may be all in all.[d]

***Practical Arguments.**** 29Otherwise, what
will people accomplish by having themselves baptized for the dead?* If the dead are
not raised at all, then why are they having
themselves baptized for them?

30* Moreover, why are we endangering ourselves all the time?[e] 31Every day I face death;
I swear it by the pride in you [brothers] that I
have in Christ Jesus our Lord.[f] 32If at Ephesus
I fought with beasts, so to speak, what benefit
was it to me? If the dead are not raised:

"Let us eat and drink,
for tomorrow we die."[g]

33Do not be led astray:

"Bad company corrupts good morals."

**15:17–18** The consequences for the Corinthians are grave: both forgiveness of sins and salvation are an illusion, despite their strong convictions about both. Unless Christ is risen, their faith does not save.

**15:20–28** After a triumphant assertion of the reality of Christ's resurrection (1 Cor 15:20a), Paul explains its positive implications and consequences. As a soteriological event of both human (1 Cor 15:20–23) and cosmic (1 Cor 15:24–28) dimensions, Jesus' resurrection logically and necessarily involves ours as well.

**15:20 The firstfruits**: the portion of the harvest offered in thanksgiving to God implies the consecration of the entire harvest to come. Christ's resurrection is not an end in itself; its finality lies in the whole harvest, ourselves.

**15:21–22** Our human existence, both natural and supernatural, is corporate, involves solidarity. **In Adam . . . in Christ**: the Hebrew word *'ādām* in Genesis is both a common noun for mankind and a proper noun for the first man. Paul here presents Adam as at least a literary type of Christ; the parallelism and contrast between them will be developed further in 1 Cor 15:45–49 and in Rom 5:12–21.

**15:24–28** Paul's perspective expands to cosmic dimensions, as he describes the climax of history, **the end**. His viewpoint is still christological, as in 1 Cor 15:20–23. 1 Cor 15:24, 28 describe Christ's final relations to his enemies and his Father in language that is both royal and military; 1 Cor 15:25–28 insert a proof from scripture (Ps 110:1; 8:6) into this description. But the viewpoint is also theological, for God is the ultimate agent and end, and likewise soteriological, for we are the beneficiaries of all the action.

**15:26 The last enemy . . . is death**: a parenthesis that specifies the final fulfillment of the two Old Testament texts just referred to, Ps 110:1 and Ps 8:7. Death is not just one cosmic power among many, but the ultimate effect of sin in the universe (cf. 1 Cor 15:56; Rom 5:12). Christ defeats death where it prevails, in our bodies. The destruction of the last enemy is concretely the "coming to life" (1 Cor 15:22) of "those who belong to Christ" (1 Cor 15:23).

**15:27b–28 The one who subjected everything to him**: the Father is the ultimate agent in the drama, and the final end of the process, to whom the Son and everything else is ordered (1 Cor 15:24, 28). **That God may be all in all**: his reign is a dynamic exercise of creative power, an outpouring of life and energy through the universe, with no further resistance. This is the supremely positive meaning of "subjection": that God may fully be God.

**15:29–34** Paul concludes his treatment of logical inconsistencies with a listing of miscellaneous Christian practices that would be meaningless if the resurrection were not a fact.

**15:29 Baptized for the dead**: this practice is not further explained here, nor is it necessarily mentioned with approval, but Paul cites it as something in their experience that attests in one more way to belief in the resurrection.

**15:30–34** A life of sacrifice, such as Paul describes in 1 Cor 4:9–13 and 2 Corinthians, would be pointless without the prospect of resurrection; a life of pleasure, such as that expressed in the Epicurean slogan of 1 Cor 15:32, would be far more consistent. **I fought with beasts**: since Paul does not elsewhere mention a combat with beasts at Ephesus, he may be speaking figuratively about struggles with adversaries.

*w:* Rom 8:11; Col 1:18; 1 Thes 4:14. *x:* Gn 3:17–19; Rom 5:12–19. *y:* 1 Thes 4:15–17. *z:* Eph 1:22. *a:* Ps 110:1. *b:* Rom 6:9; 2 Tm 1:10; Rev 20:14; 21:4. *c:* Ps 8:7; Eph 1:22; Phil 3:21. *d:* Eph 4:6; Col 3:11. *e:* 2 Cor 4:8–12; 11:23–27. *f:* Ps 44:23; Rom 8:36. *g:* 4:9; 2 Cor 4:10–11 / Wis 2:5–7; Is 22:13.

34 Become sober as you ought and stop sinning. For some have no knowledge of God;
I say this to your shame.[h]

## C. The Manner of the Resurrection*

35* But someone may say, "How are the dead
raised? With what kind of body will they
come back?"

*The Resurrection Body.* 36* You fool!
What you sow is not brought to life unless it
dies.[i] 37 And what you sow is not the body
that is to be but a bare kernel of wheat, perhaps, or of some other kind; 38[j] but God
gives it a body as he chooses, and to each of
the seeds its own body. 39* Not all flesh is the
same, but there is one kind for human beings, another kind of flesh for animals, another kind of flesh for birds, and another for
fish. 40 There are both heavenly bodies and
earthly bodies, but the brightness of the
heavenly is one kind and that of the earthly
another. 41 The brightness of the sun is one
kind, the brightness of the moon another,
and the brightness of the stars another. For
star differs from star in brightness.
42* So also is the resurrection of the dead.
It is sown corruptible; it is raised incorruptible. 43 It is sown dishonorable; it is raised
glorious. It is sown weak; it is raised powerful.[k] 44 It is sown a natural body; it is raised a
spiritual body. If there is a natural body,
there is also a spiritual one.
45 So, too, it is written, "The first man,
Adam,* became a living being," the last
Adam a life-giving spirit.[l] 46 But the spiritual
was not first; rather the natural and then the
spiritual. 47 The first man was from the earth,
earthly; the second man, from heaven. 48 As
was the earthly one, so also are the earthly,
and as is the heavenly one, so also are the
heavenly. 49 Just as we have borne the image
of the earthly one, we shall also bear the image* of the heavenly one.[m]

*The Resurrection Event.* 50* This I declare, brothers: flesh and blood cannot inherit the kingdom of God, nor does corruption* inherit incorruption.[n] 51* Behold, I tell
you a mystery. We shall not all fall asleep,

**15:35–58** Paul imagines two objections that the Corinthians could raise: one concerning the manner of the resurrection (**how**?), the other pertaining to the qualities of the risen body (**what kind**?). These questions probably lie behind their denial of the resurrection (1 Cor 15:12), and seem to reflect the presumption that no kind of body other than the one we now possess would be possible. Paul deals with these objections in inverse order, in 1 Cor 15:36–49 and 1 Cor 15:50–58. His argument is fundamentally theological and its appeal is to the understanding.

**15:35–49** Paul approaches the question of the nature of the risen body (**what kind of body**?) by means of two analogies: the seed (1 Cor 15:36–44) and the first man, Adam (1 Cor 15:45–49).

**15:36–38** The analogy of the seed: there is a change of attributes from seed to plant; the old life-form must be lost for the new to emerge. By speaking about the seed as a **body** that dies and comes to life, Paul keeps the point of the analogy before the reader's mind.

**15:39–41** The expression "its own body" (1 Cor 15:38) leads to a development on the marvelous diversity evident in bodily life.

**15:42–44** The principles of qualitative difference before and after death (1 Cor 15:36–38) and of diversity on different levels of creation (1 Cor 15:39–41) are now applied to the human body. Before: a body animated by a lower, natural life-principle (*psychē*) and endowed with the properties of natural existence (corruptibility, lack of glory, weakness). After: a body animated by a higher life-principle (*pneuma*; cf. 1 Cor 15:45) and endowed with other qualities (incorruptibility, glory, power, spirituality), which are properties of God himself.

**15:45** The analogy of **the first man, Adam,** is introduced by a citation from Gn 2:7. Paul alters the text slightly, adding the adjective **first**, and translating the Hebrew *'ādām* twice, so as to give it its value both as a common noun (**man**) and as a proper name (**Adam**). 1 Cor 15:45b then specifies similarities and differences between the two Adams. **The last Adam**, Christ (cf. 1 Cor 15:21–22) has become **a . . . spirit** (*pneuma*), a life-principle transcendent with respect to the natural soul (*psychē*) of the first Adam (on the terminology here, cf. note on 1 Cor 3:1). Further, he is not just alive, but life-giving, a source of life for others.

**15:49 We shall also bear the image**: although it has less manuscript support, this reading better fits the context's emphasis on futurity and the transforming action of God; on future transformation as conformity to the image of the Son, cf. Rom 8:29; Phil 3:21. The majority reading, "let us bear the image," suggests that the image of the heavenly man is already present and exhorts us to conform to it.

**15:50–57** These verses, an answer to the first question of 1 Cor 15:35, explain theologically how the change of properties from one image to another will take place: God has the power to transform, and he will exercise it.

**15:50–53 Flesh and blood . . . corruption**: living persons and the corpses of the dead, respectively. In both cases, the gulf between creatures and God is too wide to be bridged unless God himself transforms us.

**15:51–52 A mystery**: the last moment in God's plan is disclosed; cf. notes on 1 Cor 2:1, 7–10a. The final trumpet and the awakening of the dead are stock details of the apocalyptic scenario. **We shall not all fall asleep**: Paul expected that some of

*h:* Mt 22:29; Mk 12:24. *i:* Jn 12:24. *j:* Gn 1:11. *k:* Phil 3:20–21; Col 3:4. *l:* Gn 2:7 / Jn 5:21–29; 2 Cor 3:6, 17. *m:* Gn 5:3 / Rom 8:29; Phil 3:21. *n:* Jn 3:3–6. *o:* 1 Thes 4:14–17.

but we will all be changed,[o] 52in an instant,
in the blink of an eye, at the last trumpet. For
the trumpet will sound, the dead will be
raised incorruptible, and we shall be
changed.[p] 53For that which is corruptible
must clothe itself with incorruptibility, and
that which is mortal must clothe itself with
immortality.[q] 54* And when this which is
corruptible clothes itself with incorruptibility and this which is mortal clothes itself
with immortality, then the word that is written shall come about:[r]

"Death is swallowed up in victory.
55 Where, O death, is your victory?
Where, O death, is your sting?"[s]

56The sting of death is sin,* and the power of
sin is the law.[t] 57But thanks be to God who
gives us the victory through our Lord Jesus
Christ.[u]

58Therefore, my beloved brothers, be
firm, steadfast, always fully devoted to the
work of the Lord, knowing that in the Lord
your labor is not in vain.

## VI. Conclusion

### CHAPTER 16

See RG 372

***The Collection.**** 1Now in regard to the
collection* for the holy ones, you also
should do as I ordered the churches of Galatia.[v] 2On the first day of the week each of
you should set aside and save whatever one
can afford, so that collections will not be going on when I come. 3And when I arrive, I
shall send those whom you have approved
with letters of recommendation to take your
gracious gift to Jerusalem. 4If it seems fitting
that I should go also,* they will go with me.

***Paul's Travel Plans.**** 5I shall come to you
after I pass through Macedonia (for I am going to pass through Macedonia),[w] 6and perhaps I shall stay or even spend the winter
with you, so that you may send me on my
way wherever I may go. 7For I do not wish
to see you now just in passing, but I hope to
spend some time with you, if the Lord permits.[x] 8* I shall stay in Ephesus[y] until Pentecost, 9because a door has opened for me
wide and productive for work, but there are
many opponents.[z]

10If Timothy comes, see that he is without
fear in your company, for he is doing the
work of the Lord just as I am.[a] 11Therefore no
one should disdain him. Rather, send him on
his way in peace that he may come to me, for
I am expecting him with the brothers. 12Now
in regard to our brother Apollos, I urged him
strongly to go to you with the brothers, but it
was not at all his will that he go now. He will
go when he has an opportunity.[b]

***Exhortation and Greetings.*** 13Be on your
guard, stand firm in the faith, be courageous,
be strong. 14Your every act should be done
with love.

15I urge you, brothers—you know that the
household of Stephanas[c] is the firstfruits of
Achaia and that they have devoted them-

his contemporaries might still be alive at Christ's return; after the death of Paul and his whole generation, copyists altered this statement in various ways. **We will all be changed**: the statement extends to all Christians, for Paul is not directly speaking about anyone else. Whether they have died before the end or happen still to be alive, all must be transformed.

**15:54–55 Death is swallowed up in victory**: scripture itself predicts death's overthrow. **O death**: in his prophetic vision Paul may be making Hosea's words his own, or imagining this cry of triumph on the lips of the risen church.

**15:56 The sting of death is sin**: an explanation of Hosea's metaphor. Death, scorpion-like, is equipped with a sting, sin, by which it injects its poison. Christ defeats sin, the cause of death (Gn 3:19; Rom 5:12).

**16:1–4** This paragraph contains our earliest evidence for a project that became a major undertaking of Paul's ministry. The collection for the church at Jerusalem was a symbol in his mind for the unity of Jewish and Gentile Christianity. Cf. Gal 2:10; Rom 15:25–29; 2 Cor 8–9 and the notes to this last passage.

**16:1 In regard to the collection**: it has already begun in Galatia and Macedonia (cf. 2 Cor 8), and presumably he has already instructed the Corinthians about its purpose.

**16:4 That I should go also**: presumably Paul delivered the collection on his final visit to Jerusalem; cf. Rom 15:25–32; Acts 24:14.

**16:5–12** The travel plans outlined here may not have materialized precisely as Paul intended; cf. 2 Cor 1:8–2:13; 7:4–16.

**16:8 In Ephesus until Pentecost**: this tells us the place from which he wrote the letter and suggests he may have composed it about Easter time (cf. 1 Cor 5:7–8).

*p:* Jl 2:1; Zec 9:14; Mt 24:31; Rev 11:15–18. *q:* 2 Cor 5:2–4. *r:* Is 25:8; 2 Cor 5:4; 2 Tm 1:10; Heb 2:14–15. *s:* Hos 13:14. *t:* Rom 4:15; 7:7, 13. *u:* Jn 16:33; 1 Jn 5:4. *v:* Acts 24:17; Rom 15:25–32; 2 Cor 8–9; Gal 2:10. *w:* Acts 19:21; Rom 15:26; 2 Cor 1:15–16. *x:* Acts 18:21. *y:* 15:32; Acts 18:19; 19:1–10. *z:* Acts 14:27; 2 Cor 2:12. *a:* 4:17; Acts 16:1; 19:22; Phil 2:19–23. *b:* 1:12; 3:4–6, 22; Acts 18:24–28. *c:* 1:16.

selves to the service of the holy ones— 16be
subordinate to such people and to everyone
who works and toils with them. 17I rejoice in
the arrival of Stephanas, Fortunatus, and
Achaicus, because they made up for your
absence, 18for they refreshed my spirit as
well as yours. So give recognition to such
people.[d]
19* The churches of Asia send you greetings. Aquila and Prisca together with the
church at their house send you many greetings in the Lord.[e] 20All the brothers greet
you. Greet one another with a holy kiss.[f]
21I, Paul, write you this greeting in my
own hand.[g] 22If anyone does not love the
Lord, let him be accursed.* *Marana tha.*[h]
23The grace of the Lord Jesus be with you.[i]
24My love to all of you in Christ Jesus.

**16:19–24** These paragraphs conform to the normal epistolary conclusion, but their language is overlaid with liturgical coloration as well. The **greetings** of the Asian churches are probably to be read, along with the letter, in the liturgy at Corinth, and the union of the church is to be expressed by a holy kiss (1 Cor 16:19–20). Paul adds to this his own greeting (1 Cor 16:21) and blessings (1 Cor 16:23–24).

**16:22 Accursed**: literally, "anathema." This expression (cf. 1 Cor 12:3) is a formula for exclusion from the community; it may imply here a call to self-examination before celebration of the Eucharist, in preparation for the Lord's coming and judgment (cf. 1 Cor 11:17–34). ***Marana tha***: an Aramaic expression, probably used in the early Christian liturgy. As understood here ("O Lord, come!"), it is a prayer for the early return of Christ. If the Aramaic words are divided differently (*Maran atha*, "Our Lord has come"), it becomes a credal declaration. The former interpretation is supported by what appears to be a Greek equivalent of this acclamation in Rev 22:20 "Amen. Come, Lord Jesus!"

*d*: 1 Thes 5:12–13. *e*: Acts 18:2, 18, 26; Rom 16:3–5. *f*: Rom 16:16; 2 Cor 13:12; 1 Thes 5:26; 1 Pt 5:14. *g*: Gal 6:11; Col 4:18; 2 Thes 3:17. *h*: 12:3; Rom 9:3; Gal 1:8–9; Rev 22:20. *i*: Rom 16:20.

See RG 375–82

# The Second Letter to the Corinthians

The Second Letter to the Corinthians is the most personal of all of Paul's extant writings, and it reveals much about his character. In it he deals with one or more crises that have arisen in the Corinthian church. The confrontation with these problems caused him to reflect deeply on his relationship with the community and to speak about it frankly. One moment he is venting his feelings of frustration and uncertainty, the next he is pouring out his relief and affection. The importance of the issues at stake between them calls forth from him an enormous effort of personal persuasion, as well as doctrinal considerations that are of great value for us. Paul's ability to produce profound theological foundations for what may at first sight appear to be rather commonplace circumstances is perhaps nowhere better exemplified than in Second Corinthians. The emotional tone of the letter, its lack of order, and our ignorance of some of its background do not make it easy to follow, but it amply repays the effort required of the reader.

Second Corinthians is rich and varied in content. The interpretation of Exodus in chapter 3, for instance, offers a striking example of early apologetic use of the Old Testament. Paul's discussion of the collection in chaps. 8–9 contains a theology of sharing of possessions, of community of goods among Christian churches, which is both balanced and sensitive. Furthermore, the closing chapters provide an illustration of early Christian invective and polemic, because the conflict with intruders forces Paul to assert his authority. But in those same chapters Paul articulates the vision and sense of values that animate his own apostolate, revealing his faith that Jesus' passion and resurrection are the pattern for all Christian life and expressing a spirituality of ministry unsurpassed in the New Testament.

The letter is remarkable for its rhetoric. Paul falls naturally into the style and argumentation of contemporary philosophic preachers, employing with ease the stock devices of the "diatribe." By a barrage of questions, by challenges both serious and ironic, by paradox heaped upon paradox, even by insults hurled at his opponents, he strives to awaken in his hearers a true sense of values and an appropriate response. All his argument centers on the destiny of Jesus, in which a paradoxical reversal of values is revealed. But Paul appeals to his own personal experience as well. In passages of great rhetorical power (2 Cor 4:7–15; 6:3–10; 11:21–29; 12:5–10; 13:3–4) he enumerates the circumstances of his ministry and the tribulations he has had to endure for Jesus and the gospel, in the hope of illustrating the pattern of Jesus' existence in his own and of drawing the Corinthians into a reappraisal of the values they cherish. Similar passages in the same style in his other letters (cf. especially Rom 8:31–39; 1 Cor 1:26–31; 4:6–21; 9:1–27; 13:1–13; Phil 4:10–19) confirm Paul's familiarity with contemporary rhetoric and demonstrate how effectively it served to express his vision of Christian life and ministry.

Second Corinthians was occasioned by events and problems that developed after Paul's first letter reached Corinth. We have no information about these circumstances except what is contained in the letter itself, which of course supposes that they are known to the readers. Consequently the reconstruction of the letter's background is an uncertain enterprise about which there is not complete agreement.

The letter deals principally with these three topics: (1) a crisis between Paul and the Corinthians, occasioned at least partially by changes in his travel plans (2 Cor 1:12–2:13), and the successful resolution of that crisis (2 Cor 7:5–16); (2) further directives and encouragement in regard to the collection for the church in Jerusalem (2 Cor 8:1–9:15); (3) the definition and defense of Paul's ministry as an apostle. Paul's reflections on this matter are occasioned by visitors from other churches who passed through Corinth, missionaries who differed from Paul in a variety of ways, both in theory and in practice. Those differences led to comparisons. Either the visitors themselves or some of the local church members appear to have sown confusion among the Corinthians with regard to Paul's authority or his style, or both. Paul deals at length with aspects of this situation in 2 Cor 2:14–7:4 and again in 2 Cor 10:1–13:10, though the manner of treatment and the thrust of the argument differ in each of these sections.

Scholars have noticed a lack of continuity in this document. For example, the long section of 2 Cor 2:14–7:4 seems abruptly spliced into the narrative of a crisis and its resolution. Identical or similar topics, moreover, seem to be treated several times during the letter (compare 2 Cor 2:14–7:4 with 2 Cor 10:1–13:10, and 2 Cor 8:1–24 with 2 Cor 9:1–15). Many judge, therefore, that this letter as it stands incorporates several briefer letters sent to Corinth over a certain span of time. If this is so, then Paul himself or, more likely, some other editor clearly took care to gather those letters together and impose some literary unity upon the collection, thus producing the document that has come down to us as the Second Letter to the Corinthians. Others continue to regard it as a single letter, attributing its inconsistencies to changes of perspective in Paul that may have been occasioned by the arrival of fresh news from Corinth during its composition. The letter, or at least some sections of it, appears to have been composed in Macedonia (2 Cor 2:12–13; 7:5–6; 8:1–4; 9:2–4). It is generally dated about the autumn of A.D. 57; if it is a compilation, of course, the various parts may have been separated by intervals of at least some months.

The principal divisions of the Second Letter to the Corinthians are the following:

I. Address (1:1–11)
II. The Crisis Between Paul and the Corinthians (1:12–7:16)
  A. Past Relationships (1:12–2:13)
  B. Paul's Ministry (2:14–7:4)
  C. Resolution of the Crisis (7:5–16)
III. The Collection for Jerusalem (8:1–9:15)
IV. Paul's Defense of His Ministry (10:1–13:10)
V. Conclusion (13:11–13)

# I. Address

## CHAPTER 1

See RG 376–77

*Greeting.* 1* Paul, an apostle of Christ Jesus by the will of God, and Timothy our brother, to the church of God that is in Corinth, with all the holy ones throughout Achaia:[a] 2 grace to you and peace from God our Father and the Lord Jesus Christ.

**1:1–11** The opening follows the usual Pauline form, except that the thanksgiving takes the form of a doxology or glorification of God (2 Cor 1:3). This introduces a meditation on the experience of suffering and encouragement shared by Paul and the Corinthians (2 Cor 1:4–7), drawn, at least in part, from Paul's reflections on a recent affliction (2 Cor 1:8–10). The section ends with a modified and delayed allusion to thanksgiving (2 Cor 1:11).

*a:* Eph 1:1; Col 1:1 / 1 Cor 1:19; Acts 16 / Rom 1:7; 1 Cor 1:2.

***Thanksgiving.*** 3b Blessed be the God and Father of our Lord Jesus Christ, the Father of compassion and God of all encouragement,* 4 who encourages us in our every affliction, so that we may be able to encourage those who are in any affliction with the encouragement with which we ourselves are encouraged by God.[c] 5 For as Christ's sufferings overflow to us, so through Christ* does our encouragement also overflow. 6 If we are afflicted, it is for your encouragement and salvation; if we are encouraged, it is for your encouragement, which enables you to endure the same sufferings that we suffer. 7 Our hope for you is firm, for we know that as you share in the sufferings, you also share in the encouragement.*

8 We do not want you to be unaware, brothers, of the affliction that came to us in the province of Asia;* we were utterly weighed down beyond our strength, so that we despaired even of life.[d] 9 Indeed, we had accepted within ourselves the sentence of death,* that we might trust not in ourselves but in God who raises the dead.[e] 10 He rescued us from such great danger of death, and he will continue to rescue us; in him we have put our hope [that] he will also rescue us again,[f] 11 as you help us with prayer, so that thanks may be given by many on our behalf for the gift granted us through the prayers of many.[g]

## II. The Crisis Between Paul and the Corinthians

### A. Past Relationships*

***Paul's Sincerity and Constancy.*** 12* For our boast is this, the testimony of our conscience that we have conducted ourselves in the world, and especially toward you, with the simplicity and sincerity of God, [and] not by human wisdom but by the grace of God. 13 For we write you nothing but what you can read and understand, and I hope that you will understand completely, 14 as you have come to understand us partially, that we are your boast as you also are ours, on the day of [our] Lord Jesus.[h]

15 With this confidence I formerly intended to come* to you so that you might receive a double favor, 16 namely, to go by way of you to Macedonia, and then to come to you again on my return from Macedonia, and have you send me on my way to Judea.[i] 17 So when I intended this, did I act lightly?*

**1:3 God of all encouragement**: Paul expands a standard Jewish blessing so as to state the theme of the paragraph. The theme of "encouragement" or "consolation" (*paraklēsis*) occurs ten times in this opening, against a background formed by multiple references to "affliction" and "suffering."

**1:5 Through Christ**: the Father of compassion is the Father of our Lord Jesus (2 Cor 1:3); Paul's sufferings and encouragement (or "consolation") are experienced in union with Christ. Cf. Lk 2:25: the "consolation of Israel" is Jesus himself.

**1:7 You also share in the encouragement**: the eschatological reversal of affliction and encouragement that Christians expect (cf. Mt 5:4; Lk 6:24) permits some present experience of reversal in the Corinthians' case, as in Paul's.

**1:8 Asia**: a Roman province in western Asia Minor, the capital of which was Ephesus.

**1:9–10 The sentence of death**: it is unclear whether Paul is alluding to a physical illness or to an external threat to life. The result of the situation was to produce an attitude of faith in God alone. **God who raises the dead**: rescue is the constant pattern of God's activity; his final act of encouragement is the resurrection.

**1:12–2:13** The autobiographical remarks about the crisis in Asia Minor lead into consideration of a crisis that has arisen between Paul and the Corinthians. Paul will return to this question, after a long digression, in 2 Cor 7:5–16. Both of these sections deal with travel plans Paul had made, changes in the plans, alternative measures adopted, a breach that opened between him and the community, and finally a reconciliation between them.

**1:12–14** Since Paul's own conduct will be under discussion here, he prefaces the section with a statement about his habitual behavior and attitude toward the community. He protests his openness, single-mindedness, and conformity to God's grace; he hopes that his relationship with them will be marked by mutual understanding and pride, which will constantly increase until it reaches its climax at the judgment. Two references to boasting frame this paragraph (2 Cor 1:12, 14), the first appearances of a theme that will be important in the letter, especially in 2 Cor 10–13; the term is used in a positive sense here (cf. note on 1 Cor 1:29–31).

**1:15 I formerly intended to come**: this plan reads like a revision of the one mentioned in 1 Cor 16:5. Not until 2 Cor 1:23–2:1 will Paul tell us something his original readers already knew, that he has canceled one or the other of these projected visits.

**1:17 Did I act lightly?**: the subsequent change of plans casts suspicion on the original intention, creating the impression that Paul is vacillating and inconsistent or that **human considera-**

*b:* 1 Cor 15:24; Eph 1:3; 1 Pt 1:3 / Rom 15:5. *c:* 7:6–7, 13; 1 Thes 3:6–8; 2 Thes 2:16. *d:* Acts 20:18–19; 1 Cor 15:32. *e:* 4:7–11; Rom 4:17. *f:* 2 Tm 4:18. *g:* 4:15; 9:12. *h:* Phil 2:16; 1 Thes 2:19–20. *i:* 1 Cor 16:5–9; Acts 19:21. *j:* Mt 5:37; Jas 5:12.

Or do I make my plans according to human considerations, so that with me it is "yes, yes" and "no, no"?[j] [18]As God is faithful,* our word to you is not "yes" and "no." [19]For the Son of God, Jesus Christ, who was proclaimed to you by us, Silvanus and Timothy and me, was not "yes" and "no," but "yes" has been in him.[k] [20]For however many are the promises of God, their Yes is in him; therefore, the Amen from us also goes through him to God for glory.[l] [21]* But the one who gives us security with you in Christ and who anointed us is God;[m] [22]he has also put his seal upon us and given the Spirit in our hearts as a first installment.[n]

***Paul's Change of Plan.*** [23][o] But I call upon God as witness, on my life, that it is to spare you that I have not yet gone to Corinth.* [24]Not that we lord it over your faith; rather, we work together for your joy, for you stand firm in the faith.

## CHAPTER 2

See RG 377–78

[1]For I decided not to come to you again in painful circumstances. [2]For if I inflict pain upon you, then who is there to cheer me except the one pained by me? [3]And I wrote as I did* so that when I came I might not be pained by those in whom I should have rejoiced, confident about all of you that my joy is that of all of you. [4]For out of much affliction and anguish of heart I wrote to you with many tears, not that you might be pained but that you might know the abundant love I have for you.

***The Offender.**** [5]If anyone has caused pain, he has caused it not to me, but in some measure (not to exaggerate) to all of you. [6]This punishment by the majority is enough for such a person, [7]so that on the contrary you should forgive and encourage him instead, or else the person may be overwhelmed by excessive pain.[p] [8]Therefore, I urge you to reaffirm your love for him. [9]For this is why I wrote, to know your proven character, whether you were obedient in everything.[q] [10]Whomever you forgive anything, so do I. For indeed what I have forgiven, if I have forgiven anything, has been for you in the presence of Christ, [11]so that we might not be

**tions** keep dictating shifts in his goals and projects (cf. the counterclaim of 2 Cor 1:12). **"Yes, yes" and "no, no"**: stating something and denying it in the same or the next breath; being of two minds at once, or from one moment to the next.

**1:18–22 As God is faithful**: unable to deny the change in plans, Paul nonetheless asserts the firmness of the original plan and claims a profound constancy in his life and work. He grounds his defense in God himself, who is firm and reliable; this quality can also be predicated in various ways of those who are associated with him. Christ, Paul, and the Corinthians all participate in analogous ways in the constancy of God. A number of the terms here, which appear related only conceptually in Greek or English, would be variations of the same root, *'mn*, in a Semitic language, and thus naturally associated in a Semitic mind, such as Paul's. These include the words **yes** (2 Cor 1:17–20), **faithful** (2 Cor 1:18), **Amen** (2 Cor 1:20), **gives us security** (2 Cor 1:21), **faith, stand firm** (2 Cor 1:24).

**1:21–22** The commercial terms **gives us security, seal, first installment** are here used analogously to refer to the process of initiation into the Christian life, perhaps specifically to baptism. The passage is clearly trinitarian. The Spirit is the **first installment** or "down payment" of the full messianic benefits that God guarantees to Christians. Cf. Eph 1:13–14.

**1:23–24 I have not yet gone to Corinth**: some suppose that Paul received word of some affair in Corinth, which he decided to regulate by letter even before the first of his projected visits (cf. 2 Cor 1:16). Others conjecture that he did pay the first visit, was offended there (cf. 2 Cor 2:5), returned to Ephesus, and sent a letter (2 Cor 2:3–9) in place of the second visit. The expressions **to spare you** (2 Cor 1:23) and **work together for your joy** (2 Cor 1:24) introduce the major themes of the next two paragraphs, which are remarkable for insistent repetition of key words and ideas. These form two clusters of terms in the English translation: (1) cheer, rejoice, encourage, joy; (2) pain, affliction, anguish. These clusters reappear when Paul resumes treatment of this subject in 2 Cor 7:5–16.

**2:3–4 I wrote as I did**: we learn for the first time about the sending of a letter in place of the proposed visit. Paul mentions the letter in passing, but emphasizes his motivation in sending it: to avoid being saddened by them (cf. 1 Cor 2:1), and to help them realize the depth of his love. Another motive will be added in 2 Cor 7:12: to bring to light their own concern for him. **With many tears**: it has been suggested that we may have all or part of this "tearful letter" somewhere in the Corinthian correspondence, either in 1 Cor 5 (the case of the incestuous man), or in 1 Corinthians as a whole, or in 2 Cor 2:10–13. None of these hypotheses is entirely convincing. See note on 2 Cor 13:1.

**2:5–11** The nature of the **pain** (2 Cor 2:5) is unclear, though some believe an individual at Corinth rejected Paul's authority, thereby scandalizing many in the community. In any case, action has been taken, and Paul judges the measures adequate to right the situation (2 Cor 2:6). The follow-up directives he now gives are entirely positive: forgive, encourage, love. **Overwhelmed** (2 Cor 2:7): a vivid metaphor (literally "swallowed") that Paul employs positively at 2 Cor 5:4 and in 1 Cor 15:54 (2 Cor 2:7). It is often used to describe satanic activity (cf. 1 Pt 5:8); note the reference to Satan here in 2 Cor 2:11.

*k:* Acts 16:1–3; 1 Thes 1:1; 2 Thes 1:1. *l:* 1 Cor 14:16; Rev 3:14. *m:* 1 Jn 2:20, 27. *n:* Eph 1:13–14; 4:30 / 2 Cor 5:5; Rom 5:5; 8:16, 23. *o:* 13:2. *p:* Col 3:13. *q:* 7:15.

taken advantage of by Satan, for we are not
unaware of his purposes.[r]
*Paul's Anxiety.** 12 When I went to Troas
for the gospel of Christ, although a door was
opened for me in the Lord,[s] 13* I had no relief in my spirit because I did not find my
brother Titus.[t] So I took leave of them and
went on to Macedonia.

## B. Paul's Ministry*

*Ministers of a New Covenant.* 14* But thanks
be to God,* who always leads us in triumph
in Christ* and manifests through us the odor
of the knowledge of him* in every place.
15 For we are the aroma of Christ for God
among those who are being saved and
among those who are perishing,[u] 16 to the latter an odor of death that leads to death, to the
former an odor of life that leads to life. Who
is qualified* for this? 17 For we are not like
the many who trade on the word of God; but
as out of sincerity, indeed as from God and
in the presence of God, we speak in Christ.[v]

### CHAPTER 3

See RG 378

1* [w] Are we beginning to commend
ourselves again? Or do we need, as some do,
letters of recommendation to you or from
you? 2 You are our letter,* written on our
hearts, known and read by all, 3* [x] shown to

**2:12–13 I had no relief**: Paul does not explain the reason for his anxiety until he resumes the thread of his narrative at 2 Cor 7:5: he was waiting to hear how the Corinthians would respond to his letter. Since 2 Cor 7:5–16 describes their response in entirely positive terms, we never learn in detail why he found it necessary to defend and justify his change of plans, as in 2 Cor 1:15–24. Was this portion of the letter written before the arrival of Titus with his good news (2 Cor 7:6–7)?

**2:13 Macedonia**: a Roman province in northern Greece.

**2:14–7:4** This section constitutes a digression within the narrative of the crisis and its resolution (2 Cor 1:12–2:13 and 2 Cor 7:5–16). The main component (2 Cor 2:14–6:10) treats the nature of Paul's ministry and his qualifications for it; this material bears some similarity to the defense of his ministry in chaps. 10–13, but it may well come from a period close to the crisis. This is followed by a supplementary block of material quite different in character and tone (2 Cor 6:14–7:1). These materials may have been brought together into their present position during final editing of the letter; appeals to the Corinthians link them to one another (2 Cor 6:11–13) and lead back to the interrupted narrative (2 Cor 7:2–4).

**2:14–6:10** The question of Paul's adequacy (2 Cor 2:16; cf. 2 Cor 3:5) and his credentials (2 Cor 3:1–2) has been raised. Paul responds by an extended treatment of the nature of his ministry. It is a ministry of glory (2 Cor 3:7–4:6), of life (2 Cor 4:7–5:10), of reconciliation (2 Cor 5:11–6:10).

**2:14–16a** The initial statement plunges us abruptly into another train of thought. Paul describes his personal existence and his function as a preacher in two powerful images (2 Cor 2:14) that constitute a prelude to the development to follow.

**2:14a Leads us in triumph in Christ**: this metaphor of a festive parade in honor of a conquering military hero can suggest either a positive sharing in Christ's triumph or an experience of defeat, being led in captivity and submission (cf. 2 Cor 4:8–11; 1 Cor 4:9). Paul is probably aware of the ambiguity, as he is in the case of the next metaphor.

**2:14b–16a The odor of the knowledge of him**: incense was commonly used in triumphal processions. The metaphor suggests the gradual diffusion of the knowledge of God through the apostolic preaching. **The aroma of Christ**: the image shifts from the fragrance Paul diffuses to the aroma that he is. Paul is probably thinking of the "sweet odor" of the sacrifices in the Old Testament (e.g., Gn 8:21; Ex 29:18) and perhaps of the metaphor of wisdom as a sweet odor (Sir 24:15).

**Death . . . life**: the aroma of Christ that comes to them through Paul is perceived differently by various classes of people. To some his preaching and his life (cf. 1 Cor 1:17–2:6) are perceived as death, and the effect is death for them; others perceive him, despite appearances, as **life**, and the effect is life for them. This fragrance thus produces a separation and a judgment (cf. the function of the "light" in John's gospel).

**2:16b–17 Qualified**: Paul may be echoing either the self-satisfied claims of other preachers or their charges about Paul's deficiencies. No one is really qualified, but the apostle contrasts himself with those who dilute or falsify the preaching for personal advantage and insists on his totally good conscience: his ministry is from God, and he has exercised it with fidelity and integrity (cf. 2 Cor 3:5–6).

**3:1** Paul seems to allude to certain preachers who pride themselves on their written credentials. Presumably they reproach him for not possessing similar credentials and compel him to spell out his own qualifications (2 Cor 4:2; 5:12; 6:4). The Corinthians themselves should have performed this function for Paul (2 Cor 5:12; cf. 2 Cor 12:11). Since he is forced to find something that can recommend him, he points to them: their very existence constitutes his **letter** of recommendation (2 Cor 3:1–2). Others who engage in self-commendation will also be mentioned in 2 Cor 10:12–18.

**3:2–3** Mention of "letters of recommendation" generates a series of metaphors in which Paul plays on the word "letter": (1) the community is Paul's letter of recommendation (2 Cor 3:2a); (2) they are a letter engraved on his affections for all to see and read (2 Cor 3:2b); (3) they are a letter from Christ that Paul merely delivers (2 Cor 3:3a); (4) they are a letter written by the Spirit on the tablets of human hearts (2 Cor 3:3b). One image dissolves into another.

**3:3b** This verse contrasts Paul's letter with those **written . . . in ink** (like the credentials of other preachers) and those **written . . . on tablets of stone** (like the law of Moses). These contrasts suggest that the other preachers may have claimed special relationship with Moses. If they were Judaizers zealous for the Mosaic law, that would explain the detailed contrast between the old and the new covenants (2 Cor 3:6; 4:7–6:10). If they were charismatics who claimed Moses as their model, that

*r:* Eph 4:27. *s:* Acts 16:8. *t:* 7:6; 1 Tm 1:3. *u:* 4:3; 1 Cor 1:18. *v:* 4:2; 1 Cor 5:8. *w:* Acts 18:27; Rom 16:1; 1 Cor 16:3. *x:* Ex 24:12; 31:18; 32:15–19 / Jer 31:33; Ez 11:19; 36:26–27.

be a letter of Christ administered by us, written not in ink but by the Spirit of the living
God, not on tablets of stone but on tablets
that are hearts of flesh.
4* Such confidence we have through
Christ toward God. 5 Not that of ourselves
we are qualified to take credit for anything
as coming from us; rather, our qualification
comes from God,[y] 6 who has indeed qualified
us as ministers of a new covenant, not of letter but of spirit;[z] for the letter brings death,
but the Spirit gives life.*

***Contrast with the Old Covenant.*** 7* Now
if the ministry of death,* carved in letters on
stone, was so glorious that the Israelites
could not look intently at the face of Moses
because of its glory that was going to fade,[a]
8 how much more* will the ministry of the
Spirit be glorious? 9 For if the ministry of
condemnation was glorious, the ministry of
righteousness will abound much more in
glory. 10 Indeed, what was endowed with
glory has come to have no glory in this respect because of the glory that surpasses it.
11 For if what was going to fade was glorious,
how much more will what endures be glorious.

12 Therefore, since we have such hope,* we
act very boldly 13 and not like Moses,* who
put a veil over his face so that the Israelites
could not look intently at the cessation of
what was fading. 14 Rather, their thoughts
were rendered dull, for to this present day* the
same veil remains unlifted when they read the
old covenant, because through Christ it is
taken away. 15 To this day, in fact, whenever
Moses is read, a veil lies over their hearts,[b]
16 but whenever a person turns to the Lord the
veil is removed.[c] 17 Now the Lord is the
Spirit,* and where the Spirit of the Lord is,

would explain the extended treatment of Moses himself and his glory (2 Cor 3:7–4:6). **Hearts of flesh**: cf. Ezekiel's contrast between the heart of flesh that the Spirit gives and the heart of stone that it replaces (Ez 36:26); the context is covenant renewal and purification that makes observance of the law possible.

**3:4–6** These verses resume 2 Cor 2:1–3:3. Paul's confidence (2 Cor 3:4) is grounded in his sense of God-given mission (2 Cor 2:17), the specifics of which are described in 2 Cor 3:1–3. 2 Cor 3:5–6 return to the question of his qualifications (2 Cor 2:16), attributing them entirely to God. 2 Cor 3:6 further spells out the situation described in 2 Cor 3:3b and "names" it: Paul is living within **a new covenant**, characterized by the Spirit, which **gives life**. The usage of a **new covenant** is derived from Jer 31:31–33 a passage that also speaks of writing on the heart; cf. 2 Cor 3:2.

**3:6b** This verse serves as a topic sentence for 2 Cor 3:7–6:10. For the contrast between **letter** and **spirit**, cf. Rom 2:29; 7:5–6.

**3:7–4:6** Paul now develops the contrast enunciated in 2 Cor 3:6b in terms of the relative glory of the two covenants, insisting on the greater glory of the new. His polemic seems directed against individuals who appeal to the glorious Moses and fail to perceive any comparable glory either in Paul's life as an apostle or in the gospel he preaches. He asserts in response that Christians have a glory of their own that far surpasses that of Moses.

**3:7 The ministry of death**: from his very first words, Paul describes the Mosaic covenant and ministry from the viewpoint of their limitations. They lead to **death** rather than life (2 Cor 3:6–7; cf. 2 Cor 4:7–5:10), to **condemnation** rather than reconciliation (2 Cor 3:9; cf. 2 Cor 5:11–6:10). **Was so glorious**: the basic text to which Paul alludes is Ex 34:29–35 to which his opponents have undoubtedly laid claim. **Going to fade**: Paul concedes the glory of Moses' covenant and ministry, but grants them only temporary significance.

**3:8–11 How much more**: the argument "from the less to the greater" is repeated three times (2 Cor 3:8, 9, 11). 2 Cor 3:10 expresses another point of view: the difference in glory is so great that only the new covenant and ministry can properly be called "glorious" at all.

**3:12 Such hope**: the glory is not yet an object of experience, but that does not lessen Paul's confidence. **Boldly**: the term *parrēsia* expresses outspoken declaration of Christian conviction (cf. 2 Cor 4:1–2). Paul has nothing to hide and no reason for timidity.

**3:13–14a Not like Moses**: in Exodus Moses veiled his face to protect the Israelites from God's reflected glory. Without impugning Moses' sincerity, Paul attributes another effect to the veil. Since it lies between God's glory and the Israelites, it explains how they could fail to notice the glory disappearing. **Their thoughts were rendered dull**: the problem lay with their understanding. This will be expressed in 2 Cor 3:14b–16 by a shift in the place of the veil: it is no longer over Moses' face but over their perception.

**3:14b–16** The parallelism in these verses makes it necessary to interpret corresponding parts in relation to one another. **To this present day**: this signals the shift of Paul's attention to his contemporaries; his argument is typological, as in 1 Cor 10. The Israelites of Moses' time typify the Jews of Paul's time, and perhaps also Christians of Jewish origin or mentality who may not recognize the temporary character of Moses' glory. **When they read the old covenant**: the lasting dullness prevents proper appraisal of Moses' person and covenant. When his writings are read in the synagogue, a veil still impedes their understanding. **Through Christ**: i.e., in the new covenant. **Whenever a person turns to the Lord**: Moses in Exodus appeared before God without the veil and gazed on his face unprotected. Paul applies that passage to converts to Christianity: when they turn to the Lord fully and authentically, the impediment to their understanding is removed.

**3:17 The Lord is the Spirit**: the "Lord" to whom the Christian turns (2 Cor 3:16) is the Spirit of whom Paul has been speaking, the life-giving Spirit of the living God (2 Cor 3:6, 8), the in-

*y:* Jn 3:27. *z:* Eph 3:7 / Jer 31:31–34. *a:* Ex 34:29–35. *b:* Rom 11:7–10. *c:* Ex 34:34.

there is freedom. 18* All of us, gazing with unveiled face on the glory of the Lord, are being
transformed into the same image from glory
to glory, as from the Lord who is the Spirit.[d]

## CHAPTER 4

See RG 378–79

*Integrity in the Ministry.* 1* Therefore,
since we have this ministry through the mercy
shown us, we are not discouraged. 2Rather,
we have renounced shameful, hidden things;
not acting deceitfully or falsifying the word
of God, but by the open declaration of the
truth we commend ourselves to everyone's
conscience in the sight of God.[e] 3And even
though our gospel is veiled,* it is veiled for
those who are perishing,[f] 4in whose case the
god of this age has blinded the minds of the
unbelievers, so that they may not see the light
of the gospel of the glory of Christ, who is the
image of God.[g] 5For we do not preach ourselves* but Jesus Christ as Lord, and ourselves as your slaves for the sake of Jesus.
6* For God who said, "Let light shine out of
darkness," has shone in our hearts to bring to
light the knowledge of the glory of God on
the face of [Jesus] Christ.[h]

*The Paradox of the Ministry.* 7* But we
hold this treasure* in earthen vessels, that the
surpassing power may be of God and not
from us. 8* We are afflicted in every way, but
not constrained; perplexed, but not driven to
despair;[i] 9persecuted, but not abandoned;
struck down, but not destroyed; 10* [j] always
carrying about in the body the dying of
Jesus, so that the life of Jesus may also be
manifested in our body. 11For we who live
are constantly being given up to death for
the sake of Jesus, so that the life of Jesus
may be manifested in our mortal flesh.[k]
12* So death is at work in us, but life in

augurator of the new covenant and ministry, who is also the Spirit of Christ. **The Spirit of the Lord**: the Lord here is the living God (2 Cor 3:3), but there may also be an allusion to Christ as Lord (2 Cor 3:14, 16). **Freedom**: i.e., from the ministry of death (2 Cor 3:7) and the covenant that condemned (2 Cor 3:9).

**3:18** Another application of the veil image. **All of us . . . with unveiled face**: Christians (Israelites from whom the veil has been removed) are like Moses, standing in God's presence, beholding and reflecting his glory. **Gazing**: the verb may also be translated "contemplating as in a mirror"; 2 Cor 4:6 would suggest that the mirror is Christ himself. **Are being transformed**: elsewhere Paul speaks of transformation, conformity to Jesus, God's image, as a reality of the end time, and even 2 Cor 3:12 speaks of the glory as an object of hope. But the life-giving Spirit, the distinctive gift of the new covenant, is already present in the community (cf. 2 Cor 1:22, the "first installment"), and the process of transformation has already begun. **Into the same image**: into the image of God, which is Christ (2 Cor 4:4).

**4:1–2** A ministry of this sort generates confidence and forthrightness; cf. 2 Cor 1:12–14; 2:17.

**4:3–4 Though our gospel is veiled**: the final application of the image. Paul has been reproached either for obscurity in his preaching or for his manner of presenting the gospel. But he confidently asserts that there is no veil over his gospel. If some fail to perceive its light, that is because of unbelief. The veil lies over their eyes (2 Cor 3:14), a blindness induced by Satan, and a sign that they are headed for destruction (cf. 2 Cor 2:15).

**4:5 We do not preach ourselves**: the light seen in his gospel is the glory of Christ (2 Cor 4:4). Far from preaching himself, the preacher should be a transparent medium through whom Jesus is perceived (cf. 2 Cor 4:10–11). **Your slaves**: Paul draws attention away from individuals as such and toward their role in relation to God, Christ, and the community; cf. 1 Cor 3:5; 2 Cor 4:1.

**4:6** Autobiographical allusion to the episode at Damascus clarifies the origin and nature of Paul's service; cf. Acts 9:1–19; 22:3–16; 26:2–18. **"Let light shine out of darkness"**: Paul seems to be thinking of Gn 1:3 and presenting his apostolic ministry as a new creation. There may also be an allusion to Is 9:1 suggesting his prophetic calling as servant of the Lord and light to the nations; cf. Is 42:6, 16; 49:6; 60:1–2, and the use of light imagery in Acts 26:13–23. **To bring to light the knowledge**: Paul's role in the process of revelation, expressed at the beginning under the image of the odor and aroma (2 Cor 2:14–15), is restated now, at the end of this first moment of the development, in the imagery of light and glory (2 Cor 4:3–6).

**4:7–5:10** Paul now confronts the difficulty that his present existence does not appear glorious at all; it is marked instead by suffering and death. He deals with this by developing the topic already announced in 2 Cor 3:3, 6, asserting his faith in the presence and ultimate triumph of life, in his own and every Christian existence, despite the experience of death.

**4:7 This treasure**: the glory that he preaches and into which they are being transformed. **In earthen vessels**: the instruments God uses are human and fragile; some imagine small terracotta lamps in which light is carried.

**4:8–9** A catalogue of his apostolic trials and afflictions. Yet in these the negative never completely prevails; there is always some experience of rescue, of salvation.

**4:10–11** Both the negative and the positive sides of the experience are grounded christologically. The logic is similar to that of 2 Cor 1:3–11. His sufferings are connected with Christ's, and his deliverance is a sign that he is to share in Jesus' resurrection.

**4:12–15** His experience does not terminate in himself, but in others (2 Cor 4:12, 15; cf. 2 Cor 1:4–5). Ultimately, everything is ordered even beyond the community, toward God (2 Cor 4:15; cf. 2 Cor 1:11).

---

*d:* Rom 8:29–30; 12:2; Gal 4:19; Phil 3:10, 20–21 / 2 Cor 4:4–6; 1 Cor 15:49; Col 1:15; 3:9–11; 1 Jn 3:2. *e:* 2:17; 1 Thes 2:4–7. *f:* 2:15–16; 2 Thes 2:10. *g:* Jn 12:31–36 / 1 Tm 1:11. *h:* Gn 1:3; Is 9:1; Acts 26:13–23; Gal 1:15–16 / Jn 8:12; Heb 1:3. *i:* 6:4–10; 1 Cor 4:9–13. *j:* Col 1:24. *k:* Rom 8:36; 1 Cor 15:31.

you. 13* Since, then, we have the same spirit
of faith, according to what is written, "I believed, therefore I spoke," we too believe and
therefore speak,[l] 14knowing that the one who
raised the Lord Jesus will raise us also with
Jesus and place us with you in his presence.[m]
15Everything indeed is for you, so that the
grace bestowed in abundance on more and
more people may cause the thanksgiving to
overflow for the glory of God.[n]
16* Therefore, we are not discouraged;*
rather, although our outer self is wasting
away, our inner self is being renewed day by
day.[o] 17For this momentary light affliction is
producing for us an eternal weight of glory
beyond all comparison,[p] 18as we look not to
what is seen but to what is unseen; for what
is seen is transitory, but what is unseen is
eternal.[q]

## CHAPTER 5

See RG 379

*Our Future Destiny.* 1r For we know
that if our earthly dwelling,* a tent, should be
destroyed, we have a building from God, a
dwelling not made with hands, eternal in
heaven. 2* For in this tent we groan, longing to
be further clothed with our heavenly habitation[s] 3if indeed, when we have taken it off,* we
shall not be found naked. 4For while we are in
this tent we groan and are weighed down, because we do not wish to be unclothed* but to be
further clothed, so that what is mortal may be
swallowed up by life.[t] 5Now the one who has
prepared us for this very thing is God,[u] who
has given us the Spirit as a first installment.*
6* So we are always courageous, although
we know that while we are at home in the
body we are away from the Lord, 7for we

**4:13–14** Like the Psalmist, Paul clearly proclaims his faith, affirming life within himself despite death (2 Cor 4:10–11) and the life-giving effect of his experience upon the church (2 Cor 4:12, 14–15). **And place us with you in his presence**: Paul imagines God presenting him and them to Jesus at the parousia and the judgment; cf. 2 Cor 11:2; Rom 14:10.

**4:16–18** In a series of contrasts Paul explains the extent of his faith in life. Life is not only already present and revealing itself (2 Cor 4:8–11, 16) but will outlast his experience of affliction and dying: it is eternal (2 Cor 4:17–18).

**4:16 Not discouraged**: i.e., despite the experience of death. Paul is still speaking of himself personally, but he assumes his faith and attitude will be shared by all Christians. **Our outer self**: the individual subject of ordinary perception and observation, in contrast to the interior and hidden self, which undergoes renewal. **Is being renewed day by day**: this suggests a process that has already begun; cf. 2 Cor 3:18. The renewal already taking place even in Paul's dying is a share in the life of Jesus, but this is recognized only by faith (2 Cor 4:13, 18; 2 Cor 5:7).

**5:1 Our earthly dwelling**: the same contrast is restated in the imagery of a dwelling. The language recalls Jesus' saying about the destruction of the temple and the construction of another building **not made with hands** (Mk 14:58), a prediction later applied to Jesus' own body (Jn 2:20).

**5:2–5** 2 Cor 5:2–3 and 4 are largely parallel in structure. **We groan, longing**: see note on 2 Cor 5:5. **Clothed with our heavenly habitation**: Paul mixes his metaphors, adding the image of the garment to that of the building. **Further clothed**: the verb means strictly "to put one garment on over another." Paul may desire to put the resurrection body on over his mortal body, without dying; 2 Cor 5:2, 4 permit this meaning but do not impose it. Or perhaps he imagines the resurrection body as a garment put on over the Christ-garment first received in baptism (Gal 3:27) and preserved by moral behavior (Rom 13:12–14; Col 3:12; cf. Mt 22:11–13). Some support for this interpretation may be found in the context; cf. the references to baptism (2 Cor 5:5), to judgment according to works (2 Cor 5:10), and to present renewal (2 Cor 4:16), an idea elsewhere combined with the image of "putting on" a new nature (Eph 4:22–24; Col 3:1–5, 9–10).

**5:3 When we have taken it off**: the majority of witnesses read "when we have put it on," i.e., when we have been clothed (in the resurrection body), then we shall not be without a body (naked). This seems mere tautology, though some understand it to mean: whether we are "found" (by God at the judgment) clothed or naked depends upon whether we have preserved or lost our original investiture in Christ (cf. the previous note). In this case to "put it on" does not refer to the resurrection body, but to keeping intact the Christ-garment of baptism. The translation follows the western reading (Codex Bezae, Tertullian), the sense of which is clear: to "take it off" is to shed our mortal body in death, after which we shall be clothed in the resurrection body and hence not "naked" (cf. 1 Cor 15:51–53).

**5:4 We do not wish to be unclothed**: a clear allusion to physical death (2 Cor 4:16; 5:1). Unlike the Greeks, who found dissolution of the body desirable (cf. Socrates), Paul has a Jewish horror of it. He seems to be thinking of the "intermediate period," an interval between death and resurrection. **Swallowed up by life**: cf. 1 Cor 15:54.

**5:5** God has created us for resurrected bodily life and already prepares us for it by the gift of the Spirit in baptism. **The Spirit as a first installment**: the striking parallel to 2 Cor 5:1–5 in Rom 8:17–30 describes Christians who have received the "firstfruits" (cf. "first installment" here) of the Spirit as "groaning" (cf. 2 Cor 5:2, 4 here) for the resurrection, the complete redemption of their bodies. In place of clothing and building, Rom 8 uses other images for the resurrection: adoption and conformity to the image of the Son.

**5:6–9** Tension between present and future is expressed by

*l:* Ps 116:10. *m:* Rom 4:24–25; 8:11; 1 Cor 6:14; 1 Thes 4:14. *n:* 1:11. *o:* 4:1. *p:* Mt 5:11–12; Rom 8:18. *q:* Rom 8:24–25; Heb 11:1. *r:* Is 38:12 / Col 3:1–4 / Mk 14:58; Col 2:11; Heb 9:11, 24. *s:* Rom 8:23 / 1 Cor 15:51–54. *t:* Is 25:8; 1 Cor 15:54. *u:* 1:22.

walk by faith, not by sight. [8]Yet we are courageous, and we would rather leave the body
and go home to the Lord.[v] [9]Therefore, we aspire to please him, whether we are at home or
away. [10]For we must all appear* before the
judgment seat of Christ, so that each one may
receive recompense, according to what he did
in the body, whether good or evil.[w]

***The Ministry of Reconciliation.*** [11]* Therefore, since we know the fear of the Lord, we
try to persuade others; but we are clearly apparent to God, and I hope we are also apparent to your consciousness.[x] [12]We are not
commending ourselves to you again but giving you an opportunity to boast of us, so that
you may have something to say to those who
boast of external appearance rather than of
the heart.[y] [13]For if we are out of our minds,*
it is for God; if we are rational, it is for you.
[14]* For the love of Christ impels us, once we
have come to the conviction that one died
for all; therefore, all have died.[z] [15]He indeed
died for all, so that those who live might no
longer live for themselves but for him who
for their sake died and was raised.[a]
[16]Consequently,* from now on we regard
no one according to the flesh; even if we
once knew Christ according to the flesh, yet
now we know him so no longer. [17b] So whoever is in Christ is a new creation: the old
things have passed away; behold, new things
have come. [18]* And all this is from God, who
has reconciled us to himself through Christ
and given us the ministry of reconciliation,
[19]namely, God was reconciling the world to
himself in Christ, not counting their trespasses against them and entrusting to us the
message of reconciliation.[c] [20]So we are ambassadors for Christ, as if God were appealing through us. We implore you on behalf of
Christ, be reconciled to God.[d] [21]* For our
sake he made him to be sin who did not
know sin,[e] so that we might become the righteousness of God in him.

## CHAPTER 6

See RG 377–78

***The Experience of the Ministry.***
[1]* Working together,[f] then, we appeal to you
not to receive the grace of God in vain.* [2]For
he says:

another spatial image, the metaphor of the country and its citizens. At present we are like citizens in exile or far away from home. The Lord is the distant homeland, believed in but unseen (2 Cor 5:7).

**5:10 We must all appear**: the verb is ambiguous: we are scheduled to "appear" for judgment, at which we will be "revealed" as we are (cf. 2 Cor 11; 2:14; 4:10–11).

**5:11–15** This paragraph is transitional. Paul sums up much that has gone before. Still playing on the term "appearance," he reasserts his transparency before God and the Corinthians, in contrast to the self-commendation, boasting, and preoccupation with externals that characterize some others (cf. 2 Cor 1:12–14; 2:14; 3:1; 3:7–4:6). 2 Cor 5:14 recalls 2 Cor 3:7–4:6, and sums up 2 Cor 4:7–5:10.

**5:13 Out of our minds**: this verse confirms that a concern for ecstasy and charismatic experience may lie behind the discussion about "glory" in 2 Cor 3:7–4:6. Paul also enjoys such experiences but, unlike others, does not make a public display of them or consider them ends in themselves. **Rational**: the Greek virtue *sōphrosynē*, to which Paul alludes, implies reasonableness, moderation, good judgment, self-control.

**5:14–15** These verses echo 2 Cor 4:14 and resume the treatment of "life despite death" from 2 Cor 4:7–5:10.

**5:16–17 Consequently**: the death of Christ described in 2 Cor 5:14–15 produces a whole new order (2 Cor 5:17) and a new mode of perception (2 Cor 5:16). **According to the flesh**: the natural mode of perception, characterized as "fleshly," is replaced by a mode of perception proper to the Spirit. Elsewhere Paul contrasts what Christ looks like according to the old criteria (weakness, powerlessness, folly, death) and according to the new (wisdom, power, life); cf. 2 Cor 5:15, 21; 1 Cor 1:17–3:3. Similarly, he describes the paradoxical nature of Christian existence, e.g., in 2 Cor 4:10–11, 14. **A new creation**: rabbis used this expression to describe the effect of the entrance of a proselyte or convert into Judaism or of the remission of sins on the Day of Atonement. The new order created **in Christ** is the new covenant (2 Cor 3:6).

**5:18–21** Paul attempts to explain the meaning of God's action by a variety of different categories; his attention keeps moving rapidly back and forth from God's act to his own ministry as well. **Who has reconciled us to himself**: i.e., he has brought all into oneness. **Not counting their trespasses**: the reconciliation is described as an act of justification (cf. "righteousness," 2 Cor 5:21); this contrasts with the covenant that condemned (2 Cor 3:8). **The ministry of reconciliation**: Paul's role in the wider picture is described: entrusted with the message of reconciliation (2 Cor 5:19), he is Christ's ambassador, through whom God appeals (2 Cor 5:20a). In v 20b Paul acts in the capacity just described.

**5:21** This is a statement of God's purpose, expressed paradoxically in terms of sharing and exchange of attributes. As Christ became our righteousness (1 Cor 1:30), we become God's righteousness (cf. 2 Cor 5:14–15).

**6:1–10** This paragraph is a single long sentence in the Greek, interrupted by the parenthesis of 2 Cor 5:2. The one main verb is "we appeal." In this paragraph Paul both exercises his min-

*v:* Phil 1:21–23. *w:* Mt 16:27; 25:31–46; Rom 2:16; 14:10–11. *x:* 1:12–14. *y:* 3:1 / 2 Cor 1:14; Phil 1:26. *z:* Rom 6:1–6. *a:* Rom 4:25; 6:4–11; 14:9; Col 3:3–4. *b:* Gal 6:15; Eph 2:15 / Is 43:18–21; Rev 21:5. *c:* Rom 5:10–11; Col 1:20. *d:* Eph 6:20; Phlm 9. *e:* Is 53:6–9; Gal 3:13 / Rom 3:24–26; 1 Cor 1:30; 1 Pt 2:24; 1 Jn 3:5–8. *f:* 1 Cor 3:9; 1 Thes 3:2. *g:* Is 49:8.

"In an acceptable time* I heard you,
and on the day of salvation I helped
you."[g]

Behold, now is a very acceptable time; behold, now is the day of salvation. 3[h] We
cause no one to stumble* in anything, in order that no fault may be found with our ministry; 4* on the contrary, in everything we
commend ourselves as ministers of God,
through much endurance,* in afflictions,
hardships, constraints,[i] 5 beatings, imprisonments, riots, labors, vigils, fasts;[j] 6* by purity, knowledge, patience, kindness, in a
holy spirit, in unfeigned love,[k] 7 in truthful
speech, in the power of God; with weapons
of righteousness at the right and at the left;[l]
8 through glory and dishonor, insult and
praise. We are treated as deceivers and yet
are truthful;* 9 as unrecognized and yet acknowledged; as dying and behold we live; as
chastised and yet not put to death;[m] 10 as sorrowful yet always rejoicing; as poor yet enriching many; as having nothing and yet
possessing all things.[n]

11* We have spoken frankly to you, Corinthians; our heart is open wide. 12 You are not
constrained by us; you are constrained by your
own affections.[o] 13 As recompense in kind (I
speak as to my children), be open yourselves.[p]

*Call to Holiness.* 14* Do not be yoked with
those who are different, with unbelievers.*
For what partnership do righteousness and
lawlessness have? Or what fellowship does
light have with darkness? 15 What accord has
Christ with Beliar? Or what has a believer in
common with an unbeliever? 16[q] What
agreement has the temple of God with idols?
For we are the temple of the living God; as
God said:

istry of reconciliation (cf. 2 Cor 5:20) and describes how his ministry is exercised: the "message of reconciliation" (2 Cor 5:19) is lived existentially in his apostolic experience.

**6:1 Not to receive . . . in vain**: i.e., conform to the gift of justification and new creation. The context indicates how this can be done concretely: become God's righteousness (2 Cor 5:21), not live for oneself (2 Cor 5:15) be reconciled with Paul (2 Cor 6:11–13; 7:2–3).

**6:2 In an acceptable time**: Paul cites the Septuagint text of Is 49:8; the Hebrew reads "in a time of favor"; it is parallel to "on the day of salvation." **Now**: God is bestowing favor and salvation at this very moment, as Paul is addressing his letter to them.

**6:3 Cause no one to stumble**: the language echoes that of 1 Cor 8–10 as does the expression "no longer live for themselves" in 2 Cor 5:15. **That no fault may be found**: i.e., at the eschatological judgment (cf. 1 Cor 4:2–5).

**6:4a** This is the central assertion, the topic statement for the catalogue that follows. **We commend ourselves**: Paul's self-commendation is ironical (with an eye on the charges mentioned in 2 Cor 3:1–3) and paradoxical (pointing mostly to experiences that would not normally be considered points of pride but are perceived as such by faith). Cf. also the self-commendation in 2 Cor 11:23–29. **As ministers of God**: the same Greek word, *diakonos*, means "minister" and "servant"; cf. 2 Cor 11:23, the central assertion in a similar context, and 1 Cor 3:5.

**6:4b–5 Through much endurance**: this phrase functions as a subtitle; it is followed by an enumeration of nine specific types of trials endured.

**6:6–7a** A list of virtuous qualities in two groups of four, the second fuller than the first.

**6:8b–10** A series of seven rhetorically effective antitheses, contrasting negative external impressions with positive inner reality. Paul perceives his existence as a reflection of Jesus' own and affirms an inner reversal that escapes outward observation. The final two members illustrate two distinct kinds of paradox or apparent contradiction that are characteristic of apostolic experience.

**6:11–13** Paul's tone becomes quieter, but his appeal for acceptance and affection is emotionally charged. References to the heart and their mutual relations bring the development begun in 2 Cor 2:14–3:3 to an effective conclusion.

**6:14–7:1** Language and thought shift noticeably here. Suddenly we are in a different atmosphere, dealing with a quite different problem. Both the vocabulary and the thought, with their contrast between good and evil, are more characteristic of Qumran documents or the Book of Revelation than they are of Paul. Hence, critics suspect that this section was inserted by another hand.

**6:14–16a** The opening injunction to separate from unbelievers is reinforced by five rhetorical questions to make the point that Christianity is not compatible with paganism. Their opposition is emphasized also by the accumulation of five distinct designations for each group. These verses are a powerful statement of God's holiness and the exclusiveness of his claims.

**6:16c–18** This is a chain of scriptural citations carefully woven together. God's covenant relation to his people and his presence among them (2 Cor 6:16) is seen as conditioned on cultic separation from the profane and cultically impure (2 Cor 6:17); that relation is translated into the personal language of the parent-child relationship, an extension to the community of the language of 2 Sm 7:14 (2 Cor 6:18). Some remarkable parallels to this chain are found in the final chapters of Revelation. God's presence among his people (Rev 21:22) is expressed there, too, by applying 2 Sm 7:14 to the community (Rev 21:7). There is a call to separation (Rev 18:4) and exclusion of the unclean from the community and its liturgy (Rev 21:27). The title "Lord Almighty" (*Pantokratōr*) occurs in the New Testament only here in 2 Cor 6:18 and nine times in Revelation.

*h:* 1 Cor 9:12; 10:32 / 2 Cor 8:20–21. *i:* 4:8–11; 11:23–27; 1 Cor 4:9–13. *j:* Acts 16:23. *k:* Gal 5:22–23. *l:* 10:4; Rom 13:12; Eph 6:11–17. *m:* 4:10–11; Rom 8:36. *n:* Rom 8:32; 1 Cor 3:21. *o:* 7:3. *p:* Gal 4:19. *q:* 1 Cor 10:20–21 / 1 Cor 3:16–17; 6:19 / Ex 25:8; 29:45; Lv 26:12; Jer 31:1; 32:38; Ez 37:27.

"I will live with them and move among
them,*
and I will be their God
and they shall be my people.
17 Therefore, come forth from them
and be separate," says the Lord,
"and touch nothing unclean;
then I will receive you[r]
18 and I will be a father to you,
and you shall be sons and daughters to
me,
says the Lord Almighty."[s]

See RG 379

CHAPTER 7

1 Since we have these promises,
beloved, let us cleanse ourselves from every
defilement of flesh and spirit, making holiness perfect in the fear of God.
2* Make room for us; we have not
wronged anyone, or ruined anyone, or taken
advantage of anyone. 3 I do not say this in
condemnation, for I have already said that
you are in our hearts, that we may die together and live together.[t] 4 I have great confidence in you, I have great pride in you; I am
filled with encouragement, I am overflowing with joy all the more because of all our
affliction.

## C. Resolution of the Crisis*

***Paul's Joy in Macedonia.*** 5* For even when
we came into Macedonia,* our flesh had no
rest, but we were afflicted in every way—
external conflicts, internal fears.[u] 6 But God,
who encourages the downcast, encouraged
us by the arrival of Titus,[v] 7 and not only by
his arrival but also by the encouragement
with which he was encouraged in regard to
you, as he told us of your yearning, your
lament, your zeal for me, so that I rejoiced
even more. 8* For even if I saddened you by
my letter, I do not regret it; and if I did regret
it ([for] I see that that letter saddened you, if
only for a while),[w] 9 I rejoice now, not because you were saddened, but because you
were saddened into repentance; for you were
saddened in a godly way, so that you did not
suffer loss in anything because of us. 10 For
godly sorrow produces a salutary repentance
without regret, but worldly sorrow produces
death. 11 For behold what earnestness this
godly sorrow has produced for you, as well
as readiness for a defense, and indignation,
and fear, and yearning, and zeal, and punishment. In every way you have shown yourselves to be innocent in the matter. 12 So then
even though I wrote to you, it was not on account of the one who did the wrong, or on
account of the one who suffered the wrong,
but in order that your concern for us might
be made plain to you in the sight of God.[x]
13 For this reason we are encouraged.

And besides our encouragement,* we rejoice even more because of the joy of Titus,
since his spirit has been refreshed by all of
you. 14 For if I have boasted to him about
you, I was not put to shame. No, just as
everything we said to you was true, so our
boasting before Titus proved to be the truth.
15 And his heart goes out to you all the more,

**7:2–4** These verses continue the thought of 2 Cor 6:11–13, before the interruption of 2 Cor 6:14–7:1. 2 Cor 7:4 serves as a transition to the next section: the four themes it introduces (confidence; pride or "boasting"; encouragement; joy in affliction) are developed in 2 Cor 7:5–16. All have appeared previously in the letter.

**7:5–16** This section functions as a peroration or formal summing up of the whole first part of the letter, 2 Cor 1–7. It deals with the restoration of right relations between Paul and the Corinthians, and it is marked by fullness and intensity of emotion.

**7:5–7** Paul picks up the thread of the narrative interrupted at 2 Cor 2:13 (2 Cor 7:5) and describes the resolution of the tense situation there depicted (2 Cor 7:6–7). Finally Titus arrives and his coming puts an end to Paul's restlessness (2 Cor 2:13; 2 Cor 7:5), casts out his fears, and reverses his mood. The theme of encouragement and affliction is reintroduced (cf. 2 Cor 1:3–11); here, too, encouragement is traced back to God and is described as contagious (2 Cor 7:6). The language of joy and sorrow also reappears in 2 Cor 7:7 (cf. 2 Cor 1:23–2:1 and the note on 2 Cor 1:23–24).

**7:5 Macedonia**: see note on 2 Cor 2:13.

**7:8–12** Paul looks back on the episode from the viewpoint of its ending. The goal of their common activity, promotion of their joy (2 Cor 1:24), has been achieved, despite and because of the sorrow they felt. That sorrow was God-given. Its salutary effects are enumerated fully and impressively in 2 Cor 7:10–11; not the least important of these is that it has revealed to them the attachment they have to Paul.

**7:13–16** Paul summarizes the effect of the experience on Titus: encouragement, joy, love, relief. Finally, he describes its effects on himself: encouragement, joy, confidence, pride or "boasting" (i.e., the satisfaction resulting from a boast that proves well-founded; cf. 2 Cor 7:4; 1:12, 14).

*r:* Is 52:11; Ez 20:34, 41; Rev 18:4; 21:27. *s:* 2 Sm 7:14; Ps 2:7; Is 43:6; Jer 31:9; Rev 21:7 / Rev 4:8; 11:17; 15:3; 21:22. *t:* 6:11–13. *u:* 2:13. *v:* 7:13–14; 1 Thes 3:6–8. *w:* 2:2–4; Heb 12:11. *x:* 2:3, 9; 7:8. *y:* 2:9.

as he remembers the obedience of all of you, when you received him with fear and trembling.[y] 16I rejoice, because I have confidence in you in every respect.

## III. The Collection for Jerusalem*

### CHAPTER 8

See RG 379–80

*Generosity in Giving.* 1* We want you to know, brothers,* of the grace of God* that has been given to the churches of Macedonia,[z] 2* for in a severe test of affliction, the abundance of their joy and their profound poverty overflowed in a wealth of generosity on their part. 3* For according to their means, I can testify, and beyond their means, spontaneously, 4they begged us insistently for the favor of taking part in the service to the holy ones,[a] 5and this, not as we expected, but they gave themselves first to the Lord and to us* through the will of God, 6so that we urged Titus* that, as he had already begun, he should also complete for you this gracious act also.[b]
7* Now as you excel in every respect, in faith, discourse, knowledge, all earnestness, and in the love we have for you,[c] may you excel in this gracious act also.
8I say this not by way of command, but to test the genuineness of your love by your concern for others. 9* [d] For you know the gracious act of our Lord Jesus Christ, that for your sake he became poor although he

**8:1–9:15** Paul turns to a new topic, the collection for the church in Jerusalem. There is an early precedent for this project in the agreement mentioned in Gal 2:6–10. According to Acts, the church at Antioch had sent Saul and Barnabas to Jerusalem with relief (Acts 11:27–30). Subsequently Paul organized a project of relief for Jerusalem among his own churches. Our earliest evidence for it comes in 1 Cor 16:1–4—after it had already begun (see notes there); by the time Paul wrote Rom 15:25–28 the collection was completed and ready for delivery. 2 Cor 8–9 contain what appear to be two letters on the subject. In them Paul gives us his fullest exposition of the meaning he sees in the enterprise, presenting it as an act of Christian charity and as an expression of the unity of the church, both present and eschatological. These chapters are especially rich in the recurrence of key words, on which Paul plays; it is usually impossible to do justice to these wordplays in the translation.

**8:1–24** This is a letter of recommendation for Titus and two unnamed companions, written from Macedonia probably at least a year later than 1 Cor 16. The recommendation proper is prefaced by remarks about the ideals of sharing and equality within the Christian community (2 Cor 8:1–15). Phil 4:10–20 shows that Paul has reflected on his personal experience of need and relief in his relations with the community at Philippi; he now develops his reflections on the larger scale of relations between his Gentile churches and the mother church in Jerusalem.

**8:1–5** The example of the Macedonians, a model of what ought to be happening at Corinth, provides Paul with the occasion for expounding his theology of "giving."

**8:1 The grace of God**: the fundamental theme is expressed by the Greek noun *charis*, which will be variously translated throughout these chapters as "grace" (2 Cor 8:1; 9:8, 14), "favor" (2 Cor 8:4), "gracious act" (2 Cor 8:6, 7, 9) or "gracious work" (2 Cor 8:19), to be compared to "gracious gift" (1 Cor 16:3). The related term, *eucharistia*, "thanksgiving," also occurs at 2 Cor 9:11, 12. The wordplay is not superficial; various mutations of the same root signal inner connection between aspects of a single reality, and Paul consciously exploits the similarities in vocabulary to highlight that connection.

**8:2** Three more terms are now introduced. **Test** (*dokimē*): the same root is translated as "to test" (2 Cor 8:8) and "evidence" (2 Cor 9:13); it means to be tried and found genuine. **Abundance**: variations on the same root lie behind "overflow" (2 Cor 8:2; 9:12), "excel" (2 Cor 8:7), "surplus" (2 Cor 8:14), "superfluous" (2 Cor 9:1) "make abundant" and "have an abundance" (2 Cor 9:8). These expressions of fullness contrast with references to need (2 Cor 8:14; 9:12). **Generosity**: the word *haplotēs* has nuances of both simplicity and sincerity; here and in 2 Cor 9:11, 13 it designates the singleness of purpose that manifests itself in generous giving.

**8:3–4** Paul emphasizes the spontaneity of the Macedonians and the nature of their action. **They begged us insistently**: the same root is translated as "urge," "appeal," "encourage" (2 Cor 8:6, 17; 9:5). **Taking part**: the same word is translated "contribution" in 2 Cor 9:13 and a related term as "partner" in 2 Cor 8:23. **Service** (*diakonia*): this word occurs also in 2 Cor 9:1, 13 as "service"; in 2 Cor 9:12 it is translated "administration," and in 2 Cor 8:19, 20 the corresponding verb is rendered "administer."

**8:5 They gave themselves . . . to the Lord and to us**: on its deepest level their attitude is one of self-giving.

**8:6 Titus**: 1 Cor 16 seemed to leave the organization up to the Corinthians, but apparently Paul has sent Titus to initiate the collection as well; 2 Cor 8:16–17 will describe Titus' attitude as one of shared concern and cooperation.

**8:7** The charitable service Paul is promoting is seen briefly and in passing within the perspective of Paul's theology of the charisms. **Earnestness** (*spoudē*): this or related terms occur also in 2 Cor 8:22 ("earnest") and 2 Cor 8:8, 16, 17 ("concern").

**8:9** The dialectic of Jesus' experience, expressed earlier in terms of life and death (2 Cor 5:15), sin and righteousness (2 Cor 5:21), is now rephrased in terms of poverty and wealth. Many scholars think this is a reference to Jesus' preexistence with God (his "wealth") and to his incarnation and death (his "poverty"), and they point to the similarity between this verse and Phil 2:6–8. Others interpret the wealth and poverty as succeeding phases of Jesus' earthly existence, e.g., his sense of intimacy with God and then the desolation and the feeling of abandonment by God in his death (cf. Mk 15:34).

*z:* 11:9; Rom 15:26. *a:* Acts 24:17; Rom 15:31. *b:* 2:13; 7:6–7, 13–14; 8:16, 23; 12:18. *c:* 1 Cor 1:5. *d:* 6:10; Phil 2:6–8.

was rich, so that by his poverty you might become rich. [10]And I am giving counsel in this matter, for it is appropriate for you who began not only to act but to act willingly last year:[e] [11]complete it now, so that your eager* willingness may be matched by your completion of it out of what you have. [12]* For if the eagerness is there, it is acceptable according to what one has, not according to what one does not have; [13]not that others should have relief while you are burdened, but that as a matter of equality [14]your surplus at the present time should supply their needs, so that their surplus may also supply your needs, that there may be equality. [15]As it is written:

> "Whoever had much did not have more,
> and whoever had little did not have
> less."[f]

***Titus and His Collaborators.**** [16]But thanks be to God who put the same concern for you into the heart of Titus, [17]for he not only welcomed our appeal but, since he is very concerned, he has gone to you of his own accord. [18]With him we have sent the brother* who is praised in all the churches for his preaching of the gospel.[g] [19]And not only that, but he has also been appointed our traveling companion by the churches in this gracious work administered by us for the glory of the Lord [himself] and for the expression of our eagerness.[h] [20]This we desire to avoid, that anyone blame us* about this lavish gift administered by us, [21]for we are concerned for what is honorable not only in the sight of the Lord but also in the sight of others.[i]

[22]And with them we have sent our brother whom we often tested in many ways and found earnest, but who is now much more earnest because of his great confidence in you. [23]As for Titus, he is my partner and co-worker for you; as for our brothers, they are apostles of the churches, the glory of Christ. [24]So give proof before the churches of your love and of our boasting about you to them.*

## CHAPTER 9

See RG 379–80

***God's Indescribable Gift.**** [1]Now about the service to the holy ones, it is superfluous for me to write to you, [2]for I know your eagerness, about which I boast of you to the Macedonians, that Achaia* has been ready since last year; and your zeal has stirred up most of them.[j] [3]Nonetheless, I sent the brothers* so that our boast about you might not prove empty in this case, so that you might be ready, as I said, [4]for fear that if any Macedonians come with me and find you not ready we might be put to shame (to say nothing of you) in this conviction. [5]So I thought it necessary to encourage the brothers to go on ahead to you and arrange in advance for your promised gift, so that in this

**8:11 Eager**: the word *prothymia* also occurs in 2 Cor 8:12, 19; 9:2.

**8:12–15** Paul introduces the principle of **equality** into the discussion. The goal is not impoverishment but sharing of resources; balance is achieved at least over the course of time. In 2 Cor 8:15 Paul grounds his argument unexpectedly in the experience of Israel gathering manna in the desert: equality was achieved, independently of personal exertion, by God, who gave with an even hand according to need. Paul touches briefly here on the theme of "living from God."

**8:16–24** In recommending Titus and his companions, Paul stresses their personal and apostolic qualities, their good dispositions toward the Corinthians, and their authority as messengers of the churches and representatives of Christ.

**8:18 The brother**: we do not know the identity of this coworker of Paul, nor of the third companion mentioned below in 2 Cor 8:22.

**8:20–22 That anyone blame us**: 2 Cor 12:16–18 suggests that misunderstandings may indeed have arisen concerning Paul's management of the collection through the messengers mentioned here, but those same verses seem to imply that the Corinthians by and large would recognize the honesty of Paul's conduct in this area as in others (cf. 2 Cor 6:3).

**8:24** As Paul began by holding up the Macedonians as examples to be imitated, he closes by exhorting the Corinthians to show their love (by accepting the envoys and by cooperating as the Macedonians do), thus justifying the pride Paul demonstrates because of them before other churches.

**9:1–15** Quite possibly this was originally an independent letter, though it deals with the same subject and continues many of the same themes. In that case, it may have been written a few weeks later than 2 Cor 8, while the delegation there mentioned was still on its way.

**9:2 Achaia**: see note on Rom 15:26.

**9:3 I sent the brothers**: the Greek aorist tense here could be epistolary, referring to the present; in that case Paul would be sending them now, and 2 Cor 9 would merely conclude the letter of recommendation begun in 2 Cor 8. But the aorist may also refer to a sending that is past as Paul writes; then 2 Cor 9, with its apparently fresh beginning, is a follow-up message entrusted to another carrier.

*e:* 9:2; 1 Cor 16:1–4. *f:* Ex 16:18. *g:* 12:18. *h:* 1 Cor 16:3–4. *i:* Rom 12:17. *j:* 8:10; Rom 15:26.

way it might be ready as a bountiful gift and
not as an exaction.
6 Consider this: whoever sows sparingly
will also reap sparingly, and whoever sows
bountifully will also reap bountifully.[k] 7 Each
must do as already determined, without sadness or compulsion, for God loves a cheerful
giver.[l] 8* Moreover, God is able to make
every grace abundant for you, so that in all
things, always having all you need, you may
have an abundance for every good work. 9 As
it is written:

“He scatters abroad, he gives to the poor;
his righteousness endures forever.”[m]

10 The one who supplies seed to the sower
and bread for food will supply and multiply
your seed and increase the harvest of your
righteousness.[n]
11* You are being enriched in every way
for all generosity, which through us produces thanksgiving to God, 12 for the administration of this public service is not only
supplying the needs of the holy ones but is
also overflowing in many acts of thanksgiving to God. 13 Through the evidence of this
service, you are glorifying God for your
obedient confession of the gospel of Christ
and the generosity of your contribution to
them and to all others,[o] 14 while in prayer on
your behalf they long for you, because of the
surpassing grace of God upon you. 15 Thanks
be to God for his indescribable gift![p]

## IV. Paul’s Defense of His Ministry*

### CHAPTER 10

See RG 380–81

*Accusation of Weakness.** 1 Now I myself, Paul, urge you through the gentleness
and clemency of Christ,* I who am humble
when face to face with you, but brave toward
you when absent, 2* [q] I beg you that, when
present, I may not have to be brave with that
confidence with which I intend to act boldly

**9:8–10** The behavior to which he exhorts them is grounded in God’s own pattern of behavior. God is capable of overwhelming generosity, as scripture itself attests (2 Cor 9:9), so that they need not fear being short. He will provide in abundance, both supplying their natural needs and increasing their righteousness. Paul challenges them to godlike generosity and reminds them of the fundamental motive for encouragement: God himself cannot be outdone.

**9:11–15** Paul’s vision broadens to take in all the interested parties in one dynamic picture. His language becomes liturgically colored and conveys a sense of fullness. With a final play on the words *charis* and *eucharistia* (see note on 2 Cor 8:1), he describes a circle that closes on itself: the movement of grace overflowing from God to them and handed on from them through Paul to others is completed by the prayer of praise and thanksgiving raised on their behalf to God.

**10:1–13:10** These final chapters have their own unity of structure and theme and could well have formed the body of a separate letter. They constitute an *apologia* on Paul’s part, i.e., a legal defense of his behavior and his ministry; the writing is emotionally charged and highly rhetorical. In the central section (2 Cor 11:16–12:10), the *apologia* takes the form of a boast. This section is prepared for by a prologue (2 Cor 11:1–15) and followed by an epilogue (2 Cor 12:11–18), which are similar in content and structure. These sections, in turn, are framed by an introduction (2 Cor 10:1–18) and a conclusion (2 Cor 12:19–13:10), both of which assert Paul’s apostolic authority and confidence and define the purpose of the letter. The structure that results from this disposition of the material is chiastic, i.e., the first element corresponds to the last, the second to the second last, etc., following the pattern a b c b¹, a¹.

**10:1–18** Paul asserts his apostolic authority and expresses the confidence this generates in him. He writes in response to certain opinions that have arisen in the community and certain charges raised against him and in preparation for a forthcoming visit in which he intends to set things in order. This section gives us an initial glimpse of the situation in Corinth that Paul must address; much of its thematic material will be taken up again in the finale (2 Cor 12:19–13:10).

**10:1–2** A strong opening plunges us straight into the conflict. Contrasts dominate here: presence versus absence, gentleness-clemency-humility versus boldness-confidence-bravery. **Through the gentleness and clemency of Christ**: the figure of the gentle Christ, presented in a significant position before any specifics of the situation are suggested, forms a striking contrast to the picture of the bold and militant Paul (2 Cor 10:2–6); this tension is finally resolved in 2 Cor 13:3–4. **Absent . . . present**: this same contrast, with a restatement of the purpose of the letter, recurs in 2 Cor 13:10, which forms an inclusion with 2 Cor 10:1–2.

**10:2b–4a Flesh**: the Greek word *sarx* can express both the physical life of the body without any pejorative overtones (as in “we are in the flesh,” 3) and our natural life insofar as it is marked by limitation and weakness (as in the other expressions) in contrast to the higher life and power conferred by the Spirit; cf. note on 1 Cor 3:1. The wordplay is intended to express the paradoxical situation of a life already taken over by the Spirit but not yet seen as such except by faith. Lack of empirical evidence of the Spirit permits misunderstanding and misjudgment, but Paul resolutely denies that his behavior and effectiveness are as limited as some suppose.

---

*k:* Prv 11:24–25. *l:* Prv 22:8 LXX. *m:* Ps 112:9. *n:* Is 55:10. *o:* 8:4; Rom 15:31. *p:* Rom 5:15–16. *q:* 13:2, 10; 1 Cor 4:21.

against some who consider us as acting according to the flesh. [3]For, although we are in
the flesh, we do not battle according to the
flesh,* [4]for the weapons of our battle are not
of flesh but are enormously powerful, capable of destroying fortresses. We destroy arguments[r] [5]and every pretension raising itself
against the knowledge of God, and take
every thought captive in obedience to Christ,
[6]and we are ready to punish every disobedience, once your obedience is complete.[s]
[7t] Look at what confronts you. Whoever
is confident of belonging to Christ should
consider that as he belongs to Christ, so do
we.* [8u] And even if I should boast a little
too much of our authority, which the Lord
gave for building you up and not for tearing
you down, I shall not be put to shame.
[9*] May I not seem as one frightening you
through letters. [10]For someone will say,
"His letters are severe and forceful, but his
bodily presence is weak, and his speech
contemptible."[v] [11]Such a person must understand that what we are in word through
letters when absent, that we also are in action when present.[w]
[12*] Not that we dare to class or compare
ourselves with some of those who recommend themselves. But when they measure
themselves by one another and compare
themselves with one another, they are without understanding.[x] [13]But we will not boast
beyond measure but will keep to the limits*
God has apportioned us, namely, to reach
even to you. [14]For we are not overreaching
ourselves, as though we did not reach you;
we indeed first came to you with the gospel
of Christ. [15]We are not boasting beyond
measure, in other people's labors; yet our
hope is that, as your faith increases, our influence among you may be greatly enlarged,
within our proper limits, [16]so that we may
preach the gospel even beyond you, not
boasting of work already done in another's
sphere.[y] [17z] "Whoever boasts, should boast
in the Lord."* [18]For it is not the one who recommends himself who is approved,* but the
one whom the Lord recommends.[a]

## CHAPTER 11

See RG 381

***Preaching Without Charge.**** [1]If only
you would put up with a little foolishness

**10:3b–6** Paul is involved in combat. The strong military language and imagery are both an assertion of his confidence in the divine power at his disposal and a declaration of war against those who underestimate his resources. The threat is echoed in 2 Cor 13:2–3.

**10:7–8 Belonging to Christ . . . so do we**: these phrases already announce the pattern of Paul's boast in 2 Cor 11:21b–29, especially 2 Cor 11:22–23. **For building you up and not for tearing you down**: Paul draws on the language by which Jeremiah described the purpose of the prophetic power the Lord gave to him (Jer 1:9–10; 12:16–17; 24:6). Though Paul's power may have destructive effects on others (2 Cor 10:2–6), its intended effect on the community is entirely constructive (cf. 2 Cor 13:10). **I shall not be put to shame**: his assertions will not be refuted; they will be revealed as true at the judgment.

**10:9–10** Paul cites the complaints of some who find him lacking in personal forcefulness and holds out the threat of a personal *parousia* (both "return" and "presence") that will be forceful, indeed will be a demonstration of Christ's own power (cf. 2 Cor 13:2–4).

**10:12–18** Paul now qualifies his claim to boldness, indicating its limits. He distinguishes his own behavior from that of others, revealing those "others" as they appear to him: as self-recommending, immoderately boastful, encroaching on territory not assigned to them, and claiming credit not due to them.

**10:13 Will keep to the limits**: the notion of proper limits is expressed here by two terms with overlapping meanings, *metron* and *kanōn*, which are played off against several expressions denoting overreaching or expansion beyond a legitimate sphere.

**10:17 Boast in the Lord**: there is a legitimate boasting, in contrast to the immoderate boasting to which 2 Cor 10:13, 15 allude. God's work through Paul in the community is the object of his boast (2 Cor 10:13–16; 2 Cor 1:12–14) and constitutes his recommendation (2 Cor 3:1–3). Cf. notes on 2 Cor 1:12–14 and 1 Cor 1:29–31.

**10:18 Approved**: to be approved is to come successfully through the process of testing for authenticity (cf. 2 Cor 13:3–7 and the note on 2 Cor 8:2). **Whom the Lord recommends**: self-commendation is a premature and unwarranted anticipation of the final judgment, which the Lord alone will pass (cf. 1 Cor 4:3–5). Paul alludes to this judgment throughout 2 Cor 10–13, frequently in final or transitional positions; cf. 2 Cor 11:15; 12:19a; 13:3–7.

**11:1–15** Although these verses continue to reveal information about Paul's opponents and the differences he perceives between them and himself, 2 Cor 11:1 signals a turn in Paul's thought. This section constitutes a prologue to the boasting that he will undertake in 2 Cor 11:16–12:10, and it bears remarkable similarities to the section that follows the central boast, 2 Cor 12:11–18.

**11:1 Put up with a little foolishness from me**: this verse indicates more clearly than the general statement of intent in 2 Cor 10:13 the nature of the project Paul is about to undertake. He alludes ironically to the Corinthians' toleration for others. **Foolishness**: Paul qualifies his project as folly from beginning to end; see note on 2 Cor 11:16–12:10.

*r:* 6:7; 13:2–3; 1 Cor 1:25; Eph 6:10–14. *s:* 2:9. *t:* 1 Cor 1:12. *u:* 13:10. *v:* 1 Cor 2:3. *w:* 13:1–2. *x:* 3:1–2; 4:2; 5:12; 6:4; 10:18; 12:11. *y:* Rom 15:20–21. *z:* Jer 9:22–23; 1 Cor 1:31. *a:* 13:3–9. *b:* 11:21; 12:11.

from me!* Please put up with me.[b] 2* For I
am jealous of you with the jealousy of God,
since I betrothed you to one husband to present you as a chaste virgin to Christ.[c] 3But I
am afraid that, as the serpent deceived Eve*
by his cunning, your thoughts may be corrupted from a sincere [and pure] commitment to Christ.[d] 4For if someone comes and
preaches another Jesus* than the one we
preached,[e] or if you receive a different spirit
from the one you received or a different
gospel from the one you accepted, you put
up with it well enough. 5* [f] For I think that I
am not in any way inferior to these "superapostles." 6Even if I am untrained in speaking, I am not so in knowledge;[g] in every way
we have made this plain to you in all things.*
7* Did I make a mistake when I humbled
myself so that you might be exalted, because
I preached the gospel of God to you without
charge?[h] 8I plundered other churches by accepting from them in order to minister to
you. 9And when I was with you and in need,
I did not burden anyone, for the brothers
who came from Macedonia supplied my
needs. So I refrained and will refrain from
burdening you in any way.[i] 10By the truth of
Christ in me, this boast of mine shall not be
silenced in the regions of Achaia.[j] 11* And
why? Because I do not love you? God
knows I do![k]
12And what I do I will continue to do, in
order to end this pretext of those who seek a
pretext for being regarded as we are in the
mission of which they boast. 13* For such
people are false apostles, deceitful workers,
who masquerade as apostles of Christ.
14And no wonder, for even Satan masquerades as an angel of light. 15So it is not
strange that his ministers also masquerade as
ministers of righteousness. Their end will
correspond to their deeds.

**11:2** Paul gives us a sudden glimpse of the theological values that are at stake. **The jealousy of God**: the perspective is that of the covenant, described in imagery of love and marriage, as in the prophets; cf. 1 Cor 10:22. **I betrothed you**: Paul, like a father (cf. 2 Cor 12:14), betroths the community to Christ as his bride (cf. Eph 5:21–33) and will present her to him at his second coming. Cf. Mt 25:1–13 and the nuptial imagery in Rev 21.

**11:3 As the serpent deceived Eve**: before Christ can return for the community Paul fears a repetition of the primal drama of seduction. Corruption of minds is satanic activity (see 2 Cor 2:11; 4:4). Satanic imagery recurs in 2 Cor 11:13–15, 20; 12:7b, 16–17; see notes on these passages.

**11:4 Preaches another Jesus**: the danger is specified, and Paul's opponents are identified with the cunning serpent. The battle for minds has to do with the understanding of Jesus, the Spirit, the gospel; the Corinthians have flirted with another understanding than the one that Paul handed on to them as traditional and normative.

**11:5 These "superapostles"**: this term, employed again in 2 Cor 12:11b, designates the opponents of whom Paul has spoken in 2 Cor 10 and again in 2 Cor 11:4. They appear to be intruders at Corinth. Their preaching is marked at least by a different emphasis and style, and they do not hesitate to accept support from the community. Perhaps these itinerants appeal to the authority of church leaders in Jerusalem and even carry letters of recommendation from them. But it is not those distant leaders whom Paul is attacking here. The intruders are "superapostles" not in the sense of the "pillars" at Jerusalem (Gal 2), but in their own estimation. They consider themselves superior to Paul as apostles and ministers of Christ, and they are obviously enjoying some success among the Corinthians. Paul rejects their claim to be apostles in any superlative sense (*hyperlian*), judging them bluntly as "false apostles," ministers of Satan masquerading as apostles of Christ (2 Cor 11:13–15). On the contrary, he himself will claim to be a superminister of Christ (*hyper egō*, 2 Cor 11:23).

**11:6** Apparently found deficient in both rhetorical ability (cf. 2 Cor 10:10) and knowledge (cf. 2 Cor 10:5), Paul concedes the former charge but not the latter. **In every way**: in all their contacts with him revelation has been taking place. Paul, through whom God reveals the knowledge of himself (2 Cor 2:14), and in whom the death and life of Jesus are revealed (2 Cor 4:10–11; cf. 2 Cor 6:4), also demonstrates his own role as the bearer of true knowledge. Cf. 1 Cor 1:18–2:16.

**11:7–10** Abruptly Paul passes to another reason for complaints: his practice of preaching without remuneration (cf. 1 Cor 9:3–18). He deftly defends his practice by situating it from the start within the pattern of Christ's own self-humiliation (cf. 2 Cor 10:1) and reduces objections to absurdity by rhetorical questions (cf. 2 Cor 12:13).

**11:11–12** Paul rejects lack of affection as his motive (possibly imputed to him by his opponents) and states his real motive, a desire to emphasize the disparity between himself and the others (cf. 2 Cor 11:19–21). The topic of his gratuitous service will be taken up once more in 2 Cor 12:13–18. 1 Cor 9:15–18 gives a different but complementary explanation of his motivation.

**11:13–15** Paul picks up again the imagery of 2 Cor 11:3 and applies it to the opponents: they are false apostles of Christ, really serving another master. **Deceitful . . . masquerade**: deception and simulation, like cunning (2 Cor 11:3), are marks of the satanic. **Angel of light**: recalls the contrast between light and darkness, Christ and Beliar at 2 Cor 6:14–15. **Ministers of righteousness**: recalls the earlier contrast between the ministry of condemnation and that of righteousness (2 Cor 3:9). **Their end**: the section closes with another allusion to the judgment, when all participants in the final conflict will be revealed or unmasked and dealt with as they deserve.

*c:* Hos 2:21–22; Eph 5:26–27. *d:* Gn 3:1–6. *e:* Gal 1:6–9. *f:* 12:11. *g:* 1 Cor 1:5, 17; 2:1–5. *h:* 12:13–18; Acts 18:3; 1 Cor 9:6–18. *i:* Phil 4:15, 18. *j:* 1 Cor 9:15. *k:* 12:15.

***Paul's Boast: His Labors.*** 16* I repeat, no
one should consider me foolish;* but if you
do, accept me as a fool, so that I too may
boast a little.* 17 What I am saying I am not
saying according to the Lord but as in foolishness, in this boastful state. 18 Since many
boast according to the flesh, I too will boast.
19 For you gladly put up with fools, since you
are wise yourselves. 20* For you put up with
it if someone enslaves you, or devours you,
or gets the better of you, or puts on airs, or
slaps you in the face. 21 To my shame I say
that we were too weak!*

But what anyone dares to boast of (I am
speaking in foolishness) I also dare. 22* Are
they Hebrews? So am I. Are they Israelites?
So am I. Are they descendants of Abraham?
So am I.[l] 23* Are they ministers of Christ? (I
am talking like an insane person.)[m] I am still
more,* with far greater labors, far more imprisonments, far worse beatings, and numerous brushes with death. 24 Five times at the
hands of the Jews I received forty lashes minus one.[n] 25 Three times I was beaten with
rods, once I was stoned, three times I was
shipwrecked, I passed a night and a day on
the deep;[o] 26 on frequent journeys, in dangers
from rivers, dangers from robbers, dangers
from my own race, dangers from Gentiles,
dangers in the city, dangers in the wilderness, dangers at sea, dangers among false
brothers; 27 in toil and hardship, through
many sleepless nights, through hunger and
thirst, through frequent fastings, through
cold and exposure.[p] 28 And apart from these
things, there is the daily pressure upon me of
my anxiety for all the churches. 29 Who is
weak, and I am not weak? Who is led to sin,
and I am not indignant?[q]

***Paul's Boast: His Weakness.**** 30 If I must
boast, I will boast of the things that show my
weakness. 31* The God and Father of the
Lord Jesus knows, he who is blessed forever,
that I do not lie. 32 At Damascus, the governor under King Aretas guarded the city of
Damascus, in order to seize me, 33 but I was
lowered in a basket through a window in the
wall and escaped his hands.[r]

## CHAPTER 12

See RG 380–81

1 I* must boast; not that it is profitable,
but I will go on to visions and revelations of

**11:16–12:10** Paul now accepts the challenge of his opponents and indulges in boasting similar to theirs, but with differences that he has already signaled in 2 Cor 10:12–18 and that become clearer as he proceeds. He defines the nature of his project and unmistakably labels it as folly at the beginning and the end (2 Cor 11:16–23; 12:11). Yet his boast does not spring from ignorance (2 Cor 11:21; 12:6) nor is it concerned merely with human distinctions (2 Cor 11:18). Paul boasts "in moderation" (2 Cor 10:13, 15) and "in the Lord" (2 Cor 10:17).

**11:16–29** The first part of Paul's boast focuses on labors and afflictions, in which authentic service of Christ consists.

**11:16–21** These verses recapitulate remarks already made about the foolishness of boasting and the excessive toleration of the Corinthians. They form a prelude to the boast proper.

**11:20** Paul describes the activities of the "others" in terms that fill out the picture drawn in vv 3–4, 13–15. Much of the vocabulary suggests fleshly or even satanic activity. **Enslaves**: cf. Gal 2:4. **Devours**: cf. 1 Pt 5:8. **Gets the better**: the verb *lambanō* means "to take," but is used in a variety of senses; here it may imply financial advantage, as in the English colloquialism "to take someone." It is similarly used at 2 Cor 12:16 and is there connected with cunning and deceit. **Puts on airs**: the same verb is rendered "raise oneself" (2 Cor 10:5) and "be too elated" (2 Cor 12:7).

**11:21** Paul ironically concedes the charge of personal weakness from 2 Cor 10:1–18 but will refute the other charge there mentioned, that of lack of boldness, accepting the challenge to demonstrate it by his boast.

**11:22** The opponents apparently pride themselves on their "Jewishness." Paul, too, can claim to be a Jew by race, religion, and promise. **Descendants of Abraham**: elsewhere Paul distinguishes authentic from inauthentic heirs of Abraham and the promise (Rom 4:13–18; 9:7–13; 11:1; Gal 3:9, 27–29; cf. Jn 8:33–47). Here he grants his opponents this title in order to concentrate on the principal claim that follows.

**11:23a Ministers of Christ . . . I am still more**: the central point of the boast (cf. note on 2 Cor 11:5). **Like an insane person**: the climax of his folly.

**11:23b–29** Service of the humiliated and crucified Christ is demonstrated by trials endured for him. This rhetorically impressive catalogue enumerates many of the labors and perils Paul encountered on his missionary journeys.

**11:30–12:10** The second part of Paul's boast, marked by a change of style and a shift in focus. After recalling the project in which he is engaged, he states a new topic: his weaknesses as matter for boasting. Everything in this section, even the discussion of privileges and distinctions, will be integrated into this perspective.

**11:31–32** The episode at Damascus is symbolic. It aptly illustrates Paul's weakness but ends in deliverance (cf. 2 Cor 4:7–11).

**12:1–4 In the body or out of the body**: he seemed no longer confined to bodily conditions, but he does not claim to understand the mechanics of the experience. **Caught up**: i.e., in ecstasy. **The third heaven . . . Paradise**: ancient cosmolo-

*l:* Acts 22:3 / Rom 11:1; Phil 3:5–6. *m:* 6:5; Acts 16:22–24; 1 Cor 15:31–32. *n:* Dt 25:2–3. *o:* Acts 14:19; 27:43–44. *p:* 1 Cor 4:11. *q:* 1 Cor 9:22. *r:* Acts 9:23–25.

the Lord. 2I know someone in Christ who,
fourteen years ago (whether in the body or
out of the body I do not know, God knows),
was caught up to the third heaven. 3And I
know that this person (whether in the body
or out of the body I do not know, God
knows) 4was caught up into Paradise and
heard ineffable things, which no one may utter.[s] 5About this person* I will boast, but
about myself I will not boast, except about
my weaknesses. 6Although if I should wish
to boast, I would not be foolish, for I would
be telling the truth. But I refrain, so that no
one may think more of me than what he sees
in me or hears from me 7because of the
abundance of the revelations. Therefore, that
I might not become too elated,* a thorn in the
flesh was given to me, an angel of Satan, to
beat me, to keep me from being too elated.[t]
8Three times* I begged the Lord about this,
that it might leave me,[u] 9* but he said to me,
"My grace is sufficient for you, for power is
made perfect in weakness." I will rather
boast most gladly of my weaknesses,* in order that the power of Christ may dwell with
me.[v] 10Therefore, I am content with weaknesses, insults, hardships, persecutions, and
constraints, for the sake of Christ;[w] for when
I am weak, then I am strong.*

*Selfless Concern for the Church.** 11I have
been foolish. You compelled me, for I ought
to have been commended by you. For I am
in no way inferior to these "superapostles,"[x]
even though I am nothing. 12* The signs of

gies depicted a multitiered universe. Jewish intertestamental literature contains much speculation about the number of heavens. Seven is the number usually mentioned, but the Testament of Levi (2:7–10; 3:1–4) speaks of three; God himself dwelt in the third of these. Without giving us any clear picture of the cosmos, Paul indicates a mental journey to a nonearthly space, set apart by God, in which secrets were revealed to him. **Ineffable things**: i.e., privileged knowledge, which it was not possible or permitted to divulge.

**12:5–7 This person**: the indirect way of referring to himself has the effect of emphasizing the distance between that experience and his everyday life, just as the indirect **someone in Christ** (2 Cor 12:2) and all the passive verbs emphasize his passivity and receptivity in the experience. The revelations were not a personal achievement, nor were they meant to draw attention to any quality of his own.

**12:7 That I might not become too elated**: God assures that there is a negative component to his experience, so that he cannot lose proper perspective; cf. 2 Cor 1:9; 4:7–11. **A thorn in the flesh**: variously interpreted as a sickness or physical disability, a temptation, or a handicap connected with his apostolic activity. But since Hebrew "thorn in the flesh," like English "thorn in my side," refers to persons (cf. Nm 33:55; Ez 28:24), Paul may be referring to some especially persistent and obnoxious opponent. The language of 2 Cor 12:7–8 permits this interpretation. If this is correct, the frequent appearance of singular pronouns in depicting the opposition may not be merely a stylistic variation; the singular may be provoked and accompanied by the image of one individual in whom criticism of Paul's preaching, way of life, and apostolic consciousness is concentrated, and who embodies all the qualities Paul attributes to the group. **An angel of Satan**: a personal messenger from Satan; cf. the satanic language already applied to the opponents in 2 Cor 11:3, 13–15, 20.

**12:8 Three times**: his prayer was insistent, like that of Jesus in Gethsemane, a sign of how intolerable he felt the thorn to be.

**12:9 But he said to me**: Paul's petition is denied; release and healing are withheld for a higher purpose. The Greek perfect tense indicates that Jesus' earlier response still holds at the time of writing. **My grace is sufficient for you**: this is not a statement about the sufficiency of grace in general. Jesus speaks directly to Paul's situation. **Is made perfect**: i.e., is given most fully and manifests itself fully.

**12:9b–10a** Paul draws the conclusion from the autobiographical anecdote and integrates it into the subject of this part of the boast. **Weaknesses**: the apostolic hardships he must endure, including active personal hostility, as specified in a final catalogue (2 Cor 12:10a). **That the power of Christ may dwell with me**: Paul pinpoints the ground for the paradoxical strategy he has adopted in his self-defense.

**12:10 When I am weak, then I am strong**: Paul recognizes a twofold pattern in the resolution of the weakness-power (and death-life) dialectic, each of which looks to Jesus as the model and is experienced in him. The first is personal, involving a reversal in oneself (Jesus, 2 Cor 13:4a; Paul, 2 Cor 1:9–10; 4:10–11; 6:9). The second is apostolic, involving an effect on others (Jesus, 2 Cor 5:14–15; Paul, 2 Cor 1:6; 4:12; 13:9). The specific kind of "effectiveness in ministry" that Paul promises to demonstrate on his arrival (2 Cor 13:4b; cf. 2 Cor 10:1–11) involves elements of both; this, too, will be modeled on Jesus' experience and a participation in that experience (2 Cor 9; 13:3b).

**12:11–18** This brief section forms an epilogue or concluding observation to Paul's boast, corresponding to the prologue in 2 Cor 11:1–15. A four-step sequence of ideas is common to these two sections: Paul qualifies his boast as folly (2 Cor 11:1; 12:11a), asserts his noninferiority to the "superapostles" (2 Cor 11:5; 12:11b), exemplifies this by allusion to charismatic endowments (2 Cor 11:6; 12:12), and finally denies that he has been a financial burden to the community (2 Cor 11:7–12; 12:13–18).

**12:12** Despite weakness and affliction (suggested by the mention **of endurance**), his ministry has been accompanied by demonstrations of power (cf. 1 Cor 2:3–4). **Signs of an apostle**: visible proof of belonging to Christ and of mediating Christ's power, which the opponents require as touchstones of apostleship (2 Cor 12:11; cf. 2 Cor 13:3).

*s:* Lk 23:43; Rev 2:7. *t:* Nm 33:55; Jos 23:13; Ez 28:24. *u:* Mt 26:39–44. *v:* 4:7. *w:* 6:4–5; Rom 5:3 / Phil 4:13. *x:* 11:5.

an apostle were performed among you with
all endurance, signs and wonders, and
mighty deeds.[y] 13* In what way were you
less privileged than the rest of the churches,
except that on my part I did not burden you?
Forgive me this wrong![z]
14 Now I am ready to come to you this
third time. And I will not be a burden, for I
want not what is yours, but you. Children
ought not to save for their parents, but parents for their children. 15 I will most gladly
spend and be utterly spent for your sakes. If
I love you more, am I to be loved less? 16 But
granted that I myself did not burden you, yet
I was crafty and got the better of you by deceit.[a] 17 Did I take advantage of you through
any of those I sent to you? 18 I urged Titus to
go and sent the brother with him. Did Titus
take advantage of you? Did we not walk in
the same spirit? And in the same steps?[b]

***Final Warnings and Appeals.**** 19 Have you
been thinking all along that we are defending* ourselves before you? In the sight of
God we are speaking in Christ, and all for
building you up, beloved. 20 For I fear that*
when I come I may find you not such as I
wish, and that you may find me not as you
wish; that there may be rivalry, jealousy,
fury, selfishness, slander, gossip, conceit,
and disorder.[c] 21 I fear that when I come
again* my God may humiliate me before
you, and I may have to mourn over many of
those who sinned earlier and have not repented of the impurity, immorality, and licentiousness they practiced.

## CHAPTER 13

See RG 380-81

1 This third time I am coming* to you.
"On the testimony of two or three witnesses
a fact shall be established."[d] 2 I warned
those who sinned earlier* and all the others,
and I warn them now while absent, as I did
when present on my second visit, that if I
come again I will not be lenient, 3* since
you are looking for proof of Christ speaking in me. He is not weak toward you but

**12:13–18** Paul insists on his intention to continue refusing support from the community (cf. 2 Cor 11:8–12). In defending his practice and his motivation, he once more protests his love (cf. 2 Cor 11:11) and rejects the suggestion of secret self-enrichment. He has recourse here again to language applied to his opponents earlier: "cunning" (2 Cor 11:3), "deceit" (2 Cor 11:13), "got the better of you" (see note on 2 Cor 11:20), "take advantage" (2 Cor 2:11).

**12:19–13:10** This concludes the development begun in 2 Cor 10. In the chiastic arrangement of the material (see note on 2 Cor 10:1–13:10), this final part corresponds to the opening; there are important similarities of content between the two sections as well.

**12:19** This verse looks back at the previous chapters and calls them by their proper name, a defense, an *apologia* (cf. 1 Cor 9:3). Yet Paul insists on an important distinction: he has indeed been speaking for their benefit, but the ultimate judgment to which he submits is God's (cf. 1 Cor 4:3–5). This verse also leads into the final section, announcing two of its themes: judgment and building up.

**12:20 I fear that . . .**: earlier Paul expressed fear that the Corinthians were being victimized, exploited, seduced from right thinking by his opponents (2 Cor 11:3–4, 19–21). Here he alludes unexpectedly to moral disorders among the Corinthians themselves. The catalogue suggests the effects of factions that have grown up around rival apostles.

**12:21 Again**: one can also translate, "I fear that when I come my God may again humiliate me." Paul's allusion to the humiliation and mourning that may await him recall the mood he described in 2 Cor 2:1–4, but there is no reference here to any individual such as there is in 2 Cor 2:5–11. The crisis of 2 Cor 2 has happily been resolved by integration of the offender and repentance (2 Cor 7:4–16), whereas 2 Cor 12:21 is preoccupied with still unrepentant sinners. The sexual sins recall 1 Cor 5–7.

**13:1 This third time I am coming**: designation of the forthcoming visit as the "third" (cf. 2 Cor 12:14) may indicate that, in addition to his founding sojourn in Corinth, Paul had already made the first of two visits mentioned as planned in 2 Cor 1:15, and the next visit will be the long-postponed second of these. If so, the materials in 2 Cor 1:12–2:13 plus 2 Cor 7:4–16 and 2 Cor 10–13 may date from the same period of time, presumably of some duration, between Paul's second and third visit, though it is not clear that they are addressing the same crisis. The chronology is too unsure and the relations between sections of 2 Corinthians too unclear to yield any certainty. The hypothesis that 2 Cor 10–13 are themselves the "tearful letter" mentioned at 2 Cor 2:3–4 creates more problems than it solves.

**13:2 I warned those who sinned earlier**: mention of unrepentant sinners (2 Cor 12:21 and here) and of an oral admonition given them on an earlier visit complicates the picture at the very end of Paul's development. It provides, in fact, a second explanation for the show of power that has been threatened from the beginning (2 Cor 10:1–6), but a different reason for it, quite unsuspected until now. It is not clear whether Paul is merely alluding to a dimension of the situation that he has not previously had occasion to mention, or whether some other community crisis, not directly connected with that behind 2 Cor 10–13, has influenced the final editing. **I will not be lenient**: contrast Paul's hesitation and reluctance to inflict pain in 2 Cor 1:23 and 2 Cor 2:1–4. The next visit will bring the showdown.

**13:3–4** Paul now gives another motive for severity when he comes, the charge of weakness leveled against him as an apos-

*y:* Rom 15:19; 1 Thes 1:5. *z:* 11:9–12. *a:* 11:3, 13. *b:* 2:13; 8:16, 23. *c:* 1 Cor 1:11; 3:3. *d:* Dt 19:15; Mt 18:16; Jn 8:17; Heb 10:28.

powerful in you. 4 For indeed he was crucified out of weakness, but he lives by the
power of God. So also we are weak in him,
but toward you we shall live with him by
the power of God.
5* Examine yourselves to see whether you
are living in faith. Test yourselves. Do you
not realize that Jesus Christ is in you?—unless, of course, you fail the test. 6 I hope you
will discover that we have not failed. 7 But
we pray to God that you may not do evil, not
that we may appear to have passed the test
but that you may do what is right, even
though we may seem to have failed. 8 For we
cannot do anything against the truth, but
only for the truth. 9 For we rejoice when we
are weak but you are strong. What we pray
for is your improvement.
10* [e] I am writing this while I am away, so
that when I come I may not have to be severe
in virtue of the authority that the Lord has
given me to build up and not to tear down.

## V. Conclusion*

11 Finally, brothers, rejoice. Mend your ways,
encourage one another, agree with one another, live in peace, and the God of love and
peace will be with you. 12 Greet one another
with a holy kiss. All the holy ones greet you.[f]
13 The grace of the Lord Jesus Christ and
the love of God and the fellowship of the
holy Spirit be with all of you.[g]

tle. The motive echoes more closely the opening section (2 Cor 10:1–18) and the intervening development (especially 2 Cor 11:30–12:10). **Proof of Christ speaking in me**: the threat of 2 Cor 10:1–2 is reworded to recall Paul's conformity with the pattern of Christ, his insertion into the interplay of death and life, weakness and power (cf. note on 2 Cor 12:10b).

**13:5–9** Paul turns the challenge mentioned in 2 Cor 13:3 on them: they are to put themselves to the test to demonstrate whether Christ is in them. These verses involve a complicated series of plays on the theme of *dokimē* (testing, proof, passing and failing a test). Behind this stands the familiar distinction between present human judgment and final divine judgment. This is the final appearance of the theme (cf. 2 Cor 10:18; 11:15; 12:19).

**13:10 Authority . . . to build up and not to tear down**: Paul restates the purpose of his letter in language that echoes 2 Cor 10:2, 8, emphasizing the positive purpose of his authority in their regard. This verse forms an inclusion with the topic sentence of the section (2 Cor 12:19), as well as with the opening of this entire portion of the letter (2 Cor 10:1–2).

**13:11–13** These verses may have originally concluded 2 Cor 10–13, but they have nothing specifically to do with the material of that section. It is also possible to consider them a conclusion to the whole of 2 Corinthians in its present edited form. The exhortations are general, including a final appeal for peace in the community. The letter ends calmly, after its many storms, with the prospect of ecclesial unity and divine blessing. The final verse is one of the clearest trinitarian passages in the New Testament.

*e:* 10:8. *f:* Rom 16:16; 1 Cor 16:20 / Phil 4:22; 1 Thes 5:26; 1 Pt 5:14. *g:* Rom 16:20; 1 Cor 16:23.

See RG 382-90

# The Letter to the Galatians

The Galatians to whom the letter is addressed were Paul's converts, most likely among the descendants of Celts who had invaded western and central Asia Minor in the third century B.C. and had settled in the territory around Ancyra (modern Ankara, Turkey). Paul had passed through this area on his second missionary journey (Acts 16:6) and again on his third (Acts 18:23). It is less likely that the recipients of this letter were Paul's churches in the southern regions of Pisidia, Lycaonia, and Pamphylia where he had preached earlier in the Hellenized cities of Perge, Iconium, Pisidian Antioch, Lystra, and Derbe (Acts 13:13–14:27); this area was part of the Roman province of Galatia, and some scholars think that South Galatia was the destination of this letter.

If it is addressed to the Galatians in the north, the letter was probably written around A.D. 54 or 55, most likely from Ephesus after Paul's arrival there for a stay of several years on his third missionary journey (Acts 19; 20:31). On the South Galatian theory, the date would be earlier, perhaps A.D. 48–50. Involved is the question of how one relates the events of Gal 2:1–10 to the "Council of Jerusalem" described in Acts 15 (see notes on each passage).

In any case, the new Christians whom Paul is addressing were converts from paganism (Gal 4:8–9) who were now being enticed by other missionaries to add the observances of the Jewish law, including the rite of circumcision, to the cross of Christ as a means of salvation. For, since Paul's visit, some other interpretation of Christianity had been brought to these neophytes, probably by converts from Judaism (the name "Judaizers" is sometimes applied to them); it has specifically been suggested that they were Jewish Christians who had come from the austere Essene sect.

These interlopers insisted on the necessity of following certain precepts of the Mosaic law along with faith in Christ. They were undermining Paul's authority also, asserting that he had not been trained by Jesus himself, that his gospel did not agree with that of the original and true apostles in Jerusalem, that he had kept from his converts in Galatia the necessity of accepting circumcision and other key obligations of the Jewish law, in order more easily to win them to Christ, and that his gospel was thus not the full and authentic one held by "those of repute" in Jerusalem (Gal 2:2). Some scholars also see in Galatians 5; 6 another set of opponents against whom Paul writes, people who in their emphasis on the Spirit set aside all norms for conduct and became libertines in practice.

When Paul learned of the situation, he wrote this defense of his apostolic authority and of the correct understanding of the faith. He set forth the unique importance of Christ and his redemptive sacrifice on the cross, the freedom that Christians enjoy from the old burdens of the law, the total sufficiency of Christ and of faith in Christ as the way to God and to eternal life, and the beauty of the new life of the Spirit. Galatians is thus a summary of basic Pauline theology. Its themes were more fully and less polemically developed in the Letter to the Romans.

Autobiographically, the letter gives us Paul's own accounts of how he came to faith (Gal 1:15–24), the agreement in "the truth of the gospel" (Gal 2:5, 14) that he shared with the Jewish Christian leaders in Jerusalem, James, Cephas, and John (Gal 2:1–10), and the rebuke he had to deliver to Cephas in Antioch for inconsistency, contrary to the gospel, on the issue of table fellowship in the racially mixed church of Jewish and Gentile Christians in Antioch (Gal 2:11–14; cf. Gal 2:15–21). At the conclusion of the letter (Gal 6:11–18), Paul wrote in his own hand (cf. 2 Thes 3:17–18) a vivid summary of the message to the Galatians.

In his vigorous emphasis on the absolute preeminence of Christ and his cross as God's way to salvation and holiness, Paul stresses Christian freedom and the ineffectiveness of the Mosaic law for gaining divine favor and blessings (Gal 3:19–29). The pious Jew saw in the law a way established by God to win divine approval by a life of meticulous observance of ritual, social, and moral regulations. But Paul's profound insight into the higher designs of God in Christ led him to understand and welcome the priority of promise and faith (shown in the experience of Abraham, Gal 3:6–18) and the supernatural gifts of the Spirit (Gal 3:2–5; 5:16–6:10). His enthusiasm for this new vision of the life of grace in Christ and of the uniquely salvific role of Christ's redemptive death on the cross shines through this whole letter.

The principal divisions of the Letter to the Galatians are the following:

I. Address (1:1–5)
II. Loyalty to the Gospel (1:6–10)
III. Paul's Defense of His Gospel and His Authority (1:11–2:21)
IV. Faith and Liberty (3:1–4:31)
V. Exhortation to Christian Living (5:1–6:10)
VI. Conclusion (6:11–18)

---

## I. Address

### CHAPTER 1

See RG 385-86

*Greeting.** [1a] Paul, an apostle* not
from human beings nor through a human being but through Jesus Christ and God the Father who raised him from the dead,[b] [2*] and all
the brothers who are with me, to the churches
of Galatia: [3] grace to you and peace from God
our Father and the Lord Jesus Christ, [4*] who

**1:1–5** See note on Rom 1:1–7, concerning the greeting.

**1:1 Apostle**: because of attacks on his authority in Galatia, Paul defends his apostleship. He is not an apostle commissioned by a congregation (Phil 2:25; 2 Cor 8:23) or even by prophets (1 Tm 1:18; 4:14) but **through Jesus Christ and God the Father**.

**1:2 All the brothers**: fellow believers in Christ, male and female; cf. Gal 3:27–28. Paul usually mentions the co-sender(s) at the start of a letter, but the use of **all** is unique, adding weight to the letter. **Galatia**: central Turkey more likely than the Roman province of Galatia; see Introduction.

**1:4** The greeting in Gal 1:3 is expanded by a christological

*a:* Rom 1:1–7; 1 Cor 1:1–3. *b:* 1:11–12. *c:* 2:20; Eph 5:2; 1 Tm 2:6 / 1 Jn 5:19 / Rom 12:2; Eph 5:16; Heb 10:10.

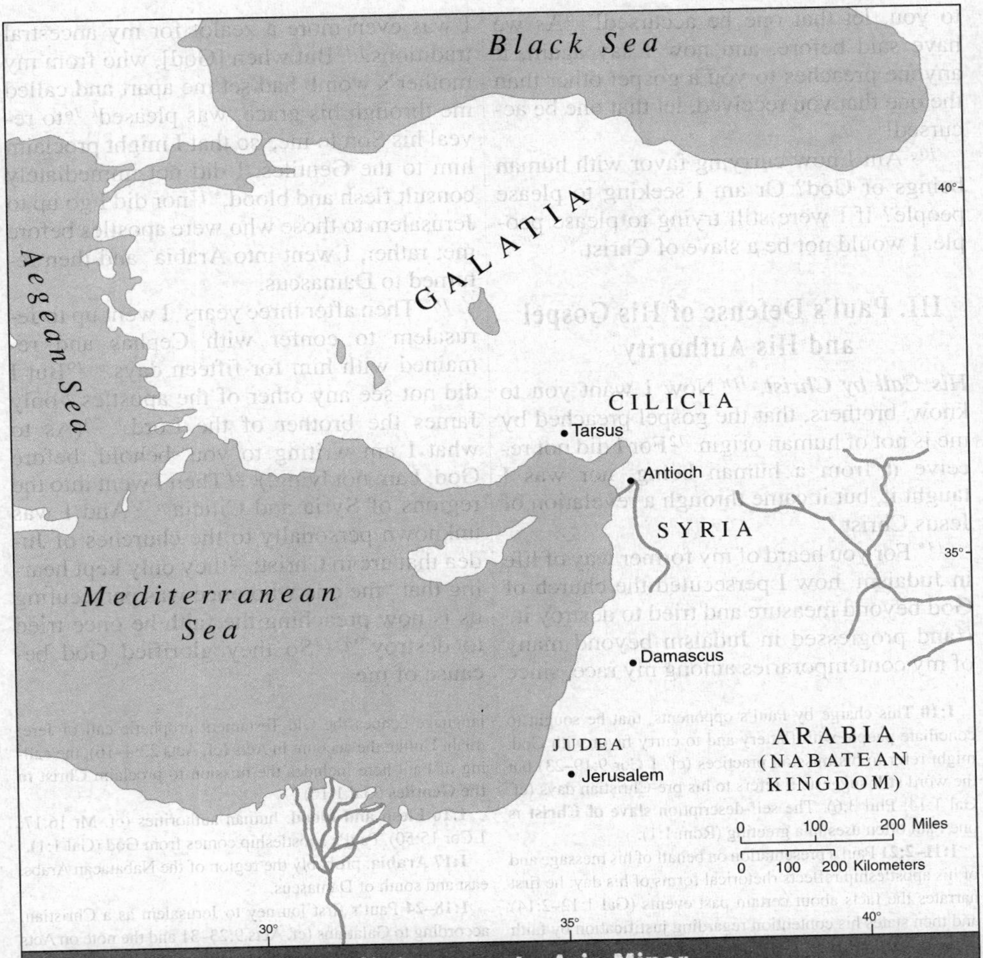


Paul's Journeys to Asia Minor

gave himself for our sins that he might rescue
us from the present evil age in accord with
the will of our God and Father,[c] 5 to whom be
glory forever and ever. Amen.[d]

## II. Loyalty to the Gospel*

6[e] I am amazed that you are so quickly forsaking the one who called you* by [the]
grace [of Christ] for a different gospel 7 (not
that there is another). But there are some
who are disturbing you and wish to pervert
the gospel of Christ. 8[f] But even if we or an
angel from heaven should preach [to you] a
gospel other than the one that we preached

formula that stresses deliverance through the Lord Jesus from a world dominated by Satan; cf. 2 Cor 4:4; Eph 2:2; 6:12.

**1:6–10** In place of the usual thanksgiving (see note on Rom 1:8), Paul, with little to be thankful for in the Galatian situation, expresses amazement at the way his converts are deserting the gospel of Christ for a perverted message. He reasserts the one gospel he has preached (Gal 1:7–9) and begins to defend himself (Gal 1:10).

**1:6 The one who called you**: God or Christ, though in actuality Paul was the divine instrument to call the Galatians.

**1:8 Accursed:** in Greek, *anathema*; cf. Rom 9:3; 1 Cor 12:3; 16:22.

*d:* Rom 16:27; 2 Tm 4:18. *e:* 5:8, 10; Acts 15:1, 24; 2 Cor 11:4. *f:* 1 Cor 16:22 / Gal 5:3, 21; 2 Cor 13:2.

to you, let that one be accursed!* 9 As we
have said before, and now I say again, if
anyone preaches to you a gospel other than
the one that you received, let that one be accursed!

10[g] Am I now currying favor with human
beings or God? Or am I seeking to please
people? If I were still trying to please people, I would not be a slave of Christ.*

## III. Paul's Defense of His Gospel and His Authority*

***His Call by Christ.*** 11[h] Now I want you to
know, brothers, that the gospel preached by
me is not of human origin. 12 For I did not receive it from a human being, nor was I
taught it, but it came through a revelation of
Jesus Christ.*

13* For you heard of my former way of life
in Judaism, how I persecuted the church of
God beyond measure and tried to destroy it,[i]
14 and progressed in Judaism beyond many
of my contemporaries among my race, since
I was even more a zealot for my ancestral
traditions.[j] 15 But when [God], who from my
mother's womb had set me apart and called
me through his grace, was pleased[k] 16 to reveal his Son to me,[l] so that I might proclaim
him to the Gentiles, I did not immediately
consult flesh and blood,* 17 nor did I go up to
Jerusalem to those who were apostles before
me; rather, I went into Arabia* and then returned to Damascus.

18* Then after three years* I went up to Jerusalem to confer with Cephas and remained with him for fifteen days.[m] 19 But I
did not see any other of the apostles,[n] only
James the brother of the Lord.* 20 (As to
what I am writing to you, behold, before
God, I am not lying.)[o] 21 Then I went into the
regions of Syria and Cilicia.[p] 22 And I was
unknown personally to the churches of Judea that are in Christ; 23 they only kept hearing that "the one who once was persecuting
us is now preaching the faith he once tried
to destroy."[q] 24 So they glorified God because of me.

**1:10** This charge by Paul's opponents, that he sought to conciliate people with flattery and to curry favor with God, might refer to his mission practices (cf. 1 Cor 9:19–23) but the word **still** suggests it refers to his pre-Christian days (cf. Gal 1:14; Phil 3:6). The self-description **slave of Christ** is one Paul often uses in a greeting (Rom 1:1).

**1:11–2:21** Paul's presentation on behalf of his message and of his apostleship reflects rhetorical forms of his day: he first narrates the facts about certain past events (Gal 1:12–2:14) and then states his contention regarding justification by faith as the gospel message (Gal 2:15–21). Further arguments follow from both experience and scripture in Galatians 3; 4, before he draws out the ethical consequences (Gal 5:1–6:10). The specific facts that he takes up here to show that his gospel is not a human invention (Gal 1:11) but **came through a revelation of Jesus Christ** (Gal 1:12) deal with his own calling as a Christian missionary (Gal 1:13–17), his initial relations with the apostles in Jerusalem (Gal 1:18–24), a later journey to Jerusalem (Gal 2:1–10), and an incident in Antioch involving Cephas and persons from James (Gal 2:11–14). The content of Paul's revealed gospel is then set forth in the heart of the letter (Gal 2:15–21).

**1:12** Although Paul received his gospel **through a revelation** from Christ, this did not exclude his use of early Christian confessional formulations. See note on Gal 1:4.

**1:13–17** Along with Phil 3:4–11, which also moves from autobiography to its climax in a discussion on justification by faith (cf. Gal 2:15–21), this passage is Paul's chief account of the change from his **former way of life** (Gal 1:13) to service as a Christian missionary (Gal 1:16); cf. Acts 9:1–22; 22:4–16; 26:9–18. Paul himself does not use the term "conversion" but stresses revelation (Gal 1:12, 16). In Gal 1:15 his language echoes the Old Testament prophetic call of Jeremiah. Unlike the account in Acts (cf. Acts 22:4–16), the calling of Paul here includes the mission to proclaim Christ **to the Gentiles** (Gal 1:16).

**1:16 Flesh and blood**: human authorities (cf. Mt 16:17; 1 Cor 15:50). Paul's apostleship comes from God (Gal 1:1).

**1:17 Arabia**: probably the region of the Nabataean Arabs, east and south of Damascus.

**1:18–24** Paul's first journey to Jerusalem as a Christian, according to Galatians (cf. Acts 9:23–31 and the note on Acts 12:25). He is quite explicit about contacts there, testifying under oath (Gal 1:20). On returning to **Syria** (perhaps specifically Damascus, cf. Gal 1:17) **and Cilicia** (including his home town Tarsus, cf. Acts 9:30; 22:3), Paul most likely engaged in missionary work. He underscores the fact that Christians in Judea knew of him only by reputation.

**1:18 After three years**: two years and more, since Paul's call. To **confer with** Cephas may mean simply "pay a visit" or more specifically "get information from" him about Jesus, over a two-week period. **Cephas**: Aramaic name of Simon (Peter); cf. Mt 16:16–18 and the notes there.

**1:19 James the brother of the Lord**: not one of the Twelve, but a brother of Jesus (see note on Mk 6:3). He played an important role in the Jerusalem church (see note on Gal 2:9), the leadership of which he took over from Peter (Acts 12:17). Paul may have regarded James as an apostle.

*g:* 2 Cor 5:11 / 1 Thes 2:4. *h:* 1 Cor 15:1 / Gal 1:1; Eph 3:3. *i:* Acts 8:1–3; 9:1–2; 1 Cor 15:9. *j:* Acts 26:4–5. *k:* Is 49:1; Jer 1:4. *l:* 1:11–12; Rom 1:5; 1 Cor 15:10; Acts 9:3–9 / Gal 2:2, 7 / Mt 16:17. *m:* Acts 9:26–30 / Jn 1:42. *n:* 2:9; Mt 13:55; Acts 12:17. *o:* Rom 9:1; 2 Cor 11:31. *p:* Acts 9:30. *q:* 1:13.

## CHAPTER 2

See RG 386–87

*The Council of Jerusalem.** 1 Then after fourteen years I again went up to Jerusalem with Barnabas,* taking Titus along also.[r]
2 I went up in accord with a revelation,* and
I presented to them the gospel that I preach
to the Gentiles—but privately to those of repute—so that I might not be running, or have
run, in vain.[s] 3 Moreover, not even* Titus,
who was with me, although he was a Greek,
was compelled to be circumcised,[t] 4 but because of the false brothers* secretly brought
in, who slipped in to spy on our freedom that
we have in Christ Jesus,[u] that they might enslave us— 5 to them we did not submit even
for a moment, so that the truth of the gospel*
might remain intact for you.[v] 6 But from
those who were reputed to be important
(what they once were makes no difference to
me; God shows no partiality)—those of repute made me add nothing.[w] 7* On the contrary, when they saw that I had been entrusted with the gospel to the uncircumcised,
just as Peter to the circumcised,[x] 8 for the one
who worked in Peter for an apostolate to the
circumcised worked also in me for the Gentiles, 9 and when they recognized the grace
bestowed upon me, James and Cephas and
John,* who were reputed to be pillars, gave
me and Barnabas their right hands in partnership, that we should go to the Gentiles
and they to the circumcised.[y] 10 Only, we
were to be mindful of the poor,* which is the
very thing I was eager to do.[z]

*Peter's Inconsistency at Antioch.** 11 [a] And
when Cephas came to Antioch, I opposed him
to his face because he clearly was wrong.*

**2:1–10** Paul's second journey to Jerusalem, according to Galatians, involved a private meeting with **those of repute** (Gal 2:2). At issue was a Gentile, Titus, and the question of circumcision, which **false brothers** (Gal 2:4) evidently demanded for him. Paul insists that the gospel he preaches (Gal 2:2; cf. Gal 1:9, 11) remained intact with no addition by those of repute (Gal 2:6); that **Titus** was not **compelled** to accept circumcision (Gal 2:3); and that he and the reputed **pillars** in Jerusalem agreed on how each would advance the missionary task (Gal 1:7–10). Usually, Gal 1:1–10 is equated with the "Council of Jerusalem," as it is called, described in Acts 15. See notes on Acts 15:6–12, 13–35, the latter concerning the "decree" that Paul does not mention.

**2:1 After fourteen years**: thirteen or more years, probably reckoned from the return to Syria and Cilicia (Gal 1:21), though possibly from Paul's calling as a Christian (Gal 1:15). **Barnabas**: cf. Gal 2:9, 13; 1 Cor 9:6. A Jewish Christian missionary, with whom Paul worked (Acts 4:36–37; 11:22, 25, 30; 12:25; 13:1–3; 15:2). **Titus**: a missionary companion of Paul (2 Cor 2:13; 7:6, 13–15; 8:6, 16, 23; 12:18), non-Jewish (Gal 2:3), never mentioned in Acts.

**2:2 A revelation**: cf. Gal 1:1, 12. Paul emphasizes it was God's will, not Jerusalem authority, that led to the journey. Acts 15:2 states that the church in Antioch appointed Paul and Barnabas for the task. **Those of repute**: leaders of the Jerusalem church; the term, while positive, may be slightly ironic (cf. Gal 1:6, 9). **Run, in vain**: while Paul presents a positive picture in what follows, his missionary work in Galatia would have been to no purpose if his opponents were correct that circumcision is needed for complete faith in Christ.

**2:3 Not even** a Gentile Christian like Titus was compelled to receive the rite of circumcision. The Greek text could be interpreted that he voluntarily accepted circumcision, but this is unlikely in the overall argument.

**2:4 False brothers**: Jewish Christians who took the position that Gentile Christians must first become Jews through circumcision and observance of the Mosaic law in order to become Christians; cf. Acts 15:1.

**2:5 The truth of the gospel**: the true gospel, in contrast to the false one of the opponents (Gal 1:6–9); the gospel of grace, used as a norm (Gal 2:14).

**2:7–9** Some think that actual "minutes" of the meeting are here quoted. Paul's apostleship to the Gentiles (Gal 1:16) is recognized alongside that of Peter to the Jews. Moreover, the right to proclaim the gospel without requiring circumcision and the Jewish law is sealed by a handshake. That Paul and colleagues **should go to the Gentiles** did not exclude his preaching to the Jews as well (Rom 1:13–16) or Cephas to Gentile areas.

**2:9 James and Cephas and John**: see notes on Gal 1:18, 19; on Peter and John as leaders in the Jerusalem church, cf. Acts 3:1 and 8:14. The order here, with James first, may reflect his prominence in Jerusalem after Peter (Cephas) departed (Acts 12:17).

**2:10 The poor**: Jerusalem Christians or a group within the church there (cf. Rom 15:26). The collection for them was extremely important in Paul's thought and labor (cf. Rom 15:25–28; 1 Cor 16:1–4; 2 Cor 8–9).

**2:11–14** The decision reached in Jerusalem (Gal 2:3–7) recognized the freedom of Gentile Christians from the Jewish law. But the problem of table fellowship between Jewish Christians, who possibly still kept kosher food regulations, and Gentile believers was not yet settled. When Cephas first came to the racially mixed community of Jewish and Gentile Christians in Antioch (Gal 2:12), he ate with non-Jews. Pressure from persons arriving later from Jerusalem caused him and Barnabas to draw back. Paul therefore publicly rebuked Peter's inconsistency toward the gospel (Gal 2:14). Some think that what Paul said on that occasion extends through Gal 2:16 or 2:21.

**2:11 Clearly was wrong**: literally, "stood condemned," by himself and also by Paul. His action in breaking table fellow-

*r:* Acts 15:2. *s:* 1:11–12, 16 / 1:16 / Phil 2:16. *t:* 2 Cor 2:13; 7:6–7; 8:16–17; 12:18; Ti 1:4 / Gal 2:14; 6:12. *u:* 5:1; Acts 15:1, 24. *v:* 2:14; 4:16. *w:* Dt 10:17; Rom 2:11. *x:* 1:15–16; Acts 9:15; 15:12; 22:21; Rom 1:5. *y:* Rom 15:15 / Gal 1:18–19; Jn 1:42; Acts 12:17 / Gal 2:1. *z:* Acts 11:29–30; Rom 15:25–28; 1 Cor 16:1–4; 2 Cor 8:9. *a:* 1:18 / Acts 11:19–30; 15:1–2.

[12]For, until some people came from James,*
he used to eat with the Gentiles; but when
they came, he began to draw back and separated himself, because he was afraid of the
circumcised.[b] [13]And the rest of the Jews*
[also] acted hypocritically along with him,
with the result that even Barnabas was carried
away by their hypocrisy.[c] [14]But when I saw
that they were not on the right road in line
with the truth of the gospel, I said to Cephas
in front of all,[d] "If you, though a Jew, are living like a Gentile and not like a Jew, how can
you compel the Gentiles to live like Jews?"*
*Faith and Works.** [15]We, who are Jews by
nature and not sinners from among the Gentiles, [16][e] [yet] who know that a person is not
justified by works of the law but through faith
in Jesus Christ, even we have believed in
Christ Jesus that we may be justified by faith
in Christ and not by works of the law, because
by works of the law no one will be justified.*
[17]But if, in seeking to be justified in Christ,
we ourselves are found to be sinners, is Christ
then a minister of sin?* Of course not! [18]But if
I am building up again those things that I tore
down, then I show myself to be a transgressor.* [19]For through the law I died to the law,*
that I might live for God. I have been crucified with Christ;[f] [20]yet I live, no longer I, but
Christ lives in me; insofar as I now live in the
flesh, I live by faith in the Son of God who
has loved me and given himself up for me.[g]
[21]I do not nullify the grace of God; for if justification comes through the law, then Christ
died for nothing.[h]

## IV. Faith and Liberty

### CHAPTER 3

See RG 387–88

*Justification by Faith.** [1]O stupid* Galatians! Who has bewitched you, before
whose eyes Jesus Christ was publicly portrayed as crucified?[i] [2]I want to learn only this
from you:[j] did you receive the Spirit from
works of the law, or from faith in what you
heard?* [3]Are you so stupid?[k] After beginning
with the Spirit, are you now ending with the
flesh?* [4]Did you experience so many things*

ship was especially grievous if the eating involved the meal at the Lord's supper (cf. 1 Cor 11:17–25).

**2:12 Some people came from James**: strict Jewish Christians (cf. Acts 15:1, 5; 21:20–21), either sent by James (Gal 1:19; 2:9) or claiming to be from the leader of the Jerusalem church. **The circumcised**: presumably Jewish Christians, not Jews.

**2:13 The Jews**: Jewish Christians, like Barnabas. **Hypocrisy**: literally, "pretense," "play-acting"; moral insincerity.

**2:14 Compel the Gentiles to live like Jews**: that is, conform to Jewish practices, such as circumcision (Gal 2:3–5) or regulations about food (Gal 2:12).

**2:15–21** Following on the series of incidents cited above, Paul's argument, whether spoken to Cephas at Antioch or only now articulated, is pertinent to the Galatian situation, where believers were having themselves circumcised (Gal 6:12–13) and obeying other aspects of Jewish law (Gal 4:9–10; 5:1–4). He insists that salvation is by faith in Christ, not by works of the law. His teaching on the gospel concerns justification by faith (Gal 2:16) in relation to sin (Gal 2:17), law (Gal 2:19), life in Christ (Gal 2:19–20), and grace (Gal 2:21).

**2:16 No one will be justified**: Ps 143:2 is reflected.

**2:17 A minister of sin**: literally, "a servant of sin" (cf. Rom 15:8), an agent of sin, one who promotes it. This is possibly a claim by opponents that justification on the basis of faith in Christ makes Christ an abettor of sin when Christians **are found to be sinners**. Paul denies the conclusion (cf. Rom 6:1–4).

**2:18** To return to observance of the law as the means to salvation would entangle one not only in inevitable transgressions of it but also in the admission that it was wrong to have abandoned the law in the first place.

**2:19 Through the law I died to the law**: this is variously explained: the law revealed sin (Rom 7:7–9) and led to death and then to belief in Christ; or, the law itself brought the insight that law cannot justify (Gal 2:16; Ps 143:2); or, the "law of Christ" (Gal 6:2) led to abandoning the Mosaic law; or, the law put Christ to death (cf. Gal 3:13) and so provided a way to our salvation, through baptism into Christ, through which we die (**crucified with Christ**; see Rom 6:6). Cf. also Gal 3:19–25 on the role of the law in reference to salvation.

**3:1–14** Paul's contention that justification comes not through the law or the works of the law but by faith in Christ and in his death (Gal 2:16, 21) is supported by appeals to Christian experience (Gal 3:1–5) and to scripture (Gal 3:6–14). The gift of God's Spirit to the Galatians came from the gospel received in faith, not from doing what the law enjoins. The story of Abraham shows that faith in God brings **righteousness** (Gal 3:6; Gn 15:6). The promise to Abraham (Gal 3:8; Gn 12:3) extends to the Gentiles (Gal 3:14)

**3:1 Stupid**: not just senseless, for they were in danger of deserting their salvation.

**3:2 Faith in what you heard**: Paul's message received with faith. The Greek can also mean "the proclamation of the faith" or "a hearing that comes from faith."

**3:3** On the contrast of **Spirit** and **flesh**, cf. Rom 8:1–11. Having received the Spirit, they need not be circumcised now.

**3:4 Experience so many things**: probably the **mighty deeds** of Gal 1:5 but possibly the experience of sufferings.

---

*b:* Acts 10:15, 28; 11:3. *c:* 2:1, 9. *d:* 2:5 / 1:18; 2:9 / 2:3. *e:* 3:2, 11; Ps 143:1–2; Rom 3:20, 28; 4:5; 11:6; Eph 2:8–9; Phil 3:9. *f:* 6:14; Rom 6:6, 8, 10; 7:6. *g:* 1:4; Rom 8:10–11; Col 3:3–4. *h:* 5:2. *i:* 5:7; 1 Cor 1:23. *j:* 2:16 / 3:14; Rom 10:17. *k:* 5:16–18.

in vain?—if indeed it was in vain. 5 Does,
then, the one who supplies the Spirit to you
and works mighty deeds among you do so
from works of the law or from faith in what
you heard?[l] 6 Thus Abraham "believed God,[m]
and it was credited to him as righteousness."*
7* Realize then that it is those who have
faith who are children of Abraham.[n] 8 Scripture, which saw in advance that God would
justify the Gentiles by faith, foretold the
good news to Abraham, saying, "Through
you shall all the nations be blessed."[o] 9 Consequently, those who have faith are blessed
along with Abraham who had faith.[p] 10* For
all who depend on works of the law are under a curse; for it is written, "Cursed be
everyone who does not persevere in doing
all the things written in the book of the
law."[q] 11 And that no one is justified before
God by the law is clear, for "the one who is
righteous by faith will live."[r] 12 But the law
does not depend on faith; rather, "the one
who does these things will live by them."[s]
13 Christ ransomed us from the curse of the
law by becoming a curse for us, for it is written, "Cursed be everyone who hangs on a
tree,"[t] 14 that the blessing of Abraham might
be extended to the Gentiles through Christ
Jesus, so that we might receive the promise
of the Spirit through faith.[u]

***The Law Did Not Nullify the Promise.***
15* Brothers, in human terms I say that no
one can annul or amend even a human will
once ratified.[v] 16 Now the promises were
made to Abraham and to his descendant.* It
does not say, "And to descendants," as referring to many, but as referring to one, "And to
your descendant," who is Christ.[w] 17 This is
what I mean: the law, which came four hundred and thirty years afterward,* does not
annul a covenant previously ratified by God,
so as to cancel the promise.[x] 18 For if the inheritance comes from the law,[y] it is no longer
from a promise; but God bestowed it on
Abraham through a promise.*
19* Why, then, the law? It was added for

**3:6 Abraham . . . righteousness**: see Gn 15:6; Rom 4:3. The Galatians like Abraham heard with faith and experienced justification. This first argument forms the basis for the further scriptural evidence that follows.

**3:7–9 Faith** is what matters, for **Abraham** and the **children of Abraham**, in contrast to the claims of the opponents that circumcision and observance of the law are needed to bring the promised blessing of Gn 12:3; cf. Gn 18:18; Sir 44:21; Acts 3:25.

**3:10–14** Those **who depend** not on promise and faith but **on works of the law are under a curse** because they do **not persevere in doing all the things written in the book of the law** (Gal 3:10; Dt 27:26) in order to gain life (Gal 3:12; Lv 18:5; cf. Rom 10:5). But scripture teaches that **no one is justified before God by the law** (Gal 3:11; Heb 2:4, adapted from the Greek version of Habakkuk; cf. Rom 1:17; Heb 10:38). Salvation, then, depends on faith in Christ who died on the cross (Gal 3:13), taking upon himself a curse found in Dt 21:23 (about executed criminals hanged in public view), to free us from **the curse of the law** (Gal 3:13). That the Gentile Galatians have received the promised Spirit (Gal 3:14) by faith and in no other way returns the argument to the experience cited in Gal 3:1–5.

**3:15–18** A third argument to support Paul's position that salvation is not through the law but by promise (Gal 3:1–14) comes from legal practice and scriptural history. A legal agreement or **human will**, duly **ratified**, is unalterable (Gal 3:15). God's **covenant** with **Abraham** and its repeated promises (Gn 12:2–3, 7; 13:15; 17:7–8; 22:16–18; 24:7) is not superseded by **the law**, which came much later, in the time of Moses. **The inheritance** (of the Spirit and the blessings) is by promise, not by law (Gal 3:18). Paul's argument hinges on the fact that the same Greek word, *diathēkē*, can be rendered as **will** or testament (Gal 3:15) and as **covenant** (Gal 3:17).

**3:16 Descendant**: literally, "and to his seed." The Hebrew, as in Gn 12:7; 15:18; 22:17–18, is a collective singular, traditionally rendered as a plural, **descendants**, but taken by Paul in its literal number to refer to **Christ** as descendant of Abraham.

**3:17 Four hundred and thirty years afterward**: follows Ex 12:40 in the Greek (Septuagint) version, in contrast to Gn 15:13 and Acts 7:6, for chronology.

**3:18** This refutes the opponents' contention that the promises of God are fulfilled only as a reward for human observance of the law.

**3:19–22** A digression: if the Mosaic law, then, does not save or **bring life**, why was it given? Elsewhere, Paul says the law served to show what sin is (Rom 3:20; 7:7–8). Here the further implication is that the law in effect served to produce transgressions. Moreover, it was received at second hand **by angels**, through a **mediator**, not directly from God (Gal 3:19). The law does not, however, oppose God's purposes, for it carries out its function (Gal 3:22), so that **righteousness** comes by **faith** and **promise**, not by human works of the law.

**3:19 The descendant**: Christ (Gal 3:16). **By angels**: Dt 33:2–4 stressed their presence as enhancing the importance of the law; Paul uses their role to diminish its significance (cf. Acts 7:38, 53). **A mediator**: Moses. But in a covenant of promise, where all depends on the one God, no mediator is needed (Gal 3:20).

---

*l:* 2:16. *m:* Gn 15:6; Rom 4:3; Jas 2:23. *n:* 3:29; Rom 4:11–12 / Sir 44:19–21. *o:* Gn 12:3; 18:17–19; Acts 3:25. *p:* Rom 4:16. *q:* Dt 27:26; Jas 2:10. *r:* 2:16; Heb 2:4; Rom 1:17. *s:* Lv 18:5; Rom 10:5. *t:* Dt 21:23; Rom 8:3; 2 Cor 5:21. *u:* 3:2–3, 5; Is 44:3; Jl 3:1–2; Acts 2:33. *v:* Rom 3:5 / Heb 9:16–17. *w:* Gn 12:7; 13:15; 17:8; 22:17; 24:7; Mt 1:1. *x:* Ex 12:40. *y:* Rom 4:16; 11:6.

transgressions, until the descendant* came to whom the promise had been made; it was promulgated by angels at the hand of a mediator.[z] 20Now there is no mediator when only one party is involved, and God is one.[a] 21Is the law then opposed to the promises [of God]? Of course not! For if a law had been given that could bring life, then righteousness would in reality come from the law.[b] 22But scripture confined all things under the power of sin, that through faith in Jesus Christ the promise might be given to those who believe.[c]

***What Faith Has Brought Us.**** 23Before faith came, we were held in custody under law, confined for the faith that was to be revealed.[d] 24Consequently, the law was our disciplinarian* for Christ, that we might be justified by faith.[e] 25But now that faith has come, we are no longer under a disciplinarian.[f] 26For through faith you are all children of God* in Christ Jesus.[g] 27* For all of you who were baptized into Christ[h] have clothed yourselves with Christ.* 28There is neither Jew nor Greek, there is neither slave nor free person, there is not male and female; for you are all one in Christ Jesus.[i] 29And if you belong to Christ, then you are Abraham's descendant, heirs according to the promise.[j]

## CHAPTER 4

See RG 388

***God's Free Children in Christ.**** 1I mean that as long as the heir is not of age,* he is no different from a slave, although he is the owner of everything, 2but he is under the supervision of guardians and administrators until the date set by his father. 3[k] In the same way we also, when we were not of age, were enslaved to the elemental powers of the world.* 4But when the fullness of time had come, God sent his Son, born of a woman, born under the law,[l] 5to ransom those under the law, so that we might receive adoption.[m] 6As proof that you are children,* God sent the spirit of his Son into our hearts, crying out, "Abba, Father!"[n] 7So you are no longer a slave but a child, and if a child then also an heir, through God.[o]

***Do Not Throw This Freedom Away.**** 8[p] At a time when you did not know God, you became slaves to things that by nature are not

**3:23–29** Paul adds a further argument in support of righteousness or justification by faith and through God's promise rather than by works of the law (Gal 2:16; 3:22): as **children of God, baptized into Christ**, the Galatians are all **Abraham's descendant** and **heirs** of **the promise** to Abraham (Gal 3:8, 14, 16–18, 29). The teaching in Gal 3:23–25, that since **faith** (Christianity) **has come, we are no longer under** the law, could be taken with the previous paragraph on the role of the Mosaic law, but it also fits here as a contrast between the situation **before faith** (Gal 3:23) and the results after faith has come (Gal 3:25–29).

**3:24–25 Disciplinarian**: the Greek *paidagōgos* referred to a slave who escorted a child to school but did not teach or tutor; hence, a guardian or monitor. Applying this to the law fits the role of the law described in Gal 3:19–25.

**3:26 Children of God**: literally "sons," in contrast to the young child under the disciplinarian in Gal 3:24–25. The term includes males and females (Gal 3:28).

**3:27–28** Likely a formula used at baptism that expresses racial, social-economic, and sexual equality in Christ (cf. Col 3:11).

**3:27 Clothed yourselves with Christ**: literally, "have put on Christ"; cf. Rom 13:14; Eph 4:24; Col 3:10. Baptismal imagery, traceable to the Old Testament (Jb 29:14; Is 59:17) but also found in pagan mystery cults.

**4:1–7** What Paul has argued in Gal 3:26–29 is now elaborated in terms of the Christian as **the heir** (Gal 4:1, 7; cf. Gal 3:18, 29) freed from control by others. Again, as in Gal 3:2–5, the proof that Christians are children of God is the gift of the Spirit of Christ relating them intimately to God.

**4:1, 3 Not of age**: an infant or minor.

**4:3 The elemental powers of the world**: while the term can refer to the "elements" like earth, air, fire, and water or to elementary forms of religion, the sense here is more likely that of celestial beings that were thought in pagan circles to control the world; cf. Gal 4:8; Col 2:8, 20.

**4:6 Children**: see note on Gal 3:26; here in contrast to the infant or young person **not of age** (Gal 3:1, 3). **Abba**: cf. Mk 14:36 and the note; Rom 8:15.

**4:8–11** On the basis of the arguments advanced from Gal 3:1 through Gal 4:7, Paul now launches his appeal to the Galatians with the question, **how can you turn back** to the slavery of the law (Gal 4:9)? The question is posed with reference to bondage to the **elemental powers** (see note on Gal 4:3) because the Galatians had originally been converted to Christianity from paganism, not Judaism (Gal 4:8). The use of the direct question is like Gal 3:3–5.

**4:8 Things that by nature are not gods**: or "gods that by nature do not exist."

*z:* Rom 4:15; 5:20; 7:7, 13 / Acts 7:38, 53. *a:* Dt 6:4. *b:* Rom 7:7, 10; 8:2–4. *c:* Rom 3:9–20, 23; 11:32. *d:* 4:3–5; 5:18. *e:* 2:16. *f:* Rom 10:4. *g:* 4:5–7; Jn 1:12; Rom 8:14–17. *h:* Rom 6:3; 13:14; Eph 4:24. *i:* Rom 10:12; 1 Cor 12:13; Col 3:11. *j:* 3:7, 14, 16, 18; Rom 4:16–17; 9:7 / Gal 4:1, 7; Rom 4:13–14; 8:17; Heb 6:12; Jas 2:5. *k:* 3:23 / 4:9; Col 2:20. *l:* Mk 1:15. *m:* 3:13, 26. *n:* 3:26; Rom 8:15. *o:* 3:29; Rom 8:16–17. *p:* 1 Cor 12:2.

gods;* 9but now that you have come to know
God, or rather to be known by God, how can
you turn back again to the weak and destitute elemental powers? Do you want to be
slaves to them all over again?[q] 10You are observing days,[r] months, seasons, and years.*
11I am afraid on your account that perhaps I
have labored for you in vain.*

*Appeal to Former Loyalty.** 12I implore
you, brothers, be as I am, because I have also
become as you are.* You did me no wrong;[s]
13you know that it was because of a physical
illness* that I originally preached the gospel
to you, 14and you did not show disdain or
contempt because of the trial caused you by
my physical condition, but rather you received me as an angel of God, as Christ
Jesus. 15Where now is that blessedness of
yours?* Indeed, I can testify to you that, if it
had been possible, you would have torn out
your eyes and given them to me. 16So now
have I become your enemy by telling you
the truth? 17They show interest in you, but
not in a good way; they want to isolate you,*
so that you may show interest in them.[t]
18Now it is good to be shown interest for
good reason at all times, and not only when
I am with you. 19My children, for whom I
am again in labor until Christ be formed in
you![u] 20I would like to be with you now and
to change my tone, for I am perplexed because of you.

*An Allegory on Christian Freedom.** 21Tell
me, you who want to be under the law, do
you not listen to the law? 22For it is written
that Abraham had two sons, one by the slave
woman and the other by the freeborn
woman.[v] 23The son of the slave woman was
born naturally, the son of the freeborn
through a promise.[w] 24Now this is an allegory. These women represent two covenants. One was from Mount Sinai, bearing
children for slavery; this is Hagar.[x] 25Hagar
represents Sinai,* a mountain in Arabia; it
corresponds to the present Jerusalem, for she
is in slavery along with her children. 26But
the Jerusalem above is freeborn, and she is
our mother.[y] 27For it is written:

"Rejoice, you barren one who bore no
children;[z]
break forth and shout, you who were
not in labor;
for more numerous are the children of the
deserted one
than of her who has a husband."*

**4:10** This is likely a reference to ritual observances from the Old Testament, promoted by opponents: sabbaths or Yom Kippur, new moon, Passover or Pentecost, sabbatical years.

**4:11** Cf. Gal 2:2. If the Galatians become **slaves . . . all over again** to the law (Gal 4:9), Paul will have worked in vain among them.

**4:12–20** A strongly personal section. Paul appeals to past ties between the Galatians and himself. He speaks sharply of the opponents (Gal 4:17–18) and pastorally to the Galatians (Gal 4:19–20).

**4:12 Because I have also become as you are**: a terse phrase in Greek, meaning "Be as I, Paul, am," i.e., living by faith, independent of the law, for, in spite of my background in Judaism (Gal 1:13), I have become as you Galatians are now, a brother in Christ.

**4:13 Physical illness**: because its nature is not described, some assume an eye disease (Gal 4:15); others, epilepsy; some relate it to 2 Cor 12:7–9. **Originally**: this may also be translated "formerly" or "on the first (of two) visit(s)"; cf. Acts 16:6; 18:23.

**4:15 That blessedness of yours**: possibly a reference to the Galatians' initial happy reception of Paul (Gal 4:14) and of his gospel (Gal 1:6; 3:1–4) and their felicitation at such blessedness, but the phrase could also refer ironically to earlier praise by Paul of the Galatians, no longer possible when they turn from the gospel to the claims of the opponents (Gal 4:17–18; 1:7). If the word is a more literal reference to a beatitude, Gal 3:26–28 may be in view.

**4:17 Isolate you**: that is, from the blessings of the gospel and/or from Paul.

**4:21–31** Paul supports his appeal for the gospel (Gal 4:9; 1:6–9; 2:16; 3:2) by a further argument from scripture (cf. Gal 3:6–18). It involves the relationship of **Abraham** (Gal 3:6–16) to his wife, Sarah, the **freeborn woman**, and to Hagar, **the slave woman**, and the contrast between the sons born to each, **Isaac**, child of promise, and Ishmael, son of Hagar (Gn 16; 21). Only through Isaac is the promise of God preserved. This **allegory** (Gal 4:24), with its equation of the Sinai covenant and Mosaic law with slavery and of the promise of God with freedom, Paul uses only in light of previous arguments. His quotation of Gn 21:10 at Gal 4:30 suggests on a scriptural basis that the Galatians should expel those who are troubling them (Gal 1:7).

**4:25 Hagar represents Sinai . . .** : some manuscripts have what seems a geographical note, "For Sinai is a mountain in Arabia."

**4:27** Is 54:1 in the Septuagint translation is applied to Sarah as the **barren one** (in Gn 15) who ultimately becomes the mother not only of Isaac but now of numerous children, i.e., of all those who believe, the **children of the promise** (Gal 4:28).

---

*q:* 4:3; Col 2:20. *r:* Col 2:16–20. *s:* 1 Cor 11:1. *t:* 1:7; 6:12; Acts 20:30. *u:* 1 Cor 4:14–15; 2 Cor 6:13; 1 Thes 2:7–8. *v:* Gn 16:15; 21:2–3. *w:* Gn 17:16; Rom 4:19–20; 9:7–9. *x:* 3:17 / Ex 19:20 / Gn 16:1. *y:* Heb 12:22; Rev 21:2. *z:* Is 54:1.

28 Now you, brothers, like Isaac, are children of the promise.[a] 29 But just as then the child of the flesh persecuted the child of the spirit, it is the same now. 30 But what does the scripture say?

"Drive out the slave woman and her son!
For the son of the slave woman shall
not share the inheritance with the
son"[b]

of the freeborn. 31 Therefore, brothers, we are children not of the slave woman but of the freeborn woman.[c]

## V. Exhortation to Christian Living

### CHAPTER 5

See RG 389

***The Importance of Faith.*** * 1 For freedom* Christ set us free; so stand firm and do not submit again to the yoke of slavery.[d]

2 It is I, Paul, who am telling you that if you have yourselves circumcised, Christ will be of no benefit to you.[e] 3 Once again I declare to every man who has himself circumcised[f] that he is bound to observe the entire law.* 4 You are separated from Christ, you who are trying to be justified by law; you have fallen from grace. 5[g] For through the Spirit, by faith, we await the hope of righteousness. 6[h] For in Christ Jesus, neither circumcision nor uncircumcision counts for anything, but only faith working through love.*

***Be Not Misled.*** * 7 You were running well;* who hindered you from following [the] truth? 8[i] That enticement does not come from the one who called you.* 9 A little yeast leavens the whole batch of dough.[j] 10 I am confident of you in the Lord that you will not take a different view, and that the one who is troubling you will bear the condemnation, whoever he may be.[k] 11 As for me, brothers, if I am still preaching circumcision,* why am I still being persecuted? In that case, the stumbling block of the cross has been abolished.[l] 12 Would that those who are upsetting you might also castrate themselves!*

***Freedom for Service.*** * 13 For you were called for freedom, brothers.[m] But do not use this freedom as an opportunity for the flesh; rather, serve* one another through love. 14 For the whole law[n] is fulfilled in one statement, namely, "You shall love your neighbor as yourself."* 15 But if you go on biting and devouring one another, beware that you are not consumed by one another.

16[o] I say, then: live by the Spirit and you will certainly not gratify the desire of the

**5:1–6** Paul begins the exhortations, continuing through Gal 6:10, with an appeal to the Galatians to side with freedom instead of slavery (Gal 5:1). He reiterates his message of justification or righteousness by faith instead of law and circumcision (Gal 5:2–5); cf. Gal 2:16; 3:3. Faith, not circumcision, is what counts (Gal 5:6).

**5:1 Freedom**: Paul stresses as the conclusion from the allegory in Gal 4:21–31 this result of Christ's work for us. It is a principle previously mentioned (Gal 2:4), the responsible use of which Gal 5:13 will emphasize.

**5:3** Cf. Gal 3:10–12. Just as those who seek to live by the law must carry out all its contents, so those who have faith and live by promise must stand firm in their freedom (Gal 5:1, 13).

**5:6** Cf. Rom 2:25–26; 1 Cor 7:19; Gal 6:15. The Greek for **faith working through love** or "faith expressing itself through love" can also be rendered as "faith energized by (God's) love."

**5:7–12** Paul addresses the Galatians directly: with questions (Gal 5:7, 11), a proverb (Gal 5:9), a statement (Gal 5:8), and biting sarcasm (Gal 5:12), seeking to persuade the Galatians to break with those trying to add law and circumcision to Christ as a basis for salvation.

**5:7 Running well**: as in an athletic contest; cf. Gal 2:2; 1 Cor 9:24–26; Phil 2:16; 3:14.

**5:8 The one who called you**: see note on Gal 1:6.

**5:11 Preaching circumcision**: this could refer to Paul's pre-Christian period (possibly as a missionary for Judaism); more probably it arose as a charge from opponents, based perhaps on the story in Acts 16:1–3 that Paul had circumcised Timothy "on account of the Jews." Unlike the Gentile Titus in Gal 2:3, Timothy was the son of a Jewish mother. **The stumbling block of the cross**: cf. 1 Cor 1:23.

**5:12** A sarcastic half-wish that their knife would go beyond mere circumcision; cf. Phil 3:2 and the note there.

**5:13–26** In light of another reminder of the freedom of the gospel (Gal 5:13; cf. Gal 5:1), Paul elaborates on what believers are called to do and be: they fulfill the law by love of neighbor (Gal 5:14–15), walking in the Spirit (Gal 5:16–26), as is illustrated by concrete **fruit of the Spirit** in their lives.

**5:13 Serve . . . through love**: cf. Gal 5:6.

**5:14** Lv 19:18, emphasized by Jesus (Mt 22:39; Lk 10:27); cf. Rom 13:8–10.

**5:16–25 Spirit . . . flesh**: cf. Gal 3:3 and the note on Rom 8:1–13.

*a:* Rom 9:8. *b:* Gn 21:10. *c:* 3:29; Jn 8:35. *d:* 2:4; 4:5, 9; Jn 8:32, 36. *e:* 2:21; Acts 15:1–29. *f:* 3:10; Rom 2:25; Jas 2:10. *g:* Rom 8:23, 25. *h:* 3:28; 6:15; 1 Cor 7:19. *i:* 1:6. *j:* 1 Cor 5:6. *k:* 1:7. *l:* 6:12, 14; 1 Cor 1:23. *m:* 5:1 / Rom 6:18; 1 Cor 8:9; 1 Pt 2:16. *n:* Lv 19:18; Mt 22:39; Rom 13:8–10. *o:* 5:24–25; Rom 8:5.

flesh.* 17For the flesh has desires against the Spirit, and the Spirit against the flesh; these are opposed to each other, so that you may not do what you want.[p] 18But if you are guided by the Spirit, you are not under the law.[q] 19* Now the works of the flesh are obvious: immorality, impurity, licentiousness,[r] 20idolatry, sorcery, hatreds, rivalry, jealousy, outbursts of fury, acts of selfishness, dissensions, factions,[s] 21occasions of envy,* drinking bouts, orgies, and the like. I warn you, as I warned you before, that those who do such things will not inherit the kingdom of God. 22In contrast, the fruit of the Spirit is love, joy, peace, patience, kindness, generosity, faithfulness,[t] 23gentleness, self-control. Against such there is no law.[u] 24Now those who belong to Christ [Jesus] have crucified their flesh with its passions and desires.[v] 25If we live in the Spirit, let us also follow the Spirit.[w] 26Let us not be conceited, provoking one another, envious of one another.[x]

## CHAPTER 6

See RG 389

***Life in the Community of Christ.**** 1Brothers, even if a person is caught in some transgression, you who are spiritual should correct that one in a gentle spirit, looking to yourself, so that you also may not be tempted.[y] 2Bear one another's burdens,[z] and so you will fulfill the law of Christ.* 3[a] For if anyone thinks he is something when he is nothing, he is deluding himself. 4* Each one must examine his own work, and then he will have reason to boast with regard to himself alone, and not with regard to someone else; 5for each will bear his own load.[b]

6[c] One who is being instructed in the word should share all good things with his instructor.* 7Make no mistake: God is not mocked, for a person will reap only what he sows, 8because the one who sows for his flesh will reap corruption from the flesh, but the one who sows for the spirit will reap eternal life from the spirit.[d] 9Let us not grow tired of doing good, for in due time we shall reap our harvest, if we do not give up.[e] 10So then, while we have the opportunity, let us do good to all,[f] but especially to those who belong to the family of the faith.*

## VI. Conclusion

***Final Appeal.**** 11See with what large letters* I am writing to you in my own hand![g] 12* It is those who want to make a good appearance in the flesh who are trying to compel you to

**5:19–23** Such lists of vices and virtues (cf. Rom 1:29–31; 1 Cor 6:9–10) were common in the ancient world. Paul contrasts **works of the flesh** (Gal 5:19) with **fruit** (not "works") **of the Spirit** (Gal 5:22). Not law, but the Spirit, leads to such traits.

**5:21 Occasions of envy**: after the Greek word *phthonoi*, "envies," some manuscripts add a similar sounding one, *phonoi*, "murders."

**6:1–10** The ethical exhortations begun at Gal 5:1 continue with a variety of admonitions to the community (**brothers**: see note on Gal 1:2). Nearly every sentence contains a separate item of practical advice; the faith and freedom of the gospel underlie each maxim. Tensions and temptation within communal life have previously been addressed in Gal 5:15, 26, and Gal 6:1 continues with a case in which a **person is caught in some transgression** such as those in Gal 5:19–21; cf. Gal 2:17.

**6:2 The law of Christ**: cf. Rom 8:2; 1 Cor 9:21; Gal 5:14. The principle of love for others is meant. To **bear one another's burdens** is to "serve one another through love" (Gal 5:13).

**6:4–5** Self-examination is the cure for self-deception. Compare what you are with what you were before, and give the glory to God; cf. Rom 6:19–22. **Load**: used elsewhere of a soldier's pack. Correcting one's own conduct avoids burdening others with it.

**6:6** Implies oral instruction in the faith by catechists; these are to be remunerated for their service; cf. Rom 15:27.

**6:10 The family of the faith**: the Christian household or church. Doing good has a universal object (**to all**), but the local community makes specific the reality of those to be served.

**6:11–18** A postscript in Paul's own hand, as was his practice (see 1 Cor 16:21; 2 Thes 3:17). Paul summarizes his appeal against his opponents (Gal 6:12–13), then returns to his message of glorying in the cross, not in circumcision, as the means of salvation (Gal 6:14–15; cf. Gal 5:11). A benediction follows at Gal 6:16. In the polemical spirit that the attack on his apostleship called forth (Gal 1:11–2:21), Paul reasserts his missionary credentials (Gal 6:17) before giving a final benediction (Gal 6:18).

**6:11 Large letters**: in contrast to the finer hand of the scribe who wrote the letter up to this point. The larger Greek letters make Paul's message even more emphatic. Some find a hint of poor eyesight on Paul's part. See note on Gal 4:13.

**6:12–15** The Jewish Christian opponents wished **not to be persecuted**, possibly by Jews. But since Judaism seems to

*p:* Rom 7:15, 23; 8:6. *q:* Rom 6:14; 8:14. *r:* Rom 1:29–31; 1 Cor 6:9–10; Col 3:5–6, 8. *s:* Rev 22:15. *t:* Eph 5:9 / 1 Cor 13:4–7; 2 Cor 6:6; 1 Tm 4:12; 2 Pt 1:6. *u:* 1 Tm 1:9. *v:* 2:19; Rom 6:6; 8:13. *w:* 5:16. *x:* Phil 2:3. *y:* Mt 18:15; Jas 5:19 / 1 Cor 10:12–13. *z:* Col 3:13 / 1 Cor 9:21. *a:* 1 Cor 3:18; 8:2; 2 Cor 12:11. *b:* Rom 14:12. *c:* 1 Cor 9:14. *d:* Prv 11:18; Rom 8:6, 13. *e:* 2 Thes 3:13; Heb 12:1–3. *f:* 1 Thes 5:15. *g:* 1 Cor 16:21.

have yourselves circumcised, only that they may not be persecuted for the cross of Christ.[h] 13 Not even those having themselves circumcised* observe the law themselves; they only want you to be circumcised so that they may boast of your flesh. 14 But may I never boast except in the cross of our Lord Jesus Christ, through which* the world has been crucified to me, and I to the world.[i] 15 For neither does circumcision mean anything, nor does uncircumcision,[j] but only a new creation.* 16 Peace and mercy be to all who follow this rule* and to the Israel of God.[k]

17 From now on, let no one make troubles for me; for I bear the marks of Jesus* on my body.[l]

18 The grace of our Lord Jesus Christ be with your spirit, brothers. Amen.[m]

have had a privileged status as a religion in the Roman empire, circumcised Christians might, if taken as Jews, thereby avoid persecution from the Romans. In any case, Paul instead stresses conformity with **the cross of our Lord Jesus Christ**; cf. Gal 2:19–21; 5:11.

**6:13 Those having themselves circumcised**: other manuscripts read, "those who have had themselves circumcised."

**6:14 Through which**: or "through whom."

**6:15 New creation**: or "new creature"; cf. 2 Cor 5:17.

**6:16 This rule**: the principle in Gal 6:14–15. **The Israel of God**: while the church may be meant (the phrase can be translated "to all who follow this rule, even the Israel of God"; cf. Gal 6:10; 1 Cor 10:18), the reference may also be to God's ancient people, Israel; cf. Ps 125:5; 128:6.

**6:17 The marks of Jesus**: slaves were often branded by marks (stigmata) burned into their flesh to show to whom they belonged; so also were devotees of pagan gods. Paul implies that instead of outdated circumcision, his body bears the scars of his apostolic labors (2 Cor 11:22–31), such as floggings (Acts 16:22; 2 Cor 11:25) and stonings (Acts 14:19), that mark him as belonging to the Christ who suffered (cf. Rom 6:3; 2 Cor 4:10; Col 1:24) and will protect his own.

*h*: 5:2, 11. *i*: 2:20; 1 Cor 2:2. *j*: 5:6; 1 Cor 7:19 / 2 Cor 5:17. *k*: Ps 125:5; 128:6. *l*: 2 Cor 4:10. *m*: Phil 4:23; 2 Tm 4:22; Phlm 25.

See RG 390–95

# The Letter to the Ephesians

Ephesians is the great Pauline letter about the church. It deals, however, not so much with a congregation in the city of Ephesus in Asia Minor as with the worldwide church, the head of which is Christ (Eph 4:15), the purpose of which is to be the instrument for making God's plan of salvation known throughout the universe (Eph 3:9–10). Yet this ecclesiology is anchored in God's saving love, shown in Jesus Christ (Eph 2:4–10), and the whole of redemption is rooted in the plan and accomplishment of the triune God (Eph 1:3–14). The language is often that of doxology (Eph 1:3–14) and prayer (cf. Eph 1:15–23; 3:14–19), indeed of liturgy and hymns (Eph 3:20–21; 5:14).

The majestic chapters of Ephesians emphasize the unity in the church of Christ that has come about for both Jews and Gentiles within God's household (Eph 1:15–2:22, especially Eph 2:11–22) and indeed the "seven unities" of church, Spirit, hope; one Lord, faith, and baptism; and the one God (Eph 4:4–6). Yet the concern is not with the church for its own sake but rather as the means for mission in the world (Eph 3:1–4:24). The gifts Christ gives its members are to lead to growth and renewal (Eph 4:7–24). Ethical admonition is not lacking either; all aspects of human life and relationships are illumined by the light of Christ (Eph 4:25–6:20).

The letter is seemingly addressed by Paul to Christians in Ephesus (Eph 1:1), a place where the apostle labored for well over two years (Acts 19:10). Yet there is a curiously impersonal tone to the writing for a community with which Paul was so intimately acquainted (cf. Eph 3:2 and Eph 4:21). There are no personal greetings (cf. Eph 6:23). More significantly, important early manuscripts omit the words "in Ephesus" (see note on Eph 1:1). Many therefore regard the letter as an encyclical or "circular letter" sent to a number of churches in Asia Minor, the addressees to be designated in each place by its bearer, Tychicus (Eph 6:21–22). Others think that Ephesians is the letter referred to in Col 4:16 as "to the Laodiceans."

Paul, who is designated as the sole author at Eph 1:1, is described in almost unparalleled terms with regard to the significant role he has in God's plan for bringing the Gentiles to faith in Christ (Eph 3:1–12). Yet at the time of writing he is clearly in prison (Eph 3:1; 4:1; 6:20), suffering afflictions (Eph 3:13). Traditionally this "Captivity Epistle" has, along with Colossians, Philippians, and Philemon, been dated to an imprisonment in Rome, likely in A.D. 61–63. Others appeal to an earlier imprisonment, perhaps in Caesarea (Acts 23:27–27:2). Since the early nineteenth century, however, much of critical scholarship has considered the letter's style and use of words (especially when compared with Colossians), its concept of the church, and other points of doctrine put forward by the writer as grounds for serious doubt about authorship by Paul. The letter may then be the work of a secretary writing at the apostle's direction or of a later disciple who sought to develop Paul's ideas for a new situation around A.D. 80–100.

The principal divisions of the Letter to the Ephesians are the following:

I. Address (1:1–14)
II. Unity of the Church in Christ (1:15–2:22)
III. World Mission of the Church (3:1–4:24)
IV. Daily Conduct, an Expression of Unity (4:25–6:20)
V. Conclusion (6:21–24).

# I. Address

## CHAPTER 1

See RG 391-92

*Greeting.** 1 Paul, an apostle of Christ Jesus by the will of God, to the holy ones who are [in Ephesus]* faithful in Christ Jesus:[a] 2 grace to you and peace from God our Father and the Lord Jesus Christ.[b]

*The Father's Plan of Salvation.* 3* Blessed be the God and Father of our Lord Jesus Christ,[c] who has blessed us in Christ with every spiritual blessing in the heavens,* 4 as he chose us in him, before the foundation of the world, to be holy and without blemish before him.[d] In love 5 he destined us for adoption to himself through Jesus Christ, in accord with the favor of his will,[e] 6 for the praise of the glory of his grace that he granted us in the beloved.[f]

*Fulfillment Through Christ.* 7 In him we have redemption by his blood, the forgiveness of transgressions, in accord with the riches of his grace[g] 8 that he lavished upon us. In all wisdom and insight,[h] 9 he has made known to us the mystery* of his will in accord with his favor that he set forth in him[i] 10 as a plan for the fullness of times, to sum up all things in Christ, in heaven and on earth.[j]

*Inheritance Through the Spirit.* 11 In him we were also chosen, destined in accord with the purpose of the One who accomplishes all things according to the intention of his will,[k] 12 so that we might exist for the praise of his glory, we who first hoped* in Christ. 13 In him you also, who have heard the word of truth, the gospel of your salva-

**1:1–2** For the epistolary form used at the beginning of letters, see note on Rom 1:1–7. Twenty-two of the thirty Greek words in Eph 1:1–2 also occur in Col 1:1–2.

**1:1 [In Ephesus]**: the phrase is lacking in important early witnesses such as P46 (3rd cent.), and Sinaiticus and Vaticanus (4th cent.), appearing in the latter two as a fifth-century addition. Basil and Origen mention its absence from manuscripts. See Introduction. Without the phrase, the Greek can be rendered, as in Col 1:2, "to the holy ones and faithful brothers in Christ."

**1:3–14** While a Pauline letter usually continues after the greeting with a prayer of thanksgiving, as in Eph 1:15–23 below, Ephesians first inserts a blessing of God for the blessings Christians have experienced, as in 2 Cor 1:3–4 and 1 Pt 1:3–12. The blessing here, akin to a Jewish *berakah*, is rich in images almost certainly drawn from hymns and liturgy. Many ideas here are also found in Col 1:3–23. Certain phrases are frequently repeated, such as **in Christ** (Eph 1:3, 10, 12) or **in him** (Eph 1:4, 7, 9, 11, 13) or **in the beloved** (Eph 1:6) and **(for) the praise of (his) glory** (Eph 1:6, 12, 14). Some terms like **chose** (Eph 1:4) and **destined** (Eph 1:5) reflect Old Testament theology (Dt 7:7; 9:4–6; 23:5) or Pauline themes (**redemption**, Eph 1:7, 14; **grace**, Eph 1:6, 7) or specific emphases in Colossians (**forgiveness**, Col 1:14). A triadic structure is discernible in Eph 1:3–14: **God** the **Father** (Eph 1:3–6, 8, 11), **Christ** (Eph 1:3, 5, 7–10, 12), and the **Spirit** (Eph 1:13–14). The spiritual blessings Christians have received through Christ (Eph 1:3) are gratefully enumerated: the call to holiness (Eph 1:4; cf. Col 1:22); the gift of divine **adoption** establishing a unique spiritual relationship with God the Father through Christ (Eph 1:5; cf. Gal 4:5); liberation from sin through Christ's sacrificial death (Eph 1:7); revelation of God's plan of salvation in Christ (Eph 1:9; cf. Eph 3:3–4; Rom 16:25); the gift of election and faith in Christ bestowed upon Jewish Christians (see note on Eph 1:12, **we who first hoped in Christ**); and finally, the same gift granted to Gentiles (Eph 1:13, **you also**). In the Christ-centered faith and existence of the Christian communities the apostle sees the predetermined **plan** of God to bring all creation under the final rule of Christ (Eph 1:4–5, 9–10) being **made known** (Eph 1:9) and carried through, to God's **glory** (Eph 1:6, 12, 14).

**1:3 In the heavens**: literally, "in the heavenlies" or "in the heavenly places," a term in Ephesians for the divine realm.

**1:9 Mystery**: as in Rom 16:25; Col 1:26–27 and elsewhere, a secret of God now revealed in the **plan** to save and **sum up all things in Christ** (Eph 1:10); cf. Eph 3:3–6.

**1:12 We who first hoped**: probably Jewish Christians (con-

*a:* Rom 1:7; 1 Cor 1:1–2; Col 1:1. *b:* Col 1:2. *c:* 2:6; 2 Cor 1:3. *d:* 5:27; Jn 15:16; 17:24; Rom 8:29; 2 Thes 2:13. *e:* Jn 1:12; 1 Jn 3:1. *f:* Mt 3:17; Col 1:13. *g:* 2:7–13; Rom 3:24; Col 1:14, 20. *h:* Col 1:9. *i:* 3:3, 9; Rom 16:25. *j:* Gal 4:4; Col 1:16, 20. *k:* Is 46:10; Rom 8:28; Col 1:12; Rev 4:11.

tion, and have believed in him, were sealed*
with the promised holy Spirit,[l] 14 which is the
first installment* of our inheritance toward
redemption as God's possession, to the
praise of his glory.[m]

## II. Unity of the Church in Christ

*The Church as Christ's Body.** 15 Therefore, I,
too, hearing of your faith in the Lord Jesus
and of your love* for all the holy ones,[n] 16 do
not cease giving thanks for you, remembering you in my prayers,[o] 17 that the God of our
Lord Jesus Christ, the Father of glory, may
give you a spirit of wisdom and revelation resulting in knowledge of him.[p] 18 May the eyes
of [your] hearts be enlightened, that you may
know what is the hope that belongs to his
call, what are the riches of glory in his inheritance among the holy ones,[q] 19 and what is
the surpassing greatness of his power for us
who believe, in accord with the exercise of
his great might,[r] 20 which he worked in
Christ, raising him from the dead and seating
him at his right hand in the heavens,[s] 21 far
above every principality, authority, power,
and dominion, and every name that is named
not only in this age but also in the one to
come.[t] 22 And he put all things beneath his
feet and gave him as head over all things to
the church,[u] 23 which is his body,* the fullness
of the one who fills all things in every way.[v]

### CHAPTER 2*

See RG 392

*Generosity of God's Plan.** 1[w] You
were dead in your transgressions and sins*
2 in which you once lived following the age

trast Eph 1:13, **you**, the Gentiles); possibly the people of Israel, "we who already enjoyed the hope of Christ," or perhaps present hope in contrast to future redemption (cf. Eph 1:14).

**1:13 Sealed**: by God, in baptism; cf. Eph 4:30; 2 Cor 1:22.

**1:14 First installment**: down payment by God on full salvation, as at 2 Cor 1:22.

**1:15–23** See note on Rom 1:8 for the thanksgiving form in a letter. Much of the content parallels thoughts in Col 1:3–20. The prayer moves from God and Christ (Eph 1:17, 20–21) to the Ephesians (Eph 1:17–19) and the church (Eph 1:22–23). Paul asks that the blessing imparted by God the Father (Eph 1:3) to the Ephesians will be strengthened in them through the message of the gospel (Eph 1:13, 17–19). Those blessings are seen in the context of God's **might** in establishing the sovereignty of Christ over all other creatures (Eph 1:19–21) and in appointing him **head** of the church (Eph 1:22–23). For the allusion to angelic spirits in Eph 1:21, see Rom 8:38 and Col 1:16. Here, as in 1 Cor 15:24–25 and Col 2:15, every such **principality** and **power** is made subject to Christ.

**1:15 Your faith . . . your love**: some manuscripts omit the latter phrase, but cf. Col 1:4.

**1:23 His body**: the church (Eph 1:22); cf. note on Col 1:18. Only in Ephesians and Colossians is Christ the **head** of the **body**, in contrast to the view in 1 Cor 12 and Rom 12:4–8 where Christ is equated with the entire body or community. **Fullness**: see note on Col 1:19. Some take **the one who fills** as God, others as Christ (cf. Eph 4:10). If in Christ "dwells the fullness of the deity bodily" (Col 2:9), then, as God "fills" Christ, Christ in turn fills the church and the believer (Eph 3:19; 5:18). But the difficult phrases here may also allow the church to be viewed as the "complement" of Christ who is "being filled" as God's plan for the universe is carried out through the church (cf. Eph 3:9–10).

**2:1–22** The gospel of **salvation** (Eph 1:13) that God **worked in Christ** (Eph 1:20) is reiterated in terms of what God's **great love** (Eph 2:4), expressed in Christ, means for us. The passage sometimes addresses **you**, Gentiles (Eph 2:1–2, 8, 11–13, 19, 22), but other times speaks of **all of us** who believe (Eph 2:3–7, 10, 14, 18). In urging people to **remember** their grim past when they were **dead** in sins (Eph 2:1–3, 11–12) and what they are **now in Christ** (Eph 2:4–10, 13), the author sees both Jew and Gentile reconciled with God, now **one new person**, a new humanity, **one body**, **the household of God**, **a temple** and **dwelling place** of God's Spirit (Eph 2:15–16, 19–22). The presentation falls into two parts, the second stressing more the meaning for the church.

**2:1–10** The recipients of Paul's letter have experienced, in their redemption from **transgressions and sins**, the effect of Christ's supremacy over the power of the devil (Eph 2:1–2; cf. Eph 6:11–12), who rules not from the netherworld but from the **air** between God in heaven and human beings on earth. Both Jew and Gentile have experienced, through Christ, God's free gift of salvation that already marks them for a future heavenly destiny (Eph 2:3–7). The language **dead**, **raised us up**, and **seated us . . . in the heavens** closely parallels Jesus' own passion and Easter experience. The terms in Eph 2:8–9 describe salvation in the way Paul elsewhere speaks of justification: **by grace, through faith, the gift of God, not from works**; cf. Gal 2:16–21; Rom 3:24–28. Christians are a newly created people in Christ, fashioned by God for a life of goodness (Eph 2:10).

**2:1–7** These verses comprise one long sentence in Greek, the main verb coming in Eph 2:5, God **brought us to life**, the object you/us **dead in . . . transgressions** being repeated in Eph 2:1, 5; cf. Col 2:13.

**2:2 Age of this world**: or "aeon," a term found in gnostic thought, possibly synonymous with the **rulers of this world**, but also reflecting the Jewish idea of "two ages," this present evil age and "the age to come"; cf. 1 Cor 3:19; 5:10; 7:31; Gal 1:4; Ti 2:12. **The disobedient**: literally, "the sons of disobedience," a Semitism as at Is 30:9.

*l:* 4:30; Acts 2:33; Col 1:5–6. *m:* 2 Cor 1:22; 5:5. *n:* Col 1:3–4; Phlm 4–5. *o:* Col 1:3, 9. *p:* 3:14, 16; Col 1:9–10; 1 Jn 5:20. *q:* 4:4; Col 1:12, 27. *r:* 2 Cor 13:4; Col 1:11; 2:12. *s:* Ps 110:1; Heb 1:3. *t:* Phil 2:9; Col 1:16; 1 Pt 3:22. *u:* 4:15; Ps 8:7; Mt 28:18; Col 1:18. *v:* 4:10, 12; Rom 12:5; 1 Cor 12:27; Col 1:19. *w:* Col 1:21; 2:13. *x:* 6:12; Jn 12:31; Col 1:13.

of this world,* following the ruler of the
power of the air, the spirit that is now at
work in the disobedient.[x] 3 All of us once
lived among them in the desires of our flesh,
following the wishes of the flesh and the im-
pulses, and we were by nature children of
wrath, like the rest.[y] 4 But God, who is rich in
mercy, because of the great love he had for
us, 5 [z] even when we were dead in our transgressions, brought us to life with Christ* (by
grace you have been saved), 6 raised us up
with him, and seated us with him in the
heavens in Christ Jesus,[a] 7 that in the ages to
come he might show the immeasurable
riches of his grace in his kindness to us in
Christ Jesus.[b] 8 For by grace you have been
saved through faith, and this is not from you;
it is the gift of God;[c] 9 it is not from works, so
no one may boast.[d] 10 For we are his handiwork, created in Christ Jesus for the good
works that God has prepared in advance,
that we should live in them.[e]

*One in Christ.** 11 Therefore, remember
that at one time you, Gentiles in the flesh,
called the uncircumcision by those called
the circumcision, which is done in the flesh
by human hands, 12 were at that time without
Christ, alienated from the community of Israel* and strangers to the covenants of promise, without hope and without God in the
world.[f] 13 But now in Christ Jesus you who
once were far off have become near by the
blood of Christ.[g]

14* For he is our peace, he who made both
one and broke down the dividing wall of enmity, through his flesh,[h] 15 abolishing the law
with its commandments and legal claims,
that he might create in himself one new person* in place of the two, thus establishing
peace,[i] 16 and might reconcile both with God,
in one body, through the cross, putting that
enmity to death by it.[j] 17 He came and
preached peace to you who were far off and
peace to those who were near,[k] 18 for through
him we both have access in one Spirit to the
Father.[l]

19 So then you are no longer strangers
and sojourners, but you are fellow citizens
with the holy ones and members of the
household of God,[m] 20 built upon the foundation of the apostles and prophets,[n] with
Christ Jesus himself as the capstone.*
21 Through him the whole structure is held
together and grows into a temple sacred in
the Lord;[o] 22 in him you also are being built
together into a dwelling place of God in the
Spirit.[p]

# III. World Mission of the Church

## CHAPTER 3

See RG 392–93

### *Commission to Preach God's Plan.**
1 Because of this,[q] I, Paul, a prisoner of

**2:5** Our relation through baptism **with Christ**, the risen Lord, is depicted in terms of realized eschatology, as already exaltation, though Eph 2:7 brings in the future aspect too.

**2:11–22** The Gentiles lacked Israel's messianic expectation, lacked the various **covenants** God made with **Israel**, lacked **hope** of salvation and knowledge of the true **God** (Eph 2:11–12); but through Christ all these religious barriers between Jew and Gentile have been transcended (Eph 2:13–14) by the abolition of the Mosaic covenant-law (Eph 2:15) for the sake of uniting Jew and Gentile into a single religious community (Eph 2:15–16), imbued with the same holy **Spirit** and worshiping the same **Father** (Eph 2:18). The Gentiles are now included in God's **household** (Eph 2:19) as it arises upon the **foundation** of **apostles** assisted by those endowed with the prophetic gift (Eph 3:5), the preachers of Christ (Eph 2:20; cf. 1 Cor 12:28). With Christ as the **capstone** (Eph 2:20; cf. Is 28:16; Mt 21:42), they are being built into the holy **temple** of God's people where the divine presence dwells (Eph 2:21–22).

**2:12 The community of Israel**: or "commonwealth"; cf. Eph 4:18. **The covenants**: cf. Rom 9:4: with Abraham, with Moses, with David.

**2:14–16** The elaborate imagery here combines pictures of Christ as **our peace** (Is 9:5), his crucifixion, the ending of the Mosaic law (cf. Col 2:14), reconciliation (2 Cor 5:18–21), and the destruction of **the dividing wall** such as kept people from God in the temple or a barrier in the heavens.

**2:15 One new person**: a corporate body, the Christian community, made up of Jews and Gentiles, replacing ancient divisions; cf. Rom 1:16.

**2:20 Capstone**: the Greek can also mean cornerstone or keystone.

**3:1–13** Paul reflects on his mission to the Gentiles. He alludes to his call and appointment to the apostolic office (Eph 3:2–3) and how his **insight** through revelation, as well as that of the other apostles and charismatic prophets in the church (Eph 3:4–5), has

*y:* Col 3:6–7. *z:* Rom 5:8; 6:13; Col 2:13. *a:* Rom 8:10–11; Phil 3:20; Col 2:12. *b:* 1:7. *c:* Rom 3:24; Gal 2:16. *d:* 1 Cor 1:29. *e:* 4:24; Ti 2:14. *f:* Rom 9:4; Col 1:21, 27. *g:* 2:17; Is 57:19; Col 1:20. *h:* Gal 3:28. *i:* 2 Cor 5:17; Col 2:14. *j:* Col 1:20, 22. *k:* Is 57:19; Zec 9:10. *l:* 3:12. *m:* Heb 12:22–23. *n:* Is 28:16; Rev 21:14. *o:* 1 Cor 3:16; Col 2:19. *p:* 1 Pt 2:5. *q:* Phil 1:7, 13; Col 1:24–29; 4:18; Phlm 9; 2 Tm 2:9.

Christ* [Jesus] for you Gentiles— 2if, as I
suppose, you have heard of the stewardship*
of God's grace that was given to me for your
benefit,[r] 3[namely, that] the mystery* was
made known to me by revelation, as I have
written briefly earlier.[s] 4When you read this
you can understand my insight into the mystery of Christ, 5which was not made known
to human beings in other generations as it
has now been revealed to his holy apostles
and prophets by the Spirit,[t] 6that the Gentiles
are coheirs, members of the same body, and
copartners in the promise in Christ Jesus
through the gospel.[u]

7Of this I became a minister by the gift of
God's grace that was granted me in accord
with the exercise of his power.[v] 8To me, the
very least of all the holy ones, this grace was
given, to preach to the Gentiles the inscrutable
riches of Christ,[w] 9and to bring to light [for
all]* what is the plan of the mystery hidden
from ages past in God who created all things,[x]
10so that the manifold wisdom of God might
now be made known through the church to the
principalities and authorities* in the heavens.[y]
11This was according to the eternal purpose
that he accomplished in Christ Jesus our Lord,
12in whom we have boldness of speech and
confidence of access through faith in him.[z]
13So I ask you not to lose heart over my afflictions for you; this is your glory.[a]

*Prayer for the Readers.** 14For this reason
I kneel before the Father, 15from whom
every family* in heaven and on earth is
named, 16that he may grant you in accord
with the riches of his glory to be strengthened with power through his Spirit in the inner self,[b] 17and that Christ may dwell in your
hearts through faith; that you, rooted and
grounded in love,[c] 18may have strength to
comprehend with all the holy ones what is
the breadth and length and height and
depth,[d] 19and to know the love of Christ that
surpasses knowledge, so that you may be
filled with all the fullness of God.[e]

20Now to him who is able to accomplish
far more than all we ask or imagine, by the
power at work within us,[f] 21to him be glory
in the church and in Christ Jesus to all generations, forever and ever. Amen.

## CHAPTER 4

See RG 392–93

*Unity in the Body.* 1* I, then, a prisoner for the Lord, urge you to live in a manner worthy of the call you have received,[g]
2with all humility and gentleness, with pa-

deepened understanding of God's plan of salvation in Christ. Paul is the special herald (Eph 3:7) of a new **promise** to the **Gentiles** (Eph 3:6): that the divine plan includes them in the spiritual benefits promised to Israel. Not only is this unique apostolic role his; Paul also has been given the task of explaining to all the divine **plan** of salvation (Eph 3:8–9), once **hidden**. Through **the church**, God's plan to save through Christ is becoming manifest to angelic beings (Eph 3:10; cf. Eph 1:21), in accord with God's **purpose** (Eph 3:11). The fulfillment of the plan in Christ gives the whole church more **confidence** through **faith** in God (Eph 3:12). The readers of this letter are also thereby encouraged to greater confidence despite Paul's imprisonment (Eph 3:13).

**3:1 A prisoner of Christ**: see Introduction. Paul abruptly departs from his train of thought at the end of Eph 3:1, leaving an incomplete sentence.

**3:2 Stewardship**: the Greek is the same term employed at Eph 1:10 for the **plan** that God administers (Col 1:25) and in which Paul plays a key role.

**3:3–4 The mystery**: God's resolve to deliver Gentiles along with Israel through Christ; cf. notes on Eph 1:10; 3:9.

**3:9 [For all]**: while some think this phrase was added so as to yield the sense "to enlighten all about the plan . . . ," it is more likely that some manuscripts and Fathers omitted it accidentally or to avoid the idea that **all** conflicted with Paul's assignment to preach to **the Gentiles** (Eph 3:8) specifically.

**3:10 Principalities and authorities**: see note on Eph 1:15–23 regarding Eph 3:21.

**3:14–21** The apostle prays that those he is addressing may, like the rest of the church, deepen their understanding of God's plan of salvation in Christ. It is a plan that affects the whole universe (Eph 3:15) with **the breadth and length and height and depth** of God's love in Christ (Eph 3:18) or possibly the universe in all its dimensions. The apostle prays that they may perceive the redemptive love of Christ for them and be completely immersed in the fullness of God (Eph 3:19). The prayer concludes with a doxology to God (Eph 3:20–21).

**3:14–15 Every family**: in the Greek there is wordplay on the word for **the Father** (*patria, patēr*). The phrase could also mean "God's whole family" (cf. Eph 2:21).

**4:1–16** A general plea for unity in the church. Christians have been fashioned through the **Spirit** into a single harmonious religious community (**one body**, Eph 4:4, 12; cf. Eph 4:16), belonging to a single **Lord** (in contrast to the many gods of the pagan world), and by one way of salvation through **faith**, brought out especially by the significance of **baptism** (Eph 4:1–6; cf. Rom 6:1–11). But Christian unity is

*r:* Col 1:25. *s:* 1:9–10; Col 1:26. *t:* Col 1:26. *u:* 2:13, 18–19. *v:* Rom 15:15; Col 1:25, 29. *w:* 1 Cor 15:8–10; Gal 1:16; 2:7–9. *x:* Rom 16:25; Col 1:26–27. *y:* 1 Pt 1:12. *z:* Rom 5:1–2; Heb 4:16. *a:* Col 1:22, 24; 2 Tm 2:10. *b:* 6:10; Rom 7:22; 2 Cor 4:16; Col 1:11. *c:* Jn 14:23; Col 1:23; 2:7. *d:* Col 2:2. *e:* Col 2:3, 9. *f:* Rom 16:25–27; Col 1:29. *g:* 3:1; Col 1:10. *h:* Col 3:12–13.

tience, bearing with one another through love,[h] 3 striving to preserve the unity of the spirit through the bond of peace:[i] 4* one body and one Spirit, as you were also called to the one hope of your call;[j] 5 one Lord, one faith, one baptism;[k] 6 one God and Father of all, who is over all and through all and in all.[l]

***Diversity of Gifts.*** 7 But grace was given to each of us according to the measure of Christ's gift.[m] 8 Therefore, it says:

"He ascended* on high and took
prisoners captive;
he gave gifts to men."[n]

9 What does "he ascended" mean except that he also descended into the lower [regions] of the earth? 10 The one who descended is also the one who ascended far above all the heavens, that he might fill all things.

11* And he gave some as apostles, others as prophets, others as evangelists, others as pastors and teachers,[o] 12 to equip the holy ones for the work of ministry,* for building up the body of Christ, 13 until we all attain to the unity of faith and knowledge of the Son of God, to mature manhood,* to the extent of the full stature of Christ,[p] 14 so that we may no longer be infants, tossed by waves and swept along by every wind of teaching arising from human trickery, from their cunning in the interests of deceitful scheming.[q] 15 Rather, living the truth in love, we should grow in every way into him who is the head,[r] Christ,* 16 from whom the whole body, joined and held together by every supporting ligament, with the proper functioning of each part, brings about the body's growth and builds itself up in love.[s]

***Renewal in Christ.**** 17 So I declare and testify in the Lord that you must no longer live as the Gentiles do, in the futility of their minds;[t] 18 darkened in understanding, alienated from the life of God because of their ignorance, because of their hardness of heart,[u] 19 they have become callous and have handed themselves over to licentiousness for the practice of every kind of impurity to excess.[v] 20 That is not how you learned Christ, 21 assuming that you have heard of him and were taught in him, as truth is in Jesus, 22 that you should put away the old self of your former way of life, corrupted through deceitful desires,[w] 23 and be renewed in the spirit of your minds,[x] 24 and put on* the new self, created in God's way in righteousness and holiness of truth.[y]

more than adherence to a common belief. It is manifested in the exalted Christ's gifts to individuals to serve so as to make the community more Christlike (Eph 4:11–16). This teaching on Christ as the source of the gifts is introduced in Eph 4:8 by a citation of Ps 68:18, which depicts Yahweh triumphantly leading Israel to salvation in Jerusalem. It is here understood of Christ, ascending **above all the heavens**, the **head** of the church; through his redemptive death, resurrection, and ascension he has become the source of the church's spiritual gifts. The "descent" of Christ (Eph 4:9–10) refers more probably to the incarnation (cf. Phil 2:6–8) than to Christ's presence after his death in the world of the dead (cf. 1 Pt 3:19).

**4:4–6** The "seven unities" (church, **Spirit**, **hope**; **Lord**, **faith** in Christ [Eph 1:13], **baptism**; **one God**) reflect the triune structure of later creeds in reverse.

**4:8–10** While the emphasis is on an ascension and gift-giving by Christ, there is also a reference in taking **prisoners captive** to the aeons and powers mentioned at Eph 1:21; 2:2; 3:10; 6:12.

**4:11** Concerning this list of ministers, cf. 1 Cor 12:28 and Rom 12:6–8. **Evangelists**: missionary preachers (cf. Acts 21:8; 2 Tm 4:5), not those who wrote gospels. **Pastors and teachers**: a single group in the Greek, shepherding congregations.

**4:12** The ministerial leaders in Eph 4:11 are to equip the whole people of God for their **work of ministry**.

**4:13 Mature manhood**: literally, "a perfect man" (cf. Col 1:28), possibly the "one new person" of Eph 2:15, though there *anthrōpos* suggests humanity, while here *anēr* is the term for male. This personage becomes visible in the church's growing to its fullness in the unity of those who believe in Christ.

**4:15–16 The head, Christ**: cf. Col 1:18 and contrast 1 Cor 12:12–27 and Rom 12:4–5 where Christ is identified with the whole body, including the head. The imagery may derive from ancient views in medicine, the **head** coordinating and caring for the body, each **ligament** (perhaps the ministers of Eph 4:11) supporting the whole. But as at Eph 2:19–22, where the temple is depicted as a growing organism, there may also be the idea here of growing toward the capstone, Christ.

**4:17–24** Paul begins to indicate how the new life in Christ contrasts with the Gentiles' old way of existence. Literally, **the old self** (Eph 4:22) and **the new self** (Eph 4:24) are "the old man" and "the new man" (*anthrōpos*, person), as at Eph 2:15; cf. note on Eph 4:13.

**4:24 Put on**: in baptism. See note on Gal 3:27.

---

*i:* Col 3:14–15. *j:* Rom 12:5; 1 Cor 10:17; 12:12–13. *k:* 1 Cor 8:6. *l:* 1 Cor 12:6. *m:* Rom 12:3, 6; 1 Cor 12:28. *n:* Ps 68:19; Col 2:15. *o:* 1 Cor 12:28. *p:* Col 1:28. *q:* 1 Cor 14:20; Col 2:4, 8; Heb 13:9; Jas 1:6. *r:* 1 Cor 11:3; Col 1:18; 2:19. *s:* Col 2:19. *t:* Rom 1:21. *u:* Col 1:21; 1 Pt 1:14. *v:* Col 3:5. *w:* Rom 8:13; Gal 6:8; Col 3:9. *x:* Rom 12:2. *y:* Gn 1:26–27; Col 3:10.

## IV. Daily Conduct, an Expression of Unity*

***Rules for the New Life.*** 25 Therefore, putting away falsehood, speak the truth, each one to his neighbor, for we are members one of another.[z] 26 Be angry but do not sin;[a] do not let the sun set on your anger,* 27 and do not leave room for the devil.[b] 28 The thief must no longer steal, but rather labor, doing honest work* with his [own] hands, so that he may have something to share with one in need.[c] 29 No foul language should come out of your mouths, but only such as is good for needed edification, that it may impart grace to those who hear.[d] 30 And do not grieve the holy Spirit of God, with which you were sealed for the day of redemption.* 31 All bitterness, fury, anger, shouting, and reviling must be removed from you, along with all malice.[e] 32 [And] be kind to one another, compassionate, forgiving one another as God has forgiven you in Christ.[f]

### CHAPTER 5

See RG 393

1 So be imitators of God,* as beloved children,[g] 2 and live in love, as Christ loved us and handed himself over for us as a sacrificial offering to God for a fragrant aroma.[h] 3 Immorality or any impurity or greed must not even be mentioned among you, as is fitting among holy ones,[i] 4 no obscenity or silly or suggestive talk, which is out of place, but instead, thanksgiving.[j] 5 Be sure of this, that no immoral or impure or greedy person, that is, an idolater, has any inheritance in the kingdom of Christ and of God.[k]

***Duty to Live in the Light.*** 6[l] Let no one deceive you with empty arguments, for because of these things the wrath of God is coming upon the disobedient.* 7 So do not be associated with them. 8 For you were once darkness, but now you are light in the Lord. Live as children of light,[m] 9 for light produces every kind of goodness and righteousness and truth.[n] 10 Try to learn what is pleasing to the Lord.[o] 11 Take no part in the fruitless works of darkness; rather expose them,[p] 12 for it is shameful even to mention the things done by them in secret; 13 but everything exposed by the light becomes visible,[q] 14 for everything that becomes visible is light. Therefore, it says:[r]

"Awake, O sleeper,
and arise from the dead,
and Christ will give you light."*

15* Watch carefully then how you live, not as foolish persons but as wise,[s] 16 making the most of the opportunity, because the days are evil. 17 Therefore, do not continue in ignorance, but try to understand what is the will of the Lord. 18 And do not get drunk on wine, in which lies debauchery, but be filled with the Spirit,[t] 19 addressing one another [in] psalms and hymns and spiritual songs, singing and playing to the Lord in your hearts,[u] 20 giving thanks always and for everything in the name of our Lord Jesus Christ to God the Father.[v]

**4:25–6:20** For similar exhortations to a morally good life in response to God's gift of faith, see notes on Rom 12:1–13:14 and Gal 5:13–26.

**4:26** If angry, seek reconciliation that day, not giving the devil (Eph 6:11) opportunity to lead into sin.

**4:28 Honest work**: literally, "the good." **His [own] hands**: some manuscripts have the full phrase as in 1 Cor 4:12.

**4:30** See note on Eph 1:13.

**5:1 Imitators of God**: in forgiving (Eph 4:32) and in loving (as exhibited in how **Christ loved us**).

**5:6** See note on Eph 2:2.

**5:14** An early Christian hymn, possibly from a baptismal liturgy. For the content compare Eph 2:5–6; 3:9 and Is 60:1.

**5:15–16, 19–20** The wording is similar to Col 4:5 and Eph 3:16–17.

**5:21–6:9** Cf. notes on Col 3:18–4:1 and 1 Pt 2:18–3:7 for a similar listing of household duties where the inferior is admonished first (**wives**, Eph 5:22; **children**, Eph 6:1; **slaves**, Eph 6:5), then the superior (**husbands**, Eph 5:25; **fathers**, Eph 6:4; **masters**, Eph 6:9). Paul varies this pattern by an emphasis on mutuality (see Eph 5:20); use of Old Testament material about **father and mother** in Eph 6:2; the judgment to come for slave-owners (**you have a Master in heaven**, Eph 6:9); and above all the initial principle of subordination **to one another** under **Christ**, thus effectively undermining exclusive claims to domination by one party. Into the section on **wives** and **husbands** an elaborate teach-

*z:* Zec 8:16. *a:* Ps 4:5 LXX; Mt 5:22. *b:* 2 Cor 2:11. *c:* 1 Thes 4:11. *d:* 5:4; Col 3:16; 4:6. *e:* Col 3:8. *f:* Mt 6:14; Col 3:12–13. *g:* Mt 5:45, 48. *h:* Ex 29:18; Ps 40:7; Gal 2:20; 1 Jn 3:16. *i:* Gal 5:19; Col 3:5. *j:* 4:29; Col 3:8. *k:* 1 Cor 6:9–10; Gal 5:21; Col 3:5. *l:* Rom 1:18; Col 2:4, 8. *m:* 2:11–13; Jn 12:36; Col 1:12–13. *n:* Gal 5:22. *o:* Rom 12:2. *p:* Rom 13:12. *q:* Jn 3:20–21. *r:* Is 26:19; 60:1. *s:* Col 4:5. *t:* Prv 23:31 LXX; Lk 21:34. *u:* Ps 33:2–3; Col 3:16. *v:* Col 3:17. *w:* 1 Pt 5:5.

*Wives and Husbands.* 21* Be subordinate to
one another[w] out of reverence for Christ.*
22 Wives should be subordinate to their husbands as to the Lord.[x] 23 For the husband is
head of his wife just as Christ is head of the
church, he himself the savior of the body.[y]
24 As the church is subordinate to Christ, so
wives should be subordinate to their husbands
in everything. 25 Husbands, love your wives,
even as Christ loved the church and handed
himself over for her[z] 26 to sanctify her, cleansing her by the bath of water with the word,[a]
27 that he might present to himself the church
in splendor, without spot or wrinkle or any
such thing, that she might be holy and without
blemish.[b] 28 So [also] husbands should love
their wives as their own bodies. He who loves
his wife loves himself. 29 For no one hates his
own flesh but rather nourishes and cherishes
it, even as Christ does the church, 30 because
we are members of his body.[c]

31 "For this reason a man shall leave [his]
father and [his] mother
and be joined to his wife,
and the two shall become one flesh."[d]

32 This is a great mystery, but I speak in reference to Christ and the church.[e] 33 In any
case, each one of you should love his wife as
himself, and the wife should respect her husband.

## CHAPTER 6

See RG 393–94

*Children and Parents.* 1 Children,
obey your parents [in the Lord], for this is
right.[f] 2 "Honor your father and mother."[g]
This is the first commandment with a promise, 3 "that it may go well with you and that
you may have a long life on earth." 4 Fathers,
do not provoke your children to anger, but
bring them up with the training and instruction of the Lord.[h]

*Slaves and Masters.* 5 Slaves, be obedient
to your human masters with fear and trembling, in sincerity of heart, as to Christ,[i] 6 not
only when being watched, as currying favor,
but as slaves of Christ, doing the will of God
from the heart,[j] 7 willingly serving the Lord
and not human beings, 8 knowing that each
will be requited from the Lord for whatever
good he does, whether he is slave or free.
9 Masters, act in the same way toward them,
and stop bullying, knowing that both they
and you have a Master in heaven and that
with him there is no partiality.[k]

*Battle Against Evil.* 10* Finally, draw your
strength from the Lord and from his mighty
power. 11 Put on the armor of God so that you
may be able to stand firm against the tactics
of the devil.[l] 12 For our struggle is not with
flesh and blood but with the principalities,
with the powers, with the world rulers of this
present darkness, with the evil spirits in the
heavens.[m] 13 Therefore, put on the armor of
God, that you may be able to resist on the evil
day and, having done everything, to hold
your ground.[n] 14 So stand fast with your loins
girded in truth, clothed with righteousness as
a breastplate,[o] 15 and your feet shod in readiness for the gospel of peace.[p] 16 In all circumstances, hold faith as a shield, to quench all
[the] flaming arrows of the evil one.[q] 17 And
take the helmet of salvation and the sword of
the Spirit, which is the word of God.[r]

*Constant Prayer.* 18 With all prayer and
supplication, pray at every opportunity in

ing on **Christ** and **the church** has been woven (Eph 5:22–33).

**5:21–33** The apostle exhorts married Christians to a strong mutual love. Holding with Gn 2:24 that marriage is a divine institution (Eph 5:31), Paul sees Christian marriage as taking on a new meaning symbolic of the intimate relationship of love between Christ and the church. The wife should serve her husband in the same spirit as that of the church's service to Christ (Eph 5:22, 24), and the husband should care for his wife with the devotion of Christ to the church (Eph 5:25–30). Paul gives to the Genesis passage its highest meaning in the light of the union of Christ and the church, of which Christlike loyalty and devotion in Christian marriage are a clear reflection (Eph 5:31–33).

**6:10–20** A general exhortation to courage and prayer. Drawing upon the imagery and ideas of Is 11:5; 59:16–17; and Wis 5:17–23, Paul describes the Christian in terms of the dress and equipment of Roman soldiers. He observes, however, that the Christian's readiness for combat is not directed against human beings but against the spiritual powers of evil (Eph 6:10–17; cf. Eph 1:21; 2:2; 3:10). Unique importance is placed upon prayer (Eph 6:18–20).

*x:* Col 3:18–4:1; 1 Pt 3:1–7. *y:* 1 Cor 11:3; Col 1:18. *z:* Col 3:19; 1 Tm 2:6. *a:* Rom 6:4; Ti 3:5–7. *b:* 2 Cor 11:2; Col 1:22. *c:* Rom 12:5; 1 Cor 6:15. *d:* Gn 2:24; Mt 19:5; Mk 10:7–8. *e:* Rev 19:7. *f:* Prv 6:20; Sir 3:1–6; Col 3:20. *g:* Ex 20:12; Dt 5:16. *h:* Col 3:21–22. *i:* Col 3:22–25; 1 Tm 6:1–2; Ti 2:9–10. *j:* 1 Pt 2:18. *k:* Col 4:1. *l:* Rom 13:12; 2 Cor 6:7; 10:4; Jas 4:7. *m:* 1:21; 2:2; Col 1:13. *n:* Rom 13:12. *o:* Wis 5:17–20; Is 11:5; Lk 12:35; 1 Thes 5:8. *p:* Is 52:7. *q:* 1 Pt 5:9. *r:* Is 59:17; 1 Thes 5:8.

the Spirit. To that end, be watchful with all
perseverance and supplication for all the
holy ones[s] 19and also for me, that speech
may be given me to open my mouth, to make
known with boldness the mystery of the
gospel[t] 20for which I am an ambassador in
chains, so that I may have the courage to
speak as I must.[u]

### V. Conclusion

*A Final Message.** 21So that you also may
have news of me and of what I am doing,
Tychicus, my beloved brother and trustworthy minister in the Lord, will tell you
everything.[v] 22I am sending him to you for
this very purpose, so that you may know
about us and that he may encourage your
hearts.[w]

23Peace be to the brothers, and love with
faith, from God the Father and the Lord
Jesus Christ. 24Grace be with all who love
our Lord Jesus Christ in immortality.[x]

**6:21–24 Tychicus**: the bearer of the letter; see note on Col 4:7. Eph 6:21–22 parallel Col 4:7–8, often word for word. If Ephesians is addressed to several Christian communities (see Introduction), it is understandable that no greetings to individual members of these communities should have been included in it.

*s:* Mt 26:41; Col 4:2–3. *t:* Acts 4:29; Col 4:3; 2 Thes 3:1. *u:* 2 Cor 5:20; Col 4:4. *v:* Acts 20:4; Col 4:7; 2 Tm 4:12. *w:* Col 4:8. *x:* 1 Pt 1:8.

See RG 395–99

# The Letter to the Philippians

Philippi, in northeastern Greece, was a city of some importance in the Roman province of Macedonia. Lying on the great road from the Adriatic coast to Byzantium, the Via Egnatia, and in the midst of rich agricultural plains near the gold deposits of Mt. Pangaeus, it was in Paul's day a Roman town (Acts 16:21), with a Greek-Macedonian population and a small group of Jews (see Acts 16:13). Originally founded in the sixth century B.C. as Krenides by the Thracians, the town was taken over after 360 B.C. by Philip II of Macedon, the father of Alexander the Great, and was renamed for himself, "Philip's City." The area became Roman in the second century B.C. On the plains near Philippi in October 42 B.C., Antony and Octavian decisively defeated the forces of Brutus and Cassius, the slayers of Julius Caesar. Octavian (Augustus) later made Philippi a Roman colony and settled many veterans of the Roman armies there.

Paul, according to Acts (Acts 16:9–40), established at Philippi the first Christian community in Europe. He came to Philippi, via its harbor town of Neapolis (modern Kavalla), on his second missionary journey, probably in A.D. 49 or 50, accompanied by Silas and Timothy (Acts 15:40; 16:3; cf. Phil 1:1) and Luke, if he is to be included in the "we" references of Acts 16:10–17. The Acts account tells of the conversion of a business woman, Lydia; the exorcism of a slave girl; and, after an earthquake, while Paul and Silas were imprisoned in Philippi, the faith and baptism of a jailer and his family. None of these persons, however, is directly mentioned in Philippians (cf. the notes on Phil 4:2 and Phil 4:3). Acts 16 concludes its account by describing how Paul (and Silas), asked by the magistrates to leave Philippi, went on to Thessalonica (Acts 17:1–10), where several times his loyal Philippians continued to support him with financial aid (Phil 4:16). Later, Paul may have passed through Philippi on his way from Ephesus to Greece (Acts 20:1–2), and he definitely stopped there on his fateful trip to Jerusalem (Acts 20:6).

Paul's letter to the Christians at Philippi was written while he was in a prison somewhere (Phil 1:7, 13, 14, 17), indeed in danger of death (Phil 1:20–23). Although under guard for preaching Christ, Paul rejoices at the continuing progress of the gospel (Phil 1:12–26) and expresses gratitude for the Philippians' renewed concern and help in an expression of thanks most clearly found at Phil 4:10–20. Much of the letter is devoted to instruction about unity and humility within the Christian community at Philippi (Phil 1:27–2:18) and exhortations to growth, joy, and peace in their life together (Phil 4:1–9). The letter seems to be drawing to a close at the end of what we number as Phil 2, as Paul reports the plans of his helper Timothy and of Epaphroditus (whom the Philippians had sent to aid Paul) to come to Philippi (Phil 2:19–3:1), and even Paul's own expectation that he will go free and come to Philippi (Phil 1:25–26; 2:24). Yet quite abruptly at Phil 3:2, Paul erupts into warnings against false teachers who threaten to impose on the Philippians the burdens of the Mosaic law, including circumcision. The section that follows, Phil 3:2–21, is a vigorous attack on these Judaizers (cf. Gal 2:11–3:29) or Jewish Christian teachers (cf. 2 Cor 11:12–23), giving us insights into Paul's own life story (Phil 3:4–6) and into the doctrine of justification, the Christian life, and ultimate hope (Phil 3:7–21).

The location of Paul's imprisonment when he wrote to the Philippians, and thus the date of the letter, are uncertain. The traditional view has been that it stems from Paul's confinement in Rome, between A.D. 59 and 63 (cf. Acts 28:14–31). One modern view suggests the period when he was imprisoned at Caesarea, on the coast of Palestine, A.D. 57 or 58 (Acts 23:23–26:32); another suggests Corinth (cf. 2 Cor 11:9). Much recent scholarship favors Ephesus, around A.D. 55, a situation referred to in 2 Cor 1:8 concerning "the affliction that came to us" in Asia Minor (cf. also 1 Cor 15:32). The reference at Phil 1:13 to the "praetorium" (cf. also Phil 4:22) can be understood to mean the imperial guard or government house at Ephesus (or Caesarea), or the praetorian camp in Rome. Involved in a decision are the several journeys back and forth between Philippi and wherever Paul is imprisoned, mentioned in the letter (Phil 2:25–28; 4:14); this factor causes many to prefer Ephesus because of its proximity to Philippi. The Ephesian hypothesis dates the composition of Philippians to the mid-50s when most of Paul's major letters were written.

There is also a likelihood, according to some scholars, that the letter as we have it is a composite from parts of three letters by Paul to the Philippians. Seemingly Phil 4:10–20 is a brief note of appreciation for help sent through Epaphroditus. The long section from Phil 1:3 to Phil 3:1 is then another letter, with news of Paul's imprisonment and reports on Timothy and Epaphroditus (who has fallen ill while with Paul), along with exhortations to the Philippians about Christian conduct; and Phil 3:2–21 a third communication warning about threats to Philippian Christianity. The other verses in Phil 4 and Phil 1:1–2, are variously assigned by critics to these three underlying letters, which an editor presumably put together to produce a picture of Paul writing earnestly from prison (Phil 1–2), facing opponents of the faith (Phil 3), and with serene joy advising and thanking his Philippians (Phil 4). If all four chapters were originally a unity, then one must assume that a break occurred between the writing of Phil 3:1 and Phil 3:2, possibly involving the receipt of bad news from Philippi, and that Paul had some reasons for delaying his words of thanks for the aid brought by Epaphroditus till the end of his letter.

This beautiful letter is rich in insights into Paul's theology and his apostolic love and concern for the gospel and his converts. In Philippians, Paul reveals his human sensitivity and tenderness, his enthusiasm for Christ as the key to life and death (Phil 1:21), and his deep feeling for those in Christ who dwell in Philippi. With them he shares his hopes and convictions, his anxieties and fears, revealing the total confidence in Christ that constitutes faith (Phil 3:8–10). The letter incorporates a hymn about the salvation that God has brought about through Christ (Phil 2:6–11), applied by Paul to the relations of Christians with one another (Phil 2:1–5). Philippians has been termed "the letter of joy" (Phil 4:4, 10). It is the rejoicing of faith, based on true understanding of Christ's unique role in the salvation of all who profess his lordship (Phil 2:11; 3:8–12, 14, 20–21).

The principal divisions of the Letter to the Philippians are the following:

I. Address (1:1–11)
II. Progress of the Gospel (1:12–26)
III. Instructions for the Community (1:27–2:18)
IV. Travel Plans of Paul and His Assistants (2:19–3:1)
V. Polemic: Righteousness and the Goal in Christ (3:2–21)
VI. Instructions for the Community (4:1–9)
VII. Gratitude for the Philippians' Generosity (4:10–20)
VIII. Farewell (4:21–23)

## I. Address

### CHAPTER 1

See RG 396–97

*Greeting.** 1Paul and Timothy, slaves*
of Christ Jesus, to all the holy ones in Christ
Jesus who are in Philippi, with the overseers
and ministers:[a] 2[b] grace to you and peace
from God our Father and the Lord Jesus
Christ.*
*Thanksgiving.** 3I give thanks to my God
at every remembrance of you,[c] 4praying always with joy in my every prayer for all of
you, 5because of your partnership for the
gospel from the first day until now. 6[d] I am
confident of this, that the one who began a
good work in you will continue to complete
it until the day of Christ Jesus.* 7It is right
that I should think this way about all of you,
because I hold you in my heart, you who are
all partners with me in grace, both in my
imprisonment and in the defense and confirmation of the gospel. 8For God is my witness, how I long for all of you with the affection of Christ Jesus.[e] 9And this is my
prayer: that your love may increase ever
more and more in knowledge and every
kind of perception,[f] 10to discern what is of
value, so that you may be pure and blameless for the day of Christ,[g] 11filled with the
fruit of righteousness that comes through
Jesus Christ for the glory and praise of
God.[h]

## II. Progress of the Gospel*

12[i] I want you to know, brothers, that my situation has turned out rather to advance the
gospel, 13so that my imprisonment has become well known in Christ throughout the
whole praetorium* and to all the rest,[j] 14* and
so that the majority of the brothers, having
taken encouragement in the Lord from my

**1:1–2** See note on Rom 1:1–7, concerning the greeting.

**1:1 Slaves**: Paul usually refers to himself at the start of a letter as an apostle. Here he substitutes a term suggesting the unconditional obligation of himself and Timothy to the service of Christ, probably because, in view of the good relationship with the Philippians, he wishes to stress his status as a co-servant rather than emphasize his apostolic authority. Reference to Timothy is a courtesy: Paul alone writes the letter, as the singular verb throughout shows (Phil 1:3–26), and the reference (Phil 2:19–24) to Timothy in the third person. **Overseers**: the Greek term *episkopos* literally means "one who oversees" or "one who supervises," but since the second century it has come to designate the "bishop," the official who heads a local church. In New Testament times this office had not yet developed into the form that it later assumed, though it seems to be well on the way to such development in the Pastorals; see 1 Tm 3:2 and Ti 1:7, where it is translated bishop. At Philippi, however (and at Ephesus, according to Acts 20:28), there was more than one *episkopos*, and the precise function of these officials is uncertain. In order to distinguish this office from the later stages into which it developed, the term is here translated as **overseers**. **Ministers**: the Greek term *diakonoi* is used frequently in the New Testament to designate "servants," "attendants," or "ministers." Paul refers to himself and to other apostles as "ministers of God" (2 Cor 6;4) or "ministers of Christ" (2 Cor 11:23). In the Pastorals (1 Tm 3:8, 12) the *diakonos* has become an established official in the local church; hence the term is there translated as **deacon**. The *diakonoi* at Philippi seem to represent an earlier stage of development of the office; we are uncertain about their precise functions. Hence the term is here translated as **ministers**. See Rom 16:1, where Phoebe is described as a *diakonos* (minister) of the church of Cenchreae.

**1:2** The gifts come **from** Christ the Lord, not simply through him from the Father; compare the christology in Phil 2:6–11.

**1:3–11** As in Rom 1:8–15 and all the Pauline letters except Galatians, a thanksgiving follows, including a direct prayer for the Philippians (Phil 1:9–11); see note on Rom 1:8. On their **partnership for the gospel** (Phil 1:5), cf. Phil 1:29–30; 4:10–20. Their devotion to the faith and to Paul made them his pride and joy (Phil 4:1). The characteristics thus manifested are evidence of the community's continuing preparation for the Lord's parousia (Phil 1:6, 10). Paul's especially warm relationship with the Philippians is suggested here (Phil 1:7–8) as elsewhere in the letter. The eschatology serves to underscore a concern for ethical growth (Eph 1:9–11), which appears throughout the letter.

**1:6 The day of Christ Jesus**: the parousia or triumphant return of Christ, when those loyal to him will be with him and share in his eternal glory; cf. Phil 1:10; 2:16; 3:20–21; 1 Thes 4:17; 5:10; 2 Thes 1:10; 1 Cor 1:8.

**1:12–26** The body of the letter begins with an account of Paul's present **situation**, i.e., his **imprisonment** (Phil 1:12–13; see Introduction), and then goes on with advice for the Philippians (Phil 1:27–2:18). The **advance** of **the gospel** (Phil 1:12) and the **progress** of the Philippians **in the faith** (Phil 1:25) frame what is said.

**1:13 Praetorium**: either the praetorian guard in the city where Paul was imprisoned or the governor's official residence in a Roman province (cf. Mk 15:16; Acts 23:35). See Introduction on possible sites.

**1:14–18** Although Paul is imprisoned, Christians there nonetheless go on preaching Christ. But they do so with varied motives, **some** with personal hostility toward Paul, others out of personal ambition.

*a:* Rom 1:1; 2 Cor 1:1; 1 Thes 1:1; Phlm 1 / 1 Tm 3:1–13. *b:* Rom 1:7; Gal 1:3; Phlm 3. *c:* Rom 1:8; 1 Cor 1:4; 1 Thes 1:2. *d:* 2:13 / 1:10; 2:16; 1 Cor 1:8. *e:* Rom 1:9; 2 Cor 1:23; 1 Thes 2:5. *f:* Eph 3:14–19; Col 1:9–10; Phlm 6. *g:* Rom 2:18; 12:2 / 1:6. *h:* Jn 15:8. *i:* Eph 3:1; 6:20; 2 Tm 2:9; Phlm 9. *j:* 4:22.

imprisonment, dare more than ever to proclaim the word fearlessly.

15 Of course, some preach Christ from envy and rivalry, others from good will. 16 The latter out of love, aware that I am here for the defense of the gospel; 17 the former proclaim Christ out of selfish ambition, not from pure motives, thinking that they will cause me trouble in my imprisonment. 18 What difference does it make, as long as in every way, whether in pretense or in truth, Christ is being proclaimed?[k] And in that I rejoice.*

Indeed I shall continue to rejoice, 19* for I know that this will result in deliverance for me* through your prayers and support from the Spirit of Jesus Christ.[l] 20 My eager expectation and hope is that I shall not be put to shame in any way, but that with all boldness, now as always, Christ will be magnified in my body, whether by life or by death.[m] 21 For to me life is Christ, and death is gain.[n] 22 If I go on living in the flesh, that means fruitful labor for me. And I do not know which I shall choose.[o] 23 I am caught between the two. I long to depart this life and be with Christ, [for] that is far better.[p] 24 Yet that I remain [in] the flesh is more necessary for your benefit. 25 And this I know with confidence, that I shall remain and continue in the service of all of you for your progress and joy in the faith, 26 so that your boasting in Christ Jesus may abound on account of me when I come to you again.

## III. Instructions for the Community

***Steadfastness in Faith.**** 27 Only, conduct yourselves in a way worthy of the gospel of Christ, so that, whether I come and see you or am absent, I may hear news of you, that you are standing firm in one spirit, with one mind struggling together for the faith of the gospel,[q] 28 not intimidated in any way by your opponents. This is proof to them of destruction, but of your salvation. And this is God's doing. 29 For to you has been granted, for the sake of Christ, not only to believe in him but also to suffer for him.[r] 30 Yours is the same struggle[s] as you saw in me and now hear about me.*

### CHAPTER 2

See RG 397

***Plea for Unity and Humility.**** 1 If there is any encouragement in Christ, any solace in love, any participation in the Spirit, any compassion and mercy, 2 complete my joy by being of the same mind, with the same love, united in heart, thinking one thing.[t] 3 Do nothing out of selfishness or out of vainglory; rather, humbly regard others as more important than yourselves,[u] 4 each looking out not for his own interests, but [also] everyone for those of others.[v]

5 Have among yourselves the same attitude that is also yours in Christ Jesus,*

**1:18 Rejoice**: a major theme in the letter; see Introduction.

**1:19–25** Paul earnestly debates his prospects of martyrdom or continued missionary labor. While he may **long to depart this life** and thus **be with Christ** (Phil 1:23), his overall and final expectation is that he will be delivered from this imprisonment and **continue in the service** of the Philippians and of others (Phil 1:19, 25; Phil 2:24). In either case, Christ is central (Phil 1:20–21); if to live means Christ for Paul, death means to be united with Christ in a deeper sense.

**1:19 Result in deliverance for me**: an echo of Jb 13:16, hoping that God will turn suffering to ultimate good and deliverance from evil.

**1:27–30** Ethical admonition begins at this early point in the letter, emphasizing steadfastness and congregational unity in the face of possible suffering. The **opponents** (Phil 1:28) are those in Philippi, probably pagans, who oppose the gospel cause. **This is proof** . . . (Phil 1:28) may refer to the whole outlook and conduct of the Philippians, turning out for their salvation but to the judgment of the opponents (cf. 2 Cor 2:15–16), or possibly the sentence refers to the opinion of the opponents, who hold that the obstinacy of the Christians points to the destruction of such people as defy Roman authority (though in reality, Paul holds, such faithfulness leads to salvation).

**1:30** A reference to Paul's earlier imprisonment in Philippi (Acts 16:19–24; 1 Thes 2:2) and to his present confinement.

**2:1–11** The admonition to likemindedness and unity (Phil 2:2–5) is based on the believers' threefold experience with Christ, God's love, and the Spirit. The appeal to humility (Phil 2:3) and to obedience (Phil 2:12) is rooted in christology, specifically in a statement about Christ Jesus (Phil 2:6–11) and his humbling of self and obedience to the point of death (Phil 2:8).

**2:5 Have . . . the same attitude that is also yours in Christ Jesus**: or, "that also Christ Jesus had." While it is often held that Christ here functions as a model for moral imitation, it is

*k:* 4:10. *l:* Jb 13:16 / 2 Cor 1:11. *m:* 1 Cor 6:20; 1 Pt 4:16. *n:* Gal 2:20. *o:* Rom 1:13. *p:* 2 Cor 5:8. *q:* Eph 4:1; Col 1:10; 1 Thes 2:12 / 4:3. *r:* Mt 5:10; 10:38; Mk 8:34; Acts 5:41. *s:* 1:13; Acts 16:22–24. *t:* Rom 15:5; 1 Cor 1:10. *u:* Rom 12:3, 10; Gal 5:26. *v:* 1 Cor 10:24, 33; 13:5.

6 Who,* though he was in the form of God,[w]
did not regard equality with God
something to be grasped.*
7 Rather, he emptied himself,
taking the form of a slave,
coming in human likeness;*
and found human in appearance,[x]
8 he humbled himself,[y]
becoming obedient to death,
even death on a cross.*
9 Because of this, God greatly exalted him
and bestowed on him the name*
that is above every name,[z]
10 that at the name of Jesus
every knee should bend,*
of those in heaven and on earth and
under the earth,[a]
11 and every tongue confess that
Jesus Christ is Lord,*
to the glory of God the Father.[b]

***Obedience and Service in the World.****
12c So then, my beloved, obedient as you
have always been, not only when I am present but all the more now when I am absent,
work out your salvation with fear and trembling.* 13 For God is the one who, for his good
purpose, works in you both to desire and to
work.[d] 14 Do everything without grumbling
or questioning,[e] 15 that you may be blameless
and innocent, children of God without blemish in the midst of a crooked and perverse
generation,* among whom you shine like
lights in the world,[f] 16 as you hold on to the
word of life, so that my boast for the day of
Christ may be that I did not run in vain or labor in vain.[g] 17 But, even if I am poured out as
a libation* upon the sacrificial service of your
faith, I rejoice and share my joy with all of
you.[h] 18 In the same way you also should rejoice and share your joy with me.[i]

## IV. Travel Plans of Paul and His Assistants*

***Timothy and Paul.*** 19 I hope, in the Lord
Jesus, to send Timothy* to you soon, so that
I too may be heartened by hearing news of

not the historical Jesus but the entire Christ event that Phil 2:6–11 depict. Therefore, the appeal is to have in relations among yourselves that same relationship you have in Jesus Christ, i.e., serving one another as you serve Christ (Phil 2:4).

**2:6–11** Perhaps an early Christian hymn quoted here by Paul. The short rhythmic lines fall into two parts, Phil 2:6–8 where the subject of every verb is Christ, and Phil 2:9–11 where the subject is God. The general pattern is thus of Christ's humiliation and then exaltation. More precise analyses propose a division into six three-line stanzas (Phil 2:6; 7abc, 7d–8, 9, 10, 11) or into three stanzas (Phil 2:6–7ab, 7cd–8, 9–11). Phrases such as **even death on a cross** (Phil 2:8c) are considered by some to be additions (by Paul) to the hymn, as are Phil 2:10c, 11c.

**2:6** Either a reference to Christ's preexistence and those aspects of divinity that he was willing to give up in order to serve in human form, or to what the man Jesus refused to grasp at to attain divinity. Many see an allusion to the Genesis story: unlike Adam, Jesus, **though . . . in the form of God** (Gn 1:26–27), did not reach out for **equality with God**, in contrast with the first Adam in Gn 3:5–6.

**2:7 Taking the form of a slave, coming in human likeness**: or ". . . taking the form of a slave. // Coming in human likeness, and found human in appearance." While it is common to take Phil 2:6–7 as dealing with Christ's preexistence and Phil 2:8 with his incarnate life, so that lines Phil 2:7b–7c are parallel, it is also possible to interpret so as to exclude any reference to preexistence (see note on Phil 2:6) and to take Phil 2:6–8 as presenting two parallel stanzas about Jesus' human state (Phil 2:6–7b; 7cd–8); in the latter alternative, **coming in human likeness** begins the second stanza and parallels Phil 2:6a to some extent.

**2:8** There may be reflected here language about the servant of the Lord, Is 52:13–53:12 especially Is 53:12.

**2:9 The name**: "Lord" (Phil 2:11), revealing the true nature of the one who is named.

**2:10–11 Every knee should bend . . . every tongue confess**: into this language of Is 45:23 there has been inserted a reference to the three levels in the universe, according to ancient thought, **heaven, earth, under the earth**.

**2:11 Jesus Christ is Lord**: a common early Christian acclamation; cf. 1 Cor 12:3; Rom 10:9. But doxology to God the Father is not overlooked here (Phil 2:11c) in the final version of the hymn.

**2:12–18** Paul goes on to draw out further ethical implications for daily life (Phil 2:14–18) from the salvation God works in Christ.

**2:12 Fear and trembling**: a common Old Testament expression indicating awe and seriousness in the service of God (cf. Ex 15:16; Jdt 2:28; Ps 2:11; Is 19:16).

**2:15–16 Generation . . . as you hold on to . . .**: or ". . . generation. Among them shine like lights in the world because you hold the word of life. . . ."

**2:17 Libation**: in ancient religious ritual, the pouring out on the ground of a liquid offering as a sacrifice. Paul means that he may be facing death.

**2:19–3:1** The plans of Paul and his assistants for future

*w:* Jn 1:1–2; 17:5; Col 2:9; Heb 1:3. *x:* Is 53:3, 11; Jn 1:14; Rom 8:3; 2 Cor 8:9; Gal 4:4; Heb 2:14, 17. *y:* Mt 26:39; Jn 10:17; Heb 5:8; 12:2. *z:* Acts 2:33; Mt 23:12; Eph 1:20–21; Heb 1:3–4. *a:* Is 45:23; Jn 5:23; Rom 14:11; Rev 5:13. *b:* Acts 2:36; Rom 10:9; 1 Cor 12:3. *c:* Ps 2:11; 1 Cor 2:3; 2 Cor 7:15. *d:* 1:6; 1 Cor 12:6; 15:10; 2 Cor 3:5. *e:* 1 Cor 10:10; 1 Pt 4:9. *f:* 1 Thes 3:13 / Dt 32:5; Mt 10:16; Acts 2:40 / Dn 12:3; Mt 5:14, 16; Eph 5:8. *g:* 1 Thes 2:19 / Is 49:4; 65:23; Gal 2:2. *h:* Rom 15:16; 2 Tm 4:6. *i:* 3:1; 4:4. *j:* Acts 16:1–3; 17:14–15; 1 Cor 4:17; 16:10.

you.[j] [20]For I have no one comparable to him for genuine interest in whatever concerns you. [21]For they all seek their own interests, not those of Jesus Christ.[k] [22]But you know his worth, how as a child with a father he served along with me in the cause of the gospel. [23]He it is, then, whom I hope to send as soon as I see how things go with me, [24]but I am confident in the Lord that I myself will also come soon.*

*Epaphroditus.* [25]With regard to Epaphroditus,* my brother and co-worker and fellow soldier, your messenger and minister in my need, I consider it necessary to send him to you.[l] [26]For he has been longing for all of you and was distressed because you heard that he was ill. [27]He was indeed ill, close to death; but God had mercy on him, not just on him but also on me, so that I might not have sorrow upon sorrow. [28]I send him therefore with the greater eagerness, so that, on seeing him, you may rejoice again, and I may have less anxiety. [29]Welcome him then in the Lord with all joy and hold such people in esteem,[m] [30]because for the sake of the work of Christ he came close to death, risking his life to make up for those services to me that you could not perform.

### CHAPTER 3

See RG 397–98

*Concluding Admonitions.* [1]Finally, my brothers, rejoice* in the Lord. Writing the same things to you is no burden for me but is a safeguard for you.[n]

## V. Polemic: Righteousness and the Goal in Christ*

*Against Legalistic Teachers.* [2]* Beware of the dogs! Beware of the evil-workers![o] Beware of the mutilation!* [3]For we are the circumcision,* we who worship through the Spirit of God, who boast in Christ Jesus and do not put our confidence in flesh,[p] [4]although I myself have grounds for confidence even in the flesh.[q]

*Paul's Autobiography.* If anyone else thinks he can be confident in flesh, all the more can I. [5]Circumcised on the eighth day,* of the race of Israel, of the tribe of Benjamin, a Hebrew of Hebrew parentage, in observance of the law a Pharisee,[r] [6]in zeal I per-

travel are regularly a part of a Pauline letter near its conclusion; cf. Rom 15:22–29; 1 Cor 16:5–12.

**2:19 Timothy**: already known to the Philippians (Acts 16:1–15; cf. 1 Cor 4:17; 16:10).

**2:24 I myself will also come soon**: cf. Phil 1:19–25 for the significance of this statement.

**2:25 Epaphroditus**: sent by the Philippians as their **messenger** (literally, "apostle") to aid Paul in his imprisonment, he had fallen seriously ill; Paul commends him as he sends him back to Philippi.

**3:1 Finally . . . rejoice**: the adverb often signals the close of a letter; cf. Phil 4:8; 2 Cor 13:11. While the verb could also be translated "good-bye" or "farewell," although it is never so used in Greek epistolography, the theme of joy has been frequent in the letter (Phil 1:18; 2:2, 18); note also Phil 4:4 and the addition of "always" there as evidence for the meaning "rejoice." To write **the same things** may refer to what Paul has previously taught in Philippi or to what he has just written or to what follows.

**3:2–21** An abrupt change in content and tone, either because Paul at this point responds to disturbing news he has just heard about a threat to the faith of the Philippians in the form of false teachers, or because part of another Pauline letter was inserted here; see Introduction. The chapter describes these teachers in strong terms as **dogs**. The persons meant are evidently different from the rival preachers of Phil 1:14–18 and the opponents of Phil 1:28. Since Phil 3:2–4 emphasize Jewish terms like **circumcision** (Phil 3:2–3, 5), some relate them to the "Judaizers" of the Letter to the Galatians. Other phrases make them appear more like the false teachers of 2 Cor 11:12–15, the **evil-workers**. The latter part of the chapter depicts the **many** who are **enemies** of Christ's cross in terms that may sound more Gentile or even "gnostic" than Jewish (Phil 3:18–19). Accordingly, some see two groups of false teachers in Phil 3, others one group characterized by a claim of having attained "perfect maturity" (Phil 3:12–15).

**3:2–11** Paul sets forth the Christian claim, especially using personal, autobiographical terms that are appropriate to the situation. He presents his own experience in coming to know Christ Jesus in terms of **righteousness** or justification (cf. Rom 1:16–17; 3:21–5:11; Gal 2:5–11), contrasting the **righteousness from God** through faith and that of one's own **based on the law** as two exclusive ways of pleasing God.

**3:2 Beware of the mutilation**: literally, "incision," an ironic wordplay on "circumcision"; cf. Gal 5:12. There may be an association with the self-inflicted mutilations of the prophets of Baal (1 Kgs 18:28) and of devotees of Cybele who slashed themselves in religious frenzy.

**3:3 We are the circumcision**: the true people of God, seed and offspring of Abraham (Gal 3:7, 29; 6:15). **Spirit of God**: some manuscripts read "worship God by the Spirit."

**3:5 Circumcised on the eighth day**: as the law required (Gn 17:12; Lv 12:3).

*k:* 1 Cor 13:5; 2 Tm 4:10. *l:* 4:10–11, 15–16, 18. *m:* 1 Cor 16:18. *n:* 2:18; 4:4. *o:* Ps 22:17, 21; Rev 22:15 / 2 Cor 11:13 / Gal 5:6, 12. *p:* Rom 2:28–29; Col 2:11. *q:* 2 Cor 11:18, 21–23. *r:* Lk 1:59; 2:21 / Acts 22:3; 23:6; 26:5.

secuted the church, in righteousness based on the law I was blameless.[s]

*Righteousness from God.* [7][But] whatever gains I had, these I have come to consider a loss* because of Christ.[t] [8]More than that, I even consider everything as a loss because of the supreme good of knowing Christ Jesus my Lord. For his sake I have accepted the loss of all things and I consider them so much rubbish, that I may gain Christ [9]and be found in him, not having any righteousness of my own based on the law but that which comes through faith in Christ,[u] the righteousness from God, depending on faith [10]to know him and the power of his resurrection and [the] sharing of his sufferings by being conformed to his death,[v] [11]if somehow I may attain the resurrection from the dead.[w]

*Forward in Christ.** [12x] It is not that I have already taken hold of it or have already attained perfect maturity,* but I continue my pursuit in hope that I may possess it, since I have indeed been taken possession of by Christ [Jesus]. [13]Brothers, I for my part do not consider myself to have taken possession. Just one thing: forgetting what lies behind but straining forward to what lies ahead, [14]I continue my pursuit toward the goal, the prize of God's upward calling, in Christ Jesus.[y] [15]Let us, then, who are "perfectly mature" adopt this attitude. And if you have a different attitude, this too God will reveal to you. [16]Only, with regard to what we have attained, continue on the same course.*

*Wrong Conduct and Our Goal.** [17]Join with others in being imitators of me,* brothers, and observe those who thus conduct themselves according to the model you have in us.[z] [18]For many, as I have often told you and now tell you even in tears, conduct themselves as enemies of the cross of Christ.[a] [19]Their end is destruction. Their God is their stomach; their glory is in their "shame." Their minds are occupied with earthly things.[b] [20]But our citizenship* is in heaven, and from it we also await a savior, the Lord Jesus Christ.[c] [21]He will change our lowly body to conform with his glorified body by the power that enables him also to bring all things into subjection to himself.[d]

## VI. Instructions for the Community*

### CHAPTER 4

See RG 398

*Live in Concord.* [1]Therefore, my brothers, whom I love and long for, my joy and crown, in this way stand firm in the Lord, beloved.[e]

[2]I urge Euodia and I urge Syntyche* to come to a mutual understanding in the Lord. [3]Yes, and I ask you also, my true yokemate,* to help them, for they have struggled at my

**3:7 Loss**: his knowledge of Christ led Paul to reassess the ways of truly pleasing and serving God. His reevaluation indicates the profound and lasting effect of his experience of the meaning of Christ on the way to Damascus some twenty years before (Gal 1:15–16; Acts 9:1–22).

**3:12–16** To be **taken possession of by Christ** does not mean that one has already arrived at perfect spiritual maturity. Paul and the Philippians instead press on, trusting in God.

**3:12 Attained perfect maturity**: possibly an echo of the concept in the mystery religions of being an initiate, admitted to divine secrets.

**3:16** Some manuscripts add, probably to explain Paul's cryptic phrase, "thinking alike."

**3:17–21** Paul and those who live a life centered in Christ, envisaging both his suffering and resurrection, provide a model that is the opposite of opponents who reject Christ's cross (cf. 1 Cor 1:23).

**3:17 Being imitators of me**: not arrogance, but humble simplicity, since all his converts know that Paul is wholly dedicated to imitating Christ (1 Cor 11:1; cf. also Phil 4:9; 1 Thes 1:6; 2 Thes 3:7, 9; 1 Cor 4:6).

**3:20 Citizenship**: Christians constitute a colony of heaven, as Philippi was a *colonia* of Rome (Acts 16:12). The hope Paul expresses involves the final coming of Christ, not a status already attained, such as the opponents claim.

**4:1–9** This series of ethical admonitions rests especially on the view of Christ and his coming (cf. Phil 4:5) in Phil 3:20–21. Paul's instructions touch on unity within the congregation, joy, prayer, and the Christian outlook on life.

**4:2 Euodia . . . Syntyche**: two otherwise unknown women in the Philippian congregation; on the advice to them, cf. Phil 2:2–4.

**4:3 Yokemate**: or "comrade," although the Greek *syzygos* could also be a proper name. **Clement**: otherwise unknown, although later writers sought to identify him with Clement, bishop of Rome (Eusebius, *Ecclesiastical History* 3, 15, 1).

*s:* Acts 8:3; 22:4; 26:9–11. *t:* Mt 13:44, 46; Lk 14:33. *u:* Rom 3:21–22. *v:* Rom 6:3–5; 8:17; Gal 6:17. *w:* Jn 11:23–26; Acts 4:2; Rev 20:5–6. *x:* 1 Tm 6:12, 19. *y:* 1 Cor 9:24–25; 2 Tm 4:7. *z:* 1 Cor 4:16; 11:1; 1 Thes 1:7; 1 Pt 5:3. *a:* 1 Cor 1:17, 23; Gal 6:12. *b:* Rom 8:5–6; 16:18. *c:* Eph 2:6, 19; Col 3:1–3; Heb 12:22. *d:* Rom 8:23, 29; 1 Cor 15:42–57; 2 Cor 3:18; 5:1–5 / 1 Cor 15:27–28. *e:* 1 Thes 2:19–20. *f:* Ex 32:32–33; Ps 69:29; Dn 12:1; Lk 10:20; Rev 3:5; 13:8; 17:8; 20:12, 15; 21:27.

side in promoting the gospel, along with Clement and my other co-workers, whose names are in the book of life.[f]

*Joy and Peace.* [4]Rejoice* in the Lord always. I shall say it again: rejoice![g] [5]Your kindness* should be known to all. The Lord is near.[h] [6]Have no anxiety at all, but in everything, by prayer and petition, with thanksgiving, make your requests known to God.[i] [7]Then the peace of God that surpasses all understanding will guard your hearts and minds in Christ Jesus.[j]

[8][k] Finally, brothers, whatever is true, whatever is honorable, whatever is just, whatever is pure, whatever is lovely, whatever is gracious, if there is any excellence and if there is anything worthy of praise, think about these things.* [9]Keep on doing what you have learned and received and heard and seen in me.[l] Then the God of peace will be with you.*

## VII. Gratitude for the Philippians' Generosity*

[10]I rejoice greatly in the Lord that now at last you revived your concern for me. You were, of course, concerned about me but lacked an opportunity.[m] [11]Not that I say this because of need, for I have learned, in whatever situation I find myself, to be self-sufficient.[n] [12]I know indeed how to live in humble circumstances; I know also how to live with abundance. In every circumstance and in all things I have learned the secret of being well fed and of going hungry, of living in abundance and of being in need. [13]I have the strength for everything through him who empowers me.[o] [14]Still, it was kind of you to share in my distress.

[15]You Philippians indeed know that at the beginning of the gospel,* when I left Macedonia, not a single church shared with me in an account of giving and receiving, except you alone. [16]For even when I was at Thessalonica you sent me something for my needs, not only once but more than once. [17]It is not that I am eager for the gift; rather, I am eager for the profit that accrues to your account. [18]I have received full payment and I abound. I am very well supplied because of what I received from you through Epaphroditus, "a fragrant aroma," an acceptable sacrifice,* pleasing to God.[p] [19]My God will fully supply whatever you need, in accord with his glorious riches in Christ Jesus.[q] [20]To our God and Father, glory forever and ever. Amen.[r]

## VIII. Farewell*

[21]Give my greetings to every holy one in Christ Jesus. The brothers who are with me send you their greetings; [22][s] all the holy ones send you their greetings, especially those of Caesar's household.* [23]The grace of the Lord Jesus Christ be with your spirit.

**4:4 Rejoice**: see note on Phil 3:1.

**4:5 Kindness**: considerateness, forbearance, fairness. **The Lord is near**: most likely a reference to Christ's parousia (Phil 1:6, 10; 3:20–21; 1 Cor 16:22), although some sense an echo of Ps 119:151 and the perpetual presence of the Lord.

**4:8** The language employs terms from Roman Stoic thought.

**4:9** Cf. note on Phil 3:17.

**4:10–20** Paul, more directly than anywhere else in the letter (cf. Phil 1:3–5), here thanks the Philippians for their gift of money sent through Epaphroditus (Phil 2:25). Paul's own policy was **to be self-sufficient** as a missionary, supporting himself by his own labor (1 Thes 2:5–9; 1 Cor 9:15–18; cf. Acts 18:2–3). In spite of this reliance on self and on God to provide (Phil 4:11–13) Paul accepted gifts from the Philippians **not only once but more than once** (Phil 4:16) when he was in Thessalonica (Acts 17:1–9), as he does now, in prison (**my distress**, Phil 4:14). While commercial terms appear in the passage, like **an account of giving and receiving** (Phil 4:15) and **received full payment** (Phil 4:18), Paul is most concerned about the spiritual growth of the Philippians (Phil 4:10, 17, 19); he emphasizes that God will care for their needs, through Christ.

**4:15 The beginning of the gospel**: it was at Philippi that Paul first preached Christ in Europe, going on from there to Thessalonica and Beroea (Acts 16:9–17:14).

**4:18 Aroma . . . sacrifice**: Old Testament cultic language (cf. Gn 8:21; Ex 29:18, 25, 41; Lv 1:9, 13; Ez 20:41) applied to the Philippians' gift; cf. Eph 5:2; 2 Cor 2:14–16.

**4:21–23** On the usual greetings at the conclusion of a letter, see note on 1 Cor 16:19–24. Inclusion of greetings from **all the holy ones** in the place from which Paul writes would involve even the Christians of Phil 1:14–18 who had their differences with Paul.

**4:22 Those of Caesar's household**: minor officials or even slaves and freedmen, found in Ephesus or Rome, among other places.

---

*g:* 2:18; 3:1. *h:* Ti 3:2 / Ps 145:18; Heb 10:37; Jas 5:8–9. *i:* Mt 6:25–34; 1 Pt 5:7 / Col 4:2. *j:* Jn 14:27; Col 3:15. *k:* Rom 12:17. *l:* 1 Thes 4:1 / Rom 15:33; 16:20; 1 Cor 14:33; 1 Thes 5:23. *m:* 1:18; 2:25; 1 Cor 9:11; 2 Cor 11:9. *n:* 1 Cor 4:11; 2 Cor 6:10; 11:27 / 2 Cor 12:9–10. *o:* Col 1:29; 2 Tm 4:17. *p:* Gn 8:21; Ex 29:18; Eph 5:2; Heb 13:16. *q:* 1 Thes 3:11, 13. *r:* Rom 16:27; Eph 5:20. *s:* 1:13.

See RG 399–403

# The Letter to the Colossians

This letter is addressed to a congregation at Colossae in the Lycus Valley in Asia Minor, east of Ephesus. At the time of writing, Paul had not visited there, the letter says (Col 1:4; 2:1). The community had apparently been established by Epaphras of Colossae (Col 1:7; 4:12; Phlm 23). Problems, however, had arisen, brought on by teachers who emphasized Christ's relation to the universe (cosmos). Their teachings stressed angels (Col 2:18; "principalities and powers," Col 2:15), which were connected with astral powers and cultic practices (see note on Col 2:16) and rules about food and drink and ascetical disciplines (Col 2:16, 18). These teachings, Paul insists, detract from the person and work of Christ for salvation as set forth magnificently in a hymnic passage at Col 1:15–20 and reiterated throughout the letter. Such teachings are but "shadows"; Christ is "reality" (Col 2:17).

For help in dealing with these problems that the new teachers posed at Colossae, Epaphras sought out Paul, who was then imprisoned (Col 4:10, 18) at a place that the letter does not mention. Paul, without entering into debate over the existence of angelic spirits or their function, simply affirms that Christ possesses the sum total of redemptive power (Col 1:19) and that the spiritual renewal of the human person occurs through contact in baptism with the person of Christ, who died and rose again (Col 2:9–14). It is unnecessary for the Christian to be concerned about placating spirits (Col 2:15) or avoiding imagined defilement through ascetical practices in regard to food and drink (Col 2:20–23). True Christian asceticism consists in the conquering of personal sins (Col 3:5–10) and the practice of love of neighbor in accordance with the standard set by Christ (Col 3:12–16).

Paul commends the community as a whole (Col 1:3–8); this seems to indicate that, though the Colossians have been under pressure to adopt the false doctrines, they have not yet succumbed. The apostle expresses his prayerful concern for them (Col 1:9–14). His preaching has cost him persecution, suffering, and imprisonment, but he regards these as reflective of the sufferings of Christ, a required discipline for the sake of the gospel (see note on 1:24; cf. 1:29; 2:1). His instructions to the Christian family and to slaves and masters require a new spirit of reflection and action. Love, obedience, and service are to be rendered "in the Lord" (Col 3:18–4:1).

Colossians follows the outline of a typical Pauline letter. It is distinguished by the poetic lines in Col 1:15–20 concerning who Christ is and what Christ means in creation and redemption. This hymn may be compared with similar passages in Phil 2:6–11; 1 Tm 3:16; and Jn 1:1–18. It was apparently familiar liturgical material to the author, the audience, and the false teachers. In Col 1:21–2:7, however, Paul interprets the relation between the body of Christ, which he insists is the church (Col 1:18), and the world or cosmos to be one not simply of Christ's preexistence and rule but one of missionary advance into the world by the spreading of the word (Col 1:25, 28). In this labor of the missionary body of Christ, Paul as a minister plays a prime part in bringing Christ and the gospel as hope to the Gentiles (Col 1:23, 25, 27). To "every creature under heaven" the word is to be proclaimed, so that everyone receives Christ, is established in faith, and walks in Christ (Col 1:28; 2:6, 7).

Paul wrote the Letter to the Colossians while in prison, but his several imprisonments leave the specific place and date of composition uncertain. On this point the same problem exists as with Ephesians and Philippians (see the Introductions to these letters). Traditionally the house arrest at Rome, in which Paul enjoyed a certain restricted freedom in preaching (see Acts 28:16–28), or a second Roman imprisonment has been claimed as the setting. Others suggest a still earlier imprisonment at Caesarea (see Acts 23:12–27:1) or in Ephesus (see Acts 19). Still others regard the letter as the work of some pupil or follower of Paul, writing in his name. In any case, the contents are often closely paralleled by thoughts in Ephesians.

The principal divisions of the Letter to the Colossians are the following:

I. Address (1:1–14)
II. The Preeminence of Christ (1:15–2:3)
III. Warnings Against False Teachers (2:4–23)
IV. The Ideal Christian Life in the World (3:1–4:6)
V. Conclusion (4:7–18)

# I. Address

## CHAPTER 1

See RG 400-401

*Greeting.** 1 Paul, an apostle of Christ
Jesus by the will of God, and Timothy our
brother,[a] 2 to the holy ones and faithful brothers in Christ in Colossae: grace to you and
peace from God our Father.

*Thanksgiving.** 3 We always give thanks to
God, the Father of our Lord Jesus Christ,
when we pray for you,[b] 4 for we have heard
of your faith in Christ Jesus and the love that
you have for all the holy ones 5 because of
the hope reserved for you in heaven. Of this
you have already heard through the word of
truth, the gospel,[c] 6 that has come to you. Just
as in the whole world it is bearing fruit and
growing, so also among you, from the day
you heard it and came to know the grace of
God in truth, 7[d] as you learned it from Epaphras* our beloved fellow slave, who is a
trustworthy minister of Christ on your behalf 8 and who also told us of your love in the
Spirit.

*Prayer for Continued Progress.** 9 Therefore, from the day we heard this, we do not
cease praying for you and asking that you
may be filled with the knowledge of his will
through all spiritual wisdom and understanding[e] 10 to live in a manner worthy of the
Lord, so as to be fully pleasing, in every
good work bearing fruit and growing in the
knowledge of God, 11 strengthened with
every power, in accord with his glorious
might, for all endurance and patience, with
joy 12* giving thanks to the Father, who has
made you fit to share in the inheritance of
the holy ones in light.[f] 13 He delivered us
from the power of darkness and transferred
us to the kingdom of his beloved Son, 14 in
whom we have redemption, the forgiveness
of sins.[g]

# II. The Preeminence of Christ

## His Person and Work

15 * He is the image* of the invisible God,
the firstborn of all creation.[h]
16 For in him* were created all things in
heaven and on earth,
the visible and the invisible,

**1:1–2** For the epistolary form used by Paul at the beginning of his letters, see note on Rom 1:1–7. On **holy ones** or "God's people," see note on Rom 1:7. Awareness of their calling helps this group to be **faithful brothers** and sisters **in Christ**, i.e., dedicated to the tasks implied in their calling.

**1:3–8** On thanksgiving at the start of a letter, see note on Rom 1:8. The apostle, recalling his own prayers for them and the good report about them he has received (Col 1:3–4), congratulates the Colossians upon their acceptance of Christ and their faithful efforts to live the gospel (Col 3:6–8). To encourage them he mentions the success of the gospel elsewhere (Col 1:6) and assures them that his knowledge of their community is accurate, since he has been in personal contact with Epaphras (Col 1:7–8), who likely had evangelized Colossae and other cities in the Lycus Valley of Asia Minor (cf. Col 4:12, 13; Phlm 23). On **faith, love,** and **hope** (Col 1:4, 5, 8), see note on 1 Cor 13:13; cf. 1 Thes 1:3; 5:8.

**1:7 Epaphras**: now with Paul but a Colossian, founder of the church there.

**1:9–14** Moved by Epaphras' account, the apostle has prayed and continues to pray fervently for the Colossians that, in their response to the gospel, they **may be filled with the knowledge of** God's **will** (Col 1:9; cf. Col 3:10). Paul expects a mutual interaction between their life according to the gospel and this knowledge (Col 1:10), yielding results (**fruit**, Col 1:10; cf. Col 1:6) **in every good work**: growth, strength, **endurance**, **patience**, **with joy** (Col 1:11), and the further giving of thanks (Col 1:12).

**1:12–14** A summary about **redemption** by **the Father** precedes the statement in Col 1:15–20 about the **beloved Son** who is God's love in person (Col 1:13). Christians share **the inheritance . . . in light** with **the holy ones**, here probably the angels (Col 1:12). The imagery reflects the Exodus (**delivered . . . transferred**) and Jesus' theme of the **kingdom. Redemption** is explained as **forgiveness of sins** (cf. Acts 2:38; Rom 3:24–25; Eph 1:7).

**1:15–20** As the poetic arrangement indicates, these lines are probably an early Christian hymn, known to the Colossians and taken up into the letter from liturgical use (cf. Phil 2:6–11; 1 Tm 3:16). They present Christ as the mediator of creation (Col 1:15–18a) and of redemption (Col 1:18b–20). There is a parallelism between **firstborn of all creation** (Col 1:15) and **firstborn from the dead** (Col 1:18). While many of the phrases were at home in Greek philosophical use and even in gnosticism, the basic ideas also reflect Old Testament themes about Wisdom found in Prv 8:22–31; Wis 7:22–8:1; and Sir 1:4. See also notes on what is possibly a hymn in Jn 1:1–18.

**1:15 Image**: cf. Gn 1:27. Whereas the man and the woman were originally created in the image and likeness of God (see also Gn 1:26), Christ as image (2 Cor 4:4) of **the invisible God** (Jn 1:18) now shares this new nature in baptism with those redeemed (cf. Col 3:10–11).

**1:16–17** Christ (though not mentioned by name) is preeminent and supreme as God's agent in the creation of **all things** (cf. Jn 1:3), as prior to **all things** (Col 1:17; cf. Heb 1:3).

*a:* Eph 1:1. *b:* Eph 1:15–16; Phlm 4–5. *c:* Eph 1:13, 18; 1 Pt 1:4. *d:* Phlm 23. *e:* Eph 1:15–17; 5:17; Phil 1:9. *f:* 3:17; Jn 8:12; Acts 26:18; 1 Tm 6:16; 1 Pt 2:9. *g:* Eph 1:7. *h:* Ps 89:28; Jn 1:3, 18; 2 Cor 4:4.

whether thrones or dominions or
principalities or powers;
all things were created through him
and for him.[i]
17 He is before all things,
and in him all things hold together.
18 He is the head of the body, the church.*
He is the beginning, the firstborn from
the dead,
that in all things he himself might be
preeminent.[j]
19 For in him all the fullness* was pleased
to dwell,
20 and through him to reconcile all things
for him,
making peace by the blood of his
cross*
[through him], whether those on earth
or those in heaven.[k]

21* And you who once were alienated and
hostile in mind because of evil deeds[l] 22 he
has now reconciled in his fleshly body
through his death, to present you holy, without blemish, and irreproachable before him,
23 provided that you persevere in the faith,
firmly grounded, stable, and not shifting
from the hope of the gospel that you heard,
which has been preached to every creature
under heaven, of which I, Paul, am a minister.

***Christ in Us.**** 24 Now I rejoice in my sufferings for your sake, and in my flesh I am
filling up what is lacking* in the afflictions
of Christ on behalf of his body, which is the
church, 25 of which I am a minister in accordance with God's stewardship given to me
to bring to completion for you the word of
God, 26 the mystery hidden from ages and
from generations past. But now it has been
manifested to his holy ones,[m] 27 to whom
God chose to make known the riches of the
glory of this mystery among the Gentiles; it
is Christ in you, the hope for glory.[n] 28 It is
he whom we proclaim, admonishing everyone and teaching everyone with all wisdom,
that we may present everyone perfect in
Christ.[o] 29 For this I labor and struggle, in accord with the exercise of his power working
within me.[p]

**1:18 Church**: such a reference seemingly belongs under "redemption" in the following lines, not under the "creation" section of the hymn. Stoic thought sometimes referred to the world as "the body of Zeus." Pauline usage is to speak of the church as the body of Christ (1 Cor 12:12–27; Rom 12:4–5). Some think that the author of Colossians has inserted the reference to the church here so as to define "head of the body" in Paul's customary way. See Col 1:24. **Preeminent**: when Christ was raised by God as **firstborn from the dead** (cf. Acts 26:23; Rev 1:5), he was placed over the community, the church, that he had brought into being, but he is also indicated as crown of the whole new creation, over **all things**. His further role is to **reconcile all things** (Col 1:20) for God or possibly "to himself."

**1:19 Fullness**: in gnostic usage this term referred to a spiritual world of beings above, between God and the world; many later interpreters take it to refer to **the fullness of the deity** (Col 2:9); the reference could also be to the fullness of grace (cf. Jn 1:16).

**1:20 The blood of his cross**: the most specific reference in the hymn to redemption through Christ's death, a central theme in Paul; cf. Col 2:14–15; 1 Cor 1:17, 18, 23. **[Through him]**: the phrase, lacking in some manuscripts, seems superfluous but parallels the reference to reconciliation through Christ earlier in the verse.

**1:21–23** Paul, in applying this hymn to the Colossians, reminds them that they have experienced the reconciling effect of Christ's death. He sees the effects of the cross in the redemption of human beings, not of cosmic powers such as those referred to in Col 1:16, 20 (**all things**). Paul also urges adherence to Christ in faith and begins to point to his own role as minister (Col 1:23), sufferer (Col 1:24), and proclaimer (Col 1:27–28) of this gospel.

**1:24–2:3** As the community at Colossae was not personally known to Paul (see Introduction), he here invests his teaching with greater authority by presenting a brief sketch of his apostolic ministry and sufferings as they reflect those of Christ on behalf of the church (Col 1:24). The preaching of God's word (Col 1:25) carries out the divine plan (**the mystery**, Col 1:26) to make Christ known to the Gentiles (Col 1:27). It teaches the God-given wisdom about Christ (Col 1:28), whose power works mightily in the apostle (Col 1:29). Even in those communities that do not know him personally (Col 2:1), he can increase the perception of God in Christ, unite the faithful more firmly in love, and so bring encouragement to them (Col 2:2). He hopes that his apostolic authority will make the Colossians perceive more readily the defects in the teaching of others who have sought to delude them, the next concern in the letter.

**1:24 What is lacking**: although variously interpreted, this phrase does not imply that Christ's atoning death on the cross was defective. It may refer to the apocalyptic concept of a quota of "messianic woes" to be endured before the end comes; cf. Mk 13:8, 19–20, 24 and the note on Mt 23:29–32. Others suggest that Paul's mystical unity with Christ allowed him to call his own **sufferings the afflictions of Christ**.

*i:* 1 Cor 8:6; Eph 1:10, 21. *j:* 1 Cor 11:3; 12:12, 27; 15:20; Eph 1:22–23; Rev 1:5. *k:* 2 Cor 5:18–19; Eph 1:10. *l:* Eph 2:14–16. *m:* Rom 16:25–26; 1 Cor 2:7; Eph 3:3, 9. *n:* 3:4; Rom 8:10. *o:* Eph 4:13. *p:* 2:1; 4:12; Phil 4:13.

## CHAPTER 2

See RG 401

1 For I want you to know how great a struggle I am having for you and for those in Laodicea* and all who have not seen me face to face, 2 that their hearts may be encouraged as they are brought together in love, to have all the richness of fully assured understanding, for the knowledge of the mystery of God, Christ,[q] 3 in whom are hidden all the treasures of wisdom and knowledge.[r]

## III. Warnings Against False Teachers*

*A General Admonition.* 4 I say this so that no one may deceive you by specious arguments.[s] 5 For even if I am absent in the flesh, yet I am with you in spirit, rejoicing as I observe your good order and the firmness of your faith in Christ.[t] 6 So, as you received Christ Jesus the Lord, walk in him, 7 rooted in him and built upon him and established in the faith as you were taught, abounding in thanksgiving.[u] 8 See to it that no one captivate you with an empty, seductive philosophy according to human tradition, according to the elemental powers of the world* and not according to Christ.[v]

*Sovereign Role of Christ.* 9[w] For in him dwells the whole fullness of the deity* bodily, 10 and you share in this fullness in him, who is the head of every principality and power. 11[x] In him* you were also circumcised with a circumcision not administered by hand, by stripping off the carnal body, with the circumcision of Christ. 12 You were buried with him in baptism, in which you were also raised with him through faith in the power of God, who raised him from the dead.[y] 13[z] And even when you were dead [in] transgressions and the uncircumcision of your flesh, he brought you to life along with him, having forgiven us all our transgressions; 14* obliterating the bond against us, with its legal claims, which was opposed to us, he also removed it from our midst, nailing it to the cross;[a] 15 despoiling the principalities and the powers, he made a public spectacle of them,[b] leading them away in triumph by it.*

*Practices Contrary to Faith.* 16[c] Let no one, then, pass judgment on you in matters of food and drink or with regard to a festival or new moon or sabbath.* 17 These are shad-

**2:1 Laodicea**: chief city in Phrygia, northwest of Colossae; cf. Col 4:13, 16; Rev 3:14–22.

**2:4–23** In face of the threat posed by false teachers (Col 2:4), the Colossians are admonished to adhere to the gospel as it was first preached to them (Col 2:6), steeping themselves in it with grateful hearts (Col 2:7). They must reject religious teachings originating in any source except the gospel (Col 2:8) because in Christ alone will they have access to God, **the deity** (Col 2:9). So fully has Christ enlightened them that they need no other source of religious knowledge or virtue (Col 2:10). They do not require **circumcision** (Col 2:11), for **in baptism** their whole being has been affected by Christ (Col 2:12) through forgiveness of sin and resurrection to a new life (Col 2:13; cf. Col 3:1 and Rom 6:1–11).

On the cross Christ canceled the record of the debt that stood against us with all its claims (Col 2:14), i.e., he eliminated the law (cf. Eph 2:15) that human beings could not observe—and that could not save them. He forgave sins against the law (Col 2:14) and exposed as false and misleading (Col 2:15) all other powers (cf. Col 1:16) that purport to offer salvation. Therefore, the Colossians are not to accept judgments from such teachers on **food and drink** or to keep certain religious festivals or engage in certain cultic practices (Col 2:16), for the Colossians would thereby risk severing themselves from Christ (Col 2:19). If, when they accepted the gospel, they believed in Christ as their savior, they must be convinced that their salvation cannot be achieved by appeasing ruling spirits through dietary practices or through a wisdom gained simply by means of harsh asceticism (Col 2:20–23).

**2:8 Elemental powers of the world**: see note on Gal 4:3.

**2:9 Fullness of the deity**: the divine nature, not just attributes; see note on Col 1:19.

**2:11** A description of baptism (Col 2:12) in symbolic terms of the Old Testament rite for entry into the community. The false teachers may have demanded physical circumcision of the Colossians.

**2:14** The elaborate metaphor here about how God canceled the legal claims against us through Christ's cross depicts not Christ being nailed to the cross by men but **the bond . . . with its legal claims** being nailed to the cross by God.

**2:15** The picture derives from the **public spectacle** and **triumph** of a Roman emperor's victory parade, where captives marched in subjection. **The principalities and the powers** are here conquered, not reconciled (cf. Col 1:16, 20). An alternate rendering for **by it** (the cross) is "by him" (Christ).

**2:16 Festival or new moon or sabbath**: yearly, monthly, and weekly observances determined by religious powers associated with a calendar set by the heavenly bodies, sun, moon, and stars (cf. Col 2:8).

*q:* 1:26–27; Eph 3:18–19. *r:* Prv 2:4–5; Is 45:3; Rom 11:33; 1 Cor 1:30. *s:* Eph 4:14. *t:* 1 Cor 5:3; Phil 1:27. *u:* Eph 2:20–22; 3:17. *v:* Gal 4:3; Eph 5:6. *w:* 1:19; Eph 3:19. *x:* 1:22; Jer 4:4; Rom 2:25–29; Phil 3:3. *y:* Rom 6:3–4. *z:* Eph 2:1, 5. *a:* Eph 2:14–15. *b:* 1:16, 20; 2 Cor 2:14; Eph 1:21. *c:* Rom 14:3–4; 1 Tm 4:3. *d:* Heb 8:5; 10:1.

ows of things to come; the reality belongs to Christ.[d] [18]Let no one disqualify you, delighting in self-abasement and worship of angels, taking his stand on visions,* inflated without reason by his fleshly mind,[e] [19]and not holding closely to the head, from whom the whole body, supported and held together by its ligaments and bonds, achieves the growth that comes from God.[f]

[20]If you died with Christ to the elemental powers of the world, why do you submit to regulations as if you were still living in the world? [21]"Do not handle! Do not taste! Do not touch!" [22]These are all things destined to perish with use; they accord with human precepts and teachings.[g] [23]While they have a semblance of wisdom in rigor of devotion and self-abasement [and] severity to the body, they are of no value against gratification of the flesh.

## IV. The Ideal Christian Life in the World

### CHAPTER 3

See RG 401–402

*Mystical Death and Resurrection.** [1]If then you were raised with Christ, seek what is above, where Christ is seated at the right hand of God.[h] [2]Think of what is above, not of what is on earth. [3]For you have died, and your life is hidden with Christ in God.[i] [4]When Christ your life appears, then you too will appear with him in glory.

*Renunciation of Vice.** [5]Put to death, then, the parts of you that are earthly:[j] immorality, impurity, passion, evil desire, and the greed that is idolatry.* [6]Because of these the wrath of God* is coming [upon the disobedient].[k] [7]By these you too once conducted yourselves, when you lived in that way. [8]But now you must put them all away:* anger, fury, malice, slander, and obscene language out of your mouths.[l] [9]Stop lying to one another, since you have taken off the old self with its practices[m] [10]* and have put on the new self, which is being renewed, for knowledge, in the image of its creator.[n] [11]Here there is not Greek and Jew, circumcision and uncircumcision, barbarian, Scythian,* slave, free; but Christ is all and in all.[o]

[12]Put on then, as God's chosen ones, holy and beloved, heartfelt compassion, kindness, humility, gentleness, and patience,[p] [13]bearing with one another and forgiving one another, if one has a grievance against another; as the Lord has forgiven you, so must you also do.[q] [14]And over all these put on love, that is, the bond of perfection.[r] [15]And let the peace of Christ control your hearts, the peace into which you were also called in one body. And be thankful.[s] [16]Let the word of Christ dwell in you richly, as in all wisdom you teach and admonish one another, singing psalms, hymns, and spiritual songs with gratitude in your hearts to God.[t] [17]And whatever you do, in word or in deed, do everything in the name of the Lord Jesus, giving thanks to God the Father through him.[u]

***The Christian Family.*** [18]* Wives, be sub-

**2:18** Ascetic practices encouraged by the false teachers included subjection of self humbly to their rules, worship of angels, and cultivation of visions, though exact details are unclear.

**3:1–4** By retaining the message of the gospel that the risen, living Christ is the source of their salvation, the Colossians will be free from false religious evaluations of the things of the world (Col 3:1–2). They have died to these; but one day **when Christ . . . appears**, they will live with Christ in the presence of God (Col 3:3–4).

**3:5–17** In lieu of false asceticism and superstitious festivals, the apostle reminds the Colossians of the moral life that is to characterize their response to God through Christ. He urges their participation in the liturgical hymns and prayers that center upon God's plan of salvation in Christ (Col 3:16).

**3:5, 8** The two lists of five vices each are similar to enumerations at Rom 1:29–31 and Gal 5:19–21.

**3:6 The wrath of God**: see note on Rom 1:18. Many manuscripts add, as at Eph 5:6, "upon the disobedient."

**3:8–10 Put . . . away; have taken off; have put on**: the terms may reflect baptismal practice, taking off garments and putting on new ones after being united with Christ, here translated into ethical terms.

**3:10 Image**: see note on Col 1:15.

**3:11 Scythian**: a barbarous people from north of the Black Sea.

**3:18–4:6** After general recommendations that connect family life and the social condition of slavery with the service of Christ (Col 3:18–4:1), Paul requests prayers for himself, especially in view of his imprisonment (Col 3:2–3), and rec-

*e:* 2:23; Mt 24:4. *f:* Eph 2:21–22; 4:16. *g:* Is 29:13. *h:* 2:12; Ps 110:1; Phil 3:20; Eph 2:6. *i:* Rom 6:2–5. *j:* Mt 15:19; Rom 1:29–30; Gal 5:19–21; Eph 5:3, 5. *k:* Rom 1:18. *l:* Eph 4:22, 25, 31. *m:* Rom 6:4, 6; Eph 4:22–25; Heb 12:1; 1 Pt 2:1; 4:2. *n:* Gn 1:26–27. *o:* 1 Cor 12:13; Gal 3:27–28. *p:* Eph 4:1–2, 32; 1 Thes 5:15. *q:* Mt 6:14; 18:21–35; Eph 4:32. *r:* Rom 13:8–10. *s:* Rom 12:5; 1 Cor 12:12; Eph 2:16; 4:3–4; Phil 4:7. *t:* Eph 5:19–20. *u:* 1 Cor 10:31. *v:* Eph 5:22; Ti 2:5; 1 Pt 3:1.

ordinate to your husbands, as is proper in the Lord.[v] 19Husbands, love your wives, and avoid any bitterness toward them. 20Children, obey your parents in everything, for this is pleasing to the Lord.[w] 21Fathers, do not provoke your children, so they may not become discouraged.[x]

***Slaves and Masters.*** 22Slaves,* obey your human masters in everything, not only when being watched, as currying favor, but in simplicity of heart, fearing the Lord.[y] 23Whatever you do, do from the heart, as for the Lord and not for others, 24knowing that you will receive from the Lord the due payment of the inheritance; be slaves of the Lord Christ. 25For the wrongdoer will receive recompense for the wrong he committed, and there is no partiality.[z]

### CHAPTER 4

See RG 401–402

1Masters, treat your slaves justly and fairly, realizing that you too have a Master in heaven.

***Prayer and Apostolic Spirit.*** 2Persevere in prayer, being watchful in it with thanksgiving;[a] 3at the same time, pray for us, too, that God may open a door to us for the word, to speak of the mystery of Christ, for which I am in prison,[b] 4that I may make it clear, as I must speak. 5Conduct yourselves wisely toward outsiders, making the most of the opportunity.[c] 6Let your speech always be gracious, seasoned with salt, so that you know how you should respond to each one.

## V. Conclusion*

***Tychicus and Onesimus.*** 7Tychicus,* my beloved brother, trustworthy minister, and fellow slave in the Lord, will tell you all the news of me.[d] 8I am sending him to you for this very purpose, so that you may know about us and that he may encourage your hearts, 9together with Onesimus, a trustworthy and beloved brother, who is one of you. They will tell you about everything here.[e]

***From Paul's Co-Workers.*** 10Aristarchus,* my fellow prisoner, sends you greetings, as does Mark the cousin of Barnabas (concerning whom you have received instructions; if he comes to you, receive him),[f] 11and Jesus,* who is called Justus, who are of the circumcision; these alone are my co-workers for the kingdom of God, and they have been a comfort to me. 12Epaphras* sends you greetings; he is one of you, a slave of Christ [Jesus], always striving for you in his prayers so that you may be perfect and fully assured in all the will of God.[g] 13For I can testify that he works very hard for you and for those in Laodicea* and those in Hierapolis. 14Luke* the beloved physician sends greetings, as does Demas.[h]

***A Message for the Laodiceans.*** 15Give greetings to the brothers in Laodicea and to Nympha and to the church in her house.* 16And when this letter is read before you, have it read also in the church of the Laodiceans, and you yourselves read the one from

ommends friendly relations and meaningful discussions of Christian teaching with **outsiders**, i.e., non-Christians (Col 3:5–6). See note on Eph 5:21–6:9.

**3:22–25 Slaves**: within this table of duties in family and societal relations, involving wives and husbands, children and parents (Col 3:18–21), such as also appears in Eph 5:22–6:9, slaves here receive special attention because of the case of Onesimus the slave returning to his master (Col 4:9; Phlm 10–12).

**4:7–18** Paul concludes with greetings and information concerning various Christians known to the Colossians.

**4:7 Tychicus**: Acts 20:4 mentions his role in the collection for Jerusalem; Eph 6:21 repeats what is said here; see also 2 Tm 4:12; Ti 3:12.

**4:10 Aristarchus**: a Thessalonian who was with Paul at Ephesus and Caesarea and on the voyage to Rome (Acts 19:29; 20:4; 27:2). **Mark**: also referred to at Phlm 24 and 2 Tm 4:11 and, as "John Mark," in Acts (Acts 12:12, 25; 13:13; 15:37–40). See also 1 Pt 5:13 and the note there. Traditionally the author of the second gospel.

**4:11 Jesus**: a then common Jewish name, the Greek form of Joshua.

**4:12 Epaphras**: see notes on Col 1:3–8 and Col 1:7.

**4:13 Laodicea**: see note on Col 2:1. **Hierapolis**: a city northeast of Laodicea and northwest of Colossae.

**4:14 Luke**: only here described as a medical doctor; cf. Phlm 24 and 2 Tm 4:11. Traditionally the author of the third gospel. **Demas**: cf. Phlm 24; he later deserted Paul (2 Tm 4:10).

**4:15 Nympha and . . . her house**: some manuscripts read a masculine for the house-church leader, "Nymphas and . . . his house."

**4:16 The one from Laodicea**: either a letter by Paul that

*w:* Eph 6:1. *x:* Eph 6:4. *y:* Eph 6:5; 1 Tm 6:1; Ti 2:9–10; 1 Pt 2:18. *z:* Rom 2:11. *a:* Lk 18:1; Rom 12:12; Eph 6:18–20; 1 Thes 5:17. *b:* Rom 15:30; 1 Cor 16:9; Eph 6:19; 2 Thes 3:1. *c:* Eph 5:15–16. *d:* Acts 20:4; Eph 6:21–22; Phil 1:12. *e:* Phlm 10–11. *f:* Acts 19:29; 20:4; 27:2 / Acts 12:12, 25; 13:13; 15:37, 40; 2 Tm 4:11; Phlm 24; 1 Pt 5:13. *g:* 1:7; Rom 15:30. *h:* Phlm 24; 2 Tm 4:10–11.

Laodicea.* 17And tell Archippus, "See that
you fulfill the ministry* that you received in
the Lord."[i]
18The greeting is in my own hand,*
Paul's. Remember my chains. Grace be with
you.[j]

has been lost or the Letter to the Ephesians (cf. note on Eph 1:1 **in Ephesus**).

**4:17 Fulfill the ministry**: usually taken to mean that **Archippus**, the son of Philemon and Apphia (Phlm 1–2), is "pastor" at Colossae. An alternate interpretation is that Archippus, not Philemon, is the owner of the slave Onesimus and that Paul is asking Archippus to complete the service he has received in the Lord by sending Onesimus back to minister to Paul in his captivity (cf. Phlm 20).

**4:18 My own hand**: a postscript in Paul's own hand was his custom; cf. Gal 6:11–18 and 2 Thes 3:17–18.

*i:* Phlm 2. *j:* 1 Cor 16:21; Gal 6:11; Eph 3:1; 2 Thes 3:17.

See RG 403–406

# The First Letter to the Thessalonians

When Paul parted from Barnabas (Acts 15:36–41) at the beginning of what is called his second missionary journey, he chose Silvanus (Silas) as his traveling companion. Soon afterwards he took Timothy along with him (Acts 16:1–3). Paul was now clearly at the head of his own missionary band. About A.D. 50, he arrived in Greece for the first time. In making converts in Philippi and, soon afterwards, in Thessalonica, he was beset by persecution from Jews and Gentiles alike. Moving on to Beroea, he was again harassed by enemies from Thessalonica and hurriedly left for Athens (Acts 16:11–17:15). Silvanus and Timothy remained behind for a while. Paul soon sent Timothy back to Thessalonica to strengthen that community in its trials (1 Thes 3:1–5). Timothy and Silvanus finally returned to Paul when he reached Corinth (Acts 18:1–18), probably in the early summer of A.D. 51. Timothy's return with a report on conditions at Thessalonica served as the occasion for Paul's first letter (1 Thes 3:6–8).

The letter begins with a brief address (1 Thes 1:1) and concludes with a greeting (1 Thes 5:26–28). The body of the letter consists of two major parts. The first (1 Thes 1:2–3:13) is a set of three sections of thanksgiving connected by two *apologiae* (defenses) dealing, respectively, with the missionaries' previous conduct and their current concerns. Paul's thankful optimism regarding the Thessalonians' spiritual welfare is tempered by his insistence on their recognition of the selfless love shown by the missionaries. In an age of itinerant peddlers of new religions, Paul found it necessary to emphasize not only the content of his gospel but also his manner of presenting it, for both attested to God's grace as freely bestowed and powerfully effected.

The second part of the letter (1 Thes 4:1–5:25) is specifically hortatory or parenetic. The superabundant love for which Paul has just prayed (1 Thes 3:12–13) is to be shown practically by living out the norms of conduct that he has communicated to them. Specific "imperatives" of Christian life, principles for acting morally, stem from the "indicative" of one's relationship to God through Christ by the sending of the holy Spirit. Thus, moral conduct is the practical, personal expression of one's Christian faith, love, and hope.

The principal divisions of the First Letter to the Thessalonians are the following:

I. Address (1:1–10)
II. Previous Relations with the Thessalonians (2:1–3:13)
III. Specific Exhortations (4:1–5:25)
IV. Final Greeting (5:26–28)

## I. Address

### CHAPTER 1

See RG 404

*Greeting.* 1* [a] Paul, Silvanus, and Timothy to the church of the Thessalonians in
God the Father and the Lord Jesus Christ:
grace to you and peace.
***Thanksgiving for Their Faith.*** 2We give
thanks to God always for all of you, remembering you in our prayers, unceasingly[b]
3calling to mind your work of faith and labor

**1:1** On the address, see note on Rom 1:1–7.

**1:3 Faith . . . love . . . hope**: this, along with 1 Thes 5:8, is the earliest mention in Christian literature of the three "theological virtues" (see 1 Cor 13:13). The order here stresses eschatological hope, in line with the letter's emphasis on the Lord's second, triumphal coming, or parousia (1 Thes 1:10;

*a:* Acts 15:40; 16:1–3, 19; 17:14–15; 2 Thes 1:1–2. *b:* 2 Thes 1:3.

of love and endurance in hope* of our Lord Jesus Christ, before our God and Father, 4 knowing, brothers loved by God, how you were chosen.[c] 5 For our gospel did not come to you in word alone, but also in power and in the holy Spirit and [with] much conviction. You know what sort of people we were [among] you for your sake.[d] 6 And you became imitators* of us and of the Lord, receiving the word in great affliction, with joy from the holy Spirit, 7 so that you became a model for all the believers in Macedonia and in Achaia.[e] 8 For from you the word of the Lord has sounded forth not only in Macedonia and [in] Achaia, but in every place your faith in God has gone forth, so that we have no need to say anything.[f] 9 For they themselves openly declare about us what sort of reception we had among you, and how you turned to God from idols to serve the living and true God[g] 10 and to await his Son from heaven, whom he raised from [the] dead, Jesus, who delivers us from the coming wrath.[h]

## II. Previous Relations with the Thessalonians

### CHAPTER 2

See RG 404–405

***Paul's Ministry Among Them.*** 1 For you yourselves know, brothers, that our reception among you was not without effect. 2 Rather, after we had suffered and been insolently treated, as you know, in Philippi, we drew courage through our God to speak to you the gospel of God with much struggle.[i] 3 Our exhortation was not from delusion or impure motives, nor did it work through deception. 4 But as we were judged worthy* by God to be entrusted with the gospel, that is how we speak, not as trying to please human beings, but rather God, who judges our hearts.[j] 5 Nor, indeed, did we ever appear with flattering speech, as you know, or with a pretext for greed—God is witness— 6 nor did we seek praise from human beings, either from you or from others,[k] 7 although we were able to impose our weight as apostles of Christ. Rather, we were gentle* among you, as a nursing mother cares for her children. 8 With such affection for you, we were determined to share with you not only the gospel of God, but our very selves as well, so dearly beloved had you become to us. 9 You recall, brothers, our toil and drudgery. Working night and day in order not to burden any of you, we proclaimed to you the gospel of God.[l] 10 You are witnesses, and so is God, how devoutly and justly and blamelessly we behaved toward you believers. 11 As you know, we treated each one of you as a father treats his children,[m] 12 exhorting and encouraging you and insisting that you conduct yourselves as worthy of the God who calls you into his kingdom and glory.[n]

***Further Thanksgiving.*** 13 And for this reason we too give thanks to God unceasingly, that, in receiving the word of God from hearing us, you received not a human word but, as it truly is, the word of God, which is now at work in you who believe. 14* For you, brothers, have become imitators of the churches of God that are in Judea in Christ Jesus. For you suffer the same things from your compatriots as they did from the Jews, 15* who killed both the Lord Jesus and the prophets and perse-

2:12, 19; 3:13; 4:13–5:11; 5:23).

**1:6 Imitators**: the Pauline theme of "imitation" (see 1 Thes 2:14; 1 Cor 4:16; 11:1; 2 Thes 3:9) is rooted in Paul's view of solidarity in Christ through sharing in Jesus' cross and in the Spirit of the risen Lord.

**2:4 Judged worthy**: Paul regards "worthiness" not as grounded in one's own talent or moral self-righteousness but in God's discernment of genuinely selfless attitudes and actions (see 2 Cor 10:17–18).

**2:7 Gentle**: many excellent manuscripts read "infants" (*nēpioi*), but "gentle" (*ēpioi*) better suits the context here.

**2:14** Luke's picture of the persecutions at Philippi (by Gentiles) and in Thessalonica and Beroea (by Jews) seems to be considerably schematized (Acts 16:11–40; 17:1–15). Paul pictures the Thessalonian community as composed of converts from paganism (1 Thes 1:9) and speaks here of persecution by their (pagan) compatriots rather than by Jews.

**2:15–16** Paul is speaking of historical opposition on the part of Palestinian Jews in particular and does so only some twenty years after Jesus' crucifixion. Even so, he quickly proceeds to depict the persecutors typologically, in apocalyptic terms. His remarks give no grounds for anti-Semitism to those willing to understand him, especially in view of Paul's

*c:* 2 Thes 2:13. *d:* Acts 13:52; 17:1–9. *e:* 2 Thes 1:4; 1 Cor 4:16; 11:1 / 2:14; Phil 3:17. *f:* Rom 1:8. *g:* Acts 14:15; Gal 4:8 / 4:5. *h:* Rom 2:1–16; 5:9; 13:4 / 5:9. *i:* Acts 16:19–17:10. *j:* Gal 1:10. *k:* Jn 5:41, 44; 1 Cor 10:31; 2 Cor 4:17. *l:* Acts 20:34; 1 Cor 4:12; 9:3–18; 2 Thes 3:7–9. *m:* Acts 20:31. *n:* 1 Pt 5:10 / 4:7; 2 Thes 2:14.

cuted us; they do not please God, and are opposed to everyone,[o] 16 trying to prevent us
from speaking to the Gentiles that they may
be saved, thus constantly filling up the measure of their sins. But the wrath of God has finally begun to come upon them.[p]
*Paul's Recent Travel Plans.* 17 Brothers,
when we were bereft of you for a short time,
in person, not in heart, we were all the more
eager in our great desire to see you in person.[q] 18 We decided to go to you—I, Paul, not
only once but more than once—yet Satan
thwarted us.[r] 19 For what is our hope or joy or
crown to boast of in the presence of our Lord
Jesus at his coming if not you yourselves?[s]
20 For you are our glory and joy.

### CHAPTER 3

See RG 404–405

1 That is why, when we could bear it
no longer, we decided to remain alone in
Athens[t] 2 and sent Timothy, our brother and
co-worker for God in the gospel of Christ, to
strengthen and encourage you in your faith,[u]
3 so that no one be disturbed in these afflictions. For you yourselves know that we are
destined* for this. 4 For even when we were
among you, we used to warn you in advance
that we would undergo affliction, just as has
happened, as you know.[v] 5 For this reason,
when I too could bear it no longer, I sent to
learn about your faith, for fear that somehow
the tempter had put you to the test and our
toil might come to nothing.
6 But just now Timothy has returned to us
from you, bringing us the good news of your
faith and love, and that you always think
kindly of us and long to see us as we long to
see you. 7 Because of this, we have been reassured about you, brothers, in our every distress and affliction, through your faith. 8 For
we now live, if you stand firm in the Lord.
*Concluding Thanksgiving and Prayer.*
9* What thanksgiving, then, can we render to
God for you, for all the joy we feel on your
account before our God? 10 Night and day we
pray beyond measure to see you in person
and to remedy the deficiencies of your faith.
11 Now may God himself, our Father, and our
Lord Jesus direct our way to you, 12 and may
the Lord make you increase and abound in
love for one another and for all, just as we
have for you,[w] 13 so as to strengthen your
hearts, to be blameless in holiness before our
God and Father at the coming of our Lord
Jesus with all his holy ones. [Amen.][x]

## III. Specific Exhortations

### CHAPTER 4

See RG 405–406

*General Exhortations.* 1 Finally, brothers, we earnestly ask and exhort you in the
Lord Jesus that, as you received from us how
you should conduct yourselves to please
God—and as you are conducting yourselves—you do so even more. 2 For you
know what instructions* we gave you
through the Lord Jesus.
*Holiness in Sexual Contact.** 3 This is the

pride in his own ethnic and religious background (Rom 9:1–5; 10:1; 11:1–3; Phil 3:4–6). Sinful conduct (1 Thes 2:16) is itself an anticipation of the ultimate wrath or judgment of God (Rom 1:18–2:5), whether or not it is perceived as such.

**3:3 We are destined**: the Greek phraseology and the context suggest Paul's concern to alert his readers to difficulties he knew they would necessarily face and to enable them to see their present experience in the light of what he warned them would happen in the future. This line of thought is followed in 2 Thes 2:1–15.

**3:9–10** The tension between Paul's optimism concerning the Thessalonians' faith and his worries about their perseverance remains unresolved. Perhaps this is accounted for not only by the continuing harassment but also by the shortness of his own stay in Thessalonica (even if that were over twice as long as the conventional three weeks that Luke assigns to it, Acts 17:2).

**4:2 Instructions**: these include specific guidelines on the basis of the Lord's authority, not necessarily sayings Jesus actually uttered. More profoundly, as 1 Thes 4:8 implies, the instructions are practical principles that Paul worked out in accordance with his understanding of the role of the Spirit.

**4:3–8** Many think that this passage deals with a variety of moral regulations (fornication, adultery, sharp business practices). It can be more specifically interpreted as bringing general norms to bear on a specific problem, namely, marriage within degrees of consanguinity (as between uncle and niece) forbidden in Jewish law but allowed according to a Greek heiress law, which would insure retention of an inheritance within the family and perhaps thereby occasion divorce. In that case, "immorality" (1 Thes 4:3) should be rendered as "unlawful marriage" and "this matter" (1 Thes 4:6) as "a lawsuit." The phrase in 1 Thes 4:4, "acquire a wife for himself," has often been interpreted to mean "control one's body."

*o:* Acts 2:23; 7:52. *p:* Gn 15:16; 2 Mc 6:14 / Rom 1:18; 2:5–6. *q:* 3:10; Rom 1:10–11. *r:* Rom 15:22. *s:* 2 Cor 1:14; Phil 2:16; 4:1. *t:* Acts 17:14. *u:* Acts 16:1–2; 1 Cor 3:5–9. *v:* Acts 14:22; 2 Thes 2:5–7; 2 Tm 3:12. *w:* 4:9–10; 2 Thes 1:3. *x:* 5:23; 1 Cor 1:8.

will of God, your holiness: that you refrain from immorality, 4that each of you know how to acquire a wife for himself in holiness and honor, 5not in lustful passion as do the Gentiles who do not know God;[y] 6not to take advantage of or exploit a brother in this matter, for the Lord is an avenger in all these things, as we told you before and solemnly affirmed. 7For God did not call us to impurity but to holiness. 8Therefore, whoever disregards this, disregards not a human being but God, who [also] gives his holy Spirit to you.[z]

*Mutual Charity.* 9On the subject of mutual charity you have no need for anyone to write you, for you yourselves have been taught by God to love one another.[a] 10Indeed, you do this for all the brothers throughout Macedonia. Nevertheless we urge you, brothers, to progress even more,[b] 11and to aspire to live a tranquil life, to mind your own affairs, and to work with your [own] hands, as we instructed you, 12that you may conduct yourselves properly toward outsiders and not depend on anyone.

*Hope for the Christian Dead.* 13We do not want you to be unaware, brothers, about those who have fallen asleep, so that you may not grieve like the rest, who have no hope. 14For if we believe that Jesus died and rose, so too will God, through Jesus, bring with him those who have fallen asleep.[c] 15Indeed, we tell you this, on the word of the Lord, that we who are alive, who are left until the coming of the Lord,* will surely not precede those who have fallen asleep.[d] 16For the Lord himself, with a word of command, with the voice of an archangel and with the trumpet of God, will come down from heaven, and the dead in Christ will rise first.[e] 17Then we who are alive, who are left, will be caught up together* with them in the clouds to meet the Lord in the air. Thus we shall always be with the Lord. 18Therefore, console one another with these words.

### CHAPTER 5

See RG 405–406

*Vigilance.* 1Concerning times and seasons, brothers, you have no need for anything to be written to you.[f] 2For you yourselves know very well that the day of the Lord will come like a thief at night.[g] 3When people are saying, "Peace and security," then sudden disaster comes upon them, like labor pains upon a pregnant woman, and they will not escape.

4But you, brothers, are not in darkness, for that day to overtake you like a thief.[h] 5For all of you are children of the light* and children of the day. We are not of the night or of darkness. 6Therefore, let us not sleep as the rest do, but let us stay alert and sober.[i] 7Those who sleep go to sleep at night, and those who are drunk get drunk at night. 8But since we are of the day, let us be sober, putting on the breastplate of faith and love and the helmet that is hope for salvation.[j] 9For God did not destine us for wrath, but to gain salvation through our Lord Jesus Christ, 10who died for us, so that whether we are awake or asleep we may live together with him.* 11Therefore, encourage one another and build one another up, as indeed you do.[k]

*Church Order.* 12We ask you, brothers, to respect those who are laboring among you and who are over you in the Lord and who

**4:15 Coming of the Lord**: Paul here assumes that the second coming, or parousia, will occur within his own lifetime but insists that the time or season is unknown (1 Thes 5:1–2). Nevertheless, the most important aspect of the parousia for him was the fulfillment of union with Christ. His pastoral exhortation focuses first on hope for the departed faithful, then (1 Thes 5:1–3) on the need of preparedness for those who have to achieve their goal.

**4:17 Will be caught up together**: literally, snatched up, carried off; cf. 2 Cor 12:2; Rev 12:5. From the Latin verb here used, *rapiemur*, has come the idea of "the rapture," when believers will be transported away from the woes of the world; this construction combines this verse with Mt 24:40–41 (see note there) // Lk 17:34–35 and passages from Revelation in a scheme of millennial dispensationalism.

**5:5 Children of the light**: that is, belonging to the daylight of God's personal revelation and expected to achieve it (an analogous development of imagery that appears in Jn 12:36).

**5:10** Characteristically, Paul plays on words suggesting ultimate and anticipated death and life. Union with the crucified and risen Lord at his parousia is anticipated in some measure in contrasted states of our temporal life. The essential element he urges is our indestructible personal union in Christ's own life (see Rom 5:1–10).

*y:* Ps 79:6; Jer 10:25; 2 Thes 1:8; 1 Pt 3:7. *z:* Lk 10:16. *a:* Jn 6:45; 13:34; 1 Jn 2:20–21, 27; 4:7. *b:* 2 Thes 3:6–12. *c:* 1 Cor 15:3–4, 12, 20. *d:* 1 Cor 15:51; Rev 14:13; 20:4–6. *e:* Mt 24:31; 1 Cor 15:23, 52. *f:* Mt 24:36–45. *g:* 2 Pt 3:10. *h:* Eph 5:8–9. *i:* Mt 24:42; Rom 13:12–13; 1 Pt 5:8. *j:* Is 59:17; Rom 13:11–14; Eph 6:11, 14–17. *k:* Rom 15:2; 1 Cor 8:1; 14:12, 26; Eph 4:29.

admonish you, 13 and to show esteem for them with special love on account of their work. Be at peace among yourselves.

14 We urge you, brothers, admonish the idle, cheer the fainthearted, support the weak, be patient with all. 15 See that no one returns evil for evil; rather, always seek what is good [both] for each other and for all.[l] 16 Rejoice always. 17 Pray without ceasing. 18 In all circumstances give thanks, for this is the will of God for you in Christ Jesus.[m] 19* Do not quench the Spirit. 20 Do not despise prophetic utterances. 21 Test everything; retain what is good. 22 Refrain from every kind of evil.

*Concluding Prayer.* 23* May the God of peace himself make you perfectly holy and may you entirely, spirit, soul, and body, be preserved blameless for the coming of our Lord Jesus Christ.[n] 24 The one who calls you is faithful, and he will also accomplish it. 25 Brothers, pray for us [too].

## IV. Final Greeting

26 Greet all the brothers with a holy kiss.* 27 I adjure you by the Lord that this letter be read to all the brothers. 28 The grace of our Lord Jesus Christ be with you.

**5:19–21** Paul's buoyant encouragement of charismatic freedom sometimes occasioned excesses that he or others had to remedy (see 1 Cor 14; 2 Thes 2:1–15; 2 Pt 3:1–16).

**5:23** Another possible translation is, "May the God of peace himself make you perfectly holy and sanctify your spirit fully, and may both soul and body be preserved blameless for the coming of our Lord Jesus Christ." In either case, Paul is not offering an anthropological or philosophical analysis of human nature. Rather, he looks to the wholeness of what may be called the supernatural and natural aspects of a person's service of God.

**5:26 Kiss**: the holy embrace (see Rom 16:16; 1 Cor 16:20; 2 Cor 13:12; 1 Pt 5:14) was a greeting of respect and affection, perhaps given during a liturgy at which Paul's letter would have been read.

*l:* Prv 20:22; Mt 5:38–42; Rom 12:17. *m:* Eph 5:20. *n:* 2 Thes 3:16.

See RG 407–409

# The Second Letter to the Thessalonians

This letter is addressed to the same church as the letter that precedes it in the canon and contains many expressions parallel to those in the First Letter to the Thessalonians, indeed verbatim with them. Yet other aspects of the contents of the Second Letter to the Thessalonians suggest a more impersonal tone and changed circumstances in the situation at Thessalonica.

The letter begins with an address (2 Thes 1:1–2) that expands only slightly on that of 1 Thes 1:1. It ends with a greeting insisting on its Pauline authority in the face of false claims made in Paul's name (see note on 2 Thes 2:2). The body of the letter falls into three short parts, of which the second is notoriously difficult (2 Thes 2).

The opening thanksgiving and prayer (2 Thes 1:3–12) speak of the Thessalonians' increasing faith and love in the face of outside persecution. God's eventual judgment against persecutors and his salvation for the faithful are already evidenced by the very fact of persecution. The second part (2 Thes 2:1–17), the heart of the letter, deals with a problem threatening the faith of the community. A message involving a prophetic oracle and apparently a forged letter, possibly presented at a liturgical gathering (cf. 2 Thes 2:2 and 1 Cor 14:26–33), to the effect that the day of the Lord and all that it means have already come, has upset the life of the Thessalonian church.

The writer counters their preoccupation with the date of the parousia (or coming again of the Lord Jesus from heaven, 2 Thes 2:1) by recalling Paul's teaching concerning what must happen first and by going on to describe what will happen at the Lord's coming (2 Thes 2:8); he indicates the twofold process by which the "activity of Satan" and God's actions (2 Thes 2:9–11) are working out, namely, a growing division between believers and those who succumb to false prophecy and "the lie." He concludes by insisting on Pauline traditions and by praying for divine strength (2 Thes 2:13–17). The closing part of the letter (2 Thes 3:1–16) deals in particular with the apostle's directives and model style of life and with correction of disorderly elements within the community.

Traditional opinion holds that this letter was written shortly after 1 Thessalonians. Occasionally it has been argued that 2 Thessalonians was written first or that the two letters are addressed to different segments within the church at Thessalonica (2 Thessalonians being directed to the Jewish Christians there) or even that 2 Thessalonians was originally written to some other nearby place where Paul carried out mission work, such as Philippi or Beroea. Increasingly in recent times, however, the opinion has been advanced that 2 Thessalonians is a pseudepigraph, that is, a letter written authoritatively in Paul's name, to maintain apostolic traditions in a later period, perhaps during the last two decades of the first century.

In any case, the presumed audience of Second Thessalonians and certain features of its style and content require that it be read and studied in a Pauline context, particularly that provided by 1 Thessalonians. At the same time, and especially if the letter is regarded as not by Paul himself, its apocalyptic presentation of preconditions for the parousia (2 Thes 2:1–12) may profit from and require recourse to a wider biblical basis for interpretation, namely Old Testament books such as Daniel and Isaiah and especially, in the New Testament, the synoptic apocalyptic discourse (Mk 13; Mt 24–25; Lk 21:5–36) and the Book of Revelation.

The principal divisions of the Second Letter to the Thessalonians are the following:

I. Address (1:1–12)
II. Warning Against Deception Concerning the Parousia (2:1–17)
III. Concluding Exhortations (3:1–16)
IV. Final Greetings (3:17–18)

## I. Address

### CHAPTER 1

See RG 408

***Greeting.**** 1 Paul, Silvanus, and Timothy to the church of the Thessalonians in
God our Father and the Lord Jesus Christ:[a]
2 grace to you and peace from God [our] Father and the Lord Jesus Christ.

***Thanksgiving.*** 3* We ought to thank God
always for you, brothers, as is fitting, because your faith flourishes ever more, and
the love of every one of you for one another
grows ever greater.[b] 4 Accordingly, we ourselves boast of you in the churches of God
regarding your endurance and faith in all
your persecutions and the afflictions you endure.

5 This is evidence of the just judgment of
God, so that you may be considered worthy of the kingdom of God for which you
are suffering.[c] 6 For it is surely just on
God's part to repay with afflictions those
who are afflicting you, 7 and to grant rest
along with us to you who are undergoing
afflictions, at the revelation of the Lord
Jesus from heaven with his mighty angels,
8 in blazing fire, inflicting punishment on
those who do not acknowledge God and
on those who do not obey the gospel of our
Lord Jesus.[d] 9 These will pay the penalty of
eternal ruin, separated from the presence
of the Lord and from the glory of his
power,[e] 10 when he comes to be glorified
among his holy ones* and to be marveled
at on that day among all who have believed, for our testimony to you was believed.[f]

***Prayer.*** 11 To this end, we always pray for
you, that our God may make you worthy of
his calling and powerfully bring to fulfillment every good purpose and every effort of
faith,[g] 12* that the name of our Lord Jesus
may be glorified in you, and you in him,[h] in
accord with the grace of our God and Lord
Jesus Christ.

**1:1–2** On the address, see note on Rom 1:1–7 and cf. 1 Thes 1:1.

**1:3–12** On the thanksgiving, see note on Rom 1:8 and cf. 1 Thes 1:2–10. Paul's gratitude to God for the faith and love of the Thessalonians (2 Thes 1:3) and his Christian pride in their faithful endurance (2 Thes 1:4–5) contrast with the condemnation announced for those who afflict them, a judgment to be carried out at the parousia (2 Thes 1:6–10), which is described in vivid language drawn from Old Testament apocalyptic. A prayer for the fulfillment of God's purpose in the Thessalonians (2 Thes 1:11–12) completes the section, as is customary in a Pauline letter (cf. 1 Thes 1:2–3).

**1:10 Among his holy ones**: in the Old Testament, this term can refer to an angelic throng (cf. also Jude 14), but here, in parallel with **among all who have believed**, it can refer to the triumphant people of God.

**1:12 The grace of our God and Lord Jesus Christ**: the Greek can also be translated, "the grace of our God and of the Lord Jesus Christ."

*a:* 1 Thes 1:1. *b:* 1 Cor 1:4; 1 Thes 1:2; 3:12. *c:* Phil 1:28; 1 Thes 2:12. *d:* Ps 79:5–6; Is 66:15; Jer 10:25. *e:* Is 2:10, 19, 21. *f:* Ps 89:8; Dn 7:18–22, 27; 1 Thes 3:13. *g:* 1 Thes 1:2–3. *h:* Is 66:5.

## II. Warning Against Deception Concerning the Parousia

### CHAPTER 2

See RG 408

***Christ and the Lawless One.**** 1We ask
you, brothers, with regard to the coming of
our Lord Jesus Christ and our assembling
with him,[i] 2not to be shaken out of your
minds suddenly, or to be alarmed either by a
"spirit,"* or by an oral statement, or by a letter allegedly from us to the effect that the
day of the Lord is at hand.[j] 3Let no one deceive you in any way. For unless the apostasy comes first and the lawless one is revealed,* the one doomed to perdition,
4[k]who opposes and exalts himself above
every so-called god and object of worship,
so as to seat himself in the temple of God,*
claiming that he is a god— 5do you not recall that while I was still with you I told you
these things? 6And now you know what is
restraining,* that he may be revealed in his
time. 7* For the mystery of lawlessness is al-

**2:1–17** The Thessalonians have been **shaken** by a message purporting to come from Paul himself that **the day of the Lord** is already present. He warns against this deception in eschatology by citing a scenario of events that must first occur (2 Thes 2:3–12) before the end will come. The overall point Paul makes is the need to reject such lies as Satan sends; he also reaffirms the Thessalonians in their calling (2 Thes 2:13–14). They are to uphold what Paul himself has taught (2 Thes 2:15). There is a concluding prayer for their strengthening (2 Thes 2:16–17). As in 2 Thes 1:8–10, the Old Testament provides a good deal of coloring; cf. especially Is 14:13–14; 66:15, 18–21; Ez 28:2–9; Dn 11:36–37. The contents of 2 Thes 2:3b–8 may come from a previously existing apocalypse. The details have been variously interpreted.

An alternative to the possibilities noted below understands that an oracular utterance, supposedly coming from a prophetic spirit (2 Thes 2:2–3a), has so disrupted the community's thinking that its effects may be compared to those of the mania connected with the worship of the Greek god Dionysus. On this view, the writer seems to allude in 2 Thes 2:6–8 to Dionysiac "seizure," although, of course, ironically, somewhat as Paul alludes to witchcraft ("an evil eye") in Gal 3:1 in speaking of the threat to faith posed by those disturbing the Galatians (Gal 1:6–7; 5:10b). On this view of 2 Thes 2, the Greek participles *katechon* (rendered above as **what is restraining**) and *katechōn* (**the one who restrains**) are to be translated "the seizing power" in 2 Thes 2:6 and "the seizer" in 2 Thes 2:7. They then allude to a pseudocharismatic force or spirit of Dionysiac character that has suddenly taken hold of the Thessalonian community (see 2 Thes 2:2). The addressees **know** (2 Thes 2:6) this force or spirit because of the problem it is causing. This pseudocharismatic force or spirit is a kind of anticipation and advance proof of the ultimate, climactic figure (**the lawless one** or the rebel, 2 Thes 2:3), of which the community has been warned (see note on 1 Thes 3:3). It is, however, only the beginning of the end that the latter's manifestation entails; the end is not yet. For in the course of **the mystery of lawlessness** (2 Thes 2:7), false prophetism, after it ceases in the Thessalonian community, will be manifested in the world at large (2 Thes 2:8–12), where it will also be eliminated in turn by the Lord Jesus.

**2:2 "Spirit"**: a Spirit-inspired utterance or ecstatic revelation. **An oral statement**: literally, a "word" or pronouncement, not necessarily of ecstatic origin. **A letter allegedly sent by us**: possibly a forged letter, so that Paul calls attention in 2 Thes 3:17 to his practice of concluding a genuine letter with a summary note or greeting in his own hand, as at Gal 6:11–18 and elsewhere.

**2:3b–5** This incomplete sentence (anacoluthon, 2 Thes 2:4) recalls what the Thessalonians had already been taught, an apocalyptic scenario depicting, in terms borrowed especially from Dn 11:36–37 and related verses, human self-assertiveness against God in **the temple of God** itself. **The lawless one** represents the climax of such activity in this account.

**2:4 Seat himself in the temple of God**: a reflection of the language in Dn 7:23–25; 8:9–12; 9:27; 11:36–37; 12:11 about the attempt of Antiochus IV Epiphanes to set up a statue of Zeus in the Jerusalem temple and possibly of the Roman emperor Caligula to do a similar thing (Mk 13:14). Here the imagery suggests an attempt to install someone in the place of God, **claiming that he is a god** (cf. Ez 28:2). Usually, it is the Jerusalem temple that is assumed to be meant; on the alternative view sketched above (see note on 2 Thes 2:1–17), **the temple** refers to the Christian community.

**2:6–7 What is restraining . . . the one who restrains**: neuter and masculine, respectively, of a force and person holding back the lawless one. The Thessalonians know what is meant (2 Thes 2:6), but the terms, seemingly found only in this passage and in writings dependent on it, have been variously interpreted. Traditionally, 2 Thes 2:6 has been applied to the Roman empire and 2 Thes 2:7 to the Roman emperor (in Paul's day, Nero) as bulwarks holding back chaos (cf. Rom 13:1–7). A second interpretation suggests that cosmic or angelic powers are binding Satan (2 Thes 2:9) and so restraining him; some relate this to an anti-Christ figure (1 Jn 2:18) or to Michael the archangel (Rev 12:7–9; 20:1–3). A more recent view suggests that it is the preaching of the Christian gospel that restrains the end, for in God's plan the end cannot come until the gospel is preached to all nations (Mk 13:10); in that case, Paul as missionary preacher par excellence is "the one who restrains," whose removal (death) will bring the end (2 Thes 2:7). On the alternative view (see note on 2 Thes 2:1–17), the phrases should be referred to that which and to him who seizes (a prophet) in ecstasy so as to have him speak pseudo-oracles.

**2:7–12 The lawless one** and **the one who restrains** are involved in an activity or process, **the mystery of lawlessness**, behind which **Satan** stands (2 Thes 2:9). The action of the **Lord [Jesus]** in overcoming the lawless one is described in

*i:* 1 Thes 4:13–17. *j:* Mt 24:6; 1 Cor 14:26, 32–33; 1 Thes 5:1–2. *k:* Dn 11:36–37; Ez 28:2. *l:* Mt 13:36–43; Acts 20:29; Gal 5:10; 2 Pt 2:1; Rev 22:11.

ready at work. But the one who restrains is to do so only for the present, until he is removed from the scene.[l] 8 And then the lawless one will be revealed, whom the Lord [Jesus] will kill with the breath of his mouth and render powerless by the manifestation of his coming,[m] 9 the one whose coming springs from the power of Satan in every mighty deed and in signs and wonders that lie,[n] 10 and in every wicked deceit for those who are perishing because they have not accepted the love of truth so that they may be saved. 11 Therefore, God is sending them a deceiving power so that they may believe the lie, 12 that all who have not believed the truth but have approved wrongdoing may be condemned.

13 But we ought to give thanks to God for you always, brothers loved by the Lord, because God chose you as the firstfruits* for salvation through sanctification by the Spirit and belief in truth.[o] 14 To this end he has [also] called you through our gospel to possess the glory of our Lord Jesus Christ.[p] 15 Therefore, brothers, stand firm and hold fast to the traditions that you were taught, either by an oral statement or by a letter of ours.*

16 May our Lord Jesus Christ himself and God our Father, who has loved us and given us everlasting encouragement and good hope through his grace, 17 encourage your hearts and strengthen them in every good deed and word.

## III. Concluding Exhortations*

### CHAPTER 3

See RG 408–409

***Request for Prayers.*** 1 Finally, brothers, pray for us, so that the word of the Lord may speed forward and be glorified, as it did among you,[q] 2 and that we may be delivered from perverse and wicked people, for not all have faith. 3 But the Lord is faithful; he will strengthen you and guard you from the evil one.[r] 4 We are confident of you in the Lord that what we instruct you, you [both] are doing and will continue to do.[s] 5 May the Lord direct your hearts to the love of God and to the endurance of Christ.

***Neglect of Work.*** 6 We instruct you, brothers, in the name of [our] Lord Jesus Christ, to shun any brother who conducts himself in a disorderly way and not according to the tradition they received from us.* 7 For you know how one must imitate us. For we did not act in a disorderly way among you, 8 nor did we eat food received free from anyone. On the contrary, in toil and drudgery, night and day we worked, so as not to burden any of you.[t] 9 Not that we do not have the right. Rather, we wanted to present ourselves as a model for you, so that you might imitate us.[u] 10 In fact, when we were with you, we instructed you that if anyone was unwilling to work, neither should that one eat.[v] 11 We hear that some are conducting themselves among you in a

Old Testament language (**with the breath of his mouth**; cf. Is 11:4; Jb 4:9; Rev 19:15). His **coming** is literally the Lord's "parousia." The biblical concept of the "holy war," eschatologically conceived, may underlie the imagery.

**2:13 As the firstfruits**: there is also strong manuscript evidence for the reading, "God chose you from the beginning," thus providing a focus on God's activity from beginning to end; **firstfruits** is a Pauline term, however; cf. Rom 8:23; 11:16; 16:5 among other references.

**2:15** Reference to **an oral statement** and **a letter** (2 Thes 2:2) and the content here, including a formula of conclusion (cf. 1 Cor 16:13; Gal 5:1), suggest that 2 Thes 2:1–15 or even 2 Thes 2:1–17 are to be taken as a literary unit, notwithstanding the incidental thanksgiving formula in 2 Thes 2:13.

**3:1–18** The final chapter urges the Thessalonians to pray for Paul and his colleagues (2 Thes 3:1–2) and reiterates confidence in the Thessalonians (2 Thes 3:3–5), while admonishing them about a specific problem in their community that has grown out of the intense eschatological speculation, namely, not to work but to become instead disorderly busybodies (2 Thes 3:6–15). A benediction (2 Thes 3:16) and postscript in Paul's own hand round out the letter. On 2 Thes 3:17–18, cf. note on 2 Thes 2:2.

**3:6** Some members of the community, probably because they regarded the parousia as imminent or the new age of the Lord to be already here (2 Thes 2:2), had apparently ceased to work for a living. The disciplinary problem they posed could be rooted in distorted thinking about Paul's own teaching (cf. 1 Thes 2:16; 3:3–4; 5:4–5) or, more likely, in a forged letter (2 Thes 2:2) and the type of teaching dealt with in 2 Thes 2:1–15. The apostle's own moral teaching, reflected in his selfless labors for others, was rooted in a deep doctrinal concern for the gospel message (cf. 1 Thes 2:3–10).

*m:* Is 11:4; Rev 19:15. *n:* Mt 24:24; Rev 13:13. *o:* 1 Thes 2:13; 5:9. *p:* Rom 5:1–10; 8:29–30; 1 Thes 4:7; 5:9. *q:* Eph 6:19; Col 4:3. *r:* 1 Thes 5:24 / 1 Cor 16:13 / Mt 6:13. *s:* 2 Cor 7:16; 1 Thes 4:1–2. *t:* 1 Thes 2:9. *u:* Mt 10:10; Phil 3:17. *v:* 1 Thes 4:11.

disorderly way, by not keeping busy but minding the business of others.[w] 12 Such people we instruct and urge in the Lord Jesus Christ to work quietly and to eat their own food. 13 But you, brothers, do not be remiss in doing good. 14 If anyone does not obey our word as expressed in this letter, take note of this person not to associate with him, that he may be put to shame. 15 Do not regard him as an enemy but admonish him as a brother.[x] 16 May the Lord of peace himself give you peace at all times and in every way. The Lord be with all of you.[y]

## IV. Final Greetings

17 This greeting is in my own hand, Paul's. This is the sign in every letter; this is how I write.[z] 18 The grace of our Lord Jesus Christ be with all of you.

*w:* 1 Thes 5:14. *x:* 2 Cor 2:7; Gal 6:1. *y:* Jn 14:27; Rom 15:33. *z:* 1 Cor 16:21; Gal 6:11.

See RG 410–14

# The First Letter to Timothy

The three letters, First and Second Timothy and Titus, form a distinct group within the Pauline corpus. In the collection of letters by the Apostle to the Gentiles, they differ from the others in form and contents. All three suggest they were written late in Paul's career. The opponents are not "Judaizers" as in Galatians but false teachers stressing "knowledge" (*gnōsis*; see note on 1 Tm 6:20–21). Attention is given especially to correct doctrine and church organization. Jesus' second coming recedes into the background compared to references in Paul's earlier letters (though not Colossians and Ephesians). The three letters are addressed not to congregations but to those who shepherd congregations (Latin, *pastores*). These letters were first named "Pastoral Epistles" in the eighteenth century because they all are concerned with the work of a pastor in caring for the community or communities under his charge.

The first of the Pastorals, 1 Timothy, is presented as having been written from Macedonia. Timothy, whom Paul converted, was of mixed Jewish and Gentile parentage (Acts 16:1–3). He was the apostle's companion on both the second and the third missionary journeys (Acts 16:3; 19:22) and was often sent by him on special missions (Acts 19:22; 1 Cor 4:17; 1 Thes 3:2). In 1 Timothy (1 Tm 1:3), he is described as the administrator of the entire Ephesian community.

The letter instructs Timothy on his duty to restrain false and useless teaching (1 Tm 1:3–11; 4:1–5; 6:3–16) and proposes principles pertaining to his relationship with the older members of the community (1 Tm 5:1–2) and with the presbyters (1 Tm 5:17–22). It gives rules for aid to widows (1 Tm 5:3–8) and their selection for charitable ministrations (1 Tm 5:9–16) and also deals with liturgical celebrations (1 Tm 2:1–15), selections for the offices of bishop and deacon (1 Tm 3:1–13), relation of slaves with their masters (1 Tm 6:1–2), and obligations of the wealthier members of the community (1 Tm 6:17–19). This letter also reminds Timothy of the prophetic character of his office (1 Tm 1:12–20) and encourages him in his exercise of it (1 Tm 4:6–16). The central passage of the letter (1 Tm 3:14–16) expresses the principal motive that should guide the conduct of Timothy—preservation of the purity of the church's doctrine against false teaching. On this same note the letter concludes (1 Tm 6:20–21).

From the late second century to the nineteenth, Pauline authorship of the three Pastoral Epistles went unchallenged. Since then, the attribution of these letters to Paul has been questioned. Most scholars are convinced that Paul could not have been responsible for the vocabulary and style, the concept of church organization, or the theological expressions found in these letters. A second group believes, on the basis of statistical evidence, that the vocabulary and style are Pauline, even if at first sight the contrary seems to be the case. They state that the concept of church organization in the letters is not as advanced as the questioners of Pauline authorship hold since the notion of hierarchical order in a religious community existed in Israel before the time of Christ, as evidenced in the Dead Sea Scrolls. Finally, this group sees affinities between the theological thought of the Pastorals and that of the unquestionably genuine letters of Paul. Other scholars, while conceding a degree of validity to the positions mentioned above, suggest that the apostle made use of a secretary who was responsible for the composition of the letters. A fourth group of scholars believes that these letters are the work of a compiler, that they are based on traditions about Paul in his later years, and that they include, in varying amounts, actual fragments of genuine Pauline correspondence.

If Paul is considered the more immediate author, the Pastorals are to be dated between the end of his first Roman imprisonment (Acts 28:16) and his execution under Nero (A.D. 63–67); if they are regarded as only more remotely Pauline, their date may be as late as the early second century. In spite of these problems of authorship and dating, the Pastorals are illustrative of early Christian life and remain an important element of canonical scripture.

The principal divisions of the First Letter to Timothy are the following:

I. Address (1:1–2)
II. Sound Teaching (1:3–20)
III. Problems of Discipline (2:1–4:16)
IV. Duties Toward Others (5:1–6:2a)
V. False Teaching and True Wealth (6:2b–19)
VI. Final Recommendation and Warning (6:20–21)

# I. Address

## CHAPTER 1

See RG 411-12

*Greeting.** 1 Paul, an apostle of Christ
Jesus by command of God our savior and of
Christ Jesus our hope,[a] 2 to Timothy, my true
child in faith: grace, mercy, and peace from
God the Father and Christ Jesus our Lord.[b]

# II. Sound Teaching

*Warning Against False Doctrine.* 3* I repeat
the request I made of you when I was on my
way to Macedonia,[c] that you stay in Ephesus
to instruct certain people not to teach false
doctrines 4* or to concern themselves with
myths and endless genealogies, which promote speculations rather than the plan of
God that is to be received by faith.[d] 5 The aim
of this instruction is love from a pure heart,
a good conscience, and a sincere faith.[e]
6 Some people have deviated from these and
turned to meaningless talk,[f] 7 wanting to be
teachers of the law, but without understanding either what they are saying or what they
assert with such assurance.

8* We know that the law is good, provided
that one uses it as law,[g] 9 with the understanding that law is meant not for a righteous
person but for the lawless and unruly, the
godless and sinful, the unholy and profane,
those who kill their fathers or mothers, murderers, 10 the unchaste, sodomites,* kidnappers, liars, perjurers, and whatever else is
opposed to sound teaching,[h] 11 according to
the glorious gospel of the blessed God, with
which I have been entrusted.[i]

*Gratitude for God's Mercy.** 12 I am grateful
to him who has strengthened me, Christ
Jesus our Lord, because he considered me
trustworthy in appointing me to the ministry.[j]

**1:1–2** For the Pauline use of the conventional epistolary form, see note on Rom 1:1–7.

**1:3–7** Here Timothy's initial task **in Ephesus** (cf. Acts 20:17–35) is outlined: to suppress the idle religious speculations, probably about Old Testament figures (1 Tm 1:3–4, but see note on 1 Tm 6:20–21), which do not contribute to the development of love within the community (1 Tm 1:5) but rather encourage similar useless conjectures (1 Tm 1:6–7).

**1:4** The **plan of God that is to be received by faith**: the Greek may also possibly mean "God's trustworthy plan" or "the training in faith that God requires."

**1:8–11** Those responsible for the speculations that are to be suppressed by Timothy do not present the Old Testament from the Christian viewpoint. The Christian values the Old Testament not as a system of law but as the first stage in God's revelation of his saving plan, which is brought to fulfillment in the good news of salvation through faith in Jesus Christ.

**1:10 Sodomites**: see 1 Cor 6:9 and the note there.

**1:12–17** Present gratitude for the Christian apostleship leads Paul to recall an earlier time when he had been a fierce persecutor of the Christian communities (cf. Acts 26:9–11) until his conversion by intervention of divine mercy through the appearance of Jesus. This and his subsequent apostolic experience testify to the saving purpose of Jesus' incarnation. The fact of his former ignorance of the truth has not kept the apostle from regarding himself as having been the worst of sinners (1 Tm 1:15). Yet he was chosen to be an apostle, that God might manifest his firm will to save sinful humanity through Jesus Christ (1 Tm 1:16). The recounting of so great a mystery leads to a spontaneous outpouring of adoration (1 Tm 1:17).

*a:* 2:3; Lk 1:47; Ti 1:3; 2:10 / Col 1:27. *b:* 2 Tm 1:2; Ti 1:4. *c:* Acts 20:1. *d:* 4:7; Ti 1:14; 3:9; 2 Pt 1:16. *e:* Rom 13:10. *f:* 6:4, 20; Ti 1:10. *g:* Rom 7:12, 16. *h:* 4:6; 6:3; 2 Tm 4:3; Ti 1:9; 2:1. *i:* Ti 1:3. *j:* Phil 4:13 / Acts 9:15; Gal 1:15–16.

13I was once a blasphemer and a persecutor
and an arrogant man, but I have been mercifully treated because I acted out of ignorance
in my unbelief.[k] 14Indeed, the grace of our
Lord has been abundant, along with the faith
and love that are in Christ Jesus.[l] 15This saying is trustworthy* and deserves full acceptance: Christ Jesus came into the world to
save sinners. Of these I am the foremost.[m]
16But for that reason I was mercifully treated,
so that in me, as the foremost, Christ Jesus
might display all his patience as an example
for those who would come to believe in him
for everlasting life. 17To the king of ages,* incorruptible, invisible, the only God, honor
and glory forever and ever. Amen.[n]
***Responsibility of Timothy.**** 18I entrust this
charge to you, Timothy, my child, in accordance with the prophetic words once spoken
about you.* Through them may you fight a
good fight[o] 19by having faith and a good
conscience. Some, by rejecting conscience,
have made a shipwreck of their faith,[p]
20among them Hymenaeus* and Alexander,
whom I have handed over to Satan to be
taught not to blaspheme.[q]

# III. Problems of Discipline

## CHAPTER 2

See RG 412-13

***Prayer and Conduct.*** 1* First of all,
then, I ask that supplications, prayers, petitions, and thanksgivings be offered for
everyone,[r] 2for kings and for all in authority,
that we may lead a quiet and tranquil life in
all devotion and dignity. 3This is good and
pleasing to God our savior,[s] 4who wills
everyone to be saved and to come to knowledge of the truth.[t]

5 For there is one God.
There is also one mediator between God
and the human race,
Christ Jesus, himself human,[u]
6 who gave himself as ransom for all.

This was the testimony* at the proper time.[v]
7For this I was appointed preacher and apostle (I am speaking the truth, I am not lying),
teacher of the Gentiles in faith and truth.[w]
8* It is my wish, then, that in every place
the men should pray, lifting up holy hands,
without anger or argument. 9Similarly, [too,]

**1:15 This saying is trustworthy**: this phrase regularly introduces in the Pastorals a basic truth of early Christian faith; cf. 1 Tm 3:1; 4:9; 2 Tm 2:11; Ti 3:8.

**1:17 King of ages**: through Semitic influence, the Greek expression could mean "everlasting king"; it could also mean "king of the universe."

**1:18–20** Timothy is to be mindful of his calling, which is here compared to the way Barnabas and Saul were designated by Christ as prophets for missionary service; cf. Acts 13:1–3. Such is probably the sense of the allusion to the prophetic words (1 Tm 1:18). His task is not to yield, whether in doctrine or in conduct, to erroneous opinions, taking warning from what has already happened at Ephesus in the case of Hymenaeus and Alexander (1 Tm 1:19–20).

**1:18 The prophetic words once spoken about you**: the Greek may also be translated, "the prophecies that led (me) to you." It probably refers to testimonies given by charismatic figures in the Christian communities. **Fight a good fight**: this translation preserves the play on words in Greek. The Greek terms imply a lengthy engagement in battle and might well be translated "wage a good campaign."

**1:20 Hymenaeus**: mentioned in 2 Tm 2:17 as saying that the resurrection has already taken place (in baptism). **Alexander**: probably the Alexander mentioned in 2 Tm 4:14 as the coppersmith who "did me a great deal of harm." **Whom I have handed over to Satan**: the same terms are used in the condemnation of the incestuous man in 1 Cor 5:5.

**2:1–7** This marked insistence that the liturgical prayer of the community concern itself with the needs of all, whether Christian or not, and especially of those in authority, may imply that a disposition existed at Ephesus to refuse prayer for pagans. In actuality, such prayer aids the community to achieve peaceful relationships with non-Christians (1 Tm 2:2) and contributes to salvation, since it derives its value from the presence within the community of Christ, who is the one and only savior of all (1 Tm 2:3–6). The vital apostolic mission to the Gentiles (1 Tm 2:7) reflects Christ's purpose of universal salvation. 1 Tm 2:5 contains what may well have been a very primitive creed. Some interpreters have called it a Christian version of the Jewish *shema*: "Hear, O Israel, the LORD is our God, the LORD alone . . ." (Dt 6:4–5). The assertion in 1 Tm 2:7, "I am speaking the truth, I am not lying," reminds one of similar affirmations in Rom 9:1; 2 Cor 11:31; and Gal 1:20.

**2:6 The testimony**: to make sense of this overly concise phrase, many manuscripts supply "to which" (or "to whom"); two others add "was given." The translation has supplied "this was."

**2:8–15** The prayer of the community should be unmarred by internal dissension (1 Tm 2:8); cf. Mt 5:21–26; 6:14; Mk 11:25. At the liturgical assembly the dress of women should be appro-

---

*k:* Acts 8:3; 9:1–2; 1 Cor 15:9; Gal 1:13. *l:* Rom 5:20; 2 Tm 1:13. *m:* Lk 15:2; 19:10. *n:* Rom 16:27. *o:* 4:14 / 6:12; 2 Tm 4:7; Jude 3. *p:* 3:9. *q:* 2 Tm 2:17; 4:14 / 1 Cor 5:5. *r:* Eph 6:18; Phil 4:6. *s:* 1:1; 4:10. *t:* 2 Tm 3:7; 2 Pt 3:9. *u:* 1 Cor 8:6; Heb 8:6; 9:15; 12:24 / Rom 5:15. *v:* Mk 10:45; Gal 1:4; 2:20; Eph 5:25; Ti 2:14. *w:* Acts 9:15; 1 Cor 9:1; Gal 2:7–8.

women should adorn themselves with
proper conduct, with modesty and self-control, not with braided hairstyles and gold ornaments, or pearls, or expensive clothes,[x]
10 but rather, as befits women who profess
reverence for God, with good deeds.[y] 11 A
woman must receive instruction silently and
under complete control.[z] 12 I do not permit a
woman to teach or to have authority over a
man.* She must be quiet. 13 For Adam was
formed first, then Eve.[a] 14 Further, Adam was
not deceived, but the woman was deceived
and transgressed.[b] 15 But she will be saved
through motherhood, provided women persevere in faith and love and holiness, with
self-control.[c]

## CHAPTER 3

See RG 412-13

### *Qualifications of Various Ministers.*

1* This saying is trustworthy:* whoever as-
pires to the office of bishop desires a noble
task.[d] 2 Therefore, a bishop must be irreproachable, married only once, temperate,
self-controlled, decent, hospitable, able to
teach, 3 not a drunkard, not aggressive, but
gentle, not contentious, not a lover of
money.[e] 4 He must manage his own household well, keeping his children under control
with perfect dignity; 5 for if a man does not
know how to manage his own household,
how can he take care of the church of God?
6 He should not be a recent convert, so that he
may not become conceited and thus incur the
devil's punishment.* 7 He must also have a
good reputation among outsiders, so that he
may not fall into disgrace, the devil's trap.[f]
8* Similarly, deacons must be dignified,
not deceitful, not addicted to drink, not
greedy for sordid gain, 9 holding fast to the
mystery of the faith with a clear conscience.
10 Moreover, they should be tested first; then,
if there is nothing against them, let them
serve as deacons. 11 Women,* similarly,
should be dignified, not slanderers, but temperate and faithful in everything.[g] 12 Deacons
may be married only once and must manage
their children and their households well.
13 Thus those who serve well as deacons gain
good standing and much confidence in their
faith in Christ Jesus.

*The Mystery of Our Religion.** 14 I am writing you about these matters, although I hope
to visit you soon. 15 But if I should be delayed,
you should know how to behave in the house-

priate to the occasion (1 Tm 2:9); their chief adornment is to be reputation for good works (1 Tm 2:10). Women are not to take part in the charismatic activity of the assembly (1 Tm 2:11–12; cf. 1 Cor 14:34) or exercise authority; their conduct there should reflect the role of man's helpmate (1 Tm 2:13; cf. Gn 2:18) and not the later relationship of Eve to Adam (1 Tm 2:14; cf. Gn 3:6–7). As long as women perform their role as wives and mothers in faith and love, their salvation is assured (1 Tm 2:15).

**2:12 A man**: this could also mean "her husband."

**3:1–7** The passage begins by commending those who aspire to the office of bishop (*episkopos*; see note on Phil 1:1) within the community, but this first sentence (1 Tm 3:1) may also imply a warning about the great responsibilities involved. The writer proceeds to list the qualifications required: personal stability and graciousness; talent for teaching (1 Tm 3:2); moderation in habits and temperament (1 Tm 3:3); managerial ability (1 Tm 3:4); and experience in Christian living (1 Tm 3:5–6). Moreover, the candidate's previous life should provide no grounds for the charge that he did not previously practice what he now preaches. No list of qualifications for presbyters appears in 1 Timothy. The presbyter-bishops here and in Titus (see note on Ti 1:5–9) lack certain functions reserved here for Paul and Timothy.

**3:1 This saying is trustworthy**: the saying introduced is so unlike others after this phrase that some later Western manuscripts read, "This saying is popular." It is understood by some interpreters as concluding the preceding section (1 Tm 2:8–15). **Bishop**: literally, "overseer"; see note on Phil 1:1.

**3:6 The devil's punishment**: this phrase could mean the punishment once incurred by the devil (objective genitive) or a punishment brought about by the devil (subjective genitive).

**3:8–13** Deacons, besides possessing the virtue of moderation (1 Tm 3:8), are to be outstanding for their faith (1 Tm 3:9) and well respected within the community (1 Tm 3:10). Women in the same role, although some interpreters take them to mean wives of deacons, must be dignified, temperate, dedicated, and not given to malicious talebearing (1 Tm 3:11). Deacons must have shown stability in marriage and have a good record with their families (1 Tm 3:12), for such experience prepares them well for the exercise of their ministry on behalf of the community (1 Tm 3:13). See further the note on Phil 1:1.

**3:11 Women**: this seems to refer to women deacons but may possibly mean wives of deacons. The former is preferred because the word is used absolutely; if deacons' wives were meant, a possessive "their" would be expected. Moreover, they are also introduced by the word "similarly," as in 1 Tm 3:8; this parallel suggests that they too exercised ecclesiastical functions.

**3:14–16** In case there is some delay in the visit to Timothy at Ephesus planned for the near future, the present letter is being sent on ahead to arm and enlighten him in his task of preserving sound Christian conduct in the Ephesian church. The care he must exercise over this community is required by the profound nature of Christianity. It centers in Christ, appear-

*x:* 1 Pt 3:3–5. *y:* 5:10; 1 Pt 3:1. *z:* 1 Cor 14:34–35. *a:* Gn 1:27; 2:7, 22; 1 Cor 11:8–9. *b:* Gn 3:6, 13; 2 Cor 11:3. *c:* 5:14. *d:* Ti 1:6–9. *e:* Heb 13:5. *f:* 2 Cor 8:21; 2 Tm 2:26. *g:* Ti 2:3.

hold of God, which is the church of the living God, the pillar and foundation of truth.[h] 16 Undeniably great is the mystery of devotion,

Who* was manifested in the flesh,
vindicated in the spirit,
seen by angels,
proclaimed to the Gentiles,
believed in throughout the world,
taken up in glory.[i]

See RG 412–13

## CHAPTER 4

*False Asceticism.** 1 Now the Spirit explicitly says that in the last times some will turn away from the faith by paying attention to deceitful spirits and demonic instructions[j] 2 through the hypocrisy of liars with branded consciences. 3 They forbid marriage and require abstinence from foods that God created to be received with thanksgiving by those who believe and know the truth.[k] 4 For everything created by God is good, and nothing is to be rejected when received with thanksgiving,[l] 5 for it is made holy by the invocation of God in prayer.*

*Counsel to Timothy.* 6* If you will give these instructions to the brothers, you will be a good minister of Christ Jesus, nourished on the words of the faith and of the sound teaching you have followed. 7 Avoid profane and silly myths. Train yourself for devotion,[m] 8 for, while physical training is of limited value, devotion is valuable in every respect, since it holds a promise of life both for the present and for the future.[n] 9 This saying is trustworthy and deserves full acceptance.[o] 10 For this we toil and struggle,* because we have set our hope on the living God, who is the savior of all, especially of those who believe.[p]

11* Command and teach these things. 12 Let no one have contempt for your youth,* but set an example for those who believe, in speech, conduct, love, faith, and purity.[q] 13 Until I arrive, attend to the reading,* exhortation, and teaching. 14 Do not neglect the gift you have, which was conferred on you through the prophetic word* with the imposition of hands of the presbyterate.[r] 15 Be diligent in these matters, be absorbed in them, so that your progress may be evident

ing in human flesh, vindicated by the holy Spirit; the mystery of his person was revealed to the angels, announced to the Gentiles, and accepted by them in faith. He himself was taken up (through his resurrection and ascension) to the divine glory (1 Tm 3:16). This passage apparently includes part of a liturgical hymn used among the Christian communities in and around Ephesus. It consists of three couplets in typical Hebrew balance: flesh-spirit (contrast), seen-proclaimed (complementary), world-glory (contrast).

**3:16 Who**: the reference is to Christ, who is himself "the mystery of our devotion." Some predominantly Western manuscripts read "which," harmonizing the gender of the pronoun with that of the Greek word for mystery; many later (eighth/ninth century on), predominantly Byzantine manuscripts read "God," possibly for theological reasons.

**4:1–5** Doctrinal deviations from the true Christian message within the church have been prophesied, though the origin of the prophecy is not specified (1 Tm 4:1–2); cf. Acts 20:29–30. The letter warns against a false asceticism that prohibits marriage and regards certain foods as forbidden, though they are part of God's good creation (1 Tm 4:3).

**4:5 The invocation of God in prayer**: literally, "the word of God and petition." The use of "word of God" without an article in Greek suggests that it refers to the name of God being invoked in blessing rather than to the "word of God" proclaimed to the community.

**4:6–10** Timothy is urged to be faithful, both in his teaching and in his own life, as he looks only to God for salvation.

**4:10 Struggle**: other manuscripts and patristic witnesses read "suffer reproach."

**4:11–16** Timothy is urged to preach and teach with confidence, relying on the gifts and the mission that God has bestowed on him.

**4:12 Youth**: some commentators find this reference a sign of pseudepigraphy. Timothy had joined Paul as a missionary already in A.D. 49, some fifteen years before the earliest supposed date of composition.

**4:13 Reading**: the Greek word refers to private or public reading. Here, it probably designates the public reading of scripture in the Christian assembly.

**4:14 Prophetic word**: this may mean the utterance of a Christian prophet designating the candidate or a prayer of blessing accompanying the rite. **Imposition of hands**: this gesture was used in the Old Testament to signify the transmission of authority from Moses to Joshua (Nm 27:18–23; Dt 34:9). The early Christian community used it as a symbol of installation into an office: the Seven (Acts 6:6) and Paul and Barnabas (Acts 13:3). **Of the presbyterate**: this would mean that each member of the college of presbyters imposed hands and appears to contradict 2 Tm 1:6, in which Paul says that he imposed hands on Timothy. This latter text, however, does not exclude participation by others in the rite. Some prefer to translate "for the presbyterate," and thus understand it to designate the office into which Timothy was installed rather than the agents who installed him.

*h:* Eph 2:19–22. *i:* Jn 1:14; Rom 1:3–4. *j:* 2 Tm 3:1; 4:3; 2 Pt 3:3; Jude 18. *k:* Gn 9:3; Rom 14:6; 1 Cor 10:30–31. *l:* Gn 1:31; Acts 10:15. *m:* 1:4; 2 Tm 2:16; Ti 1:14. *n:* 6:6. *o:* 1:15; 2 Tm 2:11; Ti 3:8. *p:* 2:4; Ti 2:11. *q:* 1 Cor 16:11; Ti 2:15 / Phil 3:17. *r:* 5:22; Acts 6:6; 8:17; 2 Tm 1:6.

to everyone. 16 Attend to yourself and to your teaching; persevere in both tasks, for by doing so you will save both yourself and those who listen to you.

## IV. Duties Toward Others

### CHAPTER 5

See RG 413

1* Do not rebuke an older man, but appeal to him as a father. Treat younger men as brothers,[s] 2 older women as mothers, and younger women as sisters with complete purity.

***Rules for Widows.*** 3 Honor widows who are truly widows. 4 But if a widow has children or grandchildren, let these first learn to perform their religious duty to their own family and to make recompense to their parents, for this is pleasing to God. 5 The real widow, who is all alone, has set her hope on God and continues in supplications and prayers night and day.[t] 6 But the one who is self-indulgent is dead while she lives. 7 Command this, so that they may be irreproachable. 8 And whoever does not provide for relatives and especially family members has denied the faith and is worse than an unbeliever.

9 Let a widow be enrolled if she is not less than sixty years old, married only once, 10 with a reputation for good works, namely, that she has raised children, practiced hospitality, washed the feet of the holy ones, helped those in distress, involved herself in every good work.[u] 11 But exclude younger widows, for when their sensuality estranges them from Christ, they want to marry 12 and will incur condemnation for breaking their first pledge. 13 And furthermore, they learn to be idlers, going about from house to house, and not only idlers but gossips and busybodies as well, talking about things that ought not to be mentioned.[v] 14 So I would like younger widows to marry, have children, and manage a home, so as to give the adversary no pretext for maligning us.[w] 15 For some have already turned away to follow Satan. 16 If any woman believer* has widowed relatives, she must assist them; the church is not to be burdened, so that it will be able to help those who are truly widows.

***Rules for Presbyters.**** 17 Presbyters who preside well deserve double honor, especially those who toil in preaching and teaching.[x] 18 For the scripture says, "You shall not muzzle an ox when it is threshing," and, "A worker deserves his pay."[y] 19 Do not accept an accusation against a presbyter unless it is supported by two or three witnesses.[z] 20 Reprimand publicly those who do sin, so that the rest also will be afraid.[a] 21 I charge you before God and Christ Jesus and the elect angels to keep these rules without prejudice, doing nothing out of favoritism. 22 Do not lay hands too readily on anyone, and do not share in an-

**5:1–16** After a few words of general advice based on common sense (1 Tm 5:1–2), the letter takes up, in its several aspects, the subject of widows. The first responsibility for their care belongs to the family circle, not to the Christian community as such (1 Tm 5:3–4, 16). The widow left without the aid of relatives may benefit the community by her prayer, and the community should consider her material sustenance its responsibility (1 Tm 5:5–8). Widows who wish to work directly for the Christian community should not be accepted unless they are well beyond the probability of marriage, i.e., sixty years of age, married only once, and with a reputation for good works (1 Tm 5:9–10). Younger widows are apt to be troublesome and should be encouraged to remarry (1 Tm 5:11–15).

**5:16 Woman believer**: some early Latin manuscripts and Fathers have a masculine here, while most later manuscripts and patristic quotations conflate the two readings, perhaps to avoid unfair restriction to women.

**5:17–25** The function of presbyters is not exactly the same as that of the *episkopos*, "bishop" (1 Tm 3:1); in fact, the relation of the two at the time of this letter is obscure (but cf. note on Ti 1:5–9). The Pastorals seem to reflect a transitional stage that developed in many regions of the church into the monarchical episcopate of the second and third centuries. The presbyters possess the responsibility of preaching and teaching, for which functions they are supported by the community (1 Tm 5:17–18). The realization that their position subjects them to adverse criticism is implied in the direction to Timothy (1 Tm 5:19–20) to make sure of the truth of any accusation against them before public reproof is given. He must be as objective as possible in weighing charges against presbyters (1 Tm 5:21), learning from his experience to take care in selecting them (1 Tm 5:22). Some scholars take 1 Tm 5:22 as a reference not to ordination of presbyters but to reconciliation of public sinners. The letter now sounds an informal note of personal concern in its advice to Timothy not to be so ascetic that he even avoids wine (1 Tm 5:23). Judgment concerning the fitness of candidates to serve as presbyters is easy with persons of open conduct, more difficult and prolonged with those of greater reserve (1 Tm 5:24–25).

*s:* Lv 19:32; Ti 2:2. *t:* Jer 49:11; Lk 2:37; 18:7. *u:* Jn 13:14; Heb 13:2. *v:* 2 Thes 3:11. *w:* 1 Cor 7:9. *x:* 1 Cor 16:18; Phil 2:29. *y:* Dt 25:4; 1 Cor 9:8 / Mt 10:10; Lk 10:7. *z:* Dt 17:6; 19:15; Mt 18:16; 2 Cor 13:1. *a:* Gal 2:14; Eph 5:11; 2 Tm 4:2; Ti 1:9, 13.

other's sins. Keep yourself pure.[b] [23]Stop drinking only water, but have a little wine for the sake of your stomach and your frequent illnesses. [24]Some people's sins are public, preceding them to judgment; but other people are followed by their sins. [25]Similarly, good works are also public; and even those that are not cannot remain hidden.

See RG 413

CHAPTER 6

*Rules for Slaves.* [1*] Those who are under the yoke of slavery must regard their masters as worthy of full respect, so that the name of God and our teaching* may not suffer abuse.[c] [2*] Those whose masters are believers must not take advantage of them because they are brothers but must give better service because those who will profit from their work are believers and are beloved.[d]

## V. False Teaching and True Wealth

Teach and urge these things. [3]Whoever teaches something different and does not agree with the sound words of our Lord Jesus Christ and the religious teaching[e] [4]is conceited, understanding nothing, and has a morbid disposition for arguments and verbal disputes. From these come envy, rivalry, insults, evil suspicions, [5]and mutual friction among people with corrupted minds, who are deprived of the truth, supposing religion to be a means of gain.[f] [6*] Indeed, religion with contentment is a great gain.[g] [7]For we brought nothing into the world, just as we shall not be able to take anything out of it.[h] [8]If we have food and clothing, we shall be content with that.[i] [9]Those who want to be rich are falling into temptation and into a trap and into many foolish and harmful desires, which plunge them into ruin and destruction.[j] [10]For the love of money is the root of all evils, and some people in their desire for it have strayed from the faith and have pierced themselves with many pains.

*Exhortations to Timothy.** [11]But you, man of God,* avoid all this. Instead, pursue righteousness, devotion, faith, love, patience, and gentleness.[k] [12]Compete well for the faith. Lay hold of eternal life, to which you were called when you made the noble confession in the presence of many witnesses.[l] [13]I charge [you] before God, who gives life to all things, and before Christ Jesus, who gave testimony under Pontius Pilate for the noble confession,[m] [14]to keep the commandment without stain or reproach until the appearance of our Lord Jesus Christ [15]that the blessed and only ruler will make manifest at the proper time, the King of kings and Lord of lords,[n] [16]who alone has immortality, who dwells in unapproachable light, and whom no human being has seen or can see. To him be honor and eternal power. Amen.[o]

*Right Use of Wealth.** [17]Tell the rich in the present age not to be proud and not to rely on so uncertain a thing as wealth but rather on God, who richly provides us with all things for our enjoyment.[p] [18]Tell them to do good, to be rich in good works, to be generous, ready to share, [19]thus accumulating as treasure a good foundation for the future, so as to win the life that is true life.[q]

**6:1–2** Compare the tables for household duties, such as that of Col 3:18–4:1. Domestic relationships derive new meaning from the Christian faith.

**6:1 Our teaching**: this refers to the teaching of the Christian community.

**6:2b–10** Timothy is exhorted to maintain steadfastly the position outlined in this letter, not allowing himself to be pressured into any other course. He must realize that false teachers can be discerned by their pride, envy, quarrelsomeness, and greed for material gain. 1 Tm 6:6 is rather obscure and is interpreted, and therefore translated, variously. The suggestion seems to be that the important gain that religion brings is spiritual, but that there is material gain, too, up to the point of what is needed for physical sustenance (cf. 1 Tm 6:17–19).

**6:6 Contentment**: the word *autarkeia* is a technical Greek philosophical term for the virtue of independence from material goods (Aristotle, Cynics, Stoics).

**6:11–16** Timothy's position demands total dedication to God and faultless witness to Christ (1 Tm 6:11–14) operating from an awareness, through faith, of the coming revelation in Jesus of the invisible God (1 Tm 6:15–16).

**6:11 Man of God**: a title applied to Moses and the prophets (Dt 33:1; 1 Sm 2:27; 1 Kgs 12:22; 13:1; etc.).

**6:17–19** Timothy is directed to instruct the rich, advising them to make good use of their wealth by aiding the poor.

*b:* 4:14; 2 Tm 1:6. *c:* Eph 6:5; Ti 2:9–10. *d:* Phlm 16. *e:* Gal 1:6–9; 2 Tm 1:13; Ti 1:1. *f:* 2 Tm 3:8; 4:4; Ti 1:14. *g:* 4:8; Phil 4:11–12; Heb 13:5. *h:* Jb 1:21; Eccl 5:14. *i:* Prv 30:8. *j:* Prv 23:4; 28:22. *k:* 2 Tm 2:22. *l:* 1 Cor 9:26; 2 Tm 4:7. *m:* Jn 18:36–37; 19:11. *n:* 2 Mc 13:4; Rev 17:14. *o:* Ex 33:20; Ps 104:2. *p:* Ps 62:11; Lk 12:20. *q:* Mt 6:20.

## VI. Final Recommendation and Warning*

[20]O Timothy, guard what has been entrusted
to you. Avoid profane babbling and the absurdities of so-called knowledge.[r] [21]By professing it, some people have deviated from the faith.

Grace be with all of you.[s]

**6:20–21** A final solemn warning against the heretical teachers, with what seems to be a specific reference to gnosticism, the great rival and enemy of the church for two centuries and more (the Greek word for "knowledge" is *gnōsis*). If gnosticism is being referred to here, it is probable that the warnings against "speculations" and "myths and genealogies" (cf. especially 1 Tm 1:4; Ti 3:9) involve allusions to that same kind of heresy. Characteristic of the various gnostic systems of speculation was an elaborate mythology of innumerable superhuman intermediaries, on a descending scale ("genealogies"), between God and the world. Thus would be explained the emphasis upon Christ's being the one mediator (as in 1 Tm 2:5). Although fully developed gnosticism belonged to the second and later centuries, there are signs that incipient forms of it belonged to Paul's own period.

*r:* 2 Tm 1:14 / 1 Tm 4:7. *s:* 1:6; 2 Tm 2:18.

See RG 414–17

# The Second Letter to Timothy

The authorship and date of this letter, as one of the Pastoral Epistles, are discussed in the Introduction to the First Letter to Timothy.

The tone here is more personal than in First Timothy, for this letter addresses Timothy in vivid terms (2 Tm 1:6–14; 2:1–13) and depicts Paul's courage and hope in the face of discouragements late in the course of his apostolic ministry (2 Tm 1:15–18; 3:10–17; 4:9–18). Indeed, the letter takes on the character of a final exhortation and testament from Paul to the younger Timothy (2 Tm 4:1–8). Paul is portrayed as a prisoner (2 Tm 1:8, 16; 2:9) in Rome (2 Tm 1:17), and there is a hint that Timothy may be in Ephesus (2 Tm 2:17). The letter reveals that, with rare exceptions, Christians have not rallied to Paul's support (2 Tm 1:15–18) and takes a pessimistic view of the outcome of his case (2 Tm 4:6). It describes Paul as fully aware of what impends, looking to God, not to human beings, for his deliverance (2 Tm 4:3–8, 18). It recalls his mission days with Timothy (2 Tm 1:3–5; cf. Acts 16:1–4). It points to his preaching of the gospel as the reason for his imprisonment and offers Timothy, as a motive for steadfastness, his own example of firmness in faith despite adverse circumstances (2 Tm 1:6–14). The letter suggests that Timothy should prepare others to replace himself as Paul has prepared Timothy to replace him (2 Tm 2:1–2). Paul urges him not to desist out of fear from preserving and spreading the Christian message (2 Tm 2:3–7). It presents the resurrection of Jesus and his messianic role as the heart of the gospel for which Paul has been ready to lay down his life (2 Tm 2:8–9) and thus not only to express his own conviction fully but to support the conviction of others (2 Tm 2:10–13).

This letter, like the preceding one, urges Timothy to protect the community from the inevitable impact of false teaching (2 Tm 2:14–3:9), without fear of the personal attacks that may result (2 Tm 3:10–13). It recommends that he rely on the power of the scriptures, on proclamation of the word, and on sound doctrine (2 Tm 3:14–4:2), without being troubled by those who do not accept him (2 Tm 4:3–5). The letter poignantly observes in passing that Paul has need of his reading materials and his cloak (2 Tm 4:13) and, what will be best of all, a visit from Timothy.

On the theory of authorship by Paul himself, Second Timothy appears to be the last of the three Pastoral Epistles. The many scholars who argue that the Pastorals are products of the Pauline school often incline toward Second Timothy as the earliest of the three and the one most likely to have actual fragments of material from Paul himself.

The principal divisions of the Second Letter to Timothy are the following:

I. Address (1:1–5)
II. Exhortations to Timothy (1:6–2:13)
III. Instructions Concerning False Teaching (2:14–4:8)
IV. Personal Requests and Final Greetings (4:9–22)

## I. Address

### CHAPTER 1

See RG 415

***Greeting.*** * 1 Paul, an apostle of Christ Jesus by the will of God[a] for the promise of life in Christ Jesus,* 2 to Timothy, my dear child: grace, mercy, and peace from God the Father and Christ Jesus our Lord.

***Thanksgiving.*** 3[b] I am grateful to God, whom I worship with a clear conscience as my ancestors did,* as I remember you constantly in my prayers, night and day. 4* I yearn to see you again, recalling your tears, so that I may be filled with joy, 5 as I recall your sincere faith that first lived in your grandmother Lois and in your mother Eunice and that I am confident lives also in you.[c]

## II. Exhortations to Timothy

***The Gifts Timothy Has Received.*** 6 For this reason, I remind you to stir into flame the gift of God* that you have through the imposition of my hands.[d] 7 For God did not give us a spirit of cowardice but rather of power and love and self-control.[e] 8 So do not be ashamed of your testimony to our Lord,* nor of me, a prisoner for his sake; but bear your share of hardship for the gospel with the strength that comes from God.[f]

9* He saved us and called us to a holy life, not according to our works but according to his own design and the grace bestowed on us in Christ Jesus before time began,[g] 10 but now made manifest through the appearance of our savior Christ Jesus, who destroyed death and brought life and immortality to light through the gospel,[h] 11* for which I was appointed preacher and apostle[i] and teacher. 12* On this account I am suffering these things; but I am not ashamed,[j] for I know him in whom I have believed and am confident that he is able to guard what has been entrusted to me until that day. 13 Take as your norm the sound words that you heard from me, in the faith and love that are in Christ Jesus.[k] 14 Guard this rich trust with the help of the holy Spirit that dwells within us.[l]

***Paul's Suffering.*** 15* [m] You know that everyone in Asia deserted me, including Phygelus and Hermogenes. 16* May the Lord grant mercy to the family of Onesiphorus[n] because he often gave me new heart and was not ashamed of my chains. 17 But when he came to Rome, he promptly searched for me and found me. 18 May the Lord grant him

**1:1–2** For the formula of address and greeting, see note on Rom 1:1–7.

**1:1 The promise of life in Christ Jesus**: that God grants through union with Christ in faith and love; cf. Col 3:4; 1 Tm 4:8.

**1:3 As my ancestors did**: this emphasizes the continuity of Judaism and Christianity; for a similar view, see Rom 9:3–5; Phil 3:4–6.

**1:4–5** Purportedly written from prison in Rome (2 Tm 1:8, 17; 4:6–8) shortly before the writer's death, the letter recalls the earlier sorrowful parting from Timothy, commending him for his faith and expressing the longing to see him again.

**1:6 The gift of God**: the grace resulting from the conferral of an ecclesiastical office. **The imposition of my hands**: see note on 1 Tm 4:14.

**1:8 Do not be ashamed of your testimony to our Lord**: i.e., of preaching and suffering for the sake of the gospel.

**1:9–10** Redemption from sin and the call to holiness of life are not won by personal deeds but are freely and graciously bestowed according to God's eternal plan; cf. Eph 1:4.

**1:11 Teacher**: the overwhelming majority of manuscripts and Fathers read "teacher of the nations," undoubtedly a harmonization with 1 Tm 2:7.

**1:12 He is able to guard . . . until that day**: the intervening words can also be translated "what I have entrusted to him" (i.e., the fruit of his ministry) as well as "what has been entrusted to me" (i.e., the faith). The same difficult term occurs in 2 Tm 1:14, where it is modified by the adjective "rich" and used without a possessive.

**1:15** Keen disappointment is expressed, here and later (2 Tm 4:16), that the Christians of the province of Asia, especially Phygelus and Hermogenes, should have abandoned the writer and done nothing to defend his case in court.

**1:16–18 The family of Onesiphorus because he . . . of my chains**: Onesiphorus seems to have died before this letter was written. His family is mentioned twice (here and in 2 Tm 4:19), though it was Onesiphorus himself who was helpful to Paul in prison and rendered much service to the community of Ephesus. Because the apostle complains of abandonment by all in Asia during his second imprisonment and trial, the assistance of Onesiphorus seems to have been given to Paul during his first Roman imprisonment (A.D. 61–63).

*a:* 1 Tm 4:8. *b:* 1 Tm 3:9 / Phil 3:5. *c:* 1 Tm 1:5 / Acts 16:1. *d:* 1 Tm 4:14; 5:22 / Acts 6:6; 8:17. *e:* Rom 5:5; 8:15; 1 Cor 2:4. *f:* 2:3, 15; Rom 1:16. *g:* Eph 2:8–9; Ti 3:5 / Eph 1:4; Ti 1:2. *h:* Rom 16:26; 1 Pt 1:20 / 1 Tm 6:14 / Phil 3:20; Ti 1:4; 2:13; 2 Pt 1:11 / 1 Cor 15:54–55; Heb 2:14 / 1 Cor 15:53–54. *i:* 1 Tm 2:7. *j:* 1 Pt 4:16 / 1 Tm 1:10–11. *k:* 1 Tm 1:14. *l:* 1 Tm 6:20 / Rom 8:11. *m:* 4:16. *n:* 4:19. *o:* Jude 21.

to find mercy from the Lord* on that day.
And you know very well the services he rendered in Ephesus.[o]

## CHAPTER 2

See RG 415-16

*Timothy's Conduct.* 1* So you, my
child, be strong in the grace that is in Christ
Jesus. 2 And what you heard from me
through many witnesses entrust to faithful
people who will have the ability to teach
others as well. 3 Bear your share of hardship
along with me like a good soldier of Christ
Jesus.[p] 4 To satisfy the one who recruited
him, a soldier does not become entangled in
the business affairs of life.[q] 5 Similarly, an
athlete cannot receive the winner's crown
except by competing according to the rules.[r]
6 The hardworking farmer ought to have the
first share of the crop.[s] 7 Reflect on what I am
saying, for the Lord will give you understanding in everything.[t]

8* Remember Jesus Christ, raised from the
dead, a descendant of David: such is my
gospel,[u] 9 for which I am suffering, even to the
point of chains, like a criminal. But the word
of God is not chained.[v] 10 Therefore, I bear
with everything for the sake of those who are
chosen, so that they too may obtain the salvation that is in Christ Jesus, together with eternal glory.[w] 11 This saying is trustworthy:

If we have died with him
we shall also live with him;[x]
12 if we persevere
we shall also reign with him.
But if we deny him
he will deny us.[y]
13 If we are unfaithful
he remains faithful,
for he cannot deny himself.[z]

## III. Instructions Concerning False Teaching

***Warning against Useless Disputes.*** 14* Remind people of these things and charge them
before God* to stop disputing about words.
This serves no useful purpose since it harms
those who listen.[a] 15 Be eager to present
yourself as acceptable to God, a workman
who causes no disgrace, imparting the word
of truth without deviation.[b] 16 Avoid profane,
idle talk, for such people will become more
and more godless,[c] 17 and their teaching will
spread like gangrene. Among them are Hymenaeus and Philetus,[d] 18 who have deviated
from the truth by saying that [the] resurrection has already taken place and are upsetting the faith of some.[e] 19 Nevertheless,
God's solid foundation stands, bearing this
inscription, "The Lord knows those who are
his"; and, "Let everyone who calls upon the
name of the Lord avoid evil."[f]

20 In a large household there are vessels
not only of gold and silver but also of wood
and clay, some for lofty and others for hum-

**1:18 Lord . . . Lord**: the first "Lord" here seems to refer to Christ, the second "Lord" to the Father.

**2:1–7** This passage manifests a characteristic deep concern for safeguarding the faith and faithfully transmitting it through trustworthy people (2 Tm 2:1–2; cf. 2 Tm 1:14; 1 Tm 6:20; Ti 1:9). Comparisons to the soldier's detachment, the athlete's sportsmanship, and the farmer's arduous work as the price of recompense (2 Tm 2:4–6) emphasize the need of singleness of purpose in preaching the word, even at the cost of hardship, for the sake of Christ (2 Tm 2:3).

**2:8–13** The section begins with a sloganlike summary of Paul's gospel about Christ (2 Tm 2:8) and concludes with what may be part of an early Christian hymn (2 Tm 2:11b–12a; most exegetes include the rest of 2 Tm 2:12 and all of 2 Tm 2:13 as part of the quotation). The poetic lines suggest that through baptism Christians die spiritually with Christ and hope to live with him and reign with him forever, but the Christian life includes endurance, witness, and even suffering, as the final judgment will show and as Paul's own case makes clear; while he is imprisoned for preaching the gospel (2 Tm 2:9), his sufferings are helpful to the elect for obtaining the salvation and glory available in Christ (2 Tm 2:10), who will be true to those who are faithful and will disown those who deny him (2 Tm 2:12–13).

**2:14–19** For those who dispute about mere words (cf. 2 Tm 2:23–24) and indulge in irreligious talk to the detriment of their listeners (2 Tm 2:16–19), see notes on 1 Tm 1:3–7; 6:20–21. Hymenaeus and Philetus (2 Tm 2:17), while accepting the Christian's mystical death and resurrection in Christ through baptism, claimed that baptized Christians are already risen with Christ in this life and thus that there is no future bodily resurrection or eternal glory to come. The first quotation in 2 Tm 2:19 is from Nm 16:5; the other quotation is from some unidentified Jewish or Christian writing.

**2:14 Before God**: many ancient manuscripts read "before the Lord."

*p:* 1:8; 4:5; Phlm 2. *q:* 1 Cor 9:6. *r:* 1 Cor 9:25. *s:* 1 Cor 9:7–10. *t:* Prv 2:6. *u:* Rom 1:3; 1 Cor 15:4, 20 / Rom 2:16; Gal 1:11; 2:2. *v:* Phil 1:12–14. *w:* Col 1:24; 1 Tm 1:15. *x:* Rom 6:8. *y:* Mt 10:22, 33; Lk 12:9. *z:* Nm 23:19; Rom 3:3–4; 1 Cor 10:13; Ti 1:2. *a:* 1 Tm 6:4. *b:* 1:8; 2 Cor 6:7; Eph 1:13; Col 1:5. *c:* 1 Tm 4:7. *d:* 1 Tm 1:20. *e:* 2 Thes 2:2. *f:* Is 28:16; 1 Cor 3:10–15 / Nm 16:5; Jn 10:14.

ble use. 21 If anyone cleanses himself of these
things, he will be a vessel for lofty use, dedicated, beneficial to the master of the house,
ready for every good work.[g] 22 So turn from
youthful desires and pursue righteousness,
faith, love, and peace, along with those who
call on the Lord* with purity of heart.[h]
23 Avoid foolish and ignorant debates, for
you know that they breed quarrels.[i] 24 A slave
of the Lord should not quarrel, but should be
gentle with everyone, able to teach, tolerant,[j]
25 correcting opponents with kindness. It
may be that God will grant them repentance
that leads to knowledge of the truth.[k] 26* and
that they may return to their senses out of the
devil's snare,[l] where they are entrapped by
him, for his will.

## CHAPTER 3

See RG 415–16

*The Dangers of the Last Days.** 1 But
understand this: there will be terrifying
times in the last days.[m] 2 People will be self-
centered and lovers of money, proud,
haughty, abusive, disobedient to their parents, ungrateful, irreligious,[n] 3 callous, implacable, slanderous, licentious, brutal, hating what is good, 4 traitors, reckless,
conceited, lovers of pleasure rather than
lovers of God, 5 as they make a pretense of
religion but deny its power. Reject them.[o]
6 For some of these slip into homes and make
captives of women weighed down by sins,
led by various desires,[p] 7 always trying to
learn but never able to reach a knowledge of
the truth.[q] 8 Just as Jannes and Jambres opposed Moses, so they also oppose the
truth—people of depraved mind, unqualified in the faith.[r] 9 But they will not make
further progress, for their foolishness will be
plain to all, as it was with those two.

*Paul's Example and Teaching.** 10 You
have followed my teaching, way of life, purpose, faith, patience, love, endurance, 11 persecutions, and sufferings, such as happened
to me in Antioch, Iconium, and Lystra, persecutions that I endured. Yet from all these
things the Lord delivered me.[s] 12 In fact, all
who want to live religiously in Christ Jesus
will be persecuted.[t] 13 But wicked people and
charlatans will go from bad to worse, deceivers and deceived. 14 But you, remain
faithful to what you have learned and believed, because you know from whom you
learned it,[u] 15 and that from infancy you have
known [the] sacred scriptures, which are capable of giving you wisdom for salvation
through faith in Christ Jesus.[v] 16* All scripture[w] is inspired by God and is useful for
teaching, for refutation, for correction, and
for training in righteousness,* 17 so that one
who belongs to God may be competent,
equipped for every good work.[x]

## CHAPTER 4

See RG 416

*Solemn Charge.** 1 I charge you in the
presence of God and of Christ Jesus, who will

**2:22 Those who call on the Lord**: those who believe in Christ and worship him as Lord, i.e., Christians (Acts 9:14–16, 20–21; Rom 10:12–13; cf. 2 Tm 2:19, literally, "Everyone who names the name of the Lord").

**2:26** Some interpreters would render this passage, "Thus they may come to their senses and, forced to do his (i.e., God's) will, may escape the devil's trap." This interpretation of the Greek is possible, but the one accepted in the text seems more likely.

**3:1–9** The moral depravity and false teaching that will be rampant in the last days are already at work (2 Tm 3:1–5). The frivolous and superficial, too, devoid of the true spirit of religion, will be easy victims of those who pervert them by falsifying the truth (2 Tm 3:6–8), just as Jannes and Jambres, Pharaoh's magicians of Egypt (Ex 7:11–12, 22), discredited the truth in Moses' time. Exodus does not name the magicians, but the two names are widely found in much later Jewish, Christian, and even pagan writings. Their origins are legendary.

**3:10–17** Paul's example for Timothy includes persecution, a frequent emphasis in the Pastorals. Timothy is to be steadfast to what he has been taught and to scripture. The scriptures are the source of wisdom, i.e., of belief in and loving fulfillment of God's word revealed in Christ, through whom salvation is given.

**3:16–17 Useful for teaching . . . every good work**: because as God's word the scriptures share his divine authority. It is exercised through those who are ministers of the word.

**3:16 All scripture is inspired by God**: this could possibly also be translated, "All scripture inspired by God is useful for. . . ." In this classic reference to inspiration, God is its principal author, with the writer as the human collaborator. Thus the scriptures are the word of God in human language. See also 2 Pt 1:20–21.

**4:1–5** The gravity of the obligation incumbent on Timothy

*g:* 3:17. *h:* Gal 5:22; 1 Tm 6:11 / Rom 10:13; 1 Cor 1:2. *i:* 1 Tm 1:4; 4:7; 6:4; Ti 3:9. *j:* 1 Tm 3:2–3. *k:* 3:7; 1 Tm 2:4. *l:* 1 Tm 3:7. *m:* 1 Tm 4:1; 2 Pt 3:3; Jude 18. *n:* Rom 1:29–31. *o:* Rom 2:20–22; Ti 1:16. *p:* Ti 1:11. *q:* 2:25. *r:* Ex 7:11, 22; 1 Tm 6:5. *s:* Acts 13:50; 14:5, 19 / Ps 34:20. *t:* Jn 15:20; Acts 14:22. *u:* 2:2. *v:* Jn 5:39. *w:* Rom 15:4; 2 Pt 1:19–21. *x:* 2:21. *y:* 1 Tm 5:21; 6:14 / Acts 10:42; Rom 14:9–10; 1 Pt 4:5.

judge the living and the dead, and by his appearing and his kingly power:[y] 2 proclaim the word; be persistent whether it is convenient or inconvenient; convince, reprimand, encourage through all patience and teaching.[z] 3 For the time will come when people will not tolerate sound doctrine but, following their own desires and insatiable curiosity,* will accumulate teachers[a] 4 and will stop listening to the truth and will be diverted to myths.[b] 5 But you, be self-possessed in all circumstances; put up with hardship; perform the work of an evangelist; fulfill your ministry.

***Reward for Fidelity.*** 6* [c] For I am already being poured out like a libation, and the time of my departure is at hand. 7* I have competed well; I have finished the race;[d] I have kept the faith. 8* From now on the crown of righteousness awaits me, which the Lord, the just judge, will award to me on that day,[e] and not only to me, but to all who have longed for his appearance.

## IV. Personal Requests and Final Greetings

***Paul's Loneliness.*** 9* Try to join me soon, 10 for Demas, enamored of the present world, deserted me and went to Thessalonica, Crescens to Galatia,* and Titus to Dalmatia.[f] 11 Luke is the only one with me. Get Mark and bring him with you, for he is helpful to me in the ministry.[g] 12 I have sent Tychicus to Ephesus.[h] 13 When you come, bring the cloak I left with Carpus in Troas, the papyrus rolls, and especially the parchments.[i]

14 Alexander* the coppersmith did me a great deal of harm; the Lord will repay him according to his deeds.[j] 15 You too be on guard against him, for he has strongly resisted our preaching.

16 At my first defense no one appeared on my behalf, but everyone deserted me. May it not be held against them![k] 17 But the Lord stood by me and gave me strength, so that through me the proclamation might be completed and all the Gentiles might hear it. And I was rescued from the lion's mouth.[l] 18 The Lord will rescue me from every evil threat and will bring me safe to his heavenly kingdom. To him be glory forever and ever. Amen.[m]

***Final Greeting.*** 19 Greet Prisca and Aquila*

to preach the word can be gauged from the solemn adjuration: in the presence of God, and of Christ coming as universal judge, and by his appearance and **his kingly power** (2 Tm 4:1). Patience, courage, constancy, and endurance are required despite the opposition, hostility, indifference, and defection of many to whom the truth has been preached (2 Tm 4:2–5).

**4:3 Insatiable curiosity**: literally, "with itching ears."

**4:6** The apostle recognizes his death through martyrdom to be imminent. He regards it as an act of worship in which his blood will be poured out in sacrifice; cf. Ex 29:38–40; Phil 2:17.

**4:7** At the close of his life Paul could testify to the accomplishment of what Christ himself foretold concerning him at the time of his conversion, "I will show him what he will have to suffer for my name" (Acts 9:16).

**4:8** When the world is judged at the parousia, all who have eagerly looked for the Lord's appearing and have sought to live according to his teachings will be rewarded. The crown is a reference to the laurel wreath placed on the heads of victorious athletes and conquerors in war; cf. 2 Tm 2:5; 1 Cor 9:25.

**4:9–13** Demas either abandoned the work of the ministry for worldly affairs or, perhaps, gave up the faith itself (2 Tm 4:10). Luke (2 Tm 4:11) may have accompanied Paul on parts of his second and third missionary journeys (Acts 16:10–12; 20:5–7). Notice the presence of the first personal pronoun "we" in these Acts passages, suggesting to some that Luke (or at least some traveling companion of Paul's) was the author of Acts. Mark, once rejected by Paul (Acts 13:13; 15:39), is now to render him a great service (2 Tm 4:11); cf. Col 4:10; Phlm 24. For Tychicus, see Eph 6:21; cf. also Acts 20:4; Col 4:7.

**4:10 Galatia**: some manuscripts read "Gaul" or "Gallia."

**4:14–18 Alexander**: an opponent of Paul's preaching (2 Tm 4:14–15), perhaps the one who is mentioned in 1 Tm 1:20. Despite Paul's abandonment by his friends in the province of Asia (cf. 2 Tm 1:15–16), the divine assistance brought this first trial to a successful issue, even to the point of making the gospel message known to those who participated in or witnessed the trial (2 Tm 4:16–17).

**4:19 Prisca and Aquila**: they assisted Paul in his ministry in Corinth (Acts 18:2–3) and Ephesus (Acts 18:19, 26; 1 Cor 16:19). They risked death to save his life, and all the Gentile communities are indebted to them (Rom 16:3–5).

*z:* Acts 20:20, 31; 1 Tm 5:20. *a:* 1 Tm 4:1. *b:* 1 Tm 1:4; 4:7; Ti 1:14. *c:* Phil 2:17. *d:* 1 Tm 1:18; 6:12; Jude 3 / Acts 20:24; 1 Cor 9:24; Heb 12:1. *e:* 2:5; Wis 5:16; 1 Cor 9:25; Phil 3:14; Jas 1:12; 1 Pt 5:4; Rev 2:10. *f:* Col 4:14; Phlm 24 / 2 Cor 2:13; 7:6–7; 8:23; Gal 2:3; Ti 1:4. *g:* Col 4:14; Phlm 24 / Col 4:10; Phlm 24. *h:* Acts 20:4; Eph 6:21; Col 4:7. *i:* Acts 16:8; 20:6. *j:* 1 Tm 1:20 / 2 Sm 3:39; Ps 28:4; 62:12; Prv 24:12; Rom 2:6. *k:* 1:15. *l:* Acts 23:11; 27:23; Phil 4:13 / 1 Mc 2:60; Ps 22:22; Dn 6:23. *m:* 2 Cor 1:10 / Rom 16:27.

and the family of Onesiphorus.[n] 20 Erastus* remained in Corinth, while I left Trophimus sick at Miletus.[o] 21 Try to get here before winter. Eubulus, Pudens, Linus,* Claudia, and all the brothers send greetings.

22 The Lord be with your spirit. Grace be with all of you.[p]

**4:20 Erastus**: he was the treasurer of the city of Corinth (Rom 16:24); cf. also Acts 19:22. **Trophimus**: from the province of Asia, he accompanied Paul from Greece to Troas (Acts 20:4–5).

**4:21 Linus**: Western tradition sometimes identified this Linus with the supposed successor of Peter as bishop of Rome, and Claudia as the mother of Linus (*Apostolic Constitutions*, fourth century).

*n:* Acts 18:2; Rom 16:3; 1 Cor 16:19 / 2 Tm 1:16. *o:* Acts 19:22; Rom 16:24 / Acts 20:4; 21:29. *p:* Gal 6:18; Phil 4:23; Col 4:18; 1 Tm 6:21; Ti 3:15.

See RG 417–19

# The Letter to Titus

The third of the Pastoral Epistles in the New Testament is addressed to a different co-worker of Paul than are First and Second Timothy. The situation is different, too, for Titus is addressed as the person in charge of developing the church on the large Mediterranean island of Crete (Ti 1:5), a place Paul had never, according to the New Testament, visited. The tone is closer to that of First Timothy as three topics of church life and structure are discussed: presbyter-bishops (see note on Ti 1:5–9), groups with which one must work in the church (Ti 2:1–10), and admonitions for conduct based on the grace and love of God that appeared in Jesus Christ (Ti 2:11–3:10). The warmer personal tone of Second Timothy is replaced by emphasis on church office and on living in the society of the day, in which deceivers and heretics abound (Ti 1:10–16; 3:9–10).

The Pauline assistant who is addressed, Titus, was a Gentile Christian, but we are nowhere informed of his place of birth or residence. He went from Antioch with Paul and Barnabas to Jerusalem (Gal 2:1; cf. Acts 15:2). According to 2 Corinthians (2 Cor 2:13; 7:6, 13–14), he was with Paul on his third missionary journey; his name, however, does not appear in Acts. Besides being the bearer of Paul's severe letter to the Corinthians (2 Cor 7:6–8), he had the responsibility of taking up the collection in Corinth for the Christian community of Jerusalem (2 Cor 8:6, 16–19, 23). In the present letter (Ti 1:5), he is mentioned as the administrator of the Christian community in Crete, charged with the task of organizing it through the appointment of presbyters and bishops (Ti 1:5–9; here the two terms refer to the same personages).

The letter instructs Titus about the character of the assistants he is to choose in view of the pastoral difficulties peculiar to Crete (Ti 1:5–16). It suggests the special individual and social virtues that the various age groups and classes in the Christian community should be encouraged to acquire (Ti 2:1–10). The motivation for transformation of their lives comes from christology, especially the redemptive sacrifice of Christ and his future coming, as applied through baptism and justification (Ti 2:11–14; 3:4–8). The community is to serve as a leaven for Christianizing the social world about it (Ti 3:1–3). Good works are to be the evidence of their faith in God (Ti 3:8); those who engage in religious controversy are, after suitable warning, to be ignored (Ti 3:9–11).

The authorship and date of the Letter to Titus are discussed in the Introduction to 1 Timothy. Those who assume authorship by Paul himself usually place Titus after 1 Timothy and before 2 Timothy. Others see it as closely related to 1 Timothy, in a growing emphasis on church structure and opposition to heresy, later than the letters of Paul himself and 2 Timothy. It has also been suggested that, if the three Pastorals once circulated as a literary unit, Titus was meant to be read ahead of 1 and 2 Timothy.

The principal divisions of the Letter to Titus are the following:

I. Address (1:1–4)
II. Pastoral Charge (1:5–16)
III. Teaching the Christian Life (2:1–3:15)

## I. Address

### CHAPTER 1

See RG 418

*Greeting.*[*] [1]Paul, a slave of God and apostle of Jesus Christ for the sake of the faith of God's chosen ones and the recognition of religious truth,[a] [2]in the hope of eternal life that God, who does not lie, promised before time began,[b] [3]who indeed at the proper time revealed his word in the proclamation with which I was entrusted by the command of God our savior,[c] [4]to Titus, my true child in our common faith: grace and peace from God the Father and Christ Jesus our savior.[d]

## II. Pastoral Charge

*Titus in Crete.* [5][*] For this reason I left you in Crete so that you might set right what remains to be done and appoint presbyters in every town, as I directed you, [6][e] on condition that a man be blameless, married only once, with believing children who are not accused of licentiousness or rebellious. [7]For a bishop as God's steward must be blameless, not arrogant, not irritable, not a drunkard, not aggressive, not greedy for sordid gain, [8]but hospitable, a lover of goodness, temperate, just, holy, and self-controlled, [9]holding fast to the true message as taught so that he will be able both to exhort with sound doctrine and to refute opponents.[f] [10][*] For there are also many rebels, idle talkers and deceivers, especially the Jewish Christians.[*] [11]It is imperative to silence them, as they are upsetting whole families by teaching for sordid gain what they should not. [12]One of them, a prophet of their own, once said, "Cretans have always been liars, vicious beasts, and lazy gluttons."[*] [13]That testimony is true. Therefore, admonish them sharply, so that they may be sound in the faith,[g] [14]instead of paying attention to Jewish myths and regulations of people who have repudiated the truth.[h] [15]To the clean all things are clean, but to those who are defiled and unbelieving nothing is clean; in fact, both their minds and their consciences are tainted.[i] [16]They claim to know God, but by their deeds they deny him. They are vile and disobedient and unqualified for any good deed.

## III. Teaching the Christian Life

### CHAPTER 2

See RG 418–19

*Christian Behavior.*[*] [1]As for yourself, you must say what is consistent with sound doctrine, namely,[j] [2]that older men should be temperate, dignified, self-controlled, sound in faith, love, and endurance. [3]Similarly, older women should be reverent in their behavior, not slanderers, not addicted to drink, teaching what is good, [4]so that they may train younger women to love their husbands and children, [5]to be self-controlled, chaste, good homemakers, under the control of their husbands, so that the word of God may not be discredited.[k]

**1:1–4** On the epistolary form, see note on Rom 1:1–7. The apostolate is the divinely appointed mission to lead others to the true faith and through it to eternal salvation (Ti 1:1–3).

**1:5–9** This instruction on the selection and appointment of presbyters, substantially identical with that in 1 Tm 3:1–7 on a bishop (see note there), was aimed at strengthening the authority of Titus by apostolic mandate; cf. Ti 2:15. In Ti 1:5, 7 and Acts 20:17, 28, the terms *episkopos* and *presbyteros* ("bishop" and "presbyter") refer to the same persons. Deacons are not mentioned in Titus. See also note on Phil 1:1.

**1:10–16** This adverse criticism of the defects within the community is directed especially against certain Jewish Christians, who busy themselves with useless speculations over persons mentioned in the Old Testament, insist on the observance of Jewish ritual purity regulations, and thus upset whole families by teaching things they have no right to teach; cf. Ti 3:9; 1 Tm 1:3–10.

**1:10 Jewish Christians**: literally, "those of the circumcision."

**1:12 Cretans . . . gluttons**: quoted from Epimenides, a Cretan poet of the sixth century B.C.

**2:1–10** One of Titus' main tasks in Crete is to become acquainted with the character of the Cretans and thereby learn to cope with its deficiencies (see Ti 1:12). The counsel is not only for Titus himself but for various classes of people with whom he must deal: older men and women (Ti 2:2–4), younger women and men (Ti 2:4–7), and slaves (Ti 2:9–10); cf. Eph 6:1–9; Col 3:18–4:1.

*a:* 1 Tm 2:4; 4:3; 2 Tm 2:25; 3:7; Heb 10:26. *b:* 3:7; 2 Tm 1:1; 1 Jn 2:25. *c:* 2:10; 3:4; Ps 24:5; 1 Tm 1:1; 2:3; 4:10; Jude 25. *d:* 2:13; 3:6; Phil 3:20; 2 Tm 1:10; 2 Pt 1:1, 11; 2:20; 3:2, 18. *e:* 1 Tm 3:2–7; 2 Tm 2:24–26. *f:* 1:13; 2:1–2, 8; 1 Tm 1:10; 6:3; 2 Tm 1:13; 4:3. *g:* 1:9. *h:* 3:9; 1 Tm 1:4; 4:7; 2 Tm 4:4; 2 Pt 1:16. *i:* Mk 7:18–23; Acts 10:15; Rom 14:14–23. *j:* 1:9, 13; 2:8; 1 Tm 1:10; 6:3; 2 Tm 1:13; 4:3. *k:* 1 Cor 11:3; 14:34; Eph 5:22–24; Col 3:18; 1 Tm 2:11–15; 1 Pt 3:1–6.

6 Urge the younger men, similarly, to control themselves, 7 showing yourself as a model of good deeds in every respect, with integrity in your teaching, dignity, 8 and sound speech that cannot be criticized, so that the opponent will be put to shame without anything bad to say about us.

9 Slaves are to be under the control of their masters in all respects, giving them satisfaction, not talking back to them[l] 10 or stealing from them, but exhibiting complete good faith, so as to adorn the doctrine of God our savior in every way.[m]

***Transformation of Life.*** 11* For the grace of God has appeared, saving all[n] 12 and training us to reject godless ways and worldly desires and to live temperately, justly, and devoutly in this age, 13 as we await the blessed hope, the appearance* of the glory of the great God and of our savior Jesus Christ,[o] 14 who gave himself for us to deliver us from all lawlessness and to cleanse for himself a people as his own, eager to do what is good.[p]

15 Say these things. Exhort and correct with all authority. Let no one look down on you.[q]

See RG 418–19

## CHAPTER 3

1* Remind them to be under the control of magistrates and authorities,* to be obedient, to be open to every good enterprise.[r] 2 They are to slander no one, to be peaceable, considerate, exercising all graciousness toward everyone. 3 For we ourselves were once foolish, disobedient, deluded, slaves to various desires and pleasures, living in malice and envy, hateful ourselves and hating one another.[s]

4 But when the kindness and generous love
of God our savior appeared,[t]
5 not because of any righteous deeds we had done
but because of his mercy,
he saved us through the bath of rebirth
and renewal by the holy Spirit,[u]
6 whom he richly poured out on us
through Jesus Christ our savior,[v]
7 so that we might be justified by his grace
and become heirs in hope of eternal life.[w]

8 This saying is trustworthy.

***Advice to Titus.**** I want you to insist on these points, that those who have believed in God be careful to devote themselves to good works; these are excellent and beneficial to others.[x] 9* Avoid foolish arguments, genealogies, rivalries, and quarrels about the law,[y] for they are useless and futile. 10 After a first and second warning, break off contact with a heretic,[z] 11 realizing that such a person is perverted and sinful and stands self-condemned.

***Directives, Greetings, and Blessing.**** 12 When I send Artemas to you, or Tychicus, try to join me at Nicopolis, where I have de-

**2:11–15** Underlying the admonitions for moral improvement in Ti 2:1–10 as the moving force is the constant appeal to God's revelation of salvation in Christ, with its demand for transformation of life.

**2:13 The blessed hope, the appearance**: literally, "the blessed hope and appearance," but the use of a single article in Greek strongly suggests an epexegetical, i.e., explanatory sense. **Of the great God and of our savior Jesus Christ**: another possible translation is "of our great God and savior Jesus Christ."

**3:1–8** The list of Christian duties continues from Ti 2:9–10, undergirded again as in Ti 2:11–13 by appeal to what God in Christ has done (Ti 2:4–7; cf. Ti 2:11–14). The spiritual renewal of the Cretans, signified in God's merciful gift of baptism (Ti 3:4–7), should be reflected in their improved attitude toward civil authority and in their Christian relationship with all (Ti 3:1–3).

**3:1 Magistrates and authorities**: some interpreters understand these terms as referring to the principalities and powers of the heavenly hierarchy. **To be open to every good enterprise**: this implies being good citizens. It could also be translated "ready to do every sort of good work" (as Christians); cf. Ti 3:14.

**3:8–11** In matters of good conduct and religious doctrine, Titus is to stand firm.

**3:9** See note on 1 Tm 6:20–21.

**3:12–15 Artemas** or **Tychicus** (2 Tm 4:12) is to replace

*l:* 1 Cor 7:21–22; Eph 6:5–8; Col 3:22–25; 1 Tm 6:1–2; 1 Pt 2:18. *m:* 1:3; 3:4; Ps 24:5; 1 Tm 1:1; 2:3; 4:10; Jude 25. *n:* 1 Tm 2:4; 4:10. *o:* 1 Cor 1:7; Phil 3:20; 1 Thes 1:10 / 2 Tm 1:10 / Ti 1:4; 3:6; 2 Pt 1:11; 2:20; 3:2, 18. *p:* Gal 1:4; 2:20; Eph 5:2, 25; 1 Tm 2:6; 1 Pt 1:18–19 / Ps 130:8. *q:* 1 Tm 4:12. *r:* Rom 13:1–7; 1 Tm 2:1–2; 1 Pt 2:13–14. *s:* 1 Cor 6:9–11; Eph 2:1–3; 5:8; Col 3:5–7; 1 Pt 4:3. *t:* 1:3; 2:10; Ps 24:5; 1 Tm 1:1; 2:3; 4:10; Jude 25. *u:* Dt 9:5; Eph 2:4–5, 8–9; 2 Tm 1:9. *v:* 1:4; 2:13; Phil 3:20; 2 Tm 1:10; 2 Pt 1:1, 11; 2:20; 3:2, 18. *w:* 1:2; 2 Tm 1:1; 1 Jn 2:25. *x:* 1 Tm 1:15; 3:1; 4:9; 2 Tm 2:11. *y:* 1 Tm 1:4; 4:7; 2 Tm 2:23. *z:* Mt 18:15–18; Rom 16:17; 1 Cor 5:11; 2 Thes 3:6, 14–15. *a:* Acts 20:4; Eph 6:21; Col 4:7; 2 Tm 4:12.

cided to spend the winter.[a] [13]Send Zenas the lawyer and Apollos on their journey soon, and see to it that they have everything they need.[b] [14]But let our people, too, learn to devote themselves to good works to supply urgent needs, so that they may not be unproductive.[c]

[15]All who are with me send you greetings. Greet those who love us in the faith.

Grace be with all of you.[d]

Titus, who will join Paul in his winter sojourn at Nicopolis in Epirus, on the western coast of Greece.

*b:* Acts 18:24–26; 1 Cor 1:12; 3:4–6, 22; 4:6; 16:12. *c:* 2:14; 3:8; Heb 10:24; 1 Pt 3:13. *d:* Heb 13:25.

See RG 420-22

# The Letter to Philemon

This short letter addressed to three specific individuals was written by Paul during an imprisonment, perhaps in Rome between A.D. 61 and 63 (see the Introduction to Colossians for other possible sites). It concerns Onesimus, a slave from Colossae (Col 4:9), who had run away from his master, perhaps guilty of theft in the process (Phlm 18). Onesimus was converted to Christ by Paul (Phlm 10). Paul sends him back to his master (Phlm 12) with this letter asking that he be welcomed willingly by his old master (Phlm 8–10, 14, 17) not just as a slave but as a brother in Christ (Phlm 16). Paul uses very strong arguments (especially Phlm 19) in his touching appeal on behalf of Onesimus. It is unlikely that Paul is subtly hinting that he would like to retain Onesimus as his own slave, lent to Paul by his master. Rather, he suggests he would like to have Onesimus work with him for the gospel (Phlm 13, 20–21). There is, however, little evidence connecting this Onesimus with a bishop of Ephesus of the same name mentioned by Ignatius of Antioch (ca. A.D. 110).

Paul's letter deals with an accepted institution of antiquity, human slavery. But Paul breathes into this letter the spirit of Christ and of equality within the Christian community. He does not attack slavery directly, for this is something the Christian communities of the first century were in no position to do, and the expectation that Christ would soon come again militated against social reforms. Yet Paul, by presenting Onesimus as "brother, beloved . . . to me, but even more so to you" (Phlm 16), voiced an idea revolutionary in that day and destined to break down worldly barriers of division "in the Lord."

---

See RG 420-21

***Address and Greeting.*** [1]* Paul, a prisoner for Christ Jesus, and Timothy our brother, to Philemon, our beloved and our co-worker,[a] [2]to Apphia our sister,* to Archippus our fellow soldier, and to the church at your house.[b] [3]Grace to you and peace* from God our Father and the Lord Jesus Christ.[c]

***Thanksgiving.*** [4]* [d]I give thanks to my God always, remembering you in my prayers, [5]as I hear of the love and the faith you have in the Lord Jesus and for all the holy ones,* [6]so that your partnership in the faith may become effective in recognizing every good there is in us* that leads to Christ.[e]

***Plea for Onesimus.*** [7]For I have experienced much joy and encouragement* from your love, because the hearts of the holy

**1 Prisoner**: as often elsewhere (cf. Romans, 1 Corinthians, Galatians especially), the second word in Greek enunciates the theme and sets the tone of the letter. Here it is the prisoner appealing rather than the apostle commanding.

**2 Apphia our sister**: sister is here used (like brother) to indicate a fellow Christian. **The church at your house: your** here is singular. It more likely refers to Philemon than to the last one named, Archippus; Philemon is then the owner of the slave Onesimus (Phlm 10). An alternate view is that the actual master of the slave is Archippus and that the one to whom the letter is addressed, Philemon, is the most prominent Christian there; see note on Col 4:17.

**3 Grace . . . and peace**: for this greeting, which may be a combination of Greek and Aramaic epistolary formulae, see note on Rom 1:1–7.

**4 In my prayers**: literally, "at the time of my prayers."

**5 Holy ones**: a common term for members of the Christian community (so also Phlm 7).

**6 In us**: some good ancient manuscripts have *in you* (plural). **That leads to Christ: leads to** translates the Greek preposition *eis*, indicating direction or purpose.

**7 Encouragement**: the Greek word *paraklēsis* is cognate with the verb translated "urge" in Phlm 9–10, and serves as an introduction to Paul's plea. **Hearts**: literally, "bowels," expressing in Semitic fashion the seat of the emotions, one's

*a:* 9; Eph 3:1; 4:1; Phil 1:7, 13. *b:* Col 4:17. *c:* Rom 1:7; Gal 1:3; Phil 1:2. *d:* Rom 1:8–9; Eph 1:15–16. *e:* Phil 1:9; Col 1:9.

ones have been refreshed by you, brother.[f] 8 Therefore, although I have the full right* in Christ to order you to do what is proper, 9 I rather urge you out of love, being as I am, Paul, an old man,* and now also a prisoner for Christ Jesus.[g] 10 I urge you on behalf of my child Onesimus, whose father I have become in my imprisonment,[h] 11 who was once useless to you but is now useful* to [both] you and me. 12 I am sending him, that is, my own heart, back to you. 13 I should have liked to retain him for myself, so that he might serve* me on your behalf in my imprisonment for the gospel,[i] 14 but I did not want to do anything without your consent, so that the good you do might not be forced but voluntary.[j] 15 Perhaps this is why he was away from* you for a while, that you might have him back forever, 16 no longer as a slave but more than a slave, a brother, beloved especially to me, but even more so to you, as a man* and in the Lord.[k] 17 So if you regard me as a partner, welcome him as you would me. 18* And if he has done you any injustice or owes you anything, charge it to me. 19 I, Paul, write this in my own hand: I will pay. May I not tell you that you owe me your very self.[l] 20 Yes, brother, may I profit from you in the Lord. Refresh my heart in Christ.

21 With trust in your compliance I write to you, knowing that you will do even more than I say. 22 At the same time prepare a guest room for me, for I hope to be granted to you through your prayers.[m]

***Final Greetings.*** 23 Epaphras,* my fellow prisoner in Christ Jesus, greets you,[n] 24 as well as Mark, Aristarchus, Demas, and Luke, my co-workers. 25 The grace of the Lord Jesus Christ be with your spirit.[o]

"inmost self." The same Greek word is used in Phlm 12 and again in Phlm 20, where it forms a literary inclusion marking off the body of the letter.

**8 Full right**: often translated "boldness," the Greek word *parrēsia* connotes the full franchise of speech, as the right of a citizen to speak before the body politic, claimed by the Athenians as their privilege (Euripides).

**9 Old man**: some editors conjecture that Paul here used a similar Greek word meaning "ambassador" (cf. Eph 6:20). This conjecture heightens the contrast with "prisoner" but is totally without manuscript support.

**11 Useless . . . useful**: here Paul plays on the name Onesimus, which means "useful" or "beneficial." The verb translated "profit" in Phlm 20 is cognate.

**13 Serve**: the Greek *diakoneō* could connote a ministry.

**15 Was away from**: literally, "was separated from," but the same verb means simply "left" in Acts 18:1. It is a euphemism for his running away.

**16 As a man**: literally, "in the flesh." With this and the following phrase, Paul describes the natural and spiritual orders.

**18–19 Charge it to me . . . I will pay**: technical legal and commercial terms in account keeping and acknowledgment of indebtedness.

**23–24 Epaphras**: a Colossian who founded the church there (Col 1:7) and perhaps also in Laodicea and Hierapolis (Col 2:1; 4:12–13). **Aristarchus**: a native of Thessalonica and fellow worker of Paul (Acts 19:29; 20:4; 27:2). For Mark, Demas, and Luke, see 2 Tm 4:9–13 and the note there.

*f:* 2 Cor 7:4. *g:* 1; Eph 3:1; 4:1; Phil 1:7, 13. *h:* 1 Cor 4:14–15; Gal 4:19; Col 4:9. *i:* Phil 2:30. *j:* 2 Cor 9:7; 1 Pt 5:2. *k:* 1 Tm 6:2. *l:* Gal 6:11; 2 Thes 3:17. *m:* Heb 13:19. *n:* Col 1:7; 4:12–13. *o:* Acts 12:12, 15; 13:13; 15:37–39; 19:29; 20:4; 27:2; Col 4:10, 14; 2 Tm 4:10–13.

See RG 422–28

# The Letter to the Hebrews

As early as the second century, this treatise, which is of great rhetorical power and force in its admonition to faithful pilgrimage under Christ's leadership, bore the title "To the Hebrews." It was assumed to be directed to Jewish Christians. Usually Hebrews was attached in Greek manuscripts to the collection of letters by Paul. Although no author is mentioned (for there is no address), a reference to Timothy (Heb 13:23) suggested connections to the circle of Paul and his assistants. Yet the exact audience, the author, and even whether Hebrews is a letter have long been disputed.

The author saw the addressees in danger of apostasy from their Christian faith. This danger was due not to any persecution from outsiders but to a weariness with the demands of Christian life and a growing indifference to their calling (Heb 2:1; 4:14; 6:1–12; 10:23–32). The author's main theme, the priesthood and sacrifice of Jesus (Heb 3–10), is not developed for its own sake but as a means of restoring their lost fervor and strengthening them in their faith. Another important theme of the letter is that of the pilgrimage of the people of God to the heavenly Jerusalem (Heb 11:10; 12:1–3, 18–29; 13:14). This theme is intimately connected with that of Jesus' ministry in the heavenly sanctuary (Heb 9:11–10:22).

The author calls this work a "message of encouragement" (Heb 13:22), a designation that is given to a synagogue sermon in Acts 13:15. Hebrews is probably therefore a written homily, to which the author gave an epistolary ending (Heb 13:22–25).

The author begins with a reminder of the preexistence, incarnation, and exaltation of Jesus (Heb 1:3) that proclaimed him the climax of God's word to humanity (Heb 1:1–3). He dwells upon the dignity of the person of Christ, superior to the angels (Heb 1:4–2:2). Christ is God's final word of salvation communicated (in association with accredited witnesses to his teaching: cf. Heb 2:3–4) not merely by word but through his suffering in the humanity common to him and to all others (Heb 2:5–16). This enactment of salvation went beyond the pattern known to Moses, faithful prophet of God's word though he was, for Jesus as high priest expiated sin and was faithful to God with the faithfulness of God's own Son (Heb 2:17–3:6).

Just as the infidelity of the people thwarted Moses' efforts to save them, so the infidelity of any Christian may thwart God's plan in Christ (Heb 3:6–4:13). Christians are to reflect that it is their humanity that Jesus took upon himself, with all its defects save sinfulness, and that he bore the burden of it until death out of obedience to God. God declared this work of his Son to be the cause of salvation for all (Heb 4:14–5:10). Although Christians recognize this fundamental teaching, they may grow weary of it and of its implications, and therefore require other reflections to stimulate their faith (Heb 5:11–6:20).

Therefore, the author presents to the readers for their reflection the everlasting priesthood of Christ (Heb 7:1–28), a priesthood that fulfills the promise of the Old Testament (Heb 8:1–13). It also provides the meaning God ultimately intended in the sacrifices of the Old Testament (Heb 9:1–28): these pointed to the unique sacrifice of Christ, which alone obtains forgiveness of sins (Heb 10:1–18). The trial of faith experienced by the readers should resolve itself through their consideration of Christ's ministry in the heavenly sanctuary and his perpetual intercession there on their behalf (Heb 7:25; 8:1–13). They should also be strengthened by the assurance of his foreordained parousia, and by the fruits of faith that they have already enjoyed (Heb 10:19–39).

It is in the nature of faith to recognize the reality of what is not yet seen and is the object of hope, and the saints of the Old Testament give striking example of that faith (Heb 11:1–40). The perseverance to which the author exhorts the readers is shown forth in the early life of Jesus. Despite the afflictions of his ministry and the supreme trial of his suffering and death, he remained confident of the triumph that God would bring him (Heb 12:1–3). The difficulties of human life have meaning when they are accepted as God's discipline (Heb 12:4–13), and if Christians persevere in fidelity to the word in which they have believed, they are assured of possessing forever the unshakable kingdom of God (Heb 12:14–29).

The letter concludes with specific moral commandments (Heb 13:1–17), in the course of which the author recalls again his central theme of the sacrifice of Jesus and the courage needed to associate oneself with it in faith (Heb 13:9–16).

As early as the end of the second century, the church of Alexandria in Egypt accepted Hebrews as a letter of Paul, and that became the view commonly held in the East. Pauline authorship was contested in the West into the fourth century, but then accepted. In the sixteenth century, doubts about that position were again raised, and the modern consensus is that the letter was not written by Paul. There is, however, no widespread agreement on any of the other suggested authors, e.g., Barnabas, Apollos, or Prisc(ill)a and Aquila. The document itself has no statement about its author.

Among the reasons why Pauline authorship has been abandoned are the great difference of vocabulary and style between Hebrews and Paul's letters, the alternation of doctrinal teaching with moral exhortation, the different manner of citing the Old Testament, and the resemblance between the thought of Hebrews and that of Alexandrian Judaism. The Greek of the letter is in many ways the best in the New Testament.

Since the letter of Clement of Rome to the Corinthians, written about A.D. 96, most probably cites Hebrews, the upper limit for the date of composition is reasonably certain. While the letter's references in the present tense to the Old Testament sacrificial worship do not necessarily show that temple worship was still going on, many older commentators and a growing number of recent ones favor the view that it was and that the author wrote before the destruction of the temple of Jerusalem in A.D. 70. In that case, the argument of the letter is more easily explained as directed toward Jewish Christians rather than those of Gentile origin, and the persecutions they have suffered in the past (cf. Heb 10:32–34) may have been connected with the disturbances that preceded the expulsion of the Jews from Rome in A.D. 49 under the emperor Claudius. These were probably caused by disputes between Jews who accepted Jesus as the Messiah and those who did not.

The principal divisions of the Letter to the Hebrews are the following:

I. Introduction (1:1–4)
II. The Son Higher than the Angels (1:5–2:18)
III. Jesus, Faithful and Compassionate High Priest (3:1–5:10)
IV. Jesus' Eternal Priesthood and Eternal Sacrifice (5:11–10:39)
V. Examples, Discipline, Disobedience (11:1–12:29)
VI. Final Exhortation, Blessing, Greetings (13:1–25)

# I. Introduction*

## CHAPTER 1

See RG 424-25

1 In times past, God spoke in partial and
various ways to our ancestors through the
prophets; 2 in these last days, he spoke to us
through a son, whom he made heir of all things
and through whom he created the universe,[a]

3 who is the refulgence of his glory,
the very imprint of his being,
and who sustains all things by his mighty word.
When he had accomplished purification from sins,
he took his seat at the right hand of the Majesty on high,[b]
4 as far superior to the angels
as the name he has inherited is more excellent than theirs.[c]

# II. The Son Higher Than the Angels

***Messianic Enthronement.**** 5 For to which of
the angels did God ever say:

"You are my son; this day I have begotten you"?[d]

Or again:

"I will be a father to him, and he shall be a son to me"?

---

**1:1–4** The letter opens with an introduction consisting of a reflection on the climax of God's revelation to the human race in his Son. The divine communication was initiated and maintained during Old Testament times in fragmentary and varied ways through **the prophets** (Heb 1:1), including Abraham, Moses, and all through whom God spoke. But now **in these last days** (Heb 1:2) the final age, God's revelation of his saving purpose is achieved **through a son**, i.e., one who is Son, whose role is redeemer and mediator of creation. He was made **heir of all things** through his death and exaltation to glory, yet he existed before he appeared as man; through him God **created the universe**. Heb 1:3–4, which may be based upon a liturgical hymn, assimilate the Son to the personified Wisdom of the Old Testament as **refulgence of** God's **glory** and **imprint of his being** (Heb 1:3; cf. Wis 7:26). These same terms are used of the Logos in Philo. The author now turns from the cosmological role of the preexistent Son to the redemptive work of Jesus: he brought about purification from sins and has been exalted to the right hand of God (see Ps 110:1). The once-humiliated and crucified Jesus has been declared God's Son, and this name shows his superiority to the angels. The reason for the author's insistence on that superiority is, among other things, that in some Jewish traditions angels were mediators of the old covenant (see Acts 7:53; Gal 3:19). Finally, Jesus' superiority to the angels emphasizes the superiority of the new covenant to the old because of the heavenly priesthood of Jesus.

**1:5–14** Jesus' superiority to the angels is now demonstrated by a series of seven Old Testament texts. Some scholars see in the stages of Jesus' exaltation an order corresponding to that of enthronement ceremonies in the ancient Near East, especially in Egypt, namely, elevation to divine status (Heb 1:5–6); presentation to the angels and proclamation of everlasting lordship (Heb 1:7–12); enthronement and conferral of royal power (Heb 1:13). The citations from the Psalms in Heb 1:5, 13 were traditionally used of Jesus' messianic sonship (cf. Acts 13:33) through his resurrection and exaltation (cf. Acts 2:33–35); those in Heb 1:8, 10–12 are concerned with his divine kingship and his creative

*a:* Is 2:2; Jer 23:20; Ez 38:16; Dn 10:14 / Jn 3:17; Rom 8:3; Gal 4:4 / Prv 8:30; Wis 7:22; Jn 1:3; 1 Cor 8:6; Col 1:16. *b:* Wis 7:26; 2 Cor 4:4; Col 1:15 / Heb 8:1; 10:12; 12:2; Mk 16:19; Acts 2:33; 7:55–56; Rom 8:34; Eph 1:20; Col 3:1; 1 Pt 3:22. *c:* Eph 1:21; Phil 2:9–11. *d:* Ps 2:7 / 2 Sm 7:14.

6 And again, when he leads* the first-born into the world, he says:

"Let all the angels of God worship him."[e]

7 Of the angels he says:

"He makes his angels winds
and his ministers a fiery flame";[f]

8 but of the Son:

"Your throne, O God,* stands forever and ever;
and a righteous scepter is the scepter of your kingdom.[g]
9 You loved justice and hated wickedness;
therefore God, your God, anointed you
with the oil of gladness above your companions";

10 and:

"At the beginning, O Lord, you established the earth,[h]
and the heavens are the works of your hands.
11 They will perish, but you remain;
and they will all grow old like a garment.
12 You will roll them up like a cloak,
and like a garment they will be changed.
But you are the same, and your years will have no end."

13 But to which of the angels has he ever said:

"Sit at my right hand
until I make your enemies your footstool"?[i]

14 Are they not all ministering spirits sent to serve, for the sake of those who are to inherit salvation?[j]

## CHAPTER 2

See RG 424–25

***Exhortation to Faithfulness.**** 1 Therefore, we must attend all the more to what we
have heard, so that we may not be carried
away. 2 For if the word announced through
angels proved firm, and every transgression
and disobedience received its just recompense,[k] 3 how shall we escape if we ignore so
great a salvation? Announced originally
through the Lord, it was confirmed for us by
those who had heard.[l] 4 God added his testimony by signs, wonders, various acts of
power, and distribution of the gifts of the
holy Spirit according to his will.[m]
***Exaltation Through Abasement.**** 5 For it
was not to angels that he subjected the world
to come, of which we are speaking. 6 Instead,
someone has testified somewhere:

"What is man that you are mindful of him,

function. The central quotation in Heb 1:7 serves to contrast the angels with the Son. The author quotes it according to the Septuagint translation, which is quite different in meaning from that of the Hebrew ("You make the winds your messengers, and flaming fire your ministers"). The angels are only **sent to serve . . . those who are to inherit salvation** (Heb 1:14).

**1:6 And again, when he leads**: the Greek could also be translated "And when he again leads" in reference to the parousia.

**1:8–12 O God**: the application of the name "God" to the Son derives from the preexistence mentioned in Heb 1:2–3; the psalmist had already used it of the Hebrew king in the court style of the original. See note on Ps 45:7. It is also important for the author's christology that in Heb 1:10–12 an Old Testament passage addressed to God is redirected to Jesus.

**2:1–4** The author now makes a transition into exhortation, using an a fortiori argument (as at Heb 7:21–22; 9:13–14; 10:28–29; 12:25). The **word announced through angels** (Heb 2:2), the Mosaic law, is contrasted with the more powerful word that Christians have received (Heb 2:3–4). Christ's supremacy strengthens Christians against being **carried away** from their faith.

**2:5–18** The humanity and the suffering of Jesus do not constitute a valid reason for relinquishing the Christian faith. Ps 8:6–7 is also applied to Jesus in 1 Cor 15:27; Eph 1:22; and probably 1 Pt 3:22. This christological interpretation, therefore, probably reflects a common early Christian tradition, which may have originated in the expression **the son of man** (Heb 2:6). The psalm contrasts God's greatness with man's relative insignificance but also stresses the superiority of man to the rest of creation, of which he is lord. Hebrews applies this christologically: Jesus lived a truly human existence, **lower than the angels**, in the days of his earthly life, particularly in his suffering and death; now, **crowned with glory and honor**, he is raised above all creation. The author considers all things as already **subject to him** because of his exaltation (Heb 2:8–9), though **we do not see** this yet. The reference to Jesus as **leader** (Heb 2:10) sounds the first note of an important leitmotif in Hebrews: the journey of the people of God to the sabbath rest (Heb 4:9), the heavenly sanctuary, following Jesus, their "forerunner" (Heb 6:20). It was fitting that God should make him **perfect through suffering**, consecrated by obedient suffering. Because he is perfected as high priest, Jesus is then able to consecrate his people (Heb 2:11); access to God is

*e:* Dt 32:43 LXX; Ps 97:7. *f:* Ps 104:4 LXX. *g:* Ps 45:7–8. *h:* Ps 102:26–28. *i:* Ps 110:1. *j:* Ps 91:11; Dn 7:10. *k:* Acts 7:38, 53; Gal 3:19. *l:* 10:29; 12:25. *m:* Mk 16:20; Acts 14:3; 19:11.

or the son of man that you care for
him?[n]
7 You made him for a little while lower
than the angels;
you crowned him with glory and honor,
8 subjecting all things under his feet."

In "subjecting" all things [to him], he left
nothing not "subject to him." Yet at present
we do not see "all things subject to him,"[o]
9 but we do see Jesus "crowned with glory
and honor" because he suffered death, he
who "for a little while" was made "lower
than the angels," that by the grace of God he
might taste death for everyone.[p]
10 For it was fitting that he, for whom and
through whom all things exist, in bringing
many children to glory, should make the
leader to their salvation perfect through suffering.[q] 11 He who consecrates and those who
are being consecrated all have one origin.
Therefore, he is not ashamed to call them
"brothers," 12 saying:

"I will proclaim your name to my
brothers,
in the midst of the assembly I will
praise you";[r]

13 and again:

"I will put my trust in him";

and again:

"Behold, I and the children God has
given me."[s]

14 Now since the children share in blood and
flesh, he likewise shared in them, that
through death he might destroy the one who
has the power of death, that is, the devil,[t]
15 and free those who through fear of death
had been subject to slavery all their life.
16 Surely he did not help angels but rather the
descendants of Abraham; 17 therefore, he had
to become like his brothers in every way,
that he might be a merciful and faithful high
priest before God to expiate the sins of the
people.[u] 18 Because he himself was tested
through what he suffered, he is able to help
those who are being tested.

## III. Jesus, Faithful and Compassionate High Priest

### CHAPTER 3

See RG 425–26

***Jesus, Superior to Moses.**** 1 Therefore,
holy "brothers," sharing in a heavenly calling, reflect on Jesus, the apostle and high
priest of our confession, 2 who was faithful to
the one who appointed him, just as Moses
was "faithful in [all] his house."[v] 3 But he is

made possible by each of these two consecrations. If Jesus is able to help human beings, it is because he has become one of us; we are his "brothers." The author then cites three Old Testament texts as proofs of this unity between ourselves and the Son. Ps 22:23 is interpreted so as to make Jesus the singer of this lament, which ends with joyful praise of the Lord in the assembly of "brothers." The other two texts are from Is 8:17, 18. The first of these seems intended to display in Jesus an example of the trust in God that his followers should emulate. The second curiously calls these followers "children"; probably this is to be understood to mean children of Adam, but the point is our solidarity with Jesus. By sharing human nature, including the ban of death, Jesus broke the power of the devil over death (Heb 2:14); the author shares the view of Hellenistic Judaism that death was not intended by God and that it had been introduced into the world by the devil. The **fear of death** (Heb 2:15) is a religious fear based on the false conception that death marks the end of a person's relations with God (cf. Ps 115:17–18; Is 38:18). Jesus deliberately allied himself with the **descendants of Abraham** (Heb 2:16) in order to be a **merciful and faithful high priest**. This is the first appearance of the central theme of Hebrews, Jesus the great high priest expiating the **sins of the people** (Heb 2:17), as one who experienced the same tests as they (Heb 2:18).

**3:1–6** The author now takes up the two qualities of Jesus mentioned in Heb 2:17, but in inverse order: faithfulness (Heb 3:1–4:13) and mercy (Heb 4:14–5:10). Christians are called **holy "brothers"** because of their common relation to him (Heb 2:11), **the apostle**, a designation for Jesus used only here in the New Testament (cf. Jn 13:16; 17:3), meaning one sent as God's final word to us (Heb 1:2). He is compared with Moses probably because he is seen as mediator of the new covenant (Heb 9:15) just as Moses was of the old (Heb 9:19–22, including his sacrifice). But when the author of Hebrews speaks of Jesus' sacrifice, he does not consider Moses as the Old Testament antitype, but rather the high priest on the Day of Atonement (Heb 9:6–15). Moses' faithfulness **"in [all] his house"** refers back to Nm 12:7, on which this section is a midrashic commentary. In Heb 3:3–6, the author does not indicate that he thinks of either Moses or Christ as the founder of the household. **His house** (Heb 3:2, 5, 6) means God's house, not that of Moses or Christ; in the case of Christ, compare Heb 3:6 with Heb 10:21. The **house** of Heb 3:6

*n:* Ps 8:5–7. *o:* Mt 28:18; 1 Cor 15:25–28; Eph 1:20–23; Phil 3:21; 1 Pt 3:22. *p:* Phil 2:6–11. *q:* 12:2; Is 53:4 / Rom 11:36; 1 Cor 8:6. *r:* Ps 22:23. *s:* Is 8:17, 18. *t:* Is 25:8; Hos 13:14; Jn 12:31; Rom 6:9; 1 Cor 15:54–55; 2 Tm 1:10; Rev 12:10. *u:* 4:15; 5:1–3. *v:* Nm 12:7. *w:* 2 Cor 3:7–8.

worthy of more "glory" than Moses, as the
founder of a house has more "honor" than the
house itself.[w] 4 Every house is founded by
someone, but the founder of all is God. 5 Moses was "faithful in all his house" as a "servant" to testify to what would be spoken, 6* [x]
but Christ was faithful as a son placed over
his house. We are his house, if [only] we hold
fast to our confidence and pride in our hope.

***Israel's Infidelity a Warning.*** 7* Therefore,
as the holy Spirit says:

"Oh, that today you would hear his voice,[y]
8 'Harden not your hearts as at the
rebellion
in the day of testing in the desert,
9 where your ancestors tested and
tried me
and saw my works[z] 10 for forty years.
Because of this I was provoked with
that generation
and I said, "They have always been
of erring heart,
and they do not know my ways."
11 As I swore in my wrath,
"They shall not enter into my
rest." ' "

12 Take care, brothers, that none of you may
have an evil and unfaithful heart, so as to
forsake the living God. 13 Encourage yourselves daily while it is still "today," so that
none of you may grow hardened by the deceit of sin. 14 We have become partners of
Christ if only we hold the beginning of the
reality firm until the end,[a] 15 for it is said:

"Oh, that today you would hear his
voice:
'Harden not your hearts as at the
rebellion.' "[b]

16c Who were those who rebelled when they
heard? Was it not all those who came out of
Egypt under Moses? 17 With whom was he
"provoked for forty years"? Was it not those
who had sinned, whose corpses fell in the
desert?[d] 18 And to whom did he "swear that
they should not enter into his rest," if not to
those who were disobedient?[e] 19 And we see
that they could not enter for lack of faith.

## CHAPTER 4

See RG 425–26

***The Sabbath Rest.*** 1 Therefore, let us
be on our guard while the promise of entering into his rest remains, that none of you
seem to have failed. 2 For in fact we have received the good news just as they did. But
the word that they heard did not profit them,
for they were not united in faith with those
who listened. 3 For we who believed enter
into [that] rest, just as he has said:[f]

"As I swore in my wrath,
'They shall not enter into my rest,' "

is the Christian community; the author suggests its continuity with Israel by speaking not of two houses but of only one. Heb 3:6 brings out the reason why Jesus is superior to Moses: the latter was the faithful **servant** laboring **in** the house founded by God, but Jesus is God's **son**, placed **over** the house.

**3:6** The majority of manuscripts add "firm to the end," but these words are not found in the three earliest and best witnesses and are probably an interpolation derived from Heb 3:14.

**3:7–4:13** The author appeals for steadfastness of faith in Jesus, basing his warning on the experience of Israel during the Exodus. In the Old Testament the Exodus had been invoked as a symbol of the return of Israel from the Babylonian exile (Is 42:9; 43:16–21; 51:9–11). In the New Testament the redemption was similarly understood as a new exodus, both in the experience of Jesus himself (Lk 9:31) and in that of his followers (1 Cor 10:1–4). The author cites Ps 95:7–11, a salutary example of hardness of heart, as a warning against the danger of growing weary and giving up the journey. To call God **living** (Heb 3:12) means that he reveals himself in his works (cf. Jos 3:10; Jer 10:11). The **rest** (Heb 3:11) into which Israel was to enter was only a foreshadowing of that rest to which Christians are called. They are to remember the example of Israel's revolt in the desert that cost a whole generation the loss of the promised land (Heb 3:15–19; cf. Nm 14:20–29). In Heb 4:1–11, the symbol of **rest** is seen in deeper dimension: because the promise to the ancient Hebrews foreshadowed that given to Christians, it is **good news**; and because the promised land was the place of rest that God provided for his people, it was a share in his own rest, which he enjoyed after he had finished his creative work (Heb 3:3–4; cf. Gn 2:2). The author attempts to read this meaning of God's rest into Ps 95:7–11 (Heb 3:6–9). The Greek form of the name of Joshua, who led Israel into the promised land, is Jesus (Heb 3:8). The author plays upon the name but stresses the superiority of Jesus, who leads his followers into heavenly rest. Heb 3:12, 13 are meant as a continuation of the warning, for the word of God brings judgment as well as salvation. Some would capitalize **the word of God** and see it as a personal title of Jesus, comparable to that of Jn 1:1–18.

*x:* 10:21; Eph 2:19; 1 Tm 3:15; 1 Pt 4:17. *y:* Ps 95:7–11. *z:* Ex 17:7; Nm 20:2–5. *a:* Rom 8:17. *b:* Ps 95:7–8. *c:* Nm 14:1–38; Dt 1:19–40. *d:* Nm 14:29. *e:* Nm 14:22–23; Dt 1:35. *f:* 3:11; Ps 95:11.

and yet his works were accomplished at the foundation of the world. 4 For he has spoken somewhere about the seventh day in this manner, "And God rested on the seventh day from all his works";[g] 5 and again, in the previously mentioned place, "They shall not enter into my rest."[h] 6 Therefore, since it remains that some will enter into it, and those who formerly received the good news did not enter because of disobedience, 7 he once more set a day, "today," when long afterwards he spoke through David, as already quoted:[i]

"Oh, that today you would hear his voice:
'Harden not your hearts.' "

8 Now if Joshua had given them rest, he would not have spoken afterwards of another day.[j] 9 Therefore, a sabbath rest still remains for the people of God. 10 And whoever enters into God's rest, rests from his own works as God did from his. 11 Therefore, let us strive to enter into that rest, so that no one may fall after the same example of disobedience.

12 Indeed, the word of God is living and effective, sharper than any two-edged sword, penetrating even between soul and spirit, joints and marrow, and able to discern reflections and thoughts of the heart.[k] 13 No creature is concealed from him, but everything is naked and exposed to the eyes of him to whom we must render an account.[l]

***Jesus, Compassionate High Priest.*** 14* Therefore, since we have a great high priest who has passed through the heavens, Jesus, the Son of God, let us hold fast to our confession.[m] 15 For we do not have a high priest who is unable to sympathize with our weaknesses, but one who has similarly been tested in every way, yet without sin.[n] 16 So let us confidently approach the throne of grace to receive mercy and to find grace for timely help.[o]

## CHAPTER 5

See RG 425-27

1* Every high priest is taken from among men and made their representative before God, to offer gifts and sacrifices for sins.* 2 He is able to deal patiently* with the ignorant and erring, for he himself is beset by weakness 3 and so, for this reason, must make sin offerings for himself as well as for the people.[p] 4 No one takes this honor upon himself but only when called by God, just as Aaron was.[q] 5 In the same way, it was not Christ who glorified himself in becoming high priest, but rather the one who said to him:

"You are my son;
this day I have begotten you";[r]

6 just as he says in another place:*

"You are a priest forever
according to the order of Melchizedek."[s]

**4:14–16** These verses, which return to the theme first sounded in Heb 2:16–3:1, serve as an introduction to the section that follows. The author here alone calls Jesus **a great high priest** (Heb 4:14), a designation used by Philo for the Logos; perhaps he does so in order to emphasize Jesus' superiority over the Jewish high priest. He has **been tested in every way, yet without sin** (Heb 4:15); this indicates an acquaintance with the tradition of Jesus' temptations, not only at the beginning (as in Mk 1:13) but throughout his public life (cf. Lk 22:28). Although the reign of the exalted Jesus is a theme that occurs elsewhere in Hebrews, and Jesus' throne is mentioned in Heb 1:8, **the throne of grace** (Heb 4:16) refers to the throne of God. The similarity of Heb 4:16 to Heb 10:19–22 indicates that the author is thinking of our confident access to God, made possible by the priestly work of Jesus.

**5:1–10** The true humanity of Jesus (see note on Heb 2:5–18) makes him a more rather than a less effective high priest to the Christian community. In Old Testament tradition, the high priest was identified with the people, guilty of personal sin just as they were (Heb 5:1–3). Even so, the office was of divine appointment (Heb 5:4), as was also the case with the sinless Christ (Heb 5:5). For Heb 5:6, see note on Ps 110:4. Although Jesus was Son of God, he was destined as a human being to learn obedience by accepting the suffering he had to endure (Heb 5:8). Because of his perfection through this experience of human suffering, he is the cause of salvation for all (Heb 5:9), a **high priest according to the order of Melchizedek** (Heb 5:10; cf. Heb 5:6 and Heb 7:3).

**5:1 To offer gifts and sacrifices for sins**: the author is thinking principally of the Day of Atonement rite, as is clear from Heb 9:7. This ritual was celebrated to atone for "all the sins of the Israelites" (Lv 16:34).

**5:2 Deal patiently**: the Greek word *metriopathein* occurs only here in the Bible; this term was used by the Stoics to designate the golden mean between excess and defect of passion. Here it means rather the ability to sympathize.

**5:6–8** The author of Hebrews is the only New Testament writer to cite Ps 110:4, here and in Heb 7:17, 21, to show that Jesus has been called by God to his role as priest. Heb 5:7–8 deal with his ability to sympathize with sinners, because of his own experience of the trials and weakness of human nature, especially fear of death. In his present exalted state,

*g:* Gn 2:2. *h:* Ps 95:11. *i:* 3:7–8, 15; Ps 95:7–8. *j:* Dt 31:7; Jos 22:4. *k:* Wis 18:15–16; Is 49:2; Eph 6:17; Rev 1:16; 2:12. *l:* Jb 34:21–22; Ps 90:8; 139:2–4. *m:* 9:11, 24. *n:* 2:17–18; 5:2. *o:* 8:1; 10:19, 22, 35; 12:2; Eph 3:12. *p:* Lv 9:7; 16:15–17, 30, 34. *q:* Ex 28:1. *r:* Ps 2:7. *s:* Ps 110:4.

7 In the days when he was in the flesh, he offered prayers and supplications with loud
cries and tears to the one who was able to
save him from death,* and he was heard because of his reverence.[t] 8 Son though he
was,* he learned obedience from what he
suffered;[u] 9 and when he was made perfect,
he became the source of eternal salvation for
all who obey him,[v] 10 declared by God high
priest according to the order of Melchizedek.[w]

## IV. Jesus' Eternal Priesthood and Eternal Sacrifice

***Exhortation to Spiritual Renewal.***
11* About this we have much to say, and it is
difficult to explain, for you have become
sluggish in hearing. 12 Although you should
be teachers by this time, you need to have
someone teach you again the basic elements of the utterances of God. You need
milk, [and] not solid food.[x] 13 Everyone who
lives on milk lacks experience of the word
of righteousness, for he is a child. 14 But
solid food is for the mature, for those
whose faculties are trained by practice to
discern good and evil.

### CHAPTER 6

See RG 426–27

1 Therefore, let us leave behind the basic teaching about Christ and advance to maturity, without laying the foundation all over
again: repentance from dead works and faith
in God,[y] 2 instruction about baptisms* and
laying on of hands, resurrection of the dead
and eternal judgment.[z] 3 And we shall do
this, if only God permits. 4 For it is impossible in the case of those who have once been
enlightened and tasted the heavenly gift* and
shared in the holy Spirit[a] 5 and tasted the
good word of God and the powers of the age
to come,* 6 and then have fallen away, to
bring them to repentance again, since they
are recrucifying the Son of God for themselves* and holding him up to contempt.[b]
7 Ground that has absorbed the rain falling
upon it repeatedly and brings forth crops
useful to those for whom it is cultivated receives a blessing from God.[c] 8 But if it produces thorns and thistles, it is rejected; it will
soon be cursed and finally burned.[d]

weakness is foreign to him, but he understands what we suffer because of his previous earthly experience.

**5:7 He offered prayers . . . to the one who was able to save him from death**: at Gethsemane (cf. Mk 14:35), though some see a broader reference (see note on Jn 12:27).

**5:8 Son though he was**: two different though not incompatible views of Jesus' sonship coexist in Hebrews, one associating it with his exaltation, the other with his preexistence. The former view is the older one (cf. Rom 1:4).

**5:11–6:20** The central section of Hebrews (5:11–10:39) opens with a reprimand and an appeal. Those to whom the author directs his teaching about Jesus' priesthood, which is **difficult to explain**, have become **sluggish in hearing** and forgetful of even **the basic elements** (Heb 5:12). But rather than treating of basic teachings, the author apparently believes that the challenge of more advanced ones may shake them out of their inertia (**therefore**, Heb 6:1). The six examples of **basic teaching** in Heb 6:1–3 are probably derived from a traditional catechetical list. No effort is made to address apostates, for their very hostility to the Christian message cuts them off completely from Christ (Heb 6:4–8). This harsh statement seems to rule out repentance after apostasy, but perhaps the author deliberately uses hyperbole in order to stress the seriousness of abandoning Christ. With Heb 6:9 a milder tone is introduced, and the criticism of the community (Heb 6:1–3, 9) is now balanced by an expression of confidence that its members are living truly Christian lives, and that God will justly reward their efforts (Heb 6:10). The author is concerned especially about their persevering (Heb 6:11–12), citing in this regard the achievement of Abraham, who relied on God's promise and on God's oath (Heb 6:13–18; cf. Gn 22:16), and proposes to them as a firm anchor of Christian hope the high priesthood of Christ, who is now living with God (Heb 6:19–20).

**6:2 Instruction about baptisms**: not simply about Christian baptism but about the difference between it and similar Jewish rites, such as proselyte baptism, John's baptism, and the washings of the Qumran sectaries. **Laying on of hands**: in Acts 8:17; 19:6 this rite effects the infusion of the holy Spirit; in Acts 6:6; 13:3; 1 Tm 4:14; 5:22; 2 Tm 1:6 it is a means of conferring some ministry or mission in the early Christian community.

**6:4 Enlightened and tasted the heavenly gift**: this may refer to baptism and the Eucharist, respectively, but more probably means the neophytes' enlightenment by faith and their experience of salvation.

**6:5 Tasted the good word of God and the powers of the age to come**: the proclamation of the **word of God** was accompanied by signs of the Spirit's power (1 Thes 1:5; 1 Cor 2:4).

**6:6 They are recrucifying the Son of God for themselves**: a colorful description of the malice of apostasy, which is portrayed as again crucifying and deriding the Son of God.

---

*t:* Mt 26:38–44; Mk 14:34–40; Lk 22:41–46; Jn 12:27. *u:* Rom 5:19; Phil 2:8. *v:* 7:24–25, 28. *w:* 6:20; Ps 110:4. *x:* 1 Cor 3:1–3. *y:* 9:14. *z:* 9:10; Mk 7:4 / Acts 6:6; 8:17; 13:3; 19:6; 1 Tm 4:14; 5:22; 2 Tm 1:6. *a:* 10:26, 32; Ps 34:6; 2 Cor 4:6. *b:* 2 Pt 2:21. *c:* Gn 1:11–12; Dt 11:11. *d:* Gn 3:17–18; Mt 7:16; 13:7; Mk 4:7; Lk 8:7.

[9]But we are sure in your regard, beloved,
of better things related to salvation, even
though we speak in this way. [10]For God is
not unjust so as to overlook your work and
the love you have demonstrated for his name
by having served and continuing to serve the
holy ones. [11]We earnestly desire each of you
to demonstrate the same eagerness for the
fulfillment of hope until the end,[e] [12]so that
you may not become sluggish, but imitators
of those who, through faith and patience,[f] are
inheriting the promises.[*]

***God's Promise Immutable.*** [13*] [g] When God
made the promise to Abraham, since he had
no one greater by whom to swear, "he swore
by himself," [14]and said, "I will indeed bless
you and multiply" you.[h] [15]And so, after patient waiting,[i] he obtained the promise.[*]
[16]Human beings swear by someone greater
than themselves; for them an oath serves as a
guarantee and puts an end to all argument.
[17]So when God wanted to give the heirs of
his promise an even clearer demonstration of
the immutability of his purpose, he intervened with an oath,[j] [18]so that by two immutable things,[*] in which it was impossible
for God to lie, we who have taken refuge
might be strongly encouraged to hold fast to
the hope that lies before us.[k] [19]This we have
as an anchor of the soul,[l] sure and firm,
which reaches into the interior behind the
veil,[*] [20]where Jesus has entered on our behalf
as forerunner, becoming high priest forever
according to the order of Melchizedek.[m]

## CHAPTER 7

See RG 426–27

***Melchizedek, a Type of Christ.*** [1*] This
"Melchizedek, king of Salem and priest of
God Most High,"[*] "met Abraham as he returned from his defeat of the kings" and
"blessed him."[n] [2*] And Abraham apportioned to him "a tenth of everything." His
name first means righteous king, and he was
also "king of Salem," that is, king of peace.
[3]Without father, mother, or ancestry, without
beginning of days or end of life,[*] thus made
to resemble the Son of God, he remains a
priest forever.[o]

[4*] See how great he is to whom the patriarch "Abraham [indeed] gave a tenth" of his
spoils.[p] [5]The descendants of Levi who receive the office of priesthood have a com-

**6:12 Imitators of those . . . inheriting the promises**: the author urges the addressees to imitate the faith of the holy people of the Old Testament, who now possess the promised goods of which they lived in hope. This theme will be treated fully in Heb 6:11.

**6:13 He swore by himself**: God's promise to Abraham, which he confirmed by an oath ("I swear by myself," Gn 22:16) was the basis for the hope of all Abraham's descendants.

**6:15 He obtained the promise**: this probably refers not to Abraham's temporary possession of the land but to the eschatological blessings that Abraham and the other patriarchs have now come to possess.

**6:18 Two immutable things**: the promise and the oath, both made by God.

**6:19 Anchor . . . into the interior behind the veil**: a mixed metaphor. The Holy of Holies, beyond the veil that separates it from the Holy Place (Ex 26:31–33), is seen as the earthly counterpart of the heavenly abode of God. This theme will be developed in Heb 9.

**7:1–3** Recalling the meeting between Melchizedek and Abraham described in Gn 14:17–20, the author enhances the significance of this priest by providing the popular etymological meaning of his name and that of the city over which he ruled (Heb 7:2). Since Genesis gives no information on the parentage or the death of Melchizedek, he is seen here as a type of Christ, representing a priesthood that is unique and eternal (Heb 7:3).

**7:1** The author here assumes that Melchizedek was a priest of the God of Israel (cf. Gn 14:22 and the note there).

**7:2** In Gn 14, the Hebrew text does not state explicitly who gave tithes to whom. The author of Hebrews supplies Abraham as the subject, according to a contemporary interpretation of the passage. This supports the argument of the midrash and makes it possible to see in Melchizedek a type of Jesus. The messianic blessings of righteousness and peace are foreshadowed in the names "Melchizedek" and "Salem."

**7:3 Without father, mother, or ancestry, without beginning of days or end of life**: this is perhaps a quotation from a hymn about Melchizedek. The rabbis maintained that anything not mentioned in the Torah does not exist. Consequently, since the Old Testament nowhere mentions Melchizedek's ancestry, birth, or death, the conclusion can be drawn that he **remains . . . forever**.

**7:4–10** The tithe that Abraham gave to Melchizedek (Heb 7:4), a practice later followed by the levitical priesthood (Heb 7:5), was a gift (Heb 7:6) acknowledging a certain superiority in Melchizedek, the foreign priest (Heb 7:7). This is further indicated by the fact that the institution of the levitical priesthood was sustained by hereditary succession in the tribe of Levi, whereas the absence of any mention of Melchizedek's death in Genesis implies that his personal priesthood is permanent (Heb 7:8). The levitical priesthood itself, through Abraham, its ancestor, paid tithes to Melchizedek, thus acknowledging the superiority of his priesthood over its own (Heb 7:9–10).

*e:* 3:14. *f:* 5:11; Gal 3:14; Eph 1:13–14. *g:* Gn 22:16. *h:* Gn 22:17. *i:* 6:12; Rom 4:20. *j:* 6:12. *k:* Nm 23:19; 1 Sm 15:29; Jn 8:17; 2 Tm 2:13. *l:* 10:20; Ex 26:31–33; Lv 16:2. *m:* 5:10; Ps 110:4. *n:* Gn 14:17–20. *o:* 4:14; 6:6; 10:29. *p:* Gn 14:20. *q:* Nm 18:21 / Gn 35:11.

mandment according to the law to exact
tithes from the people, that is, from their
brothers, although they also have come from
the loins of Abraham.[q] 6But he who was not
of their ancestry received tithes from Abraham and blessed him who had received the
promises. 7Unquestionably, a lesser person
is blessed by a greater.* 8In the one case,
mortal men receive tithes; in the other, a man
of whom it is testified that he lives on. 9One
might even say that Levi* himself, who receives tithes, was tithed through Abraham,
10for he was still in his father's loins when
Melchizedek met him.
11* If, then, perfection came through the
levitical priesthood, on the basis of which
the people received the law, what need
would there still have been for another priest
to arise according to the order of
Melchizedek, and not reckoned according to
the order of Aaron?[r] 12When there is a
change of priesthood, there is necessarily a
change of law as well. 13Now he of whom
these things are said* belonged to a different
tribe, of which no member ever officiated at
the altar. 14It is clear that our Lord arose
from Judah,* and in regard to that tribe Moses said nothing about priests.[s] 15* It is even
more obvious if another priest is raised up
after the likeness of Melchizedek, 16who has
become so, not by a law expressed in a commandment concerning physical descent but
by the power of a life that cannot be destroyed.* 17For it is testified:

"You are a priest forever
according to the order of
Melchizedek."[t]

18On the one hand, a former commandment
is annulled because of its weakness and uselessness,[u] 19for the law brought nothing to
perfection; on the other hand, a better hope*
is introduced, through which we draw near
to God. 20* And to the degree that this happened not without the taking of an oath*—
for others became priests without an oath,
21but he with an oath, through the one who
said to him:

"The Lord has sworn, and he will not
repent:[v]
'You are a priest forever' "—

**7:7 A lesser person is blessed by a greater**: though this sounds like a principle, there are some examples in the Old Testament that do not support it (cf. 2 Sm 14:22; Jb 31:20). The author may intend it as a statement of a liturgical rule.

**7:9 Levi**: for the author this name designates not only the son of Jacob mentioned in Genesis but the priestly tribe that was thought to be descended from him.

**7:11–14** The levitical priesthood was not typified by the priesthood of Melchizedek, for Ps 110:4 speaks of a priesthood of a new order, the order of Melchizedek, to arise in messianic times (Heb 7:11). Since the levitical priesthood served the Mosaic law, a new priesthood (Heb 7:12) would not come into being without a change in the law itself. Thus Jesus was not associated with the Old Testament priesthood, for he was a descendant of the tribe of Judah, which had never exercised the priesthood (Heb 7:13–14).

**7:13 He of whom these things are said**: Jesus, the priest "according to the order of Melchizedek." According to the author's interpretation, Ps 110 spoke prophetically of Jesus.

**7:14 Judah**: the author accepts the early Christian tradition that Jesus was descended from the family of David (cf. Mt 1:1–2, 16, 20; Lk 1:27; 2:4; Rom 1:3). The Qumran community expected two Messiahs, one descended from Aaron and one from David; Hebrews shows no awareness of this view or at least does not accept it. Our author's view is not attested in contemporaneous Judaism.

**7:15–19** Jesus does not exercise a priesthood through family lineage but through his immortal existence (Heb 7:15–16), fulfilling Ps 110:4 (Heb 7:17; cf. Heb 7:3). Thus he abolishes forever both the levitical priesthood and the law it serves, because neither could effectively sanctify people (Heb 7:18) by leading them into direct communication with God (Heb 7:19).

**7:16 A life that cannot be destroyed**: the life to which Jesus has attained by virtue of his resurrection; it is his exaltation rather than his divine nature that makes him priest. The Old Testament speaks of the Aaronic priesthood as eternal (see Ex 40:15); our author does not explicitly consider this possible objection to his argument but implicitly refutes it in Heb 7:23–24.

**7:19 A better hope**: this hope depends upon the sacrifice of the Son of God; through it we "approach the throne of grace" (Heb 4:16); cf. Heb 6:19, 20.

**7:20–25** As was the case with the promise to Abraham (Heb 6:13), though not with the levitical priesthood, the eternal priesthood of the order of Melchizedek was confirmed by God's oath (Heb 7:20–21); cf. Ps 110:4. Thus Jesus becomes the guarantee of a permanent covenant (Heb 7:22) that does not require a succession of priests as did the levitical priesthood (Heb 7:23) because his high priesthood is eternal and unchangeable (Heb 7:24). Consequently, Jesus is able to save all who draw near to God through him since he is their everliving intercessor (Heb 7:25).

**7:20 An oath**: God's oath in Ps 110:4.

*r:* 5:6; Ps 110:4. *s:* Gn 49:10; Is 11:1; Mt 1:1–2, 16, 20; 2:6; Lk 1:27; 2:4; Rom 1:3; Rev 5:5. *t:* 5:6; Ps 110:4. *u:* 10:1. *v:* Ps 110:4.

22[w] to that same degree has Jesus [also] become the guarantee of an [even] better covenant.* 23Those priests were many because they were prevented by death from remaining in office, 24but he, because he remains forever, has a priesthood that does not pass away.[x] 25* Therefore, he is always able to save those who approach God through him, since he lives forever to make intercession for them.[y]

26[z] It was fitting that we should have such a high priest:* holy, innocent, undefiled, separated from sinners, higher than the heavens.* 27He has no need, as did the high priests, to offer sacrifice day after day,*[a] first for his own sins and then for those of the people; he did that once for all when he offered himself. 28For the law appoints men subject to weakness to be high priests, but the word of the oath, which was taken after the law, appoints a son, who has been made perfect forever.[b]

## CHAPTER 8

See RG 426–27

***Heavenly Priesthood of Jesus.**** 1The main point of what has been said is this: we have such a high priest, who has taken his seat at the right hand of the throne of the Majesty in heaven,[c] 2a minister of the sanctuary* and of the true tabernacle that the Lord, not man, set up.[d] 3Now every high priest is appointed to offer gifts and sacrifices; thus the necessity for this one also to have something to offer.[e] 4If then he were on earth, he would not be a priest, since there are those who offer gifts according to the law.[f] 5They worship in a copy and shadow of the heavenly sanctuary, as Moses was warned when he was about to erect the tabernacle. For he says, "See that you make everything according to the pattern shown you on the mountain."[g] 6Now he has obtained so much more excellent a ministry as he is mediator of a better covenant, enacted on better promises.[h]

***Old and New Covenants.**** 7For if that first covenant had been faultless, no place would have been sought for a second one. 8But he finds fault with them and says:*

**7:22 An [even] better covenant**: better than the Mosaic covenant because it will be eternal, like the priesthood of Jesus upon which it is based. Heb 7:12 argued that a change of priesthood involves a change of law; since "law" and "covenant" are used correlatively, a new covenant is likewise instituted.

**7:25 To make intercession**: the intercession of the exalted Jesus, not the sequel to his completed sacrifice but its eternal presence in heaven; cf. Rom 8:34.

**7:26** This verse with its list of attributes is reminiscent of Heb 7:3 and is perhaps a hymnic counterpart to it, contrasting the exalted Jesus with Melchizedek.

**7:26–28** Jesus is precisely the high priest whom the human race requires, holy and sinless, installed far above humanity (Heb 7:26); one having no need to offer sacrifice daily for sins but making a single offering of himself (Heb 7:27) once for all. The law could only appoint high priests with human limitations, but the fulfillment of God's oath regarding the priesthood of Melchizedek (Ps 110:4) makes the Son of God the perfect priest forever (Heb 7:28).

**7:27** Such daily sacrifice is nowhere mentioned in the Mosaic law; only on the Day of Atonement is it prescribed that the high priest must **offer sacrifice . . . for his own sins and then for those of the people** (Lv 16:11–19). **Once for all**: this translates the Greek words *ephapax/hapax* that occur eleven times in Hebrews.

**8:1–6** The Christian community has in Jesus the kind of high priest described in Heb 7:26–28. In virtue of his ascension Jesus has taken his place at God's right hand in accordance with Ps 110:1 (Heb 8:1), where he presides over the heavenly sanctuary established by God himself (Heb 8:2). Like every high priest, he has his offering to make (Heb 8:3; cf. Heb 9:12, 14), but it differs from that of the levitical priesthood in which he had no share (Heb 8:4) and which was in any case but a shadowy reflection of the true offering in the heavenly sanctuary (Heb 8:5). But Jesus' ministry in the heavenly sanctuary is that of mediator of a superior covenant that accomplishes what it signifies (Heb 8:6).

**8:2 The sanctuary**: the Greek term could also mean "holy things" but bears the meaning "sanctuary" elsewhere in Hebrews (Heb 9:8, 12, 24, 25; 10:19; 13:11). **The true tabernacle**: the heavenly tabernacle **that the Lord . . . set up** is contrasted with the earthly tabernacle that Moses set up in the desert. **True** means "real" in contradistinction to a mere "copy and shadow" (Heb 8:5); compare the Johannine usage (e.g., Jn 1:9; 6:32; 15:1). The idea that the earthly sanctuary is a reflection of a heavenly model may be based upon Ex 25:9, but probably also derives from the Platonic concept of a real world of which our observable world is merely a shadow.

**8:7–13** Since the first covenant was deficient in accomplishing what it signified, it had to be replaced (Heb 8:7), as Jeremiah (Jer 31:31–34) had prophesied (Heb 8:8–12). Even in the time of Jeremiah, the first covenant was antiquated (Heb 8:13). In Heb 7:22–24, the superiority of the new covenant was seen in the permanence of its priesthood; here the superiority is based on better promises, made explicit in the citation of Jer 31:31–34 (LXX: 38), namely, in the immediacy of the people's knowledge of God (Heb 8:11) and in the forgiveness of sin (Heb 8:12).

*w:* 8:6–10; 9:15–20; 10:29; 12:24; 13:20. *x:* 5:6; 13:8. *y:* Rom 8:34; 1 Jn 2:1; Rev 1:18. *z:* 4:14, 15. *a:* 5:3; 9:12, 25–28; 10:11–14; Ex 29:38–39; Lv 16:6, 11, 15–17; Nm 28:3–4; Is 53:10; Rom 6:10. *b:* 5:1, 2, 9. *c:* 1:3; 4:14; 7:26–28. *d:* 9:11; Ex 33:7; Nm 24:6 LXX. *e:* 5:1. *f:* 7:13. *g:* 9:23; Ex 25:40; Acts 7:44; Col 2:17. *h:* 7:22; 9:15. *i:* Jer 31:31–34.

"Behold, the days are coming, says the
Lord,[i]
when I will conclude a new covenant
with the house of Israel and the
house of Judah.
9 It will not be like the covenant I made
with their fathers
the day I took them by the hand to lead
them forth from the land of
Egypt;
for they did not stand by my covenant
and I ignored them, says the Lord.
10 But this is the covenant I will establish
with the house of Israel
after those days, says the Lord:
I will put my laws in their minds
and I will write them upon their hearts.
I will be their God,
and they shall be my people.[j]
11 And they shall not teach, each one his
fellow citizen
and kinsman, saying, 'Know the
Lord,'
for all shall know me,
from least to greatest.
12 For I will forgive their evildoing
and remember their sins no more."

13* [k] When he speaks of a "new" covenant,
he declares the first one obsolete. And what
has become obsolete and has grown old is
close to disappearing.

## CHAPTER 9

See RG 426–27

### *The Worship of the First Covenant.**

1 Now [even] the first covenant had regulations for worship and an earthly sanctuary.
2 For a tabernacle was constructed, the outer
one,* in which were the lampstand, the table,
and the bread of offering; this is called the
Holy Place.[l] 3* Behind the second veil was
the tabernacle called the Holy of Holies,[m] 4 in
which were the gold altar of incense* and the
ark of the covenant entirely covered with
gold. In it were the gold jar containing the
manna, the staff of Aaron that had sprouted,
and the tablets of the covenant.[n] 5* Above it
were the cherubim of glory overshadowing
the place of expiation. Now is not the time to
speak of these in detail.[o]
6 With these arrangements for worship, the
priests, in performing their service,* go into
the outer tabernacle repeatedly,[p] 7 but the
high priest alone goes into the inner one
once a year, not without blood* that he offers

**8:8–12** In citing Jeremiah the author follows the Septuagint; some apparent departures from it may be the result of a different Septuagintal text rather than changes deliberately introduced.

**8:13 Close to disappearing**: from the prophet's perspective, not that of the author of Hebrews.

**9:1–10** The regulations for worship under the old covenant permitted all the priests to enter the Holy Place (Heb 2:6), but only the high priest to enter the Holy of Holies and then only once a year (Heb 9:3–5, 7). The description of the sanctuary and its furnishings is taken essentially from Ex 25–26. This exclusion of the people from the Holy of Holies signified that they were not allowed to stand in God's presence (Heb 9:8) because their offerings and sacrifices, which were merely symbols of their need of spiritual renewal (Heb 9:10), could not obtain forgiveness of sins (Heb 9:9).

**9:2 The outer one**: the author speaks of **the outer tabernacle** (Heb 9:6) and **the inner one** (Heb 9:7) rather than of one Mosaic tabernacle divided into two parts or sections.

**9:3 The second veil**: what is meant is the veil that divided the Holy Place from the Holy of Holies. It is here called **the second**, because there was another veil at the entrance to the Holy Place, or "outer tabernacle" (Ex 26:36).

**9:4 The gold altar of incense**: Ex 30:6 locates this altar in the Holy Place, i.e., the first tabernacle, rather than in the Holy of Holies. Neither is there any Old Testament support for the assertion that the jar of manna and the staff of Aaron were in the ark of the covenant. For the tablets of the covenant, see Ex 25:16.

**9:5 The place of expiation**: the gold "mercy seat" (Greek *hilastērion*, as in Rom 3:25), where the blood of the sacrificial animals was sprinkled on the Day of Atonement (Lv 16:14–15). This rite achieved "expiation" or atonement for the sins of the preceding year.

**9:6 In performing their service**: the priestly services that had to be performed regularly in the Holy Place or **outer tabernacle** included burning incense on the incense altar twice each day (Ex 30:7), replacing the loaves on the table of the bread of offering once each week (Lv 24:8), and constantly caring for the lamps on the lampstand (Ex 27:21).

**9:7 Not without blood**: blood was essential to Old Testament sacrifice because it was believed that life was located in the blood. Hence blood was especially sacred, and its outpouring functioned as a meaningful symbol of cleansing from sin and reconciliation with God. Unlike Hebrews, the Old Testament never says that the blood is "offered." The author is perhaps retrojecting into his description of Mosaic ritual a concept that belongs to the New Testament antitype, as Paul does when he speaks of the Israelites' passage through the sea as a "baptism" (1 Cor 10:2).

*j:* 10:16–17. *k:* Rom 10:4. *l:* Ex 25:23–30. *m:* Ex 26:31–34. *n:* Ex 16:32–34; 25:10, 16, 21; 30:1–10; Lv 16:12–13; Nm 17:2–7, 16–26. *o:* Ex 25:16–22; 26:34; Lv 16:14–15. *p:* Ex 27:21; 30:7; Lv 24:8.

for himself and for the sins of the people.[q]
8 In this way the holy Spirit shows that the
way into the sanctuary had not yet been revealed while the outer tabernacle still had its
place. 9 This is a symbol of the present time,*
in which gifts and sacrifices are offered that
cannot perfect the worshiper in conscience
10 but only in matters of food and drink and
various ritual washings: regulations concerning the flesh, imposed until the time of
the new order.[r]

*Sacrifice of Jesus.* 11* But when Christ
came as high priest of the good things that
have come to be,* passing through the greater
and more perfect tabernacle not made by
hands, that is, not belonging to this creation,[s]
12 he entered once for all into the sanctuary,
not with the blood of goats and calves but
with his own blood, thus obtaining eternal redemption.[t] 13 For if the blood of goats and
bulls and the sprinkling of a heifer's ashes*
can sanctify those who are defiled so that
their flesh is cleansed,[u] 14 how much more
will the blood of Christ, who through the
eternal spirit* offered himself unblemished to
God, cleanse our consciences from dead
works to worship the living God.[v]

15* For this reason he is mediator of a new
covenant: since a death has taken place for
deliverance from transgressions under the
first covenant, those who are called may receive the promised eternal inheritance.[w]
16* Now where there is a will, the death of the
testator must be established. 17 For a will
takes effect only at death; it has no force
while the testator is alive. 18 Thus not even
the first covenant was inaugurated without
blood. 19* When every commandment had
been proclaimed by Moses to all the people
according to the law, he took the blood of
calves [and goats], together with water and
crimson wool and hyssop, and sprinkled both
the book itself and all the people,[x] 20 saying,
"This is 'the blood of the covenant which
God has enjoined upon you.' "[y] 21 In the same
way, he sprinkled also the tabernacle* and all

**9:9 The present time**: this expression is equivalent to the "present age," used in contradistinction to the "age to come."

**9:11–14** Christ, the high priest of the spiritual blessings foreshadowed in the Old Testament sanctuary, has actually entered the true sanctuary of heaven that is not of human making (Heb 9:11). His place there is permanent, and his offering is his own blood that won eternal redemption (Heb 9:12). If the sacrifice of animals could bestow legal purification (Heb 9:13), how much more effective is the blood of the sinless, divine Christ who spontaneously offered himself to purge the human race of sin and render it fit for the service of God (Heb 9:14).

**9:11 The good things that have come to be**: the majority of later manuscripts here read "the good things to come"; cf. Heb 10:1.

**9:13 A heifer's ashes**: ashes from a red heifer that had been burned were mixed with water and used for the cleansing of those who had become ritually defiled by touching a corpse; see Nm 19:9, 14–21.

**9:14 Through the eternal spirit**: this expression does not refer either to the holy Spirit or to the divine nature of Jesus but to the life of the risen Christ, "a life that cannot be destroyed" (Heb 7:16).

**9:15–22** Jesus' role as **mediator of the new covenant** is based upon his sacrificial **death** (cf. Heb 8:6). His death has effected **deliverance from transgressions**, i.e., deliverance from sins committed under the old covenant, which the Mosaic sacrifices were incapable of effacing. Until this happened, the **eternal inheritance** promised by God could not be obtained (Heb 9:15). This effect of his work follows the human pattern by which a last will and testament becomes effective only with the death of the testator (Heb 9:16–17). The Mosaic covenant was also associated with death, for Moses made use of blood to seal the pact between God and the people (Heb 9:18–21). In Old Testament tradition, guilt could normally not be remitted without the use of blood (Heb 9:22; cf. Lv 17:11).

**9:16–17 A will . . . death of the testator**: the same Greek word *diathēkē*, meaning "covenant" in Heb 9:15, 18, is used here with the meaning **will**. The new covenant, unlike the old, is at the same time a will that requires the **death of the testator.** Jesus as eternal Son is the one who established the new covenant together with his Father, author of both covenants; at the same time he is the testator whose death puts his **will** into effect.

**9:19–20** A number of details here are different from the description of this covenant rite in Ex 24:5–8. Exodus mentions only calves ("young bulls," NAB), not goats (but this addition in Hebrews is of doubtful authenticity), says nothing of the use of **water and crimson wool and hyssop** (these features probably came from a different rite; cf. Lv 14:3–7; Nm 19:6–18), and describes Moses as splashing blood on the altar, whereas Hebrews says he sprinkled it on the book (but both book and altar are meant to symbolize the agreement of God). The words of Moses are also slightly different from those in Exodus and are closer to the words of Jesus at the Last Supper in Mk 14:24 // Mt 26:28.

**9:21** According to Exodus, the tabernacle did not yet exist at the time of the covenant rite. Moreover, nothing is said of sprinkling it with blood at its subsequent dedication (Ex 40:9–11).

---

*q:* Ex 30:10; Lv 16:1–14. *r:* 13:9; Lv 11; 14:8; Nm 19:11–21; Col 2:16. *s:* 4:14; 10:1, 20. *t:* 7:27; Mt 26:28. *u:* 10:4; Lv 16:6–16; Nm 19:9, 14–21. *v:* 10:10; Rom 5:9; 1 Tm 3:9; Ti 2:14; 1 Pt 1:18–19; 1 Jn 1:7; Rev 1:5. *w:* 1 Tm 2:5. *x:* 9:12–13. *y:* Ex 24:3–8; Mt 26:28; Mk 14:24. *z:* Ex 40:9; Lv 8:15, 19.

the vessels of worship with blood.[z] 22* According to the law almost everything is purified by blood,[a] and without the shedding of
blood there is no forgiveness.
23* Therefore, it was necessary for the
copies of the heavenly things to be purified
by these rites, but the heavenly things themselves by better sacrifices than these.[b] 24 For
Christ did not enter into a sanctuary made by
hands, a copy of the true one, but heaven itself, that he might now appear before God
on our behalf.[c] 25 Not that he might offer
himself repeatedly, as the high priest enters
each year into the sanctuary with blood that
is not his own; 26 if that were so, he would
have had to suffer repeatedly from the foundation of the world. But now once for all he
has appeared at the end of the ages* to take
away sin by his sacrifice.[d] 27 Just as it is appointed that human beings die once, and after this the judgment,[e] 28 so also Christ, offered once to take away the sins of many,*
will appear a second time, not to take away
sin but to bring salvation to those who eagerly await him.[f]

## CHAPTER 10

See RG 426–27

### *One Sacrifice Instead of Many.*

1* Since the law has only a shadow of the
good things to come,* and not the very image of them, it can never make perfect those
who come to worship by the same sacrifices
that they offer continually each year.[g] 2 Otherwise, would not the sacrifices have ceased
to be offered, since the worshipers, once
cleansed, would no longer have had any
consciousness of sins? 3 But in those sacrifices there is only a yearly remembrance of
sins,[h] 4 for it is impossible that the blood of
bulls and goats take away sins.[i] 5 For this
reason, when he came into the world, he
said:*

"Sacrifice and offering you did not
desire,[j]
but a body you prepared for me;

**9:22 Without the shedding of blood there is no forgiveness**: in fact, ancient Israel did envisage other means of obtaining forgiveness; the Old Testament mentions contrition of heart (Ps 51:17), fasting (Jl 2:12), and almsgiving (Sir 3:29). The author is limiting his horizon to the sacrificial cult, which did always involve the shedding of blood for its expiatory and unitive value.

**9:23–28** Since the blood of animals became a cleansing symbol among Old Testament prefigurements, it was necessary that the realities foreshadowed be brought into being by a shedding of blood that was infinitely more effective by reason of its worth (Heb 9:23). Christ did not simply prefigure the heavenly realities (Heb 9:24) by performing an annual sacrifice with a blood not his own (Heb 9:25); he offered the single sacrifice of himself as the final annulment of sin (Heb 9:26). Just as death is the unrepeatable act that ends a person's life, so Christ's offering of himself for all is the unrepeatable sacrifice that has once for all achieved redemption (Heb 9:27–28).

**9:26 At the end of the ages**: the use of expressions such as this shows that the author of Hebrews, despite his interest in the Platonic concept of an eternal world above superior to temporal reality here below, nevertheless still clings to the Jewish Christian eschatology with its sequence of "the present age" and "the age to come."

**9:28 To take away the sins of many**: the reference is to Is 53:12. Since the Greek verb *anapherō* can mean both "to take away" and "to bear," the author no doubt intended to play upon both senses: Jesus took away sin by bearing it himself. See the similar wordplay in Jn 1:29. **Many** is used in the Semitic meaning of "all" in the inclusive sense, as in Mk 14:24. **To those who eagerly await him**: Jesus will appear **a second time** at the parousia, as the high priest reappeared on the Day of Atonement, emerging from the Holy of Holies, which he had entered **to take away sin**. This dramatic scene is described in Sir 50:5–11.

**10:1–10** Christian faith now realizes that the Old Testament sacrifices did not effect the spiritual benefits to come but only prefigured them (Heb 10:1). For if the sacrifices had actually effected the forgiveness of sin, there would have been no reason for their constant repetition (Heb 10:2). They were rather a continual reminder of the people's sins (Heb 10:3). It is not reasonable to suppose that human sins could be removed by the blood of animal sacrifices (Heb 10:4). Christ, therefore, is here shown to understand his mission in terms of Ps 40:6–8, cited according to the Septuagint (Heb 10:5–7). Jesus acknowledged that the Old Testament sacrifices did not remit the sins of the people and so, perceiving the will of God, offered his own body for this purpose (Heb 10:8–10).

**10:1 A shadow of the good things to come**: the term **shadow** was used in Heb 8:5 to signify the earthly counterpart of the Platonic heavenly reality. But here it means a prefiguration of what is to come in Christ, as it is used in the Pauline literature; cf. Col 2:17.

**10:5–7** A passage from Ps 40:7–9 is placed in the mouth of the Son at his incarnation. As usual, the author follows the Septuagint text. There is a notable difference in Heb 10:5 (Ps 40:6), where the Masoretic text reads "ears you have dug for me" ("ears open to obedience you gave me," NAB), but most Septuagint manuscripts have "a body you prepared for me," a reading obviously more suited to the interpretation of Hebrews.

*a:* Lv 17:11. *b:* Jb 15:15. *c:* 7:25; Rom 8:34; 1 Jn 2:1–2. *d:* 7:27; Jn 1:29; Gal 4:4. *e:* Gn 3:19. *f:* 10:10; Is 53:12. *g:* 8:5; Col 2:17. *h:* Lv 16:21; Nm 5:15 LXX. *i:* Is 1:11; Mi 6:6–8. *j:* Ps 40:7–9.

6 holocausts and sin offerings you took no
delight in.
7 Then I said, 'As is written of me in the
scroll,
Behold, I come to do your will, O God.' "

8 First he says, "Sacrifices and offerings,
holocausts and sin offerings,* you neither desired nor delighted in." These are offered according to the law.[k] 9 Then he says, "Behold,
I come to do your will." He takes away the
first to establish the second.[l] 10 By this "will,"
we have been consecrated through the offering of the body of Jesus Christ once for all.[m]
11* Every priest stands daily at his ministry, offering frequently those same sacrifices
that can never take away sins.[n] 12 But this one
offered one sacrifice for sins, and took his
seat forever at the right hand of God;[o]
13* now he waits until his enemies are made
his footstool. 14 For by one offering he has
made perfect forever those who are being
consecrated.[p] 15* The holy Spirit also testifies to us, for after saying:

16 "This is the covenant I will establish with
them after those days, says the
Lord:
'I will put my laws in their hearts,
and I will write them upon their
minds,' "[q]
17 he also says:*
"Their sins and their evildoing
I will remember no more."[r]
18 Where there is forgiveness of these, there
is no longer offering for sin.

*Recalling the Past.** 19 Therefore, brothers,
since through the blood of Jesus we have
confidence of entrance into the sanctuary[s]
20* by the new and living way he opened for
us through the veil,[t] that is, his flesh, 21* [u] and

**10:8 Sacrifices and offerings, holocausts and sin offerings**: these four terms taken from the preceding passage of Ps 40 (with the first two changed to plural forms) are probably intended as equivalents to the four principal types of Old Testament sacrifices: peace offerings (Lv 3, here called **sacrifices**); cereal offerings (Lv 2, here called **offerings**); **holocausts** (Lv 1); and **sin offerings** (Lv 4–5). This last category includes the guilt offerings of Lv 5:14–19.

**10:11–18** Whereas the levitical priesthood offered daily sacrifices that were ineffectual in remitting sin (Heb 10:11), Jesus offered a single sacrifice that won him a permanent place at God's right hand. There he has only to await the final outcome of his work (Heb 10:12–13; cf. Ps 110:1). Thus he has brought into being in his own person the new covenant prophesied by Jeremiah (Jer 31:33–34) that has rendered meaningless all other offerings for sin (Heb 10:14–18).

**10:13 Until his enemies are made his footstool**: Ps 110:1 is again used; the reference here is to the period of time between the enthronement of Jesus and his second coming. The identity of the **enemies** is not specified; cf. 1 Cor 15:25–27.

**10:15–17** The testimony of the scriptures is now invoked to support what has just preceded. The passage cited is a portion of the new covenant prophecy of Jer 31:31–34, which the author previously used in Heb 8:8–12.

**10:17 He also says**: these words are not in the Greek text, which has only *kai*, "also," but the expression **"after saying"** in Heb 10:15 seems to require such a phrase to divide the Jeremiah text into two sayings. Others understand "the Lord says" of Heb 10:16 (here rendered **says the Lord**) as outside the quotation and consider Heb 10:16b as part of the second saying. Two ancient versions and a number of minuscules introduce the words "then he said" or a similar expression at the beginning of Heb 10:17.

**10:19–39** Practical consequences from these reflections on the priesthood and the sacrifice of Christ should make it clear that Christians may now have direct and confident access to God through the person of Jesus (Heb 10:19–20), who rules God's house as high priest (Heb 10:21). They should approach God with sincerity and faith, in the knowledge that through baptism their sins have been remitted (Heb 10:22), reminding themselves of the hope they expressed in Christ at that event (Heb 10:23). They are to encourage one another to Christian love and activity (Heb 10:24), not refusing, no matter what the reason, to participate in the community's assembly, especially in view of the parousia (Heb 10:25; cf. 1 Thes 4:13–18). If refusal to participate in the assembly indicates rejection of Christ, no sacrifice exists to obtain forgiveness for so great a sin (Heb 10:26); only the dreadful judgment of God remains (Heb 10:27). For if violation of the Mosaic law could be punished by death, how much worse will be the punishment of those who have turned their backs on Christ by despising his sacrifice and disregarding the gifts of the holy Spirit (Heb 10:28–29). Judgment belongs to the Lord, and he enacts it by his living presence (Heb 10:30–31). There was a time when the spirit of their community caused them to welcome and share their sufferings (Heb 10:32–34). To revitalize that spirit is to share in the courage of the Old Testament prophets (cf. Is 26:20; Heb 2:3–4), the kind of courage that must distinguish the faith of the Christian (Heb 10:35–39).

**10:20 Through the veil, that is, his flesh**: the term **flesh** is used pejoratively. As the temple veil kept people from entering the Holy of Holies (it was rent at Christ's death, Mk 15:38), so the flesh of Jesus constituted an obstacle to approaching God.

**10:21 The house of God**: this refers back to Heb 3:6, "we are his house."

*k:* 10:5–6; Ps 40:7. *l:* 7; Ps 40:8; Mt 26:39; Mk 14:36; Lk 22:42; Jn 6:38. *m:* 9:12, 14. *n:* 7:27; Dt 10:8; 18:7. *o:* Ps 110:1. *p:* 9:28. *q:* 8:10; Jer 31:33. *r:* 8:12; Jer 31:34. *s:* 3:6; 4:16; 6:19–20; Eph 1:7; 3:12. *t:* Jn 14:6 / Heb 6:19–20; 9:8, 11–12; Mt 27:51; Mk 15:38; Lk 23:45. *u:* 3:6.

since we have "a great priest over the house
of God," 22 let us approach with a sincere
heart and in absolute trust, with our hearts
sprinkled clean from an evil conscience* and
our bodies washed in pure water.[v] 23 Let us
hold unwaveringly to our confession that
gives us hope, for he who made the promise
is trustworthy.[w] 24 We must consider how to
rouse one another to love and good works.
25 We should not stay away from our assembly,* as is the custom of some, but encourage
one another, and this all the more as you see
the day drawing near.[x]
26* [y] If we sin deliberately after receiving
knowledge of the truth, there no longer remains sacrifice for sins 27 but a fearful
prospect of judgment and a flaming fire that
is going to consume the adversaries.[z]
28 Anyone who rejects the law of Moses* is
put to death without pity on the testimony of
two or three witnesses.[a] 29 Do you not think
that a much worse punishment is due the
one who has contempt for the Son of God,
considers unclean the covenant-blood by
which he was consecrated, and insults the
spirit of grace?[b] 30 We know the one who
said:

"Vengeance is mine; I will repay,"

and again:

"The Lord will judge his people."[c]

31 It is a fearful thing to fall into the hands of
the living God.[d]
32 Remember the days past when, after you
had been enlightened,* you endured a great
contest of suffering.[e] 33 At times you were
publicly exposed to abuse and affliction; at
other times you associated yourselves with
those so treated.[f] 34 You even joined in the
sufferings of those in prison and joyfully accepted the confiscation of your property,
knowing that you had a better and lasting
possession.[g] 35 Therefore, do not throw away
your confidence; it will have great recompense.[h] 36 You need endurance to do the will
of God and receive what he has promised.[i]

37 "For, after just a brief moment,*
he who is to come shall come;
he shall not delay.[j]
38 But my just one shall live by faith,
and if he draws back I take no pleasure
in him."[k]

39 We are not among those who draw back
and perish, but among those who have faith
and will possess life.

## V. Examples, Discipline, Disobedience

### CHAPTER 11*

See RG 427

*Faith of the Ancients.* 1 Faith is the realization of what is hoped for and evidence*

**10:22 With our hearts sprinkled clean from an evil conscience**: as in Heb 9:13 (see note there), the sprinkling motif refers to the Mosaic rite of cleansing from ritual impurity. This could produce only an external purification, whereas sprinkling with the blood of Christ (Heb 9:14) cleanses the **conscience. Washed in pure water**: baptism is elsewhere referred to as a washing; cf. 1 Cor 6:11; Eph 5:26.

**10:25 Our assembly**: the liturgical **assembly** of the Christian community, probably for the celebration of the Eucharist. **The day**: this designation for the parousia also occurs in the Pauline letters, e.g., Rom 2:16; 1 Cor 3:13; 1 Thes 5:2.

**10:26 If we sin deliberately**: verse 29 indicates that the author is here thinking of apostasy; cf. Heb 3:12; 6:4–8.

**10:28 Rejects the law of Moses**: evidently not any sin against the law, but idolatry. Dt 17:2–7 prescribed capital punishment for idolaters who were convicted on the testimony of two or three witnesses.

**10:32 After you had been enlightened**: "enlightenment" is an ancient metaphor for baptism (cf. Eph 5:14; Jn 9:11), but see Heb 6:4 and the note there.

**10:37–38** In support of his argument, the author uses Hb 2:3–4 in a wording almost identical with the text of the Codex Alexandrinus of the Septuagint but with the first and second lines of Heb 10:4 inverted. He introduces it with a few words from Is 26:20: **after just a brief moment**. Note the Pauline usage of Hb 2:4 in Rom 1:17; Gal 3:11.

**11:1–40** This chapter draws upon the people and events of the Old Testament to paint an inspiring portrait of religious faith, firm and unyielding in the face of any obstacles that confront it. These pages rank among the most eloquent and lofty to be found in the Bible. They expand the theme announced in Heb 6:12, to which the author now returns (Heb 10:39). The material of this chapter is developed chronologically. Heb 11:3–7 draw upon the first nine chapters of Genesis (Gn 1–9);

*v:* 9:13–14; Ez 36:25; 1 Cor 6:11; Ti 3:5; 1 Pt 3:21. *w:* 3:1, 6; 4:14; 1 Cor 10:13. *x:* Rom 13:12; 1 Cor 3:13. *y:* 3:12; 6:4–8. *z:* 10:31; 9:27; Is 26:11 LXX; Zep 1:18. *a:* Dt 17:6. *b:* 6:6. *c:* Dt 32:35, 36; Rom 12:19. *d:* 10:27; Mt 10:28; Lk 12:4–5. *e:* 6:4. *f:* 1 Cor 4:9. *g:* 13:3; Mt 6:19–20; Lk 12:33–34. *h:* 4:16. *i:* Lk 21:19. *j:* Is 26:20; Heb 2:3. *k:* Heb 2:4; Rom 1:17; Gal 3:11.

of things not seen.[l] 2 Because of it the ancients were well attested. 3[m] By faith we understand that the universe was ordered by the word of God,* so that what is visible came into being through the invisible. 4* By faith Abel offered to God a sacrifice greater than Cain's. Through this he was attested to be righteous, God bearing witness to his gifts, and through this, though dead, he still speaks.[n] 5 By faith Enoch was taken up so that he should not see death, and "he was found no more because God had taken him." Before he was taken up, he was attested to have pleased God.[o] 6* But without faith it is impossible to please him,[p] for anyone who approaches God must believe that he exists and that he rewards those who seek him. 7 By faith Noah, warned about what was not yet seen, with reverence built an ark for the salvation of his household. Through this he condemned the world and inherited the righteousness that comes through faith.[q]

8 By faith Abraham obeyed when he was called to go out to a place that he was to receive as an inheritance; he went out, not knowing where he was to go.[r] 9 By faith he sojourned in the promised land as in a foreign country, dwelling in tents with Isaac and Jacob, heirs of the same promise;[s] 10 for he was looking forward to the city with foundations, whose architect and maker is God.[t] 11 By faith he received power to generate, even though he was past the normal age—and Sarah herself was sterile—for he thought that the one who had made the promise was trustworthy.[u] 12 So it was that there came forth from one man, himself as good as dead, descendants as numerous as the stars in the sky and as countless as the sands on the seashore.[v]

13 All these died in faith. They did not receive what had been promised but saw it and greeted it from afar and acknowledged themselves to be strangers and aliens on earth,[w] 14 for those who speak thus show that they are seeking a homeland. 15 If they had been thinking of the land from which they had come, they would have had opportunity to return. 16 But now they desire a better homeland, a heavenly one. Therefore, God is not ashamed to be called their God, for he has prepared a city for them.[x]

17 By faith Abraham, when put to the test, offered up Isaac, and he who had received the promises was ready to offer his only son,[y] 18 of whom it was said, "Through Isaac descendants shall bear your name."[z] 19* He reasoned that God was able to raise even

Heb 11:8–22, upon the period of the patriarchs; Heb 11:23–31, upon the time of Moses; Heb 11:32–38, upon the history of the judges, the prophets, and the Maccabean martyrs. The author gives the most extensive description of faith provided in the New Testament, though his interest does not lie in a technical, theological definition. In view of the needs of his audience he describes what authentic faith does, not what it is in itself. Through faith God guarantees the blessings to be hoped for from him, providing evidence in the gift of faith that what he promises will eventually come to pass (Heb 11:1). Because they accepted in faith God's guarantee of the future, the biblical personages discussed in Heb 11:3–38 were themselves commended by God (Heb 11:2). Christians have even greater reason to remain firm in faith since they, unlike the Old Testament men and women of faith, have perceived the beginning of God's fulfillment of his messianic promises (Heb 11:39–40).

**11:1 Faith is the realization . . . evidence**: the author is not attempting a precise definition. There is dispute about the meaning of the Greek words *hypostasis* and *elenchos*, here translated **realization** and **evidence**, respectively. *Hypostasis* usually means "substance," "being" (as translated in Heb 1:3), or "reality" (as translated in Heb 3:14); here it connotes something more subjective, and so **realization** has been chosen rather than "assurance" (RSV). *Elenchos*, usually "proof," is used here in an objective sense and so translated **evidence** rather than the transferred sense of "(inner) conviction" (RSV).

**11:3 By faith . . . God**: this verse does not speak of the faith of the Old Testament men and women but is in the first person plural. Hence it seems out of place in the sequence of thought.

**11:4** The "Praise of the Ancestors" in Sir 44:1–50:21 gives a similar list of heroes. The Cain and Abel narrative in Gn 4:1–16 does not mention Abel's faith. It says, however, that God "looked with favor on Abel and his offering" (Gn 4:4); in view of Heb 11:6 the author probably understood God's favor to have been activated by Abel's faith. **Though dead, he still speaks**: possibly because his blood "cries out to me from the soil" (Gn 4:10), but more probably a way of saying that the repeated story of Abel provides ongoing witness to faith.

**11:6** One must believe not only that God *exists* but that he is concerned about human conduct; the Old Testament defines folly as the denial of this truth; cf. Ps 52:2.

**11:19 As a symbol**: Isaac's "return from death" is seen as

*l:* 1:3; 3:14; Rom 8:24; 2 Cor 4:18. *m:* Gn 1:3; Ps 33:6; Wis 9:1; Jn 1:3. *n:* 12:24; Gn 4:4, 10. *o:* Gn 5:24; Sir 44:16. *p:* Wis 4:10. *q:* Gn 6:8–22; Sir 44:17–18; Mt 24:37–39; Lk 17:26–27; 1 Pt 3:20; 2 Pt 2:5. *r:* Gn 12:1–4; 15:7–21; Sir 44:19–22; Acts 7:2–8; Rom 4:16–22. *s:* Gn 12:8; 13:12; 23:4; 26:3; 35:27. *t:* 12:22; 13:14; Rev 21:10–22. *u:* Gn 17:19; 21:2; Rom 4:19–21 / 1 Cor 10:13. *v:* Gn 15:5; 22:17; 32:13; Ex 32:13; Dt 10:22; Dn 3:36 LXX. *w:* Gn 23:4; Ps 39:13. *x:* 13:14; Ex 3:6. *y:* Gn 22:1–10; Sir 44:20; 1 Mc 2:52; Jas 2:21. *z:* Gn 21:12 LXX; Rom 9:7. *a:* Rom 4:16–22.

from the dead,[a] and he received Isaac back
as a symbol. 20 By faith regarding things still
to come Isaac* blessed Jacob and Esau.[b]
21 By faith Jacob, when dying, blessed each
of the sons of Joseph and "bowed in worship, leaning on the top of his staff."[c] 22 By
faith Joseph, near the end of his life, spoke
of the Exodus of the Israelites and gave instructions about his bones.[d]

23[e] By faith Moses was hidden by his parents for three months after his birth, because
they saw that he was a beautiful child, and
they were not afraid of the king's edict.
24* By faith Moses, when he had grown up,
refused to be known as the son of Pharaoh's
daughter;[f] 25 he chose to be ill-treated along
with the people of God rather than enjoy the
fleeting pleasure of sin. 26 He considered the
reproach of the Anointed greater wealth than
the treasures of Egypt, for he was looking to
the recompense. 27 By faith he left Egypt, not
fearing the king's fury, for he persevered as
if seeing the one who is invisible.[g] 28 By faith
he kept the Passover and sprinkled the
blood, that the Destroyer of the firstborn
might not touch them.[h] 29 By faith they
crossed the Red Sea as if it were dry land,
but when the Egyptians attempted it they
were drowned.[i] 30 By faith the walls of Jericho fell after being encircled for seven days.[j]
31 By faith Rahab the harlot did not perish
with the disobedient, for she had received
the spies in peace.[k]

32 What more shall I say? I have not time
to tell of Gideon, Barak, Samson, Jephthah,
of David and Samuel and the prophets,[l]
33 who by faith conquered kingdoms, did
what was righteous, obtained the promises;
they closed the mouths of lions,[m] 34 put out
raging fires, escaped the devouring sword;
out of weakness they were made powerful,
became strong in battle, and turned back foreign invaders.[n] 35 Women received back their
dead through resurrection. Some were tortured and would not accept deliverance, in
order to obtain a better resurrection.[o] 36 Others endured mockery, scourging, even
chains and imprisonment.[p] 37 They were
stoned, sawed in two, put to death at sword's
point; they went about in skins of sheep or
goats, needy, afflicted, tormented.[q] 38 The
world was not worthy of them. They wandered about in deserts and on mountains, in
caves and in crevices in the earth.[r]

39 Yet all these, though approved because
of their faith, did not receive what had been
promised. 40 God had foreseen something
better for us, so that without us they should
not be made perfect.*

## CHAPTER 12

See RG 427

*God Our Father.** 1 Therefore, since
we are surrounded by so great a cloud of witnesses, let us rid ourselves of every burden
and sin that clings to us* and persevere in
running the race that lies before us 2 while
keeping our eyes fixed on Jesus, the leader
and perfecter of faith. For the sake of the joy

a **symbol** of Christ's resurrection. Others understand the words *en parabolē* to mean "in figure," i.e., the word **dead** is used figuratively of Isaac, since he did not really die. But in the one other place that *parabolē* occurs in Hebrews, it means symbol (Heb 9:9).

**11:20–22** Each of these three patriarchs, Isaac, Jacob, and Joseph, had faith in the future fulfillment of God's promise and renewed this faith when near death.

**11:24–27** The reason given for Moses' departure from Egypt differs from the account in Ex 2:11–15. The author also gives a christological interpretation of his decision to share the trials of his people.

**11:40 So that without us they should not be made perfect**: the heroes of the Old Testament obtained their recompense only after the saving work of Christ had been accomplished. Thus they already enjoy what Christians who are still struggling do not yet possess in its fullness.

**12:1–13** Christian life is to be inspired not only by the Old Testament men and women of faith (Heb 12:1) but above all by Jesus. As the architect of Christian faith, he had himself to endure the cross before receiving the glory of his triumph (Heb 12:2). Reflection on his sufferings should give his followers courage to continue the struggle, if necessary even to the shedding of blood (Heb 12:3–4). Christians should regard their own sufferings as the affectionate correction of the Lord, who loves them as a father loves his children.

**12:1 That clings to us**: the meaning is uncertain, since the Greek word *euperistatos*, translated **cling**, occurs only here. The papyrus P46 and one minuscule read *euperispastos*, "easily distracting," which also makes good sense.

*b:* Gn 27:27–40. *c:* Gn 27:38–40; 47:31 LXX; 48:15–16. *d:* Gn 50:24–25. *e:* Ex 2:2; Acts 7:20. *f:* Ex 2:10–15; Acts 7:23–29. *g:* Ex 2:15; Acts 7:29. *h:* Ex 12:21–23; Wis 18:25; 1 Cor 10:10. *i:* Ex 14:22–28. *j:* Jos 6:12–21. *k:* Jos 2:1–21; 6:22–25; Jas 2:25. *l:* Jgs 4:6–22; 6:11–8:32; 11:1–12:7. *m:* Dn 6:23. *n:* Dn 3:22–25, 49–50. *o:* 1 Kgs 17:17–24; 2 Kgs 4:18–37; 2 Mc 6:18–7:42. *p:* 2 Chr 36:16; Jer 20:2; 37:15. *q:* 2 Chr 24:21. *r:* 1 Mc 2:28–30.

that lay before him he endured the cross, despising its shame, and has taken his seat at
the right of the throne of God.[s] 3 Consider
how he endured such opposition from sinners, in order that you may not grow weary
and lose heart. 4 In your struggle against sin
you have not yet resisted to the point of
shedding blood. 5 You have also forgotten
the exhortation addressed to you as sons:

"My son, do not disdain the discipline of
the Lord[t]
or lose heart when reproved by him;
6 for whom the Lord loves, he disciplines;
he scourges every son he
acknowledges."

7 Endure your trials as "discipline"; God
treats you as sons. For what "son" is there
whom his father does not discipline?[u] 8 If you
are without discipline, in which all have
shared, you are not sons but bastards. 9 Besides this, we have had our earthly fathers to
discipline us, and we respected them. Should
we not [then] submit all the more to the Father of spirits and live?[v] 10 They disciplined
us for a short time as seemed right to them,
but he does so for our benefit, in order that
we may share his holiness. 11 At the time, all
discipline seems a cause not for joy but for
pain, yet later it brings the peaceful fruit of
righteousness to those who are trained by it.[w]
12 So strengthen your drooping hands and
your weak knees.[x] 13 Make straight paths for
your feet, that what is lame may not be dislocated but healed.[y]

***Penalties of Disobedience.*** 14[z] Strive for
peace with everyone, and for that holiness
without which no one will see the Lord.
15* See to it that no one be deprived of the
grace of God, that no bitter root spring up
and cause trouble, through which many may
become defiled,[a] 16 that no one be an immoral or profane person like Esau, who sold
his birthright for a single meal.[b] 17 For you
know that later, when he wanted to inherit
his father's blessing, he was rejected because he found no opportunity to change his
mind, even though he sought the blessing
with tears.[c]

18* You have not approached that which
could be touched*[d] and a blazing fire and
gloomy darkness and storm 19 and a trumpet
blast and a voice speaking words such that
those who heard begged that no message be
further addressed to them,[e] 20 for they could
not bear to hear the command: "If even an
animal touches the mountain, it shall be
stoned."[f] 21 Indeed, so fearful was the spectacle that Moses said, "I am terrified and trembling."[g] 22 No, you have approached Mount
Zion and the city of the living God, the
heavenly Jerusalem, and countless angels in
festal gathering,[h] 23 and the assembly of the
firstborn enrolled in heaven,* and God the
judge of all, and the spirits of the just made
perfect,[i] 24 and Jesus, the mediator of a new

**12:15–17** Esau serves as an example in two ways: his **profane** attitude illustrates the danger of apostasy, and his inability to secure a blessing afterward illustrates the impossibility of repenting after falling away (see Heb 6:4–6).

**12:18–29** As a final appeal for adherence to Christian teaching, the two covenants, of Moses and of Christ, are compared. The Mosaic covenant, the author argues, is shown to have originated in fear of God and threats of divine punishment (Heb 12:18–21). The covenant in Christ gives us direct access to God (Heb 12:22), makes us members of the Christian community, God's children, a sanctified people (Heb 12:23), who have Jesus as mediator to speak for us (Heb 12:24). Not to heed the voice of the risen Christ is a graver sin than the rejection of the word of Moses (Heb 12:25–26). Though Christians fall away, God's kingdom in Christ will remain and his justice will punish those guilty of deserting it (Heb 12:28–29).

**12:18** This remarkably beautiful passage contrasts two great assemblies of people: that of the Israelites gathered at Mount Sinai for the sealing of the old covenant and the promulgation of the Mosaic law, and that of the followers of Jesus gathered at **Mount Zion, the heavenly Jerusalem**, the assembly of the **new covenant**. This latter scene, marked by the presence of **countless angels** and of **Jesus** with his redeeming **blood**, is reminiscent of the celestial liturgies of the Book of Revelation.

**12:23 The assembly of the firstborn enrolled in heaven**: this expression may refer to the angels of Heb 12:22, or to the heroes of the Old Testament (see Heb 11), or to the entire assembly of the new covenant.

**12:24 Speaks more eloquently**: the blood of Abel, the first human blood to be shed, is contrasted with that of Jesus. Abel's blood cried out from the earth for vengeance, but the blood of Jesus has opened the way for everyone, providing cleansing and access to God (Heb 10:19).

*s:* 2:10; Ps 110:1; Phil 2:6–8. *t:* Prv 3:11–12 / Dt 8:5; 1 Cor 11:32. *u:* Prv 13:24; Sir 30:1. *v:* Nm 16:22; 27:16 LXX. *w:* 2 Cor 4:17; Phil 1:11; Jas 3:18. *x:* Is 35:3; Sir 25:23; Jb 4:3–4. *y:* Prv 4:26 LXX. *z:* Rom 12:18; 14:19. *a:* Dt 29:18 (17 LXX). *b:* Gn 25:33. *c:* Gn 27:34–38. *d:* Ex 19:12–14; Dt 4:11; 5:22–23. *e:* Ex 19:16, 19; 20:18–19. *f:* Ex 19:12–13. *g:* Dt 9:19. *h:* Gal 4:26; Rev 21:2. *i:* Lk 10:20; Rev 5:11. *j:* 7:22; 8:6; 9:15 / 11:4; Gn 4:10.

covenant, and the sprinkled blood that speaks more eloquently* than that of Abel.[j]

25 See that you do not reject the one who speaks. For if they did not escape when they refused the one who warned them on earth, how much more in our case if we turn away from the one who warns from heaven.[k] 26 His voice shook the earth at that time, but now he has promised, "I will once more shake not only earth but heaven."[l] 27 That phrase, "once more," points to [the] removal of shaken, created things, so that what is unshaken may remain.[m] 28 Therefore, we who are receiving the unshakable kingdom should have gratitude, with which we should offer worship pleasing to God in reverence and awe.[n] 29 For our God is a consuming fire.[o]

## VI. Final Exhortation, Blessing, Greetings

### CHAPTER 13

See RG 427–28

1* Let mutual love continue. 2 Do not neglect hospitality, for through it some have unknowingly entertained angels.[p] 3 Be mindful of prisoners as if sharing their imprisonment, and of the ill-treated as of yourselves, for you also are in the body.[q] 4 Let marriage be honored among all and the marriage bed be kept undefiled, for God will judge the immoral and adulterers.[r] 5 Let your life be free from love of money but be content with what you have, for he has said, "I will never forsake you or abandon you."[s] 6 Thus we may say with confidence:

"The Lord is my helper,
[and] I will not be afraid.
What can anyone do to me?"[t]

7 Remember your leaders who spoke the word of God to you. Consider the outcome of their way of life and imitate their faith. 8 Jesus Christ is the same yesterday, today, and forever.[u]

9 Do not be carried away by all kinds of strange teaching.* It is good to have our hearts strengthened by grace and not by foods, which do not benefit those who live by them.[v] 10 We have an altar* from which those who serve the tabernacle have no right to eat. 11 The bodies of the animals whose blood the high priest brings into the sanctuary as a sin offering are burned outside the camp.[w] 12 Therefore, Jesus also suffered outside the gate, to consecrate the people by his own blood.[x] 13 Let us then go to him outside the camp, bearing the reproach that he bore. 14 For here we have no lasting city, but we seek the one that is to come.[y] 15 Through him [then] let us continually offer God a sacrifice of praise, that is, the fruit of lips that confess his name.[z] 16 Do not neglect to do good and to share what you have; God is pleased by sacrifices of that kind.[a]

17* Obey your leaders and defer to them, for they keep watch over you and will have to give an account, that they may fulfill their task with joy and not with sorrow, for that would be of no advantage to you.

18 Pray for us, for we are confident that we have a clear conscience, wishing to act rightly in every respect. 19 I especially ask for

**13:1–16** After recommendations on social and moral matters (Heb 13:1–6), the letter turns to doctrinal issues. The fact that the original leaders are dead should not cause the recipients of this letter to lose their faith (Heb 13:7), for Christ still lives and he remains always the same (Heb 13:8). They must not rely for their personal sanctification on regulations concerning foods (Heb 13:9), nor should they entertain the notion that Judaism and Christianity can be intermingled (Heb 13:10; cf. notes on Gal 2:11–14; 2:15–21). As Jesus died separated from his own people, so must the Christian community remain apart from the religious doctrines of Judaism (Heb 13:11–14). Christ must be the heart and center of the community (Heb 13:15–16).

**13:9 Strange teaching**: this doctrine about **foods** probably refers to the Jewish food laws; in view of Heb 13:10, however, the author may be thinking of the Mosaic sacrificial banquets.

**13:10 We have an altar**: this does not refer to the Eucharist, which is never clearly mentioned in Hebrews, but to the sacrifice of Christ.

**13:17–25** Recommending obedience to the leaders of the community, the author asks for prayers (Heb 13:17–19). The letter concludes with a blessing (Heb 13:20–21), a final request for the acceptance of its message (Heb 13:22), information regarding Timothy (Heb 13:23), and general greetings (Heb 13:24–25).

---

*k:* Ex 20:19. *l:* Ex 19:18; Jgs 5:4–5; Ps 68:9; Hg 2:6. *m:* Is 66:22; Mt 24:35; Mk 13:31; Lk 21:33. *n:* Dn 7:14, 18 / Rom 1:9. *o:* Dt 4:24; Is 33:14. *p:* Gn 18:3; 19:2–3; Jgs 6:11–22; Tb 5:4. *q:* Mt 25:36. *r:* 1 Cor 5:13; Eph 5:5. *s:* Dt 31:6, 8; Jos 1:5. *t:* Ps 27:1–3; 118:6. *u:* 1:12; 7:24; Rev 1:17. *v:* Rom 14:17; 1 Cor 8:8; Eph 4:14; Col 2:16. *w:* Ex 29:14; Lv 16:27. *x:* Mt 21:39; Mk 12:8; Lk 20:15; Jn 19:17. *y:* 11:10, 14. *z:* Hos 14:3. *a:* Phil 4:18.

your prayers that I may be restored to you
very soon.
20* May the God of peace, who brought up
from the dead the great shepherd of the sheep
by the blood of the eternal covenant, Jesus our
Lord,[b] 21 furnish you with all that is good, that
you may do his will. May he carry out in you
what is pleasing to him through Jesus Christ,
to whom be glory forever [and ever]. Amen.
22 Brothers, I ask you to bear with this
message of encouragement, for I have written to you rather briefly. 23 I must let you
know that our brother Timothy has been set
free. If he comes soon, I shall see you together with him.[c] 24 Greetings to all your
leaders and to all the holy ones. Those from
Italy send you greetings. 25 Grace be with all
of you.[d]

**13:20–21** These verses constitute one of the most beautiful blessings in the New Testament. The resurrection of Jesus is presupposed throughout Hebrews, since it is included in the author's frequently expressed idea of his exaltation, but this is the only place where it is explicitly mentioned.

*b:* Is 63:11; Zec 9:11; Jn 10:11; Acts 2:24; Rom 15:33. *c:* Acts 16:1. *d:* Ti 3:15.

# THE CATHOLIC LETTERS

See RG 429–55

In addition to the thirteen letters attributed to Paul and the Letter to the Hebrews, the New Testament contains seven other letters. Three of these are attributed to John, two to Peter, and one each to James and Jude, all personages of the apostolic age. The term "catholic letter" first appears, with reference only to 1 John, in the writings of Apollonius of Ephesus, a second-century apologist, known only from a citation in Eusebius's *Ecclesiastical History*. Eusebius himself (A.D. 260–340) used the term to refer to all seven letters.

The reason for the term "catholic," which means "universal," was the perception that these letters, unlike those of Paul, which were directed to a particular local church, were apparently addressed more generally to the universal church. This designation is not entirely accurate, however. On the one hand, Hebrews has no specifically identified addressees, and originally this was probably true of Ephesians as well. On the other hand, 3 John is addressed to a named individual, 2 John to a specific, though unnamed, community, and 1 Peter to a number of churches that are specified as being located in Asia Minor.

While all seven of these writings begin with an epistolary formula, several of them do not appear to be real letters in the modern sense of the term. In the ancient world it was not unusual to cast an exhortation in the form of a letter for literary effect, a phenomenon comparable to the "open letter" that is sometimes used today.

With the exception of 1 Peter and 1 John, the ancient church showed reluctance to include the catholic letters in the New Testament canon. The reason for this was widespread doubt whether they had actually been written by the apostolic figures to whom they are attributed. The early Christians saw the New Testament as the depository of apostolic faith; therefore, they wished to include only the testimony of apostles. Today we distinguish more clearly between the authorship of a work and its canonicity: even though written by other, later witnesses than those whose names they bear, these writings nevertheless testify to the apostolic faith and constitute canonical scripture. By the late fourth or early fifth centuries, most objections had been overcome in both the Greek and Latin churches (though not in the Syriac), and all seven of the catholic letters have since been acknowledged as canonical.

# The Letter of James

See RG 429–34

The person to whom this letter is ascribed can scarcely be one of the two members of the Twelve who bore the name James (see Mt 10:2–3; Mk 3:17–18; Lk 6:14–15), for he is not identified as an apostle but only as "slave of God and of the Lord Jesus Christ" (Jas 1:1). This designation most probably refers to the third New Testament personage named James, a relative of Jesus who is usually called "brother of the Lord" (see Mt 13:55; Mk 6:3). He was the leader of the Jewish Christian community in Jerusalem whom Paul acknowledged as one of the "pillars" (Gal 2:9). In Acts he appears as the authorized spokesman for the Jewish Christian position in the early Church

(Acts 12:17; 15:13–21). According to the Jewish historian Josephus (*Antiquities* 20:201–203), he was stoned to death by the Jews under the high priest Ananus II in A.D. 62.

The letter is addressed to "the twelve tribes in the dispersion." In Old Testament terminology the term "twelve tribes" designates the people of Israel; the "dispersion" or "diaspora" refers to the non-Palestinian Jews who had settled throughout the Greco-Roman world (see Jn 7:35). Since in Christian thought the church is the new Israel, the address probably designates the Jewish Christian churches located in Palestine, Syria, and elsewhere. Or perhaps the letter is meant more generally for all Christian communities, and the "dispersion" has the symbolic meaning of exile from our true home, as it has in the address of 1 Peter (1 Pt 1:1). The letter is so markedly Jewish in character that some scholars have regarded it as a Jewish document subsequently "baptized" by a few Christian insertions, but such an origin is scarcely tenable in view of the numerous contacts discernible between the Letter of James and other New Testament literature.

From the viewpoint of its literary form, James is a letter only in the most conventional sense; it has none of the characteristic features of a real letter except the address. It belongs rather to the genre of parenesis or exhortation and is concerned almost exclusively with ethical conduct. It therefore falls within the tradition of Jewish wisdom literature, such as can be found in the Old Testament (Proverbs, Sirach) and in the extracanonical Jewish literature (Testaments of the Twelve Patriarchs, the Books of Enoch, the Manual of Discipline found at Qumran). More specifically, it consists of sequences of didactic proverbs, comparable to Tb 4:5–19, to many passages in Sirach, and to sequences of sayings in the synoptic gospels. Numerous passages in James treat of subjects that also appear in the synoptic sayings of Jesus, especially in Matthew's Sermon on the Mount, but the correspondences are too general to establish any literary dependence. James represents a type of early Christianity that emphasized sound teaching and responsible moral behavior. Ethical norms are derived not primarily from christology, as in Paul, but from a concept of salvation that involves conversion, baptism, forgiveness of sin, and expectation of judgment (Jas 1:17; 4:12).

Paradoxically, this very Jewish work is written in an excellent Greek style, which ranks among the best in the New Testament and appears to be the work of a trained Hellenistic writer. Those who continue to regard James of Jerusalem as its author are therefore obliged to suppose that a secretary must have put the letter into its present literary form. This assumption is not implausible in the light of ancient practice. Some regard the letter as one of the earliest writings in the New Testament and feel that its content accurately reflects what we would expect of the leader of Jewish Christianity. Moreover, they argue that the type of Jewish Christianity reflected in the letter cannot be situated historically after the fall of Jerusalem in A.D. 70.

Others, however, believe it more likely that James is a pseudonymous work of a later period. In addition to its Greek style, they observe further that (a) the prestige that the writer is assumed to enjoy points to the later legendary reputation of James; (b) the discussion of the importance of good works seems to presuppose a debate subsequent to that in Paul's own day; (c) the author does not rely upon prescriptions of the Mosaic law, as we would expect from the historical James; (d) the letter contains no allusions to James's own history and to his relationship with Jesus or to the early Christian community of Jerusalem. For these reasons, many recent interpreters assign James to the period A.D. 90–100.

The principal divisions of the Letter of James are the following:

I. Address (1:1)
II. The Value of Trials and Temptation (1:2–18)
III. Exhortations and Warnings (1:19–5:12)
IV. The Power of Prayer (5:13–20)

# I. Address

## CHAPTER 1

See RG 430–31

1* James, a slave of God and of the
Lord Jesus Christ, to the twelve tribes in the
dispersion, greetings.[a]

# II. The Value of Trials and Temptation

***Perseverance in Trial.*** 2[b] Consider it all joy,
my brothers, when you encounter various
trials,* 3 for you know that the testing* of
your faith produces perseverance. 4 And let
perseverance be perfect, so that you may be
perfect and complete, lacking in nothing.
5 But if any of you lacks wisdom,* he should
ask God who gives to all generously and ungrudgingly, and he will be given it.[c] 6 But he
should ask in faith, not doubting, for the one
who doubts is like a wave of the sea that is
driven and tossed about by the wind.[d] 7 For
that person must not suppose that he will receive anything from the Lord, 8 since he is a
man of two minds, unstable in all his ways.
9 The brother in lowly circumstances*
should take pride in his high standing,[e] 10 and
the rich one in his lowliness, for he will pass
away "like the flower of the field."[f] 11 For the
sun comes up with its scorching heat and
dries up the grass, its flower droops, and the
beauty of its appearance vanishes. So will
the rich person fade away in the midst of his
pursuits.

***Temptation.*** 12[g] Blessed is the man who
perseveres in temptation,* for when he has
been proved he will receive the crown of life
that he promised to those who love him.
13* No one experiencing temptation should
say, "I am being tempted by God"; for God
is not subject to temptation to evil, and he
himself tempts no one.[h] 14 Rather, each person is tempted when he is lured and enticed
by his own desire. 15 Then desire conceives
and brings forth sin, and when sin reaches
maturity it gives birth to death.
16* Do not be deceived, my beloved brothers: 17 all good giving and every perfect gift*
is from above, coming down from the Father
of lights, with whom there is no alteration or
shadow caused by change. 18[i] He willed to
give us birth by the word of truth that we
may be a kind of firstfruits of his creatures.*

**1:1 James, a slave of God and of the Lord Jesus Christ**: a declaration of the writer's authority for instructing the Christian communities; cf. Rom 1:1. Regarding the identity of the author, see Introduction. **Dispersion**: see Introduction.

**1:2 Consider it all joy . . . various trials**: a frequent teaching of the New Testament derived from the words and sufferings of Jesus (Mt 5:10–12; Jn 10:11; Acts 5:41).

**1:3–8** The sequence of testing, perseverance, and being perfect and complete indicates the manner of attaining spiritual maturity and full preparedness for the coming of Christ (Jas 5:7–12; cf. 1 Pt 1:6–7; Rom 5:3–5). These steps require wisdom (Jas 1:5).

**1:5 Wisdom**: a gift that God readily grants to all who ask in faith and that sustains the Christian in times of trial. It is a kind of knowledge or understanding not accessible to the unbeliever or those who doubt, which gives the recipient an understanding of the real importance of events. In this way a Christian can deal with adversity with great calm and hope (cf. 1 Cor 2:6–12).

**1:9–11** Throughout his letter (see Jas 2:5; 4:10, 13–16; 5:1–6), the author reaffirms the teaching of Jesus that worldly prosperity is not necessarily a sign of God's favor but can even be a hindrance to proper humility before God (cf. Lk 6:20–25; 12:16–21; 16:19–31).

**1:12 Temptation**: the Greek word used here is the same one used for "trials" in Jas 1:2. **The crown of life**: in ancient Palestine, crowns or wreaths of flowers were worn at festive occasions as signs of joy and honor. In the Hellenistic world, wreaths were given as a reward to great statesmen, soldiers, athletes. **Life**: here means eternal life. **He promised**: some manuscripts read "God" or "the Lord," while the best witnesses do not specify the subject of "promised."

**1:13–15** It is contrary to what we know of God for God to be the author of human temptation (Jas 1:13). In the commission of a sinful act, one is first beguiled by passion (Jas 1:14), then consent is given, which in turn causes the sinful act. When sin permeates the entire person, it incurs the ultimate penalty of death (Jas 1:15).

**1:16–18** The author here stresses that God is the source of all good and of good alone, and the evil of temptation does not come from him.

**1:17 All good giving and every perfect gift** may be a proverb written in hexameter. **Father of lights**: God is here called the Father of the heavenly luminaries, i.e., the stars, sun, and moon that he created (Gn 1:14–18). Unlike orbs moving from nadir to zenith, he never changes or diminishes in brightness.

**1:18** Acceptance of the gospel message, **the word of truth**, constitutes new birth (Jn 3:5–6) and makes the recipient the **firstfruits** (i.e., the cultic offering of the earliest grains, symbolizing the beginning of an abundant harvest) of a new creation; cf. 1 Cor 15:20; Rom 8:23.

---

*a:* Jn 7:35; 1 Pt 1:1. *b:* Rom 5:3–5; 1 Pt 1:6; 4:13–16. *c:* Prv 2:2–6; Wis 9:4, 9–12. *d:* Mt 7:7; Mk 11:24. *e:* 2:5. *f:* Is 40:6–7. *g:* 1 Cor 9:25; 2 Tm 4:8; 1 Pt 5:4; Rev 2:10. *h:* Sir 15:11–20; 1 Cor 10:13. *i:* Jn 1:12–13; 1 Pt 1:23.

## III. Exhortations and Warnings

*Doors of the Word.* 19Know this, my dear
brothers: everyone should be quick to hear,*
slow to speak, slow to wrath,[j] 20for the wrath
of a man does not accomplish the righteousness of God.[k] 21Therefore, put away all filth
and evil excess and humbly welcome the
word that has been planted in you and is able
to save your souls.[l]
22Be doers of the word and not hearers
only, deluding yourselves.[m] 23For if anyone
is a hearer of the word and not a doer, he is
like a man who looks at his own face in a
mirror. 24He sees himself, then goes off and
promptly forgets what he looked like. 25But
the one who peers into the perfect law* of
freedom and perseveres, and is not a hearer
who forgets but a doer who acts, such a one
shall be blessed in what he does.[n]
26* If anyone thinks he is religious and
does not bridle his tongue* but deceives his
heart, his religion is vain.[o] 27Religion that is
pure and undefiled before God and the Father is this: to care for orphans and widows*
in their affliction and to keep oneself unstained by the world.[p]

### CHAPTER 2

See RG 431–32

*Sin of Partiality.** 1My brothers, show
no partiality as you adhere to the faith in our
glorious Lord Jesus Christ. 2For if a man
with gold rings on his fingers and in fine
clothes comes into your assembly, and a
poor person in shabby clothes also comes in,
3and you pay attention to the one wearing
the fine clothes and say, "Sit here, please,"
while you say to the poor one, "Stand there,"
or "Sit at my feet," 4have you not made distinctions among yourselves and become
judges with evil designs?*
5Listen, my beloved brothers. Did not God
choose those who are poor* in the world to be
rich in faith and heirs of the kingdom that he
promised to those who love him?[q] 6But you
dishonored the poor person. Are not the rich
oppressing you? And do they themselves not
haul you off to court? 7Is it not they who blaspheme the noble name that was invoked over
you?[r] 8However, if you fulfill the royal* law
according to the scripture, "You shall love
your neighbor as yourself," you are doing
well.[s] 9But if you show partiality, you commit
sin, and are convicted by the law as transgressors.[t] 10For whoever keeps the whole law,
but falls short in one particular, has become
guilty in respect to all of it.[u] 11For he who
said, "You shall not commit adultery," also
said, "You shall not kill."[v] Even if you do not
commit adultery but kill, you have become a
transgressor of the law. 12[w] So speak and so
act as people who will be judged by the law

**1:19–25** To **be quick to hear** the gospel is to accept it readily and to act in conformity with it, removing from one's soul whatever is opposed to it, so that it may take root and effect salvation (Jas 1:19–21). To listen to the gospel message but not practice it is failure to improve oneself (Jas 1:22–24). Only conformity of life to the perfect law of true freedom brings happiness (Jas 1:25).

**1:25 Peers into the perfect law**: the image of a person doing this is paralleled to that of hearing God's word. The **perfect law** applies the Old Testament description of the Mosaic law to the gospel of Jesus Christ that brings freedom.

**1:26–27** A practical application of Jas 1:22 is now made.

**1:26** For control of the tongue, see note on Jas 3:1–12.

**1:27** In the Old Testament, orphans and widows are classical examples of the defenseless and oppressed.

**2:1–13** In the Christian community there must be no discrimination or favoritism based on status or wealth (Jas 2:2–4; cf. Mt 5:3; 11:5; 23:6; 1 Cor 1:27–29). Divine favor rather consists in God's election and promises (Jas 2:5). The rich who oppress the poor blaspheme the name of Christ (Jas 2:6–7). By violating one law of love of neighbor, they offend against the whole law (Jas 2:8–11). On the other hand, conscious awareness of the final judgment helps the faithful to fulfill the whole law (Jas 2:12).

**2:4** When Christians show favoritism to the rich they are guilty of the worst kind of prejudice and discrimination. The author says that such Christians set themselves up as judges who judge not by divine law but by the basest, self-serving motives.

**2:5** The poor, "God's poor" of the Old Testament, were seen by Jesus as particularly open to God for belief in and reliance on him alone (Lk 6:20). God's law cannot tolerate their oppression in any way (Jas 2:9).

**2:8 Royal**: literally, "kingly"; because the Mosaic law came from God, the universal king. There may be an allusion to Jesus' uses of this commandment in his preaching of the kingdom of God (Mt 22:39; Mk 12:31; Lk 10:27).

**2:12–13** The law upon which the last judgment will be based is the law of freedom. As Jesus taught, mercy (which participates in God's own loving mercy) includes forgiveness of those who wrong us (see Mt 6:12, 14–15).

*j:* Prv 14:17; Sir 5:11. *k:* Eph 4:26. *l:* Col 3:8. *m:* Mt 7:26; Rom 2:13. *n:* 2:12; Ps 19:8; Rom 8:2. *o:* 3:2; Ps 34:14. *p:* Ex 22:21. *q:* 1 Cor 1:26–28; Rev 2:9. *r:* 1 Pt 4:4. *s:* Lv 19:18; Mt 22:39; Rom 13:9. *t:* Dt 1:17. *u:* Gal 3:10. *v:* Ex 20:13–14; Dt 5:17–18. *w:* 1:25; Rom 8:2.

of freedom.* 13For the judgment is merciless
to one who has not shown mercy; mercy triumphs over judgment.[x]
***Faith and Works.**** 14What good is it, my
brothers, if someone says he has faith but
does not have works? Can that faith save
him?[y] 15If a brother or sister has nothing to
wear and has no food for the day, 16and one
of you says to them, "Go in peace, keep
warm, and eat well," but you do not give
them the necessities of the body, what good
is it?[z] 17So also faith of itself, if it does not
have works, is dead.
18Indeed someone may say, "You have
faith and I have works." Demonstrate your
faith to me without works, and I will demonstrate my faith to you from my works. 19You
believe that God is one. You do well. Even the
demons believe that and tremble. 20Do you
want proof, you ignoramus, that faith without
works is useless? 21Was not Abraham our father justified by works when he offered his
son Isaac upon the altar?[a] 22You see that faith
was active along with his works, and faith
was completed by the works. 23Thus the
scripture was fulfilled that says, "Abraham
believed God, and it was credited to him as
righteousness," and he was called "the friend
of God."[b] 24See how a person is justified by
works and not by faith alone. 25And in the
same way, was not Rahab the harlot also justified by works when she welcomed the messengers and sent them out by a different
route?[c] 26For just as a body without a spirit is
dead, so also faith without works is dead.

## CHAPTER 3

See RG 432–33

***Power of the Tongue.**** 1Not many of
you should become teachers, my brothers, for
you realize that we will be judged more
strictly, 2for we all fall short in many respects.
If anyone does not fall short in speech, he is a
perfect man, able to bridle his whole body
also.[d] 3If we put bits into the mouths of horses
to make them obey us, we also guide their
whole bodies. 4It is the same with ships: even
though they are so large and driven by fierce
winds, they are steered by a very small rudder
wherever the pilot's inclination wishes. 5In
the same way the tongue is a small member
and yet has great pretensions.
Consider how small a fire can set a huge
forest ablaze. 6The tongue is also a fire. It
exists among our members as a world of
malice, defiling the whole body and setting
the entire course of our lives on fire, itself set
on fire by Gehenna. 7For every kind of beast
and bird, of reptile and sea creature, can be
tamed and has been tamed by the human
species, 8but no human being can tame the
tongue. It is a restless evil, full of deadly poison.[e] 9With it we bless the Lord and Father,
and with it we curse human beings who are
made in the likeness of God. 10From the
same mouth come blessing and cursing. This
need not be so, my brothers. 11Does a spring
gush forth from the same opening both pure
and brackish water? 12Can a fig tree, my
brothers, produce olives, or a grapevine
figs? Neither can salt water yield fresh.[f]
***True Wisdom.**** 13Who among you is wise
and understanding? Let him show his works
by a good life in the humility that comes
from wisdom.[g] 14But if you have bitter jealousy and selfish ambition in your hearts, do
not boast and be false to the truth. 15Wisdom
of this kind does not come down from above
but is earthly, unspiritual, demonic. 16For

**2:14–26** The theme of these verses is the relationship of faith and works (deeds). It has been argued that the teaching here contradicts that of Paul (see especially Rom 4:5–6). The problem can only be understood if the different viewpoints of the two authors are seen. Paul argues against those who claim to participate in God's salvation because of their good deeds as well as because they have committed themselves to trust in God through Jesus Christ (Paul's concept of faith). Paul certainly understands, however, the implications of true faith for a life of love and generosity (see Gal 5:6, 13–15). The author of James is well aware that proper conduct can only come about with an authentic commitment to God in faith (Jas 2:18, 26). Many think he was seeking to correct a misunderstanding of Paul's view.

**3:1–12** The use and abuse of the important role of teaching in the church (Jas 3:1) are here related to the good and bad use of the tongue (Jas 3:9–12), the instrument through which teaching was chiefly conveyed (see Sir 5:11–6:1; 28:12–26).

**3:13–18** This discussion of true wisdom is related to the previous reflection on the role of the teacher as one who is in control of his speech. The qualities of the wise man endowed from above are detailed (Jas 3:17–18; cf. Gal 5:22–23), in contrast to the qualities of earthbound wisdom (Jas 3:14–16; cf. 2 Cor 12:20).

*x:* Mt 5:7; 6:14–15; 18:32–33. *y:* Mt 25:31–46; Gal 5:6. *z:* 1 Jn 3:17. *a:* Gn 22:9–12; Heb 11:17. *b:* Gn 15:6; Rom 4:3; Gal 3:6 / 2 Chr 20:7; Is 41:8. *c:* Jos 2:1–21. *d:* 1:26; Prv 13:3; Sir 28:12–26. *e:* Ps 140:4. *f:* Mt 7:16–17. *g:* Eph 4:1–2.

where jealousy and selfish ambition exist,
there is disorder and every foul practice.
17But the wisdom from above is first of all
pure, then peaceable, gentle, compliant, full
of mercy and good fruits, without inconstancy or insincerity.[h] 18And the fruit of righteousness is sown in peace for those who
cultivate peace.[i]

See RG 432–34

## CHAPTER 4

***Causes of Division.**** 1Where do the
wars and where do the conflicts among you
come from? Is it not from your passions* that
make war within your members?[j] 2You
covet but do not possess. You kill and envy
but you cannot obtain; you fight and wage
war. You do not possess because you do not
ask. 3You ask but do not receive, because
you ask wrongly, to spend it on your passions. 4Adulterers!* Do you not know that to
be a lover of the world means enmity with
God? Therefore, whoever wants to be a
lover of the world makes himself an enemy
of God.[k] 5Or do you suppose that the scripture speaks without meaning when it says,
"The spirit that he has made to dwell in us
tends toward jealousy"?* 6But he bestows a
greater grace; therefore, it says:[l]

"God resists the proud,
but gives grace to the humble."*

7So submit yourselves to God. Resist the
devil, and he will flee from you.[m] 8Draw
near to God, and he will draw near to you.
Cleanse your hands, you sinners, and purify
your hearts, you of two minds.[n] 9Begin to
lament, to mourn, to weep. Let your laughter
be turned into mourning and your joy into
dejection. 10Humble yourselves before the
Lord and he will exalt you.[o]

11Do not speak evil of one another, brothers. Whoever speaks evil of a brother or
judges his brother speaks evil of the law and
judges the law.* If you judge the law, you are
not a doer of the law but a judge. 12There is
one lawgiver and judge who is able to save
or to destroy. Who then are you to judge
your neighbor?[p]

***Warning Against Presumption.**** 13Come
now, you who say, "Today or tomorrow we
shall go into such and such a town, spend a
year there doing business, and make a
profit"— 14you have no idea what your life
will be like tomorrow.* You are a puff of
smoke that appears briefly and then disappears.[q] 15Instead you should say, "If the Lord
wills it,* we shall live to do this or that."

**4:1–12** The concern here is with the origin of conflicts in the Christian community. These are occasioned by love **of the world**, which **means enmity with God** (Jas 4:4). Further, the conflicts are bound up with failure to pray properly (cf. Mt 7:7–11; Jn 14:13; 15:7; 16:23), that is, not asking God at all or using God's kindness only for one's pleasure (Jas 4:2–3). In contrast, the proper dispositions are submission to God, repentance, humility, and resistance to evil (Jas 4:7–10).

**4:1–3 Passions**: the Greek word here (literally, "pleasures") does not indicate that pleasure is evil. Rather, as the text points out (Jas 4:2–3), it is the manner in which one deals with needs and desires that determines good or bad. The motivation for any action can be wrong, especially if one does not pray properly but seeks only selfish enjoyment (Jas 4:3).

**4:4 Adulterers**: a common biblical image for the covenant between God and his people is the marriage bond. In this image, breaking the covenant with God is likened to the unfaithfulness of adultery.

**4:5** The meaning of this saying is difficult because the author of James cites, probably from memory, a passage that is not in any extant manuscript of the Bible. Other translations of the text with a completely different meaning are possible: "The Spirit that he (God) made to dwell in us yearns (for us) jealously," or, "He (God) yearns jealously for the spirit that he has made to dwell in us." If this last translation is correct, the author perhaps had in mind an apocryphal religious text that echoes the idea that God is zealous for his creatures; cf. Ex 20:5; Dt 4:24; Zec 8:2.

**4:6** The point of this whole argument is that God wants the happiness of all, but that selfishness and pride can make that impossible. We must work with him in humility (Jas 4:10).

**4:11** Slander of a fellow Christian does not break just one commandment but makes mockery of the authority of law in general and therefore of God.

**4:13–17** The uncertainty of life (Jas 4:14), its complete dependence on God, and the necessity of submitting to God's will (Jas 4:15) all help one know and do what is right (Jas 4:17). To disregard this is to live in pride and arrogance (Jas 4:16); failure to do what is right is a sin (Jas 4:17).

**4:14** Some important Greek manuscripts here have, "You who have no idea what tomorrow will bring. Why, what is your life?"

**4:15 If the Lord wills it**: often in piety referred to as the "*conditio Jacobaea*," the condition James says we should employ to qualify all our plans.

*h:* 1:17; Wis 7:22–23. *i:* Mt 5:9. *j:* Rom 7:23; 1 Pt 2:11. *k:* Mt 6:24; Lk 16:13; Rom 8:7; 1 Jn 2:15–16. *l:* Jb 22:29; Prv 3:34; Mt 23:12; 1 Pt 5:5. *m:* 1 Pt 5:8–9. *n:* Zec 1:3; Mal 3:7. *o:* Jb 5:11; Mt 23:12; Lk 14:11; 18:14; 1 Pt 5:6. *p:* Mt 7:1; Rom 2:1; 14:4. *q:* Prv 27:1 / Ps 39:6–7.

16 But now you are boasting in your arrogance. All such boasting is evil. 17[r] So for
one who knows the right thing to do and
does not do it, it is a sin.*

## CHAPTER 5

See RG 433–34

***Warning to the Rich.**** 1 Come now,
you rich, weep and wail over your impending miseries.[s] 2 Your wealth has rotted away,
your clothes have become moth-eaten,[t]
3 your gold and silver have corroded, and that
corrosion will be a testimony against you; it
will devour your flesh like a fire. You have
stored up treasure for the last days.[u] 4 Behold, the wages you withheld from the
workers who harvested your fields are crying aloud, and the cries of the harvesters
have reached the ears of the Lord of hosts.[v]
5 You have lived on earth in luxury and
pleasure; you have fattened your hearts for
the day of slaughter.[w] 6 You have condemned; you have murdered the righteous
one;[x] he offers you no resistance.*

***Patience and Oaths.*** 7* Be patient, therefore, brothers, until the coming of the Lord.
See how the farmer waits for the precious
fruit of the earth, being patient with it until it
receives the early and the late rains.* 8 You
too must be patient. Make your hearts firm,
because the coming of the Lord is at hand.[y]
9 Do not complain, brothers, about one another, that you may not be judged. Behold,
the Judge is standing before the gates.
10 Take as an example of hardship and patience, brothers, the prophets who spoke in
the name of the Lord. 11 Indeed we call
blessed those who have persevered. You
have heard of the perseverance of Job, and
you have seen the purpose of the Lord, because "the Lord is compassionate and merciful."[z]

12[a] But above all, my brothers, do not
swear, either by heaven or by earth or with
any other oath, but let your "Yes" mean
"Yes" and your "No" mean "No," that you
may not incur condemnation.*

## IV. The Power of Prayer

***Anointing of the Sick.*** 13 Is anyone among
you suffering? He should pray. Is anyone in
good spirits? He should sing praise. 14 Is anyone among you sick?* He should summon
the presbyters of the church, and they should
pray over him and anoint [him] with oil in
the name of the Lord,[b] 15 and the prayer of
faith will save the sick person, and the Lord
will raise him up. If he has committed any
sins, he will be forgiven.*

***Confession and Intercession.*** 16 Therefore,
confess your sins to one another and pray for
one another, that you may be healed. The
fervent prayer of a righteous person is very

**4:17 It is a sin**: those who live arrogantly, forgetting the contingency of life and our dependence on God (Jas 4:13–16), are guilty of sin.

**5:1–6** Continuing with the theme of the transitory character of life on earth, the author points out the impending ruin of the godless. He denounces the unjust rich, whose victims cry to heaven for judgment on their exploiters (Jas 5:4–6). The decay and corrosion of the costly garments and metals, which symbolize wealth, prove them worthless and portend the destruction of their possessors (Jas 5:2–3).

**5:6** The author does not have in mind any specific crime in his readers' communities but rather echoes the Old Testament theme of the harsh oppression of the righteous poor (see Prv 1:11; Wis 2:10, 12, 20).

**5:7–11** Those oppressed by the unjust rich are reminded of the need for patience, both in bearing the sufferings of human life (Jas 5:9) and in their expectation of the coming of the Lord. It is then that they will receive their reward (Jas 5:7–8, 10–11; cf. Heb 10:25; 1 Jn 2:18).

**5:7 The early and the late rains**: an expression related to the agricultural season in ancient Palestine (see Dt 11:14; Jer 5:24; Jl 2:23).

**5:12** This is the threat of condemnation for the abuse of swearing oaths (cf. Mt 5:33–37). **By heaven or by earth**: these words were substitutes for the original form of an oath, to circumvent its binding force and to avoid pronouncing the holy name of God (see Ex 22:10).

**5:14** In case of sickness a Christian should ask for the presbyters of the church, i.e., those who have authority in the church (cf. Acts 15:2, 22–23; 1 Tm 5:17; Ti 1:5). They are to pray over the person and anoint with oil; oil was used for medicinal purposes in the ancient world (see Is 1:6; Lk 10:34). In Mk 6:13, the Twelve anoint the sick with oil on their missionary journey. **In the name of the Lord**: by the power of Jesus Christ.

**5:15** The results of the prayer and anointing are physical health and forgiveness of sins. The Roman Catholic Church (Council of Trent, Session 14) declared that this anointing of the sick is a sacrament "instituted by Christ and promulgated by blessed James the apostle."

*r:* Lk 12:47. *s:* Lk 6:24. *t:* Mt 6:19. *u:* Ps 21:10; Prv 11:4; Jdt 16:17. *v:* Lv 19:13; Dt 24:14–15; Mal 3:5. *w:* Jer 12:3; Lk 16:19–25. *x:* Wis 2:10–20. *y:* Lk 21:19; Heb 10:36 / Heb 10:25; 1 Pt 4:7. *z:* Ex 34:6; Ps 103:8. *a:* Mt 5:34–37. *b:* Mk 6:13.

powerful. [17]Elijah was a human being like
us; yet he prayed earnestly that it might not
rain, and for three years and six months it did
not rain upon the land.[c] [18]Then he prayed
again, and the sky gave rain and the earth
produced its fruit.[d]

*Conversion of Sinners.* [19e]My brothers, if
anyone among you should stray from the truth
and someone bring him back, [20f]he should
know that whoever brings back a sinner from
the error of his way will save his soul from
death and will cover a multitude of sins.*

**5:20** When a Christian is instrumental in the conversion of a sinner, the result is forgiveness of sins and a reinstatement of the sinner to the life of grace.

*c:* 1 Kgs 17:1; Lk 4:25. *d:* 1 Kgs 18:45. *e:* Mt 18:15; Gal 6:1. *f:* Prv 10:12; 1 Pt 4:8.

See RG 435–40

# The First Letter of Peter

This letter begins with an address by Peter to Christian communities located in five provinces of Asia Minor (1 Pt 1:1), including areas evangelized by Paul (Acts 16:6–7; 18:23). Christians there are encouraged to remain faithful to their standards of belief and conduct in spite of threats of persecution. Numerous allusions in the letter suggest that the churches addressed were largely of Gentile composition (1 Pt 1:14, 18; 2:9–10; 4:3–4), though considerable use is made of the Old Testament (1 Pt 1:24; 2:6–7, 9–10, 22; 3:10–12).

The contents following the address both inspire and admonish these "chosen sojourners" (1 Pt 1:1) who, in seeking to live as God's people, feel an alienation from their previous religious roots and the society around them. Appeal is made to Christ's resurrection and the future hope it provides (1 Pt 1:3–5) and to the experience of baptism as new birth (1 Pt 1:3, 23–25; 3:21). The suffering and death of Christ serve as both source of salvation and example (1 Pt 1:19; 2:21–25; 3:18). What Christians are in Christ, as a people who have received mercy and are to proclaim and live according to God's call (1 Pt 2:9–10), is repeatedly spelled out for all sorts of situations in society (1 Pt 2:11–17), work (even as slaves, 1 Pt 2:18–20), the home (1 Pt 3:1–7), and general conduct (1 Pt 3:8–12; 4:1–11). But over all hangs the possibility of suffering as a Christian (1 Pt 3:13–17). In 1 Pt 4:12–19 persecution is described as already occurring, so that some have supposed the letter was addressed both to places where such a "trial by fire" was already present and to places where it might break out.

The letter constantly mingles moral exhortation (*paraklēsis*) with its catechetical summaries of mercies in Christ. Encouragement to fidelity in spite of suffering is based upon a vision of the meaning of Christian existence. The emphasis on baptism and allusions to various features of the baptismal liturgy suggest that the author has incorporated into his exposition numerous homiletic, credal, hymnic, and sacramental elements of the baptismal rite that had become traditional at an early date.

From Irenaeus in the late second century until modern times, Christian tradition regarded Peter the apostle as author of this document. Since he was martyred at Rome during the persecution of Nero between A.D. 64 and 67, it was supposed that the letter was written from Rome shortly before his death. This is supported by its reference to "Babylon" (1 Pt 5:13), a code name for Rome in the early church.

Some modern scholars, however, on the basis of a number of features that they consider incompatible with Petrine authenticity, regard the letter as the work of a later Christian writer. Such features include the cultivated Greek in which it is written, difficult to attribute to a Galilean fisherman, together with its use of the Greek Septuagint translation when citing the Old Testament; the similarity in both thought and expression to the Pauline literature; and the allusions to widespread persecution of Christians, which did not occur until at least the reign of Domitian (A.D. 81–96). In this view the letter would date from the end of the first century or even the beginning of the second, when there is evidence for persecution of Christians in Asia Minor (the letter of Pliny the Younger to Trajan, A.D. 111–12).

Other scholars believe, however, that these objections can be met by appeal to use of a secretary, Silvanus, mentioned in 1 Pt 5:12. Such secretaries often gave literary expression to the author's thoughts in their own style and language. The persecutions may refer to local harassment rather than to systematic repression by the state. Hence there is nothing in the document incompatible with Petrine authorship in the 60s.

Still other scholars take a middle position. The many literary contacts with the Pauline literature, James, and 1 John suggest a common fund of traditional formulations rather than direct dependence upon Paul. Such liturgical and catechetical traditions must have been very ancient and in some cases of Palestinian origin.

Yet it is unlikely that Peter addressed a letter to the Gentile churches of Asia Minor while Paul was still alive. This suggests a period after the death of the two apostles, perhaps A.D. 70–90. The author would be a disciple of Peter in Rome, representing a Petrine group that served as a bridge between the Palestinian origins of Christianity and its flowering in the Gentile world. The problem addressed would not be official persecution but the difficulty of living the Christian life in a hostile, secular environment that espoused different values and subjected the Christian minority to ridicule and oppression.

The principal divisions of the First Letter of Peter are the following:

I. Address (1:1–2)
II. The Gift and Call of God in Baptism (1:3–2:10)
III. The Christian in a Hostile World (2:11–4:11)
IV. Advice to the Persecuted (4:12–5:11)
V. Conclusion (5:12–14)

## I. Address

### CHAPTER 1

See RG 436–38

_Greeting._* 1Peter, an apostle of Jesus
Christ, to the chosen sojourners of the dispersion* in Pontus, Galatia, Cappadocia,
Asia, and Bithynia,[a] 2in the foreknowledge
of God the Father, through sanctification by
the Spirit, for obedience and sprinkling with
the blood of Jesus Christ: may grace and
peace be yours in abundance.[b]

## II. The Gift and Call of God in Baptism

_Blessing._ 3* Blessed be the God and Father of
our Lord Jesus Christ, who in his great mercy
gave us a new birth to a living hope through
the resurrection of Jesus Christ from the dead,[c]
4to an inheritance that is imperishable, undefiled, and unfading, kept in heaven for you[d]
5who by the power of God are safeguarded
through faith, to a salvation that is ready to be
revealed in the final time. 6* In this you rejoice, although now for a little while you may
have to suffer through various trials,[e] 7so that
the genuineness of your faith, more precious
than gold that is perishable even though tested
by fire, may prove to be for praise, glory, and
honor at the revelation of Jesus Christ.[f] 8Al-
though you have not seen him you love him;
even though you do not see him now yet believe in him, you rejoice with an indescribable
and glorious joy,[g] 9as you attain the goal of
[your] faith, the salvation of your souls.
10* Concerning this salvation, prophets

**1:1–2** The introductory formula names **Peter** as the writer (but see Introduction). In his comments to the presbyters (1 Pt 5:1), the author calls himself a "fellow presbyter." He addresses himself to the Gentile converts of Asia Minor. Their privileged status as a **chosen** and sanctified people makes them worthy of God's **grace** and **peace**. In contrast is their actual existence as aliens and **sojourners**, scattered among pagans, far from their true country.

**1:1 Dispersion**: literally, diaspora; see Jas 1:1 and Introduction to that letter. **Pontus . . . Bithynia**: five provinces in Asia Minor, listed in clockwise order from the north, perhaps in the sequence in which a messenger might deliver the letter.

**1:3–5** A prayer of praise and thanksgiving to God who bestows the gift of new life and hope in baptism **(new birth,** 1 Pt 1:3) **through the resurrection of Jesus Christ from the dead.** The new birth is a sign of an **imperishable inheritance** (1 Pt 1:4), of **salvation** that is still in the future **(to be revealed in the final time**, 1 Pt 1:5).

**1:6–9** As the glory of Christ's resurrection was preceded by his sufferings and death, the new life of faith that it bestows is to be subjected to many **trials** (1 Pt 1:6) while achieving its goal: the glory of the fullness of **salvation** (1 Pt 1:9) at the coming of Christ (1 Pt 1:7).

**1:10–12** The **Spirit of Christ** (1 Pt 1:11) is here shown to have been present in the prophets, moving them to search, investigate, and prophesy about the **grace** of **salvation** that was to come (1 Pt 1:10), and in the apostles impelling them to preach the fulfillment of salvation in the message of Christ's sufferings and glory (1 Pt 1:12).

*a:* Jas 1:1. *b:* Rom 8:29. *c:* Ti 3:5. *d:* Mt 6:19–20. *e:* Jas 1:2–3. *f:* 1 Cor 3:13. *g:* 2 Cor 5:6–7.

who prophesied about the grace that was to
be yours searched and investigated it, 11 investigating the time and circumstances that
the Spirit of Christ within them indicated
when it testified in advance to the sufferings
destined for Christ and the glories to follow
them.[h] 12 It was revealed to them that they
were serving not themselves but you with regard to the things that have now been announced to you by those who preached the
good news to you [through] the holy Spirit
sent from heaven, things into which angels
longed to look.

*Obedience.* 13* Therefore, gird up the loins
of your mind,* live soberly, and set your
hopes completely on the grace to be brought
to you at the revelation of Jesus Christ.
14 Like obedient children, do not act in compliance with the desires of your former ignorance* 15 but, as he who called you is holy, be
holy yourselves in every aspect of your conduct,[i] 16 for it is written, "Be holy because I
[am] holy."[j]

*Reverence.* 17 Now if you invoke as Father
him who judges impartially according to
each one's works, conduct yourselves with
reverence during the time of your sojourning,[k] 18 realizing that you were ransomed
from your futile conduct, handed on by your
ancestors, not with perishable things like silver or gold[l] 19 but with the precious blood of
Christ[m] as of a spotless unblemished lamb.*
20 He was known before the foundation of
the world but revealed in the final time for
you, 21 who through him believe in God who
raised him from the dead and gave him
glory, so that your faith and hope are in God.

*Mutual Love.** 22 Since you have purified
yourselves by obedience to the truth for sincere mutual love, love one another intensely
from a [pure] heart.[n] 23 You have been born
anew,[o] not from perishable but from imperishable seed, through the living and abiding
word of God,* 24 for:

"All flesh is like grass,
and all its glory like the flower of the
field;
the grass withers,
and the flower wilts;[p]
25 but the word of the Lord remains
forever."

This is the word that has been proclaimed to
you.

## CHAPTER 2

See RG 437-38

*God's House and People.* 1* Rid yourselves of all malice and all deceit, insincerity, envy, and all slander;[q] 2 like newborn infants, long for pure spiritual milk so that
through it you may grow into salvation,
3[r] for you have tasted that the Lord is good.*
4 Come to him, a living stone,* rejected by
human beings but chosen and precious in the
sight of God,[s] 5 and, like living stones, let
yourselves be built* into a spiritual house to
be a holy priesthood to offer spiritual sacri-

**1:13–25** These verses are concerned with the call of God's people to holiness and to mutual love by reason of their redemption through the blood of Christ (1 Pt 1:18–21).

**1:13 Gird up the loins of your mind**: a figure reminiscent of the rite of Passover when the Israelites were in flight from their oppressors (Ex 12:11), and also suggesting the vigilance of the Christian people in expectation of the parousia of Christ (Lk 12:35).

**1:14–16** The **ignorance** here referred to (1 Pt 1:14) was their former lack of knowledge of God, leading inevitably to godless conduct. Holiness (1 Pt 1:15–16), on the contrary, is the result of their call to the knowledge and love of God.

**1:19** Christians have received the redemption prophesied by Isaiah (Is 52:3), through the blood (Jewish symbol of life) of the spotless lamb (Is 53:7, 10; Jn 1:29; Rom 3:24–25; cf. 1 Cor 6:20).

**1:22–25** The new birth of Christians (1 Pt 1:23) derives from Christ, the **imperishable seed** or sowing that produces a new and lasting existence in those who accept the gospel (1 Pt 1:24–25), with the consequent duty of loving **one another** (1 Pt 1:22).

**1:23 The living and abiding word of God**: or, "the word of the living and abiding God."

**2:1–3** Growth toward salvation is seen here as two steps: first, stripping away all that is contrary to the new life in Christ; second, the nourishment (**pure spiritual milk**) that the newly baptized have received.

**2:3 Tasted that the Lord is good**: cf. Ps 34:9.

**2:4–8** Christ is the cornerstone (cf. Is 28:16) that is the foundation of the spiritual edifice of the Christian community (1 Pt 2:5). To unbelievers, Christ is an obstacle and a stumbling block on which they are destined to fall (1 Pt 2:8); cf. Rom 11:11.

**2:5 Let yourselves be built**: the form of the Greek word could also be indicative passive, "you are being built" (cf. 1 Pt 2:9).

*h:* Is 52:13–53:12; Dn 9:24. *i:* Mt 5:48; 1 Jn 3:3. *j:* Lv 11:44; 19:2. *k:* 2:11. *l:* Is 52:3; 1 Cor 6:20. *m:* Ex 12:5; Jn 1:29; Heb 9:14. *n:* Rom 12:10. *o:* 1 Jn 3:9. *p:* Is 40:6–8. *q:* Jas 1:21. *r:* Ps 34:9. *s:* Ps 118:22; Mt 21:42; Acts 4:11. *t:* Eph 2:21–22.

fices acceptable to God through Jesus
Christ.[t] 6For it says in scripture:

"Behold, I am laying a stone in Zion,
a cornerstone, chosen and precious,
and whoever believes in it shall not be
put to shame."[u]

7Therefore, its value is for you who have
faith, but for those without faith:

"The stone which the builders rejected
has become the cornerstone,"[v]

8and

"A stone that will make people stumble,
and a rock that will make them fall."

They stumble by disobeying the word, as is
their destiny.[w]
9* But you are "a chosen race, a royal
priesthood, a holy nation, a people of his
own, so that you may announce the praises"
of him who called you out of darkness into
his wonderful light.[x]

10 Once you were "no people"
but now you are God's people;
you "had not received mercy"
but now you have received mercy.[y]

## III. The Christian in a Hostile World

***Christian Examples.*** 11* Beloved, I urge you
as aliens and sojourners* to keep away from
worldly desires that wage war against the
soul.[z] 12Maintain good conduct among the
Gentiles, so that if they speak of you as evildoers, they may observe your good works
and glorify God on the day of visitation.
***Christian Citizens.**** 13Be subject to every
human institution for the Lord's sake,
whether it be to the king as supreme[a] 14or to
governors as sent by him for the punishment
of evildoers and the approval of those who
do good. 15For it is the will of God that by
doing good you may silence the ignorance of
foolish people. 16Be free, yet without using
freedom as a pretext for evil, but as slaves of
God.[b] 17Give honor to all, love the community, fear God, honor the king.[c]
***Christian Slaves.*** 18* Slaves, be subject to
your masters with all reverence, not only to
those who are good and equitable but also to
those who are perverse.[d] 19For whenever
anyone bears the pain of unjust suffering because of consciousness of God, that is a
grace. 20But what credit is there if you are

**2:9–10** The prerogatives of ancient Israel mentioned here are now more fully and fittingly applied to the Christian people: "a chosen race" (cf. Is 43:20–21) indicates their divine election (Eph 1:4–6); "a royal priesthood" (cf. Ex 19:6) to serve and worship God in Christ, thus continuing the priestly functions of his life, passion, and resurrection; "a holy nation" (Ex 19:6) reserved for God, a people he claims for his own (cf. Mal 3:17) in virtue of their baptism into his death and resurrection. This transcends all natural and national divisions and unites the people into one community to glorify the one who led them from the darkness of paganism to the light of faith in Christ. From being "no people" deprived of all mercy, they have become the very people of God, the chosen recipients of his mercy (cf. Hos 1:9; 2:25).

**2:11–3:12** After explaining the doctrinal basis for the Christian community, the author makes practical applications in terms of the virtues that should prevail in all the social relationships of the members of the community: good example to Gentile neighbors (1 Pt 2:11–12); respect for human authority (1 Pt 2:13–17); obedience, patience, and endurance of hardship in domestic relations (1 Pt 2:18–25); Christian behavior of husbands and wives (1 Pt 3:1–7); mutual charity (1 Pt 3:8–12).

**2:11 Aliens and sojourners**: no longer signifying absence from one's native land (Gn 23:4), this image denotes rather their estrangement from the world during their earthly pilgrimage (see also 1 Pt 1:1, 17).

**2:13–17** True Christian freedom is the result of being servants of God (1 Pt 2:16; see note on 1 Pt 2:18–23). It includes reverence for God, esteem for every individual, and committed love for fellow Christians (1 Pt 2:17). Although persecution may threaten, subjection to human government is urged (1 Pt 2:13, 17) and concern for the impact of Christians' conduct on those who are not Christians (1 Pt 2:12, 15).

**2:18–21** Most of the labor in the commercial cities of first-century Asia Minor was performed by a working class of slaves. The sense of freedom contained in the gospel undoubtedly caused great tension among Christian slaves: witness the special advice given concerning them here and in 1 Cor 7:21–24; Eph 6:5–8; Col 3:22–25; Phlm. The point made here does not have so much to do with the institution of slavery, which the author does not challenge, but with the nonviolent reaction (1 Pt 2:20) of slaves to unjust treatment. Their patient suffering is compared to that of Jesus (1 Pt 2:21), which won righteousness for all humanity.

*u:* Is 28:16. *v:* Ps 118:22; Mt 21:42; Lk 20:17; Acts 4:11. *w:* Is 8:14; Rom 9:33. *x:* Ex 19:6; Is 61:6; Rev 1:6; 20:6. *y:* Hos 1:9; 2:25 / Hos 1:6. *z:* Gal 5:24. *a:* Rom 13:1–7. *b:* Gal 5:13. *c:* Prv 24:21; Mt 22:21. *d:* Eph 6:5.

patient when beaten for doing wrong? But if
you are patient when you suffer for doing
what is good, this is a grace before God.
21 For to this you have been called, because
Christ also suffered* for you, leaving you an
example that you should follow in his footsteps.[e]

22 "He committed no sin,[f]
and no deceit was found in his mouth."*
23 When he was insulted, he returned no insult; when he suffered, he did not threaten;
instead, he handed himself over to the one
who judges justly.[g] 24 He himself bore our
sins in his body upon the cross, so that, free
from sin, we might live for righteousness.
By his wounds you have been healed.[h] 25 For
you had gone astray like sheep,[i] but you
have now returned to the shepherd and
guardian of your souls.*

See RG 438–39

## CHAPTER 3

*Christian Spouses.* 1* Likewise, you
wives should be subordinate to your husbands so that, even if some disobey the
word, they may be won over without a word
by their wives' conduct 2 when they observe
your reverent and chaste behavior.[j] 3 Your
adornment should not be an external one:
braiding the hair, wearing gold jewelry, or
dressing in fine clothes,[k] 4 but rather the hidden character of the heart, expressed in the
imperishable beauty of a gentle and calm
disposition, which is precious in the sight of
God. 5 For this is also how the holy women
who hoped in God once used to adorn themselves and were subordinate to their husbands; 6 thus Sarah obeyed Abraham, calling
him "lord." You are her children when you
do what is good and fear no intimidation.
7 Likewise, you husbands should live
with your wives in understanding, showing
honor to the weaker female sex, since we are
joint heirs of the gift of life, so that your
prayers may not be hindered.*

*Christian Conduct.** 8 Finally, all of you,
be of one mind, sympathetic, loving toward
one another, compassionate, humble. 9 Do
not return evil for evil, or insult for insult;
but, on the contrary, a blessing, because to
this you were called, that you might inherit a
blessing.[m] 10 For:

"Whoever would love life[n]
and see good days
must keep the tongue from evil
and the lips from speaking deceit,
11 must turn from evil and do good,
seek peace and follow after it.
12 For the eyes of the Lord are on the
righteous
and his ears turned to their prayer,
but the face of the Lord is against
evildoers."

*Christian Suffering.** 13 Now who is going
to harm you if you are enthusiastic for what

**2:21 Suffered**: some ancient manuscripts and versions read "died" (cf. 1 Pt 3:18).

**2:22–25** After the quotation of Is 53:9b, the passage describes Jesus' passion with phrases concerning the Suffering Servant from Is 53:4–12, perhaps as employed in an early Christian confession of faith; cf. 1 Pt 1:18–21 and 1 Pt 3:18–22.

**2:25 The shepherd and guardian of your souls**: the familiar shepherd and flock figures express the care, vigilance, and love of God for his people in the Old Testament (Ps 23; Is 40:11; Jer 23:4–5; Ez 34:11–16) and of Jesus for all humanity in the New Testament (Mt 18:10–14; Lk 15:4–7; Jn 10:1–16; Heb 13:20).

**3:1–6** The typical marital virtues of women of the ancient world, obedience, reverence, and chastity (1 Pt 3:1–2), are outlined here by the author, who gives them an entirely new motivation: Christian wives are to be virtuous so that they may be instrumental in the conversion of their husbands. In imitation of **holy women** in the past (1 Pt 3:5) they are to cultivate the interior life (1 Pt 3:4) instead of excessive concern with their appearance (1 Pt 3:3).

**3:7** Husbands who do not respect their wives will have as little success in prayer as those who, according to Paul, have no love: their prayers will be "a resounding gong or a clashing cymbal" (1 Cor 13:1). Consideration for others is shown as a prerequisite for effective prayer also in Mt 5:23–24; 1 Cor 11:20–22; Jas 4:3. After all, whatever the social position of women in the world and in the family, they are equal recipients of the gift of God's salvation. Paul is very clear on this point, too (see 1 Cor 11:11–12; Gal 3:28).

**3:8–12** For the proper ordering of Christian life in its various aspects as described in 1 Pt 2:11–3:9, there is promised the blessing expressed in Ps 34:13–17. In the Old Testament this refers to longevity and prosperity; here, it also refers to eternal life.

**3:13–22** This exposition, centering on 1 Pt 3:17, runs as follows: by his suffering and death Christ the righteous one saved the unrighteous (1 Pt 3:18); by his resurrection he received new life in the spirit, which he communicates to be-

*e:* Mt 16:24. *f:* Is 53:9. *g:* Mt 5:39. *h:* Is 53:4, 12 / Is 53:5. *i:* Is 53:6. *j:* 1 Cor 7:12–16; Eph 5:22–24; Col 3:18; 1 Tm 2:9–15. *k:* 1 Tm 2:9–10. *l:* Eph 5:25–33; Col 3:19. *m:* Mt 5:44; Lk 6:28; Rom 12:14. *n:* Ps 34:13–17.

is good? 14But even if you should suffer because of righteousness, blessed are you. Do
not be afraid or terrified with fear of them,
15but sanctify Christ as Lord in your hearts.
Always be ready to give an explanation to
anyone who asks you for a reason for your
hope,[o] 16but do it with gentleness and reverence, keeping your conscience clear, so that,
when you are maligned, those who defame
your good conduct in Christ may themselves
be put to shame. 17For it is better to suffer for
doing good, if that be the will of God, than
for doing evil.

18For Christ also suffered* for sins once,
the righteous for the sake of the unrighteous,
that he might lead you to God. Put to death
in the flesh, he was brought to life in the
spirit.[p] 19In it he also went to preach to the
spirits in prison,* 20who had once been disobedient while God patiently waited in the
days of Noah during the building of the ark,
in which a few persons, eight in all, were
saved through water.[q] 21This prefigured baptism, which saves you now. It is not a removal of dirt from the body but an appeal to
God* for a clear conscience, through the resurrection of Jesus Christ,[r] 22who has gone
into heaven and is at the right hand of God,
with angels, authorities, and powers subject
to him.[s]

## CHAPTER 4

See RG 438–39

***Christian Restraint.**** 1Therefore, since
Christ suffered in the flesh, arm yourselves
also with the same attitude (for whoever suffers in the flesh has broken with sin), 2so as not
to spend what remains of one's life in the flesh
on human desires, but on the will of God. 3For
the time that has passed is sufficient for doing
what the Gentiles like to do: living in debauchery, evil desires, drunkenness, orgies,
carousing, and wanton idolatry.[t] 4They are
surprised that you do not plunge into the same
swamp of profligacy, and they vilify you; 5but
they will give an account to him who stands
ready to judge the living and the dead.[u] 6For
this is why the gospel was preached even to
the dead* that, though condemned in the flesh
in human estimation, they might live in the
spirit in the estimation of God.

***Christian Charity.**** 7The end of all things
is at hand. Therefore, be serious and sober
for prayers. 8[v] Above all, let your love for
one another be intense, because love covers
a multitude of sins.* 9Be hospitable to one
another without complaining.[w] 10As each
one has received a gift, use it to serve one
another as good stewards of God's varied
grace.[x] 11Whoever preaches, let it be with the
words of God; whoever serves, let it be with

lievers through the baptismal bath that cleanses their consciences from sin. As Noah's family was saved **through water**, so Christians are saved through the waters of baptism (1 Pt 3:19–22). Hence they need not share the fear of sinners; they should rather rejoice in suffering because of their hope in Christ. Thus their innocence disappoints their accusers (1 Pt 3:13–16; cf. Mt 10:28; Rom 8:35–39).

**3:18 Suffered**: very many ancient manuscripts and versions read "died." **Put to death in the flesh**: affirms that Jesus truly died as a human being. **Brought to life in the spirit**: that is, in the new and transformed existence freed from the limitations and weaknesses of natural human life (cf. 1 Cor 15:45).

**3:19 The spirits in prison**: it is not clear just who these spirits are. They may be the spirits of the sinners who died in the flood, or angelic powers, hostile to God, who have been overcome by Christ (cf. 1 Pt 3:22; Gn 6:4; Enoch 6–36, especially 21:6; 2 Enoch 7:1–5).

**3:21 Appeal to God**: this could also be translated "pledge," that is, a promise on the part of Christians to live with a good conscience before God, or a pledge from God of forgiveness and therefore a good conscience for us.

**4:1–6** Willingness to suffer with Christ equips the Christian with the power to conquer sin (1 Pt 4:1). Christ is here portrayed as the judge to whom those guilty of pagan vices must render an account (1 Pt 4:5; cf. Jn 5:22–27; Acts 10:42; 2 Tm 4:1).

**4:6 The dead**: these may be the sinners of the flood generation who are possibly referred to in 1 Pt 3:19. But many scholars think that there is no connection between these two verses, and that **the dead** here are Christians who have died since hearing the preaching of the gospel.

**4:7–11** The inner life of the eschatological community is outlined as **the end** (the parousia of Christ) and the judgment draws near in terms of seriousness, sobriety, prayer, and love expressed through hospitality and the use of one's gifts for the glory of God and of Christ.

**4:8 Love covers a multitude of sins**: a maxim based on Prv 10:12; see also Ps 32:1; Jas 5:20.

*o:* Is 8:12. *p:* 1 Cor 15:45. *q:* Gn 7:7, 17; 2 Pt 2:5. *r:* Eph 5:26; Heb 10:22. *s:* Eph 1:20–21. *t:* Eph 2:2–3; 4:17–19; Col 3:7; Ti 3:3. *u:* Acts 10:42; 2 Tm 4:1. *v:* Prv 10:12; Jas 5:20. *w:* Heb 13:2. *x:* Rom 12:6–8; 1 Cor 12:4–11.

the strength that God supplies, so that in all things God may be glorified through Jesus Christ,[y] to whom belong glory and dominion forever and ever. Amen.*

## IV. Advice to the Persecuted

***Trial of Persecution.**** 12 Beloved, do not be surprised that a trial by fire is occurring among you, as if something strange were happening to you.[z] 13 But rejoice to the extent that you share in the sufferings of Christ, so that when his glory is revealed you may also rejoice exultantly.[a] 14 If you are insulted for the name of Christ, blessed are you, for the Spirit of glory and of God rests upon you.[b] 15 But let no one among you be made to suffer as a murderer, a thief, an evildoer, or as an intriguer. 16 But whoever is made to suffer as a Christian should not be ashamed but glorify God because of the name. 17 For it is time for the judgment to begin with the household of God; if it begins with us, how will it end for those who fail to obey the gospel of God?[c]

18 "And if the righteous one is barely
saved,
where will the godless and the sinner
appear?"[d]

19 As a result, those who suffer in accord with God's will hand their souls over to a faithful creator as they do good.

See RG 439

### CHAPTER 5

***Advice to Presbyters.**** 1 So I exhort the presbyters* among you, as a fellow presbyter and witness to the sufferings of Christ and one who has a share in the glory to be revealed. 2 Tend the flock of God in your midst, [overseeing] not by constraint but willingly, as God would have it, not for shameful profit but eagerly.[e] 3 Do not lord it over those assigned to you, but be examples to the flock. 4[f] And when the chief Shepherd is revealed, you will receive the unfading crown of glory.*

***Advice to the Community.**** 5 Likewise, you younger members,* be subject to the presbyters. And all of you, clothe yourselves with humility in your dealings with one another, for:

"God opposes the proud
but bestows favor on the humble."[g]

6 So humble yourselves under the mighty hand of God, that he may exalt you in due time.[h] 7 Cast all your worries upon him because he cares for you.[i]

8 Be sober and vigilant. Your opponent the devil is prowling around like a roaring lion looking for [someone] to devour.[j] 9 Resist him, steadfast in faith, knowing that your fellow believers throughout the world undergo the same sufferings. 10 The God of all grace who called you to his eternal glory through Christ [Jesus] will himself restore, confirm, strengthen, and establish you after you have suffered a little.[k] 11 To him be dominion forever. Amen.

**4:11** Some scholars feel that this doxology concludes the part of the homily addressed specifically to the newly baptized, begun in 1 Pt 1:3; others that it concludes a baptismal liturgy. Such doxologies do occur within a New Testament letter, e.g., Rom 9:5. Some propose that 1 Pt 4:11 was an alternate ending, with 1 Pt 4:12–5:14 being read in places where persecution was more pressing. But such doxologies usually do not occur at the end of letters (the only examples are 2 Pt 3:18, Jude 25, and Rom 16:27, the last probably a liturgical insertion).

**4:12–19** The suffering to which the author has already frequently referred is presented in more severe terms. This has led some scholars to see these verses as referring to an actual persecution. Others see the heightening of the language as only a rhetorical device used at the end of the letter to emphasize the suffering motif.

**5:1–4** In imitation of Christ, the chief shepherd, those entrusted with a pastoral office are to tend the flock by their care and example.

**5:1 Presbyters**: the officially appointed leaders and teachers of the Christian community (cf. 1 Tm 5:17–18; Ti 1:5–8; Jas 5:14).

**5:4** See note on 1 Pt 2:25.

**5:5–11** The community is to be subject to the presbyters and to show humility toward one another and trust in God's love and care (1 Pt 5:5–7). With sobriety, alertness, and steadfast faith they must resist the evil one; their sufferings are shared with Christians everywhere (1 Pt 5:8–9). They will be strengthened and called to eternal glory (1 Pt 5:10–11).

**5:5 Younger members**: this may be a designation for office-holders of lesser rank.

*y:* 1 Cor 10:31. *z:* 1:6–7; 3:14, 17. *a:* Rom 5:3–5; 8:17; 2 Tm 2:12. *b:* Acts 5:41 / Is 11:2. *c:* Lk 23:31; 2 Thes 1:8. *d:* Prv 11:31 LXX. *e:* Acts 20:28; Ti 1:7. *f:* Wis 5:15–16; 1 Cor 9:25; 2 Tm 4:8; Jas 1:12. *g:* Prv 3:34. *h:* Jb 22:29; Jas 4:10. *i:* Ps 55:23; Mt 6:25–33; Lk 12:22–31; Phil 4:6. *j:* 1 Thes 5:6. *k:* Rom 8:18; 2 Cor 4:17.

## V. Conclusion

12 I write you this briefly through Silvanus,*
whom I consider a faithful brother, exhorting you and testifying that this is the true
grace of God. Remain firm in it. 13 The chosen one* at Babylon sends you greeting, as
does Mark, my son. 14 Greet one another
with a loving kiss. Peace to all of you who
are in Christ.[l]

**5:12 Silvanus**: the companion of Paul (see 2 Cor 1:19; 1 Thes 1:1; 2 Thes 1:1). Jews and Jewish Christians, like Paul, often had a Hebrew name (Saoul, Silas) and a Greek or Latin name (Paul, Silvanus). On Silvanus's possible role as amanuensis, see Introduction.

**5:13 The chosen one**: feminine, referring to the Christian community (*ekklēsia*) at **Babylon**, the code name for Rome in Rev 14:8; 17:5; 18:2. **Mark, my son**: traditionally a prominent disciple of Peter and co-worker at the church in Rome, perhaps the John Mark referred to in Acts 12:12, 25; 13:5, 13; and in Acts 15:37–39, a companion of Barnabas. Perhaps this is the same Mark mentioned as Barnabas's cousin in Col 4:10, a co-worker with Paul in Phlm 24 (see also 2 Tm 4:11).

*l*: Rom 16:16; 1 Cor 16:20; 2 Cor 13:12.

See RG 440–44

# The Second Letter of Peter

This letter can be appreciated both for its positive teachings and for its earnest warnings. It seeks to strengthen readers in faith (2 Pt 1:1), hope for the future (2 Pt 3:1–10), knowledge (2 Pt 1:2, 6, 8), love (2 Pt 1:7), and other virtues (2 Pt 1:5–6). This aim is carried out especially by warning against false teachers, the condemnation of whom occupies the long central section of the letter (2 Pt 2:1–22). A particular crisis is the claim by "scoffers" that there will be no second coming of Jesus, a doctrine that the author vigorously affirms (2 Pt 3:1–10). The concept of God's "promises" is particularly precious in the theology of 2 Peter (2 Pt 1:4; 3:4, 9, 13). Closing comments at 2 Pt 3:17–18 well sum up the twin concerns: that you not "be led into" error and "fall" but instead "grow in grace" and "knowledge" of Jesus Christ.

Second Peter is clearly structured in its presentation of these points. It reminds its readers of the divine authenticity of Christ's teaching (2 Pt 1:3–4), continues with reflections on Christian conduct (2 Pt 1:5–15), then returns to the exalted dignity of Jesus by incorporating into the text the apostolic witness to his transfiguration (2 Pt 1:16–18). It takes up the question of the interpretation of scripture by pointing out that it is possible to misunderstand the sacred writings (2 Pt 1:19–21) and that divine punishment will overtake false teachers (2 Pt 2:1–22). It proclaims that the parousia is the teaching of the Lord and of the apostles and is therefore an eventual certainty (2 Pt 3:1–13). At the same time, it warns that the meaning of Paul's writings on this question should not be distorted (2 Pt 3:14–18).

In both content and style this letter is very different from 1 Peter, which immediately precedes it in the canon. The opening verse attributes it to "Symeon Peter, a slave and apostle of Jesus Christ." Moreover, the author in 2 Pt 3:1 calls his work a "second letter," referring probably to 1 Peter as his first, and in 2 Pt 1:18 counts himself among those present at the transfiguration of Jesus.

Nevertheless, acceptance of 2 Peter into the New Testament canon met with great resistance in the early church. The oldest certain reference to it comes from Origen in the early third century. While he himself accepted both Petrine letters as canonical, he testifies that others rejected 2 Peter. As late as the fifth century some local churches still excluded it from the canon, but eventually it was universally adopted. The principal reason for the long delay was the persistent doubt that the letter stemmed from the apostle Peter.

Among modern scholars there is wide agreement that 2 Peter is a pseudonymous work, i.e., one written by a later author who attributed it to Peter according to a literary convention popular at the time. It gives the impression of being more remote in time from the apostolic period than 1 Peter; indeed, many think it is the latest work in the New Testament and assign it to the first or even the second quarter of the second century.

The principal reasons for this view are the following. The author refers to the apostles and "our ancestors" as belonging to a previous generation, now dead (2 Pt 3:2–4). A collection of Paul's letters exists and appears to be well known, but disputes have arisen about the interpretation of them

(2 Pt 3:14–16). The passage about false teachers (2 Pt 2:1–18) contains a number of literary contacts with Jude 4–16, and it is generally agreed that 2 Peter depends upon Jude, not vice versa. Finally, the principal problem exercising the author is the false teaching of "scoffers" who have concluded from the delay of the parousia that the Lord is not going to return. This could scarcely have been an issue during the lifetime of Simon Peter.

The Christians to whom the letter is addressed are not identified, though it may be the intent of 2 Pt 3:1 to identify them with the churches of Asia Minor to which 1 Peter was sent. Except for the epistolary greeting in 2 Pt 1:1–2, 2 Peter does not have the features of a genuine letter at all, but is rather a general exhortation cast in the form of a letter. The author must have been a Jewish Christian of the dispersion for, while his Jewish heritage is evident in various features of his thought and style, he writes in the rather stilted literary Greek of the Hellenistic period. He appeals to tradition against the twin threat of doctrinal error and moral laxity, which appear to reflect an early stage of what later developed into full-blown gnosticism. Thus he forms a link between the apostolic period and the church of subsequent ages.

The principal divisions of the Second Letter of Peter are the following:

I. Address (1:1–2)
II. Exhortation to Christian Virtue (1:3–21)
III. Condemnation of the False Teachers (2:1–22)
IV. The Delay of the Second Coming (3:1–16)
V. Final Exhortation and Doxology (3:17–18)

# I. Address

## CHAPTER 1

See RG 441–42

*Greeting.* 1* Symeon Peter, a slave
and apostle of Jesus Christ, to those who
have received a faith of equal value to ours
through the righteousness of our God and
savior Jesus Christ: 2 may grace and peace be
yours in abundance through knowledge* of
God and of Jesus our Lord.

# II. Exhortation to Christian Virtue

***The Power of God's Promise.**** 3 His divine
power has bestowed on us everything that
makes for life and devotion, through the
knowledge of him[a] who called us by his own
glory and power.* 4 Through these, he has bestowed on us the precious and very great
promises, so that through them you may come
to share in the divine nature, after escaping
from the corruption that is in the world because of evil desire.[b] 5* For this very reason,
make every effort to supplement your faith
with virtue, virtue with knowledge,[c] 6 knowledge with self-control, self-control with endurance, endurance with devotion, 7 devotion
with mutual affection, mutual affection with
love. 8 If these are yours and increase in abundance, they will keep you from being idle or
unfruitful in the knowledge of our Lord Jesus
Christ. 9[d] Anyone who lacks them is blind and
shortsighted, forgetful of the cleansing of his
past sins. 10* Therefore, brothers, be all the

**1:1 Symeon Peter**: on the authorship of 2 Peter, see Introduction; on the spelling here of the Hebrew name *Sim'ôn*, cf. Acts 15:14. The greeting is especially similar to those in 1 Peter and Jude. The words translated **our God and savior Jesus Christ** could also be rendered "our God and the savior Jesus Christ"; cf. 2 Pt 1:11; 2:20; 3:2, 18.

**1:2 Knowledge**: a key term in the letter (2 Pt 1:3, 8; 2:20; 3:18), perhaps used as a Christian emphasis against gnostic claims.

**1:3–4** Christian life in its fullness is a gift of divine power effecting a knowledge of Christ and the bestowal of divine promises (2 Pt 3:4, 9). **To share in the divine nature**, escaping from a corrupt world, is a thought found elsewhere in the Bible but expressed only here in such Hellenistic terms, since it is said to be accomplished through knowledge (2 Pt 1:3); cf. 2 Pt 1:2; 2:20; but see also Jn 15:4; 17:22–23; Rom 8:14–17; Heb 3:14; 1 Jn 1:3; 3:2.

**1:3 By his own glory and power**: the most ancient papyrus and the best codex read "through glory and power."

**1:5–9** Note the climactic gradation of qualities (2 Pt 1:5–7), beginning with faith and leading to the fullness of Christian life, which is love; cf. Rom 5:3–4; Gal 5:6, 22 for a similar series of "virtues," though the program and sense here are different than in Paul. The fruit of these is knowledge of Christ (2 Pt 1:8) referred to in 2 Pt 1:3; their absence is spiritual blindness (2 Pt 1:9).

**1:10–11** Perseverance in the Christian vocation is the best preventative against losing it and the safest provision for attaining its goal, the kingdom. **Kingdom of . . . Christ**, instead of "God," is unusual; cf. Col 1:13 and Mt 13:41, as well as the **righteousness of . . . Christ** (2 Pt 1:1).

*a:* 2 Cor 4:6; 1 Pt 2:9. *b:* 2 Cor 7:1; 1 Jn 2:15. *c:* Gal 5:22–23. *d:* 1 Jn 2:9, 11.

more eager to make your call and election firm, for, in doing so, you will never stumble. [11]For, in this way, entry into the eternal kingdom of our Lord and savior Jesus Christ will be richly provided for you.

*Apostolic Witness.* [12]* Therefore, I will always remind you of these things, even though you already know them and are established in the truth you have. [13]I think it right, as long as I am in this "tent,"* to stir you up by a reminder, [14]since I know that I will soon have to put it aside, as indeed our Lord Jesus Christ has shown me.[e] [15]I shall also make every effort to enable you always to remember these things after my departure.

[16]We did not follow cleverly devised myths when we made known to you the power and coming* of our Lord Jesus Christ, but we had been eyewitnesses of his majesty.[f] [17]For he received honor and glory from God the Father* when that unique declaration came to him from the majestic glory, "This is my Son, my beloved, with whom I am well pleased."[g] [18]We* ourselves heard this voice come from heaven while we were with him on the holy mountain. [19h] Moreover, we possess the prophetic message that is altogether reliable. You will do well to be attentive to it, as to a lamp shining in a dark place, until day dawns and the morning star rises in your hearts. [20]* Know this first of all, that there is no prophecy of scripture that is a matter of personal interpretation, [21]for no prophecy ever came through human will; but rather human beings moved by the holy Spirit spoke under the influence of God.

## III. Condemnation of the False Teachers

### CHAPTER 2

See RG 442

*False Teachers.** [1]There were also false prophets among the people, just as there will be false teachers among you, who will introduce destructive heresies and even deny the Master who ransomed them, bringing swift destruction on themselves.[i] [2]Many will follow their licentious ways, and because of them the way of truth will be reviled.[j] [3]In their greed they will exploit you with fabrications, but from of old their condemnation has not been idle and their destruction does not sleep.[k]

*Lessons from the Past.* [4]* For if God did not

**1:12–19** The purpose in writing is to call to mind the apostle's witness to the truth, even as he faces the end of his life (2 Pt 1:12–15), his eyewitness testimony to Christ (1 Pt 1:16–18), and the true prophetic message (2 Pt 1:19) through the Spirit in scripture (2 Pt 1:20–21), in contrast to what false teachers are setting forth (2 Pt 2).

**1:13 Tent**: a biblical image for transitory human life (Is 38:12), here combined with a verb that suggests not folding or packing up a tent but its being discarded in death (cf. 2 Cor 5:1–4).

**1:16 Coming**: in Greek *parousia*, used at 2 Pt 3:4, 12 of the second coming of Christ. The word was used in the extrabiblical writings for the visitation of someone in authority; in Greek cult and Hellenistic Judaism it was used for the manifestation of the divine presence. That the apostles **made known** has been interpreted to refer to Jesus' transfiguration (2 Pt 1:17) or to his entire first coming or to his future coming in power (2 Pt 3).

**1:17** The author assures the readers of the reliability of the apostolic message (including Jesus' power, glory, and coming; cf. note on 2 Pt 1:16) by appeal to the transfiguration of Jesus in glory (cf. Mt 17:1–8 and parallels) and by appeal to the prophetic message (2 Pt 1:19; perhaps Nm 24:17). Here, as elsewhere, the New Testament insists on continued reminders as necessary to preserve the historical facts about Jesus and the truths of the faith; cf. 2 Pt 3:1–2; 1 Cor 11:2; 15:1–3. **My Son, my beloved**: or, "my beloved Son."

**1:18 We**: at Jesus' transfiguration, referring to Peter, James, and John (Mt 17:1).

**1:20–21** Often cited, along with 2 Tm 3:16, on the "inspiration" of scripture or against private interpretation, these verses in context are directed against the false teachers of 2 Pt 2 and clever tales (2 Pt 1:16). The prophetic word in scripture comes admittedly through **human beings** (2 Pt 1:21), but **moved by the holy Spirit**, not from their own interpretation, and is a matter of what the author and Spirit intended, not the **personal interpretation** of false teachers. Instead of **under the influence of God**, some manuscripts read "holy ones of God."

**2:1–3** The pattern of **false prophets** among the Old Testament people of God will recur through **false teachers** in the church. Such destructive opinions of heretical sects bring loss of faith in Christ, contempt for the way of salvation (cf. 2 Pt 2:21), and immorality.

**2:4–6** The false teachers will be punished just as surely and as severely as were the fallen **angels** (2 Pt 2:4; cf. Jude 6; Gn 6:1–4), the sinners of Noah's day (2 Pt 2:5; Gn 7:21–23), and the inhabitants of the cities of the Plain (2 Pt 2:6; Jude 7; Gn 19:25). Whereas there are three examples in Jude 5–7 (Exodus and wilderness; rebellious angels; Sodom and Gomorrah), 2 Peter omitted the first of these, has inserted a new illustration about Noah (2 Pt 2:5) between Jude's second and third examples, and listed the resulting three examples in their Old Testament order (Gn 6; 7; 19).

**2:4 Chains of Tartarus**: cf. Jude 6; other manuscripts in

*e:* Is 38:12; Jn 21:18–19. *f:* Lk 9:28–36; Jn 1:14. *g:* Ps 2:7; Mt 17:4–6. *h:* Lk 1:78–79; Rev 2:28. *i:* Mt 24:11, 24; 1 Tm 4:1; Jude 4. *j:* Is 52:5. *k:* Rom 16:18.

spare the angels when they sinned, but condemned them to the chains of Tartarus* and handed them over to be kept for judgment;[l] 5* and if he did not spare the ancient world, even though he preserved Noah, a herald of righteousness, together with seven others, when he brought a flood upon the godless world;[m] 6 and if he condemned the cities of Sodom and Gomorrah [to destruction], reducing them to ashes, making them an example for the godless [people] of what is coming;[n] 7 and if he rescued Lot, a righteous man oppressed by the licentious conduct of unprincipled people 8 (for day after day that righteous man living among them was tormented in his righteous soul at the lawless deeds that he saw and heard), 9 then the Lord knows how to rescue the devout from trial and to keep the unrighteous under punishment for the day of judgment,[o] 10 and especially those who follow the flesh with its depraved desire and show contempt for lordship.[p]

*False Teachers Denounced.** Bold and arrogant, they are not afraid to revile glorious beings,* 11* whereas angels,[q] despite their superior strength and power, do not bring a reviling judgment against them from the Lord. 12 But these people, like irrational animals born by nature for capture and destruction, revile things that they do not understand, and in their destruction they will also be destroyed,[r] 13 suffering wrong* as payment for wrongdoing. Thinking daytime revelry a delight, they are stains and defilements as they revel in their deceits while carousing with you.[s] 14 Their eyes are full of adultery and insatiable for sin. They seduce unstable people, and their hearts are trained in greed. Accursed children! 15 Abandoning the straight road, they have gone astray, following the road of Balaam, the son of Bosor,* who loved payment for wrongdoing,[t] 16 but he received a rebuke for his own crime: a mute beast spoke with a human voice and restrained the prophet's madness.[u]

17 These people are waterless springs and mists driven by a gale; for them the gloom of darkness has been reserved.[v] 18 For, talking empty bombast, they seduce with licentious desires of the flesh those who have barely escaped* from people who live in error.[w] 19 They promise them freedom, though they themselves are slaves of corruption, for a person is a slave of whatever overcomes him.[x] 20 For if they, having escaped the defilements of the world through the knowledge of [our] Lord and savior Jesus Christ, again become entangled and overcome by them, their last condition is worse than their first.[y] 21 For it would have been better for them not to have known the way of righteousness than after knowing it to turn back from the holy commandment handed down* to them.[z] 22* What is expressed in the true

2 Peter read "pits of Tartarus." **Tartarus**: a term borrowed from Greek mythology to indicate the infernal regions.

**2:5–10a** Although God did not spare the sinful, he kept and saved the righteous, such as **Noah** (2 Pt 2:5) and **Lot** (2 Pt 2:7), and **he knows how to rescue the devout** (2 Pt 2:9), who are contrasted with the false teachers of the author's day. On Noah, cf. Gn 5:32–9:29, especially 7:1. On Lot, cf. Gn 13 and 19.

**2:10b–22** Some take 2 Pt 2:10b, 11 with the preceding paragraph. Others begin the new paragraph with 2 Pt 2:10a, supplying from 2 Pt 2:9 **The Lord knows how . . . to keep . . . under punishment**, with reference to God and probably specifically Christ (2 Pt 2:1). The conduct of the false teachers is described and condemned in language similar to that of Jude 8–16. This arrogance knows no bounds; animal-like, they are due to be caught and destroyed. They seduce even those who have knowledge of Christ (2 Pt 2:20).

**2:10b Glorious beings**: literally, "glories"; cf. Jude 8. While some think that illustrious personages are meant or even political officials behind whom (fallen) angels stand, it is more likely that the reference is to glorious angelic beings (cf. Jude 9).

**2:11 From the Lord**: some manuscripts read "before the Lord"; cf. Jude 9.

**2:13 Suffering wrong**: some manuscripts read "receiving a reward." **In their deceits**: some manuscripts read "in their love feasts" (Jude 12).

**2:15 Balaam, the son of Bosor**: in Nm 22:5, Balaam is said to be the son of Beor, and it is this name that turns up in a few ancient Greek manuscripts by way of "correction" of the text. Balaam is not portrayed in such a bad light in Nm 22. His evil reputation and his **madness** (2 Pt 2:16), and possibly his surname Bosor, may have come from a Jewish tradition about him in the first/second century, of which we no longer have any knowledge.

**2:18 Barely escaped**: some manuscripts read "really escaped."

**2:21 Commandment handed down**: cf. 2 Pt 3:2 and Jude 3.

**2:22** The second proverb is of unknown origin, while the first appears in Prv 26:11.

*l:* Jude 6. *m:* Gn 8:15–19; Heb 11:7. *n:* Gn 19:24–25; Jude 7. *o:* 1 Cor 10:13; Rev 3:10. *p:* Jude 8. *q:* Jude 9. *r:* Ps 49:13–15; Jude 10. *s:* Jude 12. *t:* Nm 31:16; Jude 11. *u:* Nm 22:28–33. *v:* Jude 12–13. *w:* Jude 16. *x:* Jn 8:34; Rom 6:16–17. *y:* Mt 12:45. *z:* Ez 3:20. *a:* Prv 26:11.

proverb has happened to them,[a] "The dog returns to its own vomit," and "A bathed sow returns to wallowing in the mire."

## IV. The Delay of the Second Coming

### CHAPTER 3

See RG 442–44

***Denial of the Parousia.*** 1* This is now, beloved, the second letter I am writing to you; through them by way of reminder I am trying to stir up your sincere disposition, 2 to recall the words previously spoken by the holy prophets and the commandment of the Lord and savior through your apostles.[b] 3 Know this first of all, that in the last days scoffers* will come [to] scoff, living according to their own desires[c] 4 and saying, "Where is the promise of his coming?* From the time when our ancestors fell asleep, everything has remained as it was from the beginning of creation."[d] 5 They deliberately ignore the fact that the heavens existed of old and earth was formed out of water and through water* by the word of God;[e] 6 through these the world that then existed was destroyed,[f] deluged with water.* 7 The present heavens and earth have been reserved by the same word for fire, kept for the day of judgment and of destruction of the godless.[g]

8* But do not ignore this one fact, beloved, that with the Lord one day is like a thousand years* and a thousand years like one day.[h] 9 The Lord does not delay his promise, as some regard "delay," but he is patient with you, not wishing that any should perish but that all should come to repentance.[i] 10 But the day of the Lord will come like a thief,* and then the heavens will pass away with a mighty roar and the elements will be dissolved by fire, and the earth and everything done on it will be found out.[j]

***Exhortation to Preparedness.**** 11 Since everything is to be dissolved in this way, what sort of persons ought [you] to be, conducting yourselves in holiness and devotion,[k] 12* waiting for and hastening the coming of the day of God,[l] because of which the heavens will be dissolved in

**3:1–4** The false teachers not only flout Christian morality (cf. Jude 8–19); they also deny the second coming of Christ and the judgment (2 Pt 3:4; cf. 2 Pt 3:7). They seek to justify their licentiousness by arguing that the promised return of Christ has not been realized and the world is the same, no better than it was before (2 Pt 3:3–4). The author wishes to strengthen the faithful against such errors by reminding them in this **second letter** of the instruction in 1 Peter and of the teaching of the **prophets** and of Christ, conveyed through the **apostles** (2 Pt 3:1–2; cf. Jude 17); cf. 1 Pt 1:10–12, 16–21, especially 16–21; Eph 2:20.

**3:3 Scoffers**: cf. Jude 18, where, however, only the passions of the scoffers are mentioned, not a denial on their part of Jesus' parousia.

**3:4–7** The false teachers tried to justify their immorality by pointing out that the promised **coming** (*parousia*) of the Lord has not yet occurred, even though early Christians expected it in their day. They thus insinuate that God is not guiding the world's history anymore, since nothing has changed and the first generation of Christians, **our ancestors** (2 Pt 3:4), has all died by this time. The author replies that, just as God destroyed the earth by water in the flood (2 Pt 3:5–6, cf. 2 Pt 2:5), so he will destroy it along with the false teachers on judgment day (2 Pt 3:7). **The word of God**, which called the world into being (Gn 1; Ps 33:6) and **destroyed** it by the waters of a flood, will destroy it again by fire on **the day of judgment** (2 Pt 3:5–7).

**3:5 Formed out of water and through water**: Gn 1:2, 6–8 is reflected as well as Greek views that water was the basic element from which all is derived.

**3:6 Destroyed, deluged with water**: cf. 2 Pt 2:5; Gn 7:11–8:2.

**3:8–10** The scoffers' objection (2 Pt 3:4) is refuted also by showing that **delay** of the Lord's second coming is not a failure to fulfill his word but rather a sign of his patience: God is giving time for repentance before the final judgment (cf. Wis 11:23–26; Ez 18:23; 33:11).

**3:8** Cf. Ps 90:4.

**3:10 Like a thief**: Mt 24:43; 1 Thes 5:2; Rev 3:3. **Will be found out**: cf. 1 Cor 3:13–15. Some few versions read, as the sense may demand, "will not be found out"; many manuscripts read "will be burned up"; there are further variants in other manuscripts, versions, and Fathers. Total destruction is assumed (2 Pt 3:11).

**3:11–16** The second coming of Christ and the judgment of the world are the doctrinal bases for the moral exhortation to readiness through vigilance and a virtuous life; cf. Mt 24:42, 50–51; Lk 12:40; 1 Thes 5:1–11; Jude 20–21.

**3:12 Flames . . . fire**: although this is the only New Testament passage about a final conflagration, the idea was common in apocalyptic and Greco-Roman thought. **Hastening**: eschatology is here used to motivate ethics (2 Pt 3:11), as elsewhere in the New Testament. Jewish sources and Acts 3:19–20 assume that proper ethical conduct can help bring the promised day of the Lord; cf. 2 Pt 3:9. Some render the phrase, however, "desiring it earnestly."

*b:* Jude 17. *c:* 1 Tm 4:1; 2 Tm 3:1; Jude 18. *d:* Is 5:19. *e:* Gn 1:2, 6, 8; Ps 24:2. *f:* Gn 7:21. *g:* Is 51:6; Mt 3:12. *h:* Ps 90:4. *i:* Ez 18:23; 1 Tm 2:4. *j:* Is 66:15–16; Mt 24:29. *k:* Acts 3:19–21. *l:* Is 34:4; Heb 10:27.

flames and the elements melted by fire.
13But according to his promise we await
new heavens and a new earth* in which
righteousness dwells.[m]
14Therefore, beloved, since you await
these things, be eager to be found without
spot or blemish before him, at peace. 15And
consider the patience of our Lord as salvation, as our beloved brother Paul, according
to the wisdom given to him, also wrote to
you,[n] 16speaking of these things* as he does
in all his letters. In them there are some
things hard to understand that the ignorant
and unstable distort to their own destruction,
just as they do the other scriptures.

## V. Final Exhortation and Doxology*

17Therefore, beloved, since you are forewarned, be on your guard not to be led into
the error of the unprincipled and to fall from
your own stability.[o] 18But grow in grace and
in the knowledge of our Lord and savior
Jesus Christ. To him be glory now and to the
day of eternity. [Amen.][p]

**3:13 New heavens and a new earth**: cf. Is 65:17; 66:22. The divine promises will be fulfilled after the day of judgment will have passed. The universe will be transformed by the reign of God's **righteousness** or justice; cf. Is 65:17–18; Acts 3:21; Rom 8:18–25; Rev 21:1.

**3:16 These things**: the teachings of this letter find parallels in Paul, e.g., God's will to save (Rom 2:4; 9:22–23; 1 Cor 1:7–8), the coming of Christ (1 Thes 4:16–17; 1 Cor 15:23–52), and preparedness for the judgment (Col 1:22–23; Eph 1:4–14; 4:30; 5:5–14). **Other scriptures**: used to guide the faith and life of the Christian community. The letters of Paul are thus here placed on the same level as books of the Old Testament. Possibly other New Testament writings could also be included.

**3:17–18** To avoid the dangers **of error** and loss of **stability**, Christians are **forewarned** to be **on guard** and to **grow in grace and knowledge** (2 Pt 1:2) of Christ. The doxology (2 Pt 3:18) recalls 1 Pt 4:11. Some manuscripts add **Amen.**

*m:* Is 65:17; 66:22; Rom 8:21; Rev 21:1, 27. *n:* Rom 8:19; Jude 24. *o:* Mk 13:5; Heb 2:1. *p:* Rom 16:27.

See RG 444–49

# The First Letter of John

Early Christian tradition identified this work as a letter of John the apostle. Because of its resemblance to the fourth gospel in style, vocabulary, and ideas, it is generally agreed that both works are the product of the same school of Johannine Christianity. The terminology and the presence or absence of certain theological ideas in 1 John suggest that it was written after the gospel; it may have been composed as a short treatise on ideas that were developed more fully in the fourth gospel. To others, the evidence suggests that 1 John was written after the fourth gospel as part of a debate on the proper interpretation of that gospel. Whatever its relation to the gospel, 1 John may be dated toward the end of the first century. Unlike 2 and 3 John, it lacks in form the salutation and epistolary conclusion of a letter. These features, its prologue, and its emphasis on doctrinal teaching make it more akin to a theological treatise than to most other New Testament letters.

The purpose of the letter is to combat certain false ideas, especially about Jesus, and to deepen the spiritual and social awareness of the Christian community (1 Jn 3:17). Some former members (1 Jn 2:19) of the community refused to acknowledge Jesus as the Christ (1 Jn 2:22) and denied that he was a true man (1 Jn 4:2). The specific heresy described in this letter cannot be identified exactly, but it is a form of docetism or gnosticism; the former doctrine denied the humanity of Christ to insure that his divinity was untainted, and the latter viewed the appearance of Christ as a mere stepping-stone to higher knowledge of God. These theological errors are rejected by an appeal to the reality and continuity of the apostolic witness to Jesus. The author affirms that authentic Christian love, ethics, and faith take place only within the historical revelation and sacrifice of Jesus Christ. The fullness of Christian life as fellowship with the Father must be based on true belief and result in charitable living; knowledge of God and love for one another are inseparable, and error in one area inevitably affects the other. Although the author recognizes that Christian doctrine presents intangible mysteries of faith about Christ, he insists that the concrete Christian life brings to light the deeper realities of the gospel.

The structure and language of the letter are straightforward yet repetitious. The author sets forth the striking contrasts between light and darkness, Christians and the world, and truth and error to illustrate the threats and responsibilities of Christian life. The result is not one of theological argument but one of intense religious conviction expressed in simple truths. The letter is of particular value for its declaration of the humanity and divinity of Christ as an apostolic teaching and for its development of the intrinsic connection between Christian moral conduct and Christian doctrine.

The principal divisions of the First Letter of John are the following:

I. Prologue (1:1–4)
II. God as Light (1:5–3:10)
III. Love for One Another (3:11–5:12)
IV. Epilogue (5:13–21)

---

# I. Prologue

## CHAPTER 1

### *The Word of Life**

See RG 446

1 What was from the beginning,
what we have heard,
what we have seen with our eyes,
what we looked upon
and touched with our hands
concerns the Word of life—[a]
2 for the life was made visible;
we have seen it and testify to it
and proclaim to you the eternal life
that was with the Father and was made
visible to us—[b]
3 what we have seen and heard
we proclaim now to you,
so that you too may have fellowship
with us;
for our fellowship is with the Father
and with his Son, Jesus Christ.[c]
4 We are writing this so that our joy may
be complete.[d]

# II. God as Light

***God Is Light.*** 5 Now this is the message that
we have heard from him and proclaim to
you: God is light,* and in him there is no
darkness at all. 6 If we say, "We have fellowship with him," while we continue to walk in
darkness, we lie and do not act in truth.[e] 7 But
if we walk in the light as he is in the light,
then we have fellowship with one another,
and the blood of his Son Jesus cleanses us
from all sin.[f] 8 If we say, "We are without
sin," we deceive ourselves,* and the truth is
not in us.[g] 9 If we acknowledge our sins, he is
faithful and just and will forgive our sins and
cleanse us from every wrongdoing.[h] 10 If we
say, "We have not sinned," we make him a
liar, and his word is not in us.[i]

## CHAPTER 2

See RG 446–47

***Christ and His Commandments.*** 1 My
children,* I am writing this to you so that you
may not commit sin. But if anyone does sin,
we have an Advocate with the Father, Jesus
Christ the righteous one.[j] 2 He is expiation
for our sins, and not for our sins only but for
those of the whole world.[k] 3 The way we may

**1:1–4** There is a striking parallel to the prologue of the gospel of John (Jn 1:1–18), but the emphasis here is not on the preexistent Word but rather on the apostles' witness to the incarnation of life by their experience of the historical Jesus. He is **the Word of life** (1 Jn 1:1; cf. Jn 1:4), **the eternal life that was with the Father and was made visible** (1 Jn 1:2; cf. Jn 1:14), and was **heard**, **seen**, **looked upon**, and **touched** by the apostles. The purpose of their teaching is to share that **life**, called **fellowship . . . with the Father and with his Son, Jesus Christ**, with those who receive their witness (1 Jn 1:3; Jn 1:14, 16).

**1:5–7 Light** is to be understood here as truth and goodness; **darkness** here is error and depravity (cf. Jn 3:19–21; 17:17; Eph 5:8). To **walk** in light or darkness is to live according to truth or error, not merely intellectual but moral as well. Fellowship with God and with one another consists in a life according to the truth as found in God and in Christ.

**1:8–10** Denial of the condition of sin is self-deception and even contradictory of divine revelation; there is also the continual possibility of sin's recurrence. Forgiveness and deliverance from sin through Christ are assured through acknowledgment of them and repentance.

**2:1 Children**: like the term "beloved," this is an expression of pastoral love (cf. Jn 13:33; 21:5; 1 Cor 4:14). **Advocate**: for the use of the term, see Jn 14:16. Forgiveness of sin is assured through Christ's intercession and expiation or "offering"; the death of Christ effected the removal of sin.

---

*a:* 2:13; Jn 1:1, 14; 20:20, 25, 27. *b:* Jn 15:27; 17:5. *c:* Jn 17:21; Acts 4:20. *d:* Jn 15:11; 2 Jn 12. *e:* Jn 12:35. *f:* Mt 26:28; Rom 3:24–25; Heb 9:14; 1 Pt 1:19; Rev 1:5. *g:* 2 Chr 6:36; Prv 20:9. *h:* Prv 28:13; Jas 5:16. *i:* 5:10. *j:* Jn 14:16; Heb 7:25. *k:* 4:10.

be sure* that we know him is to keep his
commandments.[l] 4 Whoever says, "I know
him," but does not keep his commandments
is a liar, and the truth is not in him.[m] 5 But
whoever keeps his word, the love of God is
truly perfected in him. This is the way we
may know that we are in union with him:[n]
6 whoever claims to abide in him ought to
live [just] as he lived.

*The New Commandment.** 7 Beloved, I
am writing no new commandment to you
but an old commandment that you had from
the beginning. The old commandment is
the word that you have heard.[o] 8 And yet I
do write a new commandment to you,
which holds true in him and among you,*
for the darkness is passing away, and the
true light is already shining.[p] 9 Whoever
says he is in the light, yet hates his brother,
is still in the darkness.[q] 10 Whoever loves
his brother remains in the light, and there is
nothing in him to cause a fall.[r] 11 Whoever
hates his brother is in darkness; he walks in
darkness and does not know where he is going because the darkness has blinded his
eyes.

*Members of the Community.** 12 I am writing to you, children, because your sins have
been forgiven[s] for his name's sake.*
13 I am writing to you, fathers, because
you know him who is from the beginning.
I am writing to you, young men, because
you have conquered the evil one.[t]
14 I write to you, children, because you
know the Father.
I write to you, fathers, because you know
him who is from the beginning.
I write to you, young men, because you
are strong and the word of God remains in
you, and you have conquered the evil one.
15 Do not love the world or the things of the
world.* If anyone loves the world, the love of
the Father is not in him.[u] 16 For all that is in the
world, sensual lust,* enticement for the eyes,
and a pretentious life, is not from the Father
but is from the world. 17 Yet the world and its
enticement are passing away. But whoever
does the will of God remains forever.[v]

*Antichrists.* 18 Children, it is the last hour;*
and just as you heard that the antichrist was
coming, so now many antichrists have appeared. Thus we know this is the last hour.[w]
19 They went out from us, but they were not
really of our number;* if they had been, they
would have remained with us. Their desertion shows that none of them was of our
number. 20 But you have the anointing that
comes from the holy one,* and you all have

**2:3–6 The way we may be sure**: to those who claim, "I have known Christ and therefore I know him," our author insists on not mere intellectual knowledge but obedience to God's commandments in a life conformed to the example of Christ; this confirms our knowledge of him and is **the love of God . . . perfected.** Disparity between moral life and the commandments proves improper belief.

**2:7–11** The author expresses the continuity and freshness of mutual charity in Christian experience. Through Christ the commandment of love has become the **light** defeating the **darkness** of evil in a new age. All hatred as darkness is incompatible with the light and Christian life. Note also the characteristic Johannine polemic in which a positive assertion is emphasized by the negative statement of its opposite.

**2:8 Which holds true in him and among you**: literally, "a thing that holds true in him and in you."

**2:12–17** The Christian community that has experienced the grace of God through forgiveness of sin and knowledge of Christ is armed against the evil one.

**2:12 For his name's sake**: because of Christ our sins are forgiven.

**2:15 The world**: all that is hostile toward God and alienated from him. Love of the **world** and love of God are thus mutually exclusive; cf. Jas 4:4.

**2:16 Sensual lust**: literally, "the lust of the flesh," inordinate desire for physical gratification. **Enticement for the eyes**: literally, "the lust of the eyes," avarice or covetousness; the eyes are regarded as the windows of the soul. **Pretentious life**: literally, "pride of life," arrogance or ostentation in one's earthly style of life that reflects a willful independence from God and others.

**2:18 It is the last hour**: literally, "a last hour," the period between the death and resurrection of Christ and his second coming. **The antichrist**: opponent or adversary of Christ; the term appears only in 1 John–2 John, but "pseudochrists" (translated "false messiahs") in Mt 24:24 and Mk 13:22, and Paul's "lawless one" in 2 Thes 2:3, are similar figures. **Many antichrists**: Matthew, Mark, and Revelation seem to indicate a collectivity of persons, here related to the false teachers.

**2:19 Not really of our number**: the apostate teachers only proved their lack of faith by leaving the community.

**2:20 The anointing that comes from the holy one**: this anointing is in the Old Testament sense of receiving the Spirit of God. The **holy one** probably refers to Christ. True knowledge is the gift of the Spirit (cf. Is 11:2), and the function of the Spirit is to lead Christians to the truth (Jn 14:17, 26; 16:13).

*l:* Jn 14:15; 15:10. *m:* 4:20. *n:* Jn 14:23. *o:* 3:11; Dt 6:5; Mt 22:37–40. *p:* Jn 13:34 / Jn 1:5; Rom 13:12. *q:* Jn 8:12. *r:* Eccl 2:14; Jn 11:10. *s:* 1 Cor 6:11. *t:* 1:1; Jn 1:1. *u:* Rom 8:7–8; Jas 4:4; 2 Pt 1:4. *v:* Is 40:8; Mt 7:21; 1 Cor 7:31; 1 Pt 4:2. *w:* 1 Tm 4:1. *x:* Jn 14:26.

knowledge.[x] [21]I write to you not because you
do not know the truth but because you do,
and because every lie is alien to the truth.[y]
[22*] Who is the liar? Whoever denies that
Jesus is the Christ. Whoever denies the Father and the Son, this is the antichrist.[z] [23]No
one who denies the Son has the Father, but
whoever confesses the Son has the Father as
well.[a]

*Life from God's Anointing.* [24b] Let what
you heard from the beginning remain in you.
If what you heard from the beginning remains in you, then you will remain in the
Son and in the Father.* [25]And this is the
promise that he made us: eternal life.[c] [26]I
write you these things about those who
would deceive you. [27]As for you, the anointing that you received from him remains in
you, so that you do not need anyone to teach
you. But his anointing teaches you about
everything and is true and not false; just as it
taught you, remain in him.

*Children of God.* [28*] And now, children,
remain in him, so that when he appears we
may have confidence and not be put to
shame by him at his coming. [29]If you consider that he is righteous, you also know that
everyone who acts in righteousness is begotten by him.

### CHAPTER 3

See RG 446–47

[1*] See what love the Father has bestowed on us that we may be called the children of God. Yet so we are. The reason the
world does not know us is that it did not
know him.[d] [2]Beloved, we are God's children
now; what we shall be has not yet been revealed. We do know that when it is revealed*
we shall be like him, for we shall see him as
he is.[e] [3]Everyone who has this hope based on
him makes himself pure, as he is pure.[f]

*Avoiding Sin.* [4]Everyone who commits sin
commits lawlessness, for sin is lawlessness.*
[5]You know that he was revealed to take
away sins, and in him there is no sin.[g] [6]No
one who remains in him sins; no one who
sins has seen him or known him. [7]Children,
let no one deceive you. The person who acts
in righteousness is righteous, just as he is
righteous. [8]Whoever sins belongs to the
devil, because the devil has sinned from the
beginning. Indeed, the Son of God was revealed to destroy the works of the devil.[h]
[9]No one who is begotten by God commits
sin, because God's seed remains in him; he
cannot sin because he is begotten by God.*
[10]In this way, the children of God and the
children of the devil are made plain; no one
who fails to act in righteousness belongs to
God, nor anyone who does not love his
brother.

## III. Love for One Another

[11*] For this is the message you have heard
from the beginning: we should love one another,[i] [12]unlike Cain who belonged to the

**2:22–23** Certain gnostics denied that the earthly Jesus was the Christ; to deny knowledge of the Son is to deny the Father, since only through the Son has God been fully revealed (Jn 1:18; 14:8–9).

**2:24** Continuity with the apostolic witness as proclaimed in the prologue is the safeguard of right belief.

**2:28–29** Our confidence at his judgment is based on the daily assurance of salvation. Our actions reflect our true relation to him.

**3:1–3** The greatest sign of God's love is the gift of his Son (Jn 3:16) that has made Christians true children of God. This relationship is a present reality and also part of the life to come; true knowledge of God will ultimately be gained, and Christians prepare themselves now by virtuous lives in imitation of the Son.

**3:2 When it is revealed**: or "when he is revealed" (the subject of the verb could be Christ).

**3:4 Lawlessness**: a reference to the activity of the antichrist, so it is expressed as hostility toward God and a rejection of Christ. The author goes on to contrast the states of sin and righteousness. Christians do not escape sin but realize that when they sin they cease to have fellowship with God. Virtue and sin distinguish the children of God from the children of the devil.

**3:9** A habitual sinner is a child of the devil, while a child of God, who by definition is in fellowship with God, cannot sin. **Seed**: Christ or the Spirit who shares the nature of God with the Christian.

**3:11–18** Love, even to the point of self-sacrifice, is the point of the commandment. The story of Cain and Abel (1 Jn 3:12–15; Gn 4:1–16) presents the rivalry of two brothers, in a contrast of evil and righteousness, where envy led to murder. For Christians, proof of deliverance is love toward others, after the example of Christ. This includes concrete acts of charity, out of our material abundance.

*y:* 3:19; 2 Pt 1:12. *z:* 2 Thes 2:4. *a:* Jn 14:7–9. *b:* Jn 14:23. *c:* Jn 5:24; 10:28; 17:2. *d:* Jn 1:12; Eph 1:5 / Jn 15:21; 17:25. *e:* Phil 3:21. *f:* 2:6. *g:* Is 53:9; Jn 1:29; 8:46; 1 Pt 2:22. *h:* Jn 8:44; 12:31–32. *i:* 2:7; Jn 13:34; 15:12, 17.

evil one and slaughtered his brother. Why did he slaughter him? Because his own works were evil, and those of his brother righteous.[j] 13 Do not be amazed, [then,] brothers, if the world hates you.[k] 14 We know that we have passed from death to life because we love our brothers. Whoever does not love remains in death.[l] 15 Everyone who hates his brother is a murderer, and you know that no murderer has eternal life remaining in him.[m] 16 The way we came to know love was that he laid down his life for us; so we ought to lay down our lives for our brothers.[n] 17 If someone who has worldly means sees a brother in need and refuses him compassion, how can the love of God remain in him?[o] 18 Children, let us love not in word or speech but in deed and truth.[p]

***Confidence Before God.**** 19 [Now] this is how we shall know that we* belong to the truth and reassure our hearts before him 20 in whatever our hearts condemn, for God is greater than our hearts and knows everything. 21 Beloved, if [our] hearts do not condemn us, we have confidence in God 22 and receive from him whatever we ask, because we keep his commandments and do what pleases him.[q] 23 And his commandment is this: we should believe in the name of his Son, Jesus Christ, and love one another just as he commanded us.[r] 24 Those who keep his commandments remain in him, and he in them, and the way we know that he remains in us is from the Spirit that he gave us.[s]

## CHAPTER 4

See RG 447–48

***Testing the Spirits.**** 1 Beloved, do not trust every spirit but test the spirits to see whether they belong to God, because many false prophets have gone out into the world.[t] 2 This is how you can know the Spirit of God: every spirit that acknowledges Jesus Christ come in the flesh belongs to God,[u] 3 and every spirit that does not acknowledge Jesus* does not belong to God. This is the spirit of the antichrist that, as you heard, is to come, but in fact is already in the world.[v] 4 You belong to God, children, and you have conquered them, for the one who is in you is greater than the one who is in the world. 5 They belong to the world; accordingly, their teaching belongs to the world, and the world listens to them.[w] 6 We belong to God, and anyone who knows God listens to us, while anyone who does not belong to God refuses to hear us. This is how we know the spirit of truth and the spirit of deceit.[x]

***God's Love and Christian Life.*** 7* Beloved, let us love one another, because love is of God; everyone who loves is begotten by God and knows God. 8 Whoever is without love does not know God, for God is love. 9 In this way the love of God was revealed to us: God sent his only Son into the world so that we might have life through him.[y] 10 In this is love: not that we have loved God, but that he loved us and sent his Son as expiation for our sins.[z] 11 Beloved, if God so loved us, we also must love one another. 12 No one has ever

**3:19–24** Living a life of faith in Jesus and of Christian love assures us of abiding in God no matter what our feelings may at times tell us. Our obedience gives us confidence in prayer and trust in God's judgment. This obedience includes our belief in Christ and love for one another.

**3:19b–20** This difficult passage may also be translated "we shall be at peace before him in whatever our hearts condemn, for . . ." or "and before God we shall convince our hearts, if our hearts condemn us, that God is greater than our hearts."

**4:1–6** Deception is possible in spiritual phenomena and may be tested by its relation to Christian doctrine (cf. 1 Cor 12:3): those who fail to acknowledge Jesus Christ in the flesh are false prophets and belong to the antichrist. Even though these false prophets are well received in the world, the Christian who belongs to God has a greater power in the truth.

**4:3 Does not acknowledge Jesus**: some ancient manuscripts add "Christ" and/or "to have come in the flesh" (cf. 1 Jn 4:2), and others read "every spirit that annuls (or severs) Jesus."

**4:7–12** Love as we share in it testifies to the nature of God and to his presence in our lives. One who loves shows that one is a child of God and knows God, for God's very being is love; one without love is without God. The revelation of the nature of God's love is found in the free gift of his Son to us, so that we may share life with God and be delivered from our sins. The love we have for one another must be of the same sort: authentic, merciful; this unique Christian love is our proof that we know God and can "see" the invisible God.

*j:* Gn 4:8; Jude 11. *k:* Mt 24:9; Jn 15:18; 17:14. *l:* Lv 19:17; Jn 5:24. *m:* Jn 8:44. *n:* Mt 20:28; Jn 10:11; 15:13. *o:* Dt 15:7, 11; Jas 2:15–16. *p:* Jas 1:22. *q:* 5:15; Mt 7:7–11; 21:22; Jn 14:13–14. *r:* Jn 13:34; 15:17. *s:* 4:13; Jn 14:21–23. *t:* 2:18; Mt 24:24. *u:* 1 Cor 12:3; 1 Thes 5:21. *v:* 3:22. *w:* Jn 15:19. *x:* Jn 8:47; 10:16. *y:* Jn 3:16. *z:* Rom 5:8. *a:* Jn 1:18; 1 Tm 6:16.

seen God. Yet, if we love one another, God remains in us, and his love is brought to perfection in us.[a]

[13]* This is how we know that we remain in him and he in us, that he has given us of his Spirit. [14]Moreover, we have seen and testify that the Father sent his Son as savior of the world. [15]Whoever acknowledges that Jesus is the Son of God, God remains in him and he in God. [16]We have come to know and to believe in the love God has for us.

God is love, and whoever remains in love remains in God and God in him. [17]In this is love brought to perfection among us, that we have confidence on the day of judgment because as he is, so are we in this world.[b] [18]There is no fear in love, but perfect love drives out fear because fear has to do with punishment, and so one who fears is not yet perfect in love. [19]We love because he first loved us. [20]If anyone says, "I love God," but hates his brother, he is a liar; for whoever does not love a brother whom he has seen cannot love God* whom he has not seen.[c] [21]This is the commandment we have from him: whoever loves God must also love his brother.[d]

## CHAPTER 5

See RG 447–48

***Faith Is Victory over the World.***

[1]* Everyone who believes that Jesus is the Christ is begotten by God, and everyone who loves the father loves [also] the one begotten by him.[e] [2]In this way we know that we love the children of God when we love God and obey his commandments. [3]For the love of God is this, that we keep his commandments. And his commandments are not burdensome,[f] [4]for whoever is begotten by God conquers the world. And the victory that conquers the world is our faith.[g] [5]Who [indeed] is the victor over the world but the one who believes that Jesus is the Son of God?[h]

[6]This is the one who came through water and blood,* Jesus Christ, not by water alone, but by water and blood. The Spirit is the one that testifies, and the Spirit is truth.[i] [7]So there are three that testify, [8]the Spirit, the water, and the blood, and the three are of one accord.[j] [9]If we accept human testimony, the testimony of God is surely greater. Now the testimony of God is this, that he has testified on behalf of his Son.[k] [10]Whoever believes in the Son of God has this testimony within himself. Whoever does not believe God has made him a liar by not believing the testimony God has given about his Son.[l] [11]And this is the testimony: God gave us eternal life, and this life is in his Son.[m] [12]Whoever possesses the Son has life; whoever does not possess the Son of God does not have life.

## IV. Epilogue*

***Prayer for Sinners.*** [13]I write these things to you so that you may know that you have

**4:13–21** The testimony of the Spirit and that of faith join the testimony of love to confirm our knowledge of God. Our love is grounded in the confession of Jesus as the Son of God and the example of God's love for us. Christian life is founded on the knowledge of God as love and on his continuing presence that relieves us from fear of judgment (1 Jn 4:16–18). What Christ is gives us confidence, even as we live and love in this world. Yet Christian love is not abstract but lived in the concrete manner of love for one another.

**4:20 Cannot love God**: some ancient manuscripts read "how can he love . . . ?"

**5:1–5** Children of God are identified not only by their love for others (1 Jn 4:7–9) and for God (1 Jn 5:1–2) but by their belief in the divine sonship of Jesus Christ. Faith, the acceptance of Jesus in his true character and the obedience in love to God's commands (1 Jn 5:3), is the source of the Christian's power in the world and conquers the world of evil (1 Jn 5:4–5), even as Christ overcame the world (Jn 16:33).

**5:6–12 Water and blood** (1 Jn 5:6) refers to Christ's baptism (Mt 3:16–17) and to the shedding of his blood on the cross (Jn 19:34). **The Spirit** was present at the baptism (Mt 3:16; Mk 1:10; Lk 3:22; Jn 1:32, 34). **The testimony** to Christ as the Son of God is confirmed by divine witness (1 Jn 5:7–9), greater by far than the two legally required human witnesses (Dt 17:6). To deny this is to deny God's truth; cf. Jn 8:17–18. The gist of the divine witness or **testimony** is that **eternal life** (1 Jn 5:11–12) is given in Christ and nowhere else. To **possess the Son** is not acceptance of a doctrine but of a person who lives now and provides life.

**5:13–21** As children of God we have confidence in prayer because of our intimate relationship with him (1 Jn 5:14–15). In love, we pray (1 Jn 5:16–17) for those who are in **sin**, but not in **deadly sin** (literally, "sin unto death"), probably referring to apostasy or activities brought on under the antichrist; cf. Mk 3:29; Heb 6:4–6; 10:26–31. Even in the latter case, however, prayer, while not enjoined, is not forbidden. The letter concludes with a summary of the themes of the letter (1 Jn 5:18–20). There is a sharp antithesis between the children of God and those belonging to the world and to the evil one. The

*b:* 2:28. *c:* 2:4. *d:* Jn 13:34; 14:15, 21; 15:17. *e:* Jn 8:42; 1 Pt 1:23. *f:* Jn 14:15. *g:* Jn 16:33. *h:* 1 Cor 15:57. *i:* Jn 15:26; 19:34. *j:* Jn 5:32, 36; 15:26. *k:* Jn 5:32, 37. *l:* Jn 3:33. *m:* 1:2; Jn 1:4; 5:21, 26; 17:3.

eternal life, you who believe in the name of the Son of God.[n] 14 And we have this confidence in him, that if we ask anything according to his will, he hears us.[o] 15 And if we know that he hears us in regard to whatever we ask, we know that what we have asked him for is ours. 16 If anyone sees his brother sinning, if the sin is not deadly, he should pray to God and he will give him life. This is only for those whose sin is not deadly. There is such a thing as deadly sin, about which I do not say that you should pray.[p] 17 All wrongdoing is sin, but there is sin that is not deadly.

18 We know that no one begotten by God sins; but the one begotten by God he protects, and the evil one cannot touch him. 19 We know that we belong to God, and the whole world is under the power of the evil one. 20 We also know that the Son of God has come and has given us discernment to know the one who is true. And we are in the one who is true, in his Son Jesus Christ. He is the true God and eternal life.[q] 21 Children, be on your guard against idols.

Son reveals the God of truth; Christians dwell in the true God, **in his Son**, and have eternal life. The final verse (1 Jn 5:21) voices a perennial warning about **idols**, any type of rival to God.

*n:* Jn 1:12; 20:31. *o:* 3:21–22; Mt 7:7; Jn 14:13–14. *p:* Mt 12:31. *q:* Jer 24:7; Jn 17:3; Eph 1:17.

See RG 449–51

# The Second Letter of John

Written in response to similar problems, the Second and Third Letters of John are of the same length, perhaps determined by the practical consideration of the writing space on one piece of papyrus. In each letter the writer calls himself "the Presbyter," and their common authorship is further evidenced by internal similarities in style and wording, especially in the introductions and conclusions. The literary considerations that link 2 John and 3 John also link them with the First Letter and the Gospel of John. The concern with "truth," christology, mutual love, the new commandment, antichrist, and the integrity of witness to the earthly Jesus mark these works as products of the Johannine school. The identity of the Presbyter is problematic. The use of the title implies more than age, and refers to his position of leadership in the early church. The absence of a proper name indicates that he was well known and acknowledged in authority by the communities to which he writes. Although traditionally attributed to John the apostle, these letters were probably written by a disciple or scribe of an apostle. The traditional place and date of composition, Ephesus at the end of the first century, are plausible for both letters.

The Second Letter is addressed to "the chosen Lady" and "to her children." This literary image of a particular Christian community reflects the specific destination and purpose of the letter. Unlike 1 John, this brief letter is not a theological treatise but a reply to problems within the church. The Johannine themes of love and truth are used to support practical advice on Christian living. The Presbyter encourages community members to show their Christianity by adhering to the great commandment of mutual love and to the historical truth about Jesus. The false teaching present among them is a spiritualizing christology that may tempt some members to discount teachings about the incarnation and death of Jesus the Christ; cf. 1 Jn 4:2. For their protection the Presbyter forbids hospitality toward unknown or "progressive" Christians to prevent their infiltration of the community. The Second Letter preserves the Johannine concerns of doctrinal purity and active love in the form of pastoral advice to a threatened community.

See RG 449–51

1* [a] The Presbyter to the chosen Lady and to her children whom I love in truth—

**1 The chosen Lady**: literally, "elected"; this could also be translated "Kyria (a woman's name) chosen (by God)" or "the lady Electa" or "Electa Kyria." The adjective "chosen" is applied to all Christians at the beginning of other New Testament letters (1 Pt 1:1; Ti 1:1). The description is of a specific community with "children" who are its members. **The truth**: the affirmation of Jesus in the flesh and in contrast to false teaching (2 Jn 7).

*a:* Jn 8:32; 3 Jn 1.

and not only I but also all who know the truth— 2because of the truth that dwells in us and will be with us forever. 3Grace, mercy, and peace* will be with us from God the Father and from Jesus Christ the Father's Son in truth and love.

4I rejoiced greatly to find some of your children* walking in the truth just as we were commanded by the Father.[b] 5But now, Lady, I ask you, not as though I were writing a new commandment but the one we have had from the beginning: let us love one another.[c] 6For this is love, that we walk according to his commandments;* this is the commandment, as you heard from the beginning, in which you should walk.[d]

7[e] Many deceivers have gone out into the world, those who do not acknowledge Jesus Christ as coming in the flesh; such is the deceitful one and the antichrist.* 8Look to yourselves that you* do not lose what we worked for but may receive a full recompense. 9[f] Anyone who is so "progressive"* as not to remain in the teaching of the Christ does not have God; whoever remains in the teaching has the Father and the Son. 10* If anyone comes to you and does not bring this doctrine, do not receive him in your house or even greet him;[g] 11for whoever greets him shares in his evil works.

12* Although I have much to write to you, I do not intend to use paper and ink. Instead, I hope to visit you and to speak face to face so that our joy may be complete.[h] 13The children of your chosen sister* send you greetings.

**3 Grace, mercy, and peace**: like 1 Timothy; 2 Timothy this letter adds **mercy** to the terms used frequently in a salutation to describe Christian blessing; it appears only here in the Johannine writings. The author also puts the blessing in relation to **truth** and **love**, the watchwords of the Johannine teaching. **The Father's Son**: the title that affirms the close relationship of Christ to God; similar variations of this title occur elsewhere (Jn 1:14; 3:35), but the precise wording is not found elsewhere in the New Testament.

**4 Some of your children**: this refers to those whom the Presbyter has recently encountered, but it may also indicate the presence of false doctrine in the community: the Presbyter encourages those who have remained faithful. **Walking in the truth**: an expression used in the Johannine writings to describe a way of living in which the Christian faith is visibly expressed; cf. 1 Jn 1:6–7; 2:6, 11; 3 Jn 3.

**6 His commandments**: cf. 1 Jn 3:23; 2:7–8; 4:21; obedience to the commandment of faith and love includes all others.

**7 The antichrist**: see 1 Jn 2:18–19, 22; 4:3.

**8 You** (plural): it is not certain whether this means the Christians addressed or includes the Presbyter, since some of the ancient Greek manuscripts and Greek Fathers have "we."

**9 Anyone who is so "progressive"**: literally, "Anyone who goes ahead." Some gnostic groups held the doctrine of the Christ come in the flesh to be a first step in belief, which the more advanced and spiritual believer surpassed and abandoned in his knowledge of the spiritual Christ. The author affirms that fellowship with God may be gained only by holding to the complete doctrine of Jesus Christ (1 Jn 2:22–23; 4:2; 5:5–6).

**10–11** At this time false teachers were considered so dangerous and divisive as to be shunned completely. From this description they seem to be wandering preachers. We see here a natural suspicion of early Christians concerning such itinerants and can envisage the problems faced by missionaries such as those mentioned in 3 Jn 10.

**12 Our joy**: a number of other Greek manuscripts read "your joy."

**13 Chosen sister**: the community of which the Presbyter is now a part greets you (singular), the community of the Lady addressed.

*b:* 3 Jn 3. *c:* Jn 13:34; 15:12; 1 Jn 4:7. *d:* Jn 13:34; 14:15; 1 Jn 5:3. *e:* 1 Jn 2:22; 4:2. *f:* Jn 8:31; 1 Jn 2:23; 4:15. *g:* Rom 16:17; 2 Thes 3:6. *h:* Jn 15:11; 1 Jn 1:4; 3 Jn 13.

See RG 451–52

# The Third Letter of John

The Third Letter of John preserves a brief glimpse into the problems of missionary activity and local autonomy in the early church. In contrast to the other two letters of John, this work was addressed to a specific individual, Gaius. This letter is less theological in content and purpose. The author's goal was to secure hospitality and material support for his missionaries, and the Presbyter is writing to another member of the church who has welcomed missionaries in the past. The Presbyter commends Gaius for his hospitality and encourages his future help. He indicates he may come to challenge the policy of Diotrephes that is based on evil gossip.

The problems of the Presbyter in this short letter provide us with valuable evidence of the flexible and personal nature of authority in the early church. The Presbyter writes to Gaius, whom perhaps he had converted or instructed, on the basis of their personal links. The brothers have also confirmed him as a loyal Christian in action and belief. Gaius accepted the missionaries from the Presbyter and presumably will accept Demetrius on the Presbyter's recommendation. In contrast, Diotrephes refuses to receive either letters or friends of the Presbyter. Although he is portrayed as ambitious and hostile, he perhaps exemplifies the cautious and sectarian nature of early Christianity; for its own protection the local community mistrusted missionaries as false teachers. Most interestingly, Diotrephes seems comfortable in ignoring the requests of the Presbyter. The Presbyter seems to acknowledge that only a personal confrontation with Diotrephes will remedy the situation (3 Jn 10). The division, however, may also rest on doctrinal disagreement in which Gaius and the other "friends" accept the teaching of the Presbyter, and Diotrephes does not; the missionaries are not received for suspicion of theological error. Diotrephes has thus been viewed by some as an overly ambitious local upstart trying to thwart the advance of orthodox Christianity, by others as an orthodox church official suspicious of the teachings of the Presbyter and those in the Johannine school who think as he does, or by still others as a local leader anxious to keep the debates in the Johannine community out of his own congregation.

This brief letter and the situation that it mirrors show us how little we know about some details of early development in the church: schools of opinion existed around which questions of faith and life were discussed, and personal ties as well as doctrine and authority played a role in what happened amid divisions and unity.

See RG 451–52

1* The Presbyter to the beloved Gaius
whom I love in truth.[a]
2 Beloved, I hope you are prospering in
every respect and are in good health, just as
your soul is prospering. 3 I rejoiced greatly
when some of the brothers* came and testified to how truly you walk in the truth.[b]
4 Nothing gives me greater joy than to hear
that my children are walking in the truth.[c]
5 Beloved, you are faithful in all you do*
for the brothers, especially for strangers;[d]
6 they have testified to your love before the
church.[e] Please help them in a way worthy of
God to continue their journey.* 7 For they
have set out for the sake of the Name* and
are accepting nothing from the pagans.
8 Therefore, we ought to support such persons, so that we may be co-workers in the
truth.
9 I wrote to the church, but Diotrephes,
who loves to dominate,* does not acknowledge us. 10 Therefore, if I come,* I will draw
attention to what he is doing, spreading evil
nonsense about us. And not content with
that, he will not receive the brothers, hinder-
ing those who wish to do so and expelling
them from the church.
11 Beloved, do not imitate evil* but imitate
good. Whoever does what is good is of God;
whoever does what is evil has never seen
God.[f] 12 Demetrius* receives a good report
from all, even from the truth itself. We give
our testimonial as well, and you know our
testimony is true.[g]

**1 Beloved Gaius**: a frequent form of address for fellow Christians in New Testament epistolary literature.

**3 The brothers**: in this letter, the term may refer to Christians who have been missionaries and received hospitality from Gaius (3 Jn 5–6). **Walk in the truth**: the common Johannine term to describe Christian living; this description presents Gaius as following the teachings of the Presbyter in contrast to Diotrephes.

**5 You are faithful in all you do**: Gaius's aid to the missionaries is a manifestation of his true Christian faith.

**6 Help them . . . to continue their journey**: the Presbyter asks Gaius not only to continue to welcome the missionaries to his community but also to equip them for further travels.

**7 The Name**: of Jesus Christ (cf. Acts 5:41; 1 Jn 2:12; 3:23; 5:13). **Accepting nothing**: not expecting support from the pagans to whom they preach the gospel, so that they will not be considered as beggars; they required support from other Christians; cf. Paul's complaints to the Corinthians (1 Cor 9:3–12).

**9 Who loves to dominate**: the Presbyter does not deny Diotrephes' place as leader but indicates that his ambition may have caused him to disregard his letter and his influence.

**10 If I come**: the Presbyter may visit the community to challenge the actions of Diotrephes toward himself and the missionaries. **Will not receive the brothers**: Diotrephes may have been critical of the teachings of the Presbyter and sought to maintain doctrinal purity; cf. 1 Jn 2:19 and 2 Jn 10–11.

**11 Do not imitate evil**: Gaius should not be influenced by the behavior of Diotrephes.

**12 Demetrius**: because of the fear of false teachers,

*a:* 2 Jn 1. *b:* 5; Gal 6:10; 2 Jn 4. *c:* 1 Thes 2:11–12; 1 Tm 1:2; 2 Tm 1:2; 1 Jn 2:1; 2 Jn 4. *d:* Rom 12:13; Gal 6:10; Heb 13:2. *e:* Acts 15:3; Col 1:10; 1 Thes 2:12. *f:* 1 Jn 2:29; 3:6, 10. *g:* Jn 19:35; 21:24; 1 Tm 3:7.

[13]I have much to write to you, but I do not wish to write with pen and ink.[h] [14]Instead, I hope to see you soon, when we can talk face to face. [15]Peace be with you. The friends greet you; greet the friends* there each by name.[i]

Demetrius, perhaps the bearer of the letter, is provided with a recommendation from the Presbyter; cf. 2 Cor 3:1; Rom 16:1. **Even from the truth itself**: this refers probably to the manner of Demetrius's life that testifies to his true belief; cf. Gaius above (3 Jn 3).

**15 Friends**: although a Johannine term for Christians (Jn 15:15), the word here may refer to those in the community loyal to the Presbyter and to Gaius.

*h:* 2 Jn 12. *i:* Jn 20:19, 21, 26; Eph 6:23; 1 Pt 5:14.

See RG 452–55

# The Letter of Jude

This letter is by its address attributed to "Jude, a slave of Jesus Christ and brother of James" (Jude 1). Since he is not identified as an apostle, this designation can hardly be meant to refer to the Jude or Judas who is listed as one of the Twelve (Lk 6:16; Acts 1:13; cf. Jn 14:22). The person intended is almost certainly the other Jude, named in the gospels among the relatives of Jesus (Mt 13:55; Mk 6:3), and the James who is listed there as his brother is the one to whom the Letter of James is attributed (see the Introduction to James). Nothing else is known of this Jude, and the apparent need to identify him by reference to his better-known brother indicates that he was a rather obscure personage in the early church.

The letter is addressed in the most general terms to "those who are called, beloved in God the Father and kept safe for Jesus Christ" (Jude 1), hence apparently to all Christians. But since its purpose is to warn the addressees against false teachers, the author must have had in mind one or more specific Christian communities located in the unidentified region where the errors in question constituted a danger. While the letter contains some Semitic features, there is nothing to identify the addressees specifically as Jewish Christians; indeed, the errors envisaged seem to reflect an early form of gnosticism, opposed to law, that points rather to the cultural context of the Gentile world. Like James and 2 Peter, the Letter of Jude manifests none of the typical features of the letter form except the address.

There is so much similarity between Jude and 2 Peter, especially Jude 4–16 and 2 Pt 2:1–18, that there must be a literary relationship between them. Since there is no evidence for the view that both authors borrowed from the same source, it is usually supposed that one of them borrowed from the other. Most scholars believe that Jude is the earlier of the two, principally because he quotes two apocryphal Jewish works, the Assumption of Moses (Jude 9) and the Book of Enoch (Jude 14–15) as part of his structured argument, whereas 2 Peter omits both references. Since there was controversy in the early church about the propriety of citing noncanonical literature that included legendary material, it is more probable that a later writer would omit such references than that he would add them.

Many interpreters today consider Jude a pseudonymous work dating from the end of the first century or even later. In support of this view they adduce the following arguments: (a) the apostles are referred to as belonging to an age that has receded into the past (Jude 17–18); (b) faith is understood as a body of doctrine handed down by a process of tradition (Jude 3); (c) the author's competent Greek style shows that he must have had a Hellenistic cultural formation; (d) the gnostic character of the errors envisaged fits better into the early second century than into a period several decades earlier. While impressive, these arguments are not entirely compelling and do not completely rule out the possibility of composition around the year A.D. 80, when the historical Jude may still have been alive.

This little letter is an urgent note by an author who intended to write more fully about salvation to an unknown group of readers, but who was forced by dangers from false teachers worming their way into the community (Jude 3–4) to dash off a warning against them (Jude 5–16) and to deliver some pressing Christian admonitions (Jude 17–23). The letter is justly famous for its majestic closing doxology ( Jude 24–25).

See RG 452–55

*Address and Greeting.* [1]* Jude, a slave of Jesus Christ and brother of James, to those who are called, beloved in God the Father and kept safe for Jesus Christ:[a] [2]may mercy, peace, and love be yours in abundance.[b]

*Occasion for Writing.* [3]Beloved, although I was making every effort to write to you about our common salvation,* I now feel a need to write to encourage you to contend for the faith that was once for all handed down to the holy ones.[c] [4]For there have been some intruders, who long ago were designated for this condemnation, godless persons, who pervert the grace of our God into licentiousness and who deny our only Master and Lord, Jesus Christ.[d]

*The False Teachers.* [5e] I wish to remind you, although you know all things, that [the] Lord who once saved a people from the land of Egypt later destroyed those who did not believe.* [6f] The angels too, who did not keep to their own domain but deserted their proper dwelling, he has kept in eternal chains, in gloom, for the judgment of the great day.* [7]Likewise, Sodom, Gomorrah, and the surrounding towns, which, in the same manner as they, indulged in sexual promiscuity and practiced unnatural vice,* serve as an example by undergoing a punishment of eternal fire.[g]

[8]Similarly, these dreamers* nevertheless also defile the flesh, scorn lordship, and revile glorious beings. [9]Yet the archangel Michael, when he argued with the devil in a dispute over the body of Moses, did not venture to pronounce a reviling judgment* upon him but said, "May the Lord rebuke you!"[h] [10]But these people revile what they do not understand and are destroyed by what they know by nature like irrational animals.[i] [11]Woe to them![j] They followed the way of Cain, abandoned themselves to Balaam's error for the sake of gain, and perished in the rebellion of Korah.* [12]These are blemishes on your love feasts,* as they carouse fearlessly and look after them-

**1 Jude . . . brother of James**: for the identity of the author of this letter, see Introduction. **To those who are called**: the vocation to the Christian faith is God's free gift to those whom he loves and whom he safely protects in Christ until the Lord's second coming.

**3–4 Our common salvation**: the teachings of the Christian faith derived from the apostolic preaching and to be kept by the Christian community.

**5** For this first example of divine punishment on those who had been saved but did not then keep faith, see Nm 14:28–29 and the note there. Some manuscripts have the word "once" (*hapax* as at Jude 3) after "you know"; some commentators have suggested that it means "knowing one thing" or "you know all things once for all." Instead of "[the] Lord" manuscripts vary, having "Jesus," "God," or no subject stated.

**6** This second example draws on Gn 6:1–4 as elaborated in the apocryphal Book of Enoch (cf. Jude 14): heavenly beings came to earth and had sexual intercourse with women. God punished them by casting them out of heaven into darkness and bondage.

**7 Practiced unnatural vice**: literally, "went after alien flesh." This example derives from Gn 19:1–25, especially 4–11, when the townsmen of Sodom violated both hospitality and morality by demanding that Lot's two visitors (really messengers of Yahweh) be handed over to them so that they could abuse them sexually. **Unnatural vice**: this refers to the desire for intimacies by human beings with angels (the reverse of the example in Jude 6). Sodom (whence "sodomy") and Gomorrah became proverbial as object lessons for God's punishment on sin (Is 1:9; Jer 50:40; Am 4:11; Mt 10:15; 2 Pt 2:6).

**8 Dreamers**: the writer returns to the false teachers of Jude 4, applying charges from the three examples in Jude 5, 6, 7. This may apply to claims they make for revelations they have received by night (to the author, hallucinations). **Defile the flesh**: this may mean bodily pollutions from the erotic dreams of sexual license (Jude 7). **Lordship . . . glorious beings**: these may reflect the Lord (Jude 5; Jesus, Jude 4) whom they spurn and the angels (Jude 6; cf. note on 2 Pt 2:10, here, as there, literally, "glories").

**9 The archangel Michael . . . judgment**: a reference to an incident in the apocryphal Assumption of Moses. Dt 34:6 had said of Moses, literally in Greek, "they buried him" or "he (God?) buried him" (taken to mean "he was buried"). The later account tells how Michael, who was sent to bury him, was challenged by the devil's interest in the body. Our author draws out the point that if an archangel refrained from reviling even the devil, how wrong it is for mere human beings to revile glorious beings (angels).

**11 Cain . . . Balaam . . . Korah**: examples of rebellious men and of the punishment their conduct incurred; cf. Gn 4:8–16; Nm 16:1–35; 31:16. See note on 2 Pt 2:15.

**12 Blemishes on your love feasts**: or "hidden rocks" or "submerged reefs" (cf. Jude 13). The opponents engaged in scandalous conduct in connection with community gatherings called **love feasts** (agape meals), which were associated with eucharistic celebrations at certain stages of early Christian practice; cf. 1 Cor 11:18–34 and the note on 2 Pt 2:13.

*a:* Mt 13:55; Mk 6:3; Acts 12:17; Rom 1:7. *b:* Gal 6:16; 1 Tm 1:2; 2 Pt 1:2. *c:* 17, 20; 1 Tm 6:12. *d:* Gal 2:4; 2 Tm 3:6; 2 Pt 2:1. *e:* Nm 14:35; 1 Cor 10:5; Heb 3:16, 17. *f:* 2 Pt 2:4, 9. *g:* Dt 29:22–24; Mt 25:41; 2 Thes 1:8–9; 2 Pt 2:6; 3:7. *h:* Dn 10:21; 12:1. *i:* 2 Pt 2:12. *j:* Gn 4:8–16; 1 Jn 3:12 / Nm 31:15–16; 2 Pt 2:15; Rev 2:14 / Nm 16:19–35. *k:* 2 Pt 2:13, 17.

selves. They are waterless clouds blown about
by winds, fruitless trees in late autumn, twice
dead and uprooted.[k] 13 They are like wild
waves of the sea, foaming up their shameless
deeds, wandering stars for whom the gloom of
darkness has been reserved forever.
14* Enoch, of the seventh generation from
Adam, prophesied also about them when he
said,[l] "Behold, the Lord has come with his
countless holy ones 15 to execute judgment
on all and to convict everyone for all the
godless deeds that they committed and for
all the harsh words godless sinners have uttered against him." 16 These people are com-
plainers, disgruntled ones who live by their
desires; their mouths utter bombast as they
fawn over people to gain advantage.[m]
***Exhortations.*** 17 But you, beloved, remember the words spoken beforehand by the apostles of our Lord Jesus Christ,[n] 18 for they told
you,[o] "In [the] last time there will be scoffers
who will live according to their own godless
desires."* 19 These are the ones who cause divisions; they live on the natural plane, devoid
of the Spirit.[p] 20 But you, beloved, build yourselves up in your most holy faith; pray in the
holy Spirit.[q] 21 Keep yourselves in the love of
God and wait for the mercy of our Lord Jesus
Christ that leads to eternal life.[r] 22 On those
who waver, have mercy;* 23 save others by
snatching them out of the fire; on others have
mercy with fear,* abhorring even the outer
garment stained by the flesh.
***Doxology.**** 24 To the one who is able to
keep you from stumbling and to present you
unblemished and exultant, in the presence of
his glory,[s] 25 to the only God, our savior,
through Jesus Christ our Lord be glory,
majesty, power, and authority from ages
past, now, and for ages to come. Amen.[t]

**14–15** Cited from the apocryphal Book of Enoch 1:9.

**18** This is the substance of much early Christian preaching rather than a direct quotation of any of the various New Testament passages on this theme (see Mk 13:22; Acts 20:30; 1 Tm 4:1–3; 2 Pt 3:3).

**22 Have mercy**: some manuscripts read "convince," "confute," or "reprove." Others have "even though you waver" or "doubt" instead of **who waver**.

**23 With fear**: some manuscripts connect the phrase "with fear" with the imperative "save" or with the participle "snatching." Other manuscripts omit the phrase "on others have mercy," so that only two groups are envisioned. Rescue of those led astray and caution in the endeavor are both enjoined. **Outer garment stained by the flesh**: the imagery may come from Zec 3:3–5, just as that of **snatching . . . out of the fire** comes from Zec 3:2; the very garments of the godless are to be abhorred because of their contagion.

**24–25** With this liturgical statement about the power of God to keep the faithful from stumbling, and praise to him through Jesus Christ, the letter reaches its conclusion by returning to the themes with which it began (Jude 1–2).

*l:* Mt 16:27; Heb 12:22–23. *m:* 18; 1 Cor 10:10; 2 Pt 2:10, 18. *n:* Heb 2:3; 2 Pt 3:2. *o:* 1 Tm 4:1; 2 Tm 3:1–5; 2 Pt 3:3. *p:* 1 Cor 2:14; Jas 3:15. *q:* 2; Eph 6:18; Col 2:7. *r:* Ti 2:13. *s:* 2 Cor 4:14; 1 Pt 4:13. *t:* Rom 11:36; 1 Tm 1:17.

See RG 455–62

# The Revelation to John

The Apocalypse, or Revelation to John, the last book of the Bible, is one of the most difficult to understand because it abounds in unfamiliar and extravagant symbolism, which at best appears unusual to the modern reader. Symbolic language, however, is one of the chief characteristics of apocalyptic literature, of which this book is an outstanding example. Such literature enjoyed wide popularity in both Jewish and Christian circles from ca. 200 B.C. to A.D. 200.

This book contains an account of visions in symbolic and allegorical language borrowed extensively from the Old Testament, especially Ezekiel, Zechariah, and Daniel. Whether or not these visions were real experiences of the author or simply literary conventions employed by him is an open question.

This much, however, is certain: symbolic descriptions are not to be taken as literal descriptions, nor is the symbolism meant to be pictured realistically. One would find it difficult and repulsive to visualize a lamb with seven horns and seven eyes; yet Jesus Christ is described in precisely such words (Rev 5:6). The author used these images to suggest Christ's universal (seven) power (horns) and knowledge (eyes). A significant feature of apocalyptic writing is the use of symbolic colors, metals, garments (Rev 1:13–16; 3:18; 4:4; 6:1–8; 17:4; 19:8), and numbers (*four* signifies the world, *six* imperfection, *seven* totality or perfection, *twelve* Israel's tribes or the apostles, *one thousand* immensity). Finally the vindictive language in the book (Rev 6:9–10; 18:1–19:4) is also to be understood symbolically and not literally. The cries for vengeance on the lips of Christian martyrs that sound so harsh are in fact literary devices the author employed to evoke in the reader and hearer a feeling of horror for apostasy and rebellion that will be severely punished by God.

The lurid descriptions of the punishment of Jezebel (Rev 2:22) and of the destruction of the great harlot, Babylon (Rev 16:9–19:2), are likewise literary devices. The metaphor of Babylon as harlot would be wrongly construed if interpreted literally. On the other hand, the stylized figure of the woman clothed with the sun (Rev 12:1–6), depicting the New Israel, may seem to be a negative stereotype. It is necessary to look beyond the literal meaning to see that these images mean to convey a sense of God's wrath at sin in the former case and trust in God's providential care over the church in the latter.

The Book of Revelation cannot be adequately understood except against the historical background that occasioned its writing. Like Daniel and other apocalypses, it was composed as resistance literature to meet a crisis. The book itself suggests that the crisis was ruthless persecution of the early church by the Roman authorities; the harlot Babylon symbolizes pagan Rome, the city on seven hills (Rev 17:9). The book is, then, an exhortation and admonition to Christians of the first century to stand firm in the faith and to avoid compromise with paganism, despite the threat of adversity and martyrdom; they are to await patiently the fulfillment of God's mighty promises. The triumph of God in the world of men and women remains a mystery, to be accepted in faith and longed for in hope. It is a triumph that unfolded in the history of Jesus of Nazareth and continues to unfold in the history of the individual Christian who follows the way of the cross, even, if necessary, to a martyr's death.

Though the perspective is eschatological—ultimate salvation and victory are said to take place at the end of the present age when Christ will come in glory at the parousia—the book presents the decisive struggle of Christ and his followers against Satan and his cohorts as already over. Christ's overwhelming defeat of the kingdom of Satan ushered in the everlasting reign of God (Rev 11:15; 12:10). Even the forces of evil unwittingly carry out the divine plan (Rev 17:17), for God is the sovereign Lord of history.

The Book of Revelation had its origin in a time of crisis, but it remains valid and meaningful for Christians of all time. In the face of apparently insuperable evil, either from within or from without, all Christians are called to trust in Jesus' promise, "Behold, I am with you always, until the end of the age" (Mt 28:20). Those who remain steadfast in their faith and confidence in the risen Lord need have no fear. Suffering, persecution, even death by martyrdom, though remaining impenetrable mysteries of evil, do not comprise an absurd dead end. No matter what adversity or sacrifice Christians may endure, they will in the end triumph over Satan and his forces because of their fidelity to Christ the victor. This is the enduring message of the book; it is a message of hope and consolation and challenge for all who dare to believe.

The author of the book calls himself John (Rev 1:1, 4, 9; 22:8), who because of his Christian faith has been exiled to the rocky island of Patmos, a Roman penal colony. Although he never claims to be John the apostle, whose name is attached to the fourth gospel, he was so identified by several of the early church Fathers, including Justin, Irenaeus, Clement of Alexandria, Tertullian, Cyprian, and Hippolytus. This identification, however, was denied by other Fathers, including Denis of Alexandria, Eusebius of Caesarea, Cyril of Jerusalem, Gregory Nazianzen, and John Chrysostom. Indeed, vocabulary, grammar, and style make it doubtful that the book could have been put into its present form by the same person(s) responsible for the fourth gospel. Nevertheless, there are definite linguistic and theological affinities between the two books. The tone of the letters to the seven churches (Rev 1:4–3:22) is indicative of the great authority the author enjoyed over the Christian communities in Asia. It is possible, therefore, that he was a disciple of John the apostle, who is traditionally associated with that part of the world. The date of the book in its present form is probably near the end of the reign of Domitian (A.D. 81–96), a fierce persecutor of the Christians.

The principal divisions of the Book of Revelation are the following:

I. Prologue (1:1–3)

---

# I. Prologue*

## CHAPTER 1

See RG 457–58

1 The revelation of Jesus Christ, which God gave to him, to show his servants what must happen soon. He made it known by sending his angel to his servant John,[a] 2 who gives witness to the word of God and to the testimony of Jesus Christ by reporting what he saw. 3 Blessed is the one* who reads aloud and blessed are those who listen to this prophetic message and heed what is written in it, for the appointed time is near.[b]

# II. Letters to the Churches of Asia

***Greeting.**** 4 John, to the seven churches in Asia:* grace to you and peace from him who is and who was and who is to come, and from the seven spirits before his throne,[c] 5 and from Jesus Christ, the faithful witness, the firstborn of the dead and ruler of the kings of the earth. To him who loves us and has freed us* from our sins by his blood,[d] 6 who has made us into a kingdom, priests for his God and Father, to him be glory and power forever [and ever]. Amen.[e]

7 Behold, he is coming amid the clouds,
and every eye will see him,
even those who pierced him.
All the peoples of the earth will lament him.
Yes. Amen.[f]

8 "I am the Alpha and the Omega,"* says the Lord God, "the one who is and who was and who is to come, the almighty."[g]

***The First Vision.**** 9 I, John, your brother, who share with you the distress, the kingdom, and the endurance we have in Jesus, found myself on the island called Patmos* because I proclaimed God's word and gave testimony to Jesus. 10 I was caught up in spirit on the Lord's day* and heard behind me a voice as loud as a trumpet, 11 which said, "Write on a scroll* what you see and send it to the seven churches: to Ephesus, Smyrna, Pergamum, Thyatira, Sardis, Phila-

---

**1:1–3** This prologue describes the source, contents, and audience of the book and forms an inclusion with the epilogue (Rev 22:6–21), with its similar themes and expressions.

**1:3 Blessed is the one**: this is the first of seven beatitudes in this book; the others are in Rev 14:13; 16:15; 19:9; 20:6; 22:7, 14. **This prophetic message**: literally, "the words of the prophecy"; so Rev 22:7, 10, 18, 19 by inclusion. **The appointed time**: when Jesus will return in glory; cf. Rev 1:7; 3:11; 22:7, 10, 12, 20.

**1:4–8** Although Revelation begins and ends (Rev 22:21) with Christian epistolary formulae, there is nothing between Rev 4; 22 resembling a letter. The author here employs the standard word order for greetings in Greek letter writing: "N. to N., greetings . . ."; see note on Rom 1:1.

**1:4 Seven churches in Asia**: Asia refers to the Roman province of that name in western Asia Minor (modern Turkey); these representative churches are mentioned by name in Rev 1:11, and each is the recipient of a message (Rev 2:1–3:22). **Seven** is the biblical number suggesting fullness and completeness; thus the seer is writing for the whole church.

**1:5 Freed us**: the majority of Greek manuscripts and several early versions read "washed us"; but "freed us" is supported by the best manuscripts and fits well with Old Testament imagery, e.g., Is 40:2.

**1:8 The Alpha and the Omega**: the first and last letters of the Greek alphabet. In Rev 22:13 the same words occur together with the expressions "the First and the Last, the Beginning and the End"; cf. Rev 1:17; 2:8; 21:6; Is 41:4; 44:6.

**1:9–20** In this first vision, the seer is commanded to write what he sees to the seven churches (Rev 1:9–11). He sees Christ in glory, whom he depicts in stock apocalyptic imagery (Rev 1:12–16), and hears him describe himself in terms meant to encourage Christians by emphasizing his victory over death (Rev 1:17–20).

**1:9 Island called Patmos**: one of the Sporades islands in the Aegean Sea, some fifty miles south of Ephesus, used by the Romans as a penal colony. **Because I proclaimed God's word**: literally, "on account of God's word."

**1:10 The Lord's day**: Sunday. **As loud as a trumpet**: the imagery is derived from the theophany at Sinai (Ex 19:16, 19; cf. Heb 12:19 and the trumpet in other eschatological settings in Is 27:13; Jl 2:1; Mt 24:31; 1 Cor 15:52; 1 Thes 4:16).

**1:11 Scroll**: a papyrus roll.

---

*a:* 22:6–8, 20; Dn 2:28 / Rev 19:10. *b:* 22:7 / Lk 11:28. *c:* 8; 4:8; 11:17; 16:5; Ex 3:14. *d:* 3:14; 1 Cor 15:20; Col 1:18 / Heb 9:14; 1 Pt 1:19; 1 Jn 1:7. *e:* Ex 19:6; 1 Pt 2:9. *f:* Dn 7:13 / Zec 12:10; Mt 24:30; Jn 19:37. *g:* 17; 21:6; 22:13; Is 41:4; 44:6; 48:12.

delphia, and Laodicea." [12]* Then I turned to
see whose voice it was that spoke to me, and
when I turned, I saw seven gold lampstands
[13]and in the midst of the lampstands one like
a son of man,* wearing an ankle-length robe,
with a gold sash around his chest.[h] [14]The
hair of his head was as white as white wool
or as snow,* and his eyes were like a fiery
flame. [15]His feet were like polished brass refined in a furnace,* and his voice was like the
sound of rushing water. [16]In his right hand
he held seven stars.* A sharp two-edged
sword came out of his mouth, and his face
shone like the sun at its brightest.[i]
[17]When I caught sight of him, I fell down
at his feet as though dead.* He touched me
with his right hand and said, "Do not be
afraid. I am the first and the last,[j] [18]the one
who lives. Once I was dead, but now I am
alive forever and ever. I hold the keys to
death and the netherworld.* [19]Write down,
therefore, what you have seen, and what is
happening, and what will happen afterwards.* [20]This is the secret meaning* of the
seven stars you saw in my right hand, and of
the seven gold lampstands: the seven stars
are the angels of the seven churches, and the
seven lampstands are the seven churches.

## CHAPTER 2

See RG 458–59

***To Ephesus.*** [1]* "To the angel of the
church* in Ephesus,* write this:
" 'The one who holds the seven stars in
his right hand and walks in the midst of the
seven gold lampstands says this: [2]"I know
your works, your labor, and your endurance,
and that you cannot tolerate the wicked; you
have tested those who call themselves apostles but are not, and discovered that they are
impostors.* [3]Moreover, you have endurance
and have suffered for my name, and you
have not grown weary. [4]Yet I hold this
against you: you have lost the love you had
at first. [5]Realize how far you have fallen.
Repent, and do the works you did at first.
Otherwise, I will come to you and remove

**1:12–16** A symbolic description of Christ in glory. The metaphorical language is not to be understood literally; cf. Introduction.

**1:13 Son of man**: see note on Mk 8:31. **Ankle-length robe**: Christ is priest; cf. Ex 28:4; 29:5; Wis 18:24; Zec 3:4. **Gold sash**: Christ is king; cf. Ex 28:4; 1 Mc 10:89; 11:58; Dn 10:5.

**1:14 Hair . . . as white as white wool or as snow**: Christ is eternal, clothed with the dignity that belonged to the "Ancient of Days"; cf. Rev 1:18; Dn 7:9. **His eyes were like a fiery flame**: Christ is portrayed as all-knowing; cf. Rev 2:23; Ps 7:10; Jer 17:10; and similar expressions in Rev 2:18; 19:12; cf. Dn 10:6.

**1:15 His feet . . . furnace**: Christ is depicted as unchangeable; cf. Ez 1:27; Dn 10:6. The Greek word translated "refined" is unconnected grammatically with any other word in the sentence. **His voice . . . water**: Christ speaks with divine authority; cf. Ez 1:24.

**1:16 Seven stars**: in the pagan world, Mithras and the Caesars were represented with seven stars in their right hand, symbolizing their universal dominion. **A sharp two-edged sword**: this refers to the word of God (cf. Eph 6:17; Heb 4:12) that will destroy unrepentant sinners; cf. Rev 2:16; 19:15; Wis 18:15; Is 11:4; 49:2. **His face . . . brightest**: this symbolizes the divine majesty of Christ; cf. Rev 10:1; 21:23; Jgs 5:31; Is 60:19; Mt 17:2.

**1:17** It was an Old Testament belief that for sinful human beings to see God was to die; cf. Ex 19:21; 33:20; Jgs 6:22–23; Is 6:5.

**1:18 Netherworld**: Greek Hades, Hebrew Sheol, the abode of the dead; cf. Rev 20:13–14; Nm 16:33.

**1:19 What you have seen, and what is happening, and what will happen afterwards**: the three parts of the Book of Revelation, the vision (Rev 1:10–20), the situation in the seven churches (Rev 2–3), and the events of Rev 6–22.

**1:20 Secret meaning**: literally, "mystery." **Angels**: these are the presiding spirits of the seven churches. Angels were thought to be in charge of the physical world (cf. Rev 7:1; 14:18; 16:5) and of nations (Dn 10:13; 12:1), communities (the seven churches), and individuals (Mt 18:10; Acts 12:15). Some have seen in the "angel" of each of the seven churches its pastor or a personification of the spirit of the congregation.

**2:1–3:22** Each of the seven letters follows the same pattern: address; description of the exalted Christ; blame and/or praise for the church addressed; threat and/or admonition; final exhortation and promise to all Christians.

**2:1–7** The letter to Ephesus praises the members of the church there for their works and virtues, including discerning false teachers (Rev 2:2–3), but admonishes them to repent and return to their former devotion (Rev 2:4–5). It concludes with a reference to the Nicolaitans (see note on Rev 2:6) and a promise that the victor will have access to eternal life (Rev 2:7).

**2:1 Ephesus**: this great ancient city had a population of ca. 250,000; it was the capital of the Roman province of Asia and the commercial, cultural, and religious center of Asia. The other six churches were located in the same province, situated roughly in a circle; they were selected for geographical reasons rather than for the size of their Christian communities. **Walks in the midst of the seven gold lampstands**: this signifies that Christ is always present in the church; see note on Rev 1:4.

**2:2 Who call themselves . . . impostors**: this refers to unauthorized and perverse missionaries; cf. Acts 20:29–30.

*h:* Dn 7:13; 10:5. *i:* Heb 4:12. *j:* Dn 8:18 / Rev 1:8.

your lampstand from its place, unless you
repent. 6But you have this in your favor: you
hate the works of the Nicolaitans,* which I
also hate.

7" ' "Whoever has ears ought to hear what
the Spirit says to the churches. To the victor*
I will give the right to eat from the tree of life
that is in the garden of God." '[k]

*To Smyrna.** 8"To the angel of the church
in Smyrna,* write this:

" 'The first and the last, who once died
but came to life, says this: 9"I know your
tribulation and poverty, but you are rich.* I
know the slander of those who claim to be
Jews and are not, but rather are members of
the assembly of Satan.[l] 10Do not be afraid of
anything that you are going to suffer. Indeed,
the devil will throw some of you into prison,
that you may be tested, and you will face an
ordeal for ten days. Remain faithful until
death, and I will give you the crown of life.

11" ' "Whoever has ears ought to hear
what the Spirit says to the churches.[m] The
victor shall not be harmed by the second
death." '*

*To Pergamum.** 12"To the angel of the
church in Pergamum,* write this:

" 'The one with the sharp two-edged
sword says this: 13"I know that you live
where Satan's throne* is, and yet you hold
fast to my name and have not denied your
faith in me, not even in the days of Antipas,
my faithful witness, who was martyred
among you, where Satan lives. 14* Yet I have
a few things against you. You have some
people there who hold to the teaching of Balaam, who instructed Balak to put a stumbling block before the Israelites: to eat food
sacrificed to idols and to play the harlot.[n]
15Likewise, you also have some people who
hold to the teaching of [the] Nicolaitans.
16Therefore, repent. Otherwise, I will come
to you quickly and wage war against them
with the sword of my mouth.

17" ' "Whoever has ears ought to hear
what the Spirit says to the churches. To the
victor I shall give some of the hidden
manna;* I shall also give a white amulet upon
which is inscribed a new name, which no one
knows except the one who receives it." '[o]

**2:6 Nicolaitans**: these are perhaps the impostors of Rev 2:2; see note on Rev 2:14–15. There is little evidence for connecting this group with Nicolaus, the proselyte from Antioch, mentioned in Acts 6:5.

**2:7 Victor**: referring to any Christian individual who holds fast to the faith and does God's will in the face of persecution. **The tree of life that is in the garden of God**: this is a reference to the tree in the primeval paradise (Gn 2:9); cf. Rev 22:2, 14, 19. The decree excluding humanity from the tree of life has been revoked by Christ.

**2:8–11** The letter to Smyrna encourages the Christians in this important commercial center by telling them that although they are impoverished, they are nevertheless rich, and calls those Jews who are slandering them members of the assembly of Satan (Rev 2:9). There is no admonition; rather, the Christians are told that they will suffer much, even death, but the time of tribulation will be short compared to their eternal reward (Rev 2:10), and they will thus escape final damnation (Rev 2:11).

**2:8 Smyrna**: modern Izmir, ca. thirty miles north of Ephesus, and the chief city of Lydia, with a temple to the goddess Roma. It was renowned for its loyalty to Rome, and it also had a large Jewish community very hostile toward Christians.

**2:9–10** The church in Smyrna was materially poor but spiritually rich. Accusations made by Jewish brethren there occasioned the persecution of Christians; cf. Acts 14:2, 19; 17:5, 13.

**2:11 The second death**: this refers to the eternal death, when sinners will receive their final punishment; cf. Rev 20:6, 14–15; 21:8.

**2:12–17** The letter to Pergamum praises the members of the church for persevering in their faith in Christ even in the midst of a pagan setting and in face of persecution and martyrdom (Rev 2:13). But it admonishes them about members who advocate an unprincipled morality (Rev 2:14; cf. 2 Pt 2:15; Jude 11) and others who follow the teaching of the Nicolaitans (Rev 2:15; see note there). It urges them to repent (Rev 2:16) and promises them the hidden manna and Christ's amulet (Rev 2:17).

**2:12 Pergamum**: modern Bergama, ca. forty-five miles northeast of Smyrna, a center for various kinds of pagan worship. It also had an outstanding library (the word *parchment* is derived from its name).

**2:13 Satan's throne**: the reference is to emperor worship and other pagan practices that flourished in Pergamum, perhaps specifically to the white marble altar erected and dedicated to Zeus by Eumenes II (197–160 B.C.).

**2:14–15** Like Balaam, the biblical prototype of the religious compromiser (cf. Nm 25:1–3; 31:16; 2 Pt 2:15; Jude 11), the Nicolaitans in Pergamum and Ephesus (Rev 2:6) accommodated their Christian faith to paganism. They abused the principle of liberty enunciated by Paul (1 Cor 9:19–23).

**2:17 The hidden manna**: this is the food of life; cf. Ps 78:24–25. **White amulet**: literally, "white stone," on which was written a magical name, whose power could be tapped by one who knew the secret name. It is used here as a symbol of victory and joy; cf. Rev 3:4–5. **New name**: this is a reference to the Christian's rebirth in Christ; cf. Rev 3:12; 19:12; Is 62:2; 65:15.

---

*k:* 11, 17, 29; 3:6, 13, 22; 13:9; Mt 11:15. *l:* Jas 2:5. *m:* 20:6, 14; 21:8. *n:* Nm 22–24; 25:1–3; 31:16; 2 Pt 2:15; Jude 11. *o:* Is 62:2; 65:15.

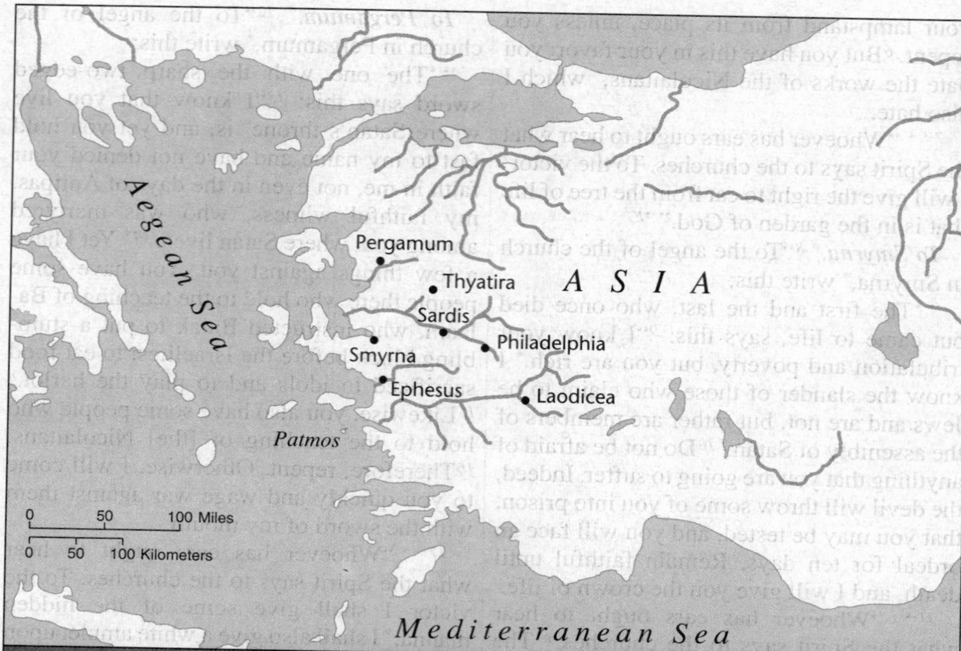


**The Seven Churches**

*To Thyatira.** [18]"To the angel of the
church in Thyatira,* write this:
" 'The Son of God, whose eyes are like a
fiery flame and whose feet are like polished
brass, says this: [19]"I know your works, your
love, faith, service, and endurance, and that
your last works are greater than the first. [20]Yet
I hold this against you, that you tolerate the
woman Jezebel, who calls herself a prophetess, who teaches and misleads my servants to
play the harlot and to eat food sacrificed to
idols.* [21]I have given her time to repent, but she
refuses to repent of her harlotry. [22]So I will cast
her on a sickbed and plunge those who commit
adultery with her into intense suffering unless
they repent of her works. [23]I will also put her
children* to death. Thus shall all the churches
come to know that I am the searcher of hearts
and minds and that I will give each of you what
your works deserve.[p] [24]But I say to the rest of
you in Thyatira, who do not uphold this teaching and know nothing of the so-called deep secrets of Satan:* on you I will place no further
burden, [25]except that you must hold fast to
what you have until I come.

[26]" ' "To the victor,* who keeps to my
ways* until the end,

**2:18–29** The letter to Thyatira praises the progress in virtue of this small Christian community (Rev 2:19) but admonishes them for tolerating a false prophet who leads them astray (Rev 2:20). Her fate is sealed, but there is hope of repentance for her followers (Rev 2:21–22). Otherwise, they too shall die (Rev 2:23). They are warned against Satanic power or knowledge (Rev 2:24–25). Those who remain faithful will share in the messianic reign, having authority over nations (Rev 2:26–27), and will in fact possess Christ himself (Rev 2:8).

**2:18 Thyatira**: modern Akhisar, ca. forty miles southeast of Pergamum, a frontier town famous for its workers' guilds (cf. Acts 16:14), membership in which may have involved festal meals in pagan temples.

**2:20** The scheming and treacherous Jezebel of old (cf. 1 Kgs 19:1–2; 21:1–14; 2 Kgs 9:22, 30–34) introduced pagan customs into the religion of Israel; this new Jezebel was doing the same to Christianity.

**2:23 Children**: spiritual descendants.

**2:24 The so-called deep secrets of Satan**: literally, "the deep things of Satan," a scathing reference to the perverse teaching of the Nicolaitans (Rev 2:15).

**2:26–28** The Christian who perseveres in faith will share in

*p*: 1 Sm 16:7; Jer 11:20; 17:10. *q*: 12:5; Ps 2:8–9.

I will give authority over the nations.[q]
27 He will rule them with an iron rod.
Like clay vessels will they be
smashed,
28 just as I received authority from my Father.
And to him I will give the morning star.
29 " 'Whoever has ears ought to hear
what the Spirit says to the churches." '

## CHAPTER 3

See RG 458–59

*To Sardis.** 1 "To the angel of the
church in Sardis,* write this:
" 'The one who has the seven spirits of
God and the seven stars says this: "I know
your works, that you have the reputation of
being alive, but you are dead. 2 Be watchful
and strengthen what is left, which is going to
die, for I have not found your works complete
in the sight of my God. 3 Remember then how
you accepted and heard; keep it, and repent. If
you are not watchful, I will come like a thief,
and you will never know at what hour I will
come upon you.[r] 4 However, you have a few
people in Sardis who have not soiled their
garments; they will walk with me dressed in
white, because they are worthy.[s]
5 " 'The victor will thus be dressed in
white,* and I will never erase his name from
the book of life but will acknowledge his
name in the presence of my Father and of his
angels.[t]
6 " 'Whoever has ears ought to hear what
the Spirit says to the churches." '
*To Philadelphia.** 7 "To the angel of the
church in Philadelphia,* write this:
" 'The holy one, the true,
who holds the key of David,
who opens and no one shall close,
who closes and no one shall open,[u]
says this:
8 " 'I know your works (behold, I have
left an open door* before you, which no one
can close). You have limited strength, and
yet you have kept my word and have not denied my name. 9 Behold, I will make those of
the assembly of Satan who claim to be Jews
and are not, but are lying, behold I will make
them come and fall prostrate at your feet,
and they will realize that I love you.[v] 10 Because you have kept my message of endurance,* I will keep you safe in the time of
trial that is going to come to the whole world
to test the inhabitants of the earth. 11 I am
coming quickly. Hold fast to what you have,
so that no one may take your crown.[w]
12 " 'The victor I will make into a pillar*

Christ's messianic authority (cf. Ps 2:8–9) and resurrection victory over death, symbolized by the morning star; cf. Rev 22:16.

**2:26 Who keeps to my ways**: literally, "who keeps my works."

**3:1–6** The letter to Sardis does not praise the community but admonishes its members to watchfulness, mutual support, and repentance (Rev 3:2–3). The few who have remained pure and faithful will share Christ's victory and will be inscribed in the book of life (Rev 3:4–5).

**3:1 Sardis**: this city, located ca. thirty miles southeast of Thyatira, was once the capital of Lydia, known for its wealth at the time of Croesus (6th century B.C.). Its citadel, reputed to be unassailable, was captured by surprise, first by Cyrus and later by Antiochus. The church is therefore warned to be on guard.

**3:5 In white**: white is a sign of victory and joy as well as resurrection; see note on Rev 2:17. **The book of life**: the roll in which the names of the redeemed are kept; cf. Rev 13:8; 17:8; 20:12, 15; 21:27; Phil 4:3; Dn 12:1. They will be acknowledged by Christ in heaven; cf. Mt 10:32.

**3:7–13** The letter to Philadelphia praises the Christians there for remaining faithful even with their limited strength (Rev 3:8). Members of the assembly of Satan are again singled out (Rev 3:9; see Rev 2:9). There is no admonition; rather, the letter promises that they will be kept safe at the great trial (Rev 3:10–11) and that the victors will become pillars of the heavenly temple, upon which three names will be inscribed: God, Jerusalem, and Christ (Rev 3:12).

**3:7 Philadelphia**: modern Alasehir, ca. thirty miles southeast of Sardis, founded by Attalus II Philadelphus of Pergamum to be an "open door" (Rev 3:8) for Greek culture; it was destroyed by an earthquake in A.D. 17. Rebuilt by money from the Emperor Tiberius, the city was renamed Neo-Caesarea; this may explain the allusions to "name" in Rev 3:12. **Key of David**: to the heavenly city of David (cf. Is 22:22), "the new Jerusalem" (Rev 3:12), over which Christ has supreme authority.

**3:8 An open door**: opportunities for sharing and proclaiming the faith; cf. Acts 14:27; 1 Cor 16:9; 2 Cor 2:12.

**3:10 My message of endurance**: this does not refer to a saying of Jesus about patience but to the example of Christ's patient endurance. **The inhabitants of the earth**: literally, "those who live on the earth." This expression, which also occurs in Rev 6:10; 8:13; 11:10; 13:8, 12, 14; 17:2, 8, always refers to the pagan world.

**3:12 Pillar**: this may be an allusion to the rebuilding of the city; see note on v 7. **New Jerusalem**: it is described in Rev 21:10–22:5.

*r:* Mt 24:42–44; Mk 13:33; 1 Thes 5:2; 2 Pt 3:10. *s:* 7:13–14. *t:* Ps 69:29; Dn 12:1 / Mt 10:32. *u:* Is 22:22; Mt 16:19. *v:* 2:9 / Is 45:14; 60:14. *w:* 2:25; 22:7, 20.

in the temple of my God, and he will never
leave it again. On him I will inscribe the
name of my God and the name of the city of
my God, the new Jerusalem, which comes
down out of heaven from my God, as well as
my new name.[x]
13" ' "Whoever has ears ought to hear
what the Spirit says to the churches." '

*To Laodicea.** 14"To the angel of the
church in Laodicea,* write this:

" 'The Amen, the faithful and true witness, the source of God's creation, says this:[y]
15"I know your works; I know that you are
neither cold nor hot.* I wish you were either
cold or hot. 16* So, because you are lukewarm, neither hot nor cold, I will spit you
out of my mouth. 17* [z] For you say, 'I am rich
and affluent and have no need of anything,'
and yet do not realize that you are wretched,
pitiable, poor, blind, and naked. 18I advise
you to buy from me gold refined by fire* so
that you may be rich, and white garments to
put on so that your shameful nakedness may
not be exposed, and buy ointment to smear
on your eyes so that you may see. 19Those
whom I love, I reprove and chastise. Be
earnest, therefore, and repent.[a]
20" ' "Behold, I stand at the door and
knock. If anyone hears my voice and opens
the door, [then] I will enter his house and
dine with him, and he with me.* 21I will give
the victor the right to sit with me on my
throne, as I myself first won the victory and
sit with my Father on his throne.[b]
22" ' "Whoever has ears ought to hear
what the Spirit says to the churches." ' "

## III. God and the Lamb in Heaven

### CHAPTER 4

See RG 459

*Vision of Heavenly Worship.** 1After
this I had a vision of an open door* to heaven,
and I heard the trumpetlike voice that had spoken to me before, saying, "Come up here and
I will show you what must happen afterwards." 2* At once I was caught up in spirit.[c] A
throne was there in heaven, and on the throne
sat 3one whose appearance sparkled like
jasper and carnelian. Around the throne was a
halo as brilliant as an emerald. 4Surrounding
the throne I saw twenty-four other thrones on
which twenty-four elders* sat, dressed in
white garments and with gold crowns on their
heads.[d] 5From the throne came flashes of

**3:14–22** The letter to Laodicea reprimands the community for being lukewarm (Rev 3:15–16), but no particular faults are singled out. Their material prosperity is contrasted with their spiritual poverty, the violet tunics that were the source of their wealth with the white robe of baptism, and their famous eye ointment with true spiritual perception (Rev 3:17–18). But Christ's chastisement is inspired by love and a desire to be allowed to share the messianic banquet with his followers in the heavenly kingdom (Rev 3:9–21).

**3:14 Laodicea**: ca. forty miles southeast of Philadelphia and ca. eighty miles east of Ephesus, a wealthy industrial and commercial center, with a renowned medical school. It exported fine woolen garments and was famous for its eye salves. It was so wealthy that it was proudly rebuilt without outside aid after the devastating earthquake of A.D. 60/61. **The Amen**: this is a divine title (cf. Hebrew text of Is 65:16) applied to Christ; cf. 2 Cor 1:20. **Source of God's creation**: literally, "the beginning of God's creation," a concept found also in Jn 1:3; Col 1:16–17; Heb 1:2; cf. Prv 8:22–31; Wis 9:1–2.

**3:15–16** Halfhearted commitment to the faith is nauseating to Christ; cf. Rom 12:11.

**3:16 Spit**: literally, "vomit." The image is that of a beverage that should be either hot or cold. Perhaps there is an allusion to the hot springs of Hierapolis across the Lycus river from Laodicea, which would have been lukewarm by the time they reached Laodicea.

**3:17** Economic prosperity occasioned spiritual bankruptcy.

**3:18 Gold . . . fire**: God's grace. **White garments**: symbol of an upright life; the city was noted for its violet/purple cloth. **Ointment . . . eyes**: to remove spiritual blindness; one of the city's exports was eye ointment (see note on Rev 3:14).

**3:20** Christ invites all to the messianic banquet in heaven; cf. Is 25:6; Lk 14:15; 22:30.

**4:1–11** The seer now describes a vision of the heavenly court in worship of God enthroned. He reverently avoids naming or describing God but pictures twenty-four elders in priestly and regal attire (Rev 4:4) and God's throne and its surroundings made of precious gems and other symbols that traditionally express the majesty of God (Rev 4:5–6). Universal creation is represented by the four living creatures (Rev 4:6–7). Along with the twenty-four elders, they praise God unceasingly in humble adoration (Rev 4:8–11).

**4:1** The ancients viewed heaven as a solid vault, entered by way of actual doors.

**4:2–8** Much of the imagery here is taken from Ez 1; 10.

**4:4 Twenty-four elders**: these represent the twelve tribes of Israel and the twelve apostles; cf. Rev 21:12–14.

**4:5 Flashes of lightning, rumblings, and peals of thunder**: as in other descriptions of God's appearance or activity; cf. Rev 8:5; 11:19; 16:18; Ex 19:16; Ez 1:4, 13. **The seven spirits of God**: the seven "angels of the presence" as in Rev 8:2 and Tb 12:15.

*x:* 21:2–3; Ez 48:35 / Rev 19:13. *y:* 1:5. *z:* Prv 13:7; Lk 12:21. *a:* Prv 3:11–12; 1 Cor 11:32; Heb 12:5–11. *b:* Lk 22:28–30; Mt 19:28. *c:* Is 6:1 / Ez 1:26–28. *d:* Is 24:23.

lightning, rumblings, and peals of thunder.*
Seven flaming torches burned in front of the
throne, which are the seven spirits of God.
6[e] In front of the throne was something that resembled a sea of glass like crystal.*
In the center and around the throne, there
were four living creatures covered with eyes
in front and in back. 7The first creature resembled a lion, the second was like a calf,
the third had a face like that of a human being, and the fourth looked like an eagle* in
flight. 8The four living creatures, each of
them with six wings,* were covered with
eyes inside and out. Day and night they do
not stop exclaiming:

"Holy, holy, holy is the Lord God almighty,
who was, and who is, and who is to
come."[f]

9Whenever the living creatures give glory
and honor and thanks to the one who sits on
the throne, who lives forever and ever, 10the
twenty-four elders fall down before the one
who sits on the throne and worship him, who
lives forever and ever. They throw down
their crowns before the throne, exclaiming:

11 "Worthy are you, Lord our God,
to receive glory and honor and power,
for you created all things;
because of your will they came to be
and were created."[g]

## CHAPTER 5

See RG 459

*The Scroll and the Lamb.** 1I saw a
scroll* in the right hand of the one who sat on
the throne. It had writing on both sides and
was sealed with seven seals.[h] 2Then I saw a
mighty angel who proclaimed in a loud
voice, "Who is worthy to open the scroll and
break its seals?" 3But no one in heaven or on
earth or under the earth was able to open the
scroll or to examine it. 4I shed many tears
because no one was found worthy to open
the scroll or to examine it. 5One of the elders
said to me, "Do not weep. The lion of the
tribe of Judah, the root of David,* has triumphed, enabling him to open the scroll
with its seven seals."[i]

6Then I saw standing in the midst of the
throne and the four living creatures and the
elders, a Lamb* that seemed to have been
slain. He had seven horns and seven eyes;
these are the [seven] spirits of God sent out
into the whole world.[j] 7He came and received the scroll from the right hand of the
one who sat on the throne. 8When he took it,
the four living creatures and the twenty-four
elders fell down before the Lamb. Each of
the elders held a harp and gold bowls filled
with incense, which are the prayers of the
holy ones. 9They sang a new hymn:

"Worthy are you to receive the scroll
and to break open its seals,

**4:6 A sea of glass like crystal**: an image adapted from Ez 1:22–26. **Four living creatures**: these are symbols taken from Ez 1:5–21; they are identified as cherubim in Ez 10:20. **Covered with eyes**: these suggest God's knowledge and concern.

**4:7 Lion . . . calf . . . human being . . . eagle**: these symbolize, respectively, what is noblest, strongest, wisest, and swiftest in creation. **Calf**: traditionally translated "ox," the Greek word refers to a heifer or young bull. Since the second century, these four creatures have been used as symbols of the evangelists Mark, Luke, Matthew, and John, respectively.

**4:8 Six wings**: like the seraphim of Is 6:2.

**5:1–14** The seer now describes a papyrus roll in God's right hand (Rev 5:1) with seven seals indicating the importance of the message. A mighty angel asks who is worthy to open the scroll, i.e., who can accomplish God's salvific plan (Rev 5:2). There is despair at first when no one in creation can do it (Rev 5:3–4). But the seer is comforted by an elder who tells him that Christ, called the lion of the tribe of Judah, has won the right to open it (Rev 5:5). Christ then appears as a Lamb, coming to receive the scroll from God (Rev 5:6–7), for which he is acclaimed as at a coronation (Rev 5:8–10). This is followed by a doxology of the angels (Rev 5:11–12) and then finally by the heavenly church united with all of creation (Rev 5:13–14).

**5:1 A scroll**: a papyrus roll possibly containing a list of afflictions for sinners (cf. Ez 2:9–10) or God's plan for the world. **Sealed with seven seals**: it is totally hidden from all but God. Only the Lamb (Rev 5:7–9) has the right to carry out the divine plan.

**5:5 The lion of the tribe of Judah, the root of David**: these are the messianic titles applied to Christ to symbolize his victory; cf. Rev 22:16; Gn 49:9; Is 11:1, 10; Mt 1:1.

**5:6** Christ is the Paschal Lamb without blemish, whose blood saved the new Israel from sin and death; cf. Ex 12; Is 53:7; Jn 1:29, 36; Acts 8:32; 1 Pt 1:18–19. This is the main title for Christ in Revelation, used twenty-eight times. **Seven horns and seven eyes**: Christ has the fullness (see note on Rev 1:4) of power (horns) and knowledge (eyes); cf. Zec 4:7. **[Seven] spirits**: as in Rev 1:4; 3:1; 4:5.

*e:* Ex 24:10. *f:* Is 6:2–3 / Rev 1:4, 8; 11:17; 16:5. *g:* Rom 4:17; 16:27. *h:* Is 29:11. *i:* Is 11:1, 10; Rom 15:12. *j:* Jn 1:29.

for you were slain and with your blood
you purchased for God
those from every tribe and tongue,
people and nation.
10 You made them a kingdom and priests
for our God,
and they will reign on earth."[k]

11 I looked again and heard the voices of
many angels who surrounded the throne and
the living creatures and the elders. They
were countless* in number,[l] 12 and they cried
out in a loud voice:

"Worthy is the Lamb that was slain
to receive power and riches, wisdom
and strength,
honor and glory and blessing."

13 Then I heard every creature in heaven and
on earth and under the earth and in the sea,
everything in the universe, cry out:

"To the one who sits on the throne and to
the Lamb
be blessing and honor, glory and
might,
forever and ever."

14 The four living creatures answered,
"Amen," and the elders fell down and worshiped.

## IV. The Seven Seals, Trumpets, and Plagues, with Interludes*

### CHAPTER 6*

See RG 459–60

*The First Six Seals.* 1* Then I watched
while the Lamb broke open the first of the
seven seals, and I heard one of the four living creatures cry out in a voice like thunder,
"Come forward." 2 I looked, and there was a
white horse, and its rider had a bow.* He was
given a crown, and he rode forth victorious
to further his victories.[m]
3 When he broke open the second seal, I
heard the second living creature cry out,
"Come forward." 4* [n] Another horse came
out, a red one. Its rider was given power to
take peace away from the earth, so that people would slaughter one another. And he was
given a huge sword.
5 When he broke open the third seal, I
heard the third living creature cry out,
"Come forward." I looked, and there was a
black horse,* and its rider held a scale in his
hand. 6 I heard what seemed to be a voice in
the midst of the four living creatures. It said,
"A ration of wheat costs a day's pay,* and
three rations of barley cost a day's pay. But
do not damage the olive oil or the wine."[o]
7 When he broke open the fourth seal, I

**5:11 Countless**: literally, "100,000,000 plus 1,000,000," used by the author to express infinity.

**6:1–16:21** A series of seven disasters now begins as each seal is broken (Rev 6:1–8:1), followed by a similar series as seven trumpets sound (Rev 8:2–11:19) and as seven angels pour bowls on the earth causing plagues (Rev 15:1–16:21). These gloomy sequences are interrupted by longer or shorter scenes suggesting the triumph of God and his witnesses (e.g., Rev 7; 10; 11; 12; 13; 14).

**6:1–17** This chapter provides a symbolic description of the contents of the sealed scroll. The breaking of the first four seals reveals four riders. The first rider (of a white horse) is a conquering power (Rev 6:1–2), the second (red horse) a symbol of bloody war (Rev 6:3–4), the third (black horse) a symbol of famine (Rev 6:5–6), the fourth (pale green horse) a symbol of Death himself, accompanied by Hades (the netherworld) as his page (Rev 6:7–8). Rev 6:8b summarizes the role of all four riders. The breaking of the fifth seal reveals Christian martyrs in an attitude of sacrifice as blood poured out at the foot of an altar begging God for vindication, which will come only when their quota is filled; but they are given a white robe symbolic of victory (Rev 6:9–11). The breaking of the sixth seal reveals typical apocalyptic signs in the sky and the sheer terror of all people at the imminent divine judgment (Rev 6:12–17).

**6:1–8** The imagery is adapted from Zec 1:8–10; 6:1–8.

**6:2 White horse . . . bow**: this may perhaps allude specifically to the Parthians on the eastern border of the Roman empire. Expert in the use of the bow, they constantly harassed the Romans and won a major victory in A.D. 62; see note on Rev 9:13–21. But the Old Testament imagery typifies the history of oppression of God's people at all times.

**6:4 Huge sword**: this is a symbol of war and violence; cf. Ez 21:14–17.

**6:5 Black horse**: this is a symbol of famine, the usual accompaniment of war in antiquity; cf. Lv 26:26; Ez 4:12–13. The **scale** is a symbol of shortage of food with a corresponding rise in price.

**6:6 A day's pay**: literally, "a denarius," a Roman silver coin that constitutes a day's wage in Mt 20:2. Because of the famine, food was rationed and sold at an exorbitant price. A liter of flour was considered a day's ration in the Greek historians Herodotus and Diogenes Laertius. **Barley**: food of the poor (Jn 6:9, 13; cf. 2 Kgs 7:1, 16, 18); it was also used to feed animals; cf. 1 Kgs 5:8. **Do not damage**: the olive and the vine are to be used more sparingly in time of famine.

*k:* 1:6; Ex 19:6; Is 61:6. *l:* Dn 7:10; Jude 14–15. *m:* Zec 1:8–10; 6:1–3. *n:* Ez 21:14–16. *o:* Lv 26:26; Ez 4:16–17.

heard the voice of the fourth living creature
cry out, "Come forward." 8 I looked, and there
was a pale green* horse. Its rider was named
Death, and Hades accompanied him. They
were given authority over a quarter of the
earth, to kill with sword, famine, and plague,
and by means of the beasts of the earth.[p]
9 When he broke open the fifth seal, I saw
underneath the altar* the souls of those who
had been slaughtered because of the witness
they bore to the word of God. 10 They cried
out in a loud voice, "How long will it be, holy
and true master,* before you sit in judgment
and avenge our blood on the inhabitants of
the earth?" 11 Each of them was given a white
robe, and they were told to be patient a little
while longer until the number was filled of
their fellow servants and brothers who were
going to be killed as they had been.
12* Then I watched while he broke open
the sixth seal, and there was a great earthquake; the sun turned as black as dark sackcloth* and the whole moon became like
blood.[q] 13 The stars in the sky fell to the earth
like unripe figs* shaken loose from the tree
in a strong wind. 14 Then the sky was divided* like a torn scroll curling up, and every
mountain and island was moved from its
place.[r] 15 The kings of the earth, the nobles,*
the military officers, the rich, the powerful,
and every slave and free person hid themselves in caves and among mountain crags.
16 They cried out to the mountains and the
rocks, "Fall on us and hide us from the face
of the one who sits on the throne and from
the wrath of the Lamb,[s] 17 because the great
day of their* wrath has come and who can
withstand it?"

## CHAPTER 7*

See RG 459–60

***The 144,000 Sealed.*** 1 After this I saw
four angels standing at the four corners of
the earth,* holding back the four winds of the
earth so that no wind could blow on land or
sea or against any tree.[t] 2 Then I saw another
angel come up from the East,* holding the
seal of the living God. He cried out in a loud
voice to the four angels who were given
power to damage the land and the sea, 3 "Do
not damage the land or the sea or the trees
until we put the seal on the foreheads of the
servants of our God."[u] 4 I heard the number
of those who had been marked with the seal,
one hundred and forty-four thousand
marked* from every tribe of the Israelites:[v]
5 twelve thousand were marked from the

**6:8 Pale green**: symbol of death and decay; cf. Ez 14:21.

**6:9 The altar**: this altar corresponds to the altar of holocausts in the temple in Jerusalem; see also Rev 11:1. **Because of the witness . . . word of God**: literally, "because of the word of God and the witness they had borne."

**6:10 Holy and true master**: Old Testament usage as well as the context indicates that this is addressed to God rather than to Christ.

**6:12–14** Symbolic rather than literal description of the cosmic upheavals attending the day of the Lord when the martyrs' prayer for vindication (Rev 6:10) would be answered; cf. Am 8:8–9; Is 34:4; 50:3; Jl 2:10; 3:3–4; Mt 24:4–36; Mk 13:5–37; Lk 21:8–36.

**6:12 Dark sackcloth**: for mourning, sackcloth was made from the skin of a black goat.

**6:13 Unripe figs**: literally, "summer (or winter) fruit."

**6:14 Was divided**: literally, "was split," like a broken papyrus roll torn in two, each half then curling up to form a roll on either side.

**6:15 Nobles**: literally, "courtiers," "grandees." **Military officers**: literally, "commanders of 1,000 men," used in Josephus and other Greek authors as the equivalent of the Roman *tribunus militum*. The listing of various ranks of society represents the universality of terror at the impending doom.

**6:17 Their**: this reading is attested in the best manuscripts, but the vast majority read "his" in reference to the wrath of the Lamb in the preceding verse.

**7:1–17** An interlude of two visions precedes the breaking of the seventh seal, just as two more will separate the sixth and seventh trumpets (Rev 10). In the first vision (Rev 7:1–8), the elect receive the seal of the living God as protection against the coming cataclysm; cf. Rev 14:1; Ez 9:4–6; 2 Cor 1:22; Eph 1:13; 4:30. The second vision (Rev 7:9–17) portrays the faithful Christians before God's throne to encourage those on earth to persevere to the end, even to death.

**7:1 The four corners of the earth**: the earth is seen as a table or rectangular surface.

**7:2 East**: literally, "rising of the sun." The east was considered the source of light and the place of paradise (Gn 2:8). **Seal**: whatever was marked by the impression of one's signet ring belonged to that person and was under his protection.

**7:4–9 One hundred and forty-four thousand**: the square of twelve (the number of Israel's tribes) multiplied by a thousand, symbolic of the new Israel (cf. Rev 14:1–5; Gal 6:16; Jas 1:1) that embraces people **from every nation, race, people, and tongue** (Rev 7:9).

**7:5–8** Judah is placed first because of Christ; cf. "the Lion of the tribe of Judah" (Rev 5:5). Dan is omitted because of a later tradition that the antichrist would arise from it.

*p:* Ez 14:21. *q:* Jl 3:4; Mt 24:29. *r:* Is 34:4 / Rev 16:20. *s:* Is 2:19; Hos 10:8; Lk 23:30. *t:* Jer 49:36; Zec 6:5. *u:* Ex 12:7–14; Ez 9:4; 2 Cor 1:22; Eph 1:13; 4:30. *v:* 14:1.

tribe of Judah,* twelve thousand from the tribe of Reuben, twelve thousand from the tribe of Gad, 6 twelve thousand from the tribe of Asher, twelve thousand from the tribe of Naphtali, twelve thousand from the tribe of Manasseh, 7 twelve thousand from the tribe of Simeon, twelve thousand from the tribe of Levi, twelve thousand from the tribe of Issachar, 8 twelve thousand from the tribe of Zebulun, twelve thousand from the tribe of Joseph, and twelve thousand were marked from the tribe of Benjamin.

***Triumph of the Elect.*** 9 After this I had a vision of a great multitude, which no one could count, from every nation, race, people, and tongue. They stood before the throne and before the Lamb, wearing white robes and holding palm branches* in their hands. 10 They cried out in a loud voice:

"Salvation comes from* our God, who is
seated on the throne,
and from the Lamb."

11 All the angels stood around the throne and around the elders and the four living creatures. They prostrated themselves before the throne, worshiped God, 12 and exclaimed:

"Amen. Blessing and glory, wisdom and
thanksgiving,
honor, power, and might
be to our God forever and ever. Amen."

13 Then one of the elders spoke up and said to me, "Who are these wearing white robes, and where did they come from?" 14 I said to him, "My lord, you are the one who knows." He said to me, "These are the ones who have survived the time of great distress;* they have washed their robes and made them white in the blood of the Lamb.[w]

15 "For this reason they stand before God's
throne
and worship him day and night in his
temple.
The one who sits on the throne will
shelter them.
16 They will not hunger or thirst anymore,
nor will the sun or any heat strike
them.[x]
17 For the Lamb who is in the center of the
throne will shepherd them
and lead them to springs of life-giving
water,*
and God will wipe away every tear
from their eyes."[y]

## CHAPTER 8*

See RG 459–60

***The Seven Trumpets.*** 1 When he broke open the seventh seal, there was silence in heaven* for about half an hour.[z] 2 And I saw that the seven angels who stood before God were given seven trumpets.[a]

***The Gold Censer.*** 3 Another angel came and stood at the altar,* holding a gold censer. He was given a great quantity of incense to offer, along with the prayers of all the holy ones, on the gold altar that was before the throne.[b] 4 The smoke of the incense along with the prayers of the holy ones went up before God from the hand of the angel. 5 Then the angel took the censer, filled it with burning coals from the altar, and hurled it down to the earth. There were peals of thunder, rumblings, flashes of lightning, and an earthquake.[c]

***The First Four Trumpets.*** 6 The seven an-

**7:9 White robes . . . palm branches**: symbols of joy and victory; see note on Rev 3:5.

**7:10 Salvation comes from**: literally, "(let) salvation (be ascribed) to." A similar hymn of praise is found at the fall of the dragon (Rev 12:10) and of Babylon (Rev 19:1).

**7:14 Time of great distress**: fierce persecution by the Romans; cf. Introduction.

**7:17 Life-giving water**: literally, "the water of life," God's grace, which flows from Christ; cf. Rev 21:6; 22:1, 17; Jn 4:10, 14.

**8:1–13** The breaking of the seventh seal produces at first silence and then seven symbolic disasters, each announced by a trumpet blast, of which the first four form a unit as did the first four seals. A minor liturgy (Rev 8:3–5) is enclosed by a vision of seven angels (Rev 8:2, 6). Then follow the first four trumpet blasts, each heralding catastrophes modeled on the plagues of Egypt affecting the traditional prophetic third (cf. Ez 5:12) of the earth, sea, fresh water, and stars (Rev 8:7–12). Finally, there is a vision of an eagle warning of the last three trumpet blasts (Rev 8:13).

**8:1 Silence in heaven**: as in Zep 1:7, a prelude to the eschatological woes that are to follow; cf. Introduction.

**8:3 Altar**: there seems to be only one altar in the heavenly temple, corresponding to the altar of holocausts in Rev 6:9, and here to the altar of incense in Jerusalem; cf. also Rev 9:13; 11:1; 14:18; 16:7.

*w:* Mt 24:21. *x:* Is 49:10. *y:* 21:4; Is 25:8. *z:* Heb 2:20; Zep 1:7; Zec 2:17. *a:* 4:5; Tb 12:15. *b:* Ps 141:2; Tb 12:12. *c:* Ez 10:2; Ps 11:6 / Rev 4:5; 11:19; 16:18. *d:* 16:1–21.

gels who were holding the seven trumpets
prepared to blow them.[d]
7 When the first one blew his trumpet,
there came hail and fire mixed with blood,
which was hurled down to the earth. A third
of the land was burned up, along with a third
of the trees and all green grass.*
8* When the second angel blew his trumpet, something like a large burning mountain
was hurled into the sea. A third of the sea
turned to blood,[e] 9 a third of the creatures living in the sea* died, and a third of the ships
were wrecked.
10 When the third angel blew his trumpet,
a large star burning like a torch fell from the
sky. It fell on a third of the rivers and on the
springs of water.[f] 11 The star was called
"Wormwood,"* and a third of all the water
turned to wormwood. Many people died
from this water, because it was made bitter.[g]
12 When the fourth angel blew his trumpet,
a third of the sun, a third of the moon, and a
third of the stars were struck, so that a third
of them became dark. The day lost its light
for a third of the time, as did the night.[h]
13 Then I looked again and heard an eagle
flying high overhead cry out in a loud voice,
"Woe! Woe! Woe* to the inhabitants of the
earth from the rest of the trumpet blasts that
the three angels are about to blow!"

## CHAPTER 9

See RG 459–60

*The Fifth Trumpet.** 1 Then the fifth
angel blew his trumpet, and I saw a star* that
had fallen from the sky to the earth. It was
given the key for the passage to the abyss. 2 It
opened the passage to the abyss,[i] and smoke
came up out of the passage like smoke from
a huge furnace. The sun and the air were
darkened by the smoke from the passage.[j]
3 Locusts came out of the smoke onto the
land, and they were given the same power as
scorpions* of the earth.[k] 4 They were told not
to harm the grass of the earth or any plant or
any tree, but only those people who did not
have the seal of God on their foreheads.
5 They were not allowed to kill them but only
to torment them for five months;* the torment they inflicted was like that of a scorpion when it stings a person. 6 During that
time these people will seek death but will
not find it, and they will long to die but death
will escape them.[l]
7* The appearance of the locusts was like
that of horses ready for battle. On their
heads they wore what looked like crowns of
gold; their faces were like human faces,[m]
8 and they had hair like women's hair. Their
teeth were like lions' teeth,[n] 9 and they had
chests like iron breastplates. The sound of
their wings was like the sound of many
horse-drawn chariots racing into battle.
10 They had tails like scorpions, with
stingers; with their tails they had power to
harm people for five months. 11 They had as
their king the angel of the abyss, whose
name in Hebrew is Abaddon* and in Greek
Apollyon.
12 The first woe has passed, but there are
two more to come.

**8:7** This woe resembles the seventh plague of Egypt (Ex 9:23–24); cf. Jl 3:3.

**8:8–11** The background of these two woes is the first plague of Egypt (Ex 7:20–21).

**8:9 Creatures living in the sea**: literally, "creatures in the sea that had souls."

**8:11 Wormwood**: an extremely bitter and malignant plant symbolizing the punishment God inflicts on the ungodly; cf. Jer 9:12–14; 23:15.

**8:13 Woe! Woe! Woe**: each of the three woes pronounced by the angel represents a separate disaster; cf. Rev 9:12; 11:14. The final woe, released by the seventh trumpet blast, includes the plagues of Rev 16.

**9:1–12** The fifth trumpet heralds a woe containing elements from the eighth and ninth plagues of Egypt (Ex 10:12–15, 21–23) but specifically reminiscent of the invasion of locusts in Jl 1:4–2:10.

**9:1 A star**: late Judaism represented fallen powers as stars (Is 14:12–15; Lk 10:18; Jude 13), but a comparison with Rev 1:20 and Rev 20:1 suggests that here it means an angel. **The passage to the abyss**: referring to Sheol, the netherworld, where Satan and the fallen angels are kept for a thousand years, to be cast afterwards into the pool of fire; cf. Rev 20:7–10. The abyss was conceived of as a vast subterranean cavern full of fire. Its only link with the earth was a kind of passage or mine shaft, which was kept locked.

**9:3 Scorpions**: their poisonous sting was proverbial; Ez 2:6; Lk 11:12.

**9:5 For five months**: more or less corresponding to the life-span of locusts.

**9:7–10** Eight characteristics are listed to show the eschatological and diabolical nature of these locusts.

**9:11 Abaddon**: Hebrew (more precisely, Aramaic) for destruction or ruin. **Apollyon**: Greek for the "Destroyer."

*e:* Ex 7:20. *f:* Is 14:12. *g:* Jer 9:14. *h:* Ex 10:21–23. *i:* 20:1. *j:* Gn 19:28. *k:* Ex 10:12–15; Wis 16:9. *l:* Jb 3:21. *m:* Jl 2:4. *n:* Jl 1:6.

*The Sixth Trumpet.** [13]Then the sixth angel blew his trumpet, and I heard a voice coming from the [four]* horns of the gold altar before God,[o] [14]telling the sixth angel who held the trumpet, "Release the four angels* who are bound at the banks of the great river Euphrates." [15]So the four angels were released, who were prepared for this hour, day, month, and year to kill a third of the human race. [16]The number of cavalry troops was two hundred million; I heard their number. [17]Now in my vision this is how I saw the horses and their riders. They wore red, blue, and yellow breastplates,* and the horses' heads were like heads of lions, and out of their mouths came fire, smoke, and sulfur.[p] [18]By these three plagues of fire, smoke, and sulfur that came out of their mouths a third of the human race was killed. [19]For the power of the horses is in their mouths and in their tails; for their tails are like snakes, with heads that inflict harm.

[20]The rest of the human race, who were not killed by these plagues, did not repent of the works of their hands,* to give up the worship of demons and idols made from gold, silver, bronze, stone, and wood, which cannot see or hear or walk.[q] [21]Nor did they repent of their murders, their magic potions, their unchastity, or their robberies.

See RG 459–60

## CHAPTER 10

### *The Angel with the Small Scroll.*

[1]* Then I saw another mighty angel come down from heaven wrapped in a cloud, with a halo around his head; his face was like the sun and his feet were like pillars of fire. [2]In his hand he held a small scroll that had been opened. He placed his right foot on the sea and his left foot on the land,* [3]and then he cried out in a loud voice as a lion roars. When he cried out, the seven thunders* raised their voices, too.[r] [4]When the seven thunders had spoken, I was about to write it down; but I heard a voice from heaven say, "Seal up what the seven thunders have spoken, but do not write it down." [5]Then the angel I saw standing on the sea and on the land raised his right hand to heaven [6]and swore by the one who lives forever and ever, who created heaven and earth and sea* and all that is in them, "There shall be no more delay.[s] [7]At the time when you hear the seventh angel blow his trumpet, the mysterious plan of God* shall be fulfilled, as he promised to his servants the prophets."[t]

[8]Then the voice that I had heard from heaven spoke to me again and said, "Go, take the scroll that lies open in the hand of the angel who is standing on the sea and on the land." [9]So I went up to the angel and told him to give me the small scroll. He said to me, "Take and swallow it. It will turn your stomach sour, but in your mouth it will taste as sweet* as honey." [10]I took the small scroll from the angel's hand and swallowed it. In

**9:13–21** The sixth trumpet heralds a woe representing another diabolical attack symbolized by an invasion by the Parthians living east of the Euphrates; see note on Rev 6:2. At the appointed time (Rev 9:15), the frightful horses act as God's agents of judgment. The imaginative details are not to be taken literally; see Introduction and the note on Rev 6:12–14.

**9:13 [Four]**: many Greek manuscripts and versions omit the word. The horns were situated at the four corners of the altar (Ex 27:2; 30:2–3); see note on Rev 8:3.

**9:14–15 The four angels**: they are symbolic of the destructive activity that will be extended throughout the universe.

**9:17 Blue**: literally, "hyacinth-colored." **Yellow**: literally, "sulfurous."

**9:20 The works of their hands**: i.e., the gods their hands had made.

**10:1–11:14** An interlude in two scenes (Rev 10:1–11 and Rev 11:1–14) precedes the sounding of the seventh trumpet; cf. Rev 7:1–17. The first vision describes an angel astride sea and land like a colossus, with a small scroll open, the contents of which indicate that the end is imminent (Rev 10). The second vision is of the measuring of the temple and of two witnesses, whose martyrdom means that the kingdom of God is about to be inaugurated.

**10:2 He placed . . . on the land**: this symbolizes the universality of the angel's message, as does the figure of the small scroll open to be read.

**10:3 The seven thunders**: God's voice announcing judgment and doom; cf. Ps 29:3–9, where thunder, as the voice of Yahweh, is praised seven times.

**10:6 Heaven and earth and sea**: the three parts of the universe. **No more delay**: cf. Dn 12:7; Heb 2:3.

**10:7 The mysterious plan of God**: literally, "the mystery of God," the end of the present age when the forces of evil will be put down (Rev 17:1–19:4, 11–21; 20:7–10; cf. 2 Thes 2:6–12; Rom 16:25–26), and the establishment of the reign of God when all creation will be made new (Rev 21:1–22:5).

**10:9–10** The small scroll was sweet because it predicted the final victory of God's people; it was sour because it also announced their sufferings. Cf. Ez 3:1–3.

*o:* Ex 30:1–3. *p:* Jb 41:10–13. *q:* Ps 135:15–17; Is 17:8; Dn 5:4. *r:* Ps 29:3–9; Jer 25:30; Am 3:8. *s:* Dt 32:40; Dn 12:7 / Ez 12:28. *t:* Am 3:7. *u:* Ez 3:1–3.

my mouth it was like sweet honey, but when
I had eaten it, my stomach turned sour.[u]
11 Then someone said to me, "You must
prophesy again about many peoples, nations, tongues, and kings."*

## CHAPTER 11

See RG 459–60

*The Two Witnesses.* 1* [v] Then I was
given a measuring rod like a staff and I was
told, "Come and measure the temple of God
and the altar, and count those who are worshiping in it. 2 But exclude the outer court* of
the temple; do not measure it, for it has been
handed over to the Gentiles, who will trample the holy city for forty-two months. 3 I
will commission my two witnesses* to
prophesy for those twelve hundred and sixty
days, wearing sackcloth." 4[w] These are the
two olive trees and the two lampstands* that
stand before the Lord of the earth. 5* If anyone wants to harm them, fire comes out of
their mouths and devours their enemies. In
this way, anyone wanting to harm them is
sure to be slain. 6 They have the power to
close up the sky so that no rain can fall during the time of their prophesying. They also
have power to turn water into blood and to
afflict the earth with any plague as often as
they wish.[x]
7 When they have finished their testimony,
the beast that comes up from the abyss* will
wage war against them and conquer them
and kill them.[y] 8 Their corpses will lie in the
main street of the great city,* which has the
symbolic names "Sodom" and "Egypt,"
where indeed their Lord was crucified.
9* Those from every people, tribe, tongue,
and nation will gaze on their corpses for
three and a half days, and they will not allow
their corpses to be buried. 10 The inhabitants
of the earth will gloat over them and be glad
and exchange gifts because these two prophets tormented the inhabitants of the earth.
11 But after the three and a half days, a breath
of life from God entered them. When they
stood on their feet, great fear fell on those
who saw them.[z] 12 Then they heard a loud
voice from heaven say to them, "Come up
here." So they went up to heaven in a cloud
as their enemies looked on.[a] 13 At that moment there was a great earthquake, and a
tenth of the city fell in ruins. Seven thousand
people* were killed during the earthquake;
the rest were terrified and gave glory to the
God of heaven.
14 The second woe has passed, but the
third is coming soon.
*The Seventh Trumpet.** 15 Then the seventh

**10:11** This further prophecy is contained in chaps. 12–22.

**11:1** The temple and altar symbolize the new Israel; see note on Rev 7:4–9. The worshipers represent Christians. The measuring of the temple (cf. Ez 40:3–42:20; 47:1–12; Zec 2:5–6) suggests that God will preserve the faithful remnant (cf. Is 4:2–3) who remain true to Christ (Rev 14:1–5).

**11:2 The outer court**: the Court of the Gentiles. **Trample . . . forty-two months**: the duration of the vicious persecution of the Jews by Antiochus IV Epiphanes (Dn 7:25; 12:7); this persecution of three and a half years (half of seven, counted as 1260 days in Rev 11:3; 12:6) became the prototype of periods of trial for God's people; cf. Lk 4:25; Jas 5:17. The reference here is to the persecution by the Romans; cf. Introduction.

**11:3** The two witnesses, wearing sackcloth symbolizing lamentation and repentance, cannot readily be identified. Do they represent Moses and Elijah, or the Law and the Prophets, or Peter and Paul? Most probably they refer to the universal church, especially the Christian martyrs, fulfilling the office of witness (two because of Dt 19:15; cf. Mk 6:7; Jn 8:17).

**11:4 The two olive trees and the two lampstands**: the martyrs who stand in the presence of the Lord; the imagery is taken from Zec 4:8–14, where the olive trees refer to Zerubbabel and Joshua.

**11:5–6** These details are derived from stories of Moses, who turned **water into blood** (Ex 7:17–20), and of Elijah, who called down fire from heaven (1 Kgs 18:36–40; 2 Kgs 1:10) and closed up the sky for three years (1 Kgs 17:1; cf. 18:1).

**11:7 The beast . . . from the abyss**: the Roman emperor Nero, who symbolizes the forces of evil, or the antichrist (Rev 13:1, 8; 17:8); cf. Dn 7:2–8, 11–12, 19–22 and Introduction.

**11:8 The great city**: this expression is used constantly in Revelation for Babylon, i.e., Rome; cf. Rev 14:8; 16:19; 17:18; 18:2, 10, 21. **"Sodom" and "Egypt"**: symbols of immorality (cf. Is 1:10) and oppression of God's people (cf. Ex 1:11–14). **Where indeed their Lord was crucified**: not the geographical but the symbolic Jerusalem that rejects God and his witnesses, i.e., Rome, called Babylon in Rev 16–18; see note on Rev 17:9 and Introduction.

**11:9–12** Over the martyrdom (Rev 11:7) of the two witnesses, now called prophets, the ungodly rejoice **for three and a half days**, a symbolic period of time; see note on Rev 11:2. Afterwards they go in triumph to heaven, as did Elijah (2 Kgs 2:11).

**11:13 Seven thousand people**: a symbolic sum to represent all social classes (seven) and large numbers (thousands); cf. Introduction.

**11:15–19** The seventh trumpet proclaims the coming of God's reign after the victory over diabolical powers; see note on Rev 10:7.

*v*: Ez 40:3–5 / Zec 2:5–9. *w*: Zec 4:3, 14. *x*: Ex 7:17. *y*: Dn 7:21. *z*: Ez 37:5, 10. *a*: 2 Kgs 2:11.

angel blew his trumpet. There were loud
voices in heaven, saying, "The kingdom of
the world now belongs to our Lord and to his
Anointed, and he will reign forever and
ever." [16]The twenty-four elders who sat on
their thrones before God prostrated themselves and worshiped God [17]and said:

"We give thanks to you, Lord God
almighty,
who are and who were.
For you have assumed your great power
and have established your reign.
[18] The nations raged,
but your wrath has come,
and the time for the dead to be
judged,
and to recompense your servants, the
prophets,
and the holy ones and those who fear
your name,
the small and the great alike,
and to destroy those who destroy the
earth."[b]

[19]Then God's temple in heaven was opened,
and the ark of his covenant could be seen in
the temple. There were flashes of lightning,
rumblings, and peals of thunder, an earthquake, and a violent hailstorm.

## CHAPTER 12

See RG 459–60

*The Woman and the Dragon.* [1]* A
great sign appeared in the sky, a woman*
clothed with the sun, with the moon under
her feet, and on her head a crown of twelve
stars.[c] [2]She was with child and wailed aloud
in pain as she labored to give birth.* [3]Then
another sign appeared in the sky; it was a
huge red dragon,* with seven heads and ten
horns, and on its heads were seven diadems.[d]
[4]Its tail swept away a third of the stars in the
sky and hurled them down to the earth. Then
the dragon stood before the woman about to
give birth, to devour her child when she gave
birth.[e] [5]She gave birth to a son, a male child,
destined to rule all the nations with an iron
rod.* Her child was caught up to God and his
throne.[f] [6]The woman herself fled into the
desert where she had a place prepared by
God, that there she might be taken care of for
twelve hundred and sixty days.*

[7]* Then war broke out in heaven; Michael* and his angels battled against the
dragon. The dragon and its angels fought
back, [8]but they did not prevail and there was
no longer any place for them in heaven. [9]The
huge dragon, the ancient serpent,* who is
called the Devil and Satan, who deceived the
whole world, was thrown down to earth, and

**12:1–14:20** This central section of Revelation portrays the power of evil, represented by a dragon, in opposition to God and his people. First, the dragon pursues the woman about to give birth, but her son is saved and "caught up to God and his throne" (Rev 12:5). Then Michael and his angels cast the dragon and his angels out of heaven (Rev 12:7–9). After this, the dragon tries to attack the boy indirectly by attacking members of his church (Rev 12:13–17). A beast, symbolizing the Roman empire, then becomes the dragon's agent, mortally wounded but restored to life and worshiped by all the world (Rev 13:1–10). A second beast arises from the land, symbolizing the antichrist, which leads people astray by its prodigies to idolize the first beast (Rev 13:11–18). This is followed by a vision of the Lamb and his faithful ones, and the proclamation of imminent judgment upon the world in terms of the wine of God's wrath (Rev 14:1–20).

**12:1–6** The woman adorned with the sun, the moon, and the stars (images taken from Gn 37:9–10) symbolizes God's people in the Old and the New Testament. The Israel of old gave birth to the Messiah (Rev 12:5) and then became the new Israel, the church, which suffers persecution by the dragon (Rev 12:6, 13–17); cf. Is 50:1; 66:7; Jer 50:12. This corresponds to a widespread myth throughout the ancient world that a goddess pregnant with a savior was pursued by a horrible monster; by miraculous intervention, she bore a son who then killed the monster.

**12:2** Because of Eve's sin, the woman gives birth in distress and pain (Gn 3:16; cf. Is 66:7–14).

**12:3 Huge red dragon**: the Devil or Satan (cf. Rev 12:9; 20:2), symbol of the forces of evil, a mythical monster known also as Leviathan (Ps 74:13–14) or Rahab (Jb 26:12–13; Ps 89:11). **Seven diadems**: these are symbolic of the fullness of the dragon's sovereignty over the kingdoms of this world; cf. Christ with many diadems (Rev 19:12).

**12:5 Rule . . . iron rod**: fulfilled in Rev 19:15; cf. Ps 2:9. **Was caught up to God**: reference to Christ's ascension.

**12:6** God protects the persecuted church in the desert, the traditional Old Testament place of refuge for the afflicted, according to the typology of the Exodus; see note on Rev 11:2.

**12:7–12** Michael, mentioned only here in Revelation, wins a victory over the dragon. A hymn of praise follows.

**12:7 Michael**: the archangel, guardian and champion of Israel; cf. Dn 10:13, 21; 12:1; Jude 9. In Hebrew, the name Michael means "Who can compare with God?"; cf. Rev 13:4.

**12:9 The ancient serpent**: who seduced Eve (Gn 3:1–6), mother of the human race; cf. Rev 20:2; Eph 6:11–12. **Was thrown down**: allusion to the expulsion of Satan from heaven; cf. Lk 10:18.

*b:* Ps 2:1, 5 / Am 3:7. *c:* Gn 37:9. *d:* Dn 7:7. *e:* Dn 8:10. *f:* Is 66:7 / Ps 2:9. *g:* Gn 3:1–4; Lk 10:18.

its angels were thrown down with it.[g] 10 Then
I heard a loud voice in heaven say:

"Now have salvation and power come,
and the kingdom of our God
and the authority of his Anointed.
For the accuser* of our brothers is cast
out,
who accuses them before our God day
and night.
11 They conquered him by the blood of the
Lamb
and by the word of their testimony;
love for life did not deter them from
death.
12 Therefore, rejoice, you heavens,
and you who dwell in them.
But woe to you, earth and sea,
for the Devil has come down to you in
great fury,
for he knows he has but a short time."

13 When the dragon saw that it had been
thrown down to the earth, it pursued the
woman who had given birth to the male
child.[h] 14 But the woman was given the two
wings of the great eagle,* so that she could
fly to her place in the desert, where, far from
the serpent, she was taken care of for a year,
two years, and a half-year.[i] 15 The serpent,*
however, spewed a torrent of water out of his
mouth after the woman to sweep her away
with the current. 16 But the earth helped the
woman and opened its mouth and swallowed the flood that the dragon spewed out
of its mouth. 17 Then the dragon became angry with the woman and went off to wage
war against the rest of her offspring, those
who keep God's commandments and bear
witness to Jesus.* 18 It took its position* on
the sand of the sea.[j]

## CHAPTER 13

See RG 459–60

*The First Beast.** 1 Then I saw a beast
come out of the sea with ten horns and seven
heads; on its horns were ten diadems, and on
its heads blasphemous name[s].[k] 2 The beast
I saw was like a leopard, but it had feet like
a bear's, and its mouth was like the mouth of
a lion.*[l] To it the dragon gave its own power
and throne, along with great authority. 3 I
saw that one of its heads seemed to have
been mortally wounded, but this mortal
wound was healed.* Fascinated, the whole
world followed after the beast. 4 They worshiped the dragon because it gave its authority to the beast; they also worshiped the
beast* and said, "Who can compare with the
beast or who can fight against it?"
5* The beast was given a mouth uttering
proud boasts and blasphemies,[m] and it was
given authority to act for forty-two months.*
6 It opened its mouth to utter blasphemies
against God, blaspheming his name and his
dwelling and those who dwell in heaven. 7 It
was also allowed to wage war against the
holy ones and conquer them, and it was
granted authority over every tribe, people,
tongue, and nation.[n] 8 All the inhabitants of

**12:10 The accuser**: the meaning of the Hebrew word "Satan," found in Rev 12:9; Jb 1–2; Zec 3:1; 1 Chr 21:1; he continues to accuse Christ's disciples.

**12:14 Great eagle**: symbol of the power and swiftness of divine help; cf. Ex 19:4; Dt 32:11; Is 40:31.

**12:15** The serpent is depicted as the sea monster; cf. Rev 13:1; Is 27:1; Ez 32:2; Ps 74:13–14.

**12:17** Although the church is protected by God's special providence (Rev 12:16), the individual Christian is to expect persecution and suffering.

**12:18 It took its position**: many later manuscripts and versions read "I took my position," thus connecting the sentence to the following paragraph.

**13:1–10** This wild beast, combining features of the four beasts in Dn 7:2–28, symbolizes the Roman empire; the seven heads represent the emperors; see notes on Rev 17:10 and Rev 17:12–14. The blasphemous names are the divine titles assumed by the emperors.

**13:2** Satan (Rev 12:9), the prince of this world (Jn 12:31), commissioned the beast to persecute the church (Rev 13:5–7).

**13:3** This may be a reference to the popular legend that Nero would come back to life and rule again after his death (which occurred in A.D. 68 from a self-inflicted stab wound in the throat); cf. Rev 13:14; Rev 17:8. Domitian (A.D. 81–96) embodied all the cruelty and impiety of Nero. Cf. Introduction.

**13:4 Worshiped the beast**: allusion to emperor worship, which Domitian insisted upon and ruthlessly enforced. **Who can compare with the beast**: perhaps a deliberate parody of the name Michael; see note on Rev 12:7.

**13:5–6** Domitian, like Antiochus IV Epiphanes (Dn 7:8, 11, 25), demanded that he be called by divine titles such as "our lord and god" and "Jupiter." See note on Rev 11:2.

**13:5 Forty-two months**: this is the same duration as the profanation of the holy city (Rev 11:2), the prophetic mission of the two witnesses (Rev 11:3), and the retreat of the woman into the desert (Rev 12:6, 14).

*h:* Gn 3:15. *i:* Ex 19:4; Dn 7:25; 12:7. *j:* Gn 3:15. *k:* 2 Thes 2:3–12. *l:* Dn 7:3–6. *m:* Dn 7:8, 11, 25; 8:14; 9:27; 11:36; 12:7. *n:* Dn 7:21.

the earth will worship it, all whose names were not written from the foundation of the world in the book of life, which belongs to the Lamb who was slain.[o]

9 Whoever has ears ought to hear these
words.[p]
10 Anyone destined for captivity goes into
captivity.
Anyone destined to be slain by the sword
shall be slain by the sword.[q]

Such is the faithful endurance of the holy ones.

***The Second Beast.**** 11 Then I saw another beast come up out of the earth; it had two horns like a lamb's but spoke like a dragon.
12 It wielded all the authority of the first beast in its sight and made the earth and its inhabitants worship the first beast, whose mortal wound had been healed. 13 It performed great signs, even making fire come down from heaven to earth in the sight of everyone.[r] 14 It deceived the inhabitants of the earth with the signs it was allowed to perform in the sight of the first beast, telling them to make an image for the beast who had been wounded by the sword and revived. 15 It was then permitted to breathe life into the beast's image, so that the beast's image could speak and [could] have anyone who did not worship it put to death.[s] 16 It forced all the people, small and great, rich and poor, free and slave, to be given a stamped image on their right hands or their foreheads,[t] 17 so that no one could buy or sell except one who had the stamped image of the beast's name or the number that stood for its name.

18* [u] Wisdom is needed here; one who understands can calculate the number of the beast, for it is a number that stands for a person. His number is six hundred and sixty-six.

## CHAPTER 14

See RG 459-60

***The Lamb's Companions.**** 1 Then I looked and there was the Lamb standing on Mount Zion,* and with him a hundred and forty-four thousand who had his name and his Father's name written on their foreheads.[v] 2 I heard a sound from heaven like the sound of rushing water or a loud peal of thunder. The sound I heard was like that of harpists playing their harps. 3 They were singing [what seemed to be] a new hymn before the throne, before the four living creatures and the elders. No one could learn this hymn except the hundred and forty-four thousand who had been ransomed from the earth.[w] 4 These are they who were not defiled with women; they are virgins* and these are the ones who follow the Lamb wherever he goes. They have been ransomed as the firstfruits of the human race for God and the Lamb.[x] 5 On their lips no deceit* has been found; they are unblemished.[y]

***The Three Angels.**** 6 Then I saw another an-

**13:11–18** The second beast is described in terms of the false prophets (cf. Rev 16:13; 19:20; 20:10) who accompany the false messiahs (the first beast); cf. Mt 24:24; Mk 13:22; 2 Thes 2:9; cf. also Dt 13:2–4. Christians had either to worship the emperor and his image or to suffer martyrdom.

**13:18** Each of the letters of the alphabet in Hebrew as well as in Greek has a numerical value. Many possible combinations of letters will add up to 666, and many candidates have been nominated for this infamous number. The most likely is the emperor Caesar Nero (see note on Rev 13:3), the Greek form of whose name in Hebrew letters gives the required sum. (The Latin form of this name equals 616, which is the reading of a few manuscripts.) Nero personifies the emperors who viciously persecuted the church. It has also been observed that "6" represents imperfection, falling short of the perfect number "7," and is represented here in a triple or superlative form.

**14:1–5** Now follows a tender and consoling vision of the Lamb and his companions.

**14:1 Mount Zion**: in Jerusalem, the traditional place where the true remnant, the Israel of faith, is to be gathered in the messianic reign; cf. 2 Kgs 19:30–31; Jl 3:5; Ob 17; Mi 4:6–8; Zep 3:12–20. **A hundred and forty-four thousand**: see note on Rev 7:4–9. **His Father's name . . . foreheads**: in contrast to the pagans who were marked with the name or number of the beast (Rev 13:16–17).

**14:4 Virgins**: metaphorically, because they never indulged in any idolatrous practices, which are considered in the Old Testament to be adultery and fornication (Rev 2:14–15, 20–22; 17:1–6; cf. Ez 16:1–58; 23:1–49). The parallel passages (Rev 7:3; 22:4) indicate that the 144,000 whose foreheads are sealed represent all Christian people.

**14:5 No deceit**: because they did not deny Christ or do homage to the beast. Lying is characteristic of the opponents of Christ (Jn 8:44), but the Suffering Servant spoke no falsehood (Is 53:9; 1 Pt 2:22). **Unblemished**: a cultic term taken from the vocabulary of sacrificial ritual.

**14:6–13** Three angels proclaim imminent judgment on the pagan world, calling all peoples to worship God the creator.

*o:* 3:5; 17:8; 20:12. *p:* Mt 13:9. *q:* Jer 15:2. *r:* Dt 13:2–4; Mt 24:24; 2 Thes 2:9–10. *s:* Dn 3:5–7, 15. *t:* 14:9; 16:2; 19:20; 20:4. *u:* 17:9. *v:* Jl 3:5; Ob 17; Acts 2:21. *w:* Ps 33:3; 96:1; 98:1; Is 42:10. *x:* Jer 2:2; Jas 1:18. *y:* Zep 3:13.

gel flying high overhead, with everlasting good news* to announce to those who dwell on earth, to every nation, tribe, tongue, and people. 7He said in a loud voice, "Fear God and give him glory, for his time has come to sit in judgment. Worship him who made heaven and earth and sea and springs of water."[z]

8A second angel followed, saying:

"Fallen, fallen is Babylon the great,[a]
that made all the nations drink
the wine of her licentious passion."*

9A third angel followed them and said in a loud voice, "Anyone who worships the beast or its image, or accepts its mark on forehead or hand, 10will also drink the wine of God's fury,* poured full strength into the cup of his wrath, and will be tormented in burning sulfur before the holy angels and before the Lamb. 11The smoke of the fire that torments them will rise forever and ever, and there will be no relief day or night for those who worship the beast or its image or accept the mark of its name."[b] 12Here is what sustains the holy ones who keep God's commandments[c] and their faith in Jesus.*

13[d]I heard a voice from heaven say, "Write this: Blessed are the dead who die in the Lord from now on." "Yes," said the Spirit, "let them find rest from their labors, for their works accompany them."*

***The Harvest of the Earth.**** 14Then I looked and there was a white cloud, and sitting on the cloud one who looked like a son of man, with a gold crown on his head and a sharp sickle in his hand.[e] 15Another angel came out of the temple, crying out in a loud voice to the one sitting on the cloud, "Use your sickle and reap the harvest, for the time to reap has come, because the earth's harvest is fully ripe."[f] 16So the one who was sitting on the cloud swung his sickle over the earth, and the earth was harvested.

17Then another angel came out of the temple in heaven who also had a sharp sickle. 18Then another angel [came] from the altar,* [who] was in charge of the fire, and cried out in a loud voice to the one who had the sharp sickle, "Use your sharp sickle and cut the clusters from the earth's vines, for its grapes are ripe." 19So the angel swung his sickle over the earth and cut the earth's vintage. He threw it into the great wine press of God's fury.[g] 20The wine press was trodden outside the city and blood poured out of the wine press to the height of a horse's bridle for two hundred miles.*

## CHAPTER 15

See RG 459–60

***The Seven Last Plagues.*** 1* Then I saw in heaven another sign,* great and awe-inspiring: seven angels with the seven last plagues, for through them God's fury is accomplished.

2Then I saw something like a sea of glass mingled with fire.* On the sea of glass were

Babylon (Rome) will fall, and its supporters will be tormented forever.

**14:6 Everlasting good news**: that God's eternal reign is about to begin; see note on Rev 10:7.

**14:8** This verse anticipates the lengthy dirge over Babylon (Rome) in Rev 18:1–19:4. The oracle of Is 21:9 to Babylon is applied here.

**14:10–11 The wine of God's fury**: image taken from Is 51:17; Jer 25:15–16; 49:12; 51:7; Ez 23:31–34. Eternal punishment in the fiery pool of burning sulfur (or "fire and brimstone"; cf. Gn 19:24) is also reserved for the Devil, the beast, and the false prophet (Rev 19:20; 20:10; 21:8).

**14:12** In addition to **faith in Jesus**, the seer insists upon the necessity and value of works, as in Rev 2:23; 20:12–13; 22:12; cf. Mt 16:27; Rom 2:6.

**14:13** See note on Rev 1:3. According to Jewish thought, people's actions followed them as witnesses before the court of God.

**14:14–20** The reaping of the harvest symbolizes the gathering of the elect in the final judgment, while the reaping and treading of the grapes symbolizes the doom of the ungodly (cf. Jl 4:12–13; Is 63:1–6) that will come in Rev 19:11–21.

**14:18 Altar**: there was only one altar in the heavenly temple; see notes above on Rev 6:9; 8:3; 11:1.

**14:20 Two hundred miles**: literally sixteen hundred stades. The *stadion*, a Greek unit of measurement, was about 607 feet in length, approximately the length of a furlong.

**15:1–16:21** The seven bowls, the third and last group of seven after the seven seals and the seven trumpets, foreshadow the final cataclysm. Again, the series is introduced by a heavenly prelude, in which the victors over the beast sing the canticle of Moses (Rev 15:2–4).

**15:1–4** A vision of the victorious martyrs precedes the vision of woe in Rev 15:5–16:21; cf. Rev 7:9–12.

**15:2 Mingled with fire**: fire symbolizes the sanctity involved in facing God, reflected in the trials that have prepared the victorious Christians or in God's wrath.

*z:* 2:10; Mt 10:28. *a:* 18:2–3; Is 21:9; Jer 51:8 / Is 51:17; Jer 25:15–17. *b:* 19:3. *c:* 12:17. *d:* Mt 11:28–29; 2 Thes 1:7; Heb 4:10. *e:* 1:7; Dn 7:13. *f:* Jl 4:13; Mt 13:36–43. *g:* 19:15; Is 63:1–6.

standing those who had won the victory over the beast and its image and the number that signified its name. They were holding God's harps,[h] 3 and they sang the song of Moses,* the servant of God, and the song of the Lamb:

"Great and wonderful are your works,
Lord God almighty.
Just and true are your ways,
O king of the nations.[i]
4 Who will not fear you, Lord,
or glorify your name?
For you alone are holy.
All the nations will come
and worship before you,
for your righteous acts have been revealed."[j]

5* After this I had another vision. The temple that is the heavenly tent of testimony* opened, 6 and the seven angels with the seven plagues came out of the temple. They were dressed in clean white linen, with a gold sash around their chests.[k] 7 One of the four living creatures gave the seven angels seven gold bowls filled with the fury of God, who lives forever and ever. 8 Then the temple became so filled with the smoke from God's glory and might that no one could enter it until the seven plagues of the seven angels had been accomplished.[l]

See RG 459–60

## CHAPTER 16

*The Seven Bowls.** 1 I heard a loud voice speaking from the temple to the seven angels, "Go and pour out the seven bowls of God's fury upon the earth."

2 The first angel went and poured out his bowl on the earth. Festering and ugly sores broke out on those who had the mark of the beast or worshiped its image.*

3* The second angel poured out his bowl on the sea. The sea turned to blood like that from a corpse; every creature living in the sea died.

4 The third angel poured out his bowl on the rivers and springs of water. These also turned to blood.[m] 5 Then I heard the angel in charge of the waters say:

"You are just, O Holy One,
who are and who were,
in passing this sentence.[n]
6 For they have shed the blood of the holy ones and the prophets,
and you [have] given them blood to drink;
it is what they deserve."[o]

7 Then I heard the altar cry out,

"Yes, Lord God almighty,
your judgments are true and just."[p]

8 The fourth angel poured out his bowl on the sun. It was given the power to burn people with fire. 9 People were burned by the scorching heat and blasphemed the name of God who had power over these plagues, but they did not repent or give him glory.[q]

10[r] The fifth angel poured out his bowl on the throne of the beast.* Its kingdom was plunged into darkness, and people bit their tongues in pain 11 and blasphemed the God of heaven because of their pains and sores. But they did not repent of their works.[s]

12 The sixth angel emptied his bowl on the great river Euphrates. Its water was dried up to prepare the way for the kings of the East.* 13 I saw three unclean spirits like frogs* come

**15:3 The song of Moses**: the song that Moses and the Israelites sang after their escape from the oppression of Egypt (Ex 15:1–18). The martyrs have escaped from the oppression of the Devil. **Nations**: many other Greek manuscripts and versions read "ages."

**15:5–8** Seven angels receive the bowls of God's wrath.

**15:5 Tent of testimony**: the name of the meeting tent in the Greek text of Ex 40. Cf. 2 Mc 2:4–7.

**16:1–21** These seven bowls, like the seven seals (Rev 6:1–17; 8:1) and the seven trumpets (Rev 8:2–9:21; 11:15–19), bring on a succession of disasters modeled in part on the plagues of Egypt (Ex 7–12). See note on Rev 6:12–14.

**16:2** Like the sixth Egyptian plague (Ex 9:8–11).

**16:3–4** Like the first Egyptian plague (Ex 7:20–21). The same woe followed the blowing of the second trumpet (Rev 8:8–9).

**16:10 The throne of the beast**: symbol of the forces of evil. **Darkness**: like the ninth Egyptian plague (Ex 10:21–23); cf. Rev 9:2.

**16:12 The kings of the East**: Parthians; see notes on Rev 6:2 and Rev 17:12–13. **East**: literally, "rising of the sun," as in Rev 7:2.

**16:13 Frogs**: possibly an allusion to the second Egyptian

*h:* 7:9, 14; 13:15–18. *i:* Ps 92:6; 98:1 / Dt 32:4; Ps 145:17. *j:* Ps 86:9–10; Jer 10:7. *k:* 19:8. *l:* 1 Kgs 8:10; Is 6:4. *m:* Ex 7:14–24. *n:* 1:4. *o:* Ez 35:6; Mt 23:34–35. *p:* Dn 3:27; Tb 3:2. *q:* Am 4:6. *r:* Ex 10:21–23. *s:* Ex 9:8–11 / Jer 5:3. *t:* Ex 8:2–3.

from the mouth of the dragon, from the mouth of the beast, and from the mouth of the false prophet.[t] [14]These were demonic spirits who performed signs. They went out to the kings of the whole world to assemble them for the battle on the great day of God the almighty.[u] [15](“Behold, I am coming like a thief.”* Blessed is the one who watches and keeps his clothes ready, so that he may not go naked and people see him exposed.)[v] [16]They then assembled the kings in the place that is named Armageddon* in Hebrew.

[17]The seventh angel poured out his bowl into the air. A loud voice came out of the temple from the throne, saying, “It is done.”[w] [18]Then there were lightning flashes, rumblings, and peals of thunder, and a great earthquake. It was such a violent earthquake that there has never been one like it since the human race began on earth.[x] [19]The great city* was split into three parts, and the gentile cities fell. But God remembered great Babylon, giving it the cup filled with the wine of his fury and wrath. [20*] Every island fled, and mountains disappeared. [21]Large hailstones like huge weights came down from the sky on people, and they blasphemed God for the plague of hail because this plague was so severe.[y]

## V. The Punishment of Babylon and the Destruction of Pagan Nations

### CHAPTER 17

See RG 460-61

***Babylon the Great.*** [1*] Then one of the seven angels who were holding the seven bowls came and said to me, “Come here. I will show you the judgment on the great harlot* who lives near the many waters.[z] [2*] The kings of the earth have had intercourse with her,[a] and the inhabitants of the earth became drunk on the wine of her harlotry.” [3]Then he carried me away in spirit to a deserted place where I saw a woman seated on a scarlet beast* that was covered with blasphemous names, with seven heads and ten horns.[b] [4]The woman was wearing purple and scarlet and adorned with gold, precious stones, and pearls.[c] She held in her hand a gold cup that was filled with the abominable and sordid deeds of her harlotry. [5]On her forehead was written a name, which is a mystery, “Babylon the great, the mother of harlots and of the abominations of the earth.” [6*] I saw that the woman was drunk on the blood of the holy ones and on the blood of the witnesses to Jesus.

***Meaning of the Beast and Harlot.**** When I saw her I was greatly amazed. [7]The angel said to me, “Why are you amazed? I will explain to you the mystery of the woman and of the beast that carries her, the beast with the seven heads and the ten horns. [8* d] The beast that you saw existed once but now exists no longer. It will come up from the abyss and is headed for destruction. The inhabitants of the earth whose names have not been written in the book of life from the foundation of the world shall be amazed when they see the beast, because it existed once but exists no longer, and yet it

plague (Ex 7:26–8:11). **The false prophet**: identified with the two-horned second beast (Rev 13:11–18 and the note there).

**16:15 Like a thief**: as in Rev 3:3 (cf. Mt 24:42–44; 1 Thes 5:2). **Blessed**: see note on Rev 1:3.

**16:16 Armageddon**: in Hebrew, this means “Mountain of Megiddo.” Since Megiddo was the scene of many decisive battles in antiquity (Jgs 5:19–20; 2 Kgs 9:27; 2 Chr 35:20–24), the town became the symbol of the final disastrous rout of the forces of evil.

**16:19 The great city**: Rome and the empire.

**16:20–21** See note on Rev 6:12–14. **Hailstones**: as in the seventh Egyptian plague (Ex 9:23–24); cf. Rev 8:7. **Like huge weights**: literally, “weighing a talent,” about one hundred pounds.

**17:1–19:10** The punishment of Babylon is now described as a past event and, metaphorically, under the image of the great harlot who leads people astray into idolatry.

**17:1–6** Babylon, the symbolic name (Rev 17:5) of Rome, is graphically described as “the great harlot.”

**17:2 Intercourse . . . harlotry**: see note on Rev 14:4. The pagan kings subject to Rome adopted the cult of the emperor.

**17:3 Scarlet beast**: see note on Rev 13:1–10. **Blasphemous names**: divine titles assumed by the Roman emperors; see note on Rev 13:5–6.

**17:6** Reference to the great wealth and idolatrous cults of Rome.

**17:6b–18** An interpretation of the vision is here given.

**17:8** Allusion to the belief that the dead Nero would return to power (Rev 17:11); see note on Rev 13:3.

*u:* 1 Cor 1:8. *v:* Mt 24:42–44 / 3:17. *w:* Is 66:6. *x:* Mk 13:19. *y:* Ex 9:22–26. *z:* Jer 50:38; 51:13. *a:* Jer 51:7. *b:* 13:1. *c:* 18:16. *d:* 13:3–4 / 3:5; 13:8; 20:12.

will come again. [9]Here is a clue* for one who has wisdom. The seven heads represent seven hills upon which the woman sits. They also represent seven kings:[e] [10]five have already fallen, one still lives, and the last has not yet come,* and when he comes he must remain only a short while. [11]The beast* that existed once but exists no longer is an eighth king, but really belongs to the seven and is headed for destruction. [12]The ten horns that you saw represent ten kings who have not yet been crowned;* they will receive royal authority along with the beast for one hour.[f] [13]They are of one mind and will give their power and authority to the beast. [14]They will fight with the Lamb, but the Lamb will conquer them, for he is Lord of lords and king of kings, and those with him are called, chosen, and faithful."[g]

[15]Then he said to me, "The waters that you saw where the harlot lives represent large numbers of peoples, nations, and tongues. [16]The ten horns* that you saw and the beast will hate the harlot; they will leave her desolate and naked; they will eat her flesh and consume her with fire.[h] [17]For God has put it into their minds to carry out his purpose and to make them come to an agreement to give their kingdom to the beast until the words of God are accomplished. [18]The woman whom you saw represents the great city that has sovereignty over the kings of the earth."

## CHAPTER 18

See RG 460–61

***The Fall of Babylon.**** [1]After this I saw another angel coming down from heaven, having great authority, and the earth became illumined by his splendor.[i] [2]* He cried out in a mighty voice:

"Fallen, fallen is Babylon the great.[j]
She has become a haunt for demons.
She is a cage for every unclean spirit,
a cage for every unclean bird,
[a cage for every unclean] and
disgusting [beast].
[3] For all the nations have drunk*
the wine of her licentious passion.
The kings of the earth had intercourse
with her,
and the merchants of the earth grew
rich from her drive for luxury."[k]

[4]Then I heard another voice from heaven say:

"Depart from her,* my people,
so as not to take part in her sins
and receive a share in her plagues,[l]
[5] for her sins are piled up to the sky,
and God remembers her crimes.[m]
[6] Pay her back as she has paid others.
Pay her back double for her deeds.
Into her cup pour double what she
poured.[n]
[7] To the measure of her boasting and
wantonness

**17:9 Here is a clue**: literally, "Here a mind that has wisdom." **Seven hills**: of Rome.

**17:10** There is little agreement as to the identity of the Roman emperors alluded to here. The number seven (Rev 17:9) suggests that all the emperors are meant; see note on Rev 1:4.

**17:11 The beast**: Nero; see note on Rev 17:8.

**17:12–13 Ten kings who have not yet been crowned**: perhaps Parthian satraps who are to accompany the revived Nero (the beast) in his march on Rome to regain power; see note on Rev 13:3. In Rev 19:11–21, the Lamb and his companions will conquer them.

**17:16–18 The ten horns**: the ten pagan kings (Rev 17:12) who unwittingly fulfill God's will against harlot Rome, the great city; cf. Ez 16:37.

**18:1–19:4** A stirring dirge over the fall of Babylon-Rome. The perspective is prophetic, as if the fall of Rome had already taken place. The imagery here, as elsewhere in this book, is not to be taken literally. The vindictiveness of some of the language, borrowed from the scathing Old Testament prophecies against Babylon, Tyre, and Nineveh (Is 23; 24; 27; Jer 50–51; Ez 26–27), is meant to portray symbolically the inexorable demands of God's holiness and justice; cf. Introduction. The section concludes with a joyous canticle on the future glory of heaven.

**18:2** Many Greek manuscripts and versions omit **a cage for every unclean . . . beast.**

**18:3–24** Rome is condemned for her immorality, symbol of idolatry (see note on Rev 14:4), and for persecuting the church; cf. Rev 19:2.

**18:4 Depart from her**: not evacuation of the city but separation from sinners, as always in apocalyptic literature.

*e:* 13:18. *f:* Dn 7:24. *g:* 19:11–21; 2 Mc 13:4; 1 Tm 6:15 / Rom 1:6; 1 Pt 2:9; Jude 1. *h:* Ez 16:37–41; 23:25–29. *i:* Ez 43:2. *j:* 14:8; Is 21:9; Jer 50:2–3; 51:8. *k:* 17:2; Jer 51:7. *l:* Is 48:20; Jer 50:8. *m:* Jer 51:9. *n:* Jer 50:15 / Jer 16:18. *o:* Is 47:8–9.

repay her in torment and grief;
for she said to herself,
'I sit enthroned as queen;
I am no widow,
and I will never know grief.'[o]
8 Therefore, her plagues will come in one day,
pestilence, grief, and famine;
she will be consumed by fire.
For mighty is the Lord God who judges her."

9The kings of the earth who had intercourse
with her in their wantonness will weep and
mourn over her when they see the smoke of
her pyre. 10They will keep their distance for
fear of the torment inflicted on her, and they
will say:

"Alas, alas, great city,
Babylon, mighty city.
In one hour your judgment has come."

11The merchants of the earth will weep and
mourn for her, because there will be no more
markets* for their cargo: 12their cargo of
gold, silver, precious stones, and pearls; fine
linen, purple silk, and scarlet cloth; fragrant
wood of every kind, all articles of ivory and
all articles of the most expensive wood,
bronze, iron, and marble; 13cinnamon,
spice,* incense, myrrh, and frankincense;
wine, olive oil, fine flour, and wheat; cattle
and sheep, horses and chariots, and slaves,
that is, human beings.

14 "The fruit you craved
has left you.
All your luxury and splendor are gone,
never again will one find them."[p]

15The merchants who deal in these goods,
who grew rich from her, will keep their distance for fear of the torment inflicted on her.
Weeping and mourning, 16they cry out:

"Alas, alas, great city,
wearing fine linen, purple and scarlet,
adorned [in] gold, precious stones, and pearls.[q]
17 In one hour this great wealth has been ruined."

Every captain of a ship, every traveler at sea,
sailors, and seafaring merchants stood at a
distance 18and cried out when they saw the
smoke of her pyre, "What city could compare with the great city?" 19[r] They threw
dust on their heads and cried out, weeping
and mourning:

"Alas, alas, great city,
in which all who had ships at sea
grew rich from her wealth.
In one hour she has been ruined.
20 Rejoice over her, heaven,
you holy ones, apostles, and prophets.
For God has judged your case against her."[s]

21A mighty angel picked up a stone like a
huge millstone and threw it into the sea and
said:

"With such force will Babylon the great city be thrown down,
and will never be found again.[t]
22 No melodies of harpists and musicians,
flutists and trumpeters,
will ever be heard in you again.
No craftsmen in any trade
will ever be found in you again.
No sound of the millstone
will ever be heard in you again.[u]
23 No light from a lamp
will ever be seen in you again.
No voices of bride and groom
will ever be heard in you again.
Because your merchants were the great ones of the world,
all nations were led astray by your magic potion.[v]
24 In her was found the blood of prophets and holy ones
and all who have been slain on the earth."[w]

**18:11** Ironically, the merchants weep not so much for Babylon-Rome, but for their lost markets; cf. Ez 27:36.
**18:13 Spice**: an unidentified spice plant called in Greek *amōmon*.

*p:* Hos 10:5 / Am 6:7. *q:* 17:4. *r:* Ez 27:27–32. *s:* 19:1–2; Dt 32:43. *t:* Jer 51:63–64; Ez 26:21. *u:* Is 24:8; Ez 26:13. *v:* Jer 7:34; 16:9; 25:10. *w:* 16:6.

## CHAPTER 19

See RG 460–61

1 After this I heard what sounded like
the loud voice of a great multitude in
heaven, saying:

"Alleluia!*
Salvation, glory, and might belong to our
God,
2 for true and just are his judgments.
He has condemned the great harlot
who corrupted the earth with her
harlotry.
He has avenged on her the blood of his
servants."[x]

3 They said a second time:

"Alleluia! Smoke will rise from her
forever and ever."[y]

4 The twenty-four elders and the four living
creatures fell down and worshiped God who
sat on the throne, saying, "Amen. Alleluia."

***The Victory Song.**** 5 A voice coming from
the throne said:

"Praise our God, all you his servants,
[and] you who revere him, small and
great."[z]

6 Then I heard something like the sound of a
great multitude or the sound of rushing water or mighty peals of thunder, as they said:

"Alleluia!
The Lord has established his reign,
[our] God, the almighty.
7 Let us rejoice and be glad
and give him glory.
For the wedding day of the Lamb* has
come,
his bride has made herself ready.[a]
8 She was allowed to wear
a bright, clean linen garment."[b]

(The linen represents the righteous deeds of
the holy ones.)*

9 Then the angel said to me, "Write this:
Blessed* are those who have been called to
the wedding feast of the Lamb." And he said
to me, "These words are true; they come
from God."[c] 10 I fell at his feet to worship
him. But he said to me, "Don't! I am a fellow servant of yours and of your brothers
who bear witness to Jesus. Worship God.[d]
Witness to Jesus is the spirit of prophecy."*

***The King of Kings.*** 11* Then I saw the
heavens opened, and there was a white
horse; its rider was [called] "Faithful and
True." He judges and wages war in righteousness.[e] 12 His eyes were [like] a fiery
flame, and on his head were many diadems.
He had a name* inscribed that no one knows
except himself.[f] 13 He wore a cloak that had
been dipped in* blood, and his name was
called the Word of God.[g] 14 The armies of
heaven followed him, mounted on white
horses and wearing clean white linen.[h] 15 Out
of his mouth came a sharp sword to strike
the nations. He will rule them with an iron
rod, and he himself will tread out in the wine
press* the wine of the fury and wrath of God

**19:1, 3, 4, 6 Alleluia**: found only here in the New Testament, this frequent exclamation of praise in the Hebrew psalms was important in Jewish liturgy.

**19:5–10** A victory song follows, sung by the entire church, celebrating the marriage of the Lamb, the union of the Messiah with the community of the elect.

**19:7 The wedding day of the Lamb**: symbol of God's reign about to begin (Rev 21:1–22:5); see note on Rev 10:7. **His bride**: the church; cf. 2 Cor 11:2; Eph 5:22–27. Marriage is one of the biblical metaphors used to describe the covenant relationship between God and his people; cf. Hos 2:16–22; Is 54:5–6; 62:5; Ez 16:6–14. Hence, idolatry and apostasy are viewed as adultery and harlotry (Hos 2:4–15; Ez 16:15–63); see note on Rev 14:4.

**19:8** See note on Rev 14:12.

**19:9 Blessed**: see note on Rev 1:3.

**19:10 The spirit of prophecy**: as the prophets were inspired to proclaim God's word, so the Christian is called to give witness to the Word of God (Rev 19:13) made flesh; cf. Rev 1:2; 6:9; 12:17.

**19:11–16** Symbolic description of the exalted Christ (cf. Rev 1:13–16) who together with the armies of heaven overcomes the beast and its followers; cf. Rev 17:14.

**19:12 A name**: in Semitic thought, the name conveyed the reality of the person; cf. Mt 11:27; Lk 10:22.

**19:13 Had been dipped in**: other Greek manuscripts and versions read "had been sprinkled with"; cf. Rev 19:15. **The Word of God**: Christ is the revelation of the Father; cf. Jn 1:1, 14; 1 Jn 2:14.

**19:15** The treading of the wine press is a prophetic symbol used to describe the destruction of God's enemies; cf. Is 63:1–6; Jl 4:13.

---

*x:* Dn 3:27 / Jer 51:48–49. *y:* 14:11; Is 34:10. *z:* 11:18; Ps 115:13. *a:* Mt 22:9; Eph 5:27. *b:* 15:6; Is 61:10; Mt 22:11–12. *c:* Mt 8:11; Lk 14:15. *d:* 22:8–9. *e:* Is 11:4. *f:* 1:14–16; 2:18 / Lk 10:22. *g:* Is 63:1 / Jn 1:1. *h:* 15:6; 19:8. *i:* 14:20; Is 63:3.

the almighty.[i] 16 He has a name written on his cloak and on his thigh, "King of kings and Lord of lords."[j]

17* Then I saw an angel standing on the sun. He cried out [in] a loud voice to all the birds flying high overhead, "Come here. Gather for God's great feast, 18 to eat the flesh of kings, the flesh of military officers, and the flesh of warriors, the flesh of horses and of their riders, and the flesh of all, free and slave, small and great."[k] 19 Then I saw the beast and the kings of the earth and their armies gathered to fight against the one riding the horse and against his army. 20 The beast was caught and with it the false prophet* who had performed in its sight the signs by which he led astray those who had accepted the mark of the beast and those who had worshiped its image. The two were thrown alive into the fiery pool burning with sulfur.[l] 21 The rest were killed by the sword that came out of the mouth of the one riding the horse, and all the birds gorged themselves on their flesh.

## CHAPTER 20

See RG 460–61

*The Thousand-year Reign.* 1* Then I saw an angel come down from heaven, holding in his hand the key to the abyss* and a heavy chain.[m] 2 He seized the dragon, the ancient serpent, which is the Devil or Satan,* and tied it up for a thousand years[n] 3 and threw it into the abyss, which he locked over it and sealed, so that it could no longer lead the nations astray until the thousand years are completed. After this, it is to be released for a short time.

4 Then I saw thrones; those who sat on them were entrusted with judgment. I also saw the souls of those who had been beheaded for their witness to Jesus and for the word of God, and who had not worshiped the beast or its image nor had accepted its mark* on their foreheads or hands. They came to life and they reigned with Christ for a thousand years.[o] 5 The rest of the dead did not come to life until the thousand years were over. This is the first resurrection. 6 Blessed* and holy is the one who shares in the first resurrection. The second death has no power over these; they will be priests of God and of Christ, and they will reign with him for [the] thousand years.

7* When the thousand years are completed, Satan will be released from his prison. 8 He will go out to deceive the nations at the four corners of the earth, Gog and Magog,* to gather them for battle; their number is like the sand of the sea.[p] 9 They invaded the breadth of the earth* and surrounded the camp of the holy ones and the beloved city. But fire came down from heaven and consumed them.[q] 10 The Devil who had led them astray was thrown into the pool of fire and sulfur, where the beast and the false prophet were. There they will be tormented day and night forever and ever.

*The Large White Throne.** 11 Next I saw a large white throne and the one who was sitting on it. The earth and the sky fled from his

**19:17–21** The certainty of Christ's victory is proclaimed by an angel, followed by a reference to the mustering of enemy forces and a fearsome description of their annihilation. The gruesome imagery is borrowed from Ez 39:4, 17–20.

**19:20 Beast . . . false prophet**: see notes on Rev 13. **The fiery pool . . . sulfur**: symbol of God's punishment (Rev 14:10; 20:10, 14–15), different from the abyss; see note on Rev 9:1.

**20:1–6** Like the other numerical values in this book, the thousand years are not to be taken literally; they symbolize the long period of time between the chaining up of Satan (a symbol for Christ's resurrection-victory over death and the forces of evil) and the end of the world. During this time God's people share in the glorious reign of God that is present to them by virtue of their baptismal victory over death and sin; cf. Rom 6:1–8; Jn 5:24–25; 16:33; 1 Jn 3:14; Eph 2:1.

**20:1 Abyss**: see note on Rev 9:1.

**20:2 Dragon . . . serpent . . . Satan**: see notes on Rev 12:3, 9, 10, 15.

**20:4 Beast . . . mark**: see Rev 13 and its notes.

**20:6 Blessed**: see note on Rev 1:3. **Second death**: see note on Rev 2:11. **Priests**: as in Rev 1:6; 5:10; cf. 1 Pt 2:9.

**20:7–10** A description of the symbolic battle to take place when Satan is released at the end of time, when the thousand years are over; see note on Rev 20:1–6.

**20:8 Gog and Magog**: symbols of all pagan nations; the names are taken from Ez 38:1–39:20.

**20:9 The breadth of the earth**: Palestine. **The beloved city**: Jerusalem; see note on Rev 14:1.

**20:11–15** A description of the final judgment. After the intermediate reign of Christ, all the dead are raised and judged, thus inaugurating the new age.

*j:* 17:14; 2 Mc 13:4. *k:* Ez 39:17–20. *l:* 14:10. *m:* 9:1. *n:* Gn 3:1. *o:* Mt 19:28. *p:* Ez 38:2, 9, 16. *q:* Ez 38:22.

presence and there was no place for them.[r] 12 I saw the dead, the great and the lowly, standing before the throne, and scrolls were opened. Then another scroll was opened, the book of life.* The dead were judged according to their deeds, by what was written in the scrolls.[s] 13 The sea gave up its dead; then Death and Hades* gave up their dead. All the dead were judged according to their deeds. 14[t] Then Death and Hades were thrown into the pool of fire. (This pool of fire is the second death.*) 15 Anyone whose name was not found written in the book of life was thrown into the pool of fire.

## VI. The New Creation*

### CHAPTER 21

See RG 461

*The New Heaven and the New Earth.*

1[u] Then I saw a new heaven and a new earth. The former heaven and the former earth had passed away, and the sea was no more.* 2 I also saw the holy city, a new Jerusalem,* coming down out of heaven from God, prepared as a bride adorned for her husband.[v] 3 I heard a loud voice from the throne saying, "Behold, God's dwelling is with the human race.[w] He will dwell with them and they will be his people* and God himself will always be with them [as their God].* 4 He will wipe every tear from their eyes, and there shall be no more death or mourning, wailing or pain, [for] the old order has passed away."[x]

5 The one who sat on the throne* said, "Behold, I make all things new." Then he said, "Write these words down, for they are trustworthy and true."[y] 6 He said to me, "They are accomplished.* I [am] the Alpha and the Omega, the beginning and the end. To the thirsty I will give a gift from the spring of life-giving water.[z] 7 The victor* will inherit these gifts, and I shall be his God, and he will be my son.[a] 8 But as for cowards,* the unfaithful, the depraved, murderers, the unchaste, sorcerers, idol-worshipers, and deceivers of every sort, their lot is in the burning pool of fire and sulfur, which is the second death."[b]

*The New Jerusalem.** 9 One of the seven angels who held the seven bowls filled with the seven last plagues came and said to me, "Come here. I will show you the bride, the wife of the Lamb."* 10 He took me in spirit to a great, high mountain and showed me the holy city Jerusalem coming down out of heaven from God.[c] 11 It gleamed with the splendor of God. Its radiance was like that of a precious stone, like jasper, clear as crystal.[d] 12 It had a massive, high wall, with twelve gates where twelve angels were stationed and on which names were inscribed, [the names] of the twelve tribes of the Israelites. 13 There were three gates facing east, three north, three south, and three west.[e] 14 The wall of the city had twelve courses of stones as its foundation, on which were inscribed the twelve names of the twelve apostles* of the Lamb.[f]

**20:12 The book of life**: see note on Rev 3:5. **Judged . . . scrolls**: see note on Rev 14:12.

**20:13 Hades**: the netherworld; see note on Rev 1:18.

**20:14 Second death**: see note on Rev 2:11.

**21:1–22:5** A description of God's eternal kingdom in heaven under the symbols of a new heaven and a new earth; cf. Is 65:17–25; 66:22; Mt 19:28.

**21:1 Sea . . . no more**: because as home of the dragon it was doomed to disappear; cf. Jb 7:12.

**21:2 New Jerusalem . . . bride**: symbol of the church (Gal 4:26); see note on Rev 19:7.

**21:3–4** Language taken from Ez 37:27; Is 25:8; 35:10; cf. Rev 7:17.

**21:3 People**: other ancient manuscripts read a plural, "peoples."

**21:5 The one . . . on the throne**: God himself; cf. Rev 4:1–11.

**21:6 They are accomplished**: God's reign has already begun; see note on Rev 20:1–6. **Alpha . . . Omega**: see note on Rev 1:8. **Life-giving water**: see note on Rev 7:17.

**21:7 The victor**: over the forces of evil; see the conclusions of the seven letters (Rev 2:7, 11, 17, 26; 3:5, 12, 21). **He will be my son**: the victorious Christian enjoys divine affiliation by adoption (Gal 4:4–7; Rom 8:14–17); see note on Rev 2:26–28.

**21:8 Cowards**: their conviction is so weak that they deny Christ in time of trial and become traitors. **Second death**: see note on Rev 2:11.

**21:9–22:5** Symbolic descriptions of the new Jerusalem, the church. Most of the images are borrowed from Ez 40–48.

**21:9 The bride, the wife of the Lamb**: the church (Rev 21:2), the new Jerusalem (Rev 21:10); cf. 2 Cor 11:2.

**21:14 Courses of stones . . . apostles**: literally, "twelve foundations"; cf. Eph 2:19–20.

*r:* 2 Pt 3:7, 10, 12. *s:* Rom 2:6. *t:* 1 Cor 15:26, 54–55. *u:* Is 65:17; 66:22; Rom 8:19–23; 2 Pt 3:13. *v:* 19:7–9. *w:* Ez 37:27. *x:* 7:17; Is 25:8; 35:10. *y:* Is 43:19; 2 Cor 5:17. *z:* 22:17; Ps 36:8–9; Is 55:1. *a:* 2 Sm 7:14. *b:* 22:15; Rom 1:29–32. *c:* Ez 40:2. *d:* Heb 11:10. *e:* Ez 48:31–35. *f:* Eph 2:20.

15* The one who spoke to me held a gold
measuring rod to measure the city, its gates,
and its wall. 16 The city was square, its length
the same as [also] its width. He measured the
city with the rod and found it fifteen hundred
miles* in length and width and height. 17 He
also measured its wall: one hundred and
forty-four cubits* according to the standard
unit of measurement the angel used. 18* The
wall was constructed of jasper, while the city
was pure gold, clear as glass. 19 The foundations of the city wall were decorated with
every precious stone; the first course of
stones was jasper, the second sapphire, the
third chalcedony, the fourth emerald,[g] 20 the
fifth sardonyx, the sixth carnelian, the seventh chrysolite, the eighth beryl, the ninth
topaz, the tenth chrysoprase, the eleventh
hyacinth, and the twelfth amethyst. 21 The
twelve gates were twelve pearls, each of the
gates made from a single pearl; and the
street of the city was of pure gold, transparent as glass.
22* [h] I saw no temple in the city, for its temple is the Lord God almighty and the Lamb.
23* The city had no need of sun or moon to
shine on it,[i] for the glory of God gave it light,
and its lamp was the Lamb. 24 The nations
will walk by its light,* and to it the kings of
the earth will bring their treasure.[j] 25 During
the day its gates will never be shut, and there
will be no night there. 26 The treasure and
wealth of the nations will be brought there,
27 but nothing unclean will enter it, nor
any[one] who does abominable things or
tells lies. Only those will enter whose names
are written in the Lamb's book of life.[k]

## CHAPTER 22

See RG 461

1 Then the angel showed me the river
of life-giving water,* sparkling like crystal,
flowing from the throne of God and of the
Lamb[l] 2 down the middle of its street. On either side of the river grew the tree of life*
that produces fruit twelve times a year, once
each month; the leaves of the trees serve as
medicine for the nations. 3 Nothing accursed
will be found there anymore. The throne of
God and of the Lamb will be in it, and his
servants will worship him. 4 They will look
upon his face,* and his name will be on their
foreheads. 5 Night will be no more, nor will
they need light from lamp or sun, for the
Lord God shall give them light, and they
shall reign forever and ever.[m]

## VII. Epilogue*

6 And he said to me, "These words are trustworthy and true, and the Lord, the God of
prophetic spirits, sent his angel to show his
servants what must happen soon."[n] 7* "Behold, I am coming soon."* Blessed is the one
who keeps the prophetic message of this
book.[o]
8 It is I, John, who heard and saw these
things, and when I heard and saw them I fell
down to worship at the feet of the angel who
showed them to me. 9 But he said to me,

**21:15–17** The city is shaped like a gigantic cube, a symbol of perfection (cf. 1 Kgs 6:19–20). The measurements of the city and its wall are multiples of the symbolic number twelve; see note on Rev 7:4–9.

**21:16 Fifteen hundred miles**: literally, twelve thousand stades, about 12,000 furlongs (see note on Rev 14:20); the number is symbolic: twelve (the apostles as leaders of the new Israel) multiplied by 1,000 (the immensity of Christians); cf. Introduction. **In length and width and height**: literally, "its length and width and height are the same."

**21:17 One hundred and forty-four cubits**: the cubit was about eighteen inches in length. **Standard unit of measurement the angel used**: literally, "by a human measure, i.e., an angel's."

**21:18–21** The gold and precious gems symbolize the beauty and excellence of the church; cf. Ex 28:15–21; Tb 13:16–17; Is 54:11–12.

**21:22** Christ is present throughout the church; hence, no temple is needed as an earthly dwelling for God; cf. Mt 18:20; 28:20; Jn 4:21.

**21:23 Lamp . . . Lamb**: cf. Jn 8:12.

**21:24–27** All men and women of good will are welcome in the church; cf. Is 60:1, 3, 5, 11. **The . . . book of life**: see note on Rev 3:5.

**22:1, 17 Life-giving water**: see note on Rev 7:17.

**22:2 The tree of life**: cf. Rev 22:14; see note on Rev 2:7. **Fruit . . . medicine**: cf. Ez 47:12.

**22:4 Look upon his face**: cf. Mt 5:8; 1 Cor 13:12; 1 Jn 3:2.

**22:6–21** The book ends with an epilogue consisting of a series of warnings and exhortations and forming an inclusion with the prologue by resuming its themes and expressions; see note on Rev 1:1–3.

**22:7, 12, 20 I am coming soon**: Christ is the speaker; see note on Rev 1:3.

**22:7, 14 Blessed**: see note on Rev 1:3.

---

*g:* Is 54:11–12. *h:* Jn 2:19–20. *i:* Is 60:1–2, 19–20. *j:* Is 60:11. *k:* Is 35:8; 52:1; Zec 13:2 / Rev 3:5; 20:12. *l:* Ez 47:1–12. *m:* Is 60:20. *n:* 1:1. *o:* 12, 20 / 1:3.

"Don't! I am a fellow servant of yours and of
your brothers the prophets and of those who
keep the message of this book. Worship
God."[p]
10 Then he said to me, "Do not seal up the
prophetic words of this book, for the appointed time* is near. 11 Let the wicked still
act wickedly, and the filthy still be filthy.
The righteous must still do right, and the
holy still be holy."
12 "Behold, I am coming soon. I bring with
me the recompense I will give to each according to his deeds.[q] 13 I am the Alpha and
the Omega,[r] the first and the last, the beginning and the end."*
14 Blessed are they who wash their robes
so as to have the right to the tree of life and
enter the city* through its gates.[s] 15 Outside
are the dogs, the sorcerers, the unchaste, the
murderers, the idol-worshipers, and all who
love and practice deceit.[t]
16 "I, Jesus, sent my angel to give you this
testimony for the churches. I am the root and
offspring of David,* the bright morning
star."[u]
17 The Spirit and the bride* say, "Come."
Let the hearer say, "Come." Let the one who
thirsts come forward, and the one who wants
it receive the gift of life-giving water.[v]
18 I warn everyone who hears the
prophetic words in this book: if anyone adds
to them, God will add to him the plagues described in this book, 19 and if anyone takes
away from the words in this prophetic book,
God will take away his share in the tree of
life and in the holy city described in this
book.[w]
20* [x] The one who gives this testimony
says, "Yes, I am coming soon." Amen!
Come, Lord Jesus!
21 The grace of the Lord Jesus be with
all.

**22:10 The appointed time**: see note on Rev 1:3.

**22:13** Christ applies to himself words used by God in Rev 1:8.

**22:14 The city**: heavenly Jerusalem; see note on Rev 21:2.

**22:16 The root . . . of David**: see note on Rev 5:5. **Morning star**: see note on Rev 2:26–28.

**22:17 Bride**: the church; see note on Rev 21:2.

**22:20 Come, Lord Jesus**: a liturgical refrain, similar to the Aramaic expression *Marana tha*—"Our Lord, come!"—in 1 Cor 16:22; cf. note there. It was a prayer for the coming of Christ in glory at the parousia; see note on Rev 1:3.

*p*: 19:10. *q*: 7, 20 / Ps 62:12; 2 Tm 4:14. *r*: 1:8; 21:6; Is 41:4; 44:6. *s*: 7:14–15; 22:2. *t*: 21:8; Rom 1:29–32. *u*: 1:1, 11–12; 22:6 / 2:28. *v*: 21:6; Is 55:1. *w*: Dt 4:2. *x*: 7, 12 / Acts 3:20–21; 1 Cor 15:23; 16:22.

ESSAYS

TABLES

GLOSSARY

CONCORDANCE

# THE CATECHISM OF THE CATHOLIC CHURCH

What are some of the things *The Catechism of the Catholic Church* (CCC) teaches about the Bible?

## How We Read and Understand Inspiration

The CCC teaches that because the books of the Bible are written in a human way, we must pay attention to what the authors intended and to what God wanted to reveal through them. To do this, we are attentive to what culture the writers lived in and how their culture influenced their writing. We also take into consideration the historical times and setting that influenced the writers, to how literature of their times was written, as well as how people at that time and place spoke and felt. We know that the various writers used many forms of expression in the Bible such as poetry, and the books must be read with that in mind (CCC#109–110).

The Catechism also reminds us to look at the unity of the whole of Scriptures and the message they teach together. We are told to keep in mind that the Holy Spirit helps the Church interpret Scriptures within its own tradition (CCC#111–114).

### Meanings or Senses of Scripture

The Catechism teaches that there are two "senses" to Scripture: the *literal* sense and the *spiritual* sense. The literal sense is based on scholars' study and exegesis based on sound interpretation. In the spiritual sense of Scripture, there are three traditional senses: allegorical, moral, and anagogical.

The first, the allegorical sense, shows a correspondence between the Scripture's image and a deeper meaning within it. We may, for example, see a sacramental significance in the scriptural uses of water and blood in the Old and New Testaments. They may represent Baptism or Eucharist to us as we read it.

The moral sense of Scripture, obviously, instructs us to live in a just manner, to behave ethically.

Then the anagogical sense, which comes from the Greek word that means "leading," is the sense in which all of what we read in and learn from Scripture has an eternal meaning, leading us to our final home in heaven (CCC#115–117).

### Books of the Bible

The list of books in the Catholic tradition is called the "canon" of the Scriptures. The Catholic canon has 46 Old Testament and 27 New Testament books. When Jeremiah and Lamentations are counted as one, it is obviously 45 books.

The Old Testament books are essential and have a permanent value. The Church has always opposed those who want to reject the Old Testament as unnecessary in light of the New Testament for both shed light on each other.

Within the New Testament the gospels are the heart, and Christ is their center. They tell the life of Jesus, they record what his first followers handed on orally after his ascension, and when they were written down, the truth of Jesus Christ was recorded (CCC#122–126; 139).

# CATHOLIC BELIEFS IN SCRIPTURE

It can be helpful to see the basis in Scripture for many Catholic beliefs. This list, showing where certain beliefs are found in Scripture, is useful for both individual and group study. Candidates and catechumens going through the process of preparation for the Rite of Christian Initiation will find this information especially helpful. Groups may use the index as the basis for their study and reflection. These references can also be helpful in private prayer and meditation. Choose one of the topics for reflection, slowly read through one or more of the Scripture citations, and quietly think over that passage after asking the Holy Spirit to be present. This can be an effective method of self-evangelization or spiritual formation.

Abraham
Gn 12:1–5; 15:1–8; 17:1–8; 22:1–8; Mt 8:11; Lk 16:15–31; Jn 15:23; Jn 8:51–59; Heb 11:8–16; Gal 3:1–29.

Anointing of the Sick (*see* Sacraments)

Apostles
Mk 3:13–19; Jn 6:10; 13:1; Lk 8:1; 9:12; 18:31–34; Mk 4:10–11; 11:11; 14:17, 22–30;
Mt 19:28; Acts 1:12–26; Eph 2:20.

Authority
Mk 1:14–45; Mt 3:13–17; 16:19; 17:5; 18:18; 28:18; Gal 1:1, 11–12; 1 Cor 4:1–3; Lk 10:6; Jn 17:6–7; Eph 4:11–13.

Baptism (*see* Sacraments)

Beatitudes
Mt 5:1–12; Lk 6:20–26.

Bishops/presbyters
Acts 11:29–30; 14:23; 15:2–6, 22–23; 20:17; 1 Pt 5:1–4; 1 Tm 2:8–10; 3:2; 4:1–8; 6:20; 2 Tm 1:6.

Charism
1 Cor 12:8–10, 28–30; 14:4–5; Acts 20:35; Rom 12:8.

Charity (*see* Virtues)

Chosen People
Gn 17:1–14; Ex 34:10–27; Mt 12:38–50.

Christ: God reveals himself in Christ
1 Tm 6:16; Eph 1:4–5; Lk 24:45.

Church
Jn 21:15–19; Col 3:18–4:1; Rev 12.

Communion (*see* Eucharist)

Communion of Saints
Acts 2:42; 1 Cor 12:7; Rom 14:7; 1 Cor 12:26–27; 13:5; 10:24.

Confirmation (*see* Sacraments)

Conscience
1 Tm 1:18–19.

Conversion
Acts 9:1–19.

Creation
Gn 1:1; Rom 1:19–20; 8:18–23; Jn 1:1–3; Acts 17:24–29; Eph 1:5–6; Rev 4:11.

Creed
Acts 4:5–12.

Death
Lk 10:25–28; Mt 7:13–14; 25:46; Mk 9:43–48; Rom 6:20–23; 8:1–2; Gal 2:19–20; Col 3:1–5; 2 Tm 1:9–10.

Desire of God
Acts 17:26–28; Lk 12:31–34.

Devil; Satan
1 Thes 2:18; Lk 23:3; 1 Cor 7:5.

Disciple
Jn 12:24–26; 13:13–17; 15:12–17;

1 Jn 3:16; Lk 6:40; 9:57–62; 14:25–33; Mt 8:19–22; 18:18–22; 19:17–21; Lk 5:10–11, 27–28; 18:22–30; 1 Pt 2:21–25; Eph 5:1–9.

Equality
Gal 3:28.

Eucharist (*see* Sacraments)

Extreme Unction (Anointing of the Sick; *see* Sacraments)

Faith
Mk 9:14–29; Lk 17:5; 22:32; 1 Cor 13:12; 2 Cor 5:7; Jn 3:16; Rom 1:5; 11:1–17; 15:13; 16:26.

Faith and works
Mt 25:31–46; 1 Jn 1:3–10; Jas 2:14–26.

Forgiveness
Lk 3:8–11; 6:27–36; 15:4–32; Jn 8:2–11; 20:21–23; Acts 2:32–36; Mt 18:21–35.

Freedom
Gal 2:19–20; 5:11–16; Rom 5:12–17; 6:14–15.

Fruits of the Holy Spirit
Gal 5:22–23.

God (*see* Trinity)

Grace
Gen 6:8; 18:3; 2 Kgs 15:25; Lk 1:28–30; 2:40, 52; 3:22; Jn 1:14, 16–17; Rom 5:12–17; 6:14–15; 16:20; Eph 1:6–12; 2:5–7; 4:7; 2 Cor 13:13; Col 4:8; 1 Tm 6:21; Heb 13:25.

Healing
Mt 8:1–9:6; 11:2–6; Jas 5:14–16.

Holy Spirit (*see* Trinity)

Hope (*see* Virtues)

Image of God
Lk 15:11–32; Col 1:15–20; 3:1–11; Jn 1:1–18; Lk 11:1–4; Gen 1:26–3:24; Ps 12:5; Ps 23; Wis 6:12–20.

Incarnation
Jn 1:1–5, 14–16; 3:13; 6:33; 13:3; Gal 4:4–5; 1 Jn 4:2; Phil 3:8–11.

Inspiration
Lk 10:16;2 Pt 1:12–21.

Jesus Christ (cf p. 1984 for subheads)

Joseph
Mt 2:13–23.

Justice
Ps 32:1–5; 35:6–11; 39:10–12; Is 12:4–6; Jgs 5:9–11; 1 Jn 1:8–10:2; 2 Pt 1:1–2.

Kingdom of God
Mt 5:3–11; 6:4–13; 7:21; 11:12; 20:1–15; 23:13; Mk 1:14; 9:35; Lk 9:2, 60–62; 11:20–22; 1 Thes 2:12.

Law
Ex 20:1–17; Jer 31:31–34; Heb 8:8–12.
Commandments: Mt 5:17–48; Gal 2:19–20; Rom 5:12–17.
Two Great Commandments: Mk 12:28–34; Rom 13:8–10; Jn 13:34–35; 1 Jn 2:7–11.

Love (*see* Virtues, Charity)

Mary
Lk 1:38; Jn 2:1–11; Jn 19:26–28.

Matrimony (*see* Sacraments)

Messiah
Ps 2; 71; 109; Is 45:1–8; Lev 8; Is 61:1; 42:1; Mt 3:16; Mk 1:10; Lk 3:22; Heb 1:1–12.

Ministry
2 Cor 3:1–11; Jn 10:11–17; 13:1–8; Lk 9:51–19:17.

Mission
Is 41:8–16; Lk 9:2; 10:1–9; 24:46–48; Acts 1:8; 2:22–24; 8:4; 10:42; 18:10; 20:24; 2 Cor 5:18.

New Covenant
Mt 26:14–27; Jer 24:7.

Old Covenant
Dt 11:22–25; Ex 20:1–17; Jer 31:33; Ez 11:19–20.

Orders (*see* Sacraments)

Paschal mystery
Jn 12:24–26; Mk 14:22–25; Mt 26:26–29; Lk 22:7–20; 1 Cor 11:23–25.

Plan of God
Jn 6:37–40; Mt 26:36–46; Eph 1:3–14.

Penance (*see* Sacraments, Reconciliation)

Peter
Mt 16:13–20; Mk 8:27–30; Lk 9:18–20; Jn 21:15–22.

Poverty
Lk 6:20; Mk 10:23–25; Mt 6:25–34; Lk 4:16–20; 6:20–26; Mt 8:18–20; 11:2–6; Mt 11:25–29; 18:5; 25:31–46; Jn 19:36 (cf Ps 33:21); Jn 13:10 (cf Ps 40:10); Mt 27:34, 48 (cf Ps 68:22); Phil 2:6–11; 2 Cor 8:9; Mt 5:42; 2 Cor 8:1–15.

Prayer
Lk 11:1–13; 2:39–56; 5:33; Eph 6:10–18; Jn 17; Ps 62; 96; 103.

Presence of God
Gn 15:7; Ex 3:1–6; Mt 18:20.

Priest
Gn 14:17–20; Heb 7:1–10.
Priesthood of the Faithful
Heb 7:23–28; 1 Pt 2:4–9.
Providence
Jer 1:5–10; Is 46:9–12; Eccl 42:15–25; Ps 22:77; Mt 6:25–34.
Redemption
Is 19:20–22; 43:3–5; Mt 11:2–6; 20:28; Jn 10:17–18; 1 Tm 2:6;
Rom 5:6–8; 8:1–4; Gal 3:13; Ti 2:13–14; Acts 2:32–36; 3:17–26;
1 Pt 2:19–25; 2 Cor 5:18–20; 1 Cor 6:19–20; 7:23; Lk 1:46–54, 77; 3:6; 4:16–21; Eph 1:7.
Resurrection
Lk 24:36–49; Jn 20–21; Mt 28:1–7; Mk 16:1–7; Acts 2:24–32;
Jn 20:1; Rom 4:24–26; 2 Cor 5:14–16; Eph 1:19–20; Rom 6:7–10; 1 Thes 4:13–18.
Sacraments
Anointing of the sick: Mk 6:7–13; Lk 13:10–13; 2 Tm 2:11–12; Jas 5:14–16.
Baptism: Mt 3:13–17; 28:19–20; Mk 1:9–11; Lk 3:21–22; Jn 1:29–34; 3:5; Acts 2:37–41; Rom 6:3–4.
Confirmation: Mt 3:13–17; Jn 1:33–34; 14:15–31; 16:5–15; Acts 2:1–4; 8:14–17; 2 Cor 1:21–22; Gal 5:22–23.
Eucharist: Mk 6:30–44; 14:12–25; Jn 6:1–13, 35–59.
Holy Orders: Rom 12:1–8; 1 Tm 3:1–13; Mt 10:1–4; Mk 3:14–19; Lk 6:12–16; Jn 13:1–14; Heb 4:14–5:10; Ti 1:5–9.
Matrimony: Jn 2:1–11; Mt 19:1–12; Mk 2:2–12; 1 Jn 4:4–16; 1 Cor 13; Eph 5:21–33.
Reconciliation: Mt 5:21–26, 38–48; 18:23–35; Mk 2:1–12; Lk 15:11–32; Jn 20:19–23; Rom 6.
Sacred Scripture
Dt 4:32–39; Jn 5:39; 7:22; Rom 9:4–5; Mt 5:17; 22:53; Acts 1:16; 28:25; 1 Pt 1:11; 2 Pt 1:21; Heb 3:9; 10:15; 2 Tm 3:14–16; 2 Cor 3:24–28; Mt 26:54–56; Lk 4:21; 11:37–53; Mk 7:1–23; 1 Cor 11:23; Gal 1:9–12; Col 2:6.
Sacrifice
Ex 24:1–8, 11; Heb 2:17–18; 10:5–7; Lk 18:9–14; Rom 1:9.
Salvation
Ps 68; 69; 97; Is 33:2–6; Ex 12–15; Lk 1:31, 78–79; 2:21, 30–32; 4:18–19; Mt 1:21; Rom 10:9–17;11:25–32; Heb 2:10–18; 5:7–10; Mk 5:34; 10:52; 16:12; Lk 7:50; Acts 3:23–26; Jn 11:25.
Sin
Mt 12:33–37; 15:19–20; 1 Jn 16–17; Mk 3:5–6; 10:19; Lk 5:30–32; 12:1–2; 16:19–31; 18:9–14; 19:1–10; Mk 3:29; Gal 4:3; 6:7–8; 1 Cor 8:12; 1 Jn 2:3–11; Rom 5:12–21; 6:20–23; Col 2:13–14.
Social doctrine
Mt 5:42; 6:24; 10:8; 11:5; 25:31–36; Lk 4:18; 6:20–22; 16:13; 2 Thes 3:10; 4:11; Jas 5:1–6; Mk 12:41–44; Eph 4:28.
Stewardship
Lk 21:1–4; Acts 4:32–37; 2 Cor 8–9.
Suffering
Mk 15:21–41.
Temptation
Mt 4:1–11; Mk 1:12–13; 7:14–23; Lk 4:1–13.
Tradition
Lk 1:2; 2 Pt 2:21; Jude 3; 1 Thes 2:13; 2 Thes 2:15; 3:6; Rom 6:17; Col 2:6f; 2 Tm 1:13; 1 Cor 9:14; 7:10–12:40; 11:2–6, 23, 26; Mt 28:20.
Trinity
Jn 6:40–57; 8:12–19; 12:20–28; 14:9–26; 17:4–26; Mt 28:19; 3:13–17; Rom 6:3–11; 2 Cor 1:21; 13:12–13.
Father
Jer 3:4, 19–22; Mt 2:13–15; 5:45; 6:9–13; Jn 5:30–47; 6:44–47; Lk 6:35–36; Eph 3:14.
Son
1 Jn 5:20; Jn 1:1; 5:1–20; 8:24, 28, 58; 10:22–38; Heb 1:8–9; Col 2:2; Ti 2:13; 2 Pt 1:1.
Spirit
Mt 3:13–17; Acts 1:5; 2:1–21; 4:31; 8:29–30; Jn 3:1–15; 4:21–24; 1 Jn 1:5–7; 1 Cor 3:16–17.
Truth
Jn 8:26–50; 6:32–40; 8:13–28; 10:22–30; 16:12–15; 14:16; 1 Jn 1:6; 2:4; 5:6–10; Mt 18:16.

Virtues
Cardinal
*Fortitude* Ps 118:14; Jn 16:33.
*Justice* Lev 19:15; Col 4:1.
*Prudence* Prov 14:15; 1 Pt 4:7.
*Temperance* Sir 5:2; 18:30; 37:27–31; Ti 2:12.
Theological
*Faith* Rom 1:17; Gal 5:6; Jas 2:26; Mt 10:32–33.
*Hope* Heb 10:23; Ti 3:6–7; Rom 4:18; Gen 17:4–8; 22:1–18.
*Charity* Jn 13:1; 15:9–12; Mt 5:44; 22:40; 25:40; Rom 13:8–10; 1 Cor 13:1–13; Col 3:14.

# THE BIBLE IN THE LECTIONARY

EILEEN SCHULLER

One of the enduring results of the Second Vatican Council has been a renewed emphasis on the place of the Bible within Catholic life, and greater attention to its use in worship, study, and devotion. As a Church and as individuals, we are discovering anew the truth of St. Jerome's insight that "ignorance of the Scriptures is ignorance of Christ." Still, for most Catholics, their main exposure to the Bible comes at those times when the Church gathers for liturgy, to offer together praise and worship to God through Jesus. Each time the Mass is celebrated there are two or three readings from the Bible, always one from the Gospel and others from the book of Acts, the Epistles, or the Old Testament. Whenever the sacraments are celebrated, readings from the Word of God are an integral part of the ritual. The first reading from Scripture is regularly followed by a psalm so that we might give our response in the words of Scripture. The Gospel Acclamation, the Entrance and Communion antiphons are usually taken directly from Scripture, and other prayers and texts of the Mass reflect or are based on scriptural sources (for instance, the Glory to God in the Highest, the Lamb of God, the Lord's Prayer).

Why is the Church so insistent that we read the Word of God whenever we gather to pray as Church? The *Constitution on the Sacred Liturgy (CSL)*, one of the foundational documents of the Second Vatican Council, puts it this way: "Christ is present in His Word since it is He Himself who speaks when the holy Scriptures are read in the church" *(Constitution on the Sacred Liturgy*, 7). The *Eucharistic Instruction* of 1967 elaborates at greater length "the principal modes by which the Lord is present to his Church in liturgical celebrations. First of all, Christ is present in the assembly of the faithful gathered in his name; He is also present in his word for it is He who is speaking as the sacred Scriptures are read in the Church; in the eucharistic sacrifice, He is present both in the person of the minister . . . and above all under the eucharistic elements" (9).

Roman Catholicism has traditionally placed primary emphasis (at times, almost the sole emphasis) on the eucharistic presence of Christ under the appearances of bread and wine. More recent theological reflection has emphasized that Christ is present from the moment when the people gather together in the Christian Assembly, and that He is present especially during the proclamation of the Word of God, both in the reading of Scripture and in its unfolding in the homily. The *Eucharistic Instruction* brings this all together with the beautiful imagery of food: "The Church is nourished by the bread of life, which she finds at the table both of the Word of God and the Body of Christ" (10).

## The Revision of the Lectionary

Very early on in the Second Vatican Council, the Bishops of the Church said there should be "more reading from holy Scripture," and it should be "more varied and suitable" (*CSL*, 35); or, to put it in more poetic fashion, "the treasures of the Bible are to be opened up more lavishly, so that richer fare may be provided for the faithful at the table of God's Word" (*CSL*, 51). The reforms envisaged by the Council meant not only that the readings would be in English, but that new and previously unheard sections of the Bible would be introduced both on Sundays and at weekday Masses.

The revision of the Lectionary has been one of the most extensive and significant reforms of the Council. Unfortunately, it has not always been given the attention it deserves, nor are some of its fundamental principles always well understood, either by the clergy who preach on these readings or by the laity who hear them. Our appreciation of the Scriptures in the liturgy can be greatly enriched by a more careful examination of the Lectionary.

## Why a Lectionary at All?

The decision to use a lectionary means that the readings for a given Sunday or weekday are predetermined, and therefore they are the starting point for the planning of the liturgy as a whole as well as the homily. On certain other occasions (for instance, celebrations of marriages, funerals), there are more options given for Scripture readings, and a choice is to be made of what is most appropriate to the pastoral needs of a given congregation. When a special group gathers for a one-time occasion (a Retreat Day, a meeting), it is recognized that the given readings for the day may not be appropriate, and provision is made for using readings "that are more suited to the particular celebration, provided that they are chosen from the texts of an approved lectionary" (*Masses with Special Groups,* 6e). Interestingly, the greatest flexibility is allowed in choosing readings for Masses with children, although a reading from the Gospels is always to be included (*Directory for Masses with Children*, 43).

The norm in the Roman Catholic tradition is that the Scripture readings are set; they are not the choice of the priest or anyone else in the congregation. Certainly a case can be made (and has been made in the Reform and Free Church traditions) for the freedom and spontaneity to choose readings suitable to a specific community on this occasion. But the Catholic tradition has opted for a structured and planned system of readings that "provides the faithful with a knowledge of the whole of God's Word, in a pattern suited to the purpose" (*CSL: Introduction,* 60).

## Foundational Principles of the Lectionary

On a first examination of the Lectionary, it is easy to get bogged down in a mass of details about different cycles and lists of what is read when, so that the whole thing can seem somewhat intimidating. Rather than trying to determine why certain texts are read on a certain day, it is more important to get an overall sense of the arrangement and rationale of the whole. The general principles and foundational decisions that have determined the basic shape and ordering of the Roman Lectionary will then be clear.

### The Paschal Mystery

The focal point of the whole Lectionary is Jesus Christ, especially "the paschal mystery of his blessed passion, resurrection from the dead and glorious ascension" (*CSL,* 5). Throughout the cycle of the Church's Year, the Lectionary sets before us the totality of this central mystery of the Christian life, a mystery that was not only accomplished in Jesus, but a mystery in which we now share through Baptism and faith.

Thus, primacy is given to readings from the Gospels, which speak most directly of the person of Jesus. Furthermore, we read these texts not as individuals, but as a people gathered for praise and thanksgiving. "Within the Christian assembly the proclamation of the word inevitably has a Christian aura . . . the God whom we worship in our liturgy is not, first of all, the God of the Book (which is why we freely interpret the Book by arranging it in a lectionary). Our God is the God of the Gathering" (R. Keifer, *To Hear and To Proclaim*, p. 115). At Mass, every passage of Scripture, whether from the Old or New Testament, is set in relationship to the passion and resurrection of Jesus as made present to us in the Eucharist.

### The Church Year

Not everything in the Lectionary is of equal importance. The Lectionary is divided into six parts: the major section (and the one that will be the main focus of our attention) is the Temporal Cycle, that is, the readings for Sundays and weekdays throughout the Church Year; the rest of the Lectionary contains the readings for special occasions (Proper of the Saints, Commons, Ritual Masses [e.g., readings for sacraments, funerals], Masses for Various Occasions, and Votive Masses).

Within the Temporal Cycle, not all days of the year are of equal importance. Sundays have special importance because they are the weekly celebration of the Lord's resurrection and the occasion for the gathering of the whole community; thus, "the more important biblical passages" (*CSL: Introduction*, 65) are assigned to Sundays and the Solemnities of the Lord. The Sunday cycle is set up independent from the weekday cycle which, in a sense, complements it.

The Church Year as a whole has its own rhythm. "The solemnity of Easter has the same kind of preeminence [in the year] . . . that Sunday has in the week" (*Norms for the Liturgical Year*, 18); there are six Sundays in Easter season, followed by Pentecost and Trinity Sundays. Then, next to Easter, the Church "holds most sacred the memorial of Christ's birth and early manifestation" (*Norms*, 32). There are two Sundays after Christmas, followed by Epiphany and the Sunday after it. These two major feasts, each with their preparatory period (Lent, with six Sundays, before Easter, and Advent, with four Sundays, before Christmas) are the primary seasons of the Church Year; the other thirty-four Sundays, which celebrate "the mystery of Christ in all its aspects" (*Norms*, 43), form what is called simply "Ordinary Time." (The Lectionary provides for more than fifty-two Sundays to allow for variations in the length of time after Easter, because Easter can fall anywhere from March 22 to April 25.)

#### Continuous or Chosen Readings

There are many different ways in which we could go about reading the Bible in a systematic fashion. We could start with the story of Creation and work through the events of the Old Testament chronologically, then move on to the New Testament and conclude with the book of Revelation; this would be a kind of salvation–history approach. Another option would be to organize the Scripture readings around certain great themes (grace, salvation, forgiveness, creation) or moral principles; the traditional name for this approach is *lectio electa*, "readings chosen" to suit a predetermined theme. Or, we could adopt *lectio continua,* a "continuous reading" of the Bible from beginning to end. This is the system of the Jewish synagogue in which the Torah, the first five books, are read continuously through a year; on the day that the last chapter of Deuteronomy is finished, on that same day the first chapter of Genesis is begun so that the reading of the Torah is unceasing.

The Roman Lectionary has opted for a combination of *lectio electa* (particularly in the major seasons of the Church Year) and *lectio continua* (particularly during Ordinary Time and in the weekday cycle); in fact, it is really more correct to talk of *lectio semicontinua* because no biblical book is read through in its entirety.

### Basic Arrangement of the Sunday Lectionary

The planners of the Sunday Lectionary decided on a three-year cycle. That is, there are different readings for each Sunday in Years A, B, and C (as they are commonly designated), and then the cycle starts over again. (The year begins on the First Sunday of Advent.)

For each Sunday there are three readings: one from the Old Testament (with a few exceptions, as we will note in the Sundays after Easter), one from the Epistles or the book of Revelation, and one from the Gospels. Although provision is made for an individual Conference of Bishops to allow only two readings "for pastoral reasons" (*General Instruction*, 318), three is clearly the norm.

Because there is considerable difference in the Lectionary during the major seasons of Advent–Christmas and Lent–Easter as compared with the Sundays of Ordinary Time, it is easier and less confusing to look at each separately, beginning with Ordinary Time.

#### The Gospels in Ordinary Time

One of the three Synoptic Gospels forms the central focus of each of the thirty-three (occasionally thirty-four) Sundays of each year of Ordinary Time.

Year A is always the Gospel of Matthew;
Year B, the Gospel of Mark; and
Year C, the Gospel of Luke.

The Gospel of John is not neglected, even though it does not form the core of a specific year. In accord with an ancient tradition of the Church, John has always been read during the Lent and Easter seasons "because it is the 'spiritual' Gospel in which the mystery of Christ is sounded out to greater depths" (*CSL: Introduction*, 1969, 7); in addition, because of the shortness of the Gospel of Mark, chapter 6 of John (the Bread of Life discourse) is taken up on five Sundays during Year B.

This particular arrangement of the Lectionary allows us to hear each of the Gospels in its own right; over the course of a year, we come to know the distinctive picture of Jesus presented by Matthew or Mark or Luke.

**The Epistles in Ordinary Time**

Over the Sundays of Ordinary Time, passages are selected from the Epistles for the second reading, according to the following outline:

| | | |
|---|---|---|
| Year A | 1 Corinthians 1–4 | (Sundays 2–8) |
| | Romans | (Sundays 9–24) |
| | Philippians | (Sundays 25–28) |
| | 1 Thessalonians | (Sundays 29–33) |
| Year B | 1 Corinthians 6–11 | (Sundays 2–6) |
| | 2 Corinthians | (Sundays 7–14) |
| | Ephesians | (Sundays 15–21) |
| | James | (Sundays 22–26) |
| | Hebrews 2–10 | (Sundays 27–33) |
| Year C | 1 Corinthians 12–15 | (Sundays 2–8) |
| | Galatians | (Sundays 9–14) |
| | Colossians | (Sundays 15–18) |
| | Hebrews 11–12 | (Sundays 19–22) |
| | Philemon | (Sunday 23) |
| | 1 Timothy | (Sundays 24–26) |
| | 2 Timothy | (Sundays 27–30) |
| | 2 Thessalonians | (Sundays 31–33) |

Though individual passages are quite short, and there is no attempt to read the Epistles in their entirety, over the three years the Lectionary gives a "rich and varied" exposure to the main themes and emphases of this part of Scripture. As already noted, in the Sundays in Ordinary Time, there is no direct correlation between the Gospel reading and the Epistle reading; although at times they may touch on similar aspects of the Christian mystery, they have not been picked to provide a common theme.

**The Old Testament Reading in Ordinary Time**

In contrast to the selection of the Epistle, the first reading from the Old Testament has been carefully chosen to correlate with the Gospel text of the day. Sometimes it is a common theme that binds the two readings together; at other times the Old Testament will foreshadow or suggest something that is more fully developed in the Gospel (e.g., on Sunday 16, Year C, the story of Martha and Mary giving hospitality to Jesus is paired with the story from Genesis of Abraham receiving his three guests). Often, if the Gospel quotes a verse from the Old Testament or refers to a specific incident, this passage will be the first reading (e.g., on the Third Sunday, Year A, Matthew quotes Is 8:23–9:1, and that Isaianic text serves as the first reading). At times, the single lines given before the readings in the Lectionary are most helpful (though they are not meant to be read publicly) to indicate the point of correspondence that led to the choice of a particular reading.

While the desirability of a weekly Old Testament reading is undisputed, it is probably fair to say that the selection of Old Testament passages has been the single most controversial aspect of the Lectionary. The decision to link the first reading so closely with the Gospel imposes certain limitations. Many of the most important Old Testament passages simply do not readily lend themselves to correlation with a particular Gospel passage and so are never heard in the Sunday assembly; often, such a brief or peripheral section of a major Old Testament story is read that it is difficult to get a sense of the whole picture. Furthermore, relatively little ever appears from the Wisdom literature (only three selections from Proverbs and two, both truncated, from the book of Job). The passages selected from the prophets are those that are readily seen to be fulfilled in Jesus, or which at least have christological implications, but other aspects of the prophetic message are given less prominence (e.g., the relatively few "social justice" passages read over the three years).

**The Lent–Easter Season**

As noted above, the seasons of Lent–Easter and Advent–Christmas form independent units; both cycles (the Advent even more so than the Lent) are carefully crafted so that through the Scripture readings we may be more closely initiated into the Church's understanding of these great feasts.

Easter, especially the Easter Triduum (Holy Thursday, Good Friday, and Easter Vigil on

Saturday), is "the culmination of the entire liturgical year" (*Norms for the Liturgical Year*, 18); Lent serves as a time of preparation, especially as a period of "closer attention to the Word of God" (*CSL*, 109). During Lent, "those important passages from the Gospels which were read to catechumens in the early centuries to prepare them for Baptism are proclaimed. These readings are directed to *all* the faithful because during Lent the whole Church, along with those about to be baptized, calls to mind the mystery of its initiation into Christ." Though it is not possible to examine closely all the readings for the Lent–Easter season, a few examples will illustrate the care and theological insight that finds expression in the arrangement of the Lectionary for this season.

The baptismal thrust is seen most clearly in Year A on the final three Sundays of Lent, where the great themes of water, light, and life are proclaimed through the reading from John's Gospel of the Samaritan woman at the well (Third Sunday), the curing of the man born blind (Fourth), and the raising of Lazarus from the dead (Fifth); so pivotal are these particular texts to the process of Christian initiation that they can be used in any of the three years, especially when there are candidates preparing for Baptism.

The readings for the first two Sundays of Lent are always the account of the Temptation and the Transfiguration respectively, read according to the Gospel being followed in a given year. In Year B, the Gospels for the rest of Lent focus on the cross and Resurrection; in Year C, on the process of conversion.

At first glance, the choice of Old Testament readings for the Sundays of Lent might look entirely diverse and random; certainly they are not specifically linked to the Gospel. Rather, each year, they are meant to lead us through the Old Testament, presenting "the main elements of salvation history from its beginning until the promise of the New Covenant" (*CSL: Introduction*, 97):

| | | |
|---|---|---|
| Year A | First Sunday: | Creation and fall |
| | Second Sunday: | The call of Abraham |
| | Third Sunday: | Water from the rock in the desert |
| | Fourth Sunday: | The anointing of David as king |
| | Fifth Sunday: | Promise of the restoration |
| Year B | First Sunday: | Flood and covenant |
| | Second Sunday: | Abraham's sacrifice of his son |
| | Third Sunday: | The ten commandments |
| | Fourth Sunday: | Exile and destruction of the Temple |
| | Fifth Sunday: | Promise of the new covenant |
| Year C | First Sunday: | Retelling the deliverance from Egypt |
| | Second Sunday: | The covenant with Abraham |
| | Third Sunday: | The call of Moses |
| | Fourth Sunday: | The Passover celebrated in the Promised Land |
| | Fifth Sunday: | Promise of a new exodus |

The Epistle readings during Lent highlight themes such as faith, repentance, baptismal motifs, and often are related to the first reading (e.g., on the First Sunday of Lent, A, the passage from Romans about Christ as the Second Adam corresponds to the reading about the sin of Adam in Gn 2).

The reading of the Gospel of John continues on most of the Sundays after Easter in all three years with texts about the Good Shepherd (Fourth Sunday) and from John's presentation of the Farewell Discourse and Prayer of Jesus (the Fifth to Seventh Sundays). This is the only time when there are no Old Testament readings; in keeping with a very ancient tradition, the Church turns to the Acts of the Apostles in all three years so that we ponder the work of the Spirit in the early Church. For the second reading, semi-continuous selections are taken from 1 Peter in Year A, 1 John in Year B (both rich in baptismal allusions), and from the book of Revelation (with its emphasis on heavenly worship) in Year C.

### Advent–Christmas Season

The Lectionary for Advent is very carefully planned, with a definite movement toward the celebration of Christmas. The First Sunday emphasizes the Second Coming of Christ, picking up on a theme already sounded in the final Sunday of the Church Year (the feast of Christ the King). On the Second and Third Sundays, the Gospel is always about John the Baptist, so that the focus of attention moves more to the historical coming of a Messiah. On the Fourth Sunday, we turn to the first chapters of Matthew and Luke for events immediately prior to the birth of Jesus (the Annunciation to Mary and Joseph, and the Visitation).

In keeping with a long tradition in the Church, the book of Isaiah with its messianic prophecies has a special place in both the Advent and Christmas readings. The Epistle readings are more general, offering exhortations and reflections; often, as the Advent focus moves to the birth of Jesus in time, the second reading serves to remind us of the Coming that still awaits us in the future.

Throughout the Christmas season, the Lectionary preserves many of the readings that have been traditional in the Roman Church. On the Octave of Christmas, the Solemnity of Mary, Mother of God (New Year's Day), the first reading is the priestly blessing from Numbers 6, and the other two speak more specifically of Mary.

## The Lectionary for Weekdays

The readings for weekdays throughout the year form a separate cycle, independent of the Sunday cycle. Even with only two readings, obviously more of the Bible can be covered on weekdays, although still only portions of many of the longer Old Testament books are included. The seasons of Advent–Christmas, Lent–Easter follow an annual cycle, that is, the readings are repeated every year; in Ordinary Time, the same Gospel passages are read every year, while the first reading follows a two-year cycle (designated as Year I and Year II).

The following will give a brief outline of the weekday cycle.

### Advent–Christmas Season

During the first nine days of Advent, the Lectionary follows a very ancient custom of the Church and reads (in sequence) selected passages from the prophet Isaiah; on these days, contrary to usual practice, the Gospel is chosen to relate to this first reading. After the Thursday of the Second Week of Advent, the Gospel consistently speaks of John the Baptist, while the first reading is still from Isaiah or chosen to relate to the Gospel. From December 17–24, passages are selected from the first chapters of Matthew and Luke of events leading up to the birth of Christ; the first reading presents some of the major Old Testament messianic prophecies. From December 27 on throughout the Epiphany season, there is a virtually continuous reading of 1 John. The Gospels relate various manifestations of Jesus; the whole of the first chapter of John's Gospel is read between December 31 and January 5.

### Lent–Easter Season

Throughout Lent, the Gospel and Old Testament are rather closely related to each other and present to us different aspects of the major Lenten themes of Baptism and penance. In accord with an ancient custom in the Church, the Gospel of John is read from the fourth week on; in Holy Week the focus is more specifically on Christ's passion.

During the Easter season, on weekdays as on Sundays, the Lectionary maintains the ancient custom of reading semi-continuously from the Acts of the Apostles. During the Octave of Easter, the Gospel selections recount the different occasions on which Christ appeared; over the next weeks there is semi-continuous reading of the teaching and prayer of Jesus at the Last Supper from John 13–17.

### Ordinary Time

Over the course of the year, the Gospels are read on a semi-continuous basis: Mark 1–12 in Weeks 1–9, Matthew 5–25 in Weeks 10–21, and Luke 4–21 in Weeks 22–34. The Church Year ends with those passages from Luke that talk specifically of the Second Coming.

The first reading is completely independent from the Gospel and provides the opportunity to read selections from the majority of the Old Testament books and Epistles. Longer books are sometimes divided (e.g., Genesis 1–11 is read in Weeks 5–6 of Year I, Genesis 12–50 in Weeks 12–14). At the very end of the Church Year, we read from Daniel in Year I and the book of Revelation in Year II with their eschatological themes.

## The Responsorial Psalm

The Lectionary also introduces us to the psalms in the Bible; in fact, more than 80 psalms (or verses thereof) are used in the Sunday Lectionary, and some 130 of the 150 psalms appear somewhere in the complete Lectionary. The psalm comes between the first and second reading and is considered "an integral part of the Liturgy of the Word" (*General Instruction,* 36).

The psalms are poetry, the majority of them certainly originally composed to be sung with musical accompaniment. The *Introduction* to the Lectionary strongly encourages singing the psalm at Mass, preferably by a soloist (cantor) with the congregation joining in with a refrain; if the psalm is spoken, it is "to be recited in a manner conducive to meditation on the Word" (*CSL: Introduction,* 22).

Although the psalm always serves in some way as a response to the Word of God, there is considerable diversity in terms of its precise relationship to other readings. If the first reading or the epistle or even the Gospel quotes a particular psalm verse, that psalm is usually taken up as an echo or anticipated response (e.g., the use of Psalm 91 on the First Sunday of Lent, C, when a verse from this psalm, "He has put his angels in charge of you," is quoted during the temptation story in the Gospel). Often a psalm simply picks up and carries on the mood of the first reading, whether lamentation, thanksgiving, or praise. Some psalms have a long tradition of usage on particular feasts (Psalm 47, "God goes up with shouts of joy" for the Ascension; Psalm 72, ". . . the kings of Arabia and Seba shall bring tribute. All Kings shall pay him homage, all nations shall serve him" for Epiphany). According to Lucien Deiss (a member of the committee involved in the choice of psalms when the Lectionary was compiled), some psalms that would not otherwise be used were introduced primarily so that the Christian community could become more familiar with the entire psalter (*Spirit and Song of the New Liturgy*, pp. 110–11).

## Ecumenical Importance of the Lectionary

One of the unexpected and unforeseen results of the revision of the Roman Lectionary has been its adoption (with some modifications) by many Protestant churches, including Anglican/ Episcopalian, Methodist, Presbyterian, Lutheran, and United Church of Canada. James White, a Methodist minister, in a much-quoted statement remarked that the Lectionary has become "Catholicism's greatest gift to Protestant preaching, just as Protestant biblical scholarship has given so much impetus to Catholic preaching" (*Christian Worship in Transition*, 1976, p. 139).

In recent years, many of these Churches came together under the auspices of the Consultation on Common Texts and developed the *Common Lectionary,* an order of readings for use on Sundays and a few special days of the Christian year. The *Common Lectionary* basically follows the Roman Lectionary, with some significant changes in the choice of Old Testament passages to deal with some of the problem areas noted above.

Although Catholics and Protestants do not share exactly the same Lectionary, tremendous progress has been made toward common reading of Scripture. The ecumenical import, even on a practical level, is significant already; in many places ministers of different churches gather together to reflect and prepare their Sunday sermons. And, although we are still not at the point of being able to be united at the table of the Lord's banquet, we can be united and nourished at the common table of his Word.

## Using the Lectionary for Prayer and Study

Many people, both clergy and laity, now use the Lectionary as a basic resource for daily prayer, whether or not they are able to celebrate liturgy with the Christian community every day. Consistent use of the Lectionary over a period of years will necessarily expose us to a broad expanse of Scripture and protect us against the subjective reading of the Bible spoken about earlier. The Lectionary puts us in touch with the Church's understanding of the mysteries of our faith as presented through the Church year, helping us to recover dimensions that may have been lost in popular piety (e.g., the baptismal dimension of the season of Lent as opposed to a solely ascetic focus).

Many religious educators use the Lectionary as a valuable resource in catechetics; reflection on the readings as appropriate to various age groups provides a common focus when the whole community gathers in prayer. Parish study groups or Bible studies often take the Gospel of a given year as their text for study. Often the Lectionary is used as the core of the RCIA program to introduce the new catechumens to the life of faith and community.

Though the Lectionary contains the Word of God, the particular selection of material is a human endeavor and thus only more or less perfect. It is recognized that some choices of specific readings could have been more auspicious, and certainly revisions will probably be made in time.

## Conclusion

The revision of the Lectionary stands as one of the most tangible and permanent implementations of the vision and challenge of the Second Vatican Council. In the Lectionary, "the treasures of the Bible are . . . opened up more lavishly so that a richer share in God's Word may be provided for the faithful" (*CSL*, 51). The Lectionary has the potential to shape the life of the Christian community, not only as the Word of God is proclaimed in the celebration of the liturgy, but also as it is broken open for us in the homily, in catechetics, and in private and group study and prayer that is rooted in Scripture. As the Lectionary is used over the cycle of years, and even generations, "there is reason to hope for a new awakening of the spiritual life deriving from an increased dedication to God's word which 'abides forever' [Is 40, 8]" (*Dei Verbum*,26).

### Bibliography

The text of the *Constitution on the Sacred Liturgy: Introduction to the Lectionary (CSL)* has been published by the United States Catholic Conference, Lectionary for Mass: Introduction, Liturgy Documentation Series 1, 1982.

*National Bulletin on Liturgy,* Canadian Conference of Bishops, Number 50, 1975.

*Proclaim the Word: The Lectionary for Mass,* Liturgy Study Text Series 8. Washington, DC: U.S. Catholic Conference, 1982.

Fitzsimmons, John H. *Guide to the Lectionary.* London: Mayhew-McCrimmon, 1981.

Keifer, Ralph. "To Hear and To Proclaim: Introduction." *Lectionary for Mass with Commentary for Musicians and Priests.* Washington, DC: National Association of Pastoral Musicians, 1983.

Pawlikowski, John J. and James A. Wilde, *When Catholics Speak About Jews.* Chicago: Liturgy Training Program, 1987. A discussion of some of the issues around the Bible and our relationship to the Jewish people.

Skudlarek, William. *The Word in Worship: Preaching in a Liturgical Context,* Abingdon's Preacher's Library. Nashville: Abingdon, 1981.

# LECTIONARY

## THE NEW 3-YEAR CYCLE OF READINGS FOR SUNDAY MASS

See pp. 1862–1863 for Readings of Feasts that displace the Sunday Readings.
Guide: 1 refers to Reading I; 2 refers to Reading II; 3 refers to Gospel reading.

**YEAR A**
**2011 2014 2017 2020 2023 2026 2029**

**Advent Season**

**1st Sunday of Advent**
1 Is 2:1–5
2 Rom 13:11–14
3 Mt 24:37–44

**2nd Sunday of Advent**
1 Is 11:1–10
2 Rom 15:4–9
3 Mt 3:1–12

**3rd Sunday of Advent**
1 Is 35:1–6a, 10
2 Jas 5:7–10
3 Mt 11:2–11

**4th Sunday of Advent**
1 Is 7:10–14
2 Rom 1:1–7
3 Mt 1:18–24

**Christmas Season**

**Christmas Vigil**
1 Is 62:1–5
2 Acts 13:16–17, 22–25
3 Mt 1:1–25

**Christmas (At Midnight)**
1 Is 9:1–6
2 Ti 2:11–14
3 Lk 2:1–14

**Christmas (At Dawn)**
1 Is 62:11–12
2 Ti 3:4–7
3 Lk 2:15–20

**Christmas (During the Day)**
1 Is 52:7–10
2 Heb 1:1–6
3 Jn 1:1–18

**Sunday After Christmas (Holy Family)**
1 Sir 3:3–7, 14–17a
2 Col 3:12–21
3 Mt 2:13–15, 19–23

**January 1 (Solemnity of Mary, Mother of God)**
1 Nm 6:22–27
2 Gal 4:4–7
3 Lk 2:16–21

**2nd Sunday After Christmas**
1 Sir 24:1–4, 12–16
2 Eph 1:3–6, 15–18
3 Jn 1:1–18

**Epiphany**
1 Is 60:1–6
2 Eph 3:2–3a, 5–6
3 Mt 2:1–12

**Sunday After Epiphany (Baptism of the Lord)**
1 Is 42:1–4, 6–7
2 Acts 10:34–38
3 Mt 3:13–17

**Lenten Season**

**Ash Wednesday**
1 Jl 2:12–18
2 2 Cor 5:20–6:2
3 Mt 6:1–6, 16–18

**1st Sunday of Lent**
1 Gn 2:7–9; 3:1–7
2 Rom 5:12–19
3 Mt 4:1–11

**2nd Sunday of Lent**
1 Gn 12:1–4a
2 2 Tm 1:8b–10
3 Mt 17:1–9

**3rd Sunday of Lent**
1 Ex 17:3–7
2 Rom 5:1–2, 5–8
3 Jn 4:5–42

**4th Sunday of Lent**
1 1 Sm 16:1b, 6–7, 10–13a
2 Eph 5:8–14
3 Jn 9:1–41

**5th Sunday of Lent**
1 Ez 37:12–14
2 Rom 8:8–11
3 Jn 11:1–45

**Passion Sunday (Palm Sunday)**
Procession: Mt 21:1–11
1 Is 50:4–7
2 Phil 2:6–11
3 Mt 26:14–27:66

**Easter Triduum and Easter Season**

**Mass of Lord's Supper**
1 Ex 12:1–8, 11–14
2 1 Cor 11:23–26
3 Jn 13:1–15

**Good Friday**
1 Is 52:13–53:12
2 Heb 4:14–16; 5:7–9
3 Jn 18:1–19:42

**Easter Vigil**
1 Gn 1:1–2:2
Gn 22:1–18
Ex 14:15–15:1

Is 54:5–14
Is 55:1–11
Bar 3:9–15, 32–4:4
Ez 36:16–17a, 18–28
2 Rom 6:3–11
3 Mt 28:1–10

**Easter Sunday**
1 Acts 10:34a, 37–43
2 Col 3:1–4
or 1 Cor 5:6b–8
3 Jn 20:1–9
or Mt 28:1–10
Evening: 3 Lk 24:13–35

**2nd Sunday of Easter**
1 Acts 2:42–47
2 1 Pt 1:3–9
3 Jn 20:19–31

**3rd Sunday of Easter**
1 Acts 2:14, 22–33
2 1 Pt 1:17–21
3 Lk 24:13–35

**4th Sunday of Easter**
1 Acts 2:14a, 36–41
2 1 Pt 2:20b–25
3 Jn 10:1–10

**5th Sunday of Easter**
1 Acts 6:1–7
2 1 Pt 2:4–9
3 Jn 14:1–12

**6th Sunday of Easter**
1 Acts 8:5–8, 14–17
2 1 Pt 3:15–18
3 Jn 14:15–21

**Ascension of Our Lord**
1 Acts 1:1–11
2 Eph 1:17–23
3 Mt 28:16–20

**7th Sunday of Easter**
1 Acts 1:12–14
2 1 Pt 4:13–16
3 Jn 17:1–11a

**Pentecost Vigil**
1 Gn 11:1–9
or Ex 19:3–8a, 16–20b
or Ez 37:1–14
or Jl 3:1–5
2 Rom 8:22–27
3 Jn 7:37–39

**Mass of the Day**
1 Acts 2:1–11
2 1 Cor 12:3b–7, 12–13
3 Jn 20:19–23

**Solemnities of the Lord During Ordinary Time**

**Trinity Sunday (Sunday after Pentecost)**
1 Ex 34:4b–6, 8–9
2 2 Cor 13:11–13
3 Jn 3:16–18

**Corpus Christi**
1 Dt 8:2–3, 14b–16a
2 1 Cor 10:16–17
3 Jn 6:51–58

**Sacred Heart of Jesus**
1 Dt 7:6–11
2 1 Jn 4:7–16
3 Mt 11:25–30

**Ordinary Time**

**1st Sunday**
*(See Baptism of the Lord, above)*

**2nd Sunday**
1 Is 49:3, 5–6
2 1 Cor 1:1–3
3 Jn 1:29–34

**3rd Sunday**
1 Is 8:23b–9:3
2 1 Cor 1:10–13, 17
3 Mt 4:12–23

**4th Sunday**
1 Zep 2:3; 3:12–13
2 1 Cor 1:26–31
3 Mt 5:1–12a

**5th Sunday**
1 Is 58:7–10
2 1 Cor 2:1–5
3 Mt 5:13–16

**6th Sunday**
1 Sir 15:16–21
2 1 Cor 2:6–10
3 Mt 5:17–37

**7th Sunday**
1 Lv 19:1–2, 17–18
2 1 Cor 3:16–23
3 Mt 5:38–48

**8th Sunday**
1 Is 49:14–15
2 1 Cor 4:1–5
3 Mt 6:24–34

**9th Sunday**
1 Dt 11:18, 26–28, 32
2 Rom 3:21–25a, 28
3 Mt 7:21–27

**10th Sunday**
1 Hos 6:3–6
2 Rom 4:18–25
3 Mt 9:9–13

**11th Sunday**
1 Ex 19:2–6a
2 Rom 5:6–11
3 Mt 9:36–10:8

**12th Sunday**
1 Jer 20:10–13
2 Rom 5:12–15
3 Mt 10:26–33

**13th Sunday**
1 2 Kgs 4:8–11, 14–16a
2 Rom 6:3–4, 8–11
3 Mt 10:37–42

**14th Sunday**
1 Zec 9:9–10
2 Rom 8:9, 11–13
3 Mt 11:25–30

**15th Sunday**
1 Is 55:10–11
2 Rom 8:18–23
3 Mt 13:1–23

**16th Sunday**
1 Wis 12:13, 16–19
2 Rom 8:26–27
3 Mt 13:24–43

**17th Sunday**
1 1 Kgs 3:5, 7–12
2 Rom 8:28–30
3 Mt 13:44–52

**18th Sunday**
1 Is 55:1–3
2 Rom 8:35, 37–39
3 Mt 14:13–21

**19th Sunday**
1 1 Kgs 19:9a, 11–13a
2 Rom 9:1–5
3 Mt 14:22–33

**20th Sunday**
1 Is 56:1, 6–7
2 Rom 11:13–15, 29–32
3 Mt 15:21–28

**21st Sunday**
1 Is 22:19–23
2 Rom 11:33–36
3 Mt 16:13–20

**22nd Sunday**
1 Jer 20:7–9
2 Rom 12:1–2
3 Mt 16:21–27

**23rd Sunday**
1 Ez 33:7–9
2 Rom 13:8–10
3 Mt 18:15–20

**24th Sunday**
1 Sir 27:30–28:7
2 Rom 14:7–9
3 Mt 18:21–35

**25th Sunday**
1 Is 55:6–9
2 Phil 1:20c–24, 27a
3 Mt 20:1–16a

**26th Sunday**
1 Ez 18:25–28
2 Phil 2:1–11
3 Mt 21:28–32

**27th Sunday**
1 Is 5:1–7
2 Phil 4:6–9
3 Mt 21:33–43

**28th Sunday**
1 Is 25:6–10a
2 Phil 4:12–14, 19–20
3 Mt 22:1–14

**29th Sunday**
1 Is 45:1, 4–6
2 1 Thes 1:1–5b
3 Mt 22:15–21

**30th Sunday**
1 Ex 22:20–26
2 1 Thes 1:5c–10
3 Mt 22:34–40

**31st Sunday**
1 Mal 1:14b–2:2b, 8–10
2 1 Thes 2:7b–9, 13
3 Mt 23:1–12

**32nd Sunday**
1 Wis 6:12–16
2 1 Thes 4:13–18
3 Mt 25:1–13

**33rd Sunday**
1 Prv 31:10–13, 19–20, 30–31
2 1 Thes 5:1–6
3 Mt 25:14–30

**34th Sunday (Christ the King)**
1 Ez 34:11–12, 15–17
2 1 Cor 15:20–26, 28
3 Mt 25:31–46

**YEAR B**

**2012 2015 2018 2021 2024 2027 2030**

**Advent Season**

**1st Sunday of Advent**
1 Is 63:16b–17, 19b; 64:2b–7
2 1 Cor 1:3–9
3 Mk 13:33–37

**2nd Sunday of Advent**
1 Is 40:1–5, 9–11
2 2 Pt 3:8–14
3 Mk 1:1–8

**3rd Sunday of Advent**
1 Is 61:1–2a, 10–11
2 1 Thes 5:16–24
3 Jn 1:6–8, 19–28

**4th Sunday of Advent**
1 2 Sm 7:1–5, 8b–12, 14a, 16
2 Rom 16:25–27
3 Lk 1:26–38

**Christmas Season**

**Christmas Vigil**
1 Is 62:1–5
2 Acts 13:16–17, 22–25
3 Mt 1:1–25

**Christmas (At Midnight)**
1 Is 9:1–6
2 Ti 2:11–14
3 Lk 2:1–14

**Christmas (At Dawn)**
1 Is 62:11–12
2 Ti 3:4–7
3 Lk 2:15–20

**Christmas (During the Day)**
1 Is 52:7–10
2 Heb 1:1–6
3 Jn 1:1–18

**Sunday After Christmas (Holy Family)**
1 Gn 15:1–6; 21:1–3
2 Heb 11:8, 11–12, 17–19
3 Lk 2:22–40 or 22, 39–40

**January 1 (Solemnity of Mary, Mother of God)**
1 Nm 6:22–27
2 Gal 4:4–7
3 Lk 2:16–21

**2nd Sunday After Christmas**
1 Sir 24:1–2, 8–12
2 Eph 1:3–6, 15–18
3 Jn 1:1–18

**Epiphany**
1 Is 60:1–6
2 Eph 3:2–3a, 5–6
3 Mt 2:1–12

**Sunday After Epiphany (Baptism of the Lord)**
1 Is 55:1–11
2 1 Jn 5:1–9
3 Mk 1:7–11

**Lenten Season**

**Ash Wednesday**
1 Jl 2:12–18
2 2 Cor 5:20–6:2
3 Mt 6:1–6, 16–18

**1st Sunday of Lent**
1 Gn 9:8–15
2 1 Pt 3:18–22
3 Mk 1:12–15

**2nd Sunday of Lent**
1 Gn 22:1–2, 9a, 10–13, 15–18
2 Rom 8:31b–34
3 Mk 9:2–10

**3rd Sunday of Lent**
1 Ex 20:1–17
2 1 Cor 1:22–25
3 Jn 2:13–25

**4th Sunday of Lent**
1 2 Chr 36:14–16, 19–23
2 Eph 2:4–10
3 Jn 3:14–21

**5th Sunday of Lent**
1 Jer 31:31–34
2 Heb 5:7–9
3 Jn 12:20–33

**Passion Sunday (Palm Sunday)**
Procession: Mk 11:1–10 or Jn 12:12–16
1 Is 50:4–7
2 Phil 2:6–11
3 Mk 14:1–15,47

**Easter Triduum and Easter Season**

**Mass of Lord's Supper**
1 Ex 12:1–8, 11–14
2 1 Cor 11:23–26
3 Jn 13:1–15

**Good Friday**
1 Is 52:13–53:12
2 Heb 4:14–16; 5:7–9
3 Jn 18:1–19:42

**Easter Vigil**
1 Gn 1:1–2:2
Gn 22:1–18
Ex 14:15–15:1
Is 54:5–14
Is 55:1–11
Bar 3:9–15, 32–4:4
Ez 36:16–28
2 Rom 6:3–11
3 Mk 16:1–7

**Easter Sunday**
1 Acts 10:34a, 37–43
2 Col 3:1–4 or 1 Cor 5:6b–8
3 Jn 20:1–9 or Mk 16:1–8
Evening: 3 Lk 24:13–35

**2nd Sunday of Easter**
1 Acts 4:32–35
2 1 Jn 5:1–6
3 Jn 20:19–31

**3rd Sunday of Easter**
1 Acts 3:13–15, 17–19
2 1 Jn 2:1–5a
3 Lk 24:35–48

**4th Sunday of Easter**
1 Acts 4:8–12
2 1 Jn 3:1–2
3 Jn 10:11–18

**5th Sunday of Easter**
1 Acts 9:26–31
2 1 Jn 3:18–24
3 Jn 15:1–8

**6th Sunday of Easter**
1 Acts 10:25–26, 34–35, 44–48
2 1 Jn 4:7–10
3 Jn 15:9–17

**Ascension of Our Lord**
1 Acts 1:1–11
2 Eph 1:17–23 or 4:1–13
3 Mk 16:15–20

**7th Sunday of Easter**
1 Acts 1:15–17, 20a, 20c–26
2 1 Jn 4:11–16
3 Jn 17:11b–19

**Pentecost Vigil**
1 Gn 11:1–9 or Ex 19:3–8a, 16–20b or Ez 37:1–14 or Jl 3:1–5
2 Rom 8:22–27
3 Jn 7:37–39

**Mass of the Day**
1 Acts 2:1–11
2 1 Cor 12:3b–7, 12–13
3 Jn 20:19–23
Pentecost-Optional
2 Gal 5:16–25

3 Jn 15:26–27; 16:12–15

**Solemnities of the Lord During Ordinary Time**

**Trinity Sunday (Sunday after Pentecost)**
1 Dt 4:32–34, 39–40
2 Rom 8:14–17
3 Mt 28:16–20

**Corpus Christi**
1 Ex 24:3–8
2 Heb 9:11–15
3 Mk 14:12–16, 22–26

**Sacred Heart of Jesus**
1 Hos 11:1, 3–4, 8c–9
2 Eph 3:8–12, 14–19
3 Jn 19:31–37

**Ordinary Time**

**1st Sunday**
*(See Baptism of the Lord, above)*

**2nd Sunday**
1 1 Sm 3:3b–10, 19
2 1 Cor 6:13c–15a, 17–20
3 Jn 1:35–42

**3rd Sunday**
1 Jon 3:1–5, 10
2 1 Cor 7:29–31
3 Mk 1:14–20

**4th Sunday**
1 Dt 18:15–20
2 1 Cor 7:32–35
3 Mk 1:21–28

**5th Sunday**
1 Jb 7:1–4, 6–7
2 1 Cor 9:16–19, 22–23
3 Mk 1:29–39

**6th Sunday**
1 Lv 13:1–2, 45–46
2 1 Cor 10:31–11:1
3 Mk 1:40–45

**7th Sunday**
1 Is 43:18–19, 21–22, 24b–25
2 2 Cor 1:18–22
3 Mk 2:1–12

**8th Sunday**
1 Hos 2:16b, 17b, 21–22
2 2 Cor 3:1b–6
3 Mk 2:18–22

**9th Sunday**
1 Dt 5:12–15
2 2 Cor 4:6–11
3 Mk 2:23–3:6

**10th Sunday**
1 Gn 3:9–15
2 2 Cor 4:13–5:1
3 Mk 3:20–35

**11th Sunday**
1 Ez 17:22–24
2 2 Cor 5:6–10
3 Mk 4:26–34

**12th Sunday**
1 Jb 38:1, 8–11
2 2 Cor 5:14–17
3 Mk 4:35–41

**13th Sunday**
1 Wis 1:13–15; 2:23–24
2 2 Cor 8:7, 9, 13–15
3 Mk 5:21–43

**14th Sunday**
1 Ez 2:2–5
2 2 Cor 12:7–10
3 Mk 6:1–6

**15th Sunday**
1 Am 7:12–15
2 Eph 1:3–14
3 Mk 6:7–13

**16th Sunday**
1 Jer 23:1–6
2 Eph 2:13–18
3 Mk 6:30–34

**17th Sunday**
1 2 Kgs 4:42–44
2 Eph 4:1–6
3 Jn 6:1–15

**18th Sunday**
1 Ex 16:2–4, 12–15
2 Eph 4:17, 20–24
3 Jn 6:24–35

**19th Sunday**
1 1 Kgs 19:4–8
2 Eph 4:30–5:2
3 Jn 6:41–51

**20th Sunday**
1 Prv 9:1–6
2 Eph 5:15–20
3 Jn 6:51–58

**21st Sunday**
1 Jos 24:1–2a, 15–17, 18b
2 Eph 5:21–32
3 Jn 6:60–69

**22nd Sunday**
1 Dt 4:1–2, 6–8
2 Jas 1:17–18, 21b–22, 27
3 Mk 7:1–8, 14–15, 21–23

**23rd Sunday**
1 Is 35:4–7a
2 Jas 2:1–5
3 Mk 7:31–37

**24th Sunday**
1 Is 50:5–9a
2 Jas 2:14–18
3 Mk 8:27–35

**25th Sunday**
1 Wis 2:12, 17–20
2 Jas 3:16–4:3
3 Mk 9:30–37

**26th Sunday**
1 Nm 11:25–29
2 Jas 5:1–6
3 Mk 9:38–43, 45, 47–48

**27th Sunday**
1 Gn 2:18–24
2 Heb 2:9–11
3 Mk 10:2–16

**28th Sunday**
1 Wis 7:7–11
2 Heb 4:12–13
3 Mk 10:17–30

**29th Sunday**
1 Is 53:10–11
2 Heb 4:14–16
3 Mk 10:35–45

**30th Sunday**
1 Jer 31:7–9
2 Heb 5:1–6
3 Mk 10:46–52

**31st Sunday**
1 Dt 6:2–6
2 Heb 7:23–28
3 Mk 12:28b–34

**32nd Sunday**
1 1 Kgs 17:10–16
2 Heb 9:24–28
3 Mk 12:38–44

**33rd Sunday**
1 Dn 12:1–3
2 Heb 10:11–14, 18
3 Mk 13:24–32

**34th Sunday (Christ the King)**
1 Dn 7:13–14
2 Rev 1:5–8
3 Jn 18:33b–37

**YEAR C**
**2013 2016 2019 2022 2025 2028 2031**

**Advent Season**

**1st Sunday of Advent**
1 Jer 33:14–16
2 1 Thes 3:12–4:2
3 Lk 21:25–28, 34–36

**2nd Sunday of Advent**
1 Bar 5:1–9
2 Phil 1:4–6, 8–11
3 Lk 3:1–6

**3rd Sunday of Advent**
1 Zep 3:14–18a
2 Phil 4:4–7
3 Lk 3:10–18

**4th Sunday of Advent**
1 Mi 5:1–4a
2 Heb 10:5–10
3 Lk 1:39–45

**Christmas Season**

**Christmas Vigil**
1 Is 62:1–6
2 Acts 13:16–17, 22–25
3 Mt 1:1–25

**Christmas (At Midnight)**
1 Is 9:1–6
2 Ti 2:11–14
3 Lk 2:1–14

**Christmas (At Dawn)**
1 Is 62:11–12

2 Ti 3:4–7
3 Lk 2:15–20

**Christmas (During the Day)**
1 Is 57:7–10
2 Heb 1:1–6
3 Jn 1:1–18

**Sunday After Christmas (Holy Family)**
1 1 Sm 1:20–22, 24–28
2 1 Jn 3:1–2, 21–24
3 Lk 2:41–52

**January 1 (Solemnity of Mary, Mother of God)**
1 Nm 6:22–27
2 Gal 4:4–7
3 Lk 2:16–21

**2nd Sunday After Christmas**
1 Sir 24:1–2, 8–12
2 Eph 1:3–6, 15–18
3 Jn 1:1–18

**Epiphany**
1 Is 60:1–6
2 Eph 3:2–3a, 5–6
3 Mt 2:1–12

**Sunday After Epiphany (Baptism of the Lord)**
1 Is 40:1–5, 9–11
2 Ti 2:11–14; 3:4–7
3 Lk 3:15–16, 21–22

**Lenten Season**

**Ash Wednesday**
1 Jl 2:12–18
2 2 Cor 5:20–6:2
3 Mt 6:1–6, 16–18

**1st Sunday of Lent**
1 Dt 26:4–10
2 Rom 10:8–13
3 Lk 4:1–13

**2nd Sunday of Lent**
1 Gn 15:5–12, 17–18
2 Phil 3:17–4:1
3 Lk 9:28b–36

**3rd Sunday of Lent**
1 Ex 3:1–8a, 13–15
2 1 Cor 10:1–6, 10–12
3 Lk 13:1–9

**4th Sunday of Lent**
1 Jos 5:9a, 10–12
2 2 Cor 5:17–21
3 Lk 15:1–3, 11–32

**5th Sunday of Lent**
1 Is 43:16–21
2 Phil 3:8–14
3 Jn 8:1–11

**Passion Sunday (Palm Sunday)**
Procession: Lk 19:28–40
1 Is 50:4–7
2 Phil 2:6–11
3 Lk 22:14–23:56

**Easter Triduum and Easter Season**

**Mass of Lord's Supper**
1 Ex 12:1–8, 11–14
2 1 Cor 11:23–26
3 Jn 13:1–15

**Good Friday**
1 Is 52:13–53:12
2 Heb 4:14–16; 5:7–9
3 Jn 18:1–19:42

**Easter Vigil**
1 Gn 1:1–2:2
Gn 22:1–18
Ex 14:15–15:1
Is 54:5–14
Is 55:1–11
Bar 3:9–15, 32–4:4
Ez 36:16–28
2 Rom 6:3–11
3 Lk 24:1–12

**Easter Sunday**
1 Acts 10:34a, 37–43
2 Col 3:1–4
or 1 Cor 5:6b–8
3 Jn 20:1–9
or Lk 24:1–12
Evening: 3 Lk 24:13–35

**2nd Sunday of Easter**
1 Acts 5:12–16
2 Rev 1:9–11a, 12–13, 17–19
3 Jn 20:19–31

**3rd Sunday of Easter**
1 Acts 5:27b–32, 40b–41
2 Rev 5:11–14
3 Jn 21:1–19 or 1–14

**4th Sunday of Easter**
1 Acts 13:14, 43–52
2 Rev 7:9, 14b–17
3 Jn 10:27–30

**5th Sunday of Easter**
1 Acts 14:21b–27
2 Rev 21:1–5a
3 Jn 13:31–33a, 34–35

**6th Sunday of Easter**
1 Acts 15:1–2, 22–29
2 Rev 21:10–14, 22–23
3 Jn 14:23–29

**Ascension of the Lord**
1 Acts 1:1–11
2 Eph 1:17–23 or Heb 9:24–28; 10:19–23
3 Lk 24:46–53

**7th Sunday of Easter**
1 Acts 7:55–60
2 Rev 22:12–14, 16–17, 20
3 Jn 17:20–26

**Pentecost Vigil**
1 Gn 11:1–9
or Ex 19:3–8a, 16–20b
or Ez 37:1–14
or Jl 3:1–5
2 Rom 8:22–27
3 Jn 7:37–39

**Mass of the Day**
1 Acts 2:1–11
2 1 Cor 12:3b–7, 12–13
or Rom 8:8–27
3 Jn 20:19–23
or Jn 14:15–16, 23b–26

**Solemnities of the Lord During Ordinary Time**

**Trinity Sunday (Sunday After Pentecost)**
1 Prv 8:22–31
2 Rom 5:1–5
3 Jn 16:12–15

**Corpus Christi**
1 Gn 14:18–20
2 1 Cor 11:23–26
3 Lk 9:11b–17

**Sacred Heart of Jesus**
1 Ez 34:11–16
2 Rom 5:5b–11
3 Lk 15:3–7

**Ordinary Time**

**1st Sunday**
*(See Baptism of the Lord, above)*

**2nd Sunday**
1 Is 62:1–5
2 1 Cor 12:4–11
3 Jn 2:1–12

**3rd Sunday**
1 Neh 8:2–4a, 5–6, 8–10
2 1 Cor 12:12–30
3 Lk 1:1–4; 4:14–21

**4th Sunday**
1 Jer 1:4–5, 17–19
2 1 Cor 12:31–13:13
3 Lk 4:21–30

**5th Sunday**
1 Is 6:1–2a, 3–8
2 1 Cor 15:1–11
3 Lk 5:1–11

**6th Sunday**
1 Jer 17:5–8
2 1 Cor 15:12, 16–20
3 Lk 6:17, 20–26

**7th Sunday**
1 1 Sm 26:2, 7–9, 12–13, 22–23
2 1 Cor 15:45–49
3 Lk 6:27–38

**8th Sunday**
1 Sir 27:5–8
2 1 Cor 15:54–58
3 Lk 6:39–45

**9th Sunday**
1 1 Kgs 8:41–43
2 Gal 1:1–2, 6–10
3 Lk 7:1–10

**10th Sunday**
1 1 Kgs 17:17–24
2 Gal 1:11–19
3 Lk 7:11–17

**11th Sunday**
1 2 Sm 12:7–10, 13
2 Gal 2:16, 19–21
3 Lk 7:36–8:3

**12th Sunday**
1 Zec 12:10–11
2 Gal 3:26–29
3 Lk 9:18–24

**13th Sunday**
1 1 Kgs 19:16b, 19–21
2 Gal 5:1, 13–18
3 Lk 9:51–62

**14th Sunday**
1 Is 66:10–14c
2 Gal 6:14–18
3 Lk 10:1–12, 17–20

**15th Sunday**
1 Dt 30:10–14
2 Col 1:15–20
3 Lk 10:25–37

**16th Sunday**
1 Gn 18:1–10a
2 Col 1:24–28
3 Lk 10:38–42

**17th Sunday**
1 Gn 18:20–32
2 Col 2:12–14
3 Lk 11:1–13

**18th Sunday**
1 Eccl 1:2; 2:21–23
2 Col 3:1–5, 9–11
3 Lk 12:13–31

**19th Sunday**
1 Wis 18:6–9
2 Heb 11:1–2, 8–19
3 Lk 12:32–48

**20th Sunday**
1 Jer 38:4–6, 8–10
2 Heb 12:1–4
3 Lk 12:49–53

**21st Sunday**
1 Is 66:18–21
2 Heb 12:5–7, 11–13
3 Lk 13:22–30

**22nd Sunday**
1 Sir 3:19–21, 30–31
2 Heb 12:18–19, 22–24a
3 Lk 14:1, 7–14

**23rd Sunday**
1 Wis 9:13–19
2 Phlm 9b–10, 12–17
3 Lk 14:25–33

**24th Sunday**
1 Ex 32:7–11, 13–14
2 1 Tm 1:12–17
3 Lk 15:1–32

**25th Sunday**
1 Am 8:4–7
2 1 Tm 2:1–8
3 Lk 16:1–13

**26th Sunday**
1 Am 6:1a, 4–7
2 1 Tm 6:11–16
3 Lk 16:19–31

**27th Sunday**
1 Hb 1:2–3; 2:2–4
2 2 Tm 1:6–8, 13–14
3 Lk 17:5–10

**28th Sunday**
1 2 Kgs 5:14–17
2 2 Tm 2:8–13
3 Lk 17:11–19

**29th Sunday**
1 Ex 17:8–13
2 2 Tm 3:14–4:2
3 Lk 18:1–8

**30th Sunday**
1 Sir 35:15b–17, 20–22a
2 2 Tm 4:6–8, 16–18
3 Lk 18:9–14

**31st Sunday**
1 Wis 11:23–12:2
2 2 Thes 1:11–2:2
3 Lk 19:1–10

**32nd Sunday**
1 2 Mc 7:1–2, 9–14
2 2 Thes 2:16–3:5
3 Lk 20:27–38

**33rd Sunday**
1 Mal 3:19–20a
2 2 Thes 3:7–12
3 Lk 21:5–19

**34th Sunday (Christ the King)**
1 2 Sm 5:1–3
2 Col 1:12–20
3 Lk 23:35–43

# READINGS FOR THE MAJOR FEASTS OF THE YEAR

**Feb. 2: Presentation of the Lord**
1 Mal 3:1–4
2 Heb 2:14–18
3 Lk 2:22–40

**Mar. 19: Joseph, Husband of Mary**
1 2 Sm 7:4–5a, 12–14a, 16
2 Rom 4:13, 16–18, 22
3 Mt 1:16, 18–21, 24a
or Lk 2:41–51a

**Mar. 25: Annunciation**
1 Is 7:10–14
2 Heb 10:4–10
3 Lk 1:26–28

**June 24: John the Baptist Vigil**
1 Jer 1:4–10
2 1 Pt 1:8–12
3 Lk 1:5–17

**Mass of the Day**
1 Is 49:1–6
2 Acts 13:22–26
3 Lk 1:57–66, 80

**June 29: Peter and Paul Vigil**
1 Acts 3:1–10
2 Gal 1:11–20
3 Jn 21:15–19

**Mass of the Day**
1 Acts 12:1–11
2 2 Tm 4:6–8, 17–18
3 Mt 16:13–19

**Aug. 6: Transfiguration**
1 Dn 7:9–10, 13–14
2 2 Pt 1:16–19
3 (A) Mt 7:1–9
(B) Mk 9:2–10
(C) Lk 9:28b–36

**Aug. 15: Assumption Vigil**
1 1 Chr 15:3–4, 15; 16:1–2
2 1 Cor 15:54–57
3 Lk 11:27–28

**Mass of the Day**
1 Rev 11:19a; 12:1–6a, 10ab
2 1 Cor 15:20–26
3 Lk 1:39–56

**Sept. 14: Triumph of the Cross**
1 Nm 21:4–9
2 Phil 2:6–11
3 Jn 3:13–17

**Nov. 1: All Saints**
1 Rev 7:2–4, 9–14
2 1 Jn 3:1–3
3 Mt 5:1–12a

**Nov. 2: All Souls First Mass**
1 Jb 19:1, 23–27
2 1 Cor 15:51–57
3 Jn 6:37–40

**Second Mass**
1 Wis 3:1–9
2 Phil 3:20–21
3 Jn 11:17–27

**Third Mass**
1 2 Mc 12:43–46
2 Rev 14:13
3 Jn 14:1–6
*(Other Readings may be chosen)*

**Nov. 9: Dedication of St. John Lateran**
1 2 Chr 5:6–10, 13–6:2
2 1 Cor 3:9–13, 16–17
3 Lk 19:1–10
*(Other Readings may be chosen)*

**Dec. 8: Immaculate Conception**
1 Gn 3:9–15, 20
2 Eph 1:3–6, 11–12
3 Lk 1:26–38

# WEEKDAY READINGS

**Advent Season**

**First Week of Advent**
Monday: Is 2:1–5 (Year A: Is 4:2–6); Mt 8:5–11
Tuesday: Is 11:1–10; Lk 10:21–24
Wednesday: Is 25:6–10a; Mt 15:29–37
Thursday: Is 26:1–6; Mt 7:21, 24–27
Friday: Is 29:17–24; Mt 9:27–31
Saturday: Is 30:19–21, 23–26; Mt 9:35–10:1, 6–8

**Second Week of Advent**
Monday: Is 35:1–10; Lk 5:17–26
Tuesday: Is 40:1–11; Mt 18:12–14
Wednesday: Is 40:25–31; Mt 11:28–30
Thursday: Is 41:13–20; Mt 11:11–15
Friday: Is 48:17–19; Mt 11:16–19
Saturday: Sir 48:1–4, 9–11; Mt 17:10–13

**Third Week of Advent**
Monday: Num 24:2–7, 15–17a; Mt 21:23–27
Tuesday: Zep 3:1–2, 9–13; Mt 21:28–32
Wednesday: Is 45:6b–8, 18, 21b–25; Lk 7:18b–23
Thursday: Is 54:1–10; Lk 7:24–30
Friday: Is 56:1–3a, 6–8; Jn 5:33–36
Dec. 17: Gn 49:2, 8–10; Mt 1:1–17
Dec. 18: Jer 23:5–8; Mt 1:18–24
Dec. 19: Jgs 13:2–7, 24–25a; Lk 1:5–25
Dec. 20: Is 7:10–14; Lk 1:26–38
Dec. 21: Sg 2:8–14 or Zep 3:14–18a; Lk 1:39–45
Dec. 22: 1 Sm 1:24–28; Lk 1:46–56
Dec. 23: Mal 3:1–4, 23–24; Lk 1:57–66
Dec. 24: 2 Sm 7:1–5, 8b–11, 16; Lk 1:67–79

**Christmas Season**

**Octave of Christmas**
Second day (St. Stephen): Acts 6:8–10; 7:54–59; Mt 10:17–22
Third day (St. John): 1 Jn 1:1–4; Jn 20:2–8
Fourth day (Holy Innocents): 1 Jn 1:5–2:2; Mt 2:13–18
Fifth day: 1 Jn 2:3–11; Lk 2:22–35
Sixth day: 1 Jn 2:12–17; Lk 2:36–40
Seventh day: 1 Jn 2:18–21; Jn 1:1–18
January 2: 1 Jn 2:22–28; Jn 1:19–28
January 3: 1 Jn 2:29–3:6; Jn 1:29–34
January 4: 1 Jn 3:7–10; Jn 1:35–42
January 5: 1 Jn 3:11–21; Jn 1:43–51
January 6 (if Epiphany not celebrated): 1 Jn 5:5–13; Mk 1:6b–11
Readings may vary slightly depending on when Epiphany is celebrated

**Week After Epiphany**
Monday after Epiphany: 1 Jn 3:22–4:6; Mt 4:12–17, 23–25
Tuesday after Epiphany: 1 Jn 4:7–10; Mk 6:34–44
Wednesday after Epiphany: 1 Jn 4:11–18; Mk 6:45–52
Thursday after Epiphany: 1 Jn 4:19–5:4; Lk 4:14–22a
Friday after Epiphany: 1 Jn 5:5–13; Lk 5:12–16
Saturday after Epiphany: 1 Jn 5:14–21; Jn 3:22–30

**Lenten Season**
Ash Wednesday: Jl 2:12–18; 2 Cor 5:20–6:2; Mt 6:1–6, 16–18
Thursday after Ash Wednesday: Dt 30:15–20; Lk 9:22–25
Friday after Ash Wednesday: Is 58:1–9a; Mt 9:14–15
Saturday after Ash Wednesday: Is 58:9b–14; Lk 5:27–32

**First Week of Lent**
Monday: Lv 19:1–2, 11–18; Mt 25:31–46
Tuesday: Is 55:10–11; Mt 6:7–15
Wednesday: Jon 3:1–10; Lk 11:29–32
Thursday: Est C:12, 14–16, 23–25; Mt 7:7–12
Friday: Ez 18:21–28; Mt 5:20–26
Saturday: Dt 26:16–19; Mt 5:43–48

**Second Week of Lent**
Monday: Dn 9:4b–10; Lk 6:36–38
Tuesday: Is 1:10, 16–20; Mt 23:1–12
Wednesday: Jer 18:18–20; Mt 20:17–28
Thursday: Jer 17:5–10; Lk 16:19–31
Friday: Gn 37:3–4, 12–13a, 17b–28; Mt 21:33–43, 45–46
Saturday: Mi 7:14–15, 18–20; Lk 15:1–3, 11–32

**Third Week of Lent**
Monday: 2 Kgs 5:1–15a; Lk 4:24–30
Tuesday: Dn 3:25, 34–43; Mt 18:21–35

Wednesday: Dt 4:1, 5–9; Mt 5:17–19
Thursday: Jer 7:23–28; Lk 11:14–23
Friday: Hos 14:2–10; Mk 12:28b–34
Saturday: Hos 6:1–6; Lk 18:19–24

**Fourth Week of Lent**
Monday: Is 65:17–21; Jn 4:43–54
Tuesday: Ez 47:1–9, 12; Jn 5:1–3a, 5–16
Wednesday: Is 49:8–15; Jn 5:17–30
Thursday: Ex 32:7–14; Jn 5:31–47
Friday: Wis 2:1a, 12–22; Jn 7:1–2, 10, 25–30
Saturday: Jer 11:18–20; Jn 7:40–53

**Fifth Week of Lent**
Monday: Dn 13:1–9, 15–17, 19–30, 33–62; Jn 8:1–11 (Year C: Jn 8:12–20)
Tuesday: Nm 21:4–9; Jn 8:21–30
Wednesday: Dn 3:14–20, 91–92, 95; Jn 8:31–42
Thursday: Gn 17:3–9; Jn 8:51–59
Friday: Jer 20:10–13; Jn 10:31–42
Saturday: Ez 37:21–28; Jn 11:45–56

**Holy Week**
Monday: Is 42:1–7; Jn 12:1–11
Tuesday: Is 49:1–6; Jn 13:21–33, 36–38
Wednesday: Is 50:4–9a; Mt 26:14–25
Thursday Chrism Mass: Is 61:1–3a, 6a, 8b–9; Rev 1:5–8; Lk 4:16–21

**Easter Season**

**Octave of Easter**
Monday: Acts 2:14, 22–32; Mt 28:8–15
Tuesday: Acts 2:36–41; Jn 20:11–18
Wednesday: Acts 3:1–10; Lk 24:13–35
Thursday: Acts 3:11–26; Lk 24:35–48
Friday: Acts 4:1–12; Jn 21:1–14
Saturday: Acts 4:13–21; Mk 16:9–15

**Second Week of Easter**
Monday: Acts 4:23–31; Jn 3:1–8
Tuesday: Acts 4:32–37; Jn 3:7–15
Wednesday: Acts 5:17–26; Jn 3:16–21
Thursday: Acts 5:27–33; Jn 3:31–36
Friday: Acts 5:34–42; Jn 6:1–15
Saturday: Acts 6:1–7; Jn 6:16–21

**Third Week of Easter**
Monday: Acts 6:8–15; Jn 6:22–29
Tuesday: Acts 7:51–8:1a; Jn 6:30–35
Wednesday: Acts 8:1–8; Jn 6:35–40
Thursday: Acts 8:26–40; Jn 6:44–51
Friday: Acts 9:1–20; Jn 6:52–59
Saturday: Acts 9:31–42; Jn 6:60–69

**Fourth Week of Easter**
Monday: Acts 11:1–18; Jn 10:1–10 (Year A: Jn 10:11–18)
Tuesday: Acts 11:19–26; Jn 10:22–30
Wednesday: Acts 12:24–13:5a; Jn 12:44–50
Thursday: Acts 13:13–25; Jn 13:16–20
Friday: Acts 13:26–33; Jn 14:1–6
Saturday: Acts 13:44–52; Jn 14:7–14

**Fifth Week of Easter**
Monday: Acts 14:5–18; Jn 14:21–26
Tuesday: Acts 14:19–28; Jn 14:27–31a
Wednesday: Acts 15:1–6; Jn 15:1–8
Thursday: Acts 15:7–21; Jn 15:9–11
Friday: Acts 15:22–31; Jn 15:12–17
Saturday: Acts 16:1–10; Jn 15:18–21

**Sixth Week of Easter**
Monday: Acts 16:11–15; Jn 15:26–16:4a
Tuesday: Acts 16:22–34; Jn 16:5–11
Wednesday: Acts 17:15, 22–18:1; Jn 16:12–15
Thursday: Acts 18:1–8; Jn 16:16–20
Friday: Acts 18:9–18; Jn 16:20–23a
Saturday: Acts 18:23–28; Jn 16:23b–28

**Seventh Week of Easter**
Monday: Acts 19:1–8; Jn 16:29–33
Tuesday: Acts 20:17–27; Jn 17:1–11a
Wednesday: Acts 20:28–38; Jn 17:11b–19
Thursday: Acts 22:30; 23:6–11; Jn 17:20–26
Friday: Acts 25:13–21; Jn 21:15–19
Saturday: Acts 28:16–20, 30–31; Jn 21:20–25

**Season of the Year**
*(I is the reading for Year I; II is the reading for Year II; the Gospel is the same each year)*

**Week One**
Monday: I – Heb 1:1–6; II – 1 Sm 1:1–8; Mk 1:14–20
Tuesday: I – Heb 2:5–12; II – 1 Sm 1:9–20; Mk 1:21–28
Wednesday: I – Heb 2:14–18; II – 1 Sm 3:1–10, 19–20; Mk 1:29–39
Thursday: I – Heb 3:7–14; II – 1 Sm 4:1–11; Mk 1:40–45
Friday: I – Heb 4:1–5, 11; II – 1 Sm 8:4–7, 10–22a; Mk 2:1–12
Saturday: I – Heb 4:12–16; II – 1 Sm 9:1–14, 17–19; 10:1a; Mk 2:13–17

**Week Two**
Monday: I – Heb 5:1–10; II – 1 Sm 15:16–23; Mk 2:18–22
Tuesday: I – Heb 6:10–20; II – 1 Sm 16:1–13; Mk 2:23–28
Wednesday: I – Heb 7:1–3, 15–17; II – 1 Sm 17:32–33, 37, 40–51; Mk 3:1–6
Thursday: I – Heb 7:25–8:6; II – 1 Sm 18:6–9; 19:1–7; Mk 3:7–12
Friday: I – Heb 8:6–13; II – 1 Sm 24:3–21; Mk 3:13–19

Saturday: I – Heb 9:2–3, 11–14; II – 2 Sm 1:1–4, 11–12, 19, 23–27; Mk 3:20–21

**Week Three**

Monday: I – Heb 9:15, 24–28; II – 2 Sm 5:1–7, 10; Mk 3:22–30

Tuesday: I – Heb 10:1–10; II – 2 Sm 6:12b–15, 17–19; Mk 3:31–35

Wednesday: I – Heb 10:11–18; II – 2 Sm 7:4–17; Mk 4:1–20

Thursday: I – Heb 10:19–25; II – 2 Sm 7:18–19, 24–29; Mk 4:21–25

Friday: I – Heb 10:32–39; II – 2 Sm 11:1–4a, 5–10a, 13–17; Mk 4:26–34

Saturday: I – Heb 11:1–2, 8–9; II – 2 Sm 12:1–7a, 10–17; Mk 4:35–41

**Week Four**

Monday: I – Heb 11:32–40; II – 2 Sm 15:13–14, 30; 16:5–13a; Mk 5:1–20

Tuesday: I – Heb 12:1–4; II 2 Sm 18:9–10, 14b, 24–25a, 30–19:3; Mk 5:21–43

Wednesday: I – Heb 12:4–7, 11–15; II – 2 Sm 24:2, 9–17; Mk 6:1–6

Thursday: I – Heb 12:18–19, 21–24; II – 1 Kgs 2:1–4, 10–12; Mk 6:7–13

Friday: I – Heb 13:1–8; II – Sir 47:2–11; Mk 6:14–29

Saturday: 1 – Heb 13:15–17, 20–21; II – 1 Kgs 3:4–13; Mk 6:30–34

**Week Five**

Monday: I – Gn 1:1–19; II – 1 Kgs 8:1–7, 9–13; Mk 6:53–56

Tuesday: I – Gn 1:20–2:4a; II – 1 Kgs 8:22–23, 27–30; Mk 7:1–13

Wednesday: I – Gn 2:4b–9, 15–17; II – 1 Kgs 10:1–10; Mk 7:14–23

Thursday: I – Gn 2:18–25; II – 1 Kgs 11:4–13; Mk 7:24–30

Friday: I – Gn 3:1–8; II – 1 Kgs 11:29–32; 12:19; Mk 7:31–37

Saturday: I – Gn 3:9–24; II – 1 Kgs 12:26–32; 13:33–34; Mk 8:1–10

**Week Six**

Monday: I – Gn 4:1–15, 25; II – Jas 1:1–11; Mk 8:11–13

Tuesday: I – Gn 6:5–8; 7:1–5, 10; II – Jas 1:12–18; Mk 8:14–21

Wednesday: I – Gn 8:6–13, 20–22; II – Jas 1:19–27; Mk 8:22–26

Thursday: I – Gn 9:1–13; II – Jas 2:1–9; Mk 8:27–33

Friday: I – Gn 11:1–9; II – Jas 2:14–24, 26; Mk 8:34–9:1

Saturday: I – Heb 11:1–7; II – Jas 3:1–10; Mk 9:2–13

**Week Seven**

Monday: I – Sir 1:1–10; II – Jas 3:13–18; Mk 9:14–29

Tuesday: I – Sir 2:1–11; II – Jas 4:1–10; Mk 9:30–37

Wednesday: I – Sir 4:11–19; II – Jas 4:13–17; Mk 9:38–40

Thursday: I – Sir 5:1–8; II – Jas 5:1–6; Mk 9:41–50

Friday: I – Sir 6:5–17; II – Jas 5:9–12; Mk 10:1–12

Saturday: I – Sir 17:1–15; II – Jas 5:13–20; Mk 10:13–16

**Week Eight**

Monday: I – Sir 17:19–27; II – 1 Pt 1:3–9; Mk 10:17–27

Tuesday: I – Sir 35:1–12; II – 1 Pt 1:10–16; Mk 10:28–31

Wednesday: I – Sir 36:1, 5–6, 10–17; II – 1 Pt 1:18–25; Mk 10:32–45

Thursday: I – Sir 42:15–25; II – 1 Pt 2:2–5, 9–12; Mk 10:46–52

Friday: I – Sir 44:1, 9–13; II – 1 Pt 4:7–13; Mk 11:11–26

Saturday: I – Sir 51:12b–20; II – Jude 17:20b–25; Mk 11:27–33

**Week Nine**

Monday: I – Tb 1:1a–2; 2:1–9; II – 2 Pt 1:2–7; Mk 12:1–12

Tuesday: I – Tb 2:9–14; II – 2 Pt 3:12–15a, 17–18; Mk 12:13–17

Wednesday: I – Tb 3:1–11, 16; II – 2 Tm 1:1–3, 6–12; Mk 12:18–27

Thursday: I – Tb 6:10–11; 7:1, 9–17; 8:4–7; II – 2 Tm 2:8–15; Mk 12:28b–34

Friday: I – Tb 11:5–17; II – 2 Tm 3:10–17; Mk 12:35–37

Saturday: I – Tb 12:1, 5–15, 20; II – 2 Tm 4:1–8; Mk 12:38–44

**Week Ten**

Monday: I – 2 Cor 1:1–7; II – 1 Kgs 17:1–6; Mt 5:1–12

Tuesday: I – 2 Cor 1:18–22; II – 1 Kgs 17:7–16; Mt 5:13–16

Wednesday: I – 2 Cor 3:4–11; II – 1 Kgs 18:20–39; Mt 5:17–19

Thursday: I – 2 Cor 3:15–4:1, 3–6; II – 1 Kgs 18:41–46; Mt 5:20–26

Friday: I – 2 Cor 4:7–15; II – 1 Kgs 19:9a, 11–16; Mt 5:27–32

Saturday: I – 2 Cor 5:14–21; II – 1 Kgs 19:19–21; Mt 5:33–37

**Week Eleven**

Monday: I – 2 Cor 6:1–10; II – 1 Kgs 21:1–16; Mt 5:38–42

Tuesday: I – 2 Cor 8:1–9; II – 1 Kgs 21:17–29; Mt 5:43–48

Wednesday: I – 2 Cor 9:6–11; II – 1 Kgs 2:1, 6–14; Mt 6:1–6, 16–18

Thursday: I – 2 Cor 11:1–11; II – Sir 48:1–15; Mt 6:7–15

Friday: I – 2 Cor 11:18, 21b–30; II – 2 Kgs 11:1–4, 9–18, 20; Mt 6:19–23

Saturday: I – 2 Cor 12:1–10; II – 2 Chr 24:17–25; Mt 6:24–34

**Week Twelve**

Monday: I – Gn 12:1–9; II – 2 Kgs 17:5–8, 13–15a, 18; Mt 7:1–5

Tuesday: I – Gn 13:2, 5–8; II – 2 Kgs 19:9b–11, 14–21, 31–35a, 36; Mt 7:6, 12–14

Wednesday: I – Gn 15:1–12, 17–18; II – 2 Kgs 22:8–13; 23:1–3; Mt 7:15–20

Thursday: I – Gn 16:1–12, 15–16; II – 2 Kgs 24:8–17; Mt 7:21–29

Friday: I – Gn 17:1, 9–10, 15–22; II – 2 Kgs 25:1–12; Mt 8:1–4

Saturday: I – Gn 18:1–15; II – Lam 2:2, 10–14, 18–19; Mt 8:5–17

**Week Thirteen**

Monday: I – Gn 18:16–33; II – Am 2:6–10, 13–16; Mt 8:18–22

Tuesday: I – Gn 19:15–29; II – Am 3:1–8; 4:11–12; Mt 8:23–27

Wednesday: I – Gn 21:5, 8–20; II – Am 5:14–15, 21–24; Mt 8:28–34

Thursday: I – Gn 22:1–19; II – Am 7:10–17; Mt 9:1–8

Friday: I – Gn 23:1–4, 19; 24:1–8, 62–67; II – Am 8:4–6, 9–12; Mt 9:9–13

Saturday: I – Gn 27:1–5, 15–29; II – Am 9:11–15; Mt 9:14–17

**Week Fourteen**

Monday: I – Gn 28:10–22a; II – Hos 2:16, 17b–18, 21–22; Mt 9:18–26

Tuesday: I – Gn 32:22–33; II – Hos 8:4–7, 11–13; Mt 9:32–38

Wednesday: I – Gn 41:51–57; 42:5–7a, 17–24a; II – Hos 10:1–3, 7–8, 12; Mt 10:1–7

Thursday: I – Gn 44:18–21, 23b–29; 45:1–5; II – Hos 11:1, 3–4, 8c–9; Mt 10:7–15

Friday: I – Gn 46:1–7, 28–30; II – Hos 14:2–10; Mt 10:16–23

Saturday: I – Gn 49:29–33; 50:15–24; II – Is 6:1–8; Mt 10:24–33

**Week Fifteen**

Monday: I – Ex 1:8–14, 22; II – Is 1:10–17; Mt 10:34–11:1

Tuesday: I – Ex 2:1–15a; II – Is 7:1–9; Mt 11:20–24

Wednesday: I – Ex 3:1–6, 9–12; II – Is 10:5–7, 13–16; Mt 11:25–27

Thursday: I – Ex 3:13–20; II – Is 26:7–9, 12, 16–19; Mt 11:28–30

Friday: I – Ex 11:10–12, 14; II – Is 38:1–6, 21–22, 7–8; Mt 12:1–8

Saturday: I – Ex 12:37–42; II – Mi 2:1–5; Mt 12:14–21

**Week Sixteen**

Monday: I – Ex 14:5–18; II – Mi 6:1–4, 6–8; Mt 12:38–42

Tuesday: I – Ex 14:21–15:1; II – Mi 7:14–15, 18–20; Mt 12:46–50

Wednesday: I – Ex 16:1–5, 9–15; II – Jer 1:1, 4–10; Mt 13:1–9

Thursday: I – Ex 19:1–2, 9–11, 16–20b; II – Jer 2:1–3, 7–8, 12–13; Mt 13:10–17

Friday: I – Ex 20:1–17; II – Jer 3:14–17; Mt 13:18–23

Saturday: I – Ex 24:3–8; II – Jer 7:1–11; Mt 13:24–30

**Week Seventeen**

Monday: I – Ex 32:15–24, 30–34; II – Jer 13:1–11; Mt 13:31–35

Tuesday: I – Ex 33:7–11; 34:5b–9, 28; II – Jer 14:17–22; Mt 13:36–43

Wednesday: I – Ex 34:29–34; II – Jer 15:10, 16–21; Mt 13:44–46

Thursday: I – Ex 40:16–21, 34–38; II – Jer 18:1–6; Mt 13:47–53

Friday: I – Lv 23:1, 4–11, 15–16, 27, 34b–37; II – Jer 26:1–9; Mt 13:54–58

Saturday: I – Lv 25:1, 8–17; II – Jer 26:11–16, 24; Mt 14:1–12

**Week Eighteen**

Monday: I – Nm 11:4b–15; II – Jer 28:1–17; Mt 14:13–21 or Mt 14:22–36

Tuesday: I – Nm 12:1–13; II – Jer 30:1–2, 12–15, 18–22; Mt 14:22–36 or Mt 15:1–2, 10–14

Wednesday: I – Nm 13:1–2a, 25–14:1, 26–29, 34–35; II – Jer 31:1–7; Mt 15:21–28

Thursday: I – Nm 20:1–13; II – Jer 31:31–34; Mt 16:13–23

Friday: I – Dt 4:32–40; II – Na 2:1, 3; 3:1–3, 6–7; Mt 16:24–28

Saturday: I – Dt 6:4–13; II – Hb 1:12–2:4; Mt 17:14–20

**Week Nineteen**

Monday: I – Dt 10:12–22; II – Ez 1:2–5, 24–28c; Mt 17:22–27

Tuesday: I – Dt 31:1–8; II – Ez 2:8–3:4; Mt 18:1–5, 10, 12–14

Wednesday: I – Dt 34:1–12; II – Ez 9:1–7; 10:18–22; Mt 18:15–20

Thursday: I – Jos 3:7–10a, 11, 13–17; II – Ez 12:1–12; Mt 18:21–19:1

Friday: I – Jos 24:1–13; II – Ez 16:1–15, 60, 63; Mt 19:3–12

Saturday: I – Jos 24:14–29; II – Ez 18:1–10, 13b, 30–32; Mt 19:13–15

**Week Twenty**

Monday: I – Jgs 2:11–19; II – Ez 24:15–24; Mt 19:16–22

Tuesday: I – Jgs 6:11–24a; II – Ez 28:1–10; Mt 19:23–30

Wednesday: I – Jgs 9:6–15; II – Ez 34:1–11; Mt 20:1–16a

Thursday: I – Jgs 11:29–39a; II – Ez 36:23–28; Mt 22:1–14

Friday: I – Ru 1:1, 3–6, 14b–16, 22; II – Ez 37:1–14; Mt 22:34–40

Saturday: I – Ru 2:1–3, 8–11; 4:13–17; II – Ez 43:1–7a; Mt 23:1–12

**Week Twenty-one**

Monday: I – 1 Thes 1:2b–5, 8b–10; II – 2 Thes 1:1–5, 11b–12; Mt 23:13–22

Tuesday: I – 1 Thes 2:1–8; II – 2 Thes 2:1–3a, 13–17; Mt 23:23–26

Wednesday: I – 1 Thes 2:9–13; II – 2 Thes 3:6–10, 16–18; Mt 23:27–32

Thursday: I – 1 Thes 3:7–13; II – 1 Cor 1:1–9; Mt 24:42–51

Friday: I – 1 Thes 4:1–8; II – 1 Cor 1:17–25; Mt 25:1–13

Saturday: I – 1 Thes 4:9–12; II – 1 Cor 1:26–31; Mt 25:14–30

**Week Twenty-two**
Monday: I – 1 Thes 4:13–18; II – 1 Cor 2:1–5; Lk 4:16–30
Tuesday: I – 1 Thes 5:1–6, 9–11; II – 1 Cor 2:10b–16; Lk 4:31–37
Wednesday: I – Col 1:1–8; II – 1 Cor 3:1–9; Lk 4:38–44
Thursday: I – Col 1:9–14; II – 1 Cor 3:18–23; Lk 5:1–11
Friday: I – Col 1:15–20; II – 1 Cor 4:1–5; Lk 5:33–39
Saturday: I – Col 1:21–23; II – 1 Cor 4:9–15; Lk 6:1–5

**Week Twenty-three**
Monday: I – Col 1:24–2:3; II – 1 Cor 5:1–8; Lk 6:6–11
Tuesday: I – Col 2:6–15; II – 1 Cor 6:1–11; Lk 6:12–19
Wednesday: I – Col 3:1–11; II – 1 Cor 7:25–31; Lk 6:20–26
Thursday: I – Col 3:12–17; II – 1 Cor 8:1b–7, 11–13; Lk 6:27–38
Friday: I – 1 Tm 1:1–2, 12–14; II – 1 Cor 9:16–19, 22b–27; Lk 6:39–42
Saturday: I – 1 Tm 1:15–17; II – 1 Cor 10:14–22a; Lk 6:43–49

**Week Twenty-four**
Monday: I – 1 Tm 2:1–8; II – 1 Cor 11:17–26, 33; Lk 7:1–10
Tuesday: I – 1 Tm 3:1–13; II – 1 Cor 12:12–14, 27–31a; Lk 7:11–17
Wednesday: I – 1 Tm 3:14–16; II – 1 Cor 12:31–13:13; Lk 7:31–35
Thursday: I – 1 Tm 4:12–16; II – 1 Cor 15:1–11; Lk 7:36–50
Friday: I – 1 Tm 6:2c–12; II – 1 Cor 15:12–20; Lk 8:1–3
Saturday: I – 1 Tm 6:13–16; II – 1 Cor 15:36–37, 42–49; Lk 8:4–15

**Week Twenty-five**
Monday: I – Ezr 1:1–6; II – Prv 3:27–34; Lk 8:16–18
Tuesday: I – Ezr 6:7–8, 12b, 14–20; II – Prv 21:1–6, 10–13; Lk 8:19–21
Wednesday: I – Ezr 9:5–9; II – Prv 30:5–9; Lk 9:1–6
Thursday: I – Hg 1:1–8; II – Eccl 1:2–11; Lk 9:7–9
Friday: I – Hg 1:15b–2:9; II – Eccl 3:1–11; Lk 9:18–22
Saturday: I – Zec 2:5–9a, 14–15a; II – Eccl 11:9–12:8; Lk 9:43b–45

**Week Twenty-six**
Monday: I – Zec 8:1–8; II – Jb 1:6–22; Lk 9:46–50
Tuesday: I – Zec 8:20–23; II – Jb 3:1–3, 11–17, 20–23; Lk 9:51–56
Wednesday: I – Neh 2:1–8; II – Jb 9:1–12, 14–16; Lk 9:57–62
Thursday: I – Neh 8:1–4a, 5–6, 7b–12; II – Jb 19:12–27; Lk 10:1–12
Friday: I – Bar 1:15–22; II – Jb 38:1, 12–21; 40:3–5; Lk 10:13–16
Saturday: I – Bar 4:5–12, 27–29; II – Jb 42:1–3, 5–6, 12–17; Lk 10:17–24

**Week Twenty-seven**
Monday: I – Jon 1:1–2:1, 11; II – Gal 1:6–12; Lk 10:25–37
Tuesday: I – Jon 3:1–10; II – Gal 1:13–24; Lk 10:38–42
Wednesday: I – Jon 4:1–11; II – Gal 2:1–2, 7–14; Lk 11:1–4
Thursday: I – Mal 3:13–20a; II – Gal 3:1–5; Lk 11:5–13
Friday: I – Jl 1:13–15; 2:1–2; II – Gal 3:7–14; Lk 11:15–26
Saturday: I – Jl 4:12–21; II – Gal 3:22–29; Lk 11:27–28

**Week Twenty-eight**
Monday: I – Rom 1:1–7; II – Gal 4:22–24, 26–27; Lk 11:29–32
Tuesday: I – Rom 1:16–25; II – Gal 5:1–6; Lk 11:37–41
Wednesday: I – Rom 2:1–11; II – Gal 5:18–25; Lk 11:42–46
Thursday: I – Rom 3:21–29; II – Eph 1:3–10; Lk 11:47–54
Friday: I – Rom 4:1–8; II – Eph 1:11–14; Lk 12:1–7
Saturday: I – Rom 4:13, 16–18; II – Eph 1:15–23; Lk 12:8–12

**Week Twenty-nine**
Monday: I – Rom 4:20–25; II – Eph 2:1–10; Lk 12:13–21
Tuesday: I – Rom 5:12, 15b, 17–19, 20b–21; II – Eph 2:12–22; Lk 12:35, 38
Wednesday: I – Rom 6:12–18; II – Eph 3:2–12; Lk 12:39–48
Thursday: I – Rom 6:19–23; II – Eph 3:14–21; Lk 12:49–53
Friday: I – Rom 7:18–25a; II – Eph 4:1–6; Lk 12:54–59
Saturday: I – Rom 8:1–11; II – Eph 4:7–16; Lk 13:1–9

**Week Thirty**
Monday: I – Rom 8:12–17; II – Eph 4:32–5:8; Lk 13:10–17
Tuesday: I – Rom 8:18–25; II – Eph 5:21–33; Lk 13:18–21
Wednesday: I – Rom 8:26–30; II – Eph 6:1–9; Lk 13:22–30
Thursday: I – Rom 3:31b–39; II – Eph 6:10–20; Lk 13:31–35
Friday: I – Rom 9:1–5; II – Phil 1:1–11; Lk 14:1–6
Saturday: I – Rom 11:1–2a, 11–12, 25–29; II – Phil 1:18b–26; Lk 14:1, 7–11

**Week Thirty-one**
Monday: I – Rom 11:29–36; II – Phil 2:1–4; Lk 14:12–14
Tuesday: I – Rom 12:5–16a; II – Phil 2:5–11; Lk 14:15–24
Wednesday: I – Rom 13:8–10; II – Phil 2:12–18; Lk 14:25–33
Thursday: I – Rom 14:7–12; II – Phil 3:3–8a; Lk 15:1–10
Friday: I – Rom 15:14–21; II – Phil 3:17–4:1; Lk 16:1–8
Saturday: I – Rom 16:3–9, 16, 22–27; II – Phil 4:10–19; Lk 16:9–15

**Week Thirty-two**
Monday: I – Wis 1:1–7; II – Ti 1:1–9; Lk 17:1–6
Tuesday: I – Wis 2:23–3:9; II – Ti 2:1–8, 11–14; Lk 17:7–10
Wednesday: I – Wis 6:1–11; II – Ti 3:1–7; Lk 17:11–19

Thursday: I – Wis 7:22–8:1; II – Phlm 7–20; Lk 17:20–25
Friday: I – Wis 13:1–9; II – 2 Jn 4–9; Lk 17:26–37
Saturday: I – Wis 18:14–16; 19:6–9; II – 3 Jn 5–8; Lk 18:1–8

**Week Thirty-three**
Monday: I – 1 Mc 1:10–15, 41–43, 54, 57, 62, 64; II – Rev 1:1–4; 2:1–5a; Lk 18:35–43
Tuesday: I – 2 Mc 6:18–31; II – Rev 3:1–6, 14–22; Lk 19:1–10
Wednesday: I – 2 Mc 7:1, 20–31; II – Rev 4:1–11; Lk 19:11–28
Thursday: I – 1 Mc 2:15–29; II – Rev 5:1–10; Lk 19:41–44
Friday: I – 1 Mc 4:36–37, 52–59; II – Rev 10:8–11; Lk 19:45–48
Saturday: I – 1 Mc 6:1–13; II – Rev 11:4–12; Lk 20:27–40

**Week Thirty-four**
Monday: I – Dn 1:1–6, 8–20; II – Rev 14:1–3, 4b–5; Lk 21:1–4
Tuesday: I – Dn 2:31–45; II – Rev 14:14–19; Lk 21:5–11
Wednesday: I – Dn 5:1–6, 13–14, 16–17, 23–28; II – Rev 15:1–4; Lk 21:12–19
Thursday: I – Dn 6:11–28; II – Rev 18:1–2, 21–23; 19:1–3, 9a; Lk 21:20–28
Friday: I – Dn 7:2–14; II – Rev 20:1–4; 20:11–21:2; Lk 21:29–33
Saturday: I – Dn 7:15–27; II – Rev 22:1–7; Lk 21:34–36

# CHART OF OLD TESTAMENT CANONS

## Jewish Canon

*Torah* (LAW)
Genesis
Exodus
Leviticus
Numbers
Deuteronomy

*Nevi'im* (PROPHETS)

FORMER PROPHETS
Joshua
Judges
Samuel (1 & 2)
Kings (1 & 2)

LATTER PROPHETS
Isaiah
Jeremiah
Ezekiel
The Twelve
- Hosea
- Joel
- Amos
- Obadiah
- Jonah
- Micah
- Nahum
- Habakkuk
- Zephaniah
- Haggai
- Zechariah
- Malachi

*Ketubim* (WRITINGS)
Psalms
Proverbs
Job

## Protestant Canon

PENTATEUCH
Genesis
Exodus
Leviticus
Numbers
Deuteronomy

HISTORIES
Joshua
Judges
Ruth
1 & 2 Samuel
1 & 2 Kings
1 & 2 Chronicles
Ezra
Nehemiah
Esther

POETICAL/WISDOM BOOKS
Job
Psalms
Proverbs
Ecclesiastes
Song of Solomon

PROPHETS
Isaiah
Jeremiah
Lamentations
Ezekiel
Daniel
Hosea
Joel
Amos
Obadiah
Jonah
Micah
Nahum

## Roman Catholic/ Orthodox Canon

PENTATEUCH
Genesis
Exodus
Leviticus
Numbers
Deuteronomy

HISTORIES
Joshua
Judges
Ruth
1 & 2 Samuel
1 & 2 Kings
1 & 2 Chronicles
Ezra
Nehemiah
Tobit
Judith
Esther
1 & 2 Maccabees

POETICAL/WISDOM BOOKS
Job
Psalms
Proverbs
Ecclesiastes
Song of Solomon
Wisdom of Solomon
Ben Sira

PROPHETS
Isaiah
Jeremiah
Lamentations
Baruch
Ezekiel
Daniel
Hosea

*Chart of Old Testament Canons*

| Jewish Canon | Protestant Canon | Roman Catholic/ Orthodox Canon |
|---|---|---|
| (Five Scrolls): | Habakkuk | Joel |
| Song of Solomon | Zephaniah | Amos |
| Ruth | Haggai | Obadiah |
| Lamentations | Zechariah | Jonah |
| Ecclesiastes | Malachi | Micah |
| Esther | | Nahum |
| Daniel | THE APOCRYPHA | Habakkuk |
| Ezra-Nehemiah | 1 & 2 Esdras | Zephaniah |
| Chronicles (1 & 2) | Tobit | Haggai |
| There is no Apocrypha in the Hebrew Bible | Judith | Zechariah |
| | Esther (with additions) | Malachi |
| | Wisdom of Solomon | Orthodox Canons generally include |
| | Ecclesiasticus (Ben Sira) | 1 & 2 Esdras |
| | Baruch | Prayer of Manasseh |
| | Letter of Jeremiah (Baruch ch 6) | Psalm 151 |
| | Prayer of Azariah and Song of Three | 3 Maccabees |
| | Daniel and Susanna | 4 Maccabees (as an Appendix) |
| | Daniel, Bel, & Snake | |
| | Prayer of Manasseh | |
| | 1 & 2 Maccabees | |

## TIMELINE OF BIBLICAL TIMES

# TIMELINE OF BIBLICAL TIMES

| DATE | PERIOD | EGYPT |
|---|---|---|
| Ca. 3300–2000 B.C. | EARLY BRONZE AGE | |
| 3300–3100 | Early Bronze I | Earliest forms of writing |
| 3100–2700 | Early Bronze II | Political unification; Early Dynastic period |
| 2700–2300 | Early Bronze III | Old Kingdom; Dynasties 3–5 |
| 2300–2000 | Early Bronze IV | First Intermediate Period |
| Ca. 2000–1550 B.C. | MIDDLE BRONZE AGE | |
| 2000–1650 | Middle Bronze I–II | Middle Kingdom; Dynasties 11–12 |
| 1650–1550 | Middle Bronze III | Second Intermediate/ Hyksos Period |
| Ca. 1550–1200 B.C. | LATE BRONZE AGE | New Kingdom; Dynasties 18–19: Thutmose III (1479–1425), Akenhaten (1352–1336), Seti I (1294–1279), Rameses II (1279–1213), Merneptah (1213–1203); Sea Peoples (groups including Philistines) invasions begin |
| Ca. 1200–586 B.C. | IRON AGE | |
| Ca. 1200–1025 | Iron I | Rameses III (1184–1153) |
| Ca. 1025–586 | Iron II | |
| Ca. 1025–928 | Iron IIA | |
| Ca. 928–722 | Iron IIB | Shishak I invades Palestine (925) |

| SYRIA-PALESTINE | MESOPOTAMIA, ASIA MINOR |
|---|---|
| | Earliest forms of writing;<br>Full urbanization; Sumerian culture develops |
| In Egyptian sphere | High point of Sumerian culture |
| Flourishing city-states | Sargon of Akkad; Naram-Sin of Akkad;<br>Gudea of Lagash |
| Decline/abandonment of city-states | Third Dynasty of Ur |
| Revival of urbanism; Invention of alphabet | Amorite kingdoms: Shamshi-Adad of Assyria (ca. 1813–1781); Hammurapi of Babylon (ca. 1792–1750); Rise of Hittites |
| In Egyptian sphere; Rise of Mitanni in north;<br>Ugarit flourishes; | |
| Exodus of the Hebrews from Egypt; | Hittites challenge Egypt for control of Syria; |
| Collapse of city-states | Hittite empire collapses; Trojan War |
| Israel emerges in Canaan; Philistines settle on SW coast; Small city-states develop in Phoenicia, Syria, Transjordan | Resurgence of Assyria:<br>Tiglath-pileser I (1114–1076) |
| United Monarchy in Israel: Saul (1025–1005);<br>David (1005–965); Solomon (968–928) | |
| Divided Monarchy:<br>JUDAH:<br>Rehoboam (928–911)<br>ISRAEL:<br>Jeroboam I (928–907)<br>Omri (882–871); Capital at Samaria | Rise of Neo-Assyrian Empire<br>Shalmaneser III (858–824);<br>Battle of Qarqar (853) |

| DATE | PERIOD | EGYPT |
|---|---|---|
| Ca. 722–586 | Iron IIC | Egypt conquered by Assyria (671)<br>Psammetichus I (664–610)<br><br>Neco II (610–595) |
| Ca. 586–539 | NEO-BABYLONIAN | |
| | | **GREECE AND ROME** |
| 539–332 | PERSIAN | Greeks repel Persian invasions<br><br>Peloponnesian War (431–404) |
| 332–63 | HELLENISTIC | Alexander the Great (336–323); Defeats Persians at Issus (332); Occupies the Levant and Egypt<br><br>Rome gains control over Greece (ca. 188–146); |

| SYRIA-PALESTINE | | MESOPOTAMIA, ASIA MINOR |
|---|---|---|
| | Ahab (873–852) | |
| Jehoshaphat (867–846) | Prophet Elijah (mid-ninth century) | |
| | Prophet Elisha (mid- to late ninth century) | |
| | Jehu (842–814) | |
| Athaliah (842–836) | Jehoash (800–788) | |
| Jehoash (836–798) | Jeroboam II (788–747) | Adad-nirari III (811–783) |
| | Prophet Amos (mid-eighth century) | |
| | Prophet Hosea (mid-eighth century) | Tiglath-pileser III (745–727); Assyrian conquest of the Levant |
| | Hoshea (732–722) | |
| Ahaz (743/735–727/715) | | Shalmaneser V (727–722) |
| | | Samaria captured (722) |

| SYRIA-PALESTINE | MESOPOTAMIA, ASIA MINOR |
|---|---|
| JUDAH: | |
| Prophet Isaiah (late eighth to early seventh centuries) | Sargon II (722–705) |
| Prophet Micah (late eighth century) | Sennacherib (705–681); Attack on Judah and seige of Jerusalem (701) |
| Hezekiah (727/715–698/687) | |
| Manasseh (698/687–642) | Esar-haddon (681–669) |
| Josiah (639–609) | Ashurbanipal (669–627) |
| Prophet Zephaniah (late seventh century) | |
| Prophet Jeremiah (late seventh to early sixth centuries) | Rise of Babylon |
| Jehoahaz (609) | Assyrian capital of Nineveh captured (612) |
| Jehoiakim (608–598) | |
| Jehoiachin (597) | Nebuchadrezzar II (604–562) of Babylon |
| Prophet Ezekiel (early sixth century) | |
| Zedekiah (597–586); Capture of Jerusalem (586) | |
| | Nabonidus (556–539) |

| EASTERN MEDITERRANEAN | |
|---|---|
| | Cyrus II (the Great) (559–530); Capture of Babylon |
| Some exiles return from Babylon (538) | Cambyses (530–522); Capture of Egypt (525) |
| Second Temple built (520–515) | Darius I (522–486) |
| Prophet Haggai (520); Prophet Zechariah (520–518) | Xerxes I (486–465) |
| Nehemiah governor of Judah (ca. 445–430) | Artaxerxes I (465–424) |
| Mission of Ezra the scribe (mid-fifth [or early fourth] century) | Artaxerxes II (405–359) |
| Seleucus I (312/311–281) controls Syria and Mesopotamia | |
| Ptolemy I (323–282) controls Egypt, Palestine, Phoenicia | |
| Antiochus III (223–187) gains control of southern Syria, Phoenicia, and Judea from Ptolemy IV (202–198) | |
| Ben Sira (Sirach) (early second century) | |

| DATE | PERIOD | GREECE AND ROME |
|---|---|---|
| | | Sack of Carthage and Corinth (146) |
| 63 B.C.–330 A.D. | ROMAN | Julius Caesar named dictator (49); assassinated (44)<br>Octavian (Augustus) defeats Antony at Actium (31); (Emperor 27 B.C.–14 A.D.)<br>Tiberius (14–37 CE)<br>Gaius (Caligula) (37–41)<br>Claudius (41–54)<br>Nero (54–68)<br>Vespasian (69–79)<br>Titus (79–81)<br>Domitian (81–96)<br>Nerva (96–98)<br>Trajan (98–117)<br>Hadrian (117–138) |

| EASTERN MEDITERRANEAN | MESOPOTAMIA, ASIA MINOR |
|---|---|
| Antiochus IV Epiphanes (175–164)<br>Revolt of the Maccabees (167–164)<br><br>HASMONEAN RULE OF JUDEA (165–37):<br>John Hyrcanus (135–104); Alexander Janneus (103–76);<br>Salome Alexandra (76–67) | |
| Pompey conquers the Levant (66–62); Enters Jerusalem (63)<br>Herod the Great king of Judea (37–4); Rebuilds Second Temple<br>(Herod) Antipas (4 B.C.–39 A.D.)<br>Life of Jesus of Nazareth (ca. 4 B.C.–30 A.D.)<br>Pontius Pilate governor of Judea (26–36)<br>(Herod) Agrippa I (39–44)<br>Missionary activity of Paul (mid-first century)<br>(Herod) Agrippa II (53–93)<br>First Jewish Revolt in Judea against Rome (66–73); Jerusalem is captured (70)<br><br>Jewish revolts in Egypt, Libya, Cyprus (115–118)<br>Second Jewish Revolt in Judea against Rome (132–135) | |

# MEASURES AND WEIGHTS

The modern equivalents for biblical measures and weights are presented in the following tables.

## Hebrew Measures of Capacity: Liquid Measures

| HEBREW | NAB | EQUIVALENCE | U.S. MEASURES | METRIC UNITS |
|---|---|---|---|---|
| *kor* | kor | 10 baths | 60.738 gallons | 230 liters |
| *bat* | bath | 6 hins | 6.073 gallons | 23 liters |
| *hin* | hin | 3 kabs | 1.012 gallons | 3.829 liters |
| *qab* | kab | 4 logs | 1.4349 quarts | 1.276 liters |
| *log* | log | | .674 pint | .32 liter |

## Hebrew Measures of Capacity: Dry Measures

| HEBREW | NAB | EQUIVALENCE | U.S. MEASURES | METRIC UNITS |
|---|---|---|---|---|
| *homer* | homer | 2 lethechs | 6.524 bushels | 229.7 liters |
| *kor* | measure, cor | 2 lethechs | 6.524 bushels | 229.7 liters |
| *letek* | lethech, measure | 5 ephahs | 3.262 bushels | 114.8 liters |
| *ʾepah* | ephah, measure | 3 seahs | 20.878 quarts | 22.9 liters |
| *tseʾah* | measure | 3.33 omers | 6.959 quarts | 7.7 liters |
| *ʿomer* | omer | 1.8 kabs | 2.087 quarts | 2.3 liters |
| *ʿissaron* | tenth part (of ephah) | | | |
| *qab* | kab | | 1.159 quarts | 1.3 liters |

## Measures of Capacity in the New Testament

| GREEK | NAB | EQUIVALENCE | U.S. MEASURES | METRIC UNITS |
|---|---|---|---|---|
| *batos* | measure | (Hebrew) *bat* | 6.073 gallons | 23 liters |
| *koros* | kor | (Hebrew) *kor* | 60.738 gallons or 6.524 bushels | 230 liters |
| *saton* | measure | (Hebrew) *tseʾah* | 6.959 dry quarts | 7.71 liters |
| *metretes* | measure | | 10.3 gallons | 39 liters |
| *choinix* | ration | | .98 dry quart | 1.079 liters |
| *modios* | bushel | (Latin) modius | 7.68 dry quarts | 8.458 liters |

## Hebrew Measures of Length

| HEBREW | NAB | EQUIVALENCE | U.S. MEASURES | METRIC UNITS |
|---|---|---|---|---|
| *ʾammaḥ* | cubit | 2 spans | 17.49 inches | .443 meter |
| *zeret* | span | 3 handbreadths | 8.745 inches | .221 meter |
| *topaḥ, tepaḥ* | handbreadth | 4 fingers | 2.915 inches | .074 meter |
| *ʾetsbaʿ* | finger | | .728 inch | .019 meter |

The cubit described in Ezekiel 40:5; 43:13 is equal to seven (not six) handbreadths, namely 20.405 inches.

## Measures of Length in the New Testament

| GREEK | NAB | U.S. MEASURES | METRIC UNITS |
|---|---|---|---|
| *pechus* | cubit | about 1.5 feet | .456 meter |
| *orguia* | fathom | about 72.44 inches | 1.839 meters |
| *stadion* | stade | about 606 feet | 184.7 meters |
| *milion* | mile | about 4,854 feet | 1.482 kilometers |

## Hebrew Weights

| HEBREW | NAB | EQUIVALENCE | U.S. UNITS | METRIC UNITS |
|---|---|---|---|---|
| *kikkar* | talent | 60 minas | 75.558 pounds | 34.3 kilograms |
| *maneh* | mina | 50 shekels | 20.148 ounces | 571.2 grams |
| *sheqel* | shekel | 2 bekas | 176.29 grains | 11.42 grams |
| *beqaʿ* | bekah, half a shekel | 10 gerahs | 88.14 grains | 5.71 grams |
| *gerah* | gerah | | 8.81 grains | .57 gram |

The practice of weighing unmarked ingots of metal used in commercial transactions prior to the invention of money explains that the names of the units of weight were used later as indications of value, and as names for monetary standards. There is, however, no direct relation between the shekel-weight and the weight of a shekel piece.

## Weights in the New Testament

| GREEK | NAB | EQUIVALENCE | U.S. UNITS | METRIC UNITS |
|---|---|---|---|---|
| *talenton* | talent | (Hebrew) talent | 75.558 pounds | 34.3 kilograms |
| *mna* | gold coin | (Hebrew) mina | 20.148 ounces | 571.2 grams |
| *litra* | pound | (Latin) libra | .719 pound | 326.4 grams |

# GLOSSARY

## A

**Abba** (Aram. "father"), the word Jesus (Mk 14:36 and many other places) and, following him, the early church (Rom 8:15) used to address God.

**Abaddon** (Heb. "place of destruction"), the realm of the dead (Jb 26:6; Prv 15:11; Ps 88:10–12; Rev 9:11).

**accession** the act of taking one's place as a ruler.

**acrostic** a literary device in which the first letter of each line of poetry occurs according to a predetermined pattern. In the poetry of the Hebrew Bible all acrostics are alphabetical: the individual lines of a poem (or occasionally small groups of lines) begin with the twenty-two letters of the Hebrew alphabet in order. (This would be equivalent to the first line of an English poem beginning with A, the second with B, etc.) The acrostic form, besides giving the esthetic pleasure of a pattern, may have been intended to make memorization easier. It may also have been intended as a way of expressing completeness: in Lamentations, for instance, the acrostic format of the individual chapters might have been used to express both the completeness of the outpouring of grief and its finality. The following poems in the Bible are acrostics: Psalms 9–10; 25; 34; 37; 111; 112; 119; 145; Proverbs 31:10–31; Lamentations 1; 2; 3; 4 (ch 5 is not an acrostic, but preserves part of the form by having 22 lines, the number of letters in the Hebrew alphabet); Nahum 1:2–8 (or 9) (incomplete). In the Hebrew text of Ben Sira, 51:13–30 is acrostic.

**Adonai** (Heb. "my Lord") a divine title and the word generally substituted for the tetragrammaton, **YHWH,** when the Bible is read aloud.

**allegorical** a method of reading a text as an allegory; explaining or interpreting elements in a narrative as if they stood for something else. Paul uses an allegorical method in Galatians 4:22–26. "Allegorical interpretation," such as that used by **Philo Judaeus** to draw out the meaning of the Bible, is an effort to make an allegory out of a writing that was not originally intended to be one, but that is, in the view of the interpreter, presenting a hidden meaning that the allegorical interpretation will reveal.

**allegory** an extended comparison which directly describes one reality while indirectly describing something entirely different. An allegory as a narrative uses action, setting, and characters to point symbolically to something else. Biblical allegories include the "Song of the Vineyard" in Isaiah 5, in which the story of the vineyard is also the story of Judah, and the parable of the sower in Matthew 13:1–8 and 18–23. Allegory is infrequent in present-day literature, but allegorical treatments or uses of art still occur: The statue of Justice in courthouses uses allegorical elements: a beautiful woman (justice attracts us), blindfolded (justice is indifferent to external appearance), holding balancing scales (justice weighs the merits of a case in a publicly observable way) and a sword (justice can punish), all of which express our ideals of justice.

**alleluia** a Greek and Latin form of a Hebrew verb, meaning "Praise the Lord." See **hallelujah.**

**Amorites** according to the Bible, one of the native nations of Canaan. Amorites are attested in other ancient Near Eastern documents from the third millennium and onwards as residents of Syria who migrated to Mesopotamia and other areas. They spoke a language related to Hebrew.

**anachronism** an element in a story that is out of place because it did not exist at the time of the story. Anachronisms can be valuable clues to when a particular narrative was written.

***anawim*** the Hebrew word for "the poor," "the afflicted," "the meek or humble." Often used in Psalms for the group to which the Psalmist belongs.

**anoint** touch or rub with oil. Both things and people can be anointed. Anointing was a sign that the person or thing was dedicated to God: kings (1 Kgs 1:39) and priests (Lv 8:30) were anointed, as were the bodies of those who had died (Lk 23:56).

**anthropomorphic** (Gr. "human form") language that presents God in human or human-like terms. "Your right hand, O LORD, magnificent in power, your right hand, O LORD, shattered the enemy" (Ex 15:6).

**antithesis** the contrast of ideas through closely contrasted words: "A mild answer turns back wrath, but a harsh word stirs up anger" (Prv 15:1).

**antithetic parallelism** two parallel lines related to one another by opposition (e.g., Prv 10:4, "The slack hand impoverishes, but the busy hand brings riches").

**aphorism** a short, memorable saying. Many of the Proverbs are aphorisms, as are many of Jesus' statements.

**apocalypse** (Gr. *apokalypsis,* "removal of the veil, revelation") a narrative literary genre in which an angel or other heavenly being communicates to a human being the divine plan for history and the arrangement of the supernatural order. Many apocalypses are a series of visions of heaven and earth that are then explained. Apocalypses are a feature of late biblical religion.

**apocalyptic** having the character of an apocalypse; assuming the existence of a supernatural realm closely related to the natural; maintaining the imminence of a final judgment.

**Apocrypha** (Gr. "hidden things") a group of about 20 mostly Jewish works, many of which were included in the **Septuagint,** but which were not accepted into the Jewish canon of the Bible. All of these works are extra-canonical for Protestants; some are canonical for Roman Catholics; a few more are canonical for Orthodox Christians. See **deuterocanonical.**

**apodictic law** law stated absolutely, as in the Decalogue's "you shall not," rather than casuistically, "if a person . . . " See **casuistic law.**

**apologia** (Gr. "explanation") a defense of one's actions or beliefs, usually in a formal speech or written document.

**apostasy** abandoning a set of beliefs, or the position of having abandoned them.

**apostle** (Gr. "one who is sent"), a delegate or representative. In the New Testament, an apostle was one who had known Jesus and could witness to the resurrection (Acts 1:21–22) or a preacher of the gospel who had been called by God (1 Cor 12:28; Rom 16:7).

**apostrophe** an address to an absent person or personified object. There is an apostrophe to Assyria in Isaiah 10:5.

**Aramaic** a Semitic language used widely in Mesopotamia and the Land of Israel during the Persian period, though it developed earlier. In the mid-first millennium, it eventually replaced Akkadian as the lingua franca of the ancient near eastern world. It became the ordinary language of Jews and is the language of much rabbinic commentary. The Aramaic translation of the Bible is the Targum.

**Arameans** a Semitic people living in the area of Syria from the second millennium onwards. Some biblical texts suggest particular kinship between Israel and the Arameans (see esp. Dt 26:5). Damascus was their main city.

**Ark (for the Torah)** a box or cabinet, typically of wood, in which the Torah scrolls are stored at the front of the synagogue. It is often finely decorated, reflecting the centrality of the Torah scrolls to Judaism.

**Ark of the Covenant** the chest (Heb. *'aron*) in the Tabernacle or Temple that contained the Pact (Heb. *'edut*) (Ex 40:20), or the tablets (Dt 10:2), or that served as the throne of the LORD (1 Sm 4:4).

**Armageddon** the traditional site of the final battle between good and evil (Rev 16:16), possibly derived from Megiddo, a battle site in Israel's history (Jgs 5:19; 2 Kgs 9:27).

**Asherah** (pl. Asherim) Canaanite goddess, wife or consort of El; her sacred symbol, a pole or tree, was the object of prophetic condemnation.

**Assyria** a Mesopotamian world power, in addition to Egypt and Babylonia. Its capital cities included Asshur and Nineveh. The Assyrian empire conquered the northern kingdom of Israel in 722 and exiled its people. The Assyrians were well-known for their massive building projects, and for their cruelty in war.

**'atbash** a form of cipher in which a word is transformed into a code by letter substitution, in which the last letter of the alphabet is substituted for the first, the next-to-last for the second, and so on: *alef* becomes *tav, bet* becomes *shin, gimel* becomes *resh,* and so on. (In English, A would become Z, B would become Y, etc.) Using this method, Jeremiah transforms Babylon into Sheshach (Jer 25:26; 51:41): "b–b–l" or *bet-bet-lamed* becomes "sh-sh-k" or *shin-shin-kaf*.

**atonement** the expiation for sin, or reparation for an injury committed against another. The Hebrew *kapparah* (with possible root meaning "to cover") refers to ritual cleansing of the Temple precincts.

## B

**baal** (Heb. "master," "lord," "husband") the chief god of the Canaanite religion; the storm god.

**Babylonia** a Mesopotamian world power. It often competed against Assyria, which it conquered in 612 B.C. Its major city was Babylon, Akkadian for "gate of the gods." Its main god became Marduk, and its religion and literature were extremely influential, even on its arch-rival Assyria. Babylonia destroyed the First Temple in 586, and was conquered by Cyrus the Great in 539.

**Babylonian Exile** the forced relocation of some of the population of Judah, perhaps the ruling portion of it, after the conquest by Babylonia in 595–586 B.C. The exile ended with the permitted return to the land under Cyrus (beginning ca. 538 B.C.).

**Babylonian Talmud** see **Talmud.**

**ban** (Heb. *herem*) the devotion of war booty (including people) in its entirety to the deity (see esp. Dt 20:17), or the forfeiture of goods (e.g., idols) from which no benefit is permissible. See ***herem.***

**baptism** ritual purification by immersion in water, a practice in use throughout the ancient Mediterranean world. New Testament baptism, based on the reported practice of John the Baptist (Mk 1:4) may have been derived from Jewish purification ritual (Lv 15:18), but Paul's connection of baptism with the death and resurrection of Christ (Rom 6:1–14) changed its meaning from purification to initiation into a new community and new identity.

**basilica** a church built according to an ancient Roman plan, with a rectangular nave and a semicircular apse at one end; also, a Catholic church with certain ceremonial or liturgical privileges.

**B.C.E.** before the Common Era, an alternative to B.C.

**Bedouin** an Arab nomad; in general, a member of a nomadic desert tribe.

**Beelzebul** (also Baalzebul, Baalzebub, Beelzebub) the ruler of the demons (Mt 12:24–27). It is based on the Hebrew *Baalzebul,* "lord of heaven," a title of the Phoenician god at Ekron (2 Kgs 1:2–18), transformed (probably as a derogatory name) into Baalzebub, "lord of the flies."

**behemoth** a mythical beast, sometimes identified with the hippopotamus (Jb 40:15–24) who represents violent forces in the world.

***berit*** (Heb. "treaty") a term that may be used of a treaty between two individuals, groups, or nations, or between God and Israel. See **covenant.**

**bicolon:** unit of Hebrew poetry composed of two *cola,* or lines (sometimes called a *distich*).

**Book of the Covenant** see **Covenant Collection**.

**Booths, Feast of** the final harvest festival of grapes and olives, falling usually within our month of October. It was called "Booths" because the harvesters lived in the fields in makeshift tents or booths. Also called Tabernacles, Sukkoth.

## C

**Canaan** a designation for the area roughly equivalent to the land of Israel in pre-biblical Mesopotamian and Egyptian documents. In the Bible, it most often refers to the pre-Israelite land of Israel.

**canon** (Gr. "measuring rod") the rule by which something is determined to belong or not to a category. Christian tradition uses the word for the official list of the individual books that make up the Scriptures. The canon of the Catholic church is more extensive than that of the Protestant churches, but less extensive than that of the Orthodox churches.

**canonical criticism** the interpretation of a biblical text based upon its final form, rather than interpretation built up from viewing it as an assemblage of smaller, pre-existing units.

**casemate** two parallel walls, joined by short cross-walls. The small rooms, like closets, that result were sometimes used for storage and sometimes filled with rubble or earth to strengthen them.

**casuistic law** (also called "case law") the form of law dealing with the treatment of specific cases. It is frequently in the form of "if/when . . . then" formulae. Most ancient near eastern law collections are formulated this way.

**C.E.** Common Era; equivalent to the christological term A.D.

**ceramic typology** dating different levels of an archeological site by classifying the pieces of pottery found in them according to the approximate eras in which they were made.

**chaos** complete lack of order. In ancient Near Eastern mythology, chaos was sometimes personified as divine beings who had to be conquered by other gods to establish an orderly, habitable universe.

**charisma** a gift of spiritual grace, particularly a gift of one of the manifestations of the Holy Spirit in the New Testament church.

**charismatic** (Gr. "gifted, graced") characterized by the ability to influence or lead others; personally magnetic; talented.

**cherubim** mythical, composite creatures with body parts from various animals; they often had wings and human heads. They were commonly guardians of temples and palaces in the ancient near east.

**chiasm, chiasmus** (from Gr. "chi," the letter that resembles an "X") inverting the second pair of terms in a parallel structure, so that the corresponding terms, if laid out in a square, would form an X. The resultant pattern is ABBA, ABCBA, ABCCBA, etc. "The king takes delight (A) in honest lips (B), and whoever speaks what is right (B) he loves (A)" (Prv 16:13). Chiasmus can also describe the structure of an entire passage, and it can involve several terms or parts of a passage, each of which has an analog that occurs in the reverse order of the original list of terms or sequence of parts.

**Christ** (Gr. "anointed"), the translation of the Hebrew *mashshiach,* "messiah." In the New Testament and in general usage, Christ always refers to Jesus of Nazareth, though in contrast to New Testament usage (where it is always a title, "the anointed one"), in general use today "Christ" is simply an alternative name for Jesus.

**Christian Hebraists** Christian scholars, inspired by the examples of Origen and Jerome, who taught the importance of returning to the Hebrew text of the Christian Old Testament, and who therefore studied Hebrew with rabbinic scholars and influenced Christian Bible translation and commentary to rely on the Hebrew and not on the Latin Vulgate text. The beginnings of Christian Hebraism are generally traced to Andrew of St. Victor (d. 1175), a monk at the Abbey of St. Victor in Paris, where Hugh of St. Victor (d. 1141) had established a school specializing in biblical exposition. There was a significant renaissance of Christian Hebraism during the Renaissance.

**Christology** the theological doctrines covering the nature of Christ.

**chronicle** an account of events in the order in which they occurred.

**Chronicler** the name for the unknown author of the books of Chronicles; sometimes also applied to the author of Ezra and Nehemiah.

**church fathers** see **patristic writers**.

**circumcision** the removal of the foreskin of the penis. In the Bible it is a sign of entry into the covenant community, whether the circumcision is meant literally (Jos 5:5–7) or metaphorically ("uncircumcised hearts," Lv 26:41). In the writings of Paul, "the circumcised" and "the uncircumcised" (Gal 2:7) refer to Jews and Gentiles, respectively.

**citadel** a stronghold or fortress, whether standing alone or serving as the inner fortification of a city.

**clan** a social unit of those considered to be descended from one common ancestor; several clans constitute a tribe.

**climax** (Gr. "ladder"), a series of clauses in which each succeeding clause repeats the important term from the previous clause, each clause in turn making a more important point: ". . . affliction produces endurance, and endurance, proven character, and proven character, hope" (Rom 5:3–4).

**codex** a manuscript of separate leaves of writing, bound into a unit along one edge. Modern books are a development of the codex.

**colon** (pl. *cola*) a single line of poetry (also known as a *stich*).

**colophon** (Gr. "summit," by extension "finishing touch") a notice, usually printed at the end of a book, giving information about authorship: Ben Sira 50:27.

**Community Rule** (or "Rule of the Community") a scroll from the Dead Sea community, 1QS, that sets out the communal arrangements under which the community functioned, or at least those that they held up as an ideal: holding property in common; eating, blessing, and advising one another in unity; preparing for the eschaton; and training new members of the community in their responsibilities.

**concordance** a word index to a given text, listing each occurrence of a given word along with a context line so that scholars may better see how a particular word is used.

**concubine** a woman who is the sexual partner of a man, and is legally recognized as such, but who does not have the full status of a wife.

**cosmology** any account (mythical or otherwise) of the origin of the world.

**cosmos** (Gr. "order, regularity") the created world of order, stability, relative permanence; the opposite of chaos.

**Council of Trent** the twenty-ninth ecumenical council of the Catholic Church (1545–1563), held after the Protestant Reformation had begun. Among other decisions, it defined the books that are included in the Catholic canon of Scripture.

**covenant** (Heb. ***berit***) a treaty between God and Israel. Some covenants have specific conditions or treaty stipulations, while others are covenants of grant. The biblical notion of covenant between God and Israel, especially as it appears in Deuteronomy, may reflect a theologized reworking of treaties between Assyrian kings and their vassals.

**Covenant Code** another term for **Covenant Collection**.

**Covenant Collection** Exodus 20:19–23:33, which details the terms of the covenant between God and Israel.

**cult** rituals and religious practices at a place of worship. The cult of the Jerusalem Temple means the religious practices carried out there, with no judgment about their value.

**cult prostitute** one available for sexual intercourse with worshipers at the temple of a god. The biblical accusation (Dt 23:17–18; 1 Kgs 14:24) that non-Israelite religions have cult prostitutes may be a polemical exaggeration.

**Cyrus** king of Persia (559–530 B.C.). He defeated Media in 550 and conquered most of the ancient Near East, including Babylonia, allowing the Jewish exiles in Babylonia to return to the land beginning about 538.

## D

**D** the Deuteronomic source, which covers almost the entire book of Deuteronomy (except for sections of the last few chapters).

**Davidic dynasty** the direct descendants of King David, who reigned in Jerusalem from the tenth century through the sixth. An attempt to reinstitute this dynasty after the return from exile was not successful.

**Day of Atonement** (Heb. **Yom Kippur**) commemorated on the tenth day of the seventh month in the fall. It was a day of fasting and abstinence, as well as performance of certain key Temple rituals (see Lv. 16).

**Day of the Lord** the time mentioned in many prophetic books where God appears as a warrior, sometimes fighting against Israel, sometimes against Israel's enemies. The earliest text to mention this Day is Amos 5:18.

**Dead Sea Scrolls** a group of manuscripts found in 1947 in caves near the Dead Sea, at Wadi Qumran. The scrolls were probably the library of an Essene settlement that flourished at the site from the second century B.C. until it was destroyed by the Romans in A.D. 68. The library included Hebrew manuscripts of biblical books older than those previously known, and other scrolls regulating the life of the community that shed light on the variety of Jewish belief and practice in the time of Jesus.

**decalogue** (Gr. "ten words") the traditional name for the list of commandments in Exodus 20:1–17 and Deuteronomy 5:6–21.

**defilement** a state of ritual impurity caused by contact with a corpse or other impure object. Priestly literature in the Torah is especially concerned with defilement and removing defilement.

**demon** (Gr. *daimon*, "spirit") a spiritual or nonphysical being, generally hostile to human beings, but in most Old Testament passages still under God's control (see Jb 1 and 2). A common Hebrew name was *satan*, meaning "adversary." By the time of the New Testament demons were generally regarded as hostile to God as well, and therefore evil, or the cause of bad influences—disease, mental distress—on human beings.

**demonic** marked by spiritual evil, like a demon.

**deuterocanon, deuterocanonical** (Gr. "second canon") those books or portions of books not included in the Hebrew canon but accepted as canonical by some Christian churches (Roman Catholic and Orthodox) because they were included in the Septuagint.

**Deutero-Isaiah** the general term for the portion of Isaiah beginning with chapter 40. Most scholars consider Deutero-Isaiah to consist of chapters 40–55 (or 40–54). These chapters are primarily concerned with the promise of return from exile and the events leading up to the decree of Cyrus (538 B.C.) permitting the exiles to return to Judah and rebuild their city and Temple. See **Trito-Isaiah.**

**deuteronomistic** pertaining to the editor(s) of the history comprised in the books of Joshua, Judges, Samuel, and Kings, as prefaced by the book of Deuteronomy. The term is also applied to the style of these books, reflecting concern for such matters as obedience to the laws given in Deuteronomy, centralized worship in Jerusalem, and support for the Davidic dynasty.

**Deuteronomistic History** the account in the books Deuteronomy, Joshua, Judges, Samuel, and Kings, that portrays the history of Israel as a partial failure to keep the covenant faithfully, and the consequences of that failure in the subsequent history of the people. These books show significant theological and linguistic similarities, suggesting that they have a common editor or editors.

**deuteronomistic** having the qualities or the theology of the **Deuteronomistic History.**

**diaspora** (Gr. "dispersal") the scattering of Jews outside the land of Israel.

**diatribe** an argument against a position, or one critical of a person or group. Diatribe often includes an imagined dialogue between opposing viewpoints, as in the book of Job.

**Didache** (Gr. "teaching") an early Christian writing, dating from around A.D. 150 but including earlier materials. It consists of moral exhortation, a manual of church order, and guidance for community life. It is valuable for providing insight into the concerns of early Christian communities. It contains material similar to that in the Pastoral Letters (1 and 2 Tm and Ti).

**discernment** the ability to distinguish between what is valuable and what is not, especially in the spiritual or moral realms.

**disciple** a follower, an adherent of a particular teaching.

**divination** the effort to learn about the future or the current situation, particularly such an effort undertaken by occult means, such as consulting mediums.

**divine warrior** God in the role of leader of the heavenly armies, usually seen as fighting for Israel.

**doctrine** (Lat. *doctrina,* "teaching") the beliefs or tenets held by a particular group; Christian doctrines are rooted in the person of Christ.

**documentary hypothesis** a theory about the formation of the first five books of the Bible, Genesis through Deuteronomy. The hypothesis holds that there are four traditions underlying these books, naming them after a chief characteristic of each: "J" or the "Yahwist" ("J" from the German spelling "Jahveh") uses the divine name "YHWH" (the LORD) consistently and contains much of the oldest material; "E" or the "Elohist" uses the divine name "Elohim" (God) fairly consistently and contains traditions from the northern kingdom of Israel; "P" or the "Priestly" writer is concerned largely with legal codes and matters of religious practice; and "D" or the "Deuteronomist" represents the traditions gathered mostly in Deuteronomy and continued through the deuteronomistic history in Joshua, Judges, Samuel, and Kings. There have been many modifications in the documentary hypothesis, and most scholars now agree that these "documents" are much more like streams of tradition, at least partly oral, than they are like fully-conceived, written texts that could be combined in a cut-and-paste process.

**doxology** (Gr. "word of glory") a prayer of praise to God, or one glorifying God.

**dualism** the religious view that reality consists of two basic elements, often seen as "good" and "evil." Some dualistic thought is primarily ethical, arguing that human actions ultimately fall into one category or the other; other dualistic philosophies see good and evil as the basic constituents of the nature of the universe.

**dynasty** a ruling family; when a leader dies, the next leader is always chosen from among the family members.

## E

**E** one of the four sources or traditions in the Torah, which characteristically refers to God as *elohim.* More recently, as scholars have examined the texts more closely, they speak of a JE tradition, since E as a separate source is difficult to isolate entirely. It may represent the traditions and practices of the inhabitants of the northern areas of Israel.

**early Christian writings** besides the books contained in the New Testament, many other writings from the first century or so of the Christian church are known to have survived, or are quoted or referred to by later writers. These writings include letters, gospels, narrative books like the Acts of the Apostles, apocalypses, and collections of teachings. In some cases these works provide direct evidence of teachings that were later rejected by the main body of Christians. In other cases they contain similar material, or parallel arguments, to those in parts of the New Testament, such as the instructions to local churches in the Pastoral Letters. In still other cases, they provide further examples of kinds of literature found in the New Testament.

**ecclesiology** the theological study of the church; the doctrines that concern the nature of the Christian community.

**ecumenism** (from the Greek *oikoumene,* "the whole inhabited world") any attempts to deal with the relations between different Christian groups, or to think about ways in which divisions among them might be overcome. Since the Second Vatican Council (1963–65), ecumenical activity has become a major goal of the Catholic Church.

**ecumenical** (from **ecumenism**) aimed at fostering ecumenism, or characterized by aims supporting ecumenism; having the character of ecumenism.

**Edom/Edomites** the territory and people to the south of Judah, first attested in late second millennium texts. Edom is identified in Genesis 36 with Esau, Jacob's brother. The enmity between these brothers and that between Judah and Edom mirror each other.

**eisegesis** (Gr. "lead into"; opposed to **exegesis,** "lead out of") the practice of reading into the text what one desires to find there, rather than reading out of the text to determine what it actually says.

**El** a Canaanite deity popular in the second millennium. In the texts from Ugarit, he is a significant deity, but is often depicted as old and is largely supplanted by Baal.

**Elohim** the Hebrew word usually translated "God," though its plural form is sometimes translated "gods" (e.g., Gn 6:2, "the sons of God," NAB note: "other heavenly beings"). It is originally a common noun (a god), though it is often used as a proper noun for The God of Israel, even though it is a plural form.

**Elohist** the putative author of the E source (see **E**).

**ephod** two different objects are called an ephod: (1) the linen apron worn by priests in the Temple; (2) a device used to divine the will of God. The second kind of ephod was carried in priestly garments, which may explain why the same word was used for both (1 Sm 2:18). "Ephod" in Judges 8:27 seems to be an idol rather than a priestly garment.

**Ephraim** the most important tribe of the **Northern Kingdom.**

**Epicureans** a Greek philosophical school, founded by Epicurus, who taught that human beings naturally seek pleasure, and that the best way to achieve this pursuit was in moderation, since moderation permits the longest possible life of pleasure-seeking.

**epigraph** an inscription, usually carved or etched in stone.

**Epiphanes** a title, "[God] made manifest," adopted by Antiochus IV, the ruler of the part of the Greek empire that included Israel during the second century B.C. He was the king who forced pagan worship to occur in the Jerusalem Temple, thus provoking the revolt of the Maccabees.

**epiphany** (Gr. "manifestation, appearance") usually the appearance of a god or divine being in a form that can be seen by human beings.

**epistle** a letter, sometimes intended for public reading and therefore written according to a particular literary form.

**epithet** a word or phrase that characterizes a person or thing, and that can often be used by itself to refer to the person. The name "Maccabeus," or "Hammer," is an epithet of Judas, the son of Mattathias and leader of the Jewish revolt against Antiochus IV in 167 B.C.

**eschatological, eschatology** (Gr. *eschata,* "last things") a concern with the end time, or the end of the world as we know it, whether that involves a new historical era radically discontinuous from this one, or an entirely new cosmos after the destruction of the current one.

**Essenes** a communal society in Judaism around the first century B.C. to the first century A.D. that kept the law with utmost rigor and lived apart in communities that were similar in some respects to later monastic groups. It is generally agreed that the Dead Sea Scrolls of Qumran were collected and preserved by an Essene community.

**etiology** (Gr. *aition,* "cause") an explanation for a word, an event, or a natural phenomenon. An etiological story is one that posits a particular cause (not necessarily the right cause) for some event. For example, the story at the end of Genesis 32 explains why Israelites do not eat the thigh muscle.

**Eucharist** a ritual or service of thanksgiving, centering on the sharing of bread and wine, based on the final meal Jesus shared with his followers before his trial and crucifixion; also called Communion, the Lord's Supper, and the Mass.

**euphemism** the substitution of an inoffensive word for one that is too explicit or impolite. The word "feet" in Isaiah 6:2; 7:20 (NAB: "between the legs") and possibly Ruth 3:4, 7, 8, 14 is a euphemism for "genitals."

**evangelist** (from Greek *euangelion,* "good news") the author of a gospel.

**exegesis** (Gr. "lead out of") the explanation or interpretation of the meaning of a written text.

**exhortation** urging a particular course of action or behavior by argument or advice.

**Exile** the forced removal of a people from its land, and the community in which they lived in the foreign land. The Israelites of the northern kingdom were exiled by the Assyrians in the late eighth century, and the Judeans were exiled by the Babylonians in the early sixth century. Specifically, "the Exile" is the period from 586 to approximately 539 B.C. During this time the ruling classes of Judah were forced to leave Judah and live in Babylonia. See **Babylonian Exile.**

## F

**fable** an illustrative story in which animals or plants have speaking parts. Judges 9:8–15 is a fable about the dangers of kingship in which plants speak.

**Fertile Crescent** the agriculturally fertile areas of Egypt, Israel, and Mesopotamia, forming a rough arc from the Nile through the coastal regions of Israel to the Tigris-Euphrates basin.

**Festival of Weeks** see **Shavuot.**

**festival scrolls** the five short books that are read on five holy days in the Jewish calendar: Song of Songs on Passover, Ruth on Pentecost (Weeks or Shavuot), Lamentations on 9 Ab (the date of the Temple's destruction), Ecclesiastes on Booths (Sukkoth), and Esther on Purim.

**First Temple** the Temple in Jerusalem from Solomon's time (tenth century) until the destruction of Jerusalem by the Babylonians in 586 B.C. The First Temple period extends from the tenth to sixth centuries B.C.

**form criticism** the interpretation of a text—a parable, a psalm, a proverb—with particular attention to the structure of the text and to the original setting of that form out of which it arose. Form criticism attempts to recover the original context, audience, or situation of a particular kind of literature, before the unit was made a part of a larger narrative such as a gospel or a historical book with its own context, audience, and situation.

**Former Prophets** the name in the Hebrew Bible for the first part of the longer section called "the Prophets." The Former Prophets are Joshua, Judges, Samuel, and Kings.

**fundamentalist** in its narrow meaning, a conservative Protestant who holds to the five fundamentals: the sole authority of Scripture; the Virgin Birth of Jesus Christ; the doctrine of the substitutionary atonement of the death of Christ; the physical, bodily resurrection of Christ; and the literal Second Coming of Christ to judge the world. In a wider sense, a fundamentalist is any rigidly conservative adherent to a belief system who regards all those outside the belief system as without hope of salvation and who treats the sacred text of the tradition as an infallible guide to belief and action.

## G

**Galilee** the northernmost geographical area of Israel.

**Gehenna** the place of punishment after death (e.g., see Mt 5:22). The name means "valley of Hinnom," a place south of Jerusalem that had been thought to be the area where children were burnt as sacrificial offerings: Josiah (2 Kgs 23:10) destroyed the site, but its associations with burning and evil remained and developed into the image of burning punishment that is found in the New Testament.

**genealogy** a list or history of the ancestors of an individual or group.

**genre** a form of literature with particular characteristics. The detective story is a genre. Once a genre is established, the audience for it knows what to expect and can respond more easily to any given work. Biblical genres include oracles, laments, proverbs, hymns, parables, letters, gospels, and apocalypses.

**gentile** a non-Jew.

**Gilgamesh** the Babylonian and Assyrian epic, whose hero, Gilgamesh, travels the world in search of immortality. Among the characters he encounters is Utnapishtim, whose tale of the flood has parallels with the biblical account of Noah (Gn chs 6–9). This epic explores the tension between nature and culture and addresses the mortality of human beings.

**glean** to gather or collect, usually by hand, grain that is left behind by reapers. People too poor to own their own fields were permitted to glean in the fields of those better off (Lv 19:9–10; Dt 24:19–24).

**gnosticism** (from Gk. *gnosis,* "knowledge") a philosophy that regards spirit and matter as opposites. According to gnostic teaching, human beings are spirits trapped or imprisoned in matter; the material world is an illusion or the work of an inferior, even demonic, divine being; and the purpose of life is to learn how to free oneself from material things (including the body) and attain eternal life in the spiritual realm. This is accomplished by learning specialized or secret knowledge about the nature of reality; it is from this emphasis on knowledge that gnosticism gets its name. Gnostic teachings were often in the form of secret doctrines or mysteries, and many mystery religions were gnostic. Gnosticism, though influential during the first few centuries of the Christian church's existence, was ultimately rejected by what became the main body of Christians, and most of the gnostic writings were lost or suppressed. Because gnosticism itself did not continue as an established form of Christianity, it did not develop an "orthodox" or systematic body of thought, and most of what is attributed to it as a philosophy has had to be assembled from disparate sources that do not always agree with each other in every particular.

**God, names for** see **Adonai, Elohim, YHWH.**

**Greek Bible** a general term for the variety of ancient translations of the Bible into Greek in antiquity, including the Septuagint and the translations of Aquila, Symmachus, and Theodotion.

## H

**Hades** the abode of the dead in Greek religion, used in the New Testament as the general name for the place where souls go after death (e.g., see Mt 11:23; Acts 2:27).

***haggadah*** (poss. from Heb. *huggad,* "things said" or "what is told") the nonlegal portions of the Talmud and Midrash (see ***halakhah***). Haggadah is concerned with explicating the meaning of Scripture in the moral sense, and with elaborating on the stories in the Bible. As such, it is more akin to preaching than to legal analysis, and many haggadic collections are homiletical in character. The legal sections, called *halakhah,* are concerned with understanding the obligations placed on the believer by the biblical text; *haggadah*, by contrast, contains ethical teaching as well as illustrative narrative, prayers, legends, and folklore.

***Haggadah of Pesah*** ("telling of Passover") the liturgical recitation, used at the Passover **seder;** also the book that contains the recitation and instructions of the seder.

***halakhah*** (Heb. "way," from *halakh* "go"; pl. *halakhot*) the legal portions of the Talmud, or any legal ruling according to Jewish law.

**Hallel** (Heb. "praise") Psalms 113–118, which are recited on major Jewish festivals.

**hallelujah** a Hebrew acclamation, "Praise Yah!" It is frequent in the Psalms.

**Hammurabi** Babylonian monarch (ruled 1792–1750 B.C.), responsible for the formulation of a legal collection (the Code [or Laws] of Hammurabi) that is one of the earliest collections of case law on various subjects.

**Hasidic, Hasidim** (Heb. *Hasid,* "pious one") (1) a Jewish group in the Maccabean period, concerned with re-establishing Jewish practices in ritual and purity laws. The Hasidim supported the Maccabees for a time; they may have been the precursors of the Sadducees. (2) a renewal movement that began in the mid-eighteenth century in eastern Europe under the influence of the Baal Shem Tov ("master of the good Name"), R. Yisrael ben Eliezer (ca. 1700–1760).

**Hasmonean** the dynasty descended from the Maccabee brothers. It ruled Israel from 135 to 36 B.C.; the last Hasmonean was overthrown by Herod the Great.

**Hasmonean Revolt** the uprising led by the family of Mattathias Heshmon against the Seleucid ruler Antiochus IV Epiphanes beginning in 166 B.C., particularly by Mattathias' son Judah (or Judas) Maccabeus ("the hammer"), which succeeded in liberating Jerusalem and the surrounding territory from Seleucid rule in 164. When the Temple, which had been desecrated by Antiochus, was retaken by the Jews, it was rededicated, an event commemorated in the festival of Hanukkah ("dedication").

**Hebrew Bible** a term used to refer to what Christians call the (Protestant) Old Testament. Though the two terms refer to basically the same body of writings, the order of books in the Hebrew Bible (i.e., the Jewish Bible) differs from that found in the Old Testament.

**Hellenism** a general term for the spread of Greek culture, politics, and language around the Mediterranean in the period after the conquests of Alexander the Great (d. 323 B.C.).

**Hellenistic** Greek-speaking or influenced by Greek culture after the time of Alexander.

**Hellenize** bring under the influence of Greek language and culture.

***herem*** (Heb. "ban") the total dedication of conquest to God; later, the exile or suspension of someone from the community ("excommunication").

**heresy** (Gr. *hairesis*, "choice") an opinion or belief contrary to the accepted doctrine of the Catholic Church; an unorthodox position.

**hermeneutics** (Gr. "interpretation") the theory and practice of interpretation.

**Herodian** followers and members of the court of Herod the Great and his sons (36 B.C. to A.D. 40).

**Hexateuch** (Gr. "six scrolls") a grouping of the first six books in the Bible—Genesis through Joshua—to complete the narrative with the conquest of the Land that is in Joshua. See **Pentateuch, Tetrateuch.**

**high places** shrines, usually on a hill or a raised platform, where worship, especially sacrifices, took place. Because they were outside of Jerusalem and sometimes, though not always, used for other gods, they were regularly condemned in the Deuteronomistic History, though in earlier writings, and even in the narratives in Kings, there are clear indications that sacrifice and worship took place in numerous locations throughout Israel.

**higher criticism** the effort to distinguish among the sources of biblical documents, and to trace them back to their origins, so far as that is possible; distinguished from textual criticism ("lower criticism"), which is concerned with establishing the most accurate text in its final form. See **documentary hypothesis.**

**historical-critical method** interpreting a text by trying to understand its original setting and audience, and what it would have meant when it was originally written or spoken. This method uses the tools of historical research to understand the conditions of the past, and critical tools to understand the traditions and developments that lie behind the surface of the text. It is also an umbrella term that includes such methods as form criticism and redaction criticism.

**holocaust** a sacrifice entirely consumed by fire, a whole burnt offering.

**holy war** battles conducted under divine guidance in which the LORD fought for Israel in the role of divine warrior (Jgs 6).

**homiletical** having the character or function of a sermon.

**hortatory** characteristic of writing or speech that aims at changing the behavior of the hearers or inspiring them to a particular course of action.

**hosanna** a Hebrew word, meaning "Save!" that was used as a cry of acclamation (Ps 118:26; Mt 21:9).

**household code** a list of rules or prescribed behaviors for the members of an extended family and their servants living under one roof. There are household codes in some of the New Testament letters, for instance Ephesians 5:22–6:9.

**Hyksos** the mostly Semitic rulers of Egypt during the period 1665–1560 B.C. (approximately).

**hyperbole** exaggeration for effect. "Will the LORD be pleased with thousands of rams, with myriad streams of oil?" (Mi 6:7).

**hypostasis** (Gr. "that which stands under," i.e., the real nature or essence of anything; pl. *hypostases*) a Greek philosophical term, meaning both "essential being" or what defines a thing as a member of a class of things and "individual being" or what a thing is in itself. It was used by, among others, the neo-Platonist mystics. It refers to the three constitutive orders of reality, the One, Mind, and Soul, each of which is an hypostasis.

**hyssop** a shrub related to mint. It was used as a medicine and, because of its leafy branches, for ritual sprinkling of water or blood (Ex 12:22).

## I

**idolatry** the worship of anything other than what the worshiper defines as the true God.

**Idumea** the Greek form of the name Edom; province in the Land during Persian, Hellenistic, and Roman times, located south of Judah (Yehud), between the Dead Sea and the Mediterranean.

**Ignatius, Letters of** early Christian writings of instruction. The author, Ignatius, bishop of Antioch, wrote them (seven are known to have survived) on his way to martyrdom in Rome. They are largely concerned with overcoming divisions in local churches, combating false teaching, and conducting one's life properly. They therefore are very similar to some of the canonical New Testament letters, particularly 1 and 2 Timothy and Titus. The letters of Ignatius are addressed to the Ephesians, the Magnesians, the Trallians, the Romans, the Philadelphians, and the Smyrnians, as well as one to Polycarp, bishop of Smyrna.

**impurity** a ritual state which forbade the impure individual to partake in Temple rituals. See **defilement**.

**incarnation** (Lat., "enfleshment") the belief that a divine being has become human in some form.

**incubation** the practice of sleeping in a particular place, or in contact with particular things (animal skins, the ground) to induce dreams that might provide divine guidance.

**inerrancy** the doctrine that the biblical materials are without error. In its most expansive form, as held for instance by Protestant fundamentalists, inerrancy includes the assertion that in the original manuscripts of the biblical books, there are no errors of fact, whether theological, historical, or scientific. A more restrained version of the doctrine would claim that the Bible is an inerrant guide in matters of faith but that it may contain historical errors or assertions that cannot be reconciled with present-day science. Vatican II expressed it this way: "Therefore, since everything asserted by the inspired authors or sacred writers must be held to be asserted by the Holy Spirit, it follows that the books of Scriptures must be acknowledged as teaching firmly, faithfully, and without error that truth which God wanted put into the sacred writings for the sake of our salvation" (Document on Revelation, *Dei Verbum,* n. 11). The final phrase, "for the sake of our salvation"—that is, not for the sake of giving us historical or scientific information—establishes the limits of inerrancy.

**inspiration** the belief that the words uttered by a human being are really the words of a divine being. In the ancient world, prophets and oracles were thought to be inspired. In Christian tradition, the notion of inspiration was eventually applied to the whole Bible. Inspiration in a more expanded sense speaks of an inspired tradition, in which numerous authors, anonymous contributors, editors, and others all worked together more or less consciously to create the biblical materials; in this view, God used all these people and their human traditions to express the Bible's teachings. The Second Vatican Council affirms the inspiration of Scripture, but warns that God speaks "through men in human fashion" so that careful attention must be given "to what the sacred writers really intended" (*Dogmatic Constitution on Divine Revelation,* III.12).

**interpolation** an insertion of material into a previously existent text. In the absence of textual evidence, e.g. differing forms of a manuscript for a given text, interpolation must be inferred and is often the subject of scholarly disagreement.

**interpretation** There are a number of different methods of interpreting the Bible, each meant to answer different questions. In general, the purpose of interpretation is to help make the meaning of the text clear, but this sometimes means not only understanding the sentences and paragraphs that we read today, but also understanding the possible ways by which they came to be written, trying to determine the original context of the story or saying, and looking at the different stages through which a biblical text does on its way to its final form. So interpreters are interested in examining the meanings of words used in the Bible, the historical religious, or social background of a particular story or saying, the process by which a story was written down, how groups of stories were combined into a longer narrative, how different biblical writers treated the same materials, what the original audience would have gotten out of a story, how a saying was adapted to address the concerns of later readers, and many similar paths of investigation. Terms used by biblical interpreters include: canonical criticism, documentary hypothesis, form criticism, redaction criticism, source criticism, synoptic problem, tradition criticism, textual criticism.

**interregnum** an interruption or gap between the end of one reign or dynasty and the beginning of the next.

**intertextuality** the interrelationship between

one part of a text (or collection of texts) and other parts. Intertextuality can take the form of recurrent images (the vineyard in Is 5:1–10 and 27:2–4), quotation and/or inner biblical interpretation (Jer 25:11–12 is partly quoted in Dn 9:2 before it is reinterpreted; 1 Cor 3:20 quotes Ps 94:11), or allusion (Is 54:8 alludes to the promise made to Noah in Gn 9:11).

**irony, ironic** a characteristic of literature in which the reader or listener knows more than the characters about the situation in the story. A character in an ironic situation is missing a vital piece of information that is known to the audience. By extension, an ironic aspect of a story, situation, or fact is one that from the outside looks very different than it does from the inside. Irony thus becomes a rhetorical technique in which the author's plain or literal meaning (what the words mean in the dictionary sense) is different from, even in conflict with, the author's intended meaning (what the words mean in their context, with particular emphasis, etc.). Saying "My! Don't you look lovely!" to someone dressed in old work clothes who has just finished a strenuous and messy task is an example of irony in this sense.

**Isis** the Egyptian mother-goddess, wife of Osiris, the god of vegetation and hence of regeneration.

**Israel** the name for both the kingdom of twelve tribal groups, of which David and Solomon were kings, and for the northern section of this kingdom, which split off after the death of Solomon and began a separate political existence under Jeroboam (1 Kgs 12). See **Northern Kingdom, Southern Kingdom.**

## J

**J** the posited document or narrative tradition that is one of the constituent parts of the Torah (Pentateuch), according to a scholarly hypothesis codified by J. Wellhausen and subsequently developed by numerous biblical researchers. J is usually understood to be the earliest source, and is Judean; it frequently depicts God, for whom it uses the tetragrammaton (YHWH, misvocalized Jehovah, thus J), in very anthropomorphic terms.

**Jerome** (ca. 340–420) Christian theologian and translator. Beginning in 382, he produced a Latin version of the Bible, the Old Testament of which was based not on a previous Latin version nor on the Greek text (Septuagint) but on the Hebrew. To do this, Jerome studied Hebrew with rabbis of the time, an unusual step for a Christian. His version, which became known as the **Vulgate** ("common") because it was the translation into commonly used Latin in the Western world, was completed in 405.

**Jerusalem Talmud** also called the Palestinian Talmud or the Talmud of the Land of Israel—none of these titles is fully accurate. This Talmud, mostly reflecting traditions of the Galilean rabbis of the third and fourth centuries A.D., is a commentary on several tractates of the Mishnah. It was ultimately seen as less authoritative than the longer, more comprehensive, and more carefully edited **Babylonian Talmud**. See **Talmud.**

**Joseph and Aseneth** an ancient Greek novel about Joseph's life in Egypt, his marriage to the haughty daughter of an Egyptian priest, and her conversion to faith in Joseph's God, and their triumph over a plot to kill them.

**Josephus** a Hellenistic Jewish historian who lived from about A.D. 37 to about A.D. 100. Four of his writings have survived: *The Jewish War,* an account of the rebellion against Rome in A.D. 66–70, with background information starting at about 200 B.C.; *The Antiquities of the Jews,* a complete history from the creation up to the point where *The Jewish War* begins; *Against Apion,* a defense of Judaism; and an autobiography, the *Life.* Josephus provides invaluable historical information about Judaism and its background from 200 B.C. to A.D. 100; his account of the rebellion, in which he was involved, is in part that of an eyewitness. He also provides first-hand information about the Essenes and the Pharisees, because at one time or another he was associated with both groups, as well as giving information about the Sadducees. Josephus is important to scholars in trying to understand the religious context in which Jesus lived and from which early Christianity and rabbinic Judaism developed.

**Jubilee** (Heb. *yovel,* perhaps "ram" from the sounding of the ram's horn to mark the beginning of the observance) the year of release for slaves and return of ancestral lands to their original owners (or descendants of the owners), to occur every 50 years (after seven sabbaths of years) (Lv ch 25). It is a cornerstone of Priestly ideology, but it is uncertain if it was ever practiced.

**Judah** the major tribal group of the southern kingdom. According to the biblical text, after the death of Solomon, the kingdom was divided into two, with Judah in the south and Israel in the north. The capital of Judah was Jerusalem.

**Judea** the Roman name for the area of Judah.

## K

**kabbalah** "what is received," that is, matter handed to one. In the twelfth century and later, however, *kabbalah* came to mean esoteric or in some sense mystical teaching. *Kabbalah* taught that God was inaccessible by direct experience and could only be apprehended through emanations of the Godhead; Torah in kabbalistic teaching had a hidden meaning, and meditation on texts was a method of ascent to a mystical vision.

**kaddish** (Aram. "holiness, sanctification") prayer in praise of God that is recited at the conclusion of a principal section of the synagogue service; a special type of kaddish is also recited in memory of the deceased.

**Kiddush** short for *kiddush ha-yom,* "sanctification of the day," both the ceremony and the prayer that proclaims the holiness of the Sabbath (or festival), recited over wine before the Sabbath (or festival) meal.

***kohen*** (Heb. "priest") a member of the hereditary group within the Levites, traditionally supposed to be descended from Aaron or Zadok, who alone were allowed to serve as Temple priests.

**kosher** (Heb. "fit" or "proper") a general term used in post-biblical texts for dietary laws; usually applied to food, but also to other ritual objects and practices. Most dietary laws apply to meat: It may not be consumed with blood in it, certain kinds of internal fat are not to be eaten, it may not be consumed along with dairy products, and some meats (e.g., pork), sea creatures (e.g., shellfish), and "creeping things" (e.g., snails) are not permitted.

## L

**lament** a poem of grief or mourning. See **qinah meter.**

**Latter Prophets** the canonical division of Nevi'im that includes the books of Isaiah, Jeremiah, Ezekiel, and the Twelve.

**law** the usual English translation of Hebrew *torah,* which more generally means "teaching, instruction." *Torah* is also the name for the first five books of the Hebrew Bible, Genesis through Deuteronomy.

**lectionary** a list of readings of Scripture passages for Sabbaths and holy days (in Judaism) or Sundays and holy days (in Christianity). Christian lectionaries also sometimes include readings for weekdays. Lectionaries are partly designed to read certain portions of the Bible—for instance, the Torah, in Jewish lectionaries, or the first three Gospels, in Christian lectionaries—completely through, in order, over a lectionary cycle of a year or several years. In addition, in Christian lectionaries important seasons (e.g., Christmas or Easter) have their own specific readings outside the continuous readings. In the synagogue, the Torah reading is followed by what is called a Haftarah reading (*haphtarah* is Hebrew for "conclusion, completion") from one of the prophets; in addition, the five **festival scrolls** are read on five holy days. In many Christian churches, the Gospel reading is preceded by a reading from the Hebrew Scriptures, a psalm, and a reading from elsewhere in the New Testament, usually a letter. The Gospel of John is read during Easter season.

**legate** an official representative.

**legend, legendary** a popular story, sometimes exaggerated or romanticized, about a holy or righteous person or a special place. The characters in legends can themselves be legendary, like Paul Bunyan, or they can be real historical personages about whom stories are told, like George Washington and the cherry tree. Characters that are legendary are those who are famous enough to have legends told about their exploits. Many of the stories told about Elijah and especially Elisha have legendary elements.

**leviathan** the monster of the sea in Canaanite mythology, who is defeated by Baal. It is sometimes identified with the crocodile (Jb 41:1) and represents the forces of watery chaos that must be overcome at creation (Ps 74:1–17) and that will be finally defeated at the end of time (Is 27:1). In the book of Revelation, the dragon, the enemy of God, is identified with the sea (17:1, 3), and in the new creation there is no more sea (21:1).

**levirate marriage** (from Lat. *levir,* "husband's brother") the provision that if a man died without an heir to carry on his name, his brother would marry the widow and the first son she bore would be regarded as the dead brother's heir. This practice is dealt with in Deuteronomy 25:5–10, but it is unclear whether it was actually carried out to any extent; by rabbinic times *halitzah,* the ceremony that released the levir from this obligation, was preferred.

**Levite** (from Heb. "descendant of Levi") originally the tribe or group from which priests were chosen; later, after the establishment of the Zadokites as priests (1 Kgs 1), a subordinate Temple servant who assisted the priests in their duties (see Ex 32:28; Nm 3:18; Ez 4:10–14).

***lex talionis*** (Lat. "law [of retribution] in kind") punishment fitting the crime. See **talion.**

**liminal** (Lat. *limina,* "threshhold") the term for rites or practices that governed life passages, such as entry into puberty or marriage.

**literal meaning** the "plain sense" of a text, as opposed to an allegorical, homiletical, or spiritual interpretation.

**literary criticism** the older name for **source criticism.**

**liturgy** the form or rite for communal, public worship.

**LXX** the roman numeral 70, the standard abbreviation for the **Septuagint.**

## M

**Ma'at** Egyptian goddess of reason and order; her name literally means "truth."

**malediction** curse; opposite of benediction, "blessing."

**martyr** (Gr. "witness") a person who demonstrates loyalty by remaining faithful even when being threatened with death or being killed.

**Martyrdom of Isaiah** a Greco-Roman, Jewish work that is the origin of the legend that Isaiah died by being sawn in two. It is alluded to in Hebrews 11:37.

**Masoretic text** the text of the Hebrew Bible, established by Jewish scholars (called Masoretes). (*Masorah* means "tradition.") The text consists of the Hebrew consonants, vowel signs, accent markings, and other notes. Texts derived from this effort date from circa A.D. 900 to 1000. The Masoretic text is the only complete form of the Hebrew Bible that has come down to us, though individual manuscripts of books are among the Dead Sea Scrolls.

**matrilineal** tracing descent through female ancestors. See **patrilineal.**

***matzah*** unleavened bread, associated with Passover, but also used with certain sacrifices.

**Mesopotamia** (Gr. "between the rivers") the area between the Tigris and Euphrates rivers.

**messiah** the Hebrew word for "anointed." A king could be referred to as "the LORD's anointed" (1 Sm 24:6); even a foreign king could be so called (Is 45:1). Later the term came to be used of the expected savior of the Jewish people and was taken over by Christians to refer to Jesus, whom they believed to be the messiah (Gr. *christos,* "anointed").

**Messiah** (Heb. *mashshiach,* "anointed [one]") a title for the king or other servant or agent of God (priest, prophet, or even non-Israelite Cyrus in Is 45:1).

**metaphor** a direct comparison between two things: "The LORD is my shepherd" (Ps 23:1). See **simile.**

**metonymy** a figure of speech in which a word is used in place of another word to which it is closely related. "The coastlands see, and fear;" (Is 41:5) means "the inhabitants of the coastlands," that is, foreigners.

**mezuzah** (Heb. "doorpost") a parchment on which are written the paragraphs of the Shema (Dt 6:4–9; 11:13–21), and on the back of which *sh-d-y* ("Shaddai," "Almighty") is written so as to be visible through a small opening in the case. *Sh-d-y* is interpreted as an acronym for *shomer delatot Yisrael,* "guardian of the doors of Israel."

**midrash, midrashic** (Heb. *derash* "inquire") interpretation to draw out meanings from a text that are other than, or go beyond, the "plain sense."

**Minor Prophets** (so-called because compared to the Major Prophets, Isaiah, Jeremiah, and Ezekiel, they are much shorter) the books from

Hosea through Malachi; in the Hebrew Bible they are treated as one collection, "The Book of the Twelve."

***mitzvah*** (Heb. "commandment") a religious obligation; by extension, any good deed.

**Moab/Moabites** the territory and inhabitants south and east of the Dead Sea.

**Molech** the title—"king"—of the Ammonite god. The worshipers of this god were accused of child sacrifice.

**motif** an image or character type that recurs throughout a literary work. The Servant motif occurs in Isaiah at 42:1–4; 49:1–6; 50:4–11; 52:13–53:12.

**mystery** in the New Testament, a divine truth that is kept hidden or secret by God until the right moment for it to be revealed (see Rom 16:25–26). A "mystery" in this sense is a revelation about God's plan (Eph 1:9–10). The later, theological meaning of "mystery," a religious teaching that is based on a revelation from God or other divine messenger, rather than on conclusions from reasoning, and that therefore can never be fully understood by reason alone, is not present in the New Testament.

**mystery religion** any one of various religious groups in the Greek and Roman empires that practiced secret rites of initiation. These rites often involved rituals enacting the myth of creation of other underlying teaching about the meaning of the universe according to the particular group. Mystery religions taught that the real meaning of life could not be learned without divine guidance and that such guidance was available in their secret teachings and practices. These secret rites were themselves known as "mysteries" and had the sense of a revelation from the divine realm that is similar to some of the New Testament uses of "mystery."

**myth** a story that expresses a spiritual truth or basic conviction of a culture through narrative. In particular myths give explanations of origins, often through the struggles of divine beings or superhuman creatures. Because the Bible firmly maintains the teaching that there is only one God, in biblical myths the presence of multiple deities has faded out, but the titanic struggle between good and evil is still maintained, as in the story of Paradise in Genesis 2–3, or the Tower of Babel story in Genesis 11:1–9. Such stories, for example, express the impossibility of human efforts to attain the level of God. Myths are not meant to be taken literally.

## N

**narrative** a connected, orderly account of an incident, or a longer account including many incidents. Narratives can be historical, fictional, legendary, mythical, or a combination of types.

**Negev** the high plateau south of the central hill country of Israel.

**Neoplatonism** a development of **Platonism.** It originated with Plotinus (ca. 204–270) and saw the universe as a series of emanations flowing out from the One, the unknowable source of all. The emanations, Mind, the realm of knowledge, and Soul, the realm of thought and activity, are called hypostases. All of existence is a balance between emanation, or movement outward, and contemplation or return, movement back toward the One. The individual's task is to return to the One by contemplation, involving a progressive detachment from the world of matter and sense and ultimately from all categories of thought until the One can be grasped in an indescribable void of thought. There may be early neoplatonic influences in the Wisdom of Solomon 7:25.

**Nevi'im** the Prophets, the second division of the Hebrew Scriptures.

**new moon** the beginning of any month in the Jewish calendar.

**Northern Kingdom** the political assembly of tribal groups that split off from the kingdom of Israel after Solomon's death (1 Kgs 12). This newly-formed kingdom was itself called Israel, and in some of the prophets (e.g., Hos 8:11), Ephraim, after its largest tribe.

**novel** a fictional work in prose. Ancient novels were often **romances.**

## O

**obelisk** a four-sided stone shaft, usually tapered and topped with a pyramid, characteristic of ancient Egypt.

**Old Latin** the Latin translation of the Bible based on the Greek text, the Septuagint. The Old Latin version was replaced by Jerome's Latin translation, the **Vulgate.**

**oracle** a statement uttered by a prophet or other sacred person, purporting to be the words of a deity.

**oracular** having the qualities of an oracle or sacred speech.

**Oral Torah** a synonym for the **Mishnah** and **Talmud.** According to traditional rabbinic belief, the Oral Law was given to Moses on Mount Sinai along with the written law, the Torah. The Oral Law was, however, as its name suggests, originally transmitted orally alongside the Torah, as the authoritative interpretation of the Torah. As a result of historical exigencies, it was committed to writing by the rabbis, in stages, in the first millennium A.D.

**ordination** a formal ceremony and process by which certain members of the community are set apart for religious service, for instance as priests (Lv 8:1–46).

**oxymoron** (Gr. "swift-slow") combining two terms that appear contradictory. "For the foolishness of God is wiser than human wisdom, and the weakness of God is stronger than human strength" (1 Cor 1:25).

## P

**P** the Priestly document in the Torah, comprised of both narratives and laws. It is concerned, among other things, with laws and regulations, ritual practices, the proper conduct of the Temple worship, holiness and purity, and genealogies. P may also have had a hand in the shaping or redaction of the Torah.

**paleography** the study of ancient writing, used to date manuscripts.

**Palestine** a name derived from the Roman designation *Provincia Syria Palaestina,* "Syro-Palestinian Province," which replaced *Provincia Judaea* after the revolt of A.D. 135; *Palaestina* was the Roman spelling of "Philistine," and the designation was probably intended as a derogation of Jewish claims to the territory.

**Palestinian Talmud** the **Jerusalem Talmud** or Talmud Yerushalmi; see **Talmud.**

**parable** a statement or story that uses figurative or imaginative language to evoke a reality that lies beyond the literal level of the story or statement. A parable makes its point by analogy, or the comparison of a known fact, situation, or experience with one that is less familiar. The analogy is usually not made explicit; for instance, in the parable of the Prodigal Son (Lk 15:11–32) the father is meant to represent, by analogy, the merciful action of God's forgiveness, but this is not stated. Sometimes an interpretation is added, however, as with the parable of the Sower (Mk 4:1–8, interpreted in vv. 14–20).

**paraenesis** moral exhortation.

**parallelism** a characteristic feature of biblical Hebrew poetry in which the second line of a unit in some way echoes the meaning or grammatical structure of the first line. This can take the form of a repetition of the meaning, or of a statement of opposites, or of a further statement that serves to extend or modify the first line in some way. Psalms and Proverbs are largely composed in parallelistic form and demonstrate the great degree of variation that the form permits.

**parousia** (Gr. "coming") the second coming of Christ; the expected return of the messiah at the end of the age or the end of the world.

**Paschal** pertaining to the Passover (ultimately from the Gr. *pascha,* derived from Heb. *pesah*).

**Passover** (Heb. *pesach,* prob. "protection"; others "pass over") the name of the festival commemorating the Exodus from Egypt. The first day involves the sacrifice of the lamb, which took place on the eve of the Exodus (14 Nisan); the rest of the festival, the "festival of unleavened bread," was probably originally a festival marking the beginning of the spring barley harvest.

**Passover *Haggadah, Haggadah* of Pesah** the "telling" of the Passover story in the context of the household liturgy of Pesah, which accompanies the ritual meal, the **seder.**

**patriarchs** the founding fathers of Israel: Abraham, Isaac, and Jacob.

**patrilineal** tracing one's descent through male ancestors. See **matrilineal.**

**patristic writers** the theologians of the early Christian centuries, from the time of the close of the New Testament period (sometime after A.D. 100) to about the fifth century. Clement, Irenaeus, Origen, and Jerome are patristic figures of importance to biblical studies.

**penitential psalms** Psalms 6; 32; 38; 51; 102; 130; and 143, used in Christian services of repentance from the earliest times, and by the Middle Ages in regular use during Lent.

**Pentapolis** the five cities of the **Philistines:** Ashdod, Ashkelon, Ekron, Gath, Gaza.

**Pentateuch** (Gr. "five scrolls") the first five books of the Bible—Genesis through Deuteronomy—regarded as a unit after its final editing during or after the Exile. The traditional term in Judaism for this collection of books is **Torah,** "teaching." Although these five books are traditionally grouped together, they contain markedly different kinds of writing—prehistory, narrative, law, ritual instruction, and so on—and scholars have investigated the materials of which they are composed. Deuteronomy is largely a separate work that was probably attached to the first four books at a later stage, leading some scholars to speak of a **Tetrateuch** consisting of Genesis through Numbers; and it is also the case that the actual narrative climax of the story, the conquest of the Land, is given in the book of Joshua, leading other scholars to speak of a **Hexateuch** consisting of Genesis through Joshua.

**Pentecost** (Gr. "fiftieth [day]") the Greek name for the Jewish festival of Weeks (Shavuot), which occurs 50 days after Passover. On the Pentecost after Jesus' crucifixion, according to Acts chapter 2, the Holy Spirit descended on his followers and inspired them to speak in different languages.

**Persian era** the period of domination of the Persian empire over the Near East, beginning at around 550 B.C. when Cyrus the Great, King of Persia, defeated the Medes, and lasting until about 330 B.C., when Alexander the Great of Macedon conquered the lands surrounding the Mediterranean and brought them under Greek rule. It was during the Persian era that the Israelites were allowed to return to their land from exile (537 B.C.) and rebuild the Temple (515 B.C. or thereafter).

**Persian period** the era from approximately 539–333 B.C., from the time of Cyrus the Great until the Greek conquest under Alexander.

**personification** representing an idea, a value, or other abstract thought as a person. Wisdom is personified as a woman in Proverbs 8.

**Pesach** the Hebrew word usually translated "Passover."

**Pharisees** a movement among Jews in the first century A.D., according to Josephus and the writings in the New Testament. The Pharisees were concerned to extend Jewish practice into all areas of life, and followed the tradition of interpretation (**Oral Law**) associated with the schools of Hillel and Shammai. They were thus proponents of a Jewish identity separate from the larger non-Jewish culture that surrounded Judea, but were also opponents of the more conservative Sadducees, who did not accept their traditions of oral law. See **Sadducees.**

**Philistines** a group from the "Sea Peoples," who invaded and settled on the coastal region of Canaan. They had been repulsed from an invasion of Egypt (ca. 1190 B.C.). The five major Philistine cities (the **Pentapolis**) were Ashkelon, Ashdod, Ekron, Gath, and Gaza.

**Philo Judaeus** Hellenistic Jewish philosopher (ca. 20 B.C.–A.D. 50) of Alexandria, Egypt. Philo worked out a system that tried to interpret biblical concepts and beliefs in terms of the philosophy of Plato and his followers. In this system, God cannot be known directly, but only through intermediate beings; the soul, the higher element in the human person, is always attempting to return to God, its origin, although if this task is not far enough along at the time of the individual's death, the soul may have to transmigrate into another body and try again. In Philo's view, the best insights of Greek philosophy were compatible with the religion of the Hebrew Scriptures and could be found in the Bible by means of allegorical interpretation, which he used in his own interpretive works. He influenced Jewish writers like the author of the Wisdom of Solomon and Christian theologians such as Clement, Origen, and Ambrose.

**Phoenicians** the people who lived in the area north of Israel, in part of what is present-day

Lebanon. Their chief cities were Tyre and Sidon. The Phoenicians were known throughout the eastern Mediterranean region as merchants, and for producing a reddish-purple dye, from which they apparently got their name (*phoinix* is the Greek word for the color of the dye).

**phylacteries** (Gr. *phulakterion,* "amulet," from *phulax,* "guard") see **tefillin.**

**Platonism** a particular philosophy derived from the teaching of Plato, saying that there is a profound difference, even an opposition, between the realm of matter and the realm of spirit, and that the world of sense experience is essentially an illusion, deriving what reality it has from a correspondence with a true, ultimately real world of Forms. The influence of Platonism on religious thought can be seen in the Wisdom of Solomon; it is also apparent in the thought of **Philo Judaeus** and Christian thinkers like Clement, Origen, and Augustine.

**pogrom** an officially encouraged, organized massacre of a minority group.

**polemic, polemical** (Gr. *polemos,* "war") an argument or debate in the form of an attack on one's opponent or on the opposing position. Polemical speech is characterized by verbal attacks, exaggerated language, and sometimes violent imagery.

**Polycarp, Letter of** an early Christian letter of instruction. it was written by Polycarp, bishop of Smyrna, and addressed to the church of Philippi. It gives advice about dealing with problems in the congregation, exhorts readers to behave in a moral fashion, and combats false teachings. It is therefore similar to many canonical New Testament writings, some of which (like the Gospels and Paul's letters) Polycarp seems to know.

**potsherd** a broken piece of pottery. Examination of such pieces allows archeologists to date the different levels of a site according to the type of pottery represented at a given level.

**primogeniture** the social arrangement by which the eldest son inherits a father's title or the bulk of the father's property.

**proem** a short introduction or preface to a literary text.

**prophet** (Gr. *prophetes,* "speak out" or "speak forth") the LXX translation of *nabi'* ("one who is called"), the standard Hebrew term for prophet. Synonyms include "seer," "man of God," and "visionary." Besides the authors of the prophetic books, Moses, Samuel, and others are called prophets. Prophets do not so much predict the future, as the current use would imply, as they speak about the situation of their own time and what it will result in if nothing changes.

**Prophets, The** the second division of the Hebrew Scriptures.

**proverb** (Heb. *mashal,* "comparison") a short statement of traditional wisdom, supported by long experience and expressed in memorable form. In Hebrew proverbs, generally the second line repeats or develops, sometimes by contrast, the thought of the first line. This feature is called parallelism and is common in Hebrew poetry. Proverbs are quoted in many books of the Bible, but the major collection is in the book of Proverbs. There are also proverbs in the Wisdom of Solomon and, in a longer "essay" form, in Ben Sira (Ecclesiasticus).

**psalm** (from Gr. *psalmos*) a song accompanied by musical instruments. In the Bible these songs cover a wide variety of styles and greatly differing content; psalms appear in many places (e.g., 1 Sm 2:1–10; Jon 2:1–9), but the principal collection of them is found in the book of Psalms. The Hebrew name for this book is *Tehillim,* meaning "praises," even though the majority of the psalms are not hymns of praise but spread over many other categories such as laments, prayers of thanksgiving and confidence, wisdom, and psalms of royalty.

**pseudonymous** written or published under a false name (e.g., Testaments of the Twelve Patriarchs). Most pseudonymous writing is attributed to someone much better known than the actual writer, to give the text the benefit of the presumed authority of the famous person.

**Ptolemies** the rulers of Egypt and its surrounding areas after the breakup of the Greek empire of Alexander the Great, following his death.

**Purim** the festival that commemorates the delivery of the Jews in Persia from destruction, as recounted in the book of Esther. It is celebrated on 14 or 15 Adar.

## Q

**Q** see **synoptic problem.**

**qinah meter** a metrical pattern consisting of a line with three stresses followed by a line with two stresses; it is primarily used in psalms of lament or complaint, and in the book of Lamentations, though it can also express joy (Ps 65).

**Qumran Community** the settlement near Wadi Qumran at the Dead Sea, most likely composed of Essenes. The Qumran group was a sectarian Jewish community that kept its own practices in opposition to the established community in Jerusalem and Judea; the library of this group was discovered in 1948 and is known as the Dead Sea Scrolls.

## R

**rabbi** (Aram. "teacher") a Jewish religious leader who studied Torah and its associated commentaries, particularly the Talmud, and offered his own teaching based on that study.

**reader-response criticism** analyzing a text by looking at the relationship between the text and its reader, including the clues within the text that guide the reader in drawing meaning from it.

**redaction criticism** the study of how already existing textual units—narratives of incidents, laws, proverbs, or other isolatable pieces that can be disentangled by **source criticism**—were combined into larger texts by the activities of editors called "redactors." Redaction criticism concentrates on the perspective of the editor, trying to deduce what editorial intentions can be understood from the way smaller units are arranged, expanded, and combined.

**redactor** an editor who works with already existing units to combine them into larger wholes.

**resident alien** a foreigner with legal rights living in Israel or an Israelite residing in the territory of another tribe.

**revelation** (Lat. "remove the veil," translating Gr. *apokalypsis*) belief or insight granted to a human being by a deity or heavenly being.

**rhetoric** (Gr. *rhetor,* "speaker, orator") the art or study of persuasive speech or writing.

**Roman Period** the period from 63 B.C. onwards, marking the beginning of Roman rule of Judea.

**romance** a popular storytelling technique in the ancient Mediterranean world that recounted the situation of young lovers and how they overcome obstacles to their marriage. Tobit is the purest romance in biblical literature. In early Christianity the form was modified to tell the stories of early converts and martyrs and the obstacles to their faith.

**Rosh ha-Shanah** (Heb. "head [i.e., beginning] of the year") the fall New Year in the Jewish calendar, 1 Tishri. (Rosh Ha-Shanah is now observed for two days.) The beginning of the religious calendar is 1 Nisan.

## S

**sackcloth** rough cloth, often made from animal hair. A garment made of sackcloth is uncomfortable and is worn to indicate penitence or grief.

**sacrifice** (Lat. "make holy") the practice of giving something of value to God to show one's devotion or commitment. In Israelite religion, sacrifice, usually of an animal or bird (though grain and wine were also offered), was carried out by the ritual destruction of part or all of it by fire on an altar; by chasing it off into the wilderness; by letting it fly away; or by pouring it out on the ground or against the side of the altar. By giving to God something of value, the offerer symbolized the bonding of self with God or the reunion with God after a sinful or unclean person received forgiveness and purification. Christianity took over this idea of sacrifice and applied it to the death of Jesus Christ, teaching that Christ's sacrifice was an atonement for human sin. In modern-day Christianity, sacrifice usually entails doing without things of value (money, material possessions, or time) by giving them away, to the church to promote its work of worship and service, to any organization engaged in the service of others, or directly to those in need.

**Sadducees** a movement among Jews in the first century A.D., according to Josephus and the New Testament. They held to a strict application of Torah and to maintaining Temple worship according to its mandate; to continue the Temple practices without interference, the Sadducees were apparently willing to collaborate with the occupying Roman power to some extent, including accepting Roman interference in the choice of high priest. They were opposed to the Pharisees in not accepting the traditions of oral law as a guide to Torah practices, and they were also opposed to the political activists who wished to rebel against Roman rule, fearing that any rebellion would bring an end to the limited autonomy under which they could maintain Temple worship. See **Pharisees.**

**Samaritan Pentateuch** a text of the Torah in Hebrew used by the **Samaritans.** This text disagrees with the Masoretic text at many points. Some of these disagreements reflect Samaritan beliefs (e.g., in the religious importance of Mt. Gerizim), but others are supported by the **Dead Sea Scrolls** and reflect an alternate textual tradition.

**Samaritans** the descendants of the population of Samaria (northern kingdom) after the invasion of that kingdom and the deportation of the inhabitants in 722 B.C. The Samaritans regard themselves as descended from the Jewish remnant after the deportation, but the returning exiles from the southern kingdom (after the Babylonian Exile) did not regard them as Jews, seeing them rather as descendants of foreigners who had been settled there after the Jewish population had been removed. Therefore, beginning with Ezra and Nehemiah, the leadership forbade intermarriage between Samaritans and Jews. The Samaritans maintained worship (with a Temple on Mt. Gerizim) and the Torah (but not the rest of the Bible), although their calendar is not the same as the Jewish calendar.

**Sanhedrin** (ultimately from Gr. *synedria* from *syn-* and *hedra,* "with seat," i.e., "council") the religious court, whose membership was drawn from the Jewish ruling classes, that held ruling authority over the territory of Palestine under the Roman empire. The Sanhedrin was responsible for census-taking and taxation, as well as for acting as a court that would decide cases on its own and also, after preliminary determination, send cases on to the Roman governors.

**scribe** in general, one who could write, especially official documents, and take down dictation for letters, legal proceedings, etc. In the New Testament, a scribe was a lawyer, one who was expert in the requirements and meaning of Jewish law.

**scroll** a long strip of parchment (treated leather) or papyrus (reeds split, moistened, and pressed together), on which a text was written in columns. The scroll was read by unrolling one side while rolling up the other, to expose successive columns of text.

**Second Isaiah** see **Deutero-Isaiah.**

**Second Temple** the Temple constructed ca. 515 B.C. by the returning exiles, and continued and expanded over the course of time, until its destruction by the Romans in A.D. 70.

**sect** a religious grouping that emphasizes strict adherence to particular teachings and excludes those who do not conform.

**seder** (Heb. "order") the ritual meal and recitation of Passover eve. Also, the major divisions of the Mishnah (pl. *sedarim*).

**Seleucid Empire** the political entity that ruled over Syria and (at times) Judea after the death of Alexander the Great. The Seleucid ruler Antiochus IV "Epiphanes" desecrated the Temple in 167 B.C., leading to the Maccabean revolt and the rededication of the Temple in 164 B.C., an event commemorated in the festival of Hanukkah.

**Seleucids** (after Seleucus, the general who was the first of this ruling group) the rulers of Syria and its surrounding areas after the breakup of the Greek empire of Alexander the Great, following his death.

**Septuagint** the ancient Greek translation of the Hebrew Scriptures. The Septuagint was translated over a lengthy period beginning probably in the third century B.C. Traditionally there were 72 translators, a number that is rounded off to 70 and, in roman numerals, used as the abbreviation for this translation (LXX). The Septuagint was prepared for the use of Jews who lived outside the land of Israel and whose main language was Greek. It is important for several reasons: it translated a version of the Hebrew text that is older than the currently available Hebrew (Masoretic) text (see **Masoretic text**); it contains additional works, the Apocryphal/Deuterocanonical Books, most of which were originally written in Greek; and it was the Bible of early Christians and therefore represents what they thought of as Scripture.

**Shabbat** (Heb. "cessation") the Sabbath day.

**Shavuot** the festival of "Weeks," (also "Pentecost," Gr. for "fiftieth" [day]) the spring harvest, occurring, according to Priestly texts, 50 days (seven full weeks) after Passover.

**Shekhinah** a post-biblical term for the "dwelling" or "presence" of God with Israel; by extension, the divine manifestation in the community's life, or the sense of divine immanence within the world.

**Shema** the first word, used as a title, of the exhortation (Dt 6:4), "Hear, O Israel! The LORD is our God, the LORD alone!" (or, "the LORD our God, the LORD is one"); also the name of perhaps the most important and best-known prayer in Judaism, comprised of Deuteronomy 6:4–9; 11:13–21 and Numbers 15:37–41.

**Sheol** the underworld or abode of the dead. In the Hebrew Bible (Old Testament), all deceased descended to Sheol; there is no concept of a separate heaven and hell.

**shofar** the ram's horn for ceremonial use. In ancient Israel it was sounded to announce the anointing of a king or as a summons to war or to sound an alarm; today, in the synagogue, it is sounded on the High Holy Days.

**simile** a comparison, using "like" or "as" rather than, as in metaphor, linking two things directly. "[He] made my feet like a deer's" (Ps 18:34).

**source criticism** the effort to discover the sources or documents behind a text and to explore how the sources were combined into larger units. See **documentary hypothesis.**

**Southern Kingdom** the remaining part of the undivided kingdom of Israel, after the northern tribes withdrew from Israel at Solomon's death (1 Kgs 12). It is also called Judah.

**Stoics** Greek philosophers in the Hellenistic and Roman periods, who taught that emotions should be strictly controlled by reason.

**Sukkot** (Heb. "booths") the autumn harvest festival ("festival of ingathering"), during which it is customary, following Leviticus 23:42–43, to dwell in temporary booths. See **Tabernacles, Feast of.**

**suzerain** the lord or ruler to whom loyalty is due in a covenant relationship. (Although the term is actually Old French for "sovereign," and originally applied to the feudal relationship of lord to peasant or subsidiary, it has been adapted for the ancient Near Eastern covenant system.)

**synagogue** (Gr. "coming together with") an assembly; a congregation. For Jews who were too distant from the Temple to worship at it, and for all Jews after the final destruction of the Temple by the Romans in A.D. 70, the synagogue became the only form of worship. Services consisted of prayer, song, and study of the sacred text.

**syncretism** the incorporation into one religion of practices and teachings derived from another, or the effort to combine two different religious traditions into a third, composite religion.

**synonymous parallelism** an imprecise term used for the type of **parallelism** where the second line or *colon* of a *bicolon* echoes the meaning of the first in different terms, for example, Isaiah 1:3, "An ox knows its owner, and an ass, its master's manger; But Israel does not know, my people has not understood."

**Synoptic Gospels** Matthew, Mark, and Luke. "Synoptic" means "view together" and is applied to these writings because they, unlike John, can be readily compared.

**synoptic problem** the observation that in many passages Matthew and Luke repeat with only minor changes what Mark says, yet in other passages they do not follow Mark, or include stories or sayings that Mark does not have, yet match each other very closely. (They also each include material that none of the others have, but that is not a characteristic that needs to be explained.) Many commentators, from the earliest years of Christianity, have tried to understand the relationship among the Synoptic Gospels. According to the most widely held theory, Matthew and Luke relied on Mark and on another document (now lost) that contained mostly sayings of Jesus; this second document is referred to as "Q" from the German word "Quelle," meaning "source." In addition, Matthew and Luke each had their own sources.

## T

**tabernacle** the portable sanctuary used by the Israelites during their wanderings in the wilderness. Exodus chapters 25–30 contain instructions for building it; the construction is narrated in Exodus chapters 35–40. It was eventually replaced by the Temple.

**Tabernacles, Feast of** the final harvest festival of grapes and olives, falling within our month of October. It was also called the "Feast of Booths" because the harvesters lived in the field in makeshift tents or booths. See **Sukkot.**

**tablet** a slab, typically of clay, with a smoothed surface that can be inscribed with a text.

**talion** (Lat. *talio,* "in kind" from *talis,* "like," "such like") a punishment that is of the same kind as the crime: exacting an equivalent penalty, such as an equal economic loss for theft, or death for murder, or "an eye for an eye." Talion is well-attested in Mesopotamian law, and in some biblical legal collections.

**Talmud** (Heb. "teaching") the title of the two great collections of rabbinic teaching, the Jerusalem Talmud or Talmud Yerushalmi and the Babylonian Talmud or Talmud Bavli. The Talmuds were compiled beginning after A.D. 200, as an extensive commentary on the Mishnah; they consist of comments on, and extensions of, the Mishnah sections to work out the application of Jewish teaching to everyday life, but they also include much other material, and information and teaching on a wide range of topics. The form of the Talmuds is that passages of the Mishnah are commented on by rabbinic teachings (called *gemara*). The Mishnah is not treated in its entirety. At the beginning of the Talmud's formation, the two centers of rabbinic study (the land of Israel and Babylonia) were in contact with each other and the commentary therefore reflected a common effort; later, especially with the completion of the Talmud in Israel (ca. A.D. 400), the Babylonian effort continued to refine and extend the applications, and it was the Talmud developed in Babylonia (completion after A.D. 500) that was distributed worldwide, under the auspices of the academies that continued to work in Babylon until the beginning of the second millennium A.D.

**tefillin** small black leather boxes containing biblical passages from Exodus 13:1–10; 13:11–16 and Deuteronomy 6:4–9; 11:13–21. Two are worn during weekday morning prayer: one on the head (above the space between the eyes, just below the hairline) and one on the (left) arm (see e.g., Dt 6:8). Also called "phylacteries."

**tel** a mound formed by repeated construction, occupation, and destruction of buildings on a particular site.

**Temple** the central place of worship for Israelite religion in Jerusalem, referring either to the first Temple built by Solomon or the Second Temple of Zerubbabel that was enlarged and rebuilt by Herod the Great.

**testament** (Lat. *testamentum,* "will, covenant"; translating Gr. *diatheke,* "covenant") an agreement, especially between God and human beings; also, the collections of books detailing various covenants between God and human beings: the "Old Testament" or "first covenant," that between God and Noah, Abraham, Moses, and the Israelites in general; and the "New Testament" or "new covenant" established by Jesus Christ.

**Tetrateuch** the first four books of the Bible, Genesis through Numbers, regarded as an edited collection to which Deuteronomy was then attached. See **Pentateuch.**

**Text** any fixed, written form of words; particularly, any writing that is subject to historical investigation, interpretation, exegesis, or homiletics.

**textual criticism** the effort to establish, by scholarly assessment of manuscript copies and other sources, an accurate version of a text according to what the original author had written.

**theodicy** the theological effort to justify the goodness of God in the face of suffering.

**theophany** (Gr. "appearance of god") the temporary appearance or manifestation of a divine being in a form that can be apprehended by the human senses.

**Third Isaiah** see **Trito-Isaiah.**

**Thomas, Gospel of** an early collection of sayings attributed to Jesus. It contains no miracle stories and no account of Jesus' deeds, his birth, his death, or the resurrection. Some of the sayings resemble those in the canonical Gospels, but others reflect a philosophy that regards spirit and matter as radically different and opposed to each other; in this view, life on earth is one of spirits trapped in matter, and the purpose of life is to free oneself from matter and attain eternal life in the spiritual realm. This philosophy, called **gnosticism,** was rejected by the main body of early Christians, and this may explain why the Gospel of Thomas was never accepted as canonical.

**thresh** to beat gathered stalks of grain to separate the grain from the stems and husks. See **winnow**. A threshing floor, a flat area used for threshing grain, was often built on a hilltop to catch the breeze necessary for winnowing. This hilltop location made a threshing floor an ideal location for holding sacrifices (1 Chr 21:18–27).

**threshing floor** a location where the usable portion of grain is separated from its outer covering. Grain is threshed by being beaten to crack the husks and separate the grain from the stems. It is then winnowed by being tossed in a flat basket in a breeze, allowing the husks (chaff), which are lighter, to blow away. A good location for this process is a flat area on a hilltop; this was also an ideal spot for offering sacrifice (see 1 Chr 21:18–27).

**toledoth** (Heb. "generations") lists of descendants; also, histories of ancestors and their descendants.

**Torah** (Heb. "teaching, instruction") the first division of the Hebrew Scriptures, consisting of Genesis through Deuteronomy. The word (and hence the title) is sometimes translated "law," but this translation can be misleading since the full collection of books contains much more than law codes and regulations.

**tradition** (Lat. *traditio,* "what is handed on") the means by which beliefs, customs, stories, laws, religious practices, and other cultural phenomena are handed down from one generation to the next. The Bible is in part a record of traditions, first among the Hebrew people and then among the Christians. The Bible itself was first represented in tradition: in traditional stories and beliefs, in religious practices, and so on; only later was it written down and handed on in that form. The study of tradition—of how things are handed on, and how they change or stay the same during the process—is of great importance for understanding the Bible and the beliefs that are based on it.

**tradition criticism** the interpretation of the history of a tradition, including stages such as oral transmission, the alteration of a tradition to address a changed situation, and the examination of particular kinds of traditions, such as the explanation of place names, the development of religious practices, or the growth or disuse of social practices.

**Transjordan** the area to the east of the Jordan River.

**transmission history** an account, usually inferred, of how a text came down to the present from its originator. Steps in transmission history can include oral transmission, redaction, manuscript copying, and scribal emendation.

**Trito-Isaiah** the scholarly term for chs 56–66 (or 55–66) of Isaiah. These chapters are primarily concerned with the life of the returned exiles in the province of Yehud (the Persian name for Judah) after 538 B.C. Some scholars doubt the separate existence of Trito-Isaiah; others maintain that it is not the product of one author, but a collection of diverse oracles by different members of a "school of Isaiah" collected during the Persian period.

**Twelve, Book of the** the Hebrew Bible's designation for the **Minor Prophets.**

**typology** (Gr. *typos,* the raised design on a seal for imprinting in wax, then by extension a pattern or model) understanding persons or events, especially in the New Testament, by referring them to Old Testament "types," such as the Exodus (1 Cor 10:1–6); Solomon (Lk 11:31); or narratives like that of Jonah (Lk 11:29–30).

## U

**uncircumcised, the** Gentiles (Rom 4:9; Gal 2:7).

**unleavened bread** (Heb. *matzah, matzot*) bread made without yeast; also the festival that follows **Passover.**

## V

**vassal** the underlord in a covenant relationship, who is granted power and control over people in a particular area in return for loyalty to the suzerain.

**Vatican II** the Council of Catholic bishops under the leadership of Popes John XXIII and Paul VI, held 1962–1965 in the Vatican. It undertook numerous reforms, including establishing vernacular liturgies and issuing decrees on ecumenism, relations with Judaism and other religions, and the Church and the modern world. The Council also promoted the study and reading of the Scriptures and encouraged new Catholic translations and commentaries to help the understanding of nonexperts.

**Vulgate** (Lat., "common") the Latin translation of the Bible begun by St. Jerome in the fourth century A.D., completed 405. Jerome translated his version directly from the Hebrew (unlike that of the previous Latin version [the "Old Latin" or "Vetus Latina"], which was translated from the Septuagint) and Greek texts and also separated the Old Testament text that was not part of the Hebrew Bible, but included in the Septuagint, into a separate section of "deuterocanonical" books. In the Middle Ages the Vulgate became the standard translation of the Bible for Western Christians. With the Protestant Reformation, its authority was questioned, but was reaffirmed by the Roman Catholic Church at the Council of Trent (1546).

## W

**wadi** (Arabic) a stream bed or valley that is dry for part of the year; an arroyo or gulch.

**Weeks, Feast of** Shavuot or Pentecost.

**winnow** to separate grain from its husks (called chaff) after it has been threshed. The threshed grain is placed in a wide, flat basket and tossed repeatedly into the air, allowing a breeze to blow away the lighter chaff while the grain drops back down into the basket.

**wisdom literature** Job, Proverbs, and Ecclesiastes in the Hebrew Bible; Ben Sira and Wisdom in the Septuagint; and some Psalms, for example, 37. Wisdom literature is concerned with insight, instruction, meditation of the meaning of life, and moral exhortation. It does not generally concern itself with key events in Israel's history, such as the Exodus; central teachings, such as the covenant; or focal institutions, such as the Davidic monarchy, prophecy, or the Temple.

**Writings** the third division of the Hebrew Scriptures.

## X

**xenophobia** fear of, or contempt for, foreigners; racial exclusiveness.

## Y

**Yehud** designation of the province of Judea during Persian times.

**YHWH** the name of God, which conventionally remains unpronounced and is represented in the text by the Hebrew letters *yod-he-vav-he* and the vowels for the title *Adonai,* "my Lord." In standard English translations, YHWH is represented by the word LORD written in capital and small capital letters. The original vocalization and meaning of this name is unknown, though it is connected to the verb *h-y-h,* "be" or "become," most likely in a causitive sense, "he who causes to be."

**Yom Kippur** (Heb. "day of atonement") the solemn fast observed each year on 10 Tishri, according to the command recorded in Leviticus 23:26–32. The observance involves abstention of various kinds and focuses on personal and communal repentance (teshuvah). The prayer services begin with the evening service and continue through the next day, with a morning service, an additional service, an afternoon service, and a concluding service.

## Z

**Zealot** a member of the Jewish revolutionary movement during the Roman occupation of Palestine; an advocate of armed resistance in Roman rule.

**ziggurat** a temple-tower in ancient Mesopotamia. Ziggurats are presumed to represent a mount, on the top of which the earthly and divine realms merged.

**Zion** the name of the fortified hill within Jerusalem and thus, by extension, an alternative name for Jerusalem itself.

# INDEX TO READING GUIDE

# INDEX TO READING GUIDE

**D**

**M**

# COLLABORATORS
## on the Old Testament of the *New American Bible* 1970

### BISHOPS' COMMITTEE OF THE CONFRATERNITY OF CHRISTIAN DOCTRINE

Most Rev. Charles P. Greco, D.D., *Chairman* Most Rev. Joseph T. McGucken, S.T.D. Most Rev. Vincent S. Waters, D.D.
Most Rev. Romeo Blanchette, D.D. Most Rev. Christopher J. Weldon, D.D.

### EDITORS IN CHIEF

Rev. Louis F. Hartman, C.SS.R., S.S.L., LING. OR. L., *Chairman* Rev. Msgr. Patrick W. Skehan, S.T.D., LL.D., *Vice-Chairman*
Rev. Stephen J. Hartdegen, O.F.M., S.S.L., *Secretary*

### ASSOCIATE EDITORS AND TRANSLATORS

Rev. Edward P. Arbez, S.S., S.T.D. Rev. Msgr. Edward J. Byrne, PH.D., S.T.D. Rev. Edward A. Cerny, S.S., S.T.D.
Rev. James E. Coleran, S.J., S.T.L., S.S.L. Rev. John J. Collins, S.J., M.A., S.S.L.
Sr. M. Emmanuel Collins, O.S.F., PH.D. Prof. Frank M. Cross Jr., PH.D. Rev. Patrick Cummins, O.S.B., S.T.D.
Rev. Antonine A. DeGuglielmo, O.F.M., S.T.D., S.S.L., S.S.LECT. GEN. Rev. Alexander A. Di Lella, O.F.M., S.T.L., S.S.L., PH.D.
Most Rev. John J. Dougherty, S.T.L., S.S.D. William A. Dowd, S.J., S.T.D., S.S.L. Prof. David Noel Freedman, PH.D.
Rev. Michael J. Fruenthaner, S.J., S.T.D., S.S.D. Rev. Msgr. Maurice A. Hofer, S.S.L Rev. Justin Krellner, O.S.B., S.T.D.
Rev. Joseph L. Lilly, C.M., S.T.D., S.S.L. Rev. Roderick F. MacKenzie, S.J., M.A., S.S.D.
Rev. Edward A. Mangan, C.SS.R., S.S.L. Rev. Daniel W. Martin, C.M., S.T.L., S.S.L. Rev. William H. McClellan, S.J.
Rev. James McGlinchey, C.M., S.T.D. Rev. Frederick Moriarty, S.J., S.S.L., S.T.D. Rev. Richard T. Murphy, O.P., S.T.D., S.S.D.
Rev. Roland E. Murphy, O. Carm., M.A., S.T.D., S.S.L. Rev. Msgr. William R. Newton, M.S., S.S.D.
Rev. Everhard Olinger, O.S.B. Rev. Charles H. Pickar, O.S.A., S.T.L., S.S.L.
Rev. Christopher Rehwinkel, O.F.M., S.T.D., S.S. LECT. GEN. Rev. Msgr. John R. Rowan, S.T.D., S.S.L.,
Prof. J.A. Sanders, PH.D. Rev. Edward F. Siegman, C.PP.S., S.T.D., S.S.L. Rev. Msgr. Matthew P. Stapleton, S.T.D., S.S.L.
Rev. Msgr. John E. Steinmueller, S.T.D., S.S.L. Rev. John Ujlaki, O.S.B., LITT.D.
Rev. Bruce Vawter, C.M., S.T.L., S.S.D. Rev. John B. Weisengoff, S.T.D., S.S.L.

# COLLABORATORS
## on the Revised Psalms of the *New American Bible* 1991

**BISHOPS' AD HOC COMMITTEE**

Most Rev. Enrique San Pedro, S.J.   Most Rev. Richard Sklba, D.D.   Most Rev. Donald W. Trautman, S.T.D., S.S.L.
Most Rev. Emil A. Wcela   Most Rev. John F. Whealon, S.S.L., *Chairman*

**BOARD OF EDITORS**

Rev. Richard Clifford, S.J.   Br. Aloysius Fitzgerald, F.S.C.   Rev. Joseph Jensen, O.S.B.   Rev. Roland Murphy, O.Carm.
Sr. Irene Nowell, O.S.B.   Dr. Judith Sanderson

**REVISERS**

Prof. Gary Anderson   Rev. Michael L. Barré, S.S.   Rev. Christopher T. Begg   Dr. Joseph Blenkinsopp
Rev. Anthony R. Ceresko, O.S.F.S.   Rev. Richard J. Clifford, S.J.   Rev. Aelred Cody, O.S.B.   Prof. Michael D. Coogan
Rev. Alexander A. Di Lella, O.F.M.   Dr. Robert A. Di Vito   Br. Aloysius Fitzgerald, F.S.C.   Rev. Michael D. Guinan, O.F.M.
Rev. William L. Holladay   Rev. William Irwin, C.S.B.   Rev. Joseph Jensen, O.S.B.   Rev. John S. Kselman
Rev. Leo Laberge, O.M.I.   Dr. Conrad E. L'Heureux   Dr. Paul G. Mosca   Rev. Dr. Roland E. Murphy, O.Carm.
Dr. Michael Patrick O'Connor   Rev. Brian J. Peckham, S.J.   Prof. Jimmy J. Roberts   Sr. Eileen M. Schuller, O.S.U.
Dr. Byron E. Shafer   Prof. Mark S. Smith   Prof. Matitiahu Tesvat   Dr. Eugene C. Ulrich
Prof. James C. VanderKam   Rev. Jerome T. Walsh

**ENGLISH CONSULTANTS**

Dr. Catherine Dunn
Br. Daniel Burke, F.S.C.

**BUSINESS MANAGER**

Charles A. Buggé

# COLLABORATORS
## on the Revised New Testament of the *New American Bible* 1986

### BISHOPS' AD HOC COMMITTEE

Most Rev. Theodore E. McCarrick, D.D. Most Rev. Richard J. Sklba, D.D. Most Rev. J. Francis Stafford, D.D.
Most Rev. John F. Whealon, D.D., *Chairman*

### BOARD OF EDITORS

Rev. Msgr. Myles M. Bourke Rev. Francis T. Gignac, S.J., *Chairman*
Rev. Stephen J. Hartdegen, O.F.M., *Secretary* Rev. John H. Reumann

### REVISERS

Rev. Msgr. Myles M. Bourke Rev. Frederick W. Danker Rev. Alexander A. Di Lella, O.F.M. Rev. Charles H. Giblin, S.J.
Rev. Francis T. Gignac, S.J. Rev. Stephen J. Hartdegen, O.F.M. Dr. Maurya P. Horgan Rev. John R. Keating, S.J.
Rev. John Knox Dr. Paul J. Kobelski Dr. J. Rebecca Lyman Br. Elliott C. Maloney, O.S.B. Dr. Janet A. Timbie

### CONSULTANTS

Rev. Joseph Jensen, O.S.B. Rev. Aidan Kavanagh, O.S.B. Dr. Marianne Sawicki

### BUSINESS MANAGER

Charles A. Buggé

### WORD PROCESSOR

Suzanna Jordan

# COLLABORATORS
## on the Old Testament of the *New American Bible* 2010

**BISHOPS' COMMITTEE ON DOCTRINE**
**SUBCOMMITTEE ON THE TRANSLATION OF SCRIPTURE TEXT**

Most Rev. Arthur J. Serratelli, *Chairman* Justin Cardinal Rigali Most Rev. Blase J. Cupich
Most Rev. Richard J. Sklba Most Rev. Anthony B. Taylor

**BOARD OF EDITORS**

Dr. Deirdre A. Dempsey Dr. Robert A. Di Vito Rev. Francis T. Gignac, S.J. Rev. Joseph Jensen, O.S.B., *Chairman*
Rev. Dale Launderville, O.S.B. Rev. Roland E. Murphy, O.Carm. + Dr. Kathleen S. Nash
Sr. Irene Nowell, O.S.B. Rev. James P. M. Walsh, S.J.

**REVISERS**

Dr. Gary A. Anderson Reverend Michael L. Barré, S.S. Reverend Christopher T. Begg Dr. Joseph Blenkinsopp
Reverend Lawrence Boadt, C.S.P. + Professor Edward F. Campbell Professor Anthony Ceresko, OSFS +
Reverend Richard J. Clifford, S.J. Reverend Aelred Cody, O.S.B. Dr. John J. Collins Professor Michael D. Coogan
Reverend T.J. Jeremy Corley Dr. Toni Craven Dr. James L. Crenshaw Reverend Alexander A. Di Lella, O.F.M.
Dr. Robert A. Di Vito Brother Aloysius Fitzgerald, F.S.C. + Reverend Joseph A. Fitzmyer, S.J. Dr. Carole R. Fontaine
Reverend Daniel J. Harrington, S.J. Dr. Richard S. Hess Dr. Theodore Hiebert Dr. William L. Holladay Dr. Tod Linafelt
Dr. P. Kyle McCarter, Jr. Dr. Carol Meyers Dr. Eric Meyers Dr. Patrick D. Miller, Jr.
Reverend Craig E. Morrison, O.Carm. Dr. Paul G. Mosca Dr. Kathleen S. Nash Professor Robert A. Oden, Jr.
Reverend Gregory J. Polan, O.S.B. Dr. James J.M. Roberts Dr. William M. Soll Dr. Gene M. Tucker
Dr. Eugene C. Ulrich Reverend Walter A. Vogels, W.F. Reverend Jerome T. Walsh
Reverend Addison G. Wright, S.S. Dr. David P. Wright

**BUSINESS MANAGERS**

Charles Buggé Mary Elizabeth Sperry

**WORD PROCESSORS**

Ellen Coughlin Nancy Hartnagel

# COLLABORATORS
## on the Book of Psalms of the *New American Bible* 2010

### BISHOPS' COMMITTEE ON DOCTRINE
### SUBCOMMITTEE ON THE TRANSLATION OF SCRIPTURE TEXT

Most Rev. Arthur J. Serratelli, *Chairman* Justin Cardinal Rigali Most Rev. Blase J. Cupich
Most Rev. Richard J. Sklba Most Rev. Anthony B. Taylor

### BOARD OF EDITORS

Rev. Joseph Mindling, OFM Cap. Rev. J. Edward Owens, O.SS.T.

### REVISERS

Rev. Michael L. Barré, S.S. Dr. Corrine L. Carvalho Dr. Robert A. Di Vito Dr. Robert D. Miller II, SFO
Rev. Joseph Mindling, OFM Cap. Rev. J. Edward Owens, O.SS.T. Dr. Eugene C. Ulrich

### BUSINESS MANAGER

Mary Elizabeth Sperry

# A CONCORDANCE TO THE *NEW AMERICAN BIBLE*

## SPECIAL SYMBOLS

| | |
|---|---|
| * | *GOD, *LORD and *LORD'S index the proper name of God *(Yahweh)* typeset in small capital letters (GOD, LORD, LORD's) in the NAB. |
| → | An arrow following an entry heading points to related words for additional study |
| = | An equals sign marks an alternate proper name for additional study (e.g., ISRAEL = JACOB) |

John R. Kohlenberger III

## TABLE OF ABBREVIATIONS

| | |
|---|---|
| Acts | Acts |
| Am | Amos |
| Bar. | Baruch |
| 1 Chr. | 1 Chronicles |
| 2 Chr. | 2 Chronicles |
| 1 Cor | 1 Corinthians |
| 2 Cor | 2 Corinthians |
| Col. | Colossians |
| Dn | Daniel |
| Dt | Deuteronomy |
| Eccl | Ecclesiastes |
| Eph | Ephesians |
| Est. | Esther |
| Ex | Exodus |
| Ez | Ezekiel |
| Ezr | Ezra |
| Gal | Galatians |
| Gn | Genesis |
| Hb. | Habakkuk |
| Hg | Haggai |
| Heb | Hebrews |
| Hos | Hosea |
| Is | Isaiah |
| Jas | James |
| Jgs | Judges |
| Jdt | Judith |
| Jb | Job |
| Jl. | Joel |
| Jer. | Jeremiah |
| Jn. | John |
| 1 Jn. | 1 John |
| 2 Jn. | 2 John |
| 3 Jn. | 3 John |
| Jon | Jonah |
| Jos | Joshua |
| Jude | Jude |
| 1 Kgs | 1 Kings |
| 2 Kgs | 2 Kings |
| Lam. | Lamentations |
| Lk | Luke |
| Lv. | Leviticus |
| Mal | Malachi |
| 1 Mc. | 1 Maccabees |
| 2 Mc. | 2 Maccabees |
| Mi | Micah |
| Mk | Mark |
| Mt. | Matthew |
| Na | Nahum |
| Neh. | Nehemiah |
| Nm | Numbers |
| Ob | Obadiah |
| Phil | Philippians |
| Phlm | Philemon |
| 1 Pt | 1 Peter |
| 2 Pt | 2 Peter |
| Prv | Proverbs |
| Ps. | Psalms |
| Rev | Revelation |
| Rom | Romans |
| Ru | Ruth |
| 1 Sm. | 1 Samuel |
| 2 Sm. | 2 Samuel |
| Sir | Ben Sira |
| Sg | Song of Songs |
| Tb | Tobit |
| 1 Thes | 1 Thessalonians |
| 2 Thes | 2 Thessalonians |
| Ti | Titus |
| 1 Tm. | 1 Timothy |
| 2 Tm. | 2 Timothy |
| Wis | Wisdom |
| Zec | Zechariah |
| Zep. | Zephaniah |

### OTHER

| | |
|---|---|
| S | Shorter Ending of Mark |
| Pr: | Ben Sira Prologue |

## A

**AARON**

Genealogy (Ex 6:16-20; Jos 21:4, 10; 1 Chr 6:3-15). Priesthood of (Ex 28:1; Nm 17; Heb 5:1-4; 7), vestments of (Ex 28; 39), consecration of (Ex 29), ordination of (Lv 8).

Spokesman for Moses (Ex 4:14-16, 27–31; 7:1-2). Supported Moses' hands in battle (Ex 17:8-13). Built golden calf (Ex 32; Dt 9:20). Spoke against Moses (Nm 12). Priesthood opposed (Nm 16); staff budded (Nm 17). Forbidden to enter the promised land (Nm 20:1-12). Death of (Nm 20:22-29; 33:38-39). Praise of (Sir 45:6-22).

**ABANDON** → ABANDONED

Dt 4:31 God, he will not **a** or destroy you,
2 Chr 15:2 but if you **a** him, he will **a** you.
Acts 2:27 because you will not **a** my soul

**ABANDONED** → ABANDON

Jgs 2:13 Because they had **a** the LORD
2 Chr 12:5 You have **a** me, and so I have **a** you
Sir 49:4 They **a** the Law of the Most High,
Is 54:7 For a brief moment I **a** you,

**ABBA**

Mk 14:36 he said, "**A**, Father, all things are
Rom 8:15 through which we cry, "**A**, Father!"
Gal 4:6 our hearts, crying out, "**A**, Father!"

**ABEDNEGO** → =AZARIAH

Deported to Babylon with Daniel (Dn 1:1-6). Name changed from Azariah (Dn 1:7). Refused defilement by food (Dn 1:8-20). Refused idol worship (Dn 3:1-12); saved from furnace (Dn 3:13-30).

**ABEL**

Second son of Adam (Gn 4:2). Offered acceptable sacrifice (Gn 4:4; Heb 11:4; 12:24). Murdered by Cain (Gn 4:8; Mt 23:35; Lk 11:51; 1 Jn 3:12).

**ABIATHAR**

High priest in days of Saul and David (1 Sm 22; 2 Sm 15; 1 Kgs 1–2; Mk 2:26). Escaped Saul's slaughter of priests (1 Sm 22:18-23). Supported David in Absalom's revolt (2 Sm 15:24-29). Supported Adonijah (1 Kgs 1:7-42); deposed by Solomon (1 Kgs 2:22-35; cf. 1 Sm 2:31-35).

**ABIDE**

Ps 15:1 LORD, who may **a** in your tent?
91:1 who **a** in the shade of the Almighty,
Wis 3:9 the faithful shall **a** with him in love:

**ABIGAIL**

1. Sister of David (1 Chr 2:16-17).

2. Wife of Nabal (1 Sm 25:30); pled for his life with David (1 Sm 25:14-35). Became David's wife after Nabal's death (1 Sm 25:36-42).

**ABIHU**

Son of Aaron (Ex 6:23; 24:1, 9); killed for offering illicit fire (Lv 10; Nm 3:2-4; 1 Chr 24:1-2).

**ABIJAH**

1. Second son of Samuel (1 Chr 6:28); a corrupt judge (1 Sm 8:1-5).

2. An Aaronic priest (1 Chr 24:10; Lk 1:5).

3. Son of Jeroboam I; died as prophesied by Ahijah (1 Kgs 14:1-18).

4. Son of Rehoboam, also called Abijam; king of Judah who fought Jeroboam I attempting to reunite Israel (1 Kgs 14:31–15:8; 2 Chr 12:16–14:1).

**ABILITY** → ABLE

Mt 25:15 to each according to his **a**.

**ABIMELECH**

1. King of Gerar who took Abraham's wife Sarah, believing her to be his sister (Gn 20). Covenanted with Abraham (Gn 21:22-33).

2. King of Gerar who took Isaac's wife Rebekah, believing her to be his sister (Gn 26:1-11). Covenanted with Isaac (Gn 26:12-31).

3. Son of Gideon (Jgs 8:31). Attempted to become king (Jgs 9).

**ABIRAM**

Sided with Dathan in rebellion against Moses and Aaron (Nm 16; 26:9; Dt 11:6; Sir 45:18).

**ABISHAI**

Son of Zeruiah, David's sister (1 Sm 26:6; 1 Chr 2:16). One of David's chief warriors (1 Chr 11:15-21): against Edom (1 Chr 18:12-13), Ammon (2 Sm 10), Absalom (2 Sm 18), Sheba (2 Sm 20). Wanted to kill Saul (1 Sm 26), killed Abner (2 Sm 2:18-27; 3:22-39).

**ABLE** → ABILITY

Ex 18:25 He picked out **a** men from all Israel
Jdt 11:18 of them will be **a** to withstand you.
Rom 14:4 for the Lord is **a** to make him stand.
2 Cor 9:8 God is **a** to make every grace
Eph 6:11 you may be **a** to stand firm against
2 Tm 1:12 that he is **a** to guard what has been
Heb 2:18 he is **a** to help those who are being
5:2 He is **a** to deal patiently
7:25 he is always **a** to save those who
Rev 5:3 or under the earth was **a** to open

**ABNER**

Cousin of Saul and commander of his army (1 Sm 14:50; 17:55-57; 26). Made Ish-Bosheth king after Saul (2 Sm 2:8-10), but later defected to David (2 Sm 3:6-21). Killed Asahel (2 Sm 2:18-32), for which he was killed by Joab and Abishai (2 Sm 3:22-39).

**ABOLISH** → ABOLISHING

Mt 5:17 think that I have come to **a** the law
5:17 I have come not to **a** but to fulfill.

**ABOLISHING** → ABOLISH

Dn 11:31 **a** the daily sacrifice and setting

**ABOMINABLE** → ABOMINATION

2 Chr 28:3 accordance with the **a** practices
Ez 7:20 of them they made their **a** images,

**ABOMINATION** → ABOMINABLE, ABOMINATIONS

1 Mc 6:7 they had pulled down the **a**
Prv 6:16 hates, yes, seven are an **a** to him;
Dn 9:27 be the desolating **a** until the ruin

**ABOMINATIONS** → ABOMINATION

Ez 44:7 broken my covenant by all your **a**.
Rev 17:5 of harlots and of the **a** of the earth."

**ABOUND**

Rom 6:1 we persist in sin that grace may **a**?

**ABOVE**

Dt 4:39 the LORD is God in the heavens **a**
Jn 3:7 you, 'You must be born from **a**.'
Phil 2:9 him the name that is **a** every name,
Col 3:2 Think of what is **a**, not of what is

**ABRAHAM**

Abram, son of Terah (Gn 11:26-27), husband of Sarah (Gn 11:29).

Covenant relation with the LORD (Gn 12:1-3; 13:14-17; 15; 17; 22:15-18; Ex 2:24; Neh 9:8; Ps 105; Mi 7:20; Lk 1:68-75; Rom 4; Heb 6:13-15).

Called from Ur, via Haran, to Canaan (Gn 12:1; Acts 7:2-4; Heb 11:8-10). Moved to Egypt, nearly lost Sarah to Pharoah (Gn

12:10-20). Divided the land with Lot; settled in Hebron (Gn 13). Saved Lot from four kings (Gn 14:1-16); blessed by Melchizedek (Gn 14:17-20; Heb 7:1-20). Declared righteous by faith (Gn 15:6; Rom 4:3; Gal 3:6-9; 1 Mc 2:52). Fathered Ishmael by Hagar (Gn 16).

Name changed from Abram (Gn 17:5; Neh 9:7). Circumcised (Gn 17; Rom 4:9-12). Entertained three visitors (Gn 18); promised a son by Sarah (Gn 18:9-15; 17:16). Questioned destruction of Sodom and Gomorrah (Gn 18:16-33). Moved to Gerar; nearly lost Sarah to Abimelech (Gn 20). Fathered Isaac by Sarah (Gn 21:1-7; Acts 7:8; Heb 11:11-12); sent away Hagar and Ishmael (Gn 21:8-21; Gal 4:22-30). Covenant with Abimelech (Gn 21:22-32). Tested by offering Isaac (Gn 22; Heb 11:17-19; Jas 2:21-24). Sarah died; bought field of Ephron for burial (Gn 23). Secured wife for Isaac (Gn 24). Fathered children by Keturah (Gn 25:1-6; 1 Chr 1:32-33). Death (Gn 25:7-11).

Called servant of God (Gn 26:24), friend of God (2 Chr 20:7; Is 41:8; Jas 2:23), prophet (Gn 20:7), father of Israel (Ex 3:15; Is 51:2; Mt 3:9; Jn 8:39-58). Praised (Sir 44:19–45:1).

**ABSALOM**
Son of David by Maacah (2 Sm 3:3; 1 Chr 3:2). Killed Amnon for rape of his sister Tamar; banished by David (2 Sm 13). Returned to Jerusalem; received by David (2 Sm 14). Rebelled against David (2 Sm 15–17). Killed (2 Sm 18).

**ABSENT**
1 Cor 5: 3 although **a** in body but present
Col 2: 5 For even if I am **a** in the flesh, yet I

**ABUNDANCE** → ABUNDANTLY
2 Cor 9: 8 you may have an **a** for every good

**ABUNDANTLY** → ABUNDANCE
Jn 10: 10 might have life and have it more **a**.

**ABYSS**
Lk 8: 31 not to order them to depart to the **a**.
Rom 10: 7 or 'Who will go down into the **a**?'

**ACCEPT** → ACCEPTED
Mt 19: 11 "Not all can **a** [this] word, but only
Jn 1: 11 but his own people did not **a** him.

**ACCEPTED** → ACCEPT
Lk 4: 24 no prophet is **a** in his own native

**ACCESS**
Rom 5: 2 through whom we have gained **a**
Eph 2: 18 through him we both have **a** in one

**ACCORDING**
Sir 16: 12 judges people, each **a** to their deeds.
Mt 9: 29 it be done for you **a** to your faith."
Rom 8: 4 who live not **a** to the flesh but **a**
Heb 2: 4 gifts of the holy Spirit **a** to his will.
1 Jn 5: 14 that if we ask anything **a** to his will,
Rev 20: 12 The dead were judged **a** to their

**ACCOUNT**
Mt 12: 36 of judgment people will render an **a**
Heb 4: 13 him to whom we must render an **a**.

**ACCURSED** → CURSE
Rom 9: 3 I could wish that I myself were **a**
Rev 22: 3 Nothing **a** will be found there

**ACCUSE** → ACCUSER
Zec 3: 1 stood at his right side to **a** him.
Mt 12: 10 so that they might **a** him.

**ACCUSER** → ACCUSE
Rev 12: 10 For the **a** of our brothers is cast out,

**ACHAN**
Sinned at Jericho; stoned (Jos 7; 22:20; 1 Chr 2:7).

**ACHISH**
King of Gath before whom David feigned insanity (1 Sm 21:10-15). Later "ally" of David (2 Sm 27–29).

**ACKNOWLEDGE**
Mt 10: 32 others I will **a** before my heavenly
Rom 1: 28 since they did not see fit to **a** God,

**ACT** → ACTED, ACTIVE, ACTS
Ps 37: 5 trust in him and he will **a**

**ACTED** → ACT
Ez 20: 9 I **a** for the sake of my name, that it
Acts 3: 17 that you **a** out of ignorance, just as
1 Tm 1: 13 been mercifully treated because I **a**

**ACTIVE** → ACT
Jas 2: 22 faith was **a** along with his works,

**ACTS** → ACT
Ex 6: 6 arm and with mighty **a** of judgment.
Ps 71: 15 day after day your **a** of deliverance,
Mt 7: 24 **a** on them will be like a wise man
Jas 1: 25 who forgets but a doer who **a**,

**ADAM**
First man (Tb 8:6; Gn 1:26–2:25; Rom 5:14; 1 Tm 2:13). Sin of (Gn 3; Hos 6:7 [note]; Rom 5:12-21). Children of (Gn 4:1–5:5). Death of (Gn 5:5; Rom 5:12-21; 1 Cor 15:22).

**ADD**
Dt 4: 2 you shall not **a** to what I command
Prv 30: 6 **A** nothing to his words, lest he
Lk 12: 25 of you by worrying **a** a moment

**ADMONISH**
Col 3: 16 you teach and **a** one another,

**ADONIJAH**
1. Son of David by Haggith (2 Sm 3:4; 1 Chr 3:2). Attempted to be king after David; killed at Solomon's order (1 Kgs 1–2).
2. Levite; teacher of the Law (2 Chr 17:8).

**ADOPTION**
Rom 8: 15 fear, but you received a spirit of **a**,
8: 23 within ourselves as we wait for **a**,
Gal 4: 5 the law, so that we might receive **a**.

**ADORNED** → ADORNMENT
Lk 21: 5 how the temple was **a** with costly
Rev 17: 4 purple and scarlet and **a** with gold,
21: 2 God, prepared as a bride **a** for her

**ADORNMENT** → ADORNED
Prv 3: 22 to your soul, and an **a** for your neck.

**ADULTERERS** → ADULTERY
Jer 23: 10 The land is filled with **a**;
1 Cor 6: 9 nor idolaters nor **a** nor boy

**ADULTERESS** → ADULTERY
Lv 20: 10 and the **a** shall be put to death.

**ADULTERY** → ADULTERERS, ADULTERESS
Ex 20: 14 You shall not commit **a**.
Jer 3: 9 committing **a** with stone and wood.
Mt 5: 28 lust has already committed **a**
Lk 16: 18 and marries another commits **a**,
Jn 8: 3 a woman who had been caught in **a**

**ADVANTAGE**
Rom 3: 1 What **a** is there then in being a Jew?
1 Cor 10: 24 No one should seek his own **a**,

**ADVERSARIES** → ADVERSARY
2 Sm 22: 49 you have exalted me above my **a**,

**ADVERSARY**
Zec 3: 2 angel of the LORD said to the **a**,

# CONCORDANCE

1 Tm 5: 14 so as to give the **a** no pretext

**ADVICE**
2 Chr 10: 13 Ignoring the **a** the elders had given
Tb 4: 18 do not think lightly of any useful **a**.
Prv 8: 14 Mine are counsel and **a**;
Sir 37: 11 Seek no **a** from a woman about her

**ADVOCATE**
Jn 14: 26 The **A**, the holy Spirit
15: 26 the **A** comes whom I will send you
1 Jn 2: 1 sin, we have an **A** with the Father,

**AFFLICTED** → AFFLICTION
2 Cor 4: 8 We are **a** in every way, but not

**AFFLICTION** → AFFLICTED
Dt 16: 3 the bread of **a**, so that you may
Ps 25: 18 Look upon my **a** and suffering;
2 Cor 4: 17 this momentary light **a** is producing

**AFRAID** → FEAR
Gn 3: 10 but I was **a**, because I was naked,
Ex 3: 6 face, for he was **a** to look at God.
Dt 20: 3 Do not be weakhearted or **a**,
Mt 10: 31 So do not be **a**; you are worth more
28: 10 Jesus said to them, "Do not be **a**.
Lk 12: 32 Do not be **a** any longer, little flock,
Heb 13: 6 is my helper, [and] I will not be **a**.

**AGABUS**
A Christian prophet (Acts 11:28; 21:10).

**AGAG**
King of Amalekites; not killed by Saul (1 Sm 15).

**AGAIN**
Jb 14: 14 to die, and live **a**, all the days of my
Jn 14: 3 I will come back **a** and take you
Heb 6: 6 to bring them to repentance **a**,

**AGE** → AGES
Gn 21: 2 bore Abraham a son in his old **a**,
Mt 28: 20 you always, until the end of the **a**."
Gal 1: 4 us from the present evil **a** in accord

**AGES** → AGE
1 Cor 2: 7 God predetermined before the **a**
Col 1: 26 the mystery hidden from **a**
1 Tm 1: 17 To the king of **a**, incorruptible,

**AGREE**
Mt 18: 19 you, if two of you **a** on earth
Mk 14: 56 him, but their testimony did not **a**.

**AGRIPPA**
Descendant of Herod; king before whom Paul argued his case in Caesarea (Acts 25:13–26:32).

**AHAB**
1. Son of Omri; king of Israel (1 Kgs 16:28–22:40), husband of Jezebel (1 Kgs 16:31). Promoted Baal worship (1 Kgs 16:31-33); opposed by Elijah (1 Kgs 17:1; 18; 21), a prophet (1 Kgs 20:35-43), Micaiah (1 Kgs 22:1-28). Defeated Ben-Hadad (1 Kgs 20). Killed for failing to kill Ben-Hadad and for murder of Naboth (1 Kgs 20:35–21:40).
2. A false prophet (Jer 29:21-22).

**AHASUERUS** → =ARTAXERXES
King of Persia (Ezr 4:6), husband of Esther (called Artaxerxes in Est 11:1; 12:2; 13:1; 16:1). Deposed Vashti; replaced her with Esther (Est 1–2). Sealed Haman's edict to annihilate the Jews (Est 3). Received Esther without having called her (Est 5:1-8). Honored Mordecai (Est 6). Hanged Haman (Est 7). Issued edict allowing Jews to defend themselves (Est 8). Promoted Mordecai (Est 8:1-2, 15; 9:4; 10).

**AHAZ**
Son of Jotham; king of Judah, (2 Kgs 16; 2 Chr 28; Mt 1:9). Idolatry of (2 Kgs 16:3-4, 10-18; 2 Chr 28:1-4, 22-25). Defeated by Aram and Israel (2 Kgs 16:5-6; 2 Chr 28:5-15). Sought help from Assyria rather than the LORD (2 Kgs 16:7-9; 2 Chr 28:16-21; Is 7).

**AHAZIAH** → =JEHOAHAZ
1. Son of Ahab; king of Israel (1 Kgs 22:51-2 Kgs 1:18; 2 Chr 20:35-37). Made an unsuccessful alliance with Jehoshaphat (2 Chr 20:35-37). Died for seeking Baal rather than the LORD (2 Kgs 1).
2. Son of Jehoram; king of Judah (2 Kgs 8:25-29; 9:14-29), also called Jehoahaz (2 Chr 21:17–22:9; 25:23). Killed by Jehu while visiting Joram (2 Kgs 9:14-29; 2 Chr 22:1-9).

**AHEAD**
Mt 11: 10 I am sending my messenger **a**
Phil 3: 13 but straining forward to what lies **a**,

**AHIJAH**
1. Priest during Saul's reign (1 Sm 14:3,18).
2. Prophet of Shiloh (1 Kgs 11:29-39; 14:1-18).

**AHIKAM**
Father of Gedaliah (2 Kgs 25:22), protector of Jeremiah (Jer 26:24).

**AHIMAAZ**
1. Father-in-law of Saul (1 Sm 14:50).
2. Son of Zadok, the high priest, loyal to David (2 Sm 15:27,36; 17:17-20; 18:19-33).

**AHIMELECH**
1. Priest who helped David in his flight from Saul (1 Sm 21–22).
2. One of David's warriors (1 Sm 26:6).

**AHITHOPHEL**
One of David's counselors who sided with Absalom (2 Sm 15:12, 31-37; 1 Chr 27:33-34); committed suicide when his advice was ignored (2 Sm 16:15–17:23).

**AI**
Jos 7: 4 but they fled before the army at **A**,

**AIR**
Eph 2: 2 the ruler of the power of the **a**,
1 Thes 4: 17 the clouds to meet the Lord in the **a**.
Rev 16: 17 poured out his bowl into the **a**.

**ALARMED**
Mk 13: 7 and reports of wars do not be **a**;
2 Thes 2: 2 or to be **a** either by a "spirit,"

**ALEXANDER**
1 Mc 1: 1 After **A** the Macedonian,

**ALIEN** → ALIENS
Lv 19: 34 you shall love the **a** as yourself;
Dt 24: 17 You shall not deprive the resident **a**

**ALIENS** → ALIEN
Gn 15: 13 your descendants will reside as **a**
1 Pt 2: 11 I urge you as **a** and sojourners

**ALIVE** → LIVE
Gn 6: 19 to keep them **a** along with you.
Acts 1: 3 He presented himself **a** to them
1 Thes 4: 17 Then we who are **a**, who are left,
Rev 1: 18 but now I am **a** forever and ever.
19: 20 The two were thrown **a**

**ALL**
Gn 6: 13 that the end of **a** mortals has come,
Dt 8: 3 by **a** that comes forth from the mouth
Sir 7: 29 With **a** your soul fear God
Jer 29: 13 you seek me with **a** your heart,

Lk 10:27 God, with **a** your heart, with **a** your
Rom 3:23 **a** have sinned and are deprived
6:10 death, he died to sin once and for **a**;
1 Cor 15:51 We shall not **a** fall asleep, but we will **a** be changed,
2 Cor 5:15 He indeed died for **a**, so that those
Eph 1:23 the one who fills **a** things in every
Col 3:11 but Christ is **a** and in **a**.
2 Tm 3:16 **A** scripture is inspired by God and is
2 Pt 3:9 that **a** should come to repentance.
Rev 21:5 "Behold, I make **a** things new."

**ALMIGHTY** → MIGHT
Gn 17:1 to Abram and said: I am God the **A**.
Ex 6:3 As God the **A** I appeared
Ps 91:1 who abide in the shade of the **A**,
Bar 3:1 "LORD **A**, God of Israel,
Rev 1:8 was and who is to come, the **a**."
21:22 for its temple is the Lord God **a**

**ALMS** → ALMSGIVING
Tb 12:8 It is better to give **a** than to store
Mt 6:2 When you give **a**, do not blow

**ALMSGIVING** → ALMS
Sir 7:10 Do not be impatient in prayer or neglect **a**.

**ALONE**
Gn 2:18 It is not good for the man to be **a**.
Dt 6:4 LORD is our God, the LORD **a**!
Is 2:11 and the LORD **a** will be exalted,
Mk 2:7 Who but God **a** can forgive sins?"
10:18 No one is good but God **a**.
Jas 2:24 by works and not by faith **a**.

**ALPHA**
Rev 1:8 "I am the **A** and the Omega,"
22:13 I am the **A** and the Omega, the first

**ALTAR** → ALTARS
Gn 22:9 put him on top of the wood on the **a**.
Ex 27:1 You shall make an **a** of acacia
30:1 burning incense you shall make an **a**
Ezr 3:2 began building the **a** of the God
Jdt 4:12 The **a**, too, they draped in sackcloth;
1 Mc 1:54 upon the **a** of burnt offerings,
4:47 built a new **a** like the former one.
Mt 5:24 leave your gift there at the **a**,
Heb 13:10 We have an **a** from which those
Jas 2:21 he offered his son Isaac upon the **a**?
Rev 6:9 I saw underneath the **a** the souls

**ALTARS** → ALTAR
Ex 34:13 Tear down their **a**;
Nm 3:31 the **a**, the utensils of the sanctuary
1 Mc 2:45 about and tore down the pagan **a**;

**ALWAYS**
Mt 28:20 I am with you **a**, until the end
Lk 18:1 to pray **a** without becoming weary.
Phil 4:4 Rejoice in the Lord **a**. I shall say it

**AMALEK**
Ex 17:8 Then **A** came and waged war
1 Sm 15:3 attack **A**, and put under the ban

**AMASA**
Nephew of David (1 Chr 2:17). Commander of Absalom's forces (2 Sm 17:24-27). Returned to David (2 Sm 19:13). Killed by Joab (2 Sm 20:4-13).

**AMAZED**
Mt 8:27 The men were **a** and said,
Mk 6:6 He was **a** at their lack of faith.

**AMAZIAH**
1. Son of Joash; king of Judah (2 Kgs 14; 2 Chr 25). Defeated Edom (2 Kgs 14:7; 2 Chr 25:5-13); defeated by Israel for worshiping Edom's gods (2 Kgs 14:8-14; 2 Chr 25:14-24).
2. Idolatrous priest; opposed Amos (Am 7:10-17).

**AMBASSADOR** → AMBASSADORS
Eph 6:20 for which I am an **a** in chains,

**AMBASSADORS** → AMBASSADOR
2 Cor 5:20 So we are **a** for Christ, as if God

**AMBITION**
Jas 3:14 and selfish **a** in your hearts, do not

**AMEN**
Dt 27:15 all the people shall answer, "**A**!"
2 Cor 1:20 the **A** from us also goes through him
Rev 3:14 " 'The **A**, the faithful and true

**AMMONITES**
Gn 19:38 He is the ancestor of the **A** of today.
Jer 49:6 I will restore the fortunes of the **A**—

**AMNON**
Firstborn of David (2 Sm 3:2; 1 Chr 3:1). Killed by Absalom for raping his sister Tamar (2 Sm 13).

**AMON**
1. Son of Manasseh; king of Judah (2 Kgs 21:18-26; 1 Chr 3:14; 2 Chr 33:21-25).
2. Ruler of Samaria (1 Kgs 22:26; 2 Chr 18:25).

**AMORITES**
Gn 15:16 of the **A** is not yet complete.
Nm 21:31 So Israel settled in the land of the **A**.

**AMOS**
Prophet from Tekoa (Am 1:1; 7:10-17; Tb 2:6).

**ANANIAS**
1. Early disciple; died for lying to God (Acts 5:1-11).
2. Disciple who baptized Saul (Acts 9:10-19).
3. High priest at Paul's arrest (Acts 22:30–24:1).

**ANCESTORS**
Acts 5:30 The God of our **a** raised Jesus,
Heb 1:1 ways to our **a** through the prophets;

**ANCHOR**
Heb 6:19 This we have as an **a** of the soul,

**ANCIENT**
Ps 24:7 be lifted, you **a** portals, that the king
Dn 7:9 and the **A** of Days took his throne.
Rev 20:2 He seized the dragon, the **a** serpent,

**ANDREW**
Apostle; brother of Simon Peter (Mt 4:18; 10:2; Mk 1:16-18, 29; 3:18; 13:3; Lk 6:14; Jn 1:35-44; 6:8-9; 12:22; Acts 1:13).

**ANGEL** → ANGELS, ARCHANGEL
Ex 3:2 There the **a** of the LORD appeared
23:20 I am sending an **a** before you,
Nm 22:22 and the **a** of the LORD took
1 Chr 21:15 sent an **a** to Jerusalem to destroy it;
Tb 5:4 found the **a** Raphael standing before
5:4 not know that this was an **a** of God).
1 Mc 7:41 your **a** went out and killed
Ps 34:8 The **a** of the LORD encamps
Is 37:36 the **a** of the LORD went forth
Dn 3:49 the **a** of the Lord went down
3:95 who sent his **a** to deliver
13:59 "for the **a** of God waits
14:34 when an **a** of the Lord told him,
Mt 1:20 the **a** of the Lord appeared to him
Lk 1:26 the **a** Gabriel was sent from God
Acts 5:19 the **a** of the Lord opened the doors

2 Cor 11: 14 even Satan masquerades as an **a**
Gal 1: 8 an **a** from heaven should preach

**ANGELS** → ANGEL
Gn 19: 1 The two **a** reached Sodom
Tb 11: 14 name, and blessed be all his holy **a**.
Ps 103: 20 all you his **a**, mighty in strength,
Mk 12: 25 but they are like the **a** in heaven.
Lk 4: 10 will command his **a** concerning you,
Jn 1: 51 opened and the **a** of God ascending
Acts 23: 8 say that there is no resurrection or **a**
Rom 8: 38 nor life, nor **a**, nor principalities,
1 Cor 6: 3 you not know that we will judge **a**?
Col 2: 18 in self-abasement and worship of **a**,
Heb 2: 7 for a little while lower than the **a**;
1 Pt 1: 12 things into which **a** longed to look.
2 Pt 2: 4 if God did not spare the **a** when they
Rev 1: 20 the seven stars are the **a** of the seven
7: 1 this I saw four **a** standing at the four
21: 12 gates where twelve **a** were stationed

**ANGER** → ANGRY
Ex 34: 6 slow to **a** and abounding in love
1 Kgs 16: 13 the God of Israel, to **a** by their idols.
Ps 30: 6 For his **a** lasts but a moment;
Prv 12: 16 Fools immediately show their **a**,
Is 48: 9 sake of my name I restrain my **a**,
Jl 2: 13 slow to **a**, abounding in steadfast
Jon 4: 2 slow to **a**, abounding in kindness,
Mk 3: 5 Looking around at them with **a**
Eph 4: 26 do not let the sun set on your **a**,

**ANGRY** → ANGER
Jer 3: 12 I will not remain **a** with you;
Mt 5: 22 whoever is **a** with his brother will

**ANGUISH**
Zep 1: 15 a day of distress and **a**, a day of ruin

**ANIMAL** → ANIMALS
Gn 1: 25 God made every kind of wild **a**, every kind of tame **a**,
Ps 50: 10 For every **a** of the forest is mine,

**ANIMALS** → ANIMAL
Gn 2: 19 out of the ground all the wild **a**
3: 14 this, cursed are you among all the **a**,
9: 2 come upon all the **a** of the earth

**ANNA**
1. Prophetess; spoke of the child Jesus (Lk 2:36-38).
2. Wife of Tobit (Tb 1:20; 2:1, 11).

**ANNAS**
High priest A.D. 6–15 (Lk 3:2; Jn 18:13, 24; Acts 4:6).

**ANOINT** → ANOINTED, ANOINTING
Ex 30: 30 and his sons you shall also **a**
1 Sm 15: 1 to **a** you king over his people Israel.
Ps 23: 5 You **a** my head with oil;

**ANOINTED** → ANOINT
1 Sm 2: 10 king, and exalt the horn of his **a**!"
26: 9 can lay a hand on the LORD's **a**
1 Chr 16: 22 "Do not touch my **a**, to my
Ps 2: 2 the LORD and against his **a** one:
Is 61: 1 me, because the LORD has **a** me;
Dn 9: 24 and a holy of holies will be **a**.
9: 26 sixty-two weeks an **a** one shall be
Zec 4: 14 are the two **a** ones who stand
Lk 4: 18 because he has **a** me to bring glad
Jn 1: 41 Messiah" (which is translated **A**).
12: 3 nard and **a** the feet of Jesus

**ANOINTING** → ANOINT
Ex 30: 25 and blend them into sacred **a** oil,

1 Jn 2: 27 the **a** that you received from him
2: 27 his **a** teaches you about everything

**ANOTHER**
Prv 27: 2 Let **a** praise you, not your own
Is 48: 11 My glory I will not give to **a**.
Jn 14: 16 he will give you **a** Advocate to be
Gal 1: 7 (not that there is **a**). But there are

**ANSWER** → ANSWERED
1 Kgs 18: 37 **A** me, LORD! **A** me, that this
Jb 30: 20 I cry to you, but you do not **a** me;
Prv 15: 1 A mild **a** turns back wrath,
Is 65: 24 Before they call, I will **a**;
Lk 23: 9 him at length, but he gave him no **a**.

**ANSWERED** → ANSWER
1 Chr 21: 26 who **a** him by sending down fire
Ps 118: 21 I thank you for you **a** me;

**ANT**
Prv 6: 6 Go to the **a**, O sluggard, study her

**ANTICHRIST**
1 Jn 2: 18 as you heard that the **a** was coming,
2: 22 the Father and the Son, this is the **a**.
4: 3 This is the spirit of the **a** that, as you
2 Jn 1: 7 such is the deceitful one and the **a**.

**ANTIOCH**
Acts 11: 26 it was in **A** that the disciples were
13: 1 were in the church at **A** prophets
Gal 2: 11 And when Cephas came to **A**,

**ANTIOCHUS**
Antiochus IV Epiphanes, king of the Syrian Greeks B.C. 175-164 (1 Mc 1:10-19). Plundered the temple in Jerusalem (1 Mc 1:20-28). Attempted to force the Hellenization of the Jewish people (1 Mc 1:41-53), including defiling the altar and holy place (1 Mc 1:54-64). His policies sparked the Maccabean revolt.

**ANXIETIES**
1 Cor 7: 32 I should like you to be free of **a**.

**ANYTHING**
Gn 18: 14 Is **a** too marvelous for the LORD
Jer 32: 27 Is **a** too difficult for me?
Mt 18: 19 of you agree on earth about **a**
Jn 16: 23 you will not question me about **a**.

**APART**
Rom 3: 21 God has been manifested **a**

**APOLLOS**
Christian from Alexandria, learned in the Scriptures; instructed by Aquila and Priscilla (Acts 18:24-28). At Corinth (Acts 19:1; 1 Cor 1:12; 3; Ti 3:13).

**APOSTASY**
1 Mc 2: 15 of enforcing the **a** came to the city

**APOSTLE** → APOSTLES
Rom 11: 13 then as I am the **a** to the Gentiles,
1 Cor 9: 1 Am I not an **a**? Have I not seen
2 Cor 12: 12 of an **a** were performed among you
Heb 3: 1 Jesus, the **a** and high priest of our

**APOSTLES** → APOSTLE
See also Andrew, Bartholomew, Barnabas, James, John, Judas, Matthew, Matthias, Nathanael, Paul, Peter, Philip, Simon, Thaddaeus, Thomas.
Mt 10: 2 names of the twelve **a** are these:
Lk 6: 13 Twelve, whom he also named **a**:
Acts 2: 43 and signs were done through the **a**.
1 Cor 12: 28 in the church to be, first, **a**;
Eph 2: 20 built upon the foundation of the **a**
4: 11 And he gave some as **a**, others as

Rev 21:14 names of the twelve **a** of the Lamb.

**APPEAL**
Acts 25:11 me over to them. I **a** to Caesar."
1 Pt 3:21 an **a** to God for a clear conscience,

**APPEAR** → APPEARANCE, APPEARANCES, APPEARED, APPEARING
Mt 24:30 of the Son of Man will **a** in heaven,
2 Cor 5:10 we must all **a** before the judgment
Heb 9:28 sins of many, will **a** a second time,

**APPEARANCE** → APPEAR
1 Sm 16: 7 Do not judge from his **a** or from his
16: 7 not see as a mortal, who sees the **a**.
2 Cor 5:12 who boast of external **a** rather than

**APPEARANCES** → APPEAR
Jn 7:24 Stop judging by **a**, but judge

**APPEARED** → APPEAR
1 Cor 15: 5 that he **a** to Cephas,
Heb 9:26 now once for all he has **a** at the end

**APPEARING** → APPEAR
Acts 1: 3 **a** to them during forty days

**APPETITES**
Rom 16:18 our Lord Christ but their own **a**,

**APPLE**
Dt 32:10 guarded them as the **a** of his eye.

**APPOINT** → APPOINTED
1 Sm 8: 5 your example, **a** a king over us,
Is 60:17 I will **a** peace your governor,

**APPOINTED** → APPOINT
Hb 1:12 LORD, you have **a** them for judgment,
Mk 3:16 [he **a** the twelve:] Simon, whom he
Acts 3:20 send you the Messiah already **a**
Heb 9:27 Just as it is **a** that human beings die

**APPROACH**
Heb 4:16 So let us confidently **a** the throne

**AQUILA**
Husband of Priscilla; co-worker with Paul, instructor of Apollos (Acts 18; Rom 16:3; 1 Cor 16:19; 2 Tm 4:19).

**ARABIANS**
1 Mc 5:39 they have also hired **A** to help them,

**ARAM** → ARAMAIC, ARAMEAN
Jgs 10: 6 the gods of **A**, the gods of Sidon,
2 Chr 16: 7 you relied on the king of **A** and did
16: 7 king of **A** has escaped your power.

**ARAMAIC** → ARAM
2 Kgs 18:26 "Please speak to your servants in **A**;
Ezr 4: 7 The document was written in **A**
Dn 2: 4 Chaldeans answered the king in **A**:

**ARAMEAN** → ARAM
Dt 26: 5 was a refugee **A** who went down

**ARARAT**
Gn 8: 4 came to rest on the mountains of **A**.

**ARAUNAH**
2 Sm 24:16 the threshing floor of **A** the Jebusite.

**ARCHANGEL** → ANGEL
Jude 1: 9 Yet the **a** Michael, when he argued

**ARCHITECT**
Heb 11:10 whose **a** and maker is God.

**AREOPAGUS**
Acts 17:22 Paul stood up at the **A** and said:

**ARGUMENT** → ARGUMENTS
Lk 9:46 An **a** arose among the disciples
1 Tm 2: 8 up holy hands, without anger or **a**.

**ARGUMENTS** → ARGUMENT
2 Cor 10: 4 We destroy **a**
Col 2: 4 one may deceive you by specious **a**.

**ARIMATHEA**
Jn 19:38 Joseph of **A**, secretly a disciple

**ARISE** → ARISES, RISE
Sg 2:10 lover speaks and says to me, "**A**,
Mt 24:11 Many false prophets will **a**

**ARISES** → ARISE, RISE
1 Mc 14:41 until a trustworthy prophet **a**.

**ARK**
Gn 6:14 Make yourself an **a** of gopherwood,
Ex 25:10 You shall make an **a** of acacia
1 Sm 4:11 The **a** of God was captured,
1 Kgs 8: 9 There was nothing in the **a**
2 Mc 2: 4 and the **a** should accompany him,
1 Pt 3:20 Noah during the building of the **a**,
Rev 11:19 the **a** of his covenant could be seen

**ARM** → ARMIES, ARMOR, ARMS, ARMY
Ex 6: 6 redeem you by my outstretched **a**
Dt 7:19 and outstretched **a**
2 Chr 32: 8 He has only an **a** of flesh, but we
Jb 40: 9 Have you an **a** like that of God,
Is 53: 1 whom has the **a** of the LORD been

**ARMIES** → ARM
1 Sm 17:36 because he has insulted the **a**
Lk 21:20 you see Jerusalem surrounded by **a**,
Rev 19:14 The **a** of heaven followed him,

**ARMOR** → ARM
Wis 5:17 He shall take his zeal for **a** and arm
Rom 13:12 darkness [and] put on the **a** of light;
Eph 6:11 Put on the **a** of God so that you may

**ARMS** → ARM
Prv 31:17 she exerts her **a** with vigor.
Hos 11: 3 to walk, who took them in my **a**;

**ARMY** → ARM
Ex 15: 4 and **a** he hurled into the sea;
Ps 27: 3 Though an **a** encamp against me,
33:16 A king is not saved by a great **a**,
Rev 19:19 riding the horse and against his **a**.

**AROMA**
2 Cor 2:15 For we are the **a** of Christ for God

**ARRESTED**
Mt 14: 3 Now Herod had **a** John,
26:50 they laid hands on Jesus and **a** him.

**ARROGANCE** → ARROGANT
1 Mc 1:24 much blood and spoke with great **a**.
Prv 8:13 Pride, **a**, the evil way,

**ARROGANT** → ARROGANCE
Ps 73: 3 of the **a** when I saw the prosperity
Dn 7:11 the first of the **a** words

**ARROW** → ARROWS
Ps 64: 8 God shoots an **a** at them;
Is 49: 2 He made me a sharpened **a**, in his

**ARROWS** → ARROW
1 Sm 20:20 month I will shoot **a** to the side

Eph 6: 16 to quench all [the] flaming **a**

**ARTAXERXES** → =AHASUERUS

1. King of Persia; allowed rebuilding of temple under Ezra (Ezr 4; 7), and of walls of Jerusalem under his cupbearer Nehemiah (Neh 2; 5:14; 13:6).

2. See Ahasuerus.

**ARTEMIS**

Acts 19: 27 of the great goddess **A** will be of no

**ASA**

King of Judah (1 Kgs 15:8-24; 1 Chr 3:10; 2 Chr 14–16). Godly reformer (2 Chr 15); in later years defeated Israel with help of Aram, not the LORD (1 Kgs 15:16-22; 2 Chr 16).

**ASAHEL**

Nephew of David, one of his warriors (2 Sm 23:24; 1 Chr 2:16; 11:26; 27:7). Killed by Abner (2 Sm 2); avenged by Joab (2 Sm 3:22-39).

**ASAPH**

1. Recorder to Hezekiah (2 Kgs 18:18, 37; Is 36:3, 22).

2. Levitical musician (1 Chr 6:39; 15:17-19; 16:4-7, 37), seer (2 Chr 29:30). Sons of (1 Chr 25; 2 Chr 5:12; 20:14; 29:13; 35:15; Ezr 2:41; 3:10; Neh 7:44; 11:17; 12:27-47). Psalms of (2 Chr 29:30; Ps 50; 73–83).

**ASCEND** → ASCENDING, ASCENTS

Ps 139: 8 If I **a** to the heavens, you are there;

**ASCENDING** → ASCEND

Jn 1: 51 the angels of God **a** and descending

**ASCENTS** → ASCEND

Songs of ascents (Ps 120-134).

**ASHAMED** → SHAME

Is 29: 22 No longer shall Jacob be **a**,
Mk 8: 38 Whoever is **a** of me and of my
8: 38 the Son of Man will be **a**
Rom 1: 16 For I am not **a** of the gospel.
Heb 2: 11 he is not **a** to call them "brothers,"
11: 16 God is not **a** to be called their God,

**ASHER**

Son of Jacob by Zilpah (Gn 30:13; 35:26; 46:17; Ex 1:4; 1 Chr 2:2). Tribe of blessed (Gn 49:20; Dt 33:24-25), numbered (Nm 1:40-41; 26:44-47), allotted land (Jos 10:24-31; Ez 48:2), failed to fully possess (Jgs 1:31-32), failed to support Deborah (Jgs 5:17), supported Gideon (Jgs 6:35; 7:23) and David (1 Chr 12:36), 12,000 from (Rev 7:6).

**ASHERAH** → ASHERAHS, ASTARTE

Dt 16: 21 You shall not plant an **a** of any kind
1 Kgs 18: 19 four hundred prophets of **A** who eat
2 Chr 15: 16 had made an obscene object for **A**;

**ASHERAHS** → ASHERAH

Jgs 3: 7 and served the Baals and the **A**,
2 Kgs 17: 10 They set up pillars and **a** for themselves

**ASHES**

Gn 18: 27 Lord, though I am only dust and **a**!
Jdt 4: 11 and sprinkled **a** on their heads,
Est 4: 1 put on sackcloth and **a**, and went
Jb 42: 6 have said, and repent in dust and **a**.
Jon 3: 6 himself with sackcloth, and sat in **a**.
Mt 11: 21 have repented in sackcloth and **a**.

**ASIA**

Acts 16: 6 the message in the province of **A**.
Rev 1: 4 John, to the seven churches in **A**:

**ASIDE** → SIDE

Ex 32: 8 They have quickly turned **a**
Dt 28: 14 not turning **a**, either to the right

**ASK**

Ps 2: 8 **A** it of me, and I will give you
Mt 6: 8 what you need before you **a** him.
7: 7 "**A** and it will be given to you;
Jn 16: 24 **a** and you will receive, so that your
Jas 4: 3 You **a** but do not receive,
4: 3 because you **a** wrongly, to spend it
1 Jn 5: 14 if we **a** anything according to his

**ASLEEP** → SLEEP

Jon 1: 5 hold of the ship, and lay there fast **a**.
Mt 8: 24 swamped by waves; but he was **a**.

**ASSEMBLE** → ASSEMBLY

Zep 3: 8 to **a** kingdoms, In order to pour
Rev 16: 14 of the whole world to **a** them

**ASSEMBLY** → ASSEMBLE

Neh 8: 2 priest brought the law before the **a**,
Ps 149: 1 his praise in the **a** of the faithful.
Heb 12: 23 and the **a** of the firstborn enrolled

**ASSIGNED**

1 Cor 3: 5 just as the Lord **a** each one.
7: 17 should live as the Lord has **a**, just as

**ASSYRIA**

2 Kgs 18: 11 The king of **A** then deported the Israelites to **A**
Jer 50: 18 as I once punished the king of **A**;

**ASTARTE** → ASHERAH

1 Kgs 11: 5 Solomon followed **A**, the goddess

**ASTONISHED**

Lk 2: 48 they were **a**, and his mother said

**ASTRAY** → STRAY

Dt 30: 17 but are led **a** and bow down to other
Is 53: 6 We had all gone **a** like sheep,
Mt 18: 12 sheep and one of them goes **a**,
1 Pt 2: 25 For you had gone **a** like sheep,

**ASYLUM**

Nm 35: 11 cities to serve as cities of **a**,

**ATE** → EAT

Gn 3: 6 she took some of its fruit and **a** it;
3: 6 who was with her, and he **a** it.
Ex 16: 35 The Israelites **a** the manna for forty
Ps 78: 25 Man **a** the bread of the angels;
Ez 3: 3 I **a** it, and it was as sweet as honey
Mt 14: 20 They all **a** and were satisfied,
15: 37 They all **a** and were satisfied.

**ATHALIAH**

Granddaughter of Omri; wife of Jehoram and mother of Ahaziah; encouraged their evil ways (2 Kgs 8:18, 27; 2 Chr 22:2). At death of Ahaziah she made herself queen, killing all his sons but Joash (2 Kgs 11:1-3; 2 Chr 22:10-12); killed six years later when Joash revealed (2 Kgs 11:4-16; 2 Chr 23:1-15).

**ATHLETE**

2 Tm 2: 5 an **a** cannot receive the winner's

**ATONE** → ATONEMENT, ATONING

Sir 3: 3 Those who honor their father **a** for sins;

**ATONEMENT** → ATONES

Ex 29: 36 as a purification offering, to make **a**.
32: 30 be able to make **a** for your sin."
Lv 23: 28 because it is the Day of **A**, when **a** is

**ATONING** → ATONE

Ex 30: 10 with the blood of the **a** purification offering.

**ATTAIN** → ATTAINED

Phil 3: 11 if somehow I may **a** the resurrection

**ATTAINED** → ATTAIN
Phil 3:16 with regard to what we have **a**,

**AUTHOR**
Acts 3:15 The **a** of life you put to death,

**AUTHORITIES** → AUTHORITY
Rom 13:1 be subordinate to the higher **a**,

**AUTHORITY** → AUTHORITIES
Mk 1:27 A new teaching with **a**.
Lk 5:24 the Son of Man has **a** on earth
Rom 13:1 for there is no **a** except from God,
1 Cor 11:10 a woman should have a sign of **a**
1 Tm 2:12 to teach or to have **a** over a man.
Rev 12:10 our God and the **a** of his Anointed.

**AVENGE** → VENGEANCE
Dt 32:43 he will **a** the blood of his servants,
1 Mc 2:67 observe the law, and **a** your people.
Rev 6:10 **a** our blood on the inhabitants

**AVENGER** → VENGEANCE
Nm 35:12 of asylum from the **a** of blood,
Ps 8:3 your foes, to silence enemy and **a**.
1 Thes 4:6 the Lord is an **a** in all these things,

**AVENGING** → VENGEANCE
Na 1:2 A jealous and **a** God is the LORD,

**AVOID** → AVOIDED
2 Tm 2:16 **A** profane, idle talk, for such people
Ti 3:9 **A** foolish arguments, genealogies,

**AVOIDED** → AVOID
Prv 16:6 by the fear of the LORD evil is **a**.

**AWAKE**
Ps 44:24 **A**! Why do you sleep, O Lord?
57:9 **A**, my soul; **a**, lyre and harp!
Is 51:9 **A**, **a**, put on strength,
Dn 12:2 sleep in the dust of the earth shall **a**;
Eph 5:14 "**A**, O sleeper, and arise

**AWE** → AWESOME
Is 29:23 Jacob, be in **a** of the God of Israel.
Mt 9:8 saw this they were struck with **a**
Acts 2:43 **A** came upon everyone, and many
Rom 11:20 not become haughty, but stand in **a**.

**AWESOME** → AWE
Dt 10:17 mighty and **a**, who has no favorites,
Neh 1:5 great and **a** God, you preserve your
Ps 65:6 You answer us with **a** deeds
68:36 **A** is God in his holy place, the God
Dn 9:4 great and **a** God, you who keep your

**AX**
Mt 3:10 Even now the **a** lies at the root

**AZARIAH** → =ABEDNEGO, =UZZIAH
1. King of Judah; see Uzziah (2 Kgs 15:1-7).
2. Prophet (2 Chr 15:1-8).
3. Opponent of Jeremiah (Jer 43:2).
4. Jewish exile; see Abednego (Dn 1:6-19).

**AZAZEL**
Lv 16:8 is for the LORD and which for **A**.

## B

**BAAL** → BAALS
Nm 25:3 attached itself to the **B** of Peor,
Jgs 2:13 and served **B** and the Astartes,
1 Kgs 18:25 Elijah then said to the prophets of **B**,
19:18 every knee that has not bent to **B**,
Jer 2:8 The prophets prophesied by **B**,
Rom 11:4 men who have not knelt to **B**."

**BAALS** → BAAL
Jgs 3:7 and served the **B** and the Asherahs,
1 Sm 7:4 So the Israelites removed their **B**

**BAASHA**
King of Israel (1 Kgs 15:16–16:7; 2 Chr 16:1-6).

**BABEL** → BABYLON
Gn 11:9 That is why it was called **B**,

**BABES**
Ps 8:3 with the mouths of **b** and infants.

**BABYLON** → BABEL
2 Kgs 24:15 He deported Jehoiachin to **B**,
Ps 137:1 the rivers of **B** there we sat weeping
Is 14:4 taunt-song against the king of **B**:
21:9 out and says, 'Fallen, fallen is **B**!
Jer 25:11 nations shall serve the king of **B**;
Dn 14:36 he set him down in **B** above the den.
1 Pt 5:13 chosen one at **B** sends you greeting,
Rev 14:8 "Fallen, fallen is **B** the great,

**BACK**
Gn 19:26 But Lot's wife looked **b**, and she

**BAD**
Prv 20:14 "**B**, **b**!" says the buyer, then goes
Mt 7:17 fruit, and a rotten tree bears **b** fruit.
1 Cor 15:33 "**B** company corrupts good

**BALAAM**
Prophet who attempted to curse Israel (Nm 22–24; Dt 23:4-5; 2 Pt 2:15; Jude 11; Rev 2:14). Killed in Israel's vengeance on Midianites (Nm 31:8; Jos 13:22).

**BALAK**
Moabite king who hired Balaam to curse Israel (Nm 22–24; Jos 24:9; Mi 6:5).

**BALANCE**
Is 40:12 in scales and the hills in a **b**?

**BALM**
Jer 8:22 Is there no **b** in Gilead, no healer

**BAPTISM** → BAPTIZE
Mk 1:4 in the desert proclaiming a **b**
10:38 be baptized with the **b** with which I
Lk 20:4 was John's **b** of heavenly
Acts 18:25 although he knew only the **b**
19:3 They replied, "With the **b** of John."
Rom 6:4 with him through **b** into death,
Eph 4:5 one Lord, one faith, one **b**;
Col 2:12 You were buried with him in **b**,
1 Pt 3:21 This prefigured **b**, which saves you

**BAPTISMS** → BAPTIZE
Heb 6:2 instruction about **b** and laying

**BAPTIST** → BAPTIZE
Mt 3:1 In those days John the **B** appeared,
11:11 been none greater than John the **B**;
14:8 on a platter the head of John the **B**."
16:14 "Some say John the **B**,

**BAPTIZE** → BAPTISM, BAPTISMS, BAPTIST, BAPTIZED, BAPTIZING
Mt 3:11 He will **b** you with the holy Spirit
Lk 3:16 He will **b** you with the holy Spirit
1 Cor 1:17 For Christ did not send me to **b**

**BAPTIZED** → BAPTIZE
Mt 3:13 to John at the Jordan to be **b** by him.
Acts 1:5 for John **b** with water, but in a few
2:38 "Repent and be **b**, every one
Rom 6:3 we who were **b** into Christ Jesus
6:3 Christ Jesus were **b** into his death?

1 Cor 10: 2 all of them were **b** into Moses
12: 13 in one Spirit we were all **b** into one

**BAPTIZING** → BAPTIZE
Mt 28: 19 **b** them in the name of the Father,
Jn 4: 1 and **b** more disciples than John

**BARABBAS**
Prisoner released by Pilate instead of Jesus (Mt 27:16-26; Mk 15:7-15; Lk 23:18-19; Jn 18:40).

**BARAK**
Judge who fought with Deborah against Canaanites (Jgs 4–5; 1 Sm 12:11; Heb 11:32).

**BARBARIAN**
Col 3: 11 circumcision and uncircumcision, **b**,

**BARBS**
Nm 33: 55 remain will become **b** in your eyes

**BARE** → BARED
Ps 18: 16 the world's foundations lay **b**,

**BARED** → BARE
Is 52: 10 The LORD has **b** his holy arm

**BARN** → BARNS
Lk 12: 24 they have neither storehouse nor **b**,

**BARNABAS** → =JOSEPH
Disciple, originally Joseph (Acts 4:36), prophet (Acts 13:1), apostle (Acts 14:14). Brought Paul to apostles (Acts 9:27), Antioch (Acts 11:22-29; Gal 2:1-13), on the first missionary journey (Acts 13–14). Together at Jerusalem Council, they separated over John Mark (Acts 15). Later co-workers (1 Cor 9:6; Col 4:10).

**BARNS** → BARN
Dt 28: 8 upon you, on your **b** and on all your
Ps 144: 13 May our **b** be full with every kind
Lk 12: 18 I shall tear down my **b** and build

**BARREN**
Gn 11: 30 Sarai was **b**; she had no child.
Ex 23: 26 no woman in your land will be **b**
1 Sm 2: 5 The **b** wife bears seven sons,
Is 54: 1 you **b** one who never bore a child,
Lk 1: 7 because Elizabeth was **b** and both

**BARTHOLOMEW** → =NATHANAEL?
Apostle (Mt 10:3; Mk 3:18; Lk 6:14; Acts 1:13). Possibly also called Nathanael (Jn 1:45-49; 21:2).

**BARUCH**
Jeremiah's secretary (Jer 32:12-16; 36; 43:1-6; 45:1-2). Deuterocanonical book ascribed to (Bar 1:1, 3, 8).

**BARZILLAI**
1. Gileadite who aided David during Absalom's revolt (2 Sm 17:27; 19:31-39).
2. Son-in-law of 1. (Ezr 2:61; Neh 7:63).

**BASHAN**
Nm 21: 33 king of **B**, advanced against them
Ps 22: 13 fierce bulls of **B** encircle me.
Mi 7: 14 Let them feed in **B** and Gilead,

**BASIN**
Jn 13: 5 he poured water into a **b** and began

**BASKET**
Ex 2: 3 she took a papyrus **b**, daubed it
Mt 5: 15 and then put it under a bushel **b**;
Acts 9: 25 in the wall, lowering him in a **b**.

**BATHING**
2 Sm 11: 2 From the roof he saw a woman **b**;

**BATHSHEBA**
Wife of Uriah; committed adultery with and married David (2 Sm 11; Ps 51), mother of Solomon (2 Sm 12:24; 1 Kgs 1–2; 1 Chr 3:5).

**BATTLE**
1 Sm 17: 47 For the **b** belongs to the LORD,
2 Chr 20: 15 for the **b** is not yours but God's.
Eccl 9: 11 the swift, nor the **b** by the valiant,
Rev 16: 14 them for the **b** on the great day
20: 8 and Magog, to gather them for **b**;

**BEAR** → BEARS, BIRTH, BIRTHRIGHT, BORE, BORN, CHILDBEARING, FIRSTBORN
Gn 4: 13 "My punishment is too great to **b**.
17: 19 your wife Sarah is to **b** you a son,
Is 7: 14 pregnant and about to **b** a son,
Mt 1: 23 shall be with child and **b** a son,
7: 18 A good tree cannot **b** bad fruit,
7: 18 nor can a rotten tree **b** good fruit.
Jn 15: 2 branch in me that does not **b** fruit,
Gal 6: 2 **B** one another's burdens, and so you

**BEARS** → BEAR
1 Cor 13: 7 It **b** all things, believes all things,

**BEAST** → BEASTS
Rev 11: 7 the **b** that comes up from the abyss
13: 18 can calculate the number of the **b**,
16: 2 on those who had the mark of the **b**
19: 20 The **b** was caught and with it
19: 20 who had accepted the mark of the **b**

**BEASTS** → BEAST
Dn 7: 3 which emerged four immense **b**,
Mk 1: 13 He was among wild **b**,

**BEAT** → BEATEN, BEATING
Is 2: 4 They shall **b** their swords

**BEATEN** → BEAT
2 Cor 11: 25 Three times I was **b** with rods,
1 Pt 2: 20 if you are patient when **b** for doing

**BEATING** → BEAT
Lk 22: 63 custody were ridiculing and **b** him.

**BEAUTIFUL** → BEAUTY
Gn 12: 11 "I know that you are a **b** woman.
Tb 6: 12 girl is wise, courageous, and very **b**;
Jb 42: 15 women were as **b** as the daughters
Is 52: 7 How **b** upon the mountains are
Dn 13: 2 who married a very **b**
Acts 3: 2 temple called "the **B** Gate" every
Rom 10: 15 "How **b** are the feet of those who

**BEAUTY** → BEAUTIFUL
2 Sm 14: 25 praised for his **b** than Absalom,
Jdt 16: 9 his eyes, her **b** captivated his mind,
1 Mc 2: 12 laid waste, our **b**, our glory.
Ps 27: 4 To gaze on the LORD's **b**, to visit
Prv 6: 25 Do not lust in your heart after her **b**,
31: 30 Charm is deceptive and **b** fleeting;
Wis 13: 3 in their **b** they thought them gods,
13: 3 original source of **b** fashioned them.
Sir 9: 8 do not gaze upon **b** that is not yours;
Dn 13: 56 said to him, "**b** has seduced you,
1 Pt 3: 4 in the imperishable **b** of a gentle

**BED**
Gn 47: 31 Israel bowed at the head of the **b**.
Ps 36: 5 On his **b** he hatches plots; he sets
Heb 13: 4 the marriage **b** be kept undefiled,

**BEE** → BEES
Sir 11: 3 The **b** is least among winged

Is 7: 18 and for the **b** in the land of Assyria.

**BEER-SHEBA**
Gn 21: 31 This is why the place is called **B**;
1 Sm 3: 20 Israel from Dan to **B** came to know

**BEES** → BEE
Jgs 14: 8 there was a swarm of **b** in the lion's

**BEFORE**
Ex 33: 2 Jebusites, I will send an angel **b** you
Is 43: 10 **B** me no god was formed,
65: 24 **B** they call, I will answer;
Mal 3: 1 he will prepare the way **b** me;
Mt 6: 8 what you need **b** you ask him.
Lk 22: 61 to him, "**B** the cock crows today,
Heb 12: 2 that lay **b** him he endured the cross,

**BEGGAR**
Jn 9: 8 had seen him earlier as a **b** said,

**BEGINNING**
Gn 1: 1 In the **b**, when God created
Ps 111: 10 of the LORD is the **b** of wisdom;
Prv 1: 7 the LORD is the **b** of knowledge;
Eccl 7: 8 is the end of a thing than its **b**;
Is 40: 21 Was it not told you from the **b**?
Mt 24: 8 All these are the **b** of the labor
Jn 1: 1 In the **b** was the Word,
1 Jn 1: 1 What was from the **b**, what we have
2 Jn 1: 6 as you heard from the **b**,
Rev 21: 6 and the Omega, the **b** and the end.

**BEGOT** → BEGOTTEN
Dt 32: 6 Is he not your father who **b** you,

**BEGOTTEN** → BEGOT
Acts 13: 33 are my son; this day I have **b** you.'
Heb 1: 5 are my son; this day I have **b** you"?

**BEHEADED** → HEAD
Lk 9: 9 But Herod said, "John I **b**.
Rev 20: 4 of those who had been **b** for their

**BEHEMOTH**
Jb 40: 15 Look at **B**, whom I made along

**BEHIND**
Is 38: 17 **B** your back you cast all my sins.
Mt 16: 23 turned and said to Peter, "Get **b** me,
Phil 3: 13 forgetting what lies **b** but straining

**BEING**
Gn 2: 7 life, and the man became a living **b**.
Dt 6: 5 with your whole **b**, and with your whole
1 Cor 15: 45 became a living **b**," the last Adam
Heb 1: 3 the very imprint of his **b**, and who

**BEL**

Babylonian deity (Is 46:1; Jer 50:2; 51:44; Bar 6:40; Dn 14:3-28).

**BELIEF** → BELIEVE
2 Thes 2: 13 by the Spirit and **b** in truth.

**BELIEVE** → BELIEF, BELIEVED, BELIEVER, BELIEVES
Ex 4: 5 is so they will **b** that the LORD,
Prv 14: 15 The naive **b** everything, but the
Jer 12: 6 Do not **b** them, even when they
Mt 18: 6 one of these little ones who **b** in me
24: 23 or, 'There he is!' do not **b** it.
Mk 1: 15 Repent, and **b** in the gospel."
9: 24 out, "I do **b**, help my unbelief!"
Lk 24: 25 of heart to **b** all that the prophets
Jn 1: 7 so that all might **b** through him.
3: 18 but whoever does not **b** has already
6: 29 God, that you **b** in the one he sent."
10: 38 them, even if you do not **b** me,
17: 20 those who will **b** in me through their
20: 29 to **b** because you have seen me?
Acts 16: 31 "**B** in the Lord Jesus and you
28: 24 he had said, while others did not **b**.
Rom 3: 22 faith in Jesus Christ for all who **b**.
10: 9 **b** in your heart that God raised him
1 Thes 4: 14 For if we **b** that Jesus died and rose,
Heb 11: 6 anyone who approaches God must **b**
Jas 2: 19 You **b** that God is one. You do well.
2: 19 Even the demons **b**
1 Pt 1: 8 you do not see him now yet **b**
Jude 1: 5 later destroyed those who did not **b**.

**BELIEVED** → BELIEVE
Ex 14: 31 They **b** in the LORD and in Moses
Jdt 14: 10 of Israel had done, **b** firmly in God.
Jn 12: 38 "Lord, who has **b** our preaching,
20: 8 at the tomb first, and he saw and **b**.
Acts 2: 44 All who **b** were together and had all
Rom 4: 3 "Abraham **b** God, and it was
10: 16 who has **b** what was heard
2 Cor 4: 13 is written, "I **b**, therefore I spoke,"
Gal 3: 6 Thus Abraham "**b** God, and it was
1 Tm 3: 16 Gentiles, **b** in throughout the world,
Heb 4: 3 For we who **b** enter into [that] rest,
Jas 2: 23 that says, "Abraham **b** God, and it

**BELIEVER** → BELIEVE
2 Cor 6: 15 Or what has a **b** in common

**BELIEVES** → BELIEVE
Jn 3: 15 everyone who **b** in him may have
11: 26 lives and **b** in me will never die.
Rom 9: 33 whoever **b** in him shall not be put
10: 10 For one **b** with the heart and so is
1 Cor 13: 7 It bears all things, **b** all things,

**BELLY**
Gn 3: 14 On your **b** you shall crawl, and dust
Lv 11: 42 Whether it crawls on its **b**,
Mt 12: 40 was in the **b** of the whale three days

**BELONG** → BELONGS
Jn 10: 16 sheep that do not **b** to this fold.
15: 19 because you do not **b** to the world,
1 Cor 12: 15 "Because I am not a hand I do not **b**

**BELONGS** → BELONG
Ps 22: 29 For kingship **b** to the LORD,
62: 12 I have heard: Strength **b** to God;

**BELOVED** → LOVE
Mt 3: 17 "This is my **b** Son, with whom I am
12: 18 chosen, my **b** in whom I delight;
17: 5 "This is my **b** Son, with whom I am
Col 3: 12 holy and **b**, heartfelt compassion,
Rev 20: 9 of the holy ones and the **b** city.

**BELSHAZZAR**

King of Babylon (Dn 5; Bar 1:11-12).

**BELT**
1 Sm 18: 4 dress, even his sword, bow, and **b**.
Is 11: 5 and faithfulness a **b** upon his hips.
Mk 1: 6 with a leather **b** around his waist.

**BELTESHAZZAR** → See DANIEL

**BEN-HADAD**

1. King of Syria in time of Asa (1 Kgs 15:18-20; 2 Chr 16:2-4).

2. King of Syria in time of Ahab (1 Kgs 20; 2 Kgs 6:24; 8:7-15).

3. King of Syria in time of Jehoahaz (2 Kgs 13:3, 24-25; Jer 49:27; Am 1:4).

**BENAIAH**
A commander of David's army (2 Sm 8:18; 20:23; 23:20-30); loyal to Solomon (1 Kgs 1:8–2:46; 4:4).

**BEND** → BENT
Phil 2:10 name of Jesus every knee should **b**,

**BENEFICIAL** → BENEFIT
1 Cor 6:12 for me," but not everything is **b**.
10:23 is lawful," but not everything is **b**.

**BENEFIT**
Gal 5:2 Christ will be of no **b** to you.

**BENJAMIN** → BENJAMINITE
Twelfth son of Jacob by Rachel (Gn 35:16-24; 46:19-21; 1 Chr 2:2). Jacob refused to send him to Egypt, but relented (Gn 42–45). Tribe of blessed (Gn 49:27; Dt 33:12), numbered (Nm 1:37; 26:41), allotted land (Jos 18:11-28; Ez 48:23), failed to fully possess (Jgs 1:21), nearly obliterated (Jgs 20–21), sided with Ish-Bosheth (2 Sm 2), but turned to David (1 Chr 12:2, 29). 12,000 from (Rev 7:8).

**BENJAMINITE** → BENJAMIN
Jgs 3:15 of Gera, a **B** who was left-handed.
1 Sm 9:21 "Am I not a **B**, from the smallest

**BENT** → BEND
Jn 8:6 Jesus **b** down and began to write
20:5 he **b** down and saw the burial cloths

**BEREAVES**
Lam 1:20 Outside the sword **b**—

**BESIDES**
Wis 12:13 is there any god **b** you who have
Is 45:21 **b** whom there is no other God?
Dn 14:41 and there is no other **b** you!"

**BEST** → GOOD
Dt 33:21 He saw that the **b** should be his,

**BETHANY**
Mt 26:6 when Jesus was in **B** in the house
Jn 11:1 Lazarus from **B**, the village of Mary

**BETHEL**
Gn 12:8 on to the hill country east of **B**,
28:19 He named that place **B**,
1 Sm 7:16 passing through **B**,

**BETHLEHEM**
Ru 4:11 Bestow a name in **B**!
1 Sm 17:12 an Ephrathite named Jesse from **B**
Mt 2:1 When Jesus was born in **B** of Judea,
Lk 2:15 to **B** to see this thing that has taken

**BETRAY**
Jn 13:11 For he knew who would **b** him;

**BETTER** → GOOD
1 Sm 15:22 Obedience is **b** than sacrifice,
Tb 12:8 It is **b** to give alms than to store
Ps 63:4 For your love is **b** than life;
Prv 15:16 **B** a little with fear of the LORD
27:5 **B** is an open rebuke than a love
Eccl 2:24 There is nothing **b** for mortals than
9:4 "A live dog is **b** off than a dead
Sir 40:26 exult, but **b** than either, fear of God.
Dn 1:20 he found them ten times **b** than any
Mt 5:29 It is **b** for you to lose one of your
Mk 14:21 It would be **b** for that man if he had
Jn 11:50 do you consider that it is **b** for you
Phil 1:23 be with Christ, [for] that is far **b**.
Heb 7:22 guarantee of an [even] **b** covenant.
9:23 by **b** sacrifices than these.
1 Pt 3:17 For it is **b** to suffer for doing good,

**BETWEEN**
Gn 3:15 I will put enmity **b** you
3:15 and **b** your offspring and hers;
9:13 serve as a sign of the covenant **b** me
16:5 May the LORD decide **b** you
Is 2:4 He shall judge **b** the nations, and set
Ez 34:17 I will judge **b** one sheep and another, **b** rams and goats.
Rom 10:12 For there is no distinction **b** Jew
1 Tm 2:5 one mediator **b** God and the human

**BEWARE**
Eccl 12:12 As to more than these, my son, **b**.
Phil 3:2 **B** of the dogs! **B** of the evil workers!
3:2 **B** of the mutilation!

**BEYOND**
Ps 147:5 in power, with wisdom **b** measure.
2 Cor 4:17 weight of glory **b** all comparison,

**BEZALEL**
Judahite craftsman in charge of building the tabernacle (Ex 31:1-11; 35:30–39:31).

**BILDAD**
One of Job's friends (Jb 2:11; 8; 18; 25; 42:9).

**BILHAH**
Servant of Rachel, mother of Jacob's sons Dan and Naphtali (Gn 30:1-7; 35:25; 46:23-25).

**BIND** → BINDS
Dt 6:8 **B** them on your arm as a sign
Mt 16:19 Whatever you **b** on earth shall be

**BINDS** → BIND
Jb 5:18 For he wounds, but he **b** up;

**BIRD** → BIRDS
Gn 7:3 of every **b** of the air, seven pairs,
Lv 20:25 detestable through any beast or **b**

**BIRDS** → BIRD
Gn 1:21 teems, and all kinds of winged **b**.
1:22 and let the **b** multiply on the earth.
Jer 7:33 will be food for the **b** of the sky
Mt 6:26 Look at the **b** in the sky; they do not
Rev 19:21 all the **b** gorged themselves on their

**BIRTH** → BEAR
Dt 32:18 you forgot the God who gave you **b**.
Eccl 3:2 A time to give **b**, and a time to die;
Jas 1:18 He willed to give us **b** by the word
1 Pt 1:3 his great mercy gave us a new **b**

**BIRTHRIGHT** → BEAR, RIGHT
Heb 12:16 who sold his **b** for a single meal.

**BISHOP**
1 Tm 3:1 the office of **b** desires a noble task.
Ti 1:7 For a **b** as God's steward must be

**BIT** → BITE, BITS
Ps 32:9 with **b** and bridle their temper is

**BITE** → BIT
Sir 21:2 a serpent that will **b** you if you go

**BITS** → BIT
Jas 3:3 If we put **b** into the mouths

**BITTER** → BITTERNESS
Ex 1:14 making life **b** for them with hard
12:8 with unleavened bread and **b** herbs.
15:23 drink its water, because it was too **b**.
Ru 1:13 daughters, my lot is too **b** for you,
Rev 8:11 this water, because it was made **b**.

**BITTERNESS** → BITTER
Prv 14:10 The heart knows its own **b**, and its
Eph 4:31 All **b**, fury, anger, shouting,

**BLACK**
Zec 6:2 horses, the second chariot **b** horses,
Mt 5:36 make a single hair white or **b**.
Rev 6:5 and there was a **b** horse, and its

**BLAMELESS**
Gn 17:1 Walk in my presence and be **b**.
1 Mc 4:42 He chose **b** priests,
Jb 1:1 In the land of Uz there was a **b**
Ps 37:18 LORD knows the days of the **b**;
Phil 2:15 that you may be **b** and innocent,
1 Thes 5:23 be preserved **b** for the coming
Ti 1:7 bishop as God's steward must be **b**,

**BLASPHEME** → BLASPHEMED, BLASPHEMER, BLASPHEMERS, BLASPHEMES, BLASPHEMIES, BLASPHEMOUS
Acts 26:11 in an attempt to force them to **b**;
1 Tm 1:20 over to Satan to be taught not to **b**.

**BLASPHEMED** → BLASPHEME
Ez 20:27 this way also your ancestors **b** me,
Mt 26:65 tore his robes and said, "He has **b**!

**BLASPHEMER** → BLASPHEME
1 Tm 1:13 I was once a **b** and a persecutor

**BLASPHEMERS** → BLASPHEME
Sir 3:16 who neglect their father are like **b**;

**BLASPHEMES** → BLASPHEME
Lv 24:15 who **b** God shall bear the penalty;
Lk 12:10 but the one who **b** against the holy

**BLASPHEMIES** → BLASPHEME
Mk 3:28 and all **b** that people utter will be
Rev 13:6 its mouth to utter **b** against God,

**BLASPHEMOUS** → BLASPHEME
Acts 6:11 heard him speaking **b** words against
Rev 13:1 and on its heads **b** name[s].

**BLAZING**
Heb 12:18 which could be touched and a **b** fire

**BLEMISH**
Ex 12:5 be a year-old male and without **b**.
Eph 5:27 she might be holy and without **b**.

**BLESS** → BLESSED, BLESSING, BLESSINGS
Gn 12:2 you a great nation, and I will **b** you;
17:16 I will **b** her, and I will give you
22:17 I will **b** you and make your
26:3 and I will be with you and **b** you;
Ex 20:24 I will come to you and **b** you.
Nm 6:24 The LORD **b** you and keep you!
23:20 I was summoned to **b**; I will **b**;
Dt 7:13 He will love and **b** and multiply
7:13 he will **b** the fruit of your womb
30:16 God, will **b** you in the land you are
1 Chr 29:20 "Now **b** the LORD your God!"
Tb 4:19 At all times **b** the Lord, your God,
12:6 "**B** God and give him thanks before all
Ps 5:13 For you, LORD, **b** the just one;
29:11 may the LORD **b** his people
34:2 I will **b** the LORD at all times;
103:1 **B** the LORD, my soul;
109:28 Though they curse, may you **b**;
Hg 2:19 From this day, I will **b** you.
Lk 6:28 **b** those who curse you,
Rom 12:14 **B** those who persecute [you],
1 Cor 4:12 When ridiculed, we **b**;
Jas 3:9 With it we **b** the Lord and Father,

**BLESSED** → BLESS
Gn 1:22 and God **b** them, saying:
2:3 God **b** the seventh day and made it
14:19 He **b** Abram with these words:
Nm 24:9 **B** are those who bless you,
Tb 3:11 "**B** are you, merciful God!
3:11 "**B** be your holy and honorable name
Jdt 13:17 saying with one accord, "**B** are you,
Jb 1:21 **b** be the name of the LORD!"
42:12 Thus the LORD **b** the later days
Ps 1:1 **B** is the man who does not walk
33:12 **B** is the nation whose God is
84:13 **b** the man who trusts in you!
118:26 **B** is he who comes in the name
Jer 17:7 **B** are those who trust
Dn 3:26 "**B** are you, and praiseworthy,
Mt 5:3 "**B** are the poor in spirit, for theirs
16:17 said to him in reply, "**B** are you,
Mk 10:16 Then he embraced them and **b** them,
Lk 1:42 "Most **b** are you among women,
1:42 and **b** is the fruit of your womb.
6:20 "**B** are you who are poor,
Jn 12:13 **B** is he who comes in the name
20:29 **B** are those who have not seen
Acts 20:35 said, 'It is more **b** to give than
Gal 3:8 you shall all the nations be **b**."
Eph 1:3 **B** be the God and Father of our Lord
1:3 who has **b** us in Christ with every
1 Pt 3:14 because of righteousness, **b** are you.
Rev 1:3 **B** is the one who reads aloud and **b**
22:7 **B** is the one who keeps

**BLESSING** → BLESS
Gn 12:2 name great, so that you will be a **b**.
22:18 the nations of the earth will find **b**,
27:36 and now he has taken away my **b**."
27:36 "Have you not saved a **b** for me?"
Dt 11:26 I set before you this day a **b**
Neh 13:2 our God turned the curse into a **b**."
Tb 8:15 are you, God, with every pure **b**!
Ez 34:26 in its season, the **b** of abundant rain.
Mal 3:10 down upon you **b** without measure!
Mk 14:22 he took bread, said the **b**, broke it,
1 Cor 10:16 The cup of **b** that we bless, is it not
Gal 3:14 that the **b** of Abraham might be
Eph 1:3 every spiritual **b** in the heavens,
Rev 5:12 strength, honor and glory and **b**."
7:12 "Amen. **B** and glory,

**BLESSINGS** → BLESS
Dt 28:2 All these **b** will come upon you
Jos 8:34 of the law, the **b** and the curses,
Ps 21:7 make him the pattern of **b** forever,
Prv 10:6 **B** are for the head of the just;
Rom 15:27 come to share in their spiritual **b**,
15:27 also to serve them in material **b**.

**BLIND** → BLINDED, BLINDNESS
Ex 4:11 another mute or deaf, seeing or **b**?
Dt 27:18 be anyone who misleads the **b**
Ps 146:8 the LORD gives sight to the **b**.
Is 35:5 Then the eyes of the **b** shall see,
42:19 Who is **b** but my servant, or deaf
Mt 11:5 the **b** regain their sight, the lame
Lk 6:39 "Can a **b** person guide a **b** person?
Jn 9:25 One thing I do know is that I was **b**
Rom 2:19 that you are a guide for the **b**
2 Pt 1:9 Anyone who lacks them is **b**

**BLINDED** → BLIND
Jn 12:40 "He **b** their eyes and hardened their

2 Cor 4: 4 of this age has **b** the minds

**BLINDNESS** → BLIND
Dt 28: 28 you with madness, **b** and panic,

**BLOCK**
Sir 31: 7 It is a stumbling **b** for fools;
Is 44: 19 Shall I worship a **b** of wood?"
Rom 11: 9 a stumbling **b** and a retribution
1 Cor 1: 23 crucified, a stumbling **b** to Jews

**BLOOD** → BLOODSHED
Gn 4: 10 Your brother's **b** cries out to me
9: 6 Anyone who sheds the **b** of a human being shall that one's **b** be shed;
Ex 7: 17 Nile and it will be changed into **b**.
12: 13 for you the **b** will mark the houses
12: 13 Seeing the **b**, I will pass over you;
24: 8 he took the **b** and splashed it
24: 8 "This is the **b** of the covenant
Lv 1: 5 shall offer its **b** by splashing it on all
3: 17 You shall not eat any fat or any **b**.
17: 11 since the life of the flesh is in the **b**,
17: 11 because it is the **b** as life that makes
Nm 35: 33 can have no expiation for the **b** shed
35: 33 on it except through the **b** of the one
Ps 72: 14 for precious is their **b** in his sight.
Is 1: 11 In the **b** of calves, lambs, and goats
Mt 27: 8 even today is called the Field of **B**.
Mk 14: 24 "This is my **b** of the covenant,
Lk 22: 44 sweat became like drops of **b** falling
Jn 6: 53 of the Son of Man and drink his **b**,
19: 34 immediately **b** and water flowed
Acts 2: 20 and the moon to **b**,
Rom 5: 9 since we are now justified by his **b**,
1 Cor 11: 25 cup is the new covenant in my **b**.
Eph 1: 7 him we have redemption by his **b**,
6: 12 our struggle is not with flesh and **b**
Heb 9: 12 not with the **b** of goats and calves
9: 12 goats and calves but with his own **b**,
9: 22 almost everything is purified by **b**,
9: 22 of **b** there is no forgiveness.
1 Jn 5: 6 one who came through water and **b**,
5: 6 by water alone, but by water and **b**.
Rev 1: 5 has freed us from our sins by his **b**,
5: 9 with your **b** you purchased for God
6: 12 and the whole moon became like **b**.
12: 11 conquered him by the **b** of the Lamb

**BLOODSHED** → BLOOD, SHED
Is 5: 7 He waited for judgment, but see, **b**!

**BLOSSOMS**
Ex 25: 33 shaped like almond **b**, each with its

**BLOT**
Ps 51: 3 your abundant compassion **b** out my

**BLOW**
Jl 2: 1 **B** the horn in Zion, sound the alarm
Rev 8: 6 seven trumpets prepared to **b** them.

**BOAST** → BOASTING
Prv 27: 1 Do not **b** about tomorrow, for you
Rom 2: 23 You who **b** of the law, do you
1 Cor 1: 31 boasts, should **b** in the Lord."
2 Cor 11: 30 If I must **b**, I will **b** of the things
Gal 6: 14 may I never **b** except in the cross
Eph 2: 9 is not from works, so no one may **b**.

**BOASTING** → BOAST
1 Cor 5: 6 Your **b** is not appropriate.

**BOAZ**
Bethlehemite who showed favor to Ruth (Ru 2), married her (Ru 4). Ancestor of David (Ru 4:18-22; 1 Chr 2:12-15), Jesus (Mt 1:5-16; Lk 3:23-32).

**BODIES** → BODY
Rom 12: 1 to offer your **b** as a living sacrifice,
1 Cor 6: 15 not know that your **b** are members
Heb 10: 22 and our **b** washed in pure water.

**BODILY** → BODY
Lk 3: 22 upon him in **b** form like a dove.
Col 2: 9 the whole fullness of the deity **b**,

**BODY** → BODIES, BODILY
Mi 6: 7 the fruit of my **b** for the sin of my
Mt 6: 22 "The lamp of the **b** is the eye.
Mk 14: 22 and said, "Take it; this is my **b**."
Lk 12: 4 not be afraid of those who kill the **b**
Jn 2: 21 speaking about the temple of his **b**.
Rom 7: 24 will deliver me from this mortal **b**?
1 Cor 6: 13 the Lord, and the Lord is for the **b**;
10: 17 are one **b**, for we all partake
15: 44 It is sown a natural **b**; it is raised a spiritual **b**.
2 Cor 5: 8 we would rather leave the **b** and go
Eph 4: 4 one **b** and one Spirit, as you were
Col 2: 19 from whom the whole **b**,

**BOLDNESS**
Eph 3: 12 in whom we have **b** of speech

**BONE** → BONES
Gn 2: 23 is **b** of my bones and flesh of my
Ez 37: 7 bones came together, **b** joining to **b**.

**BONES** → BONE
Ex 12: 46 You shall not break any of its **b**.
Ps 34: 21 He watches over all his **b**;

**BOOK** → BOOKS
Jos 1: 8 Do not let this **b** of the law depart
Ps 69: 29 they be blotted from the **b** of life;
Rev 21: 27 are written in the Lamb's **b** of life.

**BOOKS** → BOOK
Eccl 12: 12 making of many **b** there is no end,
Dn 7: 10 convened, and the **b** were opened.
Jn 21: 25 whole world would contain the **b**

**BOOTHS**
Lv 23: 34 month is the LORD's feast of **B**,
Ezr 3: 4 kept the feast of **B** in the manner
Zec 14: 16 and to celebrate the feast of **B**.

**BORE** → BEAR
Ps 22: 11 since my mother **b** me you are my God.
Mt 8: 17 our infirmities and **b** our diseases."
1 Pt 2: 24 He himself **b** our sins in his body

**BORN** → BEAR
Is 66: 8 or a nation be **b** in a single moment?
Lk 2: 11 of David a savior has been **b** for you
Jn 3: 7 you, 'You must be **b** from above.'
1 Cor 15: 8 as to one **b** abnormally, he appeared
1 Pt 1: 23 You have been **b** anew,

**BORROW** → BORROWER, BORROWS
Dt 28: 12 to many nations but **b** from none.
Mt 5: 42 your back on one who wants to **b**.

**BORROWER** → BORROW
Prv 22: 7 and the **b** is the slave of the lender.

**BORROWS** → BORROW
Ps 37: 21 The wicked one **b** but does not

**BOW** → BOWED
Gn 9: 13 I set my **b** in the clouds to serve as
Ex 20: 5 you shall not **b** down before them
Ps 95: 6 Enter, let us **b** down in worship;

**BOWED** → BOW
Ps 146: 8 raises up those who are **b** down;

**BOWLS**
Rev 16: 1 pour out the seven **b** of God's fury

**BOY** → BOYS
Lk 2: 43 the **b** Jesus remained behind

**BOYS** → BOY
Ex 1: 18 done this, allowing the **b** to live?"

**BRANCH** → BRANCHES
Is 4: 2 The **b** of the LORD will be beauty
Jn 15: 2 He takes away every **b** in me

**BRANCHES** → BRANCH
Jn 15: 5 I am the vine, you are the **b**.
Rom 11: 21 if God did not spare the natural **b**,

**BREAD**
Gn 3: 19 sweat of your brow you shall eat **b**,
Ex 12: 8 eating it roasted with unleavened **b**
Dt 8: 3 it is not by **b** alone that people live,
Ps 136: 25 gives **b** to all flesh, for his mercy
Eccl 11: 1 Send forth your **b** upon the face
Wis 16: 20 and furnished them **b** from heaven,
Sir 15: 3 will feed him with the **b** of learning,
Mt 6: 11 Give us today our daily **b**;
Lk 4: 4 'One does not live by **b** alone.' "
Jn 6: 35 said to them, "I am the **b** of life;
Acts 2: 42 to the breaking of the **b**
1 Cor 10: 17 Because the loaf of **b** is one, we,
11: 26 For as often as you eat this **b**

**BREAK** → BROKEN, BROKENHEARTED
Mt 6: 19 destroy, and thieves **b** in and steal.
Jn 19: 33 dead, they did not **b** his legs,

**BREASTPIECE** → BREASTPLATE
Ex 28: 15 The **b** of decision you shall

**BREASTPLATE** → BREASTPIECE
Wis 5: 18 Shall put on righteousness for a **b**,
Is 59: 17 He put on justice as his **b**, victory as
Eph 6: 14 clothed with righteousness as a **b**,

**BREATH**
Gn 2: 7 blew into his nostrils the **b** of life,
6: 17 sky in which there is the **b** of life;
Eccl 12: 7 the life **b** returns to God who gave
2 Thes 2: 8 will kill with the **b** of his mouth

**BRIBE**
Dt 16: 19 you shall not take a **b**, for a **b** blinds

**BRIDE** → BRIDEGROOM
Is 62: 5 in his **b** so shall your God rejoice
Rev 19: 7 come, his **b** has made herself ready.
21: 9 I will show you the **b**, the wife

**BRIDEGROOM** → BRIDE
Mt 9: 15 wedding guests mourn as long as the **b** is
Jn 3: 29 The one who has the bride is the **b**;

**BRIDLE**
Ps 32: 9 bit and **b** their temper is curbed,
Jas 3: 2 man, able to **b** his whole body also.

**BRIGHT** → BRIGHTNESS
Mt 17: 5 a **b** cloud cast a shadow over them,
Rev 22: 16 of David, the **b** morning star."

**BRIGHTNESS** → BRIGHT
Am 5: 20 not light, gloom without any **b**!

**BRING** → BRINGS, BROUGHT
Gn 6: 19 all living creatures you shall **b** two
Eccl 12: 14 because God will **b** to judgment
Jer 24: 6 good and **b** them back to this land,
Mt 10: 34 I have come to **b** peace
10: 34 I have come to **b** not peace
Rom 10: 15 of those who **b** [the] good news!"

**BRINGS** → BRING
Jas 5: 20 know that whoever **b** back a sinner

**BROKE** → BREAK
Ex 32: 19 **b** them on the base of the mountain.
Jer 31: 32 They **b** my covenant, though I was
Mt 14: 19 he said the blessing, **b** the loaves,
1 Cor 11: 24 he had given thanks, **b** it and said,

**BROKEN** → BREAK
Rom 11: 20 They were **b** off because

**BROKENHEARTED** → BREAK, HEART
Ps 147: 3 Healing the **b**, and binding up their
Is 61: 1 to bind up the **b**, To proclaim liberty

**BRONZE**
Nm 21: 9 Moses made a **b** serpent
Dt 28: 23 over your heads will be like **b**
Dn 10: 6 and feet looked like burnished **b**,

**BROOD**
Mt 3: 7 he said to them, "You **b** of vipers!
Lk 13: 34 a hen gathers her **b** under her wings,

**BROTHER** → BROTHER'S, BROTHER-IN-LAW, BROTHERS
Gn 4: 8 Cain attacked his **b** Abel and killed
Mt 5: 24 first and be reconciled with your **b**,
10: 21 **B** will hand over **b** to death,

**BROTHER'S** → BROTHER
Dt 25: 7 does not want to marry his **b** wife,
25: 7 to perpetuate his **b** name in Israel
Mk 6: 18 for you to have your **b** wife."

**BROTHER-IN-LAW** → BROTHER
Gn 38: 8 in fulfillment of your duty as **b**,

**BROTHERS** → BROTHER
Gn 9: 25 of slaves shall he be to his **b**."
37: 11 So his **b** were furious at him but his
Mk 3: 33 "Who are my mother and [my] **b**?"
Lk 22: 32 back, you must strengthen your **b**."
Heb 2: 11 he is not ashamed to call them "**b**,"

**BROUGHT** → BRING
Gn 15: 7 I am the LORD who **b** you
Jgs 2: 1 I **b** you up from Egypt and led you
2 Chr 36: 18 princes, all these he **b** to Babylon.
Ezr 6: 5 and **b** to Babylon be sent back;
1 Tm 6: 7 For we **b** nothing into the world,

**BUILD** → BUILDERS, BUILDING, BUILDS, BUILT, REBUILD
Gn 11: 4 let us **b** ourselves a city and a tower
Dt 6: 10 fine, large cities that you did not **b**,
Ps 127: 1 Unless the LORD **b** the house, they labor in vain who **b**.
Is 57: 14 **B** up, **b** up, prepare the way,
Mt 16: 18 upon this rock I will **b** my church,

**BUILDERS** → BUILD
Ps 118: 22 The stone the **b** rejected has become
Mk 12: 10 that the **b** rejected has become
1 Pt 2: 7 which the **b** rejected has become

**BUILDING** → BUILD
1 Cor 3: 9 you are God's field, God's **b**.
2 Cor 5: 1 destroyed, we have a **b** from God,
Eph 4: 12 for **b** up the body of Christ,

**BUILDS** → BUILD
Prv 14: 1 Wisdom **b** her house, but Folly tears

1 Cor 3:10 each one must be careful how he **b**
8: 1 inflates with pride, but love **b** up.
10:23 is lawful," but not everything **b** up.

**BUILT** → BUILD
Tb 13:16 of Jerusalem will be **b** with sapphire
13:16 of Jerusalem will be **b** with gold,
1 Mc 4:47 **b** a new altar like the former one.
Prv 9: 1 Wisdom has **b** her house, she has set
Eph 2:20 **b** upon the foundation

**BULLS**
1 Chr 29:21 a thousand **b**, a thousand rams,
Ps 22:13 Many **b** surround me; fierce **b**
Heb 10: 4 it is impossible that the blood of **b**

**BURDEN** → BURDENS, BURDENSOME
Mt 11:30 my yoke is easy, and my **b** light."

**BURDENS** → BURDEN
Lk 11:46 You impose on people **b** hard
Gal 6: 2 Bear one another's **b**, and so you

**BURDENSOME** → BURDEN
1 Jn 5: 3 And his commandments are not **b**,

**BURIED** → BURY
Rom 6: 4 We were indeed **b** with him through
1 Cor 15: 4 that he was **b**; that he was raised

**BURN** → BURNED, BURNING, BURNT
Ex 3: 3 sight. Why does the bush not **b** up?"
21:25 **b** for **b**, wound for wound,
Lk 3:17 his barn, but the chaff he will **b**

**BURNED** → BURN
Jn 15: 6 them into a fire and they will be **b**.
1 Cor 3:15 But if someone's work is **b** up,

**BURNING** → BURN
Ps 79: 5 your jealous anger keep **b** like fire?
Lk 24:32 not our hearts **b** [within us] while he

**BURNT** → BURN
Ex 40: 6 Put the altar for **b** offerings in front
Lv 1: 3 If a person's offering is a **b** offering
1 Sm 15:22 "Does the LORD delight in **b** offerings
1 Mc 1:45 to prohibit **b** offerings, sacrifices,
4:56 and joyfully offered **b** offerings and
Ps 51:18 a **b** offering you would not accept.
Hos 6: 6 knowledge of God rather than **b** offerings.
Mi 6: 6 Shall I come before him with **b** offerings,
Mk 12:33 is worth more than all **b** offerings

**BURY** → BURIED
Lk 9:60 him, "Let the dead **b** their dead.

**BUSH**
Ex 3: 2 to him as fire flaming out of a **b**.
3: 2 looked, although the **b** was on fire,

**BUY** → BUYS
Rev 3:18 I advise you to **b** from me gold
3:18 **b** ointment to smear on your eyes

**BUYS** → BUY
Mt 13:44 sells all that he has and **b** that field.

**BYWORD** → WORD
Jb 17: 6 I am made a **b** of the people;
Ps 44:15 You make us a **b** among the nations;

## C

**CAESAREA**
Mt 16:13 of **C** Philippi he asked his disciples,
Acts 10: 1 Now in **C** there was a man named
25: 4 Paul was being held in custody in **C**

**CAIAPHAS**
High priest at trial of Jesus (Mt 26:3, 57; Lk 3:2; Jn 11:49; 18:13-28); at trial of disciples (Acts 4:6).

**CAIN**
Firstborn of Adam (Gn 4:1), murdered brother Abel (Gn 4:1-25; Heb 11:4; 1 Jn 3:12; Jude 11).

**CALAMITIES**
1 Sm 10:19 saves you from all your evils and **c**,

**CALEB**
Judahite who spied out Canaan (Nm 13:6); allowed to enter land (Nm 13:30–14:38; Dt 1:36; Sir 46:7-9; 1 Mc 2:56). Given Hebron (Jos 14:6–15:19).

**CALF** → CALVES
Ex 32: 4 it with a tool, made a molten **c**.
Lk 15:23 Take the fattened **c** and slaughter it.

**CALL** → CALLED, CALLING
Dt 4:26 I **c** heaven and earth this day
1 Sm 3: 5 "I did not **c** you," Eli answered.
1 Kgs 18:24 You shall **c** upon the name of your
18:24 and I will **c** upon the name
Ps 61: 3 From the ends of the earth I **c**;
Prv 8: 1 Does not Wisdom **c**,
Is 65:24 Before they **c**, I will answer;
Mt 9:13 I did not come to **c** the righteous
Lk 6:46 "Why do you **c** me, 'Lord, Lord,'
Jn 15:15 I no longer **c** you slaves,
Rom 10:12 of all, enriching all who **c** upon him.
11:29 and the **c** of God are irrevocable.

**CALLED** → CALL
2 Sm 22: 7 In my distress I **c** out: LORD!
Is 43: 1 I have **c** you by name:
Mt 23: 8 As for you, do not be **c** 'Rabbi.'
1 Cor 7:15 God has **c** you to peace.
1 Jn 3: 1 we may be **c** the children of God.

**CALLING** → CALL
Phil 3:14 the prize of God's upward **c**,

**CALVES** → CALF
1 Kgs 12:28 took counsel, made two **c** of gold,

**CAMEL**
Mt 23:24 out the gnat and swallow the **c**!
Mk 10:25 for a **c** to pass through [the] eye

**CANA**
Jn 2: 1 third day there was a wedding in **C**

**CANAAN** → CANAANITE, CANAANITES
Gn 9:25 "Cursed be **C**! The lowest of slaves
Nm 13: 2 men to reconnoiter the land of **C**,
1 Chr 16:18 "To you will I give the land of **C**,

**CANAANITE** → CANAAN
Gn 28: 1 "You shall not marry a **C** woman!
Mt 15:22 a **C** woman of that district came

**CANAANITES** → CANAAN
Ex 33: 2 Driving out the **C**, Amorites,
Jgs 3: 5 the Israelites settled among the **C**,

**CAPERNAUM**
Mt 4:13 and went to live in **C** by the sea,
Jn 6:59 teaching in the synagogue in **C**.

**CAPTIVE** → CAPTIVITY
2 Kgs 24:16 of Babylon brought **c** to Babylon.
Rom 7:23 taking me **c** to the law of sin
Eph 4: 8 on high and took prisoners **c**;

**CAPTIVITY** → CAPTIVE
Dt 28:41 with you, for they will go into **c**.

Ezr 8: 35 those who had returned from the **c**,

**CARE** → CARELESS, CARES
Ps 8: 5 a son of man that you **c** for him?
Heb 2: 6 the son of man that you **c** for him?
Jas 1: 27 to **c** for orphans and widows in their

**CARELESS** → CARE
Mt 12: 36 for every **c** word they speak.

**CARES** → CARE
1 Pt 5: 7 upon him because he **c** for you.

**CARMEL**
1 Kgs 18: 20 the prophets gather on Mount **C**.

**CARPENTER'S**
Mt 13: 55 Is he not the **c** son? Is not his

**CARRY**
Lk 14: 27 Whoever does not **c** his own cross

**CASE**
Is 41: 21 Present your **c**, says the LORD;

**CAST**
Est 9: 24 to destroy them and had **c** the *pur*,
Ps 22: 19 for my clothing they **c** lots.
55: 23 **C** your care upon the LORD,
Prv 16: 33 Into the bag the lot is **c**,
Jn 19: 24 and for my vesture they **c** lots."
1 Pt 5: 7 **C** all your worries upon him

**CAUGHT**
2 Cor 12: 2 was **c** up to the third heaven.
1 Thes 4: 17 will be **c** up together with them

**CAUSE**
Ps 9: 5 For you upheld my right and my **c**,
Jn 15: 25 fulfilled, 'They hated me without **c**.'

**CAVE**
Gn 23: 9 he will sell me the **c** of Machpelah
1 Sm 22: 1 and escaped to the **c** of Adullam.

**CEASE**
Gn 8: 22 and day and night shall not **c**.
Jer 31: 36 of Israel **c** as a people before me
1 Cor 13: 8 if tongues, they will **c**;

**CEDAR**
2 Sm 7: 2 "Here I am living in a house of **c**,
Ps 92: 13 tree, shall grow like a **c** of Lebanon.

**CELEBRATE**
1 Cor 5: 8 Therefore let us **c** the feast,

**CENSER** → CENSERS
Ez 8: 11 of Shaphan, each with **c** in hand;
Rev 8: 3 stood at the altar, holding a gold **c**.

**CENSERS** → CENSER
Lv 10: 1 Nadab and Abihu took their **c** and,

**CENSUS**
Nm 1: 2 Take a **c** of the whole community

**CENTURION**
Mt 8: 5 a **c** approached him and appealed
Lk 23: 47 The **c** who witnessed what had
Acts 10: 1 a **c** of the Cohort called the Italica,

**CEPHAS** → =PETER
Name given to the apostle Peter (Jn 1:42; 1 Cor 1:12; 3:22; 9:5; 15:5; Gal 1:18; 2:9, 11, 14).

**CHAFF**
Ps 1: 4 They are like **c** driven by the wind.
Lk 3: 17 his barn, but the **c** he will burn

**CHAINED** → CHAINS
2 Tm 2: 9 But the word of God is not **c**.

**CHAINS** → CHAINED
Eph 6: 20 for which I am an ambassador in **c**,
Heb 11: 36 even **c** and imprisonment.
2 Pt 2: 4 them to the **c** of Tartarus

**CHALDEANS**
Gn 15: 7 of the **C** to give you this land as
Dn 1: 4 the language and literature of the **C**.

**CHANGE** → CHANGED, CHANGERS
1 Kgs 8: 47 they have a **c** of heart in the land
Jas 1: 17 no alteration or shadow caused by **c**.

**CHANGED** → CHANGE
1 Cor 15: 51 all fall asleep, but we will all be **c**,
Heb 1: 12 and like a garment they will be **c**.

**CHANGERS** → CHANGE
Mk 11: 15 overturned the tables of the money **c**
Jn 2: 15 spilled the coins of the money **c**

**CHARACTER**
Rom 5: 4 endurance, proven **c**, and proven **c**,

**CHARGE**
Mk 15: 26 of the **c** against him read,
Rom 8: 33 will bring a **c** against God's chosen
1 Cor 9: 18 I offer the gospel free of **c** so as not

**CHARIOT** → CHARIOTS
2 Kgs 2: 11 a fiery **c** and fiery horses came
Ps 104: 3 You make the clouds your **c**;

**CHARIOTS** → CHARIOT
Ex 14: 28 it covered the **c** and the horsemen.
Zec 6: 1 and saw four **c** coming

**CHARM**
Prv 31: 30 **C** is deceptive and beauty fleeting;

**CHEEK**
Mt 5: 39 strikes you on (your) right **c**,

**CHEERFUL**
2 Cor 9: 7 compulsion, for God loves a **c** giver.

**CHEMOSH**
1 Kgs 11: 7 then built a high place to **C**,
Jer 48: 7 **C** shall go into exile, his priests

**CHERUB** → CHERUBIM
Ps 18: 11 Mounted on a **c** he flew,
Ez 28: 14 With a **c** I placed you; I put you

**CHERUBIM** → CHERUB
Gn 3: 24 man, stationing the **c** and the fiery
Ex 25: 18 Make two **c** of beaten gold
2 Chr 3: 11 of the **c** spanned twenty cubits:
Ps 80: 2 Seated upon the **c**, shine forth
Heb 9: 5 Above it were the **c** of glory

**CHIEF**
Mk 15: 3 The **c** priests accused him of many
1 Pt 5: 4 when the **c** Shepherd is revealed,

**CHILD** → CHILDBEARING, CHILDISH, CHILDREN
Gn 17: 17 "Can a **c** be born to a man who is
Sir 4: 10 Then God will call you his **c**,
Is 11: 6 with a little **c** to guide them.
49: 15 tenderness for the **c** of her womb?
Hos 11: 1 When Israel was a **c** I loved him,
Mt 1: 18 with **c** through the holy Spirit.
Mk 10: 15 of God like a **c** will not enter it."
1 Cor 13: 11 When I was a **c**, I used to talk as a **c**, think as a **c**, reason as a **c**;

Gal 3:27 into Christ have **c** yourselves
Rev 12: 1 in the sky, a woman **c** with the sun,

**CLOTHING** → CLOTHE
Ps 22:19 for my **c** they cast lots.

**CLOUD** → CLOUDS
Ex 13:21 of a column of **c** to show them
1 Kgs 8:10 the **c** filled the house of the LORD
18:44 "There is a **c** as small as a man's
Ez 10: 4 the temple was filled with the **c**,
Mk 9: 7 Then a **c** came, casting a shadow
9: 7 then from the **c** came a voice,
Lk 21:27 of Man coming in a **c** with power
Heb 12: 1 by so great a **c** of witnesses, let us
Rev 14:14 I looked and there was a white **c**,
14:14 on the **c** one who looked like a son

**CLOUDS** → CLOUD
Gn 9:13 my bow in the **c** to serve as a sign
Dn 7:13 with the **c** of heaven One like a son
Mt 24:30 Man coming upon the **c** of heaven
1 Thes 4:17 them in the **c** to meet the Lord
Rev 1: 7 he is coming amid the **c**, and every

**CLUSTER**
Nm 13:23 a branch with a single **c** of grapes

**COALS**
Ps 11: 6 rains upon the wicked fiery **c**
Prv 25:22 For live **c** you will heap on their
Rom 12:20 by so doing you will heap burning **c**

**COIN**
Mt 17:27 you will find a **c** worth twice
22:19 Show me the **c** that pays the census
Lk 15: 9 me because I have found the **c** that I

**COLD**
Zec 14: 6 that day there will no longer be **c**
Mt 24:12 the love of many will grow **c**.
Rev 3:16 neither hot nor **c**, I will spit you

**COLLECTOR** → COLLECTORS
Mt 10: 3 Thomas and Matthew the tax **c**;
Lk 18:10 a Pharisee and the other was a tax **c**.
19: 2 who was a chief tax **c**

**COLLECTORS** → COLLECTOR
Mt 5:46 Do not the tax **c** do the same?
11:19 a friend of tax **c** and sinners.'

**COLT**
Zec 9: 9 donkey, on a **c**, the foal of a donkey.
Jn 12:15 comes, seated upon an ass's **c**."

**COME** → COMES, COMING
Ps 144: 5 incline your heavens and **c** down;
Is 59:20 Then for Zion shall **c** a redeemer,
Zec 14: 5 will **c**, and all his holy ones
Mt 6:10 your kingdom **c**, your will be done,
Lk 7:20 ask, 'Are you the one who is to **c**,
Jn 6:37 the Father gives me will **c** to me,
Rev 1: 4 is and who was and who is to **c**,
22:20 Amen! **C**, Lord Jesus!

**COMES** → COME
Ps 118:26 Blessed is he who **c** in the name
Lk 19:38 "Blessed is the king who **c**
Jn 14: 6 No one **c** to the Father except

**COMFORT** → COMFORTED, COMFORTERS, COMFORTS
Is 40: 1 **C**, give **c** to my people, says your

**COMFORTED** → COMFORT
Mt 5: 4 they who mourn, for they will be **c**.

**COMFORTERS** → COMFORT
Jb 16: 2 Troublesome **c**, all of you!
Ps 69:21 was none, for **c**, but found none.

**COMFORTS** → COMFORT
Is 66:13 As a mother **c** her child, so I will

**COMING** → COME
Mal 3: 2 who can endure the day of his **c**?
2 Pt 3: 4 "Where is the promise of his **c**?
Rev 22:20 says, "Yes, I am **c** soon." Amen!

**COMMAND** → COMMANDED, COMMANDMENT, COMMANDMENTS
Dt 1:26 you defied the **c** of the LORD,

**COMMANDED** → COMMAND
Gn 7: 5 complied, just as the LORD had **c**.
Ex 40:32 altar, as the LORD had **c** Moses.
Jos 1:16 "We will do all you have **c** us,
Mt 28:20 to observe all that I have **c** you.
Jn 14:31 that I do just as the Father has **c** me.

**COMMANDMENT** → COMMAND
Dt 6: 1 This then is the **c**, the statutes and
Mt 22:38 This is the greatest and the first **c**.
Rom 7:12 and the **c** is holy and righteous
1 Jn 3:23 And his **c** is this: we should believe

**COMMANDMENTS** → COMMAND
Ex 20: 6 those who love me and keep my **c**.
Eccl 12:13 Fear God and keep his **c**, for this
Mt 19:17 wish to enter into life, keep the **c**."
22:40 prophets depend on these two **c**."
Jn 14:15 you love me, you will keep my **c**.
1 Cor 7:19 what matters is keeping God's **c**.
1 Jn 5: 3 of God is this, that we keep his **c**. And his **c** are not burdensome,
Rev 14:12 the holy ones who keep God's **c**

**COMMIT** → COMMITS
Dt 5:18 You shall not **c** adultery.
2 Kgs 17:21 causing them to **c** a great sin.
Mt 5:27 was said, 'You shall not **c** adultery.'

**COMMITS** → COMMIT
Jn 8:34 everyone who **c** sin is a slave of sin.

**COMMON**
Acts 2:44 together and had all things in **c**;

**COMPANY**
1 Cor 15:33 "Bad **c** corrupts good morals."

**COMPARE**
Prv 8:11 and no treasures can **c** with her.]
Lk 7:31 to what shall I **c** the people of this

**COMPASSION** → COMPASSIONATE
Ps 103:13 As a father has **c** on his children,
103:13 so the LORD has **c** on those who
Col 3:12 and beloved, heartfelt **c**, kindness,

**COMPASSIONATE** → COMPASSION
Sir 2:11 For the Lord is **c** and merciful;
Jas 5:11 Lord, because "the Lord is **c**

**COMPETING**
2 Tm 2: 5 crown except by **c** according

**COMPLAINING** → COMPLAINT
1 Pt 4: 9 hospitable to one another without **c**.

**COMPLAINT** → COMPLAINING
Jb 10: 1 I will give myself up to **c**;
Ps 142: 3 Before him I pour out my **c**,
Hb 2: 1 what answer he will give to my **c**.

**COMPLETED**
Gn 2: 2 On the seventh day God **c** the work

**CONCEITED**
Gal 5: 26 Let us not be **c**, provoking one
1 Tm 6: 4 is **c**, understanding nothing, and has
3: 6 so that he may not become **c**

**CONCEIVE**
Lk 1: 31 you will **c** in your womb and bear

**CONDEMN** → CONDEMNATION, CONDEMNED
Lk 11: 31 this generation and she will **c** them,
Jn 3: 17 Son into the world to **c** the world,
Rom 8: 34 Who will **c**? It is Christ [Jesus] who
1 Jn 3: 21 if [our] hearts do not **c** us, we have

**CONDEMNATION** → CONDEMN
Mk 12: 40 They will receive a very severe **c**."
Rom 5: 18 as through one transgression **c** came
Jas 5: 12 "No," that you may not incur **c**.

**CONDEMNED** → CONDEMN
Mt 12: 37 and by your words you will be **c**."
Jn 3: 18 believes in him will not be **c**,
3: 18 does not believe has already been **c**,
16: 11 the ruler of this world has been **c**.
1 Cor 11: 32 that we may not be **c** along

**CONDUCT**
Tb 4: 14 and discipline yourself in all your **c**.
Sir 37: 17 The root of all **c** is the heart;
Rom 13: 3 are not a cause of fear to good **c**,
1 Pt 1: 15 in every aspect of your **c**,

**CONFESS** → CONFESSES, CONFESSION
Lv 5: 5 person shall **c** the wrong committed,
16: 21 he shall **c** over it all the iniquities
Phil 2: 11 every tongue **c** that Jesus Christ is

**CONFESSES** → CONFESS
Rom 10: 10 and one **c** with the mouth and so is
1 Jn 2: 23 whoever **c** the Son has the Father as

**CONFESSION** → CONFESS
1 Tm 6: 12 when you made the noble **c**
Heb 4: 14 Son of God, let us hold fast to our **c**.

**CONFIDENCE**
Phil 3: 3 Jesus and do not put our **c** in flesh,
Heb 10: 19 of Jesus we have **c** of entrance

**CONFIRM**
2 Sm 7: 25 **c** the promise that you have spoken
Rom 15: 8 to **c** the promises to the patriarchs,

**CONFORMED**
Rom 8: 29 predestined to be **c** to the image

**CONFUSE**
Gn 11: 7 go down and there **c** their language,

**CONQUER** → CONQUERED, CONQUERS
Rev 17: 14 but the Lamb will **c** them, for he is

**CONQUERED** → CONQUER
Jn 16: 33 take courage, I have **c** the world."
Heb 11: 33 who by faith **c** kingdoms, did what
1 Jn 2: 13 because you have **c** the evil one.

**CONQUERS** → CONQUER
1 Jn 5: 4 is begotten by God **c** the world.
5: 4 victory that **c** the world is our faith.

**CONSCIENCE**
Rom 2: 15 while their **c** also bears witness
1 Cor 8: 7 to idols, their **c**, which is weak,
1 Tm 1: 5 heart, a good **c**, and a sincere faith.
1 Pt 3: 21 but an appeal to God for a clear **c**,

**CONSECRATE** → CONSECRATED
Ex 13: 2 **C** to me every firstborn;

**CONSECRATED** → CONSECRATE
2 Chr 7: 16 **c** this house that my name may be

**CONSIDER** → CONSIDERED
Jas 1: 2 **C** it all joy, my brothers, when you

**CONSIDERED** → CONSIDER
Prv 17: 28 fools, keeping silent, are **c** wise;

**CONSOLATION**
Lk 2: 25 and devout, awaiting the **c** of Israel,

**CONSULT** → CONSULTED
Is 40: 14 Whom did he **c** to gain knowledge?

**CONSULTED** → CONSULT
Ez 20: 3 not allow myself to be **c** by you!—

**CONSUME** → CONSUMED, CONSUMING
Nm 16: 21 that I may **c** them at once.
Jn 2: 17 "Zeal for your house will **c** me."

**CONSUMED** → CONSUME
Ex 3: 2 bush was on fire, it was not being **c**.
Ps 90: 7 Truly we are **c** by your anger,
Zep 3: 8 of my passion all the earth will be **c**.
Gal 5: 15 that you are not **c** by one another.

**CONSUMING** → CONSUME
Heb 12: 29 For our God is a **c** fire.

**CONTAIN**
Jn 21: 25 the whole world would **c** the books

**CONTEMPT**
Mk 9: 12 suffer greatly and be treated with **c**?
Heb 6: 6 themselves and holding him up to **c**.

**CONTEND**
Jude 1: 3 to encourage you to **c** for the faith

**CONTENT** → CONTENTMENT
Sir 29: 23 or much, be **c** with what you have:
2 Cor 12: 10 Therefore, I am **c** with weaknesses,
Heb 13: 5 money but be **c** with what you have,

**CONTENTMENT** → CONTENT
1 Tm 6: 6 religion with **c** is a great gain.

**CONTRIBUTE**
Rom 12: 13 **C** to the needs of the holy ones,

**CONTRITE**
Ps 51: 19 My sacrifice, O God, is a **c** spirit;

**CONVERT**
Mt 23: 15 traverse sea and land to make one **c**,
1 Tm 3: 6 He should not be a recent **c**,

**CONVICT**
Jude 1: 15 and to **c** everyone for all the godless

**CONVINCE** → CONVINCED
Acts 28: 23 trying to **c** them about Jesus
2 Tm 4: 2 **c**, reprimand, encourage through all

**CONVINCED** → CONVINCE
Rom 8: 38 For I am **c** that neither death,

**COPY**
Dt 17: 18 he shall write a **c** of this law
Heb 9: 24 made by hands, a **c** of the true one,

**CORDS**
2 Sm 22: 6 The **c** of Sheol tightened;
Hos 11: 4 I drew them with human **c**,

**CORNELIUS**
First Gentile Christian (Acts 10).

**CORNERSTONE** → STONE
Ps 118: 22 builders rejected has become the **c**.
Is 28: 16 A precious **c** as a sure foundation;
Lk 20: 17 builders rejected has become the **c**'?
1 Pt 2: 6 in Zion, a **c**, chosen and precious,

**CORRECTING** → CORRECTION
2 Tm 2: 25 **c** opponents with kindness.

**CORRECTION** → CORRECTING
Jer 5: 3 laid them low, but they refused **c**;
2 Tm 3: 16 refutation, for **c**, and for training

**CORRUPT** → CORRUPTION
Gn 6: 11 the earth was **c** in the view of God
Acts 2: 40 yourselves from this **c** generation."

**CORRUPTION** → CORRUPT
Acts 2: 31 netherworld nor did his flesh see **c**.
2 Pt 1: 4 escaping from the **c** that is

**COST**
1 Chr 21: 24 burnt offerings that **c** me nothing."
Lk 14: 28 and calculate the **c** to see if there is

**COUNCIL**
Jer 23: 18 has stood in the **c** of the LORD,

**COUNSEL** → COUNSELOR, COUNSELORS
Is 28: 29 wonderful is his **c** and great his

**COUNSELOR** → COUNSEL
Rom 11: 34 of the Lord or who has been his **c**?"

**COUNSELORS** → COUNSEL
Prv 11: 14 security lies in many **c**.
24: 6 and victory depends on many **c**.

**COUNT** → COUNTED
Ps 90: 12 Teach us to **c** our days aright,

**COUNTED** → COUNT
Gn 13: 16 your descendants too might be **c**.
Mt 10: 30 all the hairs of your head are **c**.

**COURAGE** → COURAGEOUS
Jn 16: 33 but take **c**, I have conquered

**COURAGEOUS** → COURAGE
1 Mc 2: 64 be **c** and strong in keeping the law,
1 Cor 16: 13 firm in the faith, be **c**, be strong.

**COURT** → COURTS
Ex 27: 9 also make a **c** for the tabernacle.
Dn 7: 10 The **c** was convened, and the books
Mt 5: 25 while on the way to **c** with him.
1 Cor 6: 6 brother goes to **c** against brother,

**COURTS** → COURT
Ps 84: 11 in your **c** than a thousand elsewhere.
96: 8 Bring gifts and enter his **c**;

**COVENANT** → COVENANTS
Gn 6: 18 I will establish my **c** with you.
9: 9 I am now establishing my **c**
15: 18 that day the LORD made a **c**
Ex 2: 24 was mindful of his **c** with Abraham,
19: 5 obey me completely and keep my **c**,
24: 7 Taking the book of the **c**, he read it
Lv 26: 42 I will remember my **c** with Jacob,
26: 42 and also my **c** with Abraham I will
Jgs 2: 1 I will never break my **c** with you,
1 Kgs 8: 23 you keep **c** and love toward your
Ezr 10: 3 enter into a **c** before our God
Jdt 9: 13 planned dire things against your **c**,
1 Mc 1: 15 and abandoned the holy **c**;
Ps 105: 8 He remembers forever his **c**,
Sir 28: 7 remember the **c** of the Most High,
Is 61: 8 an everlasting **c** I will make
Jer 31: 31 I will make a new **c** with the house
Ez 16: 60 I will remember the **c** I made
16: 60 set up an everlasting **c** with you.
Mal 3: 1 of the **c** whom you desire—
Lk 22: 20 "This cup is the new **c** in my blood,
1 Cor 11: 25 "This cup is the new **c** in my blood.
2 Cor 3: 6 qualified us as ministers of a new **c**,
Heb 7: 22 the guarantee of an [even] better **c**.
12: 24 the mediator of a new **c**,
Rev 11: 19 the ark of his **c** could be seen

**COVENANTS** → COVENANT
Rom 9: 4 glory, the **c**, the giving of the law,
Gal 4: 24 These women represent two **c**.

**COVER** → COVERED
Ex 33: 22 will **c** you with my hand until I have
Jas 5: 20 death and will **c** a multitude of sins.

**COVERED** → COVER
Ez 10: 12 wheels were **c** with eyes all around

**COVET**
Ex 20: 17 You shall not **c** your neighbor's
Rom 7: 7 I did not know what it is to **c** except
7: 7 the law said, "You shall not **c**."
Jas 4: 2 You **c** but do not possess.

**CRAFTY**
2 Cor 12: 16 yet I was **c** and got the better of you

**CRAWLING**
Gn 1: 24 tame animals, **c** things, and every kind

**CREATE** → CREATED, CREATING, CREATION, CREATOR
Ps 51: 12 A clean heart **c** for me, God;
Eph 2: 15 that he might **c** in himself one new

**CREATED** → CREATE
Gn 1: 1 when God **c** the heavens
1: 27 God **c** mankind in his image;
1: 27 in the image of God he **c** them;
1: 27 male and female he **c** them.
Sir 1: 4 all other things wisdom was **c**;
Mal 2: 10 Has not one God **c** us?
1 Cor 11: 9 nor was man **c** for woman,
Eph 2: 10 **c** in Christ Jesus for the good works
Col 1: 16 in him were **c** all things in heaven
1: 16 all things were **c** through him
1 Tm 4: 4 For everything **c** by God is good,
Rev 4: 11 and power, for you **c** all things;
4: 11 will they came to be and were **c**."

**CREATING** → CREATE
Is 65: 17 I am **c** new heavens and a new earth;

**CREATION** → CREATE
Gn 2: 3 from all the work he had done in **c**.
Mk 10: 6 But from the beginning of **c**,
Rom 8: 19 For **c** awaits with eager expectation
2 Cor 5: 17 So whoever is in Christ is a new **c**:
Gal 6: 15 uncircumcision, but only a new **c**.
Col 1: 15 invisible God, the firstborn of all **c**.
2 Pt 3: 4 as it was from the beginning of **c**."

**CREATOR** → CREATE
Eccl 12: 1 Remember your **C** in the days
Rom 1: 25 the creature rather than the **c**, who is
Col 3: 10 for knowledge, in the image of its **c**.
1 Pt 4: 19 over to a faithful **c** as they do good.

**CREATURE** → CREATURES
Rom 1:25 and worshiped the **c** rather than

**CREATURES** → CREATURE
Ps 104:24 the earth is full of your **c**.
Ez 1:5 likeness of four living **c** appeared.
Rev 4:6 there were four living **c** covered
19:4 and the four living **c** fell down

**CREDIT**
Lk 6:33 good to you, what **c** is that to you?
1 Pt 2:20 But what **c** is there if you are patient

**CRIED** → CRY
Ex 2:23 under their bondage and **c** out,
Nm 20:16 When we **c** to the LORD, he heard
Jgs 3:9 But when the Israelites **c**
Ps 22:6 To you they **c** out and they escaped;
Mt 27:46 about three o'clock Jesus **c**

**CRIMINAL** → CRIMINALS
Jn 18:30 "If he were not a **c**, we would not
2 Tm 2:9 even to the point of chains, like a **c**.

**CRIMINALS** → CRIMINAL
Lk 23:32 both **c**, were led away with him

**CROOKED**
Dt 32:5 basely, a twisted and **c** generation!
Eccl 1:15 What is **c** cannot be made straight,
Phil 2:15 without blemish in the midst of a **c**

**CROSS** → CROSSROADS
Dt 31:3 your God, who will **c** before you;
31:3 (It is Joshua who will **c** before you,
Mk 15:30 by coming down from the **c**."
Lk 14:27 Whoever does not carry his own **c**
1 Cor 1:18 The message of the **c** is foolishness
Gal 6:14 in the **c** of our Lord Jesus Christ,
Phil 2:8 obedient to death, even death on a **c**.
Col 1:20 by the blood of his **c** [through him],
Heb 12:2 lay before him he endured the **c**,

**CROSSROADS** → CROSS, ROAD
Prv 8:2 road, at the **c** she takes her stand;

**CROWD** → CROWDS
Mk 8:2 heart is moved with pity for the **c**,
14:43 accompanied by a **c** with swords

**CROWDS** → CROWD
Mt 7:28 words, the **c** were astonished at his

**CROWN** → CROWNED, CROWNS
Prv 4:9 a glorious **c** will she bestow
Jn 19:2 the soldiers wove a **c** out of thorns
Phil 4:1 my joy and **c**, in this way stand firm
2 Tm 4:8 on the **c** of righteousness awaits me,
1 Pt 5:4 you will receive the unfading **c**
Rev 6:2 He was given a **c**, and he rode forth
14:14 man, with a gold **c** on his head

**CROWNED** → CROWN
Ps 8:6 a god, **c** him with glory and honor.
Heb 2:9 but we do see Jesus "**c** with glory

**CROWNS** → CROWN
Rev 4:10 They throw down their **c** before

**CRUCIFIED** → CRUCIFY
Mt 27:22 They all said, "Let him be **c**!"
Lk 24:7 be handed over to sinners and be **c**,
Acts 4:10 Christ the Nazorean whom you **c**,
Rom 6:6 that our old self was **c** with him,
1 Cor 1:23 but we proclaim Christ **c**,
Gal 2:19 I have been **c** with Christ;

**CRUCIFY** → CRUCIFIED
Lk 23:21 continued their shouting, "**C** him!
Jn 19:15 him away, take him away! **C** him!"
19:15 said to them, "Shall I **c** your king?"

**CRUSH** → CRUSHED
Jb 6:9 that God would decide to **c** me,
Is 53:10 it was the LORD'S will to **c** him
Rom 16:20 of peace will quickly **c** Satan under

**CRUSHED** → CRUSH
Ps 34:19 saves those whose spirit is **c**.

**CRY** → CRIED, CRYING
Ex 2:23 their bondage their **c** for help went
Ps 5:3 Attend to the sound of my **c**,
Hb 1:2 must I **c** for help and you do not
1:2 Or **c** out to you, "Violence!"
Mk 15:37 Jesus gave a loud **c** and breathed his

**CRYING** → CRY
Mk 1:3 A voice of one **c** out in the desert:

**CRYSTAL**
Ez 1:22 upwards like shining **c** over their
Rev 22:1 sparkling like **c**,

**CUP**
Ps 23:5 my head with oil; my **c** overflows.
Jer 25:15 Take this **c** of the wine of wrath
Mt 10:42 And whoever gives only a **c** of cold
26:39 is possible, let this **c** pass from me;
Mk 10:38 Can you drink the **c** that I drink
Lk 22:17 Then he took a **c**, gave thanks,
1 Cor 11:25 In the same way also the **c**,
11:25 "This **c** is the new covenant in my
Rev 14:10 full strength into the **c** of his wrath,

**CURED**
Mt 8:16 spirits by a word and **c** all the sick,
Acts 5:16 unclean spirits, and they were all **c**.

**CURSE** → ACCURSED, CURSED, CURSES
Gn 12:3 bless you and **c** those who **c** you.
Lv 24:16 death for uttering the LORD'S name in a **c**.
Nm 22:12 with them and do not **c** this people,
Dt 21:23 anyone who is hanged is a **c** of God.
23:5 Pethor in Aram Naharaim, to **c** you.
Jb 2:9 **C** God and die!"
Ps 109:28 Though they **c**, may you bless;
Sir 4:5 do not give them reason to **c** you.
Mk 14:71 He began to **c** and to swear, "I do
Lk 6:28 bless those who **c** you,
Rom 12:14 [you], bless and do not **c** them.
Gal 3:13 ransomed us from the **c** of the law by becoming a **c** for us,

**CURSED** → CURSE
Gn 3:17 it, **C** is the ground because of you!
9:25 he said: "**C** be Caanan!
27:29 **C** be those who curse you,
Nm 23:8 on the one whom God has not **c**?
Jb 3:1 Job opened his mouth and **c** his day.
Mk 11:21 fig tree that you **c** has withered."
Gal 3:10 "**C** be everyone who does not
Heb 6:8 it will soon be **c** and finally burned.

**CURSES** → CURSE
2 Chr 34:24 all the **c** written in the book that was

**CUSTOM** → CUSTOMS
Jn 18:39 But you have a **c** that I release one

**CUSTOMS** → CUSTOM
1 Mc 1:42 and abandon their particular **c**.
Acts 16:21 are advocating **c** that are not lawful

**CUT**
Ps 37: 9 Those who do evil will be **c** off,
Is 53: 8 For he was **c** off from the land
Mt 3: 10 not bear good fruit will be **c** down
Mk 9: 43 your hand causes you to sin, **c** it off.
Rom 11: 22 otherwise you too will be **c** off.

**CYMBAL** → CYMBALS
1 Cor 13: 1 a resounding gong or a clashing **c**.

**CYMBALS** → CYMBAL
2 Sm 6: 5 harps, tambourines, sistrums, and **c**.
Neh 12: 27 hymns and the music of **c**, harps,
Ps 150: 5 Give praise with crashing **c**,

**CYRUS**
Persian king who allowed exiles to return (2 Chr 36:22-Ezr 1:8), to rebuild temple (Ezr 5:13–6:14), as appointed by the LORD (Is 44:28–45:13).

## D

**DAGON**
Jgs 16: 23 offer a great sacrifice to their god **D**
1 Sm 5: 2 and brought it into the temple of **D**,

**DAILY** → DAY
Mt 6: 11 Give us today our **d** bread;
Lk 9: 23 take up his cross **d** and follow me.

**DAMASCUS**
Acts 9: 3 as he was nearing **D**, a light

**DAN**
1. Son of Jacob by Bilhah (Gn 30:4-6; 35:25; 46:23). Tribe of blessed (Gn 49:16-17; Dt 33:22), numbered (Nm 1:39; 26:43), allotted land (Jos 19:40-48; Ez 48:1), failed to fully possess (Jgs 1:34-35), failed to support Deborah (Jgs 5:17), possessed Dan (Jgs 18).
2. Northernmost city in Israel (Gn 14:14; Jgs 18; 20:1).

**DANCE**
Ps 150: 4 Give praise with tambourines and **d**,
Eccl 3: 4 a time to mourn, and a time to **d**.
Lk 7: 32 the flute for you, but you did not **d**.

**DANIEL** → =BELTESHAZZAR
1. Hebrew exile to Babylon, name changed to Belteshazzar (Dn 1:6-7). Refused to eat unclean food (Dn 1:8-21). Interpreted Nebuchadnezzar's dreams (Dn 2; 4), writing on the wall (Dn 5). Thrown into lion's den (Dn 6; 14:31-42). Visions of (Dn 7–12). Saves Susanna (Dn 13). Destroys Bel and its priests (Dn 14).
2. Son of David (1 Chr 3:1).

**DARE**
Mt 22: 46 did anyone **d** to ask him any more

**DARIUS**
1. King of Persia (Ezr 4:5), allowed rebuilding of temple (Ezr 5–6).
2. Mede who conquered Babylon (Dn 5:31).

**DARK** → DARKNESS
Ps 139: 12 Darkness is not **d** for you, and night
2 Pt 1: 19 it, as to a lamp shining in a **d** place,

**DARKNESS** → DARK
Gn 1: 2 with **d** over the abyss and a mighty
Ex 10: 22 there was dense **d** throughout
Dt 5: 23 the voice from the midst of the **d**,
Zep 1: 15 desolation, A day of **d** and gloom,
Mt 4: 16 who sit in **d** have seen a great light,
6: 23 bad, your whole body will be in **d**. And if the light in you is **d**, how great will the **d** be.
Jn 1: 5 the light shines in the **d**, and the **d**
Eph 5: 8 For you were once **d**, but now you
Col 1: 13 He delivered us from the power of **d**
1 Jn 1: 5 light, and in him there is no **d** at all.

**DATHAN**
Involved in Korah's rebellion against Moses and Aaron (Nm 16:1-27; 26:9; Dt 11:6; Ps 106:17; Sir 45:18).

**DAUGHTER** → DAUGHTERS
Ex 2: 5 Pharaoh's **d** came down to bathe
Jdt 10: 12 "I am a **d** of the Hebrews, and I am
Est 2: 7 Mordecai adopted her as his own **d**.
Ps 9: 15 salvation in the gates of **d** Zion.
Lam 2: 1 in his wrath has abhorred **d** Zion,
Mi 7: 6 the **d** rises up against her mother,
Zec 9: 9 Exult greatly, O **d** Zion!
9: 9 Shout for joy, O **d** Jerusalem!
Mt 14: 6 the **d** of Herodias performed a dance
Lk 12: 53 a mother against her **d** and a **d**

**DAUGHTERS** → DAUGHTER
Gn 6: 4 with the **d** of human beings,
19: 36 Thus the two **d** of Lot became
Nm 27: 1 The **d** of Zelophehad,
Dt 12: 31 their sons and **d** to their gods.
Jb 42: 15 women were as beautiful as the **d**
Acts 2: 17 sons and your **d** shall prophesy,
2 Cor 6: 18 and you shall be sons and **d** to me,

**DAVID**
Son of Jesse (Ru 4:17-22; 1 Chr 2:13-15), ancestor of Jesus (Mt 1:1-17; Lk 3:31). Wives and children (1 Sm 18; 25:39-44; 2 Sm 3:2-5; 5:13-16; 11:27; 1 Chr 3:1-9).
Anointed king by Samuel (1 Sm 16:1-13). Musician to Saul (1 Sm 16:14-23; 18:10). Killed Goliath (1 Sm 17). Relation with Jonathan (1 Sm 18:1-4; 19-20; 23:16-18; 2 Sm 1). Disfavor of Saul (1 Sm 18:6–23:29). Spared Saul's life (1 Sm 24; 26). Among Philistines (1 Sm 21:10-14; 27-30). Lament for Saul and Jonathan (2 Sm 1).
Anointed king of Judah (2 Sm 2:1-11). Conflict with house of Saul (2 Sm 2–4). Anointed king of Israel (2 Sm 5:1-4; 1 Chr 11:1-3). Conquered Jerusalem (2 Sm 5:6-10; 1 Chr 11;4-9). Brought ark to Jerusalem (2 Sm 6; 1 Chr 13; 15–16). The LORD promised eternal dynasty (2 Sm 7; 1 Chr 17; Ps 132). Showed kindness to Mephibosheth (2 Sm 9). Adultery with Bathsheba, murder of Uriah (2 Sm 11–12). Son Amnon raped daughter Tamar; killed by Absalom (2 Sm 13). Absalom's revolt (2 Sm 14–17); death (2 Sm 18). Sheba's revolt (2 Sm 20). Victories: Philistines (2 Sm 5:17-25; 21:15-22; 1 Chr 14:8-17; 20:4-8), Ammonites (2 Sm 10; 1 Chr 19), various (2 Sm 8; 1 Chr 18). Mighty men (2 Sm 23:8-39; 1 Chr 11–12). Punished for numbering army (2 Sm 24; 1 Chr 21). Appointed Solomon king (1 Kgs 1:28–2:9). Prepared for building of temple (1 Chr 22–29). Last words (2 Sm 23:1-7). Death (1 Kgs 2:10-12; 1 Chr 29:28).
Psalmist (Mt 22:43-45), musician (Am 6:5), prophet (2 Sm 23:2-7; Acts 1:16; 2:30).
Psalms of: 2 (Acts 4:25), 3–32, 34–41, 51–65, 68–70, 86, 95 (Heb 4:7), 101, 103, 108-110, 122, 124, 131, 133, 138-145.

**DAWN** → DAWNS
Is 14: 12 O Morning Star, son of the **d**!
Hos 6: 3 as certain as the **d** is his coming.

**DAWNS** → DAWN
Ps 97: 11 Light **d** for the just, and gladness
2 Pt 1: 19 until day **d** and the morning star

**DAY** → DAILY, DAYS
Gn 1: 5 God called the light "**d**,"
1: 5 and morning followed—the first **d**.
8: 22 and **d** and night shall not cease.
Ex 13: 21 Thus they could travel both **d**
20: 8 Remember the sabbath **d**—
Jos 1: 8 Recite it by **d** and by night, that you
Ps 1: 2 on his law he meditates **d** and night.
118: 24 This is the **d** the LORD has made;
Is 66: 8 a land be brought forth in one **d**,

Jl 1:15 O! The **d**! For near is the **d**
Zec 14:1 A **d** is coming for the LORD
Mal 3:2 But who can endure the **d** of his
Mt 25:13 you know neither the **d** nor the hour.
Lk 11:3 Give us each **d** our daily bread
24:46 and rise from the dead on the third **d**
Jn 6:40 I shall raise him [on] the last **d**."
Rom 14:5 considers one **d** more important
2 Cor 6:2 on the **d** of salvation I helped you."
6:2 behold, now is the **d** of salvation.
1 Thes 5:2 the **d** of the Lord will come like
2 Pt 3:8 the Lord one **d** is like a thousand
3:8 and a thousand years like one **d**.
3:10 the **d** of the Lord will come like
1 Jn 4:17 the **d** of judgment because as he is,
Rev 1:10 caught up in spirit on the Lord's **d**
16:14 on the great **d** of God the almighty.

**DAYS** → DAY
Gn 1:14 the seasons, the **d** and the years,
7:4 seven **d** from now I will bring rain
7:4 rain down on the earth for forty **d**
Ex 24:18 He was on the mountain for forty **d**
1 Kgs 19:8 he walked forty **d** and forty nights
1 Mc 4:56 For eight **d** they celebrated
Mk 1:13 remained in the desert for forty **d**,
Eph 5:16 opportunity, because the **d** are evil.
2 Tm 3:1 will be terrifying times in the last **d**.
Heb 1:2 in these last **d**, he spoke to us

**DEACONS**
1 Tm 3:8 Similarly, **d** must be dignified,

**DEAD** → DEATH, DIE, DIED, DYING
Dt 18:11 spirits, or seeks oracles from the **d**.
Ps 115:17 The **d** do not praise the LORD,
Eccl 9:4 live dog is better off than a **d** lion."
Mt 8:22 me, and let the **d** bury their **d**."
Mk 12:27 He is not God of the **d**
Lk 24:5 seek the living one among the **d**?
Rom 6:11 of yourselves as [being] **d** to sin
Eph 2:1 You were **d** in your transgressions
Col 1:18 the firstborn from the **d**, that in all
1 Pt 4:5 ready to judge the living and the **d**.
Rev 1:5 the firstborn of the **d** and ruler
20:12 I saw the **d**, the great and the lowly,
20:12 The **d** were judged according

**DEAF**
Ex 4:11 Who makes another mute or **d**,
Is 29:18 that day the **d** shall hear the words
Lk 7:22 lepers are cleansed, the **d** hear,

**DEATH** → DEAD
Dt 30:19 I have set before you life and **d**,
Ru 1:17 if even **d** separates me from you!"
Ps 22:16 you lay me in the dust of **d**.
Prv 18:21 **D** and life are in the power
Sg 8:6 For Love is strong as **D**, longing is
Sir 15:17 Before everyone are life and **d**,
Hos 13:14 shall I redeem them from **d**?
13:14 Where are your plagues, O **d**!
Mt 16:28 who will not taste **d** until they see
Jn 5:24 but has passed from **d** to life.
Rom 6:23 For the wages of sin is **d**,
1 Cor 15:55 Where, O **d**, is your victory?
15:55 Where, O **d**, is your sting?"
2 Cor 2:16 to the latter an odor of **d** that leads to **d**,
Heb 2:14 through **d** he might destroy the one who has the power of **d**,
1 Jn 3:14 that we have passed from **d** to life
3:14 does not love remains in **d**.
Rev 1:18 I hold the keys to **d**
20:14 Then **D** and Hades were thrown
20:14 (This pool of fire is the second **d**.
21:4 and there shall be no more **d**

**DEBAUCHERY**
Eph 5:18 in which lies **d**, but be filled

**DEBORAH**
Prophetess; led victory over Canaanites (Jgs 4–5).

**DEBTS**
Dt 15:1 you shall have a remission of **d**,
Mt 6:12 and forgive us our **d**, as we forgive

**DECEIT** → DECEITFUL, DECEIVE, DECEIVED, DECEIVERS
Dt 32:4 without **d**, just and upright is he!
1 Pt 2:22 and no **d** was found in his mouth."

**DECEITFUL** → DECEIT
Ps 35:20 in the land they fashion **d** speech.
Zep 3:13 be found in their mouths a **d** tongue;
1 Tm 4:1 faith by paying attention to **d** spirits

**DECEIVE** → DECEIT
Eph 5:6 Let no one **d** you with empty
1 Jn 1:8 are without sin," we **d** ourselves,
Rev 20:8 to **d** the nations at the four corners

**DECEIVED** → DECEIT
1 Tm 2:14 Adam was not **d**, but the woman was **d** and transgressed.

**DECEIVERS** → DECEIT
Ti 1:10 idle talkers and **d**,
2 Jn 1:7 Many **d** have gone

**DECISION**
Prv 16:33 from the LORD comes every **d**.

**DECLARED**
Mk 7:19 (Thus he **d** all foods clean.)

**DECREASE**
Jn 3:30 He must increase; I must **d**."

**DECREE** → DECREED
Ps 2:7 I will proclaim the **d** of the LORD,
Lk 2:1 In those days a **d** went

**DECREED** → DECREE
Dn 9:24 "Seventy weeks are **d** for your

**DEDICATED** → DEDICATION
1 Kgs 8:63 all the Israelites **d** the house

**DEDICATION** → DEDICATED
2 Chr 7:9 they had celebrated the **d** of the altar
Ezr 6:16 celebrated the **d** of this house
1 Mc 4:56 eight days they celebrated the **d**

**DEED** → DEEDS
Jer 32:10 I had written and sealed the **d**,
Col 3:17 in word or in **d**, do everything

**DEEDS** → DEED
Dt 3:24 or on earth can perform **d**
Ps 9:2 I will declare all your wondrous **d**.
Jer 50:29 Repay them for their **d**;
Rev 19:8 linen represents the righteous **d**

**DEFEND**
Ps 72:4 he may **d** the oppressed among
Prv 31:9 justly, **d** the needy and the poor!

**DEFILE** → DEFILED
Nm 35:34 Do not **d** the land in which you live
Mk 7:15 one from outside can **d** that person;
7:15 come out from within are what **d**."

**DEFILED** → DEFILE
1 Mc 1:37 they **d** the sanctuary.
Ps 79:1 they have **d** your holy temple;

**DEFRAUD**
Mk 10:19 you shall not **d**; honor your father

**DEITY**
Col 2:9 the whole fullness of the **d** bodily,

**DELAY**
Ps 70:6 LORD, do not **d**!
Heb 10:37 to come shall come; he shall not **d**.

**DELIGHT** → DELIGHTS
1 Sm 15:22 "Does the LORD **d** in burnt
Ps 40:9 I **d** to do your will, my God;
Prv 8:30 I was his **d** day by day,
Zec 11:7 took two staffs: one I called **D**,
Rom 7:22 For I take **d** in the law of God,

**DELIGHTS** → DELIGHT
Ps 5:5 You are not a god who **d** in evil;

**DELILAH**
Philistine who betrayed Samson (Jgs 16:4-22).

**DELIVER** → DELIVERANCE, DELIVERER
Mt 27:43 let him **d** him now if he wants him.

**DELIVERANCE** → DELIVER
Est 4:14 and **d** will come to the Jews
Phil 1:19 this will result in **d** for me through

**DELIVERER** → DELIVER
Rom 11:26 "The **d** will come out of Zion,

**DEMON** → DEMONIACS, DEMONIC, DEMONS
Tb 3:8 the wicked **d** Asmodeus kept killing
6:8 a woman who is afflicted by a **d**
Mt 11:18 they said, 'He is possessed by a **d**.'
17:18 him and the **d** came out of him,
Jn 10:21 surely a **d** cannot open the eyes

**DEMONIACS** → DEMON
Mt 8:28 two **d** who were coming

**DEMONIC** → DEMON
Rev 16:14 These were **d** spirits who performed

**DEMONS** → DEMON
Dt 32:17 They sacrificed to **d**, to "no-gods,"
Bar 4:7 your Maker with sacrifices to **d**
Lk 11:18 it is by Beelzebul that I drive out **d**.
1 Cor 10:20 [they sacrifice] to **d**, not to God,
10:20 you to become participants with **d**.
Jas 2:19 Even the **d** believe that and tremble.
Rev 9:20 to give up the worship of **d**

**DEN**
Jer 7:11 become in your eyes a **d** of thieves?
Mk 11:17 you have made it a **d** of thieves."

**DENARIUS**
Mk 12:15 Bring me a **d** to look at."

**DENIED** → DENY
Mt 26:70 But he **d** it in front of everyone,
1 Tm 5:8 family members has **d** the faith
Rev 3:8 my word and have not **d** my name.

**DENIES** → DENY
Lk 12:9 whoever **d** me before others will be
1 Jn 2:22 Whoever **d** that Jesus is the Christ.
2:22 Whoever **d** the Father and the Son,

**DENY** → DENIED, DENIES
Mt 16:24 to come after me must **d** himself,
2 Tm 2:12 But if we **d** him he will **d** us.
2 Pt 2:1 even **d** the Master who ransomed

**DEPART**
Gn 49:10 The scepter shall never **d**
Phil 1:23 I long to **d** this life and be

**DEPRAVED**
2 Pt 2:10 follow the flesh with its **d** desire

**DEPRIVE**
1 Cor 7:5 Do not **d** each other, except perhaps

**DEPTH** → DEPTHS
Rom 11:33 the **d** of the riches and wisdom
Eph 3:18 breadth and length and height and **d**,

**DEPTHS** → DEPTH
Ps 130:1 Out of the **d** I call to you, LORD;
1 Cor 2:10 everything, even the **d** of God.

**DESCENDANTS**
Gn 15:18 To your **d** I give this land,
Dt 4:37 your ancestors he chose their **d**
Is 44:3 offspring, my blessing upon your **d**.
Rom 9:7 of Abraham because they are his **d**;

**DESCENDED** → DESCENDING
Eph 4:9 also **d** into the lower [regions]

**DESCENDING** → DESCENDED
Mk 1:10 the Spirit, like a dove, **d** upon him.
Jn 1:51 and **d** on the Son of Man."

**DESERT**
Ps 106:14 In the **d** they gave in to their

**DESERTED**
Mk 8:4 satisfy them here in this **d** place?"

**DESERVE**
Rev 2:23 give each of you what your works **d**.

**DESIRE** → DESIRED, DESIRES
Is 46:10 shall stand, I accomplish my every **d**.
Hos 6:6 For it is loyalty that I **d**,
Mt 9:13 meaning of the words, 'I **d** mercy,
Jas 1:14 is lured and enticed by his own **d**.

**DESIRED** → DESIRE
Lk 22:15 them, "I have eagerly **d** to eat this

**DESIRES** → DESIRE
Sir 18:30 guide, but keep your **d** in check.
2 Tm 4:3 following their own **d** and insatiable

**DESOLATE** → DESOLATING
Ex 23:29 lest the land become **d** and the wild
1 Mc 1:39 Her sanctuary became **d** as
Mt 23:38 your house will be abandoned, **d**.

**DESOLATING** → DESOLATE
Mk 13:14 you see the **d** abomination standing

**DESPAIR** → DESPAIRED
2 Cor 4:8 perplexed, but not driven to **d**;

**DESPAIRED** → DESPAIR
2 Cor 1:8 strength, so that we **d** even of life.

**DESPISE** → DESPISED
Prv 1:7 fools **d** wisdom and discipline.
Lk 16:13 be devoted to one and **d** the other.

**DESPISED** → DESPISE
1 Cor 1:28 chose the lowly and **d** of the world,

**DESTINED**
Eph 1:5 he **d** us for adoption to himself
1 Pt 1:11 to the sufferings **d** for Christ

**DESTROY** → DESTROYED, DESTROYER, DESTRUCTION
Gn 6: 13 So I am going to **d** them
Est 3: 6 he sought to **d** all the Jews,
Mt 10: 28 of the one who can **d** both soul
Jn 10: 10 only to steal and slaughter and **d**;
Jas 4: 12 judge who is able to save or to **d**.
1 Jn 3: 8 God was revealed to **d** the works

**DESTROYED** → DESTROY
1 Cor 15: 26 The last enemy to be **d** is death,
2 Cor 5: 1 should be **d**, we have a building

**DESTROYER** → DESTROY
Ex 12: 23 not let the **d** come into your houses
1 Cor 10: 10 did, and suffered death by the **d**.

**DESTRUCTION** → DESTROY
Mt 7: 13 and the road broad that leads to **d**,
Rom 9: 22 the vessels of wrath made for **d**?
2 Pt 3: 16 and unstable distort to their own **d**,

**DEVIL**
Mt 4: 1 the desert to be tempted by the **d**.
Lk 8: 12 but the **d** comes and takes away
Jn 8: 44 You belong to your father the **d**
Eph 4: 27 and do not leave room for the **d**.
6: 11 firm against the tactics of the **d**.
Heb 2: 14 the power of death, that is, the **d**,
Jas 4: 7 Resist the **d**, and he will flee
1 Pt 5: 8 Your opponent the **d** is prowling
1 Jn 3: 8 Whoever sins belongs to the **d**, because the **d** has sinned
3: 8 to destroy the works of the **d**.
Jude 1: 9 with the **d** in a dispute over the body
Rev 12: 9 who is called the **D** and Satan,
20: 2 serpent, which is the **D** or Satan,

**DEVOTED** → DEVOTION
Ps 116: 15 eyes of the LORD is the death of his **d**.
Mt 6: 24 or be **d** to one and despise the other.

**DEVOTION** → DEVOTED
Wis 10: 12 that he might know that **d** to God is
1 Tm 4: 7 Train yourself for **d**,
2 Pt 1: 3 everything that makes for life and **d**,

**DEVOUR** → DEVOURING
1 Pt 5: 8 lion looking for [someone] to **d**.
Rev 12: 4 to **d** her child when she gave birth.

**DEVOURING** → DEVOUR
Gal 5: 15 you go on biting and **d** one another,

**DEW**
Jgs 6: 37 and if **d** is on the fleece alone,

**DICTATE**
Jer 36: 18 he would **d** all these words to me,"

**DIE** → DEAD
Gn 2: 17 when you eat from it you shall **d**.
3: 4 "You certainly will not **d**!
Ex 11: 5 firstborn in the land of Egypt will **d**,
Ru 1: 17 Where you **d** I will **d**, and there be
Jb 2: 9 Curse God and **d**!"
Prv 10: 21 many, but fools **d** for want of sense.
Eccl 3: 2 A time to give birth, and a time to **d**;
Is 22: 13 and drink, for tomorrow we **d**!"
Jer 31: 30 but all shall **d** because of their own
Mt 26: 35 "Even though I should have to **d**
Jn 11: 26 and believes in me will never **d**.
Rom 14: 8 and if we **d**, we **d** for the Lord;
14: 8 whether we live or **d**, we are
1 Cor 15: 32 eat and drink, for tomorrow we **d**."
Heb 9: 27 that human beings **d** once,

**DIED** → DEAD
Rom 5: 6 yet **d** at the appointed time
1 Cor 15: 3 that Christ **d** for our sins
Gal 2: 19 For through the law I **d** to the law,

**DIFFERENT**
2 Cor 11: 4 if you receive a **d** spirit from the one
11: 4 or a **d** gospel from the one you
Gal 1: 6 [the] grace [of Christ] for a **d** gospel

**DILIGENCE**
Rom 12: 8 if one is over others, with **d**;

**DINAH**
Only daughter of Jacob, by Leah (Gn 30:21; 46:15). Raped by Shechem; avenged by Simeon and Levi (Gn 34).

**DIRECT** → DIRECTS
2 Thes 3: 5 May the Lord **d** your hearts

**DIRECTS** → DIRECT
Prv 16: 9 the way, but the LORD **d** the steps.

**DISAPPOINT**
Rom 5: 5 and hope does not **d**,

**DISCERNMENT**
1 Cor 12: 10 to another **d** of spirits;

**DISCIPLE** → DISCIPLES
Mt 10: 24 No **d** is above his teacher, no slave
Lk 14: 26 his own life, he cannot be my **d**.

**DISCIPLES** → DISCIPLE
Is 8: 16 seal the instruction with my **d**.
Mt 26: 56 Then all the **d** left him and fled.
28: 19 and make **d** of all nations,
Lk 6: 13 day came, he called his **d** to himself,
Jn 8: 31 in my word, you will truly be my **d**,
Acts 11: 26 the **d** were first called Christians.

**DISCIPLINE** → DISCIPLINED
Prv 5: 23 They will die from lack of **d**,
Heb 12: 5 do not disdain the **d** of the Lord

**DISCIPLINED** → DISCIPLINE
1 Cor 11: 32 we are being **d** so that we may not

**DISEASE** → DISEASES
Mt 4: 23 curing every **d** and illness among
9: 35 and curing every **d** and illness.

**DISEASES** → DISEASE
Ex 15: 26 any of the **d** with which I afflicted
Mt 8: 17 our infirmities and bore our **d**."

**DISGRACE**
1 Mc 4: 58 the people now that the **d** brought
Prv 11: 2 When pride comes, **d** comes;

**DISHONEST**
Lk 16: 10 the person who is **d** in very small matters is also **d** in great ones.

**DISHONOR**
Jn 8: 49 I honor my Father, but you **d** me.
Acts 5: 41 worthy to suffer **d** for the sake

**DISMAYED**
Jos 1: 9 Do not fear nor be **d**,

**DISOBEDIENT** → DISOBEY
Rom 10: 21 long I stretched out my hands to a **d**
Ti 3: 3 we ourselves were once foolish, **d**,

**DISOBEY** → DISOBEYING, DISOBEDIENT
Lv 26: 27 you **d** and continue hostile to me,

**DISOBEYING** → DISOBEDIENT
1 Pt 2: 8 They stumble by **d** the word, as is

**DISPERSION**
Jn 7:35 not going to the **d** among the Greeks

**DISQUALIFIED** → DISQUALIFY
1 Cor 9:27 to others, I myself should be **d**.

**DISQUALIFY** → DISQUALIFIED
Col 2:18 Let no one **d** you,

**DISSENSIONS**
Gal 5:20 fury, acts of selfishness, **d**, factions,

**DISTINCTION** → DISTINCTIONS
Rom 3:22 all who believe. For there is no **d**;

**DISTINCTIONS** → DISTINCTION
Jas 2:4 you not made **d** among yourselves

**DISTRESS**
Dt 4:30 In your **d**, when all these things
Jgs 2:15 and they were in great **d**.
2 Sm 22:7 In my **d** I called out: LORD!
Ps 81:8 In **d** you called and I rescued you;
Jer 30:7 A time of **d** for Jacob, though he
Rom 8:35 Will anguish, or **d**, or persecution,

**DISTRIBUTED**
Acts 4:35 they were **d** to each according

**DIVIDE** → DIVIDED
Ps 22:19 they **d** my garments among them;

**DIVIDED** → DIVIDE
Lk 11:18 And if Satan is **d** against himself,

**DIVINATION** → DIVINE
1 Sm 15:23 For a sin of **d** is rebellion,
2 Kgs 17:17 They practiced augury and **d**.

**DIVINE** → DIVINATION
2 Pt 1:4 may come to share in the **d** nature,

**DIVORCE** → DIVORCED
Dt 24:1 he writes out a bill of **d** and hands it
Is 50:1 Where is the bill of **d** with which I
Jer 3:8 her away and gave her a bill of **d**,
Mal 2:16 For I hate **d**, says the LORD,
Mt 5:31 his wife must give her a bill of **d**.'
19:3 a man to **d** his wife for any cause
1 Cor 7:11 and a husband should not **d** his wife.

**DIVORCED** → DIVORCE
Lv 21:7 nor a woman who has been **d** by her
Mt 5:32 marries a **d** woman commits

**DOCTRINE** → DOCTRINES
2 Tm 4:3 people will not tolerate sound **d** but,
Ti 1:9 be able both to exhort with sound **d**

**DOCTRINES** → DOCTRINE
Mk 7:7 me, teaching as **d** human precepts.'
1 Tm 1:3 certain people not to teach false **d**

**DOEG**
Edomite; Saul's chief shepherd; murdered 85 priests at Nob (1 Sm 21:7; 22:6-23; Ps 52).

**DOERS** → DOES, DONE
Jas 1:22 Be **d** of the word and not hearers

**DOES** → DOERS
Ps 135:6 Whatever the LORD desires he **d**
Eccl 3:14 whatever God **d** will endure forever;
Mk 3:35 [For] whoever **d** the will of God is

**DOG** → DOGS
Jgs 7:5 the water as a **d** does with its tongue
2 Pt 2:22 "The **d** returns to its own vomit,"

**DOGS** → DOG
Prv 26:11 As **d** return to their vomit, so fools
Mt 7:6 "Do not give what is holy to **d**,
15:26 the children and throw it to the **d**."
Phil 3:2 Beware of the **d**! Beware of the evil
Rev 22:15 Outside are the **d**, the sorcerers,

**DOMINION**
Gn 1:26 Let them have **d** over the fish
Ps 110:2 from Zion. Have **d** over your enemies!
Dn 7:14 His **d** is an everlasting **d** that shall

**DONE** → DOERS
Mt 6:10 come, your will be **d**, on earth as
26:42 my drinking it, your will be **d**!"
Rev 16:17 from the throne, saying, "It is **d**."

**DOOM** → DOOMED
Dt 32:35 and their **d** is rushing upon them!

**DOOMED** → DOOM
Ps 102:21 prisoners, to release those **d** to die."

**DOOR** → DOORPOSTS
Mt 7:7 and the **d** will be opened to you.
Rev 3:20 I stand at the **d** and knock.
3:20 hears my voice and opens the **d**,

**DOORPOSTS** → DOOR
Ex 12:7 apply it to the two **d** and the lintel

**DORCAS**
Disciple; raised from the dead (Acts 9:36-43).

**DOUBLE**
Dt 21:17 giving him a **d** share of whatever he
1 Sm 1:5 but he would give a **d** portion
2 Kgs 2:9 "May I receive a **d** portion of your
Rev 18:6 Pay her back **d** for her deeds.
18:6 her cup pour **d** what she poured.

**DOUBT** → DOUBTED, DOUBTING
Mt 14:31 you of little faith, why did you **d**?"

**DOUBTED** → DOUBT
Mt 28:17 him, they worshiped, but they **d**.

**DOUBTING** → DOUBT
Jas 1:6 not **d**, for the one who doubts is like

**DOUGH**
Ex 12:39 The **d** they had brought out of Egypt
Gal 5:9 yeast leavens the whole batch of **d**.

**DOVE**
Gn 8:8 Then he released a **d**, to see
Mk 1:10 like a **d**, descending upon him.

**DRAGON**
Is 27:1 he will slay the **d** in the sea.
Dn 14:23 There was a great **d**
Rev 12:3 it was a huge red **d**, with seven
20:2 He seized the **d**, the ancient serpent,

**DRANK** → DRINK
Mk 14:23 it to them, and they all **d** from it.
1 Cor 10:4 and all **d** the same spiritual drink,
10:4 for they **d** from a spiritual rock

**DRAW**
Jn 12:32 earth, I will **d** everyone to myself."
Jas 4:8 **D** near to God, and he will **d** near

**DREAM** → DREAMER, DREAMS
1 Kgs 3:5 appeared to Solomon in a **d** at night.
Dn 7:1 as Daniel lay in bed he had a **d**,
7:1 Then he wrote down the **d**;
Mt 1:20 of the Lord appeared to him in a **d**

Acts 2: 17 your old men shall **d** dreams.

**DREAMER** → DREAM
Gn 37: 19 to one another: "Here comes that **d**!

**DREAMS** → DREAM
Nm 12: 6 to them, in **d** I speak to them;
1 Sm 28: 6 neither in **d** nor by Urim nor
Sir 34: 7 For **d** have led many astray,

**DRIED** → DRY
Jos 5: 1 that the LORD had **d** up the waters
Is 51: 10 Was it not you who **d** up the sea,

**DRINK** → DRANK, DRUNK, DRUNKARD, DRUNKARDS, DRUNKENNESS
Ex 32: 6 Then they sat down to eat and **d**,
Eccl 9: 7 and **d** your wine with a merry heart,
Is 22: 13 "Eat and **d**, for tomorrow we die!"
Mt 20: 22 Can you **d** the cup that I am going to **d**?"
Jn 18: 11 Shall I not **d** the cup that the Father
Rom 14: 17 of God is not a matter of food and **d**,
1 Cor 12: 13 we were all given to **d** of one Spirit.
Rev 14: 10 will also **d** the wine of God's fury,

**DRIVE** → DROVE
Ex 23: 30 little I will **d** them out before you,
Mk 11: 15 the temple area he began to **d**

**DROSS**
Ps 119: 119 Like **d** you regard all the wicked
Is 1: 25 and refine your **d** in the furnace,
Ez 22: 18 house of Israel has become **d** to me.

**DROVE** → DRIVE
Jos 24: 18 our approach the LORD **d** out all
Mk 1: 12 At once the Spirit **d** him

**DRUNK** → DRINK
Gn 9: 21 became **d**, and lay naked inside his
1 Sm 1: 13 Eli, thinking she was **d**,
Jn 2: 10 and then when people have **d** freely,
Acts 2: 15 These people are not **d**, as you
Eph 5: 18 And do not get **d** on wine,

**DRUNKARD** → DRINK
Mt 11: 19 he is a glutton and a **d**, a friend
1 Cor 5: 11 a slanderer, a **d**, or a robber,
1 Tm 3: 3 not a **d**, not aggressive, but gentle,

**DRUNKARDS** → DRINK
Prv 23: 21 For **d** and gluttons come to poverty,

**DRUNKENNESS** → DRINK
Tb 4: 15 let **d** accompany you on your way.

**DRY** → DRIED
Gn 1: 9 basin, so that the **d** land may appear.
Ex 14: 16 may pass through the sea on **d** land.
Jos 3: 17 of the LORD stood on **d** ground
3: 17 while all Israel crossed on **d** ground,
Jgs 6: 37 while all the ground is **d**, I shall
Ez 37: 4 **D** bones, hear the word

**DUE**
1 Chr 16: 29 to the LORD the glory **d** his name!
Mal 1: 6 father, where is the honor **d** to me?
1: 6 a master, where is the fear **d** to me?
Rom 13: 7 taxes to whom taxes are **d**, toll to whom toll is **d**,

**DULL**
Is 6: 10 **d** their ears and close their eyes;
59: 1 to save, nor his ear too **d** to hear.

**DUST**
Gn 13: 16 make your descendants like the **d**
1 Sm 2: 8 He raises the needy from the **d**;
Ps 103: 14 formed, remembers that we are **d**.
Eccl 3: 20 both were made from the **d**, and to the **d** they both return.
Na 1: 3 and clouds are the **d** at his feet;
Mt 10: 14 and shake the **d** from your feet.

**DWELL** → DWELLING, DWELLS
Ex 25: 8 for me, that I may **d** in their midst.
Ps 23: 6 I will **d** in the house of the LORD
Eph 3: 17 Christ may **d** in your hearts through
Col 1: 19 all the fullness was pleased to **d**,
Rev 21: 3 He will **d** with them and they will

**DWELLING** → DWELL
Dt 12: 11 chooses as the **d** place for his name
1 Kgs 8: 27 "Is God indeed to **d** on earth?
Jn 14: 2 house there are many **d** places.
Eph 2: 22 being built together into a **d** place

**DWELLS** → DWELL
Jn 14: 10 The Father who **d** in me is doing his
Rom 7: 17 I who do it, but sin that **d** in me.
1 Cor 3: 16 and that the Spirit of God **d** in you?
Col 2: 9 in him **d** the whole fullness

**DYING** → DEAD
2 Cor 6: 9 as **d** and behold we live;

## E

**EAGLE** → EAGLES'
Ez 1: 10 an ox, and each had the face of an **e**.
17: 3 The great **e**, with wide wingspan
Rev 4: 7 the fourth looked like an **e** in flight.

**EAGLES'** → EAGLE
Is 40: 31 strength, they will soar on **e** wings;

**EAR** → EARS
Lk 22: 51 Then he touched the servant's **e**
1 Cor 2: 9 and **e** has not heard, and what has

**EARLY**
Dt 11: 14 land, the **e** rain and the late rain,
Lk 24: 22 were at the tomb **e** in the morning
Jas 5: 7 patient with it until it receives the **e**

**EARS** → EAR
Is 35: 5 see, and the **e** of the deaf be opened;
Mt 11: 15 Whoever has **e** ought to hear.
Rev 2: 7 " ' "Whoever has **e** ought to hear

**EARTH** → EARTHLY, EARTHQUAKE, EARTHQUAKES
Gn 1: 1 God created the heavens and the **e**—
6: 11 the **e** was corrupt in the view of God
Ex 19: 5 all peoples, though all the **e** is mine.
Ps 37: 11 But the poor will inherit the **e**,
47: 3 feared, the great king over all the **e**,
Sir 40: 11 All that is of **e** returns to **e**, and what
Is 6: 3 All the **e** is filled with his glory!"
65: 17 creating new heavens and a new **e**;
Jer 23: 24 Do I not fill heaven and **e**?—
Mt 24: 35 Heaven and **e** will pass away,
Lk 5: 24 of Man has authority on **e** to forgive
2 Pt 3: 13 and a new **e** in which righteousness
Rev 21: 1 I saw a new heaven and a new **e**.
21: 1 and the former **e** had passed away,

**EARTHLY** → EARTH
Jn 3: 12 If I tell you about **e** things and you
2 Cor 5: 1 For we know that if our **e** dwelling,

**EARTHQUAKE** → EARTH
1 Kgs 19: 11 after the wind, an **e**—but the LORD was not in the **e**;
Mt 28: 2 And behold, there was a great **e**;
Acts 16: 26 there was suddenly such a severe **e**

Rev 6: 12 sixth seal, and there was a great **e**;

**EARTHQUAKES** → EARTH
Mt 24: 7 famines and **e** from place to place.

**EASIER** → EASY
Mt 9: 5 Which is **e**, to say, 'Your sins are
Lk 16: 17 It is **e** for heaven and earth to pass
18: 25 For it is **e** for a camel to pass

**EAST**
Gn 2: 8 in the **e**, and placed there the man
Ps 103: 12 As far as the **e** is from the west,
Mt 2: 1 behold, magi from the **e** arrived

**EASY** → EASIER
Mt 11: 30 For my yoke is **e**, and my burden

**EAT** → ATE, EATING, EATS
Gn 2: 16 You are free to **e** from any
Ex 12: 11 This is how you are to **e** it:
12: 11 in hand, you will **e** it in a hurry.
Lv 11: 4 you shall not **e** any of the following
Eccl 2: 24 nothing better for mortals than to **e**
Mt 26: 26 it to his disciples said, "Take and **e**;
Acts 10: 13 "Get up, Peter. Slaughter and **e**."
1 Cor 10: 31 So whether you **e** or drink,

**EATING** → EAT
Lk 7: 34 The Son of Man came **e**
1 Cor 8: 4 So about the **e** of meat sacrificed

**EATS** → EAT
Jn 6: 51 whoever **e** this bread will live
1 Cor 11: 27 Therefore whoever **e** the bread

**EDEN**
Gn 2: 8 LORD God planted a garden in **E**,
Is 51: 3 wilderness he shall make like **E**,
Ez 28: 13 In **E**, the garden of God, you lived;

**EDOM** → =ESAU
Gn 25: 30 That is why he was called **E**.
Nm 20: 18 But **E** answered him, "You shall
Ob 1: 1 says the Lord GOD concerning **E**:
Mal 1: 4 If **E** says, "We have been crushed,

**EFFORT**
2 Pt 1: 5 make every **e** to supplement your

**EGYPT**
Gn 12: 10 so Abram went down to **E**
37: 28 the Ishmaelites, who took him to **E**.
47: 27 Thus Israel settled in the land of **E**,
Ex 1: 8 of Joseph, rose to power in **E**.
12: 40 had stayed in **E** was four hundred
Jos 15: 47 as far as the Wadi of **E** and the coast
Neh 9: 18 God who brought you up from **E**,'
Ps 78: 51 He struck all the firstborn of **E**,
Hos 11: 1 loved him, out of **E** I called my son.
Mt 2: 15 "Out of **E** I called my son."
Rev 11: 8 names "Sodom" and "**E**,"

**EHUD**
Judge of Israel (Jgs 3:12-30).

**ELAH**
1. Son of Baasha; king of Israel (1 Kgs 16:6-14).
2. Valley in which David fought Goliath (1 Sm 17:2, 19; 21:9).

**ELDERS**
Ex 24: 1 and seventy of the **e** of Israel.
Jgs 2: 7 of those **e** who outlived Joshua
Is 3: 14 into judgment with the people's **e**
Mt 27: 12 accused by the chief priests and **e**,
Mk 7: 3 hands, keeping the tradition of the **e**.
Rev 4: 4 thrones on which twenty-four **e** sat,

**ELEAZAR**
1. Third son of Aaron (Ex 6:23-25). Succeeded Aaron as high priest (Nm 20:26; Dt 10:6). Allotted land to tribes (Jos 14:1). Death (Jos 24:33).
2. Brother of Judas Maccabeus (1 Mc 2:5; 6:43-46).

**ELECT** → ELECTION
Mt 24: 22 sake of the **e** they will be shortened.
Mk 13: 22 mislead, if that were possible, the **e**.

**ELECTION** → ELECT
Rom 11: 28 but in respect to **e**, they are beloved
2 Pt 1: 10 eager to make your call and **e** firm,

**ELEMENTS**
Heb 5: 12 someone teach you again the basic **e**
2 Pt 3: 10 and the **e** will be dissolved by fire,

**ELEVEN**
Mt 28: 16 The **e** disciples went to Galilee,
Acts 1: 26 he was counted with the **e** apostles.

**ELI**
1. High priest in youth of Samuel (1 Sm 1–4). Blessed Hannah (1 Sm 1:12-18); raised Samuel (1 Sm 2:11-26). Prophesied against because of wicked sons (1 Sm 2:27-36). Death of Eli and sons (1 Sm 4:11-22).
2. "Eli, Eli, lema sabachthani?" (Mt 27:46).

**ELIAKIM** → =JEHOIAKIM
1. Original name of Jehoiakim (2 Kgs 23:34; 2 Chr 36:4).
2. Hezekiah's palace administrator (2 Kgs 18:17-37; 19:2; Is 36:1-22; 37:2).

**ELIEZER**
1. Servant of Abraham (Gn 15:2).
2. Son of Moses (Ex 18:4; 1 Chr 23:15-17).

**ELIHU**
A friend of Job (Jb 32–37).

**ELIJAH**
Prophet; predicted famine in Israel (1 Kgs 17:1; Jas 5:17). Fed by ravens (1 Kgs 17:2-6). Raised Sidonian widow's son (1 Kgs 17:7-24). Defeated prophets of Baal at Carmel (1 Kgs 18:16-46). Ran from Jezebel (1 Kgs 19:1-9). Prophesied death of Azariah (2 Kgs 1). Succeeded by Elisha (1 Kgs 19:19-21; 2 Kgs 2:1-18). Taken to heaven in whirlwind (2 Kgs 2:11-12; Sir 48:1-12; 1 Mc 2:58).
Return prophesied (Mal 4:5-6); equated with John the Baptist (Mt 17:9-13; Mk 9:9-13; Lk 1:17). Appeared with Moses in transfiguration of Jesus (Mt 17:1-8; Mk 9:1-8).

**ELIMELECH**
Ru 1: 3 **E**, the husband of Naomi, died,

**ELIPHAZ**
A friend of Job (Jb 4–5; 15; 22; 42:7, 9).

**ELISHA**
Prophet; successor of Elijah (1 Kgs 19:16-21; Sir 48:12-14); inherited his mantle (2 Kgs 2:1-18). Purified bad water (2 Kgs 2:19-22). Cursed young men (2 Kgs 2:23-25). Aided Israel's defeat of Moab (2 Kgs 3). Provided widow with oil (2 Kgs 4:1-7). Raised Shunammite woman's son (2 Kgs 4:8-37). Purified food (2 Kgs 4:38-41). Fed 100 men (2 Kgs 4:42-44). Healed Naaman's leprosy (2 Kgs 5). Made axhead float (2 Kgs 6:1-7). Captured Arameans (2 Kgs 6:8-23). Political adviser to Israel (2 Kgs 6:24–8:6; 9:1-3; 13:14-19), Aram (2 Kgs 8:7-15). Death (2 Kgs 13:20).

**ELIZABETH**
Mother of John the Baptist (Lk 1:5-58).

**ELKANAH**
Husband of Hannah, father of Samuel (1 Sm 1–2).

**EMMANUEL**
Is 7: 14 about to bear a son, shall name him **E**.
8: 8 will fill the width of your land, **E**!
Mt 1: 23 and they shall name him **E**,"

**EMMAUS**
Lk 24: 13 miles from Jerusalem called **E**,

**EMPTIED** → EMPTY
1 Cor 1: 17 cross of Christ might not be **e** of its
Phil 2: 7 Rather, he **e** himself,

**EMPTY** → EMPTIED, EMPTY-HANDED
Ru 3: 17 not go back to your mother-in-law **e**.' "
Eph 5: 6 one deceive you with **e** arguments,

**EMPTY-HANDED** → EMPTY, HAND
Ex 23: 15 No one shall appear before me **e**.

**ENCOURAGEMENT**
Acts 4: 36 (which is translated "son of **e**"),
Rom 15: 5 and **e** grant you to think in harmony
Phil 2: 1 If there is any **e** in Christ,

**END** → ENDS
Gn 6: 13 that the **e** of all mortals has come,
Prv 14: 12 right, but the **e** of it leads to death!
Eccl 12: 12 making of many books there is no **e**,
Mt 24: 13 perseveres to the **e** will be saved.
28: 20 you always, until the **e** of the age."
Jn 13: 1 world and he loved them to the **e**.
Rom 10: 4 For Christ is the **e** of the law
Rev 22: 13 the last, the beginning and the **e**."

**ENDOR**
1 Sm 28: 7 is a woman in **E** who is a medium."

**ENDS** → END
Ps 2: 8 your possession, the **e** of the earth.
Is 40: 28 of old, creator of the **e** of the earth.
Rom 10: 18 their words to the **e** of the world."

**ENDURANCE** → ENDURE
Rom 5: 3 knowing that affliction produces **e**,
Heb 10: 36 You need **e** to do the will of God
2 Pt 1: 6 self-control with **e**, **e** with devotion,
Rev 1: 9 and the **e** we have in Jesus,

**ENDURE** → ENDURANCE, ENDURED, ENDURES
Mal 3: 2 who can **e** the day of his coming?

**ENDURED** → ENDURE
Heb 12: 2 that lay before him he **e** the cross,

**ENDURES** → ENDURE
1 Chr 16: 41 LORD, "whose love **e** forever,"
Sir 40: 17 cut off, and righteousness **e** forever.
Bar 4: 1 of God, the law that **e** forever;
Mt 10: 22 whoever **e** to the end will be saved.
Jn 6: 27 for the food that **e** for eternal life,
1 Cor 13: 7 things, hopes all things, **e** all things.

**ENEMIES** → ENEMY
Ex 23: 22 I will be an enemy to your **e**
Jdt 8: 35 you to take vengeance upon our **e**!"
Est 9: 5 The Jews struck down all their **e**
1 Mc 4: 36 "Now that our **e** have been crushed,
Ps 110: 1 I make your **e** your footstool."
Mt 5: 44 love your **e**, and pray for those who
Lk 20: 43 I make your **e** your footstool." '
Rom 5: 10 if, while we were **e**, we were

**ENEMY** → ENEMIES, ENMITY
Mt 13: 39 the **e** who sows them is the devil.
1 Cor 15: 26 The last **e** to be destroyed is death,
Jas 4: 4 of the world makes himself an **e**

**ENJOY** → ENJOYMENT
Eccl 9: 9 **E** life with the wife you love,

**ENJOYMENT** → ENJOY
1 Tm 6: 17 provides us with all things for our **e**.

**ENLIGHTENED** → LIGHT
Eph 1: 18 May the eyes of [your] hearts be **e**,
Heb 6: 4 case of those who have once been **e**

**ENLIGHTENS** → LIGHT
Jn 1: 9 which **e** everyone, was coming

**ENMITY** → ENEMY
Gn 3: 15 I will put **e** between you
Jas 4: 4 of the world means **e** with God?

**ENOCH**
Walked with God and taken by him (Gn 5:18-24; Heb 11:5; Sir 44:16). Prophet (Jude 14).

**ENSLAVE** → SLAVE
Gal 2: 4 Christ Jesus, that they might **e** us—

**ENTER**
Ex 40: 35 Moses could not **e** the tent
Nm 20: 24 he shall not **e** the land I have given
Ps 95: 11 "They shall never **e** my rest."
Mt 5: 20 you will not **e** into the kingdom
7: 13 "**E** through the narrow gate;
7: 13 those who **e** through it are many.
Mk 10: 15 of God like a child will not **e** it."
Jn 3: 5 no one can **e** the kingdom of God
Heb 3: 11 wrath, "They shall not **e** into my
Rev 21: 27 but nothing unclean will **e** it,
21: 27 Only those will **e** whose names are

**ENTHRONED** → THRONE
1 Chr 13: 6 by the name "LORD **e**

**ENTRUSTED** → TRUST
Lk 12: 48 required of the person **e** with much,
12: 48 of the person **e** with more.
2 Tm 1: 12 to guard what has been **e** to me until

**ENVY**
Mk 7: 22 deceit, licentiousness, **e**, blasphemy,
Rom 1: 29 full of **e**, murder, rivalry, treachery,

**EPHOD**
Ex 28: 6 The **e** they shall make of gold
Jgs 8: 27 Gideon made an **e** out of the gold

**EPHRAIM**
1. Second son of Joseph (Gn 41:52; 46:20). Blessed as firstborn by Jacob (Gn 48). Tribe of numbered (Nm 1:33; 26:37), blessed (Dt 33:17), allotted land (Jos 16:4-9; Ez 48:5), failed to fully possess (Jos 16:10; Jgs 1:29).
2. Term for the Northern Kingdom (Is 7:17; Hos 5).

**EQUAL** → EQUALITY
Is 40: 25 To whom can you liken me as an **e**?
46: 5 whom would you liken me as an **e**,
Jn 5: 18 father, making himself **e** to God.

**EQUALITY** → EQUAL
Phil 2: 6 of God, did not regard **e** with God

**EQUIPPED**
2 Tm 3: 17 competent, **e** for every good work.

**ESAU** → =EDOM
Firstborn of Isaac, twin of Jacob (Gn 25:21-26). Also called Edom (Gn 25:30). Sold Jacob his birthright (Gn 25:29-34); lost blessing (Gn 27). Married Hittites (Gn 26:34), Ishmaelites (Gn 28:6-9). Reconciled to Jacob (Gn 33). Genealogy (Gn 36). The LORD chose Jacob over Esau (Mal 1:2-3), but gave Esau land (Dt 2:2-12). Descendants eventually obliterated (Ob 1-21; Jer 49:7-22).

**ESCAPE**
Ps 68:21 e from death is the LORD God's.
Rom 2:3 that you will e the judgment
1 Thes 5:3 woman, and they will not e.
Heb 12:25 they did not e when they refused

**ESTABLISH** → ESTABLISHED
Gn 6:18 I will e my covenant with you.
Dt 28:9 The LORD will e you as a holy
Ps 89:5 and e your throne through all ages."
Rom 10:3 to e their own [righteousness],

**ESTABLISHED** → ESTABLISH
Ps 89:3 For I said, "My mercy is e forever;
Jer 10:12 power, e the world by his wisdom,
2 Pt 1:12 and are e in the truth you have.

**ESTHER**
Jewess, originally named Hadassah, who lived in Persia; cousin of Mordecai (Est 2:7). Chosen queen of Xerxes (Est 2:8-18). Persuaded by Mordecai to foil Haman's plan to exterminate the Jews (Est 3–4). Revealed Haman's plans to Xerxes, resulting in Haman's death (Est 7), the Jews' preservation (Est 8–9), Mordecai's exaltation (Est 8:15; 9:4; 10). Decreed celebration of Purim (Est 9:18-32).

**ETERNAL** → ETERNITY
Mt 25:46 these will go off to e punishment,
25:46 but the righteous to e life."
Mk 10:17 what must I do to inherit e life?"
Jn 3:16 not perish but might have e life.
4:14 of water welling up to e life."
10:28 I give them e life, and they shall
Rom 5:21 e life through Jesus Christ our Lord.
2 Cor 4:17 us an e weight of glory beyond all
Heb 5:9 he became the source of e salvation
1 Jn 5:13 you may know that you have e life,

**ETERNITY** → ETERNAL
Sir 42:21 he is from all e one and the same,
2 Pt 3:18 be glory now and to the day of e.

**EUNUCH** → EUNUCHS
Acts 8:27 Now there was an Ethiopian e,

**EUNUCHS** → EUNUCH
Is 56:4 To the e who keep my sabbaths,

**EUPHRATES**
Gn 2:14 The fourth river is the E.
15:18 of Egypt to the Great River, the E,
Rev 16:12 his bowl on the great river E.

**EUTYCHUS**
Acts 20:9 and a young man named E who was

**EVANGELIST** → EVANGELISTS
Acts 21:8 we went to the house of Philip the e,
2 Tm 4:5 perform the work of an e;

**EVANGELISTS** → EVANGELIST
Eph 4:11 others as e, others as pastors

**EVE**
Gn 3:20 man gave his wife the name "E,"
4:1 had intercourse with his wife E,
Tb 8:6 you made his wife E to be his helper
2 Cor 11:3 as the serpent deceived E by his
1 Tm 2:13 For Adam was formed first, then E.

**EVENING**
Gn 1:5 E came, and morning followed—
Eccl 11:6 at e do not let your hand be idle:
Zec 14:7 night, for in the e there will be light.

**EVERLASTING** → LAST
Gn 9:16 remember the e covenant between

**EVERY** → EVERYTHING
Gn 7:23 The LORD wiped out e being
Ex 11:5 E firstborn in the land of Egypt will
Eccl 12:14 God will bring to judgment e work,
Is 45:23 To me e knee shall bend; by me e
Mt 12:25 "E kingdom divided against itself
Rom 14:11 Lord, e knee shall bend before me,
14:11 e tongue shall give praise to God."
Phil 2:10 name of Jesus e knee should bend,
2 Tm 3:17 equipped for e good work.
1 Jn 4:1 do not trust e spirit but test
Rev 21:4 He will wipe e tear from their eyes,

**EVERYTHING** → EVERY
Gn 1:31 God looked at e he had made,
Ex 19:8 together, "E the LORD has said,
Eccl 3:1 There is an appointed time for e,
1 Cor 10:31 you do, do e for the glory of God.
1 Tm 4:4 For e created by God is good,
2 Pt 1:3 has bestowed on us e that makes

**EVIL** → EVILDOERS, EVILS
Gn 6:5 was always nothing but e,
Ex 32:22 know how the people are prone to e.
Tb 12:7 good, and e will not overtake you.
Prv 8:13 fear of the LORD is hatred of e;]
8:13 Pride, arrogance, the e way,
Sir 7:1 Do no e, and e will not overtake
Is 5:20 Those who call e good, and good e,
Ez 7:5 says the Lord GOD: E upon e!
Dn 9:13 law of Moses, this e has come upon us.
Mt 6:13 test, but deliver us from the e one.
12:35 an e person brings forth e out of a store of e.
Jn 17:15 that you keep them from the e one.
Rom 12:17 Do not repay anyone e for e;
Eph 5:16 opportunity, because the days are e.
1 Pt 2:16 using freedom as a pretext for e,
1 Jn 5:18 and the e one cannot touch him.
2 Jn 1:11 greets him shares in his e works.
3 Jn 1:11 do not imitate e but imitate good.
1:11 does what is e has never seen God.

**EVILDOERS** → EVIL
Ps 34:17 The LORD's face is against e
Lk 13:27 Depart from me, all you e!'
1 Pt 2:12 so that if they speak of you as e,

**EVILS** → EVIL
1 Tm 6:10 love of money is the root of all e,

**EXALT** → EXALTED, EXALTS
Prv 4:8 Extol her, and she will e you;
Jas 4:10 before the Lord and he will e you.

**EXALTED** → EXALT
Ps 97:9 all the earth, e far above all gods.
Is 2:11 and the LORD alone will be e.
Phil 2:9 God greatly e him and bestowed

**EXALTS** → EXALT
Prv 14:34 Justice e a nation, but sin is
Sir 7:11 there is One who e and humbles.
Lk 14:11 For everyone who e himself will be

**EXAMINE**
1 Cor 11:28 A person should e himself, and so
2 Cor 13:5 E yourselves to see whether you are

**EXAMPLES**
1 Cor 10:6 These things happened as e for us,
1 Pt 5:3 to you, but be e to the flock.

**EXCELLENCE** → EXCELLENT
Phil 4:8 if there is any e and if there is

## F

| | | |
|---|---|---|
| | 5: 6 | but only **f** working through love. |
| Eph | 4: 5 | one Lord, one **f**, one baptism; |
| Phil | 3: 9 | which comes through **f** in Christ, |
| 1 Tm | 6: 11 | righteousness, devotion, **f**, love, |
| 2 Tm | 4: 7 | finished the race; I have kept the **f**. |
| Heb | 11: 1 | **F** is the realization of what is hoped |
| | 12: 2 | Jesus, the leader and perfecter of **f**. |
| Jas | 2: 17 | So also **f** of itself, if it does not have |
| | 2: 24 | by works and not by **f** alone. |
| 2 Pt | 1: 1 | those who have received a **f** of equal |
| 1 Jn | 5: 4 | that conquers the world is our **f**. |
| Jude | 1: 3 | contend for the **f** that was once |
| Rev | 2: 13 | and have not denied your **f** in me, |

**FAITHFUL** → FAITH

| | | |
|---|---|---|
| Dt | 32: 4 | A **f** God, without deceit, |
| Ps | 4: 4 | works wonders for his **f** one; |
| Wis | 3: 9 | the **f** shall abide with him in love: |
| Mi | 7: 2 | The **f** have vanished from the earth, |
| Zec | 8: 3 | Jerusalem will be called the **f** city, |
| Mt | 24: 45 | then, is the **f** and prudent servant, |
| 1 Cor | 10: 13 | God is **f** and will not let you be tried |
| 1 Thes | 5: 24 | The one who calls you is **f**, and he |
| 1 Pt | 4: 19 | over to a **f** creator as they do good. |
| 1 Jn | 1: 9 | he is **f** and just and will forgive our |
| Rev | 1: 5 | and from Jesus Christ, the **f** witness, |
| | 19: 11 | its rider was [called] "**F** and True." |

**FAITHFULNESS** → FAITH

| | | |
|---|---|---|
| Ps | 26: 3 | I walk guided by your **f**. |
| Is | 11: 5 | his waist, and **f** a belt upon his hips. |
| Lam | 3: 23 | great is your **f**! |
| Gal | 5: 22 | patience, kindness, generosity, **f**, |

**FAITHLESS** → FAITH

| | | |
|---|---|---|
| Mt | 17: 17 | reply, "O **f** and perverse generation, |

**FALL** → FALLEN, FALLING

| | | |
|---|---|---|
| Ps | 91: 7 | Though a thousand **f** at your side, |
| Prv | 16: 18 | and a haughty spirit before a **f**. |
| Sir | 28: 23 | who forsake the Lord will **f** victim |
| Lk | 10: 18 | have observed Satan **f** like lightning |
| Rom | 9: 33 | and a rock that will make them **f**, |
| 1 Cor | 10: 12 | secure should take care not to **f**. |
| Heb | 10: 31 | It is a fearful thing to **f** |

**FALLEN** → FALL

| | | |
|---|---|---|
| 2 Sm | 1: 19 | How can the warriors have **f**! |
| Is | 14: 12 | How you have **f** from the heavens, |
| | 21: 9 | He calls out and says, '**F**, **f** is |
| Rev | 9: 1 | I saw a star that had **f** from the sky |
| | 18: 2 | "**F**, **f** is Babylon the great. |

**FALLING** → FALL

| | | |
|---|---|---|
| Lk | 22: 44 | like drops of blood **f** on the ground.] |

**FALSE**

| | | |
|---|---|---|
| Mt | 7: 15 | "Beware of **f** prophets, who come |
| Mk | 13: 22 | **F** messiahs and **f** prophets will arise |
| 2 Pt | 2: 1 | also **f** prophets among the people, |
| | 2: 1 | there will be **f** teachers among you, |
| Rev | 16: 13 | and from the mouth of the **f** prophet. |
| | 20: 10 | the beast and the **f** prophet were. |

**FAMILIES** → FAMILY

| | | |
|---|---|---|
| Acts | 3: 25 | your offspring all the **f** of the earth |
| Ti | 1: 11 | as they are upsetting whole **f** |

**FAMILY** → FAMILIES

| | | |
|---|---|---|
| Gal | 6: 10 | who belong to the **f** of the faith. |
| Eph | 3: 15 | from whom every **f** in heaven |

**FAMINE**

| | | |
|---|---|---|
| Gn | 12: 10 | since the **f** in the land was severe. |
| | 41: 27 | they are seven years of **f**. |
| Ru | 1: 1 | the judges there was a **f** in the land; |
| Ps | 37: 19 | in days of **f** they will be satisfied. |
| Jer | 14: 12 | will destroy them with the sword, **f**, |
| Am | 8: 11 | when I will send a **f** upon the land: |
| Acts | 11: 28 | would be a severe **f** all over |
| Rom | 8: 35 | or persecution, or **f**, or nakedness, |

**FAR**

| | | |
|---|---|---|
| Is | 57: 19 | Peace to those who are **f** and near, |
| Jer | 23: 23 | and not a God **f** off? |
| Mk | 7: 6 | lips, but their hearts are **f** from me; |
| | 12: 34 | "You are not **f** from the kingdom |

**FAST** → FASTED, FASTING

| | | |
|---|---|---|
| Is | 58: 5 | Is this what you call a **f**, a day |
| Mt | 6: 16 | "When you **f**, do not look gloomy |
| Lk | 18: 12 | I **f** twice a week, and I pay tithes |

**FASTED** → FAST

| | | |
|---|---|---|
| Mt | 4: 2 | He **f** for forty days and forty nights, |

**FASTING** → FAST

| | | |
|---|---|---|
| Mt | 6: 16 | they may appear to others to be **f**. |

**FATE**

| | | |
|---|---|---|
| Ps | 81: 16 | him, but their **f** is fixed forever. |

**FATHER** → FATHER'S

| | | |
|---|---|---|
| Gn | 2: 24 | That is why a man leaves his **f** |
| Ex | 20: 12 | Honor your **f** and your mother, |
| | 21: 15 | Whoever strikes **f** or mother shall be |
| 2 Sm | 7: 14 | I will be a **f** to him, and he shall be |
| Ps | 89: 27 | cry to me, 'You are my **f**, my God, |
| Prv | 28: 24 | Whoever defrauds **f** or mother |
| Wis | 2: 16 | and boasts that God is his **F**. |
| Sir | 3: 3 | Those who honor their **f** atone |
| Is | 8: 4 | learns to say, "My **f**, my mother," |
| Jer | 3: 19 | would call me, "My **F**," I thought, |
| Mal | 1: 6 | A son honors his **f**, and a servant |
| | 1: 6 | I am a **f**, where is the honor due |
| Mt | 6: 9 | Our **F** in heaven, hallowed be your |
| | 28: 19 | baptizing them in the name of the **F**, |
| Lk | 18: 20 | honor your **f** and your mother.' " |
| Jn | 5: 18 | but he also called God his own **f**, |
| | 8: 44 | You belong to your **f** the devil |
| | 8: 44 | because he is a liar and the **f** of lies. |
| | 14: 6 | comes to the **F** except through me. |
| Rom | 8: 15 | through which we cry, "Abba, **F**!" |
| Gal | 4: 6 | our hearts, crying out, "Abba, **F**!" |
| Eph | 6: 2 | "Honor your **f** and mother." |
| Heb | 1: 5 | "I will be a **f** to him, and he shall be |
| | 12: 9 | all the more to the **F** of spirits |
| Jas | 1: 17 | coming down from the **F** of lights, |
| Rev | 3: 5 | his name in the presence of my **F** |

**FATHER'S** → FATHER

| | | |
|---|---|---|
| Lk | 2: 49 | that I must be in my **F** house?" |
| Jn | 1: 14 | the glory as of the **F** only Son, |
| | 2: 16 | here, and stop making my **F** house |
| | 10: 29 | can take them out of the **F** hand. |
| | 14: 2 | In my **F** house there are many |

**FAULT**

| | | |
|---|---|---|
| Sir | 11: 7 | Before investigating, do not find **f**; |
| Rom | 9: 19 | "Why (then) does he still find **f**? |

**FAVOR** → FAVORED

| | | |
|---|---|---|
| Gn | 6: 8 | But Noah found **f** with the LORD. |
| Ex | 33: 12 | You have found **f** with me. |
| Ps | 30: 6 | lasts but a moment; his **f** a lifetime. |
| Is | 49: 8 | In a time of **f** I answer you, |

**FAVORED** → FAVOR

| | | |
|---|---|---|
| Lk | 1: 28 | coming to her, he said, "Hail, **f** one! |

**FEAR** → AFRAID, FEARED, FEARS
Dt 6: 13 The LORD, your God, shall you **f**;
Ps 19: 10 The **f** of the LORD is pure,
23: 4 the shadow of death, I will **f** no evil,
27: 1 and my salvation; whom should I **f**?
Prv 1: 7 **F** of the LORD is the beginning
Eccl 12: 13 all is heard: **F** God and keep his
Sir 1: 11 The **f** of the Lord is glory and
Phil 2: 12 work out your salvation with **f**
1 Pt 3: 14 be afraid or terrified with **f** of them,
1 Jn 4: 18 There is no **f** in love, but perfect love drives out **f**
Rev 14: 7 voice, "**F** God and give him glory,

**FEARED** → FEAR
Ex 14: 31 Egypt, the people **f** the LORD.
Jb 1: 1 Job, who **f** God and avoided evil.
Hg 1: 12 thus the people **f** the LORD.

**FEARS** → FEAR
Jdt 16: 16 one who **f** the Lord is forever great.
Ps 34: 5 me, delivered me from all my **f**.
Prv 31: 30 the woman who **f** the LORD is
Sir 15: 1 Whoever **f** the LORD will do this;

**FED** → FEED
Dt 8: 16 **f** you in the wilderness with manna,
Ps 80: 6 You have **f** them the bread of tears,

**FEED** → FED, FEEDS
Jn 21: 15 He said to him, "**F** my lambs."
Rom 12: 20 "if your enemy is hungry, **f** him;

**FEEDS** → FED
Is 40: 11 Like a shepherd he **f** his flock;

**FEET** → FOOT
Ps 8: 7 of your hands, put all things at his **f**:
119: 105 Your word is a lamp for my **f**, a light
Dn 2: 33 its **f** partly iron and partly clay.
Mt 22: 44 your enemies under your **f**' "?
Lk 24: 39 Look at my hands and my **f**, that it
Jn 12: 3 nard and anointed the **f** of Jesus
13: 5 began to wash the disciples' **f**
Rom 16: 20 quickly crush Satan under your **f**.
1 Cor 15: 25 has put all his enemies under his **f**.
Rev 1: 15 His **f** were like polished brass

**FELLOWSHIP**
2 Cor 6: 14 Or what **f** does light have
1 Jn 1: 3 so that you too may have **f** with us;
1: 3 for our **f** is with the Father

**FEMALE**
Gn 1: 27 male and **f** he created them.
Mk 10: 6 'God made them male and **f**.
Gal 3: 28 free person, there is not male and **f**;

**FESTIVALS**
Lv 23: 2 declare holy days. These are my **f**:

**FEVER**
Dt 28: 22 will strike you with consumption, **f**,
Mk 1: 30 mother-in-law lay sick with a **f**.

**FEW**
Ps 105: 12 When they were **f** in number,
Mt 22: 14 Many are invited, but **f** are chosen."
Lk 13: 23 will only a **f** people be saved?"

**FIDELITY**
Tb 3: 2 All your ways are mercy and **f**;
Ps 25: 5 Guide me by your **f** and teach me,

**FIELD** → FIELDS
Prv 31: 16 She picks out a **f** and acquires it;
Mt 13: 44 is like a treasure buried in a **f**,
13: 44 sells all that he has and buys that **f**.
24: 40 Two men will be out in the **f**;
1 Cor 3: 9 you are God's **f**, God's building.

**FIELDS** → FIELD
Lk 2: 8 in that region living in the **f**
Jn 4: 35 up and see the **f** ripe for the harvest.

**FIG** → FIGS
Gn 3: 7 so they sewed **f** leaves together
Hb 3: 17 though the **f** tree does not blossom,
Mt 24: 32 "Learn a lesson from the **f** tree.
Lk 13: 6 a person who had a **f** tree planted

**FIGHT** → FOUGHT
Ex 14: 14 The LORD will **f** for you;
1 Tm 1: 18 Through them may you **f** a good **f**

**FIGS** → FIG
Jer 24: 1 of **f** placed before the temple
Lk 6: 44 For people do not pick **f**

**FILL** → FILLED, FULL, FULLNESS
Gn 1: 28 **f** the earth and subdue it.
9: 1 fertile and multiply and **f** the earth.
Ps 72: 19 may he **f** all the earth with his glory.
Jer 23: 24 Do I not **f** heaven and earth?—
Eph 4: 10 heavens, that he might **f** all things.

**FILLED** → FILL
Ex 1: 7 that the land was **f** with them.
40: 34 of the LORD **f** the tabernacle.
1 Kgs 8: 11 of the LORD had **f** the house
Ez 43: 5 glory of the LORD **f** the temple!
Lk 1: 15 He will be **f** with the holy Spirit
Acts 2: 4 they were all **f** with the holy Spirit
Eph 5: 18 debauchery, but be **f** with the Spirit,

**FILTHY**
Zec 3: 3 before the angel, clad in **f** garments.
Rev 22: 11 still act wickedly, and the **f** still be **f**.

**FIND** → FINDS, FOUND
Dt 4: 29 you shall indeed **f** him if you search
Prv 18: 22 To **f** a wife is to **f** happiness,
Jer 29: 13 you look for me, you will **f** me.
Mt 11: 29 and you will **f** rest for your selves.
16: 25 loses his life for my sake will **f** it.
Lk 11: 9 seek and you will **f**;

**FINDS** → FIND
Prv 8: 35 For whoever **f** me **f** life, and wins

**FINGER**
Dt 9: 10 by God's own **f**, with a copy of all
Mt 23: 4 they will not lift a **f** to move them.
Lk 11: 20 if it is by the **f** of God that [I] drive

**FINISHED**
Ex 40: 33 Thus Moses **f** all the work.
Jn 19: 30 taken the wine, he said, "It is **f**."

**FIRE**
Ex 3: 2 appeared to him as **f** flaming
3: 2 although the bush was on **f**, it was
13: 21 of a column of **f** to give them light.
Lv 9: 24 **F** came forth from the LORD's
Nm 11: 1 the LORD's **f** burned among them
Dt 4: 24 is a consuming **f**, a jealous God.
1 Kgs 19: 12 after the earthquake, **f**—but the LORD was not in the **f**;
19: 12 after the **f**, a light silent sound.
2 Chr 7: 1 **f** came down from heaven
Is 66: 24 die, their **f** shall not be extinguished;
Dn 3: 92 walking in the **f**, and the fourth
Mal 3: 2 For he will be like a refiner's **f**,
Mt 3: 11 you with the holy Spirit and **f**.

Mk 9:43 Gehenna, into the unquenchable **f**.
Acts 2:3 appeared to them tongues as of **f**,
1 Cor 3:13 It will be revealed with **f**, and the **f**
Heb 12:29 For our God is a consuming **f**.
Jas 3:6 The tongue is also a **f**.
3:6 itself set on **f** by Gehenna.
2 Pt 3:10 the elements will be dissolved by **f**,
Rev 20:14 were thrown into the pool of **f**.
20:14 (This pool of **f** is the second death.

**FIRM**
Is 7:9 Unless your faith is **f**, you shall not be **f**!
2 Cor 1:24 your joy, for you stand **f** in the faith.

**FIRST** → FIRSTBORN
Gn 1:5 and morning followed—the **f** day.
Is 41:4 am the **f**, and at the last I am he.
Mt 6:33 But seek **f** the kingdom (of God)
Mk 10:31 But many that are **f** will be last,
10:31 last, and [the] last will be **f**."
16:2 had risen, on the **f** day of the week,
Acts 11:26 disciples were **f** called Christians.
Rom 1:16 for Jew **f**, and then Greek.
1 Cor 15:45 it is written, "The **f** man, Adam,
1 Thes 4:16 and the dead in Christ will rise **f**.
1 Jn 4:19 We love because he **f** loved us.
Rev 1:17 not be afraid. I am the **f** and the last,
20:5 This is the **f** resurrection.

**FIRSTBORN** → BEAR, FIRST
Gn 25:34 Esau treated his right as **f** with disdain.
Ex 4:22 says the LORD: Israel is my son, my **f**.
12:29 at midnight the LORD struck down every **f**
13:2 Consecrate to me every **f**;
Ps 78:51 He struck all the **f** of Egypt,
Zec 12:10 for him as one grieves over a **f**.
Lk 2:7 and she gave birth to her **f** son.
Col 1:15 invisible God, the **f** of all creation.
Rev 1:5 the **f** of the dead and ruler of

**FISH**
Gn 1:26 Let them have dominion over the **f**
Jon 2:1 But the LORD sent a great **f**
2:1 in the belly of the **f** three days
Mt 7:10 or a snake when he asks for a **f**?
Jn 6:9 has five barley loaves and two **f**;

**FIVE**
1 Sm 17:40 David selected **f** smooth stones
Mt 14:19 Taking the **f** loaves and the two fish,
1 Cor 14:19 church I would rather speak **f** words

**FLAME** → FLAMES
Is 10:17 a **f**, That burns and consumes its
Rev 19:12 His eyes were [like] a fiery **f**,

**FLAMES** → FLAME
Dn 3:49 drove the fiery **f** out of the furnace,

**FLED** → FLEE
Ex 2:15 But Moses **f** from Pharaoh and went
Mk 14:50 And they all left him and **f**.
Rev 12:6 The woman herself **f** into the desert
20:11 and the sky **f** from his presence

**FLEE** → FLED
Ps 11:1 me, "**F** like a bird to the mountains!
139:7 From your presence, where can I **f**?
Is 30:17 if five threaten, you shall **f**.
Jas 4:7 the devil, and he will **f** from you.

**FLESH**
Gn 2:23 is bone of my bones and **f** of my **f**;
Jb 19:26 off, and from my **f** I will see God:
Mt 16:17 For **f** and blood has not revealed this
26:41 spirit is willing, but the **f** is weak."
Jn 1:14 the Word became **f** and made his
3:6 What is born of **f** is **f** and what is
Rom 8:4 who live not according to the **f**
8:13 For if you live according to the **f**,
2 Cor 12:7 a thorn in the **f** was given to me,
Gal 5:19 Now the works of the **f** are obvious:
Eph 6:12 For our struggle is not with **f**
1 Pt 1:24 "All **f** is like grass, and all its glory
1 Jn 4:2 Jesus Christ come in the **f** belongs

**FLOCK**
Is 40:11 Like a shepherd he feeds his **f**;
Mt 26:31 the sheep of the **f** will be dispersed';
Lk 12:32 little **f**, for your Father is pleased
Jn 10:16 voice, and there will be one **f**,
1 Pt 5:3 to you, but be examples to the **f**.

**FLOGGED**
Acts 5:40 they had them **f**, ordered them

**FLOOD**
Gn 7:7 ark because of the waters of the **f**.
9:15 waters will never again become a **f**
Ps 29:10 LORD sits enthroned above the **f**!
2 Pt 2:5 he brought a **f** upon the godless

**FLOW** → FLOWING
Zec 14:8 fresh water will **f** from Jerusalem,
Jn 7:38 of living water will **f** from within

**FLOWER**
Is 40:7 The grass withers, the **f** wilts,
1 Pt 1:24 all its glory like the **f** of the field;
1:24 the grass withers, and the **f** wilts;

**FLOWING** → FLOW
Ex 3:8 land, a land **f** with milk and honey,
Jos 5:6 us, a land **f** with milk and honey.
Ez 47:1 I saw water **f** out from under
Rev 22:1 **f** from the throne of God

**FOE**
Ex 23:22 to your enemies and a **f** to your foes.
Ps 60:13 Give us aid against the **f**;

**FOLLOW** → FOLLOWED
Ex 16:4 see whether they **f** my instructions
1 Kgs 18:21 If the LORD is God, **f** him; if Baal, **f** him."
Lk 9:23 and take up his cross daily and **f** me.
Jn 10:27 I know them, and they **f** me.
Rev 14:4 the ones who **f** the Lamb wherever

**FOLLOWED** → FOLLOW
Jgs 2:12 They **f** other gods, the gods
Mk 1:18 they abandoned their nets and **f** him.
Rev 13:3 the whole world **f** after the beast.

**FOLLY** → FOOL
Prv 13:16 prudently but the foolish parade **f**.
26:4 answer fools according to their **f**,
Eccl 2:13 as much profit over **f** as light has
Mk 7:22 envy, blasphemy, arrogance, **f**.

**FOOD** → FOODS
Gn 1:30 I give all the green plants for **f**.
1 Mc 1:63 to die rather than to be defiled with **f**
Mt 6:25 Is not life more than **f** and the body
Jn 6:55 For my flesh is true **f**, and my blood
1 Cor 8:8 Now **f** will not bring us closer

**FOODS** → FOOD
Mk 7:19 (Thus he declared all **f** clean.)
1 Tm 4:3 require abstinence from **f** that God

**FOOL** → FOLLY, FOOLISH, FOOLISHNESS, FOOLS
Ps 14:1 The **f** says in his heart, "There is no

Prv 15: 5 The **f** spurns a father's instruction,
20: 3 strife, while every **f** starts a quarrel.
Mt 5: 22 says, 'You **f**,' will be liable to fiery

**FOOLISH** → FOOL
Prv 17: 25 A **f** son is vexation to his father,
Jer 5: 21 to this, you **f** and senseless people,
Mt 25: 2 Five of them were **f** and five were
1 Cor 1: 20 made the wisdom of the world **f**?
Ti 3: 3 For we ourselves were once **f**,

**FOOLISHNESS** → FOOL
1 Cor 1: 18 of the cross is **f** to those who are
3: 19 wisdom of this world is **f** in the eyes

**FOOLS** → FOOL
Prv 1: 7 **f** despise wisdom and discipline.
10: 21 many, but **f** die for want of sense.
Rom 1: 22 claiming to be wise, they became **f**
1 Cor 4: 10 We are **f** on Christ's account,

**FOOT** → FEET, FOOTSTOOL
Ps 91: 12 lest you strike your **f** against a stone.
Mt 18: 8 If your hand or **f** causes you to sin,
Lk 4: 11 you dash your **f** against a stone.' "

**FOOTSTOOL** → FOOT
Ps 110: 1 while I make your enemies your **f**."
Is 66: 1 are my throne, the earth, my **f**.
Heb 10: 13 until his enemies are made his **f**.

**FOREHEAD** → FOREHEADS
Ex 13: 9 your hand and a reminder on your **f**,
1 Sm 17: 49 and struck the Philistine on the **f**.

**FOREHEADS** → FOREHEAD
Ez 9: 4 an X on the **f** of those who grieve
Rev 7: 3 put the seal on the **f** of the servants
13: 16 image on their right hands or their **f**,
20: 4 nor had accepted its mark on their **f**

**FOREIGN** → FOREIGNER, FOREIGNERS
Ps 81: 10 There shall be no **f** god among you;
Prv 2: 16 a **f** woman with her smooth words,

**FOREIGNER** → FOREIGN
Ex 12: 43 No **f** may eat of it.
1 Cor 14: 11 I shall be a **f** to one who speaks it, and one who speaks it a **f** to me.

**FOREIGNERS** → FOREIGN
1 Cor 14: 21 by the lips of **f** I will speak to this

**FOREKNEW** → KNOW
Rom 8: 29 For those he **f** he also predestined
11: 2 not rejected his people whom he **f**.

**FORERUNNER** → RUN
Heb 6: 20 Jesus has entered on our behalf as **f**,

**FORESKIN**
Gn 17: 14 flesh of his **f** has not been cut away,

**FOREVER**
Gn 3: 22 tree of life, and eats of it and lives **f**?
6: 3 shall not remain in human beings **f**,
Ex 3: 15 This is my name **f**; this is my title
2 Sm 7: 13 I will establish his royal throne **f**.
1 Chr 16: 15 He remembers **f** his covenant
Ps 19: 10 of the LORD is pure, enduring **f**.
110: 4 "You are a priest **f** in the manner
117: 2 the faithfulness of the LORD is **f**.
Eccl 3: 14 whatever God does will endure **f**;
Wis 5: 15 But the righteous live **f**,
Is 40: 8 but the word of our God stands **f**."
51: 6 My salvation shall remain **f** and my
Jn 6: 51 whoever eats this bread will live **f**;
Heb 5: 6 "You are a priest **f** according
13: 8 is the same yesterday, today, and **f**.
1 Pt 1: 25 the word of the Lord remains **f**."
Rev 1: 18 dead, but now I am alive **f** and ever.
11: 15 and he will reign **f** and ever."
22: 5 and they shall reign **f** and ever.

**FORFEIT**
Mk 8: 36 gain the whole world and **f** his life?

**FORGAVE** → FORGIVE
Ps 85: 3 You **f** the guilt of your people,

**FORGET** → FORGOT, FORGOTTEN
Dt 6: 12 be careful not to **f** the LORD,
Ps 137: 5 If I **f** you, Jerusalem, may my right hand **f**.
Prv 4: 5 Do not **f** or turn aside
Is 49: 15 Can a mother **f** her infant,
49: 15 Even should she **f**, I will never **f**

**FORGIVE** → FORGAVE, FORGIVEN, FORGIVENESS, FORGIVING
Ex 32: 32 Now if you would only **f** their sin!
Sir 5: 6 my many sins he will **f**."
Mt 6: 12 and **f** us our debts, as we **f** our
Lk 5: 24 has authority on earth to **f** sins"—
1 Jn 1: 9 just and will **f** our sins and cleanse

**FORGIVEN** → FORGIVE
Lv 4: 20 on their behalf, that they may be **f**.
Ps 32: 1 fault is removed, whose sin is **f**.
Mt 12: 31 sin and blasphemy will be **f** people,
12: 31 against the Spirit will not be **f**.
Mk 2: 9 'Your sins are **f**,' or to say, 'Rise,
Rom 4: 7 are they whose iniquities are **f**
Eph 4: 32 one another as God has **f** you

**FORGIVENESS** → FORGIVE
Mk 1: 4 of repentance for the **f** of sins.
3: 29 the holy Spirit will never have **f**,
Col 1: 14 we have redemption, the **f** of sins.
Heb 9: 22 the shedding of blood there is no **f**.

**FORGIVING** → FORGIVE
Ex 34: 7 and **f** wickedness, rebellion, and sin;
Ps 86: 5 you are good and **f**, most merciful
Eph 4: 32 **f** one another as God has forgiven

**FORGOT** → FORGET
Dt 32: 18 you **f** the God who gave you birth.
Jer 23: 27 just as their ancestors **f** my name

**FORGOTTEN** → FORGET
Ps 77: 10 Has God **f** how to show mercy,
Is 49: 14 my Lord has **f** me."
Heb 12: 5 **f** the exhortation addressed to you as

**FORM** → FORMED, FORMLESS
Gn 1: 2 and the earth was without **f** or shape,
Lk 3: 22 upon him in bodily **f** like a dove.

**FORMED** → FORM
Gn 2: 7 the LORD God **f** the man
Ps 139: 13 You **f** my inmost being; you knit me
Gal 4: 19 in labor until Christ be **f** in you!

**FORMLESS** → FORM
Wis 11: 17 the universe from **f** matter, to send

**FORSAKE** → FORSAKEN
Dt 31: 6 he will never fail you or **f** you.
Jos 1: 5 I will not leave you nor **f** you.
Jer 17: 13 all who **f** you shall be put to shame;
Heb 13: 5 said, "I will never **f** you or abandon

**FORSAKEN** → FORSAKE
Mt 27: 46 my God, why have you **f** me?"

**FORTRESS**
2 Sm 22: 2 my rock, my **f**, my deliverer,
Ps 71: 3 for you are my rock and **f**.

**FORTY**
Gn 7: 4 rain down on the earth for **f** days and **f** nights,
Nm 14: 34 reconnoitering the land—**f** days—
14: 34 one year for each day: **f** years.
1 Kgs 19: 8 he walked **f** days and **f** nights
Jon 3: 4 "**F** days more and Nineveh shall be
Mt 4: 2 He fasted for **f** days and **f** nights,
Heb 3: 17 was he "provoked for **f** years"?

**FOUGHT** → FIGHT
Jos 10: 42 the God of Israel, **f** for Israel.
Rev 12: 7 The dragon and its angels **f** back,

**FOUND** → FIND
Is 55: 6 Seek the LORD while he may be **f**,
65: 1 be **f** by those who did not seek me.
Lk 15: 24 he was lost, and has been **f**.'
Rom 10: 20 "I was **f** [by] those who were not
Rev 20: 15 whose name was not **f** written

**FOUNDATION** → FOUNDATIONS
Ezr 3: 6 though the **f** of the LORD's temple
Is 28: 16 A precious cornerstone as a sure **f**;
1 Cor 3: 11 no one can lay a **f** other than the one
Eph 2: 20 built upon the **f** of the apostles
2 Tm 2: 19 God's solid **f** stands, bearing this

**FOUNDATIONS** → FOUNDATION
1 Kgs 6: 37 The **f** of the LORD's house were
Heb 11: 10 looking forward to the city with **f**,

**FOUNTAIN**
Ps 36: 10 For with you is the **f** of life,
Prv 16: 22 Good sense is a **f** of life to those
Zec 13: 1 that day a **f** will be opened

**FOUR**
Ez 1: 5 of **f** living creatures appeared.
10: 14 Each living creature had **f** faces:
Rev 4: 6 there were **f** living creatures covered

**FOXES**
Lk 9: 58 "**F** have dens and birds of the sky

**FRAGRANT**
Ex 25: 6 anointing oil and for the **f** incense;
Eph 5: 2 offering to God for a **f** aroma.

**FRANKINCENSE** → INCENSE
Is 60: 6 shall come bearing gold and **f**,
Mt 2: 11 and offered him gifts of gold, **f**,

**FREE** → FREED, FREEDOM
Ps 146: 7 The LORD sets prisoners **f**;
Sir 15: 14 them subject to their own **f** choice.
Jn 8: 32 truth, and the truth will set you **f**."
Gal 3: 28 there is neither slave nor **f** person,
Eph 6: 8 he does, whether he is slave or **f**.

**FREED** → FREE
Rev 1: 5 has **f** us from our sins by his blood,

**FREEDOM** → FREE
2 Cor 3: 17 the Spirit of the Lord is, there is **f**.
Gal 5: 1 For **f** Christ set us free;
1 Pt 2: 16 yet without using **f** as a pretext

**FRIEND** → FRIENDS
Prv 17: 17 A **f** is a **f** at all times, and a brother
Sir 7: 18 Do not barter a **f** for money,
Mt 11: 19 a **f** of tax collectors and sinners.'
Jas 2: 23 and he was called "the **f** of God."

**FRIENDS** → FRIEND
Jb 2: 11 three of Job's **f** heard of all
Prv 18: 24 but there are true **f** more loyal
Jn 15: 13 to lay down one's life for one's **f**.
15: 15 I have called you **f**, because I have

**FRUIT** → FRUITFUL, FRUITS
Gn 3: 6 So she took some of its **f** and ate it;
Dt 28: 4 Blessed be the **f** of your womb,
Ps 1: 3 of water, that yields its **f** in season;
Prv 8: 19 My **f** is better than gold, even pure
Ez 47: 12 river every kind of **f** tree will grow;
47: 12 will not wither, nor will their **f** fail.
Mt 3: 8 Produce good **f** as evidence of your
Lk 1: 42 and blessed is the **f** of your womb.
6: 44 every tree is known by its own **f**.
Jn 15: 2 branch in me that does not bear **f**,
15: 2 he prunes so that it bears more **f**.
Gal 5: 22 contrast, the **f** of the Spirit is love,
Col 1: 10 in every good work bearing **f**
Heb 13: 15 the **f** of lips that confess his name.
Rev 22: 2 that produces **f** twelve times a year,

**FRUITFUL** → FRUIT
Ex 1: 7 the Israelites were **f** and prolific.

**FRUITS** → FRUIT
Prv 3: 9 with first **f** of all your produce;
Mt 7: 16 By their **f** you will know them.

**FULFILL** → FULFILLED
Eccl 5: 4 a vow than make it and not **f** it.
Mt 5: 17 I have come not to abolish but to **f**.
Gal 6: 2 and so you will **f** the law of Christ.
Jas 2: 8 if you **f** the royal law according

**FULFILLED** → FULFILL
Lk 24: 44 the prophets and psalms must be **f**."
Rom 8: 4 decree of the law might be **f** in us,

**FULL** → FILL
Jn 1: 14 only Son, **f** of grace and truth.

**FULLNESS** → FILL
Jn 1: 16 From his **f** we have all received,
1 Cor 10: 26 "the earth and its **f** are the Lord's."
Gal 4: 4 But when the **f** of time had come,
Eph 1: 10 as a plan for the **f** of times, to sum
3: 19 may be filled with all the **f** of God.
Col 1: 19 him all the **f** was pleased to dwell,
2: 9 him dwells the whole **f** of the deity

**FURNACE**
Is 48: 10 I tested you in the **f** of affliction.
Dn 3: 6 be instantly cast into a white-hot **f**."
3: 49 went down into the **f** with Azariah
3: 49 drove the fiery flames out of the **f**,
Mt 13: 42 will throw them into the fiery **f**,

**FURY**
Rom 2: 8 **f** to those who selfishly disobey
Rev 16: 19 the cup filled with the wine of his **f**

**FUTURE**
Prv 24: 20 For the evil have no **f**, the lamp
Jer 31: 17 There is hope for your **f**—
1 Cor 3: 22 life or death, or the present or the **f**:
1 Tm 6: 19 treasure a good foundation for the **f**,

**G**

**GABRIEL**
Angel who interpreted Daniel's visions (Dn 8:16-26; 9:20-27); announced births of John (Lk 1:11-20), Jesus (Lk 1:26-38).

**GAD**
1. Son of Jacob by Zilpah (Gn 30:9-11; 35:26; 1 Chr 2:2). Tribe

of blessed (Gn 49:19; Dt 33:20-21), numbered (Nm 1:25; 26:18), allotted land east of the Jordan (Nm 32; 34:14; Jos 18:7; 22), west (Ez 48:27-28), 12,000 from (Rev 7:5).
2. Prophet; seer of David (1 Sm 22:5; 2 Sm 24:11-19; 1 Chr 29:29).

**GAIN**
Lk 9:25 one to **g** the whole world yet lose
Phil 1:21 to me life is Christ, and death is **g**.
3:8 so much rubbish, that I may **g** Christ
1 Tm 6:5 religion to be a means of **g**.

**GALILEAN** → GALILEE
Mt 26:69 "You too were with Jesus the **G**."

**GALILEANS** → GALILEE
Acts 2:7 these people who are speaking **G**?

**GALILEE** → GALILEAN, GALILEANS
Mt 4:15 the Jordan, **G** of the Gentiles,
Jn 7:41 Messiah will not come from **G**,

**GAMALIEL**
Pharisee (Acts 5:34-39), teacher of Paul (Acts 22:5).

**GARDEN**
Gn 2:8 The LORD God planted a **g**
Ez 28:13 In Eden, the **g** of God, you lived;
Jn 19:41 he had been crucified there was a **g**, and in the **g** a new tomb,

**GARMENT** → GARMENTS
Ps 102:27 they all wear out like a **g**;

**GARMENTS** → GARMENT
Gn 3:21 for the man and his wife **g** of skin,

**GATE** → GATES
Mt 7:13 "Enter through the narrow **g**;
7:13 for the **g** is wide and the road broad
Jn 10:7 say to you, I am the **g** for the sheep.
Heb 13:12 Jesus also suffered outside the **g**,

**GATES** → GATE
Gn 24:60 of the **g** of their enemies!"
Dt 6:9 of your houses and on your **g**.
Ps 100:4 Enter his **g** with thanksgiving,
Mt 16:18 the **g** of the netherworld shall not
Rev 21:21 The twelve **g** were twelve pearls,
21:21 each of the **g** made from a single

**GATH**
1 Sm 17:4 champion named Goliath of **G** came
2 Sm 1:20 Do not report it in **G**, as good news

**GATHER** → GATHERED
Ex 16:4 to go out and **g** their daily portion;
Ru 2:7 'I would like to **g** the gleanings
Is 11:12 nations and **g** the outcasts of Israel;
Mt 12:30 and whoever does not **g** with me
Lk 13:34 to **g** your children together as a hen

**GATHERED** → GATHER
Mt 18:20 or three are **g** together in my name,

**GAVE** → GIVE
Ex 31:18 he **g** him the two tablets
Neh 9:15 heaven you **g** them in their hunger,
Eccl 12:7 life breath returns to God who **g** it.
Mt 25:35 I was hungry and you **g** me food,
25:35 I was thirsty and you **g** me drink,
Jn 1:12 who did accept him he **g** power
3:16 the world that he **g** his only Son,
Eph 4:11 And he **g** some as apostles, others as
1 Tm 2:6 who **g** himself as ransom for all.

**GEDALIAH**
Governor of Judah (2 Kgs 25:22-26; Jer 39–41).

**GEHAZI**
Servant of Elisha (2 Kgs 4:12–5:27; 8:4-5).

**GENEALOGY**
Mt 1:1 The book of the **g** of Jesus Christ,

**GENERATION** → GENERATIONS
Ex 20:6 the thousandth **g** of those who love
34:7 children to the third and fourth **g**!
Mt 12:39 evil and unfaithful **g** seeks a sign,
Lk 21:32 this **g** will not pass away until all

**GENERATIONS** → GENERATION
Is 51:8 forever, my salvation, for all **g**.

**GENEROSITY**
Rom 12:8 if one contributes, in **g**; if one is
Gal 5:22 patience, kindness, **g**, faithfulness,

**GENTILE** → GENTILES
1 Mc 1:14 according to the **G** custom.
Mt 18:17 treat him as you would a **G** or a tax
Gal 2:14 are living like a **G** and not like

**GENTILES** → GENTILE
1 Mc 1:11 a covenant with the **G** all around us;
Lk 21:24 be taken as captives to all the **G**;
21:24 underfoot by the **G** until the times
Acts 15:19 to stop troubling the **G** who turn
Rom 3:29 Does he not belong to **G**, too?
Gal 3:8 God would justify the **G** by faith,
Eph 4:17 you must no longer live as the **G** do,

**GENTLE** → GENTLENESS
1 Pt 3:4 in the imperishable beauty of a **g**

**GENTLENESS** → GENTLE
Gal 5:23 **g**, self-control. Against such there is
1 Tm 6:11 faith, love, patience, and **g**.

**GETHSEMANE**
Mk 14:32 Then they came to a place named **G**,

**GHOST**
Mt 14:26 "It is a **g**," they said, and they cried
Lk 24:39 because a **g** does not have flesh

**GIANT**
Sir 47:4 As a youth he struck down the **g**

**GIBEON**
Jos 10:12 Sun, stand still at **G**, Moon,
1 Kgs 3:5 In **G** the LORD appeared

**GIDEON**
Judge, also called Jerubbaal; freed Israel from Midianites (Jgs 6–8; Heb 11:32). The fleece (Jgs 8:36-40).

**GIFT** → GIFTS
Nm 18:7 I give you your priesthood as a **g**.
Mt 5:23 if you bring your **g** to the altar,
Jn 4:10 "If you knew the **g** of God and who
Acts 2:38 you will receive the **g** of the holy
Rom 6:23 the **g** of God is eternal life in Christ
1 Cor 7:7 each has a particular **g** from God,
Jas 1:17 and every perfect **g** is from above,
Rev 21:6 the thirsty I will give a **g**

**GIFTS** → GIFT
Mt 2:11 treasures and offered him **g** of gold,
Lk 11:13 how to give good **g** to your children,
Rom 11:29 For the **g** and the call of God are
1 Cor 12:1 Now in regard to spiritual **g**,
14:1 but strive eagerly for the spiritual **g**,
Eph 4:8 he gave **g** to men."

**GILGAL**
Jos 5:9 Therefore the place is called **G**

1 Sm 7:16 **G** and Mizpah and judging Israel

**GIRL**
Ex 1:16 but if it is a **g**, she may live."
Mk 5:41 means, "Little **g**, I say to you,

**GIVE** → GAVE, GIVEN, GIVER, GIVES
Gn 9:3 I **g** them all to you as I did the green
12:7 your descendants I will **g** this land.
1 Kgs 3:5 Whatever you ask I shall **g** you.
Tb 12:9 Those who **g** alms will enjoy a full
Prv 25:21 are hungry, **g** them food to eat,
25:21 if thirsty, **g** something to drink;
30:15 has two daughters: "**G**," and "**G**."
Ez 36:26 I will **g** you a new heart, and a new
36:26 and **g** you a heart of flesh.
Mt 6:11 **G** us today our daily bread;
7:6 "Do not **g** what is holy to dogs,
Mk 10:45 to **g** his life as a ransom for many."
Jn 10:28 I **g** them eternal life, and they shall
Acts 20:35 said, 'It is more blessed to **g** than

**GIVEN** → GIVE
Mt 7:7 "Ask and it will be **g** to you;
Mk 4:25 To the one who has, more will be **g**;
Lk 22:19 is my body, which will be **g** for you;
Rom 5:5 the holy Spirit that has been **g** to us.

**GIVER** → GIVE
2 Cor 9:7 for God loves a cheerful **g**.

**GIVES** → GIVE
2 Cor 3:6 brings death, but the Spirit **g** life.
Jas 4:6 proud, but **g** grace to the humble."

**GLAD** → GLADNESS
Ps 16:9 Therefore my heart is **g**, my soul
90:15 Make us **g** as many days as you
Mt 5:12 Rejoice and be **g**, for your reward
Acts 2:26 Therefore my heart has been **g**

**GLADNESS** → GLAD
Ps 51:14 Restore to me the **g** of your salvation;
100:2 serve the LORD with **g**;
Is 16:10 orchards are taken away joy and **g**,
Zep 3:17 Who will rejoice over you with **g**,
Heb 1:9 you with the oil of **g** above your

**GLASS**
Rev 4:6 resembled a sea of **g** like crystal.
21:18 the city was pure gold, clear as **g**.

**GLEAN**
Ru 2:2 **g** grain in the field of anyone who

**GLOOM**
Is 9:1 in a land of **g** a light has shone.
Jl 2:2 a day of darkness and **g**, a day

**GLORIFIED** → GLORY
Jn 13:31 "Now is the Son of Man **g**, and God is **g** in him.
17:4 I **g** you on earth by accomplishing
Acts 3:13 has **g** his servant Jesus whom you
Rom 8:30 and those he justified he also **g**.

**GLORIFY** → GLORY
Ps 86:12 all my heart, **g** your name forever,
Jn 17:1 son, so that your son may **g** you,
1 Cor 6:20 Therefore, **g** God in your body.
Rev 15:4 not fear you, Lord, or **g** your name?

**GLORIOUS** → GLORY
Jdt 16:13 great are you and **g**,
Dn 3:26 and **g** forever is your name.
Jas 2:1 the faith in our **g** Lord Jesus Christ.

**GLORY** → GLORIFIED, GLORIFY, GLORIOUS
Ex 24:16 The **g** of the LORD settled
33:18 said, "Please let me see your **g**!"
40:34 and the **g** of the LORD filled
1 Sm 4:21 "Gone is the **g** from Israel,"
1 Kgs 8:11 since the **g** of the LORD had filled
1 Chr 29:12 Riches and **g** are from you, and you
1 Mc 1:40 As her **g** had been, so great was her
Ps 8:6 god, crowned him with **g** and honor.
19:2 The heavens declare the **g** of God;
24:7 portals, that the king of **g** may enter.
Is 6:3 All the earth is filled with his **g**!"
40:5 Then the **g** of the LORD shall be
Bar 5:4 of justice, the **g** of God's worship.
Ez 44:4 and the **g** of the LORD filled
Hos 4:7 I will change their **g** into shame.
Mt 25:31 the Son of Man comes in his **g**,
Lk 2:14 "**G** to God in the highest
Jn 1:14 us, and we saw his **g**, the **g** as
12:41 Isaiah said this because he saw his **g**
Rom 3:23 and are deprived of the **g** of God.
8:18 compared with the **g** to be revealed
9:4 the adoption, the **g**, the covenants,
1 Cor 10:31 do, do everything for the **g** of God.
2 Cor 4:17 weight of **g** beyond all comparison,
Heb 1:3 who is the refulgence of his **g**,
2 Pt 1:17 came to him from the majestic **g**,
Rev 4:11 to receive **g** and honor and power,
21:23 for the **g** of God gave it light, and its

**GLUTTON** → GLUTTONS
Mt 11:19 'Look, he is a **g** and a drunkard,

**GLUTTONS** → GLUTTON
Prv 23:21 drunkards and **g** come to poverty,

**GNAT**
Mt 23:24 who strain out the **g** and swallow

**GO**
Ex 5:1 Let my people **g**, that they may hold
Dt 6:14 You shall not **g** after other gods,
Jos 1:9 God, is with you wherever you **g**.
Ru 1:16 "Do not press me to **g** back
1:16 Wherever you **g** I will **g**,
Mt 28:19 **G**, therefore, and make disciples
Jn 14:3 if I **g** and prepare a place for you,

**GOAT** → GOATS
Lv 16:9 The **g** that is determined by lot
Dn 8:21 The he-**g** is the king of the Greeks,

**GOATS** → GOAT
Ps 50:13 of bulls or drink the blood of he-**g**?
Mt 25:32 separates the sheep from the **g**.
Heb 10:4 blood of bulls and **g** take away sins.

**GOD** → GOD'S, GODDESS, GODLESS, GODLY, GODS
Gn 1:1 when **G** created the heavens
1:27 **G** created mankind in his image;
1:27 in the image of **G** he created them;
3:5 **G** knows well that when you eat
17:1 I am **G** the Almighty.
Ex 3:4 **G** called out to him from the bush:
15:2 This is my **G**, I praise him; the **G** of my father, I extol him.
20:5 LORD, your **G**, am a jealous **G**,
34:6 LORD, a **G** gracious and merciful,
Nm 23:19 **G** is not a human being who speaks
23:19 Is **G** one to speak and not act,
Dt 4:7 our **G**, is to us whenever we call
6:5 your **G**, with your whole heart,
Jos 22:34 among them that the LORD is **G**.
1 Sm 2:2 there is no Rock like our **G**.

**GOOD** → BEST, BETTER, GOODNESS
Gn 1:31 he had made, and found it very **g**.
2:9 delightful to look at and **g** for food,
2:9 the tree of the knowledge of **g**
3:22 like one of us, knowing **g** and evil!
50:20 God meant it for **g**, to achieve this
Dt 6:18 and **g** in the sight of the LORD,
6:18 in and possess the **g** land
30:15 today set before you life and **g**,
2 Chr 7:3 "who is so **g**, whose love endures
Ps 34:9 Taste and see that the LORD is **g**;
84:12 The LORD withholds no **g** thing
Eccl 12:14 hidden qualities, whether **g** or bad.
Is 52:7 the feet of the one bringing **g** news,
Dn 3:89 who is **g**, whose mercy endures
Mt 5:45 his sun rise on the bad and the **g**,
25:21 done, my **g** and faithful servant.
Mk 10:18 him, "Why do you call me **g**? No one is **g** but God alone.
Lk 2:10 I proclaim to you **g** news of great
6:43 "A **g** tree does not bear rotten fruit,
6:43 nor does a rotten tree bear **g** fruit.
Jn 10:11 I am the **g** shepherd. A **g** shepherd
Rom 7:16 not want, I concur that the law is **g**.
12:2 what is **g** and pleasing and perfect.
12:21 by evil but conquer evil with **g**.
Eph 2:10 in Christ Jesus for the **g** works
1 Tm 4:4 For everything created by God is **g**,
Heb 10:1 has only a shadow of the **g** things
1 Pt 3:17 For it is better to suffer for doing **g**,

**GOODNESS** → GOOD
Ps 23:6 **g** and mercy will pursue me all

**GOSHEN**
Gn 45:10 You can settle in the region of **G**,

**GOSPEL**
Mk 8:35 sake and that of the **g** will save it.
Rom 1:16 For I am not ashamed of the **g**.
1 Cor 9:16 If I preach the **g**, this is no reason
2 Cor 4:3 And even though our **g** is veiled,
Gal 1:6 grace [of Christ] for a different **g**
Phil 1:27 in a way worthy of the **g** of Christ,
1:27 together for the faith of the **g**,

**GOSSIP**
2 Cor 12:20 selfishness, slander, **g**, conceit,

**GRACE** → GRACIOUS
Wis 3:9 Because **g** and mercy are with his
Jn 1:14 only Son, full of **g** and truth.
1:16 have all received, **g** in place of **g**,
Acts 15:11 we are saved through the **g**
Rom 3:24 by his **g** through the redemption
6:1 we persist in sin that **g** may abound?
6:14 are not under the law but under **g**.
11:6 otherwise **g** would no longer be **g**.
1 Cor 15:10 But by the **g** of God I am what I am,
15:10 his **g** to me has not been ineffective.
2 Cor 12:9 to me, "My **g** is sufficient for you,
Gal 5:4 you have fallen from **g**.
Eph 2:5 Christ (by **g** you have been saved),
2 Thes 2:16 and good hope through his **g**,
Ti 2:11 For the **g** of God has appeared,
Heb 4:16 confidently approach the throne of **g**
4:16 mercy and to find **g** for timely help.
Jas 4:6 But he bestows a greater **g**;
4:6 proud, but gives **g** to the humble."
1 Pt 5:10 The God of all **g** who called you
Jude 1:4 who pervert the **g** of our God
Rev 22:21 The **g** of the Lord Jesus be with all.

**GRACIOUS** → GRACE
Ex 34:6 the LORD, a God **g** and merciful,
Nm 6:25 shine upon you, and be **g** to you!
Ps 116:5 **G** is the LORD and righteous;
Col 4:6 Let your speech always be **g**,

**GRAFTED**
Rom 11:17 were **g** in their place and have come

**GRAIN**
Dt 25:4 muzzle an ox when it treads out **g**.
Mk 2:23 he was passing through a field of **g**
2:23 a path while picking the heads of **g**.

**GRAPES**
Nm 13:23 with a single cluster of **g** on it,
Is 5:2 Then he waited for the crop of **g**, but it yielded rotten **g**.
Jer 31:29 "The parents ate unripe **g**,
Mt 7:16 Do people pick **g** from thornbushes,
Rev 14:18 the earth's vines, for its **g** are ripe."

**GRASS**
Is 40:6 "All flesh is **g**, and all their loyalty
Mt 6:30 If God so clothes the **g** of the field,
1 Pt 1:24 "All flesh is like **g**, and all its glory
1:24 the **g** withers, and the flower wilts;

**GRATIFY**
Gal 5:16 you will certainly not **g** the desire

**GRAVE** → GRAVES
Ps 49:15 Straight to the **g** they descend,
Is 53:9 was given a **g** among the wicked,

**GRAVES** → GRAVE
Ez 37:12 I am going to open your **g**;
37:12 make you come up out of your **g**,
Lk 11:44 You are like unseen **g** over

**GRAY**
Prv 16:31 **G** hair is a crown of glory;

**GREAT** → GREATER, GREATEST
Gn 1:16 God made the two **g** lights,
12:2 I will make of you a **g** nation,
12:2 I will make your name **g**,
Ex 32:11 of the land of Egypt with **g** power
Dt 10:17 the Lord of lords, the **g** God,
Neh 8:6 blessed the LORD, the **g** God,
Jdt 16:13 O Lord, **g** are you and glorious,
Ps 95:3 For the LORD is the **g** God, the **g**
Jer 10:6 you are **g**, **g** and mighty is your
Lam 3:23 **g** is your faithfulness!
Dn 9:4 Lord, **g** and awesome God, you who
Jl 2:11 How **g** is the day of the LORD!
Mt 4:16 sit in darkness have seen a **g** light,
13:46 When he finds a pearl of **g** price,
20:26 to be **g** among you shall be your
Eph 2:4 because of the **g** love he had for us,
Ti 2:13 of the glory of the **g** God and of our
Heb 2:3 if we ignore so **g** a salvation?
12:1 we are surrounded by so **g** a cloud
13:20 the dead the **g** shepherd of the sheep
Rev 14:8 fallen is Babylon the **g**, that made

**GREATER** → GREAT
Mt 12:6 something **g** than the temple is here.
Mk 12:31 other commandment **g** than these."
Jn 14:12 I do, and will do **g** ones than these,
15:13 No one has **g** love than this, to lay
1 Jn 4:4 is in you is **g** than the one who is

**GREATEST** → GREAT
Mt 22:38 This is the **g** and the first
Lk 9:48 all of you is the one who is the **g**."

1 Cor 13: 13 but the **g** of these is love.

**GREECE** → GREEK, GREEKS
1 Mc 1: 1 in his place, having first ruled in **G**.

**GREED** → GREEDY
Lk 12: 15 "Take care to guard against all **g**,
Col 3: 5 evil desire, and the **g** that is idolatry.

**GREEDY** → GREED
Prv 28: 25 The **g** person stirs up strife,
1 Cor 6: 10 thieves nor the **g** nor drunkards nor
Ti 1: 7 aggressive, not **g** for sordid gain,

**GREEK** → GREECE
Jn 19: 20 written in Hebrew, Latin, and **G**.
Rom 1: 16 for Jew first, and then **G**.
Gal 3: 28 There is neither Jew nor **G**, there is

**GREEKS** → GREECE
1 Cor 1: 22 signs and **G** look for wisdom,

**GREEN**
Gn 1: 30 I give all the **g** plants for food.
Ps 23: 2 In **g** pastures he makes me lie down;

**GREW** → GROW
1 Sm 2: 21 while young Samuel **g**
Is 53: 2 He **g** up like a sapling before him,
Lk 1: 80 The child **g** and became strong
2: 40 The child **g** and became strong,

**GRIEVE** → GRIEVED
Eph 4: 30 And do not **g** the holy Spirit of God,
1 Thes 4: 13 so that you may not **g** like the rest,

**GRIEVED** → GRIEVE
Is 63: 10 they rebelled and **g** his holy spirit;

**GRINDING**
Lk 17: 35 will be two women **g** meal together;

**GROAN**
Rom 8: 23 **g** within ourselves as we wait
2 Cor 5: 2 For in this tent we **g**, longing to be

**GROUND**
Gn 2: 7 the man out of the dust of the **g**
3: 17 it, Cursed is the **g** because of you!
Ex 3: 5 the place where you stand is holy **g**.
Mt 13: 5 Some fell on rocky **g**, where it had

**GROW** → GREW, GROWTH
Ez 47: 12 river every kind of fruit tree will **g**;
2 Pt 3: 18 But **g** in grace and in the knowledge

**GROWTH** → GROW
1 Cor 3: 7 but only God, who causes the **g**.
Col 2: 19 achieves the **g** that comes

**GUARANTEE** → GUARANTEED
Heb 7: 22 become the **g** of an [even] better

**GUARANTEED** → GUARANTEE
Rom 4: 16 and the promise may be **g** to all his

**GUARD** → GUARDIAN, GUARDS
Prv 2: 11 over you, understanding will **g** you;
2 Thes 3: 3 you and **g** you from the evil one.
2 Tm 1: 12 is able to **g** what has been entrusted

**GUARDIAN** → GUARD
1 Pt 2: 25 to the shepherd and **g** of your souls.

**GUARDS** → GUARD
Mt 28: 4 The **g** were shaken with fear of him

**GUIDANCE** → GUIDE
Prv 11: 14 For lack of **g** a people falls;

**GUIDE** → GUIDANCE
Is 58: 11 the LORD will **g** you always
Lk 6: 39 a blind person **g** a blind person?
Jn 16: 13 of truth, he will **g** you to all truth.

**GUILT** → GUILTY
Ps 32: 5 my sin to you; my **g** I did not hide.
32: 5 and you took away the **g** of my sin.
Zec 3: 9 I will take away the **g** of that land

**GUILTY** → GUILT
Ex 23: 7 to death, for I will not acquit the **g**.
Nm 14: 18 not declaring the **g** guiltless,
Dn 13: 53 and freeing the **g**, although the Lord
Mk 3: 29 but is **g** of an everlasting sin."

## H

**HABAKKUK**
Prophet to Judah (Hb 1:1; 3:1; Dn 14:33-39).

**HADASSAH** → See ESTHER

**HADES**
Rev 20: 14 **H** were thrown into the pool of fire.

**HAGAR**
Servant of Sarah, wife of Abraham, mother of Ishmael (Gn 16:1-6; 25:12). Driven away by Sarah while pregnant (Gn 16:5-16); after birth of Isaac (Gn 21:9-21; Gal 4:21-31).

**HAGGAI**
Post-exilic prophet who encouraged rebuilding of the temple (Ezr 5:1; 6:14; Hg 1–2).

**HAIL** → HAILSTONES
Ex 9: 19 will die when the **h** comes down
Rev 8: 7 there came **h** and fire mixed

**HAILSTONES** → HAIL
Jos 10: 11 these **h** than the Israelites killed
Rev 16: 21 Large **h** like huge weights came

**HAIR** → HAIRS
Jgs 16: 22 the **h** of his head began to grow as
Lk 7: 44 her tears and wiped them with her **h**.
Jn 12: 3 of Jesus and dried them with her **h**;
1 Cor 11: 6 she may as well have her **h** cut off.

**HAIRS** → HAIR
Ps 40: 13 They are more numerous than the **h**
Mt 10: 30 Even all the **h** of your head are

**HALF**
Est 5: 3 Even if it is **h** of my kingdom,
Mk 6: 23 of me, even to **h** of my kingdom."
Lk 19: 8 "Behold, **h** of my possessions,

**HALLOWED**
Mt 6: 9 Father in heaven, **h** be your name,

**HAM**
Son of Noah (Gn 5:32; 1 Chr 1:4), father of Canaan (Gn 9:18; 10:6-20; 1 Chr 1:8-16). Saw Noah's nakedness (Gn 9:20-27).

**HAMAN**
Agagite nobleman honored by Xerxes (Est 3:1-2). Plotted to exterminate the Jews because of Mordecai (Est 3:3-15). Forced to honor Mordecai (Est 5–6). Plot exposed by Esther (Est 5:1-8; 7:1-8). Hanged (Est 7:9-10).

**HANANIAH** → =SHADRACH
1. False prophet; adversary of Jeremiah (Jer 28).
2. Original name of Shadrach (Dn 1:6-19; 2:17).

**HAND** → EMPTY-HANDED, HANDED, HANDS
Ex 15: 6 in power, your right **h**, O LORD,
Dt 19: 21 tooth for tooth, **h** for **h**, and foot
1 Kgs 18: 44 a cloud as small as a man's **h** rising

Jdt 9:10 their arrogance by the **h** of a female.
Ps 110:1 "Sit at my right **h**, while I make
Prv 3:16 Long life is in her right **h**, in her left
Is 5:25 he stretches out his **h** to strike them;
5:25 back, his **h** is still outstretched.
Dn 5:5 the fingers of a human **h** appeared,
5:5 When the king saw the **h** that wrote,
Hb 2:16 the LORD's right **h** shall come
Mt 3:12 His winnowing fan is in his **h**.
Mk 9:43 If your **h** causes you to sin, cut it
Lk 20:42 said to my lord, "Sit at my right **h**
Jn 10:28 No one can take them out of my **h**.
Rom 8:34 who also is at the right **h** of God,
1 Cor 12:15 I am not a **h** I do not belong
Heb 10:12 seat forever at the right **h** of God;
Rev 1:16 In his right **h** he held seven stars.
5:1 in the right **h** of the one who sat

**HANDED** → HAND
Mt 27:26 he **h** him over to be crucified.
Rom 4:25 who was **h** over for our

**HANDS** → HAND
Ps 115:7 They have **h** but do not feel,
Is 49:16 palms of my **h** I have engraved you;
Lk 23:46 into your **h** I commend my spirit";
24:40 he showed them his **h** and his feet.
Acts 8:18 by the laying on of the apostles' **h**,
Rom 10:21 I stretched out my **h** to a disobedient
Heb 6:2 about baptisms and laying on of **h**,
10:31 to fall into the **h** of the living God.

**HANNAH**
Wife of Elkanah, mother of Samuel (1 Sm 1). Prayer at dedication of Samuel (1 Sm 2:1-10). Blessed (1 Sm 2:18-21).

**HAPPY**
Tb 13:14 **H** are those who love you,
13:14 **H** too are all who grieve over all
Prv 3:13 **H** the one who finds wisdom,
Is 30:18 of justice: **h** are all who wait for him!

**HARD** → HARDEN, HARDENED, HARDENING, HARDSHIPS
Ex 1:14 life bitter for them with **h** labor,
Mt 19:23 it will be **h** for one who is rich

**HARDEN** → HARD
Ps 95:8 Do not **h** your hearts as at Meribah,
Heb 3:8 '**H** not your hearts as

**HARDENED** → HARD
Mk 8:17 Are your hearts **h**?
Rom 11:7 the elect attained it; the rest were **h**,

**HARDENING** → HARD
Rom 11:25 a **h** has come upon Israel in part,

**HARDSHIPS** → HARD
2 Cor 12:10 weaknesses, insults, **h**, persecutions,

**HARM**
Gn 50:20 Even though you meant **h** to me,
Neh 6:2 They were planning to do me **h**.
Prv 12:21 No **h** befalls the just, but the wicked
1 Pt 3:13 Now who is going to **h** you if you

**HARP** → HARPS
Ps 150:3 the horn, praise him with **h** and lyre.
Rev 5:8 Each of the elders held a **h** and gold

**HARPS** → HARP
1 Chr 15:16 to play on musical instruments, **h**,
Neh 12:27 hymns and the music of cymbals, **h**,
Ps 137:2 in its midst we hung up our **h**.

**HARVEST**
Gn 8:22 earth, seedtime and **h**, cold and heat,
Ex 23:16 of the grain **h** with the first fruits
Mt 13:39 The **h** is the end of the age,
Mk 4:29 sickle at once, for the **h** has come."
Lk 10:2 "The **h** is abundant but the laborers
10:2 so ask the master of the **h** to send
Rev 14:15 "Use your sickle and reap the **h**,
14:15 because the earth's **h** is fully ripe."

**HASTENING**
2 Pt 3:12 and **h** the coming of the day of God,

**HATE** → HATED
Ps 45:8 You love justice and **h** wrongdoing;
97:10 You who love the LORD, **h** evil,
Eccl 3:8 A time to love, and a time to **h**;
Am 5:15 **H** evil and love good, and let justice
Mal 2:16 For I **h** divorce, says the LORD,
Mt 5:43 your neighbor and **h** your enemy.'
Lk 6:27 do good to those who **h** you,
Jn 7:7 The world cannot **h** you, but it hates
Rom 7:15 do what I want, but I do what I **h**.

**HATED** → HATE
Jn 15:18 hates you, realize that it **h** me first.
Rom 9:13 "I loved Jacob but **h** Esau."

**HATES** → HATE
Prv 6:16 There are six things the LORD **h**,
Sir 15:13 wickedness the LORD **h** and he
Jn 15:23 Whoever **h** me also **h** my Father.

**HAUGHTY**
Prv 6:17 **H** eyes, a lying tongue,
16:18 disaster, and a **h** spirit before a fall.

**HAY**
1 Cor 3:12 precious stones, wood, **h**, or straw,

**HEAD** → BEHEADED, HEADS
Is 59:17 victory as a helmet on his **h**;
Mt 8:20 of Man has nowhere to rest his **h**."
Mk 6:28 He brought in the **h** on a platter
1 Cor 11:3 that Christ is the **h** of every man,
11:3 and a husband the **h** of his wife, and God the **h** of Christ.
Eph 1:22 gave him as **h** over all things

**HEADS** → HEAD
Ez 11:21 their conduct down upon their **h**—
Rev 12:3 dragon, with seven **h** and ten horns,
12:3 and on its **h** were seven diadems.

**HEAL** → HEALED, HEALING, HEALS, HEALTH
Dt 32:39 I who inflict wounds and **h** them,
Eccl 3:3 A time to kill, and a time to **h**;
Is 57:19 says the LORD; and I will **h** them.
Jn 12:40 be converted, and I would **h** them."

**HEALED** → HEAL
Is 6:10 understand, and they turn and be **h**.
53:5 us whole, by his wounds we were **h**.
Jas 5:16 for one another, that you may be **h**.
1 Pt 2:24 By his wounds you have been **h**.

**HEALING** → HEAL
Prv 12:18 but the tongue of the wise is **h**.
1 Cor 12:9 another gifts of **h** by the one Spirit;

**HEALS** → HEAL
Ps 103:3 all your sins, and **h** all your ills,

**HEALTH** → HEAL
Sir 30:15 rather have bodily **h** than any gold,
3 Jn 1:2 in every respect and are in good **h**,

**HEAR** → HEARD, HEARERS, HEARING, HEARS
Dt 6: 4 **H**, O Israel! The LORD is our
31: 13 shall **h** and learn to fear the LORD,
Is 59: 1 to save, nor his ear too dull to **h**.
Jer 5: 21 not see, who have ears and do not **h**.
Ez 37: 4 bones, **h** the word of the LORD!
Mt 13: 17 and to **h** what you **h** but did not **h** it.
Mk 12: 29 "The first is this: '**H**, O Israel!
Lk 7: 22 the deaf **h**, the dead are raised,
Heb 3: 7 that today you would **h** his voice,

**HEARD** → HEAR
Is 40: 21 Have you not **h**? Was it not told you
Rom 10: 17 Thus faith comes from what is **h**,
10: 17 what is **h** comes through the word
1 Cor 2: 9 and ear has not **h**, and what has not
1 Jn 1: 3 seen and **h** we proclaim now to you,
Rev 22: 8 I, John, who **h** and saw these things,

**HEARERS** → HEAR
Jas 1: 22 doers of the word and not **h** only,

**HEARING** → HEAR
Am 8: 11 but for **h** the word of the LORD.
1 Cor 12: 17 were an eye, where would the **h** be?
12: 17 If the whole body were **h**,

**HEARS** → HEAR
Ps 69: 34 For the LORD **h** the poor,
Prv 15: 29 wicked, but **h** the prayer of the just.
Jn 5: 24 whoever **h** my word and believes
1 Jn 5: 14 according to his will, he **h** us.
Rev 22: 18 warn everyone who **h** the prophetic

**HEART** → BROKENHEARTED, HEART'S, HEARTLESS, HEARTS
Gn 6: 6 on the earth, and his **h** was grieved.
Dt 6: 5 with your whole **h**, and with your
30: 14 in your mouth and in your **h**, to do it.
Jos 22: 5 serve him with your whole **h**
1 Sm 16: 7 The LORD looks into the **h**.
Ps 19: 15 the thoughts of my **h** before you,
51: 12 A clean **h** create for me, God;
Prv 3: 5 Trust in the LORD with all your **h**,
7: 3 write them on the tablet of your **h**.
Sir 37: 17 The root of all conduct is the **h**;
Ez 36: 26 I will give you a new **h**, and a new
36: 26 I will remove the **h** of stone
36: 26 your flesh and give you a **h** of flesh.
Dn 3: 39 with contrite **h** and humble spirit let
Mt 5: 8 Blessed are the clean of **h**, for they
5: 28 adultery with her in his **h**.
Mk 12: 30 the Lord your God with all your **h**,
Lk 12: 34 treasure is, there also will your **h** be.
Rom 2: 29 and circumcision is of the **h**,
10: 9 in your **h** that God raised him
Heb 10: 22 let us approach with a sincere **h**

**HEART'S** → HEART
Rom 10: 1 my **h** desire and prayer to God

**HEARTLESS** → HEART
Rom 1: 31 are senseless, faithless, **h**, ruthless.

**HEARTS** → HEART
Ps 95: 8 Do not harden your **h** as at Meribah,
Jer 31: 33 them, and write it upon their **h**;
Mk 7: 6 lips, but their **h** are far from me;
Jn 14: 1 "Do not let your **h** be troubled.
Rom 2: 15 of the law are written in their **h**,
5: 5 into our **h** through the holy Spirit
Eph 3: 17 may dwell in your **h** through faith;
Col 3: 15 the peace of Christ control your **h**,
Heb 3: 8 'Harden not your **h** as
10: 16 'I will put my laws in their **h**, and I
2 Pt 1: 19 and the morning star rises in your **h**.
1 Jn 3: 20 in whatever our **h** condemn, for God is greater than our **h**
Rev 2: 23 to know that I am the searcher of **h**

**HEAVEN** → HEAVENLY, HEAVENS
Gn 14: 19 High, the creator of **h** and earth;
Ex 16: 4 to rain down bread from **h** for you.
Dt 31: 28 so may call **h** and earth to witness
Jb 16: 19 Even now my witness is in **h**,
Jer 10: 11 gods that did not make **h** and earth—
23: 24 Do I not fill **h** and earth?—
Mt 3: 2 for the kingdom of **h** is at hand!"
6: 9 Our Father in **h**, hallowed be your
24: 35 **H** and earth will pass away, but my
26: 64 and 'coming on the clouds of **h**.' "
Mk 10: 21 and you will have treasure in **h**;
Lk 19: 38 Peace in **h** and glory
24: 51 from them and was taken up to **h**.
Jn 3: 13 to **h** except the one who has come down from **h**,
Acts 1: 11 you into **h** will return in the same
1: 11 as you have seen him going into **h**."
Rom 10: 6 your heart, 'Who will go up into **h**?'
2 Cor 12: 2 was caught up to the third **h**.
Phil 3: 20 But our citizenship is in **h**,
1 Thes 1: 10 and to await his Son from **h**,
Heb 9: 24 one, but **h** itself, that he might now
2 Pt 1: 18 voice come from **h** while we were
Rev 4: 1 I had a vision of an open door to **h**,
21: 1 Then I saw a new **h** and a new earth.
21: 1 The former **h** and the former earth

**HEAVENLY** → HEAVEN
Mt 5: 48 just as your **h** Father is perfect.
2 Cor 5: 2 further clothed with our **h** habitation
Heb 3: 1 sharing in a **h** calling,

**HEAVENS** → HEAVEN
Gn 1: 1 when God created the **h**
28: 12 with its top reaching to the **h**;
Dt 10: 14 Look, the **h**, even the highest **h**,
28: 23 The **h** over your heads will be like bronze
1 Kgs 8: 27 If the **h** and the highest **h** cannot
Ps 57: 6 Be exalted over the **h**, God;
115: 16 The **h** belong to the LORD, but he
Eccl 3: 1 a time for every affair under the **h**.
Is 14: 12 How you have fallen from the **h**,
65: 17 See, I am creating new **h** and a new
Eph 4: 10 who ascended far above all the **h**,
Heb 4: 14 priest who has passed through the **h**,
2 Pt 3: 10 the **h** will pass away with a mighty

**HEAVY**
Mt 23: 4 They tie up **h** burdens [hard

**HEBREW** → HEBREWS
Jon 1: 9 "I am a **H**," he replied; "I fear
Jn 19: 20 and it was written in **H**, Latin,
Phil 3: 5 of Benjamin, a **H** of **H** parentage,

**HEBREWS** → HEBREW
Ex 3: 18 the God of the **H**, has come to meet
Jdt 10: 12 "I am a daughter of the **H**, and I am
2 Cor 11: 22 Are they **H**? So am I.

**HEBRON**
Gn 13: 18 the oak of Mamre, which is at **H**.
2 Sm 2: 11 David was king in **H** over the house

**HEEL**
Gn 3: 15 head, while you strike at their **h**.
25: 26 brother came out, gripping Esau's **h**;
Jn 13: 18 food has raised his **h** against me.'

**HEIGHT** → HIGH
Rom 8: 39 nor **h**, nor depth, nor any other
Eph 3: 18 breadth and length and **h** and depth,

**HEIGHTS** → HIGH
Ps 148: 1 praise him in the **h**.
Hb 3: 19 and enables me to tread upon the **h**.

**HEIR** → HEIRS
Gn 15: 4 No, that one will not be your **h**;
15: 4 your own offspring will be your **h**.
Gal 4: 7 a child, and if a child then also an **h**,
Heb 1: 2 whom he made **h** of all things

**HEIRS** → HEIR
Rom 8: 17 then **h**, **h** of God and joint **h**
Ti 3: 7 become **h** in hope of eternal life.
1 Pt 3: 7 since we are joint **h** of the gift

**HELMET**
Is 59: 17 victory as a **h** on his head;
Eph 6: 17 And take the **h** of salvation

**HELP** → HELPER, HELPS
1 Sm 7: 12 this place the LORD has been our **h**."
Jdt 6: 21 called upon the God of Israel for **h**.
Ps 33: 20 the LORD, he is our **h** and shield.
46: 2 an ever-present **h** in distress.
Sir 2: 6 Trust in God, and he will **h** you;
Mk 9: 24 out, "I do believe, **h** my unbelief!"
Heb 2: 18 able to **h** those who are being tested.
4: 16 and to find grace for timely **h**.

**HELPER** → HELP
Jdt 9: 11 **h** of those of little account, supporter
Ps 30: 11 mercy on me; LORD, be my **h**."
Heb 13: 6 "The Lord is my **h**, [and] I will not

**HELPS** → HELP
Ps 37: 40 The LORD **h** and rescues them,

**HERBS**
Ex 12: 8 with unleavened bread and bitter **h**.

**HERMON**
Dt 3: 8 from the Wadi Arnon to Mount **H**
Ps 133: 3 Like dew of **H** coming down

**HEROD** → HERODIANS
1. King of Judea; tried to kill Jesus (Mt 2; Lk 1:5).
2. Son of 1. Tetrarch of Galilee who arrested and beheaded John the Baptist (Mt 14:1-12; Mk 6:14-29; Lk 3:1, 19-20; 9:7-9); tried Jesus (Lk 23:6-15).
3. Grandson of 1. King of Judea who killed James (Acts 12:2); arrested Peter (Acts 12:3-19). Death (Acts 12:19-23).

**HERODIANS** → HEROD
Mk 3: 6 took counsel with the **H** against him
12: 13 and **H** to him to ensnare him in his

**HERODIAS**
Wife of Herod the Tetrarch who persuaded her daughter to ask for John the Baptist's head (Mt 14:1-12; Mk 6:14-29; Lk 3:19).

**HEWN**
Mk 15: 46 in a tomb that had been **h**

**HEZEKIAH**
King of Judah (Sir 48:17-25). Restored the temple and worship (2 Chr 29–31). Sought the LORD for help against Assyria (2 Kgs 18–19; 2 Chr 32:1-23; Is 36–37). Illness healed (2 Kgs 20:1-11; 2 Chr 32:24-26; Is 38). Judged for showing Babylonians his treasures (2 Kgs 20:12-21; 2 Chr 32:31; Is 39).

**HID** → HIDE
Gn 3: 8 and his wife **h** themselves
Ex 2: 2 he was, she **h** him for three months.
3: 6 Moses **h** his face, for he was afraid
Jos 6: 17 because she **h** the messengers we
1 Kgs 18: 13 that I **h** a hundred of the prophets
Is 49: 2 arrow, in his quiver he **h** me.
54: 8 for a moment I **h** my face from you;

**HIDDEN** → HIDE
Prv 2: 4 and like **h** treasures search her out,
Is 40: 27 "My way is **h** from the LORD,
Mk 4: 22 there is nothing **h** except to be made
Col 3: 3 your life is **h** with Christ in God.
Rev 2: 17 I shall give some of the **h** manna;

**HIDE** → HID, HIDDEN
Dt 31: 17 them and **h** my face from them;
Ps 13: 2 How long will you **h** your face
17: 8 **h** me in the shadow of your wings

**HIGH** → HEIGHT, HEIGHTS, HIGHEST, HIGHLY
Gn 14: 18 He was a priest of God Most **H**.
1 Kgs 3: 2 were sacrificing on the **h** places,
Ps 91: 1 dwell in the shelter of the Most **H**,
Mt 4: 8 took him up to a very **h** mountain,
17: 1 and led them up a **h** mountain
Mk 5: 7 me, Jesus, Son of the Most **H** God?
Eph 4: 8 "He ascended on **h** and took
Heb 2: 17 and faithful **h** priest before God
7: 26 that we should have such a **h** priest:

**HIGHEST** → HIGH
1 Kgs 8: 27 the **h** heavens cannot contain you,
Mt 21: 9 of the Lord; hosanna in the **h**."
Lk 2: 14 "Glory to God in the **h** and on earth

**HIGHLY** → HIGH
Rom 12: 3 of himself more **h** than one ought

**HILL**
Is 40: 4 every mountain and **h** made low;
Lk 3: 5 mountain and **h** shall be made low.

**HINDERED**
1 Pt 3: 7 so that your prayers may not be **h**.

**HIRAM**
King of Tyre; helped David build his palace (2 Sm 5:11-12; 1 Chr 14:1); helped Solomon build the temple (1 Kgs 5; 2 Chr 2) and his navy (1 Kgs 9:10-27; 2 Chr 8).

**HITTITE** → HITTITES
Gn 23: 10 So Ephron the **H** replied
2 Sm 11: 3 and wife of Uriah the **H**,

**HITTITES** → HITTITE
Dt 20: 17 the **H**, Amorites, Canaanites,
Ezr 9: 1 Canaanites, **H**, Perizzites, Jebusites,

**HOLD** → HOLDS
Ps 73: 23 you take **h** of my right hand.
Col 1: 17 and in him all things **h** together.

**HOLDS** → HOLD
Ps 37: 24 fall, for the LORD **h** his hand.
Rev 2: 1 " 'The one who **h** the seven stars

**HOLES**
Hg 1: 6 worker labors for a bag full of **h**.

**HOLINESS** → HOLY
Ps 89: 36 By my **h** I swore once for all:
Rom 1: 4 the spirit of **h** through resurrection
1 Tm 2: 15 persevere in faith and love and **h**,
Heb 12: 14 that **h** without which no one will see

**HOLOCAUST** → See BURNT (OFFERING)

**HOLOFERNES**
Assyrian general (Jdt 2:4). Beguiled and beheaded by Judith (Jdt 10–13).

**HOLY** → HOLINESS

Ex 3: 5 place where you stand is **h** ground.
15: 11 like you, magnificent among the **h** ones?
20: 8 the sabbath day—keep it **h**.
26: 33 which divides the **h** place from the **h**
Lv 11: 44 and keep yourselves **h**, because I am **h**.
Jos 5: 15 on which you are standing is **h**."
1 Sm 2: 2 There is no **H** One like the LORD;
1 Mc 1: 15 and abandoned the **h** covenant;
Ps 2: 6 my king on Zion, my **h** mountain."
11: 4 The LORD is in his **h** temple;
Is 6: 3 "**H**, **h**, **h** is the LORD of hosts!
40: 25 me as an equal? says the **H** One.
Dn 9: 24 for your people and for your **h** city:
9: 24 and a **h** of holies will be anointed.
Mt 1: 18 with child through the **h** Spirit.
3: 11 He will baptize you with the **h** Spirit
24: 15 in the **h** place (let the reader
Mk 1: 24 who you are—the **H** One of God!"
3: 29 blasphemes against the **h** Spirit will
Lk 3: 22 the **h** Spirit descended upon him
11: 13 in heaven give the **h** Spirit to those
Jn 14: 26 the **h** Spirit that the Father will send
Acts 2: 4 they were all filled with the **h** Spirit
2: 27 nor will you suffer your **h** one to see
5: 3 heart so that you lied to the **h** Spirit
Rom 12: 1 sacrifice, **h** and pleasing to God,
Eph 1: 4 to be **h** and without blemish before
4: 30 do not grieve the **h** Spirit of God,
Heb 6: 4 gift and shared in the **h** Spirit
1 Pt 1: 16 is written, "Be **h** because I [am] **h**."
1 Jn 2: 20 that comes from the **h** one, and you
Jude 1: 14 has come with his countless **h** ones
Rev 4: 8 "**H**, **h**, **h** is the Lord God almighty,
21: 2 I also saw the **h** city, a new
22: 11 still do right, and the **h** still be **h**."

**HOME** → HOMELESS

Dt 6: 7 Recite them when you are at **h**
Ps 68: 7 God gives a **h** to the forsaken,
2 Cor 5: 8 leave the body and go **h** to the Lord.

**HOMELESS** → HOME

Is 58: 7 afflicted and the **h** into your house;
1 Cor 4: 11 roughly treated, we wander about **h**

**HONEST**

Lv 19: 36 weights, an **h** ephah and an **h** hin.

**HONEY**

Ex 3: 8 a land flowing with milk and **h**,
Jgs 14: 8 of bees in the lion's carcass, and **h**.
Ps 19: 11 than **h** or drippings from the comb.
Mt 3: 4 His food was locusts and wild **h**.

**HONOR** → HONORABLE, HONORED, HONORS

Dt 5: 16 **H** your father and your mother,
Tb 4: 3 **H** your mother, and do not abandon
Ps 8: 6 god, crowned him with glory and **h**.
Mal 1: 6 a father, where is the **h** due to me?
Mt 13: 57 "A prophet is not without **h** except
15: 4 '**H** your father and your mother,'
Jn 12: 26 The Father will **h** whoever serves
Rom 13: 7 respect is due, **h** to whom **h** is due.
Eph 6: 2 "**H** your father and mother."
1 Tm 5: 17 who preside well deserve double **h**,
Heb 2: 7 you crowned him with glory and **h**,
Rev 4: 11 to receive glory and **h** and power,

**HONORABLE** → HONOR

Phil 4: 8 true, whatever is **h**, whatever is just,

**HONORED** → HONOR

1 Cor 12: 26 if one part is **h**, all the parts share its

**HONORS** → HONOR

Mal 1: 6 A son **h** his father, and a servant
Mt 15: 8 'This people **h** me with their lips,

**HOOFS**

Lv 11: 3 Any animal that has **h** you may eat,

**HOOK** → HOOKS

Mt 17: 27 drop in a **h**, and take the first fish

**HOOKS** → HOOK

Is 2: 4 and their spears into pruning **h**;

**HOPE** → HOPED, HOPES

Jb 17: 15 Where then is my **h**, my happiness,
Ps 62: 6 alone, from whom comes my **h**.
146: 5 of Jacob, whose **h** is in the LORD,
Prv 23: 18 and your **h** will not be cut off.
Jer 14: 8 **H** of Israel, LORD, our savior
Lam 3: 21 will call to mind; therefore I will **h**:
Dn 13: 60 God who saves those who **h** in him.
Mt 12: 21 in his name the Gentiles will **h**."
Rom 5: 5 and **h** does not disappoint,
12: 12 Rejoice in **h**, endure in affliction,
1 Cor 13: 13 So faith, **h**, love remain, these three;
Col 1: 27 it is Christ in you, the **h** for glory.
1 Thes 5: 8 the helmet that is **h** for salvation.
Heb 7: 19 other hand, a better **h** is introduced,
1 Pt 1: 3 a living **h** through the resurrection
1 Jn 3: 3 Everyone who has this **h** based

**HOPED** → HOPE

Heb 11: 1 is the realization of what is **h**
1 Pt 3: 5 how the holy women who **h** in God

**HOPES** → HOPE

1 Cor 13: 7 believes all things, **h** all things,

**HOREB** → =SINAI

Ex 3: 1 he came to the mountain of God, **H**.
Dt 5: 2 God, made a covenant with us at **H**;
1 Kgs 19: 8 nights to the mountain of God, **H**.

**HORN** → HORNS

Ps 18: 3 shield, my saving **h**, my stronghold!
Dn 7: 8 a little **h**, sprang out of their midst,
7: 8 This **h** had eyes like human eyes,
Jl 2: 15 Blow the **h** in Zion! Proclaim a fast,

**HORNS** → HORN

Gn 22: 13 ram caught by its **h** in the thicket.
Ex 27: 2 At the four corners make **h** that are
Dn 8: 3 by the river a ram with two great **h**,
Rev 5: 6 He had seven **h** and seven eyes;
9: 13 the [four] **h** of the gold altar before
17: 3 names, with seven heads and ten **h**.

**HORSE** → HORSES

Ex 15: 1 **h** and chariot he has cast
Ps 33: 17 Useless is the **h** for safety;
Zec 1: 8 on a red **h** standing in the shadows
Rev 6: 2 and there was a white **h**, and its
19: 11 opened, and there was a white **h**;

**HORSES** → HORSE

2 Kgs 2: 11 and fiery **h** came between the two
Ps 20: 8 others on **h**, but we on the name
Jl 2: 4 Their appearance is that of **h**;
Rev 9: 7 was like that of **h** ready for battle.
19: 14 mounted on white **h** and wearing

**HOSANNA**

Mk 11: 10 that is to come! **H** in the highest!"
Jn 12: 13 out to meet him, and cried out: "**H**!

**HOSEA**
Prophet whose wife and family pictured the unfaithfulness of Israel (Hos 1–3).

**HOSHEA** → =JOSHUA
1. Original name of Joshua (Nm 13:8, 16).
2. Last king of Israel (2 Kgs 15:30; 17:1-6).

**HOSPITABLE** → HOSPITALITY
1 Tm 3: 2 decent, **h**, able to teach,
Ti 1: 8 but **h**, a lover of goodness,
1 Pt 4: 9 Be **h** to one another without

**HOSPITALITY** → HOSPITABLE
Rom 12: 13 needs of the holy ones, exercise **h**.
1 Tm 5: 10 practiced **h**, washed the feet
Heb 13: 2 Do not neglect **h**, for through it

**HOST** → HOSTS
Dt 4: 19 whole heavenly **h**, do not be led astray
2 Kgs 17: 16 bowed down to all the **h** of heaven;
Lk 2: 13 of the heavenly **h** with the angel,

**HOSTILE**
Col 1: 21 and **h** in mind because of evil deeds

**HOSTS** → HOST
1 Sm 1: 3 to the LORD of **h** at Shiloh,
Ps 46: 8 The LORD of **h** is with us;
Is 48: 2 whose name is the LORD of **h**.

**HOT**
Rev 3: 15 that you are neither cold nor **h**. I wish you were either cold or **h**.

**HOUR**
Mt 24: 36 of that day and **h** no one knows,
Jn 2: 4 My **h** has not yet come."
17: 1 and said, "Father, the **h** has come.

**HOUSE** → HOUSEHOLD, HOUSES, HOUSETOP, HOUSETOPS, STOREHOUSE
Ex 20: 17 shall not covet your neighbor's **h**.
2 Sm 7: 11 the LORD will make a **h** for you:
Ezr 1: 5 up to build the **h** of the LORD
Ps 69: 10 zeal for your **h** has consumed me,
127: 1 Unless the LORD build the **h**,
Prv 9: 1 Wisdom has built her **h**, she has set
Is 56: 7 make them joyful in my **h** of prayer;
Mt 7: 24 be like a wise man who built his **h**
21: 13 'My **h** shall be a **h** of prayer,'
Mk 3: 25 And if a **h** is divided against itself,
3: 25 that **h** will not be able to stand.
Jn 2: 17 for your **h** will consume me."
14: 2 In my Father's **h** there are many
1 Pt 2: 5 a spiritual **h** to be a holy priesthood

**HOUSEHOLD** → HOUSE
Jos 24: 15 As for me and my **h**, we will serve
Mi 7: 6 enemies are members of your **h**.
Mt 10: 36 enemies will be those of his **h**.'
Eph 2: 19 ones and members of the **h** of God,
1 Tm 3: 4 He must manage his own **h** well,
3: 15 how to behave in the **h** of God,
1 Pt 4: 17 to begin with the **h** of God;

**HOUSES** → HOUSE
Ex 12: 27 who passed over the **h**
12: 27 Egyptians, he delivered our **h**.' "
Mt 19: 29 everyone who has given up **h**

**HOUSETOP** → HOUSE
Mt 24: 17 a person on the **h** must not go down

**HOUSETOPS** → HOUSE
Mt 10: 27 hear whispered, proclaim on the **h**.

**HULDAH**
Prophetess inquired by Hilkiah for Josiah (2 Kgs 22; 2 Chr 34:14-28).

**HUMAN** → HUMANKIND
Jdt 8: 16 God is not like a **h** being to be
Dn 5: 5 the fingers of a **h** hand appeared,
Hos 11: 4 I drew them with **h** cords,
Mt 15: 9 as doctrines **h** precepts.' "
1 Cor 2: 13 not with words taught by **h** wisdom,
Phil 2: 7 of a slave, coming in **h** likeness;
2: 7 and found **h** in appearance,
1 Tm 2: 5 between God and the **h** race, Christ Jesus, himself **h**,
Rev 4: 7 had a face like that of a **h** being,

**HUMBLE** → HUMBLED, HUMBLY, HUMILITY
Ps 25: 9 He guides the **h** in righteousness,
25: 9 and teaches the **h** his way.
Zep 2: 3 the LORD, all you **h** of the land,
Mt 11: 29 me, for I am meek and **h** of heart;
Jas 4: 10 **H** yourselves before the Lord and he
1 Pt 5: 5 proud but bestows favor on the **h**."

**HUMBLED** → HUMBLE
Lk 14: 11 who exalts himself will be **h**,
Phil 2: 8 he **h** himself, becoming obedient

**HUMBLY** → HUMBLE
Mi 6: 8 and to walk **h** with your God.

**HUMILITY** → HUMBLE
Prv 15: 33 wisdom, and **h** goes before honors.
Zep 2: 3 Seek justice, seek **h**;
Col 3: 12 kindness, **h**, gentleness,
1 Pt 5: 5 clothe yourselves with **h** in your

**HUNDRED**
Gn 17: 17 born to a man who is a **h** years old?
Is 65: 20 at a **h** years shall be considered
65: 20 of a **h** shall be thought accursed.
Rom 4: 19 (for he was almost a **h** years old)

**HUNG**
Ps 137: 2 in its midst we **h** up our harps.

**HUNGER** → HUNGRY
Dt 8: 3 therefore let you be afflicted with **h**,
Mt 5: 6 Blessed are they who **h** and thirst
Rev 7: 16 They will not **h** or thirst anymore,

**HUNGRY** → HUNGER
Ps 50: 12 Were I **h**, I would not tell you,
146: 7 oppressed, who gives bread to the **h**.
Prv 25: 21 If your enemies are **h**, give them
Mt 12: 1 His disciples were **h** and began
Rom 12: 20 "if your enemy is **h**, feed him;

**HUSBAND** → HUSBANDS
Gn 3: 6 and she also gave some to her **h**,
3: 16 Yet your urge shall be for your **h**,
Prv 31: 28 her **h**, too, praises her:
Sir 26: 1 Happy the **h** of a good wife;
Is 54: 5 For your **h** is your Maker;
1 Cor 7: 10 wife should not separate from her **h**
Eph 5: 23 For the **h** is head of his wife just as
Rev 21: 2 as a bride adorned for her **h**.

**HUSBANDS** → HUSBAND
Jn 4: 18 For you have had five **h**,
Eph 5: 25 **H**, love your wives, even as Christ
Col 3: 18 be subordinate to your **h**, as is
Ti 2: 4 train younger women to love their **h**
1 Pt 3: 7 you **h** should live with your wives

**HUSHAI**
Wise man of David; foiled Absalom's revolt (2 Sm 15:32-37; 16:15–17:16).

**HYMN** → HYMNS
Mt 26:30 after singing a **h**, they went

**HYMNS** → HYMN
Eph 5:19 one another [in] psalms and **h**
Col 3:16 singing psalms, **h**, and spiritual

**HYPOCRISY** → HYPOCRITE, HYPOCRITES
Mt 23:28 but inside you are filled with **h**
Mk 12:15 Knowing their **h** he said to them,

**HYPOCRITE** → HYPOCRISY
Lk 6:42 You **h**! Remove the wooden beam

**HYPOCRITES** → HYPOCRISY
Mt 6:5 do not be like the **h**, who love
23:13 to you, scribes and Pharisees, you **h**.
Mk 7:6 did Isaiah prophesy about you **h**,

**HYSSOP**
Ex 12:22 Then take a bunch of **h**, and dipping
Nm 19:6 **h** and scarlet yarn and throw them
Ps 51:9 Cleanse me with **h**, that I may be
Jn 19:29 soaked in wine on a sprig of **h**

## I

**IDLE**
Eccl 11:6 at evening do not let your hand be **i**:

**IDOL** → IDOLS
Ex 20:4 You shall not make for yourself an **i**
Is 40:19 An **i**? An artisan casts it, the smith
1 Cor 10:19 Or that an **i** is anything?

**IDOLS** → IDOL
1 Mc 1:43 they sacrificed to **i** and profaned
Ps 115:4 Their **i** are silver and gold, the work
1 Cor 8:1 in regard to meat sacrificed to **i**:

**IGNORANCE** → IGNORANT
Acts 17:30 God has overlooked the times of **i**,
1 Pt 2:15 doing good you may silence the **i**

**IGNORANT** → IGNORANCE
Heb 5:2 is able to deal patiently with the **i**
2 Pt 3:16 things hard to understand that the **i**

**ILL**
1 Cor 11:30 That is why many among you are **i**

**ILLEGITIMATE**
Jn 8:41 they said to him, "We are not **i**.

**IMAGE** → IMAGES
Gn 1:26 Let us make human beings in our **i**,
1 Cor 15:49 Just as we have borne the **i**
15:49 also bear the **i** of the heavenly one.
Col 1:15 He is the **i** of the invisible God,
Rev 20:4 or its **i** nor had accepted its mark

**IMAGES** → IMAGE
Nm 33:52 destroy all their molten **i**,

**IMITATE** → IMITATORS
Heb 13:7 of their way of life and **i** their faith.
3 Jn 1:11 Beloved, do not **i** evil but **i** good.

**IMITATORS** → IMITATE
1 Cor 11:1 Be **i** of me, as I am of Christ.
Eph 5:1 So be **i** of God, as beloved children,

**IMMORAL** → IMMORALITY
1 Cor 5:9 letter not to associate with **i** people,
Heb 12:16 that no one be an **i** or profane

**IMMORALITY** → IMMORAL
2 Cor 12:21 have not repented of the impurity, **i**,

**IMMORTAL** → IMMORTALITY
Rom 1:23 exchanged the glory of the **i** God

**IMMORTALITY** → IMMORTAL
1 Cor 15:53 is mortal must clothe itself with **i**.
1 Tm 6:16 who alone has **i**, who dwells

**IMPERISHABLE**
1 Cor 9:25 a perishable crown, but we an **i** one.
1 Pt 1:4 to an inheritance that is **i**, undefiled,

**IMPORTANCE**
1 Cor 15:3 handed on to you as of first **i** what I

**IMPOSSIBLE**
Zec 8:6 if this should seem **i** in the eyes
8:6 should it seem **i** in my eyes also?—
Mt 17:20 Nothing will be **i** for you."
Mk 10:27 "For human beings it is **i**, but not
Heb 11:6 without faith it is **i** to please him,

**IMPURE** → IMPURITY
Eph 5:5 this, that no immoral or **i** or greedy
1 Thes 2:3 was not from delusion or **i** motives,

**IMPURITY** → IMPURE
Gal 5:19 immorality, **i**, licentiousness,
1 Thes 4:7 For God did not call us to **i**

**INCENSE** → FRANKINCENSE
Ex 25:6 anointing oil and for the fragrant **i**;

**INCREASE** → INCREASED
Lk 17:5 said to the Lord, "**I** our faith."
Jn 3:30 He must **i**; I must decrease."

**INCREASED** → INCREASE
Rom 5:20 where sin **i**, grace overflowed all

**INDEPENDENT**
1 Cor 11:11 Woman is not **i** of man or man

**INFANTS**
Ps 8:3 with the mouths of babes and **i**.
Mt 21:16 the text, 'Out of the mouths of **i**
1 Cor 14:20 In respect to evil be like **i**,

**INFIRMITIES**
Mt 8:17 "He took away our **i** and bore our

**INHERIT** → INHERITANCE
Lk 10:25 what must I do to **i** eternal life?"
1 Cor 6:9 the unjust will not **i** the kingdom
Heb 1:14 sake of those who are to **i** salvation?

**INHERITANCE** → INHERIT
Col 1:12 to share in the **i** of the holy ones
Heb 9:15 may receive the promised eternal **i**.

**INIQUITIES** → INIQUITY
Lv 16:22 The goat will carry off all their **i**
Rom 4:7 are they whose **i** are forgiven

**INIQUITY** → INIQUITIES
Hos 14:2 you have stumbled because of your **i**.

**INJURY**
Lv 24:20 The same **i** that one gives another

**INJUSTICE**
Rom 9:14 Is there **i** on the part of God?

**INN**
Lk 2:7 there was no room for them in the **i**.
10:34 took him to an **i** and cared for him.

**INNER** → INWARDLY
Mt 24:26 say, ‘He is in the **i** rooms,’ do not
2 Cor 4:16 our **i** self is being renewed day

**INNOCENCE** → INNOCENT
Ps 26:6 I will wash my hands in **i** so that I
Hos 8:5 long will they be incapable of **i**

**INNOCENT** → INNOCENCE
Prv 6:17 tongue, hands that shed **i** blood,
Mt 27:24 saying, “I am **i** of this man’s blood.

**INQUIRE**
Dt 12:30 Do not **i** regarding their gods,

**INSCRIBED** → INSCRIPTION
Rev 19:12 He had a name **i** that no one knows

**INSCRIPTION** → INSCRIBED
Mk 15:26 The **i** of the charge against him
2 Tm 2:19 bearing this **i**, “The Lord knows

**INSIGHT**
Dn 12:3 But those with **i** shall shine brightly
Eph 1:8 In all wisdom and **i**,

**INSPIRED**
2 Tm 3:16 All scripture is **i** by God and is

**INSTALL**
Ex 29:9 thus shall you **i** Aaron and his sons.

**INSTITUTION**
1 Pt 2:13 every human **i** for the Lord’s sake,

**INSTRUCT** → INSTRUCTED, INSTRUCTION
1 Cor 14:19 mind, so as to **i** others also, than ten

**INSTRUCTED** → INSTRUCT
Is 40:13 LORD, or **i** him as his counselor?

**INSTRUCTION** → INSTRUCT
Prv 8:10 Take my **i** instead of silver,
15:5 The fool spurns a father’s **i**,
Mi 4:2 For from Zion shall go forth **i**,
Rom 15:4 previously was written for our **i**,
1 Tm 1:5 The aim of this **i** is love from a pure

**INSULTS**
2 Cor 12:10 I am content with weaknesses, **i**,

**INTEGRITY**
Ti 2:7 respect, with **i** in your teaching,

**INTELLIGENT**
Prv 11:12 lacks sense, but the **i** keep silent.

**INTERCEDES** → INTERCESSION
Rom 8:26 the Spirit itself **i** with inexpressible

**INTERCESSION** → INTERCEDES
Heb 7:25 he lives forever to make **i** for them.

**INTERMARRY** → MARRIAGE
Dt 7:3 You shall not **i** with them,

**INTERPRET** → INTERPRETATION, INTERPRETATIONS
Gn 41:15 a dream but there was no one to **i** it.
41:15 ‘If he hears a dream he can **i** it.’ ”
1 Cor 12:30 Do all speak in tongues? Do all **i**?

**INTERPRETATION** → INTERPRET
1 Cor 12:10 to another **i** of tongues.
2 Pt 1:20 that is a matter of personal **i**,

**INTERPRETATIONS** → INTERPRET
Gn 40:8 to them, “Do **i** not come from God?

**INVISIBLE**
Col 1:15 He is the image of the **i** God,
1 Tm 1:17 ages, incorruptible, **i**, the only God,

**INVITE** → INVITES
Lk 14:13 you hold a banquet, **i** the poor,

**INVITES** → INVITE
1 Cor 10:27 If an unbeliever **i** you and you want

**INVOKE**
1 Pt 1:17 if you **i** as Father him who judges

**INWARDLY** → INNER
Rom 2:29 one is a Jew **i**, and circumcision is

**IRON**
Ps 2:9 an **i** rod you will shepherd them,
Prv 27:17 **I** is sharpened by **i**;
Dn 2:33 its legs **i**, its feet partly **i** and partly
Rev 19:15 He will rule them with an **i** rod,

**IRREVOCABLE**
Rom 11:29 the gifts and the call of God are **i**.

**ISAAC**
Son of Abraham by Sarah (Gn 17:19; 21:1-7; 1 Chr 1:28). Abrahamic covenant perpetuated with (Gn 17:21; 26:2-5). Offered up by Abraham (Gn 22; Heb 11:17-19). Rebekah taken as wife (Gn 24). Inherited Abraham’s estate (Gn 25:5). Father of Esau and Jacob (Gn 25:19-26; 1 Chr 1:34). Nearly lost Rebekah to Abimelech (Gn 26:1-11). Covenant with Abimelech (Gn 26:12-31). Tricked into blessing Jacob (Gn 27). Death (Gn 35:27-29). Father of Israel (Ex 3:6; Dt 29:13; Rom 9:10).

**ISAIAH**
Prophet to Judah (Is 1:1). Called by the LORD (Is 6). Announced judgment to Ahaz (Is 7), deliverance from Assyria to Hezekiah (2 Kgs 19; Is 36–37), deliverance from death to Hezekiah (2 Kgs 20:1-11; Is 38). Chronicler of Judah’s history (2 Chr 26:22; 32:32).

**ISCARIOT**
Mt 10:4 and Judas **I** who betrayed him.
Lk 22:3 Judas, the one surnamed **I**, who was

**ISHBAAL**
Son of Saul; would-be king (2 Sm 2:8–4:12).

**ISHMAEL**
Son of Abraham by Hagar (Gn 16; 1 Chr 1:28). Blessed, but not son of covenant (Gn 17:18-21; Gal 4:21-31). Sent away by Sarah (Gn 21:8-21). Children (Gn 25:12-18; 1 Chr 1:29-31). Death (Gn 25:17).

**ISRAEL** → ISRAELITE, ISRAELITES, =JACOB
1. Name given to Jacob (Gn 32:28; 35:10).
2. Corporate name of Jacob’s descendants; often specifically Northern Kingdom.
Gn 49:28 All these are the twelve tribes of **I**,
Ex 28:11 with the names of the sons of **I**
Nm 24:17 and a scepter shall rise from **I**,
Dt 6:4 Hear, O **I**! The LORD is our God,
Ps 125:5 with the evildoers. Peace upon **I**!
Jer 31:31 a new covenant with the house of **I**
Hos 11:1 When **I** was a child I loved him,
Mt 2:6 is to shepherd my people **I**.’ ”
Mk 12:29 “The first is this: ‘Hear, O **I**!
Lk 22:30 judging the twelve tribes of **I**.
Acts 1:6 going to restore the kingdom to **I**?”
Rom 9:6 For not all who are of **I** are **I**,
Heb 8:8 a new covenant with the house of **I**

**ISRAELITE** → ISRAEL
Jn 1:47 and said of him, “Here is a true **I**.
Rom 11:1 For I too am an **I**, a descendant

**ISRAELITES** → ISRAEL
Ex 2:23 The **I** groaned under their bondage
29:45 I will dwell in the midst of the **I**

**ISSACHAR**

Son of Jacob by Leah (Gn 30:18; 35:23; 1 Chr 2:1). Tribe of blessed (Gn 49:14-15; Dt 33:18-19), numbered (Nm 1:29; 26:25), allotted land (Jos 19:17-23; Ez 48:25), assisted Deborah (Jgs 5:15), 12,000 from (Rev 7:7).

**ITCH**

Dt 28:27 the **i**, from none of which you can be cured.

## J

**JACKALS**

Jgs 15:4 Samson went and caught three hundred **j**,

**JACOB** → =ISRAEL

1. Son of Isaac, younger twin of Esau (Gn 26:21-26; 1 Chr 1:34). Bought Esau's birthright (Gn 26:29-34); tricked Isaac into blessing him (Gn 27:1-37). Fled to Haran (Gn 28:1-5). Abrahamic covenant perpetuated through (Gn 28:13-15; Mal 1:2). Vision at Bethel (Gn 28:10-22). Served Laban for Rachel and Leah (Gn 29:1-30). Children (Gn 29:31–30:24; 35:16-26; 1 Chr 2–9). Flocks increased (Gn 30:25-43). Returned to Canaan (Gn 31). Wrestled with God; name changed to Israel (Gn 32:22-32). Reconciled to Esau (Gn 33). Returned to Bethel (Gn 35:1-15). Favored Joseph (Gn 37:3). Sent sons to Egypt during famine (Gn 42–43). Settled in Egypt (Gn 46). Blessed Ephraim and Manasseh (Gn 48). Blessed sons (Gn 49:1-28; Heb 11:21). Death (Gn 49:29-33). Burial (Gn 50:1-14).

2. Corporate name of Jacob's descendants; often specifically Northern Kingdom.

1 Mc 1:28 all the house of **J** was clothed
Ps 135:4 For the LORD has chosen **J**
Mi 7:20 You will show faithfulness to **J**,
Rom 9:13 "I loved **J** but hated Esau."

**JAEL**

Woman who killed the Canaanite general, Sisera (Jgs 4:17-22; 5:6, 24-27).

**JAIRUS**

Synagogue ruler whose daughter Jesus raised (Mk 5:22-43; Lk 8:41-56).

**JAMES**

1. Apostle; brother of John (Mt 4:21-22; 10:2; Mk 3:17; Lk 5:1-10). At transfiguration (Mt 17:1-13; Mk 9:1-13; Lk 9:28-36). Killed by Herod (Acts 12:2).

2. Apostle (Mt 10:3; Mk 3:18; Lk 6:15).

3. Brother of Jesus (Mt 13:55; Mk 6:3; Lk 24:10; Gal 1:19) and Judas (Jude 1). With believers before Pentecost (Acts 1:13). Leader of church at Jerusalem (Acts 12:17; 15; 21:18; Gal 2:9, 12). Author of epistle (Jas 1:1).

**JAPHETH**

Son of Noah (Gn 5:32; 1 Chr 1:4-5). Blessed (Gn 9:18-28). Sons of (Gn 10:2-5).

**JAR** → JARS

1 Kgs 17:14 The **j** of flour shall not go empty,
Mk 14:3 She broke the alabaster **j** and poured
Lk 22:10 a man will meet you carrying a **j**

**JARS** → JAR

Jn 2:6 there were six stone water **j** there

**JEALOUS**

Ex 34:14 for the LORD—"**J**" his name—is a **j** God.
Nm 25:13 because he was **j** on behalf of his God
Dt 4:24 God, is a consuming fire, a **j** God.
Rom 10:19 "I will make you **j** of those who are

**JEBUSITES**

Ex 3:8 Girgashites, the Hivites and the **J**.
Jos 15:63 But the **J** who lived in Jerusalem

**JECONIAH** → See JEHOIACHIN

**JEHOAHAZ**

1. Son of Jehu; king of Israel (2 Kgs 13:1-9).

2. Son of Josiah; king of Judah (2 Kgs 23:31-34; 2 Chr 36:1-4).

**JEHOASH** → =JOASH

1. Son of Ahaziah, king of Judah (2 Kgs 12). See Joash, 1.

2. Son of Jehoahaz; king of Israel. Defeat of Aram prophesied by Elisha (2 Kgs 13:10-25). Defeated Amaziah in Jerusalem (2 Kgs 14:1-16). See Joash, 2.

**JEHOIACHIN** → =JECONIAH

Son of Jehoiakim; king of Judah exiled by Nebuchadnezzar (2 Kgs 24:8-17; 2 Chr 36:8-10; Ez 1:2). Status improved (2 Kgs 25:27-30; Jer 52:31-34).

**JEHOIADA**

Priest who sheltered Joash from Athaliah (2 Kgs 11–12; 2 Chr 22:11–24:16).

**JEHOIAKIM** → =ELIAKIM

Son of Josiah; made king of Judah by Nebuchadnezzar (2 Kgs 23:34–24:6; 2 Chr 36:4-8; Jer 22:18-23). Burned scroll of Jeremiah's prophecies (Jer 36).

**JEHORAM** → =JORAM

1. Son of Jehoshaphat; king of Judah. Prophesied against by Elijah; killed by the LORD (2 Chr 21). See Joram, 1.

2. Son of Ahab; king of Israel (2 Chr 22:5). Joined Jehoshaphat against Moab (2 Kgs 3). See Joram, 2.

**JEHOSHAPHAT**

1. Son of Asa; king of Judah. Strengthened his kingdom (2 Chr 17). Joined with Ahab against Aram (2 Kgs 22; 2 Chr 18). Established judges (2 Chr 19). Joined Joram against Moab (2 Kgs 3; 2 Chr 20).

2. Valley of judgment (Jl 3:2, 12).

**JEHU**

1. Prophet against Baasha (2 Kgs 16:1-7).

2. King of Israel. Anointed by Elijah to obliterate house of Ahab (1 Kgs 19:16-17); anointed by servant of Elisha (2 Kgs 9:1-13). Killed Joram and Ahaziah (2 Kgs 9:14-29; 2 Chr 22:7-9), Jezebel (2 Kgs 9:30-37), relatives of Ahab (2 Kgs 10:1-17; Hos 1:4), ministers of Baal (2 Kgs 10:18-29). Death (2 Kgs 10:30-36).

**JEPHTHAH**

Judge from Gilead who delivered Israel from Ammon (Jgs 10:6–12:7). Made rash vow concerning his daughter (Jgs 11:30-40).

**JEREMIAH**

Prophet to Judah (Jer 1:1-3). Called by the LORD (Jer 1). Put in stocks (Jer 20:1-3). Threatened for prophesying (Jer 11:18-23; 26). Opposed by Hananiah (Jer 28). Scroll burned (Jer 36). Imprisoned (Jer 37). Thrown into cistern (Jer 38). Forced to Egypt with those fleeing Babylonians (Jer 43).

**JERICHO**

Jos 6:2 I have delivered **J**, its king, and its
1 Kgs 16:34 his reign, Hiel from Bethel rebuilt **J**.
Lk 18:35 as he approached **J** a blind man was

**JEROBOAM**

1. Official of Solomon; rebelled to become first king of Israel (1 Kgs 11:26-40; 12:1-20; 2 Chr 10). Idolatry (1 Kgs 12:25-33; Tb 1:5; Sir 47:23); judgment for (1 Kgs 13–14; 2 Chr 13).

2. Son of Jehoash; king of Israel (1 Kgs 14:23-29).

**JERUSALEM**

2 Sm 5:5 **J** he was king thirty-three years over
15:29 took the ark of God back to **J**
2 Kgs 25:10 down the walls that surrounded **J**,
Ezr 2:1 and who came back to **J** and Judah,
Neh 2:17 how **J** lies in ruins and its gates
2:17 let us rebuild the wall of **J**,

1 Mc 1:29 he came to **J** with a strong force.
Is 40:2 Speak to the heart of **J**,
Lam 1:8 **J** has sinned grievously,
Dn 9:25 of the word that **J** was to be rebuilt
Mi 4:2 and the word of the LORD from **J**.
Zec 1:14 I am jealous for **J** and for Zion
14:8 fresh water will flow from **J**,
Mt 23:37 "**J**, **J**, you who kill the prophets
Lk 4:9 Then he led him to **J**, made him
Gal 4:25 it corresponds to the present **J**,
Heb 12:22 the heavenly **J**, and countless angels
Rev 21:2 city, a new **J**, coming down

**JESSE**

Father of David (Ru 4:17-22; 1 Sm 16; 1 Chr 2:12-17).

**JESUS**

1. Jesus the Messiah.

**LIFE:** Genealogy (Mt 1:1-17; Lk 3:21-37). Birth announced (Mt 1:18-25; Lk 1:26-45). Birth (Mt 2:1-12; Lk 2:1-40). Escape to Egypt (Mt 2:13-23). As a boy in the temple (Lk 2:41-52). Baptism (Mt 3:13-17; Mk 1:9-11; Lk 3:21-22; Jn 1:32-34). Temptation (Mt 4:1-11; Mk 1:12-13; Lk 4:1-13). Ministry in Galilee (Mt 4:12–18:35; Mk 1:14–9:50; Lk 4:14–13:9; Jn 1:35–2:11; 4; 6), Transfiguration (Mt 17:1-8; Mk 9:2-8; Lk 9:28-36), on the way to Jerusalem (Mt 19–20; Mk 10; Lk 13:10–19:27), in Jerusalem (Mt 21–25; Mk 11–13; Lk 19:28–21:38; Jn 2:12–3:36; 5; 7–12). Last supper (Mt 26:17-35; Mk 14:12-31; Lk 22:1-38; Jn 13–17). Arrest and trial (Mt 26:36–27:31; Mk 14:43–15:20; Lk 22:39–23:25; Jn 18:1–19:16). Crucifixion (Mt 27:32-66; Mk 15:21-47; Lk 23:26-55; Jn 19:28-42). Resurrection and appearances (Mt 28; Mk 16; Lk 24; Jn 20–21; Acts 1:1-11; 7:56; 9:3-6; 1 Cor 15:1-8; Rev 1:1-20).

**MIRACLES.** *Healings:* official's son (Jn 4:43-54), demoniac in Capernaum (Mk 1:23-26; Lk 4:33-35), Peter's mother-in-law (Mt 8:14-17; Mk 1:29-31; Lk 4:38-39), leper (Mt 8:2-4; Mk 1:40-45; Lk 5:12-16), paralytic (Mt 9:1-8; Mk 2:1-12; Lk 5:17-26), cripple (Jn 5:1-9), shriveled hand (Mt 12:10-13; Mk 3:1-5; Lk 6:6-11), centurion's servant (Mt 8:5-13; Lk 7:1-10), widow's son raised (Lk 7:11-17), demoniac (Mt 12:22-23; Lk 11:14), Gadarene demoniacs (Mt 8:28-34; Mk 5:1-20; Lk 8:26-39), woman's bleeding and Jairus' daughter (Mt 9:18-26; Mk 5:21-43; Lk 8:40-56), blind man (Mt 9:27-31), mute man (Mt 9:32-33), Canaanite woman's daughter (Mt 15:21-28; Mk 7:24-30), deaf man (Mk 7:31-37), blind man (Mk 8:22-26), demoniac boy (Mt 17:14-18; Mk 9:14-29; Lk 9:37-43), ten lepers (Lk 17:11-19), man born blind (Jn 9:1-7), Lazarus raised (Jn 11), crippled woman (Lk 13:11-17), man with dropsy (Lk 14:1-6), two blind men (Mt 20:29-34; Mk 10:46-52; Lk 18:35-43), Malchus' ear (Lk 22:50-51). *Other Miracles:* water to wine (Jn 2:1-11), catch of fish (Lk 5:1-11), storm stilled (Mt 8:23-27; Mk 4:37-41; Lk 8:22-25), 5,000 fed (Mt 14:15-21; Mk 6:35-44; Lk 9:10-17; Jn 6:1-14), walking on water (Mt 14:25-33; Mk 6:48-52; Jn 6:15-21), 4,000 fed (Mt 15:32-39; Mk 8:1-9), money from fish (Mt 17:24-27), fig tree cursed (Mt 21:18-22; Mk 11:12-14), catch of fish (Jn 21:1-14).

**MAJOR TEACHING:** Sermon on the Mount (Mt 5–7; Lk 6:17-49), to Nicodemus (Jn 3), to Samaritan woman (Jn 4), Bread of Life (Jn 6:22-59), at Feast of Tabernacles (Jn 7–8), woes to Pharisees (Mt 23; Lk 11:37-54), Good Shepherd (Jn 10:1-18), Olivet Discourse (Mt 24–25; Mk 13; Lk 21:5-36), Upper Room Discourse (Jn 13–16).

**PARABLES:** Sower (Mt 13:3-23; Mk 4:3-25; Lk 8:5-18), seed's growth (Mk 4:26-29), wheat and weeds (Mt 13:24-30, 36-43), mustard seed (Mt 13:31-32; Mk 4:30-32), yeast (Mt 13:33; Lk 13:20-21), hidden treasure (Mt 13:44), valuable pearl (Mt 13:45-46), net (Mt 13:47-51), house owner (Mt 13:52), good Samaritan (Lk 10:25-37), unmerciful servant (Mt 18:15-35), lost sheep (Mt 18:10-14; Lk 15:4-7), lost coin (Lk 15:8-10), prodigal son (Lk 15:11-32), dishonest manager (Lk 16:1-13), rich man and Lazarus (Lk 16:19-31), persistent widow (Lk 18:1-8), Pharisee and tax collector (Lk 18:9-14), payment of workers (Mt 20:1-16), tenants and the vineyard (Mt 21:28-46; Mk 12:1-12; Lk 20:9-19), wedding banquet (Mt 22:1-14), faithful servant (Mt 24:45-51), ten virgins (Mt 25:1-13), talents (Mt 25:14-30; Lk 19:12-27).

**DISCIPLES** see APOSTLES. Call (Jn 1:35-51; Mt 4:18-22; 9:9; Mk 1:16-20; 2:13-14; Lk 5:1-11, 27-28). Named Apostles (Mk 3:13-19; Lk 6:12-16). Twelve sent out (Mt 10; Mk 6:7-11; Lk 9:1-5). Seventy sent out (Lk 10:1-24). Defection of (Jn 6:60-71; Mt 26:56; Mk 14:50-52). Final commission (Mt 28:16-20; Jn 21:15-23; Acts 1:3-8).

Acts 9:5 "I am **J**, whom you are persecuting.
1 Cor 8:6 and one Lord, **J** Christ,
Phil 2:10 name of **J** every knee should bend,
2 Thes 2:1 to the coming of our Lord **J** Christ
1 Tm 1:15 Christ **J** came into the world to save
Heb 12:2 while keeping our eyes fixed on **J**,
13:8 **J** Christ is the same yesterday,
1 Jn 1:7 the blood of his Son **J** cleanses us
Rev 1:1 The revelation of **J** Christ,
22:20 Amen! Come, Lord **J**!

2. Disciple, also called Justus (Col 4:11).

3. Writer of Ben Sira (Sir Pr:1; 50:27; 51:1).

**JETHRO**

Father-in-law and adviser of Moses (Ex 3:1; 4:18; 18). Also known as Reuel (Ex 2:18).

**JEW → JEWS, JUDAHITE, JUDAISM**

Est 10:3 The **J** Mordecai was next in rank
Rom 1:16 for **J** first, and then Greek.
2:29 Rather, one is a **J** inwardly,
1 Cor 9:20 To the Jews I became like a **J** to win
Col 3:11 Here there is not Greek and **J**,

**JEWS → JEW**

Est 3:13 kill and annihilate all the **J**,
Mt 2:2 is the newborn king of the **J**?
27:11 him, "Are you the king of the **J**?"
Jn 4:22 because salvation is from the **J**.
Rom 3:29 Does God belong to **J** alone?

**JEZEBEL**

Sidonian wife of Ahab (1 Kgs 16:31). Promoted Baal worship (1 Kgs 16:32-33). Killed prophets of the LORD (1 Kgs 18:4, 13). Opposed Elijah (1 Kgs 19:1-2). Had Naboth killed (1 Kgs 21). Death (1 Kgs 21:17-24; 2 Kgs 9:30-37). Metaphor of immorality (Rev 2:20).

**JEZREEL**

2 Kgs 10:7 baskets, and sent them to Jehu in **J**.
Hos 1:4 Give him the name "**J**,"
1:4 house of Jehu for the bloodshed at **J**

**JOAB**

Nephew of David (1 Chr 2:16). Commander of his army (2 Sm 8:16). Victorious over Ammon (2 Sm 10; 1 Chr 19), Rabbah (2 Sm 11; 1 Chr 20), Jerusalem (1 Chr 11:6), Absalom (2 Sm 18), Sheba (2 Sm 20). Killed Abner (2 Sm 3:22-39), Amasa (2 Sm 20:1-13). Numbered David's army (2 Sm 24; 1 Chr 21). Sided with Adonijah (1 Kgs 1:17, 19). Killed by Benaiah (1 Kgs 2:5-6, 28-35).

**JOASH → =JEHOASH**

1. Son of Ahaziah; king of Judah. Sheltered from Athaliah by Jehoiada (2 Kgs 11; 2 Chr 22:10–23:21). Repaired temple (2 Chr 24). See Jehoash, 1.

2. Son of Jehoahaz, king of Israel (2 Kgs 13; 2 Chr 25:17-25). See Jehoash, 2.

**JOB**

Wealthy man from Uz; feared God (Jb 1:1-5). Integrity tested by disaster (Jb 1:6-22), personal affliction (Jb 2). Maintained innocence in debate with three friends (Jb 3–31), Elihu (Jb 32–37). Rebuked by the LORD (Jb 38–41). Vindicated and restored to greater stature by the LORD (Jb 42). Example of righteousness (Ez 14:14, 20; Sir 49:9).

**JOEL**

1. Son of Samuel (1 Sm 8:2; 1 Chr 6:28).

2. Prophet (Jl 1:1; Acts 2:16).

**JOHANAN**

1. First high priest in the temple (1 Chr 6:9-10).
2. Jewish leader who tried to save Gedaliah from assassination (Jer 40:13-14); took Jews, including Jeremiah, to Egypt (Jer 40–43).

**JOHN**

1. Son of Zechariah and Elizabeth (Lk 1). Called the Baptist (Mt 3:1-12; Mk 1:2-8). Witness to Jesus (Mt 3:11-12; Mk 1:7-8; Lk 3:15-18; Jn 1:6-35; 3:27-30; 5:33-36). Doubts about Jesus (Mt 11:2-6; Lk 7:18-23). Arrest (Mt 4:12; Mk 1:14). Execution (Mt 14:1-12; Mk 6:14-29; Lk 9:7-9). Ministry compared to Elijah (Mt 11:7-19; Mk 9:11-13; Lk 7:24-35).
2. Apostle; brother of James (Mt 4:21-22; 10:2; Mk 3:17; Lk 5:1-10). At transfiguration (Mt 17:1-13; Mk 9:1-13; Lk 9:28-36). Desire to be greatest (Mk 10:35-45). Leader of church at Jerusalem (Acts 4:1-3; Gal 2:9). Elder who wrote epistles (2 Jn 1; 3 Jn 1). Prophet who wrote Revelation (Rev 1:1; 22:8).
3. Cousin of Barnabas, co-worker with Paul, (Acts 12:12–13:13; 15:37; see Mark).
4. Son of Simon Maccabeus (1 Mc 13:53; 16).

**JOIN** → JOINED

Ez 37: 17 **J** the two sticks together so they

**JOINED** → JOIN

Mt 19: 6 what God has **j** together, no human

**JOINT** → JOINTS

Rom 8: 17 heirs of God and **j** heirs with Christ,

**JOINTS** → JOINT

Heb 4: 12 soul and spirit, **j** and marrow,

**JONAH**

Prophet in days of Jeroboam II (2 Kgs 14:25). Called to Nineveh; fled to Tarshish (Jon 1:1-3). Cause of storm; thrown into sea (Jon 1:4-16). Swallowed by fish (Jon 1:17). Prayer (Jon 2). Preached to Nineveh (Jon 3). Attitude reproved by the LORD (Jon 4). Sign of (Mt 12:39-41; Lk 11:29-32).

**JONATHAN**

1. Son of Saul (1 Sm 13:16; 1 Chr 8:33). Valiant warrior (1 Sm 13–14). Relation to David (1 Sm 18:1-4; 19–20; 23:16-18). Killed at Gilboa (1 Sm 31). Mourned by David (2 Sm 1).
2. Brother and successor of Judas Maccabeus (1 Mc 2:5; 9:28-31).

**JOPPA**

Jon 1: 3 He went down to **J**, found a ship
Acts 9: 43 And he stayed a long time in **J**

**JORAM** → =JEHORAM

1. Son of Jehoshaphat; king of Judah (2 Kgs 8:16-24). See Jehoram, 1.
2. Son of Ahab; king of Israel. Killed with Ahaziah by Jehu (2 Kgs 8:25-29; 9:14-26; 2 Chr 22:5-9). See Jehoram, 2.

**JORDAN**

Gn 13: 10 watered the whole **J** Plain was as far
Nm 34: 12 boundary will descend along the **J**
Jos 3: 17 had completed the crossing of the **J**.
Mt 3: 6 in the **J** River as they acknowledged

**JOSEPH** → =BARNABAS

1. Son of Jacob by Rachel (Gn 30:24; 1 Chr 2:2). Favored by Jacob, hated by brothers (Gn 37:3-4). Dreams (Gn 37:5-11). Sold by brothers (Gn 37:12-36). Served Potiphar; imprisoned by false accusation (Gn 39). Interpreted dreams of Pharaoh's servants (Gn 40), of Pharaoh (Gn 41:4-40). Made greatest in Egypt (Gn 41:41-57). Sold grain to brothers (Gn 42–45). Brought Jacob and sons to Egypt (Gn 46–47). Sons Ephraim and Manasseh blessed (Gn 48). Blessed (Gn 49:22-26; Dt 33:13-17). Death (Gn 50:22-26; Ex 13:19; Heb 11:22). 12,000 from (Rev 7:8).
2. Husband of Mary mother of Jesus (Mt 1:16-24; 2:13-19; Lk 1:27; 2; Jn 1:45).
3. Disciple from Arimathea; buried Jesus in his tomb (Mt 27:57-61; Mk 15:43-47; Lk 24:50-52).
4. Original name of Barnabas (Acts 4:36).

**JOSHUA** → =HOSHEA

1. Son of Nun; name changed from Hoshea (Nm 13:8, 16; 1 Chr 7:27). Fought Amalekites under Moses (Ex 17:9-14). Servant of Moses on Sinai (Ex 24:13; 32:17). Spied Canaan (Nm 13). With Caleb, allowed to enter land (Nm 14:6, 30). Succeeded Moses (Dt 1:38; 31:1-8; 34:9).

Charged Israel to conquer Canaan (Jos 1). Crossed Jordan (Jos 3–4). Circumcised sons of wilderness wanderings (Jos 5). Conquered Jericho (Jos 6), Ai (Jos 7–8), five kings at Gibeon (Jos 10:1-28), southern Canaan (Jos 10:29-43), northern Canaan (Jos 11–12). Defeated at Ai (Jos 7). Deceived by Gibeonites (Jos 9). Renewed covenant (Jos 8:30-35; 24:1-27). Divided land among tribes (Jos 13–22). Last words (Jos 23). Death (Jos 24:28-31).

2. High priest during rebuilding of temple (Hg 1–2; Zec 3:1-9; 6:11). See Jeshua.

**JOSIAH**

Son of Amon; king of Judah (2 Kgs 21:26; 1 Chr 3:14). Prophesied (1 Kgs 13:2). Book of the Law discovered during his reign (2 Kgs 22; 2 Chr 34:14-31). Reforms (2 Kgs 23:1-25; 2 Chr 34:1-13; 35:1-19; Sir 49:1-4). Killed in battle (2 Kgs 23:29-30; 2 Chr 35:20-27).

**JOTHAM**

1. Son of Gideon (Jgs 9).
2. Son of Azariah (Uzziah); king of Judah (2 Kgs 15:32-38; 2 Chr 26:21–27:9).

**JOY**

Jb 20: 5 is short and the **j** of the impious
Prv 10: 1 A wise son gives his father **j**,
21: 15 justice is done it is a **j** for the just,
Is 12: 3 With **j** you will draw water
35: 10 singing, crowned with everlasting **j**; They meet with **j** and gladness,
Lam 2: 15 in beauty and **j** of all the earth?"
Bar 5: 9 For God is leading Israel in **j**
Mk 4: 16 the word, receive it at once with **j**.
Lk 1: 44 the infant in my womb leaped for **j**.
2: 10 good news of great **j** that will be
Jn 16: 22 no one will take your **j** away
Rom 14: 17 peace, and **j** in the holy Spirit;
Gal 5: 22 the fruit of the Spirit is love, **j**,
Phil 4: 1 I love and long for, my **j** and crown,
Heb 12: 2 the **j** that lay before him he endured
Jas 1: 2 Consider it all **j**, my brothers,

**JUBILEE**

Lv 25: 10 It shall be a **j** for you, when each
Nm 36: 4 the Israelites celebrate the **j** year,

**JUDAH** → JUDAHITE, JUDEA

1. Son of Jacob by Leah (Gn 29:35; 35:23; 1 Chr 2:1). Did not want to kill Joseph (Gn 37:26-27). Among Canaanites, fathered Perez by Tamar (Gn 38). Tribe of blessed as ruling tribe (Gn 49:8-12; Dt 33:7), numbered (Nm 1:27; 26:22), allotted land (Jos 15; Ez 48:7), failed to fully possess (Jos 15:63; Jgs 1:1-20).
2. Name used for Southern Kingdom.

2 Sm 2: 4 David king over the house of **J**.
Lam 1: 3 **J** has gone into exile,
Mt 2: 6 land of **J**, are by no means least among the rulers of **J**;
Heb 7: 14 is clear that our Lord arose from **J**,
Rev 5: 5 The lion of the tribe of **J**, the root

**JUDAHITE** → JUDAH

Zec 8: 23 hold of the cloak of every **J** and say,

**JUDAISM** → JEW

Acts 13: 43 were converts to **J** followed Paul
Gal 1: 13 heard of my former way of life in **J**,

**JUDAS** → =JUDE, =THADDAEUS, MACCABEUS

1. Apostle; son of James (Lk 6:16; Jn 14:22; Acts 1:13). Probably also called Thaddaeus (Mt 10:3; Mk 3:18).

2. Brother of James and Jesus (Mt 13:55; Mk 6:3), also called Jude (Jude 1).

3. Christian prophet (Acts 15:22-32).

4. Apostle, also called Iscariot, who betrayed Jesus (Mt 10:4; 26:14-56; Mk 3:19; 14:10-50; Lk 6:16; 22:3-53; Jn 6:71; 12:4; 13:2-30; 18:2-11). Suicide of (Mt 27:3-5; Acts 1:16-25).

5. Leader of the Maccabean revolt (1 Mc 2:4, 66). Recaptured Jerusalem and rededicated the temple and altar (1 Mc 4:36-61). Death of (1 Mc 9).

**JUDE** → See JUDAS, 2

**JUDEA** → JUDAH
Mt 2: 1 Jesus was born in Bethlehem of **J**,
Lk 3: 1 Pontius Pilate was governor of **J**,
Acts 1: 8 throughout **J** and Samaria,

**JUDGE** → JUDGED, JUDGES, JUDGMENT, JUDGMENTS
Ex 2: 14 appointed you ruler and **j** over us?
Is 11: 3 Not by appearance shall he **j**,
Ez 34: 17 I will **j** between one sheep
Jn 7: 24 by appearances, but **j** justly."
18: 31 and **j** him according to your law."
Rom 3: 6 For how else is God to **j** the world?
1 Cor 6: 2 that the holy ones will **j** the world?
2 Tm 4: 1 who will **j** the living and the dead,
Heb 12: 23 and God the **j** of all, and the spirits
Jas 5: 9 the **J** is standing before the gates.

**JUDGED** → JUDGE
Mt 7: 1 judging, that you may not be **j**.
Jas 3: 1 that we will be **j** more strictly,
Rev 20: 12 The dead were **j** according to their

**JUDGES** → JUDGE
Jgs 2: 16 the LORD raised up **j** to save them
1 Sm 2: 10 the LORD **j** the ends of the earth.
Sir 16: 12 he **j** people, each according to their
Lk 11: 19 Therefore they will be your **j**.
Acts 4: 19 you rather than God, you be the **j**.
Jas 4: 11 **j** his brother speaks evil of the law and **j** the law.
Rev 19: 11 He **j** and wages war

**JUDGMENT** → JUDGE
Ex 6: 6 arm and with mighty acts of **j**.
Ps 1: 5 the wicked will not arise at the **j**,
Eccl 12: 14 God will bring to **j** every work,
Jer 25: 31 he enters into **j** against all flesh:
Dn 7: 22 **j** was pronounced in favor
Mal 3: 5 I will draw near to you for **j**, and I
Mt 11: 24 on the day of **j** than for you."
Rom 14: 10 we shall all stand before the **j** seat
2 Cor 5: 10 we must all appear before the **j** seat
Heb 9: 27 beings die once, and after this the **j**,
10: 27 a fearful prospect of **j** and a flaming
Jas 2: 13 For the **j** is merciless to one who has
2: 13 mercy triumphs over **j**.
1 Pt 4: 17 it is time for the **j** to begin
1 Jn 4: 17 on the day of **j** because as he is,
Rev 18: 10 In one hour your **j** has come."

**JUDGMENTS** → JUDGE
Rom 11: 33 How inscrutable are his **j** and how
Rev 19: 2 for true and just are his **j**.

**JUDITH**

Virtuous widow and heroine of the deuterocanonical book of Judith (Jdt 8–16).

**JUST** → JUSTICE, JUSTIFICATION, JUSTIFIED, JUSTIFY
Dt 32: 4 without deceit, **j** and upright is he!
Tb 3: 2 Lord, and all your deeds are **j**;
1 Jn 1: 9 he is faithful and **j** and will forgive
Rev 15: 3 **J** and true are your ways, O king

**JUSTICE** → JUST
Jb 37: 23 abundant in **j**, who never oppresses.
Ps 33: 5 He loves **j** and right. The earth is
Prv 21: 15 When **j** is done it is a joy
Is 30: 18 For the LORD is a God of **j**:
42: 4 be bruised until he establishes **j**
Am 5: 24 Rather let **j** surge like waters,

**JUSTIFICATION** → JUST
Rom 4: 25 and was raised for our **j**.
Gal 2: 21 for if **j** comes through the law,

**JUSTIFIED** → JUST
Rom 3: 24 They are **j** freely by his grace
5: 1 since we have been **j** by faith,
10: 10 believes with the heart and so is **j**,
1 Cor 6: 11 you were **j** in the name of the Lord
Gal 2: 16 know that a person is not **j** by works
2: 16 Jesus that we may be **j** by faith
Jas 2: 24 See how a person is **j** by works

**JUSTIFY** → JUST
Rom 3: 30 will **j** the circumcised on the basis
Gal 3: 8 that God would **j** the Gentiles

## K

**KADESH** → KADESH-BARNEA
Nm 20: 1 month, and the people stayed at **K**.
Dt 1: 46 had to stay as long as you did at **K**.

**KADESH-BARNEA** → KADESH
Nm 32: 8 I sent them from **K** to reconnoiter

**KEEP** → KEEPER, KEEPS, KEPT
Gn 17: 9 you must **k** my covenant throughout
Ex 19: 5 me completely and **k** my covenant,
Nm 6: 24 The LORD bless you and **k** you!
Dt 5: 10 love me and **k** my commandments.
Neh 1: 5 you and **k** your commandments.
Prv 7: 2 **K** my commands and live, and my
Eccl 3: 6 a time to **k**, and a time to cast away.
12: 13 Fear God and **k** his commandments,
Sir 1: 26 wisdom, **k** the commandments,
Jude 1: 24 the one who is able to **k** you
Rev 22: 9 of those who **k** the message of this

**KEEPER** → KEEP
Gn 4: 9 Am I my brother's **k**?"

**KEEPS** → KEEP
Jas 2: 10 For whoever **k** the whole law,

**KEPT** → KEEP
Jn 17: 6 to me, and they have **k** your word.
2 Tm 4: 7 finished the race; I have **k** the faith.

**KEY** → KEYS
Is 22: 22 I will place the **k** of the House
Lk 11: 52 You have taken away the **k**
Rev 3: 7 the true, who holds the **k** of David,

**KEYS** → KEY
Mt 16: 19 I will give you the **k** to the kingdom
Rev 1: 18 I hold the **k** to death

**KIDRON**
2 Sm 15: 23 the king crossed the Wadi **K** with all
Jn 18: 1 his disciples across the **K** valley

**KILL**
Ex 4: 23 to let him go, I will **k** your son,
Eccl 3: 3 A time to **k**, and a time to heal;

Mt 10: 28 afraid of those who **k** the body but cannot **k** the soul;

**KIND** → KINDNESS, KINDS
Gn 6: 20 Of every **k** of bird, of every **k** of animal,
1 Cor 13: 4 Love is patient, love is **k**. It is not
Eph 4: 32 [And] be **k** to one another,

**KINDNESS** → KIND
Rom 2: 4 that the **k** of God would lead you
Gal 5: 22 joy, peace, patience, **k**, generosity,

**KINDS** → KIND
Lv 19: 19 yours with two different **k** of seed;
19: 19 with two different **k** of thread.

**KING** → KINGDOM, KINGS
Ex 1: 8 Then a new **k**, who knew nothing
Dt 17: 14 "I will set a **k** over me, like all
1 Sm 8: 7 They are rejecting me as their **k**.
2 Sm 2: 4 anointed David **k** over the house
Jdt 9: 12 waters, **K** of all you have created,
Ps 2: 6 "I myself have installed my **k**
10: 16 The LORD is **k** forever;
Is 6: 5 and my eyes have seen the **K**,
Jer 10: 10 the eternal **K**, Before whose anger
Mt 2: 2 "Where is the newborn **k**
27: 37 This is Jesus, the **K** of the Jews.
Lk 19: 38 "Blessed is the **k** who comes
Jn 1: 49 you are the **K** of Israel."
1 Tm 1: 17 To the **k** of ages, incorruptible,
Rev 19: 16 "**K** of kings and Lord of lords."

**KINGDOM** → KING
Ex 19: 6 You will be to me a **k** of priests,
2 Sm 7: 12 your loins, and I will establish his **k**.
1 Kgs 11: 31 to tear the **k** out of Solomon's hand
Wis 10: 10 Showed him the **k** of God and gave
Mt 4: 17 for the **k** of heaven is at hand."
5: 3 spirit, for theirs is the **k** of heaven.
6: 10 your **k** come, your will be done,
13: 24 "The **k** of heaven may be likened
Mk 1: 15 The **k** of God is at hand.
6: 23 ask of me, even to half of my **k**."
10: 24 how hard it is to enter the **k** of God!
12: 34 are not far from the **k** of God."
13: 8 rise against nation and **k** against **k**.
Lk 17: 21 the **k** of God is among you."
22: 16 there is fulfillment in the **k** of God."
Jn 3: 5 you, no one can enter the **k** of God
18: 36 "My **k** does not belong to this
Acts 1: 6 going to restore the **k** to Israel?"
Rom 14: 17 For the **k** of God is not a matter
1 Cor 6: 9 the unjust will not inherit the **k**
Eph 5: 5 any inheritance in the **k** of Christ
Col 1: 13 us to the **k** of his beloved Son,
1 Thes 2: 12 of the God who calls you into his **k**
Heb 12: 28 the unshakable **k** should have
2 Pt 1: 11 entry into the eternal **k** of our Lord
Rev 11: 15 "The **k** of the world now belongs

**KINGS** → KING
Gn 17: 6 **k** will stem from you.
Ps 2: 2 **K** on earth rise up and princes plot
138: 4 All the **k** of earth will praise you,
Prv 8: 15 By me **k** reign, and rulers enact
Is 52: 15 nations, **k** shall stand speechless;
Dn 7: 24 The ten horns shall be ten **k** rising
7: 24 him, who shall lay low three **k**.
Acts 4: 26 The **k** of the earth took their stand
1 Tm 6: 15 the King of **k** and Lord of lords,
Rev 19: 16 "King of **k** and Lord of lords."

**KISS**
Sg 1: 2 Let him **k** me with kisses of his
Mt 26: 48 "The man I shall **k** is the one;
2 Cor 13: 12 Greet one another with a holy **k**.

**KNEE**
Is 45: 23 To me every **k** shall bend;
Rom 14: 11 Lord, every **k** shall bend before me,
Phil 2: 10 name of Jesus every **k** should bend,

**KNEEL** → KNELT
Ps 95: 6 let us **k** before the LORD who

**KNELT** → KNEEL
2 Chr 6: 13 it, Solomon **k** in the presence

**KNEW** → KNOW
Dt 34: 10 whom the LORD **k** face to face,
Jer 1: 5 I formed you in the womb I **k** you,
Mt 7: 23 to them solemnly, 'I never **k** you.
Rom 1: 21 for although they **k** God they did not

**KNOCK**
Lk 11: 9 **k** and the door will be opened

**KNOW** → FOREKNEW, KNEW, KNOWING, KNOWLEDGE, KNOWN, KNOWS
Gn 22: 12 For now I **k** that you fear God,
Ex 6: 7 and you will **k** that I, the LORD,
1 Kgs 8: 39 their ways, you who **k** every heart;
Jb 19: 25 for me, I **k** that my vindicator lives,
Eccl 8: 16 I applied my heart to **k** wisdom
Is 1: 3 But Israel does not **k**, my people has
Jer 31: 34 and relatives, "**K** the LORD!"
31: 34 from least to greatest, shall **k** me—
Mt 6: 3 let your left hand **k** what your right
24: 42 For you do not **k** on which day your
Lk 11: 13 **k** how to give good gifts to your
22: 34 deny three times that you **k** me."
Jn 10: 14 and I **k** mine and mine **k** me,
13: 35 This is how all will **k** that you are
21: 24 and we **k** that his testimony is true.
Acts 1: 7 "It is not for you to **k** the times
Rom 8: 28 We **k** that all things work for good
1 Cor 8: 2 he does not yet **k** as he ought to **k**.
13: 12 At present I **k** partially; then I shall
13: 12 then I shall **k** fully, as I am fully
Eph 3: 19 to **k** the love of Christ that surpasses
Phil 3: 10 to **k** him and the power of his
Ti 1: 16 They claim to **k** God, but by their
Heb 8: 11 and kinsman, saying, '**K** the Lord,' for all shall **k** me, from least to greatest.
1 Jn 2: 4 Whoever says, "I **k** him," but does
3: 16 The way we came to **k** love was
Rev 3: 3 you will never **k** at what hour I will

**KNOWING** → KNOW
Gn 3: 22 like one of us, **k** good and evil!
Jn 18: 4 **k** everything that was going
Phil 3: 8 good of **k** Christ Jesus my Lord.

**KNOWLEDGE** → KNOW
Gn 2: 9 the tree of the **k** of good and evil.
Ps 94: 10 one who teaches man not have **k**?
Prv 1: 7 of the LORD is the beginning of **k**;
8: 10 silver, and **k** rather than choice gold.
Eccl 1: 18 whoever increases **k** increases grief.
Is 11: 2 a spirit of **k** and of fear
Hos 4: 6 My people are ruined for lack of **k**! Since you have rejected **k**,
Lk 11: 52 You have taken away the key of **k**.
Rom 11: 33 riches and wisdom and **k** of God!
1 Cor 8: 1 we realize that "all of us have **k**";
Eph 3: 19 the love of Christ that surpasses **k**,
Col 2: 3 all the treasures of wisdom and **k**.

1 Tm 6:20 and the absurdities of so-called **k**.
2 Pt 1:5 your faith with virtue, virtue with **k**,
1 Jn 2:20 the holy one, and you all have **k**.

**KNOWN** → KNOW
Lk 6:44 For every tree is **k** by its own fruit.
1 Cor 2:16 For "who has **k** the mind
Eph 1:9 he has made **k** to us the mystery

**KNOWS** → KNOW
Ps 1:6 the LORD **k** the way of the just,
103:14 For he **k** how we are formed,
Mt 6:8 Your Father **k** what you need before
24:36 "But of that day and hour no one **k**,
Rom 8:27 who searches hearts **k** what is
2 Tm 2:19 "The Lord **k** those who are his";
1 Jn 4:7 loves is begotten by God and **k** God.

**KORAH** → KORAHITES
Levite; led rebels against Moses (Nm 16; Jude 11).

**KORAHITES** → KORAH
Psalms of: Ps 42; 44–49; 84; 85; 87; 88.

**L**

**LABAN**
Brother of Rebekah (Gn 24:29), father of Rachel and Leah (Gn 29:16). Received Abraham's servant (Gn 24:29-51). Provided daughters as wives for Jacob in exchange for Jacob's service (Gn 29:1-30). Provided flocks for Jacob's service (Gn 30:25-43). Pursued and covenanted with Jacob (Gn 31).

**LABOR** → LABORER
Ex 1:11 to oppress them with forced **l**.
20:9 Six days you may **l** and do all your
1 Cor 15:58 that in the Lord your **l** is not in vain.

**LABORER** → LABOR
Lv 19:13 overnight the wages of your **l**.
Lk 10:7 you, for the **l** deserves his payment.

**LACKING**
Col 1:24 filling up what is **l** in the afflictions

**LAID** → LAY
Is 53:6 the LORD **l** upon him the guilt
Mk 16:6 Behold the place where they **l** him.
1 Jn 3:16 love was that he **l** down his life

**LAMB** → LAMBS
Is 53:7 Like a **l** led to slaughter or a sheep
Mk 14:12 when they sacrificed the Passover **l**,
Jn 1:29 "Behold, the **L** of God, who takes
1 Cor 5:7 For our paschal **l**, Christ, has been
1 Pt 1:19 as of a spotless unblemished **l**.
Rev 5:12 "Worthy is the **L** that was slain
19:7 the wedding day of the **L** has come,
21:23 gave it light, and its lamp was the **L**.

**LAMBS** → LAMB
Ex 12:21 and procure **l** for your families,
Is 40:11 in his arms he gathers the **l**,
Jn 21:15 He said to him, "Feed my **l**."

**LAME**
Is 35:6 Then the **l** shall leap like a stag,
Zep 3:19 I will save the **l**, and assemble
Mt 11:5 blind regain their sight, the **l** walk,

**LAMP** → LAMPS, LAMPSTAND, LAMPSTANDS
Ps 18:29 For you, LORD, give light to my **l**;
119:105 Your word is a **l** for my feet,
Pr 13:9 but the **l** of the wicked goes out.
31:18 her **l** is never extinguished at night.
Mt 5:15 Nor do they light a **l** and then put it
6:22 "The **l** of the body is the eye.
Rev 21:23 and its **l** was the Lamb.
22:5 nor will they need light from **l**

**LAMPS** → LAMP
Ex 25:37 You shall then make seven **l** for it
25:37 set up the **l** that they give their light
Mt 25:1 be like ten virgins who took their **l**

**LAMPSTAND** → LAMP, MENORAH
1 Mc 4:50 altar and lighted the lamps on the **l**,
Zec 4:2 I replied, "I see a **l** all of gold,

**LAMPSTANDS** → LAMP
Rev 1:20 right hand, and of the seven gold **l**:
1:20 the seven **l** are the seven churches.
11:4 the two **l** that stand before the Lord

**LAND**
Gn 1:10 God called the dry **l** "earth,"
12:7 your descendants I will give this **l**.
Ex 3:8 lead them up from that **l** into a good and spacious **l**,
20:2 brought you out of the **l** of Egypt,
Nm 13:2 men to reconnoiter the **l** of Canaan,
Jos 11:23 Thus Joshua took the whole **l**,
11:23 And the **l** had rest from war.
2 Kgs 17:5 of Assyria occupied the whole **l**
25:21 death in Riblah, in the **l** of Hamath.
2 Chr 7:14 pardon their sins and heal their **l**.
Jer 22:29 O **l**, **l**, **l**, hear the word
Dn 11:41 He shall enter the glorious **l**

**LANGUAGE**
Acts 2:6 heard them speaking in his own **l**.

**LASHES**
2 Cor 11:24 Jews **l** received forty **l** minus one.

**LAST** → EVERLASTING
2 Sm 23:1 These are the **l** words of David:
Is 44:6 I am the first, I am the **l**; there is no
Mt 19:30 But many who are first will be **l**, and the **l** will be first.
Mk 9:35 first, he shall be the **l** of all
1 Cor 15:26 The **l** enemy to be destroyed is
15:52 the blink of an eye, at the **l** trumpet.
2 Tm 3:1 will be terrifying times in the **l** days.
Heb 1:2 in these **l** days, he spoke to us
1 Jn 2:18 Children, it is the **l** hour; and just as
2:18 Thus we know this is the **l** hour.
Rev 1:17 I am the first and the **l**,

**LAUGH** → LAUGHINGSTOCK, LAUGHTER
Gn 18:13 "Why did Sarah **l** and say, 'Will I
Eccl 3:4 A time to weep, and a time to **l**;
Lk 6:21 are now weeping, for you will **l**.

**LAUGHINGSTOCK** → LAUGH
Lam 3:14 I have become a **l** to all my people,

**LAUGHTER** → LAUGH
Ps 126:2 Then our mouths were filled with **l**;
Jas 4:9 Let your **l** be turned into mourning

**LAW** → LAWFUL, LAWLESSNESS
Dt 1:5 Moses undertook to explain this **l**:
31:9 Moses had written down this **l**,
Jos 1:8 Do not let this book of the **l** depart
1 Mc 2:48 They saved the **l** from the hands
Ps 1:2 the **l** of the LORD is his joy;
1:2 on his **l** he meditates day and night.
Jer 31:33 I will place my **l** within them,
Mt 5:17 that I have come to abolish the **l**
23:23 the weightier things of the **l**:
Lk 24:44 written about me in the **l** of Moses
Jn 1:17 because while the **l** was given

Rom 2: 15 the demands of the **l** are written
6: 14 since you are not under the **l**
10: 4 the end of the **l** for the justification
Gal 2: 19 For through the **l** I died to the **l**,
Heb 10: 1 Since the **l** has only a shadow
Jas 2: 10 For whoever keeps the whole **l**,

**LAWFUL** → LAW
Mt 12: 12 So it is **l** to do good
1 Cor 6: 12 "Everything is **l** for me," but not
10: 23 "Everything is **l**," but not

**LAWLESSNESS** → LAW
2 Thes 2: 7 the mystery of **l** is already at work.
1 Jn 3: 4 who commits sin commits **l**, for sin is **l**.

**LAY** → LAID
Mt 28: 6 Come and see the place where he **l**.
Jn 10: 15 I will **l** down my life for the sheep.
1 Cor 3: 11 no one can **l** a foundation other than

**LAZARUS**
1. Poor man in Jesus' parable (Lk 16:19-31).
2. Brother of Mary and Martha whom Jesus raised from the dead (Jn 11:1–12:19).

**LAZY**
Ex 5: 17 He answered, "**L**! You are **l**!

**LEAD** → LEADER, LEADERS, LEADS, LED
Ex 32: 34 **l** the people where I have told you.
Rom 2: 4 of God would **l** you to repentance?

**LEADER** → LEAD
1 Chr 28: 4 For he chose Judah as **l**, then one

**LEADERS** → LEAD
Is 3: 12 My people, your **l** deceive you,
Lk 19: 47 and the **l** of the people, meanwhile,
Heb 13: 7 Remember your **l** who spoke

**LEADS** → LEAD
Rom 6: 16 either of sin, which **l** to death,
6: 16 which **l** to righteousness?

**LEAH**
Wife of Jacob (Gn 29:16-30); bore six sons and one daughter (Gn 29:31–30:21; 34:1; 35:23; Ru 4:11).

**LEAPED** → LEAPING
Lk 1: 41 greeting, the infant **l** in her womb,

**LEAPING** → LEAPED
1 Chr 15: 29 and when she saw King David **l**

**LEARN** → LEARNED, LEARNING
Dt 4: 10 that they may **l** to fear me as long as
Is 1: 17 **l** to do good. Make justice your aim:

**LEARNED** → LEARN
Phil 4: 11 for I have **l**, in whatever situation I

**LEARNING** → LEARN
Acts 26: 24 much **l** is driving you mad."

**LEAST** → LESS
Mt 2: 6 are by no means **l** among the rulers
5: 19 one of the **l** of these commandments
5: 19 do so will be called **l** in the kingdom
Lk 9: 48 the one who is **l** among all of you is

**LEAVE** → LEFT
Nm 11: 20 'Why did we ever **l** Egypt?' "
Mk 10: 7 this reason a man shall **l** his father
Jn 14: 18 I will not **l** you orphans; I will come

**LEAVEN** → LEAVENS
Ex 12: 15 will have your houses clear of all **l**.

**LEAVENS** → LEAVEN
Gal 5: 9 A little yeast **l** the whole batch

**LEAVES**
Gn 3: 7 so they sewed fig **l** together
Ez 47: 12 their **l** will not wither, nor will their
47: 12 for food, and their **l** for healing."
Rev 22: 2 the **l** of the trees serve as medicine

**LEBANON**
Dt 11: 24 from the wilderness and the **L**,
Is 40: 16 **L** would not suffice for fuel, nor its

**LED** → LEAD
Is 53: 7 Like a lamb **l** to slaughter or a sheep
Mt 4: 1 Jesus was **l** by the Spirit
27: 31 and **l** him off to crucify him.
Rom 8: 14 For those who are **l** by the Spirit

**LEFT** → LEAVE
Dt 28: 14 either to the right or to the **l**,
Mt 6: 3 do not let your **l** hand know what
25: 33 on his right and the goats on his **l**.
Lk 17: 34 one will be taken, the other **l**.

**LEGION**
Lk 8: 30 He replied, "**L**," because many

**LEGS**
Jn 19: 33 dead, they did not break his **l**,

**LENDER**
Prv 22: 7 the borrower is the slave of the **l**.

**LEPER** → LEPERS
Mt 8: 2 And then a **l** approached, did him
26: 6 Bethany in the house of Simon the **l**,

**LEPERS** → LEPER
Lk 7: 22 the lame walk, **l** are cleansed,

**LESS** → LEAST
Ex 30: 15 nor shall the poor give **l**,
Ezr 9: 13 have made **l** of our sinfulness than it

**LETTER**
Mt 5: 18 not the smallest **l** or the smallest part of a **l** will pass
2 Cor 3: 6 new covenant, not of **l** but of spirit;
3: 6 for the **l** brings death, but the Spirit

**LEVI** → LEVITES, LEVITICAL, =MATTHEW
1. Son of Jacob by Leah (Gn 29:34; 46:11; 1 Chr 2:1). With Simeon avenged rape of Dinah (Gn 34). Tribe of blessed (Gn 49:5-7; Dt 33:8-11), chosen as priests (Nm 3–4), numbered (Nm 3:39; 26:62), given cities, but not land (Nm 18; 35; Dt 10:9; Jos 13:14; 21), land (Ez 48:8-22), 12,000 from (Rev 7:7).
2. See Matthew.

**LEVIATHAN**
Ps 74: 14 You crushed the heads of **L**,

**LEVITES** → LEVI
Nm 1: 53 but the **L** shall camp around
1: 53 The **L** shall keep guard over
Jos 14: 4 But the **L** were given no share
Neh 8: 9 and the **L** who were instructing

**LEVITICAL** → LEVI
Heb 7: 11 came through the **l** priesthood,

**LIAR** → LIE
Prv 19: 22 rather be poor than a **l**.
Jn 8: 44 because he is a **l** and the father
Rom 3: 4 though every human being is a **l**,

1 Jn 2:22 Who is the l? Whoever denies

**LIARS** → LIE
1 Tm 1:10 sodomites, kidnapers, l, perjurers,

**LIBERTY**
Lv 25:10 You shall proclaim l in the land
Is 61: 1 To proclaim l to the captives,
1 Cor 8: 9 make sure that this l of yours in no

**LICENTIOUSNESS**
Mk 7:22 malice, deceit, l, envy, blasphemy,
Gal 5:19 immorality, impurity, l,
Jude 1: 4 pervert the grace of our God into l

**LIE** → LIAR, LIARS, LIES, LYING
Is 11: 6 the leopard shall l down
1 Jn 2:21 because every l is alien to the truth.

**LIES** → LIE
Phil 3:13 forgetting what l behind
3:13 straining forward to what l ahead,

**LIFE** → LIVE
Gn 2: 7 blew into his nostrils the breath of l,
2: 9 with the tree of l in the middle
9: 5 demand an accounting for human l.
Ex 21:23 injury ensues, you shall give l for l,
Dt 12:23 for blood is l; you shall not eat that l
30:19 I have set before you l and death,
30:19 Choose l, then, that you and your
Ps 34:13 Who is the man who delights in l,
Prv 18:21 and l are in the power of the tongue;
Eccl 7:12 is profitable because wisdom gives l
Sir 4:12 Those who love her love l;
Is 53:10 By making his l as a reparation
Mt 7:14 constricted the road that leads to l.
10:39 Whoever finds his l will lose it,
10:39 whoever loses his l for my sake will
20:28 to give his l as a ransom for many."
Mk 10:30 and eternal l in the age to come.
Jn 1: 4 through him was l, and this l was
3:15 in him may have eternal l."
6:35 said to them, "I am the bread of l;
11:25 "I am the resurrection and the l;
14: 6 am the way and the truth and the l.
Acts 3:15 The author of l you put to death,
Rom 5:21 eternal l through Jesus Christ our
8:11 the dead will give l to your mortal
8:38 that neither death, nor l, nor angels,
2 Cor 3: 6 brings death, but the Spirit gives l.
Phil 4: 3 whose names are in the book of l.
1 Jn 3:14 to l because we love our brothers.
5:20 He is the true God and eternal l.
Rev 2: 8 who once died but came to l,
20: 4 They came to l and they reigned
20:12 scroll was opened, the book of l.
22: 2 of the river grew the tree of l

**LIFT** → LIFTED
Ps 119:28 l me up acccording to your word.

**LIFTED** → LIFT
Jn 3:14 just as Moses l up the serpent
3:14 so must the Son of Man be l up,

**LIGHT** → ENLIGHTENED, ENLIGHTENS, LIGHTS
Gn 1: 3 Let there be l, and there was l.
Ex 13:21 of a column of fire to give them l.
Ps. 27: 1 The LORD is my l and my
Prv 4:18 the path of the just is like shining l,
Eccl 2:13 over folly as l has over darkness.
Is 42: 6 for the people, a l for the nations,
60: 1 for your l has come, the glory
Mt 4:16 sit in darkness have seen a great l,
4:16 by death l has arisen."
5:14 You are the l of the world.
11:30 my yoke is easy, and my burden l."
Jn 1: 9 The true l, which enlightens
8:12 saying, "I am the l of the world.
8:12 but will have the l of life."
Rom 13:12 [and] put on the armor of l;
2 Cor 11:14 Satan masquerades as an angel of l.
1 Pt 2: 9 out of darkness into his wonderful l.
1 Jn 1: 7 if we walk in the l as he is in the l,
Rev 22: 5 nor will they need l from lamp
22: 5 for the Lord God shall give them l,

**LIGHTNING**
Ex 19:16 there were peals of thunder and l,
Dn 10: 6 his face shone like l, his eyes were
Lk 10:18 "I have observed Satan fall like l
Rev 4: 5 From the throne came flashes of l,

**LIGHTS** → LIGHT
Gn 1:16 God made the two great l,
Jas 1:17 coming down from the Father of l,

**LIKE** → LIKENESS
Gn 3: 5 be opened and you will be l gods,
Ex 15:11 Who is l you among the gods,
15:11 Who is l you, magnificent among
2 Sm 7:22 There is no one l you, no God
Ps 113: 5 Who is l the LORD our God,
Is 46: 9 I am God, there is none l me.
Jer 10: 6 No one is l you, LORD, you are
Lk 13:18 "What is the kingdom of God l?
Rev 1:13 the lampstands one l a son of man,
10: 1 his face was l the sun and his feet
10: 1 and his feet were l pillars of fire.
16:15 ("Behold, I am coming l a thief."

**LIKENESS** → LIKE
Gn 1:26 beings in our image, after our l.
Rom 8: 3 his own Son in the l of sinful flesh
Phil 2: 7 form of a slave, coming in human l;

**LINEN**
Ex 26: 1 of ten sheets woven of fine l twined
Dn 10: 5 I saw a man dressed in l with a belt
Rev 19: 8 to wear a bright, clean l garment."
19: 8 (The l represents the righteous

**LION** → LION'S, LIONS'
1 Sm 17:34 whenever a l or bear came to carry
Eccl 9: 4 live dog is better off than a dead l."
Is 11: 7 the l shall eat hay like the ox.
Dn 7: 4 The first was like a l,
Rev 4: 7 The first creature resembled a l,
5: 5 The l of the tribe of Judah, the root

**LION'S** → LION
2 Tm 4:17 I was rescued from the l mouth.

**LIONS'** → LION
Dn 6:20 morning and hastened to the l den.

**LIPS**
Is 6: 5 For I am a man of unclean l,
6: 5 living among a people of unclean l,
Mt 15: 8 'This people honors me with their l,
Heb 13:15 the fruit of l that confess his name.

**LISTEN** → LISTENS
Jos 24:24 our God, and will l to his voice."
2 Kgs 17:40 But they did not l; they continued
Mk 9: 7 is my beloved Son. L to him."
Lk 16:31 'If they will not l to Moses

Acts 3:22 to him you shall **l** in all that he may

**LISTENS** → LISTEN
Jn 18:37 belongs to the truth **l** to my voice."
1 Jn 4:6 and anyone who knows God **l** to us,

**LITTLE**
Ex 16:18 a small amount did not have too **l**.
Ps 8:6 Yet you have made him **l** less than
Prv 15:16 Better a **l** with fear of the LORD
Sir 29:23 Whether **l** or much, be content
Mt 8:26 are you terrified, O you of **l** faith?"
2 Cor 8:15 whoever had **l** did not have less."
Gal 5:9 A **l** yeast leavens the whole batch

**LIVE** → ALIVE, LIFE, LIVES, LIVING
Ex 1:16 but if it is a girl, she may **l**."
33:20 my face, for no one can see me and **l**.
Dt 8:3 not by bread alone that people **l**,
Wis 5:15 But the righteous **l** forever,
Hb 2:4 is righteous because of faith shall **l**.
Mt 4:4 'One does not **l** by bread alone,
Jn 11:25 in me, even if he dies, will **l**,
Rom 1:17 who is righteous by faith will **l**."
14:8 For if we **l**, we **l** for the Lord,
14:8 so then, whether we **l** or die, we are
2 Cor 5:15 that those who **l** might no longer **l**
Gal 3:12 one who does these things will **l**

**LIVES** → LIVE
Gn 3:22 of life, and eats of it and **l** forever?
Tb 13:1 Blessed be God who **l** forever,
Jb 19:25 I know that my vindicator **l**,
Ps 18:47 The LORD **l**! Blessed be my rock!
Jn 11:26 everyone who **l** and believes in me
Rom 6:10 as to his life, he **l** for God.
1 Jn 3:16 to lay down our **l** for our brothers.
Rev 15:7 fury of God, who **l** forever and ever.

**LIVING** → LIVE
Gn 2:7 life, and the man became a **l** being.
3:20 she was the mother of all the **l**.
6:19 all **l** creatures you shall bring two
Dt 5:26 the voice of the **l** God speaking
Jer 2:13 forsaken me, the source of **l** waters;
Mt 16:16 the Messiah, the Son of the **l** God."
Jn 4:10 he would have given you **l** water."
6:51 I am the **l** bread that came down
Rom 12:1 to offer your bodies as a **l** sacrifice,
2 Cor 6:16 For we are the temple of the **l** God;
Heb 4:12 the word of God is **l** and effective,
1 Pt 2:4 Come to him, a **l** stone,

**LOAVES**
Mk 6:41 broke the **l**, and gave them to [his]
8:6 taking the seven **l** he gave thanks,

**LOCK**
Mt 23:13 You **l** the kingdom of heaven before

**LOCUST** → LOCUSTS
Jl 2:25 what the swarming **l** has eaten,

**LOCUSTS** → LOCUST
Ex 10:4 tomorrow I will bring **l** into your
2 Chr 6:28 mildew, or **l** swarm, or caterpillars;
Mt 3:4 His food was **l** and wild honey.
Rev 9:3 **L** came out of the smoke onto

**LONG** → LONGING
Ex 20:12 you may have a **l** life in the land
Ps 13:2 How **l** will you hide your face
Prv 3:16 **L** life is in her right hand, in her left
1 Cor 11:14 man wears his hair **l** it is a disgrace
1 Pt 2:2 **l** for pure spiritual milk so

Rev 6:10 in a loud voice, "How **l** will it be,

**LONGING** → LONG
2 Cor 5:2 **l** to be further clothed with our

**LOOK** → LOOKED, LOOKS
Ex 3:6 face, for he was afraid to **l** at God.
Ps 80:15 **l** down from heaven and see;
Lk 24:39 **L** at my hands and my feet, that it is

**LOOKED** → LOOK
Gn 19:26 But Lot's wife **l** back, and she was

**LOOKS** → LOOK
1 Sm 16:7 The LORD **l** into the heart.
Ps 14:2 The LORD **l** down from heaven
Mt 5:28 everyone who **l** at a woman

**LORD** → LORD'S, LORDS
Gn 18:27 I am presuming to speak to my **L**,
Ex 4:10 to the **L**, "If you please, my **L**,
Dt 10:17 the God of gods, the **L** of lords,
Jdt 6:19 "**L**, God of heaven, look at their
Ps 16:2 I say to the **L**, you are my **L**,
110:1 The LORD says to my **l**: "Sit at my
Sir 1:1 All wisdom is from the **L**
Is 6:1 I saw the **L** seated on a high
Dn 2:47 is the God of gods and **L** of kings
3:57 Bless the **L**, all you works of the **L**,
Mi 1:2 Let the **L** GOD be witness against
Mt 7:22 Many will say to me on that day, '**L**, **L**, did we not prophesy
12:8 Son of Man is **L** of the sabbath."
Mk 1:3 'Prepare the way of the **L**,
12:29 The **L** our God is **L** alone!
Lk 2:11 born for you who is Messiah and **L**.
10:27 "You shall love the **L**, your God,
19:38 who comes in the name of the **L**.
Jn 20:28 said to him, "My **L** and my God!"
Acts 2:34 'The **L** said to my **L**, "Sit at my
Rom 4:24 the one who raised Jesus our **L**
10:12 the same **L** is **L** of all, enriching all
1 Cor 2:16 "who has known the mind of the **L**,
8:6 we exist, and one **L**, Jesus Christ,
12:3 "Jesus is **L**," except by the holy
2 Cor 3:17 Now the **L** is the Spirit, and where
Eph 4:5 one **L**, one faith, one baptism;
Phil 2:11 confess that Jesus Christ is **L**,
4:5 be known to all. The **L** is near.
Col 3:13 as the **L** has forgiven you, so must
1 Thes 4:15 are left until the coming of the **L**,
1 Tm 6:15 the King of kings and **L** of lords,
Heb 12:14 without which no one will see the **L**.
Jas 4:10 Humble yourselves before the **L**
1 Pt 3:15 sanctify Christ as **L** in your hearts.
2 Pt 3:9 The **L** does not delay his promise,
Jude 1:4 who deny our only Master and **L**,
Rev 4:8 holy is the **L** God almighty,
19:16 "King of kings and **L** of lords."
22:20 Amen! Come, **L** Jesus!

***LORD** → *GOD, *LORD'S
Gn 2:7 the **L** God formed the man
13:4 and there Abram invoked the **L**
18:14 too marvelous for the **L** to do?
22:14 the mountain the **L** will provide."
Ex 3:15 The **L**, the God of your ancestors,
5:2 "Who is the **L**, that I should obey
5:2 I do not know the **L**, and I will not
6:7 the **L**, am your God who has freed
15:3 The **L** is a warrior, **L** is his name!
34:6 So the **L** passed before him
34:6 The **L**, the **L**, a God gracious
Lv 19:2 for I, the **L** your God, am holy.

Nm 6:24 The **L** bless you and keep you!
14:18 'The **L** is slow to anger
Dt 6:4 The **L** is our God, the **L** alone!
Jos 24:15 household, we will serve the **L**."
1 Sm 2:2 There is no Holy One like the **L**;
1 Kgs 8:11 glory of the **L** had filled the house of the **L**.
18:21 If the **L** is God, follow him;
1 Chr 16:11 Rely on the mighty **L**;
Ezr 7:10 practice of the law of the **L**
Neh 8:10 for today is holy to our **L**.
8:10 in the **L** is your strength!"
Jb 1:21 The **L** gave and the **L** has taken
1:21 blessed be the name of the **L**!"
42:12 Thus the **L** blessed the later days
Ps 1:2 Rather, the law of the **L** is his joy;
10:16 The **L** is king forever;
18:2 I love you, **L**, my strength,
23:1 The **L** is my shepherd;
33:12 is the nation whose God is the **L**,
84:12 For a sun and shield is the **L** God,
84:12 The **L** withholds no good thing
110:1 The **L** says to my lord: "Sit at my
113:5 Who is like the **L** our God,
125:2 the **L** surrounds his people both
128:1 Blessed are all who fear the **L**,
145:18 The **L** is near to all who call
150:6 has breath give praise to the **L**!
Prv 1:7 Fear of the **L** is the beginning
3:5 Trust in the **L** with all your heart,
19:23 The fear of the **L** leads to life;
21:2 but it is the **L** who weighs hearts.
Is 2:11 and the **L** alone will be exalted,
6:3 holy, holy is the **L** of hosts!
33:22 For the **L** is our judge, the **L** is our lawgiver, the **L** is our king;
53:6 the **L** laid upon him the guilt of us
64:8 Do not be so very angry, **L**, do not
Jer 4:4 Be circumcised for the **L**,
31:34 and relatives, "Know the **L**!"
32:27 I am the **L**, the God of all
Lam 3:25 The **L** is good to those who trust
Ez 3:23 of the **L** was standing there like
10:18 the glory of the **L** left the threshold
37:4 Dry bones, hear the word of the **L**!
44:4 of the **L** filled the LORD's house!
48:35 of the city is "The **L** is there."
Jl 1:15 For near is the day of the **L**,
Am 5:6 Seek the **L**, that you may live,
Ob 1:15 day of the **L** against all the nations!
Na 1:3 The **L** is slow to anger, yet great
1:3 the **L** will not leave the guilty
Zep 1:14 Near is the great day of the **L**,
Zec 14:9 The **L** will be king over the whole
14:9 that day the **L** will be the only one,
Mal 3:6 For I, the **L**, do not change,

**LORD'S** → LORD
Rom 14:8 whether we live or die, we are the **L**.
1 Cor 10:26 earth and its fullness are the **L**."

***LORD'S** → *LORD
Nm 11:23 Is this beyond the **L** reach?
Dt 32:9 But the **L** portion was his people;
Ps 24:1 The earth is the **L** and all it holds,
Ob 1:21 and the kingship shall be the **L**.

**LORDS** → LORD
Dt 10:17 gods, the Lord of **l**, the great God,
Ps 136:3 Praise the Lord of **l**; for his mercy
1 Cor 8:5 sure, many "gods" and many "**l**"),
Rev 19:16 "King of kings and Lord of **l**."

**LOSE** → LOSS, LOST
Mk 8:35 wishes to save his life will **l** it,
Heb 12:3 may not grow weary and **l** heart.
2 Jn 1:8 that you do not **l** what we worked

**LOSS** → LOSE
1 Cor 3:15 is burned up, that one will suffer **l**;
Phil 3:8 consider everything as a **l** because
3:8 his sake I have accepted the **l** of all

**LOST** → LOSE
Ps 119:176 I have wandered like a **l** sheep;
Jer 50:6 **L** sheep were my people,
Ez 34:16 The **l** I will search out, the strays I
Mt 10:6 Go rather to the **l** sheep of the house
Lk 15:6 because I have found my **l** sheep.'
19:10 to seek and to save what was **l**."

**LOT** → LOT'S, LOTS

1. Nephew of Abraham (Gn 11:27; 12:5). Chose to live in Sodom (Gn 13). Rescued from four kings (Gn 14). Rescued from Sodom (Gn 19:1-29; 2 Pt 2:7). Fathered Moab and Ammon (Gn 19:30-38).

2. Object cast to make decisions.

Nm 33:54 the land among yourselves by **l**,
33:54 Wherever anyone's **l** falls, there
Est 3:7 or **l**, was cast in Haman's presence
Prv 16:33 Into the bag the **l** is cast,
Acts 1:26 and the **l** fell upon Matthias, and he

**LOT'S** → LOT, 1
Gn 19:26 But **L** wife looked back, and she

**LOTS** → LOT, 2
Ps 22:19 for my clothing they cast **l**.
Jon 1:7 let us cast **l** to discover on whose
Mt 27:35 divided his garments by casting **l**;

**LOVE** → BELOVED, LOVED, LOVER, LOVERS, LOVES
Ex 20:6 showing **l** down to the thousandth generation of those who **l** me
Lv 19:18 You shall **l** your neighbor as
Dt 6:5 Therefore, you shall **l** the LORD,
Neh 1:5 of mercy with those who **l** you
1 Mc 4:33 by the sword of those who **l** you,
Ps 18:2 I **l** you, LORD, my strength,
116:1 I **l** the LORD, who listened to my
119:97 How I **l** your law, Lord! I study it
Prv 5:19 whose **l** you will ever have your fill,
8:17 Those who **l** me I also **l**, and those
Eccl 3:8 A time to **l**, and a time to hate;
Sg 1:2 for your **l** is better than wine,
8:6 For **L** is strong as Death, longing is
Sir 2:15 those who **l** him keep his ways.
4:12 Those who **l** her **l** life;
7:30 With all your strength **l** your Maker
Is 54:8 with enduring **l** I take pity on you,
Dn 9:4 show mercy toward those who **l** you
14:38 not forsaken those who **l** you."
Hos 11:4 with human cords, with bands of **l**;
Mal 1:2 I **l** you, says the LORD; but you say, "How do you **l** us?"
Mt 5:44 But I say to you, **l** your enemies,
6:24 will either hate one and **l** the other,
Mk 12:31 'You shall **l** your neighbor as
Lk 6:32 Even sinners **l** those who **l** them.
10:27 said in reply, "You shall **l** the Lord,
Jn 13:34 a new commandment: **l** one another.
14:15 "If you **l** me, you will keep my
15:13 No one has greater **l** than this, to lay
21:16 son of John, do you **l** me?"
21:16 Lord, you know that I **l** you."
Rom 5:5 because the **l** of God has been

5: 8 God proves his **l** for us in that while
12: 9 Let **l** be sincere; hate what is evil,
13: 8 to anyone, except to **l** one another;
1 Cor 8: 1 inflates with pride, but **l** builds up.
13: 4 **L** is patient, **l** is kind.
13: 13 So faith, hope, **l** remain, these three;
13: 13 but the greatest of these is **l**.
Gal 5: 6 but only faith working through **l**.
5: 22 the fruit of the Spirit is **l**, joy, peace,
Eph 2: 4 because of the great **l** he had for us,
3: 19 and to know the **l** of Christ
5: 25 Husbands, **l** your wives, even as
Col 3: 14 And over all these put on **l**, that is,
1 Thes 5: 8 on the breastplate of faith and **l**
1 Tm 6: 10 For the **l** of money is the root of all
Ti 2: 2 sound in faith, **l**, and endurance.
Heb 10: 24 how to rouse one another to **l**
13: 5 Let your life be free from **l**
Jas 2: 8 "You shall **l** your neighbor as
1 Pt 1: 8 you have not seen him you **l** him;
2 Pt 1: 7 affection, mutual affection with **l**.
1 Jn 2: 15 Do not **l** the world or the things
2: 15 the **l** of the Father is not in him.
3: 1 See what **l** the Father has bestowed
3: 16 The way we came to know **l** was
4: 7 Beloved, let us **l** one another, because **l** is of God;
4: 8 Whoever is without **l** does not know God, for God is **l**.
5: 3 For the **l** of God is this, that we keep
2 Jn 1: 6 For this is **l**, that we walk according
Jude 1: 21 Keep yourselves in the **l** of God
Rev 2: 4 you have lost the **l** you had at first.

**LOVED** → LOVE
Jer 31: 3 With age-old love I have **l** you;
Hos 11: 1 When Israel was a child I **l** him,
Jn 3: 16 For God so **l** the world that he gave
13: 1 He **l** his own in the world and he **l**
Gal 2: 20 in the Son of God who has **l** me
Eph 5: 2 as Christ **l** us and handed himself
1 Jn 4: 19 We love because he first **l** us.

**LOVER** → LOVE
Ps 99: 4 O mighty king, **l** of justice,
1 Tm 3: 3 not contentious, not a **l** of money.

**LOVERS** → LOVE
Jer 3: 1 played the prostitute with many **l**,
2 Tm 3: 2 be self-centered and **l** of money,

**LOVES** → LOVE
Ps 33: 5 He **l** justice and right. The earth is
Prv 3: 12 whom the LORD **l** he reproves,
Mt 10: 37 "Whoever **l** father or mother more
10: 37 and whoever **l** son or daughter more
Lk 7: 47 to whom little is forgiven, **l** little."
Rom 13: 8 the one who **l** another has fulfilled
Eph 5: 28 He who **l** his wife **l** himself.
Heb 12: 6 for whom the Lord **l**, he disciplines;
1 Jn 4: 7 everyone who **l** is begotten by God
Rev 1: 5 To him who **l** us and has freed us

**LOW** → LOWER, LOWLY
Is 40: 4 up, every mountain and hill made **l**;
Lk 3: 5 mountain and hill shall be made **l**.

**LOWER** → LOW
Heb 2: 7 for a little while **l** than the angels;

**LOWLY** → LOW
Jdt 9: 11 You are God of the **l**,
Lk 1: 52 from their thrones but lifted up the **l**.
Rom 12: 16 be haughty but associate with the **l**;

**LOYAL**
Dn 11: 32 but those who remain **l** to their God

**LUKE**
Associate of Paul (Col 4:14; 2 Tm 4:11; Phlm 24).

**LUKEWARM**
Rev 3: 16 because you are **l**, neither hot nor

**LUST** → LUSTS
Mt 5: 28 **l** has already committed adultery

**LUSTS** → LUST
Rom 1: 24 impurity through the **l** of their hearts

**LYDIA**
Acts 16: 14 them, a woman named **L**, a dealer

**LYING** → LIE
1 Kgs 22: 23 the LORD has put a **l** spirit
Prv 6: 17 Haughty eyes, a **l** tongue,
Wis 1: 11 and a **l** mouth destroys the soul.
Hos 4: 2 Swearing, **l**, murder,

**LYRE**
Ps 33: 2 on the ten-stringed **l** offer praise.

**M**

**MACCABEUS** → JUDAS
1 Mc 2: 66 And Judas **M**, a mighty warrior

**MACEDONIA**
Acts 16: 9 "Come over to **M** and help us."

**MADE** → MAKE
Gn 1: 31 God looked at everything he had **m**,
3: 21 The LORD God **m** for the man
15: 18 day the LORD **m** a covenant
Ex 20: 11 six days the LORD **m** the heavens
20: 11 the sabbath day and **m** it holy.
36: 8 doing the work **m** the tabernacle
Ps 8: 6 Yet you have **m** him little less than
118: 24 This is the day the LORD has **m**;
139: 14 you, because I am wonderfully **m**;
Jer 27: 5 It was I who **m** the earth,
Mk 2: 27 them, "The sabbath was **m** for man,
Acts 2: 36 that God has **m** him both Lord
Rev 14: 7 Worship him who **m** heaven

**MADNESS**
Dt 28: 28 the LORD will strike you with **m**,
Eccl 9: 3 and **m** is in their hearts during life;

**MAGDALENE**
Mt 27: 56 Among them were Mary **M**

**MAGICIANS**
Ex 7: 11 and they also, the **m** of Egypt,
Dn 2: 2 So he ordered that the **m**,

**MAGNIFY**
Ps 34: 4 **M** the LORD with me; and let us

**MAJESTIC** → MAJESTY
2 Pt 1: 17 came to him from the **m** glory,

**MAJESTY** → MAJESTIC
1 Chr 29: 11 are greatness and might, **m**, victory,
Ps 93: 1 The LORD is king, robed with **m**;
Heb 1: 3 at the right hand of the **M** on high,
2 Pt 1: 16 we had been eyewitnesses of his **m**.

**MAKE** → MADE, MAKER
Gn 1: 26 Let us **m** human beings in our
2: 18 I will **m** a helper suited to him.
12: 2 I will **m** of you a great nation,
12: 2 I will **m** your name great,
Ex 32: 1 **m** us a god who will go before us;

Is 61: 8 an everlasting covenant I will **m**
Jer 31: 31 when I will **m** a new covenant
Mt 28: 19 and **m** disciples of all nations,
Mk 1: 17 and I will **m** you fishers of men."

**MAKER** → MAKE
Jb 4: 17 be more blameless than their **M**?
Is 54: 5 For your husband is your **M**;

**MAKING** → MAKE
Gn 6: 6 the LORD regretted **m** human beings
Is 66: 22 heavens and the new earth which I am **m**

**MALACHI**
Post-exilic prophet (Mal 1:1).

**MALE**
Gn 1: 27 **m** and female he created them.
17: 10 every **m** among you shall be
Lv 20: 13 If a man lies with a **m** as
Mt 19: 4 the Creator 'made them **m**
Rev 12: 5 She gave birth to a son, a **m** child,

**MALICE**
Rom 1: 29 of wickedness, evil, greed, and **m**;
1 Cor 5: 8 the yeast of **m** and wickedness,

**MAN** → MEN
Gn 2: 7 the LORD God formed the **m**
2: 7 and the **m** became a living being.
2: 18 It is not good for the **m** to be alone.
1 Sm 13: 14 sought out a **m** after his own heart
Ps 8: 5 What is **m** that you are mindful of him, and a son of **m** that you care
Mt 9: 6 the Son of **M** has authority on earth
Lk 6: 5 them, "The Son of **M** is lord
Jn 9: 35 "Do you believe in the Son of **M**?"
1 Cor 11: 3 that Christ is the head of every **m**,
Rev 1: 13 the lampstands one like a son of **m**,
14: 14 one who looked like a son of **m**,

**MANAGE**
1 Tm 3: 4 He must **m** his own household well,
5: 14 and **m** a home, so as to give

**MANASSEH**
1. Firstborn of Joseph (Gn 41:51; 46:20). Blessed by Jacob but not as firstborn (Gn 48). Tribe of blessed (Dt 33:17), numbered (Nm 1:35; 26:34), half allotted land east of Jordan (Nm 32; Jos 13:8-33), half west (Jos 16; Ez 48:4), failed to fully possess (Jos 17:12-13; Jgs 1:27), 12,000 from (Rev 7:6).
2. Son of Hezekiah; king of Judah (2 Kgs 21:1-18; 2 Chr 33:1-20). Judah exiled for his detestable sins (2 Kgs 21:10-15). Repented (2 Chr 33:12-19).

**MANGER**
Lk 2: 12 clothes and lying in a **m**."

**MANNA**
Ex 16: 31 house of Israel named this food **m**.
Jos 5: 12 produce of the land, the **m** ceased.
Jn 6: 49 Your ancestors ate the **m**
Rev 2: 17 I shall give some of the hidden **m**;

**MANTLE**
2 Kgs 2: 8 Elijah took his **m**, rolled it

**MANY**
Is 53: 12 give him his portion among the **m**,
53: 12 Bore the sins of **m**, and interceded
Mt 22: 14 **M** are invited, but few are chosen."
Mk 10: 45 to give his life as a ransom for **m**."
Jn 20: 30 Now Jesus did **m** other signs
Rom 12: 5 though **m**, are one body in Christ

**MARAH**
Ex 15: 23 Hence this place was called **M**.

**MARK** → MARKED, MARKS
1. Cousin of Barnabas (Acts 12:12; 15:37-39; Col 4:10; 2 Tm 4:11; Phlm 24; 1 Pt 5:13), see John.
2. Brand or symbol:
Gn 4: 15 So the LORD put a **m** on Cain,
Rev 14: 9 or accepts its **m** on forehead
19: 20 astray those who had accepted the **m**

**MARKED** → MARK
Ez 9: 6 do not touch anyone **m** with the X.

**MARKET** → MARKETPLACE
1 Cor 10: 25 Eat anything sold in the **m**,

**MARKETPLACE** → MARKET
Jn 2: 16 making my Father's house a **m**."

**MARKS** → MARK
Gal 6: 17 for I bear the **m** of Jesus on my

**MARRIAGE** → INTERMARRY, MARRIED, MARRIES
Mt 22: 30 neither marry nor are given in **m**
Heb 13: 4 Let **m** be honored among all and the **m** bed be kept undefiled,

**MARRIED** → MARRIAGE
Mal 2: 11 has **m** a daughter of a foreign god.
Mk 12: 23 For all seven had been **m** to her."
1 Tm 3: 2 be irreproachable, **m** only once,
Ti 1: 6 a man be blameless, **m** only once,

**MARRIES** → MARRIAGE
Mk 10: 11 **m** another commits adultery against
1 Cor 7: 28 an unmarried woman sin if she **m**;

**MARTHA**
Sister of Mary and Lazarus (Lk 10:38-42; Jn 11; 12:2).

**MARVELOUS**
Ps 98: 1 LORD, for he has done **m** deeds.

**MARY**
1. Mother of Jesus (Mt 1:16-25; Lk 1:27-56; 2:1-40). With Jesus at temple (Lk 2:41-52), at the wedding in Cana (Jn 2:1-5), questioning his sanity (Mk 3:21), at the cross (Jn 19:25-27). Among disciples (Acts 1:14).
2. Magdalene; former demoniac (Lk 8:2). Helped support Jesus' ministry (Lk 8:1-3). At the cross (Mt 27:56; Mk 15:40; Jn 19:25), burial (Mt 27:61; Mk 15:47). Saw angel after resurrection (Mt 28:1-10; Mk 16:1-9; Lk 24:1-12); also Jesus (Jn 20:1-18).
3. Sister of Martha and Lazarus (Jn 11). Washed Jesus' feet (Jn 12:1-8).
4. Mother of James and Joses; witnessed crucifixion (Mt 27:56; Mk 15:40) and empty tomb (Mk 16:1; Lk 24:10).

**MASTER** → MASTERS
Mal 1: 6 his father, and a servant fears his **m**;
1: 6 And if I am a **m**, where is the fear
Mt 25: 21 His **m** said to him, 'Well done,
Jn 15: 20 'No slave is greater than his **m**.'
2 Pt 2: 1 and even deny the **M** who ransomed

**MASTERS** → MASTER
Mt 6: 24 "No one can serve two **m**.

**MATTANIAH** → See ZEDEKIAH

**MATTATHIAS**
Priest who started the Maccabean revolt (1 Mc 2).

**MATTHEW** → =LEVI
Apostle; former tax collector (Mt 9:9-13; 10:3; Mk 3:18; Lk 6:15; Acts 1:13). Also called Levi (Mk 2:14-17; Lk 5:27-32).

**MATTHIAS**
Disciple chosen to replace Judas (Acts 1:23-26).

**MATURE**
1 Cor 2: 6 speak a wisdom to those who are **m**,
Phil 3: 15 who are "perfectly **m**" adopt this
Heb 5: 14 But solid food is for the **m**, for those

**MEAN** → MEANING
Ex 12: 26 'What does this rite of yours **m**?'
Jos 4: 6 'What do these stones **m** to you?'

**MEANING** → MEAN
Gn 40: 5 and each dream with its own **m**.

**MEASURE**
Mk 4: 24 The **m** with which you **m** will be
Lk 6: 38 For the **m** with which you **m** will

**MEAT**
Rom 14: 21 it is good not to eat **m** or drink wine

**MEDIATOR**
Gal 3: 19 by angels at the hand of a **m**.
1 Tm 2: 5 There is also one **m** between God
Heb 8: 6 more excellent a ministry as he is **m**

**MEDIUM**
Lv 20: 27 man or a woman who acts as a **m**

**MEEK**
Mt 5: 5 Blessed are the **m**, for they will

**MEET** → MEETING
Ex 30: 36 tent of meeting where I will **m** you.
Am 4: 12 prepare to **m** your God, O Israel!
1 Thes 4: 17 the clouds to **m** the Lord in the air.

**MEETING** → MEET
Ex 27: 21 before the LORD in the tent of **m**,
40: 34 the cloud covered the tent of **m**,

**MELCHIZEDEK**
Gn 14: 18 **M**, king of Salem, brought out bread
Ps 110: 4 priest forever in the manner of **M**."
Heb 7: 1 This "**M**, king of Salem and priest

**MELT**
Ps 97: 5 The mountains **m** like wax before

**MEMBERS**
Rom 7: 23 I see in my **m** another principle
7: 23 the law of sin that dwells in my **m**.
1 Cor 6: 15 that your bodies are **m** of Christ?
6: 15 make them the **m** of a prostitute?

**MEMORIAL**
Jos 4: 7 are to serve as a perpetual **m**

**MEN** → MAN
Gn 18: 2 he saw three **m** standing near him.
Dn 3: 92 "I see four **m** unbound and unhurt,
Lk 9: 30 two **m** were conversing with him,

**MENAHEM**
King of Israel (2 Kgs 15:14-23).

**MENE**
Dn 5: 25 **M**, TEKEL, and PERES.

**MENORAH** → LAMPSTAND
Ex 25: 31 You shall make a **m** of pure beaten gold

**MEPHIBOSHETH**
Son of Jonathan shown kindness by David (2 Sm 4:4; 9; 21:7). Accused of siding with Absalom (2 Sm 16:1-4; 19:24-30).

**MERCIFUL** → MERCY
Dt 4: 31 is a **m** God, he will not abandon
Ps 111: 4 gracious and **m** is the LORD.
Sir 2: 11 the Lord is compassionate and **m**;
Jer 3: 12 For I am **m**, oracle of the LORD,
Mt 5: 7 Blessed are the **m**, for they will be
Lk 6: 36 Be **m**, just as [also] your Father is **m**.
Heb 2: 17 that he might be a **m** and faithful

**MERCY** → MERCIFUL
1 Chr 21: 13 the LORD, whose **m** is very great,
Ps 136: 1 he is good; for his **m** endures forever;
Lam 3: 22 The LORD's acts of **m** are not exhausted,
Zec 1: 12 how long will you be without **m**
Mt 9: 13 words, 'I desire **m**, not sacrifice.'
23: 23 judgment and **m** and fidelity.
Rom 9: 15 "I will show **m** to whom I will,
Eph 2: 4 who is rich in **m**,
Ti 3: 5 we had done but because of his **m**,
Heb 4: 16 the throne of grace to receive **m**
Jas 2: 13 to one who has not shown **m**;

**MERIBAH**
Ex 17: 7 place was named Massah and **M**,
Ps 95: 8 Do not harden your hearts as at **M**,

**MESHACH** → =MISHAEL
Hebrew exiled to Babylon; name changed from Mishael (Dn 1:6-7). Refused defilement by food (Dn 1:8-20). Refused to worship idol (Dn 3:1-18); saved from furnace (Dn 3:19-30).

**MESSAGE** → MESSENGER
1 Cor 1: 18 The **m** of the cross is foolishness
2 Cor 5: 19 to us the **m** of reconciliation.

**MESSENGER** → MESSAGE
Is 42: 19 servant, or deaf like the **m** I send?
Mt 11: 10 I am sending my **m** ahead of you;

**MESSIAH** → CHRIST, MESSIAHS
Mt 16: 16 "You are the **M**, the Son
Lk 2: 11 has been born for you who is **M**
Acts 2: 36 has made him both Lord and **M**,
Rom 9: 5 according to the flesh, is the **M**.

**MESSIAHS** → MESSIAH
Mk 13: 22 False **m** and false prophets will arise

**MICAH**
1. Idolater from Ephraim (Jgs 17–18).
2. Prophet from Moresheth (Jer 26:18-19; Mi 1:1).

**MICAIAH**
Prophet of the LORD who spoke against Ahab (1 Kgs 22:1-28; 2 Chr 18:1-27).

**MICHAEL**
Archangel (Jude 9); warrior in angelic realm, protector of Israel (Dn 10:13, 21; 12:1; Rev 12:7).

**MICHAL**
Daughter of Saul, wife of David (1 Sm 14:49; 18:20-28). Warned David of Saul's plot (1 Sm 19). Saul gave her to Paltiel (1 Sm 25:44); David retrieved her (2 Sm 3:13-16). Criticized David for dancing before the ark (2 Sm 6:16-23; 1 Chr 15:29).

**MIDDLE**
Gn 3: 3 the tree in the **m** of the garden
Rev 22: 2 down the **m** of its street.

**MIDIAN** → MIDIANITES
Ex 18: 1 the priest of **M**, heard of all

**MIDIANITES** → MIDIAN
Gn 37: 36 The **M**, meanwhile, sold Joseph
Nm 31: 2 Avenge the Israelites on the **M**,

**MIDWIVES**
Ex 1: 17 The **m**, however, feared God;

**MIGHT** → ALMIGHTY, MIGHTY
1 Chr 29: 11 Yours, LORD, are greatness and **m**,
2 Chr 20: 6 In your hand is power and **m**,

Zec 4: 6 Not by **m**, and not by power,

**MIGHTY** → MIGHT
Gn 49: 24 the power of the **M** One of Jacob,
1 Chr 16: 11 Rely on the **m** LORD; constantly seek
Ps 99: 4 O **m** king, lover of justice, you have
Lk 1: 49 The **M** One has done great things
Rev 18: 8 **m** is the Lord God who judges her."

**MILE**
Mt 5: 41 press you into service for one **m**,

**MILK**
Ex 3: 8 a land flowing with **m** and honey,
Heb 5: 12 You need **m**, [and] not solid food.
1 Pt 2: 2 pure spiritual **m** so that through it

**MILLSTONE** → STONE
Lk 17: 2 him if a **m** were put around his neck

**MIND** → MINDFUL, MINDS
Mt 22: 37 all your soul, and with all your **m**.
Rom 1: 28 their undiscerning **m** to do what is
1 Cor 2: 16 But we have the **m** of Christ.
2: 16 "who has known the **m** of the Lord,

**MINDFUL** → MIND
Ps 8: 5 What is man that you are **m** of him,
Heb 2: 6 is man that you are **m** of him,

**MINDS** → MIND
2 Cor 4: 4 of this age has blinded the **m**
Eph 4: 23 be renewed in the spirit of your **m**,
Phil 4: 7 your hearts and **m** in Christ Jesus.

**MINISTER** → MINISTERS, MINISTRY
Ex 28: 43 or approach the altar to **m**

**MINISTERS** → MINISTER
2 Cor 3: 6 who has indeed qualified us as **m**
11: 15 masquerade as **m** of righteousness.

**MINISTRY** → MINISTER
2 Cor 5: 18 and given us the **m** of reconciliation,
Eph 4: 12 the holy ones for the work of **m**,
Heb 8: 6 so much more excellent a **m** as he is

**MIRACLES** → See JESUS: MIRACLES

**MIRIAM**
Sister of Moses and Aaron (Nm 26:59). Led dancing at Red Sea (Ex 15:20-21). Struck with leprosy for criticizing Moses (Nm 12). Death (Nm 20:1).

**MIRROR**
1 Cor 13: 12 as in a **m**, but then face to face.
Jas 1: 23 who looks at his own face in a **m**.

**MISHAEL** → See MESHACH

**MOAB**
Gn 19: 37 birth to a son whom she named **M**,
Ru 1: 1 sons to reside on the plateau of **M**.
Is 15: 1 Oracle on **M**: Laid waste in a night,

**MOANING**
Ex 2: 24 God heard their **m** and God was mindful

**MOCK** → MOCKED
Ps 22: 8 All who see me **m** me;
Mk 10: 34 who will **m** him, spit upon him,

**MOCKED** → MOCK
Gal 6: 7 God is not **m**, for a person will reap

**MOLECH**
Lv 18: 21 your offspring for immolation to **M**,

**MOMENT** → MOMENTARY
Ex 33: 5 up in your company even for a **m**,
Ps 30: 6 For his anger lasts but a **m**;
Is 54: 7 For a brief **m** I abandoned you,
66: 8 or a nation be born in a single **m**?

**MOMENTARY** → MOMENT
2 Cor 4: 17 this **m** light affliction is producing

**MONEY**
Eccl 10: 19 but **m** answers for everything.
Mk 11: 15 the tables of the **m** changers
1 Tm 3: 3 not contentious, not a lover of **m**.
6: 10 the love of **m** is the root of all evils,
Heb 13: 5 Let your life be free from love of **m**

**MONTH**
Ex 12: 2 you will reckon it the first **m**
Ez 47: 12 Every **m** they will bear fresh fruit
Rev 22: 2 twelve times a year, once each **m**;

**MOON** → MOONS
Gn 37: 9 the **m** and eleven stars were bowing
Dt 17: 3 the **m** or any of the host of heaven,
Jos 10: 13 The sun stood still, the **m** stayed,
Acts 2: 20 and the **m** to blood,
Rev 6: 12 and the whole **m** became like blood.
21: 23 no need of sun or **m** to shine on it,

**MOONS** → MOON
2 Chr 8: 13 at the new **m**, and on the fixed

**MORALS**
1 Cor 15: 33 "Bad company corrupts good **m**."

**MORDECAI**
Benjamite exile who raised Esther (Est 2:5-15). Mordecai's dream (Est 11; 10:4-13). Exposed plot to kill Xerxes (Est 2:19-23; 12:1-6). Refused to honor Haman (Est 3:1-6; 5:9-14). Mordecai's prayer (Est 13). Charged Esther to foil Haman's plot against the Jews (Est 4). Xerxes forced Haman to honor Mordecai (Est 6). Mordecai exalted (Est 8–10). Established Purim (Est 9:18-32).

**MORE** → MOST
Ps 19: 11 **M** desirable than gold, than a hoard
69: 32 please the LORD **m** than oxen,
Mk 4: 25 the one who has, **m** will be given;
Lk 12: 23 For life is **m** than food and the body
1 Cor 12: 31 show you a still **m** excellent way.
Rev 21: 4 and there shall be no **m** death

**MORIAH**
Gn 22: 2 you love, and go to the land of **M**.
2 Chr 3: 1 LORD in Jerusalem on Mount **M**,

**MORNING**
Gn 1: 5 Evening came, and **m** followed—
Lam 3: 23 They are renewed each **m**—
Lk 24: 22 they were at the tomb early in the **m**
2 Pt 1: 19 and the **m** star rises in your hearts.
Rev 22: 16 of David, the bright **m** star."

**MORTAL**
1 Cor 15: 53 which is **m** must clothe itself
2 Cor 5: 4 so that what is **m** may be swallowed

**MOSES**
Levite; brother of Aaron (Ex 6:20; 1 Chr 6:3). Put in basket into Nile; discovered and raised by Pharaoh's daughter (Ex 2:1-10). Fled to Midian after killing Egyptian (Ex 2:11-15). Married to Zipporah, fathered Gershom (Ex 2:16-22).

Called by the LORD to deliver Israel (Ex 3–4). Pharaoh's resistance (Ex 5). Ten plagues (Ex 7–11). Passover and Exodus (Ex 12–13). Led Israel through Red Sea (Ex 14). Song of deliverance (Ex 15:1-21). Brought water from rock (Ex 17:1-7). Raised hands to defeat Amalekites (Ex 17:8-16). Delegated judges (Ex 18; Dt 1:9-18).

Received Law at Sinai (Ex 19–23; 25–31; Jn 1:17). Announced Law to Israel (Ex 19:7-8; 24; 35). Broke tablets because of golden calf (Ex 32; Dt 9). Saw glory of the LORD (Ex 33–34). Supervised building of tabernacle (Ex 36–40). Set apart Aaron and priests (Lv 8–9). Numbered tribes (Nm 1–4; 26). Opposed by Aaron and Miriam (Nm 12). Sent spies into Canaan (Nm 13). Announced forty years of wandering for failure to enter land (Nm 14). Opposed by Korah (Nm 16). Forbidden to enter land for striking rock (Nm 20:1-13; Dt 1:37). Lifted bronze snake for healing (Nm 21:4-9; Jn 3:14). Final address to Israel (Dt 1–33). Succeeded by Joshua (Nm 27:12-23; Dt 34). Death and burial by God (Dt 34:5-12). Praise of (Sir 45).

Law of (1 Kgs 2:3; Ezr 3:2; Mk 12:26; Lk 24:44). Book of (2 Chr 25:12; Neh 13:1). Song of (Ex 15:1-21; Rev 15:3). Prayer of (Ps 90).

**MOST** → MORE
Gn 14:18 He was a priest of God **M** High.
Ps 91:1 dwell in the shelter of the **M** High,
Mk 5:7 me, Jesus, Son of the **M** High God?
Col 4:5 making the **m** of the opportunity.
Jude 1:20 yourselves up in your **m** holy faith;

**MOTH**
Mt 6:19 earth, where **m** and decay destroy,

**MOTHER** → MOTHER'S, MOTHERS
Gn 2:24 why a man leaves his father and **m**
3:20 because she was the **m** of all
Ex 20:12 Honor your father and your **m**,
Jgs 5:7 arose, when I arose, a **m** in Israel.
Tb 4:3 Honor your **m**, and do not abandon
Prv 31:1 the instruction his **m** taught him:
Sir 3:6 who obey the Lord honor their **m**.
Is 66:13 As a **m** comforts her child, so I will
Mt 10:37 or **m** more than me is not worthy
Lk 14:26 me without hating his father and **m**,
Jn 2:3 ran short, the **m** of Jesus said to him,
19:27 to the disciple, "Behold, your **m**."
Gal 4:26 above is freeborn, and she is our **m**.
Eph 5:31 [his] **m** and be joined to his wife,
Rev 17:5 the great, the **m** of harlots

**MOTHER'S** → MOTHER
Jb 1:21 I came forth from my **m** womb,
Prv 1:8 and reject not your **m** teaching;
Jn 3:4 he cannot reenter his **m** womb

**MOTHERS** → MOTHER
Mk 10:30 and sisters and **m** and children

**MOUNT** → MOUNTAIN, MOUNTAINS
Ex 19:20 LORD came down upon **M** Sinai,
Dt 11:29 **M** Gerizim you shall pronounce the blessing, on **M** Ebal, the curse.
Ps 78:68 of Judah, **M** Zion which he loved.
Mi 4:7 shall be king over them on **M** Zion,
Zec 14:4 feet will stand on the **M** of Olives,
14:4 The **M** of Olives will be split in two
Mk 13:3 the **M** of Olives opposite the temple
Heb 12:22 you have approached **M** Zion
Rev 14:1 was the Lamb standing on **M** Zion,

**MOUNTAIN** → MOUNT
Ex 3:1 he came to the **m** of God, Horeb.
24:18 He was on the **m** for forty days
Is 2:2 The **m** of the LORD's house shall be established as the highest **m**
Dn 2:45 from the **m** without a hand being put
Mt 4:8 devil took him up to a very high **m**,
17:20 you will say to this **m**,
2 Pt 1:18 we were with him on the holy **m**.

**MOUNTAINS** → MOUNT
Gn 7:20 cubits higher than the submerged **m**.
Ps 125:2 As **m** surround Jerusalem,
Is 52:7 beautiful upon the **m** are the feet
1 Cor 13:2 if I have all faith so as to move **m**

Rev 16:20 island fled, and **m** disappeared.

**MOURN** → MOURNING
Eccl 3:4 a time to **m**, and a time to dance.
Sir 7:34 who weep, but **m** with those who **m**.
Zec 12:10 they will **m** for him as one mourns
Mt 5:4 Blessed are they who **m**, for they

**MOURNING** → MOURN
Ps 30:12 You changed my **m** into dancing;
Is 61:3 them oil of gladness instead of **m**,
Rev 21:4 there shall be no more death or **m**,

**MOUTH** → MOUTHS
Dt 8:3 forth from the **m** of the LORD.
Ps 19:15 the words of my **m** be acceptable,
Mt 4:4 comes forth from the **m** of God.' "
15:11 It is not what enters one's **m**
15:11 out of the **m** is what defiles one."
Jas 3:10 From the same **m** come blessing
Rev 19:15 Out of his **m** came a sharp sword

**MOUTHS** → MOUTH
Ps 115:5 They have **m** but do not speak,

**MUCH**
Eccl 12:12 in **m** study there is weariness
Lk 12:48 **M** will be required of the person entrusted with **m**,
Jn 12:24 but if it dies, it produces **m** fruit.

**MULTIPLY**
Gn 1:28 Be fertile and **m**; fill the earth
9:7 Be fertile, then, and **m**;

**MULTITUDE**
Jas 5:20 death and will cover a **m** of sins.
1 Pt 4:8 because love covers a **m** of sins.

**MURDER** → MURDERER, MURDERERS
Hos 4:2 lying, **m**, stealing and adultery break

**MURDERER** → MURDER
Nm 35:16 that person is a **m**, and the **m** must
Jn 8:44 He was a **m** from the beginning

**MURDERERS** → MURDER
Rev 21:8 the depraved, **m**, the unchaste,

**MUSTARD**
Mt 17:20 you have faith the size of a **m** seed,
Mk 4:31 It is like a **m** seed that, when it is

**MUTUAL**
Rom 12:10 love one another with **m** affection;
Heb 13:1 Let **m** love continue.

**MYRRH**
Mt 2:11 gifts of gold, frankincense, and **m**.
Mk 15:23 gave him wine drugged with **m**,

**MYSTERY**
Dn 2:19 During the night the **m** was revealed
Rom 11:25 want you to be unaware of this **m**,
1 Cor 15:51 Behold, I tell you a **m**. We shall not
Eph 3:4 my insight into the **m** of Christ,
1 Tm 3:9 holding fast to the **m** of the faith
Rev 17:5 which is a **m**, "Babylon the great,

**MYTHS**
2 Pt 1:16 did not follow cleverly devised **m**

## N

**NAAMAN**
Aramean general whose leprosy was cleansed by Elisha (2 Kgs 5; Lk 4:27).

**NABAL**

Wealthy Carmelite the LORD killed for refusing to help David (1 Sm 25). David married Abigail, his widow (1 Sm 25:39-42).

**NABOTH**

Jezreelite killed for his vineyard (1 Kgs 21). Ahab's family punished (1 Kgs 21:17-24; 2 Kgs 9:21-37).

**NADAB**

1. Firstborn of Aaron (Ex 6:23); killed with Abihu for offering unauthorized fire (Lv 10; Nm 3:4).

2. Son of Jeroboam I; king of Israel (1 Kgs 15:25-32).

**NAHUM**

Prophet against Nineveh (Na 1:1; Tb 14:4).

**NAILING** → NAILS
Col 2: 14 it from our midst, **n** it to the cross;

**NAILS** → NAILING
Jn 20: 25 I see the mark of the **n** in his hands

**NAKED** → NAKEDNESS
Gn 2: 25 The man and his wife were both **n**,
Jb 1: 21 "**N** I came forth from my mother's womb, and **n** shall I go back there.
2 Cor 5: 3 taken it off, we shall not be found **n**.

**NAKEDNESS** → NAKED
Rom 8: 35 or famine, or **n**, or peril,

**NAME** → NAMES
Gn 2: 19 each living creature was then its **n**.
4: 26 began to invoke the LORD by **n**.
12: 2 I will make your **n** great, so that you
Ex 3: 15 This is my **n** forever; this is my title
20: 7 anyone who invokes his **n** in vain.
34: 5 him there and proclaimed the **n**,
Dt 12: 11 place for his **n** you shall bring all
Ps 9: 11 Those who know your **n** trust
Prv 18: 10 The **n** of the LORD is a strong
Is 42: 8 I am the LORD, LORD is my **n**;
Zec 14: 9 and the LORD's **n** the only one.
Mt 1: 21 a son and you are to **n** him Jesus,
6: 9 in heaven, hallowed be your **n**,
28: 19 them in the **n** of the Father,
Jn 1: 12 God, to those who believe in his **n**,
20: 31 belief you may have life in his **n**.
Acts 4: 12 is there any other **n** under heaven
Phil 2: 9 bestowed on him the **n** that is above every **n**,
Rev 13: 17 the stamped image of the beast's **n** or the number that stood for its **n**.
19: 13 his **n** was called the Word of God.
22: 4 and his **n** will be on their foreheads.

**NAMES** → NAME
Gn 2: 20 The man gave **n** to all the tame
Ex 28: 9 engrave on them the **n** of the sons
Mt 10: 2 The **n** of the twelve apostles are
Rev 21: 14 were inscribed the twelve **n**

**NAOMI**

Wife of Elimelech, mother-in-law of Ruth (Ru 1:2, 4). Left Bethlehem for Moab during famine (Ru 1:1). Returned a widow, with Ruth (Ru 1:6-22). Advised Ruth to seek marriage with Boaz (Ru 2:17–3:4). Cared for Ruth's son Obed (Ru 4:13-17).

**NAPHTALI**

Son of Jacob by Bilhah (Gn 30:8; 35:25; 1 Chr 2:2). Tribe of blessed (Gn 49:21; Dt 33:23), numbered (Nm 1:43; 26:50), allotted land (Jos 19:32-39; Ez 48:3), failed to fully possess (Jgs 1:33), supported Deborah (Jgs 4:10; 5:18), David (1 Chr 12:34), 12,000 from (Rev 7:6).

**NARROW**
Lk 13: 24 "Strive to enter through the **n** door,

**NATHAN**

Prophet and chronicler of Israel's history (1 Chr 29:29; 2 Chr 9:29). Announced the Davidic covenant (2 Sm 7; 1 Chr 17). Denounced David's sin with Bathsheba (2 Sm 12). Supported Solomon (1 Kgs 1).

**NATHANAEL** → =BARTHOLOMEW?

Apostle (Jn 1:45-49; 21:2). Probably also called Bartholomew (Mt 10:3).

**NATION** → NATIONS
Gn 12: 2 I will make of you a great **n**, and I
Ex 32: 10 Then I will make of you a great **n**.
Ps 33: 12 Blessed is the **n** whose God is
Prv 14: 34 Justice exalts a **n**, but sin is
Is 2: 4 One **n** shall not raise the sword
66: 8 or a **n** be born in a single moment?
Mt 24: 7 **N** will rise against **n**, and kingdom
1 Pt 2: 9 a holy **n**, a people of his own,

**NATIONS** → NATION
Gn 18: 18 and all the **n** of the earth are to find
2 Kgs 17: 15 the surrounding **n** whom
Ps 47: 9 God rules over the **n**; God sits
Is 2: 2 All **n** shall stream toward it.
42: 1 he shall bring forth justice to the **n**.
Am 9: 12 and all **n** claimed in my name—
Mt 28: 19 and make disciples of all **n**,
Rom 4: 18 become "the father of many **n**,"
Rev 22: 2 the trees serve as medicine for the **n**.

**NATURAL** → NATURE
Rom 11: 21 if God did not spare the **n** branches,

**NATURE** → NATURAL
2 Pt 1: 4 may come to share in the divine **n**,

**NAZARETH**
Mt 2: 23 went and dwelt in a town called **N**,
Jn 1: 46 anything good come from **N**?"

**NAZIRITE**
Nm 6: 2 women solemnly take the **n** vow

**NEAR**
Dt 30: 14 No, it is something very **n** to you,
Is 55: 6 found, call upon him while he is **n**.
Zep 1: 14 **N** is the great day of the LORD,
Jas 4: 8 Draw **n** to God, and he will draw **n**
Rev 22: 10 book, for the appointed time is **n**.

**NEBUCHADNEZZAR**

Babylonian king, also spelled Nebuchadrezzar. Subdued and exiled Judah (2 Kgs 24–25; 2 Chr 36; Jer 39). Dreams interpreted by Daniel (Dn 2; 4). Worshiped God (Dn 3:28-29; 4:34-37).

**NECK** → STIFF-NECKED
Prv 3: 22 soul, and an adornment for your **n**.
Mt 18: 6 a great millstone hung around his **n**

**NECO**

Pharaoh who killed Josiah (2 Kgs 23:29-30; 2 Chr 35:20-22), deposed Jehoahaz (2 Kgs 23:33-35; 2 Chr 36:3-4).

**NEED** → NEEDY
Mt 6: 8 knows what you **n** before you ask
1 Cor 12: 21 head to the feet, "I do not **n** you."
1 Jn 2: 27 you do not **n** anyone to teach you.

**NEEDLE**
Lk 18: 25 pass through the eye of a **n** than

**NEEDY** → NEED
1 Sm 2: 8 He raises the **n** from the dust;
Ps 113: 7 He raises the **n** from the dust,

**NEGLECT**
1 Tm 4: 14 Do not **n** the gift you have,

**NEHEMIAH**
Cupbearer of Artaxerxes (Neh 2:1); governor of Israel (Neh 8:9). Returned to Jerusalem to rebuild walls (Neh 2–6). With Ezra, reestablished worship (Neh 8). Prayer confessing nation's sin (Neh 9). Dedicated wall (Neh 12). Story of the miraculous fire (2 Mc 1).

**NEIGHBOR**
Lv 19: 18 You shall love your **n** as yourself.
Dt 5: 20 dishonest witness against your **n**.
Mt 19: 19 shall love your **n** as yourself.' "
Jas 2: 8 shall love your **n** as yourself,"

**NESTS**
Mt 8: 20 dens and birds of the sky have **n**,

**NEVER**
Ps 15: 5 acts like this shall **n** be shaken.
Dn 2: 44 a kingdom that shall **n** be destroyed
Mt 7: 23 to them solemnly, 'I **n** knew you.
Jn 10: 28 eternal life, and they shall **n** perish.
1 Cor 13: 8 Love **n** fails. If there are prophecies,
Heb 13: 5 "I will **n** forsake you or abandon

**NEW**
Ex 1: 8 Then a **n** king, who knew nothing
Ps 33: 3 Sing to him a **n** song;
Eccl 1: 9 Nothing is **n** under the sun!
Is 43: 19 See, I am doing something **n**!
65: 17 See, I am creating **n** heavens and a **n** earth;
Jer 31: 31 I will make a **n** covenant
Ez 36: 26 I will give you a **n** heart, and a **n** spirit I will put within you.
Mt 9: 17 People do not put **n** wine into old
9: 17 Rather, they pour **n** wine into fresh
Mk 1: 27 A **n** teaching with authority.
Lk 22: 20 "This cup is the **n** covenant in my
Jn 13: 34 I give you a **n** commandment:
2 Cor 3: 6 us as ministers of a **n** covenant,
Col 3: 10 and have put on the **n** self, which is
Heb 8: 8 I will conclude a **n** covenant
1 Pt 1: 3 his great mercy gave us a **n** birth
2 Pt 3: 13 we await **n** heavens and a **n** earth in which righteousness
1 Jn 2: 7 I am writing no **n** commandment
Rev 21: 1 Then I saw a **n** heaven and a **n** earth.
21: 2 saw the holy city, a **n** Jerusalem,
21: 5 said, "Behold, I make all things **n**."

**NEWS**
Is 52: 7 the feet of the one bringing good **n**,
Mt 11: 5 poor have the good **n** proclaimed

**NICODEMUS**
Pharisee who visted Jesus at night (Jn 3). Argued for fair treatment of Jesus (Jn 7:50-52). With Joseph, prepared Jesus for burial (Jn 19:38-42).

**NIGHT** → NIGHTS
Gn 1: 5 and the darkness he called "**n**."
Ex 13: 21 at **n** by means of a column of fire
13: 21 they could travel both day and **n**.
Jos 1: 8 Recite it by day and by **n**, that you
Mt 24: 43 the house had known the hour of **n**
1 Thes 5: 2 the Lord will come like a thief at **n**.
Rev 22: 5 **N** will be no more, nor will they

**NIGHTS** → NIGHT
Gn 7: 12 forty **n** heavy rain poured down
Ex 24: 18 mountain for forty days and forty **n**.
1 Kgs 19: 8 and forty **n** to the mountain of God,
Mt 4: 2 He fasted for forty days and forty **n**,
12: 40 of the whale three days and three **n**,
12: 40 of the earth three days and three **n**.

**NINEVEH**
Jon 1: 2 Set out for the great city of **N**,
Na 1: 1 Oracle concerning **N**. The book
Mt 12: 41 the men of **N** will arise with this

**NOAH**
Righteous man (Ez 14:14, 20) called to build ark (Gn 6–8; Heb 11:7; 1 Pt 3:20; 2 Pt 2:5). God's covenant with (Gn 9:1-17). Drunkenness of (Gn 9:18-23). Blessed sons, cursed Canaan (Gn 9:24-27). Praised (Sir 44:17-18).

**NOISE**
Ex 32: 17 Joshua heard the **n** of the people

**NOON**
Mk 15: 33 At **n** darkness came over the whole

**NORTH**
Jer 4: 6 Disaster I bring from the **n**,
Dn 11: 6 to the king of the **n** to carry

**NOTHING**
Eccl 1: 9 **N** is new under the sun!
Sir 39: 20 To him, **n** is small or insignificant,
39: 20 and **n** too wonderful or hard
Jer 32: 17 **n** is too difficult for you.
Mt 17: 20 **N** will be impossible for you."
Jn 15: 5 because without me you can do **n**.
1 Cor 13: 2 but do not have love, I am **n**.

**NULLIFY**
Rom 3: 3 Will their infidelity **n** the fidelity
Gal 2: 21 I do not **n** the grace of God;

**NUMBER** → NUMBERED, NUMEROUS
Rom 11: 25 part, until the full **n** of the Gentiles
Rev 13: 18 who understands can calculate the **n**
13: 18 His **n** is six hundred and sixty-six.

**NUMBERED** → NUMBER
2 Sm 24: 10 David regretted having **n** the people.

**NUMEROUS** → NUMBER
Ex 1: 9 and become more **n** than we are!
Zec 10: 8 and they will be as **n** as before.

## O

**OATH**
Dt 7: 8 his fidelity to the **o** he had sworn
Ps 132: 11 The LORD swore an **o** to David
Heb 7: 20 not without the taking of an **o**—
7: 20 others became priests without an **o**,

**OBADIAH**
1. Believer who sheltered 100 prophets from Jezebel (1 Kgs 18:1-16).
2. Prophet against Edom (Ob 1).

**OBEDIENCE** → OBEY
Rom 5: 19 so through the **o** of one the many
Heb 5: 8 he learned **o** from what he suffered;

**OBEDIENT** → OBEY
Phil 2: 8 himself, becoming **o** to death,

**OBEY** → OBEDIENCE, OBEDIENT, OBEYED
Acts 5: 29 "We must **o** God rather than men.
Eph 6: 1 **o** your parents [in the Lord], for this

**OBEYED** → OBEY
Heb 11: 8 faith Abraham **o** when he was called

**OBSERVE**
Lv 20: 8 careful, therefore, to **o** my statutes.

**OBSTACLE**
1 Cor 9: 12 so as not to place an **o** to the gospel

**OBTAIN** → OBTAINED
2 Tm 2: 10 they too may **o** the salvation that is

**OBTAINED** → OBTAIN
Heb 8: 6 Now he has **o** so much more

**ODOR**
Gn 8: 21 the LORD smelled the sweet **o**,

**OFFENSE**
Mk 6: 3 And they took **o** at him.

**OFFER** → OFFERING, OFFERINGS
Ps 4: 6 **O** fitting sacrifices and trust
Heb 9: 25 that he might **o** himself repeatedly,

**OFFERING** → OFFER
Gn 4: 4 with favor on Abel and his **o**,
Ps 40: 7 Sacrifice and **o** you do not want;
Eph 5: 2 over for us as a sacrificial **o** to God
Heb 10: 14 one **o** he has made perfect forever

**OFFERINGS** → OFFER
Mk 12: 33 is worth more than all burnt **o**

**OFFSPRING**
Gn 3: 15 and between your **o** and hers;

**OHOLIAB**
Craftsman who worked on the tabernacle (Ex 31:6; 35:34; 36:1-2; 38:23).

**OIL**
Ex 25: 6 **o** for the light;
25: 6 spices for the anointing **o**
Dt 14: 23 wine and **o**, as well as the firstlings
Ps 23: 5 You anoint my head with **o**;
Heb 1: 9 anointed you with the **o** of gladness
Jas 5: 14 anoint [him] with **o** in the name

**OLD**
Gn 21: 7 have borne him a son in his **o** age."
Ps 74: 12 are my king from of **o**,
Dn 13: 61 They rose up against the two **o** men,
Mk 2: 22 pours new wine into **o** wineskins.
Rom 4: 19 he was almost a hundred years **o**)
Eph 4: 22 you should put away the **o** self

**OLIVE** → OLIVES
Zec 4: 3 And beside it are two **o** trees,
Rom 11: 17 a wild **o** shoot, were grafted in their
11: 17 to share in the rich root of the **o** tree,
Rev 11: 4 These are the two **o** trees

**OLIVES** → OLIVE
Zec 14: 4 feet will stand on the Mount of **O**,
14: 4 The Mount of **O** will be split in two
Mt 24: 3 he was sitting on the Mount of **O**,

**OMEGA**
Rev 1: 8 "I am the Alpha and the **O**,"

**OMRI**
King of Israel (1 Kgs 16:21-26).

**ONCE** → ONE
Ex 30: 10 **O** a year Aaron shall purge its
Rom 6: 10 death, he died to sin **o** and for all;
Heb 7: 27 he did that **o** for all when he offered
9: 27 appointed that human beings die **o**,

**ONE** → FIRST, ONCE
Gn 2: 24 and the two of them become **o** body.
Zec 14: 9 day the LORD will be the only **o**,
14: 9 and the LORD's name the only **o**.
Jn 10: 30 The Father and I are **o**."
1 Cor 12: 13 in **o** Spirit we were all baptized into **o** body,
12: 13 were all given to drink of **o** Spirit.
Gal 3: 28 for you are all **o** in Christ Jesus.
Eph 4: 5 **o** Lord, **o** faith, **o** baptism;

**ONLY**
Gn 22: 2 Take your son Isaac, your **o** one,
1 Kgs 18: 22 "I am the **o** remaining prophet
Jn 1: 14 the glory as of the Father's **o** Son,
3: 16 the world that he gave his **o** Son,
1 Tm 1: 17 invisible, the **o** God,
1 Jn 4: 9 God sent his **o** Son into the world so

**OPEN** → OPENED, OPENS
Is 53: 7 he submitted and did not **o** his mouth;
Rev 5: 2 "Who is worthy to **o** the scroll

**OPENED** → OPEN
Gn 3: 7 the eyes of both of them were **o**,
Dn 7: 10 convened, and the books were **o**.
Lk 11: 9 knock and the door will be **o** to you.
Heb 10: 20 living way he **o** for us through
Rev 20: 12 the throne, and scrolls were **o**.
20: 12 Then another scroll was **o**, the book

**OPENS** → OPEN
Rev 3: 7 who **o** and no one shall close,

**OPPORTUNITY**
Mt 26: 16 he looked for an **o** to hand him over.
Gal 5: 13 do not use this freedom as an **o**

**OPPRESS** → OPPRESSED, OPPRESSION
2 Sm 7: 10 nor shall the wicked ever again **o**

**OPPRESSED** → OPPRESS
Gn 15: 13 and **o** for four hundred years.
Ex 1: 12 Yet the more they were **o**, the more
Ps 146: 7 secures justice for the **o**, who gives

**OPPRESSION** → OPPRESS
Ez 45: 9 Put away violence and **o**, and do

**ORDER**
Heb 5: 10 according to the **o** of Melchizedek.

**ORIGIN**
Mt 21: 26 'Of human **o**,' we fear the crowd,
Acts 5: 38 or this activity is of human **o**, it will

**ORNAMENTS**
Ex 33: 6 the Israelites stripped off their **o**.

**ORPHANS**
Jas 1: 27 to care for **o** and widows in their

**OTHER** → OTHERS
Ex 20: 3 shall not have **o** gods beside me.
Jgs 2: 19 their ancestors, following **o** gods,
2 Kgs 17: 7 They venerated **o** gods,
Is 45: 5 there is no **o**, there is no God
Mt 6: 24 will either hate one and love the **o**,
6: 24 be devoted to one and despise the **o**.

**OTHERS** → OTHER
Lk 6: 31 Do to **o** as you would have them do
Phil 2: 3 humbly regard **o** as more important

**OTHNIEL**
Nephew of Caleb (Jos 15:15-19; Jgs 1:12-15). Judge who freed Israel from Aram (Jgs 3:7-11).

**OUTSIDE**
Lk 11: 39 Although you cleanse the **o**
Heb 13: 12 Jesus also suffered **o** the gate,
Rev 22: 15 **O** are the dogs, the sorcerers,

**OUTSTRETCHED** → STRETCH
Ex 6: 6 I will redeem you by my **o** arm
Ps 136: 12 With mighty hand and **o** arm, for his
Jer 27: 5 by my great power, with my **o** arm;

**OVERCOME**
Jn 1: 5 and the darkness has not **o** it.

**OVERSEERS**
Acts 20: 28 the holy Spirit has appointed you **o**,

**OVERSHADOW**
Lk 1: 35 power of the Most High will **o** you.

**OWE**
Mt 18: 28 demanding, 'Pay back what you **o**.'
Rom 13: 8 **O** nothing to anyone, except to love

**OWN**
Is 53: 6 like sheep, all following our **o** way;
Jer 31: 30 shall die because of their **o** iniquity:
Jn 1: 11 He came to what was his **o**, but his **o** people did not accept him.
10: 18 from me, but I lay it down on my **o**.
1 Cor 6: 19 God, and that you are not your **o**?

**OX**
Dt 25: 4 You shall not muzzle an **o** when it
Is 65: 25 and the lion shall eat hay like the **o**—
Ez 1: 10 the face of an **o**, and each had
1 Tm 5: 18 "You shall not muzzle an **o** when it

## P

**PAGANS**
1 Cor 12: 2 how, when you were **p**, you were

**PAIN** → PAINS
Gn 3: 16 in **p** you shall bring forth children.
Is 53: 4 our **p** that he bore, our sufferings
1 Pt 2: 19 For whenever anyone bears the **p**
Rev 21: 4 wailing or **p**, [for] the old order has

**PAINS** → PAIN
Rom 8: 22 groaning in labor **p** even until now;
1 Thes 5: 3 them, like labor **p** upon a pregnant

**PALM** → PALMS
Jn 12: 13 they took **p** branches and went
Rev 7: 9 holding **p** branches in their hands.

**PALMS** → PALM
Is 49: 16 the **p** of my hands I have engraved

**PARABLE** → PARABLES
Mt 13: 18 "Hear then the **p** of the sower.

**PARABLES** → PARABLE; See also JESUS: PARABLES
Mt 13: 35 "I will open my mouth in **p**, I will

**PARADISE**
Lk 23: 43 today you will be with me in **P**."
2 Cor 12: 4 was caught up into **P** and heard

**PARALYTIC** → PARALYZED
Mt 9: 2 he said to the **p**, "Courage,

**PARALYZED** → PARALYTIC
Acts 8: 7 many **p** and crippled people were

**PARCHMENTS**
2 Tm 4: 13 papyrus rolls, and especially the **p**.

**PARDON**
Ex 34: 9 yet **p** our wickedness and sins,

**PARENTS**
Eph 6: 1 Children, obey your **p** [in the Lord],

**PARTAKE**
1 Cor 10: 17 body, for we all **p** of the one loaf.

**PARTIALITY**
Prv 24: 23 To show **p** in judgment is not good.
Rom 2: 11 There is no **p** with God.

**PARTNERSHIP**
2 Cor 6: 14 For what **p** do righteousness

**PASHHUR**
Priest; opponent of Jeremiah (Jer 20:1-6).

**PASS** → PASSED, PASSING
Ex 12: 13 Seeing the blood, I will **p** over you;
33: 19 make all my goodness **p** before you,
Am 5: 17 when I **p** through your midst,
Mt 24: 35 Heaven and earth will **p** away,
24: 35 but my words will not **p** away.
2 Pt 3: 10 then the heavens will **p** away

**PASSED** → PASS
Gn 15: 17 which **p** between those pieces.
Ex 12: 27 who **p** over the houses
33: 22 you with my hand until I have **p** by.
2 Cor 5: 17 the old things have **p** away;
1 Jn 3: 14 We know that we have **p** from death
Rev 21: 4 [for] the old order has **p** away."

**PASSING** → PASS
1 Cor 7: 31 world in its present form is **p** away.
1 Jn 2: 17 and its enticement are **p** away.

**PASSIONS**
Gal 5: 24 have crucified their flesh with its **p**

**PASSOVER**
Ex 12: 11 it in a hurry. It is the LORD's **P**.
Dt 16: 1 by keeping the **P** of the LORD,
Mk 14: 12 when they sacrificed the **P** lamb,
14: 12 and prepare for you to eat the **P**?"

**PASTORS**
Eph 4: 11 others as **p** and teachers,

**PASTURES**
Ps 23: 2 In green **p** he makes me lie down;

**PATH** → PATHS
Ps 16: 11 You will show me the **p** to life,
119: 105 lamp for my feet, a light for my **p**.
Mt 13: 4 some seed fell on the **p**, and birds

**PATHS** → PATH
Prv 3: 6 and he will make straight your **p**.
Mt 3: 3 the Lord, make straight his **p**.' "
Heb 12: 13 Make straight **p** for your feet,

**PATIENCE** → PATIENT
Mi 2: 7 of Jacob, "Is the LORD short of **p**;
Rom 2: 4 and **p** in low esteem,
Gal 5: 22 joy, peace, **p**, kindness, generosity,
2 Pt 3: 15 And consider the **p** of our Lord as

**PATIENT** → PATIENCE
1 Cor 13: 4 Love is **p**, love is kind. It is not
2 Pt 3: 9 but he is **p** with you, not wishing

**PATTERN**
Ex 25: 40 them according to the **p** shown you
Heb 8: 5 according to the **p** shown you

**PAUL** → =SAUL
Also called Saul (Acts 13:9). Pharisee from Tarsus (Acts 9:11; Phil 3:5). Apostle (Gal 1). At stoning of Stephen (Acts 8:1). Persecuted Church (Acts 9:1-2; Gal 1:13). Vision of Jesus on road to Damascus (Acts 9:4-9; 26:12-18). In Arabia (Gal 1:17). Preached

in Damascus; escaped death through the wall in a basket (Acts 9:19-25). In Jerusalem; back to Tarsus (Acts 9:26-30).

Brought to Antioch by Barnabas (Acts 11:22-26). First missionary journey to Cyprus and Galatia (Acts 13–14). Stoned at Lystra (Acts 14:19-20). At Jerusalem council (Acts 15). Split with Barnabas over Mark (Acts 15:36-41).

Second missionary journey with Silas (Acts 16–20). Called to Macedonia (Acts 16:6-10). Freed from prison in Philippi (Acts 16:16-40). In Thessalonica (Acts 17:1-9). Speech in Athens (Acts 17:16-33). In Corinth (Acts 18). In Ephesus (Acts 19). Return to Jerusalem (Acts 20). Farewell to Ephesian elders (Acts 20:13-38). Arrival in Jerusalem (Acts 21:1-26). Arrested (Acts 21:27-36). Addressed crowds (Acts 22), Sanhedrin (Acts 23:1-11). Sent to Caesarea (Acts 23:12-35). Trial before Felix (Acts 24), Festus (Acts 25:1-12). Before Agrippa (Acts 25:13–26:32). Voyage to Rome; shipwreck (Acts 27). Arrival in Rome (Acts 28).

**PAVEMENT**
Jn 19: 13 bench in the place called Stone **P**,

**PAY** → REPAY
Dt 24: 15 day you shall **p** the servant's wages
Mt 22: 17 Is it lawful to **p** the census tax
Rom 13: 7 **P** to all their dues, taxes to whom

**PEACE** → PEACEMAKERS
Lv 26: 6 I will establish **p** in the land,
Ps 122: 6 For the **p** of Jerusalem pray:
Is 26: 3 With firm purpose you maintain **p**; in **p**, because of our trust
57: 19 creating words of comfort. **P**!
57: 21 There is no **p** for the wicked!
Jer 6: 14 "**P**, **p**!" they say, though there is no **p**.
Lk 2: 14 and on earth **p** to those on whom his
Jn 14: 27 **P** I leave with you; my **p** I give
Rom 16: 20 of **p** will quickly crush Satan under
1 Cor 14: 33 is not the God of disorder but of **p**.
Gal 5: 22 of the Spirit is love, joy, **p**, patience,
Eph 4: 3 of the spirit through the bond of **p**:
Phil 4: 7 Then the **p** of God that surpasses all
2 Tm 2: 22 and **p**, along with those who call

**PEACEMAKERS** → PEACE
Mt 5: 9 Blessed are the **p**, for they will be

**PEARL** → PEARLS
Mt 13: 46 When he finds a **p** of great price,
Rev 21: 21 of the gates made from a single **p**;

**PEARLS** → PEARL
Mt 7: 6 or throw your **p** before swine,

**PEKAH**
King of Israel (2 Kgs 15:25-31; 2 Chr 28:6; Is 7:1).

**PEKAHIAH**
Son of Menahem; king of Israel (2 Kgs 15:22-26).

**PENALTY**
Rom 1: 27 their own persons the due **p** for their

**PENTECOST**
Acts 2: 1 When the time for **P** was fulfilled,

**PEOPLE** → PEOPLES
Ex 5: 1 Let my **p** go, that they may hold
33: 13 this nation is indeed your own **p**.
Dt 4: 20 that you might be his **p**, his heritage,
Ru 1: 16 Your **p** shall be my **p** and your God,
2 Sm 5: 2 You shall shepherd my **p** Israel;
Ps 29: 11 the LORD give might to his **p**; may the LORD bless his **p**
125: 2 LORD surrounds his **p** both now
Is 40: 1 give comfort to my **p**, says your
42: 6 and set you as a covenant for the **p**,
53: 8 living, struck for the sins of his **p**.
Jer 50: 6 Lost sheep were my **p**,
Dn 9: 24 weeks are decreed for your **p**
Zec 13: 9 "They are my **p**," and they will
Mt 1: 21 because he will save his **p**
Jn 11: 50 one man should die instead of the **p**,
18: 14 man should die rather than the **p**.
Rom 9: 25 who were not my **p** I will call 'my **p**,'
Heb 8: 10 their God, and they shall be my **p**.
1 Pt 2: 9 a holy nation, a **p** of his own,

**PEOPLES** → PEOPLE
Gn 17: 16 and rulers of **p** will issue from her.
Ps 117: 1 Extol him, all you **p**!

**PERFECT** → PERFECTER
Ps 19: 8 The law of the LORD is **p**,
Mt 5: 48 So be **p**, just as your heavenly Father is **p**.
Rom 12: 2 what is good and pleasing and **p**.
2 Cor 12: 9 for power is made **p** in weakness."
Heb 5: 9 and when he was made **p**,
1 Jn 4: 18 **p** love drives out fear because fear
4: 18 and so one who fears is not yet **p**

**PERFECTER** → PERFECT
Heb 12: 2 on Jesus, the leader and **p** of faith.

**PERISH** → PERISHABLE
Jos 23: 13 until you **p** from this good land
Est 4: 16 contrary to the law. If I **p**, I **p**!"
Jn 3: 16 who believes in him might not **p**
2 Pt 3: 9 not wishing that any should **p**

**PERISHABLE** → PERISH
1 Cor 9: 25 They do it to win a **p** crown, but we
1 Pt 1: 23 not from **p** but from imperishable

**PERSECUTE** → PERSECUTED, PERSECUTION
Mt 5: 44 and pray for those who **p** you,
Rom 12: 14 Bless those who **p** [you],

**PERSECUTED** → PERSECUTE
Jn 15: 20 If they **p** me, they will
2 Cor 4: 9 **p**, but not abandoned;
2 Tm 3: 12 religiously in Christ Jesus will be **p**.

**PERSECUTION** → PERSECUTE
Mt 13: 21 or **p** comes because of the word,
Rom 8: 35 or distress, or **p**, or famine,

**PERSEVERE**
Rom 12: 12 endure in affliction, **p** in prayer.

**PERSIA**
Ezr 1: 1 spirit of Cyrus king of **P** to issue

**PESTILENCE**
Dt 32: 24 and consuming fever and bitter **p**,
Ps 91: 6 Nor the **p** that roams in darkness,

**PETER** → =CEPHAS, =SIMON
Apostle, brother of Andrew, also called Simon (Mt 10:2; Mk 3:16; Lk 6:14; Acts 1:13), and Cephas (Jn 1:42). Confession of Christ (Mt 16:13-20; Mk 8:27-30; Lk 9:18-27). At transfiguration (Mt 17:1-8; Mk 9:2-8; Lk 9:28-36; 2 Pt 1:16-18). Caught fish with coin (Mt 17:24-27). Denial of Jesus predicted (Mt 26:31-35; Mk 14:27-31; Lk 22:31-34; Jn 13:31-38). Denied Jesus (Mt 26:69-75; Mk 14:66-72; Lk 22:54-62; Jn 18:15-27). Commissioned by Jesus to shepherd his flock (Jn 21:15-23).

Speech at Pentecost (Acts 2). Healed beggar (Acts 3:1-10). Speech at temple (Acts 3:11-26), before Sanhedrin (Acts 4:1-22). In Samaria (Acts 8:14-25). Sent by vision to Cornelius (Acts 10). Announced salvation of Gentiles in Jerusalem (Acts 11; 15). Freed from prison (Acts 12). Inconsistency at Antioch (Gal 2:11-21). At Jerusalem Council (Acts 15).

**PHARAOH** → PHARAOH'S
Gn 41: 14 **P** therefore had Joseph summoned,

Ex 3: 11 "Who am I that I should go to **P**
14: 17 I will receive glory through **P**
Rom 9: 17 For the scripture says to **P**, "This is

**PHARAOH'S** → PHARAOH
Heb 11: 24 be known as the son of **P** daughter;

**PHARISEE** → PHARISEES
Lk 11: 37 a **P** invited him to dine at his home.
Jn 3: 1 there was a **P** named Nicodemus,
Acts 5: 34 But a **P** in the Sanhedrin named
Phil 3: 5 in observance of the law a **P**,

**PHARISEES** → PHARISEE
Mt 5: 20 surpasses that of the scribes and **P**,
16: 6 beware of the leaven of the **P**
23: 13 you, scribes and **P**, you hypocrites.

**PHILEMON**
Phlm 1: 1 brother, to **P**, our beloved and our

**PHILIP**
1. Apostle (Mt 10:3; Mk 3:18; Lk 6:14; Jn 1:43-48; 14:8; Acts 1:13).
2. Deacon (Acts 6:1-7); evangelist in Samaria (Acts 8:4-25), to Ethiopian (Acts 8:26-40).

**PHILISTINE** → PHILISTINES
1 Sm 17: 37 me from the hand of this **P**."

**PHILISTINES** → PHILISTINE
Gn 26: 1 Abimelech, king of the **P** in Gerar.
1 Sm 5: 1 The **P**, having captured the ark
17: 1 The **P** rallied their forces for battle
2 Sm 8: 1 David defeated the **P** and subdued
Am 1: 8 and the last of the **P** shall perish,

**PHILOSOPHERS** → PHILOSOPHY
Acts 17: 18 Stoic **p** engaged him in discussion.

**PHILOSOPHY** → PHILOSOPHERS
Col 2: 8 seductive **p** according to human

**PHINEHAS**
1. Grandson of Aaron (Ex 6:25; Jos 22:30-32). Zeal for the LORD (Nm 25:7-13; Ps 106:30).
2. A wicked priest (1 Sm 1:3; 2:12-17; 4:1-19).

**PHOEBE**
Rom 16: 1 I commend to you **P** our sister,

**PHYSICAL**
1 Tm 4: 8 while **p** training is of limited value,

**PHYSICIAN**
Mt 9: 12 who are well do not need a **p**,
Col 4: 14 Luke the beloved **p** sends greetings,

**PIECES**
Gn 15: 17 which passed between those **p**.
Lk 20: 18 on that stone will be dashed to **p**;

**PIERCED**
Jn 19: 37 look upon him whom they have **p**."
Rev 1: 7 will see him, even those who **p** him.

**PIG**
Dt 14: 8 And the **p**, which indeed has

**PILATE**
Governor of Judea. Questioned Jesus (Mt 27:1-26; Mk 15:15; Lk 22:66–23:25; Jn 18:28–19:16); sent him to Herod (Lk 23:6-12); consented to his crucifixion when crowds chose Barabbas (Mt 27:15-26; Mk 15:6-15; Lk 23:13-25; Jn 19:1-10).

**PILLAR**
Gn 19: 26 and she was turned into a **p** of salt.

**PIT**
Ps 103: 4 Who redeems your life from the **p**,

**PITY**
Dt 7: 16 You are not to look on them with **p**,
Hos 1: 6 I will no longer feel **p** for the house

**PLACE** → PLACES
Ex 26: 33 divides the holy **p** from the holy
Ps 24: 3 Who can stand in his holy **p**?
Jn 14: 3 And if I go and prepare a **p** for you,

**PLACES** → PLACE
Lv 26: 30 I will demolish your high **p**,
Ps 78: 58 They enraged him with their high **p**,

**PLAGUE** → PLAGUES
Zec 14: 12 this will be the **p**
Rev 11: 6 with any **p** as often as they wish.

**PLAGUES** → PLAGUE
Hos 13: 14 Where are your **p**, O death!
Rev 15: 1 seven angels with the seven last **p**,
22: 18 to him the **p** described in this book,

**PLAIN**
Gn 13: 12 settled among the cities of the **P**,
Is 40: 4 The rugged land shall be a **p**,

**PLANNED**
Is 46: 11 I have **p** it, and I will do it.

**PLANT** → PLANTED
Gn 1: 29 I give you every seed-bearing **p**
Eccl 3: 2 a time to **p**, and a time to uproot the **p**.

**PLANTED** → PLANT
Gn 2: 8 The LORD God **p** a garden
Ps 1: 3 He is like a tree **p** near streams
1 Cor 3: 6 I **p**, Apollos watered, but God

**PLEASE** → PLEASED, PLEASES, PLEASING, PLEASURE
Ps 69: 32 will **p** the LORD more than oxen,
Sir 2: 16 who fear the Lord seek to **p** him;
Rom 8: 8 who are in the flesh cannot **p** God.
15: 3 For Christ did not **p** himself;
1 Cor 10: 33 just as I try to **p** everyone in every
1 Thes 4: 1 conduct yourselves to **p** God—
Heb 11: 6 faith it is impossible to **p** him,

**PLEASED** → PLEASE
Mi 6: 7 Will the LORD be **p**
Mt 3: 17 Son, with whom I am well **p**."
Col 1: 19 him all the fullness was **p** to dwell,
2 Pt 1: 17 beloved, with whom I am well **p**."

**PLEASES** → PLEASE
1 Jn 3: 22 commandments and do what **p** him.

**PLEASING** → PLEASE
Ps 104: 34 May my meditation be **p** to him;
Eph 5: 10 Try to learn what is **p** to the Lord.
Phil 4: 18 an acceptable sacrifice, **p** to God.

**PLEASURE** → PLEASE
Prv 21: 17 The lover of **p** will suffer want;
Ez 18: 32 For I find no **p** in the death
2 Tm 3: 4 lovers of **p** rather than lovers

**PLOWSHARES**
Is 2: 4 They shall beat their swords into **p**

**PLUNDERED**
Ez 39: 10 plundering those who **p** them,

**POISON**
Jas 3: 8 It is a restless evil, full of deadly **p**.

**POLE**
Nm 21: 8 Make a seraph and mount it on a **p**,

**POOR** → POVERTY
1 Sm 2: 8 from the ash heap lifts up the **p**,
Jb 29: 16 I was a father to the **p**; the complaint
Ps 113: 7 dust, lifts the **p** from the ash heap,
Prv 19: 22 rather be **p** than a liar.
Mt 5: 3 "Blessed are the **p** in spirit,
Mk 10: 21 give to [the] **p** and you will have
12: 42 A **p** widow also came and put
Jn 12: 8 You always have the **p** with you,
2 Cor 6: 10 as **p** yet enriching many;
8: 9 sake he became **p** although he was
Jas 2: 5 Did not God choose those who are **p**

**PORTION**
Dt 32: 9 But the LORD's **p** was his people;
Ps 142: 6 my **p** in the land of the living.
Lam 3: 24 The LORD is my **p**, I tell myself,

**POSSESS** → POSSESSED, POSSESSION, POSSESSIONS
Is 60: 21 for all time they will **p** the land;

**POSSESSED** → POSSESS
Mt 8: 16 they brought him many who were **p**

**POSSESSION** → POSSESS
Ex 19: 5 will be my treasured **p** among all
Jos 1: 11 your God, is giving as your **p**.' "
Ps 2: 8 and, as your **p**, the ends of the earth.

**POSSESSIONS** → POSSESS
Lk 12: 15 one's life does not consist of **p**."

**POSSIBLE**
Mt 19: 26 but for God all things are **p**."
26: 39 if it is **p**, let this cup pass from me;

**POTIPHAR**
Egyptian who bought Joseph (Gn 37:36; 39:1-6), sent him to prison (Gn 39:7-30).

**POTTER** → POTTER'S
Sir 33: 13 Like clay in the hands of a **p**, to be
Rom 9: 21 does not the **p** have a right over

**POTTER'S** → POTTER
Jer 18: 2 Arise and go down to the **p** house;
Mt 27: 7 it to buy the **p** field as a burial place

**POUR** → POURED
Dt 12: 16 but must **p** it out on the ground like
Is 44: 3 I will **p** out my spirit upon your
Ez 39: 29 once I **p** out my spirit upon the house of
Acts 2: 17 'that I will **p** out a portion of my
Rev 16: 1 **p** out the seven bowls of God's fury

**POURED** → POUR
Acts 2: 33 Spirit from the Father and **p** it forth,
Rom 5: 5 the love of God has been **p**
Ti 3: 6 whom he richly **p** out on us through

**POVERTY** → POOR
Prv 30: 8 me, give me neither **p** nor riches;
Sir 11: 14 evil, life and death, **p** and riches—
Mk 12: 44 from her **p**, has contributed all she
2 Cor 8: 9 by his **p** you might become rich.

**POWER** → POWERFUL, POWERS
Ex 9: 16 to show you my **p** and to make my
15: 6 magnificent in **p**, your right hand,
Jdt 9: 14 are God, the God of all **p** and might,
Ps 68: 35 Confess the **p** of God,
68: 35 Israel, whose **p** is in the sky.
Prv 18: 21 and life are in the **p** of the tongue;
Mt 22: 29 know the scriptures or the **p** of God.
Mk 13: 26 coming in the clouds' with great **p**
Rom 1: 20 his invisible attributes of eternal **p**
1 Cor 15: 24 and every authority and **p**.
Eph 1: 19 of his **p** for us who believe,
Phil 3: 10 him and the **p** of his resurrection
2 Tm 3: 5 a pretense of religion but deny its **p**.
2 Pt 1: 3 His divine **p** has bestowed on us
1: 3 called us by his own glory and **p**.
Rev 20: 6 second death has no **p** over these;

**POWERFUL** → POWER
1 Cor 1: 26 not many were **p**, not many were

**POWERS** → POWER
Rom 8: 38 things, nor future things, nor **p**,
Eph 6: 12 with the **p**, with the world rulers

**PRACTICE** → PRACTICES
Sir 50: 29 If they put them into **p**, they can
Mt 23: 3 For they preach but they do not **p**.

**PRACTICES** → PRACTICE
Col 3: 9 have taken off the old self with its **p**

**PRAISE** → PRAISED, PRAISES
Ex 15: 2 This is my God, I **p** him; the God
Ps 56: 5 I **p** the word of God; I trust in God,
150: 6 has breath give **p** to the LORD!
Prv 27: 2 Let another **p** you, not your own
31: 31 let her deeds **p** her at the city gates.
Mt 21: 16 you have brought forth **p**'?"
1 Cor 14: 15 I will sing **p** with the spirit, but I will also sing **p** with the mind.
Rev 19: 5 "**P** our God, all you his servants,

**PRAISED** → PRAISE
Ps 48: 2 and highly **p** in the city of our God:

**PRAISES** → PRAISE
Sir 24: 1 Wisdom sings her own **p**,

**PRAY** → PRAYED, PRAYER, PRAYERS, PRAYING, PRAYS
1 Sm 12: 23 the LORD by ceasing to **p** for you
2 Chr 7: 14 humble themselves and **p**, and seek
Ps 5: 3 For to you I will **p**, LORD;
122: 6 For the peace of Jerusalem **p**:
Sir 37: 15 **p** to God to make your steps firm
Mt 5: 44 and **p** for those who persecute you,
6: 5 "When you **p**, do not be like
6: 5 to stand and **p** in the synagogues
Lk 11: 1 **p** just as John taught his disciples."
Rom 8: 26 do not know how to **p** as we ought,
1 Cor 14: 15 I will **p** with the spirit, but I will also **p** with the mind.
1 Thes 5: 17 **P** without ceasing.
Jas 5: 16 one another and **p** for one another,

**PRAYED** → PRAY
Mk 1: 35 off to a deserted place, where he **p**.
14: 35 **p** that if it were possible the hour

**PRAYER** → PRAY
Ps 6: 10 the LORD will receive my **p**.
Prv 15: 29 wicked, but hears the **p** of the just.
Is 56: 7 make them joyful in my house of **p**;
56: 7 house shall be called a house of **p**
Mt 21: 13 'My house shall be a house of **p**,'
Mk 11: 24 all that you ask for in **p**,
Rom 12: 12 endure in affliction, persevere in **p**.
Jas 5: 16 The fervent **p** of a righteous person

**PRAYERS** → PRAY
Mk 12: 40 and, as a pretext, recite lengthy **p**.
Heb 5: 7 he offered **p** and supplications
Rev 5: 8 which are the **p** of the holy ones.

**PRAYING** → PRAY
2 Mc 15: 12 was **p** with outstretched arms

**PRAYS** → PRAY
2 Mc 15: 14 Jews and fervently **p** for the people

**PREACHING**
1 Tm 5: 17 especially those who toil in **p**

**PRECEPTS**
Ps 19: 9 The **p** of the LORD are right,
119: 15 I will ponder your **p** and consider
Mt 15: 9 teaching as doctrines human **p**.' "

**PRECIOUS**
Ps 72: 14 for **p** is their blood in his sight.
Prv 3: 15 She is more **p** than corals, and no
Is 28: 16 tested, A **p** cornerstone as a sure
1 Pt 1: 19 with the **p** blood of Christ as
2: 6 chosen and **p**, and whoever believes

**PREDESTINED**
Rom 8: 30 And those he **p** he also called;

**PREPARE** → PREPARED
Mal 3: 1 he will **p** the way before me;
Mt 3: 3 the desert, '**P** the way of the Lord,
Jn 14: 2 that I am going to **p** a place for you?

**PREPARED** → PREPARE
1 Cor 2: 9 what God has **p** for those who love

**PRESENCE**
Ps 139: 7 From your **p**, where can I flee?

**PRESENT**
Rom 6: 13 do not **p** the parts of your bodies
6: 13 **p** yourselves to God as raised
1 Cor 3: 22 life or death, or the **p** or the future:
Eph 5: 27 he might **p** to himself the church
2 Tm 2: 15 Be eager to **p** yourself as acceptable

**PREVAIL**
1 Sm 2: 9 for not by strength does one **p**.

**PRICE**
Mt 27: 9 value of a man with a **p** on his head,
1 Cor 6: 20 For you have been purchased at a **p**.

**PRIDE** → PROUD
Prv 16: 18 **P** goes before disaster,
Sir 10: 7 Odious to the Lord and to mortals is **p**,

**PRIEST** → PRIESTHOOD, PRIESTS
Gn 14: 18 He was a **p** of God Most High.
Ex 2: 16 Now the **p** of Midian had seven
Ps 110: 4 "You are a **p** forever in the manner
Mk 14: 63 At that the high **p** tore his garments
Heb 3: 1 and high **p** of our confession,
5: 10 God high **p** according to the order
7: 3 Son of God, he remains a **p** forever.
10: 21 we have "a great **p** over the house

**PRIESTHOOD** → PRIEST
Ex 29: 9 Thus shall the **p** be theirs
Heb 7: 24 has a **p** that does not pass away.
1 Pt 2: 5 to be a holy **p** to offer spiritual

**PRIESTS** → PRIEST
Ex 28: 1 Israelites, that they may be my **p**:
Dt 31: 9 it to the levitical **p** who carry the ark
Mi 3: 11 for a bribe, the **p** teach for pay,
Mk 15: 3 The chief **p** accused him of many
Heb 7: 27 as did the high **p**, to offer sacrifice
Rev 20: 6 they will be **p** of God and of Christ,

**PRINCE** → PRINCES
Ez 37: 25 David my servant as their **p** forever.
Dn 10: 21 these except Michael, your **p**.

**PRINCES** → PRINCE
Dn 8: 25 he rises against the Prince of **p**,

**PRISCILLA**
Wife of Aquila, also called Prisca; co-worker with Paul (Acts 18; Rom 16:3; 1 Cor 16:19; 2 Tm 4:19); instructor of Apollos (Acts 18:24-28).

**PRISON** → PRISONER, PRISONERS
Mt 14: 10 and he had John beheaded in the **p**.
Acts 12: 5 Peter thus was being kept in **p**,

**PRISONER** → PRISON
Mk 15: 6 to them one **p** whom they requested.
Eph 3: 1 I, Paul, a **p** of Christ [Jesus] for you

**PRISONERS** → PRISON
Ps 146: 7 The LORD sets **p** free;
Is 61: 1 to the captives, release to the **p**,

**PRIZE**
1 Cor 9: 24 in the race, but only one wins the **p**?
Phil 3: 14 goal, the **p** of God's upward calling,

**PROCLAIM**
Ps 97: 6 The heavens **p** his justice;
Mt 10: 27 hear whispered, **p** on the housetops.
Mk 16: 15 and **p** the gospel to every creature.
Lk 4: 19 to **p** a year acceptable to the Lord."

**PRODUCE** → PRODUCES
Jos 5: 11 they ate of the **p** of the land
Prv 3: 9 wealth, with first fruits of all your **p**;

**PRODUCES** → PRODUCE
2 Cor 7: 10 For godly sorrow **p** a salutary
7: 10 regret, but worldly sorrow **p** death.
Jas 1: 3 testing of your faith **p** perseverance.

**PROFANE**
Lv 22: 32 Do not **p** my holy name,
1 Mc 1: 45 to **p** the sabbaths and feast days,

**PROFIT**
Sir 29: 11 that will **p** you more than the gold.
Mt 16: 26 What **p** would there be for one

**PROMISE** → PROMISED, PROMISES
Acts 2: 39 For the **p** is made to you and to your
Eph 2: 12 and strangers to the covenants of **p**,
1 Tm 4: 8 since it holds a **p** of life both
2 Pt 3: 9 The Lord does not delay his **p**,

**PROMISED** → PROMISE
Dt 1: 11 times over, and bless you as he **p**!
Eph 1: 13 were sealed with the **p** holy Spirit,

**PROMISES** → PROMISE
Ps 12: 7 The **p** of the LORD are sure,
2 Cor 1: 20 For however many are the **p** of God,
Heb 8: 6 better covenant, enacted on better **p**.

**PROOFS**
Acts 1: 3 by many **p** after he had suffered,

**PROPHECIES** → PROPHESY
1 Cor 13: 8 If there are **p**, they will be brought

**PROPHECY** → PROPHESY
Acts 21: 9 four virgin daughters gifted with **p**.
1 Cor 12: 10 to another **p**; to another discernment
2 Pt 1: 20 that there is no **p** of scripture that is

**PROPHESY** → PROPHECIES, PROPHECY, PROPHET, PROPHETS
Mt 7: 22 Lord, did we not **p** in your name?
1 Cor 13: 9 know partially and we **p** partially,

Rev 11: 3 commission my two witnesses to **p**

**PROPHET** → PROPHESY
Ex 7: 1 Aaron your brother will be your **p**.
Dt 18: 18 for them a **p** like you from among
18: 18 my words into the mouth of the **p**;
1 Mc 4: 46 of a **p** who could determine what
Lk 4: 24 no **p** is accepted in his own native
20: 6 are convinced that John was a **p**."
Rev 16: 13 and from the mouth of the false **p**.
20: 10 the beast and the false **p** were.

**PROPHETS** → PROPHESY
Nm 11: 29 the people of the LORD were **p**!
1 Kgs 18: 40 said to them, "Seize the **p** of Baal.
1 Mc 9: 27 had not been since the time **p** ceased
Ps 105: 15 ones, to my **p** do no harm."
Mt 5: 17 come to abolish the law or the **p**.
22: 40 law and the **p** depend on these two
Lk 24: 44 and in the **p** and psalms must be
1 Cor 12: 28 second, **p**; third, teachers;
Eph 2: 20 the foundation of the apostles and **p**,
4: 11 others as **p**, others as evangelists,
Rev 11: 10 because these two **p** tormented
18: 20 you holy ones, apostles, and **p**.

**PROSPERITY** → PROSPERS
Ps 73: 3 when I saw the **p** of the wicked.

**PROSPERS** → PROSPERITY
Ps 1: 3 whatever he does **p**.

**PROSTITUTE** → PROSTITUTES
1 Cor 6: 15 and make them the members of a **p**?

**PROSTITUTES** → PROSTITUTE
Mt 21: 31 **p** are entering the kingdom of God
1 Cor 6: 9 adulterers nor boy **p** nor sodomites

**PROTECTION** → PROTECTS
Eccl 7: 12 For the **p** of wisdom is as the **p** of money;

**PROTECTS** → PROTECTION
Ps 116: 6 The LORD **p** the simple;

**PROUD** → PRIDE
Ps 94: 2 give the **p** what they deserve!
Prv 21: 4 Haughty eyes and a **p** heart—
Sir 10: 9 Why are dust and ashes **p**?
Jas 4: 6 "God resists the **p**, but gives grace

**PROVERBS**
Prv 1: 1 The **p** of Solomon, the son
Eccl 12: 9 scrutinized and arranged many **p**.

**PROVIDE** → PROVIDES
Gn 22: 8 "God will **p** the sheep for the burnt
1 Cor 10: 13 the trial he will also **p** a way out,

**PROVIDES** → PROVIDE
1 Tm 6: 17 who richly **p** us with all things

**PROVOKE** → PROVOKED
Dt 32: 21 with a foolish nation I will **p** them.
Jer 25: 6 do not **p** me with the works of your

**PROVOKED** → PROVOKE
Ps 78: 41 God, **p** the Holy One of Israel.

**PRUNES**
Jn 15: 2 does he **p** so that it bears more fruit.

**PSALMS**
Lk 24: 44 prophets and **p** must be fulfilled."
Eph 5: 19 addressing one another [in] **p**

**PUBLIC**
Col 2: 15 he made a **p** spectacle of them,

**PUNISH** → PUNISHMENT
Ex 32: 34 When it is time for me to **p**, I will **p**
Jer 21: 14 I will **p** you—

**PUNISHMENT** → PUNISH
Gn 4: 13 "My **p** is too great to bear.
Mt 25: 46 And these will go off to eternal **p**,
1 Jn 4: 18 fear because fear has to do with **p**,

**PURE** → PURIFICATION, PURIFIED, PURITY
Ps 19: 10 The fear of the LORD is **p**,
Hb 1: 13 Your eyes are too **p** to look
Phil 4: 8 whatever is **p**, whatever is lovely,
1 Jn 3: 3 hope based on him makes himself **p**, as he is **p**.

**PURIFICATION** → PURE
Heb 1: 3 he had accomplished **p** from sins,

**PURIFIED** → PURE
Dn 12: 10 Many shall be refined, **p**, and tested,
1 Pt 1: 22 Since you have **p** yourselves

**PURIM**
Est 9: 26 so these days have been named **P**

**PURITY** → PURE
2 Cor 6: 6 by **p**, knowledge, patience,

**PURPLE**
Ex 25: 4 violet, **p**, and scarlet yarn;
Mk 15: 17 They clothed him in **p** and,

**PURPOSE**
Rom 8: 28 who are called according to his **p**.
Eph 3: 11 the eternal **p** that he accomplished

**PURSUE** → PURSUED, PURSUES
Ps 34: 15 and do good; seek peace and **p** it.
Rom 14: 19 Let us then **p** what leads to peace
1 Tm 6: 11 Instead, **p** righteousness, devotion,

**PURSUED** → PURSUE
Ps 18: 38 I **p** my enemies and overtook them;

**PURSUES** → PURSUE
Prv 21: 21 Whoever **p** justice and kindness will
Sir 31: 5 whoever **p** money will be led astray

**PUT**
Is 42: 1 Upon him I have **p** my spirit;
Ez 36: 27 I will **p** my spirit within you so
Eph 6: 11 **P** on the armor of God so that you

## Q

**QUARRELED**
Ex 17: 7 because the Israelites **q** there

**QUEEN**
1 Kgs 10: 1 The **q** of Sheba, having heard
Est 2: 17 and made her **q** in place of Vashti.
Mt 12: 42 the judgment the **q** of the south will
Rev 18: 7 said to herself, 'I sit enthroned as **q**;

**QUESTIONS**
2 Chr 9: 1 Jerusalem to test him with subtle **q**,
Mt 22: 46 anyone dare to ask him any more **q**.

**QUICK** → QUICKLY
Jas 1: 19 everyone should be **q** to hear,

**QUICKLY** → QUICK
Jn 13: 27 "What you are going to do, do **q**."
Rom 9: 28 **q** will the Lord execute sentence
Gal 1: 6 you are so **q** forsaking the one who

**QUIET**
1 Tm 2: 2 that we may lead a **q** and tranquil

**QUIVER**
Is 49: 2 sharpened arrow, in his **q** he hid me.

## R

**RABBI**
Mt 23: 8 As for you, do not be called '**R**.'
Jn 1: 38 him, "**R**" (which translated means

**RACE**
Eccl 9: 11 under the sun that the **r** is not won
1 Cor 9: 24 in the stadium all run in the **r**,
Heb 12: 1 in running the **r** that lies before us
1 Pt 2: 9 But you are "a chosen **r**, a royal

**RACHEL**
Daughter of Laban (Gn 29:16); wife of Jacob (Gn 29:28); bore two sons (Gn 30:22-24; 35:16-24; 46:19). Stole Laban's gods (Gn 31:19, 32–35). Death (Gn 35:19-20).

**RAHAB**
Prostitute who hid Israelite spies (Jos 2; 6:22-25; Heb 11:31; Jas 2:25). Mother of Boaz (Mt 1:5).

**RAIN** → RAINED, RAINS
Gn 7: 4 now I will bring **r** down on the earth
1 Kgs 17: 1 be no dew or **r** except at my word."
Is 45: 8 like gentle **r** let the clouds drop it
Mt 5: 45 and causes **r** to fall on the just
Rev 11: 6 so that no **r** can fall during the time

**RAINED** → RAIN
Gn 19: 24 and the LORD **r** down sulfur
Ex 9: 23 the LORD **r** down hail

**RAINS** → RAIN
Jas 5: 7 it receives the early and the late **r**.

**RAISE** → RISE
Dt 18: 15 **r** up for you from among your own
2 Mc 7: 9 the King of the universe will **r** us
Jn 2: 19 and in three days I will **r** it up."
2 Cor 4: 14 who raised the Lord Jesus will **r** us

**RAISED** → RISE
Mt 17: 23 and he will be **r** on the third day."
Acts 2: 24 But God **r** him up, releasing him
Rom 4: 25 and was **r** for our justification.
1 Cor 15: 4 that he was **r** on the third day

**RAM** → RAMS
Gn 22: 13 saw a single **r** caught by its horns
22: 13 and took the **r** and offered it up as
Ex 29: 22 from this **r** you shall take its fat:
29: 22 since this is the **r** for installation;
Dn 8: 3 the river a **r** with two great horns,

**RAMS** → RAM
1 Sm 15: 22 to listen, better than the fat of **r**.

**RANSOM** → RANSOMED
Mt 20: 28 to give his life as a **r** for many."
1 Tm 2: 6 who gave himself as **r** for all.

**RANSOMED** → RANSOM
Is 35: 10 the **r** of the LORD shall return,

**RAVENS**
1 Kgs 17: 6 **R** brought him bread and meat
Lk 12: 24 Notice the **r**: they do not sow

**READ** → READING
Ex 24: 7 he **r** it aloud to the people,
Jos 8: 34 were **r** aloud all the words
Neh 8: 8 Ezra **r** clearly from the book
8: 8 all could understand what was **r**.
Lk 4: 16 on the sabbath day. He stood up to **r**
2 Cor 3: 15 whenever Moses is **r**, a veil lies

**READING** → READ
Acts 8: 30 and heard him **r** Isaiah the prophet
8: 30 you understand what you are **r**?"

**READY**
Rev 19: 7 come, his bride has made herself **r**.

**REAP**
Gal 6: 7 a person will **r** only what he sows,
Rev 14: 15 "Use your sickle and **r** the harvest,
14: 15 for the time to **r** has come,

**REBEKAH**
Sister of Laban, secured as bride for Isaac (Gn 24). Mother of Esau and Jacob (Gn 25:19-26). Taken by Abimelech as sister of Isaac; returned (Gn 26:1-11). Encouraged Jacob to trick Isaac out of blessing (Gn 27:1-17).

**REBEL** → REBELLED, REBELLION
Ex 23: 21 Do not **r** against him, for he will not
1 Sm 12: 14 and do not **r** against the LORD's

**REBELLED** → REBEL
Nm 20: 24 because you both **r** against my

**REBELLION** → REBEL
1 Sm 15: 23 For a sin of divination is **r**,

**REBUILD** → BUILD
Neh 2: 17 let us **r** the wall of Jerusalem,
Acts 15: 16 return and **r** the fallen hut of David;
15: 16 from its ruins I shall **r** it and raise it

**REBUKE**
Prv 27: 5 Better is an open **r** than a love
Zec 3: 2 "May the LORD **r** you,
Mk 8: 32 took him aside and began to **r** him.

**RECEIVE** → RECEIVED
Jn 3: 27 said, "No one can **r** anything except
16: 24 ask and you will **r**, so that your joy
20: 22 and said to them, "**R** the holy Spirit.
Acts 2: 38 you will **r** the gift of the holy Spirit.
20: 35 more blessed to give than to **r**.'"
1 Cor 4: 7 you boasting as if you did not **r** it?
Rev 4: 11 to **r** glory and honor and power,

**RECEIVED** → RECEIVE
Mt 6: 2 say to you, they have **r** their reward.
1 Cor 11: 23 For I **r** from the Lord what I

**RECONCILE** → RECONCILED, RECONCILIATION
Acts 7: 26 and tried to **r** them peacefully,
Col 1: 20 through him to **r** all things for him,

**RECONCILED** → RECONCILE
Mt 5: 24 go first and be **r** with your brother,
1 Cor 7: 11 single or become **r** to her husband—

**RECONCILIATION** → RECONCILE
Rom 5: 11 whom we have now received **r**.
2 Cor 5: 18 and given us the ministry of **r**,

**RED**
Ex 15: 4 officers were drowned in the **R** Sea.
Mt 16: 3 for the sky is **r** and threatening.'
Rev 12: 3 it was a huge **r** dragon, with seven

**REDEEMED** → REDEMPTION
2 Sm 7: 23 whom you **r** for yourself
Ps 107: 2 that be the prayer of the LORD's **r**,

**REDEEMER** → REDEMPTION
Ps 19: 15 you, LORD, my rock and my **r**.
Is 48: 17 your **r**, the Holy One of Israel:

**REDEMPTION** → REDEEMED, REDEEMER
Lk 21: 28 raise your heads because your **r** is

Rom 3: 24 by his grace through the **r** in Christ
Eph 1: 7 In him we have **r** by his blood,
Heb 9: 12 own blood, thus obtaining eternal **r**.

**REFINE** → REFINED
Zec 13: 9 I will **r** them as one refines silver,

**REFINED** → REFINE
Dn 12: 10 Many shall be **r**, purified,

**REFUGE**
Prv 30: 5 a shield to those who take **r** in him.
Jer 16: 19 fortress, my **r** in the day of distress!

**REGARD**
Phil 2: 6 of God, did not **r** equality with God

**REGRET**
Nm 23: 19 nor a mortal, who feels **r**. Is God

**REGULATIONS**
Col 2: 20 why do you submit to **r** as if you
Heb 9: 10 **r** concerning the flesh,

**REHOBOAM**
Son of Solomon (1 Kgs 11:43; 1 Chr 3:10). Harsh treatment of subjects caused divided kingdom (1 Kgs 12:1-24; 14:21-31; 2 Chr 10–12).

**REIGN**
Ex 15: 18 May the LORD **r** forever and ever!
Ps 146: 10 The LORD shall **r** forever,
1 Cor 15: 25 For he must **r** until he has put all his
2 Tm 2: 12 persevere we shall also **r** with him.
Rev 11: 15 and he will **r** forever and ever."
22: 5 and they shall **r** forever and ever.

**REJECT** → REJECTED
Is 30: 12 Because you **r** this word, And put

**REJECTED** → REJECT
Ps 60: 3 O God, you **r** us, broke our
118: 22 stone the builders **r** has become
Mt 21: 42 that the builders **r** has become
1 Pt 2: 4 **r** by human beings but chosen

**REJOICE** → REJOICING
Ps 118: 24 let us **r** in it and be glad.
Is 62: 5 his bride so shall your God **r** in you.
Zep 3: 17 Who will **r** over you with gladness,
Lk 6: 23 **R** and leap for joy on that day!
Phil 4: 4 **R** in the Lord always. I shall say it again: **r**!

**REJOICING** → REJOICE
2 Cor 6: 10 as sorrowful yet always **r**;

**RELEASE**
Is 61: 1 to the captives, **r** to the prisoners,
Mt 27: 15 the governor was accustomed to **r**

**RELENT**
Jl 2: 14 Perhaps he will again **r** and leave

**RELIGION**
Jas 1: 27 **R** that is pure and undefiled before

**RELY**
Prv 3: 5 on your own intelligence do not **r**;
Sir 5: 1 Do not **r** on your wealth, or say,

**REMAIN** → REMAINS
1 Cor 7: 20 Everyone should **r** in the state
Heb 1: 11 They will perish, but you **r**;

**REMAINS** → REMAIN
Heb 7: 3 Son of God, he **r** a priest forever.
10: 26 there no longer **r** sacrifice for sins

**REMEMBER** → REMEMBERED, REMEMBERS
Ex 20: 8 **R** the sabbath day—keep it holy.
Dt 8: 18 **R** then the LORD, your God,
Jb 10: 9 **r** that you fashioned me from clay!
Eccl 12: 1 **R** your Creator in the days of your
Jer 31: 34 iniquity and no longer **r** their sin.
2 Tm 2: 8 **R** Jesus Christ, raised from the dead,
Heb 8: 12 evildoing and **r** their sins no more."

**REMEMBERED** → REMEMBER
Ps 78: 35 They **r** that God was their rock,
106: 45 For their sake he **r** his covenant
Rev 16: 19 But God **r** great Babylon, giving it

**REMEMBERS** → REMEMBER
Ps 111: 5 fear him, he **r** his covenant forever.

**REMNANT**
Gn 45: 7 of you to ensure for you a **r** on earth
Is 10: 21 A **r** will return, the **r** of Jacob,
Jer 50: 20 for I will forgive the **r** I preserve.
Rom 9: 27 of the sea, only a **r** will be saved;

**RENEW** → RENEWED
Is 40: 31 in the LORD will **r** their strength,

**RENEWED** → RENEW
2 Cor 4: 16 our inner self is being **r** day by day.
Eph 4: 23 and be **r** in the spirit of your minds,

**REPARATION**
Lv 5: 15 to the sanctuary shekel, as a **r** offering.

**REPAY** → PAY
Ps 28: 4 **R** them for their deeds, for the evil
Rom 12: 17 Do not **r** anyone evil for evil;

**REPENT** → REPENTANCE
Jb 42: 6 I have said, and **r** in dust and ashes.
Jon 3: 9 God may again **r** and turn from his blazing
Mt 3: 2 [and] saying, "**R**, for the kingdom
Acts 2: 38 [said] to them, "**R** and be baptized,
Rev 16: 9 but they did not **r** or give him glory.

**REPENTANCE** → REPENT
Mk 1: 4 desert proclaiming a baptism of **r**
Lk 3: 8 good fruits as evidence of your **r**;
Rom 2: 4 of God would lead you to **r**?
2 Cor 7: 10 produces a salutary **r** without regret,
2 Pt 3: 9 perish but that all should come to **r**.

**REPROVE**
Rev 3: 19 Those whom I love, I **r** and chastise.

**RESCUE** → RESCUED, RESCUES
Ps 22: 9 if he loves him, let him **r** him."
2 Pt 2: 9 the Lord knows how to **r** the devout

**RESCUED** → RESCUE
Prv 11: 8 The just are **r** from a tight spot,

**RESCUES** → RESCUE
Ps 37: 40 The LORD helps and **r** them,

**RESIST**
Jas 4: 7 **R** the devil, and he will flee

**RESPECT**
Rom 13: 7 toll is due, **r** to whom **r** is due,

**REST** → RESTED
Ex 31: 15 day is the sabbath of complete **r**,
2 Sm 7: 11 I will give you **r** from all your
Ps 95: 11 "They shall never enter my **r**."
Mt 11: 28 are burdened, and I will give you **r**.
Heb 4: 10 And whoever enters into God's **r**,

**RESTED** → REST
Gn 2: 2 he **r** on the seventh day from all
Ex 20: 11 but on the seventh day he **r**.

**RESTORE**
Ps 51: 14 **R** to me the gladness of your
Mt 17: 11 will indeed come and **r** all things;

**RESURRECTION**
Mt 22: 30 At the **r** they neither marry nor are
Mk 12: 18 who say there is no **r**, came to him
Jn 11: 25 told her, "I am the **r** and the life;
1 Cor 15: 12 some among you say there is no **r**
Phil 3: 10 the power of his **r** and [the] sharing
Rev 20: 5 years were over. This is the first **r**.

**RETAIN**
Jn 20: 23 and whose sins you **r** are retained."

**RETURN**
Gn 3: 19 eat bread, Until you **r** to the ground,
3: 19 you are dust, and to dust you shall **r**.
Dt 30: 2 and **r** to the LORD, your God,
Mal 3: 7 **R** to me, that I may **r** to you,

**REUBEN**
Firstborn of Jacob by Leah (Gn 29:32; 46:8; 1 Chr 2:1). Attempted to rescue Joseph (Gn 37:21-30). Lost birthright for sleeping with Bilhah (Gn 35:22; 49:4). Tribe of blessed (Gn 49:3-4; Dt 33:6), numbered (Nm 1:21; 26:7), allotted land east of Jordan (Nm 32; 34:14; Jos 13:15), west (Ez 48:6), failed to help Deborah (Jgs 5:15-16), supported David (1 Chr 12:37), 12,000 from (Rev 7:5).

**REVEAL** → REVEALED, REVELATION, REVELATIONS
Mt 11: 27 to whom the Son wishes to **r** him.

**REVEALED** → REVEAL
Is 40: 5 the glory of the LORD shall be **r**,
Mt 16: 17 and blood has not **r** this to you,
Lk 17: 30 be on the day the Son of Man is **r**.
Rom 1: 17 in it is **r** the righteousness of God
1 Jn 3: 2 what we shall be has not yet been **r**.
3: 2 when it is **r** we shall be like him,

**REVELATION** → REVEAL
1 Cor 14: 6 if I do not speak to you by way of **r**,
Eph 3: 3 was made known to me by **r**, as I
Rev 1: 1 The **r** of Jesus Christ, which God

**REVELATIONS** → REVEAL
2 Cor 12: 1 go on to visions and **r** of the Lord.

**REVERENCE**
Eph 5: 21 to one another out of **r** for Christ.

**REWARD** → REWARDED, REWARDS
Ps 19: 12 obeying them brings much **r**.
Is 40: 10 Here is his **r** with him,
Mt 6: 5 to you, they have received their **r**.
Lk 6: 23 your **r** will be great in heaven.

**REWARDED** → REWARD
2 Sm 22: 21 **r** my clean hands.

**REWARDS** → REWARD
Heb 11: 6 and that he **r** those who seek him.

**RIB**
Gn 2: 22 built the **r** that he had taken

**RICH** → RICHES
Mt 19: 23 one who is **r** to enter the kingdom
Lk 12: 21 is not **r** in what matters to God."
2 Cor 8: 9 he became poor although he was **r**,
8: 9 by his poverty you might become **r**.
Eph 2: 4 But God, who is **r** in mercy,
1 Tm 6: 18 good, to be **r** in good works, to be
Jas 1: 10 and the **r** one in his lowliness, for he

**RICHES** → RICH
Prv 30: 8 me, give me neither poverty nor **r**;
Lk 8: 14 are choked by the anxieties and **r**
Rom 11: 33 the depth of the **r** and wisdom

**RID**
1 Pt 2: 1 **R** yourselves of all malice and all

**RIDER** → RIDES, RIDING
Rev 19: 11 its **r** was [called] "Faithful

**RIDES** → RIDER
Dt 33: 26 who **r** the heavens in his power,
33: 26 who **r** the clouds in his majesty;

**RIDING** → RIDER
Zec 9: 9 and **r** on a donkey, on a colt,

**RIGHT** → BIRTHRIGHT
Ex 15: 6 magnificent in power, your **r** hand,
Dt 6: 18 Do what is **r** and good in the sight
Jb 4: 17 anyone be more in the **r** than God?
Ps 110: 1 "Sit at my **r** hand, while I make
Prv 14: 12 Sometimes a way seems **r**,
Mt 25: 33 He will place the sheep on his **r**
Acts 2: 34 said to my Lord, "Sit at my **r** hand
Heb 1: 13 "Sit at my **r** hand until I make your

**RIGHTEOUS** → RIGHTEOUSNESS
Jer 23: 5 I will raise up a **r** branch for David;
Mk 2: 17 I did not come to call the **r**
Rom 1: 17 "The one who is **r** by faith will
5: 19 of one the many will be made **r**.
1 Jn 2: 1 the Father, Jesus Christ the **r** one.
Rev 19: 8 (The linen represents the **r** deeds

**RIGHTEOUSNESS** → RIGHTEOUS
Gn 15: 6 attributed it to him as an act of **r**.
Mt 5: 6 are they who hunger and thirst for **r**,
Jn 16: 8 the world in regard to sin and **r**
Rom 3: 22 the **r** of God through faith in Jesus
Gal 3: 6 and it was credited to him as **r**."
Eph 6: 14 truth, clothed with **r** as a breastplate,
1 Pt 2: 24 free from sin, we might live for **r**.
2 Pt 3: 13 and a new earth in which **r** dwells.
Rev 19: 11 He judges and wages war in **r**.

**RIPE**
Jn 4: 35 and see the fields **r** for the harvest.
Rev 14: 15 the earth's harvest is fully **r**."

**RISE** → ARISE, RAISE, RAISED, ROSE
Nm 24: 17 and a scepter shall **r** from Israel,
2 Mc 12: 44 not expecting the fallen to **r** again,
Ps 94: 2 **R** up, O judge of the earth;
Dn 12: 13 you shall **r** for your reward
1 Thes 4: 16 and the dead in Christ will **r** first.

**RIVER** → RIVERS
Ps 46: 5 Streams of the **r** gladden the city
Is 48: 18 your peace would be like a **r**,
Ez 47: 12 Along each bank of the **r** every kind
Mt 3: 6 the Jordan **R** as they acknowledged
Rev 22: 1 Then the angel showed me the **r**

**RIVERS** → RIVER
Ps 137: 1 By the **r** of Babylon there we sat
Rev 8: 10 It fell on a third of the **r**

**ROAD** → CROSSROADS
Mt 7: 13 the **r** broad that leads to destruction,

**ROARING** → ROARS
1 Pt 5: 8 around like a **r** lion looking

**ROARS** → ROARING
Jer 25:30 The LORD **r** from on high,
25:30 Mightily he **r** over his sheepfold,
Hos 11:10 the LORD, who **r** like a lion;
11:10 When he **r**, his children shall come

**ROB** → ROBBER
Mal 3:8 Can anyone **r** God? But you are
3:9 for you, the whole nation, **r** me.

**ROBBER** → ROB
1 Cor 5:11 or a **r**, not even to eat with such

**ROBE** → ROBED, ROBES
Ex 28:4 an ephod, a **r**, a brocade tunic,
Lk 15:22 'Quickly bring the finest **r** and put it
Rev 6:11 Each of them was given a white **r**,

**ROBED** → ROBE
Ps 93:1 The LORD is king, **r** with majesty;
93:1 the LORD is **r**, girded with might.

**ROBES** → ROBE
Mk 12:38 who like to go around in long **r**
Rev 22:14 are they who wash their **r** so as

**ROCK**
Ex 17:6 Strike the **r**, and the water will flow
Nm 20:8 forth water from the **r** for them,
1 Sm 2:2 there is no **R** like our God.
Ps 19:15 LORD, my **r** and my redeemer.
Is 44:8 There is no other **R**, I know of none!
Mt 16:18 upon this **r** I will build my church,
Mk 15:46 that had been hewn out of the **r**.
1 Pt 2:8 and a **r** that will make them fall."

**ROD**
2 Sm 7:14 I will reprove him with a human **r**
Ps 2:9 an iron **r** you will shepherd them,
23:4 your **r** and your staff comfort me.
Prv 13:24 Whoever spares the **r** hates
Rev 2:27 He will rule them with an iron **r**.

**ROLL**
Mk 16:3 "Who will **r** back the stone for us

**ROOF**
Jos 2:6 Now, she had led them to the **r**,
2 Sm 11:2 the **r** he saw a woman bathing;
Mk 2:4 they opened up the **r** above him.

**ROOM**
Mk 14:15 show you a large upper **r** furnished
Rom 12:19 revenge but leave **r** for the wrath;
Eph 4:27 and do not leave **r** for the devil.

**ROOT** → ROOTED
Is 11:10 On that day, The **r** of Jesse,
Rom 11:16 and if the **r** is holy, so are
15:12 "The **r** of Jesse shall come,
1 Tm 6:10 love of money is the **r** of all evils,
Rev 5:5 of the tribe of Judah, the **r** of David,

**ROOTED** → ROOT
Eph 3:17 that you, **r** and grounded in love,

**ROSE** → RISE
1 Thes 4:14 if we believe that Jesus died and **r**,

**ROUGH**
Is 40:4 land shall be a plain, the **r** country,
Lk 3:5 and the **r** ways made smooth,

**ROYAL**
Jas 2:8 you fulfill the **r** law according
1 Pt 2:9 are "a chosen race, a **r** priesthood,

**RUBBISH**
1 Cor 4:13 We have become like the world's **r**,
Phil 3:8 and I consider them so much **r**,

**RUINS**
Ezr 9:9 house of our God and restore its **r**,
Neh 2:17 how Jerusalem lies in **r** and its gates
Acts 15:16 from its **r** I shall rebuild it and raise

**RULE** → RULER, RULERS, RULES
Rev 19:15 He will **r** them with an iron rod,

**RULER** → RULE
Ex 2:14 "Who has appointed you **r**
Wis 8:3 with God; even the **R** of all loved her.
Mt 2:6 since from you shall come a **r**,
Rev 1:5 dead and **r** of the kings of the earth.

**RULERS** → RULE
Is 40:23 makes the **r** of the earth as nothing.
Eph 6:12 the world **r** of this present darkness,

**RULES** → RULE
Ps 66:7 who **r** by his might forever,
Is 40:10 GOD, who **r** by his strong arm;
2 Tm 2:5 by competing according to the **r**.

**RUN** → FORERUNNER, RUNNERS
Is 40:31 They will **r** and not grow weary,
Gal 2:2 not be running, or have **r**, in vain.

**RUNNERS** → RUN
1 Cor 9:24 that the **r** in the stadium all run

**RUTH**
Moabitess; widow who went to Bethlehem with mother-in-law Naomi (Ru 1). Gleaned in field of Boaz; shown favor (Ru 2). Proposed marriage to Boaz (Ru 3). Married (Ru 4:1-12); bore Obed, ancestor of David (Ru 4:13-22), Jesus (Mt 1:5).

## S

**SABBATH**
Ex 20:8 Remember the **s** day—keep it holy.
1 Mc 1:43 to idols and profaned the **s**.
Mt 12:1 through a field of grain on the **s**.
Mk 2:28 Son of Man is lord even of the **s**."

**SACKCLOTH**
Dn 9:3 petition, with fasting, **s**, and ashes.
Mt 11:21 would long ago have repented in **s**

**SACRED**
Ex 28:2 you shall have **s** vestments made.
34:13 smash their **s** stones, and cut down

**SACRIFICE** → SACRIFICED, SACRIFICES
Ex 12:27 'It is the Passover **s** for the LORD,
1 Sm 15:22 Obedience is better than **s**, to listen,
Ps 40:7 **S** and offering you do not want;
Prv 15:8 The **s** of the wicked is
Dn 9:27 Half the week he shall abolish **s**
Hos 6:6 not **s**, and knowledge of God rather
Mt 9:13 of the words, 'I desire mercy, not **s**.'
Phil 4:18 an acceptable **s**, pleasing to God.
Heb 13:15 let us continually offer God a **s**

**SACRIFICED** → SACRIFICE
1 Cor 5:7 paschal lamb, Christ, has been **s**.
8:1 Now in regard to meat **s** to idols:

**SACRIFICES** → SACRIFICE
Mk 12:33 than all burnt offerings and **s**."

**SADDUCEES**
Mt 16:6 the leaven of the Pharisees and **S**."
Mk 12:18 Some **S**, who say there is no

**SAFE**
Prv 18:10 the just run to it and are s.

**SALT**
Gn 19:26 and she was turned into a pillar of s.
Mt 5:13 "You are the s of the earth. But if s

**SALVATION** → SAVE
Ps 27:1 The LORD is my light and my s;
51:14 to me the gladness of your s;
Is 12:3 draw water from the fountains of s,
52:7 news, announcing s, saying to Zion,
Lk 3:6 all flesh shall see the s of God.' "
Acts 4:12 There is no s through anyone else,
2 Cor 6:2 and on the day of s I helped you."
6:2 behold, now is the day of s.
Phil 2:12 work out your s with fear
Heb 2:3 we escape if we ignore so great a s?
2 Pt 3:15 the patience of our Lord as s, as our
Rev 19:1 S, glory, and might belong to our

**SAMARIA** → SAMARITAN
1 Kgs 16:24 then bought the mountain of S
16:24 the mountain the city he named S,
2 Kgs 17:6 the king of Assyria took S,
Jn 4:4 He had to pass through S.
Acts 1:8 throughout Judea and S,

**SAMARITAN** → SAMARIA
Lk 10:33 But a S traveler who came upon him

**SAME**
Rom 10:12 the s Lord is Lord of all,
1 Cor 12:4 of spiritual gifts but the s Spirit;
Heb 13:8 Jesus Christ is the s yesterday,

**SAMSON**
Danite judge. Birth promised (Jgs 13). Married a Philistine, but his wife given away (Jgs 14). Vengeance on the Philistines (Jgs 15). Betrayed by Delilah (Jgs 16:1-22). Death (Jgs 16:23-31). Feats of strength: killed lion (Jgs 14:6), 30 Philistines (Jgs 14:19), 1,000 Philistines with jawbone (Jgs 15:13-17), carried off gates of Gaza (Jgs 16:3), pushed down temple of Dagon (Jgs 16:25-30; Heb 11:32).

**SAMUEL**
Ephraimite judge and prophet (Heb 11:32). Birth prayed for (1 Sm 1:10-18). Dedicated to temple by Hannah (1 Sm 1:21-28). Raised by Eli (1 Sm 2:11, 18-26). Called as prophet (1 Sm 3). Led Israel to victory over Philistines (1 Sm 7). Asked by Israel for a king (1 Sm 8). Anointed Saul as king (1 Sm 9–10). Farewell speech (1 Sm 12). Rebuked Saul for sacrifice (1 Sm 13). Announced rejection of Saul (1 Sm 15). Anointed David as king (1 Sm 16). Protected David from Saul (1 Sm 19:18-24). Death (1 Sm 25:1). Returned from dead to condemn Saul (1 Sm 28).

**SANCTIFICATION** → SANCTIFIED
Rom 6:19 as slaves to righteousness for s.

**SANCTIFIED** → SANCTIFICATION
1 Cor 6:11 you were s, you were justified

**SANCTUARY**
Ex 25:8 They are to make a s for me, that I
1 Chr 22:19 to build the s of the LORD God,
1 Mc 1:21 He insolently entered the s and took
4:36 let us go up to purify the s
Ez 37:26 and put my s among them forever.
Dn 9:26 shall destroy the city and the s.
Heb 9:24 Christ did not enter into a s made

**SAND**
Mt 7:26 like a fool who built his house on s.

**SANDALS**
Ex 3:5 Remove your s from your feet,
Mt 3:11 I am not worthy to carry his s.

**SARAH**
1. Wife of Abraham, originally named Sarai; barren (Gn 11:29-31; 1 Pt 3:6). Taken by Pharaoh as Abraham's sister; returned (Gn 12:10-20). Gave Hagar to Abraham; sent her away in pregnancy (Gn 16). Name changed; Isaac promised (Gn 17:15-21; 18:10-15; Heb 11:11). Taken by Abimelech as Abraham's sister; returned (Gn 20). Isaac born; Hagar and Ishmael sent away (Gn 21:1-21; Gal 4:21-31). Death (Gn 23).
2. Daughter of Raguel, wife of Tobias (Tb 3; 6–8; 10–12).

**SATAN**
1 Chr 21:1 A s rose up against Israel, and he
Jb 1:6 the s also came among them.
Mt 4:10 Jesus said to him, "Get away, S!
12:26 And if S drives out S, he is divided
16:23 said to Peter, "Get behind me, S!
2 Cor 11:14 for even S masquerades as an angel
Rev 12:9 who is called the Devil and S,
20:7 S will be released from his prison.

**SATISFY**
Is 55:2 your wages for what does not s?

**SAUL** → =PAUL
1. Benjamite; anointed by Samuel as first king of Israel (1 Sm 9–10). Defeated Ammonites (1 Sm 11). Rebuked for offering sacrifice (1 Sm 13:1-15). Defeated Philistines (1 Sm 14). Rejected as king for failing to annihilate Amalekites (1 Sm 15). Soothed from evil spirit by David (1 Sm 16:14-23). Sent David against Goliath (1 Sm 17). Jealousy and attempted murder of David (1 Sm 18:1-11). Gave David Michal as wife (1 Sm 18:12-30). Second attempt to kill David (1 Sm 19). Anger at Jonathan (1 Sm 20:26-34). Pursued David: killed priests at Nob (1 Sm 22), went to Keilah and Ziph (1 Sm 23), life spared by David at En Gedi (1 Sm 24) and in his tent (1 Sm 26). Rebuked by Samuel's spirit for consulting witch at Endor (1 Sm 28). Wounded by Philistines; took his own life (1 Sm 31; 1 Chr 10). Lamented by David (2 Sm 1:17-27). Children (1 Sm 14:49-51; 1 Chr 8).
2. See Paul.

**SAVE** → SALVATION, SAVED, SAVIOR
Ps 54:3 O God, by your name s me.
Is 59:1 of the LORD is not too short to s,
Mt 1:21 because he will s his people
16:25 wishes to s his life will lose it,
Lk 19:10 to seek and to s what was lost."
Heb 7:25 s those who approach God through

**SAVED** → SAVE
Mt 10:22 endures to the end will be s.
Mk 15:31 themselves and said, "He s others;
Lk 13:23 will only a few people be s?"
Acts 2:21 everyone shall be s who calls
16:30 "Sirs, what must I do to be s?"
Rom 10:13 on the name of the Lord will be s."
Eph 2:8 grace you have been s through faith,

**SAVIOR** → SAVE
Is 49:26 LORD, am your s, your redeemer,
Hos 13:4 do not know; there is no s but me.
Lk 2:11 the city of David a s has been born
Acts 13:23 has brought to Israel a s, Jesus.
1 Tm 4:10 the living God, who is the s of all,
Ti 2:13 great God and of our s Jesus Christ,
2 Pt 3:18 of our Lord and s Jesus Christ.

**SCARLET**
Is 1:18 Though your sins be like s,
Mt 27:28 threw a s military cloak about him.

**SCATTER** → SCATTERED
Dt 4:27 The LORD will s you among

**SCATTERED** → SCATTER
Dt 30: 3 the LORD, your God, has s you.
Jer 31: 10 The One who s Israel, now gathers

**SCEPTER**
Gn 49: 10 The s shall never depart from Judah,
Heb 1: 8 and a righteous s is the s of your

**SCOFFERS**
Ps 1: 1 sinners, nor sit in company with s.
2 Pt 3: 3 the last days s will come [to] scoff,

**SCRIBES**
Mt 7: 29 having authority, and not as their s.
23: 13 "Woe to you, s and Pharisees,

**SCRIPTURE** → SCRIPTURES
Lk 4: 21 "Today this s passage is fulfilled
Jn 10: 35 came, and s cannot be set aside,
2 Tm 3: 16 All s is inspired by God and is

**SCRIPTURES** → SCRIPTURE
Mt 22: 29 because you do not know the s
Lk 24: 45 their minds to understand the s.
Jn 5: 39 You search the s, because you think
1 Cor 15: 3 our sins in accordance with the s;

**SCROLL**
Lk 4: 17 and was handed a s of the prophet
4: 17 He unrolled the s and found
Rev 5: 2 "Who is worthy to open the s

**SEA**
Gn 1: 26 dominion over the fish of the s,
Ex 15: 1 and chariot he has cast into the s.
Dt 30: 13 "Who will cross the s to get it
Ps 95: 5 The s and dry land belong to God,
Mi 7: 19 into the depths of the s all our sins;
Rev 4: 6 resembled a s of glass like crystal.
13: 1 come out of the s with ten horns
21: 1 away, and the s was no more.

**SEAL** → SEALS
2 Cor 1: 22 he has also put his s upon us
Rev 7: 3 or the trees until we put the s
22: 10 "Do not s up the prophetic words

**SEALS** → SEAL
Rev 5: 2 to open the scroll and break its s?"

**SEARCH** → SEARCHES
Dt 4: 29 indeed find him if you s after him
1 Chr 28: 9 If you s for him, he will be found;

**SEARCHES** → SEARCH
Rom 8: 27 the one who s hearts knows what is

**SEASON** → SEASONS
Ps 1: 3 of water, that yields its fruit in s;

**SEASONS** → SEASON
Gal 4: 10 days, months, s, and years.
1 Thes 5: 1 Concerning times and s, brothers,

**SEAT** → SEATED
Rom 14: 10 shall all stand before the judgment s
2 Cor 5: 10 all appear before the judgment s

**SEATED** → SEAT
Lk 22: 69 of Man will be s at the right hand

**SECOND** → TWO
Mt 22: 39 The s is like it: You shall love your
Rev 20: 14 (This pool of fire is the s death.

**SECURITY**
1 Thes 5: 3 "Peace and s," then sudden disaster

**SEE** → SEEN, SIGHT
Ex 33: 20 But you cannot s my face, for no one can s me and live.
Ps 115: 5 but do not speak, eyes but do not s.
Jn 9: 25 is that I was blind and now I s."
1 Cor 13: 12 At present we s indistinctly,
1 Jn 3: 2 like him, for we shall s him as he is.
Rev 1: 7 and every eye will s him, even those

**SEED** → SEEDS
Mt 17: 20 have faith the size of a mustard s,
1 Pt 1: 23 perishable but from imperishable s,

**SEEDS** → SEED
Mk 4: 31 the smallest of all the s on the earth.

**SEEK**
Ps 34: 11 but those who s the LORD lack no
119: 10 With all my heart I s you; do not let
Sir 2: 16 Those who fear the Lord s to please
Is 55: 6 S the LORD while he may be
Lk 19: 10 For the Son of Man has come to s
Heb 11: 6 that he rewards those who s him.

**SEEMS**
Prv 16: 25 Sometimes a way s right,
Heb 12: 11 all discipline s a cause not for joy

**SEEN** → SEE
Jn 1: 18 No one has ever s God.
14: 9 Whoever has s me has s the Father.
20: 29 to believe because you have s me?
20: 29 Blessed are those who have not s
1 Pt 1: 8 you have not s him you love him;

**SELF-CONTROL** → SELF-CONTROLLED
1 Cor 7: 5 tempt you through your lack of s.
2 Pt 1: 6 knowledge with s, s with endurance,

**SELF-CONTROLLED** → SELF-CONTROL
Ti 1: 8 temperate, just, holy, and s,
2: 5 to be s, chaste, good homemakers,

**SELFISH** → SELFISHNESS
Phil 1: 17 proclaim Christ out of s ambition,
Jas 3: 14 and s ambition in your hearts,

**SELFISHNESS** → SELFISH
2 Cor 12: 20 jealousy, fury, s, slander, gossip,

**SELL**
Prv 23: 23 Buy truth and do not s:
Mk 10: 21 Go, s what you have, and give

**SEND** → SENT
Ex 33: 2 I will s an angel before you
Is 6: 8 the Lord saying, "Whom shall I s?
6: 8 "Here I am," I said; "s me!"
Jn 3: 17 God did not s his Son into the world
14: 26 that the Father will s in my name—

**SENNACHERIB**
Assyrian king; siege of Jerusalem was overthrown by the LORD following prayer of Hezekiah and Isaiah (2 Kgs 18:13–19:37; 2 Chr 32:1-21; Is 36–37).

**SENT** → SEND
Ex 3: 14 I AM has s me to you.
Lk 10: 16 me rejects the one who s me."
Jn 17: 18 As you s me into the world, so I s
20: 21 As the Father has s me, so I send
1 Jn 4: 10 s his Son as expiation for our sins.

**SEPARATE** → SEPARATED
Mt 19: 6 together, no human being must s."
Rom 8: 35 What will s us from the love
1 Cor 7: 10 A wife should not s from her

**SEPARATED** → SEPARATE
Heb 7: 26 undefiled, s from sinners,

**SERPENT** → SERPENTS
Nm 21: 9 Accordingly Moses made a bronze s
21: 9 and whenever the s bit someone,
2 Cor 11: 3 that, as the s deceived Eve by his
Rev 20: 2 the ancient s, which is the Devil

**SERPENTS** → SERPENT
Mt 10: 16 so be shrewd as s and simple as

**SERVANT** → SERVANTS
Ps 19: 12 By them your s is warned;
Is 42: 1 Here is my s whom I uphold,
53: 11 My s, the just one, shall justify
Zec 3: 8 I will surely bring my s the Branch.
Acts 3: 13 has glorified his s Jesus whom you
Heb 3: 5 in all his house" as a "s" to testify

**SERVANTS** → SERVANT
2 Kgs 17: 23 as he had declared through all his s,
Rev 7: 3 the foreheads of the s of our God."

**SERVE**
Ex 20: 5 not bow down before them or s them.
Jos 24: 15 choose today whom you will s,
24: 15 household, we will s the LORD."
Ps 100: 2 s the LORD with gladness;
Mt 6: 24 "No one can s two masters.
6: 24 You cannot s God and mammon.
Mk 10: 45 to s and to give his life as a ransom
1 Pt 4: 10 it to s one another as good stewards

**SETH**
Gn 4: 25 birth to a son whom she called S.

**SETTLE**
Nm 33: 53 possession of the land and s in it,

**SEVEN** → SEVENTH
Gn 7: 2 take with you s pairs, a male and its
Ex 25: 37 You shall then make s lamps for it
Jos 6: 4 s priests carrying ram's horns ahead
6: 4 day march around the city s times,
Dn 9: 25 ruler, there shall be s weeks.
Mt 18: 22 say to you, not s times but s times.
Rev 1: 12 I turned, I saw s gold lampstands
5: 1 sides and was sealed with s seals.
8: 2 the s angels who stood before God
8: 2 before God were given s trumpets.
12: 3 dragon, with s heads and ten horns,
12: 3 and on its heads were s diadems.
15: 1 s angels with the s last plagues,

**SEVENTH** → SEVEN
Gn 2: 2 the s day God completed the work
2: 2 he rested on the s day from all
Ex 20: 10 the s day is a sabbath of the LORD
23: 11 the s year you shall let the land lie
Heb 4: 4 God rested on the s day from all his

**SEVENTY** → SEVENTY-SEVEN
Gn 46: 27 Egypt amounted to s persons in all.
2 Chr 36: 21 have rest while s years are fulfilled.
Jer 25: 12 but when the s years have elapsed,
Dn 9: 24 "S weeks are decreed for your

**SEVENTY-SEVEN** → SEVENTY
Mt 18: 22 to you, not seven times but s times.

**SHADOW**
2 Kgs 20: 11 He made the s go back the ten steps
Ps 17: 8 hide me in the s of your wings

**SHADRACH** → =HANANIAH
Hebrew exiled to Babylon; name changed from Hananiah (Dn 1:6-7). Refused defilement by food (Dn 1:8-20). Refused to worship idol (Dn 3:1-18); saved from furnace (Dn 3:19-30).

**SHALLUM**
King of Israel (2 Kgs 15:10-16).

**SHALMANESER**
King of Assyria; conquered and deported Israel (2 Kgs 17:3-4; 18:9; Tb 1:2).

**SHAME** → ASHAMED, SHAMEFUL
1 Cor 1: 27 foolish of the world to s the wise,
1: 27 weak of the world to s the strong,
Heb 12: 2 despising its s, and has taken his
1 Jn 2: 28 not be put to s by him at his coming.

**SHAMEFUL** → SHAME
2 Cor 4: 2 we have renounced s, hidden things;
Eph 5: 12 for it is s even to mention the things

**SHAMGAR**
Judge; killed 600 Philistines (Jgs 3:31; 5:6).

**SHARE**
Lk 3: 11 "Whoever has two tunics should s
Rom 15: 27 the Gentiles have come to s in their
Col 1: 12 who has made you fit to s
Heb 12: 10 in order that we may s his holiness.

**SHARP** → SHARPENS, SHARPER
Prv 5: 4 as s as a two-edged sword.
Rev 19: 15 his mouth came a s sword to strike

**SHARPENS** → SHARP
Prv 27: 17 one person s another.

**SHARPER** → SHARP
Heb 4: 12 s than any two-edged sword,

**SHEBA**
1. Benjamite; rebelled against David (2 Sm 20).
2. Queen of Sheba (1 Kgs 10; 2 Chr 9; Mt 12:42; Lk 11:31).

**SHECHEM**
1. Raped Jacob's daughter Dinah; killed (Gn 34).
2. City where Joshua renewed the covenant (Jos 24). Abimelech as king (Jgs 9).

**SHED** → BLOODSHED, SHEDDING
Gn 9: 6 being shall that one's blood be s;
Prv 6: 17 tongue, hands that s innocent blood,
Mt 23: 35 you all the righteous blood s
Rev 16: 6 For they have s the blood

**SHEDDING** → SHED
Heb 9: 22 without the s of blood there is no
12: 4 yet resisted to the point of s blood.

**SHEEP** → SHEEPFOLD
1 Kgs 22: 17 like s without a shepherd,
Is 53: 6 We had all gone astray like s,
Ez 34: 15 I myself will pasture my s;
Zec 13: 7 that the s may be scattered;
Mt 9: 36 like s without a shepherd.
Lk 15: 4 man among you having a hundred s
Jn 10: 7 I say to you, I am the gate for the s.
10: 15 I will lay down my life for the s.
Heb 13: 20 great shepherd of the s by the blood
1 Pt 2: 25 For you had gone astray like s,

**SHEEPFOLD** → SHEEP
Jn 10: 1 does not enter a s through the gate

**SHELTER**
Ps 91: 1 dwell in the s of the Most High,
Rev 7: 15 who sits on the throne will s them.

**SHEM**
Son of Noah (Gn 5:32; 6:10). Blessed (Gn 9:26). Descendants (Gn 10:21-31; 11:10-32; Lk 3:36).

**SHEOL**
Ps 139: 8 if I lie down in S, there you are.

**SHEPHERD** → SHEPHERDS
Ps 23: 1 The LORD is my s;
Is 40: 11 Like a s he feeds his flock;
Mt 2: 6 who is to s my people Israel.' "
26: 31 'I will strike the s, and the sheep
Jn 10: 11 I am the good s. A good s lays down
Heb 13: 20 the dead the great s of the sheep
1 Pt 5: 4 And when the chief S is revealed,

**SHEPHERDS** → SHEPHERD
Ez 34: 2 prophesy against the s of Israel.
34: 2 Should not s pasture the flock?
Lk 2: 8 Now there were s in that region

**SHIELD** → SHIELDS
Gn 15: 1 I am your s; I will make your
Ps 7: 11 God is a s above me saving
Eph 6: 16 hold faith as a s, to quench all

**SHIELDS** → SHIELD
Jdt 9: 14 no other who s the people of Israel

**SHILOH**
1 Sm 1: 24 at the house of the LORD in S.

**SHIMEI**
Cursed David (2 Sm 16:5-14); spared (2 Sm 19:16-23). Killed by Solomon (1 Kgs 2:8-9, 36-46).

**SHINE** → SHINES, SHINING
Nm 6: 25 The LORD let his face s upon you,
Is 60: 1 Arise! S, for your light has come,
Dn 12: 3 with insight shall s brightly like
Mt 5: 16 your light must s before others,

**SHINES** → SHINE
Jn 1: 5 the light s in the darkness,

**SHINING** → SHINE
2 Pt 1: 19 as to a lamp s in a dark place,
1 Jn 2: 8 away, and the true light is already s.

**SHOFAR**
Ex 19: 16 mountain, and a very loud blast of the s,

**SHORT**
Is 59: 1 of the LORD is not too s to save,

**SHOUT**
Ps 47: 2 s to God with joyful cries.
Zec 9: 9 S for joy, O daughter Jerusalem!

**SHOW** → SHOWED
Gn 12: 1 house to a land that I will s you.
Ps 85: 8 S us, LORD, your mercy;
Jn 14: 8 "Master, s us the Father,
1 Cor 12: 31 I shall s you a still more excellent
Rev 4: 1 and I will s you what must happen

**SHOWED** → SHOW
Dt 34: 1 and the LORD s him all the land—
Jn 20: 20 he s them his hands and his side.

**SHUT**
Is 22: 22 opens, no one will s, what he shuts,

**SICK** → SICKNESS
Mt 8: 16 spirits by a word and cured all the s,
9: 12 not need a physician, but the s do.
Jas 5: 14 Is anyone among you s?

**SICKLE**
Rev 14: 14 his head and a sharp s in his hand.

**SICKNESS** → SICK
Ex 23: 25 I will remove s from your midst;

**SIDE** → ASIDE
Ps 91: 7 Though a thousand fall at your s,
Jn 19: 34 soldier thrust his lance into his s,

**SIFT**
Lk 22: 31 behold Satan has demanded to s all

**SIGHT** → SEE
Ps 72: 14 for precious is their blood in his s.
Mt 11: 5 the blind regain their s, the lame
2 Cor 5: 7 for we walk by faith, not by s.
1 Pt 3: 4 which is precious in the s of God.

**SIGN** → SIGNS
Gn 9: 12 This is the s of the covenant that I
Is 7: 14 the Lord himself will give you a s;
Mt 24: 3 what s will there be of your coming,
Mk 8: 12 does this generation seek a s?
8: 12 say to you, no s will be given to this

**SIGNS** → SIGN
Ex 7: 3 despite the many s and wonders
Mt 16: 3 you cannot judge the s of the times.]
Jn 20: 30 Now Jesus did many other s
1 Cor 1: 22 For Jews demand s and Greeks look
Rev 16: 14 demonic spirits who performed s.

**SILAS**
Prophet (Acts 15:22-32); co-worker with Paul on second missionary journey (Acts 16–18; 2 Cor 1:19). Co-writer with Paul (1 Thes 1:1; 2 Thes 1:1); Peter (1 Pt 5:12).

**SILENT**
Is 53: 7 or a sheep s before shearers, he did
Mk 14: 61 But he was s and answered nothing.
1 Cor 14: 34 women should keep s

**SILVER**
Ps 66: 10 us, O God, tried us as s tried by fire.
Prv 8: 10 Take my instruction instead of s,
Is 48: 10 See, I refined you, but not like s;
Zec 13: 9 I will refine them as one refines s,
Mt 26: 15 They paid him thirty pieces of s,
Acts 3: 6 "I have neither s nor gold, but what
1 Cor 3: 12 on this foundation with gold, s,

**SIMEON** → =SIMON
1. Son of Jacob by Leah (Gn 29:33; 35:23; 1 Chr 2:1). With Levi killed Shechem for rape of Dinah (Gn 34:25-29). Held hostage by Joseph in Egypt (Gn 42:24–43:23). Tribe of blessed (Gn 49:5-7), numbered (Nm 1:23; 26:14), allotted land (Jos 19:1-9; Ez 48:24), 12,000 from (Rev 7:7).
2. Godly Jew who blessed the infant Jesus (2:25-35).
3. See Peter (Acts 15:14; 2 Pt 1:1).

**SIMON** → =PETER, =SIMEON
1. See Peter.
2. Apostle; the Zealot (Mt 10:4; Mk 3:18; Lk 6:15; Acts 1:13).
3. Samaritan sorcerer (Acts 8:9-24).

**SIMPLE**
Ps 19: 8 trustworthy, giving wisdom to the s.

**SIN** → SINFUL, SINNED, SINNER, SINNERS, SINS
Gn 4: 7 but if not, s lies in wait at the door:
Ex 32: 32 if you would only forgive their s!
Nm 32: 23 of your s will overtake you.
1 Kgs 8: 46 "When they s against you (for there is no one who does not s),
Tb 12: 10 those who commit s and do evil are
Ps 119: 11 that I may not s against you.

**SLEEPING** → SLEEP
Mt 9: 24 The girl is not dead but s."

**SLEEPS** → SLEEP
Ps 121: 4 of Israel never slumbers nor s.

**SLING**
1 Sm 17: 50 triumphed over the Philistine with s

**SLOW**
Ex 34: 6 s to anger and abounding in love
Nm 14: 18 'The LORD is s to anger
Ps 145: 8 s to anger and abounding in mercy.
Na 1: 3 The LORD is s to anger, yet great
Lk 24: 25 How s of heart to believe all

**SMALL** → SMALLEST
Jas 3: 5 same way the tongue is a s member
3: 5 Consider how s a fire can set a huge

**SMALLEST** → SMALL
Mk 4: 31 is the s of all the seeds on the earth.

**SMOKE** → SMOKING
Ex 19: 18 was completely enveloped in s,
Is 6: 4 and the house was filled with s.
Rev 15: 8 filled with the s from God's glory

**SMOKING** → SMOKE
Gn 15: 17 there appeared a s fire pot
Ex 20: 18 of the shofar and the mountain s,

**SNAKE**
Gn 3: 1 Now the s was the most cunning of all
Lk 11: 11 among you would hand his son a s

**SNARE**
Jgs 2: 3 for you, and their gods a s for you.

**SNOW**
Ps 51: 9 me, and I will be whiter than s.
Is 1: 18 they may become white as s;
Dn 7: 9 His clothing was white as s, the hair
Rev 1: 14 was as white as white wool or as s,

**SOBER**
1 Thes 5: 6 rest do, but let us stay alert and s.

**SODOM**
Gn 19: 24 LORD rained down sulfur upon S
Is 1: 9 We would have become as S,
Lk 10: 12 it will be more tolerable for S
Rev 11: 8 which has the symbolic names "S"

**SOLDIERS**
Mt 28: 12 gave a large sum of money to the s,
Jn 19: 23 When the s had crucified Jesus,

**SOLID**
1 Cor 3: 2 I fed you milk, not s food,
Heb 5: 14 But s food is for the mature,

**SOLITARY**
Lam 1: 1 How s sits the city, once filled

**SOLOMON**

Son of David by Bathsheba; king of Judah (2 Sm 12:24; 1 Chr 3:5, 10). Appointed king by David (1 Kgs 1); adversaries Adonijah, Joab, Shimei killed by Benaiah (1 Kgs 2). Asked for wisdom (1 Kgs 3; 2 Chr 1). Judged between two prostitutes (1 Kgs 3:16-28). Built temple (1 Kgs 5–7; 2 Chr 2–5); prayer of dedication (1 Kgs 8; 2 Chr 6). Visited by Queen of Sheba (1 Kgs 10; 2 Chr 9). Wives turned his heart from God (1 Kgs 11:1-13). Jeroboam rebelled against (1 Kgs 11:26-40). Death (1 Kgs 11:41-43; 2 Chr 9:29-31).

Proverbs of (1 Kgs 4:32; Prv 1:1; 10:1; 25:1); psalms of (Ps 72; 127); song of (Sg 1:1).

**SON** → SONS
Gn 21: 2 bore Abraham a s in his old age,
Ex 4: 23 Let my s go, that he may serve me.
4: 23 I will kill your s, your firstborn.
2 Sm 7: 14 to him, and he shall be a s to me.
Ps 2: 7 he said to me, "You are my s;
Is 7: 14 pregnant and about to bear a s,
Mt 1: 23 shall be with child and bear a s,
2: 15 "Out of Egypt I called my s."
3: 17 "This is my beloved S, with whom
12: 8 For the S of Man is Lord
16: 16 Messiah, the S of the living God."
Mk 10: 45 For the S of Man did not come to be
Lk 1: 35 will be called holy, the S of God.
20: 44 him 'lord,' how can he be his s?"
Jn 1: 34 testified that he is the S of God."
3: 16 the world that he gave his only S,
Rom 8: 29 be conformed to the image of his S,
1 Thes 1: 10 and to await his S from heaven,
Heb 1: 2 he spoke to us through a s, whom he
1: 5 "You are my s; this day I have
1: 5 to him, and he shall be a s to me"?
2 Pt 1: 17 glory, "This is my S, my beloved,
1 Jn 4: 9 God sent his only S into the world
Rev 12: 5 She gave birth to a s, a male child,
14: 14 the cloud one who looked like a s

**SONG** → SING
Ex 15: 1 and the Israelites sang this s
Dt 31: 21 them, this s will speak to them as
Ps 40: 4 And puts a new s in my mouth,
Rev 15: 3 and they sang the s of Moses,
15: 3 of God, and the s of the Lamb:

**SONGS** → SING
Col 3: 16 and spiritual s with gratitude in your

**SONS** → SON
Gn 6: 2 the s of God saw how beautiful
35: 22 The s of Jacob were now twelve.
Dt 7: 3 to their s nor taking their daughters for your s.
Acts 2: 17 Your s and your daughters shall
2 Cor 6: 18 you shall be s and daughters to me,

**SOON**
Rev 22: 20 says, "Yes, I am coming s." Amen!

**SORCERERS** → SORCERY
Rev 22: 15 are the dogs, the s, the unchaste,

**SORCERY** → SORCERERS
Gal 5: 20 idolatry, s, hatreds, rivalry,

**SORROW** → SORROWFUL
Est 9: 22 was turned for them from s into joy,
Eccl 1: 18 in much wisdom there is much s;
Is 35: 10 gladness, s and mourning flee away.

**SORROWFUL** → SORROW
2 Cor 6: 10 as s yet always rejoicing;

**SOUL** → SOULS
Ps 16: 9 my heart is glad, my s rejoices;
25: 1 To you, O LORD, I lift up my s,
42: 2 of water, so my s longs for you,
Sir 7: 29 With all your s fear God and revere
Mi 6: 7 fruit of my body for the sin of my s?
Mt 10: 28 kill the body but cannot kill the s;
10: 28 of the one who can destroy both s
Heb 4: 12 penetrating even between s
Jas 5: 20 his way will save his s from death
3 Jn 1: 2 health, just as your s is prospering.

**SOULS** → SOUL
1 Pt 2: 25 the shepherd and guardian of your s.

**SOUND**
Ez 1:24 Then I heard the s of their wings,
1 Cor 15:52 For the trumpet will s, the dead will
2 Tm 4:3 will not tolerate s doctrine but,
Ti 1:9 able both to exhort with s doctrine
Rev 1:15 his voice was like the s of rushing

**SOW** → SOWED, SOWER, SOWS
Ex 23:10 For six years you may s your land
Eccl 11:6 In the morning s your seed,
Hos 10:12 "S for yourselves justice,
Mt 13:3 "A sower went out to s.
1 Cor 15:36 What you s is not brought to life

**SOWED** → SOW
Mt 13:24 a man who s good seed in his field.

**SOWER** → SOW
Mk 4:14 The s sows the word.

**SOWS** → SOW
Jn 4:37 the saying is verified that 'One s
2 Cor 9:6 whoever s sparingly will also reap
9:6 and whoever s bountifully will

**SPAN**
Is 40:12 marked off the heavens with a s,
Mt 6:27 add a single moment to your l-s?

**SPARE**
Rom 11:21 God did not s the natural branches,
11:21 [perhaps] he will not s you either.
2 Pt 2:4 God did not s the angels when they

**SPARROWS**
Lk 12:7 You are worth more than many s.

**SPEAK** → SPEAKING, SPEECH, SPOKE
Gn 18:27 "See how I am presuming to s
Nm 12:8 face to face I s to him,
12:8 fear to s against my servant Moses?
Dt 18:20 if a prophet presumes to s a word
18:22 it is a word the LORD did not s.
Jb 13:3 But I would s with the Almighty;
Eccl 3:7 a time to be silent, and a time to s.
Mt 13:13 This is why I s to them in parables,
Acts 2:4 and began to s in different tongues,
1 Cor 12:30 Do all s in tongues?
Jas 1:19 to hear, slow to s, slow to wrath,

**SPEAKING** → SPEAK
1 Cor 14:39 and do not forbid s in tongues,

**SPEAR** → SPEARS
1 Sm 19:10 to pin David to the wall with the s,
19:10 and the s struck only the wall,

**SPEARS** → SPEAR
Mi 4:3 and their s into pruning hooks;

**SPECTACLE**
1 Cor 4:9 since we have become a s

**SPEECH** → SPEAK
Ex 4:10 but I am slow of s and tongue."
Sir 4:29 Do not be haughty in your s, or lazy
1 Tm 4:12 for those who believe, in s, conduct,
1 Jn 3:18 let us love not in word or s

**SPICES**
Ex 25:6 s for the anointing oil
Jn 19:40 with burial cloths along with the s,

**SPIES**
Jos 2:1 secretly sent out two s from Shittim,

**SPIRIT** → SPIRITS, SPIRITUAL
Gn 6:3 My s shall not remain in human
Nm 11:25 Taking some of the s that was
11:25 and as the s came to rest on them,
2 Kgs 2:9 receive a double portion of your s."
Neh 9:20 Your good s you bestowed on them,
Jb 33:4 For the s of God made me,
Ps 31:6 Into your hands I commend my s;
51:19 My sacrifice, O God, is a contrite s;
Prv 16:18 and a haughty s before a fall.
Is 42:1 Upon him I have put my s;
Ez 36:26 and a new s I will put within you.
Mt 1:18 found with child through the holy S.
5:3 "Blessed are the poor in s, for theirs
12:31 blasphemy against the S will not be
26:41 The s is willing, but the flesh is
Mk 1:8 will baptize you with the holy S."
Jn 3:5 without being born of water and S.
4:24 God is S, and those who worship him must worship in S
6:63 It is the s that gives life,
6:63 words I have spoken to you are s
14:26 the holy S that the Father will send
Acts 2:4 they were all filled with the holy S
2:4 as the S enabled them to proclaim.
2:38 will receive the gift of the holy S.
Rom 8:9 you are in the s, if only the S of God
8:26 the S too comes to the aid of our
8:26 but the S itself intercedes
1 Cor 6:19 is a temple of the holy S within you,
12:4 of spiritual gifts but the same S;
2 Cor 3:6 new covenant, not of letter but of s;
3:6 brings death, but the S gives life.
Gal 4:6 God sent the s of his Son into our
5:22 the fruit of the S is love, joy, peace,
Eph 1:13 sealed with the promised holy S,
2:18 have access in one S to the Father.
4:30 do not grieve the holy S of God,
5:18 debauchery, but be filled with the S,
1 Thes 5:19 Do not quench the S.
Heb 4:12 even between soul and s,
1 Jn 4:1 do not trust every s but test
Rev 1:10 caught up in s on the Lord's day

**SPIRITS** → SPIRIT
Nm 16:22 God of the s of all living creatures,
Dt 18:11 consults ghosts and s, or seeks
Lk 4:36 power he commands the unclean s,
1 Cor 12:10 to another discernment of s;
Rev 1:4 from the seven s before his throne,

**SPIRITUAL** → SPIRIT
Rom 7:14 We know that the law is s; but I am
1 Cor 2:13 describing s realities in s terms.
12:1 Now in regard to s gifts, brothers,
14:1 but strive eagerly for the s gifts,
15:46 But the s was not first;
15:46 rather the natural and then the s.
Eph 1:3 Christ with every s blessing
Col 1:9 of his will through all s wisdom
1 Pt 2:2 long for pure s milk so that through
2:5 let yourselves be built into a s house
2:5 to offer s sacrifices acceptable

**SPIT**
Mk 14:65 Some began to s on him.
Rev 3:16 cold, I will s you out of my mouth.

**SPLENDOR**
Eph 5:27 present to himself the church in s,

**SPOKE** → SPEAK
Mk 4:33 many such parables he s the word
Heb 1:1 God s in partial and various ways
2 Pt 1:21 the holy Spirit s under the influence

**SPOT**
Eph 5:27 without s or wrinkle or any such
2 Pt 3:14 be eager to be found without s

**SPRING**
Is 45:8 let righteousness s up with them!
Jn 4:14 become in him a s of water welling
Rev 21:6 gift from the s of life-giving water.

**SPRINKLE** → SPRINKLED
Nm 8:7 S them with the water
Ez 36:25 I will s clean water over you

**SPRINKLED** → SPRINKLE
Lv 8:11 he s some of the oil seven times
Heb 10:22 with our hearts s clean from an evil

**STAFF**
Ex 4:4 of it, and it became a s in his hand.
Ps 23:4 your rod and your s comfort me.
Zec 11:10 I took my s Delight and snapped it

**STAND** → STANDING
Ex 14:13 S your ground and see the victory
Jb 19:25 he will at last s forth upon the dust.
Mt 12:25 house divided against itself will s.
Rom 14:4 for the Lord is able to make him s.
14:10 we shall all s before the judgment
Eph 6:11 be able to s firm against the tactics

**STANDARDS**
1 Cor 1:26 many of you were wise by human s,

**STANDING** → STAND
1 Cor 10:12 thinks he is s secure should take
Jas 5:9 the Judge is s before the gates.

**STAR** → STARS
Nm 24:17 A s shall advance from Jacob,
Is 14:12 O Morning S, son of the dawn!
Mt 2:2 We saw his s at its rising and have
2 Pt 1:19 the morning s rises in your hearts.
Rev 9:1 I saw a s that had fallen
22:16 of David, the bright morning s."

**STARS** → STAR
Gn 1:16 one to govern the night, and the s.
Jb 38:7 While the morning s sang together
Ps 148:3 praise him, all shining s.
Dn 12:3 to justice shall be like the s forever.
Rev 1:16 In his right hand he held seven s.
12:4 away a third of the s in the sky

**STATUE**
Dn 2:31 O king, you saw a s, very large

**STATUTES**
Dt 4:1 hear the s and ordinances I am
Neh 9:13 laws, good s and commandments;

**STEADFAST**
Ps 57:8 My heart is s, God, my heart is s.
1 Pt 5:9 Resist him, s in faith,

**STEAL**
Ex 20:15 You shall not s.
Mt 6:19 destroy, and thieves break in and s.
Jn 10:10 A thief comes only to s

**STEPHEN**
Early church leader (Acts 6:5). Arrested (Acts 6:8-15). Speech to Sanhedrin (Acts 7). Stoned (Acts 7:54-60; 8:2; 11:19; 22:20).

**STEPS**
Prv 16:9 way, but the LORD directs the s.

**STIFF-NECKED** → NECK
Ex 32:9 seen this people, how s they are,
Acts 7:51 "You s people,

**STILL**
Ex 14:14 you have only to keep s."
Jos 10:13 The sun stood s, the moon stayed,
Ps 46:11 "Be s and know that I am God!
Mk 4:39 Be s!" The wind ceased and there
Rom 5:8 while we were s sinners Christ died
Heb 11:4 this, though dead, he s speaks.

**STING**
1 Cor 15:55 Where, O death, is your s?"

**STONE** → CORNERSTONE, MILLSTONE, STONED, STONES
Gn 28:18 the next morning Jacob took the s
Ex 28:10 six of their names on one s,
28:10 of the remaining six on the other s,
31:18 the s tablets inscribed by God's own
1 Sm 17:50 over the Philistine with sling and s;
Ps 118:22 The s the builders rejected has
Is 28:16 See, I am laying a s in Zion, a s
Mt 4:6 you dash your foot against a s.' "
Mk 12:10 'The s that the builders rejected has
16:3 "Who will roll back the s for us
Rom 9:32 They stumbled over the s
2 Cor 3:3 not on tablets of s but on tablets
1 Pt 2:4 a living s, rejected by human beings

**STONED** → STONE
2 Chr 24:21 at the king's command they s him
Acts 14:19 They s Paul and dragged him
Heb 11:37 They were s, sawed in two,

**STONES** → STONE
Jos 4:3 "Take up twelve s from this spot
1 Sm 17:40 David selected five smooth s
Mt 3:9 children to Abraham from these s.
Lk 19:40 they keep silent, the s will cry out!"
1 Cor 3:12 gold, silver, precious s, wood, hay,
1 Pt 2:5 like living s, let yourselves be built

**STORE** → STOREHOUSE, STORING
Mt 6:19 "Do not s up for yourselves

**STOREHOUSE** → HOUSE, STORE
Mal 3:10 Bring the whole tithe into the s,

**STORING** → STORE
Rom 2:5 you are s up wrath for yourself

**STRAIGHT**
Prv 3:6 him, and he will make s your paths.
Sir 2:6 make your ways s and hope in him.
Is 40:3 Make s in the wasteland a highway
Mt 3:3 of the Lord, make s his paths.' "
Acts 9:11 go to the street called S and ask

**STRANGE** → STRANGER, STRANGERS
Dt 32:16 With s gods they incited him,
1 Cor 14:21 "By people speaking s tongues

**STRANGER** → STRANGE
Mt 25:35 drink, a s and you welcomed me,

**STRANGERS** → STRANGE
Eph 2:12 and s to the covenants of promise,
Heb 11:13 acknowledged themselves to be s

**STRAW**
Ex 5:10 'I will not provide you with s.
1 Cor 3:12 precious stones, wood, hay, or s,

**STRAY** → ASTRAY
Ps 119:10 do not let me s from your

**STREAM** → STREAMS
Is 2:2 All nations shall s toward it.

Am 5: 24 righteousness like an unfailing s.

**STREAMS** → STREAM
Ps 1: 3 He is like a tree planted near s
42: 2 As the deer longs for s of water,

**STREET**
Prv 1: 20 Wisdom cries aloud in the s,
Mt 6: 5 on s corners so that others may see
Rev 21: 21 the s of the city was of pure gold,

**STRENGTH** → STRONG
Ex 15: 2 My s and my refuge is the LORD,
Neh 8: 10 rejoicing in the LORD is your s!"
Jdt 9: 11 "Your s is not in numbers, nor does
1 Mc 3: 19 but on s that comes from Heaven.
Ps 46: 2 God is our refuge and our s,
Prv 31: 25 She is clothed with s and dignity,
Is 40: 31 in the LORD will renew their s,
Mk 12: 30 all your mind, and with all your s.'
1 Cor 1: 25 of God is stronger than human s.

**STRENGTHEN** → STRONG
Jgs 16: 28 S me only this once that I may
Lk 22: 32 back, you must s your brothers."
Heb 12: 12 So s your drooping hands and your

**STRETCH** → OUTSTRETCHED, STRETCHED
Mk 3: 5 said to the man, "S out your hand."

**STRETCHED** → STRETCH
2 Sm 24: 16 the angel s forth his hand toward

**STRIFE** → STRIVE
Prv 23: 29 Who have s? Who have anxiety?

**STRIKE**
Gn 3: 15 They will s at your head, while you
3: 15 your head, while you s at their heel.
Ex 17: 6 S the rock, and the water will flow
Zec 13: 7 S the shepherd that the sheep may
Mk 14: 27 'I will s the shepherd, and the sheep
Rev 19: 15 came a sharp sword to s the nations.

**STRIVE** → STRIFE
1 Cor 12: 31 S eagerly for the greatest spiritual

**STRONG** → STRENGTH, STRENGTHEN, STRONGHOLD
Ex 6: 1 For by a s hand, he will let them go;
Ps 140: 8 my master, my s deliverer,
Prv 18: 10 name of the LORD is a s tower;
Rom 15: 1 We who are s ought to put
1 Cor 1: 27 weak of the world to shame the s,
2 Cor 12: 10 for when I am weak, then I am s.

**STRONGHOLD** → STRONG
Ps 9: 10 The LORD is a s for the oppressed, a s in times of trouble.

**STRUGGLE**
Eph 6: 12 For our s is not with flesh and blood
Heb 12: 4 your s against sin you have not yet

**STUBBORN**
Hos 4: 16 For like a s cow, Israel is s;

**STUDY**
Ezr 7: 10 Ezra had set his heart on the s
Eccl 12: 12 in much s there is weariness

**STUMBLE** → STUMBLING
Ps 37: 24 May s, but he will never fall,
Prv 4: 12 and should you run, you will not s.
Rom 9: 33 in Zion that will make people s
1 Pt 2: 8 "A stone that will make people s,
2: 8 They s by disobeying the word, as is

**STUMBLING** → STUMBLE
Rom 11: 9 a s block and a retribution for them;
1 Cor 8: 9 in no way becomes a s block

**STUMP**
Is 11: 1 shall sprout from the s of Jesse,

**SUBDUE**
Gn 1: 28 fill the earth and s it.
1 Chr 17: 10 And I will s all your enemies.

**SUBJECTED**
Rom 8: 20 but because of the one who s it,
1 Cor 15: 28 When everything is s to him,
15: 28 be s to the one who s everything

**SUBMIT**
Gal 5: 1 and do not s again to the yoke

**SUCCEED**
Prv 15: 22 but they s when advisers are many.

**SUDDENLY**
Mal 3: 1 the lord whom you seek will come s
Mk 13: 36 May he not come s and find you

**SUFFER** → SUFFERED, SUFFERING, SUFFERINGS, SUFFERS
Lk 22: 15 this Passover with you before I s,
24: 46 is written that the Messiah would s
Rom 8: 17 if only we s with him so that we
Heb 9: 26 he would have had to s repeatedly
1 Pt 3: 17 For it is better to s for doing good,

**SUFFERED** → SUFFER
1 Pt 2: 21 because Christ also s for you,

**SUFFERING** → SUFFER
Jb 2: 13 for they saw how great was his s.
Is 53: 3 by men, a man of s, knowing pain,

**SUFFERINGS** → SUFFER
Rom 8: 18 that the s of this present time are as
1 Pt 4: 13 that you share in the s of Christ,

**SUFFERS** → SUFFER
1 Cor 12: 26 If [one] part s, all the parts suffer

**SUFFICIENT**
2 Cor 12: 9 said to me, "My grace is s for you,

**SULFUR**
Rev 21: 8 is in the burning pool of fire and s,

**SUMMED**
Rom 13: 9 there may be, are s up in this saying,

**SUN**
Jos 10: 13 The s stood still, the moon stayed,
Ps 84: 12 For a s and shield is the LORD
Eccl 1: 9 Nothing is new under the s!
Mt 5: 45 for he makes his s rise on the bad
Acts 2: 20 The s shall be turned to darkness,
Rev 1: 16 and his face shone like the s at its
19: 17 I saw an angel standing on the s.
22: 5 will they need light from lamp or s,

**SUPERIOR**
Heb 1: 4 as far s to the angels as the name he

**SUPPLICATION** → SUPPLICATIONS
Eph 6: 18 With all prayer and s, pray at every
6: 18 and s for all the holy ones

**SUPPLICATIONS** → SUPPLICATION
1 Tm 2: 1 then, I ask that s, prayers, petitions,
Heb 5: 7 offered prayers and s with loud cries

**SUPPORT**
Ps 18:19 distress, but the LORD was my s.
Rom 11:18 consider that you do not s the root;

**SURE**
Nm 32:23 you can be s that the consequences
Is 28:16 cornerstone as a s foundation;
Heb 6:19 as an anchor of the soul, s and firm,

**SURPASSES** → SURPASSING
Sir 25:11 Fear of the Lord s all else.
Eph 3:19 the love of Christ that s knowledge,
Phil 4:7 s all understanding will guard your

**SURPASSING** → SURPASSES
2 Cor 9:14 because of the s grace of God

**SURPRISED**
1 Pt 4:12 do not be s that a trial by fire is

**SURROUNDED** → SURROUNDS
Lk 21:20 you see Jerusalem s by armies,
Heb 12:1 since we are s by so great a cloud
Rev 20:9 and s the camp of the holy ones

**SURROUNDS** → SURROUNDED
Ps 125:2 the LORD s his people both now

**SURVIVORS**
Ez 14:22 there will still be some s in it who

**SUSA**
Neh 1:1 year, I was in the citadel of S
Est 1:2 throne in the royal precinct of S,

**SUSANNA**
Righteous woman wrongly accused of immorality (Dn 13:1-44); vindicated by Daniel (Dn 13:45-64).

**SUSTAINS**
Heb 1:3 who s all things by his mighty word.

**SWALLOW** → SWALLOWED
Mt 23:24 strain out the gnat and s the camel!

**SWALLOWED** → SWALLOW
Gn 41:7 and the thin ears s up the seven fat,
Nm 16:32 earth opened its mouth and s them
1 Cor 15:54 "Death is s up in victory.

**SWEAR** → SWORE, SWORN
Dt 10:20 fast and by his name shall you s.
Mt 5:34 But I say to you, do not s at all;

**SWEAT**
Gn 3:19 By the s of your brow you shall eat
Lk 22:44 that his s became like drops

**SWEET** → SWEETER
Ps 119:103 How s to my tongue is your promise,
Ez 3:3 it was as s as honey in my mouth.
Rev 10:10 In my mouth it was like s honey,

**SWEETER** → SWEET
Jgs 14:18 said to him, "What is s than honey,
Ps 19:11 S also than honey or drippings

**SWIFT**
Eccl 9:11 sun that the race is not won by the s,
2 Pt 2:1 them, bringing s destruction

**SWINE**
1 Mc 1:47 to sacrifice s and unclean animals,
Mt 7:6 or throw your pearls before s,
Mk 5:12 with him, "Send us into the s.

**SWORD** → SWORDS
Gn 3:24 and the fiery revolving s east
1 Sm 17:47 shall learn that it is not by s or spear
1 Chr 21:30 he was fearful of the s of the angel
Sir 21:3 lawlessness is like a two-edged s;
Is 2:4 shall not raise the s against another,
49:2 my mouth like a sharp-edged s,
Mt 10:34 come to bring not peace but the s.
Lk 2:35 you yourself a s will pierce) so
Eph 6:17 of salvation and the s of the Spirit,
Heb 4:12 sharper than any two-edged s,
Rev 1:16 A sharp two-edged s came
19:15 his mouth came a sharp s to strike

**SWORDS** → SWORD
Is 2:4 They shall beat their s

**SWORE** → SWEAR
Ex 6:8 into the land which I s to give
32:13 and how you s to them by your own
Ps 132:11 The LORD s an oath to David
Heb 6:13 whom to swear, "he s by himself,"

**SWORN** → SWEAR
Ps 110:4 The LORD has s and will not
Heb 7:21 "The Lord has s, and he will not

**SYMPATHIZE**
Heb 4:15 have a high priest who is unable to s

**SYNAGOGUE** → SYNAGOGUES
Lk 4:16 into the s on the sabbath day.
8:41 an official of the s, came forward.
Acts 18:26 He began to speak boldly in the s;

**SYNAGOGUES** → SYNAGOGUE
Mt 4:23 teaching in their s,

## T

**TABERNACLE**
Lv 26:11 I will set my t in your midst,

**TABITHA** → See DORCAS

**TABLE** → TABLES
Ex 25:23 shall also make a t of acacia wood,
Ps 23:5 You set a t before me in front of my

**TABLES** → TABLE
Mk 11:15 He overturned the t of the money

**TABLETS**
Ex 31:18 Sinai, he gave him the two t
31:18 the stone t inscribed by God's own
2 Cor 3:3 not on t of stone but on t that are

**TAKE** → TAKEN, TAKES
Mt 11:29 T my yoke upon you and learn
Mk 8:34 must deny himself, t up his cross,

**TAKEN** → TAKE
Sir 44:16 walked with the LORD and was t,
Heb 11:5 By faith Enoch was t up so that he
11:5 no more because God had t him."

**TAKES** → TAKE
Jn 1:29 who t away the sin of the world.
10:18 No one t it from me, but I lay it
Rev 22:19 if anyone t away from the words

**TALENT**
Mt 25:25 off and buried your t in the ground.

**TAMAR**
1. Wife of Judah's sons Er and Onan (Gn 38:1-10). Children by Judah (Gn 38:11-30; Mt 1:3).
2. Daughter of David, raped by Amnon (2 Sm 13).

**TASTE** → TASTED
Mt 16:28 here who will not t death until they
Col 2:21 Do not t! Do not touch!"

**TASTED** → TASTE
Heb 6: 4 enlightened and **t** the heavenly gift
1 Pt 2: 3 for you have **t** that the Lord is good.

**TAUGHT** → TEACH
Is 40: 14 Who **t** him the path of judgment,
Jn 6: 45 'They shall all be **t** by God.'

**TAX** → TAXES
Mt 11: 19 a friend of **t** collectors and sinners.'
Lk 18: 10 and the other was a **t** collector.

**TAXES** → TAX
Rom 13: 7 all their dues, **t** to whom **t** are due,

**TEACH** → TAUGHT, TEACHER, TEACHERS, TEACHING
Ps 90: 12 **T** us to count our days aright,
Jer 31: 34 They will no longer **t** their friends
Jn 14: 26 he will **t** you everything and remind
Col 3: 16 richly, as in all wisdom you **t**
1 Tm 2: 12 I do not permit a woman to **t**
1 Jn 2: 27 you do not need anyone to **t** you.

**TEACHER** → TEACH
Mt 10: 24 No disciple is above his **t**, no slave
Jn 1: 38 (which translated means **T**),

**TEACHERS** → TEACH
Ps 119: 99 I have more insight than all my **t**,
1 Cor 12: 28 third, **t**; then, mighty deeds;
Eph 4: 11 evangelists, others as pastors and **t**,
Jas 3: 1 Not many of you should become **t**,

**TEACHING** → TEACH
Mk 1: 27 A new **t** with authority.
Ti 1: 11 are upsetting whole families by **t**
2 Jn 1: 9 in the **t** of the Christ does not have
1: 9 remains in the **t** has the Father

**TEAR** → TORN
Mk 2: 21 from the old, and the **t** gets worse.
Rev 7: 17 God will wipe away every **t**

**TEETH** → TOOTH
Mt 8: 12 will be wailing and grinding of **t**."

**TEKEL**
Dn 5: 27 **T**, you have been weighed

**TELL**
Ps 50: 12 I would not **t** you, for mine is
1 Cor 15: 51 Behold, I **t** you a mystery.

**TEMPERATE**
1 Tm 3: 2 irreproachable, married only once, **t**,
Ti 2: 2 that older men should be **t**,

**TEMPLE**
1 Sm 3: 3 in the **t** of the LORD where the ark
1 Mc 4: 48 the interior of the **t** and consecrated
Ps 11: 4 The LORD is in his holy **t**;
Mt 4: 5 him stand on the parapet of the **t**,
12: 6 something greater than the **t** is here.
Jn 2: 21 speaking about the **t** of his body.
1 Cor 3: 16 not know that you are the **t** of God,
Eph 2: 21 grows into a **t** sacred in the Lord;
Rev 21: 22 I saw no **t** in the city, for its **t** is

**TEMPTATION** → TEMPTED, TEMPTER
1 Tm 6: 9 who want to be rich are falling into **t**
Jas 1: 12 is the man who perseveres in **t**,

**TEMPTED** → TEMPTATION
Mk 1: 13 the desert for forty days, **t** by Satan.
Gal 6: 1 so that you also may not be **t**.

**TEMPTER** → TEMPTATION
Mt 4: 3 The **t** approached and said to him,

1 Thes 3: 5 fear that somehow the **t** had put you

**TEN** → TENTH
Ex 34: 28 words of the covenant, the **t** words.
Dn 7: 24 The **t** horns shall be **t** kings rising
Mt 25: 1 will be like **t** virgins who took their
Rev 17: 12 The **t** horns that you saw represent **t**

**TENDER**
Lk 1: 78 because of the **t** mercy of our God

**TENT**
Ex 27: 21 the LORD in the **t** of meeting,
2 Sm 7: 2 but the ark of God dwells in a **t**!"
2 Cor 5: 1 dwelling, a **t**, should be destroyed,

**TENTH** → TEN
Gn 14: 20 Abram gave him a **t** of everything.
Is 6: 13 If there remain a **t** part in it,

**TERROR**
Ps 91: 5 You shall not fear the **t** of the night

**TEST** → TESTED, TESTING
Dt 6: 16 God, to the **t**, as you did at Massah.
Lk 4: 12 the Lord, your God, to the **t**.' "
10: 25 of the law who stood up to **t** him
2 Cor 13: 5 you are living in faith. **T** yourselves.
13: 5 unless, of course, you fail the **t**.
1 Jn 4: 1 but **t** the spirits to see whether they

**TESTED** → TEST
Ps 78: 41 Again and again they **t** God,
Heb 4: 15 but one who has similarly been **t**

**TESTIFIED** → TESTIFY
Jn 1: 15 John **t** to him and cried out, saying,
1 Pt 1: 11 them indicated when it **t** in advance

**TESTIFIES** → TESTIFY
1 Jn 5: 6 The Spirit is the one that **t**,

**TESTIFY** → TESTIFIED, TESTIFIES, TESTIMONIES, TESTIMONY
Jn 15: 26 from the Father, he will **t** to me.
1 Jn 5: 7 So there are three that **t**,

**TESTIMONIES** → TESTIFY
Ps 119: 2 Blessed those who keep his **t**,

**TESTIMONY** → TESTIFY
Mk 14: 59 Even so their **t** did not agree.
Rev 1: 9 God's word and gave **t** to Jesus.

**TESTING** → TEST
Jas 1: 3 that the **t** of your faith produces

**THADDAEUS** → =JUDAS
Apostle (Mt 10:3; Mk 3:18); probably also known as Judas son of James (Lk 6:16; Acts 1:13).

**THANK** → THANKS, THANKSGIVING
2 Chr 29: 31 and **t** offerings for the house
29: 31 the sacrifices and **t** offerings and all

**THANKS** → THANK
1 Chr 16: 8 Give **t** to the LORD, invoke his
Ps 107: 1 "Give **t** to the LORD for he is
Rom 1: 21 him glory as God or give him **t**.
1 Cor 11: 24 after he had given **t**, broke it
2 Cor 9: 15 **T** be to God for his indescribable
Rev 4: 9 **t** to the one who sits on the throne,

**THANKSGIVING** → THANK
Lv 7: 12 If someone offers it for **t**,
Ps 100: 4 Enter his gates with **t**,
Phil 4: 6 with **t**, make your requests known
Rev 7: 12 and glory, wisdom and **t**, honor,

**THEFT** → THIEF
Mt 15:19 adultery, unchastity, **t**, false witness,

**THIEF** → THEFT, THIEVES
Ex 22: 1 If a **t** is caught in the act
Jn 10:10 A **t** comes only to steal
1 Thes 5: 2 the Lord will come like a **t** at night.
Rev 16:15 ("Behold, I am coming like a **t**."

**THIEVES** → THIEF
Mt 6:19 destroy, and **t** break in and steal.

**THINK** → THINKING, THOUGHT, THOUGHTS
Rom 12: 3 I tell everyone among you not to **t** more highly than one ought to **t**,

**THINKING** → THINK
1 Cor 14:20 stop being childish in your **t**.
14:20 like infants, but in your **t** be mature.

**THIRD** → THREE
Hos 6: 2 on the **t** day he will raise us up,
Mt 26:44 withdrew again and prayed a **t** time,
Lk 18:33 him, but on the **t** day he will rise."
2 Cor 12: 2 was caught up to the **t** heaven.

**THIRST** → THIRSTY
Mt 5: 6 who hunger and **t** for righteousness,
Rev 7:16 They will not hunger or **t** anymore,

**THIRSTY** → THIRST
Mt 25:35 I was **t** and you gave me drink,

**THOMAS**
Apostle (Mt 10:3; Mk 3:18; Lk 6:15; Jn 11:16; 14:5; 21:2; Acts 1:13). Doubted resurrection (Jn 20:24-28).

**THORN** → THORNS
2 Cor 12: 7 a **t** in the flesh was given to me,

**THORNS** → THORN
Gn 3:18 **T** and thistles it shall bear for you,
Mt 13: 7 Some seed fell among **t**, and the **t**
Jn 19: 2 the soldiers wove a crown out of **t**

**THOUGHT** → THINK
2 Cor 10: 5 take every **t** captive in obedience

**THOUGHTS** → THINK
Is 55: 8 For my **t** are not your **t**, nor are your
1 Cor 3:20 "The Lord knows the **t** of the wise,
Heb 4:12 reflections and **t** of the heart.

**THOUSAND** → THOUSANDS
Ps 90: 4 A **t** years in your eyes are merely
2 Pt 3: 8 the Lord one day is like a **t** years
3: 8 a **t** years and a **t** years like one day.
Rev 20: 4 reigned with Christ for a **t** years.

**THOUSANDS** → THOUSAND
1 Sm 18: 7 "Saul has slain his **t**, David his tens of **t**."
Dn 7:10 **T** upon **t** were ministering to him,

**THREE** → THIRD
Gn 18: 2 up, he saw **t** men standing near him.
Ex 23:14 **T** times a year you shall celebrate
Mt 18:20 **t** are gathered together in my name,
26:34 crows, you will deny me **t** times."
Mk 8:31 and be killed, and rise after **t** days.
2 Cor 12: 8 **T** times I begged the Lord
1 Jn 5: 7 So there are **t** that testify,

**THRONE** → THRONES
2 Sm 7:13 I will establish his royal **t** forever.
Ps 45: 7 Your **t**, O God, stands forever;
Is 6: 1 Lord seated on a high and lofty **t**,
Jer 33:21 descendant to act as king upon his **t**,
Mt 19:28 of Man is seated on his **t** of glory,
Heb 4:16 So let us confidently approach the **t**
12: 2 his seat at the right of the **t** of God.
Rev 4:10 before the one who sits on the **t**
4:10 down their crowns before the **t**,
20:11 Next I saw a large white **t**

**THRONES** → THRONE
Dn 7: 9 **T** were set up and the Ancient
Rev 4: 4 the throne I saw twenty-four other **t**

**THROW** → THROWN
Ex 1:22 "**T** into the Nile every boy that is
Mt 7: 6 or **t** your pearls before swine,

**THROWN** → THROW
Rev 20:10 Devil who had led them astray was **t**

**THUMMIM**
Ex 28:30 you shall put the Urim and **T**,

**THUNDER** → THUNDERS
Ex 9:23 the LORD sent forth peals of **t**
Rev 4: 5 lightning, rumblings, and peals of **t**.

**THUNDERS** → THUNDER
Rev 10: 3 out, the seven **t** raised their voices,

**TIBNI**
King of Israel (1 Kgs 16:21-22).

**TIE**
Mt 23: 4 They **t** up heavy burdens [hard

**TIME** → TIMES
Est 4:14 perhaps it was for a **t** like this
Eccl 3: 1 and a **t** for every affair under
Rom 5: 6 at the appointed **t** for the ungodly.
2 Cor 6: 2 "In an acceptable **t** I heard you,
6: 2 Behold, now is a very acceptable **t**;
Gal 4: 4 when the fullness of **t** had come,
Rev 22:10 book, for the appointed **t** is near.

**TIMES** → TIME
Jos 6: 4 day march around the city seven **t**,
Mt 16: 3 you cannot judge the signs of the **t**.]
18:22 you, not seven **t** but seventy-seven **t**.
Mk 14:30 twice you will deny me three **t**."

**TIMOTHY**
Believer from Lystra (Acts 16:1). Joined Paul on second missionary journey (Acts 16–20). Sent to settle problems at Corinth (1 Cor 4:17; 16:10). Led church at Ephesus (1 Tm 1:3). Co-writer with Paul (1 Thes 1:1; 2 Thes 1:1; Phlm 1).

**TITHE**
Dt 12:17 partake of your **t** of grain or wine
Mal 3:10 Bring the whole **t**

**TITUS**
Gentile co-worker of Paul (Gal 2:1-3; 2 Tm 4:10); sent to Corinth (2 Cor 2:13; 7–8; 12:18), Crete (Ti 1:4-5).

**TOBIAH**
Enemy of Nehemiah (Neh 2:10-19; 4; 6; 13:4-9).

**TOBIT**
Tb 1: 1 This book tells the story of **T**,

**TODAY**
Dt 30:15 See, I have **t** set before you life
Ps 2: 7 are my son; **t** I have begotten you.
Lk 23:43 **t** you will be with me in Paradise."
Heb 13: 8 Jesus Christ is the same yesterday, **t**,

**TOGETHER**
Mt 19: 6 what God has joined **t**, no human

**TOIL**
Gn 3:16 I will intensify your **t** in childbearing;

**TOLA**
A judge of Israel (Jgs 10:1-2).

**TOMB**
Mk 15: 46 laid him in a **t** that had been hewn
15: 46 a stone against the entrance to the **t**.
Lk 24: 2 the stone rolled away from the **t**;

**TOMORROW**
Is 22: 13 "Eat and drink, for **t** we die!"
Mt 6: 34 Do not worry about **t**; **t** will take
Jas 4: 14 no idea what your life will be like **t**.

**TONGUE** → TONGUES
Ex 4: 10 but I am slow of speech and **t**."
Ps 139: 4 Even before a word is on my **t**,
Prv 18: 21 and life are in the power of the **t**;
Is 45: 23 by me every **t** shall swear,
1 Cor 14: 19 also, than ten thousand words in a **t**.
Phil 2: 11 every **t** confess that Jesus Christ is
Jas 3: 8 but no human being can tame the **t**.

**TONGUES** → TONGUE
Acts 2: 3 there appeared to them **t** as of fire,
1 Cor 12: 10 to another varieties of **t**; to another interpretation of **t**.
14: 5 I should like all of you to speak in **t**,
14: 5 is greater than one who speaks in **t**,

**TOOTH** → TEETH
Ex 21: 24 eye for eye, **t** for **t**, hand for hand,
Mt 5: 38 'An eye for an eye and a **t** for a **t**.'

**TORCHES**
Dn 10: 6 his eyes were like fiery **t**, his arms
Rev 4: 5 Seven flaming **t** burned in front

**TORMENTED**
Rev 20: 10 There they will be **t** day and night

**TORN** → TEAR
1 Sm 28: 17 he has **t** the kingdom from your
Lk 23: 45 the temple was **t** down the middle.

**TORTURED**
Heb 11: 35 Some were **t** and would not accept

**TOUCH**
Gn 3: 3 'You shall not eat it or even **t** it,
Mt 9: 21 "If only I can **t** his cloak, I shall be
Lk 24: 39 **T** me and see, because a ghost does
Col 2: 21 Do not taste! Do not **t**!"

**TOWER**
Gn 11: 4 a city and a **t** with its top in the sky,
Prv 18: 10 name of the LORD is a strong **t**;

**TRADITION**
Mt 15: 2 "Why do your disciples break the **t**
Col 2: 8 philosophy according to human **t**,

**TRAIN** → TRAINING
Prv 22: 6 **T** the young in the way they should
1 Tm 4: 7 **T** yourself for devotion,

**TRAINING** → TRAIN
1 Tm 4: 8 while physical **t** is of limited value,
2 Tm 3: 16 and for **t** in righteousness,

**TRAITOR**
Lk 6: 16 and Judas Iscariot, who became a **t**.

**TRANSFIGURED**
Mt 17: 2 And he was **t** before them;

**TRANSFORMED**
Rom 12: 2 be **t** by the renewal of your mind,
2 Cor 3: 18 are being **t** into the same image

**TRANSGRESSION**
Dn 9: 24 Then **t** will stop and sin will end,
Gal 6: 1 even if a person is caught in some **t**,

**TRAP**
Lk 20: 20 to be righteous who were to **t** him
Rom 11: 9 their table become a snare and a **t**,

**TREAD** → TREADING, TREADS
Rev 19: 15 and he himself will **t** out in the wine

**TREADING** → TREAD
Mi 7: 19 on us, **t** underfoot our iniquities?
1 Cor 9: 9 shall not muzzle an ox while it is **t**

**TREADS** → TREAD
Dt 25: 4 not muzzle an ox when it **t** out grain.

**TREASURE** → TREASURES
Ps 119: 11 In my heart I **t** your promise, that I
Mt 6: 21 For where your **t** is, there also will
2 Cor 4: 7 we hold this **t** in earthen vessels,

**TREASURES** → TREASURE
Col 2: 3 in whom are hidden all the **t**

**TREE** → TREES
Gn 3: 24 to guard the way to the **t** of life.
Dt 21: 23 shall not remain on the **t** overnight.
Mt 12: 33 "Either declare the **t** good and its
12: 33 or declare the **t** rotten and its fruit is
Acts 5: 30 him killed by hanging him on a **t**.
Rom 11: 24 what is by nature a wild olive **t**,
11: 24 grafted back into their own olive **t**.
Rev 22: 2 side of the river grew the **t** of life

**TREES** → TREE
Ps 96: 12 Then let all the **t** of the forest rejoice
Zec 4: 11 "What are these two olive **t**,
Rev 11: 4 These are the two olive **t**

**TREMBLE** → TREMBLED, TREMBLING
Ps 114: 7 **T**, earth, before the Lord,
Hb 3: 6 he looked and made the nations **t**.

**TREMBLED** → TREMBLE
Ex 20: 18 smoking, they became afraid and **t**.

**TREMBLING** → TREMBLE
Ps 2: 11 exult with **t**, Accept correction lest
Phil 2: 12 out your salvation with fear and **t**.

**TRESPASSES**
2 Cor 5: 19 not counting their **t** against them

**TRIAL** → TRIALS
2 Pt 2: 9 how to rescue the devout from **t**
Rev 3: 10 safe in the time of **t** that is going

**TRIALS** → TRIAL
Jas 1: 2 when you encounter various **t**,
1 Pt 1: 6 have to suffer through various **t**,

**TRIBE** → TRIBES
Nm 1: 4 there shall be a man from each **t**,
Ps 78: 68 God chose the **t** of Judah,
Rev 5: 5 The lion of the **t** of Judah, the root

**TRIBES** → TRIBE
Gn 49: 28 All these are the twelve **t** of Israel,
Ex 24: 4 stones for the twelve **t** of Israel.
Mt 19: 28 judging the twelve **t** of Israel.
Rev 21: 12 of the twelve **t** of the Israelites.

**TRIUMPHS**
Jas 2: 13 mercy **t** over judgment.

**TROUBLE** → TROUBLED
Jb 14: 1 woman is short-lived and full of **t**,
Ps 9: 10 a stronghold in times of **t**.
Sir 51: 10 Do not abandon me in time of **t**,
Is 33: 2 morning, our salvation in time of **t**!

**TROUBLED** → TROUBLE
Jn 14: 1 "Do not let your hearts be **t**.

**TRUE** → TRUTH
Jn 1: 9 The **t** light, which enlightens
21: 24 and we know that his testimony is **t**.
Rom 3: 4 God must be **t**, though every human
1 Jn 5: 20 to know the one who is **t**. And we are in the one who is **t**,
5: 20 He is the **t** God and eternal life.
Rev 3: 14 the faithful and **t** witness, the source
19: 11 rider was [called] "Faithful and **T**."
22: 6 "These words are trustworthy and **t**,

**TRUMPET** → TRUMPETS
1 Cor 15: 52 in the blink of an eye, at the last **t**.
15: 52 For the **t** will sound, the dead will
1 Thes 4: 16 an archangel and with the **t** of God,

**TRUMPETS** → TRUMPET
Nm 10: 2 Make two **t** of silver, making them
Rev 8: 2 before God were given seven **t**.

**TRUST** → ENTRUSTED, TRUSTED, TRUSTS, TRUSTWORTHY
Nm 14: 11 How long will they not **t** me, despite
Ps 9: 11 Those who know your name **t**
37: 3 **T** in the LORD and do good
119: 42 with a word, for I **t** in your word.
Prv 3: 5 **T** in the LORD with all your heart,
Sir 2: 6 **T** in God, and he will help you;
Jer 17: 7 Blessed are those who **t** in the LORD; the LORD will be their **t**.
Heb 2: 13 and again: "I will put my **t** in him";

**TRUSTED** → TRUST
Ps 22: 5 In you our fathers **t**; they **t** and you
Dn 3: 95 to deliver the servants that **t** in him;
13: 35 she **t** in the Lord wholeheartedly.

**TRUSTS** → TRUST
Ps 86: 2 save your servant who **t** in you.

**TRUSTWORTHY** → TRUST
1 Cor 7: 25 as one who by the Lord's mercy is **t**.
Rev 22: 6 to me, "These words are **t** and true,

**TRUTH** → TRUE
Prv 23: 23 Buy **t** and do not sell:
Jn 1: 17 and **t** came through Jesus Christ.
4: 23 worship the Father in Spirit and **t**;
8: 32 and you will know the **t**, and the **t**
14: 6 "I am the way and the **t** and the life.
14: 17 the Spirit of **t**, which the world
16: 13 the Spirit of **t**, he will guide you to all **t**.
Eph 4: 15 Rather, living the **t** in love,
1 Tm 3: 15 God, the pillar and foundation of **t**.
2 Tm 2: 15 the word of **t** without deviation.

**TUNIC**
Lk 9: 3 and let no one take a second **t**.
Jn 19: 23 They also took his **t**, but the **t** was

**TURN**
Is 6: 10 and they **t** and be healed.
45: 22 **T** to me and be safe, all you ends
Lk 1: 17 of Elijah to **t** the hearts of fathers

**TWELVE**
Gn 49: 28 All these are the **t** tribes of Israel,
Ex 24: 4 and **t** sacred stones for the **t** tribes
Jos 4: 3 "Take up **t** stones from this spot
Mt 10: 1 he summoned his **t** disciples
Lk 9: 17 up, they filled **t** wicker baskets.
Rev 21: 12 with **t** gates where **t** angels were
21: 12 [the names] of the **t** tribes
22: 2 that produces fruit **t** times a year,

**TWO** → TWO-EDGED
Gn 1: 16 God made the **t** great lights,
6: 19 all living creatures you shall bring **t**
Ex 31: 18 he gave him the **t** tablets
Dt 17: 6 Only on the testimony of **t** or three
Mt 6: 24 "No one can serve **t** masters.
19: 5 and the **t** shall become one flesh'?

**TWO-EDGED** → TWO
Heb 4: 12 effective, sharper than any **t** sword,
Rev 1: 16 A sharp **t** sword came out of his

**TYRE**
Ez 28: 12 raise a lament over the king of **T**,
Mt 11: 22 it will be more tolerable for **T**

## U

**UNBELIEF** → UNBELIEVER, UNBELIEVERS
Mk 9: 24 out, "I do believe, help my **u**!"
Rom 11: 20 They were broken off because of **u**,
1 Tm 1: 13 I acted out of ignorance in my **u**.

**UNBELIEVER** → UNBELIEF
1 Cor 10: 27 If an **u** invites you and you want
2 Cor 6: 15 a believer in common with an **u**?

**UNBELIEVERS** → UNBELIEF
2 Cor 6: 14 with those who are different, with **u**.

**UNCIRCUMCISED** → UNCIRCUMCISION
Ex 12: 48 But no one who is **u** may eat of it.
1 Mc 1: 48 to leave their sons **u**, and to defile
Acts 7: 51 people, **u** in heart and ears,
Rom 4: 11 through faith while he was **u**.
4: 11 the father of all the **u** who believe,

**UNCIRCUMCISION** → UNCIRCUMCISED
1 Cor 7: 19 nothing, and **u** means nothing;
Gal 5: 6 neither circumcision nor **u** counts

**UNCLEAN**
Lv 5: 2 it, touches any **u** thing, such as
5: 2 creature, and thus is **u** and guilty;
Is 52: 11 go out from there, touch nothing **u**!
Mk 3: 11 whenever **u** spirits saw him they
Rev 21: 27 but nothing **u** will enter it,

**UNDER**
Acts 4: 12 any other name **u** heaven given
Rom 6: 14 since you are not **u** the law but **u**

**UNDERSTAND** → UNDERSTANDING
Jb 42: 3 I have spoken but did not **u**;
Prv 2: 5 will you **u** the fear of the LORD;
Mt 13: 15 with their ears and **u** with their heart
Lk 24: 45 their minds to **u** the scriptures.
Acts 8: 30 "Do you **u** what you are reading?"
Eph 5: 17 try to **u** what is the will of the Lord.

**UNDERSTANDING** → UNDERSTAND
Ex 36: 1 **u** in knowing how to do all the work
Prv 2: 6 his mouth come knowledge and **u**;
Is 40: 14 or showed him the way of **u**?
Lk 2: 47 heard him were astounded at his **u**
Phil 4: 7 that surpasses all **u** will guard your
2 Tm 2: 7 for the Lord will give you **u**

**UNFAITHFUL**
Rom 3: 3 What if some were **u**?

**UNGODLY**
Rom 5: 6 died at the appointed time for the **u**.

**UNITY**
Eph 4: 3 preserve the **u** of the spirit through

**UNJUST**
Rom 3: 5 Is God **u**, humanly speaking,
Heb 6: 10 God is not **u** so as to overlook your

**UNLEAVENED**
Ex 12: 17 the custom of the **u** bread, since it
Mt 26: 17 first day of the Feast of **U** Bread,

**UNPRODUCTIVE**
1 Cor 14: 14 spirit is at prayer but my mind is **u**.
Ti 3: 14 needs, so that they may not be **u**.

**UNRIGHTEOUS**
2 Pt 2: 9 to keep the **u** under punishment

**UPHOLD**
Is 42: 1 Here is my servant whom I **u**,

**UPRIGHT**
Jb 1: 1 a blameless and **u** man named Job,

**UR**
Gn 15: 7 LORD who brought you from **U**

**URIAH**
Hittite husband of Bathsheba, killed (2 Sm 11).

**URIM**
Ex 28: 30 of decision you shall put the **U**

**USE** → USEFUL
Gal 5: 13 But do not **u** this freedom as
2 Tm 2: 20 for lofty and others for humble **u**.

**USEFUL** → USE
2 Tm 3: 16 by God and is **u** for teaching,

**UZZIAH** → =AZARIAH
Son of Amaziah; king of Judah also known as Azariah (2 Kgs 15:1-7; 1 Chr 6:24; 2 Chr 26). Struck with leprosy because of pride (2 Chr 26:16-23).

## V

**VAIN** → VANITY
Lv 26: 16 You will sow your seed in **v**,
Ps 2: 1 and the peoples conspire in **v**?
Mt 15: 9 in **v** do they worship me, teaching as
Phil 2: 16 that I did not run in **v** or labor in **v**.

**VALLEY**
Ps 23: 4 Even though I walk through the **v**
Is 40: 4 Every **v** shall be lifted up,
40: 4 plain, the rough country, a broad **v**.
Lk 3: 5 Every **v** shall be filled and every

**VALUE**
Rom 3: 1 Or what is the **v** of circumcision?
1 Tm 4: 8 physical training is of limited **v**,

**VANITY** → VAIN
Eccl 1: 2 **V** of vanities, says Qoheleth,
1: 2 **v** of vanities! All things are **v**!
12: 8 **V** of vanities, says Qoheleth,
12: 8 says Qoheleth, all things are **v**!

**VASHTI**
Persian queen replaced by Esther (Est 1–2).

**VEIL**
Ex 34: 33 with them, he put a **v** over his face.
2 Cor 3: 15 is read, a **v** lies over their hearts,

**VENGEANCE** → AVENGE, AVENGER, AVENGING
Is 34: 8 For the LORD has a day of **v**,
Na 1: 2 The LORD takes **v** on his

**VICTORY**
Prv 21: 31 day of battle, but **v** is the LORD'S.
1 Cor 15: 54 "Death is swallowed up in **v**.
1 Jn 5: 4 the **v** that conquers the world is our

**VINDICATED** → VINDICATION
Mt 11: 19 But wisdom is **v** by her works."
1 Tm 3: 16 in the flesh, **v** in the spirit,

**VINDICATION** → VINDICATED
Is 48: 18 your **v** like the waves of the sea,

**VINE** → VINEYARD
Ps 80: 9 You brought a **v** out of Egypt;
Jer 2: 21 But I had planted you as a choice **v**,
2: 21 so obnoxious to me, a spurious **v**?
Jn 15: 1 "I am the true **v**, and my Father is the **v** grower.

**VINEYARD** → VINE
1 Kgs 21: 1 Naboth the Jezreelite had a **v**
Is 5: 1 my beloved's song about his **v**.
Mt 21: 33 was a landowner who planted a **v**,

**VIOLENCE**
Hb 2: 17 For the **v** done to Lebanon shall
2: 17 and **v** done to the land, to the city

**VIPERS**
Mt 23: 33 you brood of **v**, how can you flee

**VIRGIN**
Jer 31: 21 Turn back, **v** Israel, turn back
Mt 1: 23 the **v** shall be with child and bear
2 Cor 11: 2 present you as a chaste **v** to Christ.

**VISION** → VISIONS
Is 22: 1 Oracle on the Valley of **V**:
Dn 8: 26 As for the **v** of the evenings
8: 26 But you, keep this **v** secret: it is
Acts 26: 19 not disobedient to the heavenly **v**.

**VISIONS** → VISION
Nm 12: 6 you, in **v** I reveal myself to them,
Ez 1: 1 opened, and I saw divine **v**.—
Dn 1: 17 to Daniel the understanding of all **v**
Acts 2: 17 your young men shall see **v**,

**VOICE**
Is 40: 3 A **v** proclaims: In the wilderness
Jn 1: 23 "I am 'the **v** of one crying
10: 3 and the sheep hear his **v**, as he calls
Heb 3: 7 that today you would hear his **v**,
Rev 3: 20 If anyone hears my **v** and opens

**VOW** → VOWS
Eccl 5: 4 better not to make a **v** than make it
Sir 18: 23 Before making a **v** prepare yourself;

**VOWS** → VOW
Ps 22: 26 my **v** I will fulfill before those who

## W

**WAGES**
Rom 6: 23 For the **w** of sin is death, but the gift

**WAIT**
Ps 27: 14 **W** for the LORD, take courage;
27: 14 be stouthearted, **w** for the LORD!
Sir 2: 7 that fear the Lord, **w** for his mercy,
Hb 2: 3 If it delays, **w** for it, it will surely
Rom 8: 23 groan within ourselves as we **w**

**WALK** → WALKED, WALKING
Gn 17: 1 **W** in my presence and be blameless.
Ps 23: 4 Even though I **w** through the valley
Is 2: 5 let us **w** in the light of the LORD!
40: 31 grow weary, **w** and not grow faint.
Jer 6: 16 and **w** it; thus you will find rest
6: 16 But they said, "We will not **w** it."
Jn 8: 12 Whoever follows me will not **w**
2 Cor 5: 7 for we **w** by faith, not by sight.
Rev 21: 24 The nations will **w** by its light,

**WALKED** → WALK
Gn 5: 24 Enoch **w** with God, and he was no

**WALKING** → WALK
Mt 14: 26 the disciples saw him **w** on the sea

**WALL**
Jos 6: 20 The **w** collapsed, and the people
Neh 2: 17 let us rebuild the **w** of Jerusalem,
Eph 2: 14 and broke down the dividing **w**

**WAR** → WARRIOR, WARS
Ps 24: 8 and mighty, the LORD, mighty in **w**.
Eccl 3: 8 a time of **w**, and a time of peace.
Dn 9: 26 until the end of the **w**, which is
Rom 7: 23 my members another principle at **w**
Rev 19: 11 and wages **w** in righteousness.

**WARRIOR** → WAR
Ex 15: 3 The LORD is a **w**, LORD is his

**WARS** → WAR
Mt 24: 6 You will hear of **w** and reports of **w**;

**WASH** → WASHED
Ps 51: 9 **w** me, and I will be whiter than
Jn 13: 5 began to **w** the disciples' feet
Rev 22: 14 are they who **w** their robes so as

**WASHED** → WASH
1 Cor 6: 11 but now you have had yourselves **w**,

**WATCH**
Lk 2: 8 keeping the night **w** over their flock.
Heb 13: 17 for they keep **w** over you and will

**WATER** → WATERS
Ex 17: 1 But there was no **w** for the people
Nm 20: 2 Since the community had no **w**,
Jer 2: 13 broken cisterns that cannot hold **w**.
Ez 36: 25 I will sprinkle clean **w** over you
Mk 1: 8 I have baptized you with **w**;
Jn 2: 9 the headwaiter tasted the **w** that had
2: 9 who had drawn the **w** knew),
3: 5 of God without being born of **w**
4: 10 he would have given you living **w**."
1 Jn 5: 6 This is the one who came through **w**
5: 6 not by **w** alone, but by **w** and blood.
Rev 22: 1 me the river of life-giving **w**,

**WATERS** → WATER
Gn 7: 7 ark because of the **w** of the flood.
Eccl 11: 1 your bread upon the face of the **w**;

**WAY** → WAYS
Ps 1: 6 Because the LORD knows the **w**
1: 6 the **w** of the wicked leads to ruin.
86: 11 your **w** that I may walk in your
Prv 12: 15 The **w** of fools is right in their own
22: 6 the young in the **w** they should go;
Is 40: 3 the wilderness prepare the **w**
Mal 3: 1 he will prepare the **w** before me;
Mt 3: 3 desert, 'Prepare the **w** of the Lord,
Jn 14: 6 "I am the **w** and the truth
Acts 9: 2 or women who belonged to the **W**,
1 Cor 12: 31 show you a still more excellent **w**.
Heb 10: 20 living **w** he opened for us through

**WAYS** → WAY
Dt 10: 12 to follow in all his **w**, to love
Sir 2: 15 those who love him keep his **w**.
Ez 22: 31 bringing down their **w** upon their heads—
Rev 15: 3 Just and true are your **w**, O king

**WEAK** → WEAKNESS, WEAKNESSES
Mt 26: 41 spirit is willing, but the flesh is **w**."
Rom 14: 1 Welcome anyone who is **w** in faith,
1 Cor 1: 27 and God chose the **w** of the world
2 Cor 12: 10 for when I am **w**, then I am strong.

**WEAKNESS** → WEAK
Rom 8: 26 Spirit too comes to the aid of our **w**;

**WEAKNESSES** → WEAK
2 Cor 12: 10 I am content with **w**, insults,
Heb 4: 15 is unable to sympathize with our **w**,

**WEALTH**
Ps 49: 7 Of those who trust in their **w**
Prv 19: 4 **W** adds many friends, but the poor
Sir 5: 1 Do not rely on your **w**, or say,

**WEAPONS**
2 Cor 6: 7 with **w** of righteousness at the right

**WEAR**
Mt 6: 31 or 'What are we to **w**?'

**WEARY**
Is 40: 31 They will run and not grow **w**,
Heb 12: 3 in order that you may not grow **w**

**WEDDING**
Jn 2: 1 the third day there was a **w** in Cana

**WEEKS**
Ex 34: 22 You shall keep the feast of **W**
Lv 23: 15 you shall count seven full **w**;
Dn 9: 24 "Seventy **w** are decreed for your

**WEEP** → WEEPING
Eccl 3: 4 A time to **w**, and a time to laugh;
Rom 12: 15 who rejoice, **w** with those who **w**.

**WEEPING** → WEEP
Ps 30: 6 At dusk **w** comes for the night;
Mt 2: 18 Rachel **w** for her children, and she

**WEIGHED**
Dn 5: 27 you have been **w** on the scales

**WELL**
Mt 3: 17 Son, with whom I am **w** pleased."
17: 5 Son, with whom I am **w** pleased;
2 Pt 1: 17 with whom I am **w** pleased."

**WEST**
Ps 103: 12 As far as the east is from the **w**,
Is 43: 5 from the **w** I will gather you.

**WHEAT**
Mt 13: 25 and sowed weeds all through the **w**,
Lk 22: 31 demanded to sift all of you like **w**,
Jn 12: 24 you, unless a grain of **w** falls
12: 24 dies, it remains just a grain of **w**;

**WHIRLWIND** → WIND
2 Kgs 2: 11 and Elijah went up to heaven in a **w**,

**WHITE** → WHITER
Dn 7: 9 His clothing was **w** as snow, the hair
Mt 5: 36 for you cannot make a single hair **w**
Rev 1: 14 hair of his head was as **w** as **w** wool
20: 11 Next I saw a large **w** throne

**WHITER** → WHITE
Ps 51: 9 wash me, and I will be **w** than snow.

**WHOLE**
Dt 6: 5 love the LORD, your God, with your **w** heart, and with your **w** being, and with your **w** strength.

**WICKED** → WICKEDNESS
Gn 13: 13 the inhabitants of Sodom were **w**,
Ps 1: 5 Therefore the **w** will not arise
73: 3 when I saw the prosperity of the **w**.
Is 48: 22 There is no peace for the **w**,
Ez 18: 23 find pleasure in the death of the **w**—
Dn 12: 10 tested, but the **w** shall prove **w**;

**WICKEDNESS** → WICKED
Gn 6: 5 the LORD saw how great the **w**

**WIDE**
Mt 7: 13 for the gate is **w** and the road broad

**WIDOW** → WIDOWS
Ps 146: 9 to the aid of the orphan and the **w**,
1 Tm 5: 4 if a **w** has children or grandchildren,
Rev 18: 7 I am no **w**, and I will never know

**WIDOWS** → WIDOW
1 Tm 5: 3 Honor **w** who are truly **w**.
Jas 1: 27 for orphans and **w** in their affliction

**WIFE** → WIVES
Gn 2: 24 and mother and clings to his **w**,
Ex 20: 17 shall not covet your neighbor's **w**,
Tb 8: 6 you made his **w** Eve to be his helper
Prv 18: 22 To find a **w** is to find happiness,
Sir 26: 3 A good **w** is a generous gift
Mt 5: 32 whoever divorces his **w** (unless
19: 3 a man to divorce his **w** for any cause
Eph 5: 28 He who loves his **w** loves himself.
Rev 21: 9 you the bride, the **w** of the Lamb."

**WILD**
Ex 32: 25 were running **w** because Aaron had
Mk 1: 13 He was among **w** beasts,
Rom 11: 17 off, and you, a **w** olive shoot,

**WILDERNESS**
Is 40: 3 In the **w** prepare the way of the LORD!

**WILL** → WILLING
Ps 40: 9 I delight to do your **w**, my God;
143: 10 Teach me to do your **w**, for you are
Is 53: 10 it was the LORD's **w** to crush him
Mt 6: 10 kingdom come, your **w** be done,
Lk 22: 42 still, not my **w** but yours be done."
Jn 4: 34 to do the **w** of the one who sent me
Rom 9: 19 For who can oppose his **w**?"
Eph 6: 6 doing the **w** of God from the heart,
1 Jn 5: 14 we ask anything according to his **w**,

**WILLING** → WILL
Mt 26: 41 The spirit is **w**, but the flesh is
Lk 22: 42 if you are **w**, take this cup away

**WIND** → WHIRLWIND
1 Kgs 19: 11 violent **w** rending the mountains
19: 11 but the LORD was not in the **w**;
Ps 1: 4 They are like chaff driven by the **w**.
Eccl 1: 14 all is vanity and a chase after **w**.
Jn 3: 8 The **w** blows where it wills, and you
Acts 2: 2 sky a noise like a strong driving **w**,

**WINE**
Dt 7: 13 your soil, your grain and **w** and oil,
Ps 104: 15 **w** to gladden their hearts,
Prv 20: 1 **W** is arrogant, strong drink is
Sg 1: 2 for your love is better than **w**,
Sir 40: 20 **W** and strong drink delight the soul,
Mt 9: 17 People do not put new **w** into old
9: 17 the skins burst, the **w** spills out,
9: 17 Rather, they pour new **w** into fresh
Jn 2: 9 tasted the water that had become **w**,
Eph 5: 18 And do not get drunk on **w**,
Rev 18: 3 all the nations have drunk the **w**

**WINGS**
Ex 19: 4 how I bore you up on eagles' **w**
Ps 17: 8 hide me in the shadow of your **w**
Lk 13: 34 a hen gathers her brood under her **w**,

**WIPE** → WIPED
Is 25: 8 Lord GOD will **w** away the tears
Rev 21: 4 He will **w** every tear from their

**WIPED** → WIPE
Acts 3: 19 that your sins may be **w** away,

**WISDOM** → WISE
Dt 4: 6 for this is your **w** and discernment
1 Kgs 7: 14 He was endowed with **w**, understanding,
Jb 11: 6 And tell you the secrets of **w**,
Prv 1: 20 **W** cries aloud in the street,
9: 10 The beginning of **w** is fear
Eccl 1: 13 investigate in **w** all things that are
Wis 6: 12 Resplendent and unfading is **W**,
Sir 1: 1 All **w** is from the Lord and remains
24: 1 **W** sings her own praises, among her
Mt 13: 54 "Where did this man get such **w**
Lk 2: 52 And Jesus advanced [in] **w** and age
Rom 11: 33 the depth of the riches and **w**
1 Cor 1: 19 "I will destroy the **w** of the wise,
Col 2: 3 are hidden all the treasures of **w**
Jas 3: 17 the **w** from above is first of all pure,
Rev 5: 12 power and riches, **w** and strength,

**WISE** → WISDOM
Dt 4: 6 "This great nation is truly a **w**
Prv 3: 7 Do not be **w** in your own eyes,
13: 20 Walk with the **w** and you become **w**,
Eccl 12: 11 The sayings of the **w** are like goads;
Mt 25: 2 them were foolish and five were **w**.
1 Cor 1: 26 of you were **w** by human standards,
Eph 5: 15 live, not as foolish persons but as **w**,

**WITHER** → WITHERED, WITHERS
Ps 1: 3 Its leaves never **w**; whatever he does

**WITHERED** → WITHER
Mt 13: 6 scorched, and it **w** for lack of roots.
21: 19 And immediately the fig tree **w**.

**WITHERS** → WITHER
1 Pt 1: 24 the grass **w**, and the flower wilts;

**WITHOUT**
2 Chr 18: 16 mountains, like sheep **w** a shepherd,
Prv 19: 2 Desire **w** knowledge is not good;
Mt 9: 36 abandoned, like sheep **w** a shepherd.
Eph 2: 12 were at that time **w** Christ,
2: 12 **w** hope and **w** God in the world.
Heb 4: 15 been tested in every way, yet **w** sin.

**WITNESS** → EYEWITNESSES, WITNESSES
Dt 19: 15 One **w** alone shall not stand against
Jb 16: 19 Even now my **w** is in heaven,
Rom 2: 15 also bears **w** and their conflicting
Rev 1: 5 the faithful **w**, the firstborn

**WITNESSES** → WITNESS
Mt 26: 60 though many false **w** came forward.
Heb 12: 1 surrounded by so great a cloud of **w**,
Rev 11: 3 I will commission my two **w**

**WRAPPED**
Mk 15:46 **w** him in the linen cloth and laid
Lk 2:7 She **w** him in swaddling clothes

**WRATH**
Ps 2:5 his anger, in his **w** he terrifies them:
6:2 LORD, nor punish me in your **w**.
Prv 15:1 A mild answer turns back **w**,
Sir 16:11 and forgives, but also pours out **w**.
Lam 4:11 his anger, poured out his blazing **w**;
Zep 1:15 A day of **w** is that day, a day
Mt 3:7 you to flee from the coming **w**?
Rom 1:18 The **w** of God is indeed being
Eph 2:3 we were by nature children of **w**,
1 Thes 1:10 who delivers us from the coming **w**.
Rev 6:17 the great day of their **w** has come

**WRITE** → WRITING, WRITTEN, WROTE
Ex 34:27 **W** down these words,
Dt 6:9 **W** them on the doorposts of your
Prv 7:3 **w** them on the tablet of your heart.
Jer 31:33 them, and **w** it upon their hearts;
Heb 8:10 and I will **w** them upon their hearts.
Rev 21:5 he said, "**W** these words down,

**WRITING** → WRITE
Dn 5:7 "Whoever reads this **w** and tells me

**WRITTEN** → WRITE
Jos 23:6 observe all that is **w** in the book
Dn 12:1 everyone who is found **w**
Lk 24:44 that everything **w** about me
Jn 21:25 contain the books that would be **w**.
Rev 21:27 those will enter whose names are **w**

**WRONG** → WRONGDOING
Nm 5:7 person shall confess the **w** that has
Acts 23:9 "We find nothing **w** with this man.

**WRONGDOING** → WRONG
1 Jn 5:17 All **w** is sin, but there is sin that is

**WROTE** → WRITE
Ex 24:4 **w** down all the words of the LORD
34:28 he **w** on the tablets the words
Jn 5:46 me, because he **w** about me.

## Y

**YEAR** → YEARS
Ex 23:14 Three times a **y** you shall celebrate
Heb 10:1 that they offer continually each **y**.

**YEARS** → YEAR
Gn 1:14 the seasons, the days and the **y**,
Ex 12:40 was four hundred and thirty **y**.
Nm 14:34 one year for each day: forty **y**.
2 Chr 36:21 rest while seventy **y** are fulfilled.
Ps 90:4 A thousand **y** in your eyes are
Jer 25:12 when the seventy **y** have elapsed,
Dn 9:2 was to lie in ruins for seventy **y**.
Gal 4:10 days, months, seasons, and **y**.
2 Pt 3:8 Lord one day is like a thousand **y**
3:8 **y** and a thousand **y** like one day.
Rev 20:2 and tied it up for a thousand **y**

**YEAST**
Gal 5:9 A little **y** leavens the whole batch

**YESTERDAY**
Heb 13:8 Jesus Christ is the same **y**, today,

**YOKE**
Mt 11:30 For my **y** is easy, and my burden
Gal 5:1 not submit again to the **y** of slavery.

**YOUNG** → YOUTH
Ps 119:9 How can the **y** keep his way without
Acts 2:17 your **y** men shall see visions,

**YOUTH** → YOUNG
Ps 71:5 my trust, GOD, from my **y**.
Eccl 12:1 your Creator in the days of your **y**,

## Z

**ZACCHAEUS**
Lk 19:2 Now a man there named **Z**, who was

**ZEAL** → ZEALOUS
1 Mc 2:26 Thus he showed his **z** for the law,
Ps 69:10 Because **z** for your house has
Is 37:32 The **z** of the LORD of hosts shall
Jn 2:17 "**Z** for your house will consume
Rom 10:2 to them that they have **z** for God,
Phil 3:6 in **z** I persecuted the church,

**ZEALOUS** → ZEAL
1 Kgs 19:10 "I have been most **z**
Ez 39:25 of Israel; I am **z** for my holy name.

**ZEBULUN**
Son of Jacob by Leah (Gn 30:20; 35:23; 1 Chr 2:1). Tribe of blessed (Gn 49:13; Dt 33:18-19), numbered (Nm 1:31; 26:27), allotted land (Jos 19:10-16; Ez 48:26), failed to fully possess (Jgs 1:30), supported Deborah (Jgs 4:6-10; 5:14, 18), David (1 Chr 12:33), 12,000 from (Rev 7:8).

**ZECHARIAH**
1. Son of Jeroboam II; king of Israel (2 Kgs 15:8-12).
2. Post-exilic prophet who encouraged rebuilding of temple (Ezr 5:1; 6:14; Zec 1:1).

**ZEDEKIAH** → =MATTANIAH
1. False prophet (1 Kgs 22:11-24; 2 Chr 18:10-23).
2. Mattaniah, son of Josiah (1 Chr 3:15), made king of Judah by Nebuchadnezzar (2 Kgs 24:17–25:7; 2 Chr 36:10-14; Jer 37–39; 52:1-11).

**ZEPHANIAH**
Prophet; descendant of Hezekiah (Zep 1:1).

**ZERUBBABEL**
Descendant of David (1 Chr 3:19; Mt 1:3). Led return from exile (Ezr 2:2; Neh 7:7). Governor of Israel; helped rebuild temple (Ezr 3; Hg 1–2; Zec 4).

**ZIMRI**
King of Israel (1 Kgs 16:9-20).

**ZION**
2 Sm 5:7 captured the fortress of **Z**, which is
Ps 2:6 myself have installed my king on **Z**,
48:3 Mount **Z**, the heights of Zaphon,
78:68 of Judah, Mount **Z** which he loved.
Is 28:16 I am laying a stone in **Z**, a stone
Mi 4:2 from **Z** shall go forth instruction,
Zec 9:9 Exult greatly, O daughter **Z**!
Mt 21:5 "Say to daughter **Z**, 'Behold,
Rom 11:26 "The deliverer will come out of **Z**,
1 Pt 2:6 "Behold, I am laying a stone in **Z**,
Rev 14:1 was the Lamb standing on Mount **Z**,

**ZIPPORAH**
Daughter of Reuel; wife of Moses (Ex 2:21-22; 4:20-26; 18:1-6).

**ZOPHAR**
One of Job's friends (Jb 2:11; 11; 20; 42:9).

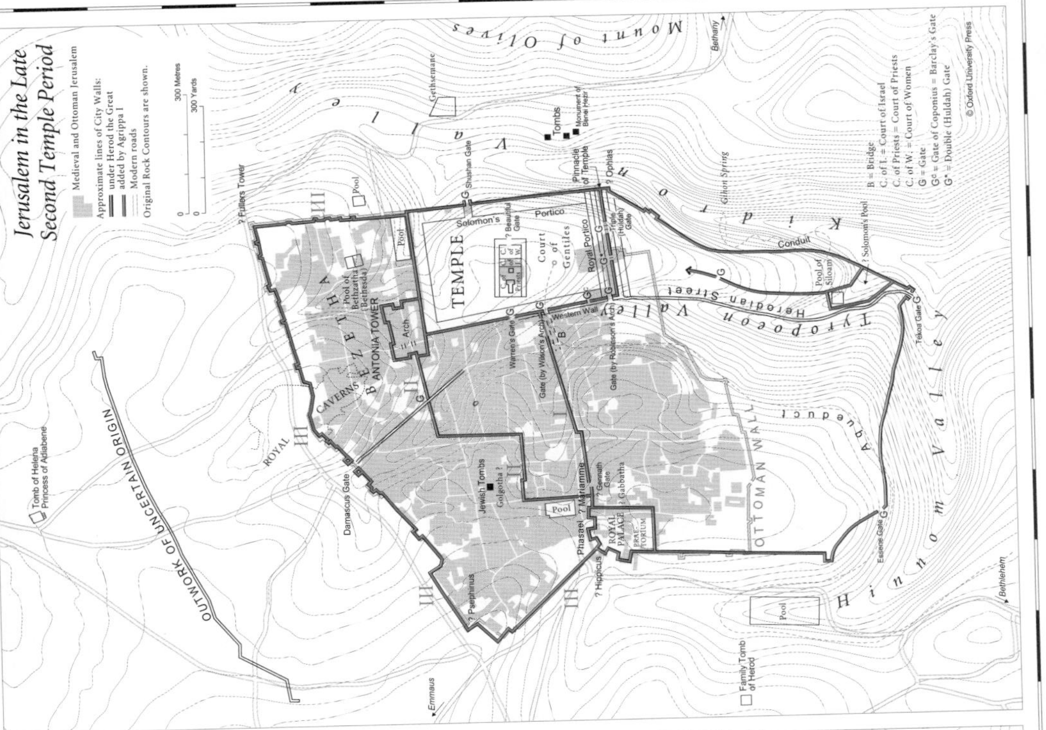


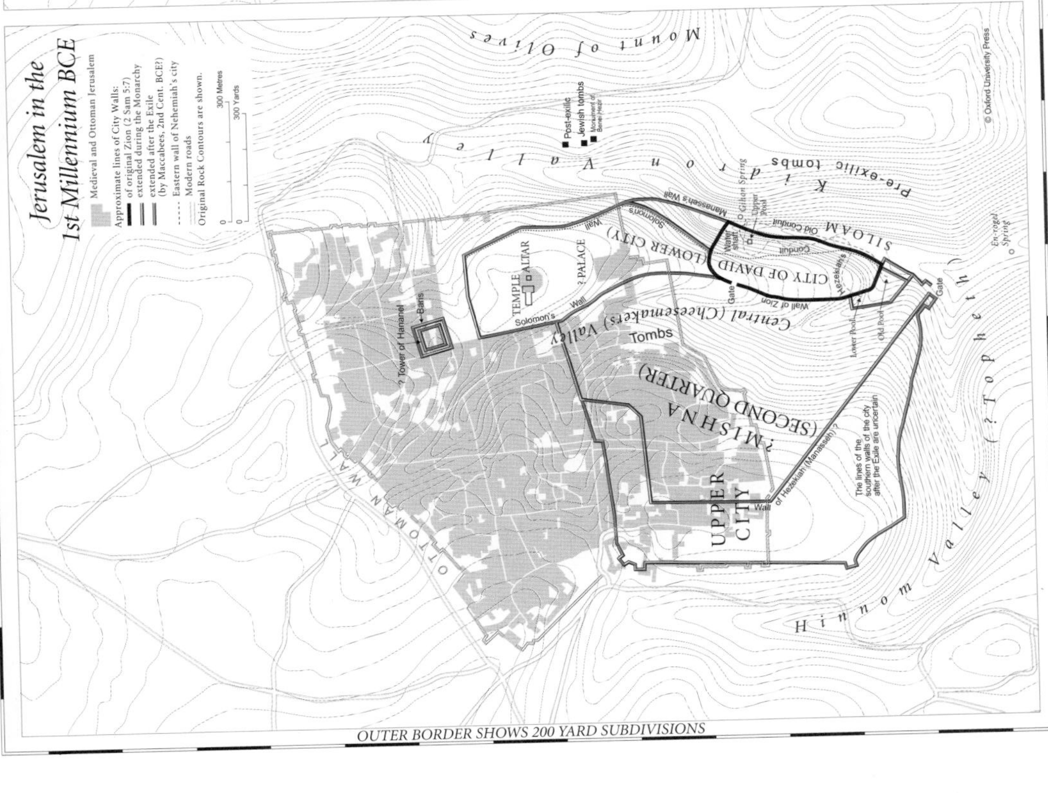


OUTER BORDER SHOWS 200 YARD SUBDIVISIONS

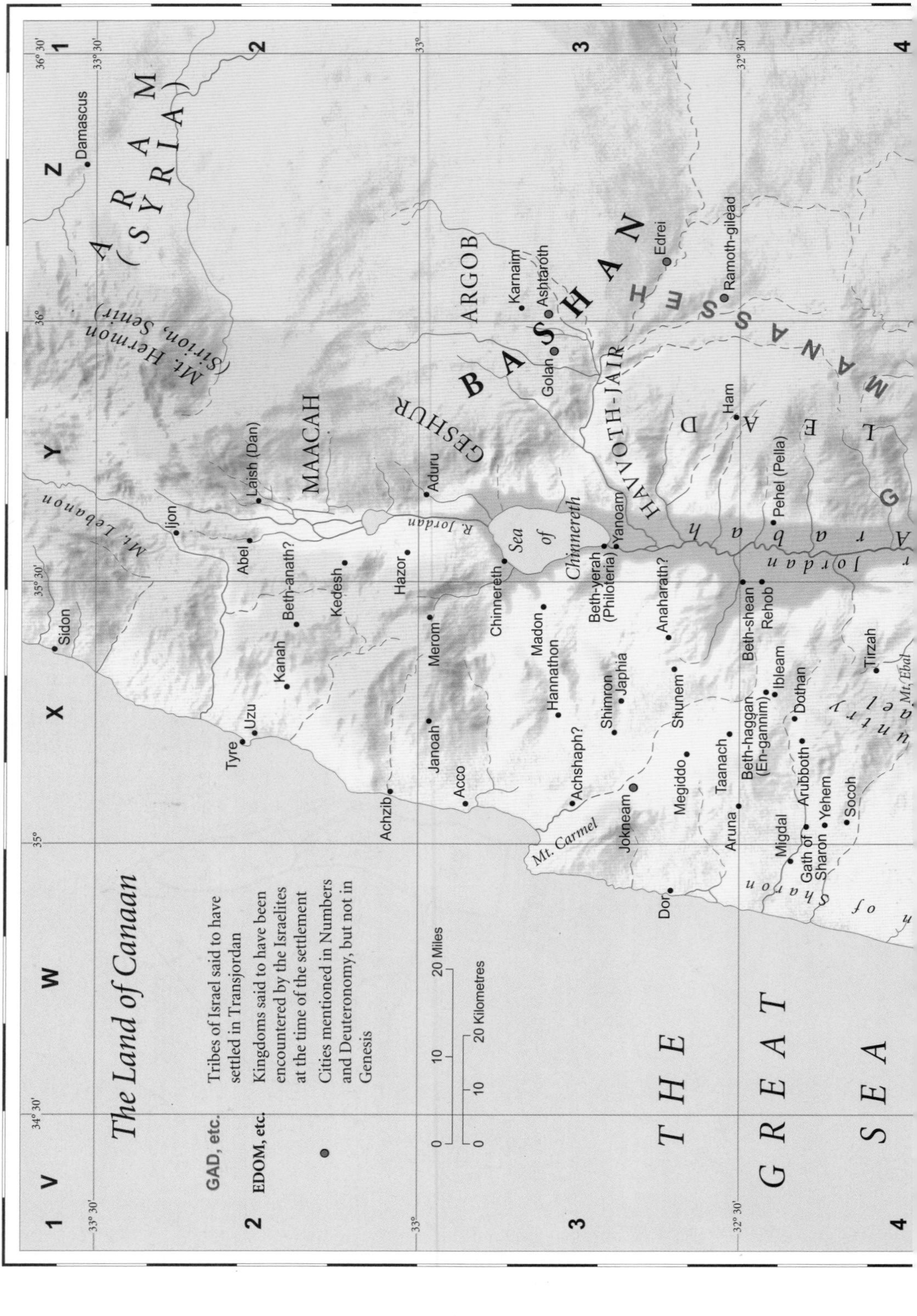
The Land of Canaan
GAD, etc. Tribes of Israel said to have settled in Transjordan
EDOM, etc. Kingdoms said to have been encountered by the Israelites at the time of the settlement
Cities mentioned in Numbers and Deuteronomy, but not in Genesis
0 10 20 Miles
0 10 20 Kilometres
THE GREAT SEA
ARAM (SYRIA)
Damascus
Mt. Hermon (Sirion, Senir)
Mt. Lebanon
Sidon
Tyre
Uzu
Ijon
Abel
Laish (Dan)
MAACAH
GESHUR
ARGOB
BASHAN
HAVVOTH-JAIR
Karnaim
Ashtaroth
Edrei
Golan
Ramoth-gilead
Aduru
Hazor
Kedesh
Beth-anath?
Kanah
Merom
Janoah
Achzib
Acco
R. Jordan
Sea of Chinnereth
Chinnereth
Beth-yerah (Philoteria)
Yanoam
Madon
Hannathon
Achshaph?
Shimron
Japhia
Anaharath?
Shunem
Mt. Carmel
Jokneam
Megiddo
Taanach
Beth-haggan (En-gannim)
Ibleam
Dothan
Beth-shean
Rehob
Pehel (Pella)
Ham
Dor
Aruna
Migdal
Gath of Sharon
Arubboth
Yehem
Socoh
Tirzah
Mt. Ebal
Plain of Sharon
Jordan
Arabah
GAD
MANASSEH
34° 30'
35°
35° 30'
36°
36° 30'
33° 30'
33°
32° 30'
V
W
X
Y
Z
1
2
3
4

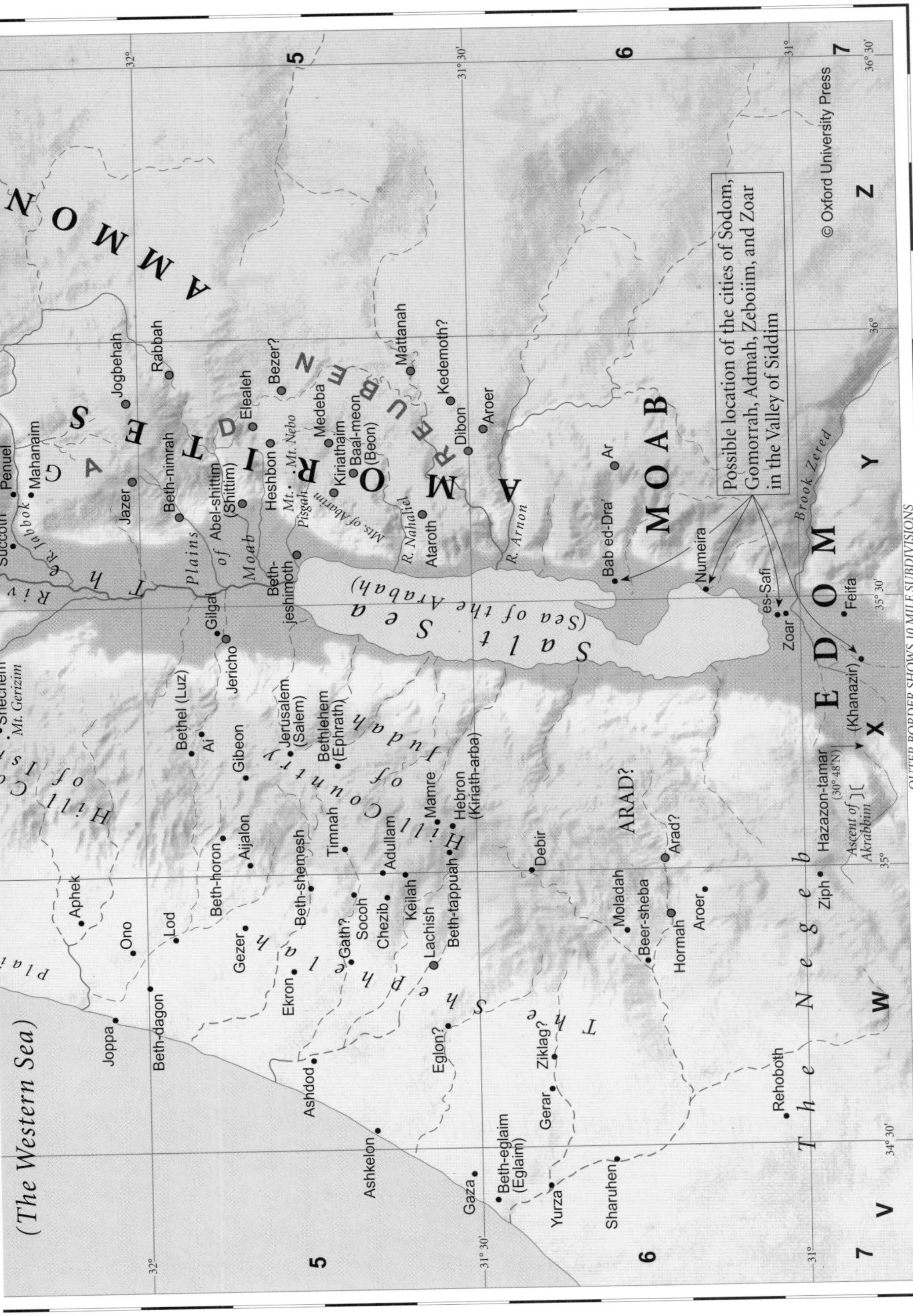

AMMON
GADITES
AMORITES
REUBEN
MOAB
EDOM
ARAD?
(The Western Sea)
Salt Sea
(Sea of the Arabah)
The Shephelah
The Negeb
Hill Country of Judah
Plains of Moab
Mts. of Abarim
R. Jabbok
R. Arnon
R. Nahaliel
Brook Zered
Possible location of the cities of Sodom, Gomorrah, Admah, Zeboiim, and Zoar in the Valley of Siddim
Succoth
Penuel
Mahanaim
Jogbehah
Rabbah
Jazer
Beth-nimrah
Abel-shittim (Shittim)
Elealeh
Heshbon
Bezer?
Mt. Nebo
Mt. Pisgah
Medeba
Kiriathaim
Baal-meon (Beon)
Mattanah
Kedemoth?
Dibon
Aroer
Ataroth
Ar
Bab ed-Dra'
Numeira
es-Safi
Zoar
Feifa
(Khanazir)
Beth-jeshimoth
Gilgal
Jericho
Shechem
Mt. Gerizim
Bethel (Luz)
Ai
Gibeon
Jerusalem (Salem)
Bethlehem (Ephrath)
Mamre
Hebron (Kiriath-arba)
Beth-tappuah
Aijalon
Beth-horon
Timnah
Adullam
Keilah
Beth-shemesh
Socoh
Chezib
Lachish
Gath?
Gezer
Lod
Ono
Aphek
Ekron
Joppa
Beth-dagon
Ashdod
Eglon?
Ashkelon
Gaza
Beth-eglaim (Eglaim)
Yurza
Gerar
Ziklag?
Sharuhen
Rehoboth
Debir
Moladah
Beer-sheba
Arad?
Hormah
Aroer
Ziph
Hazazon-tamar
(30° 48'N)
Ascent of Akrabbim
V
W
X
Y
Z
5
6
7
31°
31° 30'
32°
34° 30'
35°
35° 30'
36°
36° 30'
© Oxford University Press
OUTER BORDER SHOWS 10 MILE SUBDIVISIONS

MAP 3

The Setting of the Exodus and Wilderness Traditions
ASIA
THE GREAT
EGYPT
Western Desert
River Nile
GOSHEN
Wilderness
(Rosetta)
Buto
Busiris
Athribis
Zoan (Tanis)
Rameses (Qantir)
Pi-beseth (Bubastis)
Pithom
Succoth
Lake Timsah
Great Bitter Lake
Little Bitter Lake
Baal-zephon
Lake Menzaleh
Pelusium (Sin)
Zilu (Tjaru)
Mons Casius
Lake Sirbonis
The Way to the Land of the
Possible Northern
Traditional Exodus route
(Tell el-Yahudiyeh)
Heliopolis (On)
Saqqarah
Memphis (Noph)
Lake Moeris
Heracleopolis
Beni-hasan
Gulf of
Possible route reflected in the Exodus story
Possible alternative routes
Line of border fortresses
1
2
3
4
5
B
C

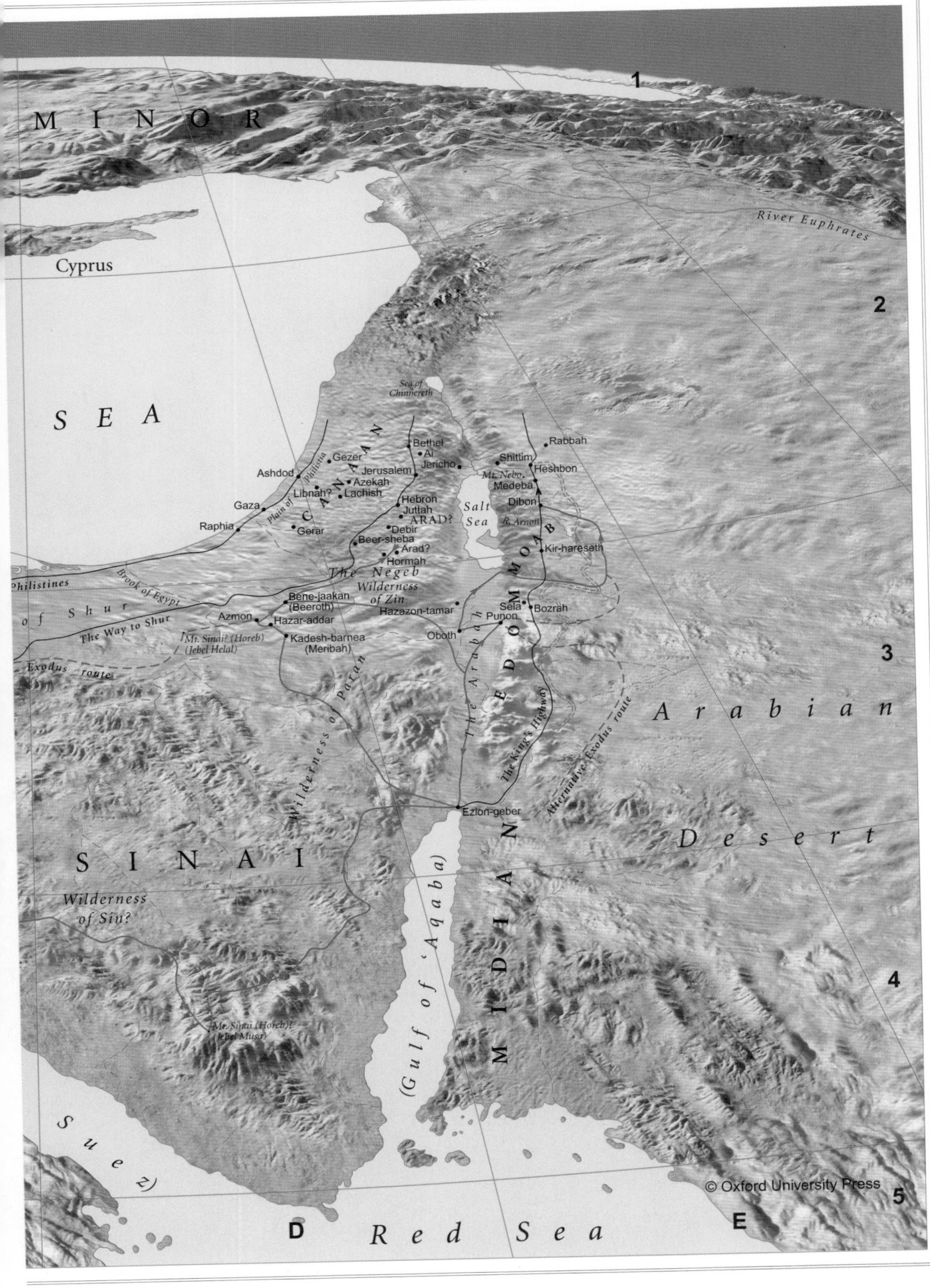
MINOR
Cyprus
SEA
River Euphrates
Sea of Chinnereth
CANAAN
Bethel
Ai
Jericho
Gezer
Ashdod
Jerusalem
Azekah
Libnah?
Lachish
Gaza
Raphia
Plain of Philistia
Hebron
Juttah
ARAD?
Debir
Gerar
Beer-sheba
Arad?
Hormah
Salt Sea
Rabbah
Shittim
Heshbon
Mt. Nebo
Medeba
Dibon
R. Arnon
MOAB
Kir-hareseth
Philistines
Brook of Egypt
The Negeb
Wilderness of Zin
of Shur
The Way to Shur
Bene-jaakan (Beeroth)
Azmon
Hazar-addar
Hazazon-tamar
Sela
Bozrah
Punon
Oboth
Mt. Sinai? (Horeb) (Jebel Helal)
Kadesh-barnea (Meribah)
Exodus route
EDOM
The Arabah
The King's Highway
Alternative Exodus route
Wilderness of Paran
Arabian
Desert
Ezion-geber
SINAI
MIDIAN
Wilderness of Sin?
(Gulf of 'Aqaba)
Mt. Sinai (Horeb)? Jebel Musa
Suez)
Red Sea
1
2
3
4
5
D
E

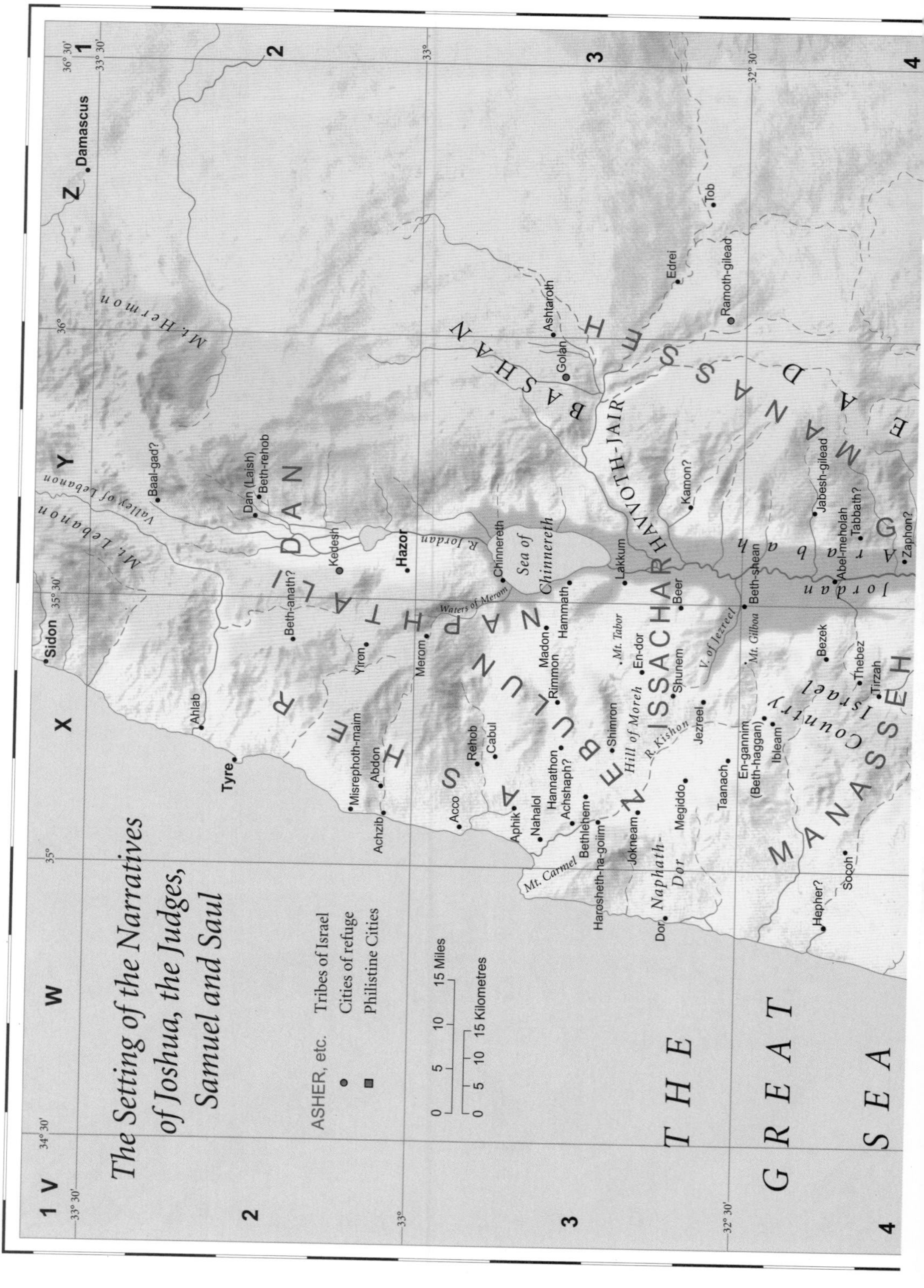
The Setting of the Narratives of Joshua, the Judges, Samuel and Saul
ASHER, etc. Tribes of Israel
Cities of refuge
Philistine Cities
0 5 10 15 Miles
0 5 10 15 Kilometres
THE GREAT SEA
Damascus
Mt. Hermon
Mt. Lebanon
Valley of Lebanon
Baal-gad?
Sidon
Ahlab
Tyre
Dan (Laish)
Beth-rehob
Beth-anath?
Kedesh
Hazor
Yiron
Merom
Waters of Merom
R. Jordan
Chinnereth
Sea of Chinnereth
Hammath
Lakkum
Madon
Rimmon
Mt. Tabor
En-dor
Shunem
Beer
Misrephoth-maim
Abdon
Achzib
Acco
Rehob
Cabul
Aphik
Nahalol
Hannathon
Achshaph?
Bethlehem
Shimron
Hill of Moreh
R. Kishon
Jezreel
V. of Jezreel
Mt. Gilboa
Beth-shean
Jokneam
Megiddo
Taanach
En-gannim (Beth-haggan)
Ibleam
Harosheth-ha-goiim
Mt. Carmel
Naphath-Dor
Dor
Hepher?
Socoh
Tirzah
Thebez
Bezek
Abel-meholah
Tabbath?
Zaphon?
Jabesh-gilead
Kamon?
Ashtaroth
Golan
Edrei
Tob
Ramoth-gilead
BASHAN
HAVVOTH-JAIR
ASHER
NAPHTALI
DAN
ZEBULUN
ISSACHAR
MANASSEH
GAD
Israel Country
Arabah
Jordan
V W X Y Z
1 2 3 4
33° 30'
33°
32° 30'
34° 30'
35°
35° 30'
36°
36° 30'

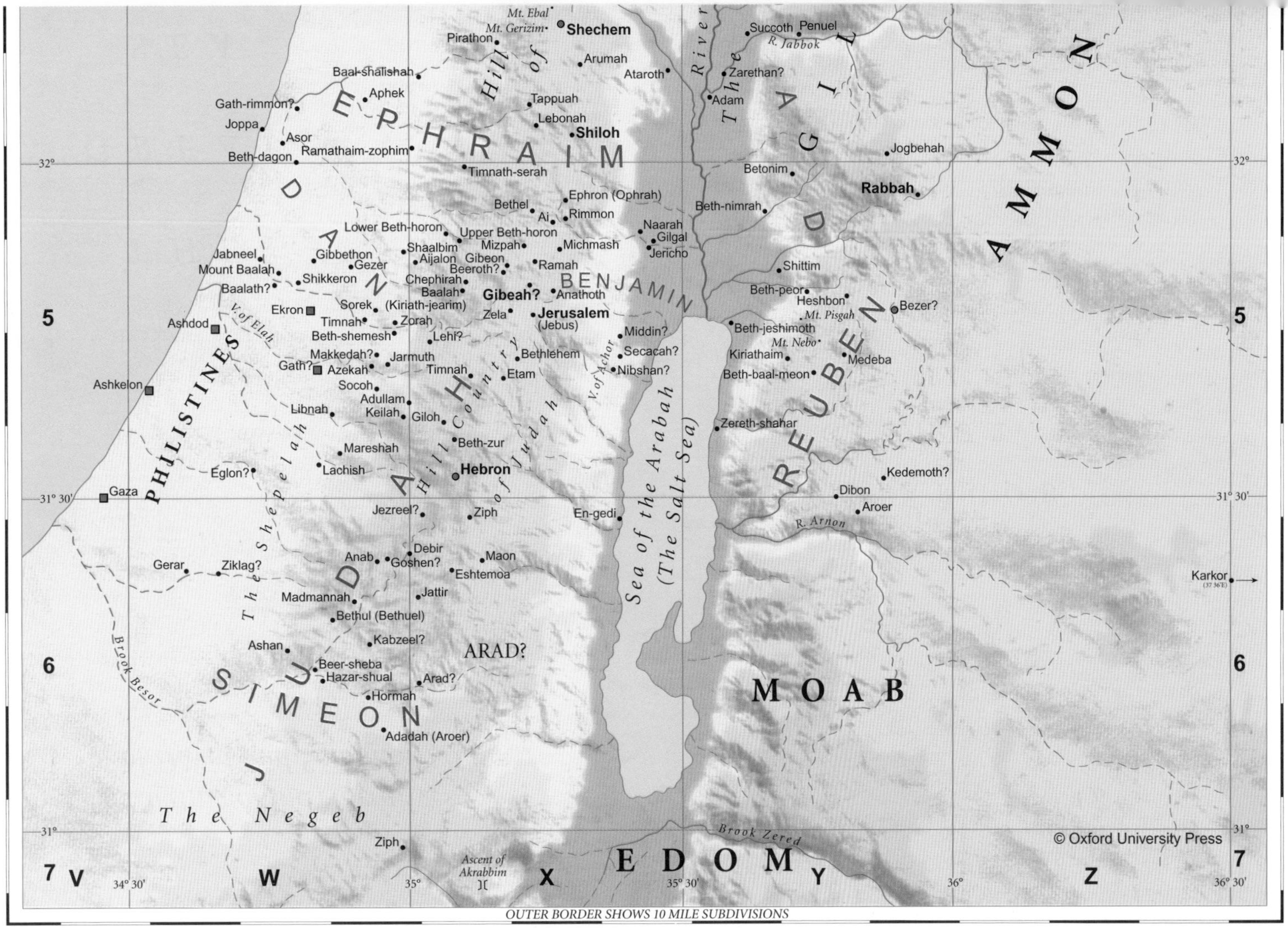

Mt. Ebal
Mt. Gerizim
Shechem
Pirathon
Hill of Ephraim
Arumah
Ataroth
The River
Succoth
Penuel
R. Jabbok
Zarethan?
Adam
GILEAD
AMMON
Baal-shalishah
Aphek
Gath-rimmon?
Joppa
Asor
Beth-dagon
Ramathaim-zophim
EPHRAIM
Tappuah
Lebonah
Shiloh
Jogbehah
Timnath-serah
Betonim
Rabbah
DAN
Bethel
Ai
Ephron (Ophrah)
Rimmon
Beth-nimrah
Lower Beth-horon
Upper Beth-horon
Mizpah
Michmash
Naarah
Gilgal
Jericho
Jabneel
Mount Baalah
Baalath?
Gibbethon
Gezer
Shikkeron
Shaalbim
Aijalon
Gibeon
Beeroth?
Ramah
Chephirah
Baalah
Shittim
BENJAMIN
Gibeah?
Anathoth
Beth-peor
Heshbon
Mt. Pisgah
Bezer?
Ekron
Sorek
(Kiriath-jearim)
Zela
Jerusalem
(Jebus)
Ashdod
V. of Elah
Timnah
Zorah
Beth-shemesh
Lehi?
Middin?
Beth-jeshimoth
Mt. Nebo
REUBEN
Makkedah?
Jarmuth
Bethlehem
Secacah?
Kiriathaim
Medeba
Gath?
Azekah
Timnah
Etam
V. of Achor
Nibshan?
Beth-baal-meon
Ashkelon
Socoh
Adullam
Libnah
Keilah
Giloh
Hill Country of Judah
PHILISTINES
Zereth-shahar
Beth-zur
Mareshah
JUDAH
Sea of the Arabah
(The Salt Sea)
Lachish
Hebron
Eglon?
Kedemoth?
Gaza
Dibon
Aroer
Jezreel?
Ziph
En-gedi
R. Arnon
The Shephelah
Anab
Debir
Goshen?
Maon
Eshtemoa
Gerar
Ziklag?
Karkor
(37 36'E)
Madmannah
Jattir
Bethul (Bethuel)
Brook Besor
Ashan
Kabzeel?
ARAD?
Beer-sheba
Hazar-shual
Arad?
SIMEON
MOAB
Hormah
Adadah (Aroer)
The Negeb
Brook Zered
Ziph
Ascent of Akrabbim
EDOM
© Oxford University Press
32°
31° 30'
31°
34° 30'
35°
35° 30'
36°
36° 30'
5
6
7
V
W
X
Y
Z
OUTER BORDER SHOWS 10 MILE SUBDIVISIONS

# The Setting of the Narratives of David and Solomon

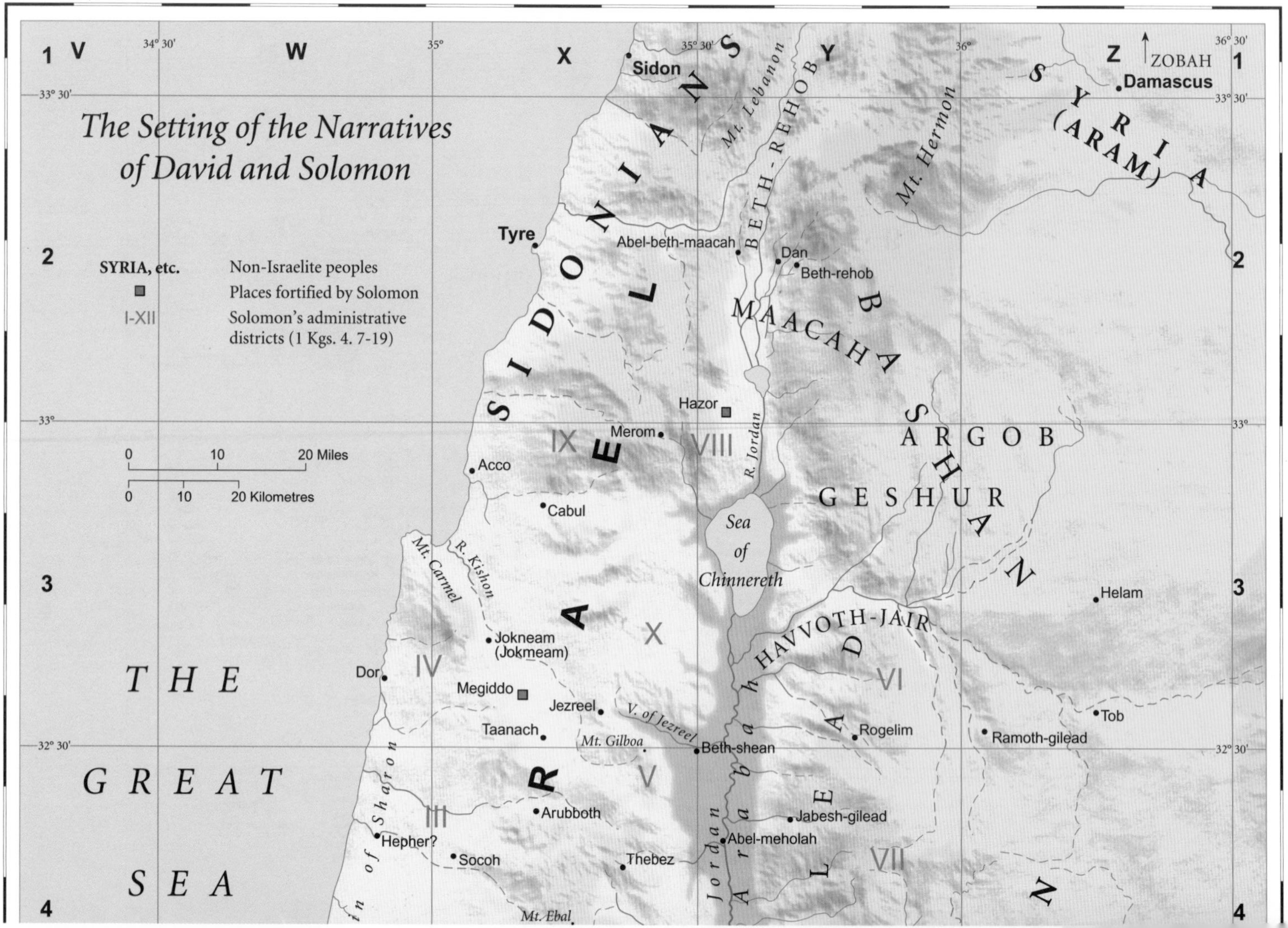

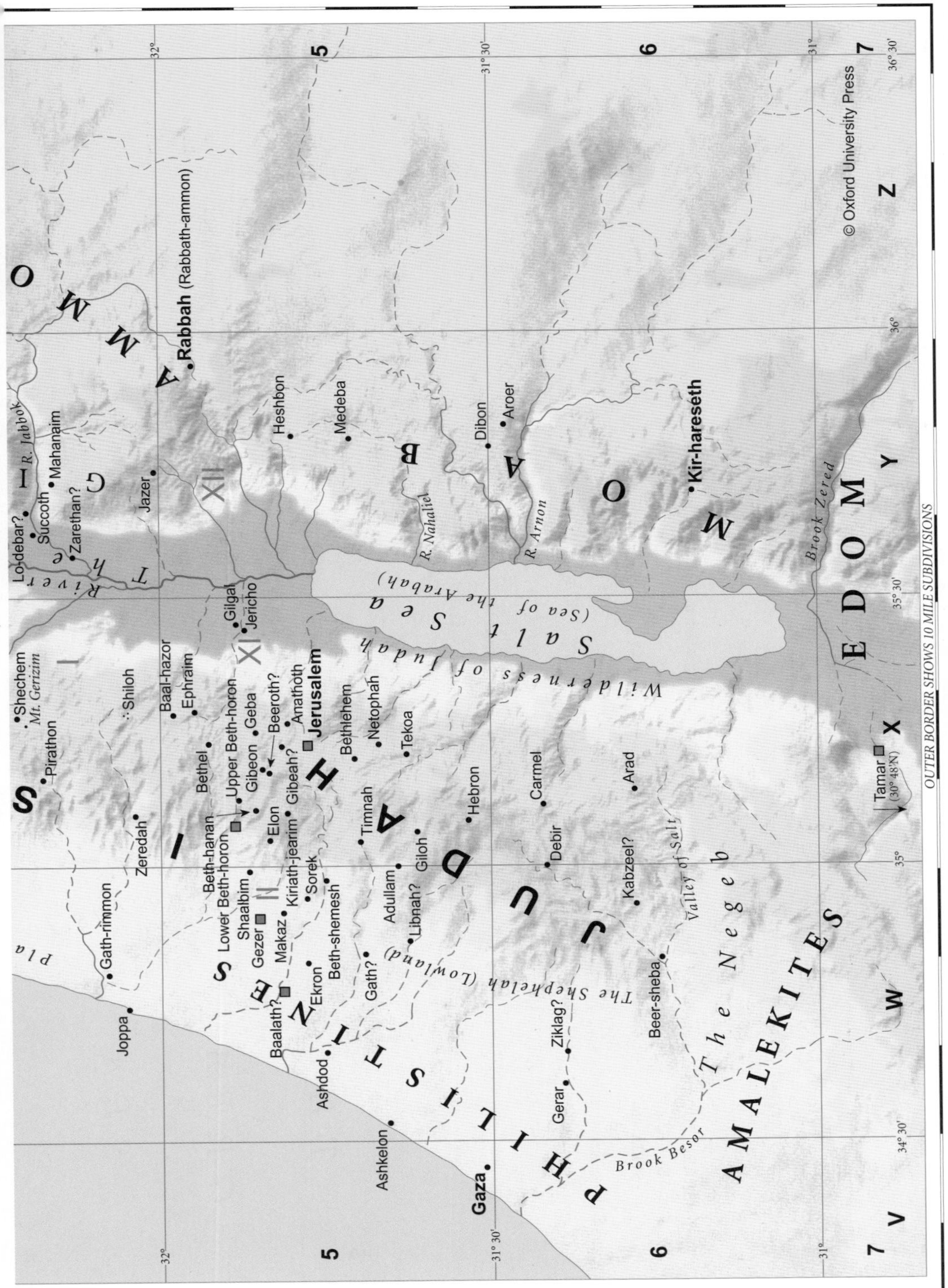

AMMON
GILEAD
SAMARIA
PHILISTINES
JUDAH
MOAB
EDOM
AMALEKITES
Rabbah (Rabbath-ammon)
R. Jabbok
Mahanaim
Succoth
Lo-debar?
Zarethan?
Jazer
Heshbon
Medeba
Dibon
Aroer
Kir-hareseth
R. Nahaliel
R. Arnon
Brook Zered
The River Jordan
Salt Sea
(Sea of the Arabah)
Wilderness of Judah
Shechem
Mt. Gerizim
Pirathon
Shiloh
Baal-hazor
Ephraim
Gilgal
Jericho
Bethel
Upper Beth-horon
Lower Beth-horon
Beth-hanan
Gibeon
Geba
Beeroth?
Anathoth
Gibeah?
Jerusalem
Elon
Kiriath-jearim
Zeredah
Shaalbim
Gezer
Makaz
Sorek
Beth-shemesh
Bethlehem
Netophah
Tekoa
Timnah
Hebron
Carmel
Arad
Debir
Giloh
Adullam
Libnah?
Kabzeel?
Gath-rimmon
Joppa
Baalath?
Ekron
Gath?
Ashdod
Ashkelon
Gaza
Ziklag?
Gerar
Beer-sheba
The Shephelah (Lowland)
The Negeb
Valley of Salt
Brook Besor
Tamar (30° 48'N)
Pla
XI
XII
32°
31° 30'
31°
34° 30'
35°
35° 30'
36°
36° 30'
V
W
X
Y
Z
5
6
7
© Oxford University Press
OUTER BORDER SHOWS 10 MILE SUBDIVISIONS

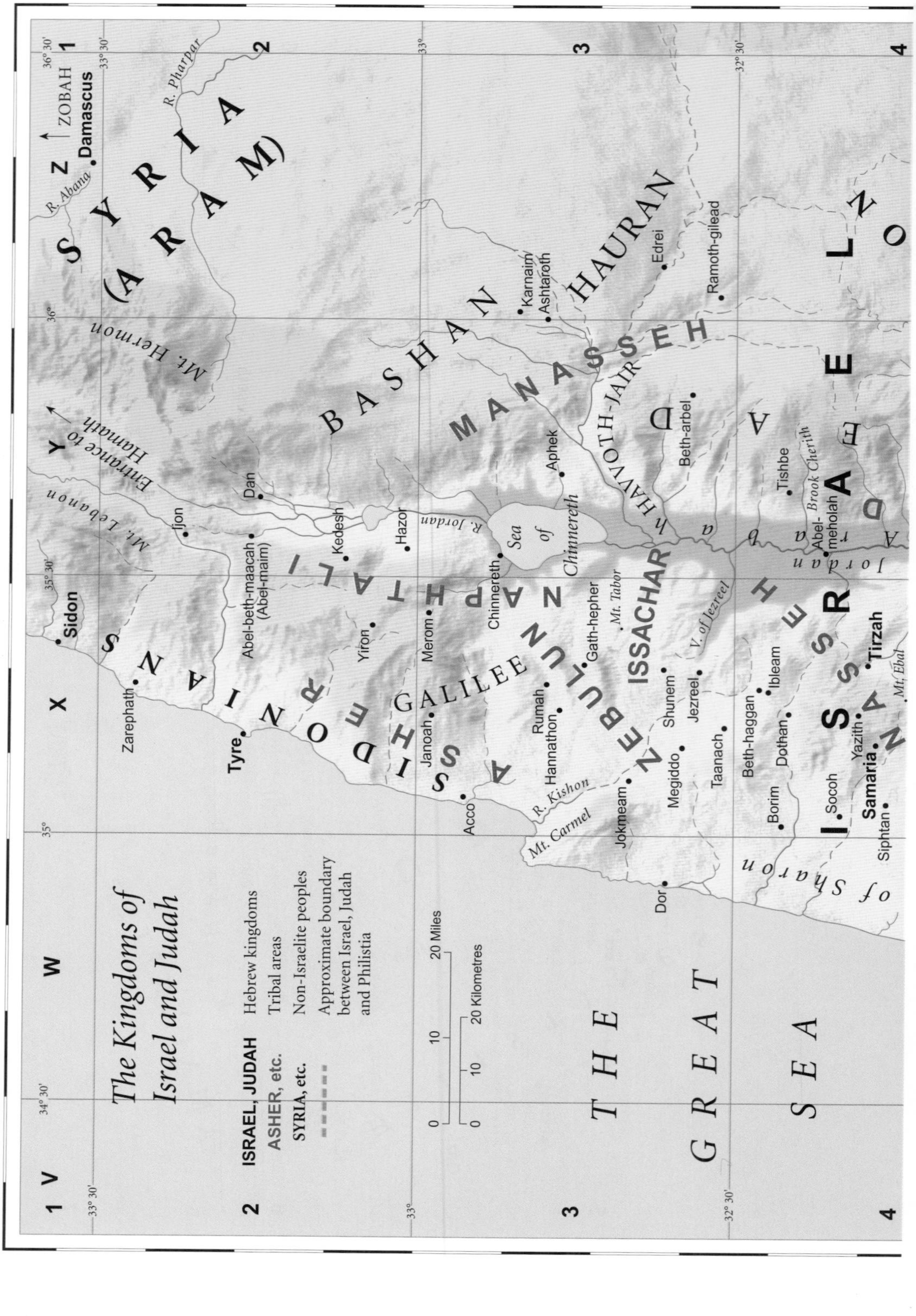
The Kingdoms of Israel and Judah
ISRAEL, JUDAH Hebrew kingdoms
ASHER, etc. Tribal areas
SYRIA, etc. Non-Israelite peoples
Approximate boundary between Israel, Judah and Philistia
0 10 20 Miles
0 10 20 Kilometres
THE GREAT SEA
SYRIA (ARAM)
ZOBAH
Damascus
R. Abana
R. Pharpar
Mt. Hermon
Entrance to Hamath
Mt. Lebanon
BASHAN
HAURAN
MANASSEH
HAVVOTH-JAIR
GAD
GILEAD
Karnaim
Ashtaroth
Edrei
Ramoth-gilead
Beth-arbel
Aphek
Tishbe
Brook Cherith
Abel-meholah
SIDONIANS
Sidon
Zarephath
Tyre
Ijon
Dan
Abel-beth-maacah (Abel-maim)
Kedesh
Hazor
R. Jordan
Sea of Chinnereth
Chinnereth
NAPHTALI
ASHER
Yiron
Merom
Janoah
GALILEE
ZEBULUN
ISSACHAR
Gath-hepher
Mt. Tabor
Rumah
Hannathon
Shunem
Jezreel
V. of Jezreel
Acco
R. Kishon
Mt. Carmel
Jokmeam
Megiddo
Taanach
Beth-haggan
Ibleam
Dothan
Borim
Socoh
Samaria
Yazith
Siphtan
Tirzah
Mt. Ebal
MANASSEH
ISRAEL
Jordan
Arabah
Dor
of Sharon
V W X Y Z
1 2 3 4
33° 30'
33°
32° 30'
34° 30'
35°
35° 30'
36°
36° 30'

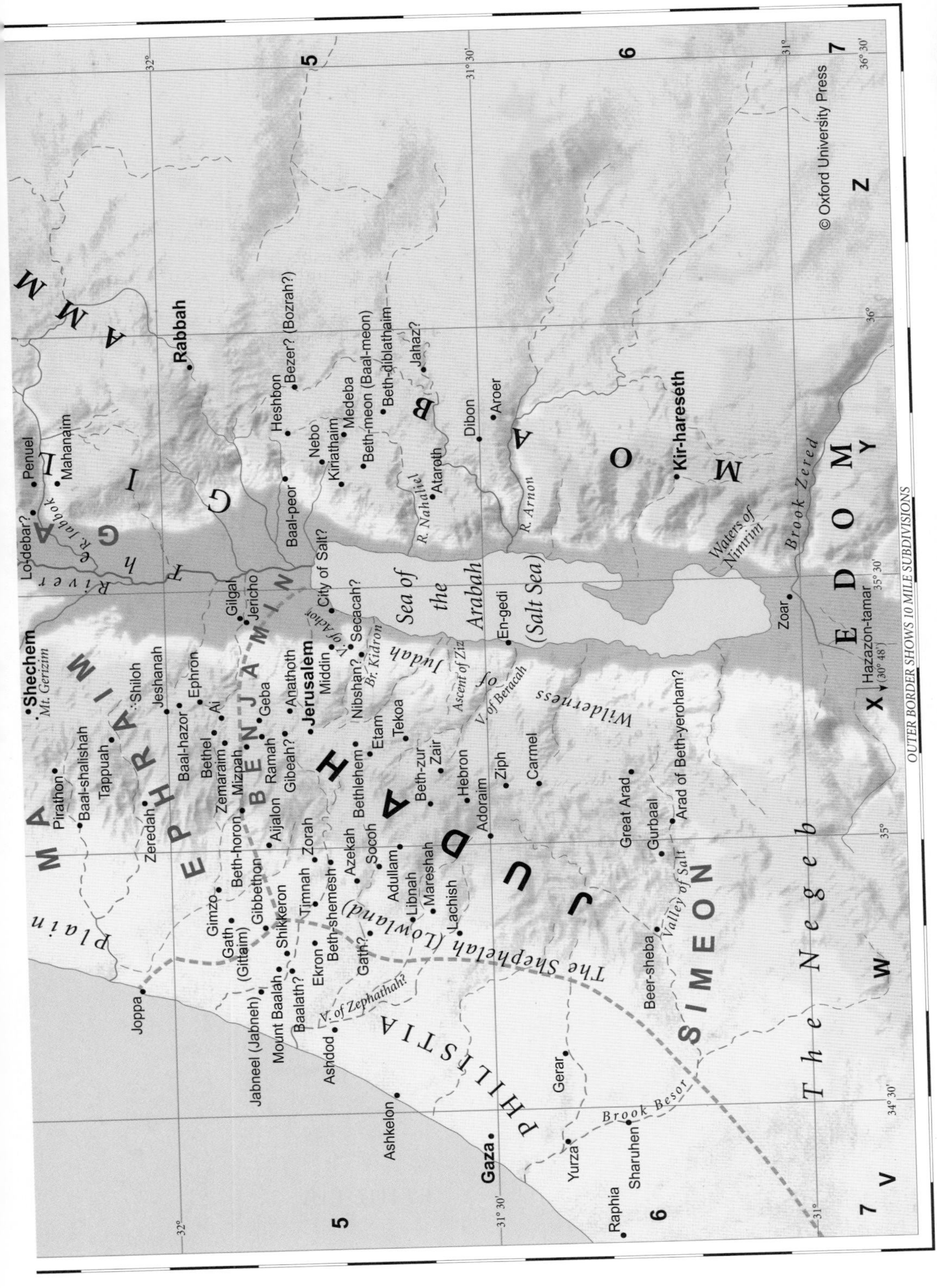
AMMON
GILEAD
EPHRAIM
MANASSEH
BENJAMIN
JUDAH
MOAB
EDOM
SIMEON
PHILISTIA
Plain
The Negeb
The Shephelah (Lowland)
Wilderness of Judah
Sea of the Arabah (Salt Sea)
River Jordan
R. Jabbok
R. Nahaliel
R. Arnon
Brook Zered
Brook Besor
Waters of Nimrim
V. of Achor
Br. Kidron
Ascent of Ziz
V. of Beracah
Valley of Salt
V. of Zephathah?
Shechem
Mt. Gerizim
Shiloh
Penuel
Mahanaim
Lo-debar?
Rabbah
Heshbon
Bezer? (Bozrah?)
Nebo
Baal-peor
Kiriathaim
Medeba
Beth-meon (Baal-meon)
Beth-diblathaim
Jahaz?
Ataroth
Dibon
Aroer
Kir-hareseth
Zoar
Hazazon-tamar (30° 48')
Pirathon
Baal-shalishah
Tappuah
Zeredah
Jeshanah
Ephron
Baal-hazor
Bethel
Ai
Zemaraim
Mizpah
Gilgal
Jericho
Geba
Anathoth
Ramah
Gibeah?
Jerusalem
Middin
City of Salt?
Secacah?
Nibshan?
Etam
Tekoa
Bethlehem
Beth-zur
Zair
Hebron
En-gedi
Ziph
Carmel
Adoraim
Great Arad
Gurbaal
Arad of Beth-yeroham?
Beth-horon
Aijalon
Zorah
Gimzo
Gibbethon
Gath (Gittaim)
Timnah
Beth-shemesh
Azekah
Socoh
Adullam
Libnah
Mareshah
Lachish
Shikkeron
Ekron
Gath?
Joppa
Jabneel (Jabneh)
Mount Baalah
Baalath?
Ashdod
Ashkelon
Gaza
Gerar
Yurza
Sharuhen
Beer-sheba
Raphia
32°
31° 30'
31°
34° 30'
35°
35° 30'
36°
36° 30'
5
6
7
V
W
X
Y
Z
© Oxford University Press
OUTER BORDER SHOWS 10 MILE SUBDIVISIONS

MAP 7

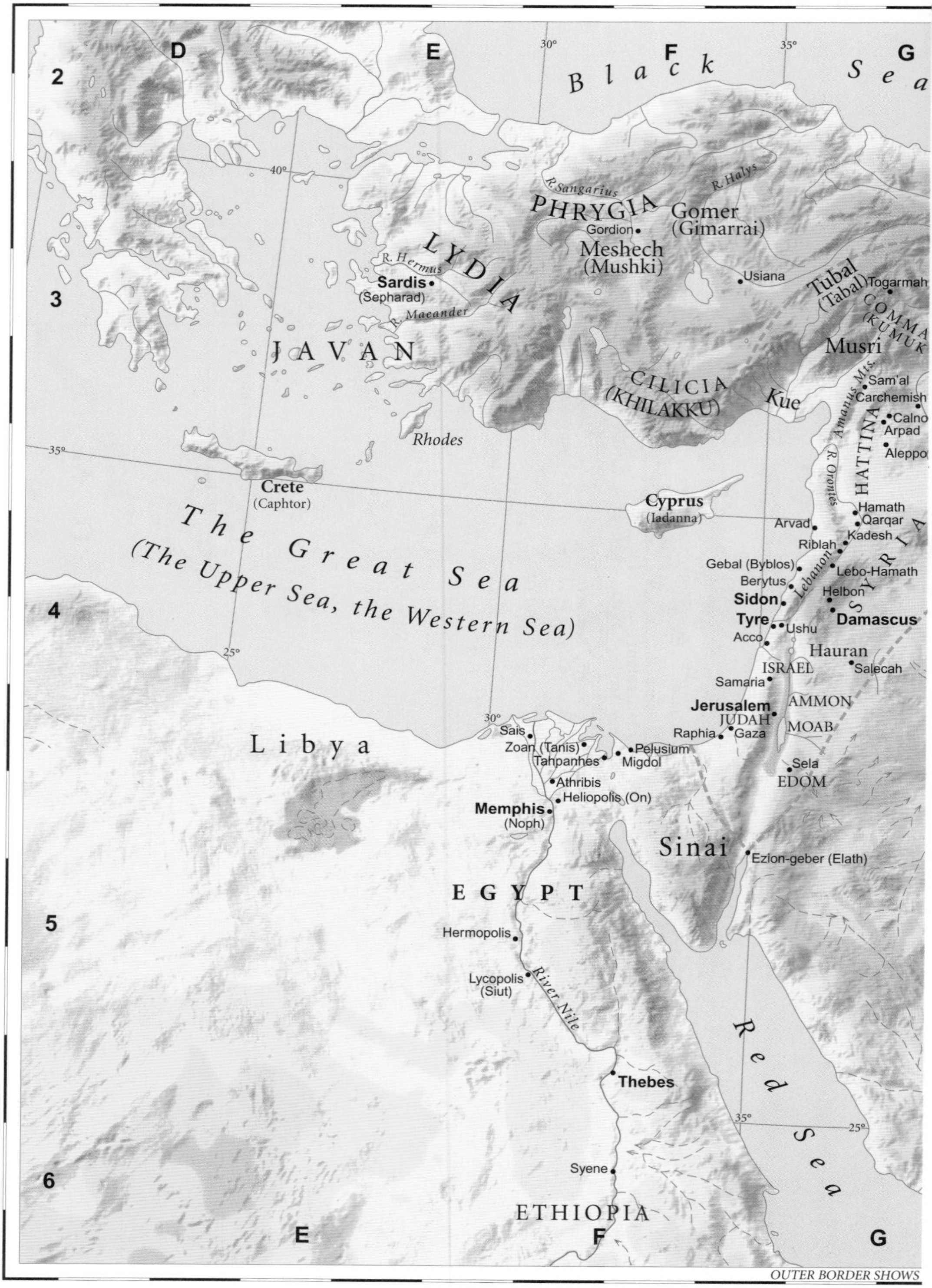


OUTER BORDER SHOWS

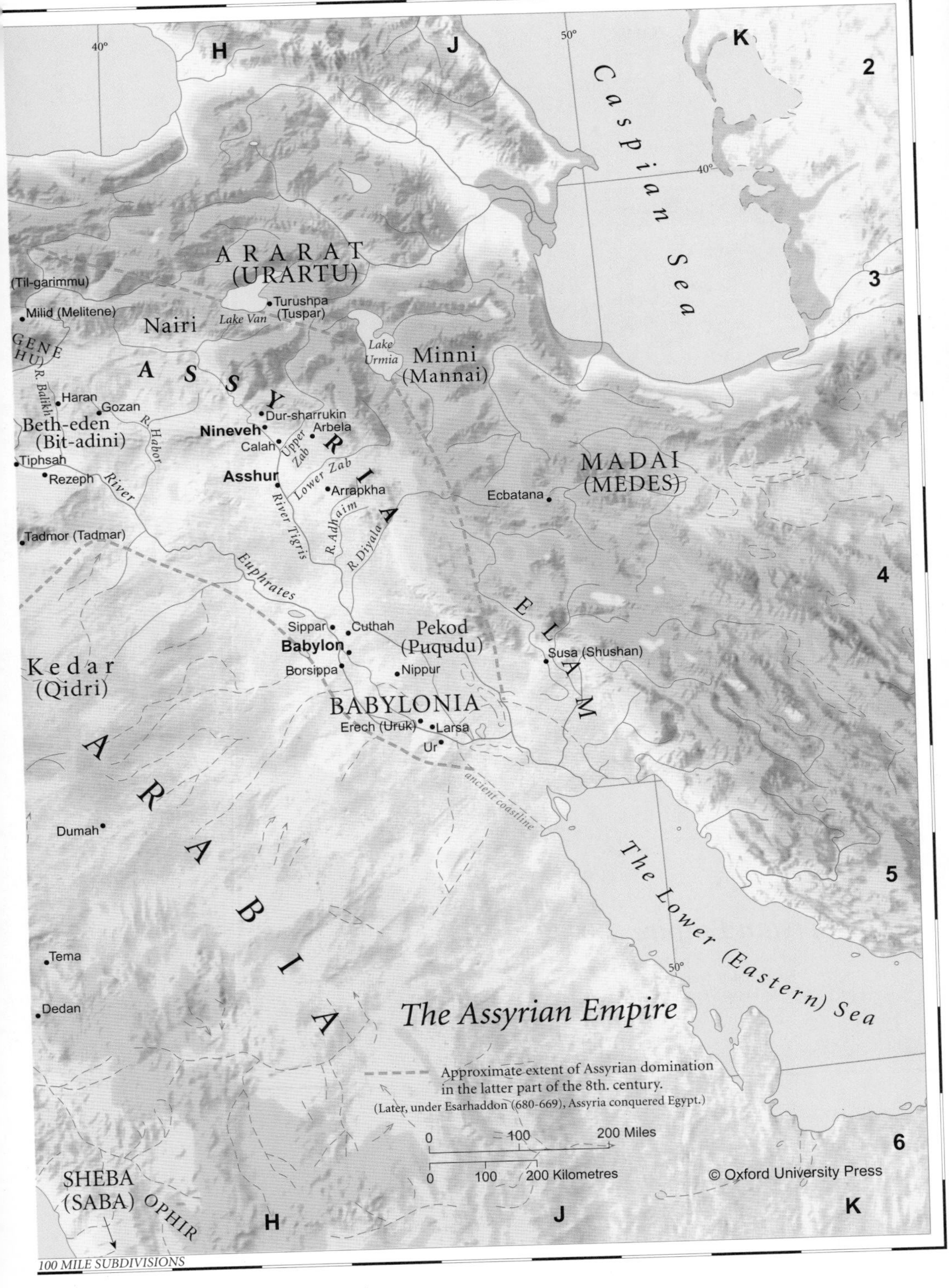
The Assyrian Empire
Approximate extent of Assyrian domination in the latter part of the 8th. century.
(Later, under Esarhaddon (680-669), Assyria conquered Egypt.)
0
100
200 Miles
0
100
200 Kilometres
© Oxford University Press
100 MILE SUBDIVISIONS
H
J
K
2
3
4
5
6
40°
50°
Caspian Sea
ARARAT (URARTU)
(Til-garimmu)
Milid (Melitene)
Nairi
Lake Van
Turushpa (Tuspar)
Lake Urmia
Minni (Mannai)
GENE HU
ASSYRIA
R. Balikh
Haran
Gozan
Beth-eden (Bit-adini)
R. Habor
Dur-sharrukin
Nineveh
Arbela
Calah
Upper Zab
Lower Zab
Tiphsah
Rezeph
River
Asshur
Arrapkha
River Tigris
R. Adhaim
R. Diyala
MADAI (MEDES)
Ecbatana
Tadmor (Tadmar)
Euphrates
ELAM
Sippar
Cuthah
Pekod (Puqudu)
Babylon
Borsippa
Nippur
Susa (Shushan)
Kedar (Qidri)
BABYLONIA
Erech (Uruk)
Larsa
Ur
ancient coastline
ARABIA
Dumah
The Lower (Eastern) Sea
Tema
Dedan
SHEBA (SABA)
OPHIR

MAP 8

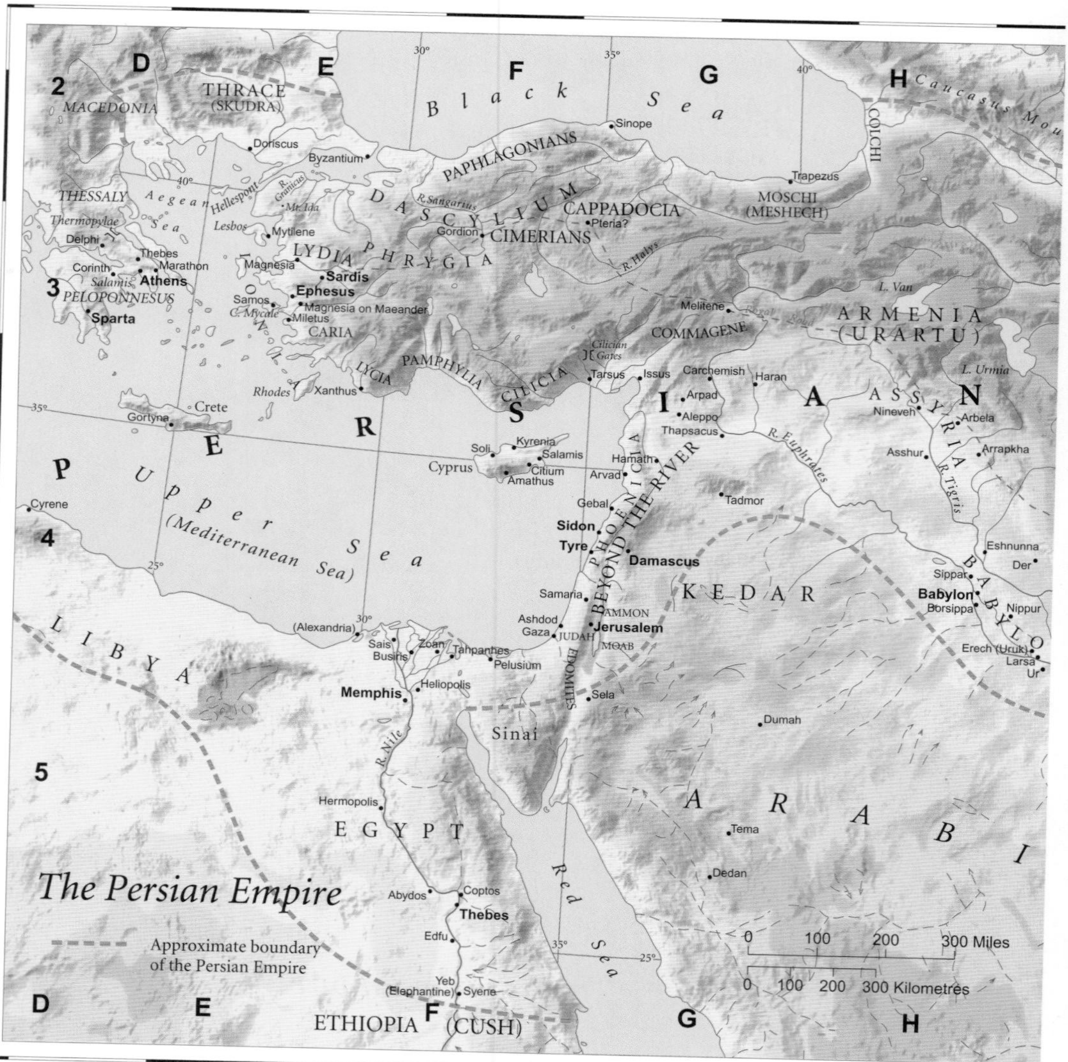


OUTER BORDER SHOWS

## MAP 8

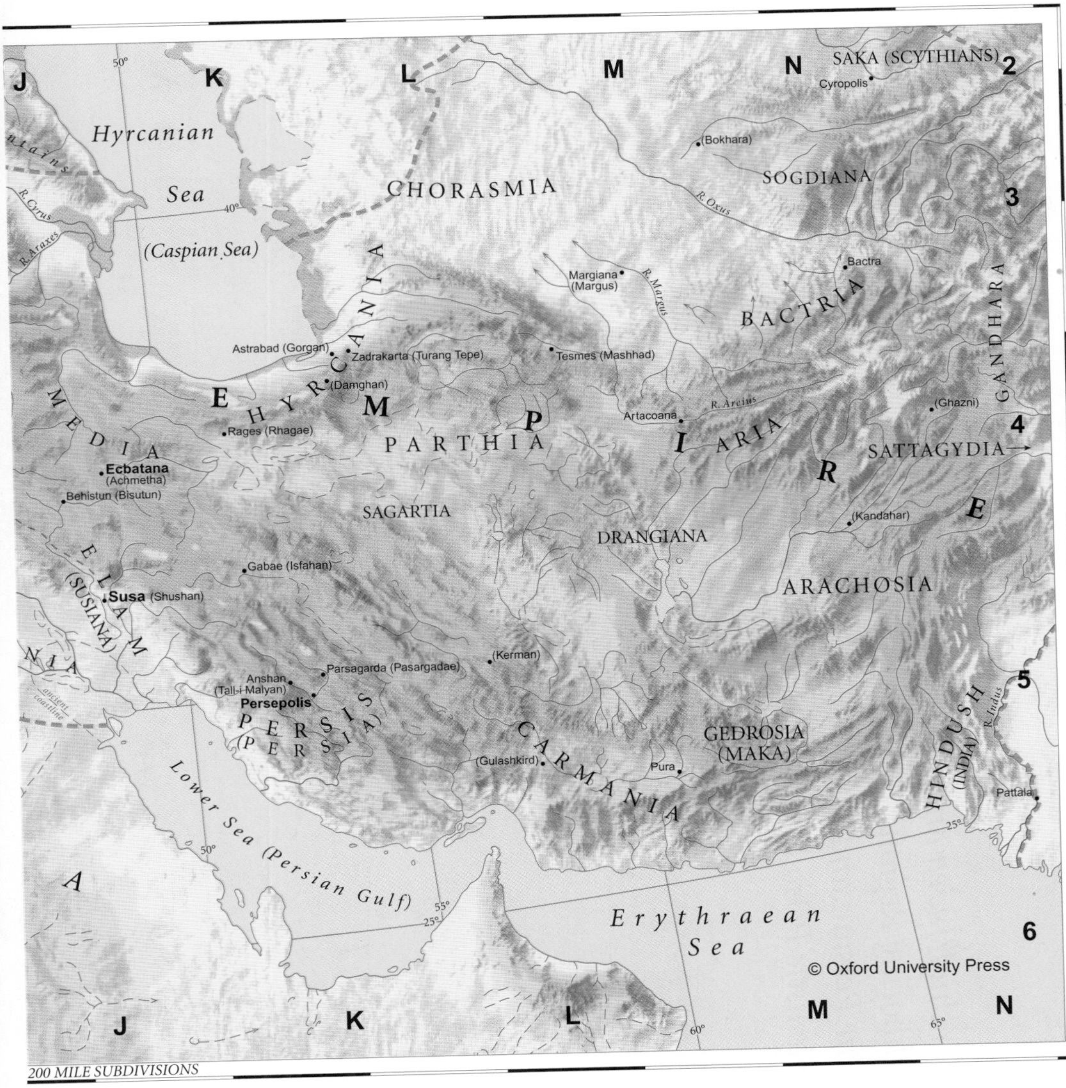
J
K
L
M
N
2
3
4
5
6
50°
40°
55°
25°
60°
65°
Hyrcanian
Sea
(Caspian Sea)
R. Cyrus
R. Araxes
CHORASMIA
SAKA (SCYTHIANS)
Cyropolis
(Bokhara)
SOGDIANA
R. Oxus
Bactra
BACTRIA
GANDHARA
Margiana
(Margus)
R. Margus
HYRCANIA
Astrabad (Gorgan)
Zadrakarta (Turang Tepe)
Tesmes (Mashhad)
(Damghan)
E M P I R E
MEDIA
Rages (Rhagae)
PARTHIA
Artacoana
R. Areius
ARIA
(Ghazni)
SATTAGYDIA
Ecbatana
(Achmetha)
Behistun (Bisutun)
SAGARTIA
DRANGIANA
(Kandahar)
ARACHOSIA
ELAM
(SUSIANA)
Gabae (Isfahan)
Susa (Shushan)
(Kerman)
Anshan
(Tall-i Malyan)
Parsagarda (Pasargadae)
Persepolis
PERSIS
(PERSIA)
ancient coastline
CARMANIA
GEDROSIA
(MAKA)
Pura
(Gulashkird)
HINDUSH
(INDIA)
R. Indus
Pattala
Lower Sea (Persian Gulf)
A
Erythraean
Sea
© Oxford University Press
200 MILE SUBDIVISIONS

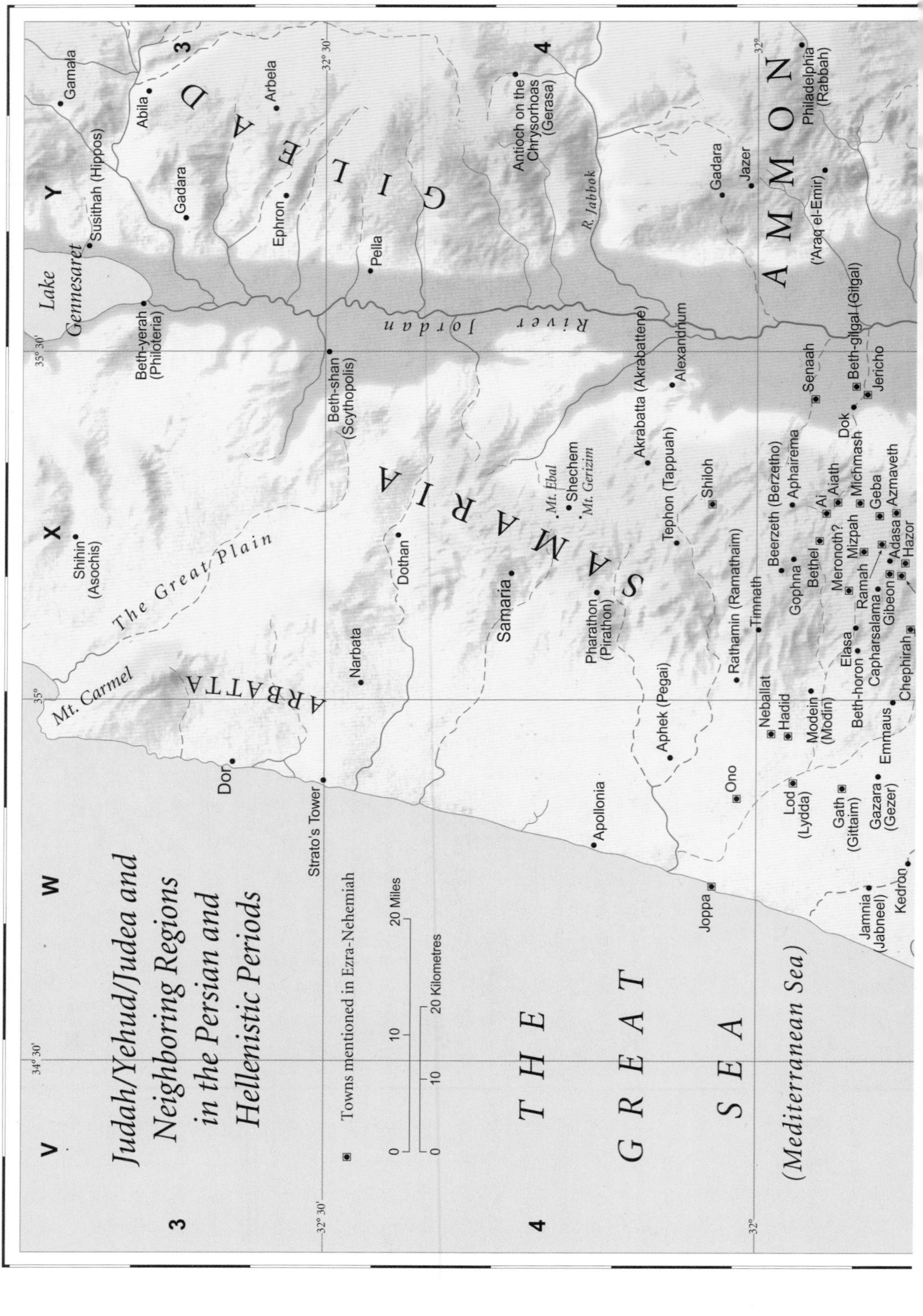

Judah/Yehud/Judea and Neighboring Regions in the Persian and Hellenistic Periods
Towns mentioned in Ezra-Nehemiah
0
10
20 Miles
0
10
20 Kilometres
V
W
X
Y
3
4
34° 30'
35°
35° 30'
32° 30'
32°
THE GREAT SEA
(Mediterranean Sea)
ARBATTA
SAMARIA
GILEAD
AMMON
The Great Plain
Mt. Carmel
Lake Gennesaret
Jordan River
R. Jabbok
Mt. Ebal
Mt. Gerizim
Gamala
Abila
Arbela
Susithah (Hippos)
Gadara
Ephron
Pella
Antioch on the Chrysorhoas (Gerasa)
Gadara
Jazer
Philadelphia (Rabbah)
('Araq el-Emir)
Beth-yerah (Philoteria)
Beth-shan (Scythopolis)
Shihin (Asochis)
Dothan
Narbata
Samaria
Shechem
Akrabatta (Akrabattene)
Alexandrium
Beth-gilgal (Gilgal)
Jericho
Senaah
Dok
Michmash
Aiath
Ai
Geba
Azmaveth
Tephon (Tappuah)
Shiloh
Aphairema
Beerzeth (Berzetho)
Bethel
Meronoth?
Mizpah
Ramah
Adasa
Hazor
Gophna
Gibeon
Capharsalama
Chephirah
Elasa
Beth-horon
Pharathon (Pirathon)
Timnath
Rathamin (Ramathaim)
Aphek (Pegai)
Neballat
Hadid
Modein (Modin)
Emmaus
Lod (Lydda)
Ono
Gath (Gittaim)
Gazara (Gezer)
Dor
Strato's Tower
Apollonia
Joppa
Jamnia (Jabneel)
Kedron

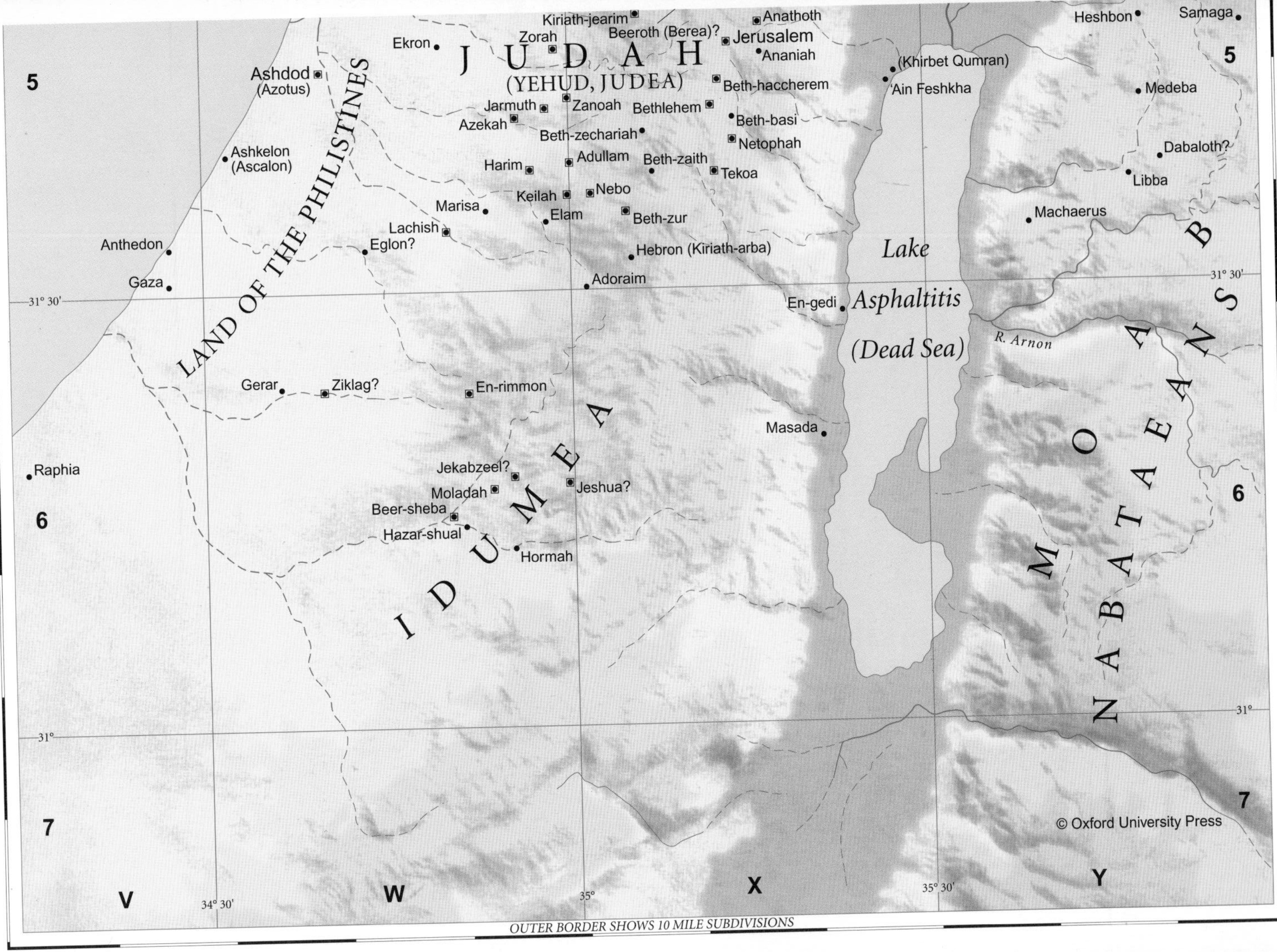
JUDAH
(YEHUD, JUDEA)
LAND OF THE PHILISTINES
IDUMEA
MOAB
NABATAEANS
Lake Asphaltitis
(Dead Sea)
R. Arnon
Kiriath-jearim
Zorah
Ekron
Beeroth (Berea)?
Anathoth
Jerusalem
Ananiah
Ashdod
(Azotus)
Beth-haccherem
Jarmuth
Zanoah
Bethlehem
Azekah
Beth-zechariah
Beth-basi
Netophah
Ashkelon
(Ascalon)
Harim
Adullam
Beth-zaith
Tekoa
Keilah
Nebo
Marisa
Elam
Beth-zur
Lachish
Eglon?
Hebron (Kiriath-arba)
Anthedon
Gaza
Adoraim
En-gedi
Gerar
Ziklag?
En-rimmon
Masada
Raphia
Jekabzeel?
Jeshua?
Moladah
Beer-sheba
Hazar-shual
Hormah
(Khirbet Qumran)
'Ain Feshkha
Heshbon
Samaga
Medeba
Dabaloth?
Libba
Machaerus
31° 30'
31°
34° 30'
35°
35° 30'
5
6
7
V
W
X
Y
© Oxford University Press
OUTER BORDER SHOWS 10 MILE SUBDIVISIONS

MAP 10

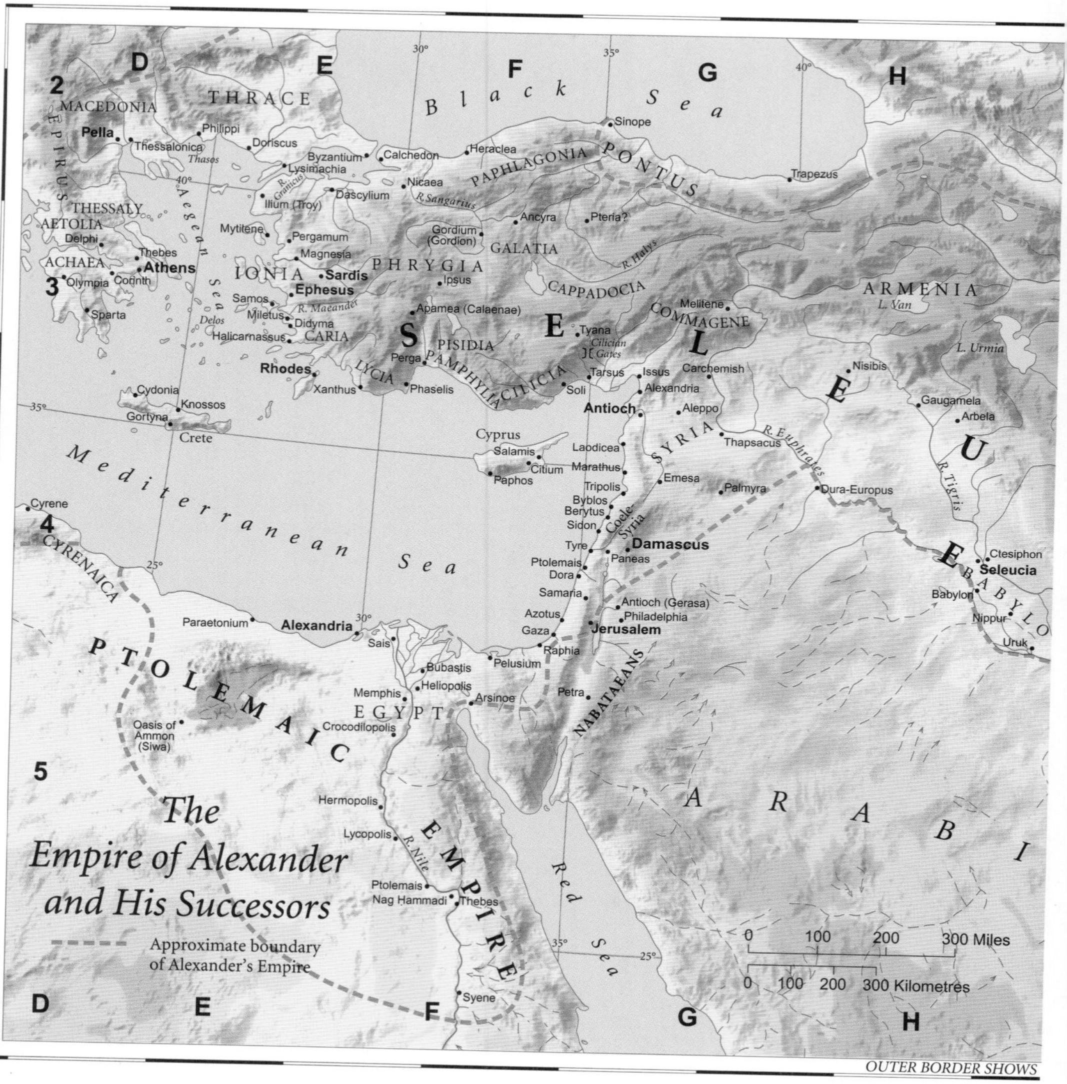


OUTER BORDER SHOWS

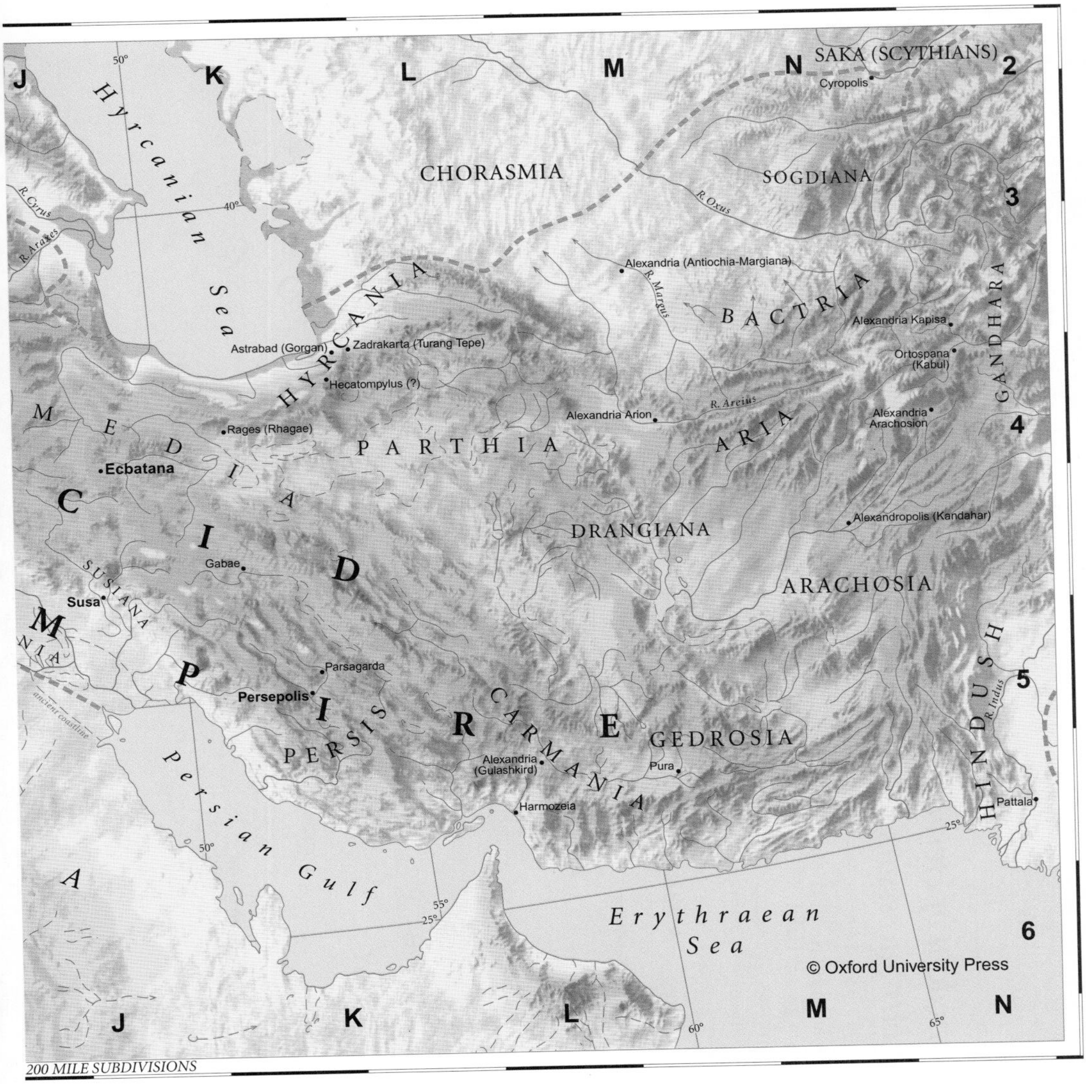
J
K
L
M
N
2
3
4
5
6
SAKA (SCYTHIANS)
Cyropolis
Hyrcanian Sea
R. Cyrus
R. Araxes
50°
40°
CHORASMIA
SOGDIANA
R. Oxus
Alexandria (Antiochia-Margiana)
R. Margus
BACTRIA
Alexandria Kapisa
Ortospana (Kabul)
GANDHARA
HYRCANIA
Astrabad (Gorgan)
Zadrakarta (Turang Tepe)
Hecatompylus (?)
Alexandria Arion
R. Areius
ARIA
Alexandria Arachosion
MEDIA
Rages (Rhagae)
Ecbatana
PARTHIA
DRANGIANA
Alexandropolis (Kandahar)
ARACHOSIA
ACHAEMENID EMPIRE
Gabae
SUSIANA
Susa
Parsagarda
Persepolis
PERSIS
CARMANIA
GEDROSIA
HINDUSH
R. Indus
Alexandria (Gulashkird)
Pura
Harmozeia
Pattala
ancient coastline
Persian Gulf
A
50°
55°
25°
25°
Erythraean Sea
60°
65°
© Oxford University Press
200 MILE SUBDIVISIONS

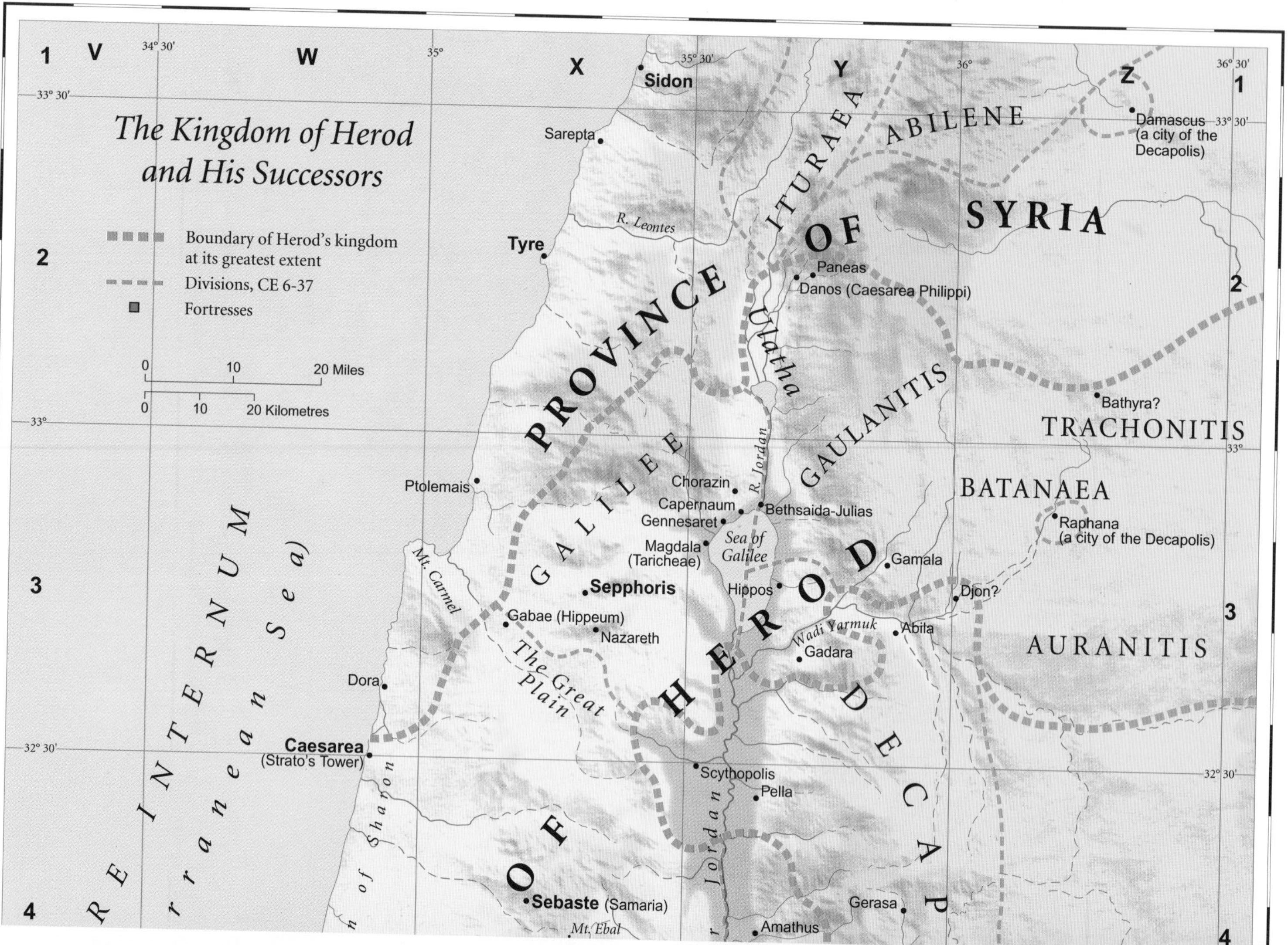
The Kingdom of Herod and His Successors
Boundary of Herod's kingdom at its greatest extent
Divisions, CE 6-37
Fortresses
0 10 20 Miles
0 10 20 Kilometres
PROVINCE OF SYRIA
ABILENE
ITURAEA
TRACHONITIS
BATANAEA
AURANITIS
GAULANITIS
GALILEE
HEROD
OF HEROD
DECAP
REINTERNUM
rranean Sea)
Ulatha
R. Leontes
R. Jordan
Jordan
Sea of Galilee
Wadi Yarmuk
The Great Plain
Mt. Carmel
Mt. Ebal
of Sharon
Sidon
Sarepta
Tyre
Ptolemais
Dora
Caesarea
(Strato's Tower)
Sebaste (Samaria)
Damascus
(a city of the Decapolis)
Paneas
Danos (Caesarea Philippi)
Bathyra?
Raphana
(a city of the Decapolis)
Chorazin
Capernaum
Gennesaret
Bethsaida-Julias
Magdala
(Taricheae)
Sepphoris
Hippos
Gamala
Djon?
Abila
Gadara
Gabae (Hippeum)
Nazareth
Scythopolis
Pella
Gerasa
Amathus
34° 30'
35°
35° 30'
36°
36° 30'
33° 30'
33°
32° 30'
V
W
X
Y
Z
1
2
3
4

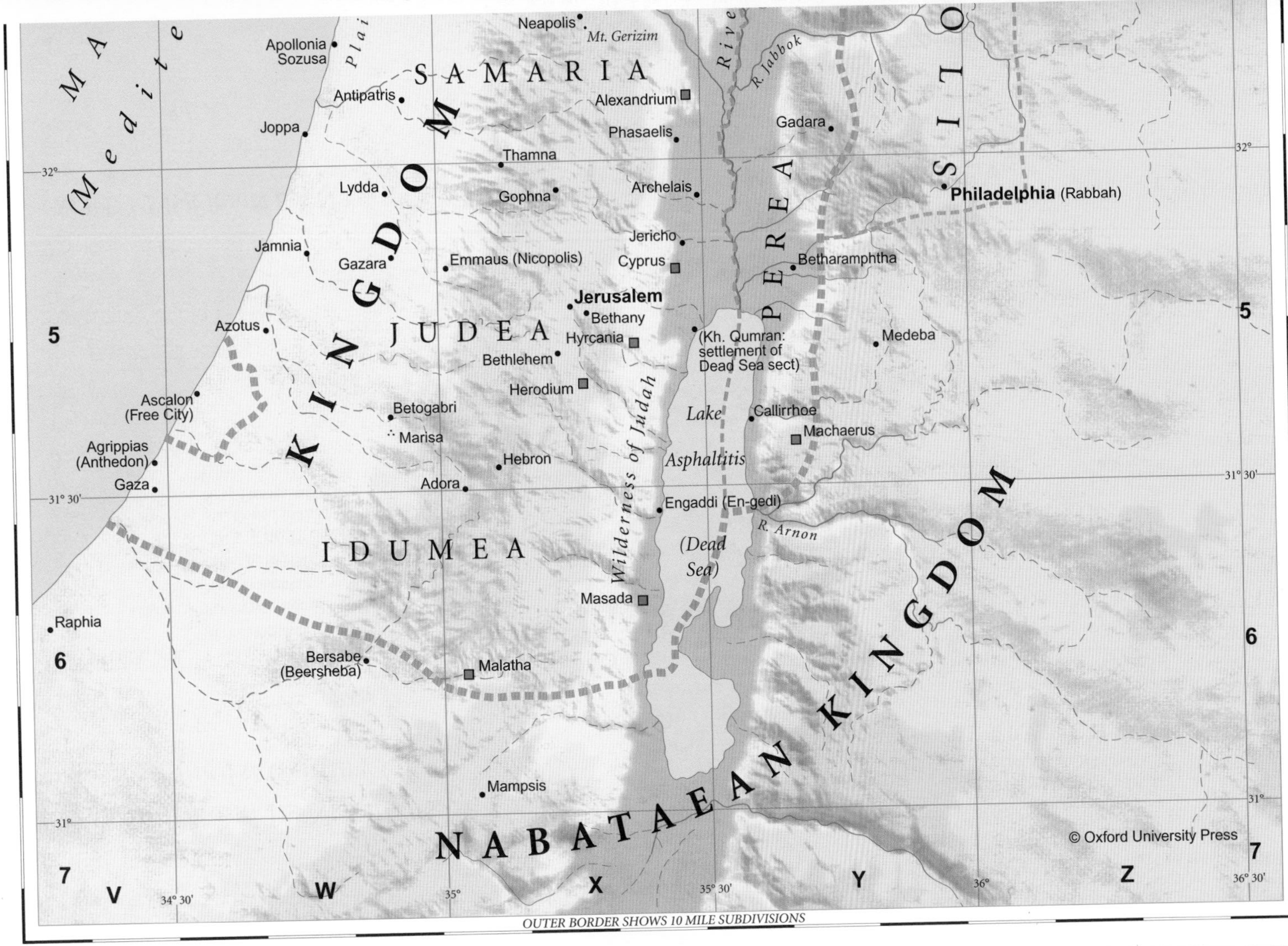

Neapolis
Mt. Gerizim
Apollonia
Sozusa
Plai
SAMARIA
Antipatris
Alexandrium
Joppa
Phasaelis
Gadara
R. Jabbok
River
Thamna
Lydda
Gophna
Archelais
Philadelphia (Rabbah)
Jamnia
Gazara
Emmaus (Nicopolis)
Jericho
Cyprus
Betharamphtha
PEREA
Jerusalem
Bethany
Azotus
JUDEA
Hyrcania
(Kh. Qumran: settlement of Dead Sea sect)
Medeba
Bethlehem
Herodium
Ascalon (Free City)
Betogabri
Marisa
Lake Asphaltitis
Callirrhoe
Machaerus
Agrippias (Anthedon)
Hebron
Gaza
Adora
Wilderness of Judah
Engaddi (En-gedi)
R. Arnon
KINGDOM
IDUMEA
(Dead Sea)
Masada
Raphia
Bersabe (Beersheba)
Malatha
Mampsis
NABATAEAN KINGDOM
(Medite
MA
OLIS
© Oxford University Press
32°
31° 30'
31°
34° 30'
35°
35° 30'
36°
36° 30'
5
6
7
V
W
X
Y
Z
OUTER BORDER SHOWS 10 MILE SUBDIVISIONS

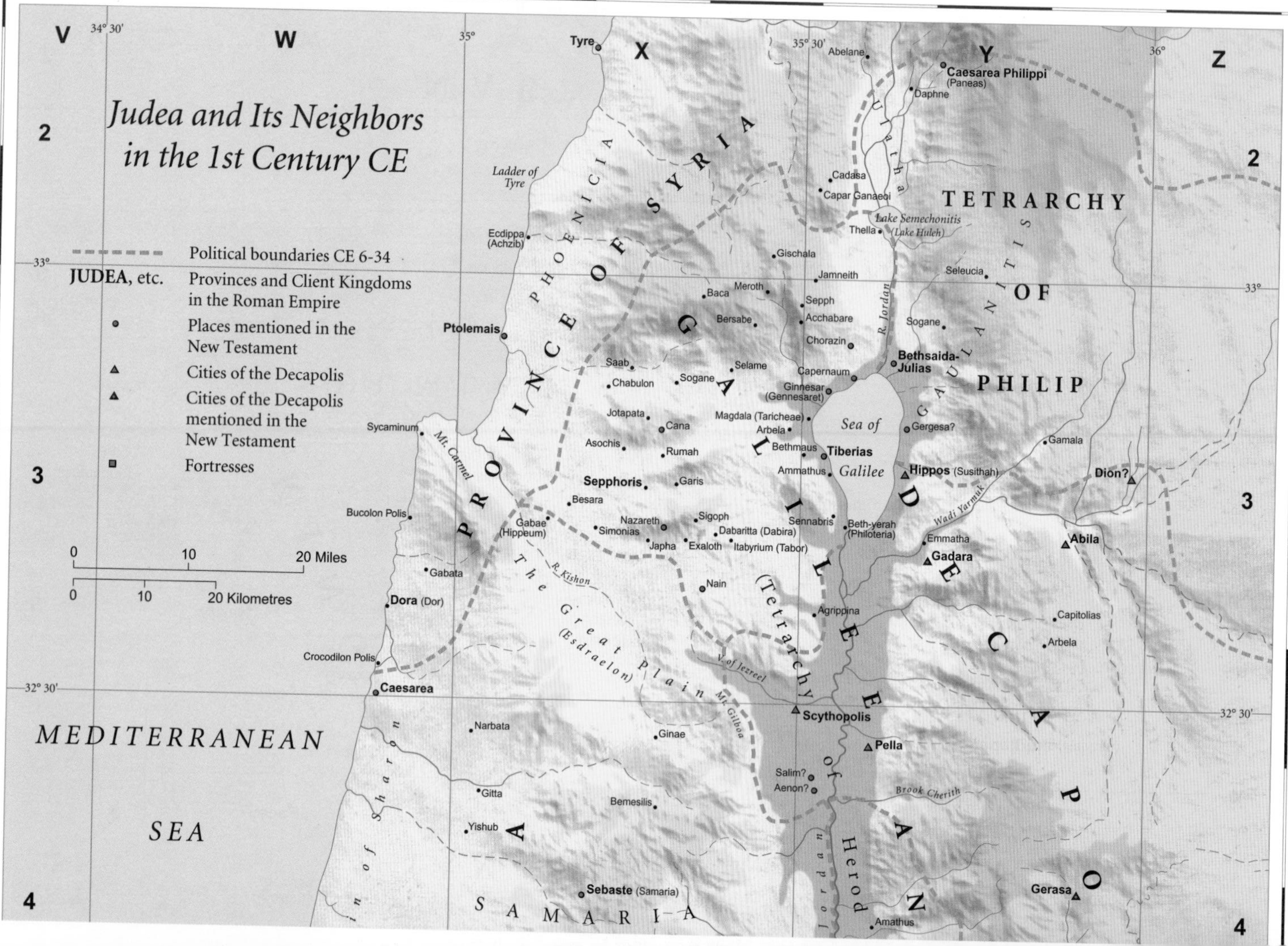
Judea and Its Neighbors in the 1st Century CE
Political boundaries CE 6-34
JUDEA, etc. Provinces and Client Kingdoms in the Roman Empire
Places mentioned in the New Testament
Cities of the Decapolis
Cities of the Decapolis mentioned in the New Testament
Fortresses
0 10 20 Miles
0 10 20 Kilometres
V
W
X
Y
Z
2
3
4
34° 30'
35°
35° 30'
36°
33°
32° 30'
MEDITERRANEAN SEA
PROVINCE OF SYRIA
PHOENICIA
GALILEE
(Tetrarchy of Herod
TETRARCHY OF PHILIP
GAULANITIS
DECAPOLIS
SAMARIA
Ulatha
Plain of Sharon
The Great Plain (Esdraelon)
Tyre
Ladder of Tyre
Ecdippa (Achzib)
Ptolemais
Sycaminum
Mt. Carmel
Bucolon Polis
Gabata
Dora (Dor)
Crocodilon Polis
Caesarea
Narbata
Gitta
Yishub
Sebaste (Samaria)
Bemesilis
Ginae
Gabae (Hippeum)
R. Kishon
Besara
Sepphoris
Garis
Simonias
Nazareth
Japha
Exaloth
Sigoph
Dabaritta (Dabira)
Itabyrium (Tabor)
Nain
Saab
Chabulon
Sogane
Selame
Jotapata
Cana
Asochis
Rumah
Baca
Meroth
Bersabe
Gischala
Jamneith
Sepph
Acchabare
Chorazin
Capernaum
Ginnesar (Gennesaret)
Magdala (Taricheae)
Arbela
Bethmaus
Tiberias
Ammathus
Sea of Galilee
Sennabris
Beth-yerah (Philoteria)
Agrippina
V. of Jezreel
Mt. Gilboa
Scythopolis
Salim?
Aenon?
Pella
Brook Cherith
Jordan
Amathus
Gerasa
Abelane
Caesarea Philippi (Paneas)
Daphne
Cadasa
Capar Ganaeoi
Lake Semechonitis (Lake Huleh)
Thella
R. Jordan
Seleucia
Sogane
Bethsaida-Julias
Gergesa?
Hippos (Susithah)
Gamala
Dion?
Wadi Yarmuk
Emmatha
Gadara
Abila
Capitolias
Arbela

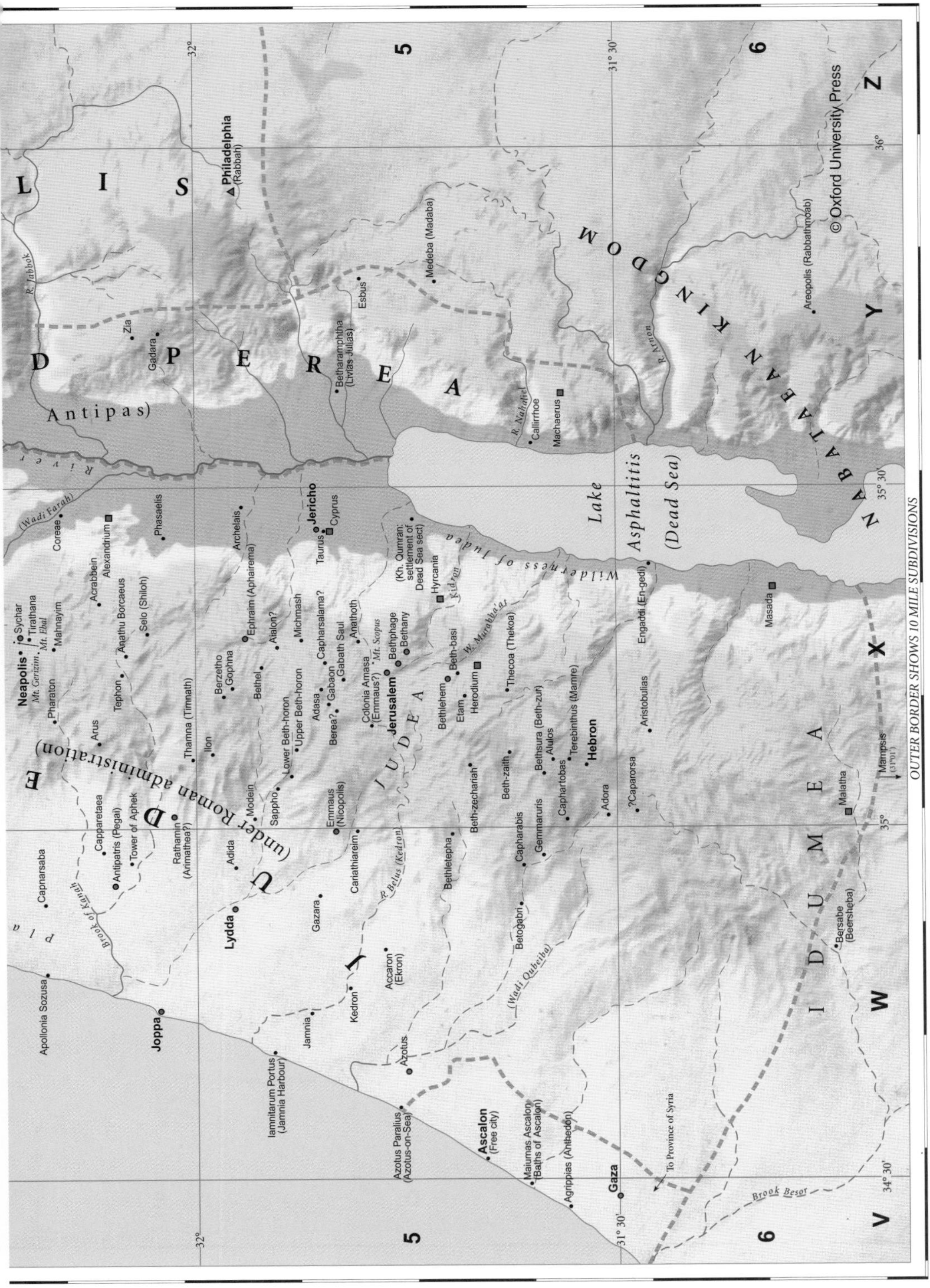
D E C A P O L I S
P E R E A
(under Roman administration)
Antipas)
J U D E A
I D U M E A
N A B A T A E A N K I N G D O M
Philadelphia (Rabbah)
Zia
Gadara
Betharamphtha (Livias Julias)
Esbus
Medeba (Madaba)
Callirrhoe
Machaerus
R. Nahaliel
R. Arnon
Areopolis (Rabbathmoab)
R. Jabbok
River
Lake Asphaltitis (Dead Sea)
Wilderness of Judea
(Wadi Farah)
Coreae
Alexandrium
Phasaelis
Archelais
Jericho
Cyprus
Taurus
(Kh. Qumran: settlement of Dead Sea sect)
Hyrcania
Kidron
W. Murabba'at
Engaddi (En-gedi)
Masada
Neapolis
Sychar
Tirathana
Mt. Gerizim
Mt. Ebal
Mahnayim
Acrabbein
Selo (Shiloh)
Anathu Borcaeus
Ephraim (Aphairema)
Aialon?
Michmash
Capharsalama?
Anathoth
Mt. Scopus
Bethphage
Bethany
Pharaton
Tephon
Arus
Berzetho
Gophna
Bethel
Thamna (Timnath)
Ilon
Lower Beth-horon
Upper Beth-horon
Adasa
Gabaon
Gabath Saul
Berea?
Colonia Amasa (Emmaus?)
Jerusalem
Bethlehem
Beth-basi
Etam
Herodium
Thecoa (Thekoa)
Bethsura (Beth-zur)
Alulos
Terebinthus (Mamre)
Hebron
Aristobulias
Capharsaba
Capparetaea
Antipatris (Pegai)
Tower of Aphek
Rathamin (Arimathea?)
Modein
Sappho
Adida
Emmaus (Nicopolis)
Cariathiareim
Beth-zechariah
Beth-zaith
Caphartobas
Adora
?Caparorsa
Lydda
Gazara
R. Belus (Kedron)
Bethletepha
Capharabis
Gemmaruris
Betogabri
Brook of Kanah
Apollonia Sozusa
Joppa
Jamnia
Kedron
Accaron (Ekron)
(Wadi Qubeiba)
Iamnitarum Portus (Jamnia Harbour)
Azotus
Azotus Paralius (Azotus-on-Sea)
Ascalon (Free city)
Maiumas Ascalon (Baths of Ascalon)
Agrippias (Anthedon)
Gaza
To Province of Syria
Brook Besor
Bersabe (Beersheba)
Malatha
Mampsis
32°
31° 30'
34° 30'
35°
35° 30'
36°
5
6
V
W
X
Y
Z
© Oxford University Press
OUTER BORDER SHOWS 10 MILE SUBDIVISIONS

MAP 13

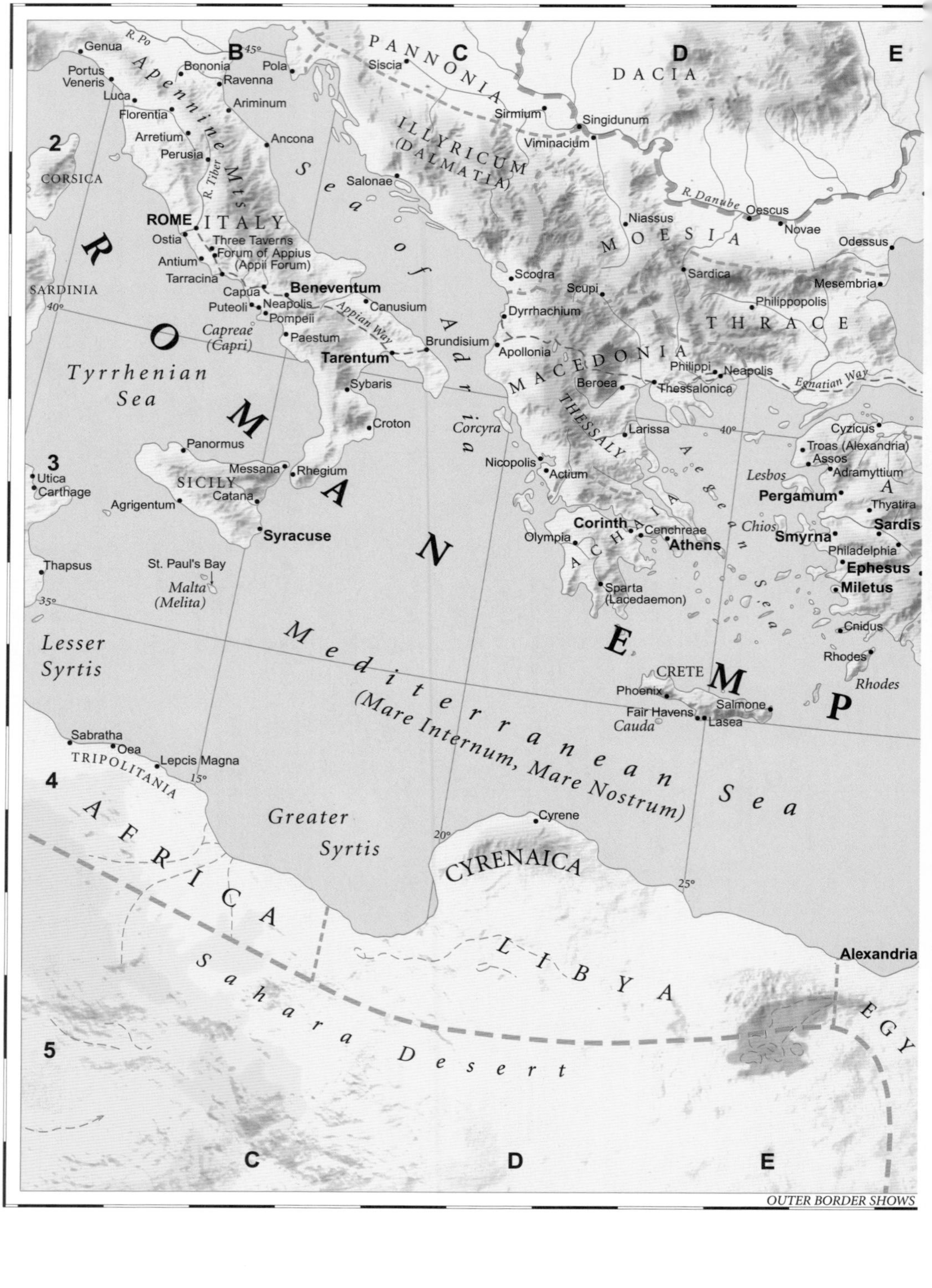


OUTER BORDER SHOWS

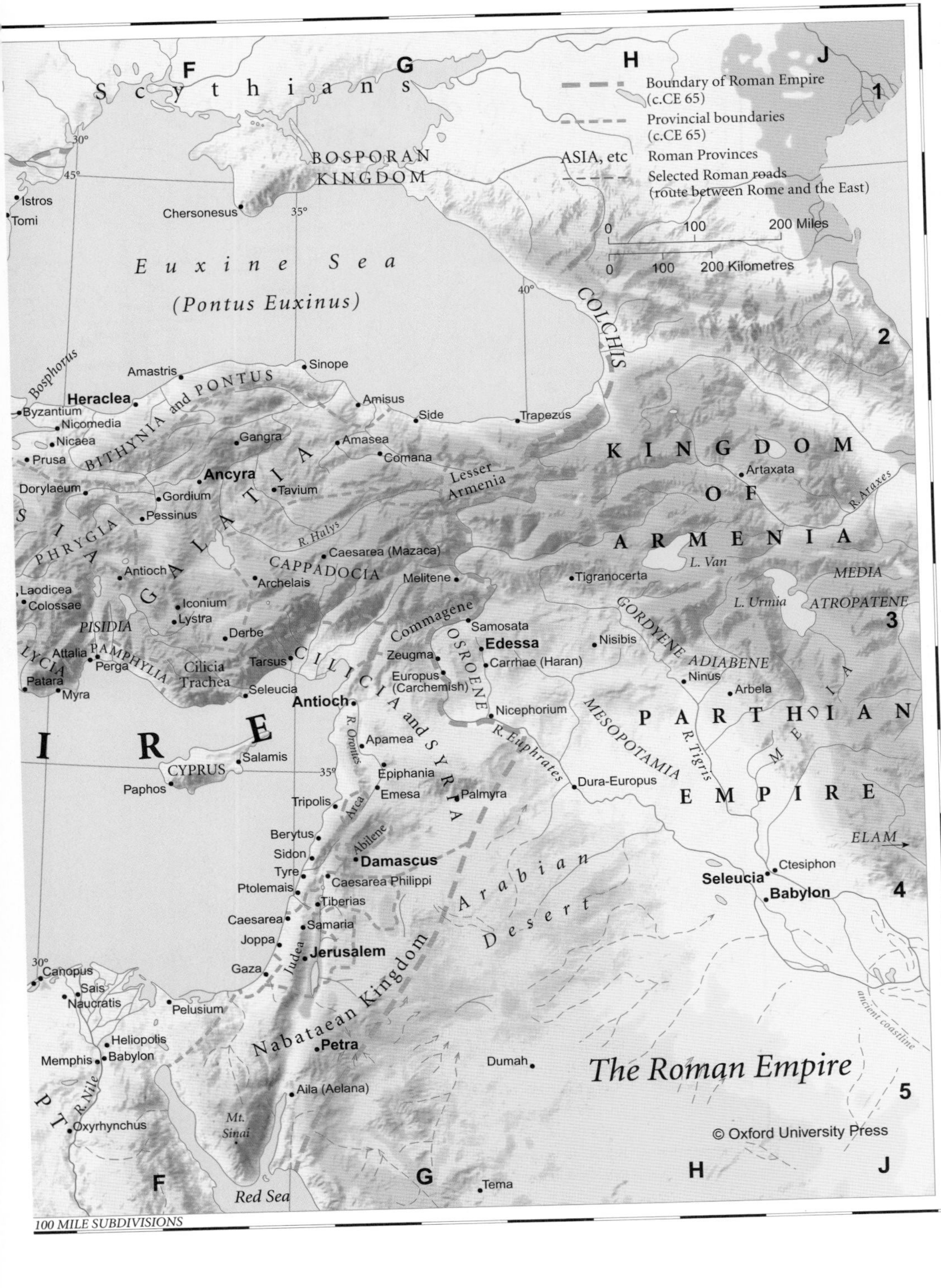
F
G
H
J
S c y t h i a n s
1
2
3
4
5
Boundary of Roman Empire (c.CE 65)
Provincial boundaries (c.CE 65)
ASIA, etc
Roman Provinces
Selected Roman roads (route between Rome and the East)
0
100
200 Miles
0
100
200 Kilometres
BOSPORAN KINGDOM
30°
45°
35°
40°
Istros
Tomi
Chersonesus
E u x i n e S e a
(Pontus Euxinus)
COLCHIS
Bosphorus
Amastris
Sinope
Heraclea
Byzantium
Nicomedia
Nicaea
Prusa
BITHYNIA and PONTUS
Amisus
Side
Trapezus
Gangra
Amasea
Comana
Ancyra
Tavium
Dorylaeum
Gordium
Pessinus
G A L A T I A
Lesser Armenia
K I N G D O M O F A R M E N I A
Artaxata
R. Araxes
R. Halys
PHRYGIA
Caesarea (Mazaca)
CAPPADOCIA
Melitene
Tigranocerta
L. Van
MEDIA
L. Urmia
ATROPATENE
Antioch
Archelais
Laodicea
Colossae
Iconium
Lystra
PISIDIA
Derbe
Commagene
Samosata
GORDYENE
Edessa
Nisibis
LYCIA
Attalia
PAMPHYLIA
Perga
Patara
Myra
Cilicia Trachea
Tarsus
Seleucia
CILICIA and SYRIA
Zeugma
Europus (Carchemish)
OSROENE
Carrhae (Haran)
ADIABENE
Ninus
Arbela
Antioch
Nicephorium
MESOPOTAMIA
P A R T H I A N E M P I R E
MEDIA
R. Tigris
I R E
CYPRUS
Salamis
Paphos
R. Orontes
Apamea
Epiphania
Emesa
Palmyra
R. Euphrates
Dura-Europus
Tripolis
Arca
Berytus
Sidon
Abilene
Damascus
Tyre
Ptolemais
Caesarea Philippi
Tiberias
Caesarea
Samaria
Joppa
Jerusalem
Judea
Gaza
A r a b i a n D e s e r t
ELAM
Ctesiphon
Seleucia
Babylon
Canopus
Sais
Naucratis
Pelusium
Nabataean Kingdom
Heliopolis
Memphis
Babylon
Petra
Dumah
The Roman Empire
ancient coastline
R. Nile
Aila (Aelana)
Mt. Sinai
Oxyrhynchus
© Oxford University Press
Red Sea
Tema
100 MILE SUBDIVISIONS

# MAP 14

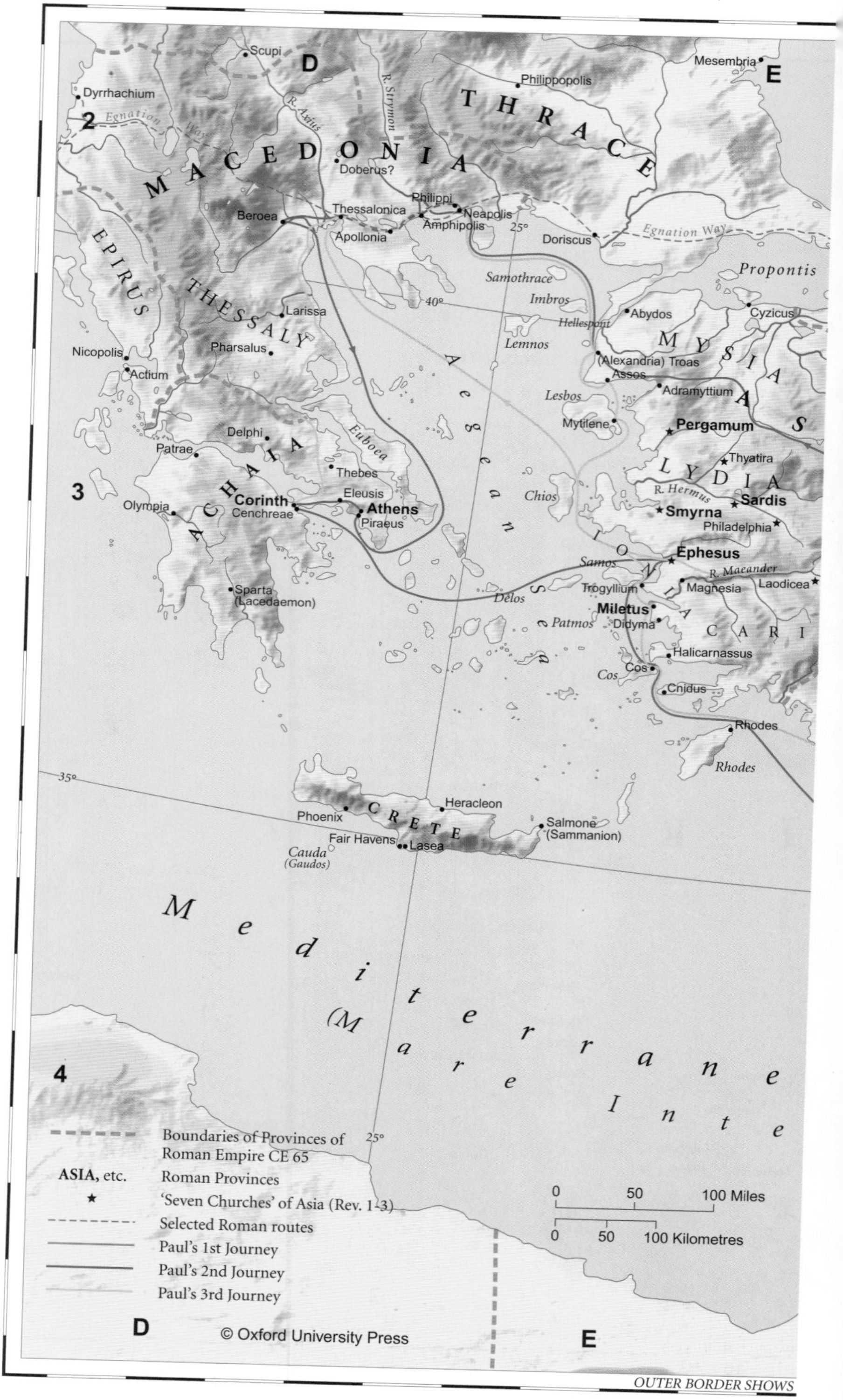




OUTER BORDER SHOWS

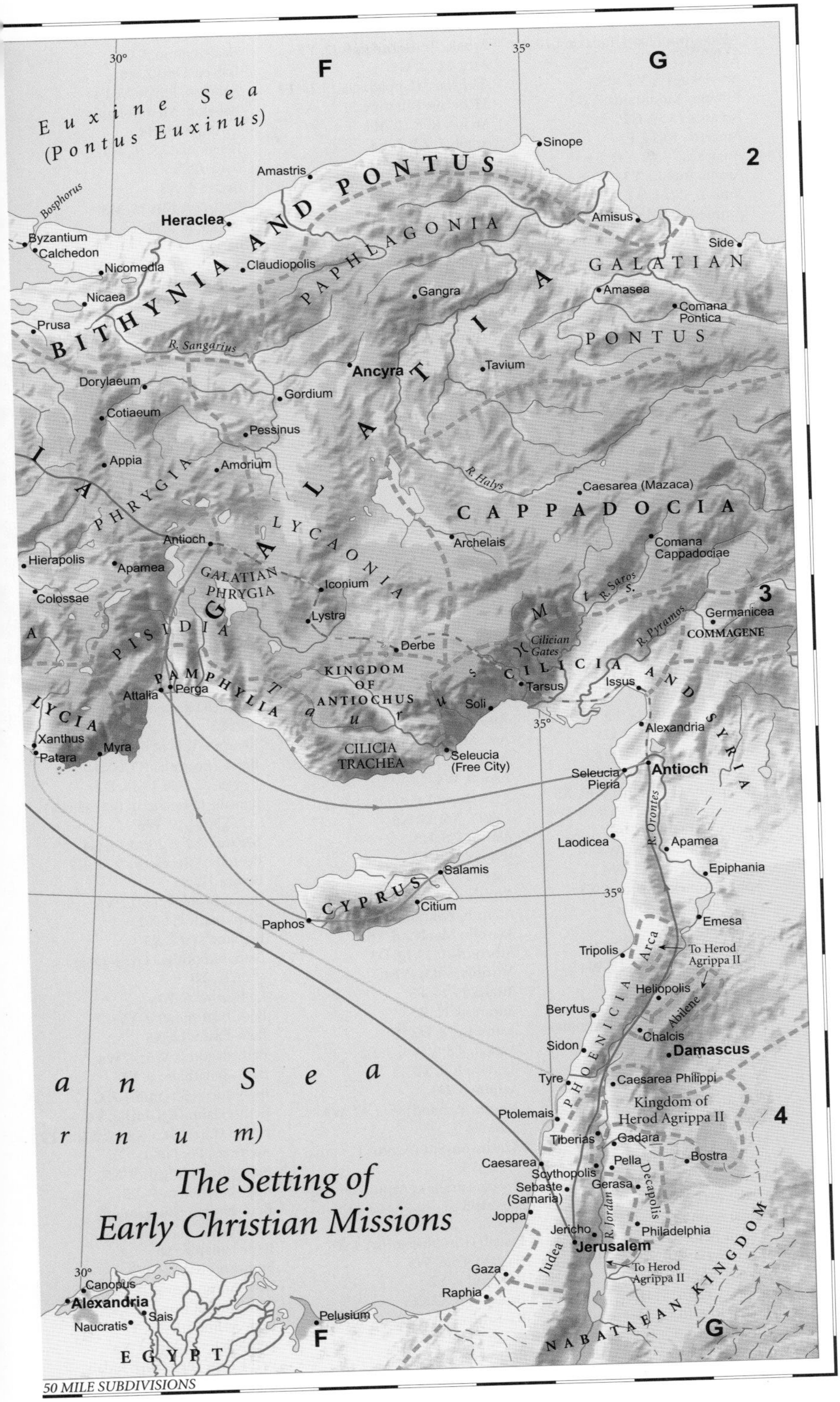
The Setting of Early Christian Missions
50 MILE SUBDIVISIONS
F
G
2
3
4
30°
35°
Euxine Sea
(Pontus Euxinus)
Bosphorus
Sinope
Amastris
BITHYNIA AND PONTUS
Heraclea
Byzantium
Calchedon
Nicomedia
Claudiopolis
Nicaea
Prusa
PAPHLAGONIA
Amisus
Side
GALATIAN
Amasea
Comana Pontica
PONTUS
Gangra
GALATIA
R. Sangarius
Ancyra
Tavium
Dorylaeum
Gordium
Cotiaeum
Pessinus
Appia
Amorium
PHRYGIA
R. Halys
Caesarea (Mazaca)
CAPPADOCIA
Antioch
LYCAONIA
Archelais
Comana Cappadociae
Hierapolis
Apamea
GALATIAN PHRYGIA
Iconium
R. Saros
Colossae
Lystra
Germanicea
COMMAGENE
PISIDIA
R. Pyramos
Cilician Gates
Derbe
KINGDOM OF ANTIOCHUS
CILICIA
Tarsus
Issus
PAMPHYLIA
Attalia
Perga
Taurus Mt
Soli
LYCIA
Alexandria
CILICIA AND SYRIA
Xanthus
Myra
Patara
CILICIA TRACHEA
Seleucia (Free City)
Seleucia Pieria
Antioch
R. Orontes
Laodicea
Apamea
Epiphania
Salamis
CYPRUS
Citium
Paphos
Emesa
Tripolis
Arca
To Herod Agrippa II
Heliopolis
Abilene
Berytus
PHOENICIA
Chalcis
Sidon
Damascus
Tyre
Caesarea Philippi
Kingdom of Herod Agrippa II
Ptolemais
Tiberias
Gadara
Bostra
Caesarea
Pella
Scythopolis
Decapolis
Sebaste (Samaria)
Gerasa
R. Jordan
Joppa
Jericho
Philadelphia
Jerusalem
Judea
To Herod Agrippa II
Gaza
Raphia
NABATAEAN KINGDOM
Canopus
Alexandria
Sais
Pelusium
Naucratis
EGYPT

# INDEX TO MAPS